2024
BRG BUSINESS
REFERENCE GUIDE

The essential guide to pricing businesses & franchises

Compiled & published by Business Brokerage Press

Important note

This publication is designed to provide accurate and authoritative information with regard to the subject matter covered. It is sold with the understanding that the authors, editors and publisher are not engaged in rendering legal, accounting or other professional advice. If legal advice or other expert assistance is required, the services of a competent professional should be sought.

ISBN: 978-1-7328971-6-8

Printed and bound in the USA

BUSINESS BROKERAGE PRESS, PUBLISHERS
Wilmington, North Carolina

In loving memory of Tom West,
June 17, 1936–December 4, 2022

Thanks to Our Sponsors

AICPA

BizComps

BusinessBroker.net

Business Valuation Resources

DealStream, Inc.

Deal Studio

Diamond Financial

Ed Legum's *Being a Business Broker*

Glen Cooper on Business Brokerage

International Business Brokers Association

International Society of Business Appraisers

The Lease Coach

Transworld Business Advisors

For more information on any of these resources, please see the glossy pages in the center section of this *Guide*.

Table of Contents

Thanks to IBISWorld

The following data included in the *Guide* comes from IBISWorld and is used with their permission:

Profit, Wages, Annual Growth Future (2023–2028), Annual Growth Past (2018–2023)—and, under Benchmark Data—Statistics, Products and Services Segmentation, Major Market Segmentation, Industry Costs, and Market Share.

Go to https://www.ibisworld.com to learn more about this valued resource.

Using the *Guide*

We've added a considerable number of industries to the *Guide* again this year, notably in the manufacturing and wholesale trade sectors. We now have compiled information on 800 industries, all of which are included in the online edition, and approximately 650, in this print *Guide*.

Much of the information we present comes from our Industry Experts, who are listed at the back of this book. We attempt to remain true to the original source, but we make some changes in grammar and punctuation to improve readability.

The online edition contains additional sections including General Information, Advantages, Disadvantages, Revenue, Expert Ratings, Executive Summary (from IBISWorld), and Downloads.

INDUSTRY MULTIPLES

The Industry Multiples section is categorized into three sections, Under $1 Million Net Sales, $1 Million–$5 Million Net Sales, and Over $5 Million Net Sales. Below is the explanation and citation; within the listings, we've included a shortened citation.

MVIC (Market Value of Invested Capital) = Also known as the selling price, the MVIC is the total consideration paid to the seller and includes any cash, notes and/or securities that were used as a form of payment plus any interest-bearing liabilities assumed by the buyer.

Net Sales = Annual Gross Sales, net of returns and discounts allowed, if any.

Gross Profit = Net Sales - Cost of Goods Sold

SDE = Operating Profit + Depreciation + Amortization + Owner's Compensation

EBITDA = Operating Profit + Depreciation & Amortization

Source: DealStats (formerly Pratt's Stats), 2023 (Portland, OR: Business Valuation Resources, LLC). DealStats is a robust online database of acquired private company transactions sourced from business brokers, M&A advisors, and SEC filings. Learn more at www.bvresources.com/dealstats or visit www.bvresources.com/contribute to become part of the Contributor Network.

PRICING METHODS

Pricing methods such as multiples of Seller's Discretionary Earnings (SDE), Earnings Before Interest and Taxes (EBIT), and Earnings Before Interest, Taxes, Depreciation, and Amortization (EBITDA) all have two things in common: each requires that the actual earnings be calculated, and then a multiple based on many factors relating to the business must also be calculated. Multiplying the two should then produce the price for that business. Unfortunately, these methods are based on the figures being calculated and by the person doing the pricing.

The other method calls for a multiple of sales. The big advantage to this method is that it doesn't call for calculating the figures. One simply takes the total annual sales (less sales taxes) and multiplies it by a percentage that "people in the know" are comfortable with, based on their knowledge and experience. In many cases there is a universal rule of thumb for the multiple, based on many transactions. The annual sales of a business are usually a provable figure; although an argument could be made, especially in very small businesses, that the owner could be "taking money off the top," thus reducing sales. However, unless the owner is really stealing from the business, small amounts shouldn't influence the price dramatically.

The purpose of the above information is to show that, although multipliers may stay about the same, the final result is based on figures that do reflect the impact of the economy. Sales are down and costs go up, especially in relation to sales. Therefore, we are comfortable with the final pricing results. As we keep saying, rules of thumb are just that. The purpose in supplying other information and data is so the user can adjust the rule of thumb up or down based on such information.

For the most part, the pricing of a business is based on the sales and earnings; however, another major factor is whether the seller will finance a portion of the selling price. If he/she won't provide some financing, the price will generally be lower than if he/she will. The rule is usually the lower the down payment, the higher the full price; and the seller who demands an all-cash transaction will receive, in most cases, a lower full price.

The price of a business is ultimately what someone will pay for it—it is market driven. Or, as the old saying goes, the price is what a buyer will pay and the seller will accept.

USING THE RULES OF THUMB

Despite all the caveats about using rules of thumb in pricing businesses, they are commonly used to do just that. The reason is quite simple—they are very easy to use. But how accurate are they? A lot more accurate than many people think. They may supply a quick assessment, but if used properly, they can come pretty close to what the business will ultimately sell for.

Rules of thumb usually come in two formats. The most commonly used rule of thumb is simply a percentage of the annual sales, or, better yet, the last 12 months of sales/revenues. For example, if the total sales were $100,000 for last year, and the multiple for the particular business is 40 percent of annual sales, then the price based on the rule of thumb would be $40,000.

Quite a few experts have said that revenue multiples are likely to be more reliable than earnings multiples. The reason is that most multiples of earnings are based on add-backs to the earnings, which can be a judgment call, as can the multiple. Sales or revenues are essentially a fixed figure. One might want to subtract sales taxes if they have not been deducted, but the sales are the sales. The only judgment then is the percentage. When it is supplied by an expert, the percentage multiplier becomes much more reliable.

The second rule of thumb used is a multiple of earnings. In small businesses, the multiple is used against what is termed Seller's Discretionary Earnings (SDE). SDE is also called Seller's or Owner's Cash Flow and similar names. It is usually based on a multiple (generally between 1 and 5), and this number is then used as a multiple against the earnings of the business. Many of the entries also contain a multiple of EBIT and/or EBITDA.

Seller's Discretionary Earnings (SDE): The earnings of a business prior to the following items:

- income taxes
- nonrecurring income and expenses
- nonoperating income and expenses
- depreciation and amortization
- interest expense or income

- owner's total compensation for one owner/operator, after adjusting the total compensation of all owners to market value.

The above definition of Seller's Discretionary Earnings, although accurate, is a bit confusing. If you change the words "prior to the" and substitute the word "plus," it may be easier to understand. We would also suggest that the highest salary be used in the calculation of SDE. The reason is that we must assume that the buyer will replace the highest compensated employee or owner—at least for the SDE calculation.

Keep in mind that the multiples for the different earnings acronyms mentioned above will be different than the multiple of SDE. The rules contained in the *Guide* are specific about what is being used. They will say *2.5 times SDE* or *4 times EBIT*, etc.

THE BASICS

The businesses are arranged alphabetically. In some cases, the business may go by two name descriptions, for example, gas stations or service stations. We use the one that we feel is the most common. If you can't find what you are looking for, see if it is listed under another name. If there is a particular franchise you are working on and it's not in the rules, check the type of business for more information. For example, if the franchise is an ice cream shop, check the name of the franchise; and if it's not there, go to ice cream shops and other ice cream franchises. If the business is not listed, find a similar business and start there.

The number of Businesses/Units is the approximate number of businesses of that type in the U.S. Where there is an IBISWorld report, we generally use that number. IBISWorld provides excellent reports on many different businesses. Most of these reports are well over 20 pages and are most informative. They are well worth the price.

We have also provided—where available—the North American Industry Classification System (NAICS) and Standard Industrial Classification (SIC) codes. For NAICS and SIC codes, go to https://www.census.gov/naics/.

THE RULES OF THUMB

The price, based on the rule of thumb, does not include inventory (unless it specifically states that it does), or real estate or other balance-sheet items such as cash and accounts receivable. We have noticed an increase in Industry Experts telling us that inventory is included in the multiples. The price derived from the rule of thumb is for the operating assets of the business plus goodwill. It also assumes that the business will be delivered free and clear of any debt. If any debt is to be assumed by a purchaser, it is subtracted from the price based on the rule of thumb method.

In other words, the rules, unless mentioned otherwise, create a price that includes goodwill; furniture, fixtures, & equipment (FF&E); and leasehold improvements, less outstanding debt, including accounts payable, loans on FF&E, bank loans, etc. The business, unless otherwise mentioned, is assumed delivered to a purchaser free and clear of any debt or encumbrances.

Accounts receivable are not included, as they are generally handled outside of any transaction and almost always belong to the seller. Work in progress, prepaid memberships, etc. also normally belong to the seller. Items such as these may be divided between buyer and seller. For example, in a dry-cleaning business, the seller may have taken in a customer's clothing for dry cleaning, but the buyer may take over the business before the work has been completed and delivered back to the customer. This is generally handled outside the transaction and does not usually figure in a pricing or valuation.

PRICING TIPS

These provide information from industry experts and other sources. They are intended to amplify the rules themselves. We include lots of new information every year, while maintaining important information from prior years.

BENCHMARK DATA

We feel it is very important, in analyzing and pricing a business, that you compare it to similar businesses, or benchmarks, that are unique to this type of business. One common benchmark unique to each business is the expenses. We have included as many of these as we could find. Many have been contributed by Industry Experts. If no source is mentioned, then you can assume that an Industry Expert(s) has supplied them. In many cases we have used a breakdown of expenses from IBISWorld.

The figures in the Expenses (% of Annual Sales) tables may not always add up to 100 percent. We provide only the major categories, and there may be other expense items not included which would make up any difference. Also, in many cases, we have had to meld the figures from several different Industry Experts or sources. This may also cause some totals to slightly exceed 100 percent.

We mentioned that if the rule of thumb was used properly, the price derived could be more accurate than simply multiplying the sales by the percentage rule or the SDE multiple. Reviewing market-driven data, one can reasonably assume that a 10 percent swing (that's our number; yours may be higher or lower) on either side of the percentage multiple would allow for the additions or subtractions to arrive at a more accurate multiple of annual sales. Using our example above, the 40 percent figure, and then using available benchmark data could lower or raise that percentage by 10 percent. The multiple then might be more accurate.

Critics of rules of thumb claim that a rule is simply an average and doesn't allow for the variables of each individual business. Comparing the business under review with industry standards—benchmarks—can allow one to raise or lower the percentage accordingly. A 40 percent figure then could be as low as 30 percent, or as high as 50 percent.

The Benchmark Data section can help you look at the vital signs of the business and compare them to similar businesses. Looking at the expenses as a percentage of annual sales can be a good start. For example, if the business under review has an occupancy percentage of 12 percent against an average 8 percent benchmark, perhaps the price then should be reduced to compensate for the higher rent. The rent is pretty much a fixed expense; but the higher the rent, the lower the profit. Certainly, a new owner could lower some of the expenses, but a trained labor force, for example, is hard to replace. Obviously, reducing the percentage multiple is a judgment call; but let's face it, even business valuation is not a science, but an art—and judgment plays a large part in it.

INDUSTRY EXPERTS' COMMENTS

This section allows our Industry Experts to add their own personal comments about this type of business. These comments may amplify a particular area or provide additional pricing information. Many times, these Industry Experts provide information or data that can't be found anywhere else. Some Industry Experts who own or manage an office with associates list themselves under more than one business. It may just mean that one or more agents in that office are experts in that industry.

RESOURCES

This section includes websites of companies, publications, and trade associations related to the particular types of businesses. Some are very informative; others are really only for members. However, many of the associations offer books or pamphlets or studies that can be informative. Every year, we find that more and more associations are charging nonmembers a high price for research materials that members can receive free or at a much lower price. *Nation's Restaurant News, Franchise Times, Auto Laundry News,* and *Convenience Store News* are examples of excellent resources, providing surveys and up-to-the-minute news about their industries. Don't forget that IBISWorld has great reports on many, many different businesses including franchises and many mom-and-pop type businesses.

FRANCHISES

We've included a List of Franchises in these introductory pages. Under the individual franchise entries, under Resources, we include parent companies, and from these sites, you may find additional franchises not in the *Guide*. Also, in addition to the specific franchises, there is a generalized Franchises entry.

If you can't find a rule of thumb for the franchise you are looking for, see if there is a similar type of franchise that has one. If that fails, go to the particular type of business that the franchise represents. You may add to or subtract from that rule of thumb based on your assessment of the value of the franchise—is it a plus or a minus? Even if there is a rule of thumb, it is always wise to refer to the type of business for more information.

For franchises, the value for Businesses/Units represents the number of U.S. franchises. Information about franchises comes from *Entrepreneur, Franchise Opportunities Guide, Franchise Times, Nation's Restaurant News*, and the websites of the franchises themselves.

FINAL NOTES

Some associations conduct their studies and surveys only every other year or even less frequently. In some cases, we have completed a particular section prior to the new data becoming available; however, we attempt to keep the information as current as possible.

We know that some of the information may be contradictory, but since we get it from those whom we believe to be experts, we still include it. The more information you have to sort through, the better your final conclusion. We think the information and data are reliable, but occasionally we find an error after the book has been printed.

Also, keep in mind that rules of thumb can vary by area and even by location. For example, businesses on the West Coast tend to sell for a higher price than the East Coast businesses, which sell for a higher price than the Midwest ones.

THANKS TO OUR INDUSTRY EXPERTS

We want to thank all who contributed rules of thumb, industry data, and information. It is a tribute to them that they are willing to contribute not only a rule of thumb, but also their knowledge on pricing.

We are focusing on the Industry Experts and in gratitude for their contribution are offering to put them on our website, provide BBP industry logos, and do anything else we can do to set them apart. We also give them complimentary use of the online version of the *Business Reference Guide*. If you're interested and feel that you are qualified, go to www.businessbrokeragepress.com and click on Services/Industry Experts.

AND WHEN ALL ELSE FAILS

Keep in mind that if it's not in the *Guide*, we really don't have a rule of thumb for that business. We get calls from people asking for a rule of thumb for some odd-ball type of business like Elephant Training Schools (not really). Honestly, if we knew of one, it would be in the *Guide*. We're always happy to help if we can, but unless there is sufficient sales data, there generally isn't a rule of thumb available. If you can't find what you need, here are some suggestions.

- Call a similar business in your area and see if they are aware of one.
- Check with a vendor, distributor, or equipment manufacturer and see if someone there can help.
- Call a trade association for that particular industry and see if they can direct you to someone who can help. Don't do it by email or fax, but call and speak to someone. Trade associations really don't want to get involved, but an individual might get you to the next step.

If none of the above helps, then we're afraid you have to accept the fact that there just may not be one for the business you are checking on.

List of Businesses

List of Franchises

Business Profiles

A&W Restaurants (A&W Root Beer) (Franchise)

| NAICS 722513 | SIC 5812-06 | Businesses/Units 503

Rules of Thumb

- 45% annual sales plus inventory

INDUSTRY MULTIPLES

Acquisition multiples below are calculated medians using US private industry transactions. Data updated annually. Last update: August 2023.

VALUATION MULTIPLE (MEDIAN VALUE)

UNDER $1 MILLION NET SALES

MVIC/Net Sales.	0.31
MVIC/Gross Profit	0.48
MVIC/SDE	1.67
MVIC/EBITDA	2.21

$1 MILLION–$5 MILLION NET SALES

MVIC/Net Sales.	0.39
MVIC/Gross Profit	0.60
MVIC/SDE	2.43
MVIC/EBITDA	2.98

OVER $5 MILLION NET SALES

MVIC/Net Sales.	0.89
MVIC/Gross Profit	2.08
MVIC/SDE	4.98
MVIC/EBITDA	12.81

Source: DealStats (formerly Pratt's Stats), 2023 (Portland, OR: Business Valuation Resources, LLC), www.bvresources.com/dealstats

PRICING TIPS

Approx. Total Investment: $276,000 to $1,469,554

BENCHMARK DATA

Recommended square footage is between 1,500 and 2,000 square feet.

RESOURCES

- A&W Restaurants: https://awrestaurants.com
- Franchise information: https://awfranchising.com

AAMCO (Franchise)

| NAICS 811114 | SIC 7537-01 | Businesses/Units 549

Rules of Thumb

- 40%–42% annual sales includes inventory

INDUSTRY MULTIPLES

Acquisition multiples below are calculated medians using US private industry transactions. Data updated annually. Last update: August 2023.

A

VALUATION MULTIPLE (MEDIAN VALUE)

UNDER $1 MILLION NET SALES

MVIC/Net Sales.	0.40
MVIC/Gross Profit	0.47
MVIC/SDE	1.60
MVIC/EBITDA	12.57

$1 MILLION–$5 MILLION NET SALES	N/A
OVER $5 MILLION NET SALES	N/A

Source: DealStats (formerly Pratt's Stats), 2023 (Portland, OR: Business Valuation Resources, LLC), www.bvresources.com/dealstats

PRICING TIPS

Approx. Total Investment: $223,600 to $330,500

"As a candidate, you should have a minimum of $65,000 in liquid capital and a net worth of at least $250,000 to get started."

Source: https://franchises.aamco.com/auto-franchise-cost/

BENCHMARK DATA

EXPENSES (% OF ANNUAL SALES)

Production labor costs	20%
Sales/Labor.	08% to 10%
Occupancy	06% to 10%
Profit (estimated pretax)	10% to 20%

COST OF SALES

Parts & Fluids	22%
Production Labor (All Technical Employees)	20%
Towing	01%
Misc. Production Supplies	03%
Total Cost of Sales	46%

SALES & ADMINISTRATION EXPENSES

Salaries (Center Mgr. & Office)	10%
Rent.	08%
Insurance	03%
Utilities	01%
Advertising-Yellow Pages	08%
Telephone	01%
Legal/Accounting	01%
Bank Fees/Bad Debt	01%
Training	01%
Total Sales & Administration Expenses	34%
Net Profit	20%

QUESTIONS

- Does the shop meet AAMCO standards?
- Historic sales and change in demographics?
- What is ratio of major to minor repairs?
- Ratio of general auto to transmission repair?
- Ratio of fleet (commercial) vs. retail?
- Percentage of "comebacks" (warranty repairs)?
- Is the manager following the AAMCO spiel?

EXPERT COMMENTS

The Internet has changed the marketing and advertising model—lowering cost but making it more difficult for the small independent to compete with the franchises in the major market areas.

- AAMCO: https://www.aamco.com
- Franchise information: https://franchises.aamco.com

A

Accounting Firms/CPAs

	NAICS 541211		SIC 8721-01		Businesses/Units 92,900
	Profit $26 B		Wages $56.2 B		Annual Growth Future 1.0%
					Annual Growth Past 1.7%

Rules of Thumb
- 100%–125% annual revenues plus inventory
- 2.2 x EBITDA
- 2–3 x SDE plus inventory

INDUSTRY MULTIPLES

Acquisition multiples below are calculated medians using US private industry transactions. Data updated annually. Last update: August 2023.

VALUATION MULTIPLE (MEDIAN VALUE)

UNDER $1 MILLION NET SALES
MVIC/Net Sales.	0.97
MVIC/Gross Profit	1.00
MVIC/SDE	2.04
MVIC/EBITDA	2.92

$1 MILLION–$5 MILLION NET SALES
MVIC/Net Sales.	0.98
MVIC/Gross Profit	1.07
MVIC/SDE	2.75
MVIC/EBITDA	4.95

OVER $5 MILLION NET SALES	N/A

Source: DealStats (formerly Pratt's Stats), 2023 (Portland, OR: Business Valuation Resources, LLC), www.bvresources.com/dealstats

PRICING TIPS

The two most important factors in valuations for these firms continues to be location and profitability.

The percent of annual gross varies from 0.7 to 1.3 times gross depending on the SDE (cash flow to owner), which can vary widely but is generally 40 to 50 percent of gross revenue for a tax practice or CPA firm with staff. For the sole practitioner with no staff, which is common, the achieved percent of gross revenue may be much higher, especially if the practice is operated from a home office. Buyers want staff with an acquisition, due to the shortage of accountants in both industry and public practice. We carefully look to the type of services performed, such as financial accounting, attestation, and tax reporting/compliance and planning. The higher the average fees for the Form 1040, 1120S, 1120, 1065, 990, etc., the higher the multiple of gross. If most of the work is performed during the first four months of the calendar year, then the practice is not as desirable. Work performed throughout the year—which includes quarterly compiled financial statements, quarterly tax reporting, extended tax returns, and tax planning and consulting—all can entice a prospective buyer. The location is very important!

A Practices in outlying and remote areas are more difficult to locate a willing and able buyer. The accounting profession is really changing! The younger practitioners want to perform services remotely, sometimes from out of state, and use technology to the maximum for labor efficiency. The old-timers who have not embraced technology and taken their practice paperless may find that they will have to transfer their practice on what is called the old earnout, which was the standard in the 70s, 80s, and 90s before SBA financing limits on goodwill were greatly increased. Earnouts can take the appearance of a pay as you go for the buyer. Example: I will pay you 20 percent a year of what I collect on your clients over a five-year period. No interest and greater risk to the practitioner.

Accounting firms generally sell for 100 to 130 percent of annual revenue. There are circumstances in very rural markets or major metro areas where firms will sell outside of this range. Virtual firms tend to sell for the very high end of market value.

Geographic location is the first consideration when determining market value. Practices located in major metropolitan areas will naturally be priced higher than those located in rural areas. Businesses with higher percentages of business clients, or those with recurring monthly revenue, tend to have higher market values, as well.

Values paid for firms can run between 0.8 x revenue and as high as 1.75 x annual revenue, but most sales fall in the 1.0 to 1.3 multiple of annual revenue range.

Multiples range from 1.0 to 1.4 x annual gross billings. Typically based on a client retention calculation.

BENCHMARK DATA

STATISTICS (ACCOUNTING SERVICES)

Number of Establishments	92,900
Average Profit Margin	18.0%
Revenue per Employee	$244,000
Average Number of Employees	6.5
Average Wages per Employee	$94,682

PRODUCTS AND SERVICES SEGMENTATION

Financial auditing	36.6%
Individual tax preparation	16.8%
Other	14.7%
Corporate tax preparation	14.5%
General accounting	11.6%
Financial statement review	2.0%
Other financial assurance services	2.0%
Tax planning and consulting	1.8%

MAJOR MARKET SEGMENTATION

Finance sector	24.9%
Individuals	16.8%
Other businesses	14.3%
Utilities and mining sector	11.4%
Manufacturing and industrial sector	11.1%
Public sector	10.2%
Retail sector	5.6%
Nonprofit organizations	5.3%

INDUSTRY COSTS

Profit	18.0%
Wages	38.9%
Purchases	3.1%

Depreciation	1.3%
Marketing	1.0%
Rent & Utilities	4.2%
Other	33.5%

MARKET SHARE

Deloitte Touche Tohmatsu Ltd.	9.8%
EY	4.0%
PricewaterhouseCoopers LLP	3.9%
KPMG International	2.5%

Employee should be able to bill out $100K to $150K. Partners, $200K.

EXPENSES (% OF ANNUAL SALES)

Cost of Goods	.0% to 05%
Occupancy Costs	05% to 15%
Payroll/Labor Costs.	25% to 35%
Profit (pretax)	30% to 40%

QUESTIONS

- Listen carefully to what their ideal transition would look like. Who is their ideal buyer and how to they want to work with them after a sale? What things are most important to them regarding a sale?
- Get a feel for the seller's clientele: general ages of clients, types of businesses, size of businesses, etc. Ask about how the seller conducts business, or inter- acts, with the clients: in-person meetings (seller's office or client's), by mail, electronic transmission.
- What is your transition plan? What are you planning on doing after the sale? Why are you selling? How capable is the staff?
- What do your clients expect from you and do they get a good deal of face time with you? What is the average age of your clients? How do you bill and how quickly do you get paid? Are your clients categorized by A, B, and C. If so, how many fall into each category?
- Buyers should review historical financials/tax returns. They should ask if staff is expected to stay when the firm is sold. They should ask if any large clients are growing very fast or getting ready to sell/retire. There are too many questions to list here. Every acquisition opportunity will have its own questions that should be asked, and some may be unique to the firm being considered for acquisition.
- What are the plans for the staff?—plan to leave, or stay with a buyer? What are the qualifications of those employees? How much interaction with the clients is done by the owner versus by those employees?
- Do the employees have noncompetes in place? Will you sign a noncompete? Why have the revenues increased/decreased the last few years?
- Questions related to tax software, operations, staffing, and marketing are all great questions for a buyer. Be sure to review concentration issues within the book. Sometimes concentration is not with an individual or entity but a series of entities and individuals that are somehow related. Make sure that your bill rate matches the buyers' or is within reason. Clients don't stick around for large price increases after an ownership change. Spend time developing a transition program with the seller. As a buyer, you need to know how long the seller can stick around to help with client transitions.
- What characteristics would be important to successfully service your clients? Are your clients aging, or fairly young? How have you been able to grow your clientele?

A

- Where do your clients come from?—advertising, referrals, community involvement, etc. What services are offered, and what are the average fees? Do you have any clients that represent more than 10 percent of annual revenue? Do you consider your practice to be a niche or specialized business, or do you have a certain industry that represents a large percent of the clientele?
- Any out-of-state clients? Has the owner or staff had any disciplinary issues with their CPA/EA license? Is the staff aware of the sale? Are there any clients the owner feels they should fire, or any problem clients? What is the A/R of the firm? Does the seller use engagement letters?

INDUSTRY TREND

Shift to more of subscription model pricing with more advisory services. More remote work and flexibility for employees, and more access to overseas workers. AI will be a factor in streamlining accounting processes and in allowing accountants to focus on more value-add services.

Market has become somewhat saturated, and multiples have been dropping.

We expect the market for selling small accounting firms to continue to be strong the next several years. There are more sellers entering the market, but there is still very high demand for many firms in major metro areas.

"Traditionally, reconciling financial statements at the end of a reporting period—whether monthly, quarterly, or annually—has been a labor-intensive process that can take weeks to complete....But one of accounting's most ambitious goals aims to change that: A zero-day close leverages intelligent automation and continuously available, up-to-date information to close the books at any time, dramatically accelerating the pace of internal reporting and data analysis. No wonder 86% of finance executives say they've set their sights on achieving a faster, real-time close by 2025, according to Gartner, with more than half of respondents already deploying investments such as general ledger technology and workflow automation."

Source: "3 trends that will reshape accounting and finance in 2023" by Philippa Lawrence, March 15, 2023, https://www.journalofaccountancy.com/news/2023/mar/3-trends-reshape-accounting-finance-2023.html

Demand for these businesses remains strong. Changes in tax legislation, extended tax seasons, etc., have forced some CPAs to consider selling sooner than they had planned for. Buyers are still eager to grow through acquisition—just as aggressively as in recent years.

With baby boomers continuing to retire at a rapid pace, the availability of firms for sale all over the country should remain high.

Market activity has been fairly consistent over the last 25 years.

Tax practices with high average fees are in demand, and staffing issues continue to be a problem for the CPA profession, so a strong staff is critical to creating intrinsic value and creating interest with the buyers.

There is a rising cost of human capital. It's extremely difficult to find qualified staff. Look for costs to increase in this area. There is also a substantial amount of outsourcing to India and other foreign countries, as well as outsourcing the input functions of the return and bookkeeping process to technology. OCR technology and AI are quickly taking hold in the industry due to staffing shortages.

Larger firms are diversifying revenue streams away from just tax and accounting. Much more emphasis has been placed on wealth management, IT, consulting, law, and insurance, to name a few different mixes we have seen in the last few years.

It is an aging profession; more existing practitioners are at, or beyond, retirement age than those that are younger getting into the business.

"Profit has decreased during the period due to increases in competition combined with recovery following the pandemic. Advisory and consulting operations are the fastest-growing segments for the largest operators. Several large operators have made extensive capital investments to boost productivity. The industry is expected to benefit from an increasing number of businesses. Operators will primarily focus on purchasing smaller, highly profitable companies. Most accounting companies are expected to only continue servicing high-wealth individuals. Increased demand for industry services has drastically outpaced the number of new accountants entering the industry."

Source: IBISWorld Industry at a Glance

EXPERT COMMENTS

Advice for buyers: develop a clear plan for transitioning the business, and allow yourself enough time before the next tax season. Acquiring a firm with the same software will save you a lot of headaches. Advice for sellers: prepare a revenue breakdown by service and return type, and have a list of clients with the type of work performed and the billings for the last couple years. Timing of when you list is very important and should line up with your exit goals.

For sellers, understand the process can take some time to find the right buyer under the right terms; don't wait until you get to the point that you can't do this any longer. For buyers, understand that no two practices, or sellers, are alike; find opportunities that fit your skill set and sellers that you feel confident in working with through the transition, and possibly beyond.

Do not be the cheapest tax preparer on the block.

Be interested in serving others.

The one silver lining from the recent pandemic is that practitioners and clients have been forced to work in a more virtual manner. As such, efficiencies and profitability have increased.

Study the Rosenberg averages.

Advice to sellers: Hire a broker that specializes in the sale of these firms. Running a professional process helps ensure the firm is sold at the higher end of market value.

Advice to buyers: Perform solid due diligence, and do not make a lot of change in a firm you acquire before you have built solid relationships with the staff and clients.

The market for selling firms in major metro areas continues to be very active. Rural firms can take longer to sell.

The CPA professional who effectively communicates with clients and staff to deliver proactive advice to help individuals and businesses navigate the accounting, taxes, and management of life's challenges will always be in high demand—and the market is strong for growth and profitability of their firm. Lifelong continuing education is a must.

Buyers: it's a rapidly changing and consolidating industry with incredible recurring income. Treat your clients right and build trust with your clients. This will allow you to sell into other revenue streams and diversify and grow your business. Set up the business with a high degree of technology, and think through staffing to avoid production problems down the road. Sellers: it's still a seller's market.

It's likely that you will be able to sell your business in the way you want to sell it. There is a high degree of demand for practices.

Buyer should understand the staffing needs intimately before acquisition. Make sure to understand how the seller is using technology and outsourcing.

Sellers: prepare; don't wait until you are to the point you can't go through another tax season. Keep overhead costs in line; don't overpay staff to complete work that could be done by the owner.

Buyers: be prepared to move quickly on the listings that fit your requirements. At least have a conversation with a lender to get an idea of the listings that should be targeted. If it is your first acquisition, start small and take incremental steps on future ones.

FINANCING

Seller usually provides a one- or two-year look-back assurance and will carry 10 percent of the sale price.

Terms vary depending on location of the selling firm and the seller's circumstances. It's not uncommon to see deals structured with 80 to 90 percent or more of the purchase price paid at closing for firms where the seller is able to provide transitional assistance and the firm is in a major metro area. At the same time, deals where a sole practitioner or one firm owner dies or has a major health event and cannot service the clients will sometimes be structured with little to no money paid up front and the balance in some form of seller note.

The majority of the transactions we do are structured with down payments of 50 to 100 percent of the purchase price. Many buyers utilize third-party financing with SBA loans. There is some conventional financing available, also.

Typically 80 percent bank, 20 percent seller; 50 to 100 percent paid at closing

Small businesses (less than $200,000) are generally completed with a down and seller financing. Generally there is some variable to purchase price (often revenue) where a clawback is possible if the clients don't effectively make the move to the buying firm. Larger firms are almost always down, seller carry of 10 to 30 percent, and a bank. Conventional programs specializing in CPA acquisitions are available, as well as SBA.

A mix of each, depending upon the size of the transaction and the expectations of the seller, which may be driven geographically. Typically, sellers see significant down payments (70 to 80 percent) with the balance held in a note. At times, this is driven by a lender to keep LTV ratios within their credit policy.

RESOURCES

- IBISWorld, January 2023: https://www.ibisworld.com
- Accounting Practice Exchange: https://accountingpracticeexchange.com/
- Accounting Today: https://www.accountingtoday.com
- AICPA—American Institute of CPAs: https://www.aicpa.org
- Arizona State Board of Accountancy: https://www.azaccountancy.gov
- ASCPA—Arizona Society of CPAs: https://www.ascpa.com
- COCPA—Colorado Society of CPAs: https://www.cocpa.org
- eCPAn—Entrepreneurial CPAs Network: https://www.ecpan.org
- MNCPA—Minnesota Society of CPAs: https://www.mncpa.org
- MAPA—Minnesota Association of Public Accountants: https://mapa-mn.com

Accounting Firms/Practices

| NAICS 541219 | SIC 8721-01

Rules of Thumb

- 2.5–3.5 x SDE plus inventory (if any)
- 1–1.25 x annual revenues (non-CPA) plus inventory
- 3–4 x EBIT
- 3–4 x EBITDA

INDUSTRY MULTIPLES

Acquisition multiples below are calculated medians using US private industry transactions. Data updated annually. Last update: August 2023.

VALUATION MULTIPLE (MEDIAN VALUE)

UNDER $1 MILLION NET SALES

MVIC/Net Sales	0.85
MVIC/Gross Profit	0.85
MVIC/SDE	2.22
MVIC/EBITDA	4.32

$1 MILLION–$5 MILLION NET SALES

MVIC/Net Sales	0.99
MVIC/Gross Profit	1.09
MVIC/SDE	3.56
MVIC/EBITDA	4.17

OVER $5 MILLION NET SALES

MVIC/Net Sales	1.33
MVIC/Gross Profit	1.97
MVIC/SDE	N/A
MVIC/EBITDA	N/A

Source: DealStats (formerly Pratt's Stats), 2023 (Portland, OR: Business Valuation Resources, LLC), www.bvresources.com/dealstats

PRICING TIPS

Accounting firms generally sell for 100 to 130 percent of annual revenue. There are circumstances in very rural markets or major metro areas where firms will sell outside of this range. Virtual firms tend to sell for the very high end of market value.

Pricing for these businesses varies based on their profitability, size, and revenue mix. Highly profitable firms with several business clients subscribing to recurring cloud-based services and lower employee costs can earn a higher multiple, while practices that are focused on nonrecurring individual tax preparation services with lower margins earn lower multiples.

BENCHMARK DATA

On average, billing per CPA should be at least $150,000 to $250,000.

Number of repeat clients on the book; it usually takes at least 250–350 to break even, and above that to be profitable.

EXPENSES (% OF ANNUAL SALES)

Cost of Goods	.0% to 10%
Occupancy Costs	10% to 20%
Payroll/Labor Costs	30% to 40%
Profit (pretax)	35% to 45%

QUESTIONS

- Buyers should review historical financials/tax returns. They should ask a seller why they are selling. They should ask if staff is expected to stay when the firm is sold. They should ask if any large clients are growing very fast or getting ready to sell/retire. There are too many questions to list here. Every acquisition opportunity will have its own questions that should be asked, and some may be unique to the firm being considered for acquisition.
- Revenue mix, opportunities for growth, contractual relationships with clients, and client retention issues
- How long will the seller be willing to stay involved? Should be at least one tax season.
- Learn about the employees, price of services, and niches.

INDUSTRY TREND

We expect the market for selling small accounting firms to continue to be strong the next several years. There are more sellers entering the market, but there is still very high demand for many firms in major metro areas.

Outsourcing and technology solutions will drive margins up but also disrupt the business model for practices that are not prepared for the transition.

EXPERT COMMENTS

There are many brokers that serve this industry that can provide information and expertise on these transactions. Deals are structured many different ways. Whether buying or selling an accounting firm, I would suggest speaking with someone who has experience working on these types of transactions.

These businesses are in high demand, especially if they have implemented the technology tools and processes to scale quickly. Certifications like CPA and EA help with tax preparation services; however, bookkeeping and fractional CFO services are viable options for accounting professionals to grow with a profitable recurring revenue model.

FINANCING

Terms vary depending on location of the selling firm and the seller's circumstances. It's not uncommon to see deals structured with 80 to 90 percent or more of the purchase price paid at closing for firms where the seller is able to provide transitional assistance and the firm is in a major metro area. At the same time, deals where a sole practitioner or one firm owner dies or has a major health event and cannot service the clients will sometimes be structured with little to no money paid up front and the balance in some form of seller note.

Seller financing is common in this business, and typical terms include 20 percent seller financing with the remaining coming from the buyer or third-party sources.

RESOURCES

- Buying a Practice by Leon Faris and Vance Wingo: https://www.cpasales.com/buyer-manual
- NSA—National Society of Accountants: https://www.nsacct.org
- TXCPA San Antonio: https://www.tx.cpa/sanantonio/

Accounting/Tax Practices

	NAICS 541213		SIC 7291-01		Businesses/Units 149,371
	Profit $2.7 B		Wages $4.6 B		Annual Growth Future 1.2%
					Annual Growth Past 3.9%

Rules of Thumb

- 1–1.35 x annual revenues plus inventory
- 2–3 x SDE plus inventory
- 5–7 x EBIT
- 4–6 x EBITDA

INDUSTRY MULTIPLES

Acquisition multiples below are calculated medians using US private industry transactions. Data updated annually. Last update: August 2023.

VALUATION MULTIPLE (MEDIAN VALUE)

UNDER $1 MILLION NET SALES	
MVIC/Net Sales.	0.89
MVIC/Gross Profit	0.89
MVIC/SDE	1.88
MVIC/EBITDA	3.05
$1 MILLION–$5 MILLION NET SALES	
MVIC/Net Sales.	0.53
MVIC/Gross Profit	0.64
MVIC/SDE	1.90
MVIC/EBITDA	3.02
OVER $5 MILLION NET SALES	
MVIC/Net Sales.	1.83
MVIC/Gross Profit	1.83
MVIC/SDE	5.75
MVIC/EBITDA	6.31

Source: DealStats (formerly Pratt's Stats), 2023 (Portland, OR: Business Valuation Resources, LLC), www.bvresources.com/dealstats

PRICING TIPS

The most reliable multiple is net revenue—revenue after discounts and refunds. The range of this multiple is from 0.9 to 1.15 and takes into consideration location, visibility, average net fee, growth trend, retention, and walkout rate. In a mature store, a growth rate of around 5 percent is healthy, and the return count growth should be fairly close to the revenue growth. If the revenue growth is significantly higher than the return count growth, the owner has raised pricing perhaps too much and retention will suffer.

Tax and audit services are recurring, thereby resulting in a higher multiple.

Firms sell primarily as a multiple of gross recurring revenue and sell between 0.75 and 1.25, while 0.75 to 1 x revenue are firms in rural or small markets with low demand. Firms in metro areas sell between 1 and 1.25 x gross revenue on average, although there are situations (very low margin or very high margin) which cause sales outside of this general area. We see firms with SDE margins between 30 and 70 percent with the 30 and 70 percent on the flat portion of the bell curve. Most firms have SDE margins in the 40 to 60 percent range.

Average fees per type of tax return prepared are important. Buyers generally are looking for revenue that is spread throughout the year, including profitable consulting and write-up work. Longevity of staff is of great value when retaining clients. Paperless and cloud-based is of importance to buyer vs. paper-based practices.

BENCHMARK DATA

STATISTICS (TAX PREPARATION SERVICES)

Number of Establishments	149,371
Average Profit Margin	18.9%
Revenue per Employee	$48,600
Average Number of Employees. . . .	2.0
Average Wages per Employee . . .	$15,554

PRODUCTS AND SERVICES SEGMENTATION

Standard tax preparation	59.1%
Full-service tax preparation. . . .	31.8%
Basic tax preparation	6.4%
Tax-related financial products . . .	2.7%

INDUSTRY COSTS

Profit	18.9%
Wages	32.0%
Purchases	3.5%
Depreciation	1.6%
Marketing	1.2%
Rent & Utilities	4.9%
Other	37.9%

MARKET SHARE

Intuit Inc.	4.2%
RSM US LLP	2.7%
H&R Block Inc.	2.5%
Crowe Global	0.9%

Average net fee = $275 to $375; 50 to 55 percent retention is normal; 3 to 5 percent walkout rate is normal.

Employee should be able to bill out $100K to $200K.

Firms sell primarily as a multiple of gross recurring revenue and sell between 0.75 and 1.25, while 0.75 to 1 x revenue are firms in rural or small markets with low demand. Firms in metro areas sell between 1 and 1.25 x gross revenue on average, although there are situations (very low margin or very high margin) which cause sales outside of this general area. We see firms with SDE margins between 30 and 70 percent with the 30 and 70 percent on the flat portion of the bell curve. Most firms have SDE margins in the 40 to 60 percent range.

EXPENSES (% OF ANNUAL SALES)

Cost of Goods	02%
Occupancy Costs	05% to 10%
Payroll/Labor Costs.	25% to 35%
Profit (pretax)	30% to 40%

QUESTIONS

- The status of the lease—is it transferable and/or renewable? Will the franchisor transfer the exiting franchise agreement to the buyer? Who are your key employees and are they happy? The age of the computers and networking hardware, and how much life do they have?
- Who are your customers exactly? How many audits do you conduct? Do you audit any publicly traded companies? How many CPAs do you have in your practice?

- Why are you leaving the industry? Do you have nonsolicits with staff? Age of staff? Average age of clients? Wealth management relationships?
- Are they selling the complete practice or retaining work?
- Why are you selling? What do you plan to do after you sell? When was your last fee increase? History of the firm—all organic growth or some acquisition growth? Are there any clients that make up more than 5 percent of the revenue of the practice? Do employees have employment agreements including nonsolicitation agreements?
- How much of revenue is earned from tax return preparation and how much from accounting or bookkeeping? What type of work does your staff do? What tax and accounting software do you use? What is the billing rate per hour? Do you bill by hour or project? How long have your clients been with this firm? How long have the employees been with this firm?
- What is the breakdown between tax, write-up, consulting, and audit revenues? Also, who else in the firm can do the tax and write-up work? Who reviews the work?

INDUSTRY TREND

The big four franchises (Liberty Tax, Jackson Hewitt, ATAX, and H&R Block) will take market share from mom-and-pop tax and accounting firms in the low-income individual tax prep industry. The mom-and-pop firms will shift to small business tax returns and higher-income individuals and not compete in the lower-income market as time goes forward.

Historically more buyers than sellers, but this ratio is changing.

Shifting from a seller's market several years ago to a buyer's market. Sellers need to be willing to make some concessions like a holdback for nonreturning clients, staying on to work as a production arm of the firm after sale, and others. Few buyers have extra capacity, so it's imperative that sellers remain flexible in their role after sale. Staying helps keep clients and staff in place until new relationships can be established with the buying firm.

Some buyers now are demanding interviews and contracts with employees prior to sale—very difficult negotiation point.

"Major companies have adapted their business model to incorporate e-filing software. Using online filing software is more affordable and less time-consuming for individuals. Demand for tax preparation services is influenced by general economic conditions. High economic growth will keep revenue growth positive. Industry businesses will need to focus on strategies which integrate online and offline service. The industry will become more consolidated. Major players have adapted to a digital environment by modifying price structures and business models."

Source: IBISWorld Industry at a Glance

EXPERT COMMENTS

As with any business, cash flow is king. Other important things to evaluate are the retention of employees and customers, the location, the average net fee, and the state of the office FF&E.

Pay attention to noncompete issues and capacity! Buyers should complete an onsite review of tax returns to make sure quality work papers exist.

Experience is very important.

FINANCING

SBA will finance this franchise with proper cash flow, and seller financing is very common.

Typically a combination of buyer, bank, and seller financed, depending on the size of the acquisition.

Deals under $250K are mostly buyer down and seller carry with the seller note carrying some retentive variables. Larger firms have a seller carry (also retentive) and buyer down, but the bank sits in the middle with the largest part of the deal. Bank subordination notes have become very difficult to deal with.

RESOURCES

- IBISWorld, January 2023: https://www.ibisworld.com
- AAFA—American Association of Finance & Accounting: https://aafa.com
- AICPA—American Institute of CPAs: https://www.aicpa.org
- American Accounting Association: https://aaahq.org
- ASCPA—Arizona Society of Certified Public Accountants: https://www.ascpa.com
- COCPA—Colorado Society of CPAs: https://www.cocpa.org
- eCPAn—Entrepreneurial CPA's Network: https://www.ecpan.org
- IMA—Institute of Management Accountants: https://www.imanet.org
- NAEA—National Association of Enrolled Agents: https://www.naea.org
- NATP—National Association of Tax Professionals: https://www.natptax.com/Pages/default.aspx
- NSA—National Society of Accountants: https://www.nsacct.org
- NSTP—National Society of Tax Professionals: https://www.nstp.org

Ace Hardware (Franchise)

| NAICS 444140 | SIC 5251-04 | Businesses/Units 4,645

Rules of Thumb

- 45% annual sales plus inventory

INDUSTRY MULTIPLES

Acquisition multiples below are calculated medians using US private industry transactions. Data updated annually. Last update: August 2023.

VALUATION MULTIPLE (MEDIAN VALUE)

UNDER $1 MILLION NET SALES

MVIC/Net Sales	0.54
MVIC/Gross Profit	1.32
MVIC/SDE	3.67
MVIC/EBITDA	4.70

$1 MILLION–$5 MILLION NET SALES

MVIC/Net Sales	0.38
MVIC/Gross Profit	1.01
MVIC/SDE	3.19
MVIC/EBITDA	5.59

OVER $5 MILLION NET SALES — N/A

Source: DealStats (formerly Pratt's Stats), 2023 (Portland, OR: Business Valuation Resources, LLC), www.bvresources.com/dealstats

PRICING TIPS

Approx. Total Investment: $292,000 to $2,119,230

Sales seem to indicate that smaller sales bring a higher multiple (50%+) than stores with sales over $1 million, which seem to bring lower multiples. Price is plus inventory, and that may be the reason for lower multiples for larger stores.

RESOURCES

- Ace Hardware: https://www.acehardware.com
- Franchise information: https://myace.com

ACE Cash Express

| NAICS 522390 | SIC 6099-03 | Businesses/Units 850 |

Rules of Thumb

- 1.25 x annual sales plus inventory

INDUSTRY MULTIPLES

Acquisition multiples below are calculated medians using US private industry transactions. Data updated annually. Last update: August 2023.

VALUATION MULTIPLE (MEDIAN VALUE)

UNDER $1 MILLION NET SALES
MVIC/Net Sales.	0.42
MVIC/Gross Profit	0.47
MVIC/SDE	1.28
MVIC/EBITDA	0.82

$1 MILLION–$5 MILLION NET SALES
MVIC/Net Sales.	0.15
MVIC/Gross Profit	0.49
MVIC/SDE	1.92
MVIC/EBITDA	1.97

OVER $5 MILLION NET SALES
MVIC/Net Sales.	0.04
MVIC/Gross Profit	1.66
MVIC/SDE	N/A
MVIC/EBITDA	7.90

Source: DealStats (formerly Pratt's Stats), 2023 (Portland, OR: Business Valuation Resources, LLC), www.bvresources.com/dealstats

PRICING TIPS

This company is publicly held, and their annual report is available online and is an excellent resource.

RESOURCES

- ACE Cash Express: https://www.acecashexpress.com

Adhesive Manufacturing

| NAICS 325520 | Businesses/Units 418 |

| Profit $1.2 B | Wages $2.3 B | Annual Growth Future 2.1% |
| | | Annual Growth Past 0.4% |

INDUSTRY MULTIPLES

Acquisition multiples below are calculated medians using US private industry transactions. Data updated annually. Last update: August 2023.

VALUATION MULTIPLE (MEDIAN VALUE)

UNDER $1 MILLION NET SALES	N/A
$1 MILLION–$5 MILLION NET SALES	
MVIC/Net Sales	0.97
MVIC/Gross Profit	3.45
MVIC/SDE	14.52
MVIC/EBITDA	11.44
OVER $5 MILLION NET SALES	
MVIC/Net Sales	3.11
MVIC/Gross Profit	9.09
MVIC/SDE	N/A
MVIC/EBITDA	N/A

Source: DealStats (formerly Pratt's Stats), 2023 (Portland, OR: Business Valuation Resources, LLC), www.bvresources.com/dealstats

BENCHMARK DATA

STATISTICS (ADHESIVE MANUFACTURING)

Number of Establishments	596
Average Profit Margin	6.3%
Revenue per Employee	$673,000
Average Number of Employees	49.0
Average Wages per Employee	$80,287

PRODUCTS AND SERVICES SEGMENTATION

Nonstructural caulking components	32.4%
Synthetic resin and rubber adhesives	24.9%
Other	17.8%
Structural sealants	15.6%
Natural-based glues and adhesives	9.4%

MAJOR MARKET SEGMENTATION

Manufacturers	54.4%
Wholesalers	23.5%
Construction	13.3%
Other	8.8%

INDUSTRY COSTS

Profit	6.3%
Wages	11.9%
Purchases	46.0%
Depreciation	1.7%
Marketing	0.3%
Rent & Utilities	1.8%
Other	32.0%

MARKET SHARE

Henkel Ag & Co. Kgaa	13.4%
3M Company	6.0%
Fuller H B Co	4.7%

INDUSTRY TREND

"The reopening of businesses caused a spike in need for adhesives. The price of plastic material and resin skyrocketed in 2021 following major supply chain disruptions. Automobile and aircraft manufacturing will remain a critical market for adhesive manufacturers. While imports are set to expand slightly, their share of domestic demand is set to drop. Nonresidential construction markets will offer a breath of fresh air for manufacturers. The prices of plastic materials and resin have been highly volatile, attributed to fluctuations in the price of crude oil and natural gas."

Source: IBISWorld Industry at a Glance

RESOURCES

• IBISWorld, January 2023: https://www.ibisworld.com

Advertising Agencies

	NAICS 541810		SIC 7311-01		Businesses/Units 88,225
	Profit $5.1 B		Wages $22.9 B		Annual Growth Future 1.3%
					Annual Growth Past 2.5%

INDUSTRY MULTIPLES

Acquisition multiples below are calculated medians using US private industry transactions. Data updated annually. Last update: August 2023.

VALUATION MULTIPLE (MEDIAN VALUE)

UNDER $1 MILLION NET SALES
MVIC/Net Sales 0.68
MVIC/Gross Profit 1.09
MVIC/SDE 2.26
MVIC/EBITDA 2.62

$1 MILLION–$5 MILLION NET SALES
MVIC/Net Sales 0.57
MVIC/Gross Profit 1.03
MVIC/SDE 3.13
MVIC/EBITDA 4.80

OVER $5 MILLION NET SALES
MVIC/Net Sales 0.73
MVIC/Gross Profit 2.05
MVIC/SDE 3.91
MVIC/EBITDA 7.49

Source: DealStats (formerly Pratt's Stats), 2023 (Portland, OR: Business Valuation Resources, LLC), www.bvresources.com/dealstats

BENCHMARK DATA

STATISTICS (ADVERTISING AGENCIES)

Number of Establishments 92,584
Average Profit Margin 6.9%
Revenue per Employee $273,000
Average Number of Employees 2.9
Average Wages per Employee $85,538

PRODUCTS AND SERVICES SEGMENTATION

Bundled creative and placement services 60.0%
Creative services 23.9%
Media buying and planning services 8.4%
All other services 6.0%
Sales promotion services 0.9%
Public relations services 0.8%

MAJOR MARKET SEGMENTATION

Other	25.2%
Technology, media and telecommunication	18.3%
Food and beverage producers	13.5%
Automotive	13.3%
Consumer packaged goods	10.0%
Financial Services	8.7%
Retail	7.0%
Travel and entertainment	4.0%

INDUSTRY COSTS

Profit	6.9%
Wages	31.2%
Purchases	6.8%
Depreciation	0.8%
Marketing	5.3%
Rent & Utilities	7.3%
Other	41.8%

MARKET SHARE

Omnicom Group Inc.	7.0%
WPP PLC	5.2%
WPP Alliance Data Systems Corp.	1.8%
Publicis Groupe SA	.1.3%

INDUSTRY TREND

"Larger companies demanded creative services for new COVID-19-focused marketing campaigns. The internet provides a more cost-effective advertising method. Niche agencies specializing in digital advertising benefit from this fragmentation. Large technology companies will steal revenue from small- and medium-sized advertising agencies. Profit for advertising agencies will benefit from viral marketing. Growth in connected TV advertising will be a boon for advertising agencies. Rising demand for digital services has motivated more companies to enter the industry."

Source: IBISWorld Industry at a Glance

RESOURCES

- IBISWorld, January 2023: https://www.ibisworld.com
- 4A's: https://www.aaaa.org

AIM Mail Centers (Franchise)

| NAICS 561431 | Businesses/Units 44

Rules of Thumb

- 44% annual sales
- 2 x SDE

INDUSTRY MULTIPLES

Acquisition multiples below are calculated medians using US private industry transactions. Data updated annually. Last update: August 2023.

VALUATION MULTIPLE (MEDIAN VALUE)

UNDER $1 MILLION NET SALES

MVIC/Net Sales	0.49
MVIC/Gross Profit	0.86
MVIC/SDE	2.12
MVIC/EBITDA	2.78

$1 MILLION–$5 MILLION NET SALES

MVIC/Net Sales.	0.13
MVIC/Gross Profit	0.69
MVIC/SDE	1.89
MVIC/EBITDA	6.02

OVER $5 MILLION NET SALES

MVIC/Net Sales.	0.79
MVIC/Gross Profit	3.45
MVIC/SDE	6.91
MVIC/EBITDA	7.44

Source: DealStats (formerly Pratt's Stats), 2023 (Portland, OR: Business Valuation Resources, LLC), www.bvresources.com/dealstats

PRICING TIPS

Approx. Total Investment: $196,000 to $275,950

RESOURCES

- AIM Mail Centers: https://www.aimmailcenters.com
- Franchise information: https://www.aimmailcenters.com/franchising/requirements
- Annex Brands: https://www.annexbrands.com

Air and Gas Compressor Manufacturing

| NAICS 333912 | Businesses/Units 235

| Profit $390 M | Wages $1.6 B | Annual Growth Future 1.3%

| | | Annual Growth Past -6.8%

INDUSTRY MULTIPLES

Acquisition multiples below are calculated medians using US private industry transactions. Data updated annually. Last update: August 2023.

VALUATION MULTIPLE (MEDIAN VALUE)

UNDER $1 MILLION NET SALES

MVIC/Net Sales.	0.77
MVIC/Gross Profit	3.42
MVIC/SDE	10.76
MVIC/EBITDA	17.15

$1 MILLION–$5 MILLION NET SALES

MVIC/Net Sales.	0.76
MVIC/Gross Profit	0.76
MVIC/SDE	2.27
MVIC/EBITDA	N/A

OVER $5 MILLION NET SALES   N/A

Source: DealStats (formerly Pratt's Stats), 2023 (Portland, OR: Business Valuation Resources, LLC), www.bvresources.com/dealstats

BENCHMARK DATA

STATISTICS (AIR AND GAS COMPRESSOR MANUFACTURING)

Number of Establishments	264
Average Profit Margin	4.7%
Revenue per Employee	$438,000
Average Number of Employees.	73.0
Average Wages per Employee	$82,332

PRODUCTS AND SERVICES SEGMENTATION

Air compressors	.30.8%
Other	.19.2%
Industrial and specialty gas compressors	.17.5%
Aftermarket parts and accessories	.15.0%
Industrial spraying equipment	9.6%
Vacuum pumps	7.9%

MAJOR MARKET SEGMENTATION

Process industries	.28.3%
Other	.27.2%
Manufacturing industries	.25.1%
Utilities and construction	.19.4%

INDUSTRY COSTS

Profit	4.7%
Wages	.18.9%
Purchases	.55.6%
Depreciation	1.6%
Marketing	0.3%
Rent & Utilities	1.4%
Other	.17.5%

MARKET SHARE

Trane Technologies	.30.8%
Atlas Copco Ab	9.5%

INDUSTRY TREND

"The COVID-19 pandemic is expected to have an adverse effect on the industry. Industry performance has been mixed during the five-year period. Several larger companies have focused on acquiring smaller competitors. Various domestic industries will underpin demand for air and gas compressors. Demand for industry products is forecast to grow steadily. Exports have traditionally been a key driver of the industry's performance. Deteriorating demand from the domestic and foreign energy sectors have hurt the industry."

Source: IBISWorld Industry at a Glance

RESOURCES

• IBISWorld, March 2023: https://www.ibisworld.com

Aircraft Cleaning

| NAICS 561720 | SIC 4581-04

Rules of Thumb

• 100% annual sales plus inventory
• 3 x SDE plus inventory

INDUSTRY MULTIPLES

Acquisition multiples below are calculated medians using US private industry transactions. Data updated annually. Last update: August 2023.

VALUATION MULTIPLE (MEDIAN VALUE)

UNDER $1 MILLION NET SALES

MVIC/Net Sales	0.59
MVIC/Gross Profit	0.76

```
MVIC/SDE  .   .   .   .   .   .   .   .   .   .   .   . 2.03
MVIC/EBITDA  .   .   .   .   .   .   .   .   .   . 2.92
```
$1 MILLION–$5 MILLION NET SALES
```
MVIC/Net Sales.   .   .   .   .   .   .   .   .   .   . 0.45
MVIC/Gross Profit  .   .   .   .   .   .   .   .   . 1.02
MVIC/SDE  .   .   .   .   .   .   .   .   .   .   .   . 2.86
MVIC/EBITDA  .   .   .   .   .   .   .   .   .   . 4.05
```
OVER $5 MILLION NET SALES
```
MVIC/Net Sales.   .   .   .   .   .   .   .   .   .   . 0.53
MVIC/Gross Profit  .   .   .   .   .   .   .   .   . 2.26
MVIC/SDE  .   .   .   .   .   .   .   .   .   .   .   . 4.26
MVIC/EBITDA  .   .   .   .   .   .   .   .   .   . 5.48
```

Source: DealStats (formerly Pratt's Stats), 2023 (Portland, OR: Business Valuation Resources, LLC), www.bvresources.com/dealstats

PRICING TIPS

Minimum 3 years in business, 2.5 x net if owner operated, as much as 4 x net if work is performed by a crew or crews

BENCHMARK DATA

Labor should run approximately 25% of sales.

Corporate aircraft cleaning is a very specialized service; if it survived the first 18 months, chances are it will do well.

All services are mobile.

EXPENSES (% OF ANNUAL SALES)

Cost of Goods	05% to 10%
Occupancy Costs	10%
Payroll/Labor Costs.	25% to 35%
Profit (pretax)	55% to 60%

QUESTIONS

- Number of accounts? How long servicing those accounts? Percentage of sales from which accounts?
- How many aircraft do you service per week, per month? Number of employees? The buyer is going to need to keep the employees.

INDUSTRY TREND

"'Of course, we cleaned aircraft cabins before COVID, but obviously we've stepped up,' said Dr. Paulo Alves, global director for aviation health at MedAire. 'Methods like ionizing machines, UV light and residual disinfectants bear a cost, but I believe they've become additional services commercial operators provide to offer passengers comfort and peace of mind.' Alves acknowledged 'with the benefit of hindsight, we now know that we perhaps overreached in some areas,' as subsequent research determined the risk of spreading the disease through contaminated surfaces is relatively low. However, he expects such measures to continue for some time to come. 'If it eases your passengers' concerns, then why not?' said Alves. 'I don't really see any way to step back from it in the short term.'"

Source: "Business Flying after COVID-19," July/August 2021, https://nbaa.org/news/business-aviation-insider/2021-july-august/business-flying-covid-19/

RESOURCES

- NBAA—National Business Aviation Association: https://nbaa.org

Aircraft Manufacturing

| NAICS 336411 | Businesses/Units 2,458

| Profit $26.8 B | Wages $43.9 B | Annual Growth Future 2.6%

| Annual Growth Past 3.7%

INDUSTRY MULTIPLES

Acquisition multiples below are calculated medians using US private industry transactions. Data updated annually. Last update: August 2023.

VALUATION MULTIPLE (MEDIAN VALUE)

UNDER $1 MILLION NET SALES	N/A
$1 MILLION–$5 MILLION NET SALES	
MVIC/Net Sales	5.24
MVIC/Gross Profit	2.19
MVIC/SDE	N/A
MVIC/EBITDA	N/A
OVER $5 MILLION NET SALES	
MVIC/Net Sales	1.87
MVIC/Gross Profit	12.04
MVIC/SDE	N/A
MVIC/EBITDA	27.19

Source: DealStats (formerly Pratt's Stats), 2023 (Portland, OR: Business Valuation Resources, LLC), www.bvresources.com/dealstats

BENCHMARK DATA

STATISTICS (AIRCRAFT, ENGINE & PARTS MANUFACTURING)

Number of Establishments	2,458
Average Profit Margin	8.3%
Revenue per Employee	$588,000
Average Number of Employees	233
Average Wages per Employee	$80,284

PRODUCTS AND SERVICES SEGMENTATION

Aircraft	59.8%
Aircraft engines and engine parts	22.2%
Other aircraft parts and auxiliary equipment	18.0%

MAJOR MARKET SEGMENTATION

Civil market	68.4%
Defense market	31.6%

INDUSTRY COSTS

Profit	8.3%
Wages	13.6%
Purchases	45.9%
Depreciation	2.7%
Marketing	0.1%
Rent & Utilities	0.9%
Other	28.6%

MARKET SHARE

Raytheon Technologies	11.4%
Boeing Co	9.3%
GE Aviation UK	6.1%
Lockheed Martin	5.2%
Textron Inc.	1.0%

"Heightened usage of planes increases wear and tear, increasing demand. Other countries expanded their air travel options over the past decade. Federal funding allocated to defense budgets initially increased but has tapered off. New higher-cost jets will begin to replace older models. Aircraft manufacturers will benefit from widespread demand for UAVs. Domestic trips by US residents and international trips will both rise. Manufacturers that serve as defense contractors have been subject to inconsistent funding."

Source: IBISWorld Industry at a Glance

RESOURCES

• IBISWorld, January 2023: https://www.ibisworld.com

Aircraft Manufacturing: Parts, Supplies, Engines, etc. (Kit-Built & Ultralight Aircraft Industry)

| NAICS 336412 | SIC 3724

Rules of Thumb

• 40%–70% annual sales includes value of equipment
• 4 x EBIT

INDUSTRY MULTIPLES

Acquisition multiples below are calculated medians using US private industry transactions. Data updated annually. Last update: August 2023.

VALUATION MULTIPLE (MEDIAN VALUE)

UNDER $1 MILLION NET SALES	N/A
$1 MILLION–$5 MILLION NET SALES	N/A
OVER $5 MILLION NET SALES	
MVIC/Net Sales	0.89
MVIC/Gross Profit	5.88
MVIC/SDE	N/A
MVIC/EBITDA	10.20

Source: DealStats (formerly Pratt's Stats), 2023 (Portland, OR: Business Valuation Resources, LLC), www.bvresources.com/dealstats

PRICING TIPS

When evaluating aerospace manufacturing firms, the first attribute in determining value is the company's position in the supply chain, and the value thereof. Further attributes are if the company is an original equipment manufacturer (OEM) supplier or a value-added reseller (VAR), or a subcontractor. The supplier's likely value and leverage diminish the further downline it is to the end user (e.g., Boeing, Airbus, Northrop Grumman, Lockheed Martin, GE, Bell, or Sikorsky, etc.). Other major value factors are if the company owns its intellectual property or is licensing it; if it is contracted with long-term contracts or if it is an approved job shop (in which case it is likely only a subcontractor); if the end user is passenger vs. military aircraft; fixed-wing airplanes vs. rotary-driven helicopters, etc. In determining its leverage, it's meaningful to determine if it is a single-source supplier of a part number or category, what that part's lead time is, and how mission critical it is (e.g., do 3 different approved firms manufacture it, and does it take 1 week to product—or is the company the only supplier, and the product requires a 6-month lead time due to testing requirements throughout the production process). Finally, companies in this segment often have one end user. This creates concentration issues, but it also streamlines production and improves margins. Being an approved vendor with several coveted major manufacturers (e.g., Boeing & Airbus) dramatically increases value over reliance on one.

To become an approved direct supplier of a mission-critical component to these manufacturers is no small feat. As such, a company directly possessing qualifications (received an approval) for one or more parts substantially increases value—with the amount being a function of that particular part (e.g., a wing fastener is more valuable than a fuse pin, pawl bolt, or door rivet). Competition is fierce for any major component, with Precision Castparts Corp. (PCC) being a fierce competitor on any bids. From a sales standpoint, the major manufacturers' contracts will require not only their consent but also regular assurances of performance, and facility inspections. These assurances will evaluate the manufacturers' liquidity in addition to their volume and quality capabilities.

BENCHMARK DATA

Revenue per employee should be at least $100,000 per annum.

EXPENSES (% OF ANNUAL SALES)

Cost of Goods	35%
Occupancy Costs	20%
Payroll/Labor Costs	35%
Profit (pretax)	10%

QUESTIONS

- Are you an OEM, job shop, or multipurpose machine shop? If you are an approved supplier, who are you directly approved with, and at what level? What volume of business do you do with each of your part numbers, and who do you compete against on those same items?
- Approvals and contracts
- What is the reputation of the aircraft or related product being sold? What is the reputation of the company? What about accidents—any deaths? A company with a great reputation may be worth little because of their product—or, vice versa.

INDUSTRY TREND

"As airline travel returns to pre-pandemic levels, airplane manufacturers are rethinking sustainability metrics, going deep and wide across the lifecycle of millions of parts that comprise the airplanes that people fly in every day. So far, getting to carbon neutral has translated into the pursuit of fuel efficiencies from lighter-weight machine and engine designs, and rightly so—airplanes produce the highest percentage of CO_2 footprint while in flight. Even as these efforts continue, manufacturers see the next horizon in sustainability that touches the entire aviation supply and production chain from airplane design and production to business operations and beyond."

Source: "Sustainability Takes Flight across Aviation Industry" by Susan Galer, August 9, 2022, https://www.forbes.com/sites/sap/2022/08/09/sustainability-takes-flight-across-aviation-industry/

EXPERT COMMENTS

Beware that job or machine shops often indicate they are direct suppliers when they are, in fact, subcontractors. The challenge is that many large shops have more substantive equipment or in-house testing labs, which has forced many of the smaller ones to close. As a result, it's not uncommon for owner-operated shops to come to market; they are not economically viable, however, without a full-time working owner working as a supervisor or machinist. Worst, many that used to thrive own their real estate, and now subsidize jobs to get work by not paying themselves rent—which is obviously not a sustainable model. In years past, the major aerospace manufacturers drove many smaller players out of the market due to lengthy terms, nonpayment, or insistence on razor-thin margins. Since then, some leverage has shifted to the OEMs with substantial resources that weathered that storm.

FINANCING

Conventional or SBA financing is a challenge in the industry due to common concentration issues and lengthy or cumbersome approval requirements should a firm intend to grow into new product categories or gain additional vendor supplier approvals.

Airport Operations

	NAICS 488119		SIC 4581-06		Businesses/Units 1,164
	Profit $647.5 M		Wages $5 B		Annual Growth Future 1.8%
					Annual Growth Past 3.4%

Rules of Thumb

- 90%–100% annual sales includes inventory
- 4–5 x SDE includes inventory
- 4 x EBIT
- 5 x EBITDA

INDUSTRY MULTIPLES

Acquisition multiples below are calculated medians using US private industry transactions. Data updated annually. Last update: August 2023.

VALUATION MULTIPLE (MEDIAN VALUE)

UNDER $1 MILLION NET SALES	
MVIC/Net Sales	0.50
MVIC/Gross Profit	1.00
MVIC/SDE	2.78
MVIC/EBITDA	4.21
$1 MILLION–$5 MILLION NET SALES	N/A
OVER $5 MILLION NET SALES	
MVIC/Net Sales	0.08
MVIC/Gross Profit	N/A
MVIC/SDE	1.01
MVIC/EBITDA	N/A

Source: DealStats (formerly Pratt's Stats), 2023 (Portland, OR: Business Valuation Resources, LLC), www.bvresources.com/dealstats

PRICING TIPS

Pricing would be highly dependent on the sector. In certain segments there is a lot of personal goodwill. A prospective buyer should separate the personal good-will from the business goodwill in calculating a purchase price. Many smaller businesses are highly dependent upon the owner's talent or specialty. These businesses should be valued with consideration to an earnout or employment contact to ensure ongoing stability.

FBOs and MROs are about real estate. Revenues per square foot can be a good metric, but most transactions above $3MM use a multiple of EBITDA plus inventory.

BENCHMARK DATA

STATISTICS (AIRPORT OPERATIONS)

Number of Establishments	2,469
Average Profit Margin	5.0%
Revenue per Employee	$86,500
Average Number of Employees	61.8
Average Wages per Employee	$33,918

PRODUCTS AND SERVICES SEGMENTATION

Aeronautical services	44.3%
Parking and ground transportation services	25.1%
Other services	14.8%
Car rental services	10.7%
Retail stores and hospitality services	5.1%

MAJOR MARKET SEGMENTATION

Individual consumers	54.5%
Passenger airlines	33.4%
Other	12.1%

INDUSTRY COSTS

Profit	5.0%
Wages	39.0%
Purchases	15.7%
Depreciation	32.1%
Marketing	0.1%
Rent & Utilities	1.5%
Other	6.7%

MARKET SHARE

The Port Authority of New York and New Jersey	19.1%
Chicago Department of Aviation	0.2%

For FBO, labor costs should be 20 to 35 percent. Occupancy could be variable depending on the airport and real estate costs. Rent + utilities, 14 percent.

Standard & Poor's benchmarks are a good starting place. Premiums placed on location, e.g., Van Nuys, CA, or major cities.

EXPENSES (% OF ANNUAL SALES)

Cost of Goods	30% to 40%
Occupancy Costs	05% to 10%
Payroll/Labor Costs	20% to 30%
Profit (pretax)	10% to 20%

QUESTIONS

- Type of aircraft, hangar size, special needs, etc.
- Why sell? How long is lease with city? Any renewable lease clauses? If so, at what rate?
- Insurance can be a major cost component. What is the company's safety record? Does the business operate under any FAA certificates (i.e., 135 charter or 141 flight school)? Is maintenance involved with the FBO? How many IAs and A&Ps are employed? Are they contract workers? Is it an FAA certified

repair station? Is it an authorized repair station for an OEM? What is the hangar occupancy rate? Is there a waiting list? How long? What are the average rates per square foot?

INDUSTRY TREND

Supply exceeds demand. More airparks to continue being developed.

"The pandemic has significantly disrupted domestic business activity, leading to a rise in unemployment and tapering of consumer spending activity. If travel restrictions are lifted following mass immunization, travel demand will rebound. In recent years, a growing disparity has emerged between small and large airports. The rapid transition to remote working may reduce business-related travel. As both industry revenue and profit recover over the five years to 2027, many competing enterprises are expected to expand workforces and increase wages. NextGen air traffic control technology will increase the efficiency of aircraft movement. The industry is characterized by a disparity between operator sizes and government involvement."

Source: IBISWorld Industry at a Glance

EXPERT COMMENTS

Know market temperature and value of location; amenities; room for future and development and growth.

A major source of income is from fuel sales. Margins vary greatly depending on competition. Smaller FBOs are harder to market because most require owner operators with a passion for aviation. FBOs are difficult to duplicate as the property is generally owned and controlled by some government entity. The number of operators allowed at any given airfield is limited.

FINANCING

Majority with investors is cash sales.

Outside and partial seller financing

RESOURCES

- IBISWorld, January 2023: https://www.ibisworld.com
- AEA—Aircraft Electronics Association: https://aea.net
- AOPA—Aircraft Owners and Pilots Association: https://www.aopa.brg
- ARSA—Aeronautical Repair Station Association: https://arsa.org
- ASA—Aviation Suppliers Association: https://www.aviationsuppliers.org
- GAMA—General Aviation Manufacturers Association: https://gama.aero
- IATA—International Air Transport Association: https://www.iata.org
- NATA—National Air Transportation Association: https://www.nata.aero

Allegra Marketing•Print•Mail (Franchise)

| NAICS 323111 | Businesses/Units 192

Rules of Thumb

- 60%–65% annual sales plus inventory

INDUSTRY MULTIPLES

Acquisition multiples below are calculated medians using US private industry transactions. Data updated annually. Last update: August 2023.

VALUATION MULTIPLE (MEDIAN VALUE)

UNDER $1 MILLION NET SALES

MVIC/Net Sales.	0.50
MVIC/Gross Profit	0.70
MVIC/SDE	2.36
MVIC/EBITDA	3.17

$1 MILLION–$5 MILLION NET SALES

MVIC/Net Sales.	0.40
MVIC/Gross Profit	0.62
MVIC/SDE	2.81
MVIC/EBITDA	4.35

OVER $5 MILLION NET SALES

MVIC/Net Sales.	0.70
MVIC/Gross Profit	1.50
MVIC/SDE	3.73
MVIC/EBITDA	4.76

Source: DealStats (formerly Pratt's Stats), 2023 (Portland, OR: Business Valuation Resources, LLC), www.bvresources.com/dealstats

PRICING TIPS

Approx. Total Investment: $128,194 to $410,695

RESOURCES

- Allegra Marketing•Print•Mail: https://www.allegramarketingprint.com
- Franchise information: https://allegrafranchise.com
- Alliance Franchise Brands: https://alliancefranchisebrands.com

AlphaGraphics (Franchise)

| NAICS 541430 | SIC 7336-02 | Businesses/Units 241 |

Rules of Thumb

- 60%–65% annual sales plus inventory

INDUSTRY MULTIPLES

Acquisition multiples below are calculated medians using US private industry transactions. Data updated annually. Last update: August 2023.

VALUATION MULTIPLE (MEDIAN VALUE)

UNDER $1 MILLION NET SALES

MVIC/Net Sales.	0.44
MVIC/Gross Profit	0.75
MVIC/SDE	2.15
MVIC/EBITDA	5.19

$1 MILLION–$5 MILLION NET SALES

MVIC/Net Sales.	0.46
MVIC/Gross Profit	2.17
MVIC/SDE	3.14
MVIC/EBITDA	4.59

OVER $5 MILLION NET SALES

MVIC/Net Sales.	1.42
MVIC/Gross Profit	3.65
MVIC/SDE	N/A
MVIC/EBITDA	14.60

Source: DealStats (formerly Pratt's Stats), 2023 (Portland, OR: Business Valuation Resources, LLC), www.bvresources.com/dealstats

PRICING TIPS

Approx. Total Investment: $281,500 to $389,450

RESOURCES

- AlphaGraphics: https://www.alphagraphics.com
- Franchise information: https://alphagraphicsfranchise.com
- MBE Worldwide: https://www.mbecorporate.com

Aluminum Extruded Products Manufacturing

| NAICS 331318

- Rules of Thumb
- 50% annual sales plus inventory
- 6 x SDE plus inventory
- 5 x EBIT
- 4 x EBITDA

INDUSTRY MULTIPLES

Acquisition multiples below are calculated medians using US private industry transactions. Data updated annually. Last update: August 2023.

VALUATION MULTIPLE (MEDIAN VALUE)

UNDER $1 MILLION NET SALES	
MVIC/Net Sales.	0.42
MVIC/Gross Profit	1.35
MVIC/SDE	N/A
MVIC/EBITDA	N/A
$1 MILLION–$5 MILLION NET SALES	
MVIC/Net Sales.	0.51
MVIC/Gross Profit	0.90
MVIC/SDE	N/A
MVIC/EBITDA	N/A
OVER $5 MILLION NET SALES	
MVIC/Net Sales.	0.31
MVIC/Gross Profit	1.93
MVIC/SDE	3.79
MVIC/EBITDA	4.57

Source: DealStats (formerly Pratt's Stats), 2023 (Portland, OR: Business Valuation Resources, LLC), www.bvresources.com/dealstats

PRICING TIPS

It depends on the nature of the contract with metal supplier; this is a low-added-value business.

BENCHMARK DATA

EXPENSES (% OF ANNUAL SALES)

Cost of Goods	70%
Occupancy Costs	05%
Payroll/Labor Costs.	35%
Profit (pretax)	08%

QUESTIONS

- Customer base, nature of metal contracts

INDUSTRY TREND

"Aluminum...Transportation applications accounted for 35% of domestic consumption; the remainder was used in packaging, 23%; building, 16%; electrical, 10%; machinery, 7%; consumer durables, 6%; and other, 3%."

Source: U.S. Geological Survey, "Mineral Commodity Summaries 2023," January 2023, https://pubs.usgs.gov/periodicals/mcs2023/mcs2023.pdf

RESOURCES

• MetalMiner: https://agmetalminer.com
• The Aluminum Association: https://www.aluminum.org

Aluminum Manufacturing

| NAICS 331315 | Businesses/Units 515

| Profit $2.1 B | Wages $5.1 B | Annual Growth Future -0.5%

| | | Annual Growth Past -2.7%

INDUSTRY MULTIPLES

Acquisition multiples below are calculated medians using US private industry transactions. Data updated annually. Last update: August 2023.

VALUATION MULTIPLE (MEDIAN VALUE)

UNDER $1 MILLION NET SALES

MVIC/Net Sales.	0.27
MVIC/Gross Profit	0.70
MVIC/SDE	1.52
MVIC/EBITDA	2.50

$1 MILLION–$5 MILLION NET SALES

MVIC/Net Sales.	1.40
MVIC/Gross Profit	2.44
MVIC/SDE	4.51
MVIC/EBITDA	6.06

OVER $5 MILLION NET SALES

MVIC/Net Sales.	0.69
MVIC/Gross Profit	21.09
MVIC/SDE	N/A
MVIC/EBITDA	8.68

Source: DealStats (formerly Pratt's Stats), 2023 (Portland, OR: Business Valuation Resources, LLC), www.bvresources.com/dealstats

BENCHMARK DATA

STATISTICS (ALUMINUM MANUFACTURING)

Number of Establishments	515
Average Profit Margin	4.7%
Revenue per Employee	$625,000
Average Number of Employees.	134
Average Wages per Employee	$72,717

PRODUCTS AND SERVICES SEGMENTATION

Aluminum sheet, plate and foil	44.0%
Aluminum extrusions	31.9%
Secondary aluminum	17.0%
Primary aluminum	5.2%
Alumina	1.5%
Other	0.4%

MAJOR MARKET SEGMENTATION

Transportation equipment, including defense	35.0%
Packaging and containers	23.0%
Construction	16.0%
Electrical applications	9.0%
Consumer durables	7.0%
Industrial manufacturing	7.0%
Other	3.0%

INDUSTRY COSTS

Profit	4.7%
Wages	11.5%
Purchases	61.8%
Depreciation	1.9%
Marketing	0.0%
Rent & Utilities	4.2%
Other	15.9%

MARKET SHARE

Novelis Inc.	14.2%
Arconic Corporation	11.2%
Kaiser Aluminum Corporation	5.8%
Constellium NV	5.8%
Alcoa Corp	3.6%
Cass, Inc	0.2%

INDUSTRY TREND

"The price of aluminum has increased 24% over the past six months to more than $3,100 a metric ton, approaching a decade high....Energy can account for as much as half the cost of making aluminum, which is why traders call the commodity congealed electricity....Rising aluminum costs are an added expense for buyers such as auto makers, already grappling with supply-chain constraints including a global computer-chip shortage."

Source: "Ukraine, Gas Costs Lift Aluminum Prices" by Rhiannon Hoyle and Joe Wallace, *Wall Street Journal*, January 31, 2022

"Persistent price volatility for aluminum has proved challenging for industry operators. Import restrictions have supported industry operators since 2018. Rising energy costs limit average profit margins. Demand from transportation equipment-related industries will likely remain the key driver of revenue growth. Government trade restrictions will continue to support the industry. Aluminum manufacturers may struggle in a high interest rate environment. Aluminum prices reached record highs due to limited supply from China, Russia and other major producers."

Source: IBISWorld Industry at a Glance

RESOURCES

• IBISWorld, January 2023: https://www.ibisworld.com

Aluminum Smelting Machinery

| NAICS 331314

Rules of Thumb

• 70% annual sales plus inventory
• 5 x EBITDA

A

INDUSTRY MULTIPLES

Acquisition multiples below are calculated medians using US private industry transactions. Data updated annually. Last update: August 2023.

VALUATION MULTIPLE (MEDIAN VALUE)

UNDER $1 MILLION NET SALES	
MVIC/Net Sales.	0.95
MVIC/Gross Profit	1.21
MVIC/SDE	2.09
MVIC/EBITDA	5.60
$1 MILLION–$5 MILLION NET SALES	N/A
OVER $5 MILLION NET SALES	N/A

Source: DealStats (formerly Pratt's Stats), 2023 (Portland, OR: Business Valuation Resources, LLC), www.bvresources.com/dealstats

PRICING TIPS

If balance sheet is sound, business is worth an average between twice net assets and 5 times EBITDA.

BENCHMARK DATA

$250,000 per employee

EXPENSES (% OF ANNUAL SALES)

Cost of Goods	70%
Occupancy Costs	05%
Payroll/Labor Costs.	25%
Profit (pretax)	10%

QUESTIONS

• Indebtedness? Officers' loan or debt? Backlog and list of references.

INDUSTRY TREND

"In 2022, three companies operated six primary aluminum smelters in five states....Domestic smelters were operating at about 52% of capacity of 1.64 million tons per year at year-end 2022. Estimated primary production decreased by 3% compared with that in 2021 but estimated secondary production from new and old scrap increased by 3% compared with that in 2021."

Source: U.S. Geological Survey, "Mineral Commodity Summaries 2023," January 2023, https://pubs.usgs.gov/periodicals/mcs2023/mcs2023.pdf

EXPERT COMMENTS

Highly specialized market. Vendor must establish himself on short list of major EPCMs through references. Spare parts market captive and profitable.

RESOURCES

• The Aluminum Association: https://www.aluminum.org

Ambulance Services

NAICS 62191	SIC 4119-02	Businesses/Units 28,212
Profit $1.9 B	Wages $9.7 B	Annual Growth Future 1.8%
		Annual Growth Past 0.5%

Rules of Thumb

- 40% annual revenues plus inventory
- 2–4.0 x SDE includes inventory
- 2.7–5.2 x EBITDA

INDUSTRY MULTIPLES

Acquisition multiples below are calculated medians using US private industry transactions. Data updated annually. Last update: August 2023.

VALUATION MULTIPLE (MEDIAN VALUE)

UNDER $1 MILLION NET SALES

MVIC/Net Sales.	0.53
MVIC/Gross Profit	0.87
MVIC/SDE	2.02
MVIC/EBITDA	1.54

$1 MILLION–$5 MILLION NET SALES

MVIC/Net Sales.	0.49
MVIC/Gross Profit	0.73
MVIC/SDE	2.80
MVIC/EBITDA	3.63

OVER $5 MILLION NET SALES

MVIC/Net Sales.	0.93
MVIC/Gross Profit	0.93
MVIC/SDE	7.94
MVIC/EBITDA	15.54

Source: DealStats (formerly Pratt's Stats), 2023 (Portland, OR: Business Valuation Resources, LLC), www.bvresources.com/dealstats

PRICING TIPS

Every company is different, and the pricing can vary significantly (25 to 35 percent) depending on many factors and business characteristics—types of contracts, tenure, average cost per run, and many other factors. Companies are challenging to get to closing without a highly knowledgeable adviser working on the seller's behalf. Very high chance of deal falling apart in due diligence if proper info is not disclosed and known during negotiations. County/city 911 operations have different ratios and cost structures than NE operations.

BENCHMARK DATA

STATISTICS (AMBULANCE SERVICES)

Number of Establishments .	28,212
Average Profit Margin	9.5%
Revenue per Employee .	$94,500
Average Number of Employees.	7.6
Average Wages per Employee .	$46,007

PRODUCTS AND SERVICES SEGMENTATION

Emergency surface ambulance.	65.0%
Nonemergency surface ambulance	17.5%
Emergency air ambulance (fixed wing).	10.1%
Other services	4.5%
Nonemergency air ambulance .	2.2%
Standby ambulance or first-aid services	0.7%

MAJOR MARKET SEGMENTATION

Other	22.2%
Open wound, including head, neck and back	18.6%
Contusions and superficial injuries.	17.0%
Head, neck and back injury, excluding fractures and open wounds	15.9%

Fractures, including head, neck and back 12.5%
Sprains or strains, excluding head, neck and back. 8.7%
Burns and poisoning 5.1%

INDUSTRY COSTS

Profit 9.5%
Wages 48.7%
Purchases 7.6%
Depreciation 4.3%
Marketing 0.6%
Rent & Utilities 2.1%
Other 27.1%

Most owners are former medics/EMTs and lack proper skill sets to grow companies over $3M to $4M in sales. They also lack logistics management and billing
expertise. As such, EBITDA in this industry averages 8 to 9 percent, but well-
run operations can generate 18 to 23 percent EBITDA consistently with proper
management, contracts, payer mix, and good logistics management and proper
billing expertise.

EXPENSES (% OF ANNUAL SALES)

Cost of Goods . . . . 02% to 12%
Occupancy Costs . . . . 01% to 03%
Payroll/Labor Costs. . . . . 50% to 60%
Profit (pretax) . . . . 07% to 22%

QUESTIONS

- Payor mix, market share, patient demographic data.
- Knowledge of medical billing; logistics management; attention to details.
- Except regular financial due diligence, buyers should be watching for lawsuits
  against the company and traffic tickets. High level of lawsuits and traffic tickets
  indicates that the business doesn't have good driver education and discipline
  in place.
- Who does billing: in-house or sub out to third party? What software is used?
  What systems do you have in place and utilize for billing and logistics?

INDUSTRY TREND

Labor market is very tight and getting tougher each year. This is driving up
payroll costs.

"Privatization has enabled many ambulance providers to focus on developing
innovative technologies. Many local ambulance providers have struggled to generate revenue amid high operational costs. Low Medicare reimbursement rates
have become an issue for the industry. Continued private equity investment in
the ambulatory care arena will likely define the outlook period. The industry will
require more employees to provide dispatch services. Consolidation will likely enable the industry to strengthen its distribution network. Many private ambulance
providers have scrambled to provide short response times."

Source: IBISWorld Industry at a Glance

EXPERT COMMENTS

Labor costs are rising; larger companies have a big advantage over smaller companies due to recruitment and financial stability, etc.

FINANCING

50 to 80 percent cash at closing, but every deal is different and has different risk
factors; also there is almost always an escrow amount held at closing for 12 to 24
months due to potential liabilities and risk factors, plus for R&Ws.

- IBISWorld, January 2023: https://www.ibisworld.com
- AAA—American Ambulance Association—primarily for members: https://ambulance.org/
- CAAS—Commission on Accreditation of Ambulance Services: https://www.caas.org
- EMS World: https://www.emsworld.com

A

Ambulatory Surgery Centers

| NAICS 621493 | Businesses/Units 12,452

| Profit $10.8 B | Wages $11.8 B | Annual Growth Future 3.7%

| Annual Growth Past 2.3%

Rules of Thumb
- 78% annual sales plus inventory
- 2.7 x SDE plus inventory
- 6.3 x EBIT
- 5.6 x EBITDA

INDUSTRY MULTIPLES

Acquisition multiples below are calculated medians using US private industry transactions. Data updated annually. Last update: August 2023.

VALUATION MULTIPLE (MEDIAN VALUE)

UNDER $1 MILLION NET SALES

MVIC/Net Sales	0.45
MVIC/Gross Profit	0.40
MVIC/SDE	1.96
MVIC/EBITDA	5.52

$1 MILLION–$5 MILLION NET SALES

MVIC/Net Sales	0.64
MVIC/Gross Profit	0.67
MVIC/SDE	2.22
MVIC/EBITDA	20.38

OVER $5 MILLION NET SALES

MVIC/Net Sales	1.23
MVIC/Gross Profit	1.23
MVIC/SDE	N/A
MVIC/EBITDA	5.27

Source: DealStats (formerly Pratt's Stats), 2023 (Portland, OR: Business Valuation Resources, LLC), www.bvresources.com/dealstats

PRICING TIPS

High-margin business, but multiple Centers for Medicare & Medicaid Services restrictions on who can own shares in them, generally being either a physician or a management company.

BENCHMARK DATA

STATISTICS (AMBULATORY SURGERY CENTERS)

Number of Establishments	12,452
Average Profit Margin	25.0%
Revenue per Employee	$230,000

Average Number of Employees. 15.6
Average Wages per Employee $63,376

PRODUCTS AND SERVICES SEGMENTATION

Other 24.6%
Digestive system diseases 20.5%
Musculoskeletal system and connective tissue diseases . . 20.0%
Nervous system and sense organ diseases 11.7%
Injury and poisoning 7.7%
Symptoms, signs and ill-defined conditions 6.3%
Respiratory system diseases 5.6%
Infectious and parasitic diseases 3.6%

MAJOR MARKET SEGMENTATION

Private insurers 39.0%
Government insurers 33.3%
Other 21.4%
Out-of-pocket payments 6.3%

INDUSTRY COSTS

Profit 25.0%
Wages 27.4%
Purchases 18.7%
Depreciation 3.2%
Marketing 0.4%
Rent & Utilities 4.1%
Other 21.2%

EXPENSES (% OF ANNUAL SALES)

Cost of Goods . . . . 11% to 15% .
Payroll/Labor Costs. 05%
Profit (pretax) . . . . 22% to 27%
Occupancy Costs 12%

QUESTIONS

- How many of the doctors are remaining at the center? Have any doctors announced retirement or that they are planning on retiring? Get a listing of patient billings per physician.

INDUSTRY TREND

These will continue to be in high demand as CMS is moving more surgical procedures out of hospitals.

"ASCs have inundated the healthcare sector since the 1970s. About 61.0% of ASCs are physician-only owned. ASCs contend with regulation at both the federal and state levels. ASC will likely continue to provide low-cost services. The aging population drives demand for ASCs. Many hospitals will likely form joint partnerships with ASCs. The cost-competitive nature of industry services and relatively low operational costs have heightened industry profitability."

Source: IBISWorld Industry Outlook

EXPERT COMMENTS

Get experience working for one before buying, or engage a healthcare consultant to assist in lifestyle and economic concerns.

FINANCING

Outside financing and bank; very little seller financing

- IBISWorld, January 2023: https://www.ibisworld.com
- ASCA—Ambulatory Surgery Center Association: https://www.ascassociation.org
- Becker's ASC Review: https://www.beckersasc.com/

A

Animal Food Production

NAICS 31111	Businesses/Units 3,978	
Profit $3.5 B	Wages $4.2 B	Annual Growth Future 0.5%
		Annual Growth Past 0.9%

INDUSTRY MULTIPLES

Acquisition multiples below are calculated medians using US private industry transactions. Data updated annually. Last update: August 2023.

VALUATION MULTIPLE (MEDIAN VALUE)

UNDER $1 MILLION NET SALES
MVIC/Net Sales.	0.36
MVIC/Gross Profit	0.36
MVIC/SDE	1.38
MVIC/EBITDA	4.92

$1 MILLION–$5 MILLION NET SALES
MVIC/Net Sales.	1.53
MVIC/Gross Profit	4.28
MVIC/SDE	4.82
MVIC/EBITDA	6.47

OVER $5 MILLION NET SALES
MVIC/Net Sales.	1.01
MVIC/Gross Profit	6.01
MVIC/SDE	3.65
MVIC/EBITDA	10.70

Source: DealStats (formerly Pratt's Stats), 2023 (Portland, OR: Business Valuation Resources, LLC), www.bvresources.com/dealstats

BENCHMARK DATA

STATISTICS (ANIMAL FOOD PRODUCTION)
Number of Establishments .	3,978
Average Profit Margin	4.8%
Revenue per Employee .	$1,149,000
Average Number of Employees.	15.9
Average Wages per Employee .	$67,444

PRODUCTS AND SERVICES SEGMENTATION
Dog food	33.3%
Poultry feeds	19.5%
Cattle feeds .	17.3%
Cat food .	12.5%
Other animal foods .	9.6%
Pig feeds	7.8%

MAJOR MARKET SEGMENTATION
Farm supplies wholesalers .	38.9%
General line and supermarket wholesalers	34.4%
Pet stores	26.7%

Profit	4.8%
Wages	5.8%
Purchases	62.7%
Depreciation	1.7%
Marketing	0.2%
Rent & Utilities	1.3%
Other	23.4%

INDUSTRY TREND

"Demand for luxury products that cater to specific needs of dogs and cats has increased. Adverse weather conditions have severely disrupted standard input prices. Increased trade activity following COVID-19 has spurned purchasing of US-based animal food. Rising pet ownership will bring higher demand for pet food. Exports will continue to grow over the next five years. Technological innovation and automation implementation are limited. The United States is a net exporter of animal food products."

Source: IBISWorld Industry at a Glance

RESOURCES

• IBISWorld, January 2023: https://www.ibisworld.com

Antique Shops/Dealers

| NAICS 453310 | SIC 5932-02

Rules of Thumb

• 20% annual sales plus inventory

INDUSTRY MULTIPLES

Acquisition multiples below are calculated medians using US private industry transactions. Data updated annually. Last update: August 2023.

VALUATION MULTIPLE (MEDIAN VALUE)

UNDER $1 MILLION NET SALES

MVIC/Net Sales	0.36
MVIC/Gross Profit	0.61
MVIC/SDE	1.83
MVIC/EBITDA	3.20

$1 MILLION–$5 MILLION NET SALES

MVIC/Net Sales	0.47
MVIC/Gross Profit	0.75
MVIC/SDE	2.74
MVIC/EBITDA	4.10

OVER $5 MILLION NET SALES

MVIC/Net Sales	0.36
MVIC/Gross Profit	2.50
MVIC/SDE	N/A
MVIC/EBITDA	9.10

Source: DealStats (formerly Pratt's Stats), 2023 (Portland, OR: Business Valuation Resources, LLC), www.bvresources.com/dealstats

INDUSTRY TREND

"The pandemic has created a bit of a perfect storm for the used and antique furniture business. All this time at home has made people yearn for a fresh look.

The spike in home remodeling and all the moving around people have done created new spaces to fill. Frustrated consumers still waiting for a headboard and bedside tables they ordered six months ago are increasingly willing to buy previously owned sofas, just as they are willing to scoop up used Hondas and Chanel bags."

A

Source: "Antique and vintage sales have soared,

thanks to supply chain issues" by Jura Koncius, January 26, 2022,

https://www.washingtonpost.com/home/2022/01/26/antiques-vintage-furniture-popular-during-pandemic/

RESOURCES

- ACNA—Antiques & Collectibles National Association: https://acna.us

Anytime Fitness (Franchise)

| NAICS 713940 | Businesses/Units 2,325

Rules of Thumb

- 2.5 x SDE plus inventory
- 75% annual sales

INDUSTRY MULTIPLES

Acquisition multiples below are calculated medians using US private industry transactions. Data updated annually. Last update: August 2023.

VALUATION MULTIPLE (MEDIAN VALUE)

UNDER $1 MILLION NET SALES

MVIC/Net Sales	0.53
MVIC/Gross Profit	0.55
MVIC/SDE	2.26
MVIC/EBITDA	2.81

$1 MILLION–$5 MILLION NET SALES

MVIC/Net Sales	0.61
MVIC/Gross Profit	0.69
MVIC/SDE	2.48
MVIC/EBITDA	3.99

OVER $5 MILLION NET SALES

MVIC/Net Sales	2.23
MVIC/Gross Profit	3.25
MVIC/SDE	N/A
MVIC/EBITDA	12.19

Source: DealStats (formerly Pratt's Stats), 2023 (Portland, OR: Business Valuation Resources, LLC), www.bvresources.com/dealstats

PRICING TIPS

Approx. Total Investment: $474,552 to $970,097

QUESTIONS

- How much in prepaid memberships?

FINANCING

2 years

RESOURCES

- Anytime Fitness: https://www.anytimefitness.com

- Franchise information: https://www.anytimefitness.com/franchise/
- Self Esteem Brands: https://www.sebrands.com

Apartment Rental

| | NAICS 531110 | | SIC 6531-11 | | Businesses/Units 766,555 |

| | Profit $81.1 B | | Wages $31.8 B | | Annual Growth Future -0.1% |

| | | | | | Annual Growth Past 0.9% |

Rules of Thumb

- 80% annual revenues of $1M+

INDUSTRY MULTIPLES

Acquisition multiples below are calculated medians using US private industry transactions. Data updated annually. Last update: August 2023.

VALUATION MULTIPLE (MEDIAN VALUE)

UNDER $1 MILLION NET SALES
MVIC/Net Sales	0.73
MVIC/Gross Profit	1.37
MVIC/SDE	2.91
MVIC/EBITDA	2.62

$1 MILLION–$5 MILLION NET SALES
MVIC/Net Sales	0.70
MVIC/Gross Profit	0.95
MVIC/SDE	6.98
MVIC/EBITDA	N/A

OVER $5 MILLION NET SALES
MVIC/Net Sales	12.01
MVIC/Gross Profit	16.34
MVIC/SDE	N/A
MVIC/EBITDA	25.52

Source: DealStats (formerly Pratt's Stats), 2023 (Portland, OR: Business Valuation Resources, LLC), www.bvresources.com/dealstats

PRICING TIPS

This is generally a secondary revenue source to real estate sales.

A real estate license is required for the operation of this business in many states.

BENCHMARK DATA

STATISTICS (APARTMENT RENTAL)

Number of Establishments	766,555
Average Profit Margin	32.3%
Revenue per Employee	$243,000
Average Number of Employees	1.3
Average Wages per Employee	$30,958

PRODUCTS AND SERVICES SEGMENTATION

Rental of 1-unit structures	32.1%
Rental of 2-to-4-unit structures	16.3%
Rental of 10-to-19-unit structures	14.6%
Rental of 50-or-more-unit structures	12.4%
Rental of 5-to-9-unit structures	11.5%
Rental of 20-to-49-unit structures	9.1%
Rental of manufactured homes, mobile homes, or trailers	4.0%

One person	. 38.3%
Two persons	. 28.0%
Four or more persons	. 19.2%
Three persons	. 14.5%

INDUSTRY COSTS

Profit	. 32.3%
Wages	. 12.7%
Purchases	. 2.1%
Depreciation	. 19.2%
Marketing	. 1.0%
Rent & Utilities	. 3.6%
Other	. 29.1%

Fees are most often paid by the apartment owner, usually about 10% to 15% or one month's rent.

INDUSTRY TREND

"Rob Warnock, a senior research associate at Apartment List, said nationwide 'affordability-driven migration' is common due to a higher cost of living, increased moving costs, and inflation....Nationwide migration patterns suggest that renters are looking to move from more expensive places to less expensive ones, Warnock said. California and New York—the two states with the largest population declines between 2020 and 2022, according to Apartment List—are indicative of this trend..."

Source: "Boston renters looking to move away want to go here" by Vivi Smilgius, February 24, 2023,
https://www.boston.com/real-estate/renting/2023/02/24/metro-boston-renters-want-to-move-here/

"As the central bank raises interest rates to cool down the economy and contain rapid inflation, it is also pushing up mortgage costs, putting home purchases out of reach for many first-time buyers. If people who would have otherwise bought a home remain waylaid in apartments and rented houses, it could compound already-booming demand—keeping pressure on rental prices. While it is tough to predict how big or how lasting that Fed-induced bump in rental demand might prove, it could ironically make it more difficult for the central bank to wrestle inflation lower in the near term. Rent-related costs make up nearly a third of the closely tracked Consumer Price Index inflation measure, so anything that helps to keep them climbing at an unusually brisk pace is likely to perpetuate rapid inflation."

Source: "Relief Eludes Many Renters as Fed Raises Interest Rates"
by Jeanna Smialek and Conor Dougherty, July 11, 2022,
https://www.nytimes.com/2022/07/11/business/economy/rent-inflation-interest-rates.html

"In the mid-1980s, about one in five people in America moved annually, most of them within the same county. By 2021, that number had fallen to one in 12....And renters are renewing their leases at record levels."

Source: "When the Best Available Home Is the One You Already Have" by Emily Badger, May 27, 2022,
https://www.nytimes.com/2022/05/27/upshot/housing-market-slow-moving.html

"The industry is expected to suffer a wave of evictions as unemployment remains high. Demographic shifts have fueled a buying bonanza in the homeownership market, specifically in single-family detached homes. 2020 is considered a turning point for the real estate sector overall and the Apartment Rental industry specifically. Increases in rental vacancy will diminish landlords' effective pricing power. As evictions rise amid recessionary conditions, the number of available units will also rise. In addition to young adults and singles, retiring baby boomers are expected to continue supporting industry demand. Since the subprime mortgage crisis, the industry has undergone structural change."

Source: IBISWorld Industry at a Glance

RESOURCES
• IBISWorld, March 2023: https://www.ibisworld.com

Apparel Knitting Mills

| NAICS 315120 | Businesses/Units 185

| Profit $33.5 M | Wages $315.3 M | Annual Growth Future 1.3%

| Annual Growth Past -5.4%

BENCHMARK DATA

STATISTICS (APPAREL KNITTING MILLS)

Number of Establishments .	185
Average Profit Margin .	3.1%
Revenue per Employee .	$119,000
Average Number of Employees.	49.1
Average Wages per Employee .	$34,479

PRODUCTS AND SERVICES SEGMENTATION

Men's and boys' hosiery and socks.	41.7%
Women's and girls' hosiery and socks .	24.3%
Contract knitting and other .	14.8%
Hats, caps, gloves and mittens .	5.9%
Sweaters .	4.0%
Men and boy's sport and leisure wear .	3.6%
Infant clothing .	3.6%
Outerwear .	2.1%

MAJOR MARKET SEGMENTATION

E-commerce and online auctions .	56.2%
Department stores .	20.8%
Discount stores and mass merchandisers .	18.6%
All other general merchandise .	3.2%
Lingerie stores .	1.2%

INDUSTRY COSTS

Profit .	3.1%
Wages .	29.2%
Purchases .	47.4%
Depreciation .	1.0%
Marketing .	0.5%
Rent & Utilities .	4.2%
Other .	14.7%

INDUSTRY TREND

"As lockdowns and social distancing in 2020 restricted expenditure on professional apparel, revenue plummeted. Supply chain woes have led to surging costs for key inputs like cotton. Domestic manufacturers have had to reduce their markup to maintain sales and remain buoyant. While manufacturers won't recover from work-from-home policies and changing fashion trends, favorable trade conditions will provide a boost. Manufacturers must begin producing products that enable them to differentiate themselves from low-cost imports. As cotton prices continue to climb, price-based competition will remain high and hinder profit growth. High import penetration has forced manufacturers to reduce their markup to maintain sales and remain buoyant, negatively impacting profit."

Source: IBISWorld Industry at a Glance

RESOURCES
• IBISWorld, May 2023: https://www.ibisworld.com

Appliance Stores

| NAICS 449210 | SIC 5064

Rules of Thumb
• 2 x monthly sales plus inventory

INDUSTRY MULTIPLES

Acquisition multiples below are calculated medians using US private industry transactions. Data updated annually. Last update: August 2023.

VALUATION MULTIPLE (MEDIAN VALUE)

UNDER $1 MILLION NET SALES	
MVIC/Net Sales	0.50
MVIC/Gross Profit	1.21
MVIC/SDE	2.23
MVIC/EBITDA	3.86
$1 MILLION–$5 MILLION NET SALES	N/A
OVER $5 MILLION NET SALES	N/A

Source: DealStats (formerly Pratt's Stats), 2023 (Portland, OR: Business Valuation Resources, LLC), www.bvresources.com/dealstats

BENCHMARK DATA

Markup is about 27 percent with some discounters working on a 25 percent markup.

INDUSTRY TREND

"Since its inception, AVB's ServiceSource has chronicled and addressed a litany of industry shortfalls, many compounded by the COVID-19 pandemic, including a dearth of trained techs, insufficient labor rates, a scarcity of parts, and increased service demand. The 'Major Appliances Blues Survey,' conducted late last year for BrandSource partner Allstate Protection Plans, provides a look at the impact those factors are having on homeowners.

"Among the findings, 78 percent of respondents waited more than three days from scheduling to receive an appointment...and 28 percent of all on-site repairs require more than one visit to complete....Nearly all homeowners (95 percent) report having a major appliance stop working at some point, with over half (52 percent) of malfunctions occurring within five years of purchase. Malfunctions occurred most frequently in washers (29 percent), followed by refrigerators/ freezers (27 percent); clothes dryers (16 percent); and dishwashers (14 percent)."

Source: "Appliance Repair Biz in Need of Fixing: Survey" by Alan Wolf, April 18, 2022, https://yoursourcenews.com/2022/04/appliance-repair-biz-in-need-of-fixing-survey/

RESOURCES

- Professional Service Association (PSA)/North American Retail Dealers Association (NARDA): http://psaworld.org/narda.php

Appraisal (Valuation Services)

| NAICS 541990　　| SIC 7389

| Profit $3.5 B

Rules of Thumb

- 1.25–1.50 x EBITDA

INDUSTRY MULTIPLES

Acquisition multiples below are calculated medians using US private industry transactions. Data updated annually. Last update: August 2023.

VALUATION MULTIPLE (MEDIAN VALUE)

UNDER $1 MILLION NET SALES

MVIC/Net Sales	1.12
MVIC/Gross Profit	1.36
MVIC/SDE	2.01
MVIC/EBITDA	2.53

$1 MILLION–$5 MILLION NET SALES

MVIC/Net Sales	1.38
MVIC/Gross Profit	1.06
MVIC/SDE	2.73
MVIC/EBITDA	3.73

OVER $5 MILLION NET SALES

MVIC/Net Sales	3.31
MVIC/Gross Profit	4.55
MVIC/SDE	13.35
MVIC/EBITDA	17.46

Source: DealStats (formerly Pratt's Stats), 2023 (Portland, OR: Business Valuation Resources, LLC), www.bvresources.com/dealstats

PRICING TIPS

Through training, certification, and support, IEV assists with consulting to bidding and selling an equipment appraisal, of which the broker retains all of the assignment fees, which can range from $1,000 to $100,000+ per equipment appraisal.

BENCHMARK DATA

STATISTICS (REAL ESTATE APPRAISAL)

Number of Establishments	43,722
Average Profit Margin	18.5%
Revenue per Employee	$184,000
Average Number of Employees	1.5
Average Wages per Employee	$50,853

PRODUCTS AND SERVICES SEGMENTATION

Real estate appraisal – residential	49.6%
Real estate appraisal – commercial	26.4%
Appraisal management	21.7%
Consulting and other services	2.3%

MAJOR MARKET SEGMENTATION

Financial institutions and brokers	55.3%
Law offices	16.3%
Private owners	12.5%
Accountants	8.2%
Government and other	7.7%

INDUSTRY COSTS

Profit	18.5%
Wages	27.8%
Purchases	2.9%
Depreciation	1.0%
Marketing	1.5%
Rent & Utilities	5.2%
Other	43.2%

MARKET SHARE

CBRE Group, Inc.	3.2%
BGC Partners, Inc.	0.2%

STATISTICS (BUSINESS VALUATION FIRMS)

Number of Establishments	74,557
Average Profit Margin	11.4%
Revenue per Employee	$130,000
Average Number of Employees	1.2
Average Wages per Employee	$50,508

PRODUCTS AND SERVICES SEGMENTATION

Capitalization of income valuation	44.8%
Asset valuation	35.1%
Owner benefit valuation	13.1%
Market valuation	7.0%

MAJOR MARKET SEGMENTATION

Private firms	65.7%
Individuals and households	18.9%
Government institutions	10.0%
Nonprofit organizations	5.4%

INDUSTRY COSTS

Profit	11.4%
Wages	39.5%
Purchases	5.8%
Depreciation	1.1%
Marketing	1.6%
Rent & Utilities	4.3%
Other	36.3%

INDUSTRY TREND

Whether the economy is going up or down, or staying consistent, equipment appraisers are always busy and landing assignments. Equipment appraisal is a wonderful niche and not regulated by any state or federal authority but follows USPAP.

"Housing starts, existing home sales and the value of residential construction expanded significantly in 2020 and 2021. Residential and nonresidential activity continues to fall due to unfavorable economic conditions. The 2008 financial crisis forced the government to change the process for real estate loans. The nonresidential sector will likely expand over the following years. The Federal Reserve has announced its intentions to continue raising the interest rate. Mortgage rates will continue to fluctuate but remain higher than pre-pandemic levels.

As downstream markets continue to struggle, revenue and profit will fall. Despite positive demand trends, COVID-19 pushed revenue into decline. Surging IPOs boosted revenue during the recovery. High investor uncertainty has constrained downstream demand. Rising corporate profit and falling investor uncertainty will support revenue growth during the outlook period. Accountants and new software will continue to remain a major sources of competition. New innovations may bring corporations back into the industry's fold. Demand for business valuation services grows in line with corporate profit and M&A activity."

Source: IBISWorld Industry at a Glance

EXPERT COMMENTS

There are approximately 460 equipment appraisers across the U.S.; brokers have businesses that have equipment, but they do not know what the equipment really is worth, which can kill a deal, or attract buyers if the equipment is valued by a certified equipment appraiser.

RESOURCES

- IBISWorld, April 2023: https://www.ibisworld.com
- IBISWorld, February 2023: https://www.ibisworld.com
- AI—Appraisal Institute: https://www.appraisalinstitute.org
- ASA: https://www.appraisers.org
- IEV—Institute of Equipment Valuation: https://www.equipmentvaluation.institute
- NAA—National Association of Appraisers: https://www.naappraisers.org
- NACVA—National Association of Certified Valuators and Analysts: https://www.nacva.com

Arcade, Food, & Entertainment Complexes

| NAICS 713120 | SIC 7993-03

| Profit $441.4 M | Wages $938.6 M | Annual Growth Future 1.4%

| | | Annual Growth Past -8.2%

Rules of Thumb

- 25% annual sales includes inventory
- 3 x SDE includes inventory
- 3–3.5 x EBITDA plus vehicle value (over 15 vehicles)

INDUSTRY MULTIPLES

Acquisition multiples below are calculated medians using US private industry transactions. Data updated annually. Last update: August 2023.

VALUATION MULTIPLE (MEDIAN VALUE)

UNDER $1 MILLION NET SALES	
MVIC/Net Sales	0.54
MVIC/Gross Profit	0.70
MVIC/SDE	1.98
MVIC/EBITDA	1.62
$1 MILLION–$5 MILLION NET SALES	
MVIC/Net Sales	0.16
MVIC/Gross Profit	0.18

```
MVIC/SDE    .    .    .    .    .    .    .    .    .    .    .    .    N/A
MVIC/EBITDA    .    .    .    .    .    .    .    .    .    .    .    N/A
```
OVER $5 MILLION NET SALES   N/A

Source: DealStats (formerly Pratt's Stats), 2023 (Portland, OR: Business Valuation Resources, LLC), www.bvresources.com/dealstats

PRICING TIPS

Make sure the equipment is either owned and is in current, fashionable condition, or make sure there is an attractive lease arrangement that enables simple trade-in for more current gaming. These games are only as valuable as the current trend. There are stability games such as air hockey, certain pinball games and redemption games where you can win toy prizes straight from the machine. The store must have a mix of current trend equipment and the stability games. Stability games are the work horses but the trendy games are very expensive to stay on top of.

This industry is not for everyone! Although, if you are an experienced retailer and have a stomach for high rent-to-gross sales percentages, this could be a great opportunity for you to enter into a fun and rewarding industry! It is a simple business model and can be improved significantly by introducing customer promotions combining game tokens with redemption prize incentives and local food retailers.

BENCHMARK DATA

STATISTICS (ARCADE, FOOD & ENTERTAINMENT COMPLEXES)

Number of Establishments .	7,392
Average Profit Margin	13.6%
Revenue per Employee .	$42,600
Average Number of Employees.	10.5
Average Wages per Employee .	$12,436

PRODUCTS AND SERVICES SEGMENTATION

Game and ride admissions .	52.1%
Food and beverages	25.8%
General admissions.	16.3%
Event services	2.2%
Other	3.6%

INDUSTRY COSTS

Profit	13.6%
Wages	28.9%
Purchases	5.1%
Depreciation	4.7%
Marketing	3.4%
Rent & Utilities	10.1%
Other	34.2%

STATISTICS (GOLF DRIVING RANGES AND FAMILY FUN CENTERS)

Number of Establishments .	62,146
Average Profit Margin	9.7%
Revenue per Employee .	$62,300
Average Number of Employees.	4.3
Average Wages per Employee .	$19,919

PRODUCTS AND SERVICES SEGMENTATION

Amusement and recreation services	61.0%
Coin operated games and rides	13.0%
Other	10.0%
Coin operated games and rides	7.0%

Meals and beverages 5.0%
Registration for tournaments and matches. 4.0%

INDUSTRY COSTS

Profit 9.7%
Wages 31.5%
Purchases 5.3%
Depreciation 6.4%
Marketing 3.5%
Rent & Utilities 10.5%
Other 33.2%

MARKET SHARE

Topgolf International Inc. 0.7%

EXPENSES (% OF ANNUAL SALES)

Cost of Goods . . . . 05% to 10%
Occupancy Costs . . . . 40% to 50%
Payroll/Labor Costs. 15%
Profit (pretax) . . . . 15% to 20%

INDUSTRY TREND

"The effects of the COVID-19 pandemic greatly diminished industry growth. By expanding its appeal toward young adults, the industry has broadened its consumer base. The push toward classic games not only appeals to adults, but also increases the industry-wide profit margin. Positive consumer sentiment coupled with a rebounding economy bodes well for revenue growth. The expected shift in demand from consumers is poised to present an excellent opportunity for an increasing number of establishments nationwide. With the worst of COVID-19 in the rearview mirror, consumers will have a renewed desire to visit entertainment complexes. Alcoholic beverage and food sales have become increasingly important to the industry. Increases in per capita disposable income revitalized revenue after the COVID-19 pandemic. Small, independent driving ranges face price pressure from in-market entertainment companies. Increased fitness awareness has affected the industry. Recreation expenditure contraction pressures companies to reduce prices. Technology based games such as laser-tag have grown. Topgolf has attracted new and older clients to its golf and entertainment centers. More prominent service providers with varied entertainment portfolios commanded a large share of industry revenue."

Source: IBISWorld Industry at a Glance

EXPERT COMMENTS

Games must also be attractive/specific to area demographics. Interestingly, my clients that owned a chain of stores in and around New York City found that the Asian neighborhoods demand more high-tech, challenging games and they will correspondingly pay a higher price per use. This is not a business that a client should jump into ill-informed or insufficiently researched. Only buy tried-and-true locations. Don't build new locations unless on a massive scale like Dave & Buster's. They are one-stop entertainment supercenters including food, bowling, and usually booze. The smaller locations in malls and plazas are way too risky given the fact that kids don't need to leave the home anymore to get the most current and challenging gaming. So, if there is a location that has withstood the transition to home-based gaming through the 80s, 90s and up to now, it is likely a winner. These arcade formats only now work in certain neighborhoods, need high volume given the price of commercial real estate, etc. Get a long lease.

Location is key. This is a capital-intensive industry but a proven location is a very valuable semi-absentee opportunity. If you are buying existing units, you can use the assets in the purchase to back part of the financing.

RESOURCES

- IBISWorld, January 2023: https://www.ibisworld.com
- IAAPA—International Association of Amusement Parks and Attractions: https://www.iaapa.org

Architectural Firms

	NAICS 541310		SIC 8712-02		Businesses/Units 80,225
	Profit $3.8 B		Wages $17.6 B		Annual Growth Future -0.3%
					Annual Growth Past 2.7%

Rules of Thumb

- 40% annual sales plus inventory

INDUSTRY MULTIPLES

Acquisition multiples below are calculated medians using US private industry transactions. Data updated annually. Last update: August 2023.

VALUATION MULTIPLE (MEDIAN VALUE)

UNDER $1 MILLION NET SALES
MVIC/Net Sales	0.66
MVIC/Gross Profit	0.67
MVIC/SDE	1.76
MVIC/EBITDA	2.70

$1 MILLION–$5 MILLION NET SALES
MVIC/Net Sales	0.40
MVIC/Gross Profit	0.55
MVIC/SDE	1.84
MVIC/EBITDA	4.82

OVER $5 MILLION NET SALES
MVIC/Net Sales	0.65
MVIC/Gross Profit	6.39
MVIC/SDE	4.16
MVIC/EBITDA	7.78

Source: DealStats (formerly Pratt's Stats), 2023 (Portland, OR: Business Valuation Resources, LLC), www.bvresources.com/dealstats

BENCHMARK DATA

STATISTICS (ARCHITECTS)
Number of Establishments	80,225
Average Profit Margin	6.4%
Revenue per Employee	$239,000
Average Number of Employees	3.0
Average Wages per Employee	$71,400

PRODUCTS AND SERVICES SEGMENTATION
All other nonresidential building projects	22.8%
Architectural services for residential building projects	15.3%
Office building project	12.6%
Architectural services for all other projects	11.6%
Hospitals and clinical buildings	11.4%

College and university school projects	8.9%
Primary and secondary school projects	8.7%
Retail and restaurant projects	8.7%

MAJOR MARKET SEGMENTATION

All other private businesses and organizations	50.4%
Governmental bodies	21.0%
Construction, engineering and architectural firms and all other	10.8%
Household consumers and individuals	10.0%
Nonprofit organizations	7.8%

INDUSTRY COSTS

Profit	6.4%
Wages	29.4%
Purchases	9.0%
Depreciation	1.0%
Marketing	0.5%
Rent & Utilities	4.4%
Other	49.5%

INDUSTRY TREND

"Architectural companies were able to invest in the healthcare market. The economic recovery led to a surge in spending in key areas, such as residential markets. Since architects thrive on a high level of construction in these markets, elevated rates have threatened revenue for the industry. GDP growth will likely increase at a steady rate, resulting in a modest rise in per capita incomes every year. Developers have been building new structures in accordance with the LEED Green Building Rating System. Construction companies, developers and government agencies are expected to build sustainable structures. Despite some challenges, architects operating in residential markets performed well."

Source: IBISWorld Industry at a Glance

RESOURCES
• IBISWorld, February 2023: https://www.ibisworld.com
• AIA—The American Institute of Architects: https://www.aia.org

Art Galleries and Dealers

	NAICS 459920		SIC 5999-69		Businesses/Units 20,051
	Profit $1.2 B		Wages $1.4 B		Annual Growth Future 1.4%
					Annual Growth Past 0.3%

Rules of Thumb
• 30% annual revenues plus inventory

PRICING TIPS

In some galleries, much of the artwork may be on consignment.

BENCHMARK DATA

STATISTICS (ART DEALERS)

Number of Establishments	20,051
Average Profit Margin	9.7%
Revenue per Employee	$387,000
Average Number of Employees	1.6
Average Wages per Employee	$42,811

PRODUCTS AND SERVICES SEGMENTATION

Paintings	38.0%
Prints	20.9%
Drawings	19.9%
Other media	9.8%
Sculptures	7.6%
Photography	3.8%

MAJOR MARKET SEGMENTATION

Modern art	29.9%
Postwar art	18.1%
Resale to other dealers	16.5%
Contemporary art	15.7%
19th century art	7.9%
Old masters	7.1%
All other	4.8%

INDUSTRY COSTS

Profit	9.7%
Wages	11.2%
Purchases	47.2%
Depreciation	0.6%
Marketing	1.6%
Rent & Utilities	6.4%
Other	23.3%

INDUSTRY TREND

"This industry will expand its digital space and use its capabilities to exhibit, promote, and sell pieces of art through cutting-edge instruments, allowing for a wider reach and greater efficiency. Aside from that, digital space allows customers from all over the world to participate in online exhibitions and become more acquainted with the available lots."

Source: "The Role of Art Dealers: Past, Present, and Future Trends" by Nancy Howard, February 20, 2022, https://artbusinessnews.com/2022/02/the-role-of-art-dealers-past-present-and-future-trends/

"The industry has benefited from record-high selling prices during the period. Industry operators have refined and developed online sales and auction platforms. The number of industry operators is expected to decline during the period. Growth in the overall economy and disposable income will benefit the industry. The already high level of globalization of this industry is expected to continue to rise. The number of industry enterprises is projected to increase. Growth for this industry has traditionally been driven by growth in the number of sales and not by inflation in selling prices."

Source: IBISWorld Industry at a Glance

RESOURCES

- IBISWorld, March 2023: https://www.ibisworld.com
- ADAA—Art Dealers Association of America: https://artdealers.org
- ArtBusiness.com: https://www.artbusiness.com

Art Supplies

| NAICS 453998 | SIC 5999-65

Rules of Thumb

- 25%–30% annual sales plus inventory

INDUSTRY MULTIPLES

Acquisition multiples below are calculated medians using US private industry transactions. Data updated annually. Last update: August 2023.

VALUATION MULTIPLE (MEDIAN VALUE)

UNDER $1 MILLION NET SALES

MVIC/Net Sales.	0.54
MVIC/Gross Profit	0.90
MVIC/SDE	2.34
MVIC/EBITDA	3.10

$1 MILLION–$5 MILLION NET SALES

MVIC/Net Sales.	0.50
MVIC/Gross Profit	0.99
MVIC/SDE	2.69
MVIC/EBITDA	4.11

OVER $5 MILLION NET SALES

MVIC/Net Sales.	1.29
MVIC/Gross Profit	3.18
MVIC/SDE	1.91
MVIC/EBITDA	10.61

Source: DealStats (formerly Pratt's Stats), 2023 (Portland, OR: Business Valuation Resources, LLC), www.bvresources.com/dealstats

PRICING TIPS

Many hobby stores and related businesses may carry a line of art supplies. A store specializing in just art supplies requires an owner with the appropriate knowledge.

BENCHMARK DATA

For Benchmark Information see Retail Stores (Small Specialty)

RESOURCES

• Art Materials Retailer: https://artmaterialsretailer.com

Arts & Crafts/Retail Stores

NAICS 4591	SIC 5085	Businesses/Units 30,388
Profit $183.2 M	Wages $692.3 M	Annual Growth Future -0.4%
		Annual Growth Past -1.1%

Rules of Thumb

• 35% annual sales plus inventory
• 2 x SDE plus inventory

INDUSTRY MULTIPLES

Acquisition multiples below are calculated medians using US private industry transactions. Data updated annually. Last update: August 2023.

VALUATION MULTIPLE (MEDIAN VALUE)

UNDER $1 MILLION NET SALES	N/A

$1 MILLION–$5 MILLION NET SALES

MVIC/Net Sales.	0.56
MVIC/Gross Profit	3.08
MVIC/SDE	5.43

MVIC/EBITDA 6.58

OVER $5 MILLION NET SALES   N/A

Source: DealStats (formerly Pratt's Stats), 2023 (Portland, OR: Business Valuation Resources, LLC), www.bvresources.com/dealstats

PRICING TIPS

Inventory should be priced separately and should include any costs associated with shipping the inventory to the place of business. Also, any needed labor required to repackage product should be part of COGS and not part of labor. As with most other business valuations, look hard at attractors and detractors to the 36 percent rule of thumb.

BENCHMARK DATA

STATISTICS (FABRIC, CRAFT & SEWING SUPPLIES STORES)

Number of Establishments	.30,388
Average Profit Margin	. 4.0%
Revenue per Employee	$74,700
Average Number of Employees. . . .	.2.0
Average Wages per Employee . . .	$11,346

PRODUCTS AND SERVICES SEGMENTATION

Fabrics	. 58.7%
Sewing and craft supplies	. 39.5%
Patterns and other	. 1.8%

INDUSTRY COSTS

Profit	. 4.0%
Wages	. 15.1%
Purchases	. 52.0%
Depreciation	. 0.9%
Marketing	. 2.0%
Rent & Utilities	. 6.2%
Other	. 19.9%

MARKET SHARE

Michaels Companies, Inc.	. 25.3%
Hobby Lobby Stores Inc.	. 22.2%
Jo-Ann Stores Inc.	. 22.1%

Rent at 10 percent of GAS (gross annual sales). Sales per square foot at $150–$175. Sales per employee at $75,000–$125,000. Advertising at 3 to 4 percent of GAS.

EXPENSES (% OF ANNUAL SALES)

Cost of Goods	. 50%
Occupancy Costs	. 15%
Payroll/Labor Costs.	. 15%
Profit (pretax)	. 20%

INDUSTRY TREND

"Strong competition from discount department stores and online retailers has eroded demand for industry products. Discount department stores and e-commerce retailers have been attracting a large number of crafting consumers, pressuring this industry's sales. Demand from baby boomers, who account for nearly one-fifth of industry sales, has increased. As the US economy begins to recover from the coronavirus, household disposable income levels are expected to increase. The ease of finding a desired item will present a strong incentive for customers to switch to online retailers. Contributing to profit growth, the price of cotton is expected to decrease. Increased consolidation is expected to drive contractions in industry employment, wages and pressure establishment growth."

Source: IBISWorld Industry at a Glance

RESOURCES

- IBISWorld, April 2023: https://www.ibisworld.com
- Craft Industry Alliance: https://craftindustryalliance.org
- Handmade Business magazine: https://handmade-business.com
- NAMTA—International Art Materials Association: https://www.namta.org

Assisted Living Facilities/Retirement Communities (with Nursing Care)

	NAICS 623311		SIC 8361-05		Businesses/Units 34,912
	Profit $15 B		Wages $65.5 B		Annual Growth Future 2.6%
					Annual Growth Past 0.7%

Rules of Thumb

- 100%–150% annual sales
- 3–4 x SDE
- 3 x EBIT

INDUSTRY MULTIPLES

Acquisition multiples below are calculated medians using US private industry transactions. Data updated annually. Last update: August 2023.

VALUATION MULTIPLE (MEDIAN VALUE)

UNDER $1 MILLION NET SALES	
MVIC/Net Sales	0.60
MVIC/Gross Profit	0.83
MVIC/SDE	2.34
MVIC/EBITDA	2.58
$1 MILLION–$5 MILLION NET SALES	
MVIC/Net Sales	0.53
MVIC/Gross Profit	0.53
MVIC/SDE	1.67
MVIC/EBITDA	6.86
OVER $5 MILLION NET SALES	
MVIC/Net Sales	2.76
MVIC/Gross Profit	3.56
MVIC/SDE	N/A
MVIC/EBITDA	N/A

Source: DealStats (formerly Pratt's Stats), 2023 (Portland, OR: Business Valuation Resources, LLC), www.bvresources.com/dealstats

PRICING TIPS

The main way that any assisted living or skilled nursing facility is valued is based on a cap rate on NOI. Another term you'll hear is EBITDAR, with the "R" standing for rent. In these projects, you always add back rent in the cash flow calculation as it's just an internal transfer into a real estate holding company, which is essentially rent paid to themselves—or for those homes that hold the entire ownership in one entity, it's still the same thing with rent being paid to themselves. The HUD

232 analysis, the basis for all valuation modeling, states that a home should have proprietary income. This is most simply calculated with what is called a 5 percent management fee that is subtracted from EBITDAR to get a NOI. It is the NOI that you then apply a cap rate to, which will range from 5 to 9 percent with nursing homes in the 9 to 12 percent range. Another key rule of thumb is price per unit (not bed but per unit or doorknob). In ALFs, you're talking as high as $175,000 per bed (current rates around $157,000/unit) and nursing homes typically in the $50,000 to $80,000 range. Many factors can swing these unit rates up or down depending on deferred maintenance, private bathrooms, fancy coffee shops that might be in assisted livings, etc. Almost all of these deals include the real estate. Sometimes a seller will want to retain the real estate (sort of like a REIT) to generate income for themselves. This changes the entire valuing for just the business that would typically go back to a 3 to 4 x multiple on cash flow.

Value of the real estate needs to be considered separately from the business. Cap rates are sometimes considered with larger facilities rather than a group home of 16 beds or under.

Annual gross sales percentage is not the way you value these businesses, nor is SDE or even using EBITDA. The HUD 232 analysis is a guide that is followed by valuation experts. It takes EBITDA, subtracts capex and what's called a proprietary income, which is what HUD believes the business should make. Valuation people state this reduction as 5 percent of gross sales, which is much easier to calculate. Once you do this, you arrive at NOI, or net operating income, and to that you apply industry standard cap rates (capitalization). These can vary significantly, depending on the size of your facility and whether it's state of the art, private bathrooms, etc. Turn to nic.org for the latest cap rate information. Their information is for larger homes with a minimum of a few million in value. ALFs value the highest, currently around 6 percent cap. SNFs, around 10 percent. However, you can see ALF range all the way up to 12 or 14 percent if you have a small facility or mansion-style home. SNFs, same thing, but can go as low as 16 percent for struggling facilities.

BENCHMARK DATA

STATISTICS (NURSING CARE)

Number of Establishments	34,912
Average Profit Margin	9.9%
Revenue per Employee	$95,400
Average Number of Employees	45.8
Average Wages per Employee	$41,284

PRODUCTS AND SERVICES SEGMENTATION

For-profit skilled nursing facilities	43.6%
For-profit nursing homes	33.0%
Nonprofit skilled nursing facilities	10.3%
Nonprofit nursing homes	7.8%
Government nursing homes and skilled nursing facilities	4.7%
Hospice centers	0.6%

INDUSTRY COSTS

Profit	9.9%
Wages	43.0%
Purchases	6.4%
Depreciation	2.4%
Marketing	0.2%
Rent & Utilities	6.1%
Other	31.9%

A Assisted livings: $150,000 to 175,000 per unit (doorknob). Nursing homes: $50,000 to $80,000 per unit (doorknob). If multiple-bed rooms (2 beds to a room), per-unit rates will drop.

Value of the real estate needs to be considered separately form the business. Cap rates are sometimes considered with larger facilities rather than group home of 16 beds or under.

Census is key in any of these businesses. If you're looking at an ALF (assisted living), 75% is good 80% is excellent. Beyond that, fantastic! Below 70% and ALFs begin to struggle to be profitable. SNFs (skilled nursing) run a higher census. 85% is good. If they're pushing 90% or higher, this is excellent. Below 80% and they struggle to be profitable.

EXPENSES (% OF ANNUAL SALES)

Cost of Goods	25% to 30%
Occupancy Costs	10% to 20%
Payroll/Labor Costs.	40% to 50%
Profit (pretax)	10% to 20%

QUESTIONS

- Ask for 3 years of census with payor mix (private, Medicaid, and Medicare), last 3 surveys, cost reports so you can see Medicare and Medicaid rates, current rate sheet and what their private pay rate is, and licensed bed count.
- Why are they selling? What are the age and health stages or categories of each of your tenants? How many are on Medicaid? Ask for all licenses and inspections.
- Ask for last 3 or 5 years of state surveys. Especially in nursing homes, being a 5-star Medicare home is golden. Being a 2-star home means big problems. A low-rated home will struggle with attracting new residents, and that creates a low census. F-tags and G-tags in nursing homes are bad! Doesn't mean the home can't fix the problems—and oftentimes it has fixed them—but survey after survey with the same problems indicates a systemic issue.

INDUSTRY TREND

Staffing challenges rank as the highest challenge. Reimbursement rates from Medicare and Medicaid are always challenging. Families are trying to keep loved ones at home longer, and this is delaying the time when residents are ready for assisted living or nursing homes. Businesses building vertically to include things like home health and adult day care can try and keep some of those dollars in their pockets.

"Facilities with a diverse and dynamic menu tend to do well as compared to those with a static menu. Having a dietician or nutritionist onboard is linked to increased satisfaction levels among the residents when it comes to physical and mental health....Unlike other industries, the healthcare sector is facing an attrition rate of over 30%."

Source: "5 Assisted Living Industry Trends That Every Owner Needs to Know," August 4, 2023, https://www.xenia.team/articles/5-assisted-living-industry-trends

More and more group homes rather than large assisted living facilities. Small group homes are able to give better care.

Tremendous pressure on staffing. ALFs have it a little better because they don't run with a lot of nurses. SNFs on the other hand have no choice. We've seen big players in the market offering huge bonuses in trying to steal quality staff from smaller homes. Census numbers have rebounded after COVID and seem to remain strong. We have seen Medicaid come up a bit in rate, and that is helping homes (SNFs) that run a high Medicaid residency.

"The group of adults in the age demographic of 65 and older has steadily grown. Many nursing homes have pivoted to providing specialized care. Shifting consumer preferences have placed pressure on nursing care facilities. Regulatory changes attempting to curtail government spending on healthcare will just barely affect revenue growth. Nursing care facilities can expand services through consolidation. States will trim benefits and turn to private insurance companies to provide managed care. The growing share of senior adults has propelled the need for services offered by nursing care facilities."

Source: IBISWorld Industry at a Glance

EXPERT COMMENTS

Census, census, census. It drives profits, and that drives value since valuations are a multiple of cash flow. A weak or inconsistent census is typically a red flag to either poor care, a not so nice looking facility, or poor screening of new residents that is causing large turnover. Buyers should ask for 3 years of census and for the number of discharges and admissions each year. That will show you the turnover rate the home is having. Likewise, sellers want to make sure they go into a sale with a solid census track record; proper staffing levels; and good, clean surveys. Buyers will always ask for the last few surveys to see how many violations a home had, if they were serious, and if these same violations showed up in future surveys indicating a potential systemic problem.

Buyers: know what you're getting into. This is 24/7 business dealing with end-of-life issues. Make sure you're emotionally prepared for this and that you're prepared to make a big time commitment out of the gate, unless the home you're buying is turnkey with management in place.

Sellers: census, census, census. Don't bring a home with a struggling census to market. You'll leave a ton of money on the table. Tired properties also push values down. It's very much like selling your home. Good curb appeal and a strong census will mean strong profits and a big payday!

Most states have moratoriums on new licenses. This makes the resale of a facility quite valuable. Staffing is a real struggle right now and is driving up costs and robbing bottom-line profits.

FINANCING

Some seller financing is probably evident in half the deals, but typically not more than 10 percent. SBA lending is a very good source for these projects, and with the new SOP out from the SBA, slightly larger deals can now fit in under their program.

Personal conventional loans, SBA 7a, and some seller financing for short term of 2 to 3 years. SBA 10 years and up to 24 years with real estate.

For deals under $5 million, most are being done via SBA lending. If the buyer is strong—and especially if they have any direct industry experience or at least healthcare experience—seller financing will not be required. However, we still see most smaller deals having some seller financing.

RESOURCES

- IBISWorld, January 2023: https://www.ibisworld.com
- A Place for Mom: https://www.aplaceformom.com
- American Health Care Association (AHCA)/National Center for Assisted Living (NCAL): https://www.ahcancal.org/Assisted-Living/Pages/default.aspx
- Argentum: https://www.argentum.org
- Argentum: https://www.argentum.org
- ASHA—American Seniors Housing Association: https://www.ashaliving.org
- LeadingAge: https://leadingage.org
- NIC—National Investment Center for Seniors Housing & Care: https://www.nic.org

Assisted Living Facilities/Retirement Communities (without Nursing Care)

| NAICS 623312 | Businesses/Units 27,922

| Profit $6.8 B | Wages $34.5 B | Annual Growth Future 2.4%

| | | Annual Growth Past 2.8%

Rules of Thumb

- 75% annual sales

INDUSTRY MULTIPLES

Acquisition multiples below are calculated medians using US private industry transactions. Data updated annually. Last update: August 2023.

VALUATION MULTIPLE (MEDIAN VALUE)

UNDER $1 MILLION NET SALES

MVIC/Net Sales	0.58
MVIC/Gross Profit	0.61
MVIC/SDE	2.23
MVIC/EBITDA	6.90

$1 MILLION–$5 MILLION NET SALES

MVIC/Net Sales	0.27
MVIC/Gross Profit	0.28
MVIC/SDE	1.62
•MVIC/EBITDA	2.39

OVER $5 MILLION NET SALES .... N/A

Source: DealStats (formerly Pratt's Stats), 2023 (Portland, OR: Business Valuation Resources, LLC), www.bvresources.com/dealstats

BENCHMARK DATA

STATISTICS (RETIREMENT COMMUNITIES)

Number of Establishments	27,922
Average Profit Margin	7.2%
Revenue per Employee	$91,800
Average Number of Employees	36.7
Average Wages per Employee	$33,736

PRODUCTS AND SERVICES SEGMENTATION

Continuing care retirement communities	46.5%
Assisted living facilities and homes for the elderly	44.0%
Other	9.5%

INDUSTRY COSTS

Profit	7.2%
Wages	36.6%
Purchases	5.7%
Depreciation	9.8%
Marketing	0.6%
Rent & Utilities	6.6%
Other	33.5%

MARKET SHARE

Brookdale Senior Living Inc.	2.8%
AlerisLife Inc.	1.9%
Sunrise Senior Living Inc.	1.3%

INDUSTRY TREND

"Seniors aren't looking for one-size-fits-all solutions. Instead, they're looking for a lifestyle with personalized and customized options that includes housing, wellness, health care and personal care....Today, retirement has a completely different look than it did for previous generations....Retirement is seen more often these days as a chance to pursue your passions."

Source: "Senior Living Trends 2022: What to Expect in the Future," August 4, 2022, https://www.whereyoulivematters.org/senior-living-trends-2022/

"An aging population and growing needs for memory care are driving demand. Occupancy rates remain below pre-pandemic totals, but pent-up demand for senior care has offset this. The number and types of regulations industry operators are subject to are anticipated to continue to intensify. An aging population will continue to drive resident numbers at retirement homes. Healthcare reform will become a more pertinent topic as the government contends with steeper budget deficits. Technological advances and new architectural designs will help operators compete. The rising medical needs of aging population currently characterize trends in the broader healthcare sector."

Source: IBISWorld Industry at a Glance

RESOURCES

- IBISWorld, January 2023: https://www.ibisworld.com
- ASHA—American Seniors Housing Association: https://www.ashaliving.org

Audio and Film Companies

| NAICS 512120

Rules of Thumb

- 4–6 x EBITDA

INDUSTRY MULTIPLES

Acquisition multiples below are calculated medians using US private industry transactions. Data updated annually. Last update: August 2023.

VALUATION MULTIPLE (MEDIAN VALUE)

UNDER $1 MILLION NET SALES	N/A
$1 MILLION–$5 MILLION NET SALES	N/A
OVER $5 MILLION NET SALES	
MVIC/Net Sales	1.13
MVIC/Gross Profit	1.48

| MVIC/SDE | . | . | . | . | . | . | . | . | . | . | N/A |
| MVIC/EBITDA | . | . | . | . | . | . | . | . | . | N/A |

Source: DealStats (formerly Pratt's Stats), 2023 (Portland, OR: Business Valuation Resources, LLC), www.bvresources.com/dealstats

BENCHMARK DATA

STATISTICS (AUDIO PRODUCTION STUDIOS)

Number of Establishments	22,461
Average Profit Margin	.11.0%
Revenue per Employee	$64,600
Average Number of Employees.	1.2
Average Wages per Employee	$18,989

PRODUCTS AND SERVICES SEGMENTATION

Music Recording	.46.4%
Postproduction, sound editing and design	.32.9%
Spoken word recording	. 8.6%
Radio recording	. 8.1%
Other sound editing and production	. 4.0%

MAJOR MARKET SEGMENTATION

Music industry clients	.46.4%
Advertising clients	.27.3%
Spoken word clients	. 8.6%
Radio programming clients	. 8.1%
Television and film clients	. 5.6%
Other clients	. 4.0%

INDUSTRY COSTS

Profit	.11.0%
Wages	.29.1%
Purchases	. 2.4%
Depreciation	. 1.7%
Marketing	. 1.8%
Rent & Utilities	.11.8%
Other	.42.2%

STATISTICS (MOVIE & VIDEO PRODUCTION)

Number of Establishments	. 6,505
Average Profit Margin	.12.9%
Revenue per Employee	. $634,000
Average Number of Employees.	7.0
Average Wages per Employee	. $121,727

PRODUCTS AND SERVICES SEGMENTATION

Action and adventure	.66.5%
Thriller and horror	.12.0%
Comedy	.11.3%
Drama	. 8.3%
Other	. 1.9%

MAJOR MARKET SEGMENTATION

TV licensing	.44.6%
Foreign distribution	.19.8%
Physical copy sales	.12.5%
Digital streaming and video on demand	.12.0%
Domestic box office	.11.1%

INDUSTRY COSTS

Profit	.12.9%
Wages	.19.6%
Purchases	. 2.0%

```
Depreciation  .    .    .    .    .    .    . 2.5%
Marketing  .    .    .    .    .    .    . 7.0%
Rent & Utilities .    .    .    .    .    .    . 5.6%
Other   .    .    .    .    .    .    . .50.5%
```

MARKET SHARE

```
The Walt Disney Company .    .    .    . .16.2%
ViacomCBS Inc..    .    .    .    .    . .15.5%
NBCUniversal Media LLC  .    .    .    . .11.9%
AT&T Inc.    .    .    .    .    .    .    . 9.8%
Sony Corporation  .    .    .    .    .    . 8.3%
```

INDUSTRY TREND

"To preserve margins, industry operators have tried to cut costs by lowering wages. Major and independent music record labels have maintained a meaningful relationship with production studios. As internet access expands in the United States, film and TV producers will shift their production needs. The music industry as a whole has been experiencing a shift in its business model. The Audio Production Studios industry benefits from various revenue streams. Disposable income will rise, which will encourage the spread of recording equipment to consumers that wish to record content. Recent technological improvements have enabled artists to take more control over their content. Limited box office sales have made studios more risk-averse. Amid competition mostly among major studios, new entry into the industry has been difficult over the past five years. The industry's focus on blockbusters has reduced the number of flops. Strong growth in foreign distribution is forecast to propel projected revenue growth. When an expected blockbuster flops, the repercussions are devastating for the studio. For the major studios, new digital players could prove disruptive. Studio revenue has become more reliant on blockbusters, especially those based on existing creative properties."

Source: IBISWorld Industry at a Glance

FINANCING

3 to 7 years

RESOURCES

* IBISWorld, March 2023: https://www.ibisworld.com
* IBISWorld, February 2023: https://www.ibisworld.com

Audio and Video Equipment Manufacturing

| NAICS 334310 | Businesses/Units 485

| Profit $229.7 M | Wages $816.7 M | Annual Growth Future -0.4%

                                    | Annual Growth Past 0.6%

INDUSTRY MULTIPLES

Acquisition multiples below are calculated medians using US private industry transactions. Data updated annually. Last update: August 2023.

VALUATION MULTIPLE (MEDIAN VALUE)

UNDER $1 MILLION NET SALES   N/A

$1 MILLION–$5 MILLION NET SALES
MVIC/Net Sales. 0.86

MVIC/Gross Profit 1.50
MVIC/SDE 13.16
MVIC/EBITDA . . . . N/A

OVER $5 MILLION NET SALES
MVIC/Net Sales. 1.93
MVIC/Gross Profit 4.63
MVIC/SDE . . . . N/A
MVIC/EBITDA 12.04

Source: DealStats (formerly Pratt's Stats), 2023 (Portland, OR: Business Valuation Resources, LLC),
www.bvresources.com/dealstats

BENCHMARK DATA

STATISTICS (AUDIO AND VIDEO EQUIPMENT MANUFACTURING)

Number of Establishments 485
Average Profit Margin 5.8%
Revenue per Employee $397,000
Average Number of Employees. 20.3
Average Wages per Employee $82,110

PRODUCTS AND SERVICES SEGMENTATION

Other consumer audio and video equipment 48.3%
Commercial sound equipment 28.2%
Speakers 17.7%
TVs and accessories 3.2%
Automotive audio equipment 2.6%

MAJOR MARKET SEGMENTATION

Exports 42.5%
Retailers and wholesalers 29.3%
Other 19.1%
Manufacturers 9.1%

INDUSTRY COSTS

Profit 5.8%
Wages 20.6%
Purchases 44.6%
Depreciation 1.3%
Marketing 1.7%
Rent & Utilities 1.9%
Other 24.1%

MARKET SHARE

Samsung Electronics Co 17.1%
Hon Hai Precision Industry 8.6%
JVC Kenwood Corporation 7.5%
Vizio 6.1%
Voxx International Corporation 5.9%
Zte Corp 5.1%
Hikvision Digital Technology Company. 4.7%
Shure 4.3%
Zhejiang Dahua Technology Company 3.9%
Peavey Electronics 3.3%

INDUSTRY TREND

"Increased per capita disposable income levels during the pandemic led to increased demand for industry products. Demand from the consumer electronics market has continued to shift. Semiconductor supply remains a concern throughout the industry. Rising interest rates will alter demand within the industry. Political tensions between Taiwan and China threaten industry operations. Industry demand will be sustained by new opportunities moving forward. Domestic operators have focused on cost-cutting strategies and product differentiation to compete with multinational corporations."

Source: IBISWorld Industry at a Glance

RESOURCES

- IBISWorld, January 2023: https://www.ibisworld.com

Audio/Video Conferencing

| NAICS 518210 | SIC 4822-06

Rules of Thumb

- 3–4 x EBITDA

INDUSTRY MULTIPLES

Acquisition multiples below are calculated medians using US private industry transactions. Data updated annually. Last update: August 2023.

VALUATION MULTIPLE (MEDIAN VALUE)

UNDER $1 MILLION NET SALES

MVIC/Net Sales.	1.41
MVIC/Gross Profit	2.15
MVIC/SDE	3.67
MVIC/EBITDA	11.90

$1 MILLION–$5 MILLION NET SALES

MVIC/Net Sales.	1.05
MVIC/Gross Profit	2.28
MVIC/SDE	3.54
MVIC/EBITDA	5.88

OVER $5 MILLION NET SALES

MVIC/Net Sales.	2.93
MVIC/Gross Profit	4.59
MVIC/SDE	8.27
MVIC/EBITDA	23.30

Source: DealStats (formerly Pratt's Stats), 2023 (Portland, OR: Business Valuation Resources, LLC), www.bvresources.com/dealstats

QUESTIONS

- How long are the contracts? What services are being provided?

EXPERT COMMENTS

Cost of setting up public centers is substantial. Industry is upgrading services and equipment.

Auto Auctions

| NAICS 425120

Rules of Thumb

- 33% annual sales
- 2.2 x SDE
- 2.5 x EBIT
- 2.7 x EBITDA

INDUSTRY MULTIPLES

Acquisition multiples below are calculated medians using US private industry transactions. Data updated annually. Last update: August 2023.

VALUATION MULTIPLE (MEDIAN VALUE)

UNDER $1 MILLION NET SALES	
MVIC/Net Sales.	0.72
MVIC/Gross Profit	1.10
MVIC/SDE	2.39
MVIC/EBITDA	6.57
$1 MILLION–$5 MILLION NET SALES	
MVIC/Net Sales.	0.34
MVIC/Gross Profit	1.39
MVIC/SDE	2.42
MVIC/EBITDA	3.64
OVER $5 MILLION NET SALES	
MVIC/Net Sales.	0.35
MVIC/Gross Profit	1.38
MVIC/SDE	2.70
MVIC/EBITDA	3.10

Source: DealStats (formerly Pratt's Stats), 2023 (Portland, OR: Business Valuation Resources, LLC), www.bvresources.com/dealstats

BENCHMARK DATA

Cars per auction is critical to profitability. The percentage of cars entered to cars sold should be 55 to 60 percent. A lower percentage is a red flag.

EXPENSES (% OF ANNUAL SALES)

Cost of Goods	02%
Occupancy Costs	06%
Payroll/Labor Costs.	30%
Profit (pretax)	25%

QUESTIONS

• How could they grow the business? What services could be added?— auto body repair, mechanical repair.

INDUSTRY TREND

Impacted by economic cycles

EXPERT COMMENTS

Great business for someone with people skills

National auto auctions are contracting with the major auto dealers. Smaller and regional auto auctions are focusing on the used car dealers, where they can maintain margins.

FINANCING

Combination of seller and outside financing. Buyers want to be assured that the business is not tied to the seller.

RESOURCES

• AutoNation Auto Auctions: https://www.autonationautoauction.com
• Manheim: https://www.manheim.com
• NAAA—National Auto Auction Association: https://www.naaa.com
• NIAA—National Independent Auto Association: http://www.independentauctions.org

Auto Body Repair

	NAICS 811121		SIC 7532-01		Businesses/Units 87,534
	Profit $4.6 B		Wages $16.9 B		Annual Growth Future 0.9%
					Annual Growth Past 0.5%

Rules of Thumb
- 1.5–2.3 x SDE plus inventory
- 3 x EBIT
- 2–4 x EBITDA
- 25%–35% annual sales includes inventory
- 3 x SDE

INDUSTRY MULTIPLES

Acquisition multiples below are calculated medians using US private industry transactions. Data updated annually. Last update: August 2023.

VALUATION MULTIPLE (MEDIAN VALUE)

UNDER $1 MILLION NET SALES
MVIC/Net Sales	0.50
MVIC/Gross Profit	0.81
MVIC/SDE	2.01
MVIC/EBITDA	3.24

$1 MILLION–$5 MILLION NET SALES
MVIC/Net Sales	0.35
MVIC/Gross Profit	0.62
MVIC/SDE	2.49
MVIC/EBITDA	5.26

OVER $5 MILLION NET SALES
MVIC/Net Sales	0.72
MVIC/Gross Profit	2.15
MVIC/SDE	12.29
MVIC/EBITDA	13.66

Source: DealStats (formerly Pratt's Stats), 2023 (Portland, OR: Business Valuation Resources, LLC), www.bvresources.com/dealstats

PRICING TIPS

3 times cash flow including seller's discretionary earnings

MSOs set the market value. Due to the closely held nature of this industry, financial reports are only a portion of the value of a collision center's worth from a buyer's perspective. There are lots of variations that cannot be compiled here, such as DRP relations, ranking, variety, capacity, and gross sales. Net profit and SDE are understood from the experienced buyer's perspective even if they cannot be found by a financial analyst. This is a closed industry and not for the faint of heart, as an unknowing broker will not do their client justice. The largest M&A brokerages in the world, which take their same approach to this industry, miss the mark nearly every time.

BENCHMARK DATA

STATISTICS (CAR BODY SHOPS)

Number of Establishments	87,534
Average Profit Margin	7.8%
Revenue per Employee	$177,000
Average Number of Employees	3.9
Average Wages per Employee	$50,171

A

Body repair services	61.1%
Glass replacement and repair	16.5%
Painting services	14.6%
Upholstery and interior repair	2.5%
Merchandise sales	2.2%
Detailing services and body conversions .	1.6%
Other services	1.5%

INDUSTRY COSTS

Profit	7.8%
Wages	28.6%
Purchases	9.4%
Depreciation	1.5%
Marketing	1.9%
Rent & Utilities	5.8%
Other	45.1%

MARKET SHARE

The Boyd Group Inc.	4.3%
Driven Brands, Inc.	2.5%
Caliber Collision Center	2.2%
Service King.	1.9%
Gerber Collision & Glass	0.6%

$150,000.00 to $250,000.00 per employee

EXPENSES (% OF ANNUAL SALES)

Cost of Goods	35% to 45%
Occupancy Costs	05% to 15%
Payroll/Labor Costs.	15% to 20%
Profit (pretax)	10% to 20%

QUESTIONS

- Provide 3 years of tax returns.
- Ask for the sales by source data, and be sure the income is spread out among insurers.
- How much of their time does the owner work on cars? When does your paint supplier contract expire? Lease terms? Worker's comp mode rate?
- Percentage of volume that is DRP contracts (insurance contracts)? Percentage of rent to gross sales? How much space is there indoors for car storage?
- Do you supply loan cars? If so, do you get rebates from rental companies for the loaners? When will a job be booked as a sale? Do you have steady referrals from dealerships? When are initial assessments made? Is any charge made for them? After the initial estimate is made, how are contacts made with the insurance company?

INDUSTRY TREND

Shops that have sales over $750,000.00 are sold to large body shops.

"More vehicles on the road will translate to more revenue. The coronavirus pandemic significantly disrupted industry operations. Competition within the industry has been increasing. Demand for industry services will increase in line with improving economic conditions. New car sales will increase, posing a potential threat to the industry. Industry operators will have to compete for highly skilled workers. Recovery in the average industry profit margin has been constrained by ongoing supply chain disruptions."

Source: IBISWorld Industry at a Glance

EXPERT COMMENTS

2 to 3 years in advance, a seller should have the business appraised, and every year moving forward.

Have experience and cash. Search for a great location and don't settle for a low-trafficked site. Execute a 10- to 15-year lease with assignment rights, and three or more 5-year lease extensions.

The industry is dominated by insurance companies. Contracts are not assumable by buyers. Without a contract, your volume is going to be very small.

FINANCING

Equity-owned groups and bank loans are the primary sources of financing in this industry.

RESOURCES

- IBISWorld, January 2023: https://www.ibisworld.com
- ASA—Automotive Service Association: https://www.asashop.org
- AutoBizBrokers: http://autobizbrokers.com
- Autobody News: https://www.autobodynews.com
- AutoInc.: https://www.autoinc.org
- BodyShop Business—publication and website; also offers back issues: https://www.bodyshopbusiness.com
- Collision Industry Foundation: https://www.collisionindustryfoundation.org
- CollisionWeek: https://collisionweek.com
- FenderBender: https://www.fenderbender.com
- I-CAR: https://www.i-car.com/s/
- RDN—Repairer Driven News: https://www.repairerdrivennews.com

---

Auto Brake Services

| NAICS 811118 | SIC 7539-14

Rules of Thumb

- 30% annual sales plus inventory
- 4 x monthly sales plus inventory

INDUSTRY MULTIPLES

Acquisition multiples below are calculated medians using US private industry transactions. Data updated annually. Last update: August 2023.

VALUATION MULTIPLE (MEDIAN VALUE)

UNDER $1 MILLION NET SALES	
MVIC/Net Sales	0.33
MVIC/Gross Profit	0.49
MVIC/SDE	1.48
MVIC/EBITDA	1.96
$1 MILLION–$5 MILLION NET SALES	
MVIC/Net Sales	0.54
MVIC/Gross Profit	0.91
MVIC/SDE	2.25
MVIC/EBITDA	3.74
OVER $5 MILLION NET SALES	N/A

Source: DealStats (formerly Pratt's Stats), 2023 (Portland, OR: Business Valuation Resources, LLC), www.bvresources.com/dealstats

A

Auto Dealerships, New Cars

	NAICS 441110		SIC 5511-02		Businesses/Units 22,201
	Profit $19.1 B		Wages $83.7 B		Annual Growth Future -0.4%
					Annual Growth Past 0.4%

Rules of Thumb
- 25%–30% annual sales
- 4–5 x SDE
- 7 x EBIT
- 8–9 x EBITDA

INDUSTRY MULTIPLES

Acquisition multiples below are calculated medians using US private industry transactions. Data updated annually. Last update: August 2023.

VALUATION MULTIPLE (MEDIAN VALUE)

UNDER $1 MILLION NET SALES
MVIC/Net Sales	0.57
MVIC/Gross Profit	0.82
MVIC/SDE	2.94
MVIC/EBITDA	11.32

$1 MILLION–$5 MILLION NET SALES
MVIC/Net Sales	0.36
MVIC/Gross Profit	22.15
MVIC/SDE	1.81
MVIC/EBITDA	N/A

OVER $5 MILLION NET SALES
MVIC/Net Sales	0.14
MVIC/Gross Profit	1.22
MVIC/SDE	4.07
MVIC/EBITDA	7.84

Source: DealStats (formerly Pratt's Stats), 2023 (Portland, OR: Business Valuation Resources, LLC), www.bvresources.com/dealstats

PRICING TIPS

The key elements in the sale of a franchise dealership:

1. Goodwill/blue sky: The value of blue sky is one of the most highly negotiated components of the sale due to the multitude of influencing factors and its subjective nature. Based on both external and internal factors, a multiple of the weighted average adjusted cash flow composes the blue sky calculation. Adjusted cash flow is the net operating income of the business after adding back lender-recognized items such as depreciation, interest expense (non–floor plan), and discretionary or one-time items. The weighting references a cash flow over a period of time (say 3 to 4 years) with more weight being placed on more current performance.

2. Parts inventory: The appraised or market value of the current OEM parts catalog inventory. Some buyers will specify those part numbers which have sold in the last 12 months. An independent appraisal will determine this value.

3. Furniture, fixtures, and equipment (FFE): The market value of the FFE which, as a general rule, is approximately 50 percent of the original acquisition cost. An independent appraisal will determine this value.

4. Real estate: If a loan is involved, the bank will require a professional real estate appraisal from a company familiar with valuing special use properties such as an automotive dealership. A Phase 1 environmental assessment is also required.

5. Used vehicles: Generally this asset is excluded from the offering, but the buyer is able to purchase the used vehicles at their own election using one of the industry-recognized pricing guidelines to determine valuation.

6. New vehicles: New vehicle inventory is floor-planned and transferred from the seller's banking source to the buyer's source at dealer cost and, therefore, not included in the sales price.

There is a great deal of variation for multiples of adjusted cash flow based on geography, brand, vehicle segmentation, and other factors (competitive density, rural versus metro, facility image compliance). For example, a domestic franchise like Ford will have a higher multiple in Texas (where truck segmentation is high) than in California (higher preference for import cars). Conversely, a BMW store will carry a higher multiple in New York (high import market) than in Detroit.

BENCHMARK DATA

STATISTICS (NEW CAR DEALERS)

Number of Establishments	22,201
Average Profit Margin	1.7%
Revenue per Employee	$889,000
Average Number of Employees	56.5
Average Wages per Employee	$66,468

PRODUCTS AND SERVICES SEGMENTATION

New vehicles	48.3%
Used vehicles	35.5%
Parts and repair services	11.7%
Finance and insurance	4.5%

INDUSTRY COSTS

Profit	1.7%
Wages	7.4%
Purchases	80.7%
Depreciation	0.2%
Marketing	0.9%
Rent & Utilities	1.0%
Other	8.1%

Revenue per employee, $875,000; wages per employee, $65,000

Return on sales is best operating measure. Average dealership is always around 2.5 percent, perhaps a bit higher now with the margin windfalls mentioned earlier. Any number over 3 percent is a high-performing store. Service absorption (degree that fixed operations covers expenses) should run 85 to 100 percent. Fixed expenses as a percent of dealership gross (sales less COGS) should be around 30 percent.

Selling gross by department—new vehicles, 45%; used, 50%; parts, 60%; service, 45%; fixed expenses, 30% of total gross

EXPENSES (% OF ANNUAL SALES)

Cost of Goods	75% to 85%
Occupancy Costs	05% to 10%
Payroll/Labor Costs. . . .	05% to 10%
Profit (pretax)	01.5% to 03%

QUESTIONS

- What is your breakeven sales point? What is your service absorption? Tell me about the management talent in place and their compensation plans? What is it like working with the OEM? What are your working capital requirements? Facility costs and lease/buy parameters? Does facility meet OEM requirements?
- What are the top three growth opportunities for your store? The typical due diligence questions with financials and market effectiveness
- Wholesale floor plan source, marketing plans, owner loyalty, retail/commercial mix, labor rates
- Any factory requirements?
- How many cars per month do they sell? How is their CSI rating?
- What is your motivation for selling? Any family members part of your succession plan? Are you interested in holding the real property—or selling with a carryback note? What tax attributes are associated with your business (LIFO, Goodwill, etc.)?
- Staff that will stay on?

INDUSTRY TREND

Additional consolidation; the number of outlets will be pretty constant, but there will be fewer owners. Presently the top 150 dealership groups sell 25 percent of the vehicles; this is up 0.5 points from a year ago and will continue to increase.

The near-term outlook is favorable with the pent-up demand caused by the microchip storage. The higher interest rates will moderate demand somewhat, but the law of supply and demand will win out, and margins and cash flow will remain strong for the next 3 to 4 years.

"A recent Cox Automotive study found that 55% of customers have shifted to an online car buying experience....A recent study found that 82% of consumers prefer contactless transactions. Dealerships are responding by providing support for mobile wallets, tap-and-go cards and disabling signature requirements on some purchases....When it comes to convenience, customers might prefer digitally signing required documents and notarizing title and registration forms online."

Source: "Tech Trends for Car Dealerships in 2022" by Jennifer Gustavson, March 16, 2022, https://www.notarize.com/blog/tech-trends-for-car-dealerships-in-2022

Aging of the boomers, industry disruption (electrification, autonomous, ride sharing), and further consolidation will drive a lot of buy–sell activity.

"COVID-19 spurred a shortage of new vehicles, driving car prices through the roof. Tighter credit markets will likely begin affecting automobile purchases after interest rate hikes in 2022. Online car dealers increase competition. Borrowing costs remain elevated, hurting demand. Car prices will stabilize as inventories grow. Global trade disputes surrounding semiconductors may keep car prices elevated. Most consumers finance new and used vehicle purchases, exposing the industry to changing interest rates."

Source: IBISWorld Industry at a Glance

EXPERT COMMENTS

Work with an experienced automotive-knowledgeable broker who can help you navigate the business purchase and the OEM application/approval process. These deals are complex, with lots of negotiations within the negotiation, and unique conventions for valuing and pricing the business.

The automotive category is undergoing great disruption with the migration from internal combustion engines to electric vehicles, the threat of OEM direct selling, the aggressive consolidation underway at all levels to achieve scale efficiencies, and the demographic aging of the dealer population. With the shortage of microchips over the last two years, dealers have experienced record profits due to very high gross margins on new vehicle and an extremely robust used vehicle market. The auto category is clearly a seller's market at present, but as the microchip shortage sorts out and the higher interest rate environment kicks in, demand will normalize somewhat, leading some dealers to exit the market at the top of the cycle. That said, natural pent-up demand and the aging of the vehicle park will sustain business performance for the foreseeable future for those who remain.

Franchise dealerships require high capital and a certain level of prior ownership and management experience in order to become approved by the OEM. The well-located, high-demand brand dealerships are highly sought.

FINANCING

Very little seller financing is ever offered. Funding comes from either buyer assets or outside lending sources.

Financing is almost 100 percent from outside sources.

RESOURCES

- IBISWorld, January 2023: https://www.ibisworld.com
- AIADA—American International Automobile Dealers Association: https://www.aiada.org
- Automotive News: https://www.autonews.com
- BVR—Business Valuation Resources: https://www.bvresources.com
- CBT News: https://www.cbtnews.com
- NADA—National Automobile Dealers Association: https://www.nada.org
- WardsAuto: https://www.wardsauto.com

Auto Dealerships, Used Cars

NAICS 441120	SIC 5511-03	Businesses/Units 156,199
Profit $4.9 B	Wages $12.3 B	Annual Growth Future 1.2%
		Annual Growth Past 5.1%

INDUSTRY MULTIPLES

Acquisition multiples below are calculated medians using US private industry transactions. Data updated annually. Last update: August 2023.

VALUATION MULTIPLE (MEDIAN VALUE)

UNDER $1 MILLION NET SALES

MVIC/Net Sales	0.29
MVIC/Gross Profit	0.77
MVIC/SDE	1.82
MVIC/EBITDA	1.60

$1 MILLION–$5 MILLION NET SALES

MVIC/Net Sales.	0.06
MVIC/Gross Profit	0.42
MVIC/SDE	0.90
MVIC/EBITDA	0.70

OVER $5 MILLION NET SALES

MVIC/Net Sales.	0.08
MVIC/Gross Profit	0.42
MVIC/SDE	1.81
MVIC/EBITDA	3.58

Source: DealStats (formerly Pratt's Stats), 2023 (Portland, OR: Business Valuation Resources, LLC), www.bvresources.com/dealstats

BENCHMARK DATA

STATISTICS (USED CAR DEALERS)

Number of Establishments .	156,199
Average Profit Margin	2.7%
Revenue per Employee .	$529,000
Average Number of Employees.	2.2
Average Wages per Employee .	$36,389

PRODUCTS AND SERVICES SEGMENTATION

Used vans, minivans, trucks and buses	67.5%
Used cars	18.1%
Parts and repair services	10.0%
Financing and insurance	4.4%

INDUSTRY COSTS

Profit	2.7%
Wages	6.8%
Purchases	79.5%
Depreciation	0.2%
Marketing	0.9%
Rent & Utilities	1.0%
Other	8.9%

MARKET SHARE

CarMax Inc..	13.3%

QUESTIONS

- What types of sales transactions did you have for the year under examination? Any sales at auctions? Any sales to wholesalers? Any sales to other dealers? Any consignment sales? Any scrap sales? Any in-house dealer financing sales? Any third-party financing sales? Did you have any other types of sales transactions? Did you have any sales that resulted in a loss on the sale? What sales did you have to relatives or family friends during the year?

INDUSTRY TREND

"'After a huge run-up in 2021, last year was a reality check,' said Chris Frey, senior manager of economic and industry insights at Cox Automotive, a market research firm. 'The used market now faces a challenging year as demand weakens.' According to Cox, used-car values fell 14 percent in 2022 and are expected to fall more than 4 percent this year. That shift means many dealers may have no choice but to sell some vehicles for less than they paid...."

"The used-car business is made up of thousands of small outlets, many of them family businesses. CarMax is the largest player in the market but accounts for only a sliver of total sales."

Source: "The Pandemic Used-Car Boom Is Coming to an Abrupt End" by Neal E. Boudette, January 31, 2023, https://www.nytimes.com/2023/01/30/business/economy/used-cars-carmax-carvana.html

"CDK Global said there are a lot of assumptions made about Gen Z—loosely defined as individuals born between 1997 and 2012—and the need for instant gratification, from simple online purchase experiences to real-time social media engagement. However, when it comes to buying a vehicle, CDK Global discovered Gen Z seems to be more thoughtful and spends more time weighing decisions, while finding the experience of buying a new car more frustrating than any other generation....With Gen Z most interested in understanding all their options (81%) compared to millennials (73%), Gen X (60%) and baby boomers (45%), the need for education—both online and from a knowledgeable representative at the dealership—proves to be critical, according to the CDK Global study."

Source: "CDK Global survey uncovers 4 traits of Gen Z vehicle shoppers," July 1, 2022, https://www.autoremarketing.com/trends/cdk-global-survey-uncovers-4-traits-gen-z-vehicle-shoppers

"Many industry operators offer in-house BHPH financing arrangements. Used car dealers are working to further reduce reliance on credit-issuing companies. Mobile apps have increased competition among industry operators. To meet rising demand, the number of used car dealerships is projected to increase. Competition from new car dealers will likely intensify. This industry will continue to be disrupted by the rise of business conducted online. Rising disposable income and greater access to credit enabled more consumers to afford industry products."

Source: IBISWorld Industry at a Glance

RESOURCES

- IBISWorld, March 2023: https://www.ibisworld.com
- NIADA—National Independent Automobile Dealers Association: https://www.niada.com
- UCN—Used Car News: https://usedcarnews.com

Auto Detailing

| NAICS 811192 | SIC 7542-03

Rules of Thumb

- 40%–45% annual sales plus inventory

INDUSTRY MULTIPLES

Acquisition multiples below are calculated medians using US private industry transactions. Data updated annually. Last update: August 2023.

VALUATION MULTIPLE (MEDIAN VALUE)

UNDER $1 MILLION NET SALES

MVIC/Net Sales.	0.70
MVIC/Gross Profit	0.76
MVIC/SDE	2.56
MVIC/EBITDA	2.52

$1 MILLION–$5 MILLION NET SALES

MVIC/Net Sales.	1.00
MVIC/Gross Profit	1.58
MVIC/SDE	4.12
MVIC/EBITDA	4.99

OVER $5 MILLION NET SALES

MVIC/Net Sales.	1.37
MVIC/Gross Profit	2.02
MVIC/SDE	N/A
MVIC/EBITDA	4.07

Source: DealStats (formerly Pratt's Stats), 2023 (Portland, OR: Business Valuation Resources, LLC), www.bvresources.com/dealstats

BENCHMARK DATA

DETAILER TYPE

Freestanding Detail Shop	50%
Full-Service Conveyor Car Wash	23%
Mobile Detailing	14%
Self-Serve Car Wash	9%
Exterior-Only Car Wash.	5%
Oil Change/Lube	5%

OPERATING COSTS AS PERCENTAGE OF REVENUE

Rent.	15.7%
Equipment/Supplies/Maintenance	6.0%
Chemicals (incl. soap, wax, compound, etc.)	5.8%
Labor	38.5%
Utilities (incl. water/sewer).	6.0%
Advertising & Promotion	3.5%
Insurance	5.0%
Customer Claims	0.1%

AVERAGE NUMBER OF CARS DETAILED ANNUALLY

Freestanding	1,052

AVERAGE PACKAGE PRICES: RETAIL, FREE-STANDING

Complete Interior/Exterior Detail	$331.75
Interior Detail Only.	$204.25
Exterior Detail Only.	$231.13

Source for the above four charts: "Results from the *Auto Laundry News* 2023 Detailing Survey," https://carwashmag.com/wp-content/uploads/2022/12/Detail-Survey-2023-for-the-web.pdf

RESOURCES

• ALN—Auto Laundry News: https://www.carwashmag.com

Auto Glass Repair/Replacement

| NAICS 811122 | SIC 5231-10 | Businesses/Units 14,753 |

Rules of Thumb

• 45%–50% annual sales plus inventory
• 1.8–3 x SDE plus inventory

INDUSTRY MULTIPLES

Acquisition multiples below are calculated medians using US private industry transactions. Data updated annually. Last update: August 2023.

VALUATION MULTIPLE (MEDIAN VALUE)

UNDER $1 MILLION NET SALES

MVIC/Net Sales.	0.53
MVIC/Gross Profit	0.58
MVIC/SDE	1.65
MVIC/EBITDA	2.26

$1 MILLION–$5 MILLION NET SALES

MVIC/Net Sales.	0.32
MVIC/Gross Profit	0.73
MVIC/SDE	4.02
MVIC/EBITDA	5.57

OVER $5 MILLION NET SALES — N/A

Source: DealStats (formerly Pratt's Stats), 2023 (Portland, OR: Business Valuation Resources, LLC), www.bvresources.com/dealstats

PRICING TIPS

For larger shops with SDE of $500K the multiple would be 3.5. For SDE of $150K the multiple decreases down to around 2.5, with the multiple increasing as SDE increases. If you have mobile service capability, the multiple can be on the high end of the range. If you have a specialized service such as construction equipment, buses, tractor trailers, etc., the multiple is on the higher end of the range. If most of your business is insurance reliant, then the multiple will be less than those businesses that rely less on insurance for payment.

BENCHMARK DATA

STATISTICS (AUTO GLASS REPAIR & REPLACEMENT FRANCHISES)

Number of Establishments	1,107
Average Profit Margin	8.0%
Revenue per Employee	$88,300
Average Number of Employees.	2.3
Average Wages per Employee	$25,415

PRODUCTS AND SERVICES SEGMENTATION

Windshield replacement	61.4%
Windshield repair	16.2%
Window replacement	15.3%
Window repair	4.1%
Other (including headlight restoration).	3.0%

INDUSTRY COSTS

Profit	8.0%
Wages	28.6%
Purchases	9.1%
Depreciation	1.9%
Marketing	1.8%
Rent & Utilities	5.6%
Other	44.9%

MARKET SHARE

Super Glass	24.47%
Novus	11.95%
Glass Doctor	10.42%

STATISTICS (AUTO WINDSHIELD REPAIR SERVICES)

Number of Establishments	13,646
Average Profit Margin	11.3%
Revenue per Employee	$155,000
Average Number of Employees.	3.1
Average Wages per Employee	$39,382

PRODUCTS AND SERVICES SEGMENTATION

Other	38.7%
Windshield repair and replacement for cars	33.7%
Windshield repair and replacement for light duty trucks	25.0%
Windshield repair and replacement for heavy trucks, buses and motor	2.1%
Merchandise sales	0.5%

INDUSTRY COSTS

Profit	11.3%
Wages	25.4%
Purchases	9.1%
Depreciation	1.9%
Marketing	1.8%
Rent & Utilities	5.6%
Other	44.9%

MARKET SHARE

Belron	48.5%

EXPENSES (% OF ANNUAL SALES)

Cost of Goods	23%

INDUSTRY TREND

"Windshield repairers are expected to benefit from the effects of pent-up demand. Insurance coverage of windshield repairs is expected to have benefited windshield repairers. Volatile profit and lack of growth opportunities has resulted in increased consolidation. An increase in motor vehicle registrations translates to a great number of cars. The industry will be marked by increasing consolidation activity. Operators may struggle to service the same number of customers. Improving economic conditions have preserved industry growth."

Source: IBISWorld Industry at a Glance

EXPERT COMMENTS

It's a competitive business but there is always a need for auto glass replacement. Regardless of economic cycle, auto glass gets dinged and cracked and needs to be replaced. Ease of replication is hard because of specialized and sometimes costly equipment, especially if you perform mobile services, which are almost a must to stay competitive.

RESOURCES

- IBISWorld, October 2022: https://www.ibisworld.com
- IBISWorld, June 2022: https://www.ibisworld.com
- NGA—National Glass Association with GANA (Glass Association of North America): https://www.glass.org
- NWRD—National Windshield Repair Division: https://nwrassn.org

Auto Lube/Oil Change

NAICS 811191	SIC 7549-03	Businesses/Units 34,036
Profit $1.6 B	Wages $2.9 B	Annual Growth Future 1.5%
		Annual Growth Past 5.0%

Rules of Thumb

- 40% annual sales (tune-up) plus inventory
- 3 x EBIT (tune-up)
- 45% annual sales (only auto lube businesses) plus inventory
- 1.5–2.25 x SDE plus inventory

INDUSTRY MULTIPLES

Acquisition multiples below are calculated medians using US private industry transactions. Data updated annually. Last update: August 2023.

VALUATION MULTIPLE (MEDIAN VALUE)

UNDER $1 MILLION NET SALES	
MVIC/Net Sales	0.49
MVIC/Gross Profit	0.71
MVIC/SDE	2.83
MVIC/EBITDA	5.82

$1 MILLION–$5 MILLION NET SALES	
MVIC/Net Sales	0.54
MVIC/Gross Profit	1.01
MVIC/SDE	3.65
MVIC/EBITDA	3.59

OVER $5 MILLION NET SALES	N/A

Source: DealStats (formerly Pratt's Stats), 2023 (Portland, OR: Business Valuation Resources, LLC), www.bvresources.com/dealstats

BENCHMARK DATA

STATISTICS (OIL CHANGE SERVICES)

Number of Establishments	34,036
Average Profit Margin	15.2%
Revenue per Employee	$147,000
Average Number of Employees	2.1
Average Wages per Employee	$40,272

PRODUCTS AND SERVICES SEGMENTATION

Semi-synthetic oil changes	33.3%
Conventional oil changes	30.5%
Full synthetic oil changes	21.0%
High-mileage oil changes	5.7%
Diesel oil changes	4.8%
Maintenance services	4.7%

INDUSTRY COSTS

Profit	15.2%
Wages	27.6%
Purchases	8.1%
Depreciation	2.4%
Marketing	1.6%
Rent & Utilities	5.0%
Other	40.1%

INDUSTRY TREND

"Growth in the profit margin has been subdued. Historically volatile crude oil prices affect consumer driving behaviors and purchase costs. A convergence of factors has supported rising demand for regular auto maintenance. Normalizing conditions post-pandemic will support steady industry growth. Price-based competition is slated to accelerate moving forward. External competition will likely affect growth as major retailers continue to pose price competition. One rising threat to oil change servicers will be the growing popularity of electric vehicles."

Source: IBISWorld Industry at a Glance

FINANCING

4 years

RESOURCES

- IBISWorld, January 2023: https://www.ibisworld.com
- ASA—Automotive Service Association: https://www.asashop.org
- AutoInc.: https://www.autoinc.org
- NOLN—National Oil and Lube News: https://www.noln.net

Auto Mufflers

| NAICS 811112 | SIC 7533-01

Rules of Thumb

- 35%–40% annual sales plus inventory
- 1–1.5 x SDE plus inventory

INDUSTRY MULTIPLES

Acquisition multiples below are calculated medians using US private industry transactions. Data updated annually. Last update: August 2023.

VALUATION MULTIPLE (MEDIAN VALUE)

UNDER $1 MILLION NET SALES	
MVIC/Net Sales.	0.35
MVIC/Gross Profit	0.78
MVIC/SDE	2.47
MVIC/EBITDA	2.86
$1 MILLION–$5 MILLION NET SALES	N/A
OVER $5 MILLION NET SALES	N/A

Source: DealStats (formerly Pratt's Stats), 2023 (Portland, OR: Business Valuation Resources, LLC), www.bvresources.com/dealstats

Auto Parts and Accessories Retail Stores

NAICS 441330	SIC 5531-11	Businesses/Units 67,475
Profit $6 B	Wages $13.5 B	Annual Growth Future 1.0%
		Annual Growth Past 2.0%

Rules of Thumb

- 40% annual sales plus inventory

PRICING TIPS

New cost of fixtures and equipment plus inventory at wholesale cost, nothing for goodwill. The inventory should turn over 4 to 6 times per year.

BENCHMARK DATA

STATISTICS (AUTO PARTS STORES)

Number of Establishments .	67,475
Average Profit Margin .	7.4%
Revenue per Employee .	$185,000
Average Number of Employees.	6.6
Average Wages per Employee .	$30,744

PRODUCTS AND SERVICES SEGMENTATION

Critical parts (new) .	42.8%
Maintenance parts .	35.5%
Performance parts .	11.2%
Critical parts (used).	6.1%
Vehicle accessories.	4.4%

MAJOR MARKET SEGMENTATION

Households in the bottom 40.0% of income	26.9%
Repair shops	22.8%
Households in the middle 40.0% of income	22.0%
Households in the top 20.0% of income	17.9%
Retailers and wholesalers for resale	5.7%
Other	4.7%

INDUSTRY COSTS

Profit	7.4%
Wages .	16.6%
Purchases .	48.4%
Depreciation .	1.0%
Marketing .	0.9%
Rent & Utilities .	3.2%
Other	22.4%

MARKET SHARE

AutoZone Inc. .	17.7%
O'Reilly Automotive Inc..	16.1%
Genuine Parts Co .	13.5%
Advance Auto Parts, Inc.	12.5%
Average store size .	6,350 square feet

EXPENSES (% OF ANNUAL SALES)

Cost of Goods .	61.3%
Occupancy Costs .	03.4%
Payroll/Labor Costs.	19.9%
Profit (pretax) .	05.3%

INDUSTRY TREND

"The average age of vehicles on the road rose to 12.2 years last year, according to S&P Global Mobility, a record high....Trips to auto-parts retailers have risen steadily since 2020, and in the first quarter they were 54% higher than in the same period in 2020, according to INRIX, a traffic-data provider. The Auto Care Association is forecasting that the U.S. automotive aftermarket will grow by 5% in 2023, lower than the breakneck pace seen in 2021 and 2022, but still higher than the annual growth rate seen before 2020."

Source: "Auto-Parts Growth Story Still Adds Up" by Jinjoo Lee, April 27, 2023,
https://www.wsj.com/articles/auto-parts-growth-story-still-adds-up-c5a6471c

"The industry is in a period of long-term stagnation, with little room for substantial revenue expansion. The industry is highly influenced by fluctuations in per capita disposable income, the average age of the vehicle fleet and the number of new car sales. Earnings vary significantly between large national or global players and small, independently run shops. The industry is expected to be supported by investment in existing cars. The increased popularity of fuel-efficient vehicles, coupled with rising regulations, has encouraged many consumers to purchase electric vehicles. The industry is anticipated to experience heightened consolidation, limiting new enterprise growth from being greater. The industry remains in an era of long-term sluggish movement, with profit declining overall and little room for substantial revenue expansion."

Source: IBISWorld Industry at a Glance

RESOURCES
• IBISWorld, April 2023: https://www.ibisworld.com
• Auto Care Association: https://www.autocare.org

Auto Rental

	NAICS 532111		SIC 7514-01		Businesses/Units 15,080
	Profit $5.1 B		Wages $6.8 B		Annual Growth Future 2.0%
					Annual Growth Past 7.5%

Rules of Thumb
• 45% annual sales plus inventory

INDUSTRY MULTIPLES

Acquisition multiples below are calculated medians using US private industry transactions. Data updated annually. Last update: August 2023.

VALUATION MULTIPLE (MEDIAN VALUE)

UNDER $1 MILLION NET SALES
MVIC/Net Sales.	0.79
MVIC/Gross Profit	1.07
MVIC/SDE	1.34
MVIC/EBITDA	1.75

$1 MILLION–$5 MILLION NET SALES
MVIC/Net Sales.	0.32
MVIC/Gross Profit	0.81
MVIC/SDE	1.15
MVIC/EBITDA	1.24

OVER $5 MILLION NET SALES
MVIC/Net Sales.	1.70
MVIC/Gross Profit	1.94
MVIC/SDE	3.90
MVIC/EBITDA	9.92

Source: DealStats (formerly Pratt's Stats), 2023 (Portland, OR: Business Valuation Resources, LLC), www.bvresources.com/dealstats

BENCHMARK DATA

STATISTICS (CAR RENTAL)

Number of Establishments .	.15,080
Average Profit Margin .	6.8%
Revenue per Employee .	$470,000
Average Number of Employees.	11.0
Average Wages per Employee .	$42,852

PRODUCTS AND SERVICES SEGMENTATION

Leisure car rental 50.5%
Car leasing 24.3%
Business car rental 16.9%
Other sales and services 6.6%
Car sharing 1.7%

MAJOR MARKET SEGMENTATION

Airport Customers 50.9%
Car leasing 24.4%
Off-airport customers 21.8%
Car sharing 2.9%

INDUSTRY COSTS

Profit 6.8%
Wages 9.1%
Purchases 7.2%
Depreciation 28.2%
Marketing 1.4%
Rent & Utilities 8.4%
Other 39.0%

MARKET SHARE

Enterprise Holdings Inc. 14.0%
Hertz Global Holdings Inc. 9.9%
Avis Budget Group Inc. 9.5%

2022 U.S. CAR RENTAL MARKET: FLEET, LOCATIONS AND REVENUE

Company	U.S. Cars in Service (Avg.) 2022	Number of U.S. Locations	2022 U.S. Revenue Est. (millions)
Enterprise Holdings (includes Alamo Rent A Car, Enterprise Rent-A-Car, National Car Rental)	1,200,000	5,500	$19,915
Avis Budget Group (includes Payless, not Zipcar)	425,000	3,000	$8,430
Hertz (includes Dollar & Thrifty)	365,000	3,900	$5,700
SIXT	29,000	98	$970
Fox Europcar	18,571	27	$391
ACE Rent A Car	12,000	75	$120
NP Auto Group (Priceless & NextCar)	7,350	101	$62
Green Motion U-Save Group	8,500	84	$40
Rent-A-Wreck of America	1,500	60	$15
Independents	45,000	3,800	$450
Totals	2,111,921	16,645	$36,093

Source: "Auto Rental News Fact Book 2023," https://autorentalnews.mydigitalpublication.com

EXPENSES (% OF ANNUAL SALES)

Cost of Goods 82%
Occupancy Costs 04%
Payroll/Labor Costs. . . . . 08% to 10%
Profit (pretax) 06%

QUESTIONS

- Relationships with franchisor; license agreement and royalty rate

INDUSTRY TREND

"In response to demand declines, industry operators have sought various measures to stay afloat. Industry profit has been pressured by a considerable drop in industry revenue in 2020. The industry has experienced growing competition from the emerging peer-to-peer car-sharing market. The industry's largest companies are expected to retain their competitive advantage. The increasing popularity of ride-sharing services presents alternatives to car rental services. The industry is likely to remain dominated by the same major companies. Due to shelter-in-place orders, the industry has endured vanishing demand."

Source: IBISWorld Industry at a Glance

RESOURCES

- IBISWorld, January 2023: https://www.ibisworld.com
- ARN—Auto Rental News: https://www.autorentalnews.com

Auto Repair (Auto Service Centers)

NAICS 811111	SIC 7514-01	Businesses/Units 289,271
Profit $4.7 B	Wages $23.1 B	Annual Growth Future 2.0%
		Annual Growth Past -0.8%

Rules of Thumb

- 30%–40% annual sales plus inventory
- 1–2.5 x SDE plus inventory ($75,000 to $100,000 SDE)
- 3 x SDE plus inventory ($150,000 + SDE)
- 3–4 x EBITDA
- 2.5–3 x EBIT
- 2.5–3.5 x SDE

INDUSTRY MULTIPLES

Acquisition multiples below are calculated medians using US private industry transactions. Data updated annually. Last update: August 2023.

VALUATION MULTIPLE (MEDIAN VALUE)

UNDER $1 MILLION NET SALES
MVIC/Net Sales	0.38
MVIC/Gross Profit	0.60
MVIC/SDE	2.11
MVIC/EBITDA	2.87

$1 MILLION–$5 MILLION NET SALES
MVIC/Net Sales	0.39
MVIC/Gross Profit	0.74
MVIC/SDE	2.25
MVIC/EBITDA	3.65

OVER $5 MILLION NET SALES
MVIC/Net Sales	0.57
MVIC/Gross Profit	1.40
MVIC/SDE	3.82
MVIC/EBITDA	8.75

Source: DealStats (formerly Pratt's Stats), 2023 (Portland, OR: Business Valuation Resources, LLC), www.bvresources.com/dealstats

PRICING TIPS

Size matters. Larger shops with larger volumes will have larger multiples than smaller shops with lower volumes. One to three bays are owner-operated, usually with a mechanic owner. Four bays or more could support an owner-operator who is not necessarily a mechanic working on cars. Post-Covid, this industry has done well due to the shortage of new cars, the need to maintain the existing car, and the fact auto repair was considered an essential service in many jurisdictions.

If the owner is also a technician, the value is lower. SDE multiples could be in the 2.0 to 2.5 range. If the owner is an administrator that isn't required to be there all of the time—for example, not a service writer or a technician—the multiple of SDE can be in the 3.0 to 3.25 range. Shops with more bays and lifts than technicians are more desirable, to allow for techs to work on other vehicles while waiting on parts.

Number of service bays per tech means a lot. Two bays per service tech are preferred, so for instance, if one vehicle is on a lift waiting for parts, the tech can work on another vehicle. Aboveground lifts are preferred over in-ground lifts. Key metrics to look at are how many ROs (repair orders) are written per day and per month; what are the average hours per RO; and what are the average dollars per RO. A repair shop should gross 35 to 40 percent on parts and 66 to 70 percent on labor. Anything at the high end of this range might result in a premium in price. Shops on the lower end might sell for less. Typical SDE multiples I've seen are 3 to 3.5. If the owner doesn't have to write service and routinely wait on customers, that is a plus. That allows the owner to focus on overall business management.

BENCHMARK DATA

AUTO REPAIR (AUTO MECHANICS)

Number of Establishments	289,271
Average Profit Margin	6.1%
Revenue per Employee	$128,000
Average Number of Employees	2.1
Average Wages per Employee	$38,509

PRODUCTS AND SERVICES SEGMENTATION

Scheduled and preventative repair and maintenance services	31.0%
Powertrain repair services	18.1%
Brake repair services	17.4%
Other repair and maintenance services	10.6%
Wheel alignment and repair services	8.1%
Electrical system repair services	6.4%
Heating repair services	4.9%
Muffler and exhaust repair services	3.5%

INDUSTRY COSTS

Profit	6.1%
Wages	30.1%
Purchases	9.2%
Depreciation	1.6%
Marketing	1.9%
Rent & Utilities	5.6%
Other	45.4%

Sales per bay should be over $200,000.

Average of $100,000 to $125,000 revenue per employee

A $200,000 to $250,000 sales per employee, excluding owner

Exceptional shops can gross $25K to $30K per month per bay. Six to ten service bays are preferred.

The average size is 3000 square feet.

EXPENSES (% OF ANNUAL SALES)

Cost of Goods	30% to 40%
Occupancy Costs	05% to 15%
Payroll/Labor Costs.	25% to 35%
Profit (pretax)	10% to 20%

QUESTIONS

- Will they help with the transition for the bigger customers?
- Questions related to their views on customer service and employee relations will give you a good idea of the culture of the shop. Since recruiting staff is the number one challenge in this industry, knowing that the prior owner valued the staff and customers is a great indication of value.
- How many bays and lifts? How many technicians? How many repair orders do you average per week? What services do you not provide? What's your most profitable service? What's your least profitable service? Where do you get your parts? How many new customers do you service in an average month? How long has your average customer been your customer?
- Dollars per repair order? Hours per RO? Sales per technician? How are the technicians paid? How are the service advisors paid? What kind of advertising do you do? How do you handle come-back repairs? What are the seller's duties in the shop? How many hours do they work? How do they find technicians and service advisors?
- What is the turnover of your staff? How long has your oldest employee been with you? A high turnover is likely an indication of reputation issues.
- What are the chances of the techs and manager remaining with the business after the sale? Will the seller stay on for six months as an employee if needed? What is the shop's hourly rate? Does the business have the proper licenses in place to service vehicles? Are there any hazardous waste/environmental issues?
- Have you had any unions or attempts at organization at this location? What is the record of the location for workplace accidents?

INDUSTRY TREND

"California, the state with the largest number of automotive technicians and 39% of all EVs in the U.S, has begun to see the effects of EVs on these jobs. Since 2014, the number of licensed independent auto shops in the state has dropped by more than 13%."

Source: "The future of the auto industry is electric. Will mechanics be out of work?" by Cara Korte, April 21, 2023, https://www.cbsnews.com/news/auto-industry-future-electric-will-mechanics-be-out-of-work/

There is the need for high-tech-trained technicians/electricians due to an increase in hybrid and electric cars.

There will continue to be a demand for a good, local auto repair shop. People like to shop close to where they either work or live, and people are keeping their vehicles longer. I don't see electric cars taking over the market anytime soon, and a good local shop will not only attract more customers, it will attract higher quality service writers and technicians.

With the new technology, you will need higher-skilled technicians.

Independent shops that have a good reputation for honesty and dependable service will outperform other shops in the industry and will retain a higher percentage of their customers. Vehicle owners are always looking for alternatives to high-cost dealership service centers.

"Consumers are expected to sharply increase car usage for trips. The decline in new car sales is expected to generally benefit industry operators. Industry profit has experienced volatility over the past five years. The average age of the vehicle fleet is projected to increase. Vehicles will likely acquire less wear and tear related damage. Rising operating costs are also expected to negatively affect profit. Rising labor and material costs constrain profit growth."

Source: IBISWorld Industry at a Glance

EXPERT COMMENTS

Be cautious as to why someone is getting out of the business and how much work the current owner does.

If the current operator does not have a good reputation and staff, it will be very difficult to grow.

Don't think it's easy money; it requires a lot of hard work. However, if you treat your employees right, they'll take care of your customers. If you take care of your customers, they'll be loyal to your shop. Don't be greedy and don't be cheap. If you focus on providing quality and dependable service rather than making money, you'll make money.

There's a lot of competition, but customers tend to stay loyal to an auto repair shop they trust. Clean facilities and a comfortable waiting room with nice furnishings are a plus. During tougher economic times, people tend to keep their current vehicles longer, which helps the repair industry. Ease of replication is difficult because of the amount of equipment involved and the current trend of it being harder to find quality auto technicians.

This is a customer service business; be ready to put in some hours. It does become addictive, so if you are thinking of selling the business, please make sure you know what are you going to do next in your life.

With Covid-19, the past several years took a toll on the industry. People drove less; vehicles did not need servicing as much; and worst of all, it was very hard to find technicians and staff. Boosted higher pay rates today and a little less profitability. All in all, industry remains strong and is in high demand.

It's a very competitive industry, and there's always price pressure due to the number of repair shops. Finding quality technicians is the most difficult part. A shop with a reputation of honest dealings with customers and good technicians can be very profitable over the long term. The key is to have good people who are properly trained to take care of customers, and not to price gouge or oversell.

FINANCING

I don't think sellers should provide more than 10 to 15 percent seller financing. This is an industry that can be lender financed for a well-established repair shop and a buyer with established business management experience. 10 to 15 percent down, with the rest outside financing to cash out the seller, is most typical of the transactions I've completed.

RESOURCES

- IBISWorld, April 2023: https://www.ibisworld.com
- AIA Canada—Automotive Industries Association of Canada: https://www.aiacanada.com
- AMRA—Automotive Maintenance & Repair Association: https://www.amra.org
- ASA—Automotive Service Association: https://www.asashop.org
- ASCCA—Automotive Service Councils of California: https://www.ascca.com
- ASE—National Institute for Automotive Service Excellence: https://www.ase.com
- AutoInc.: https://www.autoinc.org
- Automotive Aftermarket: https://automotiveaftermarket.org
- CARS—Canadian Auto Repair & Service Magazine: https://www.autoserviceworld.com/carsmagazine/
- MOTOR Magazine: https://www.motor.com/magazine/
- RepairPal: https://repairpal.com
- RW—Ratchet+Wrench: https://www.ratchetandwrench.com
- WMDA/CAR: https://www.wmda.net

Auto Transmission Centers

| NAICS 811113 | SIC 7537-01

Rules of Thumb

- 35%–45% annual sales includes inventory
- 1.5–2 x SDE includes inventory
- 3 x EBITDA

INDUSTRY MULTIPLES

Acquisition multiples below are calculated medians using US private industry transactions. Data updated annually. Last update: August 2023.

VALUATION MULTIPLE (MEDIAN VALUE)

UNDER $1 MILLION NET SALES	
MVIC/Net Sales.	0.26
MVIC/Gross Profit	0.57
MVIC/SDE	1.88
MVIC/EBITDA	2.40
$1 MILLION–$5 MILLION NET SALES	
MVIC/Net Sales.	0.51
MVIC/Gross Profit	0.93
MVIC/SDE	2.20
MVIC/EBITDA	4.28
OVER $5 MILLION NET SALES	N/A

Source: DealStats (formerly Pratt's Stats), 2023 (Portland, OR: Business Valuation Resources, LLC), www.bvresources.com/dealstats

PRICING TIPS

Look at present staffing and labor cost; focus on developing a pro forma with present and realistic data for each expense. Ratio of general repair vs. transmission? Are they using remanufactured units?

As the SDE increases, so will the multiple—e.g., SDE $50,000, the multiple will be 1.5 times; SDE $200,000, the multiple will be 2 times—all include inventory.

This industry is changing. Going forward, general auto repair is a significant part as well as using remanufactured parts as an alternative to rebuilding. Independent shops in major markets have a hard time competing with established franchises, and in some markets finding experienced technical employees is hard.

EXPENSES (% OF ANNUAL SALES)

Cost of Goods	18% to 24%
Occupancy Costs	08% to 15%
Payroll/Labor Costs.	20% to 25%
Profit (pretax)	10% to 20%

QUESTIONS

- Why are you selling? What is the ratio of transmission to general auto? What are the demographics and tenure of employees? What is your job function?

INDUSTRY TREND

Franchises will dominate and small shops revert to general auto repair. Long term, with improved quality, the industry will change.

EXPERT COMMENTS

Build a pro forma alternative to trying to analyze historic records.

Advertising online is important; parts cost should be in the 20 percent for transmission only.

FINANCING

Seller financing 50 percent down, 5 years

RESOURCES

- ATRA—Automatic Transmission Rebuilders Association: https://www.atra.com
- Gears Magazine: https://gearsmagazine.com
- Transmission Digest: https://www.transmissiondigest.com

Auto Wrecking/Recyclers/Dismantlers/Scrap/Salvage Yards (Auto Parts: Used & Rebuilt)

| NAICS 441310 | SIC 5015-02

| Profit $493.8 M | Wages $1.2 B | Annual Growth Future 2.8%

                                             | Annual Growth Past 0.3%

Rules of Thumb

- 100% annual gross sales including inventory
- 2.5 x EBITDA
- 2 x SDE

INDUSTRY MULTIPLES

Acquisition multiples below are calculated medians using US private industry transactions. Data updated annually. Last update: August 2023.

VALUATION MULTIPLE (MEDIAN VALUE)

UNDER $1 MILLION NET SALES

MVIC/Net Sales	0.55
MVIC/Gross Profit	0.99
MVIC/SDE	2.73
MVIC/EBITDA	3.07

$1 MILLION–$5 MILLION NET SALES

MVIC/Net Sales	0.40
MVIC/Gross Profit	1.15
MVIC/SDE	2.85
MVIC/EBITDA	4.34

OVER $5 MILLION NET SALES

MVIC/Net Sales	0.44
MVIC/Gross Profit	1.40
MVIC/SDE	3.28
MVIC/EBITDA	3.85

Source: DealStats (formerly Pratt's Stats), 2023 (Portland, OR: Business Valuation Resources, LLC), www.bvresources.com/dealstats

BENCHMARK DATA

STATISTICS (USED CAR PARTS WHOLESALING)

Number of Establishments	2,855
Average Profit Margin	6.8%
Revenue per Employee	$301,000
Average Number of Employees	8.7
Average Wages per Employee	$48,064

PRODUCTS AND SERVICES SEGMENTATION

General auto recycling	54.7%
Specialized motor vehicle dismantling and parts sales	36.5%
Other	8.8%

MAJOR MARKET SEGMENTATION

Direct to end users	65.9%
Retail/wholesale resale	25.5%
Government and other	8.6%

INDUSTRY COSTS

Profit	6.8%
Wages	16.0%
Purchases	66.7%
Depreciation	1.0%
Marketing	0.9%
Rent & Utilities	0.8%
Other	7.8%

MARKET SHARE

LKQ Corp. 23.6%

Approximate expenses are difficult to estimate, as vehicle purchases are 70 percent of COGS but parts expenses are 10 percent. Each wrecking yard has to be looked at as a separate business.

EXPENSES (% OF ANNUAL SALES)

Cost of Goods	40% to 50%
Occupancy Costs	14%
Payroll/Labor Costs	10%
Profit (pretax)	25%

- Good records are needed to establish profits.

A

The business should remain constant as we continue to be a vehicle-driven economy.

"Industry demand was curbed in early 2020. The lack of new car sales bodes well for used auto parts wholesalers. The rise in input prices has raised demand for comparatively cheaper used goods, as the price of new parts has risen. With more cars on the road, demand for repair work will increase. As disposable income rises, more consumers will likely be able to afford used auto parts. Increased consolidation is likely to take place. Input prices and supply chain disruptions have constrained profit margins across the industry."

Source: IBISWorld Industry at a Glance

EXPERT COMMENTS

Newer vehicles and parts are the key to success.

FINANCING

Seller financing. 50 percent down; 4-year note at 5 or 6 percent. Tax returns usually don't justify an SBA loan.

RESOURCES

- IBISWorld, March 2023: https://www.ibisworld.com
- ARA—Automotive Recyclers Association: https://www.a-r-a.org
- ARANY—Automotive Recyclers Association of New York: https://www.arany.com
- ISRI—Institute of Scrap Recycling Industries, Inc.: https://www.isri.org
- SAS Forks: https://www.sasforks.com

Automobile Manufacturing

| NAICS 336110 | Businesses/Units 241

| Profit $6.2 B | Wages $17.5 B | Annual Growth Future 2.1%

| Annual Growth Past -2.9%

BENCHMARK DATA

STATISTICS (AUTOMOBILE & LIGHT DUTY MOTOR VEHICLE MANUFACTURING)

Number of Establishments	241
Average Profit Margin	1.9%
Revenue per Employee	$1,642,000
Average Number of Employees. . . .	857.0
Average Wages per Employee . . .	$87,311

PRODUCTS AND SERVICES SEGMENTATION

Crossovers	43.6%
Pickup Trucks	20.8%
Cars	19.8%
SUVs.	11.9%
Vans	3.9%

MAJOR MARKET SEGMENTATION

Wholesale	56.4%
Retail to Dealers	32.3%
Rental	4.8%
Commercial	4.0%
Government	2.5%

INDUSTRY COSTS

Profit	1.9%
Wages	5.4%
Purchases	77.2%
Depreciation	2.1%
Marketing	0.0%
Rent & Utilities	0.3%
Other	13.1%

MARKET SHARE

General Motors Company	33.5%
Toyota Motor Corp	22.4%
Ford Motor Co.	15.2%
Stellantis N.V.	10.4%
Honda Motor Co Ltd	4.1%
Mitsubishi Motors Corp.	2.5%
Mazda Motor Corp	1.5%

INDUSTRY TREND

"Lockdowns resulted in cars being driven sparingly, reducing overall wear and lengthening their lifespans, to the detriment of manufacturers. Tightening restrictions have pushed manufacturers to invest heavily in research and development, resulting in the fast improvement of EV technology. The pandemic disrupted all supply chains, dragging down vehicle manufacturers along with the rest of the world's industries. Improving trade conditions will continue to lift the industry. Manufacturers are racing to revamp their facilities to focus on electric vehicles. Persistently high inflation has caused concern, threatening to derail the widespread economic growth the United States has enjoyed recently. The auto sector is changing drastically, forcing adaptation from its participants to stay relevant."

Source: IBISWorld Industry at a Glance

RESOURCES

• IBISWorld, May 2023: https://www.ibisworld.com

Bagel Shops

| NAICS 722513 | SIC 546101

Rules of Thumb

• 30%–35% annual sales plus inventory
• 2.5 x SDE plus inventory

INDUSTRY MULTIPLES

Acquisition multiples below are calculated medians using US private industry transactions. Data updated annually. Last update: August 2023.

B

UNDER $1 MILLION NET SALES

MVIC/Net Sales	0.31
MVIC/Gross Profit	0.48
MVIC/SDE	1.67
MVIC/EBITDA	2.21

$1 MILLION–$5 MILLION NET SALES

MVIC/Net Sales	0.39
MVIC/Gross Profit	0.60
MVIC/SDE	2.43
MVIC/EBITDA	2.98

OVER $5 MILLION NET SALES

MVIC/Net Sales	0.89
MVIC/Gross Profit	2.08
MVIC/SDE	4.98
MVIC/EBITDA	12.81

Source: DealStats (formerly Pratt's Stats), 2023 (Portland, OR: Business Valuation Resources, LLC), www.bvresources.com/dealstats

PRICING TIPS

Generally worth one-third of gross sales volume, with a decent rent. Higher rent or upcoming increase will lower price.

Rent a large factor; hand-rolled or frozen product?

BENCHMARK DATA

For additional Benchmark Information see also Restaurants—Fast Food

Rent and payroll the most important factors

EXPENSES (% OF ANNUAL SALES)

Cost of Goods	10%
Occupancy Costs	20%
Payroll/Labor Costs	25%
Profit (pretax)	20%

INDUSTRY TREND

"'Jerusalem bagels seem to be gaining a lot more popularity in the States in recent years, but it's not something you would typically find in an everyday bagel shop,' Breanne Kostyk, owner of Flour Moon Bagels in New Orleans, tells *The Takeout*."

Source: "Jerusalem Bagels Are on the Rise" by Micheline Maynard, September 22, 2023, https://thetakeout.com/jerusalem-bagel-vs-regular-bagel-yom-kippur-break-fast-1850861648

"The owner of Popupbagels, Adam Goldberg, thinks that there has been little recent innovation in New York bagels, and that the current crop of offerings isn't up to past standards. 'I think there is unlimited room for great bagel shops anywhere in any town in America, including in New York City,' he said."

Source: "A New York Bagel from an Unexpected Borough: Connecticut" by Priya Krishna, April 29, 2022, https://www.nytimes.com/2022/04/29/dining/popup-bagels-connecticut.html

EXPERT COMMENTS

Easy to duplicate. Setup cost expensive. Most shopping centers already have a bagel shop.

RESOURCES

• National Bagel Association: http://www.bagels.org

Bait and Tackle Shops

| NAICS 451110 | SIC 5941-01

Rules of Thumb

• 30% annual sales plus inventory

INDUSTRY MULTIPLES

Acquisition multiples below are calculated medians using US private industry transactions. Data updated annually. Last update: August 2023.

VALUATION MULTIPLE (MEDIAN VALUE)

UNDER $1 MILLION NET SALES

MVIC/Net Sales.	0.50
MVIC/Gross Profit	1.01
MVIC/SDE	2.56
MVIC/EBITDA	3.93

$1 MILLION–$5 MILLION NET SALES

MVIC/Net Sales.	0.37
MVIC/Gross Profit	1.03
MVIC/SDE	2.71
MVIC/EBITDA	4.08

OVER $5 MILLION NET SALES

MVIC/Net Sales.	0.46
MVIC/Gross Profit	1.33
MVIC/SDE	2.95
MVIC/EBITDA	7.63

Source: DealStats (formerly Pratt's Stats), 2023 (Portland, OR: Business Valuation Resources, LLC), www.bvresources.com/dealstats

BENCHMARK DATA

For Benchmark Information see Sporting Goods Stores

INDUSTRY TREND

"In 2022, 54.5 million Americans ages 6 and over took to the nation's waterways to enjoy recreational fishing, a 4 percent increase from 2021."

Source: "2023 Special Report on Fishing," https://outdoorindustry.org/resource/2023-fishing-report/

RESOURCES

• ASA—American Sportfishing Association: https://asafishing.org

Bakeries

| NAICS 445291 | SIC 5461-02

| Profit $807.6 M | Wages $2.3 B | Annual Growth Future 3.6%

| | | | Annual Growth Past -2.9%

Rules of Thumb

• 40%–45% annual sales plus inventory
• 2 x SDE plus inventory

INDUSTRY MULTIPLES

Acquisition multiples below are calculated medians using US private industry transactions. Data updated annually. Last update: August 2023.

VALUATION MULTIPLE (MEDIAN VALUE)

UNDER $1 MILLION NET SALES

MVIC/Net Sales	0.34
MVIC/Gross Profit	0.46
MVIC/SDE	1.97
MVIC/EBITDA	3.34

$1 MILLION–$5 MILLION NET SALES

MVIC/Net Sales	0.70
MVIC/Gross Profit	0.90
MVIC/SDE	1.45
MVIC/EBITDA	1.55

OVER $5 MILLION NET SALES   N/A

Source: DealStats (formerly Pratt's Stats), 2023 (Portland, OR: Business Valuation Resources, LLC), www.bvresources.com/dealstats

PRICING TIPS

Receivables; years in business; scope of market; new state-of-the-art equipment vs. old

BENCHMARK DATA

EXPENSES (% OF ANNUAL SALES)

Cost of goods sold (Food)	05% to 10%
Payroll/Labor Costs	30% to 35%
Occupancy Cost	06% to 08%
Other Overhead	10% to 15%
Profit (estimated)	20%+

INDUSTRY TREND

"The expansion of natural food grocery store chains has diverted demand. Rapidly growing appeal for organic foods has supported revenue during periods of volatile demand. The number of companies operating in this industry has declined due to increasing competition. Operators are expected to continue to experience escalating competition. Consumers are expected to purchase a greater share of higher-quality food products. The industry will continue experiencing intense competition from other retail channels. Diet-conscious consumers have helped to support industry revenue."

Source: IBISWorld Industry at a Glance

RESOURCES

- IBISWorld, January 2022: https://www.ibisworld.com
- IBA—Independent Bakers Association: https://www.ibabaker.com
- SN—Supermarket News:
  https://www.supermarketnews.com/product-categories/bakery

Bakeries, Commercial

NAICS 311812	SIC 5149-02	Businesses/Units 35,822
Profit $2.4 B	Wages $10.6 B	Annual Growth Future 0.3%
		Annual Growth Past 0.2%

Rules of Thumb

- 60%–70% annual sales plus inventory
- 3–5 x EBITDA

B

- 2–3 x SDE
- 5.5 x EBIT

INDUSTRY MULTIPLES

Acquisition multiples below are calculated medians using US private industry transactions. Data updated annually. Last update: August 2023.

VALUATION MULTIPLE (MEDIAN VALUE)

UNDER $1 MILLION NET SALES

MVIC/Net Sales.	0.37
MVIC/Gross Profit	0.74
MVIC/SDE	1.97
MVIC/EBITDA	2.73

$1 MILLION–$5 MILLION NET SALES

MVIC/Net Sales.	0.48
MVIC/Gross Profit	0.59
MVIC/SDE	2.92
MVIC/EBITDA	4.38

OVER $5 MILLION NET SALES

MVIC/Net Sales.	0.25
MVIC/Gross Profit	1.29
MVIC/SDE	4.59
MVIC/EBITDA	4.83

Source: DealStats (formerly Pratt's Stats), 2023 (Portland, OR: Business Valuation Resources, LLC), www.bvresources.com/dealstats

PRICING TIPS

It's been my experience that bakeries—both retail and wholesale—typically sell in the 2.5 to 3.25 multiple of SDE, depending on some very important drivers, such as percentage of sales retail vs. wholesale, and types of products being produced (bread vs. cake vs. other treats). The assets package? Is there any automation? Is the owner working in the back of the house or just operations? Staffing? Longevity of client list? Are they co-packing? Quality of books and records? Location, lease, and expandability? Purchasing power with vendors? All of these very important issues come into play when pricing such a business. Note that I have found that multiples for franchised/retail outfits are far less than that of a privately owned bakery.

Develop hard statistics on pounds of flour, water, and power (gas or electric?) usage over the past year. Find out if retail business is also conducted out of the bakery, and if so, the volume of such.

BENCHMARK DATA

How does the bakery receive its inventory of flour...by the 50-lb bag?...or by bulk delivery? Get a measure of this for a proper evaluation, as a check on the represented bakery volume.

Credit policy with established, and new, customers; receivables policy with customers

STATISTICS (BREAD PRODUCTION)

Number of Establishments	35,822
Average Profit Margin	4.6%
Revenue per Employee	$186,000
Average Number of Employees.	7.9
Average Wages per Employee	$37,592

PRODUCTS AND SERVICES SEGMENTATION

Bread (white, wheat, rye, etc.), including frozen	.31.3%
Rolls, bagels and croissants	.22.2%
Other	.16.1%
Fresh baked desserts	.15.8%
Frozen cakes, pies and other frozen desserts	.14.6%

MAJOR MARKET SEGMENTATION

Supermarkets and grocery stores	.53.8%
Food service and institutional customers	.24.5%
Local bakeries (direct to consumer)	. 8.0%
Convenience stores.	. 5.4%
Other	. 4.5%
Exports	. 3.8%

INDUSTRY COSTS

Profit	. 4.6%
Wages	.20.1%
Purchases	.35.9%
Depreciation	. 2.8%
Marketing	. 0.4%
Rent & Utilities	. 3.1%
Other	.33.1%

MARKET SHARE

Grupo Bimbo Sab De Cv	.20.7%
Flowers Foods, Inc.	. 9.8%

EXPENSES (% OF ANNUAL SALES)

Cost of Goods	. 25% to 30%
Occupancy Costs	. 10% to 20%
Payroll/Labor Costs.	. 30% to 40%
Profit (pretax)	. 15% to 20%

QUESTIONS

- What percentage of sales is retail vs. wholesale? What functions does the seller perform exactly? Describe the management team and/or top employee positions. Are any of your clients or vendor relationships personal friends? Wholesalers: Describe your clients; what industries are they in? Are you co-packing for anyone?
- Ask about the staffing—how many employed, how long has each worked, and are there any green card employees?
- Ask for flour, water, and utility bills; aging of receivables?
- Any special prices given to special customers? Is there any one customer controlling more than 10 percent of the bakery's volume?

INDUSTRY TREND

The small commercial bakeries will likely disappear/consolidate as time goes by since the cost of distribution increases annually, and many giants of the industry (Bimbo, Flowers, etc.) provide good commercial products at very competitive prices compared to the small guys!

"Operators encountered mounting external competition from imports. Significant merger and acquisition activity has increased market concentration. The industry's proactive response to evolving health trends has helped offset greater revenue declines. The continued development of healthier bread varieties will aid industry performance. Stronger demand for fresh, handmade or all-natural bread products will benefit operators. Due to intensified external competition, industry profitability is expected to be challenged. Producers have contended with America's ever-changing palate."

Source: IBISWorld Industry at a Glance

EXPERT COMMENTS

Automation is key to raising the bottom line. Be sure to understand the assets being sold.

Retail bakeries seem to come and go, but every now and then someone gets a good idea and knows how to market properly. For example, some retailers specialize in Bundt cakes, some in custom-designed cakes with fancy fondant— but others try to do it all, which usually doesn't work out due to lack of proper staffing. Wholesalers that have automated their kitchens seem to expand quickly while lowering payroll costs, while others—old schoolers—tend to drown in their own batter.

Consider buying a commercial bakery that makes a decent (35+) percent of its sales from the retail sector.

FINANCING

Wholesalers are typically sold via SBA financing with the seller holding at least a 10 percent second.

Seller financing—with monthly notes proportionate to the net income the business generates monthly.

RESOURCES

- IBISWorld, January 2023: https://ibisworld.com
- American Bakers Association: https://www.americanbakers.org
- American Society of Baking: https://asbe.org/

Ball Bearing Manufacturing

| NAICS 332991 | Businesses/Units 169

| Profit $360.4 M | Wages $1 B | Annual Growth Future 0.9%

                                 | Annual Growth Past -6.2%

INDUSTRY MULTIPLES

Acquisition multiples below are calculated medians using US private industry transactions. Data updated annually. Last update: August 2023.

VALUATION MULTIPLE (MEDIAN VALUE)

UNDER $1 MILLION NET SALES	N/A
$1 MILLION–$5 MILLION NET SALES	
MVIC/Net Sales	0.47
MVIC/Gross Profit	1.26
MVIC/SDE	21.24
MVIC/EBITDA	N/A
OVER $5 MILLION NET SALES	
MVIC/Net Sales	2.66
MVIC/Gross Profit	7.16
MVIC/SDE	N/A
MVIC/EBITDA	23.76

Source: DealStats (formerly Pratt's Stats), 2023 (Portland, OR: Business Valuation Resources, LLC), www.bvresources.com/dealstats

B

BENCHMARK DATA

STATISTICS (BALL BEARING MANUFACTURING)

Number of Establishments	169
Average Profit Margin	6.4%
Revenue per Employee	$362,000
Average Number of Employees	92.2
Average Wages per Employee	$65,990

PRODUCTS AND SERVICES SEGMENTATION

Ball bearings, unmounted	43.0%
Roller bearings, unmounted	37.3%
Parts and components for roller and ball bearings	12.5%
Mounted roller and ball bearings	7.2%

MAJOR MARKET SEGMENTATION

Industrial equipment	42.1%
Automotive and transportation	39.1%
Off-highway and heavy equipment	11.8%
Aerospace and defense	7.0%

INDUSTRY COSTS

Profit	6.4%
Wages	18.4%
Purchases	37.3%
Depreciation	2.5%
Marketing	0.0%
Rent & Utilities	2.6%
Other	32.8%

MARKET SHARE

Timken Co	21.5%
Schaeffler Ag	14.9%
Aktiebolaget Skf	14.4%
NSK Ltd.	10.2%
Jtekt Corp	4.6%
NTN Corporation	3.3%

INDUSTRY TREND

"Industry players have also had to contend with a deteriorating export market. On top of sometimes lukewarm demand, the industry has experienced significant foreign competition. To capitalize on increasing activity in downstream industrial markets, operators have been engaging in merger and acquisition activity. The US auto market is expected to rebound from coronavirus-induced lows. Domestic producers have dealt with rising import competition for years, with the majority of imports coming from Japan, China and Germany. Industry employment is projected to rise slowly as successful incumbents expand operations. An appreciating dollar and a competitive global landscape have made US exports less competitive."

Source: IBISWorld Industry at a Glance

RESOURCES

• IBISWorld, March 2023: https://www.ibisworld.com

Banks, Commercial

	NAICS 522110		SIC 6021-01		Businesses/Units 79,881
	Profit $462.6 B		Wages $308.2 B		Annual Growth Future -0.6%
					Annual Growth Past 3.2%

Rules of Thumb
- 1–2 x book value
- 15 x SDE includes inventory
- 15 x EBIT

INDUSTRY MULTIPLES

Acquisition multiples below are calculated medians using US private industry transactions. Data updated annually. Last update: August 2023.

VALUATION MULTIPLE (MEDIAN VALUE)

UNDER $1 MILLION NET SALES	N/A
$1 MILLION–$5 MILLION NET SALES	
MVIC/Net Sales.	3.22
MVIC/Gross Profit	3.78
MVIC/SDE	N/A
MVIC/EBITDA	22.05
OVER $5 MILLION NET SALES	
MVIC/Net Sales.	4.14
MVIC/Gross Profit	4.67
MVIC/SDE	9.09
MVIC/EBITDA	14.12

Source: DealStats (formerly Pratt's Stats), 2023 (Portland, OR: Business Valuation Resources, LLC), www.bvresources.com/dealstats

PRICING TIPS

The value of a bank is based primarily on the quality of the loan portfolio and the ability to attract deposits.

BENCHMARK DATA

STATISTICS (COMMERCIAL BANKING)

Number of Establishments .	79,881
Average Profit Margin	38.2%
Revenue per Employee .	$525,000
Average Number of Employees.	27.6
Average Wages per Employee .	$137,177

PRODUCTS AND SERVICES SEGMENTATION

Real estate loans	34.1%
Depository services and other noninterest–generating products.	27.5%
Commercial and industrial loans	15.6%
Other	10.7%
Loans to individuals excluding credit cards	6.4%
Credit card loans	5.7%

MAJOR MARKET SEGMENTATION

Retail customers	43.8%
Corporate clients	39.8%
Other clients	16.4%

INDUSTRY COSTS

Profit	38.2%
Wages	25.5%
Purchases	1.4%
Depreciation	0.9%
Marketing	1.7%
Rent & Utilities	1.5%
Other	30.8%

MARKET SHARE

Citigroup Inc.	7.4%
Wells Fargo & Company	6.6%
JPMorgan Chase & Co.	6.6%
Bank of America Corporation . . .	3.1%
BMO Harris Bank NA	2.5%
Deutsche Bank Ag	1.5%

Loan and deposit growth, return on equity, and delinquency rate

EXPENSES (% OF ANNUAL SALES)

Cost of Goods	25%
Occupancy Costs	05% to 10%
Payroll/Labor Costs.	35%
Profit (pretax)	25%

QUESTIONS

- Why are you selling? Time frame? What are the selling objectives?
- Provide all the financial statements and tax returns for at least three years.

INDUSTRY TREND

"The financial services sector has...been one of the keenest early adopters of AI, where its role in the automation of repetitive processes, risk assessment, and fraud prevention is well established....Established banks face competition from more directions than ever before–with fintech startups, big retailers, and tech giants like Google, Amazon and Apple all signing up customers to services that would traditionally have been their domain....Worldwide, IDC predicts that the financial services industry will be second only to retail when it comes to spending on AI between 2021 and 2025, accounting for nearly 14% of the $204 billion that will be spent annually by the end of that period. One further area where growth will be apparent is the use of AI to ensure fair and equitable treatment of credit applicants."

Source: "The 5 Biggest Financial Services Tech Trends In 2022" by Bernard Marr, January 14, 2022, https://www.forbes.com/sites/bernardmarr/2022/01/14/ the-5-biggest-financial-services-tech-trends-in-2022/

"Lingering supply chain issues and global energy crisis have created historically high inflation. The current rate hikes are decreasing the quantity of house loans. Consolidation has been occurring since the 2008 financial crisis. The Fed has indicated it will pursue higher interest rates going forward. Technology is becoming essential to modern banking operations. Quality customer service will increase as Commercial Banks compete against other banks. Commercial Banks are expected to benefit from the increased rates."

Source: IBISWorld Industry at a Glance

EXPERT COMMENTS

Have a written plan, and mutual understanding with investors and/or board of directors.

FINANCING

Sale is either cash, stock, or a combination of both.

RESOURCES

- IBISWorld, January 2023: https://www.ibisworld.com
- ABA—American Bankers Association: https://www.aba.com
- RMA–The Risk Management Association: https://www.rmahq.org/Default.aspx
- State Bankers Association Alliance Contact List: https://www.aba.com/advocacy/state-association-alliance/state-association-contacts

Barbershops

NAICS 812111	SIC 7241-01	Businesses/Units 155,839
Profit $732.4 M	Wages $2.8 B	Annual Growth Future 0.6%
		Annual Growth Past 0.6%

Rules of Thumb

- 10%–25% SDE plus inventory; add $1500 per chair

INDUSTRY MULTIPLES

Acquisition multiples below are calculated medians using US private industry transactions. Data updated annually. Last update: August 2023.

VALUATION MULTIPLE (MEDIAN VALUE)

UNDER $1 MILLION NET SALES

MVIC/Net Sales	0.33
MVIC/Gross Profit	0.77
MVIC/SDE	1.96
MVIC/EBITDA	2.00

$1 MILLION–$5 MILLION NET SALES

MVIC/Net Sales	0.37
MVIC/Gross Profit	0.38
MVIC/SDE	4.32
MVIC/EBITDA	34.13

OVER $5 MILLION NET SALES   N/A

Source: DealStats (formerly Pratt's Stats), 2023 (Portland, OR: Business Valuation Resources, LLC), www.bvresources.com/dealstats

BENCHMARK DATA

For Benchmark data see Beauty Salons

STATISTICS (BARBERSHOPS)

Number of Establishments	155,839
Average Profit Margin	15.0%
Revenue per Employee	$28,400
Average Number of Employees	1.1
Average Wages per Employee	$16,438

PRODUCTS AND SERVICES SEGMENTATION

Basic haircuts	70.0%
Haircuts with shave	25.1%
Merchandise	2.2%
Other	2.1%
Other hair services	0.6%

INDUSTRY COSTS

Profit	. 15.0%
Wages	. 57.6%
Purchases	. 3.8%
Depreciation	. 1.8%
Marketing	. 0.8%
Rent & Utilities	. 2.4%
Other	. 18.7%

INDUSTRY TREND

"Rapid economic recovery post-pandemic fuels demand for haircuts. Consistent rise in adult population creates diverse customer base for operators. The rise of the internet and social media accelerated marketability of specialized service hairstyles. Stable economic conditions set to provide crucial respite for customers. Growth in broader domestic population poised to provide important revenue stabilizer. The growing prevalence of social media marketing will provide advantage for barbers to differentiate themselves. The use of social media to market barber shop services helped bolster core revenue streams."

Source: IBISWorld Industry at a Glance

RESOURCES

- IBISWorld, May 2023: https://www.ibisworld.com
- ABA—American Barber Association: https://americanbarber.org

Bare Printed Circuit Board Manufacturing

| NAICS 334412 | Businesses/Units 409

| Profit $217.5 M | Wages $1.3 B | Annual Growth Future 0.6%

                                            | Annual Growth Past -0.4%

INDUSTRY MULTIPLES

Acquisition multiples below are calculated medians using US private industry transactions. Data updated annually. Last update: August 2023.

VALUATION MULTIPLE (MEDIAN VALUE)

UNDER $1 MILLION NET SALES	
MVIC/Net Sales.	0.60
MVIC/Gross Profit	1.09
MVIC/SDE	3.07
MVIC/EBITDA	7.81
$1 MILLION–$5 MILLION NET SALES	N/A
OVER $5 MILLION NET SALES	
MVIC/Net Sales.	0.89
MVIC/Gross Profit	3.26
MVIC/SDE	3.44
MVIC/EBITDA	7.38

Source: DealStats (formerly Pratt's Stats), 2023 (Portland, OR: Business Valuation Resources, LLC), www.bvresources.com/dealstats

BENCHMARK DATA

STATISTICS (BARE PRINTED CIRCUIT BOARD MANUFACTURING)

Number of Establishments	409
Average Profit Margin	4.5%

Revenue per Employee	$222,000
Average Number of Employees.	53.6
Average Wages per Employee	$58,719

PRODUCTS AND SERVICES SEGMENTATION

Other circuit boards with four to six layers	26.4%
Flex printed circuit boards	24.2%
High density interconnect circuit boards	17.2%
Other circuit boards with either or more layers	16.1%
Glass printed circuit boards	16.1%

MAJOR MARKET SEGMENTATION

Industrial, medical and defense manufacturers	47.7%
Communications equipment manufacturers	28.8%
Exports	17.2%
Embedded computing and storage equipment manufacturers	6.3%

INDUSTRY COSTS

Profit	4.5%
Wages	26.6%
Purchases	40.6%
Depreciation	2.1%
Marketing	0.2%
Rent & Utilities	3.2%
Other	22.7%

MARKET SHARE

TTM Technologies	13.1%

INDUSTRY TREND

"Operators serving military and defense markets were largely unaffected by the pandemic. Demand for bare printed circuit boards has become increasingly satisfied by low-cost imports. Rapid globalization and heightened competition have had a negative influence on the industry's operations. A significant share of domestic demand will likely continue to be satisfied by imports. The industry is expected to exhibit more subdued trade changes. Operations are expected to continue contracting due to supply and demand imbalances. Operators have contended with volatile commodity prices, resulting in lower profit."

Source: IBISWorld Industry at a Glance

RESOURCES

• IBISWorld, April 2022: https://www.ibisworld.com

Bars

NAICS 722410	SIC 5813-01	Businesses/Units 71,194	
Profit $2.3 B	Wages $10.9 B	Annual Growth Future 0.9%	
		Annual Growth Past 2.2%	

Rules of Thumb

• 35%–45% annual sales-business only plus inventory
• 2–3 x SDE plus inventory
• 1.5–2.5 x EBIT
• 2–2.5 x EBITDA
• 4 x monthly sales + game revenue (net) plus inventory
• 4 x monthly sales + liquor license and inventory

INDUSTRY MULTIPLES

Acquisition multiples below are calculated medians using US private industry transactions. Data updated annually. Last update: August 2023.

B

VALUATION MULTIPLE (MEDIAN VALUE)

UNDER $1 MILLION NET SALES

MVIC/Net Sales	0.37
MVIC/Gross Profit	0.63
MVIC/SDE	2.04
MVIC/EBITDA	2.59

$1 MILLION–$5 MILLION NET SALES

MVIC/Net Sales	0.33
MVIC/Gross Profit	0.57
MVIC/SDE	2.65
MVIC/EBITDA	2.84

OVER $5 MILLION NET SALES

MVIC/Net Sales	0.41
MVIC/Gross Profit	0.52
MVIC/SDE	0.10
MVIC/EBITDA	5.59

Source: DealStats (formerly Pratt's Stats), 2023 (Portland, OR: Business Valuation Resources, LLC), www.bvresources.com/dealstats

PRICING TIPS

You have to understand the value of a liquor license if in a control state; in our market that can be $80K to $500K, which impacts the business.

You have to be able to read between the lines of creative accounting. Many times owners want to minimize tax consequences and end up running many personal expenses through the business. It's important to be able to back up these expenses. Oftentimes employees not on the books create a challenge when adjusting expenses.

A bar serving alcohol only should have a higher profit margin than one selling food. It is a cash business. A lot of due diligence is necessary to verify cash expenses and receipts.

BENCHMARK DATA

STATISTICS (BARS & NIGHTCLUBS)

Number of Establishments	71,194
Average Profit Margin	6.3%
Revenue per Employee	$60,400
Average Number of Employees	8.5
Average Wages per Employee	$18,316

PRODUCTS AND SERVICES SEGMENTATION

Sale of distilled spirit drinks	35.0%
Sale of beer and ale	33.7%
Sale of meals and nonalcoholic beverages	14.5%
Sale of wine drinks	7.5%
Accommodation, cigarettes, rentals and packaged liquor	6.9%
Admissions to special events and nightclubs, including cover charges	2.4%

INDUSTRY COSTS

Profit	6.3%
Wages	30.0%
Purchases	39.8%
Depreciation	2.1%
Marketing	1.8%

Rent & Utilities 7.4%
Other 12.6%

Liquor pouring costs should be at 25% or less. Beer and wine at 33%.

Food costs under 34% helpful.

High rents have been the cause of many failures.

Small, easily operated bars are the most desirable. Rent at 10%–12% (or less) of sales help.

Benchmarks vary widely with markets and types of establishments; food costs tend to be 25%–33%; however, productivity per square foot is a function of size and location (and subsequent lease rate).

EXPENSES (% OF ANNUAL SALES)

Cost of Goods	20% to 30%
Occupancy Costs	10% to 20%
Payroll/Labor Costs. . . .	20% to 30%
Profit (pretax)	10% to 20%

QUESTIONS

- Have they ever had any fighting or calls to the police?
- If you were to stay, or were 20 years younger, what would you do differently?
- You first need to find out about any money, grants, or programs they took advantage of—and, outstanding debts. It's imperative, if leasing, to make sure that they actually have a valid lease.
- Do you have any violations? How do you get along with the neighbors? Tell me about the customers that come to your bar. Tell me about your bartenders.
- Financials—P&Ls and associated tax returns.
- Length of time employees have been at work, number of employees, tax audits?
- Please provide me with a copy of the permit or conditional use permit, as provided by the city and the state Alcohol Control Board.
- What conditions have been placed on the license restricting the hours, use, or entertainment associated with the license?
- Number of licenses in town; length of lease; percent of food sales; percent of liquor sales; entertainment costs, if any. Watch for ratios that are out of industry standards.

INDUSTRY TREND

We see more creative offerings.

More experiential places, reasons to come, and attention to detail in the ingredients. Have nonalcoholic selections as well. Customers want to know where their products are coming from.

"The severity of the coronavirus pandemic and its effects on the industry will likely hurt overall revenue growth. The rising popularity of craft beer, cider, specialty cocktails and wine has helped the industry. Industry profit growth can largely be attributed to the post-coronavirus economic recovery. Premiumization will likely continue to benefit industry operators. Traditional bars that have not updated business concepts tend to experience the greatest competitive threat. Establishments will likely need to anticipate and respond quickly to beverage trends. Tight profit forced many operators to close establishments permanently in 2020."

Source: IBISWorld Industry at a Glance

EXPERT COMMENTS

There is high demand for a bar for sale. Buyers should be prepared to pay all cash. Buyer should not be an active drinker.

Owners have to be great at social media marketing with their businesses and know how to work with the influencers to help with sales.

I think with labor costs and employee challenges, it's a tougher market. Also, shortages of supplies and rising costs have to be considered.

Keep good records. Follow the ABC regulations; they offer courses you can take. Stay away from drinking when at the business.

FINANCING

Seller financing, outside financing hard to get.

Seeing many SBA deals.

We don't see seller financing. Sometimes SBA deals, 401K ROBS conversions.

All cash

RESOURCES

- IBISWorld, February 2023: https://www.ibisworld.com
- BarProducts.com: https://barproducts.com

Bars with Slot Machines

| NAICS 722410

Rules of Thumb

- 3 x SDE plus inventory

INDUSTRY MULTIPLES

Acquisition multiples below are calculated medians using US private industry transactions. Data updated annually. Last update: August 2023.

VALUATION MULTIPLE (MEDIAN VALUE)

UNDER $1 MILLION NET SALES	
MVIC/Net Sales	0.37
MVIC/Gross Profit	0.63
MVIC/SDE	2.04
MVIC/EBITDA	2.59
$1 MILLION–$5 MILLION NET SALES	
MVIC/Net Sales	0.33
MVIC/Gross Profit	0.57
MVIC/SDE	2.65
MVIC/EBITDA	2.84
OVER $5 MILLION NET SALES	
MVIC/Net Sales	0.41
MVIC/Gross Profit	0.52
MVIC/SDE	0.10
MVIC/EBITDA	5.59

Source: DealStats (formerly Pratt's Stats), 2023 (Portland, OR: Business Valuation Resources, LLC), www.bvresources.com/dealstats

PRICING TIPS

Drinks are free to slot players. Pay close attention to only the net, providing other operating costs are in line.

EXPENSES (% OF ANNUAL SALES)

Cost of Goods	32%
Occupancy Costs	10%
Payroll/Labor Costs.	30%
Profit (pretax)	17% (estimated)

Bars/Nightclubs

| NAICS 722410

Rules of Thumb

- 30%–40% annual sales
- 2–2.5 x SDE plus inventory
- 2.3–3 x EBIT
- 2–2.5 x EBITDA

INDUSTRY MULTIPLES

Acquisition multiples below are calculated medians using US private industry transactions. Data updated annually. Last update: August 2023.

VALUATION MULTIPLE (MEDIAN VALUE)

UNDER $1 MILLION NET SALES	
MVIC/Net Sales.	0.37
MVIC/Gross Profit	0.63
MVIC/SDE	2.04
MVIC/EBITDA	2.59

$1 MILLION–$5 MILLION NET SALES	
MVIC/Net Sales.	0.33
MVIC/Gross Profit	0.57
MVIC/SDE	2.65
MVIC/EBITDA	2.84

OVER $5 MILLION NET SALES	
MVIC/Net Sales.	0.41
MVIC/Gross Profit	0.52
MVIC/SDE	0.10
MVIC/EBITDA	5.59

Source: DealStats (formerly Pratt's Stats), 2023 (Portland, OR: Business Valuation Resources, LLC), www.bvresources.com/dealstats

PRICING TIPS

It is important to understand, and factor in, the add-backs for this type of business. The add-backs can be substantial.

The conditions or potential restrictions on the liquor license are paramount. Are there abbreviated hours? Are happy hours or door fees allowed? What is the security guard to patron ratio? Does a significant percentage of sales need to be derived from food sales?

BENCHMARK DATA

Percentage breakdown of sales by category—beer, wine, and spirits

EXPENSES (% OF ANNUAL SALES)

Cost of Goods	25% to 35%
Occupancy Costs	07% to 15%
Payroll/Labor Costs.	25% to 35%
Profit (pretax)	10% to 20%

QUESTIONS

- Experience, capital to invest/borrowing ability, price range, locations. Have they made attempts to purchase any prior to this point? What happened? How long have they been looking?
- Specific type of liquor license—beer, wlne, spirits, or combination of all three? Cost on the open market for license and the yearly fees?

INDUSTRY TREND

We believe it is on the up.

EXPERT COMMENTS

Check first with the landlord to make sure that the seller is not in default.

You have to understand this type of business.

Verify financials and all beer, wine, and liquor purchases to help determine volume.

Clubs are rated along socioeconomic lines. Some are very high end, some bottom end, though profits do not always follow these levels.

FINANCING

With the pandemic in our market, I didn't see much seller financing; now we are seeing a shift in this. We are seeing outside financing, but it is getting trickier.

RESOURCES

- ANA—American Nightlife Association: https://www.nightlifeassociation.org
- Bar & Restaurant: https://www.barandrestaurant.com

Baskin-Robbins (Franchise)

| NAICS 722515 | SIC 2024-98 | Businesses/Units 2,276

Rules of Thumb

- 46%–56% annual sales plus inventory

INDUSTRY MULTIPLES

Acquisition multiples below are calculated medians using US private industry transactions. Data updated annually. Last update: August 2023.

VALUATION MULTIPLE (MEDIAN VALUE)

UNDER $1 MILLION NET SALES	
MVIC/Net Sales.	0.44
MVIC/Gross Profit	0.62
MVIC/SDE	2.20
MVIC/EBITDA	2.82
$1 MILLION–$5 MILLION NET SALES	
MVIC/Net Sales.	0.41
MVIC/Gross Profit	0.69
MVIC/SDE	2.82
MVIC/EBITDA	5.94
OVER $5 MILLION NET SALES	
MVIC/Net Sales.	3.89
MVIC/Gross Profit	4.87
MVIC/SDE	N/A
MVIC/EBITDA	N/A

Source: DealStats (formerly Pratt's Stats), 2023 (Portland, OR: Business Valuation Resources, LLC), www.bvresources.com/dealstats

PRICING TIPS

Approx. Total Investment: $293,840 to $636,360

RESOURCES

- Baskin-Robbins: https://www.baskinrobbins.com/en
- Franchise information: https://www.baskinrobbinsfranchising.com
- Inspire Brands: https://inspirebrands.com

Batteries Plus (Franchise)

| NAICS 441330 | Businesses/Units 618

Rules of Thumb

- 30%–35% annual sales plus inventory

INDUSTRY MULTIPLES

Acquisition multiples below are calculated medians using US private industry transactions. Data updated annually. Last update: August 2023.

VALUATION MULTIPLE (MEDIAN VALUE)

UNDER $1 MILLION NET SALES
MVIC/Net Sales	0.55
MVIC/Gross Profit	0.99
MVIC/SDE	2.73
MVIC/EBITDA	3.07

$1 MILLION–$5 MILLION NET SALES
MVIC/Net Sales	0.40
MVIC/Gross Profit	1.15
MVIC/SDE	2.85
MVIC/EBITDA	4.34

OVER $5 MILLION NET SALES
MVIC/Net Sales	0.44
MVIC/Gross Profit	1.40
MVIC/SDE	3.28
MVIC/EBITDA	3.85

Source: DealStats (formerly Pratt's Stats), 2023 (Portland, OR: Business Valuation Resources, LLC), www.bvresources.com/dealstats

PRICING TIPS

Approx. Total Investment: $197,400 to $465,600

RESOURCES

- Batteries Plus: https://www.batteriesplus.com
- Franchise information: https://www.batteriesplusfranchise.com
- Freeman Spogli & Co.: https://www.freemanspogli.com

Beauty Salons

NAICS 812112	SIC 7231-06	Businesses/Units 1,423,726
Profit $4.8 B	Wages $33 B	Annual Growth Future 0.9%
		Annual Growth Past -2.4%

Rules of Thumb

- 35% annual revenues; add fixtures, equipment, & inventory
- 2 x SDE plus inventory
- 4 x monthly sales plus inventory
- 2.5 x EBIT
- 4 x EBITDA

B

INDUSTRY MULTIPLES

Acquisition multiples below are calculated medians using US private industry transactions. Data updated annually. Last update: August 2023.

VALUATION MULTIPLE (MEDIAN VALUE)

UNDER $1 MILLION NET SALES

MVIC/Net Sales.	0.31
MVIC/Gross Profit	0.39
MVIC/SDE	1.60
MVIC/EBITDA	2.11

$1 MILLION–$5 MILLION NET SALES

MVIC/Net Sales.	0.29
MVIC/Gross Profit	0.39
MVIC/SDE	2.30
MVIC/EBITDA	3.05

OVER $5 MILLION NET SALES	N/A

Source: DealStats (formerly Pratt's Stats), 2023 (Portland, OR: Business Valuation Resources, LLC), www.bvresources.com/dealstats

PRICING TIPS

Multiples vary significantly, based on size of the company. The multiples above are for product businesses, not service-based businesses like hair salons. Product businesses command significantly higher multiples than service-based businesses. Growth and distribution channels are the primary drivers of value. Online direct to consumer distribution is attractive, given the higher margins, although retail distribution brings larger scale. Distribution through spas and salons is less attractive given the likely margins that need to be shared with distributors in these industries. Strength of brand is important.

BENCHMARK DATA

STATISTICS (HAIR & NAIL SALONS)

Number of Establishments .	1,423,726
Average Profit Margin	7.1%
Revenue per Employee .	$33,500
Average Number of Employees.	.1.4
Average Wages per Employee .	$16,535

PRODUCTS AND SERVICES SEGMENTATION

Haircut and styling services	45.5%
Hair coloring and tinting services	17.1%
Nail care services	15.9%
Merchandise sales .	7.2%
Other beauty care services .	6.1%
Other hair care services	4.7%
Skin care services	3.5%

INDUSTRY COSTS

Profit	7.1%
Wages	48.9%
Purchases	6.3%

B

Depreciation 1.8%
Marketing 1.3%
Rent & Utilities 3.9%
Other 30.7%

EXPENSES (% OF ANNUAL SALES)

Cost of Goods . . . . . . 06% to 12%
Occupancy Costs . . . . . 10% to 20%
Payroll/Labor Costs. . . . . 50% to 60%
Profit (pretax) . . . . . . 07% to 15%

QUESTIONS

- How much of the sales belong to your performance? Will you stay on? If the buyer is a stylist and so is the seller, will the clientele slowly flow to the buyer? How long have the employees been with you? What is the turnover of technicians? Commission or rental? What type of products do you use, and how old is the product on your shelf? How often, and where, do you advertise? Who does your website, Facebook page? Where do you find your employees? How often do you offer education classes, and from what company?

INDUSTRY TREND

"From independent solo artist to the largest upscale chain, salon owners and stylists everywhere are looking to combat the dual threat of rising costs and shrinking margins. And yet, across the industry, professionals often overlook a valuable and largely untapped asset: the male clients we so quickly usher in and out of our salons....

"According to data from a new survey recently published by Boulevard, the opportunity for growth in men's salon services is significant:

Male clients visit the salon with far greater regularity than female clients: 68% visiting at least once a month and 38% coming in at least once a week.

Male clients are far more likely than female clients to seek multiple services in a single visit (67% vs. 49%).

Male clients are far more likely than female clients to buy products at the salon (69% vs. 31%) and to be heavily influenced by the recommendations of their stylist (63% vs 37%)."

Source: "Why Male Clients Are the Salon Industry's Most Overlooked Asset"
by Shanalie Wijesinghe, February 25, 2022,
https://www.modernsalon.com/1080343/why-male-clients-are-the-salon-industrys-most-overlooked-asset

"As salons began reopening amid the removal of pandemic restrictions, they slowly got back into the swing of things. Many nail salons are striving to reduce water waste through the end of 2023 by going waterless. Cosmetic companies have continued to remove harmful chemicals from many nail salon products. Consumers are expected to indulge more often in higher value hair and nail services. Nail salons are expected to continue promoting natural polish products over the next five years. Operators will further implement websites and social media to promote service offerings. Reduced demand stemming from the pandemic has weighed on revenue and profit significantly."

Source: IBISWorld Industry at a Glance

EXPERT COMMENTS

Significant number of acquisitions of indie beauty brands, at high multiples, by large strategists and PEGs (private equity groups)

FINANCING

Seller financing is suggested in this industry as most banks do not lend money to the majority of these businesses. Never take less than 50 percent down payment. I typically see 75 percent down payment or all cash balance over 2 to 3 years.

RESOURCES

- IBISWorld, January 2023: https://www.ibisworld.com
- Modern Salon: https://www.modernsalon.com
- PBA—Professional Beauty Association: https://www.probeauty.org
- Salon Today: https://www.salontoday.com

Bed and Mattress Stores

	NAICS 449110		SIC 5712-09		Businesses/Units 67,928
	Profit $5.2 B		Wages $17.2 B		Annual Growth Future 1.1%
					Annual Growth Past 2.0%

Rules of Thumb

- 35% annual sales plus inventory

INDUSTRY MULTIPLES

Acquisition multiples below are calculated medians using US private industry transactions. Data updated annually. Last update: August 2023.

VALUATION MULTIPLE (MEDIAN VALUE)

UNDER $1 MILLION NET SALES
MVIC/Net Sales	0.32
MVIC/Gross Profit	0.65
MVIC/SDE	1.53
MVIC/EBITDA	1.81

$1 MILLION–$5 MILLION NET SALES
MVIC/Net Sales	0.38
MVIC/Gross Profit	0.89
MVIC/SDE	2.44
MVIC/EBITDA	3.25

OVER $5 MILLION NET SALES
MVIC/Net Sales	0.98
MVIC/Gross Profit	1.95
MVIC/SDE	5.46
MVIC/EBITDA	10.70

Source: DealStats (formerly Pratt's Stats), 2023 (Portland, OR: Business Valuation Resources, LLC), www.bvresources.com/dealstats

PRICING TIPS

More retail locations equal more favorable manufacturer pricing.

BENCHMARK DATA

STATISTICS (BED AND MATTRESS STORES)
Number of Establishments	67,928
Average Profit Margin	4.0%
Revenue per Employee	$337,000
Average Number of Employees	5.8
Average Wages per Employee	$44,550

PRODUCTS AND SERVICES SEGMENTATION

Queen-sized mattresses	41.4%
Full-sized mattresses	18.0%
King-sized mattresses	17.8%
Twin-sized mattresses	17.2%
Other mattresses, foundations and bedding	5.6%

INDUSTRY COSTS

Profit	4.0%
Wages	13.2%
Purchases	49.8%
Depreciation	0.9%
Marketing	3.5%
Rent & Utilities	5.8%
Other	22.8%

MARKET SHARE

Steinhoff International Holdings N.V.	3.3%
Sleep Number Corporation	1.7%

EXPENSES (% OF ANNUAL SALES)

Cost of Goods	25%
Occupancy Costs	20%
Payroll/Labor Costs.	10%
Profit (pretax)	45%

QUESTIONS

• What is the reason for selling? Where do you stand in terms of your relationships with the major bedding suppliers? What customer service issues might be pending?

INDUSTRY TREND

"After a century or so of being dominated by just a few big brands, there are now 175 online mattress brands alone. The prevalence of online mattress companies reflects one of the biggest ongoing trends in the mattress industry: Mattress shoppers are increasingly researching and purchasing mattresses online. This trend has been accelerated by the Covid-19 pandemic. As people increasingly prioritize a good night's sleep, they're developing particular preferences around mattress type, firmness, and so on. In some cases, these preferences break down along generational lines. The mattress industry is booming, and it shows no signs of slowing down."

Source: "The Mattress Industry Is Evolving for the Future: Statistics and Trends" by Laura Newcomer, January 4, 2022, https://www.mattressclarity.com/news/mattress-industry-statistics/

"The product offerings of mattress stores have expanded greatly. Employment has strengthened during the period to keep up with demand. Boosts in the number of bedbug infestations induced higher demand for new mattresses. Continued innovations will further support revenue expansion. The continued spread of bedbugs and additional media exposure will also boost industry sales. Bed and mattress stores' new technologies are helping them win over customers that were previously holdouts. More competitors have entered the industry to capitalize on the growing portfolio of products and expanding business."

Source: IBISWorld Industry at a Glance

Bedding continues to be a needed product and the consumer now has a perceived need for enhanced comfort and a better night's rest.

RESOURCES

- IBISWorld, July 2023: https://www.ibisworld.com
- BedTimes: https://bedtimesmagazine.com
- ISPA—International Sleep Products Association: https://sleepproducts.org
- Furniture Today: https://www.furnituretoday.com/category/mattress-bedding-news/

Bed-and-Breakfasts

NAICS 721191	SIC 7011-07	Businesses/Units 15,563
Profit $118.6 M	Wages $781.3 M	Annual Growth Future 2.2%
		Annual Growth Past 3.5%

Rules of Thumb

- 400%–450% annual sales includes inventory and real estate
- 8–9 x SDE includes inventory and real estate

INDUSTRY MULTIPLES

Acquisition multiples below are calculated medians using US private industry transactions. Data updated annually. Last update: August 2023.

VALUATION MULTIPLE (MEDIAN VALUE)

UNDER $1 MILLION NET SALES	
MVIC/Net Sales	1.06
MVIC/Gross Profit	1.22
MVIC/SDE	0.55
MVIC/EBITDA	0.87
$1 MILLION–$5 MILLION NET SALES	N/A
OVER $5 MILLION NET SALES	N/A

Source: DealStats (formerly Pratt's Stats), 2023 (Portland, OR: Business Valuation Resources, LLC), www.bvresources.com/dealstats

PRICING TIPS

B&B buyers must make both a lifestyle and a financial purchase decision. Innkeeping is one of the few businesses where you want to live where you work! For the past 20+ years, we have had smaller B&Bs sold/converted back to homes than we've had homes being converted to inns! Start-ups are more difficult to accomplish today versus the mid-1980s primarily due to rising real estate values, high conversion cost, zoning restrictions, tougher lending practices, and a lack of market demand for innkeeping (during a strong economy). Some of the smaller inns in less popular areas were converted to alternative uses, and a minority of inns closed for avoidance of taxes from capital gains and depreciation recapture.

The majority of the B&Bs and inns are supplemental income businesses. The innkeeping industry was created and replenished by the baby boomer generation. Those folks have gotten too old for innkeeping. Many of the next generation have limited financial capacity and interest in innkeeping. The lack of profitable inns and the lack of buyers have created a very low rate of inn sales.

BENCHMARK DATA

STATISTICS (BED & BREAKFAST & HOSTEL ACCOMMODATIONS)

Number of Establishments	15,563
Average Profit Margin	4.1%
Revenue per Employee	$79,900
Average Number of Employees. . . .	2.4
Average Wages per Employee . . .	$21,693

PRODUCTS AND SERVICES SEGMENTATION

Bed & Breakfast accommodations . . .	47.7%
Hostels and other accommodations . .	39.7%
Food and alcohol	8.1%
Other products and services	4.5%

MAJOR MARKET SEGMENTATION

Property website	49.7%
Online travel agency	24.1%
Direct bookings	24.0%
Travel agency	2.2%

INDUSTRY COSTS

Profit	4.1%
Wages	27.0%
Purchases	22.5%
Depreciation	4.8%
Marketing	2.5%
Rent & Utilities	0.4%
Other	38.7%

EXPENSES (% OF ANNUAL SALES)

Cost of Goods	15%
Occupancy Costs	10%
Payroll/Labor Costs.	.9% to 10%
Profit (pretax)	10%

QUESTIONS

- Can you show me how your B&B will work for me financially and in lifestyle?

INDUSTRY TREND

"Falling recreational expenditures has adversely influenced demand for accommodations. A wave of industry operators has left the industry permanently in 2020 as a result of the pandemic. Demand for hostels is driven by international visitors and US residents who want to travel. Inbound trips by non-US residents and domestic trips by US residents are both projected to increase. Hostels will be able to offer some significant competitive advantages to maintain their market share. The industry's footprint is expected to recover over the next five years as travel demand rises. More baby boomers entering the retirement threshold has raised demand for industry services."

Source: IBISWorld Industry at a Glance

EXPERT COMMENTS

Unless the B&B is in a high-occupancy area, it is difficult to cash flow with fewer than 6 rooms.

RESOURCES

- IBISWorld, January 2023: https://www.ibisworld.com
- ALP—Association of Lodging Professionals: https://www.alplodging.org

- MBBA—Michigan Bed and Breakfast Association: https://laketolake.com
- Vrbo: https://www.vrbo.com

Beekeeping

| NAICS 112910 | Businesses/Units 16,619

| Profit $28.1 M | Wages $171.9 M | Annual Growth Future -0.8%

| | | Annual Growth Past -6.7%

INDUSTRY MULTIPLES

Acquisition multiples below are calculated medians using US private industry transactions. Data updated annually. Last update: August 2023.

VALUATION MULTIPLE (MEDIAN VALUE)

UNDER $1 MILLION NET SALES	
MVIC/Net Sales.	0.87
MVIC/Gross Profit	1.95
MVIC/SDE	N/A
MVIC/EBITDA	N/A
$1 MILLION–$5 MILLION NET SALES	N/A
OVER $5 MILLION NET SALES	N/A

Source: DealStats (formerly Pratt's Stats), 2023 (Portland, OR: Business Valuation Resources, LLC), www.bvresources.com/dealstats

BENCHMARK DATA

STATISTICS (BEEKEEPING)

Number of Establishments .	16,619
Average Profit Margin .	4.5%
Revenue per Employee .	$35,900
Average Number of Employees.	1.0
Average Wages per Employee .	$10,155

PRODUCTS AND SERVICES SEGMENTATION

Honey	50.0%
Pollination services .	40.7%
Other products .	9.3%

MAJOR MARKET SEGMENTATION

Processors .	70.4%
Farmer's markets	19.4%
Brokers .	10.2%

INDUSTRY COSTS

Profit	4.5%
Wages .	27.5%
Purchases .	25.5%
Depreciation	4.8%
Marketing .	0.8%
Rent & Utilities .	10.5%
Other	26.4%

INDUSTRY TREND

"'Anybody who eats food needs bees,' said Noah Wilson-Rich, co-founder, CEO and chief scientific officer of the Boston-based Best Bees company, which contracts with the government to take care of the honeybee hives at the New

Hampshire courthouse and at some other federal buildings....Best Bees tests the plant DNA in the honey to get an idea of the plant diversity and health in the area, Wilson-Rich said, and they have found that bees that forage on a more diverse diet seem to have better survival and productivity outcomes."

Source: "Honeybee health blooms at federal facilities across the country," June 4, 2023, https://www.boston.com/news/environment/2023/06/04/ honeybee-health-blooms-at-federal-facilities-across-the-country/

"The United States no longer imports large volumes of honey from China. This industry experiences a high level of import competition. US beekeepers have increased their sales to other farmers within the agricultural sector. As a result of international competition, industry establishments may turn to new or niche products. The use of bee products in medicine may influence demand for the industry's products. The growth of agricultural industries is expected to lead to higher demand for bee pollination purposes. Due to the rising cost of pollination services, industry profit has decreased."

Source: IBISWorld Industry at a Glance

RESOURCES

- IBISWorld, May 2023: https://www.ibisworld.com
- ABF—American Beekeeping Federation: https://www.abfnet.org

Beer & Wine Stores

| NAICS 445320 | SIC 5921-04

Rules of Thumb

- 4 x monthly sales plus inventory

INDUSTRY MULTIPLES

Acquisition multiples below are calculated medians using US private industry transactions. Data updated annually. Last update: August 2023.

VALUATION MULTIPLE (MEDIAN VALUE)

UNDER $1 MILLION NET SALES
MVIC/Net Sales	0.40
MVIC/Gross Profit	1.41
MVIC/SDE	3.33
MVIC/EBITDA	4.64

$1 MILLION–$5 MILLION NET SALES
MVIC/Net Sales	0.43
MVIC/Gross Profit	1.59
MVIC/SDE	3.50
MVIC/EBITDA	6.49

OVER $5 MILLION NET SALES
MVIC/Net Sales	0.31
MVIC/Gross Profit	1.33
MVIC/SDE	3.76
MVIC/EBITDA	7.85

Source: DealStats (formerly Pratt's Stats), 2023 (Portland, OR: Business Valuation Resources, LLC), www.bvresources.com/dealstats

BENCHMARK DATA

For Benchmark data see Liquor Stores

Beer Taverns, Beer & Wine

| NAICS 722410

Rules of Thumb

- 6 x monthly sales plus inventory
- 1–1.5 x annual EBIT
- 55% annual sales plus inventory

INDUSTRY MULTIPLES

Acquisition multiples below are calculated medians using US private industry transactions. Data updated annually. Last update: August 2023.

VALUATION MULTIPLE (MEDIAN VALUE)

UNDER $1 MILLION NET SALES	
MVIC/Net Sales.	0.37
MVIC/Gross Profit	0.63
MVIC/SDE	2.04
MVIC/EBITDA	2.59
$1 MILLION–$5 MILLION NET SALES	
MVIC/Net Sales.	0.33
MVIC/Gross Profit	0.57
MVIC/SDE	2.65
MVIC/EBITDA	2.84
OVER $5 MILLION NET SALES	
MVIC/Net Sales.	0.41
MVIC/Gross Profit	0.52
MVIC/SDE	0.10
MVIC/EBITDA	5.59

Source: DealStats (formerly Pratt's Stats), 2023 (Portland, OR: Business Valuation Resources, LLC), www.bvresources.com/dealstats

PRICING TIPS

There are 1,980 ounces in a keg, less 10 percent waste, about 1,700 net ounces per keg. If there are 12 ounces (net) in a glass of beer, divide 12 ounces into 1,700 net ounces per keg to determine cost and number of glasses that should be poured from that keg. Determine what a 12-ounce glass of beer is selling for, then multiply that times the number of glasses that is poured from the keg. This will give you the total gross per keg.

RESOURCES

- Beer Institute: https://www.beerinstitute.org

Beer Wholesaling

	NAICS 424810		SIC 5181-01		Businesses/Units 4,437
	Profit $3.8 B		Wages $7.4 B		Annual Growth Future 1.3%
					Annual Growth Past 0.9%

Rules of Thumb

- 35% annual sales

INDUSTRY MULTIPLES

Acquisition multiples below are calculated medians using US private industry transactions. Data updated annually. Last update: August 2023.

VALUATION MULTIPLE (MEDIAN VALUE)

UNDER $1 MILLION NET SALES

MVIC/Net Sales	12.11
MVIC/Gross Profit	N/A
MVIC/SDE	N/A
MVIC/EBITDA	N/A

$1 MILLION–$5 MILLION NET SALES

MVIC/Net Sales	0.38
MVIC/Gross Profit	N/A
MVIC/SDE	4.67
MVIC/EBITDA	N/A

OVER $5 MILLION NET SALES

MVIC/Net Sales	0.24
MVIC/Gross Profit	1.95
MVIC/SDE	N/A
MVIC/EBITDA	8.82

Source: DealStats (formerly Pratt's Stats), 2023 (Portland, OR: Business Valuation Resources, LLC), www.bvresources.com/dealstats

PRICING TIPS

You have to know if the owner is selling to tavern accounts, and the percentage of retail traffic in the store.

The two most important characteristics are (1) the brands carried, and (2) the territory.

Brands vary considerably in market sales, and also vary regionally. Territories that are densely populated tend to be serviced more efficiently.

1 U.S. BBL (beer barrel) = 31 U.S. gallons = 13.778 = 24/12-oz. cases

BENCHMARK DATA

STATISTICS (BEER WHOLESALING)

Number of Establishments	4,437
Average Profit Margin	4.2%
Revenue per Employee	$766,000
Average Number of Employees	26.7
Average Wages per Employee	$63,543

PRODUCTS AND SERVICES SEGMENTATION

Cans of beer and ale	46.1%
Bottles of beer and ale	35.2%
Barrels and kegs of beer and ale	10.4%
Other malt beverages and brewing products	8.3%

MAJOR MARKET SEGMENTATION

Liquor stores	42.5%
Grocery stores and supermarkets	30.9%
Downstream wholesalers	14.6%
Restaurants, drinking establishments and hotels	9.9%
Other	2.1%

INDUSTRY COSTS

Profit	4.2%
Wages	8.6%

```
Purchases  .    .    .    .    .    .    . 64.5%
Depreciation   .    .    .    .    .    .    8.5%
Marketing   .    .    .    .    .    .    .    1.4%
Rent & Utilities .    .    .    .    .    .    1.0%
Other    .    .    .    .    .    .    . 11.8%
```

MARKET SHARE

```
Reyes Beverage Group Inc. .    .    .    . 36.5%
Columbia Distributing  .    .    .    .    .    0.6%
DBI Beverage Inc.   .    .    .    .    .    .    0.2%
Straub Distributing .    .    .    .    .    .    0.2%
```

EXPENSES (% OF ANNUAL SALES)

```
Cost of Goods  .    .    .    .    .    .    25%
Occupancy Costs   .    .    .    .    .    09%
Payroll/Labor Costs.   .    .    .    .    24%
Profit (pretax)   .    .    .    .    .    .    28%
```

QUESTIONS

• You have to know as much about the operations as they do. Seller requirements with licensing past records in our state need to be disclosed.

INDUSTRY TREND

"The National Beer Wholesalers Association (NBWA), the leading voice for America's 3,000 local, independent beer distributors, celebrates the results of the latest Gallup Consumption Habits poll showing that most Americans reach for a cold beer as their alcohol beverage of choice. The poll found that 37% percent of U.S. adults say they drink beer most frequently, compared to 31% for liquor and 29% for wine."

Source: "New Gallup Poll: Beer Continues to Be Americans' Drink of Choice," August 16, 2023, https://nbwa.org/press-release/new-gallup-poll-beer-continues-to-be-americans-drink-of-choice/

Very bullish. Drinking didn't go away with the pandemic; it has been altered.

"Beer excise taxes are usually put onto retailers. Consumers are showing growing interest in craft beers. The sustained success of wholesalers has depended heavily on the alcohol distribution system. Increased interest in craft beers will support industry growth. Strict regulation at the state level will likely preserve the industry's overall fragmentation. There have been attempts to remove the three-tiered system. Small-scale craft breweries have become increasingly popular among consumers."

Source: IBISWorld Industry Outlook

EXPERT COMMENTS

With the pandemic, beer distributors are very popular at least in our state.

FINANCING

Make sure you hire someone who is experienced. Check first with the landlord to make sure that the seller is not in default.

We have a checklist of items that a seller needs to provide. You have to know as much about the operations as they do. Seller requirements with licensing past records in our state need to be disclosed.

RESOURCES

• IBISWorld, January 2023: https://www.ibisworld.com
• BA—Brewers Association: https://www.brewersassociation.org

- Beer Institute: https://www.beerinstitute.org
- Beer Marketer's Insights: https://www.beerinsights.com
- Brewbound: https://www.brewbound.com
- NBWA—National Beer Wholesalers Association: https://www.nbwa.org

Ben & Jerry's (Franchise)

| NAICS 722515 | SIC 2024-98 | Businesses/Units 216

Rules of Thumb

- 35%–40% annual sales plus inventory

INDUSTRY MULTIPLES

Acquisition multiples below are calculated medians using US private industry transactions. Data updated annually. Last update: August 2023.

VALUATION MULTIPLE (MEDIAN VALUE)

UNDER $1 MILLION NET SALES

MVIC/Net Sales	0.44
MVIC/Gross Profit	0.62
MVIC/SDE	2.20
MVIC/EBITDA	2.82

$1 MILLION–$5 MILLION NET SALES

MVIC/Net Sales	0.41
MVIC/Gross Profit	0.69
MVIC/SDE	2.82
MVIC/EBITDA	5.94

OVER $5 MILLION NET SALES

MVIC/Net Sales	3.89
MVIC/Gross Profit	4.87
MVIC/SDE	N/A
MVIC/EBITDA	N/A

Source: DealStats (formerly Pratt's Stats), 2023 (Portland, OR: Business Valuation Resources, LLC), www.bvresources.com/dealstats

PRICING TIPS

Approx. Total Investment: $152,200 to $565,300

RESOURCES

- Ben & Jerry's: https://www.benjerry.com
- Franchise information: https://www.benjerry.com/about-us/open-a-franchise

Between Rounds Bakery Sandwich Café (Franchise)

| NAICS 722513 | SIC 5461-01 | Businesses/Units 1

Rules of Thumb

- 40%–45% annual sales plus inventory

INDUSTRY MULTIPLES

Acquisition multiples below are calculated medians using US private industry transactions. Data updated annually. Last update: August 2023.

VALUATION MULTIPLE (MEDIAN VALUE)

UNDER $1 MILLION NET SALES

MVIC/Net Sales	0.31
MVIC/Gross Profit	0.48
MVIC/SDE	1.67
MVIC/EBITDA	2.21

$1 MILLION–$5 MILLION NET SALES

MVIC/Net Sales	0.39
MVIC/Gross Profit	0.60
MVIC/SDE	2.43
MVIC/EBITDA	2.98

OVER $5 MILLION NET SALES

MVIC/Net Sales	0.89
MVIC/Gross Profit	2.08
MVIC/SDE	4.98
MVIC/EBITDA	12.81

Source: DealStats (formerly Pratt's Stats), 2023 (Portland, OR: Business Valuation Resources, LLC), www.bvresources.com/dealstats

PRICING TIPS

Approx. Total Investment: $165,500 to $525,000

RESOURCES

- Between Rounds: https://betweenroundsbagels.com
- Franchise information: https://betweenroundsbagels.com/franchise-home/

Bicycle Shops

NAICS 459110	SIC 5941-41	Businesses/Units 11,204
Profit $366.8 M	Wages $845.9 M	Annual Growth Future 0.2%
		Annual Growth Past 5.3%

Rules of Thumb

- 30%–40% annual sales plus inventory
- 2–3 x SDE plus inventory
- 2–3 x EBIT
- 3 x EBITDA

INDUSTRY MULTIPLES

Acquisition multiples below are calculated medians using US private industry transactions. Data updated annually. Last update: August 2023.

VALUATION MULTIPLE (MEDIAN VALUE)

UNDER $1 MILLION NET SALES

MVIC/Net Sales	0.50
MVIC/Gross Profit	1.01
MVIC/SDE	2.56
MVIC/EBITDA	3.93

$1 MILLION–$5 MILLION NET SALES

MVIC/Net Sales	0.37
MVIC/Gross Profit	1.03
MVIC/SDE	2.71
MVIC/EBITDA	4.08

OVER $5 MILLION NET SALES

MVIC/Net Sales.	0.46
MVIC/Gross Profit	1.33
MVIC/SDE	2.95
MVIC/EBITDA	7.63

Source: DealStats (formerly Pratt's Stats), 2023 (Portland, OR: Business Valuation Resources, LLC), www.bvresources.com/dealstats

PRICING TIPS

Make sure the inventory is current; the tech is changing quickly.

E-bikes are important. Figure out if the shop has built a segment of their business with e-bikes, both sales and service.

The key to success is returning customers, and that is directly related to the sales experience and even more to the service experience. The service business drives the success of bike shops. Second to the service department is the accessory sales business. Will clients come in to pick up bottles, bags, bike jerseys? If yes, then you have a profitable source of revenue. Bike sales are low margin.

BENCHMARK DATA

STATISTICS (BICYCLE DEALERSHIP AND REPAIR)

Number of Establishments	11,204
Average Profit Margin	4.5%
Revenue per Employee	$107,000
Average Number of Employees.	6.8
Average Wages per Employee	$11,074

PRODUCTS AND SERVICES SEGMENTATION

Mountain bicycles	28.4%
Road bicycles	21.0%
Electric bicycles	16.3%
Hybrid bicycles	11.6%
Youth bicycles	8.9%
Parts and repairs	8.2%
Lifestyle bicycles	3.8%
BMX bicycles	1.8%

INDUSTRY COSTS

Profit	4.5%
Wages	10.4%
Purchases	71.9%
Depreciation	0.8%
Marketing	0.9%
Rent & Utilities	1.1%
Other	10.3%

EXPENSES (% OF ANNUAL SALES)

Cost of Goods	50% to 60%
Occupancy Costs	08% to 11%
Profit (pretax)	08% to 15%
Payroll/Labor Costs.	15% to 20%

QUESTIONS

- Understand the expertise of the employees. Do they have a successful e-bike business? What is the strength of the service business?

INDUSTRY TREND

2020 was a springboard year for these businesses. The big question is how much will stick. Businesses that offer e-bikes and have a strong service and accessories business are likely to continue to grow, though slower than 2020. A youth segment of the business will also continue to grow.

E-commerce will grow.

"Health-focused and eco-friendly trends have contributed to cycling's rising appeal. A wide range of consumers have turned to cycling due to its perceived advantages. Industry profit benefits from consumers investing in higher-end bikes. Mass merchandisers will continue to be a source of external competition. Electric bicycles are expected to emerge as the fastest-growing revenue stream. Profit for the average industry operator is anticipated to remain relatively stable. Enthusiasts willing to pay higher prices for premium bikes have supported profit growth."

Source: IBISWorld Industry at a Glance

EXPERT COMMENTS

Make sure that there are e-bikes in the store, that it has a great location, that there is a solid service business, and that it is available for e-commerce opportunities.

FINANCING

Outside financing via the SBA is common, with some seller financing involved. Most buyers have to finance the purchase, since the value of inventory can be very high.

RESOURCES

- IBISWorld, February 2023: https://www.ibisworld.com
- BRAIN—Bicycle Retailer and Industry News: https://www.bicycleretailer.com
- NBDA—National Bicycle Dealers Association: https://nbda.com
- The League of American Bicyclists: https://www.bikeleague.org
- PeopleForBikes: https://www.peopleforbikes.org

Big O Tires (Franchise)

| NAICS 441340 | Businesses/Units 434

Rules of Thumb

- 35% annual sales plus inventory

INDUSTRY MULTIPLES

Acquisition multiples below are calculated medians using US private industry transactions. Data updated annually. Last update: August 2023.

VALUATION MULTIPLE (MEDIAN VALUE)

UNDER $1 MILLION NET SALES	
MVIC/Net Sales	0.33
MVIC/Gross Profit	0.65
MVIC/SDE	2.37
MVIC/EBITDA	2.47
$1 MILLION–$5 MILLION NET SALES	
MVIC/Net Sales	0.37
MVIC/Gross Profit	0.69
MVIC/SDE	2.69
MVIC/EBITDA	3.65

OVER $5 MILLION NET SALES

MVIC/Net Sales	0.50
MVIC/Gross Profit	1.23
MVIC/SDE	3.14
MVIC/EBITDA	7.46

Source: DealStats (formerly Pratt's Stats), 2023 (Portland, OR: Business Valuation Resources, LLC), www.bvresources.com/dealstats

PRICING TIPS

Approx. Total Investment: $333,500 to $1,441,800

RESOURCES

- Big O Tires: https://www.bigotires.com
- Franchise information: https://www.bigofranchise.com
- TBC Corporation: https://www.tbccorp.com

Billboard Advertising Companies (Outdoor Advertising)

	NAICS 541850		SIC 7312-01		Businesses/Units 12,499
	Profit $1.2 B		Wages $1.8 B		Annual Growth Future -7.3%
					Annual Growth Past -2.3%

Rules of Thumb

- 12 x EBITDA
- 500% annual sales

INDUSTRY MULTIPLES

Acquisition multiples below are calculated medians using US private industry transactions. Data updated annually. Last update: August 2023.

VALUATION MULTIPLE (MEDIAN VALUE)

UNDER $1 MILLION NET SALES

MVIC/Net Sales	0.98
MVIC/Gross Profit	1.49
MVIC/SDE	2.74
MVIC/EBITDA	4.00

$1 MILLION–$5 MILLION NET SALES

MVIC/Net Sales	2.39
MVIC/Gross Profit	5.86
MVIC/SDE	N/A
MVIC/EBITDA	N/A

OVER $5 MILLION NET SALES

MVIC/Net Sales	4.77
MVIC/Gross Profit	10.04
MVIC/SDE	N/A
MVIC/EBITDA	18.86

Source: DealStats (formerly Pratt's Stats), 2023 (Portland, OR: Business Valuation Resources, LLC), www.bvresources.com/dealstats

PRICING TIPS

"Billboard companies are usually worth surprisingly high prices in the market. Buyers and sellers rely almost exclusively on market multiples that are widely recognized as the best measures of fair market value. Discount rates and capitalization rates in this industry are more closely aligned with real estate yields than returns on operating businesses."

Source: "Appraising Billboard Companies" by Jeffrey P. Wright, ASA, CFA, Business Valuation Review

B

BENCHMARK DATA

STATISTICS (BILLBOARD & OUTDOOR ADVERTISING)

Number of Establishments	12,499
Average Profit Margin	13.5%
Revenue per Employee	$237,000
Average Number of Employees	2.8
Average Wages per Employee	$49,434

PRODUCTS AND SERVICES SEGMENTATION

Static billboards	45.7%
Digital billboards	19.6%
Transit displays	13.0%
Street furniture and other urban fixture displays	12.5%
Alternative and other leased displays	9.2%

MAJOR MARKET SEGMENTATION

Services	30.3%
Retail and consumer goods	23.1%
Entertainment	21.0%
Health/Medical	10.5%
Manufacturing	7.3%
Government	2.8%
Nonprofit organizations	2.7%
Household consumers and individuals	2.3%

INDUSTRY COSTS

Profit	13.5%
Wages	20.4%
Purchases	7.3%
Depreciation	5.9%
Marketing	5.0%
Rent & Utilities	6.8%
Other	41.1%

MARKET SHARE

Lamar Advertising Company	22.2%
Outfront Media Inc.	16.1%
Clear Channel Outdoor Holdings Inc.	12.5%
Intersection Co.	5.6%
Young Electric Sign Company	2.3%
JCDecaux SA	1.3%

EXPENSES (% OF ANNUAL SALES)

Cost of Goods	05%
Occupancy Costs	10%
Payroll/Labor Costs	05%
Profit (pretax)	45%

QUESTIONS

- Net revenue, cash flow, lease costs, and occupancy levels

INDUSTRY TREND

"Volatility has increased concentration. Operators generate revenue by selling advertisements on display faces. Revenue has declined overall because of COVID-19. Increased consumer spending will encourage businesses to spend on advertising. Competition from substitutes will create major problems for operators. Operators hope that recent innovations will help them fight off external competition. Revenue fluctuates with changes in corporate profit."

Source: IBISWorld Industry at a Glance

EXPERT COMMENTS

Industry growing, difficult to build new billboards

FINANCING

5 years

RESOURCES
- IBISWorld, April 2023: https://www.ibisworld.com
- OAAA—Out of Home Advertising Association of America: https://oaaa.org

Billiards

	NAICS 713990		SIC 7999-12		Businesses/Units 843
	Profit $69.5 M		Wages $179.8 M		Annual Growth Future 2.3%
					Annual Growth Past -9.2%

Rules of Thumb
- 50% annual sales plus inventory

INDUSTRY MULTIPLES

Acquisition multiples below are calculated medians using US private industry transactions. Data updated annually. Last update: August 2023.

VALUATION MULTIPLE (MEDIAN VALUE)

UNDER $1 MILLION NET SALES
MVIC/Net Sales.	0.69
MVIC/Gross Profit	0.76
MVIC/SDE	2.37
MVIC/EBITDA	2.99

$1 MILLION–$5 MILLION NET SALES
MVIC/Net Sales.	0.69
MVIC/Gross Profit	0.86
MVIC/SDE	3.06
MVIC/EBITDA	3.71

OVER $5 MILLION NET SALES
MVIC/Net Sales.	0.58
MVIC/Gross Profit	1.27
MVIC/SDE	3.09
MVIC/EBITDA	3.27

Source: DealStats (formerly Pratt's Stats), 2023 (Portland, OR: Business Valuation Resources, LLC), www.bvresources.com/dealstats

BENCHMARK DATA

STATISTICS (POOL & BILLIARD HALLS)
Number of Establishments .	843
Average Profit Margin	10.9%
Revenue per Employee .	$85,200
Average Number of Employees.	9.6
Average Wages per Employee .	$22,789

Table rentals for open play	38.6%
Food and drink	32.3%
Table rentals for league play	18.1%
Other	11.0%

INDUSTRY COSTS

Profit	10.9%
Wages	28.2%
Purchases	5.2%
Depreciation	6.1%
Marketing	3.5%
Rent & Utilities	10.4%
Other	35.7%

INDUSTRY TREND

"Rising external competition for consumers' leisure time has put pressure on industry operators. Pool halls have competed by upgrading tables, lowering prices and expanding their merchandise offerings. As industry revenue plummeted and profit wavered, many operators have exited the industry. Pool and billiard halls will likely continue to have difficulty attracting younger customers. Industry revenue is anticipated to recover to the levels experienced prior to the pandemic. Operators are projected to continue exiting the industry, albeit at a slower rate. Revenue and profit will likely suffer from the mandatory closure of nonessential businesses."

Source: IBISWorld Industry at a Glance

RESOURCES

- IBISWorld, November 2021: https://www.ibisworld.com
- BCA—Billiard Congress of America: https://home.bca-pool.com/

Blimpie (Franchise)

| | NAICS 722513 | | SIC 5812-19 | | Businesses/Units 162 |

Rules of Thumb

- 45%–50% annual sales plus inventory

INDUSTRY MULTIPLES

Acquisition multiples below are calculated medians using US private industry transactions. Data updated annually. Last update: August 2023.

VALUATION MULTIPLE (MEDIAN VALUE)

UNDER $1 MILLION NET SALES

MVIC/Net Sales	0.31
MVIC/Gross Profit	0.48
MVIC/SDE	1.67
MVIC/EBITDA	2.21

$1 MILLION–$5 MILLION NET SALES

MVIC/Net Sales	0.39
MVIC/Gross Profit	0.60
MVIC/SDE	2.43
MVIC/EBITDA	2.98

OVER $5 MILLION NET SALES

MVIC/Net Sales	0.89
MVIC/Gross Profit	2.08

MVIC/SDE 4.98
MVIC/EBITDA 12.81

Source: DealStats (formerly Pratt's Stats), 2023 (Portland, OR: Business Valuation Resources, LLC), www.bvresources.com/dealstats

PRICING TIPS

Approx. Total Investment: $74,780 to $422,200

BENCHMARK DATA

For Benchmark data see Sandwich Shops

RESOURCES

- Blimpie: https://www.blimpie.com
- Franchise information: https://www.blimpiefranchise.com
- MTY Group: https://mtygroup.com

Blind and Shade Manufacturing

| NAICS 337920 | Businesses/Units 304

| Profit $77.3 M | Wages $584 M | Annual Growth Future 0.9%

| | | Annual Growth Past -4.3%

INDUSTRY MULTIPLES

Acquisition multiples below are calculated medians using US private industry transactions. Data updated annually. Last update: August 2023.

VALUATION MULTIPLE (MEDIAN VALUE)

UNDER $1 MILLION NET SALES
MVIC/Net Sales. 0.29
MVIC/Gross Profit 1.31
MVIC/SDE 1.61
MVIC/EBITDA 3.59

$1 MILLION–$5 MILLION NET SALES
MVIC/Net Sales. 0.36
MVIC/Gross Profit 0.73
MVIC/SDE 3.30
MVIC/EBITDA 4.74

OVER $5 MILLION NET SALES   N/A

Source: DealStats (formerly Pratt's Stats), 2023 (Portland, OR: Business Valuation Resources, LLC), www.bvresources.com/dealstats

BENCHMARK DATA

STATISTICS (BLIND AND SHADE MANUFACTURING)

Number of Establishments 304
Average Profit Margin 3.4%
Revenue per Employee $262,000
Average Number of Employees. 28.9
Average Wages per Employee $66,727

PRODUCTS AND SERVICES SEGMENTATION

Window shades 57.7%
Other blinds and shades, including fixtures and accessories 34.6%
Venetian blinds 7.7%

MAJOR MARKET SEGMENTATION

Wholesalers. 32.9%
Home improvement stores 30.6%
Other retailers 18.5%
Home furnishing stores. 16.4%
Exports 1.6%

INDUSTRY COSTS

Profit 3.4%
Wages 25.7%
Purchases 44.1%
Depreciation 1.1%
Marketing 1.6%
Rent & Utilities 1.6%
Other 22.4%

MARKET SHARE

Hunter Douglas N.V. 44.5%
Springs Window Fashions, LLC. . . . 7.6%
The Shade Store LLC 4.5%
3 Day Blinds Corp 3.4%
Blinds.com 1.1%
Smith & Noble Home, Inc. 1.0%
Somfy Systems Inc. 0.3%

INDUSTRY TREND

"The industry has been volatile. The current period's influx of import competition from abroad has posed a serious challenge for business owners in the industry. Blind and shade manufacturers have been forced to implement a number of cost-cutting strategies. Sales of industry items are expected to increase. The industry is expected to keep going global. It's likely that growing material costs will make it challenging for industry manufacturers to control operating expenses. Similar to other producers of household goods, the industry has experienced volatility over the past five years."

Source: IBISWorld Industry at a Glance

RESOURCES

• IBISWorld, March 2023: https://www.ibisworld.com

Boat Dealerships

NAICS 441222	SIC 5551-04	Businesses/Units 99,528
Profit $2.4 B	Wages $3.6 B	Annual Growth Future 1.4%
		Annual Growth Past 5.0%

Rules of Thumb

• 2–3 x SDE includes used boat inventory, parts, and FF&E

INDUSTRY MULTIPLES

Acquisition multiples below are calculated medians using US private industry transactions. Data updated annually. Last update: August 2023.

VALUATION MULTIPLE (MEDIAN VALUE)

UNDER $1 MILLION NET SALES

MVIC/Net Sales.	0.41
MVIC/Gross Profit	0.80
MVIC/SDE	2.59
MVIC/EBITDA	6.22

$1 MILLION–$5 MILLION NET SALES

MVIC/Net Sales.	0.37
MVIC/Gross Profit	1.08
MVIC/SDE	2.47
MVIC/EBITDA	3.23

OVER $5 MILLION NET SALES

MVIC/Net Sales.	0.58
MVIC/Gross Profit	1.97
MVIC/SDE	0.73
MVIC/EBITDA	3.35

Source: DealStats (formerly Pratt's Stats), 2023 (Portland, OR: Business Valuation Resources, LLC), www.bvresources.com/dealstats

PRICING TIPS

Boat dealerships in the Pacific Northwest typically sell for 2–3 times SDE, which includes used boat inventory, parts, and FF&E.

BENCHMARK DATA

STATISTICS (BOAT DEALERSHIP AND REPAIR)

Number of Establishments	99,528
Average Profit Margin	6.9%
Revenue per Employee	$245,000
Average Number of Employees.	1.5
Average Wages per Employee	$25,554

PRODUCTS AND SERVICES SEGMENTATION

New boats	69.5%
Parts and repair services	16.1%
Used boats	14.4%

INDUSTRY COSTS

Profit	6.9%
Wages	10.4%
Purchases	70.0%
Depreciation	1.0%
Marketing	0.8%
Rent & Utilities	1.1%
Other	9.6%

INDUSTRY TREND

"As boat use increases, demand for repair and maintenance will also increase. Low fuel costs and interest rates have aided in consumers' decision to purchase a boat. The increase in boat usage has spurred demand for boat repair services. Per capita disposable income will increase, making large-scale purchases, like boats, more feasible. Boat rental companies will also gain popularity. Boat dealers employ numerous marine mechanics to provide repair and maintenance services. Favorable consumer conditions have enabled individuals to spend more on recreational activities."

Source: IBISWorld Industry at a Glance

RESOURCES
- IBISWorld, January 2023: https://www.ibisworld.com
- ABYC—The American Boat & Yacht Council: https://abycinc.org
- Boating Industry: https://boatingindustry.com
- NMMA—National Marine Manufacturers Association: https://www.nmma.org
- Trade Only Today: https://www.tradeonlytoday.com

B

Boiler & Heat Exchanger Manufacturing

| NAICS 332410 | Businesses/Units 301

| Profit $429 M | Wages $1.7 B | Annual Growth Future 0.7%

| | | Annual Growth Past 1.7%

BENCHMARK DATA

STATISTICS (BOILER & HEAT EXCHANGER MANUFACTURING)

Number of Establishments	301
Average Profit Margin	4.3%
Revenue per Employee	$394,000
Average Number of Employees	83.4
Average Wages per Employee	$69,245

PRODUCTS AND SERVICES SEGMENTATION

Heat exchangers and steam condensers	59.3%
Nuclear reactor supply systems	25.5%
Power boilers and parts/attachments	15.2%

MAJOR MARKET SEGMENTATION

Vehicular	50.0%
Commercial	38.0%
Heating and refrigeration	8.0%
Other	4.0%

INDUSTRY COSTS

Profit	4.3%
Wages	17.5%
Purchases	45.7%
Depreciation	2.1%
Marketing	0.1%
Rent & Utilities	1.4%
Other	28.9%

MARKET SHARE

Kawasaki Heavy Industries Ltd	6.6%
Spx Corp	4.3%
Chart Industries, Inc.	1.9%
Power Mechanical Inc.	0.5%
Alfa Laval Ab	0.2%
Bharat Heavy Electricals Limited	0.2%
Mersen Corporate Services SAS	0.1%

INDUSTRY TREND

"Tariffs on Chinese-produced boilers and heat exchangers caused import values to fall. High steel prices enabled revenue growth as manufacturers passed down production costs. Domestic operators are increasingly relying on their comparative technological advantages. Falling steel prices will enable manufacturers to increase profit. A weakening US dollar will boost sales in markets abroad. The US government plans to revisit trade discussions with Chine to lift or reduce tariffs. Industry exports have declined due to the appreciation of the US dollar."

Source: IBISWorld Industry at a Glance

RESOURCES

• IBISWorld, March 2023: https://www.ibisworld.com

Book, Periodical, and Newspaper Merchant Wholesalers

| NAICS 424920 | Businesses/Units 3,179

| Profit $363.8 M | Wages $1.1 B | Annual Growth Future -5.8%

| Annual Growth Past -8.9%

INDUSTRY MULTIPLES

Acquisition multiples below are calculated medians using US private industry transactions. Data updated annually. Last update: August 2023.

VALUATION MULTIPLE (MEDIAN VALUE)

UNDER $1 MILLION NET SALES	N/A
$1 MILLION–$5 MILLION NET SALES	
MVIC/Net Sales.	0.87
MVIC/Gross Profit	2.05
MVIC/SDE	3.15
MVIC/EBITDA	3.15
OVER $5 MILLION NET SALES	
MVIC/Net Sales.	0.37
MVIC/Gross Profit	1.35
MVIC/SDE	N/A
MVIC/EBITDA	3.73

Source: DealStats (formerly Pratt's Stats), 2023 (Portland, OR: Business Valuation Resources, LLC), www.bvresources.com/dealstats

BENCHMARK DATA

STATISTICS (BOOK, MAGAZINE & NEWSPAPER WHOLESALING)

Number of Establishments	3,179
Average Profit Margin	4.0%
Revenue per Employee	$463,000
Average Number of Employees.	5.8
Average Wages per Employee	$54,496

PRODUCTS AND SERVICES SEGMENTATION

Books	75.3%
Periodicals and newspapers	15.6%
Other printed materials	5.7%
Other	3.4%

MAJOR MARKET SEGMENTATION

Bookstores	46.7%
Other	13.2%
Grocery and convenience stores	11.2%
General merchandisers.	10.3%
Public sector customers	8.9%
Gas stations.	3.8%

Other retailers 3.0%
Pharmacies 2.9%

INDUSTRY COSTS

Profit 4.0%
Wages 11.9%
Purchases 73.0%
Depreciation 0.6%
Marketing 0.2%
Rent & Utilities 0.9%
Other 9.7%

MARKET SHARE

Ingram Industries Inc. 30.8%
ReaderLink Distribution Services LLC . . 16.5%

INDUSTRY TREND

"Digital competition has also eroded demand for books wholesaled by the industry. Many distressed magazine publishers have adopted a strategy of offering steep promotional discounts. Retailers that once moved much of magazine publishers' inventory have reduced shelf space for low-margin magazines. Industry profit is also expected to continue declining over the next five years. Continued adoption of tablet devices will also likely turn consumers away from printed material. The number of industry establishments is projected to fall over the next five years. As stay-at-home orders are lifted, consumers will likely be afforded more options for entertainment, lessening demand for books."

Source: IBISWorld Industry at a Glance

RESOURCES

• IBISWorld, March 2023: https://www.ibisworld.com

Bookstores, New Books

	NAICS 459210		SIC 5942-01		Businesses/Units 17,145
	Profit -$149.9 M		Wages $1.9 B		Annual Growth Future 1.7%
					Annual Growth Past 2.0%

Rules of Thumb

• 15%–20% annual sales plus inventory
• 1.5–2 x SDE plus inventory

PRICING TIPS

The underlying lease is very important. The inventory turns should be between 4 and 5 times. It is important that the store is diligently returning new book inventory as allowed.

We don't use EBIT or EBITDA because the owner pretty much always works in the business. Normalizing for an industry standard expense would drive EBIT or EBITDA towards zero, making the multiple unrealistic. One note is that gift certificates outstanding need to be accounted for and treated as a liability. Lots of negotiation around this point.

BENCHMARK DATA

STATISTICS (BOOKSTORES)

Number of Establishments 17,145	
Average Profit Margin . . . . . . -1.1%	
Revenue per Employee $171,000	
Average Number of Employees. 4.7	
Average Wages per Employee . . . $23,026	

PRODUCTS AND SERVICES SEGMENTATION

Trade books 59.3%	
PreK through 12 books 16.4%	
Higher education books 12.6%	
Professional books 7.0%	
Other 4.7%	

INDUSTRY COSTS

Profit . . . . -1.1%	
Wages 13.7%	
Purchases 56.0%	
Depreciation 1.1%	
Marketing 2.2%	
Rent & Utilities 6.6%	
Other 21.4%	

MARKET SHARE

Barnes & Noble Inc.. . . . . . 20.6%	
Barnes & Nobles Education, Inc. . . 11.5%	
Follett Higher Education Group Inc. . . 5.2%	

EXPENSES (% OF ANNUAL SALES)

Cost of Goods . . . . . . 30% to 35%	
Occupancy Costs . . . . . 06% to 10%	
Payroll/Labor Costs. . . . . 20% to 25%	
Profit (pretax) . . . . . . 02% to 04%	

QUESTIONS

- Sales trends? Community standing? Online sales? Website condition? Staffing quality? Tenure of staff? Number of events? Social media exposure? Program of inventory returns? Seasonality? Is there a frequent-buyer program in place?

INDUSTRY TREND

"The New England Independent Booksellers Association, which typically sees just a few new stores open each year, saw its new store membership go up by 30 in 2022. The renaissance mirrors a revival that has also been happening nationally in recent years."

Source: "Boston's bookstore boom continues in 2023 with two more new shops" by Dialynn Dwyer, January 9, 2023, https://www.boston.com/news/business/2023/01/09/bostons-bookstore-boom-continues-in-2023-with-two-more-new-shops/

"Two years ago, the future of independent book selling looked bleak. As the coronavirus forced retailers to shut down, hundreds of small booksellers around the United States seemed doomed. Bookstore sales fell nearly 30 percent in 2020, U.S. Census Bureau data showed. The publishing industry was braced for a blow to its retail ecosystem, one that could permanently reshape the way readers discover and buy books. Instead, something unexpected happened: Small booksellers not only survived the pandemic, but many are thriving.

"'It's kind of shocking when you think about what dire straits the stores were in in 2020,' said Allison Hill, the chief executive of the American Booksellers Association, a trade organization for independent bookstores. 'We saw a rally like we've never seen before.' The association now has 2,023 member stores in 2,561 locations, up from 1,689 in early July of 2020. Some of the growth reflects the renewal of memberships by existing stores that put off doing it last year amid the uncertainly caused by the pandemic. But there has also been a sharp and sustained rise in new bookshops, and more than 200 additional stores are preparing to open in the next year or two, Ms. Hill said....

"The rapid growth of physical bookshops is especially surprising at a time when brick and mortar stores face crushing competition from Amazon and other online retailers."

Source: "Some Surprising Good News: Bookstores Are Booming and Becoming More Diverse" by Alexandra Alter and Elizabeth A. Harris, July 10, 2022, https://www.nytimes.com/2022/07/10/books/bookstores-diversity-pandemic.html

"Retailers selling textbooks and other educational products have experienced the most intense competitive pressure. Rising competition is pressuring book stores. Local support keeps small, indie book shops alive. Online retailers will experience the most growth, hindering industry revenue. Large companies will continue to struggle due to high operating costs and increasing competition. Plateauing e-book sales and less focus on e-readers will benefit operators. Online sales of print books will continue growing."

Source: IBISWorld Industry at a Glance

FINANCING

Usually, these stores are sold to wealthy buyers for cash. If there is any financing, it is typically from the sellers. Due to the high risk in the industry, seller financing is limited.

RESOURCES

- IBISWorld, April 2023: https://www.ibisworld.com
- Paz & Associates: http://pazbookbiz.com
- ABA—American Booksellers Association: https://www.bookweb.org
- NewPages: https://www.newpages.com
- PW—Publishers Weekly: https://www.publishersweekly.com

Bookstores, Rare and Used

| NAICS 459210 | SIC 5932-01

PRICING TIPS

Used bookstores seem to be a vanishing business. Many owners of these stores have closed them and now offer their books online. Rare bookstores would have the same multiple as used stores, perhaps a bit higher. The real value is the inventory.

RESOURCES

- ABAA—The Antiquarian Booksellers' Association of America: https://www.abaa.org
- IOBA—Independent Online Booksellers Association: https://www.ioba.org/pages/

Bottled Water Production

| NAICS 312112 | Businesses/Units 676

| Profit $257.5 M | Wages $1 B | Annual Growth Future 0.4%

| Annual Growth Past -0.1%

INDUSTRY MULTIPLES

Acquisition multiples below are calculated medians using US private industry transactions. Data updated annually. Last update: August 2023.

VALUATION MULTIPLE (MEDIAN VALUE)

UNDER $1 MILLION NET SALES

MVIC/Net Sales.	0.90
MVIC/Gross Profit	1.81
MVIC/SDE	4.48
MVIC/EBITDA	3.89

$1 MILLION–$5 MILLION NET SALES	N/A

OVER $5 MILLION NET SALES

MVIC/Net Sales.	1.08
MVIC/Gross Profit	1.86
MVIC/SDE	N/A
MVIC/EBITDA	9.51

Source: DealStats (formerly Pratt's Stats), 2023 (Portland, OR: Business Valuation Resources, LLC), www.bvresources.com/dealstats

BENCHMARK DATA

STATISTICS (BOTTLED WATER PRODUCTION)

Number of Establishments.	676
Average Profit Margin	3.1%
Revenue per Employee.	$497,000
Average Number of Employees.	25.0
Average Wages per Employee	$60,367

PRODUCTS AND SERVICES SEGMENTATION

Still water	62.6%
Sparkling water.	17.2%
Bulk products	10.9%
Manufactured ice	9.3%

MAJOR MARKET SEGMENTATION

Food service and drinking establishments.	29.6%
Warehouse clubs and supercenters	28.8%
Gas stations and convenience stores	21.6%
Supermarkets and grocery stores	18.3%
Vending machine operators	1.7%

INDUSTRY COSTS

Profit	3.1%
Wages	12.2%
Purchases	41.9%
Depreciation	4.8%
Marketing	0.5%
Rent & Utilities	3.5%
Other	34.1%

"Americans are drinking a lot of water, but they are on the fence about how best to do it. More than $2 billion in reusable water bottles were sold in the United States in 2022, up from around $1.5 billion in 2020, according to Greg Williamson, the president of CamelBak, which is a maker of reusable bottles.

"And sales of single-serving water bottles have been rising steadily, too, reaching 11.3 billion gallons in 2022, according to the most recent data from the Beverage Marketing Association, which tracks beverage sales."

Source: "'We're All Water-Bottle Freaks'" by Matt Richtel, August 11, 2023, https://www.nytimes.com/2023/08/11/health/water-bottles-beverages.html

"Industry revenue influenced by high price volatility of plastic materials and resin. Impact on consumer demand from COVID-19 changed industry's strategic plans. Push toward sustainable materials weathered worse revenue losses for the industry. Improved economic outlook from consumers poised to benefit industry growth. Promotion of sustainability from companies set to save money, improve consumer relations for companies. Supply chain snarls expected to dampen revenue growth for the industry. The industry has contended with changing consumer behaviors."

Source: IBISWorld Industry at a Glance

RESOURCES

• IBISWorld, January 2023: https://www.ibisworld.com

Bowling Centers

NAICS 713950	SIC 7933-01		Businesses/Units 3,489
Profit $303.8 M	Wages $1 B		Annual Growth Future 0.8%
			Annual Growth Past -6.0%

Rules of Thumb

• 150%–200% annual sales plus inventory
• Maybe 2 x annual sales in highly exceptional situation
• 5–7 x SDE plus inventory
• 5–7 x EBITDA
• 8–10 x EBIT

INDUSTRY MULTIPLES

Acquisition multiples below are calculated medians using US private industry transactions. Data updated annually. Last update: August 2023.

VALUATION MULTIPLE (MEDIAN VALUE)

UNDER $1 MILLION NET SALES	N/A
$1 MILLION–$5 MILLION NET SALES	N/A
OVER $5 MILLION NET SALES	
MVIC/Net Sales	2.56
MVIC/Gross Profit	4.10
MVIC/SDE	N/A
MVIC/EBITDA	31.38

Source: DealStats (formerly Pratt's Stats), 2023 (Portland, OR: Business Valuation Resources, LLC), www.bvresources.com/dealstats

PRICING TIPS

Physical condition of building and equipment, demographics of primary market area

BENCHMARK DATA

STATISTICS (BOWLING CENTERS)

Number of Establishments	3,489
Average Profit Margin	9.3%
Revenue per Employee	$40,500
Average Number of Employees . . .	22.2
Average Wages per Employee . . .	$13,111

PRODUCTS AND SERVICES SEGMENTATION

Bowling	56.7%
Food and beverages	32.3%
Nonbowling games and activities . .	9.5%
Other	1.5%

INDUSTRY COSTS

Profit	9.3%
Wages	32.0%
Purchases	5.1%
Depreciation	5.7%
Marketing	3.3%
Rent & Utilities	10.1%
Other	34.4%

MARKET SHARE

Bowlero Corp.	19.4%

Sales per square foot: 66,000+ equals success.

Profitable with as little as $50 in sales per square foot. Most profit is in bowling, shoe rental, and arcade sales.

EXPENSES (% OF ANNUAL SALES)

Cost of Goods	20% to 30%
Occupancy Costs	10% to 20%
Payroll/Labor Costs.	25% to 30%
Profit (pretax)	20% to 30%

QUESTIONS

- Access to all financials and legal?
- Physical condition of facility? Status of employees?
- Stability of leagues?

INDUSTRY TREND

Continuing to add profit centers such as arcades/redemption centers; small ball games; string pinsetters; and the latest technology in visual, lighting, and computerization. Improved food and beverage offerings.

More conversions of traditional centers into FECs

"The industry's changing client base drives the industry's shift from primarily providing bowling services to providing many different recreation options. New industry entrants are predominately locating in urban and suburban environments. The average industry profit margin has declined. The number of industry establishments is forecast to decline. More urban residents will likely increase demand for bowling centers located in urban areas. Bowling centers are anticipated to continue to shift toward multi-use facilities. The industry has been transitioning toward centers that either cater to families or young adults interested in upscale restaurants and bars."

Source: IBISWorld Industry at a Glance

EXPERT COMMENTS

Buying: get finances in order and due diligence.

Selling: prepare to sell by having clear financial statements; refresh the center. Get advice on pricing, and hire a specialist to sell.

FINANCING

Outside financing. Equity 15 to 30 percent. SBA usually best bet.

RESOURCES

- IBISWorld, March 2023: https://www.ibisworld.com
- BPAA: https://bpaa.com
- International Bowling Industry magazine: https://www.bowlingindustry.com
- Mischel & Company: https://mischelcompany.com
- The Hansell Group: https://thehansellgroup.com

Bread Production

| NAICS 31181 | Businesses/Units 35,822

| Profit $2.4 B | Wages $10.6 B | Annual Growth Future 0.3%

                                                      | Annual Growth Past 0.2%

INDUSTRY MULTIPLES

Acquisition multiples below are calculated medians using US private industry transactions. Data updated annually. Last update: August 2023.

VALUATION MULTIPLE (MEDIAN VALUE)

UNDER $1 MILLION NET SALES

MVIC/Net Sales	0.40
MVIC/Gross Profit	0.63
MVIC/SDE	1.94
MVIC/EBITDA	2.72

$1 MILLION–$5 MILLION NET SALES

MVIC/Net Sales	0.46
MVIC/Gross Profit	0.70
MVIC/SDE	3.04
MVIC/EBITDA	4.41

OVER $5 MILLION NET SALES

MVIC/Net Sales	0.47
MVIC/Gross Profit	1.49
MVIC/SDE	3.86
MVIC/EBITDA	5.90

Source: DealStats (formerly Pratt's Stats), 2023 (Portland, OR: Business Valuation Resources, LLC), www.bvresources.com/dealstats

BENCHMARK DATA

STATISTICS (BREAD PRODUCTION)

Number of Establishments	35,822
Average Profit Margin	4.6%

Revenue per Employee $186,000
Average Number of Employees. 7.9
Average Wages per Employee $37,592

PRODUCTS AND SERVICES SEGMENTATION

Bread (white, wheat, rye, etc.) including frozen 31.3%
Rolls, bagels and croissants 22.2%
Other 16.1%
Fresh baked desserts 15.8%
Frozen cakes, pies and other frozen desserts 14.6%

MAJOR MARKET SEGMENTATION

Supermarkets and grocery stores 53.8%
Food service and institutional customers 24.5%
Local bakeries (direct to consumer) 8.0%
Convenience stores. 5.4%
Other 4.5%
Exports 3.8%
Profit 4.6%
Wages 20.1%
Purchases 35.9%
Depreciation 2.8%
Marketing 0.4%
Rent & Utilities 3.1%
Other 33.1%

INDUSTRY TREND

"Operators encountered mounting external competition from imports. Significant merger and acquisition activity has increased market concentration. The industry's proactive response to evolving health trends has helped offset greater revenue declines. The continued development of healthier bread varieties will aid industry performance. Stronger demand for fresh, handmade or all-natural bread products will benefit operators. Due to intensified external competition, industry profitability is expected to be challenged. Producers have contended with America's ever-changing palate."

Source: IBISWorld Industry at a Glance

RESOURCES

• IBISWorld, January 2023: https://www.ibisworld.com

Breweries

| NAICS 312120 | Businesses/Units 10,878

| Profit $738.2 M | Wages $4.8 B | Annual Growth Future 1.6%

| Annual Growth Past -2.1%

INDUSTRY MULTIPLES

Acquisition multiples below are calculated medians using US private industry transactions. Data updated annually. Last update: August 2023.

VALUATION MULTIPLE (MEDIAN VALUE)

UNDER $1 MILLION NET SALES
MVIC/Net Sales. 0.63
MVIC/Gross Profit 0.92
MVIC/SDE 3.83
MVIC/EBITDA 7.15

$1 MILLION–$5 MILLION NET SALES

MVIC/Net Sales.	1.41
MVIC/Gross Profit	2.69
MVIC/SDE	4.34
MVIC/EBITDA	8.44

OVER $5 MILLION NET SALES

MVIC/Net Sales.	0.84
MVIC/Gross Profit	1.74
MVIC/SDE	4.12
MVIC/EBITDA	5.56

Source: DealStats (formerly Pratt's Stats), 2023 (Portland, OR: Business Valuation Resources, LLC), www.bvresources.com/dealstats

PRICING TIPS

There is regional and national variation to pricing craft breweries. Breweries in states with fewer breweries per capita sell at a higher multiple, e.g., 0.3 to 0.7. Craft breweries typically fall into annual production ranges, with improved profitability (and pricing) as production increases through thresholds of 500, 1000, 2000, and 5000 BBLs. A key to higher valuations is the transition of the role of the brewer. Craft breweries typically start with the owner/founder/partners brewing beer. As the business grows and becomes profitable, brewer-employees are hired and trained. A typical 1000 BBL brewery should have 1 head brewer and 1 to 2 assistant brewers. Once this transition is reached and sustained for a year or two, the business will command a higher multiple. Equipment does not depreciate as in food service industries. The brewhouse, fermenter tanks, and related equipment typically hold their value. Pay particular attention to distribution arrangements. For most craft breweries, other than the initial payment for the distribution rights (varies by state), brewers typically get sideways with their distributors. The distributors typically take on many breweries and have little incentive to sell one beer over another of their manufacturers. Ideally, the agreement should have been negotiated with an industry-specialist attorney. Many brewery owners mistakenly believe that distribution is the key to success. A distribution agreement with clear responsibilities, advertising allowances, and penalties/termination provisions for nonperformance by either side, is more important (but rarely seen). Permits and licenses vary by state. In some states, these have their own value (e.g., New Mexico, Massachusetts), but in others, they are relatively inexpensive and have little value (e.g., Texas, Oklahoma). Regional and national breweries are typically interested in craft breweries that have minimum production, e.g., 10,000 BBLs, but more importantly, have a great story, brand following, and destination facility to support future scaling and expansion.

BENCHMARK DATA

STATISTICS (BREWERIES)

Number of Establishments .	10,878
Average Profit Margin	2.2%
Revenue per Employee .	$301,000
Average Number of Employees.	10.5
Average Wages per Employee .	$43,899

PRODUCTS AND SERVICES SEGMENTATION

Premium beer	45.6%
Sub-premium beer .	17.8%
Super-premium beer	16.1%
Craft beer	14.1%
Malt .	6.4%

MAJOR MARKET SEGMENTATION

Restaurants and bars	35.0%
Convenience stores.	18.2%
Supermarkets, grocery stores and drug stores.	16.7%
Clubs and event spaces	16.0%
Liquor stores	14.1%

INDUSTRY COSTS

Profit	2.2%
Wages	14.3%
Purchases	33.8%
Depreciation	6.1%
Marketing	0.4%
Rent & Utilities	2.2%
Other	41.0%

INDUSTRY TREND

Continued growth trend. States with fewer breweries per capita are experiencing biggest share of growth.

"The industry is highly concentrated, with few historically dominant global operators controlling the majority of industry revenue. The Breweries industry is exposed to global trends through heightened trade volumes and an increasing share of foreign ownership. Demand for alcoholic beverages typically remains high and steady during periods of economic or social disruption. As the economy begins to recover from the coronavirus pandemic, pent-up demand for industry products is expected to drive growth. The industry's largest brewers will likely continue to seek out automation methods that require minimal use of labor. A depreciating US dollar will be the main influence on demand for industry exports and the ability of imports to compete with local brewers. The coronavirus created significant volatility as demand from off-premise channels spiked while demand from on-premise channels plummeted."

Source: IBISWorld Industry at a Glance

FINANCING

Bank financing is readily available. Seller financing not needed, unless poor books and records. If bank requires seller financing, typical is 10 percent of sales price, financed for 2 to 5 years, subordinated to bank note.

RESOURCES

- IBISWorld, January 2023: https://www.ibisworld.com
- BA—Brewers Association: https://www.brewersassociation.org

Brewpubs

| NAICS 722410 | Businesses/Units 11,131 |

| Profit $332.3 M | Wages $995.7 M | Annual Growth Future 0.6% |

| | | Annual Growth Past -1.4% |

Rules of Thumb

- 40% annual sales plus inventory
- 4.5 x SDE plus inventory

INDUSTRY MULTIPLES

Acquisition multiples below are calculated medians using US private industry transactions. Data updated annually. Last update: August 2023.

B

VALUATION MULTIPLE (MEDIAN VALUE)

UNDER $1 MILLION NET SALES

MVIC/Net Sales.	0.37
MVIC/Gross Profit	0.63
MVIC/SDE	2.04
MVIC/EBITDA	2.59

$1 MILLION–$5 MILLION NET SALES

MVIC/Net Sales.	0.33
MVIC/Gross Profit	0.57
MVIC/SDE	2.65
MVIC/EBITDA	2.84

OVER $5 MILLION NET SALES

MVIC/Net Sales.	0.41
MVIC/Gross Profit	0.52
MVIC/SDE	0.10
MVIC/EBITDA	5.59

Source: DealStats (formerly Pratt's Stats), 2023 (Portland, OR: Business Valuation Resources, LLC), www.bvresources.com/dealstats

PRICING TIPS

These business are very location specific and product specific. You need to know, do they serve food? If so, is it through a kitchen or a food truck? Do they own the food truck, or are they leasing space? Are they selling only on-site, or do they have a distribution network set up?

BENCHMARK DATA

STATISTICS (CRAFT BEER PRODUCTION)

Number of Establishments .	11,131
Average Profit Margin	4.3%
Revenue Per Employee .	$439,000
Average Number of Employees.	1.6
Average Wages per Employee .	$58,486

PRODUCTS AND SERVICES SEGMENTATION

IPA	46.0%
Pale and amber ale .	10.0%
Seasonal	10.0%
Wheat	10.0%
Other	7.1%
Sour and fruit	6.6%
Stout	6.2%
Lager	4.1%

INDUSTRY COSTS

Profit	4.3%
Wages	12.9%
Purchases	33.5%
Depreciation	5.9%
Marketing	0.4%
Rent & Utilities .	2.1%
Other	40.9%

MARKET SHARE

Boston Beer Company, Inc..	18.7%
D.G. Yuengling & Son Inc.	6.1%

INDUSTRY TREND

"The industry has experienced operational difficulties amid the coronavirus pandemic. Many operators that entered the industry within the past decade have expanded operations. Many operators have struggled or have not attempted to expand to international markets. Industry saturation is anticipated to slow any potential revenue growth. Craft breweries will likely become larger, sprouting additional facilities. The industry will likely play an increasingly prominent role in the global market for beer. Though the industry has experienced detrimental operating conditions, industry revenue has risen."

Source: IBISWorld Industry at a Glance

EXPERT COMMENTS

The quality of the product is a major factor and should be reflected in the revenues. This industry is really trendy in most major metropolitan areas.

FINANCING

Outside financing with a mix of seller financing or an earnout. Two of our last three carried earnouts and kept one of the owners on contract for at least a year.

RESOURCES

- IBISWorld, January 2023: https://www.ibisworld.com
- BA—Brewers Association: https://www.brewersassociation.org

Bridal Shops

	NAICS 458110		SIC 5621-04		Businesses/Units 6,025
	Profit $1.7 B		Wages $373.9 M		Annual Growth Future -0.3%
					Annual Growth Past -1.7%

Rules of Thumb

- 10%–15% annual sales plus inventory

INDUSTRY MULTIPLES

Acquisition multiples below are calculated medians using US private industry transactions. Data updated annually. Last update: August 2023.

VALUATION MULTIPLE (MEDIAN VALUE)

UNDER $1 MILLION NET SALES	
MVIC/Net Sales	0.27
MVIC/Gross Profit	0.53
MVIC/SDE	1.03
MVIC/EBITDA	1.03
$1 MILLION–$5 MILLION NET SALES	
MVIC/Net Sales	0.66
MVIC/Gross Profit	1.09
MVIC/SDE	4.47
MVIC/EBITDA	5.69
OVER $5 MILLION NET SALES	
MVIC/Net Sales	4.35
MVIC/Gross Profit	5.17
MVIC/SDE	N/A
MVIC/EBITDA	N/A

Source: DealStats (formerly Pratt's Stats), 2023 (Portland, OR: Business Valuation Resources, LLC), www.bvresources.com/dealstats

PRICING TIPS

Special-order gowns require deposits. Many bridal stores don't put the deposits aside but commingle funds during the normal course of operations (a liability issue that could be deadly for a new buyer unless appropriate safeguards are in place). A bridal store's inventory is made of samples and the samples should be considered amortized over the ordering life of the gown style.

BENCHMARK DATA

STATISTICS (BRIDAL STORES)

Number of Establishments	6,025
Average Profit Margin	6.6%
Revenue per Employee	$1,393,000
Average Number of Employees	3.1
Average Wages per Employee	$19,985

PRODUCTS AND SERVICES SEGMENTATION

Wedding gowns	45.0%
Bridesmaid dresses	24.5%
Mother-of-the-bride dress	16.9%
Accessories	6.4%
Bridegroom and groomsmen tuxedos and suits	5.5%
Flower girl dress	1.7%

INDUSTRY COSTS

Profit	6.6%
Wages	1.4%
Purchases	56.5%
Depreciation	1.1%
Marketing	2.0%
Rent & Utilities	8.1%
Other	24.2%

INDUSTRY TREND

"Samantha Brown, a professional stylist in New York, sees bridal swimwear as a trend that's likely here to stay. 'We used to see brides wearing gigantic gowns on the beach, which never made any sense,' she said. 'They were heavy, dragging through the sand and out of place for the venue. Now, people are trying to find unique touch points that make their wedding memorable and photographically beautiful.'"

Source: "The Bridal Industry Is Having a Swimsuit Moment" by Alix Strauss, June 22, 2023, https://www.nytimes.com/2023/06/22/style/bridal-swimsuits.html

"Soon after Queen Victoria of England wore a white satin gown at her 1840 marriage to Prince Albert, the shade became synonymous with wedding dresses, which before then were more vibrant....A study published in November by Brides and Investopedia, which surveyed 1,000 people who are planning to wed in the next two years, found that 28 percent of participants want to ditch the white gown and classic suit for an atypical alternative....Andrew Kwon, a fashion designer in New York who has made yellow and green dresses for his bridal collections, says a benefit of wearing a colored gown is that it can easily be repurposed after a wedding day."

Source: "Saying Goodbye to the Plain White Wedding Gown" by Danielle Braff, April 11, 2022, https://www.nytimes.com/2022/04/11/style/wedding-dress-bridal-gown-color.html

"In an effort to boost sales and profit, many bridal gown manufacturers are opting to sell directly to consumers. Demand for bridal stores is heavily dependent on the number of wedding ceremonies conducted each year. Traditional retailers in the Bridal Stores industry have experienced rising competitive pressure from upstream manufacturers. The industry continues to struggle amid a falling marriage rate and rising external competition. Rising mobile usage to compare, shop and research bridal trends is expected to grow increasingly prominent. Competition from manufacturers and alternative retailers is projected to intensify. Strong consumer buying power has benefited industry revenue, but the falling marriage rate limited overall demand."

Source: IBISWorld Industry at a Glance

RESOURCES
- IBISWorld, July 2023: https://www.ibisworld.com
- The Wedding Report: https://wedding.report

Bruster's Real Ice Cream (Franchise)

| NAICS 722515 | Businesses/Units 192

Rules of Thumb
- 40%–45% annual sales plus inventory

INDUSTRY MULTIPLES

Acquisition multiples below are calculated medians using US private industry transactions. Data updated annually. Last update: August 2023.

VALUATION MULTIPLE (MEDIAN VALUE)

UNDER $1 MILLION NET SALES
MVIC/Net Sales	0.44
MVIC/Gross Profit	0.62
MVIC/SDE	2.20
MVIC/EBITDA	2.82

$1 MILLION–$5 MILLION NET SALES
MVIC/Net Sales	0.41
MVIC/Gross Profit	0.69
MVIC/SDE	2.82
MVIC/EBITDA	5.94

OVER $5 MILLION NET SALES
MVIC/Net Sales	3.89
MVIC/Gross Profit	4.87
MVIC/SDE	N/A
MVIC/EBITDA	N/A

Source: DealStats (formerly Pratt's Stats), 2023 (Portland, OR: Business Valuation Resources, LLC), www.bvresources.com/dealstats

PRICING TIPS

Approx. Total Investment: $318,000 to $2,236,500

RESOURCES
- Bruster's Real Ice Cream: https://brusters.com
- Franchise information: https://www.brustersfranchise.com

Budget Blinds (Franchise)

| NAICS 449122 | Businesses/Units 1,258

Rules of Thumb

- 2 x annual EBIT plus inventory & equipment
- 50%–55% annual sales plus inventory

INDUSTRY MULTIPLES

Acquisition multiples below are calculated medians using US private industry transactions. Data updated annually. Last update: August 2023.

VALUATION MULTIPLE (MEDIAN VALUE)

UNDER $1 MILLION NET SALES	N/A
$1 MILLION–$5 MILLION NET SALES	N/A
OVER $5 MILLION NET SALES	
MVIC/Net Sales	0.40
MVIC/Gross Profit	1.27
MVIC/SDE	2.28
MVIC/EBITDA	3.70

Source: DealStats (formerly Pratt's Stats), 2023 (Portland, OR: Business Valuation Resources, LLC), www.bvresources.com/dealstats

PRICING TIPS

Approx. Total Investment: $140,500 to $211,750

RESOURCES

- Budget Blinds: https://budgetblinds.com
- Franchise information: https://franchise.budgetblinds.com
- HFC—Home Franchise Concepts: https://www.homefranchiseconcepts.com

Burger King (Franchise)

| NAICS 722513 | Businesses/Units 7,054

Rules of Thumb

- 35% annual sales plus inventory

INDUSTRY MULTIPLES

Acquisition multiples below are calculated medians using US private industry transactions. Data updated annually. Last update: August 2023.

VALUATION MULTIPLE (MEDIAN VALUE)

UNDER $1 MILLION NET SALES	
MVIC/Net Sales	0.31
MVIC/Gross Profit	0.48
MVIC/SDE	1.67
MVIC/EBITDA	2.21
$1 MILLION–$5 MILLION NET SALES	
MVIC/Net Sales	0.39
MVIC/Gross Profit	0.60
MVIC/SDE	2.43
MVIC/EBITDA	2.98
OVER $5 MILLION NET SALES	
MVIC/Net Sales	0.89
MVIC/Gross Profit	2.08
MVIC/SDE	4.98
MVIC/EBITDA	12.81

Source: DealStats (formerly Pratt's Stats), 2023 (Portland, OR: Business Valuation Resources, LLC), www.bvresources.com/dealstats

PRICING TIPS

Approx. Total Investment: $1,790,800 to $4,194,700

RESOURCES

- Burger King: https://www.bk.com
- Franchise information: https://franchising.bk.com
- RBI—Restaurant Brands International: https://www.rbi.com

Bus Companies (Charter, School, & Scheduled)

| | NAICS 485510 | | SIC 4142-01 | | Businesses/Units 18,755 |

Rules of Thumb

- 35% revenues plus asset value of buses plus inventory

INDUSTRY MULTIPLES

Acquisition multiples below are calculated medians using US private industry transactions. Data updated annually. Last update: August 2023.

VALUATION MULTIPLE (MEDIAN VALUE)

UNDER $1 MILLION NET SALES

MVIC/Net Sales	0.71
MVIC/Gross Profit	1.04
MVIC/SDE	1.33
MVIC/EBITDA	3.32

$1 MILLION–$5 MILLION NET SALES

MVIC/Net Sales	0.48
MVIC/Gross Profit	1.26
MVIC/SDE	1.36
MVIC/EBITDA	1.50

OVER $5 MILLION NET SALES   N/A

Source: DealStats (formerly Pratt's Stats), 2023 (Portland, OR: Business Valuation Resources, LLC), www.bvresources.com/dealstats

BENCHMARK DATA

STATISTICS (SCHEDULED AND CHARTER BUS SERVICES)

Number of Establishments	7,315
Average Profit Margin	8.8%
Revenue per Employee	$74,600
Average Number of Employees	9.4
Average Wages per Employee	$27,104

PRODUCTS AND SERVICES SEGMENTATION

Charter bus services	57.3%
Scheduled bus services	41.8%
Other services (including rural transit)	0.9%

MAJOR MARKET SEGMENTATION

Long-distance travel	59.7%
Local travel	27.4%
All other including business travel	1.6%

INDUSTRY COSTS

Profit	8.8%
Wages	36.2%
Purchases	9.8%

Depreciation 9.8%
Marketing 0.5%
Rent & Utilities 4.0%
Other 30.7%

MARKET SHARE

Coach USA Inc. 10.9%
Global Charter Services Ltd 4.5%
Academy Bus LLC 3.8%
Easton Coach Company 2.8%

STATISTICS (PUBLIC SCHOOL BUS SERVICES)

Number of Establishments 11,440
Average Profit Margin 6.5%
Revenue per Employee $47,500
Average Number of Employees. . . . 24.1
Average Wages per Employee . . . $22,878

PRODUCTS AND SERVICES SEGMENTATION

School busing for public schools . . . 63.9%
School busing for private schools . . . 31.6%
Employee bus services 2.5%
Other transportation and services . . . 2.0%

MAJOR MARKET SEGMENTATION

Public schools 89.7%
Private schools 6.8%
Other 3.5%

INDUSTRY COSTS

Profit 6.5%
Wages 47.9%
Purchases 7.7%
Depreciation 10.6%
Marketing 0.4%
Rent & Utilities 3.3%
Other 23.7%

MARKET SHARE

FirstGroup PLC 19.1%
National Express Group PLC 11.7%
Student Transportation Inc.. . . . . 4.7%

INDUSTRY TREND

"Traditional scheduled bus service providers serving bus depots have been in a state of long-term stagnation. Curbside low-cost scheduled bus services have been successful in the Mid-Atlantic and New England regions. Diesel prices rising meant operators passed on part of this cost to consumers. Low ticket prices are the main reason for the success of low-cost curbside carriers. Wages will likely increase in the coming years, especially for drivers working for larger companies and in urban areas. The price of diesel, a significant industry cost, will likely rise in the coming years, hindering profitability. The COVID-19 pandemic has had a significant effect on scheduled and charter bus services. As contracts have been renegotiated and services suspended, industry revenue declined. Lower receipts from income taxes, sales taxes and other revenue sources caused much of the funding deficits. Slow revenue growth and aggressive acqui-sitions resulted in stagnation in the number of operators. Cost-cutting measures or reduced growth in various budgets may affect the industry negatively. The growing number of students enrolled in K–12 education presents an opportunity for the industry. Strong revenue growth is expected to prevent declines in profit.

To sustain profitability, many companies have mounted aggressive campaigns to increase contract retention rates."

Source: IBISWorld Industry at a Glance

FINANCING

3 years

RESOURCES

- IBISWorld, February 2023: https://www.ibisworld.com
- ABA—American Bus Association: https://www.buses.org/aba-foundation
- BUSRide magazine: https://busride.com
- UMA—United Motorcoach Association: https://www.uma.org

Business Brokerage Offices

	NAICS 531210		SIC 7389-22		Businesses/Units 6,179
	Profit $243.1 M		Wages $879.6 M		Annual Growth Future 1.1%
					Annual Growth Past -2.2%

Rules of Thumb

- 50% annual commissions
- 1.4–2.5 x SDE
- 2–4 x EBITDA
- 60–100% annual sales
- 2–4 x EBIT

INDUSTRY MULTIPLES

Acquisition multiples below are calculated medians using US private industry transactions. Data updated annually. Last update: August 2023.

VALUATION MULTIPLE (MEDIAN VALUE)

UNDER $1 MILLION NET SALES

MVIC/Net Sales	0.46
MVIC/Gross Profit	0.64
MVIC/SDE	1.94
MVIC/EBITDA	2.36

$1 MILLION–$5 MILLION NET SALES

MVIC/Net Sales	0.23
MVIC/Gross Profit	0.67
MVIC/SDE	1.92
MVIC/EBITDA	3.67

OVER $5 MILLION NET SALES

MVIC/Net Sales	2.20
MVIC/Gross Profit	5.19
MVIC/SDE	2.54
MVIC/EBITDA	2.99

Source: DealStats (formerly Pratt's Stats), 2023 (Portland, OR: Business Valuation Resources, LLC), www.bvresources.com/dealstats

PRICING TIPS

Usually requires a portion of the purchase price to be tied to future results—an earnout.

BENCHMARK DATA

B

STATISTICS (BUSINESS BROKERS)

Number of Establishments	6,179
Average Profit Margin	. 13.1%
Revenue per Employee	$94,400
Average Number of Employees. . . .	.3.2
Average Wages per Employee . . .	$45,605

PRODUCTS AND SERVICES SEGMENTATION

Valuation	. 46.9%
Due diligence	. 22.7%
Other services	. 17.4%
Advertising	. 13.0%

MAJOR MARKET SEGMENTATION

Restaurants	. 19.4%
Personal services	. 18.3%
Consumer goods and retail	. 14.0%
Business services	. 14.0%
Construction and engineering . . .	. 10.8%
Other	. 10.5%
Manufacturing	6.5%
Biotech and healthcare	6.5%

INDUSTRY COSTS

Profit	. 13.1%
Wages	. 47.4%
Purchases	8.3%
Depreciation	1.0%
Marketing	1.4%
Rent & Utilities	3.9%
Other	. 25.0%

A good business broker should have 25 to 30 good listings. Each associated agent/broker should have 25 to 30 listings. All listings should be posted on all of the top websites advertising businesses for sale.

EXPENSES (% OF ANNUAL SALES)

Cost of Goods	.0% to 20%
Payroll/Labor Costs.	10% to 20%
Occupancy Costs	05% to 10%
Profit (pretax)	50% to 60%

QUESTIONS

- Average annual sales? Average annual net?
- Ask the seller if they think the buyer can be successful in the business; most will give a straight answer.
- The depth and breadth of the potential client pipeline? How long will you stay with the buyer to effectively transfer their potential client and referral base?
- How would you pay for the business if you wanted to buy it? What is your relevant background and training? Can you function without hierarchal supervision?

INDUSTRY TREND

Currently things are growing and getting larger.

Excellent, as baby boomers, who own the majority of privately held businesses, will be divesting them because of health issues, retirement, terminal illnesses, burnout, etc.

Change in fees charged, and the amount of effort to sell a business, will increase.

"The industry has grown due to more mergers and acquisitions and increased access to credit. Given the decrease in wages and other costs, industry profit has risen. Business brokers may increasingly focus on purchases of smaller, localized businesses. Increased borrowing costs and external competition are expected to mitigate industry revenue growth. Growth in the number of businesses generally provides greater opportunity for brokerage services. Industry profit is expected to slowly decrease during the outlook period. Sustained demand for industry services has resulted in increased industry profit."

Source: IBISWorld Industry at a Glance

EXPERT COMMENTS

It takes a good bit of time with a start-up to get to the point of generating cash, and even longer to get to positive cash flowing. A good business brokerage franchise, like Sunbelt, is well worth the money.

Join an association or an established brokerage.

Make sure you have the necessary sales and accounting skills to operate this kind of business. I would suggest working for another brokerage prior to starting your own business or buying one from another broker.

Get as much business broker education as possible. Join and participate in industry trade groups, the International Business Brokers Association (IBBA), and any local/regional affiliate, and take advantage of the education and relationships provided. Obtain the industry standard designation of professional business brokers, the Certified Business Intermediary (CBI).

FINANCING

Larger portion of seller financing

Purchaser's cash and seller financing

RESOURCES

- IBISWorld, April 2023: https://www.ibisworld.com
- IBBA—International Business Brokers Association: https://www.ibba.org
- AM&AA—Alliance of Merger & Acquisition Advisors: https://amaaonline.com
- BBF—Business Brokers of Florida: https://bbfmls.com
- BBN—Business Brokers Network: http://www.bbnbrokers.com
- BBU—Business Buyers University: https://www.businessbuyersuniversity.com
- CABB—California Association of Business Brokers: https://cabb.org
- CVBBA—Carolinas–Virginia Business Brokers Association: https://www.cvbba.com
- M&A Source: https://masource.org
- Sunbelt: https://www.sunbeltnetwork.com
- TABB, Inc.—Texas Association of Business Brokers: https://tabb.org

Call Centers

NAICS 561421	SIC 7389-12	Businesses/Units 37,044
Profit $1.8 B	Wages $18.5 B	Annual Growth Future 2.7%
		Annual Growth Past 0.9%

Rules of Thumb

- 10–12 x current monthly billings for larger services; may require earnout
- 5–7 x current monthly billings for smaller services; may require earnout

INDUSTRY MULTIPLES

Acquisition multiples below are calculated medians using US private industry transactions. Data updated annually. Last update: August 2023.

VALUATION MULTIPLE (MEDIAN VALUE)

UNDER $1 MILLION NET SALES	
MVIC/Net Sales	1.01
MVIC/Gross Profit	1.01
MVIC/SDE	5.24
MVIC/EBITDA	21.15

$1 MILLION–$5 MILLION NET SALES	
MVIC/Net Sales	0.48
MVIC/Gross Profit	0.49
MVIC/SDE	N/A
MVIC/EBITDA	5.86

OVER $5 MILLION NET SALES	N/A

Source: DealStats (formerly Pratt's Stats), 2023 (Portland, OR: Business Valuation Resources, LLC), www.bvresources.com/dealstats

BENCHMARK DATA

STATISTICS (TELEMARKETING & CALL CENTERS)

Number of Establishments	37,044
Average Profit Margin	5.7%
Revenue per Employee	$65,700
Average Number of Employees	13.0
Average Wages per Employee	$39,405

PRODUCTS AND SERVICES SEGMENTATION

Customer service	68.4%
Technical support	15.7%
Telemarketing	8.0%
Other	5.6%
Debt collection	2.3%

MAJOR MARKET SEGMENTATION

Telecommunications and IT	32.8%
Other	24.6%
Retail	13.4%
Financial services	9.9%
Government	9.7%
Healthcare	9.6%

INDUSTRY COSTS

Profit	5.7%
Wages	60.2%
Purchases	11.5%
Depreciation	1.7%
Marketing	1.6%
Rent & Utilities	1.9%
Other	17.4%

MARKET SHARE

TD SYNNEX Corporation	9.5%
Intrado Inc.	6.7%
TTEC Services Corporation	5.6%
HCL Technologies Limited	2.9%

Qualfon Data Services Group LLC . . . 2.8%
Red Ventures, LLC 2.3%

INDUSTRY TREND

"Many smaller operators do not have established offshore operations. New technology enables operators to reduce input costs and boost revenue. Inbound call centers can be a source of revenue and profit. Rising consumer spending will aid clients' efforts to grow their customer bases. The continued implementation of interactive voice response systems will heighten efficiency. Domestic call centers will seek to boost revenue by providing more value-added services. Industry profit remained relatively stable, despite setbacks incurred amid the pandemic."

Source: IBISWorld Industry at a Glance

RESOURCES

- IBISWorld, January 2023: https://ibisworld.com
- ICMI: https://www.icmi.com
- TAS Marketing—a telephone answering service brokerage firm: https://tasmarketing.com

Camera Stores

	NAICS 443130		SIC 5946-01		Businesses/Units 1,232
	Profit $53.7 M		Wages $218.4 M		Annual Growth Future -1.7%
					Annual Growth Past -4.7%

Rules of Thumb

- 10%–15% annual revenues plus fixtures, equipment, & inventory

BENCHMARK DATA

STATISTICS (CAMERA STORES)

Number of Establishments	1,232
Average Profit Margin	1.7%
Revenue per Employee	$716,000
Average Number of Employees. . . .	3.5
Average Wages per Employee . . .	$48,887

PRODUCTS AND SERVICES SEGMENTATION

Non-reflex interchangeable cameras .	44.3%
Interchangeable lenses.	40.4%
Single-reflex interchangeable cameras.	9.6%
Built-in lens cameras	5.7%

INDUSTRY COSTS

Profit	1.7%
Wages	6.9%
Purchases	69.1%
Depreciation	1.2%
Marketing	1.5%
Rent & Utilities	3.5%
Other	16.1%

INDUSTRY TREND

"Demand for personal cameras from everyday consumers has remained relatively low. Many operators are exiting the industry, and many of those that remain are laying off workers. Competing retailers are able to sell higher volumes of goods at lower prices, undercutting industry operators. Post-pandemic temporary growth has provided relief, but does not aid standalone cameras against outside competition. Smartphones will likely cut considerably into the industry's market. Camera stores will likely focus on serving niche markets. The industry has declined for over a decade and will likely continue to do so."

Source: IBISWorld Industry at a Glance

RESOURCES

- IBISWorld, June 2023: https://ibisworld.com

Campgrounds

	NAICS 721211		SIC 7033-01		Businesses/Units 16,751
	Profit $1.2 B		Wages $2.3 B		Annual Growth Future 1.9%
					Annual Growth Past 0.1%

Rules of Thumb

- 8.5 x EBITDA
- 8.5–8.9 x SDE; add store inventory

INDUSTRY MULTIPLES

Acquisition multiples below are calculated medians using US private industry transactions. Data updated annually. Last update: August 2023.

VALUATION MULTIPLE (MEDIAN VALUE)

UNDER $1 MILLION NET SALES
MVIC/Net Sales	1.04
MVIC/Gross Profit	1.23
MVIC/SDE	3.61
MVIC/EBITDA	4.61

$1 MILLION–$5 MILLION NET SALES
MVIC/Net Sales	1.06
MVIC/Gross Profit	1.07
MVIC/SDE	1.82
MVIC/EBITDA	N/A

OVER $5 MILLION NET SALES
MVIC/Net Sales	2.25
MVIC/Gross Profit	2.29
MVIC/SDE	N/A
MVIC/EBITDA	5.44

Source: DealStats (formerly Pratt's Stats), 2023 (Portland, OR: Business Valuation Resources, LLC), www.bvresources.com/dealstats

PRICING TIPS

Often owners feel they need a lot of negotiating room. This is not necessary. The astute prospective buyer will immediately recognize the value being correct, and may likely assume if they don't jump on this quickly, someone else will. Another common feeling is "we can always come down in price, but we cannot go up." Although this sounds very logical, with an unrealistic price tag you could be missing many qualified and cash buyers even viewing your business. Another negative could be the possibility of becoming market stale and having prospective buyers wondering "Why has this campground been for sale so long?"

BENCHMARK DATA

STATISTICS (CAMPGROUNDS & RV PARKS)

Number of Establishments	16,751
Average Profit Margin	14.1%
Revenue per Employee	$132,000
Average Number of Employees	4.1
Average Wages per Employee	$35,138

PRODUCTS AND SERVICES SEGMENTATION

Overnight recreational camps	45.8%
RV parks and campgrounds	38.7%
Other unit accommodations and service fees	15.5%

INDUSTRY COSTS

Profit	14.1%
Wages	26.6%
Purchases	18.7%
Depreciation	8.1%
Marketing	2.0%
Rent & Utilities	0.3%
Other	30.1%

EXPENSES (% OF ANNUAL SALES)

Cost of Goods	10%
Occupancy Costs	40%
Payroll/Labor Costs	10%
Profit (pretax)	40%

QUESTIONS

- Will you carry a contract? Do you have a database of customers? Age and condition of all utilities? We always would ask about roof, sewer, property lines, and permits.

INDUSTRY TREND

"In 2022, 92 million American households identified as campers and 58 million households camped at least once last year."

Source: "Key Findings of the 2023 North American Camping & Outdoor Hospitality Report,"
https://koa.com/north-american-camping-report/

"The industry exhibited strong declines due to travel restrictions and stay-at-home orders, despite a temporary surge in RV sales. Younger customer groups are expanding as camping has increased in popularity. Many RV parks and campgrounds have improved amenities to attract visitors. Volatility in both fuel prices and demand from RV dealers is expected to further contribute to a tempered recovery. The rising popularity of luxury camping or "glamping", is expected to drive millennials to spend time at industry sites. Operators are expected to benefit from increasing demand and the ability to charge premium fees for more amenities. An increasing amount of time spent on leisure and travel has contributed to strong growth for industry operators."

Source: IBISWorld Industry at a Glance

EXPERT COMMENTS

Start to plan three years before selling. The price is directly tied to cash flow.

Difficult start-up business due to lakeshore and PCA regulations. Typically seasonal businesses.

Sellers: Buyers are more sophisticated now and want to see credible valuation information to support the asking price and a business plan that shows the future. Have documentation about repairs and maintenance, permits and zoning and other issues that could limit the future. If you have a bank loan now, talk with your banker to see what they will require for a new owner.

Buyers: You will need to work hard for the first few years but at a realistic pace. If the current owner is completely worn out, you may want to watch their labor costs and deferred maintenance. Financing can take time and the bankers will need to see plenty of working capital in addition to the down payment. Take time up-front to understand valuation before you get caught up in negotiating based on feelings. Leased property has a far lower value. The great locations will cost more but will also provide a much better future. Different campgrounds will have a different type of customer too. Look for a location that caters to customers that you can relate to.

FINANCING

The majority of campgrounds are sold with a combination of owner and bank financing. When the closing date is set as it relates to their season can complicate things. If the closing is in the fall and the campground is closed for the winter, it could mean several months of payments without income. We often see delayed closings to make it realistic.

RESOURCES

- IBISWorld, January 2023: https://www.ibisworld.com
- ARVC—National Association of RV Parks & Campgrounds: https://www.arvc.org

Camps

	NAICS 721214		SIC 7032-03		Businesses/Units 6,648
	Profit $251.1 M		Wages $1.4 B		Annual Growth Future 1.9%
					Annual Growth Past -1.3%

Rules of Thumb

- 2 x annual sales plus inventory
- 3.3–6 x SDE plus inventory
- 3.3 x EBITDA

INDUSTRY MULTIPLES

Acquisition multiples below are calculated medians using US private industry transactions. Data updated annually. Last update: August 2023.

VALUATION MULTIPLE (MEDIAN VALUE)

UNDER $1 MILLION NET SALES	
MVIC/Net Sales	0.99
MVIC/Gross Profit	1.02
MVIC/SDE	2.83
MVIC/EBITDA	9.83
$1 MILLION–$5 MILLION NET SALES	N/A
OVER $5 MILLION NET SALES	N/A

Source: DealStats (formerly Pratt's Stats), 2023 (Portland, OR: Business Valuation Resources, LLC), www.bvresources.com/dealstats

PRICING TIPS

Make certain to get the last three years of financials and that revenue is trending upward each of those years.

Children's overnight camps use a multiple of earnings of 4.5.

BENCHMARK DATA

Average cost per child per week

STATISTICS (SUMMER CAMPS)

Number of Establishments	6,648
Average Profit Margin	6.2%
Revenue per Employee	$109,000
Average Number of Employees	5.7
Average Wages per Employee	$37,268

PRODUCTS AND SERVICES SEGMENTATION

Sports Camps	42.9%
Wilderness camps	21.5%
Team-building camps	19.2%
Community service camps	10.5%
Farming/ranching, gardening camps	5.9%

MAJOR MARKET SEGMENTATION

Adolescents aged 10 to 12	37.6%
Adolescents aged 13 to 17	29.7%
Children aged nine and younger	28.8%
Adults	3.9%

INDUSTRY COSTS

Profit	6.2%
Wages	34.0%
Purchases	18.7%
Depreciation	5.8%
Marketing	2.0%
Rent & Utilities	7.9%
Other	25.4%

EXPENSES (% OF ANNUAL SALES)

Cost of Goods	15% to 20%
Occupancy Costs	20% to 30%
Payroll/Labor Costs	25% to 35%
Profit (pretax)	10% to 20%

QUESTIONS

- Will they stay on for a month during the season?
- What percentage of your campers renew from year to year?

INDUSTRY TREND

"Amanda Lenhart, a researcher who has studied summer care, wasn't surprised to hear about the balancing act that parents have to pull to manage child care over the summer months.... Increasingly, families in the U.S. have both parents working outside of the home, which means they have to rely on a mix of summer camps, daycare, and support from friends and family....

"As vital as summer camps are for many families, the business model isn't ideal for parents or providers, Lenhart said. Camps are expensive to run and require a lot of seasonal workers, which means the supply doesn't meet the demand. 'To do it affordably, it needs to be subsidized,' she said. 'Certainly in my own community, the camps that fill up immediately are the local recreation department camps that are affordable and offer care for kids that doesn't cost very much.'"

Source: "For readers with young children, summer is no vacation" by Zipporah Osei, June 28, 2023, https://www.boston.com/community/readers-say/for-readers-with-young-children-summer-is-no-vacation/

Generally very good

"Industry revenue is anticipated to decline due to temporary camp closures. Due to rising demand, the number of specialty and niche camps has expanded. The number of households earning more than $100,000 has increased, expanding a potential customer base. Spending on recreation services is anticipated to grow. Camps designed around specific activities will likely proliferate, raising the number of industry operators. Overnight camps will likely lower their prices to offer relatively better bargains. Competition from instructional day camps has increased, limiting revenue growth."

Source: IBISWorld Industry at a Glance

EXPERT COMMENTS

Competition is increasing year to year.

FINANCING

Outside financing usually can be found due to the fact that there is a great deal of real estate involved in the deal.

RESOURCES

- IBISWorld, April 2023: https://www.ibisworld.com
- ACA—American Camp Association: https://www.acacamps.org

Candy Production

| NAICS 311340 | Businesses/Units 1,469 |

| Profit $516.2 M | Wages $1.8 B | Annual Growth Future 1.2% |

| | | Annual Growth Past 1.4% |

INDUSTRY MULTIPLES

Acquisition multiples below are calculated medians using US private industry transactions. Data updated annually. Last update: August 2023.

VALUATION MULTIPLE (MEDIAN VALUE)

UNDER $1 MILLION NET SALES	
MVIC/Net Sales .	0.53
MVIC/Gross Profit .	0.82
MVIC/SDE .	2.68
MVIC/EBITDA .	3.72
$1 MILLION–$5 MILLION NET SALES	N/A
OVER $5 MILLION NET SALES	N/A

Source: DealStats (formerly Pratt's Stats), 2023 (Portland, OR: Business Valuation Resources, LLC), www.bvresources.com/dealstats

BENCHMARK DATA

STATISTICS (CANDY PRODUCTION)

Number of Establishments .	1,469
Average Profit Margin .	4.0%

Revenue per Employee $471,000
Average Number of Employees. . . . 18.9
Average Wages per Employee . . . $64,086

PRODUCTS AND SERVICES SEGMENTATION

Chewy candy 34.1%
Gums and mints. 28.4%
Specialty 20.3%
Other 9.5%
Sugar free 7.7%

MAJOR MARKET SEGMENTATION

Grocery stores 31.2%
Convenience stores. 26.3%
Confectionery wholesalers 25.0%
Drugstores 11.8%
Exports 5.7%

INDUSTRY COSTS

Profit 4.0%
Wages 13.6%
Purchases 48.6%
Depreciation 2.8%
Marketing 1.4%
Rent & Utilities 2.7%
Other 27.0%

INDUSTRY TREND

"Operators have been able to raise prices due to strong demand driven by growing disposable incomes. Industry operators have expanded their product mix over the past five years. External competition from the Chocolate Production industry and imports has intensified. The largest industry operators are expected to accelerate their development of low-sugar products. Industry gains will likely be limited by imports and the growing popularity of chocolate. Profit growth will be aided by the heavy marketing of premium products. Volatile commodity prices have continuously challenged the industry over the past five years."

Source: IBISWorld Industry at a Glance

RESOURCES

• IBISWorld, January 2023: https://www.ibisworld.com

Candy Stores

| NAICS 445292 | SIC 5441-01

| Profit $149.4 M | Wages $263.1 M | Annual Growth Future 0.1%

| Annual Growth Past -0.8%

Rules of Thumb

• 30%–35% annual sales plus inventory
• 1.7 x SDE plus inventory

INDUSTRY MULTIPLES

Acquisition multiples below are calculated medians using US private industry transactions. Data updated annually. Last update: August 2023.

VALUATION MULTIPLE (MEDIAN VALUE)

UNDER $1 MILLION NET SALES

MVIC/Net Sales.	0.41
MVIC/Gross Profit	0.56
MVIC/SDE	2.13
MVIC/EBITDA	3.79

$1 MILLION–$5 MILLION NET SALES

MVIC/Net Sales.	0.58
MVIC/Gross Profit	0.66
MVIC/SDE	2.33
MVIC/EBITDA	1.97

OVER $5 MILLION NET SALES — N/A

Source: DealStats (formerly Pratt's Stats), 2023 (Portland, OR: Business Valuation Resources, LLC), www.bvresources.com/dealstats

BENCHMARK DATA

See Food Stores—Specialty for additional Benchmark information

STATISTICS (CHOCOLATE STORES)

Number of Establishments .	7,546
Average Profit Margin	10.5%
Revenue per Employee .	$88,900
Average Number of Employees.	2.1
Average Wages per Employee .	$16,379

PRODUCTS AND SERVICES SEGMENTATION

Milk chocolate .	46.8%
Dark chocolate .	39.2%
Other	7.7%
White chocolate.	6.3%

INDUSTRY COSTS

Profit	10.5%
Wages .	18.5%
Purchases .	55.9%
Depreciation	2.6%
Marketing	0.6%
Rent & Utilities .	2.3%
Other	9.6%

MARKET SHARE

See's Candies	27.0%
Chocoladefabriken Lindt & Sprüngli AG	14.5%

EXPENSES (% OF ANNUAL SALES)

Payroll/Labor Costs.	55.6%

INDUSTRY TREND

"Health consciousness has been particularly beneficial for demand for dark chocolate. Recent innovations include collaborations with other craft food and beverage companies. Major players have been the greatest beneficiaries of favorable industry conditions. Higher incomes will likely contribute to increasing industry demand. Innovation and demand for premium chocolates will likely go beyond flavors. IBISWorld expects the number of chocolate stores to increase. Industry performance has been somewhat constrained by declining sweets consumption."

Source: IBISWorld Industry at a Glance

RESOURCES

- IBISWorld, June 2023: https://www.ibisworld.com
- Candy Industry: https://www.candyindustry.com
- NCA—National Confectioners Association: https://www.candyusa.com

Canned Fruit & Vegetable Processing

| NAICS 311421 | Businesses/Units 3,985

| Profit $665.7 M | Wages $4.9 B | Annual Growth Future -0.5%

                                              | Annual Growth Past -0.2%

INDUSTRY MULTIPLES

Acquisition multiples below are calculated medians using US private industry transactions. Data updated annually. Last update: August 2023.

VALUATION MULTIPLE (MEDIAN VALUE)

UNDER $1 MILLION NET SALES

MVIC/Net Sales	1.05
MVIC/Gross Profit	1.05
MVIC/SDE	2.89
MVIC/EBITDA	2.89

$1 MILLION–$5 MILLION NET SALES   N/A

OVER $5 MILLION NET SALES

MVIC/Net Sales	2.49
MVIC/Gross Profit	6.85
MVIC/SDE	N/A
MVIC/EBITDA	N/A

Source: DealStats (formerly Pratt's Stats), 2023 (Portland, OR: Business Valuation Resources, LLC), www.bvresources.com/dealstats

BENCHMARK DATA

STATISTICS (CANNED FRUIT & VEGETABLE PROCESSING)

Number of Establishments	3,985
Average Profit Margin	1.4%
Revenue per Employee	$637,000
Average Number of Employees	18.8
Average Wages per Employee	$65,113

PRODUCTS AND SERVICES SEGMENTATION

Canned fruits and vegetables	28.6%
Other	20.9%
Soups, stews and bouillon	14.1%
Ketchup and other tomato-based sauces	10.8%
Fruit and vegetable juices	8.5%
Dried and dehydrated fruits and vegetables	8.0%
Pickled products	5.1%
Jams and jellies	4.0%

MAJOR MARKET SEGMENTATION

Retail stores	52.3%
Independent grocery wholesalers	32.4%
Food service and manufacturing customers	9.6%
Households and other	5.7%

INDUSTRY COSTS

Profit	1.4%
Wages	10.2%
Purchases	50.5%
Depreciation	2.7%
Marketing	0.8%
Rent & Utilities	2.3%
Other	32.0%

INDUSTRY TREND

"Recent inflationary pressures exacerbated the bulk-food trend. The negative perception associated with canned and processed food has been producers' largest hurdle. New companies continue to enter the industry to take advantage of the organic boom. Substantial declines in the value of the US dollar will raise the relative cost of imported canned products. The effects of the continued rise of organic are twofold. Companies will look to wages to as a means of cutting costs. Rising disposable incomes will likely have consumers trading up to fresher products."

Source: IBISWorld Industry at a Glance

RESOURCES

• IBISWorld, January 2023: https://www.ibisworld.com

Car Washes, Coin Operated/Self-Service

| NAICS 811192 | SIC 7542-05

Rules of Thumb

• 2–3 x cap rate
• 4 x annual sales

INDUSTRY MULTIPLES

Acquisition multiples below are calculated medians using US private industry transactions. Data updated annually. Last update: August 2023.

VALUATION MULTIPLE (MEDIAN VALUE)

UNDER $1 MILLION NET SALES

MVIC/Net Sales	0.70
MVIC/Gross Profit	0.76
MVIC/SDE	2.56
MVIC/EBITDA	2.52

$1 MILLION–$5 MILLION NET SALES

MVIC/Net Sales	1.00
MVIC/Gross Profit	1.58
MVIC/SDE	4.12
MVIC/EBITDA	4.99

OVER $5 MILLION NET SALES

MVIC/Net Sales	1.37
MVIC/Gross Profit	2.02
MVIC/SDE	N/A
MVIC/EBITDA	4.07

Source: DealStats (formerly Pratt's Stats), 2023 (Portland, OR: Business Valuation Resources, LLC), www.bvresources.com/dealstats

"At the lowest end, you may be able to purchase a car wash facility for $100,000 or less. At the high end you could be paying millions of dollars...."

"In-bay automatic car washes and self-service car washes do not cost much to operate each year and therefore you get to keep a great deal of your profit. Conveyor and full-service car washes cost more to operate but the revenue is higher."

Source: "How to Buy a Car Wash Business and How Much It Costs," May 11, 2022, https://pitcrew.com/how-to-buy-a-car-wash-business-and-how-much-it-costs/

INDUSTRY TREND

"The average monthly gross income per bay was $1,810."

Source: "Results from the *Auto Laundry News* 2023 Self-Service Survey," *Auto Laundry News*, May 2023, https://carwashmag.com/wp-content/uploads/2023/04/SELF-SURVEY-2023-high-res-for-web.pdf

RESOURCES

- ALN—Auto Laundry News: https://www.carwashmag.com
- ICA—International Carwash Association: https://www.carwash.org

Car Washes, Full-Service/Exterior

NAICS 811192		SIC 7542-01		Businesses/Units 59,780
Profit $2.3 B		Wages $4.5 B		Annual Growth Future 1.8%
				Annual Growth Past -1.0%

Rules of Thumb

- 0.80–1 x annual sales plus inventory
- 32% annual sales includes inventory
- 3 x SDE includes inventory
- 2–3 x EBIT
- 3.75–4.75 x EBITDA
- 4–6 x owner's provable net income includes income

INDUSTRY MULTIPLES

Acquisition multiples below are calculated medians using US private industry transactions. Data updated annually. Last update: August 2023.

VALUATION MULTIPLE (MEDIAN VALUE)

UNDER $1 MILLION NET SALES

MVIC/Net Sales.	0.70
MVIC/Gross Profit	0.76
MVIC/SDE	2.56
MVIC/EBITDA	2.52

$1 MILLION–$5 MILLION NET SALES

MVIC/Net Sales.	1.00
MVIC/Gross Profit	1.58
MVIC/SDE	4.12
MVIC/EBITDA	4.99

OVER $5 MILLION NET SALES

MVIC/Net Sales.	1.37
MVIC/Gross Profit	2.02
MVIC/SDE	N/A
MVIC/EBITDA	4.07

Source: DealStats (formerly Pratt's Stats), 2023 (Portland, OR: Business Valuation Resources, LLC), www.bvresources.com/dealstats

C

PRICING TIPS

Mostly sold with real estate; a cash business; not easy to verify income numbers.

Tax returns are not easily available, and estimating is generally the rule; therefore, using water bills, etc., to figure out the sales is one common method.

BENCHMARK DATA

STATISTICS (CAR WASH & AUTO DETAILING)

Number of Establishments	59,780
Average Profit Margin	16.1%
Revenue per Employee	$73,700
Average Number of Employees	3.4
Average Wages per Employee	$22,462

PRODUCTS AND SERVICES SEGMENTATION

Full-service clean (conveyor car washes)	30.9%
Detailing services	19.6%
Exterior only clean (conveyor car washes)	19.5%
In-bay automatic car washes	15.4%
Self-service bays	9.7%
Hand washing services	4.9%

INDUSTRY COSTS

Profit	16.1%
Wages	30.7%
Purchases	6.5%
Depreciation	8.5%
Marketing	1.3%
Rent & Utilities	4.0%
Other	33.0%

EXPENSES (% OF ANNUAL SALES)

Cost of Goods	05% to 10%
Occupancy Costs	10% to 20%
Payroll/Labor Costs	42.5%
Profit (pretax)	25%

QUESTIONS

- How many vehicles per month do they do? Summer vs. winter? The average ticket on each vehicle? Any environmental issues? The length of the lease and the rent factor? Is there at least one manager? You need to ask the seller the name and age of the equipment. Is the car wash brush or brushless? Any problems with the system?

INDUSTRY TREND

"Average gross revenue per car (car wash sales only): $20.71"

Source: "Results from the *Auto Laundry News* 2023 Full/Flex Survey," *Auto Laundry News*, March 2023, https://carwashmag.com/wp-content/uploads/2023/02/FullFlex-Survey-2023-All-pages.pdf

"Economic volatility negatively impacts customer demand and dampens consumer sentiment. Increasing rate of consumption of do-it-yourself (DIY) services dampens industry demand. Adding purchasable products like drying towels, floor mats and air fresheners boosts the industry's revenue stream. Increased number of vehicle registrations will fuel industry growth. Implementation of new environmental policies will alter consumer behavior. Municipal regulations are also expected to boost demand for the industry's services. Companies diversified their offerings to build a stronger customer base, implementing value-added services."

Source: IBISWorld Industry at a Glance

EXPERT COMMENTS

Good weather brings forth more sales; summer is generally a better season than winter. There is some seasonality in this business; best time to purchase is early summer or late spring. Have working capital and cash flow in reserve for the winter months.

Location, marketing, management, and visual appeal

In some areas replication is easy, and in others it's difficult due to the local restrictions on the usability of water and recycling it, plus the traffic problems.

FINANCING

Virtually no outside financing or SBA available because of figures, and lack of bookkeeping

RESOURCES

- IBISWorld, March 2023: https://www.ibisworld.com
- ALN—Auto Laundry News: https://www.carwashmag.com
- ICA—International Carwash Association: https://www.carwash.org
- WashTrends Magazine: https://www.washtrends.com/site/

Cardboard Box & Container Manufacturing

| NAICS 32221 | Businesses/Units 1,922

| Profit $3.7 B | Wages $10.6 B | Annual Growth Future 2.0%

| Annual Growth Past 0.1%

INDUSTRY MULTIPLES

Acquisition multiples below are calculated medians using US private industry transactions. Data updated annually. Last update: August 2023.

VALUATION MULTIPLE (MEDIAN VALUE)

UNDER $1 MILLION NET SALES

MVIC/Net Sales	1.01
MVIC/Gross Profit	3.18
MVIC/SDE	N/A
MVIC/EBITDA	N/A

$1 MILLION–$5 MILLION NET SALES

MVIC/Net Sales	0.59
MVIC/Gross Profit	2.51
MVIC/SDE	3.89
MVIC/EBITDA	4.06

OVER $5 MILLION NET SALES

MVIC/Net Sales	1.34
MVIC/Gross Profit	5.28
MVIC/SDE	N/A
MVIC/EBITDA	9.00

Source: DealStats (formerly Pratt's Stats), 2023 (Portland, OR: Business Valuation Resources, LLC), www.bvresources.com/dealstats

BENCHMARK DATA

STATISTICS (CARDBOARD BOX & CONTAINER MANUFACTURING)

Number of Establishments	1,922
Average Profit Margin	4.5%
Revenue per Employee	$567,000
Average Number of Employees	76.6
Average Wages per Employee	$73,138

PRODUCTS AND SERVICES SEGMENTATION

Corrugated and solid fiber boxes	54.5%
Other paperboard containers	24.5%
Folding paperboard boxes	21.0%

MAJOR MARKET SEGMENTATION

Food, beverage and agricultural producers	55.1%
Retail and wholesale	30.5%
Paper and chemical products	14.4%

INDUSTRY COSTS

Profit	4.5%
Wages	13.0%
Purchases	64.0%
Depreciation	2.4%
Marketing	0.0%
Rent & Utilities	2.3%
Other	13.7%

MARKET SHARE

Westrock Co	24.0%
International Paper Company	18.4%
Pratt Industries, Inc.	4.5%
Transpak Corp	1.0%

INDUSTRY TREND

"Consistent downstream demand is an important factor influencing how successful manufacturers will be. Evolving consumer trends can affect cardboard manufacturers. The COVID-19 pandemic created temporary volatility throughout international markets. Downstream markets like food and beverage manufacturers will have enlarged consumer demand. Many industry manufacturers will look abroad to lower labor costs. The increased adoption of automated technology will ensure industry growth remains strong. The continued expansion of online retailers has significantly contributed to industry growth."

Source: IBISWorld Industry at a Glance

RESOURCES

- IBISWorld, January 2023: https://www.ibisworld.com

Carl's Jr. (Franchise)

| | NAICS 722513 | | SIC 5812-06 | | Businesses/Units 1,020 |

Rules of Thumb

- 40% annual sales plus inventory

INDUSTRY MULTIPLES

Acquisition multiples below are calculated medians using US private industry transactions. Data updated annually. Last update: August 2023.

VALUATION MULTIPLE (MEDIAN VALUE)

UNDER $1 MILLION NET SALES

MVIC/Net Sales.	0.31
MVIC/Gross Profit	0.48
MVIC/SDE	1.67
MVIC/EBITDA	2.21

$1 MILLION–$5 MILLION NET SALES

MVIC/Net Sales.	0.39
MVIC/Gross Profit	0.60
MVIC/SDE	2.43
MVIC/EBITDA	2.98

OVER $5 MILLION NET SALES

MVIC/Net Sales.	0.89
MVIC/Gross Profit	2.08
MVIC/SDE	4.98
MVIC/EBITDA	12.81

Source: DealStats (formerly Pratt's Stats), 2023 (Portland, OR: Business Valuation Resources, LLC), www.bvresources.com/dealstats

PRICING TIPS

Approx. Total Investment: $1,334,670 to $2,256,000

RESOURCES

- Carl's Jr.: https://www.carlsjr.com
- Franchise information: https://ckefranchise.com
- CKE Restaurants: https://www.ckr.com

Carpenters

| NAICS 238350 | Businesses/Units 218,432

| Profit $1.4 B | Wages $11.4 B | Annual Growth Future 0.2%

| Annual Growth Past -1.7%

INDUSTRY MULTIPLES

Acquisition multiples below are calculated medians using US private industry transactions. Data updated annually. Last update: August 2023.

VALUATION MULTIPLE (MEDIAN VALUE)

UNDER $1 MILLION NET SALES

MVIC/Net Sales.	0.45
MVIC/Gross Profit	0.73
MVIC/SDE	2.43
MVIC/EBITDA	4.52

$1 MILLION–$5 MILLION NET SALES

MVIC/Net Sales.	0.38
MVIC/Gross Profit	0.85
MVIC/SDE	2.35
MVIC/EBITDA	3.10

OVER $5 MILLION NET SALES

MVIC/Net Sales.	0.34
MVIC/Gross Profit	1.06

```
MVIC/SDE  .   .   .   .   .   .   .   .   .   .   .   .   .   3.15
MVIC/EBITDA  .   .   .   .   .   .   .   .   .   .   .   .   2.16
```

Source: DealStats (formerly Pratt's Stats), 2023 (Portland, OR: Business Valuation Resources, LLC), www.bvresources.com/dealstats

BENCHMARK DATA

STATISTICS (CARPENTERS)

Number of Establishments	218,432
Average Profit Margin	3.4%
Revenue per Employee	$118,000
Average Number of Employees.	1.6
Average Wages per Employee	$33,534

PRODUCTS AND SERVICES SEGMENTATION

Finish carpentry.	85.0%
Other contractor services	11.4%
Framing carpentry	3.6%

MAJOR MARKET SEGMENTATION

Residential building construction (single-family) . . .	54.8%
Commercial building construction	18.7%
Other nonresidential building construction . . .	12.8%
Municipal building construction	6.9%
Residential building construction (multifamily) . . .	6.8%

INDUSTRY COSTS

Profit	3.4%
Wages	28.5%
Purchases	43.3%
Depreciation	1.0%
Marketing	1.0%
Rent & Utilities	5.4%
Other	17.3%

INDUSTRY TREND

"DIY projects have become increasingly popular among home owners, hurting industry demand. A declining value of private nonresidential construction segment has slowed industry revenue growth. The number of industry enterprises has increased over the five years to 2021. Growing demand in the nonresidential building market is forecast to support the industry's expansion over the next five years. As income levels improve, homeowners will likely be more inclined to invest in larger projects. Positive demand conditions are expected to continue encouraging more operators to enter the industry. The value of nonresidential construction has declined, further weakening industry demand."

Source: IBISWorld Industry at a Glance

RESOURCES

• IBISWorld, March 2023: https://www.ibisworld.com

Carpet Cleaning

NAICS 561740	SIC 7217-04	Businesses/Units 33,572
Profit $942.4 M	Wages $1.9 B	Annual Growth Future 1.0%
		Annual Growth Past 3.9%

Rules of Thumb
- 60% annual revenue plus inventory
- 1.5 x SDE plus inventory

INDUSTRY MULTIPLES

Acquisition multiples below are calculated medians using US private industry transactions. Data updated annually. Last update: August 2023.

VALUATION MULTIPLE (MEDIAN VALUE)

UNDER $1 MILLION NET SALES	
MVIC/Net Sales.	0.60
MVIC/Gross Profit	0.73
MVIC/SDE	1.88
MVIC/EBITDA	2.69

$1 MILLION–$5 MILLION NET SALES	
MVIC/Net Sales.	0.56
MVIC/Gross Profit	0.56
MVIC/SDE	3.07
MVIC/EBITDA	4.55

OVER $5 MILLION NET SALES	N/A

Source: DealStats (formerly Pratt's Stats), 2023 (Portland, OR: Business Valuation Resources, LLC), www.bvresources.com/dealstats

BENCHMARK DATA

STATISTICS (CARPET CLEANING)

Number of Establishments	33,572
Average Profit Margin	14.3%
Revenue per Employee	$108,000
Average Number of Employees.	1.9
Average Wages per Employee	$30,175

PRODUCTS AND SERVICES SEGMENTATION

Residential carpet cleaning.	42.0%
Other	22.8%
Commercial carpet cleaning	20.1%
Offsite cleaning services	15.1%

INDUSTRY COSTS

Profit	14.3%
Wages	28.2%
Purchases	26.7%
Depreciation	2.8%
Marketing	1.7%
Rent & Utilities	2.3%
Other	23.9%

INDUSTRY TREND

"As the pandemic increased sensitivity to contaminants, demand for auxiliary services is estimated to rise. The rise in popularity of laminate flooring has hampered demand for carpet cleaning services. The industry has experienced an increasing proportion of small-scale operators. With improving economic conditions, more consumers will be able to hire industry services. The industry endures stiff competition from janitorial companies that offer carpet cleaning. Rising wage and fuel costs are expected to hamper stronger profit growth. Increased cleaning frequency for businesses is anticipated to boost revenue."

Source: IBISWorld Industry at a Glance

- IBISWorld, March 2023: https://www.ibisworld.com
- CRI—The Carpet and Rug Institute: https://carpet-rug.org
- RIA—Restoration Industry Association: https://www.restorationindustry.org

Carpet/Floor Coverings

| NAICS 442210	| SIC 5713-05	| Businesses/Units 36,589
| Profit $1.3 B	| Wages $6.7 B	| Annual Growth Future -0.1%
		| Annual Growth Past 1.1%

Rules of Thumb
- 20% annual sales plus inventory

INDUSTRY MULTIPLES

Acquisition multiples below are calculated medians using US private industry transactions. Data updated annually. Last update: August 2023.

VALUATION MULTIPLE (MEDIAN VALUE)

UNDER $1 MILLION NET SALES	
MVIC/Net Sales.	0.19
MVIC/Gross Profit	0.44
MVIC/SDE	1.45
MVIC/EBITDA	1.49
$1 MILLION–$5 MILLION NET SALES	
MVIC/Net Sales.	0.28
MVIC/Gross Profit	0.70
MVIC/SDE	2.18
MVIC/EBITDA	3.08
OVER $5 MILLION NET SALES	
MVIC/Net Sales.	0.29
MVIC/Gross Profit	1.24
MVIC/SDE	2.25
MVIC/EBITDA	2.44

Source: DealStats (formerly Pratt's Stats), 2023 (Portland, OR: Business Valuation Resources, LLC), www.bvresources.com/dealstats

BENCHMARK DATA

STATISTICS (FLOOR COVERING STORES)

Number of Establishments .	36,589
Average Profit Margin	2.8%
Revenue per Employee .	$328,000
Average Number of Employees.	3.9
Average Wages per Employee .	$47,871

PRODUCTS AND SERVICES SEGMENTATION

Other hard-surface floor coverings.	45.4%
Carpets and other soft-surface floor coverings	35.0%
Hardwood flooring	15.2%
Other services	4.4%

MAJOR MARKET SEGMENTATION

Do-it-yourself customers	39.8%
Building contractors	28.8%
Do-it-for-me customers .	16.7%
Other markets	14.7%

Profit	2.8%
Wages	14.4%
Purchases	50.0%
Depreciation	0.6%
Marketing	3.5%
Rent & Utilities	5.8%
Other	22.8%

INDUSTRY TREND

"Even as COVID-19 swept through the United States, demand for flooring remained heightened. High interest rates further disrupted demand from nonresidential markets. Retailers are in direct competition with nationwide stores like Lowe's and the Home Depot. The two crucial downstream market indicators for floor covering stores are residential and nonresidential. The largest threat for floor covering stores is the encroachment of big-box home improvement stores. A crucial indicator of demand is per capita disposable income levels. Despite major slowdowns, floor covering stores' revenue has been growing."

Source: IBISWorld Industry at a Glance

RESOURCES

- IBISWorld, March 2023: https://www.ibisworld.com
- FCW—Floor Covering Weekly: https://www.floorcoveringweekly.com
- Floor Covering News: https://www.fcnews.net
- Floor Daily: https://www.floordaily.net

Carvel (Franchise)

| | NAICS 722515 | | SIC 2024-98 | | Businesses/Units 326 |

Rules of Thumb

- 2.25–2.5 x SDE plus inventory

INDUSTRY MULTIPLES

Acquisition multiples below are calculated medians using US private industry transactions. Data updated annually. Last update: August 2023.

VALUATION MULTIPLE (MEDIAN VALUE)

UNDER $1 MILLION NET SALES	
MVIC/Net Sales	0.44
MVIC/Gross Profit	0.62
MVIC/SDE	2.20
MVIC/EBITDA	2.82
$1 MILLION–$5 MILLION NET SALES	
MVIC/Net Sales	0.41
MVIC/Gross Profit	0.69
MVIC/SDE	2.82
MVIC/EBITDA	5.94
OVER $5 MILLION NET SALES	
MVIC/Net Sales	3.89
MVIC/Gross Profit	4.87
MVIC/SDE	N/A
MVIC/EBITDA	N/A

Source: DealStats (formerly Pratt's Stats), 2023 (Portland, OR: Business Valuation Resources, LLC), www.bvresources.com/dealstats

PRICING TIPS

Approx. Total Investment: $111,250 to $518,400

BENCHMARK DATA

EXPENSES (% OF ANNUAL SALES)

Cost of Goods	26%
Occupancy Costs	11%
Payroll/Labor Costs.	21%
Profit (pretax)	25%

FINANCING

3 to 5 years

RESOURCES

- Carvel: https://www.carvel.com
- Franchise information: https://development.focusbrands.com/carvel/
- Focus Brands: https://www.focusbrands.com

Casinos/Casino Hotels

NAICS 713210	SIC 7993-02	Businesses/Units 1,032

INDUSTRY MULTIPLES

Acquisition multiples below are calculated medians using US private industry transactions. Data updated annually. Last update: August 2023.

VALUATION MULTIPLE (MEDIAN VALUE)

UNDER $1 MILLION NET SALES	
MVIC/Net Sales.	0.36
MVIC/Gross Profit	0.43
MVIC/SDE	N/A
MVIC/EBITDA	N/A
$1 MILLION–$5 MILLION NET SALES	N/A
OVER $5 MILLION NET SALES	
MVIC/Net Sales.	1.94
MVIC/Gross Profit	3.59
MVIC/SDE	N/A
MVIC/EBITDA	9.20

Source: DealStats (formerly Pratt's Stats), 2023 (Portland, OR: Business Valuation Resources, LLC), www.bvresources.com/dealstats

BENCHMARK DATA

STATISTICS (CASINO HOTELS)

Number of Establishments .	655
Average Profit Margin	13.1%
Revenue per Employee .	$128,000
Average Number of Employees.	975.0
Average Wages per Employee .	$36,111

PRODUCTS AND SERVICES SEGMENTATION

Gambling machines.	55.5%
Accommodation	13.3%
Food and alcohol	13.2%
Table games.	12.6%
Other services	3.9%
Entertainment	1.5%

INDUSTRY COSTS

Profit	13.1%
Wages	27.9%
Purchases	19.1%
Depreciation	6.6%
Marketing	2.0%
Rent & Utilities	0.3%
Other	31.0%

MARKET SHARE

MGM Resorts International.	14.8%
Caesars Entertainment, Inc.	14.1%

STATISTICS (NON-HOTEL CASINOS)

Number of Establishments	377
Average Profit Margin	20.7%
Revenue per Employee	$208,000
Average Number of Employees.	311.0
Average Wages per Employee	$39,114

PRODUCTS AND SERVICES SEGMENTATION

Gambling machines.	76.0%
Table wagering games	15.2%
Food and beverages	6.2%
Other	2.2%
Lotteries.	0.4%

INDUSTRY COSTS

Profit	20.7%
Wages	18.8%
Purchases	5.4%
Depreciation	5.0%
Marketing	3.6%
Rent & Utilities	10.9%
Other	35.6%

MARKET SHARE

Caesars Entertainment, Inc.	33.0%
Penn National Gaming, Inc..	9.8%

INDUSTRY TREND

"Commercial gaming revenue reached $60.4 billion in 2022, passing the previous record of $53.0 billion set in 2021."

Source: "State of the States 2023" by American Gaming Association, May 16, 2023,
https://www.americangaming.org/resources/state-of-the-states-2023/

"Operators have attempted to attract younger generations. Casinos have boosted budgets for live concert events, parties and other large events. Online gambling has grown in popularity. Travel spending is projected to grow in line with an improving economy. Vulnerable casinos will need to prioritize improving ameni-ties to remain in business. Occurring internally and externally, the industry will contend with hackers. High industry profit has been maintained due to upgrades on machines on the gaming floor. Existing casinos struggle to stay afloat due to increased competition from casinos with lodging accommodations attached. Casinos have become an increasingly popular way for cash-strapped states to raise funds. The effects of the COVID-19 pandemic have made online gambling a much more sensible form of play. Domestic trips by US residents and consumer spending will increase, benefiting casinos. New casinos will open because of changes in state-based legislation. The industry will need to catch up to growth in profit as rising competition puts downward pressure on the revenue of existing casinos. Tourism trends significantly affect casino revenue because consumers tend to spend their income on gambling while on vacation."

Source: IBISWorld Industry at a Glance

RESOURCES

- IBISWorld, February 2023: https://www.ibisworld.com
- IBISWorld, January 2023: https://www.ibisworld.com
- AGA—American Gaming Association: https://www.americangaming.org
- GGB—Global Gaming Business Magazine: https://ggbmagazine.com
- Indian Gaming: https://www.indiangaming.com
- NASPL—North American Association of State and Provincial Lotteries: https://www.naspl.org
- National Indian Gaming Association: http://www.indiangaming.org
- World Casino News: https://news.worldcasinodirectory.com/

Caterers/Catering

	NAICS 722320		SIC 5812-12		Businesses/Units 88,799
	Profit $594 M		Wages $3.6 B		Annual Growth Future 1.0%
					Annual Growth Past -6.7%

Rules of Thumb

- 35%–40% annual sales plus inventory

INDUSTRY MULTIPLES

Acquisition multiples below are calculated medians using US private industry transactions. Data updated annually. Last update: August 2023.

VALUATION MULTIPLE (MEDIAN VALUE)

UNDER $1 MILLION NET SALES
MVIC/Net Sales.	0.26
MVIC/Gross Profit	0.38
MVIC/SDE	1.49
MVIC/EBITDA	2.17

$1 MILLION–$5 MILLION NET SALES
MVIC/Net Sales.	0.27
MVIC/Gross Profit	0.49
MVIC/SDE	3.02
MVIC/EBITDA	4.14

OVER $5 MILLION NET SALES
MVIC/Net Sales.	0.38
MVIC/Gross Profit	0.93
MVIC/SDE	1.19
MVIC/EBITDA	1.34

Source: DealStats (formerly Pratt's Stats), 2023 (Portland, OR: Business Valuation Resources, LLC), www.bvresources.com/dealstats

BENCHMARK DATA

STATISTICS (CATERERS)

Number of Establishments .	88,799
Average Profit Margin .	5.5%
Revenue per Employee .	$42,300
Average Number of Employees.	2.9
Average Wages per Employee .	$14,140

PRODUCTS AND SERVICES SEGMENTATION

Food served at events on customer's premises or third-party's premises.	35.7%
Food served at events on caterer's premises .	26.5%
Other services .	11.9%
No-service catering .	10.0%
Alcohol beverages .	8.3%
Food prepared for immediate consumption .	7.6%

INDUSTRY COSTS

Profit .	5.5%
Wages .	33.0%
Purchases .	39.1%
Depreciation .	1.9%
Marketing .	1.9%
Rent & Utilities .	7.5%
Other .	11.2%

INDUSTRY TREND

"Improvements in household earnings have supported industry demand. Operators have sought to distinguish themselves in this highly competitive industry. The industry is expected to experience an uptick in profit margins. Household demand is expected to increase in line with consumer spending growth. More restaurants are growing their catering services in direct response to consumer trends. Operators are expected to respond to a culinary environment that has become increasingly innovative. With relatively low barriers to entry, this industry experiences high competition."

Source: IBISWorld Industry at a Glance

RESOURCES

- IBISWorld, January 2023: https://www.ibisworld.com
- Catersource magazine: https://www.catersource.com
- ICA—International Caterers Association: https://www.internationalcaterers.org
- NACE—National Association for Catering & Events: https://www.nace.net

Catering Trucks

NAICS 722330	Businesses/Units 68,407

Profit $175.7 M	Wages $737.8 M	Annual Growth Future 0.5%
		Annual Growth Past 8.8%

Rules of Thumb

- 40% annual sales plus inventory

INDUSTRY MULTIPLES

Acquisition multiples below are calculated medians using US private industry transactions. Data updated annually. Last update: August 2023.

VALUATION MULTIPLE (MEDIAN VALUE)

UNDER $1 MILLION NET SALES

MVIC/Net Sales	0.64
MVIC/Gross Profit	0.83
MVIC/SDE	0.86
MVIC/EBITDA	1.04

$1 MILLION–$5 MILLION NET SALES — N/A

OVER $5 MILLION NET SALES

MVIC/Net Sales	3.43
MVIC/Gross Profit	9.59
MVIC/SDE	N/A
MVIC/EBITDA	N/A

Source: DealStats (formerly Pratt's Stats), 2023 (Portland, OR: Business Valuation Resources, LLC), www.bvresources.com/dealstats

BENCHMARK DATA

STATISTICS (STREET VENDORS)

Number of Establishments	68,407
Average Profit Margin	6.3%
Revenue per Employee	$34,400
Average Number of Employees	1.2
Average Wages per Employee	$9,344

PRODUCTS AND SERVICES SEGMENTATION

American	28.7%
Mixed ethnicity	21.7%
Other	13.1%
Central and South American	10.9%
Asian	8.5%
Desserts	7.8%
Seafood	6.2%
Greek Mediterranean	3.1%

INDUSTRY COSTS

Profit	6.3%
Wages	26.5%
Purchases	42.5%
Depreciation	2.9%
Marketing	2.0%
Rent & Utilities	8.1%
Other	11.8%

INDUSTRY TREND

"Street vendors survived 2020 as an alternative to indoor dining in restaurants. Demand for street vendor products will continue to expand as more people return to office buildings. Higher prices of key inputs, including food ingredients and energy, have pushed down profit. A return to urbanization, population density and office settings will provide opportunities. Street vendor revenue will steadily expand despite ongoing competition. Higher interest rates weighing on consumer spending may limit revenue expansion. Profit is expected to struggle due to higher input prices, while revenue surges."

Source: IBISWorld Industry at a Glance

RESOURCES

• IBISWorld, March 2023: https://www.ibisworld.com

Cement Manufacturing

| NAICS 327310 | Businesses/Units 161

| Profit $465.8 M | Wages $1.1 B | Annual Growth Future 1.1%

| Annual Growth Past 0.1%

INDUSTRY MULTIPLES

Acquisition multiples below are calculated medians using US private industry transactions. Data updated annually. Last update: August 2023.

VALUATION MULTIPLE (MEDIAN VALUE)

UNDER $1 MILLION NET SALES	N/A
$1 MILLION–$5 MILLION NET SALES	N/A
OVER $5 MILLION NET SALES	
MVIC/Net Sales.	4.31
MVIC/Gross Profit	34.74
MVIC/SDE	N/A
MVIC/EBITDA	15.27

Source: DealStats (formerly Pratt's Stats), 2023 (Portland, OR: Business Valuation Resources, LLC), www.bvresources.com/dealstats

BENCHMARK DATA

STATISTICS (CEMENT MANUFACTURING)

Number of Establishments .	161
Average Profit Margin .	4.5%
Revenue per Employee .	$918,000
Average Number of Employees.	71.0
Average Wages per Employee .	$97,393

PRODUCTS AND SERVICES SEGMENTATION

Portland and masonry cement .	54.9%
Clinker cement .	44.1%
Other	1.0%

MAJOR MARKET SEGMENTATION

Ready-mixed concrete producers .	69.6%
Other	17.1%
Concrete product manufacturers .	11.5%
Exports .	1.8%

INDUSTRY COSTS

Profit	4.5%
Wages .	10.7%
Purchases .	22.4%
Depreciation	3.7%
Marketing .	0.0%
Rent & Utilities .	15.0%
Other	43.7%

MARKET SHARE

CEMEX S.A.B. de C.V. .	15.7%
LafargeHolcim .	12.6%
Martin Marietta Materials, Inc. .	4.9%
Heidelbergcement Ag .	3.3%

INDUSTRY TREND

"Periods of construction growth have driven demand for related cement products. Companies have undertaken energy-saving initiatives to reduce operating costs. The appreciating US dollar has increased the pricing advantage of imports. Rebounding construction activity will drive demand for related cement products. The industry will continue consolidating as bigger players vie for market share. The depreciation of the US dollar will make domestic cement products more competitive. Revenue has remained stable as construction shifts to nonresidential projects."

Source: IBISWorld Industry at a Glance

RESOURCES

• IBISWorld, February 2023: https://www.ibisworld.com

Cemeteries

	NAICS 812220		SIC 6553-02		Businesses/Units 7,358
	Profit $591.8 M		Wages $1.8 B		Annual Growth Future 1.6%
					Annual Growth Past 2.8%

Rules of Thumb

• 6 x SDE includes real estate
• 8 x EBIT includes real estate
• 6 x EBITDA includes real estate

INDUSTRY MULTIPLES

Acquisition multiples below are calculated medians using US private industry transactions. Data updated annually. Last update: August 2023.

VALUATION MULTIPLE (MEDIAN VALUE)

UNDER $1 MILLION NET SALES	
MVIC/Net Sales.	0.75
MVIC/Gross Profit	0.82
MVIC/SDE	2.94
MVIC/EBITDA	6.11
$1 MILLION–$5 MILLION NET SALES	N/A
OVER $5 MILLION NET SALES	
MVIC/Net Sales.	3.89
MVIC/Gross Profit	9.32
MVIC/SDE	N/A
MVIC/EBITDA	N/A

Source: DealStats (formerly Pratt's Stats), 2023 (Portland, OR: Business Valuation Resources, LLC), www.bvresources.com/dealstats

PRICING TIPS

Valuations will vary depending on the strategic fit of the buyer. A local funeral home is generally the best strategic fit and should, therefore, be willing to pay the most.

STATISTICS (CEMETERY SERVICES)

Number of Establishments	7,358
Average Profit Margin	9.6%
Revenue per Employee	$172,000
Average Number of Employees. . . .	.4.9
Average Wages per Employee . . .	$50,443

PRODUCTS AND SERVICES SEGMENTATION

Sale of graves, plots and other spaces . .	43.0%
Sales of funeral goods	20.7%
Interment services	19.7%
Pre-burial services	5.3%
Cemetery maintenance services . . .	5.1%
Cremation services	4.2%
Other	2.0%

INDUSTRY COSTS

Profit	9.6%
Wages	29.3%
Purchases	8.6%
Depreciation	3.3%
Marketing	1.7%
Rent & Utilities	5.3%
Other	42.2%

MARKET SHARE

Service Corporation International . . .	34.3%

QUESTIONS

• Trust fund information is critical. What are the liabilities? Are they properly funded? Is there a successful sales organization/program in place?

INDUSTRY TREND

"The number of US deaths is the predominant driver for the industry. Cremation services have become increasingly more popular than traditional burials. The industry's largest companies steadily consolidated in recent years. Increased merger and acquisition activity is expected to continue among the industry's largest operators. Cremation will continue to become more prevalent over the next five years. Operators will continue to rely on client-family relationships and referrals fostered at the local level. With improving economic conditions, families have increased their purchases of high-profit funeral merchandise and services."

Source: IBISWorld Industry at a Glance

RESOURCES

• IBISWorld, February 2023: https://www.ibisworld.com

Ceramics Manufacturing

| NAICS 327110 | Businesses/Units 1,897

| Profit $142.9 M | Wages $657.5 M | Annual Growth Future 1.4%

| Annual Growth Past 0.5%

INDUSTRY MULTIPLES

Acquisition multiples below are calculated medians using US private industry transactions. Data updated annually. Last update: August 2023.

VALUATION MULTIPLE (MEDIAN VALUE)

UNDER $1 MILLION NET SALES

MVIC/Net Sales .	0.39
MVIC/Gross Profit .	0.47
MVIC/SDE .	N/A
MVIC/EBITDA .	N/A

$1 MILLION–$5 MILLION NET SALES N/A

OVER $5 MILLION NET SALES

MVIC/Net Sales .	3.37
MVIC/Gross Profit .	6.66
MVIC/SDE .	N/A
MVIC/EBITDA .	25.56

Source: DealStats (formerly Pratt's Stats), 2023 (Portland, OR: Business Valuation Resources, LLC), www.bvresources.com/dealstats

BENCHMARK DATA

STATISTICS (CERAMICS MANUFACTURING)

Number of Establishments .	1,897
Average Profit Margin .	4.7%
Revenue per Employee .	$236,000
Average Number of Employees.	7.0
Average Wages per Employee .	$50,697

PRODUCTS AND SERVICES SEGMENTATION

Advanced ceramics.	38.5%
Plumbing fixtures and other ceramic bathroom accessories .	38.3%
Other pottery .	15.0%
Porcelain kitchenware, earthenware and pottery products .	8.2%

MAJOR MARKET SEGMENTATION

Domestic high-tech devices and equipment manufacturing .	40.0%
Residential and nonresidential construction and remodeling .	36.7%
Other .	14.9%
Households, food service, and hospitality .	8.4%

INDUSTRY COSTS

Profit .	4.7%
Wages .	21.6%
Purchases .	27.3%
Depreciation .	1.7%
Marketing .	0.3%
Rent & Utilities .	3.3%
Other .	41.1%

MARKET SHARE

Coorstek Inc. .	12.5%
Kohler Co. .	10.8%
Morgan Advanced Materials PLC .	10.5%
Mansfield Plumbing Products LLC .	3.6%
Zurn Industries LLC. .	2.2%
3M Company .	2.0%
Sloan Valve Company .	1.5%

INDUSTRY TREND

"Professional construction and maintenance have been steady sources of demand. Revenue growth during the current period has been stifled by the persistently high import rate. Operators have been forced to cut costs to salvage profit and compete with low-cost imports. Changes in imports or exports have a substantial effect on industry revenue. Despite imports remaining high, smaller operators are expected to increase as they find niches. Demand for advanced ceramics is expected to be supported by high-tech and innovative markets. The level of regulation is expected to increase, further burdening operators."

Source: IBISWorld Industry at a Glance

RESOURCES

• IBISWorld, April 2023: https://www.ibisworld.com

Cereal Production

| NAICS 311230 | Businesses/Units 99

| Profit $859.5 M | Wages $980.6 M | Annual Growth Future 0.2%

| Annual Growth Past 0.1%

INDUSTRY MULTIPLES

Acquisition multiples below are calculated medians using US private industry transactions. Data updated annually. Last update: August 2023.

VALUATION MULTIPLE (MEDIAN VALUE)

UNDER $1 MILLION NET SALES
MVIC/Net Sales.	31.94
MVIC/Gross Profit	N/A
MVIC/SDE	N/A
MVIC/EBITDA	N/A

$1 MILLION–$5 MILLION NET SALES   N/A

OVER $5 MILLION NET SALES
MVIC/Net Sales.	2.77
MVIC/Gross Profit	7.83
MVIC/SDE	N/A
MVIC/EBITDA	15.51

Source: DealStats (formerly Pratt's Stats), 2023 (Portland, OR: Business Valuation Resources, LLC), www.bvresources.com/dealstats

BENCHMARK DATA

STATISTICS (CEREAL PRODUCTION)

Number of Establishments .	.99
Average Profit Margin	6.9%
Revenue per Employee .	$1,139,000
Average Number of Employees.	111.0
Average Wages per Employee .	$89,679

PRODUCTS AND SERVICES SEGMENTATION

Ready-to-eat corn breakfast cereals	.29.2%
Ready-to-eat oat breakfast cereals .	.20.1%
Other ready-to-eat grain breakfast cereals .	.17.9%
Ready-to-eat wheat breakfaster cereals	.16.8%
Hot cereal foods	8.1%
Ready-to-eat rice breakfast cereals.	7.9%

MAJOR MARKET SEGMENTATION

Supermarkets and grocery stores . . . 44.8%
Warehouse clubs and supercenters . . 35.2%
Grocery wholesalers 17.5%
Convenience stores. 2.5%

INDUSTRY COSTS

Profit 6.9%
Wages 7.9%
Purchases 53.4%
Depreciation 3.8%
Marketing 7.6%
Rent & Utilities 1.4%
Other 19.0%

INDUSTRY TREND

"Children's preferences are crucial to success in the industry. Cereal producers are expanding distribution networks to serve a wider array of markets. Cereal producers have struggled with the rising price of agricultural inputs. External competition will intensify over the next five years. More companies are expected engage in merger and acquisition activity. Improved foreign demand is expected to slightly boost industry revenue. Prominent acquisition activity by major players has kept the industry trending toward consolidation."

Source: IBISWorld Industry at a Glance

RESOURCES

• IBISWorld, January 2023: https://www.ibisworld.com

CertaPro Painters (Franchise)

| NAICS 238320 | SIC 1721-01 | Businesses/Units 342

Rules of Thumb

• 45% annual sales plus inventory

INDUSTRY MULTIPLES

Acquisition multiples below are calculated medians using US private industry transactions. Data updated annually. Last update: August 2023.

VALUATION MULTIPLE (MEDIAN VALUE)

UNDER $1 MILLION NET SALES
MVIC/Net Sales. 0.49
MVIC/Gross Profit 0.64
MVIC/SDE 1.37
MVIC/EBITDA 2.90

$1 MILLION–$5 MILLION NET SALES
MVIC/Net Sales. 0.44
MVIC/Gross Profit 0.95
MVIC/SDE 2.07
MVIC/EBITDA 2.56

OVER $5 MILLION NET SALES
MVIC/Net Sales. 0.62
MVIC/Gross Profit 1.98
MVIC/SDE 1.31
MVIC/EBITDA 2.48

Source: DealStats (formerly Pratt's Stats), 2023 (Portland, OR: Business Valuation Resources, LLC), www.bvresources.com/dealstats

PRICING TIPS
Approx. Total Investment: $155,650 to $232,400

RESOURCES

- CertaPro Painters: https://certapro.com
- Franchise information: https://certapro.com/franchise/
- FirstService Brands: https://www.fsvbrands.com

Charleys (Franchise)

| NAICS 722513 | Businesses/Units 574

Rules of Thumb

- 35% annual sales

INDUSTRY MULTIPLES

Acquisition multiples below are calculated medians using US private industry transactions. Data updated annually. Last update: August 2023.

VALUATION MULTIPLE (MEDIAN VALUE)

UNDER $1 MILLION NET SALES	
MVIC/Net Sales	0.31
MVIC/Gross Profit	0.48
MVIC/SDE	1.67
MVIC/EBITDA	2.21
$1 MILLION–$5 MILLION NET SALES	
MVIC/Net Sales	0.39
MVIC/Gross Profit	0.60
MVIC/SDE	2.43
MVIC/EBITDA	2.98
OVER $5 MILLION NET SALES	
MVIC/Net Sales	0.89
MVIC/Gross Profit	2.08
MVIC/SDE	4.98
MVIC/EBITDA	12.81

Source: DealStats (formerly Pratt's Stats), 2023 (Portland, OR: Business Valuation Resources, LLC), www.bvresources.com/dealstats

PRICING TIPS

Approx. Total Investment: $251,637 to $1,002,700

RESOURCES

- Charleys: https://www.charleys.com
- Franchise information: https://charleysfranchise.com

Check Cashing Services

| NAICS 522390 | SIC 6099-03

Rules of Thumb

- 75% annual revenues of $1M+
- 2 x SDE

Acquisition multiples below are calculated medians using US private industry transactions. Data updated annually. Last update: August 2023.

C

VALUATION MULTIPLE (MEDIAN VALUE)

UNDER $1 MILLION NET SALES
MVIC/Net Sales.	0.42
MVIC/Gross Profit	0.47
MVIC/SDE	1.28
MVIC/EBITDA	0.82

$1 MILLION–$5 MILLION NET SALES
MVIC/Net Sales.	0.15
MVIC/Gross Profit	0.49
MVIC/SDE	1.92
MVIC/EBITDA	1.97

OVER $5 MILLION NET SALES
MVIC/Net Sales.	0.04
MVIC/Gross Profit	1.66
MVIC/SDE	N/A
MVIC/EBITDA	7.90

Source: DealStats (formerly Pratt's Stats), 2023 (Portland, OR: Business Valuation Resources, LLC), www.bvresources.com/dealstats

BENCHMARK DATA

See Payday Loans for additional Benchmark data.

SERVICES/PRODUCTS OFFERINGS & VOLUMES
Check Cashing	96%
Money Orders	96%
Money Transfers	96%
Bill Payments	96%
Prepaid Debit Cards	88%
Payday Advances	58%
Traveler's Checks	04%
Installment Loans	25%
Other Financial Products	63%

Check cashing should provide the owner with 1% of total gross sales as owner's discretionary income.

EXPENSES (% OF ANNUAL SALES)
Cost of Goods	99%
Occupancy Costs	01%
Payroll/Labor Costs.	01%
Profit (pretax)	01%

Chemical Product Manufacturing

NAICS 32599	SIC 2899-05	Businesses/Units 4,472
Profit $2.5 B	Wages $7.2 B	Annual Growth Future -0.4%
		Annual Growth Past 3.9%

Rules of Thumb
- 0.5–2 x annual sales includes inventory
- 4–9 x EBITDA

INDUSTRY MULTIPLES

Acquisition multiples below are calculated medians using US private industry transactions. Data updated annually. Last update: August 2023.

VALUATION MULTIPLE (MEDIAN VALUE)

UNDER $1 MILLION NET SALES

MVIC/Net Sales	0.78
MVIC/Gross Profit	1.16
MVIC/SDE	3.65
MVIC/EBITDA	4.09

$1 MILLION–$5 MILLION NET SALES

MVIC/Net Sales	1.76
MVIC/Gross Profit	3.78
MVIC/SDE	4.57
MVIC/EBITDA	6.81

OVER $5 MILLION NET SALES

MVIC/Net Sales	1.76
MVIC/Gross Profit	6.47
MVIC/SDE	N/A
MVIC/EBITDA	13.01

Source: DealStats (formerly Pratt's Stats), 2023 (Portland, OR: Business Valuation Resources, LLC), www.bvresources.com/dealstats

BENCHMARK DATA

STATISTICS (CHEMICAL PRODUCT MANUFACTURING)

Number of Establishments	4,472
Average Profit Margin	4.3%
Revenue per Employee	$622,000
Average Number of Employees	20.9
Average Wages per Employee	$77,870

PRODUCTS AND SERVICES SEGMENTATION

Other	42.9%
Custom compounding of resins	27.3%
Photographic films, papers, and plates	10.0%
Water-treating compounds	8.4%
Evaporated salt	4.3%
Automotive chemicals	4.2%
Gelatin	2.9%

MAJOR MARKET SEGMENTATION

Manufacturing sector	26.7%
Automobile industry	0.2%
Households	18.7%
Construction sector	16.1%
Exports	14.3%
Other	4.0%

INDUSTRY COSTS

Profit	4.3%
Wages	12.3%
Purchases	49.4%
Depreciation	1.8%
Marketing	0.2%
Rent & Utilities	2.2%
Other	29.8%

MARKET SHARE

Lubrizol Corp	5.4%
Fujifilm Holdings Corp	4.9%
Mark IV Industries Inc.	3.2%

| ICL Group 1.8%
| Rockwater Energy Solutions, Inc. . . . 1.1%

| Cost of Goods 25%
| Profit (pretax) 10%

QUESTIONS

- Normal due diligence–type issues plus environmental/regulatory issues, which are somewhat unique to the industry, and impact of overseas competition

INDUSTRY TREND

"The industry has experienced a decline in demand from several key end markets. The photo chemicals and materials segment has continued its long-term decline. Volatile raw material costs have created a tumultuous environment for operators. Developments in the consumer appliance sector are expected to stimulate demand. Industry operators will have to cope with changing environmental regulations. Imports are expected to fall due to a decrease in the value of the dollar. Chemical manufacturers rely heavily on downstream demand from the manufacturing sector."

Source: IBISWorld Industry at a Glance

"26% of the total construction spending by the U.S. manufacturing sector in 2022 involved the business of chemistry."

Source: *The Business of Chemistry by the Numbers*, https://www.americanchemistry.com/chemistry-in-america/data-industry-statistics/the-business-of-chemistry-by-the-numbers

RESOURCES

- IBISWorld, March 2023: https://www.ibisworld.com
- ACC—American Chemistry Council: https://www.americanchemistry.com
- C&EN—Chemical & Engineering News: https://cen.acs.org
- Chemical Week: https://chemweek.com/cw/
- SOCMA—The Society of Chemical Manufacturers & Affiliates: https://www.socma.org

---

Chick-fil-A (Franchise)

| NAICS 722513 | SIC 5812-06 | Businesses/Units 2,628

Rules of Thumb

- 60%–70% annual sales plus inventory

INDUSTRY MULTIPLES

Acquisition multiples below are calculated medians using US private industry transactions. Data updated annually. Last update: August 2023.

VALUATION MULTIPLE (MEDIAN VALUE)

UNDER $1 MILLION NET SALES
| MVIC/Net Sales. 0.31
| MVIC/Gross Profit 0.48
| MVIC/SDE 1.67
| MVIC/EBITDA 2.21

$1 MILLION–$5 MILLION NET SALES
| MVIC/Net Sales. 0.39
| MVIC/Gross Profit 0.60

MVIC/SDE	2.43
MVIC/EBITDA	2.98

OVER $5 MILLION NET SALES

MVIC/Net Sales	0.89
MVIC/Gross Profit	2.08
MVIC/SDE	4.98
MVIC/EBITDA	12.81

Source: DealStats (formerly Pratt's Stats), 2023 (Portland, OR: Business Valuation Resources, LLC), www.bvresources.com/dealstats

PRICING TIPS

Approx. Total Investment: $435,500 to $2,701,000

RESOURCES

- Chick-fil-A: https://www.chick-fil-a.com
- Franchise information: https://www.chick-fil-a.com/franchising

---

Children's and Infants' Clothing Stores

| NAICS 458110 | Businesses/Units 18,957

| Profit $231.2 M | Wages $1.2 B | Annual Growth Future 0.6%

| Annual Growth Past -8.1%

Rules of Thumb

- 25%–30% annual sales plus inventory

INDUSTRY MULTIPLES

Acquisition multiples below are calculated medians using US private industry transactions. Data updated annually. Last update: August 2023.

VALUATION MULTIPLE (MEDIAN VALUE)

UNDER $1 MILLION NET SALES

MVIC/Net Sales	0.27
MVIC/Gross Profit	0.53
MVIC/SDE	1.03
MVIC/EBITDA	1.03

$1 MILLION–$5 MILLION NET SALES

MVIC/Net Sales	0.66
MVIC/Gross Profit	1.09
MVIC/SDE	4.47
MVIC/EBITDA	5.69

OVER $5 MILLION NET SALES

MVIC/Net Sales	4.35
MVIC/Gross Profit	5.17
MVIC/SDE	N/A
MVIC/EBITDA	N/A

Source: DealStats (formerly Pratt's Stats), 2023 (Portland, OR: Business Valuation Resources, LLC), www.bvresources.com/dealstats

BENCHMARK DATA

STATISTICS (CHILDREN'S & INFANTS' CLOTHING STORES)

Number of Establishments	18,957
Average Profit Margin	3.1%
Revenue per Employee	$83,600

Average Number of Employees. 4.7
Average Wages per Employee . . . $13,653

PRODUCTS AND SERVICES SEGMENTATION

Girls' clothing 40.5%
Boys' clothing 23.6%
Other 22.7%
Infants' and toddlers' clothing 13.2%

INDUSTRY COSTS

Profit 3.1%
Wages 16.4%
Purchases 49.4%
Depreciation 1.1%
Marketing 1.8%
Rent & Utilities 7.1%
Other 21.2%

MARKET SHARE

Carter's Inc.. . . . . 18.2%
Ascena Retail Group Inc. 15.1%
The Children's Place Inc. 11.3%

INDUSTRY TREND

"Instability of consumers' purchasing power influenced lower rate of shopping. High e-commerce adoption rate shifts consumer propensity away from brick-and-mortar retailers. Volatile commodity prices impact broader supply chain. Strong economic recovery offsets larger revenue losses. Continuous appeal of e-commerce sites harms core revenue streams. High external competition threatens future children's and infants' clothing stores viability. Stores have been shifting their focus away from selling in physical locations in favor of e-commerce, which is detrimental."

Source: IBISWorld Industry at a Glance

RESOURCES

• IBISWorld, April 2023: https://www.ibisworld.com

Children's Educational Franchises

| NAICS 611691

Rules of Thumb

• 2.5–3.5 x SDE
• 2–3 x EBIT
• 2–4 x EBITDA
• 55% annual sales includes inventory

INDUSTRY MULTIPLES

Acquisition multiples below are calculated medians using US private industry transactions. Data updated annually. Last update: August 2023.

VALUATION MULTIPLE (MEDIAN VALUE)

UNDER $1 MILLION NET SALES
MVIC/Net Sales. 0.45
MVIC/Gross Profit 0.49
MVIC/SDE 1.85
MVIC/EBITDA 3.33

$1 MILLION–$5 MILLION NET SALES

MVIC/Net Sales.	0.75
MVIC/Gross Profit	1.32
MVIC/SDE	3.11
MVIC/EBITDA	4.54

OVER $5 MILLION NET SALES   N/A

Source: DealStats (formerly Pratt's Stats), 2023 (Portland, OR: Business Valuation Resources, LLC), www.bvresources.com/dealstats

PRICING TIPS

Depends upon the size/licensed capacity of the childcare facility. Generally, fewer than 50 children, 1 x EBITDA; 50–100 children, 2 x EBITDA; 100–150 children, 3 x EBITDA; 4 x EBITDA for anything larger.

BENCHMARK DATA

35 square feet of space required for each child. Food costs are 3 to 6 percent. Labor expense (including PR taxes and excluding owner's salary) is 35 to 50 percent.

EXPENSES (% OF ANNUAL SALES)

Cost of Goods	05% to 15%
Occupancy Costs	15% to 20%
Payroll/Labor Costs.	35% to 45%
Profit (pretax)	10% to 20%

QUESTIONS

- Once a letter of intent is agreed to and the buyer is doing due diligence, the buyer should look at records for each and every child enrolled in the center.
- Any violations and strikes against the license or the facility? Is the director staying post-acquisition? Are the teachers fully compliant in terms of background and education requirements for early childhood education?
- How old is the roof? HVAC? How long has your director been with you? How old is the building? How stable are your employees? How many elementary schools are in the area? Do they offer after-school care? How many do you pick up from? What government subsidies do you accept?

INDUSTRY TREND

In demand

EXPERT COMMENTS

Covid-19 hurt the childcare industry and increased buyers' perception of the amount of risk in the industry. Values are down because of Covid-19.

FINANCING

10 percent equity injection, 5 percent seller financing, 85 percent SBA loan

RESOURCES

- Childcare Brokers: https://www.ChildcareBrokers.com
- GCCA—Georgia Child Care Association: https://www.georgiachildcare.org
- NAEYC—National Association for the Education of Young Children: https://www.naeyc.org

Children's Indoor Play Areas

| NAICS 713990 | Businesses/Units 62,146

| Profit $1.6 B | Wages $5.3 B | Annual Growth Future 1.0%

| Annual Growth Past -0.1%

INDUSTRY MULTIPLES

Acquisition multiples below are calculated medians using US private industry transactions. Data updated annually. Last update: August 2023.

VALUATION MULTIPLE (MEDIAN VALUE)

UNDER $1 MILLION NET SALES

MVIC/Net Sales.	0.69
MVIC/Gross Profit	0.76
MVIC/SDE	2.37
MVIC/EBITDA	2.99

$1 MILLION–$5 MILLION NET SALES

MVIC/Net Sales.	0.69
MVIC/Gross Profit	0.86
MVIC/SDE	3.06
MVIC/EBITDA	3.71

OVER $5 MILLION NET SALES

MVIC/Net Sales.	0.58
MVIC/Gross Profit	1.27
MVIC/SDE	3.09
MVIC/EBITDA	3.27

Source: DealStats (formerly Pratt's Stats), 2023 (Portland, OR: Business Valuation Resources, LLC), www.bvresources.com/dealstats

BENCHMARK DATA

STATISTICS (GOLF DRIVING RANGES & FAMILY FUN CENTERS)

Number of Establishments .	62,146
Average Profit Margin	9.7%
Revenue per Employee .	$62,300
Average Number of Employees.	4.3
Average Wages per Employee .	$19,919

PRODUCTS AND SERVICES SEGMENTATION

Amusement and recreation services	61.0%
Coin operated games and rides	13.0%
Other	10.0%
Amateur sports teams and club services	7.0%
Meals and beverages	5.0%
Registration for tournaments and matches.	4.0%

INDUSTRY COSTS

Profit	9.7%
Wages	31.5%
Purchases	5.3%
Depreciation	6.4%
Marketing	3.5%
Rent & Utilities .	10.5%
Other	33.2%

MARKET SHARE

Topgolf International Inc.	0.7%

INDUSTRY TREND

"Increases in per capita disposable income revitalized revenue after the COVID-19 pandemic. Small, independent driving ranges face price pressure from in-market entertainment companies. Increased fitness awareness has affected the industry. Recreation expenditure contraction pressures companies to reduce prices. Technology based games such as laser-tag have grown. Topgolf has attracted new and older clients to its golf and entertainment centers. More prominent service providers with varied entertainment portfolios commanded a large share of industry revenue."

Source: IBISWorld Industry at a Glance

RESOURCES

• IBISWorld, January 2023: https://www.ibisworld.com

Chiropractic Practices

	NAICS 621310		SIC 8041-01		Businesses/Units 72,247
	Profit $3.8 B		Wages $6.8 B		Annual Growth Future 2.3%
					Annual Growth Past 0.4%

Rules of Thumb

• 70%–80% annual sales includes inventory
• 1.5–2.5 x SDE includes inventory
• 1.5–2 x EBITDA
• 1.5–2 x EBIT

INDUSTRY MULTIPLES

Acquisition multiples below are calculated medians using US private industry transactions. Data updated annually. Last update: August 2023.

VALUATION MULTIPLE (MEDIAN VALUE)

UNDER $1 MILLION NET SALES

MVIC/Net Sales	0.45
MVIC/Gross Profit	0.56
MVIC/SDE	1.18
MVIC/EBITDA	2.14

$1 MILLION–$5 MILLION NET SALES

MVIC/Net Sales	0.77
MVIC/Gross Profit	0.78
MVIC/SDE	2.37
MVIC/EBITDA	3.87

OVER $5 MILLION NET SALES   N/A

Source: DealStats (formerly Pratt's Stats), 2023 (Portland, OR: Business Valuation Resources, LLC), www.bvresources.com/dealstats

PRICING TIPS

Using gross revenue figures for estimating the price of a chiropractic practice is often inaccurate due to the fact that these methods seem to best apply to the average chiropractic practice. This would assume that the business was average in terms of gross income, expenses, profits, equipment, staffing, location, etc. In reality, it is the rare practice that is average in all of these areas. Because of the wide range of overhead and profitability, gross income calculations can vary widely compared to price estimates that focus on profits or bottom-line income.

Most rule of thumb valuations tend to work best to arrive at a ballpark figure for chiropractic businesses that fall into the midrange or for statistically average practices. However, there is a wide discrepancy in businesses in the profession in terms of owner income, with the lowest percentage of chiropractic businesses earning only a small fraction of what successful practices do. Unfortunately, this leads many brokers, CPAs, and those with general business valuation experience to significantly over- or undervalue chiropractic practices if they do not have a working knowledge and/or experience with chiropractic practice sales. Finding someone with valuation or appraisal experience in the chiropractic industry may be critical to the successful appraisal or sale of a chiropractic business.

There are a lot of variabilities based on the size of the practice, the location, and the profitability.

BENCHMARK DATA

STATISTICS (CHIROPRACTORS)

Number of Establishments	72,247
Average Profit Margin	19.6%
Revenue per Employee	$104,000
Average Number of Employees	2.7
Average Wages per Employee	$38,343

PRODUCTS AND SERVICES SEGMENTATION

General chiropractic care	64.0%
Other	14.0%
Family chiropractic care	13.0%
Sports and rehabilitation chiropractic care	9.0%

MAJOR MARKET SEGMENTATION

Patients paying out of pocket	41.6%
Private health insurance	30.4%
Medicare and Medicaid	14.2%
Other	13.8%

INDUSTRY COSTS

Profit	19.6%
Wages	34.9%
Purchases	8.0%
Depreciation	1.7%
Marketing	1.4%
Rent & Utilities	8.2%
Other	26.1%

High variability in practice settings, from solo docs with no staff, to highly leveraged multispecialty institutions

There are many subspecialty modalities, often described by chiropractors as straights versus mixers, i.e., straights do just spinal manipulation, whereas mixers add other modalities; so benchmarks vary.

COMPONENTS OF CHIROPRACTIC PRACTICE

Direct patient care	52.9%
Documentation	18.9%
Patient education	15.1%
Business management	13.2%

The majority of chiropractic practices have less than $300,000 in annual collections, and a business in the top 25 percent may be collecting only $500,000 per year. The top 5 to 10 percent of the profession will be collecting $750,000 per year, with the top 5 percent over $1 million in gross revenues. The average owner income for the profession is approximately $71,000, but there are chiropractors whose incomes are significantly higher (and lower) than the average.

REIMBURSEMENT CATEGORIES, MANAGED CARE, AND REFERRAL

Private Insurance	21.5%
Private pay/cash	21.2%
Managed care	19.4%
Personal injury	13.6%
Medicare	10.8%
Workers' Comp	7.8%
Pro Bono	3.9%
Medicaid	1.8%

EXPENSES (% OF ANNUAL SALES)

Cost of Goods	02% to 12%
Occupancy Costs	05% to 15%
Payroll/Labor Costs.	15% to 25%
Profit (pretax)	25% to 50%

QUESTIONS

- Why are you selling? What is the breakdown of your revenue between payor sources? What is the balance/structure of your prepaid services? How do you get new patients? Are any of your insurance panels closed to new providers?
- State and federal law compliance? Mix of patients? Type of services rendered?

INDUSTRY TREND

"Our Salary & Expense Survey attracted a wide range of doctors across the nation, with responses from practitioners between the ages of 25 to more than 70 years old, and from those who have been in practice for less than a year to 30 years or more....

"Our average respondent:
- owns one clinic (90%)
- prefers to practice in the suburbs (56%)
- sees 154 patients a week; patient-visit average (PVA) of 60.3
- attracts eight new patients each week
- and sees patients about 31–40 hours a week (45%)....

"This typical respondent spends roughly $30,509 per year on office leases or mortgages, $16,512 on advertising, and $3,372 on malpractice insurance."

Source: "Dips and Jumps in 2023: The 26th Annual Salary & Expense Survey" by Allison M. Payne, June 7, 2023, https://www.chiroeco.com/dips-and-jumps-the-26th-annual-salary-expense-survey/

Overall, the chiropractic profession continues to grow faster than average for healthcare professions. The increasing number of baby boomers who seek natural remedies for the very common problem of back pain will continue to fuel the demand for chiropractic services for at least the next decade or more. In addition, chiropractic is also a benefit for most health insurance plans, which further increases the expansion of the profession.

The interest in natural healthcare, and the need for more affordable options for pain management and preventative health measures, are growing. The main challenges are the decreasing insurance reimbursements for chiropractors and the high student loan debt they are graduating with.

There's significant consolidation happening in this industry right now. Many sellers are retiring. Buyers are quite hesitant due to enormous student loan debt.

"Consumer spending encouraged patients to make out-of-pocket payments, keeping the industry profit margin steady. By offering coverage, private health-care insurers and Medicare and Medicaid validate chiropractors' treatments. Despite disruption related to the COVID-19 pandemic, recovery in the economy contributed to an uptick in patient volume. Other healthcare providers will ramp up their efforts to regain lost market share or grab new clients. The structure of the industry is changing. The industry generates most of its revenue through out-of-pocket payments. The face of the chiropractor's office is changing and concentration is the expected outcome."

Source: IBISWorld Industry at a Glance

EXPERT COMMENTS

Be sure to find a business broker or valuation specialist who is a chiropractor and/or has specific working knowledge and experience with the chiropractic profession. Valuations done by general business brokers or even accountants with no experience in chiropractic tend to be wildly inaccurate, or at least inconsistent.

Chiropractic practices are very complex to buy/sell because there are so many practice models, philosophies, and techniques—and they typically have been run without an intentional business strategy due to the doctors' primary focus on patient care. So it's very important to put in extra effort up front to prepare the business for sale, or understand the business you are buying. Working with a broker that specializes in chiropractic is invaluable to avoid missing things that could turn into huge problems later.

Buying an existing clinic is a great way to mitigate risk and have a professional income from the start. Because there are many, many data points due to the variability in types of chiropractic practices, however, it can be a very in-depth sales process.

FINANCING

The trend continues to shift towards outside financing, with SBA financing as the most popular route for lending.

Both outside financing and seller financing are readily seen, although outside financing (typically via SBA loans) is becoming more popular and now represents the majority of practice sales.

We see very little seller financing, but it is very common when the seller represents themselves, as chiropractic can be outside of many banks' lending parameters.

RESOURCES

- IBISWorld, January 2023: https://www.ibisworld.com
- ACA—American Chiropractic Association: https://www.acatoday.org
- CE—Chiropractic Economics: https://www.chiroeco.com
- Dynamic Chiropractic: https://www.dynamicchiropractic.com
- International Chiropractors Association: https://www.chiropractic.org
- MGMA—Medical Group Management Association: https://www.mgma.com
- NBCE—National Board of Chiropractic Examiners: https://www.nbce.org
- NCMIC: https://www.ncmic.com
- NSCHBC—National Society of Certified Healthcare Business Consultants: https://www.nschbc.org
- Strategic Chiropractor: https://www.strategicdc.com

Chocolate Production

| NAICS 31135 | | Businesses/Units 3,340 |

| Profit $2.8 B | | Wages $2.8 B | | Annual Growth Future 0.1% |

| | | | | Annual Growth Past -0.6% |

INDUSTRY MULTIPLES

Acquisition multiples below are calculated medians using US private industry transactions. Data updated annually. Last update: August 2023.

VALUATION MULTIPLE (MEDIAN VALUE)

UNDER $1 MILLION NET SALES

MVIC/Net Sales.	0.55
MVIC/Gross Profit	1.15
MVIC/SDE	2.61
MVIC/EBITDA	7.81

$1 MILLION–$5 MILLION NET SALES

MVIC/Net Sales.	0.54
MVIC/Gross Profit	0.91
MVIC/SDE	4.57
MVIC/EBITDA	5.58

OVER $5 MILLION NET SALES

MVIC/Net Sales.	0.37
MVIC/Gross Profit	1.27
MVIC/SDE	N/A
MVIC/EBITDA	12.02

Source: DealStats (formerly Pratt's Stats), 2023 (Portland, OR: Business Valuation Resources, LLC), www.bvresources.com/dealstats

BENCHMARK DATA

STATISTICS (CHOCOLATE PRODUCTION)

Number of Establishments .	3,340
Average Profit Margin	13.9%
Revenue per Employee .	$392,000
Average Number of Employees.	15.2
Average Wages per Employee .	$54,450

PRODUCTS AND SERVICES SEGMENTATION

Chocolate bars, plain	53.1%
Chocolate molded with candy, fruit, nut, or granola	33.2%
Chocolate coatings .	7.0%
Cocoa butter, liquor, and syrup .	3.4%
Cocoa powder .	3.3%

MAJOR MARKET SEGMENTATION

Supermarkets and grocery stores .	58.4%
Confectionery wholesalers .	26.9%
Exports .	10.2%
Specialty retailers .	4.5%

INDUSTRY COSTS

Profit	13.9%
Wages .	13.8%
Purchases .	54.2%
Depreciation	2.1%
Marketing	0.8%
Rent & Utilities .	3.2%
Other	11.9%

"The introduction of healthier and more nutritious chocolate products has helped producers secure revenue. The prices of inputs, especially cacao beans and sugar, have been extremely volatile. The benefits of consolidation have encouraged players to undergo more mergers and acquisitions. Higher volume sales of mainstream and premium brands are expected to drive revenue growth. Rising cocoa prices are anticipated to negatively affect small chocolate producers. Exports are expected to increase as the US dollar depreciates. The industry has seen highly volatile raw input prices over the past five years, which has had varied implications for operators."

Source: IBISWorld Industry at a Glance

RESOURCES

• IBISWorld, January 2023: https://www.ibisworld.com

Cigarette & Tobacco Manufacturing

| NAICS 312230　　| Businesses/Units 134

| Profit $21 B　　| Wages $974.9 M　　| Annual Growth Future -1.5%

　　　　　　　　　　　　　　　　　　| Annual Growth Past -1.5%

INDUSTRY MULTIPLES

Acquisition multiples below are calculated medians using US private industry transactions. Data updated annually. Last update: August 2023.

VALUATION MULTIPLE (MEDIAN VALUE)

UNDER $1 MILLION NET SALES	N/A
$1 MILLION–$5 MILLION NET SALES	
MVIC/Net Sales	5.40
MVIC/Gross Profit	11.89
MVIC/SDE	N/A
MVIC/EBITDA	N/A
OVER $5 MILLION NET SALES	
MVIC/Net Sales	2.73
MVIC/Gross Profit	6.03
MVIC/SDE	N/A
MVIC/EBITDA	13.70

Source: DealStats (formerly Pratt's Stats), 2023 (Portland, OR: Business Valuation Resources, LLC), www.bvresources.com/dealstats

BENCHMARK DATA

STATISTICS (CIGARETTE & TOBACCO MANUFACTURING)

Number of Establishments	134
Average Profit Margin	39.8%
Revenue per Employee	$5,168,000
Average Number of Employees	76.1
Average Wages per Employee	$94,902

PRODUCTS AND SERVICES SEGMENTATION

Regular cigarettes	51.8%
Menthol cigarettes	30.4%
Smokeless tobacco	11.4%
Other	4.3%
Cigars	2.1%

MAJOR MARKET SEGMENTATION

Cigarette and tobacco wholesalers. . . 52.3%
Gas stations with convenience stores . . 36.1%
Convenience stores. 8.0%
Supermarkets and grocery stores . . . 3.1%
Grocery distributors and wholesalers . . 0.5%

INDUSTRY COSTS

Profit 39.8%
Wages 1.8%
Purchases 14.7%
Depreciation 0.5%
Marketing 0.1%
Rent & Utilities 0.3%
Other 42.8%

MARKET SHARE

Altria Group, Inc. 45.5%
Reynolds American Inc.. . . . . 7.1%
Imperial Brands PLC 6.8%

INDUSTRY TREND

"Consumer demand for cigarette and tobacco products rises during high-stress periods, like the COVID-19 pandemic. Cigarette and tobacco manufacturers can't attract enough customers to maintain profit. Excise taxes have been particularly damaging to cigarette sales. Moving forward, an increasing number of smokers will turn to substitute products. Large manufacturers will focus on marketing secondary products, like machine-made cigars and smokeless tobacco. Domestic manufacturers will continue to face major resistance from foreign companies. The COVID-19 pandemic has significantly increased tobacco consumption."

Source: IBISWorld Industry at a Glance

RESOURCES

• IBISWorld, February 2023: https://www.ibisworld.com

Claims Adjusting

| NAICS 524291

| Profit $15.6 B | Wages $3.8 B | Annual Growth Future 0.6%
| Annual Growth Past 3.3%

INDUSTRY MULTIPLES

Acquisition multiples below are calculated medians using US private industry transactions. Data updated annually. Last update: August 2023.

VALUATION MULTIPLE (MEDIAN VALUE)

UNDER $1 MILLION NET SALES
MVIC/Net Sales. 0.34
MVIC/Gross Profit . . . . . . N/A
MVIC/SDE 0.56
MVIC/EBITDA . . . . N/A

$1 MILLION–$5 MILLION NET SALES
MVIC/Net Sales. 0.92
MVIC/Gross Profit 1.33
MVIC/SDE 5.81
MVIC/EBITDA . . . . N/A

MVIC/Net Sales.	1.03
MVIC/Gross Profit	3.05
MVIC/SDE	N/A
MVIC/EBITDA	N/A

Source: DealStats (formerly Pratt's Stats), 2023 (Portland, OR: Business Valuation Resources, LLC), www.bvresources.com/dealstats

BENCHMARK DATA

STATISTICS (REINSURANCE CARRIERS)

Number of Establishments	876
Average Profit Margin	13.2%
Revenue per Employee	$6,581,000
Average Number of Employees.	20.7
Average Wages per Employee	$214,857

PRODUCTS AND SERVICES SEGMENTATION

Property and casualty reinsurance	52.5%
Life and health reinsurance.	20.5%
Investment activities	19.0%
Other	8.0%

MAJOR MARKET SEGMENTATION

Direct insurers (except life, health, and medical) . . .	64.7%
Life and health insurers.	25.4%
Other	9.9%

INDUSTRY COSTS

Profit	13.2%
Wages	3.2%
Purchases	4.8%
Marketing	2.9%
Rent & Utilities	2.7%
Other	72.4%

MARKET SHARE

Berkshire Hathaway.	17.6%
Reinsurance Group Of America, Incorporated	6.9%

INDUSTRY TREND

"The industry is truly global with foreign reinsurers capturing more than half of US reinsurance demand. Demand for industry operators' services steadily increased in the early portion of the five-year period to 2023. Reinsurers' exposure to unpredictable catastrophe losses still exposes operators to extreme volatility in profitability. Increased investment income from rising interest rates and stock prices will help to offset profit-eroding effects. Reinsurers will use reserves to stabilize their bottom lines. Increased demand for industry operators' services is expected to sustain operators' profitability. Demand for underwriting in downstream markets drastically declined in 2020."

Source: IBISWorld Industry at a Glance

RESOURCES

- IBISWorld, March 2023: https://www.ibisworld.com
- ACP—Association of Claims Professionals: https://claimsprofession.org

Closet Factory (Franchise)

| NAICS 238390 | Businesses/Units 69

Rules of Thumb

- 45%–50% annual sales plus inventory

INDUSTRY MULTIPLES

Acquisition multiples below are calculated medians using US private industry transactions. Data updated annually. Last update: August 2023.

VALUATION MULTIPLE (MEDIAN VALUE)

UNDER $1 MILLION NET SALES

MVIC/Net Sales	0.43
MVIC/Gross Profit	0.94
MVIC/SDE	2.56
MVIC/EBITDA	3.54

$1 MILLION–$5 MILLION NET SALES

MVIC/Net Sales	0.55
MVIC/Gross Profit	1.10
MVIC/SDE	2.31
MVIC/EBITDA	2.72

OVER $5 MILLION NET SALES

MVIC/Net Sales	0.59
MVIC/Gross Profit	1.32
MVIC/SDE	3.62
MVIC/EBITDA	4.92

Source: DealStats (formerly Pratt's Stats), 2023 (Portland, OR: Business Valuation Resources, LLC), www.bvresources.com/dealstats

PRICING TIPS

Approx. Total Investment: $273,500 to $466,000

RESOURCES

- Closet Factory: https://www.closetfactory.com
- Franchise information: https://www.closetfactory.com/about/franchise/

Closets by Design (Franchise)

| NAICS 238390 | SIC 1521-20 | Businesses/Units 65

Rules of Thumb

- 45% annual sales plus inventory

INDUSTRY MULTIPLES

Acquisition multiples below are calculated medians using US private industry transactions. Data updated annually. Last update: August 2023.

VALUATION MULTIPLE (MEDIAN VALUE)

UNDER $1 MILLION NET SALES

MVIC/Net Sales	0.43
MVIC/Gross Profit	0.94
MVIC/SDE	2.56
MVIC/EBITDA	3.54

$1 MILLION–$5 MILLION NET SALES

MVIC/Net Sales	0.55

```
MVIC/Gross Profit  .    .    .    .    .    .    . 1.10
MVIC/SDE  .    .    .    .    .    .    .    .    . 2.31
MVIC/EBITDA  .    .    .    .    .    .    .    . 2.72
```

OVER $5 MILLION NET SALES
```
MVIC/Net Sales.    .    .    .    .    .    .    . 0.59
MVIC/Gross Profit  .    .    .    .    .    .    . 1.32
MVIC/SDE  .    .    .    .    .    .    .    .    . 3.62
MVIC/EBITDA  .    .    .    .    .    .    .    . 4.92
```

Source: DealStats (formerly Pratt's Stats), 2023 (Portland, OR: Business Valuation Resources, LLC), www.bvresources.com/dealstats

PRICING TIPS

Approx. Total Investment: $152,000 to $503,000

RESOURCES

• Closets by Design: https://www.closetsbydesign.com
• Franchise information: https://www.closetsbydesign.com/franchise/

Clothing Accessories Stores

| NAICS 458110 | Businesses/Units 78,820

| Profit $2.6 B | Wages $3.4 B | Annual Growth Future 4.0%

                                     | Annual Growth Past 2.7%

INDUSTRY MULTIPLES

Acquisition multiples below are calculated medians using US private industry transactions. Data updated annually. Last update: August 2023.

VALUATION MULTIPLE (MEDIAN VALUE)

UNDER $1 MILLION NET SALES
```
MVIC/Net Sales.    .    .    .    .    .    .    . 0.27
MVIC/Gross Profit  .    .    .    .    .    .    . 0.53
MVIC/SDE  .    .    .    .    .    .    .    .    . 1.03
MVIC/EBITDA  .    .    .    .    .    .    .    . 1.03
```

$1 MILLION–$5 MILLION NET SALES
```
MVIC/Net Sales.    .    .    .    .    .    .    . 0.66
MVIC/Gross Profit  .    .    .    .    .    .    . 1.09
MVIC/SDE  .    .    .    .    .    .    .    .    . 4.47
MVIC/EBITDA  .    .    .    .    .    .    .    . 5.69
```

OVER $5 MILLION NET SALES
```
MVIC/Net Sales.    .    .    .    .    .    .    . 4.35
MVIC/Gross Profit  .    .    .    .    .    .    . 5.17
MVIC/SDE  .    .    .    .    .    .    .    .    . N/A
MVIC/EBITDA  .    .    .    .    .    .    .    . N/A
```

Source: DealStats (formerly Pratt's Stats), 2023 (Portland, OR: Business Valuation Resources, LLC), www.bvresources.com/dealstats

BENCHMARK DATA

STATISTICS (HANDBAG, LUGGAGE & ACCESSORY STORES)
```
Number of Establishments .    .    .    . .78,820
Average Profit Margin  .    .    .    .    . 9.4%
Revenue per Employee .    .    .    . $11,000
Average Number of Employees.    .    . .2.2
Average Wages per Employee .    .    . $21,100
```

PRODUCTS AND SERVICES SEGMENTATION

Women's accessories	41.0%
Men's accessories	22.5%
Luggage and leather goods	15.7%
Costume and novelty jewelry	14.4%
Other clothing accessories	6.4%

INDUSTRY COSTS

Profit	9.4%
Wages	12.4%
Purchases	47.5%
Depreciation	1.5%
Marketing	1.9%
Rent & Utilities	7.1%
Other	20.3%

MARKET SHARE

Tapestry, Inc.	13.3%
Capri Holdings Limited	4.1%

INDUSTRY TREND

"Travel has paved the way for product innovation within the industry. Efforts to provide a service-oriented shopping experience has increased total wage costs. External competition from alternative retailers has intensified over the past five years. There is an expected surge in the number of fashion rental companies. The growing market of younger consumers is also expected to increase demand for eco-friendly faux-leather accessories. Time-strapped consumers will opt for the convenience of online shopping. Despite growth, industry revenue has been pressured by heightened levels of competition."

Source: IBISWorld Industry at a Glance

RESOURCES

- IBISWorld, April 2023: https://www.ibisworld.com

Clothing Stores, Used

| NAICS 459510 | SIC 5932-05

Rules of Thumb

- 20% annual sales plus inventory unless it is on consignment

INDUSTRY TREND

"The global secondhand apparel market is expected to grow 3x faster on average than the global apparel market overall....Online resale is expected to reach $38 billion by 2027, growing 2x faster than secondhand overall."

Source: "thredUP Resale Report 2023," https://www.thredup.com/resale/

RESOURCES

- NARTS—The Association of Resale Professionals: https://www.narts.org
- thredUP: https://www.thredup.com/resale

Coated & Laminated Paper Manufacturing

| NAICS 322220 | Businesses/Units 694

| Profit $1.2 B | Wages $3.7 B | Annual Growth Future -1.2%

| Annual Growth Past -2.5%

INDUSTRY MULTIPLES

Acquisition multiples below are calculated medians using US private industry transactions. Data updated annually. Last update: August 2023.

VALUATION MULTIPLE (MEDIAN VALUE)

UNDER $1 MILLION NET SALES	N/A
$1 MILLION–$5 MILLION NET SALES	N/A
OVER $5 MILLION NET SALES	
MVIC/Net Sales.	1.51
MVIC/Gross Profit	8.81
MVIC/SDE	N/A
MVIC/EBITDA	N/A

Source: DealStats (formerly Pratt's Stats), 2023 (Portland, OR: Business Valuation Resources, LLC), www.bvresources.com/dealstats

BENCHMARK DATA

STATISTICS (COATED & LAMINATED PAPER MANUFACTURING)

Number of Establishments .	694
Average Profit Margin	4.7%
Revenue per Employee .	$472,000
Average Number of Employees.	75.0
Average Wages per Employee .	$71,444

PRODUCTS AND SERVICES SEGMENTATION

Pressure-sensitive products	47.3%
Coated and laminated packaging paper	21.2%
Uncoated and coated paper bags and sacks	15.4%
Coated and laminated paper not for packaging	10.0%
Surface-coated paperboard	4.7%
Other	1.4%

MAJOR MARKET SEGMENTATION

Food and beverage sector .	50.7%
Financial and professional services	22.8%
Printers and media .	9.7%
Other manufacturers	8.5%
Retailers and wholesalers .	8.3%

INDUSTRY COSTS

Profit	4.7%
Wages	15.1%
Purchases	56.8%
Depreciation	2.3%
Marketing	0.1%
Rent & Utilities .	2.7%
Other	18.3%

MARKET SHARE

Domtar Corp.	6.1%
Avery Dennison Corporation	4.9%
Verso Corporation .	4.8%
Uline, Inc.	0.9%

INDUSTRY TREND

"Digital advertising has become far more lucrative for publications than print. Import penetration has ramped up in recent years. Enterprises have fallen off quicker than establishments. The continued shift from plastic to paper will uplift manufacturers. Print publications like magazines will continue to struggle with a decline in readership. The trade-weighted index will fall moving forward, making imports comparatively more expensive. The steady rise of environmental consciousness bodes well for the industry."

Source: IBISWorld Industry at a Glance

RESOURCES

- IBISWorld, January 2023: https://www.ibisworld.com

Cocktail Lounges

| NAICS 722410 | SIC 5813-03

Rules of Thumb

- 40% annual sales plus inventory
- 3–4 x monthly sales; add license (where applicable) and plus inventory
- 1.5–2 x SDE; add fixtures, equipment and inventory

INDUSTRY MULTIPLES

Acquisition multiples below are calculated medians using US private industry transactions. Data updated annually. Last update: August 2023.

VALUATION MULTIPLE (MEDIAN VALUE)

UNDER $1 MILLION NET SALES

MVIC/Net Sales.	0.37
MVIC/Gross Profit	0.63
MVIC/SDE	2.04
MVIC/EBITDA	2.59

$1 MILLION–$5 MILLION NET SALES

MVIC/Net Sales.	0.33
MVIC/Gross Profit	0.57
MVIC/SDE	2.65
MVIC/EBITDA	2.84

OVER $5 MILLION NET SALES

MVIC/Net Sales.	0.41
MVIC/Gross Profit	0.52
MVIC/SDE	0.10
MVIC/EBITDA	5.59

Source: DealStats (formerly Pratt's Stats), 2023 (Portland, OR: Business Valuation Resources, LLC), www.bvresources.com/dealstats

BENCHMARK DATA

EXPENSES (% OF ANNUAL SALES)

Cost of Goods—Food	30%–40%
Cost of Goods—Beverages	18%–22%
Occupancy	08%
Payroll/Labor	25%
Profit (pretax)	10%

Coffee Shops

NAICS 722515	SIC 5812-28	Businesses/Units 91,607
Profit $1.9 B	Wages $16.5 B	Annual Growth Future 0.9%
		Annual Growth Past 1.4%

C

Rules of Thumb

- 3.5–4 x monthly sales plus inventory
- 35%–40% annual sales plus inventory
- 2–2.2 x SDE plus inventory
- 3 x EBITDA

INDUSTRY MULTIPLES

Acquisition multiples below are calculated medians using US private industry transactions. Data updated annually. Last update: August 2023.

VALUATION MULTIPLE (MEDIAN VALUE)

UNDER $1 MILLION NET SALES	
MVIC/Net Sales	0.44
MVIC/Gross Profit	0.62
MVIC/SDE	2.20
MVIC/EBITDA	2.82
$1 MILLION–$5 MILLION NET SALES	
MVIC/Net Sales	0.41
MVIC/Gross Profit	0.69
MVIC/SDE	2.82
MVIC/EBITDA	5.94
OVER $5 MILLION NET SALES	
MVIC/Net Sales	3.89
MVIC/Gross Profit	4.87
MVIC/SDE	N/A
MVIC/EBITDA	N/A

Source: DealStats (formerly Pratt's Stats), 2023 (Portland, OR: Business Valuation Resources, LLC), www.bvresources.com/dealstats

PRICING TIPS

The exact pricing depends on multiple factors—location, size, profitability, product offering, if the company roasts coffee on premises (their own brand of roasted coffee increases value), innovation, technology, service, outside seating, inside seating capacity, etc. I view multiples more as general guidelines and the fine-tuning more as an art, which depends on the factors I listed above. As a general rule—larger businesses tend to earn higher multiples; more profitable businesses go for larger multiples; and businesses that stay on trend and whose offerings match the customers' demands earn higher multiples. It's hard to underestimate the importance of location and availability of foot traffic. Also, different types of coffee establishments would earn different multiples—coffee kiosks and carts would be valued at lower multiples, in general. Also, EBIT and EBITDA are less applicable in the case of a small owner-operator business.

1. Terms and conditions of lease

2. Days and times open

3. Number and type of employees

4. Cooking or noncooking facility

5. Franchise or nonfranchise

6. Location

STATISTICS (COFFEE AND SNACK SHOPS)

Number of Establishments 91,607	
Average Profit Margin 3.4%	
Revenue per Employee $58,500	
Average Number of Employees. . . . 10.2	
Average Wages per Employee . . . $17,817	

PRODUCTS AND SERVICES SEGMENTATION

Beverages consumed in-store 26.4%	
Beverages ordered via drive-through . . 18.8%	
Beverages taken to-go 17.5%	
Food consumed in-store 17.0%	
Food taken to-go 11.9%	
Food ordered via drive-through. . . . 6.9%	
Other 1.5%	

INDUSTRY COSTS

Profit 3.4%	
Wages 30.2%	
Purchases 41.1%	
Depreciation 3.6%	
Marketing 2.0%	
Rent & Utilities 8.0%	
Other 11.7%	

MARKET SHARE

Starbucks Corporation 38.3%	
Krispy Kreme Doughnuts Inc. 3.5%	

Rent of 15 percent is acceptable; however, a good rate would be 10 percent. Profit before tax—anything below 5 percent equals poor performance; 10 percent is good; 20 percent would be considered very good. It's very important to establish a good inventory system and a smart purchasing policy, and minimize waste. Waste can be the difference between a shop with good gross profit margins and a shop with bad gross profit margins. The gross profit margin depends on the sale mix, as a lot of coffee shops offer food or snacks as well as coffee. While a 70 percent gross profit margin would be considered very good, in reality that number is around 60 percent.

If you can keep your rent to 10 percent of gross, and labor to 20 percent of gross, you are doing quite well!

EXPENSES (% OF ANNUAL SALES)

Cost of Goods . . . . . . 28% to 35%	
Occupancy Costs . . . . . 08% to 15%	
Payroll/Labor Costs. 25%	
Profit (pretax) . . . . . . 15% to 20%	

QUESTIONS

- Why selling? Turnover of employees? Key employees? Any employee-related issues in the past? Any future employee raises or other commitments? Key lease terms? Competition? Any information on new competitors coming to the area? Competitive advantages and disadvantages? What's the hardest thing about running this business? Request thorough review of financial information for the past 3 years and the latest interim period. Who is your customer? Existing marketing practices?
- Length of time in the business? What is your role in the business?

"Low rainfall in Brazil and global supply chain disruptions resulted in surging coffee prices. Fluctuations in consumer confidence, consumer spending and the unemployment rate directly affect the industry. There has been a growing focus on the quality of beans. Most coffee shops will return with new strategies and menu options. Larger chains that endured limited growth in domestic profit will double down on international expansion. Many coffee shops need to shift part of their focus to aesthetics and function. Increases in consumer spending led to increased spending at industry locations."

Source: IBISWorld Industry at a Glance

EXPERT COMMENTS

Buyers: Do your due diligence and make it a risk-based approach. Understand the risks associated with the industry and the particular business, and address those risk in your due diligence review.

Sellers: Do your research and get a professional valuation of your business prior to putting it on the market.

I expect that industry will continue to grow at a slow pace. The production of premium coffee (specialty coffee) is the fastest growing segment of the coffee industry.

The market is undoubtedly saturated. Successful businesses in this industry will have to address several aspects:

Branding. Compelling branding and identity will be very important for future success. Experiences are becoming as important as products, which should be a part of successful branding. A successful owner should not underestimate the importance of social networks and perceptions/reputational drivers—Generation Z likes to work from coffee shops where they can see and be seen. This generation is forming its opinions, to a big extent, under the influence of social networks.

Be environmentally friendly and sustainable. Sustainability will play a significant part in the coffee market as the world begins to move past the pandemic. Coffee shop owners will have to concentrate on what is important to their customers—recyclable cups, reusable straws, coffee bag recycling, and other environmentally friendly initiatives. GlobalData's most recent consumer survey found that 43 percent of global consumers said that how ethical, environmentally friendly, or socially responsible the product or service is, always or often influences their product choice.

Multiformat. More and more specialists (especially due to Covid-19) are working remotely or becoming freelancers, which means they need a workspace. Coffee shops are often used for this purpose. Therefore, now it is not enough to make an Instagram-friendly design; there also should be excellent Wi-Fi, comfortable furniture, and a menu with snacks.

Current and adaptable product offering and product innovations. Coffee shop owners will have to follow their customers and offer products which are trending—in the nearest future, those include Snapchilled coffee, healthy coffee, nondairy milk, ready-to-drink coffee, coffee subscriptions, specialty drinks, and coffee-infused drinks. A firm grip of the latest market trends and adaptability will be the key to win new clients and keep them. At the same time, classic offerings will be the key to keep existing loyal clientele.

Know your customers and their habits. According to the National Coffee Association:

Coffee drinkers age 60+ are more than twice as likely to consume traditional, "non-gourmet" coffee than 18–24-year-olds.

Drinkers age 25–39 led the increase in espresso-based beverages, which are favored by 27.5% of Americans under 40, compared to 17% for seniors.

Nine out of 10 older coffee drinkers have coffee at breakfast, compared to 7 out of 10 of the youngest drinkers, who are almost twice as likely to drink coffee at lunchtime than their older counterparts.

Since 2015, consumption is up 40% among drinkers age 18–24, and nearly 25% for drinkers age 25–39.

For smaller coffee shops which are not part of big chains, it's important to create clientele loyalty programs, and dialogue with your customers—through reviews and feedback—about any prizes, seasonal offerings, or newsletters. The more personal it gets, the more chances that this customer will come back. Quality of service is becoming more and more important.

Up-to-date technology. It's also important to be technologically advanced—a lot of coffee shops adopted no-cash systems to speed customer service and for safety reasons. Having proper apps, cashless systems, such as Apple Pay or Samsung Pay, tap options for credit cards, prepaid cards, etc., would be a standard. I would expect this trend to continue and to add gamification through promotions, cash back, grades of memberships, and other promotions.

I can say that overall there is strong competition within the industry for new customers, premium locations, etc., but overall the industry is saturated, settled, and stable, which allows almost all of the competitors to yield good margins. I asses risk as average because a lot of risk factors are within an owner's control. Common risks include a poor location, high rent, a poor design, bad service, poor or outdated product offering, and poor marketing. Location is one of the key factors in the success of a coffee shop—significant foot traffic, busy street, and be on the right side of a busy street. All of these aspects can make or break a coffee shop. Marketability is very good for this industry. Especially with the new generation—which looks at going to a coffee shop as a cultural norm—a well-branded, well-marketed, and well-promoted business has all chances for success. Industry outlook is good; there are certain trends which a coffee shop owner would be watching for, and I described them above. There are a lot of resources available related to coffee shops, success factors, and financial aspects. It's not too hard to replicate, but the difficulty comes when there is a personal touch or idea, which is much harder to replicate than bland market standards.

FINANCING

For most businesses sold nowadays, it's typically done though SBA loans (unless the business is too big and hits an SBA threshold, but that would be not typical for coffee shops). Terms are attractive. SBA lenders do not require a mandatory seller financing any longer, eliminating the need for it. Occasionally, buyers insist on a certain portion of seller financing but mostly because they want a seller to have some skin in the game to make sure they are buying what the seller tells them they are buying.

RESOURCES

- IBISWorld, January 2023: https://www.ibisworld.com

- CRG—Coffee Roasters Guild: https://crg.coffee
- GCA—Green Coffee Association: https://greencoffeeassociation.org
- ICO—International Coffee Organization: https://www.ico.org
- NCA—National Coffee Association USA: https://www.ncausa.org
- OTA—Organic Trade Association: https://ota.com
- SCA—Specialty Coffee Association: https://sca.coffee

Coin Laundries

NAICS 812310	SIC 7215-01	Businesses/Units 19,124
Profit $1.3 B	Wages $1.1 B	Annual Growth Future -0.1%
		Annual Growth Past -1.4%

Rules of Thumb

- 1–1½ x annual sales plus inventory
- 1–1½ x annual sales plus inventory
- 3–5 x SDE includes inventory (higher multiple for newer equipment and long lease)
- 4–5 x SDE plus inventory-assumes long-term lease (10+ years) and newer equipment (3–5 years old).
- 3–6 x EBIT
- 3–6 x EBITDA

INDUSTRY MULTIPLES

Acquisition multiples below are calculated medians using US private industry transactions. Data updated annually. Last update: August 2023.

VALUATION MULTIPLE (MEDIAN VALUE)

UNDER $1 MILLION NET SALES	
MVIC/Net Sales	0.91
MVIC/Gross Profit	0.97
MVIC/SDE	2.82
MVIC/EBITDA	2.95
$1 MILLION–$5 MILLION NET SALES	
MVIC/Net Sales	1.62
MVIC/Gross Profit	1.64
MVIC/SDE	5.05
MVIC/EBITDA	5.47
OVER $5 MILLION NET SALES	N/A

Source: DealStats (formerly Pratt's Stats), 2023 (Portland, OR: Business Valuation Resources, LLC), www.bvresources.com/dealstats

PRICING TIPS

10-year lease

5-year-old equipment

Minimal competition

BENCHMARK DATA

STATISTICS (LAUNDROMATS)

Number of Establishments	19,124
Average Profit Margin	22.1%

```
Revenue per Employee .    .    .    .    . $114,000
Average Number of Employees.   .    .    . .2.8
Average Wages per Employee .    .    . $19,994
```

PRODUCTS AND SERVICES SEGMENTATION

```
Washer services     .    .    .    .    .    . 47.8%
Dryer services  .    .    .    .    .    .    . 30.3%
Other    .    .    .    .    .    .    .    . 17.5%
Self-service dry cleaning  .    .    .    .    3.1%
Commercial laundry services   .    .    .    1.3%
```

MAJOR MARKET SEGMENTATION

```
Renters using laundromats .    .    .    .    . 37.7%
Renters using on-site laundry facilities .    . 21.9%
Commercial and industrial clients  .    .    . 16.9%
Colleges and universities   .    .    .    . 14.6%
Homeowners    .    .    .    .    .    .    8.9%
```

INDUSTRY COSTS

```
Profit     .    .    .    .    .    .    .    . 22.1%
Wages    .    .    .    .    .    .    .    . 17.6%
Purchases  .    .    .    .    .    .    .    7.7%
Depreciation   .    .    .    .    .    .    9.3%
Marketing   .    .    .    .    .    .    .    1.6%
Rent & Utilities .    .    .    .    .    .    4.8%
Other    .    .    .    .    .    .    .    . 37.1%
```

MARKET SHARE

CSC ServiceWorks, Inc. 17.4%

EXPENSES (% OF ANNUAL SALES)

```
Cost of Goods  .    .    .    .    .    .    .    . .0%
Occupancy Costs  .    .    .    .    . 14% to 25%
Payroll/Labor Costs.   .    .    .    . 09% to 12%
Profit (pretax)   .    .    .    . .    25% to 35%
```

QUESTIONS

- How long will you train me? Who services the equipment?
- Who are the key employees? What are the growth opportunities? Get details on commercial accounts.
- Occupational license? Water and sewer impact (connection) fees? Organizational skills?
- Area crime rate? Review utility bills. New development or competition in trade area?
- Request copies of utility bills for at least 12 months. Request model numbers and age of washers and dryers, and ask for maintenance records. Especially request information on water heating systems, as this is probably the one single point of failure that can easily be the most costly repair item.

INDUSTRY TREND

"Laundromat sales have struggled because of increased competition. The COVID-19 pandemic hurt laundromats. Laundromats' success is dependent on proximity to consumers. Competition from substitute products and services will increase, resulting in a drop in overall sales. The average industry profit margin will decrease. Laundromats will invest in energy-efficient equipment to reduce utility costs. The industry is highly competitive, as there needs to be more differentiation between laundromats in terms of service and price."

Source: IBISWorld Industry at a Glance

EXPERT COMMENTS

Cleanliness, not price, is the deciding factor for the public to use a coin laundry!

FINANCING

Sellers should be prepared to hold a note for 10%–25% of the selling price. There are financing entities in the marketplace that would finance a coin laundry.

RESOURCES

- IBISWorld, February 2023: https://www.ibisworld.com
- American Coin-Op magazine: https://americancoinop.com
- American Laundry News: https://americanlaundrynews.com
- CLA—Coin Laundry Association: https://www.coinlaundry.org
- DLI—Drycleaning & Laundry Institute International: https://www.dlionline.org
- Entrepreneur: https://www.entrepreneur.com
- LaundroMatAdvisor: https://www.laundromatadvisor.com
- LCNi—Laundry and Cleaning News International: http://www.laundryandcleaningnews.com

---

Cold Stone Creamery (Franchise)

| NAICS 722515 | SIC 2024-98 | Businesses/Units 894 |

Rules of Thumb

- 30% annual sales plus inventory
- 1.5–2 x SDE plus inventory

INDUSTRY MULTIPLES

Acquisition multiples below are calculated medians using US private industry transactions. Data updated annually. Last update: August 2023.

VALUATION MULTIPLE (MEDIAN VALUE)

UNDER $1 MILLION NET SALES	
MVIC/Net Sales.	0.44
MVIC/Gross Profit	0.62
MVIC/SDE	2.20
MVIC/EBITDA	2.82

$1 MILLION–$5 MILLION NET SALES	
MVIC/Net Sales.	0.41
MVIC/Gross Profit	0.69
MVIC/SDE	2.82
MVIC/EBITDA	5.94

OVER $5 MILLION NET SALES	
MVIC/Net Sales.	3.89
MVIC/Gross Profit	4.87
MVIC/SDE	N/A
MVIC/EBITDA	N/A

Source: DealStats (formerly Pratt's Stats), 2023 (Portland, OR: Business Valuation Resources, LLC), www.bvresources.com/dealstats

PRICING TIPS

Approx. Total Investment: $310,375 to $580,650

BENCHMARK DATA

Food cost is low at 20 percent; rent is typically above 10 percent since it is location dependent. Leases must be at least 15 years to provide value and time for ROI long term.

EXPENSES (% OF ANNUAL SALES)

Cost of Goods	20%
Occupancy Costs	12%
Payroll/Labor Costs.	22%
Profit (pretax)	22%

QUESTIONS

- Will you finance? How is the store managed? Do you have a production staff, separate from your counter staff? Are there any wholesale or outside accounts?

RESOURCES

- Cold Stone Creamery: https://www.coldstonecreamery.com
- Franchise information: https://coldstonecreameryfranchise.com
- MTY Group: https://mtygroup.com

Collectibles Stores

| NAICS 453220 | SIC 5947-05

Rules of Thumb

- 20% annual sales plus inventory

INDUSTRY MULTIPLES

Acquisition multiples below are calculated medians using US private industry transactions. Data updated annually. Last update: August 2023.

VALUATION MULTIPLE (MEDIAN VALUE)

UNDER $1 MILLION NET SALES	
MVIC/Net Sales.	0.51
MVIC/Gross Profit	0.75
MVIC/SDE	2.28
MVIC/EBITDA	3.32
$1 MILLION–$5 MILLION NET SALES	
MVIC/Net Sales.	0.30
MVIC/Gross Profit	0.86
MVIC/SDE	2.31
MVIC/EBITDA	2.72
OVER $5 MILLION NET SALES	
MVIC/Net Sales.	0.49
MVIC/Gross Profit	1.15
MVIC/SDE	2.63
MVIC/EBITDA	5.60

Source: DealStats (formerly Pratt's Stats), 2023 (Portland, OR: Business Valuation Resources, LLC), www.bvresources.com/dealstats

BENCHMARK DATA

For Benchmark Information see Retail Stores (Small Specialty)

"Wooden furniture, colorful quilts, and early-American wares are particularly hot right now, say a mix of esteemed collectors....

"Increasing numbers of people are turning to antiques and vintage items for furniture, décor, and gift-giving, and experts know why. Namely, home items produced from mass manufacturers simply don't match the quality level of those from bygone eras—and then, of course, there's the notion of personalization."

Source: "These Are the 9 Antique Trends New—and Experienced—
Collectors Need to Know About in 2023" by Blythe Copeland, January 23, 2023,
https://www.marthastewart.com/8360440/collecting-antique-trends

Collection Agencies

NAICS 561440	SIC 7322-01	Businesses/Units 6,858
Profit $2.6 B	Wages $6.7 B	Annual Growth Future 1.4%
		Annual Growth Past 1.6%

Rules of Thumb

- 75%–125% annual revenues of $1M+
- 100% annual revenues includes inventory
- 4–6 x EBIDTA
- 2.5–3 x SDE plus inventory
- 5 x EBIT

INDUSTRY MULTIPLES

Acquisition multiples below are calculated medians using US private industry transactions. Data updated annually. Last update: August 2023.

VALUATION MULTIPLE (MEDIAN VALUE)

UNDER $1 MILLION NET SALES

MVIC/Net Sales	0.26
MVIC/Gross Profit	0.65
MVIC/SDE	2.15
MVIC/EBITDA	1.93

$1 MILLION–$5 MILLION NET SALES

MVIC/Net Sales	0.40
MVIC/Gross Profit	0.46
MVIC/SDE	4.06
MVIC/EBITDA	20.08

OVER $5 MILLION NET SALES

MVIC/Net Sales	3.18
MVIC/Gross Profit	6.80
MVIC/SDE	N/A
MVIC/EBITDA	8.87

Source: DealStats (formerly Pratt's Stats), 2023 (Portland, OR: Business Valuation Resources, LLC),
www.bvresources.com/dealstats

PRICING TIPS

Consumer debt is a higher risk exposure than business debt collections in terms of regulatory oversight.

BENCHMARK DATA

STATISTICS (DEBT COLLECTION AGENCIES)

Number of Establishments	6,858
Average Profit Margin	.13.0%
Revenue per Employee	$147,000
Average Number of Employees	20.1
Average Wages per Employee	$48,634

PRODUCTS AND SERVICES SEGMENTATION

Other contingency collections services	.64.6%
Contingency collections services by letter and email	.23.3%
Early-out receivables services	7.3%
Other	3.1%
Portfolio acquisition	1.7%

MAJOR MARKET SEGMENTATION

Healthcare	.24.7%
Other	.20.6%
Household consumers and individuals	.19.7%
Government agencies	.13.5%
Financial services	.12.8%
Retail	8.7%

INDUSTRY COSTS

Profit	.13.0%
Wages	.33.1%
Purchases	.13.5%
Depreciation	1.3%
Marketing	2.5%
Rent & Utilities	3.5%
Other	.33.1%

MARKET SHARE

Alorica, Inc.	7.1%
Encore Capital Group, Inc.	6.8%
GC Services Limited Partnership	1.5%

EXPENSES (% OF ANNUAL SALES)

Cost of Goods	10%
Occupancy Costs	05% to 10%
Payroll/Labor Costs	40% to 50%
Profit (pretax)	15% to 20%

QUESTIONS

- Understand the quality of the accounts receivable portfolio, backoff technology, history of compliance violations.
- Do you have any long-term contracts with your clients, or can they cancel at any time? Do you have any open lawsuits? Have you had any CFPB complaints filed against you? How were they resolved? Do you use an auto dialer?

INDUSTRY TREND

"High interest rates will increase the potential for delinquency. Borrowing related to financing mortgages on homes drove a significant share of aggregate debt during COVID. The CFPB ensures debt collectors provide required disclosures to consumers. Steady increases in household debt will improve the debt collection recovery rate. Regulation will bring higher compliance costs. State-of-the-art automated accounts receivables platforms increase competition. Changes in the recurring debt pool create revenue volatility."

Source: IBISWorld Industry at a Glance

EXPERT COMMENTS

When selling, be sure you have well-documented standard operating procedures and an up-to-date collection management software system. Also, a track record of few lawsuits and consumer complaints is a big plus.

The regulatory and compliance risk is great. There are numerous regulatory bodies that have jurisdiction, and often their rules conflict. One minor violation by an employee can result in a $5,000+ fine. Operational excellence, technology, and a focus on compliance are central to success. Hiring and keeping good employees can be a challenge, as often it is not pleasant to ask for money and listen to the hardship stories.

FINANCING

Seller financing is not very common in this industry.

RESOURCES

- IBISWorld, January 2023: https://www.ibisworld.com
- ACA International: https://www.acainternational.org/default
- iA—insideARM: https://www.insidearm.com
- IACC—International Association of Commercial Collectors, Inc.: https://www.commercialcollector.com
- Receivables Advisor: https://collectionadvisor.com

Comfort Keepers (Franchise)

| NAICS 621610 | Businesses/Units 553

Rules of Thumb

- 37% annual sales
- 2.3 x SDE

INDUSTRY MULTIPLES

Acquisition multiples below are calculated medians using US private industry transactions. Data updated annually. Last update: August 2023.

VALUATION MULTIPLE (MEDIAN VALUE)

UNDER $1 MILLION NET SALES	
MVIC/Net Sales.	0.40
MVIC/Gross Profit	0.69
MVIC/SDE	2.53
MVIC/EBITDA	4.62
$1 MILLION–$5 MILLION NET SALES	
MVIC/Net Sales.	0.52
MVIC/Gross Profit	0.80
MVIC/SDE	2.99
MVIC/EBITDA	4.81
OVER $5 MILLION NET SALES	
MVIC/Net Sales.	1.09
MVIC/Gross Profit	2.37
MVIC/SDE	5.31
MVIC/EBITDA	9.36

Source: DealStats (formerly Pratt's Stats), 2023 (Portland, OR: Business Valuation Resources, LLC), www.bvresources.com/dealstats

PRICING TIPS

Approx. Total Investment: $91,161 to $144,964

RESOURCES

- Comfort Keepers: https://www.comfortkeepers.com
- Franchise information: https://www.comfortkeepersfranchise.com

Comic Book Stores

| NAICS 459210 | SIC 5942-05

Rules of Thumb

- 12%–15% annual sales plus inventory

INDUSTRY TREND

"*PW*'s annual comics retailer survey offers an anecdotal look into the comics retail landscape....While nearly every bookseller *PW* spoke with is upbeat about the market, some comics shops dealt with a slight downturn on the single-issue comic side in 2022, with the broader graphic novel channel offsetting that dip. Sales there were driven by manga and adult graphic novels."

Source: "Comics Retailers Navigate a New Normal" by David Harper, March 3, 2023, https://www.publishersweekly.com/pw/by-topic/industry-news/comics/article/91678-comics-retailers-navigate-a-new-normal.html

Commercial Air, Rail, and Water Transportation Equipment Rental and Leasing

| NAICS 532411 | Businesses/Units 5,928

| Profit $13.5 B | Wages $7.5 B | Annual Growth Future 0.5%

| | | Annual Growth Past 1.3%

INDUSTRY MULTIPLES

Acquisition multiples below are calculated medians using US private industry transactions. Data updated annually. Last update: August 2023.

VALUATION MULTIPLE (MEDIAN VALUE)

UNDER $1 MILLION NET SALES	N/A
$1 MILLION–$5 MILLION NET SALES	
MVIC/Net Sales	1.86
MVIC/Gross Profit	3.72
MVIC/SDE	17.76
MVIC/EBITDA	29.51
OVER $5 MILLION NET SALES	N/A

Source: DealStats (formerly Pratt's Stats), 2023 (Portland, OR: Business Valuation Resources, LLC), www.bvresources.com/dealstats

BENCHMARK DATA

STATISTICS (HEAVY EQUIPMENT RENTAL)

Number of Establishments	5,928
Average Profit Margin	25.7%

Revenue per Employee $657,000
Average Number of Employees. 13.6
Average Wages per Employee $93,990

PRODUCTS AND SERVICES SEGMENTATION

Construction, mining and forestry equipment 52.2%
Air transportation equipment 22.5%
Commercial and industrial equipment 13.9%
Rail transportation equipment 10.5%
Water transportation equipment 0.9%

MAJOR MARKET SEGMENTATION

Construction, industrial, mining, and forestry operations . 66.1%
Transportation operations 33.9%

INDUSTRY COSTS

Profit 25.7%
Wages 14.2%
Purchases 4.2%
Depreciation 23.8%
Marketing 0.9%
Rent & Utilities 5.1%
Other 26.0%

MARKET SHARE

United Rentals 14.4%
Sunbelt Rentals Exchange 12.4%
GE Capital Aviation Services 4.5%
Wells Fargo Rail 1.8%
Ahern Rentals 1.5%
McGrath RentCorp 1.1%
Herc Holdings 0.9%
Holt Texas 0.7%
Ashtead 0.6%
Cashman Equipment Co 0.5%

INDUSTRY TREND

"Due to the coronavirus pandemic, beneficial trends receded in 2020. Airlines have expanded their fleet sizes to meet rising demand and leased more aircraft as a result. With new project investments helping downstream industries, industry participation has recovered from previous lows during 2020. Industry profit will likely rise due to operators being able to charge higher rental rates. Demand for rented or leased mining equipment is expected to increase. Supply chain challenges are expected to continue disrupting industry operations. Rising demand from downstream markets has supported industry revenue growth."

Source: IBISWorld Industry at a Glance

RESOURCES

• IBISWorld, January 2023: https://www.ibisworld.com

Computer Consulting

NAICS 541512	SIC 7379-05	Businesses/Units 487,647
Profit $42.6 B	Wages $285.2 B	Annual Growth Future 2.2%
		Annual Growth Past 2.0%

Rules of Thumb

- 50%–65% annual sales plus inventory

INDUSTRY MULTIPLES

Acquisition multiples below are calculated medians using US private industry transactions. Data updated annually. Last update: August 2023.

VALUATION MULTIPLE (MEDIAN VALUE)

UNDER $1 MILLION NET SALES

MVIC/Net Sales	0.70
MVIC/Gross Profit	1.04
MVIC/SDE	2.17
MVIC/EBITDA	6.46

$1 MILLION–$5 MILLION NET SALES

MVIC/Net Sales	0.70
MVIC/Gross Profit	1.00
MVIC/SDE	3.39
MVIC/EBITDA	4.58

OVER $5 MILLION NET SALES

MVIC/Net Sales	1.21
MVIC/Gross Profit	3.31
MVIC/SDE	5.86
MVIC/EBITDA	16.58

Source: DealStats (formerly Pratt's Stats), 2023 (Portland, OR: Business Valuation Resources, LLC), www.bvresources.com/dealstats

PRICING TIPS

Many consulting businesses are one-man operations or are headed by someone who has the contacts and may basically be the business. This person may be the goodwill, and without his or her presence the business may not be worth much. If this person stays while the business is slowly being transferred and an earnout is in place, the value may still be there.

BENCHMARK DATA

STATISTICS (IT CONSULTING)

Number of Establishments	487,647
Average Profit Margin	6.4%
Revenue per Employee	$265,000
Average Number of Employees	5.3
Average Wages per Employee	$113,125

PRODUCTS AND SERVICES SEGMENTATION

Other services	31.6%
Custom services	27.1%
Technical consulting	12.3%
Computer systems development	11.0%
Technical support	9.2%
IT infrastructure	8.8%

MAJOR MARKET SEGMENTATION

Manufacturing and retail companies	22.0%
Financial services companies	21.4%
Public sector and nonprofit organizations	18.8%
Communications, media and technology companies	14.7%
Healthcare companies	13.0%
Other sectors	10.1%

INDUSTRY COSTS

Profit	6.4%
Wages	42.8%
Purchases	7.1%
Depreciation	0.7%
Marketing	1.3%
Rent & Utilities	2.6%
Other	39.0%

INDUSTRY TREND

"The industry has experienced an uptick in demand. Cloud computing trends have benefited industry operators. The current five-year period has been characterized by extensive M&A activity. Demand for industry services will likely remain high. Large operators are expected to continue acquiring smaller businesses. New companies are expected to continue entering the industry at a steady pace. Shifting technology trends have boosted demand for new services."

Source: IBISWorld Industry at a Glance

RESOURCES

- IBISWorld, January 2023: https://www.ibisworld.com
- TechServe Alliance: https://www.techservealliance.org

Computer Services

| NAICS 811212	| SIC 7378-01	| Businesses/Units 46,932
| Profit $1.1 B	| Wages $7.2 B	| Annual Growth Future -2.3%
		| Annual Growth Past -1.7%

Rules of Thumb

- 55% annual sales, plus fixtures, equipment and inventory

INDUSTRY MULTIPLES

Acquisition multiples below are calculated medians using US private industry transactions. Data updated annually. Last update: August 2023.

VALUATION MULTIPLE (MEDIAN VALUE)

UNDER $1 MILLION NET SALES

MVIC/Net Sales	0.57
MVIC/Gross Profit	0.73
MVIC/SDE	1.89
MVIC/EBITDA	1.88

$1 MILLION–$5 MILLION NET SALES

MVIC/Net Sales	0.84
MVIC/Gross Profit	1.13
MVIC/SDE	2.79
MVIC/EBITDA	30.59

OVER $5 MILLION NET SALES

MVIC/Net Sales	0.73
MVIC/Gross Profit	N/A
MVIC/SDE	4.25
MVIC/EBITDA	N/A

Source: DealStats (formerly Pratt's Stats), 2023 (Portland, OR: Business Valuation Resources, LLC), www.bvresources.com/dealstats

BENCHMARK DATA

STATISTICS (ELECTRONIC & COMPUTER REPAIR SERVICES)

Number of Establishments .	46,932
Average Profit Margin .	. 5.6%
Revenue per Employee .	. $140,000
Average Number of Employees.	. 2.9
Average Wages per Employee .	. $51,582

PRODUCTS AND SERVICES SEGMENTATION

Other electronic equipment (including medical equipment) repairs .	47.1%
Computer and office machine repairs .	26.4%
Communications equipment repairs .	17.7%
Consumer electronics (including radio, TV and VCR) repairs .	. 8.8%

MAJOR MARKET SEGMENTATION

Businesses and not-for-profit organizations .	55.5%
Households .	29.4%
Federal, state, and local governments .	. 9.3%
Other .	. 5.8%

INDUSTRY COSTS

Profit .	. 5.6%
Wages .	36.6%
Purchases .	. 8.4%
Depreciation .	. 1.3%
Marketing .	. 1.7%
Rent & Utilities .	. 5.2%
Other .	41.3%

INDUSTRY TREND

"Widespread vaccine distribution, business reopenings and return-to-office measures has increased demand. Qualified technicians are now required for most repairs. Declining industry establishment figures suggests consolidation among players. Declining prices may lead to a higher rate of product replacement. New product introductions and consumer demand for the latest models will constrain growth in the long term. The number of electrical and electronic installers and repairers is forecast to contract. Recent price hikes and long lead times for installation is likely to increase industry demand."

Source: IBISWorld Industry at a Glance

RESOURCES

• IBISWorld, June 2022: https://ibisworld.com

Computer Stores

	NAICS 443120		SIC 5734-07		Businesses/Units 16,822
	Profit $2.2 B		Wages $4.9 B		Annual Growth Future 0.6%
					Annual Growth Past 0.2%

Rules of Thumb

• 30% annual sales plus inventory

STATISTICS (COMPUTER STORES)

Number of Establishments	16,822
Average Profit Margin	5.5%
Revenue per Employee	$361,000
Average Number of Employees. . . .	6.6
Average Wages per Employee . . .	$44,286

PRODUCTS AND SERVICES SEGMENTATION

Computers and related equipment . . .	65.1%
TV and other electronics	29.1%
Software	4.0%
Repair services	1.8%

INDUSTRY COSTS

Profit	5.5%
Wages	12.4%
Purchases	62.5%
Depreciation	0.5%
Marketing	1.4%
Rent & Utilities	3.1%
Other	14.6%

INDUSTRY TREND

"The industry is subject to a strong level of external competition from other industries that sell computers. E-commerce has enabled more consumers to purchase computers directly from manufacturers. The industry has become an increasingly marginal component of the US economy. The cost savings associated with investments in automation will drive demand from business users. The entire retail sector is likely to shift toward an online economy at the expense of brick-and-mortar establishments. As revenue continues to decrease, industry operators are expected to reduce their employment numbers to minimize costs. The number of industry enterprises has declined as e-commerce sales have drawn revenue away."

Source: IBISWorld Industry at a Glance

RESOURCES

• IBISWorld, April 2023: https://www.ibisworld.com

Computer Systems Design

| NAICS 541512 | SIC 7373-98

Rules of Thumb

• 50% annual sales plus inventory
• 2–4 x SDE plus inventory
• 3–6 x EBIT
• 3–7 x EBITDA

INDUSTRY MULTIPLES

Acquisition multiples below are calculated medians using US private industry transactions. Data updated annually. Last update: August 2023.

VALUATION MULTIPLE (MEDIAN VALUE)

UNDER $1 MILLION NET SALES

MVIC/Net Sales	0.70
MVIC/Gross Profit	1.04
MVIC/SDE	2.17
MVIC/EBITDA	6.46

$1 MILLION–$5 MILLION NET SALES

MVIC/Net Sales	0.70
MVIC/Gross Profit	1.00
MVIC/SDE	3.39
MVIC/EBITDA	4.58

OVER $5 MILLION NET SALES

MVIC/Net Sales	1.21
MVIC/Gross Profit	3.31
MVIC/SDE	5.86
MVIC/EBITDA	16.58

Source: DealStats (formerly Pratt's Stats), 2023 (Portland, OR: Business Valuation Resources, LLC), www.bvresources.com/dealstats

PRICING TIPS

Very workforce intensive. Make sure the business can prosper without the owner. Contracts are important.

System design firms are often classified as programming firms. More work is being done by temporary employment firms, renting IT professional staff.

Highly variable valuations. Biggest component of valuation is the management structure. Midmarket companies with excellent management structure can get very good multiples but a small operation which is highly owner driven may get very little. Having contracts with large customers can improve valuation significantly.

BENCHMARK DATA

$100,000 or more in revenues per technician and $200,000 or more per engineer

Revenue and profit growth are more important than stability of earnings. Sales per employee is a key metric.

EXPENSES (% OF ANNUAL SALES)

Cost of Goods	20%
Occupancy Costs	05%
Payroll/Labor Costs	50% to 55%
Profit (pretax)	20%

QUESTIONS

• Reasons for the exit? Strategic growth plans? Customer retention plans? Employee-specific compensation issues?
• Who is (are) the key employee(s) who drive(s) the sales? Are there any critical technical roles?

INDUSTRY TREND

Continuing growth as technology and tools become indispensable for businesses and individuals.

EXPERT COMMENTS

Talented people can easily leave and start their own gig. Contracts with a very wide customer base can be very important. Corporate clients are more valuable than consumer clients.

Design firms are being acquired by the large consulting houses. May be attractive for strategic reasons, such as industry niches and/or package familiarity.

Highly knowledge driven industry. Risk can be very high depending on the importance of the role played by the current owner. If the owner's role is noncritical, then the business can be very lucrative.

Computer Terminal and Other Computer Peripheral Equipment Manufacturing

| NAICS 334118 | Businesses/Units 528

| Profit $613.6 M | Wages $2.2 B | Annual Growth Future 1.7%

| Annual Growth Past 0.7%

INDUSTRY MULTIPLES

Acquisition multiples below are calculated medians using US private industry transactions. Data updated annually. Last update: August 2023.

VALUATION MULTIPLE (MEDIAN VALUE)

UNDER $1 MILLION NET SALES	N/A
$1 MILLION–$5 MILLION NET SALES	
MVIC/Net Sales	0.24
MVIC/Gross Profit	0.71
MVIC/SDE	2.71
MVIC/EBITDA	3.09
OVER $5 MILLION NET SALES	
MVIC/Net Sales	1.83
MVIC/Gross Profit	4.23
MVIC/SDE	N/A
MVIC/EBITDA	26.36

Source: DealStats (formerly Pratt's Stats), 2023 (Portland, OR: Business Valuation Resources, LLC), www.bvresources.com/dealstats

BENCHMARK DATA

STATISTICS (COMPUTER PERIPHERAL MANUFACTURING IN THE US)

Number of Establishments	528
Average Profit Margin	4.3%
Revenue per Employee	$636,000
Average Number of Employees	43.8
Average Wages per Employee	$97,195

PRODUCTS AND SERVICES SEGMENTATION

Computer storage devices	40.9%
Computer peripheral equipment	25.8%
Parts, subassemblies, accessories for computer peripheral equipment	13.9%
Parts and attachments for computer storage devices	9.7%
Computer terminals	4.2%
Other	3.9%
Parts and attachments for computer terminals	1.0%
Parts and attachments for POS terminals	0.6%

MAJOR MARKET SEGMENTATION

Original equipment manufacturers	75.0%
Distributors	14.0%
Retailers	11.0%

INDUSTRY COSTS

Profit	4.3%
Wages	15.5%
Purchases	40.8%
Depreciation	1.3%
Marketing	0.1%
Rent & Utilities	1.0%
Other	37.0%

MARKET SHARE

HP Inc.	21.6%
Gigabyte Technology Co. Ltd.	4.8%
Dell Technologies Inc.	3.1%

INDUSTRY TREND

"The industry's performance is partially tied to the performance of the Computer Manufacturing industry. The price of computers and related equipment has fallen steadily over time. Mergers and acquisitions increased industry consolidation by creating larger, more integrated companies to compete with other companies. The number of enterprises will drop. Technological advancements in computer peripherals will likely continue. Industry wages are estimated to increase. Manufacturers have improved their core products and reduced prices in response to tighter competition."

Source: IBISWorld Industry at a Glance

RESOURCES

• IBISWorld, January 2023: https://www.ibisworld.com

Confectionery Merchant Wholesalers

| NAICS 424450 | Businesses/Units 4,007 |

| Profit $2.4 B | Wages $3.3 B | Annual Growth Future 0.5% |

| | | Annual Growth Past 2.0% |

INDUSTRY MULTIPLES

Acquisition multiples below are calculated medians using US private industry transactions. Data updated annually. Last update: August 2023.

VALUATION MULTIPLE (MEDIAN VALUE)

UNDER $1 MILLION NET SALES

MVIC/Net Sales	0.47
MVIC/Gross Profit	1.53
MVIC/SDE	2.56
MVIC/EBITDA	5.06

$1 MILLION–$5 MILLION NET SALES

MVIC/Net Sales	0.22
MVIC/Gross Profit	1.24
MVIC/SDE	2.61
MVIC/EBITDA	2.74

OVER $5 MILLION NET SALES

MVIC/Net Sales	0.16
MVIC/Gross Profit	1.77
MVIC/SDE	4.96
MVIC/EBITDA	7.17

Source: DealStats (formerly Pratt's Stats), 2023 (Portland, OR: Business Valuation Resources, LLC), www.bvresources.com/dealstats

BENCHMARK DATA

C

STATISTICS (CONFECTIONERY WHOLESALING)

Number of Establishments	4,007
Average Profit Margin	3.5%
Revenue per Employee	$1,524,000
Average Number of Employees	11.4
Average Wages per Employee	$72,382

PRODUCTS AND SERVICES SEGMENTATION

Other	46.7%
Chocolate	30.5%
Nonchocolate candy	18.3%
Gum and mints	4.5%

MAJOR MARKET SEGMENTATION

Other wholesalers	39.8%
Other	18.8%
Grocery stores and mass merchandisers	18.2%
Convenience stores	16.3%
Drug stores	6.9%

INDUSTRY COSTS

Profit	3.5%
Wages	4.8%
Purchases	81.8%
Depreciation	0.8%
Marketing	0.2%
Rent & Utilities	0.8%
Other	8.1%

MARKET SHARE

Frito-Lay North America, Inc.	18.6%
Performance Food Group Co	18.4%
Mars Inc.	15.1%
Hershey Co.	13.1%
McLane Company Inc.	9.6%
Mondelez International, Inc.	5.5%
Core-Mark Holding Company, Inc.	1.6%

INDUSTRY TREND

"Rising health consciousness has constrained demand for candy bars and other key products. Ongoing supply chain disruptions have led to higher transportation costs. Smaller confectionary wholesalers have experienced heightened competition from manufacturers. Premium confectioneries will become an even more powerful segment. Rising sugar prices and continued supply chain issues will likely limit average industry profit margins. Customers will avoid wholesalers as the percentage of business conducted online grows. Diversification in candy and snack products shielded the industry from substantial declines."

Source: IBISWorld Industry at a Glance

RESOURCES

• IBISWorld, February 2023: https://www.ibisworld.com

Concrete Contractors

| NAICS 238110 | Businesses/Units 83,127

| Profit $5.4 B | Wages $19.5 B | Annual Growth Future 0.8%

| Annual Growth Past 0.6%

INDUSTRY MULTIPLES

Acquisition multiples below are calculated medians using US private industry transactions. Data updated annually. Last update: August 2023.

VALUATION MULTIPLE (MEDIAN VALUE)

UNDER $1 MILLION NET SALES
MVIC/Net Sales.	0.51
MVIC/Gross Profit	1.51
MVIC/SDE	2.18
MVIC/EBITDA	1.94

$1 MILLION–$5 MILLION NET SALES
MVIC/Net Sales.	0.43
MVIC/Gross Profit	1.70
MVIC/SDE	2.53
MVIC/EBITDA	5.76

OVER $5 MILLION NET SALES
MVIC/Net Sales.	0.45
MVIC/Gross Profit	1.54
MVIC/SDE	3.83
MVIC/EBITDA	4.80

Source: DealStats (formerly Pratt's Stats), 2023 (Portland, OR: Business Valuation Resources, LLC), www.bvresources.com/dealstats

BENCHMARK DATA

STATISTICS (CONCRETE CONTRACTORS)

Number of Establishments .	83,127
Average Profit Margin	7.1%
Revenue per Employee .	$238,000
Average Number of Employees.	3.9
Average Wages per Employee .	$60,721

PRODUCTS AND SERVICES SEGMENTATION

New nonresidential construction	45.8%
New residential construction	34.3%
Additions, alterations, and reconstruction .	14.7%
Other services	5.2%

MAJOR MARKET SEGMENTATION

Residential building construction	38.1%
Commercial building construction .	34.2%
Municipal building construction	8.2%
Other nonresidential building construction	7.8%
Nonbuilding construction	6.1%
Industrial building construction	5.6%

INDUSTRY COSTS

Profit	7.1%
Wages	25.5%
Purchases	45.8%
Depreciation	2.2%
Marketing	0.2%
Rent & Utilities .	4.5%
Other	14.8%

"Accelerated construction activity has enabled heightened demand for industry contractors. The nature of work done by contractors enabled the industry to avoid the worst of the COVID-19 pandemic. Public spending flexibility has dwindled due to tighter state budgets. Growth in downstream commercial construction markets will benefit industry contractors. Rising interest rates will slow demand for new residential construction. Infusion of funding from the federal government will alleviate tight fiscal budgets for states to the benefit of contractors. Concrete contracting's outdoor work setting and high demand from a spike in housing projects in 2020 boosted revenue."

Source: IBISWorld Industry at a Glance

RESOURCES

- IBISWorld, January 2023: https://www.ibisworld.com

Consignment Shops

| NAICS 453310 | SIC 5932-04

Rules of Thumb

- 15%–20% annual sales

INDUSTRY MULTIPLES

Acquisition multiples below are calculated medians using US private industry transactions. Data updated annually. Last update: August 2023.

VALUATION MULTIPLE (MEDIAN VALUE)

UNDER $1 MILLION NET SALES

MVIC/Net Sales	0.36
MVIC/Gross Profit	0.61
MVIC/SDE	1.83
MVIC/EBITDA	3.20

$1 MILLION–$5 MILLION NET SALES

MVIC/Net Sales	0.47
MVIC/Gross Profit	0.75
MVIC/SDE	2.74
MVIC/EBITDA	4.10

OVER $5 MILLION NET SALES

MVIC/Net Sales	0.36
MVIC/Gross Profit	2.50
MVIC/SDE	N/A
MVIC/EBITDA	9.10

Source: DealStats (formerly Pratt's Stats), 2023 (Portland, OR: Business Valuation Resources, LLC), www.bvresources.com/dealstats

BENCHMARK DATA

For additional Benchmark data see Used Goods

INDUSTRY TREND

"Resale is expected to grow 9x faster than the broader retail clothing sector by 2027."

Source: "thredUP Resale Report 2023," https://www.thredup.com/resale/

- IBISWorld, May 2022: https://www.ibisworld.com
- NARTS—The Association of Resale Professionals: https://www.narts.org

Construction and Mining (except Oil Well) Machinery and Equipment Merchant Wholesalers

| NAICS 423810 | Businesses/Units 4,841

| Profit $6.5 B | Wages $9.4 B | Annual Growth Future 1.0%

| Annual Growth Past 1.4%

INDUSTRY MULTIPLES

Acquisition multiples below are calculated medians using US private industry transactions. Data updated annually. Last update: August 2023.

VALUATION MULTIPLE (MEDIAN VALUE)

UNDER $1 MILLION NET SALES	N/A
$1 MILLION–$5 MILLION NET SALES	N/A
OVER $5 MILLION NET SALES	
MVIC/Net Sales	0.70
MVIC/Gross Profit	2.11
MVIC/SDE	4.75
MVIC/EBITDA	5.79

Source: DealStats (formerly Pratt's Stats), 2023 (Portland, OR: Business Valuation Resources, LLC), www.bvresources.com/dealstats

BENCHMARK DATA

STATISTICS (CONSTRUCTION & MINING EQUIPMENT WHOLESALING)

Number of Establishments	4,841
Average Profit Margin	5.0%
Revenue per Employee	$1,182,000
Average Number of Employees	21.9
Average Wages per Employee	$89,382

PRODUCTS AND SERVICES SEGMENTATION

Other new equipment	33.1%
Parts and supplies	31.0%
New construction and mining equipment	24.2%
Used construction and mining equipment	11.7%

MAJOR MARKET SEGMENTATION

Construction projects	33.1%
Mining operations	29.2%
Businesses for use in own operations, not for re-sale or production	11.8%
Other wholesalers	10.1%
Retailers	5.9%
Miscellaneous other markets	5.1%
Federal, state, and local governments	3.4%
Farms	1.4%

INDUSTRY COSTS

Profit	5.0%
Wages	7.5%
Purchases	68.3%
Depreciation	1.5%
Marketing	0.3%

Rent & Utilities 1.1%
Other 16.2%

MARKET SHARE

Komatsu. 3.6%
Volvo 1.2%
Liebherr. 0.7%
Vermeer. 0.3%
Tigercat Industries 0.1%

INDUSTRY TREND

"Mining activity has grown substantially over the past five years. Large wholesalers often control the price of products. The Construction sector is a major source of revenue for this industry. Demand from mining is projected to decline. The value of utilities construction is projected to rise. Part of the incline in revenue will be consumed by increasing employment. Growing demand for the construction and mining industries directly increases the demand for industry products."

Source: IBISWorld Industry at a Glance

RESOURCES

• IBISWorld, January 2023: https://www.ibisworld.com

Construction: Buildings

| NAICS 236

| Profit $7.4 B | Wages $16.9 B | Annual Growth Future 0.1%
| | | Annual Growth Past 1.5%

Rules of Thumb

• 20%–30% annual sales plus inventory
• 1–2 x SDE plus inventory
• 1–3 x EBITDA
• 3 x EBIT

INDUSTRY MULTIPLES

Acquisition multiples below are calculated medians using US private industry transactions. Data updated annually. Last update: August 2023.

VALUATION MULTIPLE (MEDIAN VALUE)

UNDER $1 MILLION NET SALES
MVIC/Net Sales. 0.38
MVIC/Gross Profit 0.68
MVIC/SDE 1.65
MVIC/EBITDA 2.08

$1 MILLION–$5 MILLION NET SALES
MVIC/Net Sales. 0.37
MVIC/Gross Profit 0.96
MVIC/SDE 2.54
MVIC/EBITDA 2.86

OVER $5 MILLION NET SALES
MVIC/Net Sales. 0.40
MVIC/Gross Profit 2.10
MVIC/SDE 2.65
MVIC/EBITDA 4.89

Source: DealStats (formerly Pratt's Stats), 2023 (Portland, OR: Business Valuation Resources, LLC), www.bvresources.com/dealstats

BENCHMARK DATA

STATISTICS (HOME BUILDERS)

Number of Establishments	385,547
Average Profit Margin	6.0%
Revenue per Employee	$198,000
Average Number of Employees	1.7
Average Wages per Employee	$26,990

PRODUCTS AND SERVICES SEGMENTATION

Stucco exterior homes	26.7%
Vinyl siding exterior homes	26.1%
Fiber cement exterior homes	22.2%
Brick exterior homes	18.7%
Wood exterior homes	4.3%
Other exterior homes	2.0%

MAJOR MARKET SEGMENTATION

Property developers for private sector clients	84.4%
Households	14.0%
State or locally funded projects	1.1%
Federally funded projects	0.5%

INDUSTRY COSTS

Profit	6.0%
Wages	13.6%
Purchases	70.5%
Depreciation	0.5%
Marketing	0.5%
Rent & Utilities	3.2%
Other	5.8%

MARKET SHARE

NVR, Inc.	7.5%

EXPENSES (% OF ANNUAL SALES)

Cost of Goods	20% to 30%
Occupancy Costs	05% to 10%
Payroll/Labor Costs	25%
Profit (pretax)	25% to 45%

QUESTIONS

- The buyer should understand the licensing requirements and require the seller to keep their license active during the transition period. Ask about employers, suppliers, and contracts that are still in progress. How will the funds be allocated for those projects that are currently active?

INDUSTRY TREND

"According to McKinsey, construction is the largest industry in the world....Read on to learn about some of the most important trends in the construction industry.

"1. The virtual construction market sees rapid growth....It's estimated that reworks of faulty or incorrect builds account for nearly 30% of construction industry costs. Virtual design helps cut down on this by allowing builders to first build structures in a virtual environment....

2. Prefabrication and modular construction change how structures are built.

3. Smart cities change the way construction companies operate.

4. Green building helps tackle environmental issues.

5. Living building materials go mainstream.

6. The construction industry benefits heavily from drone technology....Using drones to measure stockpiles of building materials in real time has resulted in a 61% increase in measurement accuracy....As a result of drone technology, the construction industry has seen a 55% increase in safety standards....

7. Tech solutions improve safety.

8. Construction firms face major labor shortage.

9. Material costs soar as shortages remain.

10. 3D printing use increases.

11. Construction robotics and automation enhance productivity."

Source: "11 Construction Industry Trends to Watch (2022–2025)" by Josh Howarth, August 17, 2022, https://explodingtopics.com/blog/construction-industry-trends

"Homebuilders received a large chunk of the Paycheck Protection Program. Interest rates increased toward the end of the period to fight off inflationary concerns. Many cities have affordable housing programs. Housing starts are set to dip. Increasing tuition costs will only discourage students from purchasing homes. More affordable housing projects will provide a source of relief for homebuilders. Home builders also cut expenses and raised profit by hiring subcontractors."

Source: IBISWorld Industry at a Glance

EXPERT COMMENTS

Research the industry well prior to evaluating a business. Avoid companies that rely on large customers or any one particular segment. Analyze the financials carefully.

FINANCING

Typically, we are seeing 20 percent seller financing along with an SBA loan.

RESOURCES

- IBISWorld, January 2023: https://www.ibisworld.com
- ABC—Associated Builders and Contractors: https://www.abc.org
- AGC—Associated General Contractors of America: https://www.agc.org
- CFMA—Construction Financial Management Association: https://www.cfma.org

Construction: Excavation (Site Preparation)

| NAICS 238910 | Businesses/Units 50,209

| Profit $5.8 B | Wages $25.5 B | Annual Growth Future 1.0%

Rules of Thumb

- 25% annual sales plus inventory
- 2.2 x SDE plus inventory
- 1.8 x EBIT
- 2 x EBITDA

INDUSTRY MULTIPLES

Acquisition multiples below are calculated medians using US private industry transactions. Data updated annually. Last update: August 2023.

VALUATION MULTIPLE (MEDIAN VALUE)

UNDER $1 MILLION NET SALES

MVIC/Net Sales	0.77
MVIC/Gross Profit	0.90
MVIC/SDE	2.17
MVIC/EBITDA	2.80

$1 MILLION–$5 MILLION NET SALES

MVIC/Net Sales	0.73
MVIC/Gross Profit	1.25
MVIC/SDE	3.48
MVIC/EBITDA	4.38

OVER $5 MILLION NET SALES

MVIC/Net Sales	0.60
MVIC/Gross Profit	1.82
MVIC/SDE	2.59
MVIC/EBITDA	3.09

Source: DealStats (formerly Pratt's Stats), 2023 (Portland, OR: Business Valuation Resources, LLC), www.bvresources.com/dealstats

PRICING TIPS

Adjust for age/condition of equipment.

BENCHMARK DATA

STATISTICS (EXCAVATION CONTRACTORS)

Number of Establishments	50,209
Average Profit Margin	7.2%
Revenue per Employee	$255,000
Average Number of Employees	6.4
Average Wages per Employee	$81,218

PRODUCTS AND SERVICES SEGMENTATION

Excavation work for residential buildings	37.9%
Excavation work for nonresidential buildings	28.8%
Foundation Digging	16.0%
Trenching	11.2%
Nonbuilding construction excavation	6.1%

MAJOR MARKET SEGMENTATION

Residential building market	37.5%
Nonbuilding construction market	34.0%
Nonresidential building market	28.5%

INDUSTRY COSTS

Profit	7.2%
Wages	31.6%
Purchases	33.5%
Depreciation	4.1%
Marketing	0.2%
Rent & Utilities	8.6%
Other	14.8%

EXPENSES (% OF ANNUAL SALES)

Cost of Goods	25%
Occupancy Costs	10%
Payroll/Labor Costs	40%
Profit (pretax)	25%

QUESTIONS

- Customer lists, future contracts, condition of equipment, and any lawsuits?

"Revenue will slow down in 2022 as the value of residential construction declines. Government support has benefited industry operators. Industry participation and employment growth have remained steady. Demand for excavation work is projected to accelerate slightly in the nonresidential building market. Rising government funding trend is expected to spur an increase in demand for excavation. Industry operators are expected to increase hiring to expand their capacity. The industry has been fueled by a strong residential housing market."

Source: IBISWorld Industry at a Glance

RESOURCES

• IBISWorld, January 2023: https://www.ibisworld.com

Construction: In General

| NAICS 23 | | Businesses/Units 3,883,347 |

| Profit $90.1 B | | Wages $575.8 B | | Annual Growth Future 0.7% |

| | | | | Annual Growth Past -1.3% |

Rules of Thumb

• 30%–50% annual sales plus inventory
• 3–4 x SDE plus inventory
• 2–3.5 x EBIT
• 2–4 x EBITDA

INDUSTRY MULTIPLES

Acquisition multiples below are calculated medians using US private industry transactions. Data updated annually. Last update: August 2023.

VALUATION MULTIPLE (MEDIAN VALUE)

UNDER $1 MILLION NET SALES

MVIC/Net Sales	0.44
MVIC/Gross Profit	0.74
MVIC/SDE	1.89
MVIC/EBITDA	2.79

$1 MILLION–$5 MILLION NET SALES

MVIC/Net Sales	0.43
MVIC/Gross Profit	0.94
MVIC/SDE	2.57
MVIC/EBITDA	3.66

OVER $5 MILLION NET SALES

MVIC/Net Sales	0.52
MVIC/Gross Profit	1.65
MVIC/SDE	3.15
MVIC/EBITDA	4.38

Source: DealStats (formerly Pratt's Stats), 2023 (Portland, OR: Business Valuation Resources, LLC), www.bvresources.com/dealstats

PRICING TIPS

Each opportunity needs to be reviewed separately. The metrics are going to vary based on subindustries due to the significant differences between each business. Examples of these variations include general contractors, underground utility contractors, and residential plumbers. Some considerations to keep in mind are the scope/scale of the projects undertaken, labor expenses based on skill level or specializations required, and overhead costs including equipment maintenance, insurance, and administrative expenses. Additionally, factors relating to equipment value and age, tenure of the company, number of employees, and growth opportunities will have impacts of differing degrees.

Commercial is a premium over residential. Design/build companies a stronger sell than just general contractor.

There is a significant difference between companies doing $10M to $20M a year in revenue and companies doing $2M to $3M a year; they don't price the same at all. A smaller company is going to be valued primarily on cash flow, while a larger company is going to valued on EBITDA. A larger company will command a much higher multiple (5 to 8 x EBITDA). Economy of scale and high-level management are key factors in the difference, but also risk. Risk is significantly mitigated in bigger companies and this has a significant effect on value and salability. Point is, larger companies and small companies are priced differently, and by a large margin.

There is a lot of variety when it comes to construction in general. Much of the determination of value is influenced by the amount of direct involvement of the owner. When a company is primarily run by a team of people, most specifically a general manager, the value and the salability are significantly increased.

EBITDA seems to be the best indicator of value when revenues are about $2M to $3M or higher, whereas cash flow is a better indicator under $2M.

Relatively little inventory with most companies since they buy materials by job; however, they can have substantial investment in equipment and vehicles. Specialty trades (mechanical/HVAC, electrical, plumbing) trade at a premium over general contractors.

BENCHMARK DATA

STATISTICS (CONSTRUCTION)

Number of Establishments	3,883,347
Average Profit Margin	3.4%
Revenue per Employee	$263,000
Average Number of Employees	2.6
Average Wages per Employee	$57,514

PRODUCTS AND SERVICES SEGMENTATION

Specialty trade contracting	42.5%
Building construction	39.9%
Heavy and civil engineering construction	14.4%
All other activities	3.2%

MAJOR MARKET SEGMENTATION

Residential building construction	32.9%
Commercial building construction	26.2%
Nonbuilding construction	21.9%
Municipal building construction	12.6%
Industrial building construction	6.4%

INDUSTRY COSTS

Profit	3.4%
Wages	21.7%
Purchases	52.1%
Depreciation	1.2%

Marketing 0.3%
Rent & Utilities 3.9%
Other 17.4%

MARKET SHARE

DR Horton Inc. 1.2%
EMCOR Group Inc. 0.4%
Turner Construction Company 0.3%
Fluor Corporation 0.2%

A key benchmark is timely completion and project management effectiveness. This can directly impact customer retention rates and the rate of won bids which leads to overall business growth.

EXPENSES (% OF ANNUAL SALES)

Cost of Goods . . . . . . 30% to 40%
Occupancy Costs . . . . . 05% to 10%
Payroll/Labor Costs. . . . . 25% to 35%
Profit (pretax) . . . . . . 15% to 25%

QUESTIONS

- What about any debt or financing on the business? How are banks treating you in these times? What impact, if any, are you seeing from talk of recession? Is business slowing down? Based on present information, are you able to prepare a 13-week cash flow forecast? Are you able to accurately forecast 2023 and 2024 revenue? Discuss your managers or management team. How stable have they been? Are you having difficulty recruiting or filling key positions? If you were 20 years younger, what would you do to grow the business? What licensing is required?
- How experienced are estimator and foremen? Do all employees have Social Security numbers?
- What do you do on a day-to-day basis? If you went away for two weeks, would anything change about the business?
- Are your books accurate? How many hours a week are you involved, on average?
- Who are key management team members, and are they staying with the company following the sale? If the buyer doesn't have the required license, is there someone else in the company who does? Employment contracts with these employees is a good idea.
- Many times the seller is the key salesperson. How do they acquire new business? Do they have varied sources of referrals, or is it predominantly word of mouth? How much work is done with in-house tradesmen versus subcontractors?
- What's your turnover rate? How has the opioid crisis affected your ability to hire? What's the longest vacation you've taken in recent years?
- What is your quick ratio? What is the percent complete of each job? What amount of working capital does the business have in cash? Who are your major clients?

INDUSTRY TREND

I think it is going to be a bit of a slog. While supply chains are easing up, global disorder and tension remain heightened. Inflation and labor challenges are easing but significant macro shifts take a long time and it can be painful along the way.

One trend we have seen accelerate over the past 6 months is that given the negative headlines, seller sentiment has turned negative and therefore fewer sellers are listing.

When interest rates spiked, and a recession loomed, interest in buying construction companies (especially for private equity groups) slowed significantly. With a strong economic outlook now the market has picked back up.

I see the residential side of construction leveling out, but not declining too much. Commercial is limited to region; some areas are booming and others are stone dead. Industrial-related construction appears to be increasing steadily, and according to reports and agendas, it should continue to grow for years to come. The infrastructure in growing states is years behind where it should be. Construction has some catching up to do.

There is a general upward trend in the construction industry, more so on the residential side versus the commercial side. In most locales, there is a shortage of housing; when you add to that the growing remodel market, the current market bodes well for business owners in the construction industry.

Increasing, especially for a skilled-trade construction company. The U.S. just is not producing enough trained electricians, plumbers, and HVAC technicians.

"The value of private nonresidential construction grew in the years prior to the pandemic. The COVID-19 pandemic has sent construction revenue into decline. The supply chain issues that have come in the wake of the pandemic have risen costs for materials. High interest rates will raise the capital needed for construction. As supply chain issues ease, contractor profit will rebound. An expected rise in demand for construction services will likely increase the rate of entry for operators. The Construction sector has benefited from relatively low interest rates, providing an accommodative borrowing environment."

Source: IBISWorld Industry at a Glance

EXPERT COMMENTS

Almost unexpectedly over the past 6 to 9 months, the market has shifted back strongly in favor of sellers. This is due to low supply of quality businesses combined with strong buyer cash positions and demand. Q1 2023 results showed that construction was among the top 3 industries that had closed deals. The buyer pool has thinned a bit due to the headlines and fear; however, those that remain are often aggressive. My top advice to a seller is that if price and deal structure are important to you, do not work with the buyer that calls you up. Work with a broker/advisor that can stir up a well-run limited auction-style bidding process.

Spend a lot of time looking at the quality of the books when buying a construction company. It's not difficult to hide weaknesses in the messy books of a construction business. If the books are inconsistent and expenses are hard to trace, you might want to look elsewhere. Bad bookkeeping is a strong sign of a business with hidden issues.

Risk is always a major consideration when looking at construction. This results primarily from the bidding nature of construction—there is no guarantee of work when bidding jobs, and there is the potential of not hitting margins by bidding too low. The more a company does repeat work, such as fire and water damage or having ongoing contracts in place with heavily funded clients (apartment complex owners, for example), the less risk and thus the greater desirability of the business.

The value of a company is affected by how good its estimation process is.

Economic downturns affect the commercial construction industry later in the cycle since the planning and construction life cycle is long.

Skilled-trades companies (HVAC, electrical) can also have reoccurring revenue streams by having maintenance contracts.

FINANCING

Most of our transactions are < $5M in enterprise value and the buyer utilizes SBA 7a financing. As a rule of thumb, I would say most deals are 10 percent buyer equity (cash), 10 percent seller note (usually over a period of 1 to 5 years), and 80 percent bank financing. Very rarely do we see no bank involved. Earnouts are disallowed by the SBA and disliked by sellers so we rarely see them; however, we believe this will change in the immediate future and we are already seeing earnouts becoming a part of our current deals. Deals that are larger than $10M have increasingly become a challenge due to the return targets of more sophisticated buyers. Basically, interest rates have squeezed the returns that private equity had been used to and many are still adjusting. Along these lines, the best buyers for larger or more middle-market transactions are to identify buyers that have a dedicated roll-up strategic; they will pay more than they want to in the face of competition.

Typically some seller financing (5 to 20 percent) at just below market rate. SBA financing is popular for smaller operations.

For smaller companies, the deals are almost exclusively buyer cash and a seller note. For larger companies with a good track record, conventional financing and SBA are viable options.

Seller financing is more typical in construction-related businesses, for the simple fact that much of construction is bid-driven revenue. Some banks are set up to fund construction business acquisitions, but most shy away from them.

Some seller financing if the company is small enough for an owner-operator purchase. Outside financing is typically the bulk of debt stack.

RESOURCES

- IBISWorld, January 2023: https://www.ibisworld.com
- Florida DBPR—Department of Business & Professional Regulation: http://www.myfloridalicense.com/DBPR/
- AGC—Associated General Contractors of America: https://www.agc.org
- AGC—Associated General Contractors of America: https://www.agc.org
- CMAA—Construction Management Association of America: https://www.cmaanet.org
- ConstructConnect: https://www.constructconnect.com
- NAHB—National Association of Home Builders: https://www.nahb.org
- TCBA—Treasure Coast Builders Association: https://www.treasurecoastba.com
- USGBC—U.S. Green Building Council: https://www.usgbc.org
- The National Association of the Remodeling Industry: https://www.nari.org
- Contractor Talk: https://www.contractortalk.com

Construction: Masonry

| NAICS 238140	| SIC 1741-01	| Businesses/Units 96,602
| Profit $2.1 B	| Wages $10.3 B	| Annual Growth Future 1.0%
		| Annual Growth Past -0.3%

Rules of Thumb

- 27% annual sales includes inventory
- 1–2 x SDE includes inventory

INDUSTRY MULTIPLES

Acquisition multiples below are calculated medians using US private industry transactions. Data updated annually. Last update: August 2023.

VALUATION MULTIPLE (MEDIAN VALUE)

UNDER $1 MILLION NET SALES

MVIC/Net Sales	0.49
MVIC/Gross Profit	0.58
MVIC/SDE	1.84
MVIC/EBITDA	2.22

$1 MILLION–$5 MILLION NET SALES

MVIC/Net Sales	0.33
MVIC/Gross Profit	0.85
MVIC/SDE	2.54
MVIC/EBITDA	3.22

OVER $5 MILLION NET SALES

MVIC/Net Sales	0.60
MVIC/Gross Profit	3.51
MVIC/SDE	5.07
MVIC/EBITDA	5.81

Source: DealStats (formerly Pratt's Stats), 2023 (Portland, OR: Business Valuation Resources, LLC), www.bvresources.com/dealstats

PRICING TIPS

Commercial masonry is worth more than residential masonry.

Home masonry will go for 1 x SDE, and B2B will go for 1.5 x SDE.

BENCHMARK DATA

STATISTICS (MASONRY)

Number of Establishments	96,602
Average Profit Margin	6.4%
Revenue per Employee	$151,000
Average Number of Employees	2.3
Average Wages per Employee	$46,989

PRODUCTS AND SERVICES SEGMENTATION

Masonry contracting using brick, block or concrete	58.2%
Masonry contracting using other materials	19.1%
Pointing, cleaning and caulking	9.5%
Stucco contracting	9.0%
Stone contracting	4.2%

MAJOR MARKET SEGMENTATION

Residential building construction	37.1%
Commercial building construction	34.7%

Municipal building construction . . . 18.4%
Nonbuilding construction 6.0%
Industrial building construction . . . 3.8%

INDUSTRY COSTS

Profit	. 6.4%
Wages	. 31.1%
Purchases	. 33.5%
Depreciation	. 1.3%
Marketing	. 0.2%
Rent & Utilities	. 4.1%
Other	. 23.4%

EXPENSES (% OF ANNUAL SALES)

Cost of Goods	20%
Occupancy Costs	10% to 15%
Payroll/Labor Costs.	50%
Profit (pretax)	15% to 20%

QUESTIONS

- What percentage of bids do they get?
- Union or nonunion labor?
- Relationships to the customers, are the contracts assignable, and when will you introduce the buyer to customers before closing?
- Make sure they have good foremen in place to run the crews going forward with a new buyer.
- Understand the builders' contracts in place.

INDUSTRY TREND

"Masonry contractors enjoyed the low-interest rate environment of 2020 and 2021. Rising interest rates disincentivized investment into commercial building construction and hindered growth. Price-based competition rose alongside falling demand. Companies will begin expansionary projects that were delayed because of the outbreak of COVID-19. Private spending on home improvements will fall as disposable income growth slows. High wage costs, compounded by lower efficiencies, will weigh down on profit. Falling nonresidential construction activity offset gains in the residential market."

Source: IBISWorld Industry at a Glance

RESOURCES

- IBISWorld, January 2023: https://www.ibisworld.com
- NCMA—National Concrete Masonry Association: https://ncma.org

Construction: Municipal

| NAICS 236220 | Businesses/Units 39,070

| Profit $4.2 B | Wages $10.3 B | Annual Growth Future 1.4%

| Annual Growth Past -2.6%

INDUSTRY MULTIPLES

Acquisition multiples below are calculated medians using US private industry transactions. Data updated annually. Last update: August 2023.

VALUATION MULTIPLE (MEDIAN VALUE)

UNDER $1 MILLION NET SALES

MVIC/Net Sales	0.46
MVIC/Gross Profit	0.87
MVIC/SDE	1.40
MVIC/EBITDA	2.44

$1 MILLION–$5 MILLION NET SALES

MVIC/Net Sales	0.39
MVIC/Gross Profit	1.02
MVIC/SDE	2.97
MVIC/EBITDA	3.92

OVER $5 MILLION NET SALES

MVIC/Net Sales	0.33
MVIC/Gross Profit	1.67
MVIC/SDE	2.46
MVIC/EBITDA	3.66

Source: DealStats (formerly Pratt's Stats), 2023 (Portland, OR: Business Valuation Resources, LLC), www.bvresources.com/dealstats

BENCHMARK DATA

STATISTICS (MUNICIPAL BUILDING CONSTRUCTION)

Number of Establishments	39,070
Average Profit Margin	2.1%
Revenue per Employee	$1,437,000
Average Number of Employees	3.7
Average Wages per Employee	$73,509

PRODUCTS AND SERVICES SEGMENTATION

General contracting	50.3%
Construction management	23.2%
Remodeling contracting	17.5%
Other construction activities	9.0%

MAJOR MARKET SEGMENTATION

Educational building construction	51.2%
Healthcare facilities construction	27.5%
Recreational building construction	14.1%
Public safety facilities construction	5.7%
Religious building construction	1.5%

INDUSTRY COSTS

Profit	2.1%
Wages	5.2%
Purchases	70.4%
Depreciation	0.4%
Marketing	0.1%
Rent & Utilities	2.1%
Other	19.8%

INDUSTRY TREND

"The industry has been supported by a slight increase in state and local government investment. The cost of certain building materials has increased amid supply chain disruptions caused by coronavirus and the Russian invasion of Ukraine. Poor operating conditions, driven by rising interest rates and input prices in 2021 and 2022, have caused declines in industry participation. Growth in the private sector will result in more public-private partnerships. Public borrowing will likely be hindered by rising interest rates. Declining purchasing costs for the industry and the overall improvement of nonresidential construction activity are expected to alleviate pressure on profit. The industry was supported by surging demand for industry-relevant healthcare construction in 2020 following the outbreak of coronavirus cases."

Source: IBISWorld Industry at a Glance

RESOURCES

- IBISWorld, January 2023: https://www.ibisworld.com

Construction: Specialty Trades

| NAICS 238 | SIC 1799-99

Rules of Thumb
- 40%–50% annual gross sales plus inventory
- 2–4 x SDE plus inventory
- 3–5 x EBIT
- 3–5 x EBITDA

PRICING TIPS

Above ratios are for SDE $1M range. SDE < $1M being discounted from this work mix is important. New construction is less valued than service work. Companies with negotiated time and materials rates for > 90 percent of their business will value at a premium of 0.5 to 1 x. Companies that bid 100 percent of their work will discount 1 to 2 x licensing requirements, which can limit pool of buyers. Non–license holders' ability to own licensed companies varies by state; advisors must know the state licensing requirements as part of the valuation. Some trades are driven by environmental factors, e.g. roof replacement and gutters. If companies are located in storm-prone areas, sales may be lumpy (due to major hail storm, for example). For these type of companies, use 3 to 5 year averages sales/earnings when using rules of thumb. Post-Covid, skilled labor shortages and employee retention have been hot factors for purchasers. Premiums should be given if trained workforce has long seniority, e.g., > 10 years for majority of technicians. Customer base is critical. Companies who mainly supply tract home builders will be heavily discounted due to cyclical nature of tract home builders. For retail customers, superior companies find pricing model to offer some type of recurring revenue and sticky customer. Gutter cleaning/inspection for gutter companies, HVAC system semiannual checkups for $99, etc., creates relationship with the customer so that they are called first when a major (profitable) breakdown occurs. Companies have been experiencing higher profitability post-Covid due to availability of money, ERTC's, PPP money, etc. Consumers have been spending their Covid-relief money on home improvements.

Size of business is a crucial factor in most businesses, and especially so in specialty trades construction. There is a major difference in the approach to valuing a large company ($5M and up in revenues) and a smaller company (less than $2M in revenues). The multiples for both revenue and cash flow are considerably higher for larger companies.

There is no one-size-fits-all. Some business owners are hiring independent contractors to do the work so it lowers their workers' comp risk, plus labor is currently hard to find. Another important factor to understand is works in progress (WIP). Some construction projects can take months to complete. The financial statements of the business, therefore, need to be detailed as well as have an accurate accounting breakdown of WIP so it's clear what part of the project the seller has completed and what part the buyer will complete.

Select sellers who have their financials in order, allow you to work with their accountant or CPA directly, and have timely tax returns that closely mirror their financials. Know the financials, dig in before you take to market. Identify any inconsistencies and be prepared to defend or correct. Some businesses may need a little more support in getting their financials cleaned up and market ready. I determine the integrity of the seller and overall value of the business before taking on a more complex engagement. I devour comps and work tirelessly to find the best and most closely related businesses. If I am working on a highly niche business, I work through it with the owner; often they know an owner of a similar business who sold a business recently. I fastidiously value businesses because the results speak for themselves. I average an annual 90 percent close ratio (higher Main Street and lower middle market), and offers/closing price is within 5 to 10 percent of ask. I have prepared the seller that any offer within 20 percent of list price is worth consideration and possibly negotiation. Discuss pricing with the seller and explain why their business is worth what it is worth. I rarely encounter a seller who is unrealistic once they have all of the information to make good decisions. Recently, I picked up an expired listing from another broker. After digging in with the residential services business seller and receiving a pre-qual from an SBA lender, we increased the price $700K. Ultimately the business sold to a national company at $500K over what another broker had listed it. Doing your homework and managing expectations up front—before the listing agreement—makes a world of difference in the deals I do now versus 5 years ago. A few more nonfinancial questions that buyers always ask and that definitely impact value: Strength of employees? Key employees staying? Will owner stay on? How long? Commercial vs. residential? Percent contracts? Recurring revenue? How does the company get paid? Useful life remaining and maintenance of vehicle and equipment? Supplier concentration growth opportunities? Local competition and market share (if known)?

I'm assuming each job is bid and each client may be a repeat or one-time client. The SDE multiplier is lower than recurring or quick-bid service work. The profit margins should be 25 percent gross profit and 10 percent net profit or 15 percent net profit plus SDE. If the owner of the company is the only salesperson, I would discount the price 5 to 10 percent, as it takes many years to become proficient in selling specialty construction services. If the business is generating less than $150,000 SDE, I would discount the price another 5 to 10 percent, as these very small businesses rely too much on the owner.

BENCHMARK DATA

The best benchmark is the customer concentration—look for companies that don't have a single customer representing over 10 percent of sales. It's common, however, to have a large customer one year that is not the same largest customer the next year because of a single job.

EXPENSES (% OF ANNUAL SALES)

Cost of Goods	30% to 40%
Occupancy Costs	02% to 10%
Payroll/Labor Costs	25% to 35%
Profit (pretax)	15% to 25%

- Are there any factors in this current market you foresee could negatively affect the value of this company over the coming months? (Get the answer in writing from the seller.)
- What are the company's greatest strengths/selling points? Are there any changes in your industry that a buyer would want to know? Are you an absentee owner? If so, what are you paying a general manager annually, including all benefits and bonuses, to run this business profitably? Does each employee have a valid I-9?
- History of business? Reputation? Strength of financials? Staff loyalty and longevity? How do they find sales and get paid for their work? Marketing efforts? Dedicated sales person(s)? Depending on specialty, commercial vs. residential, contracts, and recurring revenue? Any lawsuits or workers' comp issues, past, present, or anticipated? Licenses? Taxes? Fees? Permits in good standing? Working capital requirements? Trends? Markets served?
- How much of the revenue is dependent on your personal connections and can this be successfully transferred?
- What is the distribution of customers? How large is the largest client? How long is the sales cycle?
- What is your role in the business, and how often are you there?

INDUSTRY TREND

Current consumer spending levels aren't sustainable. We expect a construction recession in the next 12 to 24 months.

Specialty trades is a growing industry, especially roofing and HVAC. No matter what the economy does, some specialty trades continue to grow with the population increase. I see this industry trending up over the next 5 years.

A positive for the industry is the federal government's passage of the Inflation Reduction Act and its focus on incentivizing green industries and boosting energy efficiency.

Continued growth in demand for services; difficulty staffing labor positions (new regulations/laws); supplier price stabilization; continued consolidation

Steady growth based upon increasing construction

Demand for specialty trades will continue to grow as fewer general contractors will be able to self-perform. Also many contractors and end users (either homeowners or business owners) will hire the specialty subcontractor over a general contractor to minimize the middleman. Fewer owners are able to perform any work on their own property because of the special skills and tools required.

EXPERT COMMENTS

If you are selling a specialty trades company, be certain you have a full time manager in place. If the company is primarily managed by you the owner, buyers will apply a major discount to the value. Also, clean up the books and leave nothing for the buyer to discover on their own. The more diligent you are to make everything clear and disclosed, the more you will sell for and the easier the process will be. If you are buying a specialty trades company, be certain you audit the company's books with a fine tooth comb. Assume nothing, verify everything. Books will tell the story of value, not the seller's testimony. Also, get to the know the manager. If you don't work well with him or her, there is a good chance you'll have a difficult time running the company profitably.

Make sure you have the skills to run the business and keep the seller long enough for training and a smooth transition.

If the customer is a professional (a business), the sales force, and likely the owner of the company, would need to be extremely well versed in the product. If the customer is a consumer (or homeowner or end user), then the salesperson only needs to know more than the customer. B2B may be more technical than B2C relationships.

The barrier to entry is usually very high for these businesses as the skills needed are harder for a businessperson to obtain. Most technical experts in these businesses are not risk-takers nor are they business minded.

There is a brutal amount of competition in this industry. The highest on the food chain often are the ones who market the most and consistently deliver high-quality services.

FINANCING

Bank financing is readily available. Seller financing not needed, unless poor books and records. If bank requires seller financing, typical is 10 percent of sales price, financed for 2 to 5 years, subordinated to bank note, unless poor books and records. If bank requires seller financing, typical is 10 percent of sales price, financed for 2 to 5 years, subordinated to bank note.

As in most industries, financing is a factor of the size of the company for sale. Larger businesses with full management in place, valued on a multiple of EBITDA, can be financed by conventional or SBA loans, or investor equity. Smaller companies are almost always financed by buyer cash and a seller note.

Because the seller of the business cannot predict the success of the buyer, a seller wants to be paid in full as opposed to carrying any seller finance.

Smaller deals: SBA, sometimes a seller held note.

Midsized: a mix of cash, bank, seller held.

Larger deals: investors, equity, corporate purchase—cash at close.

Combination: usually 20 percent seller financing, 50 to 60 percent outside financing.

Outside (SBA financing is most common). If the buyer is concerned about any risk (warranty, loss of skilled employees, owner leaving with too much knowledge in his head), then seller financing or escrow for up to 15 percent of the business price is common.

Construction: Steel Fabrication

| NAICS 238120 | Businesses/Units 15,472

| Profit $1 B | Wages $7.4 B | Annual Growth Future 0.0%

| | | Annual Growth Past 2.7%

Rules of Thumb
- 15% annual sales includes inventory
- 3 x SDE plus inventory
- 4.5 x EBIT
- 4 x EBITDA

INDUSTRY MULTIPLES

Acquisition multiples below are calculated medians using US private industry transactions. Data updated annually. Last update: August 2023.

VALUATION MULTIPLE (MEDIAN VALUE)

UNDER $1 MILLION NET SALES	N/A
$1 MILLION–$5 MILLION NET SALES	
MVIC/Net Sales.	0.47
MVIC/Gross Profit	1.10
MVIC/SDE	3.10
MVIC/EBITDA	2.90
OVER $5 MILLION NET SALES	
MVIC/Net Sales.	0.37
MVIC/Gross Profit	1.59
MVIC/SDE	2.50
MVIC/EBITDA	4.29

Source: DealStats (formerly Pratt's Stats), 2023 (Portland, OR: Business Valuation Resources, LLC), www.bvresources.com/dealstats

PRICING TIPS

The quality of fabrication backlog and the risks involved in the open contracts are big drivers of enterprise value. A buyer will typically have to provide bonding, and most PE buyers will have to post a letter of credit to secure the bonding; therefore, PE buyers are often less interested than strategic buyers, who usually have a bonding program in place. Valuation of the assumed contracts and the related estimate of cost to complete is a key element of the diligence leading to a sale and can prove to be a point of contention between buyer and seller if not managed effectively.

BENCHMARK DATA

STATISTICS (STEEL FRAMING)

Number of Establishments .	15,472
Average Profit Margin	4.0%
Revenue per Employee .	$247,000
Average Number of Employees.	6.4
Average Wages per Employee .	$72,678

PRODUCTS AND SERVICES SEGMENTATION

Structural steel erection	61.9%
Steel fabrication.	20.4%
Precast concrete installation	8.9%
Additions and alterations to existing structures	8.8%

MAJOR MARKET SEGMENTATION

Commercial building construction .	34.3%
Nonbuilding construction	25.0%
Municipal building construction	12.5%
Industrial building construction	11.8%
Other nonresidential building construction	10.5%
Residential building construction .	5.9%

INDUSTRY COSTS

Profit	4.0%
Wages .	28.8%
Purchases	32.6%
Depreciation	1.5%
Marketing	0.1%
Rent & Utilities .	5.7%
Other Costs .	27.2%

EXPENSES (% OF ANNUAL SALES)

Cost of Goods	90%
Payroll/Labor Costs.	25%
Profit (pretax)	05%

QUESTIONS

- Are there any open claims? How is revenue recognized (percent complete, or value shipped)? What is the historical workforce turnover rate? Does the company have a succession plan or any retention/noncompete agreements?

INDUSTRY TREND

The growth and profitability of the steel fabrication segment is dependent on construction growth rates and demand. Currently (Q1, 2020), the industry is on a path of expansion driven by high construction demand.

"Steel framing companies are often contracted by local and federal government for their services. Nonresidential construction was stable at the onset of the period. The Biden administration has remained committed to investing in improving infrastructure. The price of steel is forecast to consistently fall. The benefit of falling steel prices allows operators to cut costs and maximize profit. Bridge, tunnel, highway and street construction is expected to grow, benefiting the industry. The industry is in a vulnerable position due to its conformity to macroeconomic trends."

Source: IBISWorld Industry at a Glance

EXPERT COMMENTS

Business that are well prepared for a sale (large backlog, current receivables, no excess or obsolete inventory, diverse customer list, facilities well equipped and maintained) bring much better selling prices.

Explanation of high risk rating—steel fabricators are typically employed by general contractors who issue contracts that serve to assign most risk for the performance of work to the steel fabricator. Common clauses state that the fabricator is due additional time but no compensation for certain changes. Indemnity clauses also serve to shift more risk to the steel fabricator.

FINANCING

Seller financing is typically involved for only the smaller companies (under $5M enterprise value). Larger sales are typically made to cash buyers.

RESOURCES

- IBISWorld, January 2023: https://www.ibisworld.com
- AISC—American Institute of Steel Construction: https://www.aisc.org/
- AWS—American Welding Society: https://www.aws.org/
- Bolt Council: RCSC—Research Council on Structural Connections: http://boltcouncil.org
- SSPC—Steel Structures Painting Counsel: https://www.sspc.org/

Consumer Electronics and Appliances Rental

| NAICS 532210 | Businesses/Units 6,494

| Profit $1.2 B | Wages $1.2 B | Annual Growth Future 1.4%

| | | | Annual Growth Past 1.2%

INDUSTRY MULTIPLES

Acquisition multiples below are calculated medians using US private industry transactions. Data updated annually. Last update: August 2023.

C

VALUATION MULTIPLE (MEDIAN VALUE)

UNDER $1 MILLION NET SALES

MVIC/Net Sales.	1.88
MVIC/Gross Profit	2.15
MVIC/SDE	N/A
MVIC/EBITDA	2.26

$1 MILLION–$5 MILLION NET SALES   N/A

OVER $5 MILLION NET SALES

MVIC/Net Sales.	1.75
MVIC/Gross Profit	6.79
MVIC/SDE	N/A
MVIC/EBITDA	21.09

Source: DealStats (formerly Pratt's Stats), 2023 (Portland, OR: Business Valuation Resources, LLC), www.bvresources.com/dealstats

BENCHMARK DATA

STATISTICS (CONSUMER ELECTRONICS & APPLIANCES RENTAL)

Number of Establishments .	6,494
Average Profit Margin	13.0%
Revenue per Employee .	$352,000
Average Number of Employees.	4.17
Average Wages per Employee .	$43,849

PRODUCTS AND SERVICES SEGMENTATION

Appliances .	52.4%
Electronics .	20.7%
Household furnishings .	14.4%
Computers .	11.9%
Other	0.6%

MAJOR MARKET SEGMENTATION

Household incomes between $24,000 and $50,000	55.0%
Household incomes between $15,000 and $24,000	28.0%
Household incomes less than $15,000.	13.0%
Household incomes between $50,000 and $75,000	3.0%
Household incomes greater than $75,000 .	1.0%

INDUSTRY COSTS

Profit	13.0%
Wages .	12.6%
Purchases .	7.6%
Depreciation	15.2%
Marketing	1.5%
Rent & Utilities .	8.9%
Other	41.3%

MARKET SHARE

Rent-A-Center .	25.1%
PROG Holdings .	21.7%
Aaron's .	16.9%

INDUSTRY TREND

"The industry has been relatively unaffected by federal legislation. All three major industry companies have pursued aggressive cost-cutting measures. Increased use of algorithmic decision-making for LTO application approvals has increased the efficiency of companies in the industry. The Federal Reserve will continue to hike interest rates to curb inflation. The industry may be subject to increasing regulatory scrutiny because of the nature of industry operations. The industry's competitive landscape will continue to be dominated by its largest companies. The industry has been reshaped by the spinoff of Progressive Leasing into PROG Holdings Inc. from Aaron's Inc."

Source: IBISWorld Industry at a Glance

RESOURCES

• IBISWorld, February 2023: https://www.ibisworld.com

Contract Manufacturing

| NAICS 332710 | SIC 3999-06

Rules of Thumb

- 4–7 x EBIT
- 3–5 x EBITDA plus reasonable owner's compensation
- 2–4 x SDE plus inventory
- 95% annual sales includes inventory

INDUSTRY MULTIPLES

Acquisition multiples below are calculated medians using US private industry transactions. Data updated annually. Last update: August 2023.

VALUATION MULTIPLE (MEDIAN VALUE)

UNDER $1 MILLION NET SALES

MVIC/Net Sales	0.73
MVIC/Gross Profit	1.29
MVIC/SDE	3.11
MVIC/EBITDA	4.25

$1 MILLION–$5 MILLION NET SALES

MVIC/Net Sales	0.70
MVIC/Gross Profit	1.56
MVIC/SDE	3.34
MVIC/EBITDA	4.33

OVER $5 MILLION NET SALES

MVIC/Net Sales	0.97
MVIC/Gross Profit	2.05
MVIC/SDE	3.76
MVIC/EBITDA	5.55

Source: DealStats (formerly Pratt's Stats), 2023 (Portland, OR: Business Valuation Resources, LLC), www.bvresources.com/dealstats

PRICING TIPS

Discounts for high sales concentration in a few customers; discounts for old equipment

BENCHMARK DATA

$300,000 revenue per employee

EXPENSES (% OF ANNUAL SALES)

Cost of Goods	45% to 60%
Occupancy Costs	05% to 15%

Payroll/Labor Costs. . . . .   15% to 20%
Profit (pretax) . . . . . .   10% to 20%

QUESTIONS

- Ask about the relationships with the present customers and any communications from them about the volume of future business. Ask about his or her growth vision and upcoming capital equipment purchase needs.

INDUSTRY TREND

Increase in defense spending, increase in CPI, and growth of GDP will all contribute to growth for this industry.

EXPERT COMMENTS

Get professional help to sell while you focus on keeping the business growing and profitable. When buying, use a team to advise you: broker, equipment appraiser, CPA, etc.; don't try to do it alone.

Cost of capital equipment and availability of skilled labor are barriers to entry.

FINANCING

Bank financing is typical.

RESOURCES

- FMA—Fabricators and Manufacturers Association: https://www.fmamfg.org

Convenience Stores

NAICS 445120	SIC 5411-03	Businesses/Units 52,780
Profit $924.8 M	Wages $4.1 B	Annual Growth Future 1.8%
		Annual Growth Past 2.8%

Rules of Thumb

- 10%–20% annual sales plus inventory
- 2–2.5 x SDE plus inventory
- 2–3 x EBITDA plus inventory—C-store only
- 6–8 x EBITDA plus inventory—real estate + business
- 5 x EBITDA less cosmetic renovation to receive a national brand of fuel; inventory is separate and above

INDUSTRY MULTIPLES

Acquisition multiples below are calculated medians using US private industry transactions. Data updated annually. Last update: August 2023.

VALUATION MULTIPLE (MEDIAN VALUE)

UNDER $1 MILLION NET SALES

MVIC/Net Sales.	0.23
MVIC/Gross Profit	0.61
MVIC/SDE	1.55
MVIC/EBITDA	2.03

$1 MILLION–$5 MILLION NET SALES

MVIC/Net Sales.	0.23
MVIC/Gross Profit	0.56
MVIC/SDE	2.88
MVIC/EBITDA	2.78

OVER $5 MILLION NET SALES

MVIC/Net Sales.	0.18
MVIC/Gross Profit	1.57
MVIC/SDE	2.80
MVIC/EBITDA	7.84

Source: DealStats (formerly Pratt's Stats), 2023 (Portland, OR: Business Valuation Resources, LLC), www.bvresources.com/dealstats

PRICING TIPS

If the annual gross sales (lotto/lottery, check cashing, money orders not to be included in total gross sales) are over $1,200,000, the price can be 1 x gross sales. If records reflect all sales and the business is bank financeable, price can be up to 3 x SDE.

BENCHMARK DATA

STATISTICS (CONVENIENCE STORES)

Number of Establishments .	.52,780
Average Profit Margin	2.1%
Revenue per Employee .	$21,211
Average Number of Employees.	.3.5
Average Wages per Employee .	$22,686

PRODUCTS AND SERVICES SEGMENTATION

Tobacco products	.38.7%
Food service	.18.8%
Packaged beverages	.16.9%
Beer.	.11.2%
Candy and snacks	9.8%
Other	4.6%

INDUSTRY COSTS

Profit	2.1%
Wages	9.4%
Purchases	.67.9%
Depreciation	1.0%
Marketing	0.7%
Rent & Utilities	2.7%
Other	.16.2%

MARKET SHARE

Alimentation Couche-Tard Inc. .	.33.8%
7-Eleven Inc.	.28.9%
Wawa, Inc. .	.16.0%

There has to be a good product mix. Liquor/wine sales should not be more than 50 percent of total sales, as markups are very competitive. General grocery items need to be at least 50 percent of total sales, as markups can be 100 percent also.

Business only: anywhere from 1.6 to 3 SDE (this market has driven values up). The higher the inside sales and SDE, the higher the multiple of SDE. When real estate is included, anywhere from 1.5 to 4 x; many factors make this range very wide.

EXPENSES (% OF ANNUAL SALES)

Cost of Goods	65% or less
Occupancy Costs	07% to 15%
Payroll/Labor Costs.	14% to 20%
Profit (pretax)	10% to 15%

QUESTIONS

- Would the seller buy the same store if he were a buyer? Understand the real reason for the sale, the relationship with the landlord, and the nature of customer complaints.
- Any previous environmental issue?
- Amount of gross that's tobacco related? Lottery sales? Any employee or customer thefts?

INDUSTRY TREND

Demand is continuing to increase, and there's the continuation of off market sales transactions. The majority I've sold over the past several years were not marketed publicly.

"The coronavirus had a negative effect on the industry in 2020. Because convenience stores rely heavily on foot traffic, social distancing regulations and work-from-home operations caused a decrease in demand for industry operators. Increased competition and changing consumer preferences have caused operators to adjust their operating strategies. This includes stores expanding their product offerings with healthier options and adopting digital innovations, like contactless payments, to increase customer satisfaction."

Source: IBISWorld Key Takeaways

EXPERT COMMENTS

Do a thorough due diligence before buying. Have sufficient working capital. Always watch the competition. Have great customer service. Keep good records for growth and cost analysis.

Street visibility and location near apartment buildings significantly affect profitability.

FINANCING

80 percent have some level of seller financing, even if it's only the inventory on hand at the time of the sale. If real estate is included, majority is bank financed. If it's a business only, most buyers pay 80 to 90 percent down and the seller finances the balance short term, typically 6 to 9 months.

RESOURCES

- IBISWorld, August 2023: https://www.ibisworld.com
- Convenience Store News: https://csnews.com
- CStore Decisions: https://cstoredecisions.com
- NACS: https://www.convenience.org
- Petroleum News: https://www.petroleumnews.com
- North Carolina Petroleum and Convenience Marketers: https://www.ncpcm.org
- South Carolina Convenience & Petroleum Marketers Association: https://sccpma.com

Cookie, Cracker & Pasta Production

NAICS 31182	Businesses/Units 2,005	
Profit $1.3 B	Wages $3.3 B	Annual Growth Future 0.3%
		Annual Growth Past 0.9%

INDUSTRY MULTIPLES

Acquisition multiples below are calculated medians using US private industry transactions. Data updated annually. Last update: August 2023.

VALUATION MULTIPLE (MEDIAN VALUE)

UNDER $1 MILLION NET SALES

MVIC/Net Sales	0.74
MVIC/Gross Profit	1.04
MVIC/SDE	2.07
MVIC/EBITDA	4.05

$1 MILLION–$5 MILLION NET SALES	N/A

OVER $5 MILLION NET SALES

MVIC/Net Sales	4.02
MVIC/Gross Profit	10.86
MVIC/SDE	N/A
MVIC/EBITDA	29.77

Source: DealStats (formerly Pratt's Stats), 2023 (Portland, OR: Business Valuation Resources, LLC), www.bvresources.com/dealstats

BENCHMARK DATA

STATISTICS (COOKIE, CRACKER & PASTA PRODUCTION)

Number of Establishments	2,005
Average Profit Margin	4.6%
Revenue per Employee	$538,000
Average Number of Employees	26.0
Average Wages per Employee	$62,329

PRODUCTS AND SERVICES SEGMENTATION

Flour mixes and dough	35.8%
Cookies, wafers, ice cream cones	26.8%
Crackers and biscuits	18.7%
Dry pasta	17.1%
Other	1.6%

MAJOR MARKET SEGMENTATION

Supermarkets, convenience stores, and grocery stores	62.2%
Warehouse clubs & supercenters	24.9%
Grocery wholesalers	12.9%

INDUSTRY COSTS

Profit	4.6%
Wages	11.6%
Purchases	47.3%
Depreciation	3.0%
Marketing	1.0%
Rent & Utilities	2.0%
Other	30.4%

INDUSTRY TREND

"Some cookie, cracker and pasta producers have reformulated products. Cookie, cracker and pasta consumption typically doesn't drop during economic downturns. Larger industry producers boosted their scale to provide a greater range of options. Time-strapped consumers will find convenience in cooking meals requiring low preparation, like pasta. US households may turn away from imported pasta and cookies. Cookie, cracker and pasta producers will continue innovating and introducing healthier brand extensions. Intensified competition has limited producers' ability to pass expanded costs of premium inputs along to customers."

Source: IBISWorld Industry at a Glance

C

Cosmetic & Beauty Products Manufacturing

| NAICS 325620 | Businesses/Units 4,390

| Profit $2.8 B | Wages $3.9 B | Annual Growth Future 1.2%

                                     | Annual Growth Past -2.7%

Rules of Thumb

• 200% annual sales

INDUSTRY MULTIPLES

Acquisition multiples below are calculated medians using US private industry transactions. Data updated annually. Last update: August 2023.

VALUATION MULTIPLE (MEDIAN VALUE)

UNDER $1 MILLION NET SALES

MVIC/Net Sales	0.65
MVIC/Gross Profit	0.96
MVIC/SDE	2.54
MVIC/EBITDA	2.12

$1 MILLION–$5 MILLION NET SALES

MVIC/Net Sales	0.64
MVIC/Gross Profit	3.83
MVIC/SDE	7.66
MVIC/EBITDA	5.33

OVER $5 MILLION NET SALES

MVIC/Net Sales	1.29
MVIC/Gross Profit	3.29
MVIC/SDE	N/A
MVIC/EBITDA	14.47

Source: DealStats (formerly Pratt's Stats), 2023 (Portland, OR: Business Valuation Resources, LLC), www.bvresources.com/dealstats

PRICING TIPS

Successful players will demonstrate growth, and ability to generate sales via their own online channels, via Amazon, and via traditional wholesale channels.

BENCHMARK DATA

STATISTICS (COSMETIC & BEAUTY PRODUCTS MANUFACTURING)

Number of Establishments	4,390
Average Profit Margin	5.7%
Revenue per Employee	$868,000
Average Number of Employees	13.0
Average Wages per Employee	$69,527

PRODUCTS AND SERVICES

Cosmetics	34.8%
Creams, lotions and oils	25.4%
Hair preparations	17.5%
Perfumes, toilet waters, and colognes	10.5%
Dentifrices, mouthwashes, gargles, and rinses	10.2%
Other	1.6%

INDUSTRY COSTS

Profit 5.7%
Wages 8.0%
Purchases 39.0%
Depreciation 1.6%
Marketing 1.4%
Rent & Utilities 1.0%
Other 43.3%

MARKET SHARE

Procter & Gamble Co. 13.9%
Estée Lauder Companies Inc. 8.7%
L'Oréal USA Inc.. . . . . . 8.5%
Unilever N V. 8.2%
Coty Inc.. . . . . . . 1.2%
Mana Products Inc.. . . . . . 0.9%

EXPENSES (% OF ANNUAL SALES)

Cost of Goods 20%

INDUSTRY TREND

"A tighter monetary policy has affected budgets and decreased disposable income. The number of adults aged 50 and older has increased in recent years. Manufacturers have adjusted marketing budgets as consumers changed their purchasing behavior. The increased production of organic and all-natural beauty products will continue. Substituting plastic for paper in cosmetic and beauty packaging is under development. Rising e-commerce and social media platforms will prevent sudden decreases in exports. Increasing awareness of innovative, inclusive, technical and sustainable products has been the trend for consumers."

Source: IBISWorld Industry at a Glance

FINANCING

Limited seller financing

RESOURCES

- IBISWorld, January 2023: https://www.ibisworld.com
- CEW—Cosmetic Executive Women: https://www.cew.org
- WWD—Women's Wear Daily: https://wwd.com/

Cost Cutters Hair Salon (Franchise)

| NAICS 812112 | SIC 7241-01 | Businesses/Units 602

Rules of Thumb

- 55%–60% annual sales plus inventory

INDUSTRY MULTIPLES

Acquisition multiples below are calculated medians using US private industry transactions. Data updated annually. Last update: August 2023.

VALUATION MULTIPLE (MEDIAN VALUE)

UNDER $1 MILLION NET SALES
MVIC/Net Sales. 0.31
MVIC/Gross Profit 0.39
MVIC/SDE 1.60
MVIC/EBITDA 2.11

$1 MILLION–$5 MILLION NET SALES

MVIC/Net Sales.	0.29
MVIC/Gross Profit	0.39
MVIC/SDE	2.30
MVIC/EBITDA	3.05

OVER $5 MILLION NET SALES   N/A

Source: DealStats (formerly Pratt's Stats), 2023 (Portland, OR: Business Valuation Resources, LLC), www.bvresources.com/dealstats

PRICING TIPS

Approx. Total Investment: $150,466 to $308,558

RESOURCES

- Cost Cutters: https://www.costcutters.com
- Franchise information:
  https://www.regiscorp.com/franchise/franchise-opportunities.html
- Regis Corporation: https://www.regiscorp.com

Country/General Stores

| NAICS 452319 | SIC 5399-02

Rules of Thumb

- 20% annual sales plus inventory

INDUSTRY MULTIPLES

Acquisition multiples below are calculated medians using US private industry transactions. Data updated annually. Last update: August 2023.

VALUATION MULTIPLE (MEDIAN VALUE)

UNDER $1 MILLION NET SALES

MVIC/Net Sales.	0.42
MVIC/Gross Profit	0.70
MVIC/SDE	2.48
MVIC/EBITDA	2.54

$1 MILLION–$5 MILLION NET SALES

MVIC/Net Sales.	0.31
MVIC/Gross Profit	0.88
MVIC/SDE	2.39
MVIC/EBITDA	3.18

OVER $5 MILLION NET SALES

MVIC/Net Sales.	0.26
MVIC/Gross Profit	0.55
MVIC/SDE	N/A
MVIC/EBITDA	N/A

Source: DealStats (formerly Pratt's Stats), 2023 (Portland, OR: Business Valuation Resources, LLC), www.bvresources.com/dealstats

INDUSTRY TREND

"The general story of rural general stores is not necessarily a happy one. Unless you've got someone doing it purely for the love of it, it's a hard road for young entrepreneurs. Which is why the locally-supported model may offer a path for-ward—a community deciding there is a value to having a store that goes beyond the bottom line."

Source: "Preserving general stores, the heart of small towns" by Conor Knighton, April 16, 2023, https://www.cbsnews.com/news/preserving-general-stores-the-heart-of-small-towns/

- NGA—National Grocers Association: https://www.nationalgrocers.org
- VAICS—Vermont Alliance of Independent Country Stores: https://vtrga.org/vermont-alliance-of-independent-country-store/

Couriers and Express Delivery Services

| NAICS 492110 | Businesses/Units 464,224

| Profit $10.2 B | Wages $43.9 B | Annual Growth Future 3.6%

| Annual Growth Past 6.9%

INDUSTRY MULTIPLES

Acquisition multiples below are calculated medians using US private industry transactions. Data updated annually. Last update: August 2023.

VALUATION MULTIPLE (MEDIAN VALUE)

UNDER $1 MILLION NET SALES
MVIC/Net Sales	0.76
MVIC/Gross Profit	1.43
MVIC/SDE	2.37
MVIC/EBITDA	5.32

$1 MILLION–$5 MILLION NET SALES
MVIC/Net Sales	0.72
MVIC/Gross Profit	2.03
MVIC/SDE	2.94
MVIC/EBITDA	4.01

OVER $5 MILLION NET SALES
MVIC/Net Sales	0.75
MVIC/Gross Profit	1.91
MVIC/SDE	4.12
MVIC/EBITDA	3.63

Source: DealStats (formerly Pratt's Stats), 2023 (Portland, OR: Business Valuation Resources, LLC), www.bvresources.com/dealstats

BENCHMARK DATA

STATISTICS (COURIERS & LOCAL DELIVERY SERVICES)
Number of Establishments	464,224
Average Profit Margin	6.7%
Revenue per Employee	$131,000
Average Number of Employees	2.58
Average Wages per Employee	$38,450

PRODUCTS AND SERVICES SEGMENTATION
Ground deliveries	60.4%
Air transit services	38.6%
Other services including messengers and local deliveries	1.0%

MAJOR MARKET SEGMENTATION
Business-to-consumers including households	52.0%
Business-to-business	41.5%
All other	6.5%

INDUSTRY COSTS
Profit	6.7%
Wages	29.0%

Purchases 7.8%
Depreciation 1.6%
Marketing 0.3%
Rent & Utilities 4.1%
Other 50.6%

MARKET SHARE

United Parcel Service 51.9%
FedEx 22.6%
Deutsche Post Ag 1.9%
Culligan International Co 0.1%

INDUSTRY TREND

"Volatile input costs constrain profit growth. Larger couriers have used technology as a way for customers to track packages and verify deliveries. The robust growth of the e-commerce sector has benefited industry operators. Industry customers are expected to continue integrating vertically, decreasing demand. Consumers expected to continue shifting to online shopping. Increasing demand for same-day delivery is expected to lead to new business locations. Over the past five years, developments in the e-commerce and online retailing space have driven industry growth."

Source: IBISWorld Industry at a Glance

RESOURCES

• IBISWorld, October 2022: https://www.ibisworld.com

Court Reporting Services

| NAICS 561492 | SIC 7338-01 | Businesses/Units 37,272

| Profit $434.4 M | Wages $868.4 M | Annual Growth Future -0.5%

| Annual Growth Past -1.5%

Rules of Thumb

• 30%–35% annual revenues includes inventory

INDUSTRY MULTIPLES

Acquisition multiples below are calculated medians using US private industry transactions. Data updated annually. Last update: August 2023.

VALUATION MULTIPLE (MEDIAN VALUE)

UNDER $1 MILLION NET SALES	N/A
$1 MILLION–$5 MILLION NET SALES	
MVIC/Net Sales.	2.02
MVIC/Gross Profit	4.05
MVIC/SDE	8.03
MVIC/EBITDA	8.03
OVER $5 MILLION NET SALES	
MVIC/Net Sales.	1.13
MVIC/Gross Profit	1.13
MVIC/SDE	6.40
MVIC/EBITDA	9.26

Source: DealStats (formerly Pratt's Stats), 2023 (Portland, OR: Business Valuation Resources, LLC), www.bvresources.com/dealstats

BENCHMARK DATA

STATISTICS (STENOGRAPHIC SERVICES)

Number of Establishments	37,272
Average Profit Margin	12.8%
Revenue per Employee	$72,400
Average Number of Employees	1.3
Average Wages per Employee	$18,530

PRODUCTS AND SERVICES SEGMENTATION

Additional services	33.3%
Local government stenographic services	24.0%
State government stenographic services	22.9%
Other stenographic services	19.8%

MAJOR MARKET SEGMENTATION

Other customers	53.1%
Local courts	24.0%
State courts	22.9%

INDUSTRY COSTS

Profit	12.8%
Wages	25.6%
Purchases	33.7%
Depreciation	1.3%
Marketing	1.7%
Rent & Utilities	2.4%
Other	22.4%

INDUSTRY TREND

"The proliferation of technology has continued to make big waves within the industry. High reliance on digital recording systems poses some potential risks. Industry operator exits have reduced internal competition. Stenographers will be forced to find opportunities outside the courtroom. Closed-captioning efforts are anticipated to facilitate demand for stenographic services. External competition from technology is expected to restrict the industry's expansion. Digital recording systems have slowly pushed stenographers out of the courtroom."

Source: IBISWorld Industry at a Glance

RESOURCES

- IBISWorld, October 2022: https://www.ibisworld.com
- AAERT—American Association of Electronic Reporters and Transcribers: https://www.aaert.org
- Court Reporting Insider: https://www.courtreportinginsider.com
- NCRA—The Association for Court Reporters and Captioners: https://www.ncra.org
- TheJCR.com: https://www.thejcr.com
- USCRA—United States Court Reporters Association®: http://www.uscra.org

Coverall (Commercial Cleaning) (Franchise)

| NAICS 561720 | Businesses/Units 6,507

Rules of Thumb

- 2–3 x monthly volume
- 4 x EBITDA

INDUSTRY MULTIPLES

Acquisition multiples below are calculated medians using US private industry transactions. Data updated annually. Last update: August 2023.

VALUATION MULTIPLE (MEDIAN VALUE)

UNDER $1 MILLION NET SALES

MVIC/Net Sales.	0.59
MVIC/Gross Profit	0.76
MVIC/SDE	2.03
MVIC/EBITDA	2.92

$1 MILLION–$5 MILLION NET SALES

MVIC/Net Sales.	0.45
MVIC/Gross Profit	1.02
MVIC/SDE	2.86
MVIC/EBITDA	4.05

OVER $5 MILLION NET SALES

MVIC/Net Sales.	0.53
MVIC/Gross Profit	2.26
MVIC/SDE	4.26
MVIC/EBITDA	5.48

Source: DealStats (formerly Pratt's Stats), 2023 (Portland, OR: Business Valuation Resources, LLC), www.bvresources.com/dealstats

PRICING TIPS

Approx. Total Investment: $15,570 to $40,320

EXPENSES (% OF ANNUAL SALES)

Cost of Goods	80%
Occupancy Costs	01%
Payroll/Labor Costs.	04%
Profit (pretax)	10%

RESOURCES

- Coverall: https://www.coverall.com
- Franchise information: https://www.coverall.com/franchise-opportunities

Crop Services

NAICS 11511	Businesses/Units 68,285	
Profit $2.3 B	Wages $5.2 B	Annual Growth Future -0.4%
		Annual Growth Past 8.9%

INDUSTRY MULTIPLES

Acquisition multiples below are calculated medians using US private industry transactions. Data updated annually. Last update: August 2023.

VALUATION MULTIPLE (MEDIAN VALUE)

UNDER $1 MILLION NET SALES

MVIC/Net Sales.	0.94
MVIC/Gross Profit	1.02
MVIC/SDE	3.80
MVIC/EBITDA	4.42
$1 MILLION–$5 MILLION NET SALES	N/A

OVER $5 MILLION NET SALES

MVIC/Net Sales.	0.38
MVIC/Gross Profit	3.14
MVIC/SDE	N/A
MVIC/EBITDA	7.31

Source: DealStats (formerly Pratt's Stats), 2023 (Portland, OR: Business Valuation Resources, LLC), www.bvresources.com/dealstats

BENCHMARK DATA

STATISTICS (CROP SERVICES)

Number of Establishments	68,285
Average Profit Margin	6.0%
Revenue per Employee	$241,000
Average Number of Employees.	2.3
Average Wages per Employee	$33,618

PRODUCTS AND SERVICES SEGMENTATION

Postharvest crop activities	37.7%
Soil preparation, planting, and cultivating	21.0%
Cotton ginning	17.9%
Farm labor contractors and crew leaders	17.3%
Farm management services	5.6%
Crop harvesting by machine	0.5%

MAJOR MARKET SEGMENTATION

Fruit and vegetable growers	45.5%
Grain and oilseed growers	37.7%
Other field crop growers	14.5%
Cotton growers	2.3%

INDUSTRY COSTS

Profit	6.0%
Wages	13.7%
Purchases	37.3%
Depreciation	2.7%
Marketing	0.8
Rent & Utilities	17.8%
Other	21.8%

INDUSTRY TREND

"As states implemented shelter-in-place policies, demand for agricultural products shifted from restaurants to grocery stores. Revenue is primarily generated from labor-oriented services. Labor-intensive services of the industry have declined as a share of revenue. Crop prices set by farmers are expected to increase. Wage costs have been increasing and will continue to grow. Farm wage costs are expected to decrease modestly. As farms with surpluses still required services to maintain their crops and avoid long-term production declines, profit ultimately grew."

Source: IBISWorld Industry at a Glance

RESOURCES

• IBISWorld, February 2023: https://www.ibisworld.com

Current-Carrying Wiring Device Manufacturing

| NAICS 335931 | Businesses/Units 551

| Profit $890.2 M | Wages $2.6 B | Annual Growth Future 0.7%

                                      | Annual Growth Past -2.1%

INDUSTRY MULTIPLES

Acquisition multiples below are calculated medians using US private industry transactions. Data updated annually. Last update: August 2023.

VALUATION MULTIPLE (MEDIAN VALUE)

UNDER $1 MILLION NET SALES	N/A
$1 MILLION–$5 MILLION NET SALES	N/A
OVER $5 MILLION NET SALES	
MVIC/Net Sales	0.71
MVIC/Gross Profit	2.58
MVIC/SDE	N/A
MVIC/EBITDA	5.48

Source: DealStats (formerly Pratt's Stats), 2023 (Portland, OR: Business Valuation Resources, LLC), www.bvresources.com/dealstats

BENCHMARK DATA

STATISTICS (WIRING DEVICE MANUFACTURING)

Number of Establishments	551
Average Profit Margin	5.6%
Revenue per Employee	$408,000
Average Number of Employees	71.4
Average Wages per Employee	$66,076

PRODUCTS AND SERVICES SEGMENTATION

Current-carrying wiring devices and supplies	30.8%
Pole line and transmission hardware	18.9%
Electrical conduit and conduit fittings	16.5%
Current-carrying wire connectors for electrical circuitry	12.9%
Other noncurrent-carrying wiring device and supplies	11.6%
Current-carrying switches for electrical circuitry	9.3%

MAJOR MARKET SEGMENTATION

Exports	32.6%
Construction	27.8%
Industrial and other manufacturing	13.2%
Telecom	9.4%
Machinery	7.5%
Government and institutional	4.8%
Aircraft and vehicle manufacturing	4.7%

INDUSTRY COSTS

Profit	5.6%
Wages	16.2%
Purchases	42.1%
Depreciation	1.8%
Marketing	0.2%
Rent & Utilities	1.5%
Other	32.5%

MARKET SHARE

TE Connectivity Ltd.	20.3%
Hubbell Inc.	10.5%

Legrand 4.3%
Leviton Manufacturing Co. Inc.. . . . . 1.6%

INDUSTRY TREND

"The industry has been adversely affected by the economic effects of the pandemic. Sharp declines in oil and natural gas prices dragged on capital expenditures. Exports have dropped as demand markets for top trade partners have waned. Increasing spending on automation will promote demand for wiring devices. Increasing demand is expected to enable some operators to expand profit slightly. IBISWorld expects industry imports to decrease due to expected downward pressure on imports. Import penetration from low-cost manufacturing regions has hurt industry profit."

Source: IBISWorld Industry at a Glance

RESOURCES

• IBISWorld, March 2023: https://www.ibisworld.com

Cut and Sew Manufacturers

| NAICS 315210 | Businesses/Units 11,764

| Profit $113.9 M | Wages $665.5 M | Annual Growth Future -1.8%

| Annual Growth Past -3.9%

INDUSTRY MULTIPLES

Acquisition multiples below are calculated medians using US private industry transactions. Data updated annually. Last update: August 2023.

VALUATION MULTIPLE (MEDIAN VALUE)

UNDER $1 MILLION NET SALES	
MVIC/Net Sales.	0.63
MVIC/Gross Profit	1.01
MVIC/SDE	3.20
MVIC/EBITDA	5.88
$1 MILLION–$5 MILLION NET SALES	N/A
OVER $5 MILLION NET SALES	
MVIC/Net Sales.	2.27
MVIC/Gross Profit	6.62
MVIC/SDE	N/A
MVIC/EBITDA	13.94

Source: DealStats (formerly Pratt's Stats), 2023 (Portland, OR: Business Valuation Resources, LLC), www.bvresources.com/dealstats

BENCHMARK DATA

STATISTICS (CUT AND SEW MANUFACTURERS)

Number of Establishments .	11,764
Average Profit Margin	5.4%
Revenue per Employee .	$74,000
Average Number of Employees.	2.4
Average Wages per Employee .	$23,136

PRODUCTS AND SERVICES SEGMENTATION

Other	33.6%
Women's and girls' shirts and blouses .	14.6%

Men's and boys' sweaters and pants 11.2%
Women's and girls' coats, jackets and pants 10.4%
Underwear, nightwear, uniforms and infant apparel . . . 8.6%
Men's and boys' shirts, excluding work shirts 8.3%
Men's and boys' work clothes, coats and jackets 6.8%
Women's, girls', and infants' dresses 6.5%

MAJOR MARKET SEGMENTATION

Women's and girls apparel companies 35.0%
Men's and boys apparel companies 26.0%
Costume, uniform and infant apparel companies 13.5%
Clothing retailers 11.6%
Direct orders 8.6%
Other 5.3%

INDUSTRY COSTS

Profit 5.4%
Wages 31.5%
Purchases 37.6%
Depreciation 0.7%
Marketing 1.0%
Rent & Utilities 4.0%
Other 19.9%

INDUSTRY TREND

"The trend of outsourcing to developing countries with low labor costs has increased. Industry operators are electing to serve the popular and niche denim markets. Fragmentation of the industry and steadily decreasing revenue has led many operators to close facilities. Manufacturers are expected to reap the benefits of the industry's realignment. Domestic clothing companies will likely invest more in production facilities abroad. Unprofitable enterprises will likely continue to leave the industry. Price pressures from abroad have encouraged many operators to exit the industry."

Source: IBISWorld Industry at a Glance

RESOURCES

• IBISWorld, March 2022: https://www.ibisworld.com

Cutting Tool and Machine Tool Accessory Manufacturing

| NAICS 333515 | Businesses/Units 1,137

| Profit $360 M | Wages $1.9 B | Annual Growth Future -0.1%

| | Annual Growth Past -0.6%

INDUSTRY MULTIPLES

Acquisition multiples below are calculated medians using US private industry transactions. Data updated annually. Last update: August 2023.

VALUATION MULTIPLE (MEDIAN VALUE)

UNDER $1 MILLION NET SALES	N/A
$1 MILLION–$5 MILLION NET SALES	
MVIC/Net Sales	1.21
MVIC/Gross Profit	2.59
MVIC/SDE	3.02
MVIC/EBITDA	4.50

OVER $5 MILLION NET SALES

MVIC/Net Sales	1.19
MVIC/Gross Profit	3.41
MVIC/SDE	N/A
MVIC/EBITDA	12.57

Source: DealStats (formerly Pratt's Stats), 2023 (Portland, OR: Business Valuation Resources, LLC), www.bvresources.com/dealstats

BENCHMARK DATA

STATISTICS (CUTTING TOOL & MACHINE TOOL ACCESSORY MANUFACTURING)

Number of Establishments	1,137
Average Profit Margin	5.5%
Revenue per Employee	$222,000
Average Number of Employees . .	25.9
Average Wages per Employee . .	$63,802

PRODUCTS AND SERVICES SEGMENTATION

Cutting tool accessories	48.5%
Other tools and services	35.3%
Tool holders and taps	16.2%

MAJOR MARKET SEGMENTATION

Engineering	32.3%
Mining and Other	26.6%
Exports	17.2%
Automotive	13.9%
Aerospace	6.5%
Energy	3.5%

INDUSTRY COSTS

Profit	5.5%
Wages	28.7%
Purchases	33.8%
Depreciation	3.2%
Marketing	0.3%
Rent & Utilities	3.1%
Other	25.3%

MARKET SHARE

Sandvik AB	11.8%

INDUSTRY TREND

"Demand is generated from the automotive, aerospace, energy and mining industries. Numerous US companies have shifted manufacturing operations overseas. Most enterprises only run one location. Demand from major downstream markets will help offset declines associated with offshoring and import competition. Manufacturers must differentiate their products through price or quality. Cutting tool and machine tool accessory manufacturers will struggle to cut costs. External competition has dragged down industry growth and mitigated profit growth."

Source: IBISWorld Industry at a Glance

RESOURCES

• IBISWorld, January 2023: https://www.ibisworld.com

Dairy Product (except Dried or Canned) Merchant Wholesalers

| NAICS 424430 | Businesses/Units 3,295

| Profit $1.4 B | Wages $3.1 B | Annual Growth Future 0.1%

| Annual Growth Past 2.6%

INDUSTRY MULTIPLES

Acquisition multiples below are calculated medians using US private industry transactions. Data updated annually. Last update: August 2023.

VALUATION MULTIPLE (MEDIAN VALUE)

UNDER $1 MILLION NET SALES

MVIC/Net Sales.	0.39
MVIC/Gross Profit	0.81
MVIC/SDE	1.39
MVIC/EBITDA	1.36

$1 MILLION–$5 MILLION NET SALES

MVIC/Net Sales.	0.23
MVIC/Gross Profit	N/A
MVIC/SDE	N/A
MVIC/EBITDA	N/A

OVER $5 MILLION NET SALES

MVIC/Net Sales.	0.66
MVIC/Gross Profit	1.90
MVIC/SDE	5.43
MVIC/EBITDA	6.36

Source: DealStats (formerly Pratt's Stats), 2023 (Portland, OR: Business Valuation Resources, LLC), www.bvresources.com/dealstats

BENCHMARK DATA

STATISTICS (DAIRY WHOLESALING)

Number of Establishments .	3,295
Average Profit Margin	1.2%
Revenue per Employee .	$2,669,000
Average Number of Employees.	13.3
Average Wages per Employee .	$71,046

PRODUCTS AND SERVICES SEGMENTATION

Cheese .	24.8%
Other dairy products	20.1%
Ice cream and frozen dairy products	18.7%
Raw milk and cream	16.0%
Packaged fluid milk and cream .	12.9%
Yogurt	5.0%
Butter	2.5%

MAJOR MARKET SEGMENTATION

Other wholesalers .	44.5%
Retailers.	32.6%
Food service outlets	10.2%
Other markets	6.4%
Food manufacturers and processors	6.3%

INDUSTRY COSTS

Profit	1.2%
Wages	2.5%
Purchases	86.1%
Depreciation	0.7%

Marketing 0.2%
Rent & Utilities 0.8%
Other 8.5%

MARKET SHARE

Dairy Farmers of America, Inc. 6.4%
Dean Foods Company 5.7%
Gordon Food Service 3.3%
Land O'Lakes, Inc. 1.2%

INDUSTRY TREND

"Dairy wholesalers benefited from rising prices that ushered in heightened revenue. New tech has boosted efficiency and lifted profit. Vegan-friendly milk substitutes have found success and tempered growth. The consumption of dairy products will decline every year over the next five years. Dairy wholesalers will face falling prices to capture lessened demand. Value-added services will become more important as wholesalers try to stay relevant in the supply chain. Falling demand and stagnating prices will place the industry back under pressure."

Source: IBISWorld Industry at a Glance

RESOURCES

• IBISWorld, March 2023: https://www.ibisworld.com

Dairy Product Production

| NAICS 31151 | Businesses/Units 1,297

| Profit $5.1 B | Wages $9.3 B | Annual Growth Future 0.3%

     | Annual Growth Past 4.5%

INDUSTRY MULTIPLES

Acquisition multiples below are calculated medians using US private industry transactions. Data updated annually. Last update: August 2023.

VALUATION MULTIPLE (MEDIAN VALUE)

UNDER $1 MILLION NET SALES	N/A
$1 MILLION–$5 MILLION NET SALES	N/A
OVER $5 MILLION NET SALES	
MVIC/Net Sales	2.44
MVIC/Gross Profit	5.28
MVIC/SDE	N/A
MVIC/EBITDA	32.66

Source: DealStats (formerly Pratt's Stats), 2023 (Portland, OR: Business Valuation Resources, LLC), www.bvresources.com/dealstats

BENCHMARK DATA

STATISTICS (DAIRY PRODUCT PRODUCTION)

Number of Establishments	1,297
Average Profit Margin	3.1%
Revenue per Employee	$1,099,000
Average Number of Employees. . . .	115.0
Average Wages per Employee . . .	$62,934

PRODUCTS AND SERVICES SEGMENTATION

Cheese 57.0%
Fluid milk and milk-based products 28.1%
Dry, condensed, and evaporated milk products 11.5%
Butter 3.4%

MAJOR MARKET SEGMENTATION

Wholesalers. 44.1%
Retail stores. 25.8%
Other 12.4%
Food service establishments 11.4%
Exports 6.3%

INDUSTRY COSTS

Profit 3.1%
Wages 5.7%
Purchases 67.3%
Depreciation 2.1%
Marketing 0.2%
Rent & Utilities 1.6%
Other 20.0%

INDUSTRY TREND

"Operators typically benefit from higher input prices. Industry exports account for an important share of revenue. Amid growing milk production from cooperatives, the number of employees has risen. Industry profitability will stagnate. As a result of expected increases in demand for premium products, industry participation is anticipated to rise. Imports will become comparatively more expensive. Industry costs have risen, pressuring industry profitability during the period."

Source: IBISWorld Industry at a Glance

RESOURCES

• IBISWorld, January 2023: https://www.ibisworld.com

Data Processing Services

	NAICS 518210		SIC 7374-01		Businesses/Units 76,379
	Profit $23.4 B		Wages $101.9 B		Annual Growth Future 6.5%
					Annual Growth Past 8.9%

Rules of Thumb

• 15% annual sales plus inventory
• 2.2 x SDE plus inventory
• 2 x EBIT
• 2.2 x EBITDA

INDUSTRY MULTIPLES

Acquisition multiples below are calculated medians using US private industry transactions. Data updated annually. Last update: August 2023.

VALUATION MULTIPLE (MEDIAN VALUE)

UNDER $1 MILLION NET SALES
MVIC/Net Sales. 1.41
MVIC/Gross Profit 2.15

MVIC/SDE	3.67
MVIC/EBITDA	11.90

MVIC/Net Sales	1.05
MVIC/Gross Profit	2.28
MVIC/SDE	3.54
MVIC/EBITDA	5.88

OVER $5 MILLION NET SALES

MVIC/Net Sales	2.93
MVIC/Gross Profit	4.59
MVIC/SDE	8.27
MVIC/EBITDA	23.30

Source: DealStats (formerly Pratt's Stats), 2023 (Portland, OR: Business Valuation Resources, LLC), www.bvresources.com/dealstats

PRICING TIPS

A proprietary software component could raise the multiple to as much as 10 x.

BENCHMARK DATA

STATISTICS (DATA PROCESSING & HOSTING SERVICES)

Number of Establishments	76,379
Average Profit Margin	7.2%
Revenue per Employee	$443,000
Average Number of Employees	10.4
Average Wages per Employee	$137,461

PRODUCTS AND SERVICES SEGMENTATION

Other services	23.3%
Web hosting services	22.5%
Business process management	22.4%
Application service provisioning	21.2%
Data storage and management services	10.6%

MAJOR MARKET SEGMENTATION

Other	49.5%
Bankin	13.5%
Telecommunication	11.1%
Individuals & households	10.6%
Professional services	7.8%
Manufacturing	7.5%

INDUSTRY COSTS

Profit	7.2%
Wages	31.3%
Purchases	6.8%
Depreciation	2.3%
Marketing	4.9%
Rent and Utilities	4.3%
Other	43.3%

MARKET SHARE

International Business Machines Corporation	7.8%
Amazon.com, Inc.	7.4%
Salesforce.com, Inc.	7.2%
NTT DATA Corp.	3.1%

EXPENSES (% OF ANNUAL SALES)

Cost of Goods	N/A
Occupancy Costs	N/A
Payroll/Labor Costs	35%
Profit (pretax)	40%

- Ask for resumes of employees and a meeting with a few top customers during due diligence.

D

INDUSTRY TREND

"The popularization of cloud computing has contributed to revenue growth. While outsourcing has contributed to revenue expansion, offshoring has decelerated revenue growth. COVID-19 has had a mixed effect on industry performance. Outsourcing will enable businesses to take advantage of lower costs. As the US economy becomes increasingly digital, demand for data management and web hosting services will grow. Revenue growth will depend on the economic performance. The advent and popularization of cloud computing has led to greater demand."

Source: IBISWorld Industry at a Glance

RESOURCES

- IBISWorld, November 2022: https://www.ibisworld.com

Dating Services

NAICS 812990	SIC 7299-26	Businesses/Units 372
Profit $512 M	Wages $937.6 M	Annual Growth Future 0.8%
		Annual Growth Past 2.1%

Rules of Thumb

- 30%–35% annual sales

INDUSTRY MULTIPLES

Acquisition multiples below are calculated medians using US private industry transactions. Data updated annually. Last update: August 2023.

VALUATION MULTIPLE (MEDIAN VALUE)

UNDER $1 MILLION NET SALES
MVIC/Net Sales.	0.66
MVIC/Gross Profit	0.85
MVIC/SDE	2.29
MVIC/EBITDA	3.49

$1 MILLION–$5 MILLION NET SALES
MVIC/Net Sales.	0.74
MVIC/Gross Profit	1.42
MVIC/SDE	2.72
MVIC/EBITDA	4.36

OVER $5 MILLION NET SALES
MVIC/Net Sales.	0.80
MVIC/Gross Profit	3.83
MVIC/SDE	N/A
MVIC/EBITDA	24.78

Source: DealStats (formerly Pratt's Stats), 2023 (Portland, OR: Business Valuation Resources, LLC), www.bvresources.com/dealstats

BENCHMARK DATA

STATISTICS (DATING SERVICES)

Number of Establishments	372
Average Profit Margin	11.9%
Revenue per Employee	$651,000
Average Number of Employees. . . .	18.0
Average Wages per Employee . . .	$141,029

PRODUCTS AND SERVICES SEGMENTATION

Mobile dating	40.4%
Online dating	21.8%
Matchmakers	21.0%
Singles events	11.5%
Other	5.3%

INDUSTRY COSTS

Profit	11.9%
Wages	21.8%
Purchases	9.5%
Depreciation	2.0%
Marketing	1.9%
Rent & Utilities	5.9%
Other	47.0%

MARKET SHARE

Match Group Inc.	42.1%
eharmony Inc.	16.5%

INDUSTRY TREND

"Today, dating apps are more popular than ever. There were an estimated 26.6 million users of online dating services in the United States alone in 2020, with projected growth to reach 30.5 million users in 2024....

"One of the most significant trends in dating apps is the growing desire to build meaningful bonds, with two-thirds of Generation Z ready to switch to in-real-life (IRL) because they can't find 'true love' online. Many users are tired of the superficial nature of online dating, where people often present a carefully curated version of themselves that doesn't reflect who they truly are."

Source: "From Machine Learning to Unfiltered Videos, These Online Dating Trends Are Set to Improve the Tricky World of Dating" by Marina Anderson, March 8, 2023, https://www.entrepreneur.com/science-technology/these-trends-are-set-to-enhance-online-dating/446359

"The COVID-19 pandemic accelerated movement toward destigmatizing online dating. Industry operators that have remained competitive have kept pace with digital advances. Most industry players do not seem overly threatened by Facebook's online dating service. Demand for online dating will expand further as internet penetration continues to rise. Revenue from mobile dating is projected to continue rising over the next five years. Industry regulations are expected to become more stringent over the outlook period. Demand has grown due to fading social stigmas associated with online dating and busy work schedules that limit ways of meeting potential partners."

Source: IBISWorld Industry at a Glance

RESOURCES

- IBISWorld, February 2023: https://www.ibisworld.com
- Online Dating Magazine: https://www.onlinedatingmagazine.com

Day Care Centers/Adult

	NAICS 624120		SIC 8322-10		Businesses/Units 38,573
	Profit $252.5 M		Wages $3.6 B		Annual Growth Future 2.7%
					Annual Growth Past 0.9%

Rules of Thumb

- 70%–75% annual sales
- 2.5 x SDE plus inventory

INDUSTRY MULTIPLES

Acquisition multiples below are calculated medians using US private industry transactions. Data updated annually. Last update: August 2023.

VALUATION MULTIPLE (MEDIAN VALUE)

UNDER $1 MILLION NET SALES

MVIC/Net Sales.	0.48
MVIC/Gross Profit	0.66
MVIC/SDE	2.12
MVIC/EBITDA	3.07

$1 MILLION–$5 MILLION NET SALES

MVIC/Net Sales.	0.45
MVIC/Gross Profit	0.78
MVIC/SDE	2.76
MVIC/EBITDA	3.87

OVER $5 MILLION NET SALES

MVIC/Net Sales.	0.47
MVIC/Gross Profit	0.78
MVIC/SDE	3.62
MVIC/EBITDA	2.97

Source: DealStats (formerly Pratt's Stats), 2023 (Portland, OR: Business Valuation Resources, LLC), www.bvresources.com/dealstats

PRICING TIPS

The mix of payers is important. What is the percent of private pay vs. Medicaid vs. VA vs. county programs? The higher the private pay component, the higher the value, as the business is not subject to governmental pricing changes. If an adult day care center also provides in-home nonmedical care for their clients, this adds to the value of the enterprise. If an adult day care center has its own transportation available to clients, this adds to the value of the enterprise.

BENCHMARK DATA

STATISTICS (ADULT DAY CARE)

Number of Establishments.	38,573
Average Profit Margin	3.8%
Revenue per Employee.	$41,300
Average Number of Employees.	4.3
Average Wages per Employee.	$22,734

PRODUCTS AND SERVICES SEGMENTATION

Social and medical model	48.5%
Social services model	31.3%
Medical services model	20.2%

INDUSTRY COSTS

Profit	3.8%
Wages	54.6%
Purchases	3.9%
Depreciation	2.2%
Marketing	0.4%
Rent & Utilities	3.9%
Other	31.2%

EXPENSES (% OF ANNUAL SALES)

Occupancy Costs	12% to 20%
Payroll/Labor Costs.	25% to 35%
Profit (pretax)	20% to 25%

QUESTIONS

- What is your mix of payors? What is your employee to participant ratio? Should be 1 to 5 or less to ensure good service is provided. How do clients get to the center? Your own transportation, regional senior transport, adult children or spouses dropping participants off at the center?

INDUSTRY TREND

"Competitive advantages over other long-term care providers resulted in industry growth. Medicaid has expanded, enabling more individuals to obtain funding for industry services. Small operators are entering the industry, while larger companies are consolidating. Aging baby boomers will increase demand for adult day care services. The projected growth in government healthcare funding will benefit industry operators. Larger operators will expand by entering new markets and acquiring smaller companies. The prevalence of physical and mental diseases will increase, raising demand for industry services."

Source: IBISWorld Industry at a Glance

EXPERT COMMENTS

This is a great industry to invest in, as the growth trend line is positive and the margins are solid if the operation is run properly, not unlike any other Main Street business.

FINANCING

Similar to other Main Street businesses, there is a mix of outside financing and seller financing. Typically sellers will carry a small percentage (10 to 20 percent) of the transaction value.

RESOURCES

- IBISWorld, May 2023: https://www.ibisworld.com
- NADSA—National Adult Day Services Association: https://www.nadsa.org

Day Care Centers/Children

NAICS 624410	SIC 8351-01	Businesses/Units 634,809
Profit $5.7 B	Wages $28.3 B	Annual Growth Future 1.1%
		Annual Growth Past 1.4%

Rules of Thumb

- 60%–70% annual sales includes inventory
- 3–5 x EBIT
- 4–6 x EBITDA
- 2–4 x SDE includes inventory. Most childcare centers are acquired with the real estate.

INDUSTRY MULTIPLES

Acquisition multiples below are calculated medians using US private industry transactions. Data updated annually. Last update: August 2023.

VALUATION MULTIPLE (MEDIAN VALUE)

UNDER $1 MILLION NET SALES

MVIC/Net Sales.	0.52
MVIC/Gross Profit	0.64
MVIC/SDE	2.28
MVIC/EBITDA	3.77

$1 MILLION–$5 MILLION NET SALES

MVIC/Net Sales.	0.58
MVIC/Gross Profit	0.62
MVIC/SDE	2.85
MVIC/EBITDA	4.28

OVER $5 MILLION NET SALES

MVIC/Net Sales.	1.61
MVIC/Gross Profit	6.83
MVIC/SDE	N/A
MVIC/EBITDA	35.51

Source: DealStats (formerly Pratt's Stats), 2023 (Portland, OR: Business Valuation Resources, LLC), www.bvresources.com/dealstats

PRICING TIPS

Centres need to have high occupancy rates above 80 percent, and they require a long lease of more than 15 years, generally 20 to 30 years. The quality of the building is super important, with new competitions spending in excess of $1M on playgrounds alone. Rent should be 12 to 15 percent of turnover at a maximum.

Typically, most buyers are after centres in excess of 60 kids. Corporate prefers 80+.Pricing is typically on a multiple of EBITDA (4 to 5). Smaller centres will get a lower multiple maybe (3 to 4).The key drivers (this will effect salability):- Wages run at around 55 to 65 percent of turnover (the better centres with higher daily fees may have lower wages).- Government license and accreditation is important, as is local council approval (often the two approvals are for different numbers of children; must calculate on lowest).- Check competition and their occupancy levels (if your centre is full and all the competitors are not, maybe some personal goodwill).- Quality of the building needs to be considered; many centres are now due for major capital injection and upgrading.

$8,000 to $10,000 per enrolled student

Lease term and amount of rent including CAM charges are major factors in profitability of day cares. Also, the center capacity, number of enrolled kids, the amount tuition charged per kids, and director education, expertise, and conduct are important factors. Brand recognition is also very important.

Very much depends upon if there is real estate involved, which there usually is, and depends upon size of center.

BENCHMARK DATA

STATISTICS (DAY CARE)

Number of Establishments	634,809
Average Profit Margin	9.3%
Revenue per Employee	$39,900
Average Number of employees	2.4
Average Wages per Employee	$18,520

PRODUCTS AND SERVICES SEGMENTATION

Center-based day care	73.0%
Pre-primary grade instructional programs	18.4%
In-home day care	4.9%
Other services and programs	3.7%

INDUSTRY COSTS

Profit	9.3%
Wages	46.7%
Purchases	4.1%
Depreciation	2.4%
Marketing	0.4%
Rent & Utilities	4.2%
Other	33.1%

Keep your fees at the high end of your competitors'; low fees will attract fewer children! Rent up to 13 percent or so, wages 55 to 65 percent; the key is to manage them.

EXPENSES (% OF ANNUAL SALES)

Cost of Goods	02% to 15%
Occupancy Costs	10% to 20%
Payroll/Labor Costs	45% to 55%
Profit (pretax)	10% to 20%

QUESTIONS

- History of staff? Owner involvement? Forward bookings?
- Why do you want to sell your business? What will you do after selling this business? Will you provide training and support after closing? Do the center and teachers have accreditation? How many classes do you have? What is the center capacity? How many kids are currently enrolled in each class? Can I look at your financial reports and tax returns? Have you had any incident or litigation? What is your projection for the coming year?
- How much of the revenue is private pay? How much is government subsidized? Do you accept cash payments? How many years of experience does the director have? Will she/he stay in the event of a sale? How is your relationship with the state regulating agency?
- Are you a member of the USDA food program? Are you willing to owner finance a small portion? A redacted roll sheet to prove the enrollment? Good building inspection?
- Occupancy reports

INDUSTRY TREND

Interest rates have a major effect on the value of childcare centres. Banks are keen to lend; however, the cost of funding does drive down the price.

The cost of building material and labour has increased; therefore, the barriers to entry for new players have increased. Government assistance is still high.

There will be more public childcare facilities than private. The market is reducing the number of private facilities. Once you learn the system, then you will be very successful in childcare. There are a lot of buyers buying childcare facilities now because of the rate of return.

Flat

We believe this industry will experience growth during the next few years. Since many parents have been working from home, however, and this trend for many of them may become a norm, growth might not be as strong as expected before Covid. But in general, demand for day care will continue to be strong.

"The industry is particularly susceptible to changes in per capita disposable income. A more substantial annualized expansion was subdued by a 12.6% revenue contraction in 2020 alone. Industry employment has decreased over the past five years in-line with the substantial contraction in competing enterprise figures. The majority of industry revenue comes directly from enrolled children's families. Public attention to day care accessibility and early learning is likely to endure over the next five years. The industry landscape is expected to remain fairly constant even as revenue recovers toward pre-pandemic levels. Child care centers have been slow to reopen after the COVID-19 pandemic."

Source: IBISWorld Industry at a Glance

EXPERT COMMENTS

Documentation: buyers need to see the local government approval and ensure the business is operating within the rules, i.e., approval to operate 7:00 a.m. to 6:00 p.m. for 80 kids; check that the centre is not running from 7:00 a.m. to 7:00 p.m., for example. The sellers should have all records, occupancy reports, profit and loss, and lease.

The cost of building a new centre and getting approvals is extensive.

Seller: maintain a track of clean financial records, and contact an experienced broker about one year before selling your business. It is important to know the value of your business before listing, and this is the service that we provide.

Buyer: review financials, and make sure the franchisor has a good reputation and franchisees are happy.

Inspect the building carefully, including all the systems (electrical, HVAC, plumbing, septic, etc.).

FINANCING

Smaller locations: mix of seller financing and SBA

Larger locations: attractive to larger national and regional chains that are cash buyers

We have done much financing for buyers or future owners of day care through SBA and conventional loan lenders with excellent terms. With current SBA rules, a buyer with 10 percent cash can acquire a day care or start a new franchise. It is important to make sure the leverage is not too high; a high leverage creates more risk.

RESOURCES

- IBISWorld, June 2022: https://www.ibisworld.com
- Association for Early Learning Leaders: https://www.earlylearningleaders.org

- CCSA—Child Care Services Association: https://www.childcareservices.org
- Child Care Aware® of America: https://www.childcareaware.org
- Childcare Brokers: http://childcarebrokers.com
- Council for Professional Recognition: https://www.cdacouncil.org/resources/find-ece-organizations
- DECAL—Georgia Dept of Early Care and Learning: http://www.decal.ga.gov
- Exchange Press: https://www.childcareexchange.com
- GCCA—Georgia Child Care Association: https://www.georgiachildcare.org
- NAEYC—National Association for the Education of Young Children: https://www.naeyc.org
- NAFCC—National Association for Family Child Care: https://www.nafcc.org
- NCCA—National Child Care Association: https://www.nccanet.org
- Schools For Sale: http://schoolsforsale.com
- SECA—Southern Early Childhood Association: https://www.seca.info/

Del Taco (Franchise)

| NAICS 722513 | Businesses/Units 306

Rules of Thumb

- 70% annual sales plus inventory

INDUSTRY MULTIPLES

Acquisition multiples below are calculated medians using US private industry transactions. Data updated annually. Last update: August 2023.

VALUATION MULTIPLE (MEDIAN VALUE)

UNDER $1 MILLION NET SALES

MVIC/Net Sales.	0.31
MVIC/Gross Profit	0.48
MVIC/SDE	1.67
MVIC/EBITDA	2.21

$1 MILLION–$5 MILLION NET SALES

MVIC/Net Sales.	0.39
MVIC/Gross Profit	0.60
MVIC/SDE	2.43
MVIC/EBITDA	2.98

OVER $5 MILLION NET SALES

MVIC/Net Sales.	0.89
MVIC/Gross Profit	2.08
MVIC/SDE	4.98
MVIC/EBITDA	12.81

Source: DealStats (formerly Pratt's Stats), 2023 (Portland, OR: Business Valuation Resources, LLC), www.bvresources.com/dealstats

PRICING TIPS

Approx. Total Investment: $862,700 to $2,368,000

RESOURCES

- Del Taco: https://deltaco.com
- Franchise information: https://deltacofranchise.com

Delicatessens

| NAICS 445110 | SIC 5812-09 |

D

Rules of Thumb

- 40% annual sales plus inventory
- 2 x SDE plus inventory

INDUSTRY MULTIPLES

Acquisition multiples below are calculated medians using US private industry transactions. Data updated annually. Last update: August 2023.

VALUATION MULTIPLE (MEDIAN VALUE)

UNDER $1 MILLION NET SALES

MVIC/Net Sales.	0.30
MVIC/Gross Profit	0.68
MVIC/SDE	2.06
MVIC/EBITDA	2.72

$1 MILLION–$5 MILLION NET SALES

MVIC/Net Sales.	0.20
MVIC/Gross Profit	0.71
MVIC/SDE	2.46
MVIC/EBITDA	4.75

OVER $5 MILLION NET SALES

MVIC/Net Sales.	0.37
MVIC/Gross Profit	1.46
MVIC/SDE	4.70
MVIC/EBITDA	10.22

Source: DealStats (formerly Pratt's Stats), 2023 (Portland, OR: Business Valuation Resources, LLC), www.bvresources.com/dealstats

INDUSTRY TREND

"Mix-and-match meal preparation, changing employment patterns, and a surge in at-home entertaining are among the factors creating deli department sales opportunities....One-quarter of shoppers are buying more prepared foods versus a year ago, according to FMI, The Food Industry Association. That's especially true for men, city dwellers, employees with hybrid office/work-from-home schedules, and households with kids, per FMI."

Source: "Destination Deli" by A . Elizabeth Sloan, June 1, 2023, https://www.ift.org/news-and-publications/food-technology-magazine/issues/2023/june/columns/consumer-trends-destination-deli

RESOURCES

- Deli Business: https://delibusiness.com
- IDDBA—International Dairy Deli Bakery Association: https://www.iddba.org
- FMI—The Food Industry Association: https://www.fmi.org

Delivery Services (Courier Services)

NAICS 492210	SIC 4212-05	Businesses/Units 464,224
Profit $10.2 B	Wages $43.9 B	Annual Growth Future 3.6%
		Annual Growth Past 6.9%

Rules of Thumb

- 70% annual sales plus inventory (if any)
- 3 x SDE including inventory
- 2 x EBITDA for businesses under $1M
- 3 x EBITDA for businesses from $1M to $5M
- 4 x EBITDA for businesses over $5M
- 3–4 x EBIT

INDUSTRY MULTIPLES

Acquisition multiples below are calculated medians using US private industry transactions. Data updated annually. Last update: August 2023.

VALUATION MULTIPLE (MEDIAN VALUE)

UNDER $1 MILLION NET SALES

MVIC/Net Sales	0.89
MVIC/Gross Profit	0.98
MVIC/SDE	2.79
MVIC/EBITDA	3.01

$1 MILLION–$5 MILLION NET SALES

MVIC/Net Sales	0.66
MVIC/Gross Profit	0.85
MVIC/SDE	2.92
MVIC/EBITDA	3.34

OVER $5 MILLION NET SALES

MVIC/Net Sales	4.56
MVIC/Gross Profit	5.62
MVIC/SDE	N/A
MVIC/EBITDA	N/A

Source: DealStats (formerly Pratt's Stats), 2023 (Portland, OR: Business Valuation Resources, LLC), www.bvresources.com/dealstats

PRICING TIPS

Given the wide range of compensation that owners of routes take, they are not typically sold based on EBIT or EBITDA multiples but usually on SDE. In former years, these routes sold for a multiple of revenues—typically 100 percent—but due to the change of contracts and the more sophisticated investor/owners coming into this market, that pricing structure is rarely used.

BENCHMARK DATA

STATISTICS (COURIERS AND LOCAL DELIVERY SERVICES)

Number of Establishments	464,224
Average Profit Margin	6.7%
Revenue per Employee	$131,000
Average Number of Employees	2.6
Average Wages per Employee	$38,450

PRODUCTS AND SERVICES SEGMENTATION

Ground deliveries	60.4%
Air transit services	38.6%
Other services including messengers and local deliveries	1.0%

MAJOR MARKET SEGMENTATION

Business-to-consumers, including households	52.0%
Business-to-business	41.5%
All other	6.5%

Profit	. 6.7%
Wages	. 29.0%
Purchases	. 7.8%
Depreciation	. 1.6%
Marketing	0.3%
Rent & Utilities	. 4.1%
Other	. 50.6%

MARKET SHARE

United Parcel Service, Inc.	. 51.8%
FedEx Corporation	. 22.6%

The most common measurement is stops per route, which will vary depending on rural versus urban, the mix of business and residential, and the distance the route is from the dispatching terminal.

EXPENSES (% OF ANNUAL SALES)

Cost of Goods	. 42%
Occupancy Costs	. .0%
Payroll/Labor Costs.	35% to 45%
Profit (pretax)	24% to 28%

QUESTIONS

• Maintenance logs on vehicles; tenure and safety record of business and individual drivers

INDUSTRY TREND

Continued growth due to e-commerce. Route owners who are overlapped, operate routes in densely populated areas, and hold their drivers to high stop-per-day standards will win.

"Volatile input costs constrain profit growth. Larger couriers have used technology as a way for customers to track packages and verify deliveries. The robust growth of the e-commerce sector has benefited industry operators. Industry customers are expected to continue integrating vertically, decreasing demand. Consumers expected to continue shifting to online shopping. Increasing demand for same-day delivery is expected to lead to new business locations. Over the past five years, developments in the e-commerce and online retailing space have driven industry growth."

Source: IBISWorld Industry at a Glance

EXPERT COMMENTS

With the increase of e-commerce, there is good news and bad news. The good news is volume has significantly increased; the bad news is the volume is driven by residential deliveries, which pay less than business deliveries. To overcome that reality, route owners need to ensure they are operating both Ground and Home Delivery in their route areas, thereby creating density and efficiencies.

FINANCING

SBA financing can be procured if the previous route owners kept clean books and records; this is becoming more common with recent investor-owned routes. But older contractors did not always present well for financing. Seller financing is rare, as the former owner has only the trucks to collateralize the seller note; the contract is not lienable.

RESOURCES

- IBISWorld, October 2022: https://www.ibisworld.com
- Amazon Delivery Service Partner (DSP) program: https://logistics.amazon.com
- CLDA—Customized Logistics and Delivery Association: https://clda.org
- eTruckBiz: https://www.etruckbiz.com

Dental Equipment and Supplies Manufacturing

| NAICS 339114 | Businesses/Units 542

| Profit $495.2 M | Wages $1.2 B

| Annual Growth Future 0.9%

| Annual Growth Past -0.1%

INDUSTRY MULTIPLES

Acquisition multiples below are calculated medians using US private industry transactions. Data updated annually. Last update: August 2023.

VALUATION MULTIPLE (MEDIAN VALUE)

UNDER $1 MILLION NET SALES

MVIC/Net Sales	1.98
MVIC/Gross Profit	1.98
MVIC/SDE	N/A
MVIC/EBITDA	N/A

$1 MILLION–$5 MILLION NET SALES .... N/A

OVER $5 MILLION NET SALES

MVIC/Net Sales	3.52
MVIC/Gross Profit	5.57
MVIC/SDE	N/A
MVIC/EBITDA	19.24

Source: DealStats (formerly Pratt's Stats), 2023 (Portland, OR: Business Valuation Resources, LLC), www.bvresources.com/dealstats

BENCHMARK DATA

STATISTICS (DENTAL CLINICAL INSTRUMENT MANUFACTURING)

Number of Establishments	542
Average Profit Margin	9.6%
Revenue per Employee	$306,000
Average Number of Employees	31.0
Average Wages per Employee	$68,308

PRODUCTS AND SERVICES SEGMENTATION

Diagnostic, imaging, and procedural instruments	24.8%
Implants	17.6%
Dental laboratory equipment	17.5%
Orthodontic instruments	15.4%
Impression materials and cements	10.9%
Other	8.5%
Storage and cleaning systems	5.3%

MAJOR MARKET SEGMENTATION

Dental clinics	38.7%
Wholesalers	37.3%
Exports	21.5%
Dental laboratories	2.5%

INDUSTRY COSTS

Profit	9.6%
Wages	22.3%
Purchases	29.0%
Depreciation	2.5%
Marketing	1.2%
Rent & Utilities	1.4%
Other	34.0%

MARKET SHARE

Envista Holdings	25.6%
Dentsply Sirona	23.8%

INDUSTRY TREND

"The aging of the US population has contributed to increased demand. While the essential nature of dental services has supported demand, falling demand from overseas has hurt industry companies. While competition has grown overseas, many domestic operators have refocused on the domestic market. Companies will focus on maintaining their highly trained research and development employees. High-value, high-margin clinical instruments will boost industry-wide profit. The improving economic climate and aging US population will continue to boost revenue. New product development will likely set the pace for growth over the next five years."

Source: IBISWorld Industry at a Glance

RESOURCES

• IBISWorld, September 2022: https://www.ibisworld.com

Dental Laboratories

NAICS 339116	SIC 8072-01	Businesses/Units 9,592
Profit $446.8 M	Wages $2.2 B	Annual Growth Future -1.0%
		Annual Growth Past 2.1%

Rules of Thumb

• 45% annual sales plus inventory
• 1 x SDE plus equipment and inventory
• 2 x SDE includes equipment & inventory

INDUSTRY MULTIPLES

Acquisition multiples below are calculated medians using US private industry transactions. Data updated annually. Last update: August 2023.

VALUATION MULTIPLE (MEDIAN VALUE)

UNDER $1 MILLION NET SALES

MVIC/Net Sales	0.51
MVIC/Gross Profit	0.95
MVIC/SDE	1.70
MVIC/EBITDA	2.84

$1 MILLION–$5 MILLION NET SALES

MVIC/Net Sales	0.63
MVIC/Gross Profit	1.20
MVIC/SDE	3.11
MVIC/EBITDA	3.78

D

MVIC/Net Sales	0.61
MVIC/Gross Profit	1.09
MVIC/SDE	5.82
MVIC/EBITDA	4.77

Source: DealStats (formerly Pratt's Stats), 2023 (Portland, OR: Business Valuation Resources, LLC), www.bvresources.com/dealstats

BENCHMARK DATA

STATISTICS (DENTAL LABORATORIES)

Number of Establishments	9,592
Average Profit Margin	6.5%
Revenue per Employee	$158,000
Average Number of Employees	4.5
Average Wages per Employee . . .	$49,323

PRODUCTS AND SERVICES

Inlays, onlays, and veneers	62.3%
Crowns, bridges, and dentures . . .	26.4%
Implants	11.3%

INDUSTRY COSTS

Profit	6.5%
Wages	31.4%
Purchases	22.2%
Depreciation	1.8%
Marketing	0.7%
Rent & utilities	2.8%
Other	34.2%

INDUSTRY TREND

"While elderly patients require more dental services, they are more price sensitive. The population with dental benefits has expanded over the past decade. Technology has played an important role in this industry over the past five years. Revenue will decline in the next five years, but a longer-term outlook remains positive. The expanding number of individuals aged 65 and older will present new challenges and opportunities. Continued adoption of computer-aided design and 3D printing will contribute to profit growth. The outbreak of COVID-19 has resulted in historically high revenue volatility."

Source: IBISWorld Industry at a Glance

RESOURCES

- IBISWorld, March 2023: https://www.ibisworld.com
- DPR—Dental Products Report: https://www.dentalproductsreport.com
- NADL—National Association of Dental Laboratories: https://nadl.org/index.cfm

Dental Practices

NAICS 621210	SIC 8021-01	Businesses/Units 201,254
Profit $26.8 B	Wages $63.7 B	Annual Growth Future 2.8%
		Annual Growth Past 1.0%

Rules of Thumb

- 65%–85% annual sales includes inventory
- 1.3–3 x SDE includes inventory
- 2–4 x EBIT
- 3–5 x EBITDA
- 50%–70% annual collections

D

INDUSTRY MULTIPLES

Acquisition multiples below are calculated medians using US private industry transactions. Data updated annually. Last update: August 2023.

VALUATION MULTIPLE (MEDIAN VALUE)

UNDER $1 MILLION NET SALES

MVIC/Net Sales.	0.65
MVIC/Gross Profit	0.69
MVIC/SDE	1.58
MVIC/EBITDA	2.74

$1 MILLION–$5 MILLION NET SALES

MVIC/Net Sales.	0.67
MVIC/Gross Profit	0.75
MVIC/SDE	1.40
MVIC/EBITDA	2.26

OVER $5 MILLION NET SALES

MVIC/Net Sales.	0.72
MVIC/Gross Profit	1.28
MVIC/SDE	1.56
MVIC/EBITDA	9.00

Source: DealStats (formerly Pratt's Stats), 2023 (Portland, OR: Business Valuation Resources, LLC), www.bvresources.com/dealstats

PRICING TIPS

Consistent overhead of 60 percent or less tends to drive a higher practice value. Dental service organizations (DSOs) are always willing to pay a higher multiple of earnings for the practice; however, the selling doc is usually required to sign a lengthy employment contract.

Pricing is different for a corporate or DSO transaction than for an individual buyer. DSOs will pay slightly higher prices. Some areas are more competitive than others and will get a higher price.

What kind of equipment and technology are used in the dental practice? Age of equipment?

Another factor that affects price is metropolitan vs. rural practice.

BENCHMARK DATA

STATISTICS (DENTISTS)

Number of Establishments .	201,254
Average Profit Margin	15.6%
Revenue per Employee .	$150,000
Average Number of Employees.	5.7
Average Wages per Employee .	$55,726

PRODUCTS AND SERVICES SEGMENTATION

Restorative dental services .	23.9%
Preventative services	15.6%
Dental consultations and diagnostic services .	15.2%
Other	13.4%

Prosthodontics (fixed and removable) 10.1%
Orthodontics 9.9%
Surgical oral and maxillofacial services 6.9%
Nonsurgical endodontic services 5.0%

INDUSTRY COSTS

Profit 15.6%
Wages 37.1%
Purchases 13.8%
Depreciation 3.0%
Marketing 1.6%
Rent & Utilities 7.0%
Other 21.9%

Profit margin 35 percent

Revenues should be $20,000 per employee. Revenues can also be $50,000 per operatory.

EXPENSES (% OF ANNUAL SALES)

Cost of Goods . . . . 07% to 15%
Occupancy Costs . . . . 04% to 10%
Payroll/Labor Costs. . . . . 20% to 30%
Profit (pretax) . . . . 30% to 40%

QUESTIONS

- How long are you willing to stay? Key sources of referrals? What target marketing do you do? Lease renewal/terms and the like?
- Where do you get your patients from? Which staff members are good, which are great, and which need to be replaced? Do you own your building? Is it for sale if you own? What's been your best marketing source for new patients?
- How many repeat patients? Average ticket? Which procedures are specialty? Term of transition?
- Why are you selling? What procedures do you refer out?

INDUSTRY TREND

More acquisitions of solo practices and small groups by DSOs and other.

Margins will get compressed as product and salary inflation will hit dentists hard, while they will not be able to negotiate higher reimbursement rates from insurance companies to offset these costs.

"Industry revenue is significantly tied to the level of disposable income and unemployment rate. Increased coverage has driven demand for industry operators. More recent graduates have joined existing dental practices, causing large offices to grow. Nearly all states offer dental benefits to their Medicaid population. Dental practitioners will become more involved in identifying symptoms of chronic conditions. There will be downward pressure on the dentist-to-patient ratio, exacerbating the need for dentists. The industry is expected to continue expanding, with more operators entering the field."

Source: IBISWorld Industry at a Glance

EXPERT COMMENTS

Be prepared to work hard, market, and stay close with the financial side of the business to create and maintain profitability.

Dentistry is a recession-resistant business. People in pain will always seek out a dentist to provide care; simply ignoring the pain doesn't make it go away. Therefore, dentists will always have demand and should do well. School is getting extremely expensive, and the younger dentists today are likely more inclined to work for a larger group practice rather than purchase right out of school.

Good time to sell at the moment; there are a lot of buyers, both individuals and corporate. Also a good time to buy; there are a lot of dentists getting out of the business.

FINANCING

Combination of buyer fully financed alone or in combination with seller financing.

Banks love to lend on these deals. If a bank disapproves the deal, it's a bad deal— run away.

RESOURCES
- IBISWorld, January 2023: https://www.ibisworld.com
- ADA—American Dental Association: https://www.ada.org/en
- AGD—Academy of General Dentistry: https://www.agd.org
- CDA—California Dental Association: https://www.cda.org
- DE—Dental Economics: https://www.dentaleconomics.com
- Dentaltown: https://www.dentaltown.com
- FDA—Florida Dental Association: https://www.floridadental.org
- NAPB—National Association of Practice Brokers: https://www.dentalpracticebroker.org
- ODA—Oregon Dental Association: https://www.oregondental.org
- SFDDA—South Florida District Dental Association: https://www.sfdda.org
- WSDA—Washington State Dental Association: https://www.wsda.org

Diagnostic Imaging Centers

| NAICS 621512 | Businesses/Units 11,735

| Profit $3.6 B | Wages $8 B | Annual Growth Future 2.4%

| Annual Growth Past 0.8%

Rules of Thumb
- 100% annual sales includes inventory
- 4–5.5 x SDE includes inventory
- 4 x EBIT
- 5 x EBITDA

INDUSTRY MULTIPLES

Acquisition multiples below are calculated medians using US private industry transactions. Data updated annually. Last update: August 2023.

VALUATION MULTIPLE (MEDIAN VALUE)

UNDER $1 MILLION NET SALES

MVIC/Net Sales	1.08
MVIC/Gross Profit	1.09
MVIC/SDE	2.72
MVIC/EBITDA	3.49

$1 MILLION–$5 MILLION NET SALES

MVIC/Net Sales	0.91
MVIC/Gross Profit	1.12
MVIC/SDE	3.11
MVIC/EBITDA	7.28

D

MVIC/Net Sales	2.39
MVIC/Gross Profit	3.17
MVIC/SDE	3.72
MVIC/EBITDA	7.76

Source: DealStats (formerly Pratt's Stats), 2023 (Portland, OR: Business Valuation Resources, LLC), www.bvresources.com/dealstats

BENCHMARK DATA

STATISTICS (DIAGNOSTIC IMAGING CENTERS)

Number of Establishments	11,735
Average Profit Margin	15.1%
Revenue per Employee	$226,000
Average Number of Employees	9.1
Average Wages per Employee	$76,114

PRODUCTS AND SERVICES SEGMENTATION

Computed tomography (CT) scanning	27.5%
Magnetic resonance imaging scans	27.1%
All other diagnostic imaging	21.4%
Ultrasound imaging	10.8%
Radiographic imaging (including x-rays)	10.0%
Other services	3.2%

MAJOR MARKET SEGMENTATION

Private insurance payments	51.3%
Medicare and medicaid payments	20.5%
Other	16.3%
Out-of-pocket payments	11.9%

INDUSTRY COSTS

Profit	15.1%
Wages	33.8%
Purchases	11.1%
Depreciation	4.9%
Marketing	0.7%
Rent & Utilities	4.5%
Other	30.0%

EXPENSES (% OF ANNUAL SALES)

Cost of Goods	10%
Occupancy Costs	05% to 10%
Payroll/Labor Costs	25%
Profit (pretax)	40%

QUESTIONS

• Payor mix, market share, patient demographic data

INDUSTRY TREND

"Patient and payer demand for lower cost and more convenient care has buoyed freestanding imaging clinics. Steadying patient volumes and recession concerns will likely dent consumer spending on elective medical services. As competition increases, tech advances at diagnostic imaging centers will become vital from a clinical and patient standpoint. An aging population will translate into a higher consumption of healthcare services. Growth in the number of people with private health insurance coverage will stunt private insurers' spending on healthcare services. Diagnostic imaging centers will continue to operate in a fragmented landscape. The COVID-19 pandemic has exacerbated chronic staffing shortages and staff burnout at diagnostic imaging centers."

Source: IBISWorld Industry at a Glance

FINANCING

Outside financing

RESOURCES

- IBISWorld, February 2023: https://www.ibisworld.com

Dialysis Centers

| NAICS 621492 | Businesses/Units 9,444

| Profit $5.6 B | Wages $8.2 B | Annual Growth Future 3.5%

| Annual Growth Past 2.4%

Rules of Thumb

- 5–10 x EBITDA
- 78% annual sales
- 2.7 x SDE

PRICING TIPS

Patient mix (types of payer sources) is key; geography is also important given differences in reimbursement in different areas and regulations.

BENCHMARK DATA

STATISTICS (DIALYSIS CENTERS)

Number of Establishments	9,444
Average Profit Margin	15.6%
Revenue per Employee	N/A
Average Number of Employees. . .	14.6
Average Wages per Employee . .	$62,186

PRODUCTS AND SERVICES SEGMENTATION

Outpatient hemodialysis	78.7%
Peritoneal dialysis	9.9%
Home-based hemodialysis	7.5%
Hospital inpatient hemodialysis . .	3.9%

MAJOR MARKET SEGMENTATION

Private insurance	42.9%
Medicare	34.1%
Other	14.2%
Other government	6.4%
Medicaid	1.8%
Patient out-of-pocket	0.6%

INDUSTRY COSTS

Profit	15.6%
Wages	22.8%
Purchases	26.4%
Depreciation	3.1%
Marketing	0.5%
Rent & Utilities	4.9%
Other	26.7%

MARKET SHARE

Fresenius Medical Care AG & Co. KGaA	46.3%
DaVita HealthCare Partners Inc.	37.2%

EXPENSES (% OF ANNUAL SALES)

Cost of Goods	13%
Payroll/Labor Costs.	06%
Profit (pretax)	05% to 15%

QUESTIONS

• Whether they are the medical director, and what relationships they have with patient referral sources; whether they would continue to work in the unit post-transaction, etc.

INDUSTRY TREND

"Decreased profit is likely due to the increased costs of operating over the coronavirus pandemic. IBISWorld estimates that the number of people with private health insurance has decreased. Employment and wages in the industry are expected to grow. Industry profit is expected to remain slightly dampened. New companies are expected to enter the industry to take advantage of high profit. Downstream technological change will support doctors in the prevention and diagnosis of kidney disease. Potential changes to the PPACA could result in a further decline in private insurance enrollment."

Source: IBISWorld Industry at a Glance

RESOURCES

• IBISWorld, February 2023: https://www.ibisworld.com

Diners

| NAICS 722511

Rules of Thumb

• 30%–35% annual sales plus inventory

INDUSTRY MULTIPLES

Acquisition multiples below are calculated medians using US private industry transactions. Data updated annually. Last update: August 2023.

VALUATION MULTIPLE (MEDIAN VALUE)

UNDER $1 MILLION NET SALES

MVIC/Net Sales.	0.29
MVIC/Gross Profit	0.43
MVIC/SDE	1.73
MVIC/EBITDA	1.98

$1 MILLION–$5 MILLION NET SALES

MVIC/Net Sales.	0.32
MVIC/Gross Profit	0.53
MVIC/SDE	2.20
MVIC/EBITDA	2.94

OVER $5 MILLION NET SALES

MVIC/Net Sales.	0.64
MVIC/Gross Profit	1.01
MVIC/SDE	2.72
MVIC/EBITDA	6.58

Source: DealStats (formerly Pratt's Stats), 2023 (Portland, OR: Business Valuation Resources, LLC), www.bvresources.com/dealstats

INDUSTRY TREND

"Restaurant owners—like [Ann] Redding of Thai Diner, Samuel Yoo of NYC's Chinatown-influenced Golden Diner, and Sofia Baltopoulos of the Tasty vegan diner in Philadelphia—are beginning to expand the definition of what a diner can be. But the survival of diners has long depended on their association with this down-home, ordinary imagery, where folks from different walks of life can put aside their differences and find common ground over sandwich platters."

Source: "The Myth of the American Diner" by Jaya Saxena, June 12, 2023, https://www.eater.com/23753429/diner-history-restaurant-democracy-politics-symbol

Direct Health and Medical Insurance Carriers

| NAICS 524114 | Businesses/Units 6,519

| Profit $103.5 B | Wages $61.2 B | Annual Growth Future 0.9%

| Annual Growth Past 2.3%

INDUSTRY MULTIPLES

Acquisition multiples below are calculated medians using US private industry transactions. Data updated annually. Last update: August 2023.

VALUATION MULTIPLE (MEDIAN VALUE)

UNDER $1 MILLION NET SALES	N/A
$1 MILLION–$5 MILLION NET SALES	N/A
OVER $5 MILLION NET SALES	
MVIC/Net Sales.	0.70
MVIC/Gross Profit	2.30
MVIC/SDE	N/A
MVIC/EBITDA	15.86

Source: DealStats (formerly Pratt's Stats), 2023 (Portland, OR: Business Valuation Resources, LLC), www.bvresources.com/dealstats

BENCHMARK DATA

STATISTICS (HEALTH AND MEDICAL INSURANCE)

Number of Establishments	6,519
Average Profit Margin	8.3%
Revenue per Employee	$2,220,000
Average Number of Employees.	86.9
Average Wages per Employee	$108,657

PRODUCTS AND SERVICES SEGMENTATION

Pharmacy benefit management (PBM)	29.1%
Preferred provider organization (PPO) plans	27.6%
High-deductible health plans (HDHPs).	18.8%
Health maintenance organization (HMO) plans	11.9%
Managed care plans	7.5%
Point-of-service (POS) plans	4.4%
Fee-for-service (FFS) plans	0.7%

MAJOR MARKET SEGMENTATION

Consumers with employer-sponsored health insurance	53.4%
Consumers with Medicare	18.0%

Consumers with Medicaid 17.4%
Consumers with direct-purchased health insurance . . .10.2%
Consumers with other insurance plans 1.0%

INDUSTRY COSTS

Profit	8.3%
Wages	4.9%
Purchases	5.0%
Depreciation	0.7%
Marketing	3.0%
Rent & Utilities	2.8%
Other	75.3%

MARKET SHARE

UnitedHealth	25.7%
CVS Health	20.9%
Anthem	12.2%
Humana	7.5%
Cigna	3.7%
Independence Health	0.6%
Prime Therapeutics Llc	0.5%
Delta Dental Insurance	0.5%
MedImpact Healthcare Systems	0.2%

INDUSTRY TREND

"The CARES Act expanded the federal Medicaid matching rate. Larger insurers benefit from mergers and acquisitions. Health insurance issued by employers is back to healthy levels. More people will need medical coverage as baby boomers age. Large life insurers will likely continue to consolidate to boost revenue. The repeal of further provisions of the Affordable Care Act (ACA) threatens revenue. As unemployment increased, many people lost their employer-sponsored health insurance, causing limited growth in 2020."

Source: IBISWorld Industry at a Glance

RESOURCES

• IBISWorld, January 2023: https://www.ibisworld.com

Direct Life Insurance Carriers

	NAICS 524113		Businesses/Units 8,326	
	Profit $242.2 B		Wages $50 B		Annual Growth Future 0.5%
					Annual Growth Past 2.5%

INDUSTRY MULTIPLES

Acquisition multiples below are calculated medians using US private industry transactions. Data updated annually. Last update: August 2023.

VALUATION MULTIPLE (MEDIAN VALUE)

UNDER $1 MILLION NET SALES	N/A
$1 MILLION–$5 MILLION NET SALES	N/A
OVER $5 MILLION NET SALES	
MVIC/Net Sales	1.72
MVIC/Gross Profit	2.25
MVIC/SDE	N/A
MVIC/EBITDA	9.71

Source: DealStats (formerly Pratt's Stats), 2023 (Portland, OR: Business Valuation Resources, LLC), www.bvresources.com/dealstats

BENCHMARK DATA

STATISTICS (LIFE INSURANCE & ANNUITIES)

Number of Establishments	8,326
Average Profit Margin	21.6%
Revenue per Employee	$3,078,000
Average Number of Employees	43.6
Average Wages per Employee	$137,268

PRODUCTS AND SERVICES SEGMENTATION

Investment income	34.8%
Individual annuities	21.4%
Individual life insurance premiums	14.8%
Group annuities	14.4%
Other	10.8%
Group life insurance premiums	3.8%

MAJOR MARKET SEGMENTATION

Individuals aged 35 to 54	37.7%
Individuals aged 65 and older	24.4%
Individuals aged 55 to 64	19.5%
Individuals aged 34 and younger	18.4%

INDUSTRY COSTS

Profit	21.6%
Wages	4.5%
Purchases	4.3%
Depreciation	1.5%
Marketing	2.5%
Rent & Utilities	2.3%
Other	63.3%

MARKET SHARE

Massachusetts Mutual Life Insurance Co	3.2%
Northwestern Mutual Life Insurance Co	3.1%
Guardian Life Insurance Co of America	2.2%
MetLife	2.1%
Manulife Financial	0.5%

INDUSTRY TREND

"Ongoing rate hikes increases investor uncertainty. Larger insurers benefit from mergers and acquisitions. Larger companies can raise capital more easily than their smaller counterparts. Millennials will become a more significant market. Consolidation is likely to continue. A significant portion of revenue comes from investment income. Many companies rely on life insurers for capital and liquidity."

Source: IBISWorld Industry at a Glance

RESOURCES

- IBISWorld, January 2023: https://www.ibisworld.com

Direct Mail Advertising

NAICS 541860	SIC 7331-05	Businesses/Units 1,810
Profit $667.5 M	Wages $2.2 B	Annual Growth Future -4.0%
		Annual Growth Past -2.4%

Rules of Thumb

- 40%–50% annual revenues plus inventory
- 2–2.5 x SDE not including inventory

INDUSTRY MULTIPLES

Acquisition multiples below are calculated medians using US private industry transactions. Data updated annually. Last update: August 2023.

VALUATION MULTIPLE (MEDIAN VALUE)

UNDER $1 MILLION NET SALES

MVIC/Net Sales.	0.42
MVIC/Gross Profit	0.99
MVIC/SDE	2.83
MVIC/EBITDA	3.39

$1 MILLION–$5 MILLION NET SALES

MVIC/Net Sales.	0.42
MVIC/Gross Profit	0.68
MVIC/SDE	2.53
MVIC/EBITDA	5.62

OVER $5 MILLION NET SALES

MVIC/Net Sales.	1.01
MVIC/Gross Profit	4.07
MVIC/SDE	N/A
MVIC/EBITDA	8.22

Source: DealStats (formerly Pratt's Stats), 2023 (Portland, OR: Business Valuation Resources, LLC), www.bvresources.com/dealstats

BENCHMARK DATA

STATISTICS (DIRECT MAIL ADVERTISING)

Number of Establishments .	1,810
Average Profit Margin	6.6%
Revenue per Employee .	$302,000
Average Number of Employees.	17.7
Average Wages per Employee .	$66,913

PRODUCTS AND SERVICES SEGMENTATION

Full direct mail services.	68.5%
Lettershop services.	14.9%
Other Services	9.4%
Printing and fulfillment services	7.2%

MAJOR MARKET SEGMENTATION

Retail stores and catalogs	42.1%
Finance, banking, and insurance providers	32.1%
Government, NGOs, and households	19.4%
Telecommunications and cable service providers .	4.5%
Travel	1.9%

INDUSTRY COSTS

Profit	6.6%
Wages	22.2%
Purchases	7.3%
Depreciation	2.7%
Marketing	5.7%
Rent & Utilities .	7.9%
Other	47.6%

EXPENSES (% OF ANNUAL SALES)

Cost of Goods	65%
Occupancy Costs	05%

Payroll/Labor Costs.   .   .   .   .   05% to 10%
Profit (pretax)   .   .   .   .   .   20% to 25%

QUESTIONS

- How many recurring agreements are in place? How large is your biggest client?
- How many active clients? What is your average net profit?

INDUSTRY TREND

"More major players in the industry have extended their services to the internet. USPS' close relationship with the industry has negatively affected other industry operators. Increased external competition from e-marketing services has pressured profit. Companies will branch out into other operations that are related to existing industry operations. Industry operators are anticipated to increasingly invest in environmentally friendly materials. Profit will fall due to increased consolidation and continued external competition. Recent innovations in direct mail advertising technology have kept the industry relevant."

Source: IBISWorld Industry at a Glance

RESOURCES

- IBISWorld, January 2023: https://www.ibisworld.com
- ANA—Data Marketing & Analytics: https://thedma.org
- DMN: https://www.dmnews.com

Direct Title Insurance Carriers

| NAICS 524127 | Businesses/Units 5,593

| Profit $3.5 B | Wages $7.9 B | Annual Growth Future -0.8%

| Annual Growth Past 8.9%

INDUSTRY MULTIPLES

Acquisition multiples below are calculated medians using US private industry transactions. Data updated annually. Last update: August 2023.

VALUATION MULTIPLE (MEDIAN VALUE)

UNDER $1 MILLION NET SALES

MVIC/Net Sales.	0.79
MVIC/Gross Profit	0.62
MVIC/SDE	2.00
MVIC/EBITDA	2.64

$1 MILLION–$5 MILLION NET SALES

MVIC/Net Sales.	1.59
MVIC/Gross Profit	1.44
MVIC/SDE	2.95
MVIC/EBITDA	3.31

OVER $5 MILLION NET SALES

MVIC/Net Sales.	0.54
MVIC/Gross Profit	N/A
MVIC/SDE	N/A
MVIC/EBITDA	N/A

Source: DealStats (formerly Pratt's Stats), 2023 (Portland, OR: Business Valuation Resources, LLC), www.bvresources.com/dealstats

STATISTICS (TITLE INSURANCE)

Number of Establishments	5,593
Average Profit Margin	12.5%
Revenue per Employee	$419,000
Average Number of Employees	11.7
Average Wages per Employee	$120,484

PRODUCTS AND SERVICES SEGMENTATION

Agency title insurance premiums	46.0%
Direct title insurance premiums	40.1%
Title search, title reconveyance, and title abstract service fees	9.8%
Other	2.3%
Investment income	1.8%

MAJOR MARKET SEGMENTATION

Real estate buyers	37.8%
Real estate sellers	31.6%
Real estate agents and mortgage lenders	30.6%

INDUSTRY COSTS

Profit	12.5%
Wages	28.6%
Purchases	3.4%
Depreciation	0.6%
Marketing	2.0%
Rent & Utilities	1.8%
Other	51.0%

MARKET SHARE

Fidelity National Financial, Inc.	26.3%
First American Financial Corporation	25.3%
Old Republic International Corporation	13.3%
Stewart Information Services Corp	8.3%

INDUSTRY TREND

"Improving access to credit has increased real estate transactions. Industry operators have benefited from a rising Federal Funds Rate. Low rates have reduced investment returns, but encouraged spending on housing. There will likely be a slowdown in the overall housing market. A rising mortgage rate is expected to subdue revenue growth in the outlook. Title insurers do not receive any direct assistance from the federal government. Strong growth in residential construction has supported industry revenue growth."

Source: IBISWorld Industry at a Glance

RESOURCES

• IBISWorld, March 2023: https://www.ibisworld.com

Directory and Mailing List Publishers

| NAICS 513140 | Businesses/Units 680

| Profit $241.1 M | Wages $1.5 B | Annual Growth Future -8.7%

| Annual Growth Past -7.6%

BENCHMARK DATA

STATISTICS (DATABASE & DIRECTORY PUBLISHING)

Number of Establishments	680
Average Profit Margin	3.7%
Revenue per Employee	$418,000
Average Number of Employees. . .	20.8
Average Wages per Employee . . .	$94,747

PRODUCTS AND SERVICES SEGMENTATION

Online publications	71.3%
Print directories.	25.4%
Other	3.3%

MAJOR MARKET SEGMENTATION

Subscriptions	70.7%
Sale of advertising space	13.7%
Other	12.6%
Rental or sale of mailing lists	3.0%

INDUSTRY COSTS

Profit	3.7%
Wages	22.5%
Depreciation	2.0%
Marketing	4.6%
Rent & Utilities	3.1%
Other	49.6%

MARKET SHARE

Thryv	2.9%

INDUSTRY TREND

"Directory and database publishers earn modest revenue by selling advertising space to businesses. Search engines and social media sites act as more convenient substitutes for industry services. Thryv owns the industry's only recognizable brands. Declining print advertising expenditure will be driven by the shift of consumer preferences to digital and online formats. More consumers are expected to conduct business searches while on Google, Facebook and similar general-interest sites. Publishers are anticipated to continue merger and acquisition activity. Institutional clients and consumers have continued their shift to online resources."

Source: IBISWorld Industry at a Glance

RESOURCES

- IBISWorld, March 2023: https://www.ibisworld.com

Distilleries

	NAICS 312140		Businesses/Units 2,399		
	Profit $2.9 B		Wages $1.4 B		Annual Growth Future 1.1%
					Annual Growth Past 3.4%

INDUSTRY MULTIPLES

Acquisition multiples below are calculated medians using US private industry transactions. Data updated annually. Last update: August 2023.

VALUATION MULTIPLE (MEDIAN VALUE)

UNDER $1 MILLION NET SALES

MVIC/Net Sales	1.89
MVIC/Gross Profit	2.25
MVIC/SDE	10.49
MVIC/EBITDA	15.40

$1 MILLION–$5 MILLION NET SALES

MVIC/Net Sales	5.21
MVIC/Gross Profit	17.59
MVIC/SDE	N/A
MVIC/EBITDA	N/A

OVER $5 MILLION NET SALES

MVIC/Net Sales	2.75
MVIC/Gross Profit	7.01
MVIC/SDE	N/A
MVIC/EBITDA	18.97

Source: DealStats (formerly Pratt's Stats), 2023 (Portland, OR: Business Valuation Resources, LLC), www.bvresources.com/dealstats

BENCHMARK DATA

STATISTICS (DISTILLERIES)

Number of Establishments	2,399
Average Profit Margin	15.7%
Revenue per Employee	$798,000
Average Number of Employees	9.9
Average Wages per Employee	$61,956

PRODUCTS AND SERVICES SEGMENTATION

Whiskey	30.8%
Vodka	18.1%
Tequila	17.8%
RTD cocktails	17.3%
Cordials	7.5%
Rum	6.0%
Gin	2.5%

MAJOR MARKET SEGMENTATION

Retail and liquor stores	49.5%
Wholesalers	34.5%
Food-service establishments	13.4%
Other	2.6%

INDUSTRY COSTS

Profit	15.7%
Wages	7.6%
Purchases	29.7%
Depreciation	3.3%
Marketing	1.0%
Rent & Utilities	1.2%
Other	41.6%

MARKET SHARE

Diageo PLC	48.4%
Brown-Forman Corporation	7.8%
Sazerac Company, Inc.	3.1%
Beam Suntory Inc.	2.9%

"Per capita expenditure on alcohol is expected to fall. Larger operators tend to experience far higher margins than the industry average. Operators at all levels experience substantial competition from imports. Steady growth is anticipated to attract new distilleries. The industry is projected to continue experiencing fierce competition. Consolidation is anticipated to keep larger operators' profit high. Pent-up demand for on-premise establishments contributed to additional revenue growth."

Source: IBISWorld Industry at a Glance

RESOURCES

- IBISWorld, January 2023: https://www.ibisworld.com

Distribution/Wholesale: Apparel

| NAICS 424350

Rules of Thumb

- 20% annual sales
- 2 x SDE
- 4.5 x EBIT
- 4 x EBITDA

PRICING TIPS

Management and sales teams are key to maintaining and driving value. Beware of large inventory positions and low marketing spending in this very competitive, fast moving industry with low barriers to entry. Factory ownership is rare, but a plus.

EXPENSES (% OF ANNUAL SALES)

Cost of Goods	50%
Payroll/Labor Costs.	30%
Profit (pretax)	06%

INDUSTRY TREND

I don't forecast significant growth for the industry overall due to the continued (albeit unsustainable) fast fashion giant retailers. Marketing and product differentiation, product quality, sustainable practices, excellency of customer service, and meeting promised delivery times will be the key to outperforming the trend.

EXPERT COMMENTS

The process of designing and producing clothing is complex and highly labor intensive. The knowledge and skills are very specific to the industry, and good employees can be hard to come by.

RESOURCES

- AAFA—American Apparel & Footwear Association: https://www.aafaglobal.org
- Apparel Magazine: https://apparelmag.com/
- California Apparel News: https://www.apparelnews.net/
- The Business of Fashion: https://www.businessoffashion.com/
- Women's Wear Daily: https://wwd.com/

Distribution/Wholesale: Durable Goods

| NAICS 423

Rules of Thumb

- 4 x EBITDA
- 2–2.5 x SDE plus inventory
- 4.5 x EBIT

INDUSTRY MULTIPLES

Acquisition multiples below are calculated medians using US private industry transactions. Data updated annually. Last update: August 2023.

VALUATION MULTIPLE (MEDIAN VALUE)

UNDER $1 MILLION NET SALES

MVIC/Net Sales	0.50
MVIC/Gross Profit	1.16
MVIC/SDE	2.61
MVIC/EBITDA	3.55

$1 MILLION–$5 MILLION NET SALES

MVIC/Net Sales	0.45
MVIC/Gross Profit	1.25
MVIC/SDE	3.14
MVIC/EBITDA	4.80

OVER $5 MILLION NET SALES

MVIC/Net Sales	0.52
MVIC/Gross Profit	1.88
MVIC/SDE	4.13
MVIC/EBITDA	7.21

Source: DealStats (formerly Pratt's Stats), 2023 (Portland, OR: Business Valuation Resources, LLC), www.bvresources.com/dealstats

PRICING TIPS

Inventory (durable or nondurable) is critical to the sale and must be current and well managed with appropriate controls and real-time valuation processes in place.

BENCHMARK DATA

Distribution costs are sensitive to energy prices. Direct competition from manufacturers is increasing, which creates a challenge for many distributors and a need to find service and delivery differentiation for the clients.

EXPENSES (% OF ANNUAL SALES)

Cost of Goods	70% to 80%
Occupancy Costs	03% to 08%
Payroll/Labor Costs	10% to 20%
Profit (pretax)	08% to 15%

QUESTIONS

- Does the business belong to any distributor buying groups/co-ops?

EXPERT COMMENTS

There are significant competitive cost barriers to entry into this industry, where size does matter along with quantity and quality of product lines, adequate logistical distribution channels, good supplier pricing and terms, adequate facilities sizing and location. Solid, well-diversified customer base mitigates risk and wards off competitive challenges.

FINANCING

Banks like the industry and will generally provide SBA 7(a) credit to qualified buyer and where consistent cash flow is evident.

RESOURCES

- NAW—National Association of Wholesaler-Distributors: https://www.naw.org

Distribution/Wholesale: Electrical Products

| NAICS 423610 | Businesses/Units 18,584

| Profit $10 B | Wages $21.4 B | Annual Growth Future 1.0%

| Annual Growth Past 0.2%

Rules of Thumb

- 35% annual revenues plus inventory
- 6 x SDE
- 5 x EBITDA

INDUSTRY MULTIPLES

Acquisition multiples below are calculated medians using US private industry transactions. Data updated annually. Last update: August 2023.

VALUATION MULTIPLE (MEDIAN VALUE)

UNDER $1 MILLION NET SALES

MVIC/Net Sales	0.66
MVIC/Gross Profit	1.58
MVIC/SDE	1.95
MVIC/EBITDA	3.90

$1 MILLION–$5 MILLION NET SALES

MVIC/Net Sales	0.48
MVIC/Gross Profit	1.26
MVIC/SDE	3.22
MVIC/EBITDA	6.79

OVER $5 MILLION NET SALES

MVIC/Net Sales	0.65
MVIC/Gross Profit	2.49
MVIC/SDE	3.27
MVIC/EBITDA	7.57

Source: DealStats (formerly Pratt's Stats), 2023 (Portland, OR: Business Valuation Resources, LLC), www.bvresources.com/dealstats

BENCHMARK DATA

STATISTICS (ELECTRICAL EQUIPMENT WHOLESALING)

Number of Establishments	18,584
Average Profit Margin	4.6%
Revenue per Employee	$916,000
Average Number of Employees	13.0
Average Wages per Employee	$89,724

PRODUCTS AND SERVICES SEGMENTATION

Communications and security	43.1%
Lighting products	32.7%
Electrical distribution	9.5%
Wire, cable, and conduit	9.1%
Automation and controls	3.1%
Other	2.5%

MAJOR MARKET SEGMENTATION

Construction	46.9%
Wholesalers	26.4%
Other	10.7%
Manufacturers	8.1%
Retailers	7.9%

INDUSTRY COSTS

Profit	4.6%
Wages	9.8%
Purchases	72.1%
Depreciation	0.5%
Marketing	0.8%
Rent & Utilities	0.8%
Other	11.4%

MARKET SHARE

Consolidated Electrical Distributors, Inc.	4.0%
Wesco International, Inc.	3.3%
Sonepar	2.2%
Anixter International Inc.	1.3%
Graybar Services, Inc.	1.2%
Rexel Inc.	1.2%

EXPENSES (% OF ANNUAL SALES)

Cost of Goods	25%
Payroll/Labor Costs	18%
Profit (pretax)	05%

QUESTIONS

- Does the seller have a strategic plan? Is there a succession plan in place? Does the seller forecast sales, profits, and gross profit, and do they track the forecast year to year? Are the forecasts accurate? Does the seller have an HR process? Does the seller have a good handle on inventory, AR, and AP?

INDUSTRY TREND

"Companies are expected to remain hesitant to begin costly commercial construction projects. An increase in housing starts has supported revenue growth. Employment growth has largely followed industry revenue growth during the period. Companies and individuals are forecast to increase their expenditures on efficiency upgrades. Greater private investment in computers and software is anticipated to stimulate revenue growth. Large operators will likely benefit from a variety of competitive advantages. Revenue is expected to rise in 2023 as improving economic performance invigorates demand."

Source: IBISWorld Industry at a Glance

More and more difficult due to online sales, but adding services could dramatically increase the value of the enterprise (value-added services, delivery services to job site, delivery to factory floor, etc.).

EXPERT COMMENTS

Sellers need to prepare 3 to 5 years in advance of a transaction to get maximum value or even attain a number that will allow them to live in a style in which they are accustomed.

Easy to replicate as long as there is capital. It is a capital-intensive business that needs to be managed.

FINANCING

The best middle-market electrical distributors are now sold to private equity.

RESOURCES

- IBISWorld, January 2023: https://www.ibisworld.com
- EW—Electrical Wholesaling®: https://www.ewweb.com/
- NAED—National Association of Electrical Distributors: https://www.naed.org/

Distribution/Wholesale: Fruits and Vegetables

	NAICS 424480		SIC 5148-01		Businesses/Units 8,165
	Profit $3.8 B		Wages $6.7 B		Annual Growth Future 0.4%
					Annual Growth Past 1.8%

Rules of Thumb

- 25% annual sales plus inventory
- 0.50–1 x SDE plus inventory
- 0.75 x EBIT
- 0.75 x EBITDA

INDUSTRY MULTIPLES

Acquisition multiples below are calculated medians using US private industry transactions. Data updated annually. Last update: August 2023.

VALUATION MULTIPLE (MEDIAN VALUE)

UNDER $1 MILLION NET SALES
MVIC/Net Sales.	0.20
MVIC/Gross Profit	0.65
MVIC/SDE	5.01
MVIC/EBITDA	0.54

$1 MILLION–$5 MILLION NET SALES
MVIC/Net Sales.	0.24
MVIC/Gross Profit	1.26
MVIC/SDE	8.08
MVIC/EBITDA	2.18

OVER $5 MILLION NET SALES
MVIC/Net Sales.	1.73
MVIC/Gross Profit	5.61
MVIC/SDE	6.49
MVIC/EBITDA	17.08

Source: DealStats (formerly Pratt's Stats), 2023 (Portland, OR: Business Valuation Resources, LLC), www.bvresources.com/dealstats

PRICING TIPS

What is the average per basket or package profit the company normally charges/expects?

BENCHMARK DATA

STATISTICS (FRUIT & VEGETABLE WHOLESALING)

Number of Establishments	8,165
Average Profit Margin	3.1%
Revenue per Employee	$1,036,000
Average Number of Employees. . . .	14.0
Average Wages per Employee . . .	$57,656

PRODUCTS AND SERVICES SEGMENTATION

Fruits	56.6%
Vegetables	40.2%
Other products	3.2%

MAJOR MARKET SEGMENTATION

Retailers.	40.0%
Other wholesalers	36.6%
Food service providers	15.0%
Other customers	8.4%

INDUSTRY COSTS

Profit	3.1%
Wages	5.5%
Purchases	81.4%
Depreciation	0.6%
Marketing	0.2%
Rent & Utilities	0.8%
Other	8.5%

MARKET SHARE

Sysco Corporation	4.5%

EXPENSES (% OF ANNUAL SALES)

Cost of Goods	40% to 50%
Occupancy Costs	10%
Payroll/Labor Costs.	30%
Profit (pretax)	10% to 20%

INDUSTRY TREND

"The widespread closure of restaurants amid the COVID-19 pandemic hindered revenue growth. Wholesalers have worked to increase the speed of acquiring produce. Price increases in fruits and vegetables helped outweigh declines in per capita consumption. Volatile weather conditions have made the cost of grow-ing crops more expensive. The increase in the price of fertilizers will translate to growing vegetable prices. High costs and higher consolidation will discourage new companies from entering the market. A significant part of this industry relies on servicing food service providers."

Source: IBISWorld Industry Outlook

EXPERT COMMENTS

It is perhaps one of the least expensive businesses to start and operate, but just as easy to destroy without a strong paying customer base. One can grow this business through adding multiple delivery trucks and yet not even have to rent warehouse space.

FINANCING

Both outside financing and seller financing, depending on what the corporate tax returns look like and the amount/age of equipment owned by the company.

RESOURCES
• IBISWorld, January 2023: https://www.ibisworld.com

D

Distribution/Wholesale: Grocery Products/Full Line

NAICS 424990	SIC 5141-05	Businesses/Units 5,222
Profit $6.3 B	Wages $12 B	Annual Growth Future 0.8%
		Annual Growth Past 1.1%

Rules of Thumb
• 3–4 x SDE
• 3–4 x EBIT
• 4–4.5 x EBITDA

INDUSTRY MULTIPLES

Acquisition multiples below are calculated medians using US private industry transactions. Data updated annually. Last update: August 2023.

VALUATION MULTIPLE (MEDIAN VALUE)

UNDER $1 MILLION NET SALES	
MVIC/Net Sales.	0.59
MVIC/Gross Profit	1.14
MVIC/SDE	1.43
MVIC/EBITDA	1.99

$1 MILLION–$5 MILLION NET SALES	
MVIC/Net Sales.	0.66
MVIC/Gross Profit	1.63
MVIC/SDE	3.10
MVIC/EBITDA	5.73

OVER $5 MILLION NET SALES	
MVIC/Net Sales.	0.45
MVIC/Gross Profit	1.49
MVIC/SDE	3.11
MVIC/EBITDA	3.42

Source: DealStats (formerly Pratt's Stats), 2023 (Portland, OR: Business Valuation Resources, LLC), www.bvresources.com/dealstats

PRICING TIPS

Good books and records need to be maintained, and tax returns should show enough SDE to qualify the business for an SBA loan.

BENCHMARK DATA

STATISTICS (GROCERY WHOLESALING)

Number of Establishments .	5,222
Average Profit Margin	2.3%
Revenue per Employee .	$1,650,000
Average Number of Employees.	32.1
Average Wages per Employee .	$72,207

PRODUCTS AND SERVICES SEGMENTATION

Fresh meat and meat products .	22.9%
Other	21.1%
Canned food	15.1%
Frozen food .	13.7%

Dairy products 9.3%
Specialty food 7.0%
Fresh fruits and vegetables. 5.8%
Paper and plastic products 5.1%

MAJOR MARKET SEGMENTATION

Food service outlets 49.7%
Supermarkets and other grocery retailers 31.9%
Other wholesalers 10.1%
Other 8.3%

INDUSTRY COSTS

Profit 2.3%
Wages 4.4%
Purchases 83.5%
Depreciation 0.5%
Marketing 0.2%
Rent & Utilities 0.8%
Other 8.4%

MARKET SHARE

Sysco Corporation 2.1%
Performance Food Group Co 1.7%
C&S Wholesale Grocers, Inc. 1.3%
US Foods Holding Corp. 1.3%

EXPENSES (% OF ANNUAL SALES)

Cost of Goods . . . . 80% to 83%
Occupancy Costs . . . . 05% to 15%
Payroll/Labor Costs. . . . . 12% to 15%
Profit (pretax) . . . . 07% to 08%

QUESTIONS

• Tax returns, P&Ls, and any other documents to prove the SDE

INDUSTRY TREND

"Improving economic conditions have prompted industry revenue to grow. The industry experienced growing sales from grocery retailers and other wholesalers. The industry has experienced large levels of consolidation. Competition among industry participants will continue to intensify. Wholesalers will experience revived demand from food service customers. Retail chains with their own distribution facilities are projected to increase in number and size. The disproportionate size of industry players has contributed to industry consolidation over the past decade."

Source: IBISWorld Industry at a Glance

EXPERT COMMENTS

Food distribution businesses tend to do better than most businesses in recessions.

FINANCING

If the owner is smart enough to report enough income so an SBA loan is possible, that is the best situation. If the tax returns don't qualify, seller financing is typically 50 percent down and a 4-year note for 50 percent.

RESOURCES

• IBISWorld, January 2023: https://www.ibisworld.com
• IFDA—International Foodservice Distributors Association:

https://www.ifdaonline.org
- NPFDA—National Poultry & Food Distributors Association: https://www.npfda.org

Distribution/Wholesale: In General

| NAICS 42

Rules of Thumb
- 3–4 x SDE plus inventory
- 3–4 x EBIT
- 3–5 x EBITDA
- 60%–65% annual sales includes inventory

INDUSTRY MULTIPLES

Acquisition multiples below are calculated medians using US private industry transactions. Data updated annually. Last update: August 2023.

VALUATION MULTIPLE (MEDIAN VALUE)

UNDER $1 MILLION NET SALES	
MVIC/Net Sales.	0.50
MVIC/Gross Profit	1.16
MVIC/SDE	2.64
MVIC/EBITDA	3.72
$1 MILLION–$5 MILLION NET SALES	
MVIC/Net Sales.	0.44
MVIC/Gross Profit	1.26
MVIC/SDE	3.14
MVIC/EBITDA	4.71
OVER $5 MILLION NET SALES	
MVIC/Net Sales.	0.49
MVIC/Gross Profit	2.05
MVIC/SDE	4.07
MVIC/EBITDA	7.57

Source: DealStats (formerly Pratt's Stats), 2023 (Portland, OR: Business Valuation Resources, LLC), www.bvresources.com/dealstats

PRICING TIPS

An important way to determine a value on the higher end is if the business has invested in innovation and intellectual property (IP).

Multiples based on revenue are not a good indicator of value in the distribution/wholesale industry. Buyers will focus on SDE/EBITDA and the value, condition, and saleability of the inventory. For transactions < $2M, buyers are generally not sophisticated enough to present the idea of a working capital PEG. They will generally expect enough inventory to be left in the business to conduct the operation normally, with the seller keeping AR/AP, cash, and long-term debt. For larger distribution/wholesale transactions, the buyers will generally value the business, including sufficient working capital (in line with historical averages), which is determined after examining 12 to 18 monthly balance sheets. For unprofitable or marginally profitable businesses, an up-to-date inventory and equipment appraisal is invaluable; generally, buyers will agree to pay some discount on the tangible inventory/asset value, generally, 20 to 30+ percent depending on whether the business is break-even or losing money rapidly. Overall, sellers should expect to finance 10 to 20 percent of the transaction. Regardless of whether the buyer requests seller financing, most lenders are going to want to see some seller skin in the game. Customer concentration in excess of 50 percent will almost always mean the seller will have to accept some form of earnout where part of the purchase price is paid based on future company performance or perhaps tied to a specific large customer. Overall, the market method (EBITDA multiplier method) will be utilized by nearly 100 percent of buyers, regardless of the size of the transaction. The income method (DCF model) will be utilized by sophisticated financial buyers (PE and family office) primarily for larger distribution/wholesale opportunities (excess of $2M EBITDA) that have a demonstrated history of growth.

This industry is very sensitive to the economy in general, and often sensitive to industry specialties if they are being particularly hard hit. For example, Covid created a shortage due to global supply chain problems. A second example is a strike at major ports, preventing goods being landed and moved into the economy, for example, auto parts and related services, IT chips, and food products.

We focus on EBITDA, and the range can be 3 to 10.

BENCHMARK DATA

Sales per employee is typically around $800K to $1M.

EXPENSES (% OF ANNUAL SALES)

Cost of Goods	60% to 70%
Occupancy Costs	05% to 10%
Payroll/Labor Costs	17% to 25%
Profit (pretax)	10% to 15%

QUESTIONS

- What are your AR and AP terms?
- What feedback have you received from your major customers in terms of how the current environment has affected them?
- How is your supply chain holding up? Are you sensing areas of stress? Breakdown?
- What about any debt or financing on the business? How are banks treating you in these times?
- What impact, if any, are you seeing from the talk of recession? Is business slowing down?
- Based on present information, are you able to prepare a 13-week cash flow forecast?
- Are you able to accurately forecast 2023 and 2024 revenue?
- Discuss your managers or management team. How stable have they been? Are you having difficulty recruiting or filling key positions?
- If you were 20 years younger, what would you do to grow the business?
- Concentration of customers? Number of redundant suppliers and the length of those relationships? What is the turn of the inventory/raw materials?
- Do you have sales forecasts going back at least 3 years and a record of meeting your forecasts? Do you have an audit or review of your financials (third-party validation reduces the perception of risk)? Do you have a succession plan for your management team, and could you show it to me in writing?

INDUSTRY TREND

Regionally and industry based—look for patterns with what's happening within the region and the specific industry.

I think it is going to be a bit of a slog. While supply chains are easing up, global disorder and tension remain heightened. Inflation and labor challenges are easing, but significant macro shifts take a long time and it can be painful along the way.

One trend we have seen accelerate over the past 6 months is that, given the negative headlines, seller sentiment has turned negative, and therefore fewer sellers are listing. This has created a shortage of quality distribution/wholesale opportunities, which is boosting buyer interest and keeping multiples elevated even against a much higher rate environment.

Businesses that create a unique offering with value-added services that will be difficult to duplicate will set the successful business well above the rest.

More and more difficult as big online retailers are looking for, and will exploit, wholesale distribution, even OEMs.

The implementation of further technology will be a driver over the next few years, as competition for labor will continue to be an issue. Also, securing a consistent source of goods will be critical, so as not to affect the end buyer's business in a negative fashion.

EXPERT COMMENTS

Almost unexpectedly over the past 6 to 9 months, the market has shifted back strongly in favor of sellers. This is due to low supply of quality businesses combined with strong buyer cash positions and demand. We have seen multiples remain high, and we are oftentimes receiving more offers on our sellers than in 2021 and 2022. The buyer pool has thinned a bit due to the headlines and fear; however, those that remain are often aggressive. My top advice to a seller is that if price and deal structure are important to you, do not work with the buyer that calls you up. Work with a broker/M&A advisor that can stir up a well-run limited auction-style bidding process.

Make sure the business is dependent on the owner when buying.

Most of what we see are private equity and synergistic buyers. They have their own financing. If your business demonstrates significant risk factors, no strategic plan, no real HR plan, and no succession planning, for example, then the selling price will be significantly reduced.

Own your customers; don't let the principal own your customers. If you get big customers, the principal will want to own the customers, and when your margins get in the way of the principal's profits, you will lose the customers to the principal direct.

Have a good, reliable source of product. Avoid too much customer or supplier concentration.

Requires a reliable and steady stream of inventory, so barrier to entry is typically harder.

FINANCING

With the rise in interest rate, we're seeing a larger percent of seller financing.

Most of our transactions are < $5M in enterprise value, and the buyer utilizes SBA 7a financing. As a rule of thumb, I would say most deals are 10 percent buyer equity (cash), 10 percent seller note, and 80 percent bank financing. Very rarely do we see no bank involved. Earnouts are disallowed by the SBA and disliked by sellers, so we rarely see them; however, we believe this will change in the immediate future, and we are already seeing earnouts becoming a part of our current deals. Deals that are larger than $10M have increasingly become a challenge due to the return targets of more sophisticated buyers. Basically, interest rates have squeezed the returns that private equity had been used to, and many are still adjusting. Along these lines, the best buyers for larger or more middle-market transactions are to identify buyers that have a dedicated roll-up strategy; they will pay more than they want to in the face of competition.

RESOURCES

- ASA—American Supply Association: https://www.asa.net
- MDM—Modern Distribution Management: https://www.mdm.com
- NAW—National Association of Wholesaler-Distributors: https://www.naw.org

Distribution/Wholesale: Industrial Supplies

| NAICS 423840 | Businesses/Units 11,993

| Profit $4 B | Wages $8.6 B | Annual Growth Future 1.3%

| | | Annual Growth Past -2.2%

Rules of Thumb

- 50% annual revenues plus inventory
- 4–5 x EBITDA

INDUSTRY MULTIPLES

Acquisition multiples below are calculated medians using US private industry transactions. Data updated annually. Last update: August 2023.

VALUATION MULTIPLE (MEDIAN VALUE)

UNDER $1 MILLION NET SALES	
MVIC/Net Sales	0.43
MVIC/Gross Profit	1.16
MVIC/SDE	2.75
MVIC/EBITDA	2.88
$1 MILLION–$5 MILLION NET SALES	
MVIC/Net Sales	0.40
MVIC/Gross Profit	1.23
MVIC/SDE	3.15
MVIC/EBITDA	4.28
OVER $5 MILLION NET SALES	
MVIC/Net Sales	0.67
MVIC/Gross Profit	2.39
MVIC/SDE	4.86
MVIC/EBITDA	8.84

Source: DealStats (formerly Pratt's Stats), 2023 (Portland, OR: Business Valuation Resources, LLC), www.bvresources.com/dealstats

PRICING TIPS

Many distributorships for larger equipment do not order high dollar inventory until they receive a request from a customer to order that equipment. Therefore, inventory levels may not be extremely high as they try to not hold excess inventory. If the business you are evaluating is not operated this way and there is a large amount of inventory, you may need to consider that in your working capital calculations.

BENCHMARK DATA

STATISTICS (INDUSTRIAL SUPPLIES WHOLESALING)

Number of Establishments	11,993
Average Profit Margin	4.5%
Revenue per Employee	$842,000
Average Number of Employees	9.1
Average Wages per Employee	$80,703

PRODUCTS AND SERVICES SEGMENTATION

Abrasives, strapping and tape	34.5%
Industrial containers	22.7%
Mechanical power transmission supplies	19.5%
Industrial valves and fittings	17.7%
Other supplies	3.7%
Iron and steel pipes and tubing	1.9%

MAJOR MARKET SEGMENTATION

Industrial users for production inputs	34.4%
Other wholesalers for resale	30.3%
Other	15.5%
Businesses for end use	11.3%
Building contractors	4.4%
Retailers for resale	4.1%

INDUSTRY COSTS

Profit	4.5%
Wages	9.6%
Purchases	67.7%
Depreciation	0.8%
Marketing	0.3%
Rent & Utilities	1.1%
Other	15.9%

MARKET SHARE

Genuine Parts Co.	4.6%
W.W. Grainger, Inc.	3.9%
MSC Industrial Direct Co., Inc.	2.3%
Crown Holdings, Inc.	2.1%

QUESTIONS

- Who are your distributor agreements with? What restrictions do you have regarding geography and other products? How many additional products can your current sales force add to their sales book?

INDUSTRY TREND

"Companies in need of equipment used to manufacture ventilators boosted the industry. Improving corporate profit encouraged investment in the repair of heavy industrial facilities. The largest industry companies have expanded, reaching more strategic markets. Growing demand from the Manufacturing sector will support industry revenue. Small independent operators will continue to be squeezed for revenue by larger operators. Manufacturers are likely to become vertically integrated, maintaining their own distribution operations. Fluctuations in the US dollar affect the export performance of key markets and thus the industry indirectly."

Source: IBISWorld Industry at a Glance

EXPERT COMMENTS

Companies that represent quality lines of products are desired. Contracts with customers to consistently provide their equipment or supplies or maintenance are a major plus.

RESOURCES

- IBISWorld, January 2023: https://www.ibisworld.com
- ISA—Industrial Supply Association: https://www.isapartners.org

---

Distribution/Wholesale: Janitorial

| NAICS 423850 | Businesses/Units 2,525

| Profit $593.5 M | Wages $1.8 B | Annual Growth Future -1.3%

| Annual Growth Past 2.2%

Rules of Thumb

- 30%–40% annual sales plus inventory

INDUSTRY MULTIPLES

Acquisition multiples below are calculated medians using US private industry transactions. Data updated annually. Last update: August 2023.

VALUATION MULTIPLE (MEDIAN VALUE)

UNDER $1 MILLION NET SALES	
MVIC/Net Sales	0.31
MVIC/Gross Profit	0.94
MVIC/SDE	2.70
MVIC/EBITDA	6.88

$1 MILLION–$5 MILLION NET SALES	
MVIC/Net Sales	0.40
MVIC/Gross Profit	1.38
MVIC/SDE	3.62
MVIC/EBITDA	4.99

OVER $5 MILLION NET SALES	
MVIC/Net Sales	0.61
MVIC/Gross Profit	2.27
MVIC/SDE	5.08
MVIC/EBITDA	7.28

Source: DealStats (formerly Pratt's Stats), 2023 (Portland, OR: Business Valuation Resources, LLC), www.bvresources.com/dealstats

BENCHMARK DATA

STATISTICS (CLEANING & MAINTENANCE SUPPLIES DISTRIBUTORS)

Number of Establishments	2,525
Average Profit Margin	4.5%
Revenue per Employee	$436,000
Average Number of Employees	11.4
Average Wages per Employee	$62,194

PRODUCTS AND SERVICES SEGMENTATION

All janitorial products, supplies, and accessories	56.0%
Janitorial and industrial cleaning equipment	21.3%
Other janitorial products	11.1%
Paper and plastics products	9.3%
Chemical supplies	2.3%

MAJOR MARKET SEGMENTATION

Businesses for their own use 60.2%	
Construction, manufacturing and government.	19.5%
Other	14.1%
Retailers for resale	6.2%

INDUSTRY COSTS

Profit	4.5%
Wages	14.0%
Purchases	64.1%
Depreciation	0.6%
Marketing	0.3%
Rent & Utilities	1.1%
Other	15.4%

MARKET SHARE

Essendant Inc.	11.9%
SupplyWorks Inc.	11.1%
Veritiv Corporation	9.9%

INDUSTRY TREND

"Industry operators have struggled to compete with external operators. Industry participants' input costs have risen during the period. Consolidation has been witnessed among some of the industry's largest operators. The industry will benefit from several demographic trends. Economic growth will likely boost demand for cleaning services from expanding businesses. Price competition is anticipated to continue to weigh on the industry. Consolidation is expected to influence the decline in the number of industry operators."

Source: IBISWorld Industry at a Glance

RESOURCES

- IBISWorld, March 2023: https://www.ibisworld.com

Distribution/Wholesale: Medical Equipment & Supplies

| NAICS 423450 | Businesses/Units 15,948

| Profit $16.6 B | Wages $42 B | Annual Growth Future 3.4%

| | | Annual Growth Past 3.9%

Rules of Thumb

- 50%–60% annual revenues plus inventory
- 3.5–4 x SDE
- 4 x EBITDA
- 3 x EBIT

INDUSTRY MULTIPLES

Acquisition multiples below are calculated medians using US private industry transactions. Data updated annually. Last update: August 2023.

VALUATION MULTIPLE (MEDIAN VALUE)

UNDER $1 MILLION NET SALES

MVIC/Net Sales	0.77
MVIC/Gross Profit	1.29
MVIC/SDE	3.17
MVIC/EBITDA	2.83

D

MVIC/Net Sales .	0.65
MVIC/Gross Profit	1.34
MVIC/SDE	3.34
MVIC/EBITDA	8.28

OVER $5 MILLION NET SALES

MVIC/Net Sales .	0.61
MVIC/Gross Profit	1.62
MVIC/SDE	3.24
MVIC/EBITDA	5.52

Source: DealStats (formerly Pratt's Stats), 2023 (Portland, OR: Business Valuation Resources, LLC), www.bvresources.com/dealstats

PRICING TIPS

SDE is an important number in this industry. Depending upon the size, the seller's salary may not be an add-back or will need to be adjusted to the market value of the tasks they complete in the business.

It is important to look at the licensing issues to determine who can legally purchase the business. If it is restricted to a doctor or licensed professional, then the buyer pool is smaller and the multiple needs to be reduced.

BENCHMARK DATA

STATISTICS (MEDICAL SUPPLIES WHOLESALING)

Number of Establishments .	15,948
Average Profit Margin	4.7%
Revenue per Employee .	$1,179,000
Average Number of Employees.	19.2
Average Wages per Employee .	$140,737

PRODUCTS AND SERVICES SEGMENTATION

Surgical, medical, and hospital instruments and equipment	53.4%
Surgical, medical, and hospital supplies	24.1%
Orthopedic and prosthetic appliances and supplies	10.4%
Dental equipment, instruments, and supplies .	6.5%
Other	4.2%
Pharmaceuticals, cosmetics, and toiletries	1.4%

MAJOR MARKET SEGMENTATION

Hospitals	63.8%
Primary care physicians and specialists	20.3%
Other medical care providers	15.9%

INDUSTRY COSTS

Profit	4.7%
Wages	11.9%
Purchases	63.8%
Depreciation	0.7%
Marketing	1.1%
Rent & Utilities .	1.0%
Other	16.9%

MARKET SHARE

Cardinal Health, Inc.	9.1%
Henry Schein Inc.	2.6%
McKesson Corporation .	1.2%

EXPENSES (% OF ANNUAL SALES)

Cost of Goods	14%

"Industry wholesalers worked with government agencies to better coordinate where and how to distribute supplies. The eliminated PPACA medical device tax has hurt industry profit growth. Consolidation trends in the healthcare sector have led to the creation of larger and more sophisticated healthcare providers. Changing demographics in the US population will have a favorable effect on the industry. Budgetary and political pressures on government programs will possibly limit revenue and profit growth. Largely due to decreasing profit, medical supplies-related industries will likely continue to consolidate. Demand for healthcare products will surge as restrictions on nonessential services are lifted."

Source: IBISWorld Industry at a Glance

EXPERT COMMENTS

Use an attorney familiar with the industry.

FINANCING

Fairly easy to get outside financing, but there is often a small earnout or seller carry component.

RESOURCES

• IBISWorld, January 2023: https://www.ibisworld.com

Distribution/Wholesale: Paper

| NAICS 424120 | Businesses/Units 866

| Profit $106.7 M | Wages $746.7 M | Annual Growth Future -12.3%

| Annual Growth Past -21.8%

Rules of Thumb
• 3–4 x SDE plus inventory
• 4–5 x EBIT
• 5 x EBITDA

INDUSTRY MULTIPLES

Acquisition multiples below are calculated medians using US private industry transactions. Data updated annually. Last update: August 2023.

VALUATION MULTIPLE (MEDIAN VALUE)

UNDER $1 MILLION NET SALES
MVIC/Net Sales	0.51
MVIC/Gross Profit	0.70
MVIC/SDE	2.90
MVIC/EBITDA	5.81

$1 MILLION–$5 MILLION NET SALES
MVIC/Net Sales	0.33
MVIC/Gross Profit	0.73
MVIC/SDE	2.99
MVIC/EBITDA	4.02

OVER $5 MILLION NET SALES   N/A

Source: DealStats (formerly Pratt's Stats), 2023 (Portland, OR: Business Valuation Resources, LLC), www.bvresources.com/dealstats

PRICING TIPS

Use 25 to 30 percent of GPM (gross profit margin) times 4 to arrive at goodwill price including all FF&E. To this number, add the dollar amount of net working capital to be included in the sale.

BENCHMARK DATA

STATISTICS (PAPER WHOLESALING)

Number of Establishments	866
Average Profit Margin	1.9%
Revenue per Employee	$680,000
Average Number of Employees	8.6
Average Wages per Employee	$90,397

PRODUCTS AND SERVICES SEGMENTATION

Printing and writing paper	50.7%
Fine roll paper	26.9%
Other	12.2%
Packaging materials	5.4%
Newsprint	2.7%
Personal care	2.1%

MAJOR MARKET SEGMENTATION

Other Wholesalers	49.4%
Businesses	30.1%
Paper Retailers	15.4%
Other buyers of industry products	5.1%

INDUSTRY COSTS

Profit	1.9%
Wages	13.3%
Purchases	71.1%
Depreciation	0.6%
Marketing	0.2%
Rent & Utilities	1.3%
Other	11.8%

MARKET SHARE

Veritiv Corporation	34.3%
Central National Gottesman Inc.	30.3%

EXPENSES (% OF ANNUAL SALES)

Cost of Goods	70% to 75%
Occupancy Costs	04%
Payroll/Labor Costs	10%
Profit (pretax)	08% to 10%

QUESTIONS

- Stability of gross profit margins, number of inventory turns per year. Percentage of slow moving inventory and the need for adjustments thereof.

INDUSTRY TREND

"Advertisers are increasingly transferring their funds to internet pages instead of printed ones. Many companies in the industry have either left, merged or been acquired. Operators are continuing to search for other avenues through which they can sustain demand. Industry operators will introduce new paper products to assist with business presentations. The costs of electricity, gasoline and paper are expected to increase, raising expenses for wholesalers. Industry operators will increasingly move into the global sphere. Operators have closed underper-forming facilities to reduce their reliance on labor."

Source: IBISWorld Industry at a Glance

D

RESOURCES

* IBISWorld, March 2023: https://www.ibisworld.com
* Fastmarkets: https://www.fastmarkets.com

Distribution/Wholesale: Metal

| NAICS 423510 | Businesses/Units 10,779

| Profit $10.8 B | Wages $13.3 B | Annual Growth Future -0.5%

     | Annual Growth Past -1.3%

INDUSTRY MULTIPLES

Acquisition multiples below are calculated medians using US private industry transactions. Data updated annually. Last update: August 2023.

VALUATION MULTIPLE (MEDIAN VALUE)

UNDER $1 MILLION NET SALES

MVIC/Net Sales.	0.31
MVIC/Gross Profit	0.62
MVIC/SDE	2.40
MVIC/EBITDA	3.68

$1 MILLION–$5 MILLION NET SALES

MVIC/Net Sales.	0.45
MVIC/Gross Profit	1.35
MVIC/SDE	3.00
MVIC/EBITDA	5.44

OVER $5 MILLION NET SALES

MVIC/Net Sales.	0.34
MVIC/Gross Profit	1.24
MVIC/SDE	5.62
MVIC/EBITDA	11.67

Source: DealStats (formerly Pratt's Stats), 2023 (Portland, OR: Business Valuation Resources, LLC), www.bvresources.com/dealstats

BENCHMARK DATA

STATISTICS (METAL WHOLESALING)

Number of Establishments .	10,779
Average Profit Margin	4.7%
Revenue per Employee .	$1,559,000
Average Number of Employees.	13.6
Average Wages per Employee .	$89,925

PRODUCTS AND SERVICES SEGMENTATION

Iron and steel products .	51.0%
Aluminum products.	18.4%
Stainless steel and alloys	14.1%
Other nonferrous metals and products.	12.3%
Copper and brass products.	4.2%

MAJOR MARKET SEGMENTATION

Manufacturing and mining industries .	42.5%
Other wholesalers for resale	26.3%

Other markets 11.2%
Building contractors 10.7%
Businesses for end use 9.3%

INDUSTRY COSTS

Profit 4.7%
Wages 5.8%
Purchases 80.2%
Depreciation 0.8%
Marketing 0.1%
Rent & Utilities 0.7%
Other 7.7%

MARKET SHARE

Reliance Steel & Aluminum Co. . . . 6.0%
O'Neal Industries, Inc. 1.3%

RESOURCES

• IBISWorld, January 2023: https://www.ibisworld.com

Distribution/Wholesale: Tools

| NAICS 423710 | Businesses/Units 6,819

| Profit $5.7 B | Wages $7.2 B | Annual Growth Future 0.4%

| | | Annual Growth Past 2.2%

Rules of Thumb

• 55% annual sales includes inventory
• 3.7 x SDE includes inventory

INDUSTRY MULTIPLES

Acquisition multiples below are calculated medians using US private industry transactions. Data updated annually. Last update: August 2023.

VALUATION MULTIPLE (MEDIAN VALUE)

UNDER $1 MILLION NET SALES
MVIC/Net Sales. 0.71
MVIC/Gross Profit 1.53
MVIC/SDE 2.74
MVIC/EBITDA 6.56

$1 MILLION–$5 MILLION NET SALES
MVIC/Net Sales. 0.38
MVIC/Gross Profit 1.08
MVIC/SDE 3.44
MVIC/EBITDA . . . . N/A

OVER $5 MILLION NET SALES
MVIC/Net Sales. 1.03
MVIC/Gross Profit 2.57
MVIC/SDE 5.21
MVIC/EBITDA 9.13

Source: DealStats (formerly Pratt's Stats), 2023 (Portland, OR: Business Valuation Resources, LLC), www.bvresources.com/dealstats

PRICING TIPS

Higher multiples for the higher net profit industries

BENCHMARK DATA

STATISTICS (TOOL AND HARDWARE WHOLESALING)

Number of Establishments 6,819
Average Profit Margin 6.2%
Revenue per Employee $973,000
Average Number of Employees. 14.0
Average Wages per Employee $75,319

PRODUCTS AND SERVICES SEGMENTATION

Bolts, nuts, rivets, and other fasteners (excludes nails) . . 32.9%
Power Tools 26.4%
Other 22.2%
Hand tools 12.6%
Plywood, panels, and millwork 3.8%
Paint, paint supplies, and wallpaper 1.2%
Cutlery 0.9%

MAJOR MARKET SEGMENTATION

Retailers for resale 38.9%
Wholesalers and distributors for resale 31.2%
Manufacturing and mining industrial users 9.5%
Construction industries. 8.0%
Businesses for use in their operations 5.4%
All other customers 4.0%
Government bodies 1.7%
Repair shops for use in repair work. 1.3%

INDUSTRY COSTS

Profit 6.2%
Wages 7.8%
Purchases 67.6%
Depreciation 0.6%
Marketing 0.5%
Rent & Utilities 1.4%
Other 15.8%

EXPENSES (% OF ANNUAL SALES)

Cost of Goods 74%
Occupancy Costs 01%
Payroll/Labor Costs. 08%
Profit (pretax) 15%

QUESTIONS

• Do you need a mechanical background or inclination to be successful?

INDUSTRY TREND

"The industry will suffer a decrease in demand due to the pandemic, despite being considered essential. Strong growth in consumer spending driven by rising disposable income has contributed to increased demand for industry products at the retail level. Despite increasing revenue, the number of operators has declined. Disposable income growth during the period will promote private spending on home improvements. The number of households is expected to increase, which will likely support growth in construction industries. Operators will continue to differentiate themselves based on price. Increased consumer spending at downstream retailers during the period has driven revenue growth."

Source: IBISWorld Industry at a Glance

EXPERT COMMENTS

Location is not typically important since there is not much drop-in traffic.

RESOURCES

• IBISWorld, January 2023: https://www.ibisworld.com

Document Destruction

| | NAICS 561990 | | Businesses/Units 1,734 |

| | Profit $546.5 M | | Wages $2.5 B | | Annual Growth Future 2.2% |

| | Annual Growth Past 2.2% |

Rules of Thumb

• 150%–200% annual sales includes inventory
• 4 x SDE includes inventory
• 6 x EBIT
• 4.5–6 x EBITDA

INDUSTRY MULTIPLES

Acquisition multiples below are calculated medians using US private industry transactions. Data updated annually. Last update: August 2023.

VALUATION MULTIPLE (MEDIAN VALUE)

UNDER $1 MILLION NET SALES

MVIC/Net Sales	0.77
MVIC/Gross Profit	0.80
MVIC/SDE	2.43
MVIC/EBITDA	3.72

$1 MILLION–$5 MILLION NET SALES

MVIC/Net Sales	0.52
MVIC/Gross Profit	0.37
MVIC/SDE	2.60
MVIC/EBITDA	3.83

OVER $5 MILLION NET SALES

MVIC/Net Sales	0.66
MVIC/Gross Profit	1.78
MVIC/SDE	2.70
MVIC/EBITDA	7.51

Source: DealStats (formerly Pratt's Stats), 2023 (Portland, OR: Business Valuation Resources, LLC), www.bvresources.com/dealstats

PRICING TIPS

The industry norm is to calculate a business value based upon a multiple of EBIT-DA or seller's discretionary earnings (SDE). The percentage of gross revenue method is a rule of thumb based upon dividing gross revenue by the value obtained using the EBITDA or SDE values. In other words, the 2 times total revenue valuation rule of thumb must be verified using the EBITDA or SDE valuation.

BENCHMARK DATA

STATISTICS (DOCUMENT MANAGEMENT SERVICES)

| Number of Establishments | 1,734 |
| Average Profit Margin | 7.0% |

```
Revenue per Employee .    .    .    .    . $100,000
Average Number of Employees.    .    .    45.9
Average Wages per Employee .    .    . $31,731
```

PRODUCTS AND SERVICES SEGMENTATION

```
Records management services.    .    .    . 56.2%
Data destruction    .    .    .    .    .    . 31.9%
Data protection and recovery services .    . 11.9%
```

MAJOR MARKET SEGMENTATION

```
Financial Services  .    .    .    .    .    .    . 67.2%
Government.    .    .    .    .    .    .    . 13.3%
Other    .    .    .    .    .    .    .    . 10.3%
Legal    .    .    .    .    .    .    .    .    4.9%
Healthcare  .    .    .    .    .    .    .    4.3%
```

INDUSTRY COSTS

```
Profit    .    .    .    .    .    .    .    .    7.0%
Wages  .    .    .    .    .    .    .    . 31.7%
Purchases  .    .    .    .    .    .    . 24.2%
Depreciation    .    .    .    .    .    .    2.7%
Marketing  .    .    .    .    .    .    .    2.1%
Rent & Utilities .    .    .    .    .    .    2.9%
Other    .    .    .    .    .    .    .    . 29.3%
```

MARKET SHARE

```
Iron Mountain Inc. .    .    .    .    .    . 12.7%
Stericycle Inc.  .    .    .    .    .    .    . 9.9%
Esquire Deposition Solutions LLC .    .    . 1.0%
```

$250,000 of revenue generated per shredding truck

EXPENSES (% OF ANNUAL SALES)

```
Cost of Goods  .    .    .    .    .    . 30% to 40%
Occupancy Costs  .    .    .    .    . 10% to 20%
Payroll/Labor Costs.    .    .    .    . 15% to 25%
Profit (pretax)  .    .    .    .    .    . 25% to 30%
```

QUESTIONS

- What is your annual regularly scheduled recurring route revenue? What is your total one-time-purge annual revenue? What is the annual purge revenue generated from route customers? How much annual revenue do you generate from recycled paper? How many tons of paper are shredded on an annual basis? How many, and what type of, shredding trucks do you own or lease? Do you offer on-site and off-site shredding?
- Age of fleet and the output of plant facilities are important. Industry standard equipment is a must.

INDUSTRY TREND

Customers are leaving the majors and returning to independent operators for better service.

"The industry generally experiences steady demand. Competition has historically been high in this industry. Demand for the electronic conversion of medical records has benefited the industry. The industry will face sustained demand because of stricter records management. Consolidation will slow as increased demand for digitizing records attracts new entrants. Operators will continue to lean on storage revenue from the financial services market. Competition has decreased as larger industry operators have increasingly acquired regional operators."

Source: IBISWorld Industry Outlook

EXPERT COMMENTS

Someone considering entry in this space should seriously consider acquiring an existing operation as opposed to starting from scratch.

FINANCING

Seller financing

RESOURCES

- IBISWorld, March 2023: https://www.ibisworld.com
- i-SIGMA—International Secure Information Governance & Management Association: https://isigmaonline.org
- MSA—Mobile Shredding Alliance: https://mobileshreddingalliance.com
- Recycling Today: https://www.recyclingtoday.com/magazine/
- Security Shredding News: https://www.securityshreddingnews.com

Dog Kennels

| NAICS 812910　　| SIC 0752-05

Rules of Thumb

- 1 x annual sales plus inventory
- 2–3 x SDE plus inventory
- 2.7 x EBIT
- 4.5 x EBITDA

INDUSTRY MULTIPLES

Acquisition multiples below are calculated medians using US private industry transactions. Data updated annually. Last update: August 2023.

VALUATION MULTIPLE (MEDIAN VALUE)

UNDER $1 MILLION NET SALES	
MVIC/Net Sales	0.58
MVIC/Gross Profit	0.66
MVIC/SDE	2.10
MVIC/EBITDA	3.07
$1 MILLION–$5 MILLION NET SALES	
MVIC/Net Sales	1.26
MVIC/Gross Profit	1.31
MVIC/SDE	3.81
MVIC/EBITDA	4.92
OVER $5 MILLION NET SALES	N/A

Source: DealStats (formerly Pratt's Stats), 2023 (Portland, OR: Business Valuation Resources, LLC), www.bvresources.com/dealstats

BENCHMARK DATA

Overnight boarding annual occupancy rate should be above 50 percent.

Labor is the largest expense; should be around 30 to 35 percent but can be as high as 50 percent.

EXPENSES (% OF ANNUAL SALES)

Cost of Goods	03%
Occupancy Costs	10% to 17%
Payroll/Labor Costs	35% to 40%
Profit (pretax)	20% to 30%

QUESTIONS

- Describe your daily and weekly duties. What exactly do you do at the business? (Sellers are the biggest risk factors in a sale in this industry.)
- Do you have direct client contact? If yes, how much?
- History of staffing, to learn of turnover?

INDUSTRY TREND

Consolidation from corporate buyers. The industry will continue to grow due to consumers' affection for their pets. Rover.com will take some of the market.

EXPERT COMMENTS

Buyers: learn about dogs and pack management as it's a risk mitigation tool. Volunteer at a facility to really experience what it means to work in the environment; this industry is quite romanticized and often different from what one expects. Understand the staffing structure and the needs of clients who are emotionally tied to their dogs. Sellers: minimize your involvement. Don't directly generate income (grooming, training). Hire a GM.

FINANCING

SBA financing as long as business cash flow qualifies. Corporate buyers pay cash.

RESOURCES

- IBPSA—International Boarding & Pet Services Association: https://www.ibpsa.com
- National Association of Professional Pet Sitters: https://petsitters.org
- Pet Boarding and Daycare Magazine: https://www.petboardinganddaycare.com

Doll, Toy, and Game Manufacturing

| NAICS 339930 | Businesses/Units 498

| Profit $115.6 M | Wages $350.4 M | Annual Growth Future 0.8%

| Annual Growth Past -2.6%

INDUSTRY MULTIPLES

Acquisition multiples below are calculated medians using US private industry transactions. Data updated annually. Last update: August 2023.

VALUATION MULTIPLE (MEDIAN VALUE)

UNDER $1 MILLION NET SALES	N/A
$1 MILLION–$5 MILLION NET SALES	N/A
OVER $5 MILLION NET SALES	
MVIC/Net Sales	0.72
MVIC/Gross Profit	2.50
MVIC/SDE	N/A
MVIC/EBITDA	11.24

Source: DealStats (formerly Pratt's Stats), 2023 (Portland, OR: Business Valuation Resources, LLC), www.bvresources.com/dealstats

BENCHMARK DATA

STATISTICS (TOY, DOLL & GAME MANUFACTURING)

Number of Establishments	498
Average Profit Margin	7.2%

```
Revenue per Employee .   .    .    .    .    .    .    .    .    .    .    . $285,000
Average Number of Employees.  .    .    .    .    .    .    .    .    .    . . 11.6
Average Wages per Employee .   .    .    .    .    .    .    .    .    .    . $61,620
```

PRODUCTS AND SERVICES SEGMENTATION

```
Electronic toys .   .    .    .    .    .    .    .    .    .    .    .    .    .    39.1%
Nonelectronic games and puzzles, including parts and pet toys .   .    .    .    22.4%
Models and crafts .   .    .    .    .    .    .    .    .    .    .    .    .    19.6%
Dolls and action figures.   .    .    .    .    .    .    .    .    .    .    .    13.1%
Baby carriages and children's vehicles.   .    .    .    .    .    .    .    .    . 5.8%
```

MAJOR MARKET SEGMENTATION

```
Mass Merchandise .   .    .    .    .    .    .    .    .    .    .    .    .    .    42.2%
Other Stores & Retailers   .    .    .    .    .    .    .    .    .    .    .    .    38.8%
Wholesalers.   .    .    .    .    .    .    .    .    .    .    .    .    .    .    12.4%
Hobby & Toy Stores .   .    .    .    .    .    .    .    .    .    .    .    .    . 6.6%
```

INDUSTRY COSTS

```
Profit    .    .    .    .    .    .    .    .    .    .    .    .    .    .    .    .    . 7.2%
Wages  .    .    .    .    .    .    .    .    .    .    .    .    .    .    .    .    21.8%
Purchases  .    .    .    .    .    .    .    .    .    .    .    .    .    .    .    51.7%
Depreciation   .    .    .    .    .    .    .    .    .    .    .    .    .    .    . 1.3%
Marketing   .    .    .    .    .    .    .    .    .    .    .    .    .    .    .    . 1.6%
Rent & Utilities .   .    .    .    .    .    .    .    .    .    .    .    .    .    . 2.8%
Other    .    .    .    .    .    .    .    .    .    .    .    .    .    .    .    .    13.6%
```

MARKET SHARE

```
Cartamundi .   .    .    .    .    .    .    .    .    .    .    .    .    .    .    . 4.4%
```

INDUSTRY TREND

"US-based toy, doll, and game manufacturers simply cannot compete with the low prices offered by overseas factories. Age compression can be temporarily abated by multipurpose toys, which has led to prominent increases in the electronic toy product segment. Tarnished consumer confidence in imported goods has helped US manufacturers stay relevant among global competition. A decrease in imports will allow operators to reclaim downstream business in their region. Wholesaling has steadily decreased as mass merchandisers and hobby stores have opted to go straight to manufacturer. Tensions with China and concerns over the safety of some products will bring some operators back to the US. American toy manufacturers simply can't keep up with the low prices offered by import competition."

Source: IBISWorld Industry at a Glance

RESOURCES

- IBISWorld, January 2023: https://www.ibisworld.com

Dollar Stores

NAICS 455219	Businesses/Units 74,273	
Profit $5.3 B	Wages $10.7 B	Annual Growth Future 0.9%
		Annual Growth Past 3.9%

Rules of Thumb

- 15%–20% annual sales plus inventory
- 2–2.5 x SDE plus inventory

- 2–2.5 x EBITDA
- 1.5–2 x EBIT

PRICING TIPS

With the increase in competition, margins must be looked into carefully.

BENCHMARK DATA

STATISTICS (DOLLAR AND VARIETY STORES)

Number of Establishments	74,273
Average Profit Margin	4.6%
Revenue per Employee	$192,000
Average Number of Employees	8.1
Average Wages per Employee	$18,173

PRODUCTS AND SERVICES SEGMENTATION

Others	30.9%
Groceries	21.4%
Kitchenware and home furnishings	19.0%
Menswear, women's wear, and other textile products	13.0%
Drugs, health aids, and beauty cosmetics	9.5%
Soaps, detergents, cleaning supplies, and paper-related products	6.2%

INDUSTRY COSTS

Profit	4.6%
Wages	9.4%
Purchases	62.5%
Depreciation	0.9%
Marketing	0.8%
Rent and Utilities	5.5%
Other	16.2%

MARKET SHARE

Dollar General Corporation	34.2%
Dollar Tree Stores, Inc.	26.0%
Big Lots, Inc.	6.2%

EXPENSES (% OF ANNUAL SALES)

Cost of Goods	70% to 75%
Occupancy Costs	10%
Payroll/Labor Costs	15% to 17%
Profit (pretax)	20% to 25%

QUESTIONS

- Tax returns and all invoices
- Paperwork, and sit and observe
- Margins and vendor contacts

INDUSTRY TREND

"Value propositions as a competitive edge are amplified during periods of economic contraction. The COVID-19 pandemic carries mixed effects for dollar and variety stores. Industry operators were unable to sustain growth in light of fierce internal and external competition. Many smaller chains and single-branch stores will likely find it increasingly difficult to compete. Industry operators are expected to invest in new technology such as computers. Efficiency and productivity will also likely become important competitive factors. Expansion in industry product portfolios has enabled larger operators to compete with other discount retailers."

Source: IBISWorld Industry at a Glance

EXPERT COMMENTS

Not too difficult to replicate; needs a large amount of inventory; the larger the store, the better the variety and the sales.

RESOURCES

- IBISWorld, March 2023: https://www.ibisworld.com
- Dollar$tores: https://www.buckstore.com

Domino's Pizza (Franchise)

	NAICS 722513		SIC 5812-22		Businesses/Units 6,185

INDUSTRY MULTIPLES

Acquisition multiples below are calculated medians using US private industry transactions. Data updated annually. Last update: August 2023.

VALUATION MULTIPLE (MEDIAN VALUE)

UNDER $1 MILLION NET SALES

MVIC/Net Sales.	0.31
MVIC/Gross Profit	0.48
MVIC/SDE	1.67
MVIC/EBITDA	2.21

$1 MILLION–$5 MILLION NET SALES

MVIC/Net Sales.	0.39
MVIC/Gross Profit	0.60
MVIC/SDE	2.43
MVIC/EBITDA	2.98

OVER $5 MILLION NET SALES

MVIC/Net Sales.	0.89
MVIC/Gross Profit	2.08
MVIC/SDE	4.98
MVIC/EBITDA	12.81

Source: DealStats (formerly Pratt's Stats), 2023 (Portland, OR: Business Valuation Resources, LLC), www.bvresources.com/dealstats

PRICING TIPS

Approx. Total Investment: $144,450 to $582,500

RESOURCES

- Domino's Pizza: https://biz.dominos.com
- Franchise information: https://biz.dominos.com/about-us/franchising/

Donut Shops

	NAICS 722515		SIC 5461-05		Businesses/Units 15,373
	Profit $303.5 M		Wages $1.6 B		Annual Growth Future 1.3%
					Annual Growth Past 0.7%

Rules of Thumb

- 45%–50% annual sales plus inventory (and can go much higher for a great store)
- 2–2.5 x SDE plus inventory

INDUSTRY MULTIPLES

Acquisition multiples below are calculated medians using US private industry transactions. Data updated annually. Last update: August 2023.

VALUATION MULTIPLE (MEDIAN VALUE)

UNDER $1 MILLION NET SALES

MVIC/Net Sales.	0.44
MVIC/Gross Profit	0.62
MVIC/SDE	2.20
MVIC/EBITDA	2.82

$1 MILLION–$5 MILLION NET SALES

MVIC/Net Sales.	0.41
MVIC/Gross Profit	0.69
MVIC/SDE	2.82
MVIC/EBITDA	5.94

OVER $5 MILLION NET SALES

MVIC/Net Sales.	3.89
MVIC/Gross Profit	4.87
MVIC/SDE	N/A
MVIC/EBITDA	N/A

Source: DealStats (formerly Pratt's Stats), 2023 (Portland, OR: Business Valuation Resources, LLC), www.bvresources.com/dealstats

PRICING TIPS

Higher coffee sales (60 percent of sales) produce higher value. Very low coffee sales produce lower values.

Length and cost of lease? Retail vs. wholesale business?

BENCHMARK DATA

STATISTICS (DOUGHNUT STORES)

Number of Establishments .	15,373
Average Profit Margin	4.1%
Revenue per Employee .	$63,000
Average Number of Employees.	7.7
Average Wages per Employee .	$14,079

PRODUCTS AND SERVICES SEGMENTATION

Full-size doughnuts.	66.9%
Assorted/multipack doughnuts.	13.5%
Other	12.0%
Doughnut holes.	6.9%
Other doughnuts	0.7%

MAJOR MARKET SEGMENTATION

Consumers aged 31 to 54 years old	44.4%
Consumers aged over 55	24.5%
Consumers aged under 30 .	22.6%
Businesses and other	8.5%

INDUSTRY COSTS

Profit	4.1%
Wages	22.2%
Purchases	45.7%
Depreciation	3.6%
Marketing	2.2%
Rent & Utilities .	8.8%
Other	13.4%

Krispy Kreme Doughnuts Inc. 6.5%

EXPENSES (% OF ANNUAL SALES)

Cost of Goods	21% food
Occupancy Costs	10%
Payroll/Labor Costs.	20% to 23%

INDUSTRY TREND

"Major franchises such as Krispy Kreme have fueled establishment growth. The industry has benefited from greater consumer spending on breakfast. The industry is labor intensive. The popularity of doughnuts as a dessert item is witnessed even at the restaurant level. Independent operators will receive a boost from shifting consumer preferences. The profit margin is expected to remain unchanged for most operators. The national presence of successful chains, such as Krispy Kreme Doughnuts Inc., has proliferated industry expansion."

Source: IBISWorld Industry at a Glance

RESOURCES

• IBISWorld, April 2023: https://www.ibisworld.com

Doors, Sales

| NAICS 444180

Rules of Thumb

• 70% annual sales plus inventory
• 5 x SDE plus inventory
• 6 x EBIT
• 6 x EBITDA

INDUSTRY MULTIPLES

Acquisition multiples below are calculated medians using US private industry transactions. Data updated annually. Last update: August 2023.

VALUATION MULTIPLE (MEDIAN VALUE)

UNDER $1 MILLION NET SALES

MVIC/Net Sales.	0.44
MVIC/Gross Profit	0.89
MVIC/SDE	2.10
MVIC/EBITDA	3.98

$1 MILLION–$5 MILLION NET SALES

MVIC/Net Sales.	0.36
MVIC/Gross Profit	1.00
MVIC/SDE	2.98
MVIC/EBITDA	3.53

OVER $5 MILLION NET SALES

MVIC/Net Sales.	0.46
MVIC/Gross Profit	1.35
MVIC/SDE	4.33
MVIC/EBITDA	5.83

Source: DealStats (formerly Pratt's Stats), 2023 (Portland, OR: Business Valuation Resources, LLC), www.bvresources.com/dealstats

EXPENSES (% OF ANNUAL SALES)

Cost of Goods	55%
Occupancy Costs	26%
Payroll/Labor Costs	04%
Profit (pretax)	06%

INDUSTRY TREND

Consolidation of distribution of the product is leading to great emphasis on service. There is vertical integration of large multinational suppliers/vendors, growing competition from companies in adjacent industries (HVAC, access controls, etc.), and a shift away from mechanical/electrical to digital systems and software-based customer decisions.

FINANCING

Combination of outside and seller financing. Deals involve cash, sellers' notes (multiyear), and, frequently, earnouts for the owners over a few years based on results.

RESOURCES

- ID&OI Magazine: https://doors.org/resources/id-oi-magazine
- DHI: https://www.dhi.org/
- Door + Access Systems magazine: https://www.dasma.com/dasma-pages/D-AS-magazine.asp
- IDA—International Door Association: https://www.doors.org/

Doors, Service

| NAICS 238290 | SIC 5211-02

| Profit $19.4 M | Wages $87.3 M | Annual Growth Future 0.2%

| | | | Annual Growth Past 0.1%

Rules of Thumb

- 25% annual sales plus inventory
- 6 x SDE
- 7 x EBIT
- 7 x EBITDA

INDUSTRY MULTIPLES

Acquisition multiples below are calculated medians using US private industry transactions. Data updated annually. Last update: August 2023.

VALUATION MULTIPLE (MEDIAN VALUE)

UNDER $1 MILLION NET SALES

MVIC/Net Sales	0.52
MVIC/Gross Profit	1.15
MVIC/SDE	1.60
MVIC/EBITDA	1.90

$1 MILLION–$5 MILLION NET SALES

MVIC/Net Sales	0.15
MVIC/Gross Profit	N/A

MVIC/SDE 1.08
MVIC/EBITDA . . . . N/A

OVER $5 MILLION NET SALES
MVIC/Net Sales 0.60
MVIC/Gross Profit 1.88
MVIC/SDE 3.26
MVIC/EBITDA 4.13

Source: DealStats (formerly Pratt's Stats), 2023 (Portland, OR: Business Valuation Resources, LLC), www.bvresources.com/dealstats

PRICING TIPS

Most pricing is driven by EBITDA multiples. This is not an extremely heavy investment business, therefore EBIT and EBITDA are frequently comparable. The greater the percentage of businesses driven by service (as opposed to new construction) will drive higher valuation and greater multiples. These types of businesses are attractive to private equity buyers and vertically integrated manufacturers of industry equipment.

BENCHMARK DATA

STATISTICS (GARAGE DOOR INSTALLATION)

Number of Establishments	181
Average Profit Margin	6.1%
Revenue per Employee	$308,000
Average Number of Employees	5.8
Average Wages per Employee . .	$83,635

PRODUCTS AND SERVICES SEGMENTATION

Residential, 2-car garage	40.9%
Commercial garage installation . .	30.7%
Maintenance	12.9%
Residential, 3-car garage or more . .	11.6%
Residential, 1-car garage	3.9%

MAJOR MARKET SEGMENTATION

Residential construction	59.0%
Retail merchants	30.7%
Utilities construction	10.3%

INDUSTRY COSTS

Profit	6.1%
Wages	27.5%
Purchases	28.0%
Depreciation	1.3%
Marketing	0.2%
Rent & Utilities	2.9%
Other	34.1%

MARKET SHARE

Precision Door Service	40.2%
Sanwa Holdings Corp.	30.5%

Some benchmarks include DSO +/- 45 days (less for residential, higher for commercial); $350K +/- sales per service vehicle; $180K +/- sales per full-time headcount; $75K +/- gross profit per full-time headcount.

EXPENSES (% OF ANNUAL SALES)

Cost of Goods	44%
Occupancy Costs	03%
Payroll/Labor Costs.	32%
Profit (pretax)	06%

QUESTIONS

- Who has or holds the contractors' license? Ratio of service to new construction; history of the labor force, suppliers, and relationships; competition analysis; where they see the industry going.

INDUSTRY TREND

"Operators benefited from increased consumer spending on home improvements. A decline in the commercial market was particularly severe throughout the pandemic. Robust demand has enabled companies to expand operations. Stronger investment in home improvements will offset slowing housing starts. Businesses are expected to increase their investment in existing structures. Garage door installers are slated to expand more rapidly over the next five years. Spending on home improvements has kept the industry positive over the past five years."

Source: IBISWorld Industry at a Glance

EXPERT COMMENTS

Embrace technology. Develop repair and maintenance business over new construction. Utilize field service technology. Focus on smart/connective devices and home automation—doors and docks are increasingly software driven.

There are growing shifts in the use of smart and connected devices in both home automation and the Internet of Things, which drives commercial businesses. In addition, adjacent industries such as HVAC, electrical, plumbing, access controls, and security are blurring industry lines. These technology and industry factors lead to a growing opportunity with little to no regulation of the industry. Gross profit margins continue to rise for businesses that are embracing service and technology shifts.

FINANCING

Combination of outside and seller financing. Deals involve cash, sellers' notes (multiyear), and, frequently, earnouts for the owners over a few years based on results.

RESOURCES

- IBISWorld, March 2023: https://www.ibisworld.com
- ID&OI Magazine: https://doors.org/resources/id-oi-magazine
- Door + Access Systems magazine: https://www.dasma.com/dasma-pages/D-AS-magazine.asp
- IDA—International Door Association: https://www.doors.org

DQ (Dairy Queen) (Franchise)

| NAICS 722513 | SIC 2024-98 | Businesses/Units 4,305 |

Rules of Thumb

- Price = 0.45 x sales for leased facility. Rent = variable item

INDUSTRY MULTIPLES

Acquisition multiples below are calculated medians using US private industry transactions. Data updated annually. Last update: August 2023.

UNDER $1 MILLION NET SALES

MVIC/Net Sales	0.31
MVIC/Gross Profit	0.48
MVIC/SDE	1.67
MVIC/EBITDA	2.21

$1 MILLION–$5 MILLION NET SALES

MVIC/Net Sales	0.39
MVIC/Gross Profit	0.60
MVIC/SDE	2.43
MVIC/EBITDA	2.98

OVER $5 MILLION NET SALES

MVIC/Net Sales	0.89
MVIC/Gross Profit	2.08
MVIC/SDE	4.98
MVIC/EBITDA	12.81

Source: DealStats (formerly Pratt's Stats), 2023 (Portland, OR: Business Valuation Resources, LLC), www.bvresources.com/dealstats

PRICING TIPS

Approx. Total Investment: $1,461,200 to $2,426,990

EXPENSES (% OF ANNUAL SALES)

Cost of Goods	31%
Occupancy Costs	08%
Payroll/Labor Costs	25%
Profit (pretax)	15%

QUESTIONS

• Leased facility—rent important; owned facility—loan and taxes important

EXPERT COMMENTS

• Many players in this market

RESOURCES

• DQ (Dairy Queen): https://www.dairyqueen.com/en-us/
• Franchise information: https://www.dairyqueenfranchising.com

Drive-in Restaurants

| NAICS 722513

Rules of Thumb

• 40%–45% annual sales plus inventory
• 5–6 x monthly sales plus inventory

INDUSTRY MULTIPLES

Acquisition multiples below are calculated medians using US private industry transactions. Data updated annually. Last update: August 2023.

VALUATION MULTIPLE (MEDIAN VALUE)

UNDER $1 MILLION NET SALES

MVIC/Net Sales	0.31
MVIC/Gross Profit	0.48
MVIC/SDE	1.67
MVIC/EBITDA	2.21

MVIC/Net Sales.	0.39
MVIC/Gross Profit	0.60
MVIC/SDE	2.43
MVIC/EBITDA	2.98

OVER $5 MILLION NET SALES

MVIC/Net Sales.	0.89
MVIC/Gross Profit	2.08
MVIC/SDE	4.98
MVIC/EBITDA	12.81

Source: DealStats (formerly Pratt's Stats), 2023 (Portland, OR: Business Valuation Resources, LLC), www.bvresources.com/dealstats

D

Dry Cleaners

NAICS 812320	SIC 7212-01	Businesses/Units 30,387
Profit $387.4 M	Wages $2.6 B	Annual Growth Future 1.2%
		Annual Growth Past -6.7%

Rules of Thumb

- 80%–100% sales plus inventory. Plants with on-site laundry equipment will get a higher multiple.
- 2.5–3.5 x SDE plus inventory
- 2–3 x EBIT
- 2.5–3.5 x EBITDA

INDUSTRY MULTIPLES

Acquisition multiples below are calculated medians using US private industry transactions. Data updated annually. Last update: August 2023.

VALUATION MULTIPLE (MEDIAN VALUE)

UNDER $1 MILLION NET SALES

MVIC/Net Sales.	0.61
MVIC/Gross Profit	0.72
MVIC/SDE	2.19
MVIC/EBITDA	2.75

$1 MILLION–$5 MILLION NET SALES

MVIC/Net Sales.	0.65
MVIC/Gross Profit	0.82
MVIC/SDE	2.91
MVIC/EBITDA	4.69

OVER $5 MILLION NET SALES

MVIC/Net Sales.	0.47
MVIC/Gross Profit	1.39
MVIC/SDE	7.77
MVIC/EBITDA	12.69

Source: DealStats (formerly Pratt's Stats), 2023 (Portland, OR: Business Valuation Resources, LLC), www.bvresources.com/dealstats

PRICING TIPS

I ask the seller to provide me 4 years of tax returns (since the effects of Covid I base the price off of 4 years of income vs. 3 years) I create annual net profit or cash flow before owner's notes, draws, salary, depreciation, auto expense, insurance, and all other discretionary expenses. I add the 4 years cash flow, then divide by 4 and multiply by 3. This will be the purchase price plus inventory. For manufacturing, dry cleaning, and auto repair business, if the equipment is under 5 years old, I add on to the price for the equipment cost. This formula is used also by bankers and the buyer must have experience in the industry he or she is looking to buy into.

Gross sales plus equipment value

EBITDA plus equipment

The multiple should be 2.5 to 3 x SDE, depending on the size of the cleaner, the equipment, etc.

BENCHMARK DATA

STATISTICS (DRY CLEANERS)

Number of Establishments	30,387
Average Profit Margin	5.1%
Revenue per Employee	$59,700
Average Number of Employees	4.2
Average Wages per Employee	$20,174

PRODUCTS AND SERVICES SEGMENTATION

Retail dry cleaning services	64.8%
Commercial full-service laundry	15.0%
Other	8.3%
Commercial dry cleaning services	6.5%
Retail full-service laundry services	5.4%

MAJOR MARKET SEGMENTATION

Households earning $100K or more	38.6%
Commercial	21.5%
Households earning less than $50K	21.1%
Households earning between $50K and $100K	10.6%
Nonprofits and other institutional clients	8.2%

INDUSTRY COSTS

Profit	5.1%
Wages	34.1%
Purchases	8.5%
Depreciation	2.3%
Marketing	1.7%
Rent & Utilities	5.2%
Other	43.1%

Keep employee cost below 30 percent; this can be done via automation.

Sales per employee

EXPENSES (% OF ANNUAL SALES)

Cost of Goods	05% to 15%
Occupancy Costs	10% to 20%
Payroll/Labor Costs	25% to 35%
Profit (pretax)	25% to 35%

QUESTIONS

- What do you like about this business? What do you dislike about this business?
- Marketing? Employee experience? Premise lease? Landlord experience?
- Is it easy to find employees? How old is the equipment? What chemicals are they using? What can I do to grow this business?
- Make sure to see financial statements that they can support.
- Buyer: are you willing to work in the business?

- How many hours do you work weekly? Any environmental problems?

INDUSTRY TREND

I don't see much change. I think dry cleaners and similar service-type businesses will always have a place and continue to hold their ground.

People need clean clothes. New fabrics are demanding professional care. The industry will grow.

The dry cleaning industry is consolidating. The larger ones remain but the smaller ones are closing. Hopefully, employees will be returning to work soon and more will use dry cleaning services.

"Operators will likely experience divergent conditions. The industry has experienced increasingly challenging and unfavorable operating conditions. Industry profit has historically been low, but is generally shielded from significant volatility. Intensifying external competition will likely significantly constrain demand. The most successful operators will likely be those that expand their presence beyond a local community. Tougher environmental regulations are expected to drive up operating and capital expenses. Work-from-home policies have resulted in an even greater shift to casual attire."

Source: IBISWorld Industry at a Glance

EXPERT COMMENTS

The seller has to have a proper valuation done on the business and the buyer should also make sure to verify all documents with their accountant.

Training in all areas of the business should be Included in the purchase contract.

I have been in the dry-clean and laundry industry for 56 years. The industry is excellent at stepping up to the plate and changing directions in garment care. The latest is meeting the needs of the environment and developing the wet cleaning process to eliminate the use of chemicals that were harmful in some cases. Shopping center owners are starting to cooperate better when it comes to location in their centers. They are recognizing the need for drive-up doors, as an example.

This billion-dollar industry is going through a major paradigm shift from small mom-and-pop operators to sophisticated businesspeople with centralized automated plants, computerized inventory, and many changes that were not known of 10 or 20 years ago. We work with the new breed of dry cleaning entrepreneurs to assist with their growth and operations. Commenting on all of the industry is difficult, as the quality levels, price points, the economy of scale, and markets served are so different! Modern dry cleaning operations are growing into light industrial production and distribution operations.

FINANCING

Outside financing: we always make sure to secure an SBA approved lender for our clients. Buyer must have experience.

RESOURCES

- IBISWorld, February 2023: https://www.ibisworld.com
- American Drycleaner: https://americandrycleaner.com
- DLI—Drycleaning & Laundry Institute International: https://www.dlionline.org
- National Clothesline: https://www.nationalclothesline.com
- NCA—National Cleaners Association: https://www.nca-i.com

- WSDLA—Western States Drycleaners & Launderers Association: https://www.wsdla.org

Drywall & Insulation Installers

| NAICS 238310 | Businesses/Units 21,075

| Profit $4 B | Wages $18.1 B | Annual Growth Future 0.4%

INDUSTRY MULTIPLES

Acquisition multiples below are calculated medians using US private industry transactions. Data updated annually. Last update: August 2023.

VALUATION MULTIPLE (MEDIAN VALUE)

UNDER $1 MILLION NET SALES

MVIC/Net Sales.	0.44
MVIC/Gross Profit	0.76
MVIC/SDE	1.34
MVIC/EBITDA	7.18

$1 MILLION–$5 MILLION NET SALES

MVIC/Net Sales.	0.27
MVIC/Gross Profit	0.88
MVIC/SDE	1.47
MVIC/EBITDA	2.26

OVER $5 MILLION NET SALES

MVIC/Net Sales.	0.57
MVIC/Gross Profit	1.38
MVIC/SDE	3.06
MVIC/EBITDA	2.90

Source: DealStats (formerly Pratt's Stats), 2023 (Portland, OR: Business Valuation Resources, LLC), www.bvresources.com/dealstats

BENCHMARK DATA

STATISTICS (DRYWALL & INSULATION INSTALLERS)

Number of Establishments	.21,075
Average Profit Margin	6.8%
Revenue per Employee	$206,000
Average Number of Employees.	13.8
Average Wages per Employee	$63,791

PRODUCTS AND SERVICES SEGMENTATION

Drywall contracting	51.2%
Other	21.6%
Insulation contracting	12.8%
Acoustical contracting	9.2%
Lath and plaster contracting	4.5%
Stucco contracting	0.7%

MAJOR MARKET SEGMENTATION

Commercial building construction	45.6%
Residential building construction	35.3%
Municipal building construction	13.8%
Other nonresidential construction	2.7%
Industrial building construction	2.6%

INDUSTRY COSTS

Profit	6.8%
Wages	31.0%
Purchases	38.3%

```
Depreciation  .   .   .   .   .   .   . 0.5%
Marketing  .   .   .   .   .   .   .   . 0.2%
Rent & Utilities  .   .   .   .   .   .   . 3.1%
Other  .   .   .   .   .   .   .   . . 20.0%
```

D

INDUSTRY TREND

"COVID-19 reduced the need for commercial space and drywall and insulation installers. Low interest rates and improved access to credit spurred consumer mortgage originations. Government incentives designed to enhance energy efficiency in homes has stimulated demand. An increasing the cost of borrowing will cool down construction activity. Strong consumer spending allows corporate profit to increase. COVID-19 outbreaks and the continued conflict in Ukraine will cause supply chain disruptions. Industry profit has remained steady due to volatile demand."

Source: IBISWorld Industry at a Glance

RESOURCES

• IBISWorld, January 2023: https://www.ibisworld.com

Dunkin' (Franchise)

| NAICS 722515 | SIC 5812-06 | Businesses/Units 9,244

Rules of Thumb

• 60%–100% annual sales plus inventory
• 4 x SDE plus inventory
• 5 x EBITDA

INDUSTRY MULTIPLES

Acquisition multiples below are calculated medians using US private industry transactions. Data updated annually. Last update: August 2023.

VALUATION MULTIPLE (MEDIAN VALUE)

UNDER $1 MILLION NET SALES	
MVIC/Net Sales.	0.44
MVIC/Gross Profit	0.62
MVIC/SDE	2.20
MVIC/EBITDA	2.82
$1 MILLION–$5 MILLION NET SALES	
MVIC/Net Sales.	0.41
MVIC/Gross Profit	0.69
MVIC/SDE	2.82
MVIC/EBITDA	5.94
OVER $5 MILLION NET SALES	
MVIC/Net Sales.	3.89
MVIC/Gross Profit	4.87
MVIC/SDE	N/A
MVIC/EBITDA	N/A

Source: DealStats (formerly Pratt's Stats), 2023 (Portland, OR: Business Valuation Resources, LLC), www.bvresources.com/dealstats

PRICING TIPS

Approx. Total Investment: $437,500 to $1,787,700

The higher values are ascribed to units with a greater percentage of coffee sales.

BENCHMARK DATA

EXPENSES (% OF ANNUAL SALES)

Cost of Goods + Supplies . .	23% to 24% + 4%
Occupancy Costs	08% to 10%
Payroll/Labor Costs.	22%
Profit (pretax)	15% to 20%

QUESTIONS

- When are remodels due? Lease details are critical, and length of time remaining on the franchise agreements. Does the seller have expansion rights in adjacent areas?
- What percent of sales is beverages?

EXPERT COMMENTS

It is a well-known franchise, but there is stiff competition from Starbucks and McDonald's.

The marketability is not as high as one would expect for such a profitable and growing business. The reason is that the franchisor has very strict requirements to approve a buyer.

FINANCING

7 years—usually are bank/SBA financed

RESOURCES

- Dunkin': https://www.dunkindonuts.com/en
- Franchise information: https://www.dunkinfranchising.com
- Inspire Brands: https://inspirebrands.com

E-Cigarette Stores/Vapor Stores

| NAICS 459991

Rules of Thumb

- 1.7 x SDE plus inventory

PRICING TIPS

The relative cost of the products is cheap, allowing a sizeable margin of profit.

EXPENSES (% OF ANNUAL SALES)

Cost of Goods	20%
Occupancy Costs	25%
Payroll/Labor Costs.	15%
Profit (pretax)	40%

QUESTIONS

- Why are you selling?

INDUSTRY TREND

"Sales of e-cigarettes rose by nearly 47 percent from January 2020, just before the pandemic hit the United States, to December 2022, according to an analysis released on Thursday by the Centers for Disease Control and Prevention.... Sales were still growing through May of last year, but then dropped by 12 percent through December. Researchers attributed the decline to several possible factors, including state or local bans on flavored products; government enforcement; and the introduction of devices that offered thousands of 'puffs' in a single device."

Source: "E-Cigarette Sales Tapered Off Last Year After Big Surge" by Christina Jewett, June 22, 2023, https://www.nytimes.com/2023/06/22/health/e-cigarette-sales-cdc-vaping.html

EXPERT COMMENTS

Don't let the tidal effects of legislation and regulation wear you down. Many are certain that this industry will weather the storm and come out more lucrative than ever.

E-Commerce (Internet Sales)

NAICS 454111	SIC 5731-24	Businesses/Units 378,363
Profit $55.1 B	Wages $36.4 B	Annual Growth Future 7.7%
		Annual Growth Past 16.1%

Rules of Thumb

- 30%–50% annual sales includes inventory
- 2–4 x SDE includes inventory
- 3–6 x EBITDA
- 3–4.5 x EBIT

PRICING TIPS

Inventory and the age of inventory are critical. Shipping details—FBA or type of shipping. How the company maintains a competitive advantage can play in to valuation.

Retail (B2C) is perceived as riskier than wholesale e-commerce (B2B).

BENCHMARK DATA

STATISTICS (E-COMMERCE & ONLINE AUCTIONS)

Number of Establishments	378,363
Average Profit Margin	5.9%
Revenue per Employee	$1,016,000
Average Number of Employees	2.6
Average Wages per Employee	$40,260

PRODUCTS AND SERVICES SEGMENTATION

Other merchandise	22.3%
Home and office	17.7%
Clothing, footwear and accessories	17.2%
Computers, electronics and appliances	14.4%
Medication and health aids	11.2%
Sporting goods, toys, hobby items and games	8.3%
Media	5.0%
Food, beer and wine	3.9%

MAJOR MARKET SEGMENTATION

Consumers under age 34	38.2%
Consumers aged 35 to 54	32.7%
Consumers aged 55 and older	29.1%

INDUSTRY COSTS

Profit	5.9%
Wages	3.9%
Purchases	64.1%
Depreciation	0.7%
Marketing	4.0%
Rent & Utilities	1.6%
Other	19.8%

MARKET SHARE

Walmart Inc..	4.0%

Net profit and SDE are best indicators of a successful venture.

EXPENSES (% OF ANNUAL SALES)

Cost of Goods	40%
Occupancy Costs	10%
Payroll/Labor Costs.	25%
Profit (pretax)	15%

QUESTIONS

- Proof of sales? Special software for updating pricing on a very regular basis? Where do sellers buy inventory? Are there any special pricing agreements in place, and will they continue postsale?
- Will your online accounts transfer? Who handles fulfillment; and can I, or would I want to, change that after the sale? Will vendors offer current pricing postsale for inventory? What type of warranty do you offer, and any outstanding claims? How much working capital is needed on a weekly, monthly, or annual basis? How many inventory turns are there per year?
- How do you get paid? What are the 10 largest customers? How much is automated? Turnover of vendors, suppliers, and employees? What is the most significant bottleneck in your operations? When evaluating contracts and seller agreements with larger platforms (Amazon, etc.), what are the returns/allowance holdbacks?

INDUSTRY TREND

Growing yet more competitive.

"Large companies have increased investment in artificial intelligence technology. Increased industry competition puts pressure on online retailers to differentiate themselves from industry rivals. Many operators have had success by selling niche products for specific customer segments. Wage growth will slightly outpace revenue growth, offsetting a stronger dollar. General consumer spending is expected to continue to rise, aiding revenue growth. Consumers and legislators have criticized the size of some major players is resulting in anticompetitive practices. Wages have been outpaced by revenue growth as new technology has increased per-employee productivity."

Source: IBISWorld Industry at a Glance

EXPERT COMMENTS

Understand how algorithms work for pricing, as that can make or break the business in many instances.

Online/e-commerce sales have become critical, and buyers and sellers know this. Ease of replication seems very easy; it's not!

Understanding the website (Amazon, Etsy, eBay, etc) rules and regulations for the specific type of inventory that a buyer plans to sell is very important, as is understanding how the seller's current accounts will or won't transfer to a buyer.

Almost anyone can set up an online business; the trick is understanding pricing, inventory, fulfillment, and customer service.

Few barriers to entry (establishing a marketplace for sales); however, marketing and SEO can be complicated and may require outsourcing.

FINANCING

Seller finance is not uncommon; 25 percent plus of sale price would be a common ask of buyers.

RESOURCES

- IBISWorld, September 2022: https://www.ibisworld.com
- Digital Commerce 360: https://www.digitalcommerce360.com/internet-retailer/
- E-Commerce Times: https://www.ecommercetimes.com
- GRA—Global Retail Alliance: https://www.gra.world
- IA—Internet Association: https://internetassociation.org

Eagle Transmission (Franchise)

| NAICS 811114 | SIC 7537-01 | Businesses/Units 28 |

Rules of Thumb

- 40% annual sales
- 2.5 x SDE

INDUSTRY MULTIPLES

Acquisition multiples below are calculated medians using US private industry transactions. Data updated annually. Last update: August 2023.

VALUATION MULTIPLE (MEDIAN VALUE)

UNDER $1 MILLION NET SALES	
MVIC/Net Sales.	0.40
MVIC/Gross Profit	0.47
MVIC/SDE	1.60
MVIC/EBITDA	12.57
$1 MILLION–$5 MILLION NET SALES	N/A
OVER $5 MILLION NET SALES	N/A

Source: DealStats (formerly Pratt's Stats), 2023 (Portland, OR: Business Valuation Resources, LLC), www.bvresources.com/dealstats

PRICING TIPS

Approx. Total Investment: $229,000 to $492,500

RESOURCES

- Eagle Transmission: https://www.eagletransmission.com
- Franchise information: https://www.eagletransmission.com/franchise-info

Electric Motor Repair

| NAICS 811310 | SIC 7694

Rules of Thumb

- 30%–40% of annual sales for fixed assets and goodwill without real estate, plus inventory
- 3 x SDE plus inventory, mom-and-pop shops
- 4–5 x EBITDA for businesses under $1,000,000 EBITDA
- 5–7 x EBITDA for businesses over $1,000,000 EBITDA

INDUSTRY MULTIPLES

Acquisition multiples below are calculated medians using US private industry transactions. Data updated annually. Last update: August 2023.

VALUATION MULTIPLE (MEDIAN VALUE)

UNDER $1 MILLION NET SALES	
MVIC/Net Sales.	0.69
MVIC/Gross Profit	0.92
MVIC/SDE	2.39
MVIC/EBITDA	4.60
$1 MILLION–$5 MILLION NET SALES	
MVIC/Net Sales.	0.47
MVIC/Gross Profit	1.22
MVIC/SDE	2.70
MVIC/EBITDA	4.89
OVER $5 MILLION NET SALES	
MVIC/Net Sales.	0.47
MVIC/Gross Profit	1.44
MVIC/SDE	3.25
MVIC/EBITDA	3.67

Source: DealStats (formerly Pratt's Stats), 2023 (Portland, OR: Business Valuation Resources, LLC), www.bvresources.com/dealstats

PRICING TIPS

3 x SDE plus inventory for mom-and-pop shops; 4 to 5 x EBITDA for businesses under $1,000,000 EBITDA; 5 to 7 x EBITDA for businesses over $1,000,000 EBITDA; 33 percent of annual value-added (repair and service) sales for fixed assets and goodwill without real estate plus inventory.

This aftermarket industry consists of the field service and repair (value-added sales) of electromechanical apparatus and the distribution of related parts and apparatus (product sales). Size and mix are critical in the valuation. Companies under $2 million in sales will be valued on SDE. For companies with sales over $2 million, the enterprise will be valued on EBITDA. Enterprise is defined as fixed assets without real estate, goodwill, net working capital without cash, and no interest-bearing debt. The EBITDA multiple of 4 to 5 x is typical for smaller companies under $1 million EBITDA and 5 to 7 x for larger companies with over $1 million EBITDA. This assumes the company is making a profit. For companies with 70 percent or higher of value-added sales, the value of the fixed assets (excluding real estate) and goodwill will typically be between 25 and 40 percent of the value-added sales. The product sales for these companies generally arise from the repair vs. replace economic decision for inoperable apparatus. For companies with less than 70 percent value-added sales, some additional premium is afforded the product sales as these begin to be pure distribution sales, not the result of the repair vs. replace decision.

Size and growth are primary value drivers in the electric motor repair industry. The key consideration for attracting a buyer is who is going to run the business after a sale is completed. The median number of employees in the industry is approximately 11.

Businesses smaller than the median sell based on SDE multiple often to an individual.

Larger businesses with EBITDA under $1,000,000 are often sold to regional, multibranch companies in the same, or very similar, industrial repair and service industries. They are seeking to expand their geographic footprint.

Buyers for business with EBITDA over $1,000,000 are national or international companies in the same, or very similar, industries, or private equity firms that may or may not have an established footprint in the industry.

A large concentration of business with only a few customers, a run-down condition, obsolete equipment, and lack of modern testing capabilities are value inhibitors.

BENCHMARK DATA

The mix of business in the industry is between value-added (labor-added) repairs and services versus off-the-shelf product sales that will arise when repair of the customer's equipment is not economically feasible.

Typical shops have a mix of 70 percent value-added sales versus 30 percent product sales. Under that ratio, the sales per total number of employees is approximately $250,000 to $330,000 per year.

The labor component of cost of goods sold (COGS) is measured by several methods within the industry: direct labor at the employee's hourly rate; direct labor with a small burden rate to cover other employee costs only; direct labor with a full burden rate; and sometimes direct labor will go into operating expenses below the total COGS line.

EXPENSES (% OF ANNUAL SALES)

Cost of Goods	30% to 40%
Occupancy Costs	05% to 10%
Payroll/Labor Costs.	25% to 35%
Profit (pretax)	05% to 10%

QUESTIONS

- Sales mix, customer concentration, labor rates, amount of overtime, technical skills of workforce. Tenure of key employees: shop, office, and sales.
- Who is going to run the business?
- Electric motor repair requires technical skills and industry experience. Any buyer coming in without the skills must be very sure of the continuation of the current employees that have those skills.
- Other important questions are the condition of the equipment, terms of the lease, condition of the inventory, and turnover of employees.

INDUSTRY TREND

Larger shops over $1,000,000 EBITDA are frequently being acquired by private equity companies. Sometimes these buyers already own one or more electric motor repair businesses. Since private equity firms typically have a five year or less cycle from buying to selling, the availability of capital expenditure monies for organic expansion is typically limited. Their typical goal is for a 25 to 30 percent annual return on the cash invested. Noncash financing mechanisms are often used by private equity firms to substitute for cash at closing, including earnouts, roll-ups, seller notes, and others. Sellers should be very aware of the differences between private equity buyers and long-term strategic buyers looking to buy, hold, and grow the acquired companies over a longer-term horizon.

Assuming no upcoming recession, a 5 to 10 percent growth per year.

There is a resurgence in the industry as manufacturing jobs have moved back to the United States. Steel mills, a large segment of the motor repair industry, have and will continue to increase production domestically. There is a shortage of new skilled labor with industry experience, and the experienced workforce is aging quickly—a trend not untypical of many industries. For the first time in over a decade, the industry has some customer pricing power to capture the value of their skilled labor.

The use of electronics to monitor and adjust motors operating in the customer's facility in real time is growing. Customers are demanding more sophisticated testing methods and testing equipment with real-time feedback.

EXPERT COMMENTS

Be careful of how warranty costs are handled from work completed before the sale.

A significant amount of capital is required for the equipment and inventory. The industry should benefit from companies onshoring their manufacturing.

Electric motor repair is a mature industry dominated by small businesses. As the cost of labor increases and productivity of electric motor manufacturing improves, the horsepower threshold when a standard motor can be economically repaired rises. New motors—it's more cost-effective to replace the malfunctioning motors, and the population of repairable motors decreases.

Success in the industry is dependent on finding new markets and additional value-added services. Larger industrial customers have reduced their maintenance and repair head count and rely more on purchased outside services. This is the door of opportunity for this industry.

Valuing companies that are profitable in the industry is done almost exclusively based on a multiple of EBITDA, compared to pretax earnings, which was used in the past.

Companies with no income are valued on the discounted market value of the equipment and inventory. A small adder may be applied to this discounted value for the revenue stream and the geographic location, but not much.

RESOURCES
• EA—Electrical Apparatus magazine:
  http://barks.com/for-readers/about-electrical-apparatus-magazine/
• EASA: https://easa.com

Electric Power Transmission

| NAICS 221121 | Businesses/Units 9,158 |

| Profit $56.1 B | Wages $56.7 B | Annual Growth Future 0.7% |
| | | Annual Growth Past 0.7% |

INDUSTRY MULTIPLES

Acquisition multiples below are calculated medians using US private industry transactions. Data updated annually. Last update: August 2023.

E

VALUATION MULTIPLE (MEDIAN VALUE)

UNDER $1 MILLION NET SALES	N/A
$1 MILLION–$5 MILLION NET SALES	N/A

OVER $5 MILLION NET SALES

MVIC/Net Sales	11.34
MVIC/Gross Profit	N/A
MVIC/SDE	N/A
MVIC/EBITDA	16.80

Source: DealStats (formerly Pratt's Stats), 2023 (Portland, OR: Business Valuation Resources, LLC), www.bvresources.com/dealstats

BENCHMARK DATA

STATISTICS (ELECTRIC POWER TRANSMISSION)

Number of Establishments	9,158
Average Profit Margin	11.1%
Revenue per Employee	$1,256,000
Average Number of Employees	44.2
Average Wages per Employee	$141,455

PRODUCTS AND SERVICES SEGMENTATION

Natural gas-generated electricity	33.6%
Coal-generated electricity	23.2%
Renewable sources	22.6%
Nuclear-generated electricity	20.3%
Petroleum-generated electricity	0.3%

MAJOR MARKET SEGMENTATION

Residential	50.6%
Commercial sector	33.3%
Industrial sector	15.9%
Transportation sector	0.2%

INDUSTRY COSTS

Profit	11.1%
Wages	11.2%
Purchases	42.3%
Depreciation	6.5%
Marketing	0.2%
Rent & Utilities	1.1%
Other	27.5%

INDUSTRY TREND

"The use of electric vehicles as a source of power has intrigued electric utility executives, including Pedro Pizarro, who heads the board of the Edison Electric Institute, the industry's main trade organization, and is the chief executive of Edison International, which provides power to millions of homes and businesses in Southern California. Mr. Pizarro's company and other utilities are testing whether it is practical and safe to send power from electric vehicles to the grid. By soaking up power when it's abundant and releasing it when it is scarce, electric vehicles, he said, could serve as 'a bigger rubber band to absorb the shocks and manage them day to day and week to week.'"

Source: "A New Job for Electric Vehicles: Powering Homes During Blackouts" by Ivan Penn, July 16, 2023, https://www.nytimes.com/2023/07/16/business/energy-environment/electric-vehicles-backup-power.html

"Many office spaces are starting to use less electricity. Advanced metering technology, also known as smart grids, has risen in popularity. Government incentives like tax credits have led more businesses and households to switch to renewable energy. The IRA extends investment tax credits for construction projects up to 2025. New power infrastructure helps reduce operating costs. New tax credits and lower production costs will entice consumers to switch to EVs. Industry profit has remained relatively unchanged overall."

Source: IBISWorld Industry at a Glance

RESOURCES

- IBISWorld, January 2023: https://www.ibisworld.com
- EEI—Edison Electric Institute: https://www.eei.org

Electricians

| NAICS 238210 | Businesses/Units 222,943 |

| Profit $14.8 B | Wages $70.6 B | Annual Growth Future 0.9% |

| Annual Growth Past 0.4% |

Rules of Thumb

- 2–3 x SDE plus inventory
- 90% annual sales includes inventory
- 3.8 x EBIT
- 3.5 x EBITDA

INDUSTRY MULTIPLES

Acquisition multiples below are calculated medians using US private industry transactions. Data updated annually. Last update: August 2023.

VALUATION MULTIPLE (MEDIAN VALUE)

UNDER $1 MILLION NET SALES

MVIC/Net Sales	0.49
MVIC/Gross Profit	0.80
MVIC/SDE	2.08
MVIC/EBITDA	2.70

$1 MILLION–$5 MILLION NET SALES

MVIC/Net Sales	0.48
MVIC/Gross Profit	0.99
MVIC/SDE	2.39
MVIC/EBITDA	3.20

OVER $5 MILLION NET SALES

MVIC/Net Sales	0.46
MVIC/Gross Profit	1.48
MVIC/SDE	3.19
MVIC/EBITDA	4.78

Source: DealStats (formerly Pratt's Stats), 2023 (Portland, OR: Business Valuation Resources, LLC), www.bvresources.com/dealstats

PRICING TIPS

Find out exactly why the owner is selling to ensure it isn't because of something that will have a negative impact on future business.

BENCHMARK DATA

STATISTICS (ELECTRICIANS)

Number of Establishments 222,943
Average Profit Margin 6.2%
Revenue per Employee $223,000
Average Number of Employees. 4.9
Average Wages per Employee $65,991

PRODUCTS AND SERVICES SEGMENTATION

Electric power and systems installation and servicing. 69.7%
Telecommunications installation and servicing 9.9%
Fire and security system installation and servicing 5.9%
All other services 5.4%
Electronic control system installation and servicing 5.1%
Highway, street, or bridge lighting and signal installation and servicing . . . 4.0%

MAJOR MARKET SEGMENTATION

Institutional, educational and civic organizations and facilities 26.3%
Commercial buildings 21.7%
Office buildings 17.8%
Infrastructure and utilities 13.9%
Residential structures 12.3%
Hotels, motels and tourist cabins 2.9%
All other nonresidential building projects 2.7%
Industrial buildings 2.4%

INDUSTRY COSTS

Profit 6.2%
Wages 29.5%
Purchases 37.9%
Depreciation 0.9%
Marketing 0.2%
Rent & Utilities 3.3%
Other 21.9%

Each service truck/van produces approximately $50,000/year net revenue.

EXPENSES (% OF ANNUAL SALES)

Cost of Goods . . . . 55% to 65%
Occupancy Costs . . . . N/A
Payroll/Labor Costs. . . . . 30% to 35%
Profit (pretax) . . . . 06% to 10%

QUESTIONS

- Are all the current apprentices, wiremen, and journeymen employees?
- What is the seller's customer database? What percentage are repeat customers, both residential and commercial?
- Details of job costs, current and bids? List of staff? Experience? Time with business?

INDUSTRY TREND

An increase in demand for installation/service of generators and solar

"The unexpected housing explosion in 2020 and 2021 gave electricians a fantastic year. The growth in green energy policy and projects has needed electricians to be helpful to the public. Fluid fuels have been the primary building-wide heating and transportation method since the late 19th century. Housing prices collapsed in 2023 and the market is anticipated to remain relaxed through 2024. Few commercial real estate investors expect to build new properties in 2023 as cash flow for this market cools. Electricians are returning to wiring installation in buildings and roads. The Electricians industry differentiates itself by providing an economically essential service."

Source: IBISWorld Industry at a Glance

EXPERT COMMENTS

There must be a plan in place for who will hold the master electrician license for the business, as the license is the lifeblood of an electrical company. Without it, the business cannot operate, and banks know this so require a solid plan in place before approving the loan.

FINANCING

Outside financing with approximately 5 to 10 percent seller Financing

RESOURCES

- IBISWorld, February 2023: https://www.ibisworld.com
- IBEW—International Brotherhood of Electrical Workers: https://www.ibew.org
- IEC—Independent Electrical Contractors: https://www.ieci.org
- NECA—National Electrical Contractors Association: https://www.necanet.org

Embroidery Services/Shops

| NAICS 314999 | SIC 7389-42

Rules of Thumb

- 55%–60% annual sales plus inventory
- 4 x SDE

INDUSTRY MULTIPLES

Acquisition multiples below are calculated medians using US private industry transactions. Data updated annually. Last update: August 2023.

VALUATION MULTIPLE (MEDIAN VALUE)

UNDER $1 MILLION NET SALES	
MVIC/Net Sales	0.55
MVIC/Gross Profit	0.83
MVIC/SDE	1.90
MVIC/EBITDA	3.38
$1 MILLION–$5 MILLION NET SALES	
MVIC/Net Sales	0.44
MVIC/Gross Profit	0.73
MVIC/SDE	3.50
MVIC/EBITDA	4.92
OVER $5 MILLION NET SALES	
MVIC/Net Sales	0.72
MVIC/Gross Profit	3.17
MVIC/SDE	N/A
MVIC/EBITDA	7.69

Source: DealStats (formerly Pratt's Stats), 2023 (Portland, OR: Business Valuation Resources, LLC), www.bvresources.com/dealstats

PRICING TIPS

40 to 50 percent of annual revenue, last three years

BENCHMARK DATA

$150,000 to $180,000 per employee

QUESTIONS

• Transition period by seller available?

INDUSTRY TREND

8 percent growth

EXPERT COMMENTS

Roll-up M&A is the fastest way to scaling distribution.

FINANCING

Cash—private investment

RESOURCES

• ASI—Advertising Specialty Institute: https://www.asicentral.com
• ETA—Embroidery Trade Association: https://embroiderytrade.org
• PRINTING United Alliance: https://www.printing.org

Engineering Services

| NAICS 541330　| Businesses/Units 157,518

| Profit $34.6 B　| Wages $150.7 B　| Annual Growth Future 1.7%

| Annual Growth Past 3.3%

Rules of Thumb

• 40%–50% annual sales
• 2.5 x SDE
• 5.5 x EBITDA

INDUSTRY MULTIPLES

Acquisition multiples below are calculated medians using US private industry transactions. Data updated annually. Last update: August 2023.

VALUATION MULTIPLE (MEDIAN VALUE)

UNDER $1 MILLION NET SALES	
MVIC/Net Sales	0.73
MVIC/Gross Profit	0.77
MVIC/SDE	2.24
MVIC/EBITDA	3.38
$1 MILLION–$5 MILLION NET SALES	
MVIC/Net Sales	0.73
MVIC/Gross Profit	1.09
MVIC/SDE	2.43
MVIC/EBITDA	4.54
OVER $5 MILLION NET SALES	
MVIC/Net Sales	0.67
MVIC/Gross Profit	2.40
MVIC/SDE	3.53
MVIC/EBITDA	8.23

Source: DealStats (formerly Pratt's Stats), 2023 (Portland, OR: Business Valuation Resources, LLC), www.bvresources.com/dealstats

PRICING TIPS

Larger firms demand a premium. Be wary of firms with only one principal (licensed professional).

With engineering firms, the employees are just as important. Revenue is derived from an employee's billable hours. Pay attention to the key employees by noting the licenses held, time in the industry, time with the company, and the likelihood the key employees will remain with the new owner after the sale. Losing a key employee or employees could dramatically impact the company's revenue and earnings.

BENCHMARK DATA

STATISTICS (ENGINEERING SERVICES)

Number of Establishments	157,518
Average Profit Margin	9.6%
Revenue per Employee	$265,000
Average Number of Employees	8.9
Average Wages per Employee	$110,698

PRODUCTS AND SERVICES SEGMENTATION

Other	29.0%
Industrial, commercial and institutional projects	24.2%
Consulting and project management	17.4%
Transportation projects	15.5%
Residential and municipal utility projects	9.1%
Telecom and broadcasting systems projects	2.7%
Power transmission and distribution projects	2.1%

MAJOR MARKET SEGMENTATION

Business	61.0%
Government	38.3%
Other	0.7%

INDUSTRY COSTS

Profit	9.6%
Wages	41.9%
Purchases	7.8%
Depreciation	1.2%
Marketing	0.4%
Rent and Utilities	3.7%
Other	35.4%

Utilization rate of professionals

The company should be generating between $100,000 and $150,000 in revenue per person.

EXPENSES (% OF ANNUAL SALES)

Cost of Goods	0%
Payroll/Labor Costs	30%
Profit (pretax)	20%

QUESTIONS

- Loyalty of staff? How many are licensed?
- What does your pipeline look like? (View it.) If you were 10 years younger, how would you grow the business? How long have your top clients been clients? What percentage of sales is from each product (environmental, civil, structural, MEP)? How would you categorize your clients (i.e.,municipal, private, consumer) and what percentage of sales do they make?

INDUSTRY TREND

Fairly constant

Overall, the industry is stable with a positive outlook due to the recently passed infrastructure bill. As a profession, the industry is very fragmented.

"High inflation has resulted in increased raw material and labor costs. COVID-19 has indirectly impacted engineers by affecting the businesses and organizations that are clients. Engineering companies have increasingly focused on developing sustainable technologies and infrastructure. Engineers' growth will be influenced by economic conditions. Demand for projects related to renewable energy and waste reduction will increase. There will be increased demand for engineering services related to digital technologies. More companies have focused on developing environmental initiatives."

Source: IBISWorld Industry at a Glance

EXPERT COMMENTS

Understand if the clients will transfer if the owner leaves. Understand the business development function of the firm.

Look closely at the pipeline of future work (signed contracts). Determine if the key employees are likely to stay after the sale. Require the seller to sign an employment agreement.

FINANCING

Some owner Financing

Typically the buyer puts at least 10 percent down. The seller should expect to provide a loan for 10 percent plus help with working capital. The bank makes up the difference.

RESOURCES

- IBISWorld, January 2023: https://www.ibisworld.com
- ASEE—American Society for Engineering Education: https://www.asee.org
- NAE—National Academy of Engineering: https://www.nae.edu
- NSPE—National Society of Professional Engineers: https://www.nspe.org

Environmental Testing

| NAICS 541380

| Profit $4.1 B | Wages $12.3 B | Annual Growth Future 1.0%

| Annual Growth Past 3.1%

Rules of Thumb

- 60% annual sales plus inventory
- 2–2.5 x SDE plus inventory

INDUSTRY MULTIPLES

Acquisition multiples below are calculated medians using US private industry transactions. Data updated annually. Last update: August 2023.

VALUATION MULTIPLE (MEDIAN VALUE)

UNDER $1 MILLION NET SALES

MVIC/Net Sales	0.88
MVIC/Gross Profit	0.66
MVIC/SDE	2.30
MVIC/EBITDA	4.96

$1 MILLION–$5 MILLION NET SALES

MVIC/Net Sales	1.23
MVIC/Gross Profit	1.54
MVIC/SDE	3.82
MVIC/EBITDA	4.49

OVER $5 MILLION NET SALES

MVIC/Net Sales	1.46
MVIC/Gross Profit	3.75
MVIC/SDE	3.15
MVIC/EBITDA	9.67

Source: DealStats (formerly Pratt's Stats), 2023 (Portland, OR: Business Valuation Resources, LLC), www.bvresources.com/dealstats

PRICING TIPS

Be sure the accounting is on the accrual method so there is no confusion as to how values are arrived at.

BENCHMARK DATA

STATISTICS (LABORATORY TESTING SERVICES)

Number of Establishments	12,292
Average Profit Margin	13.5%
Revenue per Employee	$190,000
Average Number of Employees	13.0
Average Wages per Employee	$77,694

PRODUCTS AND SERVICES SEGMENTATION

Environmental and biological testing	39.0%
Commercial and construction testing	32.7%
Miscellaneous testing	19.7%
Agricultural and food product testing	8.6%

MAJOR MARKET SEGMENTATION

Construction and restoration companies	50.1%
Consumer and industrial product manufacturers	40.2%
Government	8.8%
Other	0.9%

INDUSTRY COSTS

Profit	13.5%
Wages	40.8%
Purchases	7.0%
Depreciation	3.5%
Marketing	0.4%
Rent & Utilities	3.3%
Other	31.6%

MARKET SHARE

Intertek Group PLC	4.7%
Eurofins Scientific	3.6%
Golder Associates Corporation	2.6%
Pace Analytical Services Inc.	1.4%
Bureau Veritas S A	1.4%

Cost of Goods	02%
Occupancy Costs	03%
Payroll/Labor Costs.	30%
Profit (pretax)	16%

QUESTIONS

• Why did you get in the business and why are you getting out at this time?

INDUSTRY TREND

"Government regulation across a range of industries has stimulated demand. One of the most important drivers of industry demand is clients' investment in R&D. Much of the industry's growth is attributable to greater environmental regulation. Growth in R&D spending from public and private sectors will benefit demand. Prevalence of disruptive technologies will help drive demand for laboratory testing. More-rigorous lab testing for GM foods and other agricultural products will continue to bolster demand for industry services. The industry has thrived due to higher government regulation of consumer and food products."

Source: IBISWorld Industry at a Glance

EXPERT COMMENTS

Owners and their contacts are more the driving, networking force than the location or the facilities.

RESOURCES

• IBISWorld, April 2023: https://www.ibisworld.com
• EBI—Environmental Business International Inc.: https://ebionline.org

Event Planning

| NAICS 561920 | SIC 7389-44

Rules of Thumb

• 3 x EBITDA plus asset value

INDUSTRY MULTIPLES

Acquisition multiples below are calculated medians using US private industry transactions. Data updated annually. Last update: August 2023.

VALUATION MULTIPLE (MEDIAN VALUE)

UNDER $1 MILLION NET SALES	
MVIC/Net Sales.	0.66
MVIC/Gross Profit	0.85
MVIC/SDE	2.29
MVIC/EBITDA	3.49
$1 MILLION–$5 MILLION NET SALES	
MVIC/Net Sales.	0.74
MVIC/Gross Profit	1.42
MVIC/SDE	2.72
MVIC/EBITDA	4.36
OVER $5 MILLION NET SALES	
MVIC/Net Sales.	0.80
MVIC/Gross Profit	3.83

MVIC/SDE . . . . N/A
MVIC/EBITDA 24.78

Source: DealStats (formerly Pratt's Stats), 2023 (Portland, OR: Business Valuation Resources, LLC), www.bvresources.com/dealstats

PRICING TIPS

Are there events on the books going forward? How many repeat clients?

BENCHMARK DATA

STATISTICS (TRADE SHOW AND CONFERENCE PLANNING)

Number of Establishments	7,713
Average Profit Margin	6.6%
Revenue per Employee	$194,000
Average Number of Employees.	14.9
Average Wages per Employee	$35,453

PRODUCTS AND SERVICES SEGMENTATION

Exhibit sales and design services	46.2%
Shipping, logistics and other services	30.6%
Registration, analytics and show services	13.3%
Sponsorships, entertainment and advertising sales	9.9%

MAJOR MARKET SEGMENTATION

Consumer goods, sporting goods, travel and other consumer services . .	22.8%
Medical and healthcare.	21.2%
Other	19.2%
Business services	16.9%
Communication and information technology	10.9%
Producers of commodities, chemicals and engineered materials	9.0%

INDUSTRY COSTS

Profit	6.6%
Wages	18.2%
Purchases	38.8%
Depreciation	1.3%
Marketing	1.9%
Rent & Utilities	2.5%
Other	30.8%

MARKET SHARE

Freeman Company LLC.	11.8%
George P. Johnson Company	3.2%
Viad Corp.	2.6%
Direct Travel Inc.	2.0%
CWT Global B.V..	1.8%
ITA Group, Inc.	1.3%

STATISTICS (PARTY & EVENT PLANNERS)

Number of Establishments	110,407
Average Profit Margin	12.2%
Revenue per Employee	$44,400
Average Number of Employees.	1.2
Average Wages per Employee	$11,657

PRODUCTS AND SERVICES SEGMENTATION

Corporate social events.	60.4%
Weddings	18.7%
Birthday parties	12.3%
Other	8.6%

Profit	12.2%
Wages	26.6%
Purchases	8.7%
Depreciation	2.0%
Marketing	1.8%
Rent & Utilities	5.4%
Other	43.3%

INDUSTRY TREND

"Rising industry participation has been facilitated by low barriers to entry. Corporate profit levels initially declined as a result of the COVID-19 pandemic. Industry performance is dependent on the ability for both domestic and international professionals to attend trade show events. Private investment is expected to increase, benefiting industry revenue growth. Industry employment is expected to increase. Industry operators must be willing to incorporate new technology into service offerings to remain competitive. As air travel and event attendance resumed, industry performance rebounded. A change in the number of ceremonies and receptions affects demand for party planning services. Low barriers to entry enable industry operators to enter or exit the market easily. Inflation and rising input costs have decreased industry profit over the period. Despite returning to growth, industry revenue is expected to be largely stagnant. Increased demand from businesses will become a primary revenue growth driver. The continuously declining marriage rate will partially curb growing demand. Increasing per capita disposable income and consumer confidence have boosted demand for event planners from the household market."

Source: IBISWorld Industry at a Glance

FINANCING

2 ½ years

RESOURCES

- IBISWorld, March 2023: https://www.ibisworld.com
- IBISWorld, January 2023: https://www.ibisworld.com

Fabric Stores

NAICS 459130	SIC 5949-02	Businesses/Units 30,388
Profit $183.2 M	Wages $692.3 M	Annual Growth Future -0.4%
		Annual Growth Past -1.1%

Rules of Thumb

- 3 x monthly sales plus inventory

INDUSTRY MULTIPLES

Acquisition multiples below are calculated medians using US private industry transactions. Data updated annually. Last update: August 2023.

VALUATION MULTIPLE (MEDIAN VALUE)

UNDER $1 MILLION NET SALES

MVIC/Net Sales	0.46
MVIC/Gross Profit	0.78

MVIC/SDE	2.38
MVIC/EBITDA	3.69

$1 MILLION–$5 MILLION NET SALES

MVIC/Net Sales.	0.41
MVIC/Gross Profit	0.86
MVIC/SDE	2.91
MVIC/EBITDA	3.38

OVER $5 MILLION NET SALES   N/A

Source: DealStats (formerly Pratt's Stats), 2023 (Portland, OR: Business Valuation Resources, LLC), www.bvresources.com/dealstats

BENCHMARK DATA

STATISTICS (FABRIC, CRAFT & SEWING SUPPLIES STORES)

Number of Establishments	.30,388
Average Profit Margin	4.0%
Revenue per Employee	$74,700
Average Number of Employees. . .	.2.0
Average Wages per Employee . .	$11,346

PRODUCTS AND SERVICES SEGMENTATION

Fabrics	. 58.7%
Sewing and craft supplies . . .	. 39.5%
Patterns and other	. 1.8%

MAJOR MARKET SEGMENTATION

Men	. 24.3%
Women aged 24 or younger . . .	. 23.9%
Women aged 45 to 64	. 19.7%
Women aged 25 to 44	. 19.4%
Women aged 65 and older	. 12.7%

INDUSTRY COSTS

Profit	. 4.0%
Wages	. 15.1%
Purchases	. 52.0%
Depreciation	. 0.9%
Marketing	. 2.0%
Rent & Utilities	. 6.2%
Other	. 19.9%

MARKET SHARE

Michaels Companies, Inc.	. 25.3%
Hobby Lobby Stores Inc.	. 22.2%
Jo-Ann Stores Inc.	. 22.1%

INDUSTRY TREND

"Strong competition from discount department stores and online retailers has eroded demand for industry products. Discount department stores and e-commerce retailers have been attracting a large number of crafting consumers, pressuring this industry's sales. Demand from baby boomers, who account for nearly one-fifth of industry sales, has increased. As the US economy begins to recover from the coronavirus, household disposable income levels are expected to increase. The ease of finding a desired item will present a strong incentive for customers to switch to online retailers. Contributing to profit growth, the price of cotton is expected to decrease. Increased consolidation is expected to drive contractions in industry employment, wages and pressure establishment growth."

Source: IBISWorld Industry at a Glance

F

Family Clothing Stores

	NAICS 458110		SIC 5651		Businesses/Units 69,948
	Profit $6.2 B		Wages $27.3 B		Annual Growth Future 3.3%
					Annual Growth Past 2.4%

Rules of Thumb

- 0.75–1.5 x SDE plus inventory
- 2.4–2.8 x SDE includes inventory
- 40%–45% annual sales includes inventory

INDUSTRY MULTIPLES

Acquisition multiples below are calculated medians using US private industry transactions. Data updated annually. Last update: August 2023.

VALUATION MULTIPLE (MEDIAN VALUE)

UNDER $1 MILLION NET SALES

MVIC/Net Sales.	0.27
MVIC/Gross Profit	0.53
MVIC/SDE	1.03
MVIC/EBITDA	1.03

$1 MILLION–$5 MILLION NET SALES

MVIC/Net Sales.	0.66
MVIC/Gross Profit	1.09
MVIC/SDE	4.47
MVIC/EBITDA	5.69

OVER $5 MILLION NET SALES

MVIC/Net Sales.	4.35
MVIC/Gross Profit	5.17
MVIC/SDE	N/A
MVIC/EBITDA	N/A

Source: DealStats (formerly Pratt's Stats), 2023 (Portland, OR: Business Valuation Resources, LLC), www.bvresources.com/dealstats

PRICING TIPS

Women's apparel—try 23 percent of annual sales + inventory and/or 1.1 times SDE.

BENCHMARK DATA

STATISTICS (FAMILY CLOTHING STORES)

Number of Establishments .	69,948
Average Profit Margin	3.2%
Revenue per Employee .	$147,000
Average Number of Employees.	19.6
Average Wages per Employee .	$20,901

PRODUCTS AND SERVICES SEGMENTATION

Women's clothing	39.8%
Men's clothing	25.4%
Footwear	13.1%
Children's clothing	12.1%
Accessories.	9.6%

MAJOR MARKET SEGMENTATION

Consumers aged 25 to 44	43.9%
Consumers aged 45 to 64	34.3%
Consumers aged 24 and younger	13.1%
Consumers aged 65 and older	8.7%

INDUSTRY COSTS

Profit	3.2%
Wages	14.2%
Purchases	55.4%
Depreciation	1.1%
Marketing	1.7%
Rent & Utilities	5.6%
Other	18.8%

MARKET SHARE

Ross Stores, Inc.	11.1%
The TJX Companies Inc.	10.9%
Gap, Inc..	3.0%
Abercrombie & Fitch Co.	1.2%

EXPENSES (% OF ANNUAL SALES)

Cost of Goods	46% to 52%
Occupancy Costs	06% to 10%
Payroll/Labor Costs.	14% to 18%
Profit (pretax)	12% to 15%

INDUSTRY TREND

"Revenue growth has been subdued by mounting competition from large department stores. Some struggling enterprises have been unable to recover from the effects of e-commerce competition. The negative effects of the COVID-19 pandemic are expected to subside as consumer spending rebounds. IBISWorld anticipates consumers to return to making more discretionary clothing purchases. Some apparel manufacturers are expected to be able to price their items competitively. The industry will experience increasing competition from the E-Commerce and Online Auctions industry. Industry operators contend with intense and growing competition from external sources."

Source: IBISWorld Industry at a Glance

FINANCING

5 to 10 years

RESOURCES

• IBISWorld, April 2023: https://www.ibisworld.com

Family Entertainment Centers

| NAICS 713120

Rules of Thumb

• 3 x EBITDA

INDUSTRY MULTIPLES

Acquisition multiples below are calculated medians using US private industry transactions. Data updated annually. Last update: August 2023.

UNDER $1 MILLION NET SALES	
MVIC/Net Sales.	0.54
MVIC/Gross Profit	0.70
MVIC/SDE	1.98
MVIC/EBITDA	1.62

$1 MILLION–$5 MILLION NET SALES	
MVIC/Net Sales.	0.16
MVIC/Gross Profit	0.18
MVIC/SDE	N/A
MVIC/EBITDA	N/A

OVER $5 MILLION NET SALES	N/A

Source: DealStats (formerly Pratt's Stats), 2023 (Portland, OR: Business Valuation Resources, LLC), www.bvresources.com/dealstats

Fantastic Sams (Franchise)

| NAICS 812112 | Businesses/Units Businesses/Units 605

Rules of Thumb

- 35%–40% annual sales plus inventory

INDUSTRY MULTIPLES

Acquisition multiples below are calculated medians using US private industry transactions. Data updated annually. Last update: August 2023.

VALUATION MULTIPLE (MEDIAN VALUE)

UNDER $1 MILLION NET SALES	
MVIC/Net Sales.	0.31
MVIC/Gross Profit	0.39
MVIC/SDE	1.60
MVIC/EBITDA	2.11

$1 MILLION–$5 MILLION NET SALES	
MVIC/Net Sales.	0.29
MVIC/Gross Profit	0.39
MVIC/SDE	2.30
MVIC/EBITDA	3.05

OVER $5 MILLION NET SALES	N/A

Source: DealStats (formerly Pratt's Stats), 2023 (Portland, OR: Business Valuation Resources, LLC), www.bvresources.com/dealstats

PRICING TIPS

Approx. Total Investment: $139,000 to $301,000

RESOURCES

- Fantastic Sams: https://www.fantasticsams.com
- Franchise information: https://fantasticsamsfranchise.com

Farm and Garden Machinery and Equipment Merchant Wholesalers

| NAICS 423820 | Businesses/Units 9,234

| Profit $3.5 B | Wages $7.7 B | Annual Growth Future 0.3%

| Annual Growth Past -3.2%

INDUSTRY MULTIPLES

Acquisition multiples below are calculated medians using US private industry transactions. Data updated annually. Last update: August 2023.

VALUATION MULTIPLE (MEDIAN VALUE)

UNDER $1 MILLION NET SALES

MVIC/Net Sales	0.49
MVIC/Gross Profit	0.85
MVIC/SDE	N/A
MVIC/EBITDA	1.72

$1 MILLION–$5 MILLION NET SALES

MVIC/Net Sales	0.48
MVIC/Gross Profit	1.63
MVIC/SDE	2.86
MVIC/EBITDA	4.94

OVER $5 MILLION NET SALES

MVIC/Net Sales	0.30
MVIC/Gross Profit	1.00
MVIC/SDE	2.88
MVIC/EBITDA	3.42

Source: DealStats (formerly Pratt's Stats), 2023 (Portland, OR: Business Valuation Resources, LLC), www.bvresources.com/dealstats

BENCHMARK DATA

STATISTICS (FARM, LAWN & GARDEN EQUIPMENT WHOLESALING)

Number of Establishments	9,234
Average Profit Margin	3.4%
Revenue per Employee	$994,000
Average Number of Employees	11.2
Average Wages per Employee	$74,826

PRODUCTS AND SERVICES SEGMENTATION

Farm machinery and equipment	47.5%
Lawn and garden equipment	19.8%
Parts and supplies	19.0%
Used equipment and parts and Other	13.7%

MAJOR MARKET SEGMENTATION

Agricultural market	38.9%
Wholesalers and distributors for resale	31.8%
Retailers for resale	12.3%
Commercial use	8.5%
Household consumers and individuals	4.7%
Other	3.8%

INDUSTRY COSTS

Profit	3.4%
Wages	7.5%
Purchases	70.9%
Depreciation	0.7%
Marketing	0.4%
Rent & Utilities	1.2%
Other	16.3%

MARKET SHARE

Horizon Distributors	0.9%

INDUSTRY TREND

"Investment into machinery and construction was high, which benefited whole-salers. Demand caused agricultural prices to skyrocket, benefiting industry revenue. Rising interest rates are causing farmers to purchase less equipment. The TWI is expected to decrease, increasing farm production and demand. The large increases in agricultural prices following the COVID-19 pandemic are not expected to persist. Interest rates are expected to be higher during the outlook period. Agricultural markets are equipment wholesalers' main source of demand."

Source: IBISWorld Industry at a Glance

RESOURCES

• IBISWorld, January 2023: https://www.ibisworld.com

Farm Supplies Merchant Wholesalers

| NAICS 424910 | Businesses/Units 12,536

| Profit $3.7 B | Wages $10.6 B | Annual Growth Future 0.5%

                                    | Annual Growth Past 1.3%

INDUSTRY MULTIPLES

Acquisition multiples below are calculated medians using US private industry transactions. Data updated annually. Last update: August 2023.

VALUATION MULTIPLE (MEDIAN VALUE)

UNDER $1 MILLION NET SALES
MVIC/Net Sales	0.31
MVIC/Gross Profit	2.04
MVIC/SDE	2.13
MVIC/EBITDA	4.84

$1 MILLION–$5 MILLION NET SALES
MVIC/Net Sales	0.43
MVIC/Gross Profit	1.06
MVIC/SDE	3.73
MVIC/EBITDA	4.83

OVER $5 MILLION NET SALES
MVIC/Net Sales	0.58
MVIC/Gross Profit	3.76
MVIC/SDE	3.96
MVIC/EBITDA	16.32

Source: DealStats (formerly Pratt's Stats), 2023 (Portland, OR: Business Valuation Resources, LLC), www.bvresources.com/dealstats

BENCHMARK DATA

STATISTICS (FARM SUPPLIES WHOLESALING)

Number of Establishments	12,536
Average Profit Margin	2.0%
Revenue per Employee	$1,404,000
Average Number of Employees	10.5
Average Wages per Employee	$81,094

PRODUCTS AND SERVICES SEGMENTATION

Fertilizers	39.0%
Seeds and plant bulbs	25.5%
Herbicides and soil conditioners	12.0%
Other	9.7%
Animal feed	7.3%
Fungicides and insecticides	6.5%

MAJOR MARKET SEGMENTATION

Livestock farmers	45.7%
Wheat, corn, soybean and general cash grains	28.1%
Other field crops and specialty crops	26.2%

INDUSTRY COSTS

Profit	2.0%
Wages	5.7%
Purchases	78.8%
Depreciation	1.5%
Marketing	0.2%
Rent & Utilities	0.9%
Other	10.7%

MARKET SHARE

CHS Inc..	20.0%
Land O'Lakes, Inc.	5.9%
Growmark, Inc.	2.2%

INDUSTRY TREND

"The COVID-19 pandemic has fueled a broad macroeconomic contraction. As input costs for fertilizer production increase, farm supplies wholesalers raise prices to attempt to maintain profit. Demand for insecticides, fungicides and herbicides may be further reduced. Low commodity prices during the beginning of the period are expected to keep fertilizer prices in check over the next five years. The movement against genetically modified products has created a niche for the GM-free and pesticide-free markets. Imports and exports for upstream suppliers will grow as the global economy becomes stronger and demand for premium foods rises. Industry profit has declined as input prices have remained volatile."

Source: IBISWorld Industry at a Glance

RESOURCES

• IBISWorld, February 2023: https://www.ibisworld.com

Fast-Fix Jewelry and Watch Repairs (Franchise)

| NAICS 811490 | SIC 7631-01 | Businesses/Units 124

Rules of Thumb

• 80%–85% annual sales plus inventory

INDUSTRY MULTIPLES

Acquisition multiples below are calculated medians using US private industry transactions. Data updated annually. Last update: August 2023.

VALUATION MULTIPLE (MEDIAN VALUE)

UNDER $1 MILLION NET SALES	
MVIC/Net Sales	0.51
MVIC/Gross Profit	0.64
MVIC/SDE	1.88
MVIC/EBITDA	2.50
$1 MILLION–$5 MILLION NET SALES	
MVIC/Net Sales	0.43
MVIC/Gross Profit	1.42

| MVIC/SDE . . . . 1.90 |
| MVIC/EBITDA . . . . 2.18 |

F

Source: DealStats (formerly Pratt's Stats), 2023 (Portland, OR: Business Valuation Resources, LLC), www.bvresources.com/dealstats

PRICING TIPS

Approx. Total Investment: $178,111 to $357,931

RESOURCES

- Fast-Fix Jewelry and Watch Repairs: https://www.fastfix.com
- Franchise information: https://www.fastfix.com/franchise-opportunities

FASTSIGNS (Franchise)

NAICS 541890	SIC 3993-02	Businesses/Units 673

Rules of Thumb

- 42%–46% annual sales plus inventory

INDUSTRY MULTIPLES

Acquisition multiples below are calculated medians using US private industry transactions. Data updated annually. Last update: August 2023.

VALUATION MULTIPLE (MEDIAN VALUE)

UNDER $1 MILLION NET SALES

| MVIC/Net Sales. . . . . 0.55 |
| MVIC/Gross Profit . . . . 0.94 |
| MVIC/SDE . . . . 1.83 |
| MVIC/EBITDA . . . . 3.22 |

$1 MILLION–$5 MILLION NET SALES

| MVIC/Net Sales. . . . . 0.49 |
| MVIC/Gross Profit . . . . 1.35 |
| MVIC/SDE . . . . 3.01 |
| MVIC/EBITDA . . . . 3.66 |

OVER $5 MILLION NET SALES

| MVIC/Net Sales. . . . . 0.93 |
| MVIC/Gross Profit . . . . 1.37 |
| MVIC/SDE . . . . N/A |
| MVIC/EBITDA . . . . 8.53 |

Source: DealStats (formerly Pratt's Stats), 2023 (Portland, OR: Business Valuation Resources, LLC), www.bvresources.com/dealstats

PRICING TIPS

Approx. Total Investment: $234,317 to $324,489

RESOURCES

- FASTSIGNS: https://www.fastsigns.com
- Franchise information: https://www.fsfastsigns.com
- Propelled Brands: https://www.propelledbrands.com

Fertility Clinics

NAICS 621410	Businesses/Units 499	
Profit $792.3 M	Wages $3.2 B	Annual Growth Future 1.4%
		Annual Growth Past 2.1%

Rules of Thumb

- 78% annual revenues plus inventory
- 2.7 x SDE plus inventory
- 3 x EBIT
- 2.9 x EBITDA

BENCHMARK DATA

STATISTICS (FERTILITY CLINICS)

Number of Establishments .	499
Average Profit Margin .	10.0%
Revenue per Employee .	$188,000
Average Number of Employees.	85.0
Average Wages per Employee .	$76,083

PRODUCTS AND SERVICES SEGMENTATION

Assisted reproductive technology and artificial insemination .	56.7%
Fertility medications	25.4%
Other fertility services .	13.0%
Fertility testing and consultations .	4.9%

INDUSTRY COSTS

Profit	10.0%
Wages	40.1%
Purchases	12.3%
Depreciation	2.9%
Marketing	0.4%
Rent & Utilities	4.2%
Other	30.1%

MARKET SHARE

IntegraMed America Inc.	9.3%
Planned Parenthood Federation of America Inc.	2.5%

EXPENSES (% OF ANNUAL SALES)

Cost of Goods	10%
Payroll/Labor Costs.	04%
Profit (pretax)	12%

INDUSTRY TREND

"Many fertility clinics ceased operation at the outset of the pandemic lockdown period. Industry revenue is broadly contingent on income levels and the personal savings rate. Major companies often engage in strategic acquisition activity. Improving insurance coverage will expand access to fertility clinics. The improving success rate of infertility treatments will encourage more couples to use them. Fertility clinics will adopt tech advances. The industry experienced significant disruption from the coronavirus pandemic."

Source: IBISWorld Industry at a Glance

Outside Financing

RESOURCES

- IBISWorld, March 2023: https://www.ibisworld.com
- NFPRHA—National Family Planning & Reproductive Health Association: https://www.nationalfamilyplanning.org
- NWHN—National Women's Health Network: https://nwhn.org/

Fiber-Optic Cable Manufacturing

| NAICS 335921 | Businesses/Units 102

| Profit $109.3 M | Wages $487.3 M | Annual Growth Future 2.2%

| Annual Growth Past 0.9%

BENCHMARK DATA

STATISTICS (FIBER-OPTIC CABLE MANUFACTURING)

Number of Establishments	102
Average Profit Margin	3.0%
Revenue per Employee	$617,000
Average Number of Employees	59.1
Average Wages per Employee	$81,767

PRODUCTS AND SERVICES SEGMENTATION

Single-mode-fiber cable	57.5%
Multimode-fiber cable	26.8%
Other fiber cable	15.7%

MAJOR MARKET SEGMENTATION

Enterprise Customers	25.2%
Internet Service Providers	23.2%
Wireless Telecommunications Carriers	23.1%
Cable Providers	17.6%
Wired Telecommunications Carriers	10.9%

INDUSTRY COSTS

Profit	3.0%
Wages	13.4%
Purchases	61.4%
Depreciation	1.7%
Marketing	0.1%
Rent & Utilities	1.3%
Other	19.1%

MARKET SHARE

Corning Inc.	17.7%
OFS Fitel, LLC	11.6%
AFL Telecommunications LLC	8.2%

INDUSTRY TREND

"Wireless carriers continue to invest in upgrading their networks to meet demand. Major operators have begun to overhaul their traditionally copper-based infrastructure. The number of industry enterprises is expected to increase as demand for inexpensive and reliable optical communications equipment has boomed. International trade of industry products is anticipated to climb. Wireless carriers will likely experience greater competition. The threat of low-cost foreign substitutes is expected to stifle industry entrance. Despite strong domestic demand for fiber-optic cable, manufacturers have grappled with mounting competition from foreign operators."

Source: IBISWorld Industry at a Glance

RESOURCES

• IBISWorld, April 2023: https://www.ibisworld.com

Financial Transactions Processing, Reserve, and Clearinghouse Activities

| NAICS 522320 | Businesses/Units 6,576

| Profit $19.4 B | Wages $41.1 B | Annual Growth Future 3.6%

| Annual Growth Past 5.2%

INDUSTRY MULTIPLES

Acquisition multiples below are calculated medians using US private industry transactions. Data updated annually. Last update: August 2023.

VALUATION MULTIPLE (MEDIAN VALUE)

UNDER $1 MILLION NET SALES
MVIC/Net Sales.	1.71
MVIC/Gross Profit	1.73
MVIC/SDE	2.17
MVIC/EBITDA	2.15

$1 MILLION–$5 MILLION NET SALES
MVIC/Net Sales.	1.53
MVIC/Gross Profit	3.00
MVIC/SDE	3.49
MVIC/EBITDA	8.96

OVER $5 MILLION NET SALES
MVIC/Net Sales.	2.61
MVIC/Gross Profit	5.62
MVIC/SDE	20.22
MVIC/EBITDA	19.73

Source: DealStats (formerly Pratt's Stats), 2023 (Portland, OR: Business Valuation Resources, LLC), www.bvresources.com/dealstats

BENCHMARK DATA

STATISTICS (CREDIT CARD PROCESSING & MONEY TRANSFERRING)

Number of Establishments .	6,576
Average Profit Margin	15.2%
Revenue per Employee .	$633,000
Average Number of Employees.	31.8
Average Wages per Employee .	$204,301

PRODUCTS AND SERVICES SEGMENTATION

Debit card services .	36.3%
Credit card services.	35.0%
Other	14.9%
Automated clearinghouse products	13.8%

MAJOR MARKET SEGMENTATION

Merchants	70.6%
Banks	26.8%
Government.	2.6%

INDUSTRY COSTS

Profit	15.2%
Wages	32.2%
Purchases	1.7%
Depreciation	1.6%
Marketing	2.2%
Rent & Utilities	1.7%
Other	45.5%

MARKET SHARE

Visa	21.9%
U.S. Bancorp	20.3%
Truist Financial	19.2%
Fiserv	18.9%
Mastercard	17.2%
Block	13.8%
PayPal Holdings.	12.9%
Fidelity National Information Services . .	10.6%
NCR	5.2%
American Express Co.	3.9%

INDUSTRY TREND

"The industry is characterized by the adoption of innovative payment methods. Electronic transactions have increasingly replaced cash and check purchases. Rising wage costs and increased regulation have reduced the average industry profit margin. Merchants' reliance on electronic payment forms will likely continue to accelerate. Mobile protection is the largest concern among industry operators. Wage growth is expected to keep pace with revenue growth. The industry's quick shift toward contactless payments has reduced profit."

Source: IBISWorld Industry at a Glance

RESOURCES

• IBISWorld, January 2023: https://www.ibisworld.com

Flooring Installers

	NAICS 238330		Businesses/Units 119,029

	Profit $1.7 B		Wages $6.2 B		Annual Growth Future -0.1%

	Annual Growth Past 0.2%

INDUSTRY MULTIPLES

Acquisition multiples below are calculated medians using US private industry transactions. Data updated annually. Last update: August 2023.

VALUATION MULTIPLE (MEDIAN VALUE)

UNDER $1 MILLION NET SALES

MVIC/Net Sales.	0.30
MVIC/Gross Profit	0.63
MVIC/SDE	1.44
MVIC/EBITDA	3.97

$1 MILLION–$5 MILLION NET SALES

MVIC/Net Sales	0.35
MVIC/Gross Profit	0.89
MVIC/SDE	1.92
MVIC/EBITDA	2.42

OVER $5 MILLION NET SALES

MVIC/Net Sales	0.45
MVIC/Gross Profit	1.43
MVIC/SDE	2.91
MVIC/EBITDA	3.31

Source: DealStats (formerly Pratt's Stats), 2023 (Portland, OR: Business Valuation Resources, LLC), www.bvresources.com/dealstats

BENCHMARK DATA

STATISTICS (FLOORING INSTALLERS)

Number of Establishments	119,029
Average Profit Margin	5.7%
Revenue per Employee	$158,000
Average Number of Employees	1.6
Average Wages per Employee	$33,785

PRODUCTS AND SERVICES SEGMENTATION

Other resilient material flooring	47.9%
Carpet and rug flooring	35.2%
Hardwood flooring	7.4%
Vinyl sheet and tile flooring	6.9%
Laminate flooring	2.6%

MAJOR MARKET SEGMENTATION

Residential building construction	46.3%
Commercial building construction	22.8%
Municipal building construction	14.8%
Other building construction	13.6%
Industrial building construction	2.5%

INDUSTRY COSTS

Profit	5.7%
Wages	21.3%
Purchases	48.5%
Depreciation	0.5%
Marketing	0.3%
Rent & Utilities	3.6%
Other	19.9%

INDUSTRY TREND

"Low interest rates led to increased residential construction activity. The COVID-19 pandemic significantly halted activity within the nonresidential building market. Institutional building construction provide a significant source of demand for flooring services. The increased cost of financing will be a larger detriment to new housing starts. Remodeling and retrofit projects in commercial buildings will provide steady work. Floor installers will continue to contend with external competition. Profit has marginally decreased due to labor costs outpacing revenue growth."

Source: IBISWorld Industry at a Glance

RESOURCES

• IBISWorld, February 2023: https://www.ibisworld.com

Fire & Flood Restoration

| NAICS 236118

INDUSTRY MULTIPLES

Acquisition multiples below are calculated medians using US private industry transactions. Data updated annually. Last update: August 2023.

VALUATION MULTIPLE (MEDIAN VALUE)

UNDER $1 MILLION NET SALES

MVIC/Net Sales.	0.36
MVIC/Gross Profit	0.64
MVIC/SDE	1.83
MVIC/EBITDA	2.08

$1 MILLION–$5 MILLION NET SALES

MVIC/Net Sales.	0.36
MVIC/Gross Profit	0.96
MVIC/SDE	2.43
MVIC/EBITDA	2.48

OVER $5 MILLION NET SALES

MVIC/Net Sales.	0.35
MVIC/Gross Profit	1.26
MVIC/SDE	2.72
MVIC/EBITDA	3.25

Source: DealStats (formerly Pratt's Stats), 2023 (Portland, OR: Business Valuation Resources, LLC), www.bvresources.com/dealstats

RESOURCES

- IICRC—Institute of Inspection Cleaning and Restoration Certification: https://iicrc.org

Fire Suppression Systems, Sales & Services

| NAICS 238220

Rules of Thumb

- 80% annual sales plus inventory
- 2.2 x SDE plus inventory

INDUSTRY MULTIPLES

Acquisition multiples below are calculated medians using US private industry transactions. Data updated annually. Last update: August 2023.

VALUATION MULTIPLE (MEDIAN VALUE)

UNDER $1 MILLION NET SALES

MVIC/Net Sales.	0.42
MVIC/Gross Profit	0.73
MVIC/SDE	1.84
MVIC/EBITDA	2.80

$1 MILLION–$5 MILLION NET SALES

MVIC/Net Sales.	0.46
MVIC/Gross Profit	0.96
MVIC/SDE	2.85
MVIC/EBITDA	4.43

OVER $5 MILLION NET SALES

MVIC/Net Sales.	0.55
MVIC/Gross Profit	1.53

MVIC/SDE 3.91
MVIC/EBITDA 4.24

Source: DealStats (formerly Pratt's Stats), 2023 (Portland, OR: Business Valuation Resources, LLC), www.bvresources.com/dealstats

PRICING TIPS

Business does not have to be profitable to obtain price, but must have good accounts, preferably with contracts in place.

The value of the customers can depend on whether the owner is the primary contact or the employees.

Most of these businesses are small and run by a family. There are larger companies that are actively seeking to roll up smaller companies. Their primary interest is retaining the current customers and the pricing of the products and services. They are more focused on gross sales than SDE or EBITDA.

BENCHMARK DATA

EXPENSES (% OF ANNUAL SALES)

Cost of Goods 20%
Occupancy Costs . . . . . 05% to 06%
Payroll/Labor Costs. 24%
Profit (pretax) 15%

QUESTIONS

- Revenue per customer? Are there contracts in place for service? Employees interact with customers, so questions about their capabilities are important. Ask questions about relationships with local fire marshals and fire departments which can be very important. You want them on your side because they are often the enforcement arm for fire safety compliance.

RESOURCES

- FSSA—Fire Suppression Systems Association: https://www.fssa.net
- NFPA—National Fire Protection Association: https://www.nfpa.org
- NFSA—National Fire Sprinkler Association: https://nfsa.org

Fish and Seafood Merchant Wholesalers

| NAICS 424460 | Businesses/Units 3,664

| Profit $543.4 M | Wages $1.3 B | Annual Growth Future 1.0%

| Annual Growth Past 0.6%

INDUSTRY MULTIPLES

Acquisition multiples below are calculated medians using US private industry transactions. Data updated annually. Last update: August 2023.

VALUATION MULTIPLE (MEDIAN VALUE)

UNDER $1 MILLION NET SALES
MVIC/Net Sales. 0.56
MVIC/Gross Profit 2.48
MVIC/SDE 13.78
MVIC/EBITDA . . . . N/A

$1 MILLION–$5 MILLION NET SALES

MVIC/Net Sales.	0.18
MVIC/Gross Profit	0.76
MVIC/SDE	1.86
MVIC/EBITDA	2.13

OVER $5 MILLION NET SALES

MVIC/Net Sales.	0.32
MVIC/Gross Profit	3.10
MVIC/SDE	N/A
MVIC/EBITDA	12.32

Source: DealStats (formerly Pratt's Stats), 2023 (Portland, OR: Business Valuation Resources, LLC), www.bvresources.com/dealstats

BENCHMARK DATA

STATISTICS (FISH & SEAFOOD WHOLESALING)

Number of Establishments	3,664
Average Profit Margin	2.3%
Revenue per Employee	$898,000
Average Number of Employees	7.3
Average Wages per Employee	$50,563

PRODUCTS AND SERVICES SEGMENTATION

Fresh shellfish	44.1%
Fresh finfish	42.1%
Frozen fish and seafood	10.8%
Cured fish and other	3.0%

MAJOR MARKET SEGMENTATION

Wholesale establishments for resale	40.9%
Retailers for resale	27.4%
Restaurants, hotels, food services and contract feeding	25.3%
Other markets	6.4%

INDUSTRY COSTS

Profit	2.3%
Wages	5.7%
Purchases	82.5%
Depreciation	0.3%
Marketing	0.2%
Rent & Utilities	0.8%
Other	8.3%

MARKET SHARE

US Foods Holding Corp.	27.9%
Sysco Corporation	13.2%
Bumble Bee Foods LLC.	1.1%

INDUSTRY TREND

"Demand from grocery stores has been the strongest supporter of industry activity, although beneficial trends have been sidetracked by the virus. For the largest companies in this industry, vertical integration has been a successful strategy. Seafood restaurants cater to wealthier consumers that are more likely to pay high prices to satisfy their seafood tastes. Consumers' health-related perceptions concerning seafood will likely remain an important factor in sustaining demand. Despite anticipated increases in the price of seafood and in per capita seafood consumption, these increases are expected to be small. Competition among fish and seafood wholesalers will continue to intensify. Much of the revenue growth during the current period is a result of significant cost inflation."

Source: IBISWorld Industry at a Glance

RESOURCES
- IBISWorld, January 2023: https://www.ibisworld.com

Fish & Seafood Markets

| NAICS 445250 | Businesses/Units 4,601

| Profit $208 M | Wages $486.3 M | Annual Growth Future 1.3%

| | | Annual Growth Past 3.4%

Rules of Thumb
- 20%–25% annual sales plus inventory

INDUSTRY MULTIPLES

Acquisition multiples below are calculated medians using US private industry transactions. Data updated annually. Last update: August 2023.

VALUATION MULTIPLE (MEDIAN VALUE)

UNDER $1 MILLION NET SALES	
MVIC/Net Sales	0.31
MVIC/Gross Profit	0.59
MVIC/SDE	1.31
MVIC/EBITDA	2.12
$1 MILLION–$5 MILLION NET SALES	
MVIC/Net Sales	0.36
MVIC/Gross Profit	1.07
MVIC/SDE	2.98
MVIC/EBITDA	N/A
OVER $5 MILLION NET SALES	N/A

Source: DealStats (formerly Pratt's Stats), 2023 (Portland, OR: Business Valuation Resources, LLC), www.bvresources.com/dealstats

BENCHMARK DATA

STATISTICS (FISH AND SEAFOOD MARKETS)

Number of Establishments	4,601
Average Profit Margin	4.9%
Revenue per Employee	$269,000
Average Number of Employees	3.4
Average Wages per Employee	$30,719

PRODUCTS AND SERVICES SEGMENTATION

Fresh finfish	55.0%
Fresh shellfish	36.3%
Prepared fish	3.3%
Other	2.9%
Frozen seafood	2.5%

MAJOR MARKET SEGMENTATION

Third & Fourth Highest Income Quintile	27.6%
Highest Income Quintile	23.2%
Lowest & Second Lowest Income Quintile	21.3%
Wholesalers	10.6%
Restaurants	9.7%
Retailers	7.2%
Other	0.4%

Profit 4.9%
Wages 11.5%
Purchases 63.6%
Depreciation 1.5%
Marketing 0.6%
Rent & Utilities 2.7%
Other 15.2%

INDUSTRY TREND

"Fish and seafood market revenue has benefited from a swell in the price of seafood. Expanded fresh and frozen seafood processors' product prices has forced seafood markets to boost prices. Many fish markets have boosted wages as a means to keep up with expanding demand. Per capita seafood consumption will expand relatively slowly. Competitive pressures from big-box retailers will swell. Consistent demand for fish and seafood products will keep fish and seafood market demand steady. Health and nutrition trends that emphasize the importance of eating seafood have driven industry growth."

Source: IBISWorld Industry at a Glance

RESOURCES

• IBISWorld, April 2023: https://www.ibisworld.com

Fitness Centers

	NAICS 713940		SIC 7991-01		Businesses/Units 124,013
	Profit $3.5 B		Wages $11.6 B		Annual Growth Future 0.7%
					Annual Growth Past -6.7%

Rules of Thumb

• 50%–100% annual sales plus inventory
• 2–3.5 x SDE plus inventory
• 4–5 x EBIT
• 3–5 x EBITDA

INDUSTRY MULTIPLES

Acquisition multiples below are calculated medians using US private industry transactions. Data updated annually. Last update: August 2023.

VALUATION MULTIPLE (MEDIAN VALUE)

UNDER $1 MILLION NET SALES
MVIC/Net Sales. 0.53
MVIC/Gross Profit 0.55
MVIC/SDE 2.26
MVIC/EBITDA 2.81

$1 MILLION–$5 MILLION NET SALES
MVIC/Net Sales. 0.61
MVIC/Gross Profit 0.69
MVIC/SDE 2.48
MVIC/EBITDA 3.99

OVER $5 MILLION NET SALES
MVIC/Net Sales. 2.23
MVIC/Gross Profit 3.25

```
MVIC/SDE   .    .    .    .    .    .    .    .    N/A
MVIC/EBITDA   .    .    .    .    .    .    .    12.19
```

Source: DealStats (formerly Pratt's Stats), 2023 (Portland, OR: Business Valuation Resources, LLC), www.bvresources.com/dealstats

PRICING TIPS

A very common marker of pricing is a multiple (11 to 13 x) of the pre-authorized monthly payments. This provides a good estimate of monthly profitability if the facility has kept the cost of both occupancy and staffing in-line.

BENCHMARK DATA

STATISTICS (GYM, HEALTH & FITNESS CLUBS)

Number of Establishments	124,013
Average Profit Margin	11.2%
Revenue per Employee	$34,100
Average Number of Employees. . .	7.4
Average Wages per Employee . . .	$12,845

PRODUCTS AND SERVICES SEGMENTATION

Membership fees	68.1%
Personal trainers	12.9%
Other	5.6%
Meals and beverages	5.4%
Guest admission	3.9%
Merchandise sales	2.6%
Spa services	1.5%

MAJOR MARKET SEGMENTATION

Consumers aged 18 to 34	27.5%
Consumers older than 50	25.4%
Consumers aged 35 to 50	25.2%
Consumers younger than 18 . . .	21.9%

INDUSTRY COSTS

Profit	11.2%
Wages	37.5%
Purchases	4.3%
Depreciation	7.1%
Marketing	2.9%
Rent & Utilities	8.7%
Other	28.3%

MARKET SHARE

Fitness International LLC	5.6%
Life Time Inc.	4.9%
24 Hour Fitness USA Inc.	3.8%
Equinox Holdings Inc.	3.1%
Curves International, Inc.	1.4%
Planet Fitness, Inc.	1.3%
Gold's Gym International Inc. . . .	1.0%

Generally, there are only two significant expenses to consider—payroll and rent. If payroll is greater than 40 percent of gross sales, it's a bad sign. Similarly, if rent is more than 33 percent of gross sales, it's a bad sign. The most common benchmark that I see missed is the payroll one. Too many owners who want to run the studio absentee struggle to compete against the studios who are run by owner-operators. They end up with bloated payrolls and employees who don't care as much about the business as owners do. Following are some pricing benchmarks. The average revenue per client per visit should be a minimum of $10; class package options should be higher than that; and drop-in options the highest. Generally, two-thirds of revenue should be recurring monthly memberships, otherwise there is likely a pricing/sales issue. New-student conversion should be at least 20 percent of intro offers converted into recurring revenue membership.

EXPENSES (% OF ANNUAL SALES)

Cost of Goods	05% to 15%
Occupancy Costs	20% to 30%
Payroll/Labor Costs.	25% to 35%
Profit (pretax)	10% to 20%

QUESTIONS

- Common questions should include role and responsibility of owners: are they teaching, leading teacher trainings, handling finances, working at the front desk, etc.? Oftentimes, owners in this industry wear all of the hats, and it is so important to make sure that the business doesn't leave with that person. Other important questions: what kind of relationship does the owner have with the instructors, and the landlord? How many outstanding packages/memberships? Are employees paid as employees or independent contractors? How different are those rules/regulations in the specific state the business is in? How does the rent compare to the market? How long is the lease term for? Does the lease allow for assignment? How much? Personal guaranty, etc.?
- Do you have proper zoning and parking? What is the tenure of coaches? What are the trends in revenue per member?
- What percentage of your revenue is derived from pre-authorized debit?
- What percentage of new members purchase premium services (like training)? What techniques are used to promote retention? How is personal technology being utilized?

INDUSTRY TREND

"Post-pandemic, the surge in the popularity of weight training has helped the gym industry recover. The number of gym memberships in the United States increased 3.6% in 2021 from pre-pandemic levels, according to the latest data from IHRSA, a trade association for the fitness industry. Strength training has been the most popular exercise class booked during the past two years, according to ClassPass, a subscription-based fitness app. In 2022, there was a 94% increase in strength training classes from the year prior....

"Changes in how people exercise have forced gyms to adapt, with new gym designs featuring more dumbbell and squat racks and open areas for lunges, deadlifts and other weighted exercises. 'In the past it was "let's cram as much equipment into these rooms as possible,"' said Daniel Allen, an architect who has designed residential and commercial gyms around the country. 'Now it's "how much free space can we add?"'"

Source: "Americans have changed the way they exercise.
Here's how gyms are adapting" by Nathaniel Meyersohn, March 1, 2023,
https://www.cnn.com/2023/02/28/business/gym-exercise-free-weights-cardio/index.html

Many midsize facilities have closed due to the ever-increasing cost of occupancy and the relatively small movement in the membership costs. Owner-operator personal training centers are on the rise, and large multilocation seem to have the upper hand.

"Pilates is once again booming. Most market researchers don't track it separately from yoga, but the International Health, Racquet & Sportsclub Association ranked it as the most popular gym activity for women. It now includes a wide array of offerings, from small private studios with one-on-one instruction and national Pilates franchises to app-based virtual classes and amped up 'power' Pilates."

Source: "Is Pilates As Good As Everyone Says?" by Danielle Friedman, July 22, 2022, https://www.nytimes.com/2022/07/22/well/move/pilates-exercise-flexibility.html

"The population aged 20 to 64 is the largest consumer niche that experienced rapid growth. One of the silver linings has been the diversification of the industry. The increased demand for gym memberships has played a role in influencing the industry landscape. Accelerating healthcare costs bode well for the industry. Market share concentration in the industry has been declining. Recent growth in employee subsidies is an integral factor that will help the industry. Growing consumer demand for low-cost monthly memberships has constrained profit for gyms with low member retention rates."

Source: IBISWorld Industry at a Glance

EXPERT COMMENTS

Sellers are focused on past performance, while buyers are looking to a new future with Covid-19. It's all about appealing to the right buyer who has the right risk tolerance for the price. I am generally continuing to list at traditional valuations, and hoping for the best.

Be prepared to spend significant time marketing.

As a seller, be prepared to provide a significant amount of vendor financing.

Competition comes not only from other fitness centers but also from fitness-related boutiques, roving trainers, municipal and corporate facilities, even online offerings. Fitness is now a commodity. The future is wellness.

FINANCING

Selling a fitness center of substantial size (7000 square feet, 1000 members) often requires both outside financing and a vendor note.

RESOURCES
- IBISWorld, January 2023: https://www.ibisworld.com
- BCRPA—BC Recreation and Parks Association: https://www.bcrpa.bc.ca/
- CrossFit: https://www.crossfit.com/
- FBA—Fitness Business Association: https://www.fbafitness.com
- IDEA Health & Fitness Association: https://www.ideafit.com
- IHRSA: https://www.ihrsa.org

Flower Shops (Florists)

| NAICS 459310 | SIC 5992-01 | Businesses/Units 36,918 |

Rules of Thumb
- 30%–35% annual sales includes inventory
- 2 x EBITDA

INDUSTRY MULTIPLES

Acquisition multiples below are calculated medians using US private industry transactions. Data updated annually. Last update: August 2023.

UNDER $1 MILLION NET SALES	
MVIC/Net Sales	0.31
MVIC/Gross Profit	0.49
MVIC/SDE	1.61
MVIC/EBITDA	2.00

$1 MILLION–$5 MILLION NET SALES	
MVIC/Net Sales	0.46
MVIC/Gross Profit	0.64
MVIC/SDE	2.72
MVIC/EBITDA	3.38

OVER $5 MILLION NET SALES	N/A

Source: DealStats (formerly Pratt's Stats), 2023 (Portland, OR: Business Valuation Resources, LLC), www.bvresources.com/dealstats

PRICING TIPS

Review the profit and loss statement to determine if wire service revenues and expenses (FTD, Teleflora, etc.) are tracked on separate line items to ensure that the sales are not overstated and cost of goods is not understated.

A premium should be given for stores with a significant number of commercial accounts (especially if there is a credit card on file for ease of billing) which helps protect revenues from big box stores that also sell flowers and plants.

BENCHMARK DATA

STATISTICS (FLORISTS)

Number of Establishments	34,320
Average Profit Margin	5.4%
Revenue per Employee	$109,000
Average Number of Employees	2.4
Average Wages per Employee	$20,864

PRODUCTS AND SERVICES SEGMENTATION

Arranged cut flowers	64.0%
Unarranged cut flowers	13.1%
Potted plants	13.1%
Giftware and other	9.8%

INDUSTRY COSTS

Profit	5.4%
Wages	19.2%
Purchases	44.5%
Depreciation	1.5%
Marketing	1.5%
Rent & Utilities	6.1%
Other	21.9%

STATISTICS (ONLINE FLOWER SHOPS)

Number of Establishments	2,598
Average Profit Margin	8.4%
Revenue per Employee	$1,914,000
Average Number of Employees	3.3
Average Wages per Employee	$48,610

PRODUCTS AND SERVICES SEGMENTATION

Potted plants	36.4%
Arranged cut flowers	22.9%
Unarranged cut flowers	18.3%
Gift baskets and others	15.4%
Floral network services	7.0%

MAJOR MARKET SEGMENTATION

Consumers aged 30-49	40.0%
Consumers aged 50-64	31.8%
Consumers under age 29	28.2%

INDUSTRY COSTS

Profit	8.4%
Wages	2.5%
Purchases	63.1%
Depreciation	1.2%
Marketing	3.9%
Rent & Utilities	1.6%
Other	19.3%

MARKET SHARE

1-800-Flowers.com Inc..	10.9%
FTD Companies, Inc.	3.1%

EXPENSES (% OF ANNUAL SALES)

Cost of Goods	33%
Occupancy Costs	10%
Payroll/Labor Costs.	20%
Profit (pretax)	20%

QUESTIONS

- Percentage of local business versus wire service?

INDUSTRY TREND

"(Based on consumer purchases of fresh flowers and plants for holidays at all outlets.) Valentine's Day is the number one holiday for florists and for floral purchases, and second to Christmas/Chanukah in dollars spent....In 2022, 22% of Americans bought fresh flowers or plants as gifts for Valentine's day. "

Source: "Valentine's Day Floral Statistics,"
https://safnow.org/aboutflowers/holidays-occasions/valentines-day/valentines-day-floral-statistics/

"Demand from wedding services will inch down while retail trade will strengthen in 2023. Supermarket floral sales have remained relatively stable at the expense of local florists. Budget-conscious consumers have expansively opted for low-cost or unarranged flowers. Demand from wedding services and funeral homes will strengthen. With continued external pressure, some traditional florists will continue to exit the industry. Florists will introduce new products and marketing plans to draw in younger clientele. As social distancing guidelines continue to ease, industry revenue is expected to recover. The industry has benefited from increases in the number of services conducted online. The industry is highly competitive. The industry has been able to quickly adapt to changing opportunities. External competition will stem from Amazon adding flowers to its product portfolio. Both internal and external competition will remain high for the industry. As per capita disposable income increases, demand for flowers will likely increase also. Over the past five years, an increase in the number of industry operators has increased internal competition."

Source: IBISWorld Industry at a Glance

EXPERT COMMENTS

Owning a flower shop continues to be a desirable lifestyle business for creative entrepreneurs who wish to provide an artistic and meaningful contribution to their community.

FINANCING

2 to 5 years

RESOURCES

- IBISWorld, August 2023: https://www.ibisworld.com
- IBISWorld, April 2023: https://www.ibisworld.com
- About Flowers: https://aboutflowers.com
- Florists' Review: https://floristsreview.com
- SAF—Society of American Florists: https://safnow.org
- WFFSA—Wholesale Florist & Florist Supplier Association: https://www.wffsa.org

Flower, Nursery Stock, and Florists' Supplies Merchant Wholesalers

| NAICS 424930 | Businesses/Units 9,888

| Profit $695.5 M | Wages $2.3 B | Annual Growth Future 0.3%

| Annual Growth Past -0.5%

INDUSTRY MULTIPLES

Acquisition multiples below are calculated medians using US private industry transactions. Data updated annually. Last update: August 2023.

VALUATION MULTIPLE (MEDIAN VALUE)

UNDER $1 MILLION NET SALES

MVIC/Net Sales.	0.36
MVIC/Gross Profit	0.71
MVIC/SDE	1.84
MVIC/EBITDA	2.18

$1 MILLION–$5 MILLION NET SALES

MVIC/Net Sales.	0.14
MVIC/Gross Profit	0.45
MVIC/SDE	1.89
MVIC/EBITDA	2.55

OVER $5 MILLION NET SALES

MVIC/Net Sales.	0.44
MVIC/Gross Profit	1.62
MVIC/SDE	10.21
MVIC/EBITDA	9.32

Source: DealStats (formerly Pratt's Stats), 2023 (Portland, OR: Business Valuation Resources, LLC), www.bvresources.com/dealstats

BENCHMARK DATA

STATISTICS (FLOWER & NURSERY STOCK WHOLESALING)

Number of Establishments	9,888
Average Profit Margin	4.3%
Revenue per Employee	$288,000
Average Number of Employees	5.7
Average Wages per Employee	$41,698

PRODUCTS AND SERVICES SEGMENTATION

Bedding/garden potted plants	27.9%
Potted flowering plants	16.7%
Flats	15.3%

Herbaceous perennials 12.0%
Other supplies and growing materials . . 10.9%
Hanging baskets 10.3%
Cut flowers 5.5%
Cut greens 1.4%

MAJOR MARKET SEGMENTATION

Retail florists 60.7%
Supermarkets and grocery stores . . . 20.3%
Event planners and venues 12.2%
Garden and nursery centers 3.0%
Other 3.0%
Home improvement stores 0.9%

INDUSTRY COSTS

Profit 4.3%
Wages 14.5%
Purchases 70.7%
Depreciation 1.0%
Marketing 0.2%
Rent & Utilities 0.9%
Other 8.5%

INDUSTRY TREND

"Wholesalers have struggled to remain relevant within the supply chain. Wholesalers must compete among themselves and with external operators to secure business. Operators are engaging in new activities to include sales of competing and complementary items. Industry operators will be challenged by additional encroachment from external operators. More companies are expanding their offices to gain control of their supply chain. Wholesalers will attempt to sustain growth by expanding operations into value-added services. Many industry operators have cut prices to remain competitive as they struggle to retain profit."

Source: IBISWorld Industry at a Glance

RESOURCES

• IBISWorld, January 2023: https://www.ibisworld.com

Food Service Contractors

| NAICS 722310 | Businesses/Units 91,293

| Profit $4.7 B | Wages $22 B | Annual Growth Future 1.3%

| | | Annual Growth Past 2.8%

Rules of Thumb

• 35%–45% annual sales plus inventory
• 2.5–3.5 x SDE plus inventory
• 2.5–3.5 x EBIT
• 3.5–4 x EBITDA

INDUSTRY MULTIPLES

Acquisition multiples below are calculated medians using US private industry transactions. Data updated annually. Last update: August 2023.

UNDER $1 MILLION NET SALES

MVIC/Net Sales.	0.72
MVIC/Gross Profit	1.06
MVIC/SDE	1.71
MVIC/EBITDA	2.82

$1 MILLION–$5 MILLION NET SALES

MVIC/Net Sales.	0.69
MVIC/Gross Profit	1.78
MVIC/SDE	3.21
MVIC/EBITDA	4.31

OVER $5 MILLION NET SALES

MVIC/Net Sales.	0.26
MVIC/Gross Profit	1.14
MVIC/SDE	5.49
MVIC/EBITDA	8.46

Source: DealStats (formerly Pratt's Stats), 2023 (Portland, OR: Business Valuation Resources, LLC), www.bvresources.com/dealstats

PRICING TIPS

Location is indeed an important factor in determining the success of a business, both the physical placement of a building or establishment, and location within the building.

One person occupying a building for every 200 square feet of total building space is a rough estimate used to assess the potential customer capacity.

Calculating the frequency rate based on the building usage and mix is crucial for understanding the number of customers that can be expected and estimating potential sales. Factors such as customer count and average ticket price play a key role in determining the revenue generated by the business.

This is a retail-related business, so it is possible to be very precise for projections.

In cases where there are multiple buildings in a center:

The guidelines suggest that for every 450 square feet of additional buildings, located no more than 125 yards away from the primary building, one person is expected to frequent the shop. These guidelines take into account the potential foot traffic generated by nearby tenants in other buildings, and bad weather. Another factor is whether you have an outside door, or does the customer walk through the lobby. It is worth noting that the impact of location depends on various factors, including the type of business occupying the building, target market, competition, and local demographics. A well-selected location can indeed contribute to increased sales.

Achieving a 25 to 30 percent boost in sales solely through a better operator is a significant claim I hear often but rarely happens. Additional strategies, marketing efforts, customer service enhancements, or other factors may be required to achieve such results.

BENCHMARK DATA

STATISTICS (FOOD SERVICE CONTRACTORS)

Number of Establishments .	91,293
Average Profit Margin	7.1%
Revenue per Employee .	$69,600
Average Number of Employees.	10.5
Average Wages per Employee .	$23,438

PRODUCTS AND SERVICES SEGMENTATION

Cafeteria dining services	35.5%
Retail outlets and concessions	31.9%
Catering and banquet	13.2%
Food and nutrition services	10.3%
Other	5.4%
On-site restaurants	3.7%

MAJOR MARKET SEGMENTATION

Educational institutions	32.6%
Business and industry	26.5%
Healthcare	22.1%
Sports and entertainment	13.1%
Other	5.7%

INDUSTRY COSTS

Profit	7.1%
Wages	33.2%
Purchases	37.6%
Depreciation	1.6%
Marketing	1.8%
Rent & Utilities	7.4%
Other	11.3%

MARKET SHARE

Compass Group PLC	2.5%
ISS A	1.7%
Aramark Corp	1.2%
Sodexo SA	1.1%

The new owner should have prior experience in the food industry and running a business. Of all the retail operations that an inexperienced person could buy, this would be good for a first-time owner.

It is important to note that sales may not increase significantly unless the new operation can effectively compete with the retail establishments in the surrounding area.

The primary objective is to establish a retail operation within a below-retail occupancy structure. Additionally, explore opportunities for vending machines and other food services that the building management can provide, such as catering, coffee, and snacks.

Consider the proximity to other restaurants as a crucial factor. Also, keep in mind that convenience stores (C-stores) are competitors due to the expanded offerings they now provide. If the competition is within walking distance, it should be considered a significant threat; otherwise, it may be a marginal concern.

Cost control is vital in this type of operation. Additional sales generated from vending machines and catering services can make a significant difference between merely making a living and achieving real success.

It is advisable to target buildings with a total area of over 110,000 square feet. This size ensures a higher volume of potential customers, as 2 to 3 visits per day are common. It is important to emphasize that snacks are just as important as lunch in this business model.

EXPENSES (% OF ANNUAL SALES)

Cost of Goods	31% to 39%
Occupancy Costs	05% to 15%
Payroll/Labor Costs	16% to 25%
Profit (pretax)	12% to 20%

QUESTIONS

- Obtain a copy of the lease agreement and carefully read it.
- Obtain a copy of the agreement with the company and review it thoroughly.
- Determine the sales trends for the past two years.
- Assess the necessary improvements or repairs needed for the restaurant.
- Count the number of people in the building during peak hours.
- Gather information about the current employees.
- Create a spreadsheet outlining compatible operations within the market.
- Evaluate the value of an outside seating area. If not available, explore the possibility of adding one.
- Assess your personal opinion of the food they sell.
- Identify the required equipment and determine if there is sufficient space for it.
- Ensure that the common areas are well-maintained.
- Inquire about the number of hours the owner currently works.
- Contact the health department to schedule an inspection promptly.
- Explore the possibility of extending operating hours.
- Determine the age of the equipment and its condition.
- Inquire about the last time the seller implemented a price increase. This is meant to help guide your evaluation of the restaurant business in a closed-market environment, which covers essential aspects related to the lease, agreements, sales trends, necessary improvements, personnel, operations, seating options, food quality, equipment, maintenance, owner's involvement, health inspections, and pricing.

INDUSTRY TREND

The restaurant industry in closed-market environments is expected to experience a surge in demand from healthcare sector clients. As healthcare facilities continue to consolidate, smaller companies specializing in niche markets are likely to enter the industry to meet specific needs.

There has been a steady increase in demand for food services from various sectors, including correctional facilities, health institutions, educational institutions, recreational facilities, and sports venues. These establishments require reliable and quality food services to cater to their patrons.

The aging population in the United States contributes to a consistent demand for healthcare services, which includes the need for food services. As the population ages, the demand for specialized and nutritionally balanced meals is expected to increase.

Air travel rates are projected to recover, driven in part by the release of pent-up demand from travelers. This recovery will create opportunities for the restaurant industry in closed-market environments, as airports and other transportation hubs seek to provide dining options for passengers.

Food waste reduction has become a prominent focus for industry operators. With growing concerns about sustainability and environmental impact, restaurants are implementing strategies to minimize food waste through efficient inventory management, portion control, and recycling initiatives.

The industry has benefited from an increase in spending on discretionary items by downstream customers. As consumers have more disposable income, they are willing to spend it on dining out experiences, including restaurants within closed-market environments.

"Food preparation experiences high volatility while earning a thin margin. The COVID-19 pandemic limited industry growth. Demand from correctional, health, educational, recreational and sports facilities has increased steadily. The aging US population will contribute to steady healthcare demand and a need for food services. Overall growth for site-specific food establishments will remain limited. Industry operators are placing a higher focus on food waste reduction. Food service contractors are challenged by multiyear contracts, high costs and variable demand."

Source: IBISWorld Industry at a Glance

EXPERT COMMENTS

If you're considering buying a small restaurant in a closed market, here are some pieces of advice to consider:

Thorough market research: Before making any investment, conduct a comprehensive market analysis. Evaluate the competition, customer preferences, and the overall demand for restaurants in the area. Determine if there are any growth opportunities or if the market is saturated.

Unique selling proposition (USP): Identify a unique aspect that differentiates your restaurant from others in the closed market. It could be a special cuisine, a specific theme, outstanding service, or a creative concept. Developing a strong USP can attract customers and set you apart from the competition.

Understand customer base: Study the demographics and preferences of the target customer base in the area. Adapt your menu, ambiance, pricing, and marketing strategies accordingly to cater to their tastes and needs.

Financial due diligence: Conduct a thorough financial analysis of the restaurant you plan to purchase. Review the financial statements, cash flow, and profitability. Consider hiring a professional accountant or financial advisor to help you assess the current and potential financial health of the business.

Evaluate existing infrastructure: Inspect the existing infrastructure, equipment, and facilities of the restaurant. Assess if any upgrades or renovations are necessary and factor in the associated costs. Ensure that the restaurant meets health and safety regulations.

Build relationships: If the market is closed and established, it may have existing suppliers, vendors, or local partners. Develop good relationships with these stakeholders to leverage their experience, negotiate better deals, and access valuable resources.

Marketing and promotion: Develop a comprehensive marketing and promotion strategy to create awareness about your restaurant. Utilize both traditional and digital marketing channels to reach your target audience. Consider offering promotional discounts or special events to attract customers initially.

Operational efficiency: Focus on streamlining operations to maximize efficiency and minimize costs. Optimize staffing, inventory management, and workflow processes. Efficient operations can lead to higher profitability, customer satisfaction, and sustainable growth.

Customer experience: Prioritize providing excellent customer service and a memorable dining experience. Train your staff to deliver top-notch service and create a welcoming atmosphere. Encourage customer feedback and take it into account for continuous improvement.

Adaptability and innovation: In a closed market, it's important to stay adaptable and innovative. Monitor trends in the industry, be open to feedback, and continuously evolve your offerings. Introduce new dishes, seasonal menus, or themed events to keep customers engaged and interested. Remember, buying a small restaurant in a closed market can be both challenging and rewarding. Thoroughly assess the risks and opportunities, create a solid business plan, and seek advice from industry experts or mentors. It's much more time-consuming than you would ever think; you'd better have a real love for it.

FINANCING

There is very little outside, third-party financing for sales, and lack of increased sales volume prohibits banks from participating in the financing. Will most likely be owner financing, 20 to 30 percent down, 3 points above market rate. Balloon within 3 to 5 years (with a 10-year term).

RESOURCES

- IBISWorld, January 2023: https://www.ibisworld.com
- Frontier Energy: https://fishnick.com

Food Service Equipment and Supplies

| NAICS 423440

Rules of Thumb

- 45% annual sales plus inventory
- 2.5 x SDE plus inventory
- 4.5–5 x EBIT
- 5–6 x EBITDA

INDUSTRY MULTIPLES

Acquisition multiples below are calculated medians using US private industry transactions. Data updated annually. Last update: August 2023.

VALUATION MULTIPLE (MEDIAN VALUE)

UNDER $1 MILLION NET SALES	
MVIC/Net Sales.	0.35
MVIC/Gross Profit	0.71
MVIC/SDE	1.73
MVIC/EBITDA	2.52
$1 MILLION–$5 MILLION NET SALES	
MVIC/Net Sales.	0.32
MVIC/Gross Profit	0.93
MVIC/SDE	2.18
MVIC/EBITDA	3.85
OVER $5 MILLION NET SALES	
MVIC/Net Sales.	0.47
MVIC/Gross Profit	1.90
MVIC/SDE	4.71
MVIC/EBITDA	6.81

Source: DealStats (formerly Pratt's Stats), 2023 (Portland, OR: Business Valuation Resources, LLC), www.bvresources.com/dealstats

PRICING TIPS

10 times EBITDA for dealerships

All assets saleable? Obsolete equipment?

EXPENSES (% OF ANNUAL SALES)

Cost of Goods	30%
Occupancy Costs	05% to 07%
Payroll/Labor Costs.	30%
Profit (pretax)	10%

RESOURCES

- Foodservice Equipment & Supplies: https://www.fesmag.com
- Foodservice Equipment Reports: https://www.fermag.com

Food Stores, Specialty

| NAICS 4452 | Businesses/Units 49,342

| Profit $866.1 M | Wages $2.6 B | Annual Growth Future 1.8%

| Annual Growth Past 0.8%

INDUSTRY MULTIPLES

Acquisition multiples below are calculated medians using US private industry transactions. Data updated annually. Last update: August 2023.

VALUATION MULTIPLE (MEDIAN VALUE)

UNDER $1 MILLION NET SALES

MVIC/Net Sales.	0.36
MVIC/Gross Profit	0.63
MVIC/SDE	2.03
MVIC/EBITDA	3.34

$1 MILLION–$5 MILLION NET SALES

MVIC/Net Sales.	0.30
MVIC/Gross Profit	0.68
MVIC/SDE	2.11
MVIC/EBITDA	3.19

OVER $5 MILLION NET SALES

MVIC/Net Sales.	0.40
MVIC/Gross Profit	1.17
MVIC/SDE	3.02
MVIC/EBITDA	4.09

Source: DealStats (formerly Pratt's Stats), 2023 (Portland, OR: Business Valuation Resources, LLC), www.bvresources.com/dealstats

PRICING TIPS

This category also includes the following retail businesses: confectionery products, gourmet foods, organic and health foods, packaged nuts, spices and soft drinks.

BENCHMARK DATA

STATISTICS (SPECIALTY FOOD STORES)

Number of Establishments	.49,342
Average Profit Margin	6.8%
Revenue Per Employee	$92,700
Average Number of Employees. . .	.2.8
Average Wages per Employee . . .	$18,742

PRODUCTS AND SERVICES SEGMENTATION

Other	.51.1%
Candy, chocolate and snacks . . .	.19.2%

Bakery Products. 17.6%
Dairy products and eggs 6.9%
Meat and seafood 5.2%

MAJOR MARKET SEGMENTATION

Consumers aged 23 to 41 . . . . . 28.2%
Consumers aged 42 to 53 . . . . . 25.9%
Consumers aged 18 to 22 . . . . . 25.3%
Consumers aged 54 to 72 . . . . . 20.6%

INDUSTRY COSTS

Profit 6.8%
Wages 20.4%
Purchases 54.8%
Depreciation 2.1%
Marketing 0.6%
Rent & Utilities 2.3%
Other 13.1%

INDUSTRY TREND

"The expansion of natural food grocery store chains has diverted demand. Rapidly growing appeal for organic foods has supported revenue during periods of volatile demand. The number of companies operating in this industry has declined due to increasing competition. Operators are expected to continue to experience escalating competition. Consumers are expected to purchase a greater share of higher-quality food products. The industry will continue experiencing intense competition from other retail channels. Diet-conscious consumers have helped to support industry revenue."

Source: IBISWorld Industry at a Glance

RESOURCES

- IBISWorld, March 2023: https://www.ibisworld.com
- INFRA—Independent Natural Food Retailers Association: https://www.naturalfoodretailers.net
- SFA—Specialty Food Association: https://www.specialtyfood.com
- Winsight Grocery Business: https://www.winsightgrocerybusiness.com

Food Trucks

| NAICS 722330 | Businesses/Units 37,555 |

| Profit $95.5 M | Wages $408.1 M | Annual Growth Future 1.2% |

| | | Annual Growth Past 4.9% |

Rules of Thumb

- 25%–30% annual sales plus inventory

INDUSTRY MULTIPLES

Acquisition multiples below are calculated medians using US private industry transactions. Data updated annually. Last update: August 2023.

VALUATION MULTIPLE (MEDIAN VALUE)

UNDER $1 MILLION NET SALES
MVIC/Net Sales. 0.64
MVIC/Gross Profit 0.83

MVIC/SDE 0.86
MVIC/EBITDA 1.04

$1 MILLION–$5 MILLION NET SALES   N/A

OVER $5 MILLION NET SALES
MVIC/Net Sales. 3.43
MVIC/Gross Profit 9.59
MVIC/SDE . . . . N/A
MVIC/EBITDA . . . . N/A

Source: DealStats (formerly Pratt's Stats), 2023 (Portland, OR: Business Valuation Resources, LLC), www.bvresources.com/dealstats

BENCHMARK DATA

STATISTICS (FOOD TRUCKS)

Number of Establishments 37,555
Average Profit Margin 6.4%
Revenue per Employee $33,400
Average Number of Employees. 1.2
Average Wages per Employee $9,314

PRODUCTS AND SERVICES SEGMENTATION

American 34.0%
Asian 18.3%
Desserts 13.8%
Central and South American 12.0%
Other 11.8%
Mixed Ethnicity 6.4%
Greek Mediterranean 3.7%

MAJOR MARKET SEGMENTATION

Consumers aged 25 to 44 . . . . . .38.3%
Consumers aged 55 and over 26.5%
Consumers aged 45 to 54 . . . . .21.7%
Consumers under age 25 . . . . .13.5%

INDUSTRY COSTS

Profit 6.4%
Wages 27.3%
Purchases 43.1%
Depreciation 2.0%
Marketing 2.1%
Rent & Utilities 8.2%
Other 10.8%

INDUSTRY TREND

"Savvy food truck vendors are responding to shifting consumer preferences. Food trucks are regulated at the local level. COVID-19 restrictions required dine-in food service providers to close. Vendors that continue to offer unique food options are carving out a niche that develops a loyal customer base. Food supplies have not kept up with demand. Food trucks are dependent upon high foot traffic. Despite strong industry-wide performance, some vendors have been held back by municipal regulations and low profit."

Source: IBISWorld Industry at a Glance

RESOURCES

- IBISWorld, January 2023: https://www.ibisworld.com
- Mobile Cuisine: https://mobile-cuisine.com
- NFTA—National Food Truck Association: https://nationalfoodtrucks.org

- NYFTA—New York Food Truck Association: https://nyfta.org
- FoodTruckOperator.com: https://www.foodtruckoperator.com

F

Forest Support Services

| NAICS 115310 | Businesses/Units 15,523

| Profit $626.5 M | Wages $1.3 B | Annual Growth Future -5.0%

| Annual Growth Past 8.8%

INDUSTRY MULTIPLES

Acquisition multiples below are calculated medians using US private industry transactions. Data updated annually. Last update: August 2023.

VALUATION MULTIPLE (MEDIAN VALUE)

UNDER $1 MILLION NET SALES

MVIC/Net Sales.	1.02
MVIC/Gross Profit	1.13
MVIC/SDE	1.98
MVIC/EBITDA	3.39

$1 MILLION–$5 MILLION NET SALES

MVIC/Net Sales.	1.39
MVIC/Gross Profit	1.39
MVIC/SDE	N/A
MVIC/EBITDA	N/A

OVER $5 MILLION NET SALES	N/A

Source: DealStats (formerly Pratt's Stats), 2023 (Portland, OR: Business Valuation Resources, LLC), www.bvresources.com/dealstats

BENCHMARK DATA

STATISTICS (FOREST SUPPORT SERVICES)

Number of Establishments .	15,523
Average Profit Margin	13.6%
Revenue per Employee .	$129,000
Average Number of Employees.	1.97
Average Wages per Employee .	$39,743

PRODUCTS AND SERVICES SEGMENTATION

Forest firefighting and pest control.	62.3%
Forest research and consulting	27.9%
Timber resource estimating and mapping .	9.8%

MAJOR MARKET SEGMENTATION

Government clients .	53.8%
Timber tract operators .	33.4%
Logging businesses	12.8%

INDUSTRY COSTS

Profit	13.6%
Wages	29.2%
Purchases .	26.1%
Depreciation	3.6%
Marketing	0.6%
Rent & Utilities .	12.5%
Other	14.3%

INDUSTRY TREND

"Industry revenue is estimated to increase due to favorable conditions largely caused by market distortions. The value of residential construction, which reflects the value of new construction, has increased. Industry demand has been bolstered by the resurgence of the mountain pine beetle. Forest support service providers are expected to generate some revenue from outsourced firefighting. A drop in price of downstream industry products will lead to a drop in industry revenue. An increasing provision of firefighting and pest-control services will likely temper growth in industry profit. Demand for new residential construction has surged during the period."

Source: IBISWorld Industry at a Glance

RESOURCES

• IBISWorld, July 2022: https://www.ibisworld.com

Formal Wear and Costume Rental

| NAICS 532281 | Businesses/Units 1,135

| Profit $25.8 M | Wages $243.2 M | Annual Growth Future -1.6%

| Annual Growth Past -3.7%

INDUSTRY MULTIPLES

Acquisition multiples below are calculated medians using US private industry transactions. Data updated annually. Last update: August 2023.

VALUATION MULTIPLE (MEDIAN VALUE)

UNDER $1 MILLION NET SALES	
MVIC/Net Sales	0.61
MVIC/Gross Profit	0.64
MVIC/SDE	2.56
MVIC/EBITDA	3.18
$1 MILLION–$5 MILLION NET SALES	
MVIC/Net Sales	0.18
MVIC/Gross Profit	N/A
MVIC/SDE	N/A
MVIC/EBITDA	N/A
OVER $5 MILLION NET SALES	N/A

Source: DealStats (formerly Pratt's Stats), 2023 (Portland, OR: Business Valuation Resources, LLC), www.bvresources.com/dealstats

BENCHMARK DATA

STATISTICS (FORMAL WEAR & COSTUME RENTAL)

Number of Establishments	1,135
Average Profit Margin	3.8%
Revenue per Employee	$103,000
Average Number of Employees	5.71
Average Wages per Employee	$36,817

PRODUCTS AND SERVICES SEGMENTATION

Men's formal wear, costumes and accessories rental	66.6%
Women's formal wear, costumes and accessories rental	25.5%
Consumer goods rental	4.4%
Other	3.5%

MAJOR MARKET SEGMENTATION

Consumers aged 25 to 54	57.6%
Consumers aged 55 and older	30.9%
Consumers under the age of 25	11.5%

INDUSTRY COSTS

Profit	3.8%
Wages	35.8%
Purchases	6.7%
Depreciation	7.4%
Marketing	1.3%
Rent & Utilities	7.9%
Other	37.1%

MARKET SHARE

Tailored Brands	41.4%

INDUSTRY TREND

"The trend toward sustainable fashion has bolstered demand for industry services. More businesses have expanded their online presence. The coronavirus pandemic has diminished industry demand significantly. The shift in wedding destination preferences heavily influences industry demand. Industry demand will likely contend with the expansion of online-based competitors. The overall size of the industry is expected to continue declining. Competition from online-based rental companies has been intensifying over the past five years."

Source: IBISWorld Industry at a Glance

RESOURCES

• IBISWorld, June 2022: https://www.ibisworld.com

Franchise Food Businesses

| NAICS 722

Rules of Thumb

• 30%–40% annual sales
• 4 x EBIT
• 3–3.5 x EBITDA
• 2–3 x SDE

INDUSTRY MULTIPLES

Acquisition multiples below are calculated medians using US private industry transactions. Data updated annually. Last update: August 2023.

VALUATION MULTIPLE (MEDIAN VALUE)

UNDER $1 MILLION NET SALES

MVIC/Net Sales	0.32
MVIC/Gross Profit	0.49
MVIC/SDE	1.81
MVIC/EBITDA	2.21

$1 MILLION–$5 MILLION NET SALES

MVIC/Net Sales	0.33
MVIC/Gross Profit	0.55
MVIC/SDE	2.31
MVIC/EBITDA	2.98

MVIC/Net Sales. 0.69
MVIC/Gross Profit 1.20
MVIC/SDE 2.72
MVIC/EBITDA 8.49

Source: DealStats (formerly Pratt's Stats), 2023 (Portland, OR: Business Valuation Resources, LLC), www.bvresources.com/dealstats

PRICING TIPS

Franchise resales can skew these metrics higher depending on the quality of the franchise or the current hotness of the franchise concept.

Rule of thumb: will list for 60 percent of gross and sell for 60 percent of list. Add cost of franchise fee on top of selling price. Nontraditional sites—very lease dependent!

Check the franchise agreement. Who pays transfer and training fees? Does the franchisor have the first right to purchase the business? Will the transition require the facilities to be upgraded to franchisor's current standards? If yes, the upgrade cost can be substantial.

BENCHMARK DATA

EXPENSES (% OF ANNUAL SALES)

Cost of Goods	30% to 40%
Occupancy Costs	07% to 12%
Payroll/Labor Costs.	20% to 25%
Profit (pretax)	05% to 15%

QUESTIONS

• What is the process to be approved by the head office? What are initial franchise fees and costs? Royalty fees? Marketing fees? What are the future plans of the franchisor?

INDUSTRY TREND

"One measure of the industry's progress can be seen in the increasing amount of dining options and diverse business models available to franchisees. Which is also helping to dispel one of the most common myths associated with franchising—that it's mostly made up of fast-food outlets. In reality, these quick-service restaurants (QSRs) actually account for less than a quarter of all franchised establishments. There are also FSRs—full-service restaurants, fast-casual, fine dining, ghost kitchens, mobile food trucks, and other franchise models that specialize in catering, employee training, and food delivery. In today's restaurant and hospitality industry, some franchise owners may never see the inside of a kitchen at all."

Source: "Today's Restaurant Franchise Trends" by Jeff Cheatham, June 9, 2022, https://www.entrepreneur.com/franchise/todays-restaurant-franchise-trends/428977

EXPERT COMMENTS

Seller—price it fairly. Buyer—engage good lawyer and accountant.

FINANCING

Bank financing. No seller financing in Canada.

RESOURCES

• CFA—Canadian Franchise Association: https://cfa.ca
• We Sell Restaurants: https://blog.wesellrestaurants.com

Franchises

PRICING TIPS

Franchises are valued by multiple factors including brand, locations, and management setup.

Most existing franchises will sell between 2 and 3 times SDE. If they are profitable with managers in place, it will be on the higher end; if they are losing money, it could be 1 or less.

"Pricing the franchise resale obviously depends on the franchise. Is the franchise value added or—as in some cases—value subtracted? Does franchising add value to the business or would the same business—independent of a franchise label—bring as high a price in the marketplace? When calculating a multiple of annual sales, is it before subtracting the royalty fees, or are they included in the annual sales? After all, 6 percent of just $500,000 in annual revenues is $30,000, but just $12,000 at 40 percent of annual sales. The $12,000 probably doesn't have much of an impact on pricing unless the sales are really astronomical.

"Some prospective business buyers like the security and the support of a franchise. Still others want the independence of owning and controlling their own business. Buying an independent business provides just that. No answering to the franchisor, no royalties and no heavy advertising fees, no forced purchasing from certain suppliers—and no politics. Owning your own independent business also allows you to expand, change, add or delete products and/or services. Independent businesses can be very quick to adjust to changes. Franchises, especially large ones, are very cumbersome and slow to adapt to new trends and ideas.

"As for pricing a franchise, we don't see much of a difference between an independent business and the franchised one, except for the very big players, where the franchise label probably adds a lot of value, maybe 10 to 20 percent, based on the same gross. On the other hand, the fledgling franchise with just a few units has some real problems on the resale side. If it's fairly new, there are plenty of new units available, the name doesn't really mean anything yet, and the age old question is asked—why is the business for sale? In cases like this, the percentage multiples might be reduced by the same figure as is added for the well-known brand name-most likely lower.

"Despite what the franchise industry would like us to believe, not all franchises are successful. What has always struck us as strange is the buyer who is very number-oriented and turns down a very good business due to some slight anomaly in the financial statement from two years ago, but will be the same buyer who purchases a franchise (a new one) where he has seen no books and records and has no idea whether the location will work out or not."

Source: *The Business Broker* (Business Brokerage Press)

Keep in mind that rules of thumb are just that. Every business is different and rules of thumb will never take the place of a business valuation or even an opinion of value, but, everything else being equal, they will give you a rough idea of what the business might sell for. A rule of thumb will tell you whether a seller is in the ballpark when he or she tells you what they think their business is worth or what they want to sell it for. For up-to-date information, go to the websites of the specific companies.

Several other factors can greatly influence the selling price of a franchise. One is the question of the transfer fee levied by the franchisor and who pays it. This amount can be substantial, so find out the information on this prior to going to market. Another factor is the franchisor requiring a major change in outside appearance and a change in the interior of the unit—or both. This should also be investigated before attempting to sell it. The costs involved in either requirement can be substantial.

BENCHMARK DATA

Franchisee unit profitability, consistent revenue growth

QUESTIONS

- Will the current owner train the new owner? What will the continued training look like? Do other franchisees consider any close-by franchisee a competitor or a resource? Will the current key employees remain with the new owners? Prove the financials. Inspect the inventory if that is a key factor. Inspect the furniture, fixtures, and equipment. Read and understand the lease and the advantages and disadvantages of the current location and ask if there is there any flexibility to continuing or exiting the current location. If you are not versed on lease issues, hire someone to help you.
- Ask for access to P&L statements for past years through the current time as well as tax returns for the same time period. Ask about the industry and future predictions for it. Ask about competition. Ask about growth potential. Ask about the franchise agreement/license and the term remaining. I don't believe any question should be off limits—ask anything and everything!
- Financial results, level and types of franchisor support, franchise costs to franchisor (royalties, marketing fees, product costs, mandatory upgrades)
- Important questions include whether the franchise must undergo a remodel, and how the terms of the new franchise agreement will differ from those in the seller's agreement. Will royalties increase? Any change in the franchise territory, etc.?
- Are you happy? Are you making money? If you had your money back, would you make this investment again? Are you getting the support you deserve from the franchise company for the royalty and/or marketing dues you are paying them? What has been your biggest concern/negative/issue with this business/industry?

INDUSTRY TREND

"Like any industry, franchising is not immune to change. It adapts and thrives on innovation, consumer preferences, and market demands. That's why understanding emerging trends and staying ahead of the curve is crucial for both franchisees and franchisors....

Cultivating and enhancing customer experience

Services becoming easier and more readily available

Small businesses will join the franchise landscape

The pet industry will continue to grow

Leaving the corporate job to follow passions

Natural disasters cement the need for home restoration services

AI is here to stay

Private equity investors will grow home service franchises

Innovative technology in the restaurant industry

A chicken industry surge

Restaurants continue to adapt to the pandemic and post-pandemic needs

Hotels and restaurants partner up"

Source: "'More Crucial Now Than Ever Before,' The Biggest Franchise Trends of 2023, According to 17 Top Franchise Executives" by Clarissa Buch Zilberman, June 20, 2023, https://www.entrepreneur.com/franchises/the-biggest-franchise-trends-of-2023/452334

"The popularity of multi-unit franchise ownership is no overnight phenomenon. In fact, interest in owning more than one unit appears to have happened over the last decade. Not only are single-unit owners looking to expand their territorial footprint, but this proposition has picked up interest among the investor class. For multi-unit franchise operations (MUOs), the average number of units rose from 4.8% to 5.1% over the past 10 years."

Source: "5 Encouraging Facts to Know about Multi-Unit Franchising" by Jeff Cheatham, January 26, 2022, https://www.entrepreneur.com/franchise/5-encouraging-facts-to-know-about-multi-unit-franchising/414553

EXPERT COMMENTS

Love what the franchisor does. Enjoy the business and what it does. Understand the model and how it gives advantage over starting up as an independent. Read the franchise agreement ask questions and then have an attorney that is an expert in the franchise industry read and give advice on the advantages and pitfalls of the agreement before you sign. Understand the franchisor commitment to training and ongoing support.

Ask every question and present those questions to both the franchisor and a number of franchisees. Hear the good, hear the bad, and make an informed decision based on what you learn. Also, be prepared to work! The franchise company provides the proven model, the system, the training—but they do not run your business for you. It's up to the franchisee to execute and manage the day-to-day operations of the business.

Do your research, read carefully the UFOC (Uniform Franchise Offering Circular), speak with multiple franchise owners of varying sizes and demographics.

FINANCING

Outside funding is more typical—retirement fund rollovers and SBA loans are among the most popular funding methods. I do, however, see more partial seller funding happening.

RESOURCES

- 1851 Franchise Magazine: https://1851franchise.com
- AAFD—American Association of Franchisees & Dealers: https://www.aafd.org
- Blue MauMau: https://www.bluemaumau.org
- Entrepreneur: https://www.entrepreneur.com
- Franchise Gator: https://www.franchisegator.com
- Franchise Grade: https://www.franchisegrade.com
- Franchise Matchmakers: https://franchisematchmakers.com
- Franchise Times: https://www.franchisetimes.com
- FranchiseKnowHow: https://www.franchiseknowhow.com
- Franchising.com: https://www.franchising.com
- FRANdata: https://www.frandata.com
- FranNet: https://frannet.com
- IFA—International Franchise Association: https://www.franchise.org
- Unhappy Franchisee: https://www.unhappyfranchisee.com

Freight Forwarding

NAICS 488510	SIC 4731-04	Businesses/Units 100,459
Profit $5.2 B	Wages $26.4 B	Annual Growth Future 2.9%
		Annual Growth Past 6.2%

Rules of Thumb
- 50% annual sales
- 2.6 x SDE

INDUSTRY MULTIPLES

Acquisition multiples below are calculated medians using US private industry transactions. Data updated annually. Last update: August 2023.

VALUATION MULTIPLE (MEDIAN VALUE)

UNDER $1 MILLION NET SALES

MVIC/Net Sales.	0.28
MVIC/Gross Profit	0.74
MVIC/SDE	1.36
MVIC/EBITDA	3.86

$1 MILLION–$5 MILLION NET SALES

MVIC/Net Sales.	0.26
MVIC/Gross Profit	0.96
MVIC/SDE	1.75
MVIC/EBITDA	2.96

OVER $5 MILLION NET SALES

MVIC/Net Sales.	0.32
MVIC/Gross Profit	1.16
MVIC/SDE	3.90
MVIC/EBITDA	7.32

Source: DealStats (formerly Pratt's Stats), 2023 (Portland, OR: Business Valuation Resources, LLC), www.bvresources.com/dealstats

BENCHMARK DATA

STATISTICS (FREIGHT FORWARDING BROKERAGES & AGENCIES)

Number of Establishments .	100,459
Average Profit Margin	4.3%
Revenue per Employee .	$275,000
Average Number of Employees.	4.5
Average Wages per Employee	$59,680

PRODUCTS AND SERVICES SEGMENTATION

Domestic freight transportation arrangement services	53.2%
International freight forwarding and customs brokerage services.	37.6%
Nonvessel operating common carrier services	8.3%
Other	0.9%

MAJOR MARKET SEGMENTATION

Manufacturers .	35.8%
Exporters	19.2%
Wholesalers.	17.8%
Importers	17.3%
Other domestic industries .	9.9%

INDUSTRY COSTS

Profit	4.3%
Wages	21.7%

Purchases 46.4%
Depreciation 0.6%
Marketing 0.2%
Rent & Utilities 4.3%
Other 22.4%

QUESTIONS
- Do you need a customs license?

INDUSTRY TREND

"Operators have benefited from growth in emerging markets and key trade partners. Rising consumer spending boosted US retail sales and manufacturing output over the past five years, contributing to higher freight volumes. Among the small companies are several start-ups aiming to disrupt the industry. Domestic freight volumes will climb, boosting industry demand. With trade values rising, players will expand their trade-related service lines. Large companies will continue to expand operations and include value-added services. As total US trade volumes have increased, demand for international freight services that require brokerage has risen."

Source: IBISWorld Industry at a Glance

RESOURCES
- IBISWorld, January 2023: https://www.ibisworld.com
- Forwarder Magazine: https://forwardermagazine.com

Freight Trucking, Local

| NAICS 484110 | Businesses/Units 332,181

| Profit $5.9 B | Wages $27.6 B | Annual Growth Future 0.6%

| Annual Growth Past 6.6%

INDUSTRY MULTIPLES

Acquisition multiples below are calculated medians using US private industry transactions. Data updated annually. Last update: August 2023.

VALUATION MULTIPLE (MEDIAN VALUE)

UNDER $1 MILLION NET SALES
MVIC/Net Sales.	0.57
MVIC/Gross Profit	0.77
MVIC/SDE	2.15
MVIC/EBITDA	2.91

$1 MILLION–$5 MILLION NET SALES
MVIC/Net Sales.	0.44
MVIC/Gross Profit	0.75
MVIC/SDE	2.71
MVIC/EBITDA	5.16

OVER $5 MILLION NET SALES
MVIC/Net Sales.	0.84
MVIC/Gross Profit	1.48
MVIC/SDE	4.61
MVIC/EBITDA	6.83

Source: DealStats (formerly Pratt's Stats), 2023 (Portland, OR: Business Valuation Resources, LLC), www.bvresources.com/dealstats

BENCHMARK DATA

STATISTICS (LOCAL FREIGHT TRUCKING)

Number of Establishments	332,181
Average Profit Margin	6.4%
Revenue per Employee	$143,000
Average Number of Employees	1.9
Average Wages per Employee	$43,786

PRODUCTS AND SERVICES

Truckload Transportation	31.8%
Other	26.9%
Less-than-truckload transportation	16.7%
Intermodal transportation	19.1%
Dry-bulk transportation	5.5%

MAJOR MARKET SEGMENTATION

Other manufacturing	30.8%
Lumber and construction materials and machinery wholesalers/retailer	19.7%
Miscellaneous durable goods wholesalers/retailers	18.5%
Food manufacturers	14.3%
Other wholesalers and retailers	10.5%
Beverage and tobacco manufacturers	6.2%

INDUSTRY COSTS

Profit	6.4%
Wages	30.1%
Purchases	30.7%
Depreciation	4.9%
Marketing	0.2%
Rent & utilities	4.6%
Other	23.1%

MARKET SHARE

XPO Logistics, Inc.	10.7%
Knight-Swift Transportation Holdings Inc.	7.7%
Werner Enterprises, Inc.	2.7%
Hunt J B Transport Services Inc.	1.6%

EXPENSES (% OF ANNUAL SALES)

Payroll & Labor	40% to 60%
Profit (pretax)	08% to 15%

INDUSTRY TREND

"A boost in e-commerce offset declines in production to cause revenue to grow. Freight truckers are in a unique place to benefit from heightened industrial production. Many truckers are upping their intermodal transportation services. Growth in consumer spending will be more stable. Most companies can't afford to haul their cargo and will continue to outsource transportation. Gas prices are set to decline after the volatile past five years. Rising fuel prices allowed trucking companies to implement fuel surcharges."

Source: IBISWorld Industry at a Glance

RESOURCES

• IBISWorld, January 2023: https://www.ibisworld.com

Freight Trucking, Long Distance

| NAICS 484121 | Businesses/Units 603,456

| Profit $14.3 B | Wages $70.8 B | Annual Growth Future 0.9%

| Annual Growth Past -0.5%

Rules of Thumb

- 40%–60% annual sales includes inventory
- 3–5 x EBIT
- 2–4 x EBITDA
- 2–4 x SDE plus Inventory

INDUSTRY MULTIPLES

Acquisition multiples below are calculated medians using US private industry transactions. Data updated annually. Last update: August 2023.

VALUATION MULTIPLE (MEDIAN VALUE)

UNDER $1 MILLION NET SALES

MVIC/Net Sales	0.51
MVIC/Gross Profit	0.59
MVIC/SDE	1.73
MVIC/EBITDA	2.20

$1 MILLION–$5 MILLION NET SALES

MVIC/Net Sales	0.58
MVIC/Gross Profit	1.14
MVIC/SDE	3.21
MVIC/EBITDA	5.46

OVER $5 MILLION NET SALES

MVIC/Net Sales	0.46
MVIC/Gross Profit	2.00
MVIC/SDE	4.22
MVIC/EBITDA	5.72

Source: DealStats (formerly Pratt's Stats), 2023 (Portland, OR: Business Valuation Resources, LLC), www.bvresources.com/dealstats

PRICING TIPS

The quality of the earnings (contracts, longevity, size, concentration), the condition of the trucks and trailers, and the workforce all are important—and potential deal breakers if the information is not detailed and accurate.

For asset-intensive companies, FMV of all assets except cash and goodwill

BENCHMARK DATA

STATISTICS (LONG-DISTANCE FREIGHT TRUCKING)

Number of Establishments	603,456
Average Profit Margin	5.5%
Revenue per Employee	$186,000
Average Number of Employees. . . .	2.4
Average Wages per Employee . . .	$50,979

PRODUCTS AND SERVICES SEGMENTATION

Truckload carriers	67.9%
Less-than-truckload carriers	29.0%
Other transportation services	3.1%

MAJOR MARKET SEGMENTATION

Manufacturing 41.0%
Retail and wholesale trade 31.6%
Other 27.4%

INDUSTRY COSTS

Profit 5.5%
Wages 27.2%
Purchases 31.8%
Depreciation 6.6%
Marketing 0.2%
Rent & Utilities 4.8%
Other 23.9%

$161,000 revenue per employee

Revenue per employee $2,000,000

EXPENSES (% OF ANNUAL SALES)

Cost of Goods 0%
Occupancy Costs . . . . . 01% to 05%
Payroll/Labor Costs. . . . . 50% to 60%
Profit (pretax) . . . . . . 08% to 15%

QUESTIONS

- What is your marketing mix, and what percent of sales is produced by your largest customer? What is your break-even point in sales dollars and miles per power unit? What is your driver turnover rate? If union, when does your current labor contract expire?
- Average rate per loaded mile, average rate per total miles driven, number of empty trucks, average equipment trade cycle
- Carrier type—truckload, LTL, household goods, van, flatbed, refrigerated local, long-distance, heavy hauling. What niche does the carrier fit into?
- Equipment—type, average age, how and where maintained, appearance, owned, leased
- Financing—amount of debt, interest rate, and debt service
- Facilities—location as related to customers, owned, leased
- Employees—longevity, quality
- Driver history—be sure to interview each driver and employee. It's important to be sure no after-sale promises have been made by the seller, i.e., pay increase, vacation time, profit sharing, and the like.
- Where do you park, and do you offer warehousing?

INDUSTRY TREND

"A shortage of truck drivers is frequently cited as an explanation for shortages of many other things—from construction supplies to electronics to clothing.... The average trucking company has a turnover rate of roughly 95%, meaning that it must replace nearly all of its workforce in the course of a year....'This shortage narrative is industry lobbying rhetoric,' said Steve Viscelli, a labor expert at the University of Pennsylvania who previously worked as a truck driver. 'There is no shortage of truck drivers. These are just really bad jobs.'"

Source: "The real reason America doesn't have enough truck drivers" by Peter S. Goodman, February 9, 2022, https://www.boston.com/news/national-news/2022/02/09/the-real-reason-america-doesnt-have-enough-truck-drivers/

Increased demand, but pressure on margins due to driver shortage requiring an increase in hiring wages to retain drivers

"During periods of high fuel prices, fuel surcharges enable industry revenue to rise while limiting increases in operating costs. Larger companies have regularly contracted nonemployers to satisfy excess capacity for larger contracts. Rising industry wage costs and competitive pricing have limited profit expansion. Industry profit is expected to moderately decline as a share of industry revenue during the outlook period. Economic policies pursued by the federal government are expected to be favorable to industry operators. Many fleet owners will likely seek to acquire hybrid-electric vehicles to mitigate the uncertainty of fuel prices. Operators have been forced to offer competitive compensation to attract and retain drivers."

Source: IBISWorld Industry at a Glance

EXPERT COMMENTS

If you are selling, do not provide a significant amount of seller financing. High risk and high break-even point business. If you are a buyer, make sure you are well capitalized primarily with equity capital.

It can be easy to open a trucking company; the challenge seems to be the operations side—gaining customers, keeping drivers, and providing quality customer service and on-time deliveries at a fair price.

Very capital intensive. Those that can successfully navigate this obstacle do very well.

FINANCING

Seller financing is pretty common. Very important to know about the truck and trailer financing—leased or owned. Find out at the beginning if those contracts are assignable and if there are any early payoff fees. That is really important to know for a broker taking a listing; those fees can be thousands of dollars.

RESOURCES

- IBISWorld, January 2023: https://www.ibisworld.com
- AITA—America's Independent Truckers' Association, Inc.: https://www.aitaonline.com
- ATA—American Trucking Associations: https://trucking.org/
- ATRI—American Transportation Research Institute: https://truckingresearch.org
- Transport Topics: https://www.ttnews.com/

Frozen Food Production

| | NAICS 311412 | | Businesses/Units 732 |

| | Profit $887.6 M | | Wages $5.4 B | | Annual Growth Future 2.3% |
| | | | | | Annual Growth Past 2.2% |

INDUSTRY MULTIPLES

Acquisition multiples below are calculated medians using US private industry transactions. Data updated annually. Last update: August 2023.

VALUATION MULTIPLE (MEDIAN VALUE)

UNDER $1 MILLION NET SALES

MVIC/Net Sales	0.62
MVIC/Gross Profit	1.43
MVIC/SDE	2.65
MVIC/EBITDA	3.61

$1 MILLION–$5 MILLION NET SALES

MVIC/Net Sales	0.38
MVIC/Gross Profit	0.77
MVIC/SDE	3.47
MVIC/EBITDA	4.81

OVER $5 MILLION NET SALES

MVIC/Net Sales	1.35
MVIC/Gross Profit	3.95
MVIC/SDE	N/A
MVIC/EBITDA	12.53

Source: DealStats (formerly Pratt's Stats), 2023 (Portland, OR: Business Valuation Resources, LLC), www.bvresources.com/dealstats

BENCHMARK DATA

STATISTICS (FROZEN FOOD PRODUCTION)

Number of Establishments	732
Average Profit Margin	2.0%
Revenue per Employee	$465,000
Average Number of Employees	132.0
Average Wages per Employee	$56,455

PRODUCTS AND SERVICES SEGMENTATION

Frozen prepared foods and entrees	41.6%
Frozen vegetables	31.4%
Frozen pizza	18.6%
Frozen fruit and juice concentrates	8.4%

MAJOR MARKET SEGMENTATION

Food service establishments	43.1%
Retailers	32.5%
Grocery wholesalers	24.4%

INDUSTRY COSTS

Profit	2.0%
Wages	12.1%
Purchases	51.8%
Depreciation	2.4%
Marketing	0.2%
Rent & Utilities	2.3%
Other	29.1%

INDUSTRY TREND

"Many frozen food producers have introduced healthier alternatives because of expanded health consciousness. Frozen food producers have invested in more machinery and equipment to automate packaging. Frozen food exports have remained relatively low, primarily because of the large size of the domestic market. New opportunities will spur mild growth in the number of frozen food enterprises. Frozen food producers will begin to include more costly and healthy ingredients. Despite US manufacturers' strong domestic position, imports from Mexico will push upward because of its proximity. Growing health concerns have caused some consumers to purchase fewer frozen foods."

Source: IBISWorld Industry at a Glance

- IBISWorld, March 2023: https://www.ibisworld.com

F

Fruit & Nut Farming

| NAICS 11133 | Businesses/Units 79,159

| Profit $1.5 B | Wages $6.6 B | Annual Growth Future 0.6%

                                                  | Annual Growth Past -1.8%

INDUSTRY MULTIPLES

Acquisition multiples below are calculated medians using US private industry transactions. Data updated annually. Last update: August 2023.

VALUATION MULTIPLE (MEDIAN VALUE)

UNDER $1 MILLION NET SALES	
MVIC/Net Sales.	3.96
MVIC/Gross Profit	4.03
MVIC/SDE	1.96
MVIC/EBITDA	1.96
$1 MILLION–$5 MILLION NET SALES	N/A
OVER $5 MILLION NET SALES	
MVIC/Net Sales.	0.42
MVIC/Gross Profit	3.66
MVIC/SDE	N/A
MVIC/EBITDA	14.76

Source: DealStats (formerly Pratt's Stats), 2023 (Portland, OR: Business Valuation Resources, LLC), www.bvresources.com/dealstats

BENCHMARK DATA

STATISTICS (FRUIT & NUT FARMING)

Number of Establishments .	79,159
Average Profit Margin	6.7%
Revenue per Employee .	$112,000
Average Number of Employees.	2.5
Average Wages per Employee .	$32,717

PRODUCTS AND SERVICES SEGMENTATION

Other (including pistachios)	24.4%
Grapes .	19.6%
Almonds.	18.2%
Strawberries	13.4%
Apples	10.7%
Cherries, blueberries, and cranberries .	8.2%
Pecans and walnuts	5.5%

MAJOR MARKET SEGMENTATION

Other	62.0%
Fruit and nut processors	16.2%
Fresh fruit markets and supermarkets .	13.7%
Wine manufacturers	8.1%

INDUSTRY COSTS

Profit	6.7%
Wages .	29.3%

Purchases	23.9%
Depreciation	5.8%
Marketing	1.0%
Rent & Utilities	19.5%
Other	13.7%

INDUSTRY TREND

"Demand for non-citrus fruit has been flagging, in line with flagging levels of per capita fruit and vegetable consumption. The rising costs of irrigation and pollination services have been a significant challenge. Imports play a big part in the industry, providing off-season non-citrus fruits to consumers. More consumers are expected to spend on premium and organic fruits and nuts. The continuation of healthy eating programs is expected to support the industry. Operators will benefit from improvements in domestic yields and overseas expansion. Compounded by weak demand growth, the value of non-citrus fruits has declined."

Source: IBISWorld Industry at a Glance

RESOURCES

- IBISWorld, January 2023: https://www.ibisworld.com

Fruit & Vegetable Markets

| NAICS 445230 | Businesses/Units 2,057

| Profit $219.3 M | Wages $603 M | Annual Growth Future 0.8%

| Annual Growth Past 2.2%

Rules of Thumb

- 35%–40% annual sales

INDUSTRY MULTIPLES

Acquisition multiples below are calculated medians using US private industry transactions. Data updated annually. Last update: August 2023.

VALUATION MULTIPLE (MEDIAN VALUE)

UNDER $1 MILLION NET SALES	
MVIC/Net Sales.	0.31
MVIC/Gross Profit	0.67
MVIC/SDE	1.99
MVIC/EBITDA	1.61
$1 MILLION–$5 MILLION NET SALES	
MVIC/Net Sales.	0.12
MVIC/Gross Profit	0.47
MVIC/SDE	2.31
MVIC/EBITDA	1.57
OVER $5 MILLION NET SALES	
MVIC/Net Sales.	0.55
MVIC/Gross Profit	1.41
MVIC/SDE	3.02
MVIC/EBITDA	6.28

Source: DealStats (formerly Pratt's Stats), 2023 (Portland, OR: Business Valuation Resources, LLC), www.bvresources.com/dealstats

STATISTICS (FRUIT AND VEGETABLE MARKETS)

Number of Establishments	2,057
Average Profit Margin	3.4%
Revenue per Employee	$278,000
Average Number of Employees	11.3
Average Wages per Employee	$25,523

PRODUCTS AND SERVICES SEGMENTATION

Vegetables	54.6%
Fruit	27.6%
Food dry goods and other foods purchased for future consumption	10.2%
Fresh meat and poultry	2.5%
Frozen foods	2.5%
Fresh fish and seafood	1.3%
Other	1.3%

MAJOR MARKET SEGMENTATION

Consumers aged 19 to 30	23.8%
Consumers aged 18 and under	23.6%
Consumers aged 31 to 50	15.8%
Consumers aged 51 to 70	14.2%
Consumers aged 71 and older	11.4%
Retailers, wholesalers and distributors that resell products	6.9%
Food service and hospitality industry	3.4%
All other customers	0.9%

INDUSTRY COSTS

Profit	3.4%
Wages	9.3%
Purchases	67.0%
Depreciation	0.8%
Marketing	0.7%
Rent & Utilities	2.9%
Other	16.0%

INDUSTRY TREND

"Industry operators have been exploring new opportunities by widening their customer base. Organic products are expected to help industry players offset any negative effects of competition. Operator efficiency has risen as a result of vendors' increased use of technology. Rising consumer spending will likely bolster revenue growth. The rising number of companies is expected to spur demand for employees. Operators are expected to experience significant external competition. Widespread adoption of EBT payment equipment has had a significant effect on the industry."

Source: IBISWorld Industry at a Glance

RESOURCES

- IBISWorld, April 2023: https://www.ibisworld.com
- The Packer: https://www.thepacker.com

Fuel Dealers (Wholesale)

| NAICS 424720 | Businesses/Units 13,521 |

| Profit $1.5 B | Wages $6.8 B | Annual Growth Future -5.4% |

| Annual Growth Past 4.9% |

Rules of Thumb

- 1.5 x SDE plus inventory
- 1.5 x EBITDA plus vehicle value (over 15 vehicles)

INDUSTRY MULTIPLES

Acquisition multiples below are calculated medians using US private industry transactions. Data updated annually. Last update: August 2023.

VALUATION MULTIPLE (MEDIAN VALUE)

UNDER $1 MILLION NET SALES

MVIC/Net Sales	0.68
MVIC/Gross Profit	N/A
MVIC/SDE	4.41
MVIC/EBITDA	N/A

$1 MILLION–$5 MILLION NET SALES

MVIC/Net Sales	0.74
MVIC/Gross Profit	1.67
MVIC/SDE	6.02
MVIC/EBITDA	7.51

OVER $5 MILLION NET SALES

MVIC/Net Sales	0.24
MVIC/Gross Profit	2.00
MVIC/SDE	5.85
MVIC/EBITDA	8.70

Source: DealStats (formerly Pratt's Stats), 2023 (Portland, OR: Business Valuation Resources, LLC), www.bvresources.com/dealstats

BENCHMARK DATA

STATISTICS (FUEL DEALERS)

Number of Establishments	13,521
Average Profit Margin	2.7%
Revenue per Employee	$476,000
Average Number of Employees	8.1
Average Wages per Employee	$60,063

PRODUCTS AND SERVICES SEGMENTATION

Heating oil	47.8%
Propane	31.3%
All other fuels and services	6.8%
Diesel	5.9%
Other household fuels	5.1%
Gasoline	2.5%
Other automotive fuels	0.6%

MAJOR MARKET SEGMENTATION

Households	67.7%
Commercial businesses	10.3%
Retailers and wholesalers	8.7%
Agriculture	3.8%
Manufacturing	3.8%
Construction	3.2%
Other customers	2.5%

INDUSTRY COSTS

Profit	2.7%
Wages	12.2%
Purchases	59.5%
Depreciation	1.9%
Marketing	3.3%
Rent & Utilities	1.5%
Other	18.9%

AmeriGas Partners LP 4.4%

F

INDUSTRY TREND

"Declines in the world price of crude oil have dampened industry revenue growth. The industry is expected to contend with little internal disruption due to COVID-19. Industry operators earn a relatively low average profit margin. Fuel dealers will fare better against electric companies than natural gas providers. Heightened competition will likely lead to greater M&A activity. Revenue volatility is expected to fluctuate with changing oil prices. The Fuel Dealers industry has experienced rough results over the past five years due to volatility in oil and natural gas prices."

Source: IBISWorld Industry Outlook

RESOURCES

- IBISWorld, March 2023: https://ibisworld.com
- BPN—Butane–Propane News: https://bpnews.com
- NPGA—National Propane Gas Association: https://www.npga.org

Funeral Homes/Services

	NAICS 812210		SIC 7261-02		Businesses/Units 29,232
	Profit $2.3 B		Wages $5 B		Annual Growth Future 0.8%
					Annual Growth Past 1.5%

Rules of Thumb

- 200% annual sales includes inventory and real estate
- 1.5–3 x SDE
- 4–7 x EBIT
- 5 x EBITDA

INDUSTRY MULTIPLES

Acquisition multiples below are calculated medians using US private industry transactions. Data updated annually. Last update: August 2023.

VALUATION MULTIPLE (MEDIAN VALUE)

UNDER $1 MILLION NET SALES

MVIC/Net Sales.	1.18
MVIC/Gross Profit	1.37
MVIC/SDE	5.96
MVIC/EBITDA	8.77

$1 MILLION–$5 MILLION NET SALES

MVIC/Net Sales.	1.04
MVIC/Gross Profit	1.46
MVIC/SDE	3.15
MVIC/EBITDA	6.48

OVER $5 MILLION NET SALES

MVIC/Net Sales.	2.94
MVIC/Gross Profit	4.18
MVIC/SDE	N/A
MVIC/EBITDA	13.89

Source: DealStats (formerly Pratt's Stats), 2023 (Portland, OR: Business Valuation Resources, LLC), www.bvresources.com/dealstats

PRICING TIPS

The standard within the industry is to use a multiple of EBITDA to determine a purchase price. The average funeral home, including all real estate, vehicles, inventory, goodwill, etc., will sell between 4 and 6 times EBITDA. The EBITDA as a percentage of net revenue (revenue less all cash advance items) should be estimated between 25 and 30 percent. While it is possible to run at a higher EBITDA percentage for a short time, it typically means they are charging too much to the public, underpaying employees, and neglecting capex and vehicles. Large funeral homes ($5 million+ in revenue) with multilocations and management in place can get a higher EBITDA multiple as they are attractive to PE-backed consolidators and the public companies in the space, but this is the exception, not the norm. Most funeral homes are smaller and will require a buyer to actually work in the business.

BENCHMARK DATA

STATISTICS (FUNERAL HOMES)

Number of Establishments	29,232
Average profit Margin	12.0%
Revenue per Employee	$166,000
Average Number of Employees	4.1
Average Wages per Employee	$42,450

PRODUCTS AND SERVICES SEGMENTATION

Funeral planning services	33.2%
Resale of merchandise	20.2%
Body preparation and internment	15.5%
Other	14.7%
Cremation	11.3%
Transportation	5.1%

MAJOR MARKET SEGMENTATION

Individuals aged 65 to 84	41.9%
Individuals aged 85 and older	31.1%
Individuals aged 45 to 64	19.7%
Individuals aged 25 to 44	4.9%
Individuals aged under 25	2.4%

INDUSTRY COSTS

Profit	12.0%
Wages	25.6%
Purchases	8.6%
Depreciation	3.4%
Marketing	1.7%
Rent & Utilities	5.3%
Other	43.3%

MARKET SHARE

Service Corporation International	19.7%
Carriage Services, Inc.	2.0%
StoneMor Partners LP	1.8%

Most funeral homes can be run around a 25 to 30 percent EBITDA of net revenue. In this industry, net revenue is defined as gross revenue less any cash advance items. Cash advance items are things that the funeral home puts on the contract as a convenience for the family that are not marked up; examples would include death certificates, obituaries, clergy honorariums, crematory fees, cemetery fees, and flowers.

Revenue per employee $125,000 to $140,000

EXPENSES (% OF ANNUAL SALES)

Cost of Goods	20%
Occupancy Costs	20% to 30%
Payroll/Labor Costs.	25% to 35%
Profit (pretax)	15% to 25%

QUESTIONS

- What are your plans after the sale?
- Make sure to ask about the prepaid funeral accounts and the last time they were audited. Make sure your attorney has a clause in the purchase agreement that states you are assuming only the prepaid funeral liabilities specifically disclosed and that can be verified.
- What amount is placed in prearranged funerals? Are they fully funded? Underfunded?
- Why are you selling? What are you looking for in a buyer? Do you want to stay on? Will you help transition the relationships you have in the community over to me?
- If you could change something about your building/business, what is it and why?
- What are the demographics of the area? What competition do you face in your local community? Is the local population growing? What is the cremation rate here? How quickly is the cremation rate rising? Is the staffing sufficient to accommodate the buyer's vision?

INDUSTRY TREND

You are going to see continued consolidation in the industry as cremation rates keep rising and revenue keeps dropping. According to the National Funeral Directors Association (NFDA), the average funeral home served 113 families and has 3 full-time and 4 part-time employees. The average funeral was $7848 and the average cremation was about $2000. The national cremation rate is 60 percent, and the national burial rate is 36 percent. Based on these numbers, the average funeral home has around $500,000 in gross revenue.

The rise in cremation has resulted in lower revenue per call and less cash flow to the business. It is estimated that by 2030, over 70 percent of all deaths in the US will result in cremation. Many states are already at or above this number. Families are still willing to spend money but want experiences not merchandise. Think memorial lunches/dinners that are more a celebration of the life lived, rather than focusing on a body in a casket in a somber environment.

Cremation rate increasing, profits decreasing, smaller firms closing

The pandemic has greatly accelerated the use of technology in this industry, so firms that adapt and offer online arrangements, online payments, and webcasting of services will succeed. There will also be further consolidation in the industry to save on costs of employees and overhead. I also think we will start to see smaller buildings as families are choosing more limited services.

"Funeral homes have experienced more funerals as a result of more deaths during COVID-19. Competition has risen as alternative sales channels have emerged. Funeral homes have increasingly experienced competition from outside the industry. Cremation will continue rising in popularity. E-commerce sales, including products retailed by funeral homes, will continue to grow. An expanding senior population will continue to significantly outpace population growth. Funeral homes with proper facilities can garner revenue from cremations."

Source: IBISWorld Industry at a Glance

F

EXPERT COMMENTS

Make sure to ask about the prepaid funeral accounts and the last time they were audited. Make sure your attorney has a clause in the purchase agreement that states you are assuming only the prepaid funeral liabilities that are specifically disclosed and that can be verified.

To a buyer, I would advise them to be disciplined in how much they agree to pay; there are only so many deaths per year in a community, so the only way to increase revenue and profits is to raise prices and cut expenses, which may not go over well in the community.

To a seller, I would tell them to think and long and hard about who they are selling to; the one that offers the most money is not always the best one to sell to, especially if you are still going to live in the community after the sale. There are a lot of former owners out there that now regret their decision to sell since the new owner fired long-term employees and raised prices, and now the former owner hears about it every time he runs into a family that had a death since he sold.

Funeral homes are often long-term stable businesses in a community, and many families always use the same one each time the need arises. Therefore, it is very difficult to replicate the success of an established funeral home. The industry is seeing a rapid shift away from traditional full-service funerals to limited to no service cremation. This is causing the overall revenue to decline, and making some large funeral home buildings obsolete, as most of the building is empty most of the time. The rise in cremation is also making location less important, since families are not having visitations and funerals; this has led to new companies entering the space and offering low-cost cremation and allowing families to complete arrangements completely online. Funeral homes need to adapt to the new reality, and convert excess space into a banquet facility, or possibly build a small funeral home building and move their existing business into it and then sell their larger building to reduce overhead. They also need to reassess staffing levels; if you are not having big traditional funeral homes, you can have fewer employees. Covid-19 has forced the industry to adapt to online arrangements and the use of technology. It has also made valuation difficult, as there has been a record number of deaths in the past 2 years; the CDC estimates the death rate from 2020 to 2021 increased by 19 percent, so, many funeral homes have record years in terms of number of families served and revenue. This is not sustainable and will revert back to the mean. Using pre-Covid average number of deaths and current prices helps to come up with a reasonable valuation, but one may also want to use an earnout.

For buyers, do the due diligence on the firm. What are their reviews in the community? What is their facility like? Has it been well maintained? Is the business positioned well to use technology that is available for the business and the families served?

For sellers, plan ahead of time. Is the business ready to sell? What does retirement look like? Fully retire/semiretire?

For sellers, get all your financials in order. If possible, start planning a sale at least 3 years before you take it to market. For buyers, make sure you have at least 10 to 20 percent of the purchase available for a down payment, and then another 5 to 10 percent for working capital. While the revenue is stable over a 12+ month period, it is not uncommon to have a period of 1 to 2 months with hardly any deaths.

Profits are trending down as more and more people choose limited services and cremation, and labor costs are increasing as fewer people are going into the industry.

FINANCING

The standard is outside financing for 75 to 80 percent of the purchase price, with the seller carrying back the balance in the form of a noncompete agreement over several years. Since this is a relationship-based business, the noncompete helps to protect the buyer and ensure the seller will help to transition the relationships in the community to the new buyer.

It is very common for an owner to carry back a note on standby if done with SBA. Most buyers want a noncompete note also attached to the deal.

We typically see a buyer using an SBA loan, with 10 to 20 percent down. In addition, a noncompete agreement for 10 to 30 percent of the total purchase price paid out over 10 to 15 years with no interest is standard.

RESOURCES

- IBISWorld, January 2023: https://www.ibisworld.com
- American Funeral Director:
  https://kates-boylston.com/american-funeral-director/
- CANA—Cremation Association of North America:
  https://www.cremationassociation.org
- FCCFA—Florida Cemetery, Cremation & Funeral Association:
  https://www.thefccfa.com
- ICCFA—International Cemetery, Cremation & Funeral Association:
  https://iccfa.com
- National Monument Builders: https://monumentbuilders.org
- NFDA—National Funeral Directors Association: https://nfda.org
- Nomis Publications: https://www.nomispublications.com

Furniture Merchant Wholesalers

| NAICS 423210 | Businesses/Units 10,343

| Profit $2.9 B | Wages $5.3 B | Annual Growth Future 0.7%

| | | Annual Growth Past 1.1%

INDUSTRY MULTIPLES

Acquisition multiples below are calculated medians using US private industry transactions. Data updated annually. Last update: August 2023.

VALUATION MULTIPLE (MEDIAN VALUE)

UNDER $1 MILLION NET SALES

MVIC/Net Sales.	0.80
MVIC/Gross Profit	1.49
MVIC/SDE	3.60
MVIC/EBITDA	6.03

$1 MILLION–$5 MILLION NET SALES

MVIC/Net Sales.	0.38
MVIC/Gross Profit	0.93
MVIC/SDE	2.63
MVIC/EBITDA	2.66

MVIC/Net Sales. 0.75
MVIC/Gross Profit 1.27
MVIC/SDE . . . . N/A
MVIC/EBITDA 20.02

Source: DealStats (formerly Pratt's Stats), 2023 (Portland, OR: Business Valuation Resources, LLC), www.bvresources.com/dealstats

BENCHMARK DATA

STATISTICS (FURNITURE WHOLESALING)

Number of Establishments	.10,343
Average Profit Margin . . .	4.4%
Revenue per Employee	$930,000
Average Number of Employees. . . .	.6.9
Average Wages per Employee . . .	$74,275

PRODUCTS AND SERVICES SEGMENTATION

Office furniture	.51.8%
Household furniture	.36.8%
Commercial furniture	6.7%
Other furniture and services	4.7%

MAJOR MARKET SEGMENTATION

Private businesses	.40.4%
Retailers.	.32.6%
Other wholesalers	.14.7%
Government entities	6.5%
Other	5.8%

INDUSTRY COSTS

Profit	4.4%
Wages	8.0%
Purchases	.66.8%
Depreciation	0.5%
Marketing	0.9%
Rent & Utilities	2.1%
Other	.17.4%

INDUSTRY TREND

"Demand from businesses depends on full-time employment and corporate profit. The shift to remote working slowed demand from businesses. The trend of manufacturers' internalizing sales to retailers has created greater competition. Positive economic conditions will enable corporations to upgrade facilities. Competition will increase, pushing wholesalers to compete on price. Advances in technology have been both a blessing and a curse for the industry. Some smaller wholesalers have found it challenging to compete and have exited the industry altogether."

Source: IBISWorld Industry at a Glance

RESOURCES

• IBISWorld, January 2023: https://www.ibisworld.com

Furniture Refinishing

	NAICS 811420		SIC 7641-05		Businesses/Units 17,700
	Profit $219 M		Wages $609.9 M		Annual Growth Future 1.4%
					Annual Growth Past -1.9%

Rules of Thumb

- 50% annual sales plus inventory

INDUSTRY MULTIPLES

Acquisition multiples below are calculated medians using US private industry transactions. Data updated annually. Last update: August 2023.

VALUATION MULTIPLE (MEDIAN VALUE)

UNDER $1 MILLION NET SALES	
MVIC/Net Sales.	0.41
MVIC/Gross Profit	0.50
MVIC/SDE	1.42
MVIC/EBITDA	2.12
$1 MILLION–$5 MILLION NET SALES	N/A
OVER $5 MILLION NET SALES	N/A

Source: DealStats (formerly Pratt's Stats), 2023 (Portland, OR: Business Valuation Resources, LLC), www.bvresources.com/dealstats

BENCHMARK DATA

STATISTICS (FURNITURE REPAIR & REUPHOLSTERY)

Number of Establishments .	17,700
Average Profit Margin	.11.1%
Revenue per Employee .	$75,200
Average Number of Employees.	1.5
Average Wages per Employee .	$22,929

PRODUCTS AND SERVICES SEGMENTATION

Off-site household restoration services	.50.3%
Off-site commercial restoration services	.29.1%
On-site household restoration services	.13.1%
On-site commercial restoration services	7.5%

MAJOR MARKET SEGMENTATION

Households .	.52.2%
Businesses .	.43.4%
Government.	4.4%

INDUSTRY COSTS

Profit	.11.1%
Wages	.30.9%
Purchases	8.4%
Depreciation	1.7%
Marketing	1.7%
Rent & Utilities .	5.1%
Other	.41.1%

INDUSTRY TREND

"The industry has traditionally been considered countercyclical. An expected decline in office vacancy in 2023 is expected to lead to growth in industry revenue. Market trends that have curtailed industry revenue have also hurt industry employment. Revenue is largely dependent on consumers' propensity and means to repair furniture. The influx of low-cost imported furniture into the United States has created problems for furniture repairers and reupholsters. Demand from businesses is expected to pick up. Over the past five years, demand for the industry waned as a result of the COVID-19 pandemic."

Source: IBISWorld Industry at a Glance

RESOURCES

• IBISWorld, August 2023: https://www.ibisworld.com

Furniture Stores

	NAICS 449110		SIC 5712-16		Businesses/Units 67,608
	Profit $4.6 B		Wages $17 B		Annual Growth Future 1.6%
					Annual Growth Past 1.6%

Rules of Thumb

• 60% annual sales includes inventory

INDUSTRY MULTIPLES

Acquisition multiples below are calculated medians using US private industry transactions. Data updated annually. Last update: August 2023.

VALUATION MULTIPLE (MEDIAN VALUE)

UNDER $1 MILLION NET SALES
MVIC/Net Sales	0.32
MVIC/Gross Profit	0.65
MVIC/SDE	1.53
MVIC/EBITDA	1.81

$1 MILLION–$5 MILLION NET SALES
MVIC/Net Sales	0.38
MVIC/Gross Profit	0.89
MVIC/SDE	2.44
MVIC/EBITDA	3.25

OVER $5 MILLION NET SALES
MVIC/Net Sales	0.98
MVIC/Gross Profit	1.95
MVIC/SDE	5.46
MVIC/EBITDA	10.70

Source: DealStats (formerly Pratt's Stats), 2023 (Portland, OR: Business Valuation Resources, LLC), www.bvresources.com/dealstats

PRICING TIPS

Analyze gross profit margin and ratio of repeat clientele to new customers.

BENCHMARK DATA

STATISTICS (FURNITURE STORES)

Number of Establishments	67,608
Average Profit Margin	3.6%
Revenue per Employee	$335,000
Average Number of Employees	5.8
Average Wages per Employee	$44,446

PRODUCTS AND SERVICES SEGMENTATION

Living room furniture	37.8%
Bedroom furniture	32.8%
Dining room furniture	17.9%
Other furniture	11.5%

MAJOR MARKET SEGMENTATION

Consumers aged 45 to 54	22.3%
Consumers aged 35 to 44	20.2%
Consumers aged 25 to 34	17.3%
Consumers aged 55 to 64	14.6%
Consumers aged 65 and older	10.9%
Consumers aged 24 and younger	10.5%
Businesses and other	4.2%

INDUSTRY COSTS

Profit	3.6%
Wages	13.2%
Purchases	50.0%
Depreciation	0.9%
Marketing	3.5%
Rent & Utilities	5.9%
Other	22.8%

MARKET SHARE

Ashley Furniture Industries, Inc.	4.2%
Inter IKEA Systems B.V.	3.7%
Williams-Sonoma, Inc.	2.2%

EXPENSES (% OF ANNUAL SALES)

Cost of Goods	30%
Occupancy Costs	20%
Payroll/Labor Costs.	15%
Profit (pretax)	35%

QUESTIONS

- What is the reason for selling? Will the purchaser assume ownership of the client base? Is there already a fully functional website?

INDUSTRY TREND

"The industry is tied to the housing market. Online retailers have siphoned revenue away from the industry. Furniture stores shifted their business models to withstand consumer spending changes. Expected increases in consumer confidence will likely boost revenue growth. Demand for furniture in the residential market will likely grow. Companies are expected to focus on providing customer service. Volatile consumer confidence and increasing e-commerce sales have mitigated further industry declines."

Source: IBISWorld Industry at a Glance

RESOURCES

- IBISWorld, April 2023: https://www.ibisworld.com
- Furniture Today: https://www.furnituretoday.com

Garden Centers/Nurseries

	NAICS 444240		SIC 5261-04		Businesses/Units 21,739
	Profit $1.9 B		Wages $5.5 B		Annual Growth Future -0.2%
					Annual Growth Past 1.9%

Rules of Thumb

- 3–5 x SDE plus inventory
- 25% sales plus inventory
- 6 x EBIT
- 5 x EBITDA

INDUSTRY MULTIPLES

Acquisition multiples below are calculated medians using US private industry transactions. Data updated annually. Last update: August 2023.

VALUATION MULTIPLE (MEDIAN VALUE)

UNDER $1 MILLION NET SALES

MVIC/Net Sales.	0.42
MVIC/Gross Profit	0.73
MVIC/SDE	2.56
MVIC/EBITDA	3.03

$1 MILLION–$5 MILLION NET SALES

MVIC/Net Sales.	0.47
MVIC/Gross Profit	1.07
MVIC/SDE	2.97
MVIC/EBITDA	3.76

OVER $5 MILLION NET SALES

MVIC/Net Sales.	0.48
MVIC/Gross Profit	1.63
MVIC/SDE	4.06
MVIC/EBITDA	4.73

Source: DealStats (formerly Pratt's Stats), 2023 (Portland, OR: Business Valuation Resources, LLC), www.bvresources.com/dealstats

PRICING TIPS

Customer database indicating the amount of recurring revenue per customer

BENCHMARK DATA

STATISTICS (NURSERY AND GARDEN STORES)

Number of Establishments .	.21,739
Average Profit Margin	3.9%
Revenue per Employee .	$339,000
Average Number of Employees.	.6.7
Average Wages per Employee .	$37,913

PRODUCTS AND SERVICES SEGMENTATION

Farm and agricultural supplies .	55.2%
Home lawn and garden goods .	26.9%
Other	11.8%
Tools and equipment	3.1%
Fuels	3.0%

MAJOR MARKET SEGMENTATION

Farmers 35.1%
Consumers aged 35 to 54 . . . . . 20.0%
Consumers aged 55 and older 16.0%
Consumers aged 34 and younger . . . 12.2%
Other 9.9%
Other retailers and wholesalers . . . 6.8%

INDUSTRY COSTS

Profit 3.9%
Wages 11.2%
Purchases 62.7%
Depreciation 1.4%
Marketing 0.9%
Rent & Utilities 2.2%
Other 17.8%

MARKET SHARE

Tractor Supply Company 18.7%

EXPENSES (% OF ANNUAL SALES)

Cost of Goods . . . . . . 45% to 48%
Occupancy Costs . . . . . 05% to 07%
Payroll/Labor Costs. . . . . 28% to 30%
Profit (pretax) 04%

QUESTIONS

- Get an ag exemption if possible; also update plumbing.
- How will you pay for the business?

INDUSTRY TREND

"Rising per capita disposable income has enabled retailers to remain profitable. Big-box stores are an extreme threat to nursery and garden stores. Retailers emphasize personalized services to compensate for their typically higher prices. E-commerce companies will continue to direct sales to customers through online purchases. Retailers will shift toward higher-margin specialty products. Retailers will shift toward higher-margin specialty products. External competition has threatened the industry over the past five years."

Source: IBISWorld Industry at a Glance

EXPERT COMMENTS

Have plenty of cash and collateral. Know what you're doing on the business side.

FINANCING

Most typical is seller financing, but this is very risky for the seller.

RESOURCES

- IBISWorld, March 2023: https://www.ibisworld.com
- AmericanHort: https://www.americanhort.org/
- Garden Center magazine: https://www.gardencentermag.com/
- Green Profit: https://www.greenprofit.com
- Greenhouse Grower: https://www.greenhousegrower.com/
- IGCA—International Garden Centre Association: https://www.intgardencentre.org/
- L&GR—Lawn & Garden Retailer: https://lgrmag.com/
- The Garden Center Group: https://www.thegardencentergroup.com/

Gas Stations with Convenience Stores

NAICS 457110	SIC 5541-01	Businesses/Units 108,156
Profit $10.9 B	Wages $23.7 B	Annual Growth Future 0.9%
		Annual Growth Past 5.1%

Rules of Thumb

- 25%–35% annual sales plus inventory
- 80% annual sales with real estate plus inventory
- 3–5 x SDE plus inventory, when a full-service car wash is included (min. $250K SDE)
- 3–5 x EBIT
- 3–5 x EBITDA
- 3.5–5 x SDE

INDUSTRY MULTIPLES

Acquisition multiples below are calculated medians using US private industry transactions. Data updated annually. Last update: August 2023.

VALUATION MULTIPLE (MEDIAN VALUE)

UNDER $1 MILLION NET SALES	
MVIC/Net Sales.	0.23
MVIC/Gross Profit	0.52
MVIC/SDE	2.51
MVIC/EBITDA	1.46
$1 MILLION–$5 MILLION NET SALES	
MVIC/Net Sales.	0.10
MVIC/Gross Profit	0.62
MVIC/SDE	2.08
MVIC/EBITDA	2.76
OVER $5 MILLION NET SALES	
MVIC/Net Sales.	0.07
MVIC/Gross Profit	0.80
MVIC/SDE	2.08
MVIC/EBITDA	3.37

Source: DealStats (formerly Pratt's Stats), 2023 (Portland, OR: Business Valuation Resources, LLC), www.bvresources.com/dealstats

PRICING TIPS

There must be an understanding of gas margins, gas pricing with fuel suppliers, C-store suppliers, and lease terms if it is rented property.

Gross sales in all profit centers compared to EBITDA income provides a new buyer a realistic picture of business operating revenue.

Look up EPA history on the location. Have tanks tested before purchasing. Most stations upgraded their tanks to fiberglass in 1985. Manufacturers said they were meant to last 30 to 40 years; the EPA, 25 to 30 years; however, the historical lifespan has been closer to 20 years. Buyers beware!

Most stations/stores in AZ are sold with the real estate, owner-occupied. To get an accurate price, the real estate and business should be valued separately. Much of our real estate, especially in the Phoenix metro market, is overvalued on an historic basis. This gives a higher multiple to the business–real estate combination. While the buyer may be willing to pay the higher price, banks are reluctant to at historically high LTVs. This results in the buyer decreasing leverage, or a seller carrying a second.

Some sellers, to resolve this, are offering the business only and providing a lease for the property; however, lease rates reflect the currently high real estate prices. Lenders sometime balk at this when calculating debt service coverage.

Due to current supply and demand, there are not many quality offerings in the current marketplace. Those that make sense command a premium above the multiples.

BENCHMARK DATA

STATISTICS (GAS STATIONS WITH CONVENIENCE STORES)

Number of Establishments	108,156
Average Profit Margin	1.7%
Revenue per Employee	$719,000
Average Number of Employees	8.3
Average Wages per Employee	$26,675

PRODUCTS AND SERVICES SEGMENTATION

Regular gasoline	59.0%
Other	13.2%
Mid-grade and premium gasoline	12.2%
Groceries	10.0%
Diesel	5.6%

MAJOR MARKET SEGMENTATION

Individuals aged 35 to 54	40.5%
Individuals aged 55 to 64	17.3%
Individuals aged 25 to 34	16.5%
Individuals under age 25	12.2%
Individuals aged 65 and over	10.7%
Other consumers	2.8%

INDUSTRY COSTS

Profit	1.7%
Wages	3.7%
Purchases	82.7%
Depreciation	1.1%
Marketing	0.2%
Rent & Utilities	1.8%
Other	8.9%

MARKET SHARE

Alimentation Couche-Tard Inc.	9.0%
7-Eleven, Inc.	7.6%
Casey's General Stores, Inc.	1.8%

Fuel pooled margins run about $0.50/gal in the Phoenix metro market, and up to $1.00 in rural markets. These are not uniform throughout markets. Occupancy cost is assuming the business purchase includes the real estate, and this is financed. The occupancy cost is the debt service on an 80 percent LTV note. For leased real estate, this cost may be as much as 15 percent NNN, before NNN expenses.

Variances in locations, the business product mix (fuel sales vs. store sales, with or without a carwash, with or without a QSR, etc.) render standards for metrics unusable. For instance, some locations may have as much as 75 to 80 percent of total sales in fuel. Others, typically rural locations, may have as little as 30 to 35 percent in fuel, functioning more as a general store or small grocery with fuel as a convenience item.

Gross profit from products, 27 percent

Gas margin of 25 cents per gallon

Occupancy costs of 5 percent

EBITDA of 15 percent of investment

A brief word about net profit before tax. A good deal of revenue in the gas station/c-store business is cash, much like bars and restaurants. As such, it's commonly known that some part of gross income is unreported. Taxable income for private companies (individual or family businesses) is typically seen from 2 to 6 percent. When figuring adjustments (add-backs) for discretionary expenses, real taxable income runs 9 to 13 percent. Also, some income never makes it to the bank or the accountant—it's what I call blue jean money—right out of the register. This convention clearly understates gross sale and gross profit, and overstates cost of goods sold.

Sales per square foot, including gasoline profit, is $1000.00 to $1200.00 per square foot; food cost is usually 30 percent of sales; employees, if the gas station offers freshly prepared to order foods, is 30 percent of food sales.

EXPENSES (% OF ANNUAL SALES)

Cost of Goods	65% to 75%
Occupancy Costs	06% to 16%
Payroll/Labor Costs.	10% to 20%
Profit (pretax)	05% to 15%

QUESTIONS

- Gas gallons margin? Food service margins? Do they have a carwash or are they thinking of getting one? Relations with fuel supplier and C-store supplier? Demographic changes in the surrounding area? Competition?
- Room for improvement? What is the image of the store? Products offered or added profit centers?
- How long have you owned the business? Do you own or lease property? Is the property owned by the oil company or third party? Do you have a supply agreement, and when does the supply agreement expire? Any environmental history with the property? Are there any future plans for new competition in the area?
- Are there any contamination issues? Age of tanks?
- Sales trends? Margin of profit? Security, crime? Infrastructure improvements? Relationship to employees? Contracts between suppliers and commitments that will survive the closing?
- Who is responsible for tanks? Dealer or oil company? What kind of gas supply agreement is in place—commission, DTW, or rack?
- EPA or fire marshal issues? Liquor, beer, or wine?

INDUSTRY TREND

Gas stations will remain a high-interest business, but they must begin to accommodate electric vehicles by adding charging stations. Where do Teslas go now to recharge? It looks like Target parking lots!

Continued concentration in established communities, with new development and reimaging existing properties.

With oil prices staying on the positive side, the trend will continue to move uphill and profitability will remain high.

The uncertainties of macro public policies will continue to be a cautionary flag to new participants entering the market, or small operators expanding location.

Larger national and regional dealers will continue to expand by acquisition of smaller dealers on an opportunistic basis. The potential to convert petro-based energy at the gas station to a green energy alternative will continue to be a talking point for the next couple of years and hold the gas station industry somewhat hostage for growth and transaction activity during this period. The long-term trend will reverse in the mid-2020s, and the return to petrofuel will begin playing catch-up after four years of abandonment.

Well-sited operations will trend upward. Maintenance is a very important component to stay on top of. Experienced staff will be a solid foundation for future growth in revenue.

Margins will get thinner and the big boys will start squeezing out, or acquiring, some of the mom and pops. But gas and gas stations are here to stay for the foreseeable future.

Large-format stores with multiple streams of income. Automated tellers.

"Francis Energy—which owns and operates the nation's first comprehensive statewide network of public EV fast chargers in Oklahoma, with coverage every 50 miles—will install and operate its EV fast charging stations at 51 GoMart locations."

Source: "GoMart Enters the Electric Vehicle Charging Space," October 20, 2022, https://www.csnews.com/gomart-enters-electric-vehicle-charging-space

The most notable trend that has been in place several years now is the addition of food service in the store. Hot dogs on a roller and nacho cheese machines are being replaced by fresh made hot foods, e.g., pizza, chicken, and good-for-you salad bars. While this trend is well entrenched in larger multisite companies—even private companies—many, if not most, of the mom-and-pops have not made the upgrade. I believe this is largely an affordability issue, and an unwillingness to leverage the balance sheet for the remodeling. These are usually older and smaller stores, and are rapidly becoming economically obsolete.

A newer trend more visible in other parts of the country is the addition of alternative energy sourcing, primarily electronic charging stations. We have plentiful sourcing of LNG, CNG, and of course, propane. But charging stations haven't shown up yet. These are starting to appear in larger shopping centers, and some hotels/motels.

Internet marketing is ubiquitous now along all measures of the spectrum. This will continue. The fight for market share will be waged over the Internet. Business models should now include an IT department, staffed by a full-time employee or third-party contractor/consultant. For much of the market, if you're not online, you're not there—it doesn't matter if they can drive by and see you. The fact is, they'll drive by!

The trend is larger stores with additional services—e.g., drive-through, pick-up, and delivery of products—and multiple profit centers like a flower shop, dry cleaning pickup, made-to-order dinner items, as well as a larger wine and specialty beer offering. New fuels, such as nitrogen and biofuels, as well as EV charging.

"Gas prices, disposable income and driving habits all influence industry revenue. Regular, midgrade, premium and diesel fuels account for more than 75.0% of revenue. Establishment owners have begun to offer a wider variety of goods inside their stores. Operators will continue to offer more higher-profit goods and services. Total vehicle miles are expected to increase, driving demand for gas upward. The growing popularity of fuel-efficient cars will further restrain revenue growth. Declines in the world price of crude oil have lowered revenue but boosted profit."

Source: IBISWorld Industry at a Glance

EXPERT COMMENTS

Understand the need for constant self-analysis on what they are doing and how they can improve their business for higher profitability.

Buying: keep track of your pennies! Have good systems in place. Selling: have 3 years' financials in order.

Concentration within a trade area shows that revenues can be diluted.

Hard to compete against some national chains. Recession-proof business. Electric vehicles have very little effect on the gas business.

Competition is high; there are lots of acquisitions and mergers of large players that are making it difficult for small operators to remain competitive. Constant need to upgrade facilities puts pressure on profitability.

Make sure you are an expert in this industry; go to work for a company and run the business as management. This way, you will have firsthand knowledge that you could help your clients in a meaningful way. Be an advisor, not a salesperson.

Location and facilities: Most locations are in good condition mainly because of contractual or government oversight. Marketability: Most operators don't focus on marketing other than that provided by the dealer requirements of jobbers or oil companies. Industry trend: There is a great demand for these types of properties; they need to make significant investments in to-go services, carry-out sales, and upgrades to add EMV charging. Ease of replication: This is a very capex-intensive process with a minimum investment of $1.0 million without the cost of land. With increases in the hourly rates to $15.00 per hour, it is shrinking bottom lines.

Buyers must check who is responsible for underground tanks—oil company or dealer. If dealer, how old are the tanks? Are they fiberglass or not?

FINANCING

It can be both, depending on the people involved. In my experience, there doesn't appear to be one consistent financing outcome.

Combination of bank financing and seller financing, unless the buyer is self-funded. Terms are market rate, typically amortized, 15-to-20-year terms.

With most SBA lenders no longer financing gas stations, conventional business loans and seller financing are the only options; 3-to-5-year terms at interest rates of 8 to 10 percent.

Outside financing or cash. A small seller carryback for a short term, if needed to close, may occur.

For me, it's outside financing. Typically SBA 7(a) loans. There's a reason for this: I'm also a commercial loan originator with a mortgage broker in Scottsdale, AZ. Secondarily, since most gas station sales include the real estate, they're fairly large by small business standards. A business only that might sell for $500,000 would sell for $1.5 to $1.7 million when including the real estate. A seller carry would typically ask for 30 to 40 percent down, whereas an SBA 7(a) loan may be done with 15 percent or so down. If the historic cash flow will support 85 percent leverage, it's then a matter of affordability.

Supplier agreements (contracts) to fund transactions and secure a client for 7 to 10 years.

RESOURCES

- IBISWorld, April 2023: https://www.ibisworld.com
- API—American Petroleum Institute: https://www.api.org
- APMA—Arizona Petroleum Marketers Association: https://www.apma4u.org
- Argus: https://www.argusmedia.com/en
- Convenience Store News: https://www.csnews.com
- CSP: https://www.cspdailynews.com/
- CStore Decisions: https://cstoredecisions.com
- Fuel Oil News: https://fueloilnews.com
- GASDA—Gasoline & Automotive Service Dealers of America: https://gasda.org
- NACS: https://www.convenience.org/
- NYACS—New York Association of Convenience Stores: https://www.nyacs.org
- Oilprice.com: https://oilprice.com/
- PMAA—The Petroleum Marketers Association of America: https://www.pmaa.org/
- PPA—Pennsylvania Petroleum Association: https://www.papetroleum.org
- VAASOA—Virginia Asian American Store Owners Association: https://www.vaaasoa.com
- WPMA—Western Petroleum Marketers Association: https://www.wpma.com

Gas Stations, Full- and/or Self-Serve

NAICS 457120	SIC 5541-01	Businesses/Units 17,851
Profit $2.2 B	Wages $4.8 B	Annual Growth Future -0.4%
		Annual Growth Past 2.6%

Rules of Thumb

- 10%–15% annual sales plus inventory
- 2.5–3 x SDE plus inventory
- 2.5–3.0 x EBIT
- 2.5–3.5 x EBITDA (business only)

INDUSTRY MULTIPLES

Acquisition multiples below are calculated medians using US private industry transactions. Data updated annually. Last update: August 2023.

VALUATION MULTIPLE (MEDIAN VALUE)

UNDER $1 MILLION NET SALES

MVIC/Net Sales	0.99
MVIC/Gross Profit	1.19
MVIC/SDE	17.26
MVIC/EBITDA	17.26

$1 MILLION–$5 MILLION NET SALES

MVIC/Net Sales	0.25
MVIC/Gross Profit	0.55
MVIC/SDE	4.21
MVIC/EBITDA	2.02

OVER $5 MILLION NET SALES

MVIC/Net Sales	0.19
MVIC/Gross Profit	1.55

MVIC/SDE		7.08
MVIC/EBITDA		6.68

Source: DealStats (formerly Pratt's Stats), 2023 (Portland, OR: Business Valuation Resources, LLC), www.bvresources.com/dealstats

PRICING TIPS

Buyers are looking for high-volume gas stations; the norm is the higher the gasoline volume per month, the more attractive the business. You also need to be aware of the margin on each gallon of gas sold. Find out if the tanks underground have been inspected in the last year and meet or exceed EPA and local standards. Ask if any leaks or hazardous waste has been found/detected on the premises in the last ten years.

BENCHMARK DATA

STATISTICS (GAS STATIONS)

Number of Establishments	17,851
Average Profit Margin	1.5%
Revenue per Employee	$964,000
Average Number of Employees.	8.5
Average Wages per Employee	$31,313

PRODUCTS AND SERVICES SEGMENTATION

Diesel	46.0%
Gas	38.9%
Other	11.1%
Automotive services (e.g. repairs, car washes and general parts)	2.7%
Nonautomotive fuel	1.3%

MAJOR MARKET SEGMENTATION

Consumers, 10am-3pm	29.7%
Consumers, 3pm-7pm	26.2%
Consumers, 6am-10am	17.5%
Businesses	13.9%
Other	7.1%
Consumers, 7pm-12am	5.6%

INDUSTRY COSTS

Profit	1.5%
Wages	3.3%
Purchases	83.0%
Depreciation	1.3%
Marketing	0.2%
Rent & Utilities	1.8%
Other	8.9%

MARKET SHARE

BP PLC	2.2%

EXPENSES (% OF ANNUAL SALES)

Cost of Goods	75%
Occupancy Costs	05% to 10%
Payroll/Labor Costs.	08% to 10%
Profit (pretax)	03% to 05%

QUESTIONS

- 5 years' financial and gallonage history; phase I and II environmental reports
- Any new competition? Security and safety? Road construction? Introduction to vendors.

INDUSTRY TREND

"Growing supply in oil reserves has significantly pressured gas prices. More consumers and truck drivers have turned to retail sites that operate convenience stores on-site. Industry profit is expected to partly rebound, following the coronavirus pandemic. Growth in disposable income will likely enable consumers to purchase higher grades of vehicle fuel. Rising competition from external retailers is expected to mitigate revenue growth. Major oil companies have reduced their footprint in the gas retailing business. Despite the negative effects of the pandemic, industry revenue has shown positive trends."

Source: IBISWorld Industry at a Glance

FINANCING

3 years, on average, 8 percent interest per annum.

As much as 50 percent of sales price could be financed; 3 to 5 years typical.

RESOURCES

- IBISWorld, April 2023: https://www.ibisworld.com

Gasket, Packing, and Sealing Device Manufacturing

| NAICS 339991 | Businesses/Units 733

| Profit $630.4 M | Wages $2.3 B | Annual Growth Future: 1.8%

                                          | Annual Growth Past -3.9%

INDUSTRY MULTIPLES

Acquisition multiples below are calculated medians using US private industry transactions. Data updated annually. Last update: August 2023.

VALUATION MULTIPLE (MEDIAN VALUE)

UNDER $1 MILLION NET SALES	N/A
$1 MILLION–$5 MILLION NET SALES	
MVIC/Net Sales.	0.73
MVIC/Gross Profit	2.97
MVIC/SDE	8.79
MVIC/EBITDA	12.80
OVER $5 MILLION NET SALES	
MVIC/Net Sales.	1.90
MVIC/Gross Profit	6.35
MVIC/SDE	N/A
MVIC/EBITDA	12.77

Source: DealStats (formerly Pratt's Stats), 2023 (Portland, OR: Business Valuation Resources, LLC), www.bvresources.com/dealstats

BENCHMARK DATA

STATISTICS (GASKET & SEAL MANUFACTURING)

Number of Establishments .	733
Average Profit Margin	9.0%
Revenue per Employee .	$226,000
Average Number of Employees.	43.8
Average Wages per Employee .	$74,106

PRODUCTS AND SERVICES SEGMENTATION

Metallic gaskets. 32.4%
Nonmetallic gaskets 30.6%
Packing and seals, molded 16.0%
Axial seals 7.1%
Rotary seals 6.3%
Other seals and gaskets 4.3%
Compression packing 3.3%

MAJOR MARKET SEGMENTATION

OEM market. 80.3%
Other markets 17.6%
MRO market. 2.1%

INDUSTRY COSTS

Profit 9.0%
Wages 32.8%
Purchases 43.2%
Depreciation 1.8%
Marketing 0.1%
Rent & Utilities 2.6%
Other 10.5%

INDUSTRY TREND

"Sharp decline in manufacturing during COVID-19 hampered growth. Volatile commodity prices encourage operators to source input goods from abroad. Continued prevalence of lower-cost foreign competitors encourages operators to import at a higher rate. Full economic recovery will accelerate demand from man-ufacturers. As commodity prices stabilize, so will operators' production costs. Continued proliferation of foreign competition will influence operators' growth trends. Operators' revenue volatility is attributable to its sensitivity to commodity prices and global industrial output."

Source: IBISWorld Industry at a Glance

RESOURCES

• IBISWorld, August 2023: https://www.ibisworld.com

General Freight Trucking, Long-Distance, Less Than Truckload

| NAICS 484122 | Businesses/Units 524,903

| Profit $16.6 B | Wages $51.4 B | Annual Growth Future 0.4%

| | | Annual Growth Past 2.6%

Rules of Thumb

• 2 x SDE

INDUSTRY MULTIPLES

Acquisition multiples below are calculated medians using US private industry transactions. Data updated annually. Last update: August 2023.

VALUATION MULTIPLE (MEDIAN VALUE)

UNDER $1 MILLION NET SALES
MVIC/Net Sales. 0.46
MVIC/Gross Profit 0.46
MVIC/SDE . . . . N/A

MVIC/EBITDA	1.24

$1 MILLION–$5 MILLION NET SALES

MVIC/Net Sales.	0.33
MVIC/Gross Profit	0.47
MVIC/SDE	2.34
MVIC/EBITDA	3.11

OVER $5 MILLION NET SALES

MVIC/Net Sales.	0.38
MVIC/Gross Profit	9.62
MVIC/SDE	N/A
MVIC/EBITDA	N/A

Source: DealStats (formerly Pratt's Stats), 2023 (Portland, OR: Business Valuation Resources, LLC), www.bvresources.com/dealstats

PRICING TIPS

Asset value plus 1 to 2 x multiple is the normal valuation formula for this industry.

BENCHMARK DATA

STATISTICS (GENERAL FREIGHT TRUCKING [LESS THAN TRUCKLOAD])

Number of Establishments	524,903
Average Profit Margin	7.4%
Revenue per Employee	$202,000
Average Number of Employees. . . .	.2.1
Average Wages per Employee . . .	$46,994

PRODUCTS AND SERVICES SEGMENTATION

Flatbed	35.4%
Reefer	34.7%
Van	29.9%

MAJOR MARKET SEGMENTATION

Manufacturing	34.4%
Other	31.7%
Retail	21.4%
Service	12.5%

INDUSTRY COSTS

Profit	7.4%
Wages	22.8%
Purchases	32.8%
Depreciation	5.5%
Marketing	0.2%
Rent & Utilities	5.0%
Other	26.3%

MARKET SHARE

XPO Logistics, Inc.	0.9%
FedEx Corporation	0.6%

INDUSTRY TREND

"Growth in e-commerce activity in particular has boosted the less-than-truck-load industry. Volatile diesel fuel costs have given truckers anxiety since the beginning of the COVID-19 pandemic. An ongoing shortage of truck drivers has hurt trucking tremendously. Total trade value is expected to grow inflated by the recovery in trade activity following the COVID-19 pandemic. Buying a truck is the single-largest cost to starting a new trucking company. The price of diesel is expected to stabilize. A significant fraction of nonemployers and high depreciation costs define the less-than-truckload shipping industry."

Source: IBISWorld Industry at a Glance

RESOURCES

• IBISWorld, May 2023: https://www.ibisworld.com

General Line Grocery Merchant Wholesalers

| NAICS 424410 | Businesses/Units 5,222

| Profit $6.3 B | Wages $12 B | Annual Growth Future 0.8%

| | | Annual Growth Past 1.1%

INDUSTRY MULTIPLES

Acquisition multiples below are calculated medians using US private industry transactions. Data updated annually. Last update: August 2023.

VALUATION MULTIPLE (MEDIAN VALUE)

UNDER $1 MILLION NET SALES

MVIC/Net Sales.	0.38
MVIC/Gross Profit	1.19
MVIC/SDE	2.44
MVIC/EBITDA	1.85

$1 MILLION–$5 MILLION NET SALES

MVIC/Net Sales.	0.28
MVIC/Gross Profit	1.21
MVIC/SDE	3.86
MVIC/EBITDA	4.86

OVER $5 MILLION NET SALES

MVIC/Net Sales.	0.17
MVIC/Gross Profit	1.39
MVIC/SDE	4.28
MVIC/EBITDA	7.24

Source: DealStats (formerly Pratt's Stats), 2023 (Portland, OR: Business Valuation Resources, LLC), www.bvresources.com/dealstats

BENCHMARK DATA

STATISTICS (GROCERY WHOLESALING)

Number of Establishments.	5222
Average Profit Margin	2.3%
Revenue per Employee.	$1,650,000
Average Number of Employees.	32.1
Average Wages per Employee.	$72,207

PRODUCTS AND SERVICES SEGMENTATION

Fresh meat and meat products.	22.9%
Other	21.1%
Canned food	15.1%
Frozen food.	13.7%
Dairy products	9.3%
Specialty food	7.0%
Fresh fruits and vegetables.	5.8%
Paper and plastic products.	5.1%

MAJOR MARKET SEGMENTATION

Food service outlets	49.7%
Supermarkets and other grocery retailers.	31.9%
Other wholesalers	10.1%
Other	8.3%

INDUSTRY COSTS

Profit	2.3%
Wages	4.4%
Purchases	83.5%
Depreciation	0.5%
Marketing	0.2%
Rent & Utilities	0.8%
Other	8.4%

MARKET SHARE

Sysco	19.0%
C&S Wholesale Grocers	11.9%
US Foods Holding	10.1%
United Natural Foods	9.9%
Performance Food	9.5%
Wakefern Food	7.7%
Bunzl	0.6%

INDUSTRY TREND

"Improving economic conditions have prompted industry revenue to grow. The industry experienced growing sales from grocery retailers and other wholesalers. The industry has experienced large levels of consolidation. Competition among industry participants will continue to intensify. Wholesalers will experience revived demand from food service customers. Retail chains with their own distribution facilities are projected to increase in number and size. The disproportionate size of industry players has contributed to industry consolidation over the past decade."

Source: IBISWorld Industry at a Glance

RESOURCES

• IBISWorld, January 2023: https://www.ibisworld.com

General Warehousing and Storage

NAICS 493110		Businesses/Units 28,418	
Profit $5.9 B		Wages $15.6 B		Annual Growth Future 1.9%
				Annual Growth Past 2.7%

INDUSTRY MULTIPLES

Acquisition multiples below are calculated medians using US private industry transactions. Data updated annually. Last update: August 2023.

VALUATION MULTIPLE (MEDIAN VALUE)

UNDER $1 MILLION NET SALES

MVIC/Net Sales	1.35
MVIC/Gross Profit	1.42
MVIC/SDE	4.09
MVIC/EBITDA	19.02

$1 MILLION–$5 MILLION NET SALES

MVIC/Net Sales	1.01
MVIC/Gross Profit	1.07
MVIC/SDE	3.19
MVIC/EBITDA	4.08

OVER $5 MILLION NET SALES

MVIC/Net Sales.	4.20
MVIC/Gross Profit	0.99
MVIC/SDE	3.94
MVIC/EBITDA	21.20

Source: DealStats (formerly Pratt's Stats), 2023 (Portland, OR: Business Valuation Resources, LLC), www.bvresources.com/dealstats

BENCHMARK DATA

STATISTICS (PUBLIC STORAGE & WAREHOUSING)

Number of Establishments	28,418
Average Profit Margin	16.7%
Revenue per Employee	$113,000
Average Number of Employees. . .	11.3
Average Wages per Employee . . .	$50,224

PRODUCTS AND SERVICES SEGMENTATION

Contract storage	68.7%
Handling services	19.4%
Packing services	5.9%
Transportation services.	4.7%
Other services	1.3%

MAJOR MARKET SEGMENTATION

Retail and e-commerce.	60.1%
Manufacturing	38.5%
Other	1.4%

INDUSTRY COSTS

Profit	16.7%
Wages	44.2%
Purchases	3.8%
Depreciation	4.1%
Marketing	0.4%
Rent & Utilities	8.8%
Other	22.1%

MARKET SHARE

Deutsche Post AG	10.9%
Kenco Group, Inc.	3.7%
Ingram Micro Inc.	3.4%
Ryder System, Inc.	2.3%
CEVA Logistics AG	2.0%

INDUSTRY TREND

"Demand for industry services tends to follow trends in consumer spending. The rise of e-commerce has presented challenges for the industry. Operators have increasingly begun to use wireless and mobile internet technology. IBISWorld expects outsourcing to continue growing over the next five years. Profit growth is anticipated to be limited somewhat over the coming years. Companies are adopting new technology that can shave time off per-unit processing. Profit has been constrained due to raised wages and rental costs for operators."

Source: IBISWorld Industry at a Glance

RESOURCES

• IBISWorld, March 2023: https://www.ibisworld.com

Gift Shops

| NAICS 459420 | SIC 5947-12

Rules of Thumb

- 40%–50% annual sales plus inventory
- 2.5–3.5 x SDE includes inventory
- 3–4 x EBITDA
- Inventory @ cost + FF&E + 1–2 x SDE

INDUSTRY MULTIPLES

Acquisition multiples below are calculated medians using US private industry transactions. Data updated annually. Last update: August 2023.

VALUATION MULTIPLE (MEDIAN VALUE)

UNDER $1 MILLION NET SALES

MVIC/Net Sales	0.51
MVIC/Gross Profit	0.75
MVIC/SDE	2.28
MVIC/EBITDA	3.32

$1 MILLION–$5 MILLION NET SALES

MVIC/Net Sales	0.30
MVIC/Gross Profit	0.86
MVIC/SDE	2.31
MVIC/EBITDA	2.72

OVER $5 MILLION NET SALES

MVIC/Net Sales	0.49
MVIC/Gross Profit	1.15
MVIC/SDE	2.63
MVIC/EBITDA	5.60

Source: DealStats (formerly Pratt's Stats), 2023 (Portland, OR: Business Valuation Resources, LLC), www.bvresources.com/dealstats

PRICING TIPS

Usually the cost of goods sold is 50 percent of the retail price. Special product lines or exclusive lines can vary. Also, most businesses have to have shipping and handling available.

BENCHMARK DATA

For additional Benchmark data see Card Shops

The open hours make for a long workday. Most successful stores are owner run to keep wages in balance. Also, most stores use part-time help to keep the hours at lower wages.

EXPENSES (% OF ANNUAL SALES)

Cost of Goods	48% to 55%
Occupancy Costs	06% to 12%
Payroll/Labor Costs	07% to 17%
Profit (pretax)	15% to 25%

QUESTIONS

- How long have you owned the business? Why are you selling the business? How have you seen the changes in the market (Amazon, Covid, online shopping, etc.)? Vendor relationships?
- What have been the trends? Can they do delivery? Will the employees stay? Gift and trade shows coming up?

INDUSTRY TREND

Developing a proprietary or exclusive product line; keeping in touch with clients and customers for gift suggestions; good customer list

EXPERT COMMENTS

The store must look happy and inviting. Gifts are usually for special occasions. The business should appreciate the purpose of the gift, both for the giver and the recipient.

Selecting inventory and sourcing unique products can set you apart from other gift shops, yet always carry good sellers (college and sports related; local merchandise in competitive price ranges).

All of the retail world is impacted by Amazon and the effect of online shopping. Many retail businesses have experienced a 16 to 25 percent hit from the shift to online shopping.

FINANCING

Seller financing with a 40 percent down payment by the buyer. Usually financed for 5 to 7 years.

RESOURCES

- AFCI—Association for Creative Industries: https://creativeindustries.org
- AmericasMart: https://www.americasmart.com
- Retail Today: https://retail-today.com/

Glass & Glazing Contractors

| NAICS 238150 | Businesses/Units 27,218

| Profit $1.3 B | Wages $5 B | Annual Growth Future 0.8%

| | | Annual Growth Past 0.2%

INDUSTRY MULTIPLES

Acquisition multiples below are calculated medians using US private industry transactions. Data updated annually. Last update: August 2023.

VALUATION MULTIPLE (MEDIAN VALUE)

UNDER $1 MILLION NET SALES

MVIC/Net Sales	0.38
MVIC/Gross Profit	0.65
MVIC/SDE	1.72
MVIC/EBITDA	2.20

$1 MILLION–$5 MILLION NET SALES

MVIC/Net Sales	0.37
MVIC/Gross Profit	0.81
MVIC/SDE	2.44
MVIC/EBITDA	3.69

OVER $5 MILLION NET SALES

MVIC/Net Sales	0.39
MVIC/Gross Profit	1.22
MVIC/SDE	3.15
MVIC/EBITDA	4.21

Source: DealStats (formerly Pratt's Stats), 2023 (Portland, OR: Business Valuation Resources, LLC), www.bvresources.com/dealstats

BENCHMARK DATA

STATISTICS (GLASS & GLAZING CONTRACTORS)

Number of Establishments	27,218
Average Profit Margin	6.4%
Revenue per Employee	$229,000
Average Number of Employees	3.3
Average Wages per Employee	$57,544

PRODUCTS AND SERVICES SEGMENTATION

New construction	43.8%
Additions and alterations	23.2%
Other general contracting work	17.6%
Maintenance and repair services	12.6%
Other miscellaneous services	2.8%

MAJOR MARKET SEGMENTATION

Office building construction	34.3%
Institutional building construction	23.6%
Commercial construction	12.6%
Existing residential construction	11.9%
New residential construction	11.0%
Other nonresidential construction	2.7%
General residential contracting work	2.3%
Manufacturing and industrial building construction	1.6%

INDUSTRY COSTS

Profit	6.4%
Wages	25.1%
Purchases	43.9%
Depreciation	0.8%
Marketing	0.4%
Rent & Utilities	4.8%
Other	18.6%

INDUSTRY TREND

"Nonresidential construction activity will continue declining in 2023. Rising interest rates will hamper the residential market. Increasing home prices bode well for glass and glazing contractors. Demand for glass exteriors will increase in many commercial buildings. The level of activity within the residential building market is highly susceptible to the price of financing. The push for more environmentally sustainable building designs and inputs will have mixed implications. Strong growth throughout the first half of the current period has modestly offset pandemic-induced declines."

Source: IBISWorld Industry at a Glance

RESOURCES

- IBISWorld, January 2023: https://www.ibisworld.com

Golf Courses

NAICS 713910	SIC 7997-06	Businesses/Units 9,862	
Profit $299.6 M	Wages $10.7 B	Annual Growth Future 1.0%	
		Annual Growth Past -1.0%	

INDUSTRY MULTIPLES

Acquisition multiples below are calculated medians using US private industry transactions. Data updated annually. Last update: August 2023.

VALUATION MULTIPLE (MEDIAN VALUE)

UNDER $1 MILLION NET SALES

MVIC/Net Sales	1.48
MVIC/Gross Profit	1.43
MVIC/SDE	4.68
MVIC/EBITDA	4.39

$1 MILLION–$5 MILLION NET SALES

MVIC/Net Sales	0.25
MVIC/Gross Profit	0.33
MVIC/SDE	1.32
MVIC/EBITDA	1.35

OVER $5 MILLION NET SALES

MVIC/Net Sales	2.02
MVIC/Gross Profit	7.53
MVIC/SDE	N/A
MVIC/EBITDA	11.05

Source: DealStats (formerly Pratt's Stats), 2023 (Portland, OR: Business Valuation Resources, LLC), www.bvresources.com/dealstats

PRICING TIPS

I'm not a fan of rules of thumb in this industry as the principles of alternatives and replacements are typically at play. Additionally, the northeastern U.S. is unique to the industry in terms of seasonality, premiums on land costs and housing, weather, and value-added services such as food and beverage, banquet facilities, private vs. public, instruction, leagues, group outings vs. public daily play, etc. Economic factors resulting from the recession have had a huge impact on the industry as well, especially on private courses where we appraised three for banks' planning auctions. Two of three sold for less at auction than what we appraised them for but were bought by past members who formed a consortium hoping to get a good deal (and did). New England also has more 9-hole courses than most other areas of the country, which skews industry rules.

Personal property + equipment (FF&E) usually accounts for 3 to 10 percent of the purchase price depending on the amount of equipment leased and type of operation (daily fee vs. private). From 4 to 7 percent of price is typical.

Due to weather-related conditions, a 5-year average for cash flow should be used. Capital reserves of 5 percent should always be accounted for.

BENCHMARK DATA

STATISTICS (GOLF COURSES & COUNTRY CLUBS)

Number of Establishments	9,862
Average Profit Margin	1.1%
Revenue per Employee	$92,600
Average Number of Employees	30.2
Average Wages per Employee	$36,215

PRODUCTS AND SERVICES SEGMENTATION

Memberships	46.1%
Green fees	24.6%
Food and beverages	17.3%
Equipment rentals and sales	7.8%
Other sales and services	4.2%

MAJOR MARKET SEGMENTATION

Consumers aged 30 to 39	20.1%
Consumers aged 18 to 29	18.0%
Consumers aged 50 to 59	15.0%
Consumers aged 40 to 49	14.5%
Consumers aged 60 to 69	12.1%
Consumers under 18	11.8%
Consumers aged 70 and older	8.5%

INDUSTRY COSTS

Profit	1.1%
Wages	39.3%
Purchases	4.7%
Depreciation	9.3%
Marketing	3.1%
Rent & Utilities	9.4%
Other	33.2%

EXPENSES (% OF ANNUAL SALES)

Cost of Goods	20%
Occupancy Costs	15%
Payroll/Labor Costs	45%
Profit (pretax)	20%

QUESTIONS

- Is there adjoining acreage that could be used for golf community homes? This can greatly increase value of the golf course.

INDUSTRY TREND

"The pandemic is expected to boost enthusiasm for industry activities. Many existing establishments have been forced to close over the past five years. The stagnating popularity of golf has hampered industry expansion. Golf participation rates have been falling. Stagnating leisure time may limit the industry's success. Competing outdoor sporting activities are expected to pressure the industry. The number of people that play golf on a course has increased in recent years."

Source: IBISWorld Industry at a Glance

"The record number of people who played on a golf course for the first time in 2022:3.3 million "The industry has had nine straight years with more than 2 million beginners, with the past three topping 3 million. Prior to the pandemic-boosted totals of recent years, the previous recorded-high of 2.4 million was set in 2000, when Tiger Woods was at the height of his popularity. Retention and conversion of newcomers remains an industry focus, and obstacle."

Source: "Golf Industry Facts," https://www.ngf.org/golf-industry-research/

FINANCING

5 to 7 years

RESOURCES

- IBISWorld, January 2023: https://www.ibisworld.com
- Golf Course Industry: https://www.golfcourseindustry.com
- NGCOA—National Golf Course Owners Association: https://www.ngcoa.org
- NGF—National Golf Foundation: https://www.ngf.org

Golf Driving Ranges

	NAICS 713990		SIC 7999-31		Businesses/Units 62,146
	Profit $1.6 B		Wages $5.3 B		Annual Growth Future 1.0%
					Annual Growth Past -0.1%

INDUSTRY MULTIPLES

Acquisition multiples below are calculated medians using US private industry transactions. Data updated annually. Last update: August 2023.

VALUATION MULTIPLE (MEDIAN VALUE)

UNDER $1 MILLION NET SALES

MVIC/Net Sales.	0.69
MVIC/Gross Profit	0.76
MVIC/SDE	2.37
MVIC/EBITDA	2.99

$1 MILLION–$5 MILLION NET SALES

MVIC/Net Sales.	0.69
MVIC/Gross Profit	0.86
MVIC/SDE	3.06
MVIC/EBITDA	3.71

OVER $5 MILLION NET SALES

MVIC/Net Sales.	0.58
MVIC/Gross Profit	1.27
MVIC/SDE	3.09
MVIC/EBITDA	3.27

Source: DealStats (formerly Pratt's Stats), 2023 (Portland, OR: Business Valuation Resources, LLC), www.bvresources.com/dealstats

BENCHMARK DATA

STATISTICS (GOLF DRIVING RANGES & FAMILY FUN CENTERS)

Number of Establishments .	62,146
Average Profit Margin	9.7%
Revenue per Employee .	$62,300
Average Number of Employees.	4.3
Average Wages per Employee .	$19,919

PRODUCTS AND SERVICES SEGMENTATION

Amusement and recreation services	61.0%
Coin operated games and rides	13.0%
Other	10.0%
Amateur sports teams and club services	7.0%
Meals and beverages	5.0%
Registration for tournaments and matches.	4.0%

MAJOR MARKET SEGMENTATION

Consumers aged 25 to 44	42.1%
Consumers aged 45 to 64	40.4%
Consumers aged 65 and older .	12.7%
Consumers aged 24 and younger .	4.8%

INDUSTRY COSTS

Profit	9.7%
Wages	31.5%
Purchases	5.3%
Depreciation	6.4%
Marketing	3.5%
Rent & Utilities	10.5%
Other	33.2%

Topgolf International, Inc. 0.7%

INDUSTRY TREND

"Increases in per capita disposable income revitalized revenue after the COVID-19 pandemic. Small, independent driving ranges face price pressure from in-market entertainment companies. Increased fitness awareness has affected the industry. Recreation expenditure contraction pressures companies to reduce prices. Technology based games such as laser-tag have grown. Topgolf has attracted new and older clients to its golf and entertainment centers. More prominent service providers with varied entertainment portfolios commanded a large share of industry revenue."

Source: IBISWorld Industry at a Glance

RESOURCES

• IBISWorld, January 2023: https://www.ibisworld.com

Golf Shops

| NAICS 451110

Rules of Thumb

• 30% annual sales plus inventory

INDUSTRY MULTIPLES

Acquisition multiples below are calculated medians using US private industry transactions. Data updated annually. Last update: August 2023.

VALUATION MULTIPLE (MEDIAN VALUE)

UNDER $1 MILLION NET SALES	
MVIC/Net Sales.	0.50
MVIC/Gross Profit	1.01
MVIC/SDE	2.56
MVIC/EBITDA	3.93

$1 MILLION–$5 MILLION NET SALES	
MVIC/Net Sales.	0.37
MVIC/Gross Profit	1.03
MVIC/SDE	2.71
MVIC/EBITDA	4.08

OVER $5 MILLION NET SALES	
MVIC/Net Sales.	0.46
MVIC/Gross Profit	1.33
MVIC/SDE	2.95
MVIC/EBITDA	7.63

Source: DealStats (formerly Pratt's Stats), 2023 (Portland, OR: Business Valuation Resources, LLC), www.bvresources.com/dealstats

QUESTIONS

• Is the seller willing to allow the buyer a 10 percent rejection on the inventory (or some other fixed amount)?

RESOURCES

• NGF—National Golf Foundation: https://www.ngf.org
• PGCC—Professional Golfers Career College: https://golfcollege.edu

Grain and Field Bean Merchant Wholesalers

| NAICS 424510 | Businesses/Units 10,246

| Profit $11.3 B | Wages $3 B | Annual Growth Future -9.7%

| Annual Growth Past 4.3%

INDUSTRY MULTIPLES

Acquisition multiples below are calculated medians using US private industry transactions. Data updated annually. Last update: August 2023.

VALUATION MULTIPLE (MEDIAN VALUE)

UNDER $1 MILLION NET SALES	N/A
$1 MILLION–$5 MILLION NET SALES	N/A
OVER $5 MILLION NET SALES	
MVIC/Net Sales.	0.46
MVIC/Gross Profit	N/A
MVIC/SDE	2.54
MVIC/EBITDA	N/A

Source: DealStats (formerly Pratt's Stats), 2023 (Portland, OR: Business Valuation Resources, LLC), www.bvresources.com/dealstats

BENCHMARK DATA

STATISTICS (CORN, WHEAT & SOYBEAN WHOLESALING)

Number of Establishments .	.10,246
Average Profit Margin	4.1%
Revenue per Employee .	$4,164,000
Average Number of Employees.	.6.4
Average Wages per Employee .	$45,474

PRODUCTS AND SERVICES SEGMENTATION

Corn.	46.8%
Soybeans	32.4%
Seeds, beans and rice	11.0%
Wheat	7.9%
Sorghum	1.4%
Oats and barley .	0.5%

MAJOR MARKET SEGMENTATION

Wholesalers for resale .	58.8%
Farmers for use in farm production.	18.5%
Manufacturing and mining .	12.2%
Other	6.1%
Retailers for resale .	4.4%

INDUSTRY COSTS

Profit	4.1%
Wages	1.1%
Purchases	90.6%
Depreciation	1.4%
Marketing	0.1%
Rent & Utilities .	0.4%
Other	2.4%

MARKET SHARE

Archer-Daniels-Midland Co.	12.4%
CHS Inc..	10.7%
Cargill, Incorporated	3.7%

"Prices of corn, wheat and soybeans are key in the success of the industry. Easing supply chains have reduced revenue for wholesalers. Investment in biofuels provides a subsidy for corn and soybean distributors. Agricultural products' prices will drop as production matches the post-pandemic food spending surge. Despite their use as substitutes, soybean prices will decline due to reduced biofuel use. Wholesalers and farmers try to fight falling prices with more innovative methods. Growth has been bolstered by the price appreciation of major crops."

Source: IBISWorld Industry at a Glance

RESOURCES

- IBISWorld, January 2023: https://www.ibisworld.com

Great Clips (Franchise)

| NAICS 812112 | Businesses/Units 4,290

Rules of Thumb

- 1–1.5 x SDE plus inventory

INDUSTRY MULTIPLES

Acquisition multiples below are calculated medians using US private industry transactions. Data updated annually. Last update: August 2023.

VALUATION MULTIPLE (MEDIAN VALUE)

UNDER $1 MILLION NET SALES	
MVIC/Net Sales.	0.31
MVIC/Gross Profit	0.39
MVIC/SDE	1.60
MVIC/EBITDA	2.11
$1 MILLION–$5 MILLION NET SALES	
MVIC/Net Sales.	0.29
MVIC/Gross Profit	0.39
MVIC/SDE	2.30
MVIC/EBITDA	3.05
OVER $5 MILLION NET SALES	N/A

Source: DealStats (formerly Pratt's Stats), 2023 (Portland, OR: Business Valuation Resources, LLC), www.bvresources.com/dealstats

PRICING TIPS

Approx. Total Investment: $178,400 to $376,900

RESOURCES

- Great Clips: https://www.greatclips.com
- Franchise information: https://www.greatclipsfranchise.com

Great Harvest (bakery and café) (Franchise)

| NAICS 311811 | Businesses/Units 171

Rules of Thumb

- 3.2–3.4 x SDE plus inventory

INDUSTRY MULTIPLES

Acquisition multiples below are calculated medians using US private industry transactions. Data updated annually. Last update: August 2023.

VALUATION MULTIPLE (MEDIAN VALUE)

UNDER $1 MILLION NET SALES

MVIC/Net Sales.	0.43
MVIC/Gross Profit	0.58
MVIC/SDE	1.91
MVIC/EBITDA	2.71

$1 MILLION–$5 MILLION NET SALES

MVIC/Net Sales.	0.45
MVIC/Gross Profit	0.85
MVIC/SDE	3.06
MVIC/EBITDA	4.45

OVER $5 MILLION NET SALES

MVIC/Net Sales.	2.71
MVIC/Gross Profit	11.63
MVIC/SDE	N/A
MVIC/EBITDA	19.86

Source: DealStats (formerly Pratt's Stats), 2023 (Portland, OR: Business Valuation Resources, LLC), www.bvresources.com/dealstats

PRICING TIPS

Approx. Total Investment: $176,678 to $725,431

RESOURCES

- Great Harvest: https://www.greatharvest.com
- Franchise information: https://www.greatharvest.com/franchise

Grocery Delivery Services

| NAICS 492210

INDUSTRY MULTIPLES

Acquisition multiples below are calculated medians using US private industry transactions. Data updated annually. Last update: August 2023.

VALUATION MULTIPLE (MEDIAN VALUE)

UNDER $1 MILLION NET SALES

MVIC/Net Sales.	0.89
MVIC/Gross Profit	0.98
MVIC/SDE	2.79
MVIC/EBITDA	3.01

$1 MILLION–$5 MILLION NET SALES

MVIC/Net Sales.	0.66
MVIC/Gross Profit	0.85
MVIC/SDE	2.92
MVIC/EBITDA	3.34

OVER $5 MILLION NET SALES

MVIC/Net Sales.	4.56
MVIC/Gross Profit	5.62
MVIC/SDE	N/A
MVIC/EBITDA	N/A

Source: DealStats (formerly Pratt's Stats), 2023 (Portland, OR: Business Valuation Resources, LLC), www.bvresources.com/dealstats

INDUSTRY TREND

"Executives and backers of the companies say losses today are investments in a promising prize. Groceries are already an enormous business, and if one or two of the startups grow to dominate the market for quick groceries, the numbers could eventually turn profitable, they say....For the U.S., the startups largely have focused on New York City because its dense population is well suited for quick delivery."

Source: "Losses Plague Grocery-Delivery Startups" by Eliot Brown and Preetika Rana, *Wall Street Journal*, January 31, 2022

Guard Services

| NAICS 561612 | SIC 7381-02

Rules of Thumb

- 30% annual sales plus inventory
- 3 x SDE includes inventory
- 3 x EBITDA

INDUSTRY MULTIPLES

Acquisition multiples below are calculated medians using US private industry transactions. Data updated annually. Last update: August 2023.

VALUATION MULTIPLE (MEDIAN VALUE)

UNDER $1 MILLION NET SALES

MVIC/Net Sales	0.59
MVIC/Gross Profit	0.57
MVIC/SDE	1.50
MVIC/EBITDA	2.02

$1 MILLION–$5 MILLION NET SALES

MVIC/Net Sales	0.23
MVIC/Gross Profit	0.29
MVIC/SDE	2.03
MVIC/EBITDA	3.75

OVER $5 MILLION NET SALES

MVIC/Net Sales	0.23
MVIC/Gross Profit	2.12
MVIC/SDE	N/A
MVIC/EBITDA	24.32

Source: DealStats (formerly Pratt's Stats), 2023 (Portland, OR: Business Valuation Resources, LLC), www.bvresources.com/dealstats

PRICING TIPS

Nonunion are worth more.

If guards are 1099s, business is worth less.

BENCHMARK DATA

For additional Benchmark data see Security Services/Systems/Alarm Companies

Cost is different for an armed guard, for an event security, or 24-hour security service.

EXPENSES (% OF ANNUAL SALES)

Cost of Goods	05%
Occupancy Costs	05% to 10%
Payroll/Labor Costs.	70%
Profit (pretax)	15% to 20%

QUESTIONS

- Most guard companies have major clients; explain anything over 20 percent—could become an earnout event.
- Relationship to customers?

EXPERT COMMENTS

As crime increases, so does the need for security.

It is easy to lose a client if you have to go to bid every year.

Gun Shops and Supplies

	NAICS 451110		SIC 5941-29		Businesses/Units 19,471
	Profit $553.5 M		Wages $2.1 B		Annual Growth Future 1.1%
					Annual Growth Past 5.5%

Rules of Thumb

- 30%–35% annual sales plus inventory

INDUSTRY MULTIPLES

Acquisition multiples below are calculated medians using US private industry transactions. Data updated annually. Last update: August 2023.

VALUATION MULTIPLE (MEDIAN VALUE)

UNDER $1 MILLION NET SALES

MVIC/Net Sales.	0.50
MVIC/Gross Profit	1.01
MVIC/SDE	2.56
MVIC/EBITDA	3.93

$1 MILLION–$5 MILLION NET SALES

MVIC/Net Sales.	0.37
MVIC/Gross Profit	1.03
MVIC/SDE	2.71
MVIC/EBITDA	4.08

OVER $5 MILLION NET SALES

MVIC/Net Sales.	0.46
MVIC/Gross Profit	1.33
MVIC/SDE	2.95
MVIC/EBITDA	7.63

Source: DealStats (formerly Pratt's Stats), 2023 (Portland, OR: Business Valuation Resources, LLC), www.bvresources.com/dealstats

BENCHMARK DATA

STATISTICS (GUN & AMMUNITION STORES)

Number of Establishments	.19,471
Average Profit Margin	3.0%
Revenue per Employee	$160,000
Average Number of Employees. . . .	.6.0
Average Wage per Employee . . .	$18,086

PRODUCTS AND SERVICES SEGMENTATION

Other equipment, apparel, and supplies	28.5%
Handguns	25.0%
Ammunition	23.2%
Rifles	13.5%
Other firearms	6.5%
Shotguns	3.3%

MAJOR MARKET SEGMENTATION

Consumers aged 65 and older	28.8%
Consumers aged 30 to 49	28.0%
Consumers aged 50 to 64	25.6%
Consumers aged 18 to 29	17.6%

INDUSTRY COSTS

Profit	3.0%
Wages	11.3%
Purchases	55.1%
Depreciation	0.8%
Marketing	2.2%
Rent & Utilities	6.5%
Other	21.1%

INDUSTRY TREND

"Industry performance has been driven by consumer perceptions and prevailing economic conditions. Operators have to compete with large sporting and outdoor goods stores and department stores. As demand for guns and ammunition increased, the need for employees has also climbed. Women are expected to continue purchasing firearms at higher rates for safety and recreational activities. Industry players will likely continue to contend with large department and sporting goods stores. Profit is anticipated to slightly fall as competition intensifies and supply and demand equalize. Consumers have sought to purchase firearms and ammunition ahead of the more stringent regulatory environment."

Source: IBISWorld Industry at a Glance

RESOURCES

- IBISWorld, July 2023: https://www.ibisworld.com
- NSSF—National Shooting Sports Foundation: https://www.nssf.org

Hardware Stores

NAICS 444130	SIC 5251-04	Businesses/Units 16,051
Profit $1.3 B	Wages $4.8 B	Annual Growth Future -0.4%
		Annual Growth Past 3.0%

Rules of Thumb

- 45%–50% annual sales plus inventory
- 3–3.5 x SDE plus inventory
- 3.5 x SDE includes inventory

INDUSTRY MULTIPLES

Acquisition multiples below are calculated medians using US private industry transactions. Data updated annually. Last update: August 2023.

VALUATION MULTIPLE (MEDIAN VALUE)

UNDER $1 MILLION NET SALES

MVIC/Net Sales	0.54
MVIC/Gross Profit	1.32
MVIC/SDE	3.67
MVIC/EBITDA	4.70

$1 MILLION–$5 MILLION NET SALES

MVIC/Net Sales	0.38
MVIC/Gross Profit	1.01
MVIC/SDE	3.19
MVIC/EBITDA	5.59

OVER $5 MILLION NET SALES

	N/A

Source: DealStats (formerly Pratt's Stats), 2023 (Portland, OR: Business Valuation Resources, LLC), www.bvresources.com/dealstats

BENCHMARK DATA

STATISTICS (HARDWARE STORES)

Number of Establishments	16,051
Average Profit Margin	3.9%
Revenue per Employee	$235,000
Average Number of Employees	8.9
Average Wages per Employee	$33,089

PRODUCTS AND SERVICES SEGMENTATION

Hardware	34.8%
Other	33.5%
Paint and sundries	8.1%
Plumbing fixtures and supplies	6.6%
Hand tools and accessories	6.5%
Power tools and equipment	5.8%
Electrical supplies	4.5%
Dimensional lumber	0.2%

MAJOR MARKET SEGMENTATION

Households	60.3%
Businesses	23.1%
Contractors	12.9%
Other	2.4%
Government	1.3%

INDUSTRY COSTS

Profit	3.9%
Wages	14.0%
Purchases	60.7%
Depreciation	1.1%
Marketing	0.9%
Rent & Utilities	2.1%
Other	17.2%

EXPENSES (% OF ANNUAL SALES)

Cost of Goods	50% to 60%
Occupancy Costs	05% to 08%
Payroll/Labor Costs	12% to 15%
Profit (pretax)	01% to 03%

QUESTIONS

- How do you value your ending inventory on the books? Is there concealed inventory or understated inventory? How often do you do a physical inventory?

Does your cash register point-of-sale system read barcodes? Are your inventory counts computerized?

INDUSTRY TREND

"Online retailers have recently become a competitive threat for operators that lack e-commerce channels. Operators in localized regions have created niche markets within construction and diversified product lines. Most hardware stores are members of cooperative businesses. Despite continuing growth of spending on home improvements, interest rates pose a threat to the industry. Hardware stores are anticipated to continue to be pressured by online retailers and large operators. External competitors will likely acquire industry market share from industry operators. The industry has benefited from a strengthening economy and a growing housing market during most of the period."

Source: IBISWorld Industry at a Glance

EXPERT COMMENTS

Stores in good locations will still bring premium prices. Rural locations are often insulated from the effects of big boxes.

Reasonably profitable hardware stores sell very quickly.

FINANCING

A good, qualified buyer should bring at least 25 percent down to the table. In such cases a 10-year amortized note is fairly common.

RESOURCES

- IBISWorld, November 2022: https://www.ibisworld.com
- HBSDealer: https://www.hbsdealer.com/
- NRHA—North American Retail Hardware Association: https://nrha.org

Harley-Davidson Motorcycle Dealerships

| NAICS 441228 | SIC 5571-06

Rules of Thumb

- 1–4 x EBITDA
- 2.5–3 x SDE plus net assets plus inventory

INDUSTRY MULTIPLES

Acquisition multiples below are calculated medians using US private industry transactions. Data updated annually. Last update: August 2023.

VALUATION MULTIPLE (MEDIAN VALUE)

UNDER $1 MILLION NET SALES	
MVIC/Net Sales.	0.44
MVIC/Gross Profit	0.86
MVIC/SDE	2.22
MVIC/EBITDA	2.31
$1 MILLION–$5 MILLION NET SALES	
MVIC/Net Sales.	0.27
MVIC/Gross Profit	1.09
MVIC/SDE	2.74
MVIC/EBITDA	4.79
OVER $5 MILLION NET SALES	
MVIC/Net Sales.	0.30

MVIC/Gross Profit 1.12
MVIC/SDE 3.66
MVIC/EBITDA 4.38

Source: DealStats (formerly Pratt's Stats), 2023 (Portland, OR: Business Valuation Resources, LLC), www.bvresources.com/dealstats

BENCHMARK DATA

For Benchmark data see Motorcycle Dealerships

QUESTIONS

- Why are you selling? What are the strengths and weaknesses of your business? Are there any add-backs? What is your reputation in the marketplace? What is the upside potential?

RESOURCES

- Harley-Davidson: https://www.harley-davidson.com

Hay & Crop Farming

| NAICS 111199 | Businesses/Units 565,367

| Profit $3.7 B | Wages $2.3 B | Annual Growth Future 0.2%

| Annual Growth Past 1.4%

INDUSTRY MULTIPLES

Acquisition multiples below are calculated medians using US private industry transactions. Data updated annually. Last update: August 2023.

VALUATION MULTIPLE (MEDIAN VALUE)

UNDER $1 MILLION NET SALES	N/A
$1 MILLION–$5 MILLION NET SALES	N/A
OVER $5 MILLION NET SALES	
MVIC/Net Sales.	2.07
MVIC/Gross Profit	N/A
MVIC/SDE	N/A
MVIC/EBITDA	N/A

Source: DealStats (formerly Pratt's Stats), 2023 (Portland, OR: Business Valuation Resources, LLC), www.bvresources.com/dealstats

BENCHMARK DATA

STATISTICS (HAY & CROP FARMING)

Number of Establishments	565,367
Average Profit Margin	10.3%
Revenue per Employee	$59,600
Average Number of Employees. . .	1.1
Average Wages per Employee . .	$3,860

PRODUCTS AND SERVICES SEGMENTATION

Other Crops	64.4%
Hay	25.3%
Peanuts	4.2%
Sugar Beets	3.4%
Hops	2.0%
Maple products	0.4%
Mint	0.3%

MAJOR MARKET SEGMENTATION

Livestock farmers	25.9%
Food manufacturers	22.7%
Direct to retail	21.6%
Grocery wholesalers	20.9%
Exports	8.9%

INDUSTRY COSTS

Profit	10.3%
Wages	6.4%
Purchases	41.5%
Depreciation	8.4%
Marketing	0.6%
Rent & Utilities	20.1%
Other	12.7%

MARKET SHARE

American Crystal Sugar Company	4.2%

INDUSTRY TREND

"Hay farmers have increased their presence in the industry. Industry revenue has been most consistently supported by gains in the value of hops and field-grown marijuana. Industry operators have found an outlet for surplus product in the form of export markets. Demand for price-premium organic hay from down-stream industries is an opportunity. Organic farming is expensive, but is expected to maintain industry profit. Farmers will likely continue to diversify their crops to avoid potential losses. The industry exhibited a slight decline in revenue and profitability as a result of the pandemic."

Source: IBISWorld Industry at a Glance

RESOURCES

• IBISWorld, October 2022: https://www.ibisworld.com

Health Food Stores

	NAICS 446191		SIC 5499-01		Businesses/Units 182,511
	Profit $2.2 B		Wages $8.8 B		Annual Growth Future 0.7%
					Annual Growth Past 5.9%

Rules of Thumb

• 1–1.5 x SDE plus inventory
• 40% annual sales plus inventory

INDUSTRY MULTIPLES

Acquisition multiples below are calculated medians using US private industry transactions. Data updated annually. Last update: August 2023.

VALUATION MULTIPLE (MEDIAN VALUE)

UNDER $1 MILLION NET SALES

MVIC/Net Sales	0.49
MVIC/Gross Profit	0.91
MVIC/SDE	2.50
MVIC/EBITDA	4.05

$1 MILLION–$5 MILLION NET SALES

MVIC/Net Sales	0.53
MVIC/Gross Profit	1.16
MVIC/SDE	3.58
MVIC/EBITDA	7.18

OVER $5 MILLION NET SALES

MVIC/Net Sales	0.25
MVIC/Gross Profit	0.60
MVIC/SDE	5.99
MVIC/EBITDA	4.38

Source: DealStats (formerly Pratt's Stats), 2023 (Portland, OR: Business Valuation Resources, LLC), www.bvresources.com/dealstats

BENCHMARK DATA

STATISTICS (HEALTH STORES)

Number of Establishments	182,511
Average Profit Margin	5.0%
Revenue per Employee	$133,000
Average Number of Employees	1.8
Average Wages per Employee	$26,872

PRODUCTS AND SERVICES SEGMENTATION

Sports nutrition products	29.9%
Vitamin and mineral supplements	28.3%
Convalescent care products	22.7%
Orthopedic equipment and first-aid supplies	9.9%
Other	9.2%

MAJOR MARKET SEGMENTATION

Consumers aged 45 to 64	37.5%
Consumers aged 25 to 44	35.4%
Consumers aged 65 and older	18.3%
Consumers under the age of 25	8.8%

INDUSTRY COSTS

Profit	5.0%
Wages	20.0%
Purchases	56.6%
Depreciation	1.3%
Marketing	1.1%
Rent & Utilities	2.3%
Other	13.7%

MARKET SHARE

GNC Holdings, Inc.	3.1%
Vitamin Shoppe, Inc.	0.8%
Vitamin World	0.8%

INDUSTRY TREND

"Online retailers are increasingly competing with industry operators. Many health stores have begun selling CBD products to capture expanding demand. External competition has become an increasing threat to retailers. Millennials will drive health spending. More regulations are expected to be implemented as health concerns continue. Retailers will experience increasing external competition from big-box retailers and e-commerce. Mounting competition from alternative retailers constrains health stores."

Source: IBISWorld Industry at a Glance

- IBISWorld, March 2023: https://www.ibisworld.com
- Natural Foods Merchandiser: https://www.newhope.com/natural-foods-merchandiser
- SFA—Specialty Food Association: https://www.specialtyfood.com

Hearing Aid Clinics

NAICS 621340	SIC 5999-79	Businesses/Units 4,311
Profit $307.2 M	Wages $602.6 M	Annual Growth Future 1.3%
		Annual Growth Past 0.8%

Rules of Thumb
- 80%–100% annual revenues plus inventory
- 4–5 x EBITDA

INDUSTRY MULTIPLES

Acquisition multiples below are calculated medians using US private industry transactions. Data updated annually. Last update: August 2023.

VALUATION MULTIPLE (MEDIAN VALUE)

UNDER $1 MILLION NET SALES
MVIC/Net Sales	0.50
MVIC/Gross Profit	0.52
MVIC/SDE	1.77
MVIC/EBITDA	2.81

$1 MILLION–$5 MILLION NET SALES
MVIC/Net Sales	0.51
MVIC/Gross Profit	0.61
MVIC/SDE	2.90
MVIC/EBITDA	4.72

OVER $5 MILLION NET SALES
MVIC/Net Sales	2.64
MVIC/Gross Profit	2.97
MVIC/SDE	N/A
MVIC/EBITDA	18.93

Source: DealStats (formerly Pratt's Stats), 2023 (Portland, OR: Business Valuation Resources, LLC), www.bvresources.com/dealstats

PRICING TIPS

Larger practices will command the higher valuations, particularly if the owner is absentee and trained dispensers are in place.

BENCHMARK DATA

STATISTICS (HEARING AID CLINICS)
Number of Establishments	4,311
Average Profit Margin	12.4%
Revenue per Employee	$212,000
Average Number of Employees	2.8
Average Wages per Employee	$51,364

PRODUCTS AND SERVICES SEGMENTATION
| Digital hearing aids | 50.0% |
| Analog hearing aids | 33.0% |

Batteries and accessories 14.8%
Other 2.2%

MAJOR MARKET SEGMENTATION

Consumers aged 65 and older 41.9%
Consumers aged 55 to 64 . . . . . 25.6%
Consumers aged 45 to 54 . . . . . 14.0%
Consumers aged 18 to 34 . . . . . 7.0%
Consumers aged 35 to 44 . . . . . 7.0%
Consumers younger than 18 . . . . 4.5%

INDUSTRY COSTS

Profit 12.4%
Wages 24.3%
Purchases 47.0%
Depreciation 2.1%
Marketing 0.9%
Rent & Utilities 1.9%
Other 11.4%

MARKET SHARE

Starkey Hearing Technologies 25.5%
Amplifon USA 12.7%
Sonova Holding AG 11.1%
William Demant Holding Group. . . . 5.6%

$300K in sales per dispenser

EXPENSES (% OF ANNUAL SALES)

Cost of Goods . . . . . . 20% to 30%
Occupancy Costs . . . . . 05% to 10%
Payroll/Labor Costs. . . . . 20% to 25%
Profit (pretax) . . . . . . 18% to 20%

QUESTIONS

- Is this business free from liens/encumbrances with vendors that would prohibit the sale of the practice?
- Are any loyalty agreements or right of first refusals in place?

INDUSTRY TREND

Continuing to increase as baby boomers enter market and the stigma of wearing hearing aids decreases.

"The increasing prevalence of diabetes is attributed to rising levels of hearing loss. The industry has benefited from the growth in disposable income during the period. IBISWorld estimates that the number of industry operators has decreased. The growth of large manufacturers with a retail presence is anticipated to lead to profit expansion. Federal funding for Medicare and Medicaid is expected to rise. Industry operators will likely experience rising competition from online retailers. The industry has benefited from the expansion of federally funded healthcare."

Source: IBISWorld Industry at a Glance

EXPERT COMMENTS

Market for audiology and hearing aids is expanding as baby boomers enter the market. Franchises such as Miracle-Ear and Beltone reduce obstacles to entry and increase ease of replication.

FINANCING

Manufacturers offer financing if customers commit to purchasing their products. Many acquisitions require an earnout based on sales and/or profit.

RESOURCES

- IBISWorld, October 2022: https://www.ibisworld.com
- AAA—American Academy of Audiology: https://www.audiology.org/
- ASHA—American Speech-Language-Hearing Association: https://www.asha.org/
- AudiologyOnline: https://www.audiologyonline.com/
- MAA—Massachusetts Academy of Audiology: https://audiology-mass.org/

Heating Oil Dealers

| NAICS 454310

Rules of Thumb

- 25% annual sales plus inventory
- 2.5 x SDE plus inventory
- 3–3.5 x EBIT
- 3–4 x EBITDA

INDUSTRY MULTIPLES

Acquisition multiples below are calculated medians using US private industry transactions. Data updated annually. Last update: August 2023.

VALUATION MULTIPLE (MEDIAN VALUE)

UNDER $1 MILLION NET SALES
MVIC/Net Sales.	0.48
MVIC/Gross Profit	1.10
MVIC/SDE	1.86
MVIC/EBITDA	1.83

$1 MILLION–$5 MILLION NET SALES
MVIC/Net Sales.	0.31
MVIC/Gross Profit	0.79
MVIC/SDE	2.95
MVIC/EBITDA	4.46

OVER $5 MILLION NET SALES
MVIC/Net Sales.	0.16
MVIC/Gross Profit	1.02
MVIC/SDE	3.01
MVIC/EBITDA	5.62

Source: DealStats (formerly Pratt's Stats), 2023 (Portland, OR: Business Valuation Resources, LLC), www.bvresources.com/dealstats

PRICING TIPS

Purchase price is typically based on FMV of assets plus retained gallonage.

Gross profit per gallon is the main value driver; the higher the better.

There is slow turnover in this industry, as most dealers are 2nd or 3rd generation in the business.

BENCHMARK DATA

Less desirable companies (discounters) are very difficult to sell.

EXPENSES (% OF ANNUAL SALES)

Cost of Goods	60% to 70%
Occupancy Costs	02% to 05%
Payroll/Labor Costs.	10% to 15%
Profit (pretax)	05% to 10%

QUESTIONS

- Are there any environmental concerns; compliance with government regulations?
- 5 years' financials and gallonage history; customer base breakdown by class of customer and type of delivery (automatic or will call); asset listing; Phase I & II environmental reports.

INDUSTRY TREND

Slow decline as customers either upgrade to heating equipment which uses less heating oil or switch to other fuels

EXPERT COMMENTS

Consider the risk involved in getting into this industry as it is a mature industry on the decline.

Customers are switching to other fuels; environmental concerns, industry image; discount competitors.

FINANCING

Outside financing for the assets; seller financing for retained gallonage/intangible value

We typically get cash at closing for fixed assets, and finance the intangibles over 2 to 5 years.

RESOURCES

- API—American Petroleum Institute: https://www.api.org
- EMA—Energy Marketers of America: https://www.energymarketersofamerica.org
- ESEA—Empire State Energy Association: https://eseany.org/index.php
- Fuel Oil News: https://fueloilnews.com/
- NEFI: https://nefi.com/
- PPA—Pennsylvania Petroleum Association: https://www.papetroleum.org/

Heavy Engineering Construction

| NAICS 237990 | Businesses/Units 19,361

| Profit $863.2 M | Wages $6.7 B | Annual Growth Future 0.9%

| Annual Growth Past -4.1%

INDUSTRY MULTIPLES

Acquisition multiples below are calculated medians using US private industry transactions. Data updated annually. Last update: August 2023.

VALUATION MULTIPLE (MEDIAN VALUE)

UNDER $1 MILLION NET SALES

MVIC/Net Sales.	0.50

MVIC/Gross Profit	0.50
MVIC/SDE	2.38
MVIC/EBITDA	2.67

$1 MILLION–$5 MILLION NET SALES

MVIC/Net Sales	0.35
MVIC/Gross Profit	0.66
MVIC/SDE	2.10
MVIC/EBITDA	2.87

OVER $5 MILLION NET SALES

MVIC/Net Sales	0.73
MVIC/Gross Profit	3.98
MVIC/SDE	4.13
MVIC/EBITDA	8.80

Source: DealStats (formerly Pratt's Stats), 2023 (Portland, OR: Business Valuation Resources, LLC), www.bvresources.com/dealstats

BENCHMARK DATA

STATISTICS (HEAVY ENGINEERING CONSTRUCTION)

Number of Establishments	19,361
Average Profit Margin	3.2%
Revenue per Employee	$330,000
Average Number of Employees	4.3
Average Wages per Employee	$81,025

PRODUCTS AND SERVICES SEGMENTATION

Mass transit and railroad construction	56.0%
Conservation and development construction	19.0%
Outdoor recreational areas	12.4%
Harbor and port facilities construction	4.8%
Tunnel construction	2.6%
Other	2.2%
Hydroelectric power plant construction	1.9%
Marine construction	1.1%

MAJOR MARKET SEGMENTATION

Local and state governments	62.8%
Private sector	32.5%
Federal government	4.7%

INDUSTRY COSTS

Profit	3.2%
Wages	24.7%
Purchases	42.2%
Depreciation	3.2%
Marketing	0.1%
Rent & Utilities	4.8%
Other	22.0%

INDUSTRY TREND

"To combat high inflation, the Federal Reserve has consistently raised interest rates. The Biden administration's commitment to investment in infrastructure has reassured industry enterprises. Price surges for crucial inputs like crude oil eased during the COVID-19 pandemic. Aggregate private investment is projected to grow. Downstream freight services will grow in importance. Profit has been increasingly pressured by soaring oil and gas prices. Industry revenue has exhibited conflicting trends due to the COVID-19 pandemic."

Source: IBISWorld Industry at a Glance

RESOURCES
- IBISWorld, January 2023: https://www.ibisworld.com

Heavy Equipment Repair & Maintenance

| NAICS 811310

Rules of Thumb
- 50% SDE plus fixtures, equipment and inventory

INDUSTRY MULTIPLES

Acquisition multiples below are calculated medians using US private industry transactions. Data updated annually. Last update: August 2023.

VALUATION MULTIPLE (MEDIAN VALUE)

UNDER $1 MILLION NET SALES	
MVIC/Net Sales	0.69
MVIC/Gross Profit	0.92
MVIC/SDE	2.39
MVIC/EBITDA	4.60
$1 MILLION–$5 MILLION NET SALES	
MVIC/Net Sales	0.47
MVIC/Gross Profit	1.22
MVIC/SDE	2.70
MVIC/EBITDA	4.89
OVER $5 MILLION NET SALES	
MVIC/Net Sales	0.47
MVIC/Gross Profit	1.44
MVIC/SDE	3.45
MVIC/EBITDA	3.67

Source: DealStats (formerly Pratt's Stats), 2023 (Portland, OR: Business Valuation Resources, LLC), www.bvresources.com/dealstats

PRICING TIPS

Value is based upon fair market value of balance sheet including real estate. Low ROI is based upon required 40 percent equity.

BENCHMARK DATA

Have to look at how numbers are assembled. Manufacturers can supply specific targets as well as how they see your client. Balance sheet composition has a great deal to do with profitability.

QUESTIONS
- What are issues with the local manufacturer's representative?

EXPERT COMMENTS

Buy quality name on the sign.

Suppliers want large, professionally managed dealerships. Move is towards multiunit operations.

FINANCING

Minimal seller financing. Manufacturer may want up to 40 percent equity in the deal.

Hobby Shops

NAICS 451120	SIC 5945-08	Businesses/Units 19,761
Profit $1.1 B	Wages $2.3 B	Annual Growth Future 0.4%
		Annual Growth Past -0.9%

Rules of Thumb
- 20% annual sales plus inventory
- 1.5 x SDE plus inventory

INDUSTRY MULTIPLES

Acquisition multiples below are calculated medians using US private industry transactions. Data updated annually. Last update: August 2023.

VALUATION MULTIPLE (MEDIAN VALUE)

UNDER $1 MILLION NET SALES

MVIC/Net Sales	0.31
MVIC/Gross Profit	0.56
MVIC/SDE	2.02
MVIC/EBITDA	3.92

$1 MILLION–$5 MILLION NET SALES

MVIC/Net Sales	0.38
MVIC/Gross Profit	0.93
MVIC/SDE	3.10
MVIC/EBITDA	8.94

OVER $5 MILLION NET SALES

MVIC/Net Sales	1.10
MVIC/Gross Profit	2.96
MVIC/SDE	N/A
MVIC/EBITDA	8.73

Source: DealStats (formerly Pratt's Stats), 2023 (Portland, OR: Business Valuation Resources, LLC), www.bvresources.com/dealstats

BENCHMARK DATA

STATISTICS (HOBBY & TOY STORES)

Number of Establishments	19,761
Average Profit Margin	5.5%
Revenue per Employee	$166,000
Average Number of Employees	5.9
Average Wages per Employee	$19,449

PRODUCTS AND SERVICES SEGMENTATION

Toys	38.8%
Hobby goods	26.3%
Other	19.2%
Craft Supplies	12.3%
Games (including electronic and video games)	3.4%

MAJOR MARKET SEGMENTATION

Consumers aged 35 to 44	27.0%
Consumers aged 65 and older	21.2%
Consumers aged 45 to 54	18.1%
Consumers aged 25 to 34	18.0%
Consumers aged 55 to 64	10.4%
Consumers younger than 25	5.3%

INDUSTRY COSTS

Profit	5.5%
Wages	11.8%
Purchases	53.2%
Depreciation	0.7%
Marketing	2.1%
Rent & Utilities	6.4%
Other	20.3%

MARKET SHARE

Hobby Lobby Stores Inc.	15.6%
GameStop Corp.	13.1%
Michaels Companies, Inc.	4.7%
Walt Disney Co	2.1%

INDUSTRY TREND

"Increased competition has placed intense price pressures on traditional hobby and toy stores. Industry operators were expected to contend with potential logistics disruptions. Growth in certain product lines is expected to continue to offset the decline in others. The industry will continue to contend with challenges from e-commerce channels. Demand for hobby supplies is expected to continue to rise. IBISWorld expects small-scale industry operators to exit the industry. Large external companies have siphoned revenue away from remaining industry operators."

Source: IBISWorld Industry at a Glance

RESOURCES

- IBISWorld, April 2023: https://www.ibisworld.com
- AFCI—Association For Creative Industries: https://creativeindustries.org
- NRHSA—National Retail Hobby Stores Association: https://www.nrhsa.org

Hog & Pig Farming

	NAICS 112210		Businesses/Units 15,191

	Profit $3.4 B		Wages $821 M		Annual Growth Future -0.1%

					Annual Growth Past 2.6%

BENCHMARK DATA

STATISTICS (HOG & PIG FARMING)

Number of Establishments	15,191
Average Profit Margin	11.8%
Revenue per Employee	$711,000
Average Number of Employees	2.6
Average Wages per Employee	$20,266

PRODUCTS AND SERVICES SEGMENTATION

Market hogs	74.4%
Feeder pigs	13.6%
Breeding stock	6.8%
Cull stock	5.2%

MAJOR MARKET SEGMENTATION

Pig and hog processors	58.6%
Other pig farmers	41.3%
Export and other	0.1%

INDUSTRY COSTS

Profit	11.8%
Wages	2.9%
Purchases	31.4%
Depreciation	6.6%
Marketing	1.0%
Rent & Utilities	13.1%
Other	33.2%

INDUSTRY TREND

"The trade war with China boosted revenue, though not as much as it could have. The price of poultry, one of the industry's main substitutes, grew at nearly double the rate of the price of red meat in 2021. Droughts have raised the cost of feed and reduced profit..Declining meat prices will lower revenue. Export volumes will continue to be very low. Investments into automation and biotech will boost efficiency for farmers. Exports to China skyrocketed in 2020 and 2021 before dropping back down to pre-period levels."

Source: IBISWorld Industry at a Glance

RESOURCES

• IBISWorld, March 2023: https://www.ibisworld.com

Home Builders

	NAICS 23611		Businesses/Units 385,547	
	Profit $7.4 B		Wages $16.9 B		Annual Growth Future 0.1%
					Annual Growth Past 1.5%

INDUSTRY MULTIPLES

Acquisition multiples below are calculated medians using US private industry transactions. Data updated annually. Last update: August 2023.

VALUATION MULTIPLE (MEDIAN VALUE)

UNDER $1 MILLION NET SALES

MVIC/Net Sales	0.38
MVIC/Gross Profit	0.68
MVIC/SDE	1.83
MVIC/EBITDA	2.08

$1 MILLION–$5 MILLION NET SALES

MVIC/Net Sales	0.33
MVIC/Gross Profit	0.95
MVIC/SDE	2.42
MVIC/EBITDA	2.48

OVER $5 MILLION NET SALES

MVIC/Net Sales	0.47
MVIC/Gross Profit	2.00
MVIC/SDE	2.65
MVIC/EBITDA	6.40

Source: DealStats (formerly Pratt's Stats), 2023 (Portland, OR: Business Valuation Resources, LLC), www.bvresources.com/dealstats

BENCHMARK DATA

STATISTICS (HOME BUILDERS)

Number of Establishments	385,547
Average Profit Margin	6.0%
Revenue per Employee	$198,000
Average Number of Employees	1.7
Average Wages per Employee	$26,990

PRODUCTS AND SERVICES SEGMENTATION

Stucco exterior homes	26.7%
Vinyl siding exterior homes	26.1%
Fiber cement exterior homes	22.2%
Brick exterior homes	18.7%
Wood exterior homes	4.3%
Other exterior homes	2.0%

MAJOR MARKET SEGMENTATION

Property developers for private sector clients	84.4%
Households	14.0%
State or locally funded projects	1.1%
Federally funded projects	0.5%

INDUSTRY COSTS

Profit	6.0%
Wages	13.6%
Purchases	70.5%
Depreciation	0.5%
Marketing	0.5%
Rent & Utilities	3.2%
Other	5.8%

MARKET SHARE

NVR, Inc.	7.5%

INDUSTRY TREND

"The affordable end of the market has been squeezed from every side. Land costs have risen steeply in booming parts of the country. Construction materials and government fees have become more expensive. And communities nationwide are far more prescriptive today than decades ago about what housing should look like and how big it must be....From a builder's view, there's nothing particularly preferable about higher-end homes. Their profit margins aren't generally higher. They demand more customization. They're riskier to build in economic downtimes. Entry-level housing, on the other hand, is invariably in deep demand."

Source: "Whatever Happened to the Starter Home?" by Emily Badger, September 25, 2022, https://www.nytimes.com/2022/09/25/upshot/starter-home-prices.html

"Homebuilders received a large chunk of the Paycheck Protection Program. Interest rates increased toward the end of the period to fight off inflationary concerns. Many cities have affordable housing programs. Housing starts are set to dip. Increasing tuition costs will only discourage students from purchasing homes. More affordable housing projects will provide a source of relief for homebuilders. Home builders also cut expenses and raised profit by hiring subcontractors."

Source: IBISWorld Industry at a Glance

RESOURCES

- IBISWorld, January 2023: https://www.ibisworld.com
- NAHB—National Association of Home Builders: https://www.nahb.org

Home Centers

	NAICS 444110		Businesses/Units 8,201
	Profit $34.5 B		Wages $23 B		Annual Growth Future 0.8%
					Annual Growth Past 3.6%

Rules of Thumb

- 40%–45% annual sales includes inventory
- 2 x SDE plus inventory

INDUSTRY MULTIPLES

Acquisition multiples below are calculated medians using US private industry transactions. Data updated annually. Last update: August 2023.

VALUATION MULTIPLE (MEDIAN VALUE)

UNDER $1 MILLION NET SALES

MVIC/Net Sales	0.18
MVIC/Gross Profit	0.32
MVIC/SDE	1.62
MVIC/EBITDA	3.47

$1 MILLION–$5 MILLION NET SALES

MVIC/Net Sales	0.33
MVIC/Gross Profit	0.36
MVIC/SDE	2.33
MVIC/EBITDA	9.01

OVER $5 MILLION NET SALES

MVIC/Net Sales	0.76
MVIC/Gross Profit	1.83
MVIC/SDE	3.34
MVIC/EBITDA	8.55

Source: DealStats (formerly Pratt's Stats), 2023 (Portland, OR: Business Valuation Resources, LLC), www.bvresources.com/dealstats

PRICING TIPS

Tend to be asset value sales

BENCHMARK DATA

STATISTICS (HOME IMPROVEMENT STORES)

Number of Establishments	8,201
Average Profit Margin	13.5%
Revenue per Employee	$355,000
Average Number of Employees	88.8
Average Wages per Employee	$31,840

PRODUCTS AND SERVICES SEGMENTATION

Lumber and other building and structural materials	31.9%
Household appliances, kitchen goods and housewares	30.7%
Hardware, tools and plumbing and electrical supplies	24.1%
Lawn, garden and farm equipment supplies	13.3%

MAJOR MARKET SEGMENTATION

Professionals	79.7%
Do-it-yourself customers	20.3%

INDUSTRY COSTS

Profit	13.5%
Wages	9.0%

```
Purchases    .    .    .    .    .    .    . 57.2%
Depreciation    .    .    .    .    .    .    1.0%
Marketing   .    .    .    .    .    .    .    0.8%
Rent & Utilities .    .    .    .    .    .    1.9%
Other    .    .    .    .    .    .    .    . 16.5%
```

MARKET SHARE

```
Home Depot Inc.    .    .    .    .    .    . 53.3%
Lowe's Companies Inc. .    .    .    .    . 36.2%
Menard, Inc..    .    .    .    .    .    .    6.2%
```

EXPENSES (% OF ANNUAL SALES)

```
Cost of Goods  .    .    .    .    .    65% to 70%
Occupancy Costs   .    .    .    .    05% to 06%
Payroll/Labor Costs.    .    .    .    12% to 15%
Profit (pretax)   .    .    .    .    .    10% to 15%
```

QUESTIONS

- How do you compete with the competition? Is it through franchise-type buying power?
- Why are you selling? Are there any potential franchise or refurbishment costs that may be included in the sale?
- Does any one contractor represent more than 10 percent of your lumber business? This is a personality business. If the old owner goes, the customer might leave too.

INDUSTRY TREND

"The industry is highly sensitive to price. Profit will likely rise due to increasing demand and successful cost saving initiatives by industry operators. Demand is anticipated to normalize as projects are completed and individuals have less free time. Competition may largely mitigate industry enterprise growth. Small- and mid-sized industry operators may need to implement similar customer analytics technology to stay relevant. Consumer's access to credit is likely to fall for an unforeseeable amount of time. The industry experiences high levels of price competition."

Source: IBISWorld Industry at a Glance

EXPERT COMMENTS

The high capital costs for inventory and fixtures and the lack of good locations are significant barriers to entry.

RESOURCES

- IBISWorld, March 2023: https://www.ibisworld.com

Home Furnishing Merchant Wholesalers

| NAICS 423220 | Businesses/Units 12,807 |

| Profit $2.3 B | Wages $6.5 B | Annual Growth Future -0.2% |
| | | Annual Growth Past -1.5% |

INDUSTRY MULTIPLES

Acquisition multiples below are calculated medians using US private industry transactions. Data updated annually. Last update: August 2023.

VALUATION MULTIPLE (MEDIAN VALUE)

UNDER $1 MILLION NET SALES

MVIC/Net Sales	0.64
MVIC/Gross Profit	1.08
MVIC/SDE	2.54
MVIC/EBITDA	2.89

$1 MILLION–$5 MILLION NET SALES

MVIC/Net Sales	0.77
MVIC/Gross Profit	1.57
MVIC/SDE	3.57
MVIC/EBITDA	4.14

OVER $5 MILLION NET SALES

MVIC/Net Sales	0.59
MVIC/Gross Profit	1.81
MVIC/SDE	5.69
MVIC/EBITDA	7.23

Source: DealStats (formerly Pratt's Stats), 2023 (Portland, OR: Business Valuation Resources, LLC), www.bvresources.com/dealstats

BENCHMARK DATA

STATISTICS (HOME FURNISHING WHOLESALING)

Number of Establishments	12,807
Average Profit Margin	3.1%
Revenue per Employee	$771,000
Average Number of Employees	7.5
Average Wages per Employee	$67,890

PRODUCTS AND SERVICES SEGMENTATION

Flooring and floor coverings	48.1%
Kitchenware, pots, pans	14.2%
Decorative furnishings	13.9%
Linens, bedding and other household textiles	10.1%
Other	7.9%
Window treatments	5.8%

MAJOR MARKET SEGMENTATION

Retailers for resale	49.4%
Other wholesalers	24.9%
Building contractors and construction	12.4%
Other	8.6%
Businesses for end-use	4.7%

INDUSTRY COSTS

Profit	3.1%
Wages	8.8%
Purchases	67.0%
Depreciation	0.6%
Marketing	0.9%
Rent & Utilities	2.1%
Other	17.6%

MARKET SHARE

Shaw Industries Group, Inc.	6.4%
Mohawk Industries, Inc.	2.8%
Newell Brands Inc.	2.3%

INDUSTRY TREND

"Home improvement buoyed revenue through the COVID-19 pandemic. Falling per capita disposable income in 2022 led to a decline in investment in home improvements. Falling construction values have lessened demand for home furnishing products and led to revenue losses. Private investment in home improvement will decline. Wholesalers will continue to face brutal external competition. Profit will compress as input costs rise and price competition remains fierce. Many home furnishing manufacturers have rolled out internalized distribution processes and sold goods directly to retailers."

Source: IBISWorld Industry at a Glance

RESOURCES

• IBISWorld, February 2023: https://www.ibisworld.com

Home Health Care Rental

	NAICS 532283		SIC 5999-20		Businesses/Units 2,617
	Profit $378.8 M		Wages $1.4 B		Annual Growth Future -2.3%
					Annual Growth Past 0.8%

Rules of Thumb

• 4 x EBITDA

INDUSTRY MULTIPLES

Acquisition multiples below are calculated medians using US private industry transactions. Data updated annually. Last update: August 2023.

VALUATION MULTIPLE (MEDIAN VALUE)

UNDER $1 MILLION NET SALES
MVIC/Net Sales .	1.40
MVIC/Gross Profit	1.46
MVIC/SDE	7.71
MVIC/EBITDA	4.01

$1 MILLION–$5 MILLION NET SALES
MVIC/Net Sales .	0.61
MVIC/Gross Profit	0.79
MVIC/SDE	2.80
MVIC/EBITDA	6.81

OVER $5 MILLION NET SALES   N/A

Source: DealStats (formerly Pratt's Stats), 2023 (Portland, OR: Business Valuation Resources, LLC), www.bvresources.com/dealstats

PRICING TIPS

Payor mix (Medicare, Medicaid, commercial, etc.)? How many "capped" patients?

BENCHMARK DATA

STATISTICS (HOME MEDICAL EQUIPMENT RENTALS)
Number of Establishments .	2,617
Average Profit Margin	7.5%
Revenue per Employee .	$198,000
Average Number of Employees .	9.6
Average Wages per Employee .	$54,471

PRODUCTS AND SERVICES SEGMENTATION
Oxygen and respiratory therapy equipment	56.5%
Other medical equipment	17.4%
Mobility aid equipment .	14.3%
Diabetic therapy equipment	11.8%

MAJOR MARKET SEGMENTATION

Privately insured individuals	.39.5%
Medicare/Medicaid insured individuals	.30.2%
Uninsured individuals and other	.20.1%
State and local governments	.10.2%

INDUSTRY COSTS

Profit	. 7.5%
Wages	.27.5%
Purchases	. 4.9%
Depreciation	.26.4%
Marketing	. 0.9%
Rent & Utilities	. 5.7%
Other	.27.1%

MARKET SHARE

Lincare Holdings Inc.	.11.0%

EXPENSES (% OF ANNUAL SALES)

Cost of Goods	10%
Occupancy Costs	04%
Payroll/Labor Costs.	20%
Profit (pretax)	18%

INDUSTRY TREND

"Senior citizens and people with disabilities drive demand for industry services. The current administration has increased access to Medicare and Medicaid. While profit is high, it is not as high as it was before the bidding program. The aging population has driven demand for home care. The competitive bidding program may be expanded to Medicaid. Profit is unlikely due to the effects of the competitive bidding process. Medicare payments to operators have fallen significantly due to recent regulatory changes."

Source: IBISWorld Industry at a Glance

EXPERT COMMENTS

Industry demand is growing, but margins continue to decline as CMS (Centers for Medicare & Medicaid Services) reduces reimbursement to providers.

RESOURCES

- IBISWorld, April 2023: https://www.ibisworld.com
- HME News: http://www.hmenews.com

Home Health Care/Home Care Agencies

| NAICS 621610 | Businesses/Units 455,113 |

| Profit $10.2 B | Wages $63.1 B | Annual Growth Future 5.7% |

| | | Annual Growth Past 3.4% |

Rules of Thumb

- 50%–60% annual sales plus inventory
- 3–4 x SDE plus inventory
- 4–5 x EBIT
- 4–6 x EBITDA

INDUSTRY MULTIPLES

Acquisition multiples below are calculated medians using US private industry transactions. Data updated annually. Last update: August 2023.

VALUATION MULTIPLE (MEDIAN VALUE)

UNDER $1 MILLION NET SALES

MVIC/Net Sales.	0.40
MVIC/Gross Profit	0.69
MVIC/SDE	2.53
MVIC/EBITDA	4.62

$1 MILLION–$5 MILLION NET SALES

MVIC/Net Sales.	0.52
MVIC/Gross Profit	0.82
MVIC/SDE	3.03
MVIC/EBITDA	4.91

OVER $5 MILLION NET SALES

MVIC/Net Sales.	1.09
MVIC/Gross Profit	2.37
MVIC/SDE	5.31
MVIC/EBITDA	9.36

Source: DealStats (formerly Pratt's Stats), 2023 (Portland, OR: Business Valuation Resources, LLC), www.bvresources.com/dealstats

PRICING TIPS

Look for client census; is it increasing or on a down trend? If so, ask why.

The EBITDA multiple is the most consistent predictor of market value. Using revenue to estimate value is irrelevant due to the wide range of margins home care agencies earn in the industry.

Businesses under $1M in revenue, 2.5x SDE; businesses $1M and above, 3 to 3.5x; independent (nonfranchise) with revenues over $3M can go for 4x SDE.

Home care agencies are most commonly sold on an SDE basis, SDE being defined as net income plus noncash expenses and owner-related expenses (wages, tax on wages, travel, cars, 401k match)—and less day-to-day services that the owner provides the operation. For example, if the owner does the bookkeeping, we'd include a negative add-back for the value of that service.

Things can get murky when the add-backs become more esoteric and small. Be practical.

Certainly, the recent changes in the prime interest rate will affect the multiple. We've not seen enough closed sales in this new rate environment to understand the effect—but that will be known in time.

The valuation multiple is mostly influenced by the size of the agency; i.e., an agency with $200K SDE may trade for 3 x, while an agency with $1M SDE may trade for 4.5+ x. Staffing and customer concentration are key business issues to evaluate.

The SDE multiple tends to be the best multiple to use.

In our inventory of closed deals, the most influential metrics, in descending order of importance, are these:1. SDE amount and SDE percent of revenues. Good operators—SDE margin is in the range of 12 to 15 percent. Excellent operators achieve an SDE margin in the 15 to 20 percent range. SDE in excess of $400K to $500K provide prospective buyers with the ability to service acquisition debt, pay themselves, and hire resources for growth. 2. Qualitative elements including culture, online reputation, nonreliance on the owner for day-to-day, management strength, and recruiting and retention strategies.3. For franchised businesses, the size, density, and household income/net worth is critical to current and future success. 4. History or stable and growing top and bottom lines.

Recast the P&L and/or tax return; sellers usually mingle many of the personal expenses with the business. Look out for family-related staff members' salaries and additional bonuses. Adjust to normal market salary. If replacing the administrator, you need to calculate the salary factor for a new quality admin.

BENCHMARK DATA

STATISTICS (HOME CARE PROVIDERS)

Number of Establishments	455,113
Average Profit Margin	7.5%
Revenue per Employee	$64,800
Average Number of Employees.	4.9
Average Wages per Employee	$30,032

PRODUCTS AND SERVICES SEGMENTATION

Traditional home healthcare and home nursing care . .	.55.2%
Home hospice	.29.2%
Homemaker and personal services.	6.4%
Other	6.1%
Home therapy services	3.1%

MAJOR MARKET SEGMENTATION

Medicare	.38.0%
Medicaid	.34.7%
Private insurance	.12.9%
Out-of-pocket	.10.7%
Other	3.7%

INDUSTRY COSTS

Profit	7.5%
Wages	.46.3%
Purchases	6.8%
Depreciation	1.1%
Marketing	0.6%
Rent & Utilities	2.9%
Other	.34.8%

Healthy businesses have 15 percent and up net margin

Pay per hour to an LPN or RN; rates can vary depending upon the caregiver, ranging from patient companion at minimum wage to a certified home health aid at $20.

Cost of goods sold is generally between 45 and 55 percent of revenue. All labor-related costs from caregivers. Admin staff is usually about 10 percent of revenue. A healthy SDE percent of revenue is 15 percent. If the SDE is higher than 20 percent, it is probably understaffed.

SDE above 16 percent is quite good.

EXPENSES (% OF ANNUAL SALES)

Cost of Goods	50% to 60%
Occupancy Costs	02% to 12%
Payroll/Labor Costs.	55% to 65%
Profit (pretax)	10% to 15%

QUESTIONS

- Why are they selling? How can the business grow and how can census increase?

- Workers' comp experience? Owner hours of involvement based on how well he/she is delegating?
- What advice would you give me in running your company once I buy it? What didn't you do and why?
- What is the current census? What is the client retention? Hours serviced? Rate per hour? Caregiver retention? What are the caregiver recruitment procedures?
- Employee tenure, compensation, benefits, last pay raise? Customer concentration? Price sheet and last increase? Caregiver turnover? State license requirements? The franchise approval process for new owners, if applicable? PR and legal issues over the past 5 years? Target market (demographics and geography)?
- What percentage is private pay? How do you recruit personnel? How do you obtain clients? What licenses and/or agreements are in place? Are there territory restrictions?
- If you were to continue running your company, what changes or growth ideas would you work towards? How do you create and foster an excellent culture in your company? Tell me more about your management team, strengths, and opportunities.
- Insurance contracts in place? Any legal issues pending with the licensing and/or the agency?
- Who are the referral sources? and how transferable are they for the new owner?
- Any third-party business valuation? Tax returns? P&Ls and balance sheets? Past legal or PR issues?
- What are the risks?
- Ask about client rates, private pay vs. Medicaid rates, caregiver pay rates, and margins. Track to see if census is going up or down, or stays the same, and why.
- Have you had any deficiencies? What software system do you use? Do you provide devices for staff in the field, or do you do bring your own device (BYOD)? Any length of stay issues for hospice? Are you a certificate of need (CON) or not?

INDUSTRY TREND

These companion-care businesses are in high demand as the population ages and wants to stay home and not be in a nursing home or facility.

More investment by outsiders; more strategic partnerships; more governmental involvement

There is a high need for this business as the population ages and in-home care services are generally preferred and cost effective.

It will continue to grow and, among franchise concepts, is one of the most sustainable and stable sectors.

The aging population continues to grow, which in turn will help the industry to grow as well.

"Excess moisture, faulty structuring and bad wiring. Those are some of the common issues that arise in the seniors' homes. But the home is where seniors want to remain as they age. That's why the University of Pittsburgh is trying to push the needle forward with its healthy home lab. The project brings together researchers from multiple disciplines with the goal of improving the viability of the home environment in order to support aging in place. This means tackling some of the biggest challenges associated with aging in place and developing the right technology solutions.

"'The primary group that the initiative brings together is the health care services and technology field,' Everette James, executive director of the Healthy Home Lab, told Home Health Care News. 'We have occupational therapists, physical therapists, a lot of engineers and we've got people from nursing and people from geriatric medicine. We've got environmental experts. We've brought together this group of researchers that have been working on aging in place and supporting people with disabilities and seniors.' But these researchers are not trying to solve these challenges in a vacuum. Instead, the university purchased a 105-year-old Pittsburgh home in April. This home is a demonstration site and community laboratory that will allow them to test solutions, develop interventions and to train students to be able to care for people in the home....

"James noted that Medicare is starting to get behind the types of solutions the healthy home lab is developing."

Source: "How a University Is Using a 105-Year-Old Home to Solve Aging-in-Place Challenges" by Joyce Famakinwa, September 27, 2022, https://homehealthcarenews.com/2022/09/university-of-pittsburgh-is-using-a-105-year-home-to-solve-aging-in-place-challenges/

This industry will continue to grow; there is a cost advantage of seeing patients at their own home.

"Home care providers have expanded their role in the healthcare sector. The COVID-19 pandemic initially reduced industry demand. The industry has been thrust into the governmental spotlight. Home care providers have benefited from an aging population. The healthcare reform legislation has provided numerous benefits and drawbacks to home care. This high demand for staff is projected to increase nurses' and physical therapists' ability to command higher wages and benefits. Despite strong growth, industry profit has been under pressure."

Source: IBISWorld Industry at a Glance

EXPERT COMMENTS

Sellers: have good books and records.

Buyer: negotiate a longer-term training and transition period, even if seller needs to get paid for the additional time. Seller: prepare for a sale early, and when the business is at peak performance, choose an experienced broker who is familiar with the industry.

Companies that have medical accreditations and also personnel to handle medical care such as wound care, respiratory care—i.e., LPN or RN services—are becoming much more desirable than nonmedical care businesses. For example, it can take 18 months to apply for and receive a Medicare license, which on its own is valuable right now.

A medical background is preferred for lending, unless the business is a franchise with ample training and a well-known trusted name; however, buyers prefer non-franchised locations, which have the ability to grow in any area without restriction. An at-home agency is also more valuable than brick-and-mortar care homes due to the home being, in most cases, more costly to purchase than the business itself. Being able to stay at home and have assistance come to your personal home is preferred and much more profitable. There are many facets of medical and nonmedical businesses.

Although the general population continues to age and will need this type of service, DDD licenses are limited.

H

Nonfranchise is preferred by buyers; however, franchised locations tend to have more sales due to brand recognition and footprint. A DDD license, if obtained, adds another layer of profitability which amplifies the value. Private pay vs. Medicare, Medicaid, and/or AHCCCS is also considered, as well as the general local areas where the service is located.

It is easy to get into this business with a home care license, but it is very difficult to scale. Larger organizations tend to have a competitive advantage and require less hands-on work from the owner(s).

Engage in business exit planning as early as you can. Optimally, you should begin planning 2 to 3 years prior to selling.

For sellers, keep good records and books; for buyers, keep an eye on the census trends.

It is recommended to purchase an agency which already has signed contracts with most private insurances. Buyer must be experienced in the industry to succeed.

Barriers to entry are low; however, building a profitable agency is very hard.

For buyers—it is not an easy business to get into and become successful at. You must wear many hats and manage several areas. It is a relationship business; therefore, one should be good at relationship building, communication, etc. Also money management; it will be the foundation of the business. For sellers—make sure you have clean books and your margins are healthy. You will also want to ensure you have multiple referral sources and are well branded in your community. You want to be at the peak of your business when you want to sell, or begin to consider it. Make sure the business can operate without you in it. Do not brand yourself to the referrals and community; they should know you, but the quality of service should be the system and the people you have implementing those systems—not you.

Home care, hospice, home health, assisted living, and skilled nursing facilities are a very competitive market—and because it is patient care–based demand and primarily the elder community, there are many in the industry, so competition is very high. The best agencies providing the best quality care out there, however, will rise above the rest if they are delivering quality care through streamlined processes and systems, keeping wide margins, and hiring quality staff. Senior care is only going to increase as our aging population grows, so the industry trend is excellent.

FINANCING

SBA 7a, with some seller paper being entertained (15 to 20 percent of the time). Current terms are a mix: – 7a core loans, 10-year amortization, 1.5 to 2.5 percent interest rate margin over prime, fixed, and variable- We are now seeing some split deals with 5 years fixed, then 5 years floating.

Collateral is typical SBA.

The typical purchase structure is 80 percent SBA loan, 10 percent buyer down payment, and 10 percent seller financing. Seller keeps working capital, including A/R. The buyer does not assume any of the seller's liabilities with the purchase.

Most buyers seek SBA 7a financing for business acquisitions in this sector. Historically, buyers (and lenders) appreciated the seller offering some sort of seller note for about 10 percent of the purchase price. Buyers feel that a seller's note keeps the seller in the game and provides some form of leverage for the buyer. Advice to buyers is to avoid seller notes for two reasons: 1. Seller notes typically have shorter amortization periods (36 to 48 months). While SBA 7a loans are 10 years in amortization, there is no logical reason that a buyer should want to shorten amortization periods, since that increases the committed debt service amount. 2. Misconception of leverage: barring intentional fraud, seller notes are always guaranteed by the buyer. As such, the note cannot be used as leverage in some postclosing negotiation. The seller will simply sue the buyer for nonpayment.

Other elements of typical home care deals include these:1. Licensing—In some jurisdictions, changing ownership and securing required licenses can be a significant hurdle. 2. Franchise authorization—For franchised deals, the franchisor will have some process that buyers will need to complete.

RESOURCES

- IBISWorld, January 2023: https://www.ibisworld.com
- CAHSAH—California Association for Health Services at Home: https://cahsah.org/
- HCAOA—Home Care Association of America: https://www.hcaoa.org
- Home Health Care News: https://homehealthcarenews.com
- Homecare United: https://www.homecareunited.com
- NAHC—National Association for Home Care & Hospice: https://www.nahc.org
- SCSA—Society of Certified Senior Advisors: https://www.csa.us/
- The Joint Commission: https://www.jointcommission.org

Home Helpers (Franchise)

| NAICS 621610 | Businesses/Units 303

Rules of Thumb

- 40%–45% annual sales plus inventory

INDUSTRY MULTIPLES

Acquisition multiples below are calculated medians using US private industry transactions. Data updated annually. Last update: August 2023.

VALUATION MULTIPLE (MEDIAN VALUE)

UNDER $1 MILLION NET SALES

MVIC/Net Sales.	0.40
MVIC/Gross Profit	0.69
MVIC/SDE	2.53
MVIC/EBITDA	4.62

$1 MILLION–$5 MILLION NET SALES

MVIC/Net Sales.	0.52
MVIC/Gross Profit	0.82
MVIC/SDE	3.03
MVIC/EBITDA	4.91

OVER $5 MILLION NET SALES

MVIC/Net Sales.	1.09
MVIC/Gross Profit	2.37
MVIC/SDE	5.31
MVIC/EBITDA	9.36

Source: DealStats (formerly Pratt's Stats), 2023 (Portland, OR: Business Valuation Resources, LLC), www.bvresources.com/dealstats

Approx. Total Investment: $99,950 to $149,350

RESOURCES

- Home Helpers: https://www.homehelpershomecare.com
- Franchise information: https://www.homehelpersfranchise.com

Home Inspection

| NAICS 541350 | Businesses/Units 30,324

| Profit $477.8 M | Wages $1.8 B | Annual Growth Future -0.3%

                                          | Annual Growth Past 1.6%

Rules of Thumb

- 45% annual sales includes inventory

INDUSTRY MULTIPLES

Acquisition multiples below are calculated medians using US private industry transactions. Data updated annually. Last update: August 2023.

VALUATION MULTIPLE (MEDIAN VALUE)

UNDER $1 MILLION NET SALES

MVIC/Net Sales	0.70
MVIC/Gross Profit	0.77
MVIC/SDE	1.72
MVIC/EBITDA	3.58

$1 MILLION–$5 MILLION NET SALES

MVIC/Net Sales	0.37
MVIC/Gross Profit	0.37
MVIC/SDE	2.10
MVIC/EBITDA	2.94

OVER $5 MILLION NET SALES   N/A

Source: DealStats (formerly Pratt's Stats), 2023 (Portland, OR: Business Valuation Resources, LLC), www.bvresources.com/dealstats

BENCHMARK DATA

STATISTICS (BUILDING INSPECTORS)

Number of Establishments	30,324
Average Profit Margin	9.6%
Revenue per Employee	$110,000
Average Number of Employees	1.5
Average Wages per Employee	$40,595

PRODUCTS AND SERVICES SEGMENTATION

Home inspection services	39.5%
Other	19.4%
Commercial building inspection services	16.2%
Specific element inspection services	15.7%
New home construction inspection services	9.2%

MAJOR MARKET SEGMENTATION

Home buyers and sellers	35.0%
Commercial and other markets	31.0%
Government	18.9%
Contractors	15.1%

INDUSTRY COSTS

Profit	9.6%
Wages	36.7%
Purchases	8.7%
Depreciation	1.4%
Marketing	0.5%
Rent & Utilities	4.2%
Other	38.9%

INDUSTRY TREND

"A booming real estate market boosted demand for building inspections. Rising inflationary pressures dampen industry growth. Growth in nonemployers diversifies industry presence. Heightened inflationary pressures will negatively influence real estate markets. Strong government investment will fuel new revenue stream for the industry. Altered consumer behavior following the COVID-19 pandemic will influence inspections frequency. Rising per capita disposable income and low housing stock have bolstered demand."

Source: IBISWorld Industry at a Glance

RESOURCES

- IBISWorld, February 2023: https://www.ibisworld.com
- ASHI—American Society of Home Inspectors: https://www.homeinspector.org
- Home Inspector magazine, published by OREP, Organization of Real Estate Professionals: https://www.workingre.com/home-inspector-magazine-news/
- ISHI—International Society of Home Inspectors: http://www.ishionline.org/

Horse & Other Equine Production

| NAICS 112920 | Businesses/Units 164,385

| Profit $328.2 M | Wages $520.6 M | Annual Growth Future 0.5%

| Annual Growth Past 0.6%

INDUSTRY MULTIPLES

Acquisition multiples below are calculated medians using US private industry transactions. Data updated annually. Last update: August 2023.

VALUATION MULTIPLE (MEDIAN VALUE)

UNDER $1 MILLION NET SALES	N/A
$1 MILLION–$5 MILLION NET SALES	
MVIC/Net Sales	1.32
MVIC/Gross Profit	2.68
MVIC/SDE	11.76
MVIC/EBITDA	11.76
OVER $5 MILLION NET SALES	N/A

Source: DealStats (formerly Pratt's Stats), 2023 (Portland, OR: Business Valuation Resources, LLC), www.bvresources.com/dealstats

BENCHMARK DATA

STATISTICS (HORSE & OTHER EQUINE PRODUCTION)

Number of Establishments	164,385
Average Profit Margin	18.2%
Revenue per Employee	$10,700

Average Number of Employees. 1.0
Average Wages per Employee $3,086

PRODUCTS AND SERVICES SEGMENTATION

Recreational horses. 54.3%
Show horses 21.7%
Racehorses 15.9%
Other horses and equines 8.1%

MAJOR MARKET SEGMENTATION

Horses for farms 39.5%
Horses for personal use 38.8%
Horses for boarding. 9.3%
Horses for breeding. 7.6%
Other 2.6%
Horses for riding stables 2.2%

INDUSTRY COSTS

Profit 18.2%
Wages 28.9%
Purchases 15.0%
Depreciation 15.4%
Marketing 0.5%
Rent & Utilities 6.3%
Other 15.8%

INDUSTRY TREND

"High incomes kept revenue rising during COVID-19. Falling consumer spending has posed a threat to horse and other equine producers. Plunging exports have reduced a major revenue stream for horse farmers. Higher economic growth will boost consumer confidence. The depreciating dollar will provide a new revenue stream for horse farmers. Falling food prices will have disparate effects on the industry. Consumer confidence is key to the industry's strength."

Source: IBISWorld Industry at a Glance

RESOURCES

• IBISWorld, April 2023: https://www.ibisworld.com

Hospitals: Medical and Surgical

| NAICS 622110

Rules of Thumb

• 78% annual sales plus inventory
• 2.7 x SDE plus inventory
• 3 x EBIT

INDUSTRY MULTIPLES

Acquisition multiples below are calculated medians using US private industry transactions. Data updated annually. Last update: August 2023.

VALUATION MULTIPLE (MEDIAN VALUE)

UNDER $1 MILLION NET SALES	N/A
$1 MILLION–$5 MILLION NET SALES	
MVIC/Net Sales.	7.99
MVIC/Gross Profit	20.62

```
MVIC/SDE  .    .    .    .    .    .    .    .    N/A
MVIC/EBITDA  .    .    .    .    .    .    .    N/A
```
OVER $5 MILLION NET SALES
```
MVIC/Net Sales.    .    .    .    .    .    .    1.37
MVIC/Gross Profit  .    .    .    .    .    .    3.71
MVIC/SDE  .    .    .    .    .    .    .    .    N/A
MVIC/EBITDA  .    .    .    .    .    .    .    15.91
```

Source: DealStats (formerly Pratt's Stats), 2023 (Portland, OR: Business Valuation Resources, LLC), www.bvresources.com/dealstats

PRICING TIPS

Tremendous variation in types of hospitals today. Substantial due diligence is required to determine appropriate EBITDA multiples for a particular hospital at a particular point in time.

BENCHMARK DATA

EXPENSES (% OF ANNUAL SALES)

Cost of Goods	08%
Payroll/Labor Costs.	03%
Profit (pretax)	06%

QUESTIONS

• Payor mix, market share, patient demographic data

INDUSTRY TREND

"'The pandemic proved the need to have flexible space,' said Jim Brexler, chief executive of Doylestown Health. 'The impact of having adequate critical care space was essential, and you don't want to build all that out and not be able to use it for other purposes. This is the future of hospitals,' he added....

"'This is no different from the code updates we go through every time there is an earthquake in California,' said Carlos L. Amato, a health care architect with Cannon Design. 'The lessons learned postpandemic will eventually make it into building codes.'"

Source: "'The Future of Hospitals': Flexible Space for the Next Pandemic" by Debra Kamin, September 13, 2022, https://www.nytimes.com/2022/09/13/business/hospitals-pandemic-flexible-space.html

EXPERT COMMENTS

Due diligence is essential!

Tremendous variation in types of hospitals today. Some are profitable and growing, some are bankrupt and closing. Some have excellent state-of-the-art facilities, while others are closing due to failure to meet required standards.

FINANCING

Outside Financing

RESOURCES

• AHA—American Hospital Association: https://www.aha.org
• HFMA—Healthcare Financial Management Association: https://www.hfma.org
• Levin Associates: https://www.levinassociates.com

Hospitals: Psychiatric and Substance Abuse

| NAICS 622210 | Businesses/Units 789

| Profit $1.8 B | Wages $18.2 B | Annual Growth Future 3.6%

| Annual Growth Past 2.0%

Rules of Thumb
- 78% annual sales plus inventory
- 2.7 x SDE plus inventory
- 3 x EBIT
- 2.9 x EBITDA

INDUSTRY MULTIPLES

Acquisition multiples below are calculated medians using US private industry transactions. Data updated annually. Last update: August 2023.

VALUATION MULTIPLE (MEDIAN VALUE)

UNDER $1 MILLION NET SALES

MVIC/Net Sales	0.54
MVIC/Gross Profit	N/A
MVIC/SDE	1.49
MVIC/EBITDA	N/A

$1 MILLION–$5 MILLION NET SALES	N/A
OVER $5 MILLION NET SALES	N/A

Source: DealStats (formerly Pratt's Stats), 2023 (Portland, OR: Business Valuation Resources, LLC), www.bvresources.com/dealstats

BENCHMARK DATA

STATISTICS (PSYCHIATRIC HOSPITALS)

Number of Establishments	789
Average Profit Margin	5.4%
Revenue per Employee	$125,000
Average Number of Employees	338.0
Average Wages per Employee	$68,919

PRODUCTS AND SERVICES SEGMENTATION

Patient care for mental disorders	67.0%
Other	31.8%
Acute long-term care services	0.6%
Assisted living services	0.5%
Assisted daily living for mental rehabilitation	0.1%

MAJOR MARKET SEGMENTATION

Third-party payers	67.7%
Medicare and Medicaid	28.3%
Out-of-pocket payments	2.8%
Other	1.2%

INDUSTRY COSTS

Profit	5.4%
Wages	54.0%
Purchases	12.8%
Depreciation	2.5%
Marketing	0.2%
Rent & Utilities	1.4%
Other	23.7%

MARKET SHARE

Universal Health Services, Inc. 17.4%	

EXPENSES (% OF ANNUAL SALES)

Cost of Goods	09%
Payroll/Labor Costs.	03%
Profit (pretax)	06%

QUESTIONS

- Payor mix, market share, patient demographic data

INDUSTRY TREND

"The long-term consequences of social isolation or financial stress have increased rates of depression and anxiety. The HHS states that more than two-thirds of mental healthcare spending is generated from government-sponsored healthcare. A nationwide shortage of nurses and psychologists has increased wages. Larger healthcare conglomerates that provide health services will acquire psychiatric facilities. Greater per capita disposable income will allow patients to better pay for expensive hospitalization. The Biden Administration could increase the likelihood of employee unionization. Modernizing hospital therapies will assist in-residence treatments."

Source: IBISWorld Industry at a Glance

FINANCING

Outside Financing

RESOURCES

- IBISWorld, January 2023: https://www.ibisworld.com
- NABH—National Association for Behavioral Healthcare: https://www.nabh.org

Hospitals: Specialty

	NAICS 622310		Businesses/Units 695

| | Profit $8.8 B | | Wages $20.8 B | | Annual Growth Future 3.2% |

| | | | | | Annual Growth Past 2.1% |

Rules of Thumb

- 51% annual sales plus inventory
- 1.8 x SDE plus inventory
- 3 x EBIT

INDUSTRY MULTIPLES

Acquisition multiples below are calculated medians using US private industry transactions. Data updated annually. Last update: August 2023.

VALUATION MULTIPLE (MEDIAN VALUE)

UNDER $1 MILLION NET SALES	
MVIC/Net Sales.	0.79
MVIC/Gross Profit	N/A
MVIC/SDE	1.97
MVIC/EBITDA	N/A
$1 MILLION–$5 MILLION NET SALES	N/A

OVER $5 MILLION NET SALES

MVIC/Net Sales 3.05
MVIC/Gross Profit 4.86
MVIC/SDE . . . . N/A
MVIC/EBITDA 13.07

Source: DealStats (formerly Pratt's Stats), 2023 (Portland, OR: Business Valuation Resources, LLC), www.bvresources.com/dealstats

BENCHMARK DATA

STATISTICS (SPECIALTY HOSPITALS)

Number of Establishments 695
Average Profit Margin 14.3%
Revenue per Employee $240,000
Average Number of Employees 374.0
Average Wages per Employee $80,169

PRODUCTS AND SERVICES SEGMENTATION

Cancer treatment 21.7%
Long-term acute care 18.5%
Other 12.8%
Diagnosis 12.7%
Diseases of the circulatory system 10.1%
Diseases of the respiratory system 9.9%
Diseases of the musculoskeletal system 8.8%
Injury and poisoning 5.5%

MAJOR MARKET SEGMENTATION

Private insurance 53.1%
Government-funded healthcare programs 39.2%
Other 5.4%
Out-of-pocket payments 2.3%

INDUSTRY COSTS

Profit 14.3%
Wages 33.8%
Purchases 17.3%
Depreciation 3.2%
Marketing 0.3%
Rent & Utilities 2.4%
Other 28.7%

MARKET SHARE

Memorial Sloan Kettering Cancer Center 9.1%
Encompass Health Corporation 8.0%
Boston Children's Hospital 2.4%

EXPENSES (% OF ANNUAL SALES)

Cost of Goods 08%
Payroll/Labor Costs 03%
Profit (pretax) 06%

QUESTIONS

• Payor mix, market share, patient demographic data

INDUSTRY TREND

"Revenue was supported by COVID-19 assistance in 2020. Consolidation trends give specialty hospitals power when negotiating with health insurers. Waivers easing telemedicine requirements allow hospitals to expand into new markets. Telemedicine will allow hospitals to provide special needs in underserved markets. Continued government support through the ACA will increase revenue.

Thank You

to all of our
Business Brokerage Press, Inc.
sponsors!

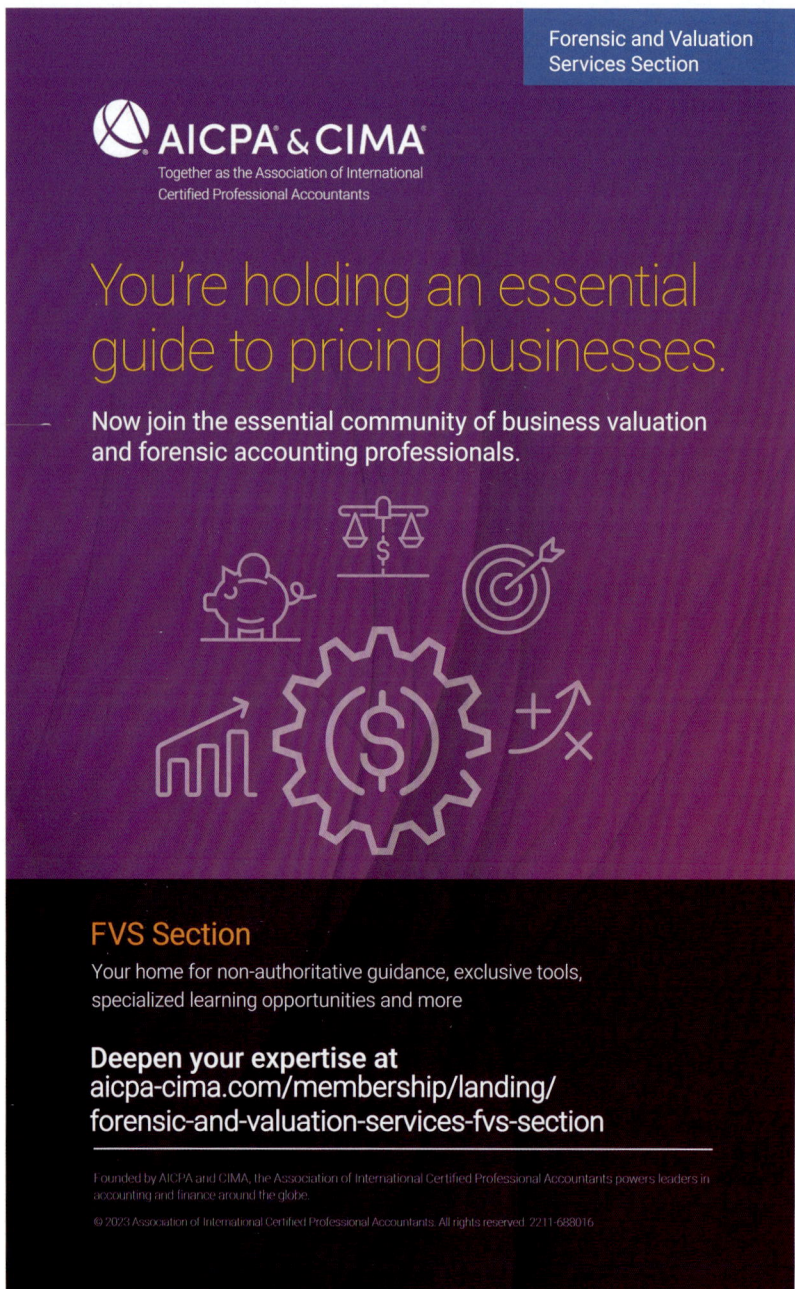
2024 BUSINESS REFERENCE GUIDE | 34TH EDITION

THE ESSENTIAL GUIDE TO PRICING BUSINESSES & FRANCHISES

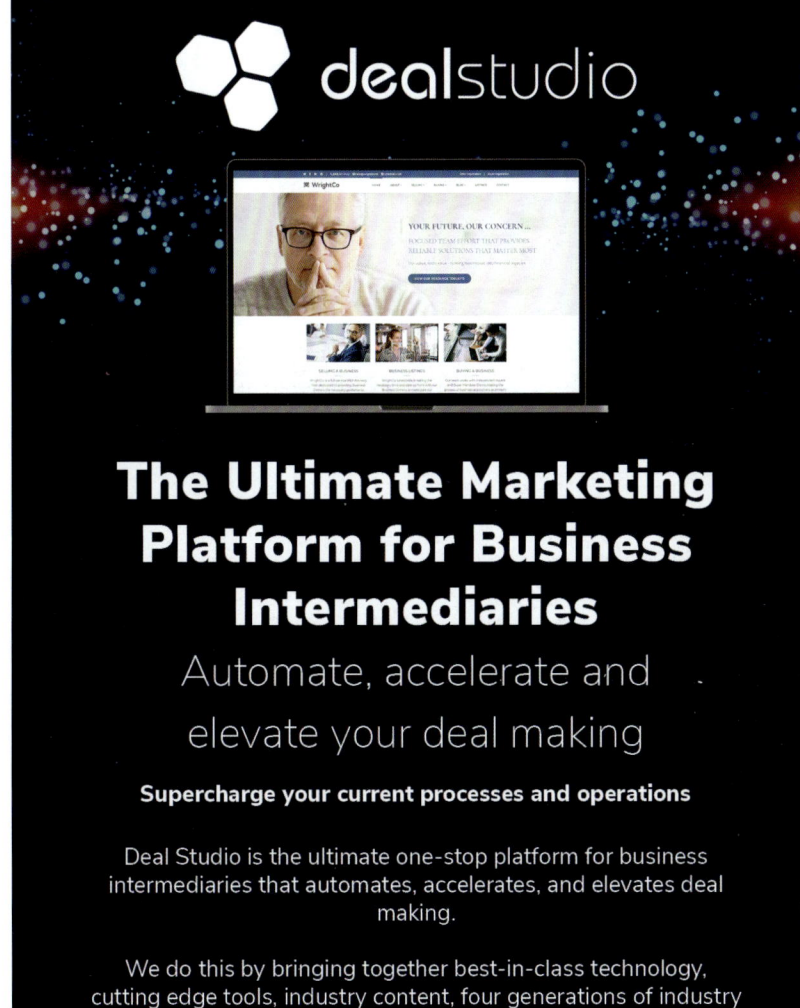
THE ESSENTIAL GUIDE TO PRICING BUSINESSES & FRANCHISES

THE ESSENTIAL GUIDE TO PRICING BUSINESSES & FRANCHISES

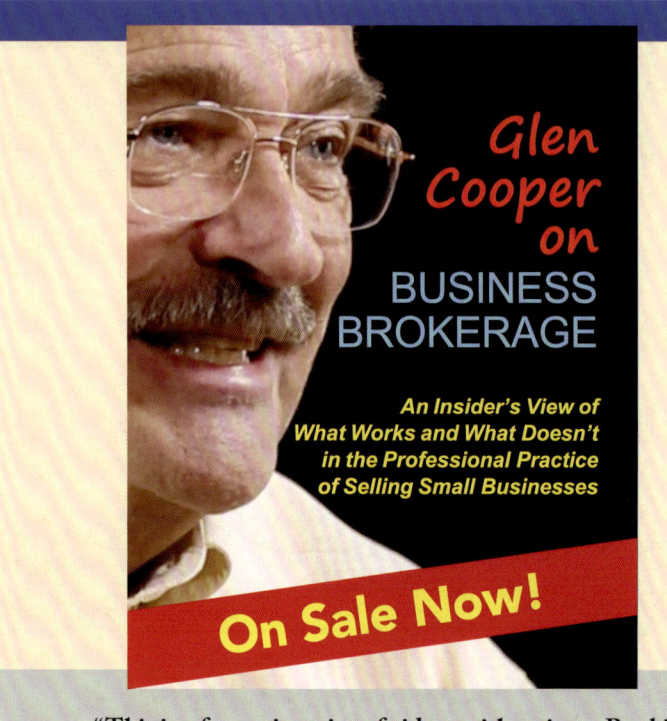

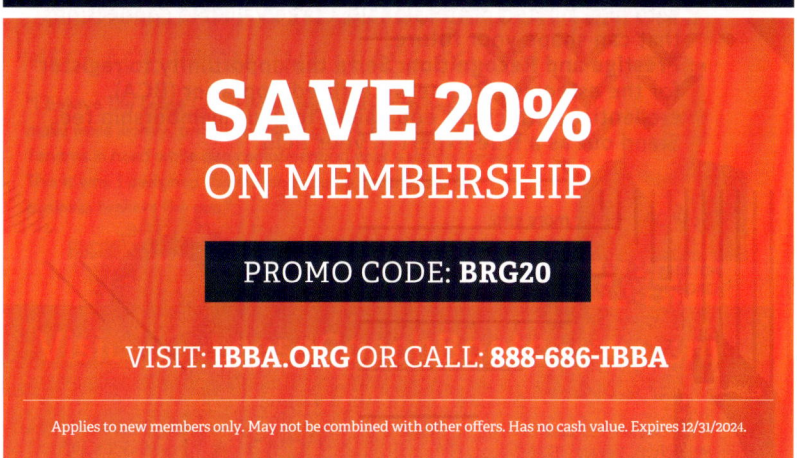

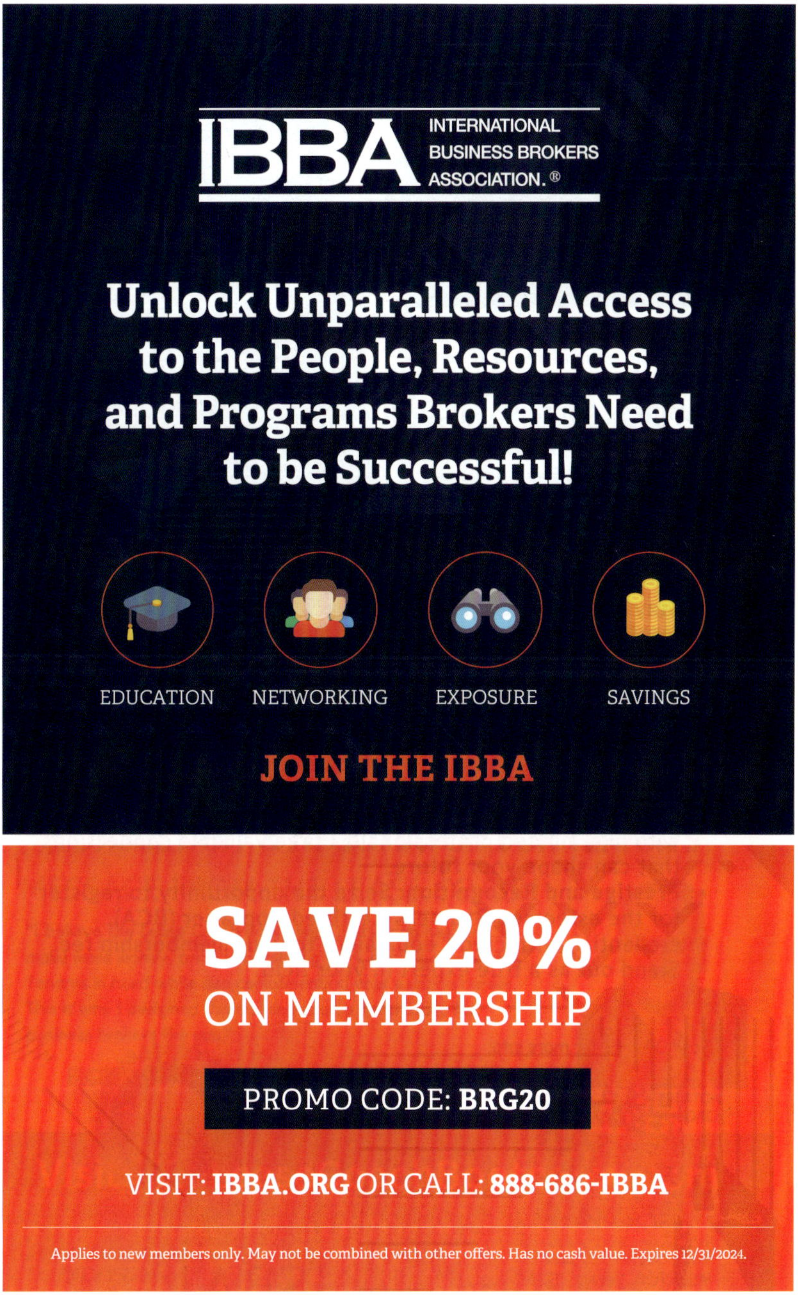
IBBA
INTERNATIONAL BUSINESS BROKERS ASSOCIATION.®
Unlock Unparalleled Access to the People, Resources, and Programs Brokers Need to be Successful!
EDUCATION
NETWORKING
EXPOSURE
SAVINGS
JOIN THE IBBA
SAVE 20%
ON MEMBERSHIP
PROMO CODE: BRG20
VISIT: IBBA.ORG OR CALL: 888-686-IBBA
Applies to new members only. May not be combined with other offers. Has no cash value. Expires 12/31/2024.

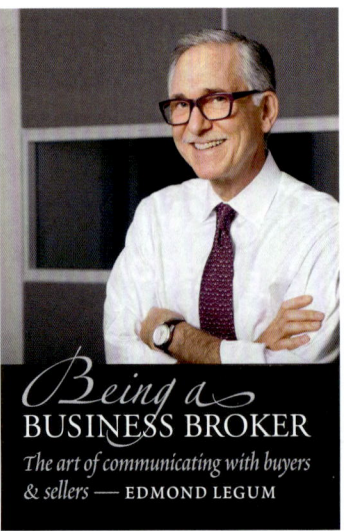

Mergers will allow larger hospitals to negotiate more favorable prices with health insurers. Sharing equipment and deploying employees over a large network brings even more cost efficiencies."

Source: IBISWorld Industry Outlook

FINANCING

Outside Financing

RESOURCES

- IBISWorld, January 2023: https://ibisworld.com
- AHA—American Hospital Association: https://www.aha.org

Hotels & Motels

NAICS 721110	SIC 7011-01	Businesses/Units 205,896
Profit $46.9 B	Wages $58.5 B	Annual Growth Future 4.6%
		Annual Growth Past 0.3%

Rules of Thumb

- 300%–400% annual sales plus inventory
- 8–10 x SDE
- 8–11 x EBITDA
- $20,000 per room
- 10%–12% cap rate
- 8–9 x EBIT

INDUSTRY MULTIPLES

Acquisition multiples below are calculated medians using US private industry transactions. Data updated annually. Last update: August 2023.

VALUATION MULTIPLE (MEDIAN VALUE)

UNDER $1 MILLION NET SALES

MVIC/Net Sales.	0.91
MVIC/Gross Profit	0.95
MVIC/SDE	1.57
MVIC/EBITDA	2.39

$1 MILLION–$5 MILLION NET SALES

MVIC/Net Sales.	0.76
MVIC/Gross Profit	0.94
MVIC/SDE	2.22
MVIC/EBITDA	1.51

OVER $5 MILLION NET SALES

MVIC/Net Sales.	2.70
MVIC/Gross Profit	6.04
MVIC/SDE	N/A
MVIC/EBITDA	13.16

Source: DealStats (formerly Pratt's Stats), 2023 (Portland, OR: Business Valuation Resources, LLC), www.bvresources.com/dealstats

PRICING TIPS

The hotel industry is a hybrid model versus general business valuations. Please note that the real estate values should be appraised by a professional. Most flagged midscale hotels currently trade around 4 times gross (multiple factors: location, size, branding, etc.).

Unfortunately, hotels are rarely priced utilizing the above metrics. EBITDA will vary from 15 to 35 percent in my experience. Wide range depends on level of services, amenities, and branding.

Most small to medium properties look at a multiple of room revenue unlike most any other industry that uses EBITDA or SDE. Larger properties will be valued on a cap rate basis.

BENCHMARK DATA

STATISTICS (HOTELS AND MOTELS)

Number of Establishments	200,353
Average Profit Margin	19.6%
Revenue per Employee	$108,000
Average Number of Employees	12.3
Average Wages per Employee	$26,111

PRODUCTS AND SERVICES SEGMENTATION

Guest room rentals from properties with between 75 and 299 rooms	44.3%
Guest room rentals from properties with under 75 rooms	20.2%
Other services	10.5%
Restaurants and Bars	9.7%
Guest room rentals from properties with over 500 rooms	8.4%
Guest room rentals from properties with between 300 and 500 rooms	6.9%

MAJOR MARKET SEGMENTATION

Domestic leisure travelers	85.7%
Business travelers	6.3%
International leisure travelers	5.2%
Meeting, events and incentive travelers	2.8%

INDUSTRY COSTS

Profit	19.6%
Wages	24.4%
Purchases	17.1%
Depreciation	8.6%
Marketing	1.8%
Rent & Utilities	3.3%
Other	25.1%

STATISTICS (BOUTIQUE HOTELS)

Number of Establishments	5,543
Average Profit Margin	17.3%
Revenue per Employee	$134,000
Average Number of Employees	31.7
Average Wages per Employee	$36,478

PRODUCTS AND SERVICES SEGMENTATION

Soft brand accommodations	46.7%
Food and beverages	20.7%
Lifestyle accommodations	16.0%
Independent boutique accommodations	13.1%
Spa and wellness services	3.4%
Other	0.1%

MAJOR MARKET SEGMENTATION

Domestic leisure travelers	81.8%
Business travelers	13.8%
International leisure travelers	4.4%

Profit 17.3%
Wages 27.3%
Purchases 17.2%
Depreciation 8.6%
Marketing 1.8%
Rent & Utilities 3.2%
Other 24.5%

MARKET SHARE

Marriott International Inc. 8.3%
InterContinental Hotels Group PLC. . . 5.2%
Hilton Worldwide Holdings Inc.. . . . 3.1%

Generally, economy or limited-service hotels don't have much in the way of COGS unless they have sundries sales, store, or restaurant onsite. These other services will affect cost of labor, as will amenities such as pools, fitness centers, greenbelts, etc. Independent operators tend to have fewer employees than flagged or franchise hotels. Noted payroll is the average I have seen over many, many years of this industry. Occupancy cost not typical of the industry, unless it is on land lease or non-arm's-length lease between affiliated owners of real estate/business. Pretax profit with a turnkey project should be 25 to 35 percent, on the high side. Can be in the midteen range depending on the brand, labor costs, geographic location, etc. For example, colder regions have much higher seasonal utility costs. Franchise fees in total could account for 10 percent of revenues (marketing/franchise).

RevPAR; occupancy rate

Compare hotel sales per employee with competitors.

PENN STATE INDEX OF U.S. HOTEL VALUES (2024)

	Value per Room	Annual Percent Change
Overall	$173,907	4.2%
Luxury	$540,041	2.3%
Upper Upscale	$269,812	3.8%
Upscale	$189,895	4.7%
Upper Midscale	$145,051	4.4%
Midscale	$92,272	3.5%
Economy	$56,944	3.5%

Source: *The Penn State Index of U.S. Hotel Values*, The Pennsylvania State University, https://hhd.psu.edu/shm/research/industry-research-and-thought-leadership/hospitality-real-estate-strategy-group/penn-1

EXPENSES (% OF ANNUAL SALES)

Cost of Goods . . . . . . 01% to 10%
Occupancy Costs . . . . . 50% to 60%
Payroll/Labor Costs. . . . . 20% to 30%
Profit (pretax) . . . . . . 10% to 30%

QUESTIONS

- PIP requirements? Ask to see the STR report. Ways to grow business?
- Are the financials correct? Are any new properties coming online in the next 12 to 18 months? Are there any major changes coming to my primary room-night

drivers? What is the ratio of weekly to nightly? What capital improvements are required in the next 12 months?
- Employee history
- Why do you want to sell your property? Are you interested in contributing toward managing the property during an interim period? Are you offering any type of seller financing?

INDUSTRY TREND

It has been increasing since 2021 but could show stabilization by Q4 of 2023 and beyond, depending on external economic factors such as increasing interest rates and potential recession. As a lender, I anticipate hotel occupancy to remain high in the short term, then stabilize or possibly decline. Operator cash flow will decline in the short term as interest rates increase debt service, but many projects are SBA financed. Thus as rates decline with no floors, cash flow will increase.

"According to an analysis for AHLA by Oxford Economics, 2023 U.S. hotel demand is projected to surpass 2019 levels while revenue is expected to reach new heights on a nominal basis."

Source: "A New Era for U.S. Hotels: The American Hotel & Lodging Association 2023 State of the Hotel Industry Report," https://www.ahla.com/sites/default/files/AHLA.SOTI_.Report.2023.final_.002.pdf

"Some industry operators had to temporarily close their operations during the pandemic. The industry has exceeded pre-pandemic revenue levels following the pandemic period. The number of new entrants in this industry has grown quickly in recent years. Investment in new boutique hotel rooms and services will continue to accelerate. Inflationary pressures and recession concerns threaten industry revenue growth. Expansion in the number of boutique hotels is anticipated to put pressure on industry profit. Travelers have begun shifting toward new and more intimate types of hotels in urban locations."

Source: IBISWorld Industry at a Glance

EXPERT COMMENTS

Seller: please provide at least 3 years of occupancy history, ADR, and RevPAR data. If you are reporting to Smith Travel Research, provide reports. Accuracy and reliability of operating history are key.

Buyer: how much cash and/or what other assets do you have?

Seek SBA financing for minimum injection, conventional financing for large injection. Conventional will have lower fees in most cases. Negotiate training into the purchase agreement regardless of experience. If selling, and asking for premium price, be prepared to provide a portion of seller financing; otherwise, lower the price.

Depending on the area, amount of competition can be high. For the most part, it is average, especially if flagged hotels are predominant, as they generally don't allow, or enter, overbuilt markets. This can lower risk, as equilibrium is key. Too much competition, lower occupancy/ADR/RevPAR, etc. Revenues were strong prepandemic, then dropped significantly in 2020. Since then, pent-up travel/leisure demand have translated into significant increases in industry metrics in most areas. The key metrics are a function of the where the facility is located, which in turn relates to marketability. Rated industry trend as good since it continues to see increased ADR/RevPAR. Occupancy could suffer with potential for looming economic slowdown due to interest rate hikes, which have had negative effect on project cash flow.

Have proper cash flow and budget for property improvement requirements.

Be prepared to hold it for 5 to 10 years before selling; make sure the PIP (property improvement plan) is completed.

H

FINANCING

Typically, financing is provided from qualified SBA lenders, or conventionally. Banks tend to use SBA financing as a credit enhancement for lower equity injection. Seller financing in conjunction with bank financing is somewhat typical, and often welcomed by the bank as it can offset risk both in LTV and in the seller still having vested interest to see the project succeed.

90 percent SBA Financing

RESOURCES

- IBISWorld, September 2023: https://www.ibisworld.com
- IBISWorld, March 2023: https://www.ibisworld.com
- AHLA—American Hotel & Lodging Association: https://www.ahla.com
- CBRE: https://pip.cbrehotels.com
- HAC—Hotel Association of Canada: http://hotelassociation.ca
- HB—Hotel Business: https://hotelbusiness.com
- HM—Hotel Management: https://www.hotelmanagement.net
- HotStats—hospitality intelligence: https://www.hotstats.com
- LODGING magazine: https://lodgingmagazine.com
- Penn State Index of U.S. Hotel Values: https://hhd.psu.edu/shm/research/industry-research-and-thought-leadership/hospitality-real-estate-strategy-group/penn-1
- STR—hotel market data & benchmarking: https://str.com

Huntington Learning Center (Franchise)

| NAICS 611691 | Businesses/Units 277

Rules of Thumb

- 60% annual sales

INDUSTRY MULTIPLES

Acquisition multiples below are calculated medians using US private industry transactions. Data updated annually. Last update: August 2023.

VALUATION MULTIPLE (MEDIAN VALUE)

UNDER $1 MILLION NET SALES

MVIC/Net Sales	0.45
MVIC/Gross Profit	0.49
MVIC/SDE	1.85
MVIC/EBITDA	3.33

$1 MILLION–$5 MILLION NET SALES

MVIC/Net Sales	0.75
MVIC/Gross Profit	1.32
MVIC/SDE	3.11
MVIC/EBITDA	4.54

OVER $5 MILLION NET SALES   N/A

Source: DealStats (formerly Pratt's Stats), 2023 (Portland, OR: Business Valuation Resources, LLC), www.bvresources.com/dealstats

Approx. Total Investment: $148,017 to $263,072

RESOURCES

- Huntington Learning Center: https://huntingtonhelps.com
- Franchise information: https://huntingtonfranchise.com

HVAC: Heating, Ventilating, & Air Conditioning

| NAICS 238220 | Businesses/Units 150,419

| Profit $6.5 B | Wages $41.7 B | Annual Growth Future -0.5%

| | | Annual Growth Past 0.4%

Rules of Thumb

- 40%–85% annual sales plus inventory
- 3–4 x SDE plus inventory
- 3–4.5 x EBIT
- 4–5 x EBITDA

INDUSTRY MULTIPLES

Acquisition multiples below are calculated medians using US private industry transactions. Data updated annually. Last update: August 2023.

VALUATION MULTIPLE (MEDIAN VALUE)

UNDER $1 MILLION NET SALES

MVIC/Net Sales.	0.42
MVIC/Gross Profit	0.73
MVIC/SDE	1.84
MVIC/EBITDA	2.80

$1 MILLION–$5 MILLION NET SALES

MVIC/Net Sales.	0.46
MVIC/Gross Profit	0.96
MVIC/SDE	2.85
MVIC/EBITDA	4.43

OVER $5 MILLION NET SALES

MVIC/Net Sales.	0.55
MVIC/Gross Profit	1.53
MVIC/SDE	3.91
MVIC/EBITDA	4.24

Source: DealStats (formerly Pratt's Stats), 2023 (Portland, OR: Business Valuation Resources, LLC), www.bvresources.com/dealstats

PRICING TIPS

A buyer may try to negotiate a price including working capital.

The upper end of the market has had so much demand that we have seen multiples as high as 1 to 13 x SDE for companies with SDE above $800K. Buyers are willing to pay a premium for businesses built purely on service, repair, and replacement and are penalized for new construction exposure.

Companies with service contracts are exceedingly more attractive. Those with high concentration of construction or new build-outs or concentration of customers are less attractive and it is often difficult to find a qualified and interested buyer. Companies with techs that are qualified and certified are attractive.

Service agreements are key to strong residential sell price.

Can realize a premium when all/most of revenue consists of residential contracts.

The 3 x SDE is for companies with an SDE of less than $300,000. Over the last 18 to 24 months, because of the interest and acquisitions from private equity firms, as that number goes up the multiple goes up drastically.

Residential, light commercial service, and replacement focus are key to higher multiples.

BENCHMARK DATA

STATISTICS (HEATING AND AIR-CONDITIONING CONTRACTORS)

Number of Establishments	150,419
Average Profit Margin	5.3%
Revenue per Employee	$186,000
Average Number of Employees	4.5
Average Wages per Employee	$63,131

PRODUCTS AND SERVICES SEGMENTATION

New construction HVAC installations	43.9%
HVAC maintenance and repairs	24.3%
Existing structure HVAC installations	19.5%
Refrigeration system installations, maintenance and repairs	12.3%

MAJOR MARKET SEGMENTATION

Other	38.6%
New Residential Construction	16.2%
Office Buildings	11.6%
Educational Buildings	9.2%
Office Manufacturing and Light Industrial Buildings	8.6%
Commercial Buildings	8.4%
Existing Residential Construction	7.4%

INDUSTRY COSTS

Profit	5.3%
Wages	33.8%
Purchases	38.8%
Depreciation	0.9%
Marketing	0.5%
Rent & Utilities	3.3%
Other	17.4%

MARKET SHARE

Emcor Group, Inc.	3.8%
Comfort Systems USA, Inc.	2.7%

10 percent NP is normal, with 20 percent NP for larger, more efficient residential HVAC contractors.

Recurring, contractual revenue—especially residential—has proven particularly attractive in recent years. Fees are climbing toward $150/man-hour, and contractors that offer installation and service can produce $200K+ per tech.

45 percent GP and 20 percent NP are key to solid multiple of earnings when selling.

Sales per employee: High = $260,000Medium = $235,000Low = $175,000

Sales per service truck: High = $350,000Medium = $300,000Low = $225,000

Focus on service and repair, high systems in place and maintenance agreements.

Most well-run businesses with employees will average a 25 to 30 percent profit margin. Those run without many employees trend to the 30 percent. Companies with strict systems in place are able to increase these figures.

Increase in inside support needed: optimal field to inside support ratio = 2/1; average = 3/1; poor = 4/1.

Harder to get consumers' attention and keep loyal customers, due to an increase in technology and consumer options.

EXPENSES (% OF ANNUAL SALES)

Cost of Goods	50% to 60%
Occupancy Costs	01% to 11%
Payroll/Labor Costs.	15% to 25%
Profit (pretax)	10% to 20%

QUESTIONS

- What does the seller do in the business? Provide a breakdown of income and how it is generated. Summaries of staff tenure? Do they offer in house warranties? How many PMAs have been paid but not completed?
- How many customers have service contracts? What is included in the service contract? How many service and how many installation crews do you have and what is the experience of the lead techs?
- How many service agreements? Look for gross profit above 45 percent before you buy.
- How well do you pay your techs and how likely is it they'll be seeking a raise on day 1 of the new company?
- Percentage of business from new construction? How many maintenance agreements do they have in place? Do they offer in-house warranties on labor? Tenure of employees?
- Number of PMAs? Average service invoice? Number of service calls per year? Average Installation invoice? Number of installations per year? Average sales per employee?
- How many residential preventative maintenance agreements have you sold over the past 3 to 5 years (recurring revenue)?What other recurring revenue streams do you have?
- Get a minimum of 5 years' worth of financial statements or tax returns.
- Get a clear understanding of staff and their motivations. Callback percentage on new installations? Hourly rate? Flat rate or TM pricing?
- What does their typical day look like? What do you do in the slow months to generate income?
- What are the seller's duties? Location of the nearest suppliers? Terms the supplier offers? Percentage of work that is residential?
- Age of fleet; age of inventory; relationship with vendors; how long with specific brand of equipment?

INDUSTRY TREND

In 2022, the Inflation Reduction Act (IRA) was signed into law. It includes about $21 billion in funding for homeowners to make energy efficiency upgrades to their homes as well as a tax credit for consumers. The tax credits and rebates will be in place for 10 years. The changes are designed to incentivize building and project owners to adopt green building principals for new buildings and retrofits, including more energy-efficient HVAC systems.

All indications are the numbers will hold constant or potentially even increase.

Demand is continuing to grow with split units more popular. Commercial HVAC will continue to be in demand as aging units need to be replaced.

Continues to be an essential service.

Contractors moving toward electric systems (heat pumps, mini-splits, etc.) will see higher demand in coming years as homeowners continue to move away from fossil fuel–powered furnaces and boilers. One-off plumbing work is falling out of favor as no one seems to want to deal with headaches like clogged pipes.

Because of the private equity interest, a potential of an economic slowdown affecting other industries, and the strong numbers in the space, I feel confident demand will continue.

Values are trending up, due to increased demand and lack of available manpower.

Trending toward two distinct types of HVAC contractors: large and small. The larger are buying up the midsize contractors to increase economies of scale.

EXPERT COMMENTS

Make sure there are quality financial statements.

Evaluate staff thoroughly.

If you are a seller, focus on four items: get out of the van; clean books and records; heavy on maintenance agreements; and stay away from new construction. If you are a buyer, I would look at the lower end of the market. There are still great deals to be had on strong businesses with low-hanging fruit.

Prepare to sell at least 3 years prior to target sale date. Expect to take 6 to 12 months to sell it, once on the market.

Selling—the market is strong. Buying—buy smaller companies. I have sold over five companies in the last year that were over 10 x SDE. The buyer competition is strong at the upper end of the market.

Look for number of recurring, written preventative maintenance agreements, with overall gross profit above 45 percent and net profit above 20 percent. If underachieving-profit business, look for higher number of preventative maintenance agreements.

Focus on residential and light commercial service and replacement.

Make sure the business can run itself well before you try to sell it.

FINANCING

I have seen that most buyers the last two years have been cash. If financing has been involved, it has been outside financing.

Most buyers require some seller notes for a small portion of financing; however, bank financing is available and implemented in most sales. Additionally, on larger transactions, sellers retain some equity.

Clean-cut financing. No seller financing required.

Typical: 10 percent seller capital, 80 percent outside financing, 10 percent seller Financing

SBA lenders, strategic buyers, and PE firms find this industry attractive, so seller financing is minimal and/or not necessary.

RESOURCES
• IBISWorld, September 2023: https://www.ibisworld.com

- HARDI—Heating Air-conditioning & Refrigeration Distributors International: https://hardinet.org/
- HVAC & Refrigeration Insider: https://hvacinsider.com/
- SMACNA—Sheet Metal & Air Conditioning Contractors' National Association: https://www.smacna.org/
- ACCA—Air Conditioning Contractors of America: https://www.acca.org/home
- ACHR News: https://www.achrnews.com/
- Air Conditioning Association of New England: https://www.acane.org
- KAMC—Kentucky Association of Master Contractors: https://www.kyamc.com
- New England Mechanical Contractors Association: https://www.nemca.org/new-england-msca.html
- PHCC—Pluming–Heating–Cooling Contractors Association: https://www.phccweb.org/
- Plumbing, Heating, and Cooling Contractors of Massachusetts: https://www.phccma.org
- SCALT—South Carolina Association of Licensed Trades: https://scalt.org
- Supply House Times: https://www.supplyht.com/
- theNEWS: https://www.achrnews.com

Ice Cream Trucks

| NAICS 722330

Rules of Thumb

- 1 x SDE plus fair market value of the truck(s) plus inventory

INDUSTRY MULTIPLES

Acquisition multiples below are calculated medians using US private industry transactions. Data updated annually. Last update: August 2023.

VALUATION MULTIPLE (MEDIAN VALUE)

UNDER $1 MILLION NET SALES	
MVIC/Net Sales	0.64
MVIC/Gross Profit	0.83
MVIC/SDE	0.86
MVIC/EBITDA	1.04
$1 MILLION–$5 MILLION NET SALES	N/A
OVER $5 MILLION NET SALES	
MVIC/Net Sales	3.43
MVIC/Gross Profit	9.59
MVIC/SDE	N/A
MVIC/EBITDA	N/A

Source: DealStats (formerly Pratt's Stats), 2023 (Portland, OR: Business Valuation Resources, LLC), www.bvresources.com/dealstats

BENCHMARK DATA

For Benchmark data see Catering Trucks

RESOURCES

- AllScream.com: https://www.allscream.com/icecreamstories.php
- IAICDV—International Association of Ice Cream Distributors & Vendors: https://www.iaicdv.org
- IDFA—International Dairy Foods Association: https://www.idfa.org

Ice Cream/Yogurt Shops

| NAICS 722515 | SIC 5812-03

Rules of Thumb

- 60% annual sales plus inventory
- 2.2–2.3 x SDE plus inventory (franchised only)
- 3 x EBIT
- 3 x EBITDA
- 15–20 x weekly sales (independent only)

INDUSTRY MULTIPLES

Acquisition multiples below are calculated medians using US private industry transactions. Data updated annually. Last update: August 2023.

VALUATION MULTIPLE (MEDIAN VALUE)

UNDER $1 MILLION NET SALES

MVIC/Net Sales.	0.44
MVIC/Gross Profit	0.62
MVIC/SDE	2.20
MVIC/EBITDA	2.82

$1 MILLION–$5 MILLION NET SALES

MVIC/Net Sales.	0.41
MVIC/Gross Profit	0.69
MVIC/SDE	2.82
MVIC/EBITDA	5.94

OVER $5 MILLION NET SALES

MVIC/Net Sales.	3.89
MVIC/Gross Profit	4.87
MVIC/SDE	N/A
MVIC/EBITDA	N/A

Source: DealStats (formerly Pratt's Stats), 2023 (Portland, OR: Business Valuation Resources, LLC), www.bvresources.com/dealstats

PRICING TIPS

Condition of the premises, lease terms, location and age of equipment, shopping center very desirable. Franchise operations have dominated the market; well-run franchise location is very desirable. Another factor is co-branding (i.e., Dunkin' & Baskin-Robbins). Since ice cream can be seasonal in some areas, this offsets the loss.

BENCHMARK DATA

Premises should be limited to 1000 to 1200 square feet or less. This is a location-driven business. Franchise locations with a minimum lease period of 10+ years remaining with transfer fee included in price are very desirable. Franchises such as Dairy Queen or A&W can add 15 to 20 percent to asking price.

STATISTICS (FROZEN YOGURT STORES)

Number of Establishments	1,659
Average Profit Margin	5.7%
Revenue per Employee	$42,400
Average Number of Employees.	8.9
Average Wages per Employee	$15,356

PRODUCTS AND SERVICES SEGMENTATION

Self-serve yogurt	70.3%
Full-service yogurt	16.7%
Toppings and other products	13.0%

MAJOR MARKET SEGMENTATION

Consumers aged 18 to 24	32.0%
Consumers aged 25 to 34	20.0%
Consumers aged 50 to 64	12.4%
Consumers aged under 18	12.4%
Consumers aged 35 to 49	11.7%
Consumers aged 65 and over	11.5%

INDUSTRY COSTS

Profits	5.7%
Wages	36.4%
Purchases	36.2%
Depreciation	3.6%
Marketing	1.6%
Rent & Utilities	6.3%
Other	10.1%

EXPENSES (% OF ANNUAL SALES)

Cost of Goods	25% to 28%
Occupancy Costs	10%
Payroll/Labor Costs.	20% to 22%
Profit (pretax)	05% to 06%

QUESTIONS

- The age and condition of the equipment
- Equipment servicing questions, employee history, historical sales
- Owner-operated or absentee? Any wholesale accounts?

INDUSTRY TREND

"As the pandemic subsides, revenue in 2021 alone is projected to increase. Higher profit, relative to other food service industries, has helped drive rapid industry expansion. More industry operators are attempting to support revenue by diversifying the food products they sell. The industry, having reached a point of oversaturation, will continue to correct itself. An increasing number of industry operators are anticipated to differentiate themselves. The industry is expected to continue to experience a slow decline in the number of establishments. Industry operators are experiencing lower revenue and are reducing their frozen yogurt store locations."

Source: IBISWorld Industry at a Glance

EXPERT COMMENTS

For the independent operator, product cost increases will hurt profitability. In franchise operations, the product may be manufactured on-site, thus cheaper cost; however, the payroll may be higher.

FINANCING

Usually outside financing. SBA provides a list of approved franchises on their website; they indicate which franchises they approve and which ones they don't.

Independent owners may consider holding a note due to the fact that they are more difficult to sell.

- IBISWorld, August 2021: https://www.ibisworld.com
- IAICDV—International Association of Ice Cream Distributors & Vendors: https://www.iaicdv.org
- IDFA—International Dairy Foods Association: https://www.idfa.org

Industrial Building Construction

| NAICS 236210 | Businesses/Units 5,206

| Profit $711.7 M | Wages $5.1 B | Annual Growth Future 1.0%

                                           | Annual Growth Past -4.0%

Rules of Thumb

- 120% annual sales

INDUSTRY MULTIPLES

Acquisition multiples below are calculated medians using US private industry transactions. Data updated annually. Last update: August 2023.

VALUATION MULTIPLE (MEDIAN VALUE)

UNDER $1 MILLION NET SALES	N/A
$1 MILLION–$5 MILLION NET SALES	
MVIC/Net Sales.	0.47
MVIC/Gross Profit	1.07
MVIC/SDE	2.55
MVIC/EBITDA	3.44
OVER $5 MILLION NET SALES	
MVIC/Net Sales.	0.27
MVIC/Gross Profit	2.42
MVIC/SDE	3.11
MVIC/EBITDA	4.89

Source: DealStats (formerly Pratt's Stats), 2023 (Portland, OR: Business Valuation Resources, LLC), www.bvresources.com/dealstats

PRICING TIPS

With today's labor, or lack of labor, especially in the trades, an established business, with employees—trained plumbers, for example—is valuable!

BENCHMARK DATA

STATISTICS (INDUSTRIAL BUILDING CONSTRUCTION)

Number of Establishments	5,206
Average Profit Margin	2.8%
Revenue per Employee	$375,000
Average Number of Employees.	13.1
Average Wages per Employee	$75,270

PRODUCTS AND SERVICES SEGMENTATION

General industrial construction.	48.9%
Renovations.	21.2%
Infrastructure and other building services	18.2%
Construction management services	11.7%

Pharmaceutical manufacturing.	.32.9%
Plastics and plastic product manufacturing	.26.8%
Chemical manufacturing	.25.4%
Mass transit.	8.6%
Aviation .	4.5%
Water transport .	1.2%
Other	0.6%

INDUSTRY COSTS

Profit	2.8%
Wages	.20.3%
Purchases	.57.7%
Depreciation	0.6%
Marketing	0.1%
Rent & Utilities .	2.2%
Other	.16.5%

MARKET SHARE

Fluor Corporation	.26.7%
AECOM .	.16.7%
DPR Construction, Inc. .	.12.8%
Gilbane Inc. .	.12.0%
Barton Malow Company	6.6%
OHL USA Inc.	5.0%
Jacobs Engineering Group Inc. .	4.3%
The Stellar Group	2.3%
Kinsley Construction Inc.	2.0%
IMC Construction	1.5%
CR Meyer	1.3%

EXPENSES (% OF ANNUAL SALES)

Cost of Goods	35%
Occupancy Costs	06%
Payroll/Labor Costs.	16%
Profit (pretax)	33%

QUESTIONS

• Where do your customers come from? How do you market your services?

INDUSTRY TREND

A lot more growth

"Government-mandated shutdowns restricted business operations, resulting in revenue loss. Early in the period, near-zero interest rates spurred new industrial building construction. Building construction in a few niche markets has driven industry growth. Industry activity is anticipated to be supported by an acceleration in the industrial production index. Increased demand from key downstream markets is expected to bolster industry performance. Industry participants often compete on price, quality and reputation. Industry revenue will most closely track with movements in manufacturing capacity utilization."

Source: IBISWorld Industry at a Glance

FINANCING

Mostly cash sale, bigger firm buying smaller firm

RESOURCES

• IBISWorld, January 2023: https://www.ibisworld.com

Industrial Machinery and Equipment Merchant Wholesalers

| NAICS 423830 | Businesses/Units 27,539

| Profit $15.7 B | Wages $33.3 B | Annual Growth Future 2.2%

| Annual Growth Past -1.0%

INDUSTRY MULTIPLES

Acquisition multiples below are calculated medians using US private industry transactions. Data updated annually. Last update: August 2023.

VALUATION MULTIPLE (MEDIAN VALUE)

UNDER $1 MILLION NET SALES

MVIC/Net Sales.	0.50
MVIC/Gross Profit	1.27
MVIC/SDE	3.22
MVIC/EBITDA	3.55

$1 MILLION–$5 MILLION NET SALES

MVIC/Net Sales.	0.44
MVIC/Gross Profit	1.28
MVIC/SDE	3.17
MVIC/EBITDA	4.11

OVER $5 MILLION NET SALES

MVIC/Net Sales.	0.62
MVIC/Gross Profit	2.28
MVIC/SDE	3.56
MVIC/EBITDA	7.42

Source: DealStats (formerly Pratt's Stats), 2023 (Portland, OR: Business Valuation Resources, LLC), www.bvresources.com/dealstats

BENCHMARK DATA

STATISTICS (INDUSTRIAL MACHINERY & EQUIPMENT WHOLESALING)

Number of Establishments .	27,539
Average Profit Margin	5.0%
Revenue per Employee .	$799,000
Average Number of Employees.	14.5
Average Wages per Employee .	$84,400

PRODUCTS AND SERVICES SEGMENTATION

General-purpose machinery and equipment	34.6%
Other industrial machinery and equipment	30.0%
Material handling equipment	10.6%
Hydraulic and pneumatic machinery and equipment .	8.2%
Oil well, refinery and pipeline machinery and equipment .	7.8%
Metalworking machinery and equipment .	6.9%
Food processing machinery	1.9%

MAJOR MARKET SEGMENTATION

Manufacturing and mining industrial users	43.0%
Wholesalers.	16.7%
Other markets	14.9%
Businesses for end use .	10.2%
Building, heavy construction and special trade contractors	5.3%
Retailers for resale .	5.3%
Repair shops	2.4%
Government bodies.	2.2%

Profit	5.0%
Wages	10.6%
Purchases	66.4%
Depreciation	0.9%
Marketing	0.3%
Rent & Utilities	1.1%
Other	15.6%

MARKET SHARE

W.W. Grainger	3.1%
Applied Industrial Technologies . . .	0.8%
MRC Global	0.7%

INDUSTRY TREND

"The industry's connection to commodity markets and crude oil production leaves it vulnerable. Spending on new industrial machinery steadily increased until the pandemic. E-commerce sales have boosted demand for machinery. Private investment in industrial machinery and equipment is set to return to growth. A growing desire for lessened reliance on foreign oil has boosted US production. Low barriers to entry allow new wholesalers to open for business. Economic recovery brought pent-up demand to wholesalers."

Source: IBISWorld Industry at a Glance

RESOURCES

• IBISWorld, January 2023: https://www.ibisworld.com

Industrial Water Treatment Companies

| NAICS 221310

Rules of Thumb

• 100%–125% annual sales
• 4 x SDE plus inventory
• 5 x EBIT
• 6 x EBITDA

INDUSTRY MULTIPLES

Acquisition multiples below are calculated medians using US private industry transactions. Data updated annually. Last update: August 2023.

VALUATION MULTIPLE (MEDIAN VALUE)

UNDER $1 MILLION NET SALES

MVIC/Net Sales.	0.58
MVIC/Gross Profit	0.81
MVIC/SDE	1.85
MVIC/EBITDA	1.82

$1 MILLION–$5 MILLION NET SALES

MVIC/Net Sales.	0.87
MVIC/Gross Profit	2.13
MVIC/SDE	3.17
MVIC/EBITDA	1.95

OVER $5 MILLION NET SALES

MVIC/Net Sales.	4.43
MVIC/Gross Profit	2.10

```
MVIC/SDE  .    .    .    .    .    .    .    .    6.96
MVIC/EBITDA  .    .    .    .    .    .    .    20.23
```

Source: DealStats (formerly Pratt's Stats), 2023 (Portland, OR: Business Valuation Resources, LLC), www.bvresources.com/dealstats

PRICING TIPS

There continues to be strong demand by experienced buyers for companies that operate in this specialized space. We see sales activity from all over the United States. The key to purchasing one of these businesses is to be in a position to act very quickly.

These rarely sell based on SDE. They are management intensive businesses and someone will need to run it. Most often sell for multiple of EBITDA. Size matters—$1M EBITDA or less sells for 4x; $1M to $2M EBITDA, 4 to 5x; $2M to $5M EBITDA, 5 to 7x. A lot will depend on quality of equipment, management, and end markets served. More recurring business is higher multiple. More project work is higher margin but lower multiple.

Industrial water treatment companies did well during the 2020–21 pandemic. Their customer base had to keep the equipment maintained. These are industrial accounts, utilities, large commercial buildings, colleges, and so on.

BENCHMARK DATA

$200K to $250K rev per employee; higher-margin businesses could do $500K rev per employee. The more niche the service, the higher the margin. Daily rate: two men and a truck should generate $3K a day on average.

Employees tend to be long-term with the company. They are paid very well, and have developed relationships with the accounts. Because industrial water treatment is so specific to accounts, the time spent at each location does vary greatly. Margins typically run 60 plus.

Our clients typically group customers into the A-B-C formula for service calls: A = yearly service, B = semiannual service, and C = quarterly service.

The benchmarks that measure success in this industry are the number of customers; types, percentage of clients under contract; the contract pricing; and the proprietary chemicals the business uses.

EXPENSES (% OF ANNUAL SALES)

Cost of Goods	30% to 40%
Occupancy Costs	03% to 10%
Payroll/Labor Costs.	20% to 30%
Profit (pretax)	20% to 30%

QUESTIONS

- How old is your equipment? How competitive is this market? What's your daily rate for two guys and a truck? How much visibility do you have into your week? Tell me about your safety record. Any insurance claims?
- Types of customers they have; what water treatment services they provide; geographic area covered; percentage of customers under contract; last price increase; what proprietary chemical formulas they own

INDUSTRY TREND

The trend for this niche business continues to be quite stable.

This marketplace will continue to trend upwards.

Excellent—always need industrial and environmental services, regardless of the economy. Remediation services tie to real estate development, so that type of business is a little cyclical.

EXPERT COMMENTS

Have a basic understanding of the product. Kind of know what you are talking about.

Generally speaking, water treatment clients have a long tenure.

If you are a buyer from outside this industry, a seller will probably not talk to you. The seller is being overcautious in protecting his/her methods, customer base, and employees. You will need an intermediary; this is a very close-knit marketplace.

These companies have been in business many years and have kept their customer base intact because of the water treatment recipes that are trade secrets of that company.

FINANCING

Our experience is that businesses are sold for 100 percent cash.

RESOURCES

- WEFTEC: https://www.weftec.org
- WWD—Water & Wastes Digest: https://www.wwdmag.com/
- WWETT Show—Water & Wastewater Equipment, Treatment & Transport Show: https://www.wwettshow.com/en/home.html

---

Information and Document Management Service Industries

| NAICS 541513 | Businesses/Units 1,734 |

| Profit $546.5 M | Wages $2.5 B | Annual Growth Future 2.2% |
| | | Annual Growth Past 2.2% |

Rules of Thumb

- 4–6 x normalized EBITDA

INDUSTRY MULTIPLES

Acquisition multiples below are calculated medians using US private industry transactions. Data updated annually. Last update: August 2023.

VALUATION MULTIPLE (MEDIAN VALUE)

UNDER $1 MILLION NET SALES
MVIC/Net Sales.	0.63
MVIC/Gross Profit	0.71
MVIC/SDE	2.09
MVIC/EBITDA	10.95

$1 MILLION–$5 MILLION NET SALES
MVIC/Net Sales.	0.95
MVIC/Gross Profit	1.30
MVIC/SDE	3.76
MVIC/EBITDA	N/A

OVER $5 MILLION NET SALES
MVIC/Net Sales. 1.80
MVIC/Gross Profit 4.97
MVIC/SDE 9.39
MVIC/EBITDA 22.92

Source: DealStats (formerly Pratt's Stats), 2023 (Portland, OR: Business Valuation Resources, LLC), www.bvresources.com/dealstats

BENCHMARK DATA

STATISTICS (DOCUMENT MANAGEMENT SERVICES)

Number of Establishments 1,734
Average Profit Margin 7.0%
Revenue per Employee $100,000
Average Number of Employees. . . . 45.9
Average Wages per Employee . . . $31,731

PRODUCTS AND SERVICES SEGMENTATION

Records management services. . . . 56.2%
Data destruction 31.9%
Data protection and recovery services . . 11.9%

MAJOR MARKET SEGMENTATION

Financial services 67.2%
Government. 13.3%
Other 10.3%
Legal 4.9%
Healthcare 4.3%

INDUSTRY COSTS

Profit 7.0%
Wages 31.7%
Purchases 24.2%
Depreciation 2.7%
Marketing 2.1%
Rent & Utilities 2.9%
Other 29.3%

MARKET SHARE

Iron Mountain Inc. 12.7%
Stericycle, Inc. 9.9%
Esquire Deposition Solutions LLC . . . 1.0%

INDUSTRY TREND

"The industry generally experiences steady demand. Competition has historically been high in this industry. Demand for the electronic conversion of medical records has benefited the industry. The industry will face sustained demand because of stricter records management. Consolidation will slow as increased demand for digitizing records attracts new entrants. Operators will continue to lean on storage revenue from the financial services market. Competition has decreased as larger industry operators have increasingly acquired regional operators."

Source: IBISWorld Industry at a Glance

RESOURCES

- IBISWorld, March 2023: https://www.ibisworld.com
- PRISM International: https://prismintl.org

Information Technology Companies

| NAICS 541512

Rules of Thumb

- 100%–150% annual sales
- 3–6 x SDE
- 3–4 x EBIT
- 3–6 x EBITDA

INDUSTRY MULTIPLES

Acquisition multiples below are calculated medians using US private industry transactions. Data updated annually. Last update: August 2023.

VALUATION MULTIPLE (MEDIAN VALUE)

UNDER $1 MILLION NET SALES

MVIC/Net Sales.	0.70
MVIC/Gross Profit	1.04
MVIC/SDE	2.17
MVIC/EBITDA	6.46

$1 MILLION–$5 MILLION NET SALES

MVIC/Net Sales.	0.70
MVIC/Gross Profit	1.00
MVIC/SDE	3.39
MVIC/EBITDA	4.58

OVER $5 MILLION NET SALES

MVIC/Net Sales.	1.21
MVIC/Gross Profit	3.31
MVIC/SDE	5.86
MVIC/EBITDA	16.58

Source: DealStats (formerly Pratt's Stats), 2023 (Portland, OR: Business Valuation Resources, LLC), www.bvresources.com/dealstats

PRICING TIPS

Major considerations in IT company valuations include: – percent of revenue that is recurring or contract based; this is the most critical element. – percent of work that is on time, and materials or project based; companies that have a high percentage of project-based work will sell at lower multiples. – skills of employees—are they highly skilled on modern platforms? – amount of customer concentration; anything above 25 percent will be scrutinized by professional buyers. – Customer base split between SMBs (usually under 50 users), midsize enterprises (51 to 200), and enterprises (200+).

Consider any off–balance sheet value, i.e., IP, government contracts, valued customer relationships, unique vendor relationships.

Is there an SLA (software license agreement) for each type/copy of software being used? Are the SLAs assignable? Has the vendor given written permission to assign them and under what conditions? Has the company been reported to the Software Consortium as a company using unlicensed software? Is the technology based on open standards and/or proprietary? Is there a complete inventory list of all software and hardware being used in the business? What third parties are hosting applications and providing IT services?

BENCHMARK DATA

On a recent deal, a team of 9, including 2 owners, could support approximately

80+ SMB clients. Cloud charges and employee costs were about 25 percent of revenue each.

Annual recurring revenue with a 2.5 multiplier applied is a benchmark for valuation. Pure book of business acquisitions will value lower and often use SDE or EBITA as the model.

EXPENSES (% OF ANNUAL SALES)

Cost of Goods	15% to 25%
Occupancy Costs	05% to 10%
Payroll/Labor Costs.	25% to 35%
Profit (pretax)	15% to 25%

QUESTIONS

- How many clients do you support? What is your split of revenue between managed services, project-based work, and time and materials? What is your average blended billing rate? How long have your employees been with you? Can you share a report of sales by client? Need to understand level of concentration. How many of your customers have signed long-term agreements? Can you provide a skills matrix for your employees? Are there certain industries or geographies you tend to excel in? How long will you be willing to stay on in a transition? Are there any key employees that are tied into accounts that can't be easily replaced? Who are you selling to—the client, CIO, director of IT, etc.? What percent of your revenue comes from security-related services?
- What are the growth opportunities that exist today?
- Explain the marketing strategy relative to the many competitors. What is the market niche?
- Client turnover and retention? Average contract value? Number of contracts? Ratio of customer support to number of technical staff?

INDUSTRY TREND

Trends for IT managed services businesses are very favorable. More companies are finding cost efficiencies in moving key systems to the cloud. IT MSPs can inexpensively add new clients and achieve higher levels of efficiencies. There will be continued consolidation in the space over the next decade.

EXPERT COMMENTS

Like all businesses, sellers need to be realistic on valuation. They need to understand that the higher the percentage of recurring revenue and contracted revenue, the higher the multiple they will receive. If they have a high percentage of revenue from projects, buyers will be less interested and pay a lower multiple. Buyers see risk in one-time revenue. Buyers seek sellers that have an extensive customer base of enterprise clients, where they can continue to expand services over time.

FINANCING

Between interest rates increasing significantly and banks tightening, outside financing has become a greater challenge over the past year. We are seeing more deals involving seller notes and earnouts.

RESOURCES

- CompTIA: https://www.comptia.org
- The ASCII Group, Inc.: https://www.ascii.com

Injection Molding

| NAICS 333249

Rules of Thumb

- 4.5–6 x EBITDA

INDUSTRY MULTIPLES

Acquisition multiples below are calculated medians using US private industry transactions. Data updated annually. Last update: August 2023.

VALUATION MULTIPLE (MEDIAN VALUE)

UNDER $1 MILLION NET SALES

MVIC/Net Sales.	0.54
MVIC/Gross Profit	0.94
MVIC/SDE	1.79
MVIC/EBITDA	2.93

$1 MILLION–$5 MILLION NET SALES

MVIC/Net Sales.	0.53
MVIC/Gross Profit	1.12
MVIC/SDE	3.22
MVIC/EBITDA	4.22

OVER $5 MILLION NET SALES

MVIC/Net Sales.	2.54
MVIC/Gross Profit	4.63
MVIC/SDE	12.50
MVIC/EBITDA	13.61

Source: DealStats (formerly Pratt's Stats), 2023 (Portland, OR: Business Valuation Resources, LLC), www.bvresources.com/dealstats

Inns

| NAICS 721110 | SIC 7011-02

Rules of Thumb

- 5–8 x SDE including inventory
- 400%–450% annual sales includes inventory

INDUSTRY MULTIPLES

Acquisition multiples below are calculated medians using US private industry transactions. Data updated annually. Last update: August 2023.

VALUATION MULTIPLE (MEDIAN VALUE)

UNDER $1 MILLION NET SALES

MVIC/Net Sales.	0.91
MVIC/Gross Profit	0.95
MVIC/SDE	1.57
MVIC/EBITDA	2.39

$1 MILLION–$5 MILLION NET SALES

MVIC/Net Sales.	0.76
MVIC/Gross Profit	0.94
MVIC/SDE	2.22
MVIC/EBITDA	1.51

OVER $5 MILLION NET SALES

MVIC/Net Sales.	2.70
MVIC/Gross Profit	6.04

```
MVIC/SDE  .   .   .   .   .   .   .   .   .   .   .   .   N/A
MVIC/EBITDA  .   .   .   .   .   .   .   .   .   .   . 13.16
```

Source: DealStats (formerly Pratt's Stats), 2023 (Portland, OR: Business Valuation Resources, LLC),
www.bvresources.com/dealstats

PRICING TIPS

The larger inns are selling for 8 (without seller financing) to 10 times (with seller
financing) SDE. Gross rent multiplier is in the 4 to 5 range.

BENCHMARK DATA

Unless the B&B is in a high-occupancy area, it is difficult to cash flow with fewer
than 6 rooms.

Operating expenses 40 to 50 percent

For additional benchmark information, see Bed and Breakfasts

EXPENSES (% OF ANNUAL SALES)

Cost of Goods (food, cleaning supplies, & linens)	15%
Occupancy Costs	07% to 10%
Payroll/Labor Costs (not including owner)	10%
Profit (pretax)	03% to 10%

QUESTIONS

• Can you show me how your inn will work for me financially and in lifestyle?

INDUSTRY TREND

"The 10 trends that are shaping the hospitality industry in 2023:

1. Bleisure travelers & hotel work spaces

2. Holistic hospitality, health & well-being

3. Digitalized guest experiences

4. Hyper-personalization

5. Experience economy & essentialism

6. Asset management strategy

7. Artificial intelligence (AI)

8. Renewable energy

9. Virtual & augmented reality (VR & AR)

10. Deal-seekers"

Source: "2023 Top Hospitality Industry Trends,"
https://hospitalityinsights.ehl.edu/hospitality-industry-trends

EXPERT COMMENTS

Buyers should have their home sold prior to buying a B&B. Contingent sale of a
buyer home is not a very compelling offer. Sellers should have a thorough understanding of the inns for sale market. They should also realistically deal with deal
killers such as needing a new roof, windows, etc.

B&B buyers must make both a lifestyle and financial purchase decision. Innkeeping is one of the few businesses in which you want to live where you work! For
the past 15+ years, we have had smaller B&Bs sold/converted back to homes
than we've had homes being converted to inns! Start-ups are more difficult to
accomplish today versus the mid-1980s primarily due to rising real estate values,

high conversion cost, zoning restrictions, tougher lending practices, and a lack of market demand for innkeeping (during a strong economy). Some of the smaller inns in less popular areas were converted to alternative uses, and a minority of inns closed for avoidance of taxes from capital gains and depreciation recapture.

FINANCING

The typical $1M+ inn sale would typically have a buyer with $200K down and the seller would typically offer a second mortgage for the gap between that amount and 70 percent of the sale/appraised price. Conventional commercial lending would provide up to 70 percent of the sale. Recently, we've seen sellers doing all the financing for inn buyers. It's a better return on the loan than alternative investments. The seller can receive a higher price by offering attractive, below-market loan terms. SBA lending has become more prevalent; lower down payment.

RESOURCES

- ALP—Association of Lodging Professionals: https://www.alplodging.org
- BB-4-Sale.com: https://bb-4-sale.com
- Michigan Bed and Breakfast Association: https://laketolake.com

---

Instrument Manufacturing for Measuring and Testing Electricity and Electrical Signals

| NAICS 334515 | Businesses/Units 726

| Profit $731 M | Wages $3.1 B | Annual Growth Future 2.3%

| | | Annual Growth Past 0.7%

INDUSTRY MULTIPLES

Acquisition multiples below are calculated medians using US private industry transactions. Data updated annually. Last update: August 2023.

VALUATION MULTIPLE (MEDIAN VALUE)

UNDER $1 MILLION NET SALES
MVIC/Net Sales.	0.56
MVIC/Gross Profit	0.88
MVIC/SDE	2.07
MVIC/EBITDA	6.64

$1 MILLION–$5 MILLION NET SALES
MVIC/Net Sales.	1.65
MVIC/Gross Profit	3.90
MVIC/SDE	2.78
MVIC/EBITDA	12.78

OVER $5 MILLION NET SALES
MVIC/Net Sales.	2.29
MVIC/Gross Profit	4.67
MVIC/SDE	12.49
MVIC/EBITDA	15.21

Source: DealStats (formerly Pratt's Stats), 2023 (Portland, OR: Business Valuation Resources, LLC), www.bvresources.com/dealstats

BENCHMARK DATA

STATISTICS (ELECTRICITY & SIGNAL TESTING INSTRUMENT MANUFACTURING)

| Number of Establishments | 726 |
| Average Profit Margin | 5.8% |

```
Revenue per Employee .    .    .    .    .    .    .    . $412,000
Average Number of Employees.    .    .    .    .    .    .    . 43.6
Average Wages per Employee .    .    .    .    .    .    . $101,311
```

PRODUCTS AND SERVICES SEGMENTATION

```
Oscilloscopes and spectrum analyzers    .    .    .    .    . 40.3%
Signal generators  .    .    .    .    .    .    .    .    .    . 21.6%
Multimeters and electrometers.    .    .    .    .    .    . 15.0%
Source measure units  .    .    .    .    .    .    .    .    . 10.0%
Handheld meters    .    .    .    .    .    .    .    .    .    . 7.1%
Parameter analyzers    .    .    .    .    .    .    .    .    . 6.0%
```

MAJOR MARKET SEGMENTATION

```
Exports .    .    .    .    .    .    .    .    .    .    .    . 50.6%
Industrial and manufacturing  .    .    .    .    .    .    . 14.5%
Semiconductors    .    .    .    .    .    .    .    .    .    . 9.2%
Communications    .    .    .    .    .    .    .    .    .    . 9.2%
Aerospace and defense.    .    .    .    .    .    .    .    . 8.6%
Medical .    .    .    .    .    .    .    .    .    .    .    . 4.6%
Retail    .    .    .    .    .    .    .    .    .    .    .    . 3.3%
```

INDUSTRY COSTS

```
Profit    .    .    .    .    .    .    .    .    .    .    .    . 5.8%
Wages  .    .    .    .    .    .    .    .    .    .    .    . 24.8%
Purchases  .    .    .    .    .    .    .    .    .    .    . 36.9%
Depreciation    .    .    .    .    .    .    .    .    .    . 1.7%
Marketing  .    .    .    .    .    .    .    .    .    .    . 0.4%
Rent & Utilities .    .    .    .    .    .    .    .    .    . 1.3%
Other    .    .    .    .    .    .    .    .    .    .    . 29.1%
```

MARKET SHARE

```
Keysight Technologies, Inc..    .    .    .    .    .    .    . 15.6%
Fortive  .    .    .    .    .    .    .    .    .    .    .    . 9.0%
National Instruments   .    .    .    .    .    .    .    .    . 5.1%
Teledyne Technologies .    .    .    .    .    .    .    .    . 2.1%
```

INDUSTRY TREND

"Many industry operators have many defense, aerospace, and government entities as clients. Increasing regulation among product standards has boosted demand for industry products. The number of industry enterprises is estimated to decline due to the appreciation of the US dollar. Internal competition is likely to drive productivity for the industry. The CHIPS and Science Act will likely increase demand for industry products. Import penetration remains an ever-present threat to the industry. Economic growth bolstered private investment and demand from the private sector during most of the period."

Source: IBISWorld Industry at a Glance

RESOURCES

• IBISWorld, October 2022: https://www.ibisworld.com

Insurance Agencies/Brokerages

| NAICS 524210	| SIC 6411-12	| Businesses/Units 424,953
| Profit $36.8 B	| Wages $75.8 B	| Annual Growth Future 0.4%
		| Annual Growth Past 1.5%

Rules of Thumb

- 200%–275% annual sales includes inventory
- 150%–200% commission revenue
- 4–6 x SDE plus inventory
- 6–8 x EBIT
- 5–7 x EBITDA

INDUSTRY MULTIPLES

Acquisition multiples below are calculated medians using US private industry transactions. Data updated annually. Last update: August 2023.

VALUATION MULTIPLE (MEDIAN VALUE)

UNDER $1 MILLION NET SALES

MVIC/Net Sales	1.64
MVIC/Gross Profit	1.77
MVIC/SDE	3.29
MVIC/EBITDA	3.98

$1 MILLION–$5 MILLION NET SALES

MVIC/Net Sales	1.96
MVIC/Gross Profit	2.12
MVIC/SDE	5.07
MVIC/EBITDA	7.58

OVER $5 MILLION NET SALES

MVIC/Net Sales	1.89
MVIC/Gross Profit	3.23
MVIC/SDE	10.11
MVIC/EBITDA	14.35

Source: DealStats (formerly Pratt's Stats), 2023 (Portland, OR: Business Valuation Resources, LLC), www.bvresources.com/dealstats

PRICING TIPS

Insurance agencies' valuations can vary depending on a number of factors, including the type of clients the agencies services. For example, if the agency services mostly low-risk clients, the multiples for selling the agency are going to be higher than if the client serves high-risk clients. High-risk clients are not as stable and typically may include only a single line, while low-risk clients have two or three lines, such as auto, home, and umbrella. For commercial insurance, this would be that the agency has lower-risk, stable clients who have the business package—workers' comp and professional liability or commercial auto with the agency. Buyers with experience are the ones who have a shot at low-risk independent agencies, as these these are the most desirable buyers for this type of agency. If you are looking for an Allstate, Farmers, or high-risk independent agency, you may have a shot without experience, though you will need to have an insurance license. Even though these agencies will entertain those without experience, it always a risk to buy any business without experience, including insurance agencies.

In the current 2023 M&A market, demand to acquire insurance agencies/broker-ages is very strong, and this will continue into the foreseeable future. Insurance agencies/brokerages routinely sell for 2.5 to 3.5 times recurring annual com-mission revenue and 6 to 8 times adjusted EBITDA. Property–casualty agencies are the most valuable versus life–health focused agencies. These pricing tips include independent insurance brokerages as well as captive insurance agen-cies where the book of business is owned by the agency owner-producer, such as Allstate and Farmers agencies. Insurance agencies/brokerages are very valuable because agency and book of business acquisitions are a primary vehicle for insurance agency growth. Another reason is that insurance agencies/brokerages have characteristics similar to that of an annuity in that the customer/policy retention range averages 85 to 95 percent, which means that year over year the agency is retaining 85 to 95 percent of its business in addition to writing new policies for new and existing customers. Most businesses start over with each new year, but insurance agencies/brokerages do not start over, via the renewal of existing policies with existing customers. Oftentimes, insurance agencies/brokerages are acquired by another existing insurance agency, sometimes a direct competitor, and these types of acquisitions can often be executed for a premium acquisition price such as 3.0 to 3.5 times annual commission revenue and 7 to 9 times adjusted EBITDA. This is because these types of acquisitions eliminate a direct competitor (strategic acquisition), and/or the existing acquiring agency is acquiring only the agency book of business revenue stream and will manage the book of business via its own existing staff and facilities and will not be retaining the existing staff or facilities of the agency book of business being acquired; and thus the impact on the acquirer's operating cost structure is very low to immaterial.

The value on an agency depends on many factors. Here are some the the most important: what companies they are appointed to sell for; what types of coverages they are selling; persistence of their block of business; claims loss ratios of their block of business; and dollar volume and size of commissions earned annually. The agency will then be ascertained by a multiple of annual earned commissions. Best-graded agencies can be valued at 4 times. Lowest grade can be valued at 0.5 to 1 times. Everything else is in between.

BENCHMARK DATA

STATISTICS (INSURANCE BROKERS AND AGENCIES)

Number of Establishments	424,953
Average Profit Margin	17.5%
Revenue per Employee	$200,000
Average Number of Employees	2.5
Average Wages per Employee	$72,061

PRODUCTS AND SERVICES SEGMENTATION

Commercial P&C insurance	29.8%
Personal P&C insurance	27.1%
Other	15.5%
Health and medical insurance	13.7%
Life and accident insurance	9.4%
Annuities	2.9%
Insurance administration and risk consulting	1.6%

MAJOR MARKET SEGMENTATION

Businesses	62.6%
Individuals and households	32.9%
Government	4.5%

INDUSTRY COSTS

Profit	17.5%
Wages	36.0%
Purchases	2.5%
Depreciation	1.3%
Marketing	1.5%
Rent & Utilities	1.4%
Other	39.6%

Marsh & McLennan Companies, Inc. . .	3.1%
Arthur J. Gallagher & Co.	2.6%
Aon PLC	2.6%
Hub International Ltd	2.1%
Brown & Brown, Inc.	1.8%

Good persistence, low claims loss ratio, high amount of earned commissions

Many industry buyers will focus on the amount of annual commissions rather than SDE.

EXPENSES (% OF ANNUAL SALES)

Cost of Goods	.0% to 15%
Occupancy Costs	05% to 15%
Payroll/Labor Costs.	55% to 65%
Profit (pretax)	20% to 30%

QUESTIONS

- Get all the financials and tax returns. Get a detailed report of the book of business. Make sure to have the seller spell out any known issues in writing.
- The buyer will need documents and information including agency tax returns, agency financial statements, retention rate, carrier and producer reports, carrier appointments, lease terms, product lines, number of customers, number of individual policies in place, years in business, policy types broken down by type of policy, as well as percentages of policies that are commercial versus personal and life versus health. Why is the agency for sale? Asking price? Have key producers and other staff signed noncompete agreements?
- Loss ratios? Typical contingencies? Any E&O issues? Key employees staying on?
- What will your clients think when you are no longer running the agency?
- Number of policies outstanding? Geographic market served?
- Any producers staying on?
- Can the seller prove all the revenue on the P&L with commission statements and bank statements?
- Do you have cash?

INDUSTRY TREND

There should be growth because of inflation, and carriers are increasing rates. This, however, can mean clients will shop; though a good agency will properly address this by being proactive, doing existing client marketing, and calling these clients. In either case, if more people are shopping, you will get more calls for insurance.

The insurance agency/brokerage industry will continue to see further consolidation and the continued entry of new participants in terms of new insurance agency/brokerage owners.

Great

Staffing is going to overseas outsourcing due to the lack of available local staff; this is also a money saver because it costs much less.

This market will continue to be very attractive for both sellers and buyers.

Always going to be interested, qualified buyers for independent agencies

More carriers are trying to write direct and eliminate the agents by using insurtech technologies.

I complete hundreds of insurance agency SBA 7(a) and conventional loan valuations every year for lenders throughout the United States, and my job is to provide a fair market valuation to ensure that the acquisition price is too high, meaning that the transaction price is far above fair market value. I rarely see a transaction that is excessively greater than actual fair market value; but I do regularly see agencies/brokerages sold for significantly less than actual, realizable fair market value. It is critically important that insurance agency owners have their agency properly appraised before signing the purchase agreement, so that they do not sell their agency for hundreds of thousands to millions of dollars less than it is worth on the open market. The cost of the agency appraisal is an investment that will also result in a transaction that is smoother, more efficient, and faster.

Have things as automated as possible. Have your financials and other records together. An agency with poor records is going to get less than one that has all its records organized and can allow for good due diligence of the buyer.

Agencies can be started and grown, though it does take time to build an agency. This is why many want to acquire an agency and pay top dollar. However, there are not enough preferred independent agencies being listed to satisfy the demand, so starting an agency may be the only option for many, unless they are willing to settle for a nonstandard or captive agency.

There are thousands of independent agencies throughout the world, and a very large number are looking to grow by acquisition.

In addition to focusing on the annual commissions, look at the SDE!

Most buyers of independent agencies are currently agency owners already, so the transition is typically smooth.

FINANCING

Outside financing via a conventional or SBA loan acquired through a traditional bank or commercial lender. Typically 5 to 10 percent cash or equity is required, as well as cash for lender fees and closing costs. Interest rate is primarily market driven and varies from lender to lender.

There is a whole network of available loan options for insurance agencies through many niche lenders.

Most of the transactions that we have seen have either been cash or more traditional financing.

RESOURCES

- IBISWorld, September 2023: https://www.ibisworld.com
- Independent Insurance Agents & Brokers of America (Big I): https://www.independentagent.com
- The PIA of Minnesota: https://www.piamn.com/
- The Council of Insurance Agents and Brokers: https://www.ciab.com
- PropertyCasualty360: https://www.NUpropertycasualty360.com/news
- PIA—Professional Insurance Agents: https://www.pia.org
- NAIC—National Association of Insurance Commissioners: https://content.naic.org/
- MIIAB—Minnesota Independent Insurance Agents and Brokers Association: https://www.miia.org/
- Insurance Journal: https://www.insurancejournal.com/
- Insurance Business America: https://www.insurancebusinessmag.com/us/

- Insurance Agency Appraisal: https://insuranceagencyappraisal.com
- IAIP—International Association of Insurance Professionals: https://www.internationalinsuranceprofessionals.org/default.aspx
- I.I.I.—Insurance Information Institute—lots of information and data: https://www.iii.org
- FAIA—Florida Association of Insurance Agents: https://www.faia.com
- Business Insurance: https://www.businessinsurance.com/
- APCIA—American Property Casualty Insurance Association: https://www.apci.org
- American Association of Insurance Management Consultants: https://www.aaimco.com
- American Agents Alliance: https://agentsalliance.com/
- Agency Equity: https://www.agencyequity.com
- Agency Equity: https://www.agencyequity.com

Insurance Companies (in General)

| NAICS 524210

Rules of Thumb

- 1–2 x capital and surplus
- 4 x SDE

INDUSTRY MULTIPLES

Acquisition multiples below are calculated medians using US private industry transactions. Data updated annually. Last update: August 2023.

VALUATION MULTIPLE (MEDIAN VALUE)

UNDER $1 MILLION NET SALES

MVIC/Net Sales.	1.64
MVIC/Gross Profit	1.77
MVIC/SDE	3.29
MVIC/EBITDA	3.98

$1 MILLION–$5 MILLION NET SALES

MVIC/Net Sales.	1.96
MVIC/Gross Profit	2.12
MVIC/SDE	5.07
MVIC/EBITDA	7.58

OVER $5 MILLION NET SALES

MVIC/Net Sales.	1.89
MVIC/Gross Profit	3.23
MVIC/SDE	10.11
MVIC/EBITDA	14.35

Source: DealStats (formerly Pratt's Stats), 2023 (Portland, OR: Business Valuation Resources, LLC), www.bvresources.com/dealstats

QUESTIONS

- Ask the seller if they think the buyer can be successful in the business. Most will give a straight answer.

INDUSTRY TREND

Excellent, as baby boomers, who own the majority of privately held businesses, will be divesting them because of health issues, retirement, terminal illnesses, burnout, etc.

Look for a good franchise.

It takes a good bit of time with a startup to get to the point of generating cash, and even longer to get to positive cash flowing.

RESOURCES

• Digital Insurance: https://www.dig-in.com

Insurance Companies: Life

| NAICS 524210 | Businesses/Units 8,326

| Profit $242.2 B | Wages $50 B | Annual Growth Future 0.5%

| Annual Growth Past 2.5%

Rules of Thumb

• 1–2.5 x capital and surplus

INDUSTRY MULTIPLES

Acquisition multiples below are calculated medians using US private industry transactions. Data updated annually. Last update: August 2023.

VALUATION MULTIPLE (MEDIAN VALUE)

UNDER $1 MILLION NET SALES	
MVIC/Net Sales	1.64
MVIC/Gross Profit	1.77
MVIC/SDE	3.29
MVIC/EBITDA	3.98
$1 MILLION–$5 MILLION NET SALES	
MVIC/Net Sales	1.96
MVIC/Gross Profit	2.12
MVIC/SDE	5.07
MVIC/EBITDA	7.58
OVER $5 MILLION NET SALES	
MVIC/Net Sales	1.89
MVIC/Gross Profit	3.23
MVIC/SDE	10.11
MVIC/EBITDA	14.35

Source: DealStats (formerly Pratt's Stats), 2023 (Portland, OR: Business Valuation Resources, LLC), www.bvresources.com/dealstats

BENCHMARK DATA

STATISTICS (LIFE INSURANCE & ANNUITIES)

Number of Establishments	8,326
Average Profit Margin	21.6%
Revenue per Employee	$3,078,000
Average Number of Employees	43.6
Average Wages per Employee	$137,268

PRODUCTS AND SERVICES SEGMENTATION

Investment income	34.8%
Individual annuities	21.4%
Individual life insurance premiums	14.8%
Group annuities	14.4%
Other	10.8%
Group life insurance premiums	3.8%

Individuals aged 35 to 54	37.7%
Individuals aged 65 and older	24.4%
Individuals aged 55 to 64	19.5%
Individuals aged 34 and younger	18.4%

INDUSTRY COSTS

Profit	21.6%
Wages	4.5%
Purchases	4.3%
Depreciation	1.5%
Marketing	2.5%
Rent & Utilities	2.3%
Other	63.3%

MARKET SHARE

New York Life Insurance Co.	0.8%
Northwestern Mutual Life Insurance Co.	0.3%
Massachusetts Mutual Life Insurance Co	0.3%
MetLife, Inc..	0.2%
Guardian Life Insurance Co of America	0.1%

INDUSTRY TREND

"Ongoing rate hikes increases investor uncertainty. Larger insurers benefit from mergers and acquisitions. Larger companies can raise capital more easily than their smaller counterparts. Millennials will become a more significant market. Consolidation is likely to continue. A significant portion of revenue comes from investment income. Many companies rely on life insurers for capital and liquidity."

Source: IBISWorld Industry at a Glance

RESOURCES

- IBISWorld, January 2023: https://www.ibisworld.com

Insurance Companies: Property & Casualty

| NAICS 524126 | Businesses/Units 15,920

| Profit $110.1 B | Wages $78.9 B | Annual Growth Future 0.3%

| Annual Growth Past 1.5%

Rules of Thumb

- 0.5–3 x capital and surplus

INDUSTRY MULTIPLES

Acquisition multiples below are calculated medians using US private industry transactions. Data updated annually. Last update: August 2023.

VALUATION MULTIPLE (MEDIAN VALUE)

UNDER $1 MILLION NET SALES

MVIC/Net Sales.	1.97
MVIC/Gross Profit	1.98
MVIC/SDE	6.37
MVIC/EBITDA	21.13

$1 MILLION–$5 MILLION NET SALES

MVIC/Net Sales.	4.34

MVIC/Gross Profit	.	.	.	.	.	.	3.87
MVIC/SDE	.	.	.	.	.	.	N/A
MVIC/EBITDA	.	.	.	.	.	.	16.05

OVER $5 MILLION NET SALES

MVIC/Net Sales.	.	.	.	.	.	.	1.57
MVIC/Gross Profit	.	.	.	.	.	.	1.80
MVIC/SDE	.	.	.	.	.	.	N/A
MVIC/EBITDA	.	.	.	.	.	.	11.53

Source: DealStats (formerly Pratt's Stats), 2023 (Portland, OR: Business Valuation Resources, LLC), www.bvresources.com/dealstats

PRICING TIPS

With a strong demand and low inventory available for P&C agencies, the values have risen sharply. Buyers are most interested in the renewal commissions that are associated with the agency. Standard line P&C agencies sell around 2.5 times commissions. Nonstandard line agencies tend to sell at lower multiples, 2.0. Other factors that positively influence the valuation: strong retention rates (85+ percent), low loss ratios, direct bill, and quality of carrier appointments. Allstate agencies tend to sell at slightly higher multiples because of the generally strong retention rates. P&C agencies that contain a strong homeowners insurance book of business are more valuable; many large buyers in the market are looking to acquire books of business.

Pricing in P&C insurance is based on commissions. Typically 1.5 to 2.0 (or a little higher if over $1M in commission). Key factors will be loss ratios.

BENCHMARK DATA

STATISTICS (PROPERTY, CASUALTY AND DIRECT INSURANCE)

Number of Establishments .	.	.	.	.15,920
Average Profit Margin	.	.	.	. 12.6%
Revenue per Employee .	.	.	.	$1,216,000
Average Number of Employees.	.	.	. 44.3
Average Wages per Employee .	.	.	$110,386

PRODUCTS AND SERVICES SEGMENTATION

Private passenger auto .	.	.	.	. 38.7%
Other	.	.	.	.	.	.	.	. 15.8%
Homeowners multiple peril.	.	.	. 14.5%
Other liability	.	.	.	.	.	9.5%
Workers compensation .	.	.	.	7.4%
Commercial multiple peril	.	.	.	6.1%
Commercial auto	.	.	.	.	6.1%
Fire .	.	.	.	.	.	.	.	1.9%

MAJOR MARKET SEGMENTATION

Other commercial market	.	.	.	. 39.7%
Private vehicle market	.	.	.	. 37.9%
Other private market	.	.	.	. 14.2%
Commercial vehicle market.	.	.	. 6.0%
Other insurance carriers	.	.	.	2.2%

INDUSTRY COSTS

Profit	.	.	.	.	.	.	.	. 12.6%
Wages	.	.	.	.	.	.	.	9.0%
Purchases	.	.	.	.	.	.	4.4%
Depreciation	.	.	.	.	.	0.8%
Marketing	.	.	.	.	.	.	2.7%
Rent & Utilities .	.	.	.	.	2.4%
Other	.	.	.	.	.	.	.	68.0%

State Farm Mutual Automobile Insurance Co	9.3%
Berkshire Hathaway Inc.	6.8%
Allstate Corp.	5.3%
Liberty Mutual Insurance Group Inc.	4.8%
The Travelers Companies, Inc.	4.1%
American International Group, Inc..	1.3%

Insurance industry has very low COGS expenses. You can estimate one service agent for every $1 million in premiums.

QUESTIONS

- 12-month renewal of commissions
- Retention rate
- List of carriers and volume of business
- Are there any large accounts that make up more than 10 percent of the book?
- Does agency accept cash payments? Direct bill or agency bill?
- What is their stockholders' equity? What management do they have?

INDUSTRY TREND

"The average cost of making damaged cars good as new has soared 36 percent since 2018, and may top $5,000 by the end of this year, according to Mitchell, a company that provides data and software to insurance companies and auto repair businesses. That big increase is the main reason that insurance premiums have been soaring—up 17 percent in the 12 months through May....

"'The modern digital architecture is so advanced that systems beyond point of impact are being disrupted,' said Ryan Mandell, director of claims performance for Mitchell. 'Getting a car back to pre-loss condition is harder than at any point in history, and will only become more challenging.'"

Source: "Why Car Repairs Have Become So Expensive" by Lawrence Ulrich, July 3, 2023, https://www.nytimes.com/2023/07/03/business/car-repairs-electric-vehicles.html

EXPERT COMMENTS

If you're selling in this industry, work with a person/company that is experienced in this industry. Buyers should contact brokers and get on as many contact lists as possible. It's a very difficult market for buyers, as there is very low inventory and lots of qualified buyers.

It's almost impossible to start a new agency from scratch. Most of the larger insurance companies (carriers) will not appoint with new start-ups. Current trend is that larger agencies are acquiring the small mom-and-pop agencies and merging the business with their current business to reduce overhead. Another factor that is having a positive influence in the insurance industry is the availability of funds. Lenders like Oak Street, PPC, and Crestmark are specialty lenders that have helped drive the market.

When selling a book of business, expect to have to carry tail insurance for 2–3 years after the deal is done. This is E+O insurance to protect the buyer from things that happened when the seller had the book of business. Also, many buyers will want to have earnouts to reduce their risk.

FINANCING

I see most deals have some seller financing (10 percent) involved. There are many specialty banks that lend to this industry. Also, cash buyers are prevalent as they are experienced buyers who currently own other agencies, hence they have the available capital to acquire.

Personal lines books tend to get a higher multiple than commercial lines. Commercial lines usually have to rebid every year and this increases the risk.

RESOURCES

- IBISWorld, September 2023: https://www.ibisworld.com

Interior Design Services

| | NAICS 541410 | | Businesses/Units 155,047 |

| | Profit $2.7 B | | Wages $4.7 B | | Annual Growth Future 1.2% |

| | | | | | Annual Growth Past 3.6% |

INDUSTRY MULTIPLES

Acquisition multiples below are calculated medians using US private industry transactions. Data updated annually. Last update: August 2023.

VALUATION MULTIPLE (MEDIAN VALUE)

UNDER $1 MILLION NET SALES
MVIC/Net Sales.	0.61
MVIC/Gross Profit	0.95
MVIC/SDE	2.78
MVIC/EBITDA	2.14

$1 MILLION–$5 MILLION NET SALES
MVIC/Net Sales.	0.52
MVIC/Gross Profit	1.22
MVIC/SDE	2.03
MVIC/EBITDA	3.50

OVER $5 MILLION NET SALES
MVIC/Net Sales.	0.29
MVIC/Gross Profit	1.32
MVIC/SDE	1.89
MVIC/EBITDA	3.96

Source: DealStats (formerly Pratt's Stats), 2023 (Portland, OR: Business Valuation Resources, LLC), www.bvresources.com/dealstats

BENCHMARK DATA

STATISTICS (INTERIOR DESIGNERS)
Number of Establishments .	155,047
Average Profit Margin	10.6%
Revenue per Employee .	$139,000
Average Number of Employees.	1.20
Average Wages per Employee .	$25,806

PRODUCTS AND SERVICES SEGMENTATION
Full-service interior design services for residential buildings .	37.3%
Other services	34.6%
Full-service interior design services for non-residential buildings.	18.6%
Interior decorating services	9.5%

MAJOR MARKET SEGMENTATION
Individuals and households.	62.9%
Corporations and businesses	18.0%
Healthcare providers	7.7%

All other .　.　.　.　.　.　.　.　.　.　.　.　. 5.8%
Hospitality providers　.　.　.　.　.　.　.　.　. 5.6%

Profit　.　.　.　.　.　.　.　.　.　.　.　.　.　.　.10.6%
Wages　.　.　.　.　.　.　.　.　.　.　.　.　.　.　.18.4%
Purchases　.　.　.　.　.　.　.　.　.　.　.　.　.　.13.8%
Depreciation　.　.　.　.　.　.　.　.　.　.　.　. 0.7%
Marketing　.　.　.　.　.　.　.　.　.　.　.　.　. 2.2%
Rent & Utilities .　.　.　.　.　.　.　.　.　.　.　. 7.7%
Other　.　.　.　.　.　.　.　.　.　.　.　.　.　.　.46.4%

MARKET SHARE

Gensler .　.　.　.　.　.　.　.　.　.　.　.　.　.　. 0.8%
Interior Architects　.　.　.　.　.　.　.　.　.　. 0.8%
HOK .　.　.　.　.　.　.　.　.　.　.　.　.　.　.　. 0.6%
Nelson & Associates Interior Design and Space Planning.　. 0.3%
HKS .　.　.　.　.　.　.　.　.　.　.　.　.　.　.　. 0.1%
Leo A Daly　.　.　.　.　.　.　.　.　.　.　.　.　. 0.1%
Hirsch　.　.　.　.　.　.　.　.　.　.　.　.　.　.　. 0.1%

INDUSTRY TREND

"The value of residential construction is expected to grow. Demand for interior design is dependent on construction activity. The industry has maintained a high level of market fragmentation. A slowdown in the US housing market could present a threat to industry growth. Growth in the value of residential construction is expected to subside. Industry designers will likely continue to have difficulty controlling large portions of market share. Heightened demand from households prevented a decline in industry revenue in 2020."

Source: IBISWorld Industry at a Glance

RESOURCES

• IBISWorld, January 2023: https://www.ibisworld.com

International Trade Financing

| NAICS 522299　　| Businesses/Units 265

| Profit $94.1 M　　| Wages $85.2 M　　　| Annual Growth Future 6.3%

　　　　　　　　　　　　　　　　　　　　　| Annual Growth Past -0.3%

BENCHMARK DATA

STATISTICS (INTERNATIONAL TRADE FINANCING)

Number of Establishments .　.　.　.　.　.　.　. 265
Average Profit Margin　.　.　.　.　.　.　.　.　.15.8%
Revenue per Employee .　.　.　.　.　.　.　. $803,000
Average Number of Employees.　.　.　.　.　. 3.15
Average Wages per Employee .　.　.　.　.　. $109,592

PRODUCTS AND SERVICES SEGMENTATION

Loans to nonfinancial businesses .　.　.　.　.　.60.1%
Other　.　.　.　.　.　.　.　.　.　.　.　.　.　.　.34.8%
Loans to financial businesses .　.　.　.　.　.　. 5.1%

US importers	60.2%
US exporters	19.9%
Foreign importers of domestic goods .	19.9%

INDUSTRY COSTS

Profit	15.8%
Wages	14.3%
Purchases	2.1%
Depreciation	0.7%
Marketing	3.6%
Rent & Utilities	2.1%
Other	61.4%

MARKET SHARE

HSBC Holdings	16.8%
Wells Fargo	12.1%
Citigroup Inc.	11.7%
Bank of America	9.7%

INDUSTRY TREND

"International trade financing companies have been crucial in reducing the riskiness of US value chains. As international trade grows, so too has demand for working capital loans. The size of the industry has largely consolidated due in part to regulatory changes. Demand for new loans is forecast to increase as global trade patterns are restored. Renewed US economic health will likely boost demand for industry loan services. Industry operators are expected to encounter increased competition from foreign banking subsidiaries. Revenue has been gained from rising demand for new trade loans that resulted from increased trade activity."

Source: IBISWorld Industry at a Glance

RESOURCES

• IBISWorld, August 2021: https://www.ibisworld.com

Investigative Services

| NAICS 561611

Rules of Thumb

• 70%–75% annual sales

INDUSTRY MULTIPLES

Acquisition multiples below are calculated medians using US private industry transactions. Data updated annually. Last update: August 2023.

VALUATION MULTIPLE (MEDIAN VALUE)

UNDER $1 MILLION NET SALES

MVIC/Net Sales	0.85
MVIC/Gross Profit	0.87
MVIC/SDE	2.45
MVIC/EBITDA	3.11

$1 MILLION–$5 MILLION NET SALES

MVIC/Net Sales	0.69
MVIC/Gross Profit	1.28
MVIC/SDE	4.57
MVIC/EBITDA	N/A

MVIC/Net Sales. 4.33
MVIC/Gross Profit 17.95
MVIC/SDE . . . . N/A
MVIC/EBITDA . . . . N/A

Source: DealStats (formerly Pratt's Stats), 2023 (Portland, OR: Business Valuation Resources, LLC), www.bvresources.com/dealstats

RESOURCES

• Professional Investigator Magazine: https://pimagazine.com

Investment Advice/Financial Planning

| NAICS 523930 | Businesses/Units 154,604

| Profit $9.8 B | Wages $18.1 B | Annual Growth Future 0.5%

| | | Annual Growth Past 3.4%

Rules of Thumb

• 5 x SDE
• 150%–250% annual sales
• 6 x EBIT
• 6 x EBITDA

INDUSTRY MULTIPLES

Acquisition multiples below are calculated medians using US private industry transactions. Data updated annually. Last update: August 2023.

VALUATION MULTIPLE (MEDIAN VALUE)

UNDER $1 MILLION NET SALES
MVIC/Net Sales. 4.23
MVIC/Gross Profit 4.33
MVIC/SDE . . . . N/A
MVIC/EBITDA 7.04

$1 MILLION–$5 MILLION NET SALES
MVIC/Net Sales. 13.10
MVIC/Gross Profit . . . . N/A
MVIC/SDE . . . . N/A
MVIC/EBITDA 23.40

OVER $5 MILLION NET SALES
MVIC/Net Sales. 1.72
MVIC/Gross Profit 2.03
MVIC/SDE . . . . N/A
MVIC/EBITDA 11.34

Source: DealStats (formerly Pratt's Stats), 2023 (Portland, OR: Business Valuation Resources, LLC), www.bvresources.com/dealstats

PRICING TIPS

Consolidation has been a trend for firms with some scale and management. A lot of fragmentation and owner dependence in this industry. Most smaller firms are built on the back of the owner and he/she owns all of the relationships with clients. Firms that command a premium have mostly eliminated owner dependence by using a team approach.

BENCHMARK DATA

STATISTICS (FINANCIAL PLANNING AND ADVICE)

Number of Establishments .	154,604
Average Profit Margin	.16.5%
Revenue per Employee .	$258,000
Average Number of Employees.	1.5
Average Wages per Employee .	$79,599

PRODUCTS AND SERVICES SEGMENTATION

Personal financial planning and investment services .	.51.7%
Financial management consulting .	.41.4%
Other	. 4.3%
Brokering and dealing .	. 2.4%
Trust services	. 0.2%

MAJOR MARKET SEGMENTATION

Individuals and households.	.51.9%
Businesses and governments .	.48.1%

INDUSTRY COSTS

Profit	.16.5%
Wages .	.30.6%
Purchases .	. 2.2%
Depreciation	. 0.8%
Marketing .	. 1.2%
Rent & Utilities .	. 2.7%
Other	.46.0%

MARKET SHARE

Ameriprise Financial Inc. 10.9%	.11.7%
Raymond James Financial Inc. .	.10.9%
Graystone Consulting .	. 0.1%

Cap rate between 4 and 15 percent

Assets under management (AUM) per advisor

The best benchmark is revenue or profit per employee. Financial services are very labor intensive and highly dependent on customer satisfaction.

EXPENSES (% OF ANNUAL SALES)

Cost of Goods .	0% to 03%
Occupancy Costs .	10% to 15%
Payroll/Labor Costs.	50% to 60%
Profit (pretax) .	25% to 30%

QUESTIONS

- Why are you selling? What are you looking for in a buyer? How many house-holds do you serve? What is average AUM per household? Who are the top ten households and AUM for each? How do you get new households? How long will you be available for a transition? What are your thoughts on a successful transition plan?
- How do you get new clients? What is your fee schedule? What are your assets under management (AUM)? How many clients do you personally work with? Do the other advisors in your firm have noncompetes? Are the clients owned by the advisor or the firm? How are advisors compensated? What is your value proposition to clients? How do you implement client portfolios?
- How does the firm monitor changes in regulations affecting the industry? What types of incentives does the company offer its portfolio and fund managers?

How does the company evaluate opportunities to expand outside its primary geographic markets?

Continued growth and consolidation

Massive growth—real estate hard assets should be in everyone's portfolio. Owners make money in their sleep. Lease space you do not use to create income. Tenants stay a long time, and pay your taxes and insurance.

"Revenue growth has been supported by a growth equity market and strong bond yields. Rising investment returns have attracted more customers to the industry. Sustained macroeconomic growth has benefited industry operators over the five years to 2021. The emergence of financial technology will likely continue to make industry services more accessible. Automated financial planning services will likely lower barriers to entry for most individuals. New operators are expected to enter the industry due to increased demand. Financial volatility is expected to affect total AUM and fees generated by industry operators in 2021."

Source: IBISWorld Industry at a Glance

There are a few trends going on in financial services.

One is the commoditization of portfolio management. Advisors are needing to differentiate with a personalized planning process.

Also, the industry is likely at the beginning of a period of fee compression as technology continues to come into financial services and drive down the fees advisors can justify.

Another is the movement toward niche practices. A lot of advisors are carving out a specialized niche as a client acquisition/retention strategy.

EXPERT COMMENTS

Get extremely clear about the owner's responsibilities and their willingness to help transition the business. Since most of these businesses are very dependent on the current owner, you will want to make sure they are committed to a successful transition.

Most firms charge a percentage of assets under management (AUM). So the firms' fees are directly tied to the performance of the markets. Decisions on growing staff and investing for growth are difficult because it must come at a time when the market is cooperating. There are low barriers to entry—it's extremely easy for an advisor to start their own firm. Usually investment advisory firms have nice offices in good locations. These businesses are very marketable as there are many firms (and consolidators) looking to grow through acquisition. There are brokerage firms dedicated to selling investment advisory practices.

To a buyer: build relationships with other advisors. Because this is a relationship business, they usually want to make sure their clients will be cared for. Therefore, they will only sell to someone they trust will take care of their clients. Also, since the transition will likely be over a longer period of time, make sure you can work well with the selling advisor.

To a seller: get to know the buyer and get comfortable with them. Can you imagine them serving your clients? Are they competent and do they have a similar approach/value set? Be creative with deal terms if you find the right buyer.

Cash flow lenders are willing to enter this space. Live Oak Bank has a department dedicated to these types of businesses. But these are usually SBA loans, which don't allow the owner to stay on past one year. So for longer transitions (which is usually a good idea in this business), sometimes you may have a seller note with a bullet payment due when the owner wants to exit the business (maybe 3–5 years, at which point an SBA loan is applied for).

RESOURCES

- IBISWorld, July 2022: https://www.ibisworld.com
- Barron's: https://www.barrons.com
- CFA Institute: https://www.cfainstitute.org/
- CFA Society New York: https://www.cfany.org/
- CFP Board—Certified Financial Planner Board of Standards: https://www.cfp.net/
- Financial Advisor Magazine: https://www.fa-mag.com
- FP—Financial Planning: https://www.financial-planning.com/
- FPA—Financial Planning Association: https://www.financialplanningassociation.org/
- InvestmentNews: https://www.investmentnews.com
- Kitces.com: https://www.kitces.com/
- Morningstar: https://www.morningstar.com

Investment Banking and Securities Dealing

| NAICS 523150 | Businesses/Units 14,160

| Profit $63.9 B | Wages $48.1 B | Annual Growth Future 3.7%

| | | Annual Growth Past 8.5%

Rules of Thumb

- 7 x SDE

BENCHMARK DATA

STATISTICS (INVESTMENT BANKING & SECURITIES DEALING)

Number of Establishments	14,160
Average Profit Margin	35.0%
Revenue per Employee	$1,586,000
Average Number of Employees	8.39
Average Wages per Employee	$417,206

PRODUCTS AND SERVICES SEGMENTATION

Trading and related services	51.6%
Advising fees	13.0%
Underwriting services (equity)	12.9%
Other	12.0%
Underwriting services (debt)	10.5%

MAJOR MARKET SEGMENTATION

Financial	36.2%
Other	29.8%
High technology	9.9%
Healthcare	8.6%
Industrial	8.2%
Energy and power	7.3%

INDUSTRY COSTS

Profit	35.0%
Wages	26.4%
Purchases	1.6%
Depreciation	0.9%
Marketing	0.9%
Rent & Utilities	2.0%
Other	33.3%

MARKET SHARE

JPMorgan Chase	20.9%
Goldman Sachs	15.5%
Morgan Stanley	15.4%
Bank of America	12.0%
Citigroup Inc.	11.0%
William Blair	1.1%

Sales per employee

EXPENSES (% OF ANNUAL SALES)

Cost of Goods	50%

QUESTIONS

• Customer base? Area of specific expertise?

INDUSTRY TREND

Continued strong growth

"Largely stemming from strong demand for IPOs, industry revenue has increased. Lower interest rates led borrowers to seek industry services to underwrite debt offerings. Smaller investment banks have increasingly shifted to M&A advising services. Industry operators are expected to benefit from rising interest rates on loans made. Improving financial markets will spur demand for equity underwriting and M&A services. Regulation of the financial sector will likely increase in the United States and Europe. Industry operators have benefited from increased trading activity on behalf of their clients."

Source: IBISWorld Industry at a Glance

EXPERT COMMENTS

Work in the field for a while to gain experience and knowledge.

FINANCING

Combination of both; noncompete; combination of equity and debt

RESOURCES

• IBISWorld, May 2022: https://www.ibisworld.com

Janitorial Services

| NAICS 561720	| SIC 7439-02	| Businesses/Units 1,256,381
| Profit $6 B	| Wages $38.4 B	| Annual Growth Future 1.3%
		| Annual Growth Past 1.2%

Rules of Thumb

- 60%–70% annual sales
- 2–3 x SDE
- 1 x one month's billings; plus fixtures, equipment and inventory
- 3–4 x monthly billings; includes fixtures, equipment and inventory
- 4 x EBITDA
- 3 x EBIT

INDUSTRY MULTIPLES

Acquisition multiples below are calculated medians using US private industry transactions. Data updated annually. Last update: August 2023.

VALUATION MULTIPLE (MEDIAN VALUE)

UNDER $1 MILLION NET SALES	
MVIC/Net Sales	0.59
MVIC/Gross Profit	0.76
MVIC/SDE	2.03
MVIC/EBITDA	2.92

$1 MILLION–$5 MILLION NET SALES	
MVIC/Net Sales	0.45
MVIC/Gross Profit	1.02
MVIC/SDE	2.86
MVIC/EBITDA	4.05

OVER $5 MILLION NET SALES	
MVIC/Net Sales	0.53
MVIC/Gross Profit	2.26
MVIC/SDE	4.26
MVIC/EBITDA	5.48

Source: DealStats (formerly Pratt's Stats), 2023 (Portland, OR: Business Valuation Resources, LLC), www.bvresources.com/dealstats

PRICING TIPS

The janitorial service field has always been a good seller especially in highly populated areas. Commercial cleaning companies tend to demand a higher price especially if their SDE is above $300K. A good sales force and low customer concentration is vital. All staff should be W-2 compliant and WC should be in place, with a good record. Residential cleaning/maid service businesses are highly dependent on the number of clients under a professional fee agreement, and typically those with 50 or more clients (100 to 200 cleans per month) sell before smaller companies. Franchise cleaning companies are much harder to sell as there simply isn't enough profit to go around and the franchisor usually owns the client. The owner should be an operator and not a cleaner! Granted a small owner/cleaner business is salable to those in need of a job or to an acquisition-minded buyer set on growth.

BENCHMARK DATA

STATISTICS (JANITORIAL SERVICES)

Number of Establishments	1,256,381
Average Profit Margin	6.7%
Revenue per Employee	$37,700
Average Number of Employees	1.9
Average Wages per Employee	$15,921

PRODUCTS AND SERVICES SEGMENTATION

Commercial cleaning services	73.4%
Residential interior cleaning services	9.2%

Damage restoration and cleaning services. 6.8%
Other 4.5%
Cleaning services for window exteriors 3.5%
Cleaning services for building exteriors 1.4%
Hard-surface floor care services 1.2%

MAJOR MARKET SEGMENTATION

Commercial 73.4%
Residential 14.3%
Government. 7.3%
Nonprofit 5.0%

INDUSTRY COSTS

Profit 6.7%
Wages 42.7%
Purchases 22.4%
Depreciation 0.9%
Marketing 1.8%
Rent & Utilities 2.5%
Other 23.0%

MARKET SHARE

ABM Industries Inc.. . . . . 4.0%
Red Coats Inc. 0.2%

EXPENSES (% OF ANNUAL SALES)

Cost of Goods . . . . 01% to 03%
Occupancy Costs . . . . 07% to 10%
Payroll/Labor Costs. . . . . 50% to 70%
Profit (pretax) . . . . 20% to 40%

INDUSTRY TREND

Labor is becoming easier to get now.

EXPERT COMMENTS

These companies should be very profitable. If they are not, then there is something wrong.

FINANCING

SBA and private equity group financing is certainly an option. Most small units are sold with at least 80 to 90 percent cash down.

RESOURCES

- IBISWorld, September 2023: https://www.ibisworld.com
- BSCAI—Building Service Contractors Association International: https://www.bscai.org
- CMM—Cleaning & Maintenance Management: https://www.cmmonline.com
- ISSA—The Worldwide Cleaning Industry Association: https://www.issa.com

Jersey Mike's Subs (Franchise)

| NAICS 722513 | SIC 5812-19 | Businesses/Units 2,379

Rules of Thumb

- 50% annual sales plus inventory

INDUSTRY MULTIPLES

Acquisition multiples below are calculated medians using US private industry transactions. Data updated annually. Last update: August 2023.

VALUATION MULTIPLE (MEDIAN VALUE)

UNDER $1 MILLION NET SALES

MVIC/Net Sales.	0.31
MVIC/Gross Profit	0.48
MVIC/SDE	1.67
MVIC/EBITDA	2.21

$1 MILLION–$5 MILLION NET SALES

MVIC/Net Sales.	0.39
MVIC/Gross Profit	0.60
MVIC/SDE	2.43
MVIC/EBITDA	2.98

OVER $5 MILLION NET SALES

MVIC/Net Sales.	0.89
MVIC/Gross Profit	2.08
MVIC/SDE	4.98
MVIC/EBITDA	12.81

Source: DealStats (formerly Pratt's Stats), 2023 (Portland, OR: Business Valuation Resources, LLC), www.bvresources.com/dealstats

PRICING TIPS

Approx. Total Investment: $194,035 to $954,611

BENCHMARK DATA

For Benchmark data see Sandwich Shops

RESOURCES

- Jersey Mike's Subs: https://www.jerseymikes.com
- Franchise information: https://www.jerseymikes.com/franchise

Jewelry and Silverware Manufacturing

| NAICS 339910 | Businesses/Units 8,306

| Profit $1.4 B | Wages $3.1 B | Annual Growth Future 1.5%

| | | Annual Growth Past -2.7%

INDUSTRY MULTIPLES

Acquisition multiples below are calculated medians using US private industry transactions. Data updated annually. Last update: August 2023.

VALUATION MULTIPLE (MEDIAN VALUE)

UNDER $1 MILLION NET SALES

MVIC/Net Sales.	0.40
MVIC/Gross Profit	0.70
MVIC/SDE	0.97
MVIC/EBITDA	2.64

$1 MILLION–$5 MILLION NET SALES

MVIC/Net Sales.	0.53
MVIC/Gross Profit	1.03
MVIC/SDE	2.01
MVIC/EBITDA	4.21

J

OVER $5 MILLION NET SALES

MVIC/Net Sales.	3.93
MVIC/Gross Profit	6.30
MVIC/SDE	N/A
MVIC/EBITDA	17.53

Source: DealStats (formerly Pratt's Stats), 2023 (Portland, OR: Business Valuation Resources, LLC), www.bvresources.com/dealstats

BENCHMARK DATA

STATISTICS (JEWELRY MANUFACTURING)

Number of Establishments	8,306
Average Profit Margin	6.4%
Revenue per Employee	$737,000
Average Number of Employees.	3.5
Average Wages per Employee	$106,874

PRODUCTS AND SERVICES SEGMENTATION

Precious metal jewelry and accessories made from gold and platinum . .	48.4%
Precious and semi-precious metal jewelry excluding gold and platinum . .	15.0%
Other	13.9%
Jewelers' materials and lapidary work manufacturing	13.3%
Costume jewelry	9.4%

MAJOR MARKET SEGMENTATION

Precious metals wholesalers	48.7%
Precious stones wholesalers	17.9%
Other	13.8%
Findings wholesalers	10.2%
Costume jewelry wholesalers	9.4%

INDUSTRY COSTS

Profit	6.4%
Wages	14.6%
Purchases	49.3%
Depreciation	1.3%
Marketing	1.4%
Rent & Utilities	2.7%
Other	24.4%

MARKET SHARE

Tiffany & Co..	8.1%

INDUSTRY TREND

"The COVID-19 pandemic resulted in falling purchases of luxury items such as jewelry. Prevalent import penetration negatively affects domestic manufacturers. Lower labor and compliance costs abroad lead to high price competition levels. The US dollar will likely stabilize as international affairs continue to resolve. The price of gold and silver will likely fall as supply chain disruptions resolve. Implementing 3D printing and design tools has lowered the need for human capital, reducing wage expenses. The rise in price competition has affected manufacturers across the board, limiting profit."

Source: IBISWorld Industry at a Glance

RESOURCES

• IBISWorld, February 2023: https://www.ibisworld.com

520   2024 BUSINESS REFERENCE GUIDE | 34TH EDITION

Jewelry Stores

	NAICS 448310		SIC 5944-09		Businesses/Units 51,333
	Profit $1.1 B		Wages $4.1 B		Annual Growth Future -1.0%
					Annual Growth Past -1.8%

Rules of Thumb
- 4–6 x EBIT if inventory included

INDUSTRY MULTIPLES

Acquisition multiples below are calculated medians using US private industry transactions. Data updated annually. Last update: August 2023.

VALUATION MULTIPLE (MEDIAN VALUE)

UNDER $1 MILLION NET SALES

MVIC/Net Sales	0.43
MVIC/Gross Profit	0.85
MVIC/SDE	1.64
MVIC/EBITDA	1.80

$1 MILLION–$5 MILLION NET SALES

MVIC/Net Sales	1.66
MVIC/Gross Profit	1.99
MVIC/SDE	5.19
MVIC/EBITDA	7.18

OVER $5 MILLION NET SALES

MVIC/Net Sales	0.77
MVIC/Gross Profit	1.49
MVIC/SDE	4.81
MVIC/EBITDA	14.75

Source: DealStats (formerly Pratt's Stats), 2023 (Portland, OR: Business Valuation Resources, LLC), www.bvresources.com/dealstats

BENCHMARK DATA

STATISTICS (JEWELRY STORES)

Number of Establishments	51,333
Average Profit Margin	3.4%
Revenue per Employee	$236,000
Average Number of Employees	2.7
Average Wages per Employee	$29,451

PRODUCTS AND SERVICES SEGMENTATION

Diamond Jewelry	35.8%
Other merchandise	22.5%
Watches	17.0%
Pearl and other gemstone jewelry	14.1%
Gold jewelry	10.6%

MAJOR MARKET SEGMENTATION

Consumers earning more than $150,000 before taxes	41.5%
Consumers earning less than $70,000 before taxes	37.0%
Consumers earning between $100,000 and $149,999 before taxes	13.5%
Consumers earning between $70,000 and $99,999 before taxes	8.0%

INDUSTRY COSTS

Profit	3.4%
Wages	12.6%
Purchases	51.4%

Depreciation 0.9%
Marketing 2.1%
Rent & Utilities 7.6%
Other 22.0%

MARKET SHARE

Signet Jewelers Limited. 15.1%
Compagnie Financière Richemont SA 6.9%
LVMH Moët Hennessy Louis Vuitton SE 5.7%
Berkshire Hathaway Inc. 3.4%
Catbird 0.1%

EXPENSES (% OF ANNUAL SALES)

Cost of Goods . . . . 55% to 58%
Occupancy Costs . . . . N/A
Payroll/Labor Costs. 22%
Profit (pretax) 06%

INDUSTRY TREND

"Industry revenue has declined due to mounting competition from external operators. Operators have increased their synthetic and man-made diamond selection to meet consumer trends. More industry operators have been aiming to grow their e-commerce platforms. The declining marriage rate is likely to pressure the industry's growth. Many operators are anticipated to exit the industry or merge with larger jewelry stores. The industry is expected to benefit from declining wage costs. Rising gold and silver prices have increased input costs for industry operators, lowering industry profit."

Source: IBISWorld Industry at a Glance

FINANCING

Not seller financed—inventory too portable—high risk

RESOURCES

- IBISWorld, June 2022: https://www.ibisworld.com
- INSTORE magazine: https://instoremag.com
- JA—Jewelers of America: https://www.jewelers.org
- National Jeweler: https://www.nationaljeweler.com

Jewelry, Watch, Precious Stone, and Precious Metal Merchant Wholesalers

| NAICS 423940 | Businesses/Units 25,255

| Profit $1.7 B | Wages $2.6 B | Annual Growth Future 0.4%

| Annual Growth Past -3.1%

INDUSTRY MULTIPLES

Acquisition multiples below are calculated medians using US private industry transactions. Data updated annually. Last update: August 2023.

VALUATION MULTIPLE (MEDIAN VALUE)

UNDER $1 MILLION NET SALES

MVIC/Net Sales. 0.43
MVIC/Gross Profit 0.66
MVIC/SDE 1.99
MVIC/EBITDA 2.43

| $1 MILLION–$5 MILLION NET SALES | N/A |
| OVER $5 MILLION NET SALES | N/A |

Source: DealStats (formerly Pratt's Stats), 2023 (Portland, OR: Business Valuation Resources, LLC), www.bvresources.com/dealstats

BENCHMARK DATA

STATISTICS (JEWELRY & WATCH WHOLESALING)

Number of Establishments 25,255
Average Profit Margin 3.1%
Revenue per Employee $932,000
Average Number of Employees. 2.3
Average Wages per Employee . . . $44,219

PRODUCTS AND SERVICES SEGMENTATION

Precious metals. 42.7%
Diamonds and diamond jewelry . . . 19.8%
Watches, clocks and parts 13.2%
Other 12.6%
Costume jewelry 5.2%
Silverware and plated jewelry 3.3%
Karat gold 3.2%

MAJOR MARKET SEGMENTATION

Wholesalers and distributors for resale . 44.1%
Retailers. 37.1%
Manufacturing and mining industries . . 11.1%
Other 4.3%
Direct sales (not for resale). 3.4%

INDUSTRY COSTS

Profit 3.1%
Wages 4.8%
Purchases 76.4%
Depreciation 0.2%
Marketing 1.1%
Rent & Utilities 1.3%
Other 13.1%

MARKET SHARE

A-Mark Precious Metals, Inc. 11.0%

RESOURCES

- IBISWorld, September 2023: https://www.ibisworld.com

Jimmy John's Sandwiches (Franchise)

| NAICS 722513 | SIC 5812-19 | Businesses/Units 2,616 |

Rules of Thumb

- 65%–70% annual sales plus inventory

INDUSTRY MULTIPLES

Acquisition multiples below are calculated medians using US private industry transactions. Data updated annually. Last update: August 2023.

VALUATION MULTIPLE (MEDIAN VALUE)

UNDER $1 MILLION NET SALES
MVIC/Net Sales. 0.31

MVIC/Gross Profit 0.48
MVIC/SDE 1.67
MVIC/EBITDA 2.21

$1 MILLION–$5 MILLION NET SALES
MVIC/Net Sales. 0.39
MVIC/Gross Profit 0.60
MVIC/SDE 2.43
MVIC/EBITDA 2.98

OVER $5 MILLION NET SALES
MVIC/Net Sales. 0.89
MVIC/Gross Profit 2.08
MVIC/SDE 4.98
MVIC/EBITDA 12.81

Source: DealStats (formerly Pratt's Stats), 2023 (Portland, OR: Business Valuation Resources, LLC), www.bvresources.com/dealstats

PRICING TIPS

Approx. Total Investment: $355,900 to $671,400

BENCHMARK DATA

For Benchmark data see Sandwich Shops

RESOURCES

- Jimmy John's Sandwiches: https://www.jimmyjohns.com
- Franchise information: https://www.jimmyjohns.com/franchising/
- Inspire Brands: https://inspirebrands.com

Juice It Up! (Franchise)

| NAICS 722515 | Businesses/Units 82

Rules of Thumb

- 20%–25% annual sales plus inventory

INDUSTRY MULTIPLES

Acquisition multiples below are calculated medians using US private industry transactions. Data updated annually. Last update: August 2023.

VALUATION MULTIPLE (MEDIAN VALUE)

UNDER $1 MILLION NET SALES
MVIC/Net Sales. 0.44
MVIC/Gross Profit 0.62
MVIC/SDE 2.20
MVIC/EBITDA 2.82

$1 MILLION–$5 MILLION NET SALES
MVIC/Net Sales. 0.41
MVIC/Gross Profit 0.69
MVIC/SDE 2.82
MVIC/EBITDA 5.94

OVER $5 MILLION NET SALES
MVIC/Net Sales. 3.89
MVIC/Gross Profit 4.87
MVIC/SDE . . . . N/A
MVIC/EBITDA . . . . N/A

Source: DealStats (formerly Pratt's Stats), 2023 (Portland, OR: Business Valuation Resources, LLC), www.bvresources.com/dealstats

PRICING TIPS

Approx. Total Investment: $226,700 to $536,745

RESOURCES

- Juice It Up!: https://juiceitup.com
- Franchise information: https://juiceitupfranchise.com

Keyrenter Property Management (Franchise)

| NAICS 531311 | Businesses/Units 40

INDUSTRY MULTIPLES

Acquisition multiples below are calculated medians using US private industry transactions. Data updated annually. Last update: August 2023.

VALUATION MULTIPLE (MEDIAN VALUE)

UNDER $1 MILLION NET SALES

MVIC/Net Sales.	0.69
MVIC/Gross Profit	1.04
MVIC/SDE	2.28
MVIC/EBITDA	3.45

$1 MILLION–$5 MILLION NET SALES

MVIC/Net Sales.	0.43
MVIC/Gross Profit	0.90
MVIC/SDE	2.83
MVIC/EBITDA	4.27

OVER $5 MILLION NET SALES

MVIC/Net Sales.	0.94
MVIC/Gross Profit	1.20
MVIC/SDE	2.99
MVIC/EBITDA	4.83

Source: DealStats (formerly Pratt's Stats), 2023 (Portland, OR: Business Valuation Resources, LLC), www.bvresources.com/dealstats

PRICING TIPS

Approx. Total Investment: $101,125 to $178,279

RESOURCES

- Keyrenter Property Management: https://keyrenter.com
- Franchise information: https://keyrenterfranchise.com

Kumon (Franchise)

| NAICS 611691 | Businesses/Units 1,620

Rules of Thumb

- 80%–90% annual sales plus inventory

INDUSTRY MULTIPLES

Acquisition multiples below are calculated medians using US private industry transactions. Data updated annually. Last update: August 2023.

VALUATION MULTIPLE (MEDIAN VALUE)

UNDER $1 MILLION NET SALES

MVIC/Net Sales	0.45
MVIC/Gross Profit	0.49
MVIC/SDE	1.85
MVIC/EBITDA	3.33

$1 MILLION–$5 MILLION NET SALES

MVIC/Net Sales	0.75
MVIC/Gross Profit	1.32
MVIC/SDE	3.11
MVIC/EBITDA	4.54

OVER $5 MILLION NET SALES	N/A

Source: DealStats (formerly Pratt's Stats), 2023 (Portland, OR: Business Valuation Resources, LLC), www.bvresources.com/dealstats

PRICING TIPS

Approx. Total Investment: $68,428 to $146,640

RESOURCES

- Kumon: https://www.kumon.com
- Franchise information: https://www.kumonfranchise.com

Land Development

	NAICS 237210		Businesses/Units 12,157
	Profit $2 B		Wages $1.7 B

	Annual Growth Future 0.8%
	Annual Growth Past -6.4%

INDUSTRY MULTIPLES

Acquisition multiples below are calculated medians using US private industry transactions. Data updated annually. Last update: August 2023.

VALUATION MULTIPLE (MEDIAN VALUE)

UNDER $1 MILLION NET SALES

MVIC/Net Sales	0.78
MVIC/Gross Profit	N/A
MVIC/SDE	1.37
MVIC/EBITDA	N/A

$1 MILLION–$5 MILLION NET SALES	N/A

OVER $5 MILLION NET SALES

MVIC/Net Sales	1.42
MVIC/Gross Profit	N/A
MVIC/SDE	N/A
MVIC/EBITDA	7.08

Source: DealStats (formerly Pratt's Stats), 2023 (Portland, OR: Business Valuation Resources, LLC), www.bvresources.com/dealstats

BENCHMARK DATA

STATISTICS (LAND DEVELOPMENT)

Number of Establishments	12,157
Average Profit Margin	17.0%
Revenue per Employee	$669,649
Average Number of Employees. . . .	1.0
Average Wages per Employee . .	$94,314

PRODUCTS AND SERVICES SEGMENTATION

Developing operator-owned land for residential use	. 45.3%
Developing and subdividing customer-owned land	.38.5%
Developing operator-owned land for nonresidential use	.16.2%

MAJOR MARKET SEGMENTATION

Nonresidential and nonbuilding	.64.5%
Residential	.20.9%
Other	.11.2%
Special trade	. 3.4%

INDUSTRY COSTS

Profit	.17.0%
Wages	.14.4%
Purchases	.43.1%
Depreciation	. 3.4%
Marketing	. 0.4%
Rent & Utilities	. 3.3%
Other	.18.4%

INDUSTRY TREND

"The residential market carried the industry through the early stages of the COVID-19 pandemic. Land developers were shielded from revenue loss in 2020 thanks to a boom in residential construction following urban flight caused by the pandemic.

"Rising material prices in response to global tensions have hindered industry growth. The ongoing Russo-Ukrainian war has placed a strain on the supply of concrete and petroleum to Western Europe, forcing the United States to divert supplies away from domestic markets.

"Rising corporate demand will buoy the industry in the coming years. US industrial concerns will have to ramp up productivity if the country wishes to retain its status as a world leader, meaning increased demand from downstream markets."

Source: IBISWorld Key Takeaways

RESOURCES

• IBISWorld, September 2023: https://www.ibisworld.com

Land Surveying Services

NAICS 541370	SIC 8713-01	Businesses/Units 17,000	
Profit $751.3 M	Wages $4.3 B	Annual Growth Future 2.7%	
		Annual Growth Past 1.6%	

Rules of Thumb

• 40%–80% annual fee revenues; plus fixtures, equipment and inventory; may require earnout

INDUSTRY MULTIPLES

Acquisition multiples below are calculated medians using US private industry transactions. Data updated annually. Last update: August 2023.

UNDER $1 MILLION NET SALES

MVIC/Net Sales.	1.04
MVIC/Gross Profit	1.09
MVIC/SDE	2.67
MVIC/EBITDA	3.72

$1 MILLION–$5 MILLION NET SALES

MVIC/Net Sales.	1.24
MVIC/Gross Profit	1.24
MVIC/SDE	3.29
MVIC/EBITDA	3.86

OVER $5 MILLION NET SALES

MVIC/Net Sales.	5.01
MVIC/Gross Profit	7.65
MVIC/SDE	N/A
MVIC/EBITDA	12.65

Source: DealStats (formerly Pratt's Stats), 2023 (Portland, OR: Business Valuation Resources, LLC), www.bvresources.com/dealstats

BENCHMARK DATA

STATISTICS (SURVEYING AND MAPPING SERVICES)

Number of Establishments .	17,000
Average Profit Margin	7.1%
General Revenue ($ Million)	$10,813,000,000
Employment (Units).	66,915
Wages ($ Million)	$4,404,000,000

PRODUCTS AND SERVICES SEGMENTATION

Cadastral, property line and boundary surveying	28.7%
Topographical and planimetric surveying and mapping	21.4%
Construction surveying .	19.8%
Other services	11.1%
Hydrographic and bathymetric services	7.5%
Subdivision layout and design services	4.4%
Geospatial processing services	4.0%
Geodetic surveying and ground control support services .	3.1%

MAJOR MARKET SEGMENTATION

Other and nonprofit .	31.5%
Construction companies	21.7%
Governmental bodies (federal, state and local)	19.7%
Professional technical companies .	15.1%
Households .	12.0%

INDUSTRY COSTS

Profit	7.1%
Wages	40.8%
Purchases	8.3%
Depreciation	3.0%
Marketing	0.4%
Rent & Utilities .	3.9%
Other	36.5%

INDUSTRY TREND

"Housing market volatility unmoors surveyors and mappers. Robust recovery after 2024 will revive surveying services. Government infrastructure investment provides a goldmine for surveyors and mappers with lucrative contracts. New technologies will improve efficiency, but at a cost. Drones aren't cheap and require skilled personnel to operate."

Source: IBISWorld Industry at a Glance

- IBISWorld, January 2023: https://www.ibisworld.com
- NSPS—National Society of Professional Surveyors: https://www.nsps.us.com/

L

Landscape Architectural Services

| NAICS 541320 | Businesses/Units 41,185

| Profit $677.1 M | Wages $2.6 B | Annual Growth Future 1.1%

| Annual Growth Past -0.5%

INDUSTRY MULTIPLES

Acquisition multiples below are calculated medians using US private industry transactions. Data updated annually. Last update: August 2023.

VALUATION MULTIPLE (MEDIAN VALUE)

UNDER $1 MILLION NET SALES

MVIC/Net Sales.	0.48
MVIC/Gross Profit	0.79
MVIC/SDE	1.87
MVIC/EBITDA	11.49

$1 MILLION–$5 MILLION NET SALES

MVIC/Net Sales.	0.29
MVIC/Gross Profit	0.29
MVIC/SDE	2.15
MVIC/EBITDA	3.30

OVER $5 MILLION NET SALES

MVIC/Net Sales.	0.37
MVIC/Gross Profit	0.92
MVIC/SDE	2.10
MVIC/EBITDA	2.60

Source: DealStats (formerly Pratt's Stats), 2023 (Portland, OR: Business Valuation Resources, LLC), www.bvresources.com/dealstats

BENCHMARK DATA

STATISTICS (LANDSCAPE DESIGN)

Number of Establishments .	41,185
Average Profit Margin	9.6%
Revenue per Employee .	$115,000
Average Number of Employees.	1.5
Average Wages per Employee .	$42,625

PRODUCTS AND SERVICES SEGMENTATION

Landscape design for residential building .	28.0%
Other services	23.6%
Landscape design for nonresidential building .	20.4%
Recreational and open space landscape design	17.8%
Urban planning services	10.2%

MAJOR MARKET SEGMENTATION

Individual property owners .	33.5%
Construction, architecture and engineering companies	24.8%
Other	23.5%
Federal, state and local government	18.2%

Profit	9.6%
Wages	37.3%
Purchases	8.8%
Depreciation	2.2%
Marketing	0.4%
Rent & Utilities	4.2%
Other	37.4%

MARKET SHARE

Brightview Holdings	9.1%
Gensler	3.9%
HDR	3.9%
Perkins and Will	3.4%
Hammel	2.9%
HKS	2.1%
HOK	0.6%
Sasaki Associates	0.4%
Kohn Pedersen Fox Associates	0.3%
NBBJ	0.1%

INDUSTRY TREND

"Landscape designers are integrating new technologies in their processes. 3D modeling and other computer software is helping designers create landscapes virtually first before forming them in the physical world. Designing accessible and inclusive outdoor spaces has become more important. This has led to an increased focus on designing wheelchair-accessible outdoor spaces and incorporating sensory elements such as scents and textures."

Source: IBISWorld Key Takeaways

RESOURCES

- IBISWorld, September 2023: https://www.ibisworld.com

Landscaping Services

| NAICS 561730	| SIC 0782-04	| Businesses/Units 672,138
| Profit $15.4 B	| Wages $35.4 B	| Annual Growth Future 3.0%
		| Annual Growth Past 8.1%

Rules of Thumb

- 45%–50% annual revenues plus inventory
- 1.5–2.5 x SDE; plus fixtures and equipment (except vehicles) & inventory
- 2–4 x EBITDA (may be higher for larger firms)

INDUSTRY MULTIPLES

Acquisition multiples below are calculated medians using US private industry transactions. Data updated annually. Last update: August 2023.

VALUATION MULTIPLE (MEDIAN VALUE)

UNDER $1 MILLION NET SALES

MVIC/Net Sales	0.60
MVIC/Gross Profit	0.75
MVIC/SDE	1.84
MVIC/EBITDA	2.29

MVIC/Net Sales.	0.58
MVIC/Gross Profit	0.93
MVIC/SDE	2.77
MVIC/EBITDA	4.22

OVER $5 MILLION NET SALES

MVIC/Net Sales.	0.42
MVIC/Gross Profit	1.05
MVIC/SDE	3.16
MVIC/EBITDA	3.75

Source: DealStats (formerly Pratt's Stats), 2023 (Portland, OR: Business Valuation Resources, LLC), www.bvresources.com/dealstats

PRICING TIPS

Customer concentration, contracts, condition of equipment, annual revenue, and profitability

BENCHMARK DATA

STATISTICS (LANDSCAPING SERVICES)

Number of Establishments .	672,138
Average Profit Margin	8.7%
Revenue per Employee .	$129,790
Average Number of Employees.	2.1
Average Wages per Employee .	$26,107

PRODUCTS AND SERVICES SEGMENTATION

Maintenance and general services, commercial	52.3%
Maintenance and general services, residential	33.2%
Design-build-installation services	9.2%
Arborist services and other services	5.3%

MAJOR MARKET SEGMENTATION

Commercial markets	47.6%
Residential markets.	42.7%
Government and institutional markets .	6.3%
Nonprofit organizations and other .	3.4%

INDUSTRY COSTS

Profit	8.7%
Wages	20.0%
Purchases	38.0%
Depreciation	3.7%
Marketing	1.9%
Rent & Utilities .	2.7%
Other	24.9%

Cost of labor, benefits, and overtime

EXPENSES (% OF ANNUAL SALES)

Cost of Goods	30% to 40%
Occupancy Costs	05%
Payroll/Labor Costs.	40% to 50%
Profit (pretax)	10% to 15%

QUESTIONS

- Management team, customer concentration, AR aging, employee retention, financials, equipment
- Does the company have contracts with its clients? Are all employees legal? How many customers are built on relationships with the seller, and what will happen to them if the business is sold?

"Getting around labor shortage continues to be a large obstacle as half of landscaping businesses surveyed (51%) said they're unable to find or hire enough staff to fill vacant positions. While that's a staggering number, it's a substantial decrease from last year's survey where 92% said they struggled to find reliable employees. In addition to hiring, retaining employees in a seasonal industry is another major issue landscapers tackle on a yearly basis. Thirty-two percent report losing a significant amount of staff members over the past year. To boost retention, businesses are increasing wages, creating employee bonus systems, and emphasizing career development."

Source: "2023 Landscape Industry Trends Survey," LMN,
https://golmn.com/blog/landscape-business-trends/

"Founded in 2018, RC Mowers manufactures remote-operated robotic mowers for commercial use. The mowers are built to safely mow steep slopes, difficult terrain and other hazardous landscapes, resulting in decreased labor costs and greater profitability. The mowers comply with, or exceed, ISO and ANSI standards."

Source: "RC Mowers breaks ground on new $4.8 million facility," May 24, 2022,
https://www.lawnandlandscape.com/article/rc-mowers-breaks-ground-new-facility/

"Residential construction boom has generated landscaping need. Low interest rates have fueled housing market growth, one of the largest markets for landscaping services. Household finances have swelled. Wealthy households purchase higher value-added landscaping services, which command higher prices. Commercial construction activity continues to drop, albeit modestly compared with prior years. Nonresidential construction activity has historically taken longer to improve post-recession and follows a lag of one to two years to that of the residential construction market."

Source: IBISWorld Key Takeaways

EXPERT COMMENTS

Lack of available water in Arizona is both a threat and an opportunity for the industry.

Competition is fierce and ease of replication is as easy as owning a lawnmower and weed whacker.

Set yourself apart from the competition. Get long-term contracts. Focus on maintenance.

FINANCING

Some seller carryback, also SBA financing available

RESOURCES

- IBISWorld, September 2023: https://www.ibisworld.com
- ALCA—Arizona Landscape Contractors Association: https://azlca.com
- APLD—Association of Professional Landscape Designers: https://www.apld.org
- Lawn & Landscape: https://www.lawnandlandscape.com
- LM—Landscape Management: https://www.landscapemanagement.net
- NALP—National Association of Landscape Professionals: https://www.landscapeprofessionals.org

Law Firms

| | NAICS 541110 | | SIC 8111-03 | | Businesses/Units 464,461

| | Profit $85.4 B | | Wages $147.4 B | | Annual Growth Future 1.0%

| | | | | | Annual Growth Past 1.6%

L

Rules of Thumb

- 90%–100% annual fee revenue; estate work approaches 100 percent; may require earnout
- 4 x SDE includes inventory
- 3.5 x EBIT
- 3.5 x EBITDA

INDUSTRY MULTIPLES

Acquisition multiples below are calculated medians using US private industry transactions. Data updated annually. Last update: August 2023.

VALUATION MULTIPLE (MEDIAN VALUE)

UNDER $1 MILLION NET SALES

MVIC/Net Sales.	0.60
MVIC/Gross Profit	0.62
MVIC/SDE	1.32
MVIC/EBITDA	2.23

$1 MILLION–$5 MILLION NET SALES

MVIC/Net Sales.	0.50
MVIC/Gross Profit	0.50
MVIC/SDE	3.31
MVIC/EBITDA	6.01

OVER $5 MILLION NET SALES

MVIC/Net Sales.	0.59
MVIC/Gross Profit	1.19
MVIC/SDE	N/A
MVIC/EBITDA	5.89

Source: DealStats (formerly Pratt's Stats), 2023 (Portland, OR: Business Valuation Resources, LLC), www.bvresources.com/dealstats

BENCHMARK DATA

STATISTICS (LAW FIRMS)

Number of Establishments .	464,461
Average Profit Margin	21.5%
Revenue per Employee .	$367,759
Average Number of employees.	2.4
Average Wages per Employee .	$135,674

PRODUCTS AND SERVICES SEGMENTATION

Commercial law services	49.5%
Criminal law, civil negligence and personal injury .	19.4%
Other services	13.3%
Real estate law .	10.6%
Labor and employment .	7.2%

MAJOR MARKET SEGMENTATION

Business and corporate clients.	68.9%
Households .	26.2%
Government and not-for-profit clients .	4.9%

INDUSTRY COSTS

Profit	21.5%
Wages	37.1%
Purchases	2.4%
Depreciation	0.7%
Marketing	2.3%
Rent & Utilities	8.4%
Other	27.6%

EXPENSES (% OF ANNUAL SALES)

Profit (pretax)	30%

QUESTIONS

- Transition timeline? Claims history? Repeat clients? Systems? Key personnel? Key clients and ability to transition?
- What is their backlog? Customer concentration?

INDUSTRY TREND

"Consolidation is increasing because of mergers and acquisitions. Law firms are increasingly expanding both domestically and internationally. Substitutes to law firms are increasing. Some states have authorized non-attorneys with certain educational requirements to assist clients in legal-related matters."

Source: IBISWorld Key Takeaways

EXPERT COMMENTS

Practices vary greatly depending on practice area, attorney, and overall firm setup.

It is difficult to replicate, as the good businesses have reputations built over many years.

FINANCING

A mix, but mostly seller financing with small to medium practices. Max 50 percent down on practices, with remaining being earnout or financed by seller.

RESOURCES

- IBISWorld, September 2023: https://www.ibisworld.com
- IBISWorld, August 2022: https://www.ibisworld.com
- Law Practice Today: https://www.lawpracticetoday.org

Lawn Maintenance & Service

| NAICS 561730 | SIC 0782-06

Rules of Thumb

- 50%–60% annual sales plus inventory
- 2–2.75 x SDE plus inventory
- 1.7–3 x EBIT
- 2–4 x EBITDA

INDUSTRY MULTIPLES

Acquisition multiples below are calculated medians using US private industry transactions. Data updated annually. Last update: August 2023.

UNDER $1 MILLION NET SALES	
MVIC/Net Sales.	0.60
MVIC/Gross Profit	0.75
MVIC/SDE	1.84
MVIC/EBITDA	2.29

$1 MILLION–$5 MILLION NET SALES	
MVIC/Net Sales.	0.58
MVIC/Gross Profit	0.93
MVIC/SDE	2.77
MVIC/EBITDA	4.22

OVER $5 MILLION NET SALES	
MVIC/Net Sales.	0.42
MVIC/Gross Profit	1.05
MVIC/SDE	3.16
MVIC/EBITDA	3.75

Source: DealStats (formerly Pratt's Stats), 2023 (Portland, OR: Business Valuation Resources, LLC), www.bvresources.com/dealstats

PRICING TIPS

Recurring revenue is a big part of the industry. Ask if the accounts have agreements or contracts, and what part is commercial vs. residential.

Multiples vary based on several factors, with the most important being the percentage of recurring revenues. Lawn care (fertilization and weed control companies) and landscape maintenance companies receive higher multiples than construction-oriented businesses. Larger companies (lawn care companies with revenues in excess of $1 million, and maintenance companies with revenues in excess of $2.5 million) tend to get higher multiples. Companies with EBITDA margins in line with industry benchmarks will usually get a higher multiple.

The age and condition of the fleet of vehicles and equipment used in the business may negatively impact the valuation if a buyer would expect to need a high level of capital expenditures.

Companies with a larger working capital requirement (more money tied up in accounts receivable) may receive a lower valuation.

Prebilling or postbilling of clients—prebill is more valuable.

BENCHMARK DATA

For additional Benchmark data see Landscaping Services

Normally, annual revenues of over $500K with personnel and managers in place

EXPENSES (% OF ANNUAL SALES)	
Cost of Goods	20% to 45%
Occupancy Costs	02% to 05%
Payroll/Labor Costs.	35% to 45%
Profit (pretax)	10% to 15%

QUESTIONS

- What is the basic monthly billing and what are the normal add-ons? Are the employees legal and are they paid on the books?
- Multiples are relatively low and so the payoff from a sale is often limited compared to the cash flow experienced owners can generate. As a result, it is very important to understand why an owner is selling, and if it is a good reason.

INDUSTRY TREND

Continued growth but very competitive

EXPERT COMMENTS

Due diligence is very important. Ask about the employees in place and what part the seller does on a daily basis.

Learn the business from the ground up.

FINANCING

Usually 80 percent down and 20 percent as a note or holdback for accounts in good standing for 90 to 360 days

RESOURCES

- AmericanHort: https://www.americanhort.org
- Lawn & Landscape: https://www.lawnandlandscape.com
- LM—Landscape Management magazine: https://www.landscapemanagement.net
- NALP—National Association of Landscape Professionals: https://www.landscapeprofessionals.org

Leather Tanning & Finishing

| NAICS 316110 | Businesses/Units 1,459

| Profit $44.3 M | Wages $155.6 M | Annual Growth Future 0.4%

| Annual Growth Past -5.4%

INDUSTRY MULTIPLES

Acquisition multiples below are calculated medians using US private industry transactions. Data updated annually. Last update: August 2023.

VALUATION MULTIPLE (MEDIAN VALUE)

UNDER $1 MILLION NET SALES

MVIC/Net Sales.	0.57
MVIC/Gross Profit	N/A
MVIC/SDE	N/A
MVIC/EBITDA	N/A
$1 MILLION–$5 MILLION NET SALES	N/A
OVER $5 MILLION NET SALES	N/A

Source: DealStats (formerly Pratt's Stats), 2023 (Portland, OR: Business Valuation Resources, LLC), www.bvresources.com/dealstats

BENCHMARK DATA

STATISTICS (LEATHER TANNING & FINISHING)

Number of Establishments .	1,459
Average Profit Margin	3.7%
Revenue per Employee .	$303,524
Average Number of Employees.	2.8
Average Wages per Employee .	$39,265

PRODUCTS AND SERVICES SEGMENTATION

Chrome tanning.	73.2%
Leather finishing	17.6%
Vegetable tanning	8.1%
Other	1.1%

Exports	56.7%
Footwear	19.1%
Automobile upholstery	10.0%
Small leather goods.	6.2%
Clothing	4.4%
Furniture upholstery	3.6%

INDUSTRY COSTS

Profit	3.7%
Wages	13.0%
Purchases	59.5%
Depreciation	0.8%
Marketing	0.1%
Rent & Utilities	1.9%
Other	20.9%

INDUSTRY TREND

"Lower downstream demand and unfavorable commodity prices have led to a drop in the industry. China, one of the industry's biggest export markets, stated a lower need for imports of leather as a result of stricter environmental regulations and a decline in demand from makers of footwear and clothing."

Source: IBISWorld Key Takeaways

RESOURCES

• IBISWorld, March 2023: https://www.ibisworld.com

Lessors of Nonresidential Buildings (except Miniwarehouses)

| NAICS 531120 | Businesses/Units 367,225

| Profit $124.1 B | Wages $25.1 B | Annual Growth Future 1.4%

| Annual Growth Past 0.4%

INDUSTRY MULTIPLES

Acquisition multiples below are calculated medians using US private industry transactions. Data updated annually. Last update: August 2023.

VALUATION MULTIPLE (MEDIAN VALUE)

UNDER $1 MILLION NET SALES

MVIC/Net Sales.	0.84
MVIC/Gross Profit	0.94
MVIC/SDE	2.78
MVIC/EBITDA	5.21

$1 MILLION–$5 MILLION NET SALES

MVIC/Net Sales.	6.99
MVIC/Gross Profit	0.07
MVIC/SDE	1.66
MVIC/EBITDA	7.14

OVER $5 MILLION NET SALES

MVIC/Net Sales.	11.46
MVIC/Gross Profit	16.78
MVIC/SDE	N/A
MVIC/EBITDA	22.27

Source: DealStats (formerly Pratt's Stats), 2023 (Portland, OR: Business Valuation Resources, LLC), www.bvresources.com/dealstats

BENCHMARK DATA

STATISTICS (COMMERCIAL LEASING)

Number of Establishments	367,225
Average Profit Margin	48.8%
Revenue per Employee	$488,939
Average Number of Employees	1.4
Average Wages per Employee	$48,346

PRODUCTS AND SERVICES SEGMENTATION

Renting office buildings	37.6%
Renting commercial buildings	29.9%
Other	11.8%
Renting industrial buildings	10.4%
Renting other nonresidential properties	8.2%
Property management and sales	2.1%

MAJOR MARKET SEGMENTATION

Office and professional buildings	42.0%
Shopping centers, retail shops and flea market spaces	33.4%
Industrial buildings	11.7%
Other nonresidential properties	9.2%
Other	3.7%

INDUSTRY COSTS

Profit	48.8%
Wages	9.9%
Purchases	1.6%
Depreciation	18.7%
Marketing	0.8%
Rent & Utilities	2.8%
Other	17.3%

INDUSTRY TREND

"Office vacancy rates remain high across the United States. As employees continue to work from home, office vacancy rates remain well above pre-pandemic levels. The industrial market has cooled off in 2023, after powering the industry through the worst of COVID-19."

Source: IBISWorld Key Takeaways

RESOURCES

• IBISWorld, September 2023: https://www.ibisworld.com

Liberty Tax (Franchise)

| NAICS 541213 | Businesses/Units 2,255

Rules of Thumb

• 45%–50% annual sales plus inventory
• 3–3.5 x SDE plus inventory
• 3.5–4 x EBIT
• 4 EBITDA

INDUSTRY MULTIPLES

Acquisition multiples below are calculated medians using US private industry transactions. Data updated annually. Last update: August 2023.

UNDER $1 MILLION NET SALES

MVIC/Net Sales.	0.89
MVIC/Gross Profit	0.89
MVIC/SDE	1.88
MVIC/EBITDA	3.05

$1 MILLION–$5 MILLION NET SALES

MVIC/Net Sales.	0.53
MVIC/Gross Profit	0.64
MVIC/SDE	1.90
MVIC/EBITDA	3.02

OVER $5 MILLION NET SALES

MVIC/Net Sales.	1.83
MVIC/Gross Profit	1.83
MVIC/SDE	5.75
MVIC/EBITDA	6.31

Source: DealStats (formerly Pratt's Stats), 2023 (Portland, OR: Business Valuation Resources, LLC), www.bvresources.com/dealstats

PRICING TIPS

The best rule of thumb is the revenue multiplier (gross revenue – discounts – free returns performed); the range for the revenue multiplier is 0.9 to 1.1. Average net fee, return count growth, customer retention, and percent of walkouts are factors when considering the range of multiple. Growth of a mature office should be 3 to 5 percent in the best offices in return count and similar for revenue. When the revenue growth is much larger than the return count growth, you should consider it a red flag in that the office may be raising their fees to obtain growth which will harm retention of customers. The system at Liberty Tax is a good system.

Approx. Total Investment: $43,700 to $78,900

BENCHMARK DATA

Rent should not exceed 25 percent of revenue and, for the very best offices, is around 12 percent. Payroll is a key metric, 18 percent to not exceeding 30 percent of revenue. Other key value indicators are the average net fee of the business's tax returns, and the number of returns. A healthy average net fee for a Liberty Tax office is above $320. The breakeven return count is a range of 400 to 475. Office productivity is also a key metric—employee hours (including marketing) per day/month/year; number of returns per day/month/year started), which should be in the range of 2 to 6, with 4.0 being ideal. Finally, the retention of customers is key—the industry standard of retention is 50 to 60 percent for average to good offices.

EXPENSES (% OF ANNUAL SALES)

Cost of Goods	.0% to 10%
Occupancy Costs	24%
Payroll/Labor Costs.	20%
Profit (pretax)	25%

QUESTIONS

- What is your average net fee? Return count? Productivity (employee hours, daily return count)? Retention?
- Who are their core employees that will return year after year? How many tax returns the current owner does; they may follow them even with a noncompete situation. How closely have they followed the Liberty System and branding recommendations? Will they closely consult at least through the first tax season of the new owner no matter when the ownership is transitioned?

Tax offices in general will need to have multiple revenue streams to be truly profitable. If the location is in a lower-income area, this might mean adding consumer loans and similar items to the offering. If the office is in a lower middle to upper middle income area, this might mean adding small business bookkeeping and tax prep to the individual tax prep offering.

Add-on services such as consumer loans, insurance, debt relief, and other financial services. More tax consultations even for lower-income clients. More options to use online and virtual tax prep with the advantage of having a local tax professional to consult, and brick and mortar as a backup, to do some or all of the prep. Customers relying on phone apps to follow their refund.

EXPERT COMMENTS

The lease is key—it needs to be transferable, allow street level marketing techniques, have a cap on HVAC repairs, and not be over 25 percent of projected revenue including CAM. To start, buyers should buy an existing business, not an undeveloped territory. Then expand by buying underperforming territories.

The Liberty Tax franchisor is putting more emphasis on uniformity of offices. Location/site selection is key to success. The tax industry has become more competitive with the growth of online do-it-yourself software. However, in my opinion, there will be a need for brick-and-mortar stores for the foreseeable future. Liberty Tax does a good job of training and support, making the site selection and marketability (two key factors) as low risk as possible.

Sellers—be prepared to finance all or a portion of the sales price and perhaps become an employee for at least one tax season to insure a smooth transition.

Buyers—make sure you know that the key metrics—average net fee, return count, customer retention, and employee productivity (returns per hours of payroll) are healthy and/or are trending that way. Make sure the closing is prior to September of a particular year—this is the time you need to really start preparing for the next tax season. If your closing is later than September, you will find yourself rushed to be prepared properly. Attend all conventions and trainings possible; you will always pick up important information to improve your business.

The franchisor has a good and proven system that balances support from the franchisor and entrepreneurship from the franchisees.

FINANCING

Seller financing, although SBA financing is available. Typical terms are 5 to 7 years at 4 to 5 points higher than prime.

RESOURCES

- Liberty Tax: https://www.libertytax.com
- Franchise information: https://www.libertytaxfranchise.com

Libraries and Archives

| NAICS 519210 | Businesses/Units 6,109 |

| Profit $93.4 M | Wages $1.1 B | Annual Growth Future -1.8% |

BENCHMARK DATA

Number of Establishments	6,109
Average Profit Margin	3.3%
Revenue per Employee	$94,785
Average Number of Employees.	4.8
Average Wages per Employee	$35,984

PRODUCTS AND SERVICES SEGMENTATION

Print material borrowing and access	47.4%
Access to computers and digital databases	34.3%
Archival institution and other services	18.3%

MAJOR MARKET SEGMENTATION

Children (Ages 0 to 14)	51.2%
Adult (Ages 25+)	38.4%
Young Adult (Ages 15 to 24)	10.4%

INDUSTRY COSTS

Profit	3.3%
Wages	37.9%
Purchases	11.3%
Depreciation	1.1%
Marketing	1.2%
Rent & Utilities	9.9%
Other	35.3%

MARKET SHARE

Library of Congress	43.0%

INDUSTRY TREND

"With their rich histories, libraries serve as vital public institutions, offering free access to costly resources and significantly aiding community development and literacy. Libraries have diversified their funding sources through grants, donations, and private partnerships, yet they continue to face a struggle in meeting their financial goals. The shift toward rapid digital information consumption presents both challenges and opportunities. Libraries are responding to intellectual property laws by advocating for fair use policies and open access initiatives while also investing in digital infrastructure and enhancing their online presence."

Source: IBISWorld Key Takeaways

RESOURCES

• IBISWorld, September 2023: https://www.ibisworld.com

Light Truck and Utility Vehicle Manufacturing

| NAICS 336110 | Businesses/Units 71

| Profit $3 B | Wages $9.2 B | Annual Growth Future 1.7%

| | | Annual Growth Past 0.1%

BENCHMARK DATA

Number of Establishments	71.0
Average Profit Margin	1.3%

Revenue per Employee $1,676,000
Average Number of Employees. . . . 1,973
Average Wages per Employee . . . $68,025

PRODUCTS AND SERVICES SEGMENTATION

CUVs 60.6%
Pickup trucks 21.8%
SUVs. 11.3%
Minivans and vans 6.3%

MAJOR MARKET SEGMENTATION

Automobile dealers 50.8%
Wholesalers. 28.6%
Government and other 7.7%
Businesses 7.5%
Exports 5.4%

INDUSTRY COSTS

Profit 1.3%
Wages 4.0%
Purchases 75.2%
Depreciation 2.2%
Marketing 0.0%
Rent & Utilities 0.2%
Other 17.0%

MARKET SHARE

Ford Motor Co 38.9%
General Motors Company 14.2%
Stellantis 9.6%
Toyota Motor 7.2%

INDUSTRY TREND

"Operators are having trouble reducing wage costs. Global concerns about greenhouse gas emissions continue to influence consumer preference. Rising wages have been a result of union power in the industry. Total industry revenue will likely be aided by the rising popularity of fuel-efficient CUVs that major companies introduced in recent years. Global trade of industry products is expected to rebound from struggles at the end of the previous period. Recovering demand is expected to benefit industry profit moving forward. Major government programs over the past five years have significantly influenced manufacturer operations."

Source: IBISWorld Industry at a Glance

RESOURCES

• IBISWorld, July 2022: https://www.ibisworld.com

Limousine Services

| NAICS 485320 | SIC 4119-03

Rules of Thumb

• 50%–55% annual revenues plus vehicles
• 2–2.5 x SDE plus vehicles
• 4 x EBITDA, companies with corporate accounts under contract plus vehicles
• 3 x EBITDA plus vehicles

INDUSTRY MULTIPLES

Acquisition multiples below are calculated medians using US private industry transactions. Data updated annually. Last update: August 2023.

L

VALUATION MULTIPLE (MEDIAN VALUE)

UNDER $1 MILLION NET SALES

MVIC/Net Sales	0.65
MVIC/Gross Profit	0.75
MVIC/SDE	1.91
MVIC/EBITDA	2.69

$1 MILLION–$5 MILLION NET SALES

MVIC/Net Sales	0.47
MVIC/Gross Profit	0.52
MVIC/SDE	2.70
MVIC/EBITDA	8.76

OVER $5 MILLION NET SALES   N/A

Source: DealStats (formerly Pratt's Stats), 2023 (Portland, OR: Business Valuation Resources, LLC), www.bvresources.com/dealstats

PRICING TIPS

You need to look at owner's discretionary cash flow (also known as seller's discretionary earnings). You also need to know whether the limousines are owned outright, financed, or leased. Depreciation expense becomes an important consideration because the owned vehicles wear down rapidly and must be replaced to keep the business looking up to date.

The figure needs to be adjusted for the fair market value of the vehicles less the outstanding debt.

Depreciation is usually considered an add-back and is therefore part of the seller's discretionary earnings/EBIT/EBITDA. However, in this type of business it should not be added back as it is a necessary business expense. Vehicles are the mainstay of the business and replacement is ongoing business.

BENCHMARK DATA

EXPENSES (% OF ANNUAL SALES)

Cost of Goods (auto purchases)	30% to 35%
Occupancy Costs	05% to 10%
Payroll/Labor Costs	25% to 35%
Profit (pretax)	10% to 20%

QUESTIONS

- Look at the repair and maintenance records for all the vehicles. Any accidents? Outstanding litigation or workers' compensation issues? What background checks and drug tests are performed on new hires?

INDUSTRY TREND

"The spread of COVID-19 resulted in closures of nonessential businesses, reducing travel plans. New technologies have altered the way operators can generate revenue. Fuel accounts for one of the industry's most significant costs. Growing demand from corporate travelers, tourists and private households is expected to stimulate expansion. The limousine segment of the industry is expected to shrink moving forward. Due to the high price of major cities' taxi medallions it has been cost prohibitive for many individuals to own a taxi license. The growth of transport network companies has been a revelation for the industry."

Source: IBISWorld Industry at a Glance

RESOURCES

- IBISWorld, August 2022: https://www.ibisworld.com
- LCT—Luxury Coach & Transportation: https://www.lctmag.com
- NLA—National Limousine Association: https://www.limo.org

Liquefied Petroleum Gas (Propane) Dealers

| NAICS 457210 | SIC 5984-01

Rules of Thumb

- 130% annual sales plus inventory
- 3–4 x SDE plus inventory
- 4 x EBIT
- 4.5–7.5 x EBITDA

PRICING TIPS

EBITDA multiples can vary from 4.5 to 7.5+ x EBITDA, depending on the size of the company, average GP price per gallon, volume, tank ownership, and other factors/business characteristics.

4.5 to 7.0 x EBITDA for companies selling under 1M gallons; larger companies can get 6 to 8 x adjusted EBITDA. Inventory at cost is added to multiple pricing, plus collectible A/R (formula to determine this).

A rule of thumb is $1.00 per propane annual gallon sold, although this varies depending on the gross margins in the region, as well as other characteristics, such as sales trends, number of customer tanks the business owns, and management depth.

BENCHMARK DATA

75 to 95 percent tank ownership; tank ownership percentage, strong management team, storage capacity, average GP price per gallon, and competition drive valuation.

SDE multiples of 3 to 6 x are the norm, with 7 to 8 x possible when the business represents a large market share that's appealing to multiple competitors. It's also helpful that facilities and trucks/tanks are newer and well-kept. A high percentage of company-owned tanks add value, since it's more difficult for customers to change suppliers and shop for lower prices. If customers don't own their tanks, they are required to purchase from the propane retailer who provided the tank. Technology advances are helpful to assist with areas like truck routing, invoicing, and on-site tank monitoring to estimate refill timing.

Can vary considerably by company, depending on customer mix between residential, commercial, farm, and industrial-type customer.

EXPENSES (% OF ANNUAL SALES)

Cost of Goods	40% to 50%
Occupancy Costs	01% to 10%
Payroll/Labor Costs.	15% to 25%
Profit (pretax)	15% to 20%

QUESTIONS

- GP margins history; storage capacity, tank ownership, breakdown of fuel sold by customer type

- Any safety violations? Do you conduct regular safety inspections of customer tanks? For company-owned tanks, what tank rental fee do you charge, and do you have customers sign a tank lease agreement? Have you kept up with available technology/software to run a better operation? Do you use remote tank monitors so you know without phone calls when customers need a refill? Do you keep customers' credit card information on file? What do you offer customers as far as discounted summer tank fills? How about prepaid contract pricing for the winter season? Are you mostly on a monthly fill schedule, or call for reorder by customer? Who does the tank sets and installs the lines to customers' houses? Are you satisfied with your primary propane suppliers?
- 5 years' financials and gallonage history; gross profit per gallon by segment of business; complete list of assets including tank inventory, bulk plants, trucks, etc.; real estate appraisal
- Customer concentration, competition, age of fleet, tenure/age of employees, reason for exit

INDUSTRY TREND

Mom and pops need to keep up with technology advances and maintain reliable delivery trucks. It's essential to have bulk tank capacity to hold sufficient backup fuel inventory during cold weather periods. Winter months require all available delivery drivers, while off-season can be very slow, other than certain agricultural fuel needs. The local companies with exceptional customer service relationships will mostly compete well with large national companies. Local small operators are often baby boomer age and ready to consider exiting the business. The industry has been, and continues to be, in a consolidation mode.

EXPERT COMMENTS

Asset-intensive business. Tank ownership plays major factor in pricing. High service levels, logistics, and management expertise are important to drive sales/growth and profitability.

Either consider being an owner-operator or be sure to hire a strong manager who is honest and has good people skills. Make sure there are no previous accidents that could be a future liability, and that the seller has followed safety procedures for tank sets and line installations, with regularly scheduled safety inspections. For sellers, make sure your books are clean and in good order.

Large regional and national companies are acquiring many of the mom and pops. Personal customer service is critical in this industry. Larger companies often don't have the customer relationships that exist with mom and pops. Gross margins are exceptionally high in some regions, while low margins exist in areas with certain competitors. Most people believe the future of propane is very bright, as it is a cleaner-burning fuel. Propane tanks are welcome in remote areas where natural gas lines are not available. Farmers, ranchers, agricultural operations, country residences, and commercial locations are the best customers. It can take years to build a substantial customer base without acquiring other propane retailers.

Hire a professional M&A advisor who has extensive experience in the propane industry, as offers for these businesses vary widely.

FINANCING

Sellers will often agree to 10 to 20 percent seller financing. The remaining is cash at closing. SBA has a high loan approval rate for the industry.

RESOURCES

- AGA—American Gas Association: https://www.aga.org/
- BPN—Butane–Propane News: https://bpnews.com
- LP Gas: https://www.lpgasmagazine.com/
- LPGas: https://www.lpgasmagazine.com
- NPGA—National Propane Gas Association: https://www.npga.org
- Propane Canada: https://www.northernstar.ab.ca
- Propane Education & Research Council: https://propane.com/

Liquor Stores/Package Stores (Beer, Wine, & Liquor Stores)

	NAICS 445320		SIC 5921-02		Businesses/Units 45,179
	Profit $3 B		Wages $5.4 B		Annual Growth Future 0.9%
					Annual Growth Past 2.6%

Rules of Thumb

- 35%–45% annual sales
- 2–4 x SDE
- 2.5–5 x EBITDA
- 3–6 x EBIT

INDUSTRY MULTIPLES

Acquisition multiples below are calculated medians using US private industry transactions. Data updated annually. Last update: August 2023.

VALUATION MULTIPLE (MEDIAN VALUE)

UNDER $1 MILLION NET SALES	
MVIC/Net Sales.	0.40
MVIC/Gross Profit	1.41
MVIC/SDE	3.33
MVIC/EBITDA	4.64
$1 MILLION–$5 MILLION NET SALES	
MVIC/Net Sales.	0.43
MVIC/Gross Profit	1.59
MVIC/SDE	3.50
MVIC/EBITDA	6.49
OVER $5 MILLION NET SALES	
MVIC/Net Sales.	0.31
MVIC/Gross Profit	1.33
MVIC/SDE	3.76
MVIC/EBITDA	7.85

Source: DealStats (formerly Pratt's Stats), 2023 (Portland, OR: Business Valuation Resources, LLC), www.bvresources.com/dealstats

PRICING TIPS

Considerations include location, occupancy expense, payroll, gross profit, competition, ordinary income, and additional income.

The rule of thumb for percent of annual sales cannot be applied to low-margin stores or discount models. That rule of thumb should be applied only with stores over 23 percent margin.

BENCHMARK DATA

STATISTICS (BEER, WINE & LIQUOR STORES)

Number of Establishments 45,179	
Average Profit Margin 3.8%	
Revenue per Employee $414,421	
Average Number of Employees. 4.2	
Average Wages per Employee . . . $28,139	

PRODUCTS AND SERVICES SEGMENTATION

Spirits 48.5%	
Wine. 22.4%	
Beer 18.7%	
Other products 10.4%	

MAJOR MARKET SEGMENTATION

Consumers aged 44 and younger . . . 37.6%	
Consumers aged 45 to 64 . . . . . 37.2%	
Consumers aged 65 and older 20.1%	
Other 5.1%	

INDUSTRY COSTS

Profit 3.8%	
Wages 6.8%	
Purchases 70.8%	
Depreciation 0.7%	
Marketing 0.5%	
Rent & Utilities 4.3%	
Other 13.1%	

MARKET SHARE

Total Wine and More 7.0%	

Pretax profit is very difficult to establish on an average basis because of product mix ratios.

Higher-margin stores will trade for higher multiples. Stores that include real estate assets will also trade at higher multiples. There has been a roll-up in the MA marketplace in this industry. Strategic buyers will pay a premium multiple over market for particular assets, i.e., high-volume stores with strong margin and underlying real estate asset.

Cost of sales varies a lot by state and location but typically runs 75 to 80 percent of sales.

EXPENSES (% OF ANNUAL SALES)

Cost of Goods . . . . . . 70% to 80%	
Occupancy Costs . . . . . 05% to 15%	
Payroll/Labor Costs. . . . . 07% to 17%	
Profit (pretax) . . . . . . 08% to 15%	

QUESTIONS

- What is payroll? Rent? Gross profit? How long established? Competition? The financials should be well documented.
- Customer ratio mix, which impacts the types of liquor sold. Do they have a license to sell retail liquor? Do they have a license to do wholesale sales to commercial accounts? Get breakdown of sales for wine, beer, liquor, and accessory sales. Do they sell lottery tickets? Do they have video game machines? Do they deliver to customers (sometimes regulated by state and/or city)?

- Crime status, length of ownership, why the store is for sale
- Product mix beer vs. liquor vs. wine; inventory cycle
- Hours owner works? Employees' length of employment? Equipment mainte-nance records, compressors, HVAC, etc.?
- Cash flow, occupancy expense, and category percentage mix?
- Is there an option on the property or is it owned by the seller? What competi-tion is nearby? Are there any other licenses available in the town? Do you owe any back taxes or fees that would hold up the transfer of the liquor license?
- What are your sales tax numbers and are you current?
- Security/surveillance system in place? Theft/shrinkage?

INDUSTRY TREND

The industry will continue to be in high demand.

As the pandemic wanes, revenues will restabilize, likely to 2019 levels.

Highly competitive industry and highly regulated by state and city governments.

"The COVID-19 pandemic was a boon for beer, wine and liquor store sales. With the closure of on-premise drinking sites, consumers flocked to liquor stores to stock up for at-home drinking. E-commerce will be an increasingly significant sales channel for beer, wine and liquor stores. Younger consumers are drifting away from heavy alcohol consumption, but online storefronts will sustain their demand. Liquor stores with broader product offerings have had the most suc-cess in recent years. Shifting consumer preferences have boosted the popularity of new beverages, like canned cocktails. Retailers that offer the latest in innova-tive beverages maintain the most foot traffic."

Source: IBISWorld Industry at a Glance

EXPERT COMMENTS

Be prepared to work long hours and become an expert knowing what products to purchase and when.

Ease of replication varies state to state. Very hard to replicate in markets where the state and licensing authorities limit the amount of licenses granted.

Must purchase existing store.

FINANCING

Outside financing is available with consistent cash flow, but seller financing is increasing with a sizable down payment (typically 50 percent) depending on the size of the deal.

RESOURCES

- IBISWorld, September 2023: https://www.ibisworld.com
- Beverage Journal: https://www.thebeveragejournal.com/
- DISCUS—Distilled Spirits Council of the United States: https://www.distilledspirits.org
- Massachusetts Package Stores Association, Inc.: https://masspack.org/
- NYSLSA—New York State Liquor Store Association: https://www.nyslsa.com
- WSWA—Wine & Spirits Wholesalers of America: https://www.wswa.org

Little Caesars (Franchise)

| NAICS 722513 | Businesses/Units 3,601

Rules of Thumb

- 55% annual sales plus inventory

INDUSTRY MULTIPLES

Acquisition multiples below are calculated medians using US private industry transactions. Data updated annually. Last update: August 2023.

VALUATION MULTIPLE (MEDIAN VALUE)

UNDER $1 MILLION NET SALES	
MVIC/Net Sales	0.31
MVIC/Gross Profit	0.48
MVIC/SDE	1.67
MVIC/EBITDA	2.21
$1 MILLION–$5 MILLION NET SALES	
MVIC/Net Sales	0.39
MVIC/Gross Profit	0.60
MVIC/SDE	2.43
MVIC/EBITDA	2.98
OVER $5 MILLION NET SALES	
MVIC/Net Sales	0.31
MVIC/Gross Profit	1.33
MVIC/SDE	3.76
MVIC/EBITDA	7.85

Source: DealStats (formerly Pratt's Stats), 2023 (Portland, OR: Business Valuation Resources, LLC), www.bvresources.com/dealstats

PRICING TIPS

Approx. Total Investment: $359,700 to $1,686,000

RESOURCES

- Little Caesars: https://littlecaesars.com/en-us/
- Franchise information: https://franchise.littlecaesars.com

Livestock Production Support Services

| NAICS 115210 | Businesses/Units 71,806

| Profit $339.6 M | Wages $2 B | Annual Growth Future -0.3%

| Annual Growth Past -2.1%

INDUSTRY MULTIPLES

Acquisition multiples below are calculated medians using US private industry transactions. Data updated annually. Last update: August 2023.

VALUATION MULTIPLE (MEDIAN VALUE)

UNDER $1 MILLION NET SALES	N/A
$1 MILLION–$5 MILLION NET SALES	N/A
OVER $5 MILLION NET SALES	
MVIC/Net Sales	2.16
MVIC/Gross Profit	9.52

MVIC/SDE . . . . N/A
MVIC/EBITDA 24.50

BENCHMARK DATA

STATISTICS (LIVESTOCK PRODUCTION SUPPORT SERVICES)

Number of Establishments 71,806
Average Profit Margin 6.7%
Revenue per Employee $59,794
Average Number of Employees. 1.2
Average Wages per Employee . . . $24,194

PRODUCTS AND SERVICES SEGMENTATION

Boarding services 47.0%
Dairy support services 21.9%
Breeding services 17.1%
Farrier services 7.2%
Livestock health services 4.7%
Spraying services 1.3%
Shearing services 0.8%

MAJOR MARKET SEGMENTATION

Beef cattle farms 27.2%
Horse owners 23.1%
Poultry and egg farms 21.6%
Dairy farms 18.7%
Hog and pig farms 9.1%
Sheep farms. 0.3%

INDUSTRY COSTS

Profit 6.7%
Wages 40.0%
Purchases 24.8%
Depreciation 2.3%
Marketing 0.5%
Rent & Utilities 11.9%
Other 13.7%

INDUSTRY TREND

"The Livestock Production Support Services industry has seen declining revenue as livestock-producing industries have experienced weak performances in recent years. Industry performance is sensitive to changes in demand from horse owners. Rising per capita disposable income has benefited demand for horse support services in recent years."

Source: IBISWorld Key Takeaways

RESOURCES

• IBISWorld, May 2023: https://www.ibisworld.com

Lock & Key Shops

NAICS 561622	SIC 7699-62	Businesses/Units 25,031
Profit $164.2 M	Wages $798.6 M	Annual Growth Future 3.4%
		Annual Growth Past -0.1%

Rules of Thumb

- 40%–45% annual sales plus inventory

INDUSTRY MULTIPLES

Acquisition multiples below are calculated medians using US private industry transactions. Data updated annually. Last update: August 2023.

VALUATION MULTIPLE (MEDIAN VALUE)

UNDER $1 MILLION NET SALES	
MVIC/Net Sales	0.60
MVIC/Gross Profit	0.87
MVIC/SDE	2.20
MVIC/EBITDA	3.11
$1 MILLION–$5 MILLION NET SALES	
MVIC/Net Sales	0.61
MVIC/Gross Profit	1.19
MVIC/SDE	2.64
MVIC/EBITDA	2.81
OVER $5 MILLION NET SALES	N/A

Source: DealStats (formerly Pratt's Stats), 2023 (Portland, OR: Business Valuation Resources, LLC), www.bvresources.com/dealstats

BENCHMARK DATA

STATISTICS (LOCKSMITHS)

Number of Establishments	25,031
Average Profit Margin	6.2%
Revenue per Employee	$77,331
Average Number of Employees	1.4
Average Wages per Employee	$23,332

PRODUCTS AND SERVICES SEGMENTATION

Nonresidential security system installation and repair	44.0%
Residential security system installation and repair	24.4%
Key cutting and duplication services	16.5%
Resale of locks and security merchandise	10.2%
Other services	3.2%
Residential and nonresidential system services with monitoring	1.7%

MAJOR MARKET SEGMENTATION

Businesses	57.4%
Households	26.6%
Government entities	9.4%
Not-for-profit organizations	6.6%

INDUSTRY COSTS

Profit	6.2%
Wages	30.2%
Purchases	34.9%
Depreciation	1.4%
Marketing	1.7%
Rent & Utilities	2.5%
Other	23.1%

INDUSTRY TREND

"The industry relies on the construction sector's performance. As interest rates climb, home sales will drop, cutting a major source of demand from rekeying, consultation and residential security and monitoring services. Locksmiths will shift to more advanced solutions as they face rising external competition.

Companies will use keyless locks, monitoring systems and other new products to distinguish from similar industries."

Source: IBISWorld Key Takeaways

RESOURCES

- IBISWorld, May 2023: https://www.ibisworld.com
- ALOA Security Professionals Association: https://www.aloa.org/index.html

Lumberyards

	NAICS 444190		SIC 5211-42		Businesses/Units 44,019
	Profit $6.9 B		Wages $19.7 B		Annual Growth Future 4.0%
					Annual Growth Past 3.4%

Rules of Thumb

- 40% annual sales includes inventory
- 4–6 x SDE includes inventory
- 4 x EBIT
- 4–6 x EBITDA

INDUSTRY MULTIPLES

Acquisition multiples below are calculated medians using US private industry transactions. Data updated annually. Last update: August 2023.

VALUATION MULTIPLE (MEDIAN VALUE)

UNDER $1 MILLION NET SALES

MVIC/Net Sales	0.44
MVIC/Gross Profit	0.89
MVIC/SDE	2.10
MVIC/EBITDA	3.98

$1 MILLION–$5 MILLION NET SALES

MVIC/Net Sales	0.36
MVIC/Gross Profit	1.00
MVIC/SDE	2.98
MVIC/EBITDA	3.53

OVER $5 MILLION NET SALES

MVIC/Net Sales	0.46
MVIC/Gross Profit	1.35
MVIC/SDE	4.33
MVIC/EBITDA	5.83

Source: DealStats (formerly Pratt's Stats), 2023 (Portland, OR: Business Valuation Resources, LLC), www.bvresources.com/dealstats

BENCHMARK DATA

STATISTICS (LUMBER & BUILDING MATERIAL STORES)

Number of Establishments	44,019
Average Profit Margin	4.5%
Revenue per Employee	$456,844
Average Number of Employees	7.5
Average Wages per Employee	$59,057

PRODUCTS AND SERVICES SEGMENTATION

Lumber and other structural building materials	34.9%
Hardware, nonpower hand tools and other building supplies	34.5%

Plumbing and electrical supplies 21.7%
Other 5.5%
Flooring 3.4%

MAJOR MARKET SEGMENTATION

Professional Contractors 50.2%
Household Customers 31.7%
Other 18.1%

INDUSTRY COSTS

Profit 4.5%
Wages 12.9%
Purchases 61.1%
Depreciation 1.0%
Marketing 0.9%
Rent & Utilities 2.1%
Other 17.6%

MARKET SHARE

Builders FirstSource Inc. 6.4%
84 Lumber Company 3.5%
Lumber Liquidators 0.5%
Carter Lumber 0.1%

EXPENSES (% OF ANNUAL SALES)

Cost of Goods 75%
Occupancy Costs . . . . 03% to 05%
Payroll/Labor Costs. 20%
Profit (pretax) . . . . 02% to 05%

QUESTIONS

- Why selling? Have audited 5 years' financials?
- Look carefully at profit, and if future earnings are possible.

INDUSTRY TREND

"COVID-19 boosted industry sales. Urban flight during the pandemic resulted in an increase in housing starts. This translated to heightened demand from downstream construction markets. External competition on the rise. External competition from big-box retailers has become an increasingly prominent detraction from industry revenue. Also, online shopping has proven detrimental to small-scale, local businesses."

Source: IBISWorld Key Takeaways

EXPERT COMMENTS

Lumberyards are very difficult to duplicate. High dollar investment keeps most competition out of a market. It also requires a minimum of 2 acres to runs a $5 million lumberyard. Cost of land these days makes it impossible to start a new store.

FINANCING

Very few sell on owner financing; the sales are generally to existing lumber dealers.

RESOURCES

- IBISWorld, August 2023: https://www.ibisworld.com
- NLBMDA—National Lumber and Building Material Dealers Association: https://www.dealer.org

Maaco (auto painting and collision repair) (Franchise)

| NAICS 811121 | Businesses/Units 402

Rules of Thumb

- 40% annual sales plus inventory
- 25% annual sales

INDUSTRY MULTIPLES

Acquisition multiples below are calculated medians using US private industry transactions. Data updated annually. Last update: August 2023.

VALUATION MULTIPLE (MEDIAN VALUE)

UNDER $1 MILLION NET SALES

MVIC/Net Sales	0.50
MVIC/Gross Profit	0.81
MVIC/SDE	2.01
MVIC/EBITDA	3.24

$1 MILLION–$5 MILLION NET SALES

MVIC/Net Sales	0.35
MVIC/Gross Profit	0.62
MVIC/SDE	2.49
MVIC/EBITDA	5.26

OVER $5 MILLION NET SALES

MVIC/Net Sales	0.72
MVIC/Gross Profit	2.15
MVIC/SDE	12.29
MVIC/EBITDA	13.66

Source: DealStats (formerly Pratt's Stats), 2023 (Portland, OR: Business Valuation Resources, LLC), www.bvresources.com/dealstats

PRICING TIPS

Approx. Total Investment: $281,000 to $495,500

RESOURCES

- Maaco: https://www.maaco.com
- Franchise information: https://maacofranchise.com
- Driven Brands: https://www.drivenbrands.com

Machine Shops

NAICS 332710	SIC 3599-03	Businesses/Units 19,084
Profit $3.4 B	Wages $17 B	Annual Growth Future -0.4%
		Annual Growth Past 1.4%

Rules of Thumb

- 50%–65% annual revenues includes inventory
- 3–5 x SDE plus inventory
- 4.5–7 x EBIT
- 3.5–5.5 x EBITDA

INDUSTRY MULTIPLES

Acquisition multiples below are calculated medians using US private industry transactions. Data updated annually. Last update: August 2023.

VALUATION MULTIPLE (MEDIAN VALUE)

UNDER $1 MILLION NET SALES

MVIC/Net Sales	0.73
MVIC/Gross Profit	1.29
MVIC/SDE	3.11
MVIC/EBITDA	4.25

$1 MILLION–$5 MILLION NET SALES

MVIC/Net Sales	0.70
MVIC/Gross Profit	1.56
MVIC/SDE	3.34
MVIC/EBITDA	4.33

OVER $5 MILLION NET SALES

MVIC/Net Sales	0.97
MVIC/Gross Profit	2.05
MVIC/SDE	3.76
MVIC/EBITDA	5.55

Source: DealStats (formerly Pratt's Stats), 2023 (Portland, OR: Business Valuation Resources, LLC), www.bvresources.com/dealstats

PRICING TIPS

Long-term contracts for mission-critical components are also a key factor in value, especially to private equity groups that are very keen on these types of companies. It is crucial that the company has a record of on-time delivery and quality that is in the 97th percentile or higher.

The more the company has in the way of tier-one clients, contracts for critical components, and a history of reliable deliveries and quality, the higher the multiple.

BENCHMARK DATA

STATISTICS (MACHINE SHOPS)

Number of Establishments	19,084
Average Profit Margin	6.4%
Revenue per Employee	$189,555
Average Number of Employees	14.3
Average Wages per Employee	$62,196

PRODUCTS AND SERVICES SEGMENTATION

Machine centers	43.0%
Other	17.8%
Turning centers and lathes	13.6%
Drills	10.9%
Grinding	10.3%
EDM and ECM	4.4%

MAJOR MARKET SEGMENTATION

Fabricated metal product markets	34.7%
Industrial machinery and equipment markets (including components)	22.4%
Other markets	15.8%
Automotive, transportation and off-highway vehicle markets	15.0%
Airline markets	5.9%
Electronics and telecommunications markets	3.3%
Medical markets	2.9%

INDUSTRY COSTS

Profit	6.4%
Wages	32.4%
Purchases	33.2%
Depreciation	3.8%
Marketing	0.2%

Rent & Utilities 3.8%
Other 20.3%

The top companies in the field have sales that equate to $200K per employee—the average range can be anything from $80K to $150K. Concentration is usually an issue with these businesses but can be a double-edged sword. As long as the major customer has a five-plus-year relationship, and is buying mission-critical parts, then most professional buyers recognize this as a plus, rather than a negative.

Geographic location is important to buyers since machinery is expensive to move.

EXPENSES (% OF ANNUAL SALES)

Cost of Goods	50% to 60%
Occupancy Costs	03% to 08%
Payroll/Labor Costs.	30% to 35%
Profit (pretax)	05% to 15%

QUESTIONS

- Concentration can be an issue in this business; sometimes 60 percent or more can be with one customer. Buyer needs to be assured that the relationship with customers is intact and will follow with a new owner.
- Does the business rely on the owner or the company?
- Are there sufficient skilled and knowledgeable supervisors/managers to help with the transition?
- How much working capital is needed during seasonable slumps or plant closures during vacations?

INDUSTRY TREND

"Strong downstream markets maintain industry growth. Since they are the strongest client for machine shops, the growth of manufacturing markets enabled industry growth. The volatility of input prices creates problems for machine shops. As increasing prices bode well for machine shops, price volatility for goods like steel creates uncertainty for short-term growth."

Source: IBISWorld Key Takeaways

EXPERT COMMENTS

As always, the seller needs to have excellent books and records, all customer reports and documentation. Buyer needs to ensure that customers are happy with quality and service and that the employees are competent. Key employees need to be retained, so buyers should offer an incentive to keep them.

Good machine shops have first-class machines, kept in good condition by competent employees. The work ethic must be, no compromise on quality or customer service.

RESOURCES

- IBISWorld, September 2023: https://www.ibisworld.com
- AMT—The Association for Manufacturing Technology: https://www.amtonline.org/index.cfm
- FMA—Fabricators & Manufacturers Association, International: https://www.fmanet.org
- Modern Machine Shop: https://www.mmsonline.com/
- PMPA—Precision Machined Products Association: https://www.pmpa.org
- SSA—Solomons Strategic Advisors: https://www.solomonsadvisors.com

Maid Brigade (Franchise)

| NAICS 561720 | Businesses/Units 338

Rules of Thumb

- 45% annual sales

INDUSTRY MULTIPLES

Acquisition multiples below are calculated medians using US private industry transactions. Data updated annually. Last update: August 2023.

VALUATION MULTIPLE (MEDIAN VALUE)

UNDER $1 MILLION NET SALES

MVIC/Net Sales.	0.59
MVIC/Gross Profit	0.76
MVIC/SDE	2.03
MVIC/EBITDA	2.92

$1 MILLION–$5 MILLION NET SALES

MVIC/Net Sales.	0.45
MVIC/Gross Profit	1.02
MVIC/SDE	2.86
MVIC/EBITDA	4.05

OVER $5 MILLION NET SALES

MVIC/Net Sales.	0.53
MVIC/Gross Profit	2.26
MVIC/SDE	4.26
MVIC/EBITDA	5.48

Source: DealStats (formerly Pratt's Stats), 2023 (Portland, OR: Business Valuation Resources, LLC), www.bvresources.com/dealstats

PRICING TIPS

Approx. Total Investment: $97,700 to $114,500

RESOURCES

- Maid Brigade: https://www.maidbrigade.com
- Franchise information: https://www.maidbrigadefranchise.com

Maid Services

| NAICS 561720

Rules of Thumb

- 35%–40% annual sales plus inventory
- 1.5 x SDE plus inventory

INDUSTRY MULTIPLES

Acquisition multiples below are calculated medians using US private industry transactions. Data updated annually. Last update: August 2023.

VALUATION MULTIPLE (MEDIAN VALUE)

UNDER $1 MILLION NET SALES

MVIC/Net Sales.	0.59
MVIC/Gross Profit	0.76
MVIC/SDE	2.03
MVIC/EBITDA	2.92

$1 MILLION–$5 MILLION NET SALES

MVIC/Net Sales.	0.45
MVIC/Gross Profit	1.02
MVIC/SDE	2.86
MVIC/EBITDA	4.05

OVER $5 MILLION NET SALES

MVIC/Net Sales.	0.53
MVIC/Gross Profit	2.26
MVIC/SDE	4.26
MVIC/EBITDA	5.48

Source: DealStats (formerly Pratt's Stats), 2023 (Portland, OR: Business Valuation Resources, LLC), www.bvresources.com/dealstats

BENCHMARK DATA

For Benchmark data see Janitorial Services

Mail and Parcel Centers (Business Centers)

NAICS 561431	SIC 7389	Businesses/Units 26,032
Profit $1.9 B	Wages $3.5 B	Annual Growth Future 0.7%
		Annual Growth Past 5.5%

Rules of Thumb

- 45%–50% annual sales includes inventory, less direct cost of goods sold (pass-throughs, e.g., stamps, money
- 2–3 x SDE for national franchises includes inventory
- 2–2.75 x EBIT
- 2–3 x EBITDA

INDUSTRY MULTIPLES

Acquisition multiples below are calculated medians using US private industry transactions. Data updated annually. Last update: August 2023.

VALUATION MULTIPLE (MEDIAN VALUE)

UNDER $1 MILLION NET SALES

MVIC/Net Sales.	0.49
MVIC/Gross Profit	0.86
MVIC/SDE	2.12
MVIC/EBITDA	2.78

$1 MILLION–$5 MILLION NET SALES

MVIC/Net Sales.	0.13
MVIC/Gross Profit	0.69
MVIC/SDE	1.89
MVIC/EBITDA	6.02

OVER $5 MILLION NET SALES

MVIC/Net Sales.	0.79
MVIC/Gross Profit	3.45
MVIC/SDE	6.91
MVIC/EBITDA	7.44

Source: DealStats (formerly Pratt's Stats), 2023 (Portland, OR: Business Valuation Resources, LLC), www.bvresources.com/dealstats

PRICING TIPS

Pricing is a function of sales and owner cash flow range. Poorly performing locations with CFO < $50K generally sell for FFE + inventory + 1 x CFO. CFO > $100K will sell for 3 x CFO.

BENCHMARK DATA

STATISTICS (BUSINESS SERVICE CENTERS)

Number of Establishments	26,032
Average Profit Margin	12.9%
Revenue per Employee	$156,460
Average Number of Employees	3.7
Average Wages per Employee	$36,663

PRODUCTS AND SERVICES SEGMENTATION

Copying and reproduction	69.5%
Postal, shipping and mailbox rental	14.5%
Packaging and labeling	9.5%
Printing	3.5%
Other	3.0%

MAJOR MARKET SEGMENTATION

Small Businesses	47.1%
Individuals and households	26.7%
Healthcare service sectors	10.8%
Financial institutions	10.6%
Government and nonprofit	4.8%

INDUSTRY COSTS

Profit	12.9%
Wages	23.5%
Purchases	34.4%
Depreciation	2.6%
Marketing	1.7%
Rent & Utilities	2.4%
Other	22.5%

MARKET SHARE

United Parcel Service, Inc.	22.2%
FedEx Corporation	8.5%
Staples Inc.	7.2%

Location is important; business does not need a lot of square footage; the rent should be kept low.

EXPENSES (% OF ANNUAL SALES)

Cost of Goods	45% to 50%
Occupancy Costs	10% to 15%
Payroll/Labor Costs	15% to 20%
Profit (pretax)	10% to 20%

QUESTIONS

- What is the price of a pack of 20 first-class stamps?
- What are the revenue splits by product lines?
- Do they have any leased equipment?
- What is their POS system (PostalMate is industry leader)?
- How much prepaid mailbox rents have been collected? Buyer should get this amount as cash back at the closing.

INDUSTRY TREND

"The desire for industry services has historically been influenced by the number of companies and the level of corporate profit, which usually has an impact on rising outsourcing costs. Factors related to the growth of digital communication and the possibility of conducting business online have put this connection under stress. However, these impacts have been mitigated by the expansion of e-commerce and a rise in the number of companies and corporate profit."

Source: IBISWorld Key Takeaways

EXPERT COMMENTS

Look for mailbox rentals > rent (including NNN).

Buyer—plan on adding on products and services. Seller—get broker price opinions from a few brokers and offer seller financing to get the highest sale price.

This is a proven successful business model; however, it's a mature industry that is always threatened with new technologies.

Ease of ownership and operation, along with endless add-on services (i.e., bookkeeping, legal documents, printing, fingerprinting, passport photos, etc.), make this a very appealing business for first-time business buyers.

FINANCING

These are readily SBA loan candidates, if the business has good books and records. Otherwise, seller financing with 30 to 50 percent down is common.

RESOURCES

- IBISWorld, March 2023: https://www.ibisworld.com
- AMBC—Association of Mail and Business Centers: https://ambc4me.org
- RSA—Retail Shipping Associates: https://www.rscentral.org/

Management Consulting

	NAICS 541611		Businesses/Units 928,251	
	Profit $34 B		Wages $157.6 B		Annual Growth Future 0.8%
					Annual Growth Past 1.1%

Rules of Thumb

- 2.5 x SDE

INDUSTRY MULTIPLES

Acquisition multiples below are calculated medians using US private industry transactions. Data updated annually. Last update: August 2023.

VALUATION MULTIPLE (MEDIAN VALUE)

UNDER $1 MILLION NET SALES	
MVIC/Net Sales	0.87
MVIC/Gross Profit	1.00
MVIC/SDE	1.93
MVIC/EBITDA	3.53

$1 MILLION–$5 MILLION NET SALES	
MVIC/Net Sales	0.61
MVIC/Gross Profit	1.04
MVIC/SDE	2.60
MVIC/EBITDA	3.69

OVER $5 MILLION NET SALES

MVIC/Net Sales	1.60
MVIC/Gross Profit	4.09
MVIC/SDE	8.08
MVIC/EBITDA	13.16

Source: DealStats (formerly Pratt's Stats), 2023 (Portland, OR: Business Valuation Resources, LLC), www.bvresources.com/dealstats

BENCHMARK DATA

STATISTICS (MANAGEMENT CONSULTING)

Number of Establishments	928,251
Average Profit Margin	10.3%
Revenue per Employee	$171,607
Average Number of Employees	2.1
Average Wages per Employee	$82,288

PRODUCTS AND SERVICES SEGMENTATION

Corporate strategy	43.3%
Organizational design	39.2%
Financial advisory	9.1%
Marketing and sales	3.3%
Process and operations management	2.6%
IT strategy	1.9%
Human resources advisory	0.6%

MAJOR MARKET SEGMENTATION

Financial services companies	32.1%
Government organizations and Not-for-profit	21.0%
Energy, resource and industrial	17.1%
Technology, media and telecommunications companies	15.0%
Healthcare and life sciences sector	10.6%
Households, consumers and individuals	4.2%

INDUSTRY COSTS

Profit	10.3%
Wages	47.8%
Purchases	2.7%
Depreciation	0.8%
Marketing	1.6%
Rent & Utilities	2.6%
Other	34.2%

MARKET SHARE

Deloitte Touche Tohmatsu	2.9%
DiscoverOrg LLC	2.7%
Accenture Plc	2.6%
Cognizant Technology Solutions Corporation	2.0%
Science Applications International Corporation	1.4%
Deutsche Post AG	1.2%
The Blackstone Group L.P.	1.2%
Marsh & McLennan Companies, Inc.	1.0%

INDUSTRY TREND

"Diversity keeps consultants busy. Diversity in downstream clients and the diversity of services offered ensures revenue growth in economic peaks and troughs. The technology tide raises demand for skilled workers. As the digital economy expands and technology infrastructure is built out, consulting practices will face increased competition for skilled workers."

Source: IBISWorld Key Takeaways

RESOURCES
• IBISWorld, September 2023: https://www.ibisworld.com

Manufacturing: Concrete Pipe & Block

| NAICS 32733 | Businesses/Units 711

| Profit $308.3 M | Wages $1.3 B | Annual Growth Future 2.6%

                                             | Annual Growth Past -2.3%

INDUSTRY MULTIPLES

Acquisition multiples below are calculated medians using US private industry transactions. Data updated annually. Last update: August 2023.

VALUATION MULTIPLE (MEDIAN VALUE)

UNDER $1 MILLION NET SALES

MVIC/Net Sales	2.77
MVIC/Gross Profit	3.86
MVIC/SDE	N/A
MVIC/EBITDA	6.16

$1 MILLION–$5 MILLION NET SALES	N/A

OVER $5 MILLION NET SALES

MVIC/Net Sales	0.82
MVIC/Gross Profit	3.12
MVIC/SDE	3.56
MVIC/EBITDA	8.35

Source: DealStats (formerly Pratt's Stats), 2023 (Portland, OR: Business Valuation Resources, LLC), www.bvresources.com/dealstats

BENCHMARK DATA

STATISTICS (CONCRETE PIPE & BLOCK MANUFACTURING)

Number of Establishments	711
Average Profit Margin	4.2%
Revenue per Employee	$391,042
Average Number of Employees	27.1
Average Wages per Employee	$65,706

PRODUCTS AND SERVICES SEGMENTATION

Concrete structural blocks	27.9%
Concrete pavers	26.8%
Other	16.7%
Concrete decorative blocks	9.1%
Concrete culvert pipes	8.3%
Concrete storm and sanitary pipes	7.1%
Concrete bricks	4.1%

MAJOR MARKET SEGMENTATION

Nonresidential building	37.9%
Infrastructure building	32.1%
Residential building	30.0%

INDUSTRY COSTS

Profit	4.2%
Wages	17.1%
Purchases	38.0%
Depreciation	3.8%

Marketing	.	.	.	.	.	.	.	.	0.7%
Rent & Utilities	.	.	.	.	.	.	.	.	2.8%
Other	.	.	.	.	.	.	.	.	33.3%

MARKET SHARE

| CRH plc | . | . | . | . | . | . | . | . | 11.9% |
| Cemex S.A.B. de C.V. | . | . | . | . | . | 6.1% |

INDUSTRY TREND

"The Infrastructure Investment and Jobs Act will benefit the industry over the next five years through higher demand from the infrastructure construction market. Green initiatives will push manufacturers to produce low-emission concretes. Concrete pipe manufacturers will face added competition from substitutions."

Source: IBISWorld Key Takeaways

RESOURCES

• IBISWorld, April 2023: https://www.ibisworld.com

Manufacturing: Custom Architectural Woodwork and Millwork

| NAICS 337212

Rules of Thumb

• 3 x SDE includes inventory

INDUSTRY MULTIPLES

Acquisition multiples below are calculated medians using US private industry transactions. Data updated annually. Last update: August 2023.

VALUATION MULTIPLE (MEDIAN VALUE)

UNDER $1 MILLION NET SALES	
MVIC/Net Sales.	0.32
MVIC/Gross Profit	0.88
MVIC/SDE	N/A
MVIC/EBITDA	2.53
$1 MILLION–$5 MILLION NET SALES	N/A
OVER $5 MILLION NET SALES	N/A

Source: DealStats (formerly Pratt's Stats), 2023 (Portland, OR: Business Valuation Resources, LLC), www.bvresources.com/dealstats

PRICING TIPS

Growth and customer list affect multiple dramatically.

EXPENSES (% OF ANNUAL SALES)

Cost of Goods	.	.	.	.	.	.	50%
Occupancy Costs	.	.	.	.	.	10%
Payroll/Labor Costs.	.	.	.	.	30%
Profit (pretax)	.	.	.	.	.	10%

Manufacturing: Electrical

NAICS 33531	Businesses/Units 1,855
Profit $2.8 B	Wages $9.4 B	Annual Growth Future -0.5%
		Annual Growth Past 0.4%

Rules of Thumb

- 5 x EBITDA

INDUSTRY MULTIPLES

Acquisition multiples below are calculated medians using US private industry transactions. Data updated annually. Last update: August 2023.

VALUATION MULTIPLE (MEDIAN VALUE)

UNDER $1 MILLION NET SALES
MVIC/Net Sales.	0.58
MVIC/Gross Profit	1.37
MVIC/SDE	2.78
MVIC/EBITDA	5.37

$1 MILLION–$5 MILLION NET SALES
MVIC/Net Sales.	1.17
MVIC/Gross Profit	2.13
MVIC/SDE	5.87
MVIC/EBITDA	8.70

OVER $5 MILLION NET SALES
MVIC/Net Sales.	1.21
MVIC/Gross Profit	3.78
MVIC/SDE	3.95
MVIC/EBITDA	6.28

Source: DealStats (formerly Pratt's Stats), 2023 (Portland, OR: Business Valuation Resources, LLC), www.bvresources.com/dealstats

PRICING TIPS

Client relationships and strength of long-term contracts are major factors. Patents and proprietary processes must be evaluated.

BENCHMARK DATA

STATISTICS (ELECTRICAL EQUIPMENT MANUFACTURING)
Number of Establishments .	1,855
Average Profit Margin	5.7%
Revenue per Employee .	$402,797
Average Number of Employees.	63.7
Average Wages per Employee .	$77,648

PRODUCTS AND SERVICES SEGMENTATION
Relays and industrial controls	28.2%
Motors and generator manufacturing	21.1%
Other	19.1%
Switchgear and switchboards	18.5%
Transformers	13.1%

MAJOR MARKET SEGMENTATION
Exports .	33.7%
Wholesalers/distributors for resale.	27.3%
Manufacturers	20.4%
Retailers.	6.6%

Other 6.0%
Businesses 6.0%

INDUSTRY COSTS

Profit 5.7%
Wages 19.1%
Purchases 51.3%
Depreciation 1.5%
Marketing 0.2%
Rent & Utilities 1.4%
Other 20.9%

MARKET SHARE

Eaton Corporation PLC 14.1%
Johnson Electric Holdings Ltd. 10.6%
Schneider Electric Se 8.8%
ABB Ltd 6.6%
General Electric Company 2.9%
Consolidated Electrical Distributors, Inc. . . . 2.2%
Westinghouse 1.7%
Rexel Inc. 1.3%
Harbor Freight Tools USA, Inc. 1.3%
Graybar Services, Inc. 1.0%

EXPENSES (% OF ANNUAL SALES)

Cost of Goods 64%
Occupancy Costs 04%
Payroll/Labor Costs. . . . . 07% to 08%
Profit (pretax) 12%

INDUSTRY TREND

"The recovery from the COVID-19 was a boon for the US economy, but electrical equipment manufacturers still face challenges. Higher interest rates have reduced demand from the construction sector, a major buyer of electrical equipment. Low input prices and weak international markets will keep revenue subdued, but major companies are attempting to innovate to buck these trends. Many manufacturers are increasing investment in renewables to improve efficiency and expand their markets."

Source: IBISWorld Key Takeaways

FINANCING

5 years

RESOURCES

• IBISWorld, September 2023: https://www.ibisworld.com

Manufacturing: Electrical Connectors

| NAICS 334510

Rules of Thumb

• 3 x EBITDA

INDUSTRY MULTIPLES

Acquisition multiples below are calculated medians using US private industry transactions. Data updated annually. Last update: August 2023.

VALUATION MULTIPLE (MEDIAN VALUE)

UNDER $1 MILLION NET SALES	
MVIC/Net Sales.	20.49
MVIC/Gross Profit	N/A
MVIC/SDE	3.09
MVIC/EBITDA	N/A

$1 MILLION–$5 MILLION NET SALES	N/A

OVER $5 MILLION NET SALES	
MVIC/Net Sales.	3.88
MVIC/Gross Profit	6.39
MVIC/SDE	4.45
MVIC/EBITDA	30.99

Source: DealStats (formerly Pratt's Stats), 2023 (Portland, OR: Business Valuation Resources, LLC), www.bvresources.com/dealstats

PRICING TIPS

Transferring the customers and good accounting of inventory are very important.

Contract manufacturing companies sell for 3 x SDE or under. Companies with proprietary products are 4–7 x SDE, depending on growth.

BENCHMARK DATA

No customer bigger than 30 percent

EXPENSES (% OF ANNUAL SALES)

Cost of Goods	40% to 45%
Occupancy Costs	10% to 15%
Payroll/Labor Costs.	30%
Profit (pretax)	10%

QUESTIONS

How much engineering work do you do?

EXPERT COMMENTS

The industry is very cyclical.

Manufacturing: Fertilizer

	NAICS 32531		Businesses/Units 851	
	Profit $1.9 B		Wages $2.3 B		Annual Growth Future 2.6%
					Annual Growth Past 7.3%

INDUSTRY MULTIPLES

Acquisition multiples below are calculated medians using US private industry transactions. Data updated annually. Last update: August 2023.

VALUATION MULTIPLE (MEDIAN VALUE)

UNDER $1 MILLION NET SALES	N/A
$1 MILLION–$5 MILLION NET SALES	N/A

OVER $5 MILLION NET SALES	
MVIC/Net Sales.	1.70
MVIC/Gross Profit	8.01
MVIC/SDE	N/A
MVIC/EBITDA	13.23

Source: DealStats (formerly Pratt's Stats), 2023 (Portland, OR: Business Valuation Resources, LLC), www.bvresources.com/dealstats

BENCHMARK DATA

Number of Establishments	851
Average Profit Margin	6.9%
Revenue per Employee	$1,108,376
Average Number of Employees. . . .	31.3
Average Wages per Employee . . .	$91,864

PRODUCTS AND SERVICES SEGMENTATION

Nitrogenous fertilizers	45.5%
Phosphate fertilizers	28.2%
Mixed fertilizers.	26.3%

MAJOR MARKET SEGMENTATION

Corn industry	46.3%
Exports	16.3%
Other industries.	16.0%
Soybean industry	12.1%
Wheat industry	5.4%
Cotton industry	3.9%

INDUSTRY COSTS

Profit	6.9%
Wages	8.4%
Purchases	41.5%
Depreciation	2.6%
Marketing	0.1%
Rent & Utilities	4.8%
Other	35.9%

MARKET SHARE

CF Industries Holdings, Inc.	31.2%
Nutrien Ltd.	27.0%
Mosaic Co	11.3%

INDUSTRY TREND

"Fertilizer prices are experiencing volatility due to the Russia-Ukraine war, the rise in natural gas prices and the lasting effects of the pandemic. Fertilizer is a commodity, meaning that global trade and the world market determines prices."

Source: IBISWorld Industry at a Glance

RESOURCES

- IBISWorld, September 2023: https://www.ibisworld.com

Manufacturing: Fiber Processing

| NAICS 313110

Rules of Thumb

- 80% annual sales includes inventory
- 3 x SDE plus inventory
- 3.5 x EBIT
- 4 x EBITDA

INDUSTRY MULTIPLES

Acquisition multiples below are calculated medians using US private industry transactions. Data updated annually. Last update: August 2023.

VALUATION MULTIPLE (MEDIAN VALUE)

UNDER $1 MILLION NET SALES

MVIC/Net Sales.	0.57
MVIC/Gross Profit	1.27
MVIC/SDE	1.89
MVIC/EBITDA	5.83

$1 MILLION–$5 MILLION NET SALES	N/A
OVER $5 MILLION NET SALES	N/A

Source: DealStats (formerly Pratt's Stats), 2023 (Portland, OR: Business Valuation Resources, LLC), www.bvresources.com/dealstats

PRICING TIPS

Very dependent on the owner's role. Is there a management team in place? Is there recurring revenue locked in with supply contracts?

EXPENSES (% OF ANNUAL SALES)

Cost of Goods	40%
Occupancy Costs	10%
Payroll/Labor Costs.	15%
Profit (pretax)	20%

QUESTIONS

- Age of equipment? Expected life of equipment? Are there chemicals that are detrimental to the equipment?

INDUSTRY TREND

High demand for good manufacturing companies. Boomers are exiting, and their businesses are in high demand if the business is doing at least $5M in revenue.

EXPERT COMMENTS

Customers tend to be a small group. Ensure the owner does not have all the relationships. If the owner does, a three-year earnout will be typical.

Manufacturing: Food

| NAICS 311

Rules of Thumb

- 4–7 x EBITDA

INDUSTRY MULTIPLES

Acquisition multiples below are calculated medians using US private industry transactions. Data updated annually. Last update: August 2023.

VALUATION MULTIPLE (MEDIAN VALUE)

UNDER $1 MILLION NET SALES

MVIC/Net Sales.	0.46
MVIC/Gross Profit	0.72
MVIC/SDE	2.27
MVIC/EBITDA	3.02

$1 MILLION–$5 MILLION NET SALES

MVIC/Net Sales.	0.49
MVIC/Gross Profit	0.98
MVIC/SDE	3.09
MVIC/EBITDA	4.45

OVER $5 MILLION NET SALES

MVIC/Net Sales.	1.23
MVIC/Gross Profit	4.79
MVIC/SDE	3.68
MVIC/EBITDA	12.14

Source: DealStats (formerly Pratt's Stats), 2023 (Portland, OR: Business Valuation Resources, LLC), www.bvresources.com/dealstats

PRICING TIPS

Brand, years in business, strong customer base and length of relationship with customers, vendor certifications (i.e., certified organic, 100 percent natural, etc.)

BENCHMARK DATA

Food manufacturing gross margins (after material costs and direct labor) should be at least 40 percent, and preferably at least 50 percent.

EXPENSES (% OF ANNUAL SALES)

Cost of Goods	30% to 40%
Occupancy Costs	05%
Payroll/Labor Costs.	10% to 15%
Profit (pretax)	05% to 10%

QUESTIONS

- Revenue? COGS? Liabilities? Owner involvement? Sales channel? Who are your customers? How long have you been supplying to these customers? Do you have contracts with clients? Any client that accounts for more than 10 percent of your sales? What is the production capacity? Type of equipment?

EXPERT COMMENTS

Food manufacturing businesses have high marketability.

FINANCING

Depends on the size of the deal. Average seller financing is 2 to 10 years.

RESOURCES

- Food Engineering: https://www.foodengineeringmag.com
- Food Manufacturing: https://www.foodmanufacturing.com

Manufacturing: Furniture/Household

NAICS 33712	SIC 2599-01	Businesses/Units 3,837
Profit $405.4 M	Wages $5.5 B	
		Annual Growth Past -4.5%

Rules of Thumb

- 4–7 x EBITDA

INDUSTRY MULTIPLES

Acquisition multiples below are calculated medians using US private industry transactions. Data updated annually. Last update: August 2023.

VALUATION MULTIPLE (MEDIAN VALUE)

UNDER $1 MILLION NET SALES

MVIC/Net Sales	0.64
MVIC/Gross Profit	1.10
MVIC/SDE	3.05
MVIC/EBITDA	4.25

$1 MILLION–$5 MILLION NET SALES

MVIC/Net Sales	0.33
MVIC/Gross Profit	0.67
MVIC/SDE	2.52
MVIC/EBITDA	5.00

OVER $5 MILLION NET SALES

MVIC/Net Sales	0.49
MVIC/Gross Profit	1.41
MVIC/SDE	2.18
MVIC/EBITDA	4.87

Source: DealStats (formerly Pratt's Stats), 2023 (Portland, OR: Business Valuation Resources, LLC), www.bvresources.com/dealstats

PRICING TIPS

Size, growth, condition of plant, how profitable it is, place in the market, and management can play a part.

BENCHMARK DATA

STATISTICS (HOUSEHOLD FURNITURE MANUFACTURING)

Number of Establishments	3,837
Average Profit Margin	1.7%
Revenue per Employee	$201,247
Average Number of Employees	32.8
Average Wages per Employee	$46,053

PRODUCTS AND SERVICES SEGMENTATION

Upholstered household furniture	52.4%
Institutional furniture	17.9%
Non-upholstered wood household furniture	13.6%
Metal household furniture	10.8%
Other	5.3%

MAJOR MARKET SEGMENTATION

Home furnishing stores	42.8%
Other retailers	19.5%
Businesses	13.4%
Other	9.8%
Independent wholesalers	8.7%
Department stores and warehouse clubs	5.8%

INDUSTRY COSTS

Profit	1.7%
Wages	23.0%
Purchases	49.2%
Depreciation	0.4%
Marketing	0.6%
Rent & Utilities	2.7%
Other	22.3%

MARKET SHARE

Ashley Furniture Industries, Inc.	20.8%
La-Z-Boy Incorporated	5.9%
Ameriwood Home	3.7%
Brown Jordan International Inc.	1.8%

Sauder Woodworking Co. 1.8%
Apex Tool Group, LLC 1.7%

INDUSTRY TREND

"Prominent import penetration harms domestic manufacturers. Domestic producers struggle to compete with lower production costs overseas, causing foreign producers to capture a large portion of US consumers. Losses in the residential market result in falling revenue. Increasing inflation and high interest rates discourage housing starts and existing home sales."

Source: IBISWorld Key Takeaways

RESOURCES

- IBISWorld, September 2023: https://www.ibisworld.com
- BIFMA—Business + Institutional Furniture Manufacturers Association: https://www.bifma.org

Manufacturing: General

| SIC 3999-03

Rules of Thumb

- 40%–60% annual sales includes inventory
- 3–4 x SDE (depending on size & quality) includes inventory
- 3–4 x SDE; must manufacture product; not be a job shop
- 3–5 x EBITDA
- 4–6 x EBIT

PRICING TIPS

Once SDE/EBITDA exceeds $1M, the multiple for sales price increases, especially if the buyer is a strategic buyer. If the construction business is not very profitable, request that the seller get a certified appraisal for their machinery and equipment, as the value could be great and the lead time to order new equipment long.

Margins for a manufacturing business can be very high depending on the customers the business has and relationships, including contracts or repeat business. Areas to watch and analyze include the following: (1) total income (revenue), (2) cost of goods sold (COGS), (3) other expenses unique to operating the business and if they are price sensitive and readily available, and (4) seller's discretionary earnings (SDE)—does the owner work in the business or have a general manager run it?

Valuation also depends on the type of product they produce. Are they making a commodity product with tons of competition and low margins, or a proprietary product with patents and premium pricing? What are the capex requirements going forward? How much working capital is required? Are they carrying a lot of inventory relative to their revenue size, or is the inventory turnover high?

Make sure you fully understand their customer base, and determine if they are heavily concentrated. The higher the customer concentration the less the value. Same with vendors. Ever since the supply chain mess, buyers are insisting on multiple vendors.

I normally use SDE for businesses with revenues in the $3 to $10 million range. The quality characteristics of the company (management team, documented

M

procedures, customer concentration, cleanliness of the facility) come into play to determine where in the 3 to 4 multiplier range that I use. To that, you need to add working capital that the buyer needs to pay for. I am seeing working capital in almost every transaction.

Type and age of equipment heavily weigh on the sale price of the business. Most smaller shops, under a few million in sales and have very old equipment with very little value. The value for the business comes almost entirely from the cash flow and has very little to do with the equipment value. This low equipment value (collateral value) increases the expected capex expenditure for the buyer and subsequently limits the multiple that buyers are willing to pay and lenders are willing to finance. Industries served by the manufacture also play into the multiple. Commodity products and industries will limit the multiple, while medical, electrical, and aerospace will help drive a higher multiple.

Customer concentration; supply chain reliability; years in business; customer consistency; age of equipment; marketing and revenue growth.

Pricing multiple will depend on the size. For $300K to $1M in EBITDA, the multiple would be 4 to 5 x EBITDA or 3 to 4 x SDE, depending on the niche, growth trends, working capital needed, ease of learning/running the business, etc. Larger businesses would get a higher multiple.

SDE x 4 for most manufacturing businesses; selling the real estate drives the loan term to 25 years. Sellers like to lease the real estate, but buying the real estate is beneficial to the buyer.

Value of the equipment has nothing to do with cash flow of the business. Banks like equipment to support their loans, but SDE must support debt service.

Manufacturing operations must leverage best practices in their respective industries and use automation where possible. Automation, process control, and quality management are paramount to an effective and efficient operation. The more automated the production process, the less risk associated with scrap and waste. The product must be something that has strong local demand and cannot easily be produced out of country. Equipment should be viewed against the latest technology to determine its FMV; older machinery may be fine for commodity manufacturing where the cost to re-equip is equally difficult for competitors. Some industries will rely on very old machinery, and that is fine as long as it is in good condition and repairable. Production equipment is a major barrier to entry, along with wages and unions. If it can be produced in China, then you will have a hard time competing, unless you have a novel process that is considered intellectual property and provides advantages in cost and efficiency. Prices will vary based on the type of product, region, and market share.

BENCHMARK DATA

The cost of rent, and its location to the market it serves, are important. The closer the proximity to the end user of the product, the lower the shipping costs and the quicker the turnaround in the manufactured product.

$100,000 to $200,000 per employee unless there is significant outsourcing of production work, in which case, it could be much higher

Revenue per employee: $500K

Quote hourly rates at $50 to $75 per hour. If special equipment is involved, add the costs of the equipment.

Make sure all equipment is producing revenue.

EXPENSES (% OF ANNUAL SALES)

Cost of Goods	45% to 55%
Occupancy Costs	05% to 10%
Payroll/Labor Costs.	20% to 30%
Profit (pretax)	10% to 15%

QUESTIONS

- How deep is your next tier of management? How dependent is your business on you either for bringing in work or in executing projects? What is your backlog of work/projects? What is your customer concentration?
- What is the business development process? Who are competitors?
- Has the company's business changed materially over the last three years? If so, how? Have there been any substantial increases or decreases in competition over the last three years, or are you aware of any competition coming to the market? If so, please explain. What is the average value of stock, supplies, or merchandise on hand for internal consumption? What is the average value of sellable inventory (at cost) on hand?
- Quality of management team? Product diversification focus? Any patents? Value of contracts on the books?
- Any employee concerns the owner has?
- What steps do I need to take to grow the business?
- How old are your machine operators? Why do customers use you over the competition? (Price alone is not a strategy as there are plenty of low-cost providers.) What industries do you serve? Have you been able to pass along cost increases to your customers? Do you have any customer concentration issues? Are there any environmental concerns with the property?
- Supply chain issues? Customer loyalty? Equipment life? Competition status? Marketing program?
- Ask about the seller's specific role in the business, and ensure that you can fit in their shoes or get the right people to help bridge any gap in skills that are necessary for the success of the business. Question their inventory management practices, and verify the working capital needs of the business.
- What would you do to grow the business if you were 20 years younger and had the working capital to invest? What are the three biggest risks of the business? Is there anything else that I should have asked?
- How involved is the owner? Are customers connecting with the owner selling, or someone on staff, that will transfer with the sale?
- Tenure of employees? How far away from the factory do employees come from to work there? Employee pay scale and benefits? Employee turnover rate? Age of equipment? Automation used to run equipment? Management system used for inventory control, production planning, shipping, financial management, customer interface, supplier interface, marketing?
- Show me your capex history and bad-debt history.
- Why do you want to sell? What is the state of your equipment, and what do you spend a year on capital equipment? What are your sale terms to customers? When would you like this to happen? Are you willing to stay for a transition period?
- What are the downside risks of your business? Ask if any of their customers or vendors are related to them.
- Are the wages paid competitive? Are your procedures and processes fully documented? Are there technologies that need to be implemented to reduce costs? Who is calling on new customers?

- What assurances are in place that the company can continue to manufacture domestically? Does the company compete on price, quality, or service, or have a process/product that is exclusive to them? Is there pending technology that could render the product or process obsolete? Can the client base be expanded? How?
- What capacity is the plant running at? Machine tool maintenance schedule? If the company has multiple products, what is the gross margin per product?

INDUSTRY TREND

With the U.S. government offering incentives for manufacturing businesses, this industry should do very well.

The U.S. economy remains resilient, but the increase in interest rates is beginning to impact the buying decisions of a lower-paid wage or salary earner. If the business, therefore, sells products to this demographic, the performance of the business will decline.

Increasing, with focus on manufacturing in U.S., inshoring of operations, and foreign businesses wanting to establish U.S. presence and move away from more volatile areas of the world.

Small growth

Industrial construction will continue to be hot, as we are seeing more onshoring and reshoring of manufacturing.

Robotics equipment is a must, and government contracts are very helpful for continued growth.

Manufacturing will continue to improve in this country. The desire for national security, better-paying jobs, and the complexity of machines/robots are just a few examples of things that will continue to improve the manufacturing environment. We will need to train the 30- to 45-year-old operators before the current 55- to 65-year-old CNC operators retire. We will also need the students coming out of postsecondary education to want to focus on the manufacturing environment, not just the computer sciences.

In general, severe supply chain issues and COGS, requiring increases in pricing, expense management, and focused marketing. These businesses may even be forced to trim marginal customers. Many who do not have strict financial and operational management systems will not survive.

I expect companies with niche products and intellectual property to do very well. Manufacturers of commodity-type products will face pressure with inflation. Demand will continue to be strong from buyers for profitable manufacturing businesses.

It seems that manufacturing is coming back to America, so demand for them should be strong.

Domestic manufacturing will do well as overseas conflicts could disrupt international manufacturing.

Good growth over the next 10 years.

"The shortage of a vital imaging agent is the latest example of the country's vulnerability to disruptions in the global supply chain and its overreliance on a small number of manufacturers for such critical products."

Source: "Patients Face Long Delays for Imaging of Cancers and Other Diseases" by Reed Abelson, May 26, 2022, https://www.nytimes.com/2022/05/26/health/dye-contrast-scan-shortage.html

Consolidation

Commodity manufacturing may suffer with competition from other countries, but "made in the USA" will still drive some consumers to overlook the price of the products. Most domestic manufacturing businesses will see an upward trend for their products, and many smaller facilities will get acquired/merged with larger flex manufacturing operations.

Manufacturing in the U.S. can rebound with appropriate protections in place from China. If it is made in China and is not proprietary, however, it will be difficult to produce in the U.S. unless its size, material, shipping, or design makes it impossible to import and make profit. Mobile homes, RVs, and storage sheds are some types of manufacturing which can be immune from imports. The trend will be to more of the niche, higher-quality products made locally, and commodity products will continue to be produced in China.

EXPERT COMMENTS

Understand the company's overall position in the industry's ecosystem.

Prepare in advance; ensure your books are clean; optimize your inventory levels and working capital. A clean and tidy operation will make a better impression on a buyer who is looking for a pleasant place to work.

Retain seller and key employees with incentives.

As a buyer, have the equipment appraised so you understand future capex needs.

Don't be a lone ranger; bring in one to two partners. It helps to make decisions as a group.

A focus by the government and large enterprises to onshoring over the last several years, along with supply chain challenges from Asian countries during Covid, have helped drive revenues higher. It is easy for a small or midsize manufacturer to grow through acquisition.

Seller: be prepared to carry paper (up to 25 percent) and commit to an extensive training and transition period for the buyer.

Be realistic in expectations. Sellers often overvalue their business, and buyers that are new to business ownership don't realize that acquiring a good business is a competitive process. Ultimately, the deal has to make sense for both sides.

You must trust the seller. Consider a clawback provision if sales decline in the first two or three years. Totally understand the cost of sales for each product. Beware if the seller does not have a good MRP system.

Most manufacturing companies have a customer concentration problem that reduces the value of the business. Inventory can be an issue. If the business has not written off and disposed of their excess and obsolete inventory, then their net income has been overstated over the years. A job shop is worth much less than a company that has proprietary products.

Employees are usually the most important asset that a manufacturing, or any, company has. Check out the company's supply chain—especially if they buy from China or other countries.

Make sure key employees stick around. Take care of key employees with bonuses.

These companies attract financing, as there are assets with the equipment. Buyers like the stuff that comes with it.

Make sure the equipment has ongoing maintenance and that this is logged for the buyer to review. This is an area that can be neglected.

Expect to have an extended transition period.

Starting a manufacturing business is capital intensive and risky. That is why buying a manufacturing business is the way to go.

Job shops have lower than average margins.

If buying: reconciling the financials is critical to determining a price. If selling: clean books that reconcile to tax returns will help drive value and decrease opposition to price.

Post-Covid, we are seeing a resurgence in demand for products in most sectors. As technology continues to drive society and business, demand for technology-driven products will continue to rise. Having a location in proximity to skilled employees for the type of manufacturing is imperative to longevity and therefore impacts business value. Recurring revenue through contracts drives business value up, along with in-demand products. Fad products are risky as consumer trends change frequently, and if the factory is set up for a niche trendy product, it will have to invest in more capex to take on additional products to stay profitable. Having a competent management team in place increases the marketability and opens up the funnel of potential buyers. Three areas to consider when analyzing manufacturing businesses; all of these impact value: (1) Are the products unique, patented, or in demand? (2) Is there a capable management team in place that is passionate about the business and that will stay on regardless of ownership? (3) Is there opportunity to further integrate technology and automation to lower costs and increase predictability?

Have more working capital than you think you need.

FINANCING

Outside financing with potentially a small amount of seller financing. Example: smaller businesses may be done with 80 percent SBA loan, 10 percent buyer equity, 0 percent seller note.

Outside financing with 10 to 15 percent seller's note only for the purpose of helping a buyer qualify for an SBA loan. The buyer and the bank will understand that the seller believes the business can transition to a new owner.

SBA and PEG buyers are more common than cash buyers these days.

If under $5M sales price, we see about 30 to 40 percent financed via SBA 7(a), with up to 20 percent being provided in seller financing.

Outside financing is very easy to find for strong businesses; 10 to 20 percent down with SBA financing is most common. Strategic acquirers can leverage the value of their own equipment and the company being acquired to gain commercial financing.

Most buyers will want seller financing to have some assurance that the seller will do their best to help them succeed. The norm of seller financing is 25 percent. Many buyers have to use SBA financing as they do not have 75 percent to put down. Sellers like this as it reduces the seller carry to only 10 percent or so.

Usually 80 percent paid in cash mainly through SBA financing with 10 to 20 percent in seller carry.

There are no trends when it comes to financing. Really depends on the size of the operation. Under $5M will most likely be financed.

- MAF—Manufacturers Association of Florida: https://www.mafmfg.com
- SME: https://www.sme.org
- Plant Engineering: https://www.plantengineering.com
- NTMA—National Tooling and Machining Association: https://ntma.org
- NED—New Equipment Digest: https://www.newequipment.com
- NAM—National Association of Manufacturers: https://www.nam.org
- MI—Manufacturing Institute: https://www.themanufacturinginstitute.org
- Manufacturing Today: https://manufacturing-today.com
- Manufacturers Alliance: https://www.manufacturersalliance.org
- AAM—Alliance for American Manufacturing:
  https://www.americanmanufacturing.org
- ISM—Institute for Supply Management: https://www.ismworld.org
- IndustryWeek: https://www.industryweek.com
- IMTS—International Manufacturing Technology Show: https://www.imts.com
- FMA—Fabricators & Manufacturers Association, International:
  https://www.fmamfg.org
- FCMA—First Coast Manufacturers Association: https://fcmaweb.com
- AME—Association for Manufacturing Excellence: https://www.ame.org
- AEM—Association of Equipment Manufacturers: https://www.aem.org

Manufacturing: General Purpose Machinery

| NAICS 3339

Rules of Thumb

- 4.5 x EBITDA

INDUSTRY MULTIPLES

Acquisition multiples below are calculated medians using US private industry transactions. Data updated annually. Last update: August 2023.

VALUATION MULTIPLE (MEDIAN VALUE)

UNDER $1 MILLION NET SALES

MVIC/Net Sales.	0.89
MVIC/Gross Profit	2.13
MVIC/SDE	3.38
MVIC/EBITDA	10.27

$1 MILLION–$5 MILLION NET SALES

MVIC/Net Sales.	0.62
MVIC/Gross Profit	1.19
MVIC/SDE	2.81
MVIC/EBITDA	4.04

OVER $5 MILLION NET SALES

MVIC/Net Sales.	1.58
MVIC/Gross Profit	4.60
MVIC/SDE	4.10
MVIC/EBITDA	13.21

Source: DealStats (formerly Pratt's Stats), 2023 (Portland, OR: Business Valuation Resources, LLC), www.bvresources.com/dealstats

Manufacturing: Glass Product

NAICS 32721	Businesses/Units 4,004	
Profit $1.8 B	Wages $5.5 B	Annual Growth Future 1.4%
		Annual Growth Past -1.8%

INDUSTRY MULTIPLES

Acquisition multiples below are calculated medians using US private industry transactions. Data updated annually. Last update: August 2023.

VALUATION MULTIPLE (MEDIAN VALUE)

UNDER $1 MILLION NET SALES	N/A
$1 MILLION–$5 MILLION NET SALES	
MVIC/Net Sales	0.88
MVIC/Gross Profit	1.10
MVIC/SDE	2.42
MVIC/EBITDA	3.13
OVER $5 MILLION NET SALES	
MVIC/Net Sales	1.18
MVIC/Gross Profit	2.88
MVIC/SDE	3.49
MVIC/EBITDA	6.09

Source: DealStats (formerly Pratt's Stats), 2023 (Portland, OR: Business Valuation Resources, LLC), www.bvresources.com/dealstats

BENCHMARK DATA

STATISTICS (GLASS PRODUCT MANUFACTURING)

Number of Establishments	4,004
Average Profit Margin	5.9%
Revenue per Employee	$343,576
Average Number of Employees	22.7
Average Wages per Employee	$61,001

PRODUCTS AND SERVICES SEGMENTATION

Glass products made from purchased glass	48.9%
Pressed or blown glass & other glass products	23.3%
Glass containers	16.7%
Flat glass	11.1%

MAJOR MARKET SEGMENTATION

Construction	40.4%
Household, appliance, food and beverage market	28.2%
Exports	16.6%
Scientific, technical and other markets	9.8%
Automotive assembly and replacement market	5.0%

INDUSTRY COSTS

Profit	5.9%
Wages	17.9%
Purchases	35.7%
Depreciation	2.5%
Marketing	0.1%
Rent & Utilities	5.5%
Other	32.4%

MARKET SHARE

Owens-Illinois, Inc.	13.5%
Cardinal Glass Industries, Inc.	6.4%

Ardagh Group S.A. 5.9%
Corning Inc. 5.8%
Berlin Packaging LLC 2.5%
Orora Limited 1.8%
Stoelzle Oberglas Gmbh 1.3%
Verallia Packaging 1.1%

INDUSTRY TREND

"The industry is still recovering from the COVID-19 pandemic. The COVID-19 pandemic took a heavy toll on downstream markets. Revenue losses resulting from restaurant closures were offset by increased demand from grocery stores. Increased competition leads to innovation. Leading manufacturers have implemented new technologies to curb emissions and increase productivity. Innovations in robotics, automation and air filtration have shaped the industry in recent years."

Source: IBISWorld Key Takeaways

RESOURCES

• IBISWorld, September 2023: https://www.ibisworld.com

Manufacturing: Guided Missile and Space Vehicle

| NAICS 336414 | Businesses/Units 115

| Profit $4 B | Wages $8.3 B | Annual Growth Future 2.1%

| | | Annual Growth Past 4.6%

Rules of Thumb

• 100+% annual sales
• 3–4 x SDE plus inventory
• 6–10 x EBIT
• 5–8 x EBITDA

INDUSTRY MULTIPLES

Acquisition multiples below are calculated medians using US private industry transactions. Data updated annually. Last update: August 2023.

VALUATION MULTIPLE (MEDIAN VALUE)

UNDER $1 MILLION NET SALES	N/A
$1 MILLION–$5 MILLION NET SALES	N/A
OVER $5 MILLION NET SALES	
MVIC/Net Sales	1.93
MVIC/Gross Profit	8.63
MVIC/SDE	N/A
MVIC/EBITDA	13.43

Source: DealStats (formerly Pratt's Stats), 2023 (Portland, OR: Business Valuation Resources, LLC), www.bvresources.com/dealstats

PRICING TIPS

Pricing is heavily impacted by third-party lending criteria and formal appraisals/evaluations. Buyers and sellers are sensitive to industry standards and trends, and a certain segment is sensitive to environmental issues and political correctness.

Usually need to sell as a stock sale due to the qualifications and licenses held by the seller.

Value increases with the company's ability to meet high quality controls and production deadlines as specified by military and military contractors. Extremely high barriers to entry in this industry keep values high.

BENCHMARK DATA

STATISTICS (SPACE VEHICLE & MISSILE MANUFACTURING)

Number of Establishments	115
Average Profit Margin	9.9%
Revenue per Employee	$653,666
Average Number of Employees	860.5
Average Wages per Employee	$134,073

PRODUCTS AND SERVICES SEGMENTATION

Missile systems	44.3%
Space systems	35.5%
Propulsion systems	11.8%
Other missile and space vehicle parts	8.4%

MAJOR MARKET SEGMENTATION

US military	62.5%
Other government agencies	30.5%
Other companies	7.0%

INDUSTRY COSTS

Profit	9.9%
Wages	20.7%
Purchases	45.9%
Depreciation	2.4%
Marketing	0.1%
Rent & Utilities	0.9%
Other	20.0%

MARKET SHARE

Raytheon Technologies Corporation	31.1%
Boeing Co	24.7%
Lockheed Martin Corporation	15.7%
Northrop Grumman Corp	6.0%

EXPENSES (% OF ANNUAL SALES)

Cost of Goods	31% to 35%
Occupancy Costs	15%
Payroll/Labor Costs	50%
Profit (pretax)	20% to 21%

QUESTIONS

- Review the long-term agreement (LTA) and supply agreements.
- Are the key employees willing to stay on postsale? Are qualifications and certifications up to current standards and valid?

INDUSTRY TREND

"Defense spending drives the industry's growth. Rising tensions across the world are a boon for companies that specialize in missile manufacturing. Companies have entered the space vehicle manufacturing niche. SpaceX and Blue Origin have developed promising reusable rockets."

Source: IBISWorld Key Takeaways

Need to be in the industry to buy in this sector.

RESOURCES
• IBISWorld, September 2023: https://www.ibisworld.com

Manufacturing: Guns & Ammunition

| NAICS 332994 | Businesses/Units 692

| Profit $2.1 B | Wages $3.8 B | Annual Growth Future 2.0%

| Annual Growth Past 5.6%

Rules of Thumb
• 5 x SDE

INDUSTRY MULTIPLES

Acquisition multiples below are calculated medians using US private industry transactions. Data updated annually. Last update: August 2023.

VALUATION MULTIPLE (MEDIAN VALUE)

UNDER $1 MILLION NET SALES
MVIC/Net Sales	0.64
MVIC/Gross Profit	1.09
MVIC/SDE	N/A
MVIC/EBITDA	N/A

$1 MILLION–$5 MILLION NET SALES   N/A

OVER $5 MILLION NET SALES
MVIC/Net Sales	2.43
MVIC/Gross Profit	6.53
MVIC/SDE	N/A
MVIC/EBITDA	36.52

Source: DealStats (formerly Pratt's Stats), 2023 (Portland, OR: Business Valuation Resources, LLC), www.bvresources.com/dealstats

PRICING TIPS

There is significant roll-up activity by major firearms manufacturers seeking to diversify their wholesale and retail product offerings into streams with higher margins than firearms. Accessories, apparel, and collectables are popular acquisition targets. Government contracts (GSA) should be priced separately as contingent payments when orders are received. Intellectual property plays a large role in valuations above 5 x owner benefit. Manufacturing dies are also priced in addition to multiple, but should be amortized to reflect useful life from a tool and product demand perspective. Sellers should have sophisticated inventory management and manufacturing processes in place. Gross profits should be extremely high.

BENCHMARK DATA

STATISTICS (GUNS & AMMUNITION MANUFACTURING)

Number of Establishments	692
Average Profit Margin	10.2%
Revenue per Employee	$454,513

M

Average Number of Employees. . . . 68.9
Average Wages per Employee . . . $82,076

PRODUCTS AND SERVICES SEGMENTATION

Small arms and machine guns 42.8%
Small arms ammunition. 29.1%
Other ammunition 22.0%
Ordnance and accessories 6.1%

MAJOR MARKET SEGMENTATION

Civilians and law enforcement 50.1%
Military 49.9%

INDUSTRY COSTS

Profit 10.2%
Wages 18.2%
Purchases 40.6%
Depreciation 2.8%
Marketing 0.4%
Rent & Utilities 2.3%
Other 25.5%

MARKET SHARE

General Dynamics Corporation. . . . 8.9%
Vista Outdoor Inc. 7.2%
Olin Corporation 6.6%
Northrop Grumman Corp 2.2%
Remington Outdoor Company Inc. . . . 2.0%
Bae Systems Plc 1.4%
Colt's Manufacturing Company LLC . . 1.3%
Sig Sauer Inc. 1.0%

EXPENSES (% OF ANNUAL SALES)

Cost of Goods 20%
Occupancy Costs 15%
Payroll/Labor Costs. 20%
Profit (pretax) 20%

QUESTIONS

• What does the company's intellectual property portfolio look like? Who competes with your products on a product-by-product basis, and what are your differentiators?

INDUSTRY TREND

"There has been uncertainty regarding gun control legislation. Consumers spend more on guns and ammunition at the perception of stricter gun control regulations. Exports will rebound for the industry as the value of the US dollar falls over the next five years. This makes US-made guns and ammunition more affordable to foreign markets."

Source: IBISWorld Key Takeaways

FINANCING

Outside financing with a component of seller financing, especially when government contracts are in place

RESOURCES

• IBISWorld, September 2023: https://www.ibisworld.com

Manufacturing: Hardware

| NAICS 332510 | Businesses/Units 567

| Profit $757.5 M | Wages $1.7 B | Annual Growth Future -0.2%

| Annual Growth Past 1.8%

INDUSTRY MULTIPLES

Acquisition multiples below are calculated medians using US private industry transactions. Data updated annually. Last update: August 2023.

VALUATION MULTIPLE (MEDIAN VALUE)

UNDER $1 MILLION NET SALES	N/A
$1 MILLION–$5 MILLION NET SALES	
MVIC/Net Sales	0.94
MVIC/Gross Profit	1.92
MVIC/SDE	2.38
MVIC/EBITDA	2.67
OVER $5 MILLION NET SALES	N/A

Source: DealStats (formerly Pratt's Stats), 2023 (Portland, OR: Business Valuation Resources, LLC), www.bvresources.com/dealstats

BENCHMARK DATA

STATISTICS (HARDWARE MANUFACTURING)

Number of Establishments	567
Average Profit Margin	6.3%
Revenue per Employee	$413,435
Average Number of Employees	51.5
Average Wages per Employee	$59,550

PRODUCTS AND SERVICES SEGMENTATION

Builder's hardware	51.6%
Motor vehicle hardware	21.3%
Miscellaneous hardware	13.8%
Other transportation equipment	7.0%
Furniture hardware	6.3%

MAJOR MARKET SEGMENTATION

Exports	32.2%
Wholesale	25.6%
Hardware and home improvement centers	22.9%
Specialty retail	17.1%
Contractors	2.2%

INDUSTRY COSTS

Profit	6.3%
Wages	14.4%
Purchases	42.4%
Depreciation	2.1%
Marketing	0.3%
Rent & Utilities	1.6%
Other	33.0%

MARKET SHARE

Allegion PLC	5.1%
Spectrum Brands Holdings, Inc.	3.9%
Fortune Brands Home & Security, Inc.	2.5%
Uline, Inc.	1.0%

INDUSTRY TREND

"Hardware Manufacturing industry operators produce a range of metal hardware goods, such as hinges, handles, keys and locks. The industry has recently seen a minor income increase due to better market circumstances in the markets for residential construction and aviation engines and parts production. Hardware manufacturers now make more money. This is due to the proliferation of new technologies, such as the Internet of Things (IoT), artificial intelligence (AI) and virtual reality (VR), as well as the rising demand for hardware products, such as sensors, processors and displays."

Source: IBISWorld Key Takeaways

RESOURCES

• IBISWorld, April 2023: https://www.ibisworld.com

Manufacturing: Inorganic Chemical

| NAICS 325180 | Businesses/Units 704

| Profit $2.3 B | Wages $5 B | Annual Growth Future 0.6%

| | | Annual Growth Past -1.9%

INDUSTRY MULTIPLES

Acquisition multiples below are calculated medians using US private industry transactions. Data updated annually. Last update: August 2023.

VALUATION MULTIPLE (MEDIAN VALUE)

UNDER $1 MILLION NET SALES

MVIC/Net Sales.	3.14
MVIC/Gross Profit	3.85
MVIC/SDE	4.11
MVIC/EBITDA	4.55

$1 MILLION–$5 MILLION NET SALES   N/A

OVER $5 MILLION NET SALES

MVIC/Net Sales.	1.73
MVIC/Gross Profit	7.68
MVIC/SDE	N/A
MVIC/EBITDA	10.22

Source: DealStats (formerly Pratt's Stats), 2023 (Portland, OR: Business Valuation Resources, LLC), www.bvresources.com/dealstats

BENCHMARK DATA

STATISTICS (INORGANIC CHEMICAL MANUFACTURING)

Number of Establishments .	704
Average Profit Margin	6.0%
Revenue per Employee .	$826,708
Average Number of Employees.	65.5
Average Wages per Employee .	$109,608

PRODUCTS AND SERVICES SEGMENTATION

Other inorganic chemicals .	50.6%
Chemical catalysts .	14.0%
Caustic soda	10.1%
Potassium, sodium and other alkali compounds	7.7%
Carbon black	7.3%

Inorganic acids 5.2%
Chlorine 5.1%

MAJOR MARKET SEGMENTATION

Other manufacturing industries 48.1%
Chemical manufacturing 26.6%
Other industries. 25.3%

INDUSTRY COSTS

Profit 6.0%
Wages 13.2%
Purchases 32.5%
Depreciation 3.0%
Marketing 0.0%
Rent & Utilities 7.4%
Other 37.9%

MARKET SHARE

Olin Corporation 10.2%
The Chemours Company 9.8%
Occidental Petroleum Corporation 8.0%
Albemarle Corporation 3.5%
Johnson Matthey Sa 2.7%
Shin-Etsu Chemical Co., Ltd. 2.5%
Akzo Nobel N.V. 1.6%
W. R. Grace & Co. 1.4%
Sinopec Group 1.2%

INDUSTRY TREND

"Energy is one of the industry's direct production costs. Manufacturers compete on the cost to maintain profitability because all producers manufacture the same basket of products. Manufacturers will be more apt to compete internationally. As domestic and global economies grow, international trade will serve as a greater industry revenue source."

Source: IBISWorld Key Takeaways

RESOURCES

• IBISWorld, February 2023: https://www.ibisworld.com

Manufacturing: Iron & Steel

| NAICS 331110 | Businesses/Units 402 |

| Profit $7.4 B | Wages $7 B | Annual Growth Future 3.6% |

| | | Annual Growth Past -6.5% |

INDUSTRY MULTIPLES

Acquisition multiples below are calculated medians using US private industry transactions. Data updated annually. Last update: August 2023.

VALUATION MULTIPLE (MEDIAN VALUE)

UNDER $1 MILLION NET SALES	
MVIC/Net Sales.	1.13
MVIC/Gross Profit	2.73
MVIC/SDE	8.00
MVIC/EBITDA	8.00
$1 MILLION–$5 MILLION NET SALES	N/A

OVER $5 MILLION NET SALES

MVIC/Net Sales.	0.35
MVIC/Gross Profit	3.61
MVIC/SDE	N/A
MVIC/EBITDA	7.00

Source: DealStats (formerly Pratt's Stats), 2023 (Portland, OR: Business Valuation Resources, LLC), www.bvresources.com/dealstats

BENCHMARK DATA

STATISTICS (IRON & STEEL MANUFACTURING)

Number of Establishments .	402
Average Profit Margin	8.4%
Revenue per Employee .	$1,408,959
Average Number of Employees.	167.6
Average Wages per Employee .	$107,805

PRODUCTS AND SERVICES SEGMENTATION

Hot-rolled sheets and strips	32.0%
Hot-rolled bars and shapes .	20.5%
Cold-rolled sheets and strips	16.0%
Steel ingots and semi-finished shapes .	13.6%
Other	12.8%
Tubular products	3.8%
Cold-finished bars and shapes .	1.3%

MAJOR MARKET SEGMENTATION

Construction	44.0%
Automotive .	28.0%
Machinery manufacturers .	9.0%
Energy .	6.0%
Appliance	5.0%
Container	3.0%
Defense .	3.0%
Other markets	2.0%

INDUSTRY COSTS

Profit	8.4%
Wages .	7.9%
Purchases .	63.8%
Depreciation	2.5%
Marketing	0.0%
Rent & Utilities .	4.5%
Other	12.9%

MARKET SHARE

Nucor Corporation .	39.6%
Cleveland-Cliffs Inc..	21.2%
Steel Dynamics, Inc.	20.9%
United States Steel Corp	15.4%
Arcelormittal	10.9%
Gerdau S.A. .	7.8%
Commercial Metals Company .	7.6%
AK Steel Holding Corp .	6.9%
Gerdau .	5.9%
Evraz PLC	3.7%

INDUSTRY TREND

"Highly volatile input prices hurt manufacturers' performance. Steel producers are directly affected by input prices, which rapidly expand and contract. Demand in downstream markets determines the need for steel products. Falling sales in the automotive and construction sectors directly affect steel sales, harming manufacturers."

Source: IBISWorld Key Takeaways

RESOURCES

• IBISWorld, September 2023: https://www.ibisworld.com

Manufacturing: Leather Good & Luggage

| NAICS 316990 | Businesses/Units 7,657

| Profit $157.4 M | Wages $940 M | Annual Growth Future -0.6%

| Annual Growth Past -1.4%

BENCHMARK DATA

STATISTICS (LEATHER GOOD & LUGGAGE MANUFACTURING)

Number of Establishments .	7,657
Average Profit Margin .	4.9%
Revenue per Employee .	$118,561
Average Number of Employees.	3.5
Average Wages per Employee .	$34,881

PRODUCTS AND SERVICES SEGMENTATION

Other	.36.0%
Women's handbags .	.22.2%
Luggage.	.12.3%
Hat bodies and fabric caps .	.11.3%
Apparel accessories	. 7.4%
Personal leather goods .	. 4.7%
Neckwear	. 3.8%
Gloves and mittens .	. 2.3%

MAJOR MARKET SEGMENTATION

Clothing and accessories stores	.56.5%
Other	.20.9%
Handbag, luggage and accessory stores	.14.1%
Clothing manufacturers.	. 8.5%

INDUSTRY COSTS

Profit	. 4.9%
Wages .	.29.3%
Purchases .	.39.6%
Depreciation	. 0.9%
Marketing .	. 1.5%
Rent & Utilities .	. 3.1%
Other	.20.8%

INDUSTRY TREND

"Wages hike as quality improves. While labor is more affordable abroad, manufacturers are using highly skilled workers to compete with foreign businesses based on product quality rather than price. Less-expensive labor costs abroad steal the spotlight. Many large businesses shift away from domestic manufacturers and instead source them from low-cost Asian countries or third-party contractors."

Source: IBISWorld Key Takeaways

RESOURCES

• IBISWorld, March 2023: https://www.ibisworld.com

Manufacturing: Machinery

| NAICS 333

Rules of Thumb

- 80%–100% annual sales includes inventory
- 4–6 x EBIT
- 3–5 x EBITDA
- 3.5–4.5 x SDE

INDUSTRY MULTIPLES

Acquisition multiples below are calculated medians using US private industry transactions. Data updated annually. Last update: August 2023.

VALUATION MULTIPLE (MEDIAN VALUE)

UNDER $1 MILLION NET SALES

MVIC/Net Sales	0.75
MVIC/Gross Profit	1.21
MVIC/SDE	2.65
MVIC/EBITDA	5.26

$1 MILLION–$5 MILLION NET SALES

MVIC/Net Sales	0.56
MVIC/Gross Profit	1.31
MVIC/SDE	3.13
MVIC/EBITDA	4.47

OVER $5 MILLION NET SALES

MVIC/Net Sales	1.41
MVIC/Gross Profit	3.95
MVIC/SDE	4.75
MVIC/EBITDA	12.54

Source: DealStats (formerly Pratt's Stats), 2023 (Portland, OR: Business Valuation Resources, LLC), www.bvresources.com/dealstats

PRICING TIPS

Each opportunity needs to be reviewed separately. The metrics are going to vary based on subindustries due to the significant differences between the products produced. Some considerations to account for are expenses based on skill level or specializations required, and the value of the manufacturer's assets, including land, buildings, machinery, and inventory. The age and maintenance of these assets are important as well, as are factors relating to equipment value and age, tenure of the company, number of employees, and market share. Multiples based on revenue are not a good indicator of value in the manufacturing industry. Buyers will focus on SDE/EBITDA and the value and condition of the equipment assets. For transactions < $2M, buyers are generally not sophisticated enough to present the ideal of a working capital PEG. They will generally expect enough inventory to be left in the business to conduct the operation normally, with the seller keeping AR/AP and long-term debt. For larger manufacturing transactions, the buyers will generally value the business including sufficient working capital (in line with historical averages), which is determined after examining 12 to 18 monthly balance sheets. For unprofitable, or marginally profitable, business-es, an up-to-date machinery and equipment appraisal is invaluable; generally, buyers will agree to pay some discount on the tangible asset value, generally, 30+ percent depending on whether the business is break-even or losing money rapidly. Overall, sellers should expect to finance 10 to 20 percent of the transac-tion. Regardless of whether the buyer requests seller financing, most lenders are going to want to see some seller skin in the game. Customer concentration in excess of 50 percent will almost always mean the seller will have to accept some form of earnout where part of the purchase price is paid based on future company performance, or perhaps tied to a specific large customer. Overall, the market method (EBITDA multiplier method) will be utilized by nearly 100 percent of buyers regardless of the size of the transaction. The income method (DCF model) will be utilized by sophisticated financial buyers (PE and family office) primarily for larger manufacturing opportunities (excess of $2M EBITDA) that have a demonstrated history of growth.

A $1M SDE or EBITDA will result in much higher multiples of offers.

Conduct an inventory count, as many of these old, owner-operator businesses typically have lots of excess raw materials that have accumulated over the years that are not necessarily captured on their balance sheet.

There is currently a premium for any manufacturing companies that were able to keep operations at, or near, capacity during Covid.

Future contracts can be taken into consideration if there are signed guarantees in place.

BENCHMARK DATA

Common benchmarks for a successful manufacturing business include revenue per employee; gross margin, which reflects profitability and production cost control; and inventory turnover, which benchmarks inventory management. Another factor is client concentration. Healthy businesses with a diversified client base face less risk and have more stability.

EXPENSES (% OF ANNUAL SALES)

Cost of Goods	60% to 65%
Occupancy Costs	01% to 05%
Payroll/Labor Costs.	15% to 25%
Profit (pretax)	05% to 15%

QUESTIONS

- What about any debt or financing on the business? How are banks treating you in these times? What impact, if any, are you seeing from talk of recession? Is business slowing down? Based on present information, are you able to prepare a 13-week cash flow forecast? Are you able to accurately forecast 2023 and 2024 revenue? Discuss your managers or management team. How stable have they been? Are you having difficulty recruiting or filling key positions? If you were 20 years younger, what would you do to grow the business?
- Customer concentration? Tenure of employees, especially the key staff? Capex spending requirements anticipated?
- Do they own their real estate (facility)? If so, is it undervalued in assets (historic value)?

INDUSTRY TREND

I think it is going to be a bit of a slog. While supply chains are easing up, global disorder and tension remain heightened. Inflation and labor challenges are easing, but significant macroshifts take a long time and it can be painful along the way.

One trend we have seen accelerate over the past 6 months is that, given the negative headlines, seller sentiment has turned negative and therefore fewer sellers are listing. This has created a shortage of quality manufacturing opportunities,

M

which is boosting buyer interest and keeping multiples elevated even against a (much) higher-rate environment.

More capital investment in 3D printing and robotics, as labor shortages are limiting growth.

With continued reshoring, the trend should be upward in this sector.

Depending on industry target, some are increasing output capacity, while others are holding steady or starting to decrease product output do to inflation.

EXPERT COMMENTS

Almost unexpectedly over the past 6 to 9 months, the market has shifted back strongly in favor of sellers. This is due to low supply of quality businesses combined with strong buyer cash positions and demand. Q2 2023 results showed that manufacturing was among the top three industries that had closed deals with $10M EV. The buyer pool has thinned a bit due to the headlines and fear; however, those that remain are often aggressive. My top advice to a seller is that if price and deal structure are important to you, do not work with the buyer that calls you up. Work with a broker/advisor that can stir up a well-run, limited-auction-style bidding process.

Pay careful attention to customer concentration—the less the better.

We're seeing a lot more reshoring of manufacturing; these companies typically have outsourced their machining and tooling.

Sell prior to the peak. With economic indicators generally trailing over multiple years, it is easy to see when a business is stagnant and potentially heading for a downturn. If you have over three years of growth, and are considering a sale, that is the time.

FINANCING

Most of our transactions are < $5M in enterprise value, and the buyer utilizes SBA 7(a) financing. As a rule of thumb, I would say most deals are 10 percent buyer equity (cash), 10 percent seller note (usually over a period of 1 to 5 years), and 80 percent bank financing. Very rarely do we see no bank involved. Earnouts disallowed by the SBA and disliked by sellers, so we rarely see them; however, we believe this will change in the immediate future, and we are already seeing earnouts becoming a part of our current deals. Deals that are larger than $10M have increasingly become a challenge due to the return targets of more sophisticated buyers. Basically, interest rates have squeezed the returns that private equity had been used to, and many are still adjusting. Along these lines, the best buyers for larger or more middle-market transactions are buyers that have a dedicated roll-up strategy; they will pay more than they want to in the face of competition.

RESOURCES

• NTMA—National Tooling & Machining Association: https://ntma.org

---

Manufacturing: Marine Products

| NAICS 336612

Rules of Thumb

• 40%–80% annual gross sales plus inventory
• 2–3 x SDE

- 3.2 x EBIT
- 3.9 x EBITDA

M

INDUSTRY MULTIPLES

Acquisition multiples below are calculated medians using US private industry transactions. Data updated annually. Last update: August 2023.

VALUATION MULTIPLE (MEDIAN VALUE)

UNDER $1 MILLION NET SALES

MVIC/Net Sales.	0.37
MVIC/Gross Profit	0.71
MVIC/SDE	2.86
MVIC/EBITDA	2.54

$1 MILLION–$5 MILLION NET SALES

MVIC/Net Sales.	0.22
MVIC/Gross Profit	0.93
MVIC/SDE	3.00
MVIC/EBITDA	N/A

OVER $5 MILLION NET SALES

MVIC/Net Sales.	1.22
MVIC/Gross Profit	5.48
MVIC/SDE	N/A
MVIC/EBITDA	9.46

Source: DealStats (formerly Pratt's Stats), 2023 (Portland, OR: Business Valuation Resources, LLC), www.bvresources.com/dealstats

PRICING TIPS

EBITDA must be adjusted to show owner's discretionary cash flow. The multiple that is used varies by industry segments, geographical location, and specific business, and must be determined in a subjective manner by one knowledgeable about current market conditions.

BENCHMARK DATA

If the marine product company has patents, this can make the business worth substantially more as it protects the business from the competition.

EXPENSES (% OF ANNUAL SALES)

Cost of Goods	30% to 40%
Occupancy Costs	06% to 08%
Payroll/Labor Costs.	25%
Profit (pretax)	21%

QUESTIONS

- Is the product truly unique patented? Is it a part that mounts on a boat, or is it related to the boating industry like a boat lift? Is the business scalable regionally or nationally? This will make a huge difference in the growth potential of the business. Is the inventory current and fresh? What is their revenue recognition method?
- Is the inventory all saleable? Do you manufacture and assemble the product? Who are your top 5 competitors, and what makes your product unique? Is the product protected by a patent? Who is the competition?
- Customer concentration and percentage of revenue from the top 10 customers
- Equipment needs to be up to date; updating equipment in this industry can be a large expense.
- Are the contracts with manufacturers transferable to the new owner?

- How is the business protected from offshore competition?
- Consider the WIP situation, as these types of products can have significant amounts invested in work in progress.
- Is the business properly insured? Consider the value and margin of the backlog and make sure it is accounted for regarding insurance needs.
- What are the capital expenditures required to maintain and grow the business?

INDUSTRY TREND

Continued solid growth that has been increased by the pandemic

EXPERT COMMENTS

Niche products are key to success and to reducing competition. Location is also key. In order to control shipping costs, it is important to be located in active boating areas. Marine-related manufacturing is typically a complex business with extensive processes creating attractive barriers to entry.

FINANCING

SBA is typical financing.

RESOURCES

- MIASF—Marine Industries Association of South Florida: https://www.miasf.org
- NMMA—National Marine Manufacturers Association: http://www.nmma.org

Manufacturing: Men's & Boys' Apparel

	NAICS 315		Businesses/Units 448		
	Profit $46 M		Wages $493.2 M		Annual Growth Future -0.2%
					Annual Growth Past -0.4%

INDUSTRY MULTIPLES

Acquisition multiples below are calculated medians using US private industry transactions. Data updated annually. Last update: August 2023.

VALUATION MULTIPLE (MEDIAN VALUE)

UNDER $1 MILLION NET SALES
MVIC/Net Sales	0.63
MVIC/Gross Profit	1.10
MVIC/SDE	2.96
MVIC/EBITDA	2.94

$1 MILLION–$5 MILLION NET SALES
MVIC/Net Sales	0.34
MVIC/Gross Profit	0.66
MVIC/SDE	1.84
MVIC/EBITDA	38.21

OVER $5 MILLION NET SALES
MVIC/Net Sales	1.38
MVIC/Gross Profit	3.38
MVIC/SDE	4.33
MVIC/EBITDA	11.63

Source: DealStats (formerly Pratt's Stats), 2023 (Portland, OR: Business Valuation Resources, LLC), www.bvresources.com/dealstats

STATISTICS (MEN'S & BOYS' APPAREL MANUFACTURING)

Number of Establishments .	448
Average Profit Margin .	2.7%
Revenue per Employee .	$115,000
Average Number of Employees.	33.2
Average Wages per Employee .	$33,351

PRODUCTS AND SERVICES SEGMENTATION

Suits.	47.2%
Work clothing	22.1%
Shirts (except work shirts) .	10.5%
Coats and jackets	9.3%
Pants and jeans (except work pants)	7.6%
Underwear and nightwear .	2.0%
Other	1.3%

MAJOR MARKET SEGMENTATION

Exports .	52.1%
Wholesalers.	15.3%
Specialty retail stores	14.3%
E-commerce	8.5%
Discount, warehouse clubs, and superstores .	6.0%
Department stores .	3.8%

INDUSTRY COSTS

Profit	2.7%
Wages	29.0%
Purchases .	45.9%
Depreciation	0.8%
Marketing	0.8%
Rent & Utilities .	2.5%
Other	18.4%

INDUSTRY TREND

"Growth prospects in the industry are generally limited given the high degree of import penetration. While input prices have declined due to plunging demand, industry profit has still fallen. There has been growing concern about the environmental footprint of the apparel manufacturing industry. Revenue is forecast to grow at a tempered rate as per capita disposable income recovers. As the industry continues to focus on the production of high-quality products, demand for highly skilled labor is expected to rise. Reshoring of apparel manufacturing has gained increased credibility. Operators have managed to differentiate their products based on quality rather than price."

Source: IBISWorld Industry at a Glance

RESOURCES

- IBISWorld, July 2022: https://www.ibisworld.com

Manufacturing: Metal Fabrication

| NAICS 331410 | SIC 1791-04

Rules of Thumb

- 50%–100% annual sales includes inventory
- 3–5 x SDE plus inventory

- 3–5 x EBIT
- 4–6 x EBITDA

PRICING TIPS

Common risks are customer concentration (large percentage of sales to one customer); succession (the founder/owner has no successor); industry concentration (example: semiconductor OEMs are very cyclical, so metal fab owners must be financially prepared for slow times); capital equipment (older equipment is slow and may take more set-up time as well as take longer for a production run); lack of enterprise software to manage all company functions, e.g., sales, purchasing, scheduling, inventory management, quality control, shipping/receiving, and accounting; and the biggest one, poor accounting records, especially when owners push revenue into the next accounting year.

Multiples based on revenue are not a good indicator of value in the metal manufacturing industry. Buyers will focus on SDE/EBITDA and the value and condition of the equipment assets. For transactions < $2M buyers are generally not sophisticated enough to present the ideal of a working capital PEG. They will generally expect enough inventory to be left in the business to conduct the operation normally, with the seller keeping AR/AP and long-term debt.

For larger manufacturing transactions, the buyers will generally value the business including sufficient working capital (in line with historical averages) that are determined after examining 12 to 18 monthly balance sheets. For unprofitable or marginally profitable businesses, an up-to-date machinery and equipment appraisal is invaluable; generally, buyers will agree to pay some discount on the tangible asset value, generally 30+ percent, depending on whether the business is break-even or losing money rapidly. Overall, sellers should expect to finance 10 to 20 percent of the transaction. Regardless of whether the buyer requests seller financing, most lenders are going to want to see some seller skin in the game. Customer concentration in excess of 50 percent will almost always mean the seller will have to accept some form of earnout where part of the purchase price is paid based on future company performance, or perhaps tied to a specific large customer.

Overall, the market method (EBITDA multiplier method) will be utilized by nearly 100 percent of buyers regardless of the size of the transaction. The income method (DCF model) will be utilized by sophisticated financial buyers (PE and family office) primarily for larger manufacturing opportunities (excess of $2M EBITDA) that have a demonstrated history of growth.

Small shops typically have one or two customers accounting for 70 to 90 percent of sales. These shops often sell for lower multiples and may have a variable price component tied to either continued business with the big customers or continued revenues regardless of who the customer is. Shops where everyone reports to the owner or, worse, where the owner is operating machines on the production floor, are very difficult to sell and only get discounted prices.

Multiples vary significantly for metal fabrication companies. Customer concentration, contracted backlog, equipment condition, and other value-added services (annealing, powder coating, surface passivation, marking) influence multiple selection. Generally, businesses with annual revenues of $1 million or less will rarely have a multiple greater than 3.5 x. Businesses with revenues greater than $1 million and gross margins of 40 percent or more—with production capacity—will sell at 3.5 x or higher, unless major capital expenditures are required to update equipment.

Well-performing metal fabrication businesses have productivity of $220,000 to $300,000 per full-time employee.

Metal fabrication companies listed for sale should be able to document preventative maintenance.

Pay attention to the scrap income line on the P&L as a clue to any income or margin anomalies.

End markets also influence multiple selection. Currently premium multiples are applied to metal fabrication companies serving the healthcare and defense markets.

BENCHMARK DATA

For additional Benchmark data see Manufacturing—Metal Stamping

$500 revenues per square foot for large facilities; $800 revenues per square foot for smaller facilities; $200,000 revenues per employee. Low-volume/high-mix companies have better margins but more volatility.

The most marketable have no single customer for more than 10 percent of sales and serve 3 or 4 vertical markets such as aerospace, medical, semiconductor equipment, industrial equipment, defense, auto, etc. Most common issue is succession—founder/president has no replacement.

Look for gross revenues per full-time employee of $220,000 to $300,000.

If direct labor exceeds 20 percent, the business is likely underperforming. Materials purchasing, pricing strategy, and inadequate employee shop floor training are often the reasons.

EXPENSES (% OF ANNUAL SALES)

Cost of Goods	50% to 60%
Occupancy Costs	05% to 15%
Payroll/Labor Costs.	10% to 20%
Profit (pretax)	10% to 20%

QUESTIONS

- What feedback have you received from your major customers in terms of how the current environment has affected them?
- How is your supply chain holding up? Are you sensing areas of stress? Breakdown?
- What about any debt or financing on the business? How are banks treating you in these times?
- What impact, if any, are you seeing from talk of recession? Is business slowing down?
- Based on present information, are you able to prepare a 13-week cash flow forecast?
- Are you able to accurately forecast 2023 and 2024 revenue?
- Discuss your managers or management team. How stable have they been? Are you having difficulty recruiting or filling key positions?
- If you were 20 years younger, what would you do to grow the business?
- Why are you selling at this time? Do you know if any of your customers are planning to discontinue product lines that may impact sales? How do you develop new business?
- Comprehensive questioning about every aspect of the business. Look for risks such as a big customer depending on a personal relationship with the seller; frequent lawsuits; old equipment; or a big concentration of sales in one or two customers.

- How have metal prices affected your margins in the past three years? What is your pricing strategy, and do you apply metal surcharges? Are all manufacturing and inspection process documented? What is your finished goods valuation policy, and when are write-downs required?
- List strengths and weaknesses; ask how to improve profits; learn the owner's duties.
- What are your preventative maintenance procedures by equipment type? Please explain in detail your inspection processes and the inspection level required.
- Sufficient noncompete?
- How long have you had these customers? When are your contracts up? How hard is it to get good welders?
- Are there upcoming technologies that would put this business at risk?

INDUSTRY TREND

I think it is going to be a bit of a slog. While supply chains are easing up, global disorder and tension remains heightened. Inflation and labor challenges are easing, but significant macro shifts take a long time and it can be painful along the way.

One trend we have seen accelerate over the past 6 months is that, given the negative headlines, seller sentiment has turned negative and, therefore, fewer sellers are listing. This has created a shortage of quality manufacturing opportunities, which is boosting buyer interest and keeping multiples elevated even against a (much) higher rate environment.

Improving productivity and reduced labor costs due to automation.

More automation and professional management are replacing seat-of-the-pants management.

EXPERT COMMENTS

Diversify your customer base among not only customers but also industries. Get your books in order. Have a premarket audit by an independent CPA (not the one doing your taxes); groom a successor to the CEO; update/replace older CNC machines and QC instruments; get ISO 9000 certifications.

Almost unexpectedly over the past 6 to 9 months, the market has shifted back strongly in favor of sellers. This is due to the low supply of quality businesses combined with strong buyer cash positions and demand. We have seen multiples remain high, and we are oftentimes receiving more offers on our sellers than in 2021 and 2022. The buyer pool has thinned a bit due to the headlines and fear; however, those that remain are often aggressive. My top advice to a seller is that if price and deal structure are important to you, do not work with the buyer that calls you up. Work with a broker/advisor that can stir up a well-run, limited, auction-style bidding process.

I believe competition is average in the industry because we continue to see a lot of manufacturing companies owned by baby boomers. These operations are facing competition from international competitors as well as larger consolidators. However, most smaller manufacturers (sales < $2M) are purchased by individuals keeping the industry somewhat fragmented. Over time, I believe there will be fewer manufacturing operations due to higher barriers to entry and more consolidation amongst private equity, family offices, and strategic buyers.

Historically, most established manufacturers that we see/work with have had healthy profit margins and do not worry too much about competition. Covid has selectively affected manufacturers. I believe relative to heavily cyclical industries like construction and low-profit sectors like retail, manufacturing remains relatively low risk.

M

Covid overall and the subsequent fallout of inflation, supply chains, and a labor force that has been spoiled by at-home work have adversely affected manufacturing relative to other industries, for example, business services.

Location and facilities are fair. Many owners have taken profits and reinvested in their facilities; however, most of those facilities are aging. There is a fair share of owners who flat out neglect their facility.

I have worked manufacturing transactions through good times and bad and they are always highly attractive in the marketplace. Presently, there is a shortage of quality manufacturing operations on the market and demand is solid, which will continue to help valuations assuming the economy charges back as anticipated.

Reshoring of manufacturing due to Covid and other secular trends revolving around supply chain control will likely keep manufacturing trends strong in the U.S.

While it is not difficult to buy a few machines and take some jobs in one's garage or pole barn, it is very difficult, capital-intensive, risky, and it takes years to build a $5M manufacturing company. Furthermore, manufacturing is foreign to most millennials and Gen Zers who might have the capital for such a venture. As a result, I believe that the barriers to entry for a sophisticated domestic manufacturer are high.

Get all accounting records in good shape by using an audit prep CPA; get accurate inventory records; get quality certifications such as ISO 9001, AS9100, ISO 13485, etc.

Owning a manufacturing company often requires continuous capital investment. Additionally, CPAs encourage owners to buy equipment, often unnecessary, to pay less in taxes. On top of this, we often see owners of manufacturing companies allured by acquiring more and more equipment. This often leads to companies being worth asset value or less when they produce marginal or no profits.

Manufacturing is also cyclical, so owners need to be ready for long periods of living frugally and long periods of feasting.

Lastly, we often see customer concentration issues with smaller manufacturing, for example, one customer making up 50 to 80 percent of sales. While this can be wonderful while it lasts, buyers see a big red flag that most often leads to a hefty earnout being part of the transaction.

The number of metal fabrication businesses appears to be shrinking as a generation of older owners (many with a machinist background) prepare to retire. Demand from strategic buyers for this declining pool of targets is high.

Ease of replication requires heavy investment in production and test equipment, workforce development, and replicating the art that is a component of this repeatable process business model.

FINANCING

Bank financing is most common.

Most of our transactions are < $5M in enterprise value and the buyer utilizes SBA 7a financing. As a rule of thumb, I would say most deals are 10 percent buyer equity (cash), 10 percent seller note, and 80 percent bank financing. Very rarely do we see no bank involved. Earnouts are disallowed by the SBA and disliked by sellers so we rarely see them; however, we believe this will change in the immediate future and we are already seeing earnouts becoming a part of our current deals.

In discussions with lenders, we are feeling that they are slow-playing things a bit given 7 straight months of negative headlines and a hawkish Fed that is intentionally trying to stymie growth. However, many banks received black eyes and long-term reputational damage based on their cold, hard plug-pulling from the last recession and we're certain that they are keeping this in the back of their minds. Additionally, it does not seem that this recession will be as brutal as past ones. Time will tell.

Senior debt, mezzanine financing, seller note, sometimes an earnout

RESOURCES

- AWS—American Welding Society: https://www.aws.org
- FMA—Fabricators & Manufacturers Association, International: https://www.fmamfg.org/
- FMA—Fabricators & Manufacturers Association, International: https://www.fmamfg.org/
- ISO: https://www.iso.org/certification.html
- MetalMiner: https://agmetalminer.com
- MMA—Michigan Manufacturers Association: https://mimfg.org/
- PMA—Precision Metalforming Association: https://www.pma.org
- SME—Society for Mining, Metallurgy & Exploration: https://www.smenet.org
- The Fabricator: https://www.thefabricator.com/

Manufacturing: Metal Pipe & Tube

| NAICS 331210 | Businesses/Units 293

| Profit $749.8 M | Wages $1.9 B | Annual Growth Future -0.2%

| | | Annual Growth Past 0.6%

INDUSTRY MULTIPLES

Acquisition multiples below are calculated medians using US private industry transactions. Data updated annually. Last update: August 2023.

VALUATION MULTIPLE (MEDIAN VALUE)

UNDER $1 MILLION NET SALES	N/A
$1 MILLION–$5 MILLION NET SALES	
MVIC/Net Sales	0.63
MVIC/Gross Profit	1.94
MVIC/SDE	9.49
MVIC/EBITDA	12.39
OVER $5 MILLION NET SALES	
MVIC/Net Sales	0.63
MVIC/Gross Profit	2.87
MVIC/SDE	N/A
MVIC/EBITDA	N/A

Source: DealStats (formerly Pratt's Stats), 2023 (Portland, OR: Business Valuation Resources, LLC), www.bvresources.com/dealstats

BENCHMARK DATA

STATISTICS (METAL PIPE & TUBE MANUFACTURING)

Number of Establishments .	293
Average Profit Margin	4.3%
Revenue per Employee .	$573,288
Average Number of Employees.	103.6
Average Wages per Employee .	$63,726

PRODUCTS AND SERVICES SEGMENTATION

Carbon steel line pipe and OCTG	21.9%
Carbon steel mechanical tubing	18.3%
Other carbon steel products	14.8%
Carbon steel, structural.	13.2%
Stainless steel tubing	12.7%
Alloy steel piping and tubing	10.2%
Carbon steel pressure tubing	8.9%

MAJOR MARKET SEGMENTATION

Oil and Gas Pipeline Construction .	39.7%
Water Sewer Line Construction	31.7%
Heavy Engineering construction	18.7%
Mining, oil and gas machinery manufacturing .	9.9%

INDUSTRY COSTS

Profit	4.3%
Wages	11.0%
Purchases	60.6%
Depreciation	1.9%
Marketing	0.0%
Rent & Utilities .	2.4%
Other	19.9%

MARKET SHARE

Tenaris SA	7.7%
United States Steel Corp	3.9%
Vallourec SA	3.9%
MRC Global .	3.4%
Northwest Pipe Company	1.2%
Webco Industries Inc.	1.1%

INDUSTRY TREND

"Industry performance is heavily influenced by oil and gas prices. Reduced consumption levels amid COVID-19 resulted in sharp declines in oil prices. Downstream utility construction plays an important role. Severe fluctuations in commodity prices have caused significant demand volatility, since it influences activity within key downstream markets. Low-cost imports continue to out compete domestic manufacturers. This rise is also attributable to lower COVID-related supply chain issues."

Source: IBISWorld Key Takeaways

RESOURCES

• IBISWorld, September 2023: https://www.ibisworld.com

THE ESSENTIAL GUIDE TO PRICING BUSINESSES & FRANCHISES 599

Manufacturing: Metal Tank

| NAICS 332420 | Businesses/Units 773

| Profit $183 M | Wages $2.6 B | Annual Growth Future -0.9%

| Annual Growth Past -1.3%

INDUSTRY MULTIPLES

Acquisition multiples below are calculated medians using US private industry transactions. Data updated annually. Last update: August 2023.

VALUATION MULTIPLE (MEDIAN VALUE)

UNDER $1 MILLION NET SALES	N/A
$1 MILLION–$5 MILLION NET SALES	N/A
OVER $5 MILLION NET SALES	
MVIC/Net Sales	0.58
MVIC/Gross Profit	3.03
MVIC/SDE	N/A
MVIC/EBITDA	4.65

Source: DealStats (formerly Pratt's Stats), 2023 (Portland, OR: Business Valuation Resources, LLC), www.bvresources.com/dealstats

BENCHMARK DATA

STATISTICS (METAL TANK MANUFACTURING)

Number of Establishments	773
Average Profit Margin	1.9%
Revenue per Employee	$265,801
Average Number of Employees	43.8
Average Wages per Employee	$72,898

PRODUCTS AND SERVICES SEGMENTATION

Pressure tanks, including liquefied petroleum gas and air receivers	32.4%
Gas cylinders and storage tanks	24.5%
Metal tanks and vessels (custom-fabricated at the factory)	20.8%
Other metal tanks	16.8%
Other	4.3%
Wholesale	1.2%

MAJOR MARKET SEGMENTATION

Petrochemical manufacturers	37.0%
Industrial manufacturers	35.2%
Biomedical manufacturers	18.4%
Exports	9.4%

INDUSTRY COSTS

Profit	1.9%
Wages	26.9%
Purchases	46.3%
Depreciation	11.0%
Marketing	0.2%
Rent & Utilities	2.2%
Other	11.6%

MARKET SHARE

Worthington Industries, Inc.	10.9%
Caldwell Tanks Inc.	2.9%
Chart Industries, Inc.	2.8%
Worley Limited	2.4%
Trinity Industries Inc.	1.9%

"The industrial manufacturing, agricultural, and dairy markets, among others, are where the industry gets the bulk of its product sales. Due to the standardization of some items, pricing has become a more important factor in business competition. As a result of these tendencies, import penetration has risen while export earnings have fallen."

Source: IBISWorld Key Takeaways

RESOURCES

- IBISWorld, February 2023: https://www.ibisworld.com

Manufacturing: Metal Valve and Pipe Fitting

| NAICS 332919

Rules of Thumb

- 7 x EBIT
- 100% annual sales

INDUSTRY MULTIPLES

Acquisition multiples below are calculated medians using US private industry transactions. Data updated annually. Last update: August 2023.

VALUATION MULTIPLE (MEDIAN VALUE)

UNDER $1 MILLION NET SALES

MVIC/Net Sales.	1.01
MVIC/Gross Profit	1.25
MVIC/SDE	1.96
MVIC/EBITDA	10.00

$1 MILLION–$5 MILLION NET SALES

MVIC/Net Sales.	0.42
MVIC/Gross Profit	1.34
MVIC/SDE	3.30
MVIC/EBITDA	3.57

OVER $5 MILLION NET SALES

MVIC/Net Sales.	0.99
MVIC/Gross Profit	2.84
MVIC/SDE	5.38
MVIC/EBITDA	5.65

Source: DealStats (formerly Pratt's Stats), 2023 (Portland, OR: Business Valuation Resources, LLC), www.bvresources.com/dealstats

BENCHMARK DATA

Four inventory turns, 50 percent gross margin

EXPENSES (% OF ANNUAL SALES)

Cost of Goods	50%
Occupancy Costs	30%
Payroll/Labor Costs.	20%
Profit (pretax)	15%

EXPERT COMMENTS

High capital investment

Manufacturing: Mineral Product

NAICS 32799	Businesses/Units 4,477
Profit $2.1 B	Wages $4.3 B	Annual Growth Future 1.0%
		Annual Growth Past 2.8%

INDUSTRY MULTIPLES

Acquisition multiples below are calculated medians using US private industry transactions. Data updated annually. Last update: August 2023.

VALUATION MULTIPLE (MEDIAN VALUE)

UNDER $1 MILLION NET SALES
MVIC/Net Sales.	0.61
MVIC/Gross Profit	0.96
MVIC/SDE	2.76
MVIC/EBITDA	4.14

$1 MILLION–$5 MILLION NET SALES
MVIC/Net Sales.	0.34
MVIC/Gross Profit	1.09
MVIC/SDE	2.15
MVIC/EBITDA	2.72

OVER $5 MILLION NET SALES
MVIC/Net Sales.	1.47
MVIC/Gross Profit	5.25
MVIC/SDE	3.98
MVIC/EBITDA	18.53

Source: DealStats (formerly Pratt's Stats), 2023 (Portland, OR: Business Valuation Resources, LLC), www.bvresources.com/dealstats

BENCHMARK DATA

STATISTICS (MINERAL PRODUCT MANUFACTURING)

Number of Establishments .	4,477
Average Profit Margin	7.7%
Revenue per Employee .	$393,966
Average Number of Employees.	15.6
Average Wages per Employee .	$61,901

PRODUCTS AND SERVICES SEGMENTATION

Mineral wood products .	31.3%
Other nonmetallic mineral products	27.1%
Cut stone and stone products	22.3%
Ground or treated mineral and earth products .	19.3%

MAJOR MARKET SEGMENTATION

Nonresidential construction	48.3%
Residential construction	38.7%
Manufacturing .	13.0%

INDUSTRY COSTS

Profit	7.7%
Wages .	15.7%
Purchases .	38.6%
Depreciation .	2.4%
Marketing	0.2%
Rent & Utilities .	4.9%
Other	30.5%

MARKET SHARE

Owens Corning 11.7%
Knauf Insulation Kft.. . . . . . . 1.7%

INDUSTRY TREND

"Revenue for mineral product manufacturers has been growing over the past five years. Operators have benefited from soaring private investment before the COVID-19 pandemic, along with strong housing market during the pandemic. The industry currently faces challenges from rising interest rates, as they reduce downstream demand from residential markets. The industry will perform well during the outlook period. Manufacturers will benefit from rising incomes, the recovering housing market, the depreciating dollar and new innovations."

Source: IBISWorld Key Takeaways

RESOURCES

• IBISWorld, April 2023: https://www.ibisworld.com

Manufacturing: Miscellaneous Electrical and Components

| NAICS 335999

Rules of Thumb

• 8 x SDE

INDUSTRY MULTIPLES

Acquisition multiples below are calculated medians using US private industry transactions. Data updated annually. Last update: August 2023.

VALUATION MULTIPLE (MEDIAN VALUE)

UNDER $1 MILLION NET SALES
MVIC/Net Sales. . . . . N/A
MVIC/Gross Profit 37.28
MVIC/SDE 3.48
MVIC/EBITDA 6.88

$1 MILLION–$5 MILLION NET SALES
MVIC/Net Sales. 0.49
MVIC/Gross Profit 0.81
MVIC/SDE 3.03
MVIC/EBITDA 3.85

OVER $5 MILLION NET SALES
MVIC/Net Sales. 1.07
MVIC/Gross Profit 4.77
MVIC/SDE 3.67
MVIC/EBITDA 10.18

Source: DealStats (formerly Pratt's Stats), 2023 (Portland, OR: Business Valuation Resources, LLC), www.bvresources.com/dealstats

PRICING TIPS

To include inventory, need to verify that materials can be used and are not outdated stock.

BENCHMARK DATA

Industrial facilities in my area are selling at $40 to $60 per square foot. Equipment and inventory are on top of that.

EXPENSES (% OF ANNUAL SALES)

Cost of Goods	50%
Occupancy Costs	15%
Payroll/Labor Costs.	25%
Profit (pretax)	10%

QUESTIONS

• Who are their customers, and how good are their contracts with those customers? If manufacturing commodity products, how easy is it for the customer to find a lower-cost supplier?

INDUSTRY TREND

Great growth opportunities as U.S. companies look to bring overseas operations back to the U.S., and foreign companies look to find locations to expand in the U.S.

EXPERT COMMENTS

Make sure the labor market will support business. Be comfortable with constant cost control.

A lot of foreign competition; however, a recent desire to on-source manufacturing makes it a good market for transactions. I am in a southeast U.S. location (NC), an area with good growth in manufacturing capabilities. Both domestic and international manufacturing companies are looking to expand in this area, so if you have a good facility and trained staff, the business will sell.

FINANCING

Combination of both on SBA-sized deals. Larger projects are mostly outside financing.

Manufacturing: Nonferrous Metal Foundry Products

| NAICS 33152 | Businesses/Units 847

| Profit $708.2 M | Wages $3.2 B | Annual Growth Future 0.1%

                                           | Annual Growth Past -3.1%

INDUSTRY MULTIPLES

Acquisition multiples below are calculated medians using US private industry transactions. Data updated annually. Last update: August 2023.

VALUATION MULTIPLE (MEDIAN VALUE)

UNDER $1 MILLION NET SALES	N/A
$1 MILLION–$5 MILLION NET SALES	N/A
OVER $5 MILLION NET SALES	
MVIC/Net Sales.	0.31
MVIC/Gross Profit	2.56
MVIC/SDE	5.32
MVIC/EBITDA	5.32

Source: DealStats (formerly Pratt's Stats), 2023 (Portland, OR: Business Valuation Resources, LLC), www.bvresources.com/dealstats

STATISTICS (NONFERROUS METAL FOUNDRY PRODUCTS MANUFACTURING)

Number of Establishments 847
Average Profit Margin 5.2%
Revenue per Employee $246,732
Average Number of Employees. 64.9
Average Wages per Employee $57,281

PRODUCTS AND SERVICES SEGMENTATION

Aluminum die-cast products 39.3%
Other aluminum foundry products 19.0%
Other 15.6%
Copper foundry products 13.1%
Die-cast products made from other nonferrous metals . .13.0%

MAJOR MARKET SEGMENTATION

Transportation equipment manufacturing 39.9%
General manufacturing 21.9%
Aerospace and defense. 19.7%
Machinery manufacturers 18.5%

INDUSTRY COSTS

Profit 5.2%
Wages 23.3%
Purchases 39.7%
Depreciation 3.0%
Marketing 0.1%
Rent & Utilities 4.0%
Other 24.9%

MARKET SHARE

Howmet Aerospace Inc. 19.3%
Precision Castparts Corp. 11.3%

INDUSTRY TREND

"Sales to automakers are being hindered by a semiconductor shortage. Automotive manufacturers' globalization is forcing foundries to reduce prices to remain relevant. A shift to partnerships enables foundries to move into niche product segments. These custom-made products are strengthening profit for nonferrous metal foundries."

Source: IBISWorld Key Takeaways

RESOURCES

• IBISWorld, January 2023: https://www.ibisworld.com

Manufacturing: Office Products

| NAICS 339940 | Businesses/Units 375

| Profit $146.2 M | Wages $469.8 M | Annual Growth Future 0.5%

| Annual Growth Past -4.1%

Rules of Thumb

• 5–8 x EBIT
• 1 x sales plus inventory

INDUSTRY MULTIPLES

Acquisition multiples below are calculated medians using US private industry transactions. Data updated annually. Last update: August 2023.

VALUATION MULTIPLE (MEDIAN VALUE)

UNDER $1 MILLION NET SALES	N/A
$1 MILLION–$5 MILLION NET SALES	
MVIC/Net Sales	2.32
MVIC/Gross Profit	2.81
MVIC/SDE	5.73
MVIC/EBITDA	10.17
OVER $5 MILLION NET SALES	N/A

Source: DealStats (formerly Pratt's Stats), 2023 (Portland, OR: Business Valuation Resources, LLC), www.bvresources.com/dealstats

PRICING TIPS

Key to higher valuation is the company's customer base. Does it include one or more office superstores, national wholesalers, or contract stationers?

BENCHMARK DATA

STATISTICS (ART & OFFICE SUPPLY MANUFACTURING IN THE U.S.)

Number of Establishments	375
Average Profit Margin	4.9%
Revenue per employee	$301,586
Average Number of Employees	27.2
Average Wages per Employee	$46,833

PRODUCTS AND SERVICES SEGMENTATION

Lead pencils and art goods	37.5%
Pens and mechanical pencils	23.3%
Carbon paper and inked ribbons	21.4%
Marking devices	17.8%

MAJOR MARKET SEGMENTATION

Wholesalers and other industries	44.0%
Retailers	43.9%
Exports	12.1%

INDUSTRY COSTS

Profit	4.9%
Wages	15.7%
Purchases	52.4%
Depreciation	1.7%
Marketing	3.0%
Rent & Utilities	1.7%
Other	20.7%

MARKET SHARE

ACCO Brands Corporation	25.6%
Newell Brands Inc.	21.5%
Pilot Corporation	10.4%
Crayola LLC	6.7%
The Smead Manufacturing Company Inc.	2.3%
Acme United Corp	2.1%
Elmer's Products, Inc.	1.4%
Industrial Packaging Supplies, Inc.	1.2%
Uline, Inc.	1.2%
MooreCo, Inc.	1.0%

INDUSTRY TREND

"Businesses all across the United States are increasingly conducting business online, which reduces their need for industry items. As work-from-home policies made the employment of digital substitutes necessary, the COVID-19 pandemic has expedited this tendency. The Art and Office Supply Manufacturing industry has been facing a decline in demand due to a combination of factors, including long-term patterns of import rivalry and a rise in the usage of electronic gadgets and communication methods as substitutes. As a result, many companies in the industry have been forced to downsize or even shut down operations entirely."

Source: IBISWorld Key Takeaways

FINANCING

If it is a good company, it is a cash deal.

RESOURCES

• IBISWorld, April 2023: https://www.ibisworld.com

Manufacturing: Organic Chemical

NAICS 32519	Businesses/Units 1,402	
Profit $7.4 B	Wages $13.3 B	Annual Growth Future -1.8%
		Annual Growth Past 2.7%

INDUSTRY MULTIPLES

Acquisition multiples below are calculated medians using US private industry transactions. Data updated annually. Last update: August 2023.

VALUATION MULTIPLE (MEDIAN VALUE)

UNDER $1 MILLION NET SALES

MVIC/Net Sales	0.78
MVIC/Gross Profit	1.01
MVIC/SDE	2.25
MVIC/EBITDA	2.73

$1 MILLION–$5 MILLION NET SALES

MVIC/Net Sales	N/A
MVIC/Gross Profit	N/A
MVIC/SDE	1.98
MVIC/EBITDA	3.76

OVER $5 MILLION NET SALES

MVIC/Net Sales	1.38
MVIC/Gross Profit	4.99
MVIC/SDE	10.54
MVIC/EBITDA	10.31

Source: DealStats (formerly Pratt's Stats), 2023 (Portland, OR: Business Valuation Resources, LLC), www.bvresources.com/dealstats

BENCHMARK DATA

STATISTICS (ORGANIC CHEMICAL MANUFACTURING)

Number of Establishments	1,402
Average Profit Margin	4.4%
Revenue per Employee	$1,415,811
Average Number of Employees	82.8
Average Wages per Employee	$113,894

M

PRODUCTS AND SERVICES SEGMENTATION

All other basic organic chemical products	53.4%
Ethyl alcohol	31.5%
Synthetic organic alcohols	. 4.5%
Cyclic crudes, coal tar, wood chemical and intermediate products . . .	. 3.8%
Fatty acids	. 3.7%
Synthetic flavor and perfume materials	. 1.8%
Bulk pesticides	. 1.3%

MAJOR MARKET SEGMENTATION

Other chemical manufacturing including agricultural chemicals	48.8%
Plastic and resin manufacturing	45.1%
Food and beverage manufacturing.	. 6.1%

INDUSTRY COSTS

Profit	. 4.4%
Wages	. 7.9%
Purchases	56.8%
Depreciation	. 3.2%
Marketing	. 0.1%
Rent & Utilities	. 4.5%
Other	23.2%

MARKET SHARE

Royal Dutch Shell PLC	. 2.7%
FMC Corporation	. 2.3%
Fresenius Medical Care AG & Co. KGaA	. 1.1%
Linde PLC	. 1.1%
Methanex Corp	. 1.1%
The Linde Group	. 1.1%

INDUSTRY TREND

"Organic chemical prices have been volatile. Fluctuating raw material prices are the most substantial cost for the industry. Manufacturers in this industry and other manufacturing-based industries that rely on crude oil will convert to renewables. This will help manufacturers lower energy costs."

Source: IBISWorld Key Takeaways

RESOURCES

• IBISWorld, January 2023: https://www.ibisworld.com

Manufacturing: Ornamental & Architectural Metal

| NAICS 332312 | SIC 3446-04

Rules of Thumb

• 3–7 x EBITDA depending on the company, industry, and buyer

INDUSTRY MULTIPLES

Acquisition multiples below are calculated medians using US private industry transactions. Data updated annually. Last update: August 2023.

VALUATION MULTIPLE (MEDIAN VALUE)

UNDER $1 MILLION NET SALES

MVIC/Net Sales.	. 0.50
MVIC/Gross Profit	. 0.74
MVIC/SDE	. 2.04
MVIC/EBITDA	. 1.99

$1 MILLION–$5 MILLION NET SALES
MVIC/Net Sales.	0.40
MVIC/Gross Profit	0.99
MVIC/SDE	2.30
MVIC/EBITDA	3.13

OVER $5 MILLION NET SALES
MVIC/Net Sales.	0.58
MVIC/Gross Profit	1.39
MVIC/SDE	3.48
MVIC/EBITDA	4.65

Source: DealStats (formerly Pratt's Stats), 2023 (Portland, OR: Business Valuation Resources, LLC), www.bvresources.com/dealstats

Manufacturing: Paint

| NAICS 325510 | Businesses/Units 1,128

| Profit $1.1 B | Wages $2.6 B | Annual Growth Future 0.2%

| Annual Growth Past -0.9%

INDUSTRY MULTIPLES

Acquisition multiples below are calculated medians using US private industry transactions. Data updated annually. Last update: August 2023.

VALUATION MULTIPLE (MEDIAN VALUE)

UNDER $1 MILLION NET SALES
MVIC/Net Sales.	0.46
MVIC/Gross Profit	0.43
MVIC/SDE	1.23
MVIC/EBITDA	2.75

$1 MILLION–$5 MILLION NET SALES
MVIC/Net Sales.	0.80
MVIC/Gross Profit	26.71
MVIC/SDE	3.11
MVIC/EBITDA	N/A

OVER $5 MILLION NET SALES
MVIC/Net Sales.	1.61
MVIC/Gross Profit	4.44
MVIC/SDE	4.93
MVIC/EBITDA	14.58

Source: DealStats (formerly Pratt's Stats), 2023 (Portland, OR: Business Valuation Resources, LLC), www.bvresources.com/dealstats

BENCHMARK DATA

STATISTICS (PAINT MANUFACTURING)
Number of Establishments .	1,128
Average Profit Margin	3.6%
Revenue per Employee .	$898,054
Average Number of Employees.	31.3
Average Wages per Employee .	$75,449

PRODUCTS AND SERVICES SEGMENTATION
Architectural coatings	45.3%
Special-purpose coatings	26.5%
Industrial coatings	18.6%
Other	9.6%

MAJOR MARKET SEGMENTATION

Wholesale	63.8%
Retail	21.9%
Exports	11.4%
Businesses for end use	2.4%
Other	0.5%

INDUSTRY COSTS

Profit	3.6%
Wages	8.4%
Purchases	52.3%
Depreciation	1.4%
Marketing	0.1%
Rent & Utilities	1.2%
Other	33.0%

MARKET SHARE

Sherwin Williams Co	58.4%
PPG Industries, Inc.	23.5%
Axalta Coating Systems Ltd.	5.7%
Akzo Nobel NV	4.6%
Masco Corporation	3.0%

INDUSTRY TREND

"The paint manufacturing industry saw its only recent year of growth in 2021. Industrial production resumed following the height of the pandemic while rising consumer confidence and disposable income led to increased spending on home improvements. The price of oil, a key input to paint, affects the industry's performance; falling oil prices prior to the COVID-19 pandemic were passed on to consumers as lower paint prices, sinking revenue. Prices can only change so fast though, so rapidly increasing oil prices (like those seen recently) have cut into industry profit."

Source: IBISWorld Key Takeaways

RESOURCES

- IBISWorld, January 2023: https://www.ibisworld.com

Manufacturing: Personal Health Products

| NAICS 325412

Rules of Thumb

- 5 x SDE plus inventory
- 6 x EBIT
- 5.5 x EBITDA

INDUSTRY MULTIPLES

Acquisition multiples below are calculated medians using US private industry transactions. Data updated annually. Last update: August 2023.

VALUATION MULTIPLE (MEDIAN VALUE)

UNDER $1 MILLION NET SALES

MVIC/Net Sales	N/A
MVIC/Gross Profit	N/A
MVIC/SDE	N/A
MVIC/EBITDA	27.90

$1 MILLION–$5 MILLION NET SALES

MVIC/Net Sales.	12.88
MVIC/Gross Profit	24.41
MVIC/SDE	2.03
MVIC/EBITDA	7.05

OVER $5 MILLION NET SALES

MVIC/Net Sales.	5.83
MVIC/Gross Profit	8.99
MVIC/SDE	N/A
MVIC/EBITDA	23.92

Source: DealStats (formerly Pratt's Stats), 2023 (Portland, OR: Business Valuation Resources, LLC), www.bvresources.com/dealstats

PRICING TIPS

30 percent of GPM (gross profit margin) x 5 should roughly equal a fair valuation.

BENCHMARK DATA

EXPENSES (% OF ANNUAL SALES)

Cost of Goods	40%
Occupancy Costs	05%
Payroll/Labor Costs.	12%
Profit (pretax)	10% to 12%

QUESTIONS

• Market share and stability of GPM

Manufacturing: Pharmaceutical Preparation & Medicine

| NAICS 32541 | Businesses/Units 5,309

Rules of Thumb

• 75% annual sales
• 5 x SDE
• 4–5 x EBIT
• 6 x EBITDA

INDUSTRY MULTIPLES

Acquisition multiples below are calculated medians using US private industry transactions. Data updated annually. Last update: August 2023.

VALUATION MULTIPLE (MEDIAN VALUE)

UNDER $1 MILLION NET SALES

MVIC/Net Sales.	N/A
MVIC/Gross Profit	N/A
MVIC/SDE	2.04
MVIC/EBITDA	16.16

$1 MILLION–$5 MILLION NET SALES

MVIC/Net Sales.	11.54
MVIC/Gross Profit	15.45
MVIC/SDE	4.31
MVIC/EBITDA	8.18

OVER $5 MILLION NET SALES

MVIC/Net Sales.	5.48
MVIC/Gross Profit	8.21
MVIC/SDE	4.41
MVIC/EBITDA	19.33

Source: DealStats (formerly Pratt's Stats), 2023 (Portland, OR: Business Valuation Resources, LLC), www.bvresources.com/dealstats

M

PRICING TIPS

Long-term contracts, updated technology platforms, partnerships, and a positive inspection record are key value drivers.

BENCHMARK DATA

STATISTICS (BRAND-NAME PHARMACEUTICAL MANUFACTURING)

Number of Establishments	3,498
Average Profit Margin	7.9%
Revenue per Employee	$865,408
Average Number of Employees	103.1
Average Wages per Employee	$106,263

PRODUCTS AND SERVICES SEGMENTATION

Other prescriptions	35.1%
Diabetes prescriptions	14.9%
Autoimmune prescriptions	12.9%
Oncology prescriptions	12.7%
Mental health and nervous system prescriptions	9.5%
Respiratory prescriptions	5.8%
Antiviral medication	5.4%
Cardiovascular prescriptions	3.7%

MAJOR MARKET SEGMENTATION

Chain pharmacies	28.5%
Healthcare providers	27.4%
Mail service retailers	23.3%
Independent retailers	10.3%
Food stores	10.3%
Other	0.2%

INDUSTRY COSTS

Profit	7.9%
Wages	12.3%
Purchases	0.0%
Depreciation	2.4%
Marketing	0.0%
Rent & Utilities	0.0%
Other	77.3%

MARKET SHARE

AbbVie Inc.	13.6%
Bristol-Myers Squibb Sa	12.9%
Johnson & Johnson	12.0%
Merck & Co	9.3%
Pfizer Inc.	9.1%
Eli Lilly and Company	7.9%
Amgen Inc.	7.2%
GlaxoSmithKline plc	5.2%
CH Boehringer Sohn AG & Ko. KG	2.5%
UCB S.A.	1.2%
Bedford Laboratories	1.1%

STATISTICS (GENERIC PHARMACEUTICAL MANUFACTURING)

Number of Establishments	1,811
Average Profit Margin	5.2%
Revenue per Employee	$1,188,119
Average Number of Employees	33.6
Average Wages per Employee	$118,252

PRODUCTS AND SERVICES SEGMENTATION

Other	51.6%
Hypertension	16.7%
Mental health	10.3%
Pain	9.5%
Lipid regulators	6.3%
Antidiabetics	5.6%

MAJOR MARKET SEGMENTATION

Third-party payers	53.0%
Medicare	31.0%
Medicaid	12.0%
Out-of-pocket payments	4.0%

INDUSTRY COSTS

Profit	5.2%
Wages	10.1%
Purchases	25.6%
Depreciation	2.4%
Marketing	0.9%
Rent & Utilities	1.1%
Other	54.7%

MARKET SHARE

Teva Pharmaceutical Industries Ltd.	7.5%
Mylan Inc.	5.7%
Hospira Inc.	3.2%
Akorn Inc.	0.9%

Mid-tier pharmaceutical manufacturing companies average 13.5 percent in SDE, 10.6 percent EBITDA.

EXPENSES (% OF ANNUAL SALES)

Cost of Goods	30% to 35%
Occupancy Costs	15% to 20%
Payroll/Labor Costs	30% to 32%
Profit (pretax)	20% to 30%

QUESTIONS

- What are your competitive advantages? How diverse is your customer base? Are any of your suppliers single sources? Are there any key customer contracts terminating within the next 24 months?

INDUSTRY TREND

"Drug expirations have had the largest effect on industry performance. Some major drugs are set to expire in 2023, harming brand name pharmaceutical producers. Growth in the US dollar has contributed to rising import penetration. This increasingly threatens domestic drug manufacturers, as consumers are increasingly opting for products manufactured overseas. Oncology, diabetes and Alzheimer's disease have been the major areas of research. These treatments often generate more revenue and face lower competition. Generic drug manufacturers have faced intense price competition, which is why many companies have invested in value-added generics and biosimilar drugs. Import penetration has been rising, driven mainly by flexible regulatory frameworks and low production costs in India and China."

Source: IBISWorld Key Takeaways

Buyers must do thorough due diligence of past records and reports. There is a lot of information often buried in documentation that could be relevant for the new owner. It's not unheard of to have a six- to nine-month closing period.

FINANCING

Outside financing represents the majority of the purchase price.

RESOURCES

- IBISWorld, September 2023: https://www.ibisworld.com
- Fierce Pharma: https://www.fiercepharma.com
- Visiongain: https://www.visiongain.com

Manufacturing: Plastic & Resin

| NAICS 325211 | Businesses/Units 1,490

| Profit $903.6 M | Wages $10.4 B | Annual Growth Future -0.9%

| Annual Growth Past 0.8%

INDUSTRY MULTIPLES

Acquisition multiples below are calculated medians using US private industry transactions. Data updated annually. Last update: August 2023.

VALUATION MULTIPLE (MEDIAN VALUE)

UNDER $1 MILLION NET SALES	N/A
$1 MILLION–$5 MILLION NET SALES	N/A
OVER $5 MILLION NET SALES	
MVIC/Net Sales	1.43
MVIC/Gross Profit	6.15
MVIC/SDE	3.66
MVIC/EBITDA	14.15

Source: DealStats (formerly Pratt's Stats), 2023 (Portland, OR: Business Valuation Resources, LLC), www.bvresources.com/dealstats

BENCHMARK DATA

STATISTICS (PLASTIC & RESIN MANUFACTURING)

Number of Establishments	1,490
Average Profit Margin	0.7%
Revenue per Employee	$1,287,490
Average Number of Employees	66.6
Average Wages per Employee	$105,103

PRODUCTS AND SERVICES SEGMENTATION

Other thermoplastics	39.8%
Thermoplastic resins and plastic materials, polyethylene	29.8%
Thermosetting resins and plastic materials	10.3%
Synthetic rubber manufacturing	8.0%

MAJOR MARKET SEGMENTATION

Manufacturing	40.1%
Wholesale	25.3%
Construction	18.7%
Other	15.9%

INDUSTRY COSTS

INDUSTRY COSTS

Profit	0.7%
Wages	8.1%
Purchases	58.6%
Depreciation	2.5%
Marketing	0.0%
Rent & Utilities	4.5%
Other	25.7%

INDUSTRY TREND

"Increasing raw material prices have increased product prices. Higher prices can help boost revenue but can cut into profit. Profit will recover as input costs decline and the construction sector grows. Reduced input costs allow manufacturers to price products aggressively and improve profit."

Source: IBISWorld Key Takeaways

RESOURCES

- IBISWorld, September 2023: https://www.ibisworld.com

Manufacturing: Plastic and Rubber Machinery

| NAICS 333249

Rules of Thumb

- 9 x EBITDA

INDUSTRY MULTIPLES

Acquisition multiples below are calculated medians using US private industry transactions. Data updated annually. Last update: August 2023.

VALUATION MULTIPLE (MEDIAN VALUE)

UNDER $1 MILLION NET SALES

MVIC/Net Sales	0.54
MVIC/Gross Profit	0.94
MVIC/SDE	1.79
MVIC/EBITDA	2.93

$1 MILLION–$5 MILLION NET SALES

MVIC/Net Sales	0.53
MVIC/Gross Profit	1.12
MVIC/SDE	3.22
MVIC/EBITDA	4.22

OVER $5 MILLION NET SALES

MVIC/Net Sales	2.54
MVIC/Gross Profit	4.63
MVIC/SDE	12.50
MVIC/EBITDA	13.61

Source: DealStats (formerly Pratt's Stats), 2023 (Portland, OR: Business Valuation Resources, LLC), www.bvresources.com/dealstats

PRICING TIPS

Look at customer concentration; determine age and condition of equipment; look at industry diversification.

EXPENSES (% OF ANNUAL SALES)

Cost of Goods	50%
Occupancy Costs	08%

Payroll/Labor Costs. 12%
Profit (pretax) 15%

Manufacturing: Plastic Bottle

| NAICS 326160 | Businesses/Units 510

| Profit $740.7 B | Wages $2.4 B | Annual Growth Future 1.1%

| Annual Growth Past 1.3%

INDUSTRY MULTIPLES

Acquisition multiples below are calculated medians using US private industry transactions. Data updated annually. Last update: August 2023.

VALUATION MULTIPLE (MEDIAN VALUE)

UNDER $1 MILLION NET SALES	N/A
$1 MILLION–$5 MILLION NET SALES	
MVIC/Net Sales.	0.46
MVIC/Gross Profit	1.71
MVIC/SDE	2.81
MVIC/EBITDA	3.60
OVER $5 MILLION NET SALES	
MVIC/Net Sales.	0.59
MVIC/Gross Profit	1.90
MVIC/SDE	3.18
MVIC/EBITDA	3.18

Source: DealStats (formerly Pratt's Stats), 2023 (Portland, OR: Business Valuation Resources, LLC), www.bvresources.com/dealstats

BENCHMARK DATA

STATISTICS (PLASTIC BOTTLE MANUFACTURING)

Number of Establishments	510
Average Profit Margin	5.1%
Revenue per Employee	$387,226
Average Number of Employees.	74.5
Average Wages per Employee	$65,397

PRODUCTS AND SERVICES SEGMENTATION

Beverage bottles	43.1%
Food bottles.	30.0%
Household product bottles	13.8%
Automotive and industrial product bottles	13.1%

MAJOR MARKET SEGMENTATION

Beverage manufacturers	43.1%
Food Manufacturers	30.0%
Automotive and industrial product manufacturers. . .	13.8%
Household product manufacturers.	13.1%

INDUSTRY COSTS

Profit	5.1%
Wages	16.8%
Purchases	51.4%
Depreciation	4.5%
Marketing	0.1%
Rent & Utilities	5.4%
Other	16.7%

MARKET SHARE

Graham Packaging Co Inc. 12.6%
Plastipak Holdings Inc. 9.5%
Loews Corp 6.6%

INDUSTRY TREND

"Imports remain a key threat to the industry. Buyers looking to cut costs have turned to less expensive foreign products or have chosen to invest in vertically integrated manufacturers. Plastic bottle manufacturers have adapted to consumer preferences. Manufacturers are creating new bottles that adhere to stricter environmental standards to compete with reusable alternatives like glass or metal."

Source: IBISWorld Key Takeaways

RESOURCES

• IBISWorld, February 2023: https://www.ibisworld.com

Manufacturing: Plastic Film, Sheet & Bag

| NAICS 32611 | Businesses/Units 1,221

| Profit $3.5 B | Wages $7.3 B | Annual Growth Future 1.0%

| Annual Growth Past 1.0%

INDUSTRY MULTIPLES

Acquisition multiples below are calculated medians using US private industry transactions. Data updated annually. Last update: August 2023.

VALUATION MULTIPLE (MEDIAN VALUE)

UNDER $1 MILLION NET SALES
MVIC/Net Sales. 1.09
MVIC/Gross Profit 1.46
MVIC/SDE 2.17
MVIC/EBITDA 2.17

$1 MILLION–$5 MILLION NET SALES
MVIC/Net Sales. 0.78
MVIC/Gross Profit 1.81
MVIC/SDE 3.52
MVIC/EBITDA 4.01

OVER $5 MILLION NET SALES
MVIC/Net Sales. 0.97
MVIC/Gross Profit 3.09
MVIC/SDE 3.00
MVIC/EBITDA 6.68

Source: DealStats (formerly Pratt's Stats), 2023 (Portland, OR: Business Valuation Resources, LLC), www.bvresources.com/dealstats

BENCHMARK DATA

STATISTICS (PLASTIC FILM, SHEET & BAG MANUFACTURING)

Number of Establishments 1,221
Average Profit Margin 6.7%
Revenue per Employee $502,578
Average Number of Employees. . . . 85.3
Average Wages per Employee . . . $70,499

PRODUCTS AND SERVICES SEGMENTATION

Plastic film and sheets (excluding packaging) 36.2%
Plastic packaging film and sheets 32.8%
Plastic bags 31.0%

MAJOR MARKET SEGMENTATION

Food beverage manufacturers and retailers 41.2%
Other markets 30.3%
Pharmaceutical, medical and hygiene manufacturers . . .14.7%
Industrial industries. 13.8%

INDUSTRY COSTS

Profit 6.7%
Wages 14.1%
Purchases 54.5%
Depreciation 2.6%
Marketing 0.1%
Rent & Utilities 3.0%
Other 18.9%

INDUSTRY TREND

"Shops, supermarkets and other vendors frequently use plastic bags and other plastic materials to package items for customers, so their demand is strong. Manufacturers have linked facilities to boost output, save overhead costs and unintentionally expand their workforce."

Source: IBISWorld Key Takeaways

RESOURCES

• IBISWorld, September 2023: https://www.ibisworld.com

Manufacturing: Plastic Pipe & Parts

| NAICS 32612 | Businesses/Units 824

| Profit $1.3 B | Wages $3 B | Annual Growth Future 1.6%

| Annual Growth Past -0.7%

INDUSTRY MULTIPLES

Acquisition multiples below are calculated medians using US private industry transactions. Data updated annually. Last update: August 2023.

VALUATION MULTIPLE (MEDIAN VALUE)

UNDER $1 MILLION NET SALES
MVIC/Net Sales. 0.57
MVIC/Gross Profit 0.73
MVIC/SDE 1.19
MVIC/EBITDA 1.98

$1 MILLION–$5 MILLION NET SALES
MVIC/Net Sales. 0.41
MVIC/Gross Profit 0.98
MVIC/SDE 5.12
MVIC/EBITDA 7.39

OVER $5 MILLION NET SALES
MVIC/Net Sales. 0.72
MVIC/Gross Profit 2.59
MVIC/SDE 9.28
MVIC/EBITDA 12.05

M

BENCHMARK DATA

STATISTICS (PLASTIC PIPE & PARTS MANUFACTURING)

Number of Establishments	824
Average Profit Margin	5.5%
Revenue per Employee	$534,949
Average Number of Employees	55.6
Average Wages per Employee	$66,653

PRODUCTS AND SERVICES SEGMENTATION

Unlaminated plastic profile extrusions and shapes	58.5%
Sewer, storm drain and other nonpressurized water pipes	15.4%
Pipe fittings and unions	14.5%
Oil and gas pipes	6.2%
Other	2.9%
Pipes for industrial and mining applications	2.5%

MAJOR MARKET SEGMENTATION

Other	22.5%
Residential construction	21.6%
Nonresidential construction	20.4%
General manufacturing	19.8%
Industrial and energy	8.7%
Utilities construction	7.0%

INDUSTRY COSTS

Profit	5.4%
Wages	12.5%
Purchases	43.4%
Depreciation	2.7%
Marketing	0.1%
Rent & Utilities	2.6%
Other	33.3%

INDUSTRY TREND

"Harmful impact of COVID-19 dampened industry performance. The negative economic effects on downstream markets harmed demand for the industry's product line. Volatility in the price of plastic materials and resin influences industry strategy. Sharp fluctuations in the price of raw goods harm industry profitability and dampen growth."

Source: IBISWorld Key Takeaways

RESOURCES

- IBISWorld, February 2023: https://www.ibisworld.com

Manufacturing: Plastic Products Miscellaneous

| NAICS 32619	| SIC 3089-10	| Businesses/Units 6,151
| Profit $5.3 B	| Wages $5.3 B	| Annual Growth Future 1.7%
		| Annual Growth Past -0.6%

Rules of Thumb

- 2.5–5 x SDE

- 70%–110% annual sales includes inventory
- 5–7 x EBIT
- 6 x EBITDA

INDUSTRY MULTIPLES

Acquisition multiples below are calculated medians using US private industry transactions. Data updated annually. Last update: August 2023.

VALUATION MULTIPLE (MEDIAN VALUE)

UNDER $1 MILLION NET SALES

MVIC/Net Sales.	0.67
MVIC/Gross Profit	1.41
MVIC/SDE	2.89
MVIC/EBITDA	6.37

$1 MILLION–$5 MILLION NET SALES

MVIC/Net Sales.	0.52
MVIC/Gross Profit	0.73
MVIC/SDE	4.45
MVIC/EBITDA	6.65

OVER $5 MILLION NET SALES

MVIC/Net Sales.	1.04
MVIC/Gross Profit	4.89
MVIC/SDE	3.88
MVIC/EBITDA	10.00

Source: DealStats (formerly Pratt's Stats), 2023 (Portland, OR: Business Valuation Resources, LLC), www.bvresources.com/dealstats

PRICING TIPS

There are various ways to get higher multiples in this industry. Some examples are, if you have a large repository of past projects that will need to be repeated as the existing product ages, so that you are likely to get the first call at that time; if you make custom products, and are known for quality; and if you have a distributor network which could be utilized to sell other things by the acquiring company.

BENCHMARK DATA

STATISTICS (PLASTIC PRODUCTS MISCELLANEOUS MANUFACTURING)

Number of Establishments .	6,151
Average Profit Margin	4.3%
Revenue per Employee .	$291,169
Average Number of Employees.	83.6
Average Wages per Employee .	$55,963

PRODUCTS AND SERVICES SEGMENTATION

Other plastic products .	22.3%
Fabricated plastic products for building applications .	20.5%
Plastic packaging	20.0%
Fabricated plastic products for consumer, industrial, institutional and commercial applications .	15.2%
Fabricated plastic products for transportation applications	15.1%
Plastic plumbing fixtures	4.8%
Fabricated plastic products for electrical/electronic applications.	2.1%

MAJOR MARKET SEGMENTATION

Hardware and home improvement wholesalers	36.9%
Motor vehicle manufacturers	24.7%
Other	21.7%
Furniture and furnishing wholesalers .	9.0%
Plumbing fixture wholesalers .	4.4%
Electrical and electronic manufacturers	3.3%

INDUSTRY COSTS

Profit	4.3%
Wages	19.2%
Purchases	46.5%
Depreciation	2.8%
Marketing	0.3%
Rent & Utilities	3.1%
Other	23.8%

In businesses where the raw materials are sheets of liner (like mine), sales per square foot is a common benchmark. Sales per man-hour and sales per machine hour are also used in various plastics operations.

Keys are bulk purchasing and cross-trained floor personnel.

EXPENSES (% OF ANNUAL SALES)

Cost of Goods	40% to 60%
Occupancy Costs	05% to 10%
Payroll/Labor Costs.	08% to 20%
Profit (pretax)	07% to 14%

QUESTIONS

- How do you ensure that your margins stay strong when prices rise? What does the price increase process look like? How often have you had them? How easy is it to flex up your workforce when demand rises? How do you flex it back down? What are your vendor relationships like? Do you have backup vendors available? How fast can they ramp up for you?
- How many shifts do you run today, and at what capacity is your facility today?
- How easily can you transfer the relationships with manufacturers' reps and heads of electronic distributorships? Over what period of time can you assist with these introductions?

INDUSTRY TREND

The industry will continue to rise until manufacturing begins to slow, which might happen if a recession sets in. As of now, the industry is showing no signs of slowing down. My personal business is up over 60 percent YoY, and I heard similar things at the SUR/FIN show from many of my peers.

"Manufacturers will face increasing pressure from lawmakers and consumers. Companies must prioritize sustainable production and recyclable products to conform to increasingly eco-conscious social trends. Manufacturers benefited from robust housing and renovation markets during the pandemic. Even so, climbing interest rates brought these markets to a standstill."

Source: IBISWorld Key Takeaways

"By 2050, the plastics industry is expected to consume 20 percent of all the oil produced. The oil industry, concerned about declining demand as the world moves toward electric cars and away from fossil fuels, has pivoted toward making more plastic—spending more than $200 billion on chemical and plastic manufacturing plants in the United States."

Source: "Maine Will Make Companies Pay for Recycling. Here's How It Works." by Winston Choi-Schagrin, August 5, 2021, https://www.nytimes.com/2021/07/21/climate/maine-recycling-law-EPR.html

EXPERT COMMENTS

The plastics market is hot right now, with all the major players (Generational Equity, Benchmark, etc.) going after midsized companies to sell to PE buyers.

Demand is through the roof, and customers have not stopped purchasing, even as prices have risen. That said, most of the industry is old, with old machines. In today's market, it would cost a fortune to build a new plant and launch a new brand, so buyers are better off purchasing an existing operation and upgrading machines where necessary.

FINANCING

Outside financing with a 10 percent seller financing option is typical. If it is an individual, 10 percent down, 10 percent seller financing, 80 percent SBA loan. If it is a corporation, 10 percent down, 10 percent seller financing, 80 percent bank loan.

RESOURCES

- IBISWorld, September 2023: https://www.ibisworld.com
- American Chemistry Council: https://www.americanchemistry.com
- MAPP—Manufacturers Association for Plastics Processors: https://www.mappinc.com
- Plastics Industry Association: https://www.plasticsindustry.org
- Plastics Machinery Magazine: https://www.plasticsmachinerymagazine.com
- Plastics Technology: https://www.ptonline.com
- Plastics Today: https://www.plasticstoday.com/
- Plastics.com: https://plastics.com
- SPE: https://www.4spe.org

Manufacturing: Precast Concrete

NAICS 327390	Businesses/Units 1,846	
Profit $1 B	Wages $3.7 B	Annual Growth Future 1.1%
		Annual Growth Past -0.4%

INDUSTRY MULTIPLES

Acquisition multiples below are calculated medians using US private industry transactions. Data updated annually. Last update: August 2023.

VALUATION MULTIPLE (MEDIAN VALUE)

UNDER $1 MILLION NET SALES	N/A
$1 MILLION–$5 MILLION NET SALES	N/A
OVER $5 MILLION NET SALES	
MVIC/Net Sales.	0.67
MVIC/Gross Profit	7.10
MVIC/SDE	3.14
MVIC/EBITDA	7.79

Source: DealStats (formerly Pratt's Stats), 2023 (Portland, OR: Business Valuation Resources, LLC), www.bvresources.com/dealstats

BENCHMARK DATA

STATISTICS (PRECAST CONCRETE MANUFACTURING)

Number of Establishments 1,846
Average Profit Margin 6.3%
Revenue per Employee $276,884
Average Number of Employees. . . . 32.2
Average Wages per Employee . . . $62,688

PRODUCTS AND SERVICES SEGMENTATION

Precast concrete products	64.8%
Precast building systems and components	17.9%
Prestressed concrete products	14.9%
Other concrete products	2.4%

MAJOR MARKET SEGMENTATION

Utilities construction	56.7%
Transport infrastructure construction	15.6%
Building construction	15.4%
Other	7.6%
Banking/security	4.7%

INDUSTRY COSTS

Profit	6.3%
Wages	22.6%
Purchases	37.4%
Depreciation	2.9%
Marketing	0.2%
Rent & Utilities	3.0%
Other	27.4%

INDUSTRY TREND

"Federal infrastructure spending drives demand from key buyers, especially as rising interest rates deter companies from starting new projects. The nation's utilities and roadways are constantly being repaired, driving the need for precast concrete structures. Green initiatives will push manufacturers to produce low-emission concretes. Precast concrete manufacturers will face added competition from substitutions."

Source: IBISWorld Key Takeaways

RESOURCES

- IBISWorld, February 2023: https://www.ibisworld.com

Manufacturing: Prefabricated Wood Buildings

| NAICS 321992 | Businesses/Units 868

| Profit $838.7 M | Wages $2.1 B | Annual Growth Future 1.4%

| Annual Growth Past -3.7%

Rules of Thumb

- 100% annual sales includes inventory

INDUSTRY MULTIPLES

Acquisition multiples below are calculated medians using US private industry transactions. Data updated annually. Last update: August 2023.

VALUATION MULTIPLE (MEDIAN VALUE)

UNDER $1 MILLION NET SALES

MVIC/Net Sales	0.28
MVIC/Gross Profit	N/A
MVIC/SDE	0.72
MVIC/EBITDA	N/A

$1 MILLION–$5 MILLION NET SALES

MVIC/Net Sales	0.48

MVIC/Gross Profit	1.79
MVIC/SDE	3.71
MVIC/EBITDA	3.71

OVER $5 MILLION NET SALES

MVIC/Net Sales.	0.80
MVIC/Gross Profit	0.80
MVIC/SDE	3.43
MVIC/EBITDA	N/A

Source: DealStats (formerly Pratt's Stats), 2023 (Portland, OR: Business Valuation Resources, LLC), www.bvresources.com/dealstats

PRICING TIPS

Modular plants sell at a premium. Log home companies sell at a discount. Dealer network is important, or, if selling direct, quality of sales staff.

BENCHMARK DATA

STATISTICS (PREFABRICATED HOME MANUFACTURING)

Number of Establishments	868
Average Profit Margin	9.2%
Revenue per Employee	$219,981
Average Number of Employees. . . .	49.8
Average Wages per Employee . . .	$49,040

PRODUCTS AND SERVICES SEGMENTATION

Prefabricated wood buildings	51.5%
Manufactured mobile homes	45.5%
Nonresidential mobile buildings . . .	3.0%

INDUSTRY COSTS

Profit	9.2%
Wages	22.5%
Purchases	51.8%
Depreciation	1.1%
Marketing	0.3%
Rent & Utilities	2.6%
Other	12.4%

MARKET SHARE

Berkshire Hathaway Inc.	46.7%
Skyline Champion Corporation . . .	20.2%
Cavco Industries Inc.	14.5%

Gross profit over 35 percent

EXPENSES (% OF ANNUAL SALES)

Cost of Goods	50%
Occupancy Costs	03% to 05%
Payroll/Labor Costs.	15%
Profit (pretax)	05%

QUESTIONS

- Warranty policy and expense—how much warranty exposure is there? Does company have a favorable reputation for taking care of warranties?
- What is your backlog? How many leads have you received over each of the last five years? How do you sell your product—through a dealer network or direct or both? What patented processes do you have? Do you have challenges meeting energy or structural/building codes? What information do you have for your sales performance by region for the last five years? How many competitors do

you have and where are they located? Do you sell internationally? Brand name, length of time in business and type of building system are extremely important.

INDUSTRY TREND

"Demand for prefabricated and modular homes has been sustained by increases in per capita disposable income and access to credit. Amid the COVID-19 pandemic, interest rates plummeted in an effort to stimulate the economy, making homes of all types, particularly prefabricated homes, more affordable. Many consumers seeking to flee congested cities turned to prefabricated homes, especially as work-from-home policies granted mobility. While a high unemployment rate and economic uncertainty mitigated industry growth, the overall effect on the industry was positive."

Source: IBISWorld Key Takeaways

EXPERT COMMENTS

Difficult to develop designs and engineering and establish a reputation, so it is not easy to start business from scratch.

RESOURCES

• IBISWorld, March 2023: https://www.ibisworld.com

Manufacturing: Products from Purchased Steel

| NAICS 3312

Rules of Thumb

• 3–5 x SDE includes inventory

INDUSTRY MULTIPLES

Acquisition multiples below are calculated medians using US private industry transactions. Data updated annually. Last update: August 2023.

VALUATION MULTIPLE (MEDIAN VALUE)

UNDER $1 MILLION NET SALES	N/A
$1 MILLION–$5 MILLION NET SALES	
MVIC/Net Sales.	0.48
MVIC/Gross Profit	1.43
MVIC/SDE	5.56
MVIC/EBITDA	7.22
OVER $5 MILLION NET SALES	
MVIC/Net Sales.	0.62
MVIC/Gross Profit	2.87
MVIC/SDE	N/A
MVIC/EBITDA	7.51

Source: DealStats (formerly Pratt's Stats), 2023 (Portland, OR: Business Valuation Resources, LLC), www.bvresources.com/dealstats

BENCHMARK DATA

Payroll costs, equipment maintenance, and age of equipment

EXPENSES (% OF ANNUAL SALES)

Cost of Goods	15%
Occupancy Costs	20%
Payroll/Labor Costs.	35%
Profit (pretax)	20%

- How many customers does the company have, and what is the percentage of the business?

INDUSTRY TREND

Very good sales should be going to $8M to $10M.

If you have a niche business, you will do well. If you are a job shop, chances are you will struggle.

EXPERT COMMENTS

Must have experience and good staff.

RESOURCES

- MetalMiner: https://agmetalminer.com

Manufacturing: Proprietary Products

Rules of Thumb

- 40%–60% annual sales
- 4 x SDE
- 5 x EBITDA
- 3–4 x EBIT

PRICING TIPS

Sellers need to understand that if they have excess equipment that is not producing revenue, then earnings are the selling price driver, not the value of the equipment.

Investment in equipment gets in the way of a seller's value of his/her business. Excess equipment gives the seller flexibility to perform many processes, but if all the equipment is not producing revenue, the value of all of the equipment could exceed the cash-generating value of the business.

BENCHMARK DATA

Gross margins should be 50 to 65 percent.

EXPENSES (% OF ANNUAL SALES)

Cost of Goods	30% to 40%
Occupancy Costs	10% to 15%
Payroll/Labor Costs.	25% to 35%
Profit (pretax)	15% to 20%

QUESTIONS

- How can this business grow?
- How well are your procedures documented? What additional capital expense is needed? What has limited the growth of the company?

INDUSTRY TREND

Businesses in the rust belt will be performing well over the next 8 to 10 years.

Business owners are adding automation (robots, custom machinery, material handling systems, ERP software).

EXPERT COMMENTS

The condition of the machinery and the building is very important to a buyer so that the replacement of machinery does not have to be considered with the term of the loan to purchase/replace equipment. Proprietary products could have patent or trade secret protection that increases the business value.

Have access to additional investors and their cash.

Continue to expand product line.

Getting new customers is always the challenge for older owners who do not want to add salespeople to cause more sales, which leads to needing to hire more employees. Manufacturers are adding automation since they cannot find good-quality manual labor.

FINANCING

Outside financing is necessary since seller financing is risky for the seller should the buyer fail during the term of the bank loan.

Banks love equipment and real estate.

RESOURCES

- AMT—The Association for Manufacturing Technology: https://www.amtonline.org
- International Manufacturing Technology Show: https://www.imts.com
- SME: https://www.sme.org

Manufacturing: Ready-Mix Concrete

| NAICS 327320 | Businesses/Units 5,953

| Profit $2.1 B | Wages $5.9 B | Annual Growth Future 0.4%

| Annual Growth Past 0.1%

Rules of Thumb

- 30%–35% SDE plus fixtures, equipment, and inventory

INDUSTRY MULTIPLES

Acquisition multiples below are calculated medians using US private industry transactions. Data updated annually. Last update: August 2023.

VALUATION MULTIPLE (MEDIAN VALUE)

UNDER $1 MILLION NET SALES	N/A
$1 MILLION–$5 MILLION NET SALES	N/A
OVER $5 MILLION NET SALES	
MVIC/Net Sales	1.40
MVIC/Gross Profit	5.11
MVIC/SDE	N/A
MVIC/EBITDA	11.69

Source: DealStats (formerly Pratt's Stats), 2023 (Portland, OR: Business Valuation Resources, LLC), www.bvresources.com/dealstats

BENCHMARK DATA

STATISTICS (READY-MIX CONCRETE MANUFACTURING)

Number of Establishments	5,953
Average Profit Margin	5.4%
Revenue per Employee	$463,016
Average Number of Employees. . . .	14.0
Average Wages per Employee . . .	$71,298

PRODUCTS AND SERVICES SEGMENTATION

Transit-mixed concrete	55.0%
Shrink-mixed concrete	25.0%
Central-mixed concrete.	20.0%

MAJOR MARKET SEGMENTATION

Nonresidential construction	36.0%
Infrastructure construction	35.0%
Residential construction	29.0%

INDUSTRY COSTS

Profit	5.4%
Wages	15.2%
Purchases	51.4%
Depreciation	4.4%
Marketing	0.1%
Rent & Utilities	2.4%
Other	21.1%

MARKET SHARE

CRH PLC	7.1%
Martin Marietta Materials, Inc. . . .	5.6%
CEMEX SAB de CV	4.7%
LafargeHolcim	2.7%

INDUSTRY TREND

"Revenue growth has been more stable than expected even though demand from nonresidential construction markets has declined. The Infrastructure Investment and Jobs Act will benefit the industry over the next five years through higher demand from the infrastructure construction market."

Source: IBISWorld Key Takeaways

RESOURCES

- IBISWorld, January 2023: https://www.ibisworld.com
- NRMCA—National Ready Mixed Concrete Association: https://www.nrmca.org

Manufacturing: Rubber Product

| NAICS 32629	| Businesses/Units 1,350	
| Profit $1 B	| Wages $3.7 B	| Annual Growth Future 1.9%
		| Annual Growth Past -3.9%

INDUSTRY MULTIPLES

Acquisition multiples below are calculated medians using US private industry transactions. Data updated annually. Last update: August 2023.

VALUATION MULTIPLE (MEDIAN VALUE)

UNDER $1 MILLION NET SALES

MVIC/Net Sales.	0.92
MVIC/Gross Profit	1.09
MVIC/SDE	3.35
MVIC/EBITDA	6.22

$1 MILLION–$5 MILLION NET SALES

MVIC/Net Sales.	0.35
MVIC/Gross Profit	0.61
MVIC/SDE	2.12
MVIC/EBITDA	3.85

OVER $5 MILLION NET SALES

MVIC/Net Sales.	4.49
MVIC/Gross Profit	6.37
MVIC/SDE	N/A
MVIC/EBITDA	13.32

Source: DealStats (formerly Pratt's Stats), 2023 (Portland, OR: Business Valuation Resources, LLC), www.bvresources.com/dealstats

BENCHMARK DATA

STATISTICS (RUBBER PRODUCT MANUFACTURING)

Number of Establishments .	1,350
Average Profit Margin	5.4%
Revenue per Employee .	$295,913
Average Number of Employees.	47.5
Average Wages per Employee .	$58,035

PRODUCTS AND SERVICES SEGMENTATION

Automotive rubber components	25.7%
Industrial rubber products .	16.2%
Other mechanical rubber components.	15.2%
Other	14.9%
Foam rubber products .	14.7%
Rubber compounds and mixtures .	13.3%

MAJOR MARKET SEGMENTATION

Automotive manufacturers .	25.7%
Industrial manufacturers	20.7%
Mechanical manufacturers .	19.6%
Rubber-based product manufacturers .	19.1%
Other	14.9%

INDUSTRY COSTS

Profit	5.4%
Wages .	19.7%
Purchases .	50.1%
Depreciation	2.0%
Marketing .	0.3%
Rent & Utilities .	2.6%
Other	19.8%

INDUSTRY TREND

"Volatility in the supply of rubber has led to drastic changes in its price. Domestic rubber product manufacturers primarily compete on the basis of price, increasing the pressure placed on the prices of industrial products. The price of natural rubber latex, the industry's main input and a key determinant of product selling prices, has been volatile during the period. Pricing pressure has stemmed from this input volatility, in addition to the continued presence of offshore rubber manufacturers that can sell similar quality rubber products at lower prices because of lower operating expenses."

Source: IBISWorld Key Takeaways

RESOURCES

• IBISWorld, September 2023: https://www.ibisworld.com

Manufacturing: Screw, Nut & Bolt

| NAICS 33272 | Businesses/Units 9,502

| Profit $2.7 B | Wages $11.3 B | Annual Growth Future -0.6%

| | | Annual Growth Past 0.9%

INDUSTRY MULTIPLES

Acquisition multiples below are calculated medians using US private industry transactions. Data updated annually. Last update: August 2023.

VALUATION MULTIPLE (MEDIAN VALUE)

UNDER $1 MILLION NET SALES

MVIC/Net Sales	0.83
MVIC/Gross Profit	0.17
MVIC/SDE	2.40
MVIC/EBITDA	1.05

$1 MILLION–$5 MILLION NET SALES

MVIC/Net Sales	1.48
MVIC/Gross Profit	3.32
MVIC/SDE	5.55
MVIC/EBITDA	8.05

OVER $5 MILLION NET SALES

MVIC/Net Sales	3.21
MVIC/Gross Profit	4.47
MVIC/SDE	7.92
MVIC/EBITDA	14.52

Source: DealStats (formerly Pratt's Stats), 2023 (Portland, OR: Business Valuation Resources, LLC), www.bvresources.com/dealstats

BENCHMARK DATA

STATISTICS (SCREW, NUT & BOLT MANUFACTURING)

Number of Establishments	9,502
Average Profit Margin	6.6%
Revenue per Employee	$216,131
Average Number of Employees	18.7
Average Wages per Employee	$61,643

PRODUCTS AND SERVICES SEGMENTATION

Other precision-turned products	46.0%
Threaded metal fasteners	22.8%
Precision-turned products for automobiles	19.4%
Aircraft fasteners, excluding plastics	8.2%
Nonthreaded metal fasteners	3.6%

MAJOR MARKET SEGMENTATION

Automotive	42.1%
Aerospace	36.0%
Construction	11.7%
General manufacturing	10.2%

INDUSTRY COSTS

Profit	6.6%
Wages	27.8%
Purchases	39.0%
Depreciation	3.5%
Marketing	0.1%
Rent & Utilities	3.3%
Other	19.6%

INDUSTRY TREND

"Rising exports will support industry growth, particularly as the US dollar declines in value. The superior quality of domestic fasteners alongside lower prices will drive foreign buyers to increase intake. The manufacturing sector's strong recovery will drive growth. Car and airplane manufacturers will be key drivers of demand though many will turn to substitutes, like adhesives."

Source: IBISWorld Key Takeaways

RESOURCES

- IBISWorld, January 2023: https://www.ibisworld.com

Manufacturing: Sheet Metal, Window & Door

| NAICS 33232 | Businesses/Units 13,413

| Profit $1.8 B | Wages $13.3 B | Annual Growth Future 0.4%

| Annual Growth Past -0.7%

INDUSTRY MULTIPLES

Acquisition multiples below are calculated medians using US private industry transactions. Data updated annually. Last update: August 2023.

VALUATION MULTIPLE (MEDIAN VALUE)

UNDER $1 MILLION NET SALES

MVIC/Net Sales	0.43
MVIC/Gross Profit	0.68
MVIC/SDE	2.38
MVIC/EBITDA	4.89

$1 MILLION–$5 MILLION NET SALES

MVIC/Net Sales	0.53
MVIC/Gross Profit	0.98
MVIC/SDE	2.98
MVIC/EBITDA	4.17

OVER $5 MILLION NET SALES

MVIC/Net Sales	0.87
MVIC/Gross Profit	3.14
MVIC/SDE	5.64
MVIC/EBITDA	9.48

Source: DealStats (formerly Pratt's Stats), 2023 (Portland, OR: Business Valuation Resources, LLC), www.bvresources.com/dealstats

BENCHMARK DATA

STATISTICS (SHEET METAL, WINDOW & DOOR MANUFACTURING)

Number of Establishments	13,413
Average Profit Margin	3.3%
Revenue per Employee	$248,261

Average Number of Employees. 16.5
Average Wages per Employee $61,509

PRODUCTS AND SERVICES SEGMENTATION

Sheet metal products 29.8%
Architectural and ornamental metal work 24.5%
Metal doors and doorframes 16.2%
Sheet metal HVAC ducts, culverts and stove pipes . . .14.7%
Metal windows, frames, and fixtures 9.2%
Other products 5.6%

MAJOR MARKET SEGMENTATION

Private construction 43.6%
Other markets 30.2%
HVAC systems and equipment 14.7%
Public construction 11.5%

INDUSTRY COSTS

Profit 3.3%
Wages 24.9%
Purchases 45.1%
Depreciation 1.9%
Marketing 0.3%
Rent & Utilities 2.5%
Other 22.0%

INDUSTRY TREND

"Success in this industry is directly tied to construction. The constantly shifting construction sector in recent years has caused revenue volatility. High input costs pressured profit. Supply has caught up following the end of pandemic-related disruptions, bringing these costs back down. Low-cost imports pose a significant threat. Domestic sheet metal, window and door manufacturers are responding to this by focusing on higher quality products."

Source: IBISWorld Key Takeaways

RESOURCES

• IBISWorld, September 2023: https://www.ibisworld.com

Manufacturing: Showcase, Partition, Shelving, and Lockers

| NAICS 337215

Rules of Thumb

• 2–3 x SDE plus inventory

INDUSTRY MULTIPLES

Acquisition multiples below are calculated medians using US private industry transactions. Data updated annually. Last update: August 2023.

VALUATION MULTIPLE (MEDIAN VALUE)

UNDER $1 MILLION NET SALES
MVIC/Net Sales. 0.48
MVIC/Gross Profit 0.19
MVIC/SDE 2.53
MVIC/EBITDA . . . . N/A

$1 MILLION–$5 MILLION NET SALES
MVIC/Net Sales. 0.26
MVIC/Gross Profit 0.79

MVIC/SDE	1.29
MVIC/EBITDA	2.41

MVIC/Net Sales.	0.69
MVIC/Gross Profit	2.46
MVIC/SDE	5.00
MVIC/EBITDA	9.54

Source: DealStats (formerly Pratt's Stats), 2023 (Portland, OR: Business Valuation Resources, LLC), www.bvresources.com/dealstats

PRICING TIPS

Customer concentration and any special skills required to operate can make for a big difference in pricing.

EXPENSES (% OF ANNUAL SALES)

Cost of Goods	35%
Occupancy Costs	15%
Payroll/Labor Costs.	40%
Profit (pretax)	10%

EXPERT COMMENTS

Economy changes the profitability very quickly here.

Manufacturing: Signs

	NAICS 339950		SIC 7389-38		Businesses/Units 29,742
	Profit $736.6 M		Wages $4.4 B		Annual Growth Future -0.1%
					Annual Growth Past -1.6%

Rules of Thumb

- 45%–50% annual sales plus inventory
- 2–2.5 x SDE plus inventory

INDUSTRY MULTIPLES

Acquisition multiples below are calculated medians using US private industry transactions. Data updated annually. Last update: August 2023.

VALUATION MULTIPLE (MEDIAN VALUE)

UNDER $1 MILLION NET SALES

MVIC/Net Sales.	0.53
MVIC/Gross Profit	0.80
MVIC/SDE	2.10
MVIC/EBITDA	3.12

$1 MILLION–$5 MILLION NET SALES

MVIC/Net Sales.	0.48
MVIC/Gross Profit	0.83
MVIC/SDE	2.98
MVIC/EBITDA	4.33

OVER $5 MILLION NET SALES

MVIC/Net Sales.	0.62
MVIC/Gross Profit	1.55
MVIC/SDE	4.60
MVIC/EBITDA	5.12

Source: DealStats (formerly Pratt's Stats), 2023 (Portland, OR: Business Valuation Resources, LLC), www.bvresources.com/dealstats

BENCHMARK DATA

STATISTICS (BILLBOARD AND SIGN MANUFACTURING)

Number of Establishments	29,742
Average Profit Margin	5.0%
Revenue per Employee	$145,236
Average Number of Employees	3.4
Average Wages per Employee	$43,651

PRODUCTS AND SERVICES SEGMENTATION

Traditional billboards and signs	43.7%
Digital billboards and signs	41.9%
Other	14.4%

MAJOR MARKET SEGMENTATION

Retail and food services	42.2%
Other	20.1%
Outdoor advertising and transportation	18.5%
Corporate and trade shows	18.5%
Exports	0.7%

INDUSTRY COSTS

Profit	5.0%
Wages	30.1%
Purchases	39.8%
Depreciation	1.9%
Marketing	0.6%
Rent & Utilities	3.3%
Other	19.5%

INDUSTRY TREND

"The COVID-19 pandemic resulted in a severe decline in traditional economic activity across downstream markets. In response, spending on new billboards and signs dropped precipitously in 2020. Digital billboards are rising in popularity because of their ability to host multiple advertisements. Their complexity makes them a high value-add product, allowing manufacturers to reap higher profits."

Source: IBISWorld Key Takeaways

RESOURCES

- IBISWorld, February 2023: https://www.ibisworld.com
- ISA—International Sign Association: https://www.signs.org

Manufacturing: Soap & Cleaning Compound

| NAICS 325611 | Businesses/Units 4,466

| Profit $2.7 B | Wages $3.8 B | Annual Growth Future -0.8%

| | | Annual Growth Past -1.8%

INDUSTRY MULTIPLES

Acquisition multiples below are calculated medians using US private industry transactions. Data updated annually. Last update: August 2023.

VALUATION MULTIPLE (MEDIAN VALUE)

UNDER $1 MILLION NET SALES

MVIC/Net Sales	0.61
MVIC/Gross Profit	0.98

```
MVIC/SDE  .   .   .   .   .   .   .   . 2.21
MVIC/EBITDA  .   .   .   .   .   .   . 2.78
```

$1 MILLION–$5 MILLION NET SALES

```
MVIC/Net Sales.   .   .   .   .   .   . 1.87
MVIC/Gross Profit  .   .   .   .   .   . 3.06
MVIC/SDE  .   .   .   .   .   .   .   . 3.23
MVIC/EBITDA  .   .   .   .   .   .   . 6.49
```

OVER $5 MILLION NET SALES

```
MVIC/Net Sales.   .   .   .   .   .   . 1.16
MVIC/Gross Profit  .   .   .   .   .   . 4.68
MVIC/SDE  .   .   .   .   .   .   .   . N/A
MVIC/EBITDA  .   .   .   .   .   .   . 12.68
```

Source: DealStats (formerly Pratt's Stats), 2023 (Portland, OR: Business Valuation Resources, LLC), www.bvresources.com/dealstats

BENCHMARK DATA

STATISTICS (SOAP & CLEANING COMPOUND MANUFACTURING)

Number of Establishments	4,466
Average Profit Margin	6.4%
Revenue per Employee	$832,004
Average Number of Employees. . .	11.4
Average Wages per Employee . . .	$73,934

PRODUCTS AND SERVICES SEGMENTATION

Household soaps and detergents . .	35.4%
Surface active agents	28.6%
Polishes and other sanitation goods .	21.0%
Commercial soaps and detergents . .	15.0%

MAJOR MARKET SEGMENTATION

Supermarkets and mass merchants .	25.9%
Independent retailers	17.0%
Exports	16.8%
Food service establishments . . .	15.2%
Lodging establishments	12.3%
Healthcare providers	11.6%
Convenience stores.	1.2%

INDUSTRY COSTS

Profit	6.4%
Wages	8.9%
Purchases	37.9%
Depreciation	1.8%
Marketing	0.1%
Rent & Utilities	1.4%
Other	43.5%

INDUSTRY TREND

"High inflation and interest rates are increasing input and capital costs for soap manufacturers significantly. Revenue for manufacturers fell quite dramatically in 2021 and 2022. Large manufacturers are investing in environmentally sustainable innovations to revive profitability. They want to appeal to younger consumers who are concerned about the planet."

Source: IBISWorld Key Takeaways

RESOURCES

• IBISWorld, September 2023: https://www.ibisworld.com

Manufacturing: Specialty Vehicle

M

| NAICS 3361

Rules of Thumb

- 4 x SDE includes inventory

PRICING TIPS

Evaluate inventory closely, as there is a tendency to accumulate difficult-to-use inventory.

Look for amount of booked business. Lead times from getting the order to shipping the finished vehicle can run 12 months or more.

Evaluate financials closely. Many in this industry do not know what their true costs are.

BENCHMARK DATA

Difficult to estimate sales per employee, but should probably be $175,000 to $200,000 per hourly production employee.

EXPENSES (% OF ANNUAL SALES)

Cost of Goods	55%
Occupancy Costs	05%
Payroll/Labor Costs.	25%
Profit (pretax)	10%

QUESTIONS

- Who has design experience in the company? Who has the manufacturing experience in the company? How do you accurately cost jobs?
- What portion of the business is municipal, corporate, and private? Who are the key employees with industry experience? What is your marketing/sales plan? What is your backlog of business?

INDUSTRY TREND

Much of the business is tied to Homeland Security. If there are attacks on our soil, demand will increase. Otherwise budget cutbacks will dampen demand.

The market for mobile command centers, bomb trucks, SWAT trucks, etc., will continue to be strong as long as the U.S. has to fight terrorists. Many corporations are developing mobile marketing vehicles, which will also help drive demand.

EXPERT COMMENTS

It is difficult to acquire the expertise to build these vehicles. Many can build them; few can build them well.

Homeland Security issues make this a growth industry. It is fairly easy to replicate the physical facility, but the real market advantage comes from experience in designing, building and using these vehicles.

RESOURCES

- SVS—Specialty Vehicle Services: https://www.vehiclesuccess.com

Manufacturing: Sporting Goods & Outdoor Products

| NAICS 339920

Rules of Thumb

- 4–6 x EBITDA
- 100% annual sales includes inventory
- 5–6 x EBIT
- 3–5 x SDE

INDUSTRY MULTIPLES

Acquisition multiples below are calculated medians using US private industry transactions. Data updated annually. Last update: August 2023.

VALUATION MULTIPLE (MEDIAN VALUE)

UNDER $1 MILLION NET SALES

MVIC/Net Sales.	0.63
MVIC/Gross Profit	1.55
MVIC/SDE	2.74
MVIC/EBITDA	3.80

$1 MILLION–$5 MILLION NET SALES

MVIC/Net Sales.	0.81
MVIC/Gross Profit	1.38
MVIC/SDE	3.66
MVIC/EBITDA	5.82

OVER $5 MILLION NET SALES

MVIC/Net Sales.	1.53
MVIC/Gross Profit	4.16
MVIC/SDE	3.71
MVIC/EBITDA	16.69

Source: DealStats (formerly Pratt's Stats), 2023 (Portland, OR: Business Valuation Resources, LLC), www.bvresources.com/dealstats

PRICING TIPS

Base valuation multiples are 4 to 5 x EBITDA. In the case of a branded product with strong market position and protected intellectual property, the multiples can range from 5 to 10 x EBITDA for companies under $25 million annual revenue.

Valuation comes down to the product category, brand strength, innovation, and differentiation.

Branded manufacturers of outdoor products can receive 5 to 6+ multiples, depending on value drivers. Those with EBITDA over 1 million may receive over 6 x. Breadth of product and diversity of customer base are factors. Walmart, Amazon, Bass Pro, and Target are common large customers. If the brand has been in-store a long time and is a category leader, it is generally worth more. IP is a major value driver, as well.

BENCHMARK DATA

For outdoors manufacturing, we like to see EBITDA margins exceeding 40 percent.

EXPENSES (% OF ANNUAL SALES)

Cost of Goods	30% to 50%
Occupancy Costs	05% to 10%
Payroll/Labor Costs.	15% to 25%
Profit (pretax)	20% to 40%

QUESTIONS

- Review the top 10 selling products. Investigate point-of-sale products. How long have the products been in-store? Do they provide healthy margins to the retailer? Is the company investing in gaining online resellers or direct to consumer? Excise tax?
- How and why they got into the business, and why they are exiting
- What is the marketing and distribution channel? What is the product life cycle, innovation cycle, position in the market (mass vs. premium), market share?

INDUSTRY TREND

Covid has created positive trends for outdoor products, with returning users and many new consumers.

EXPERT COMMENTS

Seller: don't wait for a seasonal dip to start selling; prepare early; start selling during high season so that a deal closes during low season.

Buyer: make sure you have the funds to cover low season if you buy a business which may produce most of its cash flow during a particular time of year.

Marketability is great for outdoors businesses—it attracts a lot of buyers looking to "live the dream." Replication tends to be easier because a lot of the outdoors widget companies are using Chinese manufacturers.

FINANCING

Bank financing, PEGs, and/or strategic buyers leveraging their own capital

RESOURCES

- AFFTA—American Fly Fishing Trade Association: https://affta.org
- ASA—American Sportfishing Association: https://asafishing.org/
- Inside Outdoor Magazine: https://insideoutdoor.com/
- NSSF—National Shooting Sports Foundation: https://www.nssf.org
- OIA—Outdoor Industry Association: https://outdoorindustry.org
- SNEWS: https://www.snewsnet.com

Manufacturing: Structural Metal Product

| NAICS 332312 | Businesses/Units 6,030

| Profit $2.6 B | Wages $10.7 B | Annual Growth Future 1.0%

| | | Annual Growth Past -2.5%

INDUSTRY MULTIPLES

Acquisition multiples below are calculated medians using US private industry transactions. Data updated annually. Last update: August 2023.

VALUATION MULTIPLE (MEDIAN VALUE)

UNDER $1 MILLION NET SALES

MVIC/Net Sales	0.50
MVIC/Gross Profit	0.74
MVIC/SDE	2.04
MVIC/EBITDA	1.99

$1 MILLION–$5 MILLION NET SALES

MVIC/Net Sales	0.40
MVIC/Gross Profit	0.99
MVIC/SDE	2.30
MVIC/EBITDA	3.13

OVER $5 MILLION NET SALES

MVIC/Net Sales	0.58
MVIC/Gross Profit	1.39
MVIC/SDE	3.48
MVIC/EBITDA	4.65

Source: DealStats (formerly Pratt's Stats), 2023 (Portland, OR: Business Valuation Resources, LLC), www.bvresources.com/dealstats

BENCHMARK DATA

STATISTICS (STRUCTURAL METAL PRODUCT MANUFACTURING)

Number of Establishments	6,030
Average Profit Margin	4.7%
Revenue per Employee	$348,875
Average Number of Employees	26.5
Average Wages per Employee	$67,847

PRODUCTS AND SERVICES SEGMENTATION

Fabricated structural metal products for construction. .	51.1%
Prefabricated metal building and components. . . .	17.2%
Fabricated structural metal products (nonconstruction) .	17.1%
Fabricated metal plate work products	14.6%

MAJOR MARKET SEGMENTATION

Building construction markets	39.0%
General construction and utilities infrastructure . . .	21.2%
Other	18.8%
Manufacturing	18.2%
Transport infrastructure construction	2.8%

INDUSTRY COSTS

Profit	4.7%
Wages	19.4%
Purchases	49.2%
Depreciation	3.3%
Marketing	0.1%
Rent & Utilities	2.0%
Other	21.2%

INDUSTRY TREND

"To mute the negative effects of COVID-19 and to stimulate the declining economy, the Federal Reserve lowered interest rates. Residential construction activity boomed amid the pandemic, as residential work takes a relatively short amount of time to complete and is highly susceptible to the price of financing. Nonresidential construction activity has historically taken longer to improve post-recession and follows a lag of one to two years to that of the residential construction market. Commercial work continues to dwindle. Volatile steel prices harm the industry. Rapid increases in steel costs cannot be quickly offset with increased selling prices."

Source: IBISWorld Key Takeaways

RESOURCES

- IBISWorld, September 2023: https://www.ibisworld.com

Manufacturing: Technology

| NAICS 334111

INDUSTRY MULTIPLES

Acquisition multiples below are calculated medians using US private industry transactions. Data updated annually. Last update: August 2023.

VALUATION MULTIPLE (MEDIAN VALUE)

UNDER $1 MILLION NET SALES	N/A

$1 MILLION–$5 MILLION NET SALES

MVIC/Net Sales	0.15
MVIC/Gross Profit	0.65
MVIC/SDE	1.21
MVIC/EBITDA	1.99

OVER $5 MILLION NET SALES

MVIC/Net Sales	1.21
MVIC/Gross Profit	4.07
MVIC/SDE	N/A
MVIC/EBITDA	33.37

Source: DealStats (formerly Pratt's Stats), 2023 (Portland, OR: Business Valuation Resources, LLC), www.bvresources.com/dealstats

PRICING TIPS

The technology industry is very diverse and there are many subsegments. The asset-intensive sectors tend to be mostly in the 0.5 to 1.0 times sales, but the asset-light companies can go for several times sales. However, as the industries mature, many fall in to the 3 to 7 times EBITDA range.

For specialty companies, there are no rules of thumb. Very high multiples are possible if the company has a very desirable product or technology.

BENCHMARK DATA

Revenue per employee is almost always in excess of $100,000. For some higher knowledge companies, it can be $200,000 per employee or more.

EXPENSES (% OF ANNUAL SALES)

Cost of Goods	60%
Occupancy Costs	10%
Payroll/Labor Costs	15%
Profit (pretax)	15%

QUESTIONS

- The most important things to find out are competition and the loyalty of customers.

INDUSTRY TREND

"'The empire of manufacturing in China is being shaken,' said Lior Susan, founder of Eclipse Venture Capital, which invests in hardware and manufacturing start-ups. 'More and more capital is going to pull manufacturing out of China and find an alternative.'"

Source: "Tech Companies Slowly Shift Production Away From China" by Daisuke Wakabayashi and Tripp Mickle, September 1, 2022, https://www.nytimes.com/2022/09/01/business/tech-companies-china.html

"Proposed right-to-repair laws and increased government regulation may one day force manufacturers to make the spare parts and instructions needed to fix their products available to all....'If you can design to be more modular, accessible and repairable, overall, you will get a better experience for your end users,' said Daniel O'Brien, general manager of HTC Corp.'s virtual reality Vive business for the Americas. HTC Vive last month started publishing repair manuals for its consoles and selling some replacement parts through the community repair site iFixit....

"The right-to-repair movement has caught the attention of lawmakers as a result of campaigning from consumer and environmental-protection groups. Right-to-repair laws have been proposed in a number of U.S. states from Arkansas, where a bill would make it easier for farmers to repair their own equipment, to Washington, where legislators hope to promote the 'fair servicing and repair of digital electronic products.'"

Source: "Some Companies Offer Spare Parts, Fix-It Manuals" by Katie Deighton, June 2, 2021, *Wall Street Journal*

EXPERT COMMENTS

Buyers should not consider if they do not have the technical background.

The customer relationships tend to be deep, making it difficult for competition to take away business.

FINANCING

A lot of transactions are financed with cash and earnouts.

Manufacturing: Wire & Spring

| NAICS 33261 | Businesses/Units 1,030

| Profit $708.2 M | Wages $2.1 B | Annual Growth Future 1.8%

| Annual Growth Past -2.0%

INDUSTRY MULTIPLES

Acquisition multiples below are calculated medians using US private industry transactions. Data updated annually. Last update: August 2023.

VALUATION MULTIPLE (MEDIAN VALUE)

UNDER $1 MILLION NET SALES

MVIC/Net Sales.	0.29
MVIC/Gross Profit	0.81
MVIC/SDE	1.67
MVIC/EBITDA	2.13

$1 MILLION–$5 MILLION NET SALES

MVIC/Net Sales.	0.58
MVIC/Gross Profit	0.85
MVIC/SDE	2.78
MVIC/EBITDA	7.70

OVER $5 MILLION NET SALES

MVIC/Net Sales.	1.89
MVIC/Gross Profit	4.32
MVIC/SDE	N/A
MVIC/EBITDA	22.80

Source: DealStats (formerly Pratt's Stats), 2023 (Portland, OR: Business Valuation Resources, LLC), www.bvresources.com/dealstats

BENCHMARK DATA

STATISTICS (WIRE & SPRING MANUFACTURING)

Number of Establishments	1,030
Average Profit Margin	6.5%
Revenue per Employee	$308,769
Average Number of Employees	34.9
Average Wages per Employee	$59,964

PRODUCTS AND SERVICES SEGMENTATION

Light-gauge springs	24.0%
Heavy-gauge springs	19.6%
Nonferrous wire products	15.5%
Other fabricated wire products	14.9%
Steel wire, rope and cable	13.0%
Woven wire products	7.9%
Steel nails, staples and similar products	3.0%
Steel wire fencing and fence gates	2.1%

MAJOR MARKET SEGMENTATION

Building and fencing construction	33.8%
Transportation equipment manufacturing	27.0%
Upholstered furniture and mattress manufacturing	15.6%
General manufacturing and industrial	14.8%
Other	8.8%

INDUSTRY COSTS

Profit	6.5%
Wages	19.6%
Purchases	45.3%
Depreciation	2.0%
Marketing	0.2%
Rent & Utilities	2.6%
Other	23.7%

INDUSTRY TREND

"Wire and spring manufacturers have shifted to custom-made products, enabling companies to move into niche product segments. These customized products will elevate profit for domestic manufacturers. Rising interest rates coupled with struggling downstream markets have slammed manufacturers. Infrastructure spending and rebounding exports will stabilize demand in the outlook period."

Source: IBISWorld Key Takeaways

RESOURCES

• IBISWorld, April 2023: https://www.ibisworld.com

Manufacturing: Women's, Girls' and Infants' Apparel

NAICS 315	Businesses/Units 4,446	
Profit $75.2 M	Wages $490.5 M	Annual Growth Future 1.2%
		Annual Growth Past -7.6%

INDUSTRY MULTIPLES

Acquisition multiples below are calculated medians using US private industry transactions. Data updated annually. Last update: August 2023.

VALUATION MULTIPLE (MEDIAN VALUE)

UNDER $1 MILLION NET SALES

MVIC/Net Sales.	0.63
MVIC/Gross Profit	1.10
MVIC/SDE	2.96
MVIC/EBITDA	2.94

$1 MILLION–$5 MILLION NET SALES

MVIC/Net Sales.	0.34
MVIC/Gross Profit	0.66
MVIC/SDE	1.84
MVIC/EBITDA	38.21

OVER $5 MILLION NET SALES

MVIC/Net Sales.	1.38
MVIC/Gross Profit	3.38
MVIC/SDE	4.33
MVIC/EBITDA	11.63

Source: DealStats (formerly Pratt's Stats), 2023 (Portland, OR: Business Valuation Resources, LLC), www.bvresources.com/dealstats

BENCHMARK DATA

STATISTICS (WOMEN'S, GIRLS' AND INFANTS' APPAREL MANUFACTURING)

Number of Establishments .	4,446
Average Profit Margin	2.7%
Revenue per Employee .	$209,000
Average Number of Employees.	3.1
Average Wages per Employee .	$36,085

PRODUCTS AND SERVICES SEGMENTATION

Dresses .	38.3%
Blouses and shirts	26.8%
Shorts, pants, and skirts	17.2%
Athletic and swimwear .	9.0%
Other, including coats and capes	7.5%
Infant wear .	1.2%

MAJOR MARKET SEGMENTATION

Exports .	43.0%
Clothing retailers	23.2%
General merchandise retailers .	14.3%
Wholesalers.	13.2%
Online retail .	6.3%

INDUSTRY COSTS

Profit	2.7%
Wages	17.6%
Purchases	46.3%
Depreciation	0.3%
Marketing	1.1%
Rent & Utilities .	3.8%
Other	28.1%

INDUSTRY TREND

"US apparel manufacturers have been moving most of their production due to low labor costs. Total imports have declined during the period. The price of clothing is expected to decline at the retail level. Companies that lack quality goods with strong branding will produce highly automated products domestically. IBISWorld expects industry operators will maintain relatively constant profit. Domestically exports will likely keep industry revenue from falling. The number of industry operators is estimated to fall as employment falls."

Source: IBISWorld Industry at a Glance

• IBISWorld, July 2022: https://www.ibisworld.com

Manufacturing: Wood Kitchen Cabinets and Countertops

| NAICS 337110

Rules of Thumb

• 2–2.5 x SDE plus inventory

INDUSTRY MULTIPLES

Acquisition multiples below are calculated medians using US private industry transactions. Data updated annually. Last update: August 2023.

VALUATION MULTIPLE (MEDIAN VALUE)

UNDER $1 MILLION NET SALES	
MVIC/Net Sales.	0.53
MVIC/Gross Profit	0.90
MVIC/SDE	2.15
MVIC/EBITDA	3.19
$1 MILLION–$5 MILLION NET SALES	
MVIC/Net Sales.	0.54
MVIC/Gross Profit	0.97
MVIC/SDE	2.42
MVIC/EBITDA	3.26
OVER $5 MILLION NET SALES	
MVIC/Net Sales.	0.85
MVIC/Gross Profit	3.07
MVIC/SDE	2.87
MVIC/EBITDA	9.11

Source: DealStats (formerly Pratt's Stats), 2023 (Portland, OR: Business Valuation Resources, LLC), www.bvresources.com/dealstats

PRICING TIPS

Such companies are considered light manufacturing operations, and since demand for manufacturing is at a premium, pricing may command higher multiples. Considerations must be put on how dependent on the amount of customization and specialty product the companies produce. Franchised operations are easier to assess if the owner is part of the production or part of marketing and sales. Franchised resale operations could be truly turnkey. If franchise resale, the territory scope could have a bearing on the multiples as its demographic plays a role in the profitability and scalability of the opportunity.

Some wood cabinet manufacturers have state-of-the-art equipment that increases the efficiency of the business. Analyzing and adding the value of the equipment is a component of the above.

BENCHMARK DATA

The ability to buy supplies (melamine, hardware, etc.) at a volume increases your profitability, as volume buy drives costs down.

EXPENSES (% OF ANNUAL SALES)

Cost of Goods	25%
Occupancy Costs	10%
Payroll/Labor Costs.	35%

QUESTIONS

- How easy or difficult has it been to hire the production labor? What's your turnover rate in this area? Do you do the sales? Are you in the production area or are you in the delivery area? How many vendors do you have to source the materials?
- What does the current owner do: production, or marketing and sales area? Is there a sales model in place that has been successful? How diverse is the customer base? If they are working with only 3 or 4 construction companies that do new builds, it could pose a risk; a diverse customer base is ideal.

EXPERT COMMENTS

Pricing the business accordingly will help sell the business quickly. A seller asking or waiting for a premium price might be coached to be prepared to get to closing. If the transaction is franchise resale, obtain and find out the resale process from the franchisor early in the process.

Barriers to entry could be difficult unless someone has previous experience and a good handle on sales and marketing. Once established, it could be on autopilot as long as an ongoing marketing campaign is established. This industry sector is attractive to previous corporate executives and managers who have a penchant for light manufacturing operations.

FINANCING

A high percentage will be eligible for SBA financing, so most owners/sellers are able to walk away with a good amount of cash at closing. Seller financing 10 percent at a minimum.

Manufacturing: Wood Office Furniture

| NAICS 337211 | SIC 2499-02

Rules of Thumb

- 2.5–3 x SDE includes inventory
- 2.5–3 x EBITDA
- 35% annual sales includes inventory

INDUSTRY MULTIPLES

Acquisition multiples below are calculated medians using US private industry transactions. Data updated annually. Last update: August 2023.

VALUATION MULTIPLE (MEDIAN VALUE)

UNDER $1 MILLION NET SALES	N/A
$1 MILLION–$5 MILLION NET SALES	
MVIC/Net Sales.	0.71
MVIC/Gross Profit	1.61
MVIC/SDE	3.98
MVIC/EBITDA	6.94
OVER $5 MILLION NET SALES	
MVIC/Net Sales.	0.58
MVIC/Gross Profit	1.68
MVIC/SDE	N/A
MVIC/EBITDA	N/A

Source: DealStats (formerly Pratt's Stats), 2023 (Portland, OR: Business Valuation Resources, LLC), www.bvresources.com/dealstats

PRICING TIPS

Contracts are rare in the industry but client relationships are important.
We would look at the percentage of sales to the largest clients. The value of the business increases with more dispersed clients rather than a few large clients.

Very cyclical business

BENCHMARK DATA

COGS below 30%

EXPENSES (% OF ANNUAL SALES)

Cost of Goods 40%
Occupancy Costs . . . . . 15% to 20%
Payroll/Labor Costs. . . . . 20% to 30%
Profit (pretax) . . . . . . 15% to 25%

QUESTIONS

- Look to see the client distribution of work. You'd like to see how many clients they have and the percentage distribution of work.
- How much design work? Fashion trends?

EXPERT COMMENTS

This is clearly a niche industry which requires creative employees. Once established, the base of creative employees takes a long time to duplicate, therefore the low competition.

Really depends where you are on the food chain; these vary from high- to low-margin businesses.

FINANCING

Seller financing for the business and outside financing for the real estate

RESOURCES

- BIFMA—Business + Institutional Furniture Manufacturers Association: https://www.bifma.org

Manufacturing: Wood Products

| NAICS 321912

Rules of Thumb

- 10 x SDE

INDUSTRY MULTIPLES

Acquisition multiples below are calculated medians using US private industry transactions. Data updated annually. Last update: August 2023.

VALUATION MULTIPLE (MEDIAN VALUE)

UNDER $1 MILLION NET SALES	N/A
$1 MILLION–$5 MILLION NET SALES	
MVIC/Net Sales. 0.24
MVIC/Gross Profit 0.50
MVIC/SDE 1.45
MVIC/EBITDA 3.12
OVER $5 MILLION NET SALES	N/A

Source: DealStats (formerly Pratt's Stats), 2023 (Portland, OR: Business Valuation Resources, LLC), www.bvresources.com/dealstats

M

PRICING TIPS

This is a very cyclical industry. Pricing depends on the competition within the wood basket, price of timber and lumber, annual MMBF produced, state of the equipment, and the strategic plan of the acquiring entity.

EXPENSES (% OF ANNUAL SALES)

Cost of Goods	60%
Occupancy Costs	10%
Payroll/Labor Costs.	15%
Profit (pretax)	.8%

INDUSTRY TREND

Wood products is a leading indicator for the economy, so when prices and demand fall, a recession will occur within 3 to 5 months.

EXPERT COMMENTS

Fluctuations could last for multiple quarters, making this a bad industry for the faint of heart and the capitally challenged investor/buyer.

FINANCING

Outside financing. Public corporations may pay cash.

RESOURCES

- AWC—American Wood Council: https://awc.org
- Timber Processing: https://www.timberprocessing.com
- WWPA—Western Wood Products Association: https://wwpa.org

Marco's Pizza (Franchise)

| NAICS 722513 | Businesses/Units 998

INDUSTRY MULTIPLES

Acquisition multiples below are calculated medians using US private industry transactions. Data updated annually. Last update: August 2023.

VALUATION MULTIPLE (MEDIAN VALUE)

UNDER $1 MILLION NET SALES	
MVIC/Net Sales.	0.31
MVIC/Gross Profit	0.48
MVIC/SDE	1.67
MVIC/EBITDA	2.21
$1 MILLION–$5 MILLION NET SALES	
MVIC/Net Sales.	0.39
MVIC/Gross Profit	0.60
MVIC/SDE	2.43
MVIC/EBITDA	2.98
OVER $5 MILLION NET SALES	
MVIC/Net Sales.	0.89
MVIC/Gross Profit	2.08
MVIC/SDE	4.98
MVIC/EBITDA	12.81

Source: DealStats (formerly Pratt's Stats), 2023 (Portland, OR: Business Valuation Resources, LLC), www.bvresources.com/dealstats

Approx. Total Investment: $286,852 to $805,927

RESOURCES

- Marco's Pizza: https://www.marcos.com
- Franchise information: https://www.marcos.com/franchising/

Margarine & Cooking Oil Processing

| NAICS 31122 | Businesses/Units 420

| Profit $4.1 B | Wages $2.4 B | Annual Growth Future 0.2%

                                             | Annual Growth Past 5.5%

INDUSTRY MULTIPLES

Acquisition multiples below are calculated medians using US private industry transactions. Data updated annually. Last update: August 2023.

VALUATION MULTIPLE (MEDIAN VALUE)

UNDER $1 MILLION NET SALES

MVIC/Net Sales	0.49
MVIC/Gross Profit	0.49
MVIC/SDE	N/A
MVIC/EBITDA	3.52

$1 MILLION–$5 MILLION NET SALES   N/A

OVER $5 MILLION NET SALES

MVIC/Net Sales	0.91
MVIC/Gross Profit	5.26
MVIC/SDE	N/A
MVIC/EBITDA	9.29

Source: DealStats (formerly Pratt's Stats), 2023 (Portland, OR: Business Valuation Resources, LLC), www.bvresources.com/dealstats

BENCHMARK DATA

STATISTICS (MARGARINE & COOKING OIL PROCESSING)

Number of Establishments	420
Average Profit Margin	4.6%
Revenue per Employee	$2,934,312
Average Number of Employees	72.0
Average Wages per Employee	$79,239

PRODUCTS AND SERVICES SEGMENTATION

Soybean cake and meal	32.6%
Other	20.4%
Soybean oil	15.3%
Fats and oils refining and blending	13.2%
Wet corn milling	12.4%
Other oilseed mill products	6.1%

MAJOR MARKET SEGMENTATION

Food service providers	48.5%
Food manufacturers	25.0%
Grocery retailers	19.8%
Grocery wholesalers	6.7%

Profit	4.6%
Wages	2.7%
Purchases	79.2%
Depreciation	1.3%
Marketing	0.0%
Rent & Utilities	2.0%
Other	10.2%

INDUSTRY TREND

"Margarine and cooking oil processors must adapt to changing consumer preferences. Processors have emphasized healthier cooking oils, like olive and avocado oil. The industry will continue to face strong price and product competition from foreign processors. Foreign producers dominate palm and olive oil production, two increasingly popular cooking oil and margarine options."

Source: IBISWorld Key Takeaways

RESOURCES

- IBISWorld, April 2023: https://www.ibisworld.com

Marijuana Stores

| NAICS 453998

Rules of Thumb

- 5 x SDE

INDUSTRY MULTIPLES

Acquisition multiples below are calculated medians using US private industry transactions. Data updated annually. Last update: August 2023.

VALUATION MULTIPLE (MEDIAN VALUE)

UNDER $1 MILLION NET SALES	
MVIC/Net Sales	0.54
MVIC/Gross Profit	0.90
MVIC/SDE	2.34
MVIC/EBITDA	3.10

$1 MILLION–$5 MILLION NET SALES	
MVIC/Net Sales	0.50
MVIC/Gross Profit	0.99
MVIC/SDE	2.69
MVIC/EBITDA	4.11

OVER $5 MILLION NET SALES	
MVIC/Net Sales	1.29
MVIC/Gross Profit	3.18
MVIC/SDE	1.91
MVIC/EBITDA	10.61

Source: DealStats (formerly Pratt's Stats), 2023 (Portland, OR: Business Valuation Resources, LLC), www.bvresources.com/dealstats

PRICING TIPS

Regulations for the location of the dispensary are very important factors to consider. Keeping a cash record book is essential, since most of the sales are cash sales.

BENCHMARK DATA

Ideally $40 per sale is a good benchmark.

EXPENSES (% OF ANNUAL SALES)

Cost of Goods	40% to 50%
Occupancy Costs	05% to 15%
Payroll/Labor Costs.	10% to 20%
Profit (pretax)	25% to 30%

QUESTIONS

• How good are your records? Can you prove your numbers?

INDUSTRY TREND

The industry is very fragmented because of state regulations.

This would be state specific, but I would imagine a flood of participants into the market over the next few years, which will result in competition in pricing and eventual market consolidation.

EXPERT COMMENTS

Local regulations are important to understand, as a buyer should look for cities that will limit the number of licenses and be least burdensome with taxes and regulations. Just as importantly, will the local government actively shut down illegal dispensaries?

FINANCING

Seller financing and cash, as institutional money are nonexistent, and hard money loans have high rates.

RESOURCES

• CCIA—California Cannabis Industry Association: https://www.cacannabisindustry.org
• CCMA—California Cannabis Manufacturers Association: https://cannabismanufacturers.org
• NCIA—The National Cannabis Industry Association: https://thecannabisindustry.org
• SCC—Southern California Coalition: https://southerncaliforniacoalition.com

Marinas

NAICS 713930	SIC 4493-06	Businesses/Units 9,767
Profit $1.2 B	Wages $1.5 B	Annual Growth Future 1.0%
		Annual Growth Past 0.7%

Rules of Thumb

• 10–12 x SDE plus inventory
• 10 x EBIT
• 11–12 x EBITDA

INDUSTRY MULTIPLES

Acquisition multiples below are calculated medians using US private industry transactions. Data updated annually. Last update: August 2023.

VALUATION MULTIPLE (MEDIAN VALUE)

UNDER $1 MILLION NET SALES

MVIC/Net Sales	1.91
MVIC/Gross Profit	2.93
MVIC/SDE	3.50
MVIC/EBITDA	5.59

$1 MILLION–$5 MILLION NET SALES

MVIC/Net Sales	2.86
MVIC/Gross Profit	3.58
MVIC/SDE	15.19
MVIC/EBITDA	25.28

OVER $5 MILLION NET SALES

MVIC/Net Sales	6.48
MVIC/Gross Profit	9.43
MVIC/SDE	N/A
MVIC/EBITDA	N/A

Source: DealStats (formerly Pratt's Stats), 2023 (Portland, OR: Business Valuation Resources, LLC), www.bvresources.com/dealstats

PRICING TIPS

This is a very complicated business. Estimating the selling price has many factors, such as dock leases, leases with resorts, years of operation, strength of midlevel management, survey of the vessels, competition, market, etc. Bottom line, it would be foolish to use a multiplier without a great deal of study.

BENCHMARK DATA

STATISTICS (MARINAS)

Number of Establishments	9,767
Average Profit Margin	18.2%
Revenue per Employee	$187,181
Average Number of Employees	3.6
Average Wages per Employee	$42,524

PRODUCTS AND SERVICES SEGMENTATION

Pleasure craft docking, launching, storage and utilities services	51.0%
Fuel and merchandise sales	17.3%
Repairs and maintenance services	13.5%
Other	9.7%
Food and beverage sales	8.5%

INDUSTRY COSTS

Profit	18.2%
Wages	22.8%
Purchases	4.8%
Depreciation	8.7%
Marketing	3.2%
Rent & Utilities	9.6%
Other	32.6%

A marina is usually a combination of many businesses, each with its own benchmarks. You have a storage business, a service business, a gas station, boat sales, brokerage sales and sometimes a restaurant, all with different rules of thumb.

Slip rental income and storage fees should cover 100 percent of debt service. Owner compensation and other benefits would come from sales and service charges and appreciation of real estate value(s).

EXPENSES (% OF ANNUAL SALES)

Cost of Goods	60% to 65%
Occupancy Costs	05% to 12%

Payroll/Labor Costs. 20%
Profit (pretax) . . . . . . 05% to 10%

M

QUESTIONS

- Be ready for a lot of hard work. Ask about environmental history. Be careful of new boat sales as the floor plans/interest thereon will eat you up. Competition results in razor thin margins. Stick to brokerage if possible.
- Why are you selling? Are you environmentally clean? What would you do differently if you were starting again?

INDUSTRY TREND

"Marinas sail along with increasing revenue regardless of COVID-19. Marinas will fully recover from pandemic-related losses in 2023 as economic conditions improve. Marinas based in highly populated areas have to offer additional services. There are naturally more establishments near population-dense regions, forcing marinas in the area to improve the customer experience."

Source: IBISWorld Key Takeaways

EXPERT COMMENTS

It is a tourist-related industry. If the location requires costly travel and the economy is soft, the sales will be down.

Location and facilities are critical but vary greatly.

FINANCING

It is extremely difficult to obtain bank financing, since the assets can literally float away. Large down payments and seller's financing are the rules.

RESOURCES

- IBISWorld, September 2023: https://www.ibisworld.com
- ABBRA—American Boat Builders & Repairers Association: https://www.abbra.org
- AMI—Association of Marina Industries: https://marinaassociation.org
- BoatUS—Boat Owners Association of The United States: https://www.boatus.com
- NMMA—National Marine Manufacturers Association: https://www.nmma.org

Marine/Yacht Services (Boat/Repair)

| NAICS 44122 | | Businesses/Units 97,236 | |

| Profit $2.4 B | | Wages $3.6 B | | Annual Growth Future 1.4% |

| | | | | Annual Growth Past 5.0% |

Rules of Thumb

- 100% annual sales includes inventory
- 2.3 x SDE includes inventory

INDUSTRY MULTIPLES

Acquisition multiples below are calculated medians using US private industry transactions. Data updated annually. Last update: August 2023.

VALUATION MULTIPLE (MEDIAN VALUE)

UNDER $1 MILLION NET SALES

MVIC/Net Sales	0.43
MVIC/Gross Profit	0.86
MVIC/SDE	2.22
MVIC/EBITDA	2.51

$1 MILLION–$5 MILLION NET SALES

MVIC/Net Sales	0.27
MVIC/Gross Profit	1.07
MVIC/SDE	2.47
MVIC/EBITDA	3.68

OVER $5 MILLION NET SALES

MVIC/Net Sales	0.36
MVIC/Gross Profit	1.27
MVIC/SDE	3.51
MVIC/EBITDA	4.38

Source: DealStats (formerly Pratt's Stats), 2023 (Portland, OR: Business Valuation Resources, LLC), www.bvresources.com/dealstats

PRICING TIPS

Determine value of furniture, fixtures, and equipment. Any warranty work involved?

BENCHMARK DATA

STATISTICS (BOAT DEALERSHIP AND REPAIR)

Number of Establishments	99,528
Average Profit Margin	6.9%
Revenue per Employee	$245,425
Average Number of Employees	1.5
Average Wages per Employee	$25,554

PRODUCTS AND SERVICES SEGMENTATION

New boats	69.5%
Parts and repair services	16.1%
Used boats	14.4%

INDUSTRY COSTS

Profit	6.9%
Wages	10.4%
Purchases	70.0%
Depreciation	1.0%
Marketing	0.8%
Rent & Utilities	1.1%
Other	9.8%

MARKET SHARE

MarineMax, Inc.	5.7%
BPS Direct LLC	2.4%

EXPENSES (% OF ANNUAL SALES)

Cost of Goods	30%
Occupancy Costs	07%
Payroll/Labor Costs	15%
Profit (pretax)	40%

QUESTIONS

- Customer base, length of time in industry, employee turnover, specific services performed

INDUSTRY TREND

"COVID-19 benefited boat dealerships. Boat sales increased in 2020 as consumers could participate in boating activities despite social distancing restrictions. Boat rental companies will threaten sales. Boat rental companies are increasingly popular since consumers do not have to commit to purchasing and storing a boat."

Source: IBISWorld Key Takeaways

RESOURCES

• IBISWorld, January 2023: https://www.ibisworld.com

Massage Envy (Franchise)

| NAICS 812199 | Businesses/Units 1,103

INDUSTRY MULTIPLES

Acquisition multiples below are calculated medians using US private industry transactions. Data updated annually. Last update: August 2023.

VALUATION MULTIPLE (MEDIAN VALUE)

UNDER $1 MILLION NET SALES	
MVIC/Net Sales	0.43
MVIC/Gross Profit	0.56
MVIC/SDE	1.79
MVIC/EBITDA	2.65
$1 MILLION–$5 MILLION NET SALES	
MVIC/Net Sales	0.43
MVIC/Gross Profit	0.59
MVIC/SDE	2.90
MVIC/EBITDA	5.02
OVER $5 MILLION NET SALES	
MVIC/Net Sales	1.13
MVIC/Gross Profit	3.93
MVIC/SDE	N/A
MVIC/EBITDA	N/A

Source: DealStats (formerly Pratt's Stats), 2023 (Portland, OR: Business Valuation Resources, LLC), www.bvresources.com/dealstats

PRICING TIPS

Approx. Total Investment: $614,850 to $927,000

RESOURCES

• Massage Envy: https://www.massageenvy.com
• Franchise information:
  https://www.massageenvy.com/about-us/own-a-franchise
• AMTA—American Massage Therapy Association:
  https://www.amtamassage.org

Massage Heights (Franchise)

| NAICS 812199 | Businesses/Units 105

INDUSTRY MULTIPLES

Acquisition multiples below are calculated medians using US private industry transactions. Data updated annually. Last update: August 2023.

VALUATION MULTIPLE (MEDIAN VALUE)

UNDER $1 MILLION NET SALES

MVIC/Net Sales.	0.43
MVIC/Gross Profit	0.56
MVIC/SDE	1.79
MVIC/EBITDA	2.65

$1 MILLION–$5 MILLION NET SALES

MVIC/Net Sales.	0.43
MVIC/Gross Profit	0.59
MVIC/SDE	2.90
MVIC/EBITDA	5.02

OVER $5 MILLION NET SALES

MVIC/Net Sales.	1.13
MVIC/Gross Profit	3.93
MVIC/SDE	N/A
MVIC/EBITDA	N/A

Source: DealStats (formerly Pratt's Stats), 2023 (Portland, OR: Business Valuation Resources, LLC), www.bvresources.com/dealstats

PRICING TIPS

Approx. Total Investment: $452,443 to $532,221

RESOURCES

- Massage Heights: https://www.massageheights.com
- Franchise information: https://www.massageheightsfranchise.com
- AMTA—American Massage Therapy Association: https://www.amtamassage.org

Mattress Manufacturing

| NAICS 337910 | Businesses/Units 422

| Profit $277.8 M | Wages $1.2 B | Annual Growth Future 4.1%

| Annual Growth Past -1.6%

INDUSTRY MULTIPLES

Acquisition multiples below are calculated medians using US private industry transactions. Data updated annually. Last update: August 2023.

VALUATION MULTIPLE (MEDIAN VALUE)

UNDER $1 MILLION NET SALES	N/A

$1 MILLION–$5 MILLION NET SALES

MVIC/Net Sales.	0.92
MVIC/Gross Profit	1.01
MVIC/SDE	2.25
MVIC/EBITDA	7.01

OVER $5 MILLION NET SALES

MVIC/Net Sales.	0.85
MVIC/Gross Profit	1.92
MVIC/SDE	N/A
MVIC/EBITDA	10.38

Source: DealStats (formerly Pratt's Stats), 2023 (Portland, OR: Business Valuation Resources, LLC), www.bvresources.com/dealstats

BENCHMARK DATA

STATISTICS (MATTRESS MANUFACTURING)

Number of Establishments	422
Average Profit Margin	3.4%
Revenue per Employee	$356,367
Average Number of Employees	59.2
Average Wages per Employee	$53,119

PRODUCTS AND SERVICES SEGMENTATION

Innerspring mattresses	66.9%
Other mattresses	21.0%
Foundations and bases	12.1%

MAJOR MARKET SEGMENTATION

Specialty bedding stores	30.7%
Furniture stores	21.7%
General retail stores	14.1%
Direct to consumer	12.1%
Accommodation sector	10.9%
Other	5.6%
Exports	2.8%
Healthcare sector	2.1%

INDUSTRY COSTS

Profit	3.4%
Wages	15.0%
Purchases	52.2%
Depreciation	0.9%
Marketing	2.0%
Rent & Utilities	2.1%
Other	24.5%

MARKET SHARE

Tempur Sealy International, Inc.	39.1%
Serta Simmons Bedding, LLC	21.1%
Sleep Number Corporation	9.6%
Casper Sleep Inc.	4.3%

INDUSTRY TREND

"Product innovation drove growth as consumer preferences shifted to high-quality mattresses. Companies innovated and created new products to remain competitive and differentiate themselves. Direct-to-consumer sales will spur growth by offering customers convenience. E-commerce sales and companies operating their own retail outlets will drive growth."

Source: IBISWorld Key Takeaways

RESOURCES

- IBISWorld, September 2023: https://www.ibisworld.com

McDonald's (Franchise)

| NAICS 722513 | Businesses/Units 12,772

Rules of Thumb

- 40% annual sales

Acquisition multiples below are calculated medians using US private industry transactions. Data updated annually. Last update: August 2023.

VALUATION MULTIPLE (MEDIAN VALUE)

UNDER $1 MILLION NET SALES	N/A
$1 MILLION–$5 MILLION NET SALES	
MVIC/Net Sales	0.39
MVIC/Gross Profit	0.60
MVIC/SDE	2.43
MVIC/EBITDA	2.98
OVER $5 MILLION NET SALES	
MVIC/Net Sales	0.89
MVIC/Gross Profit	2.08
MVIC/SDE	4.98
MVIC/EBITDA	12.81

Source: DealStats (formerly Pratt's Stats), 2023 (Portland, OR: Business Valuation Resources, LLC), www.bvresources.com/dealstats

PRICING TIPS

Approx. Total Investment: $1,366,000 to $2,450,000

RESOURCES

- McDonald's: https://www.mcdonalds.com/us/en-us.html
- Franchise information: https://www.mcdonalds.com/us/en-us/us-franchising.html

Meat and Meat Product Merchant Wholesalers

| NAICS 424470 | Businesses/Units 6,375

| Profit $15.4 B | Wages $27.8 B | Annual Growth Future 0.3%

| | | Annual Growth Past 2.6%

INDUSTRY MULTIPLES

Acquisition multiples below are calculated medians using US private industry transactions. Data updated annually. Last update: August 2023.

VALUATION MULTIPLE (MEDIAN VALUE)

UNDER $1 MILLION NET SALES	
MVIC/Net Sales	0.38
MVIC/Gross Profit	1.68
MVIC/SDE	3.12
MVIC/EBITDA	6.76
$1 MILLION–$5 MILLION NET SALES	
MVIC/Net Sales	0.25
MVIC/Gross Profit	1.95
MVIC/SDE	5.78
MVIC/EBITDA	9.59
OVER $5 MILLION NET SALES	
MVIC/Net Sales	0.19
MVIC/Gross Profit	1.08
MVIC/SDE	3.53
MVIC/EBITDA	4.41

Source: DealStats (formerly Pratt's Stats), 2023 (Portland, OR: Business Valuation Resources, LLC), www.bvresources.com/dealstats

BENCHMARK DATA

STATISTICS (MEAT, BEEF & POULTRY PROCESSING)

Number of Establishments .	6,375
Average Profit Margin .	5.2%
Revenue per Employee .	$509,728
Average Number of Employees.	91.9
Average Wages per Employee .	$47,953

PRODUCTS AND SERVICES SEGMENTATION

Slaughtered animal products (except poultry) .	39.4%
Poultry .	32.6%
Processed meats	25.7%
Meat byproducts	2.3%

MAJOR MARKET SEGMENTATION

Beef and pork wholesalers .	52.9%
Animal feed manufacturers.	26.1%
Frozen food production .	12.1%
Poultry wholesalers.	6.0%
Meat markets	2.9%

INDUSTRY COSTS

Profit	5.2%
Wages .	9.4%
Purchases .	0.0%
Depreciation	1.6%
Marketing	0.0%
Rent & Utilities .	0.0%
Other	83.9%

MARKET SHARE

JBS USA Holdings .	15.7%
Tyson Foods, Inc.	11.8%
Cargill, Incorporated	7.8%
Smithfield Foods Inc.	5.4%
Hormel Foods Corporation .	1.8%

INDUSTRY TREND

"Revenue jumped following COVID-19. Surging feed prices led to elevated red meat prices, which solid disposable income helped consumers afford. The high consolidation and vertical integration of the industry allowed processors to use this boon to boost profit. Trade activity has increased, especially to China as their farmers and processors dealt with a severe outbreak of the African Swine Flu and intense drought. The industry's position as a food provider secured revenue during the pandemic, and the drops in consumer confidence didn't translate to decreased spending on high-quality meat products."

Source: IBISWorld Key Takeaways

RESOURCES

• IBISWorld, September 2023: https://www.ibisworld.com

Meat Markets

| NAICS 44521 | SIC 5421-07	| Businesses/Units 9,081	
| Profit $343.9 M | Wages $1.3 B	| Annual Growth Future 0.2%	
	| Annual Growth Past 0.8%	

Rules of Thumb

- 40% annual sales plus inventory
- 2.5 x SDE includes inventory
- 5 x monthly sales plus inventory

INDUSTRY MULTIPLES

Acquisition multiples below are calculated medians using US private industry transactions. Data updated annually. Last update: August 2023.

VALUATION MULTIPLE (MEDIAN VALUE)

UNDER $1 MILLION NET SALES

MVIC/Net Sales.	0.27
MVIC/Gross Profit	0.61
MVIC/SDE	1.70
MVIC/EBITDA	3.01

$1 MILLION–$5 MILLION NET SALES

MVIC/Net Sales.	0.29
MVIC/Gross Profit	0.48
MVIC/SDE	2.05
MVIC/EBITDA	2.00

OVER $5 MILLION NET SALES

MVIC/Net Sales.	0.27
MVIC/Gross Profit	0.68
MVIC/SDE	4.42
MVIC/EBITDA	1.89

Source: DealStats (formerly Pratt's Stats), 2023 (Portland, OR: Business Valuation Resources, LLC), www.bvresources.com/dealstats

BENCHMARK DATA

STATISTICS (MEAT MARKETS)

Number of Establishments .	9,081
Average Profit Margin	3.7%
Revenue per Employee .	$207,032
Average Number of Employees.	5.2
Average Wages per Employee .	$28,343

PRODUCTS AND SERVICES SEGMENTATION

Beef .	32.1%
Other meats.	25.7%
Other products .	16.5%
Chicken .	15.0%
Pork .	8.0%
Turkey	2.7%

INDUSTRY COSTS

Profit	3.7%
Wages	13.7%
Purchases	63.0%
Depreciation	1.5%
Marketing	0.6%
Rent & Utilities .	2.6%
Other	14.8%

EXPENSES (% OF ANNUAL SALES)

Cost of Goods	50%
Occupancy Costs	10%
Payroll/Labor Costs.	15%
Profit (pretax)	15%

INDUSTRY TREND

"Value-added meat products are driving growth for butchers and delicatessens. A growing immigrant community and an expansion of time-poor consumers is prompting meat markets to offer more premarinated, preseasoned and uncommon cuts of meat. COVID-19 shifted consumer preferences to locally-sourced meat. Health concerns amid the pandemic boosted demand for high-quality, organic and fresh meat products. The pandemic also prompted consumers to support local businesses."

Source: IBISWorld Key Takeaways

RESOURCES

- IBISWorld, March 2023: https://www.ibisworld.com
- Beef.org: https://www.beef.org
- NAMI—North American Meat Institute: https://www.meatinstitute.org
- NCBA—National Cattlemen's Beef Association: https://www.ncba.org

Meat, Beef & Poultry Processing

NAICS 31161		Businesses/Units 6,375	
Profit $15.4 B		Wages $27.8 B		Annual Growth Future 0.3%
				Annual Growth Past 2.6%

INDUSTRY MULTIPLES

Acquisition multiples below are calculated medians using US private industry transactions. Data updated annually. Last update: August 2023.

VALUATION MULTIPLE (MEDIAN VALUE)

UNDER $1 MILLION NET SALES
MVIC/Net Sales	0.77
MVIC/Gross Profit	1.32
MVIC/SDE	2.60
MVIC/EBITDA	3.67

$1 MILLION–$5 MILLION NET SALES
MVIC/Net Sales	0.42
MVIC/Gross Profit	0.98
MVIC/SDE	2.50
MVIC/EBITDA	6.51

OVER $5 MILLION NET SALES
MVIC/Net Sales	0.38
MVIC/Gross Profit	4.01
MVIC/SDE	3.16
MVIC/EBITDA	10.28

Source: DealStats (formerly Pratt's Stats), 2023 (Portland, OR: Business Valuation Resources, LLC), www.bvresources.com/dealstats

BENCHMARK DATA

STATISTICS (MEAT, BEEF & POULTRY PROCESSING)
Number of Establishments	6,375
Average Profit Margin	5.2%
Revenue per Employee	$509,728
Average Number of Employees	91.9
Average Wages per Employee	$47,953

PRODUCTS AND SERVICES SEGMENTATION

Slaughtered animal products (except poultry) 39.4%
Poultry 32.6%
Processed meats 25.7%
Meat byproducts 2.3%

MAJOR MARKET SEGMENTATION

Beef and pork wholesalers 52.9%
Animal feed manufacturers. 26.1%
Frozen food production. 12.1%
Poultry wholesalers. 6.0%
Meat markets 2.9%

INDUSTRY COSTS

Profit 5.2%
Wages 9.4%
Purchases 0.0%
Depreciation 1.6%
Marketing 0.0%
Rent & Utilities 0.0%
Other 83.9%

INDUSTRY TREND

"Revenue jumped following COVID-19. Surging feed prices led to elevated red meat prices, which solid disposable income helped consumers afford. The high consolidation and vertical integration of the industry allowed processors to use this boon to boost profit. Trade activity has increased, especially to China as their farmers and processors dealt with a severe outbreak of the African Swine Flu and intense drought. The industry's position as a food provider secured revenue during the pandemic, and the drops in consumer confidence didn't translate to decreased spending on high-quality meat products."

Source: IBISWorld Key Takeaways

RESOURCES

• IBISWorld, September 2023: https://www.ibisworld.com

Medical and Diagnostic Laboratories

| NAICS 621511 | Businesses/Units 36,881

| Profit $14.2 B | Wages $23.1 B | Annual Growth Future 2.4%

| Annual Growth Past 2.4%

Rules of Thumb

• 100%–125% annual gross sales
• 3–5 x SDE plus inventory
• 4–5 x EBIT
• 4–5 x EBITDA

INDUSTRY MULTIPLES

Acquisition multiples below are calculated medians using US private industry transactions. Data updated annually. Last update: August 2023.

M

UNDER $1 MILLION NET SALES

MVIC/Net Sales.	0.69
MVIC/Gross Profit	0.71
MVIC/SDE	1.79
MVIC/EBITDA	4.48

$1 MILLION–$5 MILLION NET SALES

MVIC/Net Sales.	0.90
MVIC/Gross Profit	1.04
MVIC/SDE	3.37
MVIC/EBITDA	5.06

OVER $5 MILLION NET SALES

MVIC/Net Sales.	2.17
MVIC/Gross Profit	3.94
MVIC/SDE	13.31
MVIC/EBITDA	14.96

Source: DealStats (formerly Pratt's Stats), 2023 (Portland, OR: Business Valuation Resources, LLC), www.bvresources.com/dealstats

PRICING TIPS

Good diversity of accounts, good third-party payer contracts a must

Multiple of SDE increases with profit levels.

BENCHMARK DATA

STATISTICS (DIAGNOSTIC & MEDICAL LABORATORIES)

Number of Establishments .	36,881
Average Profit Margin	18.9%
Revenue per Employee .	$235,235
Average Number of Employees.	8.8
Average Wages per Employee .	$72,469

PRODUCTS AND SERVICES SEGMENTATION

General pathology services.	36.8%
Clinical pathology services .	18.6%
Other	17.5%
X-ray/radiography imaging .	10.3%
MRI imaging	10.0%
Anatomic pathology services	6.8%

MAJOR MARKET SEGMENTATION

Private insurance payments	39.6%
Medicare and Medicaid payments .	19.2%
Payments from healthcare providers	18.4%
Other	12.2%
Patient out-of-pocket	10.6%

INDUSTRY COSTS

Profit	18.9%
Wages	30.9%
Purchases	11.6%
Depreciation	4.6%
Marketing	0.6%
Rent & Utilities	4.6%
Other	28.8%

MARKET SHARE

Quest Diagnostics Inc. .	14.5%
Laboratory Corporation of America Holdings	12.9%
Roche Holding AG	2.8%
OPKO Health, Inc.	1.1%

EXPENSES (% OF ANNUAL SALES)

Cost of Goods	13% to 20%
Occupancy Costs	03%
Payroll/Labor Costs.	44% to 45%
Profit (pretax)	30% to 35%

INDUSTRY TREND

"Advances in medical technologies have posed a competitive threat to laboratories. Particularly, point-of-care testing has allowed hospitals to perform their own tests, avoiding medical laboratories. The healthcare sector will see a trend of consolidation among insurance plans. This will give them more bargaining power to negotiate fee arrangements with healthcare providers, including laboratories."

Source: IBISWorld Key Takeaways

EXPERT COMMENTS

It would take over four years to replicate a new diagnostic clinic and that long to obtain a good strong client base.

Difficult to acquire accounts since physician groups don't like to make changes. Third-party payer contracts are difficult to obtain.

This is a marketing business. Location, ease of service, and networking with doctors and attorneys are musts.

FINANCING

Outside financing

RESOURCES

- IBISWorld, September 2023: https://www.ibisworld.com
- Dark Daily: https://www.darkdaily.com
- Diagnostics World: https://www.diagnosticsworldnews.com
- LabMedica: https://www.labmedica.com/industry-news/

Medical Billing

NAICS 541219	Businesses/Units 3,398	
Profit $746 M	Wages $931.2 M	Annual Growth Future 3.0%
		Annual Growth Past 2.1%

Rules of Thumb

- 100%–150% annual sales plus inventory
- 2.5–4 x SDE
- 3–5 x EBIT
- 3–5 x EBITDA

INDUSTRY MULTIPLES

Acquisition multiples below are calculated medians using US private industry transactions. Data updated annually. Last update: August 2023.

VALUATION MULTIPLE (MEDIAN VALUE)

UNDER $1 MILLION NET SALES

MVIC/Net Sales.	0.85
MVIC/Gross Profit	0.85

M

MVIC/SDE	2.22
MVIC/EBITDA	4.32

$1 MILLION–$5 MILLION NET SALES

MVIC/Net Sales	0.97
MVIC/Gross Profit	1.10
MVIC/SDE	3.54
MVIC/EBITDA	4.21

OVER $5 MILLION NET SALES

MVIC/Net Sales	1.33
MVIC/Gross Profit	1.97
MVIC/SDE	N/A
MVIC/EBITDA	N/A

Source: DealStats (formerly Pratt's Stats), 2023 (Portland, OR: Business Valuation Resources, LLC), www.bvresources.com/dealstats

PRICING TIPS

Review customer concentration and length of their relationship with the medical billing company.

Medical billing valuations vary with size of the company, breadth of practice base, collection rate, and growth.

BENCHMARK DATA

STATISTICS (MEDICAL CLAIMS PROCESSING SERVICES)

Number of Establishments	3,398
Average Profit Margin	15.2%
Revenue per Employee	$399,364
Average Number of Employees	3.7
Average Wages per Employee	$76,948

PRODUCTS AND SERVICES SEGMENTATION

Claims processing	48.1%
Policy and claims examinations	22.2%
Claims investigations	21.6%
Back-office, administrative support and consulting	8.1%

MAJOR MARKET SEGMENTATION

Healthcare providers	52.5%
Private insurers	28.7%
Government insurers	18.8%

INDUSTRY COSTS

Profit	15.2%
Wages	19.0%
Purchases	3.6%
Depreciation	3.6%
Marketing	2.2%
Rent & Utilities	2.0%
Other	54.5%

MARKET SHARE

HMS Holdings Corp.	15.5%
Aon PLC	6.6%

This industry is a labor-heavy business model. There is not a conventional COGS with material cost. Facility costs have declined as many staff still are working at home post-Covid. This is an overhead reduction event for medical billing owners.

Revenues per employee range from $150 to $200,000.

Occupancy Costs . . . . . .0% to 06%
Payroll/Labor Costs. . . . . 25% to 35%
Profit (pretax) . . . . . . 15% to 30%

QUESTIONS

- How long have top twenty accounts been with company? What are the areas of medical practice focus? Rank them. Where has the growth come from? Rank them. Review any business plan for one year out.
- How many practices constituted 50 percent of your revenues? Who is the interface with the client, and do they meet on a schedule basis with clients?
- Buyers most commonly ask why a seller is looking to sell and what impact the current economic conditions have had on operations.

INDUSTRY TREND

Consolidation, driven by regional strategic buyers as well as private equity

High demand for medical billing as industry consolidation, as well as private equity groups targeting this type of revenue cycle management (RCM) business, are driving deal flow and supporting higher multiples. Medical billing works well with consolidation strategies as well as work from home models.

"Economic and demographic forces are increasing the volume of medical claims. Expanding medical needs of an aging population push more healthcare providers to outsource costly and complex medical claims. Consolidation characterizing the broader health sector is challenging medical claims processing companies. Larger health systems can keep claims in-house, making it difficult for companies to acquire customers in an already competitive environment."

Source: IBISWorld Key Takeaways

EXPERT COMMENTS

Profile the competitive market within sixty miles of the to-be-acquired company.

Create a spreadsheet detailing practices, number of medical professionals per practice, type of practice, location, collection rate, annual revenues over the past three years, and software utilized.

A barrier to entry for medical billing start-ups is the time-consuming task of developing a large enough quantity of practices to be profitable.

FINANCING

Outside financing by credit-strong companies. Few assets, so cash and industry experience are essential.

Seller financing generally not needed. Conventional lending common.

RESOURCES

- IBISWorld, April 2023: https://www.ibisworld.com
- First Choice Business Brokers, medical billing sales and acquisitions: http://www.medicalbillingbrokers.com/
- HBMA—Healthcare Business Management Association: https://www.hbma.org
- American Medical Billing Association: https://www.americanmedicalbillingassociation.com

Medical Device Manufacturing

| NAICS 33451 | Businesses/Units 1,119

| Profit $6.5 B | Wages $10.3 B | Annual Growth Future 3.0%

| Annual Growth Past -0.6%

INDUSTRY MULTIPLES

Acquisition multiples below are calculated medians using US private industry transactions. Data updated annually. Last update: August 2023.

VALUATION MULTIPLE (MEDIAN VALUE)

UNDER $1 MILLION NET SALES

MVIC/Net Sales	1.56
MVIC/Gross Profit	8.06
MVIC/SDE	2.36
MVIC/EBITDA	6.60

$1 MILLION–$5 MILLION NET SALES

MVIC/Net Sales	0.74
MVIC/Gross Profit	2.05
MVIC/SDE	3.43
MVIC/EBITDA	7.70

OVER $5 MILLION NET SALES

MVIC/Net Sales	2.48
MVIC/Gross Profit	5.75
MVIC/SDE	9.55
MVIC/EBITDA	19.64

Source: DealStats (formerly Pratt's Stats), 2023 (Portland, OR: Business Valuation Resources, LLC), www.bvresources.com/dealstats

BENCHMARK DATA

STATISTICS (MEDICAL DEVICE MANUFACTURING)

Number of Establishments	1,119
Average Profit Margin	13.0%
Revenue per Employee	$489,336
Average Number of Employees	93.1
Average Wages per Employee	$101,453

PRODUCTS AND SERVICES SEGMENTATION

Electromedical cardiovascular devices	21.7%
Irradiation apparatus	19.7%
Other	18.2%
Electromedical surgical devices	17.4%
Electromedical neuroscience devices and spinal devices	16.7%
Hearing aids	6.3%

MAJOR MARKET SEGMENTATION

General Medical and Surgical Hospitals	39.7%
Other	32.2%
Offices of Physicians	18.8%
Nursing and residential care facilities	9.3%

INDUSTRY COSTS

Profit	13.0%
Wages	20.7%
Purchases	37.2%
Depreciation	1.4%
Marketing	0.5%

Rent & Utilities 1.3%
Other 25.8%

MARKET SHARE

Medtronic PLC 15.4%
Abbott Laboratories. 12.4%
General Electric Company 10.5%
Danaher Corporation 7.5%
Boston Scientific Corporation . . . 4.6%
Johnson & Johnson 3.3%
GE HealthCare 2.9%
Endress + Hauser 2.5%
Keep Truckin, Inc. 1.7%
Asahi Kasei Corp 1.5%
Leonardo SpA 1.4%

INDUSTRY TREND

"Medical device manufacturing revenue has been declining over the past five years. The decline is explained mainly by pandemic-related disruptions. Germany remains the largest source of imports, but its role has declined. The growing prominence of other international markets with lower operating costs, such as Mexico, is creating a shift in imports. The industry has continued to consolidate. Shorter product life cycles and higher costs of developing new technology have driven industry consolidation, as both of these trends encourage large players to acquire new technologies from small companies."

Source: IBISWorld Key Takeaways

RESOURCES

• IBISWorld, September 2023: https://www.ibisworld.com

Medical Practices (Physicians)

| NAICS 621111 | SIC 8011-01

| Profit $41.6

Rules of Thumb

• 30%–50% annual sales includes inventory
• 1–3 x SDE includes inventory
• 1.5–3.5 x EBITDA
• 1.5–3.5 x EBIT

INDUSTRY MULTIPLES

Acquisition multiples below are calculated medians using US private industry transactions. Data updated annually. Last update: August 2023.

VALUATION MULTIPLE (MEDIAN VALUE)

UNDER $1 MILLION NET SALES
MVIC/Net Sales. 0.39
MVIC/Gross Profit 0.42
MVIC/SDE 1.33
MVIC/EBITDA 3.72

$1 MILLION–$5 MILLION NET SALES
MVIC/Net Sales. 0.44
MVIC/Gross Profit 0.49
MVIC/SDE 1.80
MVIC/EBITDA 3.02

MVIC/Net Sales	2.24
MVIC/Gross Profit	8.31
MVIC/SDE	3.66
MVIC/EBITDA	12.45

Source: DealStats (formerly Pratt's Stats), 2023 (Portland, OR: Business Valuation Resources, LLC), www.bvresources.com/dealstats

PRICING TIPS

Prices vary widely depending on the practice specialty type, number of providers, services provided, and profitability. Smaller practice multiples can easily range from 0.5 to 3.5 EBITDA or 15 to 80 percent of gross. A large practice with 5+ physicians can easily sell between 3.0 and 12 x EBITDA, particularly if EBITDA is over $1 million. A key data point is to understand the low/medium/high salary for a particular specialty. For some doctors, $250K per year is a decent salary. For other specialties, $600K to $750K is normal. Also, be cognizant of what a normal work week is for a specialty. For some specialties, 35 hours per week is the norm. For others, it may be 55 or 60 hours per week. You want to compare the subject practice to the industry norms/benchmarks for that particular specialty. Ask if the practice gets additional revenue from things like ACOs that might transfer to a buyer/new owner. This revenue can be significant. There is an overall shortage of physicians nationwide. More and more practices are bringing PAs and NPs to meet patient demand. Single-doctor practices can be hard to sell and often have lower multiples price/gross, though if a doctor is making considerably higher than normal income for that specialty, they can sell for premiums. Most full-time primary care doctors need about 1,500 active patients to make a living. Concierge or direct primary care practices may need only 400 or 500 active patients. Some practice types are equipment/technology heavy. For those types of practices, having old equipment is seen as a significant detriment.

Valuations are difficult as the medical industry is in flux at the moment. Many doctors are retiring as they are burned out from Covid-19, and medical students are graduating with a large amount of debt and not looking to own and operate their own practice but work in corporate medicine.

For single-physician practices, the discretionary earnings typically must exceed the market wage for a physician with that specialty, or else the practice likely has little value.

Be careful valuing a medical practice as it covers different specialties from family medicine, urgent care, to a cross section of specialties such as cosmetic surgery, med spas, neurology, physical therapy, and chiropractic, to name a few, while there are many more. The medical community is also influx-adapting to post-Covid, changes to Medicare, electronic health records, older doctors retiring and walking away from their practices, telehealth/telemedicine, and more.

For a single-MD practice, the value is the amount an owner would receive after paying fair market wages to the doctor seeing the patients. If fair market wages are $200K and the single-MD owner is taking out $150K, then there is no EBITDA and this might sell for 0.5 to 0.7 times SDE. Why would an MD "buy a job" making $150K when they have job offers for $200K+? If the practice has multiple clinicians, then the true EBITDA could sell for 2 to 3 times over and above what the MD owner makes.

Patients are under no obligation to remain with the practice after it is sold, so this can be a negative to a buyer and hurt the sales price/multiple but is alleviated somewhat by the length of time the physician has physically been practicing in that location, and the selling physician's willingness to help transition the patients.

Inventory consists of medical supplies on hand and typically ranges from $7,000 to $15,000, depending on the size of the practice. Buyers are either doctors or companies that own multiple medical clinics. Buyers are usually very interested in being able to continue the relationship with the existing insurance carriers. The selling doctor typically provides training and introduction to patients for 3 to 4 weeks following the acquisition at no additional cost. Sometimes the selling doctor is willing to stay on part-time for an extended time at the prevailing rate of locums.

Pricing rules of thumb are highly dependent upon practice specialty and size of practice. Also, once EBITDA goes above $1M, there is a whole different pricing tier. But for smaller 1 to 4 doctor practices, you'll see most primary care practices selling for about 33 percent of annual gross collections (asset sale, not stock sale). Specialty practices, like internal medicine subspecialties or surgical, tend to sell for less— 20 to 25 percent of annual gross. Some practices are hotter in the market by national consolidators, like ophthalmology. In general, hospitals and large medical organizations tend to pay less for practices than an owner-practitioner buyer. Hospitals don't like to pay for goodwill, whereas individual doctors will.

BENCHMARK DATA

STATISTICS (PRIMARY CARE DOCTORS)

Number of Establishments	162,927
Average Profit Margin	13.5%
Revenue per Employee	$29,906
Average Number of Employees	7.3
Average Wages per Employee	$125,756

PRODUCTS AND SERVICES SEGMENTATION

Internal medicine practitioners	38.7%
Family medicine and general practice doctors	38.1%
Pediatric medicine	21.3%
Geriatric medicine	1.9%

INDUSTRY COSTS

Profit	13.5%
Wages	41.9%
Purchases	11.0%
Depreciation	1.4%
Marketing	0.4%
Rent & Utilities	3.7%
Other	28.1%

STATISTICS (SPECIALIST DOCTORS)

Number of Establishments	317,797
Average Profit Margin	13.6%
Revenue per Employee	$177,113
Average Number of Employees	6.3
Average Wages per Employee	$92,963

PRODUCTS AND SERVICES SEGMENTATION

All Other	54.6%
Emergency medicine	8.4%
Obstetrics and gynecology	7.9%
Anesthesiology	7.8%

Psychiatry 7.2%
Radiology and diagnostic medicine . . 5.2%
General surgery 4.7%
Cardiovascular health 4.2%

INDUSTRY COSTS

Profit	13.6%
Wages	52.4%
Purchases	8.3%
Depreciation	1.4%
Marketing	0.2%
Rent & Utilities	2.8%
Other	21.3%

Cost of goods varies depending on specialty. For example, an allergy/immunology practice has a high cost of goods. For a family practice without obstetrics: income per FTE doctor, $920K; nonphysician provider wage costs, 18%; total staff wage costs, 43%; average rent, 6.8%; total facility cost, 7.8%; and you should expect about 5 or 6 support staff for each FTE doctor.

Single MD with no PA or NP that has SDE < market wage might sell for 0.7 to 1 x SDE. Practice with multiple MDs, PAs, and NPs, and a busy lab, sells for 1 to 3 x EBITDA and more if EBITDA > $1M.

EXPENSES (% OF ANNUAL SALES)

Cost of Goods	.0% to 10%
Occupancy Costs	05% to 15%
Payroll/Labor Costs.	30% to 40%
Profit (pretax)	35% to 45%

QUESTIONS

- Payer mix? Number hours worked per week? Number of support staff? Revenue trends? Services provided? Percentage of work/revenue from outpatient vs. inpatient?
- How many active charts? How many patients does each clinician see per day? What is the insurance panel? How much revenue is Medicaid, Medicare? Receivables 30, 60, 90, 180 days? Revenue streams, lab, etc.?
- What are their specialties and services offered? Where and how do they source their new patients? Do they have payor contracts affiliated through a hospital?
- What insurance carriers does the clinic utilize? At what hospitals do the doctors at the clinic have privileges? How many exam rooms does the clinic have?
- Explanation of revenue variances over the past 3 to 4 years? Staffing and provider levels? What policies, procedures, and compliance plans are in place? What ancillary services are provided? What revenue cycle management systems are in place? What are the new patient volume and encounter trends over the past several years? How frequently are the provider's charts being audited by management and certified professional coders, etc.?
- Hours worked by seller and number of weekly patient encounters? RVU data? Where do new patients come from (word of mouth, doctor referrals, advertising, insurance plans)?

INDUSTRY TREND

Higher demand as baby boomers grow older. More doctor shortages. More regulation. More consolidation.

This is an industry in transition.

More top-tier specialty practices will be shifting to a hybrid concierge model.

Older doctors have had a successful career and are ready to retire. Younger doctors are graduating from medical school with an enormous amount of debt. Their preference is to work in a hospital system that pays them well and provides regular hours rather than own and operate their own practice.

Continued consolidation as the smaller practices are inefficient at billing, marketing, purchasing, etc. They have no economies of scale.

Private equity firms are aggressively looking for specialty practices to roll up and partner with. This trend is working to keep the practices in demand and will continue; however, patients' stickiness will keep a check on the multiples paid.

Increased billing audits by insurance companies for providers who don't properly support the billing level submitted

Continued growth in general; however, technology and regulation can impact particular specialties. Pay attention to CMS physician fee schedule reimbursements.

"The country faces a physician shortage as the number of new doctors fails to keep pace with the aging population. Telehealth offers an alternative to in-person physician visits and has grown in popularity since the onset of the pandemic."

Source: IBISWorld Key Takeaways

EXPERT COMMENTS

Be a physician, or understand the healthcare industry. This is not for someone that owns a tanning salon and then wants to own a medical office.

Due to the lengthy process for licensing, credentialing, and cost of medical build-out, ease of replication is difficult.

There are not enough physicians to support the demand for services from a growing and aging population. Hence, the move toward nurse practitioners and physician assistants providing services that would historically be the duty of a physician.

Each medical practice runs off the skill of the physician and the back-end support they create for themselves. Do not look for a one-size-fits-all approach. Look at each practice individually.

Think about the transferability of the cash flow. A single-MD practice with the MD's name on the sign may be riskier for a buyer than an MD practice with six clinicians and a generic name like "Town & Country Family Medicine." Risk plays into how much a buyer will pay.

Most health care is very regulated and price controlled through CMMS and insurance companies. Not as much for esthetics and private pay practices. Single-MD practices are difficult to sell as they complete with the job market for MDs. Practices with multiple MDs, PAs, and NPs, and CLIA-certified labs, have more revenue streams, more EBITDA, and are harder to find for sale so they command a higher valuation.

Sellers need to be patient as it takes almost a year to sell a medical practice.

Buyers should seek practices with longer seller transitions and earnout structures (20 to 30 percent).

Medical practices are hard to sell as it depends if the practice takes health insurance, Medicare, or is cash only. If the practice takes health insurance and Medicare, it can take time to transition to the buyer as they have to qualify for this coverage and it's a slow process. A buyer may also need to get local hospital priv-

M

ileges where the selling doctor can refer patients, so be thorough prior to listing the practice for sale.

Sales price needs to be set where new buyer doctor can make at least average compensation or higher.

Healthcare demand is increasing. Highly regulated industry. The government is always trying to muck with payment models. But even if some single-payor model is implemented, people will still need care. Doctors will still need to be highly compensated. Concierge practices and direct patient care models are becoming more popular.

FINANCING

Outside financing. Up to 50 to 65 percent of gross for 100 percent financing. 10-year term. Both SBA and commercial products are available. Many lenders have divisions that specialize in funding medical practices.

Excellent finance terms are typically available to a doctor that wants to buy a medical practice.

Physicians are a preferred lending class. Banks are anxious to get their business. Practice finance divisions of major banks offer much more competitive loans for medical practice acquisitions than SBA lenders—lower closing costs, much lower interest rates, and a lot less red tape. Most of these lenders will provide a loan amount from 65 to 85 percent of gross revenues for a practice acquisition, as long as the cash flow is there to support the payments. So, the loan amount that is readily available to a buyer of a medical practice can sometimes exceed the true value of the practice being purchased.

Approximately 50 percent of the sales entail some seller financing with a down payment of at least 50 percent and a payout over 5 years at 6 percent interest.

Outside financing for competitive practices in urban areas. Some seller financing 5 to 10 percent is typical. Practices located in rural areas or poor performing practices have a higher percentage of seller financing.

RESOURCES

- IBISWorld, September 2023: https://www.ibisworld.com
- AAFP—American Academy of Family Physicians: https://www.aafp.org/home.html
- ACP—American College of Physicians—internal medicine: https://www.acponline.org
- AHA—American Hospital Association: https://www.aha.org
- AHLA—American Health Law Association: https://www.americanhealthlaw.org
- AMA—American Medical Association: https://www.ama-assn.org
- AMGA—American Medical Group Association: https://www.amga.org
- Becker's ASC Review: https://www.beckersasc.com
- CMS—Centers for Medicare & Medicaid Services: https://www.cms.gov
- HCG—The Health Care Group: https://www.healthcaregroup.com
- HFMA—Healthcare Financial Management Association: https://www.hfma.org
- Medical Economics: https://www.medicaleconomics.com
- Medscape: https://www.medscape.com
- MGMA—Medical Group Management Association: https://www.mgma.com
- NSCHBC—National Society of Certified Healthcare Business Consultants: https://www.nschbc.org
- Physicians Practice: https://www.physicianspractice.com

Medical Spas

| | NAICS 812199 | | Businesses/Units 22,621 |

| | Profit $2.3 B | | Wages $16.1 B | | Annual Growth Future 1.7% |

| | | | | | Annual Growth Past 1.1% |

Rules of Thumb

- 50% annual gross sales plus inventory
- 2–3 x SDE includes inventory
- 3.5 x EBIT
- 5 x EBITDA

INDUSTRY MULTIPLES

Acquisition multiples below are calculated medians using US private industry transactions. Data updated annually. Last update: August 2023.

VALUATION MULTIPLE (MEDIAN VALUE)

UNDER $1 MILLION NET SALES
MVIC/Net Sales	0.43
MVIC/Gross Profit	0.56
MVIC/SDE	1.79
MVIC/EBITDA	2.65

$1 MILLION–$5 MILLION NET SALES
MVIC/Net Sales	0.43
MVIC/Gross Profit	0.59
MVIC/SDE	2.90
MVIC/EBITDA	5.02

OVER $5 MILLION NET SALES
MVIC/Net Sales	1.13
MVIC/Gross Profit	3.93
MVIC/SDE	N/A
MVIC/EBITDA	N/A

Source: DealStats (formerly Pratt's Stats), 2023 (Portland, OR: Business Valuation Resources, LLC), www.bvresources.com/dealstats

PRICING TIPS

The industry finally attracted the interest of PEGs and larger investors a few years ago, completely changing the dynamics of the industry. Do not value like a standard medical practice. I regularly get higher multiples than that, even if not selling to PE.

BENCHMARK DATA

STATISTICS (HEALTH AND WELLNESS SPAS)
Number of Establishments	22,621
Average Profit Margin	8.8%
Revenue per Employee	$62,803
Average Number of Employees	16.7
Average Wages per Employee	$43,338

PRODUCTS AND SERVICES SEGMENTATION
Massage and bodywork treatments	54.2%
Skin-care treatments	12.8%
All other	12.7%
Salon services	10.8%
Retail sales	9.5%

M

Adult women under 65	. 41.8%
Adult men under 65.	. 29.1%
Seniors	. 18.9%
Teenagers and children.	. 10.2%

INDUSTRY COSTS

Profit	. 10.0%
Wages	. 69.2%
Purchases	. 2.4%
Depreciation	. 2.6%
Marketing	. 0.5%
Rent & Utilities	. 1.5%
Other	. 13.8%

Revenue per employee can vary significantly by type of provider and what services they may perform (varies from state to state). Those who can inject Botox and dermal fillers can bring in as much as $1M annually in revenue, but the average is less than half that. Those performing laser/radio frequency/cryolipolysis (CoolSculpting) can bring in as much as $500K annually, but the average is probably half that. Cost of goods is key here: injectables can average 40 to 50 percent COGS, where lasers/IPL are usually none or minimal. Retail product (50 percent COGS) sales should average about 10 percent of revenue. Rent should be under 5 percent unless the location provides significant foot/drive-by traffic in an affluent area.

EXPENSES (% OF ANNUAL SALES)

Cost of Goods	25% to 30%
Occupancy Costs	05% to 10%
Payroll/Labor Costs. . . .	30% to 35%
Profit (pretax)	15% to 30%

QUESTIONS

- When were the lasers and other devices last "pm'd" and are they on warranty? Will warranty transfer from manufacturer to new owner? Get that in writing from the manufacturer! Breakdown of revenue by area: toxins, fillers, lasers, other devices, wellness, aesthetics, etc. Specific pay plans for employees (a big minefield currently)? What they are paying (wholesale) for injectables (tox and fillers)? If the costs seem too cheap, or they are not buying directly from the manufacturers, likely illegal due to FDA rules on chain of custody or importation from outside the U.S. Ensure what buyer's attorney says in terms of state laws on who can legally do what procedure jives with the owner's answer to the same questions. Don't buy a place where lower-level folks are doing procedures that they shouldn't be doing.
- Who are your big earners, and will they stay on? Compensation plan? Many are on commission, though it is technically illegal as it is considered fee splitting and not allowed in the medical world. Who can own a med spa in your state? Must it be a physician, or can a nurse or entrepreneur directly own the med spa? If not, an MSO is probably required. Detailed COGS breakdown? What devices (lasers, etc.) are owned, and when were they last serviced?
- How many hours does each renter or commission employee work? How many chairs or rooms are available and how often aren't they in use?

INDUSTRY TREND

Lots of new entrants, including one-offs and franchises. Also, PEG-backed chains are likely to try to do de novo start-ups where supportable.

"Trips to health and wellness spas from new visitors have exploded since COVID-19. Spas are offering more services to cater to consumers with varying budgets. Health and wellness spas are contending with surging demand and a shortage of workers. Heightened demand and labor issues result in spas incorporating more technology into their offerings."

Source: IBISWorld Key Takeaways

EXPERT COMMENTS

If buying, you need the specific medical skills for the procedures done at a med spa—and a few weekend courses won't cut it. Next, if you've never been in business before and don't understand the basics of business, marketing, and accounting, then you are setting yourself up for failure.

FINANCING

Outside financing

RESOURCES

- IBISWorld, September 2023: https://www.ibisworld.com
- AmSpa—American Med Spa Association: https://www.americanmedspa.org/default.aspx
- MedEsthetics magazine: https://www.medestheticsmag.com
- SIA—Spa Industry Association: https://dayspaassociation.com
- AMTA—American Massage Therapy Association: https://www.amtamassage.org

Meineke (Franchise)

| NAICS 811114 | Businesses/Units 700

Rules of Thumb

- 30%–35% annual sales plus inventory
- 30% annual sales
- 1.75 x SDE

INDUSTRY MULTIPLES

Acquisition multiples below are calculated medians using US private industry transactions. Data updated annually. Last update: August 2023.

VALUATION MULTIPLE (MEDIAN VALUE)

UNDER $1 MILLION NET SALES	
MVIC/Net Sales	0.40
MVIC/Gross Profit	0.47
MVIC/SDE	1.60
MVIC/EBITDA	12.57
$1 MILLION–$5 MILLION NET SALES	N/A
OVER $5 MILLION NET SALES	N/A

Source: DealStats (formerly Pratt's Stats), 2023 (Portland, OR: Business Valuation Resources, LLC), www.bvresources.com/dealstats

PRICING TIPS

Approx. Total Investment: $206,774 to $561,688

RESOURCES
- Meineke: https://www.meineke.com
- Franchise information: https://meinekefranchise.com
- Driven Brands: https://www.drivenbrands.com

Men's Clothing Stores

| NAICS 458110 | Businesses/Units 13,260

| Profit $144.5 M | Wages $1.9 B | Annual Growth Future -1.0%

| | | Annual Growth Past -5.7%

INDUSTRY MULTIPLES

Acquisition multiples below are calculated medians using US private industry transactions. Data updated annually. Last update: August 2023.

VALUATION MULTIPLE (MEDIAN VALUE)

UNDER $1 MILLION NET SALES
MVIC/Net Sales.	0.27
MVIC/Gross Profit	0.53
MVIC/SDE	1.03
MVIC/EBITDA	1.03

$1 MILLION–$5 MILLION NET SALES
MVIC/Net Sales.	0.66
MVIC/Gross Profit	1.09
MVIC/SDE	4.47
MVIC/EBITDA	5.69

OVER $5 MILLION NET SALES
MVIC/Net Sales.	4.35
MVIC/Gross Profit	5.17
MVIC/SDE	N/A
MVIC/EBITDA	N/A

Source: DealStats (formerly Pratt's Stats), 2023 (Portland, OR: Business Valuation Resources, LLC), www.bvresources.com/dealstats

BENCHMARK DATA

STATISTICS (MEN'S CLOTHING STORES)

Number of Establishments .	.13,260
Average Profit Margin .	1.3%
Revenue per Employee .	$181,707
Average Number of Employees.	.6.2
Average Wages per Employee .	$31,166

PRODUCTS AND SERVICES SEGMENTATION

Casual wear.	39.0%
Suits and formal wear	20.4%
Office wear .	14.1%
Accessories.	8.3%
Sport coats and blazers.	7.3%
Overcoats and raincoats	5.7%
Other	5.2%

INDUSTRY COSTS

Profit	1.3%
Wages .	17.2%
Purchases	45.4%

Depreciation	. . . .	1.1%
Marketing	. . . .	2.0%
Rent & Utilities	. . . .	7.5%
Other	. . . .	25.5%

MARKET SHARE

| Tailored Brands Inc.. | . . . . | 8.8% |
| Destination XI Group, Inc. | . . . . | 3.1% |

INDUSTRY TREND

"Heightened interest rates at the end of the period have caused a decline in both consumer confidence and disposable income, leading to diminished demand for men's clothes. COVID-19 not only caused a massive decline in demand for men's clothing, but it also aided in the structural shift to a more casually dressed workforce."

Source: IBISWorld Key Takeaways

RESOURCES

• IBISWorld, September 2022: https://www.ibisworld.com

Mental Health and Substance Abuse Centers

| NAICS 623220 | Businesses/Units 9,012

| Profit $1.5 B | Wages $10.7 B | Annual Growth Future 4.0%

| Annual Growth Past 3.9%

Rules of Thumb

• 100% annual sales plus inventory
• 12.3 x SDE plus inventory
• 9.9 x EBIT
• 11.8 x EBITDA

BENCHMARK DATA

STATISTICS (MENTAL HEALTH & SUBSTANCE ABUSE CENTERS)

Number of Establishments .	. . . .	9,012
Average Profit Margin	. . . .	6.0%
Revenue per Employee .	. . . .	$103,185
Average Number of Employees.	. . . .	27.3
Average Wages per Employee .	. . . .	$44,379

PRODUCTS AND SERVICES SEGMENTATION

Residential treatment programs (detoxification & substance abuse) .	. .	39.9%
Residential treatment programs (mental illnesses)	. . . .	35.6%
Residential treatment with counseling services	. . . .	12.1%
All other .	. . . .	7.9%
Independent living services	. . . .	4.5%

MAJOR MARKET SEGMENTATION

Medicare and Medicaid	. . . .	45.6%
All other government funding	. . . .	24.7%
Other	. . . .	14.4%
Private insurance	. . . .	10.7%
Out-of-pocket payers	. . . .	4.6%

INDUSTRY COSTS

Profit	6.0%
Wages	43.1%
Purchases	4.2%
Depreciation	2.6%
Marketing	0.6%
Rent & Utilities	5.9%
Other	37.8%

EXPENSES (% OF ANNUAL SALES)

Cost of Goods	12%
Payroll/Labor Costs.	05%
Profit (pretax)	08%

QUESTIONS

• Payor mix, market share, patient demographic data

INDUSTRY TREND

"Government funding and assistance are essential for performance. Unable to provide telehealth, residential centers kept healthy profit and revenue because of government assistance during COVID-19 and strong funding post-COVID-19. Offering complimentary services may soften competition. As telemedicine increases in healthcare, adopting new medical technology (wearables) and offering some outpatient services may increase interest in residential drug treatment and mental illness therapy."

Source: IBISWorld Key Takeaways

FINANCING

Outside financing

RESOURCES

• IBISWorld, September 2023: https://www.ibisworld.com
• NABH—National Association for Behavioral Healthcare: https://www.nabh.org
• NIMH—National Institute of Mental Health: https://www.nimh.nih.gov

Mental Health Physicians

| NAICS 621112

Rules of Thumb

• 43% annual sales plus inventory
• 1.1 x SDE plus inventory
• 3 x EBIT
• 1.7 x EBITDA

INDUSTRY MULTIPLES

Acquisition multiples below are calculated medians using US private industry transactions. Data updated annually. Last update: August 2023.

VALUATION MULTIPLE (MEDIAN VALUE)

UNDER $1 MILLION NET SALES	
MVIC/Net Sales.	0.63
MVIC/Gross Profit	0.68
MVIC/SDE	2.03
MVIC/EBITDA	2.67

$1 MILLION–$5 MILLION NET SALES — N/A

OVER $5 MILLION NET SALES

MVIC/Net Sales	1.31
MVIC/Gross Profit	N/A
MVIC/SDE	N/A
MVIC/EBITDA	16.92

Source: DealStats (formerly Pratt's Stats), 2023 (Portland, OR: Business Valuation Resources, LLC), www.bvresources.com/dealstats

EXPENSES (% OF ANNUAL SALES)

Cost of Goods	07%
Payroll/Labor Costs	05%
Profit (pretax)	10%

QUESTIONS

- Payor mix, market share, patient demographic data

FINANCING

Outside financing

RESOURCES

- AAFP—American Academy of Family Physicians: https://www.aafp.org/home.html
- AMA—American Medical Association: https://www.ama-assn.org

Mental Health Practitioners (Except Physicians)

| NAICS 621330

Rules of Thumb

- 23% annual sales plus inventory
- 5.5 x SDE plus inventory
- 2.7 x EBIT
- 2.8 x EBITDA

INDUSTRY MULTIPLES

Acquisition multiples below are calculated medians using US private industry transactions. Data updated annually. Last update: August 2023.

VALUATION MULTIPLE (MEDIAN VALUE)

UNDER $1 MILLION NET SALES

MVIC/Net Sales	0.22
MVIC/Gross Profit	0.29
MVIC/SDE	1.44
MVIC/EBITDA	2.55

$1 MILLION–$5 MILLION NET SALES

MVIC/Net Sales	0.59
MVIC/Gross Profit	0.62
MVIC/SDE	4.44
MVIC/EBITDA	5.48

OVER $5 MILLION NET SALES

MVIC/Net Sales	4.18
MVIC/Gross Profit	8.99
MVIC/SDE	4.34
MVIC/EBITDA	5.27

Source: DealStats (formerly Pratt's Stats), 2023 (Portland, OR: Business Valuation Resources, LLC), www.bvresources.com/dealstats

EXPENSES (% OF ANNUAL SALES)

Cost of Goods	07%
Payroll/Labor Costs.	01%
Profit (pretax)	10%

QUESTIONS

• Payor mix, market share, patient demographic data

INDUSTRY TREND

"Demand for anxiety and depression treatment remains high, according to the survey results, while demand for treatment for trauma- and stress-related disorders and substance use disorders has grown....Psychologists' workload and patient load have continued to rise in response to increased demand. Most practitioners report that they no longer have openings for new patients and have longer waitlists than before the pandemic. Burnout among psychologists is persistently high, and almost half of respondents reported not being able to meet the demand from their patients."

Source: "Psychologists struggle to meet demand amid mental health crisis: 2022 COVID-19 Practitioner Impact Survey," November 2022, https://www.apa.org/pubs/reports/practitioner/2022-covid-psychologist-workload

FINANCING

Outside financing

RESOURCES

• AAFP—American Academy of Family Physicians: https://www.aafp.org/home.html
• AMA—American Medical Association: https://www.ama-assn.org

Merry Maids (Franchise)

| NAICS 561720 | Businesses/Units 950

Rules of Thumb

• 45% annual sales plus inventory

INDUSTRY MULTIPLES

Acquisition multiples below are calculated medians using US private industry transactions. Data updated annually. Last update: August 2023.

VALUATION MULTIPLE (MEDIAN VALUE)

UNDER $1 MILLION NET SALES

MVIC/Net Sales.	0.59
MVIC/Gross Profit	0.76
MVIC/SDE	2.03
MVIC/EBITDA	2.92

$1 MILLION–$5 MILLION NET SALES

MVIC/Net Sales.	0.45
MVIC/Gross Profit	1.02
MVIC/SDE	2.86
MVIC/EBITDA	4.05

OVER $5 MILLION NET SALES

MVIC/Net Sales.	0.53
MVIC/Gross Profit	2.26

```
MVIC/SDE    .    .    .    .    .    .    .    .    .    .    .    .    .    .    .    .    4.26
MVIC/EBITDA    .    .    .    .    .    .    .    .    .    .    .    .    .    .    5.48
```

Source: DealStats (formerly Pratt's Stats), 2023 (Portland, OR: Business Valuation Resources, LLC), www.bvresources.com/dealstats

PRICING TIPS

Approx. Total Investment: $94,480 to $144,425

RESOURCES

- Merry Maids: https://www.merrymaids.com
- Franchise information: https://franchise.merrymaids.com
- ServiceMaster: https://www.servicemaster.com

Metal Plating & Treating

| NAICS 33281 | Businesses/Units 5,233

| Profit $2.9 B | Wages $6.6 B | Annual Growth Future -0.3%

| Annual Growth Past -0.3%

INDUSTRY MULTIPLES

Acquisition multiples below are calculated medians using US private industry transactions. Data updated annually. Last update: August 2023.

VALUATION MULTIPLE (MEDIAN VALUE)

UNDER $1 MILLION NET SALES
```
MVIC/Net Sales.    .    .    .    .    .    .    .    .    .    .    .    .    .    .    0.82
MVIC/Gross Profit    .    .    .    .    .    .    .    .    .    .    .    .    .    1.37
MVIC/SDE    .    .    .    .    .    .    .    .    .    .    .    .    .    .    .    2.77
MVIC/EBITDA    .    .    .    .    .    .    .    .    .    .    .    .    .    .    3.44
```

$1 MILLION–$5 MILLION NET SALES
```
MVIC/Net Sales.    .    .    .    .    .    .    .    .    .    .    .    .    .    .    1.00
MVIC/Gross Profit    .    .    .    .    .    .    .    .    .    .    .    .    .    1.51
MVIC/SDE    .    .    .    .    .    .    .    .    .    .    .    .    .    .    .    2.86
MVIC/EBITDA    .    .    .    .    .    .    .    .    .    .    .    .    .    .    4.59
```

OVER $5 MILLION NET SALES
```
MVIC/Net Sales.    .    .    .    .    .    .    .    .    .    .    .    .    .    .    1.87
MVIC/Gross Profit    .    .    .    .    .    .    .    .    .    .    .    .    .    6.61
MVIC/SDE    .    .    .    .    .    .    .    .    .    .    .    .    .    .    .    5.86
MVIC/EBITDA    .    .    .    .    .    .    .    .    .    .    .    .    .    .    9.25
```

Source: DealStats (formerly Pratt's Stats), 2023 (Portland, OR: Business Valuation Resources, LLC), www.bvresources.com/dealstats

BENCHMARK DATA

STATISTICS (METAL PLATING & TREATING)
```
Number of Establishments .    .    .    .    .    .    .    .    .    .    .    .    5,233
Average Profit Margin    .    .    .    .    .    .    .    .    .    .    .    .    8.7%
Revenue per Employee .    .    .    .    .    .    .    .    .    .    .    .    $303,257
Average Number of Employees.    .    .    .    .    .    .    .    .    .    .    20.9
Average Wages per Employee .    .    .    .    .    .    .    .    .    .    $60,057
```

PRODUCTS AND SERVICES SEGMENTATION
```
Metal coating, engraving and allied services    .    .    .    .    .    .    .    56.3%
Electroplating, plating, polishing, anodizing and coloring services    .    .    .    27.1%
Metal heat-treating services    .    .    .    .    .    .    .    .    .    .    16.6%
```

Steel product and steel framing companies 55.3%
Other markets 29.7%
Metal stamping and forging companies 15.0%

INDUSTRY COSTS

Profit 8.7%
Wages 19.8%
Purchases 35.2%
Depreciation 3.4%
Marketing 0.1%
Rent & Utilities 4.8%
Other 27.9%

INDUSTRY TREND

"Rising interest rates will temper demand from key markets such as the automotive and construction industries. The Federal Reserve's attempt to curb inflation will limit businesses borrowing ability. Steel prices will fall and coincide with metal plating and treating providers charging lower prices for their services."

Source: IBISWorld Key Takeaways

RESOURCES

• IBISWorld, September 2023: https://www.ibisworld.com

Metal Stamping & Forging

| NAICS 33211 | Businesses/Units 2,064

| Profit $2.8 B | Wages $6.7 B | Annual Growth Future -0.4%

| | | Annual Growth Past 1.1%

Rules of Thumb

• 4–5 x SDE plus inventory
• 80% annual sales includes inventory
• 4 x EBIT
• 5 x EBITDA

INDUSTRY MULTIPLES

Acquisition multiples below are calculated medians using US private industry transactions. Data updated annually. Last update: August 2023.

VALUATION MULTIPLE (MEDIAN VALUE)

UNDER $1 MILLION NET SALES	N/A
$1 MILLION–$5 MILLION NET SALES	
MVIC/Net Sales	0.43
MVIC/Gross Profit	0.90
MVIC/SDE	3.26
MVIC/EBITDA	6.66
OVER $5 MILLION NET SALES	
MVIC/Net Sales	0.56
MVIC/Gross Profit	3.00
MVIC/SDE	6.37
MVIC/EBITDA	8.06

Source: DealStats (formerly Pratt's Stats), 2023 (Portland, OR: Business Valuation Resources, LLC), www.bvresources.com/dealstats

PRICING TIPS

Equipment lasts forever. Multiple-ton presses are important. Are they a high-volume shop or low-volume–high-volume mix? Changeover and tooling costs matter. Need to know who is paying for tooling. Size matters; the bigger your press capacity, the higher the margin. Good to combine with fabrication and other metal services.

BENCHMARK DATA

STATISTICS (METAL STAMPING & FORGING)

Number of Establishments	2,064
Average Profit Margin	6.5%
Revenue per Employee	$374,473
Average Number of Employees	51.9
Average Wages per Employee	$59,658

PRODUCTS AND SERVICES SEGMENTATION

Nonautomotive stamping	31.9%
Custom roll-forming	20.7%
Ferrous forging	20.5%
Other	14.4%
Powder metallurgy	6.7%
Nonferrous forging	5.8%

MAJOR MARKET SEGMENTATION

Commercial aerospace	39.4%
Off-highway and agriculture	24.8%
Industrial manufacturing	19.7%
Military aerospace	11.0%
Ordnance	3.5%
Other	1.6%

INDUSTRY COSTS

Profit	6.5%
Wages	15.7%
Purchases	51.3%
Depreciation	2.9%
Marketing	0.1%
Rent & Utilities	3.2%
Other	20.3%

EXPENSES (% OF ANNUAL SALES)

Cost of Goods	55% to 65%
Occupancy Costs	05% to 15%
Payroll/Labor Costs	15% to 20%
Profit (pretax)	08% to 18%

QUESTIONS

- How long in business? Cost of goods sold? Lease and rent? How long have employees been there? Diversification of customer base?

INDUSTRY TREND

Good; reshoring

"Metal stamping and forging were weakened by COVID-19, with crashing manufacturing interest requiring the dismissal of thousands of metallurgists. Clients in the aerospace and defense markets fared significantly better, relying on long-term contracts to keep from melting. Metal manufacturers are adding value with automation, higher-precision manufacturing, specialty alloy manipulation and tightened quality tolerances. These changes are designed to serve metal markets that prize quality, reliability and value more than sticker price, especially when lives and livelihoods are built on a framework of metal. Custom metal manufacturing technologies are reducing minimum order quantities and enabling never-before-seen metal shapes for clients. These improvements will reduce reliance on the weaker metal powder manufacturing technique."

Source: IBISWorld Key Takeaways

EXPERT COMMENTS

Confirm condition of equipment and tooling; make sure you have capable tool makers or tool repair sources.

Lots of equipment that lasts a long time; many commodity operators; always someone who will do it cheaper; hard to differentiate on value

RESOURCES

• IBISWorld, September 2023: https://www.ibisworld.com

Midas (Franchise)

| NAICS 811114 | Businesses/Units 973

Rules of Thumb

• 30%–35% annual sales plus inventory

INDUSTRY MULTIPLES

Acquisition multiples below are calculated medians using US private industry transactions. Data updated annually. Last update: August 2023.

VALUATION MULTIPLE (MEDIAN VALUE)

UNDER $1 MILLION NET SALES	
MVIC/Net Sales.	0.40
MVIC/Gross Profit	0.47
MVIC/SDE	1.60
MVIC/EBITDA	12.57
$1 MILLION–$5 MILLION NET SALES	N/A
OVER $5 MILLION NET SALES	N/A

Source: DealStats (formerly Pratt's Stats), 2023 (Portland, OR: Business Valuation Resources, LLC), www.bvresources.com/dealstats

PRICING TIPS

Approx. Total Investment: $103,650 to $885,640

RESOURCES

• Midas: https://www.midas.com
• Franchise information: https://www.midasfranchise.com
• TBC Corporation: https://www.tbccorp.com

Millwork

| NAICS 32191 | Businesses/Units 9,355

| Profit $1.5 B | Wages $5.9 B | Annual Growth Future -0.4%
| | | Annual Growth Past 0.6%

INDUSTRY MULTIPLES

Acquisition multiples below are calculated medians using US private industry transactions. Data updated annually. Last update: August 2023.

VALUATION MULTIPLE (MEDIAN VALUE)

UNDER $1 MILLION NET SALES

MVIC/Net Sales.	0.47
MVIC/Gross Profit	1.10
MVIC/SDE	1.74
MVIC/EBITDA	4.96

$1 MILLION–$5 MILLION NET SALES

MVIC/Net Sales.	0.50
MVIC/Gross Profit	0.90
MVIC/SDE	2.99
MVIC/EBITDA	4.14

OVER $5 MILLION NET SALES

MVIC/Net Sales.	0.83
MVIC/Gross Profit	4.80
MVIC/SDE	4.27
MVIC/EBITDA	9.34

Source: DealStats (formerly Pratt's Stats), 2023 (Portland, OR: Business Valuation Resources, LLC), www.bvresources.com/dealstats

BENCHMARK DATA

STATISTICS (MILLWORK)

Number of Establishments .	9,355
Average Profit Margin	4.4%
Revenue per Employee .	$282,542
Average Number of Employees.	12.8
Average Wages per Employee .	$49,758

PRODUCTS AND SERVICES SEGMENTATION

Wood windows and doors	50.2%
Flooring and other millwork products	26.8%
Cut stock, resawed lumber and planed lumber	23.0%

MAJOR MARKET SEGMENTATION

New residential construction	45.0%
Residential repair and remodeling .	43.0%
Nonresidential construction	12.0%

INDUSTRY COSTS

Profit	4.4%
Wages	17.7%
Purchases	50.1%
Depreciation	1.6%
Marketing	0.5%
Rent & Utilities	2.4%
Other	23.4%

INDUSTRY TREND

"To mute the negative effects of COVID-19 and to stimulate the declining economy, the Federal Reserve lowered interest rates. Residential construction activity boomed amid the pandemic, as residential work takes a relatively short amount of time to complete and is highly susceptible to the price of financing. Nonresidential construction activity has historically taken longer to improve post-recession and follows a lag of one to two years to that of the residential construction market. Commercial work has started to renew as COVID-19-related operational restrictions ease. Performance amid the pandemic was stellar due to low interest rates, but now in 2023 interest rates have hiked up significantly. As the economy continues to overcome COVID-19-related externalities, the Federal Reserve will spike up rates, hampering the residential market."

Source: IBISWorld Key Takeaways

RESOURCES

• IBISWorld, September 2023: https://www.ibisworld.com

Mining: Copper, Nickel, Lead & Zinc

| NAICS 212230 | Businesses/Units 65

| Profit $3.7 B | Wages $1.7 B | Annual Growth Future -1.4%

| Annual Growth Past 3.2%

INDUSTRY MULTIPLES

Acquisition multiples below are calculated medians using US private industry transactions. Data updated annually. Last update: August 2023.

VALUATION MULTIPLE (MEDIAN VALUE)

UNDER $1 MILLION NET SALES	N/A
$1 MILLION–$5 MILLION NET SALES	N/A
OVER $5 MILLION NET SALES	
MVIC/Net Sales	2.08
MVIC/Gross Profit	5.45
MVIC/SDE	N/A
MVIC/EBITDA	11.87

Source: DealStats (formerly Pratt's Stats), 2023 (Portland, OR: Business Valuation Resources, LLC), www.bvresources.com/dealstats

BENCHMARK DATA

STATISTICS (COPPER, NICKEL, LEAD & ZINC MINING)

Number of Establishments	65
Average Profit Margin	23.4%
Revenue per Employee	$815,565
Average Number of Employees	280.6
Average Wages per Employee	$89,265

PRODUCTS AND SERVICES SEGMENTATION

Copper ore mining	76.5%
Zinc ore mining	16.3%
Lead ore mining	5.0%
Nickel ore mining	2.2%

MAJOR MARKET SEGMENTATION

Exports	32.6%
Construction	32.0%
Automobile equipment manufacturers	16.0%
Metal manufacturers	12.7%
Electronic product manufacturers	4.7%
Other	2.0%

INDUSTRY COSTS

Profit	23.4%
Wages	10.7%

Purchases	. . . .	23.5%
Depreciation	. . . .	20.9%
Marketing	. . . .	0.0%
Rent & Utilities	. . . .	6.8%
Other	. . . .	14.8%

INDUSTRY TREND

"As industrial and construction activity picked back up following restrictions during the COVID-19 pandemic, demand for industry services swelled. Limited supply and high demand caused mineral prices to skyrocket, enabling industry enterprises to generate more revenue. The COVID-19 pandemic forced many mining operations to complete close or operate at reduced capacity. This hindrance cut into industry profitability. Supply chain issues and mining disruptions were most notable in China, which has significantly declined as an export destination for domestic products."

Source: IBISWorld Key Takeaways

RESOURCES

• IBISWorld, February 2023: https://www.ibisworld.com

Mining: Sand & Gravel

| NAICS 21232 | Businesses/Units 2,653

| Profit $1.5 B | Wages $3.1 B | Annual Growth Future 0.5%

| | | Annual Growth Past -2.4%

Rules of Thumb

• 100% annual sales plus inventory
• 5 x EBITDA

INDUSTRY MULTIPLES

Acquisition multiples below are calculated medians using US private industry transactions. Data updated annually. Last update: August 2023.

VALUATION MULTIPLE (MEDIAN VALUE)

| UNDER $1 MILLION NET SALES | N/A |
| $1 MILLION–$5 MILLION NET SALES | N/A |

OVER $5 MILLION NET SALES

MVIC/Net Sales	. . . .	1.99
MVIC/Gross Profit	. . . . . .	7.72
MVIC/SDE	. . . .	N/A
MVIC/EBITDA	. . . . . .	10.69

Source: DealStats (formerly Pratt's Stats), 2023 (Portland, OR: Business Valuation Resources, LLC), www.bvresources.com/dealstats

BENCHMARK DATA

STATISTICS (SAND & GRAVEL MINING)

Number of Establishments	. . . .	2,653
Average Profit Margin	. . . . .	8.5%
Revenue per Employee	. . . .	$457,074
Average Number of Employees	. . .	15.2
Average Wages per Employee	. .	$78,860

PRODUCTS AND SERVICES SEGMENTATION

Construction sand and gravel	.59.5%
Industrial sand and gravel	.31.7%
Kaolin, common clay, and other products	. 8.8%

MAJOR MARKET SEGMENTATION

Construction sector.	.63.9%
Industrial sector.	.36.1%

INDUSTRY COSTS

Profit	. 8.5%
Wages	.17.2%
Purchases	.22.3%
Depreciation	. 8.0%
Marketing	. 0.1%
Rent & Utilities	.17.0%
Other	.27.0%

MARKET SHARE

CRH PLC	. 7.7%
HeidelbergCement AG	. 5.2%
Vulcan Materials Company	. 4.1%
Granite Construction Inc.	. 1.2%

At least 150,000 tons/year is the minimum usually necessary for a profitable site.

INDUSTRY TREND

"The Infrastructure Investment and Jobs Act will aid sand and gravel miners in the coming years. The act supports investment into highway and bridge infrastructure, which both use sand and gravel. The use of industrial sand has had its ups and downs. While hydraulic fracturing has become immensely popular, environmental concerns and swings in commodity prices can impact sales."

Source: IBISWorld Key Takeaways

"Sand is used in the construction and manufacturing of everything from buildings to roadways, bridges, windows, computer screens, semiconductors and more. This has helped make sand mining the largest mining industry in the world.

"'We don't think about it like a strategic resource, and yet it is everywhere in our societies and our economies,' Louise Gallagher of the United Nations Environment Programme told CNBC. However, sand use around the world has tripled in the last twenty years as global industrialization has increased, according to UNEP. This is causing concern over a potential shortage, which could have ripple effects around the world."

Source: "Here's why the world could be facing a massive sand crisis" by Andrea Miller, May 12, 2021, https://www.cnbc.com/2021/05/12/heres-why-the-world-could-be-facing-a-massive-sand-crisis.html

RESOURCES

- IBISWorld, September 2023: https://www.ibisworld.com
- NSSGA—National Stone, Sand & Gravel Association: https://www.nssga.org

Mining: Stone

NAICS 21231	Businesses/Units 2,190	
Profit $1.8 B	Wages $3.6 B	Annual Growth Future 0.4%
		Annual Growth Past 0.1%

INDUSTRY MULTIPLES

Acquisition multiples below are calculated medians using US private industry transactions. Data updated annually. Last update: August 2023.

M

VALUATION MULTIPLE (MEDIAN VALUE)

UNDER $1 MILLION NET SALES

MVIC/Net Sales.	0.69
MVIC/Gross Profit	0.80
MVIC/SDE	4.89
MVIC/EBITDA	4.89

$1 MILLION–$5 MILLION NET SALES   N/A

OVER $5 MILLION NET SALES

MVIC/Net Sales.	3.35
MVIC/Gross Profit	16.62
MVIC/SDE	N/A
MVIC/EBITDA	20.36

Source: DealStats (formerly Pratt's Stats), 2023 (Portland, OR: Business Valuation Resources, LLC), www.bvresources.com/dealstats

BENCHMARK DATA

STATISTICS (STONE MINING)

Number of Establishments .	2,190
Average Profit Margin	8.9%
Revenue per Employee .	$476,035
Average Number of Employees.	19.4
Average Wages per Employee .	$85,591

PRODUCTS AND SERVICES SEGMENTATION

Crushed limestone and dolomite	68.4%
Crushed granite.	14.7%
Other crushed stone	8.7%
Crushed trap rock	5.9%
Dimension limestone and dimension sandstone	1.7%
Dimension granite	0.4%
Other dimension stone (e.g. marble and slate).	0.2%

MAJOR MARKET SEGMENTATION

Infrastructure construction.	70.4%
Building construction and renovation	16.8%
Product manufacturing (e.g. chemicals and metallurgical)	9.8%
Agriculture .	2.0%
Other	1.0%

INDUSTRY COSTS

Profit	8.9%
Wages .	18.0%
Purchases	18.7%
Depreciation	7.0%
Marketing	0.1%
Rent & Utilities .	9.9%
Other	37.4%

INDUSTRY TREND

"The housing market has been a boon to stone miners as infrastructure construction growth stagnated during COVID-19. The threat of a housing market crash may hurt this demand. The Infrastructure Investment and Jobs Act will be the main growth driver for stoner miners. The act supports infrastructure work in which stone miners are heavily involved."

Source: IBISWorld Key Takeaways

RESOURCES

• IBISWorld, January 2023: https://www.ibisworld.com

Minuteman Press (Franchise)

| NAICS 323111 | Businesses/Units 709

Rules of Thumb

• 60%–65% annual sales plus inventory

INDUSTRY MULTIPLES

Acquisition multiples below are calculated medians using US private industry transactions. Data updated annually. Last update: August 2023.

VALUATION MULTIPLE (MEDIAN VALUE)

UNDER $1 MILLION NET SALES

MVIC/Net Sales.	0.49
MVIC/Gross Profit	0.68
MVIC/SDE	2.35
MVIC/EBITDA	3.07

$1 MILLION–$5 MILLION NET SALES

MVIC/Net Sales.	0.40
MVIC/Gross Profit	0.62
MVIC/SDE	2.81
MVIC/EBITDA	4.35

OVER $5 MILLION NET SALES

MVIC/Net Sales.	0.70
MVIC/Gross Profit	1.50
MVIC/SDE	3.73
MVIC/EBITDA	4.76

Source: DealStats (formerly Pratt's Stats), 2023 (Portland, OR: Business Valuation Resources, LLC), www.bvresources.com/dealstats

PRICING TIPS

Approx. Total Investment: $75,900 to $187,106

RESOURCES

• Minuteman Press: https://www.minutemanpress.com
• Franchise information: https://minutemanpressfranchise.com

Miscellaneous Financial Investment Activities

| NAICS 523999 | Businesses/Units 16,310

| Profit $8.4 B | Wages $9.7 B | Annual Growth Future 1.6%

| | | Annual Growth Past 2.0%

Rules of Thumb

• 40% annual sales

INDUSTRY MULTIPLES

Acquisition multiples below are calculated medians using US private industry transactions. Data updated annually. Last update: August 2023.

VALUATION MULTIPLE (MEDIAN VALUE)

UNDER $1 MILLION NET SALES	N/A
$1 MILLION–$5 MILLION NET SALES	N/A
OVER $5 MILLION NET SALES	
MVIC/Net Sales	5.30
MVIC/Gross Profit	7.27
MVIC/SDE	N/A
MVIC/EBITDA	11.93

Source: DealStats (formerly Pratt's Stats), 2023 (Portland, OR: Business Valuation Resources, LLC), www.bvresources.com/dealstats

BENCHMARK DATA

STATISTICS (CUSTODY, ASSET & SECURITIES SERVICES)

Number of Establishments	16,310
Average Profit Margin	22.6%
Revenue per Employee	$503,000
Average Number of Employees	4.65
Average Wages per Employee	$130,615

PRODUCTS AND SERVICES SEGMENTATION

Trust and fiduciary services	36.6%
Support services for financial and commodity markets	35.7%
Brokerage and dealing services	9.2%
Financial planning and investment management	8.2%
Financing related to securities	6.4%
Other services	3.9%

MAJOR MARKET SEGMENTATION

Businesses and governments	47.9%
Households	27.8%
Other	24.3%

INDUSTRY COSTS

Profit	22.6%
Wages	26.2%
Purchases	1.7%
Depreciation	2.3%
Marketing	1.0%
Rent & Utilities	1.2%
Other	44.2%

MARKET SHARE

Bank of New York Mellon	21.0%
State Street	15.7%
Bank of America	8.0%
JPMorgan Chase	4.7%
Citigroup Inc.	2.9%

INDUSTRY TREND

Increased competition; more alliances

"Growing asset prices benefit the broader industry. Processing fees from trades across the markets have slipped due to automation. Some US custodians have aggressively expanded into foreign markets. Strong corporate performance coupled with broader economic growth will overshadow interest rate hikes. Technological advancement will be a key driver of growth. Increased federal regulation will accelerate the industry's push abroad to developing markets. A continued influx of assets under custody has led to higher fee income."

Source: IBISWorld Industry at a Glance

EXPERT COMMENTS

Seller: Develop an exit strategy as soon as possible. Consider all the ways to sell your business. Know what you are going to do after the sale. Know how to protect against risk. Buyer: Look under the hood. Know the small things as well as the large ones. Know the management of the company you are purchasing. Inventory as much as you can.

The industry is changing in regards to methods and procedures of completing a sale.

RESOURCES

• IBISWorld, January 2023: https://www.ibisworld.com

Mobile Home Parks

| NAICS 531190 | SIC 6515-01

Rules of Thumb

• 3–8 x monthly income

INDUSTRY MULTIPLES

Acquisition multiples below are calculated medians using US private industry transactions. Data updated annually. Last update: August 2023.

VALUATION MULTIPLE (MEDIAN VALUE)

UNDER $1 MILLION NET SALES	
MVIC/Net Sales	1.68
MVIC/Gross Profit	0.73
MVIC/SDE	2.56
MVIC/EBITDA	2.56
$1 MILLION–$5 MILLION NET SALES	N/A
OVER $5 MILLION NET SALES	
MVIC/Net Sales	8.65
MVIC/Gross Profit	8.56
MVIC/SDE	N/A
MVIC/EBITDA	22.50

Source: DealStats (formerly Pratt's Stats), 2023 (Portland, OR: Business Valuation Resources, LLC), www.bvresources.com/dealstats

RESOURCES

• MHI—Manufactured Housing Institute: https://www.manufacturedhousing.org

Molly Maid (Franchise)

| NAICS 561720 | Businesses/Units 488

Rules of Thumb

• 35%–40% annual sales plus inventory

INDUSTRY MULTIPLES

Acquisition multiples below are calculated medians using US private industry transactions. Data updated annually. Last update: August 2023.

VALUATION MULTIPLE (MEDIAN VALUE)

UNDER $1 MILLION NET SALES

MVIC/Net Sales	0.59
MVIC/Gross Profit	0.76
MVIC/SDE	2.03
MVIC/EBITDA	2.92

$1 MILLION–$5 MILLION NET SALES

MVIC/Net Sales	0.45
MVIC/Gross Profit	1.02
MVIC/SDE	2.86
MVIC/EBITDA	4.05

OVER $5 MILLION NET SALES

MVIC/Net Sales	0.53
MVIC/Gross Profit	2.26
MVIC/SDE	4.26
MVIC/EBITDA	5.48

Source: DealStats (formerly Pratt's Stats), 2023 (Portland, OR: Business Valuation Resources, LLC), www.bvresources.com/dealstats

PRICING TIPS

Approx. Total Investment: $127,200 to $184,450

RESOURCES

- Molly Maid: https://www.mollymaid.com
- Franchise information: https://franchise.neighborly.com/molly-maid/
- Neighborly: https://www.neighborlybrands.com

Mortgage and Nonmortgage Loan Brokers

| NAICS 522310 | Businesses/Units 18,802

| Profit $3.6 B | Wages $10.5 B | Annual Growth Future 2.5%

| Annual Growth Past 13.6%

INDUSTRY MULTIPLES

Acquisition multiples below are calculated medians using US private industry transactions. Data updated annually. Last update: August 2023.

VALUATION MULTIPLE (MEDIAN VALUE)

UNDER $1 MILLION NET SALES

MVIC/Net Sales	0.15
MVIC/Gross Profit	0.15
MVIC/SDE	N/A
MVIC/EBITDA	N/A

$1 MILLION–$5 MILLION NET SALES

MVIC/Net Sales	0.40
MVIC/Gross Profit	0.40
MVIC/SDE	N/A
MVIC/EBITDA	1.30

OVER $5 MILLION NET SALES

MVIC/Net Sales	3.04
MVIC/Gross Profit	3.28
MVIC/SDE	N/A
MVIC/EBITDA	13.60

Source: DealStats (formerly Pratt's Stats), 2023 (Portland, OR: Business Valuation Resources, LLC), www.bvresources.com/dealstats

BENCHMARK DATA

STATISTICS (LOAN BROKERS)

Number of Establishments	18,802
Average Profit Margin	15.2%
Revenue per Employee	$326,767
Average Number of Employees	4.0
Average Wages per Employee	$145,386

PRODUCTS AND SERVICES SEGMENTATION

Residential mortgages for single family residences	77.3%
Residential mortgages for multifamily residences	11.6%
Brokering and dealing products	4.2%
Commercial and industrial mortgages	3.6%
Other	2.7%
Home equity loans	0.4%
Vehicle loans	0.1%
Loans to governments	0.1%

MAJOR MARKET SEGMENTATION

Existing homebuyers	58.7%
First-time homebuyers	30.2%
Other	7.5%
Businesses	3.6%

INDUSTRY COSTS

Profit	15.2%
Wages	44.2%
Purchases	1.4%
Depreciation	0.6%
Marketing	2.0%
Rent & Utilities	1.4%
Other	35.2%

MARKET SHARE

LendingTree	5.6%

INDUSTRY TREND

"Rising interest rates are reducing loan originations, as consumers and businesses dodge the high cost of borrowing. Stiff competition with online brokerage firms is driving demand away from loan brokers, forcing them to make technological advances. Deregulation of lenders is increasing the pool of applicants for loans, enabling consumers to secure lower interest rates when they are available. Competitors also benefit from deregulation, especially commercial banks."

Source: IBISWorld Key Takeaways

RESOURCES

• IBISWorld, September 2023: https://www.ibisworld.com

Motion Picture and Video Production

NAICS 512110	Businesses/Units 6,505	
Profit $3.6 B	Wages $5.5 B	Annual Growth Future 3.3%
		Annual Growth Past -5.0%

INDUSTRY MULTIPLES

Acquisition multiples below are calculated medians using US private industry transactions. Data updated annually. Last update: August 2023.

M

VALUATION MULTIPLE (MEDIAN VALUE)

UNDER $1 MILLION NET SALES

MVIC/Net Sales	0.63
MVIC/Gross Profit	0.75
MVIC/SDE	1.48
MVIC/EBITDA	3.00

$1 MILLION–$5 MILLION NET SALES

MVIC/Net Sales	0.34
MVIC/Gross Profit	0.22
MVIC/SDE	1.39
MVIC/EBITDA	1.40

OVER $5 MILLION NET SALES

MVIC/Net Sales	3.26
MVIC/Gross Profit	7.50
MVIC/SDE	10.09
MVIC/EBITDA	7.47

Source: DealStats (formerly Pratt's Stats), 2023 (Portland, OR: Business Valuation Resources, LLC), www.bvresources.com/dealstats

BENCHMARK DATA

STATISTICS (MOVIE & VIDEO PRODUCTION)

Number of Establishments	6,505
Average Profit Margin	12.9%
Revenue per Employee	$634,233
Average Number of Employees	7.0
Average Wages per Employee	$121,727

PRODUCTS AND SERVICES SEGMENTATION

Action and adventure	66.5%
Thriller and horror	12.0%
Comedy	11.3%
Drama	8.3%
Other	1.9%

MAJOR MARKET SEGMENTATION

TV licensing	44.6%
Foreign distribution	19.8%
Physical copy sales	12.5%
Digital streaming and video on demand	12.0%
Domestic box office	11.1%

INDUSTRY COSTS

Profit	2.0%
Wages	19.6%
Purchases	2.0%
Depreciation	2.5%
Marketing	7.0%
Rent & Utilities	5.6%
Other	50.5%

MARKET SHARE

Walt Disney Co	16.2%
ViacomCBS	15.5%
NBCUniversal Media	11.9%
AT&T	9.8%
Sony	8.3%

INDUSTRY TREND

"Major movie producers lean on box office blockbusters to generate low-risk sales. Theater attendance is steadily declining as video streaming options expand. Online streaming encroaches on box office sales but provides a new revenue channel for producers. Digital distribution is quickly growing as a share of movie and video production revenue. Video producers are finding new opportunities through social media and digital streaming platforms. Platforms like Twitch and YouTube are investing in professional video producers to create content. Widespread strikes have shutdown many productions. This could continue for some time into the future."

Source: IBISWorld Key Takeaways

RESOURCES

• IBISWorld, September 2023: https://www.ibisworld.com

Motor Home Manufacturing

| NAICS 336213 | Businesses/Units 2,012

| Profit $1 B | Wages $11 B | Annual Growth Future 1.5%

| | | Annual Growth Past -1.3%

INDUSTRY MULTIPLES

Acquisition multiples below are calculated medians using US private industry transactions. Data updated annually. Last update: August 2023.

VALUATION MULTIPLE (MEDIAN VALUE)

UNDER $1 MILLION NET SALES	N/A
$1 MILLION–$5 MILLION NET SALES	N/A
OVER $5 MILLION NET SALES	
MVIC/Net Sales.	0.60
MVIC/Gross Profit	4.50
MVIC/SDE	N/A
MVIC/EBITDA	12.69

Source: DealStats (formerly Pratt's Stats), 2023 (Portland, OR: Business Valuation Resources, LLC), www.bvresources.com/dealstats

BENCHMARK DATA

STATISTICS (TRUCK, TRAILER & MOTOR HOME MANUFACTURING)

Number of Establishments	2,012
Average Profit Margin	1.8%
Revenue per Employee	$333,466
Average Number of Employees. . .	86.5
Average Wages per Employee . .	$64,118

PRODUCTS AND SERVICES SEGMENTATION

Travel trailers and campers	42.0%
Motor vehicle bodies	26.4%
Truck trailers	21.6%
Motor homes	10.0%

MAJOR MARKET SEGMENTATION

Consumers	65.0%
Exports	22.8%
Freight operators	12.2%

INDUSTRY COSTS

Profit	1.8%
Wages	19.2%
Purchases	64.5%
Depreciation	1.1%
Marketing	0.3%
Rent & Utilities	1.0%
Other	12.1%

MARKET SHARE

Thor Industries, Inc..	25.1%
Forest River Inc..	13.9%
Winnebago Industries, Inc. .	7.8%
Hyundai Motor Group	5.5%
Wabash National Corporation	1.7%
Nissan Motor Co. Ltd.	1.7%

INDUSTRY TREND

"Pandemic-related economic slowdowns suppressed demand. The need for RV transportation dropped, thereby, cutting down production. An economic recovery restored demand. A surge in consumer confidence and a steadily increasing number of domestic trips by US residents propelled operators to expand production."

Source: IBISWorld Key Takeaways

RESOURCES

• IBISWorld, February 2023: https://www.ibisworld.com

Motorcycle Dealerships

	NAICS 441228		SIC 5571-06		Businesses/Units 18,731
	Profit $1 B		Wages $3.8 B		Annual Growth Future 1.2%
					Annual Growth Past -0.1%

Rules of Thumb

• 12%–14% annual sales plus inventory
• 2–3 x SDE plus inventory
• 3–4 x EBITDA

INDUSTRY MULTIPLES

Acquisition multiples below are calculated medians using US private industry transactions. Data updated annually. Last update: August 2023.

VALUATION MULTIPLE (MEDIAN VALUE)

UNDER $1 MILLION NET SALES

MVIC/Net Sales.	0.44
MVIC/Gross Profit	0.86
MVIC/SDE	2.22
MVIC/EBITDA	2.31

$1 MILLION–$5 MILLION NET SALES

MVIC/Net Sales.	0.27
MVIC/Gross Profit	1.09
MVIC/SDE	2.74
MVIC/EBITDA	4.79

MVIC/Net Sales	0.30
MVIC/Gross Profit	1.12
MVIC/SDE	3.66
MVIC/EBITDA	4.38

Source: DealStats (formerly Pratt's Stats), 2023 (Portland, OR: Business Valuation Resources, LLC), www.bvresources.com/dealstats

PRICING TIPS

It can be sold for a little higher multiple of SDE because of the hobby aspect.

BENCHMARK DATA

STATISTICS (MOTORCYCLE DEALERSHIP AND REPAIR)

Number of Establishments	18,731
Average Profit Margin	3.0%
Revenue per Employee	$406,265
Average Number of Employees	4.4
Average Wages per Employee	$45,969

PRODUCTS AND SERVICES SEGMENTATION

Motorized sport vehicles	31.3%
Cruiser motorcycles	21.2%
Touring motorcycles	12.3%
Other motorcycles	10.7%
Other	9.3%
Sports motorcycles	9.0%
Repairs	6.2%

MAJOR MARKET SEGMENTATION

Consumers aged 18 to 34	31.3%
Consumers aged 35 to 54	25.8%
Consumers aged 55 and older	21.7%
Businesses	19.3%
Government	1.0%
Other	0.9%

INDUSTRY COSTS

Profit	3.0%
Wages	11.4%
Purchases	73.0%
Deprecation	0.6%
Marketing	0.9%
Rent & Utilities	1.1%
Other	10.0%

EXPENSES (% OF ANNUAL SALES)

Cost of Goods	77% to 85%
Occupancy Costs	01%
Payroll/Labor Costs	05%
Profit (pretax)	02% to 03%

QUESTIONS

- PG&A inventory and new vehicle value requirements for a new buyer can be the most difficult and complex aspects to understand. A good deal of time should be spent understanding what inventory there is and how much is really needed. Inventory should turn on an average of 4 to 6 times per year in a healthy dealership. Slower turns suggest the business is carrying too much inventory or is very seasonal.

INDUSTRY TREND

The floored inventory, which can run into millions of dollars, is not included; although the buyer will assume the liability, usually 100 percent of the purchase price.

"Motorcycles remain an expensive hobby. Healthy economic conditions and an increasing number of high earners are necessary to generate sufficient revenue. Target demographics are shifting. Motorcycle enthusiasts are slowly aging out of the industry, pushing dealerships to focus on brining in younger customers."

Source: IBISWorld Key Takeaways

EXPERT COMMENTS

Several years ago motorcycle dealerships were easy to sell. Some regions of the country have experienced a downward trend in sales. The southeastern U.S. is still very strong. Currently, smaller dealerships can be very difficult to sell.

The original equipment manufacturers (Honda, Harley-Davidson, Yamaha, Suzuki, Kawasaki, etc.) control the number of dealers permitted in a marketplace. An existing dealership can block the establishment of a competing dealership of the same brand within a geographical proximity to the existing dealership.

FINANCING

Seller financing, all cash

RESOURCES

- IBISWorld, April 2023: https://www.ibisworld.com
- PowerSports Business: https://powersportsbusiness.com/

Mountain Mike's Pizza (Franchise)

| NAICS 722513 | SIC 5812-22 | Businesses/Units 270

Rules of Thumb

- 30% annual sales plus inventory

INDUSTRY MULTIPLES

Acquisition multiples below are calculated medians using US private industry transactions. Data updated annually. Last update: August 2023.

VALUATION MULTIPLE (MEDIAN VALUE)

UNDER $1 MILLION NET SALES	
MVIC/Net Sales	0.31
MVIC/Gross Profit	0.48
MVIC/SDE	1.67
MVIC/EBITDA	2.21
$1 MILLION–$5 MILLION NET SALES	
MVIC/Net Sales	0.39
MVIC/Gross Profit	0.60
MVIC/SDE	2.43
MVIC/EBITDA	2.98
OVER $5 MILLION NET SALES	
MVIC/Net Sales	0.89
MVIC/Gross Profit	2.08
MVIC/SDE	4.98
MVIC/EBITDA	12.81

Source: DealStats (formerly Pratt's Stats), 2023 (Portland, OR: Business Valuation Resources, LLC), www.bvresources.com/dealstats

Approx. Total Investment: $417,850 to $798,500

RESOURCES

- Mountain Mike's Pizza: https://www.mountainmikespizza.com
- Franchise information: https://mountainmikesfranchise.com

Movie Theaters

	NAICS 512131		SIC 7832-01		Businesses/Units 4,993
	Profit $640 M		Wages $1.8 B		Annual Growth Future 1.9%
					Annual Growth Past -15.9%

Rules of Thumb

- 4 x SDE
- 4%–6% annual sales; add fixtures & equipment

INDUSTRY MULTIPLES

Acquisition multiples below are calculated medians using US private industry transactions. Data updated annually. Last update: August 2023.

VALUATION MULTIPLE (MEDIAN VALUE)

UNDER $1 MILLION NET SALES

MVIC/Net Sales.	0.20
MVIC/Gross Profit	0.33
MVIC/SDE	1.17
MVIC/EBITDA	1.17

$1 MILLION–$5 MILLION NET SALES

MVIC/Net Sales.	0.47
MVIC/Gross Profit	0.79
MVIC/SDE	2.81
MVIC/EBITDA	9.05

OVER $5 MILLION NET SALES

MVIC/Net Sales.	1.78
MVIC/Gross Profit	3.60
MVIC/SDE	N/A
MVIC/EBITDA	N/A

Source: DealStats (formerly Pratt's Stats), 2023 (Portland, OR: Business Valuation Resources, LLC), www.bvresources.com/dealstats

PRICING TIPS

Concession sales usually make up 24 percent of movie theater sales. It has been said that without concession sales, the movie theater business would not be viable.

BENCHMARK DATA

STATISTICS (MOVIE THEATERS)

Number of Establishments	4,993
Average Profit Margin	7.2%
Revenue per Employee	$44,970
Average Number of Employees	39.4
Average Wages per Employee	$9,106

PRODUCTS AND SERVICES SEGMENTATION

Admissions to feature films.	63.3%
Food and beverage sales	32.6%
All other.	2.8%
Advertising revenue.	1.3%

INDUSTRY COSTS

Profit	7.2%
Wages	34.1%
Purchases	2.7%
Depreciation	6.3%
Marketing	2.9%
Rent & Utilities	4.8%
Other	42.0%

MARKET SHARE

AMC Entertainment Holdings, Inc.	36.2%
Cinemark Holdings, Inc.	25.8%
Cineworld Group PLC	18.5%

INDUSTRY TREND

"As they struggle in a fast-changing business, multiplex operators—some carrying astounding debt because of pandemic shutdowns—have started to experiment with pricing in ways that have startled moviegoers....Because multiplex chains make most of their money from popcorn and soda, it is in their economic interest to keep ticket prices low; concession counters rely on foot traffic. But there isn't much room to raise the price of popcorn anymore, prompting some operators to look at 'creative' ticket pricing for growth."

Source: "Heads Up: A Better Movie Seat May Cost You" by Brooks Barnes, March 5, 2023, https://www.nytimes.com/2023/03/05/business/media/movie-theaters-ticket-prices.html

"The COVID-19 pandemic severely damaged industry revenue, which dropped 73.1% in 2020 as lockdown orders pushed consumers to online streaming. Revenue growth post-COVID has been sluggish as disposable income has wavered and reliance on online streaming has stayed strong. A shorter theatrical release window will damage revenue as vertically integrated production studios go to streaming to avoid piracy and boost revenue for other businesses under their ownership."

Source: IBISWorld Key Takeaways

RESOURCES

- IBISWorld, September 2023: https://www.ibisworld.com
- MPA—Motion Picture Association: https://www.motionpictures.org
- NATO—National Association of Theatre Owners: https://www.natoonline.org

Moving Services

NAICS 484210	SIC 4214-01	Businesses/Units 18,311
Profit $1.7 B	Wages $5.2 B	Annual Growth Future 1.1%
		Annual Growth Past 1.1%

Rules of Thumb

- 50% annual sales

INDUSTRY MULTIPLES

Acquisition multiples below are calculated medians using US private industry transactions. Data updated annually. Last update: August 2023.

VALUATION MULTIPLE (MEDIAN VALUE)

UNDER $1 MILLION NET SALES

MVIC/Net Sales	0.46
MVIC/Gross Profit	0.60
MVIC/SDE	2.15
MVIC/EBITDA	2.68

$1 MILLION–$5 MILLION NET SALES

MVIC/Net Sales	0.41
MVIC/Gross Profit	0.79
MVIC/SDE	2.40
MVIC/EBITDA	3.84

OVER $5 MILLION NET SALES   N/A

Source: DealStats (formerly Pratt's Stats), 2023 (Portland, OR: Business Valuation Resources, LLC), www.bvresources.com/dealstats

BENCHMARK DATA

STATISTICS (MOVING SERVICES)

Number of Establishments	18,311
Average Profit Margin	7.9%
Revenue per Employee	$200,214
Average Number of employees	6.1
Average Wages per Employee	$47,717

PRODUCTS AND SERVICES SEGMENTATION

Residential moving	64.8%
Other	19.0%
Commercial moving	11.4%
Warehousing services	4.8%

INDUSTRY COSTS

Profit	7.9%
Wages	24.0%
Purchases	34.0%
Depreciation	2.4%
Marketing	0.2%
Rent & Utilities	5.1%
Other	26.7%

MARKET SHARE

ArcBest Corporation	2.7%
UniGroup, Inc.	0.9%
Atlas World Group Inc.	0.5%

INDUSTRY TREND

"Despite severe disruption from the COVID-19 pandemic, moving companies performed well during the current period. Low-interest rates for most of the period led to a booming housing market, which boosted revenue in 2021 and 2022. The use of mobile apps to find movers will become more popular in the near future. This has the potential to replace many traditional moving service companies."

Source: IBISWorld Key Takeaways

RESOURCES

• IBISWorld, September 2023: https://www.ibisworld.com

- Moving & Storage Conference:
  https://www.trucking.org/moving-storage-conference

Music Go Round (Franchise)

| NAICS 459510 | SIC 5736-08 | Businesses/Units 37

Rules of Thumb
- 40% annual sales plus inventory

PRICING TIPS

Approx. Total Investment: $295,500 to $378,300

RESOURCES
- Music Go Round: https://www.musicgoround.com/home
- Franchise information: https://www.musicgoround.com/home/own-a-store
- Winmark: https://winmarkcorporation.com

Musical Instrument Stores

| NAICS 451140 | SIC 5736 | Businesses/Units 9,976

| Profit $239.2 M | Wages $859.9 M | Annual Growth Future 0.2%

| | | Annual Growth Past -2.9%

Rules of Thumb
- 25% annual sales

INDUSTRY MULTIPLES

Acquisition multiples below are calculated medians using US private industry transactions. Data updated annually. Last update: August 2023.

VALUATION MULTIPLE (MEDIAN VALUE)

UNDER $1 MILLION NET SALES

MVIC/Net Sales.	0.55
MVIC/Gross Profit	0.70
MVIC/SDE	2.49
MVIC/EBITDA	2.84

$1 MILLION–$5 MILLION NET SALES

MVIC/Net Sales.	0.24
MVIC/Gross Profit	N/A
MVIC/SDE	2.90
MVIC/EBITDA	N/A

OVER $5 MILLION NET SALES	N/A

Source: DealStats (formerly Pratt's Stats), 2023 (Portland, OR: Business Valuation Resources, LLC), www.bvresources.com/dealstats

BENCHMARK DATA

STATISTICS (MUSICAL INSTRUMENT AND SUPPLIES STORES)

Number of Establishments .	9,976
Average Profit Margin .	4.6%
Revenue per Employee .	$148,805

Average Number of Employees.   3.8
Average Wages per Employee $24,656

PRODUCTS AND SERVICES SEGMENTATION

New guitars .   . 42.5%
New other instruments .   . 23.9%
New pianos .   . 15.1%
Services such as lessons and repairs   . 9.3%
Used violins, drums, guitars and other instruments   . 6.0%
Other   . 2.6%
Electronic equipment   . 0.6%

MAJOR MARKET SEGMENTATION

Students and instructors   . 45.7%
Hobbyists   . 33.3%
Professionals   . 21.0%

INDUSTRY COSTS

Profit   . 4.6%
Wages   . 16.5%
Purchases   . 50.5%
Depreciation   . 1.1%
Marketing   . 2.0%
Rent & Utilities   . 6.0%
Other   . 19.3%

MARKET SHARE

Guitar Center, Inc.   . 32.3%

INDUSTRY TREND

"Music stores are being aggressively replaced by big-box retailers and online merchants. Even peer-to-peer music websites are taking notes from the historic revenue generator, music instrument stores. Technology's aggressive expansion has drawn away many younger musicians from music stores. Simultaneously, the electronic music equipment used to make popular tracks sells more readily online than in classical-focused music retail locations."

Source: IBISWorld Key Takeaways

EXPERT COMMENTS

Independent brick-and-mortar locations are a dying breed.

RESOURCES

• IBISWorld, September 2023: https://www.ibisworld.com
• NAMM: https://www.namm.org

Nail Salons

| NAICS 812113 | SIC 7231-02

Rules of Thumb

• 25% annual sales plus inventory

INDUSTRY MULTIPLES

Acquisition multiples below are calculated medians using US private industry transactions. Data updated annually. Last update: August 2023.

VALUATION MULTIPLE (MEDIAN VALUE)

UNDER $1 MILLION NET SALES
MVIC/Net Sales 0.37
MVIC/Gross Profit 0.52
MVIC/SDE 1.69
MVIC/EBITDA 2.69

$1 MILLION–$5 MILLION NET SALES
MVIC/Net Sales 0.98
MVIC/Gross Profit 1.07
MVIC/SDE 2.75
MVIC/EBITDA 4.95

OVER $5 MILLION NET SALES   N/A

Source: DealStats (formerly Pratt's Stats), 2023 (Portland, OR: Business Valuation Resources, LLC), www.bvresources.com/dealstats

BENCHMARK DATA

For additional Benchmark data see Beauty Salons.

RESOURCES

• NAILS Magazine: https://www.nailsmag.com

Nathan's Famous (Franchise)

| NAICS 722513 | Businesses/Units 168

Rules of Thumb

• 85%–90% annual sales plus inventory

INDUSTRY MULTIPLES

Acquisition multiples below are calculated medians using US private industry transactions. Data updated annually. Last update: August 2023.

VALUATION MULTIPLE (MEDIAN VALUE)

UNDER $1 MILLION NET SALES
MVIC/Net Sales 0.31
MVIC/Gross Profit 0.48
MVIC/SDE 1.67
MVIC/EBITDA 2.21

$1 MILLION–$5 MILLION NET SALES
MVIC/Net Sales 0.39
MVIC/Gross Profit 0.60
MVIC/SDE 2.43
MVIC/EBITDA 2.98

OVER $5 MILLION NET SALES
MVIC/Net Sales 0.89
MVIC/Gross Profit 2.08
MVIC/SDE 4.98
MVIC/EBITDA 12.81

Source: DealStats (formerly Pratt's Stats), 2023 (Portland, OR: Business Valuation Resources, LLC), www.bvresources.com/dealstats

PRICING TIPS

Approx. Total Investment: $501,633 to $1,170,360

BENCHMARK DATA

Units range from 120 to 3,000 square feet.

RESOURCES
- Nathan's Famous: https://www.nathansfamous.com
- Franchise information: https://franchise.nathansfamous.com

Natural Gas Distribution

| NAICS 221210　　| Businesses/Units 2,906

| Profit $14.3 B　　| Wages $14.7 B　　| Annual Growth Future -0.8%

　　　　　　　　　　　　　　　　　　　　| Annual Growth Past 3.1%

INDUSTRY MULTIPLES

Acquisition multiples below are calculated medians using US private industry transactions. Data updated annually. Last update: August 2023.

VALUATION MULTIPLE (MEDIAN VALUE)

UNDER $1 MILLION NET SALES	N/A
$1 MILLION–$5 MILLION NET SALES	
MVIC/Net Sales	1.11
MVIC/Gross Profit	2.33
MVIC/SDE	3.35
MVIC/EBITDA	20.55
OVER $5 MILLION NET SALES	
MVIC/Net Sales	3.16
MVIC/Gross Profit	5.34
MVIC/SDE	N/A
MVIC/EBITDA	14.16

Source: DealStats (formerly Pratt's Stats), 2023 (Portland, OR: Business Valuation Resources, LLC), www.bvresources.com/dealstats

BENCHMARK DATA

STATISTICS (NATURAL GAS DISTRIBUTION)

Number of Establishments	2,906
Average Profit Margin	6.6%
Revenue per Employee	$1,769,987
Average Number of Employees	39.6
Average Wages per Employee	$123,137

PRODUCTS AND SERVICES SEGMENTATION

Natural gas distribution	59.3%
Natural gas marketing and brokering	34.5%
Other	6.2%

MAJOR MARKET SEGMENTATION

Residential	35.1%
Industrial	24.6%
Electric power	22.9%
Commercial	17.2%
Transportation	0.2%

INDUSTRY COSTS

Profit	6.6%
Wages	6.7%
Purchases	44.7%
Depreciation	7.0%
Marketing	0.2%
Rent & Utilities	1.2%
Other	33.6%

INDUSTRY TREND

"International unrest has driven gas prices up. Deteriorating relations between the Western powers, Russia and China, have caused significant disruptions in the global supply of natural gas, which distributors have been able to capitalize on. Volatile gas prices drive customers toward frugality. Rapidly fluctuating natural gas prices have driven consumers to travel less and consequentially spend less on gas. Distributors have been able to retain revenue by increasing prices accordingly. Rising demand will level out the industry in years to come. Volatility caused by the COVID-19 pandemic will subside as the virus abates. Increasing demand from the manufacturing sector will bring distributors to the industry and stabilize revenue."

Source: IBISWorld Key Takeaways

RESOURCES

- IBISWorld, September 2023: https://www.ibisworld.com

Navigational Instrument Manufacturing

| NAICS 334511 | Businesses/Units 4,040

| Profit $9.3 B | Wages $32.9 B | Annual Growth Future 1.0%

| Annual Growth -0.7%

INDUSTRY MULTIPLES

Acquisition multiples below are calculated medians using US private industry transactions. Data updated annually. Last update: November 2023.

VALUATION MULTIPLE (MEDIAN VALUE)

UNDER $1 MILLION NET SALES	
MVIC/Net Sales.	2.56
MVIC/Gross Profit	8.06
MVIC/SDE	2.57
MVIC/EBITDA	3.97
$1 MILLION–$5 MILLION NET SALES	N/A
OVER $5 MILLION NET SALES	
MVIC/Net Sales.	1.69
MVIC/Gross Profit	6.04
MVIC/SDE	N/A
MVIC/EBITDA	15.93

Source: DealStats (formerly Pratt's Stats), 2023 (Portland, OR: Business Valuation Resources, LLC), www.bvresources.com/dealstats

BENCHMARK DATA

STATISTICS (NAVIGATIONAL INSTRUMENT MANUFACTURING)

Number of Establishments .	4,040
Average Profit Margin	7.2%
Revenue per Employee .	$424,571
Average Number of Employees.	77.3
Average Wages per Employee .	$106,986

PRODUCTS AND SERVICES SEGMENTATION

Search, detection and navigation instruments .	50.6%
Analytical laboratory instruments	14.0%
Other measuring and controlling devices including watches and clocks .	10.0%

Electricity measuring and testing instruments 9.7%
Industrial process control instruments 9.4%
Totalizing fluid meter and counting devices 4.0%
Automatic environmental control instruments 2.3%

MAJOR MARKET SEGMENTATION

Transportation 36.3%
Other 19.7%
Original equipment manufacturers 15.7%
Government clients 14.3%
Scientific laboratories 14.0%

INDUSTRY COSTS

Profit 7.2%
Wages 25.3%
Purchases 36.6%
Depreciation 1.7%
Marketing 0.3%
Rent & Utilities 1.3%
Other 27.5%

MARKET SHARE

UTC 5.2%
Thermo Fisher Scientific Inc. 2.9%
Honeywell International Inc. 2.9%
Keysight Technologies, Inc. 1.6%

INDUSTRY TREND

"Government spending has propped up demand for the industry. As COVID-19 crushed all other spouts of demand, funding for US defense and transportation remained. Government spending will continue to support demand moving forward. Rising interest rates will continue to restrain growth. As rates rise, manufacturers will see falling exports as the dollar appreciates and expansion of operations will be much more costly looking to the future."

Source: IBISWorld Key Takeaways

RESOURCES

• IBISWorld, September 2023: https://www.ibisworld.com

Newspaper Routes

| NAICS 454390

Rules of Thumb

• 90%–100% annual sales plus inventory

INDUSTRY MULTIPLES

Acquisition multiples below are calculated medians using US private industry transactions. Data updated annually. Last update: August 2023.

VALUATION MULTIPLE (MEDIAN VALUE)

UNDER $1 MILLION NET SALES
MVIC/Net Sales 0.59
MVIC/Gross Profit 0.81
MVIC/SDE 1.63
MVIC/EBITDA 1.45

$1 MILLION–$5 MILLION NET SALES

MVIC/Net Sales.	0.97
MVIC/Gross Profit	1.22
MVIC/SDE	1.99
MVIC/EBITDA	1.71

OVER $5 MILLION NET SALES

MVIC/Net Sales.	0.39
MVIC/Gross Profit	0.70
MVIC/SDE	3.28
MVIC/EBITDA	3.44

Source: DealStats (formerly Pratt's Stats), 2023 (Portland, OR: Business Valuation Resources, LLC), www.bvresources.com/dealstats

Nonferrous Metal Rolling & Alloying

| NAICS 33149 | Businesses/Units 992

| Profit $853.2 M | Wages $2.4 B | Annual Growth Future 1.6%

| Annual Growth Past 2.3%

INDUSTRY MULTIPLES

Acquisition multiples below are calculated medians using US private industry transactions. Data updated annually. Last update: August 2023.

VALUATION MULTIPLE (MEDIAN VALUE)

UNDER $1 MILLION NET SALES	N/A
$1 MILLION–$5 MILLION NET SALES	N/A

OVER $5 MILLION NET SALES

MVIC/Net Sales.	0.40
MVIC/Gross Profit	1.81
MVIC/SDE	3.27
MVIC/EBITDA	3.52

Source: DealStats (formerly Pratt's Stats), 2023 (Portland, OR: Business Valuation Resources, LLC), www.bvresources.com/dealstats

BENCHMARK DATA

STATISTICS (NONFERROUS METAL ROLLING & ALLOYING)

Number of Establishments .	992
Average Profit Margin	4.4%
Revenue per Employee .	$608,030
Average Number of Employees.	32.5
Average Wages per Employee .	$74,962

PRODUCTS AND SERVICES SEGMENTATION

Other primary and secondary nonferrous meta	28.2%
Secondary precious metal and precious metal alloys .	18.8%
Titanium and titanium-based alloy products	16.1%
Nickel and nickel-based alloy products	12.6%
Nonferrous metal powders, paste and flakes	11.0%
Primary precious metal mill shapes	9.2%
Zinc-based alloys	4.1%

MAJOR MARKET SEGMENTATION

Aerospace and defense manufacturing	45.9%
Other segments.	32.9%
Mining, oil and gas machinery manufacturing .	12.4%
Transportation	8.8%

INDUSTRY COSTS

Profit	4.4%
Wages	12.3%
Purchases	55.1%
Depreciation	1.4%
Marketing	0.0%
Rent & Utilities	2.6%
Other	24.1%

INDUSTRY TREND

"Rebounding demand for the aerospace sector benefits metal processors. Airlines will be more inclined to purchase new aircraft as travel activity grows, boosting titanium sales. Strong import penetration supports price competition. This has put downward pressure on revenue growth, as consumers are inclined to buy more affordable products whenever possible."

Source: IBISWorld Key Takeaways

RESOURCES

• IBISWorld, April 2023: https://www.ibisworld.com

Nursing Homes/Skilled Nursing Facilities

	NAICS 623110		SIC 8051-01		Businesses/Units 37,123
	Profit $14.7 B		Wages $59.5 B		Annual Growth Future 4.7%
					Annual Growth Past 0.7%

Rules of Thumb

• 45%–50% annual sales plus inventory
• 2.5–3 x SDE plus inventory
• 3–3.3 x EBIT
• 3.5–4 x EBITDA

INDUSTRY MULTIPLES

Acquisition multiples below are calculated medians using US private industry transactions. Data updated annually. Last update: August 2023.

VALUATION MULTIPLE (MEDIAN VALUE)

UNDER $1 MILLION NET SALES	
MVIC/Net Sales	0.40
MVIC/Gross Profit	0.31
MVIC/SDE	2.44
MVIC/EBITDA	2.53
$1 MILLION–$5 MILLION NET SALES	N/A
OVER $5 MILLION NET SALES	
MVIC/Net Sales	1.87
MVIC/Gross Profit	3.01
MVIC/SDE	N/A
MVIC/EBITDA	15.09

Source: DealStats (formerly Pratt's Stats), 2023 (Portland, OR: Business Valuation Resources, LLC), www.bvresources.com/dealstats

PRICING TIPS

This industry has really struggled with filling staffing and maintaining quality service. Companies that have a strong staff retention history can demand a higher price. The business is there and will be for some time; the key is maintaining a team that can service the need.

Pricing the value of a nursing home depends on several factors—i.e., case mix, city or rural location, state where it is located, current census, whether there a certificate of need in that area, and number of competitors close by.

First and foremost, pricing of these facilities as well as ALFs hinges on a cap rate on NOI, or net operating income, which is different from SDE or EBITDA. Also, in the industry when calculating EBITDA, you do add-back rent, so you will often see this acronym stated as EBITDAR, with the "R" being for rent. NOI takes into account a "management fee" of 5 percent (not a real management fee but, considered proprietary earnings for the business, you must calculate on gross revenue before applying any cap rate) and capex, or capital expenditures for the future, like roofs, HVAC, floors, furniture, etc. If you want to get scientific with the capex number, ask the seller for the last 5 years of capital expenditures and you can create a moving average to use. Cap rates can fluctuate significantly, depending on the type of long-term care and state of the home. Right now, SNFs are in the 10 percent cap range with ALFs in the 6 percent cap range. IL, or independent living, are traditionally about the same as ALFs. Recasting/add-backs are critical, as you will often find nonessential employees (family or just wasted positions) or possibly understaffing, which means a negative impact to cash flow, below market private pay rates or even underperforming Medicare/Medicaid rates, that could present opportunities in your marketing of the business.

BENCHMARK DATA

STATISTICS (NURSING CARE FACILITIES)

Number of Establishments	37,123
Average Profit Margin	10.4%
Revenue per Employee	$93,900
Average Number of Employees	42.6
Average Wages per Employee	$39,157

PRODUCTS AND SERVICES SEGMENTATION

For-profit skilled nursing facilities	43.6%
For-profit nursing homes	33.0%
Nonprofit skilled nursing facilities	10.3%
Nonprofit nursing homes	7.8%
Government nursing homes and skilled nursing facilities	4.7%
Hospice centers	0.6%

INDUSTRY COSTS

Profit	10.4%
Wages	42.0%
Purchases	6.7%
Depreciation	2.0%
Marketing	0.2%
Rent & Utilities	6.3%
Other	32.5%

Labor as a percentage of gross is very typical at 50 percent of gross for a strong home running a census of 85 percent or higher. Food is another good measuring barometer. You don't often find a lot of waste in a home, but what you will see is quality differences and that can move the costs up considerably. A 60-bed home can see food costs that can range from $135,000 to $180,000 annually, or $6.37/day/resident to $8.50/day/resident.

Cost of Goods	15% to 20%
Occupancy Costs	07% to 12%
Payroll/ Labor Costs.	40% to 50%
Profit (pretax)	10% to 20%

QUESTIONS

- Do you have a strong referral rate?
- Have any new facilities opened in the last two years, and/or are any new facilities approved to be built?
- Where is your business coming from? Good relationships with hospitals?
- Let me see your last three surveys. Surveys are conducted on life safety and health issues at the homes—and detail any violations and corrective measures the home took to resolve the problem. If it's an SNF, what's their CMS rating? This ranges from one star to five stars. One-star homes will have challenges getting referrals in from hospitals, as many won't refer patients to nursing homes with such a low rating.

INDUSTRY TREND

This industry will be in high demand for many years. There will be plenty of sellers for buyers as the burnout level is high for owners as they work 24/7, have high staffing issues, and in many states have excessive regulatory requirements.

Demand should rise as baby boomers age and go to nursing homes.

"The Biden administration is expected to issue a federal minimum staffing mandate for nursing homes. As the long term care sector continues to face a historic labor crisis, experts are questioning how the proposed mandate would address staffing shortages without resources or support. Many providers have already increased pay and benefits, which has been invaluable for workers and enabled nursing homes to try to compete in today's challenging job market. This raises serious questions about the ability of programs like Medicaid and Medicare Advantage to keep pace. The mandate could require an estimated $10 billion per year for caregivers' wages and benefits—and so far, the proposed mandate remains unfunded."

Source: "Experts Question How Nursing Homes Will Pay for More Staff amid Anticipated Minimum Staffing Mandate," October 7, 2022, https://www.ahcancal.org/News-and-Communications/Press-Releases/Pages/Experts-Question-How-Nursing-Homes-Will-Pay-For-More-Staff-Amid-Anticipated-Minimum-Staffing-Mandate-.aspx

The pandemic has introduced new concerns over viral spread at these types of facilities. You will see, new SNFs have to plan for more isolation rooms and better social distancing, not only to avoid pandemic issues but for more normal situations like the flu. You could even see older homes forced to make accommodations for this same thing. Required staffing in SNFs is always an issue. Oftentimes CMS will require more staffing but provide no extra revenue, thus reducing net earnings. Homes are really trying to capitalize on their rehab and PT to create higher-margin revenue streams. You are also seeing homes branch out to create a total continuum of care where they have assisted living, independent living, nursing home, home health, etc.

"Many operators have been able to capitalize on an increase in per capita disposable income. Operators have taken steps to improve the delivery of clinical and hospitality services. Shifting consumer preferences have placed pressure on nursing care facilities. Demand for nursing care facilities is expected to rise along with an aging population. Uncertainty surrounding healthcare legislation is expected to present challenges to nursing facilities. The average industry profit margin is expected to decline slightly over the next five years. The aging population is expected to return the industry to growth in 2022."

Source: IBISWorld Industry at a Glance

EXPERT COMMENTS

Make sure you know how to manage employees, and have a knack for retaining them.

Study the market for bed availability and the staffing situation.

Census is key. If census has only ramped up in the previous few months, really monitor what kind of residents have been admitted. You'd like to see a consistent census over the years at least at 88 percent. Surveys are also important, and CMS ratings. A 5-star rating means a home is top notch. Below 3 stars indicates serious issues. Buyers should request copies of surveys. "F" tags and "G" tags are bad. If you see those, you're typically looking at poor care for seniors. Anyone can make a mistake, so read surveys thoroughly and ask for the correction plan so you can see what the home did to correct it, and then ask for the reinspection report so you can see how the state saw their correction work.

In most states, there is a moratorium on new SNF licenses. This makes current licenses fairly valuable and also limits competition, at least as it relates to other SNFs. ALFs are typically not limited, so they can come into the market at any time but offer much different services than a SNF so they're not really competition. These facilities, even through the pandemic, remain highly marketable with good financing options.

FINANCING

Oftentimes there is outside financing. If a strategic buyer, they seem to have a 60/40 financing structure, which means 60 percent financed and 40 percent buyer equity. Individual buyers usually have less equity in the transaction and require 5 to 10 percent seller carry.

Outside financing. Seller financing is rare in this business.

For deals $10 million and under, you should be able to secure SBA financing. There is quite a bit of seller financing involved in these deals, but be cautious as rules have made those less favorable to the seller. SBA will give you up to 25-year fully amortized loans. If your home qualifies for HUD financing, this is ideal for the buyer with 35-year amortizations, the lowest interest rates, and no personal guarantees for the debt!

RESOURCES

- IBISWorld, August 2022: https://www.ibisworld.com
- AHCA/NCAL—American Health Care Association/National Center for Assisted Living: https://www.ahcancal.org/Pages/Default.aspx
- LeadingAge: https://leadingage.org
- McKnight's Long-Term Care News: https://www.mcknights.com
- NIC—The National Investment Center: https://www.nic.org

Office Staffing and Temporary Agencies

NAICS 561320	SIC 7363-03	Businesses/Units 42,454
Profit $12.7 B	Wages $155.8 B	Annual Growth Future 1.1%
		Annual Growth Past 1.8%

Rules of Thumb

- 6–12 x EBITDA
- 1–2 x annual sales plus inventory
- 3 x SDE plus inventory
- 2–5 x EBIT (smaller deals under $25 million)
- 5–7.5 x EBIT (larger deals over $25 million)
- 6–9 x EBIT (information technology)

INDUSTRY MULTIPLES

Acquisition multiples below are calculated medians using US private industry transactions. Data updated annually. Last update: August 2023.

VALUATION MULTIPLE (MEDIAN VALUE)

UNDER $1 MILLION NET SALES

MVIC/Net Sales.	0.47
MVIC/Gross Profit	0.59
MVIC/SDE	2.42
MVIC/EBITDA	2.42

$1 MILLION–$5 MILLION NET SALES

MVIC/Net Sales.	0.30
MVIC/Gross Profit	0.73
MVIC/SDE	2.26
MVIC/EBITDA	5.07

OVER $5 MILLION NET SALES

MVIC/Net Sales.	0.35
MVIC/Gross Profit	0.89
MVIC/SDE	2.49
MVIC/EBITDA	6.08

Source: DealStats (formerly Pratt's Stats), 2023 (Portland, OR: Business Valuation Resources, LLC), www.bvresources.com/dealstats

PRICING TIPS

Client attrition and A/R information are very important in valuing a staffing business.

BENCHMARK DATA

STATISTICS (OFFICE STAFFING & TEMP AGENCIES)

Number of Establishments	42,454
Average Profit Margin	5.1%
Revenue per Employee	$64,147
Average Number of Employees.	92.3
Average Wages per Employee	$40,284

PRODUCTS AND SERVICES SEGMENTATION

Industrial staffing	22.8%
Office, clerical and administrative staffing	17.4%
Information technology staffing	16.8%
Professional and managerial staffing	16.8%
Healthcare staffing	9.8%
Engineering and scientific staffing	9.0%
Other	7.4%

Professional, retail and other service-oriented sectors	44.3%
Technical sectors	26.5%
Industrial sectors	21.5%
Other	7.7%

INDUSTRY COSTS

Profit	5.1%
Wages	62.7%
Purchases	10.3%
Depreciation	0.2%
Marketing	1.4%
Rent & Utilities	2.0%
Other	18.4%

EXPENSES (% OF ANNUAL SALES)

Cost of Goods	10%
Occupancy Costs	10%
Payroll/Labor Costs.	50% to 60%
Profit (pretax)	08% to 10%

QUESTIONS

- Typical questions for any service business: customer concentration, staff non-competes, contracts with clients, ability to speak to next level of management when the time is right, historical growth, gross margins, etc.
- Length of service by account; gross profit by account; bad debt experience

INDUSTRY TREND

"The economy significantly impacts staffing agencies, as their demand depends on business landscape strength. In recessions, temporary worker usage declines as companies prioritize retaining permanent staff over temporary hires. The continued implementation of the Patient Protection and Affordable Care Act will drive demand for temporary labor in healthcare. Concurrently, AI technologies necessitate temp agencies to adapt, streamlining the hiring process."

Source: IBISWorld Key Takeaways

FINANCING

For the more substantial transactions ($10 million in sales and up), normally these are financed internally or with lines of credit for larger buyers. Smaller sellers, especially those with lower margins that are less desirable, may be willing to consider seller financing.

RESOURCES

- IBISWorld, September 2023: https://www.ibisworld.com
- ASA—American Staffing Association: https://americanstaffing.net
- NAPS—National Association of Personnel Services: https://www.naps360.org
- SIA—Staffing Industry Analysts: https://staffingindustry.com

Office Supplies and Stationery Stores

NAICS 453210	SIC 5943-01	Businesses/Units 8,699
Profit $808.9 M	Wages $1.3 B	Annual Growth Future -1.1%
		Annual Growth Past -2.3%

Rules of Thumb

- 25% annual sales plus inventory
- 1.5 x SDE plus inventory

INDUSTRY MULTIPLES

Acquisition multiples below are calculated medians using US private industry transactions. Data updated annually. Last update: August 2023.

VALUATION MULTIPLE (MEDIAN VALUE)

UNDER $1 MILLION NET SALES

MVIC/Net Sales.	0.36
MVIC/Gross Profit	0.62
MVIC/SDE	1.65
MVIC/EBITDA	5.49

$1 MILLION–$5 MILLION NET SALES

MVIC/Net Sales.	0.36
MVIC/Gross Profit	0.63
MVIC/SDE	2.19
MVIC/EBITDA	4.51

OVER $5 MILLION NET SALES

MVIC/Net Sales.	0.44
MVIC/Gross Profit	1.67
MVIC/SDE	N/A
MVIC/EBITDA	35.01

Source: DealStats (formerly Pratt's Stats), 2023 (Portland, OR: Business Valuation Resources, LLC), www.bvresources.com/dealstats

PRICING TIPS

Check inventory levels and FF&E carefully. Owners of these types of businesses tend to hide cash flow in excessive inventory and FF&E.

BENCHMARK DATA

STATISTICS (OFFICE SUPPLY STORES)

Number of Establishments .	8,699
Average Profit Margin	6.5%
Revenue per Employee .	$221,106
Average Number of Employees.	.6.4
Average Wages per Employee .	$23,519

PRODUCTS AND SERVICES SEGMENTATION

Miscellaneous merchandise	31.5%
Computers and computer equipment .	22.4%
Office and school supplies .	16.2%
Office equipment and furniture .	15.2%
Other products and services	7.5%
Printing services	7.2%

MAJOR MARKET SEGMENTATION

Businesses for end use .	57.4%
Households and individuals	10.7%
Hospitality and tourism industries .	9.4%
Governments	7.4%
Industrial uses .	5.8%
Wholesalers and distributors for resale	4.9%
Other	4.4%

INDUSTRY COSTS

Profit	6.5%
Wages	10.7%

Purchases	.	.	.	.	.	.	.	. 49.4%
Depreciation	.	.	.	.	.	.	. 0.7%
Marketing	.	.	.	.	.	.	. 1.7%
Rent & Utilities	.	.	.	.	.	. 6.7%
Other	.	.	.	.	.	.	. 24.3%

MARKET SHARE

Staples Inc. .	.	.	.	.	.	.	. 39.2%
The ODP Corporation	.	.	.	. 29.8%
ACCO Brands Corporation	.	.	. 4.4%

INDUSTRY TREND

"Digitization has contributed to consistent declines as there is less demand for core industry products. The industry is in the declining phase of its life cycle. Consistent revenue declines are expected to continue through the outlook period."

Source: IBISWorld Key Takeaways

RESOURCES

• IBISWorld, March 2023: https://www.ibisworld.com

Oil & Gas Field Services

| | NAICS 21311 | | Businesses/Units 27,416 |

| | Profit $8.1 B | | Wages $27.2 B | | Annual Growth Future -0.4% |

| | | | | | Annual Growth Past -5.2% |

Rules of Thumb

• 3 x SDE
• 4 x EBITDA

INDUSTRY MULTIPLES

Acquisition multiples below are calculated medians using US private industry transactions. Data updated annually. Last update: August 2023.

VALUATION MULTIPLE (MEDIAN VALUE)

UNDER $1 MILLION NET SALES	N/A
$1 MILLION–$5 MILLION NET SALES	
MVIC/Net Sales.	0.91
MVIC/Gross Profit	1.75
MVIC/SDE	3.76
MVIC/EBITDA	4.74
OVER $5 MILLION NET SALES	
MVIC/Net Sales.	1.86
MVIC/Gross Profit	4.02
MVIC/SDE	3.03
MVIC/EBITDA	7.35

Source: DealStats (formerly Pratt's Stats), 2023 (Portland, OR: Business Valuation Resources, LLC), www.bvresources.com/dealstats

PRICING TIPS

Oil field services can be cyclical with energy prices. If the particular service company is less upstream and more midstream, e.g., gasket or valve repair, then they will trade at higher multiples. Transactions often start as asset sales and convert to stock sales in order to facilitate transfer of MSAs (master service agreements). Values of site preparation, oil field construction, and roustabout service companies tend to fluctuate with boom–bust cycles, since they are typically demand-driven based on oil rig count. Monitor U.S. rig count—it is a harbinger to the owner's mood. Post-Covid, staffing and availability/retention of trained employees have been the greatest throttle to growth. Capex must be correctly factored and EBITDA adjusted (lowered) if equipment rental accounts for more than 15 percent of total sales. Water transportation and general trucking companies should be treated as commodity companies; discount the EBITDA multiple and ensure that capex is correctly reflected. Customer concentration is common. However, if 1 customer > 50 percent or top 3 > 80 percent of sales, expect to be discounted 0.5 to 2 x EBITDA; > $5M should not rely on rules of thumb. Different factors come into play, especially for strategic buyers. Need to include an average amount of net working capital (AR + prepaid expenses – AP – accrued expenses) in your deal structure.

It important to distinguish between services and suppliers, who are also service providers.

This business is very dynamic, and depending on which segment of the oil field service sector, transaction structures vary greatly. In most cases, deals are transacted based on a percent of equipment replacement value, or a multiple of EBITDA, with deductions for cash or equivalents. Most deals are currently moving in a 2 to 4 x EBITDA range.

BENCHMARK DATA

STATISTICS (OIL & GAS FIELD SERVICES)

Number of Establishments	27,416
Average Profit Margin	8.6%
Revenue per Employee	$273,046
Average Number of Employees	12.5
Average Wages per Employee	$79,219

PRODUCTS AND SERVICES SEGMENTATION

Oilfield support services	44.0%
Oil drilling services	32.8%
Natural gas well support services	11.3%
Natural gas drilling services	8.5%
Metallic ore mining support	1.4%
Coal mining support	1.1%
Nonmetallic ore mining support	0.9%

MAJOR MARKET SEGMENTATION

Oil extractors	76.8%
Gas extractors	19.8%
Metallic ore mining industry	1.4%
Coal mining industry	1.1%
Nonmetallic ore mining industry	0.9%

INDUSTRY COSTS

Profit	8.6%
Wages	28.9%
Purchases	19.6%
Depreciation	7.5%
Marketing	0.2%
Rent & Utilities	4.2%
Other	31.2%

This industry was hit hard through Covid, and while oil prices have rebounded, the companies still have weak balance sheets and little access to capital. Most smaller businesses are back making nice margins but are struggling to grow due to capital constraints. Many owners are choosing to ride this positive wave and exit while their companies are profitable.

EXPENSES (% OF ANNUAL SALES)

Cost of Goods	40% to 50%
Occupancy Costs	15%
Payroll/Labor Costs.	30%

QUESTIONS

• Years in business? Employees' seniority? Customers' loyalty? Competition differentiating factors?

INDUSTRY TREND

Stable

"Oil and gas prices drive industry performance. Energy producer hire more support services only when prices are sufficient to cover costs. Natural gas is a relatively affordable and efficient source of energy. These characteristics will make the energy source in high demand by power producers for years to come. Lower hydrocarbon prices and the growing prevalence of renewable energy are the two most significant threats to the industry in the long term. Demand for oil and gas support services will fall as interest in hydrocarbons wanes."

Source: IBISWorld Key Takeaways

EXPERT COMMENTS

Ensure qualified management in place with reasonable transition period.

FINANCING

Outside financing. Typically seller holds 10 to 20 percent.

Seller financing is common, 20 to 40 percent of selling price.

RESOURCES

• IBISWorld, September 2023: https://www.ibisworld.com

Oil & Gas Pipeline Construction

	NAICS 237120		Businesses/Units 2,215

	Profit $4.4 B		Wages $16.6 B		Annual Growth Future 1.1%

				Annual Growth Past -6.1%

INDUSTRY MULTIPLES

Acquisition multiples below are calculated medians using US private industry transactions. Data updated annually. Last update: August 2023.

VALUATION MULTIPLE (MEDIAN VALUE)

UNDER $1 MILLION NET SALES

MVIC/Net Sales.	0.76
MVIC/Gross Profit	1.23
MVIC/SDE	3.09
MVIC/EBITDA	4.97

$1 MILLION–$5 MILLION NET SALES

MVIC/Net Sales .	0.69
MVIC/Gross Profit .	1.87
MVIC/SDE .	3.13
MVIC/EBITDA .	4.85

OVER $5 MILLION NET SALES

MVIC/Net Sales .	0.89
MVIC/Gross Profit .	3.43
MVIC/SDE .	4.09
MVIC/EBITDA .	7.29

Source: DealStats (formerly Pratt's Stats), 2023 (Portland, OR: Business Valuation Resources, LLC), www.bvresources.com/dealstats

BENCHMARK DATA

STATISTICS (OIL & GAS PIPELINE CONSTRUCTION)

Number of Establishments .	2,215
Average Profit Margin .	8.9%
Revenue per Employee .	$231,210
Average Number of Employees .	97.3
Average Wages per Employee .	$78,218

PRODUCTS AND SERVICES SEGMENTATION

New pipeline construction .	57.1%
Pipeline additions and alterations .	37.2%
Pipeline maintenance .	5.7%

MAJOR MARKET SEGMENTATION

Private sector natural gas interests .	68.3%
Private sector oil interests .	24.7%
Public sector clients .	7.0%

INDUSTRY COSTS

Profit .	8.9%
Wages .	33.7%
Purchases .	24.9%
Depreciation .	2.6%
Marketing .	0.1%
Rent & Utilities .	5.3%
Other .	24.5%

INDUSTRY TREND

"The United States achieved its first-ever month as a net exporter of hydrocarbons in September 2019. This was a major accomplishment for the nation and took widescale cooperation among upstream, midstream and downstream industries. Fracking and horizontal drilling have turned the United States into an energy powerhouse. New pipelines have been constructed and old lines reverse to accommodate unprecedented flows of oil and gas from new formations. The majority of new pipeline construction is being performed in the South. Some of the most lucrative projects center on bringing US and Canadian hydrocarbons to international terminals located in the Gulf Coast."

Source: IBISWorld Key Takeaways

RESOURCES

• IBISWorld, September 2023: https://www.ibisworld.com

Oil & Gas Related Businesses

Rules of Thumb

- 2–4 x EBITDA
- 65%–100% annual sales includes inventory
- 3–5 x EBIT
- 2.5–4 x SDE plus inventory

PRICING TIPS

The oil and gas industry is very cyclical, and sometimes they are successful by accident. Care must be taken to look past the profit and ask yourself why they are truly profitable in the long term, and do they understand how they got there? If they don't have a clear vision across the organization, then after a transition to different management, they could have an unraveling of their success. It is common to have these companies show a lot of discretionary spending that is hard to quantify.

The exit timing in this highly cyclical business—added to the inventory type, age, and utilization—is a major factor in the evaluation in this industry.

You must average a 3- or 4-year time frame to get a good feel for the business risk. With the fluctuations of the market, the 3- to 4-year snapshot incorporates a truer picture of the business.

BENCHMARK DATA

Oil and gas service company should have at least $5 million to $8 million in revenue to be salable (this is a quirk about this industry).

Barrels produced per day; proven, probable, and possible reserves; lift cost (breakeven price of oil and gas)

EXPENSES (% OF ANNUAL SALES)

Cost of Goods	.0% to 10%
Occupancy Costs	02% to 10%
Payroll/Labor Costs.	30% to 40%
Profit (pretax)	30% to 40%

QUESTIONS

- Safety record report along with the SOP for safety
- What do we do to minimize cost during a downturn?
- Factor in the true depreciation or the cost of repair/replacement of the equipment. Be sure to check the rollover in the accounts. Receivables/payables from year to year? This throws off the true sales/income for the year either way (loss or profit).
- Barrels per day production? Water flooding possibilities? New well potential? Modern tanks, lines, pumps in place? Reserves estimated by a third-party petroleum engineer? What is your lift (breakeven) price of oil?

INDUSTRY TREND

Innovation is key for this industry. Oil and gas is a declining industry and needs to innovate to remain profitable.

Slowing

Because of the potential for profit and quick ROI, there is a lot of competition, and the ease of replication is very high. The amount of competition will drive down pricing in good markets and bad.

Account for the risk and fluctuations in the market in the structure of the deal.

Mineral rights leases in proven oil and gas fields are outstanding assets.

Make certain you keep your service personnel; they are usually the ones with customer connections.

FINANCING

Seller financing, specially in this environment

RESOURCES

- AAPG—American Association of Petroleum Geologists: https://www.aapg.org
- AAPL: https://www.landman.org
- The American Oil & Gas Reporter: https://www.aogr.com
- API—American Petroleum Institute: https://www.api.org
- Hart Energy: https://www.hartenergy.com
- Oil & Gas Journal: https://www.ogj.com
- SPE—Society of Petroleum Engineers: https://www.spe.org/en/
- TXOGA—Texas Oil & Gas Association: https://www.txoga.org
- USOGA—US Oil & Gas Association: https://www.usoga.org

Once Upon A Child (Franchise)

| NAICS 459510 | SIC 5932-05 | Businesses/Units 352 |

Rules of Thumb

- 25% annual sales plus inventory
- 30% annual sales includes inventory

PRICING TIPS

Approx. Total Investment: $276,200 to $417,400

RESOURCES

- Once Upon A Child: https://www.onceuponachild.com
- Franchise information: https://www.onceuponachild.com/home/own-a-store
- Winmark: https://winmarkcorporation.com

Optical Stores

NAICS 456130	Businesses/Units 25,658	
Profit $1.5 B	Wages $4.6 B	Annual Growth Future 2.5%
		Annual Growth Past 4.4%

Rules of Thumb

- 50%–60% annual sales includes inventory (Sales do not include regular exam fees.)
- 2 x SDE includes inventory (Sales do not include regular exam fees.)

INDUSTRY MULTIPLES

Acquisition multiples below are calculated medians using US private industry transactions. Data updated annually. Last update: August 2023.

VALUATION MULTIPLE (MEDIAN VALUE)

UNDER $1 MILLION NET SALES

MVIC/Net Sales.	0.25
MVIC/Gross Profit	0.46
MVIC/SDE	2.50
MVIC/EBITDA	N/A
$1 MILLION–$5 MILLION NET SALES	N/A
OVER $5 MILLION NET SALES	N/A

Source: DealStats (formerly Pratt's Stats), 2023 (Portland, OR: Business Valuation Resources, LLC), www.bvresources.com/dealstats

PRICING TIPS

Adjust price up or down depending on how updated the equipment is.

How many days do they perform exams? For whom?

BENCHMARK DATA

STATISTICS (EYEGLASSES & CONTACT LENS STORES)

Number of Establishments .	25,658
Average Profit Margin	6.4%
Revenue per Employee .	$154,387
Average Number of Employees.	5.9
Average Wages per Employee .	$30,855

PRODUCTS AND SERVICES SEGMENTATION

Prescription lenses .	31.6%
Contact lenses .	23.5%
Eye exams	20.4%
Frames .	16.3%
Readers .	4.2%
Eyeglass accessories	2.0%
Readers .	2.0%

INDUSTRY COSTS

Profit	6.4%
Wages .	19.9%
Purchases .	55.1%
Depreciation	1.4%
Marketing	1.0%
Rent & Utilities .	2.3%
Other	13.9%

MARKET SHARE

EssilorLuxottica .	21.4%
Costco Wholesale Corp.	13.7%
National Vision Inc. .	7.0%
Visionworks of America Inc.	5.4%

EXPENSES (% OF ANNUAL SALES)

Cost of Goods	35% to 45%
Occupancy Costs	15% to 20%
Payroll/Labor Costs.	10% to 15%
Profit (pretax)	25% to 30%

- Contact lens sales? Do they keep the profits from opticians?
- Probability of staff retention, number of active patient records
- Days they have exams. If only one or two, it could be tough to generate sales.
- What kind of equipment? Leased? Referral sources? Insurances accepted?

INDUSTRY TREND

"Demographic and economic trends are influencing eyewear sales. Rising incomes and an aging population are behind rising spending on eyeglasses. A challenging economic environment in 2023 will subdue sales. Online eyewear sales are reshaping the industry. E-commerce sales will be an increasingly large share of traditional brick-and-mortar sales. Advances in at-home try-on tools facilitate online sales."

Source: IBISWorld Key Takeaways

EXPERT COMMENTS

Very limited buyer pool; must have OD degree and state license

National chains seem to be weaker. Mom and pops seem to be hanging in there, so they may be keeping optometrists busy.

RESOURCES

- IBISWorld, April 2023: https://www.ibisworld.com
- EB—Eyecare Business: https://www.eyecarebusiness.com

Optometry Practices

NAICS 621320	SIC 5999-04	Businesses/Units 35,334
Profit $3 B	Wages $8 B	Annual Growth Future 2.5%
		Annual Growth Past 1.8%

Rules of Thumb

- 55%–75% annual revenues includes inventory
- 2–4 x SDE includes inventory
- 2–3 x EBIT
- 2.5–4 x EBITDA

INDUSTRY MULTIPLES

Acquisition multiples below are calculated medians using US private industry transactions. Data updated annually. Last update: August 2023.

VALUATION MULTIPLE (MEDIAN VALUE)

UNDER $1 MILLION NET SALES

MVIC/Net Sales	0.57
MVIC/Gross Profit	0.78
MVIC/SDE	1.91
MVIC/EBITDA	4.31

$1 MILLION–$5 MILLION NET SALES

MVIC/Net Sales	0.54
MVIC/Gross Profit	0.78
MVIC/SDE	2.43
MVIC/EBITDA	7.47

MVIC/Net Sales	1.86
MVIC/Gross Profit	2.45
MVIC/SDE	N/A
MVIC/EBITDA	9.33

Source: DealStats (formerly Pratt's Stats), 2023 (Portland, OR: Business Valuation Resources, LLC), www.bvresources.com/dealstats

PRICING TIPS

1 x SDE, then add tangible assets

Multidoctor practices sell for higher percentage than solo practices. Most practices have a high retail component with the optical shop: frames, lenses, contacts.

Price may be discounted for high level of competition in the practice area, for poor employee retention, unfavorable lease transferability, and need for additional equipment.

Other factors influencing the multiple include whether or not the clinic and/or equipment require significant upgrades.

AR is excluded.

BENCHMARK DATA

STATISTICS (OPTOMETRISTS)

Number of Establishments	35,334
Average Profit Margin	.13.4%
Revenue per Employee	$134,295
Average Number of Employees	4.8
Average Wages per Employee	$47,932

PRODUCTS AND SERVICES SEGMENTATION

Sales of prescription eyewear	.37.0%
Providing eye exams	.28.0%
Sales of contact lenses	.17.0%
Providing miscellaneous eye care services	.11.0%
Providing medical eye care	.7.0%

MAJOR MARKET SEGMENTATION

Out-of-pocket spending	.44.6%
Reimbursements from private healthcare providers . .	.33.9%
All other	.12.0%
Reimbursements from Medicare and Medicaid . . .	.9.5%

INDUSTRY COSTS

Profit	.13.4%
Wages	.35.6%
Purchases	.8.7%
Depreciation	.2.0%
Marketing	.1.7%
Rent & Utilities	.9.2%
Other	.29.2%

Average practice served an average of 2,163 patients.

Eyewear revenue average	38%
Eye exam revenue average	21%
Contact lens revenue average	18%

Traditional solo practices have sold for 55 to 65 percent of gross revenue. Multi-doctor practices can sell for much more. Multilocation and multidoctor practices are key targets of private equity groups.

A healthy primary care practice brings in 26% of their revenue from exams; diagnostics contribute 10%; spectacles 50%; contact lenses 12%; and miscellaneous (OTC products and optical accessories) 2%.

43 annual eye exams for every 100 active patients.

FTE staff per FTE OD = 4; new patient ratio = 30%

Equipment lease and purchase expenses should be up to 5% of sales. Established practices should have about 80% returning patients and 20% new patients.

EXPENSES (% OF ANNUAL SALES)

Cost of Goods	25% to 35%
Occupancy Costs	05% to 10%
Payroll/Labor Costs.	15% to 25%
Profit (pretax)	15% to 30%

QUESTIONS

- How does fee schedule compare to competition/industry average? Adjust for cost of living in the area. Number hours per week seeing patients? Percentage of revenue from optical frames/lenses, exams, etc.? How much medical-related work? Pre-/postsurgery? Payor mix?
- What is the wholesale value of frame/lens/contact inventory? How old is equipment? Noncompetes for associate ODs?
- Carefully examine the current marketing efforts. Many selling doctors have neglected marketing, providing an opportunity for the new doctor to get value added with a more dedicated marketing effort, including social media.
- What insurances do you currently accept, and how is your billing handled?
- Certainly the reason for selling should be standard. Also, confirm the seller will not become a competitor by continuing to practice at a nearby location. A noncompete agreement is essential.
- What are the three things I can do to either increase revenue or decrease costs?
- Administrative system; client lists; reputation, including word-of-mouth referrals
- What does your recall system consist of?
- Is there any current or pending litigation against the practice?
- What is the true cash flow for the practice? What are the demographics of the patients, and what percent of patients is new each year?

INDUSTRY TREND

"COVID-19 accelerated disruption in the optometry field. Mounting competition from online eyewear retailers picked up during the pandemic, spurring consolidation activity. Greater medical needs for an aging population translate to higher demand for optometrists. Optometrists have a growing base of patients aged 65 and older seeking preventative exams and treatment for age-related eye diseases."

Source: IBISWorld Key Takeaways

More emphasis on medical procedures

Decline in single-doctor practices; increase in group practices

More of the same; increase of group practices, and national consolidation

EXPERT COMMENTS

Be patient; it can take a year to find a buyer. Like all businesses, sell when it's doing well, not as it declines toward retirement.

Optometry practices are seeing more competition from discount online frame/contact lens sellers like Warby Parker and Zenni Optical.

Past 5 years have seen increased consolidation of optometric and ophthalmologic practices due, in large part, to rising competition and the growth of private equity firms. In a span of just two years, more than 3,000 optometrists and 660 ophthalmologists were involved in practice consolidation. There are many reasons for this trend: the increasing cost of running a practice and online competition are just a couple; however, a large reason for consolidation involves demographics.

More focus on educating patients about the need for regular eye exams. Exams screening for potential risk for eye disease like cataracts, glaucoma, macular degeneration, low vision, and diabetic retinopathy will increase annually due to the aging of baby boomers and the rise of diabetes.

Potential buyers: Work as an OD for at least two years before owning a practice. Sellers: Start early and have patience! It might take more than a year to sell.

Be sure you want to be an owner, not an associate.

Optometry practices have historically had a low failure rate. Marketability is good, especially if the gross exceeds $500,000. Marketability is best in major metropolitan areas.

Must be sold to a like- or higher-licensed professional. An optical shop could be sold to an optician, optometrist, or ophthalmologist. An optometry practice (in most states) can be sold only to an optometrist or ophthalmologist.

FINANCING

Outside financing. Specialty divisions of most large lenders handle these businesses. 10-year fixed is most common. Seller financing seems to be making a comeback.

Outside financing. Financing is very easy for an optometry practice; 10-year term, 4 to 4.5 percent.

RESOURCES

- IBISWorld, September 2023: https://www.ibisworld.com
- AAO—American Academy of Optometry: https://www.aaopt.org
- American Board of Optometry: https://americanboardofoptometry.org
- AOA—American Optometric Association: https://www.aoa.org
- NOA—National Optometric Association: https://nationaloptometricassociation.com
- ODwire.org: https://www.odwire.org
- Optometric Management: https://www.optometricmanagement.com
- Optometry Times: https://www.optometrytimes.com
- Review of Optometric Business: https://www.reviewob.com
- Review of Optometry: https://www.reviewofoptometry.com
- VM—Vision Monday: https://www.visionmonday.com

Other Activities Related to Real Estate

NAICS 531390	Businesses/Units 690,996	
Profit $35.1 B	Wages $26.6 B	Annual Growth Future -1.0%
		Annual Growth Past 3.8%

INDUSTRY MULTIPLES

Acquisition multiples below are calculated medians using US private industry transactions. Data updated annually. Last update: August 2023.

VALUATION MULTIPLE (MEDIAN VALUE)

UNDER $1 MILLION NET SALES

MVIC/Net Sales	1.00
MVIC/Gross Profit	0.86
MVIC/SDE	1.86
MVIC/EBITDA	2.63

$1 MILLION–$5 MILLION NET SALES

MVIC/Net Sales	0.36
MVIC/Gross Profit	1.00
MVIC/SDE	N/A
MVIC/EBITDA	N/A

OVER $5 MILLION NET SALES

MVIC/Net Sales	7.67
MVIC/Gross Profit	9.21
MVIC/SDE	N/A
MVIC/EBITDA	17.56

Source: DealStats (formerly Pratt's Stats), 2023 (Portland, OR: Business Valuation Resources, LLC), www.bvresources.com/dealstats

BENCHMARK DATA

STATISTICS (REAL ESTATE ASSET MANAGEMENT & CONSULTING)

Number of Establishments	690,996
Average Profit Margin	36.6%
Revenue per Employee	1.0
Average Number of Employees	$129,321
Average Wages per Employee	$36,511

PRODUCTS AND SERVICES SEGMENTATION

Household real estate consulting services	41.1%
Corporate real estate consulting services	39.8%
Real estate listing	13.4%
Other services	5.7%

MAJOR MARKET SEGMENTATION

Residential markets	48.2%
Commercial markets	40.7%
Industrial	5.4%
Other	3.3%
Real estate agents and brokers	2.4%

INDUSTRY COSTS

Profit	36.6%
Wages	27.7%
Purchases	1.2%
Depreciation	15.0%
Marketing	0.6%
Rent & Utilities	2.2%
Other	16.7%

MARKET SHARE

CBRE	1.1%
Jones Lang LaSalle	0.4%
Altisource Portfolio Solutions	0.1%

INDUSTRY TREND

"Revenue for real estate asset managers and consultants has performed well during most of the current period, as the residential sector has been strong because of low interest rates. The nonresidential market has created some volatility for the industry. High business investment and consumer confidence will increase demand from the nonresidential sector during the outlook period, but higher permanent interest rates will constrain spending from residential markets. Fewer college graduates will make finding good employees difficult also."

Source: IBISWorld Key Takeaways

RESOURCES

• IBISWorld, September 2023: https://www.ibisworld.com

Other Commercial and Industrial Machinery and Equipment, Rental and Leasing

| NAICS 532490 | Businesses/Units 10,277

| Profit $6.7 B | Wages $8.2 B | Annual Growth Future 2.0%

| Annual Growth Past -1.1%

INDUSTRY MULTIPLES

Acquisition multiples below are calculated medians using US private industry transactions. Data updated annually. Last update: August 2023.

VALUATION MULTIPLE (MEDIAN VALUE)

UNDER $1 MILLION NET SALES
MVIC/Net Sales	0.99
MVIC/Gross Profit	1.21
MVIC/SDE	2.41
MVIC/EBITDA	3.51

$1 MILLION–$5 MILLION NET SALES
MVIC/Net Sales	0.99
MVIC/Gross Profit	1.19
MVIC/SDE	3.19
MVIC/EBITDA	3.90

OVER $5 MILLION NET SALES
MVIC/Net Sales	5.62
MVIC/Gross Profit	3.08
MVIC/SDE	N/A
MVIC/EBITDA	8.22

Source: DealStats (formerly Pratt's Stats), 2023 (Portland, OR: Business Valuation Resources, LLC), www.bvresources.com/dealstats

BENCHMARK DATA

STATISTICS (INDUSTRIAL EQUIPMENT RENTAL & LEASING)
Number of Establishments	10,277
Average Profit Margin	17.3%
Revenue per Employee	$314,000
Average Number of Employees	12.2
Average Wages per Employee	$66,136

PRODUCTS AND SERVICES SEGMENTATION
General industrial equipment rental	24.6%
Light construction equipment rental	23.5%
Audiovisual equipment rental	17.3%
Medical equipment rental	11.2%

Industrial energy equipment and pumps rental 8.8%
Retail sales, product delivery and repair 7.5%
Theatrical and motion picture rental 6.8%
Rental of other products 0.3%

MAJOR MARKET SEGMENTATION

Construction markets 25.5%
Heavy industry and manufacturing markets 22.2%
Entertainment and audiovisual markets 21.6%
Healthcare markets 12.6%
Individuals 7.1%
Other markets 6.1%
Government bodies 4.9%

INDUSTRY COSTS

Profit 17.3%
Wages 21.0%
Purchases 6.0%
Depreciation 13.2%
Marketing 1.1%
Rent & Utilities 6.9%
Other 34.4%

MARKET SHARE

United Rentals 12.9%
Sunbelt Rentals Exchange 6.4%
Ashtead 3.3%
Herc Holdings 2.8%
NEP 2.3%
WCA Waste 1.2%
United Site Services 1.2%
Williams Scotsman 1.2%
Maxim Crane Works 0.9%
Cooperatieve Rabobank U.A. 0.8%

INDUSTRY TREND

"The state of the economy influences contractors' performance. With such a broad range of markets catered to, the strength of nonresidential building, industrial production and important markets such as hospitals, significantly impact performance. The industry gains from downstream markets' propensity to lease or rent equipment rather than outright purchasing to save money upfront and adjust capacity more flexibly when demand changes."

Source: IBISWorld Key Takeaways

RESOURCES

- IBISWorld, September 2023: https://www.ibisworld.com

Other Computer-Related Services

| NAICS 541519 | Businesses/Units 518,365

| Profit $44.3 B | Wages $297.7 B | Annual Growth Future 2.6%

| | | Annual Growth Past 2.8%

INDUSTRY MULTIPLES

Acquisition multiples below are calculated medians using US private industry transactions. Data updated annually. Last update: August 2023.

VALUATION MULTIPLE (MEDIAN VALUE)

UNDER $1 MILLION NET SALES

MVIC/Net Sales	0.45
MVIC/Gross Profit	0.68
MVIC/SDE	0.76
MVIC/EBITDA	N/A

$1 MILLION–$5 MILLION NET SALES   N/A

OVER $5 MILLION NET SALES

MVIC/Net Sales	0.52
MVIC/Gross Profit	3.64
MVIC/SDE	6.66
MVIC/EBITDA	23.43

Source: DealStats (formerly Pratt's Stats), 2023 (Portland, OR: Business Valuation Resources, LLC), www.bvresources.com/dealstats

BENCHMARK DATA

STATISTICS (IT CONSULTING)

Number of Establishments	518,365
Average Profit Margin	6.4%
Revenue per Employee	$279,560
Average Number of Employees	4.9
Average Wages per Employee	$120,014

PRODUCTS AND SERVICES SEGMENTATION

Other services	37.3%
Custom services	25.1%
Computer systems development	10.6%
Technical consulting	10.5%
Technical support	8.9%
IT infrastructure	7.6%

MAJOR MARKET SEGMENTATION

Manufacturing and retail companies	22.2%
Financial services companies	20.8%
Public sector and nonprofit organizations	18.8%
Communications, media and technology companies	15.0%
Healthcare companies	12.9%
Other sectors	10.3%

INDUSTRY COSTS

Profit	6.4%
Wages	43.0%
Purchases	7.1%
Depreciation	0.7%
Marketing	1.3%
Rent & Utilities	2.6%
Other	38.9%

MARKET SHARE

Dell Technologies Inc.	1.1%
Tata Consultancy Services Ltd	1.1%
Booz Allen Hamilton Inc.	1.0%
Accenture PLC	1.0%

INDUSTRY TREND

"Shifting technology trends reshape the industry as the world becomes more technology-driven. Businesses across all industries have become reliant on external IT services. As more business is conducted online, the need for the cloud network and other industry services will provide a boost to the industry.

Operators constantly modify the software they provide to customers to remain competitive."

Source: IBISWorld Key Takeaways

RESOURCES

• IBISWorld, October 2023: https://www.ibisworld.com

Other Electronic Parts and Equipment Merchant Wholesales

| NAICS 423690 | Businesses/Units 14,118

| Profit $30.3 B | Wages $41.6 B | Annual Growth Future 1.9%

| Annual Growth Past 2.9%

INDUSTRY MULTIPLES

Acquisition multiples below are calculated medians using US private industry transactions. Data updated annually. Last update: August 2023.

VALUATION MULTIPLE (MEDIAN VALUE)

UNDER $1 MILLION NET SALES

MVIC/Net Sales.	0.45
MVIC/Gross Profit	1.05
MVIC/SDE	2.20
MVIC/EBITDA	4.59

$1 MILLION–$5 MILLION NET SALES

MVIC/Net Sales.	0.77
MVIC/Gross Profit	1.29
MVIC/SDE	2.51
MVIC/EBITDA	N/A

OVER $5 MILLION NET SALES

MVIC/Net Sales.	0.61
MVIC/Gross Profit	1.80
MVIC/SDE	5.04
MVIC/EBITDA	6.00

Source: DealStats (formerly Pratt's Stats), 2023 (Portland, OR: Business Valuation Resources, LLC), www.bvresources.com/dealstats

BENCHMARK DATA

STATISTICS (ELECTRONIC PART & EQUIPMENT WHOLESALING)

Number of Establishments .	14,118
Average Profit Margin	5.5%
Revenue per Employee .	$2,192,000
Average Number of Employees.	18.1
Average Wages per Employee .	$163,751

PRODUCTS AND SERVICES SEGMENTATION

Communications equipment	47.3%
Semiconductors	16.6%
Other electronic components	13.9%
Computers and software	10.0%
Other	7.8%
Integrated circuits	4.4%

MAJOR MARKET SEGMENTATION

Other wholesalers	34.2%
Business end users .	29.4%

Other									. 12.8%
Retailers.								. 12.3%
Manufacturers .							. 11.3%

INDUSTRY COSTS

Profit								. 5.5%
Wages	.							. 7.6%
Purchases	.						. 73.2%
Depreciation							. 0.4%
Marketing	.						. 0.8%
Rent & Utilities .						. 0.8%
Other								. 11.6%

MARKET SHARE

| Arrow Electronics | . | | | | . 1.9% |
| Avnet | . | | | | | | . 0.9% |

INDUSTRY TREND

"Improvements to communication infrastructure leads to upgrades. Demand for equipment used to upgrade to 5G and devices, which use this technology, has surged. Reshoring of semiconductor production aids wholesalers. Recent legislation has incentivized US companies to produce semiconductors domestically, increasing access to them for wholesalers while bolstering tech production as a whole. The CHIPS act is expected to benefit wholesalers. By lowering the price of domestically produced electronic parts and equipment, wholesalers can offer lower prices and become more competitive."

Source: IBISWorld Key Takeaways

RESOURCES

• IBISWorld, September 2023: https://www.ibisworld.com

Other Specialized Design Services

| NAICS 541490

| Profit $316.6 M | Wages $962.7 M | Annual Growth Future 2.0%

| Annual Growth Past -0.7%

INDUSTRY MULTIPLES

Acquisition multiples below are calculated medians using US private industry transactions. Data updated annually. Last update: August 2023.

VALUATION MULTIPLE (MEDIAN VALUE)

UNDER $1 MILLION NET SALES
MVIC/Net Sales.						0.43
MVIC/Gross Profit						0.84
MVIC/SDE	.						2.00
MVIC/EBITDA	.					10.88

$1 MILLION–$5 MILLION NET SALES
MVIC/Net Sales.						0.52
MVIC/Gross Profit						1.42
MVIC/SDE	.						3.81
MVIC/EBITDA	.					7.68

OVER $5 MILLION NET SALES
MVIC/Net Sales.						4.38
MVIC/Gross Profit						4.61
MVIC/SDE	.						N/A

MVIC/EBITDA 16.16

Source: DealStats (formerly Pratt's Stats), 2023 (Portland, OR: Business Valuation Resources, LLC), www.bvresources.com/dealstats

BENCHMARK DATA

STATISTICS (FASHION DESIGNERS)

Number of Establishments 27,755	
Average Profit Margin 10.3%	
Revenue per Employee $92,000	
Average Number of Employees. . . . 1.23	
Average Wages per Employee . . . $28,929	

PRODUCTS AND SERVICES SEGMENTATION

Fashion clothing design 48.3%	
Footwear design 24.1%	
Jewelry and accessory design 13.4%	
Other design services 11.8%	
Textile design 2.4%	

MAJOR MARKET SEGMENTATION

Retailers and wholesalers 56.0%	
Individual consumers 17.6%	
Apparel manufacturers 14.4%	
Fashion houses 8.3%	
Other markets 3.7%	

INDUSTRY COSTS

Profit 10.3%	
Wages 31.3%	
Purchases 11.4%	
Depreciation 1.1%	
Marketing 1.8%	
Rent & Utilities 6.4%	
Other 37.6%	

INDUSTRY TREND

"Rising economic uncertainty has caused consumer confidence to decline, taking down consumer spending with it. The industry often follows similar trends to the overall clothing and accessories retail market. The assortment of services offered in this industry means that operators also come in a wide variety. The trend of designer collaborations with low-cost outlets has revolutionized the industry. Fast-fashion outlets are expected to increase in popularity over the next five years. As the global economy rebounds, international demand for designs created in the United States will strengthen. The increasing visibility and accessibility of fashion will bode well for industry participants."

Source: IBISWorld Industry at a Glance

RESOURCES

• IBISWorld, March 2023: https://www.ibisworld.com

Other Support Activities for Air Transportation

| NAICS 488190 | Businesses/Units 4,879

| Profit $2.9 B | Wages $9.2 B | Annual Growth Future 1.8%

| Annual Growth Past 8.9%

INDUSTRY MULTIPLES

Acquisition multiples below are calculated medians using US private industry transactions. Data updated annually. Last update: August 2023.

VALUATION MULTIPLE (MEDIAN VALUE)

UNDER $1 MILLION NET SALES	
MVIC/Net Sales.	0.58
MVIC/Gross Profit	1.31
MVIC/SDE	3.05
MVIC/EBITDA	3.66
$1 MILLION–$5 MILLION NET SALES	N/A
OVER $5 MILLION NET SALES	
MVIC/Net Sales.	1.42
MVIC/Gross Profit	3.40
MVIC/SDE	3.74
MVIC/EBITDA	9.06

Source: DealStats (formerly Pratt's Stats), 2023 (Portland, OR: Business Valuation Resources, LLC), www.bvresources.com/dealstats

BENCHMARK DATA

STATISTICS (AIRCRAFT MAINTENANCE, REPAIR & OVERHAUL)

Number of Establishments .	4,879
Average Profit Margin	8.7%
Revenue per Employee .	$260,069
Average Number of Employees.	26.7
Average Wages per Employee .	$72,946

PRODUCTS AND SERVICES SEGMENTATION

Engine MRO.	42.0%
Component MRO	19.1%
Airframe MRO	15.1%
Line maintenance	13.9%
Modifications	5.9%
Other	4.0%

MAJOR MARKET SEGMENTATION

Air transport.	42.7%
Department of Defense.	34.9%
Helicopter operators	14.0%
Business and general aviation .	8.4%

INDUSTRY COSTS

Profit	8.7%
Wages	27.8%
Purchases	38.9%
Depreciation	2.0%
Marketing	0.2%
Rent & Utilities .	3.6%
Other	18.9%

MARKET SHARE

AAR Corp	3.7%

INDUSTRY TREND

"Emphasis on economic sentiment will drive industry growth. If consumers and commercial clients lack fiscal flexibility, demand for air travel will decline, harming the industry. Gauging air travel frequency among consumers will fuel broader demand for MRO servicers. As consumers' travel propensity increases, MRO aircraft services will grow."

Source: IBISWorld Key Takeaways

RESOURCES

- IBISWorld, September 2023: https://www.ibisworld.com
- NATA—National Air Transportation Association: https://www.nata.aero
- NBAA—National Business Aviation Association: https://nbaa.org
- HAI—Helicopter Association International: https://rotor.org

Other Support Activities for Road Transportation

| NAICS 488490 | Businesses/Units 3,287

| Profit $713.4 M | Wages $1.5 B | Annual Growth Future 1.9%

                                       | Annual Growth Past 7.3%

INDUSTRY MULTIPLES

Acquisition multiples below are calculated medians using US private industry transactions. Data updated annually. Last update: August 2023.

VALUATION MULTIPLE (MEDIAN VALUE)

UNDER $1 MILLION NET SALES

MVIC/Net Sales.	0.78
MVIC/Gross Profit	0.83
MVIC/SDE	2.33
MVIC/EBITDA	2.62

$1 MILLION–$5 MILLION NET SALES

MVIC/Net Sales.	0.08
MVIC/Gross Profit	0.08
MVIC/SDE	2.69
MVIC/EBITDA	9.89

OVER $5 MILLION NET SALES

MVIC/Net Sales.	2.50
MVIC/Gross Profit	2.93
MVIC/SDE	N/A
MVIC/EBITDA	3.87

Source: DealStats (formerly Pratt's Stats), 2023 (Portland, OR: Business Valuation Resources, LLC), www.bvresources.com/dealstats

BENCHMARK DATA

STATISTICS (TOLL ROADS & WEIGH STATIONS)

Number of Establishments .	3,287
Average Profit Margin	11.3%
Revenue per Employee .	$209,000
Average Number of Employees.	9.4
Average Wages per Employee	$50,068

PRODUCTS AND SERVICES SEGMENTATION

Handling and warehousing services	46.5%
Toll road, bridge, highway and tunnel operation	20.7%
Weighing services and vehicle repair	16.8%
Other maintenance .	16.0%

MAJOR MARKET SEGMENTATION

Commercial trucks .	83.8%
Personal vehicles	15.7%
Other vehicles .	0.5%

Profit	. 11.3%
Wages	. 23.9%
Purchases	. 39.7%
Depreciation	. 3.7%
Marketing	. 0.2%
Rent & Utilities	. 3.7%
Other	. 17.5%

MARKET SHARE

Sweeping Corporation of America Inc..	. 3.8%
Joe's Sweeping Inc..	. 0.2%

INDUSTRY TREND

"Strong economic growth benefited the industry pre-pandemic. Government investment in highways rose during COVID-19. Surging fuel prices reduced revenue growth. The economic recovery will boost revenue. Government spending on highways induces revenue volatility. The adoption of innovations will generate new revenue streams for the industry. Higher disposable income benefits the industry."

Source: IBISWorld Industry at a Glance

RESOURCES

• IBISWorld, September 2023: https://www.ibisworld.com

OXXO Care Cleaners (Franchise)

| NAICS 812320 | SIC 7212-01 | Businesses/Units 39

Rules of Thumb

• 60% annual sales plus inventory

INDUSTRY MULTIPLES

Acquisition multiples below are calculated medians using US private industry transactions. Data updated annually. Last update: August 2023.

VALUATION MULTIPLE (MEDIAN VALUE)

UNDER $1 MILLION NET SALES	
MVIC/Net Sales.	. 0.61
MVIC/Gross Profit	. 0.72
MVIC/SDE	. 2.19
MVIC/EBITDA	. 2.75

$1 MILLION–$5 MILLION NET SALES	
MVIC/Net Sales.	. 0.65
MVIC/Gross Profit	. 0.82
MVIC/SDE	. 2.91
MVIC/EBITDA	. 4.69

OVER $5 MILLION NET SALES	
MVIC/Net Sales.	. 0.47
MVIC/Gross Profit	. 1.39
MVIC/SDE	. 7.77
MVIC/EBITDA	. 12.69

Source: DealStats (formerly Pratt's Stats), 2023 (Portland, OR: Business Valuation Resources, LLC), www.bvresources.com/dealstats

PRICING TIPS

Approx. Total Investment: $169,500 to $672,000

RESOURCES

- OXXO Care Cleaners: https://oxxousa.com
- Franchise information: https://oxxocarecleanersfranchise.com

Packaging (Industrial)

| NAICS 561910 | Businesses/Units 1,749

| Profit $898.5 M | Wages $2.6 B | Annual Growth Future 1.9%

| Annual Growth Past 4.3%

Rules of Thumb

- 5–6 x EBIT
- 60%–70% annual sales plus inventory

INDUSTRY MULTIPLES

Acquisition multiples below are calculated medians using US private industry transactions. Data updated annually. Last update: August 2023.

VALUATION MULTIPLE (MEDIAN VALUE)

UNDER $1 MILLION NET SALES
MVIC/Net Sales	0.48
MVIC/Gross Profit	0.84
MVIC/SDE	2.76
MVIC/EBITDA	6.02

$1 MILLION–$5 MILLION NET SALES
MVIC/Net Sales	0.69
MVIC/Gross Profit	1.16
MVIC/SDE	3.34
MVIC/EBITDA	6.58

OVER $5 MILLION NET SALES
MVIC/Net Sales	2.36
MVIC/Gross Profit	9.25
MVIC/SDE	N/A
MVIC/EBITDA	12.77

Source: DealStats (formerly Pratt's Stats), 2023 (Portland, OR: Business Valuation Resources, LLC), www.bvresources.com/dealstats

BENCHMARK DATA

STATISTICS (PACKAGING & LABELING SERVICES)
Number of Establishments	1,749
Average Profit Margin	7.6%
Revenue per Employee	$254,228
Average Number of Employees	27.3
Average Wages per Employee	$54,310

PRODUCTS AND SERVICES SEGMENTATION
Packaging services	48.6%
Other	26.8%
Assembly and fulfillment services	18.1%
Labeling services	6.5%

Food/Beverage producers	38.0%
All other	31.6%
Cosmetics and personal care product producers . . .	15.3%
Pharmaceutical and medical product manufacturers . . .	8.6%
Hardware manufacturers	2.9%
Electronic goods manufacturers	2.3%
Apparel/textile producers	1.3%

INDUSTRY COSTS

Profit	7.6%
Wages	21.6%
Purchases	44.7%
Depreciation	2.3%
Marketing	1.5%
Rent & Utilities	2.0%
Other	20.3%

EXPENSES (% OF ANNUAL SALES)

Cost of Goods	60% to 65%
Payroll/Labor Costs.	08% to 10%
Profit (pretax)	10% to 15%

QUESTIONS

- How stable is your customer base? What is your customer retention record? What percentage of total sales do your top 10 accounts represent? Is there really any free cash flow in the business?

INDUSTRY TREND

"COVID-19-related drug trials brought much-needed demand for packaging and labeling services. E-commerce sellers use contract packaging services as they seek to minimize costs. Rising e-commerce sales bolster demand for packaging and labeling services."

Source: IBISWorld Key Takeaways

RESOURCES

- IBISWorld, September 2023: https://www.ibisworld.com

Paint & Decorating (Wallpaper) Retailers

NAICS 444120	SIC 5231-07	Businesses/Units 8,747
Profit $412.1 M	Wages $2.9 B	Annual Growth Future 0.7%
		Annual Growth Past 1.5%

Rules of Thumb

- 20% annual sales plus inventory

INDUSTRY MULTIPLES

Acquisition multiples below are calculated medians using US private industry transactions. Data updated annually. Last update: August 2023.

VALUATION MULTIPLE (MEDIAN VALUE)

UNDER $1 MILLION NET SALES

MVIC/Net Sales.	0.29
MVIC/Gross Profit	0.74

MVIC/SDE	2.16
MVIC/EBITDA	2.06

$1 MILLION–$5 MILLION NET SALES

MVIC/Net Sales	0.24
MVIC/Gross Profit	0.63
MVIC/SDE	2.75
MVIC/EBITDA	N/A

OVER $5 MILLION NET SALES   N/A

Source: DealStats (formerly Pratt's Stats), 2023 (Portland, OR: Business Valuation Resources, LLC), www.bvresources.com/dealstats

PRICING TIPS

They should have a nationally known brand name plus two competitive paint lines. A wide variety of wallpaper from lesser-priced to higher-priced lines should be offered. National averages tell us these stores make from 16 to 17 percent plus reasonable wages for the owner/operators. The average markup is 40 percent. These stores are sold for fixtures, equipment plus inventory at cost.

BENCHMARK DATA

STATISTICS (PAINT STORES)

Number of Establishments	8,747
Average Profit Margin	2.6%
Revenue per Employee	$289,991
Average Number of Employees	6.3
Average Wages per Employee	$53,805

PRODUCTS AND SERVICES SEGMENTATION

Interior paint	41.7%
Exterior paint	24.1%
Painting equipment and supplies	17.9%
Stains, varnishes and other coatings	11.1%
Other	4.2%
Wallpaper and other flexible wall coverings	1.0%

MAJOR MARKET SEGMENTATION

Building contractors, heavy construction and specialty contractors	45.7%
Household consumers and individuals	32.2%
Other	11.3%
Businesses	7.0%
Repair shops	3.8%

INDUSTRY COSTS

Profit	2.6%
Wages	18.4%
Purchases	58.4%
Depreciation	0.9%
Marketing	0.9%
Rent & Utilities	2.0%
Other	16.8%

MARKET SHARE

Sherwin-Williams Co	65.0%
PPG Industries, Inc.	7.4%
Kelly-Moore Paints	6.2%

INDUSTRY TREND

"The do-it-yourself trend has boosted paint stores. Many individuals turned to home improvements during pandemic lockdown measures. Paint stores endure mounting competition from large home-improvement stores. Paint stores can't compete with the added convenience of home improvement retailers but often offer superior knowledge and service."

Source: IBISWorld Key Takeaways

RESOURCES

- IBISWorld, March 2023: https://www.ibisworld.com
- PDRA—Paint and Decorating Retailers Association: https://www.pdra.org

Pak Mail (Franchise)

| NAICS 561431 | Businesses/Units 178

Rules of Thumb

- 50% annual sales plus inventory

INDUSTRY MULTIPLES

Acquisition multiples below are calculated medians using US private industry transactions. Data updated annually. Last update: August 2023.

VALUATION MULTIPLE (MEDIAN VALUE)

UNDER $1 MILLION NET SALES

MVIC/Net Sales.	0.49
MVIC/Gross Profit	0.86
MVIC/SDE	2.12
MVIC/EBITDA	2.78

$1 MILLION–$5 MILLION NET SALES

MVIC/Net Sales.	0.13
MVIC/Gross Profit	0.69
MVIC/SDE	1.89
MVIC/EBITDA	6.02

OVER $5 MILLION NET SALES

MVIC/Net Sales.	0.79
MVIC/Gross Profit	3.45
MVIC/SDE	6.91
MVIC/EBITDA	7.44

Source: DealStats (formerly Pratt's Stats), 2023 (Portland, OR: Business Valuation Resources, LLC), www.bvresources.com/dealstats

PRICING TIPS

Approx. Total Investment: $196,000 to $275,950

RESOURCES

- Pak Mail: https://www.pakmail.com
- Franchise information: https://franchise.pakmail.com
- Annex Brands: https://www.annexbrands.com

Papa Johns (Franchise)

| NAICS 722513 | SIC 5812-22 | Businesses/Units 2,649

Rules of Thumb

- 38%–40% annual sales

INDUSTRY MULTIPLES

Acquisition multiples below are calculated medians using US private industry transactions. Data updated annually. Last update: August 2023.

VALUATION MULTIPLE (MEDIAN VALUE)

UNDER $1 MILLION NET SALES

MVIC/Net Sales.	0.31
MVIC/Gross Profit	0.48
MVIC/SDE	1.67
MVIC/EBITDA	2.21

$1 MILLION–$5 MILLION NET SALES

MVIC/Net Sales.	0.39
MVIC/Gross Profit	0.60
MVIC/SDE	2.43
MVIC/EBITDA	2.98

OVER $5 MILLION NET SALES

MVIC/Net Sales.	0.89
MVIC/Gross Profit	2.08
MVIC/SDE	4.98
MVIC/EBITDA	12.81

Source: DealStats (formerly Pratt's Stats), 2023 (Portland, OR: Business Valuation Resources, LLC), www.bvresources.com/dealstats

PRICING TIPS

Approx. Total Investment: $200,130 to $788,930

BENCHMARK DATA

See Pizza Shops

RESOURCES

- Papa Johns: https://www.papajohns.com
- Franchise information: https://www.papajohns.com/franchise/

Papa Murphy's Take 'N' Bake Pizza (Franchise)

| NAICS 722513 | Businesses/Units 1,157

Rules of Thumb

- 35%–40% annual sales plus inventory

INDUSTRY MULTIPLES

Acquisition multiples below are calculated medians using US private industry transactions. Data updated annually. Last update: August 2023.

VALUATION MULTIPLE (MEDIAN VALUE)

UNDER $1 MILLION NET SALES

MVIC/Net Sales.	0.31
MVIC/Gross Profit	0.48
MVIC/SDE	1.67
MVIC/EBITDA	2.21

$1 MILLION–$5 MILLION NET SALES

MVIC/Net Sales.	0.39
MVIC/Gross Profit	0.60
MVIC/SDE	2.43
MVIC/EBITDA	2.98

MVIC/Net Sales. 0.89
MVIC/Gross Profit 2.08
MVIC/SDE 4.98
MVIC/EBITDA 12.81

Source: DealStats (formerly Pratt's Stats), 2023 (Portland, OR: Business Valuation Resources, LLC), www.bvresources.com/dealstats

PRICING TIPS

Approx. Total Investment: $308,469 to $557,879

BENCHMARK DATA

See Pizza Shops

RESOURCES

- Papa Murphy's Take 'N' Bake Pizza: https://www.papamurphys.com
- Franchise information: https://papamurphysfranchise.com
- MTY Group: https://mtygroup.com

Parking Lot Sweeping

| NAICS 561790 | SIC 1611-04

Rules of Thumb

- 60%–65% annual sales includes inventory
- 2–2.5 x SDE includes inventory
- 5–5.5 x EBIT
- 5–6 x EBITDA

INDUSTRY MULTIPLES

Acquisition multiples below are calculated medians using US private industry transactions. Data updated annually. Last update: August 2023.

VALUATION MULTIPLE (MEDIAN VALUE)

UNDER $1 MILLION NET SALES
MVIC/Net Sales. 0.73
MVIC/Gross Profit 1.00
MVIC/SDE 2.08
MVIC/EBITDA 2.36

$1 MILLION–$5 MILLION NET SALES
MVIC/Net Sales. 0.57
MVIC/Gross Profit 0.98
MVIC/SDE 3.09
MVIC/EBITDA 4.12

OVER $5 MILLION NET SALES
MVIC/Net Sales. 1.08
MVIC/Gross Profit 1.55
MVIC/SDE 5.26
MVIC/EBITDA 8.41

Source: DealStats (formerly Pratt's Stats), 2023 (Portland, OR: Business Valuation Resources, LLC), www.bvresources.com/dealstats

EXPENSES (% OF ANNUAL SALES)

Cost of Goods 20%
Occupancy Costs 05%

Payroll/Labor Costs. 15%
Profit (pretax) . . . . 10% to 12%

QUESTIONS

- Must establish the quality of the accounts and condition of equipment, review contracts, examine labor force, etc. Is the owner tied to any special interests, people, or other connections responsible for a significant portion of the company's business? If so, how will this affect these accounts/sites? Future growth in a local area or region? Competition?

EXPERT COMMENTS

This industry has been unable to support national or regional consolidation. Mostly local, statewide, or small regional players.

RESOURCES

- NAPSA—North American Power Sweeping Association: https://www.powersweeping.org
- WorldSweeper: https://www.worldsweeper.com
- SCA—Sweeping Corp of America: https://www.sweepingcorp.com

Parking Lots and Garages

| NAICS 812930 | Businesses/Units 18,575

| Profit $793.5 M | Wages $3.2 B | Annual Growth Future 1.4%

| Annual Growth Past -7.7%

INDUSTRY MULTIPLES

Acquisition multiples below are calculated medians using US private industry transactions. Data updated annually. Last update: August 2023.

VALUATION MULTIPLE (MEDIAN VALUE)

UNDER $1 MILLION NET SALES

MVIC/Net Sales.	0.90
MVIC/Gross Profit	1.44
MVIC/SDE	N/A
MVIC/EBITDA	2.40
$1 MILLION–$5 MILLION NET SALES	N/A
OVER $5 MILLION NET SALES	N/A

Source: DealStats (formerly Pratt's Stats), 2023 (Portland, OR: Business Valuation Resources, LLC), www.bvresources.com/dealstats

BENCHMARK DATA

STATISTICS (PARKING LOTS AND GARAGES)

Number of Establishments	18,575
Average Profit Margin	9.7%
Revenue per Employee	$50,320
Average Number of Employees.	8.7
Average Wages per Employee	$19,951

PRODUCTS AND SERVICES SEGMENTATION

Hourly or daily off-street parking	38.2%
Weekly or monthly off-street parking in buildings . . .	23.3%
Valet parking	12.5%

Management fees for the operation of parking facilities . . 8.9%
Weekly or monthly off-street parking on lots 8.8%
Other and on-street parking services 8.3%

MAJOR MARKET SEGMENTATION

Commercial businesses 56.4%
Aviation 16.6%
Manufacturing facilities. 14.6%
Educational facilities 12.4%

INDUSTRY COSTS

Profit 9.7%
Wages 39.5%
Purchases 7.3%
Depreciation 3.1%
Marketing 1.5%
Rent & Utilities 4.5%
Other 34.3%

MARKET SHARE

ABM Industries Inc.. . . . . .21.9%
LAZ Parking Ltd. LLC 16.2%
Reef Technology Inc. 11.1%
SP Plus Corporation 10.4%
Impark Parking Corporation 9.2%
Propark Inc.. . . . . 6.7%
ACE Parking Management Inc.. . . . . 2.9%
Diamond Parking Inc. 2.0%

INDUSTRY TREND

"Management contracts have gained popularity among parking service operators seeking to cut costs in a highly competitive landscape. Through management contracts, parking operators can provide services without the burden of ownership or construction. Alternative transportation modes will threaten parking operators over the next five years. Public transportation, ridesharing services and self-driving cars will steer consumers away from parking services."

Source: IBISWorld Key Takeaways

RESOURCES

- IBISWorld, September 2023: https://www.ibisworld.com
- IPMI—International Parking & Mobility Institute: https://www.parking-mobility.org

---

Pawnshops

NAICS 522298	SIC 5932-29	Businesses/Units 13,218
Profit $484.2 M	Wages $1.3 B	Annual Growth Future -0.4%
		Annual Growth Past -0.3%

Rules of Thumb

- 3 x SDE includes inventory
- 3–5 x EBIT
- 3–3.5 x EBITDA
- 48% annual sales includes inventory

INDUSTRY MULTIPLES

Acquisition multiples below are calculated medians using US private industry transactions. Data updated annually. Last update: August 2023.

VALUATION MULTIPLE (MEDIAN VALUE)

UNDER $1 MILLION NET SALES

MVIC/Net Sales.	0.73
MVIC/Gross Profit	1.64
MVIC/SDE	3.53
MVIC/EBITDA	4.20

$1 MILLION–$5 MILLION NET SALES

MVIC/Net Sales.	0.95
MVIC/Gross Profit	0.74
MVIC/SDE	3.63
MVIC/EBITDA	18.99

OVER $5 MILLION NET SALES

MVIC/Net Sales.	1.67
MVIC/Gross Profit	1.67
MVIC/SDE	N/A
MVIC/EBITDA	9.57

Source: DealStats (formerly Pratt's Stats), 2023 (Portland, OR: Business Valuation Resources, LLC), www.bvresources.com/dealstats

PRICING TIPS

This business is not about inventory but money on the street. Knowing your client and loan to value on an item presented to pawn (loan) purchase an item outside of precious metals (jewelry) tend to be minimal profits.

BENCHMARK DATA

STATISTICS (PAWN SHOPS)

Number of Establishments .	13,218
Average Profit Margin	13.6%
Revenue per Employee .	$99,729
Average Number of Employees.	2.7
Average Wages per Employee .	$37,732

PRODUCTS AND SERVICES SEGMENTATION

Merchandise sales .	51.9%
Secured loans	45.3%
Other sales .	2.8%

INDUSTRY COSTS

Profit	13.6%
Wages	37.8%
Purchases	1.6%
Depreciation	0.8%
Marketing	2.0%
Rent & Utilities .	1.7%
Other	42.6%

MARKET SHARE

FirstCash Corp .	28.9%
EZCORP, Inc.	21.5%

Employees are key. They set the loan amounts based on the collateral presented.

According to the National Pawnbrokers Association, 85 percent of all customers do end up reclaiming their items.

Cost of Goods	60% to 65%
Occupancy Costs	. . 04%
Payroll/Labor Costs.	10% to 20%
Profit (pretax)	20% to 30%

QUESTIONS

- Regular due diligence questions and surveillance of the store and area so the buyer knows the type of clientele.
- Loan balance over past 24 months
- What type of software do you use to track pawn receivables and inventory? How do you value pawned items? What is the quality of your pawn receivable? How do you measure and track bad inventory? What are the state laws regarding pawn shops, gun sales, and interest rates on loans?

INDUSTRY TREND

Trending up as a recession and personal income is falling as is forecasted lower within the next 12 to 24 months.

"The industry is countercyclical and tends to benefit from poor macroeconomic performance. During the beginning of the current period, macroeconomic conditions improved steadily, resulting in lower unemployment and broad-based gains in income.

The COVID-19 pandemic negatively impacted the Pawn Shops industry. Fiscal stimulus programs initiated by the federal government amid the pandemic sterilized recession-related effects that would benefit the industry."

Source: IBISWorld Key Takeaways

EXPERT COMMENTS

Buyer: great return if you manage correctly. Why is the owner selling? You have to be all in for this industry. Seller: profits should be good. Provide your true numbers and the true reason for the sale. Usually, employees or robbery is the issue for sale.

It makes a ton of money, but be smart, as people try to rip you off all the time with fake goods.

This is the new middle-class short-term loan center, not your backroom type of business anymore.

FINANCING

Always, 100 percent cash to the buyer. Never heard of an SBA loan for this business.

RESOURCES

- IBISWorld, June 2023: https://www.ibisworld.com
- NPA—National Pawnbrokers Association: https://nationalpawnbrokers.org
- Pawn Shops Today: https://www.pawnshopstoday.com

Payday Loans

	NAICS 522291		Businesses/Units 12,998	
	Profit $3.8 B		Wages $5.7 B		Annual Growth Future -0.4%
					Annual Growth Past 1.6%

Rules of Thumb

• 70% annual sales

INDUSTRY MULTIPLES

Acquisition multiples below are calculated medians using US private industry transactions. Data updated annually. Last update: August 2023.

VALUATION MULTIPLE (MEDIAN VALUE)

UNDER $1 MILLION NET SALES

MVIC/Net Sales	0.08
MVIC/Gross Profit	0.08
MVIC/SDE	N/A
MVIC/EBITDA	N/A

$1 MILLION–$5 MILLION NET SALES

MVIC/Net Sales	0.77
MVIC/Gross Profit	0.98
MVIC/SDE	N/A
MVIC/EBITDA	1.83

OVER $5 MILLION NET SALES

MVIC/Net Sales	2.73
MVIC/Gross Profit	2.29
MVIC/SDE	N/A
MVIC/EBITDA	10.98

Source: DealStats (formerly Pratt's Stats), 2023 (Portland, OR: Business Valuation Resources, LLC), www.bvresources.com/dealstats

BENCHMARK DATA

STATISTICS (CHECK CASHING & PAYDAY LOAN SERVICES)

Number of Establishments	12,998
Average Profit Margin	18.0%
Revenue per Employee	$244,145
Average Number of Employees	6.7
Average Wages per Employee	$65,626

PRODUCTS AND SERVICES SEGMENTATION

Payday loans for recurring expenses	59.5%
Check cashing	14.9%
Payday loans for unexpected emergencies/expenses	13.6%
Payday loans for other reasons	12.0%

INDUSTRY COSTS

Profit	18.0%
Wages	27.0%
Purchases	1.8%
Depreciation	1.1%
Marketing	2.2%
Rent & Utilities	1.9%
Other	48.0%

MARKET SHARE

AARC LLC	6.1%

INDUSTRY TREND

"Heightened inflationary pressures affect consumers' fiscal flexibility. As prices for core expenses such as rent and utilities increase, consumers have less available income, increasing demand for the industry. Increasingly hawkish regulatory landscape negatively affects industry's growth prospects. As regulations increase on a state level, industry servicers have a smaller revenue stream they can generate."

Source: IBISWorld Key Takeaways

- IBISWorld, September 2023: https://www.ibisworld.com
- CFSA—Community Financial Services Association of America: https://www.cfsaa.com

P

Payroll Services

| NAICS 541214 | Businesses/Units 326,859 |

| Profit $9.2 B | Wages $39 B | Annual Growth Future 1.6% |

| | | Annual Growth Past 2.7% |

INDUSTRY MULTIPLES

Acquisition multiples below are calculated medians using US private industry transactions. Data updated annually. Last update: August 2023.

VALUATION MULTIPLE (MEDIAN VALUE)

UNDER $1 MILLION NET SALES

MVIC/Net Sales.	0.79
MVIC/Gross Profit	0.79
MVIC/SDE	2.25
MVIC/EBITDA	1.51

$1 MILLION–$5 MILLION NET SALES

MVIC/Net Sales.	1.40
MVIC/Gross Profit	1.69
MVIC/SDE	N/A
MVIC/EBITDA	N/A

OVER $5 MILLION NET SALES   N/A

Source: DealStats (formerly Pratt's Stats), 2023 (Portland, OR: Business Valuation Resources, LLC), www.bvresources.com/dealstats

BENCHMARK DATA

STATISTICS (PAYROLL AND BOOKKEEPING SERVICES)

Number of Establishments .	326,859
Average Profit Margin	13.9%
Revenue per Employee .	$86,101
Average Number of Employees.	2.4
Average Wages per Employee .	$50,497

PRODUCTS AND SERVICES SEGMENTATION

Full-service payroll services	34.5%
Bookkeeping and compilation services	19.9%
General accounting services	11.8%
Billing services .	11.6%
Tax preparation and representation services	10.9%
Payroll services sold separately	7.6%
Tax planning and consulting services	2.7%
Other services	1.0%

MAJOR MARKET SEGMENTATION

Consumer and industrial businesses	33.5%
Financial businesses and energy	25.0%
Healthcare providers	13.7%
Technology, media and telecommunications	13.6%
Individuals	13.0%

INDUSTRY COSTS

Profit	13.9%
Wages	59.0%
Purchases	1.9%
Depreciation	0.9%
Marketing	0.6%
Rent & Utilities	2.6%
Other	21.1%

MARKET SHARE

Automatic Data Processing	15.2%
Intuit	12.5%
Paychex	6.4%
Ceridian HCM Holding	1.2%
BKD LLP	0.1%
Grant Thornton LLP	0.1%

INDUSTRY TREND

"One of the key trends in the industry over the past five years has been the increased adoption of technology. This has included the use of cloud-based software and mobile apps for payroll and bookkeeping services, which have made these services more accessible and convenient for businesses and individuals. The shift toward remote work has heightened the need for mobile-friendly payroll and bookkeeping services. These solutions will allow employees to access their payroll information and perform bookkeeping tasks from anywhere, on any device."

Source: IBISWorld Key Takeaways

RESOURCES

• IBISWorld, October 2023: https://www.ibisworld.com

Pest Control

NAICS 561710	SIC 7342-01	Businesses/Units 35,306
Profit $3.4 B	Wages $8.6 B	Annual Growth Future 0.9%
		Annual Growth Past 7.0%

Rules of Thumb

• 80%–90% annual sales plus inventory
• 2–3 x SDE plus inventory
• 3–4 x EBIT
• 3–4 x EBITDA

INDUSTRY MULTIPLES

Acquisition multiples below are calculated medians using US private industry transactions. Data updated annually. Last update: August 2023.

VALUATION MULTIPLE (MEDIAN VALUE)

UNDER $1 MILLION NET SALES

MVIC/Net Sales	0.90
MVIC/Gross Profit	0.96
MVIC/SDE	2.90
MVIC/EBITDA	4.24

$1 MILLION–$5 MILLION NET SALES

MVIC/Net Sales.	0.93
MVIC/Gross Profit	1.30
MVIC/SDE	3.67
MVIC/EBITDA	6.84

OVER $5 MILLION NET SALES

MVIC/Net Sales.	1.52
MVIC/Gross Profit	2.80
MVIC/SDE	3.19
MVIC/EBITDA	19.72

Source: DealStats (formerly Pratt's Stats), 2023 (Portland, OR: Business Valuation Resources, LLC), www.bvresources.com/dealstats

PRICING TIPS

60 to 125 percent of sales, depending on profit and future outlook

BENCHMARK DATA

STATISTICS (PEST CONTROL)

Number of Establishments.	35,306
Average Profit Margin	13.1%
Revenue per Employee.	$155,341
Average Number of Employees.	4.9
Average Wages per Employee.	$51,627

PRODUCTS AND SERVICES SEGMENTATION

Insect extermination and control	51.1%
Other services	16.7%
Rodent containment and extermination	12.8%
Termite extermination control.	12.4%
Bedbugs and mosquitos	7.0%

MAJOR MARKET SEGMENTATION

Residential homes	48.9%
Commercial establishments	31.5%
Government institutions and nonprofit organizations.	19.6%

INDUSTRY COSTS

Profit	13.1%
Wages	33.0%
Purchases	19.0%
Depreciation	2.7%
Marketing	2.1%
Rent & Utilities.	3.0%
Other	27.1%

MARKET SHARE

Rollins, Inc.	10.2%
ServiceMaster Co, LLC.	7.5%
Rentokil Initial PLC	7.1%
Ecolab Inc.	2.8%

Production per technician = $100K to $150K per year. The more production per technician, the better the profit.

EXPENSES (% OF ANNUAL SALES)

Cost of Goods	05% to 15%
Occupancy Costs	03% to 10%
Payroll/Labor Costs.	25% to 35%
Profit (pretax)	20% to 30%

- How long will they take part in the transition, and will they qualify for a license if needed? Will they warrant that their accounts are in good standing and should accept and pay for their next regular service? Do they drug test, and do the employees have noncompetes?
- Would you stay for a conversion period of time, depending on size of company and categories working?
- Any recent significant changes in your business such as the loss of a major account? What portion of your business is your largest customer?
- Why are you getting out of the business? What is your employee turnover rate? Have you paid all of your federal and state taxes and can you prove it?
- Breakdown of services: commercial versus residential; general pest versus wood destroying.

INDUSTRY TREND

"The prevalence of an insecticide-resistant bedbug strain has significantly raised the demand for industry services, while concurrently enabling operators to raise their prices. In addition to causing frequent physical and mental pain, bedbugs also spread a number of infectious diseases such as Hepatitis C and Hepatitis B. Revenue growth will be balanced out by divergent trends in the growth of important external drivers. While consumer spending, per capita disposable income and demand for hotels and motels will all increase, private spending on home improvements, housing starts and existing home sales will fall."

Source: IBISWorld Key Takeaways

Big companies are buying medium and small businesses. More technicians are striking out on their own to start new businesses. That is why the industry has grown so much so fast.

EXPERT COMMENTS

Sellers need to be prepared, and you almost need a due diligence package as part of the sale. Of course you want to be as confidential as possible for sellers. Buyers need to have their financing ready and be aware of the licensing requirements. If it is an acquisition, it must be a good fit to the existing company.

Get maximum exposure to the entire market, a broker who knows what he is doing, someone who has prior experience running or owning a pest business, a specialist in pest control company sales. These may be hard to find, but you just have to look.

Know how to price a treatment. Know how to identify a pest and why the customer should treat their home. Have a good driving record. Must have a high school education and more if possible.

FINANCING

Normally 60 to 80 percent down and a note for 12 to 24 or 36 months depending on the type of deal. Usually there is a noncompete for three to five years.

RESOURCES

- IBISWorld, September 2023: https://www.ibisworld.com
- Acquisition Experts LLC: https://www.acquisitionexperts.net
- AzPPO—Arizona Pest Professional Organization: https://www.azppo.org
- A+ Business Brokers: https://www.pestcontrolbiz.com
- NPMA—National Pest Management Association: https://www.pestworld.org

- PCL—Pest Control License: https://pestcontrollicense.com
- PCT—Pest Control Technology—magazine: https://www.pctonline.com/magazine/
- PestPro Magazine: http://pestpromagazine.com
- PestWeb: https://pestweb.com

Pet Care

	NAICS 812910		SIC 0752-04		Businesses/Units 166,513
	Profit $1.4 B		Wages $5.9 B		Annual Growth Future 1.1%
					Annual Growth Past 2.8%

Rules of Thumb

- 35%–45% annual sales plus inventory
- 1.5–3 x SDE
- 5 x EBITDA

INDUSTRY MULTIPLES

Acquisition multiples below are calculated medians using US private industry transactions. Data updated annually. Last update: August 2023.

VALUATION MULTIPLE (MEDIAN VALUE)

UNDER $1 MILLION NET SALES
MVIC/Net Sales.	0.58
MVIC/Gross Profit	0.66
MVIC/SDE	2.10
MVIC/EBITDA	3.07

$1 MILLION–$5 MILLION NET SALES
MVIC/Net Sales.	1.26
MVIC/Gross Profit	1.31
MVIC/SDE	3.81
MVIC/EBITDA	4.92

OVER $5 MILLION NET SALES   N/A

Source: DealStats (formerly Pratt's Stats), 2023 (Portland, OR: Business Valuation Resources, LLC), www.bvresources.com/dealstats

PRICING TIPS

The private buyer multiplier of 3 has not changed over the years, and can be lower if there are high-risk/key person–dependent revenue streams (training and grooming). The EBITDA multiplier is effective only if sold to a consolidator through a structured auction.

BENCHMARK DATA

STATISTICS (PET GROOMING AND BOARDING)
Number of Establishments .	166,513
Average Profit Margin	11.5%
Revenue per Employee .	$37,476
Average Number of Employees.	1.9
Average Wages per Employee .	$19,137

PRODUCTS AND SERVICES SEGMENTATION
Other	46.7%
Pet boarding	38.0%

P

| Pet grooming | . . . . 12.5% |
| Pet training | . . . . 2.8% |

Profit	. . . . 11.5%
Wages	. . . . 50.4%
Purchases	. . . . 6.0%
Depreciation	. . . . . . 3.7%
Marketing	. . . . 1.2%
Rent & Utilities	. . . . . . 3.6%
Other	. . . . 23.7%

Revenues should be well over $120/square foot. Labor under 40 percent.

EXPENSES (% OF ANNUAL SALES)

Payroll/Labor Costs.	. . . . 35% to 40%
Occupancy Costs	. . . . . .0% to 10%
Profit (pretax)	. . . . . . 30% to 32%

QUESTIONS

- Do the clients have your cell phone number? Owner dependency is the biggest risk in this industry.
- What is your role? What do you do on a daily basis? Who is the main salesperson for this company? Inspection reports?

INDUSTRY TREND

Pet care is booming and will continue to do so; consumers' spending is growing for the industry. Consolidation is in its early stages.

"Demand for training and anxiety solutions is '10 times higher' than pre-pandemic levels, according to Rover Dog People Panelist and Certified Professional Dog Trainer Nicole Ellis....A growing pet industry market capitalization means more money and innovation will provide pet parents with more technology-based solutions than ever before. Dog-activated video calls, virtual vet visits, smart feeders and collars, microchip-enabled devices, and even online services—like a virtual weight-loss clinic for pets—are already a reality. Expect these new technologies to double down as pet parents seek out tech that delivers convenience, safety and health monitoring solutions in the years to come....The growing recognition that 'pets are people, too' continues to grow strong with human comforts and needs—from organic bedding to meal delivery services and telehealth and insurance—crossing over to our pets."

Source: "5 trends to watch in pet care and products," January 21, 2022,
https://www.supermarketnews.com/winning-pet-care/5-trends-watch-pet-care-and-products

"A jump in pet ownership during COVID-19 has overwhelmed pet groomers and boarders. Pet owners eager to travel and returning to the office have pushed more pet owners to pet care professionals than ever before. Rising incomes and shifting attitudes toward pets will encourage owners to spend on premium care. Pet care professionals will take advantage of this through new offerings focusing on convenience and total pet wellness."

Source: IBISWorld Key Takeaways

EXPERT COMMENTS

Volunteer at a pet care facility to really understand the stress level and what all it entails.

Main competitors are friends and family, app-based service providers (rover.com). No real barriers to entry except zoning.

FINANCING

SBA financing for solid businesses, owner financing for others

RESOURCES

- IBISWorld, September 2023: https://www.ibisworld.com
- APPA—American Pet Products Association: https://www.americanpetproducts.org
- Barkleigh Productions: https://www.barkleigh.com
- IBPSA—International Boarding & Pet Services Association: https://www.ibpsa.com
- NDGAA—National Dog Groomers Association of America, Inc.: https://nationaldoggroomers.com
- PetGroomer.com: https://petgroomer.com

Pet Stores

	NAICS 453910		SIC 5999-30		Businesses/Units 17,860
	Profit $558.8 M		Wages $4 B		Annual Growth Future 0.8%
					Annual Growth Past 4.0%

Rules of Thumb

- 25%–30% annual sales plus inventory
- 2 x SDE plus inventory

INDUSTRY MULTIPLES

Acquisition multiples below are calculated medians using US private industry transactions. Data updated annually. Last update: August 2023.

VALUATION MULTIPLE (MEDIAN VALUE)

UNDER $1 MILLION NET SALES

MVIC/Net Sales	0.36
MVIC/Gross Profit	0.74
MVIC/SDE	2.19
MVIC/EBITDA	3.49

$1 MILLION–$5 MILLION NET SALES

MVIC/Net Sales	0.40
MVIC/Gross Profit	0.93
MVIC/SDE	2.97
MVIC/EBITDA	3.93

OVER $5 MILLION NET SALES

MVIC/Net Sales	0.83
MVIC/Gross Profit	2.19
MVIC/SDE	N/A
MVIC/EBITDA	9.37

Source: DealStats (formerly Pratt's Stats), 2023 (Portland, OR: Business Valuation Resources, LLC), www.bvresources.com/dealstats

PRICING TIPS

Be sure to check inventory turnover rate to make sure inventory is salable.

Dealing with reputable breeders increases value.

BENCHMARK DATA

STATISTICS (PET STORES)

Number of Establishments 17,860	
Average Profit Margin 1.9%	
Revenue per Employee $218,834	
Average Number of Employees. 7.6	
Average Wages per Employee . . . $30,001	

PRODUCTS AND SERVICES SEGMENTATION

Pet food 40.3%	
Pet supplies 35.8%	
Other 12.9%	
Pet services 6.0%	
Live animals. 5.0%	

INDUSTRY COSTS

Profit 1.9%	
Wages 13.7%	
Purchases 50.1%	
Depreciation 1.1%	
Marketing 1.7%	
Rent & Utilities 6.8%	
Other 24.7%	

MARKET SHARE

PetSmart Inc. 22.7%	
Petco Animal Supplies Inc.. . . . . 12.9%	

EXPENSES (% OF ANNUAL SALES)

Cost of Goods . . . . . . 50% to 60%	
Occupancy Costs . . . . . 04% to 05%	
Payroll/Labor Costs. . . . . 08% to 10%	
Profit (pretax) . . . . . . 20% to 25%	

QUESTIONS

- Where do you get your puppies from and what is their guarantee?

INDUSTRY TREND

"Recovering economic conditions will boost consumer spending on premium pet products and services. Despite this anticipated growth, traditional brick-and-mortar operators will continue to struggle with mounting pricing pressures from online retailers, mass merchandisers and discount department stores. The increasing popularity of exclusive niche pet products will help diversify price competition. As almost half of the industry consists of small-scale stores, niche product marketing will become more vital because it assists pet stores in positioning themselves apart from other stores."

Source: IBISWorld Key Takeaways

EXPERT COMMENTS

Location is a key factor in pricing, as many people travel to pick out the right dog. Location to major intersections is a definite plus. Although it is fairly easy to duplicate a pet or pet supply store, knowing the mechanics of the industry can be tricky. Diseases such as parvo and kennel cough can cost quite a bit.

RESOURCES
- IBISWorld, September 2023: https://www.ibisworld.com
- APPA—American Pet Products Association: https://www.americanpetproducts.org
- PIJAC—Pet Industry Joint Advisory Council: https://pijac.org
- WPA—World Pet Association: https://worldpetassociation.org

P

Petland (Franchise)

| NAICS 459910 | Businesses/Units 75

Rules of Thumb

- 50% annual sales plus inventory

INDUSTRY MULTIPLES

Acquisition multiples below are calculated medians using US private industry transactions. Data updated annually. Last update: August 2023.

VALUATION MULTIPLE (MEDIAN VALUE)

UNDER $1 MILLION NET SALES	
MVIC/Net Sales.	0.50
MVIC/Gross Profit	0.86
MVIC/SDE	2.82
MVIC/EBITDA	3.69
$1 MILLION–$5 MILLION NET SALES	
MVIC/Net Sales.	0.37
MVIC/Gross Profit	1.15
MVIC/SDE	2.19
MVIC/EBITDA	3.20
OVER $5 MILLION NET SALES	N/A

Source: DealStats (formerly Pratt's Stats), 2023 (Portland, OR: Business Valuation Resources, LLC), www.bvresources.com/dealstats

PRICING TIPS

Approx. Total Investment: $303,000 to $1,068,000

RESOURCES

- Petland: https://petland.com
- Franchise information: https://petland.com/franchise-opportunities/

Pharmacies and Drugstores

| NAICS 456110 | SIC 5912-05 | Businesses/Units 89,184

| Profit $22.2 B | Wages $54 B | Annual Growth Future 3.7%

| | | Annual Growth Past 3.7%

Rules of Thumb

- 20%–30% annual sales
- 3–4.5 x EBIT
- 2–3 x SDE
- 3–5 x EBITDA

PRICING TIPS

Pharmacies with less than $1M in sales struggle. Pharmacies with niche products, in-store clinics, compounding labs, or 340B programs can carve out better margins.

I take a three-year average of total prescriptions written, then use a range between $12.50 and $14.00 per prescription to determine a value. Be careful if there is a one-off spike up—it can throw out the value and must be discussed in length with the owner.

It is a good method to double check the SDE value, which should be used on deals valued below $1 million.

Depending on the state and local demographics, a baseline (little to no business) pharmacy in good standing with all of the licenses and major insurance contracts has a valuation between $125,000 and $200,000.

Product mix is very important to overall profitability. Pharmacies that fill mostly generics have better margins. Specialty pharmacies (HIV, behavioral health, etc.) have better margins.

BENCHMARK DATA

STATISTICS (PHARMACIES AND DRUGSTORES)

Number of Establishments	89,184
Average Profit Margin	3.9%
Revenue per Employee	$502,537
Average Number of Employees	13.1
Average Wages per Employee	$47,482

PRODUCTS AND SERVICES SEGMENTATION

Branded prescription drugs	58.7%
Generic drugs	14.7%
Other	12.5%
Nonprescription medicines	5.2%
Groceries and food items	2.6%
Personal health supplies	2.5%
Cosmetics	2.3%
Vitamins, minerals and dietary supplements	1.5%

INDUSTRY COSTS

Profit	3.9%
Wages	9.5%
Purchases	69.3%
Depreciation	0.4%
Marketing	1.0%
Rent & Utilities	2.3%
Other	13.5%

MARKET SHARE

Walgreens Boots Alliance, Inc.	20.9%
CVS Health Corporation	18.4%
Rite Aid Corp	3.0%
Walmart Inc.	1.3%
H-E-B Grocery Company LP	1.2%

Successful pharmacies should have 25+ percent gross margins. Pharmacists can manage more than one pharmacy technician, so the ability to scale without huge labor jumps is possible, but maintaining a profitable patient/product mix is key.

Script count has been a classic measure of a successful pharmacy—typically 25K to 30K annual scripts as a breakeven, 50K annual scripts or more is much more valuable. The reimbursement from insurers, however, continues to decline, and better-run pharmacies are able to promote higher-margin products in their mix.

Successful pharmacies have sales of over $2M, lower rent, at least 80/20 generic/brand mix, and all major PBM contracts.

EXPENSES (% OF ANNUAL SALES)

Cost of Goods	70% to 80%
Occupancy Costs	01% to 07%
Payroll/Labor Costs.	06% to 10%
Profit (pretax)	03% to 11%

QUESTIONS

- Why are you selling? What marketing have you done? Where are the largest medical practices located?
- How long have you been in the industry? Have you owned a pharmacy previously? How many locations do you want?
- Where do you get most of your business from? What services do you provide to physicians to entice them to refer patients? Have you had any DEA notices or PBM audits? What does your staff do on a daily basis? How do you analyze your monthly data?
- Is the owner the primary pharmacist? If so, can a smooth transition be agreed upon? Ask to see the Rx summary or detail report. Analyze the report with data mining techniques regarding types of medications dispensed, frequencies, etc. Ask for 3 years of financial reports and tax returns. What are the lease and lease term? Do you have drive-through or delivery options? What is the tenure of the staff?
- Independently, the buyer can look at the competition, clinics, physicians, medical practices, immediate care facilities, and senior care sites in the area.
- Review pharmacy dispensary report. Do they perform compounding? Are there group homes (assisted living, senior independent living), clinics or hospitals nearby? How many deliveries per day? How is staffing—full-time and part-time? Any ancillary services provided?
- Why are sales up or down? What has changed with your patients over the years and most recently? Have you lost any insurance contracts? What part of your business is public vs. private pay?

INDUSTRY TREND

Successful pharmacies will be more specialized and offer more inclusive services, i.e., in-store clinics.

Will continue to increase due to baby boomers and the growing trend of young families. Doctors' offices are starting to look at expanding into the business—rather than allowing the pharmacy to locate close to the clinic, the clinic is setting up a pharmacy.

Generic meds will be dispensed to retain patients, but the trend is to bypass insurance reimbursements by getting better pricing from the manufacturers. Pharmacies will still need to dispense brand-name drugs at very low margins, but garnering enough volume with a patient base of generics makes a big difference in profitability.

More cash-based sales (erectile dysfunction, antiaging treatments, etc.); expanding patient offerings (vaccinations, weight loss programs/treatments, etc.); co-locating or teaming up with doctors to provide one-stop service; more sourcing of products directly from manufacturers when possible (reducing costs).

"Pharmacies being deemed essential businesses, enabled the industry to experience revenue growth even during the adverse conditions of the pandemic. As industry enterprises began offering a wider array of products they benefited from an influx of demand from health-conscious consumers and siphon demand away from non-essential businesses. The industry has adapted to price-conscious consumers and growing external threats, by using internet integration and discount incentives to market branded and generic drugs. The proliferation of price-based competition and low product differentiation has led to many smaller pharmacies struggling and succumbing to consolidation activity."

Source: IBISWorld Key Takeaways

EXPERT COMMENTS

Buyers: be open to all kinds of, and allocate money for, marketing; care for your patients but keep an eye on profits. Sellers: the pharmacy infrastructure (licensing, credentialing, build-out) is expensive; before selling, consider bringing in a marketing rep/consultant to increase business before deciding to sell.

Drug costs are regulated. Labor costs must be managed, but if the owner is a pharmacist (necessary for license), the costs can be managed.

Location to clinic is a huge advantage since your customer base is nearby. Get set up with the insurance companies for QuickPay, and it also saves the customer from having to pay you and then collect from the insurance company.

Buyers: look for ways to expand your market—long-term care facilities, small local hospitals, adding nonsterile compounding, etc.

Sellers: keep good records and don't wait to sell until your sales volume declines.

The process of accrediting a pharmacy takes anywhere from 6 to 12 months to be full operational and in network with all of the insurers. During this time they can only process scripts from a few insurers or cash patients. Meanwhile, the store expenses and salaries must be paid. It is the opportunity cost that sets the value for the start-up pharmacy. Well-established pharmacies can rely on standard cash flow metrics for valuation.

If selling: don't wait to sell until your sales are declining. If buying: look at the store's dispensing history to determine the potential for any audits or clawbacks from PBMs. Investigate the store's compliance history.

PBMs/insurance companies rule this industry. They set reimbursement rates and even what medications are dispensed. Pharmacy owners need to look at the formulary and work with the prescribers to achieve the best reimbursement. Marketing and adding more products per patient are keys to success.

FINANCING

Under $500,000 typically cash sale. Over $500,000, 50 percent seller or 50 percent bank financing.

Almost all bank financing, very little VTB. The banks love this business and make it very easy for the buyer to be prequalified.

Sales are 50/50 between cash and either seller/bank or wholesaler financing.

RESOURCES
- IBISWorld, September 2023: https://www.ibisworld.com
- AACP—American Association of Colleges of Pharmacy: https://www.aacp.org/
- APhA—American Pharmacists Association: https://www.pharmacist.com
- ASHP: https://www.ashp.org
- NABP—National Association of Boards of Pharmacy: https://nabp.pharmacy/
- NCPA—National Community Pharmacists Association: https://ncpa.org
- NPhA—National Pharmaceutical Association: https://nationalpharmaceuticalassociation.org
- PCCA—Professional Compounding Centers of America: https://www.pccarx.com/
- SCPC—Senior Care Pharmacy Coalition: https://seniorcarepharmacies.org
- U.S. Pharmacist: https://www.uspharmacist.com/

Photographers & Photographic Studios

| NAICS 541921 | Businesses/Units 266,354

| Profit $942.1 M | Wages $3.8 B | Annual Growth Future 0.3%

| | | Annual Growth Past -1.3%

Rules of Thumb
- 45%–50% SDE; add fixtures, equipment & inventory
- 2.5–3 x monthly sales; add inventory

INDUSTRY MULTIPLES

Acquisition multiples below are calculated medians using US private industry transactions. Data updated annually. Last update: August 2023.

VALUATION MULTIPLE (MEDIAN VALUE)

UNDER $1 MILLION NET SALES	
MVIC/Net Sales	0.76
MVIC/Gross Profit	0.79
MVIC/SDE	3.22
MVIC/EBITDA	31.80
$1 MILLION–$5 MILLION NET SALES	N/A
OVER $5 MILLION NET SALES	
MVIC/Net Sales	1.05
MVIC/Gross Profit	1.74
MVIC/SDE	N/A
MVIC/EBITDA	N/A

Source: DealStats (formerly Pratt's Stats), 2023 (Portland, OR: Business Valuation Resources, LLC), www.bvresources.com/dealstats

PRICING TIPS

They are usually sold for the new cost of fixtures and equipment, plus inventory, plus 30 percent of one year's net profit. National average states the gross profit usually runs about 62 percent, leaving a net profit of about 24 percent after expenses.

BENCHMARK DATA

STATISTICS (PHOTOGRAPHY)

Number of Establishments	266,354
Average Profit Margin	7.3%
Revenue per Employee	$43,520
Average Number of Employees	1.1
Average Wages per Employee	$13,076

PRODUCTS AND SERVICES SEGMENTATION

Portrait Services	52.2%
Commercial or industrial photography services	29.1%
All other services	10.5%
Wedding photography	8.2%

INDUSTRY COSTS

Profit	7.3%
Wages	29.8%
Purchases	12.6%
Depreciation	3.2%
Marketing	2.2%
Rent & Utilities	6.7%
Other	38.2%

MARKET SHARE

Shutterfly Inc.	8.6%

INDUSTRY TREND

"The quantity of amateur and professional photographers has increased since the quick development, improvement, and rising affordability of digital photography technology. There is both consumer and commercial demand. The greatest market for photographic services is comprised of households and individual consumers, but commercial photography is also frequently utilized."

Source: IBISWorld Key Takeaways

RESOURCES

- IBISWorld, September 2023: https://www.ibisworld.com
- The Imaging Alliance: https://www.theimagingalliance.com

Physical Therapy

	NAICS 621340		Businesses/Units 144,756	
	Profit $5 B		Wages $24 B		Annual Growth Future 3.2%
					Annual Growth Past 1.6%

Rules of Thumb

- 60%–75% annual sales
- 1.8–2.5 x SDE
- 1.5–2 x EBIT
- 1.5–3 x EBITDA

INDUSTRY MULTIPLES

Acquisition multiples below are calculated medians using US private industry transactions. Data updated annually. Last update: August 2023.

VALUATION MULTIPLE (MEDIAN VALUE)

UNDER $1 MILLION NET SALES

MVIC/Net Sales	0.50
MVIC/Gross Profit	0.52
MVIC/SDE	1.77
MVIC/EBITDA	2.81

$1 MILLION–$5 MILLION NET SALES

MVIC/Net Sales	0.51
MVIC/Gross Profit	0.61
MVIC/SDE	2.90
MVIC/EBITDA	4.72

OVER $5 MILLION NET SALES

MVIC/Net Sales	2.64
MVIC/Gross Profit	2.97
MVIC/SDE	N/A
MVIC/EBITDA	18.93

Source: DealStats (formerly Pratt's Stats), 2023 (Portland, OR: Business Valuation Resources, LLC), www.bvresources.com/dealstats

PRICING TIPS

Price dependent upon size/revenue. A small solo practice with a small facility is much less desirable and valuable percentagewise than a multiple-provider integrated practice with multiple modalities (PT, medical massage, chiro, sports, stem cell injection, etc.).

BENCHMARK DATA

STATISTICS (PHYSICAL THERAPISTS)

Number of Establishments	144,756
Average Profit Margin	10.3%
Revenue per Employee	$84,235
Average Number of Employees	4.1
Average Wages per Employee	$41,654

PRODUCTS AND SERVICES SEGMENTATION

Musculoskeletal conditions	44.7%
Other	36.3%
Neurological disorders	7.1%
General physical therapy	6.1%
Injuries	5.8%

INDUSTRY COSTS

Profit	10.3%
Wages	49.2%
Purchases	6.8%
Depreciation	1.0%
Marketing	1.3%
Rent & Utilities	7.4%
Other	24.0%

PT practitioners have lower compensation expectations than physician practices and thus sell for higher multiples.

No more than 45 percent of the gross income should be going to employee salaries. Well-organized practice operates at a 1-to-1 ratio, which is 1 clinical person to 1 administrative person. Practice should also be generating approximately $2500 per week per clinical staff member. Weekly patient visits should roughly equal the total square feet of office space divided by 10.

A/R aging is a critical metric to gauge the efficiency of billing procedures and the profitability of payer contracts. Median of 21 percent in the 120-day plus category for net accounts receivable (A/R excluding liens).

P

Cost of Goods	05% to 20%
Occupancy Costs	06% to 10%
Payroll/Labor Costs.	15% to 25%
Profit (pretax)	15% to 30%

QUESTIONS

- Number of new patients per month? Referral sources? Percent revenue? How far booked out to see new patient? How many PT assistants? Any massage, chiro, acupuncture? Specialty work focus like sports injuries, worker compensation, military?
- Compliance with state and federal regulations?
- Hospital contacts? Length of lease and terms?

INDUSTRY TREND

"In a move strongly supported by APTA and World Physiotherapy, the World Health Organization has adopted what it describes as a landmark resolution to strengthen rehabilitation in health systems worldwide. The statement—the first-ever official WHO acknowledgement of the global need for rehab—calls for all health systems to increase support for and access to rehabilitative services."

Source: "WHO Adopts 'Historic' Resolution to Strengthen Access to Rehab Worldwide," June 5, 2023, https://www.apta.org/news/2023/06/05/who-rehab-resolution

"There's been a quiet revolution taking place in the field of physical therapy.... 'We have gotten quite a bit more evidence for the effectiveness of exercise in both facilitating recovery and also protecting people from different kinds of injuries or diseases,' said James Gordon, chair of the division of biokinesiology and physical therapy at the University of Southern California."

Source: "What to Look for in a Physical Therapist" by Dana G. Smith, March 10, 2023, https://www.nytimes.com/article/physical-therapist-search.html

Overall growth. CMS seems to be showing trend of increasing reimbursements.

"Physical therapy has an expanding role in healthcare. Physical therapy addresses an aging population's rising medical needs and healthcare costs. An increasingly complex operating landscape accelerates consolidation activity. Cost pressures are pushing private physical therapist practices toward the group model."

Source: IBISWorld Key Takeaways

EXPERT COMMENTS

Check referral sources and source of new patients. You want new patient referral sources to be wide. Investigate any single referral source that contributes more than 5 percent of total revenue.

PT practices are harder to start up than, say, a physician primary care practice. You need referral networks form physicians, insurance agents, lawyers, etc.

FINANCING

Outside mostly, with maybe 5 to 10 percent seller carryback

RESOURCES

- IBISWorld, September 2023: https://www.ibisworld.com
- APTA—American Physical Therapy Association: https://www.apta.org
- AHLA—American Health Law Association: https://www.americanhealthlaw.org
- Medical Economics magazine: https://www.medicaleconomics.com

- MGMA: https://www.mgma.com
- NSCHBC—National Society of Certified Healthcare Business Consultants: https://nschbc.org
- HCG—The Health Care Group: https://www.healthcaregroup.com

Picture Framing Stores

	NAICS 442299		SIC 5999-27		Businesses/Units 4,734
	Profit $66.7 M		Wages $223.9 M		Annual Growth Future -1.9%
					Annual Growth Past -4.3%

Rules of Thumb

- 45% annual sales plus inventory

INDUSTRY MULTIPLES

Acquisition multiples below are calculated medians using US private industry transactions. Data updated annually. Last update: August 2023.

VALUATION MULTIPLE (MEDIAN VALUE)

UNDER $1 MILLION NET SALES

MVIC/Net Sales	0.43
MVIC/Gross Profit	0.72
MVIC/SDE	1.85
MVIC/EBITDA	2.20

$1 MILLION–$5 MILLION NET SALES

MVIC/Net Sales	0.46
MVIC/Gross Profit	1.01
MVIC/SDE	2.47
MVIC/EBITDA	3.54

OVER $5 MILLION NET SALES

MVIC/Net Sales	1.04
MVIC/Gross Profit	2.84
MVIC/SDE	3.91
MVIC/EBITDA	6.67

Source: DealStats (formerly Pratt's Stats), 2023 (Portland, OR: Business Valuation Resources, LLC), www.bvresources.com/dealstats

PRICING TIPS

Perhaps most critical is the impact of a change in ownership. If the shop is small—that is, the owner is the face of the business—rarely is the business worth any more than 10 percent of sales.

BENCHMARK DATA

STATISTICS (PICTURE FRAMING STORES)

Number of Establishments	4,734
Average Profit Margin	3.3%
Revenue per Employee	$143,000
Average Number of Employees	2.9
Average Wages per Employee	$15,767

PRODUCTS AND SERVICES SEGMENTATION

Custom framing	70.0%
Ready-made frames	13.2%
Photo frames	11.0%
Other	5.7%

INDUSTRY COSTS

Profit	3.3%
Wages	11.1%
Purchases	51.5%
Depreciation	1.0%
Marketing	3.6%
Rent & Utilities	6.1%
Other	23.5%

EXPENSES (% OF ANNUAL SALES)

Cost of Goods	25%
Occupancy Costs	10%
Payroll/Labor Costs.	12%
Profit (pretax)	14%

QUESTIONS

- In addition to the usual financial questions, you should conduct a market evaluation to determine the viability of the present pricing structure.

INDUSTRY TREND

"Even upon reopening, brick-and-mortar operators have experienced challenges. Since the marriage rate has fallen, custom frame sales from this market have decreased. Many industry operators have shifted operations from brick-and-mortar stores to online stores. Rising disposable income will likely flow through the economy to benefit of art dealers. Fewer marriages will likely curb demand for wedding photography, in turn lowering demand for framing services. External competition will likely continue to place downward pressure on industry operators. The industry has experienced increased external competition from online framing services."

Source: IBISWorld Industry at a Glance

EXPERT COMMENTS

Location and cotenancy are extremely important to value as long as lease is secure.

RESOURCES

- IBISWorld, June 2022: https://www.ibisworld.com
- PPFA—Professional Picture Framers Association: https://www.ppfa.com

Pizza Factory (Franchise)

| NAICS 722513 | Businesses/Units 103

Rules of Thumb

- 30%–35% annual sales plus inventory

INDUSTRY MULTIPLES

Acquisition multiples below are calculated medians using US private industry transactions. Data updated annually. Last update: August 2023.

VALUATION MULTIPLE (MEDIAN VALUE)

UNDER $1 MILLION NET SALES

MVIC/Net Sales.	0.31
MVIC/Gross Profit	0.48

```
MVIC/SDE  .   .   .   .   .   .   .   . 1.67
MVIC/EBITDA  .   .   .   .   .   .   . 2.21
```

$1 MILLION–$5 MILLION NET SALES
```
MVIC/Net Sales.   .   .   .   .   .   . 0.39
MVIC/Gross Profit  .   .   .   .   .   . 0.60
MVIC/SDE  .   .   .   .   .   .   .   . 2.43
MVIC/EBITDA  .   .   .   .   .   .   . 2.98
```

OVER $5 MILLION NET SALES
```
MVIC/Net Sales.   .   .   .   .   .   . 0.89
MVIC/Gross Profit  .   .   .   .   .   . 2.08
MVIC/SDE  .   .   .   .   .   .   .   . 4.98
MVIC/EBITDA  .   .   .   .   .   .   . 12.81
```

Source: DealStats (formerly Pratt's Stats), 2023 (Portland, OR: Business Valuation Resources, LLC), www.bvresources.com/dealstats

PRICING TIPS

Approx. Total Investment: $274,000 to $542,000

RESOURCES

- Pizza Factory: https://www.pizzafactory.com
- Franchise information: https://pizzafactoryfranchises.com

Pizza Shops

	NAICS 722513		SIC 5812-22		Businesses/Units 102,186
	Profit $3.3 B		Wages $19.9 B		Annual Growth Future 1.1%
					Annual Growth Past 3.0%

Rules of Thumb

- 25%–35% annual sales plus inventory for independent shops
- 38% annual sales plus inventory for franchised or chain pizza shops
- 1–2.5 x SDE; plus fixtures, equipment and inventory
- 1.2–2 x EBIT
- 1.5–2 x EBITDA
- 4 x monthly sales plus inventory
- 30%–40% annual sales

INDUSTRY MULTIPLES

Acquisition multiples below are calculated medians using US private industry transactions. Data updated annually. Last update: August 2023.

VALUATION MULTIPLE (MEDIAN VALUE)

UNDER $1 MILLION NET SALES
```
MVIC/Net Sales.   .   .   .   .   .   . 0.31
MVIC/Gross Profit  .   .   .   .   .   . 0.48
MVIC/SDE  .   .   .   .   .   .   .   . 1.67
MVIC/EBITDA  .   .   .   .   .   .   . 2.21
```

$1 MILLION–$5 MILLION NET SALES
```
MVIC/Net Sales.   .   .   .   .   .   . 0.39
MVIC/Gross Profit  .   .   .   .   .   . 0.60
MVIC/SDE  .   .   .   .   .   .   .   . 2.43
MVIC/EBITDA  .   .   .   .   .   .   . 2.98
```

OVER $5 MILLION NET SALES
```
MVIC/Net Sales.   .   .   .   .   .   . 0.89
MVIC/Gross Profit  .   .   .   .   .   . 2.08
```

```
MVIC/SDE  .   .   .   .   .   .   .   . 4.98
MVIC/EBITDA  .   .   .   .   .   .   . 12.81
```

Source: DealStats (formerly Pratt's Stats), 2023 (Portland, OR: Business Valuation Resources, LLC), www.bvresources.com/dealstats

PRICING TIPS

The multiples are strong, but the business has changed. Due to food costs, they have eliminated and reduced menu items. They also are moving toward shifting from dine-in to delivery. Labor costs have skyrocketed, and finding employees is still difficult. Delivery is substantially more profitable than dine-in. Due to the higher profit margin, the multiples are still intact.

Franchises will sell for a higher price. If the SDE is over $125,000, the multiples will be higher. If there are clean books, the multiples will be higher.

Values have increased due to high margins and the ability to raise prices above the inflation rate.

BENCHMARK DATA

STATISTICS (PIZZA RESTAURANTS)

```
Number of Establishments .   .   .   . 102,186
Average Profit Margin  .   .   .   .   .   . 5.1%
Revenue per Employee .   .   .   .   . $73,449
Average Number of Employees.   .   .   . .8.7
Average Wages per Employee .   .   . $22,456
```

PRODUCTS AND SERVICES SEGMENTATION

```
Takeout services   .   .   .   .   .   . 45.0%
Delivery services  .   .   .   .   .   . 29.6%
Dine-in services.   .   .   .   .   .   . 25.4%
```

INDUSTRY COSTS

```
Profit   .   .   .   .   .   .   .   .   . 5.1%
Wages  .   .   .   .   .   .   .   .   . 30.6%
Purchases  .   .   .   .   .   .   .   . 40.4%
Depreciation   .   .   .   .   .   .   . 2.7%
Marketing  .   .   .   .   .   .   .   . 1.8%
Rent & Utilities .   .   .   .   .   .   . 7.4%
Other   .   .   .   .   .   .   .   . 12.0%
```

The lease is an important component. Look at the rent percent and how much it will increase each year. Look at options to renew, and the total length of the lease. Keep the rent under 10 percent of revenue.

Food cost has increased by 5 to 10 percent. Labor cost is up 10 percent, based on an increase in the minimum wage; and finding employees is still difficult.

Multiples are raising in all the categories in determining the selling price. Covid showed how well this business is situated for long-term success.

Always look at the food orders—not just how much food is ordered, but are they using quality products? Pizza ovens can put out 300,000 pizzas before you need new ovens.

Marketing costs should run 5 percent to maintain growth in this business segment.

EXPENSES (% OF ANNUAL SALES)

```
Cost of Goods  .   .   .   .   .   . 25% to 35%
Occupancy Costs  .   .   .   .   . 07% to 10%
```

```
Payroll/Labor Costs.    .    .    .    .    25% to 35%
Profit (pretax)    .    .    .    .    .    .    15% to 25%
```

P

QUESTIONS

- Standard questions, but double-check the POS system and income statement. The rest is old-school investigation.
- Type of pizza software they are using for takeout? Number of customers in the database for delivery? What marketing is the present owner utilizing?
- Cash vs. credit cards? True revenue vs. IRS for 1120? Look at flour, cheese, and sauce orders—this is a way to check their retail sales. Past violation reports?
- Employee tenure? Transition period? Noncompete provisions?

INDUSTRY TREND

Less dine-in and more delivery. In-house drivers, not major food delivery companies.

Business should stay strong; however, there are many new establishments opening up.

Values going up; ability to raise menu prices; cost of the goods lags inflation.

"The number of independent pizzerias rose from 39,808 last year to 44,644 this year—that's 12.15% growth in total units. The chains, on the other hand, saw relatively flat growth in terms of units, from 35,309 last year to 35,531 in 2022, an increase of just 0.63%. In other words, we saw a mini-boom in openings of independent pizzerias. More than 4,800 new independent stores opened, compared to just 222 new chain units."

Source: "Pizza Power Report 2023: Are Independents Making a Comeback?" by Rick Hynum, https://www.pmq.com/pizza-power-report-2023/

With the acceptance of curbside pickup, delivery services, and less cash (more charges), this business will be able to increase its selling multiple above past benchmarks.

"Pizza restaurants are facing greater levels of competition, as more restaurants offer pizza and similar food items and the number of pizzerias continues to rise. Offering different food items and gourmet options is one way some are standing out from the pack. Demand for pizza remains strong, but a rise in health conscious consumers is leaving many restaurants struggling to adapt. Those with healthier options and a wider variety of choices are faring best."

Source: IBISWorld Key Takeaways

EXPERT COMMENTS

Buyers: trust but verify numbers, employees, and food costs. I ask my buyers to park outside (away) and watch customer count during lunch and dinner. Sellers: I ask my seller to tell the truth from the beginning, as the truth comes out during due diligence, and you don't want to be embarrassed and/or scare off buyers with faulty information.

Make sure you receive all the recipes, as once you change that, you have an entirely new business and potentially could lose your existing customer base.

Don't be cheap with the quality of ingredients; treat staff well; enjoy what you're doing.

It's not as easy as you think. Quality food and quality management experience will prevail.

People will pay for good food and good service. Sellers can get a premium for a well-run business, and buyers will pay for a well-run business. Takeout and pickup drive profits.

Consistency is one of the key factors when purchasing a pizza shop. Maintaining consistent recipes is very important, especially in the dough texture.

FINANCING

100 percent cash or, in larger transactions, 80 percent cash and 20 percent owner financing. Because this is a cash business (less as credit cards become the first payment option), I like the seller to take back 20 percent for 12 to 18 months, proving the cash business is as stated.

Seller financing is typically what is used in this type of industry.

RESOURCES

- IBISWorld, September 2023: https://www.ibisworld.com
- Franchise Times: https://www.franchisetimes.com
- Nation's Restaurant News: https://www.nrn.com
- PMQ Pizza Magazine: https://www.pmq.com

Plant & Flower Growing

| NAICS 111422 | Businesses/Units 42,632

| Profit $982.1 M | Wages $4.6 B | Annual Growth Future 0.6%

| | Annual Growth Past 0.9%

INDUSTRY MULTIPLES

Acquisition multiples below are calculated medians using US private industry transactions. Data updated annually. Last update: August 2023.

VALUATION MULTIPLE (MEDIAN VALUE)

UNDER $1 MILLION NET SALES	N/A
$1 MILLION–$5 MILLION NET SALES	
MVIC/Net Sales.	1.05
MVIC/Gross Profit	1.43
MVIC/SDE	N/A
MVIC/EBITDA	N/A
OVER $5 MILLION NET SALES	N/A

Source: DealStats (formerly Pratt's Stats), 2023 (Portland, OR: Business Valuation Resources, LLC), www.bvresources.com/dealstats

BENCHMARK DATA

STATISTICS (PLANT & FLOWER GROWING)

Number of Establishments	42,632
Average Profit Margin	5.3%
Revenue per Employee	$111,826
Average Number of Employees	3.9
Average Wages per Employee	$27,702

PRODUCTS AND SERVICES SEGMENTATION

Floriculture	45.2%
Horticulture	42.2%
Other	12.6%

MAJOR MARKET SEGMENTATION

Flower and nursery stock wholesalers .	. 63.5%
Intra-industry sales .	. 26.2%
Retailers.	. 10.3%

INDUSTRY COSTS

Profit	. 5.3%
Wages	. 24.8%
Purchases	. 32.7%
Depreciation	. 2.8%
Marketing	. 0.7%
Rent & Utilities	. 15.6%
Other	. 18.1%

INDUSTRY TREND

"Boosted leisure time amid COVID-19 expanded consumer desire to purchase plants and flowers. In turn, price-based competition with imports intensified among major domestic retailers such as Walmart and Home Depot. Demand from florists will grow alongside consumer spending and time spent on leisure and sports. This will push up demand for plants and flowers cultivated by industry growers."

Source: IBISWorld Key Takeaways

RESOURCES

• IBISWorld, October 2023: https://www.ibisworld.com

Play It Again Sports (Franchise)

| NAICS 459510 | Businesses/Units 248

Rules of Thumb

• 40%–45% annual sales plus paid-for inventory

PRICING TIPS

Approx. Total Investment: $292,500 to $401,300

RESOURCES

• Play It Again Sports: https://www.playitagainsports.com/home
• Franchise information: https://www.playitagainsports.com/home/own-a-store
• Winmark: https://winmarkcorporation.com

Plumbers

| NAICS 238220 | Businesses/Units 112,539

| Profit $4.9 B | Wages $39.1 B | Annual Growth Future 1.6%

| | | Annual Growth Past -0.8%

Rules of Thumb

• 3 x SDE plus inventory
• 4 x EBITDA

Acquisition multiples below are calculated medians using US private industry transactions. Data updated annually. Last update: August 2023.

VALUATION MULTIPLE (MEDIAN VALUE)

UNDER $1 MILLION NET SALES

MVIC/Net Sales	0.42
MVIC/Gross Profit	0.73
MVIC/SDE	1.84
MVIC/EBITDA	2.80

$1 MILLION–$5 MILLION NET SALES

MVIC/Net Sales	0.46
MVIC/Gross Profit	0.96
MVIC/SDE	2.85
MVIC/EBITDA	4.43

OVER $5 MILLION NET SALES

MVIC/Net Sales	0.55
MVIC/Gross Profit	1.53
MVIC/SDE	3.91
MVIC/EBITDA	4.24

Source: DealStats (formerly Pratt's Stats), 2023 (Portland, OR: Business Valuation Resources, LLC), www.bvresources.com/dealstats

PRICING TIPS

Buyers, especially private equity buyers, seek plumbing businesses which are pandemic-resilient and are not tied to new construction, which is cyclical. Plumbing businesses which serve residential clients are very much in demand. The business we sold has a few very large property management companies as clients, which increased demand, as the client serves both the property management company HOAs as well as tenants.

BENCHMARK DATA

STATISTICS (PLUMBERS)

Number of Establishments	112,539
Average Profit Margin	3.9%
Revenue per Employee	$220,548
Average Number of Employees	4.9
Average Wages per Employee	$69,107

PRODUCTS AND SERVICES SEGMENTATION

General plumbing services	53.8%
Mechanical services	34.4%
Building sprinkler system installation	6.3%
Steamfitting and piping services	3.6%
Lawn sprinkler installation	1.9%

MAJOR MARKET SEGMENTATION

Residential construction	31.1%
Other general construction	23.0%
Healthcare, public safety and educational buildings	15.9%
Office buildings	13.3%
Retail and storage spaces	8.5%
Manufacturing and industrial buildings	8.2%

INDUSTRY COSTS

Profit	3.9%
Wages	30.9%
Purchases	39.5%

Depreciation	.	.	.	.	.	.	.	0.9%
Marketing	.	.	.	.	.	.	.	0.5%
Rent & Utilities	.	.	.	.	.	.	.	3.5%
Other	.	.	.	.	.	.	.	20.8%

Buyers expect labor costs to be not more than 35 percent of sales.

EXPENSES (% OF ANNUAL SALES)

Cost of Goods	.	.	.	.	.	.	.	10%
Occupancy Costs	.	.	.	.	.	.	.	05%
Payroll/Labor Costs.	.	.	.	.	.	.	30%
Profit (pretax)	.	.	.	.	.	.	.	30%

QUESTIONS

- Customer mix (looking for concentration)? Mix of services and gross margins for each? How are financials prepared? What systems are used for order management, scheduling, financials? How many trucks? What kind of equipment? How old are vehicles? Why do customers choose this company over others? What licenses do you have? Who runs operations? Who orders parts, etc.?

INDUSTRY TREND

Plumbing services business that have developed brands in their local markets will continue to be aggressively sought by private equity looking to roll up the industry.

"Revenue from the Plumbing industry managed to grow amid the COVID-19 pandemic despite falling commercial demand. The residential market ferried the industry through the worst of the pandemic. The commercial market has rebounded from the lows of the COVID-19 pandemic. While this will help larger plumbing companies in the long run, these operators will not see any short-term stimulus. Demand from the residential market has ground to a halt as mortgage rates continue to climb. With that said, there will always be a need for plumbing services from residential clients, providing a reliable stream of income for the industry."

Source: IBISWorld Key Takeaways

EXPERT COMMENTS

Sellers need to have excellent books—likely prepared on accrual/GAAP—that will correctly reflect customer deposits and any potential warranty liability. Sellers also need to have excellent records of equipment purchases and maintenance, and be able to show minimal turnover of staff.

Businesses that have great reputations in their community, well-trained staff with clear job descriptions, and well-maintained equipment and facilities will be more in demand. Buyers will most likely keep the local brand name as it is very hard to replicate the brand loyalty that is built over decades.

FINANCING

Trend towards further industry consolidation. Private equity firms will likely use some debt to lever up returns and also ask sellers to roll over some equity, which can have advantages for the seller.

RESOURCES

- IBISWorld, September 2023: https://www.ibisworld.com
- ASPE—American Society of Plumbing Engineers: https://www.aspe.org

- IAPMO—International Association of Plumbing and Mechanical Officials: https://www.iapmo.org
- PHCC—Plumbing-Heating-Cooling Contractors Association: https://www.phccweb.org

Plumbing and Heating Equipment and Supplies (Hydronics) Merchant Wholesalers

| NAICS 423720 | Businesses/Units 7,852

| Profit $3.2 B | Wages $7.4 B

| Annual Growth Past 1.1%

INDUSTRY MULTIPLES

Acquisition multiples below are calculated medians using US private industry transactions. Data updated annually. Last update: August 2023.

VALUATION MULTIPLE (MEDIAN VALUE)

UNDER $1 MILLION NET SALES

MVIC/Net Sales	0.53
MVIC/Gross Profit	0.99
MVIC/SDE	1.87
MVIC/EBITDA	6.35

$1 MILLION–$5 MILLION NET SALES

MVIC/Net Sales	0.49
MVIC/Gross Profit	1.05
MVIC/SDE	3.48
MVIC/EBITDA	5.41

OVER $5 MILLION NET SALES

MVIC/Net Sales	0.56
MVIC/Gross Profit	1.87
MVIC/SDE	3.60
MVIC/EBITDA	5.94

Source: DealStats (formerly Pratt's Stats), 2023 (Portland, OR: Business Valuation Resources, LLC), www.bvresources.com/dealstats

BENCHMARK DATA

STATISTICS (PLUMBING & HEATING SUPPLIES WHOLESALING)

Number of Establishments	7,852
Average Profit Margin	3.7%
Revenue per Employee	$922,024
Average Number of Employees	11.7
Average Wages per Employee	$80,604

PRODUCTS AND SERVICES SEGMENTATION

Other plumbing supplies	33.2%
Pipes, fittings and valves	25.0%
Plumbing fixtures	17.2%
Furnaces and water heaters	10.9%
Sump pumps and water treatment equipment	5.1%
HVAC equipment	4.6%
Boilers, radiators and related products	4.0%

MAJOR MARKET SEGMENTATION

New residential building construction	27.3%
Residential remodeling and repairs	26.4%

New nonresidential building construction 22.4%
Other 16.8%
Nonresidential remodeling and repairs. 7.1%

INDUSTRY COSTS

Profit 3.7%
Wages 8.7%
Purchases 68.8%
Depreciation 0.6%
Marketing 0.6%
Rent & Utilities 1.5%
Other 16.2%

MARKET SHARE

Ferguson PLC 32.5%

INDUSTRY TREND

"The industry sells a range of goods. These include plumbing fixtures, hydronic and gas furnaces, gas water heaters and pipes, valves, and fittings (PVF), that are utilized in residential development and home renovation projects. All in all, the business has benefited from rising house starts and private home improvement investment. This has lessened the negative impact that the 2020 economic slowdown has had on the industry."

Source: IBISWorld Key Takeaways

RESOURCES

• IBISWorld, September 2023: https://www.ibisworld.com

Podiatrists

	NAICS 621391		SIC 8043-01		Businesses/Units 11,585
	Profit $992.7 M		Wages $2.3 B		Annual Growth Future 1.8%
					Annual Growth Past 2.3%

Rules of Thumb

• 40%–50% annual sales plus inventory
• 3–4 x SDE plus inventory
• 1.5 x EBITDA

INDUSTRY MULTIPLES

Acquisition multiples below are calculated medians using US private industry transactions. Data updated annually. Last update: August 2023.

VALUATION MULTIPLE (MEDIAN VALUE)

UNDER $1 MILLION NET SALES	
MVIC/Net Sales.	0.24
MVIC/Gross Profit	0.48
MVIC/SDE	1.86
MVIC/EBITDA	6.72
$1 MILLION–$5 MILLION NET SALES	N/A
OVER $5 MILLION NET SALES	N/A

Source: DealStats (formerly Pratt's Stats), 2023 (Portland, OR: Business Valuation Resources, LLC), www.bvresources.com/dealstats

PRICING TIPS

Smaller practices with less than $1M to $2M EBITDA rarely sell for more than 1.5 x EBITDA. Larger practices in certain specialties sell for more. Sale at greater than fair market value can trigger federal audits into whether the acquirer is buying referrals rather than just buying equity and can result in felony prosecutions, so always involve a medical practice transactions specialist attorney; referrals at https://www.nschbc.org and https://www.americanhealthlaw.org. Brokers should never try to negotiate and document a transaction, as state and federal applicable laws are complex, confusing, and illogical. Always use a specialist attorney!

BENCHMARK DATA

STATISTICS (PODIATRISTS)

Number of Establishments	11,585
Average Profit Margin	14.2%
Revenue per Employee	$165,733
Average Number of Employees	3.7
Average Wages per Employee	$54,156

PRODUCTS AND SERVICES SEGMENTATION

Musculoskeletal system and connective tissue diseases	39.9%
Skin and subcutaneous tissue diseases	21.7%
Other	12.6%
Infectious and parasitic diseases	8.2%
Endocrine, nutritional and metabolic diseases	7.6%
Circulatory system diseases	5.4%
Nervous system and sense organ diseases	2.8%
Merchandise sales	1.8%

INDUSTRY COSTS

Profit	14.2%
Wages	32.7%
Purchases	9.6%
Depreciation	1.1%
Marketing	1.7%
Rent & Utilities	10.0%
Other	30.7%

EXPENSES (% OF ANNUAL SALES)

Cost of Goods	04% to 06%
Occupancy Costs	06% to 07%
Payroll/Labor Costs	16% to 23%
Profit (pretax)	30% to 40%

QUESTIONS

- State and federal compliance
- Do you have nursing home contracts? Do you have Medicaid patients?

INDUSTRY TREND

"Consolidation is a step in the right direction for podiatrists. Multidiscipline group practice would bring cost savings, increased buyer power and greater visibility and a more extensive revenue base while enabling funding for costly innovative tools and systems. The need for services is steady, with funding bringing volatility. Demographic and lifestyle trends will keep individuals needing podiatrists' care, but the availability of funding will impact revenue growth."

Source: IBISWorld Key Takeaways

EXPERT COMMENTS

You must be a licensed podiatrist to own a practice in most states. Orthopedists sit on many hospital boards and discriminate against podiatrists getting hospital privileges. Podiatrists tend to have heavy Medicare populations.

P

FINANCING

SBA 7a 80 percent

RESOURCES

- IBISWorld, April 2023: https://www.ibisworld.com
- AAPPM—American Academy of Podiatric Practice Management: https://aappm.org
- AHLA—American Health Law Association: https://www.americanhealthlaw.org
- APMA—American Podiatric Medical Association: https://www.apma.org
- MGMA—Medical Group Management Association: https://www.mgma.com
- NSCHBC—National Society of Certified Healthcare Business Consultants: https://www.nschbc.org
- Podiatry Today: https://www.podiatrytoday.com

Pool Service (Swimming)

	NAICS 561790		SIC 7389-09		Businesses/Units 74,475
	Profit $522.4 M		Wages $1.9 B		Annual Growth Future 1.1%
					Annual Growth Past 1.9%

Rules of Thumb

- 2–3 x SDE
- 80% annual sales
- 3 x EBIT
- 3 x EBITDA

INDUSTRY MULTIPLES

Acquisition multiples below are calculated medians using US private industry transactions. Data updated annually. Last update: August 2023.

VALUATION MULTIPLE (MEDIAN VALUE)

UNDER $1 MILLION NET SALES
MVIC/Net Sales.	0.73
MVIC/Gross Profit	1.00
MVIC/SDE	2.08
MVIC/EBITDA	2.36

$1 MILLION–$5 MILLION NET SALES
MVIC/Net Sales.	0.57
MVIC/Gross Profit	0.98
MVIC/SDE	3.09
MVIC/EBITDA	4.12

OVER $5 MILLION NET SALES
MVIC/Net Sales.	1.08
MVIC/Gross Profit	1.55
MVIC/SDE	5.26
MVIC/EBITDA	8.41

Source: DealStats (formerly Pratt's Stats), 2023 (Portland, OR: Business Valuation Resources, LLC), www.bvresources.com/dealstats

PRICING TIPS

Sales price depends on if the seller is selling the entire business or just some accounts. Accounts only sell for an average of 12 times the gross monthly service billing, not including repairs. An entire business would sell for an average of 3 to 4 times SDE, depending on many other factors.

Routes are based on the monthly service rates, not including repairs.

BENCHMARK DATA

STATISTICS (SWIMMING POOL CLEANING SERVICES)

Number of Establishments 74,475
Average Profit Margin 7.3%
Revenue per Employee $76,782
Average Number of Employees. 1.3
Average Wages per Employee . . . $19,966

PRODUCTS AND SERVICES SEGMENTATION

General cleaning services 33.1%
Chemical adjustments 30.2%
Other 19.3%
Equipment cleaning and maintenance . . 17.4%

INDUSTRY COSTS

Profit 7.3%
Wages 25.9%
Purchases 29.1%
Depreciation 2.3%
Marketing 2.3%
Rent & Utilities 3.0%
Other 30.2%

Good location with long-term customers is essential.

How many pools can I service in a day? A good question, but difficult to answer. The average pool service technician will service approximately 16 full-service pools a day, while some can service 25 to 30 in a day. It depends on the individual and what type of pools he or she is servicing. The average pool service technician will service 2 pools an hour including driving time. If the accounts are chemical only, he can do many more. If the accounts are commercial, he or she will do fewer.

Source: Contributed by Frank Passantino, Pool Route Brokers, Inc.

EXPENSES (% OF ANNUAL SALES)

Cost of Goods . . . . 10% to 20%
Payroll/Labor Costs. . . . . 20% to 30%
Profit (pretax) . . . . . . 40% to 50%

QUESTIONS

- Age of accounts? Location of accounts?
- Are customers on a preventative maintenance program? Do you charge extra for chemicals? Are there any challenging customers or pools? How long have employees been with you? Do you take any vacation/time off?
- Payment history of accounts
- Where did your pools come from (did you buy the route, build it, etc.)?

INDUSTRY TREND

Always in demand. New pool construction demands service professionals.

"Pool construction boomed through COVID-19. Consumers quarantined at home looked to swimming pools as safe solutions to entertain family and friends, providing a large base of potential clients for pool cleaning services. This has offset losses from dampened consumer spending. Consumers will be better able to hire cleaning services. Rising per capita disposable income, consumer spending and the number of households with over $100,000 in annual income indicate pool owners will be more comfortable outsourcing cleaning to professional services."

Source: IBISWorld Key Takeaways

EXPERT COMMENTS

Sellers need to provide as much training and support as possible.

Buyers: review customer payment history and confirm seller support. Sellers: understand most buyers are new in the industry and will need training and support.

FINANCING

Cash for small to midsize routes. Outside financing for larger routes.

RESOURCES

- IBISWorld, September 2023: https://www.ibisworld.com
- AQUA Magazine: https://www.aquamagazine.com
- FSPA—Florida Swimming Pool Association: https://www.floridapoolpro.com
- IPSSA—Independent Pool & Spa Service Association, Inc.: https://www.ipssa.com
- PHTA—Pool & Hot Tub Alliance: https://www.phta.org
- Pool Pro: https://www.poolpro.com
- PRB—Pool Route Brokers: http://poolroutebrokers.com
- PSN—Pool and Spa News: https://www.poolspanews.com

Portable Toilet Companies

NAICS 562991	SIC 7359-22	Businesses/Units 3,582
Profit $257 M	Wages $1.7 B	Annual Growth Future 2.2%
		Annual Growth Past 10.7%

Rules of Thumb

- 4x SDE plus inventory
- 5x EBITDA

INDUSTRY MULTIPLES

Acquisition multiples below are calculated medians using US private industry transactions. Data updated annually. Last update: August 2023.

VALUATION MULTIPLE (MEDIAN VALUE)

UNDER $1 MILLION NET SALES

MVIC/Net Sales	0.78
MVIC/Gross Profit	0.89
MVIC/SDE	2.76
MVIC/EBITDA	2.60

$1 MILLION–$5 MILLION NET SALES

MVIC/Net Sales	0.89
MVIC/Gross Profit	1.19

MVIC/SDE	4.69
MVIC/EBITDA	4.69
OVER $5 MILLION NET SALES	N/A

Source: DealStats (formerly Pratt's Stats), 2023 (Portland, OR: Business Valuation Resources, LLC), www.bvresources.com/dealstats

PRICING TIPS

As with any business acquisition, a reasonable investment for this industry varies depending on cash flow margins, quality of personnel/management, condition and value of rental equipment, sales trends, level of competition, strength of trade name, search engine positioning, etc.

Strategic buyers are in the process of consolidating this industry, although there are many independently owned companies still in this space. For the companies with larger market share and size, cash flow multiples are higher, especially those with EBITDA over $1,000,000.

BENCHMARK DATA

STATISTICS (PORTABLE TOILET RENTAL)

Number of Establishments	3,582
Average Profit Margin	8.9%
Revenue per Employee	$99.552
Average Number of Employees. . . .	.8.4
Average Wages per Employee . . .	$60,175

PRODUCTS AND SERVICES SEGMENTATION

Standard portable toilet rentals. . .	.63.1%
Luxury and trailer portable toilet rentals	.23.6%
Portable toilet pumping and cleaning .	6.7%
Testing and waste collection . . .	6.6%

MAJOR MARKET SEGMENTATION

Construction sites	.47.2%
Event organizers	.28.0%
Recreation sites.	.13.7%
Other commercial entities	.11.1%

INDUSTRY COSTS

Profit	8.9%
Wages	.59.9%
Purchases	.17.1%
Depreciation	6.2%
Marketing	0.4%
Rent & Utilities	4.8%
Other	2.8%

MARKET SHARE

United Site Services Inc.	.16.7%

It's reasonable to expect the cost of rental units to equal one to two year's rental income, not including operating expenses.

EXPENSES (% OF ANNUAL SALES)

Cost of Goods	20%
Occupancy Costs	10%
Payroll/Labor Costs.	40%
Profit (pretax)	30%

- Any customer concentration? Assurance that larger customers will continue on with buyer? Get an official count of rental units included in the sale, as well as number of units currently rented or available to rent. Does the owner have an arrangement with local competitors to help out when a large event or need comes along in order to have enough available rental units?

INDUSTRY TREND

Companies are investing more in luxury toilet trailers, which often are temperature controlled and include hot and cold water. These are a considerable investment but bring in a high amount of rental revenues when in use. Portable toilet businesses tend to look for additional revenue sources, such as dumpster rentals, temporary fencing, septic installation, and various sewer and excavating services. Military bases, government projects, construction, and special events offer great cash flow opportunities for efficient operators.

"Customers can rent restrooms from the industry for a set amount of time. Construction companies, live venue service providers and providers of on-site cleanup services are examples of clients. With a growing economy, construction activity surges. This leads to a higher demand for portable toilets to serve the needs of workers. Similarly, the increase in outdoor events, such as music festivals, sporting events and fairs, has led to a surge in demand for portable toilets."

Source: IBISWorld Key Takeaways

EXPERT COMMENTS

If adjusted net cash flow is much below 20 percent of total revenues, the operating expenses are likely not in control, or there is untapped revenue potential. Although facility location is not a critical feature in this industry, having the facility and yard in well-kept and clean condition is important. If it doesn't show well to buyers, the value is often minimized.

Generally, investment risks are minimized due to the fair market value of rental equipment, most of which could be liquidated, if desired, at a reasonable value. Customer service is extremely important. Repeat business can depend on company reputation and online reviews. It's not necessary for facility locations to be visible to the public. In fact, the preferred locations are in lower-traffic areas, although convenient access for servicing and transporting rental units is a plus. Existing portable toilet businesses are the best way to enter, or expand in, the industry, as it takes time to build up regular customers in this industry.

FINANCING

These are mostly cash transactions. Sometimes the seller will hold a note for 10 to 20 percent of the purchase price.

RESOURCES

- IBISWorld, July 2023: https://www.ibisworld.com
- PSAI—Portable Sanitation Association International: https://www.psai.org

Portfolio Management

| NAICS 523940 | Businesses/Units 313,018

| Profit $200 B | Wages $145.1 B | Annual Growth Future 8.2%

| | | Annual Growth Past 7.6%

BENCHMARK DATA

STATISTICS (PORTFOLIO MANAGEMENT)

Number of Establishments	313,018
Average Profit Margin	36.1%
Revenue per Employee	$715,376
Average Number of Employees	2.5
Average Wages per Employee	$189,933

PRODUCTS AND SERVICES SEGMENTATION

Active core	30.1%
Passive	22.1%
Active specialists	17.7%
Alternatives	16.8%
Solutions	13.3%

MAJOR MARKET SEGMENTATION

Retail	41.0%
Institutional equity	29.1%
Institutional fixed income	20.3%
Institutional multi asset	7.8%
Institutional alternative	1.8%

INDUSTRY COSTS

Profit	36.1%
Wages	26.2%
Purchases	1.7%
Depreciation	1.0%
Marketing	0.8%
Rent & Utilities	1.9%
Other	32.3%

INDUSTRY TREND

"Assets under management (AUM) are trending toward a winner-take-all competitive environment, as the companies with the most assets leverage them to attract additional assets. As high inflation continues to plague the US economy, the FED has indicated it will pursue higher interest rates going forward. Lower liquidity and investor preference shifts are going to be the main obstacles for the industry in the coming years."

Source: IBISWorld Key Takeaways

RESOURCES

• IBISWorld, May 2023: https://www.ibisworld.com

Postal Service

| NAICS 491110 | Businesses/Units 30,050

| Profit -$6.5 B | Wages $52.8 B | Annual Growth Future -1.9%

| | | Annual Growth Past -1.1%

INDUSTRY MULTIPLES

Acquisition multiples below are calculated medians using US private industry transactions. Data updated annually. Last update: August 2023.

VALUATION MULTIPLE (MEDIAN VALUE)

UNDER $1 MILLION NET SALES	
MVIC/Net Sales	0.52
MVIC/Gross Profit	0.79
MVIC/SDE	2.13
MVIC/EBITDA	2.76
$1 MILLION–$5 MILLION NET SALES	
MVIC/Net Sales	0.60
MVIC/Gross Profit	N/A
MVIC/SDE	3.05
MVIC/EBITDA	N/A
OVER $5 MILLION NET SALES	
MVIC/Net Sales	6.19
MVIC/Gross Profit	8.08
MVIC/SDE	N/A
MVIC/EBITDA	28.42

Source: DealStats (formerly Pratt's Stats), 2023 (Portland, OR: Business Valuation Resources, LLC), www.bvresources.com/dealstats

BENCHMARK DATA

STATISTICS (POSTAL SERVICE)

Number of Establishments	30,050
Average Profit Margin	-8.1%
Revenue per Employee	$128,560
Average Number of Employees	20.6
Average Wages per Employee	$84,380

PRODUCTS AND SERVICES SEGMENTATION

Shipping and package services	39.9%
First-class mail	30.6%
Marketing mail (formerly standard mail)	20.4%
Other mail services	5.7%
International mail	2.2%
Periodicals	1.2%

MAJOR MARKET SEGMENTATION

Residential—city	51.8%
Residential—rural	28.8%
Residential—PO box	9.8%
Business	7.7%
Residential—highway	1.9%

INDUSTRY COSTS

Profit	-8.1%
Wages	65.6%
Purchases	7.6%
Depreciation	1.6%
Marketing	1.3%
Rent & Utilities	2.3%
Other	29.7%

MARKET SHARE

United States Postal Service	94.8%

INDUSTRY TREND

"Revenue has declined slightly during the current period. The USPS benefited from rising demand for shipping and packaging during the COVID-19 pandemic but has been hurt by falling consumer confidence recently. The USPS will enter into long-term decline during the outlook period because of external competition from email, online media and private courier service companies. The postal service will seek to use innovations to stem some of this decline."

Source: IBISWorld Key Takeaways

RESOURCES

• IBISWorld, June 2023: https://www.ibisworld.com

Power/Pressure Washing

| NAICS 561790

Rules of Thumb

• 50% annual revenues of $1M+

INDUSTRY MULTIPLES

Acquisition multiples below are calculated medians using US private industry transactions. Data updated annually. Last update: August 2023.

VALUATION MULTIPLE (MEDIAN VALUE)

UNDER $1 MILLION NET SALES
MVIC/Net Sales	0.73
MVIC/Gross Profit	1.00
MVIC/SDE	2.08
MVIC/EBITDA	2.36

$1 MILLION–$5 MILLION NET SALES
MVIC/Net Sales	0.57
MVIC/Gross Profit	0.98
MVIC/SDE	3.09
MVIC/EBITDA	4.12

OVER $5 MILLION NET SALES
MVIC/Net Sales	1.08
MVIC/Gross Profit	1.55
MVIC/SDE	5.26
MVIC/EBITDA	8.41

Source: DealStats (formerly Pratt's Stats), 2023 (Portland, OR: Business Valuation Resources, LLC), www.bvresources.com/dealstats

Printing

| NAICS 32311 | Businesses/Units 21,045

| Profit $3.4 B | Wages $20.7 B | Annual Growth Future -3.5%

| | | Annual Growth Past -3.0%

INDUSTRY MULTIPLES

Acquisition multiples below are calculated medians using US private industry transactions. Data updated annually. Last update: August 2023.

VALUATION MULTIPLE (MEDIAN VALUE)

UNDER $1 MILLION NET SALES
| MVIC/Net Sales | 0.48 |

MVIC/Gross Profit 0.80
MVIC/SDE 2.25
MVIC/EBITDA 3.22

$1 MILLION–$5 MILLION NET SALES
MVIC/Net Sales. 0.46
MVIC/Gross Profit 0.78
MVIC/SDE 2.88
MVIC/EBITDA 4.30

OVER $5 MILLION NET SALES
MVIC/Net Sales. 0.70
MVIC/Gross Profit 1.50
MVIC/SDE 3.73
MVIC/EBITDA 4.76

Source: DealStats (formerly Pratt's Stats), 2023 (Portland, OR: Business Valuation Resources, LLC),
www.bvresources.com/dealstats

BENCHMARK DATA

STATISTICS (PRINTING)

Number of Establishments 21,045
Average Profit Margin 4.1%
Revenue per Employee $212,950
Average Number of Employees. . . . 17.9
Average Wages per Employee . . . $53,543

PRODUCTS AND SERVICES SEGMENTATION

Commercial lithographic printing . . . 40.4%
Other printing 15.4%
Digital printing 14.2%
Commercial flexographic printing . . . 10.8%
Commercial screen printing 9.7%
Book printing 5.8%
Commercial gravure printing 3.7%

MAJOR MARKET SEGMENTATION

Other 26.8%
Manufacturers 25.5%
Publishing 17.5%
Advertisers 15.2%
Financial and legal firms 8.1%
Exports 6.9%

INDUSTRY COSTS

Profit 4.1%
Wages 25.0%
Purchases 39.9%
Depreciation 2.3%
Marketing 0.4%
Rent & Utilities 3.6%
Other 24.7%

INDUSTRY TREND

"Long-term decline continues among printers. The industry's decades-long decline has continued. An overall shift towards digital primacy has resulted in consistent revenue loss year-over-year. Advancements in communication negate industry demand. The industry will continue to decline as the world moves beyond physical printing. Traditional major print publications have given way to their electronic counterparts."

Source: IBISWorld Key Takeaways

RESOURCES
- IBISWorld, September 2023: https://www.ibisworld.com
- FGA—Florida Graphics Alliance: https://www.floridagraphics.org
- ISA—International Sign Association: https://signs.org
- PRINTING United Alliance: https://www.printing.org
- TLMI: https://tlmi.com/home

Printing Services

| NAICS 323120 | Businesses/Units 1,653

| Profit $120.8 M | Wages $1 B | Annual Growth Future -5.6%

| Annual Growth Past -4.7%

INDUSTRY MULTIPLES

Acquisition multiples below are calculated medians using US private industry transactions. Data updated annually. Last update: August 2023.

VALUATION MULTIPLE (MEDIAN VALUE)

UNDER $1 MILLION NET SALES

MVIC/Net Sales.	0.40
MVIC/Gross Profit	0.75
MVIC/SDE	2.70
MVIC/EBITDA	3.51
$1 MILLION–$5 MILLION NET SALES	N/A
OVER $5 MILLION NET SALES	N/A

Source: DealStats (formerly Pratt's Stats), 2023 (Portland, OR: Business Valuation Resources, LLC), www.bvresources.com/dealstats

BENCHMARK DATA

STATISTICS (PRINTING SERVICES)

Number of Establishments .	1,653
Average Profit Margin	4.3%
Revenue per Employee .	$148,276
Average Number of Employees.	10.8
Average Wages per Employee .	$53,804

PRODUCTS AND SERVICES SEGMENTATION

Prepress services	28.2%
Printing plates and cylinders	21.1%
Postpress services .	18.0%
Other	13.3%
Samples.	12.1%
Hardcover and softcover bookbinding .	7.3%

MAJOR MARKET SEGMENTATION

Printing industry	65.7%
Packaging industry .	10.8%
Book publishers.	8.9%
Magazine publishers	7.9%
Newspaper publishers .	4.4%
Exports .	2.4%

INDUSTRY COSTS

Profit	4.3%
Wages	36.2%

Purchases	.	.	.	.	.	.	. 25.6%
Depreciation	.	.	.	.	.	.	. 3.4%
Marketing	.	.	.	.	.	.	. 0.2%
Rent & Utilities	.	.	.	.	.	.	. 4.2%
Other	.	.	.	.	.	.	. 26.1%

P

INDUSTRY TREND

"Industry operators provide prepress and postpress services, such as print-plate manufacturing and bookbinding services. Demand for these services is based on the need for printed books, magazines, newspapers and print advertising. Therefore, the industry has been threatened by the shift from print to online media and advertising. The Printing Services industry is not expected to experience any revenue gains as the growth of digital media persists. While broader economic conditions are expected to improve, generating increased demand for print-based advertising and general printing will be difficult."

Source: IBISWorld Key Takeaways

RESOURCES

• IBISWorld, February 2023: https://www.ibisworld.com

Printing: Commercial Printers

| NAICS 323111 | SIC 2752-02

Rules of Thumb

• 50%–55% annual sales plus inventory
• 2–3 x SDE includes inventory
• 2.5–3 x recast EBITDA if sales under $2 million
• 2.5–3.5 x recast EBITDA if sales $2 to $5 million
• 3.5 x recast EBITDA if sales $5 to $25 million
• 4 x EBIT

INDUSTRY MULTIPLES

Acquisition multiples below are calculated medians using US private industry transactions. Data updated annually. Last update: August 2023.

VALUATION MULTIPLE (MEDIAN VALUE)

UNDER $1 MILLION NET SALES	
MVIC/Net Sales.	0.49
MVIC/Gross Profit	0.68
MVIC/SDE	2.35
MVIC/EBITDA	3.07
$1 MILLION–$5 MILLION NET SALES	
MVIC/Net Sales.	0.40
MVIC/Gross Profit	0.62
MVIC/SDE	2.81
MVIC/EBITDA	4.35
OVER $5 MILLION NET SALES	
MVIC/Net Sales.	0.70
MVIC/Gross Profit	1.50
MVIC/SDE	3.73
MVIC/EBITDA	4.76

Source: DealStats (formerly Pratt's Stats), 2023 (Portland, OR: Business Valuation Resources, LLC), www.bvresources.com/dealstats

PRICING TIPS

The printing industry is still a very fragmented cottage industry. Pricing is mostly dependent on the size of the company (earnings) and other factors. Equipment age is a big consideration. Old lithographic offset printing presses are not very efficient nowadays. Most firms have now incorporated digital printing equipment either exclusively, or as additional pieces of equipment for shorter-run work.

BENCHMARK DATA

EXPENSES (% OF ANNUAL SALES)

Cost of Goods	35% to 45%
Occupancy Costs	04% to 14%
Payroll/Labor Costs.	30% to 40%
Profit (pretax)	05% to 15%

QUESTIONS

- Do you have skilled and experienced people in place?
- Why are you leaving and are there any contracts still honored?
- Commercial account base? Outside salespeople? What role(s) does owner fill? Product mix? Specialty vs. commodity.
- Look for any niche they serve; client concentration is a risk; client contracts are rare and would be a premium multiple.
- Is production equipment leased or owned?

INDUSTRY TREND

Digital printing will continue to encroach on the more conventional lithographic offset methods of printing.

EXPERT COMMENTS

Industry buyers will be looking for terms that include a seller's note.

Digital printing has changed the industry forever, and much of the work done now is printing on demand as opposed to printing to inventory.

FINANCING

No different than other manufacturing businesses; bank financing unless there is some serious client concentration

RESOURCES

- *Handbook of Business Valuation*, 2nd ed., West & Jones: https://www.wiley.com/en-us/Handbook+of+Business+ Valuation%2C+2nd+Edition-p-9780471297871
- American Printer: https://americanprinter.com
- PIA—Printing Industries Association, Inc.: https://www.piasc.org
- Printing Impressions: https://www.piworld.com
- PRINTING United Alliance: https://www.printing.org
- TLMI—Tag and Label Manufacturers Institute: https://www.tlmi.com/home

Printing: Custom Screen

NAICS 323113	SIC 7336-09		Businesses/Units 12,350
Profit $371.7 M	Wages $2.5 B		Annual Growth Future -2.0%
			Annual Growth Past -3.0%

Rules of Thumb

- 40%–45% annual sales plus inventory
- 2.5–3 x SDE includes inventory
- 3.5–4 x EBITDA
- 3.5–4 x EBIT

INDUSTRY MULTIPLES

Acquisition multiples below are calculated medians using US private industry transactions. Data updated annually. Last update: August 2023.

VALUATION MULTIPLE (MEDIAN VALUE)

UNDER $1 MILLION NET SALES

MVIC/Net Sales	0.48
MVIC/Gross Profit	0.88
MVIC/SDE	2.24
MVIC/EBITDA	3.30

$1 MILLION–$5 MILLION NET SALES

MVIC/Net Sales	0.58
MVIC/Gross Profit	1.31
MVIC/SDE	3.69
MVIC/EBITDA	4.27

OVER $5 MILLION NET SALES	N/A

Source: DealStats (formerly Pratt's Stats), 2023 (Portland, OR: Business Valuation Resources, LLC), www.bvresources.com/dealstats

PRICING TIPS

Sales growth, market potential, age/quality of equipment, staffing, lease will determine which end of range to use.

Value of any long-term contracts that are in place. Are contracts assignable?

National/corporate accounts vs. small local accounts increases value.

BENCHMARK DATA

STATISTICS (CUSTOM SCREEN PRINTING)

Number of Establishments	12,350
Average Profit Margin	4.0%
Revenue per employee	$127,628
Average Number of Employees	5.8
Average Wages per Employee	$34,807

PRODUCTS AND SERVICES SEGMENTATION

Apparel printing	49.4%
Stationery, invitations and other paper-based printing	25.8%
Other	16.9%
Labels	7.9%

MAJOR MARKET SEGMENTATION

Manufacturers	52.1%
Advertisers	31.0%
Other	16.9%

INDUSTRY COSTS

Profit	4.0%
Wages	27.1%
Purchases	40.2%
Depreciation	2.3%
Marketing	0.4%
Rent & Utilities	3.7%
Other	22.3%

EXPENSES (% OF ANNUAL SALES)

Cost of Goods	60%
Occupancy Costs	05%
Payroll/Labor Costs.	20% to 25%
Profit (pretax)	05% to 10%

QUESTIONS

- Sales and profit trend over past 3 years, and especially over most recent 12-month period
- Monthly revenue over past 3 years to gauge seasonality of business and to analyze competitive environment
- Provide concentration of customers. Maintenance schedule for all equipment?

INDUSTRY TREND

"The industry has significantly outperformed the broader printing sector. Its lesser reliance on declining print media and advertising markets makes companies less resilient. The industry was greatly affected by reduced consumer spending. Social distancing policies implemented during the pandemic largely prevented large gatherings, like sporting games, fundraisers or concerts, where customized merchandise is often available."

Source: IBISWorld Key Takeaways

EXPERT COMMENTS

Can be high capital investment to start up.

Anyone can open a small screen printing shop or store. Most companies do screen printed and embroidered products. They also sell small signs, graphics, etc. This industry can be capital intensive. High-speed equipment is necessary to produce larger volume, and some companies add a second and third shift.

RESOURCES

- IBISWorld, September 2023: https://www.ibisworld.com
- PRINTING United Alliance: https://www.printing.org
- Screen Printing magazine: https://screenprintingmag.com

Printing: Label

| NAICS 323111

INDUSTRY MULTIPLES

Acquisition multiples below are calculated medians using US private industry transactions. Data updated annually. Last update: August 2023.

VALUATION MULTIPLE (MEDIAN VALUE)

UNDER $1 MILLION NET SALES	
MVIC/Net Sales.	0.49
MVIC/Gross Profit	0.68
MVIC/SDE	2.35
MVIC/EBITDA	3.07

$1 MILLION–$5 MILLION NET SALES	
MVIC/Net Sales.	0.40
MVIC/Gross Profit	0.62
MVIC/SDE	2.81
MVIC/EBITDA	4.35

OVER $5 MILLION NET SALES

MVIC/Net Sales.	0.70
MVIC/Gross Profit	1.50
MVIC/SDE	3.73
MVIC/EBITDA	4.76

Source: DealStats (formerly Pratt's Stats), 2023 (Portland, OR: Business Valuation Resources, LLC), www.bvresources.com/dealstats

EXPENSES (% OF ANNUAL SALES)

Cost of Goods	45%
Occupancy Costs	04%
Payroll/Labor Costs.	18%
Profit (pretax)	20%

QUESTIONS

• How do you plan to finance the deal? What are the strategic advantages?

FINANCING

Outside and privately financed

RESOURCES

• TLMI: https://tlmi.com

Printing: Quick Print

NAICS 323111	SIC 2752-02	Businesses/Units 8,603
Profit $195.5 M	Wages $843.3 M	Annual Growth Future -4.4%
		Annual Growth Past -3.0%

Rules of Thumb

• 45%–55% annual sales plus inventory
• 2.5–3.5 x SDE plus inventory
• 4 x EBIT
• 3–4 x EBITDA

INDUSTRY MULTIPLES

Acquisition multiples below are calculated medians using US private industry transactions. Data updated annually. Last update: August 2023.

VALUATION MULTIPLE (MEDIAN VALUE)

UNDER $1 MILLION NET SALES

MVIC/Net Sales.	0.49
MVIC/Gross Profit	0.68
MVIC/SDE	2.35
MVIC/EBITDA	3.07

$1 MILLION–$5 MILLION NET SALES

MVIC/Net Sales.	0.40
MVIC/Gross Profit	0.62
MVIC/SDE	2.81
MVIC/EBITDA	4.35

OVER $5 MILLION NET SALES

MVIC/Net Sales.	0.70
MVIC/Gross Profit	1.50
MVIC/SDE	3.73
MVIC/EBITDA	4.76

Source: DealStats (formerly Pratt's Stats), 2023 (Portland, OR: Business Valuation Resources, LLC), www.bvresources.com/dealstats

P

PRICING TIPS

Fair market salary adjustment required prior to calculating SDE or excess earnings.

Quick printer valuations have been on the decline.

The terms of the leases on the digital equipment will affect the operating income and price.

BENCHMARK DATA

STATISTICS (QUICK PRINTING)

Number of Establishments	8,603
Average Profit Margin	4.7%
Revenue per Employee	$176,368
Average Number of Employees. . . .	.2.6
Average Wages per Employee . . .	$36,062

PRODUCTS AND SERVICES SEGMENTATION

Bindery and finishing services	. 38.7%
Digital printing	. 29.6%
Prepress services	. 17.7%
Offset printing	. 10.9%
Other	. 3.1%

MAJOR MARKET SEGMENTATION

Other business customers	. 59.0%
In-store business customers . . .	. 24.0%
Other	. 9.1%
Household consumers	. 7.9%

INDUSTRY COSTS

Profit	. 4.7%
Wages	. 20.3%
Purchases	. 40.1%
Depreciation	. 3.8%
Marketing	. 0.4%
Rent & Utilities	. 3.7%
Other	. 27.2%

EXPENSES (% OF ANNUAL SALES)

Cost of Goods	30% to 40%
Occupancy Costs	05% to 10%
Payroll/Labor Costs. . . .	25% to 30%
Profit (pretax)	10% to 20%

QUESTIONS

- Percent of sales represented by top three to five customers?
- Describe competition, percentage of sales by category (products and customers).
- Type of equipment, lease terms, click charges. What related services do they offer? How do they get and maintain sales?

INDUSTRY TREND

"Advances in computer technology have allowed consumers and small businesses to perform tasks previously done by quick printing shops from their own locations. Affordable printers and equipment continue to bolster this trend.

Consumers favor online media and digital communications, reducing the need for traditional printed materials. Customers typically rely on quick print shops for more high-value services."

Source: IBISWorld Key Takeaways

EXPERT COMMENTS

Printing customers today do not necessarily buy on price, but they are buying small quantities and cutting back; this favors smaller printers.

Industry is equipment intensive and requires a high degree of marketing skills to succeed.

These are marketable companies suitable for corporate dropouts or general business people.

RESOURCES

- IBISWorld, September 2023: https://www.ibisworld.com
- PrintingNews: https://www.printingnews.com

Process Serving

| NAICS 541199

Rules of Thumb

- 35%–40% annual sales includes inventory

INDUSTRY MULTIPLES

Acquisition multiples below are calculated medians using US private industry transactions. Data updated annually. Last update: August 2023.

VALUATION MULTIPLE (MEDIAN VALUE)

UNDER $1 MILLION NET SALES

MVIC/Net Sales	0.68
MVIC/Gross Profit	0.77
MVIC/SDE	2.33
MVIC/EBITDA	6.06

$1 MILLION–$5 MILLION NET SALES

MVIC/Net Sales	0.84
MVIC/Gross Profit	1.59
MVIC/SDE	2.52
MVIC/EBITDA	11.42

OVER $5 MILLION NET SALES   N/A

Source: DealStats (formerly Pratt's Stats), 2023 (Portland, OR: Business Valuation Resources, LLC), www.bvresources.com/dealstats

Property Management Companies

NAICS 531311	SIC 6531-08	Businesses/Units 319,498
Profit $11.6 B	Wages $50.5 B	Annual Growth Future 1.3%
		Annual Growth Past 1.0%

Rules of Thumb

- 3–6 x EBIT
- 3–5 x EBITDA
- 2–3 x SDE plus inventory
- 70%–140% annual sales includes inventory

INDUSTRY MULTIPLES

Acquisition multiples below are calculated medians using US private industry transactions. Data updated annually. Last update: August 2023.

VALUATION MULTIPLE (MEDIAN VALUE)

UNDER $1 MILLION NET SALES

MVIC/Net Sales.	0.69
MVIC/Gross Profit	1.04
MVIC/SDE	2.28
MVIC/EBITDA	3.45

$1 MILLION–$5 MILLION NET SALES

MVIC/Net Sales.	0.43
MVIC/Gross Profit	0.90
MVIC/SDE	2.83
MVIC/EBITDA	4.27

OVER $5 MILLION NET SALES

MVIC/Net Sales.	0.94
MVIC/Gross Profit	1.20
MVIC/SDE	2.99
MVIC/EBITDA	4.83

Source: DealStats (formerly Pratt's Stats), 2023 (Portland, OR: Business Valuation Resources, LLC), www.bvresources.com/dealstats

PRICING TIPS

In the short term: Mortgage position of owners? Dollar volume of bookings with owner? Retargeting of guests—do they have a program for that? Subs, employees on staff? What are the splits with the contractors? Price per pool vs. bill; same on the lawn; cleans by room count; pest control. Are there insurance fees, e.g., damage insurance, set up? What is the average booking duration; if condos, will see fast turns, meaning more cleans (high margin). In the long term: What software? Lease durations? Owner concentration? Mortgage position of owners relative to the market rate on rent managers managing the portfolio, and how many? Are the renewals in place and current?—check the paperwork. Tenant issues; lawsuits; drive-bys of properties—must see upkeep and maintenance. Insured properly? Licensed by state law (caretaking vs. real estate—know the difference)? Sticky customers are middle-class homes—high end, hard to rent out, high turn rate.

Customer concentration/diversification, streamlined operations, opportunities for growth, and longevity are all factors that can influence pricing.

Determine if the company offers in-house maintenance and landscape services.

Mix of homes, future bookings are indicators of cash flow. Look for the mortgage position of the homeowners in vacation rentals as an indicator of tolerance to move up and down, with rates, to the market demand.

The type of properties managed affects the valuation. The management of large (100+ unit) apartment buildings is the most desirable, followed by the management of medium-sized (20–100 unit) apartments, followed by the management of single-family homes. The management of commercial properties is also very desirable, although many commercial property management companies also have revenue streams other than management fees that may or may not continue for the buyer, such as brokerage fees on property sales, construction management fees on tenant improvement projects, etc.

The management of homeowner associations (HOAs) and condominium associations (COAs) tends to be less desirable. The industry is going through a shakeup. Younger property managers don't want the stresses of HOA and COA management, and older property managers are retiring.

The term of the management contracts also makes a difference. The best property management contracts are annual contracts with automatic 12-month renewals. Month-to-month contracts with building owners may result in some buyers proposing clawback clauses in their offers. Example: the purchase price is reduced by X percent of the revenue loss if the client quits within 90 days of new ownership, and Y percent of the revenue loss if the client quits between 91 days and 180 days of new ownership.

BENCHMARK DATA

STATISTICS (PROPERTY MANAGEMENT)

Number of Establishments	319,498
Average Profit Margin	10.1%
Revenue per Employee	$128,196
Average Number of Employees	2.9
Average Wages per Employee	$56,499

PRODUCTS AND SERVICES SEGMENTATION

Residential property management	47.8%
Nonresidential property management	23.7%
Other	21.4%
Real estate agent and brokerage services	7.1%

MAJOR MARKET SEGMENTATION

Residential properties	56.8%
Nonresidential properties	43.2%

INDUSTRY COSTS

Profit	10.1%
Wages	44.0%
Purchases	2.5%
Deprecation	1.7%
Marketing	1.3%
Rent & Utilities	4.6%
Other	35.8%

It is critical to understand the mortgage position of the homeowners as it directly relates to the ability to put bookings into homes at market rate.

Number of units managed, type of properties managed, location of properties managed

EXPENSES (% OF ANNUAL SALES)

Cost of Goods	20% to 40%
Occupancy Costs	05% to 10%
Payroll/Labor Costs	30% to 40%
Profit (pretax)	30% to 40%

QUESTIONS

- You will ask about contracts; they don't exist, so forget that they are even a factor. Identify density of properties in proximity to your base of operation; time and speed matter. Understand where the bookings come from, who they are, why they book, nationality, duration, and demographic—families vs. golf vs. groups, etc.—it sets your profile.

- How is your organization structured? What types of clients do you service? How would you grow the company?
- Are any homes for sale or considering sale?
- Look at the number of units managed, types of properties managed (residential, commercial, single-family, small apartments, big apartments, HOA).
- Look at management contracts: month-to-month or annual contracts with automatic renewal?
- Location of properties managed, longevity of clients
- Staffing, owner's role
- Determine how much of the labor is performed in-house versus outsourced.
- Ask what special licenses are required to perform the work, such as real estate or community association manager (CAM) licenses.
- Ask the seller if there are any lawsuits or outstanding complaints.
- Are any of your owners in debt to you (seller), and if so, how much and for how long have they owed that money?
- Escrow account/operating account terms and transfer?
- Homeowner mortgage? How do you generate occupancy? What is the occupancy rate?

INDUSTRY TREND

I predict mergers and acquisitions remain strong in this industry along with the real estate market.

"Property value determines the success of property managers. The greater the returns owners manage, the greater the need for managers. The high cost of homeownership keeps consumers renting. Rising interest rates and darkening economic prospects prevent many from affording homes."

Source: IBISWorld Key Takeaways

EXPERT COMMENTS

Have clean books and use software. Make sure contracts are signed, clean, and up to date. Get a real estate license even for the short term; it expands your line. Books are profitable, but more and more, owners will compete with you, so build a maintenance and service model as well. Deploy AI in what you do across all platforms.

Understand who your customers are both homeowners and guests and pick a balance based upon who will get the highest occupancy.

Property management tends to be a recession-proof industry. If a building gets foreclosed in a recession, the property management company would end up managing the building for the bank. Revenues and profits tend to be stable every year. If the economy is really strong and a property management company mostly manages single-family houses as rentals, the property management company may lose clients as a result of the economy being strong because the property owner ends up selling the house for a profit. The location of the property management company doesn't matter much; it can be run out of anywhere as long as it's in reasonable proximity to the properties being managed. Building owners typically don't switch property management companies unless something is seriously wrong, which means it can be difficult for property management companies to gain new clients, making acquisition of existing property management companies very attractive as a strategy to grow one's management portfolio fast.

Combination of cash and bank financing

- IBISWorld, September 2023: https://www.ibisworld.com
- BOMA International—Building Owners and Managers Association International: https://www.boma.org
- FAVR—Florida Alliance for Vacation Rentals: https://fvrma.org
- IREM—Institute of Real Estate Management: https://www.irem.org
- NARPM—National Association of Residential Property Managers: https://www.narpm.org
- NPMA—National Property Management Association: https://www.npma.org
- OPMA—Onsite Property Management Association: https://theopma.org
- PMA—Property Management Association: https://www.pma-dc.org
- VRMA—Vacation Rental Management Association: https://www.vrma.org

Publishers: Books

	NAICS 511130		SIC 2731-01		Businesses/Units 2,227
	Profit $2.3 B		Wages $6.2 B		
					Annual Growth Past -2.3%

Rules of Thumb
- 70% annual sales plus inventory
- 4–6 x EBIT
- 4–6 x EBITDA

INDUSTRY MULTIPLES

Acquisition multiples below are calculated medians using US private industry transactions. Data updated annually. Last update: August 2023.

VALUATION MULTIPLE (MEDIAN VALUE)

UNDER $1 MILLION NET SALES

MVIC/Net Sales	0.63
MVIC/Gross Profit	N/A
MVIC/SDE	1.84
MVIC/EBITDA	N/A

$1 MILLION–$5 MILLION NET SALES

MVIC/Net Sales	18.66
MVIC/Gross Profit	N/A
MVIC/SDE	N/A
MVIC/EBITDA	N/A

OVER $5 MILLION NET SALES

MVIC/Net Sales	2.32
MVIC/Gross Profit	5.62
MVIC/SDE	N/A
MVIC/EBITDA	13.05

Source: DealStats (formerly Pratt's Stats), 2023 (Portland, OR: Business Valuation Resources, LLC), www.bvresources.com/dealstats

PRICING TIPS

Professional publishing is valued higher than educational publishing, and both are valued higher than consumer publishing. Proprietary and niche-specific publishing are most attractive.

BENCHMARK DATA

STATISTICS (BOOK PUBLISHING)

Number of Establishments	2,227
Average Profit Margin	5.7%
Revenue per Employee	$618,577
Average Number of Employees	29.7
Average Wages per Employee	$93,430

PRODUCTS AND SERVICES SEGMENTATION

Professional, technical and scholarly books	28.6%
Textbooks	25.7%
Adult trade books	22.0%
Other books and services	13.0%
Children's books	10.7%

INDUSTRY COSTS

Profit	5.7%
Wages	15.1%
Purchases	15.8%
Depreciation	1.3%
Marketing	6.8%
Rent & Utilities	5.1%
Other	50.2%

MARKET SHARE

Bertelsmann SE & Co. KGaA	7.2%
Pearson PLC	1.8%

INDUSTRY TREND

"Increasing market penetration from external threats, in the form of e-readers and self-publishing platforms, has hindered industry performance. Industry operators have shifted their priorities toward the education market as consumers opt toward abandoning brick-and-mortar bookstores. As internet use becomes omnipresent and continues to expand, industry enterprises must contend against not only online databases like Wikipedia and Google, but also Amazon, which remains the central source for e-books. The industry has negotiated for favorable e-book prices, but high paper prices have pressured profitability."

Source: IBISWorld Key Takeaways

RESOURCES

- IBISWorld, March 2023: https://www.ibisworld.com
- AAP—Association of American Publishers: https://publishers.org
- ABA—American Booksellers Association: https://www.bookweb.org
- IBPA—Independent Book Publishers Association: https://www.ibpa-online.org

Publishers (in General)

| NAICS 511130

Rules of Thumb

- 75%–100% annual sales includes inventory
- 3–6 x SDE includes inventory
- 4–6 x EBIT
- 4–7 x EBITDA

INDUSTRY MULTIPLES

Acquisition multiples below are calculated medians using US private industry transactions. Data updated annually. Last update: August 2023.

VALUATION MULTIPLE (MEDIAN VALUE)

UNDER $1 MILLION NET SALES

MVIC/Net Sales.	0.63
MVIC/Gross Profit	N/A
MVIC/SDE	1.84
MVIC/EBITDA	N/A

$1 MILLION–$5 MILLION NET SALES

MVIC/Net Sales.	18.66
MVIC/Gross Profit	N/A
MVIC/SDE	N/A
MVIC/EBITDA	N/A

OVER $5 MILLION NET SALES

MVIC/Net Sales.	2.32
MVIC/Gross Profit	5.62
MVIC/SDE	N/A
MVIC/EBITDA	13.05

Source: DealStats (formerly Pratt's Stats), 2023 (Portland, OR: Business Valuation Resources, LLC), www.bvresources.com/dealstats

PRICING TIPS

The key is to obtain a multiple for a niche. For example, local publishers have lower multiples than national publishers. Publishers with an established digital presence are considerably more valuable than those that have not established a digital presence. Larger publishers, those above $10 million in revenue and $1–$2 million in EBITDA, can expect a considerably higher multiple; 8 times is doable.

BENCHMARK DATA

Sales per employee, gross profit margin, ad rates versus the competition's. For magazines, the rank of the magazine in its niche is critical; ad dollars flow to the leading magazines.

EXPENSES (% OF ANNUAL SALES)

Cost of Goods	20% to 25%
Occupancy Costs	05% to 08%
Payroll/Labor Costs.	10% to 25%
Profit (pretax)	15% to 20%

QUESTIONS

- Get a complete set of financial statements for three years, as well as tax returns. Sales data at a granular level should be provided. Who are competitors, and where does the business being sold rank in market share? Contracts? Trademarks? Copyrights? Digital versus print and longer-term trends.

INDUSTRY TREND

There will be a continued migration to digital. Some niche areas, such as technical/scientific, have been so consolidated that little M&A activity, other than among the major players, can be anticipated. Also, some segments are closed to competitors, as private equity has built up some companies and driven competition out of the market. B2B publishers are still substantial, and certain niches are good. Consumer publishers are more difficult.

EXPERT COMMENTS

Location is not a factor for the most part. The print publishing industry has been badly damaged by digital. Publishers, without exception, must have a strong digital presence.

There has been consolidation across the publishing industry. Competition is intense. Distribution is difficult for the smaller players.

Get a valuation. Price the business properly. Work with a broker who specializes in publishing. It is a unique and difficult business.

FINANCING

Outside financing for the most part, supplemented by seller financing

RESOURCES

- AAP—Association of American Publishers: https://publishers.org
- BISG—Book Industry Study Group: https://bisg.org
- Booklist: https://www.booklistonline.com
- E&P—Editor & Publisher Magazine: https://www.editorandpublisher.com
- IBPA—Independent Book Publishers Association: https://www.ibpa-online.org
- MPA—The Association of Magazine Media: https://www.magazine.org
- PW—Publishers Weekly: https://www.publishersweekly.com
- SIIA—Software & Information Industry Association: https://www.siia.net

Publishers: Internet and Broadcasting

| NAICS 519130

Rules of Thumb

- 100% annual revenue includes inventory
- 6 x SDE includes inventory
- 6 x EBIT
- 5 x EBITDA

INDUSTRY MULTIPLES

Acquisition multiples below are calculated medians using US private industry transactions. Data updated annually. Last update: August 2023.

VALUATION MULTIPLE (MEDIAN VALUE)

UNDER $1 MILLION NET SALES	
MVIC/Net Sales	1.41
MVIC/Gross Profit	1.66
MVIC/SDE	2.07
MVIC/EBITDA	2.41
$1 MILLION–$5 MILLION NET SALES	
MVIC/Net Sales	11.10
MVIC/Gross Profit	12.00
MVIC/SDE	N/A
MVIC/EBITDA	N/A
OVER $5 MILLION NET SALES	
MVIC/Net Sales	3.59
MVIC/Gross Profit	5.18
MVIC/SDE	N/A
MVIC/EBITDA	38.64

Source: DealStats (formerly Pratt's Stats), 2023 (Portland, OR: Business Valuation Resources, LLC), www.bvresources.com/dealstats

Cost of Goods	10%
Occupancy Costs	05% to 10%
Payroll/Labor Costs.	65%
Profit (pretax)	20%

QUESTIONS

- Stability of earnings? Renewal rates? Staff turnover? Number of advertising contracts? Any revenue/customer concentration?

EXPERT COMMENTS

Ease of replication; it really depends on the content provided. The best businesses have proprietary content and/or a market niche in which they operate.

Online publishing is a popular business. The barriers to entry are low and the financial reward can be great. The key is developing something original that keeps users coming back to a site. Competition is growing, a factor that will make good sites more valuable while leading to the demise of weaker ones.

Publishers: Magazines/Periodicals

| NAICS 511120	| SIC 2721-02	| Businesses/Units 5,897
| Profit $3.4 B	| Wages $10.2 B	| Annual Growth Future -1.1%
		| Annual Growth Past -0.7%

Rules of Thumb

- 7 x SDE includes inventory
- 2–5 x EBIT
- 2–5 x EBITDA

INDUSTRY MULTIPLES

Acquisition multiples below are calculated medians using US private industry transactions. Data updated annually. Last update: August 2023.

VALUATION MULTIPLE (MEDIAN VALUE)

UNDER $1 MILLION NET SALES

MVIC/Net Sales.	0.68
MVIC/Gross Profit	0.78
MVIC/SDE	1.93
MVIC/EBITDA	2.55

$1 MILLION–$5 MILLION NET SALES

MVIC/Net Sales.	0.47
MVIC/Gross Profit	0.80
MVIC/SDE	3.19
MVIC/EBITDA	7.86

OVER $5 MILLION NET SALES

MVIC/Net Sales.	1.16
MVIC/Gross Profit	2.01
MVIC/SDE	N/A
MVIC/EBITDA	17.44

Source: DealStats (formerly Pratt's Stats), 2023 (Portland, OR: Business Valuation Resources, LLC), www.bvresources.com/dealstats

PRICING TIPS

Publications generally sell for a multiple of EBITDA and have very little inventory. Depending on the size and the industry, if it is a consumer publication or business-to-business, profitability, etc., smaller ones will sell in the 2 to 5 times range, while the large companies will sell for as much as 12 times EBITDA.

Circulation questions are key, including various details of subscriptions and newsstand: how many advertisers, number of new advertisers, share of market in the specific specialty area such as log-home or fishing magazines, number of pages and revenue dollars.

BENCHMARK DATA

STATISTICS (MAGAZINE & PERIODICAL PUBLISHING)

Number of Establishments	5,897
Average Profit Margin	8.5%
Revenue per Employee	$394,143
Average Number of Employees	17.1
Average Wages per Employee	$100,252

PRODUCTS AND SERVICES SEGMENTATION

Entertainment magazines	27.4%
Other periodicals	25.5%
Academic and professional	14.6%
Home and living magazines	13.9%
Political, social and business	13.0%
Other products and services	5.6%

INDUSTRY COSTS

Profit	8.5%
Wages	25.5%
Purchases	12.6%
Depreciation	1.2%
Marketing	4.9%
Rent & Utilities	3.8%
Other	43.6%

MARKET SHARE

Meredith Corporation	4.7%
Bonnier Group Aktiebolag	2.4%
American Media Inc.	1.3%
Time USA LLC	1.0%

EXPENSES (% OF ANNUAL SALES)

Cost of Goods	50%
Occupancy Costs	05%
Payroll/Labor Costs	35%
Profit (pretax)	10%

QUESTIONS

- What are advertisers telling you? Look at circulation trends and costs.
- What have you done to grow the company and how would you grow it in the future?

INDUSTRY TREND

"Profit has held steady thanks to staff layoffs and cutbacks on printing and ink. Digital companies still contend with the costs of managing websites and earn less advertising and subscriber revenue per reader than print-focused publishers. Some companies will focus on highly niche premium content to stay relevant in print. Others will aggregate titles to cover a broad range of topics with one magazine or periodical. Both strategies could help companies struggling in the digital space stay competitive."

Source: IBISWorld Key Takeaways

EXPERT COMMENTS

Publishing, especially trade publishing, is declining rapidly. People are looking to the Internet for trade information because it can be delivered daily and weekly and be received long before a magazine can even be produced.

RESOURCES

- IBISWorld, September 2023: https://www.ibisworld.com
- ASME—American Society of Magazine Editors: https://www.asme.media
- MPA—The Association of Magazine Media: https://www.magazine.org

Publishers: Monthly Community Magazines

| NAICS 511120

Rules of Thumb

- 50%–85% annual sales includes inventory
- 3–4 x SDE includes inventory
- 3.5–5 x EBITDA
- 3.5 x cap rate
- 4.5 x EBIT

INDUSTRY MULTIPLES

Acquisition multiples below are calculated medians using US private industry transactions. Data updated annually. Last update: August 2023.

VALUATION MULTIPLE (MEDIAN VALUE)

UNDER $1 MILLION NET SALES

MVIC/Net Sales.	0.68
MVIC/Gross Profit	0.78
MVIC/SDE	1.93
MVIC/EBITDA	2.55

$1 MILLION–$5 MILLION NET SALES

MVIC/Net Sales.	0.47
MVIC/Gross Profit	0.80
MVIC/SDE	3.19
MVIC/EBITDA	7.86

OVER $5 MILLION NET SALES

MVIC/Net Sales.	1.16
MVIC/Gross Profit	2.01
MVIC/SDE	N/A
MVIC/EBITDA	17.44

Source: DealStats (formerly Pratt's Stats), 2023 (Portland, OR: Business Valuation Resources, LLC), www.bvresources.com/dealstats

PRICING TIPS

Competition is critical in community or local magazines. As in most magazine publishing, rank in the locality is key because advertisers want to concentrate their advertising with leading publication. Of course, cost per thousand target population enters in; but for community publications, advertisers are usually focused on the success they have in driving business with a given publication. Most advertisers do not have sophisticated media buyers to guide them. Also the quality of the leads is key. For example, with home magazines, the zip codes to which the magazine goes is considered, as is the means by which the magazine selects households for distribution.

BENCHMARK DATA

Cost per thousand of target group. Cost per thousand of magazines printed. Distribution costs per thousand.

EXPENSES (% OF ANNUAL SALES)

Cost of Goods	25% to 30%
Occupancy Costs	05%
Payroll/Labor Costs.	15% to 25%
Profit (pretax)	12% to 22%

QUESTIONS

- Future forecast is critical. What is the size of the market? What is the direction of the market?
- What are the top five advertisers? How long have they been with you? Could you grow the circulation? How long have you been with your current printer? Describe your layout process.
- How long have you been publishing and what are your historical trends? How many salespeople and how long have they worked for you? Who do you consider your competition?

INDUSTRY TREND

There seems to be a downward trend. The fact is that digital products continue to supplant print.

EXPERT COMMENTS

If it is a franchise with other units in other parts of the country, speak with other owners.

FINANCING

Some seller financing is generally required. We generally offer 40 percent at a maximum. If profitable, it may be possible to get outside financing, but given the lack of hard assets, this can be a struggle.

RESOURCES

- News/Media Alliance: https://www.newsmediaalliance.org

Publishers: Newsletters

| NAICS 511120

Rules of Thumb

- 1 x annual sales

INDUSTRY MULTIPLES

Acquisition multiples below are calculated medians using US private industry transactions. Data updated annually. Last update: August 2023.

UNDER $1 MILLION NET SALES

MVIC/Net Sales.	0.68
MVIC/Gross Profit	0.78
MVIC/SDE	1.93
MVIC/EBITDA	2.55

$1 MILLION–$5 MILLION NET SALES

MVIC/Net Sales.	0.47
MVIC/Gross Profit	0.80
MVIC/SDE	3.19
MVIC/EBITDA	7.86

OVER $5 MILLION NET SALES

MVIC/Net Sales.	1.16
MVIC/Gross Profit	2.01
MVIC/SDE	N/A
MVIC/EBITDA	17.44

Source: DealStats (formerly Pratt's Stats), 2023 (Portland, OR: Business Valuation Resources, LLC), www.bvresources.com/dealstats

PRICING TIPS

A high renewal rate (70 percent plus) increases value.

Publishers: Newspapers, Weeklies/Community Papers

| NAICS 511110

Rules of Thumb

- 100% annual sales
- 3 x SDE
- 3 x EBIT
- 1 x annual income for midsized weekly newspaper

INDUSTRY MULTIPLES

Acquisition multiples below are calculated medians using US private industry transactions. Data updated annually. Last update: August 2023.

VALUATION MULTIPLE (MEDIAN VALUE)

UNDER $1 MILLION NET SALES

MVIC/Net Sales.	0.70
MVIC/Gross Profit	0.71
MVIC/SDE	2.84
MVIC/EBITDA	2.56

$1 MILLION–$5 MILLION NET SALES

MVIC/Net Sales.	0.40
MVIC/Gross Profit	0.72
MVIC/SDE	4.33
MVIC/EBITDA	4.33

OVER $5 MILLION NET SALES

MVIC/Net Sales.	0.45
MVIC/Gross Profit	1.48
MVIC/SDE	N/A
MVIC/EBITDA	5.57

Source: DealStats (formerly Pratt's Stats), 2023 (Portland, OR: Business Valuation Resources, LLC), www.bvresources.com/dealstats

BENCHMARK DATA

EXPENSES (% OF ANNUAL SALES)

Cost of Goods	25%
Occupancy Costs	05%
Payroll/Labor Costs.	25%
Profit (pretax)	20%

QUESTIONS

- How many salespeople do you have?

INDUSTRY TREND

Local merchants are looking for a cost-effective way to reach their local customers. Major dailies are too expensive and provide too much reach for the local markets.

New communities are receptive to local papers that educate them as to local restaurants, salons, etc.

EXPERT COMMENTS

Barriers to entry are low. This is a selling business. Getting good salespeople is very difficult. The buyers of this type of business should expect to spend half of their time selling.

RESOURCES

- ACP—Association of Community Publishers: https://www.communitypublishers.com
- NNPA—National Newspaper Publishers Association: https://nnpa.org

Publishers: Newspapers (in General)

| NAICS 511110 | SIC 2711-98

Rules of Thumb

- 25% annual sales includes inventory
- 3 x SDE plus inventory
- 3–5 x EBIT
- 3–5 x EBITDA

INDUSTRY MULTIPLES

Acquisition multiples below are calculated medians using US private industry transactions. Data updated annually. Last update: August 2023.

VALUATION MULTIPLE (MEDIAN VALUE)

UNDER $1 MILLION NET SALES	
MVIC/Net Sales.	0.70
MVIC/Gross Profit	0.71
MVIC/SDE	2.84
MVIC/EBITDA	2.56
$1 MILLION–$5 MILLION NET SALES	
MVIC/Net Sales.	0.40
MVIC/Gross Profit	0.72
MVIC/SDE	4.33
MVIC/EBITDA	4.33
OVER $5 MILLION NET SALES	
MVIC/Net Sales.	0.45

MVIC/Gross Profit 1.48
MVIC/SDE . . . . N/A
MVIC/EBITDA 5.57

Source: DealStats (formerly Pratt's Stats), 2023 (Portland, OR: Business Valuation Resources, LLC), www.bvresources.com/dealstats

PRICING TIPS

Price can vary greatly depending on the size and frequency of publication, i.e., weekly, daily publication; if the company has its own printing plant; and the value of printing equipment.

BENCHMARK DATA

For additional Benchmark data see Publishers—Newspapers—Dailies

EXPENSES (% OF ANNUAL SALES)

Cost of Goods	35% to 45%
Occupancy Costs	05% to 10%
Payroll/Labor Costs. . . .	25% to 35%
Profit (pretax)	15% to 25%

QUESTIONS

- What is your online market position and share of market in each market that you serve?
- Revenue by category, cash flow, paid circulation and free circulation, average advertising percentage, competition, owner's duties, who sells the ads, number of ad contracts in place and dollar value.
- What contracts do you have? How are you handling the changes in the newspaper environment? Is it an all-cash sale or is the owner willing to carry some of the sale price?

EXPERT COMMENTS

The growth of online advertising has significantly reduced profitability and gross revenues of newspapers.

Amount of competition from all media in the market is important because there is a limited amount of advertising dollars to go around. Historic performance and competition will be large factors in determining the amount of risk. Location is of minor importance because the customer rarely goes to the business. It is easy to start a new publication, but a lot more difficult to build a reader and advertising base.

FINANCING

About 50 percent of sales are financed. Larger papers generally sell for cash. Smaller papers will sell for as little as 30 percent down with terms averaging 7 years.

Seller financing is typical with terms of 5 years or longer.

RESOURCES

- CG&C—Cribb, Greene & Cope—newspaper and publication brokerage: https://cribb.com
- E&P—Editor & Publisher Magazine: https://www.editorandpublisher.com
- News/Media Alliance: https://www.newsmediaalliance.org

Publishers: Software

| NAICS 511210 | Businesses/Units 54,183 |

| Profit $149.4 B | Wages $187.8 B | Annual Growth Future 2.9% |
| | | Annual Growth Past 5.9% |

INDUSTRY MULTIPLES

Acquisition multiples below are calculated medians using US private industry transactions. Data updated annually. Last update: August 2023.

VALUATION MULTIPLE (MEDIAN VALUE)

UNDER $1 MILLION NET SALES

MVIC/Net Sales	3.43
MVIC/Gross Profit	5.09
MVIC/SDE	3.04
MVIC/EBITDA	9.61

$1 MILLION–$5 MILLION NET SALES

MVIC/Net Sales	2.37
MVIC/Gross Profit	3.64
MVIC/SDE	4.29
MVIC/EBITDA	9.69

OVER $5 MILLION NET SALES

MVIC/Net Sales	4.02
MVIC/Gross Profit	6.09
MVIC/SDE	8.80
MVIC/EBITDA	23.76

Source: DealStats (formerly Pratt's Stats), 2023 (Portland, OR: Business Valuation Resources, LLC), www.bvresources.com/dealstats

BENCHMARK DATA

STATISTICS (SOFTWARE PUBLISHING)

Number of Establishments	54,183
Average Profit Margin	31.0%
Revenue per Employee	$528,803
Average Number of Employees	17.2
Average Wages per Employee	$27,868

PRODUCTS AND SERVICES SEGMENTATION

Application software publishing	49.3%
System software publishing	22.2%
All others	14.8%
Technology consulting and training	7.0%
Resale of computer hardware and software	3.8%
Custom application design and development	2.9%

MAJOR MARKET SEGMENTATION

Businesses	66.3%
Households	24.7%
Government	9.0%

INDUSTRY COSTS

Profit	31.0%
Wages	39.0%
Purchases	1.5%
Depreciation	4.7%
Marketing	2.6%
Rent & Utilities	1.3%
Other	19.9%

MARKET SHARE

Microsoft Corporation	19.2%
International Business Machines Corporation	4.9%
Apple Inc.	3.3%
Oracle Corporation	2.5%
SAP SE	1.6%
First Data Corp	1.3%
VMware, Inc.	1.0%

INDUSTRY TREND

"Software is reaching saturation for most home user clients. Instead, developers are switching to focus on mid-size and small businesses that are currently experiencing high churn. Businesses have wrapped around software, and its use is non-negotiable in many circumstances. This dependence has enabled developers to charge high monthly fees and profit enormously."

Source: IBISWorld Key Takeaways

EXPERT COMMENTS

Market momentum of software products can change quickly, both up and down. With specialized niche firms, buyers can be international companies. This is a transnational market.

RESOURCES

• IBISWorld, September 2023: https://www.ibisworld.com

Pure Barre (Franchise)

| NAICS 713940 | Businesses/Units 643

INDUSTRY MULTIPLES

Acquisition multiples below are calculated medians using US private industry transactions. Data updated annually. Last update: August 2023.

VALUATION MULTIPLE (MEDIAN VALUE)

UNDER $1 MILLION NET SALES
MVIC/Net Sales	0.53
MVIC/Gross Profit	0.55
MVIC/SDE	2.26
MVIC/EBITDA	2.81

$1 MILLION–$5 MILLION NET SALES
MVIC/Net Sales	0.61
MVIC/Gross Profit	0.69
MVIC/SDE	2.48
MVIC/EBITDA	3.99

OVER $5 MILLION NET SALES
MVIC/Net Sales	2.23
MVIC/Gross Profit	3.25
MVIC/SDE	N/A
MVIC/EBITDA	12.19

Source: DealStats (formerly Pratt's Stats), 2023 (Portland, OR: Business Valuation Resources, LLC), www.bvresources.com/dealstats

PRICING TIPS

Approx. Total Investment: $217,845 to $487,495

RESOURCES

• Pure Barre: https://www.purebarre.com
• Franchise information: https://www.purebarre.com/franchise
• Xponential Fitness: https://www.xponential.com

Radio Networks

| NAICS 516210 | Businesses/Units 4,837

| Profit $2.3 B | Wages $5.6 B | Annual Growth Future 0.3%

| Annual Growth Past 0.1%

BENCHMARK DATA

STATISTICS (RADIO BROADCASTING)

Number of Establishments	4,837
Average Profit Margin	9.9%
Revenue per Employee	$280,000
Average Number of Employees. . .	17.5
Average Wages per Employee . .	$66,126

PRODUCTS AND SERVICES SEGMENTATION

Adult contemporary.	25.5%
Country	16.0%
Rock and alternative	14.3%
News, talk and sports	14.1%
Top 40	12.1%
Urban formats	9.6%
Other	8.4%

MAJOR MARKET SEGMENTATION

Consumers aged 50 to 64	29.3%
Consumers aged 65 and over . . .	27.7%
Consumers aged 35 to 49	24.0%
Consumers aged 18 to 34	19.0%

INDUSTRY COSTS

Profit	9.9%
Wages	23.7%
Purchases	9.6%
Depreciation	5.2%
Marketing	6.0%
Rent & Utilities	3.9%
Other	41.7%

MARKET SHARE

Sirius XM Radio	37.7%
iHeartMedia.	11.0%
Communication	5.3%
Townsquare Media	1.8%
Beasley Broadcast	1.0%
Radio One	0.5%
Saga Communications, Inc.. . . .	0.5%
Emmis Communications	0.1%

INDUSTRY TREND

"Industry growth has in most years has lagged total advertising expenditure. Satellite radio has been the industry's fastest-growing segment. Terrestrial radio stations and networks have struggled compared with satellite radio. Restructuring is expected to limit employment opportunities. Radio commercials have long been a staple in advertising budgets. Satellite radio's dual revenue streams give it an edge. Audio streaming services have been a major source of competition for radio broadcasters over the past five years."

Source: IBISWorld Industry at a Glance

RESOURCES

- IBISWorld, October 2022: https://www.ibisworld.com
- Dave Garland Media Brokerage: https://radiobroker.com

Real Estate Agencies

| NAICS 531210 | SIC 6531-18

Rules of Thumb

- 2 x SDE; may require earnout
- 25%–35% annual sales (real estate offices) includes inventory
- 3 x EBIT
- 3.5 x EBITDA

INDUSTRY MULTIPLES

Acquisition multiples below are calculated medians using US private industry transactions. Data updated annually. Last update: August 2023.

VALUATION MULTIPLE (MEDIAN VALUE)

UNDER $1 MILLION NET SALES	
MVIC/Net Sales	0.46
MVIC/Gross Profit	0.64
MVIC/SDE	1.94
MVIC/EBITDA	2.36
$1 MILLION–$5 MILLION NET SALES	
MVIC/Net Sales	0.23
MVIC/Gross Profit	0.67
MVIC/SDE	1.92
MVIC/EBITDA	3.67
OVER $5 MILLION NET SALES	
MVIC/Net Sales	2.20
MVIC/Gross Profit	5.19
MVIC/SDE	2.54
MVIC/EBITDA	2.99

Source: DealStats (formerly Pratt's Stats), 2023 (Portland, OR: Business Valuation Resources, LLC), www.bvresources.com/dealstats

PRICING TIPS

Based on gross commissions, franchise fees, operating expenses and other factors, this is a very competitive space.

BENCHMARK DATA

STATISTICS (REAL ESTATE AGENCY FRANCHISES)

Number of Establishments	28,135
Average Profit Margin	12.3%
Revenue per Employee	$469,000
Average Number of Employees	3.1
Average Wages per Employee	$194,418

PRODUCTS AND SERVICES SEGMENTATION

Residential real estate sales	.67.8%
Commercial real estate rentals	.10.3%
Transaction, advisory, and other services	9.5%
Commercial real estate sales	7.5%
Residential real estate rentals	4.9%

MAJOR MARKET SEGMENTATION

Residential buyers	.37.5%
Residential sellers	.37.3%
Lessors	.17.6%
Commercial properties	7.6%

INDUSTRY COSTS

Profit	.12.3%
Wages	.40.5%
Purchases	2.6%
Depreciation	1.7%
Marketing	1.3%
Rent and Utilities	4.7%
Other	.36.8%

STATISTICS (REAL ESTATE SALES AND BROKERAGE)

Number of Establishments	.1,209,133
Average Profit Margin	.19.1%
Revenue per Employee	$158,000
Average Number of Employees	1.2
Average Wages per Employee	$32,638

PRODUCTS AND SERVICES SEGMENTATION

Residential sales	.80.1%
Commercial sales	.19.6%
Real estate transaction, advisory and other services	0.3%

MAJOR MARKET SEGMENTATION

Married/Partnered	.56.8%
Single	.23.5%
Office and professional space	8.4%
Retail space	6.8%
Warehousing and other commercial space	2.9%
Manufacturing space	1.6%

INDUSTRY COSTS

Profit	.20.4%
Wages	.20.4%
Purchases	3.4%
Depreciation	1.7%
Marketing	1.7%
Rent & Utilities	6.0%
Other	.47.6%

EXPENSES (% OF ANNUAL SALES)

Cost of Goods	65% (commission)
Occupancy Costs	05% to 10%
Payroll/Labor Costs	20% to 30%
Profit (pretax)	14% to 20%

QUESTIONS

- Where is room to increase sales, agents, offices, and exposure? Where is growth going in next 5 years? Where is growth coming from? Why?
- Provide me with a plan that keeps the agents with the firm after the sale. Retention bonus? It's all about the sales team.

- How long in business? Number of agents? Experience of each agent? Top-producing agents? Biggest strengths/advantages of this business? Area that needs most improvement?

INDUSTRY TREND

"Overall, buyers expected to live in their homes for a median of 15 years, up from 12 years last year. For younger millennials, the expected length of time was only 10 years compared to 20 years for younger and older baby boomers."

Source: "2023 Home Buyers and Sellers Generational Trends Report," National Association of REALTORS® Research Group, https://cdn.nar.realtor/sites/default/files/documents/2023-home-buyers-and-sellers-generational-trends-report-03-28-2023.pdf

"Falling unemployment and rising incomes have helped boost activity in residential markets. Larger companies sought to increase their position in the market by acquiring others. Industry operators have been assisted by new technologies that provide lower costs. Deteriorating macroeconomic conditions are expected to limit growth in the industry. The number of businesses in the United States is expected to grow and precipitate higher demand for office buildings and other commercial spaces. Agents are projected to increase their online presence in an attempt to increase sales. Despite revenue growth, industry profit has fallen due to rising wage costs and pandemic-related pressures from compliance with new safety protocols. Commercial real estate was adversely affected by the slowdown in business activity. Operators had to innovate ways to sell residential and commercial properties. Access to credit, corporate profit and per capita disposable income influence the market. Rising home prices and greater construction are anticipated to boost revenue. Real estate agents have benefited from expansion in key markets. Part-time agents will return to the industry and bolster employee numbers. Higher interest rates will increase borrowing costs and temper demand for homeownership."

Source: IBISWorld Industry at a Glance

EXPERT COMMENTS

Know what you're getting into before doing it. Real estate is a backbiting, nasty, dog-eat-dog, greedy business.

FINANCING

Franchises = outside. Independent = seller financing.

RESOURCES

- IBISWorld, September 2022: https://www.ibisworld.com
- Inman: https://www.inman.com
- MIAMI REALTORS: https://www.miamirealtors.com
- NAR—National Association of REALTORS: https://www.nar.realtor

Record Stores

NAICS 443142	Businesses/Units 2,303	
Profit $14.1 M	Wages $101.4 M	Annual Growth Future -0.1%
		Annual Growth Past -8.9%

PRICING TIPS

Inventory of tapes, CDs, DVDs at FMV (used) is in addition to the above. Usually in a store of this kind inventory turns about twice a year. The store should be located in an area where rent will not exceed 4 percent of the gross sales. National average shows a gross profit of approximately 54 percent before expenses of wages, repairs, maintenance, advertising, bad debts, utilities, insurance, taxes, etc. National average net profit is approximately 10 to 18 percent.

BENCHMARK DATA

STATISTICS (RECORD STORES)

Number of Establishments	2,303
Average Profit Margin	1.3%
Revenue per Employee	$181,836
Average Number of Employees	3.2
Average Wages per Employee	$16,569

PRODUCTS AND SERVICES SEGMENTATION

Music	45.3%
Video	34.9%
Electronics	15.3%
Other	4.5%

INDUSTRY COSTS

Profit	1.3%
Wages	9.3%
Purchases	57.0%
Depreciation	1.6%
Marketing	2.2%
Rent & Utilities	6.7%
Other	21.8%

BUSINESS SALE INFORMATION

Average SBA Loan Amount	N/A
Average SBA Down Payment Percentage	N/A
Average Days To Sell	304 days
Average Non-Compete Length	44 days

Source: DealStats (formerly Pratt's Stats), 2023 (Portland, OR: Business Valuation Resources, LLC). DealStats is a robust online database of acquired private company transactions sourced from business brokers, M&A advisors, and SEC filings. Learn more at www.bvresources.com/dealstats or visit www.bvresources.com/contribute to become part of the Contributor Network.

INDUSTRY TREND

"Record album sales revenue grew a whopping 61% in 2021—and reached $1 billion for the first time since the 1980s—far outpacing growth rates for paid music subscriptions and streaming services like Spotify and Pandora, according to the Recording Industry Association of America.

"Record albums nearly spun into oblivion with sales overtaken by cassettes before the compact discs brushed both aside. Then came digital downloads and online piracy, Apple iPods and 99-cent downloads. Streaming services are now ubiquitous. But nostalgic baby boomers who missed thumbing through record albums in their local record stores helped to fuel a vinyl resurgence that started about 15 years ago. It coincided with the launch of Record Store Day to celebrate indie record stores, said Larry Jaffee, author of *Record Store Day: The Most Improbable Comeback of the 21st Century*. These days, though, it's more than just boomers. A younger generation is buying turntables and albums—and cassette tapes, too—and a new generation of artists like Adele, Ariana Grande and Harry Styles have been moving to vinyl, Jaffee noted."

Source: "Manufacturers Struggle to Keep Pace With Vinyl Record Demand" by David Sharp, June 24, 2022, https://www.nbcchicago.com/entertainment/entertainment-news/ manufacturers-struggle-to-keep-pace-with-vinyl-record-demand

"The Record Stores industry has struggled in recent years because of growing competition from digital platforms and discount stores, leading to a drop in revenue. COVID-19 further exacerbated this drop, negatively impacting sales in physical stores. Record stores will adapt by expanding product offerings to include specialized genres and merchandise, attracting niche consumers and slowing industry drop. This strategy focuses on retaining music enthusiasts and supporting the growing vinyl record collection trend."

Source: IBISWorld Key Takeaways

RESOURCES

• IBISWorld, June 2023: https://www.ibisworld.com

Records Management

| NAICS 541611 | Businesses/Units 1,734

| Profit $546.5 M | Wages $2.5 B | Annual Growth Future 2.2%

| Annual Growth Past 2.1%

Rules of Thumb

• 8 x SDE
• 200% annual sales

INDUSTRY MULTIPLES

Acquisition multiples below are calculated medians using US private industry transactions. Data updated annually. Last update: August 2023.

VALUATION MULTIPLE (MEDIAN VALUE)

UNDER $1 MILLION NET SALES

MVIC/Net Sales	0.87
MVIC/Gross Profit	1.00
MVIC/SDE	1.93
MVIC/EBITDA	3.53

$1 MILLION–$5 MILLION NET SALES

MVIC/Net Sales	0.61
MVIC/Gross Profit	1.04
MVIC/SDE	2.60
MVIC/EBITDA	3.69

OVER $5 MILLION NET SALES

MVIC/Net Sales	1.60
MVIC/Gross Profit	4.09
MVIC/SDE	8.08
MVIC/EBITDA	13.16

Source: DealStats (formerly Pratt's Stats), 2023 (Portland, OR: Business Valuation Resources, LLC), www.bvresources.com/dealstats

BENCHMARK DATA

STATISTICS (DOCUMENT MANAGEMENT SERVICES)

Number of Establishments	1,734
Average Profit Margin	7.0%
Revenue per Employee	$100,494
Average Number of Employees. . .	45.9
Average Wages per Employee . . .	$31,731

PRODUCTS AND SERVICES SEGMENTATION

Records management services. . .	56.2%
Data destruction	31.9%
Data protection and recovery services .	11.9%

MAJOR MARKET SEGMENTATION

Financial Services	67.2%
Government.	13.3%
Other	10.3%
Legal	4.9%
Healthcare	4.3%

INDUSTRY COSTS

Profit	7.0%
Wages	31.7%
Purchases	24.2%
Depreciation	2.7%
Marketing	2.1%
Rent & Utilities	2.9%
Other	29.3%

MARKET SHARE

Iron Mountain Inc.	9.7%
Stericycle Inc.	7.6%

EXPENSES (% OF ANNUAL SALES)

Cost of Goods	.0%
Occupancy Costs	25%
Payroll/Labor Costs.	35%
Profit (pretax)	30%

INDUSTRY TREND

"The landmark Sarbanes-Oxley Act mandated that public companies retain corporate records and work papers for seven years. These regulations have largely shielded the industry from broader economic declines. Most healthcare providers have yet to fully convert to Electronic Health Records (EHR). Instead, they have a mix of paper and electronic records, leading to increasing demand from healthcare providers."

Source: IBISWorld Key Takeaways

RESOURCES

- IBISWorld, September 2023: https://www.ibisworld.com
- i-SIGMA: https://isigmaonline.org

Recruiting Agencies

	NAICS 56131		SIC 7361-03		Businesses/Units 13,028
	Profit $4.1 B		Wages $18.1 B		Annual Growth Future 1.0%
					Annual Growth Past 11.7%

Rules of Thumb

- 50% annual revenues; may require earnout
- 1–1.5 x SDE; add fixtures equipment & inventory; may require earnout

INDUSTRY MULTIPLES

Acquisition multiples below are calculated medians using US private industry transactions. Data updated annually. Last update: August 2023.

VALUATION MULTIPLE (MEDIAN VALUE)

UNDER $1 MILLION NET SALES

MVIC/Net Sales.	0.72
MVIC/Gross Profit	0.77
MVIC/SDE	2.29
MVIC/EBITDA	3.60

$1 MILLION–$5 MILLION NET SALES

MVIC/Net Sales.	0.38
MVIC/Gross Profit	0.82
MVIC/SDE	2.31
MVIC/EBITDA	3.83

OVER $5 MILLION NET SALES

MVIC/Net Sales.	0.47
MVIC/Gross Profit	1.69
MVIC/SDE	4.87
MVIC/EBITDA	6.07

Source: DealStats (formerly Pratt's Stats), 2023 (Portland, OR: Business Valuation Resources, LLC), www.bvresources.com/dealstats

BENCHMARK DATA

STATISTICS (EMPLOYMENT AND RECRUITING AGENCIES)

Number of Establishments .	13,028
Average Profit Margin	8.7%
Revenue per Employee .	$173,818
Average Number of Employees.	20.0
Average Wages per Employee .	$68,167

PRODUCTS AND SERVICES SEGMENTATION

Permanent placement services.	45.1%
Executive search services	29.7%
Temporary staffing services	18.3%
Independent contractor placement services	4.7%
Other	2.2%

MAJOR MARKET SEGMENTATION

Industrial	37.0%
Administrative and clerical .	28.0%
Technical	13.0%
Executive and managerial .	13.0%
Healthcare .	9.0%

INDUSTRY COSTS

Profit	8.7%
Wages	38.7%
Purchases	22.3%
Depreciation	0.2%
Marketing	1.9%
Rent & Utilities	2.8%
Other	25.4%

MARKET SHARE

Randstad Holding NV	4.3%
LinkedIn Corp.	3.0%
ASGN Inc.	2.5%
Allegis Group, Inc.	1.7%
Insight Global, LLC	1.4%

INDUSTRY TREND

"The US is facing a labor shortage, with many employers struggling to find qualified workers. This has increased the demand for employment and recruiting agencies, as employers are turning to them to help them fill their open positions. Monetary tightening will limit hiring and weigh on employment and recruiting agency revenue. Employment and recruiting agencies also have to borrow money to finance their operations, so rising interest rates can increase their costs."

Source: IBISWorld Key Takeaways

FINANCING

Typically uses outside financing.

RESOURCES

• IBISWorld, October 2023: https://www.ibisworld.com

Recycling

| NAICS 562920 | Businesses/Units 1,513

| Profit $732.3 M | Wages $1.4 B | Annual Growth Future 1.8%

| | | | Annual Growth Past 5.1%

Rules of Thumb

• 3–5 x SDE includes inventory
• 3–6 x EBIT
• 3–6 x EBITDA

INDUSTRY MULTIPLES

Acquisition multiples below are calculated medians using US private industry transactions. Data updated annually. Last update: August 2023.

VALUATION MULTIPLE (MEDIAN VALUE)

UNDER $1 MILLION NET SALES

MVIC/Net Sales.	1.12
MVIC/Gross Profit	1.89
MVIC/SDE	29.98
MVIC/EBITDA	1.52

$1 MILLION–$5 MILLION NET SALES

MVIC/Net Sales.	0.81
MVIC/Gross Profit	3.72
MVIC/SDE	5.45
MVIC/EBITDA	3.98

OVER $5 MILLION NET SALES

MVIC/Net Sales.	0.23
MVIC/Gross Profit	1.78
MVIC/SDE	5.82
MVIC/EBITDA	27.56

Source: DealStats (formerly Pratt's Stats), 2023 (Portland, OR: Business Valuation Resources, LLC), www.bvresources.com/dealstats

PRICING TIPS

Value is based on land and improvements, inventory (aged), earnings, and goodwill.

Once the EBITDA exceeds $1,000,000, most buyers will assume that normal levels of inventory, A/R, and FFE will be included in the transaction as working capital. The key is to understand how the buyer is structuring their offer and how they are accounting for these values.

BENCHMARK DATA

STATISTICS (RECYCLING FACILITIES)

Number of Establishments	1,513
Average Profit Margin	7.2%
Revenue per Employee	$415,210
Average Number of Employees.	16.5
Average Wages per Employee	$59,155

PRODUCTS AND SERVICES SEGMENTATION

Recyclable material recovery and processing services	62.8%
Sale of recycled materials	32.8%
Collection services	3.7%
Other	0.7%

MAJOR MARKET SEGMENTATION

Businesses (services)	53.1%
Businesses (materials)	27.7%
Households	10.7%
Government and other	8.5%

INDUSTRY COSTS

Profit	7.2%
Wages	14.3%
Purchases	42.5%
Depreciation	4.0%
Marketing	0.3%
Rent & Utilities	2.9%
Other	28.9%

MARKET SHARE

Waste Management, Inc.	18.7%
Republic Services, Inc.	4.4%
Waste Connections, Inc.	2.9%

EXPENSES (% OF ANNUAL SALES)

Cost of Goods	50%
Occupancy Costs	10%
Payroll/Labor Costs.	12%
Profit (pretax)	08%

- What kind of contracts do you have with your paper suppliers? Are you contracted to sell your paper to certain mills or brokers? Who is your competition within 100 miles?

INDUSTRY TREND

"Recycling facilities are expanding in popularity, driven by energy and cost savings. Surging commodity prices encourage consumers and businesses to recycle and purchase more recycled goods. Surging demand from construction and manufacturing businesses is boosting demand for recyclable materials, supporting revenue. For example, recycled plastics are used to strengthen concrete structures like sidewalks and driveways."

Source: IBISWorld Key Takeaways

RESOURCES

- IBISWorld, October 2023: https://www.ibisworld.com
- ISRI—Institute of Scrap Recycling Industries: https://www.isri.org
- NERC—Northeast Recycling Council: https://nerc.org
- NWRA—National Waste & Recycling Association: https://wasterecycling.org

Red Robin (Franchise)

| NAICS 722513 | Businesses/Units 101

Rules of Thumb

- 30%–35% annual sales

INDUSTRY MULTIPLES

Acquisition multiples below are calculated medians using US private industry transactions. Data updated annually. Last update: August 2023.

VALUATION MULTIPLE (MEDIAN VALUE)

UNDER $1 MILLION NET SALES

MVIC/Net Sales	0.31
MVIC/Gross Profit	0.48
MVIC/SDE	1.67
MVIC/EBITDA	2.21

$1 MILLION–$5 MILLION NET SALES

MVIC/Net Sales	0.39
MVIC/Gross Profit	0.60
MVIC/SDE	2.43
MVIC/EBITDA	2.98

OVER $5 MILLION NET SALES

MVIC/Net Sales	0.89
MVIC/Gross Profit	2.08
MVIC/SDE	4.98
MVIC/EBITDA	12.81

Source: DealStats (formerly Pratt's Stats), 2023 (Portland, OR: Business Valuation Resources, LLC), www.bvresources.com/dealstats

PRICING TIPS

Approx. Total Investment: $1,865,000 to $4,115,000

- Red Robin: https://www.redrobin.com
- Franchise information: https://www.redrobin.com/franchise-request

R

Refrigerated Warehousing and Storage

| NAICS 493120 | Businesses/Units 2,571 |

| Profit $1.3 B | Wages $3.3 B | Annual Growth Future 2.6% |

| | Annual Growth Past 2.3% |

INDUSTRY MULTIPLES

Acquisition multiples below are calculated medians using US private industry transactions. Data updated annually. Last update: August 2023.

VALUATION MULTIPLE (MEDIAN VALUE)

UNDER $1 MILLION NET SALES
MVIC/Net Sales	0.31
MVIC/Gross Profit	N/A
MVIC/SDE	N/A
MVIC/EBITDA	N/A

$1 MILLION–$5 MILLION NET SALES
MVIC/Net Sales	0.92
MVIC/Gross Profit	1.28
MVIC/SDE	3.41
MVIC/EBITDA	3.94

OVER $5 MILLION NET SALES
MVIC/Net Sales	2.45
MVIC/Gross Profit	7.94
MVIC/SDE	N/A
MVIC/EBITDA	15.54

Source: DealStats (formerly Pratt's Stats), 2023 (Portland, OR: Business Valuation Resources, LLC), www.bvresources.com/dealstats

BENCHMARK DATA

STATISTICS (REFRIGERATED STORAGE)
Number of Establishments	2,571
Average Profit Margin	16.0%
Revenue per Employee	$144,000
Average Number of Employees	23.4
Average Wages per Employee	$57,019

PRODUCTS AND SERVICES SEGMENTATION
Storage of goods	65.7%
Handling of goods	24.9%
Other services	5.4%
Transportation of goods	4.0%

MAJOR MARKET SEGMENTATION
Food product wholesalers	38.4%
Food product manufacturers	26.9%
Food product retailers	24.0%
Other	10.7%

INDUSTRY COSTS
Profit	16.0%
Wages	39.7%

Purchases	.	.	.	.	.	.	.	3.6%
Depreciation	.	.	.	.	.	.	.	6.4%
Marketing	.	.	.	.	.	.	.	0.5%
Rent & Utilities	.	.	.	.	.	.	8.6%
Other	.	.	.	.	.	.	.	25.2%

MARKET SHARE

XPO Logistics	.	.	.	.	.	.	35.7%
Lineage Logistics Holdings.	.	.	.	28.7%
Americold Realty Trust .	.	.	.	.	23.2%
United States Cold Storage .	.	.	.	7.6%

INDUSTRY TREND

"Increasing consumer spending surges demand for refrigeration services. Increased demand for food products correlates directly with increased demand for refrigeration services. Refrigeration service companies benefit from trade activity. Operators provide refrigeration and logistic services for soon-to-be exported goods. Decreased demand from restaurants amid the COVID-19 pandemic was offset by higher grocery and frozen food demand since supermarkets and groceries were deemed essential and provided the industry with steady work."

Source: IBISWorld Key Takeaways

RESOURCES

• IBISWorld, September 2023: https://www.ibisworld.com

Registered Investment Advisors

| NAICS 523930 | Businesses/Units 154,604

| Profit $9.8 B | Wages $18.1 B | Annual Growth Future 0.5%

| | | Annual Growth Past 3.4%

Rules of Thumb

• 150%–250% annual sales
• 3–5 x SDE plus net assets plus inventory
• 6 x EBIT
• 6 x EBITDA

INDUSTRY MULTIPLES

Acquisition multiples below are calculated medians using US private industry transactions. Data updated annually. Last update: August 2023.

VALUATION MULTIPLE (MEDIAN VALUE)

UNDER $1 MILLION NET SALES

MVIC/Net Sales.	.	.	.	.	.	.	4.23
MVIC/Gross Profit	.	.	.	.	.	4.33
MVIC/SDE	.	.	.	.	.	.	N/A
MVIC/EBITDA	.	.	.	.	.	.	7.04

$1 MILLION–$5 MILLION NET SALES

MVIC/Net Sales.	.	.	.	.	.	.	13.10
MVIC/Gross Profit	.	.	.	.	.	N/A
MVIC/SDE	.	.	.	.	.	.	N/A
MVIC/EBITDA	.	.	.	.	.	.	23.40

OVER $5 MILLION NET SALES

| MVIC/Net Sales. | . | . | . | . | . | . | 1.72 |
| MVIC/Gross Profit | . | . | . | . | . | 2.03 |

```
MVIC/SDE    .    .    .    .    .    .    .    .    .    .    .    .    .    N/A
MVIC/EBITDA    .    .    .    .    .    .    .    .    .    .    .    . 11.34
```

Source: DealStats (formerly Pratt's Stats), 2023 (Portland, OR: Business Valuation Resources, LLC), www.bvresources.com/dealstats

PRICING TIPS

Recurring revenue business model, but usually very owner dependent. Any purchase needs to be accompanied by a thoughtful transition plan for client relationships.

BENCHMARK DATA

STATISTICS (FINANCIAL PLANNING AND ADVICE)

Number of Establishments	154,604
Average Profit Margin	16.5%
Revenue per Employee	$258,000
Average Number of Employees.	1.5
Average Wages per Employee	$79,599

PRODUCTS AND SERVICES SEGMENTATION

Personal financial planning and advice services . . .	51.7%
Financial management consulting	41.4%
Other	4.3%
Brokering and dealing	2.4%
Trust services	0.2%

MAJOR MARKET SEGMENTATION

Individuals and households.	51.9%
Businesses and governments	48.1%

INDUSTRY COSTS

Profit	16.5%
Wages	30.6%
Purchases	2.2%
Depreciation	0.8%
Marketing	1.2%
Rent & Utilities	2.7%
Other	46.0%

MARKET SHARE

Ameriprise Financial Inc.	11.7%
Raymond James Financial Inc.	11.0%

Since pricing is based on a percent of assets managed, a key metric in the industry is assets under management, or AUM. This typically points to the size of the firm.

EXPENSES (% OF ANNUAL SALES)

Cost of Goods	0% to 10%
Occupancy Costs	05% to 15%
Payroll/Labor Costs.	10% to 20%
Profit (pretax)	20% to 45%

QUESTIONS

- How long are you willing to stay on to transition client relationships? What is your fee structure? Do the other advisors in the firm have noncompetes? How are they compensated? How do you get new clients? Why do your clients choose to work with your firm?
- Gross commissions? Net? Broker-dealer? Overhead? Fee-based or commission-based? Average client investment, net worth?

INDUSTRY TREND

More advisors are breaking away from broker-dealers to join or launch RIA firms. And larger RIA firms are consolidating smaller ones.

EXPERT COMMENTS

Make sure the seller is committed to transitioning client relationships.

It's not difficult to start a registered investment advisory firm. There is a lot of competition, so anything that creates some differentiation is valuable. Most firms price services as a percent of assets managed. Since the market is stoking all-time highs, it may be prudent to consider factoring in a drop in asset values and how that affects profitability. As professional services firms, RIAs typically have very nice locations and facilities. The service is very marketable, and the overall financial industry is moving toward the RIA model and away from the broker-dealer model.

FINANCING

It's so dependent on the seller; there are a wide range of deal structures. SBA lenders will lend into the RIA space, so there is SBA financing available. Also, there is usually some form of seller note or amount held in escrow to ensure client relationships transfer.

RESOURCES

- IBISWorld, July 2022: https://www.ibisworld.com
- CFA Institute: https://www.cfainstitute.org
- CFP Board: https://www.cfp.net
- FA—Financial Advisor: https://www.fa-mag.com
- FPA—Financial Planning Association: https://www.financialplanningassociation.org
- NAPFA—The National Association of Personal Financial Advisors: https://www.napfa.org
- RIABiz: https://riabiz.com

Remediation Services

| NAICS 562910 | Businesses/Units 6,112

| Profit $2.4 B | Wages $6.9 B | Annual Growth Future 1.2%

| | | Annual Growth Past 2.5%

Rules of Thumb

- 4–5 x EBITDA
- 40% annual sales includes inventory
- 2–3 x SDE includes inventory

INDUSTRY MULTIPLES

Acquisition multiples below are calculated medians using US private industry transactions. Data updated annually. Last update: August 2023.

VALUATION MULTIPLE (MEDIAN VALUE)

UNDER $1 MILLION NET SALES

MVIC/Net Sales.	0.59
MVIC/Gross Profit	0.78

MVIC/SDE	. . . .	2.11
MVIC/EBITDA	. . . .	2.63

$1 MILLION–$5 MILLION NET SALES

MVIC/Net Sales.	. . . .	0.65
MVIC/Gross Profit	. . . .	0.96
MVIC/SDE	. . . .	2.82
MVIC/EBITDA	. . . .	3.69

OVER $5 MILLION NET SALES

MVIC/Net Sales.	. . . .	0.37
MVIC/Gross Profit	. . . .	1.75
MVIC/SDE	. . . .	3.44
MVIC/EBITDA	. . . .	4.74

Source: DealStats (formerly Pratt's Stats), 2023 (Portland, OR: Business Valuation Resources, LLC), www.bvresources.com/dealstats

PRICING TIPS

The most important things when pricing the restoration industry are the insurance agreements.

BENCHMARK DATA

STATISTICS (REMEDIATION & ENVIRONMENTAL CLEANUP SERVICES)

Number of Establishments	6,112
Average Profit Margin	9.8%
Revenue per Employee	$254,102
Average Number of Employees.	15.8
Average Wages per Employee	$73,227

PRODUCTS AND SERVICES SEGMENTATION

Site remediation services	52.0%
Building remediation services	26.3%
Other services	16.2%
Environmental emergency response services	5.5%

MAJOR MARKET SEGMENTATION

Businesses	64.3%
Public sector	23.1%
Other customers	12.6%

INDUSTRY COSTS

Profit	9.8%
Wages	28.7%
Purchases	27.2%
Depreciation	2.1%
Marketing	0.3%
Rent & Utilities	3.0%
Other	28.8%

MARKET SHARE

Jacobs Engineering Group Inc.	17.0%
McDermott International Inc.	5.2%
Veolia Environnement	4.4%
Tetra Tech, Inc.	2.8%
Brown & Caldwell Inc.	1.8%
ERM Group Inc.	1.6%
Performance Contracting Group	1.3%

EXPENSES (% OF ANNUAL SALES)

Cost of Goods	70%
Occupancy Costs	04% to 05%
Payroll/Labor Costs.	07% to 17%
Profit (pretax)	03% to 05%

QUESTIONS

- Have there been any Department of Environmental Protection (DEP) violations? Workers' comp claims?
- Check for hidden liabilities. Union vs. non-union is important difference. Reputation is also important—how many jobs have they abandoned or not completed on time?

INDUSTRY TREND

I see it trending upward due to more floods, tornadoes, and infrastructure failure due to age of buildings.

"Remediation and environmental cleanup companies enjoyed private sector growth. Growth in construction and mining benefitted remediation and environmental cleanup companies. Increases in public sector funding will bolster remediation and environment cleanup companies. Remediation and environmental cleanup companies will enjoy growth spurred by federal investment."

Source: IBISWorld Key Takeaways

EXPERT COMMENTS

These businesses have a high regulatory component as they deal with hazardous waste and the packaging, handling, transport, and recycling/disposal of a myriad of constituents. On top of this, the EPA, OSHA, DOT, and several others have federal rules that contractors must adhere to; also each state has its own specific regulations that reside on top of the federal rules. Affordable compliance is a competitive advantage giving higher value to businesses with a strong regulatory, compliance, and profiling department. Facilities close to, but isolated from, populous areas are best.

FINANCING

It's normally outside financing, with some owner financing included.

RESOURCES

- IBISWorld, September 2023: https://www.ibisworld.com

Rental Centers

| NAICS 532310 | SIC 7359-59

Rules of Thumb

- 95%–100% annual sales includes inventory
- 2.5–3 x SDE includes inventory
- 4 x EBITDA
- 5 x SDE (party and tent rental)
- 3 x EBIT

INDUSTRY MULTIPLES

Acquisition multiples below are calculated medians using US private industry transactions. Data updated annually. Last update: August 2023.

VALUATION MULTIPLE (MEDIAN VALUE)

UNDER $1 MILLION NET SALES

MVIC/Net Sales.	0.76
MVIC/Gross Profit	0.83

MVIC/SDE	2.35
MVIC/EBITDA	3.84

$1 MILLION–$5 MILLION NET SALES

MVIC/Net Sales.	1.42
MVIC/Gross Profit	1.67
MVIC/SDE	3.41
MVIC/EBITDA	4.08

OVER $5 MILLION NET SALES　　　　　　N/A

Source: DealStats (formerly Pratt's Stats), 2023 (Portland, OR: Business Valuation Resources, LLC), www.bvresources.com/dealstats

PRICING TIPS

Labor costs and age of inventory are key metrics that need to be looked at. The management of event rental businesses, as well, is key to the price point they receive at closing. Owners who are able to work on the business, instead of working in the business, on a daily basis typically generate a much higher multiple across all metrics listed above.

BENCHMARK DATA

A rule is that each employee should be able to generate at least $75,000 in sales. Key is that, in this industry, space is much more important than visibility. You need warehouse space to hold all the inventory and, as well, a facility that is capable of maintenance of this inventory. Most of your clients never visit your showroom; however, it is important to have a well-maintained and clean showroom in order to show off your inventory to those clients that do visit. Easy access to major roads and highways helps to reduce travel times for deliveries.

STATISTICS (TOOL AND EQUIPMENT RENTAL)

Number of Establishments	11,366
Average Profit Margin	12.0%
Revenue per Employee	$164,992
Average Number of Employees. . . .	2.5
Average Wages per Employee . . .	$43,994

PRODUCTS AND SERVICES SEGMENTATION

Contractor equipment	56.1%
Home tools and DIY equipment rental .	23.7%
Delivery, repair and other services . .	14.1%
Renting consumer goods	4.8%
Other equipment rentals	1.3%

MAJOR MARKET SEGMENTATION

Independent builders and contractors .	35.5%
Private Households	30.5%
Construction and industrial companies	26.9%
Government.	7.1%

INDUSTRY COSTS

Profit	12.0%
Wages	26.6%
Purchases	6.2%
Depreciation	12.4%
Marketing	1.2%
Rent & Utilities	7.3%
Other	34.3%

STATISTICS (PARTY SUPPLY RENTAL)

Number of Establishments	10,416
Average Profit Margin	7.8%

Revenue per Employee	$110,352
Average Number of Employees.	5.5
Average Wages per Employee	$30,720

PRODUCTS AND SERVICES SEGMENTATION

Other rentals	39.5%
Rental of tableware, decorations and balloons.	35.0%
Rental of costumes, party favors and other social event products. . . .	20.6%
Event and rental services	4.9%

INDUSTRY COSTS

Profit	7.8%
Wages	27.6%
Purchases	6.6%
Depreciation	8.9%
Marketing	1.3%
Rent & Utilities	7.7%
Other	40.1%

QUESTIONS

- Daily duties. How did they get started? What was their background before owning the business? How to keep quality employees, and so important, what should one expect as to number of hours to work in a week in both slow times and the busy season? What activities go on during the slow periods (typically after Christmas and winter)? Transition and training periods. Breakdown of every employee from what job they perform to strengths and weaknesses.
- Get a depreciation schedule and verify equipment age and condition. Do a thorough due diligence. If a stock sale, find out about lawsuits and environmental issues.

INDUSTRY TREND

"Construction markets have fluctuated through the period. The pandemic significantly shifted investments in both residential and commercial construction. This was followed by rising interest rates, which induced more volatility. Prominent rental centers have engaged in consolidation activity. Acquiring smaller businesses helps larger establishments cut operational costs and expand their customer base. Consistent slowdown in marriage rate shrinks customer base. As the marriage rate dropped, servicers lost many family customers, causing revenue to shrink. Rebound in disposable income enhances appeal of party supply rental. The consistent growth of per capita disposable income has enabled households to purchase more party supplies, strengthening recovery."

Source: IBISWorld Key Takeaways

EXPERT COMMENTS

Selling: There is no way you will ever get dollar for dollar on your inventory investment. Inventory is a tool for doing business. Without a good inventory, you have nothing to offer. Same goes with equipment purchases. The key is that you have the process and procedures in place so that when a buyer looks at the business, they can easily see themselves doing your job.

Buying: Like in any business, you are the president, but at times you are also the janitor. You have to be willing to get your hands dirty at times in order to make sure that the jobs are completed.

Replication of the event rental industry, while appearing to be the easiest, is incredibly hard. Knowing which items to purchase—and the massive number of items that need to be purchased—make it incredibly difficult to just buy your way into a high-volume business. Most established event rental businesses will easily have $1.5+ million invested in inventory, depending on the number of products and services they offer.

R

FINANCING

Every transaction I have completed in the events rental industry has had outside financing, along with a small percentage of owner carry.

RESOURCES

- IBISWorld, April 2023: https://www.ibisworld.com
- IBISWorld, February 2023: https://www.ibisworld.com
- ARA—American Rental Association: https://www.ararental.org
- NACE—National Association for Catering & Events: https://www.nace.net
- Special Events: https://www.specialevents.com

Restaurants, Fast Food

NAICS 722513	SIC 5812-08	Businesses/Units 305,902
Profit $20.2 B	Wages $99.2 B	Annual Growth Future 2.6%
		Annual Growth Past 3.4%

Rules of Thumb

- 1.5–2.5 x SDE plus inventory
- 2–5 x EBIT
- 2–5 x EBITDA
- 30%–35% annual sales
- 2 x SDE

INDUSTRY MULTIPLES

Acquisition multiples below are calculated medians using US private industry transactions. Data updated annually. Last update: August 2023.

VALUATION MULTIPLE (MEDIAN VALUE)

UNDER $1 MILLION NET SALES	
MVIC/Net Sales	0.31
MVIC/Gross Profit	0.48
MVIC/SDE	1.67
MVIC/EBITDA	2.21
$1 MILLION–$5 MILLION NET SALES	
MVIC/Net Sales	0.39
MVIC/Gross Profit	0.60
MVIC/SDE	2.43
MVIC/EBITDA	2.98
OVER $5 MILLION NET SALES	
MVIC/Net Sales	0.89
MVIC/Gross Profit	2.08
MVIC/SDE	4.98
MVIC/EBITDA	12.81

Source: DealStats (formerly Pratt's Stats), 2023 (Portland, OR: Business Valuation Resources, LLC), www.bvresources.com/dealstats

PRICING TIPS

National franchise restaurants sell for more than mom-and-pop units. Lease payments should not exceed 8 percent of gross revenue—better around 6 percent. Food and payroll costs are critical. Food costs should be less than 33 percent of sales, 28 to 33 percent. Payroll costs used to be around 22 percent of sales; now with increased wage payments required by the market, they will be higher—resulting in increased food and drink prices—but they should not be over 25 percent of total sales. SDE should be between 1.5 and 3, with 3 times limited to national franchise units.

The food cost should be near 28 to 35 percent. Above that requires a closer look at revenues reported. Business should be operating with labor cost and management at or below 35 to 38 percent because of higher wages. Rents today are 7 to 9 percent.

Add liquor license cost and value of FF&E.

BENCHMARK DATA

STATISTICS (FAST FOOD RESTAURANTS)

Number of Establishments	305,902
Average Profit Margin	5.2%
Revenue per Employee	$82,249
Average Number of Employees	15.7
Average Wages per Employee	$21,029

PRODUCTS AND SERVICES SEGMENTATION

Burgers	32.6%
Other	27.4%
Chicken	12.9%
Global	9.5%
Sandwiches	9.3%
Pizza and pasta	8.3%

INDUSTRY COSTS

Profit	5.2%
Wages	25.6%
Purchases	43.0%
Depreciation	3.2%
Marketing	2.1%
Rent & Utilities	8.2%
Other	12.7%

Good food and service; $250 to $300 per square foot; 22 to 25 percent labor cost; 25 to 27 percent food cost; 5 to 7 percent rent

Food costs vary depending on the amount of protein and use of paper. For fast casual brands with high paper costs (no dishwasher), this can add an additional 3 PPT to the COGS. For heavy meat (protein concepts) like BBQ or steak houses, COGS can also go up.

EXPENSES (% OF ANNUAL SALES)

Cost of Goods	30% to 50%
Occupancy Costs	06% to 12%
Payroll/Labor Costs	25% to 35%
Profit (pretax)	10% to 20%

QUESTIONS

- How many hours do they work a week in the restaurant? What is the employee turnover rate?

- What would you do differently, and will you finance? If a seller is not willing to finance an operationally strong, financially qualified buyer with a good background and credit, look harder.
- Tell me your story. What would you do to improve the business?
- If a franchise, get a copy of the agreement. How involved is the franchisor in the company?
- Why selling? Are there any family members working in business? Who does the cooking? What is food/beverage percent split? How does that compare to liquor license and zoning requirements? Average ticket? Which is stronger: breakfast, lunch, dinner? Is there anything in the restaurant that you do not own, e.g., dishwasher, ice machine, POS, beer draft system? Franchise transfer fees? Other franchise fees?
- Would you do it again? What are the biggest challenges?

INDUSTRY TREND

The industry has gone through a difficult period because of limited and high-cost labor and extremely high product costs. I see product cost easing slightly in 1 to 2 years, but I'm afraid the higher labor cost is here to stay. Rental costs are going to remain steady because of the availability of space and the lack of demand for space.

There will be fewer units that are not part of a national franchise network.

"Healthy and low-calorie menu items are increasingly implemented in fast food restaurants. The restaurant industry is fiercely competitive, so to contend for consumer dollars, operators must add new, exciting menu items to cater to changing consumer tastes. Restaurants are increasingly incorporating technology in their operations to contend with staffing issues and maintain profit. COVID-19 accelerated the use of technology in restaurants, with self-ordering kiosks in particular being established in restaurants."

Source: IBISWorld Key Takeaways

EXPERT COMMENTS

Be operationally qualified, have liquidity, and be prepared to work hard for your money! Buyers want training and support, and if you finance, you will want to be involved until the last payment is made.

Sellers should do a good job keeping the business maintained and running efficiently. Buyers are looking for a well-run restaurant that they can grow—and not have to fix problems.

A couple of challenges for the restaurant industry are getting qualified help and inventory shortages.

If inexperienced, get a partner that does have experience.

FINANCING

National franchise units can often be financed by banks; seller carry is likely for nonnational franchise restaurants.

Today, unfortunately, cash is the answer. Financing is difficult because of the poor financial results in recent years and the high interest rates. SBA financing is available, but the process is tedious depending on the quality and detail of the financial information and results. I tell sellers, consider owner financing if you are looking for a quick exit. With the right buyer, the results for the seller could be good.

Some seller financing will help make the business more sellable. The amount of seller financing will depend on the buyer qualifications.

Bank financing at 60 percent with seller financing. Banks do not like lending to restaurants.

RESOURCES

- IBISWorld, October 2023: https://www.ibisworld.com
- IFA—International Franchise Association: https://www.franchise.org
- National Restaurant Association: https://restaurant.org
- NRN—Nation's Restaurant News: https://www.nrn.com
- RestaurantNews.com: https://www.restaurantnews.com

Restaurants, Full Service

| NAICS 722511 | SIC 5812-08

Rules of Thumb

- 30%–50% annual sales
- 2–3 x SDE
- 2.5–3.5 x EBIT
- 3–4 x EBITDA

INDUSTRY MULTIPLES

Acquisition multiples below are calculated medians using US private industry transactions. Data updated annually. Last update: August 2023.

VALUATION MULTIPLE (MEDIAN VALUE)

UNDER $1 MILLION NET SALES
MVIC/Net Sales.	0.29
MVIC/Gross Profit	0.43
MVIC/SDE	1.73
MVIC/EBITDA	1.98

$1 MILLION–$5 MILLION NET SALES
MVIC/Net Sales.	0.32
MVIC/Gross Profit	0.53
MVIC/SDE	2.20
MVIC/EBITDA	2.94

OVER $5 MILLION NET SALES
MVIC/Net Sales.	0.66
MVIC/Gross Profit	1.05
MVIC/SDE	2.72
MVIC/EBITDA	7.33

Source: DealStats (formerly Pratt's Stats), 2023 (Portland, OR: Business Valuation Resources, LLC), www.bvresources.com/dealstats

PRICING TIPS

It is important how long the business has been established, whether the recipes are included and written down, whether it is well staffed, and whether the employees have tenure.

Every restaurant is different. Different geographic conditions present great variables. Generally the value of the lease, plus equipment in place, plus (annualized discretionary earnings x 2) will give you a benchmark. This goes up or down based on the systems, people, and any contracts the business may have. Right now the push in small operator restaurants is for operator to own, rather then rent, so these businesses earn a premium plus value of the real estate.

Be able to separate any government grants/loans, in the prior years.

The range of SDE multiples is 1.5 to 2.5 and includes inventory.

Every business is different. We look at gross revenues and costs, seller benefits. Inventory and FFE has limited value most of the time. A well-run and efficient business will bring far more profit stream than a run-down and lacking one, regardless of revenues. Labor pool is a big part of the equation now.

You have to look at the market and see what the most recent sales of a similar business sold for. Also, in this current economic environment, you may want to look at the political climate, where you have inflation, food shortages, labor, and pandemics.

In my opinion, EBIT and EBITDA are not useful in selling independent restaurants; SDE is. Restaurant buyers, however, are inherently irrational, and the SDE multiple only serves as confirmation bias for most buyers. So the story, location, look, concept, and potential are what matter.

It is important today to look at cost of goods sold as well as the labor cost. The effect of higher cost of goods reflects inadequate selling prices or control issues with the management. High labor costs reflect scheduling issues and also the market prices for labor. Be certain the business financials are based on frequent inventories so that accurate costs are shown.

For a goodwill sale where the buyer will continue on with the name and concept, use SDE as a relevant metric. For an asset sale only where the buyer will create a new concept and name, then the percent of gross sales metric is most relevant, as it provides indication of the revenue achievable at the location. The range is 30 percent plus or minus 10 percent, depending on multiple other factors.

2 to 3 times net; 33 percent of gross for a year works only if the restaurant is very profitable.

Total discretionary benefit x 2 plus inventory and real estate = likely sales price in Florida.

Volume, sales per foot, owner involvement, and management in place are all important areas to identify. Currently, buyers appear to be seeking opportunities with access to large amounts of outdoor seating and/or a model that can provide a high volume of delivery. Make sure to benchmark COGS against industry standards to make sure the provided numbers are within a range to be considered believable. It is unlikely the tax returns will be in sync with the P&L when dealing with smaller businesses. It is imperative that you understand if the local health authority or permitting body will require the facility to meet current codes with the issuance of a new food service permit!

Location and lease terms are very important when determining the value of a restaurant or bar business. Condition of the FF&E (furniture, fixtures, and equipment) also plays a critical role when putting a value on a business.

If the style of restaurant is fine dining and expensive chef, would be lower price.

2 to 3 times net profit has always been the norm in a seller's mind for the last 30 years that I have been selling restaurant businesses. Buyers always want to see numbers lower.

35 percent is a good starting point. Adjust for the condition of equipment and the lease rate (6 percent of monthly sales or less, very good; around 10 percent or more, very bad). Other factors are the profit and loss statement and taxes. Many

businesses show a loss or very low profit—it's hard to convince many buyers of the profitability of these businesses. Some owners report and document a decent income, thus allowing a buyer to obtain some financing and feel good about the purchase. It's always helpful to have a seller who carries anywhere from 20 to 40 percent as short-term financing—no longer than 2 or 3 years. Some seller financing offered in the sales advertising also gives buyers a better sense of confidence.

Since the lease is an asset, look for a good term with options to renew (if the rent is specified in the option periods, even better). A rent structure with the total gross rent (base plus CAM) that falls between 6 and 8 percent of sales is a major plus. This can add value to the business valuation. Of course, equipment that is maintained on a regular basis (plus with maintenance contracts in place) would also enhance valuation. But when all the shots are fired, it gets down always to cash flow.

Location is always important, and so is parking; rent has to be in line; condition of equipment is usually overlooked but is very important. Does the restaurant have a grease trap, and what kind? All mentioned here will affect the price.

You have to be able to add back expenses that are not related to the sale or a new buyer; that is key.

BENCHMARK DATA

STATISTICS (CHAIN RESTAURANTS)

Number of Establishments	40,363
Average Profit Margin	4.7%
Revenue per Employee	$80,954
Average Number of Employees	17.6
Average Wages per Employee	$29,119

PRODUCTS AND SERVICES SEGMENTATION

American	45.8%
Varied menus	29.5%
Italian/pizza	11.5%
Other	6.9%
Seafood	6.3%

INDUSTRY COSTS

Profit	4.7%
Wages	36.0%
Purchases	36.0%
Depreciation	2.1%
Marketing	1.8%
Rent & Utilities	7.1%
Other	12.2%

MARKET SHARE

Darden Restaurants Inc.	15.7%

STATISTICS (SINGLE-LOCATION FULL-SERVICE RESTAURANTS)

Number of Establishments	156,960
Average Profit Margin	4.2%
Revenue per Employee	$59,183
Average Number of Employees	25.3
Average Wages per Employee	$19,120

PRODUCTS AND SERVICES SEGMENTATION

US restaurants	23.3%
European restaurants	17.1%

Steakhouses	15.6%
Asian restaurants	15.1%
Seafood restaurants	11.8%
Mexican restaurants	7.1%
Pizza Restaurants	6.5%
Other	3.5%

INDUSTRY COSTS

Profit	4.2%
Wages	32.1%
Purchases	40.1%
Depreciation	2.1%
Marketing	1.9%
Rent & Utilities	7.7%
Other	11.9%

STATISTICS (PREMIUM STEAK RESTAURANTS)

Number of Establishments	4,508
Average Profit Margin	4.7%
Revenue per Employee	$66,669
Average Number of Employees	22.6
Average Wages per Employee	$19,217

PRODUCTS AND SERVICES SEGMENTATION

Classic steak restaurants	59.7%
Steak and seafood restaurants	34.8%
Other premium steak restaurants	4.0%
Premium Brazilian steak restaurants	1.5%

INDUSTRY COSTS

Profit	4.7%
Wages	28.5%
Purchases	42.1%
Depreciation	2.2%
Marketing	2.0%
Rent & Utilities	8.1%
Other	12.4%

MARKET SHARE

Darden Restaurants Inc.	6.7%
Ruth's Hospitality Group, Inc.	5.7%
Fleming's Prime Steakhouse & Wine Bar	4.1%
Fogo de Chão, Inc.	3.4%

These all went out the window during Covid. The stability of a business is now directly related to having a hands-on owner and a large employee pool.

Increase in sales and decrease in cost

Profit margin, 5 percent; revenue per employee, $50K; average wage per employee, $18K

Food costs, under 35 percent; full bar run efficiently; management in place; high traffic

Do you number weekly? The old days of monthly are over. I also watch my prime cost, food cost, and labor; the closer to 55 percent, the easier it will be for you.

In general, for mid- to high-level independent restaurants, you're doing something right if you can pay your rent with a day's (or not more than 2 days') sales, or if food and labor combined make up less than 50 percent of sales; if return business is over 50 percent monthly; if staff turnover is below 50 percent annually; if alcohol sales are over 30 percent of total, and tips over 20 percent; and if alcohol (and especially wine) inventory turns more than once a month, and food more than once a week.

Food costs and labor costs each need to be monitored and kept below 35 and 25 percent, respectively, for most restaurants and bars to be successful.

Sales per square foot have increased simply because the check averages have increased because of increased prices. The average check has grown by 15 to 20 percent over the last 18 months. Operators are managing increased costs, or the doors are closed. Higher costs are being passed along, and the consumer is understanding. Surprisingly, the revenues have increased and profits have grown in well-managed businesses, and restaurants with long-term leases in place have seen the rent factors decline.

Two key metrics are critical: (1) prime cost (total of cost of goods sold and gross labor, including payroll tax and benefits) should not exceed 68 percent, and (2) occupancy cost (including rent and associated net lease expenses like real estate tax, building insurance, and common area maintenance) should not exceed 9 percent.

As for occupancy, take the annual gross rent and divide that number by 7 percent. That represents the revenue you will need to generate in order for your occupancy to be 7 percent of sales. I see way too many new operators who negotiate leases without clearly understanding the implication of this commitment on the revenue they need to generate to be profitable.

Food cost and labor benchmark has historically been 50 to 52 percent but is rising.

Controlling food costs is one of the most important aspects of running a successful business. Food costs for quick-serve restaurants should be 30 percent or lower, while fine-dining food costs should be no higher than 40 percent.

Food cost higher for fine-dining, full-service.

Prime costs of loaded labor and cost of goods never to exceed 65 percent. Total lease costs never to exceed 10 percent.

The key to profitability and longevity is controlling costs. You can't control fixed costs like rent but you can control almost everything else. At the onset of opening a business is hiring a leasing expert who can navigate and steer the process of lease negotiation. Once a lease is signed, it's impossible to change terms, so you've got to get the rental rate down upfront and make sure you get landlord concessions like free rent, tenant improvement dollars, and, again, a reduced rental rate. Once the lease is settled, then it's time to negotiate with every vendor from insurance to the credit card processor to get the best deal. Controlling labor, food, and utilities is crucial to success and profitability.

Initially, I start out at 35 percent of gross sales as a listing price and then add for owner-owned property, condition of assets, quality of financial documentation, motivation of seller, quality of lease, etc.

For a full-service restaurant, food and beverage cost should be around 34 percent with bar cost around 18 percent.

EXPENSES (% OF ANNUAL SALES)

Cost of Goods	30% to 40%
Occupancy Costs	06% to 12%
Payroll/Labor Costs.	25% to 35%
Profit (pretax)	10% to 20%

QUESTIONS

• How much training are you willing to provide?

- Show me a typical day. Ask to see social media and visit the restaurant several times.
- Are all their government and municipal fees paid up to date? Make sure the business is not involved in any kind of litigation. Are all the staff members getting the salary they deserve? Are all taxes and VAT returns up to date?
- Would they pay whatever the list price is for your business? If they won't, that is a tough sale to a buyer.
- Where would you grow this business, if money weren't an issue?
- How old is the business?
- How many employees are there, and what are they paid?
- Will the menu and recipes be included?
- Need a copy of the lease and 3 years of tax returns
- Do they have the experience to run it? Do they have the funds to buy and run the operation? What is their plan to run the business (very important if you hold paper)?
- What would you do differently? If you had extra cash to invest in the business, what would you do with it?
- Look at the 1099-K reports from the IRS; 90 percent credit card sales today.
- How much liquid cash do you have on hand?
- What are your hours? How would you improve your business? Will you hold paper?
- How many employees are off book?
- Ask for the last 2 to 3 years of federal tax returns; profit and loss statements; a state sales tax report showing they are up-to-date on their state sales tax; a copy of the lease; an equipment list; and invoices for all food/beverage purchases, etc.
- A major question would be, do the employees desire to continue to keep working with the business? Another, how long are they willing to train and assist the buyer?
- Age, and maintenance of, equipment? Key staff? How often is the menu changed? What are the top-selling items? Percentage of beer, wine, and liquor sales?
- When was it established? How long have you been in the business? Do you have any loans? Is all your equipment in working condition, and is it all free and clear? Any secret recipe?
- How much time do you spend day-to-day, and what is your job description?
- Have you heard of any new restaurants coming to the area? Then research it on your own.
- Experience? Funds? How much do you want to make? What are you best at?
- What is the employee turnover rate? View the P&L by month to identify seasonality. How do the expenses and profitability compare with industry standards?
- Is seller in good standing with meals tax? Is seller in good standing with vendors (particularly liquor vendors)?
- Does your labor cost include all of the burdening? Are you quoting revenue net of sales tax? Is all of the payroll on the books? When was your last workers' comp claim? When was your last slip and fall claim by a customer's attorney?
- Only pay for the results on tax returns!
- How will you prove that your financials are actual?
- Ask if there are any family members working in the business and what will happen to them when the business is sold? Is there any source of income that is not recorded on the books? Look at how you can verify that money. Is there any road construction going to happen in the area? What is the maintenance program for all the refrigeration?

- Please review the income and expense report in detail. Which employees would you keep and which would you not keep?
- Ask about landlord and facility issues. Understand responsibilities of landlord and tenant based on the lease. Ask about health department open items; ABC restrictions. Are employees all paid on payroll 100 percent?
- Reason for selling, seasonal trends, food cost, social media items, list of vendors. Are you willing to give me all your recipes? Will you sign a noncompete? Are all licenses transferable? Are there any unresolved health department issues? Is the liquor license transferable? Is the lease transferable? Is anything leased?
- What is your relationship with your neighbors? What is the smartest thing you did as a restaurant operator?

INDUSTRY TREND

In spite of rising prices due to inflation, people are still going out to eat in record numbers.

Automation, smaller menus, more efficient kitchens that run on less people. Pay at table, order at table, robotics, and takeout services

Good staffing

More technology for payment, ordering, and robots cleaning floors and delivering food

The restaurant industry will continue to grow as more and more people cook less.

The number of restaurants and bars will increase each year by about 2 percent.

Emerging AI to replace labor, smaller portions, lean profits

"Citing data from Yelp, the *Wall Street Journal* reported that restaurants are now seating 10% of their diners between 2 p.m. and 5 p.m.—double the number of seatings at those times in 2019....'Most restaurants that made it through the pandemic have altered their hours and now close earlier, so some folks have pushed their eating times earlier,' Lisa Schultz, managing partner at Zingerman's Roadhouse in Ann Arbor, told *The Takeout*."

Source: "Why Early-Bird Dining Is Sweeping the Country" by Micheline Maynard, September 13, 2023, https://thetakeout.com/early-bird-dining-trend-afternoon-restaurant-reservatio-1850825080

"A few months ago, a number of serious food journalists asked out loud whether fine dining was dying, or possibly already dead. This seemed odd to me. I keep close tabs on the restaurant scene, especially in New York City, and if expensive restaurants were undergoing a mass die-off, I'd like to think I would notice. The truth, in fact, seemed to be the opposite. Fancy restaurants are opening here so quickly that there aren't enough nights in the week for me to check them all out.

"One thing I did see, though, is that the flavor of fine dining has changed a lot lately. Korean owners and chefs now run about a dozen of the city's most prominent high-end restaurants. Their rise, which has been remarkably swift, brings to an end the unquestioned supremacy of French cuisine that lasted for decades....

"With the exception of the rowdier steakhouses, almost any place where each person pays more than $100 or $125 for the meal alone, without drinks, is probably offering fine dining."

Source: "How Korean Restaurants Remade Fine Dining in New York" by Pete Wells, August 29, 2023, https://www.nytimes.com/2023/08/29/dining/korean-fine-dining-restaurants-nyc.html

More technology is utilized. Robots to deliver food orders. Different types of ordering systems to cut down on labor. Also the ability to have take-out counters, and drive-thrus if possible. More chef collaborations.

I think that a lot of the restaurants that are still around are staying open from PPP, ERC, and EIDL money. I see a lot of them going out of business soon. I see a lot of inexperienced business owners that could use my help and guidance to stay open.

Up if employees can be retained.

Shorter menus specializing in more focused cuisines, higher prices, more streamlined (read leaner) service, more attempts at plant-based food (most of which will fail), an emphasis on maximizing flavor and painting from a wider flavor palette, a relative increase in high quality QSRs, and a faster churn of full service. A move to remote, commissary kitchens and smaller finishing kitchens in restaurants using a hub and spoke self-distribution system. A move to multiple sales channels—in-house, delivery, remote, food trucks, catering, private dining, etc. Landlords of large buildings will increase TI to get the tenants they want.

Takeout and delivery has become a crucial part of the restaurant business. Those who embrace this sector and effectively manage that part of their business will do well.

I feel the trends are very good for the strong operators. I expect the good financially managed business will succeed, and even get stronger.

More carryout, delivery, ghost kitchens.

Tough going for the next couple of years. Sales are slowing at the unit level. Chains are dominating more and more. Everyone seems to want to own multiple restaurants.

So much depends on the economy as it relates to commodity prices and labor trends.

Owners being more hands-on as staffing has become difficult.

Decreased profitability, trend to franchise or multiunits to control costs.

Business should trend up significantly.

"What the new generation of tasting-menu restaurants lack in luxury trappings they make up for with nervy imagination conveyed by deeply personal food, bohemian charisma and business models that challenge assumptions about what restaurants should provide customers and employees. These restaurants have gone from micro-niche to emerging movement since the start of the pandemic, as hospitality professionals were forced to be resourceful to make ends meet....

"An advantage of tasting menus is that they enable thrift. Because they tend to require reservations and compel diners to choose and pay for their meals in advance, tasting menus allow chefs to estimate the ingredients purchased for each meal with precision. This reduces waste that is common at à la carte restaurants, which have to stock up on food that diners may not order. Fixed menus also contain fewer dishes than conventional ones, making them possible to execute with fewer employees inside the small spaces that tend to command lower rents."

Source: "The New Generation of Tasting Menus Won't Test Your Patience
(or Your Wallet)" by Brett Anderson, September 6, 2022,
https://www.nytimes.com/2022/09/06/dining/new-wave-tasting-menus-fine-dining.html

It looks like we are bouncing back; some people that lost their jobs during the pandemic are looking at business ownership as a way to have more say in life.

Fast-casual concept trading better than full-service. Locations with outdoor dining, as a Covid measure, are more desirable

I see incredible growth and rebounding for many. I can attest to many businesses we sold recently that showed no decrease in sales or profit. During a down market or shift, the key is to pivot. If your full-service and sales are down, then pivot into takeout and delivery. I have seen countless restaurants shift to different strategies to not only survive but remain profitable. Many have failed because they have changed their business model. The key is knowing when to change what you're doing and not sit on the sidelines.

Tough slog with consolidation

Since a lot of restaurants are shutting down recently, the competition will be reduced, and the owner that is a restaurateur with a lot of restaurant experience will thrive in the future.

I think buyers will want to see footprints that allow for outdoor dining, designated parking for pickup and delivery, drive-throughs, seating that can be modified, and suburban businesses.

"Many consumers have remained less willing to spend on sit-down meals. Increasing awareness of health risks has encouraged chain restaurants to update menus. As many restaurants have furloughed employees amid the pandemic, the number of industry employees is expected to increase. Despite the industry's projected return to growth, intense competition will likely persist. Despite attempts to automate, the industry is expected to remain labor-intensive. Many major restaurant chains are expected to continue their push overseas. Cost-conscious consumers are increasingly eating from a buffet of dining alternatives. Many consumers seek alternatives to industry restaurants by searching for deals online. Restaurants have expanded the number of healthy options on their menus. There is a high level of turnover among industry operators. Intense competition among industry operators and external competitors is forecast to continue. Fine dining is expected to do well due to the stable share of high-income households. Restaurants will likely engage with customers using websites and social media. The industry has been highly fragmented and exceedingly competitive. Industry demand is influenced primarily by economic factors that directly affect consumer end markets. Premium steak restaurants are popular among corporations for business events, meetings and celebrations. Wage expense as a portion of industry revenue has increased over the past five years, resulting in an overall decrease in industry profitability. As fears of a global economic recession continue, the manner in which consumers prioritize spending habits has become a main area of focus. Purchase expenses represent the largest industry expense category. A rise in domestic meat prices could potentially amplify internal competition. Industry demand is derived primarily from households that generate annual incomes above $100,000."

Source: IBISWorld Industry at a Glance

EXPERT COMMENTS

Go work in the industry to make sure you love it. If you do not love it, you will burn out quickly.

Buyers should make sure they can get training. Don't assume all of the employees will stay in a transition.

Inflation is driving food costs, and supply shortages have made some restaurants challenging. We are seeing some RRF fallout being that a few folks got sizeable amounts while others did not receive the grants. These people who received millions are able to attract employees and pay the highest wages because of this advantage which has artificially driven up labor and the ability to get people because another restaurant can afford to overpay in a position that isn't typically a certain range.

Some of the restaurants that are Main Street are too large a space for the independents. More buyers are looking for places that have a takeout segment and that are smaller and cost effective to operate.

To a buyer: get a good team together, as you'll likely need it. Nobody has all the skills it takes. If you're buying an existing restaurant, realize that the seller did all the hard work already. You just need to make it better. You couldn't build this from scratch for close to the asking price, and it would take you a year with no money coming in. The question is, what is it worth to you?

To a seller: I know how much blood, sweat and tears you put into this, and how much of yourself you see in every bit of it, but our goal here is to get you paid to move on and do something else. If you start getting sentimental, think about the days the health inspector showed up in the middle of lunch and found your walk-in is running too warm, your hot water heater broke, or your chef quit. You may think it's worth more than they're offering, but how much is it worth not to worry about the daily dramas and making payroll in the off months? What else could you do with the money they're offering?

Restaurateurs are inherently optimistic in normal times. Aspiring restaurateurs, more so. These are not normal times. The independent restaurant model is ancient and in need of innovation and disruption. The proof here is in the pudding (failure rate). To be successful, one needs to master the quality of food and service in the right location with a protected niche, cost control, and a means to scale and achieve a profit. The same person needs to manage a difficult and diverse workforce traumatized by Covid and empowered by labor shortages. They need to master marketing in the golden age of digital marketing. That being said, to those not in the industry, restaurants are sexy and more interesting than any rational business, so buyers frequently come out of corporate America looking for a fun project.

Rising food and supply costs, and rising labor costs are making it increasingly difficult to find and keep good employees.

Seller needs to maintain good books. Consider sales trends and look at 3-year averages to compensate for the pandemic. Location and lease terms play an important role when pricing a restaurant or bar business.

You need to know and love the food business. Your family and social life will be impacted! Examine the financials closely. Understand the expenses and any deviations from the normal indexes like food cost, labor costs, and rent index. Rent never goes away, it just goes higher. Triple net leases can be very costly. Know what you're buying into with the lease. Are inventories being taken regularly? Is the lease available long-term with options in place?

The market is excellent for quality operations that produce good food and provide good service to the customer. The higher product costs can be absorbed and passed along to the customer. They are prepared for the higher costs. The profit trends are up because owners are passing along higher prices not always based on higher costs of ingredients. Labor costs are down because of the lack of labor. The businesses are forced to become more efficient, so the hours of operation are reduced and less profitable portions of the operation go away. Owners are putting the labor against the most profitable share of revenues.

Selling: be patient; could take a year or more to get the right fit. Buying: find a good broker to work with who knows the restaurant business and business brokerage.

As to the decrease in historic profit trends—the increase in food costs, localized labor shortages, and the need to raise wages to both acquire and keep employees are the primary drivers. The cost to open a new restaurant is prohibitive to most buyers, which makes the purchase of an existing restaurant (either as a going business or pure asset sale) more desirable, especially at the lower end of the price spectrum (under $150K).

Ease of replication is very important. Another factor I ask about is employee retention, the biggest factor owners don't follow. More compliance to fashion the major source of business: (1) business plan, (2) budget, (3) P&L. Also, I ask my consulting clients to make a weekly sample P&L; the days of monthly P&Ls are over!

Plan on owner financing and selling to an experienced operator.

Restaurants are high potential sales because they are approachable for first-time entrepreneurs.

It is imperative that you understand if the local health authority or permitting body will require the facility to meet current codes with the issuance of a new food service permit!

For sellers, they need to keep good books if they want to realize a fair market price.

For buyers, analyze the sales and net profit trends over the past few years and identify what has affected those trends.

Create entity ahead of time; have a CPA, and contractor ready for tenant improvement; have social media savvy.

If you did not grow up in the industry, get some on-the-job education or formal education. Cannot get SBA financing unless you have restaurant experience.

Restaurants typically have the highest rate of failure; it also has the highest profit possibilities. There are a million reasons for not entering this business because of failure rate, location, trends, and economy; but there are a million reasons to enter this arena. I have personally seen countless restaurants open with no street signage or exposure, located in factory or warehouse spaces, that have lines out the door and did almost $10M in their first year of business. So the premise here is that the restaurant industry is for dreamers and those willing to take a chance. The end result can be amazing.

If it's operating successfully, I tell buyers don't change a thing for a year. Sellers can assure a buyer by offering some financing and commitment to assisting the buyer.

Existing businesses with a track record of gross income and profit says a lot about a business. Business owners can come and go; with a good business model with a following and good reputation, it is easier to continue operation without disruption.

Be patient—it takes time once the business is listed for sale. Keep your foot on the gas.

The seller should be understandable and cooperative with the buyer in this difficult time, and they have to take responsibility for PPP loan if any, and they have to provide good training after the closing of escrow. The buyer should have a lot of experience; otherwise, the chance of failing will be very high.

Food should be controlled and not wasted to keep it in line with the food cost!

It is extremely difficult to build up a restaurant from scratch with all the city and health department requirements, not to mention ABC if liquor or B&W will be served.

Make sure you hire someone who is experienced, especially in this climate. Check first with the landlord to make sure that the seller is not in default.

We see a different generation of people who want to get into the industry.

FINANCING

Depends upon the financial records. If the business has good financials and tax returns, then SBA financing is available, but if the business is not reporting some portion of the cash, then the transaction will require seller financing.

Even with SBA, you need 20 percent down; and seller most of time has skin in the game. The last three business I have sold all required some degree of owner finance.

Recently, bank financing has disappeared, and it looks like rates are going much higher; owners are required to do more financing. I would encourage more owner financing. Sellers can keep more of their capital gains by deferring payment. It will help sell the business quicker. The buyers like owner financing because it keeps the seller involved and available for advice. The buyers also feel more comfortable with the financial information when sellers are willing to finance. Terms are typically 3 to 5 years and slightly above market interest rates. Buyers are willing to accept those terms.

60 percent of the deals we do involve seller financing (typically 30 to 50 percent) over 3 to 5 year periods. Only landmark restaurants with a long successful history and consistent cash flows are likely to be financed. Even in those cases, the buyer will need to be experienced in the industry and financially strong.

RESOURCES

- IBISWorld, October 2023: https://www.ibisworld.com
- IBISWorld, September 2023: https://www.ibisworld.com
- IBISWorld, April 2023: https://www.ibisworld.com
- FRLA—Florida Restaurant & Lodging Association: https://frla.org
- Joe Vagnone—small business broker & adviser: https://jvagnone.com
- NCRLA—NC Restaurant & Lodging Association: https://www.ncrla.org
- QSR magazine: https://www.qsrmagazine.com
- We Sell Restaurants: https://www.wesellrestaurants.com
- Today's Restaurant: https://trnusa.com
- The MRA—Massachusetts Restaurant Association: https://www.themassrest.org
- The Boston Restaurant Group, Inc.: https://bostonrestaurantgroup.com
- ServSafe: https://www.servsafe.com
- RRG—Restaurant Resource Group: https://www.rrgconsulting.com
- RestaurantOwner.com: https://www.restaurantowner.com
- Restaurant Report: http://www.restaurantreport.com
- Restaurant Hospitality: https://www.restaurant-hospitality.com

- Restaurant Finance Monitor: https://www.restfinance.com
- Restaurant Business magazine: https://www.restaurantbusinessonline.com/magazine
- ORA—Ohio Restaurant Association: http://www.ohiorestaurant.org
- NRN—Nation's Restaurant News: https://www.nrn.com
- NCCR—National Council of Chain Restaurants: https://nrf.com/about-us/national-council-chain-restaurants
- National Restaurant Association: https://restaurant.org
- HM—HospitalityMaine: https://www.hospitalitymaine.com
- TRA—Texas Restaurant Association: https://txrestaurant.org

Retail Businesses (in General)

| NAICS 455

Rules of Thumb

- 25%–35% annual sales plus inventory
- 1.5–3 x SDE plus inventory
- 8–10 x EBIT
- 10–12 x EBITDA
- 25% annual sales
- 1.5 x SDE

PRICING TIPS

Accurate valuation: The first step in pricing a retail business is to conduct a comprehensive and accurate valuation. This should involve a thorough analysis of the business's financials, assets, market position, customer base, and growth potential. Utilize multiple valuation methods, such as the income approach, market approach, and asset-based approach, to arrive at a fair and realistic price range.

Consider net profit, not just revenue: While revenue is essential, it's the net profit that matters most to potential buyers. Buyers are interested in the business's profitability and its ability to generate cash flow. A high-revenue business with slim profit margins may not be as attractive as a lower-revenue business with healthier profitability.

Competitive market analysis: Research the market and compare the business with similar retail enterprises that have been recently sold. Understanding the selling prices of comparable businesses will help you determine a competitive and reasonable asking price.

Growth potential: Highlight the growth potential of the retail business when pricing it. Buyers are often willing to pay a premium for a business that has the potential for expansion and increased profitability.

Asset value: Don't overlook the value of tangible assets, such as inventory, equipment, and fixtures. These assets contribute to the overall value of the business and should be factored into the pricing.

Unique selling points: Identify and emphasize the unique selling points of the retail business. A well-established brand, loyal customer base, exclusive products, or prime location can justify a higher asking price.

Seller's discretionary earnings (SDE): In many retail businesses, the owner's compensation may be intertwined with the financials. Consider the seller's discretionary earnings, which includes the owner's salary and other perks, as it provides a more accurate representation of the business's true profitability.

Be realistic: While it's natural for sellers to have an emotional attachment to their business, it's essential to be realistic about its market value. Overpricing can deter potential buyers and prolong the selling process.

Prepare comprehensive documentation: Compile all the necessary documents and financial records well in advance. Having well-organized and transparent documentation instills confidence in buyers and can justify the asking price.

Seek professional assistance: Engage the services of an experienced business broker who specializes in retail business sales.

When pricing—in addition to valuation based on financials—consider whether it is recession-proof or how resilient it was to the pandemic, client retention risk, future projections, and terms with landlord.

BENCHMARK DATA

Sales per square foot for retail clothing, recurring revenue percent, client concentration, owner dependence.

Sales per square foot for a clothing discounter should be in excess of $200.00.

EXPENSES (% OF ANNUAL SALES)

Cost of Goods	30% to 40%
Occupancy Costs	10% to 20%
Payroll/Labor Costs.	20% to 30%
Profit (pretax)	10% to 20%

QUESTIONS

- How dependent is the business on the owner? How many clients would leave if the current owner leaves? How would they scale if they were years younger? What are the biggest challenges currently being faced?
- Percent breakdown of the different products/services? How many clients? How much repeat business? How much business in-store vs. phone or Internet? How many staff? Are they willing to stay on? Is the landlord aware of the sale? Any insight on terms for lease assignment?
- Trend of the business? Lease? Competition?
- What are their motivations for selling? What are they going to do after they leave the business? What's an average day like? What is your least favorite thing about your business?
- Sales per square foot, age of inventory, shrinkage

INDUSTRY TREND

Retail businesses seem to be less appealing and transferrable to the buyers in the private capital market due to rising costs and expanded online counterparts offering more convenience and pricing advantage.

Long-standing businesses with unique product offerings that are scalable and can incorporate an e-commerce element into the business will likely trend upwards and have strong demand. There are business owners in this space that haven't upgraded business operations with technology—and having more streamlined processes will present opportunities for cost efficiencies.

Stable

Thorough due diligence, and find a business you are passionate about. Focus on the business and not only the financials.

Retail businesses have faced increased challenges during the pandemic and are recovering slower than expected. Main obstacles are labor price/shortage, higher cost of goods, and overall concerns about the economy.

FINANCING

Seller financing and/or SBA 7(a) loans

Outside financing; seller financing with 30 percent down

RESOURCES

- Appriss Retail: https://apprissretail.com/about/partners/
- NRF—National Retail Federation: https://nrf.com

Retail Stores, Small Specialty

| NAICS 453998 | Businesses/Units 183,215

| Profit $3.9 B | Wages $8.7 B | Annual Growth Future 2.0%

| | | Annual Growth Past 6.4%

Rules of Thumb

- 15%–20% annual sales plus inventory
- 2–3 x SDE plus inventory
- 3–5 x EBIT
- 4–6 x EBITDA
- 40–60% annual sales
- 2.5–3x SDE

INDUSTRY MULTIPLES

Acquisition multiples below are calculated medians using US private industry transactions. Data updated annually. Last update: August 2023.

VALUATION MULTIPLE (MEDIAN VALUE)

UNDER $1 MILLION NET SALES

MVIC/Net Sales.	0.54
MVIC/Gross Profit	0.90
MVIC/SDE	2.34
MVIC/EBITDA	3.10

$1 MILLION–$5 MILLION NET SALES

MVIC/Net Sales.	0.50
MVIC/Gross Profit	0.99
MVIC/SDE	2.69
MVIC/EBITDA	4.11

OVER $5 MILLION NET SALES

MVIC/Net Sales.	1.29
MVIC/Gross Profit	3.18
MVIC/SDE	1.91
MVIC/EBITDA	10.61

Source: DealStats (formerly Pratt's Stats), 2023 (Portland, OR: Business Valuation Resources, LLC), www.bvresources.com/dealstats

Look at growth, competition, gross margin trend, leases.

BENCHMARK DATA

STATISTICS (SMALL SPECIALTY RETAIL STORES)

Number of Establishments	183,215
Average Profit Margin	5.3%
Revenue per Employee	$211,619
Average Number of Employees	1.9
Average Wages per Employee	$25,196

PRODUCTS AND SERVICES SEGMENTATION

Tobacco product and smokers' accessories	36.7%
Home goods	32.1%
Other	17.1%
Collectibles and monuments	10.6%
Groceries and alcoholic beverages	3.5%

INDUSTRY COSTS

Profit	5.3%
Wages	11.8%
Purchases	49.2%
Depreciation	0.9%
Marketing	1.7%
Rent & Utilities	6.7%
Other	24.3%

Stores need to generate $700 to $800 per square foot to remain viable.

Sales per square foot: $800 to $1000

EXPENSES (% OF ANNUAL SALES)

Cost of Goods	35% to 45%
Occupancy Costs	10% to 15%
Payroll/Labor Costs	30% to 35%
Profit (pretax)	05% to 15%

QUESTIONS

- In depth due diligence is an absolute requirement, including the macroeconomic environment.
- Trend of business? Status of lease? Nearby competition?
- How would you improve brick-and-mortar and online sales? How would you improve inventory turnover? What costs can be cut without hurting the business? What do you look for in a good employee hire? Will the landlord extend the lease, and at what rental? Who is your main competitor and how do you compete? What would you do to make the store more attractive to the customer? What other items would you bring in that would be highly salable?

INDUSTRY TREND

Higher rents; lower gross margins; higher wages

Difficult growth trend; online sales; customer cutbacks; potential recession

"E-cigarettes maintain sales for tobacco stores. Despite a steady decline in traditional cigarette smokers, e-cigarettes have created a new market of younger consumers. Pent-up demand following the pandemic pushed consumers to shop locally. Small specialty retailers substantially benefited from an uptick in demand as the economy reopened. Expanding environmental and health consciousness will drive consumers to specialty retailers over the next five years. Many small specialty stores source their products locally and sell products with natural ingredients."

Source: IBISWorld Key Takeaways

EXPERT COMMENTS

Make sure the business has a positive cash flow.

For a seller, make it more profitable and ensure that the recordkeeping is pristine. For a buyer, the ability to manage for profitability is key.

The specialty retail business is highly competitive, but certain stores can be attractive sellers if they show above-average growth and have limited competition, a beneficial lease, and a strong customer following.

FINANCING

30 percent down; 5-year take-back for seller financing; SBA or conventional term financing

RESOURCES

• IBISWorld, April 2023: https://www.ibisworld.com

Rocket Fizz Soda Pop & Candy Shop (Franchise)

| NAICS 445292 | Businesses/Units 83

Rules of Thumb

• 20% annual sales

INDUSTRY MULTIPLES

Acquisition multiples below are calculated medians using US private industry transactions. Data updated annually. Last update: August 2023.

VALUATION MULTIPLE (MEDIAN VALUE)

UNDER $1 MILLION NET SALES	
MVIC/Net Sales	0.41
MVIC/Gross Profit	0.56
MVIC/SDE	2.13
MVIC/EBITDA	3.79
$1 MILLION–$5 MILLION NET SALES	
MVIC/Net Sales	0.58
MVIC/Gross Profit	0.66
MVIC/SDE	2.33
MVIC/EBITDA	1.97
OVER $5 MILLION NET SALES	N/A

Source: DealStats (formerly Pratt's Stats), 2023 (Portland, OR: Business Valuation Resources, LLC), www.bvresources.com/dealstats

PRICING TIPS

Approx. Total Investment: $126,400 to $307,500

RESOURCES

• Rocket Fizz Soda Pop & Candy Shop: https://rocketfizz.com
• Franchise information: https://rocketfizz.com/own-a-franchise/

Roofing Contractors

| NAICS 238160 | Businesses/Units 79,214 |

| Profit $3.6 B | Wages $14.1 B | Annual Growth Future 1.6% |

| | | Annual Growth Past -1.3% |

INDUSTRY MULTIPLES

Acquisition multiples below are calculated medians using US private industry transactions. Data updated annually. Last update: August 2023.

VALUATION MULTIPLE (MEDIAN VALUE)

UNDER $1 MILLION NET SALES

MVIC/Net Sales.	0.43
MVIC/Gross Profit	0.70
MVIC/SDE	2.20
MVIC/EBITDA	1.86

$1 MILLION–$5 MILLION NET SALES

MVIC/Net Sales.	0.32
MVIC/Gross Profit	0.63
MVIC/SDE	1.79
MVIC/EBITDA	2.90

OVER $5 MILLION NET SALES

MVIC/Net Sales.	0.41
MVIC/Gross Profit	1.30
MVIC/SDE	2.61
MVIC/EBITDA	4.18

Source: DealStats (formerly Pratt's Stats), 2023 (Portland, OR: Business Valuation Resources, LLC), www.bvresources.com/dealstats

BENCHMARK DATA

STATISTICS (ROOFING CONTRACTORS)

Number of Establishments .	79,214
Average Profit Margin	6.4%
Revenue per Employee .	$221,497
Average Number of Employees.	3.2
Average Wages per Employee .	$55,969

PRODUCTS AND SERVICES SEGMENTATION

Asphalt roofing .	33.5%
Single-ply roofing	28.0%
Sheet metal roofing .	22.3%
Other	16.2%

MAJOR MARKET SEGMENTATION

Existing nonresidential building construction .	32.0%
Existing residential building construction .	31.4%
New nonresidential building construction .	24.6%
New residential construction	12.0%

INDUSTRY COSTS

Profit	6.4%
Wages	25.1%
Purchases	42.2%
Depreciation	1.0%
Marketing	0.5%
Rent & Utilities .	3.8%
Other	21.0%

INDUSTRY TREND

"The COVID-19 pandemic diminished commercial demand while simultaneously increasing residential demand. These trends will revert to normalcy as the pandemic continues to abate. A burgeoning market for eco-friendly alternatives to legacy roofing offerings has changed the industry landscape. Materials that reflect heat (as opposed to absorbing it) and the wider availability of solar panels have encouraged a need for specialized roofing contractors. Corporate profit will expand and contractual construction work will continue as the pandemic subsides and the economy gets up and running again. Concurrently, demand for roofing contractors will rise as industrial concerns ramp up production and require more facilities."

Source: IBISWorld Key Takeaways

RESOURCES

- IBISWorld, October 2023: https://www.ibisworld.com

Route Distribution Businesses

Rules of Thumb

- 50%–70% annual sales plus inventory
- 1–4 x SDE plus inventory
- 2–4 x EBIT
- 10–20 x weekly gross plus inventory
- 3–4 x EBITDA
- 2–3 x SDE

PRICING TIPS

To determine approximate value of a route distribution business to own, one must consider the following characteristics of that particular route: area where route is; number of days/hours it operates; coding of product being handled; any special type of vehicle needed (refrigerated, etc.) to operate route; returns policy practiced; how orders are administered (e.g., need to call customers, standard orders); whether product is of a consumer-recognized name brand; how long route has been operating; whether there is a distribution agreement in place, and if so, what its contents are; customer receivables policy; supplier payables policy; name of product distributed; whether route is contracted (franchised) or not.

SDE is used most often for pricing for pickup and delivery businesses.

Pricing depends on the quality of the fleet, the experience of the drivers and supervisors, and the stem miles from the distribution terminal to the delivery zone.

The fleet of delivery vehicles must be considered in the pricing model. Age and wear will be heavily reflected in the maintenance expense. Most of my route sales are FedEx routes, and the trucks are now used 7 days a week.

Multiples of earnings are based on many factors: the proximity of the routes to the terminal, age of fleet, tenure of drivers, current contract, and potential growth in the delivery/work areas.

BENCHMARK DATA

One would want each account on any route distribution business to generate a defined minimum ($25 to $50) gross income to make it worthwhile making the physical stop on one's route!

Each truck/route should be capable of generating $120,000 in gross revenue.

You should be working on a minimum of 20 percent profit margin.

Payroll should be between 42 and 48 percent of gross revenue.

One should be able to net (after all expenses) somewhere between $200 and $250 per day of work on any particular route. On any beverage route, one should gross a minimum of $2.00 per case, while on any produce route, one should gross a minimum of $2.50 per package.

For FedEx: $100K+ annual gross per route target; payroll over 50 percent is too high.

A typical FedEx route should be generating approx. $100,000 in gross revenue annually.

Related to FedEx route sales. Payroll should not exceed 50 percent. Profit margin, 20 percent or so. No rent or COGS, usually. Truck repairs and maintenance, 10 percent.

Route driver should handle 75–125 stops daily, depending on the route density.

Value of routes will vary by destination, quality of trucks, and whether routes are unassigned or dedicated.

EXPENSES (% OF ANNUAL SALES)

Cost of Goods	.0% to 20%
Occupancy Costs	.0% to 10%
Payroll/Labor Costs.	40% to 50%
Profit (pretax)	10% to 20%

QUESTIONS

- How long have you been operating this business? If fewer than 2 years, say "thanks, but no thanks." Is the seller willing to pinch-hit an operating route should you go away on vacation? Hard thing to solidify, but worth mentioning. Which customers have proven to be the most problematic, and what is their specific problem? On any particular customer whose receivables is outside the norm, get details as to why this is and decide whether it's worth the risk to you.
- What is the safety score? How many incidents and accidents has the business experienced in the past 3 years? How many workers' comp claims have been filed in past 3 years?
- Where (geographically) are customers located? How close (or spread out) are customer locations? What industry is the route involved in? What time does the route have to start, and how many days weekly is it operated? Returns— credit for out coded items? Is the customer base protected (via a distribution agreement) or not protected? Is preordering done, and if so, how? Size vehicle needed to make deliveries?
- Who is the party responsible for scheduling and handling fleet maintenance/ repairs? Request a list of vendors. Employee turnover? Are there manager candidates in the driver pool that can be elevated?
- What are the criteria used to hire new drivers?
- How much capacity is left before adding another truck/driver to service a territory? How many temporary drivers, and how many trucks need to be in service, during peak season and holidays?
- Is credit on stale merchandise normal? How do accounts pay you?

R

DSD (direct store distribution) is unfortunately becoming extinct. This is due to two main reasons: online buying habits, which make it less necessary for food items to be properly merchandised in brick-and-mortar stores; and overall eroding profit margins on merchandise, which dictates reducing the number of lines of distribution. In other words, the pie needs to be cut into fewer pieces!

Independent contractor model operated by FedEx will continue to take market share from UPS, USPS, and other carriers.

Down—as profit margins get tighter, the food (and nonfood) manufacturers will look to reduce the levels of distribution, to leave more profit at each level.

Expect to see the multiple of cash flow to remain steady.

What is called a DSD (direct store delivery) route will be under much pressure as the margins continue to shrink on a most product's profitability. Bottom line, the manufacturer must look for ways to cut the duplicate handling of products (known as the channels of distribution) to be sure there are dollars left on the bottom line.

Increased expectations of contractors from terminal management. Stronger vetting up front for contractor candidates. Increasing technology on vehicles with higher delivery rates per driver/truck.

In FedEx, we see larger route systems being downsized due to regulations placed on the amount of volume each contractor can handle in a given terminal.

EXPERT COMMENTS

Pay attention to the four Ps (personality; punctuality, product, and price) this expert listed as being of importance for success in the DSD industry: get what you feel is a good product line to distribute; be sure its price is competitive; and certainly be sure you have the right personality to participate in a business where you are usually meeting your customers daily or weekly!

Having an experienced manager and driver that are cross-trained are important factors.

Trust—but verify—the seller's representations.

Driving training is essential to the success.

As Amazon develops their own fleet of delivery resources, driver and truck chassis are in limited supply.

Review the numbers, especially in light of the pandemic. Review sales figures from July 2019 to March 1, 2020; then from March 1 to July 31, 2020; and from August 1, 2020, to the current date. See just how much its sales have been affected (lower, higher, or untouched), and be sure to pay the price reflective of the correct sales numbers.

Talk with other contractors about positives and negatives in the business.

As e-commerce continues to become more popular, route systems will grow. To have a product delivered to a home or business, it makes sense to put it on a truck.

Use a business broker with specific industry experience.

Maintenance records for the fleets are essential.

FINANCING

Many times (with franchised routes) financing is offered by the manufacturer of that product, such as BIMBO, Pepperidge Farm, etc. On other route selections, traditionally (if route is valued and selling over $35,000 to $50,000 in total), the down payment is 50 to 65 percent of total price with balance seller financed over enough years at an interest rate 1 to 2 points above prime, where the monthly note payment (consisting of principle and interest) is no more than 25 percent of the monthly net earnings (before taxes) of that route.

In over 100 transactions we facilitated, only a few went with SBA lending. Mostly all cash transaction with no seller financing.

If a seller is not willing to hold paper (even if you don't need/want such), walk away! This is the best way to ascertain and prequalify the stated (and verified) level of income.

Majority of transactions are cash at closing. Little to no seller financing. Limited SBA lending available.

Whole routes offerings are now very viable for SBA lending (50 percent of the time); carveout deals are seller-financed or cash deals.

RESOURCES

- FedEx: https://www.fedex.com
- Mr. Route: https://www.mrrouteinc.com
- Route Brokers Inc: https://www.routebrokers.com

RV Dealerships

NAICS 441210	SIC 5561-03	Businesses/Units 7,267
Profit $1.3 B	Wages $5 B	Annual Growth Future 1.7%
		Annual Growth Past 6.6%

Rules of Thumb

- 15% annual sales plus RV inventory & parts, etc.

INDUSTRY MULTIPLES

Acquisition multiples below are calculated medians using US private industry transactions. Data updated annually. Last update: August 2023.

VALUATION MULTIPLE (MEDIAN VALUE)

UNDER $1 MILLION NET SALES

MVIC/Net Sales	1.56
MVIC/Gross Profit	2.72
MVIC/SDE	0.80
MVIC/EBITDA	N/A

$1 MILLION–$5 MILLION NET SALES

MVIC/Net Sales	0.55
MVIC/Gross Profit	0.68
MVIC/SDE	2.05
MVIC/EBITDA	1.80

OVER $5 MILLION NET SALES

MVIC/Net Sales	0.50
MVIC/Gross Profit	1.85

| MVIC/SDE | . | . | . | . | . | . | . | 3.46 |
| MVIC/EBITDA | . | . | . | . | . | . | . | 5.85 |

Source: DealStats (formerly Pratt's Stats), 2023 (Portland, OR: Business Valuation Resources, LLC), www.bvresources.com/dealstats

PRICING TIPS

A good formula: ease of entry, big secular swings, keep the price in the 4x range for smaller, privately owned companies. Also, balance sheets generally are not critical.

BENCHMARK DATA

STATISTICS (RECREATIONAL VEHICLE DEALERS)

Number of Establishments 7,267	
Average Profit Margin 2.8%	
Revenue per Employee $735,266	
Average Number of Employees. 8.9	
Average Wages per Employee . . . $77,683	

PRODUCTS AND SERVICES SEGMENTATION

Travel trailers 52.8%	
Fifth-wheel trailers 14.5%	
Services, parts and repair 11.2%	
Class C RVs 10.3%	
Class B RVs 4.3%	
Class A RVs 4.0%	
Folding trailers 1.8%	
Truck campers 1.1%	

INDUSTRY COSTS

Profit 2.8%	
Wages 10.5%	
Purchases 74.2%	
Depreciation 0.3%	
Marketing 0.9%	
Rent & Utilities 1.2%	
Other 10.2%	

MARKET SHARE

Camping World Holdings Inc. 13.0%

QUESTIONS

• Gross margin—it's really important to have that straight.

INDUSTRY TREND

"COVID-safe travel drew in more customers. RV dealers made record sales as consumers sought to escape the house any way they could. Demographic shifts promise growth moving forward. Younger individuals and families are continually showing more interest in RVs."

Source: IBISWorld Key Takeaways

FINANCING

Outside financing and maybe some seller paper to keep the transaction kosher

RESOURCES

• IBISWorld, March 2023: https://www.ibisworld.com
• RV PRO: https://rv-pro.com
• RVDA—The National RV Dealers Association: https://www.rvda.org

RV Parks

| NAICS 721211 | SIC 7033-02

Rules of Thumb

- 3.3% annual sales plus inventory
- 8.5 x SDE plus inventory

INDUSTRY MULTIPLES

Acquisition multiples below are calculated medians using US private industry transactions. Data updated annually. Last update: August 2023.

VALUATION MULTIPLE (MEDIAN VALUE)

UNDER $1 MILLION NET SALES

MVIC/Net Sales.	1.04
MVIC/Gross Profit	1.23
MVIC/SDE	3.61
MVIC/EBITDA	4.61

$1 MILLION–$5 MILLION NET SALES

MVIC/Net Sales.	1.06
MVIC/Gross Profit	1.07
MVIC/SDE	1.82
MVIC/EBITDA	N/A

OVER $5 MILLION NET SALES

MVIC/Net Sales.	2.25
MVIC/Gross Profit	2.29
MVIC/SDE	N/A
MVIC/EBITDA	5.44

Source: DealStats (formerly Pratt's Stats), 2023 (Portland, OR: Business Valuation Resources, LLC), www.bvresources.com/dealstats

PRICING TIPS

These businesses are based on cap rates starting at 4 percent for a 5-star manufactured home community up to 12 percent for an overnight campground.

"RV parks are a very high-yielding investment, with returns from 10% to 20%+ on your money. RV parks are among the highest yielding of all real estate asset classes. So if your goal is to maximize the return on your money, RV parks are not a bad starting spot."

Source: https://www.rvparkuniversity.com/articles/is-buying-a-rv-park-worth-the-investment

BENCHMARK DATA

Gross income minus 30 to 40 percent in total expenses based on renting lots/sites and not homes/cottages

Below 5,000 camper nights per year makes it difficult to operate the business and make a profit.

See Campgrounds for additional Benchmark Data

EXPENSES (% OF ANNUAL SALES)

Cost of Goods	10%
Occupancy Costs	30% to 40%
Payroll/Labor Costs.	10%
Profit (pretax)	40%

QUESTIONS

- Show me your last 3 years of tax returns. Show me where I can increase revenues and decrease expenses.
- Ask for a complete due diligence package and if they will sign a noncompete agreement.

INDUSTRY TREND

This is a high-growth industry. Manufacturers cannot keep up with the demand for new RVs.

EXPERT COMMENTS

Currently a buyer's market. Maximize earnings a couple years before selling.

The outdoor hospitality industry has been surging since the pandemic. The pandemic changed the way people take vacations, and RV parks/campgrounds are the benefactor.

FINANCING

More typical for outside financing, but when there is seller financing, the cost is less. Outside financing 4 to 5 percent interest, 20- to 30-year terms, 5 to 10 balloons.

RESOURCES

- *Appraising Manufactured (Mobile) Home Communities and Recreational Vehicle Parks* by R. S. Saia: https://www.appraisalinstitute.org/insights-and-resources/resources/books
- ARVC—National Association of RV Parks & Campgrounds: https://www.arvc.org
- Florida RV Park & Campground Association: https://farvc.org
- FRVTA—Florida RV Trade Association: https://www.frvta.org
- Good Sam: https://www.goodsam.com
- RV Industry Association: https://www.rvia.org
- RV LIFE: https://rvlife.com
- RVBusiness: https://rvbusiness.com
- RVParkStore: https://www.rvparkstore.com
- RVU: https://www.rvparkuniversity.com
- TACO—Texas Association of Campground Owners: https://tacomembers.com
- Woodall's Campground Magazine: https://woodallscm.com

Sales Consulting

| NAICS 541613 | SIC 8748-08

Rules of Thumb

- 33% annual sales includes inventory

INDUSTRY MULTIPLES

Acquisition multiples below are calculated medians using US private industry transactions. Data updated annually. Last update: August 2023.

VALUATION MULTIPLE (MEDIAN VALUE)

UNDER $1 MILLION NET SALES

MVIC/Net Sales	0.99
MVIC/Gross Profit	1.58
MVIC/SDE	2.00
MVIC/EBITDA	2.84

$1 MILLION–$5 MILLION NET SALES

MVIC/Net Sales	0.78
MVIC/Gross Profit	0.85
MVIC/SDE	2.76
MVIC/EBITDA	4.19

OVER $5 MILLION NET SALES

MVIC/Net Sales	2.17
MVIC/Gross Profit	3.62
MVIC/SDE	N/A
MVIC/EBITDA	14.16

Source: DealStats (formerly Pratt's Stats), 2023 (Portland, OR: Business Valuation Resources, LLC), www.bvresources.com/dealstats

PRICING TIPS

Price paid should be affected by current accounts surviving the exit of the owner.

Sandwich Shops

| NAICS 722513 | SIC 5812-19

| Profit $1.2 B | Wages $6.1 B | Annual Growth Future 2.6%

| | | Annual Growth Past -1.1%

Rules of Thumb

- 40%–50% annual sales plus inventory
- 2 x SDE plus inventory
- 3 x EBIT

INDUSTRY MULTIPLES

Acquisition multiples below are calculated medians using US private industry transactions. Data updated annually. Last update: August 2023.

VALUATION MULTIPLE (MEDIAN VALUE)

UNDER $1 MILLION NET SALES

MVIC/Net Sales	0.31
MVIC/Gross Profit	0.48
MVIC/SDE	1.67
MVIC/EBITDA	2.21

$1 MILLION–$5 MILLION NET SALES

MVIC/Net Sales	0.39
MVIC/Gross Profit	0.60
MVIC/SDE	2.43
MVIC/EBITDA	2.98

OVER $5 MILLION NET SALES

MVIC/Net Sales	0.89
MVIC/Gross Profit	2.08
MVIC/SDE	4.98
MVIC/EBITDA	12.81

Source: DealStats (formerly Pratt's Stats), 2023 (Portland, OR: Business Valuation Resources, LLC), www.bvresources.com/dealstats

BENCHMARK DATA

STATISTICS (SANDWICH & SUB STORE FRANCHISES)

Number of Establishments	62,381
Average Profit Margin	5.2%
Revenue per Employee	$60,700
Average Number of Employees	6.2
Average Wages per Employee	$16,384

PRODUCTS AND SERVICES SEGMENTATION

Meals dispensed without table service for consumption on premise	59.8%
Meals prepared for immediate consumption off premise	28.3%
Nonalcoholic beverages	9.2%
Full service	2.7%

INDUSTRY COSTS

Profit	5.2%
Wages	27.2%
Purchases	42.7%
Depreciation	3.1%
Marketing	2.0%
Rent & Utilities	8.1%
Other	11.7%

MARKET SHARE

Subway	37.7%
Jimmy John's	9.0%
Jersey Mike's Franchise Systems Inc.	7.7%

EXPENSES (% OF ANNUAL SALES)

Cost of Goods	28%
Occupancy Costs	10%
Payroll/Labor Costs	22%
Profit (pretax)	20%

INDUSTRY TREND

"The industry has been more successful than fellow fast-food companies at expanding their presence. Many operators have expanded their menu options. Low barriers to entry has encouraged new players to enter the industry. Profit is also expected to improve slightly as consumers start purchasing higher-priced items. Industry operators will likely need to continually innovate menus. Many domestic franchise operators will likely continue to expand internationally. Economic slowdowns caused by the pandemic have pressured profit for industry operators."

Source: IBISWorld Industry at a Glance

RESOURCES

- IBISWorld, September 2021: https://www.ibisworld.com

Satellite Telecommunications

| NAICS 517410 | Businesses/Units 470

| Profit $845.4 M | Wages $1.4 B | Annual Growth Future 6.9%

| Annual Growth Past 3.8%

INDUSTRY MULTIPLES

Acquisition multiples below are calculated medians using US private industry transactions. Data updated annually. Last update: August 2023.

VALUATION MULTIPLE (MEDIAN VALUE)

UNDER $1 MILLION NET SALES	N/A
$1 MILLION–$5 MILLION NET SALES	N/A
OVER $5 MILLION NET SALES	
MVIC/Net Sales.	2.25
MVIC/Gross Profit	4.27
MVIC/SDE	N/A
MVIC/EBITDA	9.81

Source: DealStats (formerly Pratt's Stats), 2023 (Portland, OR: Business Valuation Resources, LLC), www.bvresources.com/dealstats

BENCHMARK DATA

STATISTICS (SATELLITE TELECOMMUNICATIONS PROVIDERS)

Number of Establishments	470
Average Profit Margin	10.0%
Revenue per Employee	$926,918
Average Number of Employees.	20.8
Average Wages per Employee	$151,811

PRODUCTS AND SERVICES SEGMENTATION

Other	45.8%
Carrier services and internet backbone services	31.6%
Private network services	22.6%

MAJOR MARKET SEGMENTATION

Telecommunications and other commercial markets	54.0%
Government.	40.0%
Other	6.0%

INDUSTRY COSTS

Profit	10.0%
Wages	16.6%
Purchases	43.2%
Depreciation	10.6%
Marketing	0.5%
Rent & Utilities	3.0%
Other	16.0%

MARKET SHARE

EchoStar Corporation	19.4%
Intelsat S.A.	9.6%
SES, LLC	6.6%

INDUSTRY TREND

"Demand for satellite telecommunication has grown. Several trends have boosted revenue, including the increased globalization of economic activities and the heightened importance of connectivity and broadband access. Competition has suppressed demand growth. This growth has been countered by continued external competition from other telecommunications providers and rising interest rates that have reduced the launch of new satellites."

Source: IBISWorld Key Takeaways

RESOURCES

• IBISWorld, September 2023: https://www.ibisworld.com

Sawmills & Wood Production

	NAICS 32111		Businesses/Units 2,752	
	Profit $3.1 B		Wages $4.8 B		Annual Growth Future 1.2%
					Annual Growth Past 1.7%

INDUSTRY MULTIPLES

Acquisition multiples below are calculated medians using US private industry transactions. Data updated annually. Last update: August 2023.

VALUATION MULTIPLE (MEDIAN VALUE)

UNDER $1 MILLION NET SALES	N/A
$1 MILLION–$5 MILLION NET SALES	
MVIC/Net Sales.	0.58
MVIC/Gross Profit	1.06
MVIC/SDE	1.97
MVIC/EBITDA	1.97
OVER $5 MILLION NET SALES	
MVIC/Net Sales.	0.68
MVIC/Gross Profit	5.57
MVIC/SDE	N/A
MVIC/EBITDA	7.98

Source: DealStats (formerly Pratt's Stats), 2023 (Portland, OR: Business Valuation Resources, LLC), www.bvresources.com/dealstats

BENCHMARK DATA

STATISTICS (SAWMILLS & WOOD PRODUCTION)

Number of Establishments	2,752
Average Profit Margin	6.7%
Revenue per Employee	$537,515
Average Number of Employees. .	31.7
Average Wages per Employee . . .	$55,777

PRODUCTS AND SERVICES SEGMENTATION

Softwood lumber	38.7%
Hardwood lumber	23.8%
Wood product preservation. . . .	15.6%
Other	14.2%
Wood chips	7.7%

MAJOR MARKET SEGMENTATION

Nonresidential construction and repair	33.5%
Millwork producers	30.1%
Residential construction and repair	28.2%
Pulp, paper and paperboard mills . .	6.9%
Rail transportation	1.3%

INDUSTRY COSTS

Profit	6.7%
Wages	10.4%
Purchases	55.4%
Depreciation	2.9%
Marketing	0.0%
Rent & Utilities	2.8%
Other	21.7%

"Sawmill wood builds homes, businesses, furniture and infrastructure. The price of wood varies mildly with the movements of durable goods in the macro-economy. When housing construction exploded in 2020 during the COVID-19 pandemic, sawmills were happy to generate record incomes. Logging occurs in the United States far north and in the southeast, but wood products from these regions vary significantly. Northern pine forests produce softwoods which are better for construction, while southern hardwoods give a denser wood more suited for furniture and flooring. One of every six trees used to make homes, businesses, paper products and railroads comes from Canada, where provincial and national governments subsidize logging heavily. Understanding import tariffs and international dynamics is critical for processing the actions of domestic sawmills managers."

Source: IBISWorld Key Takeaways

RESOURCES

- IBISWorld, September 2023: https://www.ibisworld.com

Schools: Educational & Nonvocational

| NAICS 611110

Rules of Thumb

- 50%–75% annual gross sales
- 2–4 x SDE
- 3–6 x EBITDA
- 1.5–4 x EBIT

INDUSTRY MULTIPLES

Acquisition multiples below are calculated medians using US private industry transactions. Data updated annually. Last update: August 2023.

VALUATION MULTIPLE (MEDIAN VALUE)

UNDER $1 MILLION NET SALES	
MVIC/Net Sales	0.57
MVIC/Gross Profit	0.84
MVIC/SDE	2.53
MVIC/EBITDA	4.26
$1 MILLION–$5 MILLION NET SALES	
MVIC/Net Sales	0.87
MVIC/Gross Profit	0.87
MVIC/SDE	3.51
MVIC/EBITDA	4.76
OVER $5 MILLION NET SALES	N/A

Source: DealStats (formerly Pratt's Stats), 2023 (Portland, OR: Business Valuation Resources, LLC), www.bvresources.com/dealstats

PRICING TIPS

Staffing is high percentage—50 percent. There are more professional staff with bachelor's, master's, and PhD degrees.

Schools with property are, most of the time, the best to buy: longer-term financing and better rate.

Analyze lease, curriculum. The higher the roster of students, the higher the multiple.

BENCHMARK DATA

STATISTICS (BUSINESS CERTIFICATION & IT SCHOOLS)

Number of Establishments	1,708
Average Profit Margin	7.3%
Revenue per Employee	$165,083
Average Number of Employees	12.4
Average Wages per Employee	$74,842

PRODUCTS AND SERVICES SEGMENTATION

Computer and information sciences training	56.2%
Basic education and higher academic courses	29.3%
Professional development and management training	12.5%
Other	2.0%

INDUSTRY COSTS

Profit	7.3%
Wages	45.1%
Purchases	4.2%
Depreciation	1.6%
Marketing	3.5%
Rent & Utilities	7.0%
Other	31.3%

Buyers need to understand this business from top to bottom and the state rules to operate a school.

Number of students; full-time versus part-time students

EXPENSES (% OF ANNUAL SALES)

Cost of Goods	10% to 20%
Occupancy Costs	10% to 20%
Payroll/Labor Costs	40% to 50%
Profit (pretax)	20% to 30%

QUESTIONS

- Details of operations, financials, ability to grow
- Programs offered, current staff, and payroll? Is it accredited or not?
- What is the hardest part of owning this business?
- Why is the seller selling his or her business? How long is the seller willing to stay post-acquisition? Is the director willing to stay? Is there a high turnover of teachers? Is there a waiting list?
- What to understand in the business from top to bottom: expense, staffing, care of the children, state requirements, and the list goes on.
- Please provide financial and compliance audits for the last three years. How much time is left on your accreditation? Any complaints filed with your accrediting agency, state licensing agency, or the U.S. Department of Education?

INDUSTRY TREND

The trend is up as people need training.

"Certification schools benefitted from COVID-19 layoffs. Many consumers lost their jobs through the pandemic, and the industry's online certification programs were able to capture demand from those looking to upgrade their resume. Competition has pressured certification schools. On the lower end, Massively Open Online Courses (MOOCs) have given students significantly cheaper options for obtaining basic certifications. On the upper end, colleges and universities have taken demand away from certification schools as degrees and in-depth skills have become more sought-after."

Source: IBISWorld Key Takeaways

EXPERT COMMENTS

Growing industry with a large barrier to entry

FINANCING

Mostly outside financing; some owner financing with 30 to 40 percent down

RESOURCES

- IBISWorld, March 2023: https://www.ibisworld.com
- Cognia: https://www.cognia.org
- FACCM—Florida Association for Child Care Management: https://www.faccm.org
- HLC—Higher Learning Commission: https://www.hlcommission.org
- NEASC—New England Association of Schools and Colleges: https://www.neasc.org
- SACS—Southern Association of Colleges and Schools: http://www.sacs.org

Schools: Montessori

| NAICS 611110

Rules of Thumb

- 35% annual gross sales plus inventory
- 1.5–2 x SDE
- 3–4 x EBITDA

INDUSTRY MULTIPLES

Acquisition multiples below are calculated medians using US private industry transactions. Data updated annually. Last update: October 2022.

VALUATION MULTIPLE (MEDIAN VALUE)

UNDER $1 MILLION NET SALES	
MVIC/Net Sales	0.57
MVIC/Gross Profit	0.84
MVIC/SDE	2.51
MVIC/EBITDA	4.26
$1 MILLION–$5 MILLION NET SALES	
MVIC/Net Sales	0.87
MVIC/Gross Profit	0.87
MVIC/SDE	3.51
MVIC/EBITDA	4.76
OVER $5 MILLION NET SALES	N/A

Source: DealStats (formerly Pratt's Stats), 2023 (Portland, OR: Business Valuation Resources, LLC), www.bvresources.com/dealstats

PRICING TIPS

"Examples of initial expenses include: purchase or rental of a property, construction, renovations, architect, contractor, legal and financial services, classroom furnishings, Montessori learning materials, outdoor play spaces, office equipment, technology, and marketing materials.

"As you plan, be sure to project your faculty and staff salaries. Among other expenses to include in your operating budget are: rent or mortgage, facilities maintenance, depreciation, interest on loans, taxes, insurance (health, workers' compensation, school directors and officers, commercial liability), scholarships, and financial aid. You will also want to include funds for ongoing professional development and professional memberships, such as AMS membership for your school and teachers.

"Income sources can include school tuition, application fees, extended care and/ or summer activities, and fundraising. Financing options may include personal savings, small business loans, personal loans, private investors, and/or grants."

Source: "Starting a Montessori School," https://amshq.org/Educators/Montessori-Schools/Starting-a-School#finances

EXPENSES (% OF ANNUAL SALES)

Cost of Goods	N/A
Occupancy Costs	30% to 45%
Payroll/Labor Costs.	25% to 35%
Profit (pretax)	20% to 35%

QUESTIONS

- Are any of the teachers interns that will have to be replaced or paid higher salaries later on?

EXPERT COMMENTS

Focus on why the facility is for sale and what the owner plans to do after sale.

A school is most successful if enrollment is over 200 students and it has a solid curriculum with stable teachers in a high-income area.

RESOURCES

- AMS—American Montessori Society: https://amshq.org
- The International Montessori Index: https://www.montessori.edu

Schools: Tutoring & Driving

| NAICS 611691 | Businesses/Units 205,355

| Profit $924.3 M | Wages $6.6 B | Annual Growth Future 0.5%

| | | Annual Growth Past 0.4%

Rules of Thumb

- 1 x SDE + fair market value of fixed assets
- 40%–45% annual sales + fair market value of fixed assets

INDUSTRY MULTIPLES

Acquisition multiples below are calculated medians using US private industry transactions. Data updated annually. Last update: August 2023.

VALUATION MULTIPLE (MEDIAN VALUE)

UNDER $1 MILLION NET SALES

MVIC/Net Sales.	0.45
MVIC/Gross Profit	0.49
MVIC/SDE	1.85
MVIC/EBITDA	3.33

$1 MILLION–$5 MILLION NET SALES

MVIC/Net Sales.	0.75
MVIC/Gross Profit	1.32
MVIC/SDE	3.11
MVIC/EBITDA	4.54

OVER $5 MILLION NET SALES   N/A

Source: DealStats (formerly Pratt's Stats), 2023 (Portland, OR: Business Valuation Resources, LLC), www.bvresources.com/dealstats

PRICING TIPS

High barrier to entry due to increasingly higher and stricter state regulations and standards

BENCHMARK DATA

STATISTICS (TUTORING & DRIVING SCHOOLS)

Number of Establishments	205,355
Average Profit Margin	6.84%
Revenue per Employee	$36,765
Average Number of Employees.	1.9
Average Wages per Employee	$16,866

PRODUCTS AND SERVICES SEGMENTATION

Tutoring	44.1%
Other schools	25.6%
Exam preparation	18.1%
Driving schools	12.2%

INDUSTRY COSTS

Profit	6.4%
Wages	45.6%
Purchases	4.1%
Depreciation	2.9%
Marketing	3.4%
Rent & Utilities	6.9%
Other	30.7%

INDUSTRY TREND

"Intense competition has pushed down prices. Lowered prices and the proliferation of free online walkthroughs have led to muted growth for tutors and driving schools. Some segments are facing volatility. Lifestyle-based courses are extremely sensitive to changes in consumer spending, but public school tutoring and driving schools enjoy stable demand as a result of government policy. Test prep courses are facing lowered demand. Over 1,000 universities no longer require the ACT or SAT for admission, leading many high schoolers and graduates to simply avoid the tests altogether."

Source: IBISWorld Key Takeaways

RESOURCES

• IBISWorld, April 2023: https://www.ibisworld.com

Schools: Vocational & Training

	NAICS 611210		Businesses/Units 9,137

	Profit $2.2 B		Wages $5.7 B		Annual Growth Future 0.5%

         | Annual Growth Past 0.4%

Rules of Thumb

- 75%–100% annual sales
- 2–4 x SDE plus inventory
- 3–4 x EBIT
- 4–6 x EBITDA

PRICING TIPS

Accreditation and federal student funding make the price of the school go up. Pricing is normally based on cash flow of the school.

BENCHMARK DATA

STATISTICS (TRADE AND TECHNICAL SCHOOLS)

Number of Establishments 9,137
Average Profit Margin 13.6%
Revenue per Employee $157,756
Average Number of Employees. . . . 11.4
Average Wages per Employee . . . $54,952

PRODUCTS AND SERVICES SEGMENTATION

Other technical and trade schools . . . 53.4%
Flight training schools 20.8%
Cosmetology and barber schools . . . 13.0%
Apprenticeship training schools . . . 12.8%

INDUSTRY COSTS

Profit 13.6%
Wages 34.8%
Purchases 4.2%
Depreciation 3.9%
Marketing 3.5%
Rent & Utilities 7.1%
Other 32.9%

EXPENSES (% OF ANNUAL SALES)

Cost of Goods . . . . . . 10% to 20%
Occupancy Costs . . . . . . 10% to 20%
Payroll/Labor Costs. . . . . 40% to 50%
Profit (pretax) . . . . . . 20% to 30%

QUESTIONS

- Details of operation, financials, ability to grow

MARKET TRENDS

Explain the program and look at the overall process. If you receive state funding, how can a new owner keep that?

INDUSTRY TREND

Growing trend over the next few years

"Economic growth in the wake of COVID-19 has dampened demand for vocational schools. The industry ultimately benefitted from spiking unemployment amid the pandemic, but the recovery's addition of new jobs has reduced the need for workers to upgrade their resumes. Trade and technical schools faced shutdowns amid the pandemic. While some had already integrated online platforms to augment training where possible, the high degree of hands-on instruction the industry provides forced many schools to temporarily close down entirely."

Source: IBISWorld Key Takeaways

Barrier to entry due to regulations

FINANCING

Mostly outside financing; some owner financing with 30 to 40 percent down

RESOURCES

- IBISWorld, October 2023: https://www.ibisworld.com
- RWM—Real Work Matters: https://www.rwm.org
- Schools For Sale, Inc.: https://schoolsforsale.com

S

Seafood Preparation

| NAICS 311710 | Businesses/Units 3,586

| Profit $355.8 M | Wages $1.9 B | Annual Growth Future 0.9%

| | | Annual Growth Past 0.6%

INDUSTRY MULTIPLES

Acquisition multiples below are calculated medians using US private industry transactions. Data updated annually. Last update: August 2023.

VALUATION MULTIPLE (MEDIAN VALUE)

UNDER $1 MILLION NET SALES	N/A
$1 MILLION–$5 MILLION NET SALES	
MVIC/Net Sales.	0.18
MVIC/Gross Profit	0.78
MVIC/SDE	5.81
MVIC/EBITDA	N/A
OVER $5 MILLION NET SALES	
MVIC/Net Sales.	0.71
MVIC/Gross Profit	1.90
MVIC/SDE	2.79
MVIC/EBITDA	10.70

Source: DealStats (formerly Pratt's Stats), 2023 (Portland, OR: Business Valuation Resources, LLC), www.bvresources.com/dealstats

BENCHMARK DATA

STATISTICS (SEAFOOD PREPARATION)

Number of Establishments .	3,586
Average Profit Margin	2.1%
Revenue per Employee .	$470,804
Average Number of Employees.	10.1
Average Wages per Employee .	$54,045

PRODUCTS AND SERVICES SEGMENTATION

Prepared frozen fish	35.1%
Prepared fresh fish and other fresh seafood	23.7%
Prepared frozen shellfish	19.5%
Other prepared fresh and frozen seafood	11.0%
Canned fish and seafood	10.7%

MAJOR MARKET SEGMENTATION

Fish and seafood wholesalers .	62.8%
Food service industries.	14.7%
Mass merchandisers and grocers .	11.8%

Other distributors 8.8%
Export markets 1.9%

INDUSTRY COSTS

Profit 2.1%
Wages 11.5%
Purchases 61.0%
Depreciation 1.1%
Marketing 0.3%
Rent & Utilities 2.2%
Other 21.8%

INDUSTRY TREND

"Seafood production has benefited from stable demand and rising product prices. Following the pandemic, the price of seafood soared globally. Import penetration into the industry has risen. The large fishing stocks and lower labor costs of Asian countries has enabled them to sell seafood in the American market, eroding the position of domestic producers."

Source: IBISWorld Key Takeaways

RESOURCES

• IBISWorld, September 2023: https://www.ibisworld.com

Security Services/Systems/Alarm Companies

| NAICS 561621 | SIC 7382-02

Rules of Thumb

• 50% annual sales includes inventory
• 2–3 x SDE includes inventory
• 3 x EBIT
• 4 x EBITDA

INDUSTRY MULTIPLES

Acquisition multiples below are calculated medians using US private industry transactions. Data updated annually. Last update: August 2023.

VALUATION MULTIPLE (MEDIAN VALUE)

UNDER $1 MILLION NET SALES
MVIC/Net Sales. 0.77
MVIC/Gross Profit 1.44
MVIC/SDE 2.38
MVIC/EBITDA 2.95

$1 MILLION–$5 MILLION NET SALES
MVIC/Net Sales. 0.49
MVIC/Gross Profit 0.92
MVIC/SDE 3.28
MVIC/EBITDA 5.78

OVER $5 MILLION NET SALES
MVIC/Net Sales. 1.08
MVIC/Gross Profit 2.36
MVIC/SDE 4.18
MVIC/EBITDA 15.50

Source: DealStats (formerly Pratt's Stats), 2023 (Portland, OR: Business Valuation Resources, LLC), www.bvresources.com/dealstats

PRICING TIPS

Security alarm companies generally sell on a multiple of their recurring monthly revenue. Monitoring contracts are key to the deal.

BENCHMARK DATA

STATISTICS (SECURITY ALARM SERVICES)

Number of Establishments	87,241
Average Profit Margin	5.7%
Revenue per Employee	$162,997
Average Number of Employees	2.5
Average Wages per Employee	$48,527

PRODUCTS AND SERVICES SEGMENTATION

Nonresidential security system installation services	40.6%
Nonresidential security monitoring services	24.7%
Residential security monitoring services	18.8%
Other	8.8%
Locksmith	7.1%

MAJOR MARKET SEGMENTATION

Business and commercial clients	52.2%
Residential clients	30.5%
State and local governments	7.1%
Nonprofit organizations	5.5%
Federal government	4.7%

INDUSTRY COSTS

Profit	5.7%
Wages	29.8%
Purchases	36.4%
Depreciation	1.4%
Marketing	1.7%
Rent & Utilities	2.4%
Other	22.5%

MARKET SHARE

ADT Inc.	19.5%
Johnson Controls International PLC	3.5%
API Group Corporation	1.1%

STATISTICS (SECURITY SERVICES)

Number of Establishments	14,918
Average Profit Margin	5.7%
Revenue per Employee	$54,679
Average Number of Employees	59.7
Average Wages per Employee	$32,456

PRODUCTS AND SERVICES SEGMENTATION

Unarmed security guard services	57.2%
Armed security guard services	18.0%
Investigation services	15.7%
Armored vehicle services	6.6%
Other services	2.5%

MAJOR MARKET SEGMENTATION

Other clients	53.6%
Government and NGO clients	21.1%
Banking institutions	16.2%
Retail businesses	9.1%

INDUSTRY COSTS

Profit	5.7%
Wages	59.4%
Purchases	7.9%
Depreciation	1.2%
Marketing	1.6%
Rent & Utilities	2.3%
Other	21.7%

MARKET SHARE

Allied Universal Security Services LLC.	13.7%
Securitas AB	11.1%
Contemporary Service Corporation	6.7%
Brink's Co	1.7%

Generally, there should be 500 paying monthly monitoring accounts for every one technician.

EXPENSES (% OF ANNUAL SALES)

Cost of Goods	40%
Occupancy Costs	05% to 10%
Payroll/Labor Costs.	40%
Profit (pretax)	10%

QUESTIONS

- A buyer wants to see a seller's contracts and the terms of the contracts.
- Do they own the central station? If not, do they own the phone lines that connect to central station? What percentage of their customers are contracted?
- Type of guard services and customer list. Most guard companies have one major client.

INDUSTRY TREND

"A reopening and growing economy in 2021 brought renewed demand for industry services. Governmental clients have increased investment in security systems. Large operators have acquired numerous competitors to grow their businesses. Increased residential construction activity is anticipated to drive demand for new security system installations. Demand for data analytics capabilities is anticipated to drive industry revenue. Home automation and control will likely continue to be a hotbed for product innovation. Industry profit has declined due partly to low demand for commercial property. An economic recovery in the latter half of the period has aided rising demand from downstream markets. Industry operators have pursued strategic acquisitions. State and federal government agencies represent a major market for industry operators. Major players will be able to provide enhanced and comprehensive services. The number of industry operators is expected to increase. The industry's largest operators are expected to compete by offering integrated security systems. Industry profit growth has been limited due to intense price competition."

Source: IBISWorld Industry at a Glance

EXPERT COMMENTS

There are many barriers to entry, specifically having the licenses in place to run the business. A buyer with no experience would need four years just to obtain the licensing.

An alarm company can be run from any location because all work is completed at a customer's home or business. They are very marketable and are not easy to replicate. The hurdle is that a new owner needs to hold a class C and D license for low-voltage wiring, which is a 3 to 5 year process to obtain.

FINANCING

Easily financed through SBA. In any deal, there will be a holdback of 10 to 25 percent of the deal for a period of 13 months for any customer loss.

There are industry specific financing companies that will hold contracted accounts as collateral. Also the SBA has gone to 10 years because of the RMR.

RESOURCES

- IBISWorld, September 2023: https://www.ibisworld.com
- IBISWorld, April 2023: https://www.ibisworld.com
- Alarm.org: https://alarm.org
- ASIS International: https://www.asisonline.org
- ESA—Electronic Security Association: https://esaweb.org
- SIA—Security Industry Association: https://www.securityindustry.org

---

Self-Storage (Mini Storage)

| NAICS 531130 | Businesses/Units 191,570 |

| Profit $12 B | Wages $3.1 B | Annual Growth Future 0.6% |

| | | Annual Growth Past 2.1% |

Rules of Thumb

- 1 x EBITDA

INDUSTRY MULTIPLES

Acquisition multiples below are calculated medians using US private industry transactions. Data updated annually. Last update: August 2023.

VALUATION MULTIPLE (MEDIAN VALUE)

UNDER $1 MILLION NET SALES
MVIC/Net Sales	4.03
MVIC/Gross Profit	4.40
MVIC/SDE	9.03
MVIC/EBITDA	11.65

$1 MILLION–$5 MILLION NET SALES
MVIC/Net Sales	4.73
MVIC/Gross Profit	6.83
MVIC/SDE	4.25
MVIC/EBITDA	18.58

OVER $5 MILLION NET SALES
MVIC/Net Sales	1.45
MVIC/Gross Profit	2.26
MVIC/SDE	N/A
MVIC/EBITDA	2.93

Source: DealStats (formerly Pratt's Stats), 2023 (Portland, OR: Business Valuation Resources, LLC), www.bvresources.com/dealstats

PRICING TIPS

"Current rule of thumb: land cost = 25%–30% of total development cost. State of the art facility of 60,000–80,000 net rentable sq. ft., cost over $45–$65 per sq. ft."

Source: "Self Storage Introductory Guide," Self Storage Association + SSA Online University Distance Learning Center, https://www.selfstorage.org/LinkClick.aspx?fileticket=AbINHWcUX9w%3D&portalid=0

BENCHMARK DATA

Number of Establishments	191,570
Average Profit Margin	41.0%
Revenue per Employee	$133,723
Average Number of Employees.	1.1
Average Wages per Employee	$14,127

PRODUCTS AND SERVICES SEGMENTATION

10-by-10-foot storage spaces	26.1%
10-by-20-foot storage spaces	22.1%
10-by-15-foot storage spaces	16.8%
Five-by-10-foot storage spaces	13.1%
Other	11.6%
10-by-25-foot storage spaces	5.5%
Five-by-five-foot storage spaces	3.9%
10-by-30-foot storage spaces	0.9%

MAJOR MARKET SEGMENTATION

Long-term residential customers	48.9%
Short-term residential customers	21.0%
Commercial operators	18.4%
Military	5.9%
Students	5.8%

INDUSTRY COSTS

Profit	41.0%
Wages	10.5%
Purchases	2.0%
Depreciation	13.1%
Marketing	1.1%
Rent & Utilities	3.7%
Other	28.6%

MARKET SHARE

Public Storage	1.4%
Extra Space Storage Inc.	0.7%
CubeSmart	0.4%

EXPENSES (% OF ANNUAL SALES)

Profit (pretax)	05%

QUESTIONS

- Who manages the site and are they willing to stay on? Can existing financing be assumed?
- Occupancy and waiting list
- Management turnover

INDUSTRY TREND

"This industry is in a special position to prosper in both good and bad economic times. In a strong economy, consumers accumulate more material goods. On the other side, a recession will compel people to downsize and businesses to close their doors. Both of these situations raise the demand for sector services. Going forward, increasing market saturation will lead to even higher price competition and increased customer acquisition expenditures."

Source: IBISWorld Key Takeaways

"Self-storage has long been lauded as a recession-resistant industry. A few years ago, conventional wisdom told us that a healthy supply of self-storage space lived at six net rentable square feet per capita. Today, most people in the industry will tell you that the number rests anywhere between 10 and 13 square feet per capita, depending on the region."

S

Source: "Self-storage is on a growth kick—and it's not slowing down" by Michael Baillargeon, March 30, 2022, https://rejournals.com/self-storage-is-on-a-growth-kick-and-its-not-slowing-down/

EXPERT COMMENTS

This is a real estate purchase with a business element attached to it. The value of the underlying real estate controls a large part of the value of the property. Management is more important than most people realize.

FINANCING

"85 percent owners have 3 or fewer sites.

Usually a $3,000,000 or more investment—owner equity plus local bank, insurance co., friends & family, country club friends or other invested equity

Self-storage is popular as a real estate investment trust (R.E.I.T.).

Sold on its cash flow performance: appreciation potential; continued rent increases possible"

Source: "Self Storage Introductory Guide," Self Storage Association + SSA Online University Distance Learning Center, https://www.selfstorage.org/LinkClick.aspx?fileticket=AbINHWcUX9w%3D&portalid=0

RESOURCES

- IBISWorld, October 2023: https://www.ibisworld.com
- ISS—Inside Self-Storage: https://www.insideselfstorage.com
- Self-Storage Now!: https://www.modernstoragemedia.com/selfstoragenow
- SSA—Self Storage Association—An excellent site with lots of information: https://www.selfstorage.org

Senior Helpers (Franchise)

| NAICS 621610 | Businesses/Units 332

Rules of Thumb

- 40%–45% annual sales

INDUSTRY MULTIPLES

Acquisition multiples below are calculated medians using US private industry transactions. Data updated annually. Last update: August 2023.

VALUATION MULTIPLE (MEDIAN VALUE)

UNDER $1 MILLION NET SALES

MVIC/Net Sales.	0.40
MVIC/Gross Profit	0.69
MVIC/SDE	2.53
MVIC/EBITDA	4.62

$1 MILLION–$5 MILLION NET SALES

MVIC/Net Sales.	0.52
MVIC/Gross Profit	0.82
MVIC/SDE	3.03
MVIC/EBITDA	4.91

OVER $5 MILLION NET SALES

MVIC/Net Sales.	1.09
MVIC/Gross Profit	2.37

```
MVIC/SDE  .    .    .    .    .    .    .    5.31
MVIC/EBITDA  .    .    .    .    .    .    .    9.36
```

Source: DealStats (formerly Pratt's Stats), 2023 (Portland, OR: Business Valuation Resources, LLC), www.bvresources.com/dealstats

PRICING TIPS

Approx. Total Investment: $127,800 to $171,800

RESOURCES

- Senior Helpers: https://www.seniorhelpers.com
- Franchise information: https://www.seniorhelpersfranchise.com

---

Service Businesses (in General)

Rules of Thumb

- 70%–75% annual sales
- 2–3 x SDE
- 4 x EBITDA
- 2–4 x EBIT

PRICING TIPS

The market method (SDE or EBITDA multiplier method) will be utilized by nearly 100 percent of buyers regardless of the size of the transaction. The income method (DCF model) will be utilized by sophisticated financial buyers (PE and family office) primarily for larger service opportunities (excess of $2M EBITDA) that have a demonstrated history of growth. Expect buyers to request some element of seller financing and potentially even rollover equity or an earnout as service businesses are generally asset-light and buyers want to ensure continuity post-closing.

Price is largely dependent on what the current owner's role in day-to-day operations is.

I use terms like owner benefit with the buyers and sellers. The biggest difficulty many novice brokers have is reconstructing the profit and loss statements and the taxes. Many times, the sellers have their point of view and the buyers, another. Sellers usually feel they are selling for less than the business is worth and buyers thing they are paying too much. To be a successful business broker, you need to help resolve numerous issues; it's a give-and-take task. Blatant honesty has always been the best policy. I always ask myself, "If this were my business, what is fair?" Also, if I were a buyer, "What would I pay and under what terms and conditions?" Seller assistance and training are important elements in any business sale, ensuring a smooth transfer.

The valuation multiples depend on a variety of factors, including:

Percent of recurring revenue

Risk assessment regarding usage of undocumented workers

Growth trends

Transferability of business including management, systems, relationships, and technology

Rent, lease costs have skyrocketed.

Successful businesses in the service space generally have at least a moderate barrier to entry, recurring revenue, low turnover within a skilled workforce, low capex requirements, and a proficient management team so the business is not reliant on a single owner or keyman/woman.

Revenue per employee: a higher revenue per employee generally indicates better productivity and operational efficiency. Customer retention rate: high customer retention is a sign of customer satisfaction, loyalty, and the ability to deliver consistent value. Profit margin: service businesses typically have lower overhead costs compared to retail businesses, so a healthy profit margin is crucial for sustainability and growth. Utilization rate: a high utilization rate indicates effective resource management and productivity. Average transaction value: increasing the average transaction value can lead to higher revenue without necessarily increasing the number of customers. Employee turnover rate: low turnover is generally preferable, as it signifies a stable and satisfied workforce. Customer feedback and reviews: good reviews can boost reputation, attract new customers, and lead to repeat business. Service delivery time: tracking and improving service delivery time can enhance customer experience and operational effectiveness. Client acquisition cost: lower client acquisition costs mean more efficient marketing and sales efforts. Employee training and development investment: investing in employee training and development can lead to a more skilled and motivated workforce, which ultimately benefits the service business.

EXPENSES (% OF ANNUAL SALES)

Cost of Goods	30% to 35%
Occupancy Costs	10% to 15%
Payroll/Labor Costs.	20% to 30%
Profit (pretax)	10% to 20%

QUESTIONS

- Please explain the relationships you have with your top 10 customers. Are any customers more than 20 percent of revenue?
- Please explain your day-to-day involvement in the business?
- Do you have any family in the business?
- Discuss your management team. Have you experienced significant turnover over the last five years?
- How difficult/easy is the recruitment of new employees?
- Who are your top competitors? Why do customers choose to work with you over them?
- What growth opportunities would you capitalize on if you were not selling the business?
- Experience and financial means, and motivation for buying a business
- What percentage of your revenue is recurring in nature?
- What percentage is contracted?
- How diversified is your client base in terms of geography and industry?
- What are the roles of your W2 employees and what would I need to do to retain them?
- How much time and support are you willing to provide after close? Will you agree to make yourself available as a consultant on a paid basis?
- In your opinion, what is the smoothest way to transition the business without adversely impacting our standard of service, client relationships, or our internal relationships with key employees?

- Do you use E-Verify for your employees?
- Are your subcontractors properly treated per IRS requirements? Should any of them be treated as an employee per the IRS? Have you had a lawyer review your employee and 1099 contractor classifications?

INDUSTRY TREND

Digital transformation: The ongoing trend of digital transformation is likely to continue impacting service businesses. Companies may adopt advanced technologies, automation, and artificial intelligence to streamline operations, enhance customer experience, and improve overall efficiency.

Remote work and virtual services: The Covid pandemic accelerated the adoption of remote work and virtual services. Even as the pandemic subsides, many service businesses may continue to offer remote options to cater to changing customer preferences and to access a broader talent pool.

Personalization and customer experience: Service businesses are expected to focus more on personalized customer experiences. Leveraging data analytics and customer insights, companies may tailor their services to meet individual needs and preferences, thus building stronger customer loyalty.

Sustainability and social responsibility: Consumers are increasingly conscious of environmental and social issues. Service businesses that demonstrate a commitment to sustainability and social responsibility may gain a competitive edge and attract like-minded customers.

Subscription and membership models: Subscription-based and membership models have gained popularity in various industries. Service businesses may explore offering subscription plans or membership packages to ensure recurring revenue and build long-term customer relationships.

Evolving workforce dynamics: The workforce composition is evolving, with a growing number of freelancers and independent contractors. Service businesses may embrace a more flexible workforce model to tap into specialized skills and control costs.

Data security and privacy: With the rise of digital services, data security and privacy concerns are becoming increasingly important. Service businesses will need to prioritize data protection and comply with evolving regulations to maintain customer trust.

Rise of e-learning and online training: As remote work continues to be prevalent, the demand for e-learning and online training services may increase. Service businesses catering to professional development and skill enhancement could see growth.

Hybrid service delivery: Hybrid service delivery models that combine in-person and digital interactions may become more common, providing customers with greater flexibility and convenience.

Industry-specific innovations: Each service business sector may witness unique trends and innovations depending on changing customer needs, advancements in technology, and market dynamics.

I see continued growth and consolidation of mom-and-pop businesses into larger networks that have relatively more sophisticated management, systems, and processes.

EXPERT COMMENTS

Sellers care deeply about a buyer maintaining their legacy and upholding their customer and employee commitments to satisfaction and quality service. Focus on building a personal relationship with the seller so they know you are also invested in the same. Focus on approaching businesses where you have a relevant background or can add value and have a vision for growth over the long term.

Advice for buying a business in the service industry: thorough due diligence; acquire industry-specific knowledge; consider growth potential; customer base and reputation; understand the competitive landscape and how the business differentiates itself from competitors; assess the financial health of the business, including revenue, expenses, profit margins, and cash flow; evaluate the skills and expertise of the existing team.

Advice for selling a business in the service industry: prepare comprehensive documentation (organize all financial records, customer data, contracts, and other pertinent documents in preparation for the sale); accurate valuation; enhance curb appeal (present the business in the best possible light); maintain confidentiality throughout the selling process to avoid disruption to the business and customer uncertainty; market the business effectively (utilize various marketing channels to reach potential buyers, including industry-specific platforms, business broker networks, and online marketplaces); be transparent; negotiation expertise; be prepared to support the new owner during the transition period, by providing training and assistance to ensure a smooth handover.

Come to an agreement to co-pilot the business along with the buyer/seller for 60 days after close and have the seller available on an hourly consulting agreement for another 12 months. Immediately lock in key employees by offering an immediate sign-on bonus that is paid immediately and returned to the buyer on a pro-rated basis if the employees leave within 6 months of the close. Pay close attention to the legal status of employees and 1099 subcontractors as well as the treatment of 1099 subcontractors. Quite often, some of them legally will need to be treated as employees by the business.

It's very easy to open a janitorial business. The businesses that thrive in the long term, however, have strong quality control and customer support systems in place. These businesses are rare and highly marketable.

FINANCING

As a firm, most of our transactions are < $5M in enterprise value and the buyer utilizes SBA 7(a) financing. As a rule of thumb, I would say most deals are 10 to 20 percent buyer equity (cash), 10 to 20 percent seller note, and 60 to 80 percent bank financing. Very rarely do we see no bank involved. For service businesses, we may see forgivable note structures, especially when dealing with businesses with large customer concentration or keyman risk. For larger transactions, we have also seen some buyers insisting on sellers maintaining a minority rollover equity position. Deals that are larger than $10M have increasingly become a challenge due to the return targets of more sophisticated buyers. Basically, interest rates have squeezed the returns that private equity had been used to and many are still adjusting. Along these lines, the best buyers for larger or more middle-market transactions are to identify buyers that have a dedicated roll-up strategy; they will pay more than they want to in the face of competition.

Usually, my sales are cash or some seller financing. Rarely do I use institutional financing such as SBA or other lenders. Some areas have groups that help new buyers with cash & training.

Seller financing and or SBA 7(a) loan. Typically seller financing of 20 to 35 percent paid over 12 to 24 months at WSJ prime interest.

This really depends on the growth rate of the business. The higher the growth rate, the higher the percentage of cash in the transaction. Recently, I completed a $7.1 million all-cash deal with a $300K holdback.

Lower middle market deals: 75 percent cash and 25 percent earnout/seller financing

Main Street deals: Down payment of at least 35 percent with the remainder being financed through an SBA loan

ServiceMaster Clean (Franchise)

| NAICS 561720 | Businesses/Units 2,099

Rules of Thumb

• 55%–60% annual sales plus inventory

INDUSTRY MULTIPLES

Acquisition multiples below are calculated medians using US private industry transactions. Data updated annually. Last update: August 2023.

VALUATION MULTIPLE (MEDIAN VALUE)

UNDER $1 MILLION NET SALES

MVIC/Net Sales.	0.59
MVIC/Gross Profit	0.76
MVIC/SDE	2.03
MVIC/EBITDA	2.92

$1 MILLION–$5 MILLION NET SALES

MVIC/Net Sales.	0.45
MVIC/Gross Profit	1.02
MVIC/SDE	2.86
MVIC/EBITDA	4.05

OVER $5 MILLION NET SALES

MVIC/Net Sales.	0.53
MVIC/Gross Profit	2.26
MVIC/SDE	4.26
MVIC/EBITDA	5.48

Source: DealStats (formerly Pratt's Stats), 2023 (Portland, OR: Business Valuation Resources, LLC), www.bvresources.com/dealstats

PRICING TIPS

Approx. Total Investment: $252,675 to $358,810

RESOURCES

• ServiceMaster Clean: https://www.servicemasterclean.com
• Franchise information: https://franchise.servicemasterclean.com
• ServiceMaster: https://www.servicemaster.com

SERVPRO (Franchise)

| NAICS 561720 | Businesses/Units 2,176

Rules of Thumb

- 90%–95% annual sales plus inventory

INDUSTRY MULTIPLES

Acquisition multiples below are calculated medians using US private industry transactions. Data updated annually. Last update: August 2023.

VALUATION MULTIPLE (MEDIAN VALUE)

UNDER $1 MILLION NET SALES

MVIC/Net Sales.	0.59
MVIC/Gross Profit	0.76
MVIC/SDE	2.03
MVIC/EBITDA	2.92

$1 MILLION–$5 MILLION NET SALES

MVIC/Net Sales.	0.45
MVIC/Gross Profit	1.02
MVIC/SDE	2.86
MVIC/EBITDA	4.05

OVER $5 MILLION NET SALES

MVIC/Net Sales.	0.53
MVIC/Gross Profit	2.26
MVIC/SDE	4.26
MVIC/EBITDA	5.48

Source: DealStats (formerly Pratt's Stats), 2023 (Portland, OR: Business Valuation Resources, LLC), www.bvresources.com/dealstats

PRICING TIPS

Approx. Total Investment: $236,270 to $296,775

RESOURCES

- SERVPRO: https://www.servpro.com
- Franchise information: https://www.servprofranchise.com

Shoe Stores

NAICS 458210	SIC 5661-01	Businesses/Units 37,683
Profit $2.1 B	Wages $6.8 B	Annual Growth Future 1.8%
		Annual Growth Past 0.7%

Rules of Thumb

- 15%–20% annual sales plus inventory

BENCHMARK DATA

STATISTICS (SHOE STORES)

Number of Establishments	37,683
Average Profit Margin	3.5%
Revenue per Employee	$191,963
Average Number of Employees.	8.6
Average Wages per Employee	$21,226

PRODUCTS AND SERVICES SEGMENTATION

Women's nonathletic shoes	26.6%
Men's athletic shoes	22.8%
Children's shoes	13.6%

Men's nonathletic shoes 11.7%
Women's athletic shoes. 10.5%
Clothing, accessories and other . . . 9.5%
Other shoes 5.3%

INDUSTRY COSTS

Profit 3.5%
Wages 11.1%
Purchases 51.1%
Depreciation 0.9%
Marketing 2.4%
Rent & Utilities 10.7%
Other 20.3%

MARKET SHARE

Foot Locker, Inc. 10.4%
Designer Brands Inc. 4.4%

INDUSTRY TREND

"Despite fluctuations in revenue, the industry has grown over the last few years. The COVID-19 pandemic and fluctuating consumer confidence caused growth to be inconsistent during the period, but online shopping help the industry continue to grow. Over the five years to 2028, the Shoe Stores industry's performance is expected to increase, following the declines experienced during the current period. A rise in per capita disposable income, coupled with the increasing popularity of online shopping and improvement in consumer confidence contributes to this growth."

Source: IBISWorld Key Takeaways

RESOURCES

- IBISWorld, September 2023: https://www.ibisworld.com
- FDRA—Footwear Distributors & Retailers of America: https://fdra.org/key-issues-and-advocacy/footwear-retail/
- FN—Footwear News: https://footwearnews.com
- NSRA—National Shoe Retailers Association: https://www.nsra.org

Shuttle Services

| NAICS 485999

| Profit $71.4 M | Wages $441.7 M | Annual Growth Future 6.7%

| Annual Growth Past -3.3%

Rules of Thumb

- 3 x EBITDA plus the value of the vehicles

INDUSTRY MULTIPLES

Acquisition multiples below are calculated medians using US private industry transactions. Data updated annually. Last update: August 2023.

VALUATION MULTIPLE (MEDIAN VALUE)

UNDER $1 MILLION NET SALES
MVIC/Net Sales 0.53
MVIC/Gross Profit 0.59
MVIC/SDE 1.59

MVIC/EBITDA 3.79

$1 MILLION–$5 MILLION NET SALES
MVIC/Net Sales 0.46
MVIC/Gross Profit 0.50
MVIC/SDE 2.21
MVIC/EBITDA 2.44

OVER $5 MILLION NET SALES
MVIC/Net Sales 0.42
MVIC/Gross Profit 0.42
MVIC/SDE 3.22
MVIC/EBITDA 4.34

Source: DealStats (formerly Pratt's Stats), 2023 (Portland, OR: Business Valuation Resources, LLC),
www.bvresources.com/dealstats

BENCHMARK DATA

STATISTICS (AIRPORT SHUTTLE OPERATORS)

Number of Establishments 845
Average Profit Margin 6.9%
Revenue per Employee $62,600
Average Number of Employees . . . 23.5
Average Wages per Employee . . . $25,661

PRODUCTS AND SERVICES SEGMENTATION

Local shuttle services 50.1%
Other services 28.9%
Long-distance shuttle services . . . 21.0%

INDUSTRY COSTS

Profit 6.9%
Wages 42.7%
Purchases 9.9%
Depreciation 6.3%
Marketing 0.4%
Rent & Utilities 3.0%
Other 30.8%

INDUSTRY TREND

"Shuttle operators depend on demand from passengers seeking transportation services. The industry has experienced turbulence amid heightened competition. Operators compete with other providers that offer identical or substitute services. Positive economic conditions are expected to increase consumers' propensity to travel. Price-based competition from ride-share applications will likely continue. Major cities have increased their investment in public transportation. Door-to-door services have resulted in stronger external competition."

Source: IBISWorld Industry at a Glance

RESOURCES

• IBISWorld, November 2021: https://www.ibisworld.com

Sign Companies

| NAICS 339950

Rules of Thumb

• 50%–60% annual sales includes inventory
• 2.5–3 x SDE includes inventory

- 3.5–5 x EBITDA
- 3 x EBIT

INDUSTRY MULTIPLES

Acquisition multiples below are calculated medians using US private industry transactions. Data updated annually. Last update: August 2023.

VALUATION MULTIPLE (MEDIAN VALUE)

UNDER $1 MILLION NET SALES

MVIC/Net Sales.	0.53
MVIC/Gross Profit	0.80
MVIC/SDE	2.10
MVIC/EBITDA	3.12

$1 MILLION–$5 MILLION NET SALES

MVIC/Net Sales.	0.48
MVIC/Gross Profit	0.83
MVIC/SDE	2.98
MVIC/EBITDA	4.33

OVER $5 MILLION NET SALES

MVIC/Net Sales.	0.62
MVIC/Gross Profit	1.55
MVIC/SDE	4.60
MVIC/EBITDA	5.12

Source: DealStats (formerly Pratt's Stats), 2023 (Portland, OR: Business Valuation Resources, LLC), www.bvresources.com/dealstats

PRICING TIPS

Independently owned sign companies range from 1.5 x SDE for the small, heavily owner-dependent businesses, to 3.0 x SDE for the larger businesses with lower owner dependence. Also, look for heavy concentration in industries and with individual clients; this can cause unbankability.

Rules of thumb depend on the earnings of the business. The higher the earnings, the higher the multiples. Owners in this industry need to be careful not to let one customer become too big and therefore dominate the revenue. Customer diversity is important to the valuation.

BENCHMARK DATA

STATISTICS (SIGN & BANNER MANUFACTURING FRANCHISES)

Number of Establishments	16
Average Profit Margin	4.5%
Revenue per Employee	$123,000
Average Number of Employees.	7.4
Average Wages per Employee	$45,763

PRODUCTS AND SERVICES SEGMENTATION

Banners and flags	24.6%
Building signs	23.2%
Trade show exhibits.	20.6%
Point-of-sale displays	13.6%
Electric signs	13.2%
Other	4.8%

MAJOR MARKET SEGMENTATION

Accommodation and food services	32.9%
Professional services	25.4%
Other retailers	24.5%

Car dealers and gas stations 10.3%
Other 6.9%

INDUSTRY COSTS

Profit 4.5%
Wages 36.8%
Purchases 39.8%
Depreciation 1.7%
Marketing 0.6%
Rent & Utilities 3.3%
Other 13.5%

MARKET SHARE

FASTSIGNS International Inc. 52.7%
Signarama 31.5%
Image360 . . . . 22.8%

Benchmarks vary greatly depending on what types of signs the company manufactures, if they have a retail presence, if they install themselves, and how much
they outsource.

EXPENSES (% OF ANNUAL SALES)

Cost of Goods . . . . . . 25% to 35%
Occupancy Costs . . . . . 10% to 20%
Payroll/Labor Costs. . . . . 20% to 25%
Profit (pretax) . . . . . . 15% to 25%

QUESTIONS

- Buyers should ask sellers their role in the company, and what a day in the life
  of the owner looks like today.
- Customer diversity in terms of industries served and revenue? Status of
  equipment? Tenure of employees?
- Responsibilities of the various employees?
- Are you reporting all your sales on your financials and tax returns?
- Is there any personal expense going through the business?
- What is your view on customer service?
- Tell me about your worst customer experience and how you handled it.

INDUSTRY TREND

I see the industry staying fairly level in the next few years. The demand for
signage was huge with Covid; and businesses in states that deemed the workers
essential—and that already offered online ordering—benefited greatly. Likewise,
sign businesses that were shut down lost market share and closed their doors.

The technology continues to improve, providing equipment producing high-
er-resolution prints, and at faster speeds. The implementation of flatbed printers
has greatly improved labor efficiency.

"The industry has declined despite improving demand for general signage.
Strong demand notwithstanding, franchises have been exiting the industry in
droves. The full burden of material cost increases has reduced profitability.
Domestic demand for signage is expected to rise over the next five years. Digital
products are the fastest-growing source of revenue for sign producers. High
price-based competition will inhibit industry operators from passing costs downstream. The industry's decline is structural and will likely continue regardless of
trends in demand."

Source: IBISWorld Industry at a Glance

EXPERT COMMENTS

Keep your employees happy; each one of them has the potential to cripple the business if they leave, and there isn't sufficient cross-training or backup plans.

FINANCING

Typically less than $5 million, these are great candidates for SBA 7a loans and also rollover retirement products through a company like Benetrends. They are typically asset sales unless there are government contracts.

Third-party financing is usually available for a good, profitable business in this industry. However, if not performing well, then seller financing may be required. Almost all of our sales in this industry are financed via third-party SBA-approved lenders.

RESOURCES

- IBISWorld, October 2022: https://www.ibisworld.com
- Graphics Pro: https://graphics-pro.com
- ISA—International Sign Association: https://www.signs.org
- SDG—Sign & Digital Graphics magazine: https://sdgmag.com
- SGIA—Specialty Graphic Imaging Association: https://www.sgia.org
- Signs of the Times: https://www.signsofthetimes.com

Signarama (Franchise)

| NAICS 339950 | Businesses/Units 387

Rules of Thumb

- 55%–60% annual sales plus inventory

INDUSTRY MULTIPLES

Acquisition multiples below are calculated medians using US private industry transactions. Data updated annually. Last update: August 2023.

VALUATION MULTIPLE (MEDIAN VALUE)

UNDER $1 MILLION NET SALES	
MVIC/Net Sales	0.53
MVIC/Gross Profit	0.80
MVIC/SDE	2.10
MVIC/EBITDA	3.12
$1 MILLION–$5 MILLION NET SALES	
MVIC/Net Sales	0.48
MVIC/Gross Profit	0.83
MVIC/SDE	2.98
MVIC/EBITDA	4.33
OVER $5 MILLION NET SALES	
MVIC/Net Sales	0.62
MVIC/Gross Profit	1.55
MVIC/SDE	4.60
MVIC/EBITDA	5.12

Source: DealStats (formerly Pratt's Stats), 2023 (Portland, OR: Business Valuation Resources, LLC), www.bvresources.com/dealstats

PRICING TIPS

Approx. Total Investment: $120,205 to $318,244

- Signarama: https://signarama.com
- Franchise information: https://signaramafranchise.com

Sir Speedy (printing) (Franchise)

| NAICS 323111 | Businesses/Units 130

Rules of Thumb

- 55%–60% annual sales plus inventory

INDUSTRY MULTIPLES

Acquisition multiples below are calculated medians using US private industry transactions. Data updated annually. Last update: August 2023.

VALUATION MULTIPLE (MEDIAN VALUE)

UNDER $1 MILLION NET SALES

MVIC/Net Sales	0.49
MVIC/Gross Profit	0.68
MVIC/SDE	2.35
MVIC/EBITDA	3.07

$1 MILLION–$5 MILLION NET SALES

MVIC/Net Sales	0.40
MVIC/Gross Profit	0.62
MVIC/SDE	2.81
MVIC/EBITDA	4.35

OVER $5 MILLION NET SALES

MVIC/Net Sales	0.70
MVIC/Gross Profit	1.50
MVIC/SDE	3.73
MVIC/EBITDA	4.76

Source: DealStats (formerly Pratt's Stats), 2023 (Portland, OR: Business Valuation Resources, LLC), www.bvresources.com/dealstats

PRICING TIPS

Approx. Total Investment: $257,981 to $302,981

RESOURCES

- Sir Speedy: https://www.sirspeedy.com
- Franchise information: https://www.franserv.com/franchise-ownership/
- FSI—Franchise Services, Inc.: https://www.franserv.com

Ski Shops

NAICS 532292	SIC 7011-10		Businesses/Units 377
Profit $464.6 M	Wages $1.3 B		Annual Growth Future 1.3%
			Annual Growth Past 3.7%

Rules of Thumb

- 40% gross annual sales plus inventory
- 2.5–3.5 x SDE plus inventory

PRICING TIPS

It depends if the business is retail, service, rental, or some combination of all of these offerings. We find we are able to get good multiples because of the desirability of the businesses.

Key is long-term lease, since location is so important in resort retail sales. If lease is shorter than 3 years, a heavy discount in percentage of gross sales is appropriate. The price goes down the higher the inventory, which is always in addition to price (calculated on rules of thumb). Every store is different. Be careful; the trend is for ski companies to get into the retail business and compete with independent shops.

BENCHMARK DATA

STATISTICS (SKI & SNOW BOARD RESORTS)

Number of Establishments	377
Average Profit Margin	10.2%
Revenue per Employee	$57,048
Average Number of Employees	216.2
Average Wages per Employee	$16,403

PRODUCTS AND SERVICES SEGMENTATION

Skiing facilities	67.9%
Equipment rental	11.5%
Food and beverages	9.5%
Ski schools	6.5%
Other	4.6%

INDUSTRY COSTS

Profit	10.2%
Wages	28.8%
Purchases	5.0%
Depreciation	8.0%
Marketing	3.0%
Rent & Utilities	10.1%
Other	34.8%

MARKET SHARE

Vail Resorts, Inc.	9.1%
Alterra Mountain Company	12.1%
Boyne Resorts	6.1%
Aspen Skiing Company	4.5%
Eldora Mountain Resort	1.0%

Gross profit is the single biggest benchmark for success. After that, it's sales per square foot and inventory turns that matter.

EXPENSES (% OF ANNUAL SALES)

Cost of Goods	45% to 50%
Occupancy Costs	08% to 12%
Payroll/Labor Costs	22% to 28%

INDUSTRY TREND

"The industry benefited from increased disposable income and an increase in domestic travel. But operators had to shut down resorts during the pandemic, as they were classified as nonessential. Improving economic conditions and increased domestic and international travel will boost revenue over the next five years. Also, the growing number of health-conscious consumers will benefit the industry."

Source: IBISWorld Key Takeaways

Our market tends to be competitive and the bar is set high. The businesses are expected to be very knowledgeable and have a lot of inventory in stock. We have seen a trend in retailers having difficulty in maintaining margins in order to keep or increase market share. In certain industries, having the right brands or product lines is very important.

FINANCING

3 years maximum

RESOURCES

• IBISWorld, February 2023: https://www.ibisworld.com

Smoothie King (Franchise)

| NAICS 722515 | Businesses/Units 1,074

Rules of Thumb

• 40%–45% annual sales

INDUSTRY MULTIPLES

Acquisition multiples below are calculated medians using US private industry transactions. Data updated annually. Last update: August 2023.

VALUATION MULTIPLE (MEDIAN VALUE)

UNDER $1 MILLION NET SALES	
MVIC/Net Sales	0.44
MVIC/Gross Profit	0.62
MVIC/SDE	2.20
MVIC/EBITDA	2.82
$1 MILLION–$5 MILLION NET SALES	
MVIC/Net Sales	0.41
MVIC/Gross Profit	0.69
MVIC/SDE	2.82
MVIC/EBITDA	5.94
OVER $5 MILLION NET SALES	
MVIC/Net Sales	3.89
MVIC/Gross Profit	4.87
MVIC/SDE	N/A
MVIC/EBITDA	N/A

Source: DealStats (formerly Pratt's Stats), 2023 (Portland, OR: Business Valuation Resources, LLC), www.bvresources.com/dealstats

PRICING TIPS

Approx. Total Investment: $311,601 to $1,379,150

RESOURCES

• Smoothie King: https://www.smoothieking.com
• Franchise information: https://www.smoothiekingfranchise.com

Snack Food Production

| NAICS 311919 | Businesses/Units 3,614 |

| Profit $6 B | Wages $4 B | Annual Growth Future 2.0% |

| | | Annual Growth Past -2.1% |

INDUSTRY MULTIPLES

Acquisition multiples below are calculated medians using US private industry transactions. Data updated annually. Last update: August 2023.

VALUATION MULTIPLE (MEDIAN VALUE)

UNDER $1 MILLION NET SALES
MVIC/Net Sales.	0.68
MVIC/Gross Profit	1.13
MVIC/SDE	6.43
MVIC/EBITDA	2.01

$1 MILLION–$5 MILLION NET SALES	N/A

OVER $5 MILLION NET SALES
MVIC/Net Sales.	1.00
MVIC/Gross Profit	4.79
MVIC/SDE	4.09
MVIC/EBITDA	15.48

Source: DealStats (formerly Pratt's Stats), 2023 (Portland, OR: Business Valuation Resources, LLC), www.bvresources.com/dealstats

BENCHMARK DATA

STATISTICS (SNACK FOOD PRODUCTION)
Number of Establishments .	3,614
Average Profit Margin	14.1%
Revenue per Employee .	$632,521
Average Number of Employees.	19.2
Average Wages per Employee .	$59,337

PRODUCTS AND SERVICES SEGMENTATION
Nuts and seeds .	31.9%
Potato chips.	24.8%
Tortilla and corn chips	19.9%
Other chips snacks .	18.9%
Nut butters .	4.5%

MAJOR MARKET SEGMENTATION
Supermarket and grocery stores	30.9%
Convenience stores.	28.6%
Warehouse clubs and supercenters	24.3%
Grocery wholesalers	11.9%
Exports .	4.3%

INDUSTRY COSTS
Profit	14.1%
Wages	9.4%
Purchases .	45.7%
Depreciation	1.7%
Marketing	1.3%
Rent & Utilities .	1.3%
Other	26.5%

INDUSTRY TREND

"Discretionary spending accompanies discretionary eating. Americans are snacking more than ever, benefiting from strong consumer economic health to purchase more expensive products. Health-conscious Americans are searching for nutritious options. Producers have responded by diversifying product lines and introducing healthier snacks that appeal to health-conscious consumers. Imports have historically been low, but are currently on the rise. Despite this increase, American consumers often prefer domestically produced foods that match their taste, but foreign producers are gradually adapting."

Source: IBISWorld Key Takeaways

RESOURCES

• IBISWorld, October 2023: https://www.ibisworld.com

Snap Fitness (Franchise)

| NAICS 713940 | Businesses/Units 564

Rules of Thumb

• 40% annual sales plus inventory
• 57% annual sales

INDUSTRY MULTIPLES

Acquisition multiples below are calculated medians using US private industry transactions. Data updated annually. Last update: August 2023.

VALUATION MULTIPLE (MEDIAN VALUE)

UNDER $1 MILLION NET SALES	
MVIC/Net Sales	0.53
MVIC/Gross Profit	0.55
MVIC/SDE	2.26
MVIC/EBITDA	2.81

$1 MILLION–$5 MILLION NET SALES	
MVIC/Net Sales	0.61
MVIC/Gross Profit	0.69
MVIC/SDE	2.48
MVIC/EBITDA	3.99

OVER $5 MILLION NET SALES	
MVIC/Net Sales	2.23
MVIC/Gross Profit	3.25
MVIC/SDE	N/A
MVIC/EBITDA	12.19

Source: DealStats (formerly Pratt's Stats), 2023 (Portland, OR: Business Valuation Resources, LLC), www.bvresources.com/dealstats

PRICING TIPS

Approx. Total Investment: $354,738 to $1,211,917

RESOURCES

• Snap Fitness: https://www.snapfitness.com/us/
• Franchise information:
  https://www.snapfitness.com/us/franchise-opportunities
• Lift Brands: https://www.liftbrands.com

Soft Drink Bottlers

| NAICS 312111 | | Businesses/Units 628 |

| Profit $2.2 B | | Wages $4.6 B | | Annual Growth Future -0.4% |

| | | | | Annual Growth Past -1.1% |

INDUSTRY MULTIPLES

Acquisition multiples below are calculated medians using US private industry transactions. Data updated annually. Last update: August 2023.

VALUATION MULTIPLE (MEDIAN VALUE)

UNDER $1 MILLION NET SALES

MVIC/Net Sales.	0.96
MVIC/Gross Profit	0.95
MVIC/SDE	4.31
MVIC/EBITDA	2.66

$1 MILLION–$5 MILLION NET SALES

MVIC/Net Sales.	0.18
MVIC/Gross Profit	0.49
MVIC/SDE	N/A
MVIC/EBITDA	N/A

OVER $5 MILLION NET SALES

MVIC/Net Sales.	0.99
MVIC/Gross Profit	4.87
MVIC/SDE	N/A
MVIC/EBITDA	12.58

Source: DealStats (formerly Pratt's Stats), 2023 (Portland, OR: Business Valuation Resources, LLC), www.bvresources.com/dealstats

BENCHMARK DATA

STATISTICS (SODA PRODUCTION)

Number of Establishments .	628
Average Profit Margin	5.1%
Revenue per Employee .	$567,452
Average Number of Employees.	118.5
Average Wages per Employee	$62,773

PRODUCTS AND SERVICES SEGMENTATION

Regular carbonated soft drinks.	49.5%
Mixers and other beverages	20.1%
Diet carbonated soft drinks and sparkling water	18.6%
Energy and sports drinks	11.8%

MAJOR MARKET SEGMENTATION

Grocery stores	4.6%
Warehouse clubs and supercenters	30.3%
Gas stations and convenience stores	16.0%
Vending machines	7.1%

INDUSTRY COSTS

Profit	5.1%
Wages	10.9%
Purchases	63.2%
Depreciation	2.4%
Marketing	2.0%
Rent & Utilities	2.6%
Other	13.7%

PepsiCo, Inc.	34.5%
Coca-Cola Consolidated, Inc.	14.1%
Keurig Dr Pepper Inc.	11.3%
Monster Beverage Corporation.	10.9%

S

INDUSTRY TREND

"Major soda producers have introduced new soda products, including a variety of different sweeteners, to mitigate the losses from lower consumption. Strong brand loyalty and new artisanal products have allowed producers to keep prices high while input costs fluctuated. Demand for CSDs has dipped through the end of 2023 as consumers have become more aware of the negative health effects of drinking soda. The government, media and even soft drink producers themselves have vocalized the consequences of consuming artificially sweetened diet soda and how drinking large volumes of regular soda can lead to obesity."

Source: IBISWorld Key Takeaways

RESOURCES

- IBISWorld, September 2023: https://www.ibisworld.com
- Beverage Industry: https://www.bevindustry.com

Software Companies

| NAICS 511210

Rules of Thumb

- 1–3 x revenue (trailing 12 months) plus inventory
- 6–10 x SDE
- 4.5–9 x EBITDA
- 4.5–8 x EBIT
- 100% annual sales includes inventory
- 4 x SDE plus inventory

INDUSTRY MULTIPLES

Acquisition multiples below are calculated medians using US private industry transactions. Data updated annually. Last update: August 2023.

VALUATION MULTIPLE (MEDIAN VALUE)

UNDER $1 MILLION NET SALES	
MVIC/Net Sales.	3.43
MVIC/Gross Profit	5.09
MVIC/SDE	3.04
MVIC/EBITDA	9.61
$1 MILLION–$5 MILLION NET SALES	
MVIC/Net Sales.	2.37
MVIC/Gross Profit	3.64
MVIC/SDE	4.29
MVIC/EBITDA	9.69
OVER $5 MILLION NET SALES	
MVIC/Net Sales.	4.02
MVIC/Gross Profit	6.09
MVIC/SDE	8.80
MVIC/EBITDA	23.76

Source: DealStats (formerly Pratt's Stats), 2023 (Portland, OR: Business Valuation Resources, LLC), www.bvresources.com/dealstats

S

Value-based pricing: Price software products based on the value they bring to customers rather than solely on production costs.

Competitive analysis: Research competitors' pricing to determine a competitive and attractive price point.

Tiered pricing: Offer different pricing tiers with varying features and benefits to cater to different customer segments.

Subscription model: Consider offering subscription-based pricing for recurring revenue and customer retention.

Free trials or freemium: Provide free trials or freemium versions to allow customers to experience the software before committing to a purchase.

Bundling and upselling: Bundle software products with related services or offer upsells to increase the average transaction value.

Dynamic pricing: Implement dynamic pricing strategies to adjust prices based on demand, usage, or market conditions.

Customer feedback: Collect customer feedback on pricing to assess its competitiveness and adjust accordingly.

Discounts and promotions: Use discounts and limited-time promotions strategically to boost sales and attract new customers.

Long-term contracts: Offer discounts or incentives for customers who commit to long-term contracts to encourage loyalty.

The value depends upon a few factors including type of service (on-prem, SaaS, PaaS), recurrence of income (percent of subscriber renewals), target focus and means to extend base of offerings, personnel and type of professionals employed, geography covered (if applicable), years in business, and growth rate of a primary offering. Financially, must maintain a high net margin (midmarket and smaller companies) with incremental onboarding costs being minimal for service delivery. Larger companies that house and pay for large infrastructure costs have much lower (< 4 percent) margins on very large numbers.

SDE, EBIT, and EBITDA ratios are meaningless in this industry because of the great differences in product, market, and development stage from company to company. Businesses even without profits or negative net worth can command multiples of gross revenue. Values are more focused on revenues trending upward, consistency and sustainability of the existing customer base, and potential for growth.

BENCHMARK DATA

Annual revenue growth rate: the rate at which a software company's revenue is growing year over year. Customer retention rate: the percentage of customers retained over a specific period, reflecting customer satisfaction and loyalty. Customer acquisition cost (CAC): the average cost of acquiring a new customer. Churn rate: the rate at which customers are leaving or discontinuing their subscriptions. Monthly recurring revenue (MRR): the total monthly revenue generated from recurring subscriptions. Gross profit margin: the percentage of revenue remaining after deducting the cost of goods sold. Employee productivity: measuring revenue generated per employee or profit per employee. Time to payback customer acquisition cost: the time it takes for a company to recoup its customer acquisition costs. Software development cycle time: the time it takes to develop and release new software products or updates. Customer lifetime value (CLV): the total revenue expected from a customer over their entire lifetime as a client.

Revenue per employee—larger company, around $800K per employee; smaller company, around $500K per employee

EXPENSES (% OF ANNUAL SALES)

Cost of Goods	01% to 11%
Occupancy Costs	10% to 15%
Payroll/Labor Costs.	50% to 60%
Profit (pretax)	15% to 30%

QUESTIONS

- Following are questions for a buyer to ask the seller. Financials: what are the revenues and profit margins? Customer base: who are the key customers? Technology: what is the software's scalability and technology stack? Market position: how does the business differentiate from competitors? Legal: are there any pending legal or IP issues? Growth potential: what are the growth opportunities? Team and talent: assess the expertise and stability of the team. Customer support: inquire about customer satisfaction and support. Reason for selling: understand the motivation behind the sale. Transition plan: how will the transition be facilitated?
- Discuss the evolution of the offering. Obtain a clear understanding of the target client. What is the average time of a subscriber? Professionals in this field are difficult to obtain and keep, so what strategies does the current company use to maintain a high level of professional capability? What offerings are you developing now, or R & D efforts (get basics, as they wont discuss any details in this area)?

INDUSTRY TREND

Cloud-based software solutions are expected to continue gaining popularity, offering scalability, flexibility, and cost-efficiency for businesses and consumers.

Artificial Intelligence in software products is likely to expand, enabling more advanced and personalized experiences for users.

As cyber threats increase, there will be a growing emphasis on software security and data privacy, driving demand for robust cybersecurity solutions.

Software companies may increasingly develop applications to support IoT devices, contributing to the growth of smart homes, cities, and industries.

The trend of subscription-based and Software-as-a-Service (SaaS) models is expected to continue, offering recurring revenue streams and continuous updates for users.

Rise of low-code and no-code platforms will likely empower non-technical users to create software applications, democratizing software development.

The demand for remote work and collaboration software will persist, as businesses and individuals continue to adopt flexible work arrangements.

These potential trends could significantly impact the software industry over the next few years, fostering opportunities for growth and innovation. However, it's essential to note that the software industry is highly dynamic, and new developments may arise beyond the scope of these predictions. Staying up-to-date with market trends and technological advancements is crucial for businesses to remain competitive in this fast-evolving landscape.

S oftware company values will increase, but the level of competition will grow and deflate the influence of some entities. Because of Covid, many companies moved to a virtual environment, thereby giving certain entities the ability to sell more products and services—while also battling an increasing pool of available alternatives from people who developed new applications due to being laid off, virtual work conditions, etc. The better-staffed and progressive companies will continue to improve, while the velocity of the new, emerging companies will slow down a bit as the economy goes through a downturn.

EXPERT COMMENTS

Advice for buying a business in the software industry: conduct thorough due diligence; evaluate technology, market, and financials; verify legal compliance and IP rights; assess customer base and team expertise; engage expert advisors for negotiations.

Advice for selling a business in the software industry: prepare detailed documentation; get a realistic business valuation; highlight unique selling points; maintain confidentiality; market widely and use online platforms; be transparent and flexible in negotiations; provide support during the transition; seek professional guidance throughout.

You must have a passion for businesses that work in complex IP. You need to understand the temperament of the software engineers who drive the product development—and also ensure that personnel (like content developers, UX, UI, DB, infrastructure, and others) are provided with a key means to show personal success, and allow them to participate in that success. If you have a potential high-end revenue base, consider option plans and obtain knowledge of getting other investors to help fuel future growth, keep professional staff engaged, and maintain competitiveness.

Software, as intellectual property, is very hard to duplicate, and then when created, hard to move from site to site or person to person. Mission critical attitudes are applied to known software because of the difficulty in conversion, training, and maintenance. Once a product is selected, it likely won't be considered for replacement for years—unless the cost is very low, and the training and migration time is low.

Historical trend can be low but grow exponentially. Depending on software, can be difficult to replicate.

High-risk, high-reward business

FINANCING

Mainly seller financing or SBA 7(a) loan financing. Terms for seller financing are typically driven by payment schedule, interest rate, term, down payment, and collateral.

Cash (primary); limited seller financing; sometimes earnouts due to high multiples; and in many cases, a recapitalization to afford the existing owner a stake in NewCo

RESOURCES

- ACM—Association for Computing Machinery: https://www.acm.org
- ACT—The App Association: https://actonline.org
- ASP—Association of Software Professionals: https://asp-software.org
- BSA—The Software Alliance: https://www.bsa.org

- CCIA—Computer and Communications Industry Association: https://www.ccianet.org
- CompTIA: https://www.comptia.org/membership/it-pro
- ITIC—Information Technology Industry Council: https://www.itic.org
- SIIA—Software & Information Industry Association: https://www.siia.net

Solar Panel Installation

| NAICS 238210

INDUSTRY MULTIPLES

Acquisition multiples below are calculated medians using US private industry transactions. Data updated annually. Last update: August 2023.

VALUATION MULTIPLE (MEDIAN VALUE)

UNDER $1 MILLION NET SALES	
MVIC/Net Sales.	0.49
MVIC/Gross Profit	0.80
MVIC/SDE	2.08
MVIC/EBITDA	2.70
$1 MILLION–$5 MILLION NET SALES	
MVIC/Net Sales.	0.48
MVIC/Gross Profit	0.99
MVIC/SDE	2.39
MVIC/EBITDA	3.20
OVER $5 MILLION NET SALES	
MVIC/Net Sales.	0.46
MVIC/Gross Profit	1.48
MVIC/SDE	3.19
MVIC/EBITDA	4.78

Source: DealStats (formerly Pratt's Stats), 2023 (Portland, OR: Business Valuation Resources, LLC), www.bvresources.com/dealstats

Solar Power

| NAICS 221114

Rules of Thumb

- 4 x SDE
- 5 x EBIT
- 6 x EBITDA

INDUSTRY MULTIPLES

Acquisition multiples below are calculated medians using US private industry transactions. Data updated annually. Last update: August 2023.

VALUATION MULTIPLE (MEDIAN VALUE)

UNDER $1 MILLION NET SALES	N/A
$1 MILLION–$5 MILLION NET SALES	N/A
OVER $5 MILLION NET SALES	
MVIC/Net Sales.	8.60
MVIC/Gross Profit	17.37
MVIC/SDE	N/A
MVIC/EBITDA	14.85

Source: DealStats (formerly Pratt's Stats), 2023 (Portland, OR: Business Valuation Resources, LLC), www.bvresources.com/dealstats

S

Project portfolio: Evaluate the size and diversity of the solar project portfolio. Larger and more diversified portfolios can be more attractive to buyers.

Location: Consider the geographic location of the solar projects. Solar projects in regions with high solar irradiance and favorable regulatory conditions may have a higher value.

Contractual agreements: Review any long-term power purchase agreements (PPAs) or feed-in tariffs (FiTs) in place. These contracts can provide revenue predictability.

Technical due diligence: Conduct a thorough technical due diligence to assess the condition and performance of the solar assets, including the solar panels and inverters.

Regulatory environment: Understand the local and national regulatory environment for solar energy. Changes in regulations can impact the value of solar assets.

Financial performance: Examine the historical financial performance of the business, including revenue, operating costs, and profit margins.

Energy market trends: Stay informed about market trends and developments in the solar industry, including advances in solar technology and energy storage solutions.

Maintenance and O&M costs: Evaluate the ongoing maintenance and operation costs of the solar assets, as they can impact profitability.

Environmental and sustainability factors: Highlight the environmental and sustainability benefits of the solar projects, as these factors can be attractive to socially responsible investors.

Competitive landscape: Analyze the competitive landscape for solar energy in the region, including the business's market positioning and its potential for growth.

Energy storage: Assess the presence of energy storage solutions (e.g., batteries) and their value in enhancing the reliability and profitability of solar projects.

Market demand: Consider the demand for renewable energy and the role that solar projects play in meeting that demand.

Revenue forecast: Develop a revenue forecast based on expected energy production and sales, considering market prices and energy demand.

Technology advancements: Explore any technological advancements in the solar industry that could enhance the value of the business.

Tax credits and incentives: Be aware of available tax credits, incentives, and subsidies that can affect the financial performance and value of solar assets.

Social and political factors: Consider the impact of social and political factors on the solar industry, such as public support for renewable energy.

BENCHMARK DATA

Common benchmarks for a successful business in this industry include revenue per installed megawatt (MW) of solar capacity, profitability per MW, and customer acquisition cost per installed MW.

Occupancy Costs	08%
Payroll/Labor Costs.	13%
Profit (pretax)	10%

QUESTIONS

- Buyers should ask sellers about the condition and age of solar panels, any existing warranties, contracts with power purchasers, and maintenance records/agreements.
- What is the current installation capacity and track record?
- What is the condition of the solar panels and equipment?
- Are there any pending regulatory or permitting issues?

INDUSTRY TREND

The trend over the next few years for the solar power industry is expected to be positive, with continued growth driven by increased demand for renewable energy and advancements in solar technology.

"The rooftops and parking lot space available at retail giants like Walmart, Target and Costco is massive. And these largely empty spaces are being touted as untapped potential for solar power that could help the US reduce its dependency on foreign energy, slash planet-warming emissions and save companies millions of dollars in the process....Big-box stores and shopping centers have enough roof space to produce half of their annual electricity needs from solar, according to a report from nonprofit Environment America and research firm Frontier Group.... Yet only a fraction of big-box stores in the US have solar on their rooftops or solar canopies in parking lots, the report's authors told CNN. CNN reached out to five of the top US retailers—Walmart, Kroger, Home Depot, Costco and Target—to ask: Why not invest in more rooftop solar? Many renewable energy experts point to solar as a relatively simple solution to cut down on costs and help rein in fossil fuel emissions, but the companies point to several roadblocks—regulations, labor costs and structural integrity of the rooftops themselves—that are preventing more widespread adoption."

Source: "Big-box stores could help slash emissions and save millions by putting solar panels on roofs. Why aren't more of them doing it?" by Rachel Ramirez and Nathaniel Meyersohn, March 20, 2022, https://www.cnn.com/2022/03/20/us/solar-power-on-big-box-store-rooftops-climate/index.html

EXPERT COMMENTS

Advice for someone buying or selling a business in the solar power industry would include conducting thorough due diligence on the financials, contracts, and equipment. Buyers should also assess the potential for further development and the condition of existing installations.

FINANCING

When businesses in this industry are sold, seller financing is more typical due to the high capital requirements. Terms can vary, but it's common to see a down payment followed by structured payments over several years.

RESOURCES

- SEIA—Solar Energy Industries Association: https://www.seia.org
- Solar Power World: https://www.solarpowerworldonline.com
- Renewable Energy World: https://www.renewableenergyworld.com
- PV Tech: https://www.pv-tech.org

Sound Contractors

| NAICS 238210 | SIC 5065-07

S

Rules of Thumb

- 75% annual sales includes inventory
- 5 x EBIT
- 3 x EBITDA

INDUSTRY MULTIPLES

Acquisition multiples below are calculated medians using US private industry transactions. Data updated annually. Last update: August 2023.

VALUATION MULTIPLE (MEDIAN VALUE)

UNDER $1 MILLION NET SALES	
MVIC/Net Sales.	0.49
MVIC/Gross Profit	0.80
MVIC/SDE	2.08
MVIC/EBITDA	2.70

$1 MILLION–$5 MILLION NET SALES	
MVIC/Net Sales.	0.48
MVIC/Gross Profit	0.99
MVIC/SDE	2.39
MVIC/EBITDA	3.20

OVER $5 MILLION NET SALES	
MVIC/Net Sales.	0.46
MVIC/Gross Profit	1.48
MVIC/SDE	3.19
MVIC/EBITDA	4.78

Source: DealStats (formerly Pratt's Stats), 2023 (Portland, OR: Business Valuation Resources, LLC), www.bvresources.com/dealstats

PRICING TIPS

Most contractors in this industry supply some type of music service; if it is a recurring base and the contractors are on their paperwork, then this company will have more value to a buyer.

Any inventory over 24 months is dead inventory and should not be part of the sale.

BENCHMARK DATA

EXPENSES (% OF ANNUAL SALES)

Cost of Goods	35%
Occupancy Costs	10%
Payroll/Labor Costs.	35%
Profit (pretax)	20%

QUESTIONS

- Inventory—how much is dead and on the books?
- Relationship to customers

EXPERT COMMENTS

If company is a commercial contractor, the economy does not have much effect on industry. If they give good service and have experience in technical support, business will be stable.

There are few good sound contractors with a great customer list.

5 to 8 years

S

Special Needs Transportation

| NAICS 485991

INDUSTRY MULTIPLES

Acquisition multiples below are calculated medians using US private industry transactions. Data updated annually. Last update: August 2023.

VALUATION MULTIPLE (MEDIAN VALUE)

UNDER $1 MILLION NET SALES

MVIC/Net Sales	0.71
MVIC/Gross Profit	0.83
MVIC/SDE	3.38
MVIC/EBITDA	5.88

$1 MILLION–$5 MILLION NET SALES

MVIC/Net Sales	0.60
MVIC/Gross Profit	0.80
MVIC/SDE	1.87
MVIC/EBITDA	9.80

OVER $5 MILLION NET SALES

MVIC/Net Sales	0.95
MVIC/Gross Profit	1.34
MVIC/SDE	N/A
MVIC/EBITDA	N/A

Source: DealStats (formerly Pratt's Stats), 2023 (Portland, OR: Business Valuation Resources, LLC), www.bvresources.com/dealstats

Sport Clips (Franchise)

| NAICS 812112 | Businesses/Units 1,784

Rules of Thumb

• 100% annual sales

INDUSTRY MULTIPLES

Acquisition multiples below are calculated medians using US private industry transactions. Data updated annually. Last update: August 2023.

VALUATION MULTIPLE (MEDIAN VALUE)

UNDER $1 MILLION NET SALES

MVIC/Net Sales	0.31
MVIC/Gross Profit	0.39
MVIC/SDE	1.60
MVIC/EBITDA	2.11

$1 MILLION–$5 MILLION NET SALES

MVIC/Net Sales	0.29
MVIC/Gross Profit	0.39
MVIC/SDE	2.30
MVIC/EBITDA	3.05

OVER $5 MILLION NET SALES   N/A

Source: DealStats (formerly Pratt's Stats), 2023 (Portland, OR: Business Valuation Resources, LLC), www.bvresources.com/dealstats

PRICING TIPS

Approx. Total Investment: $266,300 – $439,500

RESOURCES

- Sport Clips: https://sportclips.com
- Franchise information: https://sportclipsfranchise.com

Sporting and Recreational Goods and Supplies Merchant Wholesalers

| NAICS 423910 | Businesses/Units 20,971

| Profit $4.4 B | Wages $5.7 B | Annual Growth Future 1.1%

| Annual Growth Past 6.1%

INDUSTRY MULTIPLES

Acquisition multiples below are calculated medians using US private industry transactions. Data updated annually. Last update: August 2023.

VALUATION MULTIPLE (MEDIAN VALUE)

UNDER $1 MILLION NET SALES

MVIC/Net Sales	0.40
MVIC/Gross Profit	0.82
MVIC/SDE	2.05
MVIC/EBITDA	3.50

$1 MILLION–$5 MILLION NET SALES

MVIC/Net Sales	0.54
MVIC/Gross Profit	1.38
MVIC/SDE	3.78
MVIC/EBITDA	10.48

OVER $5 MILLION NET SALES

MVIC/Net Sales	0.31
MVIC/Gross Profit	1.53
MVIC/SDE	3.72
MVIC/EBITDA	4.97

Source: DealStats (formerly Pratt's Stats), 2023 (Portland, OR: Business Valuation Resources, LLC), www.bvresources.com/dealstats

BENCHMARK DATA

STATISTICS (SPORTING GOODS WHOLESALING)

Number of Establishments	20,971
Average Profit Margin	5.5%
Revenue per Employee	$1,152,000
Average Number of Employees	3.3
Average Wages per Employee	$82,062

PRODUCTS AND SERVICES SEGMENTATION

Hunting equipment and firearms	31.8%
Bicycles	18.1%
Pools and pool equipment	14.0%
Billiards and other	13.1%
Marine pleasure craft	8.2%
Camping and fishing equipment	8.1%
Athletic exercise and fitness equipment	4.6%
Skiing and snowboarding equipment	2.1%

Retailers for resale	. 60.3%
Wholesale establishments for resale .	. 26.3%
Other	. 13.4%

INDUSTRY COSTS

Profit	. 5.5%
Wages	. 7.1%
Purchases	. 72.1%
Depreciation	. 0.6%
Marketing	. 1.1%
Rent & Utilities	. 1.1%
Other	. 12.5%

MARKET SHARE

Pool Corporation	. 6.8%

INDUSTRY TREND

"Wholesalers are increasingly being bypassed as sporting goods manufacturers and retailers work directly with one another. This has created challenges for wholesalers to negotiate favorable prices, limiting revenue growth. The increasing popularity of niche sports has supported growth. Manufacturers of niche equipment are more likely to go through wholesalers."

Source: IBISWorld Key Takeaways

RESOURCES

• IBISWorld, September 2023: https://www.ibisworld.com

Sporting Goods Stores

| NAICS 451110	| SIC 5941-13	| Businesses/Units 38,065
| Profit $1.8 B	| Wages $6.8 B	| Annual Growth Future 0.8%
		| Annual Growth Past 3.0%

Rules of Thumb

• 25% annual sales plus inventory
• 4 x EBIT

INDUSTRY MULTIPLES

Acquisition multiples below are calculated medians using US private industry transactions. Data updated annually. Last update: August 2023.

VALUATION MULTIPLE (MEDIAN VALUE)

UNDER $1 MILLION NET SALES

MVIC/Net Sales.	0.50
MVIC/Gross Profit	1.01
MVIC/SDE	2.56
MVIC/EBITDA	3.93

$1 MILLION–$5 MILLION NET SALES

MVIC/Net Sales.	0.37
MVIC/Gross Profit	1.03
MVIC/SDE	2.71
MVIC/EBITDA	4.08

MVIC/Net Sales.	0.46
MVIC/Gross Profit	1.33
MVIC/SDE	2.95
MVIC/EBITDA	7.63

Source: DealStats (formerly Pratt's Stats), 2023 (Portland, OR: Business Valuation Resources, LLC), www.bvresources.com/dealstats

PRICING TIPS

Add or subtract based on nearby competition.

Inventory should be excluded due to rapid obsolescence.

BENCHMARK DATA

STATISTICS (SPORTING GOODS STORES)

Number of Establishments	38,065
Average Profit Margin	2.9%
Revenue per Employee	$251,913
Average Number of Employees. . . .	6.5
Average Wages per Employee . . .	$27,281

PRODUCTS AND SERVICES SEGMENTATION

Sporting equipment.	33.7%
Other	30.9%
Athletic apparel	15.0%
Firearms and hunting equipment . .	13.5%
Athletic footwear	6.9%

INDUSTRY COSTS

Profit	2.9%
Wages	10.9%
Purchases	55.4%
Depreciation	0.9%
Marketing	2.2%
Rent & Utilities	6.6%
Other	21.1%

MARKET SHARE

Dick's Sporting Goods, Inc.. . . .	15.0%
BPS Direct LLC	12.2%
Academy Sports & Outdoors . . .	7.6%
Recreational Equipment, Inc. . . .	2.9%

EXPENSES (% OF ANNUAL SALES)

Cost of Goods	45% to 55%
Occupancy Costs	15% to 20%
Payroll/Labor Costs.	17%
Profit (pretax)	08%

QUESTIONS

• Are the sales personnel knowledgeable in their specific areas?

INDUSTRY TREND

"Despite significant pressures in the overall retail sector during the pandemic as regulations forced nonessential stores to close, the Sporting Goods Stores industry expanded in 2020. This growth was driven by a surge in gun sales and other outdoor and at-home sporting equipment, such as road and stationary bicycles. The industry has benefited from more health-conscious individuals requiring sporting goods during the five-year period. The expansion of gym offerings and post-collegiate recreational sports has been and will likely continue to be a major factor for revenue growth."

Source: IBISWorld Key Takeaways

EXPERT COMMENTS

Increasing competition from online retailers

RESOURCES

- IBISWorld, September 2023: https://www.ibisworld.com
- NSGA—National Sporting Goods Association: https://www.nsga.org

Steel Framing

| NAICS 238120 | Businesses/Units 15,472

| Profit $1 B | Wages $7.4 B

| Annual Growth Past 2.7%

Rules of Thumb

- 5 x SDE plus inventory
- 5 x EBIT
- 4.5 x EBITDA

INDUSTRY MULTIPLES

Acquisition multiples below are calculated medians using US private industry transactions. Data updated annually. Last update: August 2023.

VALUATION MULTIPLE (MEDIAN VALUE)

UNDER $1 MILLION NET SALES	N/A
$1 MILLION–$5 MILLION NET SALES	
MVIC/Net Sales.	0.47
MVIC/Gross Profit	1.10
MVIC/SDE	3.10
MVIC/EBITDA	2.90
OVER $5 MILLION NET SALES	
MVIC/Net Sales.	0.37
MVIC/Gross Profit	1.59
MVIC/SDE	2.50
MVIC/EBITDA	4.29

Source: DealStats (formerly Pratt's Stats), 2023 (Portland, OR: Business Valuation Resources, LLC), www.bvresources.com/dealstats

PRICING TIPS

Most transaction prices include a target working capital to be included with the sale, and a true-up 90 days posttransaction.

BENCHMARK DATA

STATISTICS (STEEL FRAMING)

Number of Establishments .	.15,472
Average Profit Margin	4.0%
Revenue per Employee .	$247,231
Average Number of Employees.	.6.4
Average Wages per Employee .	$72,678

PRODUCTS AND SERVICES SEGMENTATION

Structural steel erection	.61.9%
Steel Fabrication	.20.4%
Precast concrete installation	. 8.9%
Additions and alterations to existing structures	. 8.8%

MAJOR MARKET SEGMENTATION

Commercial building construction	.34.3%
Nonbuilding construction	.25.0%
Municipal building construction	.12.5%
Industrial building construction	.11.8%
Other nonresidential building construction	.10.5%
Residential building construction	. 5.9%

INDUSTRY COSTS

Profit	. 4.0%
Wages	.28.8%
Purchases	.32.6%
Depreciation	. 1.5%
Marketing	. 0.1%
Rent & Utilities	. 5.7%
Other	.27.2%

Revenue of $1M per employee

EXPENSES (% OF ANNUAL SALES)

Cost of Goods	70%
Payroll/Labor Costs	25%
Profit (pretax)	05%

INDUSTRY TREND

"As pandemic-related business closures have eased, corporate profit has had a strong recovery, enabling nonresidential construction to flourish. Steel framing has seen an influx of demand from the commercial sector as delayed projects come to fruition. After taking advantage of a commodity lending environment for most of the period, high interests have begun to stymie residential construction activity. Consistent increases in the 30-year conventional mortgage from 2022 onward have siphoned demand from steel framing contractors in residential markets."

Source: IBISWorld Key Takeaways

EXPERT COMMENTS

Use careful diligence in reviewing percentage of completion of acquired contracts, and any assumed contract liability claims.

Replication of the business is difficult due to the requirement of a highly skilled workforce.

FINANCING

Typically PE buyers invest 30 to 35 percent and take the balance in bank debt.

RESOURCES

- IBISWorld, September 2023: https://www.ibisworld.com
- AISC: https://www.aisc.org

Steel Rolling & Drawing

| NAICS 33122 | Businesses/Units 575

| Profit $596.1 M | Wages $1.7 B | Annual Growth Future 0.6%

| Annual Growth Past -1.0%

INDUSTRY MULTIPLES

Acquisition multiples below are calculated medians using US private industry transactions. Data updated annually. Last update: December 2023.

VALUATION MULTIPLE (MEDIAN VALUE)

UNDER $1 MILLION NET SALES — N/A

$1 MILLION–$5 MILLION NET SALES

MVIC/Net Sales.	0.48
MVIC/Gross Profit	1.01
MVIC/SDE	1.63
MVIC/EBITDA	2.04

OVER $5 MILLION NET SALES

MVIC/Net Sales.	0.53
MVIC/Gross Profit	3.19
MVIC/SDE	N/A
MVIC/EBITDA	7.51

Source: DealStats (formerly Pratt's Stats), 2023 (Portland, OR: Business Valuation Resources, LLC), www.bvresources.com/dealstats

BENCHMARK DATA

STATISTICS (STEEL ROLLING & DRAWING)

Number of Establishments	575
Average Profit Margin	3.9%
Revenue per Employee	$576,873
Average Number of Employees	46.9
Average Wages per Employee	$64,249

PRODUCTS AND SERVICES SEGMENTATION

Cold-rolled steel sheet	27.9%
Ferrous wire products	26.1%
Cold finished bars and other shapes	19.2%
Steel wire and fencing	16.6%
Other	9.2%
Wholesale	1.0%

MAJOR MARKET SEGMENTATION

Steel service and distribution centers	32.9%
Industrial and general manufacturing	22.0%
Construction	21.0%
Automotive manufacturing	20.4%
Exports	3.7%

INDUSTRY COSTS

Profit	3.9%
Wages	11.1%
Purchases	60.7%
Depreciation	2.0%
Marketing	0.1%
Rent & Utilities	2.3%
Other	19.8%

INDUSTRY TREND

"The onset of the COVID-19 pandemic and accompanying economic turmoil created vast fluctuations in the price of steel. This compounded already-diminished demand from downstream markets. Demand returned as the world reopened in the wake of the COVID-19 pandemic. This resumption of business activity revitalized the steel manufacturing industry. Competition from China will drop in the coming years because of rising political tensions with the United States. Import tariffs on Chinese goods will remain high, creating opportunity for the domestic market to fulfill more of the demand."

Source: IBISWorld Key Takeaways

RESOURCES

• IBISWorld, March 2023: https://www.ibisworld.com

Subway (Franchise)

| NAICS 722513 | SIC 5812-06 | Businesses/Units 21,147

Rules of Thumb

• 45%–55% annual sales includes inventory
• 3–4 x SDE includes inventory
• 2.5–3.5 x EBIT
• 3–3.5 x EBITDA
• 35–40 x weekly sales
• 30%–50% annual sales

INDUSTRY MULTIPLES

Acquisition multiples below are calculated medians using US private industry transactions. Data updated annually. Last update: August 2023.

VALUATION MULTIPLE (MEDIAN VALUE)

UNDER $1 MILLION NET SALES	
MVIC/Net Sales	0.31
MVIC/Gross Profit	0.48
MVIC/SDE	1.67
MVIC/EBITDA	2.21
$1 MILLION–$5 MILLION NET SALES	
MVIC/Net Sales	0.39
MVIC/Gross Profit	0.60
MVIC/SDE	2.43
MVIC/EBITDA	2.98
OVER $5 MILLION NET SALES	
MVIC/Net Sales	0.89
MVIC/Gross Profit	2.08
MVIC/SDE	4.98
MVIC/EBITDA	12.81

Source: DealStats (formerly Pratt's Stats), 2023 (Portland, OR: Business Valuation Resources, LLC), www.bvresources.com/dealstats

PRICING TIPS

Approx. Total Investment: $222,050 to $506,900

For additional Benchmark Data see Sandwich Shops

An owner-operator-run store can see food cost at 28 to 30 percent and labor cost at 20 to 22 percent.

Gross margin ratio should be approximately 0.535.

Successful locations maintain food costs at below 32 percent and labor costs below 25 percent.

Most stores are 1,000 sq. ft., have approximately 20 seats, and are owner-operated. Food cost is controllable.

EXPENSES (% OF ANNUAL SALES)

Cost of Goods	30% to 35%
Occupancy Costs	10% to 15%
Payroll/Labor Costs.	20% to 25%
Profit (pretax)	10% to 20%

QUESTIONS

- When was the store remodeled last? Is the store in full compliance? Are you an owner-operator or do you pay a manager?
- How much time do you spend working at the location? What have you done to attract local customers?

INDUSTRY TREND

"Subway, a family-owned business of nearly 60 years that has other sandwich shops in its portfolio, has been acquired by private equity firm Roark Capital."

Source: "Subway has been sold for billions in one of the biggest fast food acquisitions ever" by Doc Louallen, August 26, 2023, https://www.usatoday.com/story/money/food/2023/08/25/subway-company-sold-roark-capital-billions/70675156007/

"Subway opened a global headquarters in Miami to supplement its existing headquarters infrastructure in Connecticut...Subway's emphasis on menu innovation and collaboration with franchisees aligns with the chain's ongoing efforts to shake up its menu and overhaul its franchise system as the chain approaches a potential sale."

Source: "Subway opens second headquarters with sandwich test station" by Aneurin Canham-Clyne, March 2, 2023, https://www.restaurantdive.com/news/Subway-Miami-HQ-opens-with-menu-innovation-center/

EXPERT COMMENTS

Three or more stores are needed before considering a general manager.

FINANCING

Bank financing is usually available with about 20 percent down, good credit, and some experience. Store must show good books and records for bank financing.

RESOURCES

- Subway: https://www.subway.com/en-us
- Franchise information: https://subwayfranchise.com/en-us
- NAASF—North American Association of Subway Franchisees: https://www.naasf.org

Sunroom and Awning Installation

| NAICS 326199 | SIC 1521-22

Rules of Thumb

- 35% annual sales plus inventory

INDUSTRY MULTIPLES

Acquisition multiples below are calculated medians using US private industry transactions. Data updated annually. Last update: August 2023.

VALUATION MULTIPLE (MEDIAN VALUE)

UNDER $1 MILLION NET SALES

MVIC/Net Sales.	0.67
MVIC/Gross Profit	1.41
MVIC/SDE	2.47
MVIC/EBITDA	6.52

$1 MILLION–$5 MILLION NET SALES

MVIC/Net Sales.	0.52
MVIC/Gross Profit	0.73
MVIC/SDE	4.45
MVIC/EBITDA	6.65

OVER $5 MILLION NET SALES

MVIC/Net Sales.	1.04
MVIC/Gross Profit	4.89
MVIC/SDE	3.88
MVIC/EBITDA	10.00

Source: DealStats (formerly Pratt's Stats), 2023 (Portland, OR: Business Valuation Resources, LLC), www.bvresources.com/dealstats

PRICING TIPS

Strong, knowledgeable managers who have been with this specialty business for a long time can add a lot of value to the company. This would also increase the buyer pool greatly. A buyer with no knowledge or experience in this business could purchase it and be successful.

BENCHMARK DATA

30+ percent net income based on gross sales

EXPENSES (% OF ANNUAL SALES)

Cost of Goods	15%
Occupancy Costs	15%
Payroll/Labor Costs.	25% to 30%
Profit (pretax)	30%

QUESTIONS

- What contracts do you have and with whom?

INDUSTRY TREND

Growing due to housing boom in area

EXPERT COMMENTS

Competition—this is a specialty business; risk—there is an abundance of work in this field; profit trend—sales have shown steady increases; location—a shop and a central location is all you need; marketability—there is a high demand for this type of work; industry trend—new housing boom and damages from hurricanes have this business booked for years; replication—this being a specialty business, most construction workers don't have the necessary knowledge to do these jobs.

RESOURCES

• NSA—National Sunroom Association: https://www.nationalsunroom.org

---

Supermarkets/Grocery Stores

	NAICS 445110		SIC 5411-05		Businesses/Units 86,251
	Profit $16.1 B		Wages $82.4 B		Annual Growth Future 0.5%
					Annual Growth Past 1.9%

Rules of Thumb

• 10%–22% annual sales plus inventory
• 2–3 x SDE; add fixtures, equipment plus inventory
• 3 x EBIT
• 3–3.5 x EBITDA

INDUSTRY MULTIPLES

Acquisition multiples below are calculated medians using US private industry transactions. Data updated annually. Last update: August 2023.

VALUATION MULTIPLE (MEDIAN VALUE)

UNDER $1 MILLION NET SALES

MVIC/Net Sales.	0.30
MVIC/Gross Profit	0.68
MVIC/SDE	2.06
MVIC/EBITDA	2.72

$1 MILLION–$5 MILLION NET SALES

MVIC/Net Sales.	0.20
MVIC/Gross Profit	0.71
MVIC/SDE	2.46
MVIC/EBITDA	4.75

OVER $5 MILLION NET SALES

MVIC/Net Sales.	0.37
MVIC/Gross Profit	1.46
MVIC/SDE	4.70
MVIC/EBITDA	10.22

Source: DealStats (formerly Pratt's Stats), 2023 (Portland, OR: Business Valuation Resources, LLC), www.bvresources.com/dealstats

PRICING TIPS

If the store fixtures are not updated, the multiples are lower, as the buyer will likely need to invest additional capital for improvements, including renewed deli/bakery departments, freezers, decor, and signage. Location and distance to competitors' stores are critical. Buyers should look at the total population of the trade area to determine the amount of grocery sales available. Your major supplier can help you compute these estimates. By knowing potential sales in the area and the market share of each competitor, the buyer can project growth potential. Store must have enough square footage and variety to compete with other stores, unless the store is in a location without nearby competitors and there is no real estate available for direct competitors to build a new facility.

STATISTICS (SUPERMARKETS AND GROCERY STORES)

Number of Establishments	.86,251
Average Profit Margin	1.9%
Revenue per Employee	$312,505
Average Number of Employees. . . .	31.4
Average Wages per Employee . . .	$30,418

PRODUCTS AND SERVICES SEGMENTATION

Other foods	. 24.1%
Other nonfood items	. 16.5%
Fresh and frozen meat	. 13.6%
Fruit and vegetables	. 12.3%
Bakery goods and prepared food . .	. 11.5%
Beverages	8.0%
Dairy and egg products	7.7%
Frozen foods	6.3%

INDUSTRY COSTS

Profit	1.9%
Wages	9.7%
Purchases	. 67.7%
Depreciation	1.0%
Marketing	0.7%
Rent & Utilities	2.7%
Other	16.3%

MARKET SHARE

The Kroger Co.	. 19.0%
Albertsons Companies, Inc. . . .	8.6%
Publix Super Markets, Inc. . .	5.9%
H-E-B Grocery Company LP . . .	3.3%
Koninklijke Ahold Delhaize N.V.. . .	2.9%
Whole Foods Market Inc.	2.1%
Trader Joe's Company	1.6%
Meijer Inc.	1.4%
Southeastern Grocers	1.2%
Wegmans Food Markets Inc. . . .	1.1%

Perimeter departments such as produce, meat, bakery, and deli have higher margins. Excelling in these departments increases overall gross margins. Labor costs must be controlled to experience acceptable net profit.

EXPENSES (% OF ANNUAL SALES)

Cost of Goods	65% to 75%
Occupancy Costs	05% to 10%
Payroll/Labor Costs.	05% to 15%
Profit (pretax)	02% to 15%

QUESTIONS

- Prove reported sales by reviewing recent sales tax reports. Some states charge sales tax on fixture purchases of an asset purchase; be sure there are no surprises here. Ask about the integrity and experience of each department manager. Have you heard of any new grocery stores considering entering the market? What payment terms do you get from your regular suppliers?

INDUSTRY TREND

"Self-checkout is nearly twice as widespread as it was before the pandemic, representing 30% of all grocery store transactions in 2021, according to an FMI-The Food Industry Association report released last week. That is up from 18% in 2018.

The machines are now at 96% of the 38,000 retail stores (across 96 companies) the group surveyed....

"With the turnover rate for grocery store employees in 2021 at 48%, down slightly from a record high in the prior year, according to FMI, industry experts believe grocers may have no choice but to expand their use in the coming months. 'We don't see the labor crisis coming to an end anytime soon,' says Mark Baum, who oversees industry relations for FMI. He adds that self-checkout machines, which cost anywhere from $14,000 to $40,000 to install, pay for themselves quickly. Stores usually only have one or two workers for every five to 10 machines, instead of one cashier per lane."

Source: "More Self-Checkout Is Coming, No Matter How Much You Hate It" by Rachel Wolfe, September 14, 2022, https://www.wsj.com/articles/more-self-checkout-is-coming-no-matter-how-much-you-hate-it-11663112381

"Supermarkets and grocery stores enjoyed price-based gains. Inflationary pressures pushing up the price of groceries and other products bolstered revenue growth despite smaller sales volumes. Supermarkets and grocery stores will continue to expand. While inflationary pressures subsiding will reduce price-based gains, higher sales volumes by consumers will offset losses."

Source: IBISWorld Key Takeaways

EXPERT COMMENTS

Competition is fierce, as there are many major national players throughout the USA and beyond. Success equals being able to purchase the correct product at the best possible pricing, while committing to a lot of community advertising.

For a single independent store buyer, being an owner-operator can be the difference between success and failure. With multistore businesses, strong management and security systems in place are essential. For sellers, don't wait until you're totally worn out from the business operations. Sell when business is thriving and growing. The situation can change quickly, such as the announcement of a new store coming in nearby.

FINANCING

Outside financing is more typical. Occasionally there is a minor amount of seller financing or earnout, but only in highly motivated seller situations.

RESOURCES

- IBISWorld, September 2023: https://www.ibisworld.com
- FMI Supermarket Facts: https://www.fmi.org/our-research/supermarket-facts
- NGA—National Grocers Association: https://www.nationalgrocers.org
- Progressive Grocer: https://progressivegrocer.com
- SN—Supermarket News: https://www.supermarketnews.com
- The Shelby Report: https://www.theshelbyreport.com

Surface Specialists (Franchise)

| NAICS 236118 | Businesses/Units 46

Rules of Thumb

- 95% annual sales
- 2.5 x SDE

INDUSTRY MULTIPLES

Acquisition multiples below are calculated medians using US private industry transactions. Data updated annually. Last update: August 2023.

VALUATION MULTIPLE (MEDIAN VALUE)

UNDER $1 MILLION NET SALES

MVIC/Net Sales	0.36
MVIC/Gross Profit	0.64
MVIC/SDE	1.83
MVIC/EBITDA	2.08

$1 MILLION–$5 MILLION NET SALES

MVIC/Net Sales	0.36
MVIC/Gross Profit	0.96
MVIC/SDE	2.43
MVIC/EBITDA	2.48

OVER $5 MILLION NET SALES

MVIC/Net Sales	0.35
MVIC/Gross Profit	1.26
MVIC/SDE	2.72
MVIC/EBITDA	3.25

Source: DealStats (formerly Pratt's Stats), 2023 (Portland, OR: Business Valuation Resources, LLC), www.bvresources.com/dealstats

PRICING TIPS

Approx. Total Investment: $43,200 to $56,000

RESOURCES

- Surface Specialists: https://www.surfacespecialists.com
- Franchise information: https://www.surfacespecialistsfranchise.com

Surgical and Medical Instrument Manufacturing

| NAICS 339112 | Businesses/Units 13,889

| Profit $7.1 B | Wages $23.3 B | Annual Growth Future 1.8%

| Annual Growth Past -0.9%

INDUSTRY MULTIPLES

Acquisition multiples below are calculated medians using US private industry transactions. Data updated annually. Last update: August 2023.

VALUATION MULTIPLE (MEDIAN VALUE)

UNDER $1 MILLION NET SALES

MVIC/Net Sales	0.67
MVIC/Gross Profit	1.17
MVIC/SDE	3.18
MVIC/EBITDA	4.69

$1 MILLION–$5 MILLION NET SALES

MVIC/Net Sales	5.57
MVIC/Gross Profit	19.64
MVIC/SDE	6.52
MVIC/EBITDA	9.02

OVER $5 MILLION NET SALES

MVIC/Net Sales	3.83
MVIC/Gross Profit	7.10

```
MVIC/SDE  .    .    .    .    .    .    .    .    .    .    .    .    5.70
MVIC/EBITDA  .    .    .    .    .    .    .    .    .    .    .  27.54
```

Source: DealStats (formerly Pratt's Stats), 2023 (Portland, OR: Business Valuation Resources, LLC), www.bvresources.com/dealstats

BENCHMARK DATA

STATISTICS (MEDICAL INSTRUMENT & SUPPLY MANUFACTURING)

Number of Establishments	13,889
Average Profit Margin	7.2%
Revenue per Employee	$353,519
Average Number of Employees.	19.4
Average Wages per Employee	$83,038

PRODUCTS AND SERVICES SEGMENTATION

Surgical instruments	41.7%
Surgical appliances	41.0%
Dental laboratories	5.8%
Dental instruments and supplies	4.9%
Personal safety equipment	4.7%
Hospital beds and other specialized hospital furniture .	1.9%

MAJOR MARKET SEGMENTATION

Hospitals	40.6%
Distributors	39.0%
Third-party healthcare providers	20.4%

INDUSTRY COSTS

Profit	7.2%
Wages	23.6%
Purchases	32.6%
Depreciation	2.0%
Marketing	0.4%
Rent & Utilities	1.3%
Other	32.8%

MARKET SHARE

Johnson & Johnson	8.2%
Stryker Corp.	7.1%
Permobil AB	4.5%
Breg, Inc.	2.9%
Coloplast Corp.	2.8%
Boston Scientific Corporation	2.4%
Laborie, Inc..	1.8%

INDUSTRY TREND

"Profit has been threatened by the growing presence of group purchasing organizations (GPO), which bulk purchase medical instruments and supplies. GPOs have high negotiating power. Demand for medical products is bolstered by favorable demographics, government and private spending on healthcare, medical technology advances and the age of in-stock capital equipment."

Source: IBISWorld Key Takeaways

RESOURCES

- IBISWorld, September 2023: https://www.ibisworld.com

Sylvan Learning (Franchise)

| NAICS 611691 | Businesses/Units 468

Rules of Thumb

- 1.7 x SDE plus inventory

INDUSTRY MULTIPLES

Acquisition multiples below are calculated medians using US private industry transactions. Data updated annually. Last update: August 2023.

VALUATION MULTIPLE (MEDIAN VALUE)

UNDER $1 MILLION NET SALES

MVIC/Net Sales.	0.45
MVIC/Gross Profit	0.49
MVIC/SDE	1.85
MVIC/EBITDA	3.33

$1 MILLION–$5 MILLION NET SALES

MVIC/Net Sales.	0.75
MVIC/Gross Profit	1.32
MVIC/SDE	3.11
MVIC/EBITDA	4.54

OVER $5 MILLION NET SALES   N/A

Source: DealStats (formerly Pratt's Stats), 2023 (Portland, OR: Business Valuation Resources, LLC), www.bvresources.com/dealstats

PRICING TIPS

Approx. Total Investment: $98,087 to $199,582

The multiples of SDE vary depending on the owner benefit. Higher owner benefits drive higher multiples.

QUESTIONS

- How much in prepaid revenues as of today?

RESOURCES

- Sylvan Learning: https://www.sylvanlearning.com
- Franchise information: https://sylvanfranchise.com
- Franchise Group, Inc.: https://franchisegrp.com

SYNERGY HomeCare (Franchise)

| NAICS 621610 | Businesses/Units 396

Rules of Thumb

- 30%–35% annual sales includes inventory

INDUSTRY MULTIPLES

Acquisition multiples below are calculated medians using US private industry transactions. Data updated annually. Last update: August 2023.

VALUATION MULTIPLE (MEDIAN VALUE)

UNDER $1 MILLION NET SALES

MVIC/Net Sales.	0.40
MVIC/Gross Profit	0.69
MVIC/SDE	2.53

| MVIC/EBITDA . . . . | 4.62 |

MVIC/Net Sales.	0.52
MVIC/Gross Profit	0.82
MVIC/SDE	3.03
MVIC/EBITDA	4.91

MVIC/Net Sales.	1.09
MVIC/Gross Profit	2.37
MVIC/SDE	5.31
MVIC/EBITDA	9.36

Source: DealStats (formerly Pratt's Stats), 2023 (Portland, OR: Business Valuation Resources, LLC), www.bvresources.com/dealstats

PRICING TIPS

Approx. Total Investment: $44,286 to $130,912

RESOURCES

- SYNERGY HomeCare: https://synergyhomecare.com
- Franchise information: https://synergyhomecarefranchise.com

Tanning Salons

NAICS 812199	SIC 7299-44	Businesses/Units 56,527
Profit $219.3 M	Wages $594.1 M	Annual Growth Future 0.6%
		Annual Growth Past -5.4%

Rules of Thumb

- 2–4 x SDE includes inventory
- 50%–60% annual sales plus inventory
- 2 x EBIT
- 2 x EBITDA

INDUSTRY MULTIPLES

Acquisition multiples below are calculated medians using US private industry transactions. Data updated annually. Last update: August 2023.

VALUATION MULTIPLE (MEDIAN VALUE)

MVIC/Net Sales.	0.43
MVIC/Gross Profit	0.56
MVIC/SDE	1.80
MVIC/EBITDA	2.61

MVIC/Net Sales.	0.43
MVIC/Gross Profit	0.59
MVIC/SDE	2.90
MVIC/EBITDA	5.02

MVIC/Net Sales.	1.13
MVIC/Gross Profit	3.93
MVIC/SDE	N/A
MVIC/EBITDA	N/A

Source: DealStats (formerly Pratt's Stats), 2023 (Portland, OR: Business Valuation Resources, LLC), www.bvresources.com/dealstats

PRICING TIPS

A big factor to add value to pricing higher than 2 times would be new or newer equipment including sun beds, tanning booths, spray-on tanning booths, red light therapy beds, etc.

The nearly zero COGS for tanning salons makes them an excellent business for first-time owners who are learning product pricing, margins, line extension, etc.

BENCHMARK DATA

STATISTICS (TANNING SALONS)

Number of Establishments	56,527
Average Profit Margin	12.0%
Revenue Per Employee	$28,169
Average Number of Employees	1.2
Average Wages per Employee	$9,027

PRODUCTS AND SERVICES SEGMENTATION

UV tanning	70.4%
Sunless tanning	25.3%
Merchandise sales	4.3%

INDUSTRY COSTS

Profit	12.0%
Wages	32.5%
Purchases	7.8%
Depreciation	2.8%
Marketing	1.6%
Rent & Utilities	4.8%
Other	38.5%

$187 to $225 sales per square foot per year and $200,000 sales per employee per year would be average to above average performance.

1,000 customers in a database for each year of full-time operations, 10 to 12 percent of which have active packages at any one time

Rent, payroll, COGS, and utilities should account for approximately 90 percent of total expenses.

It will be worthwhile to determine bed utilization, electrical power capacity utilization, sales per square foot, and percentage of sale percentages from monthly electronic fund transfers, recurring memberships or single sessions.

EXPENSES (% OF ANNUAL SALES)

Cost of Goods	05% to 10%
Occupancy Costs	10% to 20%
Payroll/Labor Costs	15% to 25%
Profit (pretax)	20% to 30%

QUESTIONS

- Buyers should request and verify the age of the beds and check the usage count/meter that most beds come with. Should check and verify remaining useful life of the lamps. Check the number of memberships and their history.
- Database content? Age and makes/models of beds? Frequency of bulb changing? Spray tan protocol? Sublets to massage therapist, nail tech, skin care, makeup artist, teeth whitening, etc.?

INDUSTRY TREND

Trends are in declining sales due to competition from hair and nail salons and gyms, and mis-information or negative sentiment from the American Academy of Dermatology. Although, before the establishment of tanning salons, dermatologists had tanning beds in their offices and prescribed light treatment for skin disorders like eczema and psoriasis.

"The expansion of products and services kept profit strong. With increasing regulations and consumer concern for safety, expansion into spray-on tanning and new products and services preserved profit. Consolidation was inevitable and at the expense of smaller independent salons. Franchisees had an advantage over smaller independent tanning salons by their ability to weather economic storms such as the COVID-19 pandemic."

Source: IBISWorld Key Takeaways

EXPERT COMMENTS

Sellers need to report all of their sales on their tax returns in order to sell the business for higher price. Buyers need to have a great salesperson at the counter who looks the part to upsell and grow the business. Check the age of the lamps and inspect the acrylics. Both of those are expensive items to replace.

Seek the help of a qualified intermediary or consultant who can help you succeed.

FINANCING

If the books and records are accurate and all the sales are reported, it is SBA financeable; otherwise, seller financing is the way to close the deal.

RESOURCES

- IBISWorld, September 2023: https://www.ibisworld.com
- ist Magazine: https://www.istmagazine.com
- NTTI—The National Tanning Training Institute: https://www.tanningtraining.com
- Smart Tan Magazine: https://www.smarttan.com

Tattoo Parlors

NAICS 812199	SIC 7299-43	Businesses/Units 27,107
Profit $157.5 M	Wages $594.3 M	Annual Growth Future 2.5%
		Annual Growth Past 2.4%

Rules of Thumb

- 50% annual sales includes inventory

INDUSTRY MULTIPLES

Acquisition multiples below are calculated medians using US private industry transactions. Data updated annually. Last update: August 2023.

VALUATION MULTIPLE (MEDIAN VALUE)

UNDER $1 MILLION NET SALES

MVIC/Net Sales.	0.43
MVIC/Gross Profit	0.56
MVIC/SDE	1.80
MVIC/EBITDA	2.61

$1 MILLION–$5 MILLION NET SALES

MVIC/Net Sales.	0.43
MVIC/Gross Profit	0.59

```
MVIC/SDE  .    .    .    .    .    .    .    .    2.90
MVIC/EBITDA  .    .    .    .    .    .    .    5.02
OVER $5 MILLION NET SALES
MVIC/Net Sales.    .    .    .    .    .    .    1.13
MVIC/Gross Profit  .    .    .    .    .    .    3.93
MVIC/SDE  .    .    .    .    .    .    .    .    N/A
MVIC/EBITDA  .    .    .    .    .    .    .    N/A
```

Source: DealStats (formerly Pratt's Stats), 2023 (Portland, OR: Business Valuation Resources, LLC),
www.bvresources.com/dealstats

BENCHMARK DATA

TATTOO STATISTICS (TATTOO ARTISTS)

```
Number of Establishments .    .    .    .    . .27,107
Average Profit Margin  .    .    .    .    .    . 9.9%
Revenue Per Employee .    .    .    .    . $41,510
Average Number of Employees.    .    .    . .1.4
Average Wages per Employee  .    .    . $15,552
```

PRODUCTS AND SERVICES SEGMENTATION

```
Custom-designed tattoos  .    .    .    .    . 59.3%
Predesigned tattoos    .    .    .    .    . 19.8%
Body piercings  .    .    .    .    .    .    . 16.8%
Other    .    .    .    .    .    .    .    . 4.1%
```

INDUSTRY COSTS

```
Profit    .    .    .    .    .    .    .    . 9.9%
Wages  .    .    .    .    .    .    .    . 37.3%
Purchases  .    .    .    .    .    .    . 7.4%
Depreciation  .    .    .    .    .    .    . 3.1%
Marketing  .    .    .    .    .    .    . 1.5%
Rent & Utilities .    .    .    .    .    . 4.5%
Other    .    .    .    .    .    .    . 36.3%
```

INDUSTRY TREND

"The growth in the number of people with tattoos is being driven by several factors, including the increasing popularity of tattoos among millennials and Gen Z, the growing acceptance of tattoos in the workplace, and the rise of social media, which has made it easier for people to share their tattoos with others. The industry is becoming more professionalized. Tattoo artists are increasingly required to have formal training and certification, and they are also subject to a number of regulations and safety standards."

Source: IBISWorld Key Takeaways

RESOURCES

• IBISWorld, September 2023: https://www.ibisworld.com

Taxicab Businesses

NAICS 485310	SIC 4121-01	Businesses/Units 1,282,503
Profit $1.3 B	Wages $18.6 B	Annual Growth Future 2.0%
		Annual Growth Past -1.5%

Rules of Thumb

• 4 x EBITDA plus value of vehicles

INDUSTRY MULTIPLES

Acquisition multiples below are calculated medians using US private industry transactions. Data updated annually. Last update: August 2023.

VALUATION MULTIPLE (MEDIAN VALUE)

UNDER $1 MILLION NET SALES

MVIC/Net Sales	0.50
MVIC/Gross Profit	0.51
MVIC/SDE	2.80
MVIC/EBITDA	5.03

$1 MILLION–$5 MILLION NET SALES

MVIC/Net Sales	0.26
MVIC/Gross Profit	0.51
MVIC/SDE	1.25
MVIC/EBITDA	0.76

OVER $5 MILLION NET SALES — N/A

Source: DealStats (formerly Pratt's Stats), 2023 (Portland, OR: Business Valuation Resources, LLC), www.bvresources.com/dealstats

PRICING TIPS

Selling price should be between one and two years' net profit, depending upon the number of cabs and their respective ages.

BENCHMARK DATA

STATISTICS (TAXI & LIMOUSINE SERVICES)

Number of Establishments	1,282,503
Average Profit Margin	2.7%
Revenue Per Employee	$39,328
Average Number of Employees	1.1
Average Wages per Employee	$15,088

PRODUCTS AND SERVICES SEGMENTATION

Taxi and taxi leasing services	67.0%
Luxury and corporate sedan services	15.3%
Stretch limousine services	11.0%
SUV, large van and other services	5.1%
Hearse rentals and other funeral services	1.6%

INDUSTRY COSTS

Profit	2.7%
Wages	37.6%
Purchases	13.1%
Depreciation	5.9%
Marketing	0.6%
Rent & Utilities	4.7%
Other	35.3%

INDUSTRY TREND

"Los Angeles joins New York City, San Francisco, and a host of other major cities around the world that feature their taxis in Uber's ridehail app. It also represents the emergence of a new and unexpected alliance between taxi owners and the tech company that vowed to disrupt their business."

Source: "How Uber learned to stop fighting and play nice with taxis" by Andrew J. Hawkins, September 26, 2023, https://www.theverge.com/2023/9/26/23888950/uber-taxi-driver-referral-third-party-los-angeles

"Rising oil prices have caused a major depression in profit levels, while prices are anticipated to drop in 2023, there is still a lot of uncertainty surrounding this.

Uber and other ride-hailing services continue to soak up demand from traditional taxi operators. This is particularly true in NYC."

Source: IBISWorld Key Takeaways

RESOURCES
- IBISWorld, September 2023: https://www.ibisworld.com

Technology Companies: Service

| NAICS 541

Rules of Thumb
- 3–7 x EBITDA
- 3 x SDE plus inventory

PRICING TIPS

The larger the business, the larger the multiple.

BENCHMARK DATA

EXPENSES (% OF ANNUAL SALES)

Cost of Goods	40% to 50%
Occupancy Costs	04% to 05%
Payroll/Labor Costs.	20% to 22%
Profit (pretax)	15% to 20%

QUESTIONS
- What are the staffing issues?
- How consistent have the margins been for specific products?
- What is your biggest challenge in operating the business?
- What would you do to grow the business in the next 12 to 18 months?

EXPERT COMMENTS

Understanding the upcoming changes in the industry and understanding competition is critical to success.

Most companies in the industry have been around a while and have their own niche; lots of long-term customers; usually good downside protection.

FINANCING

Smaller companies (less than $10M) are seller financed while others may qualify for bank or outside financing depending on inventory levels, receivable levels and past banking relationships.

SBA is difficult because most of the value is likely to be in goodwill. High cash component, seller carry and performance payouts are common.

Typically sellers get a good parity of value on earnouts, noncompetes, etc.

Telecommunications Carriers (Wired)

| NAICS 517311 | Businesses/Units 5,216

| Profit $6.5 B | Wages $12.1 B | Annual Growth Future 0.1%

| Annual Growth Past -2.6%

Rules of Thumb

- 2.5 x SDE includes inventory

INDUSTRY MULTIPLES

Acquisition multiples below are calculated medians using US private industry transactions. Data updated annually. Last update: August 2023.

VALUATION MULTIPLE (MEDIAN VALUE)

UNDER $1 MILLION NET SALES

MVIC/Net Sales	0.59
MVIC/Gross Profit	0.59
MVIC/SDE	N/A
MVIC/EBITDA	N/A

$1 MILLION–$5 MILLION NET SALES

MVIC/Net Sales	5.68
MVIC/Gross Profit	15.17
MVIC/SDE	N/A
MVIC/EBITDA	N/A

OVER $5 MILLION NET SALES

MVIC/Net Sales	2.35
MVIC/Gross Profit	3.57
MVIC/SDE	7.25
MVIC/EBITDA	9.32

Source: DealStats (formerly Pratt's Stats), 2023 (Portland, OR: Business Valuation Resources, LLC), www.bvresources.com/dealstats

PRICING TIPS

Need to understand how the carrier commission structure will impact the current client base and future sales. Trained, knowledgeable and professional sales staff is critical; this is not an order-taking environment.

BENCHMARK DATA

STATISTICS (WIRED TELECOMMUNICATIONS CARRIERS)

Number of Establishments	5,216
Average Profit Margin	9.7%
Revenue Per Employee	$595,246
Average Number of Employees	21.8
Average Wages per Employee	$104,849

PRODUCTS AND SERVICES SEGMENTATION

Long-distance voice services	32.8%
Carrier services	27.0%
Local voice services	23.3%
Private network services	12.9%
Subscriber line charges	4.0%

MAJOR MARKET SEGMENTATION

Business, government and nonprofit organizations	32.3%
Households w/adults aged 65 and older	19.1%
Households w/adults aged 35-54	18.9%

Households w/adults aged 55-64	. . . . . .	. 14.0%
Households w/adults aged 25-34	. . . . . .	. 9.4%
Households w/adults aged 18-25	. . . . . .	. 6.3%

INDUSTRY COSTS

Profit	. . . .	. 9.7%
Wages	. . . .	. 17.9%
Purchases	. . . .	. 30.9%
Depreciation	. . . .	. 10.7%
Marketing	. . . .	. 2.4%
Rent & Utilities	. . . .	. 2.7%
Other	. . . .	. 25.7%

EXPENSES (% OF ANNUAL SALES)

Cost of Goods	. . . .	. 40%
Occupancy Costs	. . . . . .	. 12%
Payroll/Labor Costs.	. . . . . .	. 24%
Profit (pretax)	. . . .	. 17%

QUESTIONS

- Trends for client counts? Cancellation rates and velocity?

INDUSTRY TREND

"External competitors have siphoned demand and revenue. Wired telecommunications carriers have faced considerable difficulties and contradictory tendencies. The transition to fiber-optic services has partially reduced external competition from wireless telecommunication carriers. Fiber-optic services will continue to become more popular."

Source: IBISWorld Key Takeaways

EXPERT COMMENTS

Very robust, competitive landscape, but a savvy operator can carve out a healthy market share.

RESOURCES

- IBISWorld, September 2023: https://www.ibisworld.com

Telecommunications Resellers

| NAICS 517121 | | Businesses/Units 5,126 |

| Profit $6.2 B | | Wages $2.4 B | | Annual Growth Future 0.8% |

| | | | | Annual Growth Past 0.9% |

BENCHMARK DATA

STATISTICS (TELECOMMUNICATIONS RESELLERS)

Number of Establishments	. 5,126
Average Profit Margin	. 25.8%
Revenue Per Employee	$675,929
Average Number of Employees.	. 7.0
Average Wages per Employee	$71,450

PRODUCTS AND SERVICES SEGMENTATION

Mobile telephony	. 57.0%
Fixed local and long-distance services.	. 22.1%
Resale of equipment and merchandise	. 7.9%

Carrier and internet backbone 7.5%
Internet and internet telephony services 3.0%
Other services 2.5%

MAJOR MARKET SEGMENTATION

Businesses 63.0%
Consumers 27.2%
Public 9.8%

INDUSTRY COSTS

Profit 25.8%
Wages 10.2%
Purchases 39.8%
Depreciation 1.4%
Marketing 4.0%
Rent & Utilities 2.5%
Other 16.3%

MARKET SHARE

América Móvil SAB de CV 39.4%
Consumer Cellular Inc. 5.2%
Duquesne Light Holdings Inc. 4.5%

INDUSTRY TREND

"The emergence of prominent upstream enterprises in the market has led to intense price-based competition. Smaller scale companies have used customization options and customer service as points of differentiation to gain a competitive edge and service niche markets looking for affordable telecommunication options. Strong demand for telecommunication services during remote work has enabled the industry to be shielded from the economic hardships of the pandemic. Revenue has continued to grow as macroeconomic conditions improved, as heightened corporate profit enabled industry enterprises to capitalize on demand from the business market."

Source: IBISWorld Key Takeaways

RESOURCES

• IBISWorld, April 2023: https://www.ibisworld.com

The Maids (Franchise)

| NAICS 561720 | Businesses/Units 1,373

Rules of Thumb

• 40%–45% annual sales plus inventory

INDUSTRY MULTIPLES

Acquisition multiples below are calculated medians using US private industry transactions. Data updated annually. Last update: August 2023.

VALUATION MULTIPLE (MEDIAN VALUE)

UNDER $1 MILLION NET SALES
MVIC/Net Sales. 0.59
MVIC/Gross Profit 0.76
MVIC/SDE 2.03
MVIC/EBITDA 2.92
$1 MILLION–$5 MILLION NET SALES
MVIC/Net Sales. 0.45

MVIC/Gross Profit 1.02
MVIC/SDE 2.86
MVIC/EBITDA 4.05

OVER $5 MILLION NET SALES
MVIC/Net Sales. 0.53
MVIC/Gross Profit 2.26
MVIC/SDE 4.26
MVIC/EBITDA 5.48

Source: DealStats (formerly Pratt's Stats), 2023 (Portland, OR: Business Valuation Resources, LLC), www.bvresources.com/dealstats

PRICING TIPS

Approx. Total Investment: $77,600 to $155,900

RESOURCES

- The Maids: https://www.maids.com
- Franchise information: https://www.maids.com/franchise/

The UPS Store (Franchise)

| NAICS 561431 | Businesses/Units 5,197

Rules of Thumb

- 35%–40% annual sales plus inventory
- 2–3 x SDE plus inventory
- 76% annual sales

INDUSTRY MULTIPLES

Acquisition multiples below are calculated medians using US private industry transactions. Data updated annually. Last update: August 2023.

VALUATION MULTIPLE (MEDIAN VALUE)

UNDER $1 MILLION NET SALES
MVIC/Net Sales. 0.49
MVIC/Gross Profit 0.86
MVIC/SDE 2.12
MVIC/EBITDA 2.78

$1 MILLION–$5 MILLION NET SALES
MVIC/Net Sales. 0.13
MVIC/Gross Profit 0.69
MVIC/SDE 1.89
MVIC/EBITDA 6.02

OVER $5 MILLION NET SALES
MVIC/Net Sales. 0.79
MVIC/Gross Profit 3.45
MVIC/SDE 6.91
MVIC/EBITDA 7.44

Source: DealStats (formerly Pratt's Stats), 2023 (Portland, OR: Business Valuation Resources, LLC), www.bvresources.com/dealstats

PRICING TIPS

Approx. Total Investment: $122,227 to $508,472

RESOURCES

- The UPS Store: https://www.theupsstore.com
- Franchise information: https://www.theupsstorefranchise.com

Third-Party Administration of Insurance and Pension Funds

| NAICS 524292 | Businesses/Units 139,497

| Profit $42.8 B | Wages $42.1 B | Annual Growth Future 1.5%

| Annual Growth Past 3.9%

INDUSTRY MULTIPLES

Acquisition multiples below are calculated medians using US private industry transactions. Data updated annually. Last update: August 2023.

VALUATION MULTIPLE (MEDIAN VALUE)

UNDER $1 MILLION NET SALES	N/A
$1 MILLION–$5 MILLION NET SALES	
MVIC/Net Sales.	1.08
MVIC/Gross Profit	1.81
MVIC/SDE	4.54
MVIC/EBITDA	5.33
OVER $5 MILLION NET SALES	
MVIC/Net Sales.	0.98
MVIC/Gross Profit	5.73
MVIC/SDE	4.70
MVIC/EBITDA	24.16

Source: DealStats (formerly Pratt's Stats), 2023 (Portland, OR: Business Valuation Resources, LLC), www.bvresources.com/dealstats

BENCHMARK DATA

STATISTICS (THIRD-PARTY ADMINISTRATORS & INSURANCE CLAIMS ADJUSTERS)

Number of Establishments .	139,497
Average Profit Margin	15.6%
Revenue Per Employee .	$414,921
Average Number of Employees.	4.9
Average Wages per Employee .	$64,692

PRODUCTS AND SERVICES SEGMENTATION

Third-party administration of health and welfare funds	83.6%
Claims adjustment services	4.2%
Consulting services for insurance .	4.0%
Third-party administration of workers' compensation funds	3.0%
Third-party administration of pension funds	2.6%
Third-party administration of self-insurance funds.	1.8%
All other .	0.8%

MAJOR MARKET SEGMENTATION

Health and medical insurance funds	35.3%
Life insurance and annuity funds	30.8%
Property and casualty insurance funds.	26.3%
Other	5.0%
Pension funds	2.6%

INDUSTRY COSTS

Profit	15.6%
Wages	15.3%
Purchases	3.8%
Depreciation	1.4%
Marketing	2.3%
Rent & Utilities	2.1%
Other	59.4%

Capgemini SE 2.4%
EmblemHealth Inc. 2.1%
Manulife Financial Corp 2.0%
Infosys Limited 1.9%

INDUSTRY TREND

"Health and medical insurance are one of the largest markets. As health and medical insurers incur increased demand from more people, including those on Medicaid and Medicare plans, claims processing for these industries has similarly increased. The concern over inflation and higher interest will create tough market conditions. Tough market conditions, characterized by more stringent underwriting criteria and less issuance of insurance policies, are important for insurers themselves, as underwriters must evaluate risk assessment and insurance prices."

Source: IBISWorld Key Takeaways

RESOURCES

• IBISWorld, September 2023: https://www.ibisworld.com

Tile Installers

| NAICS 238340 | Businesses/Units 66,575

| Profit $668.4 M | Wages $4 B | Annual Growth Future 0.4%

| Annual Growth Past -2.2%

INDUSTRY MULTIPLES

Acquisition multiples below are calculated medians using US private industry transactions. Data updated annually. Last update: August 2023.

VALUATION MULTIPLE (MEDIAN VALUE)

UNDER $1 MILLION NET SALES
MVIC/Net Sales. 0.59
MVIC/Gross Profit 0.78
MVIC/SDE 2.54
MVIC/EBITDA 3.00

$1 MILLION–$5 MILLION NET SALES
MVIC/Net Sales. 0.78
MVIC/Gross Profit 1.28
MVIC/SDE . . . . N/A
MVIC/EBITDA . . . . N/A

OVER $5 MILLION NET SALES
MVIC/Net Sales. 0.87
MVIC/Gross Profit 2.67
MVIC/SDE 4.21
MVIC/EBITDA 7.77

Source: DealStats (formerly Pratt's Stats), 2023 (Portland, OR: Business Valuation Resources, LLC), www.bvresources.com/dealstats

BENCHMARK DATA

STATISTICS (TILE INSTALLERS)

Number of Establishments 66,575
Average Profit Margin 5.2%

Revenue Per Employee $116,071
Average Number of Employees 1.7
Average Wages per Employee $35,980

PRODUCTS AND SERVICES SEGMENTATION

Tile, terrazzo and mosaic contracting 51.6%
Marble, granite, and slate contracting 39.1%
Other construction 8.0%
Nonconstruction activities (e.g. retailing) 1.3%

MAJOR MARKET SEGMENTATION

Commercial building construction 30.6%
Municipal building construction 28.4%
Single-family residential building construction 22.3%
Multifamily residential building construction 10.0%
Other nonresidential building construction 8.7%

INDUSTRY COSTS

Profit 5.2%
Wages 31.1%
Purchases 38.4%
Depreciation 1.3%
Marketing 0.4%
Rent & Utilities 5.8%
Other 17.9%

INDUSTRY TREND

"High interest rates have taken a toll on a once-flourishing residential market, siphoning away demand for tile installation. Amid an unaccommodating borrowing environment, investment in residential construction is discouraged, damaging tile installation contractors' revenue-earning potential. Nonresidential construction was depleted by pandemic-induced business closures and lockdowns, but recovering corporate profit has sustained industry contractors. As macroeconomic conditions improve and nonresidential construction activity enlivens, tile installation contractors look to capitalize on burgeoning commercial and municipal building construction."

Source: IBISWorld Key Takeaways

RESOURCES

• IBISWorld, March 2023: https://www.ibisworld.com

Tire Stores

NAICS 441320	SIC 5531-23	Businesses/Units 36,557
Profit $1.1 B	Wages $9.3 B	Annual Growth Future 1.2%
		Annual Growth Past 1.5%

Rules of Thumb

• 25% annual gross sales
• 1–3 x SDE plus inventory
• 3–4 x EBIT
• 2.5–3 x EBITDA

INDUSTRY MULTIPLES

Acquisition multiples below are calculated medians using US private industry transactions. Data updated annually. Last update: August 2023.

VALUATION MULTIPLE (MEDIAN VALUE)

UNDER $1 MILLION NET SALES

MVIC/Net Sales.	0.33
MVIC/Gross Profit	0.65
MVIC/SDE	2.37
MVIC/EBITDA	2.47

$1 MILLION–$5 MILLION NET SALES

MVIC/Net Sales.	0.37
MVIC/Gross Profit	0.69
MVIC/SDE	2.69
MVIC/EBITDA	3.65

OVER $5 MILLION NET SALES

MVIC/Net Sales.	0.50
MVIC/Gross Profit	1.23
MVIC/SDE	3.14
MVIC/EBITDA	7.46

Source: DealStats (formerly Pratt's Stats), 2023 (Portland, OR: Business Valuation Resources, LLC), www.bvresources.com/dealstats

BENCHMARK DATA

STATISTICS (TIRE DEALERS)

Number of Establishments	36,557
Average Profit Margin	2.5%
Revenue Per Employee	$221,585
Average Number of Employees.	5.7
Average Wages per Employee	$45,181

PRODUCTS AND SERVICES SEGMENTATION

Passenger car tires.	55.5%
Medium- and heavy-duty truck tires	15.0%
Light-truck tires.	12.8%
Automotive services	11.6%
Off-road tires	3.8%
Farm tires	1.3%

INDUSTRY COSTS

Profit	2.5%
Wages	20.4%
Purchases	49.0%
Depreciation	1.2%
Marketing	0.9%
Rent & Utilities	3.2%
Other	22.7%

MARKET SHARE

The Reinalt-Thomas Corporation	12.9%
Sumitomo Corporation	6.3%

EXPENSES (% OF ANNUAL SALES)

Cost of Goods	36% to 43%
Occupancy Costs	09% to 15%
Payroll/Labor Costs.	20% to 28%
Profit (pretax)	13% to 20%

- Ask the owner what their percentage of revenues is on tires vs. aftermarket services. The split for a good store would be 50 percent tires to 50 percent services; however, the average normally comes in at 70 percent tires to 30 percent services. You may also ask what is their vehicle count and average ticket on a monthly basis. Do they have a manager and key techs, the tenure of each one, are all employees W-2, and what are their benefits?
- Where do they obtain their tires from (suppliers) and what is their delivery process timewise?
- Reason for selling? What he/she does on a daily basis? Workers' comp mod rate? Upside potential?

INDUSTRY TREND

"The COVID-19 pandemic dealt a significant blow to the Tire Dealers industry. Decreased travel resulted in drastically decreased demand for new tires. Fuel-efficient tires are becoming increasingly popular. These tires are more environmentally friendly than traditional tires, and degrade much quicker, requiring more frequent replacement. The need for heavy transport to move heavy material products across the United States rose in line with industrial production. This has translated into a rise in demand for commercial tires."

Source: IBISWorld Key Takeaways

EXPERT COMMENTS

For a buyer: You want to do your books and records check along with the staff in place. Who are their suppliers and what is their proximity to the store? Are there any commercial accounts that attribute more than 20 percent of the revenues? The number of customers in their database?

For a seller: You need to have your books and tax returns in order, an operations manual, management in place, all employees on a W-2, good monthly records showing average ticket and number of vehicles for the same period. Keep your shop very clean and upgrade the customer area annually.

FINANCING

When the revenues exceed $1M, you will generally see outside financing; for the smaller-producing stores, you will generally see seller financing.

RESOURCES

- IBISWorld, September 2023: https://www.ibisworld.com
- MTD—Modern Tire Dealer: https://www.moderntiredealer.com
- Tire Business: https://www.tirebusiness.com
- Tire Review: https://www.tirereview.com

Title Abstract and Settlement Offices

NAICS 541191	SIC 6541-02	Businesses/Units 33,103
Profit $1.7 B	Wages $6.4 B	Annual Growth Future -0.5%
		Annual Growth Past -1.3%

Rules of Thumb

- 60% annual sales
- 3 x SDE
- 5 x EBIT
- 4.5 x EBITDA

INDUSTRY MULTIPLES

Acquisition multiples below are calculated medians using US private industry transactions. Data updated annually. Last update: August 2023.

VALUATION MULTIPLE (MEDIAN VALUE)

UNDER $1 MILLION NET SALES

MVIC/Net Sales	0.99
MVIC/Gross Profit	0.99
MVIC/SDE	2.33
MVIC/EBITDA	6.10

$1 MILLION–$5 MILLION NET SALES

MVIC/Net Sales	0.91
MVIC/Gross Profit	0.91
MVIC/SDE	3.29
MVIC/EBITDA	12.80

OVER $5 MILLION NET SALES

MVIC/Net Sales	0.58
MVIC/Gross Profit	N/A
MVIC/SDE	N/A
MVIC/EBITDA	3.94

Source: DealStats (formerly Pratt's Stats), 2023 (Portland, OR: Business Valuation Resources, LLC), www.bvresources.com/dealstats

PRICING TIPS

Affiliated business arrangements (ABAs) are in vogue. Make sure the ABA is transferable upon sale. Title agencies will command higher prices in states with higher filed premiums.

Criteria include the sales history and trends. Title companies' revenues are affected by interest rates, but the stronger ones will maintain profits through the ups and downs by adjustments of variable expenses.

BENCHMARK DATA

STATISTICS (CONVEYANCING SERVICES)

Number of Establishments	33,103
Average Profit Margin	9.4%
Revenue Per Employee	$190,853
Average Number of Employees	3.2
Average Wages per Employee	$66,245

PRODUCTS AND SERVICES SEGMENTATION

Title, abstract and settlement services	66.4%
Other	18.6%
Title search and other document filing services	8.4%
Process services	4.7%
Patent copyright and other intellectual property document services	1.9%

MAJOR MARKET SEGMENTATIONS

Businesses	57.2%
Individuals	40.6%
Government and nonprofit organizations	2.2%

INDUSTRY COSTS

Profit	9.4%
Wages	34.8%
Purchases	2.8%
Depreciation	1.1%
Marketing	2.9%
Rent & Utilities	10.2%
Other	38.9%

MARKET SHARE

Fidelity National Financial, Inc.	20.3%
Old Republic International Corporation	19.0%
First American Financial Corporation	16.4%
Stewart Information Services Corporation	6.1%
Epiq Systems Inc.	5.1%
Integron, Inc.	3.6%
UnitedLex Corporation	3.5%
BDO USA, LLP	3.4%
Infosys Limited	2.2%
Elevate Services, Inc.	1.4%
CRA International, Inc.	1.2%
Clarivate PLC	1.2%
Argo Group International Holdings, Ltd.	1.0%

Title companies typically retain 70 percent of the premium on title insurance policies issued, with remaining 30 percent going to the underwriter.

EXPENSES (% OF ANNUAL SALES)

Cost of Goods	30%
Occupancy Costs	07%
Payroll/Labor Costs	20%
Profit (pretax)	35%

QUESTIONS

• How many referral sources does the company have solid relationships with?

INDUSTRY TREND

"The industry grew through consistent housing starts and increased home sales. The first half of the period experienced a strong economy with a steadily rising house price index despite increasing interest rates. The housing market will become unstable. Rising interest rates, an inadequate housing supply and decreased per capita disposable income will hinder expanding real estate and construction activity."

Source: IBISWorld Key Takeaways

EXPERT COMMENTS

Although there is significant competition, this is a highly profitable industry with relatively low barriers to entry.

Buyers for title agencies have increased due to legislative changes.

RESOURCES

• IBISWorld, March 2023: https://www.ibisworld.com

Tobacco Stores

| NAICS 459991 | SIC 5993-01

Rules of Thumb

- 15%–20% annual sales plus inventory

RESOURCES

- TMA: https://www.tma.org

Tour Operators

| NAICS 561520 | SIC 4725-01 | Businesses/Units 10,910

| Profit $677.2 M | Wages $2.9 B | Annual Growth Future 3.5%

| Annual Growth Past -3.4%

Rules of Thumb

- 2–4 x SDE
- 2 x SDE for small companies
- 3–5 x EBITDA—multiple expands as profits go up
- 3 x EBIT

INDUSTRY MULTIPLES

Acquisition multiples below are calculated medians using US private industry transactions. Data updated annually. Last update: August 2023.

VALUATION MULTIPLE (MEDIAN VALUE)

UNDER $1 MILLION NET SALES

MVIC/Net Sales.	0.73
MVIC/Gross Profit	1.20
MVIC/SDE	2.30
MVIC/EBITDA	2.57

$1 MILLION–$5 MILLION NET SALES

MVIC/Net Sales.	0.36
MVIC/Gross Profit	1.00
MVIC/SDE	2.61
MVIC/EBITDA	3.51

OVER $5 MILLION NET SALES

MVIC/Net Sales.	1.26
MVIC/Gross Profit	1.53
MVIC/SDE	4.58
MVIC/EBITDA	4.85

Source: DealStats (formerly Pratt's Stats), 2023 (Portland, OR: Business Valuation Resources, LLC), www.bvresources.com/dealstats

PRICING TIPS

The majority of tour operators are valued using a multiple of their SDE or EBITDA; we don't see a percentage of annual gross sales used. We look at net profit and all add-backs that can be added back to the net profit. Things like current owner's salary and replacement costs also figure into the evaluation.

Revenue flight per hour; capex

Upscale or midgrade?

Average markup? Wholesale or direct?

BENCHMARK DATA

STATISTICS (TOUR OPERATORS)

Number of Establishments 10,910	
Average Profit Margin 6.6%	
Revenue Per Employee $231,045	
Average Number of Employees. 4.4	
Average Wages per Employee . . . $64,628	

PRODUCTS AND SERVICES SEGMENTATION

Domestic packaged tours 35.1%	
International packaged tours 30.9%	
Domestic customized tours 17.7%	
Other 8.5%	
International customized tours 7.8%	

MAJOR MARKET SEGMENTATION

Individuals 65.2%	
Travel agencies 25.2%	
Businesses 5.6%	
Other 4.0%	

INDUSTRY COSTS

Profit 6.6%	
Wages 28.0%	
Purchases 45.1%	
Depreciation 1.6%	
Rent & Utilities 1.9%	
Other 15.5%	

MARKET SHARE

Apple Leisure Group 18.5%

Many tour operators are paying staff lower salaries while increasing bonuses and commissions on sales. Locations are now becoming less important; many operate from their homes, and employees do the same. Buyers will try to lower rent or overhead by using technology or closing a location.

EXPENSES (% OF ANNUAL SALES)

Cost of Goods . . . . 80% to 90%	
Occupancy Costs . . . . . 10% to 15%	
Payroll/Labor Costs. . . . . 45% to 55%	
Profit (pretax) 20%	

QUESTIONS

- Buyer to seller: Why are you selling? Is management willing to stay? Age of the aircraft?

INDUSTRY TREND

"Intensifying competition from mobile apps and websites has aided consumers in finding lower travel options. Tour operators seeking to compete with online resources have reduced prices. Domestic and international travel is set to increase along with disposable income over the next five years, resulting in more consumers seeking luxurious travel options."

Source: IBISWorld Key Takeaways

EXPERT COMMENTS

How productive are their agents? Is the business diversified? How are sales trending? For sellers—keep expenses low, have great financial records, and understand they are in a risky industry.

Ninety percent of the buyers are in the travel and tourism industry. Being outside the industry has a strong learning curve; a buyer such as this needs to have a willing seller that will stay on and train. There are Internet courses on how to be a tour owner-operator.

Normally there are many competitors in this industry, so anyone that has a unique clientele, offers special services, has knowledgeable staff, and keeps expenses low has a great chance to sell.

Study the industry and the markets where the business is located well in advance.

FINANCING

Seller financing is most common—30 percent to 40 percent cash at close and the balance over 2 to 3 years.

Usually outside financing. Owner-operators rarely carry notes.

RESOURCES

- IBISWorld, January 2023: https://ibisworld.com/
- ATTA—Adventure Travel Trade Association: https://www.adventuretravel.biz
- HAI—Helicopter Association International: https://www.rotor.org
- IITA—International Inbound Travel Association: https://internationalinboundtravelassociation.org
- NTA—National Tour Association: https://ntaonline.com
- TravelPulse: https://www.travelpulse.com
- USTOA—United States Tour Operators Association: https://ustoa.com

Towing Companies

NAICS 488410	SIC 7549-01	Businesses/Units 10,689
Profit $853 M	Wages $3.1 B	Annual Growth Future 1.2%
		Annual Growth Past -0.3%

Rules of Thumb

- 70% annual revenues plus inventory
- 2.75 x EBITDA

INDUSTRY MULTIPLES

Acquisition multiples below are calculated medians using US private industry transactions. Data updated annually. Last update: August 2023.

VALUATION MULTIPLE (MEDIAN VALUE)

UNDER $1 MILLION NET SALES

MVIC/Net Sales	0.65
MVIC/Gross Profit	0.82
MVIC/SDE	2.78
MVIC/EBITDA	2.32

$1 MILLION–$5 MILLION NET SALES

MVIC/Net Sales	0.88
MVIC/Gross Profit	0.93
MVIC/SDE	3.11
MVIC/EBITDA	4.71

OVER $5 MILLION NET SALES   N/A

Source: DealStats (formerly Pratt's Stats), 2023 (Portland, OR: Business Valuation Resources, LLC), www.bvresources.com/dealstats

PRICING TIPS

Extreme care with adding back depreciation, and/or allowance to replace trucks. Define which segment of industry, and check to see if the insurance premium is fair market value. Small companies and those in nonconsent businesses are hard to sell.

BENCHMARK DATA

STATISTICS (AUTOMOBILE TOWING)

Number of Establishments	10,689
Average Profit Margin	9.0%
Revenue Per Employee	$141,703
Average Number of Employees	6.4
Average Wages per Employee	$47,059

PRODUCTS AND SERVICES SEGMENTATION

Commercial vehicle towing	81.2%
Passenger car towing	16.3%
Maintenance and roadside assistance	2.5%

MAJOR MARKET SEGMENTATION

State and local government	48.5%
Commercial customers	41.6%
Individuals	9.9%

INDUSTRY COSTS

Profit	9.0%
Wages	33.2%
Purchases	31.6%
Depreciation	7.5%
Marketing	0.1%
Rent & Utilities	3.0%
Other	15.7%

Drivers ought to bring in revenue of 2 to 3 times their salaries.

EXPENSES (% OF ANNUAL SALES)

Cost of Goods	10% to 20%
Occupancy Costs	08% to 10%
Payroll/Labor Costs	30%
Profit (pretax)	14% to 20%

INDUSTRY TREND

"There is a higher likelihood of car accidents or other vehicle problems as the number of vehicles on the road and average vehicle miles have risen over time, which has increased demand for towing services and roadside help. Demand for these services from businesses and governments to assist in removing vehicles that are parked illegally on their property in violation of the law has been stable."

Source: IBISWorld Key Takeaways

EXPERT COMMENTS

Be careful to use tax returns versus P&Ls to calculate EBITDA, and don't pay a higher multiple than described here.

Anybody can buy trucks, but getting contracts and hiring qualified drivers are difficult.

FINANCING

Deals under $2M in purchase price many times involve seller financing, 5 years at 6 percent. Larger deals typically are paid in full at closing.

- IBISWorld, February 2023: https://www.ibisworld.com
- TRAA—Towing and Recovery Association of America, Inc.: http://traaonline.com

Toy and Hobby Goods and Supplies Merchant Wholesalers

| NAICS 423920 | Businesses/Units 9,845

| Profit $2.1 B | Wages $4 B | Annual Growth Future 0.0%

| Annual Growth Past 1.7%

INDUSTRY MULTIPLES

Acquisition multiples below are calculated medians using US private industry transactions. Data updated annually. Last update: August 2023.

VALUATION MULTIPLE (MEDIAN VALUE)

UNDER $1 MILLION NET SALES	N/A
$1 MILLION–$5 MILLION NET SALES	
MVIC/Net Sales.	1.71
MVIC/Gross Profit	2.58
MVIC/SDE	3.41
MVIC/EBITDA	4.23
OVER $5 MILLION NET SALES	
MVIC/Net Sales.	1.78
MVIC/Gross Profit	3.93
MVIC/SDE	7.33
MVIC/EBITDA	7.81

Source: DealStats (formerly Pratt's Stats), 2023 (Portland, OR: Business Valuation Resources, LLC), www.bvresources.com/dealstats

BENCHMARK DATA

STATISTICS (TOY & CRAFT SUPPLIES WHOLESALING)

Number of Establishments	9,845
Average Profit Margin	4.5%
Revenue Per Employee	$1,067,000
Average Number of Employees.	4.39
Average Wages per Employee	$93,110

PRODUCTS AND SERVICES SEGMENTATION

Video games	44.1%
Traditional toys including children's vehicles	37.2%
Hobby and craft supplies	10.8%
Other	7.9%

MAJOR MARKET SEGMENTATION

Big-box stores	56.0%
Wholesalers and distributors for resale	28.8%
Discount department stores	9.4%
Independent specialty stores	3.9%
Direct sales	1.3%
Businesses for end use	0.6%

INDUSTRY COSTS

Profit	4.5%
Wages	8.7%

Purchases	. . . .	71.5%
Depreciation	. . . .	0.6%
Marketing	. . . .	1.1%
Rent & Utilities	. . . .	1.1%
Other	. . . .	12.5%

MARKET SHARE

| Mattel | . . . . | 8.6% |
| Hasbro | . . . . | 7.8% |

INDUSTRY TREND

"Limited in-person activities during the COVID-19 pandemic boosted demand as parents sought toys and activities for their children. Time spent indoors propelled the video game segment to surpass industry sales of traditional toys. Vertically integrated toy manufacturers constrict profit by putting significant pressure on wholesalers' pricing. However, the globalization of manufacturing solidifies the importance of wholesalers."

Source: IBISWorld Key Takeaways

RESOURCES

- IBISWorld, October 2023: https://www.ibisworld.com

Toy Stores

	NAICS 451120		SIC 5945-17		Businesses/Units 19,761
	Profit $1.1 B		Wages $2.3 B		Annual Growth Future 0.4%
					Annual Growth Past -0.9%

Rules of Thumb

- 20%–25% annual sales plus inventory

INDUSTRY MULTIPLES

Acquisition multiples below are calculated medians using US private industry transactions. Data updated annually. Last update: August 2023.

VALUATION MULTIPLE (MEDIAN VALUE)

UNDER $1 MILLION NET SALES
MVIC/Net Sales.	. . . . . .	0.31
MVIC/Gross Profit	. . . . . .	0.56
MVIC/SDE	. . . .	2.02
MVIC/EBITDA	. . . . . .	3.92

$1 MILLION–$5 MILLION NET SALES
MVIC/Net Sales.	. . . . . .	0.38
MVIC/Gross Profit	. . . . . .	0.93
MVIC/SDE	. . . .	3.10
MVIC/EBITDA	. . . . . .	8.94

OVER $5 MILLION NET SALES
MVIC/Net Sales.	. . . . . .	1.10
MVIC/Gross Profit	. . . . . .	2.96
MVIC/SDE	. . . .	N/A
MVIC/EBITDA	. . . . . .	8.73

Source: DealStats (formerly Pratt's Stats), 2023 (Portland, OR: Business Valuation Resources, LLC), www.bvresources.com/dealstats

BENCHMARK DATA

Number of Establishments	19,761
Average Profit Margin	5.5%
Revenue Per Employee	$166,414
Average Number of Employees	7.1
Average Wages per Employee	$19,449

PRODUCTS AND SERVICES SEGMENTATION

Toys	38.8%
Hobby goods	26.3%
Other	19.2%
Craft supplies	12.3%
Games (including electronic and video games)	3.4%

INDUSTRY COSTS

Profit	5.5%
Wages	11.8%
Purchases	53.2%
Depreciation	0.7%
Marketing	2.1%
Rent & Utilities	6.4%
Other	20.3%

MARKET SHARE

Hobby Lobby Stores Inc.	14.2%
GameStop Corp.	12.0%
Michaels Companies, Inc.	4.5%
Walt Disney Co.	1.9%

INDUSTRY TREND

"Over the past five years, toy demand has risen with favorable macroeconomic conditions and improving household finances. Specifically, rising per capita disposable income enabled households to increase their spending on toys and hobby products. The industry will be aided by an uptick in the number of children aged nine and younger, which is one of the industry's primary customer demographics. However, the industry will continue to contend with challenges from e-commerce channels, as these retailers persistently provide popular toy and craft items at competitive prices."

Source: IBISWorld Key Takeaways

RESOURCES

- IBISWorld, September 2023: https://www.ibisworld.com
- The Toy Association: https://www.toyassociation.org

Translation and Interpretation Services

NAICS 541930	SIC 7389-20	Businesses/Units 79,307
Profit $1.3 B	Wages $3 B	Annual Growth Future 1.2%
		Annual Growth Past 6.5%

Rules of Thumb

- 40%–45% annual sales plus inventory

INDUSTRY MULTIPLES

Acquisition multiples below are calculated medians using US private industry transactions. Data updated annually. Last update: August 2023.

VALUATION MULTIPLE (MEDIAN VALUE)

UNDER $1 MILLION NET SALES

MVIC/Net Sales	0.77
MVIC/Gross Profit	1.27
MVIC/SDE	2.08
MVIC/EBITDA	2.01

$1 MILLION–$5 MILLION NET SALES

MVIC/Net Sales	0.92
MVIC/Gross Profit	1.83
MVIC/SDE	4.75
MVIC/EBITDA	5.35

OVER $5 MILLION NET SALES

MVIC/Net Sales	3.70
MVIC/Gross Profit	11.03
MVIC/SDE	N/A
MVIC/EBITDA	N/A

Source: DealStats (formerly Pratt's Stats), 2023 (Portland, OR: Business Valuation Resources, LLC), www.bvresources.com/dealstats

BENCHMARK DATA

STATISTICS (TRANSLATION SERVICES)

Number of Establishments	79,307
Average Profit Margin	12.4%
Revenue Per Employee	$80,692
Average Number of Employees	1.7
Average Wages per Employee	$23,960

PRODUCTS AND SERVICES SEGMENTATION

Interpretation services	44.2%
Written translation services	34.5%
Other	21.3%

MAJOR MARKET SEGMENTATION

Businesses	48.8%
Government	41.1%
Nonprofit organizations	6.9%
Other	3.2%

INDUSTRY COSTS

Profit	12.4%
Wages	29.5%
Purchases	12.7%
Depreciation	0.8%
Marketing	2.1%
Rent & Utilities	5.8%
Other	36.8%

MARKET SHARE

Transperfect Global, Inc.	7.4%
Teleperformance S.A.	4.7%
Lionbridge Technologies, Inc.	2.7%
Language Services Associates Inc.	1.1%
RWS Holdings PLC	1.0%

"Translation services helped companies work through the fallout of a US–China trade war and supply chain disruptions caused by COVID-19. Translation services revenue jumped despite the 2020 drop in trade volume. Government agencies and companies will need translation services to work with Japan, Vietnam, Malaysia, Mexico and Europe. Shifting US trade policy will invest in relations with specific political allies and move away from China. Defense agencies' investment in translators to navigate US–China relations will surpass levels seen in the Middle Eastern anti-terror campaign of the 2000s. Translators focused on Mandarin Chinese, Russian, Farsi and Urdu will benefit the most."

Source: IBISWorld Key Takeaways

RESOURCES

• IBISWorld, February 2023: https://www.ibisworld.com

Transmission Line Construction

| NAICS 237130 | Businesses/Units 11,022

| Profit $4.3 B | Wages $24.6 B | Annual Growth Future 1.5%

| Annual Growth Past 2.9%

INDUSTRY MULTIPLES

Acquisition multiples below are calculated medians using US private industry transactions. Data updated annually. Last update: August 2023.

VALUATION MULTIPLE (MEDIAN VALUE)

UNDER $1 MILLION NET SALES	N/A
$1 MILLION–$5 MILLION NET SALES	
MVIC/Net Sales	0.46
MVIC/Gross Profit	0.81
MVIC/SDE	3.37
MVIC/EBITDA	3.94
OVER $5 MILLION NET SALES	
MVIC/Net Sales	0.87
MVIC/Gross Profit	2.97
MVIC/SDE	4.82
MVIC/EBITDA	5.74

Source: DealStats (formerly Pratt's Stats), 2023 (Portland, OR: Business Valuation Resources, LLC), www.bvresources.com/dealstats

BENCHMARK DATA

STATISTICS (TRANSMISSION LINE CONSTRUCTION)

Number of Establishments	11,022
Average Profit Margin	4.4%
Revenue Per Employee	$354,457
Average Number of Employees	25.4
Average Wages per Employee	$90,248

PRODUCTS AND SERVICES SEGMENTATION

Electric power transmission infrastructure construction and repair	55.5%
Power plant construction and repair	23.2%
Telecommunications infrastructure construction and repair	11.5%
Other construction services	9.8%

Private power infrastructure markets . . 72.8%
Private telecommunications markets . . 17.2%
Government. 10.0%

INDUSTRY COSTS

Profit 4.4%
Wages 25.4%
Purchases 34.0%
Depreciation 3.0%
Marketing 0.2%
Rent & Utilities 5.5%
Other 27.5%

INDUSTRY TREND

"Transmission line construction has been deemed essential to critical infrastructure and has not faced any operational disruptions amid COVID-19. Transmission
line contractors were able to operate uninhibited as the nation relies on proper
power delivery. Increased electrical usage amid COVID-19 boosted demand.
Hospitals in particular required a higher amount of electricity. Nonessential businesses are beginning to resume. This provides transmission line workers with
several recovering downstream markets."

Source: IBISWorld Key Takeaways

RESOURCES

• IBISWorld, October 2023: https://www.ibisworld.com

Transportation Equipment and Supplies (except Motor Vehicle) Merchant Wholesalers

| NAICS 423860 | Businesses/Units 3,961

| Profit $7.6 B | Wages $4.1 B | Annual Growth Future 2.0%

| Annual Growth Past 4.5%

INDUSTRY MULTIPLES

Acquisition multiples below are calculated medians using US private industry
transactions. Data updated annually. Last update: August 2023.

VALUATION MULTIPLE (MEDIAN VALUE)

UNDER $1 MILLION NET SALES
MVIC/Net Sales. 1.07
MVIC/Gross Profit 2.37
MVIC/SDE 4.20
MVIC/EBITDA 17.81

$1 MILLION–$5 MILLION NET SALES
MVIC/Net Sales. 0.36
MVIC/Gross Profit 0.94
MVIC/SDE 2.87
MVIC/EBITDA 5.40

OVER $5 MILLION NET SALES
MVIC/Net Sales. 0.48
MVIC/Gross Profit 2.65
MVIC/SDE 4.23
MVIC/EBITDA 5.82

Source: DealStats (formerly Pratt's Stats), 2023 (Portland, OR: Business Valuation Resources, LLC),
www.bvresources.com/dealstats

STATISTICS (AIRCRAFT, MARINE & RAILROAD TRANSPORTATION EQUIPMENT WHOLESALING)

Number of Establishments	3,961
Average Profit Margin	9.0%
Revenue Per Employee	$1,789,478
Average Number of Employees	13.8
Average Wages per Employee	$86,369

PRODUCTS AND SERVICES SEGMENTATION

Aircraft equipment and supplies including engines and parts	58.2%
New aircraft	20.5%
Other transportation equipment	14.5%
Marine machinery, equipment and supplies	5.9%
Service receipts and labor charges	0.9%

MAJOR MARKET SEGMENTATION

Other	70.3%
Businesses for end use in their own operation	9.4%
Wholesalers/distributors for resale	6.2%
Manufacturers	4.5%
Repair shops for use in repair work	3.8%
Government bodies	2.9%
Retailers for resale	2.9%

INDUSTRY COSTS

Profit	9.0%
Wages	4.8%
Purchases	67.9%
Depreciation	0.8%
Marketing	0.3%
Rent & Utilities	1.1%
Other	16.0%

MARKET SHARE

Aviall Inc.	6.3%

INDUSTRY TREND

"Wholesalers have contended with increased competition. Original equipment manufacturers have become more prolific in offering aftermarket services to capture more of the profitable aftermarket. The freight transportation services index will remain a significant driver of industry revenue. Generally, as freight activity increases, downstream customers like FedEx, UPS and DHL demand more substantial quantities of transportation equipment."

Source: IBISWorld Key Takeaways

RESOURCES

• IBISWorld, September 2023: https://www.ibisworld.com

Travel Agencies

NAICS 561510	SIC 4724-02	Businesses/Units 50,281
Profit $1.8 B	Wages $7.2 B	Annual Growth Future 1.2%
		Annual Growth Past -1.0%

Rules of Thumb

• 45% annual gross profit

- 1.8–3 x SDE plus inventory
- 2–3 x EBIT for small to midsize agencies
- 3–5 x EBITDA for larger agencies
- 3.5–6 x EBIT
- 3.5–5 x EBITDA

INDUSTRY MULTIPLES

Acquisition multiples below are calculated medians using US private industry transactions. Data updated annually. Last update: August 2023.

VALUATION MULTIPLE (MEDIAN VALUE)

UNDER $1 MILLION NET SALES

MVIC/Net Sales.	0.47
MVIC/Gross Profit	0.86
MVIC/SDE	2.09
MVIC/EBITDA	3.11

$1 MILLION–$5 MILLION NET SALES

MVIC/Net Sales.	0.13
MVIC/Gross Profit	0.99
MVIC/SDE	2.37
MVIC/EBITDA	3.78

OVER $5 MILLION NET SALES

MVIC/Net Sales.	7.07
MVIC/Gross Profit	7.58
MVIC/SDE	N/A
MVIC/EBITDA	N/A

Source: DealStats (formerly Pratt's Stats), 2023 (Portland, OR: Business Valuation Resources, LLC), www.bvresources.com/dealstats

PRICING TIPS

4 percent on gross sales translates to 45 percent of gross income/gross profit. Sale minus cost of sales = gross profit (not net profit).

The higher the EBIT or EBITDA, the higher the multiple. The range in travel industry is 2.5 to 5.5 times, average 3 to 4 times.

These are unusual times; after almost dead period in Covid, now business is booming. Travel agencies make profit from commissions and service fees. Very low inventory to sell; prices are going high, specially if good staff and in-house business (long-term goodwill). Shortage of good travel agencies; low availability of qualified staff. Now the demand is going through the roof.

BENCHMARK DATA

STATISTICS (TRAVEL AGENCIES)

Number of Establishments	50,281
Average Profit Margin	4.7%
Revenue Per Employee	$427,466
Average Number of Employees.	1.8
Average Wages per Employee	$80,430

PRODUCTS AND SERVICES SEGMENTATION

Tour and packaged travel	28.6%
Cruises	23.3%
Airline travel.	19.8%
Other services	18.2%
Accommodation bookings	9.0%
Car rental	1.1%

International leisure travel	.29.8%
Domestic leisure travel	.27.4%
Businesses	.25.9%
Travel agencies	.16.9%

INDUSTRY COSTS

Profit	4.7%
Wages	.19.0%
Purchases	.54.4%
Depreciation	0.3%
Marketing	1.4%
Rent & Utilities	2.0%
Other	.18.2%

MARKET SHARE

American Express Co	.65.1%
Expedia Group, Inc.	.24.7%
The American Automobile Association, Inc.	.14.6%
Travel Leaders Group, LLC	8.3%
Booking Holdings Inc.	6.8%
Carlson Wagonlit Travel.	6.5%
BCD Holdings N.V.	3.2%

$500,000 gross sales per employee

Corporate agents should provide over $1 million in volume per year; leisure agents, $600K per year.

EXPENSES (% OF ANNUAL SALES)

Cost of Goods	80% to 90%
Occupancy Costs	10% to 20%
Payroll/Labor Costs.	45% to 55%
Profit (pretax)	10% to 20%

QUESTIONS

- Quality of staff? Clientele and type of travel—luxury, middle-income, corporate clients? What percentage of corporate accounts make up your sales? It better not be that one or two clients make up 60 to 75 percent of the sales.
- What are the sustainable earnings? What keeps you up at night?
- How old are your agents? Sales trend YoY? Marketing success? Any niche products?
- The goodwill or the client base history; how to improve expand the present base; history of staff; reason to sell. Check profit and loss statements. Is most of the business in-house, or what percent is outside business?
- Last two ARC reports. Any clients about to leave?
- What are the slow months? How is cash flow; any debt? What creates lean times in your experiences?
- Do you have a solid database?

INDUSTRY TREND

Very strong. Owners are looking to retire; Covid delayed many travel related business owners' retirement plans by three years!

Bright future especially with owners on hand or with qualified personable staff. Service fees are up.

"The travel industry is facing significant labor shortages. In June, domestic employment in the leisure and hospitality sectors was down nearly 8 percent since

February 2020, according to the U.S. Bureau of Labor Statistics, leaving hotels, airlines and other travel operators ill-equipped to contend with surging demand."

Source: "Silver-Haired and Shameless about Perks: Retirees Take Part-Time Work in the Travel Industry" by Debra Kamin, August 11, 2022, https://www.nytimes.com/2022/08/11/travel/retirees-part-time-travel.html

"COVID-19 had a devastating impact on the travel industry, and travel agencies were no exception. Agencies are still recovering, and revenue is expected to continue to grow in the next 5 years as disposable income climbs. Travelers are increasingly looking for personalized travel experiences that are tailored to their unique needs and interests. This is driving demand for travel agencies that can provide customized travel plans."

Source: IBISWorld Key Takeaways

EXPERT COMMENTS

Travel agencies are becoming more profitable as many are going home based; agents are going home based. Few agents working harder as well. And if locations are kept, they have reduced their rent.

FINANCING

Seller financing; 20 to 50 percent cash down and an earnout for 2 to 3 years.

Common practice—seller financing as SBA and banks do not offer to finance the buyer. Normally 50 percent down and 2 or 3 year financing. Seller stays as a part-time consultant for the duration of payoff.

RESOURCES

- IBISWorld, October 2023: https://www.ibisworld.com
- ARC—Airlines Reporting Corporation—licensing and requirements of the travel industry: https://www2.arccorp.com
- ASTA—American Society of Travel Advisors: https://www.asta.org
- CLIA—Cruise Lines International Association: https://cruising.org/
- GBTA—Global Business Travel Association: https://www.gbta.org
- IATAN—licensing and requirements of the travel industry: https://www.iatan.org
- NTA—National Tour Association: https://ntaonline.com
- PhocusWire: https://www.phocuswire.com
- Skål International: https://www.skal.org
- Travel Agent Central: https://www.travelagentcentral.com
- Travel Weekly: https://www.travelweekly.com
- TravelAge West: https://www.travelagewest.com
- U.S. Travel Association: https://www.ustravel.org

Travel Trailer and Camper Manufacturing

| NAICS 336214 | Businesses/Units 611

| Profit $490 M | Wages $4.2 B | Annual Growth Future 2.3%

| | | Annual Growth Past -0.7%

INDUSTRY MULTIPLES

Acquisition multiples below are calculated medians using US private industry transactions. Data updated annually. Last update: August 2023.

UNDER $1 MILLION NET SALES

MVIC/Net Sales	0.65
MVIC/Gross Profit	1.66
MVIC/SDE	2.95
MVIC/EBITDA	3.65

$1 MILLION–$5 MILLION NET SALES

MVIC/Net Sales	0.48
MVIC/Gross Profit	1.52
MVIC/SDE	2.39
MVIC/EBITDA	3.96

OVER $5 MILLION NET SALES

MVIC/Net Sales	1.55
MVIC/Gross Profit	9.08
MVIC/SDE	N/A
MVIC/EBITDA	13.40

Source: DealStats (formerly Pratt's Stats), 2023 (Portland, OR: Business Valuation Resources, LLC), www.bvresources.com/dealstats

BENCHMARK DATA

STATISTICS (RECREATIONAL VEHICLE MANUFACTURING)

Number of Establishments	611
Average Profit Margin	1.8%
Revenue Per Employee	$381,949
Average Number of Employees	98.9
Average Wages per Employee	$58,310

PRODUCTS AND SERVICES SEGMENTATION

Travel trailers	44.9%
Fifth-wheel trailers	27.0%
Class A motor homes	15.0%
Class B motor homes	6.3%
Truck campers	4.2%
Folding campers	2.2%
Class C motor homes	0.4%

INDUSTRY COSTS

Profit	1.8%
Wages	15.3%
Purchases	64.3%
Depreciation	0.5%
Marketing	0.3%
Rent & Utilities	1.0%
Other	16.7%

MARKET SHARE

Thor Industries, Inc.	22.2%
Berkshire Hathaway Inc.	10.0%
Winnebago Industries, Inc.	8.7%
REV Group, Inc.	2.4%

INDUSTRY TREND

"The pandemic had a mixed impact on RV manufacturers. Poor economic sentiment led to an increase in savings, but RVs grew in popularity alongside outdoor travel interest. Greater disposable income and a rise in domestic travel activity yield a positive outlook for manufacturers. Even as high inflation and rising interest rates threaten consumer spending, US residents are taking more road trips year over year."

Source: IBISWorld Key Takeaways

- IBISWorld, September 2023: https://www.ibisworld.com

Tropical Smoothie Cafe (Franchise)

| NAICS 722515 | Businesses/Units 1,311

Rules of Thumb
- 50%–55% annual sales plus inventory
- 41.2% annual sales
- 2.39 x SDE

INDUSTRY MULTIPLES

Acquisition multiples below are calculated medians using US private industry transactions. Data updated annually. Last update: August 2023.

VALUATION MULTIPLE (MEDIAN VALUE)

UNDER $1 MILLION NET SALES	
MVIC/Net Sales.	0.44
MVIC/Gross Profit	0.62
MVIC/SDE	2.20
MVIC/EBITDA	2.82
$1 MILLION–$5 MILLION NET SALES	
MVIC/Net Sales.	0.41
MVIC/Gross Profit	0.69
MVIC/SDE	2.82
MVIC/EBITDA	5.94
OVER $5 MILLION NET SALES	
MVIC/Net Sales.	3.89
MVIC/Gross Profit	4.87
MVIC/SDE	N/A
MVIC/EBITDA	N/A

Source: DealStats (formerly Pratt's Stats), 2023 (Portland, OR: Business Valuation Resources, LLC), www.bvresources.com/dealstats

PRICING TIPS

Approx. Total Investment: $296,500 to $661,500

RESOURCES
- Tropical Smoothie Cafe: https://www.tropicalsmoothiecafe.com
- Franchise information: https://www.tropicalsmoothiefranchise.com

Truck Stops

| NAICS 447190 | SIC 5541-03

Rules of Thumb
- 75% annual sales
- 5 x SDE plus inventory; may deduct cost of cosmetic update
- 5 x EBITDA

INDUSTRY MULTIPLES

Acquisition multiples below are calculated medians using US private industry transactions. Data updated annually. Last update: August 2023.

VALUATION MULTIPLE (MEDIAN VALUE)

UNDER $1 MILLION NET SALES

MVIC/Net Sales.	0.99
MVIC/Gross Profit	1.19
MVIC/SDE	17.26
MVIC/EBITDA	17.26

$1 MILLION–$5 MILLION NET SALES

MVIC/Net Sales.	0.25
MVIC/Gross Profit	0.55
MVIC/SDE	4.21
MVIC/EBITDA	2.02

OVER $5 MILLION NET SALES

MVIC/Net Sales.	0.19
MVIC/Gross Profit	1.55
MVIC/SDE	7.08
MVIC/EBITDA	6.68

Source: DealStats (formerly Pratt's Stats), 2023 (Portland, OR: Business Valuation Resources, LLC), www.bvresources.com/dealstats

PRICING TIPS

The rule of thumb for truck stops is going to be 5 to 6 times EBITDA with the factors coming into play like the quality of the assets, and are there any environmental issues that will need to be deducted from the value of the truck stop. However, to arrive at an EBITDA one must add up all of the different profit centers that comprise the truck stop such as: income from the scales, truck wash, video games, gift shop, restaurant income or restaurant lease income if the unit is leased out, and sometimes there are other ancillary forms of income that will all need to be added together to get to the EBITDA of the truck stop.

A lot of people will try to pump up the value of a truck stop by stating how much property is comprised by the truck stop, because it takes several acres to make a truck stop, but anything beyond the basic amount of property needed that is being used to support the business should not be included as additional value. For example there may be a truck stop that sits on a 10-acre tract of ground and the seller has another 5 acres that he thinks add additional value to the truck stop, but it doesn't. Only the property that is being used at the present time.

Be sure to check to see if they have any additional profit centers such as scales and if the scales are leased or owned. Other profit centers such as gambling machines (video poker, etc.) sometimes are not included in the P&Ls due to skimming.

BENCHMARK DATA

To be a profitable truck stop it seems inevitable that there is a restaurant connected to the facility. Many of the truck stops are now partnering with Hardee's, Wendy's, McDonald's, Arby's, etc., while the others have a sit-down restaurant.

Convenience/retail combined is approximately $500 per square foot.

At a typical full-service travel plaza you will find the following:
- Convenience or retail stores
- Check cashing
- Private showers
- Free parking
- Buses welcome
- Public fax machines
- Restaurants or delis

- Platform scales
- Laundry facilities
- Truck repair
- Emergency road service
- ATM machines
- Security/local police patrol
- Load boards
- Postal service
- Truck washes
- Hotels or motels
- Driver lounges
- Recreational vehicle facilities
- On-site fast food
- Church services
- Food court
- Internet services

EXPENSES (% OF ANNUAL SALES)

Cost of Goods	63%
Occupancy Costs	02% to 03%
Payroll/Labor Costs.	08%
Profit (pretax)	04%

QUESTIONS

- Do they own the restaurant or lease it out? What is the environmental situation?
- Do they have any fuel agreements with any trucking lines? Do they have Fuelman or similar fuel agreements that would be in place to draw regional or national trucking companies to them? Any hidden income, i.e., video machines, laundry, showers, etc.?
- As much paperwork as possible, including tax returns
- When valuing the business be sure to question the seller about all of the sources of income. Most units have income from video games, which is very lucrative, but that doesn't make it to the P&L; scale income and do they own the scales or lease them, any contracts with carriers, do they have Mr. Fuel or other recognized fuel discount programs, shower income, etc.? The money is still made on the inside so the higher the fuel volume, the more people that visit the facility, the more money they will spend inside. Is the unit branded with Shell, BO, TA, etc.? If so how much time is left on the contract with them and what are their costs to them? Who do they buy their fuel from? To purchase fuel you must have a fuel purchase agreement with your supplier and what is the length of the term and the charge for the fuel? Most agreements are for 7 to 10 years and if it is a branded unit you will be required to pay them back if you do not fulfill the length of the agreement, and this can be very costly. Are there any rebates coming back from the fuel supplier? How much over rack are they charging you? Very important that you know what the cost to buy fuel is. If you are doing 400,000 gallons of fuel per month and you are paying 1 cent over the posted rack price, that is $4,000 per month plus freight to bring it to your facility. The seller will know this and the buyer should know it too.

INDUSTRY TREND

"The driver shortages are reshaping the work force, as the specter of self-driving trucks increasingly threatens to transform how the work is done. Self-driving trucks are being tested now and are viewed as the future for shipping all manner of goods across the country. As trucking evolves, the patchwork of businesses across the United States that exist to support the industry is at risk of disappearing."

Source: "Arcades, Churches and Laundromats:
A Trucker's Haven on the Precipice of Change" by Jamie Lee Taete, June 4, 2022,
https://www.nytimes.com/2022/06/04/business/truck-driver-shortage-support.html

EXPERT COMMENTS

The truck stop industry has taken a severe beating lately due to the increased diesel fuel prices. Plus, the major truck stop operators such as Love's, Petro, Flying J, and Pilot are ruthless on their competition and have decreased the fuel margins considerably. They have also made it a point to have fueling agreements with most of the major truck carriers across the country, leaving only the independent truckers who will stop at the independent truck stops.

The average return on investment for a truck stop is 6 to 8 percent. The high profit return on investment for a truck stop is 16 to 17 percent. In order for a buyer to determine a good deal, 12 to 15 percent ROI for a truck stop should provide a good rule of thumb.

FINANCING

Property and land included: 10 to 15 years (8 to 11 percent); business only: 3 to 8 years (8 to 10 percent)

RESOURCES

- AITA—America's Independent Truckers' Association, Inc.: https://www.aitaonline.com
- Fuel Oil News: https://fueloilnews.com
- NATSO: https://www.natso.com

Truck Trailer Manufacturing

| NAICS 336212 | Businesses/Units 558

| Profit $631.3 M | Wages $2.4 B | Annual Growth Future 1.2%

| Annual Growth Past 1.7%

INDUSTRY MULTIPLES

Acquisition multiples below are calculated medians using US private industry transactions. Data updated annually. Last update: August 2023.

VALUATION MULTIPLE (MEDIAN VALUE)

UNDER $1 MILLION NET SALES	N/A
$1 MILLION–$5 MILLION NET SALES	N/A
OVER $5 MILLION NET SALES	
MVIC/Net Sales	0.91
MVIC/Gross Profit	4.85
MVIC/SDE	3.12
MVIC/EBITDA	8.65

Source: DealStats (formerly Pratt's Stats), 2023 (Portland, OR: Business Valuation Resources, LLC),
www.bvresources.com/dealstats

STATISTICS (TRUCK TRAILER MANUFACTURING)

Number of Establishments	558
Average Profit Margin	4.0%
Revenue Per Employee	$366,667
Average Number of Employees.	75.9
Average Wages per Employee	$56,499

PRODUCTS AND SERVICES SEGMENTATION

Long-distance freight trailers	53.9%
Local freight trailers.	16.1%
Other	12.0%
Refrigerated trailers.	11.0%
Flatbed trailers	7.0%

MAJOR MARKET SEGMENTATION

General freight trucking	62.2%
Exports	25.9%
Specialized freight trucking.	11.9%

INDUSTRY COSTS

Profit	4.0%
Wages	15.1%
Purchases	66.1%
Depreciation	1.2%
Marketing	0.2%
Rent & Utilities	1.3%
Other	12.1%

MARKET SHARE

Wabash National Corporation	7.5%
Utility Trailer Manufacturing Company	7.2%
Great Dane LLC	7.2%

INDUSTRY TREND

"A high volume of trade will keep manufacturers trucking. The US economy relies on trucks and trailers to get exports out and distribute imports. Sustainability will continue to become the focus of trailer manufacturers. Developing lighter and more aerodynamic trailers to improve fuel economy will be paramount."

Source: IBISWorld Key Takeaways

RESOURCES

- IBISWorld, May 2023: https://www.ibisworld.com

Truck, Utility Trailer, and RV (Recreational Vehicle) Rental and Leasing

| NAICS 532120 | Businesses/Units 15,410

| Profit $3.2 B | Wages $4.3 B | Annual Growth Future 1.1%

| | | Annual Growth Past 1.4%

INDUSTRY MULTIPLES

Acquisition multiples below are calculated medians using US private industry transactions. Data updated annually. Last update: August 2023.

VALUATION MULTIPLE (MEDIAN VALUE)

UNDER $1 MILLION NET SALES

MVIC/Net Sales	0.71
MVIC/Gross Profit	1.27
MVIC/SDE	2.92
MVIC/EBITDA	3.93

$1 MILLION–$5 MILLION NET SALES

MVIC/Net Sales	0.44
MVIC/Gross Profit	0.92
MVIC/SDE	N/A
MVIC/EBITDA	N/A

OVER $5 MILLION NET SALES

MVIC/Net Sales	2.72
MVIC/Gross Profit	8.41
MVIC/SDE	N/A
MVIC/EBITDA	N/A

Source: DealStats (formerly Pratt's Stats), 2023 (Portland, OR: Business Valuation Resources, LLC), www.bvresources.com/dealstats

BENCHMARK DATA

STATISTICS (TRUCK RENTAL)

Number of Establishments	15,410
Average Profit Margin	9.5%
Revenue Per Employee	$370,000
Average Number of Employees	5.86
Average Wages per Employee	$47,683

PRODUCTS AND SERVICES SEGMENTATION

Truck and trailer leases	48.0%
Truck and trailer rentals	37.6%
Other vehicle and equipment rentals and leases	8.5%
Repairs and other services	5.9%

MAJOR MARKET SEGMENTATION

Freight businesses	49.4%
Nonfreight businesses	38.0%
Households	12.2%
Government	0.4%

INDUSTRY COSTS

Profit	9.5%
Wages	12.8%
Purchases	6.8%
Depreciation	16.1%
Marketing	1.2%
Rent & Utilities	7.5%
Other	45.2%

MARKET SHARE

Penske Truck Leasing	15.8%
Ryder System	12.7%
Amerco	11.3%
Enterprise Holdings	7.9%
Idealease	0.5%
TRAC Intermodal LLC	0.5%
Premier Trailer Leasing	0.2%
Flexi-Van Leasing	0.2%
Milestone Equipment Holdings	0.1%
Compass Holding	0.1%

"Revenue has risen has demand for vehicle rentals and leases increased. More businesses have increased their demand for industrial services to move items between warehouses, commercial locations and construction sites. Consumer demand has grown as more people have moved between homes. The expanding housing market in recent years has supported greater demand for truck rental services. Online shopping greatly benefits truck renters. The majority of online purchases are delivered via truck and renting is a more cost-effective option than buying."

Source: IBISWorld Key Takeaways

RESOURCES

- IBISWorld, September 2023: https://www.ibisworld.com

TWO MEN AND A TRUCK (Franchise)

| NAICS 484210 | Businesses/Units 291

Rules of Thumb

- 40%–45% annual sales plus inventory

INDUSTRY MULTIPLES

Acquisition multiples below are calculated medians using US private industry transactions. Data updated annually. Last update: August 2023.

VALUATION MULTIPLE (MEDIAN VALUE)

UNDER $1 MILLION NET SALES	
MVIC/Net Sales	0.46
MVIC/Gross Profit	0.60
MVIC/SDE	2.15
MVIC/EBITDA	2.68
$1 MILLION–$5 MILLION NET SALES	
MVIC/Net Sales	0.41
MVIC/Gross Profit	0.79
MVIC/SDE	2.40
MVIC/EBITDA	3.84
OVER $5 MILLION NET SALES	N/A

Source: DealStats (formerly Pratt's Stats), 2023 (Portland, OR: Business Valuation Resources, LLC), www.bvresources.com/dealstats

PRICING TIPS

Approx. Total Investment: $105,500 to $446,600

RESOURCES

- TWO MEN AND A TRUCK: https://twomenandatruck.com
- Franchise information: https://franchise.twomenandatruck.com
- ServiceMaster: https://www.servicemaster.com

Uniform Rental

| NAICS 812331 | Businesses/Units 4,008 |

| Profit $2.3 B | Wages $5.3 B | Annual Growth Future 1.4% |

| Annual Growth Past 2.8% |

Rules of Thumb

- 40–45 x weekly sales plus inventory

INDUSTRY MULTIPLES

Acquisition multiples below are calculated medians using US private industry transactions. Data updated annually. Last update: August 2023.

VALUATION MULTIPLE (MEDIAN VALUE)

UNDER $1 MILLION NET SALES

MVIC/Net Sales.	0.53
MVIC/Gross Profit	0.93
MVIC/SDE	N/A
MVIC/EBITDA	N/A

$1 MILLION–$5 MILLION NET SALES

MVIC/Net Sales.	0.41
MVIC/Gross Profit	0.89
MVIC/SDE	1.98
MVIC/EBITDA	2.31

OVER $5 MILLION NET SALES

MVIC/Net Sales.	1.55
MVIC/Gross Profit	3.14
MVIC/SDE	N/A
MVIC/EBITDA	6.83

Source: DealStats (formerly Pratt's Stats), 2023 (Portland, OR: Business Valuation Resources, LLC), www.bvresources.com/dealstats

PRICING TIPS

An industry expert says that if there are contracts with the accounts serviced, the rule of thumb will be 70 percent of gross annual sales.

BENCHMARK DATA

STATISTICS (INDUSTRIAL LAUNDRY & LINEN SUPPLY)

Number of Establishments .	4,008
Average Profit Margin	11.3%
Revenue Per Employee .	$158,187
Average Number of Employees.	32.0
Average Wages per Employee .	$41,611

PRODUCTS AND SERVICES SEGMENTATION

Uniform supply .	56.2%
Linen supply	28.4%
Other services	15.4%

MAJOR MARKET SEGMENTATION

Food service	30.0%
Manufacturing .	23.7%
Healthcare .	22.4%
Other	17.2%
Hospitality .	6.7%

INDUSTRY COSTS

Profit	11.3%
Wages	26.4%
Purchases	8.4%
Depreciation	3.8%
Marketing	1.7%
Rent & Utilities	5.1%
Other	43.3%

MARKET SHARE

Cintas Corporation	36.0%
UniFirst Corporation	9.8%
Aramark Corp	9.2%
Alsco Inc.	4.0%
Prudential Overall Supply Inc.	1.7%
ImageFIRST Healthcare Laundry Specialists LLC	1.2%

INDUSTRY TREND

"Laundry and linen supply outsourcing remained in demand despite deep disruptions to its core markets. Diversification balances industrial launderers as COVID-19 reshapes how end markets use laundry and linen services. Rising employment and higher consumer spending will push businesses to outsource more laundry services and linen supply. But, how key customers in food service, hospitality and healthcare look post-COVID will determine the industry's trajectory."

Source: IBISWorld Key Takeaways

RESOURCES

• IBISWorld, September 2023: https://www.ibisworld.com

Urgent Care Centers

| NAICS 621493 | Businesses/Units 11,316

| Profit $12.3 B | Wages $15 B | Annual Growth Future 7.0%

| Annual Growth Past 7.1%

INDUSTRY MULTIPLES

Acquisition multiples below are calculated medians using US private industry transactions. Data updated annually. Last update: August 2023.

VALUATION MULTIPLE (MEDIAN VALUE)

UNDER $1 MILLION NET SALES

MVIC/Net Sales	0.45
MVIC/Gross Profit	0.40
MVIC/SDE	1.96
MVIC/EBITDA	5.52

$1 MILLION–$5 MILLION NET SALES

MVIC/Net Sales	0.64
MVIC/Gross Profit	0.67
MVIC/SDE	2.22
MVIC/EBITDA	20.38

OVER $5 MILLION NET SALES

MVIC/Net Sales	1.23
MVIC/Gross Profit	1.23
MVIC/SDE	N/A
MVIC/EBITDA	5.27

Source: DealStats (formerly Pratt's Stats), 2023 (Portland, OR: Business Valuation Resources, LLC), www.bvresources.com/dealstats

BENCHMARK DATA

STATISTICS (URGENT CARE CENTERS)

Number of Establishments	11,316
Average Profit Margin	23.4%
Revenue Per Employee	$226,839
Average Number of Employees	21.5
Average Wages per Employee	$65,121

PRODUCTS AND SERVICES SEGMENTATION

Injury and poisoning	20.1%
Other	24.8%
Symptoms, signs and abnormal findings	16.0%
Respiratory system	11.5%
Musculoskeletal system and connective tissue	7.8%
Circulatory system	7.0%
Digestive system	6.8%
Genitourinary system	6.0%

MAJOR MARKET SEGMENTATION

Private insurers	53.2%
Government insurers	23.5%
Other patient care revenue	14.7%
Patient out-of-pocket	8.6%

INDUSTRY COSTS

Profit	23.4%
Wages	28.5%
Purchases	17.6%
Depreciation	3.2%
Marketing	0.4%
Rent & Utilities	4.5%
Other	22.5%

INDUSTRY TREND

"Industry value added has grown faster than the economy, as urgent care centers have helped patients and insurers reduce high healthcare expenses associated with emergency room visits. The shortage of primary care physicians has had a positive effect on urgent care centers and will continue to affect the industry going forward."

Source: IBISWorld Key Takeaways

RESOURCES

- IBISWorld, September 2023: https://www.ibisworld.com
- UCA—Urgent Care Association: https://www.ucaoa.org

Used Goods Stores

NAICS 459510	Businesses/Units 77,945	
Profit $2.4 B	Wages $5.1 B	Annual Growth Future 1.7%
		Annual Growth Past 4.6%

Rules of Thumb

- 20%–25% annual sales includes inventory

BENCHMARK DATA

STATISTICS (USED GOODS STORES)

Number of Establishments	77,945
Average Profit Margin	8.2%
Revenue Per Employee	$103,918
Average Number of Employees	3.9
Average Wages per Employee	$18,413

PRODUCTS AND SERVICES SEGMENTATION

Clothing, footwear and accessories	49.4%
Furniture, appliances and home furnishings	19.7%
Antiques and collectables	14.3%
Entertainment, recreation and culture products	9.5%
Other	7.1%

INDUSTRY COSTS

Profit	8.2%
Wages	17.8%
Purchases	43.8%
Depreciation	1.2%
Marketing	1.5%
Rent & Utilities	5.9%
Other	21.6%

MARKET SHARE

Savers, Inc.	3.3%

INDUSTRY TREND

"U.S. secondhand market expected to reach $70 billion by 2027."

Source: "thredUP Resale Report 2023," https://www.thredup.com/resale/

"Kaiyo, an online marketplace for pre-owned furniture, was founded in 2014 and says it has since kept more than 3.5 million pounds of furniture out of landfills. Those with furniture to unload can offer it to Kaiyo, and if the company accepts— Alpay Koralturk, the chief executive, said the company purchases about half of the pieces offered to them—it'll get picked up for free and the seller will get a check. Buyers can shop the online marketplace, and know that items shown online are always in stock. 'Everyone has a ton of furniture. Few products are as ubiquitous,' Mr. Koralturk said. 'I was trying to imagine what the 21st century solution should be.'"

Source: "'Fast Furniture' Is Cheap. And Americans Are Throwing It in the Trash." by Debra Kamin, November 2, 2022, https://www.nytimes.com/2022/10/31/realestate/fast-furniture-clogged-landfills.html

"Used goods stores typically move countercyclical to the economy, with performance generally faltering as the economy strengthens. However, despite rising incomes and recovering consumer confidence over most of the past five years, revenue continued its upward climb. Several used goods stores have created websites to boost sales. For example, Goodwill Industries International Inc. launched www.ShopGoodwill.com and MyGoodwill, an online auction site and an e-learning site for employees and associated organizations, respectively."

Source: IBISWorld Key Takeaways

- IBISWorld, March 2023: https://www.ibisworld.com
- NARTS—The Association of Resale Professionals: https://www.narts.org

Vending Machine Industry

| NAICS 454210 | SIC 2599-02 | Businesses/Units 17,381 |

| Profit $434.5 M | Wages $1.7 B | Annual Growth Future 0.5% |

| | | Annual Growth Past -0.1% |

Rules of Thumb

- 75%–85% annual sales plus inventory
- 2–3 x SDE plus inventory
- 3–4 x EBIT
- 3–5 x EBITDA

INDUSTRY MULTIPLES

Acquisition multiples below are calculated medians using US private industry transactions. Data updated annually. Last update: August 2023.

VALUATION MULTIPLE (MEDIAN VALUE)

UNDER $1 MILLION NET SALES

MVIC/Net Sales.	0.87
MVIC/Gross Profit	1.69
MVIC/SDE	2.42
MVIC/EBITDA	2.63

$1 MILLION–$5 MILLION NET SALES

MVIC/Net Sales.	0.42
MVIC/Gross Profit	0.92
MVIC/SDE	2.41
MVIC/EBITDA	3.74

OVER $5 MILLION NET SALES

MVIC/Net Sales.	1.16
MVIC/Gross Profit	6.13
MVIC/SDE	N/A
MVIC/EBITDA	N/A

Source: DealStats (formerly Pratt's Stats), 2023 (Portland, OR: Business Valuation Resources, LLC), www.bvresources.com/dealstats

PRICING TIPS

When evaluating a full list of established (2 years+ in age) full-line (consisting of beverage and snack machines) vending accounts, you must consider the following characteristics: age of machines; number machines that have credit card devices, and number that can accommodate such; what days/hours weekly the particular account can be serviced; commissions (if any) paid to that account, and review of the level of vend prices the account can generate from its customer base; geographic spread of accounts being considered to purchase.

How many machines without devices are multidrop bus (MDB), meaning they can accommodate a device should you decide to install one? Are there any existing leases on new equipment in place? Volume of business each account does, and how can that number be substantiated?

Are machines owned or leased? EPorts in place?

BENCHMARK DATA

STATISTICS (VENDING MACHINE OPERATORS)

Number of Establishments .	17,381
Average Profit Margin .	4.3%
Revenue Per Employee .	$181,945
Average Number of Employees.	3.2
Average Wages per Employee .	$31,182

PRODUCTS AND SERVICES SEGMENTATION

Food and snacks	33.0%
Cold Beverages .	24.5%
Other products .	15.5%
Candy .	13.5%
Healthy Items	10.0%
Hot beverages	3.5%

MAJOR MARKET SEGMENTATION

Manufacturing sites	31.5%
Offices .	19.5%
Retail sites .	13.0%
Schools and colleges	10.0%
Hospitals and nursing homes	8.5%
Military bases, correctional facilities and other	8.5%
Hotels and motels .	7.0%
Restaurants, bars and clubs	2.0%

INDUSTRY COSTS

Profit	4.3%
Wages .	17.1%
Purchases .	53.2%
Depreciation	4.1%
Marketing .	3.0%
Rent & Utilities .	1.4%
Other	16.9%

One should look for accounts to buy (or open) that may generate a minimum of $50 to $75 per machine per week in business. To have smaller accounts (which may be serviced EOW) makes sense if they are in close proximity to larger accounts.

The old rule of thumb for the pros in the industry is that an account doing $200 weekly on each machine is considered proper/desirable for acquisition. This expert does not accept this, for he has seen accounts that are less than that grow, and accounts that do that amount shrink in sales. More important is to review the type of location each vending machine is in—and decide whether the industry that business is in is going to grow or shrink.

One should service accounts (whether they be institutional, schools, factories, medical facilities, etc.) that produce at least $100 weekly per machine, with any account doing less very close in proximity to the previously described account. Also, when out soliciting for new accounts, use the rule of thumb that the account being considered should have either a head count of at least 35 people and/or a transient flow of people going through the facility (like at a hospital, airport, etc.).

EXPENSES (% OF ANNUAL SALES)

Cost of Goods	35% to 50%
Occupancy Costs	02% to 10%
Payroll/Labor Costs.	20% to 30%
Profit (pretax)	20% to 30%

QUESTIONS

- Need to know (and consider) the following information on the accounts/vending machines in the offering. Geographically how close are the offered accounts to each other? Commission being paid? If so, how much? Are credit card readers on the offered machines? If not, are the machines MDB (or able to accommodate such devices)? Are any accounts being shared with another vendor?
- Customer-level sales by product category; contracts; fleet information; third-party management agreements; route compensation systems; software and IT management systems in place

INDUSTRY TREND

The largest competitor in this industry is an international company called Canteen—but the very soft economy and the pandemic have seriously eroded this company's competitiveness. As food prices skyrocketed and many of its longtime employees were laid off, it has become more necessary for them to go after accounts only where sales are in the $400 to $500 weekly range. Thus it is harder for them to find/get such accounts, and in light of equipping such large accounts, it takes a long time until such an account can generate money. Overall, this fact is good for the small vending operator!

Just like in other businesses, inflation is hurting the bottom line! I always relate the story to my own customers of how 15 to 20 years ago, the vending industry experienced inflationary turmoil as it affected the price of a 12-ounce can of soda. Up until that time, the average (and customer-accepted) vend price was $0.75 per can. That vend price per unit slowly grew to $0.85, then $0.95, with all vendors afraid to pass the $1.00 per unit threshold. Well, the increasing wholesale price of cans pushed it to that level—and vending customers grew to accept the $1.00 vend price! With the increasing prices of today, this expert predicts that by early 2023, the average vend price per 12-ounce can will be $1.25. This inflation, overall, will slow the growth of the industry.

"Growing health consciousness is a detriment to several products, but it also gives operators an opportunity to capitalize on the new demand for healthy foods. A return of travel and entertainment has aided the industry in its recovery, but work-from-home has dampened potential growth."

Source: IBISWorld Key Takeaways

EXPERT COMMENTS

Be careful of scams.

Buyers falsely believe that all one needs to do is buy a vending machine or two and presto they are in the vending business! Unfortunately that is as far from the truth as imaginable. The key to getting into the business is the accounts that harbor the machines owned. You can have the best machines, but if the locations do not produce a modest ($100+ weekly per machine) cash flow, then you are wasting your time. You would still need to take the time to go to account to input product into machines and spend the time (and money) to repair the equipment within.

For the buyer, look for a seller willing to sell a small part of his business; this piece can be used as a learning experience.

If the given vending route is worth, or selling for, less than $25,000 to $30,000, it is usually a cash deal. For businesses selling for more, it is usually 50 to 65 percent down, and the balance financed for 2 to 4 years at current interest rate. It is becoming more common in the industry for financing packages as offered to buyers to be funded through the credit card devices.

One usually does not see much seller financing offered in this industry. If buyer is a recognized vendor, there are several financing companies that lend money to that prospective experienced buyer, based on the value of the equipment being transferred under the sale agreement.

There are several lenders that specifically lend money to individuals looking to buy vending accounts—with such a loan based on the machines being used for collateral. I believe, however, these lenders will give loans only to established vendors, not new owners.

RESOURCES

- IBISWorld, September 2023: https://www.ibisworld.com
- NAMA—National Automatic Merchandising Association: https://www.namanow.org
- Vending Times: https://www.vendingtimes.com
- VendingMarketWatch.com: https://www.vendingmarketwatch.com

Veterinary Hospitals

| NAICS 541940

Rules of Thumb

- 65%–70% annual revenues plus inventory

INDUSTRY MULTIPLES

Acquisition multiples below are calculated medians using US private industry transactions. Data updated annually. Last update: August 2023.

VALUATION MULTIPLE (MEDIAN VALUE)

UNDER $1 MILLION NET SALES

MVIC/Net Sales	0.67
MVIC/Gross Profit	0.84
MVIC/SDE	2.64
MVIC/EBITDA	8.66

$1 MILLION–$5 MILLION NET SALES

MVIC/Net Sales	0.75
MVIC/Gross Profit	1.31
MVIC/SDE	3.23
MVIC/EBITDA	5.78

OVER $5 MILLION NET SALES

MVIC/Net Sales	3.06
MVIC/Gross Profit	13.01
MVIC/SDE	N/A
MVIC/EBITDA	15.74

Source: DealStats (formerly Pratt's Stats), 2023 (Portland, OR: Business Valuation Resources, LLC), www.bvresources.com/dealstats

RESOURCES

- AAHA—American Animal Hospital Association: https://www.aaha.org

Veterinary Practices

	NAICS 541940		SIC 0742-01			Businesses/Units 59,859
	Profit $9.4 B		Wages $23.5 B			Annual Growth Future 1.2%
						Annual Growth Past 4.7%

Rules of Thumb

- 70%–75% annual sales includes inventory
- 2–3 x SDE for small-animal practices includes inventory
- 2–4 x EBIT
- 3–5 x EBITDA

INDUSTRY MULTIPLES

Acquisition multiples below are calculated medians using US private industry transactions. Data updated annually. Last update: August 2023.

VALUATION MULTIPLE (MEDIAN VALUE)

UNDER $1 MILLION NET SALES

MVIC/Net Sales	0.67
MVIC/Gross Profit	0.84
MVIC/SDE	2.64
MVIC/EBITDA	8.66

$1 MILLION–$5 MILLION NET SALES

MVIC/Net Sales	0.75
MVIC/Gross Profit	1.31
MVIC/SDE	3.23
MVIC/EBITDA	5.78

OVER $5 MILLION NET SALES

MVIC/Net Sales	3.06
MVIC/Gross Profit	13.01
MVIC/SDE	N/A
MVIC/EBITDA	15.74

Source: DealStats (formerly Pratt's Stats), 2023 (Portland, OR: Business Valuation Resources, LLC), www.bvresources.com/dealstats

PRICING TIPS

Small solo practices sell for lower multiples. Use SDE and price/gross for smaller practices. Often 60 to 70 percent for an average-performing practice. Larger practices, 2 or 3+ veterinarians, are highly desirable by the 30+ national consolidators. They will pay 5 to 12 x EBITDA.

Even with a strong consolidation trend over the last 15 years, the market is still very fragmented.

Some practices make significant income from ancillary profit centers like grooming, doggie daycare, boarding, rehab, retail sales, flea/tick. There may be high dollar volume of food sales, but the profit margin is very low on food sales as practices have to compete with Walmart/PetSmart/etc.

Multidoctor practices with EBIDTA of over $800K/$900K often sell for 100 to 120 percent of annual gross revenue. This is because national consolidators are snapping up bigger practices, though the small solo doctor practice is still viable.

BENCHMARK DATA

STATISTICS (VETERINARY SERVICES)

Number of Establishments	59,859
Average Profit Margin	14.4%
Revenue Per Employee	$139,875
Average Number of Employees	7.9
Average Wages per Employee	$50,257

PRODUCTS AND SERVICES SEGMENTATION

Nonsurgical treatments	26.6%
Routine examinations	23.3%
Laboratory services	17.3%
Surgical treatments	14.9%
Merchandise sales	11.0%
Boarding services	2.9%
Other	2.6%
Pet grooming services	1.4%

MAJOR MARKET SEGMENTATION

Companion animal exclusive practices	66.8%
Companion animal predominate practices	12.5%
Other	6.3%
Mixed animal practices	5.0%
Equine	4.8%
Food animal exclusive and predominate practices	4.6%

INDUSTRY COSTS

Profit	14.4%
Wages	35.7%
Purchases	10.3%
Depreciation	2.0%
Marketing	1.7%
Rent & Utilities	4.9%
Other	31.0%

MARKET SHARE

VCA Inc.	5.7%
Banfield	1.4%

Average DVM comes out of school with $160K+ in debt. Average starting salary for DVMs in private practice is mid-$90K. Companion animal practices (dog/cat) represent 70 percent of the market. Most veterinarians work about 45 to 50 hours per week. Most practices are highly dependent upon wellness exams as a main source of revenue. For companion animal practices, prescription and drug sales are usually the second biggest source of revenue, followed by laboratory services. Typical FTE DVM needs about 1500 active clients.

4 to 5 support staff for every doctor

$233 revenue per vet per hour

4426 transaction per vet per year

Each full-time vet needs about 1500 active clients to be a viable business; 1800 is better.

Most practices average about 630 new patients/year.

17 percent of gross income is the average paid to owners for revenue.

EXPENSES (% OF ANNUAL SALES)

Cost of Goods	15% to 20%
Occupancy Costs	05% to 11%

```
Payroll/Labor Costs.   .    .    .    .    20% to 30%
Profit (pretax)   .    .    .    .    .    20% to 30%
```

QUESTIONS

- Type of practice: companion, feline, ER, equine, large animal, etc. Services provided. Ancillary profit centers. Number of support staff? There should be 4 to 6 support staff for each FTE DVM. Own or lease? Any family members working in practice? Are they being paid fair market compensation? Who is your competition? What is your market radius for 90 percent of clients? Hours worked per week? Do specialists come to practice to do surgery in-house? How are they compensated?
- Number patient encounters per week? Ancillary profit centers like grooming, boarding, chiropractic, acupuncture, retail?
- The buyer needs to ask for everything related to the practice—tax returns, practice computer reports, employee information, equipment lists—and learn the local economics, including competition, of the community. Then the buyer must perform extensive due diligence.
- Types of species treated; drug inventory levels; in-house lab and equipment capabilities
- Ask what medical services they do not provide that could be added.

INDUSTRY TREND

Strong market demand for services

Strong growth, demand; limited by shortage of doctors

"Innovations bolstered growth for veterinarians. Refinements in surgeries and diagnostic practices enabled services comparable to human medicine at a higher price tag. The popularity of pet insurance is increasing. The rise of pet insurance will make the out-of-pocket cost of expensive surgeries more affordable for pet owners and bolster revenue for veterinarians."

Source: IBISWorld Key Takeaways

EXPERT COMMENTS

Buy a practice. DVMs tend to make more money. If building a hospital building, be cautious about building more than 3500 square feet.

If you can grow the practice to 3+ doctors and good profitability, they sell extremely well for good prices (120 percent of annual gross).

Veterinary/pet industry expects high growth over the next 10 years. Most practice were unaffected by Covid shutdowns. Many had their best year ever.

FINANCING

Outside financing. There are lots of specialty lenders offering up to 100 percent financing both with SBA and commercial loans.

Usually 10-year term

RESOURCES

- IBISWorld, October 2023: https://www.ibisworld.com
- AAHA—American Animal Hospital Association: https://www.aaha.org
- AVMA—American Veterinary Medical Association: https://www.avma.org
- dvm360: https://www.dvm360.com
- Veterinarian's Money Digest: https://www.vmdtoday.com
- Veterinary Practice News: https://www.veterinarypracticenews.com

- VetPartners: https://www.vetpartners.org
- VIN—Veterinary Information Network: https://www.vin.com/vin/

Waste/Garbage/Trash Collection

| | NAICS 56211 | | Businesses/Units 12,864 |

| | Profit $6.7 B | | Wages $17.4 B | | Annual Growth Future 1.2% |

| | | | | | Annual Growth Past 1.9% |

Rules of Thumb
- 95% annual sales
- 3 x SDE
- 5 x EBIT
- 4 x EBITDA

INDUSTRY MULTIPLES

Acquisition multiples below are calculated medians using US private industry transactions. Data updated annually. Last update: August 2023.

VALUATION MULTIPLE (MEDIAN VALUE)

UNDER $1 MILLION NET SALES
MVIC/Net Sales.	1.07
MVIC/Gross Profit	1.13
MVIC/SDE	3.48
MVIC/EBITDA	3.28

$1 MILLION–$5 MILLION NET SALES
MVIC/Net Sales.	0.60
MVIC/Gross Profit	1.00
MVIC/SDE	1.87
MVIC/EBITDA	4.70

OVER $5 MILLION NET SALES
MVIC/Net Sales.	1.44
MVIC/Gross Profit	2.38
MVIC/SDE	N/A
MVIC/EBITDA	10.10

Source: DealStats (formerly Pratt's Stats), 2023 (Portland, OR: Business Valuation Resources, LLC), www.bvresources.com/dealstats

PRICING TIPS

For a company with predictable repeat earnings with service contracts, price should be eleven times the last twelve months' revenue. For a company involved in the construction industry, there may be a holdback of an amount multiple to adjust for homebuilder risk. The most valued are ongoing commercial accounts, which might have an adjustment or an earnout up or down. The best buyers are the big boys in waste management.

BENCHMARK DATA

STATISTICS (WASTE COLLECTION SERVICES)
Number of Establishments .	12,864
Average Profit Margin	8.8%
Revenue Per Employee .	$307,381
Average Number of Employees.	19.4
Average Wages per Employee .	$70,237

PRODUCTS AND SERVICES SEGMENTATION

Nonresidential waste collection	51.2%
Residential waste collection	30.6%
Transfer and storage facility	16.3%
Hazardous and recyclable waste collection	1.9%

MAJOR MARKET SEGMENTATION

Commercial	34.6%
Industrial	27.4%
Individuals and households	25.9%
Government and nonprofit organizations	12.1%

INDUSTRY COSTS

Profit	8.8%
Wages	22.7%
Purchases	26.8%
Depreciation	7.3%
Marketing	0.3%
Rent & Utilities	3.3%
Other	30.8%

MARKET SHARE

Waste Management, Inc.	21.7%
Republic Services, Inc.	18.0%
Waste Connections, Inc.	6.9%
Veolia Environnement	1.5%

EXPENSES (% OF ANNUAL SALES)

Cost of Goods	20%
Occupancy Costs	05%
Payroll/Labor Costs	50%
Profit (pretax)	25%

INDUSTRY TREND

"Public awareness and governmental policies spur eco-friendly waste service expansion. However, stringent regulations and service privatization boost costs, posing challenges for smaller businesses and causing community concern. President Biden's infrastructure bill will generate a sizable increase in attracting customers for the industry. The bill will call upon large-scale construction services, which will need support from waste collection services."

Source: IBISWorld Key Takeaways

EXPERT COMMENTS

This has been a very difficult business dominated by a few large companies.

RESOURCES

- IBISWorld, October 2023: https://www.ibisworld.com
- Waste360: https://www.waste360.com

Water & Sewer Line Construction

	NAICS 237110		Businesses/Units 15,393	
	Profit $3.9 B		Wages $12.4 B		Annual Growth Future 1.2%
				Annual Growth Past 0.8%

INDUSTRY MULTIPLES

Acquisition multiples below are calculated medians using US private industry transactions. Data updated annually. Last update: August 2023.

VALUATION MULTIPLE (MEDIAN VALUE)

UNDER $1 MILLION NET SALES

MVIC/Net Sales.	0.85
MVIC/Gross Profit	1.21
MVIC/SDE	2.06
MVIC/EBITDA	1.88

$1 MILLION–$5 MILLION NET SALES

MVIC/Net Sales.	0.75
MVIC/Gross Profit	1.31
MVIC/SDE	3.61
MVIC/EBITDA	10.73

OVER $5 MILLION NET SALES

MVIC/Net Sales.	0.77
MVIC/Gross Profit	5.11
MVIC/SDE	4.86
MVIC/EBITDA	20.34

Source: DealStats (formerly Pratt's Stats), 2023 (Portland, OR: Business Valuation Resources, LLC), www.bvresources.com/dealstats

BENCHMARK DATA

STATISTICS (WATER & SEWER LINE CONSTRUCTION)

Number of Establishments .	15,393
Average Profit Margin	6.6%
Revenue Per Employee .	$386,963
Average Number of Employees.	10.3
Average Wages per Employee .	$79,717

PRODUCTS AND SERVICES SEGMENTATION

Water mains and other water supply infrastructure	34.0%
Sewer lines and other sewer infrastructure	29.3%
Sewage and water treatment plants	18.1%
Other	10.8%
Building-related construction .	6.1%
Highway-related construction .	1.7%

MAJOR MARKET SEGMENTATION

State and local government funding	96.2%
Private-sector funding .	2.3%
Federal government funding	1.5%

INDUSTRY COSTS

Profit	6.6%
Wages	20.8%
Purchases .	49.7%
Depreciation	2.9%
Marketing	0.1%
Rent & Utilities .	5.4%
Other	14.4%

INDUSTRY TREND

"Water and sewer line construction has not endured operational disruptions amid COVID-19. Contractors could operate uninhibited as the nation relies on proper water and sewage systems. Stagnant government budgets following COVID-19 limit large-scale growth. COVID-19 caused states to necessitate a surge in spending while also being short on taxes. Population growth and expansion facilitate constructing new water and sewer lines. Higher residential construction activity due to low interest rates have also boosted utility demand."

Source: IBISWorld Key Takeaways

RESOURCES

• IBISWorld, September 2023: https://www.ibisworld.com

Web Hosting

| NAICS 518210

Rules of Thumb

• 3–4 x EBITDA

INDUSTRY MULTIPLES

Acquisition multiples below are calculated medians using US private industry transactions. Data updated annually. Last update: August 2023.

VALUATION MULTIPLE (MEDIAN VALUE)

UNDER $1 MILLION NET SALES
MVIC/Net Sales	1.41
MVIC/Gross Profit	2.15
MVIC/SDE	3.67
MVIC/EBITDA	11.90

$1 MILLION–$5 MILLION NET SALES
MVIC/Net Sales	1.05
MVIC/Gross Profit	2.28
MVIC/SDE	3.54
MVIC/EBITDA	5.88

OVER $5 MILLION NET SALES
MVIC/Net Sales	2.93
MVIC/Gross Profit	4.59
MVIC/SDE	8.27
MVIC/EBITDA	23.30

Source: DealStats (formerly Pratt's Stats), 2023 (Portland, OR: Business Valuation Resources, LLC), www.bvresources.com/dealstats

BENCHMARK DATA

Most are netting between 33 and 44 percent of gross income.

EXPENSES (% OF ANNUAL SALES)

Cost of Goods	N/A
Occupancy Costs	N/A
Payroll/Labor Costs	N/A
Profit (pretax)	33%

Weight Loss Services/Centers

	NAICS 812191		SIC 7299-34		Businesses/Units 2,823
	Profit $329.5 M		Wages $817 M		Annual Growth Future -0.7%
					Annual Growth Past -2.8%

Rules of Thumb

- 50%–55% annual sales

INDUSTRY MULTIPLES

Acquisition multiples below are calculated medians using US private industry transactions. Data updated annually. Last update: August 2023.

VALUATION MULTIPLE (MEDIAN VALUE)

UNDER $1 MILLION NET SALES

MVIC/Net Sales	0.41
MVIC/Gross Profit	0.42
MVIC/SDE	2.13
MVIC/EBITDA	0.70

$1 MILLION–$5 MILLION NET SALES

MVIC/Net Sales	0.34
MVIC/Gross Profit	0.34
MVIC/SDE	3.89
MVIC/EBITDA	9.28

OVER $5 MILLION NET SALES

MVIC/Net Sales	1.18
MVIC/Gross Profit	2.24
MVIC/SDE	N/A
MVIC/EBITDA	14.31

Source: DealStats (formerly Pratt's Stats), 2023 (Portland, OR: Business Valuation Resources, LLC), www.bvresources.com/dealstats

BENCHMARK DATA

STATISTICS (WEIGHT LOSS SERVICES)

Number of Establishments	2,823
Average Profit Margin	8.7%
Revenue Per Employee	$179,598
Average Number of Employees	7.4
Average Wages per Employee	$38,626

PRODUCTS AND SERVICES SEGMENTATION

Digital Subscriptions	65.0%
In-person Consultation Subscriptions	22.7%
Other fees	10.5%
In-meeting product sales	1.8%

INDUSTRY COSTS

Profit	8.7%
Wages	21.6%
Purchases	9.9%
Depreciation	3.2%
Marketing	2.0%
Rent & Utilities	6.0%
Other	48.6%

MARKET SHARE

Medifast Inc.	25.0%
WW International Inc.	21.9%
Nutrisystem Inc.	16.2%

INDUSTRY TREND

"Some COVID-19 impacts were long lasting. Performance was compromised as consumers now familiar with remote technology and communication were exposed to substitute products and services. Technology will help reach consumers. Some regions underserved based on obesity rates and population will have greater access to services as new technology enhances the quality and reach of services."

Source: IBISWorld Key Takeaways

RESOURCES

• IBISWorld, March 2023: https://www.ibisworld.com

Wholesale Trade Agents and Brokers

| NAICS 425120 | Businesses/Units 98,099

| Profit $29.1 B | Wages $19.3 B | Annual Growth Future -0.9%

                                               | Annual Growth Past -3.3%

INDUSTRY MULTIPLES

Acquisition multiples below are calculated medians using US private industry transactions. Data updated annually. Last update: August 2023.

VALUATION MULTIPLE (MEDIAN VALUE)

UNDER $1 MILLION NET SALES

MVIC/Net Sales	0.72
MVIC/Gross Profit	1.10
MVIC/SDE	2.39
MVIC/EBITDA	6.57

$1 MILLION–$5 MILLION NET SALES

MVIC/Net Sales	0.34
MVIC/Gross Profit	1.39
MVIC/SDE	2.42
MVIC/EBITDA	3.64

OVER $5 MILLION NET SALES

MVIC/Net Sales	0.35
MVIC/Gross Profit	1.38
MVIC/SDE	2.70
MVIC/EBITDA	3.10

Source: DealStats (formerly Pratt's Stats), 2023 (Portland, OR: Business Valuation Resources, LLC), www.bvresources.com/dealstats

BENCHMARK DATA

STATISTICS (WHOLESALE TRADE AGENTS AND BROKERS)

Number of Establishments	98,099
Average Profit Margin	5.1%
Revenue Per Employee	$1,612,581
Average Number of Employees	3.6
Average Wages per Employee	$54,637

PRODUCTS AND SERVICES SEGMENTATION

Other items	30.2%
Food products	23.5%
Automotive (including parts)	21.9%
Electrical apparatuses and equipment	15.0%
Industrial machinery and commodities	9.4%

MAJOR MARKET SEGMENTATION

Retailers	42.6%
Wholesalers	26.2%
Other markets	24.8%
Manufacturers	6.4%

Profit 5.1%
Wages 3.4%
Purchases 79.8%
Depreciation 0.2%
Marketing 0.6%
Rent & Utilities 0.8%
Other 10.1%

MARKET SHARE

C&S Wholesale Grocers, Inc. 4.5%
Ferguson PLC 3.4%

INDUSTRY TREND

"The need for wholesale trade agents and brokers has declined. Companies have become more vertically integrated, cutting off the need for companies to facilitate exchanges. The continued move toward online sales has also hampered the industry. As more consumers purchase goods online, there is less need for wholesale trade agents."

Source: IBISWorld Key Takeaways

RESOURCES

• IBISWorld, September 2023: https://www.ibisworld.com

Wienerschnitzel (Franchise)

| NAICS 722513 | Businesses/Units 316

Rules of Thumb

• 30%–35% annual sales plus inventory

INDUSTRY MULTIPLES

Acquisition multiples below are calculated medians using US private industry transactions. Data updated annually. Last update: August 2023.

VALUATION MULTIPLE (MEDIAN VALUE)

UNDER $1 MILLION NET SALES
MVIC/Net Sales. 0.31
MVIC/Gross Profit 0.48
MVIC/SDE 1.67
MVIC/EBITDA 2.21

$1 MILLION–$5 MILLION NET SALES
MVIC/Net Sales. 0.39
MVIC/Gross Profit 0.60
MVIC/SDE 2.43
MVIC/EBITDA 2.98

OVER $5 MILLION NET SALES
MVIC/Net Sales. 0.89
MVIC/Gross Profit 2.08
MVIC/SDE 4.98
MVIC/EBITDA 12.81

Source: DealStats (formerly Pratt's Stats), 2023 (Portland, OR: Business Valuation Resources, LLC), www.bvresources.com/dealstats

PRICING TIPS

Approx. Total Investment: $299,100 to $1,462,100

- Wienerschnitzel: https://www.wienerschnitzel.com
- Franchise information: https://wienerschnitzelfranchise.com

Wild Birds Unlimited (Franchise)

| NAICS 459910 | Businesses/Units 339

Rules of Thumb
- 30%–35% annual sales plus inventory

INDUSTRY MULTIPLES

Acquisition multiples below are calculated medians using US private industry transactions. Data updated annually. Last update: August 2023.

VALUATION MULTIPLE (MEDIAN VALUE)

UNDER $1 MILLION NET SALES

MVIC/Net Sales.	0.50
MVIC/Gross Profit	0.86
MVIC/SDE	2.82
MVIC/EBITDA	3.69

$1 MILLION–$5 MILLION NET SALES

MVIC/Net Sales.	0.37
MVIC/Gross Profit	1.15
MVIC/SDE	2.19
MVIC/EBITDA	3.20

OVER $5 MILLION NET SALES	N/A

Source: DealStats (formerly Pratt's Stats), 2023 (Portland, OR: Business Valuation Resources, LLC), www.bvresources.com/dealstats

PRICING TIPS

Approx. Total Investment: $209,425 to $350,037

RESOURCES
- Wild Birds Unlimited: https://www.wbu.com
- Franchise information: https://franchise.wbu.com

Wind Farms (Energy)

| NAICS 221115 | Businesses/Units 962

| Profit $24.7 B | Wages $1.6 B | Annual Growth Future 3.2%

| | | | Annual Growth Past 11.8%

Rules of Thumb
- 20–30 x EBITDA
- 20 x SDE
- 25 x EBIT

INDUSTRY MULTIPLES

Acquisition multiples below are calculated medians using US private industry transactions. Data updated annually. Last update: August 2023.

UNDER $1 MILLION NET SALES	
MVIC/Net Sales.	20.60
MVIC/Gross Profit	N/A
MVIC/SDE	N/A
MVIC/EBITDA	N/A
$1 MILLION–$5 MILLION NET SALES	N/A
OVER $5 MILLION NET SALES	
MVIC/Net Sales.	6.27
MVIC/Gross Profit	7.36
MVIC/SDE	N/A
MVIC/EBITDA	8.39

Source: DealStats (formerly Pratt's Stats), 2023 (Portland, OR: Business Valuation Resources, LLC), www.bvresources.com/dealstats

PRICING TIPS

Location matters: The geographical location of the wind farm is crucial. Wind farms in areas with strong and consistent wind patterns are more valuable. Coastal or elevated locations tend to be more favorable.

Age of wind turbines: The age and condition of wind turbines significantly impact value. Newer, well-maintained turbines are more attractive to buyers and may command a higher price.

Power purchase agreements (PPAs): Long-term power purchase agreements with fixed or escalating prices provide revenue predictability and add value to wind farms. Buyers often consider the terms of these contracts.

Regulatory and permitting: An understanding of local and national regulations, permits, and compliance is essential. Having a streamlined regulatory process in place can be an asset.

Technical infrastructure: The condition and performance of turbines, electrical infrastructure, and grid connections are vital. Buyers will assess maintenance records and equipment health.

Future development potential: If there is room for expansion or technological upgrades, it can enhance the value. Buyers may pay more for a wind farm with growth opportunities.

Competitive landscape: An assessment of local and regional competition can provide insights into market dynamics and competitiveness.

Environmental and sustainability factors: Wind farms with strong sustainability practices and environmental compliance may have a competitive advantage.

Due diligence: Both buyers and sellers should conduct thorough due diligence, including financial, technical, legal, and environmental assessments.

Financing terms: Understanding the available financing options, including loans, grants, and incentives, can impact the price and terms of the sale.

Timing considerations: Market conditions and energy price trends can affect the timing of a sale. It's essential to assess the current market environment.

Experienced advisors: Working with experienced advisors who understand the energy and wind farm industry can help ensure a smooth transaction.

Energy market trends: Stay informed about energy market trends, renewable energy policies, and the evolving landscape of the wind energy sector.

Community relations: Positive community relations can be an asset, as local support and goodwill can impact the wind farm's operations.

Environmental impact: Highlighting the positive environmental impact of the wind farm can resonate with buyers and investors interested in sustainability.

These pricing tips and factors should be considered in conjunction with the specific attributes of the wind farm in question. Professional assistance and a comprehensive evaluation are recommended for accurate valuation and successful transactions in the wind energy industry.

BENCHMARK DATA

STATISTICS (WIND POWER)

Number of Establishments	962
Average Profit Margin	18.1%
Revenue Per Employee	$12,755,664
Average Number of Employees. . . .	12.4
Average Wages per Employee . .	$148,315

PRODUCTS AND SERVICES SEGMENTATION

Distributed generation	81.6%
Utility scale generation	18.3%
Other	0.1%

MAJOR MARKET SEGMENTATION

Residential sector	47.1%
Commercial sector	35.3%
Industrial users	17.4%
Transportation and other	0.2%

INDUSTRY COSTS

Profit	18.1%
Wages	1.1%
Purchases	25.7%
Depreciation	38.8%
Marketing	0.1%
Rent & Utilities	0.7%
Other	15.4%

MARKET SHARE

NextEra Energy Inc..	1.5%

The success of a wind farm is often measured by its capacity factor, which indicates how efficiently it converts wind into electricity. A common benchmark could be the capacity utilization rate, indicating how efficiently turbines are producing energy in relation to their maximum potential. An average capacity factor for a successful wind farm might be around 35 to 45 percent.

EXPENSES (% OF ANNUAL SALES)

Cost of Goods	25%
Payroll/Labor Costs.	20%

QUESTIONS

- What is the wind farm's historical capacity factor?
- What is the condition of the wind turbines and their maintenance history?
- Are there long-term power purchase agreements in place?
- What is the maintenance and repair history of the turbines?
- What are the local regulations and permitting requirements?
- Are there any pending environmental or regulatory issues?
- What is the contract duration with energy purchasers?

The wind farm industry is expected to continue growing, driven by increasing demand for renewable energy sources, supportive policies and incentives, and advancements in wind turbine technology.

"The $4 billion project, known as Vineyard Wind, is expected to start generating electricity by year's end. 'This has been really hard,' said Rachel Pachter, the chief development officer of Vineyard Offshore, the American arm of Copenhagen Infrastructure Partners, a Danish renewable energy developer that is a co-owner of the wind farm. To bring a big energy project to this point near population centers requires clearing countless regulatory hurdles and heading off potential opposition and litigation....The Biden administration wants to make offshore wind a big part of the effort to rapidly build up renewable energy and related jobs, and it gave Vineyard Wind a go-ahead in 2021.

"Constructing and installing the giant machines at sea is a fairly novel proposition in the United States. There are only a couple of other smaller offshore wind farms in the country. Another, about one-fifth Vineyard Wind's size, is expected to come online this year off Long Island, New York. Europe has thousands of offshore turbines, and so much of the expertise and equipment used in Vineyard Wind's construction, including the specialized vessels used to hammer the turbine towers into the seabed, is from across the Atlantic....

"Industry executives and analysts say building this first giant U.S. wind farm should help clear the way for similar projects."

Source: "A giant wind farm is taking root off Massachusetts" by Stanley Reed and Ivan Penn, June 27, 2023, https://www.boston.com/news/environment/2023/06/27/a-giant-wind-farm-is-taking-root-off-massachusetts/

"Wind and solar developers have long said that lease rates and fees for projects on federal lands were too high to attract investors. The new policy would cut those costs by about 50 percent, administration officials said....In a report to Congress in April, the Interior Department said it was on track to approve 48 wind, solar and geothermal energy projects with the capacity to produce an estimated 31,827 megawatts of electricity, enough to power roughly 9.5 million homes, by the end of the fiscal 2025 budget cycle."

Source: "Biden Administration to Cut Costs for Wind and Solar Energy Projects" by Lisa Friedman, June 1, 2022, https://www.nytimes.com/2022/06/01/climate/biden-solar-wind-fees-cut.html

"Government incentives have rapidly accelerated the growth of wind power companies as more entrants continue to join. 36 states have established renewable portfolio standards, pushing for greener initiatives. Lower turbine costs have made installation less expensive for consumers. This has given more markets access to wind power. Offshore wind projects are poised to play a central role in the industry's future. Despite facing rigorous regulations, harnessing the power of coastal winds has the potential to yield a substantial amount of energy."

Source: IBISWorld Key Takeaways

EXPERT COMMENTS

Buyers should conduct thorough due diligence on the wind farm's operational energy production history, potential for growth, and condition of the turbines. Sellers should prepare comprehensive documentation and financial records.

W

FINANCING

Wind farm sales often involve outside financing due to the significant capital requirements. Terms can vary based on the specifics of each deal. Both outside financing and seller financing are possible, with terms varying based on the scale of the project.

RESOURCES

- IBISWorld, September 2023: https://www.ibisworld.com
- ACP—American Clean Power: https://cleanpower.org
- Windpower Monthly: https://www.windpowermonthly.com
- American Wind Energy Association (AWEA): https://cleanpower.org/
- Global Wind Energy Council (GWEC): https://gwec.net/

Window Cleaning

| NAICS 561720

Rules of Thumb

- 60% annual sales

INDUSTRY MULTIPLES

Acquisition multiples below are calculated medians using US private industry transactions. Data updated annually. Last update: August 2023.

VALUATION MULTIPLE (MEDIAN VALUE)

UNDER $1 MILLION NET SALES
MVIC/Net Sales.	0.59
MVIC/Gross Profit	0.76
MVIC/SDE	2.03
MVIC/EBITDA	2.92

$1 MILLION–$5 MILLION NET SALES
MVIC/Net Sales.	0.45
MVIC/Gross Profit	1.02
MVIC/SDE	2.86
MVIC/EBITDA	4.05

OVER $5 MILLION NET SALES
MVIC/Net Sales.	0.53
MVIC/Gross Profit	2.26
MVIC/SDE	4.26
MVIC/EBITDA	5.48

Source: DealStats (formerly Pratt's Stats), 2023 (Portland, OR: Business Valuation Resources, LLC), www.bvresources.com/dealstats

RESOURCES

- IWCA—International Window Cleaning Association: https://www.iwca.org

Window Treatment/Draperies

| NAICS 442291 | Businesses/Units 2,082

| Profit $65 M | Wages $470.3 M | Annual Growth Future -1.0%

| Annual Growth Past 0.9%

Rules of Thumb

- 35%–40% annual sales plus inventory

INDUSTRY MULTIPLES

Acquisition multiples below are calculated medians using US private industry transactions. Data updated annually. Last update: August 2023.

VALUATION MULTIPLE (MEDIAN VALUE)

UNDER $1 MILLION NET SALES

MVIC/Net Sales	0.47
MVIC/Gross Profit	1.00
MVIC/SDE	2.04
MVIC/EBITDA	2.72

$1 MILLION–$5 MILLION NET SALES

MVIC/Net Sales	0.46
MVIC/Gross Profit	0.91
MVIC/SDE	2.93
MVIC/EBITDA	4.36

OVER $5 MILLION NET SALES

MVIC/Net Sales	0.39
MVIC/Gross Profit	0.78
MVIC/SDE	2.35
MVIC/EBITDA	3.18

Source: DealStats (formerly Pratt's Stats), 2023 (Portland, OR: Business Valuation Resources, LLC), www.bvresources.com/dealstats

BENCHMARK DATA

STATISTICS (WINDOW TREATMENT STORES)

Number of Establishments	2,082
Average Profit Margin	3.6%
Revenue Per Employee	$189,000
Average Number of Employees	4.5
Average Wages per Employee	$49,898

PRODUCTS AND SERVICES SEGMENTATION

Vertical and horizontal blinds, woven blinds and shades	61.4%
Curtains and draperies	20.1%
Ready-made and custom-made furniture coverings	3.1%
Domestics (e.g. towels, sheets, blankets, table linens)	1.2%

INDUSTRY COSTS

Profit	3.6%
Wages	26.0%
Purchases	42.2%
Depreciation	0.9%
Marketing	3.0%
Rent & Utilities	5.0%
Other	19.3%

INDUSTRY TREND

"Demand has been hampered by sales lost to big-box stores and online retailers. Green and sustainable window treatments are another popular trend in product advancement. Sales of traditional window treatments are a significant part of industry revenue. The anticipated expansion of less-expensive retailers will result in more low-priced product offerings. The rising homeownership rate is one of the most significant factors contributing to the increase in demand. Large operators are expected to benefit from increased service options. Competition from general home improvement stores and online retailers will continue to be the greatest obstacle for this industry."

Source: IBISWorld Industry at a Glance

RESOURCES

- IBISWorld, October 2022: https://www.ibisworld.com
- WCAA—Window Coverings Association of America: https://www.wcaa.org
- Window Fashion VISION: https://www.wf-vision.com

Window World (Franchise)

| NAICS 236118 | Businesses/Units 212

INDUSTRY MULTIPLES

Acquisition multiples below are calculated medians using US private industry transactions. Data updated annually. Last update: August 2023.

VALUATION MULTIPLE (MEDIAN VALUE)

UNDER $1 MILLION NET SALES
MVIC/Net Sales.	0.36
MVIC/Gross Profit	0.64
MVIC/SDE	1.83
MVIC/EBITDA	2.08

$1 MILLION–$5 MILLION NET SALES
MVIC/Net Sales.	0.36
MVIC/Gross Profit	0.96
MVIC/SDE	2.43
MVIC/EBITDA	2.48

OVER $5 MILLION NET SALES
MVIC/Net Sales.	0.35
MVIC/Gross Profit	1.26
MVIC/SDE	2.72
MVIC/EBITDA	3.25

Source: DealStats (formerly Pratt's Stats), 2023 (Portland, OR: Business Valuation Resources, LLC), www.bvresources.com/dealstats

PRICING TIPS

Approx. Total Investment: $122,857 to $328,157

RESOURCES

- Window World: https://www.windowworld.com
- Franchise information: https://www.windowworldfranchise.com

Wine and Distilled Alcoholic Beverage Merchant Wholesalers

| NAICS 424820 | Businesses/Units 7,855

| Profit $4.4 B | Wages $9.2 B | Annual Growth Future 1.2%

| | | Annual Growth Past 1.0%

INDUSTRY MULTIPLES

Acquisition multiples below are calculated medians using US private industry transactions. Data updated annually. Last update: August 2023.

VALUATION MULTIPLE (MEDIAN VALUE)

UNDER $1 MILLION NET SALES

MVIC/Net Sales	0.65
MVIC/Gross Profit	1.50
MVIC/SDE	2.65
MVIC/EBITDA	5.29

$1 MILLION–$5 MILLION NET SALES

MVIC/Net Sales	0.72
MVIC/Gross Profit	1.27
MVIC/SDE	9.48
MVIC/EBITDA	26.56

OVER $5 MILLION NET SALES

MVIC/Net Sales	1.48
MVIC/Gross Profit	7.25
MVIC/SDE	4.63
MVIC/EBITDA	18.31

Source: DealStats (formerly Pratt's Stats), 2023 (Portland, OR: Business Valuation Resources, LLC), www.bvresources.com/dealstats

BENCHMARK DATA

STATISTICS (WINE & SPIRITS WHOLESALING)

Number of Establishments	7,855
Average Profit Margin	3.4%
Revenue Per Employee	$1,289,377
Average Number of Employees	13.0
Average Wages per Employee	$90,795

PRODUCTS AND SERVICES SEGMENTATION

Table wine	33.0%
Other wine and spirits	20.2%
Whiskey	17.4%
Vodka	11.6%
Tequila	8.2%
Rum	4.0%
Dessert wine	4.0%
Gin	1.6%

MAJOR MARKET SEGMENTATION

Retailers	63.8%
Wholesalers	20.4%
Food service providers	13.2%
Other	2.6%

INDUSTRY COSTS

Profit	3.4%
Wages	7.0%
Purchases	73.1%
Depreciation	0.5%
Marketing	1.5%
Rent & Utilities	1.1%
Other	13.4%

MARKET SHARE

Southern Glazer's Wine and Spirits, LLC	17.0%
Republic National Distributing Company, LLC	10.6%
Breakthru Beverage Group, LLC	4.4%
Young's Market Company, LLC	1.5%

INDUSTRY TREND

"Consumer preferences for premium liquors has driven growth. Premium brands have a higher price tag, benefiting wine and liquor wholesaler revenue. Positive economic trends will support growth in the coming years. Increasing disposable income, consumer spending and demand from beer, wine and liquor stores will drive revenue growth."

Source: IBISWorld Key Takeaways

RESOURCES

- IBISWorld, September 2023: https://www.ibisworld.com

Wineries

NAICS 312130	SIC 2084-01	Businesses/Units 8,486
Profit $1.3 B	Wages $4.6 B	Annual Growth Future 1.0%
		Annual Growth Past 1.4%

Rules of Thumb

- 25% annual sales (does include real estate)
- 10 x SDE
- 60 x EBIT (does include real estate)
- 89 x EBITDA (does include real estate)

INDUSTRY MULTIPLES

Acquisition multiples below are calculated medians using US private industry transactions. Data updated annually. Last update: August 2023.

VALUATION MULTIPLE (MEDIAN VALUE)

UNDER $1 MILLION NET SALES	
MVIC/Net Sales	1.17
MVIC/Gross Profit	2.48
MVIC/SDE	4.33
MVIC/EBITDA	8.71
$1 MILLION–$5 MILLION NET SALES	N/A
OVER $5 MILLION NET SALES	
MVIC/Net Sales	0.73
MVIC/Gross Profit	2.02
MVIC/SDE	N/A
MVIC/EBITDA	15.53

Source: DealStats (formerly Pratt's Stats), 2023 (Portland, OR: Business Valuation Resources, LLC), www.bvresources.com/dealstats

BENCHMARK DATA

STATISTICS (WINERIES)

Number of Establishments	8,486
Average Profit Margin	4.7%
Revenue Per Employee	$327,106
Average Number of Employees	9.5
Average Wages per Employee	$56,816

PRODUCTS AND SERVICES SEGMENTATION

Zinfandel, Riesling and other blends	29.1%
Chardonnay	20.0%
Cabernet Sauvignon	19.3%
Pinot Grigio	11.9%
Sauvignon Blanc	7.0%

Merlot	6.4%
Pinot Noir	6.3%

INDUSTRY COSTS

Profit	4.7%
Wages	17.1%
Purchases	42.8%
Depreciation	5.0%
Marketing	1.0%
Rent & Utilities	2.7%
Other	26.7%

MARKET SHARE

E. & J. Gallo Winery	15.7%
Constellation Brands, Inc.	8.6%
The Wine Group, Inc.	1.8%

EXPENSES (% OF ANNUAL SALES)

Cost of Goods	59%
Occupancy Costs	20%
Payroll/Labor Costs.	20%
Profit (pretax)	10%

QUESTIONS

• Will you [the seller] stay on as a consultant?

INDUSTRY TREND

"One piece of good news that should be underlined and shouted from the rooftops is that the premium segment of the wine business has been performing quite well after the difficult year in 2020. In 2022, the premium side of the industry experienced another good year in an increasingly challenging marketplace, with revenue up 9.7 percent, on average, through September, according to the Silicon Valley Bank Peer Group Analysis Database. That is solid growth.

"The more difficult news is that for the industry as a whole, we aren't measuring up. Wine sold below $15 continues to slide, and we will have a second year of negative volume growth in the industry as a consequence."

Source: "State of the US Wine Industry 2023" by Rob McMillan, https://www.svb.com/globalassets/trendsandinsights/reports/wine/svb-state-of-the-wine-industry-report-2023.pdf

"Reopening key on-premise markets like bars and restaurants provided a necessary boost in revenue. But the increase proved to be short-lived. Profit is slim for many wineries, especially smaller producers. Wages continue rising, while input prices increase due to detrimental growing conditions and distribution interruption. Imported brands, new wineries and alternative products, like beer and spirits, mean competition is stiff. Wineries struggle to differentiate their products and appeal to shifting consumer preferences."

Source: IBISWorld Key Takeaways

EXPERT COMMENTS

Wineries take 1 to 2 years to sell if they are priced well.

RESOURCES

• IBISWorld, October 2023: https://www.ibisworld.com
• AmericanWineryGuide.com: http://www.americanwineryguide.com
• ASEV—American Society for Enology and Viticulture: https://www.asev.org
• Family Winemakers of California: https://familywinemakers.org

- New York Wine & Grape Foundation: https://newyorkwines.org
- Wine Business.com: https://www.winebusiness.com

Wingstop (Restaurants) (Franchise)

| NAICS 722513 | Businesses/Units 1,618

Rules of Thumb

- 30%–35% annual sales plus inventory

INDUSTRY MULTIPLES

Acquisition multiples below are calculated medians using US private industry transactions. Data updated annually. Last update: August 2023.

VALUATION MULTIPLE (MEDIAN VALUE)

UNDER $1 MILLION NET SALES

MVIC/Net Sales.	0.31
MVIC/Gross Profit	0.48
MVIC/SDE	1.67
MVIC/EBITDA	2.21

$1 MILLION–$5 MILLION NET SALES

MVIC/Net Sales.	0.39
MVIC/Gross Profit	0.60
MVIC/SDE	2.43
MVIC/EBITDA	2.98

OVER $5 MILLION NET SALES

MVIC/Net Sales.	0.89
MVIC/Gross Profit	2.08
MVIC/SDE	4.98
MVIC/EBITDA	12.81

Source: DealStats (formerly Pratt's Stats), 2023 (Portland, OR: Business Valuation Resources, LLC), www.bvresources.com/dealstats

PRICING TIPS

Approx. Total Investment: $315,310 to $948,080

RESOURCES

- Wingstop: https://www.wingstop.com
- Franchise information: https://www.wingstop.com/own-a-wingstop

Wireless Communications

| NAICS 517112 | SIC 5999-02

Rules of Thumb

- 30% annual gross sales
- 2–3 x SDE plus inventory
- 2.5–5 x EBITDA includes inventory

PRICING TIPS

It is important to consider revenue per customer.

Strong employee technical base/tenure desirable along with noncompetes for key personnel

Trend upward in volume and downward in service income is not abnormal.

Subscribers, physical plant capacity, client retention and gross margins

Calculating furniture, fixtures and equipment value along with any real estate involved

BENCHMARK DATA

3 x SDE is a good place to begin. Inventory/chargebacks and deactivations can be issues if not clearly discussed.

EXPENSES (% OF ANNUAL SALES)

Cost of Goods	60%
Occupancy Costs	05% to 10%
Payroll/Labor Costs.	20%
Profit (pretax)	10%

QUESTIONS

- Seller financing? Lease issues? Any problems with the carrier transferring the business to a buyer and what are those exact requirements?
- Ask if market is built out (to what percentage of population and geography) and if it is operational (how long).
- Number of activations and deactivations per month? What is advertising budget? How long at this location? Are employees on commission or salary or both? Number of locations?
- Pricing strategy and debt owed

EXPERT COMMENTS

Multistore operators with strong sales and net earnings are in demand.

The business is difficult to replicate due to its technical nature and the relationships required with myriad suppliers.

Expanding into synergistic product lines is becoming the norm.

FINANCING

1 to 2 years

RESOURCES

- CTIA: https://www.ctia.org
- RCR Wireless News: https://www.rcrwireless.com
- Wireless Dealer Magazine: http://www.wirelessdealermag.com

Women's Clothing Stores

NAICS 458110	SIC 5621-01	Businesses/Units 86,495
Profit $2.5 B	Wages $7.5 B	Annual Growth Future 2.6%
		Annual Growth Past 1.5%

Rules of Thumb

- 20% annual sales plus inventory
- 2 x monthly sales plus inventory

INDUSTRY MULTIPLES

Acquisition multiples below are calculated medians using US private industry transactions. Data updated annually. Last update: August 2023.

VALUATION MULTIPLE (MEDIAN VALUE)

UNDER $1 MILLION NET SALES

MVIC/Net Sales	0.27
MVIC/Gross Profit	0.53
MVIC/SDE	1.03
MVIC/EBITDA	1.03

$1 MILLION–$5 MILLION NET SALES

MVIC/Net Sales	0.66
MVIC/Gross Profit	1.09
MVIC/SDE	4.47
MVIC/EBITDA	5.69

OVER $5 MILLION NET SALES

MVIC/Net Sales	4.35
MVIC/Gross Profit	5.17
MVIC/SDE	N/A
MVIC/EBITDA	N/A

Source: DealStats (formerly Pratt's Stats), 2023 (Portland, OR: Business Valuation Resources, LLC), www.bvresources.com/dealstats

BENCHMARK DATA

STATISTICS (WOMEN'S CLOTHING STORES)

Number of Establishments	86,495
Average Profit Margin	3.7%
Revenue Per Employee	$206,607
Average Number of Employees	5.2
Average Wages per Employee	$22,626

PRODUCTS AND SERVICES SEGMENTATION

Tops	31.0%
Other apparel and accessories	24.2%
Bottoms	20.7%
Dresses	15.2%
Outerwear	8.9%

INDUSTRY COSTS

Profit	3.7%
Wages	11.1%
Purchases	45.7%
Depreciation	0.9%
Marketing	2.2%
Rent & Utilities	9.6%
Other	26.8%

INDUSTRY TREND

"Women's clothing stores have experienced growth over the past five years despite some challenges. Expansion was driven by higher-income consumers' willingness to spend on luxury items and the boosted popularity of specialty stores catering to niche markets. Changing consumer preferences are expected to shift women's clothing stores' strategies over the next five years. Key trends include expanding their online presence, promoting sustainable and eco-friendly products and offering unique or personalized clothing."

Source: IBISWorld Key Takeaways

EXPERT COMMENTS

Make sure there is a viable consumer base already cultivated and there is a strong marketing strategy that has proven successful in the past.

RESOURCES

- IBISWorld, September 2023: https://www.ibisworld.com

Women's, Children's, and Infants' Clothing and Accessories Merchant Wholesalers

| NAICS 424350 | Businesses/Units 19,366

| Profit $3.6 B | Wages $5 B | Annual Growth Future 1.4%

| Annual Growth Past -4.3%

BENCHMARK DATA

STATISTICS (WOMEN'S & CHILDREN'S APPAREL WHOLESALING)

Number of Establishments .	19,366
Average Profit Margin .	5.8%
Revenue Per Employee .	$683,000
Average Number of Employees.	4.79
Average Wages per Employee .	$55,060

PRODUCTS AND SERVICES SEGMENTATION

Dresses, blouses and sweaters, including unisex clothing	28.5%
Other apparel including clothing accessories .	28.4%
Outerwear including skirts, slacks and jeans	19.8%
Underwear and sleepwear .	11.0%
Children's and infants' apparel .	8.9%
Suits and coats .	3.4%

MAJOR MARKET SEGMENTATION

Family clothing stores .	45.3%
Department stores .	28.5%
Women's clothing stores	13.9%
Warehouse clubs .	10.0%
Children's clothing stores .	2.3%

INDUSTRY COSTS

Profit .	5.8%
Wages .	8.2%
Purchases .	64.1%
Depreciation .	0.3%
Marketing .	0.6%
Rent & Utilities .	0.6%
Other .	20.3%

MARKET SHARE

Hanesbrands .	2.9%

INDUSTRY TREND

"Despite falling, industry revenue has been somewhat supported by improving domestic economic conditions. Imports satisfy most of the domestic demand for apparel. Automation and advanced supply chain technologies have decreased demand for labor. Projected revenue growth will likely be driven primarily by rising per capita disposable income and consumer spending. Several adverse trends will likely continue to take their toll on industry operators. Large apparel companies are expected to continue to consolidate steps of the supply chain. The vertical integration of the supply chain for many large operators poses a threat to industry growth."

Source: IBISWorld Industry at a Glance

RESOURCES

• IBISWorld, September 2022: https://www.ibisworld.com

Wood Pallets & Skids Production

| NAICS 321920 | Businesses/Units 2,779

| Profit $617.5 M | Wages $2.7 B | Annual Growth Future 1.9%

| Annual Growth Past 1.9%

INDUSTRY MULTIPLES

Acquisition multiples below are calculated medians using US private industry transactions. Data updated annually. Last update: August 2023.

VALUATION MULTIPLE (MEDIAN VALUE)

UNDER $1 MILLION NET SALES
MVIC/Net Sales.	0.95
MVIC/Gross Profit	1.61
MVIC/SDE	3.01
MVIC/EBITDA	3.41

$1 MILLION–$5 MILLION NET SALES
MVIC/Net Sales.	0.45
MVIC/Gross Profit	1.05
MVIC/SDE	2.52
MVIC/EBITDA	3.46

OVER $5 MILLION NET SALES
MVIC/Net Sales.	0.51
MVIC/Gross Profit	1.58
MVIC/SDE	3.56
MVIC/EBITDA	3.68

Source: DealStats (formerly Pratt's Stats), 2023 (Portland, OR: Business Valuation Resources, LLC), www.bvresources.com/dealstats

BENCHMARK DATA

STATISTICS (WOOD PALLETS & SKIDS PRODUCTION)

Number of Establishments .	2,779
Average Profit Margin	4.6%
Revenue Per Employee .	$209,310
Average Number of Employees.	23.4
Average Wages per Employee	$42,459

PRODUCTS AND SERVICES SEGMENTATION

New wood pallets	65.9%
Recovered wood pallets	20.9%
Other wood containers and parts	8.4%
Nailed and lock-corner wood boxes and shook	4.8%

MAJOR MARKET SEGMENTATION

| Food and beverages | 36.9% |
| Chemicals and pharmaceuticals | 18.9% |

Metals and construction materials 17.2%
Other 9.7%
Machinery and electronics 8.6%
Paper products 5.2%
Exports 3.5%

INDUSTRY COSTS

Profit 4.6%
Wages 20.3%
Purchases 52.9%
Depreciation 1.8%
Marketing 0.1%
Rent & Utilities 3.3%
Other 17.0%

INDUSTRY TREND

"The market for wooden pallets is typically stable. This is because many different industries use pallets in their supply chains. The COVID-19 pandemic disrupted the industry in 2020. As economic activity resumed in 2021, high lumber prices were passed along to consumers, resulting in higher industry revenue. Wooden pallets face competition. The reuse of pallets of any type threatens the industry, while pallets made from materials other than wood can have advantages."

Source: IBISWorld Key Takeaways

RESOURCES

• IBISWorld, September 2023: https://www.ibisworld.com

You've Got Maids (Franchise)

| NAICS 561720 | SIC 7349-23 | Businesses/Units 70

Rules of Thumb

• 60% annual sales plus inventory

INDUSTRY MULTIPLES

Acquisition multiples below are calculated medians using US private industry transactions. Data updated annually. Last update: August 2023.

VALUATION MULTIPLE (MEDIAN VALUE)

UNDER $1 MILLION NET SALES
MVIC/Net Sales. 0.59
MVIC/Gross Profit 0.76
MVIC/SDE 2.03
MVIC/EBITDA 2.92

$1 MILLION–$5 MILLION NET SALES
MVIC/Net Sales. 0.45
MVIC/Gross Profit 1.02
MVIC/SDE 2.86
MVIC/EBITDA 4.05

OVER $5 MILLION NET SALES
MVIC/Net Sales. 0.53
MVIC/Gross Profit 2.26
MVIC/SDE 4.26
MVIC/EBITDA 5.48

Source: DealStats (formerly Pratt's Stats), 2023 (Portland, OR: Business Valuation Resources, LLC), www.bvresources.com/dealstats

PRICING TIPS

Approx. Total Investment: $36,394 to $107,537

RESOURCES

- You've Got Maids: https://www.youvegotmaids.com
- Franchise information: https://www.youvegotmaids.com/franchise

Ziebart (Auto Services) (Franchise)

| NAICS 8111 | Businesses/Units 78

Rules of Thumb

- 42% annual sales plus inventory

INDUSTRY MULTIPLES

Acquisition multiples below are calculated medians using US private industry transactions. Data updated annually. Last update: August 2023.

VALUATION MULTIPLE (MEDIAN VALUE)

UNDER $1 MILLION NET SALES

MVIC/Net Sales	0.42
MVIC/Gross Profit	0.62
MVIC/SDE	2.13
MVIC/EBITDA	2.96

$1 MILLION–$5 MILLION NET SALES

MVIC/Net Sales	0.40
MVIC/Gross Profit	0.76
MVIC/SDE	2.38
MVIC/EBITDA	4.01

OVER $5 MILLION NET SALES

MVIC/Net Sales	0.79
MVIC/Gross Profit	2.00
MVIC/SDE	3.90
MVIC/EBITDA	9.35

Source: DealStats (formerly Pratt's Stats), 2023 (Portland, OR: Business Valuation Resources, LLC), www.bvresources.com/dealstats

PRICING TIPS

Approx. Total Investment: $416,820 to $566,100

RESOURCES

- Ziebart: https://www.ziebart.com
- Franchise information: https://www.ziebart.com/franchise-opportunities

Industry Experts

We are grateful to the following Industry Experts who help make this book possible.

Their experiences and insights provide invaluable information for anyone buying, selling, or valuing a business.

For more information about the Industry Experts, visit us online at industryexpert.net/expert-directory. Also, an Industry Experts section is included, when applicable, within the industry listings in the online edition of the *Guide*.

ACCOUNTING FIRMS/CPAS

Larry Brusacoram
281-713-2468
larry@acctsales.com
acctsales.com

Chuck Hayes
ABA Advisors, LLC
4005 Senour Road
Indianapolis, IN 46250
317-862-3570
ch@AcctSales.com

Thomas Lang
303-726-7646
Thomas.joseph.lang@gmail.com
thomaslangcpabroker.com

Brian Naab
Naab Consulting, Inc.
5511 E. 82nd Street, Suite H
Indianapolis, IN 46250
888-726-6282
Brian@NaabConsulting.com
NaabConsulting.com

Matt Sobieski
612-964-8884
msobieski@sunbeltmidwest.com

ACCOUNTING FIRMS/PRACTICES

Chuck Hayes
ABA Advisors, LLC
4005 Senour Road
Indianapolis, IN 46250
317-862-3570
ch@AcctSales.com

Brian Naab
Naab Consulting, Inc.
5511 E. 82nd Street, Suite H
Indianapolis, IN 46250
888-726-6282
Brian@NaabConsulting.com
NaabConsulting.com

ACCOUNTING/TAX PRACTICES

Scott Curtis
704-649-8068
scott@fcbb.com
businessbuyingandsellingexpert.com

Chuck Hayes
ABA Advisors, LLC
4005 Senour Road
Indianapolis, IN 46250
317-862-3570
ch@AcctSales.com

Brian Naab
Naab Consulting, Inc.
5511 E. 82nd Street, Suite H
Indianapolis, IN 46250
888-726-6282
Brian@NaabConsulting.com
NaabConsulting.com

AIRCRAFT MANUFACTURING: PARTS, SUPPLIES, ENGINES, ETC. (KIT-BUILT & ULTRALIGHT AIRCRAFT INDUSTRY)

Michael Wildeveld
The Veld Group
1 Park Plaza, 600
Irvine, CA 92614
310-652-8353
michaelw@theveldgroup.com

AIRPORT OPERATIONS

Dale Pearson
830-480-9955
dalepearson1@gmail.com
nwsarealty.com

AMBULATORY SURGERY CENTERS

Jim Shaub
615-788-1006
jim@tennbusinessbrokers.com
tennbusinessbrokers.com

ASSISTED LIVING FACILITIES/ RETIREMENT COMMUNITIES (WITH NURSING CARE)

Ronald Ekstrom
978-235-3871
ronalde@georgeandco.com
georgeandco.com

AUTO DEALERSHIPS, NEW CARS

Hal Feder
Murphy Business & Financial
3 Bayberry Lane
Williamsburg, VA 23185
248-885-7804
h.feder@murphybusiness.com
murphybusiness.com

BARS

Neil Kaplan
VR Business Brokers
17100 Pioneer Blvd, Ste 195
Artesia, CA 90701-2730
310-490-3422
neilvrbb@gmail.com

Terri Sokoloff
Specialty Tavern & Restaurant Brokers
3200 McKnight East Drive, #3205
Pittsburgh, PA 15237-6423
terri@specialtygroup.com

BOWLING CENTERS

Ken Mischel
Mischel & Company
37 Tunapuna Ln.
Coronado, CA 92118
mischelco@msn.com

BREWERIES

Jeff Adam
Adam Noble Group
2000 E Lamar Blvd, Suite 600
Arlington, TX 76006
jeff@adamnoble.com

BUSINESS BROKERAGE OFFICES

Doug Robbins
Robbinex
41 Stuart Street
Hamilton, ON L8L 1B5
dmr@robbinex.com

CAR WASHES, FULL-SERVICE/ EXTERIOR

Max Friar
Calder Capital, LLC
25 Division Ave S, Suite 225
Grand Rapids, MI 49503
616-965-2771
max@caldergr.com
caldergr.com

CHIROPRACTIC PRACTICES

Tom Necela
The Strategic Chiropractor
13423 Blanco Rd #475
San Antonio, TX 78216
800-577-0321
info@strategicdc.com
strategicdc.com

CONSTRUCTION: IN GENERAL

Max Friar
Calder Capital, LLC
25 Division Ave S, Suite 225
Grand Rapids, MI 49503
616-965-2771
max@caldergr.com
caldergr.com

Rhett Kniep CBI M&AMI
Centurion 7 Business Advisors
1209 Pleasant Grove Blvd
Roseville, CA 95678
916-974-9733
rhett@centurion7.com

AJ Ramsey
ajramsey@tworld.com

Jeff Adam
Adam Noble Group
2000 E Lamar Blvd, Suite 600
Arlington, TX 76006
jeff@adamnoble.com

Carrie Duvall
Commercial Associates LLC
2431 Aloma Ave, Suite 124
Winter Park, FL 32792
407-718-8955
carrie@isellyour.biz

Greg Kells
Sunbelt Business Brokers
2821 Riverside Dr.
Ottawa, ON K1V8N4
gregkells@sunbeltcanada.com

Rhett Kniep CBI M&AMI
Centurion 7 Business Advisors
1209 Pleasant Grove Blvd
Roseville, CA 95678
916-974-9733
rhett@centurion7.com

Andrew Rogerson
Rogerson Business Services
5150 Fair Oaks Blvd, #101-198
Carmichael, CA 95608
916-570-2674
andrew@rogersonbusiness
services.com
wwwrogersonbusinessservices.com

Sara Cartee
980-722-1048
sarac@countysouth.biz
countysouth.biz

Henry Tiberi
303-271-1010
htiberi@hingeadvisors.com
hingeadvisors.com

Stephen Wray
sales@csbb.com.au

Eric Burgmaier
Hindley Burgmaier Group
eric@myabqcpa.com

Garrett Monroe
Calder Capital
586-350-6619
garrett@caldergr.com
caldergr.com

Andrew Rogerson
Rogerson Business Services
5150 Fair Oaks Blvd, #101-198
Carmichael, CA 95608
916-570-2674
andrew@rogersonbusiness
services.com
rogersonbusinessservices.com

Sam Thompson
Transitions In Business
6550 York Av. S., Suite 402
Edina, MN 55435
612-282-1750
sthompson@transitionsib.com
transitionsib.com

Richard Ehrenreich, CBI, CED, SBA
Ehrenreich & Associates/
Cleaner Broker Network
16917 MacDuff Avenue
Olney, MD 20832
301-570-3000
ehrenassoc@aol.com

David Miller
480-223-1234
dmiller@sbaphoenix.com
SBAphoenix.com

John Mikaelian
111 Kristin Circle, Unit #2
Schaumburg, IL 60195
847-867-0050
John@venturebus.com
aaaventurebusinessbrokers.com

ELECTRIC MOTOR REPAIR

C Peter Smith
205-837-4845
petesmith@value-a-business.com
value-a-business.com

ENGINEERING SERVICES

AJ Ramsey
ajramsey@tworld.com

FOOD SERVICE CONTRACTORS

Joe Vagnone
21213 Norman Shores Dr
Cornelius, NC 28031
704-577-8030
joe@jvagnone.com
jvagnone.com

FRANCHISES

Neal Patel
ACE International Brokers
1 Station Plaza
Ridgefield Park, NJ 07660
neal@agrbrokers.com

FUNERAL HOMES/SERVICES

David Deighton
810-835-1845
david.deighton@gmail.com
clearstonemp.com

Andrew Rumph
andy@thedecaingroup.com

GAS STATIONS WITH CONVENIENCE STORES

Tony Amato
Avison Young
3993 Howard Hughes Pkwy.
Suite 350
Las Vegas, NV 89169
tony.amato@avisonyoung.com

Jorge Portalea
240-305-1156
Jorge@washmbb.com
www,washmbb.com

Matthew Ody
615-417-8512
mody@gatewaypropertiestn.com
linkedin.com/in/matthew-ody-5631ab34

GENERAL FREIGHT TRUCKING, LONG-DISTANCE, LESS THAN TRUCKLOAD

Daniel Arcand
Sunbelt Business Brokers
1300 Godward Street NE
Minneapolis, MN 55413
651-402-0098
darcand@sunbeltmidwest.com
sunbeltmidwest.com

GOVERNMENT CONTRACTING

Jonathan Ring
First Choice GovCon M&A
202-681-6777
jring@govconmergers.com
GovConMergers.com

HOME HEALTH CARE/ HOME CARE AGENCIES

Vasilis Georgiou
georgiouv@crossroadsbusiness.com

Penny Papaioannou
Atlantic Business Brokers
230 Kings Hwy E, #133
Haddonfield, NJ 08033
856-524-5178
atlanticbusinessbrokers@comcast.net
atlanticbusinessbroker.com

Dallas Romanowski
910-681-1420
dallas@homecareunited.com
homecareunited.com

HOTELS & MOTELS

Neal Patel
ACE International Brokers
1 Station Plaza
Ridgefield Park, NJ 07660
neal@agrbrokers.com

HVAC: HEATING, VENTILATING, & AIR CONDITIONING

Anthony Citrollo
The NYBB Group
25 Melville Park Rd, Ste 216
Melville, NY 11747
631-390-9650
anthony@thenybbgroup.com
thenybbgroup.com

Patrick Lange
352-440-4604
patrick@businessmodification
group.com
businessmodificationgroup.com

Mike Lohbeck
MGL Business Solutions
6665 Taylor Road
Cincinnati, OH 45248
513-200-0247
mike@mglbusinesssolutions.com

Andrew Rogerson
Rogerson Business Services
5150 Fair Oaks Blvd, #101-198
Carmichael, CA 95608
916-570-2674
andrew@rogersonbusiness
services.com
rogersonbusinessservices.com

INDUSTRIAL DESIGN SERVICES

Andrew Rogerson
Rogerson Business Services
5150 Fair Oaks Blvd, #101-198
Carmichael, CA 95608
916-570-2674
andrew@rogersonbusiness
services.com
rogersonbusinessservices.com

INDUSTRIAL WATER TREATMENT COMPANIES

Frank Balzler
386-267-4398
fbalzer@hbbva.com
hbbva.com

INFORMATION TECHNOLOGY COMPANIES

Kevin Berson
kevin@kinected.com

INSURANCE AGENCIES/BROKERAGES

Robert Bourgeois
Sunbelt Business Brokers of Louisiana
4744 Jamestown Ave, Suite 200
Baton Rouge, LA 70808
andre@sunbeltnetwork.com

Sean Hayes
Chicago, IL 60601
904-655-5565
sean@insuranceagencyappraisal.com
insuranceagencyappraisal.com

Joseph Totah
650-344-9660
joe@strategicagencies.com
agencyequity.com

INVESTMENT BANKING AND SECURITIES DEALING

Don Keysser
612-710-0995
don@hannoverconsulting.com
hannoverconsulting.com

JANITORIAL SERVICES

Thomas Milana
Transworld Business Advisors
5101 NW 21st Ave, Suite 300
Ft. Lauderdale, FL 33309
tom@tworld.com

LAWN MAINTENANCE & SERVICE

James Magrogan
602-989-9960
Jmagrogan@macorassociates.com
macorassociates.com

LIQUOR STORES/PACKAGE STORES (BEER, WINE, & LIQUOR STORES)

Stephen Atkins
Atkins Business Solutions
1830 Ritchie Hwy.
Annapolis, MD 21409
atkins.steve@comcast.net

MANUFACTURING: GENERAL

John Geiwitz
904-412-5771
johng@tworld.com
thejacksonvillebusinessbroker.com

Tony Khoury
Transworld Business Advisors
100 E. 4th St.
Greenville, NC 27858
252-347-9606
tkhoury@tworld.com
transworldeast.com

Thomas Poyser
American Business Investors, Inc.
319 E. City Center Dr
Carmel, IN 46032
317-513-2898
TomAmericanBusiness@gmail.com

Vinil Ramchandran
Dream Business Brokers
2901 W Coast Hwy, Suite 200
Newport Beach, CA 92663
562-761-4689
vinilramchandran@gmail.com

AJ Ramsey
ajramsey@tworld.com

Andrew Rogerson
Rogerson Business Services
5150 Fair Oaks Blvd, #101-198
Carmichael, CA 95608
916-570-2674
andrew@rogersonbusiness
services.com
rogersonbusinessservices.com

Sam Thompson
Transitions In Business
6550 York Av. S., Suite 402
Edina, MN 55435
612-282-1750
sthompson@transitionsib.com
transitionsib.com

MANUFACTURING: MACHINERY

Max Friar
Calder Capital, LLC
25 Division Ave S, Suite 225
Grand Rapids, MI 49503
616-965-2771
max@caldergr.com
caldergr.com

MANUFACTURING: MEN'S & BOYS' APPAREL

Max Friar
Calder Capital, LLC
25 Division Ave S, Suite 225
Grand Rapids, MI 49503
616-965-2771
max@caldergr.com
caldergr.com

MANUFACTURING: METAL FABRICATION

Greg Carpenter
Horizon M&A Advisors
408-898-0393
greg@horizonmaa.com
horizonmaa.com

Max Friar
Calder Capital, LLC
25 Division Ave S, Suite 225
Grand Rapids, MI 49503
616-965-2771
max@caldergr.com
caldergr.com

MANUFACTURING: SIGNS

Max Friar
Calder Capital, LLC
25 Division Ave S, Suite 225
Grand Rapids, MI 49503
616-965-2771
max@caldergr.com
caldergr.com

MANUFACTURING: WOOD PRODUCTS

Max Friar
Calder Capital, LLC
25 Division Ave S, Suite 225
Grand Rapids, MI 49503
616-965-2771
max@caldergr.com
caldergr.com

MANUFACTURING: WOMEN'S, GIRLS' AND INFANTS' APPAREL

Max Friar
Calder Capital, LLC
25 Division Ave S, Suite 225
Grand Rapids, MI 49503
616-965-2771
max@caldergr.com
caldergr.com

MARIJUANA STORES

Ryan Parks
rjparks03@gmail.com

MEDICAL BILLING

Robert Flynn
401-744-0320
rflynn@unitedbrokersgrp.com
unitedbrokersgrp.com

MEDICAL PRACTICES (PHYSICIANS)

David Greene
719-487-9973
david@vetbroker.com
vetbroker.com

Andrew Rogerson
Rogerson Business Services
5150 Fair Oaks Blvd, #101-198
Carmichael, CA 95608
916-570-2674
andrew@rogersonbusiness
services.com
rogersonbusinessservices.com

MEDICAL SPAS

Leon Garber
757-615-7154
leon@aestheticgrowthpartners.com
aestheticgrowthpartners.com

MEDICAL TRANSCRIPTION

Tim Kruse
Kruse Acquisitions, LLC
8505 Miller Rd
Verona, WI 53593
tim@kruseacquisitions.com

MINING: METALS

Chuck Berg
801-455-0332
chuck.berg@colliers.com
colliers.com/en

MOTORCYCLE DEALERSHIPS

Ian MacLachlan
ian@business-team.com

NURSING HOMES/ SKILLED NURSING FACILITIES

Sam Thompson
Transitions In Business
6550 York Av. S., Suite 402
Edina, MN 55435
612-282-1750
sthompson@transitionsib.com
transitionsib.com

OIL & GAS FIELD SERVICES

Jeff Adam
Adam Noble Group
2000 E Lamar Blvd, Suite 600
Arlington, TX 76006
jeff@adamnoble.com

Lou Sabbagh
713-231-8995
lsabbagh@intercapusa.com
intercapusa.com

PAWNSHOPS

Ross Miller
rossthebizbroker@gmail.com

PHARMACIES AND DRUGSTORES

James McNeela
847-701-2767
jmcneela@sourceworks-inc.com
sourceworks-inc.com

PIZZA SHOPS

Paul McNally
Central Florida Business Brokerage
498 Palm Springs Drive, Suite 100
Altamonte Springs, FL 32701
407-324-5100
Paul@CFBB.biz
CFBB.biz

Ross Miller
rossthebizbroker@gmail.com

PROPERTY MANAGEMENT COMPANIES

Jeff Cushing
jeff@thetransitiongroup.biz

Michael Shea
Transworld Business Advisors
Orlando, FL 32837
mike@tworld.com

RESTAURANTS, FAST FOOD

Richard Chinappi
Read Commercial Properties, Inc.
6 Manhattan Square #102
Hampton, VA 23666
rac@readcompanies.com

Paul Hyde
Hyde Valuations, Inc.
504 Grove Avenue, PO Box 9
Parma, ID 83660-0009
prh@hydevaluations.com

RESTAURANTS, FULL SERVICE

Jeffrey Jones
jdj@advancedbb.com

Steven Josovitz
steven@shumacher.com

Michael Kinney
936 Keeney Road
Fabius, NY 13063
kinneybrokerage@gmail.com

Julie Lemke
RE/MAX Market Force
26 Spanish St
St Augustine FL 32084
904-501-6011
julie@remaxjulie.com
remaxjulie.com

Robert Leone
Acquisition Experts
50 East Ocean Blvd.
Stuart, FL 34994
772-621-0528
bobtbb@gmail.com

Paul Sanchez
paul@benchmarksa.com

Terri Sokoloff
Specialty Tavern & Restaurant Brokers
3200 McKnight East Drive, #3205
Pittsburgh, PA 15237-6423
terri@specialtygroup.com

Owen Wolf
+27-83-255-9829
owen.wolf66@gmail.com

RETAIL BUSINESSES (IN GENERAL)

Vishal Bharucha
VNB Business Brokers
845 3rd Ave, 6th Floor
New York, NY 10022
212-220-0725
vishal@vnbbrokers.com
vnbbrokers.com

RETAIL STORES, SMALL SPECIALTY

Leonard Briskman
301-938-9049
assetvaluation@comcast.net
assetvaluationadvisors.net

ROUTE DISTRIBUTION BUSINESSES

Patrick Gagliardi
Capital Business Solutions
1525 NW 3rd Street, Suite 9
Deerfield Beach, FL 33442
954-633-7278
pgagliardi@capitalbbw.com
capitalbbw.com

Kenny Leif
Route World Brokers, Inc.
99 W. Hawthorne Avenue
Valley Stream, NY 11580
RWBKRS@gmail.com

SCHOOLS: EDUCATIONAL & NONVOCATIONAL

Charles Faherty
800-371-1159
cpfaherty@aol.com
charlesfahertyandassociates.com

SCHOOLS: VOCATIONAL & TRAINING

Charles Faherty
800-371-1159
cpfaherty@aol.com
charlesfahertyandassociates.com

SERVICE BUSINESSES (IN GENERAL)

Vishal Bharucha
VNB Business Brokers
845 3rd Ave, 6th Floor
New York, NY 10022
212-220-0725
vishal@vnbbrokers.com
vnbbrokers.com

Rick Maerkle
Asheville Business Brokers
521 College Street
Asheville, NC 28801
828-989-1858
rickmaerkle21@aol.com
ashevillebusinessbrokers.biz

Ryan Parks
rjparks03@gmail.com

Sam Scharich
Calder Capital
25 Division Ave S, Suite 225
Grand Rapids, MI 49503
616-970-6124
sam@caldergr.com
caldergr.com

SIGN COMPANIES

Jennifer Broeckling
Murphy Business Sales
1200 N. Cape Rock Drive, Suite 2
Cape Girardeau, Missouri 63701
573-335-1885
j.broeckling@murphybusiness.com
murphybusiness.com/capegirardeau

SOLAR POWER

Maria Reis
ValuBridge
Rua Cláudio Manoel 489, 901
Belo Horizonte, Minas Gerais
30140-105
+31-97-112-1832
ereismarialuisa@gmail.com
linkedin.com/in/ereismarialuisa

SOFTWARE COMPANIES

Vishal Bharucha
VNB Business Brokers
845 3rd Ave, 6th Floor
New York, NY 10022
212-220-0725
vishal@vnbbrokers.com
vnbbrokers.com

TANNING SALONS

Nick Modares
Business Brokers, Inc
PO Box 840
Roswell, GA 30077
nick@nbb-web.com

VENDING MACHINE INDUSTRY

Kenny Leif
Route World Brokers, Inc.
99 W. Hawthorne Avenue
Valley Stream, NY 11580
RWBKRS@gmail.com

VETERINARY PRACTICES

David Greene
719-487-9973
david@vetbroker.com
vetbroker.com

WIND FARMS (ENERGY)

Maria Reis
ValuBridge
Rua Cláudio Manoel 489, 901
Belo Horizonte, Minas Gerais
30140-105
+31-97-112-1832
ereismarialuisa@gmail.com
linkedin.com/in/ereismarialuisa

Y0-EMJ-706

Union of Soviet Socialist Republics

Moscow

Mongolia

Harbin

Shenyang

D.P.R.

Korea

Japan

Peking

Lü-ta

Tientsin

Seoul

Nagoya

Tokyo

Yokohama

Osaka

People's Republic of China

Sian

Nanking

Shanghai

Wuhan

Teheran

Iran

Afghanistan

Chungking

Ryukyu Is.
(Japan)

Iraq

K.

Lahore

Sikkim

Bh.

Taiwan

Pakistan

Delhi

Nepal

Canton

Hong Kong
(U.K.)

United
Arab
Emirates

Karachi

Bangladesh

D.R.

B.

Q.

Calcutta

Burma

Laos

Sa'udi Arabia

'Oman

India

Viet-Nam

Yemen
A.R.

Yemen P.D.R.

Bombay

Rangoon

Thailand

Manila

Fr. Terr. Afars/Issas

Madras

Bangkok

Khmer
Rep.

R.

Philippines

Somalia

Maldives

Sri Lanka

Malaysia

Brunei
(U.K.)

opia

Singapore

(Indo.)

Indonesia

New Guinea

Jakarta

Port Timor

(Austl.)

Madagascar

Mauritius

Réunion
(Fr.)

Australia

New
Caledonia
(Fr.)

• Cities with population over 2 million

Sydney

Melbourne

New Zealand

Feet
16,000
10,000
6,000
3,000
1,500
1,000
600
300
Sea Level
Land Depression

Date Line

50°

100°

150°

0°

© Oxford University Press

THE EUROPA YEAR BOOK

1974

A WORLD SURVEY

THE
EUROPA
YEAR BOOK
1974
A WORLD SURVEY

VOLUME II

Africa, The Americas, Asia, Australasia

EUROPA PUBLICATIONS LIMITED
18 BEDFORD SQUARE LONDON WC1B 3JN

First Published 1926

© EUROPA PUBLICATIONS LIMITED 1974

All rights reserved

ISBN 0 900 36271 5

Library of Congress Catalog Card Number 59–2942

AUSTRALIA AND NEW ZEALAND
James Bennett (Collaroy) Pty. Ltd., Collaroy, N.S.W., Australia

INDIA
UBS Publishers' Distributors Pvt. Ltd., P.O.B. 1882, 5 Ansari Road, Daryaganj, Delhi 6

JAPAN
Maruzen Co. Ltd., 6 Tori-Nichome, Nihonbashi, Tokyo 103

Printed and bound in England by
STAPLES PRINTERS LIMITED
at The Stanhope Press, Rochester, Kent.

Foreword

THE second volume of the two-part EUROPA YEAR BOOK, now in its fifteenth edition, covers the countries of Asia, Australasia, Africa and the Americas. With its companion volume, which deals with international organizations and the countries of Europe, it provides a wealth of detailed information on the political, economic and commercial activity of the countries of the world.

For a more detailed account of the history and economy of countries, readers are referred to our regional books: THE MIDDLE EAST AND NORTH AFRICA, AFRICA SOUTH OF THE SAHARA and THE FAR EAST AND AUSTRALASIA.

The editor would like to acknowledge the invaluable assistance of numerous individuals and organizations throughout the world in providing current information for this edition and would like to express particular indebtedness to the following publications: the United Nations' *Demographic Yearbook*, the United Nations' *Statistical Yearbook*, the Food and Agricultural Organization of the United Nations' *Production Yearbook*, the International Institute for Strategic Studies' *The Military Balance 1973–74* and the *Bank of London and South America Review* for material on Latin America.

July 1974.

COUNTRIES AND TERRITORIES

ABBREVIATIONS

abbrev.	abbreviation
Acad.	Academician, Academy
accred.	accredited
adm., admin.	administration
ag., ags.	agency(ies)
A.G.	joint stock company (German)
a.i.	ad interim
ALM	Dutch Antillean Airlines
AM	amplitude modulation
amalg.	amalgamated
approx.	approximately
A/S	joint stock company (Norwegian)
asscn.	association
assocd.	associated
asst.	assistant
AUA	Austrian Airlines
Aug.	August
auth.	authorized
Av.	Avenue
Avda.	Avenida (Avenue)
Bd., Blv., Blvd., Bld.	Boulevard
BEA	British European Airways
Benelux	Belgium-Netherlands-Luxembourg Union
BOAC	British Overseas Airways Corporation
br.(s)	branch(es)
Brig.	Brigadier
Bt.	Baronet
C., cen.	central
c, ca.	circa
CACM	Central American Common Market
cap.	capital
Capt.	Captain
CARIFTA	Caribbean Free Trade Association
Cav.	Cavaliere
C.B.E.	Commander of (the Order of) the British Empire
CENTO	Central Treaty Organization
CFA	Communauté Financière Africaine
C.H	Companion of Honour
Chair.	Chairman
Chr.Dem.	Christian Democrat
Chr.Soc.	Christian Socialist
C.I.	Channel Islands
c.i.f.	cost, insurance and freight
C.-in-C.	Commander-in-Chief
circ.	circulation
Cmd.	Command
Cmdr.	Commander
CMEA	Council for Mutual Economic Assistance
Co.	Company, County
Col.	Colonel
Comm.	Commendatore
Commr.	Commissioner
Confed.	Confederation
Cons.-Gen.	Consul-General
Corr.	Correspondent
corresp.	corresponding
ČSA	Czechoslovak Airlines
Cttee.	Committee
cu.	cubic
curr.	current
cwt.	hundredweight

D.C.	District of Columbia
D.D.R.	Deutsche Demokratische Republik
Dec.	December
Dem.	Democratic
dep.	deposits
depos.	depositary
Dept.	Department
Dir.	Director
Div.	Division(al)
D.M.	Deutsche Mark
Dott.	Dottore
Dr., Doc.	Doctor
dr.(e)	drachma(e)
d.w.t.	dead weight tons
E.	East, Eastern
EAA	East African Airways
Econ.	Economist, Economics
EEC	European Economic Community
EFTA	European Free Trade Association
e.g.	exempli gratia (for example)
eKv.	electron kilovolt
eMv.	electron megavolt
Eng.	Engineer, Engineering
Esc.	Escuela, Escudos
est.	established, estimate, estimated
etc.	etcetera
excl.	excluding
exec.	executive
f.	founded
FAO	Food and Agriculture Organization
Feb	February
Fed.	Federation
FM	frequency modulation
fmrly.	formerly
f.o.b.	free on board
Fr.	Franc
ft.	foot (feet)
GATT	General Agreement on Tariffs and Trade
G.B.E.	Knight (or Dame) Grand Cross of (the Order of) the British Empire
G.C.M.G.	Knight Grand Cross of (the Order of) St. Michael and St. George
G.D.P.	Gross Domestic Product
G.D.R.	German Democratic Republic
Gen.	General
GeV	giga electron volts
G.m.b.H.	company with limited liability(German)
G.N.P.	Gross National Product
g.r.t.	gross registered tons
GWh	gigawatt hours
ha.	hectares
H.E.	His Eminence, His Excellency
hl.	hectolitre
H.M.	His (or Her) Majesty
Hon.	Honorary (or Honourable)
H.R.H.	His (or Her) Royal Highness
H.S.H.	His Serene Highness
IBRD	International Bank for Reconstruction and Development (World Bank)

ICC	.. ..	International Chamber of Commerce
ICSU	.. ..	International Council of Scientific Unions
IMF	.. ..	International Monetary Fund
in. (ins.)		inch (inches)
Inc., Incorp., Incd.		Incorporated
incl.	..	including
Ing.	..	Engineer
Insp.	..	Inspector
Int.	..	International
Inż.	..	Engineer
Is.	..	Islands
ISIC	.. ..	International Standard Industrial Classification
JAL	..	Japan Airlines
Jan.	..	January
JAT	..	Yugoslav Air Transport
Jnr.	..	Junior
Jr.	..	Jonkheer (Netherlands)
K.B.E.	..	Knight Commander of (the Order of) the British Empire
K.C.M.G.	..	Knight Commander of (the Order of) St. Michael and St. George
kg.	..	kilogramme
K.G.	..	Knight of (the Order of) the Garter, Kommandit Gesellschaft
kHz	..	kilohertz
KLM	..	Royal Dutch Airlines
km.	..	kilometre(s)
kWh.	..	kilowatt hours
kW.	..	kilowatt(s)
LAFTA		Latin American Free Trade Association
lb.	..	pound(s)
LOT	..	Polish Airlines
L.P.G.	..	liquefied petroleum gas
Lt., Lieut.		Lieutenant
Ltd.	..	Limited
m.	..	million
MALÉV		Hungarian Airlines
Man.	..	Manager, managing
March.	..	Marchese
M.B.E.	..	Member of (the Order of) the British Empire
m.b.H.	..	with limited liability (German)
Mc/s	..	megacycles per second
MEA	..	Middle East Airlines
mem.	..	member
MEV	..	mega electron volts
mfrs.	..	manufacturers
Mgr.	..	Monseigneur; Monsignor
MHz	..	megahertz
Mlle.	..	Mademoiselle
Mme.	..	Madame
M.P.	..	Member of Parliament
MSS	..	Manuscripts
m.t.	..	metric tons
MW	..	megawatt(s)
N.	..	North, Northern
n.a.	..	not available
NATO	..	North Atlantic Treaty Organization
n.e.s.	..	not elsewhere specified
No.	..	number
Nov.	..	November
nr.	..	near
n.r.t.	..	net registered tons
N.V.	..	limited company (Dutch)
N.Z.	..	New Zealand

OAS	.. ..	Organization of American States
OAU	.. ..	Organization of African Unity
O.B.E.	..	Officer of (the Order of) the British Empire
Oct.	..	October
On.	..	Onorevole (Honourable)
p.a.	..	per annum
P.C.	..	Privy Counsellor
per.	..	passage, street (Russian)
PIA	..	Pakistan International Airlines
P.K.	..	Post Box (Turkish)
pl.	..	platz, place, ploshchad (square)
P.O.B.	..	Post Office Box
polit.	..	political
Pres.	..	President
Prof.	..	Professor
Propr.	..	Proprietor
Prov.	..	Provisional, Provinciale (Dutch)
p.u.	..	paid up
publ.	..	publication
Q.C.	..	Queen's Counsel
q.v.	..	quod vide
reg., regd.		register, registered
Rep.	..	Republic
rep.	..	representative
reorg.	..	reorganized
res.	..	reserve(s)
retd.	..	retired
Rev.	..	Reverend
Rp.	..	Rupee(s)
R.S.F.S.R.		Russian Soviet Federative Socialist Republic
R.S.R.		Socialist Republic of Romania
Rt.	..	Right
Rt. Hon.	..	Right Honourable
S.	..	South, Southern, San.
S.A.	..	limited company (French and Spanish)
SAA	..	South African Airways
SAHSA		Honduras Air Service
SAS	..	Scandinavian Airlines System
SDR(s)	..	Special Drawing Right(s)
SEATO	..	South-East Asia Treaty Organization
Sec.	..	Secretary
Sen.	..	Senior
Sept.	..	September
S.E.R.	..	Sua Eccellenza Reverendissima (His Eminence)
Sig.	..	Signore
SITC		Standard International Trade Classification
Soc.	..	Socialist
S.p.A.	..	joint stock company (Italian)
sq.	..	square
S.S.R.	..	Soviet Socialist Republic
St.	..	Saint; Street
stds.	..	standards (timber measurement)
Ste.	..	Sainte
subs.	..	subscriptions; subscribed
Supt.	..	Superintendent
TAP	..	Portuguese Air Transport
TAROM	..	Romanian Air Transport
TASS	..	Soviet Telegraph Agency
techn.	..	technical
THY	..	Turkish Airlines
Tit.	..	Titular
Treas.	..	Treasurer
T.U.	..	Trade Union

ABBREVIATIONS

TV	.. ..	Television
TWA	.. ..	Trans World Airways
u/a	..	unit of account (European Monetary Agreement)
U.A.R.	.. ..	United Arab Republic
UIC	.. ..	International Union of Railways
Ul. (ul.)	..	Street
UN	.. ..	United Nations
UNDP	.. ..	United Nations Development Programme
UNESCO	..	United Nations Educational, Scientific and Cultural Organisation
U.K.	.. ..	United Kingdom

U.S.(A.)	..	United States (of America)
U.S.S.R.	..	Union of Soviet Socialist Republics
UTA	..	Union des Transports Aériens
VEB	..	public company (German)
VHF	..	Very High Frequency
viz.	..	videlicet
vol.(s)	..	volume(s)
W.	.. ..	West, Western
WHO	..	World Health Organization
WMO	..	World Meteorological Organization
yr.	.. ..	year

AFGHANISTAN

INTRODUCTORY SURVEY

Location, Climate, Language, Religion, Flag, Capital

The Republic of Afghanistan lies in the heart of Asia. Its neighbours are to the north the Soviet Union, to the west Iran, to the east China and to the east and south Pakistan. The climate varies sharply between the highlands and lowlands; the temperature in the south-west in summer reaches 120°F (48.8°C) and in the winter in the Hindu Kush mountains of the north-east falls far below zero. The two main languages are Pakhto (Pashtu) and Dari Persian. With the exception of small minorities of Hindus, Sikhs and Jews, all Afghans are Muslims, almost 90 per cent of them of the Sunni sect. The national flag (proportions 3 by 2) has three vertical stripes, of black, red and green, with the coat of arms in the centre. The capital is Kabul.

Recent History

During both World Wars Afghanistan was neutral and is now a staunch advocate of the policy of non-alignment, accepting economic assistance from both East and West. Relations with neighbouring Pakistan have from time to time been strained over Afghanistan's support for the creation of an autonomous area for the Pashtun tribes living in the north-west of Pakistan, to be known as "Pashtunistan". It was for this reason that trade and diplomatic relations with Pakistan were suspended between 1961 and 1963 during the premiership of Mohammad Daud, a firm supporter of Pashtunistan. The difficulties arising from this rupture (Afghanistan's trade routes run through Pakistan) led to the fall of the ten-year-old Daud administration. He was succeeded by Dr. Mohammad Yusuf (1963–65), under whom relations with Pakistan were restored and a liberal constitution was promulgated. Subsequent administrations tried to continue Dr. Yusuf's policy of economic modernization and gradual political development, but student riots, parliamentary crises and droughts led to political instability between 1968 and 1972. It seemed that Musa Shafiq, who took office at the end of 1972, might be more energetic and successful than his immediate predecessors. In July 1973, however, the Government and the monarchy were overthrown by a *coup* led by the former premier, Mohammad Daud, who was proclaimed Head of State. King Zahir Shah, a cousin of Mohammad Daud, was absent from the country at the time and abdicated in August 1973, having held the throne for 40 years. The new régime appears to have adopted a firm and austere line: reforms that will lead to greater social justice have been promised and a new constitution is under consideration.

Government

Following the *coup* of July 1973, the constitution of 1964 was abolished, except for those parts of it "not repugnant to the principles of democracy". The monarchy was therefore abolished (the King had had the power to nominate the Prime Minister and approve the Cabinet) and both Houses of the Shura (Parliament) were dissolved. The Government now comprises a thirteen-member Central Committee presided over by the Head of State.

Defence

Every able-bodied Afghan has to serve two years in the army, which numbers 80,000 men. Its equipment and training are very largely provided by the Soviet Union. The Afghan air force, which numbers 3,000, is equipped with supersonic jet aircraft. Police security forces come under the Ministry of the Interior. Para-military forces number about 13,000 men.

Economic Affairs

Agriculture remains the mainstay of the economy, in terms of both production and employment. About two-thirds of agricultural production is at subsistence level. Roughly a sixth, comprising wool, karakul skins, cotton and fruit, is exported, but it has recently been necessary to import quantities of foodstuffs, notably wheat. There are known deposits of petroleum, iron ore (with estimated reserves of over 2,000 million tons) and other minerals, but commercial exploitation is limited at present to coal, salt and lapis lazuli. The discovery of over 60,000 million cubic metres of natural gas in northern Afghanistan holds promise for the development of the unexploited minerals, and the increasing export of natural gas to the U.S.S.R., started in 1967, will have an important impact on the economy. Existing sources of energy are imported petroleum (mainly from the U.S.S.R.), hydroelectricity, coal and wood. Industry accounts for only about 7 per cent of domestic production. Major industries are cotton textiles, cement and the processing of agricultural products, but among the limited consumer industries hand-woven carpets are very valuable as export items. The Fourth Five-Year Plan (1972–76) allocates a greater proportion of funds for investment in agriculture and industry and rather less to infrastructural projects than previous plans provided.

Nearly 40 per cent of exports go to the U.S.S.R. under barter contracts, 20 per cent to India under bilateral trade agreements, and 14 per cent to the U.K., while the remainder is sold in other Western markets for convertible currencies. Imports are greatly in excess of exports and Afghanistan is dependent on the foreign aid she receives, which, however, has been declining in recent years. The main sources of foreign aid have been the U.S.S.R. and the U.S.A, with other substantial help from China and the Federal Republic of Germany. Combined with increasingly heavy debt repayments and a decline in exports, the fall in foreign aid led to a projected balance of payments deficit of $15 million in 1973–74.

Transport and Communications

Afghanistan is a land-locked country and the most convenient access to the sea lies through Pakistan. There are no railways. The United States and the Soviet Union have helped to build all-weather highways connecting the main towns, and a network of asphalted highways covers the country. A road link between Kabul and the northern provinces through the Hindu Kush was opened in 1964. There are internal and international air services and water traffic on the River Oxus.

Social Welfare

Government officials in the main towns enjoy national health insurance and all officials are entitled to an old age pension. Most private companies have their own doctor and hospitals. There are over 60 public hospitals. Disabled people are looked after in social welfare centres in the provincial capitals. China is to construct a 250-bed hospital free of charge.

Education

Primary education is free, and compulsory wherever possible; by 1970 there were 648,125 children in over 3,500 schools. The Government aims to provide basic educational facilities to 50 per cent of the population by 1980. There are two universities.

Tourism

These are Afghanistan's principal attractions: Bamian with its high statue of Buddha and thousands of painted caves; Bandi Amir with its suspended lakes; the Blue Mosque of Mazar; the walls of Kabul; Herat with its Grand Mosque and minarets; the towns of Kandahar and Girishk; Balkh (ancient Bactria), "Mother of Cities", in the north; Bagram, Hadda and Surkh Kotal (of interest to archaeologists); and the high mountains of the Hindu Kush.

Visas are required to enter Afghanistan for nationals of all countries.

Sport

The traditional sports are wrestling and buzkashi, a game played by teams of hundreds of horsemen. Athletics and ball games are sponsored by the Ministry of Education.

Public Holidays

1974: August 23rd–25th (Jashn), August 31st (Pashtunistan Day), September 19th (First Day of Ramadan), October 18th (Id ul Fitr), December 26th (Id ul Adha).

1975: January 14th (Muslim New Year), January 23rd (Ashoura, 10th day of New Year), March 26th (Mouloud, Birth of Muhammad), May 27th (Independence Day).

Weights and Measures

The metric system has been officially adopted but traditional weights are still used. One "seer" equals 16 pounds.

Currency and Exchange Rates

100 puls=2 krans=1 afghani.

Exchange rates (March 1974):

£1 sterling=143.2 afghanis;

U.S. $1=59.82 afghanis.

STATISTICAL SURVEY

AREA AND POPULATION

TOTAL AREA	ESTIMATED MID-YEAR POPULATION				DENSITY (per sq. km.) 1972
	1969	1970	1971	1972	
250,000 sq. miles (647,497 sq. km.)	16,700,000	17,087,000	17,480,000	17,878,000*	27.6

* United Nations estimate.

ETHNIC GROUPS (1963)

Pathans or Pashtuns	Tadzhiks	Uzbeks	Hazarahs	Nomads
8,800,000	4,300,000	800,000	444,000	650,000

AFGHANISTAN—(STATISTICAL SURVEY)

PROVINCES*
(1970)

	AREA (sq. km.)	POPULATION	DENSITY (per sq. km.)	CAPITAL (with population)
Uruzgan . . .	34,000	513,100	15.1	Tareenkoot (48,200)
Badghis . . .	24,700	329,500	13.3	Qala-i-nau (78,400)
Bamian . . .	19,200	356,200	18.5	Bamian (46,200)
Badakhshan . . .	42,600	354,600	8.3	Faizabad (64,700)
Baghlan . . .	18,600	641,800	34.5	Baghlan (103,600)
Balkh . . .	15,100	364,100	24.1	Mazar-i-Sharif (44,500)
Parwan . . .	5,600	913,300	163.0	Charikar (93,800)
Paktia . . .	17,600	859,100	48.8	Gardiz (40,300)
Takhar . . .	11,800	508,800	43.1	Taluqan (68,600)
Jawzjan . . .	24,700	442,100	17.9	Sheberghan (56,500)
Zabul . . .	20,000	368,600	18.4	Qalat (51,200)
Samangan . . .	16,000	213,400	13.3	Uiback (39,500)
Ghazni . . .	31,400	1,136,400	36.1	Ghazni (44,700)
Ghour . . .	35,100	333,000	9.5	Cheghcheran (62,700)
Fariab . . .	22,900	447,500	19.5	Maimana (57,100)
Farah . . .	57,800	323,500	5.6	Farah (29,600)
Kunduz . . .	7,400	417,400	56.4	Kunduz (82,500)
Kandahar . . .	45,100	763,100	16.9	Kandahar (130,800)
Kabul . . .	4,500	1,330,100	295.7	Kabul (513,000)
Kapisa . . .	5,800	354,900	78.4	Mahmoodraqi (72,700)
Kunarha . . .	10,300	339,300	32.9	Asadabad (28,900)
Laghman . . .	9,100	229,100	25.2	Meterlam (74,700)
Logar . . .	4,500	318,300	70.7	Pulialam (27,500)
Nangarhar . . .	7,600	842,100	110.8	Jelalabad (50,400)
Neemroze . . .	50,000	125,400	2.5	Zarunj (17,400)
Wardak . . .	10,300	427,900	41.5	Maidan (55,900)
Herat . . .	41,500	706,100	17.0	Herat (73,700)
Helmand . . .	59,700	325,800	5.5	Bost (29,200)
TOTAL . .	652,900†	14,284,500	21.9	

* Population figures refer to settled inhabitants only, excluding kuchies (nomads), estimated at 2,801,800 for the whole country in 1970.

† Other sources give the total area as 250,000 square miles (647,497 sq. km.).

Source: Department of Statistics, Ministry of Planning, *Statistical Pocket-Book of Afghanistan.*

PRINCIPAL CITIES
(population at July 1st, 1971)

Kabul (capital) .	. 318,094*	Herat . .	. 103,915
Kandahar .	. 133,799	Tagab . .	. 102,028
Baghlan .	. 105,944		

* Population 498,821, including suburbs.

Births and Deaths: Average annual birth rate 50.5 per 1,000; death rate 26.5 per 1,000 (UN estimates for 1965–70).

EMPLOYMENT*

	1966	1970
Agriculture . . .	2,940,000	2,960,000
Manufacturing (incl. Handi-crafts) . . .	230,000	259,000
Construction and Mining .	90,000	104,000
Transport and Communica-tions . . .	20,000	29,000
Other Production Industries	60,000	77,000
Education and Health Ser-vices . . .	20,000	40,000
Government Institutions .	60,000	67,000
Commerce . . .	100,000	107,000
Other Services . . .	100,000	108,000
Unknown . . .	340,000	640,000
TOTAL LABOUR FORCE .	3,960,000	4,391,000

*Excluding kuchies (nomads).

Source: Estimates by a Soviet advisory and planning team, during preparation of the Fourth Five-Year Plan.

Total economically active population (1970): 6,000,000, including 4,890,000 in agriculture (ILO and FAO estimates).

AGRICULTURE

LAND USE, 1968
('000 hectares)

Arable Land	7,844
Permanent Crops	136
Permanent Meadows and Pastures . .	6,020
Forest Land	2,000
Other Areas	48,750
TOTAL	64,750

Source: FAO, *Production Yearbook 1971.*

PRINCIPAL CROPS

	AREA ('000 hectares)				PRODUCTION ('000 metric tons)			
	1968	1969	1970	1971	1968	1969	1970	1971
Wheat . . .	2,063	2,105	2,176	2,350	2,354	2,401	2,081	1,915
Barley . . .	316*	319*	315	315	361	365	370	355
Maize . . .	553	559	451	460*	773	785	667	700*
Rice (Paddy) . .	205	206	202	200	402	407	366	350
Sugar Cane† . .	2	2	3	3*	57	57	60	50§
Sugar Beets† . .	5	5	5	5*	67	62	68	60§
Grapes‡ . .	60	61	61*	n.a.	200	204	210*	n.a.
Cotton Seed . .	} 55	65	54	54 {	47	57	49	52
Cotton (Lint) . .					24	29	25	27

*FAO estimate.   † Crop year ending in year stated.

‡ Production of raisins (in '000 metric tons): 32 in 1968; 32 in 1969; 33* in 1970; 33* in 1971.   § 1971–72.

Source: mainly FAO, *Production Yearbook 1971.*

1971 estimates ('000 metric tons): Total fruit 650; total vegetables 725; other oilseeds 55.

LIVESTOCK
('000)

	1967–68	1968–69	1969–70	1970–71
Cattle	3,600	3,605	3,608	3,700
Sheep†	21,453	21,668	21,880	22,900
Goats	3,186	3,187	3,219	3,300
Horses	402	410	414	300
Asses	1,328	1,341	1,360	1,275
Mules	32	33	33	25*
Buffaloes	33	33	33	35*
Camels	299	299	301	300

* FAO estimate.   † Including Karakul sheep, numbering 6.8 million in 1971.

Source: FAO, *Production Yearbook 1971.*

LIVESTOCK PRODUCTS
(metric tons)

	1968	1969	1970*	1971*
Beef, Veal and Buffalo Meat† .	32,000*	32,000*	32,000	33,000
Mutton, Lamb and Goats' Meat†	118,000*	118,000*	118,000	120,000
Cows' Milk . . .	303,000*	311,000*	311,000	315,000
Sheep's Milk . . .	212,000	215,000	218,000	220,000
Goats' Milk . . .	49,000	50,000	51,000	52,000
Buffaloes' Milk . . .	4,000	4,000	4,000	4,000
Hen Eggs . . .	11,500*	11,900*	12,300	13,000
Wool: Greasy . . .	27,500	29,500	30,000	31,000
Clean . . .	15,100	16,200	16,500	17,000

* FAO estimates.

† Meat from indigenous animals only, including the meat equivalent of exported live animals. The estimates are based on earlier years' official figures, the scope of which was unspecified, and may refer to commercial meat production only, excluding farm slaughter.

Source: FAO, *Production Yearbook 1971.*

FORESTRY
('000 cubic metres)

	ROUNDWOOD REMOVALS*			SAWNWOOD PRODUCTION		
	1969	1970	1971	1969	1970	1971
Coniferous (soft wood) . .	1,310	1,455	1,600	550	630	655
Broadleaved (hard wood) . .	6,085	6,275	6,600	163	154	168
TOTAL . . .	7,395	7,730	8,200	713	784	823

* Unofficial figures.

Source: FAO, *Yearbook of Forest Products 1970*; United Nations *Statistical Yearbook 1972.*

OTHER FOREST PRODUCTS
(metric tons)

	1968	1969	1970
Bark and other tanning materials	200	220	242
Materials for plaiting (excluding bamboo) . . .	n.a.	320	n.a.

Source: FAO, *Yearbook of Forest Products.*

Inland Fishing (1964–71): Total catch 1,500 metric tons each year (FAO estimate).

INDUSTRIAL AND MINERAL PRODUCTION
(Twelve months ending March 20th)

		1968–69	1969–70	1970–71	1971–72
Ginned Cotton . . .	'ooo tons	13.9	27.0	30.5	16.8
Cotton Fabrics . . .	million metres	48.7	49.4	57.1	62.0
Woollen Fabrics . . .	'ooo metres	445.8	663.4	433.3	284.0
Rayon Fabrics . . .	,, ,,	2,818.0	2,520.0	8,272.0	10,547.0
Cement . . .	'ooo tons	90.6	103.5	94.3	73.0
Electricity . . .	million kWh	317.4	358.8	395.0	422.6
Wheat Flour . . .	'ooo tons	58.5	40.4	51.2	92.3
Sugar . . .	,, ,,	5.3	6.1	8.6	8.5
Vegetable Oil . . .	,, ,,	3.0	2.8	4.1	4.0
Coal . . .	,, ,,	124.9	136.6	164.4	135.0
Natural Gas . . .	million cu. metres	1,681.1	2,029.0	2,583.0	2,635.4

Source: Department of Statistics, Kabul, *Survey of Progress 1971–72.*

FINANCE
100 puls = 2 krans = 1 afghani.

Coins: 25 and 50 puls; 1, 2 and 5 afghanis.

Notes: 10, 20, 50, 100, 500 and 1,000 afghanis.

Exchange rates (March 1974): £1 sterling = 107.7 afghanis (official rate) or 143.2 afghanis (free rate);
U.S. $1 = 45.00 afghanis (official rate) or 59.82 afghanis (free rate).

1,000 afghanis = £6.98 = $16.72 (free rates).

BUDGET
GOVERNMENT REVENUE AND EXPENDITURE
(million afghanis, twelve months ending March 20th)

REVENUE	1970/71	1971/72 (est.)	1972/73 (est.)
Direct Taxes . . .	467	428	565
Indirect Taxes . . .	2,818	2,976	2,904
Revenue from monopolies and other enterprises .	950	933	791
Natural Gas Revenue .	720	587	740
Revenue from other property and services . .	424	522	461
Other Revenue . .	334	375	381
TOTAL REVENUE .	5,713	5,821	5,842

EXPENDITURE	1970/71	1971/72 (est.)	1972/73 (est.)
Administration and Defence	2,127	2,116	2,175
Social Services . . .	1.030	1,116	1,230
Economic Service . .	468	473	460
Exchange Subsidies . .	240	425	410
Other Subsidies and Grants	279	229	432
Foreign Debt Service .	1,014	1,135	1,055
TOTAL ORDINARY EXPENDITURE .	5,158	5,494	5,762
Budgetary Development Expenditures* .	1,731	1,868	2,150
Extrabudgetary Expenditures . . .	—	—	250

*Excludes expenditures financed by foreign project aid.

Source: United Nations, *Quarterly Bulletin of Statistics for Asia and the Far East*, December 1971.

Budget (1972-73): Total expenditure Afs. 8,372 million.

GOLD RESERVES
Bank of Afghanistan
('ooo U.S. dollars at December 31st)

1970	.	.	32,980
1971	.	.	33,630
1972	.	.	35,410
1973	.	.	39,350

Source: IMF, International Financial Statistics.

CURRENCY IN CIRCULATION
(million afghanis at March 21st)

1970	.	.	6,144
1971	.	.	6,532
1972	.	.	6,785
1973	.	.	8,180

October 21st, 1973: 8,734 million afghanis.

Source: IMF, International Financial Statistics.

COST OF LIVING
Index Numbers of Consumer Prices
(Twelve months ending March 20th. Base: 1961–62 = 100)

	1966–67	1967–68	1968–69	1969–70	1970–71	1971–72
All Items	214	264	208	207	270	310
Cereals	247	336	234	219	318	395
Meat	217	212	191	214	223	204
Fruits	188	177	199	232	268	225
Vegetables . .	157	156	173	241	248	239
Other Food Articles . .	151	152	146	146	147	161
Non-Food Items .	111	111	105	115	117	120

Source: Department of Statistics, Ministry of Planning, Kabul, Survey of Progress 1971–72.

NATIONAL ACCOUNTS
Net Domestic Product by Origin
(million afghanis, at 1965 market prices)

Economic Activity	1967	1968	1969
Agriculture, Forestry and Fishing . . .	28,300	29,050	29,117
Mining	280	540	700
Manufacturing	5,707	5,777	6,200
Construction	860	900	990
Transportation, Communication, Utilities .	1,481	1,630	1,820
Wholesale and Retail Trade* . . .	7,122	7,350	7,650
Ownership of Dwellings . . .	4,673	4,800	4,900
Public Administration and Defence .	2,890	3,150	3,528
Other services	2,174	2,200	2,300
Net Domestic Product . . .	53,487	55,397	57,205

* Including storage, hotels and restaurants.

Source: United Nations, Quarterly Bulletin of Statistics for Asia and the Far East, December 1971.

BALANCE OF PAYMENTS

(million units of account*, twelve months ending March 20th)

	1970–71	1971–72 (est.)	1972–73 (est.)
Goods and services:			
Exports f.o.b.	81.5	100.9	90.2
Imports c.i.f.	— 112.1	— 117.9	— 129.5
Trade balance	— 30.6	— 17.0	— 39.3
Services obtained under project aid .	— 5.5	— 5.9	— 6.3
Other services (net)	5.7	6.0	6.4
TOTAL GOODS AND SERVICES .	— 30.4	— 16.9	— 39.2
Loans and grants received (net)			
Grants received and drawings on loans .	42.2	48.8	65.8
Debt service	— 23.7	— 27.5	— 33.6
TOTAL LOANS AND GRANTS .	18.5	21.3	32.2
Net errors and omissions . . .	7.9	6.3	7.0
Allocation of SDRs	4.0	3.9	—
NET BALANCE . . .	—	14.6	—
Monetary movements†			
Da Afghanistan Bank . . .	0.6	— 14.8	
Other banks	— 0.6	0.2	
TOTAL	—	— 14.6	—

* The unit of account is the value of one IMF Special Drawing Right (SDR) equivalent to U.S. $1 before December 1971. Since February 1973 the value of each unit has been U.S. $1.206.

† Increase in assets is indicated by a — sign.

FOREIGN AID

(million U.S.$)

SOURCE	1968–69	1969–70	1970–71	1971–72
U.S.A.	4.79	1.45	3.00	2.35
U.S.S.R. . . .	30.52	28.90	17.62	22.47
Germany, Federal Republic	6.47	2.30	2.66	4.04
United Nations . .	2.11	6.24	2.61	2.66
China, People's Republic .	5.53	5.56	1.10	—
TOTAL (including others)	50.20	44.22	27.58	34.32

EXTERNAL TRADE

(million afghanis, twelve months ending March 20th)

	1966–67	1967–68	1968–69	1969–70	1970–71	1971–72
Imports*	11,271	10,454	9,267	9,410	6,271	14,155
Exports	4,835	5,018	5,348	6,180	7,160	8,427

1972-73: Exports 7,214 million afghanis.

*Including imports under commodity loans and grants from foreign countries and international organizations. In recent years the value of these imports (in million afghanis) was: 4,383.5 in 1968–69; 3,940.1 in 1969–70.

PRINCIPAL COMMODITIES
(million afghanis)

IMPORTS	1967–68	1968–69	1969–70
Food	1,917.02	1,118.63	1,607.29
Wheat Meal and Flour, etc. . .	989.41	266.82	0.16
Sugar	394.20	70.39	289.64
Tea	365.11	706.19	705.04
Petroleum Products . . .	404.47	477.17	563.43
Vegetables Oils and Fat . . .	236.01	328.24	292.49
Chemicals	360.77	370.26	573.74
Medicinal and Pharmaceutical .	191.98	186.26	260.83
Rubber Tyres and Tubes . .	288.42	211.23	230.08
Textile Yarn and Thread . .	202.20	335.48	647.79
Cotton Fabrics . . .	266.32	206.67	222.85
Miscellaneous Fabrics. .	388.49	270.81	484.63
Machinery and Transport Equipment	624.01	600.46	752.18
Road Motor Vehicles and Parts .	330.78	278.29	407.90
TOTAL (incl. others)*	10,454.45	9,266.80	9,409.79

* Includes imports not distributed by commodity, valued (in million afghanis) at 4,866.55 in 1967–68; 4,120.68 in 1968–69; and 2,964.28 in 1969–70. These were most of the imports obtained under commodity loans and grants.

1970/71 (million afghanis): Tea 702.0; Rubber Tyres and Tubes 264.0; Cotton Fabrics 219.0; Miscellaneous Fabrics 453.0; Total 6,258.3 (provisional figures).

EXPORTS	1967–68	1968–69	1969–70*
Food	2,079.21	2,102.86	2,225.78
Fresh Fruits . . .	611.79 }	596.67	668.50
Prepared and Preserved Fruits .	9.42 }		
Edible Nuts	513.06	593.17	521.87
Dried Fruits . . .	841.59	814.40	891.85
Hides and Skins . . .	155.17	152.18	194.50
Fur Skins, undressed . .	1,086.99	636.49	1,004.44
Karakul	1,077.55	629.10	991.09
Oil-Seeds, Oil Nuts and Kernels .	67.86	208.50	193.78
Wool and Other Animal Hair .	367.06	520.65	505.64
Cotton	593.87	438.02	426.89
Natural Gas . . .	221.25	672.76	915.96
Carpets, etc., of wool and hair .	390.91	336.75	470.83
TOTAL (incl. others)	5,017.57	5,348.32	6,160.62

* Provisional figures. Revised total is 6,180 million afghanis.

1970/71 (million afghanis): Hides and Skins 163.0; Wool 527.3; Raw Cotton 670.7; Carpets and Rugs 427.7; Total 7,109.8 (provisional figures).

PRINCIPAL TRADING PARTNERS
(million afghanis)

IMPORTS*	1967–68	1968–69	1969–70
China, Peoples' Republic . . .	424.49	689.64	790.78
Germany, Federal Republic* . .	846.98	838.27	524.98
India	478.25	850.52	863.07
Iran	215.68	367.72	269.42
Japan	802.99	892.40	1,100.88
Pakistan	246.50	227.44	269.85
U.S.S.R.*	5,025.71	3,561.19	3,145.81
United Kingdom . . .	271.09	238.09	390.97
U.S.A.*	1,340.75	783.74	526.67
TOTAL (incl. others)	10,454.45	9,266.80	9,409.79

* Includes imports under commodity loans and grants (million afghanis):
Total 4,383.51 in 1968–69; 3,940.08 in 1969–70; of which:
Federal Republic of Germany 548.84 in 1968–69; 188.98 in 1969–70;
U.S.S.R. 2,519.56 in 1968–69; 2,201.79 in 1969–70;
U.S.A. 583.52 in 1968–69; 179.58 in 1969–70.

EXPORTS	1967–68	1968–69	1969–70*
Czechoslovakia	170.66	133.14	122.17
India	816.38	1,173.67	1,200.26
Lebanon	144.41	178.72	132.57
Pakistan	416.29	427.31	401.51
Switzerland	284.25	222.97	348.19
U.S.S.R.	1,667.86	1,978.37	2,320.69
United Kingdom . . .	805.06	552.98	965.52
U.S.A.	420.16	341.77	185.35
TOTAL (incl. others)	5,017.57	5,348.32	6,160.62

* Provisional figures. Revised total is 6,180 million afghanis.

Source for Trade tables: United Nations, *Yearbook of International Trade Statistics.*

TOURISM
INTERNATIONAL TOURIST ARRIVALS BY COUNTRY

	1969	1970	1971
Australia	1,879	2,072	2,703
France	4,709	6,536	8,130
Germany, Federal Republic . .	3,916	5,472	7,524
Pakistan	26,175	51,250	51,792
United Kingdom . . .	8,080	9,309	10,117
U.S.A.	7,644	9,572	11,965
Others	10,686	16,022	20,878
TOTAL	63,089	100,233	113,109

Receipts from Tourism: U.S. $4.3 million in 1969; $7.8 million in 1970; $11 million in 1971.

Source: Afghan Tourist Organization, Kabul.

TRANSPORT

CIVIL AVIATION
TOTAL SCHEDULED SERVICES

	1969	1970	1971
Aircraft Departures . . .	3,618	3,993	n.a.
Kilometres Flown . . .	2,872,000	3,605,000	4,624,000
Passengers Carried . . .	67,271	84,688	97,000
Passenger-km. . . .	84,888,000	115,037,000	171,000,000
Cargo Carried: metric tons .	2,359	5,599	n.a.
Cargo tonne-km. . . .	7,093,000	7,646,000	2,091,000
Mail tonne-km. . . .	72,000	101,000	75,000

Source: mainly ICAO, *Digest of Statistics.*

ROAD TRAFFIC
Motor Vehicles in Use (Kabul only)

	1969–70	1970–71	1971–72
Cars . . .	30,788	31,884	33,408
Lorries . . .	15,770	15,890	16,162
Buses . . .	2,443	2,611	2,849

COMMUNICATIONS MEDIA

Telephones in use: 21,000 at January 1st, 1972.
Radio sets in use: 248,000 in 1968.
Books published: 83 titles in 1969.
Daily newspapers: 18 in 1970 (total circulation 101,000).

EDUCATION
(1970)

	INSTITUTIONS	PUPILS
Primary Schools . .	1,189	421,163
Village Schools . . .	1,852	119,353
Middle Schools . . .	403	81,699
Lycées	133	25,910
Commercial, Agricultural and Technical Schools .	15	7,646
Teacher Training Colleges .	25	3,987
Universities and Higher Institutes	16	7,397

Note: Teachers in all institutions totalled 18,158 in 1970.

Source (unless otherwise indicated): Department of Statistics, Ministry of Planning, Kabul.

THE CONSTITUTION

On July 27th, 1973, a special ordinance stated that the 1964 Constitution was abolished except for those parts of it "not repugnant to the principles of democracy". These, for the most part, relate to the rights of the King, which are now transferred to the Head of State. On August 24th, 1973, the Head of State announced that a commission would be established to put forward proposals for a new Constitution.

THE GOVERNMENT

HEAD OF STATE
MOHAMMAD DAUD.

CABINET
(April 1974*)*

Head of State, Prime Minister, Minister of Foreign Affairs, Minister of National Defence: MOHAMMAD DAUD.

Deputy Prime Minister: Dr. MOHAMMAD HASSAN SHARQ.

Minister of Justice: Dr. ABDUL MAJID.

Minister of Finance: SAID ABDUL ELAH.

Minister of the Interior: FAIZ MOHAMMAD.

Minister of Education: Dr. NEMATULLAH PAZHWAK.

Minister of the Security of the Frontiers: (to be appointed).

Minister of Mines and Industries: ABDUL KAYOUM.

Minister of Communications: ABDUL HAMID MOHTAT.

Minister of Public Health: Dr. NAZAR MOHAMMAD SEKANDAR.

Minister of Information: Dr. ABDUR RAHIM NAWIN.

Minister of Agriculture: GHULAM JAILANI BAKHTARI.

Minister of Planning: (to be appointed).

Minister of Commerce: MOHAMMAD KHAN JALALAR.

DIPLOMATIC REPRESENTATION

EMBASSIES AND LEGATIONS ACCREDITED TO AFGHANISTAN
(Kabul unless otherwise stated).
(E) Embassy; (L) Legation.

Argentina: Teheran, Iran (E).

Australia: Islamabad, Pakistan (E).

Austria: Zarghouna Wat (E); *Ambassador:* Dr. GEORG SEYFFERTITZ.

Belgium: Teheran, Iran (L).

Brazil: Teheran, Iran (E).

Bulgaria: Wazir Akbar Khan Mena (E); *Ambassador:* IVAN HRISTOV KARATZANOV.

Burma: New Delhi, India (E).

Canada: Islamabad, Pakistan (E).

China, People's Republic: Shah Mahmoud Ghazi Wat (E); *Ambassador:* HSIEH PANG-CHIH.

Czechoslovakia: Taimani Wat, Kale Fathullah (E); *Ambassador:* JAN SUCHANIK.

Denmark: Teheran, Iran (E).

Egypt: Wazir Akbar Khan Mena (E); *Ambassador:* ABU ZAID.

Finland: Ankara, Turkey (E).

France: Nedjat Wat (E); *Ambassador:* EUGÈNE WERNERT.

Germany, Federal Republic: Wazir Akbar Khan Mena (E); *Ambassador:* Dr. J. HOFFMAN.

Ghana: New Delhi, India (E).

Greece: Teheran, Iran (E).

Hungary: Teheran, Iran (E).

India: Malalai Wat (E); *Ambassador:* K. L. MEHTA.

Indonesia: Wazir Akbar Khan Mena (E); *Ambassador:* SUYOTO SURYO-DI-PURO.

Iran: Malekyar Wat (E); *Ambassador:* DJAHANGUIR TAFAZZOLI.

Iraq: Malalai Wat, Shar-e-Nau (E); *Ambassador:* N. A. KADER HADISSI.

Italy: Khwaja Abdullah Ansari Wat (E); *Ambassador:* ITALO PAPINA.

Japan: Nawai Wat (E); *Ambassador:* KENJI NAKAO.

Jordan: Teheran, Iran (E).

Kuwait: Teheran, Iran (E).

Lebanon: Teheran, Iran (E).

Malaysia: Teheran, Iran (E).

Mexico: New Delhi, India (E).

Mongolia: Moscow, U.S.S.R. (E).

Morocco: Teheran, Iran (E).

Nepal: New Delhi, India (E).

Netherlands: Teheran, Iran (E).

Norway: Teheran, Iran (E).

Pakistan: Zarghouna Wat (E); *Ambassador:* Mr. ISPHA-HANI.

Philippines: New Delhi, India (E).

Poland: Guzargah Wat (E); *Ambassador:* TADEUSZ MARTYNOWICZ.

Romania: Teheran, Iran (E).

Saudi Arabia: Wazir Akbar Khan Mena (E); *Ambassador:* MOHAMMAD AL-AHMAD AL-SHOBAILI.

Spain: Ankara, Turkey (E).

Sri Lanka: New Delhi, India (E).

Sudan: Islamabad, Pakistan (E).

Sweden: Teheran, Iran (E).

Switzerland: Teheran, Iran (E).

Syria: New Delhi, India (E).

Thailand: New Delhi, India (L).

Turkey: Shah Mahmoud Ghazi Wat (E); *Ambassador:* FARUK ŞAHINBAŞ.

U.S.S.R.: Dar-ul-Aman Wat (E); *Ambassador:* M. POZANOV.

United Kingdom: Parwan Mena (E); *Ambassador:* J. K. DRINKALL.

U.S.A.: Khwaja Abdullah Ansari Wat (E); *Ambassador:* T. ELLIOT.

Yugoslavia: Wazir Akbar Khan Mena (E); *Ambassador:* VOJO SOBAJIC.

12

PARLIAMENT

Prior to the *coup* of July 17th, 1973, the Shura (Parliament) consisted of the Meshrano Jirgah (House of Elders) and the Wolesi Jirgah (House of the People). The Shura was dissolved on July 28th, 1973.

POLITICAL PARTIES

No political parties had been officially authorized before the *coup* of July 17th, 1973.

JUDICIAL SYSTEM

Prior to the *coup* of July 17th, 1973, the judiciary of Afghanistan consisted of the Supreme Court, the highest judicial authority, three High Courts, a Court of Appeal, 28 Provincial Courts, 216 Primary Courts and a number of Special Courts. On July 28th, 1973, the powers of the Supreme Court, which include administrative powers within the framework of the judicial organization, were transferred to a council set up within the Ministry of Justice.

RELIGION

The official religion of Afghanistan is Islam. The great majority (almost 90 per cent) are Muslims of the Sunni (Hanafi) sect, and the remainder belong to the Shi'a sect. About 20,000 Hindus are living in different parts of the country.

THE PRESS

PRINCIPAL DAILIES

Anis (*Friendship*): Kabul; f. 1927; evening; Independent; news and literary articles; Persian and Pashtu; circ. 25,000; Editor-in-Chief M. Shafi Rahgozer; Editor Abdul Hamid Mubariz.

Badakshan: Faizabad; f. 1945; Persian and Pashtu.

Bedar: Mazar-i-Sharif; f. 1920; Persian and Pashtu; circ. 1,500.

Daiwan: Sheberghan.

Ettifaqi-Islam: Herat; f. 1920; Persian and Pashtu; circ. 1,500.

Ettehadi-Baghlan: Baghlan; f. 1921; Persian and Pashtu.

Helmand: Bost; f. 1953; twice weekly; Pashtu.

Heywad: Kabul; f. 1949; Pashtu; Editor Mir Said Bariman; circ. 5,000.

Islah (*Reform*): Kabul; f. 1929; morning; Independent; but co-operating with the Government; Persian and Pashtu; circ. 25,000; Chief Editor Habiburrahman Jadeer.

Kabul Times: Kabul; f. 1962; English; Editor-in-Chief S. Rahel; circ. 5,000.

Nangarhar: Jelalabad; f. 1918; Persian and Pashtu; circ. 1,500.

Seistan: Farah; f. 1947; twice weekly.

Tuloi-Afghan: Kandahar; f. 1924; circ. 1,500.

Wolanga: Gardiz; f. 1941; Pashtu; circ. 1,000.

PERIODICALS

Adab: Kabul; f. 1953; organ of the Faculty of Literature, Univ. of Kabul.

Afghan Journal of Public Health: Institute of Public Health, Ansari Wat, Kabul; 2 per month; Editor A. Satar Ahmadi, M.D.

Afghan Mellat: Kabul; f. 1966; organ of Afghan Social Democrat Party; circ. 10,000; Editor Qudratullah Haddad.

Afghan Tebbi Mojalla: Faculty of Medicine, Kabul University; monthly.

Afghanistan: Kabul; f. 1946; quarterly; English and French; historical and cultural; Historical and Literary Society of the Afghanistan Academy, Kabul.

Akhbare Erfani: Ministry of Education, Kabul; f. 1952; fortnightly.

Aryana: Kabul; monthly; (Pashtu and Persian) cultural and historical; produced by the Historical and Literary Society of the Afghanistan Academy; Editor Dr. K. Wafaie.

Badany Rauzana: Department of Physical Education, Kabul University; quarterly.

Eqtesad: National Chamber of Commerce, Kabul; monthly.

Hawa: Afghan Air Authority, Kabul; f. 1957.

Irfan: Ministry of Education, Kabul; f. 1923; monthly; Persian.

Kabul: Pashtu Tolana, Kabul; f. 1931; 2 per month; Pashtu; literature, history, social sciences; Editor Rohili.

Kabul Pohantoon: Kabul University; monthly.

Karhana: Kabul; f. 1955; monthly; produced by the Ministry of Agriculture; circ. 2,500; Editor M. Y. Aina.

Kocheniano Zhaqh: Ministry of Education, Kabul; f. 1957; monthly.

Mairmun: Kabul; f. 1955; Persian and Pashtu; produced by the Women's Welfare Association.

Mokhaberet: Ministry of Communications, Kabul; f. 1957; monthly.

Pamir: Kabul; f. 1951; organ of the Municipality; fortnightly.

Pashtun Zhaqh: Ansari Wat, Kabul; f. 1940; programmes of broadcasts; issued by Kabul Radio; 2 per month.

Payame Haq: Ministry of Information, Kabul; f. 1953; monthly.

Payame Wejdan: Kabul; f. 1966; weekly; Editor Abdul Rauf Turkman.

Sera Miasht: Red Crescent Society, Kabul; f. 1958.

Talim wa Tarbia: Kabul; f. 1954; monthly; published by Institute of Education.

Urdu: Kabul; f. 1922; monthly; military journal; issued by the Ministry of National Defence.

Zhwandoon: Kabul; Persian; illustrated; circ. 10,000; Editor Mohammed Bashir Rafiq.

Zeru: Pashtu Tolana, Kabul; f. 1949; weekly.

NEWS AGENCIES

Bakhtar News Agency: Kabul; f. 1939; Pres. Ghulam H. Kushan.

FOREIGN BUREAUX

The following Foreign Agencies are represented in Kabul: Agence France-Presse (AFP), Deutsche Presse-Agentur (DPA), and Tass.

PRESS ASSOCIATION

Journalists' Association: c/o Department of Press and Information, Sanaii Wat, Kabul.

PUBLISHERS

Afghan Historical Society: Kabul; f. 1943 by Department of Press and Information; mainly historical works and two quarterly magazines of which one is in English and French.

Afghan Kitab: Kabul; f. 1969 by K. Ahang; books on various subjects and translations of foreign works on Afghanistan.

Baihaqi Book Publishing Institute: Kabul; f. 1971 by Government Press, Ministry of Information and Culture.

Book Publishing Institute: Kabul; f. 1966 by co-operation of the Government Press, Bakhtar News Agency and leading newspapers.

Book Publishing Institute: Herat; f. 1970 by co-operation of Government Press and citizens of Herat; books on literature, history and religion.

Book Publishing Institute: Kandahar; f. 1970 by citizens of Kandahar, supervised by Government Press; mainly books in Pashtu language.

Educational Publications: Ministry of Education, Kabul; text-books for primary and secondary schools in the Pashtu and Dari languages; also two monthly magazines, one in Pashtu and the other in Dari.

Government Press: Kabul; f. 1870 under supervision of the Ministry of Information and Culture; four daily newspapers in Kabul, one in English; sixteen journals of the private press, one of them a daily; weekly, fortnightly and monthly magazines, one of them in English and French; books on Afghan history and literature, as well as text-books for the Ministry of Education; thirteen daily newspapers in thirteen provincial centres and one journal and also magazines in three provincial centres.

Institute of Geography: Faculty of Letters, Kabul University; geographical and related works.

Pashto Tolana: Kabul; f. 1937 by the Department of Press and Information; research works on Pashtu language.

RADIO

Radio Afghanistan: P.O.B. 544, Kabul; Pres. Dr. A. L. Jalali; Prog. Chief S. Y. Waseep; the Afghan Broadcasting station is under the supervision of the Ministry of Information; Home service in Dari, Pashtu, Uzbaki, Pashahi and Balochi; Foreign service in Urdu, English, Russian, German, Dari and Pashtu.

Number of radio receivers: 450,000 in 1973.

There is no television.

FINANCE

(cap. = capital; p.u. = paid up; res. = reserves; m. = million; Afs. = Afghanis.)

BANKING

CENTRAL BANK

Afghanistan Bank (Da): Jadeh Ibne Sina Wat, Kabul; f. 1939; the central bank; main functions: banknote issue, foreign exchange control and operations, credit extensions to banks and leading enterprises and companies, government and private depository, government fiscal agency; 57 local brs.; cap. Afs. 480m.; dep. 7,426m. (April 1973); Gov. Habibullah Mali Achaczai; Deputy Gov. Dr. Mohammed Nawaz; First Deputy Gov. Mohammed Hakim; Second Deputy Gov. Faqir Mohammed Munif; Sec. Abdullah Habashzadah.

Overseas Corporations:

The Trading Company of Afghanistan Inc.: 122 West Thirtieth, New York, U.S.A.

The Trading Company of Afghanistan Ltd.: Friars House, New Broad St., London, E.C.2, England.

Pashtany Tejaraty Bank (*Afghan Commercial Bank*): Mohammad Jan Khan Wat, Kabul; f. 1954 to provide long- and short-term credits, forwarding facilities, opening letters of credit, purchase and sale of foreign exchange, transfer of capital, issuing travellers' cheques; cap. p.u. Afs. 250m.; total resources Afs. 2,249m. (March 1971); Pres. Jannat Khan Gharwal; Vice-Pres. A. R. Vall; 17 brs. in Afghanistan and abroad.

Agricultural Development Bank of Afghanistan: Kabul; f. 1955; makes available credits for farmers, co-operatives and agro-business; aid provided by IBRD and UNDP; auth. share cap. Afs. 1 billion; Pres. A. Afzal; Gen. Man. J. Dvester.

Banke Millie Afghan (*Afghan National Bank*): Head Office: Jada Ibn Sina, Kabul; f. 1932; brs. throughout Afghanistan and in Pakistan; London Office: (as Afghan National Bank Ltd.) 22 Finsbury Square, E.C.2; offices in New York and Hamburg; cap. Afs. 500m.; dep. 830m. (March 1970); Pres. Dr. A. Ghani Ghaussy.

Mortgage and Construction Bank: 2 Jade' Maiwand, Kabul; f. 1955 to provide short and long term building loans; cap. Afs. 60m.; Pres. Esmatollah Enayat Seraj.

Industrial Development Bank: Kabul; f. 1965; provides loans for industrial devt.; Pres. Dr. Mohd. Aman (acting).

There are no foreign banks operating in Afghanistan.

INSURANCE

There is one national insurance company:

Afghan Insurance Co.: P.O.B. 329, 26 Mohd. Jan Khan Wat, Kabul; f. March 1964; marine, aviation, fire, motor and accident insurance; cap. p.u. Af. 15m.; Pres. Abdul Rashid; Gen. Man. N. H. Simonds.

Three foreign insurance companies are operating in the country: *Ingosstrakh* (Russian National Company); the *Commercial Union Group* (Head Office: 24 Cornhill, London, E.C.3, England) and the *Sterling General Insurance Co. Ltd.* (Head Office: Scindia House, P.O.B. 12, New Delhi 1, India) maintain branch offices.

TRADE AND INDUSTRY

CHAMBER OF COMMERCE

Afghan Chamber of Commerce: Darul Aman Wat, Kabul; Pres. A. Ghafoor Seraj.

TRADING CORPORATIONS

Cotton Export Corporation: Kabul; formed to facilitate cotton production, improve methods of cultivation, install modern ginning and pressing plants, and export cotton.

Kandahar Woollen Factory: Kandahar; formed for the export of wool.

Livestock Improvement Organization: Kabul; f. 1952; formed to improve the quality of Karakul, campaign against animal diseases and to fix buying prices in the interests of producers.

Pashtoon Food Processors Inc.: P.O.B. 3025, Kabul; f. 1946 for the export of fresh, dry and canned fruit in particular Red Afghan raisins; 64 mems.; Pres. A. MOOSA, Mans. A. ISA, M. D. MOOSA.

Textile Company: Kabul; manufactures yarn and fabrics from cotton, rayon and other synthetic fibres at its three mills.

Herat Pistachio Company: Herat; formed for the export of pistachio nuts.

Balkh Union: export and import agency handling exports of wool, hides and karakul.

Wool Company: deals with wool exports.

Carpet Export Company: Kabul.

State Co-operative Depot: Kabul; deals with export and imports of all commodities.

Government Officials' Co-operative: Kabul; export and import company.

Office S. M. Azam Azimi: P.O.B. 498, Kabul; f. 1972; carries out import-export transactions.

TRADE UNIONS

There are no trade unions in Afghanistan.

TRANSPORT

RAILWAYS

There are no railways in Afghanistan.

ROADS

Ministry of Communication and Ministry of Public Works: Kabul; there are about 6,700 km. of all-weather tarmac and gravel roads. A modern highway from Kandahar to Kabul was completed in 1966, and the Salang road tunnel beneath the Hindu Kush opened in 1964. Road development continues with the aid of Soviet and American loans.

Afghan Motor Service and Parts Co.: Zendabanon Workshops, P.O.B. 86, Kabul; passenger services in Kabul; long-distance freight and passenger services from Kabul to most parts of the country; trucking services in all towns; Pres. HAFIZULLAH RAHIMI; Vice-Pres. KHAWJA MOENODDIN.

INLAND WATERWAYS

River ports on the Oxus are linked by road to Kabul.

CIVIL AVIATION

Civil Aviation Authority: Ansari Wat, Kabul; Pres. H.R.H. SARDAR SULTAN MAHMOUD GHAZI.

There are modern international terminals at Kandahar and Kabul.

NATIONAL AIRLINE

Ariana Afghan Airlines Co. Ltd.: P.O.B. 76, Kabul; f. 1955; internal services between Kabul and Kandahar; international services to London, Frankfurt, Istanbul, Beirut, Teheran, New Delhi, Lahore, Amritsar, Tashkent, Paris, Rome, Baghdad and Damascus; Chair. Sultan MAHMOUD GHAZI; Pres. AMINULLAH NAJIB; Exec. Vice-Pres. CHARLES H. BENNETT; Comptroller S. G. HAZRAT; Dir. of Operations AZIZ A. MALIKYAR; Commercial Dir. EHSAN GRAN.

The following airlines also operate services to Afghanistan: Aeroflot, IAC, Iran Air, Pakistan International Airways, TMA (cargo).

KLM, Lufthansa, TWA, British Airways, SAS and Pan American are also represented in Kabul.

Bakhtar Afghan Airlines: Ansari Wat, P.O.B. 3058, Kabul; f. 1968; internal services between Kabul and 17 regional locations; Pres. A. A. ETEMADI; Dir. of Operations Capt. R. NAWROZ.

TOURISM

Afghan Tourist Organization: Mohammad Jan Khan Wat, Kabul; f. 1958; Pres. A. W. TARZI; Vice-Pres. R. A. SULTANI. Publishes monthly Afghan Travel News (in English) and a quarterly Statistical bulletin.

Afghan Tour: Kabul; official travel agency; Gen. Man. ANWARULHAQ GRAN.

ATOMIC ENERGY

Atomic Energy Commission: Faculty of Science, Kabul University, Kabul; Pres. of Commission and Dean of Faculty Dr. A. G. KARKAR.

Under an agreement signed in September 1963 the U.S.S.R. was to provide Afghanistan with a nuclear reactor. No further details have yet been announced (1972).

UNIVERSITIES

Kabul University: Kabul; 924 teachers, 7,000 students.

University of Nangarhar: Jelalabad; 61 teachers, 410 students.

ALGERIA
INTRODUCTORY SURVEY

Location, Climate, Language, Religion, Flag, Capital

The Democratic and Popular Republic of Algeria borders on the Mediterranean to the north, Mali and Niger to the south, Tunisia and Libya to the east and Morocco, Spanish Sahara and Mauritania to the west. The climate on the coast is temperate, becoming more extreme in the Atlas mountains immediately to the south. The Sahara, further south, is hot and arid. The languages spoken are Arabic, Berber and French. The Muslim faith predominates. The national flag (proportions 3 by 2) has equal vertical stripes of green and white, with a red crescent moon and five-pointed red star superimposed in the centre. The capital is Algiers.

Recent History

Algeria was part of the French Republic until 1962, when rebellion by the Algerians, which began in 1954 and which was led by the *Front de Libération Nationale* (FLN), was finally successful. In 1962, by the Agreement of Evian, self-government was ceded by France. There was provision to maintain French bases in Algeria and for continued French aid to the territory. In June 1965 President Mohammed Ben Bella was deposed in a bloodless *coup d'état* and Col. Houari Boumedienne assumed control of the state as President of a Revolutionary Council. Relations with France deteriorated when French oil interests were nationalized in February 1971. Further difficulties arose over the treatment of Algerian workers in France, leading to the Algerian Government's ban on emigration to France in September 1973. Meanwhile, strong links with the Soviet Union have been formed. Algeria has taken a militant Arab nationalist position since independence, notably over Palestine, and, while remaining non-aligned, supports other countries' national liberation movements, of which about 25 have offices in Algiers. Algeria played a leading role in the non-aligned conference at Algiers in September 1973 and in the concerted Arab oil strategy during the Arab-Israeli War in October 1973.

Government

Under the 1963 Constitution Algeria is a one-party state with strong executive powers vested in the President. The National Assembly is the main legislative body, elected for five years by universal adult suffrage. The present Assembly was elected in September 1964. Since June 1965 the functions of Presidency have been exercised by the Revolutionary Council. Communal and departmental assemblies have been functioning since 1967 and 1969 respectively; the Government announced a general election for a national assembly in 1970, but none was in fact held.

Defence

The National Popular Army, formerly FLN's military wing, is now Algeria's official army. The estimated strength of the armed forces is 63,000, comprising an army of 55,000, navy 3,500 and air force 4,500. The 1972 defence budget was 450m. dinars. Both France and the Soviet Union provide military equipment and training. Military service is voluntary, and there is a gendarmerie of 10,000.

Economic Affairs

Algeria is predominantly an agricultural country; its main products are wine, wheat, olives, citrus fruit and tobacco. The present government has sought to encourage cereal production and dairy farming to replace the traditional dependence on wine exports. The U.S.S.R. is now the largest importer of Algerian wine. An agrarian reform programme has been under way since 1971. Land is to be distributed among the rural population organized into cooperatives. Large state farms account for about 75 per cent of agricultural production.

Algeria is also rich in minerals, notably iron ore, phosphates, petroleum and natural gas. An industrialization programme based on these resources is now under way. Production of crude petroleum reached 50 million metric tons in 1972. Since 1964 liquefied natural gas has been exported in quantity to the United Kingdom and France, and a large American contract was concluded in 1973. With the exception of oil and gas, production in Algeria declined after the change of régime, but many sectors recovered after 1965. However, the economy continues to be heavily bolstered by external aid. Most foreign firms have been nationalized. Attempts have been made to establish *autogestion*, a system of workers' control, but this has met with difficulties and, for the present, most industry is run on the lines of orthodox state capitalism. In 1969 Algeria joined OPEC. In February 1971 Algeria took over 51 per cent interest in the French oil companies' local operations, having previously nationalized all other oil companies. In September 1973 Algeria announced a large increase in the price of crude oil.

Transport and Communications

There are about 4,000 km. of railway, excellent coastal roads and good major roads over the mountains and into the Sahara. Algiers is one of the principal ports on the Mediterranean. There are internal and international air services.

Social Welfare

Since January 1st, 1974, all Algerian citizens have the right to free medical attention. There is a great shortage of doctors and hospitals, but the public health budget more than doubled in 1974 to 670 million dinars.

The unemployment situation has been improved by the creation of nearly half a million jobs in public works and by the opening of employment agencies. Some 30 per cent of the labour force is without work and many more are underemployed. Public works projects attempt to absorb some of the unemployed; workers are provided with food but otherwise unpaid. In 1968 an agreement was signed with France allowing 35,000 Algerian workers into France each year. In September 1973 further Algerian emigration to France was halted.

Education

In 1972 more than two million children were in schools, and 25 per cent of the state's current budget went to education. In 1972 there were 22,000 students at the three universities of Algiers, Oran and Constantine. Almost all French staff in schools have now been replaced by Arabs.

Tourism

The chief attractions for tourists are the Mediterranean coast, the Atlas mountains and the desert, and the climate. An ambitious programme for the expansion of tourist facilities began in 1968 with the object of attracting over 400,000 tourists a year by 1973.

Visas are not required to visit Algeria by nationals of the following countries: Andorra, Bahrain, Denmark, Egypt, Finland, France and the French overseas territories, Guinea, Guyana, Iraq, Italy, Jordan, Kuwait, Lebanon, Liechtenstein, Mauritius, Morocco, Norway, Oman, San Marino, Spain, Spanish Sahara, Sweden, Switzerland, Syria, Tunisia, the Yemen Arab Republic and Yugoslavia.

Sport

Football is the most popular sport. Algeria also takes part in many athletic events, and sports of all kinds are being encouraged.

Public Holidays

1974: October 18th (Id ul Fitr), November 1st (Anniversary of the Revolution), December 26th (Id ul Adha).

1975: January 1st (New Year), January 14th (Muslim New Year), January 23rd (Ashoura), March 26th (Mouloud), May 1st (Labour Day), June 19th (Ben Bella's Overthrow), July 5th (Independence Day).

Note: The European community observes the usual Christian holidays.

Weights and Measures

The metric system is in force.

Currency and Exchange Rates

100 centimes=1 Algerian dinar.

Exchange rates (April 1974):
£1 sterling=9.66 dinars;
U.S. $1=4.093 dinars.

STATISTICAL SURVEY

AREA AND POPULATION

AREA	CENSUS	POPULATION					
		MID-YEAR ESTIMATES†					
	April 4th, 1966	1969	1970	1971	1972	1973
2,381,741 sq. km.*	11,821,679	13,910,000	14,330,000	14,769,000	15,270,000	15,772,000

* 919,595 square miles.

† Including Algerian nationals living abroad, numbering 268,868 at the 1966 census.

In 1972 over 700,000 Algerians were estimated to be living in France.

LANGUAGES*
(1966 Census)

	MALES	FEMALES	TOTAL	PERCENTAGE
Arabic	4,908,100	4,826,000	9,734,100	80.43
Berber	1,123,200	1,144,100	2,267,300	18.73
French	37,500	40,100	77,600	0.64
Others	8,500	8,900	17,400	0.14
Unknown	2,600	3,000	5,600	0.05
TOTAL . .	6,079,900	6,022,100	12,102,000	100.00

* Rounded provisional figures, including Algerian nationals abroad.

POPULATION BY DEPARTMENTS

(1966 Census)

Algiers	.	1,629,019	Saida .	236,338
Annaba	.	939,378	Saoura*	209,850
Aurès	.	748,970	Sétif .	1,164,636
Constantine	.	1,469,106	Tiaret .	360,920
El Asnam	.	775,692	Tizi-Ouzou	776,588
Médéa	.	864,799	Tlemcen .	432,225
Mostaganem	.	766,216		
Oasis*	.	501,375	TOTAL	11,821,679
Oran	.	946,567		

* Enumeration took place between December 22nd, 1965, and January 20th, 1966.

CHIEF TOWNS

POPULATION (1966 Census)

Algiers (capital)	.	903,530*	Skikda .	88,000‡
Oran	.	327,493†	Mostaganem	74,876
Constantine	.	243,558	El Asnam	69,580
Annaba .	.	152,006	Batna .	68,856
Sidi Bel Abbès	.	105,000‡	Bejaia .	65,012
Sétif .	.	98,384	Biskra .	59,052
Tlemcen .	.	96,072	Médéa .	53,951
Blida .	.	93,000‡	Tizi Ouzou	53,291

* 1973 estimate 1,200,000 (including suburbs).
† 1973 estimate 325,000. ‡ Estimates.

BIRTHS, MARRIAGES AND DEATHS

	LIVE BIRTHS*		MARRIAGES		DEATHS*	
	Number	Rate (per 1,000)	Number	Rate (per 1,000)	Number	Rate (per 1,000)
1966 . . .	561,528	46.2	61,981	5.1	122,999	10.1
1967 . . .	534,904	42.7	59,549	4.7	118,325	9.4
1968 . . .	529,806	39.3	n.a.	n.a.	134,160	9.9

* Data exclude live-born infants dying before registration of birth. Death registration is estimated to be between 40 and 60 per cent complete. According to United Nations estimates, the average annual death rate was 16.9 per 1,000 in 1965–70.

ECONOMICALLY ACTIVE POPULATION*

(1966 Census)

	MALES	FEMALES†	TOTAL†
Agriculture, Forestry, Hunting and Fishing	1,270,098	23,315	1,293,413
Mining and Quarrying	21,456	414	21,870
Manufacturing	148,506	14,496	163,002
Construction	128,012	690	128,702
Electricity, Gas and Water Supply .	9,752	391	10,143
Commerce	148,500	3,775	152,275
Transport, Storage and Communications .	85,580	2,316	87,896
Services	286,134	51,778	337,912
Other Activities (not adequately described) .	83,104	2,655	85,759
TOTAL	2,181,142	99,830	2,280,972

* Excluding Algerian nationals abroad, military personnel in barracks and 283,691 persons (274,068 males and 9,623 females) seeking work for the first time.
† Excluding about 1,200,000 females, mainly occupied in agriculture.

AGRICULTURE

LAND USE, 1968
('ooo hectares)

Arable Land	6,243
Under Permanent Crops . . .	544
Permanent Meadows and Pastures .	37,416
Forest Land	2,424
Other Land and Inland Water . .	191,547
TOTAL AREA	238,174

Source: FAO, *Production Yearbook.*

PRINCIPAL CROPS
('ooo metric tons)

	1968	1969	1970	1971
Wheat	1,534	1,326	1,435	1,235
Barley	538	466	571	340
Wine	1,001	871	869	825
Olives	150*	137	130*	220*
Citrus Fruit . . .	431	492	507	471
Dates	161	79	100	n.a.
Figs	45	24	30*	n.a.

* FAO estimate.

1972 ('ooo metric tons): Wheat 1,950, Barley 720.

LIVESTOCK
(FAO Estimates)
(1970–71—'ooo)

Sheep .	8,400
Goats .	2,100
Cattle .	860
Pigs .	2
Camels .	174
Chickens .	12,800

FISHING
('ooo metric tons)

1969 . .	22.9
1970 . .	25.7
1971 . .	23.7

MINING

		1968	1969	1970	1971
Coal	'ooo metric tons	n.a.	17	15	n.a.
Iron Ore	,, ,, ,,	1,684	1,599	1,546	n.a.
Antimony	metric tons	19	60*	150*	150*
Copper Ore	,, ,,	800	600	600	500*
Lead Ore	,, ,,	5,100	7,900	6,500	4,700
Zinc Ore	,, ,,	15,400	20,900	17,000	15,800*
Phosphate Ore	'ooo metric tons	361	420	492	491*
Crude Petroleum	,, ,, ,,	42,168	44,778	48,204	37,758*
Natural Gas	million cu. metres	2,478	2,954	2,838	n.a.

* Estimates.

Source: United Nations, *Statistical Yearbook 1972.*

FINANCE

100 centimes = 1 Algerian dinar.

Coins: 1, 2, 5, 10, 20 and 50 centimes; 1 dinar.

Notes: 5, 10, 50 and 100 dinars.

Exchange rates (April 1974): £1 sterling = 9.66 dinars; U.S. $1 = 4.093 dinars.

100 Algerian dinars = £10.35 = $24.435.

BUDGET 1972
(million AD)

Current Budget	5,500
of which:	
Ministry of Primary and Secondary Education	1,233
Ministry of Defence	492
Ministry of Public Health . . .	406
Ministry of Interior	406
Construction Budget	3,495
of which:	
Education	685
Irrigation	504
Agriculture and rural development .	381
Special programmes	355

1973 Current Budget Expenditure: 6,430 million AD.

INVESTMENT EXPENDITURE

	1970	1971
Agriculture	793	1,010
Industry	3,100	3,100
Infrastructure	494	1,543
Education	784	825
Housing and Health . . .	238	220
Others	714	390
TOTAL	6,507	7,088
Add Current Expenditure . .	4,447	4,915
TOTAL EXPENDITURE . .	10,954	12,003

Investment expenditure for 1972: 9,000 million dinars; for 1973: 12,000 million dinars.

FOUR-YEAR DEVELOPMENT PLAN 1970–73
PRODUCTION

		1969 PRODUCTION (ESTIMATE)	1973 (TARGET)
Crude Petroleum	million tons	46	65
Natural Gas	million cu. metres	2,500	6,500
Liquefied Natural Gas	,, ,, ,,	2,000	5,500
Iron Ore	'000 tons	3,500	3,700
Zinc Concentrates	tons	43,000	127,000
Phosphates	,,	520,000	1,470,000
Electricity	million kWh.	1,500	2,800
Crude Steel	tons	—	430,000
Sulphuric Acid	,,	61,000	100,000
Manufactured fertilizers	,,	120,000	700,000
Refined Sugar	,,	—	160,000
Cement	,,	950,000	1,800,000
Paper Pulp	,,	17,000	70,000
Cotton, Synthetic and Wool Fabrics	million sq. metres	53	110

DEVELOPMENT PLAN 1970–73
EXPENDITURE (million AD)

Agriculture	4,140
Mineral Prospecting	1,577
Industry	10,218
Electricity	735
Dams and Water	850
Transport and Communications . .	2,177
Education and Training . . .	3,397
Health and Welfare	934
Tourism	700
Housing and Urban Affairs . . .	2,282
Administration	870
TOTAL	27,740

Source: UN (ECA) Summary of Economic Data (Algeria),
November 1972.

A new Four-Year Development Plan for the period 1974 to 1977 envisages a total expenditure of some 52,000 million AD. Priorities will be light industries and labour intensive projects and social objectives. State investment is expected to reach 50,000 million AD.

EXTERNAL TRADE
(million AD)

	1966	1967	1968	1969	1970	1971	1972*
Imports .	3,153	3,154	4,023	4,981	6,205	6,028	8,000
Exports .	3,067	3,572	4,098	4,611	4,980	4,208	6,700

* Estimates by the International Monetary Fund.

COMMODITIES
(million AD)

	IMPORTS			EXPORTS		
	1969	1970	1971	1969	1970	1971
Food, Drink and Tobacco . .	653	625	755	929	985	514
Energy and Lubricants . .	78	132	210	3,291	3,505	3,149*
Crude Products . . .	308	421	428	203	158	180
Semi-finished Goods . .	1,362	1,781	1,608	70	194	123
Capital Goods . . .	1,515	2,238	2,264	69	88	198
Consumer Goods . . .	1,065	1,008	743	49	50	43

* Includes exports of crude petroleum to the value of 2,972 million AD.

Source: UN (ECA) Summary of Economic Data (Algeria), November 1972.

COUNTRIES
('000 AD)

IMPORTS	1969	1970	1971*	EXPORTS	1969	1970	1971*
France . .	2,200,066	2,631,278	2,273,000	France . .	2,510,791	2,667,180	991,000
Germany, Fed. Rep.	457,777	619,807	568,000	Germany, Fed. Rep.	695,018	640,296	1,014,000
U.S.A. . .	438,471	497,948	503,000	U.S.S.R. .	254,544	242,045	278,000
Italy . .	419,243	451,509	515,000	United Kingdom .	200,284	204,784	153,000
U.S.S.R. .	181,529	224,591	242,000	Italy . .	169,648	209,737	317,000
Belg.-Lux. .	164,326	215,631	168,000	Belg.-Lux. .	128,200	101,464	206,000
United Kingdom .	135,084	207,488	331,000	Spain . .	47,000	125,000	170,000
				Brazil . .	30,000	99,000	154,000

*Provisional.

TRANSPORT
RAILWAYS

	1969	1970	1971
Passengers Carried ('000) . . .	7,592	6,168	n.a.
Freight Carried ('000 metric tons) . .	5,904	6,168	n.a.
Passenger-km. (million)	953	1,013	1,144
Freight ton-km. (million) . . .	1,318	1,380	1,363

Sources: Institut National de la Statistique et des Etudes Economiques, *Données Statistiques*; UN (ECA) *Summary of Economic Data (Algeria)*, November 1972.

ROADS
VEHICLES IN USE

	1969	1970	1971
Passenger Cars	121,151	142,806	149,339
Lorries and Vans	70,776	81,625	85,324
Tractors (non-agricultural) . . .	20,969	23,847	24,854
Other	10,820*	11,847	11,979

* Includes trailers.

Source: UN (ECA) *Summary of Economic Data (Algeria)*, November 1972.

SHIPPING
SEA-BORNE FREIGHT TRAFFIC
('000 metric tons, international and coastwise)

	GOODS LOADED			GOODS UNLOADED		
	1968	1969	1970	1968	1969	1970
Algiers	1,579	2,142	2,256	3,488	3,665	4,240
Annaba	3,089	2,838	2,331	461	768	1,130
Arzew	19,269	20,568	20,141	134	190	199
Bejaia	15,557	15,371	16,683	158	287	638
Oran	495	662	786	918	908	1,076
TOTAL (incl. others) .	40,037	41,680	44,260	5,752	5,820	8,085

Source: UN *Monthly Bulletin of Statistics*, December 1972 and February 1974.

CIVIL AVIATION
SCHEDULED SERVICES

	1968	1969	1970	1971
Kilometres Flown ('000) . .	7,496	8,696	10,353	12,439
Passengers Carried ('000) .	385	448	563	715
Passenger-km. (million) . .	363	418	515	634
Freight ton-km. ('000) . .	2,863	2,586	3,078	3,663
Mail ton-km. ('000) . .	564	621	647	697
Total ton-km. ('000) . .	36,116	40,782	49,983	61,354

Source: UN *Statistical Yearbook 1972.*

TOURISM
Number of Tourist Arrivals: (1970) 235,900, (1971) 367,700.

EDUCATION
(1971–72)

	Schools	Pupils	Teachers
Primary .	6,500	1,851,000	49,879 (of whom 44,839 Algerians)
Secondary .	670	287,700	12,305 (of whom 5,152 Algerians)
University .	3	22,568	n.a.

In 1968–69 there were 5,738 students in teacher-training colleges, and 820 students followed courses of higher education abroad, including 355 in France.

Source (unless otherwise stated): Direction Générale du Plan et des Etudes Economiques, Ministère de l'Economie Nationale, Algiers.

THE CONSTITUTION
(Approved by popular referendum, September 1963)

Articles 1–11; Main Aims and Principles

Algeria is a Democratic and Popular Republic. It forms part of the Arab Maghreb, the Arab World and of Africa. Islam is the official religion, but the State guarantees freedom of opinion and belief and free expression of religion. Arabic is the official language of the State. The capital of Algeria is Algiers, headquarters of the National Assembly and the Government. The National Popular Army ensures the defence of territory and takes part in the country's social and economic activities. The basic administrative unit of the Republic is the Commune.

The main aims of the Republic are to build a socialist democracy; to fight discrimination, in particular that based on race or religion and to strive for peace in the world. The Republic conforms to the Universal Declaration of the Rights of Man.

Articles 12–22; Fundamental Rights

All citizens of both sexes have the same rights and the same duties. All citizens over 19 years have the right to vote. Domicile cannot be violated and secrecy of correspondence is guaranteed to all citizens. No one can be arrested or tried except for legal offences and according to legal procedure. The Family, main unit of society, is under State protection. Education is compulsory. The Republic guarantees freedom of the Press and other means of information, freedom of association, freedom of speech and public discourse and freedom to hold meetings. Trade unionism, the right to strike, and the participation of workers in the administration of business will be upheld within the framework of the relevant laws. The Republic guarantees political asylum to all who fight for freedom.

The rights and freedoms referred to may not be used to hinder national independence, or to affect territorial integrity, national unity, the institution of the Republic, the socialist aims of the people or the principle of unity of the F.L.N.

Articles 23–26; The National Liberation Front (F.L.N.)

The F.L.N. achieves the objectives of the revolution and establishes socialism in Algeria.

Articles 27–38; Sovereign Rights—The National Assembly

Sovereign rights belong to the people. They are exercised by representatives in the National Assembly, nominated by the F.L.N. and elected for five years by direct and secret ballot.

The President of the National Assembly occupies the second highest position in the State.

The President of the Republic and Members of the Assembly have the power to initiate laws. All members of the Government have the right to attend debates and to address the Assembly. Control over Government acts is exercised by: hearings of Ministers in Committees; written questions; oral questions with or without debate.

Articles 39–59; The Executive

The executive power lies with the Head of State, the President of the Republic. He is nominated by the Party, and is elected by universal direct and secret ballot, for a five-year term. Any Moslem of Algerian origin having all civil and political rights and being 36 years of age or older, may be elected President of the Republic.

The President: signs, ratifies (in consultation with the Assembly) and ensures the execution of Treaties and other International Agreements; is Supreme Leader of the Armed Forces; declares war and draws up terms for peace, with the approval of the National Assembly; presides over the Higher Councils of Defence and the Law; exercises the right to grant a legal reprieve; nominates Ministers, of whom two-thirds must be members of the Assembly; has sole responsibility before the Assembly; defines and directs Government policies; proclaims and publishes Laws and ensures that they are executed; appoints all civil servants and defence personnel.

The President must promulgate Laws within ten days of their formal transmission by the National Assembly. Within this time limit the President can ask the Assembly to deliberate a second time, and this request cannot be refused. The period of ten days can be reduced at the request of the Assembly in matters of urgent necessity. If the President of the Republic does not proclaim the Laws within the time limit, the President of the Assembly shall do so.

A motion of censure may be tabled against the President if signed by one-third of the members of the Assembly. A majority vote in the Assembly on such a motion shall entail the resignation of the President and the automatic dissolution of the Assembly. This vote by public ballot shall take place after five clear days have expired from the time of tabling the motion.

In the case of emergency, the President can take

exceptional measures to safeguard national independence and the Institutions of the Republic. The National Assembly then has the full right to meet automatically.

Articles 60–62; Justice

Judges obey only the Law and the interests of the Socialist Revolution. Their independence is guaranteed by Law and by the existence of a Higher Council of Law.

Articles 63–64; The Constitutional Council

The Constitutional Council consists of the President of the Supreme Court, the Presidents of the Civil and Administrative Chambers of the Supreme Court, three nominated members of the National Assembly and a member nominated by the President of the Republic.

Articles 65–70; Higher Organizations

The Higher Council of the Law consists of the President, the Minister of Justice, the President and Attorney General of the Supreme Court, a Lawyer of the Supreme Court, two Magistrates, one of whom is a judge, elected by their colleagues, and six Members of the Assembly elected by the permanent Committee of Justice.

The Higher Council of Defence consists of the President, the Ministers of National Defence, the Interior, and Foreign Affairs, the President of the Assembly's Commission for National Defence, and two Members nominated by the President of the Republic.

The Higher Economic and Social Council consists of five Members of the Assembly, the Director of Economic Planning, the Governor of the Central Bank of Algeria, members of the national organizations and representatives of major national economic and social activities appointed by the President. It elects its own President.

Articles 71–74; Constitutional Alterations

The initiative for altering the Constitution lies jointly with the President of the Republic and the National Assembly. Two readings and two votes with absolute majority must be given at an interval of two months, to draft any bill. This draft shall then be submitted for approval to the People by referendum. A bill approved by the People shall be proclaimed Law within eight days of the referendum.

Articles 75–78; Temporary Measures

The national hymn is *Kassamen* until such time as an extra-constitutional law shall fix a new national hymn.

The use of French in education shall continue only until the realisation of all-Arabic education becomes possible.

After approval of the Constitution by popular referendum it shall be promulgated within eight days. The election of the President of the Republic shall take place within one month of the approval of the Constitution.

THE GOVERNMENT

REVOLUTIONARY COUNCIL

Set up in June 1965 following the arrest of President Ben Bella. With Col. HOUARI BOUMEDIENNE as its President the Council has the following members:

AHMED BELHOUCHET	BOUHEDJAR BENHADDOU	AHMED DRAIA	YAHYAOUI MOHAMMED
CHERIF BELKACEM	CHEDLI BENJEDID	AHMED KAID	SALAH
MOHAMMED BEN AHMED	ABDERRAHMAN BEN SALEM	TAYEBI LARBI	SALAH SOUFI
AHMED BENCHERIF	ABDELAZIZ BOUTEFLIKA	AHMED MEDEGHRI	

COUNCIL OF MINISTERS

(April 1974)

Prime Minister and Minister of Defence: Col. HOUARI BOUMEDIENNE.

Minister of State: CHERIF BELKACEM.

Minister of State for Transport: RABAH BITAT.

Minister of the Interior: AHMED MEDEGHRI.

Minister of Justice: BOUALEM BEN HAMOUDA.

Minister of Industry and Energy: BELAID ABDESSALEM.

Minister of Foreign Affairs: ABDELAZIZ BOUTEFLIKA.

Minister of Finance: ISMAIL MAHROUG.

Minister of Agriculture and Agrarian Reform: TAYEBI LARBI.

Minister of Primary and Secondary Education: ABDELKRIM BEN MAHMOUD.

Minister of Higher Education and Scientific Research: MOHAMMED BEN YAHIA.

Minister of General Education and Religious Affairs: MOULOUD KASSEM.

Minister of Health: OMAR BOUDJELLAB.

Minister of Public Works: ABDELKADER ZAIBEK.

Minister of Posts and Telecommunications: SAID AYAT MASSAOUDEEN.

Minister of Commerce: LAYECHI YAKER.

Minister of Labour and Social Affairs: MOHAND SAID MAZOUNI.

Minister of Youth and Sports: ABDALLAH FADEL.

Minister of Tourism: ABDELAZIZ MAAOUI.

Minister for Ex-Servicemen: MAHMOUD GUENNEZ.

Minister of Information and Culture: AHMED TALEB.

Under-Secretary of State for Planning: KAMEL ABDULLAH KHODJA.

Under-Secretary of State for Hydraulics: ABDULLAH ARBAOUI.

DIPLOMATIC REPRESENTATION

EMBASSIES ACCREDITED TO ALGERIA

(In Algiers unless otherwise stated)

Afghanistan: Cairo, Egypt.

Albania: 50 rue Oukil Mohammed, Birmandréis; *Ambassador:* RIZA TAUSHANI.

Argentina: 7 rue Hamani; *Ambassador:* MARIO RAÚL PICO.

Austria: Cité Dar el Kef, rue Shakespeare, El Mouradia; *Ambassador:* Dr. PAUL ZEDTWITZ.

Belgium: 18 ave. Claude Debussy; *Ambassador:* PAUL DENIS.

Brazil: 48 blvd. Mohammed V; *Ambassador:* DAVID SILVEIRA DA MOTA.

Bulgaria: 13 blvd. Bougara Mohammed; *Ambassador:* A. P. PACHEV.

Cameroon: 28 chemin Sheikh Bachir Brahimi; *Ambassador:* FERDINAND LEOPOLD AYONO.

Canada: *Ambassador:* CHRISTIAN HARDY.

Central African Republic: 15 Lotissement Brausifour; *Chargé d'Affaires:* M. BAKOUZOU.

China, People's Republic: 34 blvd. des Martyrs; *Ambassador:* LIN CHING.

Congo (Brazzaville): 115 rue Ziad Abdelkader; *Ambassador:* RAPHAEL ELENGA.

Cuba: 14 rue Claude Bernard, Le Golf; *Ambassador:* RAÚL FORNEL DELGADO.

Czechoslovakia: Villa Malika, Parc Gattlif; *Ambassador:* VACLAV PLESCOT.

Denmark: 23 blvd. Zirout Youcef; *Ambassador:* DIPLEV GORGEN SCHEEL.

Egypt: chemin de la Madeleine, Hydra; *Ambassador:* NAGUIB H. EL SADR.

Finland: 2 blvd. Mohammed V.; *Ambassador:* OSSI SUNEL.

France: rue Larbi Alik, Hydra; *Ambassador:* JEAN SOUTOU.

Gabon: *Ambassador:* M'BOUMBA MOUDOUNGA ETIENNE.

German Democratic Republic: *Ambassador:* SIEGFRIED KAMPF.

Germany, Federal Republic: 165 Chemin Findga; *Ambassador:* Dr. G. MOLTMANN.

Ghana: 62 rue Parmentier, Kubba; *Ambassador:* YAW ALBERT OSEBRE.

Greece: 38 rue Didouche Mourad; *Ambassador:* DIMITRI COSMADOPOULOS.

Guinea: 43 blvd. Central Said Hamdine, Hydra; *Ambassador:* NAINE NABE.

Hungary: 18 ave. Lyautey; *Ambassador:* ZSIGMOND ZOLTAN.

India: 119 rue Didouche Mourad; *Ambassador:* SAYEB SHEHABEDDIN.

Indonesia: rue Etienne Baillac, Mouradia; *Ambassador:* SOE MARMAN.

Iran: 60 rue Didouche Mourad; *Ambassador:* ALI REZA SEDAGHAT.

Iraq: 4 rue Areski, Abri-Hydra; *Ambassador:* A. EL YASSINE.

Italy: 37 chemin Sheikh Bachir Brahimi; *Ambassador:* A. M. SAREDO.

Ivory Coast: Parc Paradou, Hydra; *Ambassador:* PIERRE ANGORAN.

Japan: 3 rue du Lucien Reynard; *Ambassador:* YUKIHISA TAMURA.

Jordan: 25 blvd. Colonel Amirouche; *Chargé d'Affaires:* TARIK EL MADI.

Kenya: Cairo, Egypt.

Korea, Democratic People's Republic: 49 rue Salvandy; *Ambassador:* KANG MAN-SU.

Kuwait: rue Didouche Mourad; *Ambassador:* NOURI ABD-AL-SALAM SHUWAIB.

Lebanon: 9 rue Kaid Ahmed el Biar; *Ambassador:* KHALIL AITANI.

Libya: 15 chemin Bachir Brahimi; *Ambassador:* MUHAMMED BUSAIRI.

Madagascar: rue Abdelkadir Aonis; *Ambassador:* JUSTIN RAKOTONIAINA.

Mali: Paris, France.

Mauritania: 33 rue Vercors Bouzariah; *Ambassador:* SAAD BOUH KANE.

Mexico: Cairo, Egypt.

Mongolia: rue Marcel Suites, Hydra; *Ambassador:* BAT OCHYRIN GOTOV.

Morocco: 6 rue des Cèdres; *Ambassador:* AHMAD SENOUSSI.

Nepal: Cairo, Egypt.

Netherlands: 23 blvd. Zirout Youcef; *Ambassador:* GERHARD WOLTER BENTINCK.

Niger: *Ambassador:* DODO BOUKARI.

Nigeria: 2 rue de l'Abreuvoir; *Chargé d'Affaires:* SOKOYA JAMES.

Norway: Tunis, Tunisia.

Pakistan: 14 ave. Souidani Boudjemâa; *Ambassador:* ZAHIR MUHAMED FAROOQI.

Peru: 47 blvd. Mohamed V; *Ambassador:* E. DE LOS HEROS.

Poland: 37 ave. Mustafa Ali Khodja, El Biar; *Ambassador:* ANTONI KARAS.

Romania: 24 rue Si Areski, Hydra; *Ambassador:* MIHAT G. STEFAN.

Saudi Arabia: chemin des Glycines; *Ambassador:* RIAD AL KHATIB.

Senegal: 50 ave. Souidani Boudjemâa; *Ambassador:* THIERNO DIOP.

Somalia: *Ambassador:* ABDEL-HAMID ALI YOUSEF.

Spain: 10 rue Tirman; *Ambassador:* R. SOBREDO-RIOBOO.

Sudan: 27 rue de Carthage, Hydra; *Ambassador:* EL AMINE EL BACHIR.

Sweden: 4 blvd. Mohammed V; *Ambassador:* BENGT GUSTAVE JEAN-JACQUES DE DARDEL.

Switzerland: 27 blvd. Zirout Youcef; *Ambassador:* ETIENNE VALLOTON.

Syria: chemin de la Madeleine, El Biar; *Ambassador:* NAIM KADAH.

Tanzania: Paris, France.

Tunisia: 11 rue du Bois de Boulogne, Hydra; *Ambassador:* NADJIB AL-BOUZIRI.

Turkey: Villa dar el Ouard, blvd. Colonel Bougara; *Ambassador:* FAIK MELEK.

U.S.S.R.: chemin du Prince d'Annam, El Biar; *Ambassador:* SERGE GROUZINOV.

United Kingdom: 7 chemin des Glycines; *Ambassador:* J. A. Robinson.

Upper Volta: Hydra le Paradou, Immeuble du Bosquet; *Ambassador:* (vacant).

Vatican: 1 rue de la Basilique; *Pro-Nuncio:* Mgr. Sante Portalupi.

Venezuela: *Ambassador:* Aquiles Certad.

Viet-Nam, Democratic Republic: rue de Chenoua, Hydra; *Ambassador:* Van Ba Kiem.

Yemen Arab Republic: 74 rue Bouraba; *Ambassador:* Abdallah Barakat.

Yemen, People's Democratic Republic: rue Pasquiet Brondt, Birmondréis; *Chargé d'Affaires:* Mohsein Ali Yasser.

Yugoslavia: 7 rue d'Anjou, Hydra; *Ambassador:* Osman Djickil.

Zaire: rue 1, 12 les Crêtes, Hydra; *Ambassador:* Mutuale Tshikanke.

Algeria also has diplomatic relations with Cambodia (Government-in-exile), Costa Rica, Ecuador, Laos, and the Provisional Revolutionary Government of South Viet-Nam.

NATIONAL ASSEMBLY

General Elections were held in September 1964 when a single list of candidates presented by the FLN was returned unopposed. The Assembly has not met since 1966.

In October 1969 President Boumedienne announced that a general election would be held during 1970; none was in fact held, and by spring 1974 no firm date for an election had been announced.

There are twelve Permanent Commissions.

POLITICAL PARTIES

Government is based on a one-party system.

Front de Libération Nationale (FLN): place Emir Abdelkader, Algiers; f. 1954; socialist in outlook, the party is divided into a Secretariat, a Central Committee, Federations, Dairas and Kasmas; Secretariat: Secretary (vacant); Col. Boumedienne has announced his intention of reorganizing the FLN.

There are several small opposition groups; all are proscribed and in exile in France or in other Arab countries.

JUDICIAL SYSTEM

The highest court of justice is the Supreme Court in Algiers. Justice is exercised through 132 courts grouped on a regional basis. Three special Criminal Courts have been set up in Oran, Constantine and Algiers to deal with economic crimes against the state. From these there is no appeal. A "Revolutionary Court" was established late in 1968 with jurisdiction over political offences.

President of Supreme Court: M. Gaty.

Procurator-General: M. Mostefaï.

President of Revolutionary Court: Major Abdelghani.

RELIGION

Islam is the official religion and it is estimated that 14 million Algerians are Muslims. The Europeans, and a few Arabs, are Christians, mostly Roman Catholics.

Archbishop of Algiers: H.E. Cardinal Leon-Etienne Duval; 13 rue Khelifa Boukhalfa, Algiers.

SUFFRAGAN BISHOPS

Constantine: Jean Scotto.

Laghouat: Jean-Marie Raimbaud.

Oran: Henri Teissier.

THE PRESS

DAILIES

ALGIERS

al Chaab: 1 Place Maurice Audin; f. 1962; National information journal in Arabic.

el Moudjahid: 20 rue de la Liberté; f. 1965; F.L.N. journal in French; circ. 130,000.

CONSTANTINE

an Nasr: 100 rue Larbi Ben M'Hidi; Arabic language.

ORAN

al Joumhouria—La République: 6 rue Benjenouci Hamida; f. 1962; French language; Editor Bachir Rezzoug; circ. 80,000.

WEEKLIES AND TWICE WEEKLIES

ALGIERS

Algérie Actualité: 20 rue de la Liberté, Algiers; f. 1965; French language weekly; Dir. R. C. Youcef Ferhi.

al Moudjahid: 20 rue de la Liberté; f. 1965; FLN journal in Arabic; weekly.

Office des Nouvelles Algériennes (O.N.A.): 52 rue Didouche Mourad, Algiers; weekly; Dir. Ahmed Khelil.

Révolution Africaine: 9 blvd. Khemisti, Algiers; F.L.N. journal in French; weekly; Socialist.

Révolution et Travail: 2 rue Ballay; journal of U.G.T.A. in Arabic and French editions; weekly; Dir. Kesri Ahmed.

La Voix de la Mosquée: rue Pêcherie.

CONSTANTINE

el Hadef: 100 rue Larbi ben M'Hidi; f. 1972; weekly; sports; in French.

PERIODICALS

L'Algérie Economique: 7 blvd. de la République, Algiers; summary of items and commentaries issued by the State news agency; every two months.

el Djeich: Office de l'Armée Nationale Populaire, Algiers; f. 1963; monthly; Algerian army review; Arabic and French.

Journal Officiel de la République Algérienne Démocratique et Populaire: 7, 9 and 13 ave. A. Benbarek; f. 1962.

Nouvelles Economiques: 6 blvd. Anatole-France, Algiers; bulletin of the Algiers Chamber of Commerce; every month.

Santé: Fédération Nationale de la Santé, U.G.T.A. Maison du Peuple, place du 1 Mai, Algiers; f. 1956; devoted to the cause of medical progress in Algeria; twice monthly; French.

al Shabab: Algiers; f. 1970; published by the F.L.N. youth organization.

Situation Economique: 6 blvd. Anatole-France, Algiers; annual.

PRESS AGENCIES

Algérie Presse Service (A.P.S.): 6 rue Jules Ferry, Algiers; f. 1962; Dir. MOHAMED BOUZID.

FOREIGN BUREAUX

Algiers

ANSA: 6 rue Abdelkrim Khattabi; Bureau Chief ADRIANA ANTONIOLI BOUTI.

Associated Press: B.P. 769; Bureau Chief MICHAEL GOLD-SMITH.

Bulgarian Telegraph Agency (BTA): Zaatcha 5, Muradia; Bureau Chief GORAN GOTEV.

Czechoslovak News Agency (Četeka): 7 rue Lafayette, Imm. Lafayette.

Middle East News: 10 ave. Pasteur, B.P. 800.

Novosti: B.P. 24, Muradia.

The following are also represented: Agence France-Presse, Deutsche Presse-Agentur (DPA), Maghreb Arabe Presse, Prensa Latina, Reuters, Tass, UPI.

PUBLISHER

All privately owned publishing firms have been replaced by a single national organization:

Société Nationale d'Edition et de Diffusion (SNED): 3 blvd. Zirout Youcef, Algiers; f. 1966; publishes books of all types, and is sole importer, exporter and distributor of books and periodicals; also holds state monopoly for commercial advertising.

RADIO AND TELEVISION

RADIO

Radiodiffusion Télévision Algérienne (R.T.A.): Imm. RTA, 21 boulevard des Martyrs, Algiers; Government controlled; Dir. MOHAMMED REZZOUG.
Arabic Network: stations at Algiers, Oran, Constantine.
French Network: stations at Algiers, Constantine, Oran.
Kabyle Network: station at Algiers.
Supplementary Network: stations at Bouira, Tlemcen, Sétif, Souk Ahras, Batna, Bejaia, Touggourt, Laghouat.
There are 700,000 radio receivers.

TELEVISION

Radiodiffusion Télévision Algérienne (R.T.A.): 21 blvd. des Martyrs, Algiers; stations at Algiers, Oran, Tizi-Ouzou, Chrea and Constantine; the national network was completed during 1970. Television is taking a major part in the national education programme. Dir. (vacant).
There are 121,000 television receivers.

FINANCE

(cap. = capital; dep. = deposits; m. = million; AD = Algerian dinars; Fr. = French francs.)

BANKING

ALGIERS

CENTRAL BANK

Banque Centrale d'Algérie: 8 blvd. Zirout-Youcef, Algiers; f. 1963; cap. 40m. AD; central bank of issue; Gov. SEGHIR MOSTAFAÏ.

From November 1967 only the following nationalized banks were authorized to conduct exchange transactions and to deal with banks abroad, and by May 1972 these three banks had absorbed all foreign and private banks.

Banque Extérieure d'Algérie: 11 blvd. Colonel Amirouche, Algiers; f. 1967 by transfer of the assets of Crédit Lyonnais, Société Générale, Barclays Bank France (Ltd.), Crédit du Nord, and Banque Industrielle de l'Algérie et de la Méditerranée in Algeria; chiefly concerned with foreign trade transactions and the financing of industrial development in Algeria; cap. 60m. AD; brs. in Algiers and ten other principal cities in Algeria; Pres. and Gen. Man. BOUASRIA BELGHOULA.

Banque Nationale d'Algérie: 8 blvd. Ernesto Ché Guévara, Algiers; f. 1966 by transfer of the assets in Algeria of Crédit Foncier d'Algérie et de Tunisie, Banque de Paris et des Pays Bas, and other foreign banks; cap. 20m. AD; dep. 3,161m. AD; 138 brs.; Pres. and Gen. Man. ABDELMALEK TEMAM.

Crédit Populaire d'Algérie: 2 blvd. Colonel Amirouche, Algiers; f. 1966; re-grouping of former credit banks; brs. in Algiers, Constantine, Oran and Annaba.

SAVINGS BANK

Caisse Nationale d'Epargne et de Prévoyance: 40-42 rue Larbi Ben M'Hidi, Algiers.

INSURANCE

A state monopoly on insurance transactions was introduced in 1966.

Caisse Algérienne d'Assurance et de Réassurance: 48 rue Didouche Mourad, Algiers; f. 1963 as a public corporation; Admin.-Gen. C. BENELHADJ SAID.

Caisse Nationale de Mutualité Agricole: 24 blvd. Victor Hugo, Algiers; Dir. T. BOUDJAKDJI.

Société Algérienne d'Assurances: 5 blvd. de la République, Algiers; f. 1963; state sponsored company; Chair. and Man. Dir. MOHAMED BENSALEM.

TRADE AND INDUSTRY

CHAMBERS OF COMMERCE

Chambre de Commerce d'Alger: 6 blvd. Anatole France, Algiers; Administrator HACHEMI LARABI.

Chambre de Commerce et d'Industrie d'Annaba: Palais Consulaire, 4 rue du Cénra, Annaba; Pres. AMARA AMAR.

Chambre de Commerce de Bejaia: B.P. 105, Bejaia; f. 1892; 11 mems.; Pres. BENCHEIKH ABDERRAHMANE; Sec.-Gen. MAHDI YOUNÉS.

Chambre de Commerce et d'Industrie de Constantin: 2 ave. Zebane, Constantine; Pres. BEN MATTI ABDESSELAM.

Chambre de Commerce et d'Industrie d'Oran: 8 boulevard de la Soummam, Oran; 12 mems.; Pres. TAÏEB BRAHIM MOKHTAR; Sec.-Gen. ABDELHAK NOR'EDDINE; publs. *Rapport Economique Mensuel.*

Chambre de Commerce et d'Industrie de Mostaganem: avenue Bénaïed Bendehiba, Mostaganem; f. 1901; 8 mems.; Pres. MOHAMED BELHADJ; Sec.-Gen. HARRAG BENBERNOU.

Chambre de Commerce Espagnole: 8 rue Amjère, Algiers.

Chambre de Commerce Italienne: 6 rue Hamami, Algiers.

Jeune Chambre Economique d'Alger: rue de Nîmes, Algiers; Pres. M. DONNEAUD.

There are also Chambers of Commerce at Colomb-Béchar, Ghordaia and Tlemcen.

EMPLOYERS' ORGANIZATIONS

Chambre Française de Commerce en Algérie: 1 rue de Languedoc, Algiers; Pres. M. J. BERNARD.

Union Générale des Commerçants Algériens: Place des Martyrs, Algiers.

PRINCIPAL TRADE UNIONS

Union Générale des Travailleurs Algériens—UGTA: Maison du Peuple, Algiers; f. 1956; 300,000 mems.; Sec.-Gen. ABDELKADER BENIKOUS; publ. *Révolution et Travail* (weekly).

AFFILIATES

Fédération du Bois, du Bâtiment, des Travaux Publics et des Activités Annexes (*Federation of Building Trades Workers*): Maison du Peuple, Algiers; f. 1964; 17,000 mems.; Gen. Sec. BELHADJ BUKIR.

Fédération Nationale des Cheminots (*National Federation of Railwaymen*): 3 rue Alexandre Dumas, Algiers; Sec.-Gen. AZZI ABDELMOUDJID.

Fédération Nationale de l'Energie Electrique et du Gaz d'Algérie—FNEEGA (*National Federation of Utility Workers*): Maison du Peuple, Place du 1er Mai, Algiers; f. 1963; 5,000 mems.; Gen. Sec. CHABANE LABOU.

Fédération Nationale de la Santé (*Federation of Hospital Workers*): Maison du Peuple, Algiers; f. 1962; 15,000 mems.; Gen. Sec. DJEFFAL ABDELAZIZ.

Fédération Nationale des Travailleurs du Pétrole, du Gaz et Assimilés (*Federation of Oil and Gas Workers*): 21 blvd. Colonel Amirouche, Algiers; f. 1964; 45,000 mems.; Gen. Sec. ALI LASFER.

Fédération Nationale des Travailleurs de la Terre—FNTT (*Federation of Farm Workers*): 4 rue Arago, Algiers; f. 1964; Gen. Sec. BENMEZIANE DAOUD.

Fédération des Ports, Docks et Aéroports (*Federation of Dock and Airport Workers*): Maison du Peuple, Algiers; f. 1964; 2,500 mems.; Gen. Sec. SAID OUKALI.

Fédération des Postes et Télécommunications (*Federation of Postal and Telecommunications Workers*): Maison du Peuple, Algiers; f. 1964; 6,000 mems.; Gen. Sec. YSSAAD ABDELKADAR.

Fédération des Travailleurs de l'Alimentation et du Commerce (*Federation of Food and Commerce Workers*): Maison du Peuple, Algiers; f. 1965; 14,000 mems.; Gen. Sec. DJEBIENE MAHMOUD.

Fédération des Travailleurs de l'Education et de la Culture—FTEC (*Federation of Teachers*): Maison du Peuple, Algiers; f. 1962; 13,000 mems.; Gen. Sec. BOUAMRANE CHAIKH.

Fédération des Travailleurs des Mines et Carrières (*Federation of Mine and Quarry Workers*): Maison du Peuple, Algiers; f. 1965; Sec.-Gen. OUALI MAHOUD KAHAR.

Fédération des Travailleurs Municipaux d'Algérie (*Federation of Municipal Employees*): Maison du Peuple, Algiers; f. 1965; 15,000 mems.; Gen. Sec. AHMED ZITOUNI.

DEVELOPMENT

Banque Algérienne de Développement: Villa Joly, ave. Franklin Roosevelt, Algiers; f. 1963; Government-sponsored development fund to finance industrial and commercial enterprises and exercise credit control by means of medium- and long-term credits in the private sector.

Caisse Centrale de Coopération Economique (C.C.C.E.): 22 rue Larbi Alik, Hydra, Algiers; f. 1968; Dir. JEAN GAMBETTE.

Caisse Nationale des Marchés de l'Etat: 4 blvd. Mohammed V, Algiers; f. 1962; Dir. M. ANDRÉ.

Office Algérien d'Action Commerciale—O.F.A.L.A.C.: 40–42 rue Benmehidi Larbi, Algiers; f. 1962; quality control and technical advice to exporters; Dir. H. HANOUZ.

Organisme de Coopération Industrielle—O.C.I.: Imm. Colisée, rue Ahmed Bey, B.P. 801, Algiers; f. 1965 to carry out the duties of the *Organisme Saharien* in the field of industry; loans granted 1,000 m. A.D.; Pres. ABDERRAHMANE KHENE; Dir.-Gen. GABRIEL VAN LAETHEM.

Société Centrale pour l'Equipment du Territoire—S.C.E.T. Coopération: 8 rue Sergent Addoun, Algiers; Dir. A. GAMBRELLE.

Société Nationale d'Etudes de Gestion, de Réalisations et d'Exploitations Industrielles—S.N.E.R.I.: 50 rue Khélifa Boukhalfa, Algiers.

NATIONALIZED INDUSTRIES

Office Algérien des Pêches: Algiers; state trawling and canned sea-food organization.

Société Nationale Algérienne de Construction Mécanique (SONACOME): Algiers; sole manufacturer and importer of motor vehicles, agricultural equipment and allied products.

Société Nationale d'Edition et de Publicité (SNEP): 1 Ave. Pasteur, Algiers.

Société Nationale des Industries Textiles (SONITEX): 4–6 blvd. Mohamed V, Alger; f. 1966; 10,107 employees; Dir. Gen. BENALY CHERIF.

Société Nationale Métallique: Algiers; f. 1968.

Société Nationale des Matériaux de Construction: Algiers; f. 1968.

Société Nationale de Recherches et d'Exploitations Minières (SONAREM): 127 Blvd. Salah Bouakouir, Algiers; Dir.-Gen. MOHAMED AMIROUCHE.

STATE TRADING ORGANIZATIONS

Since 1972 all international trading has been carried out by state organizations, of which the following are the most important:

Office Algérien Interprofessionel des Céréales (OAIC): Algiers; f. 1962; monopoly of trade in wheat, rice, maize, barley and products derived from these cereals.

Office des Fruits et Légumes d'Algérie (OFLA): 12 ave. des Trois Frères Bouadou, Birmandréis, Algiers; f. 1969; division of the Ministry of Agriculture and Agrarian Reform; collects the produce from worker-controlled farms, and exports vegetables, fresh and dried fruit and associated by-products to Europe.

Office National de Commercialisation (ONACO): 31 rue Larbi Ben M'hidi, Algiers; f. 1963; monopoly of bulk trade in basic foodstuffs except cereals; brs. in over forty towns and under the fair development plan is to open a wholesale market in each *wilaya* to serve retailers.

Office National de Commercialisation des Produits Viti-Vinicoles: 112, Quai-Sud, Algiers; f. 1968; monopoly of importing and exporting products of the wine industry; exports amounted to 483,000 hectolitres in 1970, of which 224,000 hl. went to France and 179,000 hl. to the Soviet Union; Dir.-Gen. H. A. KARA TERKI.

Société Nationale de la Sidérurgie (SNS): 2 rue du Chenova, Hydra-Algiers; sole importer of most semi-finished and manufactured metal products; commissioned feasibility study of an aluminium smelter for Algiers February 1970; Dir. Gen. MOHAMMED LIASSINE.

Société Nationale des Tabacs et Allumettes (SNTA): Algiers; monopoly of manufacture and trade in tobacco and matches.

Other state buying organizations exist for dairy products, wood and wood products, textiles, footwear, and hides and skins, and more are being set up.

TRADE FAIR

Foire Internationale d'Alger: Palais des Expositions, Pins Maritimes, B.P. 571, Algiers; annual; fortnight in September.

OIL

Sonatrach (*Société nationale pour la recherche, la production, le transport, la transformation et la commercialisation des hydrocarbures*): Immeuble Maurétania, Agha, Algiers; f. 1963; state-owned organization for exploration, exploitation, transport, refining and marketing of oil and gas and their products. Became the sole marketing organization in May 1968, when the state took over all foreign marketing interests, and since April 1972 has been the sole organization with exploration rights. Built and controls oil pipelines to the coast: from Hassi Messaoud to Arzew (capacity 18 million tons p.a., to be increased to 23 million); from Hassi Messoud to Bejaia (capacity 15.4 million tons p.a.); from In Amenas to la Skirra (capacity 9.6 million tons p.a.); and, completed in 1972, from Mesdar to Haoud el Hamra (6 million tons p.a., to be increased to 18 million) to Skikda (12 million tons p.a., to be increased to 30 million); Dir. SID AHMED GHOZALI.

ALCIP: f. 1974; 51 per cent owned by SONATRACH, 49 per cent by ENI; carries out petroleum and petrochemical projects.

ALREP: f. 1971; 51 per cent owned by SONATRACH, 49 per cent owned by French company CFP, represented by *Total-Algérie*; operates oil interests formerly owned by CFP.

L'Association Coopérative (ASCOOP): 126 rue Didouche Mourad, Algiers; f. 1966 as the body controlling exploitation of Saharan oil and gas; owned by SONATRACH (51 per cent) and SOPEFAL of France, which acts through ERAP.

Société Nationale de Recherche et d'Exploitation des Pétroles en Algérie (S.N. REPAL): chemin du Réservoir, Hydra, Algiers; f. 1946; 1,663 mems.; Pres. N. AÏT LAOUSSINE; oil exploration, and development, mainly in Northern Algeria and Sahara; SONATRACH has an interest of about 37 per cent following its acquisition of the Shell interests in Algeria in 1970.

NATURAL GAS

Société d'Exploitation des Hydrocarbons de Hassi-R'Mel (SEHR): concession at Hassi-R'Mel; estimated reserves 900,000 million cubic metres equivalent to a possible annual production of 25,000 million cubic metres.

Compagnie Algérienne du Méthane Liquide (CAMEL): B.P. 11, Arzew; promotes export of liquid natural gas.

TRANSPORT

RAILWAYS

Société Nationale des Chemins de Fer Algériens: 21 blvd. Mohammed V, Algiers; f. 1959; 4,074 km. of track, of which 239 km. are electrified; daily passenger services from Algiers to the principal provincial cities, and a service to Casablanca via Oran; Dir. Gen. SADDEK BENMEHDJOUBA.

ROADS

There are about 82,000 km. of roads and tracks, of which 18,500 km. are main roads and 19,000 km. are secondary roads. The total is made up of 55,000 km. in the north, including 24,000 km. of good roads, and 27,000 km. in the south, including 3,200 km. with asphalt surface. The French administration built a good road system, partly for military purposes, which since independence has been allowed to deteriorate in parts, and only a small percentage of roads are surfaced. New roads have been built linking the Sahara oil fields with the coast, and the trans-Saharan highway is a major project. Algeria is a member of the Trans-Sahara Road Committee, organizing the building of this road, now renamed the "Road of African Unity". The first 360-km. stretch, from Hassi Marroket to In Salah, was opened in April 1973, and work has begun on the next section, which will include 420 km. inside Algeria and run into Niger.

Société Nationale des Transports Routiers: 27 rue des 3 Frères, Bouaddon, Algiers; f. 1967; holds a monopoly of goods transport by road; Dir.-Gen. HAOUSSINE EL-HADJ.

MOTORISTS' ORGANIZATION

Touring Club d'Algérie: Algiers.

SHIPPING

Algiers is the main port, with 23–29 metres anchorage in the Bay of Algiers, and anchorage for the largest vessels in Agha Bay. The port has a total quayage of 8,380 metres in three basins; the Old Port with 2.4–12 metres depth alongside, Mustapha Basin 7–11 metres depth alongside, and the Agha Basin.

Annaba's 48 hectare harbour has 9–11 metres depth with 140 metres of quayage for petrol tankers. The Inner Port (Grande Darse) has 1,850 metres of quayage with 9 metres depth alongside. Oran's 120 hectare harbour has 2,800 metres of quayage with 6–12 metres depth alongside, accommodating vessels of up to 167 metres. Arzew has 1,850 metres of quayage of which a third has 8 metres depth alongside. There are also important ports at Bedjaia, Djidjelli, Ghazaouet, Skikda (for oil), and Mostaganem.

Compagnie Nationale Algérienne de Navigation (CNAN): quai d'Ajaccio, B.P. 280, Algiers; f. 1964; State-owned company managing its own fleet and vessels on time charter; concerned in the transport of oil, gas, wine, early fruit and other goods; 5 vessels; agencies and monopoly of handling facilities in all Algerian ports; office in Marseilles and reps. in Paris, all French ports and the principal ports in many other countries.

Cie. de Navigation Mixte: 1 la Canebière, Marseilles; f. 1850; tonnage 39,292 gross; Pres. G. DE CAZALET; Dir.-Gen. J. L. MASSIERA; passenger and cargo service to Algiers and Oran.

Société d'Armement et de Navigation Ch. Schiaffino & Cie.: 90 rue de Miromesnil, Paris 8e; tonnage 29,530; Dir. LAURENT SCHIAFFINO.

CIVIL AVIATION

Algeria's main airport, Dar el Beïda at Algiers, is a class A airport of international standing. At Constantine, Annaba and Oran are smaller modern airports able to accommodate jet aircraft, and there are also 65 aerodromes of which 20 are public, and a further 125 air-strips connected with the oil industry.

Air Algérie: 1 place Maurice Audin, B.P. 858, Algiers; f. 1946; internal services and extensive services to Europe, North and West Africa, Middle East and Asia; fleet of 3 Caravelles, 4 Convair 640, 2 Boeing 727-200, 4 Boeing 737-200, 5 Nord 262; Pres. MOHAMED BOUZADA.

FOREIGN LINES

The following foreign airlines operate services to Algiers: Aeroflot, Air France, Alitalia, Aviaco (Spain), Balkan (Bulgaria), ČSA (Czechoslovakia), EgyptAir, Interflug (German Democratic Republic), Royal Air Maroc, Saudi Arabian Airlines, Swissair, Tunis Air.

TOURISM

Agence Touristique Algérienne: 2 Place Ben Badis, Algiers; f. 1962; branches in London, Paris, Frankfurt and Stockholm.

The first Pan African Cultural Festival was held in Algiers in July 1969. Thirty-five African states were represented by over 4,000 artists.

THEATRE

Théâtre National Algérien: Opéra Municipal, Algiers; performances in Arabic and French in Algiers and all main cities.

ATOMIC ENERGY

Institut d'Etudes Nucléaires d'Alger: B.P. 1147, Algiers; f. 1958; research into nuclear physics, solid and electronic physics; two Van de Graaff accelerators, 3 MeV and 2 MeV; one Sames accelerator 600 KeV and one isotope separator of the Saclay type; Dir. Prof. M. ALLAB.

UNIVERSITIES

Université d'Alger: 2 rue Didouche Mourad, Algiers; 500 teachers, 9,500 students.

Université d'Oran: rue du Colonel Lotfi, Oran.

Université de Constantine: rue Ben M'hidi, Constantine; 370 teachers, 4,600 students.

ANTARCTICA

The Continent of Antarctica is estimated to cover 5,282,000 sq. miles. There are no indigenous inhabitants, but since 1944 a number of permanent research stations have been established.

MAJOR BASES

(The following list only includes bases south of latitude 60°.)

	Latitude	Longitude
ARGENTINA		
Almirante Brown	64° 53′ S	62° 53′ W
Esperanza	63° 24′ S	57° 00′ W
General Belgrano	77° 58′ S	38° 48′ W
Orcadas	60° 45′ S	44° 43′ W
Petrel	63° 28′ S	56° 17′ W
Teniente Matienzo	64° 58′ S	60° 02′ W
Vicecomodoro Marambio	64° 16′ S	56° 45′ W
AUSTRALIA		
Casey	66° 17′ S	110° 32′ E
Davis	68° 35′ S	77° 58′ E
Mawson	67° 36′ S	62° 53′ E
CHILE		
Capitán Arturo Prat	62° 29′ S	59° 38′ W
General Bernardo O'Higgins	63° 19′ S	57° 54′ W
Presidente Frei	62° 12′ S	58° 55′ W
FRANCE		
Dumont d'Urville	66° 40′ S	140° 01′ E
JAPAN		
Syowa	69° 00′ S	39° 35′ E
NEW ZEALAND		
Scott	77° 51′ S	166° 46′ E
Vanda	77° 32′ S	161° 38′ E

	Latitude	Longitude
SOUTH AFRICA		
Sanae	70° 19′ S	2° 22′ W
Borg Massivet	72° 58′ S	3° 48′ W
U.S.S.R.		
Bellingshausen	62° 12′ S	58° 56′ W
Mirny	66° 33′ S	93° 01′ E
Molodyozhnaya	67° 40′ S	45° 51′ E
Novolazarevskaya	70° 46′ S	11° 50′ E
Vostok	78° 28′ S	106° 48′ E
UNITED KINGDOM		
Fossil Bluff	72° 21′ S	68° 17′ W
Stonington Island	68° 11′ S	67° 00′ W
Argentine Islands	65° 15′ S	64° 15′ W
Signy Island	60° 43′ S	45° 56′ W
Adelaide	67° 46′ S	68° 54′ W
Halley Bay	75° 31′ S	26° 38′ W
UNITED STATES		
Amundsen-Scott		South Pole
New Byrd	80° 01′ S	119° 32′ W
McMurdo	77° 51′ S	166° 37′ W
Palmer Station	64° 46′ S	64° 05′ W

TERRITORIAL CLAIMS

Territory	Claimant State
British Antarctic Territory	United Kingdom
Antártida Argentina	Argentina
Antártida Chilena	Chile
Dronning Maud Land	Norway
Australian Antarctic Territory	Australia
Terre Adélie	France
Ross Dependency	New Zealand

These claims are not recognized by the U.S.A. and the U.S.S.R.

No formal claims have been made in the sector of Antarctica between 90°W. and 150°W.

See also Article 4 of the Antarctic Treaty on next page.

RESEARCH

Scientific Committee on Antarctic Research (SCAR) of the **International Council of Scientific Unions (ICSU):** f. 1958 to further the co-ordination of scientific activity in Antarctica, with a view to framing a scientific programme of circumpolar scope and significance; mems. 12 countries.

President: Dr. G. DE Q. ROBIN (U.K.).

Vice-President: Prof. T. NAGATA (Japan).

THE ANTARCTIC TREATY

The Treaty was signed in Washington in December 1959 by the twelve nations co-operating in the Antarctic during the International Geophysical Year. The Treaty entered into force on June 23rd, 1961.

SIGNATORIES

Argentina	France	South Africa
Australia	Japan	U.S.S.R.
Belgium	New Zealand	United Kingdom
Chile	Norway	U.S.A.

ACCEDING STATES

Czechoslovakia	Denmark	Netherlands	Poland

ANTARCTIC TREATY CONSULTATIVE MEETINGS

Meetings of delegations from all the signatory nations of the Antarctic Treaty are held from time to time to discuss scientific and political matters. The representatives elect a Chairman and Secretary. Committees and Working Groups may be established as required.

MEETINGS

First Meeting: Canberra, July 1961.
Second Meeting: Buenos Aires, July 1962.
Third Meeting: Brussels, June 1964.
Fourth Meeting: Santiago, Nov. 1966.
Fifth Meeting: Paris, 1968.
Sixth Meeting: Tokyo, 1970.

SUMMARY OF TREATY

Article 1. Antarctica shall be used for peaceful purposes only.

Article 2. Freedom of scientific investigation and co-operation.

Article 3. Exchange of information and personnel.

Article 4. 1. Nothing contained in the present Treaty shall be interpreted as:

(a) a renunciation by any Contracting Party of previously asserted rights of or claims to territorial sovereignty in Antarctica;

(b) a renunciation or diminution by any Contracting Party of any basis of claim to territorial sovereignty in Antarctica which it may have whether as a result of its activities or those of its nationals in Antarctica, or otherwise;

(c) prejudicing the position of any Contracting Party as regards its recognition or non-recognition of any other State's right of or claim or basis of claim to territorial sovereignty in Antarctica.

2. No acts or activities taking place while the present Treaty is in force shall constitute a basis for asserting, supporting or denying a claim to territorial sovereignty in Antarctica or create any rights of sovereignty in Antarctica. No new claim, or enlargement of an existing claim, to territorial sovereignty in Antarctica shall be asserted while the present Treaty is in force.

Article 5. Any nuclear explosions in Antarctica and the disposal there of radioactive waste material shall be prohibited.

Article 6. Geographical limits.

Article 7. Designation of observers and notification of stations and expeditions.

Article 8. Jurisdiction over observers and scientists.

Article 9. Future meetings.

Articles 10–14. Upholding, interpreting, amending, notifying and depositing the Treaty.

ARGENTINA

INTRODUCTORY SURVEY

Location, Climate, Language, Religion, Flag, Capital

The Argentine Republic occupies almost the whole of South America south of the Tropic of Capricorn and east of the Andes. It has a long Atlantic coastline stretching from Uruguay and the River Plate to Tierra del Fuego. To the west lie Chile and the Andes mountains, to the north are Bolivia, Paraguay and Brazil. Argentina also claims the Falkland Islands, the Falkland Islands Dependencies and part of Antarctica. The climate varies from sub-tropical in the north to sub-arctic in Patagonia, generally with moderate summer rainfall. The language is Spanish. Nearly 90 per cent of the population are Roman Catholic and about 2 per cent Protestant. The national flag (proportions 2 by 1) has three horizontal stripes of light blue, white and light blue. The state flag (proportions 3 by 2) has the same design with, in addition, a gold "Sun of May" on the white stripe. The capital is Buenos Aires.

Recent History

In June 1966 a military *coup* overthrew Argentina's civilian administration and began nearly seven years of government by the armed forces. In 1972 the President, Lt.-Gen Alejandro Lanusse, announced that the military régime intended to restore civilian rule.

Nine candidates emerged from various alliances to contest the presidential election held in March 1973. At the same time, elections were held for the Chamber of Deputies, the Senate and many local offices. The Frente Justicialista de Liberación (Frejuli), a coalition comprising the supporters of Lt.-Gen. Juan Perón (who had been the country's President from 1946 to 1955 and, although in exile, a considerable influence on subsequent politics), won a large majority in Congress. The Justicialist candidate, Dr. Héctor J. Cámpora, became President, and military rule ended in May 1973. But it soon became clear that he was unable to maintain order in the face of continuing social upheaval and urban guerrilla activity, and, under combined pressure from the trade unions and pro-Perónist leaders of the armed forces, both Cámpora and the Vice-President, Dr. Vicente Solano Lima, resigned in July to make way for the election of Gen. Perón as President.

Gen. Perón returned to Argentina, from 18 years' exile in Spain, in June 1973. The months from July to October saw widespread violence as a result of the animosity between the right-wing Perónists (including the leadership of the CGT, the trade union organization) and the left-wing pro-socialist elements of the movement; also as a result of the activities of guerrilla groups whose kidnappings of foreign businessmen continued well into 1974. Among those assassinated during this period was the Secretary-General of the CGT, José Rucci. During the election campaign Gen. Perón announced that, due to the unstable political situation, he considered it necessary to introduce, from the date of his assumption of office, a four-year period of national emergency.

In the elections, held in September, Gen. Perón obtained 62 per cent of the votes, and he and his wife María Estela Martínez de Perón were sworn in as President and Vice-President respectively in October. A promise of stricter legislation on subversive activity and a purge of the left-wing elements of the Perónist movement were among the first acts of the new administration. Early in 1974 the Government began talks with representatives of the political parties with a view to holding elections for a constituent assembly to reform the Constitution. Gen. Perón died in July 1974, and was succeeded by his wife as President.

Government

Argentina is a Republic composed of a Federal District, twenty-two States and the National Territory of Tierra del Fuego, Antarctica and the South Atlantic Islands (Argentine jurisdiction over the Falkland Islands and part of Antarctica is disputed by the United Kingdom). The Federal Government has a separate executive, legislature and judiciary similar to that of the U.S.A. Executive power is vested in the President. The Supreme Court exercises judicial power.

Each State has its own elected Governor and Legislature. Their authority extends to all matters not delegated to the Federal Government.

Defence

A period of national service is compulsory between the ages of 20 and 45, either one year being spent in the army or air force or fourteen months in the navy. The total strength of the regular armed forces is 135,000, of which the army has 85,000 with a further 250,000 trained reservists, the navy has 33,000 and the air force 17,000 men. The defence budget for 1972 amounted to 3,470 million pesos.

Economic Affairs

Argentina is primarily an agricultural country and her prosperity rests on livestock, wool and cereals. Meat production is largely geared to the needs of Western Europe. The main crops are wheat, maize and cotton. Argentina is one of the world's largest producers of wine, and export markets are now being sought in the United Kingdom and the U.S.A. Industry is mainly concerned with meat processing, meat packing and other animal by-products. There has been rapid growth in the plastics, textile, steel, engineering and chemical industries. Oil and natural gas provide the great bulk of the country's energy. Other minerals produced include sulphur and tin; areas in the Andean zones are to be prospected for copper, and aluminium production was scheduled to begin in January 1974 from a plant at Puerto Madryn.

Despite the initial success of the Government's price control policy introduced in May 1973, and the unions' agreement not to press for higher wages until 1974, inflation is still Argentina's main economic problem. Nevertheless, there are expectations that a rising growth rate will be sustained in the period 1973–74, based on the hope that the Perón administration will be able to restore economic stability. A three-year economic plan, announced in December 1973, aims at raising the Gross National Product by 7.8 per cent a year. Included in the plan are the construction of three hydro-electric projects, investment to increase steel production and expand the petrochemical industry, and the construction of 136 ships in Argentine shipyards. Argentina is a member of the Latin American Free Trade Association and the Inter-American Development Bank.

Transport and Communications

Argentina's transport network is concentrated in the east central provinces of Buenos Aires, Santa Fé, Córdoba, San Luis and Entre Ríos. Main railways connect with Chile, Bolivia, Brazil and Paraguay and run parallel with branches of the Pan American Highway. There are 220,332 km. of roads, of which 20 per cent are paved and 137 km. are motorway. The Government is considering a three-year road-building programme (1974–76) to resurface more than 3,000 km. of existing roads, and also to include a further 7,000 km. in the national network. The plan will require investment totalling 8,300 million pesos. Other plans include the extension of the San Nicolás-Rosario motorway and the construction of the Patagonés-Viedma bridge. River steamers operate on the Plate, Paraguay, Paraná and Uruguay rivers. A treaty providing equal navigational rights to both Argentina and Uruguay on the River Plate was signed in Montevideo in November 1973. Internal air services are well developed and Aerolíneas Argentinas, as well as many foreign airlines, operate international schedules.

Social Welfare

Social welfare benefits are provided to wage-earners through trade unions and employers' associations. In 1967 all welfare services were co-ordinated under the National Council of Social Welfare, and a new Pensions Law was introduced.

Education

The adult literacy rate of about 90 per cent is regarded as the highest in Latin America. Education is free from pre-school to university level, and compulsory for all children at primary and intermediate levels, from the ages of six to fourteen. Secondary education covers a five-year period, and university courses range from one to six years. There are over 30 universities with about 300,000 students. In 1968 a plan for educational reform was approved which dispensed with the entrance examination for secondary schools and outlined a new programme for teacher training which has been raised to the level of higher education. The reform is to lead gradually to a centralized system of education.

Tourism

Argentina has yet to exploit fully her superb tourist attractions. The principal ones are the Andes mountains, the lake district of Bariloche, where there is a National Park, the Atlantic beaches, the Iguazú falls, the Pampas and the city of Buenos Aires.

Visas are not required to visit Argentina by nationals of the following countries: Austria, Belgium, Denmark, France, Federal Republic of Germany, Luxembourg, Netherlands, Norway, Sweden, Switzerland, United Kingdom, and all American countries except Cuba.

Sport

The most popular sport is football, followed by horse racing, polo, rugby, motor racing and basket-ball.

Public Holidays

The following dates are the official public holidays and are invariable: May 1st (Labour Day), May 25th (Anniversary of the 1810 Revolution), June 20th (Flag Day), July 9th (Independence Day), August 17th (Death of General San Martín), October 12th (Discovery of America), December 25th (Christmas Day).

1974-75 (the following are optional holidays on which only banks and public offices are obliged to close): August 15th (Assumption), November 1st (All Saints' Day), December 8th (Immaculate Conception), January 1st (New Year's Day), January 6th (Epiphany), February 26th, 27th (Carnival), March 27th, 28th (Maundy Thursday and Good Friday), May 29th (Corpus Christi).

Weights and Measures

The metric system is in force.

Currency and Exchange Rates

100 centavos=1 Argentine peso.

Exchange rates (April 1974):

£1 sterling=23.49 new pesos;
U.S. $1=9.98 new pesos.

STATISTICAL SURVEY

AREA AND POPULATION

AREA†	POPULATION (1968 estimates)			
	Total*	Births	Deaths	Natural Increase
2,776,889 sq. kilometres	24,286,000	509,120	213,340	295,780

* June 1972 estimate.

† Excluding the Falkland Islands and Antarctic territory claimed by Argentina.

CHIEF TOWNS

(metropolitan areas at 1970 census)

Buenos Aires (capital) .	8,352,900	Santa Fé . . .	244,579
Rosario . . .	810,840	San Juan . .	224,000
Córdoba . . .	798,663	Salta . . .	176,130
La Plata . .	506,287	Bahía Blanca . .	175,000
Mendoza . . .	470,896	Resistencia . .	142,736
San Miguel de Tucumán	365,757	Corrientes . .	131,392
Mar del Plata .	299,700	Paraná . . .	127,836

STATES

(June 1972—estimate in '000)

	POPULATION	CAPITAL		POPULATION	CAPITAL
Buenos Aires – Federal District . .	2,975		Misiones . .	458	Posadas
Buenos Aires – State .	9,107	La Plata	Neuquén . .	162	Neuquén
Catamarca . . .	173	Catamarca	Río Negro . .	275	Viedma
Córdoba . .	2,115	Córdoba	Salta . .	527	Salta
Corrientes . . .	569	Corrientes	San Juan . .	390	San Juan
Chaco . . .	571	Resistencia	San Luis . .	186	San Luis
Chubut . . .	199	Rawson	Santa Cruz . .	91	Río Gallegos
Entre Ríos . .	814	Paraná	Santa Fe . .	2,180	Santa Fe
Formosa . .	233	Formosa	Santiago del Estero .	499	Santiago del Estero
Jujuy . . .	310	Jujuy			
La Pampa . .	174	Santa Rosa	Tucumán . .	764	Tucumán
La Rioja . .	138	La Rioja	TERRITORY:		
Mendoza . . .	999	Mendoza	Tierra del Fuego .	14	Ushuaia

35

AGRICULTURE

	AREA SOWN ('ooo hectares)				PRODUCTION ('ooo metric tons)			
	1969–70	1970–71	1971–72	1972–73	1969–70	1970–71	1971–72*	1972–73*
Wheat . .	6,239	4,468	4,986	5,627	7,020	4,250	5,680	7,900
Maize . .	4,666	4,993	4,439	4,251	9,360	9,930	5,860	9,700
Oats . .	1,129	1,026	1,098	1,222	425	360	475	566
Barley . .	945	813	934	1,081	571	367	553	880
Rye . .	2,489	1,977	2,202	2,534	377	181	256	690
Linseed . .	952	973	539	509	640	680	316	330
Sunflower .	1,472	1,614	1,533	1,652	1,140	830	828	880
Cotton . .	464	388	435	536	458	285	292	402
Sugar Cane .	203	208	256	319	9,700	10,200	12,870	14,700
Rice . .	109	86	93	86	407	288	294	260
Millet . .	243	231	217	277	125	183	105	227
Tobacco . .	76	71	74	78	66	59	74	73

* Provisional.

LIVESTOCK
(1969)

Cattle .	.	.	48,298,211
Sheep .	.	.	44,319,840
Pigs .	.	.	4,097,564
Horses .	.	.	3,762,203*

*1963 figure.

LIVESTOCK SLAUGHTERINGS AND MEAT PRODUCTS

	CATTLE SOLD FOR SLAUGHTER ('ooo head)	MEAT EXPORTS (tons)
1967 . .	9,724.1	696,700
1968 . .	12,802	668,600
1969 . .	13,791	863,700

FISHING
(tons)

	1971*	1972*
Sea Fish . .	184,347	195,273
Shell Fish . .	17,399	9,561
Freshwater Fish .	5,719	6,344

MINING

	UNIT	1971	1972*
Sulphur . .	tons	37,375	35,489
Tin . .	,,	3,625	3,650
Silver and Tin .	,,	1,049	1,039
Coal . .	'ooo tons	631.8	675.4
Crude Petroleum	'ooo cu. metres	24,565.3	25,177.5

INDUSTRY

PRODUCT	UNIT	1971	1972*
Yerba Maté .	'ooo tons	126.6	127.6
Casein . .	,, ,,	10.4	12.4
Washed Wool .	,, ,,	63.3	52.4
Portland Cement	,, ,,	5,508.6	5,406.3
Quebracho Extract	,, ,,	79.3	96.5
Cotton Fibre .	,, ,,	81.9	85.5
Cellulose (Paper)	tons	212,915	240,412
Artificial Silk Yarn	,,	13,765	15,851
Diesel Oil .	'ooo cu. metres	2,198.1	2,243.9
Fuel Oil . .	tons	9,236.8	9,500.4
Gas Oil . .	'ooo cu. metres	4,424.0	4,371.5
Kerosene . .	,, ,,	929.6	927.8
Beer . .	'ooo tons	297,029	296,994
Cigarettes . .	tons	30,867.6	33,110

* Provisional.

FINANCE

100 centavos = 1 Argentine peso.

Coins: 1, 5, 10, 20 and 50 centavos.

Notes: 1, 5, 10, 50, 100, 500 and 1,000 pesos.

Exchange rates (April 1974): £1 sterling = 11.74 new pesos (official commercial rate) or 23.49 new pesos (free rate); U.S. $1 = 5.00 new pesos (official rate) or 9.98 new pesos (free rate).

100 Argentine pesos = £4.26 = $10.02 (free rates).

Note: The new peso was introduced in January 1970, replacing the old peso (official exchange rate: U.S. $1 = 350 old pesos since March 1967) at the rate of 1 new peso = 100 old pesos. From January to June 1970 the exchange rate remained at U.S. $1 = 3.50 new pesos. Between June 1970 and April 1971 the rate was $1 = 4.00 new pesos. After six more devaluations the official rate was fixed at $1 = 5.00 new pesos in August 1971. The next month a free rate was introduced, beginning at $1 = 6.70 pesos. This has been revised several times and has stood at $1 = 9.98 pesos since August 1972. In terms of sterling, the official exchange rate was £1 = 8.40 new pesos from November 1967 to June 1970; £1 = 9.60 new pesos from June 1970 to April 1971; and £1 = 13.03 new pesos from December 1971 to June 1972.

BUDGET

Revenue, 1972

('000 pesos)

Customs and Ports	4,594,014.9
Income Tax	2,175,924.0
Interest and Revenue	3,096,540.1
Sales	2,992,830.8
Stamp Duties	620,002.3
Estate Duty, Patents, Passport Fees	566,704.4
Miscellaneous Income	6,575,254.7
Others	222,849.8
Total	20,844,121.0

Total revenue in 1971 was 12,931,588,800 new pesos.

Expenditure

(million new pesos)

	CURRENT		CAPITAL		TOTAL	
	1969	1970	1969	1970	1969	1970
General Administration	497	673	486	208	983	881
Defence	1,250	1,421	272	378	1,521	1,800
Security	367	503	62	75	430	578
Health	391	483	319	342	710	825
Education	1,310	1,648	211	179	1,520	1,827
Economic Development	1,882	2,303	1,845	2,283	3,727	4,586
Social Welfare	288	604	145	341	433	945
Public Debt	237	335	429	375	666	711
Unclassified	354	45	60	186	414	231
Total	6,576	8,016	3,829	4,368	10,405	12,384

CENTRAL BANK RESERVES
(U.S.$ million at Dec. 31st)

	1970	1971	1972
Gold . . .	140	98	152
Foreign Exchange .	343	70	294
IMF Special Drawing Rights . .	59	3	19
Reserve position in IMF	130	119	—
TOTAL .	673	290	465

June 30th, 1973: Total Reserves $817 million.

CURRENCY IN CIRCULATION
(million new pesos on Dec. 31st)

1970	7,620
1971	9,930
1972	13,160

COST OF LIVING AND WAGES INDEX—
FEDERAL CAPITAL
Base 1960=100

	1972	1973
General level of cost of living .	1,466.2	2,350.5
Food	1,523.1	2,363.2
Clothing . . .	1,265.4	1,986.3
Rent	1,260.2	4,035.2
Electricity . .	799.2	1,117.8
General Expenses .	1,693.7	2,697.0
Household Goods . .	1,320.5	2,073.1
Average wages index:		
Official Worker . .	1,569.6	2,702.8
Day Labourer . .	1,646.8	2,875.7

The cost of living index is based on the expenses of an industrial worker with two school-age children.

NATIONAL ACCOUNTS
('000 million old pesos at current prices)

	1967	1968	1969
GROSS DOMESTIC PRODUCT AT FACTOR COST .	5,312.3	6,153.0	7,147.2
of which:			
Agriculture, hunting, forestry and fishing.	722.3	782.1	898.3
Mining and quarrying . . .	84.2	100.9	111.7
Manufacturing industries . . .	1,687.6	1,907.9	2,228.5
Building	241.1	305.5	359.7
Electricity, gas and water . .	132.2	161.5	167.6
Transport, storage and communications .	480.5	585.2	667.8
Wholesale and retail trade, restaurants and hotels	800.4	937.0	1,142.5
Finance, insurance and property .	181.6	245.5	306.5
Other producers and services . .	982.3	1,127.4	1,264.6
Indirect taxes net of subsidies . .	599.7	729.2	895.0
G.D.P. AT PURCHASERS' VALUES . .	5,912.0	6,882.3	8,042.2
of which:			
Private consumption . . .	4,140.7	4,870.7	5,763.6
Government consumption . .	604.7	657.9	719.6
Gross domestic investment . .	1,070.6	1,307.9	1,565.7
Balance of trade . . .	96.1	45.7	—6.7
Net income from abroad . . .	—41.3	—50.8	—59.9
GROSS NATIONAL PRODUCT . . .	5,870.7	6,831.5	7,982.3

BALANCE OF PAYMENTS
(million U.S. $)

	1971			1972*		
	Credit	Debit	Balance	Credit	Debit	Balance
Goods and Services:						
Merchandise	1,740.4	1,868.1	− 127.7	1,935.0	1,895.0	40.0
Freight and insurance .	125.2	—	125.2	127.3	—	127.3
Transport	94.6	149.8	− 55.2	87.2	121.6	− 34.4
Travel	92.5	112.8	− 20.3	79.5	78.4	1.1
Investment income . .	17.7	273.6	− 255.9	6.7	340.3	− 333.6
Government n.e.s. . .	95.9	62.3	33.6	91.0	60.6	30.4
Other services . . .	49.0	134.0	− 85.0	50.7	106.1	− 55.4
Total	2,215.3	2,600.6	− 385.3	2,377.4	2,602.0	− 224.6
Transfer Payments (net) . .	—	3.4	− 3.4	—	4.0	− 4.0
Current Balance .	2,215.3	2,604.0	− 388.7	2,377.4	2,606.0	− 228.6
Capital and Monetary Gold:						
Private long-term . .	66.1	—	66.1	143.3	—	143.3
Private short-term . .	− 400.6	− 3.0	− 397.6	− 80.9	—	− 80.9
Local government . .	3.1	—	3.1	− 3.1	—	− 3.1
Central government . .	126.7	1.4	125.3	− 49.6	35.6	− 85.2
Monetary authorities . .	216.7	− 378.2	594.9	535.5	327.5	208.0
Banks	2.5	23.4	− 20.9	− 1.2	− 45.2	44.0
Capital Balance .	14.5	− 356.4	370.9	544.0	317.9	226.1
Net Errors and Omissions . .	17.8	—	17.8	2.5		2.5

* Provisional.

EXTERNAL TRADE
TOTAL IMPORTS AND EXPORTS
(million pesos)

	1968	1969	1970	1971	1972
Imports . .	4,092.1	5,516.3	6,416.8	8,579.1	15,629.9
Exports . .	4,781.7	5,642.1	6,504.0	7,968.5	15,425.3

PRINCIPAL COMMODITIES

IMPORTS	VOLUME (tons)		VALUE ('000 pesos)	
	1971	1972	1971	1972
Animals and Animal Products . .	11,236	7,222	41,844	48,595
Vegetable Products . . .	219,602	483,204	286,793	877,034
Animal and Vegetable Fats and Oils .	19,363	8,152	27,047	28,489
Foodstuffs, Beverages and Tobacco .	63,344	51,518	121,122	173,496
Mineral Products	7,272,665	5,211,316	782,151	913,151
Chemical Products . . .	593,479	718,836	1,142,985	2,327,108
Natural and Synthetic Rubber and Plastics .	90,990	113,792	262,878	539,239
Timber, Cork, Cane and Manufactures .	640,285	431,978	331,396	424,190
Paper Goods	438,803	381,067	480,073	782,305
Textiles and Manufactures . .	59,417	53,520	220,618	344,491
Stone, Cement, Ceramic and Glassware .	53,583	43,677	110,400	182,912
Metals and Manufactures . .	1,855,598	2,010,838	1,655,198	3,215,190
Machinery, including Electrical .	119,123	124,134	2,188,926	4,256,526
Transport Material . . .	59,249	81,214	509,064	1,058,584
Precision Instruments . . .	4,840	2,940	261,502	395,400
Miscellaneous Merchandise and Products. .	3,535	1,358	157,111	63,269
TOTAL	11,505,112	9,724,766	8,579,108	15,629,979

PRINCIPAL COMMODITIES—*continued*]

EXPORTS	VOLUME (tons)		VALUE ('000 pesos)	
	1971	1972	1971	1972
Animals and Animal Products . . .	462,415	689,528	1,610,702	5,039,753
Vegetable Products	10,191,921	6,161,355	2,812,723	3,396,912
Animal and Vegetable Fats and Oils . .	353,346	238,669	370,452	424,910
Foodstuffs, Beverages and Tobacco . .	2,159,226	1,667,242	1,340,135	2,228,803
Mineral Products.	515,344	404,236	74,071	104,662
Chemical Products	137,473	147,684	268,340	572,725
Natural and Synthetic Rubber and Plastics .	22,946	25,458	41,592	96,451
Leather and Manufactures . . .	118,474	98,179	351,545	1,063,241
Textiles and Manufactures . . .	102,000	88,862	353,491	753,010
Metals and Manufactures . . .	283,731	336,134	218,388	453,418
Machinery, including Electrical . .	49,548	54,530	304,330	675,877
Transport Material	11,037	18,787	90,464	288,729
Miscellaneous Merchandise and Products	30,144	48,508	131,325	326,809
TOTAL	14,437,605	9,979,172	7,968,558	15,425,300

PRINCIPAL COUNTRIES

('000 pesos)

	IMPORTS			EXPORTS		
	1970	1971	1972	1970	1971	1972
Austria	24,044	33,027.9	56,152	5,976	8,353.4	19,957
Belgium	81,658	127,099.7	414,219	240,583	266,438.5	377,637
Brazil	696,794	912,708.0	1,429,586	511,461	495,811.2	1,469,987
British Asiatic Possessions . .	9,971	9,262.1	6,058	17,737	4,131.6	17,623
Canada	186,467	249,644.9	504,923	24,749	36,866.7	79,321
Chile	285,185	318,006.2	453,425	340,610	622,521.0	1,299,864
Czechoslovakia	10,941	17,954.2	21,188	39,286	35,581.9	59,115
France	241,313	259,624.9	632,013	258,770	338,778.4	954,779
Germany, Federal Republic . .	702,078	992,004.4	2,004,650	383,294	525,312.0	1,832,147
India	10,566	29,961.2	45,159	15,077	1,102.2	7,947
Italy	459,147	539,809.0	1,001,168	990,824	1,171,440.1	1,978,558
Japan	322,699	715,523.5	1,163,809	391,958	397,805.6	435,119
Kuwait	3,745	118,070.8	57,673	447	119.4	102
Netherlands.	122,635	153,726.9	433,485	662,570	711,489.8	896,999
Netherlands Antilles . . .	31,866	19,399.0	55,532	16,880	3,971.2	4,445
Paraguay	75,489	98,854.6	162,659	56,231	45,560.1	104,243
Peru	52,938	105,084.6	139,239	118,325	67,548.2	181,258
Sweden	130,353	166,159.5	277,427	26,673	28,414.7	54,987
United Kingdom . . .	349,884	523,531.5	1,058,647	452,384	565,218.8	1,361,945
U.S.A.	1,583,921	1,876,892.6	3,176,236	578,950	733,829.6	1,491,569
U.S.S.R.	11,679	18,384.4	21,361	98,680	132,499.2	180,046
Venezuela	114,924	127,550.7	276,863	426,268	73,410.0	92,664

TRANSPORT

RAILWAYS

	Passengers Carried (million)	Freight Carried ('000 tons)	Passenger-km. (million)	Ton-km. (million)
1970 .	443	21,862	12,828	13,356
1971 .	429	20,662	12,186	13,026
1972* .	401	17,942	12,183	12,284

ROADS
Motor Vehicles in Use, 1969
Cars	1,390,000
Goods Vehicles . .	722,000
Buses and Coaches .	32,500

SHIPPING
Tonnage of Shipping Entering Argentine Ports ('000 net registered tons)

	Total Tonnage	Buenos Aires	Other Ports
1969 . .	12,642	7,987	4,656
1970 . .	12,865	7,486	5,379
1971 . .	13,276	7,662	5,373
1972* . .	11,123	7,727	3,396

* Provisional.

CIVIL AVIATION

	Passengers Carried ('000)		Freight Carried (tons)		Kilometres Flown ('000)	
	Argentine Airlines	Foreign Airlines	Argentine Airlines	Foreign Airlines	Argentine Airlines	Foreign Airlines
1967 . .	1,415.4	527.4	13,311.4	15,611.4	40,327.2	6,377.3
1968 . .	1,530.2	591.8	16,897.9	16,512.7	44,277.9	6,717.6
1969 . .	1,783.5	663.1	22,091.3	22,612.1	44,837.3	7,485.0
1970 . .	1,871.6	735.8	23,020.2	26,019.2	47,439.5	7,740.5
1971 . .	2,278.6	722.7	26,745.1	19,326.3	50,846.6	7,506.2
1972 . .	2,472.8	683.3	35,381.6	17,777.8	56,688.7	7,242.1

EDUCATION
(1972)

	Establishments	Students	Teachers
Primary	25,881	3,699,007	202,596
Secondary and Technical . . .	4,349	1,058,945	143,234
Universities	386	297,529	19,805
Colleges of Higher Education . .	405	53,758	9,999

Sources: Dirección Nacional de Estadística y Censos, Buenos Aires; Banco Central de la República Argentina.

THE CONSTITUTION

(On August 24th, 1972, the President announced changes in the Constitution. These have been incorporated into the summary given below.)

THE Constitution of 1853 establishes a federal republican and representative form of government. The following are its main points:

Each province has the right to exercise its own administration of justice, municipal system and primary education. The Roman Catholic religion, being the faith of the majority of the nation, shall enjoy State protection; freedom of religious belief is guaranteed to all other denominations. All the inhabitants of the country have the right to work and exercise any legal trade; to petition the authorities; to leave or enter the Argentine territory, to use or dispose of their properties, to associate for a peaceable or useful purpose; to teach and acquire education, and to express freely their opinion in the press without censorship. The State does not admit any prerogative of blood, birth, privilege or titles of nobility. Equality is the basis of all duties and public offices. No citizen may be detained, except for reasons and in the manner prescribed by the law; or sentenced other than by virtue of a law existing prior to the offence and by decision of the competent tribunal after the hearing and defence of the person concerned. Private residence, property and correspondence are inviolable. No one may enter the home of a citizen or carry out any search in it without his consent, unless by a warrant from the competent authority; no one may suffer expropriation, except in case of public necessity and provided that the appropriate compensation has been paid in accordance with the provisions of the laws. In no case may the penalty of confiscation of property be imposed.

The National Constitution states, in its preamble, that its benefits will be extended to "all men, from all parts of the world, who wish to live on Argentine soil".

The Constitution may be amended in part or in its entirety if the Congress so decides by a two-thirds majority, in which case a constitutional assembly must be convened.

Congress. The Constitution provides for a bi-cameral legislature: a Senate and a Chamber of Deputies. Deputies are elected for four years, by a majority of votes, and are eligible for re-election; but half the Chamber shall be renewed every two years.

The Senate is composed of three members for each province, two representing the majority and one the minority.

Their term of office is four years and they are eligible for re-election.

The ordinary sessions of Congress take place from April 1st to November 30th. The President may extend the sessions or convene extraordinary sessions.

The powers of Congress include regulating foreign trade; fixing import and export duties; levying taxes for a specified time whenever the defence, common safety or general welfare of the State so require; contracting loans on the nation's credit; regulating the internal and external debt and the currency system of the country; fixing the budget and providing for whatever is conducive to the prosperity and well-being of the nation. Congress also approves or rejects treaties, authorizes the Executive to declare war or make peace, and establishes the strength of the armed forces in peace and war.

The Executive Power is vested in the President, who must be Argentine-born and of the Roman Catholic faith. He and the Vice-President are elected by direct popular vote for a term of four years. They may be re-elected for one further term of office.

The President is Commander-in-Chief of all the armed forces. The general administration of the country is in his hands, and he appoints, with the approval of the Senate, the judges of the Supreme Court and all other competent tribunals, ambassadors and ministers plenipotentiary, senior officers of the armed forces and bishops. He may also appoint and remove, without reference to another body, his cabinet ministers, consular officials and employees of the administration whose appointment is not otherwise governed by the Constitution. He issues the instructions and rulings necessary for the execution of the laws of the country, and himself takes part in drawing up and promulgating those laws.

The Judicial Power is exercised by the Supreme Court and all other competent tribunals. The Supreme Court is responsible for the internal administration of all tribunals and for the nomination of its junior members.

Provincial Government. The 22 States retain all the power not delegated to the Federal Government. They are governed by their own institutions and elect their own governors, legislators and officials.

THE GOVERNMENT

HEAD OF THE STATE

President of the Republic: Sra. ISABEL MARÍA ESTELA MARTÍNEZ DE PERÓN.

MINISTERS

(*March* 1974)

Minister of the Interior: Dr. BENITO P. LLAMBÍ.

Minister of Foreign Affairs: Dr. ALBERTO J. VIGNES.

Minister of Treasury and Finance: JOSÉ GELBARD.

Minister of Culture and Education: Dr. JORGE ALBERTO TAIANA.

Minister of Justice: Dr. ANTONIO JUAN BENÍTEZ.

Minister of Social Welfare: JOSÉ LÓPEZ REGA.

Minister of Labour: RICARDO OTERO.

Minister of Defence: Dr. ÁNGEL ROBLEDO.

Secretary-General of the Presidency: Dr. VICENTE SOLANO LIMA.

DIPLOMATIC REPRESENTATION

EMBASSIES ACCREDITED TO ARGENTINA
(Buenos Aires unless otherwise stated)

Afghanistan: Washington, D.C., U.S.A.

Algeria: Montevideo 1889; *Ambassador:* MUHAMMAD MESAOUD KELLOU.

Australia: Avda. Santa Fe 846, 8° piso; *Ambassador:* HUGH A. DUNN.

Austria: French 3671; *Ambassador:* Dr. KARL WOLF (also accred. to Uruguay).

Bangladesh: Avda. Alvear 1749, 2° piso; *Ambassador:* MUKSUM-UL-HAKIM.

Belgium: Defensa 113, 8° piso; *Ambassador:* RENÉ LION.

Bolivia: Corrientes 545, 2° piso; *Chargé d'Affaires a.i.:* AGUSTÍN SAAVEDRA WEISE.

Brazil: Arroyo 1142; *Ambassador:* (vacant).

Bulgaria: Manuel Obarrio 2967; *Ambassador:* CHRISTO GUEORGUIEV.

Canada: Suipacha 1111, 26° piso; *Ambassador:* ALFRED P. BISSONNET.

Chile: Tagle 2762; *Ambassador:* RENÉ ROJAS GALDAMES.

China, People's Republic: Conesa 1964; *Ambassador:* CHENG WEI-CHIH.

Colombia: Avda. Sante Fe 782; *Ambassador:* ANTONIO JOSÉ URIBE PORTOCARRERO.

Costa Rica: Avda. Libertador 1146; *Ambassador:* ALVARO MONGE UMAÑA.

Cuba: Virrey del Pino 1810; *Ambassador:* EMILIO ARAGONES NAVARRO.

Cyprus: Washington, D.C., U.S.A.

Czechoslovakia: Figueroa Alcorta 3240; *Ambassador:* LUDEK KAPITOLA.

Denmark: Avda. Leandro N. Alem 1074, 9° piso; *Ambassador:* JOHANNE NONNY HARTNACK DE WRIGHT.

Dominican Republic: Avda. Santa Fe 1206, 2°; *Ambassador:* FABIO F. HERRERA CABRAL.

Ecuador: Avda. Quintana 585, 9° piso; *Ambassador:* ALFONSO BARRERA VALVERDE.

Egypt: Guido 1530, 1° piso; *Ambassador:* AMIN HELMY HASSAN HELMY.

El Salvador: Talcahuano 1038, 2° piso; *Ambassador:* RAFAEL EGUIZÁBAL TOBÍAS.

Finland: Avda. Santa Fe 846, 5° piso; *Ambassador:* A. A. THESLEFF.

France: Cerrito 1373; *Ambassador:* JEAN-CLAUDE WINCKLER.

German Democratic Republic: Figueroa Alcorta 3297; *Ambassador:* GÜNTER BLUM.

Germany, Federal Republic: Maipú 942; *Ambassador:* Dr. HORST KRAFFT-ROBERT.

Ghana: Rio de Janeiro, Brazil.

Greece: Avda. Roque S. Peña 547, 4° y 5° pisos; *Ambassador:* JUAN S. SOSSIDIS.

Guatemala: Lavalle 1759, 6° piso; *Ambassador:* ARMANDO SANDOVAL ALARCÓN (also accred. to Paraguay).

Guinea: New York, U.S.A.

Haiti: Viamonte 1167, 8° piso; *Ambassador:* MARCEL CHARLES ANTOINE.

Honduras: R. Peña 336, 2° piso; *Ambassador:* DANIEL BREVÉ MARTÍNEZ.

Hungary: Coronel Díaz 1874; *Ambassador:* LASZLO MATYAS.

Iceland: Washington, D.C., U.S.A.

India: Paraguay 580, 3° piso; *Ambassador:* MADAN MOHAN KHURANA.

Indonesia: M. Ramón Castilla 3000; *Ambassador:* JUSUF RONODIPURO.

Iran: Ocampo 2901; *Ambassador:* ALI NOURY ESFANDIARY.

Ireland: Avda. Santa Fe 782, 7° piso; *Ambassador:* MICHAEL L. SKENTELBERY.

Israel: Arroyo 916; *Ambassador:* ELIEZER DORON.

Italy: Billinghurst 2577; *Ambassador:* GIUSEPPE DE REGE THESAURO.

Jamaica: Washington, D.C., U.S.A.

Japan: Azcuénaga 1035; *Ambassador:* MASAYUKI HARIGAI.

Jordan: Santiago, Chile.

Korea, Democratic People's Republic: Gorostiaga 2115; *Chargé d'Affaires a.i.:* MUN SONG GUK.

Korea, Republic: Figueroa Alcorta 3221; *Ambassador:* DONG SUNG KIM (also accred. to Bolivia).

Lebanon: Avda. Libertador 2354; *Ambassador:* FONAD TURK.

Libya: Caracas, Venezuela.

Liechtenstein: Consular relations through Switzerland.

Luxembourg: jointly with Belgium.

Mali: jointly with Morocco.

Mexico: Posadas 1031, 2° piso; *Ambassador:* CELSO H. DELGADO CASTILLO.

Morocco: Avda. Sante Fé 1385, 1° piso; *Ambassador:* M. BEN ABDESLEM EL FASSI EL HALFAOUI.

Nepal: Washington, D.C., U.S.A.

Netherlands: Maipú 66, 2° piso; *Ambassador:* HENDRIK JONKER.

New Zealand: Argentine Consulate-General in Washington.

Nicaragua: Paraná 552, 2° piso; *Ambassador:* NOEL SACASA SEVILLA.

Norway: Esmeralda 909, 3° piso; *Chargé d'Affaires a.i.:* OLAV H. AARRESTAD (also accred. to Uruguay).

Pakistan: Avda. Alvear 1402; *Ambassadr:* SAAD R. KHAIRI.

Panama: Corrientes 1628; *Ambassador:* R. A. ACHEEN.

Paraguay: Viamonte 1851; *Ambassador:* MANUEL AVILA.

Peru: Avda. Libertador 1720; *Ambassador:* GONZALO FERNÁNDEZ PUYO.

Philippines: Castex 3123; *Chargé d'Affaires a.i.:* C. DE A. RODOLFO A. ARIZALA.

Poland: Alejandro María de Aguado 2870; *Ambassador:* MIECZYSLAW WLODAREK.

Portugal: Córdoba 315, 3° piso; *Ambassador:* LUIS DA CÂMARA PINTO COELHO.

Romania: Arroyo 962; *Ambassador:* MIHAI BALANESCU.

Saudi Arabia: Caracas, Venezuela.

South Africa: Marcelo T. de Alvear 590, 8° piso; *Ambassador:* ROBERT A. DU PLOOY.

Spain: Mariscal Ramón Castilla 2720; *Ambassador:* LUIS GARCÍA DE LLERA Y RODRÍGUEZ.

Sudan: jointly with Egypt.

Sweden: Corrientes 330; *Ambassador:* SVEN FREDRICK HEDIN.

Switzerland: Avda. Santa Fe 846, 12° piso; *Ambassador:* MARCEL GROSSENBACHER.

Syria: Callao 956; *Ambassador:* MOHAMAD JAWDAT ATASSY.

Thailand: Belgrano 265, 9° piso; *Ambassador:* WONGSE POLNIKORN.

Trinidad and Tobago: Washington, D.C., U.S.A.

Turkey: Avda. Roque S. Peña 852; *Ambassador:* HALUK SAYINSOY (also accred. to Bolivia and Uruguay).

U.S.S.R.: R. Peña 1741; *Ambzssador:* SEMYON PETROVICH DIUKAREV.

United Kingdom: Dr. Luis Agote 2412; *Ambassador:* Sir DONALD HOPSON, K.C.M.G.

U.S.A.: Sarmiento 663; *Ambassador:* ROBERT C. HILL.

Uruguay: Las Heras 1907; *Ambassador:* ADOLFO FOLLE MARTÍNEZ.

Vatican: Avda. Alvear 1605 (Nunciature); *Apostolic Nuncio:* Rev. Monsignor Dr. LINO ZANINI.

Venezuela: Avda. Santa Fe 1461; *Ambassador:* LUCIANO NOGUERA MORA.

Viet-Nam, Republic: Córdoba 1184; *Chargé d'Affaires a.i.:* TA THAI BUU.

Yugoslavia: Marcelo T. de Alvear 1705; *Ambassador:* DRAGAN BERNADIC.

Argentina also has diplomatic relations with Albania, Andorra, Burma, Burundi, Cameroon, Central African Republic, Chad, Congo (Brazzaville), Dahomey, Ethiopia, Gabon, Gambia, Iraq, Ivory Coast, Kenya, Kuwait, Laos, Liberia, Madagascar, Malaysia, Malawi, Maldives, Mauritania, Monaco, Niger, Rwanda, San Marino, Senegal, Sierra Leone, Singapore, Somalia, Togo, Tunisia, Uganda, Upper Volta, Viet-Nam (Democratic Republic), Western Samoa, Zaire, Zambia.

PRESIDENT

PRESIDENTIAL ELECTION

(*September 23rd, 1973*)

CANDIDATES	VOTES
Lt.-Gen. JUAN DOMINGO PERÓN	7,381,249
Dr. RICARDO BALBÍN	2,905,326
FRANCISCO GUILLERMO MANRIQUE	1,445,981
JUAN CARLOS CORAL	188,227

CONGRESS

President of the Senate: SANTIAGO DÍAZ BIALET.

President of the Chamber of Deputies: Dr. RAÚL LASTIRI.

GENERAL ELECTION

(*March 1973*)

PARTY	SEATS	
	Senate	Chamber of Deputies
Frente Justicialista de Liberación (Frejuli)	43	145
Unión Cívica Radical (UCR)	12	51
Alianza Popular Federalista (APF)	5	20
Alianza Republicana Federal (ARP)	4	12
Others	5	15

POLITICAL PARTIES

In the Presidential elections held on September 23rd, 1973, the following political groupings participated:

Frente Justicialista de Liberación (Frejuli): Perónist coalition party which includes the *Partido Justicialista* (Perónist party) and the *Movimiento de Integración y Desarrollo*; Presidential and Vice-Presidential candidates Lt.-Gen. JUAN DOMINGO PERÓN and Sra. MARÍA ESTELA MARTÍNEZ DE PERÓN.

Unión Cívica Radical: moderate radicals; Presidential and Vice-Presidential candidates Dr. RICARDO BALBÍN and Dr. FERNANDO DE LA RUA.

Alianza Popular Federalista: supported by the *Partido Demócrata Progresista*; Presidential and Vice-Presidential candidates FRANCISCO GUILLERMO MANRIQUE and R. MARTÍNEZ RAYMONDA.

Partido Socialista de los Trabajadores: workers' socialist party; Presidential and Vice-Presidential candidates JUAN CARLOS CORAL and NORA SCIAPPONE.

Other parties include:

Frente de Izquierda Popular: Marxist; supported the Perónist coalition in the Presidential elections.

Fuerzas Armadas Revolucionarias (FAR): guerrilla movement, amalgamated with the *Montonero* group led by MARIO FIRMENICH; supported the Perónist coalition in the Presidential elections; Leader ROBERTO QUIETO.

Ejército Revolucionario del Pueblo (ERP): Trotskyite guerrilla group, outlawed September 1973; Leader ROBERTO MARIO SANTUCHO.

JUDICIAL SYSTEM

Supreme Court of Justice: Buenos Aires.

President: Dr. MIGUEL ANGEL BERÇAITZ.

Judges: Dr. AGUSTÍN RAMÓN ALBERTO DÍAZ BIALET, Dr. MANUEL GUILLERMO LUIS ARAUZ CASTEX, Dr. ERNESTO ABELARDO CORVALÁN NANCLARES, Dr. HÉCTOR MASNATTA.

Federal Appeal Courts: Buenos Aires, Córdoba, La Plata, Paraná, Rosario, Bahía Blanca, Mendoza, Tucumán and Resistencia.

Provincial Courts: Each with its Supreme Court and system of subsidiary courts, deals with cases originating within and confined to the provinces.

RELIGION

ROMAN CATHOLIC CHURCH

METROPOLITAN SEES

Buenos Aires: Palacio Arzobispal, Suipacha 1034; H.E. Cardinal Dr. ANTONIO CAGGIANO; Most Rev. JUAN CARLOS ARAMBURU, Assistant Archbishop.

Bahia Blanca: Colón 164; Most Rev. JORGE MAYER.

Córdoba: Hipólito Yrigoyen 98; H.E. Cardinal RAÚL FRANCISCO PRIMATESTA.

Corrientes: 9 de Julio 1543; Most Rev. JORGE M. LÓPEZ.

La Plata: Calle 14, No. 1009; Most Rev. ANTONIO JOSÉ PLAZA.

Mendoza: Catamarca 98; (vacant); Most Rev. OLIMPO SANTIAGO MARESMA, Apostolic Administrator.

Paraná: Monte Caseros 77; Most Rev. ADOLFO SERVANDO TORTOLO.

Rosario: Córdoba 1677; Most Rev. GUILLERMO BOLATTI.

Salta: España 596; Most Rev. CARLOS MARIANO PÉREZ ESLAVA.

San Juan de Cuyo: Rivadavia 46; Most Rev. ILDEFONSO MARÍA SANSIERRA ROBLA.

Santa Fe: General López 2720; Most Rev. VICENTE FAUSTINO ZAZPE.

Tucumán: Sarmiento 895; Most Rev. BLAS VICTORIO CONRERO.

PROTESTANT CHURCHES

Federación Argentina de Iglesias Evangélicas (*Argentine Federation of Evangelical Churches*): Tucumán 358-6L, Buenos Aires; f. 1958; 41 denominations; Chair. Rev. LUIS P. BUCAFUSCO.

Iglesia Congregacionalista en la República Argentina (*The Congregational Church in the Argentine*): San Martín 119, Concordia, E.R.; f. 1924; 105 congregations, 8,500 mems., 19,000 adherents (1968); Supt. Rev. HERBERT R. SCHAAL; publs. *Der Herold* (German), *Crecimiento* (Spanish).

Iglesia Evangélica del Río de la Plata: Esmeralda 162, Buenos Aires; f. 1899; 60,000 mems.; Pres. Dr. HEINZ JOACHIM HELD; publ. *Revista Parroquial*.

Iglesia Evangélica Metodista Argentina (*Methodist Church of Argentina*): Rivadavia 4044, Buenos Aires; f. 1836; 45,000 mems; Dr. CARLOS T. GATTINONI, Bishop.

JEWISH COMMUNITY

Delegación de Asociaciones Israelitas Argentinas—DAIA (*Delegation of Argentine Jewish Associations*): Pasteur 633, 5° piso, Buenos Aires; f. 1935; there are about 500,000 Jews, mostly in Buenos Aires; Pres. Dr. NEHEMÍAS RESNIZKY; Sec. Dr. JUAN GUREVICH.

THE PRESS

The major Buenos Aires newspapers have a total circulation of approximately two million. The five most important newspapers, which have a semi-national circulation are: *La Razón, Clarín, La Prensa, La Nación* and *El Mundo*.

DAILIES

BUENOS AIRES

Buenos Aires Herald: 25 de Mayo 596; English; f. 1876; morning; independent; Editor ROBERT COX; circ. 16,000.

Clarín: Piedras 1743; f. 1945; morning; independent; Editor Dr. ROBERTO NOBLE; circ. 341,744.

Crónica: morning and evening; Dir. OSCAR RUIZ.

El Cronista Comercial: Alsina 547; f. 1908; morning; Dir. RAFAEL A. PERROTTA; circ. 37,000.

El Mundo: Rio de Janeiro 300; f. 1938; morning; independent; Editor JOSÉ LUIS REEHAX; circ. 280,000 (daily), 375,000 (Sunday).

La Nación: Florida 337–347; f. 1870; morning; democratic; independent; Dir. Dr. BARTOLOMÉ MITRE; circ. 335,000.

La Prensa: Avda. de Mayo 567–75; f. 1869 by José C. Paz; morning; independent; Dir. ALBERTO GAINZA PAZ; circ. 179,367.

La Razón: Avda. de Mayo 729–41; f. 1905; evening; independent; Dir. RICARDO PERALTA-RAMOS; circ. 404,491.

PROVINCIAL DAILIES

BAHÍA BLANCA

El Atlántico: Alsina 260; circ. 18,000.

La Nueva Provincia: Sarmiento 54; f. 1898; morning; independent; Dirs. DIANA JULIO DE MASSOT and Dr. MARIO C. MARRA; circ. 31,786.

CONCORDIA

El Diario: Pellegrini 569-571; f. 1924; evening; Dir. HÉCTOR OLIVERA; circ. 1,200.

El Heraldo: San Luis; evening; Editor Carlos Lieber-MANN; circ. 4,826.

El Litoral: Entre Ríos 522; f. 1901; evening; independent; Editor José Domínguez; circ. 3,500.

Córdoba

Comercio y Justicia: 27 de Abril 536; f. 1939; economic and legal news; weekly supplement *Factor*; Dir. Jorge Raúl Eguía; circ. 10,000.

Córdoba: Avda. General Paz 410; f. 1928; evening; Dir. Jose W. Agusti; circ. 25,359.

La Voz del Interior: Avda. Colón 37; f. 1904; morning; independent; Dir. Luis F. Remonda; Gen. Admin. Dr. Juan E. Remonda; Gen. Sec. Jorge S. Remonda-Ruibal; circ. 70,000.

Los Principios: 9 de Julio 241; f. 1894; morning; Catholic, independent; Editor Victor H. Martínez; circ. 16,390.

Corrientes

El Liberal: Carlos Pellegrini 1172; f. 1909; evening; non-party; Editor Juan Francisco Torrent; circ. 4,000.

La Mañana: Buenos Aires 466; f. 1930; daily except Mondays; Dir. Eugenio Mancini; circ. 10,000.

La Plata

El Dia: Diagonal 80, No. 817–25; f. 1884; morning; democratic; independent; Editor Dr. David Kraiselburd; circ. 69,575.

Mar del Plata

El Atlántico: Bolívar 2965; f. 1938; evening; Dir. Victor Hugo Casares; circ. 20,000.

La Capital: f. 1905; Dir. Manuel de Llano; circ. 29,691.

Mendoza

Los Andes: San Martín 1049; f. 1882; morning; independent; Dir. Felipe Calle; circ. 53,164.

El Tiempo de Cuyo: Lavalle 61; f. 1956; morning; Dir. Salvador Montalvo; circ. 22,000.

Paraná

La Acción: Urquiza 814; f. 1912; morning; circ. 10,000.

El Diario: Buenos Aires y Urquiza; f. 1914; morning; democratic; Dir. Dr. Arturo J. Etchevehere; circ. 11,947.

Quilmes, B.A.

El Sol: Rivadavia 279–81; f. 1927; Editor Rodolfo Alberto Imperiali; circ. 25,000.

Rosario

La Capital: Sarmiento 763; f. 1867; morning; independent; Dirs. Carlos Lagos, Ovidio Lagos; circ. 93,920.

Crónica: Santa Fé 873–77; f. 1914; evening; independent; Propr. Editorial Crónica S.R.L.; Dir. Néstor Joaquín Lagos; office in Buenos Aires: Empresa Periodística Linari S.A.C., Esmeralda 358, 5° piso; circ. 87,096.

La Tribuna: Santa Fe 966; f. 1950; evening; circ. 30,000.

Salta

El Intransigente: Mitre 256; Dir. Martín Michel Torino; circ. 15,000.

El Tribuno: f. 1949; Dir. Roberto Romero; circ. 25,649.

Santa Fe

La Acción: circ. 40,000.

El Litoral: San Martín 2651; evening; independent; Dir. Riobo Caputto; circ. 34,598.

Santiago del Estero

El Liberal: Libertal 263; morning; Editor Dr. José F. L. Castiglione; circ. 20,161.

Tucumán

La Gaceta: Mendoza 654; f. 1912; morning; independent; Dir. Enrique García Hamilton; circ. 80,000.

El Mercurio: Buenos Aires 363; f. 1952; morning; Dir. Angel Enrique Raffo; circ. 5,500.

Noticias: Buenos Aires 363; f. 1956; evening; Dir. Angel Enrique Raffo; circ. 10,000.

PERIODICALS

Buenos Aires

Aeroespacio: Paraguay 748; monthly; Editor J. E. Nisivoccia.

El Arquitecto Constructor: Esmeralda 320, 5° piso; f. 1907; monthly; Dir. Jorge Cometta Manzoni; circ. 15,000.

ARS, Revista de Arte: Rodríguez-Peña 335; art magazine; weekly.

Ases y Motores: Esmeralda 320, 5° piso; f. 1953; circ. 50,000; Editor Alfredo Bigeschi.

Atlántida: Azopardo 579; f. 1918; monthly; general interest; illustrated; Dir. Carlos Vigil; circ. 83,550.

Auto: Rivadavia 1255; monthly; motoring; Dir. Roberto Torreiro; circ. 15,000,

Avia, Aeroespacial: Hipólito Yrigoyen 788; f. 1933; aeronautics; monthly; Dir. Miguel Angel Maccor.

Billiken: Azopardo 579; f. 1919; children's magazine; weekly; Dir. Anibal C. Vigil; circ. 200,543.

Buenos Aires Musical: Alsina 912; fortnightly.

Cámara Argentina de Comercio: Avda. Leandro N. Alem 36; monthly.

Casas y Jardines (*Houses and Gardens*): Sarmiento 643; f. 1933; monthly; publ. by Editorial Contémpora S.R.L.

La Chacra: Editorial Atlántida S.A., Azopardo 579; farm and country magazine; Dir. Constancio C. Vigil; circ. 24,780.

Comentario: Tucumán 2137 y San Martín 663; literary.

Criterio: Alsina 840; literary and arts.

Economía y Finanzas: 25 de Mayo 362, 10° piso, Casilla 2379; finance.

El Economista: Córdoba 632; financial weekly; Dir. Dr. D. Radonjic; circ. 33,000.

Gente: Editorial Atlántida S.A., Azopardo 579; news, current events; weekly; Dir. Anibal C. Vigil; circ. 325,558.

El Gráfico: Azopardo 579; weekly; sport; publ. by Editorial Atlántida S.A.; Dir. Constancio C. Vigil; circ. 217,145.

Histonium: Paraná 461; f. 1939; monthly; art and literature; Editor Della Penna.

Industria Textil Sud Americana: Avda. Roque S. Peña 825; monthly.

La Ingeniería: Avda. del Mayor 963; quarterly.

Jurisprudencia Argentina: Talcahuano 650; f. 1918; Dir. José Rufino Lastra; daily; circ. 10,000.

Mecánica Automotriz: Esmeraldo 320, 5° piso; f. 1963; Editor Luis Grajer; circ. 38,000.

Mundo Aeronáutico: Rivadavia 945-949; f. 1932; monthly; aeronautics; Dir. Francisco Cortegoso.

Nuestra Arquitectura (*Our Architecture*): Sarmiento 643; f. 1929; monthly; publ. by Editorial Contémpora S.R.L.

La Obra: Independencia 3124; monthly; magazine for teachers; Dir. Prof. EDUARDO CASTAGNINO.

Panorama: Avda. Leandro N. Alem 896; weekly.

Para Ti: Editorial Atlántida S.A., Azopardo 579; f. 1922; women's weekly; Dir. ANIBAL C. VIGIL; circ. 223,106.

La Prensa Médica Argentina: Junin 845; f. 1914; medical; weekly; Editor PABLO LÓPEZ.

Radiolandia: Avda. Roque S. Peña 1110; f. 1928; weekly; broadcasting and cinema; Editor JULIO KORN; circ. 310,000.

Review of the River Plate: Austria 1828; f. 1891; three times monthly; agricultural, financial, economic and shipping news and comment; Dir. ARCHIBALD B. NORMAN.

Revista de Quimica: Cangallo 1642; monthly.

Revista Sur: Viamonte 494, 8° piso; arts review.

Revista Textil: Avda. de Mayo 1157; monthly.

Rico Tipo: Avda. Roque S. Peña 825; f. 1944; humorous weekly of wide circulation; Dir. JOSÉ ANTONIO GUILLERMO DIVITO.

La Semana Médica: Anchorena 1267; f. 1894; bi-weekly; Dir. Prof. Dr. GUILLERMO R. JAUREGUI; circ. 7,200.

Siete Días Ilustrados: Avda. Leandro N. Alem 896; weekly.

Sur: Viamonte 494; literary monthly.

Técnica e Industria (*Technology and Industry*): Rodríguez Peña 486, 5° piso; f. 1922; monthly; Dir. DANTE R. MARCHESOTTI.

Vosotras: Belgrano 624; f. 1935; women's weekly; circ. 160,000. Monthly supplements: **Labores;** circ. 130,000; **Modas;** circ. 70,000.

Yachting Argentino: monthly.

NEWS AGENCIES
BUENOS AIRES

Agencia "Los Diarios": Sarmiento 1236; f. 1910; Dir. ALFREDO SOLANA.

TELAM: Chacabuco 142; f. 1945; Pres. A. O. ALMEIDA.

TelPress International: Perú 275; f. 1964; Dirs. RAMIRO GARCÍA, Ing. LUIS MARÍA PERFILIO.

FOREIGN BUREAUX
Buenos Aires

ANSA: Calle San Martín 326, 4° piso; Bureau Chief GIOVANNI CAMPANA.

AP: Calle San Martín 346; Bureau Chief KENNETH L. DAVIES.

EFE: Corrientes 456.

France-Press: Reconquista 379.

Inter Prensa S.R.L.: Florida 229.

Reuters: Edificio Safico, Corrientes 456, Oficina 61.

The following are also represented: Deutsche Presse-Agentur (DPA), Jiji Press, Kyodo News Service, Tass, UPI.

PRESS ASSOCIATION

Asociación de Entidades Periodísticas Argentinas: Esmeralda 356, Buenos Aires.

PUBLISHERS

BUENOS AIRES

Acme Agency S.A.: Suipacha 245, 3° piso; f. 1949; Dir. M. EDERRA.

Aguilar Argentina S.A. de Ediciones: Avda. Córdoba 2100; f. 1946; general non-fiction; Pres. ANTONIO SEMPERE; Dir. MANUEL RODRÍGUEZ.

Editorial "Albatros", S.R.L.: Lavalle 3975; technical, non-fiction and general literature; Man. R. R. CANEVARO.

Americana: Brasil 675; fine arts, history, politics, sociology.

Editorial Angel Estrada y Cia: Bolívar 462–466; f. 1869; textbooks, classics; Pres. TOMÁS J. DE ESTRADA.

Ediciones Arayú: law, sociology, economics, philosophy, pedagogy; Pres. MARTÍN J. J. BRITOS; Man. Dir. PEDRO A. FEDERICO.

Editorial Argentina Aristides Quillet, S.A.: Uruguay 1037; f. 1938; encyclopaedias; Chair. Dr. LUIS M. BAUDIZZONE; Dir. JUAN FANO.

Argos S.A. Editorial, Comercial e Industrial: San Martín 345; f. 1946; literature, arts, science; Pres. JUAN ANDRÉS CUELLO FREYRE; Man. Dir. OSCAR L. LAMELAS.

Librería "El Ateneo" Editorial: Florida 340; f. 1912; medicine, engineering, economics and general; Propr. "El Ateneo" Pedro García S.A.L.E.I.; brs. in Barcelona, Lima, Caracas, Bogotá, Mexico, Rio de Janeiro and Guatemala.

Editorial Atlántida, S.A.: Azopardo 579; f. 1918; publs. *Billiken, El Gráfico, Para Ti, La Chacra, Gente;* Founder CONSTANCIO C. VIGIL; Dir.-Gen. ANIBAL C. VIGIL.

Editorial Aurora: Doblas 1753; general, religion, children's.

S.A. Editorial Bell: Santander 735; literary, scientific, sport and technical books.

Editorial Bibliográfica Argentina, S.R.L.: Hipólito Yrigoyen 850, subsuelo; general non-fiction.

Bibliográfica Omeba: Hipólito Yrigoyen 850; scholarly and reference.

Centro Editor de América Latina: Cangallo 1228.

Centro Nacional de Documentación e Información Educativa: Madero 235; education, bibliography, directories, etc.; Dir. FLORENCIA GUEVARA DE VATTEONE.

Editorial Ciordia, S.R.L.: Belgrano 2271; general educational and fiction.

Editorial Claridad, S.A.: San José 1627; f. 1922; literature, biographies, social science, medicine, politics; Dir. ANTONIO ZAMORA.

Club de Lectores: Avda. de Mayo 624; non-fiction; Dirs. LUCÍA ELENA FONTENLA, MARÍA INÉS FONTENLA.

Editorial Codex, S.A.: Maipú 88, f. 1944; art, history, natural sciences, technology, food and the home, textbooks, encyclopedias.

Librería Colegio: del Humberto 545, 1° piso; children's textbooks.

Editorial Columba S.A.: Sarmiento 1889; general non-fiction; Pres. CLAUDIO COLUMBA.

Editorial Contémpora S.R.L.: Sarmiento 643 (R.30); publs. *Nuestra Arquitectura, Casas y Jardines*, and books on architecture, town-planning and interior decoration.

Cosmopolia S.A.R.L.: Calle Chile 474; science and technology.

Editorial Crespillo S.A.C.I.: Bolívar 369; fine arts, travel, history.

Ediciones Depalma: Talcahuano 494; f. 1955; history, politics, sociology, law and economics; Dir. ROQUE DEPALMA.

Editorial Difusión, S.A.: Sarandi 1065-67; f. 1937; Catholic; prayer books, text-books, fiction, juvenile; Dir. LUIS LUCHÍA PUIG.

Emecé Editores: Alsina 2041; f. 1939; history, drama, economics, philosophy, religion, fiction, etc.; Chair. BONIFACIO DEL CARRIL; Editor JORGE NAVEIRO.

Espasa Calpe Argentina, S.A.: Tacuarí 328; f. 1937; literature, science, dictionaries; publ. *Colección Austral*; Dir. MANUEL OLARRA GARMENDIA; br. in Mexico City.

Eudeba—Editorial Universitaria de Buenos Aires: Rivadavia 1573.

Fabril Editora: Hipólito Yrigoyen 1582; f. 1958; Editorial Man. ANDRÉS ALFONSO BRAVO; Business Man. RÓMULO AYERZA; non-fiction, science, arts, scholarly and reference.

Editorial Glem, SACIF: Santiago del Estero 1269; f. 1933; literature, technology; Pres. JOSÉ ALFREDO TUCCI.

Editorial Golova: Avda. de Mayo 863; technical and industrial.

Editorial González Porto: Hipólito Yrigoyen 851; science and technology.

Editorial Guadalupe: Mansilla 3865; children's, religious, psychology.

Editorial Hachette S.A.: Rivadavia 739-45; arts, children's, philosophy, universal and Latin American history, literature; Man. Dir. J. A. MUSSET.

Editorial Hispano-Americana S.A. (HASA): Alsina 731; f. 1942; science and technology; Pres. MARÍA LUISA MARTÍNEZ DE DUBUISSON; Dirs. ROBERTO L. MARTÍNEZ, Dr. RENATO SAENZ; publ. *Radio Técnica*.

Editorial Inter-Médica S.A.: Junín 917, 1° piso, Casilla 4625; science, medicine, dentistry, psychology.

Itinerarium, S.R.L.: Pueyrredón 1716; politics, philosophy, religion, belles-lettres.

Editorial Jackson: Maipú 257; scholarly and reference.

Editorial Kapelusz, S.A.: Moreno 372; f. 1905; text-books, audio-visual aids, juveniles, scientific works, collections; Pres. JORGE KAPELUSZ.

Guillermo Kraft, Ltda., S.A.: Moreno 872; f. 1864; publs. *Quién es Quién*, textbooks, art, science, fiction; Pres. Dr. FÉLIX A. ZÚÑIGA.

Editorial Labor S.A. Argentina: Venezuela 617; f. 1924; technology, science, art; Dir. CARLOS JOSÉ.

Luis Lasserre y Cía, S.A.: Lavalle 1101; geography, travel, maps, hygiene, school texts.

Editorial Lautaro, S.R.L.: Sánchez de Bustamente 68; f. 1942; philosophy, technology, science, literature; Dir. SARA MAGLIONE DE JORGE.

Editorial Victor Lerú: Don Bosco 3834; f. 1944; art and architecture, school books; Pres. VICTOR NEP; Dir. LEON NEP.

Carlos Lohlé SAIC: Tacuarí 1516, Casilla 3097; f. 1945; philosophy, religion, belles-lettres; Dirs. C. F. P. LOHLÉ, MARIO A. BRUNETTO, F. M. LOHLÉ.

Editorial Losada, S.A.: Alsina 1131; f. 1938; general; Dir. GONZALO LOSADA.

Editorial "Mundi", S.A.I.C. & F.: Junín 895 y Paraguay 2100; f. 1939; science, dentistry, medicine; Pres. CARLOS GARCÍA; Vice-Pres. ADELA D. DE ALVAREZ.

Editorial Musical Américo A. Vivona: San Juan 2223.

Editorial Nova S.A.: Perú 858; f. 1946; arts, science and technology; Dir. HORACIO D. ROLANDO.

Nueva Visión: Viamonte 494; art, archaeology, cinema, theatre; Man. Dir. J. GRISETTI.

Editorial Pan América Klug y Cia: Perú 677; f. 1927; technology; Dir. CÉSAR KLUG.

Peuser S.A.C. e I.: San Martín 200; children's, educational.

Plaza y Janés, S.A.: Montevideo 333; popular fiction and non-fiction, fine arts.

Editorial Poblet: Pozos 212; fiction.

Editorial Poseidon, S.R.L.: Perú 973; fiction.

Salvat Editores Argentina, S.A.: Corrientes 2777; f. 1954; sciences, technology.

Santillana S.A.C.I.F.: San José 1758; f. 1963; textbooks, general fiction, science; Pres. JESÚS POLANCO; Vice-Pres. FRANCISCO PÉREZ GONZÁLEZ.

Schapire Editor S.R.L.: Uruguay 1249; f. 1941; music, art, theatre, sociology, history, fiction; Dir. MIGUEL SCHAPIRE DALMAT.

Ediciones Siglo Veinte S.A.C. e I.: Maza 177; f. 1946; fiction, sociology, psychology; Gen. Man. I. WAINER.

Editorial Sopena Argentina, S.A.C.I. e I.: Bolívar 430, 6° piso, Casilla 1075; f. 1918; Pres. RICARDO SOPENA; publs. *Ajedrez* (monthly), classics, dictionaries.

Editorial Stella: Viamonte 1984; Prop. Asociación Educacionista Argentina; general non-fiction and textbooks.

Editorial Sudamericana, S.A.: del Humberto 545, 1° piso; f. 1939; fiction, biographies, history, essays, agriculture; magazines and reviews; UN and UNESCO Agents; Dirs. A. LÓPEZ LLAUSÁS, FERNANDO VIDAL BUZZI.

Tipográfica Editora Argentina, S.A.: Lavalle 1430; f. 1946; Dir. PEDRO GUILLERMO SAN MARTÍN; law, economics, history, sociology.

Editorial Troquel, S.A.: San José 157-9; children's, textbooks, fiction; Man. Dir. A. S. RESSIA.

Editorial Universitaria de Buenos Aires: Rivadavia 1573; f. 1958; scientific, technical, Latin American, literary and sociological; paperbacks; Exec. Dir. Dr. ANIBAL D'ANGELO RODRÍGUEZ.

Universitaria Macchi: Córdoba 2015; general publishers.

ASSOCIATION

Cámara Argentina del Libro: Paraguay 610, 7° piso, Buenos Aires; Sec. ABEL A. SALDAÑO.

RADIO AND TELEVISION

In February 1970, all broadcasting stations were placed under the direct control of the Ministry of the Interior.

Subsecretaría de Comunicaciones: Sarmiento 151, Buenos Aires; Sub-Sec. Col. Mario Augusto Desimoni; Dir. Public Relations J. A. Flores.

Administración General de Emisoras Comerciales de Radio y Televisión: Maipú 555, Buenos Aires.

RADIO

Radio Nacional: Ayacucho 1556, Buenos Aires; 16 stations on medium wave, 4 on short wave; international service Radiodifusión Argentina al Exterior, Sarmiento 151; Pres. Dr. T. E. Flores.

Asociación Radiofusoras Privadas Argentinas (A.R.P.A.): Cangallo 1561, Buenos Aires; Pres. Evaristo R. E. Alonso.

There are 99 commercial stations and 20 non commercial; 52 are privately owned. The principal ones are Radio El Mundo, Radio Libertad, Radio Belgrano, Radio Argentina, Radio Continental, Radio Mitre and Radio Splendid, all in Buenos Aires.

In 1973 there were some 11,000,000 radio receivers in use.

TELEVISION

Following a move in October 1973 by which the licences of three commercial stations were revoked, most networks are now under the control of the Government.

Canal 9-Libertad: Castex 3345, Buenos Aires; Channel 9; Dir.-Gen. Alejandro Saul Romay.

Dicon Difusión Contemporánea, S.A.: Calle Pavón 2444, Buenos Aires; Channel 11; Dir.-Gen. Héctor Ricardo García.

Difusora Marplatense S.A.: Avda. Luro 2907, Mar del Plata; Dir.-Gen. N. Paoletti.

Difusora Mendoza: Garibaldi 7, 5° piso, Mendoza; Dir.-Gen. H. Bortolamedi.

Primera Televisora Argentina: Viamonte 153, Buenos Aires; f. 1951; official service; Dir.-Gen. T. L. A. Puig.

Río de la Plata T.V., S.A.: San Juan 1170, Buenos Aires; Gen. Man. Jorge J. Alcaraz.

Servicios de Radio y Teledifusión de la Universidad Nacional de Córdoba: Rivera Indarte 170; f. 1962; government; Dir.-Gen. Omar José Robino.

Telecor S.A.C.I.: Fader 111, Cerro de las Rosas, Córdoba; Channel 12; Exec. Pres. José Domingo Bonaldi.

Televisora Universitaria: Avda. Buenos Aires 296, San Miguel de Tucumán; f. 1966; Dir.-Gen. María Lucila Padrón.

Televisora San Juan: Rivadavia 22 Este, San Juan; f. 1964; Dir. D. Rodríguez; serves 60,000 sets for 12½ hours daily.

There are 21 other stations in operation.

In 1973 there were estimated to be some 3,400,000 television receivers in use.

FINANCE

(cap.=capital; p.u.=paid up; dep.=deposits; m=million; amounts in new Argentine pesos.)

BANKING

Central Bank

Banco Central de la República Argentina: Reconquista 266, Buenos Aires; f. 1935 as a central reserve bank; it has the sole right of note issue; all capital is held by the State; cap. 100m., dep. 3,904.2m. (Mar. 1972); Pres. Dr. Alfredo Gómez Morales; Gen. Man. Rodolfo Mancini.

Buenos Aires

Banco Argentino de Comercio: Sarmiento 454-56; f. 1904; Pres. Dr. Jorge S. Oría; Gen. Man. Raúl S. Pardal.

Banco Continental: Tucumán 462-466; f. 1931; cap. 4.83m., res. 1.17m. (Dec. 1971); Pres. Miguel Joaquín de Anchorena; Gen. Man. Rodolfo Goñi.

Banco de Crédito Rural Argentino: Bartolomé Mitre 343; cap. 4.7m., dep. 182.4m. (1970).

Banco de la Ciudad de Buenos Aires: Florida 302; f. 1878; cap. 90.0m., dep. 935.3m. (Oct. 1972).

Banco Español del Río de la Plata Ltdo.: Reconquista 200; f. 1935; cap. 2.5m., dep. 847.3m. (Oct. 1971); 58 brs.; Pres. Jorge R. Vázquez Iglesias; Gen. Man. F. M. L. Mauri.

Banco Francés del Río de la Plata: Reconquista 199; f. 1886; cap. 10m., dep. 165.9m. (Aug. 1970); 12 brs.; Pres. Francisco E. Dellepiane.

Banco de Galicia y Buenos Aires: Cangallo 415-439, Casilla 86; f. 1905; cap. 32.7m., dep. 1,837.8m. (June 1972); 77 brs.; Pres. Eduardo Escasany.

Banco Ganadero Argentino: Defensa 113; f. 1964; cap. 14.2m., res. 46.1m. (Dec. 1973); Chair. Dr. Narciso Ocampo; Mans. Juan Peralta Ramos, Isidoro Fernández, Miguel A. Franzé, Oscar González, Carlos Falcone.

Banco Industrial de la República Argentina: 25 de Mayo 145; f. 1944; Pres. Carlos Pérez Companc; Gen. Man. Dr. Rodolfo A. Mancini.

Banco de Italia y Río de la Plata, S.A.: Bartolomé Mitre 402-468; f. 1872; cap. 41.7m., dep. 1,473.7m. (Nov. 1972); Pres. Edmundo Doretti; 27 brs.

Banco Mercantil Argentino, S.A.: Avda. Corrientes 1891; f. 1923; cap. 4m., dep. 377.3m. (Dec. 1973); 20 brs.; Pres. Noel Werthein.

Banco de la Nación Argentina: Bartolomé Mitre 326; f. 1891; cap. 88.2m., dep. 3,047.9m. (Aug. 1969); 417 brs.; Pres. Dr. Mario Raúl Nosiglia; Gen. Man. Walter Bernardo Stegmayer.

Banco Popular Argentino: Cangallo y Florida, Casilla 3650; f. 1887; cap. 20.4m., dep. 705.5m. (April 1972); 25 brs.; Pres. Alfonso Escamez López; Gen. Man. Antonio Campos Campos.

Banco de la Provincia de Buenos Aires: San Martín 137; f. 1822; cap. 211m., dep. 3,658.6m. (Dec. 1971); 214 brs.; Pres. Brig. R. E. Ricardo Lumi; Gen. Man. Oscar A. Pontino.

Banco Río de la Plata, S.A.: Calle 8, esq. 50, La Plata; cap. 5.8m., dep. 206.1m. (July 1971); Gen. Man. ROQUE MACCARONE.

Banco de Santander, Argentina, S.A.: Bartolomé Mitre 573; cap. 6.5m., dep. 164.7m. (1970); Gen. Man. SANTOS J. CRISERÁ.

Banco Shaw, S.A.: Sarmiento 355; f. 1944; cap. 6m., dep. 532.6m. (Sept. 1973); 20 brs.; Pres. ALEJANDRO SHAW.

Banco Supervielle de Buenos Aires, Société Générale S.A.: Reconquista 330; f. 1887; cap. 7.4m., dep. 291.9m. (June 1971); Chair. Baron ANDRÉS SUPERVIELLE; Vice-Pres. and Gen. Man. FRANCIS SENECA.

Banco Tornquist, S.A.: Bartolomé Mitre 531, Casilla 1001; f. 1960; cap. 9.4m., dep. 206.4m. (March 1973); 16 brs.; Pres. Dr. FERNANDO F. A. TORNQUIST.

Caja Nacional de Ahorro Postal (*Savings Bank*): Hipólito Yrigoyen 1750; f. 1915; dep. 18.1m. (Oct. 1971); Pres. MARIO GASTÓN TOBÍAS; Gen. Man. JUAN ALBERTO TARRUELLA.

Nuevo Banco Italiano: Reconquista 2; f. 1887; cap. 21.3m., dep. 875.5m. (June 1971); 34 brs.; Pres. EUGENIO CASTELLI; Gen. Man. ALBERT FOÁ.

DEVELOPMENT BANK

Banco Nacional de Desarrollo: 25 de Mayo 145, Buenos Aires.

FOREIGN BANKS

Banco di Napoli: H.O.: 177–178 Via Roma, Naples; Diagonal Roque S. Peña 660–700, Buenos Aires; Dir. HUMBERTO LANG.

Banco Francés e Italiano para la América del Sud (Banque Française et Italienne pour l'Amérique du Sud, S.A.): H.O.: 12 rue Halévy, Paris; Cangallo 500, Buenos Aires; Chair. J. VINCENOT; Gen. Man. V. SOZZANI.

Banco Germánico de la América del Sud: and **Dresdner Bank A.G.:** joint representation: Corrientes 311, Buenos Aires.

Banco Holandés Unido (Hollandsche Bank-Unie, N.V.): H.O.: Herengracht 434-440, Amsterdam; 25 de Mayo 81, Casilla 171, Buenos Aires; Man. (Argentina) J. C. WINK.

Banco Italo-Belga (Banque Italo-Belge, S.A.): H.O.: 48 Place de Meir, Antwerp; f. 1911; Cangallo 338, Buenos Aires; f. 1914.

Bank of America National Trust and Savings Association: 300 Montgomery St., San Francisco 20; Maipú 250, Buenos Aires; Man. D. R. DAVIS.

Bank of London and South America, Ltd.: H.O.: 40-66 Queen Victoria St., London, E.C.4; H.O. in Argentina: Reconquista 101, Buenos Aires; Dir. and Gen. Man. Argentina H. E. L. PLANT, C.B.E.

Bank of Tokyo: H.O.: Tokyo; Buenos Aires.

Banque Hypothécaire Franco-Argentine: H.O.: Paris; Reconquista 468, Buenos Aires.

Chase Manhattan Bank: Reconquista 336, Buenos Aires; Rep. DONALD L. PORTER.

First National City Bank: H.O.: 399 Park Avenue, New York, N.Y. 10022; Bartolomé Mitre 502, Buenos Aires; f. 1812; Vice-Pres. Argentina B. B. BURNQUIST.

The First National Bank of Boston: H.O.: 100 Federal St., Boston, Mass.; f. 1784; Florida 99, Buenos Aires; Pres. J. L. MORBY.

Royal Bank of Canada: H.O.: Place Ville Marie, Montreal; esq. Florida y Cangallo, Buenos Aires; f. 1869; Chair. and Pres. W. EARLE McLAUGHLIN.

BANKERS' ASSOCIATIONS

Asociación de Bancos del Interior: Lavalle 1473, Buenos Aires; 47 member banks.

Asociación de Bancos de la República Argentina: Reconquista 458, 2° piso, Buenos Aires; f. 1919; 33 member banks; Pres. Dr. JOSÉ HERIBERTO MARTÍNEZ; publ. *Boletín*.

STOCK EXCHANGES

Bolsa de Comercio: 25 de Mayo esq. Sarmiento, Buenos Aires; Pres. JUAN BAUTISTA PEÑA.

There are stock exchanges at Córdoba, San Juan, Rosario, Mendoza and Mar del Plata.

INSURANCE

La Agrícola, Compañía de Seguros: Corrientes 441, Buenos Aires; f. 1905; associated companies: El Acuerdo, La Mercantil Andina, La Regional; all classes of insurance; Pres. Dr. FERNANDO F. A. TORNQUIST; Man. Dir. LUIS R. MARCÓ.

La Anglo-Argentina S.A., Compañía de Seguros: Juncal 1319, Buenos Aires; f. 1911; fire, motor, cattle, accident, plate glass, third party risk, life, burglary, hail; Gen. Man. CONSTANTINO VILLANUSTRE.

Aseguradora de Créditos y Garantías S.A.: Cangallo 324, Buenos Aires; f. 1965; Man. CARLOS DUPONT.

Aseguradora de Río Negro y Neuquén: Villegas 316, Cipolletti, Río Negro; f. 1960; all classes; Gen. Man. ERNESTO LÓPEZ.

Aseguraciones Industriales S.A.: Maipú 471, Buenos Aires, f. 1961; all classes; Pres. NICOLÁS TRIGUB CLOVER.

La Austral: Juncal 1319, Buenos Aires; f. 1942; all classes; Man. Dir. J. D. ALCORTA; Man. C. J. VILLANUSTRE.

Boston, Compañía Argentina de Seguros, S.A.: Suipacha 268, Buenos Aires; f. 1924; fire, motor, marine, casualty, group life; Man. Dir. ALFREDO F. BRACHT.

La Buenos Aires, Compañía Argentina de Seguros, S.A.: 25 de Mayo 258, Buenos Aires; f. 1903; London Agents: W. T. Greig Ltd., 52 Lime St., E.C.3; all risks except hail; Pres. E. O. ROBERTS.

Caledonia Argentina, Compañía de Seguros (S.A.): San Martín 439, Buenos Aires; f. 1931; fire, marine, motor cars, all risks, etc.; Pres. VERNON R. DOUGALL.

Colón, Compañía de Seguros S.A.: San Martín 546-550, Buenos Aires; all classes; Gen. Man. L. D. STÜCK.

Columbia, Sociedad Anónima de Seguros: Cangallo 690, Buenos Aires; f. 1918; all classes; Man. EDUARDO BONNEU.

El Comercio, Compañía de Seguros a prima fija: Maipú 53, Buenos Aires; all classes; Man. ALBERTO COMBAL.

Compañía Aseguradora Argentina S.A. de Seguros Generales: Avda. Roque S. Peña 555, Buenos Aires; f. 1918; all classes; Man. GUIDO LUTTINI.

La Construcción, S.A.: Paseo Colón 823, Buenos Aires; f. 1948; workmen's compensation, liability, surety, personal accident, glass, bid bonds, etc.; Pres. Arq. MARCELO HÉCTOR ROGGIO; Gen. Man. F. P. FERRERO.

La Continental, Compañía de Seguros Generales S.A.: Corrientes 655, Buenos Aires; f. 1912; all classes; Man. RAÚL MASCARENHAS.

La Franco-Argentina, Compañía de Seguros: Hipólito Yrigoyen 476, Buenos Aires; f. 1896; London office: Mummery, Morse & Rimmer Ltd., Minister House, Arthur St., E.C.4; Paris office: Gastón F. Walbaum,

17 rue de la Banque; life, fire, workmen's compensation, accident, motor, plate glass, marine, hail; brs. in Asunción, Paraguay and Montevideo, Uruguay; Pres. Dr. GUILLERMO MORENO HUEYO.

Hermes, Compañia Argentina de Seguros, S.A.: Bartolomé Mitre 754-760, Buenos Aires; f. 1926; all classes; Gen. Man. M. C. CASAVILLA.

La Holando-Sudamericana, Compañia de Seguros, S.A.: Sarmiento 309, Buenos Aires; f. 1918; fire, motor, plate glass, marine, theft, accident, life, bonds; Pres. FERNANDO LEVI.

Iguazu, Compañia de Seguros, S.A.: San Martín 442, Buenos Aires; f. 1947; all classes; Gen. Man. V. A. PIOTTO.

India, Compañia de Seguros Generales, S.A.: Bolívar 173-177, Buenos Aires; f. 1950; all classes; Pres. CARLOS DE ALZAGA.

Instituto Italo-Argentino de Seguros Generales, S.A.: Avda. Roque S. Peña 890, Buenos Aires; f. 1920; all classes; Man. H. H. PINNEL.

Londres y Rio de la Plata, Compañia Argentina de Seguros: Bartolomé Mitre 441, Buenos Aires; f. 1966; part of Bank of London and South America group; Man. Dir. J. N. DE CASTRO.

La Mercantil Rosarina, Compañia de Seguros: General Mitre 575, Rosario; f. 1919; fire, accident, motor, marine, air, plate glass; Pres. JOSÉ ROSETTI; Man. Dir. JUAN BELMONTE.

La Meridional, Compañia Argentina de Seguros, S.A.: Avda. Roque S. Peña 648, Buenos Aires; f. 1949; fire, marine, motor car, burglary, plate glass, boiler and machinery, fidelity bonds, workmen's compensation, casualty, accident, life, hospitalization; Pres. RAYMOND REY.

El Mundo, Compañia de Seguros Generales, S.A.: Cangallo 555, Buenos Aires; f. 1946; general; Chair. Ing. MIGUEL A. BISONNI; Gen. Man. MARIO HÉCTOR D'ANGELO.

Patria, Compañia de Seguros Generales, S.A.: Sarmiento 354-6, Buenos Aires; f. 1922; fire, marine, motor, workmen's compensation, accident, burglary, life, etc.; Pres. THILO MARTENS; Gen. Man. GUILLERMO A. WAGNER.

Plus Ultra: San Martín 546-50, Buenos Aires; f. 1956; all classes; Gen. Man. L. D. STÜCK.

La Porteña, Compañia Argentina de Seguros, S.A.: Lavalle 465, Buenos Aires; f. 1944; fire, marine, motor, plate glass, workers' compensation, accident, etc.; Pres. Dr. MANUEL F. CASTELLO; Man. Dir. L. M. PASCUAL.

La Primera, Compañia Argentina de Seguros Generales, S.A.: Villegas y Fray Justo Santa María de Oro, Trenque Lanquen, Buenos Aires; all classes; Man. Dr. SANTIAGO M. SERRUTI.

La Rectora, Compañia Argentina de Seguros S.A.: Corrientes 848, Buenos Aires; f. 1951; all classes; Man. M. F. GONZÁLEZ.

La Rosario, Compañia Argentina de Seguros: San Lorenzo 1121, Rosario; f. 1888; fire, life, plate glass, motor, workmen's compensation, personal accident, marine, burglary, aviation, transit, miscellaneous; Pres. EDUARDO BRUERA.

El Sol Argentino, Compañia de Seguros Generales S.A.: San Martín 439, 4° piso, Buenos Aires; f. 1923; life, fire, marine, motor, accident, plate glass, theft, livestock, personal accident; Pres. JULIO A. PUEYRREDON.

Sud América, Compañia de Seguros de Vida, S.A.: Avda. Roque S. Peña 530, Buenos Aires; f. 1923; Pres. ROBERTO GUSTAVO WALLER; Man. DARIO MAZZINI.

Sud América Terrestre y Marítima S.A.: Reconquista 559, Buenos Aires; f. 1919; all classes; Pres. R. G. WALLER.

Sud Atlántica, Compañia de Seguros, S.A.: Florida 142, Buenos Aires; f. 1933; fire, marine, motor, workmen's compensation, glass, air, burglary, personal accidents, life, etc.; Chair. GILBERTO VAN TIENHOVEN; Man. Dir. PATRICIO G. WHITNEY.

Sur, Compañia Argentina de Seguros, S.A.: Paraguay 610, esq. Florida, Buenos Aires; f. 1949; fire, motor car, marine, workmen's compensation, glass, general, burglary, accident, aviation, life; Gen. Man. D. E. SALAMONESCO.

Ultramar, S.A. de Seguros: Cangallo 925, Buenos Aires; f. 1956; fire, marine, aviation, motor car, glass, burglary, livestock, accident, workmen's compensation, general; Man. J. RÉNYI.

La Unión Gremial Compañia de Seguros, S.A.: General Mitre 665-99, Rosario; f. 1908; general; Pres. Ing. SILVIO GAGLIARDI; Gen. Man. JUAN A. ELZEARD; Man. CARLOS E. ALVAREZ.

Unión Mercantil: Lavalle 445, Buenos Aires; f. 1901; fire, motor car, marine, glass, burglary, accident; Man. J. M. CAMPOS.

La Universal: Juncal 1319, Buenos Aires; f. 1905; all classes; Pres. Dr. E. MAYER.

La Uruguaya-Argentina: Maipú 535, Buenos Aires; f. 1962; life; Pres. Ing. L. M. YGARTÚA.

There are also many foreign insurance companies operating in Argentina.

SUPERVISING AUTHORITY

Superintendencia de Seguros de la Nación: Hipólito Yrigoyen 250, 9° piso, Buenos Aires; f. 1937; 219 members; Superintendent Dr. MIGUEL ANTONIO PELAEZ.

TRADE AND INDUSTRY

CHAMBERS OF COMMERCE

Cámara Argentina de Comercio: Avda. Leandro N. Alem 36, Buenos Aires; f. 1924, authorized 1927; correspondents abroad; Pres. Dr. ARTURO A. FAUVETY; Sec. JORGE F. GUIGON; publs. *Revista* (bi-monthly), *Mercurio* (fortnightly).

Similar chambers are located in most of the larger centres and there are many foreign chambers of commerce.

DEVELOPMENT ORGANIZATIONS AND STATE COUNCILS

Corporación de Empresas Nacionales: Buenos Aires; f. 1973 to control the activities of all state-owned companies and those in which the State has a majority share; administers bond issues and tax and treasury payments, centralizes the generation of external finance and controls private participation.

Instituto de Desarrollo Económico y Social (IDES): Güemes 3950, Buenos Aires; f. 1961; Pres. OSCAR ALTIMIR; Sec. JUAN V. SOURROUILLE; publ. *Desarrollo Económico, Revista de Ciencias Sociales*.

Instituto Nacional de Tecnología Agropecuaria (Inta): Buenos Aires; f. 1956; carries out a variety of research and extension programmes.

Secretaria del Consejo Nacional de Desarrollo (CONADE) (*Secretariat of the National Development Council*): Hipólito Yrigoyen 250, 8° piso, Buenos Aires; f. 1961; State organization with funds totalling 460,100,000 pesos in 1968; formulates national long-term development plans and integrates them into internal, external, economic, social and defence policies; co-ordinates with **Consejo Nacional de Seguridad**; evaluates regional development plans into the *Plan Nacional de Desarrollo y Seguridad;* checks existing organizations and creates new ones to carry out the national plans; publs. reports, etc. in *Serie B.* (internal) and *Serie C.* (public).

Consejo Federal de Inversiones: Alsina 1407, Buenos Aires.

Instituto Argentino de la Industria Exportadora de Carnes: 11 mem. companies.

Junta Nacional de Carnes: San Martín 459, Buenos Aires; national meat board; Pres. HÉCTOR A. FERNÁNDEZ MENDY.

Junta Nacional de Granos: Paseo Colón 359, Buenos Aires; national grain board; supervises commercial practices; organizes building of farm silos and port elevators.

Subsecretaría de Energía: energy and fuels.

EMPLOYERS' ORGANIZATION

Unión Industrial Argentina: Avda. de Mayo 1157, Buenos Aires.

TRADE UNIONS

Confederación General del Trabajo—CGT (*General Confederation of Labour*): Azopardo 802, Buenos Aires; f. 1930; mems. 3,500,000 (1965); Interventor ALFREDO INSAURRALDE; Sec.-Gen. ADELINO ROMERO; publ. *Weekly News, The Argentine Labour Movement* (monthly).

Acción Sindical Argentina—ASA (*Argentine Trade Union Action*): Buenos Aires; f. 1955; affiliated to the World Confederation of Labour; Sec.-Gen. JUAN CARLOS LOUREIRO.

About 19 unions are independent of the above bodies, including the large Postal and Telegraph Workers Union (*Federación Obreros y Empleados de Correos y Telecomunicaciones*).

TRANSPORT

RAILWAYS

Ferrocarriles Argentinos (FA): Avda. Ramos Mejía 1302, Buenos Aires; autonomous body consisting of representatives of the Government, railway unions and managers of the various lines; Pres. ISIDORO GONZÁLEZ; Exec. Vice-Pres. Ing. NÉSTOR E. FERNÁNDEZ.

Principal lines: General Belgrano, General Roca, General Bartolomé Mitre, General San Martín, Domingo F. Sarmiento, General Urquiza, and provincial lines. There is a direct link between Buenos Aires and Santa Cruz in Bolivia. A line linking Buenos Aires with Pôrto Alegre in Brazil was opened in March 1974.

There are about 39,500 km. of track.

Subterráneos de Buenos Aires: Bartolomé Mitre 3342, Buenos Aires; state-owned underground railway; 3 lines of 32 km.; Gen. Administrator Lt.-Col. OSCAR FERNANDO CÓRDOVA.

ROADS

Consejo Nacional de Carreteras: Secretaría de Transportes, Buenos Aires; total road length: 220,332 km. It is planned to use the toll system to construct a basic national system of automobile roads, the first stage to be developed in the coastal zone of the country, starting in the cities of Santa Fe and Mar del Plata, and inter-

connecting the cities of Rosario, San Nicolás, Buenos Aires and La Plata, with an approximate length of 900 km.

MOTORISTS' ORGANIZATION

Automóvil Club Argentino: Avda. Libertador 1850, Buenos Aires; supplies information and road maps for touring Argentina.

Autobuses Sudamericanos S.R.L.: Entre Ríos 1135, Local 8 (Casilla 463), Rosario de Santa Fe; international bus services.

INLAND WATERWAYS

Flota Fluvial del Estado: Corrientes 389, Buenos Aires; services on the Plate, Paraná, Paraguay and Uruguay rivers; Pres. Ing. FEDERICO PREUSCHE; Gen. Administrator Ing. LEANDRO J. OTERO.

There is a hydrofoil service between Buenos Aires and Colonia del Sacramento (Uruguay).

An agreement was signed in January 1967 between Argentina and Paraguay establishing equal navigational rights for merchant vessels of both countries on the Rivers Paraguay, Paraná and Plate.

SHIPPING

Administración General de Puertos: Ministerio de Obras Públicas; Avda. Julio A. Roca 734–42, Buenos Aires; f. 1956; State enterprise for exploitation and conservation of all national sea and river ports; U.S.$ 350m. is being spent over the five year period 1971–75 on the modernization of river and sea ports; Administrator-Gen. Vice-Adml. J. A. DESIMONI; publs. *Técnica y Puertos, Boletín Mensual, Nuestra Imagen.*

Capitanía del Puerto: Buenos Aires; f. 1967; co-ordination of the working of the ports; Port Captain Capitán de Navío MARIO ANDRÉS DURRIEU.

The chief State-owned organizations are:

Empresa Líneas Marítimas Argentinas (ELMA): Corrientes 389, Buenos Aires; f. 1960; operates coastal services in S. America, services to N. America and Europe.

Yacimientos Petrolíferos Fiscales (Y.P.F.): Avda. Roque S. Peña 777, Buenos Aires; fleet of tankers, cargo and tanker craft, and motor launches; Administrator Ing. DANIEL A. BRUNELLA; Marine Superintendent Ing. ERNESTO R. PETERS.

There are also private shipping companies operating on coastal and overseas routes.

CIVIL AVIATION

Ezeiza international airport, 35 km. from Buenos Aires, is one of the most important air terminals in Latin America.

Dirección Nacional de Aviación Civil: Buenos Aires.

Aerolíneas Argentinas: Paseo Colón 185, Buenos Aires; f. Dec. 1949; non-stop services to New York and Europe and via Rio de Janeiro; to Miami via Santiago and Lima; to Los Angeles via Lima, Bogotá and Mexico. Its South American services link Argentina with Chile, Colombia, Bolivia, Uruguay, Brazil, Peru and Paraguay. The internal network covers the whole country. Passengers, mail and freight are carried. Pres. Brig. CÉSAR A. GUASCO; fleet comprises four Boeing 707-387B, four 707-387C, six 737-287, two 737-287C, three Caravelle, nine HS.748.

Austral Líneas Aéreas S.A.: Florida 234, Buenos Aires; f. 1971; services to Uruguay; domestic flights linking 22 cities in Argentina; fleet includes 4 BAC 1-11 series 400, 3 BAC 1-11 series 500 and 3 YS-IIA; Pres. W. J. REYNAL.

Líneas Aéreas del Estado (LADE): Perú 710, Buenos Aires; f. 1940; controlled by the Air Ministry and operates through the Argentine Air Force. LADE operates routes in isolated regions with limited traffic which would not sustain commercial operations; this includes a route to the Falkland Islands opened in 1972 in agreement with the British Government; Dir. Brig. Higinio González; fleet comprises 11 Fokker F.27, three Douglas DC-6, seven Twin Otter.

Transportes Aéreos Buenos Aires (TABA): Suipacha 745, 4° piso, Buenos Aires; internal services; Pres. José C. Alsina; fleet includes one Fairchild F.27 and four Beech 18.

FOREIGN AIRLINES

The following airlines also serve Argentina: Air France, Alitalia, Avianca, Braniff, British Caledonian, Canadian Pacific, Cruzeiro do Sul, Iberia, KLM, Lloyd Aéreo Boliviano, LAN de Chile, Líneas Aéreas Paraguayas, Lufthansa, Pan American, Primeras Líneas Uruguayas (PLUNA), Sabena, SAS, Swissair, TAP and Varig.

TOURISM

Dirección Nacional de Turismo: Calle Suipacha 1111, Buenos Aires; Interventor Mauricio Fischer.

Confederación de Organizaciones Turísticas de la América Latina (C.O.T.A.L.): Viamonte 640, 8° piso, Buenos Aires; f. 1957; groups 20 national travel associations from south and central America; Pres. José Rodrigo Marimón (Argentina); Exec. Dir. Hector Jorge Testoni; publ. *Revista COTAL* (monthly).

Asociación Argentina de Agencias de Viajes y Turismo (AAAVYT): Viamonte 640, Buenos Aires; f. 1951; Pres. François Verger; publ. *Noticias de Turismo*.

PRINCIPAL THEATRES

Teatro Colón: Cerrito 618; Buenos Aires municipal opera house; f. 1908; has 2 orchestras, a chorus and a ballet company; Dirs. Félix Pérez Constanzó (General), Antonio Pini (Artistic); Admin. Cristobal L. Juliá.

Teatro Municipal General San Martín: Corrientes 1532; f. 1944; municipally owned; contains 6 auditoria, 1 exhibition room and 2 art galleries; Dir.-Gen. Kive Staif; Admin. Dir. Col. Alfredo Jorge Urien.

Ballet del San Martín: f. 1968; Choreographic Dir. Oscar Araíz.

Teatro Nacional de Comedia (Cervantes): Libertad 815, Buenos Aires; f. 1921; operated under the auspices of the Ministry of Education and Culture; Administrator Nestor Suárez Aboy; Artistic Director Pedro Escudero; Technical Director Mario Vanarelli.

Teatro del Pueblo: Buenos Aires; f. 1931; independent; presents classical and modern plays; Founder and Dir. Leónidas Barletta.

There are 12 symphony orchestras in Argentina, 5 of them in Buenos Aires.

ATOMIC ENERGY

Comisión Nacional de Energía Atómica: Avda. Libertador 8250, Buenos Aires; f. 1950; Departments of Raw Materials, Energy, Technology, Research, Radiological Protection and Security, Logistics and Economics. Pres. Rear Adml. Oscar Armando Quihillalt.

Argentina's first nuclear reactor, with a capacity of 319 MW, has been built at Atucha on the River Paraná de las Palmas. An agreement has been signed with Canadian and Italian companies for the construction of a second plant, with a capacity of 600 MW, at Río Tercero (Córdoba).

Research reactors: The following research reactors are in operation:

RA-1 Centro Atómico Constituyentes: maximum capacity 150 kW.

RA-2 Centro Atómico Constituyentes: maximum capacity 30W.

RA-3 Centro Atómico Ezeiza: maximum capacity 8 MW.

RA-4 Universidad Nacional de Rosario: maximum capacity 0.1 W.

In 1972 the budget of the Comisión Nacional de Energía Atómica amounted to 92 million pesos.

Universidad Nacional de Cuyo: San Luis; nuclear physics.

Universidad de Buenos Aires: Viamonte 444, Buenos Aires; the application and study of radio-isotopes and nuclear physics are carried out in the faculties of Agronomy, National Science, Medicine and Engineering.

Universidad Nacional de La Plata: La Plata; Nuclear Chemistry and Spectroscopy; Beta spectroscope, 100-channel analyser.

Universidad Nacional de Litoral: Santa Fe; Nuclear Electronics, Metallurgy, Radio-Chemistry and Mineral-Processing.

PRINCIPAL UNIVERSITIES

Universidad de Buenos Aires: Calle Viamonte 444, Buenos Aires; 9,100 teachers, 88,628 students.

Universidad Católica Argentina "Santa María de los Buenos Aires": Río Bamba 1227, Buenos Aires; 1,500 teachers, 12,000 students.

Universidad Católica de Córdoba: Trejo 323, Córdoba; 650 teachers, 3,100 students.

Universidad Católica de Santa Fe: San Martín 1966, Santa Fe; 491 teachers, 1,627 students.

Universidad Nacional de Córdoba: Calle Obispo Trejo y Sanabria 242, Córdoba.

Universidad Nacional de Cuyo: Parque General San Martín, Mendoza; 844 teachers, 7,579 students.

Universidad Nacional de La Plata: Calle 7 No. 776, La Plata; 1,209 teachers, 22,000 students.

Universidad Nacional del Litoral: Boulevard Pellegrini 2750, Santa Fe; 1,406 professors, 15,330 students.

Universidad Nacional del Nordeste: 25 de Mayo 868, Corrientes; 66 teachers, 6,879 students.

Universidad Nacional de Rosario: Córdoba 1814, Rosario; 2,053 teachers, 15,974 students.

Universidad Nacional del Sur: Avda. Colón 80, Bahía Blanca.

Universidad Nacional de Tucumán: Ayacucho 482, Tucumán; 1,756 teachers, 11,489 students.

Universidad Tecnológica Nacional: Medrano 951, Buenos Aires; 893 teachers, 9,805 students.

Universidad del Salvador: Callao 542, Buenos Aires; 960 teachers, 4,466 students.

AUSTRALIA

INTRODUCTORY SURVEY

Location, Climate, Language, Religion, Flag, Capital

The Commonwealth of Australia occupies the whole of the island continent of Australia in the South Pacific and the offshore island of Tasmania to the south-east. Its External Territories are: Papua New Guinea (which is now self-governing but not yet fully independent); Norfolk Island in the Pacific; the 27 Cocos (Keeling) Islands and Christmas Island in the Indian Ocean; Australian Antarctica, Heard Island and McDonald Islands, Coral Sea Islands Territory, MacQuarie Island and Ashmore and Cartier Islands. Australia's nearest neighbour is Indonesia, covering the long archipelago to the north and north-west. The Australian climate is hot and dry with average temperatures of about 80°F (26.8°C) rising to over 120°F (49°C) in the interior. Over half the country is desert or semi-desert with little rainfall. More than 98 per cent of the population are of European origin. English is the official language. In 1971 there were 106,000 people with 50 per cent or more Aboriginal blood. The population is mainly Christian: Anglicans 34 per cent, Roman Catholics about 26 per cent. The national flag (proportions 2 by 1) is blue with a Union Jack in the upper hoist, a large seven-pointed white star in the lower hoist and five smaller white stars in the form of the Southern Cross in the fly. The capital, Canberra, lies in one of two enclaves of Federal Territory known as the Australian Capital Territory.

Recent History

Since the war Australia has taken an important place in Pacific and Asian affairs and has strengthened her political and economic ties with India, South-East Asia and Japan. The country co-operates more closely than formerly with the U.S.A., and contributed troops to the war in Viet-Nam until 1970. As a founder-member of the Colombo Plan she has given much aid in money, materials and training to Asian countries. In 1966 Sir Robert Menzies resigned after sixteen years as Prime Minister, and was succeeded by Harold Holt, who died the next year. His successor, Senator John Gorton, resigned after a vote of no confidence and William McMahon was Prime Minister from March 1971 until December 1972, when, after 23 years in office, the Liberal-Country Party Coalition was defeated by the Labor Party, led by Gough Whitlam.

In December 1973 Papua New Guinea attained self government under a seven-man Executive Council, which has since been enlarged and reshuffled. Australia is still responsible for some internal affairs but full independence is likely to be granted in December 1974.

In May 1974 elections were held for both Houses after a crisis concerning supply funds split the Parliament. A reduced Labour majority in the House of Representatives is likely to be offset by a gain in the Senate.

Government

Australia is a Federation of six States, forming the Commonwealth of Australia. Queen Elizabeth II is Queen of Australia and is permanently represented there by a Governor-General and by a Governor in each of the six States. The Federal Government consists of two elected Houses, the Senate in which the States have equal representation, and the House of Representatives where representation is based on population.

The State Governments are autonomous except for certain powers placed under the jurisdiction of the Federal Government. All except Queensland have an Upper House, the Legislative Council, and a Lower House, the Legislative Assembly or House of Assembly. The chief ministers of the States are known as Premiers, as distinct from the Federal Prime Minister.

Defence

Australia's defence policy is based on collective security and she is a member of the British Commonwealth Strategic Reserve, the ANZUS Council (Australia, New Zealand and U.S.A.) and the South East Asia Treaty Organization (SEATO). Australia's armed forces numbered 73,330 in 1973 (army 33,100, navy 17,460, air force 22,770). There is also a civilian force, at present some 15,000 strong, which is soon to be renamed the Australian Army Reserve and doubled in size. About 20 per cent of Australia's budget is allocated to defence. In January 1973 conscription was abolished.

Under the UN Charter and Trusteeship Agreement, Australia is responsible for the defence of part of Papua New Guinea until its independence, which is provisionally set for December 1974.

Economic Affairs

Australia's traditional reliance on the agricultural sector has been eroded by the phenomenal oil and mineral discoveries of recent years. Some 70 per cent of Australia's oil requirements are now met by domestic sources. In 1970–71 agriculture contributed less than 7 per cent of Gross Domestic Product (G.D.P.) and the share of agricultural products in total export trade declined to less than 50 per cent in 1971, with wool, wheat, meat, sugar and dairy products remaining major export items. Gold, silver, lead, zinc and copper have long been exploited, but recent discoveries of vast deposits of oil, natural gas, coal, nickel, iron ore and bauxite have transformed the economy; many of these minerals are being exploited as raw materials for Japan's industries. The pattern of Australia's dependence on foreign trade has thus undergone a change, with Japan overtaking Western countries as the major market. Australia has also increased her trade with China and South-East Asian countries, and has recently reached trade agreements with the U.S.S.R. and five East European countries. Manufacturing industries contributed 27.4 per cent of G.D.P. in 1970–71 and employed nearly 1.4 million people, mainly in iron and steel and engineering. Other important industries are food processing, machinery, motor vehicles, chemicals, electrical and electronic equipment. Domestic sources of energy are coal, gas, thermal- and hydro-electricity. Oil and natural gas production totalled 119.7 million barrels and 92,801 million cu. ft. respectively during 1971–72.

Australia faces difficulties and uncertainties in economic affairs, with retail prices in the last quarter of 1973 up by over 13 per cent compared with the figure for 12 months before, and the necessity of revaluing the Australian dollar by 5 per cent in September 1973. Problems derive from such factors as increased defence spending, the uncertainties facing primary products in world markets, high transport and labour costs, and the difficulties of overall policy-making arising from the autonomy in industrial and mineral development enjoyed by the States. However, with a trade surplus for 1972–73 of $A2,000 million, the balance of payments remains strong and there is a continuing healthy inflow of foreign capital.

In June 1971, Australia became a member of OECD. The United Kingdom-Australia Trade Agreement was terminated in February 1973, following the entry into the EEC of the U.K., but new trade terms are to be established.

Transport and Communications

For her population, Australia has a well developed transport system with 25,000 miles of railway, 563,000 miles of roads and 83,000 miles of scheduled air routes. Until recently railways in some States were of different gauges, but a standard gauge system now covers almost all of the country. In the thinly populated areas of Central and Western Australia air transport is extremely important and Australia has pioneered services such as the Flying Doctor Service to overcome the problems of distance. Many of the larger sheep stations have their own aircraft. Australia is well served by international shipping and air lines. Her civil aviation industry is expanding rapidly and in 1973 Australia's domestic airlines carried some ten million passengers.

Social Welfare

Australia provides old age pensions, invalid, maternity, sickness and unemployment benefits and children's allowances. Reciprocal welfare agreements operate between Australia and New Zealand and the United Kingdom. About 30 per cent of Federal budget expenditure is allocated to welfare.

Education

Education is the responsibility of each of the six States. It is free and compulsory from the ages of six to fifteen.

In 1970 there were over two million children enrolled in government primary and secondary schools, and some 600,000 attending private schools. Special services have been developed to meet the needs of children living in the outback. Some 20,000 are enrolled in correspondence classes and in 1950 the first School of the Air was established, using two-way receiver sets. A system of one-teacher schools, which accounts for a third of all government schools, also helps meet these needs. Australia has fifteen universities with over 128,000 students.

Tourism

Australian tourism is developing with quicker and cheaper air transport. The main attractions are swimming and surfing on the Pacific beaches, sailing from Sydney and other harbours, skin-diving along the Great Barrier Reef, and winter and summer sports in the Blue Mountains.

Visas are not required by citizens of Ireland or South Africa, or by United Kingdom subjects of European descent.

Sport

Australians excel at sport, especially tennis and cricket. They play a number of codes of football and are enthusiastic followers of horse-racing. They also pursue water sports.

Public Holidays

1974: December 25th–26th (Christmas)†.

1975: January 1st, January 29th (Australia Day), March 28–31st (Easter), April 25th (Anzac Day), Queen's official Birthday.

There are also a number of State holidays.

† Boxing Day is not a public holiday in South Australia.

Weights and Measures

The imperial system of weights and measures is in force.

Currency and Exchange Rates

100 cents = 1 Australian dollar.

Exchange rates (April 1974):
£1 sterling = $A1.585;
U.S. $1 = 67.23 Australian cents.

STATISTICAL SURVEY

Note.—The Australian statistical year mostly ends in June.

AREA
(sq. km.)

Total	New South Wales	Victoria	Queensland	South Australia	Western Australia	Tasmania	Northern Territory	Australian Capital Territory
7,686,850*	801,428	227,619	1,727,522	984,377	2,527,621	68,332	1,347,519	2,432

* 2,967,909 square miles.

POPULATION
(March 31st, 1973)

Total	New South Wales	Victoria	Queensland	South Australia	Western Australia	Tasmania	Northern Territory	Australian Capital Territory
13,154,700	4,715,100	3,595,200	1,909,800	1,201,300	1,070,300	396,400	98,400	168,200

At the census of June 1971, there were 106,208 persons who considered themselves to be of Aboriginal origin.

Population (June 1973): Estimate 13,100,000.

PRINCIPAL CITIES*
Population (June 30th, 1972)

Canberra (national capital)†	174,100	Perth (capital W. Australia)	724,800
Sydney (capital N.S.W.)	2,850,630	Newcastle	354,630
Melbourne (capital Victoria)	2,544,400	Wollongong	202,830
Brisbane (capital Queensland)	888,000	Hobart (capital Tasmania)	154,720
Adelaide (capital S. Australia)	855,300	Geelong	124,550

* Statistical divisions or districts.   † Includes the municipality of Queanbeyan in New South Wales.

BIRTHS, MARRIAGES AND DEATHS
(1972)

	Births	Marriages	Deaths
New South Wales	95,278	41,520	41,652
Victoria	71,807	31,206	29,856
Queensland	39,251	16,066	16,598
S. Australia	21,844	10,829	9,764
W. Australia	22,177	9,120	7,441
Tasmania	7,824	3,426	3,227
N. Territory	2,722	490	553
Aust. Capital Ter.	4,066	1,372	669
Total	264,969	114,029	109,760

MIGRATION

	ARRIVALS			DEPARTURES			NET INCREASE
	Males	Females	Total	Males	Females	Total	
1968 . .	465,232	306,560	771,792	311,727	254,991	658,739	91,909
1969 . .	545,559	353,299	898,858	403,748	293,972	769,812	113,053
1970 . .	613,899	412,776	1,026,675	475,840	355,448	903,801	129,046
1971 . .	625,066	453,732	1,078,798	548,353	412,683	994,193	122,874
1972 . .	608,730	501,940	1,110,670	597,765	485,059	1,082,824	27,846

EMPLOYMENT*
('000 persons)

	JUNE 1971	JUNE 1972	JUNE 1973
Forestry, Fishing and Trapping . .	14.6	15.1	15.0
Mining and Quarrying	74.2	74.5	74.7
Manufacturing	1,392.0	1,369.0	1,384.5
Public Services†	115.1	116.6	117.8
Building and Construction . . .	379.0	384.0	386.3
Transport, Storage and Communication .	370.8	370.6	377.3
Commerce	746.6	764.0	804.6
Finance and Property . . .	217.3	219.2	227.9
Public Authority Activities . .	201.0	209.4	219.5
Community and Business Services‡ .	687.5	697.5	739.6
Amusement, Hotels, Personal Service .	279.7	287.1	305.4
TOTAL‡ . . .	4,477.8	4,507.0	4,652.6
Private	3,368.7	3,384.2	3,494.1
Government‡	1,109.1	1,122.8	1,158.5

* Wage and salary earners in civilian employment. Excludes defence forces and employees in agriculture and private domestic service. The agricultural labour force totalled 404,300 in 1972.

† Comprises Electricity, Gas, Water and Sanitary Services.

‡ From July 1971: excludes trainee teachers, some of whom were classified as wage and salary earners for earlier periods.

AGRICULTURE
AREA OF CROPS
('000 acres)

	1968–69	1969–70	1970–71	1971–72
Wheat	26,799	23,440	16,009	17,638
Oats	3,872	3,396	3,838	3,066
Sugar Cane . .	568	526	545	578
Barley . .	3,314	3,759	4,942	6,265
Maize	164	197	212	193
Potatoes . . .	113	107	95	100
Vineyards . . .	143	150	158	164
Fruit	310	309	305	304

PRODUCTION

		1968–69	1969–70	1970–71	1971–72
Wheat . . .	'000 bushels	543,950	387,512	289,895	312,691
Oats . . .	,, ,,	94,250	68,723	88,882	70,280
Barley . . .	,, ,,	72,588	74,901	103,650	135,153
Maize . . .	,, ,,	5,869	7,543	8,331	8,422
Sugar Cane . .	'000 tons	18,413	15,535	17,366	19,084
Wine . . .	'000 gallons	52,111	63,127	55,257	62,931

FRUIT
('ooo bushels)

	1969–70	1970–71	1971–72
Apples . .	22,259	23,238	18,913
Apricots . .	1,815	2,425	1,454
Bananas . .	5,160	5,142	5,036
Oranges . .	10,786	14,804	13,362
Peaches . .	5,513	6,012	5,745
Pears . .	9,331	9,192	9,026
Plums and Prunes	985	1,179	886

LIVESTOCK
('ooo)

	1970	1970–71	1971–72	1972–73*
Horses . . .	456	n.a.	n.a.	n.a.
Cattle . . .	22,162	24,373	27,373	29,199
Sheep . . .	180,080	177,192	162,910	142,097
Pigs . . .	2,398	2,590	3,199	3,299

* Preliminary.

MEAT
('ooo tons)

	1970–71	1971–72	1972–73*
Beef and Veal	1,031	1,149	11,412
Mutton	463	587	426
Lamb	349	354	271
Pig Meats	179	191	229

* Preliminary.

DAIRY PRODUCE

		1970–71	1971–72	1972–73*
Whole Milk . . .	million gal.	1,595	1,557	1,561
Factory Butter . . .	million lb.	448	432	408
Factory Cheese . .	,, ,,	171	175	206
Processed Milk Products (whole milk equivalent) .	million gal.	129	129	144

* Preliminary.

WOOL ('ooo lb.)

1969–70	1970–71	1971–72*	1972–73*	1973–74*†
2,035,700	1,935,300	875.4	755.6	737.3

* Million kg.   † Preliminary.

MINING (a)

		1969–70	1970–71	1971–72*
Coal (Black) . .	'ooo tons	47,732	48,935	52,703
Coal (Brown) . .	,, ,,	23,927	22,814	23,257
Bauxite . . .	,, ,,	8,163	10,869	13,481
Zircon(b) . . .	tons	246,121	273,488	254,679
Iron . . .	'ooo tons	28,223	35,537	38,634
Lead . . .	,, ,,	452	410	414
Zinc . . .	,, ,,	494	437	490
Copper . . .	,, ,,	140	170	169
Titanium(c) . .	,, ,,	790	840	741
Tin . . .	tons	8,568	8,782	10,895
Tungsten(d) . .	units of 22.4 lb.	173,229	163,439	193,270
Crude Oil . .	'ooo bls.	30,643	93,949	119,746
Natural Gas . .	million cu. ft.	27,580	69,275	92,801
Gold . . .	'ooo fine oz.	659	614	748
Silver . . .	,, ,, ,,	27,519	23,269	22,511
Nickel . . .	tons	17,762	34,366	34,997

(a) Figures for metallic minerals represent contents based on chemical assay, except figures for bauxite, which are in terms of gross quantities produced. (b) In terms of zircon ($Zr O_2$) contained in zircon concentrates. (c) In terms of $Ti O_2$ contained in rutile, ilmenite and leucoxene. (d) In terms of WO_2 contained in scheelite and wolfram concentrates.

* Preliminary.

INDUSTRY

(1971–72)

Industry Sub-Division	Establishments at End of Year	Persons Employed*	Turnover ($m.)
Food, Beverages and Tobacco	4,423	201,425	5,295.1
Textiles	873	55,267	812.1
Clothing and Footwear	3,214	116,081	1,140.4
Wood, Wood Products and Furniture . . .	5,884	81,084	1,077.5
Paper and Paper Products, Printing . . .	3,588	106,252	1,616.3
Chemical, Petroleum and Coal Products . . .	1,165	65,610	1,847.1
Non-Metallic Mineral Products	1,854	51,202	1,001.9
Basic Metal Products	628	92,760	2,659.1
Fabricated Metal Products	5,169	120,281	1,772.2
Other Machinery and Equipment	4,899	189,589	2,808.3
Transport Equipment	1,426	151,890	2,519.0
Miscellaneous Manufacturing . . .	3,022	70,857	1,093.8

* Includes working proprietors.

Note: Direct comparisons with figures for previous years are not possible because of changes in the census units, the scope of the census and the items of data.

INDUSTRIAL PRODUCTION

		1970–71	1971–72	1972–73
Steel (Ingots) .	'000 tonnes	6,800	6,585	7,230
Electric Motors (< 1 h.p.) .	'000	3,024	3,252	3,555
Clay Bricks .	million	1,669	1,749	1,874
Sulphuric Acid .	'000 tonnes	1,611	1,750	2,265
Nitric Acid .	tons	119,864	146,221	162,672
Radios .	'000	746	761	867
TV Sets .	,,	335	354	383
Motor Vehicles .	,,	453	467	454
Cotton Yarn .	million lb.	64	60	61
Cotton Cloth .	'000 sq. yds.	56,495	56,358	54,019
Tinplate .	'000 tonnes	290	309	317
Electricity .	million kWh	57,974	60,908	64,814
Cement .	'000 tonnes	4,611	4,728	4,957

FINANCE

100 cents = 1 Australian dollar ($A).

Coins: 1, 2, 5, 10, 20 and 50 cents.

Notes: 1, 2, 5, 10, 20 and 50 dollars.

Exchange rates (April 1974): £1 sterling = $A1.585; U.S. $1 = 67.23 Australian cents.

$A100 = £63.10 = U.S. $148.75.

COMMONWEALTH BUDGET

(Consolidated Revenue Fund)

($A million, twelve months ending June 30th)

REVENUE	1972–73	1973–74	EXPENDITURE	1972–73	1973–74
Income Tax .	5,723.3	7,121.8	Defence† .	1,286.7	1,402.2
Sales Tax .	765.0	889.0	Payments to or for the States	2,535.5	3,200.5
Customs .	513.5	563.8	Social Services and Welfare		
Excise .	1,268.4	1,548.9	Payments .	2,197.4	2,621.7
Payroll Tax .	6.3	9.3	Other .	3,258.6	4,172.0
Other Taxes .	77.1	71.9			
Other Revenue .	924.6	1,191.7			
TOTAL .	9,278.2	11,396.4	TOTAL .	9,278.2	11,396.4

† "Defence" excludes Loan Fund expenditure under U.S. Defence Credit arrangements.

STATE BUDGET ESTIMATES

($A million—1973–74)

	REVENUE	EXPENDITURE
New South Wales .	1,633	1,643
Victoria .	1,304	1,320
Queensland .	675	679
South Australia .	582	593
Western Australia .	469	475
Tasmania .	176	179
TOTAL .	4,541	4,589

NATIONAL ACCOUNTS
($A million)

	1969–70	1970–71	1971–72
GROSS DOMESTIC PRODUCT . . .	29,764	32,702	36,002
Indirect taxes *less* subsidies	3,031	3,312	3,703
GROSS DOMESTIC PRODUCT AT FACTOR COST .	26,733	29,390	32,299
of which:			
Agriculture, forestry and fishing .	2,193	2,040	n.a.
Mining and quarrying . . .	836	942	n.a.
Manufacturing	7,401	8,053	n.a.
Electricity, gas and water . .	940	1,004	n.a.
Building and construction . .	2,211	2,496	n.a.
Transport and communication .	2,237	2,465	n.a.
Commerce	3,668	3,893	n.a.
Public administration and defence .	1,115	1,328	n.a.
Community and business services .	2,472	2,943	n.a.
Other	3,659	4,228	n.a.
Depreciation allowances . .	2,665	2,850	3,065
DOMESTIC FACTOR INCOMES . . .	24,068	26,540	29,234
Indirect taxes *less* subsidies . .	3,031	3,312	3,703
Net income paid overseas . .	388	365	383
NATIONAL INCOME (AT MARKET PRICES) . .	26,711	29,487	32,554
EXPENDITURE ON GROSS DOMESTIC PRODUCT .	29,764	32,702	36,002
of which:			
Private final consumption expenditure .	17,702	19,419	21,325
Government final consumption expenditure	3,677	4,258	4,831
Gross fixed capital expenditure .	7,959	8,744	9,389
Increase in stocks . . .	495	445	−111
Statistical discrepancy . .	−60	−96	168
Export of goods and services . .	4,755	5,054	5,638
Less Import of goods and services .	4,764	5,122	5,238

OFFICIAL RESERVE ASSETS
(30 June—$A million)

	1971	1972	1973
Gold . . .	227	233	220
SDR's . . .	146	209	200
IMF Gold . .	186	149	143
Foreign Exchange .	1,720	3,173	3,767
TOTAL . .	2,280	3,764	4,331

CURRENCY IN CIRCULATION
(30 June—$A million)

	1971	1972	1973
Coins . . .	180.4	191.4	204.8
Notes . . .	1,369.4	1,499.1	1,757.8
TOTAL . .	1,549.8	1,690.5	1,962.6

BALANCE OF PAYMENTS
($A million)

	1970–71			1971–72		
	Credit	Debit	Balance	Credit	Debit	Balance
Goods and Services:						
Merchandise	4,216	3,790	426	4,729	3,791	938
Non-Monetary gold	15	—	15	13	—	13
Transportation	469	837	−368	496	833	−337
Travel	136	199	− 63	139	266	−127
Investment income	178	778	−600	239	852	−613
Government n.e.s.	82	127	− 45	90	124	− 34
Other services	134	234	−100	160	266	−106
Total	5,230	5,965	−735	5,866	6,131	−265
Transfer Payments:						
Private	181	134	47	226	172	54
Central Government	—	185	−185	—	205	−205
Total	181	319	−138	226	377	−151
Current Balance	—	—	−873	—	—	−416
Capital and Monetary Gold:						
Non-Monetary:						
Government transactions (net)	—	63	− 63	—	60	− 60
Private investment	1,612	95	1,517	1,499	138	1,361
Marketing authorities investment	—	43	− 43	—	45	− 45
Total	1,612	201	1,411	1,499	243	1,256
Monetary:						
Changes in official reserve assets	—	742	−742	—	1,544	−1,544
Allocation of Special Drawing Rights	64	—	64	63	—	63
Other offical monetary institutions transactions	10	—	10	8	—	8
Other	100	1	99	75	3	72
Total	174	743	−569	146	1,547	−1,401
Balancing item	33	—	33	562	—	562
Capital Balance			−873			416

Note: Any discrepancies between totals and sums of components in the above table are due to rounding.

CURRENT BALANCES—REGIONAL
($A million)

	1969–70	1970–71	1971–72		1969–70	1970–71	1971–72
United Kingdom:				*Japan:*			
Exports f.o.b.	483	486	441	Exports f.o.b.	1,018	1,182	1,352
Imports f.o.b.	774	800	762	Imports f.o.b.	472	557	606
Invisibles (net)	−393	−428	−385	Invisibles (net)	3	18	15
Balance on Current Account	−685	−743	−706	Balance on Current Account	549	644	761
Other Sterling Area:				*Other Non-sterling:*			
Exports f.o.b.	765	856	898	Exports f.o.b.	707	795	966
Imports f.o.b.	455	431	461	Imports f.o.b.	575	598	583
Invisibles (net)	−129	−170	−168	Invisibles (net)	−205	−225	−247
Balance on Current Account	181	255	269	Balance on Current Account	−71	−29	135
U.S.A.:				*Unallocated:*			
Exports f.o.b.	551	511	612	Exports f.o.b.	—	—	—
Imports f.o.b.	840	905	889	Imports f.o.b.	—	—	—
Invisibles (net)	−360	−360	−441	Invisibles (net)	2	−10	−7
Balance on Current Account	−650	−754	−718	Balance on Current Account	2	−10	−7
E.E.C.:				TOTAL:			
Exports f.o.b.	445	386	460	Exports f.o.b.	3,969	4,216	4,729
Imports f.o.b.	437	499	490	Imports f.o.b.	3,553	3,790	3,791
Invisibles (net)	−95	−124	−120	Invisibles (net)	−1,177	−1,299	−1,353
Balance on Current Account	−87	−236	−150	Balance on Current Account	−761	−873	−416

Note: Any discrepancies between totals and sums of components in the above table are due to rounding.

OVERSEAS INVESTMENT
($A million)

	U.K.	U.S.A.	Canada	Other Countries	IBRD	Total
	INFLOW					
1967–68	356	565	39	174	−23	1,110
1968–69	462	379	22	329	−24	1,171
1969–70	262	355	28	327	−20	951
1970–71	520	514	48	495	−16	1,561
1971–72	388	548	37	496	−16	1,453

	U.K.	New Zealand	U.S.A. and Canada	Papua and New Guinea	Other Countries	Total
	OUTFLOW					
1967–68	5	9	−1	21	8	42
1968–69	13	13	−2	32	5	60
1969–70	32	12	2	90	8	143
1970–71	−5	21	1	62	15	95
1971–72	−3	13	11	94	23	138

FOREIGN AID EXTENDED BY AUSTRALIA*
($A million)

	YEAR ENDED JUNE			
	1970	1971	1972	1973
Government Transfer Payments:				
Papua and New Guinea	116	131	132	158
Other Foreign Aid and Contributions	64	55	73	95
TOTAL	180	185	205	252

* Official only; excludes transfers by private persons and organizations to overseas recipients.

EXTERNAL TRADE
($A million, twelve months ending June 30th)

	1967–68	1968–69	1969–70	1970–71	1971–72	1972–73
Imports (f.o.b.)	3,264	3,469	3,881	4,150	4,008	4,120
Exports (f.o.b.)	3,045	3,374	4,137	4,376	4,896	6,220

COMMODITIES
($A'000)

IMPORTS	1970–71	1971–72	1972–73
Producers' Materials for use in:			
Building and Construction	146,947	135,533	166,951
Rural Industries	45,383	40,768	47,799
Motor Vehicle Assembly	288,100	256,379	228,520
Other Manufacturing	1,297,846	1,257,555	1,285,799
Capital Equipment:			
Producers' Equipment	981,930	915,335	855,672
Road Vehicles and Chassis	155,285	159,533	193,814
Railway Equipment, Ships, Aircraft	137,780	116,057	128,800
Finished Consumer Goods:			
Food, Beverages and Tobacco	157,234	165,121	171,241
Clothing and Accessories	57,108	76,438	88,196
Other	580,210	628,298	719,530
Fuels and Lubricants†	61,495	69,406	69,285
Auxiliary Aids to Production	99,823	100,515	93,486
Munitions, etc.	89,419	33,839	22,107
	4,098,560	3,954,775	4,071,201
Non-Merchandise Trade	51,468	53,590	48,555
TOTAL	4,150,028	4,008,365	4,119,756

† Excludes crude petroleum, which is included in "Other Producers' Materials".

EXPORTS	1970–71	1971–72	1972–73
Food and Live Animals	1,480,268	1,728,440	1,940,173
Butter	48,055	48,866	61,987
Cheese and Curd	18,382	22,421	21,688
Bacon and Hams	425	416	406
Meat of Bovine Animals	303,096	389,323	655,411
Meat of Sheep, Lambs and Goats	74,441	107,439	119,903
Pork	1,425	3,144	17,117
Dried Fruits	20,053	19,775	28,550
Preserved Fruit and Preparations	46,806	40,878	55,358
Wheat	433,000	418,529	274,274
Flour	20,051	13,712	13,112
Barley	50,820	74,344	38,512
Sugar	149,645	210,595	249,770
Beverages and Tobacco	14,590	15,616	15,242
Crude Materials, inedible, except Fuels	1,292,520	1,337,959	2,115,745
Wool (greasy)	493,073	524,518	1,067,175
Wool (scoured, etc.)	50,754	57,690	90,560
Sheep and Lamb skins (excl. pieces)	49,813	51,657	109,703
Mineral Fuels, Lubricants and Related Materials	247,862	300,425	341,110
Animal and Vegetable Oils and Fats	29,119	34,774	30,606
Chemicals	191,179	244,569	272,147
Manufactured Goods, classified chiefly by material	516,512	566,210	354,837
Machinery and Transport Equipment	325,085	374,681	498,049
Miscellaneous Manufactured Articles	73,566	100,637	98,322
Commodities and Transactions not classified according to kind	205,058	193,070	553,917
TOTAL	4,375,757	4,896,381	6,220,148

PRINCIPAL TRADING PARTNERS
($A '000)

	EXPORTS		IMPORTS	
	1971–72	1972–73	1971–72	1972–73
Belgium-Luxembourg .	43,272	60,642	28,220	36,629
Canada .	139,117	165,561	138,149	134,595
China, People's Republic of .	37,257	62,849	41,318	49,924
Egypt	86,878	40,890	88	167
Finland	11,454	10,942	17,028	24,367
France	127,900	188,606	69,136	75,530
Germany, Federal Republic of .	149,785	203,098	292,382	288,126
Hong Kong	100,386	94,930	68,121	80,307
India	36,395	37,399	35,215	31,952
Indonesia	57,209	74,629	14,312	13,586
Italy	89,391	132,923	87,368	86,586
Japan	1,360,152	1,933,946	628,569	738,633
Kuwait	13,537	15,771	33,621	30,227
Malaysia	70,111	97,921	31,030	38,430
Netherlands	56,215	63,911	66,816	55,790
New Zealand	277,125	325,622	112,264	130,115
Pakistan	6,002	7,430	7,426	4,572
Papua and New Guinea . .	156,965	134,793	23,576	24,595
Philippines	45,913	49,393	5,752	7,787
Poland	21,517	54,734	2,801	3,759
Saudi Arabia	15,383	13,695	20,010	20,206
Singapore	118,463	132,125	38,437	40,014
South Africa	79,237	10,953	21,420	20,621
Sri Lanka	8,037	95,120	11,989	9,620
Sweden	12,485	22,604	72,561	82,881
Switzerland	5,671	7,658	73,611	65,891
Taiwan	55,680	69,837	35,147	54,339
Thailand	37,305	36,285	7,415	7,034
U.S.S.R.	82,825	126,021	1,836	2,975
United Kingdom . . .	449,243	603,487	836,120	768,011
United States of America .	615,294	760,628	872,618	859,742
Viet-Nam, Republic of . .	8,017	8,823	13	34
Other Countries . . .	522,161	576,922	314,041	332,705
TOTAL . . .	4,896,381	6,220,148	4,008,365	4,119,756

TRANSPORT

		1968–69	1969–70	1970–71	1971–72
Railways:					
Route Mileage* . . .		25,095	25,060	25,022	25,055
Passengers . . .	('000)	447,437	450,122	452,530	403,816
Goods and Livestock .	('000 tons)	75,742	82,351	85,929	87,271
Roads:					
Motor Vehicles Registered* .	('000)	4,510	4,772	5,039	5,359
Overseas Shipping:					
Tonnage Entered . .	('000 tons)	36,419	44,496	50,820	53,144
Tonnage Cleared . .	('000 tons)	36,159	44,573	51,399	53,492
Air Transport, Internal Services:					
Mileage Flown . . .	('000)	60,348	66,241	71,212	72,036
Passengers Carried . . .		5,184,828	5,911,002	6,340,036	6,629,316
Freight . . .	(short tons)	89,950	100,100	100,752	99,079
Mail . . .	(short tons)	9,876	10,625	10,931	11,174
Air Transport, Overseas Services:					
Mileage Flown . . .	('000)	33,591	37,537	43,711	41,178
Passengers Carried . .		642,524	751,315	839,629	885,548
Freight . . .	(short tons)	18,537	21,165	23,650	23,105
Mail . . .	(short tons)	2,862	2,925	3,107	3,132

* June 30th.

TOURISM

	1969	1970	1971	1972
Number of Visitors (Arrivals)*	361,277	416,128	432,393	426,403

* i.e. intending to stay less than one year.

Tourist Spending (1970): $A129,000,000.

COMMUNICATIONS MEDIA
(At June 30th—'000)

	1970	1971	1972	1973
Telephones:				
Services in Operation . .	2,704	2,857	2,978	3,147
Instruments in service .	3,913	4,157	4,400	n.a.
Radio Licences* . . .	2,670	2,699	2,758	2,814
Television Licences* . .	2,758	2,845	2,939	3,013
Combined Licences . . .	2,275	2,337	2,420	2,493

* Includes combined radio and television licences.

EDUCATION
(1972)

	Number	Full-Time Teaching Staff	Students
Government Schools . . .	7,362	99,774*	2,228,941
Non-Government Schools . .	2,190	23,871	612,010
Universities . . .	15	8,216	128,668
Colleges of Advanced Education .	44	n.a.	52,170
Teachers' Colleges . . .	59	n.a.	25,754

* Preliminary.

Source: Commonwealth Bureau of Census and Statistics, Canberra 2600, A.C.T.

THE CONSTITUTION

PARLIAMENT

The legislative power of the Commonwealth is vested in a Federal Parliament, consisting of the Queen, represented by the Governor-General, a Senate, and a House of Representatives. The Governor-General may appoint such times for holding the sessions of the Parliament as he thinks fit, and may also from time to time, by Proclamation or otherwise, prorogue the Parliament, and may in like manner dissolve the House of Representatives. This power is limited by strict although unwritten constitutional understanding, and it is seldom that decisions on these matters would be made at the discretion of the Governor-General. After any general election Parliament must be summoned to meet not later than thirty days after the day appointed for the return of the writs. Parliament must meet at least once every year.

THE SENATE

The Senate is composed of ten Senators from each State, with two representing the Northern Territory and two the Australian Capital Territory, directly chosen for a period of six years by the people of the State, voting as one electorate. The Senators are elected by proportional representation. They are chosen for a term of six years and retire by rotation, half from each State on June 30th of each third year. The Senate may proceed to the dispatch of business notwithstanding the failure of any State to provide for its representation in the Senate.

If a Senator vacates his seat before the expiration of his term of service, the houses of Parliament of the State for which he was chosen shall, in joint session, choose a person to hold the place until the expiration of the term or until the election of a successor. If the State Parliament is not in session the Governor of the State appoints a Senator to hold office until Parliament reassembles, or until a new Senator is elected.

At least one-third of the members of the Senate must be present for the exercise of its powers.

THE HOUSE OF REPRESENTATIVES

In accordance with the Constitution, the total number of members of the House of Representatives must be as nearly as practicable double that of the Senate. The number in each State is in proportion to population, but under the Constitution must be at least five. At present the House of Representatives is composed of 125 members which includes 2 members for the internal Territories. Until recently these members, though able to join in all debates, were entitled to vote only on matters affecting their territories; full voting rights were extended to the member for the Australian Capital Territory in 1967 and to the member for the Northern Territory in 1968.

Members are elected by universal adult suffrage and voting is compulsory. Qualifications for Commonwealth franchise are possessed by any British subject, not under 18 years of age, subject to certain disqualifications (e.g. if of unsound mind), who has lived in Australia for six months continuously.

Members are chosen by the electors of their respective electorates by the preferential voting system.

The duration of the Parliament is limited to three years.

Qualification for membership of the House of Representatives are possessed by any British subject 18 years of age or over who has resided in the Commonwealth for at least three years and who is, or is qualified to become, an elector of the Commonwealth.

THE EXECUTIVE GOVERNMENT

The executive power of the Federal Government is vested in the Queen, and is exercised by the Governor-General, assisted by an Executive Council of Ministers of State. These Ministers are, or must become within three months, members of the Australian Parliament.

THE JUDICIAL POWER

The judicial power of the Commonwealth is vested in the High Court of Australia, in such other Federal Courts as the Australian Parliament creates, and in such other courts as it invests with Federal jurisdiction.

The High Court consists of a Chief Justice and not less than two other Justices, appointed by the Governor-General in Council. (There are at present a Chief Justice and six other Justices.) It has both an original and an appellate jurisdiction.

The High Court's original jurisdiction extends to all matters arising under any treaty, affecting representatives of other countries, in which the Commonwealth of Australia or its representative is a party, between States or between residents of different States or between a State and a resident of another State, and in which a writ of *Mandamus*, or prohibition, or an injunction is sought against an officer of the Commonwealth of Australia. It also extends to matters arising under the Constitution or involving its interpretation, and to any other matters empowered by the Australian Parliament.

The appellate jurisdiction extends to appeals from all judgments, decrees, orders and sentences of its own Justices exercising original jurisdiction, of any other Federal Court or court exercising Federal jurisdiction and of the Supreme Court of any State or any other State court from which an appeal lies to the Queen in Council. In 1968 appeals from the High Court to the Queen in Council were abolished in most, if not all, matters involving the constitution and laws passed by the Australian Parliament.

An amendment of the Conciliation and Arbitration Act assented to on June 30th, 1956 altered the structure of the arbitration machinery by separating the judicial and arbitral functions. The Commonwealth Industrial Court was set up to deal with judicial matters under the Act and the Commonwealth Conciliation and Arbitration Commission to handle the function of conciliation and arbitration.

The Commonwealth Industrial Court is composed of a Chief Judge and five other Judges. The Commonwealth Conciliation and Arbitration Commission comprises a President, not less than two Deputy Presidents, a Senior Commissioner, not less than five Commissioners, and a number of Conciliators. Also, since 1928, jurisdiction in bankruptcy and insolvency is administered by Commonwealth Bankruptcy Courts. There is a Federal Supreme Court in the Australian Capital Territory and in the Northern Territory. State courts, usually courts of summary jurisdiction, are invested with Federal judicial power, principally to deal with offences created by Federal statutes.

THE STATES

The Commonwealth Constitution safeguards the Constitution of each State by providing that it shall continue as at the establishment of the Commonwealth, except as altered in accordance with its own provisions. When a State law is inconsistent with a law of the Commonwealth, the latter prevails, and the former is invalid to the extent of the inconsistency. However, the legislation of the Commonwealth Parliament is limited to those matters which are listed in Section 51 of the Constitution, while the States possess, as well as concurrent powers in those matters, residual legislative powers enabling them to legislate in any way for "the peace, order and good Government" of their respective territories.

The States may not raise or maintain naval or military forces, or impose taxes on any property belonging to the Commonwealth, nor may the Commonwealth tax State property. The State may not coin money.

The Commonwealth may not make any law for establishing any religion or for prohibiting the exercise of any religion, and no religious test may be imposed as a qualification for any office under the Commonwealth.

The Commonwealth is charged with protecting every State against invasion, and, on the application of a State Executive Government, against domestic violence.

Provision is made under the Constitution for the admission of new States and for the establishment of new States within the Commonwealth.

ALTERATION OF THE CONSTITUTION

Proposed laws for the alteration of the Constitution must be passed by an absolute majority of each House of Parliament, and not less than two or more than six months after its passage the proposed law must be submitted in each State to the qualified electors.

In the event of one House twice rejecting a proposed law which has already received an absolute majority in the other House, the Governor-General may submit the proposed law to the electors. If, in a majority of the States a majority of the electors voting approve the proposed law and if a majority of all the electors voting also approve, it shall be presented to the Governor-General for Royal Assent.

No alteration diminishing the proportionate representation of any State in either House of the Parliament, or the minimum number of representatives of a State in the House of Representatives, or increasing, diminishing or altering the limits of the State, or in any way affecting the provisions of the Constitution in relation thereto, shall become law unless the majority of the electors voting in that State approve the proposed law.

A Constitutional Convention was held in Sydney in September 1973 to review the Constitution for the first time since it was established on January 1st, 1901. Following this, four standing committees were set up to inquire into 15 areas of the Australian Constitution. The recommendations of the committees will be submitted to the next meeting of the convention, expected to be held in 1974.

NEW SOUTH WALES

The executive power is in the hands of a Governor, appointed by the Crown, who is assisted by a Cabinet.

The Legislative Power is vested in a Parliament of two Houses, the Legislative Council and the Legislative Assembly. The former consists of sixty members, elected at a joint sitting of both Houses of Parliament, for a term of twelve years, fifteen members retiring every three years. The Legislative Assembly consists of ninety-four members, and sits for three years.

VICTORIA

The legislative authority is vested in a bicameral Parliament: the Upper House, or Legislative Council of thirty-six members, elected for six years, and the Lower House, or Legislative Assembly, of seventy-three members, elected for three years. One-half of the members of the Council retire every three years.

In the exercise of the executive the Governor is assisted by a Cabinet of responsible Ministers. Not more than five members of the Council and not more than twelve members of the Assembly may occupy salaried office at any one time.

QUEENSLAND

Legislative power rests with a unicameral Parliament composed of eighty-two members elected from eighty-two districts for a term of three years.

SOUTH AUSTRALIA

The Constitution vests the legislative power in a Parliament elected by the people and consisting of a Legislative Council and a House of Assembly. The Council is composed of twenty members, one-half of whom retire every three years. Their places are filled by new members elected from each of the five districts into which the State is divided for this purpose. The executive has no authority to dissolve this body.

The forty-seven members of the House of Assembly are elected for three years from forty-seven electoral districts.

The executive power is vested in a Governor, appointed by the Crown, and an Executive Council consisting of ten responsible Ministers.

WESTERN AUSTRALIA

In 1890 the administration was vested in the Governor, a Legislative Council and a Legislative Assembly. The Council was, at first, nominated by the Governor, but it was provided that in the event of the population of the colony reaching 60,000 it should be elective. This figure was reached in 1893.

According to the present Constitution, the Legislative Council consists of thirty members, each of the fifteen provinces returning two members. Election is for a term of six years, and one-half of the members retire every three years.

The Legislative Assembly consists of fifty-one members, elected for three years, each representing one electorate.

The entire management and control of the unalienated lands of the Crown in Western Australia is vested in the State Legislature.

TASMANIA

The administration is vested in a Governor acting upon the advice of a Legislative Council and House of Assembly. The Council consists of nineteen members who sit for six years, retiring in rotation. There is no power to dissolve the Council. The House of Assembly has thirty members elected for five years.

NORTHERN TERRITORY

By a Federal Act of 1947 a Legislative Council (sitting at Darwin) was set up, consisting of the Administrator, 7 official members and 6 elected members. At present the Council consists of an elected President, 6 nominated official members and 11 elected members. The Northern Territory is administered on behalf of the Commonwealth Government by the Administrator and the Department of the Northern Territory in Darwin. In addition the Legislative Council is given the power to make Ordinances for the peace order and good government of the Northern Territory.

AUSTRALIAN CAPITAL TERRITORY

The Australian Capital Territory within which the Seat of Government is situated, is administered by the Commonwealth Government. The main department assisting in this regard is the Department of the Australian Capital Territory. Under legislation passed by the Commonwealth Parliament the Governor-General is given power to make ordinances for the peace order and good government of the Territory. There is established in the Territory an elected Advisory Council which may advise the Government on matters affecting the Territory.

THE GOVERNMENT

(April 1974*)*

Head of State: H.M. Queen ELIZABETH II.

Governor-General: H.E. the Rt. Hon. Sir JOHN KERR, K.C.M.G., LL.B., Q.C.

FEDERAL MINISTRY

Prime Minister: Hon. E. GOUGH WHITLAM, Q.C.

Deputy Prime Minister and Minister for Defence: Hon. LANCE BARNARD.

Treasurer: Hon. FRANK CREAN.

Minister for Overseas Trade: Hon. Dr. JAMES CAIRNS.

Attorney-General, Leader in the Senate and Minister for Customs and Excise: Senator the Hon. LIONEL MURPHY, Q.C.

Minister for Immigration: Hon. ALBERT GRASSBY.

Minister for Science and Minister assisting the Minister for Foreign Affairs (in matters relating to Papua New Guinea): Hon. WILLIAM MORRISON.

Minister for Social Security: Hon. WILLIAM HAYDEN.

Minister for Northern Development and Northern Territory: Hon. Dr. REX PATTERSON.

Minister for Primary Industry: Senator the Hon. KENNETH WRIEDT.

Minister for Media: Senator the Hon. DOUGLAS McCLELLAND.

Minister for Services and Property and Leader of the House of Representatives: Hon. FREDERICK DALY.

Minister for Foreign Affairs and Deputy Leader in the Senate: Senator the Hon. DONALD WILLESEE.

Minister for Aboriginal Affairs: Senator the Hon. JAMES CAVANAGH.

Minister for Labour: Hon. CLYDE CAMERON.

Minister for Urban and Regional Development: Hon. THOMAS UREN.

Minister for Transport: Hon. CHARLES JONES.

Minister for Education: Hon. KIM BEAZLEY.

Minister for Health: Hon. Dr. DOUGLAS EVERINGHAM.

Minister for Environment and Conservation: Hon. Dr. MOSS CASS.

Postmaster-General, Special Minister of State and Minister assisting the Prime Minister: Hon. LIONEL BOWEN.

Minister for Housing and Construction: Hon. LESLIE JOHNSON.

Minister for Capital Territory: Hon. GORDON BRYANT.

Minister for Minerals and Energy: Hon. REGINALD CONNOR.

Minister for Repatriation and Minister assisting the Minister for Defence: Senator the Hon. REGINALD BISHOP.

Minister for Tourism and Recreation and Minister assisting the Treasurer: Hon. FRANCIS STEWART.

Minister for Secondary Industry and Supply: Hon. KEPPEL ENDERBY.

ADMINISTRATORS OF TERRITORIES

Northern Territory: Hon. FREDERICK C. CHANEY, C.B.E., A.F.C.

Papua New Guinea: THOMAS CRITCHLEY.

Norfolk Island: Air Commodore E. T. PICKERD, O.B.E., D.F.C.

Cocos (Keeling) Islands: C. McMANUS (Official Representative).

Christmas Island: F. S. EVATT.

CHIEFS OF STAFF

Chairman of Chiefs of Staff Committee: Admiral Sir VICTOR SMITH, K.B.E., C.B., D.S.C.

Chief of the Naval Staff: Vice-Admiral H. D. STEVENSON, C.B.E.

Chief of the Air Staff: Air Marshal C. F. READ, C.B., C.B.E., D.F.C., A.F.C.

Chief of the General Staff: Lt.-Gen. FRANK G. HASSETT, C.B., C.B.E., D.S.O., M.V.O.

DIPLOMATIC REPRESENTATION

HIGH COMMISSIONS AND EMBASSIES ACCREDITED TO AUSTRALIA
(Canberra unless otherwise stated.)
(HC) High Commission; (E) Embassy.

Argentina: 58 Mugga Way (E); *Ambassador:* J. GÓMEZ ERRAZURIZ.

*Austria: Ainslie Bldg., 39 Ainslie Ave., Civic Centre (E); *Chargé d'Affaires a.i.:* Dr. ROBERT KARAS.

Bangladesh: 43 Hampton Circuit, Yarralumla (HC); *High Commissioner:* S. A. M. S. KIBRIA.

Belgium: 19 Arkana St., Yarralumla (E); *Ambassador:* ELI LUYCKX.

*Brazil: 127 Mugga Way, Red Hill (E); *Ambassador:* LEONARDO E. DO NASCIMENTO E SILVA.

Bulgaria: 36 Imam Bondjol, Jakarta (E); *Ambassador:* P. KARAPENEV.

*Burma: 85 Mugga Way, Red Hill (E); *Ambassador:* U MAUNG MAUNG.

Canada: Commonwealth Ave. (HC); *High Commissioner:* J. J. McCARDLE (also accred. to Fiji).

Chile: P.O.B. E118 (E); *Ambassador:* JULIO REITHMULLER.

China, People's Republic: (E); *Ambassador:* WANG KUO-CHUAN.

Czechoslovakia: (E); *Ambassador:* J. PINKAVA.

Denmark: P.O.B. 111, Wellington D.I., New Zealand (E); *Ambassador:* P. VON DER HUDE.

Egypt: 125 Monaro Crescent, Red Hill (E); *Ambassador:* KHAIRY AHMED RAGHEB EL AYOUTY.

Fiji: 9 Beagle St., Red Hill (HC); *High Commissioner:* R. N. NAIR.

*Finland: 83 Endeavour St., Red Hill (E); *Ambassador:* T. MENTULA.

France: 6 Darwin Ave., Yarralumla (E); *Ambassador:* GABRIEL VAN LAETHEM.

German Democratic Republic: 12 Bengle St., Red Hill (E); *Ambassador:* H. RICHTER.

Germany, Federal Republic: Empire Circuit, Yarralumla (E); *Ambassador:* Dr. HEINZ VOIGT.

Ghana: 131 Mugga Way, Red Hill (HC); *High Commissioner:* J. OWUSU-AKYEAMPONG (also accred. to Malaysia).

*Greece: 22 Arthur Circle, Forrest (E); *Ambassador:* ALEXIS STEPHANOU.

India: 92 Mugga Way, Red Hill (HC); *High Commissioner:* J. S. DODDAMANI (acting).

*Indonesia: 8 Darwin Ave., Yarralumla (E); *Ambassador:* HER TASNING.

Iran: City Mutual Bldg., Hobart Place (E); *Ambassador:* H. T. ESHRAGHI.

*Ireland: 2nd Floor, Bank House, Civic Square (E); *Ambassador:* GERARD WOODS.

*Israel: 6 Turrana St., Yarralumla (E); *Ambassador:* M. ERELL.

Italy: 27 State Circle, Deakin (E); *Ambassador:* Dr. PAOLO CANALI.

Japan: 112 Empire Circuit, Yarralumla (E); *Chargé d'Affaires a.i.:* K. KIMURA.

Khmer Republic: 5 Canterbury Crescent, Deakin (E); *Chargé d'Affaires a.i.:* THEAM BUN SRUN.

*Korea, Republic: 55 Mugga Way, Red Hill (E); *Ambassador:* LO SUCK CHAN.

Laos: 28 Melbourne Ave., Deakin (E); *Ambassador:* K. PRADITH.

Lebanon: 1 Arkana St., Yarralumla (E); *Ambassador.* SHAFIK GHARZUDDINE.

*Malaysia: 71 State Circle, Yarralumla (HC); *High Commissioner:* A. FAIZ HAMID (acting).

Malta: 261 La Perouse St., Red Hill (HC); *High Commissioner:* J. L. FORACE.

Mexico: 1 Bengle St., Red Hill (E); *Ambassador:* J. GAMAS-TORRUCO.

Nepal: (E); *Ambassador* (*designate*): PRAKASH CHAD THAKUR.

Netherlands: 120 Empire Circuit, Yarralumla (E); *Ambassador:* R. C. PEKELHARING.

New Zealand: M.L.C. Building, London Circuit, Civic Centre (HC); *High Commissioner:* ERIC CHAPMAN.

Norway: 3 Zeehan St., Red Hill (E); *Ambassador:* A. J. JAKOBSEN.

*Pakistan: 59 Franklin St., Forrest (E); *Ambassador:* M. M. ABBAS.

Peru: P.O.B. 508, Manuka (E); *Ambassador:* G. A. BARREDA.

*Philippines: Moonah Place, Yarralumla (E); *Ambassador:* G. G. ABAD.

Poland: 10 Millen St., Hughes (E); *Chargé d'Affaires a.i.:* R. HOSZOWSKI.

Portugal: 22 Bougainville St., Manuka (E); *Ambassador:* Dr. CARLOS A. EMPIS WEMANS.

Romania: (E); *Ambassador:* N. FINANTU.

Singapore: 81 Mugga Way, Red Hill (HC); *High Commissioner:* P. COOMARASWAMY.

South Africa: Corner of State Circle and Rhodes Place, Yarralumla (E); *Ambassador:* J. B. MILLS.

Spain: 19 Beagle St., Red Hill (E); *Ambassador:* JUAN RAMÓN PARELLADA.

*Sri Lanka: 35 Empire Circuit, Forrest (HC); *High Commissioner:* JUSTIN SIRIWARDENE.

Sweden: Turrana St., Yarralumla (E); *Ambassador:* PER ANGER.

Switzerland: 44 Endeavour St., Red Hill (E); *Ambassador:* Dr. MAX KOENIG.

Thailand: 15 Mugga Way, Red Hill (E); *Ambassador:* VIVADH NA POMBEJRA.

Turkey: 60 Mugga Way, Red Hill (E); *Ambassador:* HIKMET BENSAN.

U.S.S.R.: 78 Canberra Ave., Griffith (E); *Ambassador:* D. P. MUSIN.

United Kingdom: Commonwealth Ave. (HC); *High Commissioner:* Sir MORRICE JAMES.

U.S.A.: Chancery, Yarralumla (E); *Ambassador:* MARSHALL GREEN.

Uruguay: 22 Bougainville St., Manuka (E); *Chargé d'Affaires:* F. MONTERO.

Vatican: 40 Edward St., Sydney: *Nuncio* Mgr. PARO GINO.

Viet-Nam, Republic: 39 National Circuit, Forrest (E); *Ambassador:* N. P. THIEP.

Yugoslavia: 27 Endeavour St., Red Hill (E); *Ambassador:* UROS VIDOVIC.

* Also accredited to New Zealand.

The following countries are represented by Consulates General or Consulates: Bolivia, Colombia, Costa Rica, Dominican Republic, Ecuador, Ethiopia, Guatemala, Haiti, Hungary, Iceland, Liberia, Monaco, Nauru and Panama. Diplomatic relations at ambassadorial level have been established with the Democratic Republic of Viet-Nam (North Viet-Nam).

COMMONWEALTH PARLIAMENT

Note: A General Election for both Houses was held in May 1974.

THE SENATE
(*April* 1974)

President: Senator the Hon. Sir Magnus Cameron Cormack, K.B.E.

Chairman of Committees: Senator E. W. Prowse.

Leader of the Government: Senator the Hon. Lionel K. Murphy, Q.C.

Leader of the Opposition: Senator R. G. Withers.

Leader of the Australian Democratic Labor Party: Senator F. P. McManus.

Clerk: J. R. Odgers, C.B.E.

There are ten Senators from each of the six states.

HOUSE OF REPRESENTATIVES
(*April* 1974)

Speaker: Hon. James Francis Cope.

Deputy Speaker and Chairman of Committees: G. G. D. Scholes, M.P.

Leader of the Government: Hon. Frederick Daly, M.P.

Leader of the Opposition: Rt. Hon. Billy Snedden, Q.C., M.P.

Clerk: N. J. Parkes, O.B.E.

STATE GOVERNMENTS

(L) Liberal Party; (CP) Country Party.

NEW SOUTH WALES

Governor: H.E. Sir Roden Cutler, V.C., K.C.M.G., K.C.V.O., C.B.E., K.ST.J.

Liberal-Country Coalition Ministry
(*March* 1974)

Premier and Treasurer: Hon. Sir Robert William Askin, K.C.M.G., M.L.A. (L).

Deputy Premier, Minister for Local Government and Highways: Hon. Sir Charles B. Cutler, K.B.E., E.D., M.L.A. (CP).

Minister for Education: Hon. E. A. Willis, B.A., M.L.A. (L).

Chief Secretary and Minister for Sport: Hon. I. R. Griffith, M.L.A. (L).

Minister for Youth and Community Services: Hon. R. O. Healy (L).

Minister for Agriculture: Hon. G. R. Crawford, D.C.M., M.L.A. (CP).

Attorney-General: Hon. K. M. McCaw, M.L.A. (L).

Minister for Public Works: Hon. L. A. Punch, M.L.A. (CP).

Minister for Transport: Hon. M. A. Morris, M.L.A. (L).

Minister for Decentralization and Development: Hon. J. C. Bruxner, M.L.A. (CP).

Minister for Lands and Tourism: Hon. T. L. Lewis, M.L.A. (L).

Minister for Mines and Power and Assistant Treasurer: Hon. W. C. Fife, M.L.A. (L).

Minister for Planning and Environment, and Vice-President of the Executive Council: Hon. Sir J. B. M. Fuller, M.L.C. (CP).

Minister for Housing and Minister for Co-operative Societies: Hon. L. F. McGinty, M.B.E., M.L.A. (L).

Minister for Justice: Hon. J. C. Maddison, B.A., LL.B., M.L.A. (L).

Minister for Health: Hon. J. L. Waddy, O.B.E., D.F.C., M.L.A. (L).

Minister for Labour and Industry and Consumer Affairs: Hon. F. M. Hewitt, M.L.C. (L).

Minister for Cultural Activities and Conservation: Hon. G. F. Freudenstein, M.L.A. (L).

Legislature

Legislative Council: Pres. Hon. Sir Harry Vincent Budd; Chair. of Committees Hon. Thomas S. McKay, B.A., LL.B.

Legislative Assembly: Speaker Hon. James Alexander Cameron, LL.M.; Chair. of Committees James Hill Brown.

VICTORIA

Governor: H.E. Maj.-Gen. Sir Rohan Delacombe, K.C.M.G., K.C.V.O., K.B.E., C.B., D.S.O., K.ST.J.

Liberal Ministry
(*March* 1974)

Premier, Treasurer and Minister for Arts: Hon. Rupert J. Hamer, E.D., M.L.C.

Deputy Premier and Minister for Education: Hon. L. H. S. Thompson, M.L.C.

Chief Secretary: Hon. J. F. Rossiter, M.L.A.

Minister for Transport: Hon. E. R. Meagher, M.B.E., E.D., M.L.A.

Minister for Agriculture: Hon. I. W. Smith, M.L.A.

Minister for Public Works: Hon. Roberts C. Dunstan, D.S.O., M.L.A.

Minister for Youth, Sport and Recreation and Assistant Minister for Education: Hon. B. J. Dixon, M.L.A.

Minister for Water Supply and Minister for Forests: Hon. F. J. Granter, M.L.C.

Minister for Lands, Minister for Soldier Settlement and Minister for Conservation: Hon. W. A. BORTHWICK M.L.A.

Minister for Fuel and Power and Minister for Mines: Hon. J. C. M. BALFOUR, M.L.A.

Minister for Local Government and Minister for Planning: Hon. ALAN J. HUNT, M.L.C.

Minister for State Development and Decentralization, Minister for Tourism and Minister for Immigration: Hon. MURRAY BYRNE, M.L.C.

Minister for Housing and Minister for Aboriginal Affairs: Hon. V. O. DICKIE, M.L.C.

Minister for Health: Hon. A. H. SCANLAN, M.L.A.

Minister for Labour and Industry and Minister for Consumer Affairs: Hon. J. A. RAFFERTY, M.L.A.

Minister for Social Welfare: Hon. W. V. HOUGHTON, M.L.C.

Attorney-General: Hon. V. F. WILCOX, M.L.A.

LEGISLATURE

Legislative Council: Pres. Hon. R. W. GARRETT, A.F.C., A.E.A., M.L.C.; Chair. of Committees Hon. G. J. NICOL, Clerk of the Council A. R. B. McDONNELL, J.P.

Legislative Assembly: Speaker Hon. KENNETH WHEELER, M.P.; Chairman of Committees Ian Francis McLaren, O.B.E., M.P.; Clerk of the Assembly J. H. CAMPBELL.

QUEENSLAND

Governor: H.E. Air Marshal Sir COLIN T. HANNAH, K.C.M.G., K.B.E., C.B.

LIBERAL-COUNTRY COALITION MINISTRY

(*March* 1974)

Premier: Hon. JOHANNES BJELKE-PETERSEN, M.L.A. (CP).

Treasurer and Deputy Premier: Hon. Sir GORDON W. W. CHALK, K.B.E., M.L.A. (L).

Minister for Education and Cultural Activities: Hon. Sir ALAN R. FLETCHER, M.L.A. (CP).

Minister for Development and Industrial Affairs: Hon. F. A. CAMPBELL, M.L.A. (L).

Minister for Mines and Main Roads: Hon. R. E. CAMM, M.L.A. (CP).

Minister for Health: Hon. S. D. TOOTH, M.L.A. (L).

Minister for Justice and Attorney-General: Hon. W. E. KNOX, M.L.A. (L).

Minister for Transport: Hon. K. W. HOOPER, M.L.A. (L).

Minister for Local Government and Electricity: Hon. H. A. McKECHNIE, M.L.A. (CP).

Minister for Lands and Forestry: Hon. W. A. R. RAE, M.L.A. (CP).

Minister for Tourism, Sport and Welfare Services: Hon. J. D. HERBERT, M.L.A. (L).

Minister for Works, Housing and Police: Hon. A. M. HODGES, M.L.A. (CP).

Minister for Primary Industries: Hon. V. B. SULLIVAN, M.L.A. (CP).

Minister for Conservation, Marine and Aboriginal Affairs: Hon. N. T. E. HEWITT, M.M., M.L.A. (CP).

LEGISLATURE

Legislative Assembly: Speaker Hon. W. H. LONERGAN; Chair. of Committees W. D. LICKISS; Clerk C. GEORGE.

SOUTH AUSTRALIA

Governor: H.E. Sir MARK OLIPHANT, K.B.E., F.R.S., LL.D., PH.D., F.A.A.

LABOR MINISTRY

(*March* 1974)

Premier and Treasurer: Hon. DONALD A. DUNSTAN, Q.C., M.P.

Deputy Premier, Minister of Works and Minister of Marine: Hon. JAMES DESMOND CORCORAN, M.P.

Chief Secretary and Minister of Lands, Repatriation and Irrigation: Hon. A. F. KNEEBONE, M.L.C.

Minister for Development and Mines and Minister assisting the Premier: Hon. DONALD HOPGOOD.

Minister of Agriculture and Forests: Hon. THOMAS MANNIX CASEY, M.L.C.

Minister for Conservation, Minister of Sport and Recreation and Minister of Fisheries: Hon. GLEN R. BROOMHILL, M.P.

Attorney-General and Minister of Community Welfare: Hon. LEONARD JAMES KING, Q.C., M.P.

Minister of Education: Hon. HUGH RICHARD HUDSON, M.P.

Minister of Local Government and Minister of Transport: Hon. GEOFFREY THOMAS VIRGO, M.P.

Minister of Labour and Industry: Hon. DAVID H. McKEE, M.P.

Minister of Health: Hon. D. H. L. BANFIELD, M.L.C.

LEGISLATURE

Legislative Council: Pres. and Chair. of Committees Hon. Sir LYELL McEWIN, K.B.E.; Clerk of the Parliaments and of the Legislative Council I. J. BALL, A.A.S.A., A.C.I.S.

House of Assembly: Speaker Hon. J. R. RYAN; Chair. of Committees A. R. BURDON; Clerk A. F. R. DODD.

WESTERN AUSTRALIA

Governor: H.E. Air Commodore H. EDWARDS.

LABOR MINISTRY

(*April* 1974)

Premier, Treasurer and Minister Co-ordinating Economic and Regional Development: Hon. Sir CHARLES COURT, O.B.E., M.L.A.

Deputy Premier, Minister for Agriculture: Hon. W. R. McPHARLIN, M.L.A.

Minister for Works, Water Supply and Housing: Hon. D. H. O'NEIL, M.L.A.

Minister for Justice and Leader of the Government in the Legislative Council: Hon. N. McNEILL, B.SC., M.L.A.

Minister for Transport, Traffic and Police: Hon. R. J. O'CONNOR, M.L.A.

Minister for Education, Cultural Affairs and Recreation: Hon. G. C. MACKINNON, M.L.C.

Chief Secretary, Minister for Conservation and the Environment, Fisheries and Fauna: Hon. M. E. STEPHENS, M.L.A.

Minister for Labour and Industry, Consumer Affairs, Immigration and Tourism: Hon. W. L. GRAYDEN, M.L.A.

Minister for Industrial Development, Mines, Fuel and Energy: Hon. A. MENSAROS, M.L.A.

Minister for Local Government, Urban Development and Town Planning: Hon. E. C. RUSHTON, M.L.A.

Minister for Lands, Forests and the North West: Hon. K. A. RIDGE, M.L.A.

Minister for Health and Community Welfare: Hon. N. E. BAXTER, M.L.C.

LEGISLATURE

Legislative Council: Pres. Hon. L. C. DIVER; Chair. of Committees Hon. NORMAN ERIC BAXTER; Clerk of the Council and Clerk of the Parliaments JOHN B. ROBERTS, M.B.E., E.D., J.P.

Legislative Assembly: Speaker Hon. DANIEL NORTON; Chair. of Committees THOMAS H. BATEMAN; Clerk of Assembly JOCELYN C. BARTLETT, D.F.M., J.P.

TASMANIA

Governor: H.E. the Hon. Sir STANLEY BURBURY, K.B.E., K.ST.J.

LABOR MINISTRY
(March 1974)

Premier, Treasurer and Minister for Mines: Hon. ERIC ELLIOTT REECE, M.H.A.

Deputy Premier, Attorney-General, Minister for the Environment and Minister Administering the Racing and Gambling Act: Hon. MERVYN G. EVERETT, Q.C., B.A., LL.B., M.H.A.

Chief Secretary and Minister for Transport: Hon. N. L. C. BATT, B.A., M.H.A.

Minister for Lands and Works and Local Government: Hon. MICHAEL T. C. BARNARD, M.H.A.

Minister for Agriculture and Fisheries, National Parks and Wildlife Service: Hon. LLOYD E. A. COSTELLO, M.H.A.

Minister for Industrial Development and Forests, Minister Administering the Hydro-Electric Commission and Minister Assisting the Treasurer: Hon. ROY F. FAGAN, B.A., LL.B., M.H.A.

Minister for Health, Social Welfare and Road Safety: Hon. ALLAN J. FOSTER, M.B., B.S., M.R.A.C.G.P., M.R.C.P., M.H.A.

Minister for Housing: Hon. DOUGLAS A. LOWE, M.H.A.

Minister for Education: Hon. WILLIAM A. NEILSON.

Minister for Tourism and Immigration and Minister for Police and Licensing: Hon. B. MILLER, M.L.C.

LEGISLATURE

Legislative Council: Pres. Hon. C. B. M. FENTON; Chair. of Committees J. H. DIXON; Clerk of the Council G. B. EDWARDS.

House of Assembly: Speaker Hon. ERIC W. BARNARD; Chair. of Committees GEOFFREY D. CHISHOLM; Clerk of the House, B. G. MURPHY.

NORTHERN TERRITORY
(see Constitution)

Minister for the Northern Territory: Hon. REX PATTERSON, M.P.

Administrator: Hon. FREDERICK C. CHANEY, C.B.E., A.F.C.

Directors, Land and Community Development Division: T. J. BROOKS, V. T. O'BRIEN, D. P. LAMPE (acting), G. W. GODWIN.

Directors, Resource Development Division: J. S. LAKE, B. HART, P. PURICH, R. J. McARTHUR.

Directors, Social and Commercial Affairs Division: D. T. LANGFORD (acting), J. C. McDONNELL.

Directors, Management Legislation and Planning Division: A. A. SHAKESPEARE, N. LYNAGH (acting), C. J. STEPHENS.

POLITICAL PARTIES

Australian Labor Party: Ainslie Bldg., 39 Ainslie Ave., Canberra, A.C.T. 2601; f. 1891, for the democratic socialization of industry, production, distribution and exchange; Leader of the Federal Parliamentary Labor Party, the Prime Minister, the Hon. E. GOUGH WHITLAM, Q.C., M.H.R.; Leader of the Party in the Senate, Senator the Hon. LIONEL MURPHY, Q.C.; National Pres. R. J. L. HAWKE; Gen. Sec. DAVID COMBE.

Liberal Party of Australia, The: Federal Secretariat, National Headquarters Bldg., cnr. Blackall and Macquarie Sts., Barton, Canberra 2600; f. 1944; the Party supports freedom of enterprise, social justice and initiative. It has always maintained uncompromising opposition to doctrinaire socialism and communism. The Leader of the Party is the Rt. Hon. BILLY SNEDDEN, Q.C., M.P.; the Leader in the Senate, Senator R. G. WITHERS; the Federal President is R. J. SOUTHEY, C.M.G.

Australian Country Party, The: John McEwen House, National Circuit Canberra, A.C.T. 2600; f. 1916; the principal objectives of the Party are the betterment of conditions in rural and agricultural communities through improved marketing facilities, more effective Parliamentary representation of country people, the encouragement of desirable immigrants, and the promotion of the study of all matters relating to agricultural and primary production. The Party upholds the integrity of the Commonwealth; Federal Parliamentary Leader Hon. J. DOUGLAS ANTHONY; Federal Dir. P. P. WARRICK; Gen. Sec. JAMES W. CUMING; publ. *The Countryman.*

Australian Democratic Labor Party: 561-7 George St., Sydney; formed 1956 following a split in the Australian Labor Party; Pres. J. D. BROSNAN; Gen. Sec. JOHN KANE; Parliamentary Leader Senator F. P. McMANUS; Deputy Leader Senator GORDON BYRNE.

Australia Party: G.P.O. Box 2562, Sydney 2001; f. July 1969 "to satisfy an urgent need for an alternative in the political management of Australia"; successor to the *Australian Reform Movement*; on Defence and Foreign Affairs the Party advocates an independent Australia adequately armed for defence but opposed to intervention in the internal affairs of other countries, and the development of friendly relations with all countries, especially in Asia, backed by aid and trade; on domestic issues the Party's policies include a restructured education system financed by increased Federal expenditure, parliamentary reform based on longer sessions and the establishment of standing committees along American lines, encouragement of entry of immigrants meeting specified educational standards within quota limits; mems. over 3,000 (1973); National Convenor GORDON BARTON.

Farm and Town Party: Horsham, Vic.; f. March 1972; advocates economic justice for rural people; Chair. A. C. EVERETT.

Socialist Party of Australia: 111 Sussex St., Sydney, N.S.W.; f. Dec. 1971; 1,000 mems.; aims: to bring about a socialist society in Australia by working with the trade union movement and to foster international co-operation; Pres. P. CLANCY; Gen. Sec. P. SYMON.

DEFENCE

Armed Forces (1973): Total strength 73,330; army 33,100, navy 17,460, air force 22,770; military service is voluntary.

Equipment: The army has British medium tanks and scout cars and American helicopters. Other material includes heavy artillery and light aircraft. The navy comprises mainly destroyers, minesweepers and patrol boats as well as an aircraft carrier. The air force has 210 combat aircraft mostly of British, French and American manufacture.

Defence Expenditure: Estimated defence spending for 1972 was $A1,323 million (U.S. $1,575 million).

Chair. Chiefs of Staff Committee: Admiral Sir VICTOR SMITH, K.B.E., C.B., D.S.C.

Chief of the Naval Staff: Vice-Admiral H. D. STEVENSON, C.B.E.

Chief of the Air Staff: Air Vice-Marshal C. F. READ, C.B.E., A.F.C., D.F.C.

Chief of the General Staff: Lt.-Gen. FRANK G. HASSETT, C.B., C.B.E., D.S.O., M.V.O.

JUDICIAL SYSTEM

The judicial power of the Commonwealth is vested in a Federal Supreme Court, the High Court of Australia, consisting of a Chief Justice and six Justices and such other courts as the Commonwealth Parliament may create. Parliament can also vest certain federal jurisdiction in State courts. The High Court has original jurisdiction in all matters arising under treaties or affecting representatives of other countries, and in certain matters in which the Commonwealth or the States are concerned. It also hears and determines appeals from judgments of its own Justices exercising original jurisdiction, and from judgments of any other Federal Court or of the Supreme Court of any State. In 1968 appeals from the High Court when acting in a Federal Capacity to the Privy Council Judicial Committee were ended but appeals direct from Australian States have continued.

HIGH COURT OF AUSTRALIA

Chief Justice: Rt. Hon. Sir GARFIELD BARWICK, G.C.M.G.

Justices: Rt. Hon. Sir EDWARD A. McTIERNAN, K.B.E., Rt. Hon. Sir DOUGLAS MENZIES, K.B.E., Rt. Hon. Sir NINIAN M. STEPHEN, K.B.E., Rt. Hon. Sir ANTHONY F. MASON, K.B.E., Rt. Hon. Sir CYRIL A. WALSH, K.B.E., Rt. Hon. Sir HARRY TALBOT GIBBS, K.B.E.

Principal Registrar: L. B. FOLEY, High Court of Australia, Taylor Square, Sydney.

COMMONWEALTH CONCILIATION AND ARBITRATION COMMISSION

President: Hon. Sir RICHARD C. KIRBY.

Deputy Presidents: Hon. Mr. Justice P. A. COLDHAM, Hon. Mr. Justice JOHN T. LUDEKE, Hon. Mr. Justice L. H. WILLIAMS, Hon. Mr. Justice A. P. AIRD, Hon. Mr. Justice J. G. ROBINSON, Hon. E. CHAMBERS, Hon. E. A. EVATI, Hon. J. B. SWEENEY, Hon. R. D. WILLIAMS, Hon. J. E. ISAACS.

Senior Commissioner: J. E. TAYLOR.

Commissioners: Mr. J. H. PORTUS, Mr. P. D. ALLSOP, Mr. J. L. GOUGH, Mr. L. G. MATTHEWS, Mr. E. J. CLARKSON, Mr. H. G. NEIL, Mr. J. B. HOLMES, Mr. R. H. C. WATSON, Mr. T. J. BRACK, Mr. E. G. DEVERALL, Mr. W. B. WILSON, Mr. T. W. S. McCLOGHRY, Mr. J.

STANTON, Mr. A. R. VOSTI, Mr. L. H. BOOTH, Mr. F. W. J. BROWN, Mr. M. E. HEAGNEY, Mr. M. F. LYTTLETON, Mr. N. J. MANSINI, Mr. A. S. PAINE, Mr. N. A. TAYLOR, Mr. J. E. HEFFERNAM.

COMMONWEALTH INDUSTRIAL COURT

Chief Judge: Hon. Sir JOHN SPICER.

Judges: Hon. Mr. Justice E. A. DUNPHY, Hon. Mr. Justice P. JOSKE, C.M.G., Hon. Sir R. EGGLESTON, Hon. Mr. Justice R. A. SMITHERS, Hon. Mr. Justice A. E. WOODWARD, O.B.E., Hon. Mr. Justice R. J. A. FRANKI, Hon. Sir. J. A. NIMMO, O.ST.J.

Industrial Registrar: K. D. MARSHALL, 451 Little Bourke St., Melbourne 3000.

COMMONWEALTH BANKRUPTCY ADMINISTRATION

Judges: Hon. Mr. Justice C. A. SWEENEY, Hon. Mr. Justice B. B. RILEY.

Inspector-General: J. T. JOHNSTONE, Administrative Bldg., Canberra, A.C.T. 2600.

NEW SOUTH WALES

THE SUPREME COURT

King and Elizabeth Streets, Sydney.

Chief Justice: (vacant).

President of the Court of Appeal: Hon. KENNETH SYDNEY JACOBS.

Judges of Appeal: Hons. C. McLELLAND, K. W. ASPREY, J. D. HOLMES, Sir JAMES KENNETH MANNING, A. R. MOFFITT, M. F. HARDIE, L. W. STREET, R. M. HOPE, R. G. REYNOLDS.

Puisne Judges: Hons. J. H. McCLEMENS, R. LE GAY BRERETON, H. MAGUIRE, W. H. COLLINS, R. ELSE-MITCHELL, B. P. MACFARLAN, O.B.E., J. F. NAGLE, R. L. TAYLOR, D. M. SELBY, E.D., C. E. BEGG, P. H. ALLEN, J. O'BRIEN, S. ISAACS, N. A. JENKYN, J. A. LEE, M. M. HELSHAM, C. L. D. MEARES, P. B. TOOSE, C.B.E., G. CARMICHAEL, J. P. SLATTERLY, A. LARKINS, P. M. WOODWARD, D. L. MAHONEY, K. J. HOLLAND, G. J. SAMUELS.

Prothonotary and Registrar, Court of Appeal: J. E. NOONAN.

VICTORIA

There is a Supreme Court with a Chief Justice and sixteen Puisne Judges, a County Court, Courts of Mines, Licensing Courts, Magistrates Courts and Children's Courts.

THE SUPREME COURT

Chief Justice: Hon. Sir HENRY ARTHUR WINNEKE, K.C.M.G., O.B.E., Q.C.

Puisne Judges: Hons. A. D. G. ADAM, Sir DOUGLAS M. LITTLE, Sir GEORGE A. PAPE, U. G. GOWANS, O. J. GILLARD, JOHN E. STARKE, E. H. E. BARBER, M. V. MCINERNEY, G. H. LUSH, C. I. MENHENNITT, H. R. NEWTON, F. R. NELSON, K. V. ANDERSON, W. C. CROCKETT, W. KAYE, J. G. NORRIS, B. J. DUNN, P. MURPHY, W. O. HARRIS.

Masters: C. P. JACOBS, M.B.E., S. H. COLLIE, E. N. BERGERE, G. S. BRETT.

Prothonotary: P. S. MALBON.

COUNTY COURT

Judges: G. L. DETHRIDGE, T. G. RAPKE, H. T. FREDERICO, N. A. VICKERY, A. C. ADAMS, D. W. CORSON, J. X. O'DRISCOLL, J. H. FORREST, C. W. HARRIS, E. E. HEWITT, R. J. LECKIE, G. JUST, I. F. C. FRANICH, T. B. SHILLITO, J. P. SOMERVILLE, W. J. MARTIN, I. GRAY, A. J. SOUTHWELL, J. R. O'SHEA, G. BYRNE, H. OGDEN, J. G. GORMAN, D. WRIGHT, N. S. STABEY, B. F. MCNAB, K. COLEMAN, G. M. SPENCE.

Registrar: V. G. STAFFORD.

QUEENSLAND

SUPREME COURT
Southern District (Brisbane)

Chief Justice: Hon. Sir MOSTYN HANGER, K.B.E.

Senior Puisne Judge: Hon. C. G. WANSTALL.

Puisne Judges: Hon. N. S. STABLE, Hon. G. L. HART, Hon. G. A. G. LUCAS, Hon. J. A. DOUGLAS, Hon. D. M. CAMPBELL, Hon. M. B. HOARE, C.M.G., Hon. W. B. CAMPBELL, Hon. R. H. MATTHEWS, Hon. E. S. WILLIAMS, Hon. D. G. ANDREWS.

Registrar and Prothonotary: V. G. MCMAHON.

Central District (Rockhampton)

Puisne Judge: Hon. J. L. KELLY.

Registrar: G. D. ROBERTS.

Northern District (Townsville)

Puisne Judge: Hon. J. P. G. KNEIPP.

Registrar: R. HORE.

SOUTH AUSTRALIA
SUPREME COURT

Chief Justice: Hon. J. J. BRAY, LL.D.

Judges: Hon. D. S. HOGARTH, Hon. C. H. BRIGHT, Hon. ROMA F. MITCHELL, Hon. G. H. WALTERS, Hon. H. E. ZELLING, Hon. W. A. N. WELLS, Hon. A. K. SANGSTER, Hon. S. J. JACOBS.

Master: J. BOEHM.

WESTERN AUSTRALIA
SUPREME COURT

Chief Justice: Hon. Sir LAWRENCE JACKSON, K.C.M.G.

Senior Puisne Judge: Hon. J. E. VIRTUE.

Puisne Judges: Hons. F. T. P. BURT, J. M. LAVAN, J. L. C. WICKHAM, A. R. A. WALLACE, R. E. JONES.

Master and Registrar: G. T. STAPLES.

TASMANIA
SUPREME COURT

Chief Justice: Hon. Mr. Justice G. S. M. GREEN.

Judges: Hon. Sir GEORGE H. CRAWFORD, Hon. F. M. NEASEY, Hon. D. M. CHAMBERS, Hon. R. R. NETTLEFOLD.

Master and Registrar: C. G. BRETTINGHAM-MOORE.

AUSTRALIAN CAPITAL TERRITORY
SUPREME COURT

Judges: Hon. R. W. FOX, Hon. R. A. BLACKBURN, O.B.E., Hon. F. X. L. CONNOR.

Additional Judges: Hon. E. A. DUNPHY, Hon. P. E. JOSKE, C.M.G., Hon. Sir RICHARD M. EGGLESTON, Hon. R. A. SMITHERS, Hon. A. E. WOODWARD, O.B.E., Hon. R. J. A. FRANKI, Hon. Sir JOHN A. NIMMO, C.B.E., O.ST.J.

Registrar: Z. HARTSTEIN.

NORTHERN TERRITORY
SUPREME COURT

Judges: Hon. J. R. KERR, Hon. E. A. DUNPHY, Hon. P. E. JOSKE, C.M.G., Hon. R. A. SMITHERS, Hon. W. E. S. FORSTER, Hon. Sir JOHN A. NIMMO, C.B.E., O.ST.J.

Master and Registrar-General: J. P. MORRISON.

RELIGION

CHURCH OF ENGLAND IN AUSTRALIA

There are over 4.1 million members of the Church of England in Australia. The national office of the Church of England in Australia is: General Synod Office, P.O.B. Q190, Queen Victoria Bldgs., York St., Sydney 2000.

Primate of Australia: Most Rev. FRANK WOODS, K.B.E., M.A., D.D., M.A., TH.D.

PROVINCE OF NEW SOUTH WALES

Archbishop of Sydney and Metropolitan: Most Rev. MARCUS L. LOANE, M.A., D.D.

PROVINCE OF VICTORIA

Archbishop of Melbourne and Metropolitan: Most Rev. FRANK WOODS, M.A., D.D.

PROVINCE OF QUEENSLAND

Archbishop of Brisbane and Metropolitan: Most Rev. FELIX R. ARNOTT, M.A., TH.D.

PROVINCE OF WESTERN AUSTRALIA

Archbishop of Perth and Metropolitan: Most Rev. GEOFFREY T. SAMBELL, B.A., TH.SOC.

ROMAN CATHOLIC CHURCH

There are over 2.8 million Roman Catholics in Australia.

The Apostolic Delegate: H.E. The Most Rev. GINO PARO, D.D., tit. Archbishop of Torcello, 40 Edward St., North Sydney, N.S.W.

Archbishops

Adelaide	.	Most Rev. JAMES W. GLEESON, D.D.
Brisbane	.	Most Rev. PATRICK M. O'DONNEL, D.D.
Canberra and Goulburn	.	Most Rev. THOMAS VINCENT CAHILL, D.D., PH.D.
Hobart	.	Most Rev. GUILFORD YOUNG, D.D.
Melbourne	.	Most Rev. JAMES ROBERT KNOX, D.D., J.C.D.
Perth	.	Most Rev. LAUNCELOT JOHN GOODY D.D. PH.D.
Sydney	.	Most Rev. JAMES FREEMAN, D.D. Auxiliary Bishops: Most Rev. JAMES CARROLL, D.D., Most Rev. THOMAS MULDOON, D.D., Most Rev. EDWARD KELLY, M.S.C., D.D.

OTHER CHURCHES

Baptist Union of Australia: 597 Burwood Rd., Auburn, Victoria 3122; Pres.-Gen. Rev. Dr. G. H. BLACKBURN, M.A., B.D., B.ED.; Hon. Sec. Rev. J. G. MANNING; 49,780 mems.; 700 churches, 670 ministers, 1,000 local preachers; Sunday Schools: 11,220 teachers, 72,500 scholars; Carey Grammar and King's College for boys; Strathcona and Kilvington Girls' Grammar Schools; Residential Theological Colleges in N.S.W., Victoria, Queensland, South and West Australia; Deaconess Training Institute in Victoria; Bedford Business College in N.S.W.; Aged People's Homes in all states; missionary work in Zambia, Bangladesh, Assam, Northern Australia, New Guinea, West Irian, Philippines, Hong Kong, Timor and among the aborigines of Central Australia; publ. *Australian Baptist* (weekly).

Congregational Union of Australia: 15 Russell St., Eastwood, N.S.W. 2122; f. 1892; 15,400 mems.; Pres. Rev. G. L. BARNES; Sec. Rev. H. T. WELLS; publ. *The Australian Congregationalist* (monthly).

Churches of Christ in Australia: P.O.B. 101, Essendon North, Victoria 3041; Conference Sec. A. E. WHITE.

Lutheran Church of Australia: Lutheran Church House, 58 O'Connell St., North Adelaide, South Australia 5006; f. Oct. 1966, by amalgamation of the United Evangelical Lutheran Church in Australia and the Evangelical Lutheran Church of Australia; first missionaries to aboriginals 1838; first Lutheran Church 1838; 155,000 mems., 360 clergy; Pres. Rev. L. B. GROPE, D.D.; First Vice-Pres. Rev. E. W. WIEBUSCH; Second Vice-Pres. Rev. C. I. KOCH, B.D.; Sec. Rev. H. F. W. PROEVE, B.A.; Ministry trained at Luther Seminary, North Adelaide (Principal Rev. S. P. HEBART, D.TH., M.A.); teachers and other church workers trained at Lutheran Teachers College, Highgate, S.A. (Principal Rev. R. W. MAYER, B.A., DIP. ED.); six colleges; aboriginal missions in Central Australia (Hermannsburg, Finke River Mission), South Australia (Koonibba, Yalata) and Queensland (Hope Vale, Bloomfield River), also mission activity in New Guinea; radio programme (Australian Lutheran Hour) on 44 stations; publs. *The Lutheran* (official organ; fortnightly), *Encounter* (for youth), *Lutheran Women*, *Lutheran Men*, *Children's Friend*, *Prism* (all monthly), *Lutheran Theological Journal* (quarterly), *Lutheran Year Book*.

Greek Orthodox Church: Greek Orthodox Archdiocese of Australia, 242 Cleveland St., Redfern, N.S.W. 2016; leader in Australia, Archbishop EZEKIEL; 380,000 mems.; Archdiocesan office in Melbourne, 221 Dorcas St., South Melbourne, Vic. 3205; Greek Orthodox Communities throughout Australia.

Methodist Church of Australasia: The General Conference, 130 Little Collins St., Melbourne, Vic. 3000; 1 million adherents; Pres.-Gen. Rev. R. C. MATHIAS, M.A., DIP. R. ED., 96 Yarra St., Geelong, Vic. 3220; Sec.-Gen. Rev. W. D. O'REILLY, M.A., M.ED., DIP.SOC.ST., 139 Castlereagh St., Sydney, N.S.W., 2000.

Presbyterian Church of Australia: 156 Collins St., Melbourne 3000; 1,043,570 mems.; Clerk of Gen. Assembly Rev. L. FARQUHAR GUNN, Assembly Hall, 156 Collins St., Melbourne, Vic. 3000.

Russian Orthodox Church: Clergy House, 31 Robertson Road, Centennial Park, Sydney; f. 1933; 120 mems.; Minister Very Rev. A. GILCHENKO; Hon. Sec. A. V. SERAPININ.

Salvation Army in Australia: Southern Territory (Victoria, South Australia, Western Australia, Tasmania and Northern Territory); 69 Bourke St., Melbourne 3000; Territorial Commander Commissioner HENRY J. WARREN; Chief Sec. Col. BRAMWELL LUCAS; Eastern Territory (New South Wales, Queensland and Papua New Guinea); 140 Elizabeth St., Sydney 2000; Territorial Commander Commissioner H. W. G. WILLIAMS; Chief Sec. Col. RICHARD HOLZ; London Publicity: 101 Queen Victoria St., E.C.4.

JEWISH COMMUNITY

Great Synagogue: Elizabeth St., Sydney; f. 1831; Chief Minister Rabbi RAYMOND APPLE; Sec. ISAAC N. GOODMAN, J.P., 166 Castlereagh St., Sydney, N.S.W.

Melbourne Hebrew Congregation: Toorak Rd., South Yarra; f. 1841; Chief Minister Rabbi Dr. I. RAPAPORT; Sec. H. FRIEDMAN; 1,200 mems.; publ. *Quarterly Newsletter*.

THE PRESS

Australia's legislation relating to the Press is partly based on modified British legislation, but as each state enacts its own laws, the form and severity thereof may vary.

Under the law concerning contempt of court, since the court takes jurisdiction from the time the accused is arrested, to publish names or photographs before proceedings begin may draw heavy penalties. Though accurate reporting of a case while it is being tried is privileged, and has been known to extend to a degree of scandal, a judge is empowered to ban all reports until the conclusion of the case. Though this legislation is intended to protect the interest of the accused, it frequently hinders the journalist.

Each state has its legislation against obscene publications, which is particularly severe in the state of Queensland, whose broadly defined Objectionable Literature Act of 1954 covers a wide range of offences.

The libel law, closely related to British law, ranges from seditious libel for matter liable to cause a breach of the peace, or for excessive abuse of government officials, to defamatory libel, knowing and plain. The most frequently cited defences are "fair comment and criticism" and "true and public benefit". Certain government agencies have privilege.

All newspapers in the state capitals are owned by limited companies. The trend towards concentration of ownership has led to the development of four principal groups of newspapers. Economic conditions have necessitated the extension of the activities of newspaper companies into related spheres, magazine and book publishing, radio and television, etc. The main groups are as follows:

The Herald and Weekly Times Group: 44 Flinders St., Melbourne; Chair. Sir PHILIP JONES: controls *The Herald* and *Sun News-Pictorial* (Melbourne), *The Advertiser* (Adelaide), *The Courier Mail*, *The Telegraph*, and *Sunday Mail* (Brisbane), *West Australian Daily News* (Perth), and also has holdings in several magazines and radio and television companies.

The John Fairfax Group: Broadway, Sydney; Chair. Sir WARWICK FAIRFAX; with its subsidiary Associated Newspapers Ltd., controls *The Sydney Morning Herald*, *The Sun*, *National Times*, *Australian Financial Review* and the *Sun-Herald* (Sydney), *The Canberra Times*, *The Canberra News*, *The Age* and the *National Times* together with four large magazines; also has radio and television interests.

Consolidated Press Group: 168 Castlereagh St., Sydney; controls *The Maitland Mercury*, and magazines including *The Australian Woman's Weekly* and *The Bulletin*.

Nationwide News Ltd.: 2 Holt St., Surry Hills, Sydney 2010; Chair. Sir NORMAN YOUNG; Man. Dir. RUPERT MURDOCH; controls *Adelaide News* and *Sunday Mail* (Adelaide), *The Australian*, *Sunday Australian*, *Daily Mirror* and *Sunday Mirror* (Sydney), *The News* (Darwin), *Sunday Sun* (Brisbane), *The Sydney Daily Telegraph* and *Sunday Telegraph* and *Sunday Times* (Perth); also has interests in magazines and radio companies.

The total circulation of Australia's 52 daily newspapers (18 metropolitan and 34 provincial) is very high at about 3,680,000 million copies, or one for every three citizens. Weekly papers are even more popular as they more successfully penetrate to the remoter parts of the country, whereas metropolitan dailies meet competition from small local papers. The circulation of newspapers has traditionally been almost entirely confined to the state in which each is produced. The only exceptions, which may fairly claim a national circulation, are the dailies *The Australian*, *Australian Financial Review*, and the weeklies, the *Sydney Bulletin*, the *National Times* and the fortnightly *Nation*.

The main newspaper centres are Sydney, where the morning *Daily Telegraph* competes with the *Morning Herald*, and the evening *Daily Mirror* competes with *The Sun*, and Melbourne, where *The Age* competes with *The Sun News-Pictorial*, both morning papers. Perth, Adelaide and Brisbane each have only one major morning and one major evening paper.

Among the daily papers most respected for their serious news treatment should be mentioned the *Sydney Morning Herald*, *The Age* (Melbourne), *The Australian*, *The Canberra Times* and the *Australian Financial Review*. The most popular dailies include Melbourne's *Sun News Pictorial* (654,680) and *Herald* (490,070), Sydney's *Daily Telegraph* (320,000), *Sun* (347,437) and *Daily Mirror* (349,522), *Sydney Morning Herald* (276,455) and Brisbane's *Courier Mail* (261,667), and Adelaide's *Advertiser* (220,000).

NEWSPAPERS

METROPOLITAN DAILIES

AUSTRALIAN CAPITAL TERRITORY

The Australian: Nationwide News Ltd., 2 Holt St., Surry Hills; f. 1964; national daily; edited in Sydney, published simultaneously in Sydney, Melbourne, Adelaide and Brisbane; Proprietor RUPERT MURDOCH; Editor OWEN THOMSON; circ. 141,846.

Canberra News: Mort St., Braddon, Canberra; f. 1969; afternoon; circ. 13,000; Editor P. J. WILSON.

Canberra Times, The: 18 Mort St., Braddon, Canberra; f. 1926; morning; Editor I. R. MATHEWS; circ. 36,089.

NEW SOUTH WALES

DAILIES

Australian Financial Review: 235 Jones St., Broadway. Sydney; f. 1951; Mon. to Fri.; Editor P. ROBINSON; Man. Editor V. J. CARROLL; circ. 43,000.

Daily Commercial News and Shipping List (incorporating *Airways News*): P.O.B. 1552, Sydney, N.S.W. 2001; f. 1912; News Editor G. JOHNSON.

Daily Mirror: 2 Holt St., Surry Hills, Sydney; f. 1941; evening; Man. Dir. K. R. MURDOCH; Editorial Dir. T. M. FITZGERALD; circ. 349,522.

Daily Telegraph: 2 Holt St., Surry Hills, Sydney; f. 1879; Independent, morning; Editor P. WOMBWELL; circ. 320,000.

Maitland Mercury: Maitland Mercury Newspapers and Printing Co. Pty. Ltd.; f. 1843; Editor D. W. AUSTIN.

Newcastle Morning Herald: 28–30 Bolton St., Newcastle, N.S.W. 2300; f. 1858; morning; Gen. Man. D. L. BAUMFIELD; Man. Editor I. L. ARNOLD, circ. 64,532.

Newcastle Sun, The: 28-30 Bolton St., Newcastle, N.S.W. 2300; f. 1918; evening; Gen. Man. D. L. BAUMFIELD; Man. Editor I. L. ARNOLD; Editor K. BROCK; circ. 31,880.

Sun, The: Broadway, Sydney; f. 1910; evening; Editor B. J. TIER; circ. 347,437.

Sydney Morning Herald, The: Broadway, Sydney; f. 1831; morning; Editor G. E. W. HARRIOTT; circ. 276,455.

SUNDAY AND WEEKLY NEWSPAPERS

National Times: G.P.O. Box 506, Sydney 2001; f. Feb. 1971; weekly; Editor Max Suich.

Sun-Herald: 235 Jones St., Broadway, Sydney; f. 1953; Sunday; Editor F. R. Peterson; circ. 662,996.

Sunday Mirror: 2 Holt St., Sydney; f. 1958; Editor B. Hogben; circ. 513,966.

Sunday Telegraph: 2 Holt St., Surry Hills, Sydney; f. 1938; Editor K. Watson; circ. 664,184.

VICTORIA
DAILIES

Age, The: 250 Spencer St., Melbourne (cnr. Lonsdale St.); f. 1854; Independent liberal; morning; circ. 208,807; Man. Dir. C. R. Macdonald; Editor E. Graham Perkin.

Herald, Melbourne: 44 Flinders St., Melbourne; f. 1840; evening; Editor C. Wallace; circ. 490,070.

Sun News-Pictorial: 44 Flinders St., Melbourne; f. 1922; morning; Editor L. Turnbull; circ. 654,680.

WEEKLY NEWSPAPERS

Sporting Globe: 44 Flinders St., Melbourne, Vic. 3000; f. 1922; Weds. and Sats.; Editor A. Dunn.

Truth: 44–74 Flinders St., Melbourne; f. 1902; Editor P. Edwards; circ. 369,000.

QUEENSLAND
DAILIES

Courier-Mail: Campbell St., Bowen Hills, Brisbane; f. 1933; morning; Editor J. R. Atherton; circ. 261,677.

Telegraph: Campbell Street, Bowen Hills, Brisbane; f. 1872; evening; circ. 166,430; Editor-in-Chief J. F. Wakefield, O.B.E.

SUNDAY NEWSPAPERS

Sunday Mail: Campbell Street, Bowen Hills, Brisbane; f. 1933; circ. 358,000; Editor H. G. Turner.

Sunday Sun: Mirror Newspapers Ltd., cnr. Brunswick and McLachlan Sts., Fortitude Valley, Brisbane, Queensland; f. 1971; Editor R. Richards; circ. 293,861.

SOUTH AUSTRALIA
DAILIES

Advertiser: King William St., Adelaide 5000; f. 1858; morning; circ. 220,334; Editor-in-Chief D. F. Colquhoun.

News: 116 North Terrace, Adelaide; f. 1923; evening Mon. to Sat., circ. 145,602; Man. Dir. and Editor Ronald R. Boland.

SUNDAY AND WEEKLY NEWSPAPERS

Chronicle: 121 King William St., Adelaide; f. 1858; Fri.; agricultural weekly; Editor J. B. McCartet.

Sunday Mail: 116–120 North Terrace, Adelaide; f. 1912; circ. 245,524; Editor Geoff Jones.

WESTERN AUSTRALIA
DAILIES

Daily News: 125 St. George's Terrace, Perth; f. 1882; evening, Mon.-Fri.; circ. 124,481; Editor D. O'Sullivan.

Independent Sun: cnr. Briggs and Swansea Sts., East Victoria Park, Perth, W.A. 6102; f. 1973; daily; circ. 55,000; Editor Patrick Nilon.

West Australian: Newspaper House, St. George's Terrace, Perth; f. 1833; morning; circ. 224,743; Editor M. C. Uren.

SUNDAY AND WEEKLY NEWSPAPERS

Countryman, The: Newspaper House, St. George's Terrace, Perth, f. 1885; Thurs.; a farmers' magazine, with pages for women; circ. 18,040; Editor H. W. Baker.

Independent: Perth; cnr. Briggs and Swansea Sts., East Victoria Park, W.A. 6102; f. April 1969; Sunday; Editor Patrick Nilon; circ. 68,000.

Sunday Times: 34-36 Stirling St., Perth; f. 1897; Man. Dir. M. W. James; Editor F. Dunn; circ. 207,349.

Weekend News: 125 St. George's Terrace, Perth; f. 1960; weekly (Saturday); Editor D. O'Sullivan; circ. 104,661.

TASMANIA
DAILIES

Advocate: P.O.B. 63, Burnie, Tas.; f. 1890; morning; circulates in N.W. and W. Tasmania; circ. 22,400; Editor D. J. Cherry.

Examiner: 71–75 Paterson St., Launceston; f. 1842; morning; Independent; circ. 34,896; *Sunday Examiner-Express*; f. 1924; circ. 37,313; Editor F. G. N. Ewence.

Mercury: 91–93 Macquarie St., Hobart; f. 1854; morning; circ. 54,851: Editor D. N. Hawker.

WEEKLY NEWSPAPERS

Advocate Weekender: P.O.B. 63, Burnie, Tas.; f. 1968; Saturday evening; circulates in N.W. and W. Tasmania; circ. 16,200; Man. L. J. Harris; Editor D. J. Cherry.

Saturday Evening Mercury: 91–93 Macquarie St., Hobart; f. 1954; Editor R. Saunders; circ. 40,000.

Sunday Examiner-Express: 71–75 Paterson St., Launceston; f. 1924; Editor F. G. N. Ewence; circ. 36,859.

Tasmanian Farmer: P.O.B. 63, Burnie, Tas.; f. 1946; Thurs.; Editor D. J. Cherry; circ. 5,700.

NORTHERN TERRITORY
DAILY

Northern Territory News: P.O.B. 675, Darwin; f. 1952; Mon. to Sat.; Editor J. F. Bowditch.

SELECTED PERIODICALS
WEEKLIES AND FORTNIGHTLIES

Advertising News: G.P.O. Box 606, Sydney; f. 1928; fortnightly; journal of advertising, advertising media and the graphic arts in Australia; circ. 3,267; Editor D. R. Mason.

Advocate: 143 a'Beckett St., Melbourne; f. 1868; Thurs.; Catholic; circ. 27,000; Editor D. Cunningham.

Australasian Post: 61 Flinders Lane, Melbourne, 3000; f. 1946; illustrated; factual, general interest, particularly Australiana; mainly for male readers; Mon.; circulates throughout Commonwealth; Editor J. Hughes; circ. 275,000.

Australian Miner, The: P.O.B. 349, Manuka A.C.T. 2603; f. 1969; mining and related subjects; weekly; Editor I. Huntley; circ. 18,500.

Australian Women's Weekly: 168 Castlereagh St., Sydney; f. 1933; Wed.; circ. 863,000; Editor Miss Dorothy Drain.

Australian Worker: Worker Trustees, 238–240 Castlereagh St., Sydney; f. 1891; fortnightly, Wed.; circ. 61,000; Man. H. V. Moore; Editor F. Roberts.

B & T: 340 Pitt St., P.O.B. 2608, G.P.O., Sydney; f. 1949; weekly trade magazine of advertising, marketing and media; circ. 2,600; Gen. Man. R. M. Bumpstead.

Building and Construction: 171 Hay St., East Perth; Man. Dir. J. L. WALTERS; circ. 6,750.

The Bulletin: 54 Park St., Sydney; f. 1880; Wed.; Editor D. HORNE.

Construction: 58–60 Margaret St., Sydney, N.S.W. 2000; f. 1907; official organ of the Housing Industry Asscn. of Australia; weekly N.S.W., Vic. and Qld.; News Editor FRED COLEMAN; Services Editor CHARLES SPITERI.

Countryman: 24 Collins St., Melbourne; f. 1917; monthly; circ. 26,500; Editor TREVOR PAYNE.

Current Affairs Bulletin: University of Sydney; Sydney 2006; f. 1952; monthly; Editor Dr. D. CROWLEY.

Incentive: P.O.B. 349, Manuka, A.C.T. 2603; f. June 1965; weekly; Australian and overseas economics, politics, business, money market, statistics; Editor MAXWELL NEWTON.

Land, The: 122 Cleveland St., Chippendale, Sydney; f. 1911; Thurs.; Man. Editor J. L. PARKER.

Listener-In T.V.: 44 Flinders St., Melbourne; f. 1925; Thurs.; circ. 125,000; Editor P. R. DUNSTONE.

Medical Journal of Australia, The: 71–79 Arundel St., Glebe, N.S.W. 2037; f 1914; weekly; circ 18,000; Man. J. G. ASTLES; Editor Dr. R. R. WINTON.

Nation Review: 777B George St., Sydney 2000 and P.O.B. 5312BB, Melbourne, Vic.; f. 1958; Independent, progressive; fortnightly.

New Idea: 32 Walsh St., Melbourne; weekly; women's magazine; Editor R. PERRY.

News Weekly: G.P.O. Box 66A, Melbourne 3001; f. 1943; Wed.; political and trade union affairs in Australia; National Civic Council organ; circ. 15,741; Man. Dir. G. A. MERCER; Editor E. S. MADDEN.

Pix/People: P.O.B. 164, Beaconsfield, N.S.W. 2015; f. 1938; weekly; circ. 180,000; Editor K. FINLAY.

Queensland Country Life: 432 Queen St., Brisbane; f. 1935; Thurs.; circ. 30,314; Man. Dir. WALLACE C. SKELSEY.

Stock and Land: Stock and Land Publishing Co. Pty. Ltd., Box 82, North Melbourne 3051; f. 1914; Wed.; livestock, land and wool market journal; official newspaper of Associated Stock and Station Agents of Melbourne, circ. 22,000, Man. Editor C. T. DeB. GRIFFITH.

TV Times: Australian Broadcasting Commission, Dudley Bldg., 630 George St., Sydney; f. 1958; Editor C. DAY.

TV Week: 32 Walsh St., Melbourne; f. 1957; Mon.; national; Editor FRANK CROOK.

Weekly Times: 44 Flinders St., Melbourne 3000; f. 1861; farming, gardening; Weds.; Editor J. BALFOUR BROWN; circ. 106,000.

Woman's Day: G.P.O. Box 3970, 57 Regent St., Broadway, Sydney; Mon.; circulates throughout Australia and New Zealand; circ. approx. 557,000; Editor JOAN REEDER.

Worker, The: 236–238 Elizabeth St., Brisbane; f. 1890; alternate Mons.; official organ of the Australian Workers' Union in Queensland; circ. 44,562; Editor J. P. DUNN.

MONTHLIES, QUARTERLIES, ETC.

Aircraft: 44–47 Flinders St., Melbourne, Vic. 3000; f. 1918; monthly; Editor W. D. G. ROBERTSON, O.B.E.

Archaeology and Physical Anthropology in Oceania: University of Sydney, N.S.W.; f. 1966; three issues a year; Editor A. P. ELKIN.

Architecture Building Engineering: 12 Downing St., Spring Hill, Brisbane, Qld. 4000; f. 1922; monthly.

Architecture in Australia: 33A McLaren Street, North Sydney; f. 1917; official journal of the Royal Australian Institute of Architects; 6 issues a year (Feb., April, June, Aug., Oct., Dec.); circ. 6,900; Editor ANNE LEONHARD.

Australasian Engineer, The: P.O.B. 1552, 58–60 Margaret St., Sydney 2000; f. 1908; monthly; Editor FRED COLEMAN.

Australasian Weekly Manufacturer: Maxwell Newton Pty. Ltd., 36 Carrington St., Sydney 2000; Editor FRED COLEMAN.

Australia Today: 318 Flinders St., Melbourne; f. 1905; national pictorial, literary and statistical annual; circ. 27,476; Man. Editor R. S. HARBER.

Australian Cricket: Modern Magazines Pty. Ltd., Ryrie House, 15 Boundary St., Rushcutters Bay, N.S.W. 2011; f. 1968; monthly, October–March inclusive.

Australian Current Taxation and Service: Butterworths Pty. Ltd., 586 Pacific Highway, Chatswood, 2067; f. 1936; monthly; Editors F. C. BOCK, E. F. MANNIX.

Australian Home Beautiful: 44–74 Flinders St., Melbourne; f. 1925; monthly; Editor A. J. HITCHINS.

Australian House and Garden: 142 Clarence St., Sydney; monthly; building, furnishing, decorating, handicrafts, gardening, etc.; Editor MARIA QUINN.

Australian Journal of Biological Sciences: C.S.I.R.O., 372 Albert St., East Melbourne, Vic. 3002; f. 1953; alternate months; Editor B. J. WALBY.

Australian Journal of Botany: C.S.I.R.O., Albert St., East Melbourne, Vic. 3002; f. 1953; irregularly, as accumulation of material permits; Editor B. J. WALBY.

Australian Journal of Chemistry: C.S.I.R.O., Albert St., East Melbourne, Vic. 3002; f. 1953; monthly; Editor B. J. WALBY.

Australian Journal of Optometry: 82 Bond St., Sydney; f. 1913; monthly; Editor J. L. HEWETT.

Australian Journal of Pharmacy: 18–22 St. Francis St., Melbourne; f. 1886; monthly; official journal of the associated pharmaceutical organizations of Australia; Editor J. G. DICKINSON; Man. I. G. LLOYD.

Australian Journal of Philosophy: Department of Philosophy, Australian National University, Canberra, A.C.T. 2600; f. 1923; official organ of the Australasian Association of Philosophy; 3 issues yearly; Editor ROBERT BROWN.

Australian Journal of Physios: C.S.I.R.O., 372 Albert St., East Melbourne, Vic. 3002; f. 1953; alternate months; Editor B. J. WALBY.

Australian Journal of Politics and History: University of Queensland, St. Lucia, Qld. 4067; f. 1955; 3 times a year; Editor G. GREENWOOD.

Australian Journal of Soil Research: C.S.I.R.O., 372 Albert St., East Melbourne, Vic. 3002; f. 1963; twice yearly, at irregular intervals; Editor B. J. WALBY.

Australian Journal of Zoology: C.S.I.R.O., 372 Albert St., East Melbourne, Vic. 3002; f. 1953; irregularly, as accumulation of material permits.

Australian Law Journal: 301 Kent St., Sydney; f. 1927; monthly; Editor PHILIP JEFFREY, Q.C.; Assistant Editor Dr. D. HODGSON.

Australian Left Review: Box A247, Sydney South P.O. 2000; f. 1966; bi-monthly.

Australian Quarterly: Australian Institute of Political Science, Hosking House, Penfold Place, 84½ Pitt St., Sydney, N.S.W. 2000; f. 1929; quarterly; Editor GORDON McCARTHY.

Australian University: Melbourne University Press, Carlton ,Vic. 3053; f. 1962; 3 times a year; Editor Dr. S. W. COHEN.

Commerce, Industrial and Mining Review: Invicta Publications, Box 142, Bentley, W.A. 6102; monthly; Man. M. J. MURPHY.

Economic Record: Economics and Research Dept., University of Melbourne; f. 1925; four times a year; journal of Economic Society of Australia and New Zealand; Joint Editors A. H. BOXER, Prof. S. J. TURNONSKY, Prof. L. R. WEBB.

Electronics Australia: Sun-Herald Bldg., 235 Jones St., Broadway, N.S.W. 2016; f. 1939; technical, radio, television, hi-fi and electronics; monthly; Editor-in-Chief W. N. WILLIAMS; Editor J. ROWE.

Good Gardening: 142 Clarence St., Sydney; quarterly; Editor BERYL GUERTNER.

Historical Studies: Department of History, University of Melbourne, Parkville, Victoria 3052; f. 1940; twice yearly, April and October; Editor N. D. McLACHLAN.

Industrial Review and Mining Year Book of Australia: 286 Hay St., Perth, W.A., 6000; Jan. each year.

Journal of Pacific History: Australian National University P.O.B. 4, Canberra, A.C.T. 2600; f. 1966; annual; Editors W. N. GUNSON, D. A. SCARR.

Manufacturers' Monthly: 74 Clarence St., Sydney 2000; f. 1961; circ. 11,015.

Meanjin Quarterly: University of Melbourne, Parkville 3052, Victoria; f. 1940; quarterly; literature, art, discussion; Editor C. B. CHRISTESEN, O.B.E.

Methodist, The: 139 Castlereagh St., Sydney, N.S.W.; published by the Methodist Church in N.S.W.; fortnightly on Sat.; circ. 27,500; Editor Rev. W. D. O'REILLY.

Modern Boating: 21–23 Bathurst St., Sydney; f. 1965; Editor PETER CAMPBELL; circ. 16,500.

Modern Motor: 15 Boundary St., Rushcutters Bay, N.S.W.; f. 1954; monthly; circ. 79,000; Editor ROB LUCK.

Modern Office Administration: 74 Clarence St., Sydney 2000; monthly; circ. 7,000.

New Horizons in Education: 1A Penn Corner, Glengowrie, S.A., 5044; f. 1938; published twice a year by the World Education Fellowship; Editor E. W. GOLDING.

Oceania: The University of Sydney, N.S.W.; f. 1930; social anthropology; quarterly; Editor A. P. ELKIN.

Open Road: 151 Clarence St., Sydney; f. 1927; official journal of National Roads and Motorists' Asscn. (N.R.M.A.); circ. 921,619; monthly; Editor B.GIULIANO.

Overland: G.P.O. Box 98a, Melbourne, Victoria 3001; f. 1954; literary; Editor S. MURRAY-SMITH.

Pacific Islands Monthly: 29 Alberta St., Sydney, N.S.W. 2000; f. 1930; specialist journal dealing with current affairs in the South Seas; Editor and Publisher STUART INDER; Man. S. C. HUGHES; circ. 20,100.

Public Administration: Department of Government, University of Sydney, Sydney, N.S.W. 2006; Editor Prof. R. M. SPANN.

Queensland Countrywoman: 89–95 Gregory Terrace, Brisbane; f. 1929; monthly journal of the Queensland Country Women's Association; Editor Mrs. G. J. PENNYCUICK

Queensland Geographical Journal: O'Brien House, 177-9 Ann St., Brisbane, Queensland; annual of Qld. br. of Royal Geographical Society of Australasia; Pres. JOHN J. G. CONROY; Hon. Gen. Dir., Sec. and Editor D. A. O'BRIEN, J.P., F.R.G.S.A.

Rydge's C.C.E.M. (Construction, Civil Engineering, Mining): 74 Clarence St., Sydney, N.S.W. 2000; monthly; Man. Dir. N. B. RYDGE.

Search-Science Technology and Society: Science House, 157 Gloucester St., Sydney 2000; f. 1970; journal of Australian and N.Z. Association for the Advancement of Science; monthly; Editor J. B. DAVENPORT; circ. 4,000.

South Pacific Bulletin (*Bulletin du Pacifique Sud*): South Pacific Commission Publications Bureau, 720 George St., Sydney, N.S.W. 2000; f. 1951; quarterly in English and French; official journal of the South Pacific Commission; Editor C. E. BIRCHMEIER.

Textile Journal of Australia: 142 Clarence St., Sydney; f. 1926; monthly; Editor MARJORIE McNEECE.

Walkabout: Sungravure Pty. Ltd., Box 164, Beaconsfield, N.S.W. 2014; f. 1934; monthly; magazine of Australian way of life; Published on behalf of Australian National Travel Association; Editor-in-Chief K. FINLAY; circ. 38,000.

World Review: University of Queensland Press, P.O.B. 42, Brisbane University, St. Lucia, Qld. 4067; f. 1962; three times a year; published under the auspices of the Australian Institute of International Affairs, Queensland; Editor DENIS WRIGHT.

Your Garden: 61 Flinders Lane, Melbourne, 3000; monthly; Editor N. MOODY; circ. 86,502.

PRESS AGENCIES

Australian Associated Press: 291 George St., Sydney; f. 1935; owned by principal daily newspapers of Australia; Chair. E. J. L. TURNBULL; Joint Man. Dirs. A. H. McLACHLAN and E. J. L. TURNBULL; Gen. Man. D. P. HOOPER.

Australian United Press Ltd.: 44 Flinders St., Melbourne 3000; f. 1928; Chair. A. T. SHAKESPEARE.

FOREIGN BUREAUX
Sydney

ANSA: 499 Parramatta Rd.; Bureau Chief EVASIO COSTANZO.

AP: Newspaper House, 44 Pitt St.; Bureau Chief GORDON TAIT.

New Zealand Press Association Ltd.: Brandon House, Featherston St., Wellington, New Zealand.

UPI: Caltex House, 2 Holt St., P.O.B. 5336; Man. CHARLES BERNARD.

The following are also represented: DPA, Jiji Press. Reuters, Tass.

Antara Indonesian News Agency is represented in Canberra; Kyodo News Service is represented in Melbourne.

PRESS ASSOCIATIONS

Australian Journalists Association: 58 Margaret St., Sydney, N.S.W. 2000; f. 1910; 8,000 mems.; Gen. Sec. S. P. CROSLAND; publ. *The Journalist*; circ. 7,500.

Australian Newspapers Council: C.B.C. Chambers, 100 Bathurst Street, Sydney; f. 1958; membership 13, confined to metropolitan daily or Sunday papers; Pres. B. A. WILLIAMS; Sec. B. G. OSBORNE.

Australian Provincial Press Association: 33 Rathdowne St., Carlton 3053, Vic.; f. 1906; Pres. B. A. Kaesehagen; Sec. K. B. Laurie.

New South Wales Country Press Association: Newspaper House, 44 Pitt Street. Sydney; f. 1900; 117 mems.; Sec. Colin C. Jenkins.

Provincial Press Association of South Australia Incorporated: 130 Franklin St., Adelaide; f. 1912; represents 34 South Australian country newspapers; Pres. D. Hann; Sec. J. F. Power, J.P.

Queensland Country Press Association: 307 Queen St., Brisbane; Pres. M. Eastwood; Sec. A. D. Morris.

Regional Dailies of Australia Ltd.: 247 Collins St., Melbourne 3000; f. 1936; formerly *Australian Provincial Daily Press Ltd.*; Chair. G. R. Dowling.

Tasmanian Press Association Pty. Ltd.: 71–75 Paterson Street, Launceston; Sec. L. W. P. Reeves.

Victorian Country Press Association Ltd.: 33 Rathdowne St., Carlton 3053, Vic.; f. 1910; Pres. F. V. Gannon; Exec. Dir. K. B. Laurie; 115 mems.

Western Australian Provincial Press Association: 97 Colin St., West Perth 6005; Sec. J. F. Ockerby.

PUBLISHERS

Angus and Robertson (Publishers) Pty. Ltd.: 102 Glover St., Cremorne, N.S.W. 2090; f. 1884; Dir. Richard Walsh; fiction, general, children's and educational.

Austral Printing and Publishing Co. Ltd.: 119–125 Hawke St., West Melbourne 3003; f. 1891; Dirs. N. R. Arnoti, L. J. Butler, R. P. Morris, W. A. Thompson, R. M. Walker, P. A. Williams; religious, educational and general.

Australasian Medical Publishing Co. Ltd.: 71–79 Arundel St., Glebe, N.S.W. 2037; f. 1913; medical, scientific and educational; Man. James G. Astles.

Australasian Publishing Co. Pty.: Corner of Bridge Rd. and Jersey St., Hornsby, N.S.W. 2077; f. 1937; Man. A. S. M. Harrap; fiction, educational; children's books, general.

Australian Consolidated Press: 168–174 Castlereagh Street, Sydney.

Australian Council for Educational Research: Frederick St., Hawthorn, Vic. 3122; f. 1930; educational research reports, reviews, comparative studies, tests, technical reports and manuals, teaching aids, educational journals; Dir. W. C. Radford, M.B.E., M.A., M.ED., PH.D., LL.D. (HON.), F.A.C.E.

Australian Government Publishing Service: 109 Canberra Ave., Griffith, A.C.T. 2603; Publishing Dir. B. P. Shurman.

Australian National University Press: P.O.B. 4, Canberra, A.C.T. 2600; f. 1966; scholarly; publishes 30–40 new books annually as well as *New Guinea Research Bulletin*; Dir. W. A. Wood; Editor Miss P. Croft.

S. John Bacon Publishing Co. Pty. Ltd.: Windsor Ave., Mount Waverley, Melbourne 3149, f. 1938; theology and Christian education, general educational material, greeting cards, music; Man. Dir. J. F. Bacon; Sec. N. K. Cuthbert; Man. R. M. Logan.

Brooks, William and Co. (Queensland) Pty. Ltd.: 921–929 Kingsford Smith Drive, Eagle Farm, Brisbane; f. 1888; Dirs. R. A. McWilliam, R. B. Macarthur-Onslow, R. W. Macarthur-Onslow, H. Lavery; Sec. K. Prowd; educational.

*****Butterworths Pty. Ltd.:** 586 Pacific Highway, Chatswood, N.S.W. 2067; f. 1912; law, medical, scientific and accountancy publications; Man. Dir. P. Cheeseman.

Cassell Australia Ltd.: 30–36 Curzon St. (P.O.B. 32), North Melbourne, Vic. 3051 and 76 Bay St., Broadway, N.S.W. 2000; inc. 1963; publishers of Australian fiction, general and educational titles; Man. Dir. J. R. Moad.

Cheshire Publishing Pty. Ltd.: 346 St. Kilda Rd., Melbourne 3004; also in Sydney, Brisbane, Adelaide, Wellington and London; educational at all levels; information and reference; Man. Dir. B. J. Rivers; Publishing Dir. Trevor Barr; Educational Publisher D. Drummond.

*****Collins, Wm. (Australia), Ltd.:** 36–38 Clarence St., Sydney, 351 Elizabeth St., Melbourne, 177 Edward St., Brisbane, C.M.L. Building, King William St., Adelaide, and 6 Sherwood Court, Perth; regd. in Australia 1946; fiction, non-fiction, religious, Bibles, children's, reference, paperbacks; Man. Dir. K. W. Wilder.

Currawong Publishing Co. Pty. Ltd.: 58 Margaret St., Sydney; f. 1940; Dirs. Keith P. Moss (Managing), H. F. Weston (Sec.); non-fiction, general, publishers of *The Australian Language*, etc.

Dymocks' Book Arcade Ltd.: 424 George St., Box 1521, G.P.O., Sydney.

Encyclopaedia Britannica Inc.: 300 Castlereagh St., Sydney, N.S.W. 2000; reference and education; Man. Dir. J. D. Bates.

Georgian House Pty. Ltd.: 296 Beaconsfield Parade, Middle Park, Melbourne; f. 1943; Man. Dir. B. W. Harris; fiction, natural history, poetry, biography, history, children's books.

Golden Press Pty. Ltd.: 2–12 Tennyson Rd., Gladesville, Sydney, N.S.W. 2111; children's cookery, adult non-fiction, Australiana.

The Hawthorn Press Pty. Ltd.: 601 Little Bourke St., Melbourne 3000; f. 1945; poetry, biography, history, reference, religion, secondary textbooks; Man. John Gartner.

Heinemann Educational Australia Pty. Ltd.: 24 River St., South Yarra, Vic. 3141; Chair. Alan Hill, C.B.E.; Man. Dir. Nicholas Hudson.

*****Wm. Heinemann Australia Pty. Ltd.:** 60 Inkerman St., St. Kilda, Vic.; f. 1948; Man. Dir. John Burchall; Editor Hilary Freeman.

Hicks Smith and Sons Pty. Ltd.: 301 Kent St., Sydney, N.S.W. 2000; educational and general; Dir. G. W Wallis-Smith.

*****Hodder and Stoughton (Australia) Ltd.:** Corner of Bridge Rd. and Jersey St., Hornsby, N.S.W. 2077, and 31 Coventry St., South Melbourne, Vic. 3205; Man. Dir. E. Coffey.

Horwitz Group Books Pty. Ltd.: 506 Miller St., Cammeray, N.S.W. 2062; fiction, reference, educational, Australiana, general; imprints: *Horwitz Publications*, *Martin Educational*; Man. Dir. L. J. Moore; Deputy Man. Dir. and Financial Dir. M. C. Phillips.

* Australian branch of London firm.

Hutchinson Group (Australia) Pty. Ltd.: 30–32 Cremorne St., Richmond, Victoria 3121.

Jacaranda Press: 46 Douglas St., Milton, Queensland 4064; general, fiction, juvenile, natural history, educational, technical; Chair. R. WOOD; Man. Dir. BRIAN CLOUSTON.

F. H. Johnston Publishing Co. Pty. Ltd.: 219A George St., Sydney.

Lamb Publications Pty. Ltd.: 286 Hay St. Perth, W.A, 6000; periodicals, journals and books.

Lansdowne Press: 37 Little Bourke St., Melbourne 3000; f. 1960; general books; Chief Executive PETER McGILL; Editorial Man. SALLY MILNER.

The Law Book Company Ltd.: 301 Kent St., Sydney; f. 1869; legal and commercial textbooks, legal reports and journals; Chair. Dr. J. WILLIAMS, PH.D.; Man. Dir. D. W. POTTER.

Longman Australia Pty. Ltd.: 427 Riversdale Rd., Hawthorn East, Victoria 3123; f. 1947; Man. Dir. W. P. KERR; Dirs. Sir ROGER DARVALL, B. SPRUNT.

Lothian Publishing Co. Pty. Ltd.: 4-12 Tattersalls Lane, Melbourne, 3000; f. 1905; Dirs. LOUIS A. LOTHIAN, K. A. LOTHIAN, L. N. JUPP; general, practical, educational.

McGraw-Hill Book Co. Australia Pty. Ltd.: 231 Pacific Highway, North Sydney, N.S.W. 2060; general; Exec. Dir. D. J. HINTON.

Macmillan Company of Australia Pty. Ltd.: 107 Moray St., South Melbourne; f. 1967; Man. Dir. BRIAN STONIER.

Melbourne University Press: 932 Swanson St., Carlton, Victoria 3053; f. 1923; academic, educational, Australiana (all fields except fiction and children's books); retail department (Melbourne University Bookroom). MUP agents outside Australia and New Zealand: International Scholarly Book Services, Inc. (U.S.A. and Canada); United Publishers Services (Singapore, Hong Kong, Tokyo); Angus and Robertson (U.K.) Ltd. (Britain and Europe).

Chairman Board of Management Prof. J. S. TURNER; Dir. P. A. RYAN; Asst. Dir. JEANNIE REID; Retail Man. T. S. P. UNWIN; Rights and Permissions, Miss S. HARDIMAN.

Murfett Pty. Ltd.: Keys Rd., Moorabbin, Vic. 3189; f. 1926; mem. Nat. Consolidated Group; greetings cards, souvenir postcards, games and jigsaws, etc.; Gen. Man. A. R. PAYNE.

Oak Tree Press Co. Ltd. (Inc. Bahamas): P.O.B. 34, Brickfield Hill, N.S.W. 2000; Man. Dir. ALBERT WAIDE; general, educational, technical, arts and crafts.

*****Oxford University Press:** 7 Bowen Crescent, Box 2784 Y, Melbourne 3001; f. 1908; Man. FRANK EYRE.

Penguin Books Australia Ltd.: 487/493 Maroondah Highway, Ringwood, Vic. 3134; general paperbacks; Man. Dir. J. W. MICHIE; Chief Editor J. HOOKER.

Pergamon Press (Australia) Pty. Ltd.: 19A Boundary St., Rushcutters Bay, N.S.W. 2011; educational, general, scientific; Chair. R. McLEOD; Man. Dir. Dr. ANDREW FABINYI, O.B.E.

*****Sir Isaac Pitman Aust. (Pty.) Ltd.:** 158 Bouverie St., Melbourne; f. 1968; secretarial and management sciences, art, photographic, educational, technical, general; Chair. Sir GEORGE PATON; Man. Dir. PHILIP J. HARRIS.

Ponsford, Newman and Benson Ltd.: 287–291 Burwood Rd., Hawthorn, Vic., and 348 Kent St., Sydney, also Brisbane, Adelaide and Perth; f. 1925; Man. Dir. D. MacKENZIE.

Prentice-Hall of Australia Pty. Ltd.: P.O.B. 151, Brookvale, N.S.W. 2100; textbooks, popular trade books, reference; Man. Dir. P. F. GLEESON.

Ramsay, Ware, Publishing Pty. Ltd.: 552–566 Victoria St., North Melbourne, N.1; f. 1887; Dirs. W. S. KENT HUGHES, A. W. RAMSAY, J. S. McCREERY; special editions.

Reed, A. H., and A. W., Ltd.: 51 Whiting St., Artarmon, N.S.W. 2064, and at Wellington, N.Z. (head office), Auckland and Christchurch, N.Z.; f. 1907; general books, educational books, gramophone recordings, relating to Australia, New Zealand and the South Pacific; Chair. J. H. RICHARDS; Man. Dir. Australia J. M. REED.

Rigby Ltd.: 30 North Terrace, Kent Town, S.A. 5067; f. 1859; general and educational; Chair. Sir DONALD BRADMAN; Man. Dir. J. L. TAINTON.

Ruskin Press Pty. Ltd.: 39 Leveson St., N. Melbourne, N.1; f. 1920; Dirs. R. E. HAYES, H. P. B. HARPER.

Rydge Publications Pty. Ltd.: 74 Clarence St., Sydney 2000; f. 1928; Man. Dir. NORMAN B. RYDGE Jr.; Chief Exec. T. J. STOREY.

Sydney University Press: Press Building, University of Sydney; f. 1964; scholarly, academic and educational books and journals; Dir. MALCOLM TITT.

University of Queensland Press: P.O.B. 42, St. Lucia 4067, Queensland; f. 1948; approximately 65 new titles annually of scholarly and general cultural interest; microfilm, audio-visual programmes; Man. FRANK W. THOMPSON; Senior Editor Miss ANN LAHEY.

University of Western Australia Press: Nedlands, W.A. 6009; f. 1960; educational, secondary and university, technical and scientific, scholarly, humanities; journals; Man. V. S. GREAVES.

Ure Smith Pty. Ltd.: 176 South Creek Rd., Dee Why West, Sydney, N.S.W. 2009; f. 1939; general book publishing, including art and architecture, Australiana, geographical, children's, cookery, educational, fiction, history, humour, medical, sociological, sport, natural history; Man. Dir. S. URE SMITH; a member of the Paul Hamlyn (Aust.) Group of Companies.

Whitcombe and Tombs Pty. Ltd.: 159–163 Victoria Rd., Marrickville, N.S.W. 2204; Head Office: Christchurch, N.Z.; f. 1939; Man. J. SMYTHEMAN; educational books.

Wiley, John, and Sons Australasia Pty. Ltd.: 110 Alexander St., Crows Nest, N.S.W. 2065; technical, scientific, educational; Man. Dir. P. SEARLE.

* Australian branch of London firm.

RADIO AND TELEVISION

Australian Broadcasting Control Board: 562–574 Bourke St., Melbourne; f. 1949; Chair. M. F. E. Wright; Vice-Chair. J. M. Donovan, J. E. Neary, o.b.e. (member), E. N. Williams, m.b.e., H. S. Harte (part-time members), B. J. Connolly (Sec.).

The Australian Broadcasting Control Board is responsible for planning the provision, and ensuring acceptable technical standards, of both commercial and national broadcasting and television stations and for the programme standards of the commercial broadcasting and television stations.

Australian Broadcasting Commission: 145–153 Elizabeth St., P.O.B. 487, Sydney, N.S.W. 2001; Commissioners Prof. R. I. Downing (Chair.), A. G. Lowndes, c.b.e., Mrs. D. E. A. Edwards, o.b.e., H. Lashwood, A. J. Smith, o.b.e., Dr. E. Hackett, J. Tehan, H. S. Lodge, M. A. K. Thompson; Gen. Man. T. S. Duckmanton, c.b.e.; London Office: 54 Portland Place, WIN 4DY.

The programmes for the national broadcasting and national television services are provided by the Australian Broadcasting Commission. All studio technical services are manned by the A.B.C.; transmitting stations in both broadcasting and television are manned by the Postmaster-General's Department staff. Advertisements are not broadcast over the national services which are financed by parliamentary appropriation. By January 1974, there were scheduled to be 157 national radio and television stations in operation. There are 81 medium-wave and 6 short-wave radio stations in the domestic network. The programmes of Radio Australia, the overseas service of the A.B.C., are transmitted from 9 additional short-wave and 3 booster transmitters.

The A.B.C. maintains membership of the Asian Broadcasting Union, the Commonwealth Broadcasting Conference and the British Commonwealth Newsfilm Agency (Visnews). The A.B.C. is also an Associate Member of the European Broadcasting Union.

RADIO

Federation of Australian Commercial Broadcasters: P.O.B. 294, Milsons Point, Sydney, N.S.W. 2061; Federal Dir. D. L. Foster; Federal Sec. J. H. Finlayson.

The commercial services are provided by stations operated by companies and individuals under licences granted and renewed by the Minister for the Media. They rely for their income on the broadcasting of advertisements and other publicity. On June 30th, 1973, there were 118 commercial broadcasting stations in operation.

Major Commercial Broadcasting Station Licensees

Adelaide Central Methodist Mission, Inc.: 43 Franklin St., Adelaide, S.A.; operates stations in Adelaide, Port Augusta, Whyalla and Berri.

Advertiser Broadcasting Network: 121 King William St., Adelaide; operates station 5A.D. in Adelaide and regional stations 5P.I., 5M.U. and 5S.E. in other parts of the State.

Amalgamated Wireless (Australasia) Ltd.: 47 York St., Sydney; operates stations at Sydney, Grafton, Goulburn, Albury, Bendigo, Townsville, Cairns and Launceston; Chair. Sir Lionel Hooke; Man. Dir. J. A. L. Hooke.

Associated Broadcasting Services Ltd.: 290 Latrobe St., Melbourne 3000; f. 1957; operates stations at Colac, Shepparton, Warragul and Warrnambool; Chair. Sidney J. A. Kemp; Gen. Man. R. W. Ellenby.

Commonwealth Broadcasting Corporation Pty. Ltd.: 365 Kent Street, Sydney; operating station 2UW, Sydney, key station of Commonwealth Broadcasting Network; stations at Brisbane, Toowoomba, Rockhampton and Maryborough.

Consolidated Broadcasting System (W.A.) Pty. Ltd.: 283 Rokeby Rd., Subiaco, W.A.; operates stations 6GE Geraldton, 6KG Kalgoorlie, 6AM Northam and 6PM Perth; Man. Des McDonald.

Findlays Broadcasting Services Pty. Ltd.: 28A Erina St., P.O.B. 665G, Launceston, Tasmania; operates Tasmanian Broadcasting Network radio stations 7BU-7AD-7SD, N. Tasmania, Australia.

The Herald and Weekly Times Ltd.: 44–74 Flinders St., Melbourne 3000; operates television station HSV7 and radio station 3DB.

Radio Broadcasting Network of Queensland: 363 Adelaide St., Brisbane, Qld.; operates stations at Longreach, Mount Isa, Darling Downs, Charleville and Greater Brisbane area.

Victorian Broadcasting Network Ltd.: "The Age" Chambers, 239 Collins St., Melbourne, Vic.; operates stations at Hamilton, Maryborough, Sale and Swan Hill.

2 TM Management Pty. Ltd.: Radio Centre, Calala, Tamworth, N.S.W.; controls stations 2 TM Tamworth, and 2 MO Gunnedah and operates 2AD Armidale and 2RE Taree through the New England network.

Note: In 1972 there were 8,000,000 radio receivers in use.

TELEVISION

Federation of Australian Commercial Television Stations: Suite 404, 4th Floor, Caltex House, Kent St., Sydney, 2000; General Manager A. S. Cowan.

The commercial television service is provided by stations operated by companies under licences granted and renewed by the Postmaster-General. On June 30th, 1973, there were 54 commercial television stations in operation and a total of 48 commercial translator stations on relay. *Note:* Colour transmissions are expected to start on March 1st, 1975.

Principal Commercial Television Station Licensees

Amalgamated Television Services Pty. Ltd.: T.V. Centre, Epping, N.S.W.: operates one station at Sydney, ATN7; f. 1956; Gen. Man. J. S. Doherty.

Austarama Television Pty. Ltd.: cnr. Springvale and Hawthorn Rds., Nunawading, Vic. 3131; operates station ATV-0 at Melbourne.

Ballarat and Western Victoria Television Ltd.: Box 464, Ballarat; f. 1962; operates BTV Channel 6, and translators Channel 9 (Warrnambool), Channel 11 (Portland) and Channel 7 (Nhill); Chair. A. C. Pittard; Gen. Man. J. L. Stapp.

Bendigo and Central Victoria Telecasters Ltd.: P.O.B. 240, Lily St., Bendigo, Vic.; f. 1961; operates country stations BCV-8, BCV-11 and GLV-10 Gippsland; Gen. Man. F. A. McManus.

Brisbane TV Ltd.: Box 604J, G.P.O., Brisbane; started full-scale telecasting 1959, from station BTQ; Man. Murray Norris.

Broken Hill Television Ltd.: P.O.B. 472, Broken Hill, N.S.W. 2880; commenced transmission August 1968; Chair. P. Martin; Man. Dir. J. M. Sturrock; Station Man. E. L. Downing.

Canberra Television Ltd.: P.O.B. 633, Canberra City, A.C.T.; f. 1962; Gen. Man. G. K. Barlin.

Country Television Services Ltd.: Radio and T.V. Centre, Bathurst Rd., Orange, N.S.W.; f. 1962; operates country stations CBN-8, CWN-6, 2GZ Orange and 2NZ Invereee; Gen. Man. A. Ridley.

Darling Downs TV Ltd.: Mt. Lofty, Toowoomba, Qld.; f. 1962; operates country stations DDQ-10, SDQ-4 and Channel 5, Toowoomba; Gen. Man. S. J. Fitzpatrick.

Far Northern Television Ltd.: 101 Aumuller St., Cairns, Qld.; f. 1966 to operate station FNQ; Chair. C. K. Carmody.

General Television Corporation Pty. Ltd.: 22–46 Bendigo St., P.O.B. 100, Richmond, Vic. 3121; f. 1957; operates station GVT-9 at Melbourne; Man. Dir. R. C. Packer; Chief Exec. E. W. Fisher.

Goulburn-Murray Television Ltd.: 290 Latrobe Street, Melbourne; f. 1961; operates country station GMV-6, Shepparton; Chair. Sidney J. A. Kemp; Gen. Man. Peter L. Twomey.

Herald-Sun TV Pty. Ltd.: 44–47 Flinders St., Melbourne 3000; f. 1956; operates station HSV-7 in Melbourne; parent company, The Herald and Weekly Times Ltd.; Chair. K. S. Cairns; Man. R. P. Casey.

Mackay Television Ltd.: Box 496 P.O. Mackay, Qld.; f. 1965; operation of station MVQ6 commenced August 1968; Gen. Man. R. J. H. Scott.

Murrumbidgee Television Ltd.: Remembrance Driveway, Griffith, N.S.W. 2680; f. 1965 to operate station MTN; Gen. Man. W. R. Gamble.

Newcastle Broadcasting and Television Corporation Ltd.: Mosbri Crescent, Newcastle, N.S.W.; f. 1962; operates country station NBN-3; Chair. Lawford Richardson; Gen. Man. K. W. Stone.

Northern Rivers Television Ltd.: Pacific Highway, Coff's Harbour, N.S.W.; operates stations NRN-11 and RTN-8.

Northern Television (TNT9) Pty. Ltd.: Watchorn St., Launceston, Tas.; f. 1962; operates Tasmanian country station TNT-9.

Queensland Television Ltd.: Box 72, G.P.O., Brisbane, Qld.; f. 1958; started operating station QTQ-9 in Brisbane 1959; Gen. Man. J. W. McKay.

Riverina and North East Victoria TV Ltd.: Television Centre, Lake Albert Rd., Wagga Wagga, N.S.W. 2650; f. 1964; operates country stations RVN-2 and AMV-4.

Rockhampton Television Ltd.: Dean Street, Rockhampton, Qld.; f. 1963; operates country station RTQ-7; Gen. Man. B. Saunders.

South Australian Telecasters Ltd.: Adelaide; f. 1965; operates a commercial TV station in Adelaide.

South East Telecasters Ltd.: P.O.B. 821, Mount Gambier; f. 1962; operates country station SES-8; Chair. G. T. Barnfield; Gen. Man. A. B. Noblet.

South Western Telecasters Ltd.: P.O.B. 112, Bunbury, W.A. 6230; f. 1967 to operate country stations BTW-3 and GSW-9; Man. B. F. Hopwood.

Southern Television Corporation Ltd.: 202 Tynte Street, North Adelaide; f. 1958; station NWS-9 at Adelaide; Man. Dir. W. L. C. Davies.

Spencer Gulf Telecasters Ltd.: P.O.B. 305, Port Pirie, S.A. 5540; f. 1968; stations GTS-4, 5 and 8; Man. E. L. Downing.

Sunraysia Television Ltd.: P.O.B. 1157, Mildura, Vic.; f. 1965 to operate country station STV-8; Chair. C. D. Lanyon; Gen. Man. D. M. Cain.

Swan Television Ltd.: Hayes Ave., Tuart Hill, W.A. 6060; f. 1965; operates station STW-9 in Perth; Man. Dir. L. J. Kiernan.

Tasmanian Television Limited: 52 New Town Rd., Hobart; f. 1959; started operating TVT-6 at Hobart, May 1960; Man. Dir. E. G. McRae; Station Man. D. L. Carter.

Telecasters North Queensland Ltd.: S.G.I.O. Bldg., Lower Denham St., P.O.B. 1016, Townsville, Qld. 4810; f. 1962; operates country station TNQ-7.

Television Corporation Limited: 168–174 Castlereagh Street, Sydney, N.S.W.; f. 1956; operates station TCN-9 at Sydney; Gen. Man. T. A. Miller; majority shareholding in GTV channel 9 at Melbourne; Chair. R. C. Packer.

Television New England Ltd.: P.O.B. 317, Tamworth, N.S.W.; f. 1965; operates stations NEN-9 and ECN-8; Chair. H. Joseph; Gen. Man. M. M. Moroney.

Television Wollongong Transmissions Ltd.: Fort Drummond, Mount St. Thomas, Wollongong, N.S.W.; f. 1962; operates station WIN-4, Channels 3 (Wollongong) 6 (Bega), 11 (Moruya), Gen. Man. W. Lean.

TV Broadcasters Ltd.: 125 Strangways Terrace, North Adelaide, S.A. 5006; f. 1958; station ADS-7 at Adelaide; Gen. Man. J. M. Fowler; Film Programme Man. I. Woodward; Executive Producer S. Pippos; News Editor C. Wood; Chief Engineer N. Sawyer.

TVW Limited: P.O.B. 77, Tuart Hill, W.A. 6060; commercial stations TVW-7 at Perth and SAS-10 at Adelaide, started operations 1959; Man. Dir. J. W. Cruthers.

United Telecasters Sydney Ltd.: P.O.B. 10, Lane Cove, Sydney 2066; operates station TEN; Gen. Man. I. G. Holmes.

Universal Telecasters Qld. Ltd.: Box 751, G.P.O., Brisbane 4001; f. 1965; operating TVQ, Channel O; Gen. Man. R. G. Archer.

V.B.N. Ltd.: Prince's Highway, Traralgon, Vic.; f. 1962; operates country station GLV-10.

Wide Bay-Burnett TV Ltd.: Granville, Maryborough, Qld.; f. 1965; operates station WBQ-8, Channel 1, Sunshine Coast; Gen. Man. Muir Daniel.

Note: In 1973 there were over 3 million sets in use.

FINANCE

BANKING

(cap. = capital; p.u. = paid up; dep. = deposits; m. = million)
($A = $ Australian)

CENTRAL BANK

Reserve Bank of Australia: Head Office: 65 Martin Place, Sydney, N.S.W. 2000; f. 1911; Central Bank and the sole bank of issue for Australia and Territories; has separate dept. for commodity marketing finance; cap. $A49.4m.; res. funds $A36.2m.; dep. and other accounts $A2,809m. (30 June 1972); Gov. Sir John G. PHILLIPS, K.B.E.; Dep. Gov. H. M. KNIGHT.

COMMONWEALTH BANKS

Commonwealth Banking Corporation: G.P.O. Box 2719, Pitt St., and Martin Place, Sydney, N.S.W. 2000; f. 1960; controlling body for three member banks: Commonwealth Trading Bank, Commonwealth Savings Bank and Commonwealth Development Bank (*below*); Chair. Sir ROLAND WILSON, K.B.E.; Man. Dir. B. B. CALLAGHAN, C.B.E.

Commonwealth Trading Bank of Australia: Pitt St. and Martin Place, Sydney 2000; est. 1953 to take over business of General Banking Division of Commonwealth Bank of Australia; cap. $A14.8m.; dep. $A2,359m. (June 1973); Gen. Man. J. F. LOWAN.

Commonwealth Savings Bank of Australia: Pitt St. and Martin Place, Sydney, N.S.W. 2000; est. 1912; dep. $A4,034m. (June 1973); Gen. Man. I. R. NORMAN.

Commonwealth Development Bank of Australia: Prudential Bldg., 39 Martin Place, Sydney, N.S.W. 2000; f. 1960; loans and equipment finance outstanding $A287m. (June 1973); Gen. Man. R. S. ELLIOTT.

DEVELOPMENT BANK

Australian Resources Development Bank Ltd.: 379 Collins St., Melbourne, Victoria 3000; f. 1967 by major Australian trading banks with support of Reserve Bank of Australia to marshal funds from local and overseas sources for the financing of Australian participation in projects of national importance; cap. p.u. $A3m.; dep. $A290.9m. (1972); Chair. H. McE. SCAMBLER; Gen. Man. R. G. McCROSSIN.

TRADING BANKS

Bank of Adelaide, The: 81 King William St., Adelaide, S. Australia; f. 1865; cap. p.u. $A25.203m.; dep. $A268.4m. (1973); Chair. Hon. Sir ARTHUR RYMILL, M.L.C.; Man. Dir. W. P. WRIGHT; Gen. Man. R. B. NANCARROW.

Bank of New South Wales: 60 Martin Place, Sydney, N.S.W.; f. 1817; cap. p.u. $A85m.; dep.$A3,038m. (1972); Pres. Sir JOHN CADWALLADER; Chief Gen. Man. Sir ROBERT NORMAN.

Bank of Queensland Ltd.: 115 Queen St., Brisbane; f. 1874; cap. p.u. $A2.75m.; dep. $A28m.; Chair. E W. SAVAGE; Gen. Man. A. N. MURRELL.

Commercial Bank of Australia Ltd.: 335–339 Collins St., Melbourne, Vic.; f. 1866; cap. p.u. $A24.4m.; consolidated dep. (Banking) $A1,746.707m. (June 1973); Chair. T. L. WEBB; Man. Dir. D. W. STRIDE.

Commercial Banking Co. of Sydney Ltd.: 343 George St., Sydney, N.S.W.; f. 1834; cap. p.u. $A32.092m.; dep. $A1,780.598m. (1971); Chair. G. B. KATER; Gen. Man. G. F. BOWEN.

Export Re-Finance Corporation Ltd.: Sydney; f. 1964.

National Bank of Australasia Ltd.: 271–285 Collins St., Melbourne, Victoria 3001; f. 1858; cap. p.u. $A43.7m.; dep. $A1,869.5m. (Sept. 1972); Chair. Sir JAMES FORREST; Gen. Man. T. B. C. BELL.

Rural and Industries Bank of Western Australia: 54–58 Barrack St., P.O.B. E 237, Perth, W.A. 6001; f. 1945; cap. $A22m.; dep. $A217m. (1972); Chair. C. E. COLLINS.

Rural Bank of New South Wales: Martin Place, Sydney, N.S.W.; 202 offices in N.S.W.; overseas offices in Canada, U.S.A., Fed. Rep. of Germany, Italy, Hong Kong and Japan; res. $A57.54m.; Pres. A. OLIVER, C.M.G.; Chief Man. Banking J. L. DE BOOS; Sec. BRIAN HERBERT.

State Bank of South Australia: 51 Pirie St., Adelaide, S. Australia; f. 1896; cap. $A149,699,541; dep. $A46,492,657 net (June 1973); Chair. G. F. SEAMAN, C.M.G., B.EC., A.U.A., F.A.S.A.; Gen. Man. J. C. TAYLOR.

SAVINGS BANKS

Bank of New South Wales Savings Bank Ltd.: 60 Martin Place, Sydney; f. 1955; cap. p.u. $A14m.; dep. $A1,146m. (1971); Chair. Sir JOHN CADWALLADER; Chief Man. W. TWYCROSS.

Savings Bank of South Australia, The: King William St., Adelaide; f. 1848; Chair. G. H. P. JEFFERY; Gen. Man. A. G. SHEPHERD.

Savings Bank of Tasmania: Liverpool St., Hobart, Tasmania; f. 1845; Pres. H. A. CUTHBERTSON; Gen. Man. R. H. TAYLOR.

State Savings Bank of Victoria: Cnr. Elizabeth St. and Bourke St., Melbourne 3000; f. 1842; dep. $A1,615m. (June 1972); Chair. R. G. HOBAN; Gen. Man. D. ROSS.

FOREIGN BANKS

Australia and New Zealand Banking Group Ltd.: Head Office: 71 Cornhill, London, EC3V 3PR; Australian Head Office: 351 Collins St., Melbourne; New Zealand Head Office: 196 Featherston St., Wellington; Man. Dir. C. H. RENNIE; Chief Gen. Man. M. BRUNKHORST.

Bank of New Zealand: Head Office: P.O.B. 2392, Lambton Quay, Wellington; branches at Sydney and Melbourne.

Banque Nationale de Paris: Head Office: 16 blvd. des Italiens, Paris 9; Australian Head Office: 12 Castlereagh St., Sydney; f. in Australia 1881; cap. 500m. FF.; dep. 82,000m. FF., reserves 554m. FF.; branches in Sydney, Melbourne, Perth, Brisbane; Gen. Man. J. GERBIER.

Barclays Australia Ltd.: Sydney; f. Aug. 1972; cap. £3.1m.; Chair. J. P. MARTIN.

International Commercial Bank of China: Head Office: 15 Chungshan Rd. North, Sec. II, Taipei, Taiwan; Australian branch: 40 Martin Place, Sydney.

STOCK EXCHANGES

Australian Associated Stock Exchanges: 60 Martin Place, Sydney, N.S.W. 2000; f. 1937; mems. Stock Exchanges in the six capital cities; Pres. MICHAEL McALISTER; Sec. MEALEY.

Brisbane Stock Exchange, The: M.M.I. Bldg., 344 Queen St., Brisbane; f. 1885; 45 mems.; Chair. T. R. BURRELL; Man. G. P. CHAPMAN; Sec. D. G. SLATER.

Hobart Stock Exchange: 86 Collins St., Hobart; f. 1891.

Stock Exchange of Adelaide Ltd.: 55 Exchange Place, Adelaide; f. 1887; 60 mems.; Chair. W. G. F. McCULLOCH; Man. F. L. WRAY.

Stock Exchange of Melbourne Ltd.: 351 Collins St., Melbourne; f. 1859 (inc. 1970); 169 mems.; Chair. J. C. JOHNSTON, C.B.E.; Gen. Man. R. B. LEE.

Stock Exchange of Perth Ltd.: Exchange House, 68 St. George's Terrace, Perth; f. 1889; 33 mems.; Chair. R. A. BLACK; Gen. Man. R. L. COPPEL.

Sydney Stock Exchange: 20 O'Connell St., Sydney; f. 1871; 145 mems.; Chair. J. H. VALDER; Gen. Man. D. M. BUTCHER; publ. *Australian Stock Exchange Journal* (monthly).

INSURANCE

Export Payments Insurance Corporation—EPIC: Head Office: 2 Castlereagh Street, Sydney; brs.: 224 Queen Street, Melbourne, 118 King William Street, Adelaide, 30 Herschell St., Brisbane and 37 St. George's Terrace, Perth; represented by Dept. of Trade and Industry Hobart; f. 1956 by Act of Parliament to give protection to exporters against risks of loss arising from non-payment of accounts by overseas buyers, and to investors against non-commercial losses on overseas investments; Commissioner G. A. HAWLEY, O.B.E.

A.A.S.A., A.A.I.I.: 53 Martin Place, Sydney; f. 1912; Chair. L. J. THOMPSON, F.C.A., F.C.I.S.; Gen. Man. W. J. MAHER.

Aetna Life of Australia and New Zealand Ltd.: Head Office: 2 Help St., Chatswood, N.S.W. 2067; Man. Dir. J. H. MAXWELL.

A.F.G. Insurances Ltd.: 277–287 William St., Melbourne 3000; f. 1922; fire, accident, marine; Chair. T. L. WEBB; Gen. Man. A. G. MAYNE YOUNG.

A.G.C. (Insurances) Ltd.: A.G.C. House, Philip and Hunter Sts., Sydney, N.S.W.; f. 1938; Chair. N. H. ROUTLEY, C.B.E.; Gen. Man. D. GRECIAN.

Ajax Insurance Co. Ltd.: 105 Queen St., Melbourne; f. 1934; cap. p.u. $A2 m.; Dir. F. E. BUNNY (Chair.); Gen. Man. H. L. WILLIAMS.

AMEV Life Assurance Co. Ltd.: 15 O'Connell St., Sydney; f. 1958; Chair. A. J. DE MONTFORT; Gen. Man. R. G. GLADING.

A.M.P. Fire & General Insurance Co. Ltd.: A.M.P. Bldg., Sydney Cove, N.S.W. 2000; f. 1958; Chair. Sir VINCENT FAIRFAX, C.M.G.; Man. Dir. J. K. STAVELEY.

Australasian Temperance and General Mutual Life Assurance Society Ltd., The: Cnr. Collins and Russell Streets, Melbourne; f. 1876; Gen. Man. K. T. BLAMEY.

Australian Alliance Assurance Co., The: 440 Collins St., Melbourne; f. 1862; cap. p.u. $A180,000; Man. Dir. R. A. SINCLAIR.

Australian & Eastern Insurance Co. Ltd.: 406 Collins St., Melbourne; f. 1954; fire, marine, accident, general; Man. K. GILBERT.

Australian Equitable Insurance Co. Ltd.: 4th Floor, 140 Arthur St., North Sydney 2060; f. 1952; cap. p.u. $A1.25m.; fire, marine, accident; Chair. ROBERT D. SOMERVILLE, LL.B.; Gen. Man. J. D. C. WOOD.

Australian General Insurance Co. Ltd.: 117 Pitt St., Sydney; f. 1913; cap. p.u. $A1m.; Chair. M. C. DAVIS; Man. Dir. W. F. RITCHIE.

Australian Mutual Fire Insurance Society Ltd.: 109 Pitt St., Sydney; Temple Court, 428 Collins St., Melbourne; cap. p.u. $A0.320m.; Chair. A. MACFADYEN.

Australian National Assurance Co. Ltd., The: 408/410 Collins Street, Melbourne 3000; f. 1922; Managing Dir. D. G. PETTIGREW.

Australian Natives' Association Insurance Co. Ltd.: 28–32 Elizabeth Street, Melbourne; f. 1948; fire, general; Chair. R. J. JOSEPH, O.B.E.; Man. Dir. L. D. BROOKS.

Australian Reinsurance Co. Ltd.: 325 Collins St., Melbourne, Vic. 3000; f. 1962; reinsurance; Chair. R. S. TURNER, C.B.E.; Gen. Man. J. H. WINTER.

Bankers & Traders' Insurance Company Ltd.: Head Office: 115 Pitt St., Sydney; f. 1921; Chair. J. F. R. LAWES; Gen. Man. W. H. MOLYNEUX.

C.G.A. Fire & Accident Insurance Co. Ltd.: C.G.A. House, 9-11 Hunter St., Sydney; f. 1959; fire, marine, accident; Chair. Sir ARTHUR FADDEN; Man. for Australia J. P. O'CONNELL; Sec. P. G. MEADOWS.

Chamber of Manufactures Insurance Ltd., The: 368–374 St. Kilda Rd., Melbourne 3004; f. 1914; cap. p.u. $A0.2m.; Chair. E. R. BEATTIE; Man. Dir. L. E. GRIFFITHS.

City Mutual General Insurance Ltd.: 66 Hunter St., Sydney; f. 1889; Chair. M. J. O'NEILL; Gen. Man. R. J. LAWSON.

City Mutual Life Assurance Society Ltd.: 60–66 Hunter St., Sydney, N.S.W.; incorp. 1878; Chair. Sir John O'NEILL, C.B.E.; Gen. Man. P. C. WICKENS, M.A., LL.M., F.I.A.

Colonial Mutual Fire Insurance Co. Ltd., The: 440 Collins St., Melbourne; f. 1878; cap. p.u. $A600,016; Chair. J. M. BAILLIEU; Dir. R. A. SINCLAIR.

Colonial Mutual Life Assurance Society Ltd., The: 330 Collins St., Melbourne 3000; f. 1873; total assets $A1,067m.; Chair. W. D. BROOKES, C.B.E., D.S.O., A.E.A.; Gen. Man. J. L. GREIG, F.A.S.A., F.C.I.S.

Commercial Union Assurance Co. of Australia Ltd.: Temple Court, 428 Collins Street, Melbourne; f. 1960; fire, accident, marine, life; Chair. Sir EDWARD COHEN; Gen. Man. A. MACFADYEN.

Co-operative Insurance Co. of Australia Ltd.: 528–534 Collins St., Melbourne, Vic. 3000; f. 1918; Gen. Man. J. S. HODGKINSON.

Copenhagen Reinsurance Company (Aust.) Ltd.: 280–288 George St., Sydney; f. 1961; reinsurance; Chair. F. M. D. JACKETT; Man. D. F. BURKE.

Derwent and Tamar Assurance Co. Ltd.: 28 Murray St., Hobart, Tasmania; f. 1838; Chair. Sir G. A. WALCH, K.B.E., C.V.O.

Equitable Life and General Insurance Co. Ltd.: Head Office: 80 Alfred St., North Sydney; f. 1921; cap. p.u. $A410,000; Man. Dir. R. R. M. MORGAN.

FAI Insurance Group: FAI Insurance Bldg., 185 Macquarie St., Sydney, N.S.W. 2000; f. 1960; includes Fire and All Risks Insurance Co. Ltd., Australian and International Insurances Ltd., Car Owners' Mutual Insurance Co. Ltd., The Falkirk and Stirlingshire Assurance Co. Ltd., Omnibus and Gen. Insurance Co. Ltd., Falkirk Assurance Soc. Ltd.; fire, marine, accident, aviation; Chair. L. J. ADLER; Dirs. J. BELFER, J. A. J. BARRINGTON, P. GREY, Prof. J. R. WILSON, R. L. HERMAN; Sec. R. L. HERMAN.

Farmers and Settlers' Co-operative Insurance Co. of Australia Ltd.: Regd. Office: Pearl Assurance House, 1-7 Castlereagh St., Sydney; f. 1914; Gen. Man. W. A. WILSON.

Federation Insurance Ltd., The: Federation House, 342–8 Flinders Street, Melbourne; f. 1926; Chair. Sir LEWIS BURNE; Man. Dir. and Gen. Man. C. J. CHAMPION.

Government Insurance Office of N.S.W.: 60–70 Elizabeth St., Sydney, N.S.W.; assets exceed $A481m.; Gen. Man. R. M. PORTER, A.C.I.S., A.A.S.A., A.A.I.I.

Insurance Office of Australia Ltd.: 428 Collins St., Melbourne, C.1; f. 1910; assets $A12.8m.; Chair. K. N. WARK; Man. A. MACFADYEN; fire, marine, accident.

London Guarantee & Accident Co. of Australia Ltd.: 32–34 Bridge St., Sydney; f. 1969; subsidiary of Phoenix Assurance Co. of Australia Ltd.: Dirs. L. E. TUTT, L. M. BLANTON, W. C. HARRIS; Gen. Man. H. A. PARKER.

Manchester Unity Fire Insurance Co. of Victoria Ltd.: Cnr. Swanston and Collins Streets, Melbourne; fire, accident; Chair. R. E. DAYMON; Sec. and Man. M. W. CAMPBELL.

Manufacturers' Mutual Insurance Ltd.: 12–14 O'Connell St., Sydney, N.S.W. 2000; f. 1914; Chair. J. M. BURNETI, C.B.E.; Gen. Man. F. T. GROSE.

Mercantile & General Life Reassurance Co. of Australia Ltd.: Swire House, 8 Spring St., Sydney; f. 1957; life reassurance; Chair. G. B. KATER; Gen. Man. S. R. B. FRANCE.

Mercantile Mutual Insurance Co. Ltd.: 117 Pitt St., Sydney; f. 1878; cap. p.u. $A8.8m.; Chair. M. C. DAVIS; Man. Dir. W. F. RITCHIE.

Mercantile Mutual Life Insurance Co. Ltd.: 50 Hunter St., Sydney; f. 1895; cap. p.u. $A0.2m.; Chair. M. C. DAVIS; Gen. Man. A. E. M. GEDDES, B.A., B.COM., F.I.A., A.A.S.A.

M.L.C. Fire & General Insurance Co. Ltd.: Victoria Cross, North Sydney, N.S.W. 2060; f. 1958; Chair. A. F. DEER; Man. for Australia and New Zealand C. W. LEPAGE.

Mutual Life and Citizens' Assurance Co. Ltd.: P.O.B. 200, North Sydney 2060; f. 1886; assets exceed $A1,175m.; Chair. B. J. D. PAGE, LL.B.; Gen. Man. A. F. DEER, B.A., LL.B., B.EC.

National & General Insurance Co. Ltd.: 100 New South Head Rd., Edgecliff, N.S.W.; f. 1954; fire, marine general; Chair. G. T. HARTIGAN; Gen. Man. R. W. MANN.

National Co-operative Insurance Society Ltd.: 799–801 Hunter Street, Newcastle West, N.S.W.; f. 1947; fire, householders, motor car, accident; Chair. A. F. J. SMITH; Gen. Manager L. C. BOYD.

National Mutual Casualty Insurances Ltd.: 447 Collins St., Melbourne; f. 1961; accident, sickness; Chair. G. M. NIALL; Man. P. R. SHIPMAN.

National Mutual Fire Insurance Co. Ltd.: 447 Collins Street, Melbourne; f. 1957; fire, accident, marine; Chair. G. M. NIALL; Gen. Man. H. G. WALKER, B.C.E., F.I.A.; Man. K. N. FISK, A.A.I.I.

National Mutual Life Association of Australasia Ltd.: 447 Collins St., Melbourne; f. 1869; assets $A1,227m.; Chair. G. M. NIALL; Gen. Man. R. L. BIENVENU, D.F.C., F.I.A.

New Zealand Victoria Life Ltd.: 79 Pitt St., Sydney, N.S.W.; Chair. A. G. WILSON, O.B.E.; Gen. Man. J. R. MARKLEY.

North British & Mercantile Insurance Co. of Australia Ltd.: 428 Collins Street, Melbourne; fire, marine, accident; Chair. Sir IAN POTTER; Man. A. MACFADYEN.

Northumberland Insurance Co. Ltd.: 52–58 Clarence St., Sydney, N.S.W.; f. 1955; fire, marine, accident; Chair. R. E. M. HUTCHESON; Gen. Man. T. G. WHITBREAD.

N.R.M.A. Insurance Ltd.: N.R.M.A. House, 151 Clarence St., Sydney, N.S.W. 2009; f. 1926; Chair. R. E. LUDOWICI; Gen. Man. R. J. LAMBLE.

Phoenix Assurance Co. of Australia Ltd.: 414 Collins St., Melbourne; 32–34 Bridge St., Sydney; f. 1931, name changed 1970; subsidiary companies: London Guarantee and Accident Co. of Australia Ltd., The Southern Union Commercial Insurance Co. of Australia Ltd., The Provident Fire Insurance Co. of Australia Ltd.; associate company Phoenix Life Assurance Co. of Australia Ltd.; Chair. G. A. SAMUEL; Gen. Man. H. A. PARKER.

Phoenix Life Assurance Co. of Australia Ltd.: 32–34 Bridge St. Sydney; incorporated in New South Wales, 1968; Dirs. A. S. RICHARDSON, H. H. HUTTEMEIER, W. C. HARRIS; Gen. Man. H. A. PARKER.

Provident Fire Insurance Co. of Australia Ltd.: 32–34 Bridge St., Sydney; f. 1969; subsidiary of Phoenix Assurance Co. of Australia Ltd.; Dirs. L. E. TUTT, L. M. BLANTON, W. C. HARRIS; Gen. Man. H. A. PARKER.

Queensland Insurance Co. Ltd.: 80–82 Pitt St., Sydney; f. 1886; cap. p.u. $A7.5m.; Chair. J. F. R. LAWES; Gen. Man. H. J. MOORHOUSE.

Regent Insurance Ltd.: 277–287 William St., Melbourne 3000; f. 1959; fire, general; Chair. H. F. STOKES; Chief Man. KEITH McMORRON.

Reinsurance Co. of Australasia Ltd.: 2 Hunter St., Sydney; f. 1961; reinsurance. fire, accident, marine; Chair. Sir JOHN MARKS, C.B.E.; Gen. Man. W. C. STEVENS.

Royal-Globe Life Assurance Co. Ltd.: 440 Collins Street, Melbourne; f. 1960; life; Chair. and Man. Dir. R. A. SINCLAIR.

Skandia Australia Insurance Ltd.: 220 George St., Sydney; Zone Man. and Chief Executive G. ANDREASSON.

South British United Life Assurance Co. Ltd.: 66 King St., Sydney; f. 1921; Man. Dir. W. J. DOWD.

Southern Pacific Insurance Co. Ltd.: 80 Alfred St., Milsons Point, N.S.W. 2061; f. 1935; fire, accident, marine; Chair. C. H. V. CARPENTER; Man. Dir. J. B. BAILEY.

Sun Alliance Insurance Ltd.: 22 Bridge St., Sydney 2000; office in Jakarta; fire, accident and marine insurance; Man. Dir. D. G. PETTIGREW.

Switzerland Life Assurance Society Ltd.: 457 Little Collins St., Melbourne, Vic. 3000; f. 1960; life, accident; Chair. and Man. Dir. W. W. PISTERMAN; Actuary and Gen. Sec. N. E. RENTON.

T. & G. Fire and General Insurance Co. Ltd.: Collins and Russell Sts., Melbourne; f. 1958; Chair. J. R. BURT; Gen. Man. M. A. KEMP.

Temperance and General Mutual Life Assurance Society Ltd. (The Australasian): Collins and Russell Streets, Melbourne; f. 1876; assets $A800m.; Gen. Man. K. T. BLAMEY, O.B.E., E.D.

Underwriting & Insurance Ltd.: 578 St. Kilda Rd., Melbourne 3004; f. 1930; life, fire, accident, marine; Chair. A. BOND; Gen. Man. R. J. FOREMAN.

United Insurance Co. Ltd.: George and Hunter Streets, Sydney; f. 1862; cap. p.u. $A2m.; Chair. Sir JOHN DUNLOP; Gen. Man. J. O. LEWIS.

Unity Life Assurance Ltd.: 20 Bridge St., Sydney; f. 1959; Chair. BLAKE PELLY, O.B.E.; Gen. Manager A. BARNETT.

VACC Insurance Co. Ltd.: 464 St. Kilda Rd., Melbourne, Vic. 3004; f. 1930; Chair. A. Coffey; Gen. Man. A. C. Stubbs.

Vanguard Insurance Co. Ltd.: 127 Kent St., Sydney, N.S.W.; f. 1951; fire, marine, accident; Chair. Sir P. Spender; Man. Dir. G. Comel.

Victory Reinsurance Co. of Australia Ltd., The: 491–493 Bourke St., Melbourne; f. 1956; reinsurance, fire, accident, marine, life; Chair. Sir Rupert Clarke, Bt.; Gen. Man. H. G. Ogilvie, e.d.; Sec. D. S. Battle, a.c.i.i.

Western Australian Insurance Co. (Canberra) Ltd.: Head Office: 12–14 O'Connell St., Sydney; assets $A5.4m.; workers' compensation, fire, general accident, motor and marine; Chair. J. M. Burnett, c.b.e.; Man. Dir. F. T. Grose; Gen. Man. C. R. Johnson.

ASSOCIATIONS

Australian Insurance Association: 11th Floor, 82 Pitt St., Sydney, N.S.W. 2000; f. 1968; Pres. J. B. Bailey, Southern Pacific Insurance Co. Ltd.; Sec. I. J. Frew.

Australian Insurance Institute: 87 King St., Melbourne; f. 1919; Pres. J. E. Harrison, a.c.i.i., f.a.i.i.; Sec. L. M. Trounce, 35,163 mems.

Council of Fire and Accident Underwriters of Australia, Council of Marine Underwriters of the Commonwealth of Australia: 335–337 Flinders Lane, Melbourne, Victoria 3000; also 210 George St. ,Sydney, N.S.W. 2000.

The Institute of Actuaries of Australia and New Zealand: Swire House, 8 Spring St., Sydney; f. 1897; Pres. J. G. Rutherford f.i.a.; Sec. R. V. Carey, m.a.; 575 mems.

Life Offices' Association of Australia, The: C.M.L. Bldg., 330 Collins St., Melbourne, Vic. 3000; Sec. G. D. Browne.

The Non-Tariff Insurance Association of Australia: 11th Floor, Building Society House, 307 Pitt St., Sydney, N.S.W. 2000; f. 1943; Joint Secs. R. F. Sinden, f.c.a., W. F. Rowe, f.c.a.

TRADE AND INDUSTRY

CHAMBERS OF COMMERCE

Australian Chamber of Commerce: Brisbane Ave., Barton A.C.T. 2600; f. 1901; Dir. R. Pelham Thorman, b.a. (Cantab.); membership includes Chambers of Commerce in Sydney, Melbourne, Brisbane, Adelaide, Perth, Hobart, Newcastle, Darwin, Tamworth, Ingham, and State Federations of Chambers of Commerce in N.S.W., Victoria, Queensland, South Australia, Western Australia and Tasmania.

Brisbane Chamber of Commerce Inc.: Qantas House, 288 Queen St., Brisbane, Qld.; f. 1868; Dir. C. Robertson, f.c.i.s., f.a.s.a.; publ. *The Voice of Business.*

Chamber of Commerce and Industry, South Australia, Inc.: 12–18 Pirie St., Adelaide, S.A. 5000; Gen. Man. C. W. Branson; Dir. Commerce Div. D. F. Thomas.

Hobart Chamber of Commerce: 150 Collins St., Hobart, Tasmania; f. 1851; Dir. B. A. Jennings; publ. *Hobart Commerce.*

Launceston Chamber of Commerce: 57 George St., Launceston, Tasmania; f. 1849; Pres. J. T. Scott.

Melbourne Chamber of Commerce: 60 Market St., Melbourne, Vic. 3000; f. 1851; Exec. Dir. A. L. Lovell.

Perth Chamber of Commerce (Inc.): 14 Parliament Place, Perth, West Australia; f. 1890; 1,100 mems.; Dir. P. C. Firkins.

Sydney Chamber of Commerce Inc.: 161 Clarence St., Sydney, N.S.W.; f. 1826; Dir. A. J. R. Birch, f.s.b.m.

AGRICULTURAL AND INDUSTRIAL ORGANIZATIONS

The Australian Agricultural Council: Dept. of Primary Industry, Canberra, A.C.T.; f. 1934 to provide means for regular consultation between individual States and Commonwealth in respect of agricultural production and marketing (excluding forestry and fisheries), to promote the welfare and standards of Australian agricultural industries and to foster the adoption of national policies in regard to these industries; 10 mems. comprising the 6 State Ministers for Agriculture and the Commonwealth Ministers for Primary Industry, Northern Development and the Northern Territory; Chair. The Minister for Primary Industry: Senator The Hon. K. S. Wriedt; Sec. G. C. Power.

Standing Committee on Agriculture: f. 1927; associated as an advisory body with the Australian Agricultural Council; additional functions are the co-ordination of agricultural research and of quarantine measures relating to pests and diseases of plants and animals; 13 mems. comprising the 6 State Directors of Agriculture and heads of Commonwealth Departments with a direct or indirect interest in agriculture; Chair. M. R. Irving (Dir.-Gen. Dept. of Agriculture, W.A.); Sec. W. D. Hardy.

There is also a Standing Committee on Soil Conservation associated with the Council.

Australian Dairy Produce Board: Dairy Industry House, 576 St. Kilda Rd., Melbourne, Vic. 3004; promotes export of dairy produce; Chair. A. P. Beatty.

Australian Export Development Council: c/o Dept. of Trade and Industry, Canberra, A.C.T. 2600; advises the government on all aspects of export promotion and development; Chair. D. H. Freeman; Deputy Chair. E. P. McLintock, R. V. Sewell, o.b.e.; publs. Reports and Bulletins.

Australian Industry Development Corporation: 218 Northbourne Ave., Canberra, A.C.T. 2601; f. 1970; aims to encourage the development and expansion of Australian industry by borrowing funds from abroad to finance industrial projects in Australia and, where appropriate, to provide loans to finance such industrial development; cap. p.u. $A50m.; Chair. Sir Alan Westerman; Dirs. Sir Colin Syme, John Dunlop, Sir Charles McGrath, Sir George Fisher, Gavin M. Bunning, W. M. Leonard, D. H. Freeman.

Australian Meat Board: P.O.B. 4129, Sydney, N.S.W.; Chair. Col. M. McArthur.

Australian Wheat Board: Ceres House, 528 Lonsdale St., Melbourne, Vic.; f. 1939; only internal wheat marketing authority; export wheat and flour; 15 mems.; Chair. J. P. Cass, o.b.e.; Gen. Man. L. H. Dorman, o.b.e.; publ. *Wheat Australia* (every 2 months).

Australian Wool Corporation: Wool House, 578 Bourke St., Melbourne, Vic. 3000; f. 1973; responsible for wool marketing, research and testing; board of 9 mems. (chairman, 4 wool growers, 3 from commerce, 1 Govt. mem.); Chair. A. C. B. Maiden, c.b.e.

Australian Wool Industry Conference: Da Costa Building, 68 Grenfell St., Adelaide 5000, S.A.; composed of 25 mems. each from the Australian Woolgrowers' and Graziers' Council and the Australian Wool and Meat Producers' Federation; elects the six wool growers mems. of A.W.B. and is consulted by the Minister for Primary Industry on the appointment of the three mems. from commerce; independent Chair. A. J. VASEY.

Department of National Development: Tasman House, 26–30 Farrell St., Canberra City, A.C.T. 2601; functions include the assessment and development of natural resources, mining and non-ferrous metallurgical industries; undertaking geological and geophysical surveys and investigations as well as geographical and resources mapping; Man. Dir. A. E. CREBBIN; Sec. L. F. BOTT, D.S.C.

Australian Minerals Council: Tasman House, 26–30 Farrell St., Canberra, A.C.T. 2601; functions include the progressive development of mining and minerals; Chair. Minister for National Development.

EMPLOYERS' ORGANIZATIONS

The Australian Council of Employers' Federations: 505 Little Collins St., Melbourne; f. 1905; comprises the Employers' Federation of New South Wales, Victorian Employers' Federation, Northern Territory Employers' Federation, Employers' Federation of Papua-New Guinea, the Queensland Employers' Federation, South Australian Employers' Federation, Western Australian Employers' Federation, Tasmanian Employers' Federation, A.C.T. Employers' Federation, Northern Territory Employers' Federations; Pres. D. A. NOAKES; Exec. Dir. G. POLITES.

Associated Newsagents' Co-op. Ltd.: 169 Bonds Rd., Punchbowl, N.S.W. 2196; Gen. Man. J. C. LAFOREST.

Australian Jewellers' Association: 151 Flinders St., Melbourne, C.1; f. 1906; 750 mems.; Sec. E. A. LEWIS; publ. *The Commonwealth Jeweller and Watchmaker.*

Dairy Farmers Co-operative Ltd.: 700 Harris St., Ultimo, N.S.W. 2007; Sec. J. B. SHARPE.

Film Production Association of Australia: 3rd Floor, 129 York St., Sydney, N.S.W.; f. 1972; 50 mems.; Pres. J. DANIEL; Dir. G. E. FARRAR.

Graziers' Association of New South Wales: G.P.O. Box 1068, 56 Young St., Sydney 2000; f. 1890; publs. *Muster* (monthly), *The Graziers' Annual* (biennial).

Master Builders' Association of New South Wales, The: P.O.B. 234, Newtown, N.S.W. 2042; f. 1873; 1,800 mems.; Exec. Dir. J. D. MARTIN, B.COM.; publ. *Builder N.S.W.* (monthly).

Meat and Allied Trades Federation of Australia: National Secretariat; Paul Bldgs., 33–35 Pitt St., Sydney 2000; f. 1928; Pres. T. J. JACKMAN, M.B.E.; Chief Exec. Officer E. W. HORTON; Chief Accountant L. J. LOUGHMAN.

Metal Trades Industry Association of Australia: 105 Walker St., North Sydney; National Pres. F. R. D. MORGAN; Nat. Dir. and Chief Exec. R. G. FRY.

Metropolitan and Suburban Dairymen's Association: Old Windsor Rd., Parklea, N.S.W.; f. 1903; Pres. D. H. CROSBY; Acting Sec. I. S. JENKINS.

New South Wales Flour Millers' Council: Kindersley House, Box 2125 G.P.O., 20 O'Connell St., Sydney; Sec. H. K. BRAY.

Restaurant and Catering Trades Organization of New South Wales: 58 Margaret St., Sydney; Sec. J. STAFF.

Roofing Tile-Makers Employers' Association: French Bank, 12 Castlereagh St., Sydney; Sec. G. G. TRAVIS, B.EC., F.C.A.

Timber Trade Industrial Association: 155 Castlereagh St., Sydney 2000; f. 1940; 530 mems.; Sec./Man. H. J. MCCARTHY.

United Farmers' and Woolgrowers' Association of New South Wales: 10 Castlereagh St., Sydney; f. 1962; 375 rural brs.; 24,000 mems.; direct representation on marketing boards, commodity cttees, education councils, etc.; provides co-operative buying facilities, special insurance rates, etc.; annual conference in July elects General Council of 40; Gen. Pres. R. H. BLACK; Gen. Sec. B. F. REGAN; publ. *United Farmer* (fortnightly); has own radio programme weekly.

MANUFACTURERS' ORGANIZATIONS

Australian British Trade Association: P.O.B. 141, Manuka, A.C.T. 2603; Dir. D. C. DOUGLAS, O.B.E., B.COM., A.A.S.A.; Fed. Sec. L. F. I. HAWKINS.

Associated Chambers of Manufactures of Australia: Industry House, Canberra; f. 1904; Dir.-Gen. W. J. HENDERSON; 21,000 mems.

Australian Industries Development Association: P.O.B. 1576, Canberra City, A.C.T. 2601; Dir. W. CALLAGHAN.

Australian Manufacturers' Export Council: Industry House, Canberra; f. 1955; Exec. Officer G. M. CARR.

Chamber of Commerce and Industry, South Australia Inc.: 12 Pirie St., Adelaide, S. Australia 5000; f. 1869; Gen. Man. C. W. BRANSON, B.EC., DIP.COMM., A.A.S.A. (Senior), F.A.I.M., J.P.; 3,900 mems.; publ. *Journal of Industry* (monthly).

Chamber of Manufactures of New South Wales: Norwich House, 6 O'Connell St., Sydney, N.S.W.; f. 1885; Dir. NOEL J. MASON.

Queensland Chamber of Manufactures: Manufacturers' House, 375 Wickham Terrace, Brisbane, Qld. 4000; f. 1911; 1,500 mems.; Gen. Man. R. D. BLUCHER.

Tasmanian Chamber of Manufactures: Manufacturers Bldg., Cnr. Charles and Cameron Streets, Launceston, Tasmania; f. 1898; (acting) Gen. Man. E. C. ILES.

Victorian Chamber of Manufactures, The: Manufacturers House, 370 St. Kilda Rd., Melbourne, Victoria 3004; f. 1877; 7,000 mems.; Dir. I. M. MACPHEE.

West Australian Chamber of Manufactures, Inc.: Manufacturers' Building, 212-220 Adelaide Terrace, Perth, Western Australia; f. 1899; Dir. A. J. FILEAR; Deputy Sec. F. J. MALONE.

TRADE UNIONS

Australian Council of Trade Unions (A.C.T.U.): 254 La Trobe St., Melbourne, Vic.; f. 1927; Pres. R. J. HAWKE; Sec. H. J. SOUTER; the organization includes a Branch in each State generally known as a Trades and Labour Council; over 150 Trade Unions are affiliated to the A.C.T.U. and its branches.

Australian Textile Workers' Union: Trades Hall, Goulburn St., Sydney 2000; Pres. S. P. WESTON; Gen. Sec. Hon. R. H. ERSKINE, M.L.C.; mems. 38,171.

Australian Workers' Union: MacDonell House, 321 Pitt St., Sydney, N.S.W.; f. 1886; Pres. E. WILLIAMS; Gen. Sec. F. V. MITCHELL; mems. 165,000; the A.W.U. affiliated with the A.C.T.U. in 1967.

Building Workers' Industrial Union of Australia: Box A288, Sydney South, 2000; f. 1945; Pres. T. W. CHARD; Gen. Sec. P. M. CLANCY; mems. 50,000.

Electrical Trades Union of Australia: Federal Council, 262 Castlereagh St., Sydney, N.S.W. 2000; f. 1919; Pres. U. E. INNES; Gen. Sec. C. O. DOLAN; mems. 64,000.

The Vehicle Builders Employees' Federation of Australia: 17-25 Lygon St., Carlton, Vic.; f. 1917; Pres. M. P. MCCARNEY; Sec. R. E. WILSON; mems. 40,000.

TRANSPORT

Australian Transport Advisory Council: Block A, Childers St., Turner, A.C.T.; f. 1946; Chairman Commonwealth Minister for Shipping and Transport; members Commonwealth Minister for the Interior, State Ministers of Transport; to discuss transport matters, promote coordination of development and maintain research; Committees: Standing Committee of Advisers, Advisory Committee on Safety in Vehicle Design, Advisory Committee on Vehicle Performance (weights, dimensions and operating standards), Advisory Committee on Road User Performance and Traffic Codes, Advisory Committee on Transport of Dangerous Goods, Publicity Advisory Committee on Education in Road Safety.

RAILWAYS

The Australian Government operates the railways in the Territories and also the Commonwealth Railways between Port Pirie in South Australia and Kalgoorlie in Western Australia, together with the Central Australia Railway between Port Augusta, South Australia, and Alice Springs in the Northern Territory. A new 75 km. branch line from the Trans-Australian railway near Port Augusta to Whyalla, Australia's third iron and steel city, has been opened.

The majority of railways in Australia are at present operated by the respective State Governments, and due to a total lack of co-ordination during the latter half of the nineteenth century a number of different rail gauges were adopted and a vast standardization programme was necessary to link Sydney, Perth and Brisbane with standard gauge track. Adelaide will be on the standard gauge network in a few years.

Commonwealth Railways: 325 Collins St., Melbourne, Vic. 3000; Commissioner K. A. SMITH, O.B.E.; Sec. H. N. TURNER; a statutory Authority; operates 2,234 miles of railways of 4 ft. 8½ in. and 3 ft. 6 in. gauge; a standard gauge 520-mile railway line, between Alice Springs and Tarcoola, S.A., is planned; operates Trans-Australian, Central Australia, North Australia, Australian Capital Territory and Port Augusta-Whyalla Railways.

Public Transport Commission of New South Wales: 11–31 York St., Sydney 2000; administers government transport services in N.S.W.; 9,758 km. train network, with 14 km. under construction; Chief Commissioner J. H. SHIRLEY; Sec. K. W. NEWTON.

Queensland Railways: Adelaide St., Brisbane; operates 5,841 miles of 3 ft. 6 in. track.

South Australian Railways: G.P.O. Box 2351, Adelaide, S.A. 5001; Railway Bldg., North Terrace, Adelaide; f. 1856; operates 3,884 km. of track; Railways Commissioner M. L. STOCKLEY.

Tasmanian Railways: Box 624F, G.P.O., Hobart, Collins St., Hobart; 831 km. of 1,067 mm. gauge; Acting Gen. Man. G. J. DINEEN; Sec. R. G. BARBER.

Victorian Railways: 67 Spencer St., Melbourne 3000; f. 1856; operates 4,153.79 miles of track; Chair. A. G. GIBBS; Gen. Man. E. P. ROGAN.

Western Australian Government Railways: Perth, W.A.; operates passenger and freight transport services mainly in the south of Western Australia; 3,855 route miles of track, 4,095 bus route miles and 2,115 truck route miles of road services; Commissioner R. J. PASCOE; Sec. A. E. WILLIAMS.

COMPANY-OWNED RAILWAYS

Emu Bay Railway Co. Ltd., The: 390 Lonsdale St., Melbourne 3001; London Office: 9 Park Place, St. James's, S.W.1; inc. 1897 in Tasmania; Chair. Sir EDWARD COHEN; Dirs. N. S. KIRBY, J. A. BULT; Sec. R. W. LOVE; Man. B. P. FAGAN, Burnie, Tasmania; mileage approx. 83; freight and passenger services between Burnie and Zeehan, Tasmania.

ROADS

At the end of Dec. 1970, there were 884,656 kms. of roads including 102,794 kms. of main roads.

SHIPPING

Commonwealth of Australia: Australian National Line: (Australian Coastal Shipping Commission); 65–79 Riverside Ave., South Melbourne, Victoria 3025; (P.O.B. 2238T); Chair. H. P. WEYMOUTH, C.B.E.; Gen. Man. R. D. ROBIN; Sec. and Dir. of Finance J. G. MEEHAN; services: Australian coastal trade and passenger and car services between mainland and Tasmania; overseas container services to Europe, United Kingdom and Japan; 34 vessels.

Adelaide Steamship Co. Ltd.: 17 Currie St., Adelaide, S.A.; f. 1875; authorized cap. $A16m.; ship and tug owners and builders; engineering products manufacturers, travel and shipping agents; Gen. Man. K. W. RUSSELL, Asst. Gen. Man. L. W. HANCOCK; Sec. H. R. GOODE.

Ampol Petroleum Ltd.: 84 Pacific Highway, North Sydney, N.S.W.; Chair. W. M. LEONARD; bulk carriage of oil from Indonesia to Brisbane; 4 vessels.

Associated Steamships Pty. Ltd.: Scottish House, 94 William St., Melbourne; wholly-owned subsidiary of Bulkships Ltd.; 1 container ship, 1 bulk ship, 4 general cargo ships; operates 2 container ships and 4 bulk ships on demise charter and manages 6 oil tankers.

Associated Steamships Pty. Ltd., is also a 50 per cent partner with Overseas Containers Australia Pty. Ltd. in Australia's first container transport undertaking, *Seatainer Terminals Ltd.*

Australind Steam Shipping Co. Ltd.: 12–20 Camomile St., London, E.C.3; f. 1904; Dirs. Sir CHARLES TRINDER, G.B.E., D.SC., A. G. HATCHETT, O. G. TRINDER, J. MORRIS; Sec. T. G. K. CLARKE; service: Europe–U.S.A.–Canada–Australasia; 3 motor vessels.

Bulkships Ltd.: Scottish House, 94 William St., Melbourne; associate company of McIlwraith McEacharn Ltd., The Adelaide Steamship Co. Ltd., Thomas Nationwide Transport Ltd.; 4 bulk vessels and 2 container vessels; Man. Agents Associated Steamships Pty. Ltd.

John Burke Pty. Ltd.: MacQuarrie St., Teneriffe, P.O.B. 509, Fortitude Valley; Chair. D. B. HILL; 5 vessels; coastal services.

Burns, Philp and Co. Ltd.: 7 Bridge St. (P.O.B. 543), Sydney, N.S.W.; London Office: Imperial House, 15/19 Kingsway, London, WC2B 6UN; Dirs. J. D. O. BURNS (Chair. and Man. Dir.), M. O'CONNOR (Gen. Man.).

Garnew Shipping Pty. Ltd.: 22 Mount St., Perth, W.A.; Man. Dir. R. D. G. AGNEW.

Howard Smith Industries Pty. Ltd.: 269 George St., Sydney; Chair. WM. HOWARD-SMITH; Gen. Man. N. T. GRIFFIN; 17 vessels, including 12 tugs.

McIlwraith MaEacharn Ltd.: Scottish House, 90 William St., Melbourne, Vic.; Chair. Sir IAN POTTER; Gen. Man. A. D. CAMPBELL; tug and shipowners, liner and trampship agents; agency for coal exports and coke-selling.

Mason Shipping Co. Pty. Ltd.: Smiths Creek Cairns; 4 vessels; coastal services.

Port Jackson and Manly Steamship Co. Ltd.: No. 2 Jetty Circular Quay, Sydney, N.S.W.; Chair. A. R. DICKSON; Man. Dir. J. C. NEEDHAM; 4 vessels, 4 hydrofoils; ferry service Sydney–Manly.

Western Australian Coastal Shipping Commission (State Shipping Service): 1 Short St., Fremantle, P.O.B. 394; Chair. H. L. McGUIGAN; Gen. Man. F. N. JONES.

CIVIL AVIATION

Airlines of N.S.W. (*Division of Ansett Transport Industries (Operations) Pty. Ltd.*): Kingsford Smith Airport, Mascot, Sydney, N.S.W. 2020; f. 1935; Gen. Man. P. STEDMAN; services in N.S.W.

Ansett Airlines of Australia: 489 Swanston St., Melbourne, Victoria, commercial airline operators; passenger and cargo air services throughout Australia and to Papua New Guinea; unduplicated route mileage 16,559; fleet includes Boeing 727, DC-9-30, L188FR, Friendship propjets; Chair. and Man. Dir. Sir REGINALD M. ANSETT, K.B.E.; Gen. Man. F. PASCOE, C.B.E.

Ansett Airlines of South Australia: Adelaide Airport, S. Australia; Gen. Man. L. CONNELLY; Sec. C. A. WINDOW; F.27 services in South Australia between Adelaide and Kangaroo Island, Port Lincoln, Whyalla, Ceduna and Broken Hill.

Connair Pty. Ltd.: 51 Todd St. (P.O.B. 1), Alice Springs, N.T. 5750; f. 1938; operations commenced 1939; RPT carrier operating in N. Territory and adjoining states; over 120 ports of call, 15,500 route miles; charter, aviation maintenance; Chair. E. J. CONNELLAN; Gen. Man. P. W. LEVIN.

East-West Airlines Ltd.: P.O.B. 249, Tamworth, N.S.W. 2340; f. 1947; route mileage 5,711; Chair. D. M. SHAND; Gen. Man. J. G. RILEY; operate 8 Fokker Friendships.

Illawarra Airways: Hangar 276, Bankstown Aerodrome, Bankstown, N.S.W.; f. 1959; air courier service between Bankstown and Kingsford-Smith airports, thrice daily.

MacRobertson Miller Airline Services: International House, 26 St. George's Terrace, Perth, W.A. 6000; a division of Ansett Transport Industries (Operations) Pty. Ltd.; Gen. Man. Capt. C. N. KLEINIG; Operations Man. L. J. BRITTEN; Commercial Man. J. E. KARASEK; F-28 jet services Perth–Darwin, via North West ports; mainline domestic services using F-28 and DHG6 Twin Otter throughout Western Australia and to Darwin, Gove and Groote Eylandt in the Northern Territory; Fleet: 2 DHC-6, 4 F-28.

Qantas Airways Ltd.: Qantas House, 70 Hunter Street, Sydney, N.S.W. 2000 (P.O. Box 489); f. 1920; Chair. Sir DONALD ANDERSON, C.B.E.; Gen. Man. Capt. R. J. RITCHIE, C.B.E.; services: round-the-world routes, Sydney–London via Middle East and Europe, Sydney–U.S.A. and Canada, Sydney–London via Mexico, Sydney–Japan, Sydney–Hong Kong via Port Moresby and Manila, Sydney–Johannesburg via Mauritius, various routes across the Tasman Sea to New Zealand, Sydney–Noumea and Norfolk Island; fleet: 6 Boeing 747-238B, 18 Boeing 707-338C, 2 DC-4, 1 HS.125.

Trans-Australia Airlines (TAA): 50 Franklin St. (P.O.B. 2806AA), Melbourne 3000; f. 1946; operated by Australian National Airlines Commission (Chair. Sir FREDERICK SCHERGER); routes totalling approx. 35,103 miles to 150 ports in every Australian State; Gen. Man. L. L. McKENZIE, C.B.E., D.F.C.; fleet includes 8 Boeing 727, 12 Douglas DC-9, 14 Fokker F-27 and 4 DHC Twin Otter.

The following foreign airlines serve Australia; Aer Lingus, Air Canada, Air France, Air India, Air New Zealand, Alitalia, British Airways, Canadian Pacific, Cathay Pacific, JAL, KLM, Lufthansa, MEA, Malaysian Airlines System (MAS), Northeast Orient Airlines, Olympic Airways, Pan American, South African Airways, SAS, Swissair, TWA and UTA.

TOURISM

Australian Tourist Commission: 414 St. Kilda Rd., Melbourne, Vic. 3004; f. 1967; Government organization for encouraging overseas and domestic tourists; Chair. C. A. GREENWAY; offices in Sydney, London, Auckland, Los Angeles, New York, Tokyo, Frankfurt-am-Main.

PRINCIPAL THEATRES

The Australian Ballet: 11 Mount Alexander Rd., Flemington, Victoria 3031; f. 1962 by the Australian Ballet Foundation; 50 full-time dancers; Artistic Dirs. Dame PEGGY VAN PRAAGH, D.B.E., Sir ROBERT HELPMANN, C.B.E.; Administrator PETER F. BAHEN.

Australian Elizabethan Theatre Trust: 153 Dowling St., Potts Point, N.S.W.; f. 1954 to promote drama, opera and ballet; a major financial supporter of The Australian Ballet, The Australian Opera, The Marionette Theatre of Australia, National Institute of Dramatic Art and regional drama companies in several States; financed by subsidies from Commonwealth and State Governments and city councils of approximately $A1,000,000 per annum, and private donations and subscriptions; Patron H.M. The Queen; Pres. Sir JAMES DARLING, C.M.G., O.B.E.; Vice-Presidents Sir WARWICK FAIRFAX,

MAURICE PARKER; Chair. Sir IAN POTTER; Gen. Man. JEFFRY JOYNTON-SMITH.

The Australian Opera: 569 George St., Sydney; f. 1955; full-time professional opera company, tours throughout Australia; 175 singers and staff mems.; annual seasons in each state capital, country tours; Chair. CLAUDE ALCORSO; Artistic Dir. STEPHEN C. HALL; Gen. Man. JOHN WINTHER; Musical Dir. EDWARD DOWNES.

Sydney Opera House Trust: Box 4274 G.P.O., Sydney, N.S.W. 2001; f. 1961 to manage Sydney Opera House as a performing arts complex and convention centre; Gen. Man. FRANK BARNES.

PRINCIPAL ORCHESTRAS

Australian Broadcasting Commission: Sydney, N.S.W.; f. 1932; organizes more than 700 concerts and recitals each year throughout Australia; has established a major symphony orchestra in each of the six State capitals, as well as a national training orchestra based in Sydney.

Melbourne Symphony Orchestra: Melbourne, Vic.; f. 1946; 85 mems.; subsidized by Victorian Government, Melbourne City Council and A.B.C.; Supervisor Peter Rorke; Orchestra Man. G. S. Wraith; Chief Conductor Hiroyuki Iwaki.

South Australian Symphony Orchestra: Adelaide, S.A.; f. 1949; 64 mems.; subsidized by S.A. Government, Adelaide City Council and A.B.C.

Sydney Symphony Orchestra: Sydney, N.S.W.; f. 1946; 93 mems.; subsidized by N.S.W. Government, Sydney City Council and Australian Broadcasting Commission; Conductor Moshe Atzmon.

FESTIVALS

Adelaide Festival of Arts: Box 1960, G.P.O., Adelaide, S.A. 5001; f. 1960; Patron H.M. Queen Elizabeth The Queen Mother; biennial; international; performing visual and allied arts; Dir. Louis van Eyssen.

Festival of Perth: Perth, W.A.; f. 1953; annual; concerts, plays, opera, dancing, art exhibitions, jazz, poetry and prose, by Australian and international artists; Chair. Sir Thomas Wardle; Exec. Officer J. Birman.

ATOMIC ENERGY

Australian Atomic Energy Commission: 45 Beach St., Coogee, N.S.W. 2034; Chair. R. W. Boswell, o.b.e., m.sc.; Deputy Chair. R. G. Ward, m.a., ph.d.; Mems. K. F. Alder, m.sc., f.i.m., Sir Lenox Hewitt, o.b.e., b.comm., f.a.s.a., a.c.i.s., l.c.a.; Sec. W. B. Lynch, b.a.; Research Establishment, Lucas Heights, N.S.W.; Act. Dir. J. L. Symonds, b.sc., ph.d.; publs. Annual Report, *Atomic Energy in Australia* (quarterly journal).

The Commission is concerned with scientific research, development of practical uses of atomic energy, the training of scientists and engineers, the discovery and production of uranium, the production of radioisotopes.

HIFAR: 10 mW. reactor; critical 1958; for testing materials and radio isotope production.

MOATA: 100 kW. reactor; critical 1962; provides neutron radiography, uranium analysis and general activation services and beams and irradiation space for physical chemistry and materials research.

Australian Institute of Nuclear Science and Engineering: Lucas Heights, New South Wales; the Institute supports university research and training projects in all branches of nuclear science and engineering. Its membership comprises fifteen Universities and A.A.E.C.; Pres. (1973–74) Sir Ernest Titterton; Exec. Officer E. A. Palmer.

Australian School of Nuclear Technology: Lucas Heights, N.S.W.; provides courses for Australian and overseas students in nuclear technology, radioisotope techniques and applications, health physics, siting and hazards evaluation of nuclear power plants, etc.

UNIVERSITIES

University of Adelaide: Adelaide; 590 teachers, 8,936 students.

The Australian National University: Canberra; 780 teachers, 5,272 students.

Flinders University of South Australia: Bedford Park; f. 1965; 220 teachers, 2,545 students.

James Cook University of North Queensland: Townsville, Qld.; f. 1970; 157 teachers, 1,461 students.

La Trobe University: Bundoora, Vic.; 350 teachers, 5,100 students.

Macquarie University: North Ryde, N.S.W.; 435 teachers, 7,190 students.

University of Melbourne: Parkville, Melbourne; 920 teachers, 14,500 students.

Monash University: Clayton, Victoria; f. 1961; 814 teachers, 12,147 students.

University of New England: Armidale, New South Wales; 360 teachers, 6,500 students.

The University of New South Wales: Sydney, N.S.W.; 780 teachers, 19,000 students.

University of Newcastle: Newcastle, N.S.W.; 220 teachers, 3,095 students.

University of Queensland: Brisbane; 1,141 teachers, 17,293 students.

University of Sydney: Sydney, N.S.W.; 1,097 teachers, 16,570 students.

University of Tasmania: Hobart; 253 teachers, 3,370 students.

University of Western Australia: Perth; 546 teachers, 9,077 students.

AUSTRALIAN EXTERNAL TERRITORIES

PAPUA NEW GUINEA	NORFOLK ISLAND	COCOS (KEELING) ISLANDS

CHRISTMAS ISLAND	OTHER TERRITORIES

PAPUA NEW GUINEA

Papua New Guinea consists of the eastern half of the island of New Guinea and the adjacent islands. To the west lies the Indonesian territory of Irian Jaya (formerly Netherlands New Guinea). Papua New Guinea was administered by Australia until December 1st, 1973, when it became self-governing. A date for independence is to be set by the Papua New Guinea and Australian Governments, subject to endorsement by the Papua New Guinea House of Assembly.

STATISTICS

AREA AND POPULATION

AREA (sq. miles)		POPULATION (estimate for June 30th, 1971)			
Papua	New Guinea	Papua		New Guinea	
		Indigenous	Non-indigenous	Indigenous	Non-indigenous
83,325 (mainland) 2,775 (islands)	69,095 (mainland) 23,065 (islands)	686,618	n.a.	1,845,264	n.a.

Total Population (estimate for June 30th, 1972): 2,581,000.

Administrative Capital: Port Moresby, in Papua, with a population of 66,244 (including 15,256 non-indigenous) at June 30th, 1971.

INDIGENOUS EMPLOYMENT

Papua New Guinea

(1970)

Primary Production	53,597
Mining and Quarrying	2,477
Manufacturing	9,179
Building and Construction . . .	13,303
Transport, Communications and Storage.	5,930
Commerce	13,000
Personal Service (Hotels, Cafés and Amusements)	2,959
Others	28,140
TOTAL . . .	128,585

AGRICULTURE

PRINCIPAL CROPS

Twelve months ending June 30th.

Papua	1969–70	1970–71	(tons) New Guinea	1969–70	1970–71
Copra	17,031	15,192	Copra and all Coconut Products . . .	114,727	112,249
Rubber	5,219	5,787	Cacao Beans . . .	22,877	24,958
Cacao Beans . . .	855	709	Coffee Beans . . .	28,225	26,000
Coffee Beans . . .	458	543	Tea	971	1,402

93

LIVESTOCK*
(June 30th, 1971)

Papua		New Guinea	
Cattle	12,987	Cattle	59,938
Goats	277	Goats	364
Pigs	2,360	Pigs	4,936
Sheep	174	Sheep	208
Horses	299	Horses	658

* Non-indigenous holdings only. Considerable numbers of pigs and poultry owned by indigenes.

FORESTRY
(Logs harvested, cu. metres)
Papua New Guinea

	1970	1971	1972
Hardwood .	443,570	655,770	794,110
Softwood .	71,930	75,150	75,550

FISHING
Exports (tons)
Twelve months ending June 30th, 1972.

Papua		New Guinea	
Mother of Pearl	37	Green Snail Shell	20
Trochus Shell	64	Mother of Pearl	5
Crayfish	9	Trochus Shell	289
Prawns	642	Tuna	14,212
		Prawns	121

MINING
Papua New Guinea

		1970–71	1971–72
Gold . . .	fine oz.	22,277	25,353
Silver . . .	fine oz.	16,897	18,923
Copper . .	tons	n.a.	140,779

FINANCE
Australian currency: 100 cents = 1 Australian dollar ($A).
Coins: 1, 2, 5, 10, 20 and 50 cents.
Notes: 1, 2, 5, 10, 20 and 50 dollars.
Exchange rates (April 1974): £1 sterling = $A1.585; U.S. $1 = 67.23 Australian cents.
$A100 = £63.10 = U.S. $148.75.

PAPUA NEW GUINEA BUDGET
($A, twelve months ending June 30th, 1973)

Revenue		Expenditure	
Internal Revenue . . .	93,434,754	Departmental	107,579,107
Grants from Australian Government .	82,863,354	Capital Works and Services .	51,602,541
Loans by Australian Government .	4,400,000	Other Expenditure . . .	56,984,514
Other Loans . . .	35,468,054		
Total . . .	216,166,162	Total . . .	216,166,162

AUSTRALIA—(EXTERNAL TERRITORIES)

FIVE-YEAR DEVELOPMENT PROGRAMME (1969–73)

Major aims of the programme were: substantial expansion of production in all sectors, the strengthening of the economic infrastructure, the advancement of indigenes in ownership management and employment. Total government expenditure required by the programme was of the order of $A1,000 million.

The programme was reviewed in August 1971 in a document entitled "The Development Programme Reviewed" which was endorsed by the PNG House of Assembly. The major purpose of the review was to take into account the impact of the Bougainville Copper Project.

A new *national* development programme covering 1973–74 was provided for in the Papua New Guinea budget for that year. It will be followed by a long-term Investment Programme.

EXTERNAL TRADE

Twelve months ending June 30th.

($A '000)

IMPORTS*	1970–71	1971–72	EXPORTS	1970–71	1971–72
Papua	67,495	73,377	Papua	15,194	22,035
New Guinea	184,069	179,448	New Guinea	86,738	105,146

* Excludes outside packing, with a value (in $A'000) of: 3,035 in 1970–71; 3,604 in 1971–72.

PRINCIPAL COMMODITIES

Papua New Guinea

IMPORTS	1970–71	1971–72	EXPORTS	1970–71	1971–72
Manufactures	71,214	65,342	Copper Ore	n.a.	22,284
Food, Drink, Tobacco,			Copra	14,207	9,392
Live Animals	47,778	51,385	Coconut Oil	7,805	5,880
Machinery and Transport			Cacao Beans	13,643	11,109
Equipment	101,417	93,066	Coffee Beans	20,572	20,457
Other Items	31,155	46,636	Rubber	2,297	1,995
			Plywood	2,505	1,999
			Gold	696	792
			Other Items	15,722	19,134
			Re-exports	24,485	34,139
TOTAL	251,564	256,429	TOTAL	101,932	127,181

PRINCIPAL TRADING PARTNERS

Papua New Guinea

IMPORTS	1970–71	1971–72	EXPORTS	1970–71	1971–72
Australia	130,394	141,330	Australia	43,373	53,245
Japan	43,650	38,009	United Kingdom	19,567	13,264
U.S.A.	29,554	20,232	U.S.A.	13,337	10,710
United Kingdom	9,822	11,415	Japan	11,813	21,377
Germany, Fed. Rep.	3,893	4,598	Germany, Fed. Rep.	5,377	17,590

TRANSPORT
LICENSED VEHICLES

(December 1972)

Papua		New Guinea	
Cars and Station Wagons . . .	10,007	Cars and Station Wagons . . .	10,050
Commercial Vehicles . . .	3,880	Commercial Vehicles . . .	10,793
Motor Cycles	1,090	Motor Cycles	1,957
Tractors	487	Tractors	1,434

SHIPPING
(Twelve months ending June 30th)

	PAPUA		NEW GUINEA	
	1969–70	1970–71	1969–70	1970–71
Vessels entered*	847	810	2,492	2,735
Vessels cleared*	842	779	2,464	2,655
Cargo unloaded†	365	373	923	1,124
Cargo loaded†	119	134	504	731

* ’000 gross registered tons.　　　　† ’000 long tons.

Papua New Guinea
(’000 long tons)

	1970–71	1971–72
Cargo unloaded . . .	1,498	1,620
Cargo loaded . . .	865	933

CIVIL AVIATION
(Twelve months ending June 30th, 1972)

INTERNAL FLIGHTS		OVERSEAS FLIGHTS	
Scheduled Services:		Passengers embarked . . .	207,655
Passengers embarked . .	476,506	Freight carried (short tons) . . .	3,325
Freight carried (short tons) . .	8,064	Mail carried (short tons) . . .	605
Mail carried (short tons) . .	1,077		
Charter Services:			
Passengers embarked . .	52,764		
Freight carried (short tons) . .	9,612		
Mail carried (short tons) . .	4		

ADMINISTRATION AND GOVERNMENT

From 1949 until 1973 Papua New Guinea was administered by the Australian Government through the *Papua New Guinea Act.* The Act provided for an Administrator who was charged with the duty of administering the government of Papua New Guinea on behalf of the Commonwealth of Australia. Members of the Administrator's Executive Council (A.E.C.) participated in policy-making and executive government, constituting the final decision-making authority in a wide range of internal matters.

Since 1964 Papua New Guinea has had a House of Assembly with a majority of members elected by adult residents enrolled on a common roll. (The voting age was reduced to 18 from 21 in 1971.) The current House of Assembly, elected in February/March 1972, consists of 100 elected members and 4 official members. There is provision for the nomination of 3 additional members by the House to represent special interests (none has been appointed to date). A National Coalition Government was formed under the leadership of Mr. Michael Somare, Chief Minister and Deputy Chairman of the A.E.C. The House of Assembly had 20 Ministers in August 1973, ten of them members of the A.E.C.

The Australian and Papua New Guinea Governments agreed to amendments to the *Papua New Guinea Act*, which gave Papua New Guinea self-government on December 1st, 1973. A second stage of self-government was scheduled for mid-1974 with the adoption of a constitution to be formulated by Papua New Guinea itself. A date for full independence remains to be settled between the Australian and Papua New Guinea Governments. Until then only defence matters and foreign affairs remain under Australian control.

For administrative purposes, Papua New Guinea is divided into 19 Districts, each administered by a District Commissioner. To assist development towards internal self-government, local government, first introduced in 1950–51 with the establishment of four village councils, has grown to a system of full local government. There are now 160 Councils covering more than 92 per cent of the total population.

THE GOVERNMENT

High Commissioner: Thomas Critchley.

EXECUTIVE COUNCIL
(*February* 1974)

Chief Minister: Michael T. Somare.
Minister of Lands and Environment: Thomas Kavali.
Minister of Commerce: Ebia Olewale.
Minister of Foreign Affairs and Defence: Albert M. Kiki.
Minister of Agriculture and Stock, and Deputy Chief Minister: Dr. J. Guise.
Minister of Health: D. Mola.
Minister of Mines and Energy: Paul Lapun.
Minister of Transport and Civil Aviation: Iambakey Okuk.
Minister of Justice: John Kaputin.
Minister of Forests and Fisheries: Bruce Jephcott.
Minister of Sport and Recreation: Sasakila Moses.
Minister of Finance: Julius Chan.
Minister assisting the Chief Minister in Police Matters: Pita Lus.
Minister for the Interior: J. Poe.
Minister of Education: Dr. Ruben Tareka.
Minister of National Development: Gavera Rae.
Minister of Communications: Kailbilt Diria.
Minister of State, Local Government and Development Administration: Boyamo Sali.
Minister of Public Works: Yano Belo.

PARLIAMENT
HOUSE OF ASSEMBLY

Speaker: Barry Holloway.
Official Members: (Dep. Administrator) A. P. J. Newman; T. W. Ellis, m.b.e., d.f.c., (Sec., Dept. of the Administrator); H. P. Richie, c.m.g., (Treasurer); W. J. F. Kearney (Secretary for Law).
Nominated Members: None appointed (the Papua New Guinea Act provides for the appointment of up to 3).
Elected Members: 100 (82 representing open electorates and 18 representing regional electorates).

POLITICAL PARTIES

Pangu Pati: formed 1967; an urban-based party which advocated the speedy achievement of self-government; dominant party in National Coalition; Leader Michael Somare.

People's Progress Party: formed 1970; member party in National Coalition; Chair. Julius Chan.

New Guinea National Party: P.O.B. 6545, Boroko; member party in National Coalition; Leader Thomas Kavali; Sec. Bavunke Kaman.

United Party: formed 1969 (formerly the Compass Party); a highland-based party which favoured a more cautious pace towards self-government; main opposition party in House of Assembly; Leader Matthias Toliman.

Note: The National Coalition commands between 55 and 60 seats in the House of Assembly.

DEFENCE

Under the United Nations Charter and Trusteeship Agreement Australia is reponsible for the defence of Papua New Guinea until independence. The Papua New Guinea Defence Force has two infantry battalions and five patrol boats together with supporting units.

JUDICIAL SYSTEM

Supreme Court of Papua New Guinea: Chief Justice The Hon. John P. Minogue.

Senior Puisne Judge: The Hon. Mr. Justice Frost.

Judges: The Hon. Mr. Justice Clarkson, The Hon. Mr. Justice Prentice, m.b.e., The Hon. Mr. Justice Williams, The Hon. Mr. Justice Raine, e.d.

The Supreme Court is the highest judicial authority in the country. Appeals may be made from decisions of a single judge to the Full Court and from the Full Court to the High Court of Australia by leave of the High Court. District Courts deal with summary and non-indictable offences. In addition, Local Courts have been established to deal with minor offences, including matters regulated by native custom, and are open to all races. They have limited jurisdiction in land matters. Wardens Courts have been established with jurisdiction over civil cases respecting mining or mining lands and offences against mining laws. Cases involving land are heard by the Land Titles Commission from which appeals lie to the Supreme Court. Children's Courts deal with cases involving minors.

RELIGION

The indigenous population is pantheistic. There are many Missionary Societies.

ANGLICAN

Bishop of New Guinea: Rt. Rev. G. David Hand, m.a., Box 806, Port Moresby.

ROMAN CATHOLIC

Archbishop of Madang: Most Rev. Adolph Noser, s.v.d., Catholic Mission, Alexishafen, Madang.

Archbishop of Port Moresby: Most Rev. Virgil P. Copas, m.s.c., d.d.

Archbishop of Rabaul: Most Rev. John Hoehne.

ECUMENIST

The United Church in Papua, New Guinea and the Solomon Islands: P.O.B. 3401, Port Moresby; f. 1968 by union of the Methodist Church in Melanesia, the Papua Ekalesia (formerly L.M.S.) and United Church Port Moresby; 90,000 communicant mems.

PRESS

Papua New Guinea Post-Courier: P.O.B. 85, Port Moresby; amalgamation in June 1969 of *South Pacific Post* (f. 1950) and *New Guinea Times Courier* (f. 1958); Independent; daily; Editor GRAEME D. BOYD.

Our News: Department of Information and Extension Services, Port Moresby; f. 1960; fortnightly in English and Pidgin (*Nius Bilong Yumi*); circ. 43,000.

There are numerous news sheets and magazines published by Local Government Councils, Co-operative Societies, Missions and government departments. Published variously in English, Pidgin, Police Motu and vernacular languages.

NEWS SERVICE

International News Service Papua New Guinea: P.O.B. 5050, Boroko; f. 1969; Man. Editor JOHN L. RYAN.

RADIO AND TELEVISION

National Broadcasting Commission of Papua New Guinea: P.O.B. 1359, Boroko; formed 1973 by a merger of the Papua New Guinea branch of the Australian Broadcasting Commission (ABC) and the Broadcasts Division of the Department of Information and Extension Services; the National Service has medium-wave stations at Port Moresby (9PA), Lae (9LA), Madang (9MD), Goroka (9GR), Wewak (9WK) and Rabaul (9RB), and short-wave stations at Port Moresby (VLK and VLT), Rabaul (9RA) and Wewak (9ZJ), all broadcasting in English, Pidgin and Hiri Motu; the District Service has short-wave stations at Rabaul, Wewak, Goroka, Kerema, Milne Bay, Western District (Daru), Bougainville (Kieta), Madang, Morobe (Lae), Northern District (Popondetta), Chimbu, Southern Highlands (Mendi), New Ireland (Kavieng), West New Britain (Kimbe) and Western Highlands (Mt. Hagen), broadcasting in English, Pidgin, Hiri Motu and numerous major vernaculars; programmes cover current events and news, music, drama, sport, women's interests, education and rural affairs, with special emphasis, in the latter case, on the requirements of village communities; Dir. of Programmes ALLEN HULL.

Television New Guinea: P.O.B. 5050, Boroko; f. 1970; Exec. Dir. JOHN L. RYAN.

FINANCE

Papua New Guinea is to establish its own banking system which will be independent of the Australian one. It is expected that a central bank will be established similar in function to the Reserve Bank of Australia.

CENTRAL BANK

Reserve Bank of Australia: Port Moresby.

TRADING BANKS

Australia and New Zealand Bank Limited: brs. at Port Moresby, Rabaul and Lae, Mt. Hagen, Madang and Boroko.

Bank of New South Wales: Port Moresby; Chief Man. L. J. RITSON; brs. at Boroko, Bulolo, Goroka, Kieta, Kimbe, Lae, Madang, Mount Hagen, Rabaul, Samarai; 4 agencies.

Commonwealth Trading Bank of Australia: Port Moresby, Rabaul; 11 other brs., 2 sub-brs. and 7 agencies.

National Bank of Australasia Ltd.: Head Office: 271–285 Collins St., Melbourne; brs. at Port Moresby, Boroko, Rabaul, Lae, Mount Hagen, Kieta (Bougainville) and Vila (New Hebrides).

DEVELOPMENT BANK

Papua New Guinea Development Bank: P.O.B. 500, Port Moresby; f. 1965; cap $A20.9m.; commenced operations July 1967; Man. Dir. R. V. COLE.

NATIVE LOAN FUND

The operations, assets and liabilities of the Native Loan Fund have been taken over by the Papua-New Guinea Development Bank. Formerly, under the Native Loan Fund Ordinance loans of any amount could be granted to indigenes or groups of indigenes to further economic projects in primary and secondary industries, other commercial enterprises and local government or community welfare projects. New loans to indigenes are made under the terms and conditions imposed by the Development Bank.

SAVINGS BANKS

Commonwealth Savings Bank of Australia: Port Moresby, Rabaul and 11 other brs. and 250 agencies.

Bank of New South Wales Savings Bank Ltd.: Port Moresby; Man. L. J. RITSON; brs. in Rabaul, Lae, Samarai, Madang, Bulolo, Goroka, Mt. Hagen, Boroko, Kieta, Kimbe; 5 agencies.

Australia and New Zealand Savings Bank: brs. in Port Moresby, Rabaul, Lae, Mt. Hagen, Madang and Boroko.

National Bank Savings Bank Ltd.: Headquarters: 271–285 Collins St., Melbourne; brs. in Boroko, Rabaul, Lae, Mt. Hagen and Kieta (Bougainville).

SAVINGS AND LOAN SOCIETIES

Registry of Savings and Loan Societies: P.O.B. 121, Port Moresby: 321 Savings and Loan Societies; mems. 35,886; total funds A$2,966,624; loans outstanding A$2,001,673; investments A$549,803. 152 Savings Clubs: mems. 7,942; total funds A$159,519.

INSURANCE

There are branches of four of the principal Australian and three of the main United Kingdom insurance companies in Port Moresby, Rabaul and Lae.

TRADE AND INDUSTRY

TRADE

Trade forms an integral part of Papua New Guinea's development and exports play an important part in the economic growth and prosperity of the country and its 2.5 million people.

Papua New Guinea earns most of its export income from copper concentrates and tropical commodities. The main exports are coconut products, coffee, cocoa, timber and rubber. Other export commodities include groundnuts, pyrethrum, passion fruit juice, tea, palm oil and crocodile skins.

The majority of exports go to Australia, Western Europe, the U.S.A. and Japan. Those areas also supply most of the Territory's import requirements.

MANUFACTURING

Initially manufacturing was confined largely to the processing of local raw materials for export. There is now a growing trend towards industries established to serve the internal market. The major manufacturing industries are generally those processing local raw materials largely for export, e.g. the production of coconut oil and copra by-products, plywood, desiccated coconut and pyrethrum. Nevertheless, industries serving the internal market and using mainly imported materials are numerically predominant. These industries include the manufacture of cigarettes, twist tobacco, wire products, building materials, tyre re-treading and re-lugging, concrete products, oil drums, paint, beer, furniture, glass bottles, packaging materials, assembly of electrical appliances and boat building.

In 1971–72 there were 693 factories in Papua New Guinea and the value of factory production was $A48 million, compared with 278 factories and a value of factory production of $9.9 million in 1961–62.

CO-OPERATIVES

There are more than 300 co-operatives with over 130,000 members and a total annual turnover of about $A7 million. Officers of the Department of Business Services provide extension services, helping with business expertise as required.

TRADE UNIONS

Australian Staffing Assistance (PNG) Association: P.O.B. 2083, Konedobu; Pres. T. C. Jackson; Sec. R. Philpot; 3,000 mems.

Bank Officials Association of Papua New Guinea: c/o Dept. of Labour, Port Moresby; Pres. M. S. More; Sec. D. J. Thackerah.

Goroka Workers' Association: c/o Radio Goroka, Goroka; f. 1964; Pres. M. Kautil; Sec. F. Kombugun; 91 mems.

Lae Workers' Association: P.O.B. 898, Lae; Pres. M. Kaniniba; Sec. D. Torome; 280 mems. (1969).

Madang Workers' Association: c/o Dept. of Labour, Madang; f. 1961; Pres. P. Naime; Sec. A. Malambes; 388 mems.

Manus District Workers' Association: 51 mems.

Milne Bay Workers' Association: c/o Milne Bay Native Societies Asscn. Ltd., Samurai; f. 1965; Pres. P. Matasaroro; Sec. J. Fifita; 445 mems.

New Ireland District Workers' Association: P.O.B. 25, Kavieng; Pres. A. Abom; Sec. M. Chilcott; 292 mems.

Northern District Workers' Association: c/o Dept. of Labour, Popondetta; f. 1965; Pres. P. Arek; Sec. P. Soroda; 220 mems.

Papua-New Guinea Teachers' Association: P.O.B. 8081, Waigani; f. 1973; Pres. E. Silachot; Exec. Officer R. Price; publ. *Teacher*; 10,000 mems.

Police Association of Papua New Guinea: P.O.B. 903, Port Moresby; f. 1964; Pres. Sub-Insp. L. Debessa; Gen. Sec. J. Shields; 3,000 mems.; publ. *Kumul*.

Port Moresby Workers' Association: P.O.B. 123, Port Moresby; f. 1961; Pres. Oala Oala Rarua; Sec. A. T. Chapman; 50 mems.

Public Service Association: P.O.B. 2033, Konedobu, Port Moresby; brs. at other PNG centres; f. 1947; 15,560 mems.; Pres. (a.i.) J. Aoae; Gen. Sec. J. T. Lemeki; publ. *PSA Bulletin*.

Rabaul Workers' Association: c/o Dept. of Labour, Rabaul; Pres. Thomas To Bun Bun; Sec. J. Tiniu; 514 mems.

Senior Police Officers' Guild: P.O.B. 2085, Konedobu; f. 1968; Pres. B. A. Beattie; Sec. K. R. Gascoigne; 50 mems.

Timber Workers' Association of Wau-Bulolo: P.O.B. 105, Bulolo; f. 1964; Pres. Rompier Siman; Sec. George Nimagi; 667 mems.

Western Highlands District Workers' Association: c/o Dept. of Labour, Mount Hagen; Pres. James T. Ovia; Sec. Joseph Avaka; Treas. Ben Pukare; 260 mems.

Wewak Workers' Association: c/o Dept. of Labour, Wewak; f. 1964; Pres. J. Bula; Sec. Y. Wrindima; 393 mems.

TRANSPORT

ROADS

In 1972 there were about 10,000 miles of roads in Papua New Guinea, including 350 miles of urban roads, 670 miles of highways and 1,610 miles of trunk roads.

SHIPPING

Regular passenger and cargo services to Australia are maintained by Burns Philp and Co. Ltd., Karlander New Guinea Line Ltd., Australia West Pacific Line, China Navigation Co. Ltd., Austasia Line, Amplex New Guinea Line, Keith Holland Shipping Co. Several of these companies also call at Asian ports. Other lines which provide services between Australia and East Asia are China Navigation Co. Ltd., Mitsui Osk Line K.K. and Nippon Yusen Kaisha. The Bank Line provides a regular service between the Territory and Europe, while the New Zealand Export Line operates regular services to New Zealand and the Pacific Islands.

CIVIL AVIATION

Note: A national airline is to be established in which the existing airlines (*see below*) are to be offered shares but it is eventually to become the *only* internal airline operator.

Ansett Airlines of Australia: Head Office: Melbourne, Australia; Papua New Guinea Office: P.O.B. 334, Port Moresby; regular public transport services within Australia and to Papua New Guinea.

Trans-Australia Airlines: Head Office: Melbourne, Australia; Papua and New Guinea Offices: Port Moresby, Rabaul, Kieta, Lae, Goroka, Madang, Mount Hagen, Wewak; regular public transport and charter services.

Ansett Airlines of Papua New Guinea: Head Office: Jackson's Airport, Port Moresby; P.O.B. 1213, Boroko; Papua New Guinea; regular public transport services within Papua New Guinea; Gen. Man. Capt. S. C. Middlemiss; Sec. D. R. Durrington.

Crowley Airways: P.O.B. 34, Lae; f. 1949; helicopter and aircraft charter services; bases at Lae, Rabaul, Kieta, Kavieng, Hoskins. Traffic Man. J. M. Cruikshank.

Territory Airlines Pty. Ltd.: P.O.B. 108, Goroka; f. 1952; offices at Mt. Hagen, Madang, Chimbu, Mendi, Angoram, Port Moresby and Wewak; Man. Dir. R. D. Buchanan, m.h.a.

UNIVERSITY

University of Papua New Guinea: P.O.B. 1144, Boroko, Port Moresby; 136 teachers, 1,209 students.

Papua New Guinea Institute of Technology: P.O.B. 793, Lae, New Guinea; 60 teachers, 500 students.

CHRISTMAS ISLAND

Christmas Island covers an area of about 52 square miles and lies 224 miles south of Java, between Fremantle and Singapore.

Administration was transferred from Singapore to Britain on January 1st, 1958, pending final transfer to Australia. It became an Australian territory on October 1st, 1958. The island has no indigenous population. At June 30th, 1972, the total population was 2,741 (1,376 Chinese, 1,081 Malays, 245 Europeans and 39 others). Nearly all the residents are employees of the Phosphate Commission, and their families. The recovery of phosphates is the sole economic activity, and exports were 769,031 tons of phosphates and 151,201 tons of phosphate dust for the year ending June 30th, 1972.

Administrator: F. S. EVATT.

Supreme Court: Judge: The Hon. Mr. Justice E. A. DUNPHY.

Christmas Island Phosphate Commission: 515 Collins St., Melbourne, Victoria, Australia. *Australian Commissioner:* Sir ALLEN BROWN, C.B.E. *New Zealand Commissioner:* S. C. GAINEY. *United Kingdom Commissioner:* Sir ALEXANDER WADDELL, G.C.M.G., D.S.C.; Gen. Man. W. B. MARSTON, O.B.E.; on behalf of the Governments of Australia and New Zealand and the Commissioners control the working of phosphate deposits at Christmas Island, and the distribution of phosphate from Christmas Island, Ocean Island, Nauru and other sources to Australia and New Zealand.

Transport: A regular shipping service to Singapore at 2-week intervals. Charter services to Fremantle and other Australian ports.

NORFOLK ISLAND

NORFOLK ISLAND is about 5 miles long and 3 wide and was discovered by Captain Cook in 1774. The island was used as a penal settlement from 1788 to 1813 and again from 1825 to 1855. It was a separate Crown Colony until 1896 when it became a Dependency of New South Wales. In 1913 it was transferred to the Australian Government. Area: 8,500 acres; Population (1972): 1,694.

THE GOVERNMENT
ADMINISTRATION
Administrator: Air Commodore E. T. PICKERD, O.B.E., D.F.C.

Official Secretary and Deputy Administrator: G. HITCH.

The Administrator is appointed by the Governor-General of Australia. In April 1960 the Norfolk Island Council was set up, which acts as an advisory body to the Administrator. The eight members are elected by adult franchise and certain financial matters and proposed legislation must be referred to the Council for its advice.

JUDICIAL SYSTEM
Supreme Court of Norfolk Island appeals lie to the **High Court of Australia.**

Judges: The Hon. Mr. Justice P. JOSKE, C.M.G., The Hon. Mr. Justice E. A. DUNPHY.

PRESS AND RADIO
Norfolk Islander: "Greenways Press", Queen Elizabeth Ave.; f. 1965; weekly; circ. 1,000; Co-Editors Mr. and Mrs. T. LLOYD.

Norfolk Island Broadcasting Service: Norfolk Island Administration.

ECONOMIC ACTIVITIES

The climate is suitable for the cultivation of a variety of crops and for grazing; the volcanic soil is chemically rich but presents many difficulties to the farmer, especially the steep terrain and the porosity of the soil. The situation is aggravated by over-cultivation, over-grazing and erosion. About 1,000 acres are arable. The main crops are bean seed, cereals, vegetables and fruit. Some flowers and plants are grown commercially. The Administration is increasing the area devoted to Norfolk Island pine and hardwoods. Seed of the Norfolk Island pine is exported.

Imports (year ending June 30th, 1972): $3,905,606, mainly from Australia.

Exports (1972): $385,536. A small quantity of frozen fish fillets is exported.

Budget (year ending June 30th, 1972): Revenue $748,923; Expenditure $740,919.

Banking: There are branches of the Commonwealth Trading Bank and the Commonwealth Savings Bank of Australia.

Trade Association: Norfolk Island Chamber of Commerce.

TRANSPORT

There are about 50 miles of roads, including 8 miles of sealed road. A bi-weekly air service from Sydney and Auckland. There is a regular three-weekly shipping service from Sydney en route to New Caledonia and a six-weekly service from Sydney, en route to the British Solomon Islands and other islands.

COCOS (KEELING) ISLANDS

The COCOS (KEELING) ISLANDS are 27 in number and lie about 200 nautical miles south-west of Java Head. The islands, which have an area of 5½ sq. miles, form a low-lying coral atoll, densely covered with coconut palms. The population on June 30th, 1972, was 637, comprising 139 Europeans and 498 Cocos Malays. Only two islands in the group are inhabited, these being West Island (Europeans) and Home Island (Cocos Malays and 5 Europeans).

The islands were declared a British possession in 1857 and came successively under the authority of the Governor of Ceylon (1878) and the Governor of the Straits Settlements (1886); they were annexed to the Straits Settlements and incorporated with the Settlement (later Colony) of Singapore in 1903. Administration of the islands was transferred to the Commonwealth of Australia in November 1955. In September 1972 by agreement with Mr. JOHN CLUNIES-ROSS, who owned most of the islands, Australia assumed full sovereignty over all of the islands.

Official Representative: C. MCMANUS.

Under instructions from the Minister for External Territories in Canberra the Official Representative administers the islands.

Supreme Court Cocos (Keeling) Islands: The Hon. Mr. Justice E. A. DUNPHY.

The main economic activity is the production of copra (annual exports about 200 tons). An airfield forms an important link between Australia and Asia.

An airmail and passenger flight from Australia to Cocos and return takes place every three weeks. Vessels from Australia visit the islands at regular intervals.

OTHER TERRITORIES

AUSTRALIAN ANTARCTIC TERRITORY

The AUSTRALIAN ANTARCTIC TERRITORY was established by Order in Council, dated 7 February 1933 and covers lands (other than Adélie Land) situated south of the 60th parallel of south latitude and lying between the 160th and 45th meridians of east longitude. The area is estimated at 2,472,000 sq. miles. In 1954 the Australians set up Mawson Base for scientific research. In 1957 a scientific research station was erected at Davis as part of Australia's contribution to the International Geophysical Year. This was closed down permanently in 1968. In 1968 Wilkes Station, built by the U.S.A. on the Budd Coast, was closed down and Casey Station was opened in 1969.

HEARD ISLAND AND McDONALD ISLANDS

These islands are situated south-east of the Kerguelen Islands and have been administered by the Commonwealth of Australia since December 1947, when an Australian Scientific Station was set up on Heard Island. The area is 159 sq. miles; there are no permanent inhabitants, but Australian expeditions visit the island from time to time. Heard Island is about 27 miles long and 13 wide. The McDonald Islands lie 26 miles to the west.

CORAL SEA ISLANDS TERRITORY

The Territory was created in May 1969 and is composed of a number of islands situated east of Queensland between the Great Barrier Reef and 157° 10' E. longitude. The islands had been acquired by the Commonwealth by acts of sovereignty over a number of years. All are very small and they include Cato Island, Chilcott Islet in the Coringa Group, and the Willis Group. Three members of the Commonwealth Bureau of Meteorology are stationed on one of the Willis Group, but the remainder of the islands are uninhabited.

The Bill constituting the Territory does not establish an administration on the islands but provides means of controlling the activities of those who visit them. The possibility of exploration for oil on the continental shelf and the increasing range and scope of international fishing enterprises made desirable such an administrative framework and system of law. The Governor-General is empowered to make ordinances for the peace, order and good government of the Territory, and the Supreme Court and Court of Petty Sessions of Norfolk Island have jurisdiction in relation to the Territory.

MACQUARIE ISLAND

MACQUARIE ISLAND lies about 1,000 miles south-east of Tasmania, of which it is a dependency. There are no permanent inhabitants. A scientific research station was established there in 1948.

ASHMORE AND CARTIER ISLANDS

These islands lie in the Indian Ocean, about 350 miles north of Derby, Western Australia. They were annexed to the Northern Territory in July 1938.

BAHAMA ISLANDS

INTRODUCTORY SURVEY

Location, Climate, Language, Religion, Flag, Capital

The Commonwealth of the Bahama Islands consists of nearly 700 islands and about 2,000 cays and rocks extending from off the Florida coast of the U.S.A. to just north of Cuba and Haiti. The climate is mild and sub-tropical. English is the official language. The largest religious denominations are the Baptists, Roman Catholics and Anglicans. The flag has three equal horizontal stripes of blue, gold and blue, with a black triangle at the hoist extending across half the width of the flag. The capital, Nassau, stands on the island of New Providence.

Recent History

In 1964 and 1968 the Government was granted increased responsibilities for its own affairs. In the elections of September 1972, the Progressive Liberal Party of the Prime Minister, Lynden Pindling, won a large majority of the seats. He advocated independence from Britain. Following talks in December 1972 with the British Government, the Bahamas became an independent nation within the Commonwealth on July 10th, 1973. Leaders of a secessionist movement were unsuccessful in their attempts to secure a separate agreement with the British Government for the two Abaco islands.

Government

There is a 16-member Senate, nine members appointed by the Governor-General on the advice of the Prime Minister, four by the Leader of the Opposition and three after consultation with the Prime Minister. Together with the 38-member House of Assembly, it forms a bi-cameral Parliament to which the Cabinet is responsible.

Defence

At present Britain retains responsibility for defence and the U.S. has certain base facilities, but security agreements are currently under discussion.

Economic Affairs

Economic policies introduced since 1970 have resulted in continued growth in tourism, the country's prime industry, and have established a programme of industrial diversification. These policies ensure continued government support of a free enterprise system, the tax haven status of the Bahamas and incentives to investors to start or expand industrial development projects in partnership with the Government. During 1972 tourist figures reached a record of one and a half million visitors and tourist revenue is running at some £100 million annually. Public expenditure is concentrated in three main areas: education, health and servicing the public debt. An enlargement costing B$18 million has made Nassau a major deep-water port, and an oil trans-shipment terminal due for completion in 1974 will service tankers carrying crude oil to the eastern seaboard of the United States. A B$200 million oil refinery was scheduled to produce 400,000 barrels per day by the end of 1973. Aragonite mining is gaining in importance. A five-year agriculture and livestock research programme on the island of Andros was initiated early in 1973 by the U.S. Agency for International Development (AID) as a joint venture with the Bahamas Government.

Transport and Communications

Inter-island transport is by aircraft and boat and on the larger islands there are excellent roads for motor traffic. A 225-mile submarine 1,380-channel telecommunications system has been installed between the Bahamas and the U.S.A., and there are radio telephone connections between the islands.

Social Welfare

There is a well-developed health service. There are no major tropical diseases. The health service is centralized in Nassau and operates throughout the islands. There is a government-supported old age pension scheme.

Education

The Bahamas contribute financially to the University of the West Indies, there is an extensive primary school education system, and in September 1971 over 500 Bahamian students were registered at universities and colleges overseas. In 1973 education received B$24 million out of a total estimated budgetary expenditure of B$104 million.

Tourism

Nationals of Commonwealth countries may visit the Bahamas without visas. Nationals of the following countries may visit without a visa for eight months: Belgium, Denmark, Finland, Greece, Iceland, Italy, Liechtenstein, Luxembourg, Netherlands, Norway, San Marino, Spain, Sweden, Switzerland, Turkey, U.S.A.; for three months: Austria, France, Federal Republic of Germany; and for two weeks: Mexico, Central and South American countries.

Sport

Swimming, fishing, tennis and golf are popular sports.

Public Holidays

1974: August 6th (Emancipation Day), October 12th (Discovery Day), December 25th–26th (Christmas).

1975: January 1st (New Year's Day), March 28th–31st (Easter), May 19th (Whit Monday), May 24th (Commonwealth Day), June 6th (Labour Day), July 10th (Independence Day).

Weights and Measures

The imperial system is used.

Currency and Exchange Rates

100 cents = 1 Bahamian dollar.

Exchange rates (April 1974):

£1 sterling = B$2.407;
U.S. $1 = B$1.02.

STATISTICAL SURVEY

AREA AND POPULATION

Area: 5,382 square miles.

Population: 175,192 at Census of April 7th, 1970. Latest estimate: 185,000 (July 1st, 1972).

Capital: Nassau, on New Providence Island (population of island 101,503 in 1970).

MAIN ISLANDS

	AREA (sq. miles)	POPULATION (1970)
Abaco . . .	395	6,501
Andros . . .	2,300	8,845
Cat Island . .	150	2,657
Eleuthera . . .	200	9,468
Grand Bahama . .	530	25,859
Inagua . . .	599	1,109
Long Island . .	230	3,861
New Providence . .	80	101,503

Population of other islands: Exuma 3,767; Briminis and Cay Lobos 1,509.

AGRICULTURE
(1966)

Livestock: Sheep 22,900, Goats 14,100, Pigs 10,700, Horses 3,600, Cattle 3,400, Poultry 650,000.

FINANCE

100 cents = 1 Bahamian dollar (B$).

Coins: 1, 5, 10, 15, 25 and 50 cents; 1, 2 and 5 dollars.

Notes: 50 cents; 1, 3, 5, 10, 20, 50 and 100 dollars.

Exchange rates (April 1974): £1 sterling = B$2.407; U.S.$1 = B$1.02.

B$100 = £41.55 = U.S.$98.11.

BUDGET
(B$)

	1970	1971
Revenue . . .	97,587,191	107,160,540
Expenditure . . .	97,030,221	106,522,046

EXTERNAL TRADE

Imports: (1969) B$302.3 million, (1970) B$337.5 million (including B$100 million of duty-free imports into Freeport); of which food and drink, motor vehicles, machinery, hardware, and oil and petroleum products are the chief items.

Exports: (1969) B$54.3 million, (1970) B$89.7 million, of which cement, pulpwood, rum and salt are the chief items.

Trade is mainly with the United Kingdom, the United States and Canada.

TRANSPORT

Roads (1970): Cars and other privately owned motor vehicles 52,863; Commercial vehicles 9,648.

TOURISM

Total number of visitors: (1969) 1,332,396, (1970) 1,298,344, (1971) 1,463,591, (1972) 1,511,858, (1973) 1,520,007.

EDUCATION
(1969)

	SCHOOLS	PUPILS	STAFF
GOVERNMENT SCHOOLS:			
Primary . . .	169	25,911	565
All Age . . .	137	12,422	493
Secondary . . .	13	3,335	161
PRIVATE AND DENOMI-NATIONAL SCHOOLS:			
Primary . . .	62	9,651	302
Secondary . . .	8	1,138	68

In September 1971, 520 Bahamian students were registered at universities and colleges overseas (U.K. 60, Canada 40, U.S.A. 300, University of West Indies 120).

THE CONSTITUTION

In 1968 the order in Council of 1963 was amended as a result of a Constitutional Conference giving the Bahamas internal self-government. The British Government retained responsibility for foreign affairs, defence and internal security.

After independence, the Bahamas retained the bi-cameral form of legislature and a Governor-General was appointed by the Queen. The Governor-General appoints the Prime Minister, and the Cabinet has not less than eight other ministers, of which one is the Attorney-General. The life of a Parliament is limited to five years.

The Senate (upper house) consists of 16 members of whom nine are appointed by the Governor on the advice of the Prime Minister, four members on the advice of the Opposition Leader, and three after consultation with the Prime Minister. The House of Assembly (lower house) has 38 members, but a Constituencies Commission reviews numbers and boundaries at intervals of not more than five years and can recommend alterations for approval of the House.

THE GOVERNMENT

Governor-General: Sir Milo Butler.

THE CABINET
(*March* 1974)

Prime Minister and Minister of Economic Affairs and Immigration: Hon. Lynden Oscar Pindling.

Deputy Prime Minister and Minister of Finance: Hon. Arthur D. Hanna.

Minister of Development and Agriculture and Fisheries: Hon. Carlton E. Francis.

Minister of External Affairs: Senator Paul L. Adderley (Attorney-General designate).

Minister of Home Affairs: Hon. R. F. Anthony Roberts.

Minister of Labour and National Insurance: Hon. Clifford Darling.

Minister of Transport and Telecommunications: Hon. Darrell E. Rolle.

Minister of Education and Culture: Hon. Livingstone N. Coakley.

Minister of Tourism: Hon. Clement T. Maynard.

Minister of Works: Hon. Simeon L. Bowe.

Minister of Health: Hon. A. Loftus Roker.

SENATE

President: Hon. Gerald C. Cash, o.b.e.
Nominated Members: 16.

HOUSE OF ASSEMBLY

Speaker: Hon. Arlington G. Butler.
Elected Members: 38.

GENERAL ELECTION—September 1972

Party	Seats
Progressive Liberal . .	29
Free National Movement .	9

POLITICAL PARTIES

Progressive Liberal Party: P.O.B. 1107, Nassau; supported by the black community which makes up about 80 per cent of the population; Chair. George Mackey; Parl. Leader The Hon. Arthur D. Hanna.

Free National Movement: P.O.B. N-4923, Nassau; Chair. Elwood Donaldson; Amalgamation of United Bahamian Party and eight dissident mems. of the Progressive Liberal Party.

JUDICIAL SYSTEM

The Supreme Court is composed of the Chief Justice and two Puisne Judges, and has jurisdiction similar to that of the High Court of England.

Appeals in all matters lie to the Court of Appeal, composed of three non-resident Judges, with further appeal in certain instances to Her Majesty in Council.

Magistrates Courts in New Providence and Grand Bahama are presided over by professionally qualified Stipendiary and Circuit Magistrates. The Commissioners in charge of Districts in the other islands also have Magisterial Powers. Appeals from the Stipendiary and Circuit Magistrates lie to the Supreme Court and from the Commissioners to a Stipendiary and Circuit Magistrate sitting as Circuit Justice.

Stipendiary and Circuit Magistrates have summary criminal jurisdiction of 2 years imprisonment and/or a fine of B$1,428.57, and civil jurisdiction of 2 years where the sum or value of the property in dispute does not exceed B$571.43. The Out Island Commissioners have jurisdiction in summary offences listed as such in the Penal Code, and in civil causes founded in Contract or Tort where the amount in dispute does not exceed B$571.43.

Chief Justice: Sir W. Gordon Bryce, c.b.e.
Chief Magistrate: Wilton Hercules.
Stipendiary and Circuit Magistrate: Emmanuel Osadebay.
Puisne Judges: H. C. Smith, c.b.e., J. A. Smith, c.b.e., t.d.

RELIGION

The chief religious denominations in the country are the Anglicans, Methodists, Baptists and Roman Catholics. There were in 1970 (census year) 24,201 Anglicans, 25,675 Roman Catholics, 27,236 Baptists and 10,534 Methodists.

ANGLICAN

Bishop of Nassau and the Bahamas: Right Rev. Michael Eldon, Addington House, P.O.B. 107, Nassau.

ROMAN CATHOLIC CHURCH

Bishop of Nassau: Most Rev. Paul Leonard Hagarty, o.s.b., d.d., ll.d., P.O.B. N-8187, Nassau.

THE PRESS

Freeport News: P.O.B. F7, Freeport, Grand Bahama; f. 1961; daily; Gen. Man. Bob Martin; circ. 6,000.

Nassau Guardian: P.O.B. N-3011, Nassau; f. 1844; daily; circ. 10,000; Gen. Man. Mark Bethel; London Rep. Colin Turner Ltd., 122 Shaftesbury Ave., W1.

The Tribune: Shirley St., P.O.B. N-3207, Nassau; f. 1903; daily; circ. 17,500; Editor Hon. Sir Etienne Dupuch, o.b.e., k.c.s.g., ll.d.; Publ. Editor Eileen Dupuch Caronne; London Reps. Joshua B. Powers Ltd., 27 Cockspur St., W1.

Bahamas Magazine: P.O.B. 208, Nassau; f. 1933; five times a year; Editor A. B. McDermott.

Bahamas Pictorial: P.O.B. 582, Nassau; f. 1964; monthly; Editor A. L. Roker; circ. 13,000.

Bahamas Tourist News: P.O.B. N-4855, Nassau; monthly; Editor Paul Bower; circ. 208,000 (annually).

Bahamian Review Magazine: Bay St., P.O.B. 494, Nassau; f. 1952; monthly; Editor William Cartwright; circ. 9,500.

Bahamian Times: P.O.B. 5490, Nassau; twice weekly; Editor James D. Andrews; circ. 3,000.

Official Gazette: Nassau; weekly; published by the Government.

The People: P.O.B. N-3249, Nassau; Editor Margaret Hope.

PUBLISHER

Etienne Dupuch Jr. Publications Ltd.: P.O.B. N-7513, Nassau; publish *Bahamas Handbook and Businessman's Annual*, *What To Do Magazine*, *Tadpole* (educational colouring book) series and maps.

RADIO AND TELEVISION

Broadcasting Corporation of the Bahamas: P.O.B. N-1347, Nassau; f. 1936; government owned; three channels; Gen. Man. G. F. Brickenden.

A northern (Grand Bahama) service of Radio Bahamas was established early in 1973 at Freeport. In 1972 there were 90,000 radio receivers. American television programmes can be received. There is no national television service.

FINANCE

The Bahamas is an international financial centre, and finance has become the industry second in importance to tourism. There are over 6,000 finance or financial service companies in the islands. These pay a small company tax and stamp duty, but there are no corporation, income, capital gains or withholding taxes or estate duty.

The Bahamas Monetary Authority has been responsible for regulating the use and possession of foreign currency. The Central Bank has evolved from the Monetary Authority and is responsible for issuing all coinage, for the issue and redemption of currency, for monitoring balance of payments, encouraging the growth of the capital market and acts as the Government fiscal agent in international money markets.

BANKING

PRINCIPAL BAHAMAS BANKS

(cap.=capital; dep.=deposits; m.=million; p.u.=paid up; res.=reserves; br.=branch.)

Bank of Nassau Ltd.: P.O.B. N-4901, Sassoon House, Shirley Street, Nassau.

Bank of New Providence Ltd.: P.O.B. 4723, 9 Norfolk House, Frederick St., Nassau; cap. B$3m.; dep. B$55.7m. (Nov. 1973); Pres. and Dir. JOHN WOLF; Man. BRIAN F. FREE.

Deltec Banking Corporation: P.O.B. N-3229, Marlborough and Cumberland Sts., Nassau; assets U.S. $239.2m. (March 1973).

Finance Corporation of Bahamas Ltd.: P.O.B. N-3038, Frederick St., Nassau; br. in Freeport.

International Credit Bank (Bahamas) Ltd.: P.O.B. N-4802, Beaumont House, Nassau; Pres. W. BURNETT GRAY; Man. Freeport Branch Mrs. M. MARTIN.

E. D. Sassoon Bank and Trust International Ltd.: P.O.B. N-3045, Nassau; incorporated Bahamas 1950; cap. p.u. B$1,000,000.

Roy West Banking Corporation Ltd.: P.O.B. 4889, Norfolk House, Nassau; f. 1965; cap. B$17.1m.; res. B$3.2m.

PRINCIPAL OVERSEAS BANKS

Bank of London and Montreal Ltd.: King and George Streets, P.O.B. 1262, Nassau; owned jointly by Bank of London and South America Ltd.; f. 1958; cap. issued B$21.5m.; Chair. W. H. SWEETING, C.M.G., C.B.E.

Bank of Nova Scotia: Head Office: Toronto 1, Canada; Nassau.

Barclays Bank International Ltd.: Head Office: 54 Lombard St., London, E.C.3; Bay St., Nassau (P.O.B. N-8348); 5 brs. and 2 agencies in New Providence, 1 br. and 2 agencies in Abaco, 2 brs. in Eleuthera, 1 br. and 2 agencies in Grand Bahama, 1 agency in Andros and 1 br. and 2 agencies in Turks and Caicos Islands; Local Dir. NORMAN E. IRELAND.

Canadian Imperial Bank of Commerce: Head Office: 25 King St. West, Toronto 1; P.O.B. N-7125, Nassau; f. 1867; 8 brs. in the Bahamas; Man. Nassau J. D. COCKWELL.

Chase Manhattan Bank: Head Office: New York; P.O.B. 4921, Nassau.

Cisalpine Overseas Bank Ltd.: IBM House, P.O.B. 6347, Nassau; f. 1971; assets U.S. $344.4m., dep. U.S.$317.9m. (Nov. 1973).

First National City Bank: Head Office: New York; P.O. Bag 58, Nassau.

Royal Bank of Canada: Head Office: Place Ville Marie, Montreal; f. 1869; 7 brs. and 1 sub-br. in Nassau; 4 sub-brs. in Out Islands; 2 brs. in Freeport.

TRUST COMPANIES IN THE BAHAMAS
(Nassau, unless otherwise stated)

Bahamas Commonwealth Trust Corporation Ltd.: Charlotte House, P.O.B. N-3912; Man. Dir. J. E. J. KING.

Bahamas International Trust Co. Ltd.: Bank Lane and East St.; incorporated 1957; cap. B$1m.

Bank of London and Montreal Ltd. (Trust Department): P.O.B. 1262; Man. R. M. BEASE.

Bank of Nova Scotia Trust Co. (Bahamas) Ltd.: Bernard Sunley Bldg., Rawson Square, P.O.B. 1355; subsidiaries in Trinidad, Barbados and Cayman Islands.

Chase Manhattan Trust Corporation Ltd.: Thompson Boulevard and Russell Rd., Oakes Field, P.O.B. N-3708.

First National City Trust Company (Bahamas) Ltd.: Thompson Boulevard, Oakes Field, P.O.B. N-1576.

Mercantile Bank and Trust Company Ltd.: Mercantile Bank Building, "On the Mall", P.O.B. F-2558, Freeport.

Trust Corporation of Bahamas Ltd.: West Bay Street, P.O.B. N-7788; f. 1936; Chair. A. D. CHESTERFIELD; Deputy Chair. and Man. Dir. D. R. KESTER.

World Banking Corporation Ltd.: P.O.B. N-100; f. 1963; cap. p.u., surplus and res. 10.8m.; dep. 357.9m. (Dec. 1972); Pres. R. D. H. WILMER.

SAVINGS AND LOAN ASSOCIATIONS

International Bank and Trust: P.O.B. 69, Nassau.

The People's Penny Savings Bank Ltd.: P.O.B. 1484, Nassau.

INSURANCE

The leading British and a number of U.S. and Canadian companies have agents in Nassau and Freeport.

TRADE AND INDUSTRY

Bahamas Chamber of Commerce: P.O.B. N-665, Nassau; f. 1933; 700 mems.; Pres. A. D. FARQUHARSON; Sec. FRED CADMAN; Man. Mrs. D. ALBURY.

Bahamas Development Corporation, The: Nassau Bank House, 2nd Terrace and Collins Avenue, P.O.B. 4940, Nassau; f. 1971 to promote the establishment of heavy industry and supervise agricultural development.

Nassau/Paradise Island Promotion Board: P.O.B. N-7799, Nassau; f. 1970; 27 mems.; Pres. RONALD OVEREND; Exec. Dir. RONALD MUZII.

EMPLOYERS' ASSOCIATIONS

Bahamas Association of Land Surveyors: P.O.B. N-4312, Nassau; 42 mems.; Pres. K. W. WADMAN; Sec. L. M. BOWE.

Bahamas Employers' Confederation: P.O.B. 166, Nassau; f. 1963; Pres. ORFILIA PELAEZ; Dir. P. S. C. POWER.

Bahamas Hotel Employers' Association: P.O.B. N-7799, Nassau; f. 1958; 27 mems.; Pres. STEVE NORTON; Exec. Dir. TREVELYAN COOPER.

Bahamian Contractors' Association: P.O.B. N-1969, Nassau; f. 1958; 40 mems.; Pres. HERBERT TRECO; Sec. E. A. PYFROM.

Corporation of Accountants and Auditors: P.O.B. 1673, Nassau; f. 1960; 27 mems.; Pres. LIVINGSTON COAKLEY; Sec. J. T. MILLS.

There are also Associations of Automobile Dealers and Licensed Plumbers.

TRADE UNIONS

Bahamas Federation of Trade Unions (BFTU): P.O.B. 5783, Nassau; Pres. Sen. The Hon. CALDWELL ARMBRISTER.

Affiliated to BFTU are the following:

Airport, Airline and Allied Workers' Union: P.O.B. 71, Windsor Field, Nassau; f. 1958; 550 mems.; Pres. CALDWELL ARMBRISTER; Sec.-Treas. PHILIP P. SMITH.

Bahama Islands Airlines Pilots' Association: P.O.B. 5533, Nassau International Airport; f. 1960; 51 mems.; Pres. Capt. GARTH MASSEY; Sec. Capt. D. DROST.

Bahama Islands Airline Stewardesses' Association: P.O.B. 876, Windsor Field, Nassau; f. 1960; 29 mems.; Pres. Mrs. Y. M. DEVEAUX.

Bahama Islands Licensed Aircraft Engineers and Aviation Specialists: P.O.B. 65, Windsor Field, Nassau; 17 mems.; Pres. JOHN BRUNNELL; Sec. W. L. HEARNE.

Bahamas Construction and Building Trade Union: P.O.B. 2511, Nassau; f. 1958; 200 mems.; Pres. S. P. ADDERLEY; Gen. Sec. P. FARQUHARSON.

Bahamas Hotel and Catering Workers' Union: P.O.B. 2514, Wulff Rd., Nassau; f. 1958; 695 mems.; Pres. BARTHOLOMEW BASTIAN; Gen. Sec. H. FERGUSON.

Bahamas Musicians' Union: P.O.B. 246, Nassau Court, Nassau; f. 1958; 61 mems.; Pres. CHARLES H. FISHER; Sec. I. HANNA.

Bahamas Transport, Agricultural, Distributive and Allied Workers' Trade Union: P.O.B. 451, Wulff Rd., Nassau; f. 1959; 1,362 mems.; Pres. RANDOLF FAWKES, M.H.A.; Gen. Sec. MAXWELL N. TAYLOR.

Bahamas Union of Teachers: P.O.B. 1314, Wulff Rd., Nassau; f. 1959; 292 mems.; Pres. ELCOTT JOHNSON; Sec. H. MINNIS.

United Brotherhood of Longshoremen: P.O.B. 451, Wulff Rd., Nassau; f. 1959; 157 mems.; Pres. A. MORRIS; Gen. Sec. W. SWANN.

Non-affiliated unions include:

Abaco Agricultural and Allied Workers' Union: Murphy Town, Abaco; f. 1960; 148 mems.; Sec. BENJAMIN CURRY.

Bahamas Engineering, Fuel, Service and Allied Workers' Union: P.O.B. 2535, Nassau; f. 1956; Pres. DUDLEY WILLIAMS; Sec. CARL STUBBS.

Bahamas Public Services Union: P.O.B. N-4692, Nassau; f. 1959; 1,119 mems.; Pres. THADDEUS DARLING; Sec. CIANO R. E. STRACHAN.

Bahamas Racehorse Workers' Union: Nassau; Gen. Sec. LAVARITY B. DEVEAUX.

Bahamas Workers' Council International: P.O.B. 5337 M.S., Nassau; f. 1969; Chair. DUDLEY WILLIAMS; publ. *Labour Speaks*.

TRANSPORT

ROADS

Nearly all roads in New Providence are motorable. Hot mix surfaced roads total 230 miles, water-bound macadam 65 miles, earth 44 miles. On Eleuthera there is an asphalt road, some 100 miles in length, covering the length of the island, and 105 miles of road on Grand Bahama. The Grand Bahama Motorway, a highway linking Freeport and Gold Rock Creek, is under construction. Other asphalt roads are under construction on the Out Islands.

SHIPPING

The following are the chief shipping lines calling at Nassau: Hamburg-Amerika, Independent Gulf, North German Lloyd, P. and O., Pacific Steam Navigation Co., Saguenay Shipping, Home Lines, Eastern Steamship Co., Norwegian-Caribbean Lines, Bahama Cruise Lines and Costa Lines.

CIVIL AVIATION

Nassau International Airport and Freeport International Airport are the main terminals for international and internal services.

Bahamasair: P.O.B. N-4881, Nassau; f. 1973 as national airline from merger of Flamingo Airlines Ltd. and Out Island Airways; scheduled services between Nassau, Freeport, Miami and the family islands; fleet: 3 BAC 111/400, 2 Twin Otters, 3 Aero Commanders, 3 F-227, 1 Grumman Goose, 1 Grumman Wigeon; Gen. Man. and Chief Exec. H. MAX HEALEY; Chair. WILLIAN C. ALLEN.

International Air Bahama: Beaumont House, Bay St., Nassau; f. 1966; a subsidiary of Hekla Holdings Ltd./Loftleidir HF; fleet: 2 DC-8-63; Gen. Man. and Chief Exec. SIGURDUR HELGASON.

The following airlines serve the Bahamas: Air Canada, Air Jamaica, British Airways, Delta, Eastern, Lufthansa, Mackey International, Pan American, Qantas, Shawnee, United (Freeport only).

TOURISM

The Ministry of Tourism: P.O.B. N-3701, Nassau; tourism is expanding rapidly, and there are 11,300 hotel rooms in the country.

There were 1,520,007 visitors in 1973.

The Ministry of Tourism maintains tourist offices in Atlanta, Boston, Chicago, Dallas, Detroit, Los Angeles, Miami, Montreal, New York, Toronto, Washington, London and Frankfurt.

Nassau Festival of Arts and Crafts: Nassau; registered association incorporating all art forms; Chair. and Dir. Mrs. META DAVIS.

BAHRAIN

INTRODUCTORY SURVEY

Location, Climate, Language, Religion, Flag, Capital

The State of Bahrain lies near Qatar off the west coast of the Arabian Gulf. The climate is cool and temperate from December to the end of March, becoming very hot and humid during the summer months. In August and September temperatures can rise to 42°C (108°F). The official language is Arabic, but English is widely spoken. Bahrain is a predominantly Muslim country, the population being divided between the Sunnis and Shi'ites. The Ruling Family belong to the Sunnis. The national flag (proportions 5 by 3) is scarlet, with a vertical white stripe at the hoist, the two colours separated by a serrated line. The port of Manama is the capital.

Recent History

Bahrain was a British Protected State from 1816 until 1971. In 1968 the British Government stated that all British troops would be withdrawn from "East of Suez" by the end of 1971 and the Rulers of the Gulf States, including Bahrain, drew up plans for a Federation of Arab Emirates.

On August 15th, 1971, the Amir, Sheikh Isa, declared Bahrain an independent sovereign state, having become disillusioned with efforts to create a federation of Gulf emirates. The treaties giving Britain responsibility for Bahrain's defence and foreign relations were terminated and a new friendship treaty was signed between the two countries. Shortly afterwards Bahrain became a member of the United Nations and the Arab League. In September 1972 Bahrain became a member of the World Bank.

Government

Bahrain is an independent sovereign state ruled by Sheikh Isa bin Sulman al-Khalifa through a Ministerial Cabinet system. In December 1972 the first Constituent Assembly was elected. This Assembly discussed a preliminary draft Constitution which was presented to the Amir for ratification during 1973. As a result, formal elections for a National Assembly were held in December 1973.

Defence

The 1,300 strong Bahrain Defence Force has taken over from British forces the sole responsibility for security in Bahrain. In December 1971 Bahrain agreed to the U.S. Middle East fleet using part of the naval base formerly used by Britain. Notice of the termination of this facility was given to the U.S. Government during the October 1973 Arab-Israeli war.

Economic Affairs

The traditional occupations of cattle breeding, agriculture and fishing are still practised throughout the islands. The main crops are vegetables, lucerne, other fodder crops and some dates. The Bahrain Fishing Company, jointly British and Bahraini owned, has now been operating successfully for several years.

Oil in commercial quantity was found in 1932 and has since been developed by the Bahrain Petroleum Company. Bahrain became a member of OAPEC in May 1970.

Although Bahrain's production of crude oil is relatively small it has the second largest refinery in the Middle East, which processed over 87 million U.S. barrels in 1972.

Important new communications facilities and port installations have improved Bahrain's standing in the transit trade. Storage and refrigeration facilities, a slipway and marine engineering workshops have been completed at Mina Sulman. Bahrain has a free zone in which many British, Amercian and local concerns have their headquarters. A £60 million aluminium smelter, under construction since 1969, began production in 1971 with an estimated capacity of 120,000 tons per annum. In November 1972 the Organization of Arab Petroleum Exporting Countries approved Bahrain as the site for a £40 million dry dock large enough to accept super-tankers of up to 375,000 d.w.t.

Transport and Communications

There are 30 kilometres of bitumen-surfaced roads linking most inhabited areas, and there is now a national bus system. The Bahrain Airport Terminal, designed specifically to take jumbo jets, was opened recently. The terminal building can handle the passengers of two 747s simultaneously, and is fully equipped for handling large passenger and freight aircraft; it is shortly to be enlarged to handle double its present capacity.

A new four-lane bridge between the two main islands was completed during 1972.

Social Welfare

In 1972 BD 3.1 million, 11.9 per cent of the budget, was allocated to health. With the withdrawal of British troops the R.A.F. hospital was handed over intact to the Bahrain Government. A new hospital complex at Sulmaniyah is now under construction.

Education

Education is free in Bahrain. There are 75 primary, and 35 intermediate and secondary schools. In 1972 there were 7,266 pupils at intermediate level and 6,694 at secondary and technical level. The sexes are segregated in all schools. Education took 16.2 per cent (BD 4.2 million) of the state budget in 1972.

Public Holidays

1974: September 3rd (National Day), October 17th (Id ul Fitr), December 16th (Amir's Accession Day), December 25th, 26th (Christmas Day, Boxing Day, also Id ul Adha).

1975: January 1st, January 14th (Muslim New Year), January 24th (Ashoura), March 26th (Birth of the Prophet).

Weights and Measures

The metric system is in force.

Currency and Exchange Rates

1,000 fils = 1 Bahrain dinar (BD).
Exchange rates (April 1974):
$£1$ sterling = 932.07 fils;
U.S. $1 = 394.74 fils.

STATISTICAL SURVEY

AREA AND POPULATION

AREA sq. km.	POPULATION (Census of April 3rd, 1971)		
	Total	Manama (capital)	Muharraq Town
369.6	216,078	89,399	37,732

Estimated Population: 224,000 (July 1st, 1972).

EMPLOYMENT
(1971)

Agriculture and fishing	3,990
Mining and Manufacturing . . .	4,152
Oil	4,312
Public Utilities	1,705
Construction	10,404
Wholesale and retail trade, and catering .	7,706
Transport, storage and communications .	7,743
Finance, insurance, property and business services	1,084
Community, social and personal services .	13,182
Public administration and defence . .	5,206
Other	817
TOTAL . . .	60,301

CRUDE OIL PRODUCTION
('000 metric tons)

1968	1969	1970	1971	1972
3,686	3,800	3,750	3,800	3,500

REFINERY PRODUCTION
(Output in million barrels)

1968	1969	1970	1971	1972
79.9	83.3	88.2	89.9	83.5

Note: 1 metric ton equals approx. 7.3 barrels.

Industry: Building materials, clothing, soft drinks, plastic products, industrial gases, boat building, air conditioning manufacture, flour mills and an aluminium plant.

FINANCE

1,000 fils = 1 Bahrain dinar (BD).

Coins: 1, 5, 10, 25, 50, 100, 250 and 500 fils.

Notes: 100, 250 and 500 fils; 1, 5 and 10 dinars.

Exchange rates (April 1974): £1 sterling = 932.07 fils; U.S. $1 = 394.74 fils.

100 Bahrain dinars = £107.29 = $253.44.

BUDGET
(1974-75—'000 Bahrain dinars)

REVENUE		EXPENDITURE	
Oil Payments	33,700	Amiri Expenditure	6,000
Government Dues	8,100	Finance and National Economy . .	2,400
Public Services	7,300	Development and Engineering Services .	7,000
Miscellaneous	3,900	Education and Science . . .	5,600
		Health	3,900
		Defence	2,800
		Public Security	4,000
		Non-recurring Expenditure . .	17,500
		Other	3,800
TOTAL . . .	53,000	TOTAL . . .	53,000

Currency in Circulation (Sept. 1972): BD 23,278,690. The Bahrain dinar is accepted in other Gulf States.

EXTERNAL TRADE
(B.D. '000)

	1970	1971	1972
Imports	80,126	105,005	100,103
Exports and Re-exports (excl. oil) . .	25,156	28,405	32,292

COMMODITIES

IMPORTS	1970	1971
Food and live animals	13,457.4	14,536.3
Beverages and tobacco . . .	2,634.5	2,531.8
Inedible raw materials (not fuels) . .	1,160.2	1,424.9
Mineral fuels, lubricants etc. . .	860.9	1,125.2
Animal and vegetable oils and fats . .	141.0	178.8
Chemicals	3,143.9	7,134.7
Manufactured goods . . .	22,936.5	30,624.5
Machinery and transport equipment .	23,958.2	33,332.0
Miscellaneous manufactured articles . .	11,431.0	13,983.3
Unclassified groups and transactions . .	403.2	133.4
TOTAL	80,126.9	105,004.9

RE-EXPORTS	1967	1968	1969	1970
Household goods	1,732	2,207	1,701	1,133
Cotton piece goods	1,276	2,031	1,323	1,778
Garments	1,378	2,019	2,906	2,390
Silk and silk piece goods . . .	1,114	2,000	2,273	2,773
Provisions	730	1,586	n.a.	n.a.
Machinery and oilwell supplies . .	961	980	1,231	1,908
Spices	1,008	695	751	915
Rice	967	679	547	1,238
Haberdashery and hosiery . . .	436	559	n.a.	n.a.

PRINCIPAL COUNTRIES

IMPORTS	1969	1970	1971	1972
United Kingdom	14,269	24,904	31,754	21,194
India	2,839	3,347	3,031	2,835
U.S.A.	6,171	5,812	12,630	13,079
Japan	8,269	9,972	12,793	14,869
Germany, Federal Republic .	2,394	2,684	4,155	4,678
Netherlands . . .	1,692	3,817	5,671	2,393
Pakistan	2,260	2,915	2,438	1,958
Australia	n.a.	1,108	2,590	5,978
China, People's Republic .	3,799	4,091	5,867	6,594
Hong Kong . . .	2,241	2,495	2,790	2,537

Exports and Re-Exports	1970	1971	1972
Saudi Arabia	12,544	14,016	16,523
Qatar	1,320	1,648	1,833
Iran	902	1,043	1,916
Dubai	1,510	1,442	2,204
Abu Dhabi	466	639	569
Kuwait	2,993	3,518	2,146
United Kingdom . . .	450	711	860

TRANSPORT
ROADS

Type of Licence	1969	1970	1971
Private Cars	8,156	8,960	10,400
Taxi Cabs	911	915	908
Vans and Lorries . . .	2,682	2,999	3,439
Private Buses . . .	344	381	419
Public Buses . . .	140	142	145
Motor Cycles . . .	1,377	1,529	1,772
Total (excl. motor cycles)	12,233	13,397	15,311

EDUCATION
GOVERNMENT EDUCATION 1970–72

	Schools/Colleges*		Pupils/Students	
	1970–71	1971–72	1970–71	1971–72
Primary	73	75	36,113	36,952
Intermediate	25	21	7,288	7,266
Secondary	7	11	5,242	5,322
Technical, Commercial, Religious .	3	3	1,079	1,372
Higher (incl. Teacher Training Colleges) .	5	5	289	312
Total	113	115	50,011	51,224

* There are also 7 private schools and 3 kindergartens under the supervision of the Ministry of Education.

The total number of pupils in Private Schools in 1971–72 was 3,473.

The total number of teaching staff under the Ministry of Education was 2,247 in 1971–72.

Source: Statistical Bureau, Finance Department, Bahrain Government.

THE CONSTITUTION

A new 108-article constitution was ratified in June 1973. It states that "all citizens shall be equal before the law" and guarantees freedom of speech, of the Press, of conscience and religious beliefs. Other provisions include the outlawing of the compulsory repatriation of political refugees. The constitution also states that the country's financial comptroller should be responsible to Parliament and not to the Government, and allows for national trade unions "for legally justified causes and on peaceful lines". Compulsory free primary education and free medical care are also laid down in the constitution. It is to remain in force for a minimum of five years. The constitution provides for a National Assembly, composed of the members of the Cabinet and 30 members elected by popular vote.

THE GOVERNMENT

Amir: Sheikh ISA BIN SULMAN AL-KHALIFA, K.C.M.G.

Heir Apparent: Sheikh HAMAD BIN ISA AL-KHALIFA.

THE CABINET
(March 1974)

Prime Minister: Sheikh KHALIFA BIN SULMAN AL-KHALIFAH.

Minister of Defence: Sheikh HAMAD BIN ISA AL-KHALIFAH.

Minister of Finance and National Economy: SAYED MAHMOOD AL-ALAWI.

Minister of Foreign Affairs: Sheikh MOHAMED BIN MUBARAK AL-KHALIFA.

Minister of Education: Sheikh ABDUL AZIZ MUHAMED AL-KHALIFA.

Minister of Health: Dr. ALI MOHAMED FAKHRO.

Minister of Interior: Sheikh MOHAMED BIN KHALIFA BIN HAMAD AL-KHALIFA.

Minister of Information: TARIQ ABDAR-RAHMAN AL-MUAYYAD.

Minister of Justice: Sheikh KHALID BIN MOHAMED AL-KHALIFA.

Minister of Development and Engineering: YOUSIF AHMED AL-SHIRAWI.

Minister of Labour and Social Affairs: IBRAHIM MOHAMED HASAN HUMAYDAN.

Minister of Municipalities and Agriculture: Sheikh ABDULLA BIN KHALID AL-KHALIFA.

Minister of State for Arab League Affairs: Dr. HUSSAIN MOHAMED AL-BAHARNA.

Minister of State for Cabinet Affairs: JAWAD SALIM AL-URRAYED.

DIPLOMATIC REPRESENTATION

EMBASSIES ACCREDITED TO BAHRAIN
(Manama unless otherwise stated)

Afghanistan: Baghdad, Iraq (E).

Egypt: 3105/7 Adliya (E); *Ambassador:* MOHAMED G. ABDUL-SALAM.

France: Kuwait City, Kuwait (E).

Germany, Federal Republic: Kuwait City, Kuwait (E).

India: Kuwait City, Kuwait (E).

Iran: 107 Sh. Isa Rd. (E); *Ambassador:* MANUCHEHR SEPAHBODI.

Iraq: 371/7 Sh. Isa Rd. (E); *Ambassador:* YAAKOUB KAZIM HAMDANI.

Italy: Kuwait City, Kuwait (E).

Japan: Kuwait City, Kuwait (E).

Jordan: Sh. Isa Rd. (E); *Ambassador:* Dr. SULIMAN AL-DAJANI.

Kuwait: Qudhaibiyya, nr. the new Palace (E); *Ambassador:* SULIEMAN MAJED AL-SHAHEN.

Lebanon: Kuwait City, Kuwait (E).

Morocco: Kuwait City, Kuwait (E).

Netherlands: Kuwait City, Kuwait (E).

Norway: (E); *Ambassador:* NILS JORGENSEN.

Pakistan: Sh. Essa Rd. (E); *Ambassador:* GHOULAM GHOUTH KHAN.

Saudi Arabia: Al-Mahooz (E); *Ambassador:* Shaikh ABDULLAH AL-FADHEL.

Senegal: Teheran, Iran (E).

Somalia: Jeddah, Saudi Arabia (E).

Spain: Kuwait City, Kuwait (E).

Sudan: Kuwait City, Kuwait (E).

Tunisia: Kuwait City, Kuwait (E).

United Kingdom: Al-Mathaf Square (E); *Ambassador:* ROBERT TESCH.

U.S.A.: Kuwait City, Kuwait (E).

Bahrain also has diplomatic relations with Chad, the Democratic People's Republic of Korea, Mongolia, Niger, Oman, Qatar, Syria, the U.S.S.R. and the United Arab Emirates.

NATIONAL ASSEMBLY

In December 1972 22 members were elected to seats in the 44-member Constituent Council. The remaining 22 seats were occupied by nominees of the Amir and members of the cabinet. During the first six months of 1973 the Constituent Assembly drew up the new constitution, which was ratified in June 1973. In accordance with this constitution elections to a National Assembly took place on December 8th, 1973, and the Amir opened the Assembly on December 16th, 1973. About 30,000 electors elected 30 members for a four-year term. Since political parties are not allowed, all 114 candidates stood as independents, but in practice the National Assembly is divided about equally between conservative, moderate and more radical members. In addition to the 30 elected members, the National Assembly also contains 14 members of the cabinet.

JUDICIAL SYSTEM

Minister of Justice: Sheikh KHALID BIN MOHAMED AL-KHALIFA.

Since the termination of British legal jurisdiction in 1971, intensive work has been in progress on the legislative requirements of Bahrain. The Criminal Law is at present contained in various Codes, Ordinances and Regulations.

Judges, both Bahraini and Arab, are all fully qualified, as are the lawyers that appear before the courts.

Since the end of 1971 all nationalities are subject to the jurisdiction of the Bahrain Courts which guarantee equality before the Law irrespective of nationality or creed.

RELIGION

The great majority of the people are Muslims of the Sunni and Shi'ite sects. The ruling family is Sunni.

Religious affiliation (1971 Census):

Muslims	206,708
Christians	6,590
Others	2,780
TOTAL	216,078

PRESS, RADIO AND TELEVISION

Al Bahrain Al-Yom (*Bahrain Today*): P.O.B. 253, Manama; Radio monthly; Arabic; published by the Ministry of Information Dept.; Manama; Editor AHMED KAMAL; circ. 4,000.

al Adhwaa: Arab Printing and Publishing Establishment, P.O.B. 250, Tijjar Rd., Manama; f. 1965; Arabic; weekly; Editor Mahmoud Al-Murdi, circ. 5,000.

Akhbar Al-Bahrain: f. 1972; free distribution, published by the Ministry of Information.

Arab Markets: P.O.B. 604, Bahrain; monthly; English and Arabic; Editor Abdu F. Bushara.

Awali Evening News: Published by the Bahrain Petroleum Co. Ltd.; daily; English; circ. 1,000.

Awali Magazine: Published by the Bahrain Petroleum Co. Ltd.; monthly; English; circ. 1,000.

Bahrain Trade Directory: P.O.B. 524, Manama; Publisher and Man. Dir. A. E. Ashir.

al Hiya al Tijariya (*Commerce Review*): P.O.B. 248, Manama; English and Arabic; published by Bahrain Chamber of Commerce and Industry.

Al-Mujtama Al-Jadid: P.O.B. 590; Editor Mustafa.

Commerce Review: P.O.B. 248, Manama; Chamber of Commerce Journal; monthly.

Gulf Weekly Mirror: P.O.B. 455, Manama; f. 1971; weekly; English; also circulates in Oman, Qatar, United Arab Emirates and eastern Saudi Arabia; Editor Stefan Kemball.

al Jarida al Rasmiya (*Official Gazette*): Information Department, Government of Bahrain, Manama; f. 1957; Arabic; weekly.

al Mawaquf: Manama, f. 1973; Arabic, weekly; world news, politics, arts, religion; Owner Abdulla Madani.

al Murshid: Arabian Printing and Publishing House, P.O.B. 553, Bahrain; monthly guide, including "What's on in Bahrain"; English and Arabic; Editor M. Soliman.

al Najma al Asbuia (*Weekly Star*): Awali; Arabic; weekly; published by The Bahrain Petroleum Co. Ltd.; circ. 8,000.

The New Society: P.O.B. 590, Manama; weekly.

Sada Al Usbou: P.O.B. 549, Bahrain; f. 1969; Arabic; weekly; Owner and Editor-in-Chief Ali Sayyar.

Bahrain Broadcasting Station: P.O.B. 253, Manama; f. 1955; state-owned and operated enterprise; two 10 kW. transmitters; programmes are in Arabic only, and include news, plays and talks; Dir. of Broadcasting Ibrahim Kanoo.

R.T.V. Bahrain: commenced colour TV broadcasting in 1973. The station takes advertising.

English language programmes broadcast by the U.S. Air Force in Dhahran and by ARAMCO can be received in Bahrain, as can the television service provided by the latter. The station is currently being expanded and its power increased.

In 1974 there were approximately 100,000 radio receiving sets.

FINANCE

BANKING

(cap. = capital; dep. = deposits; m. = millions; B.D. = Bahrain Dinars)

National Bank of Bahrain: P.O.B. 106, Manama; f. 1957; cap. p.u. (1972) B.D. 750,000; reserves B.D. 575,000; dep. B.D. 20.4m.; Chair. Ahmed Ali Kanoo; Gen. Man. A. S. Wood.

Foreign Banks

Arab Bank Ltd.: Amman, Jordan; P.O.B. 395, Manama; Man. Ahmed I. Jaber.

Bank of Bahrain and Kuwait: Suk-al-Tuggar, P.O.B. 597, Manama; cap. p.u. 2m B.D. subscribed by Bahraini citizens and six leading financial institutions in Kuwait.

Bank of Cairo: Manama.

Bank Melli Iran: Teheran; Government Rd., P.O.B. 785, Manama; 1 br.

British Bank of the Middle East: London; P.O.B. 57, Manama; Man. F. X. Paul.

The Chartered Bank: London; P.O.B. 29, Manama; dep. B.D. 63,678,000 (Dec. 71); Chief Man. V. R. Winton.

Chase Manhattan Bank: New York; Manama; Man. John House.

First National City Bank: New York; P.O.B. 548, Manama; 1 br.; Man. Donald L. Byram.

Habib Bank (Overseas) Ltd.: Karachi; Government Road, Manama; Man. Ch. Sajjad Ali.

National and Grindlays Bank Ltd.: London; Manama.

Rafidain Bank: Baghdad; f. 1969; P.O.B. 607, Manama; Man. T. Al-Khatib.

United Bank Ltd.: Karachi; Government Road, Manama; Man. S. M. Akhtar.

INSURANCE

Bahrain Insurance Co.: f. 1971; general accident, fire and life insurance; cap. B.D. 270,000; 66⅔ per cent Bahrain owned; 33⅓ per cent Iraq owned.

About fourteen foreign insurance companies are represented.

TRADE AND INDUSTRY

Bahrain Chamber of Commerce and Industry: P.O.B. 248, Manama; f. 1939; 1,200 mems.; Pres. Khalil Ibrahim Kamel; Dir. Yusuf Muhammad Saleh.

Michael Rice Group—Middle East: P.O.B. 551, Manama; consultants to the Governments of Bahrain and Oman and to numerous local and foreign businesses trading in Bahrain, the Gulf area, Saudi Arabia and Kuwait.

There are no Trade Unions in Bahrain.

OIL

The Bahrain Petroleum Company (BAPCO) Ltd.: Awali; the sole oil producer in Bahrain; owned jointly by Texaco and Standard Oil of California; also operates the Bahrain refinery and holds a contract to supply natural gas to the ALBA aluminium smelter; Pres. W. O. Stolz.

TRANSPORT

ROADS

Most inhabited areas of Bahrain are linked by bitumen-surfaced roads. Public transport consists of taxis and privately owned bus services. A new national bus company is being developed to provide public services throughout the country. A modern network of dual highways is being developed; the length of the paved road system rose from 4.3 kilometres in 1964 to 30 kilometres in 1968. In 1967 the rule of the road was changed from left to right.

SHIPPING

Director-General of Customs and Ports: Sheikh Daij bin Khalifa al-Khalifa.

Harbour Master: Captain J. A. Duck.

Cargo Manager: Hassan Shams.

Numerous shipping services link Bahrain and the Gulf with Britain and with Europe (Strick Line, V.N.S. "Kerk" Line, Hansa Line, Nationale Compagnie Havraise Peninsulaire and Compagnie Maritime Belge, Kuwait Shipping Company, Iraqi Maritime Transport Corporation, Lauro Line, Yugo-Linea, Polish Ocean Lines); with the East and West Coasts, of U.S.A. (Concordia Line, Nedlloyd Line); with Pakistan, India, Japan and the Far East and Australia P & O, British & India Steam Navigation Company, Maersk Line, Everett Johnson Line, "K" Line of Japan, etc.). Though predominantly cargo operators, most of the foregoing lines have some passenger accommodation available; the British India Line operates a mail service between Bombay, Karachi, Bahrain and other Gulf Ports, carrying passengers in Saloon and Deck classes; the Mogul line operates mail and passenger services between Bombay and the Gulf, and the Pan Islamic Steamship Co. between Karachi and the Gulf ports.

The deep water harbour of Mina Sulman was opened in April 1962; it has six berths capable of taking vessels of draughts up to 9 metres. In the vicinity are two slipways able to take vessels of up to 1,016 tonnes and 73 metres in length, with services available for ship repairs afloat. A trawler basin is the centre of a flourishing shrimping industry, the packaged produce being exported primarily to Europe, North America and Japan.

In November 1972 OAPEC approved Bahrain as the site for a £40 million dry dock large enough to accept super-tankers of up to 375,000 d.w.t. Engineering consultants for the scheme were appointed in July 1973.

CIVIL AVIATION

Bahrain Airport has a first-class runway, capable of taking the largest aircraft in use. A new jumbo jet airport terminal was opened in December 1971 and is due to be expanded in 1974.

Gulf Air: P.O.B. 138, Bahrain Island; f. 1950; jointly owned by the governments of Bahrain, Qatar, Abu Dhabi and Oman, and by British Airways; services from Bahrain to Kuwait, Abu Dhabi, Bandar Abbas, Dhahran, Doha, Dubai, Muscat, Sharjah, Shiraz, Karachi, Bombay and Beirut; the fleet consists of two BAC 1-11, three F27, three Skyvans, two Islanders, two Beechcraft B80 and one chartered VC 10 on Gulf-London services.

Bahrain is served by the following foreign airlines: Air India, British Airways, British Caledonian, Iran Air, Iraqi Airways, Kuwait Airways, MEA, Singapore International Airlines, PIA (Pakistan), Qantas, Saudia, TMA.

BANGLADESH

INTRODUCTORY SURVEY

Location, Climate, Language, Religion, Flag, Capital

The People's Republic of Bangladesh covers 55,126 square miles and is almost surrounded by Indian territory except for a short south-eastern frontier with Burma and a southern deltaic coast fronting the Bay of Bengal. The climate is tropical monsoon with an average temperature from October to March of 67°F (19°C) and 84°F (29°C) from May to September. Three-quarters of the annual average rainfall (74 inches) occurs between June and September. About 85 per cent of the population speak Bengali, the State language, the remainder Bihari and some Hindi. The principal religion is Islam but there is a small minority of Hindus. The national flag is green, with a red disc in the centre. The capital is Dacca.

Recent History

The origin of the modern state of Bangladesh can be traced back to the original partition of the old Indian Empire in 1947 when Pakistan was established in two parts, East Pakistan and West Pakistan, separated by a thousand miles of Indian territory. The first awakening of national consciousness grew out of the successful campaign from 1951–53 to establish Bengali as the second official language of Pakistan in addition to Urdu. Political instability in successive Central Governments from 1954 to late 1958 finally culminated in the military rule in October 1958 of General Ayub Khan which was to last for ten years. Another major cause of discontent was the economic disparity between both provinces. The amount of capital resources made available under successive Pakistan Development Plans was so inadequate that the already low standard of living of the mass of the population of East Pakistan was barely maintained. The Indo-Pakistan war of 1965 severely affected the economy, giving rise to further discontent in the East. In December 1968 popular discontent mounted with the arrest of Sheikh Mujibur Rahman, the newly elected leader of the Awami League.

Following elections held in Pakistan in December 1970, the Awami League emerged as what would have been the largest single party in a proposed National Assembly. Sheikh Mujib, now free, intensified demands for autonomy in the east. Talks with the new President, Gen. Yahya Khan, broke down and the Army took repressive measures in East Pakistan. The People's Republic of Bangladesh was proclaimed on March 26th, 1971, and civil war followed immediately. Sheikh Mujib was arrested and taken to West Pakistan. Indian assistance to the Bengali guerrilla fighters became more apparent throughout November and Indo-Pakistan border clashes intensified.

On December 3rd, 1971, the Pakistani Air Force attacked Indian airfields on the western sector, precipitating a general war. India formally recognized Bangladesh on December 6th. Pakistan set up a civilian government in Dacca under the acting premiership of Nurul Amin, a Bengali. On December 17th, General A. A. K. Niazi, Commander of the Pakistani Army in Bangladesh, surrendered to the Indians. Sheikh Mujib was freed by Pakistan's new President, Zulfikar Ali Bhutto, on January 8th, 1972. On his arrival in Dacca Mujib resigned the Presidency, to which he had been elected while in prison, and became Prime Minister. Elections held in March 1973 convincingly confirmed him in office.

The new nation quickly achieved international recognition, but was faced with the problems of freeing prisoners of war held in Pakistan, of housing the Bihari community which wished to emigrate to Pakistan, and of managing an economy deeply affected by the war, the separation from Pakistan and natural disaster, and burdened by a high rate of population growth.

Following Indo-Pakistan negotiations an agreement was signed in New Delhi on August 28th, 1973, providing for the repatriation of Pakistanis in India, of Bengalis in Pakistan and of some (but not all) non-Bengalis in Bangladesh. This three-way exchange began in September and was completed successfully in May 1974, though Pakistan still refuses to accept most of the Biharis.

Pakistan finally recognized Bangladesh on February 22nd, 1974, after pressure to do so had been brought to bear by nations attending the Islamic summit in Lahore that same month.

Government

Under the 1972 Constitution, executive authority is vested in the President while Parliament (*Jatiya Sangsad*) comprises an unicameral legislature (the Constituent Assembly) of 315 seats, fifteen of which are reserved for women. Members of Parliament are elected for a five-year term on the basis of universal suffrage exercised by those aged 18 and over. The Constituent Assembly, which first met on April 10th, 1972, comprises members of the national and provincial assemblies elected in 1970 (prior to independence) from the former province of East Pakistan. The vast majority of these representatives belong to the Awami League, led by the Prime Minister, Sheikh Mujibur Rahman.

Defence

Indian armed forces were withdrawn from Bangladesh in March 1972. The maintenance of law and order and internal security is entrusted to the regular armed forces of Bangladesh, together with a people's police force and national militia.

Economic Affairs

The economy is predominantly agricultural. The land is fertile but densely populated and average income per capita is extremely low by international standards. The disruptions arising from the war of secession and from the frequent cyclones and floods have depressed production in recent years. In 1972–73 the gross domestic product was about 13 per cent lower in real terms than in 1969–70, the last "normal" year before the war. Production of rice, which is by far the most important subsistence crop, has still not regained the level of 1969–70. This would have meant a shortage of the staple diet in any circumstances; with population growing at about 3 per cent a year the need to import rice and wheat to make up the deficiency has taxed the new country's foreign exchange resources.

Jute and tea are the main cash crops, the former being a vital sector of the economy: sales of raw jute and jute manufactures constitute 85 per cent of export earnings. Production of jute in 1972–73 was 28 per cent below the level of 1969–70, so that Bangladesh is not in a position to take advantage of the rises in price of synthetic fibres that compete with jute. Similar falls in production have taken place in nearly all the main industries, owing to damage to plant during the war, the departure of the largely non-Bengali financier and managerial class and the disappearance of many skilled Bengali workers. Rising domestic prices have stemmed from the low levels of production. Most organized industry has been nationalized and state corporations have been set up for the major commodities. Bangladesh has few mineral resources, although some natural gas has been produced, and there are the beginnings of steel and oil industries.

The separation from Pakistan meant the interruption of customary trade patterns. The tea crop was largely exported to West Pakistan before the war and attempts have been made to find new markets. However, following the recognition of Bangladesh by Pakistan in 1974, there is the possibility that the former links will be revived. Exports as a whole in 1972–73 were 30 per cent below the figure for 1969–70.

Owing to severe dislocation of the economy caused by the war of independence it seems likely that for the foreseeable future Bangladesh will remain heavily dependent on foreign aid. Total aid from October 1971 to March 1973 is estimated at U.S. $1,318 million, one-third of which was spent on food relief. Aid estimates for 1973–74 total U.S. $800 million.

The first Five-Year Plan, announced in November 1973, aimed at creating new jobs and achieving self-sufficiency in food. Of the total outlay of 44,500 million taka (about U.S. $5,560 million), nearly 40 per cent is expected to be raised in foreign loans. The plan targets, which aim at an annual rate of growth in the gross domestic product of 5.5 per cent and an annual increase of 2.5 per cent in income per capita, have been criticized by some as unrealistic. But even the planners themselves have said that if plan targets are achieved, the per capita consumption of basic items "will still represent dismal poverty" in 1977–78. This will, they say, "represent a qualitatively different situation and provide a minimum basis for further social and economic development."

Transport and Communications

Water transport is of major significance in Bangladesh, and there are about 5,000 miles of navigable waterways. It has been severely disrupted and of some 800 vessels in use prior to the war, only 500 are still serviceable. Chittagong, the principal port, has been expanded in recent years and now handles 4.3 million tons a year. There are about 1,750 miles of railway. A rapid expansion in road building has increased the length of surface roads to some 15,000 miles. There are approximately 100,000 miles of unsurfaced roads. In March 1972 *Bangladesh Biman*, the national airline, began internal services and a weekly charter service to London.

Social Welfare

The government's main task since independence has been to prevent epidemics and widespread malnutrition and to treat and rehabilitate war victims. The number of hospital beds has been increased from 8,000, prior to independence, to 13,000. A five-year health programme costing 1,660 million taka is to begin in July 1973 with priority being given to health care and population control.

Education

Since independence the Government has allocated 100 million taka (U.S. $12.5 million) for education. In March 1973 there were six universities, 296 colleges and 36,000 schools but a number were also destroyed during the war. About 15 per cent of the population is literate.

Tourism

Until further notice visas will be required by all nationals of countries which have recognized Bangladesh, but Commonwealth citizens are exempt.

Public Holidays

1974: August 26th (Autumn Bank Holiday), September 12th (Shab-i-Barat), October 11th (Jamat-ul-Wida), October 14th (Shab-i-Qadr), October 17th–18th (Id-ul-Fitr), October 24th–25th (Durga Puja), December 16th (Victory Day), December 25th (Christmas), December 26th (Id-ul-Adha).

1975: January 1st (New Year's Day), January 23rd (Ashoura), February 21st (National Mourning Day), March 26th (Independence Day and Muhammad's Birthday), April 16th (Bengali New Year Day), April 25th (Buddha Purnima), May 1st (May Day).

Weights and Measures

The imperial system of measures is in force pending the introduction of a metric system.

    1 maund = 82.27lb.

    1 seer = 2.057lb.

    1 tola = 180 grains.

Currency and Exchange Rates

    100 paisa = 1 taka.

    Exchange rates (April 1974):

        £1 sterling = 18.97 taka;

        U.S. $1 = 8.03 taka.

STATISTICAL SURVEY

AREA AND POPULATION

AREA	POPULATION					
	Official Estimates†		United Nations Estimates (mid-year)‡			
	Feb. 1st, 1961 (Census)	July 1st, 1970	1969	1970	1971	1972
55,126 sq. miles*	50,853,721	60,675,000	72,135,000	74,749,000	77,486,000	80,339,000

* 142,776 sq. km.

† Excluding adjustment for underenumeration at the 1961 census. According to the Pakistan Planning Commission (PPC), the census result understated the total population (in both wings of pre-1971 Pakistan) by about 8.3 per cent. The PPC estimated the population of East Pakistan (now Bangladesh) to be 64 million at January 1st, 1968.

‡ These projections assume a stable growth of population and take no account of the effect of natural disasters or the war of secession. An official estimate puts the mid-1973 population at 71,610,000

DIVISIONS*
(1961 Census)

Chittagong	.	.	13,629,650
Dacca	.	.	15,293,596
Khulna	.	.	10,066,900
Rajshahi	.	.	11,850,089
TOTAL	.	.	50,840,235

* Excluding aliens, who numbered 13,486 at the time of the census.

POPULATION OF CHIEF TOWNS

	1961 Census	Estimate*
Dacca (capital) . . .	556,712	915,000†
Chittagong . .	364,205	458,000
Khulna . .	127,970	403,000
Narayanganj . .	162,054	389,000

* Feb. 1st, 1971.

† 1972 estimate: 1,500,000, including Narayanganj.

ECONOMICALLY ACTIVE POPULATION
(1971 estimates)

TOTAL	AGRICULTURE	OTHERS
24,840,000	23,180,000	1,660,000

AGRICULTURE
PRINCIPAL CROPS
(Twelve months ending June 30th)

	Area Harvested ('000 acres)			Production ('000 long tons)		
	1968/69	1969/70	1970/71	1968/69	1969/70	1970/71
Wheat	289.7	296.2	311.3	92.2	103.3	109.9
Barley	70.2	72.9	90.2	18.0	19.7	25.8
Rice (cleaned) . . .	24,073.5	25,486.1	24,494.7	11,164.8	11,815.9	10,967.8
Sugar Cane	406.8	398.5	404.3	7,297.0	7,417.8	7,597.6
Potatoes	207.7	211.1	213.9	786.5	850.8	849.3
Sweet Potatoes . .	172.9	179.7	179.7	793.2	838.6	818.8
Onions	82.0	81.5	81.9	182.4	179.1	176.0
Chick-peas (Gram) . .	168.8	172.8	180.6	54.3	56.6	60.0
Bananas	107.0	106.5	96.9	755.3	733.0	584.4
Pineapples	25.6	26.7	24.1	95.3	103.8	92.4
Mangoes	99.0	102.9	102.7	444.2	393.3	414.6
Rapeseed and Mustard . .	552.0	535.9	531.3	128.3	126.1	136.3
Tea*	104.9	107.0	110.0	28.1	29.8	30.8
Tobacco	112.6	113.0	108.8	40.0	40.6	38.6
Jute	2,170.0	2,464.7	2,200.1	1,050.0	1,319.0	1,251.0

* Area figures refer to the total planted area.

Paddy Rice ('000 metric tons) 16,714 in 1970/71, 14,883 in 1971/72; Groundnuts (in shell) 46,000 metric tons in 1970.

1971/72 ('000 metric tons): Barley 27, Rice (cleaned) 9,800 (from 23 million acres), Tea 12.4 (from 110,000 acres), Jute 761 (from 1,700,000 acres).

1972/73 ('000 metric tons): Paddy Rice 14,250 (FAO estimate), Tea 23.5, Jute 1,192.

Livestock: 26,000,000 cattle (FAO estimate) in 1971/72.

Cows' Milk (estimated production, '000 metric tons): 3,250 in 1968, 3,400 in 1969, 3,530 in 1970.

FISHING

	Weight of Catch (metric tons)			Value of Landings ('000 Pakistani rupees)		
	1968	1969	1970	1968	1969	1970
Inland Waters . . .	221,000	229,500	211,900	465,923	505,283	671,920
Trout (culture) . .	1,800	5,300	4,000	4,923	15,264	11,200
Other Freshwater Fish .	214,200	219,200	203,200	428,400	457,419	629,920
Prawns and Shrimps . .	5,000	5,000	4,700*	32,600	32,600	30,800
Indian Ocean . . .	45,400	47,800	35,300	89,951	77,991	69,430
Redfishes, etc. . .	26,000	26,500	19,700	26,512	28,240	27,500
Other Marine Fish . .	11,500	16,000	11,700	11,931	15,831	14,630
Prawns and Shrimps . .	7,900	5,300	3,900	51,508	33,920	27,300
Total . . .	266,400	277,300	247,200	555,874	583,274	741,350

* FAO estimate.

Source: FAO, Yearbook of Fishery Statistics.

MINING
(metric tons)

	1968	1969	1970
Limestone Flux, etc. . .	129,000	61,000	143,000
Clay	3,000	3,000	n.a.
Salt*	442,000	432,000	n.a.

* Twelve months ending June 30th of year stated.

INDUSTRY

SELECTED PRODUCTS

(Twelve months ending June 30th)

	Unit	1968/69	1969/70	1970/71
Vegetable Oils	metric tons	6,000	6,000	n.a.
Refined Sugar	,, ,,	58,000	89,000	n.a.
Cigarettes.	million	16,851	17,787	15,554
Cotton Yarn	metric tons	43,403	47,927	n.a.
Woven Cotton Fabrics . . .	'ooo yards	60,852	59,149	52,725
Jute Fabrics	'ooo sq. metres	1,109,300	1,240,010	n.a.
Synthetic Fabrics	,, ,, ,,	5,676	4,154	n.a.
Newsprint	long tons	39,002	35,740	29,625
Other Paper and Paperboard . .	,, ,,	43,647	42,214	29,569*
Sulphuric Acid	metric tons	6,000	7,000	4,000
Caustic Soda	,, ,,	4,000	3,000	3,000
Nitrogenous Fertilizers . . .	,, ,,	39,000	45,000†	25,000†
Cement	long tons	63,000	53,000	63,000
Crude Steel	,, ,,	209,588	173,701	n.a.
Bicycles	number	26,000	18,000	n.a.

Other Products (1967/68 figures): 227,000 tyres and inner tubes for bicycles and motor cycles; 1,201 million kWh. of electric energy.

* For 9 months only.   † FAO estimate.

FINANCE

100 paisa = 1 taka.

Coins: 1, 2, 5, 10, 25 and 50 paisa.

Notes: 1, 5, 10 and 100 taka.

Exchange rates (April 1974): £1 sterling = 18.97 taka; U.S. $1 = 8.03 taka.

100 taka = £5.27 = $12.45.

Note: Since December 1971 the taka has been at par with the Indian rupee, with an official exchange rate against sterling maintained at a mid-point of £1 = 18.9677 taka. Until the "floating" of the pound in June 1972 this was equivalent to a rate of U.S. $1 = 7.279 taka.

BUDGET ESTIMATES

(million taka, July 1st to June 30th)

Revenue	1972/73	1973/74	Expenditure	1972/73	1973/74
Current Budget:			*Current Budget:*		
Income Tax, Corporation and			Civil Administration . .	879.1	1,041.9
Agricultural Income Tax .	83.6	163.8	Defence	250.0	470.0
Sales Tax	300.0	462.9	Education	450.1	584.4
Customs Receipts . . .	1,000.0	1,400.2	Health	120.7	141.7
Excise Duties . . .	620.5	1,165.2	Revenue Collecting Depart-		
Nationalized Sectors . .	102.1	280.0	ments	134.3	148.0
Interest	7.4	232.5	Other Items . . .	417.9	567.0
Other Receipts . . .	311.4	408.5			
Sub-Total . . .	2,425.0	4,113.1	Sub-Total . . .	2,252.1	2,953.0
Capital Budget:			*Capital Budget:*		
Loans and Grants . .	3,750.9	3,600.0	Development . . .	3,028.8	4,499.7
Other Receipts . .	689.7	n.a.	Reconstruction . . .	992.3	} 753.8
			Rehabilitation . . .	605.5	
			Other Items . . .	162.1	n.a.
Sub-Total . . .	4,440.6	n.a.	Sub-Total . . .	4,789.7	5,253.5*
Total Revenue .	6,865.6	n.a.	Total Expenditure .	7,041.8	8,206.5*

* Excluding non-development capital expenses.

DEVELOPMENT BUDGET
(million taka)

Expenditure	1972/73	1973/74
Agriculture	877.5	869.5
Rural Institutions	293.2	306.7
Water and Flood Control	310.8	332.0
Industries	275.3	754.1
Power, Natural Resources and Scientific Research	246.1	492.9
Transport and Communications	574.0	789.9
Physical Planning and Housing	143.7	235.4
Education and Training	173.2	349.2
Health	125.0	323.7
Social Welfare, Manpower and Employment	10.0	46.3
Total	3,028.8	4,499.7

COST OF LIVING
Consumer Price Index
(Average of monthly figures for government employees in Dacca. Base: 1963 = 100)

	1962	1964	1965	1966	1967	1968	1969	1970	1971†	1972	1973‡
Food	102.0	106.1	117.1	126.5	133.8	134.1	140.4	143.6	158.2	212.0	294.3
Fuel and Lighting	92.0	96.7	96.0	102.1	106.7	123.0	132.6	136.5	147.8	n.a.	n.a.
Clothing	92.6	102.1	103.7	111.0	117.7	120.4	130.7	133.1	137.9		
Rent*	95.2	102.5	107.3	109.4	111.7	114.0	119.0	120.5	124.3		
All Items	98.0	104.0	111.7	121.4	127.6	130.6	137.2	142.0	159.6	205.0	289.7

* Including certain household equipment.   † Average of 11 months.   ‡ For the month of June.

Gross Domestic Product (estimate): 33,500 million taka in the 12 months ending June 30th, 1972.

EXTERNAL TRADE
(million Pakistani rupees, July 1st to June 30th)
EXPORTS TO PAKISTAN

	1968/69	1969/70	1970/71
Tea	248.7	224.5	274.0
Jute Products	158.3	159.2	121.2
Paper and Paperboards	104.3	79.2	73.9
Total (incl. others)	868.5	923.4	803.8

EXPORTS TO OTHER COUNTRIES

	1968/69	1969/70	1970/71
Raw Jute	730.7	762.4	501.1
Jute Products	655.9	768.3	627.3
Leather	75.2	60.0	43.0
Total (incl. others)	1,542.7	1,670.1	1,251.1

1972/73 (estimates, million taka): Total Imports 6,900; Total Exports 3,000.

JUTE EXPORTS
('ooo long tons)

	1968/69	1969/70	1970/71	1971/72
Raw Jute . . .	589	636	396	180
Jute Products . . .	454	495	488	280

TRANSPORT
RAILWAYS

	1967	1968	1969
Passenger-kilometres (million) . .	3,343	3,549	3,319
Freight: net ton-km. (million) . .	1,316	1,185	1,570

ROAD MOTOR VEHICLES
(number in use)

	1967	1968	1969
Passenger Cars . . .	16,600	17,300	22,400
Commercial Vehicles . . .	10,800	13,400	14,400

INTERNATIONAL SEA-BORNE SHIPPING
(Twelve months ending June 30th)

	1968/69	1969/70
Vessels ('ooo net reg. tons):		
Entered	3,687.0	4,134.0
Cleared	4,475.0	3,154.0
Goods Loaded ('ooo long tons) .	1,087.7	1,126.1
Chalna	844.7	898.1
Chittagong	243.0	228.0
Goods Unloaded ('ooo long tons) .	3,901.3	3,538.0
Chalna	852.0	693.4
Chittagong	3,049.3	2,844.6

1970/71 ('ooo metric tons): Goods Loaded 825; Goods Unloaded 3,501.

EDUCATION
(1972 estimate)

	Number	Students
Primary Schools . .	} 36,000†	5,500,000*
High Schools . .		1,030,000
Technical Colleges and Institutes . .	296†	176,000
Universities . .	6	16,466

* 1968.   † March 1973.

THE CONSTITUTION

(Promulgated November 4th, 1972)

SUMMARY

Fundamental Principles of State Policy

The Constitution is based on the fundamental principles of the State, namely nationalism, socialism, democracy and secularism. It aims to establish a society free from exploitation in which the rule of law, fundamental human rights and freedoms, justice and equality are to be secured for all citizens. A socialist economic system is to be established to ensure the attainment of a just and egalitarian society through state and co-operative ownership though private property is permitted within such limits as are prescribed by law. A universal, free and compulsory system of education shall be established.

Fundamental Rights

All citizens are equal before the law and have a right to its protection. Arbitrary arrest or detention, discrimination based on race, age, sex, birth, caste or religion and forced labour are prohibited. Subject to law, public order or morality freedom of movement, of assembly and of association are recognized while freedom of conscience, of speech, of the Press and of religious worship are guaranteed.

The President

The President is the constitutional Head of State and is elected for a term of five years. He is eligible for re-election for a second term only. The supreme control of the armed forces is vested in the President. He appoints the Prime Minister and other Ministers as well as the Chief Justice and other judges.

The Executive

Executive authority is exercised by a Cabinet collectively responsible to Parliament and headed by the Prime Minister.

The Legislature

Parliament (*Jatiya Sangsad*) consists of a unicameral legislature (the Constituent Assembly), and comprises 315 seats of which 15 are reserved for women. Members of Parliament are directly elected on the basis of universal adult franchise from single territorial constituencies. Persons aged 18 and over are entitled to vote. The parliamentary term lasts for five years unless the Government resigns or a vote of no confidence is passed in which case general elections may be held (*see* under Elections). War can only be declared with the assent of Parliament. In the case of actual or imminent invasion, the President may take whatever action he may consider appropriate.

The Judiciary

The Judiciary comprises a Supreme Court with High Court and Appelate Divisions. The Supreme Court consists of a Chief Justice and such other judges as may be appointed. The High Court division has unlimited original jurisdiction to hear and determine any civil or criminal proceedings under any law and such appelate and other jurisdiction and powers as are conferred on it by the Constitution. The Appelate division has jurisdiction to determine appeals from judgments, decrees, orders or sentences of the High Court division. Subordinate courts may, in addition to the Supreme Court, be established.

Elections

An Election Commission supervises elections for the Presidency and for Parliament, delimits constituencies and prepares electoral rolls. It consists of a Chief Election Commissioner and other Commissioners as may be appointed by the President. The Election Commission is independent in the exercise of its functions and is subject to the Constitution, though Parliament may make provision as to elections where necessary.

Amendment

Any provision in the Constitution may be amended or repealed by Act of Parliament provided that it has been passed by a two-thirds majority of the votes cast of those Members of Parliament present and sitting.

THE GOVERNMENT

HEAD OF THE STATE

President: MOHAMMADULLAH (Speaker of the Constituent Assembly).

THE CABINET

(*July* 1974)

Prime Minister, Minister of Defence, Minister of Cabinet Affairs, Minister of Planning, Minister of Relief and Rehabilitation, Minister of Information and Broadcasting: Sheikh MUJIBUR RAHMAN.

Minister for Industries: SYED NAZRUL ISLAM.

Minister of Finance, Minister of Jute Affairs: TAJUDDIN AHMED.

Minister of Communications: MOHAMMAD MANSOOR ALI.

Minister of Flood Control, Power and Water Resources: KHANDAKAR MOSHTAQUE AHMED.

Minister for Trade and Commerce: A. H. M. KAMARUZ-ZAMAN.

Minister of Agriculture: MOHAMMAD ABDUS SAMAD.

Minister of Posts, Telegraphs and Communications:(vacant).

Minister of Education, Cultural Affairs and Sports: Prof. MOHAMMAD YOUSUF ALI.

Minister of Labour and Social Welfare: ZAHUR AHMED CHOUDHURY.

Minister of Food and Civil Supplies: Phani Majumdar.

Minister of Foreign Affairs: Dr. Kamal Hossain.

Minister of Home Affairs: Abdul Malek Ukil.

Minister for Local Government, Rural Development and Co-operatives: (vacant).

Minister for Housing, Works and Urban Development: Mohammad Sohrab Hussain.

Minister for Health and Family Planning: Abdul Mannan.

Minister for Land Administration, Land Reforms, Forests, Fisheries and Livestock: Abdur Rab Serniabat.

Minister for Shipping, Inland Water Transport and Airways: Gen. (vacant).

Minister for Atomic Energy, Natural Resources, Scientific and Technological Research: (vacant).

Minister of Law and Parliamentary Affairs: Manoranjan Dhar.

Minister of Jute and Jute Industries: (vacant).

Minister of Forestry, Fisheries and Livestock: (vacant).

DIPLOMATIC REPRESENTATION

HIGH COMMISSIONS AND EMBASSIES ACCREDITED TO BANGLADESH

(Dacca, unless otherwise stated)

(E) Embassy; (HC) High Commission.

Australia: Hotel Purbani, 9th Floor (HC); *High Commissioner:* J. L. Allen, o.b.e.

Austria: New Delhi, India (E).

Bulgaria: House 12, Road 127, Gulshan Model Town (E); *Chargé d'Affaires:* Kolyu Asenov.

Burma: 135-C, Dhanmondi, Residential Area, Road 5 (E); *Chargé d'Affaires:* Mrs. Thet.

Canada: 37 Indira Rd. (HC); *High Commissioner:* Robert W. Maclaren.

Czechoslovakia: 69/70 Motijheel Commercial Area (E); *Ambassador:* Adolf Panz.

Denmark: New Delhi, India (E).

France: 354 Dhanmondi, Road 28 (E); *Ambassador:* Pierre Millet.

German Democratic Republic: 32/34 Road 74, Gulshan Model Town (E); *Ambassador:* Lothar Wenzel.

Germany, Federal Republic: House Kalpana, 7 Green Rd., Dhanmondi Residential Area (E); *Ambassador:* Dr. Edwin Jungfleisch.

Hungary: Road 95, CEN-DI-4, Gulshan (E); *Chargé d'Affaires:* L. Szikra.

India: Road 2, Dhanmondi (HC); *High Commissioner:* Subimal Dutt.

Indonesia: 11 (A) C.W.S., Gulshan Model Town (E); *Chargé d'Affaires:* Soepari Tjokrohartono.

Japan: 1 Santinagar (E); *Ambassador:* Tokashi Oyamada.

Nepal: 248 Dhanmondi Residential Area, Road 21 (E); *Ambassador:* K. B. Malla.

Netherlands: Bangkok, Thailand (E).

New Zealand: New Delhi, India (HC).

Norway: New Delhi, India (E).

Poland: House 309, Road 26, Dhanmondi Residential Area (E); *Ambassador:* Zbigniew Byszewski.

Romania: 126 Gulshan Ave., Gulshan Model Town (E); *Chargé d'Affaires:* Vicentiu Ilie.

Singapore: New Delhi, India (HC).

Spain: New Delhi, India (E).

Sweden: New Delhi, India (E).

Switzerland: Kuala Lumpur, Malaysia (E).

U.S.S.R.: NE(J)9, Road 79, Gulshan (E); *Ambassador:* Andrei Fomin.

United Kingdom: DIT Building Annexe, Dilkusha (HC); *High Commissioner:* A. A. Golds.

U.S.A.: Adamjee Court, Motijheel (E); *Chargé d'Affaires:* Daniel O. Newberry.

Yugoslavia: Gulshan, Road 45 (E); *Chargé d'Affaires:* Mirco Zec.

Bangladesh also has diplomatic relations with Cuba, Italy and Malaysia and is recognized by Pakistan and the following:
Afghanistan, Algeria, Barbados, Belgium, Bhutan, Bolivia, Botswana, Brazil, Cameroon, Central African Republic, Chile, Colombia, Costa Rica, Cyprus, Dominican Republic, Ecuador, Egypt, El Salvador, Ethiopia, Fiji, Finland, Gabon, Gambia, Ghana, Greece, Guatemala, Guyana, Haiti, Honduras, Iceland, Iran, Iraq, Ireland, Israel, Jamaica, Japan, Jordan, Khmer Republic, Republic of Korea, Kuwait, Laos, Lebanon, Lesotho, Liberia, Luxembourg, Madagascar, Malawi, Maldives, Malta, Mauritania, Mauritius, Mexico, Mongolia, Morocco, Nicaragua, Niger, Panama, Paraguay, Peru, Philippines, Senegal, Sierra Leone, Sudan, Swaziland, Syria, Tanzania, Thailand, Tonga, Tunisia, Turkey, Uganda, United Arab Emirates, Upper Volta, Uruguay, Vatican, Venezuela, Democratic Republic of Viet-Nam, the Provisional Revolutionary Government of the Republic of South Viet-Nam, Western Samoa, Yemen Arab Republic, People's Democratic Republic of Yemen, Zaire and Zambia.

PARLIAMENT

Under the new Constitution Parliament comprises a unicameral legislature—the Constituent Assembly—of 315 seats. General elections were held on March 7th, 1973.

CONSTITUENT ASSEMBLY

(*Jatiya Sangsad*)

Speaker: Mohammadullah.

(General Election, March 1973)

Party	Seats	Votes Cast	% of Votes Cast
Awami League .	293	13,534,830	73
Independents .	5		
NAP(M) . .	1	4,930,170	27
NAP(B) . .	1		
	300*	18,465,000	100

* Fifteen seats are reserved for women, all Awami League Candidates who were elected unopposed in April 1973, making a total of 315.

POLITICAL PARTIES

Awami League: Dacca; f. 1967; Government Party which successfully led a campaign of regional autonomy and eventual independence; Pres. A. H. M. Kamaruzzaman.

National Awami Party (B): Dacca; f. 1956; pro-China; Pres.: Maulana Bhashani.

National Awami Party (M): Dacca; pro-Soviet; Pres. Prof. Muzaffar Ahmed.

DEFENCE

Armed Forces (1973): Total strength 17,900; army 17,000; navy 500; air force 400; military service is voluntary.

Equipment: The army has one artillery brigade. The air force has 13 combat aircraft, eight Russian and five American.

Defence Expenditure: The Defence Budget for 1973/74 is 470 million taka.

JUDICIAL SYSTEM

Chief Justice of Bangladesh: Justice A. M. Sayem.

Note: See also under the Constitution (*above*).

RELIGION

CENSUS 1961

Muslims	40,890,481
Caste Hindus	4,386,623
Scheduled Castes . . .	4,993,046
Buddhists	373,867
Christians	148,903
Tribal and others . . .	617,400

Complete freedom of religious worship is guaranteed under the Constitution (q.v.).

CHURCH OF BANGLADESH

Dacca: The Bishop of Dacca; Rt. Rev. J. D. Blair.

Formerly a diocese of the Church of Pakistan; unites Lutheran and Presbyterian denominations.

ROMAN CATHOLIC CHURCH

Archbishop of Dacca: Most Rev. Theotonius Amal Ganguly, c.s.c., Archbishop's House, Dacca 2.

THE PRESS

PRINCIPAL DAILIES

DACCA

Azad: 27A Dhakeswari Rd.; Bengali; f. 1936; Editor M. Anisuzzaman.

Banglar Bani: 81 Motijheel Commercial Area, Bengali; Editor Sheikh Fazlul Haq Mani.

Daily Ittefaq: 1 Ram Krishna Mission Rd.; f. 1953; Editor Anwar Hossain; circ. 73,325.

Dainik Bangla: Abdul Hai I, IT Ave.; Bengali; Editor Abdul Tayab Khan.

Dainik Samaj: Hathkhola; Bengali; Editor Asadul Haq.

Dainik Swadesh: 9 Gopikishan Lane; Bengali; Editor Mohd Korban Ali.

Ganakantha: 24/c Tipu Sultan Rd.; f. 1972; Bengali; Editor Al-Mahmud; circ. 25,000.

Ittefaq: 1 Ramkrishna Mission Rd.; f. 1953; Bengali.

Nabajat: 53-59 Dinnanath Sen Rd.; Bengali; Editor Saifunnesa.

Purbadesh: 33 Toynbee Circular Rd.; Bengali; Editor Ehtesham Chowdhury.

Sangbad: 263 Bangshal Rd.; Bengali; Editor Ahmadul Kabir.

OTHER TOWNS

Azadi: Anderkilla, Chittagong; f. 1960; Bengali; Editor Mohammed Khaled; circ. 14,000.

Dainik Bangladesh: Bogra Lithographic Works, Bogra; Bengali; Editor Amanullah Khan.

Dainik Michil: 20 Harish Dutta Lane, Nandankanan, Chittagong; f. 1972; Bengali; Editor M. A. Quddus; circ. 15,000.

Desh Bangla: 6 Anderkella, Chittagong; Bengali; Editor Abu Hena.

ENGLISH LANGUAGE

Bangladesh Observer: 33 Toynbee Circular Rd., Dacca; Editor Obaidul Haq.

Eastern Examiner: Chandanpura, Chittagong; Editor Khalilur Rahman.

Evening Post: 33 Topkhana Rd., Dacca; Editor Habibul Bashar.

Morning News: 1 D.I.T. Rd., Dacca; Editor A. B. M. Musa.

The People: Nippon Premises, Shahbag Ave., Dacca; Editor Abidur Rahman; circ. 25,000.

People's View: 129 Panchlaish Residential Area, Chittagong; Editor Nurul Islam.

SELECTED WEEKLIES

DACCA

Arafat: 86 Qazi Alauddin Rd.; Bengali; Editor M. A. Bari.

Begum: 66 Lyall St.; Bengali; Editor Nasiruddin Ahmed.

Bajra Kantha: 109 Hrishikesh Das Rd.; Bengali; Editor Altaf Hossain Mustafa.

Banglar Mukh: 10 Hatkhola Rd.; Bengali; Editor Siddiqur Rahman Ashrafi.

Drishtipat: 68/2 Purana Paltan; Bengali; Editor Mohd Abu Jafar Khan.

Ekata: 68/2 Purana Pultan; Bengali; Editor Sheikh Bazlur Rahman.

Express: 41 Naya Paltan; English; Editor Ghazi Shahabuddin Ahmed.

Freedom: 42/A Hatkhola Rd.; English; Editor I. Hossain.

Ganshakti: 43/1 Joginagar Lane; Bengali; Editor Mohammad Toha.

Holiday: Polwel Printing Press, Naya Paltan; English; Editor C. T. Ahmed.

Jagrata Bangla: 25 Ahsan Manzil; Bengali; Editor M. A. Majid.

Joyaddhani: 10 Purana Paltan; Bengali; Editor A. K. M. Jahangir.

Kalantar: 87 Khanjahan Ali Rd.; Bengali; Editor Noor Mohammad.

Pratibeshi: 61/1 Subas Bose Ave.; Bengali; Editor Fr. Paul Gomes; circ. 2,500.

Sonar Bangla: 109 Hrishikesh Das Rd.; Bengali; Editor Mohd Belayet Hossain.

Spokesman: 9 Hatkhola Rd.; English; Editor Faizur Rahman.

OTHER TOWNS

Banglar Darpan: (formerly *Shaptahik Bangladesh*): 34 Ramesh Sen Rd., Mymensingh; f. 1972; Bengali; Editor Mohd. Habibur Rahman Sheikh; circ. 10,000.

Kalantar: 87 Khanjahan Ali Rd., Khulna; f. 1970; Editor Noor Mohammad; circ. 7,000.

The Weekly Spulinga: Kazipara Rd., P.O.B. 18, Jessore; f. 1971; Editor Mian Abdus Sattar; circ. 8,000.

SELECTED PERIODICALS
(Dacca unless otherwise stated)

Ahmadi: 4 Bakshibazar, Dacca; Bengali; fortnightly; Editor Mohd Fazlul Karim Mollah.

Babosha Banijya (*Trade and Commerce*): Techno Trade Ltd., 59 Dilkhusha Commercial Area, P.O.B. 674; f. 1972; fortnightly; Editor Q. S. Hafiz, Ahmed Farooque; circ. 5,000.

Commercial Bulletin: Prabhati Printing Works, 148 Mitford, Dacca; English; monthly; Editor Mohd Nurul Huq.

Dacca Basi: 56/4 Bhajahari Shaha St., Dacca; f. 1972; Bengali; monthly; Editor Mohd Hanif; circ. 4,000.

Ganashiskha (*Education for the People*): Bengali; fortnightly; Editor Mohd. Zainul Abedeen Chowdhury.

Nabajug: Hitashi Press, Chandpur District, Comilla; Bengali; monthly; Editor Mahendra Adhikari.

Saogat: 66 Loyall St., Dacca; Bengali; monthly; Editor Nasiruddin Ahmed.

NEWS AGENCIES

Bangladesh Press International (B.P.I.): Dacca.

Bangladesh Sangbad Sangasta (*Bangladesh News Agency*): Dacca.

Eastern News Agency (E.N.A.): Dacca.

United Press of Bangladesh: Dacca; daily press service of news bulletins and features; Editor M. A. Ghani.

PUBLISHERS

Adeylebros & Co.: 60 Patuatuly, Dacca 1.

Anwari Publications: 5/1 Simson Rd., Dacca 1.

Banga Sahitya Bhavan: 144 Government New Market, Dacca.

Biswakosh: 316 Government New Market, Dacca.

Boighar: 149 Government New Market, Dacca.

Chalantika: 177 Government New Market, Dacca.

Continental Publications: 18-19, Dhanmandi Hawkers Market, Dacca 5; f. 1957; publishers, importers and distributors of scientific and technical books; Chief Exec. M. A. Noor.

Crescent Publishers: 77 Patuatuly, Dacca 1.

Kitabistan: 3 Liaquat Ave., Dacca.

Lekha Prokashani: 18 Pyaridas Rd., Dacca 1.

Mullick Bros.: 3/1 Bangla Bazar, Dacca; textbooks and schoolbooks.

Oxford University Press: P.O.B. 88, 114 Motijheel C.A., Dacca; f. 1952; academic and educational; Man. M. Islam.

Pak Kitab Ghar: 39 Patuatuly, Dacca.

Paramount Book Corporation: Ashraf Chamber, 66 Bangladesh Ave., Dacca; Administrator D. H. Khondker.

PUBLISHERS ASSOCIATION

The Bangladesh Publishers and Booksellers Association 3rd Floor, 3/12 Liaquat Ave., Dacca 1; Sec. Z. I. Khan.

RADIO AND TELEVISION

RADIO

Radio Bangladesh: 20 Green Rd., Dacca 5; started broadcasting December 17th, 1971; overseas service broadcasts $10\frac{3}{4}$ hours and $2\frac{1}{4}$ hours in Bengali and English, respectively; five main stations in addition to Dacca:

Radio Bangladesh: Kajla Kuthi, Rajshahi.

Radio Bangladesh: Arakan Road, Chittagong.

Radio Bangladesh: Sylhet.

Radio Bangladesh: Rangpur.

Radio Bangladesh: Khulna.

TELEVISION

Bangladesh Television Corporation: Dacca 6; originally founded 1964 but taken over by the Bangladesh authorities in December 1971; broadcasting covers (in addition to Dacca) Comilla, Tangail, Mymensingh and Faridpur districts.

FINANCE

BANKING

Central Bank

Bangladesh Bank: Dacca; f. Feb. 1972; Gov. A. N. Hamidullah.

Commercial Banks

Janata Bank: P.O.B. 468, Dacca; f. 1972; 281 brs.; Chair. Khairul Kabir.

Pubali Bank: 24-25 Dilkusha Commercial Area, Dacca 2; f. 1972; 108 brs.; Chair. M. Khaled.

Uttara Bank: 42 Dilkusha Commercial Area, Dacca 2; f. 1972; 66 brs.

Foreign Banks

American Express International Banking Corpn.: Dacca, Chittagong; **Chartered Bank:** Dacca, Chittagong; **National and Grindlays Bank:** Dacca (4 brs.), Chittagong, Khulna; **United Bank of India:** Barisal, Bogra, Brahmanbaria, Chandpur.

DEVELOPMENT FINANCE ORGANIZATIONS

House Building Finance Corporation: 24 Purana Paltan, Dacca 2; f. 1952; provides credit facilities at low interest for house-building; cap. authorized and p.u. Rs. 50m. (subscribed by the Bangladesh Government) and loans sanctioned up to Dec. 1971 total Rs. 224m.; credit facilities exist in 78 towns and villages, 11 regional and sub-regional offices.

Agricultural Development Bank: f. 1972; Motijheel Commercial Area, Dacca.

INSURANCE

The Bangladesh Government in August 1972 set up a National Insurance Corporation together with four subsidiary corporations (*see* below) to regulate all national and foreign general and life insurance companies.

NATIONAL INSURANCE COMPANIES

General Insurance:

Karnafully Insurance Corporation: Commercial Area, Dacca; f. 1972; government-owned.

Teesta Insurance Corporation: Commercial Area, Dacca; f. 1972; government-owned.

Eastern Federal Union Insurance Co. Ltd.: Dienfa Bldg., 9 Bangabandhu Ave., Dacca.

Adamjee Insurance Co. Ltd., Adamjee Insurance Bldg., 115/116 Motijheel, Commercial Area, Dacca.

Muslim Insurance Co. Ltd.: Muslim Insurance Bldg., 121 Motijheel, Dacca.

New Jubilee Insurance Co. Ltd.: 74 Motijheel Commercial Area, Dacca.

Habib Insurance Co. Ltd.: Habib Bank Bldg., 2nd Floor, Motijheel Commercial Area, Dacca.

Premier Insurance Co. Ltd.: Jang Chamber, 21 Motijheel Commercial Area, Dacca.

National Security Insurance Co. Ltd.: Elahi Chamber, 21 Motijheel Commercial Area, Dacca.

Union Insurance Co. of Bangladesh Ltd.: Red Cross Bldg., Motijheel Commercial Area, Dacca.

Bangladesh Guarantee Insurance Co. Ltd.: Malek Mansion, 128 Motijheel Commercial Area, Dacca.

United Insurance Co. of Bangladesh Ltd.: Rahman Chamber, 12-13 Motijheel Commercial Area, Dacca.

Co-operative Insurance Co. Ltd.: Rahman Chamber, 13 Motijheel Commercial Area, Dacca.

Alpha Insurance Co. Ltd.: 12 Bangabandhu Ave., Hassan Bldg., Dacca.

Eastern General Insurance Co. Ltd.: Shamabaya Sadon, 2nd Floor, 9/D Motijheel Commercial Area, Dacca.

Bangladesh Mutual Insurance Co. Ltd.: 20 Shaheed Subal Rd., Chittagong.

Bangladesh Co-operative Insurance Society: Shamabay Bima Bhaban, 24-25 Dilkusha Commercial Area, Dacca.

Eastern General Insurance Co. Ltd.: EIC House SK, Mojib Road, Chittagong.

Eastern Mercantile Insurance Co. Ltd.: 22 Dilkusha Commercial Area, Dacca 2.

Great Eastern Insurance Co. Ltd.: 4 Kilkusha Commercial Area, Dacca 2.

Homeland Insurance Co. Ltd.: 48 Dilkusha Commercial Area, Dacca 2.

Janata Insurance Co. Ltd.: Tiger Mansion, 1st Floor, 69/70 Motijheel Commercial Area, Dacca.

Popular Insurance Co. Ltd.: Corner Court, 2nd Floor, 29 Toyenbeen Circular Rd., Motijheel Commercial Area, Dacca.

National Insurance Co. Ltd.: 48 Motijheel Commercial Area, Dacca.

Bangladesh Mutual Insurance Co. Ltd.: 42 Dilkusha Commercial Area, Dacca.

Life Insurance:

Surma Life Insurance Corporation: Commercial Area, Dacca; f. 1972; government-owned.

Ruspa Life Insurance Corporation: Commercial Area, Dacca; f. 1972; government-owned.

Ideal Life Assurance Co. Ltd.: ILACO House, 24 Motijheel C/A, Dacca; f. 1972; Custodian S. U. AHMED.

Central Life Assurance Co. Ltd.: 99 Motijheel Commercial Area, Karim Chamber, 3rd Floor, Dacca.

Universal Life and General Insurance Co. Ltd.: Shamabay Sadon, 2nd Floor, 9/D Motijheel Commercial Area, Dacca.

Bangal Life and General Insurance Co. Ltd.: 1st Floor, 79 Motijheel Commercial Area, Dacca.

Eastern Life Insurance Co. Ltd.: EIC House, Sk. Mojib Rd., Chittagong.

Federal Life and General Insurance Co. Ltd.: 12 Bangabandu Ave., Dacca 2.

FOREIGN INSURANCE COMPANIES

Guardian Assurance Group: Ispahani Building, 14/15 Motijheel, P.O.B. 42, Dacca 2; Man. M. M. Z. MOGRI.

Commercial Union Assurance Co. Ltd.: Shareef Mansion, 56/57 Motijheel, Dacca 2; Man. A. AHMED; agent for *Northern Assurance* and *NZ Insurance Cos. Ltd.*

Royal Insurance Co. Ltd.: 47 Motijheel, Dacca 2; Branch Sec. M. A. SHAH; agent for *London & Lancashire Insurance Co. Ltd.*

Queensland Insurance Co. Ltd.: Adamjee Court, Motijheel, Dacca 2; Branch Sec. N. PALMER.

American International Underwriters Insurance Co. Ltd.: American Life Building, 18/20 Motijheel, Dacca 2; Man. S. K. HUSSEIN; agent for *New Hampshire Insurance Co. Ltd.*

Norwich Union Fire Insurance Society Ltd.: 10K Motijheel, Dacca 2; Man. M. G. KEBRIA; agent for *Scottish Union and Maritime Insurance Cos Ltd.*

Home Insurance Co. Ltd.: 31 Banglabandhu Ave., Dacca; Man. G. FALLEIRO.

South British Insurance Co. Ltd.: c/o Finlay House, Agrabad, Chittagong; Man. B. M. KADWANI.

TRADE AND INDUSTRY

In January 1972 the Government took over all cotton, jute and other major industrial enterprises and the tea estates. Management Boards have been appointed by the Government.

GOVERNMENT SPONSORED ORGANIZATIONS

Bangladesh Fisheries Development Corpn.: 24/25 Dilkusha Commercial Area, Dacca 2; f. 1964; to develop and exploit fish resources in the Bay of Bengal; Man. Dir. A. LATIF; Sec. L. RAHMAN.

Bangladesh Food and Allied Products Corpn.: 115/120 Motijheel Commercial Area, Dacca; f. 1972.

Bangladesh Jute Mills Corporation: Dacca; f. 1972; Chair. The Minister for Industries; controls seventy-six jute mills with over 25,000 looms.

Bangladesh Paper and Board Corpn.: Shilpa Bhavan, Motijheel C/A, Dacca; f. 1972; exports paper, paper board, newsprint, rayon, yarn and cellophane.

Bangladesh Planning Commission: Planning Commission Secretariat, Eden Bldgs., Dacca; f. 1972; responsible for all aspects of economic planning and development including the preparation of the Five-Year Plans and annual development programmes (in conjunction with appropriate government ministries), the promotion of savings and investment, the compilation of statistics and evaluation of development schemes and projects; Chair. The Prime Minister Sheikh MUJIBUR RAHMAN; Dep. Chair. Dr. NURUL ISLAM; Members Dr. MUSHARRAF HUSSAIN, Dr. MUHAMMAD ANISUR RAHMAN, RAHMAN SUBHAN.

Bangladesh Textile Industries Corpn.: Dacca; f. 1972.

Export Promotion Bureau: 122–124 Motijheel, Commercial Area, Dacca; f. 1972; promotes the export of textile goods, hosiery, lace, hessian bags, thread, spices, ceramics and handicrafts; regional offices in Chittagong, Khulna and Rajshahi; Dir.-Gen. MOSLEHUDDIN AHMED.

Trading Corporation of Bangladesh: 27th Floor, H.B.C.F. Bldg., 24 Purana Paltan, Dacca 2; f. 1972; exports and imports jute goods, tanned leather, tea, paper products, textiles and handicrafts.

CHAMBERS OF COMMERCE

Agrabad Chamber of Commerce and Industry: P.O.B. 70, Chamber Building, Bangabandhu Rd., Chittagong. Pres. W. SUTHERLAND; Vice-Pres. J. NEWLING; Sec. K. CHOUDHURY.

Bogra Chamber of Commerce and Industry: Jhawtola Rd., Bogra.

Chittagong Chamber of Commerce and Industry: Chamber House, Agrabad Commercial Area, Chittagong; f. 1963; 2,319 mems.; Pres. M. IDREES; Sec. (acting) MAHMUDUL H. CHOWDHURY; publs. *Daily Circulars, Annual Report, Trade Directory* (irregular).

Dacca Chamber of Commerce and Industry: 65–66 Motijheel Commercial Area, Dacca 2; f. 1960; 680 mems.; Pres. M. MASHIUR RAHMAN.

Khulna Chamber of Commerce and Industry: P.O.B. 26, Lower Jessore Rd., Khulna; f. 1934.

Narayanganj Chamber of Commerce and Industry: Chamber Building (2nd Floor), 122-124 Motijheel C.A., Dacca; Narayanganj Office: 137 Bangabandhu Sharak; Pres. (acting) M. ANISUDDOWLA; Sec. C. K. HYDER.

Rajshahi Chamber of Commerce and Industry: P.O. Ghoramara, Rajshahi; f. 1960; 48 mems.

Sylhet Chamber of Commerce and Industry: New Market, Sylhet.

TRADE ASSOCIATIONS

Bangladesh Jute Association: P.O.B. 59, B.J.A. Building, Narayanganj.

Bangladesh Jute Export Corporation: 14 Topkhana Road, Dacca-2; f. 1972; Chair. M. S. H. CHISHTY.

Bangladeshiyo Cha Sangsad (*Bangladesh Tea Association*): Bangabandhu Rd., Chittagong; f. 1972; Chair. N. L. SMITH; Sec. F. A. BISWAS.

CO-OPERATIVE

Chattagram Bahini Kalyan Shamabaya Samity Ltd.: 70 Agrabad Commercial Area, Osman Court, Chittagong; f. 1972.

TRANSPORT
RAILWAYS

Chairman of the Bangladesh Railway Board: A. M. CHOWDHURY.

The former Pakistan Eastern Railway, managed since 1962 by the East Pakistan Government, was taken over by the Bangladesh authorities in January 1972. The railway is mostly metre gauge and totals 1,753 miles.

ROADS

There are approximately 15,000 miles of surfaced roads and about 100,000 miles of dirt roads.

RIVERS, CANALS AND IRRIGATION

In Bangladesh there are some 5,000 miles of navigable waterways. Twenty steamers, motor vessels and launches recently re-opened seven routes linking Dacca with Barisal and Chandpur.

Bangladesh Inland Water Transport Authority: DIT Bldg., Motijahaal, Dacca 2; f. 1959 as E. Pakistan Inland Water Transport Authority; controls river conservancy and pilotage services.

SHIPPING

The chief ports are Chittagong and Chalna. At Chittagong in February 1972, a 26-mile long, 1-mile wide and 33 ft. draught channel was established, vessels of up to LOA 575 ft. can now be manoeuvred on the Karnaphuli river. A modern seaport is being developed at Mangla.

Bangladesh Steam Navigation Co. Ltd.: Batali Hills, Chittagong; coastal services; Chair. A. K. KHAN; Man. Dir. A. M. Z. KHAN.

Chittagong Port Trust: Chittagong; provides bunkering and lighterage facilities as well as provisions and drinking water supplies.

CIVIL AVIATION

Dacca and Chittagong are international airports. There are also airports at all major towns.

Bangladesh Biman (*Bangladesh Airlines*): Dacca; f. 1972; fleet of 6 Fokker Friendships and 2 Boeing 707s. A domestic service was inaugurated at the end of February 1972 using 2 Fokker Friendships. A weekly charter service using Boeing 707s began in early March 1972 to London from Dacca; services also to Rangoon, Bangkok and Calcutta.

UNIVERSITIES

Bangladesh Agricultural University: P.O.B. Mymensingh; 210 teachers, 1,600 students.

Bangladesh University of Engineering and Technology: Ramna, Dacca; 141 teachers, 1,661 students.

University of Chittagong: University Post Office, Chittagong; 98 teachers, 1,215 students.

University of Dacca: Ramna, Dacca; 500 teachers, 8,151 students.

Jahangirnagar University: Savar, Dacca; 30 teachers, 144 students.

University of Rajshahi: Rajshahi; 3,695 students.

BARBADOS

INTRODUCTORY SURVEY

Location, Climate, Language, Religion, Flag, Capital

The Dominion of Barbados is the most easterly of the Caribbean islands, lying about 200 miles north-east of Trinidad. There is a rainy season from July to November and the climate is cool during the rest of the year. The mean annual temperature is about 78°F (26°C). About 95 per cent of the population is of African descent. The language used is English and the principal religion is Christianity. The national flag (proportions 3 by 2) has three equal vertical stripes of blue, gold and blue. On the gold band is the head of a black trident. The capital is Bridgetown.

Recent History

Barbados joined the West Indies Federation on its formation in 1958, remaining a member until the dissolution of the Federation in 1962. In 1964 it was agreed that Bridgetown should become the capital of a proposed East Caribbean Federation, to include the Windward and Leeward Islands, but the Federation was never established. However, some common services, particularly transport and education, are shared with other Caribbean territories. In 1954 executive powers were transferred to a Cabinet of Ministers, and Barbados became fully independent within the Commonwealth in 1966. The Democratic Labour Party, led by Errol Barrow, has been in power since 1961. Barbados is a member of the UN and OAS.

Government

The country adopted Dominion status within the Commonwealth in November 1966. H.M. the Queen is represented by a Governor-General, and executive power is in the hands of a Cabinet consisting of a Prime Minister and not less than five other Ministers. Parliament consists of a senate of 24 members, appointed by the Governor-General, and an elected House of Assembly. Elections are by universal adult suffrage, the voting age being 18.

Defence

There is a small local volunteer force, the Barbados Regiment, but no standing armed forces.

Economic Affairs

The Commonwealth Sugar Agreement, extended until 1974, allows sugar to remain the mainstay of the country's economy. However, the Prime Minister, Errol Barrow, announced in February 1974 that Barbados would export no sugar to the United Kingdom under the agreement in the coming year. The tourist industry is rapidly expanding, and there is a small source of natural gas. Outside the harvest season there is a labour surplus and unemployment is a persistent problem, particularly among school leavers. Many Barbadians work in the United Kingdom. With Guyana and Antigua, Barbados set up in 1967 the Caribbean Free Trade Association (Carifta), and in 1973 was a founder-member of the Caribbean Community (CARIBCOM), aimed at the economic integration of member states by the establishment of a common market régime.

Transport and Communications

The situation of the island and its good harbour and airport facilities make it a natural entrepôt for the eastern Caribbean. There are 840 miles of roads, mostly bitumenized; the airport can handle jet aircraft; the harbour at Bridgetown has moorings for eight ocean-going ships.

Social Welfare

Expenditure on health services totalled EC $29.7 million in 1972–73. There are one government and three private (acute short-stay) hospitals and 21 child care clinics. The government has also undertaken the building of group housing for lower income families, and there are a number of voluntary social welfare organizations.

Education

Education is free and compulsory between the ages of five and fifteen years. The State provides for approximately 86 per cent of those eligible for primary and secondary education. The literacy rate is 98 per cent. There are nine comprehensive schools, eleven grammar schools, a community college, teacher training college, a technical institute and a polytechnic. At the Barbados branch of the University of the West Indies an in-service training programme for graduate teachers in secondary schools is run at the School of Education.

Tourism

The natural attractions of the island consist chiefly of the healthy climate and varied scenery. In addition, there are many facilities for outdoor sports of all kinds. Bathsheba on the east coast is a well-known health resort. Since 1961 the number of tourists visiting Barbados has been increasing by about 15 per cent a year. Revenue from tourism has increased from EC $13 million in 1960 to $120 million in 1972.

Visas are not required by nationals of Commonwealth countries, U.S.A., Iceland, Switzerland, Norway, Sweden, Denmark, the Federal Republic of Germany, Israel, Liechtenstein, Spain, Italy, Tunisia, Turkey, San Marino, Venezuela, Colombia, Austria, Netherlands, Luxembourg, Belgium, Surinam and Netherlands Antilles.

Sport

Sporting facilities cover golf, tennis, cricket, football, rugby, hockey, polo, riding, horse racing, motor racing, fishing, swimming, surfing and boating. Cricket is especially popular. A new National Stadium was opened in 1970.

Public Holidays

1974: August 5th (Emancipation Day), October 7th (Clerk's Day), November 30th (Independence), December 25th–26th (Christmas).

1975: January 1st (New Year), March 28th–31st (Easter), April 21st (Queen's Birthday), May 1st (May Day), May 19th (Whit Monday), May 26th (Spring Holiday).

Weights and Measures

The imperial system of weights and measures is used, with the exception of the U.S. gallon (231 cubic inches).

Currency and Exchange Rates

100 cents = 1 Barbados dollar (B$).

Exchange rates (April 1974):

£1 sterling = B$4.80;

U.S. $1 = B$2.03.

STATISTICAL SURVEY

AREA AND POPULATION

AREA	POPULATION (Census of April 7th, 1970)			
	Total	Bridgetown	St. Michael	Other Areas
166 sq. miles*	238,141	8,789	88,097	141,255

* 430 sq. km.

Estimated Population: 241,200 (Dec. 1972).

BIRTHS, MARRIAGES AND DEATHS

	1967	1968	1969	1970	1971	1972
Birth Rate (per 1,000)	22.0	22.0	20.9	20.8	21.9	20.7
Marriage Rate (per 1,000) . . .	3.92	3.86	4.09	4.58	4.5	n.a.
Death Rate (per 1,000)	8.3	8.2	8.0	8.7	8.6	8.7

EMPLOYMENT
(1970 Census)

Sugar	16,034
Other Agriculture	1,781
Mining. Quarrying, etc. . . .	295
Manufacturing	11,237
Construction	10,737
Electricity, Gas, Water . . .	1,088
Commerce	12,178
Transport and Communications . .	4,624
Services (Government) . . .	9,882
Services (Other) . . .	15,813
TOTAL	83,669

AGRICULTURE
SUGAR PRODUCTION
('000 tons)

	1969	1970	1971	1972	1973
Canes Reaped	1,264	1,433	1,214	1,043	1,072
Sugar Produced	154	154	135	111	116

SUGAR, MOLASSES AND RUM EXPORTS

	1969		1970		1971		1972	
	Quantity	Value (EC$'000)	Quantity	Value (EC$'000)	Quantity	Value (EC$'000)	Quantity	Value (EC$'000)
Sugar ('000 tons) . .	119.3	26,982	130.3	29,434	116.0	26,427.0	92.8	27,086.4
Molasses ('000 gals.) .	7,219	3,451	11,160	5,056	6,879.9	3,558.1	4,468.3	3,338.4
Rum ('000 gals.) . .	663	2,938	627	3,250	790.8	4,092.6	802.6	4,647.1

LIVESTOCK
(1971)

Cattle	Pigs	Sheep and Goats	Poultry
7,100	27,600	33,000	409,000

FISHING
('000 lb.)

	1971 (est.)
Total Catch	6,938

Mining: Natural Gas 123 million cubic feet (1972).

FINANCE

100 cents = 1 Barbados dollar (B$).

Coins: 1, 5, 10 and 25 cents

Notes: 1, 5, 10, 20 and 100 dollars.

Exchange rates (April 1974): £1 sterling = B$4.80; U.S. $ = B$2.03.

B$100 = £20.83 = U.S. $49.19.

Note: The Barbados dollar was introduced in November 1973, replacing the East Caribbean dollar (EC$) at par. Tables in this survey may include figures in the old currency.

Budget (1973–74): Revenue (est.) EC$120.7 million; Expenditure (est.) EC$146.9 million.

Development Plan (1972–76): The Plan calls for an investment of EC$42 million in housing, EC$34 million in airport and harbour improvements, EC$26 million in education, EC$10 million in health, and EC$24 million in agricultural and industrial development and export promotion. In the agricultural sector, increasing support will be given to the production of vegetables and other food products for local consumption and for export to member countries of the newly inaugurated CARICOM.

EXTERNAL TRADE
(EC$'000)

	1968	1969	1970	1971	1972
Imports (c.i.f.) .	168,057	194,554	235,005	243,685	270,436
Exports (f.o.b.) .	73,509	74,255	79,146	80,345	84,462

PRINCIPAL COMMODITIES

Imports	1971	1972	Exports	1971	1972
Food and Live Animals. .	53,350	63,002	Sugar	26,427	27,086
Beverages and Tobacco .	4,700	6,086	Molasses . . .	3,558	3,338
Raw Materials . . .	7,313	6,723	Rum	4,093	4,647
Mineral Oils . . .	15,934	15,823	Semi-Processed and Other Food		
Other Oils and Fats .	3,951	3,782	Products . . .	5,004	6,108
Chemicals . . .	18,444	23,050	Crustacea and Molluscs .	15	13
Manufactures . . .	48,240	56,039	Manufactured Goods .	11,515	16,763
Machinery . . .	56,017	54,847	Machinery and Transport		
Miscellaneous Manufactures .	28,972	33,171	Equipment . . .	8,201	6,740
Other Items . . .	6,763	7,914	Chemicals . . .	4,003	5,322
			Mineral Fuels and Lubricants .	14,526	11,349
			Other Items . . .	3,003	3,095

PRINCIPAL COUNTRIES

	IMPORTS			EXPORTS		
	1970	1971*	1972	1970	1971*	1972
United Kingdom . . .	71,495	73,178	72,572	30,485	28,025	29,019
United States . . .	49,303	44,389	51,916	15,531	8,575	10,628
Canada	24,635	24,974	27,116	3,645	4,035	4,931
West Indies . . .	22,141	24,994	30,510	15,671	17,554	21,456
Guyana	4,309	4,963	5,893	1,072	1,225	1,732

* Revised.

TOURISM

YEAR	NUMBER OF BEDS	NUMBER OF VISITORS	EXPENDITURE BY TOURISTS (EC$m.)
1970 .	7,000	156,417	63.5
1971 .	7,446	189,075	77.3
1972 .	7,773	210,349	120.0

Of the total number of tourists in 1972, 75,255 were from the U.S.A., 61,918 from Canada and 143,851 from the U.K.

EDUCATION
(1971–72)

	Schools	Pupils
Primary	118	40,732
Secondary* . . .	19	16,068
Technical	2	1,121
Teacher Training . .	1	200
Theological . . .	1	37
University College . .	1	881

* There are also 19 approved private secondary schools with 6,799 pupils.

Sources: Barbados Statistical Service, St. Michael; Government Information Service, Bridgetown.

THE CONSTITUTION

Representative institutions in Barbados date from the Royal Charter granted by Charles I in 1627. The present Constitution came into force on November 30th, 1966. Under its terms protection is afforded to individuals from slavery and forced labour, from inhuman treatment, deprivation of property, arbitrary search and entry, and racial discrimination; freedom of conscience, of expression, assembly, and movement are guaranteed.

Her Majesty's representative in Barbados is the Governor-General, who appoints the Prime Minister and, on the advice of the Prime Minister, appoints Ministers and some Senators.

The executive consists of the Prime Minister, appointed by the Governor-General as being the person best able to command a majority in the House of Assembly, and not less than five other Ministers. Provision is also made for

a Privy Council, presided over by the Governor-General.

Parliament consists of two houses, the Senate and the House of Assembly. The Senate has 21 members, 12 appointed by the Governor-General on the advice of the Prime Minister, 2 on the advice of the Leader of the Opposition, and 7 as representatives of such interests as the Governor-General considers appropriate. The House of Assembly has 24 members, elected by universal adult suffrage for a five-year term. Since 1963 the voting age has been 18.

The Constitution also provides for the establishment of a Judiciary and a Legal Service, and Service Commissions for the Judicial Service, the Public Service and the Police Service. These Commissions are exempt from legal investigation; they have executive powers to deal with appointments, dismissals and disciplinary control of the services for which they are responsible.

THE GOVERNMENT

Governor-General: Sir ARLEIGH WINSTON SCOTT, G.C.M.G., M.D., L.R.C.P., L.R.C.S.

THE CABINET
(*March* 1974)

Prime Minister, Minister of Finance: ERROL WALTON BARROW, P.C.

Minister of External Affairs, Attorney-General and Minister of Legal Affairs: Senator the Hon. GEORGE MOE.

Minister of State with Responsibility for Parliamentary Affairs and Leader of the House: The Hon. C. E. TALMA.

Minister of Housing, Lands, Labour and National Insurance: The Hon. P. M. GREAVES.

Minister of Agriculture, Science and Technology: The Hon. P. ANDERSON MORRISON.

Minister of Education, Youth Affairs, Community Development and Sport: The Hon. L. ERSKINE SANDIFORD.

Minister of Communications and Works: The Hon. F. G. SMITH.

Minister of Tourism, Information and Public Relations The Hon. P. G. MORGAN.

Minister of Health and Welfare: Dr. the Hon. R. B. CADDLE.

Minister of Trade, Industry and Commerce: Senator the Hon. B. M. TAITT.

Minister of Home Affairs: The Hon. Capt. G. G. FERGUSSON.

DIPLOMATIC REPRESENTATION

(E) Embassy; (HC) High Commission.

Austria: Caracas, Venezuela (E).

Belgium: Caracas, Venezuela (E).

Canada: Port of Spain, Trinidad (HC).

Chile: Santo Domingo, Dominican Republic (E).

China (Taiwan): P.O.B. 623c, Bridgetown (E); *Ambassador:* S. S. C. Yao.

Colombia: Washington, U.S.A. (E).

Cuba: Ottawa, Canada (E).

Cyprus: New York, U.S.A. (HC).

Dominican Republic: Kingston, Jamaica (E).

France: Port of Spain, Trinidad (E).

Germany, Federal Republic: Georgetown, Guyana (E).

Guyana: Kingston, Jamaica (HC).

India: Port of Spain, Trinidad (HC).

Israel: Caracas, Venezuela (E).

Jamaica: Port of Spain, Trinidad (HC).

Japan: Caracas, Venezuela (E).

Netherlands: Port of Spain, Trinidad (E).

Nigeria: New York, U.S.A. (HC).

Peru: Kingston, Jamaica (E).

Tanzania: New York, U.S.A. (HC).

Trinidad and Tobago: Port of Spain, Trinidad (HC).

United Kingdom: P.O.B. 676c, Bridgetown (HC); *High Commissioner:* Stuart Roberts.

U.S.A.: Bridgetown (E); *Ambassador:* Miss Eileen Donovan.

Venezuela: Barclays Bank Bldg., Broad St., Bridgetown (E).

Zambia: New York, U.S.A. (HC).

Barbados has also established diplomatic relations with Australia.

PARLIAMENT

THE SENATE

President: Sir Theodore Brancker, q.c.
The Attorney-General and 19 other members.

HOUSE OF ASSEMBLY

Speaker: Neville Maxwell.

Twenty-four elected members (one for each electoral district).

Clerk of Parliament: Chezley R. Boyce.

(*Election, September* 1971)

Party	Seats (Sept. 1971 Election)
Democratic Labour	18
Barbados Labour Party . . .	6

POLITICAL PARTIES

Democratic Labour Party: George St., Belleville, St. Michael; f. 1955; the majority party in the House of Assembly (holds 18 seats, 1971); Leader Rt. Hon. E. W. Barrow; publ. *Democrat.*

Barbados Labour Party: 111 Roebuck St., Bridgetown; f. 1938; holds 6 seats in the House of Assembly (1971); Chair. J. M. G. M. Adams; publ. *The Beacon.*

JUDICIAL SYSTEM

Supreme Court: Consists of a High Court and a Court of Appeal.

Chief Justice: Sir William Randolph Douglas.

Puisne Judges: Hon. A. J. H. Hanschell, Hon. D. H. L. Ward, Hon. D. Williams.

Registrar: C. A. Rocheford.

Magistrates' Courts: Appeals lie to a Divisional Court of the High Court.

RELIGION

There are over 90 denominations and sects. According to the 1970 census figures, Anglicans number about 150,000 and the Methodist, Moravian and Pentecostal groups are next in importance. There are about 6,500 Roman Catholics, and other Christian groups have a combined membership of 50,000.

Anglican Bishop of Barbados: Rt. Rev. Drexel Gomez, b.a.

Roman Catholic Bishop of Barbados: Rev. A. H. Dickson, St. Patrick's Cathedral, Jemmotts Lane, Bridgetown, St. Michael.

Methodist Superintendent: Rev. V. Commissiong.

Moravian Superintendent: Rev. Peter Gubi.

THE PRESS

Advocate-News: 34 Broad St., Bridgetown; f. 1895; daily; Man. Dir. and Publr. N. S. Grosvenor; Editor Robert Best; circ. 24,474.

Bajan and South Caribbean, The: Carlisle House, Hincks St., P.O.B. 718c, Bridgetown; f. 1953; monthly; illustrated magazine; Man. Editor C. E. McKenzie; circ. over 3,000.

Barbados News: Carlisle House, Hincks Street, P.O.B. 718c, Bridgetown; f. 1963; bi-monthly; tourist magazine; Man. Editor C. E. McKenzie.

Barbados Observer: Westbury Rd., Bridgetown; weekly; Editor W. A. Crawford; circ. 8,000.

The Beacon: 111 Roebuck St., Bridgetown; f. 1948; weekly; Publr. A. Maynard; Editor Ronald Mapp, circ. 2,000.

The Nation: St. Mary's Row, St. Michael; f. 1973; Editor Carl Moore; circ. over 20,000.

Official Gazette: Government Printing Office, Bay Street, St. Michael; Mons. and Thurs.

Sunday Advocate-News: 34 Broad St., Bridgetown; Man. Dir. and Publr. N. S. Grosvenor; Editor Ulric Rice; circ. 35,036.

PUBLISHER

Caribbean Universities Press (CarUP): 8 Rock Dundo Heights, Lodge Hill, Eagle Hall 15; f. 1969; 3 mems.; educational, academic and general books in English Spanish and French; Man. Dir. John Macpherson; publ. *Journal of Caribbean History.*

RADIO AND TELEVISION

RADIO

Caribbean Broadcasting Corporation: P.O.B. 900, Bridgetown; f. 1963; Gen. Man. Ian Gale.

Number of radio sets (1973): 75,000.

TELEVISION

Barbados Rediffusion Service Ltd.: River Rd., Bridgetown; f. 1934; subsidiary of Rediffusion International Ltd., London; commercial wired service with island-wide coverage; rented sets (1972): 26,283; Gen. Man. F. Duesbury.

Caribbean Broadcasting Corporation: P.O.B. 900, Bridgetown; 7 hours colour transmission daily. Educational broadcasts are made in the morning and afternoon.

Number of television sets (1973): 30,000.

FINANCE

CENTRAL BANK

Central Bank of Barbados: Fourth Floor, Treasury Building, P.O.B. 671C, Bridgetown; authorized cap. EC$5m.; Governor Dr. C. N. Blackman; Gen. Man. Tin Tun.

REGIONAL DEVELOPMENT BANK

Caribbean Development Bank: Treasury Building, P.O.B. 408, Bridgetown; equity subscribed by former British Caribbean Territories, Canada, the U.K. and Venezuela; authorized cap. U.S. $100m.; minimum loan EC$100,000; priority given to projects in agriculture, livestock, fisheries, manufacturing, mining, tourism, transport, housing and technical education; Pres. William Demas.

BANKING

Agricultural Credit Bank: Lot 60, Garrison, St. Michael; f. 1937; cap. EC $1,604,925 (May 31st, 1973); makes loans to farmers and co-operatives; Chair. E. L. Brathwaite.

Sugar Industry Development Bank: Bridgetown; f. 1907 with a grant of B.W.I.$384,000 from the U.K. Treasury to assist the sugar industry. By an Act of 1943 the Bank was authorized to make loans to sugar factories (previously loans had been made to sugar plantations and for cane cultivation only). The Bank is now empowered to make loans for diversification of crops designated by the Ministry of Agriculture; Chair. J. A. Kahon.

Barbados Development Bank: Lot 61, Garrison, P.O.B. 50, St. Michael; f. 1969; Gen. Man. Edward Pilgrim.

Barbados Savings Bank: Bridgetown; government-controlled; total credits (1972) EC $21m.

Bank of America: Broad St., Bridgetown; f. 1969; Man. John E. Osborne.

Bank of Nova Scotia: Toronto; P.O.B. 202, Bridgetown; Man. Richard Gallagher.

Barclays Bank International Ltd.: Head Office: 54 Lombard St., London, E.C.3; P.O.B. 301, Broad St., Bridgetown; f. 1837; Man. A. D. McConney; seven branches and eleven agencies in Barbados.

Canadian Imperial Bank of Commerce: Head Office: 25 King St., West Toronto 1; brs. in Speightstown, Worthing, Holetown and Bridgetown; Man. (Bridgetown) G. M. Foster.

Chase Manhattan Bank, N.A.: Nile House, Broad St., Bridgetown; f. 1971; Man. W. B. Richardson.

First National City Bank: Broad St., Bridgetown; Seawel Airport; Sunset Crest.

Royal Bank of Canada: Head Office: Place Ville Marie, Montreal; brs. in Bridgetown (Broad, Hincks and Nile Streets), Black Rock, Holetown, Speightstown, Hastings, Christ Church and Oistin; f. 1911; Man. (Bridgetown) R. I. Cox.

INSURANCE

The leading British and a number of U.S. and Canadian companies have agents in the territory. Local insurance companies include the following:

Barbados Fire Insurance Co.: Bridgetown.

Barbados Mutual Life Assurance Society: P.O.B. 104, Bridgetown; f. 1840; Chair. P. McG. Patterson; Man. D. W. Allan.

C. F. Harrison & Co. (Barbados) Ltd.: 1 & 2 Broad St., Bridgetown.

TRADE AND INDUSTRY

Barbados Industrial Development Corporation: P.O.B. 250, Bridgetown; operates industrial estates; processes applications for industrial incentives; provides information on plant location; Gen. Man. K. D. King; publ. *Operation Beehive* (quarterly).

Barbados Marketing Corporation: P.O.B. 703C, Bridgetown; Chair. E. L. Greaves.

British Development Division in the Caribbean: P.O.B. 167, Carlisle House, Hincks St., The Wharf, Bridgetown; Head Sir Bruce Greatbatch, KT., K.C.V.O., C.M.G., M.B.E.

ASSOCIATIONS

Barbados Agricultural Society: Bridgetown; Pres. O. B. K. Deane.

Barbados Chamber of Commerce: P.O.B. 189, Bridgetown; f. 1825; 287 mems.; Pres. B. L. Banfield; Sec. Keith P. Roberts; publ. *Journal* (quarterly).

Barbados Junior Chamber of Commerce: Bridgetown; Sec. Simon Angoy.

Barbados Sugar Producers' Association (Inc.): Warrens, St. Michael; Dir. E. R. L. Ward; Sec. D. H. A. Johnson.

Sugar Producers' Federation of Barbados: Warrens, St. Michael; Dir. E. R. L. Ward; Sec. D. H. A. Johnson.

West Indies Sugar Association (Inc.): Barclays Bank Building, Broad St., P.O.B. 170, Bridgetown, Barbados; f. 1942; 5 mem. associations; Chair. Sir Robert Kirkwood, K.C.M.G.; Sec. R. Norris, M.B.E.; publs. *W.I.S.A. Handbook*, *W.I.S.A. Annual Report*, *Proceedings of Meetings of W.I. Sugar Technologists*.

EMPLOYERS' ORGANIZATION

Barbados Employers' Confederation: 206 Plantations Building, Broad St., Bridgetown; f. 1960; 215 mems.; Pres. R. C. Goddard; Dir. N. D. Lewis; Sec.-Treas. Miss M. Alleyne.

TRADE UNIONS

Principal unions include:

Barbados Secondary Teachers' Union: Harrison College, Bridgetown; f. 1948; 230 mems.; Pres. Ernest Rocheford; Treas. Miss S. Pilgrim.

Barbados Workers' Union: Nelson and Fairchild Streets, Bridgetown; . 1948; 30,000 mems.; Sec.-Gen. Frank Walcott.

The National Union of Public Workers: P.O.B. 174, Bridgetown; f. 1944; 5,000 mems.; Pres. NORMAN DANIEL; Gen. Sec. O'BRIEN TROTMAN; publ. *The Worker* (quarterly).

TRANSPORT

ROADS

Ministry of Communications and Works: Chief Techn. Dir. H. L. V. GRIFFITH.

The Ministry maintains a network of 840 miles of asphalted roads.

SHIPPING

The following shipping companies operate regular services to Bridgetown: Royal Netherlands Steamship Co., Saguenay Shipping Ltd., Booth Line, Geest Line, Shaw Saville Line, Hamburg Amerika Line, French Line, P. and O., Spanish and West Indies Shipping, (K.N.S.M.) Cunaard, Bookers W.I. Shipping, Wesfal Larsen and Co. Ltd., Royal Mail Lines Ltd., Home Line. Inter-island traffic is catered for by a fortnightly service of two vessels of the West Indies Shipping Corporation operating from Trinidad as far north as Jamaica. In addition, there are many schooners and motor vessels trading from neighbouring islands with no regular schedules. Bridgetown harbour has berths for eight ships and simultaneous bunkering facilities for five.

CIVIL AVIATION

International Caribbean Airways: Seawell International Airport; Central European Office: 9 Grosvenor St., London, W1X 0EE, England; f. 1970; low-cost jet services to Luxembourg and London; Gen. Man. IAN ALLEN.

The following foreign airlines serve Barbados: Air Calypso, Air Canada, Air France, ALM (Netherlands Antilles), British Airways, BWIA (Trinidad), Carib West Airways (Venezuela), Cubana, Eastern (Puerto Rico), SAS, Ward Air (Canada).

TOURISM AND CULTURE

Barbados Tourist Board: P.O.B. 242, Bridgetown; f. 1958; Chair. D. L. BURROWES; Dir. of Tourism F. J. ODLE, M.B.E.; publ. *The Traveller* (quarterly).

OVERSEAS OFFICES

Canada: 11 King St. West, Suite 1108, 105 Ontario.
U.S.A.: 800 Second Ave., New York, N.Y. 10017.
U.K.: c/o Barbados High Commission, 6 Upper Belgrave St., London, S.W.1.

CULTURAL ORGANIZATION

Barbados Arts Council: Civic Theatre, Queen's Park, St. Michael; established to co-ordinate the activities of groups and individuals active in the field of the arts, acting as liaison between the government and the people; Pres. JOHN WICKHAM; Vice-Pres. GORDON BELLE, GRANTLEY PRESCOD; Sec. EDWARD OXLEY.

UNIVERSITY

University of the West Indies: Cave Hill Campus, Bridgetown; faculties of Arts and Science, Natural Sciences, Institute of Social and Economic Research, School of Education f. 1963; faculty of Law f. 1970; 96 teachers, 881 students.

BHUTAN

INTRODUCTORY SURVEY

Location, Climate, Language, Religion, Flag, Capital

Bhutan lies in the Himalayas, with Tibet to the north and India to the south, and covers 47,000 square kilometres. Average monthly temperature ranges from 40°F (mean January) to 62°F (mean July). Rainfall is heavy, averaging over 120 inches in a year. The official language is Dzong-Kha, spoken mainly in western Bhutan. Written Dzong-Kha is based on the Tibetan script. Lamanism (a Tibetan form of Buddhism) is the chief religion. The state flag (proportions 5 by 4) comprises two triangles, one yellow and the other maroon, divided diagonally, with a white dragon superimposed in the centre. The capital is Thimphu.

Recent History

In 1907 the *Tongsa Penlop* (governor) was elected hereditary monarch. Under a treaty concluded with the United Kingdom in 1910, the British Government obtained the right to guide Bhutan's external relations. This right passed to the Indian Government when it concluded a treaty with Bhutan in 1949. In recent years the late King Jigme Dorji Wangchuk vigorously asserted his country's sovereignty, which was exemplified by the entry of Bhutan into the UN in 1971 and her membership of the Colombo Plan a year later. The new King, Jigme Singhye Wangchuk, has stressed that Bhutan's future still depends on Indian goodwill and friendship.

Government

The system of government is unusual in that power is shared between the monarch, the Council of Ministers, the National Assembly (*Tshogdu*) and the monastic head (*Jey Khempo*) of Bhutan's 6,000 Lamas. Since June 1969, the King has been dependent on popular assent, i.e. he must seek a vote of confidence every three years. Any member of the National Assembly can table a vote of no-confidence at any time. All adults over 17 have the right to vote.

Defence

The 5,000 strong Royal Bhutanese Army is under the direct command of the King. Training facilities are provided by an Indian military training team. Though India is not directly responsible for the country's defence, the Indian Government has indicated that any act of aggression against Bhutan would be regarded as an act of aggression against India.

Economic Affairs

Economic development has been a notable feature in recent years. The country's first bank, the Bank of Bhutan, was established in 1968 and issues Bhutan's currency. The First and Second Five-Year Plans (1961–66 and 1966–71) brought about considerable improvements in roads, animal husbandry, electricity generation, coal mining and forestry. The current Third Five-Year Plan (1971–76) involves expenditure totalling Rs. 350 million, most of which is provided by India.

Transport and Communications

In 1972 there were 368 kilometres of roads, 322 kilometres of which were surfaced. In addition, rough roads now link Siliguri with the plains of Bengal and Assam, bringing the total road network to 1,000 kilometres. Paro, where the chief airport opened in 1968, is served by a weekly flight to and from Hashimara in West Bengal.

Social Welfare

The country has four hospitals, providing 166 beds, and 28 local dispensaries, staffed mainly by Indians or Indian-trained personnel. There are 20 doctors. Tuberculosis and malaria remain the major diseases.

Education

In 1963 there were only 36 primary schools, with some 2,500 pupils. By 1973 these figures increased to nearly 100 and 16,000 respectively. There are no missions or private schools in Bhutan, all schools being subsidized by the Government. About 500 Bhutanese students are receiving higher education in India on Indian Government scholarships.

Tourism

Tourism is relatively underdeveloped except that assistance may be offered to the mountaineering enthusiast. Visas are required by all visitors.

Sport

There is little sport other than football and archery.

Public Holidays

The usual Buddhist holidays are observed.

Weights and Measures

The imperial system is in operation.

Currency and Exchange Rates

Indian currency: 100 paisa = 1 rupee.

Exchange rates (April 1974):

£1 sterling = 18.97 rupees;
U.S. $1 = 8.03 rupees.

STATISTICAL SURVEY

Area: 18,000 sq. miles (6,000 sq. miles of forests).

Population: 1,034,774 (Census of November-December 1969).

PRODUCTS

Forests: Pine, spruce, larch, oaks, beech, ash, maple and cypress.

Agriculture: Rice, corn, millets, wheat, buckwheat, mustard, potatoes, chillies, cardamom, oranges and lac. Cultivated land area totals 812,382 acres.

Handicrafts: In the towns metalware (silver, bronze, copper), muzzle-loading guns, swords, hand-woven cloth, masks, thangka (religious scrolls) and wood work are produced.

Animals and Game: Elephant, rhino, tiger, cheetah, leopard, sambur, hog-deer, barking-deer (forests); bears and musk deer (mountains); ponies (domesticated); pheasants, jungle fowl and many other birds.

Minerals: Dolomite, gypsum, graphite, coal, limestone, some traces of copper deposits.

Industry: Recent development projects included a wood-work centre at Paro, weaving centres at Tashigong, Tongsa, Mongar and Thimphu, a bamboo work centre at Shemgong and a nuts and bolts factory at Samchi. Cement, matches, paper and other light industries are being set up with Indian assistance. The principal towns have electricity. The total capacity exceeds 1,500 kilowatts.

FINANCE

Mainly Indian currency: 100 paisa = 1 rupee.

Coins: 1, 2, 3, 5, 10, 25 and 50 paisa (there is one Bhutanese coin, the tikchung, worth 50 paisa).

Notes: 1, 2, 5, 10, 100, 1,000, 5,000 and 10,000 rupees.

Exchange rates (April 1974): £1 sterling = 18.97 rupees; U.S. $1 = 8.03 rupees.

100 Indian rupees = £5.27 = $12.45.

BUDGET

Revenue: 1971-72: Rs. 27.5 million; 1972-73: (n.a.).

Expenditure: 1971-72: Rs. 69.1 million; 1972-73: Rs. 71.1 million (proposed); roads, primary education, court and government expenses, construction works and establishment. Privy Purses for Royalty, and expenditure on monasteries, have been settled and curtailed.

OUTLAY BY SECTOR
(Rs. '000)

	1971–72 (actual)	1972–73 (proposed)
Agricultural Co-operatives .	15,780	15,580
Power	5,300	6,250
Industry and Mining . .	3,000	7,700
Transport and Communications .	18,450	15,250
Medical and Social Services .	20,930	19,950
Other Sectors	5,600	6,870

(a) Roads: 800 miles. Main projects: (1) 120-mile jeep road from Paro to Phuntsholing; (2) 100-mile road from Tashigong to Darrang in Assam, India; (3) 300-mile road from Paro to Tashigong (rising to 14,000 ft.).

(b) Improvement of livestock.

(c) Development of forest industries.

(d) Exploitation of coal and other mineral resources.

(e) Expansion of cottage crafts.

(f) Building of River Jaldhaka power plant.

SECOND FIVE-YEAR PLAN
(1966–71)

Actual Expenditure: Rs. 200 million.

(a) Micro hydro-electric projects; two have been completed at Thimphu and Paro, and a third is under construction at Wangdiphodrang.

(b) Industrial surveys.

(c) Horticulture.

DEVELOPMENT PLANS
FIRST FIVE-YEAR PLAN
(1961–66)

Actual Expenditure: Rs. 106 million.

THIRD FIVE-YEAR PLAN
(1971-76)

Proposed Expenditure: Rs. 350 million.

Note: India is to provide Rs. 330 milion.

AID

Up to February 1972 India gave Rs. 351 million to Bhutan in the form of financial aid. Subsidies have also been granted to the value of Rs. 763.7 million to finance projects such as road and bridge construction, an airfield, geological, power and transport surveys and the cost of services.

TRADE

All external trade is with India. The main exports are timber, fruit and coal, while textiles and light equipment are imported. Other export commodities include Bhutan Distillery products such as rum, gin, whisky and liquors; Fruit Preservation Factory products such as orange and pineapple juices, jams and marmalades.

THE GOVERNMENT

Head of State: His Majesty Druk Gyalpo JIGME SINGYE WANGCHUK (installed July 24th, 1972, at Thimphu).

Royal Advisory Council: Established 1965 and composed of eight members, one representing H.M. the King, two representing the Lamas and five regional representatives of the people.

COUNCIL OF MINISTERS

Minister of Trade, Industry and Forests: H.R.H. NAMGYAL WANGCHUK.

Home Minister: LYONPO TAMJI JAGAR.

Finance Minister: LYONPO CHOGYAL.

Minister of Foreign Affairs: LYONPO DAWA TSERING.

Minister of Communications: LYONPO SANGYE PENJOR.

(*Note:* He is absent at present. *See* Diplomatic Representation below).

NATIONAL ASSEMBLY

A National Assembly (*Tshogdu*) was established in 1953. The Assembly has a three-year term and meets twice yearly in spring and autumn. Present strength is 150 members, of whom 110 are indirectly elected by village headmen. Ten seats are reserved for the monastery (*see* Religion below) and the remainder are occupied by officials, the ministers, their deputies and the 4 chief justice members of the National Assembly. The Assembly enacts laws, advises on constitutional and political matters and debates all important issues. Both the Royal Advisory Council and the Council of Ministers are responsible to it.

The country was formerly an Absolute Monarchy but H.M. the late King, Jigme Dorji Wangchuk, voluntarily surrendered the absolute powers of the Monarchy to establish a new political system described as "Democratic Monarchy". During 1969 Assembly sessions, the Assembly was made a sovereign body under the following provisions:

1. The right of veto by the King was removed.

2. Full freedom of speech is guaranteed.

3. Power to remove the King at any time by a two-thirds majority vote.

4. A vote of confidence is to be taken in the King every three years and requires a two-thirds majority. In the event of a no-confidence vote, the King is to abdicate but the Wangchuk Dynasty is always to provide the ruler in order of succession.

5. The Assembly has the right to appoint and remove ministers.

The system of government is unusual since power is in effect shared between the monarch, the executive and legislative branches and with the *Jey Khempo* or monastic head of Bhutan's 6,000 Lamas.

LOCAL ADMINISTRATION

Provinces: There are eight Provinces each ruled by a Dzongda (District Officer).

Regions: The revenue is collected by the village headmen and remitted to the District Headquarters.

DIPLOMATIC REPRESENTATION

Permanent Representative at the United Nations: LYONPO SANGYE PENJOR.

Representative in India: LYONPO PEMA WANGCHUCK.

Representative of India in Bhutan: A. B. GOKHALE, Thimphu.

Diplomatic relations have been established with Bangladesh. H.E. Dr. A. R. MALLICK, High Commissioner of Bangladesh to India, has been accredited as Ambassador to Bhutan, and H. E. LYONPO PEMA WANGCHUCK, Representative of Bhutan in India, has been accredited to Bangladesh. No other foreign representatives are accredited to Bhutan.

POLITICAL PARTIES

There are no political parties in Bhutan. The Bhutan National Congress which operated in India, and aimed at popular government and closer relations with India, has been wound up and the party leaders and followers have returned to Bhutan after receiving the Royal pardon in November 1969.

LAW

Judicial System: Bhutan has a Civil and a Criminal Code.

High Court: Established February 1968 to review Appeals from Lower Courts; 5 Judges.

Appeal Court: The Supreme Court of Appeal is H.M. the King.

Magistrates Courts: All cases are heard by Local Magistrates. Appeals lie to the High Court.

RELIGION

Religion: The population practises a Tibetan form of Buddhism of the Mahayana branch. The sect of Buddhism supported by the dominant race (Bhutias) is the Dukpa (Red-Cap) Sect of Lamaism. Monasteries are numerous. The chief monastery is situated at Tashichho Dzong and contains 1,000 Lamas. There are some 6,000 Lamas in all headed by a monastic head (*Jey Khempo*).

THE PRESS

Kuensel: Weekly government newspaper; in English, Dzong-Kha and Nepalese.

FINANCE

Bank of Bhutan: Head Office at Phuntsholing; brs. at Thimphu, Samdrup Jongkhar and Gaylegphug; f. May 1968 under Royal Charter to provide banking facilities throughout the kingdom of Bhutan. An agreement between the Royal Government of Bhutan and the State Bank of India was concluded in early 1972 under which the State Bank of India became a 40 per cent shareholder of the Bank of Bhutan as from March 1st, 1972; auth. cap. Rs. 5m. and cap. p.u. Rs. 2m. (in Indian Rupees and Bhutanese currency in fully paid shares of Rs. 1,000 each). Branches were due to be opened at Tashigang and Chirang in 1973. Board of Directors (comprising 4 Directors, including the Chairman, nominated by the Royal Govt. of Bhutan and 3 Directors, including the Managing Director, nominated by the State Bank of India). Directors nominated by the Bhutan Govt.: H.R.H. ASHIDECHHEN WANGMO WANGCHUCK (Representative of His Majesty in the Ministry of Development), H.R.H. NAMGYAL WANGCHUCK (Minister of Trade, Industry & Forests), DASHO TSHEWANG PENJORE (Royal Advisory Councillor). Directors nominated by the State Bank of India: N. ROY, R. SINHA; Chair. LYONPO CHOGYAL (Minister of Finance, Bhutan); Managing Director H. C. VISHNOI (State Bank of India).

TRANSPORT

ROADS AND TRACKS

Main roads connect India with Western, Central and Eastern Bhutan. They are all fair weather metalled roads. A 90-km. road, completed in 1969, links the east-west road to Thimphu and Paro; also extends to the Ha Valley. Northern Bhutan has only mule tracks. In 1972 motorable roads totalled 368 kilometres.

Ponies and mules are still the chief means of transport on the rough mountain tracks.

State Transport Department: Phuntsholing; f. 1962; operates a fleet of 31 buses and 52 lorries (1972).

TOURISM

An hotel is planned in Thimphu. Tourists stay in government-run guest houses. At present tourists are only allowed into Bhutan in restricted numbers because of a lack of facilities.

CIVIL AVIATION

Bhutan's first airport was opened at Paro in March 1968. It is served by DC-3s of Jamair, an Indian airline operating weekly flights from Hashimara (West Bengal) to Paro.

EDUCATION

(1973)

Primary Schools	100
High Schools	2
Public Schools	2
Teachers' Training School	1
Agricultural Colleges	3
Junior Technical School	1
Pupils	16,000

BOLIVIA

INTRODUCTORY SURVEY

Location, Climate, Language, Religion, Flag, Capital

Bolivia is a landlocked, Andean state bordered by Chile and Peru in the west, by Brazil to the north and east and by Paraguay and Argentina to the south. Climate varies according to altitude from humid tropical below 1,500 metres to the cool and cold zones above 3,500 metres. The official language is Spanish. The Indians speak Quechua or Aymará. The people are Roman Catholics but Roman Catholicism ceased to be the official religion of the state in 1961. The national flag (proportions 3 by 2) has equal horizontal stripes of red, yellow and green. The state flag has, in addition, the national emblem in the centre. The legal capital is Sucre. The administrative capital and seat of government is La Paz.

Recent History

In 1969, Dr. Luis Adolfo Siles Salinas, the vice-president, succeeded to the presidency on the death of Gen. René Barrientos, but in September Gen. Alfredo Ovando Candía assumed power by *coup d'état* and established a left-wing military government. The American-owned Bolivian Gulf Oil Company was expropriated and nationalized, and agrarian reforms were promised. Little was achieved and opposition increased. In October 1970 Gen. Ovando was deposed and Gen. Juan José Torres Gonzales emerged as President, pledging support for agrarian reform and worker participation in management. A "People's Assembly" was allowed to meet which called for extreme socialist measures to be taken, causing disquiet in right-wing circles. Gen. Torres' failure either to purge his right-wing opponents from the army or to arm his civilian supporters led to his deposition in August 1971 by Col. Hugo Banzer Suárez, who became the country's fifty-eighth president in 146 years. Col. Banzer drew support from the right-wing Falange Socialista Boliviano and a section of the Movimiento Nacionalista Revolucionario (MNR), as well as from the army. During 1972 strains appeared in the ruling coalition and many of the MNR were arrested. The Government was re-organized in April 1973. In June, Col. Banzer announced an imminent return to constitutional government and presidential elections (the first since 1966) to be held in June 1974. In November, however, Col. Banzer stated that he would not contest the elections himself. Immediately after this announcement the Government resigned, and on November 27th eleven ministers were re-appointed to their previous posts and five portfolios were re-allocated. The MNR subsequently declared that it would withdraw its support from the Government and enter into active opposition. The leaders of the armed forces made clear their opposition to any elections, and these were subsequently postponed until 1975. A state of siege was declared in January 1974, after serious clashes between the army and peasants protesting against price rises and demanding higher wages. Bolivia is a member of the United Nations, the Alliance for Progress, the Organization of American States, LAFTA and the Andean Development Corporation.

Government

Executive power is normally vested in the President and his cabinet. The President is elected for four years by direct popular vote. The National Congress consists of a Senate and Chamber of Deputies. The 27 Senators are elected for six years, with a third renewable every two years, and the 102 Deputies for four years, with half renewable every two years. All persons of 21 or over are enfranchised.

Defence

Military service for one year is compulsory for all males at nineteen. The army numbers 20,000 men and the air force 1,800 men. Para-military forces number about 5,000 men.

Economic Affairs

The economy still depends largely on the export of tin, although progress is being made in diversifying exports; tin dropped from 80 per cent of the total in the 1950s to less than 60 per cent in 1969. Lead, wolfram, silver, zinc and other minerals are mined. Crude oil is exported via a pipeline to the Chilean port of Arica. Production was 2.5 million cubic metres in 1972. With the granting of the first foreign concession to Union Oil in March 1973, there is expected to be an intensification of petroleum exploration in the regions of Beni and La Paz. Natural gas is being exported by pipeline to Argentina. Cereals, fruits, nuts and rubber are grown. Livestock is raised, including llamas, and there is a valuable export trade in hides and skins and vicuña wool. Industry is on a small scale but development schemes are being undertaken with a view to exporting within the Andean group. At the end of 1972 the Government declared a stabilization programme, based on the devaluation of the peso and credits obtained abroad. This devaluation led, however, to an inflationary situation, causing a growing imbalance between wages and prices. Price rises of 100 per cent in 1973 were aimed at re-establishing equilibrium with international prices and rationalizing the availability of supplies, but such measures cannot succeed while the large-scale black market for primary products continues.

Transport and Communications

There are 3,700 km. of railways, linking the main towns. The road network is being lengthened. A 560 km. highway runs from Santa Cruz to Cochabamba, serving a colonization scheme on virgin lands around Santa Cruz. In 1972 the Argentine Government offered a free zone in the port of Rosario on the Paraná River, about 1,280 km. from the border and connected by rail. This gave Bolivia an independent Atlantic outlet. Internal and international air services are provided by Lloyd Aéreo Boliviano. Foreign lines also serve the country.

Social Welfare

There are benefits for unemployment, accident, sickness, old age and death.

Education

The illiteracy rate is high (60 per cent in 1960), though a ten-year campaign to combat this was introduced in 1966. Education is free and, where possible, compulsory between the ages of seven and fourteen. There are eight universities.

Tourism

Lake Titicaca, at 3,800 metres above sea-level, offers excellent fishing and on its shore stands the famous Catholic sanctuary of Copacabana. The Andes peaks include Chacaltaya, which has the highest ski-run in the world. Tourists are mainly from the U.S.A. and South American countries.

Visas are not required to visit Bolivia by nationals of Argentina, Austria, Belgium, Canada, Chile, Denmark, France, Federal Republic of Germany, Liechtenstein, Peru, Spain, Sweden, Switzerland, United Kingdom and U.S.A. All visitors require an exit permit.

Sport

Football is the most popular sport.

Public Holidays

1974: August 5th–7th (Independence), October 12th (Discovery of America), November 2nd (All Souls'), December 25th (Christmas).

1975: January 1st (New Year), February 26th–27th (Carnival), March 23rd (Memorial Day), March 27th–28th (Easter), May 1st (Labour Day), May 29th (Corpus Christi).

Weights and Measures

The metric system is officially in force.

Currency and Exchange Rates

100 centavos=1 peso Boliviano.
Exchange rates (April 1974):
£1 sterling=47.25 pesos;
U.S. $1=20.00 pesos.

STATISTICAL SURVEY

AREA AND POPULATION

AREA	ESTIMATED MID-YEAR POPULATION					
	1961	1968	1969	1970	1971	1972
1,098,581 sq. km.*	3,920,000	4,680,000	4,803,900	4,931,000	5,062,500	5,195,000

* 424,164 square miles.

Ethnic Groups (estimated): American Indian 54 per cent; Mestizo 32 per cent; European (mainly Spanish) 14 per cent.

DEPARTMENTS
(July 1st, 1971)

	POPULATION ('000)	CAPITAL
Beni . . .	200.9	Trinidad
Chuquisaca . .	474.4	Sucre
Cochabamba .	822.5	Cochabamba
La Paz . .	1,590.4	La Paz de Ayacucho
Oruro . . .	352.6	Oruro
Pando . . .	33.2	Cobija
Potosí . . .	896.1	Potosí
Santa Cruz . .	479.8	Santa Cruz de la Sierra
Tarija . . .	212.6	Tarija
TOTAL . .	5,062.5	

PRINCIPAL TOWNS

	POPULATION	
	1965	1969
La Paz de Ayacucho (administrative capital)* . . .	360,329	525,000
Cochabamba . . .	95,083	157,000
Santa Cruz de la Sierra .	80,522	108,720
Oruro	94,336	n.a.
Sucre (legal capital) . .	58,359	n.a.
Potosí	57,916	n.a.

* Population 562,500 at December 31st, 1970.

Births and Deaths (1965–70): Average annual birth rate 44.0 per 1,000, death rate 19.1 per 1,000 (United Nations estimates).

AGRICULTURE

PRINCIPAL CROPS ('ooo metric tons)

	1970–71	1971–72
Sugar cane . . .	1,001.6	1,468.4
Potatoes	698.0	703.0
Maize	292.5	260.0
Wheat	68.5	49.5
Rice. . . .	76.9	74.6

LIVESTOCK
('ooo, at October each year)

	1971	1972*
Cattle	2,220	2,300
Sheep	6,897	7,000
Goats	2,450*	2,500
Pigs	1,000*	1,000
Asses	670*	660
Horses	300*	300
Mules	88*	90
Chickens . . .	3,200*	3,300
Ducks	245*	245
Turkeys	98*	100

* FAO estimate.

Source: FAO, *Production Yearbook 1972.*

MINING

MINERAL PRODUCTION
('ooo metric tons)

	1969	1970	1971
Tin . . .	29.9	29.3	35.9
Wolfram . . .	2.3	2.3	2.5
Antimony . .	13.1	11.8	11.9
Lead . .	24.7	25.4	20.5
Zinc . .	26.3	46.5	8.3
Copper . .	7.9	8.8	7.4
Silver . .	0.1	0.1	0.0
Sulphur . .	36.1	16.3	9.1
Petroleum ('ooo cubic metres)	2,349.3	1,402.2	2,138.1

INDUSTRY
(million)

	1969	1970
Cigarettes (packets) . .	5.0	3.7
Beer (litres) . .	33.9	38.1
Flour (Kg.) . .	34.1	44.2
Cement (Kg.) . .	80.3	116.2
Refined Sugar (Kg.) . .	123.9	133.2

FINANCE

100 centavos = 1 peso Boliviano.

Coins: 10, 20, 25 and 50 centavos; 1 peso.

Notes: 1, 5, 10, 20, 50 and 100 pesos.

Exchange rates (April 1974): £1 sterling = 47.25 pesos; U.S. $1 = 20.00 pesos.

100 pesos Bolivianos = £2.12 = $5.00.

Note: Prior to October 31st, 1972, the official exchange rate was U.S. $1 = 11.875 pesos.

BUDGET
(1973—'ooo pesos Bolivianos)

REVENUE		EXPENDITURE	
Taxation	740.0	Education	711.1
Customs	600.0	Health and Social Security . .	204.4
Communications . . .	8.3	Labour	8.5
Consular . . .	12.6	Transport and Public Works . .	344.5
Royalties and Special Funds .	1,113.7	Agriculture	38.5
Government Enterprises . .	256.4	Industry and Commerce . .	32.0
Loans and Grants . . .	185.0	Defence . . .	441.4
		Administration . . .	250.5
		Public Debt . . .	596.5
TOTAL . . .	2,917.0	TOTAL . . .	2,917.0

NATIONAL ACCOUNTS
(million pesos at 1968 prices)

	1970	1971*	1972†
GROSS DOMESTIC PRODUCT . . .	11,205	11,632	12,308
of which:			
Agriculture	1,817	1,890	1,975
Mining	1,235	1,179	1,257
Petroleum exploitation . . .	252	370	439
Industry	1,564	1,608	1,669
Construction	469	487	516
Transport and fuel . . .	1,127	1,172	1,244
Commerce and finance . .	1,630	1,661	1,748
Services and rent . . .	2,145	2,242	2,376
Public administration . . .	966	1,023	1,084
Income per capita (pesos) . . .	2,272.3	2,297.7	n.a.
Income per capita (U.S. $) . . .	113.6	114.8	n.a.

* Provisional figures.   † Estimated.

RESERVES AND CURRENCY IN CIRCULATION
(December)

	1971	1972
Total Reserves (U.S. $ million) . .	57.2	69.8
of which Gold in Bolivia .	12.4	14.3
Currency in Circulation (million pesos) . .	1,699.2	2,152.6

COST OF LIVING
(Base: 1966=100)

	LA PAZ	
	1971	1972
General Index . . .	129.11	137.51
Food . . .	138.37	147.20
Housing . . .	130.69	138.01
Clothes . . .	114.27	124.58
Various . . .	107.62	113.82

BALANCE OF PAYMENTS
(U.S. $ million)

	1971			1972		
	Credit	Debit	Balance	Credit	Debit	Balance
Goods, Services and Transfer Payments:						
Goods	181.1	181.4	− 0.3	212.7	197.8	14.9
Non-monetary gold . . .	0.9	—	0.9	2.0	—	2.0
Freight and insurance . .	—	24.7	−24.7	—	29.7	−29.7
Travel and transport . .	5.5	10.4	− 4.9	10.3	20.8	−10.5
Investment income . .	1.2	19.9	−18.7	—	23.3	−23.3
Government transactions . .	4.4	4.0	0.4	5.2	4.3	0.9
Other services . . .	5.2	7.0	− 1.8	5.6	7.9	− 2.3
Transfer payments . .	7.2	0.1	7.1	6.4	0.2	6.2
CURRENT BALANCE . . .	205.4	247.5	−42.0	242.4	284.0	−41.8
Capital Movements:						
Long term . . .	75.3	28.3	47.0	138.4	50.4	88.0
Short term . . .	6.6	25.0	−18.4	16.9	32.7	−15.8
CAPITAL BALANCE . . .	81.9	53.3	28.6	155.3	83.1	72.2
Net Errors and Omissions . .	—	0.6	− 0.6	—	17.9	−17.9
Balance (Reserves movement, incl. banking system)			−14.0			−17.7

BOLIVIA—(Statistical Survey)

EXTERNAL TRADE
(U.S. $'000)

	1965	1966	1967	1968	1969	1970	1971
Imports . . .	133,847	138,425	150,946	152,846	165,037	158,529	171,283
Exports . . .	131,830	150,436	166,325	170,648	198,191	228,323	212,253

1972: Imports $185.4 million.

COMMODITIES
(U.S. $'000)

IMPORTS	1969	1970	1971	EXPORTS	1969	1970	1971
Consumer Goods .	32,435	31,710	37,015	Minerals. . .	167,200	204,700	175,700
Raw Materials .	49,292	47,619	50,797	Crude Oil . .	23,000	10,200	23,900
Capital Goods .	82,737	79,200	82,241	Others . .	8,000	13,400	12,600
Others . .	573	700	1,230				

EXPORTS OF MINING PRODUCTS
(U.S. $'000)

	1967	1968	1969	1970	1971	1972
Tin . .	90,878	92,537	102,450	101,907	82,004	89,518
Wolfram . . .	7,971	9,699	11,100	17,568	13,610	10,276
Antimony . .	6,411	6,034	10,986	30,978	9,040	9,056
Lead . .	4,922	5,133	6,831	7,808	5,949	5,705
Zinc . .	4,441	2,978	7,816	14,319	15,270	15,434
Copper . .	6,401	7,729	10,940	12,498	8,297	8,764
Silver . .	6,669	11,199	10,830	10,508	8,342	7,569
Gold . .	39	26	1,497	169	22	6

COUNTRIES
(U.S. $'000)

IMPORTS	1969	1970	1971	EXPORTS	1969	1970	1971
Argentina . .	16,937	16,272	17,581	Argentina . .	10,611	10,772	11,969
Belgium . .	1,934	1,604	2,007	Belgium . .	1,686	5,010	1,795
Brazil . .	3,122	3,000	3,241	Brazil . .	926	961	992
Canada . .	2,896	2,782	3,006	Chile . .	1,551	2,396	2,388
Chile . .	1,999	1,920	2,075	France . .	134	170	143
France . .	2,365	2,272	2,455	German Fed. Republic	5,208	6,059	5,578
German Fed. Republic	20,889	19,667	21,249	Italy . .	188	200	202
Italy . .	2,355	2,263	2,445	Japan . .	11,973	21,615	12,823
Japan . .	655	26,033	28,127	Netherlands .	6,184	6,677	6,623
Netherlands .	5,730	5,505	5,948	Peru . .	3,292	6,077	8,126
Peru . .	2,202	2,116	2,286	Switzerland .	195	234	209
Switzerland .	2,988	2,871	3,102	United Kingdom .	90,775	86,837	97,216
United Kingdom .	8,333	7,980	8,622	United States .	60,780	74,482	59,149
United States .	51,378	49,243	53,205				

TRANSPORT

Railways (1971): Passengers transported: 1,138,000;
Freight transported: 1,101,000 tons.

ROADS
(Kilometres)

	1969	1970	1971
Paved Roads . . .	779	950	1,104
Other Roads usable all year	11,591	11,640	11,486
Other Roads . . .	12,984	13,047	15,529
TOTAL .	25,354	25,637	28,119

In 1970 there were 13,982 cars, 26,025 lorries and vans,
2,224 buses, and 10,360 jeeps and motorcycles.

Civil Aviation (1971): Passengers 220,000; Freight
41,000 tons.

EDUCATION
(1970)

	SCHOOLS	TEACHERS	STUDENTS
Primary and Elementary . .	8,416	24,073	661,423
Secondary General . . .	1,028	7,837	192,435
Technical	86	915	11,491
Teacher Training. . . .	26	497	10,948

Sources (unless otherwise indicated): Instituto Nacional de Estadística, La Paz; Banco Central de Bolivia, *Memoria Anual*.

THE CONSTITUTION

Bolivia became an independent republic in 1825 and received its first Constitution in November 1826. Since that date a number of new Constitutions have been promulgated. Following the *coup d'état* of November 1964 the Constitution of 1947 was revived. Under it the executive power is vested in the President and members of his cabinet. In the revised Constitution the President is elected by direct suffrage for a four-year term and is not eligible for immediate re-election. In the event of his death or failure to assume office, the Vice-President takes his place and, failing the Vice-President, the President of the Senate.

The President has power to appoint members of the cabinet, diplomatic representatives, and archbishops and bishops from a panel proposed by the Senate. He is responsible for the conduct of foreign affairs and is also empowered to issue decrees, and initiate legislation by special messages to Congress.

Congress consists of a Senate and Chamber of Deputies and meets annually on August 6th at La Paz. Its ordinary sessions only last 90 working days, which may be extended to 120. Each of the nine departments (La Paz, Chuquisaca, Oruro, Beni, Santa Cruz, Potosí, Tarija, Cochabamba and Pando) into which the country is divided for administrative purposes, elects three senators to serve for a period of six years. One-third of the Senate retires every two years. The 102 deputies are elected for four years, half the Chamber retiring every two years.

The supreme administrative, political and military authority in each department is vested in a prefect appointed by the President. The sub-divisions of each department, known as provinces, are administered by subprefects. The provinces are further divided into cantons. There are 94 provinces and some 1,000 cantons. The capital of each department has its autonomous municipal council and controls its own revenue and expenditure.

Public order, education and roads are under national control. The armed militia has been granted the legal status of Armed Forces.

A decree issued in July 1952 conferred the franchise on all persons who had reached the age of 21, whether literate or illiterate. Previously the franchise had been restricted to literate persons.

The death penalty was restored in October 1971.

Note: The Constitution is suspended at present.

THE GOVERNMENT

HEAD OF STATE

President: Col. Hugo Banzer Suárez.

THE CABINET
(*May* 1974)

Minister of Foreign Affairs: Gen. Alberto Guzmán Soriano.

Minister of the Interior: Col. Juan Pereda Asbún.

Minister of Finance: Jaime Quiroga Matos.

Minister of Labour and Union Affairs: Alfredo Franco Guachalla.

Minister of Education and Culture: Mario Serrate Ruiz.

Minister of Transport and Communications: Ambrosio García Rivera.

Minister of Industry and Commerce: Col. Miguel Ayoroa.

Minister of Rural Affairs: Col. Ramón Azero Zanzetenea.

Minister of Agriculture: Lt.-Col. Alberto Matusch Busch.

Minister of Welfare and Public Health: Luis Leigue Suárez.

Minister of Mines: Raúl Lema Patiño.

Minister of Urban Development and Housing: Germán Azcárraga Jiménez.

Minister of Power: Col. Guillermo Jiménez Gallo.

Minister of Defence: Gen. Jaime Florentino Mendieta.

Minister of Planning: Sergio Otero Gómez.

Minister of Co-ordination: Roberto Capriles.

Minister of Information: Guillermo Bulacia Salek.

Minister without Portfolio: Dr. Alfredo Arce Carpio.

Minister-Secretary to the Presidency: Dr. Guido Valle Antelo.

DIPLOMATIC REPRESENTATION

EMBASSIES AND LEGATIONS ACCREDITED TO BOLIVIA

(La Paz unless otherwise stated)

(E) Embassy; (L) Legation.

Algeria: Buenos Aires, Argentina (E).

Argentina: Calle Aspiazu, Esquina Sánchez Lima (E); *Ambassador:* (vacant).

Austria: Lima, Peru (E).

Belgium: Lima, Peru (E).

Brazil: 494 Fernando Guachalla (E); *Ambassador:* Claudio Garcia de Souza.

Canada: Lima, Peru (E).

China (Taiwan): 240 Gabriel Gonsálvez y Avda. 6 de Agosto (E); *Ambassador:* Pablo S. K. Tseng.

Colombia: 2376 Avda. 6 de Agosto (E); *Ambassador:* Octavio Rosselli Quijano.

Costa Rica: Potosí 1130 (E); *Ambassador:* J. A. Ortiz.

Czechoslovakia: 8135 Calle 12, Calacoto (L); *Chargé d'Affaires a.i.:* Karel Vozabal.

Denmark: Lima, Peru (E).

Ecuador: 2108 Avda. Arce (E); *Ambassador:* Miguel Angel López Saa.

Egypt: 2919 Avda. 6 de Agosto (E); *Chargé d'Affaires:* Hazem Mohamed Mahmoud.

France: 2383 Avda. Arce (E); *Ambassador:* Jean Mandereau.

Germany, Federal Republic: 2395 Avda. Arce (E); *Ambassador:* Dr. Ernst August Racky.

Greece: Buenos Aires, Argentina (E).

Guatemala: Lima, Peru (E).

Hungary: 8140 Calle 13, Calacoto (L); *Chargé d'Affaires:* M. Bernat.

India: Brasilia, Brazil (E).

Israel: Potosí 1130 (E); *Ambassador:* S. Hadas.

Italy: 2575 Avda. 6 de Agosto (E); *Ambassador:* Beniamino del Giudice.

Japan: 2400 Sánchez Lima y Belisario Salinas (E); *Ambassador:* Masao Fujimoto.

Korea, Republic: Buenos Aires, Argentina (E).

Lebanon: Bogotá, Colombia (E).

Malta: Avda. Camacho, Edificio Bernardi, 3° (E); *Minister:* Carlo di Leonardis.

Mexico: 2932 Avda. 6 de Agosto (E); *Ambassador:* Humberto Martínez Romero.

Netherlands: 2915 Avda. Arce (E); *Chargé d'Affaires:* Gerardo Jansen.

Nicaragua: (address not available) (E).

Norway: Santiago, Chile (E).

Panama: 2451 Pedro Salazar y Capt. Ravelo; *Chargé d'Affaires a.i.:* Lic. Arquimides Barrios B.

Paraguay: Potosí 1285 (E); *Ambassador:* Ruben Domingo Ruiz.

Peru: 2190 Avda. 6 de Agosto (E); *Ambassador:* Felipe de Bustamante Donegri.

Poland: 7836 Calle 11, Calacoto (E); *Ambassador:* Meiczyslaw Wlodarek.

Portugal: 1800 Avda. 16 de Julio (E); *Chargé d'Affaires:* Antonio Pinto Machado.

South Africa: Buenos Aires, Argentina (E).

Spain: 2827 Avda. 6 de Agosto (E); *Ambassador:* Eduardo García Ontiveros.

Sweden: Lima, Peru (E).

Switzerland: Avda. 16 de Julio, Edificio Petrolero (E); *Ambassador:* WILLIAM FREI.

Thailand: Buenos Aires, Argentina (L).

Turkey: Buenos Aires, Argentina (E).

U.S.S.R.: 8129 Avda. Arequipa (E); *Ambassador:* ALEXEI SCHERBACHEVICH.

United Kingdom: 2732 Avda. Arce (E); *Ambassador:* R. C. HOPE-JONES, C.M.G.

U.S.A.: Calle Colón, Edificio Banco Popular del Perú (E); *Ambassador:* WILLIAM P. STEDMAN, Jr.

Uruguay: 250 Calle Loayza, Edificio Castilla (E); *Ambassador:* ALFREDO J. PLATAS.

Vatican: 2990 Avda. Arce (Apostolic Nunciature); *Apostolic Nuncio:* (vacant).

Venezuela: Isabel la Católica 2508 (E); *Ambassador:* Gen. JOSÉ ELISEO MEDINA ARELLANO.

Yugoslavia: 2683 Avda. 20 de Octubre (E); *Ambassador:* REDZAI SUROI.

Bolivia also has diplomatic relations with Bulgaria, Finland and the German Democratic Republic.

CONGRESS

Congress has been suspended indefinitely.

POLITICAL PARTIES

Frente Popular Nacionalista: formed 1971; Government coalition comprising the armed forces and the following two parties:

Falange Socialista Boliviano (FSB): Leader MARIO GUTIÉRREZ.

Movimiento Nacionalista Revolucionario (MNR): f. 1942 by Dr. Víctor Paz Estenssoro; led revolution of 1952 and remained in power for twelve years; at present in opposition to government although several members have retained their ministerial posts; Leader VÍCTOR PAZ ESTENSSORO (in exile).

Partido Demócrata Cristiano (PDC): f. 1954; left of centre; Leader BENJAMIN MIGUEL (under arrest).

Partido Comunista de Bolivia (PCB): f. 1950; illegal.

JUDICIAL SYSTEM

President of the Supreme Court: Dr. MANUEL DURAN PADILLA.

Attorney-General: Dr. ADALID HERVAS CASTRO.

Judicial power is vested in the **Supreme Court** which sits at Sucre. There are 13 members, appointed by Congress for a term of ten years. The court is divided into four sections of three justices each. Two sections deal with civil cases, the others deal with criminal cases and fraud. The President of the Supreme Court presides over all four subsidiary sections.

There is a **District Court** sitting in each Department, and additional provincial and local courts to try minor cases.

In addition to the Attorney-General at Sucre (appointed by the President), there is a District Attorney in each Department.

RELIGION

The majority of the population is Roman Catholic.

Metropolitan See:
La Paz: Most Rev. JORGE MANRIQUE HURTADO.

Suffragan Sees:
Cochabamba: Most Rev. JOSÉ ARMANDO GUTIÉRREZ GRANIER.
Oruro: Most Rev. RENÉ FERNÁNDEZ APAZA.

Metropolitan See:
Sucre: Most Rev. Cardinal JOSÉ CLEMENTE MAURER.

Suffragan Sees:
Potosí: Most Rev. BERNARDO L. FEY SCHNEIDER.
Santa Cruz de la Sierra: Most Rev. LUIS RODRÍGUEZ PARDO.
Tarija: Most Rev. JUAN NICCOLAI.

THE PRESS

DAILY NEWSPAPERS

LA PAZ

El Diario: Loayza 118, Cajón Postal 8; f. 1904; morning; Independent; Dir. JORGE CARRASCO VILLALOBOS; circ. 60,000.

Hoy: evening; independent; Dir. MARIO VARGAS; circ. 40,000.

Nueva Jornada: Calle Bequaron 605; evening; Dir. HECTOR ZAPATA; circ. 6,000.

Presencia: Casilla 1451; f. 1962; morning; Catholic; Dir. HUÁSCAR CAJÍAS K.; Gen. Man. ARMANDO MARIACA V.; circ. 55,000, Sunday 65,000.

Ultima Hora: Avda. Camacho 308; f. 1939; evening; Independent; Dir. MARIO BAPTISTA; circ. 20,000.

COCHABAMBA

Extra: circ. 6,900.

El Mundo: daily; Dirs. V. ZANNIER, C. BECCART; circ. 4,000.

Prensa Libre: Cajón Postal 482; Independent; Dir. JOSÉ CABERO AMADOR; circ. 8,000.

Los Tiempos: Independent; circ. 8,000.

ORURO

La Patria: Casilla 48; Independent; Dir. ENRIQUE MIRALLES B.; Man. CRISTÓBAL MOLINA; f. 1919; circ. 6,000.

SANTA CRUZ

La Crónica: Calle Junia 222; Independent; Dir. SERAFÍN DÍAZ G.; circ. 3,000.

El Deber: circ. 3,000.

Diario del Oriente: daily; circ. 2,000.

SUCRE

La Prensa: Grau 70; f. 1896; evening; Liberal; Dir. Armando Oropeza; circulation 4,000.

PERIODICALS

LA PAZ

Ateneo de Medicina: Casilla 549; bi-monthly.

Boletín Comercial y Minero: Casilla 549; f. 1918; monthly; Dir. Luis Llanos Aparicio; Editor Luis G. Ergueta.

El Deporte: Casilla 2320; f. 1939; official organ of the National Sports Committee and Bolivian Olympic Committee.

Kollasuyo: f. 1939; monthly; current affairs.

Litoral: Casilla 2279; f. 1952; fortnightly; sports; Dir. Dámaso Eduardo Delgado.

Minería Boliviana: Bernardo Trigo 429, Cajón Postal 2022; monthly; Man. O. B. Sánchez.

Momento: weekly; Independent; Dir. Luis Ramiro Beltrán.

Periódico Economía Boliviana: Casilla 301; fortnightly; Dir. Aldo C. Llamas.

Prensa Médica: Casilla 891; f. 1941; bi-monthly; medical, scientific; Dir. Dr. Roberto Suárez M; circ. 1,500.

El Pueblo: La Paz; Communist weekly; Prop. and Dir. Fernando Siñani Valdivieso; circ. 2,500.

Revista de Antropología: Casilla 1487; f. 1930; official organ of the Archaeological Society of Bolivia; half-yearly; Pres. Prof. Alberto Laguna Meave; Sec. Ernesto Aliaga Suárez.

Revista del Colegio de Abogados: Casilla 760; f. 1893; quarterly; non-political; Chair. Jorge Pinto de la Torre; Editor José María Baldivia; Sec. Mario Lanza Suárez.

Revista de Jurisprudencia: monthly.

Revista Militar: Venezuela 37; f. 1912; official organ of the Armed Forces; bi-monthly; Dir. Ricardo Castañón y Solaligue.

Revista de la Universidad: monthly.

Selecciones Bolivianas: Bolivian Digest, Casilla 461; monthly; Dir. Renato Tapia Caballero.

Telecom: Telégrafos del Estado; weekly; Independent; Dir. Roberto Acosta.

SANTA CRUZ

Democracia: published periodically; Independent; Dir. Rubén Darío F.

El Llano: Editorial Santa Cruz; published periodically; Independent; Dir. Carmelo Saucedo.

La Universidad: published periodically; Independent; Dir. Napoleón Rodríguez.

SUCRE

Junín: Grau 601; weekly; Independent; Dir. Luis S. Wayar.

Tribuna Universitaria: Universidad Mayor de San Francisco Xavier.

PRESS ASSOCIATION

Asociación Boliviana de Periodistas: La Paz.

FOREIGN BUREAUX

La Paz

ANSA: c/o Ultima Hora, Avda. Camacho 1372; Bureau Chief Jorge Alvestegui.

UPI: Edif. El Diario; Bureau Chief Betsy Zavala Pabón.
The following are also represented: AP, DPA, Tass.

PUBLISHERS

Editorial "Centenario": Casilla 883, La Paz; Mans. Luis Suaznábar V. and Alfredo Suaznábar V.

Editorial Don Bosco: Avda. 16 de Julio 1899, Cajón Postal 204, La Paz.

Editorial Fénix: Casilla 120, La Paz.

Editorial Juventud: Plaza Murillo 519, Casilla 1489, La Paz.

Editorial e Imprenta "Artística": Casilla 813, La Paz.

Editorial Renacimiento (R. Zumelzu & Cía.): Casilla 433, La Paz.

Empresa Editora "Universo": Casilla 1514, La Paz.

Librería y Editorial "Juventud": Casilla 1489, La Paz.

Gisbert y Cía., S.A.: Casilla 195, La Paz; f. 1906; textbooks and general.

RADIO AND TELEVISION

RADIO

Dirección General de Telecomunicaciones: Departamento de Radiodifusión, La Paz; Government-controlled broadcasting authority; Dir.-Gen. H. Azogue Galindo.

Asociación Boliviana de Radiodifusoras (ASBORA): Casilla 5028, La Paz; Pres. R. Salmon; Sec. Gen. L. Suárez B.

There are 54 short-wave and 71 medium-wave stations, the majority of which are commercial. Broadcasts take place in Spanish, Quechua, English and German.

There were estimated to be 1,350,000 radios in Bolivia in 1973.

TELEVISION

Televisión Boliviana, S.A.: La Paz; f. 1969; Dir.-Gen. A. de Latorre.

There were 11,000 television sets in Bolivia in 1973.

FINANCE

(cap. = capital; dep. = deposits; p.u. = paid up; m. = million; amounts are in Pesos Bolivianos unless otherwise stated).

BANKING

CENTRAL BANK

Banco Central de Bolivia: Ayacucho esq. Mercado, Casilla 1401, La Paz; f. 1928; bank of issue; Pres. J. Salazar Mostajo; Gen. Man. Luis Viscarra Cruz.

Banco del Estado: Ayacucho esq. Mercado, Casilla 1401, La Paz; f. 1970; state bank incorporating banking department of Banco Central de Bolivia; Pres. Lic. Armando Pinell Centellas; Gen. Man. José Luis Aparicio Carrasco.

DEVELOPMENT BANK

Banco Agrícola de Bolivia: Avda. Mariscal Santa Cruz esq. Grau, Casilla 1179, La Paz; f. 1942; cap. 76m. (Jan. 1974); Pres. Alberto Natuch Busch; Gen. Man. Lic. Luis Mayser Ardaya.

COMMERCIAL BANKS

Banco Boliviano Americano: Calle Loayza 127-131, Casilla 3059, La Paz; f. 1957; cap. and res. 13.1m., dep. 76.8m. (Dec. 1973); Pres. Luis E. Siles; Gen. Man. Mario Villarejos M.

Banco Hipotecario Nacional: Socabaya 348, Casilla 4824, La Paz; brs. in Cochabamba, Santa Cruz and Montero.

Banco Industrial, S.A.: Avda. 16 de Julio 1628, Casilla 1290, La Paz; f. 1963; industrial credit bank; cap. 994,000 U.S dollars; Pres. E. Urioste Calvo; Gen. Man. J. López Pacheco.

Banco Mercantil S.A.: Ayacucho esq. Mercado, Casilla 423, La Paz; f. 1906; cap. 5.6m., dep. 25m. (Dec. 1970); Pres. Eduardo Saenz García; Gen. Man. Guido Quiroga Quiroga.

Banco Minero de Bolivia: Calle Comercio 1290, Cajón Postal 1410, La Paz.

Banco Nacional de Bolivia: Ingavi esq. Yanacocha, Casilla 360, La Paz; f. 1871; 5 brs.; Pres. Dr. Alfredo Gutiérrez V.; Gen. Man. Dr. Hugo Arce Arce.

FOREIGN BANKS

Banco do Brasil: Brasília; Avda. Camacho 1336, Casilla 1650, La Paz; f. 1960; Man. I. P. Salgueiro.

Banco de la Nación Argentina: Bartolomé Mitre 326, Buenos Aires; br. in La Paz: Avda. Camacho 1355, Casilla 2745.

Banco Popular del Perú: esq. Beytia y Melchormalo, Lima, Peru; Mercado esq. Colón, Casilla 907, La Paz; f. 1899; cap. and res. 13,694m., dep. 109,493m. (Dec. 1971); Pres. and Gen. Man. Miguel A. Fabbri; brs. in Cochabamba, Oruro, Sucre and Santa Cruz.

Bank of America: New York; Calle Mercado 1046, Casilla 5015, La Paz.

Deutsch-Südamerikanische Bank A.G. (Banco Germánico de la América del Sud) and Dresdner Bank A.G.: H.O. Hamburg; Joint representation: Avda. Mariscal Santa Cruz 1336, 1° piso, Casilla 1077, La Paz.

First National City Bank: New York; Calle Colón 228, Casilla 260, La Paz.

SUPERVISING AUTHORITY

Superintendencia de Bancos: Edificio Sáenz, Avda. Camacho 1377, La Paz; Superintendent R. Gómez García.

INSURANCE

Compañía Boliviana de Seguros, S.A.: Calle Colón 288, La Paz; f. 1946; Pres. and Gen. Man. Orlando González Herrera.

Compañía Internacional de Seguros, S.A.: Calle Ayacucho 251, La Paz; f. 1957; Pres. L. de Alencar Z.; Gen. Man. R. Carrasco Quiroga.

Compañía Nacional de Seguros "Illimani": Avda. Camacho 1424, La Paz; in liquidation.

La Mercantil de Seguros y Reaseguros, S.A.: Calle Mercado 1121, Casilla 2727, La Paz; f. 1956; Pres. Dr. Hugo Echeverría; Gen. Man. Antonio Hernández M.

La Nacional, Compañía de Seguros, S.A.: Calle Jordán 3881 esq. Nataniel Aguirre, Casilla 810, Cochabamba; f. 1958; Pres. J. Arce Zenarruza; Man. H. Valenzuela.

There are also a number of foreign companies operating in La Paz.

TRADE AND INDUSTRY

CHAMBERS OF COMMERCE

LA PAZ

Cámara Nacional de Comercio: Avda. Camacho, Casilla No. 7; f. 1890; 30 brs. and special brs.; Pres. Marcelo Pérez; Man. René Candia Navarro; publ. *Boletín Informativo*.

Cámara Nacional de Industrias: Avda. Camacho, Casilla 611; f. 1931; Pres. René Capriles Rico.

COCHABAMBA

Cámara Departamental de Comercio: Casilla 493; f. 1922; 405 mems.; Pres. Javier Rodríguez Paz; Gen. Man. Wálter Antezana Paz.

ORURO

Cámara de Comercio: Pasaje Guachalla, Casilla 148.

DEVELOPMENT ORGANIZATIONS

Agencia Promotora de Inversiones A. Castedo Leygue: Casilla 2355, La Paz; f. 1967 to promote agricultural and industrial investment in Bolivia; Man. A. Castedo Leygue.

Corporación Boliviana de Fomento: Avda. Camacho, Casilla 2454, La Paz; f. 1942; all aspects of national development; main fields of aid include highways, agriculture, conservation of natural resources, electricity, industries, housing; cap. 480,000m. pesos; property 193,385m.; investments 156,953m. (Dec. 1966); Pres. Col. Mario Vargas Salinas.

Comisión Nacional de Estudios de Operaciones Mineras—CNEOM (*National Commission for the Study of Mineral Marketing*): Casilla 349, La Paz; Chair. The Minister of Mines; Sec.-Gen. Dr. Raul Ybarnegaray.

Corporación Minera de Bolivia—COMIBOL: Avda. Mariscal Santa Cruz 1092, Casilla 349; a government organization holding a monopoly of tin and other mineral production; Pres. Alvaro Torrico Arze.

Empresa Nacional de Fundiciones: La Paz; f. 1966; State company for the smelting of non-ferrous minerals.

Instituto Boliviano del Café: Ministerio de Agricultura, Casilla 1262; f. 1965; department controlling the export, marketing and growing policies in the coffee industry; Pres. Dr. José Ayala.

Yacimientos Petroliferos Fiscales Bolivianos—YPFB: Calle Bueno, Casilla 401, La Paz; f. 1936; state oil enterprise; Pres. Ing. Rolando Prada M.; Publ. Relations Carlos Meyer Ayala.

EMPLOYERS' ASSOCIATION

Asociación Nacional Exportadores de Bolivia (ANEB): Casilla 2355, La Paz; f. 1968, to promote exports of agricultural products and Bolivian raw materials; Pres. Guillermo Crooker; Vice-Pres. Antonio Castedo Leygue.

TRADE UNIONS

Central Obrera Boliviana—COB (*Central Labour Organization of Bolivia*): Casilla 1379, La Paz; f. 1952; 200,000 (est.) mems. and affiliating all the major unions in the country; Dir. Juan Lechín Oquendo; publs. *Rebelión* (weekly), *Voz Sindical* (monthly).

The three largest federations attached to COB are:

Federación Sindical de Trabajadores Mineros de Bolivia—FSTMB (*Trade Union Federation of Mineworkers of Bolivia*): La Paz; f. 1944; 65,000 (est.) mems.; Exec. Sec. Juan Lechín Oquendo; 69 affiliated unions.

Confederación General de Trabajadores Fabriles de Bolivia—CGTFB (*General Confederation of Factory Workers of Bolivia*): Avda. Armentia 919, Casilla 2355, La Paz; 35,000 (est.) mems.; Exec. Sec. Stanley Gamberos; Sec.-Gen. Guillermo Torrigo; 120 affiliated unions.

Confederación Sindical de Trabajadores Ferroviarios, Ramas Anexas y Transportes Aéreos de Bolivia—CSTFTAB (*Trade Union Confederation of Railroad and Related Workers and Air Transport Workers of Bolivia*): Calle Ayacucho 284, Casilla 1976, La Paz; f. 1949; 26,000 (est.) mems.; Sec.-Gen. Juan Sanjinés Ovando; publ. *El Expreso* (monthly); 9 affiliated federations with 77 affiliated unions.

Acción Sindical Boliviana—ASB (*Bolivian Trade Union Action*): Casilla 3281, La Paz; f. 1957; Christian Trade Union; Pres. José Lara S.; Sec. Luis Murillo V.; 5,000 mems.; publ. *Acción Sindical*.

TRANSPORT

An agreement has been reached with the UN Development Programme and IBRD for a general transport survey in Bolivia and the drawing up of a ten-year transport development programme.

RAILWAYS

Empresa Nacional de Ferrocarriles: Calle Bolívar 724, Casilla 428, La Paz; f. 1964; administers most of the railways in Bolivia, including the Bolivian sections of the **Antofagasta (Chili) and Bolivia Railway Company**, which were transferred under a settlement agreed in 1965, and track previously belonging to the Peruvian Corporation of Lima; Pres. Ambrosio García Riveros; Gen. Man. Ing. Carlos Belmonte Ichazo; publ. *Revista, Memoria Anual*, reports.

Western Network: Total 2,101 km.

Eastern Network: Total 1,222 km.

ex-Peruvian Corporation: Total 97 km.

Total Networks: 3,420 km.

Private Railways:

Machacamarca–Uncia (Owners: Corporación Minera de Bolivia) . . . 108 km.

Uyuni–Pulacayo (Owners: Empresa Minera Pulacayo) . . . . 52 km.

All the railways are of 1-metre gauge, with the exception of the railway from Uyuni to Pulacayo, which is 0.75-metre gauge. Some electrification has taken place.

ROADS

Bolivia has approximately 40,000 km. of roads and paths. These may be classified as follows: approximately 5,600 km. of all-weather roads, including 535 km. asphalted, and a further 8,160 km. serviceable only in the dry season; 9,500 km. of secondary departmental roads; 5,200 km. of provincial roads; and 11,300 km. of tracks and paths.

Almost the entire road network is concentrated in the *altiplano* region and the Andes valleys. New projects include the construction of a Trans-Chaco highway, linking La Paz with Asunción, capital of Paraguay.

INLAND WATERWAYS

By agreement with Paraguay in 1938 (confirmed in 1939) Bolivia has an outlet on the River Paraguay. This arrangement, together with navigation rights on the Paraná, gives her access to the River Plate and the sea. The River Paraguay is navigable for vessels of 12-foot draught for 288 km. beyond Asunción in Paraguay and for smaller boats another 960 km. to Corumbá in Brazil.

An agreement with Argentina in 1972 granted Bolivia free port facilities at Rosario for handling iron ore for export from the Mutún mines.

Bolivia has about 19,200 km. of waterways navigable by light draught vessels when the rivers are full.

Bolivian River Navigation Company: f. 1958; services from Puerto Suárez to Buenos Aires (Argentina).

CIVIL AVIATION

Lloyd Aéreo Boliviano (LAB): Casilla 132, Cochabamba; Avda. Camacho 1460, Casilla 691, La Paz; G.R. Moreno esq. Suárez de Figueroa, Santa Cruz; f. 1925; partly State-owned since 1941. Operates internal services linking the main localities in Bolivia. Joint services with other national lines to Argentina, Brazil, Chile and Peru; Pres. Guillermo Bilbao la Vieja; fleet: 5 Douglas DC-3, 2 Fairchild F-27M, 1 Boeing 727.

The following foreign airlines serve Bolivia: Aerolíneas Argentinas, Braniff, Cruzeiro do Sul, Iberia, Lufthansa and Varig.

TOURISM

Dirección Nacional de Turismo: Avda. Camacho esq. Loayza, Casilla 1868, La Paz; Dir. Juan Luzio.

Asociación Boliviana de Agencias de Viajes y Turismo: Casilla 460, La Paz; Pres. Mario Grisi.

CULTURAL ORGANIZATIONS

Consejo Nacional del Arte: Palacio de los Marqueses de Villaverde, La Paz; f. 1960 to encourage the arts and organize cultural events.

Dirección General de Cultura: La Paz; publs. *Khana, Cuadernos quincenales de poesía*.

ATOMIC ENERGY

Comisión Boliviana de Energía Nuclear: La Paz; f. 1962; Dir. Col. Federico Paz Lora; Scientific Documentation: Lic. Bruno Aparicio Gómez; Nuclear Engineering: Ing. Angel García Ontiveros; Nuclear Medicine Centre: Dr. Luis Barragán; Agriculture and Entomology: Ing. María Luisa de Fernández.

Universidad Boliviana Mayor de "San Andrés": Avda. Villazón, La Paz; conducts cosmic ray and radioisotope research in engineering, medicine and pharmacy.

Instituto de Investigaciones Físicas—Laboratorio de Física Cósmica: Universidad Mayor de San Andrés, La Paz; f. 1952; Dir. Gastón R. Mejía; Basic Physics Division: Carlos Aguirre; Applied Physics Division: Ricardo Anda; research into high energy cosmic radiation, geomagnetic and astrophysical effects, the ionosphere, higher atmosphere and meteorology, high energy nuclear physics, astronomy, solar physics, solid state physics, biophysics, electronics and solar radiation applications; publ. *Resumen de Labores*.

Facultad de Ciencias Geológicas: La Paz; Ing. Dir. Jorge Muñoz Reyes.

Academia Nacional de Ciencias: Casilla 2325, La Paz; f. 1960; Pres. Ing. Jorge Muñoz Reyes; research in cosmic physics, solar radiation, geology and archaeology.

Instituto Superior de Ciencias Básicas: Universidad Boliviana Mayor de "San Andrés," La Paz; f. 1966; Dir. Ing. Abelardo Alarcón Méndez.

UNIVERSITIES

Universidad Boliviana Mayor "Gabriel René Moreno": Plaza 24 de Setiembre, Casilla 702, Santa Cruz de la Sierra.

Universidad Boliviana "Juan Misael Saracho": Calle Marqués Campero 882, Edif. Central, Avda. de las Américas, Tarija; 180 teachers, 1,800 students.

Universidad Boliviana Mayor y Pontificia de San Francisco Xavier: Casilla 212, Sucre; 240 teachers, 1,750 students.

Universidad Boliviana Mayor de "San Andrés": Avda. Villazón 1995, La Paz; 800 teachers, 12,500 students.

Universidad Boliviana Mayor de "San Simón" de Cochabamba: Casilla 658, Cochabamba; 273 professors, 4,024 students.

Universidad Boliviana "Tomás Frias": Avda. del Estudiante, Casilla 36, Potosí; 137 teachers, 2,125 students.

Universidad Boliviana Técnica de Oruro: 6 de Octubre 1209, Casilla 49, Oruro.

Universidad Católica Boliviana: La Paz.

BOTSWANA

INTRODUCTORY SURVEY

Location, Climate, Language, Religion, Flag, Capital

The Republic of Botswana, formerly known as Bechuanaland, lies in southern Africa between the Republic of South Africa to the south and east, Rhodesia to the northeast and South West Africa (Namibia) to the west and north. A short section of the northern frontier adjoins Zambia. The climate is generally sub-tropical, with hot summers and an average rainfall of 18 inches. The territory is largely near-desert, and most of the population lives along the eastern border by the main railway line. The languages used are Tswana and English. The chief religion is Christianity. The national flag (proportions 3 by 2) consists of a central horizontal band of black edged with white, between bands of azure blue above and below. The capital is Gaborone.

Recent History

Formerly one of the British High Commission Territories in southern Africa, Bechuanaland became internally self-governing in March 1965 and, as Botswana, attained full independence within the Commonwealth in 1966. Sir Seretse Khama's Botswana Democratic Party won 28 of the 31 elected seats in the National Assembly at the general elections of March, 1965, and 24 of the seats at the elections of October, 1969. Botswana is a member of the United Nations and the Organization of African Unity, but because of the country's complete economic and geographical dependence on South Africa, on which it is totally reliant for trade and communications, the government has been unable to play an effective role in enforcing sanctions against Rhodesia or in guerrilla campaigns directed against South Africa. South Africa has exerted pressure on Botswana over its claim to have a common border with Zambia, its establishment of diplomatic relations with Czechoslovakia and the Soviet Union and its repeatedly voiced criticism of *apartheid*. Sir Seretse has refused South African aid and recently strengthened Botswana's ties with Zambia and Tanzania. Together with Lesotho and Swaziland, Botswana occupies one of the most politically delicate positions in Africa.

Government

Botswana is a Republic with a President as executive head of state and an elected National Assembly. The President has powers to delay implementation of legislation for six months; and certain matters also have to be referred to the House of Chiefs for approval though they have no power of veto. Local government is effected through nine district councils and three town councils (Gaborone, Lobatse and Francistown).

Defence

Botswana has a police force of 1,000.

Economic Affairs

The economy is based chiefly on livestock, a large proportion of trade being with South Africa. Botswana, together with Lesotho and Swaziland, is linked to South Africa in a customs union. Excise and customs duties are paid into a common pool managed by South Africa, and Botswana receives revenues in respect of its share of duties collected. A new agreement in 1970 makes provision for Botswana to levy additional duties on imports and to receive a larger share of South Africa's customs and excise revenue. The result has been a rise in revenue from this source from R1.4 million in 1968–69 to R12.5 million in 1972–73, and a projected R21 million in 1973–74. The two countries also have a common currency, the rand. There is a serious deficiency of employment in Botswana, and over half the paid employment lies in South Africa on nine-month mining contracts. Exploitation of mineral deposits offers excellent prospects for diversifying the economy. In addition to manganese and asbestos, already being produced, vast deposits of copper and copper/nickel ore have been located, and the development of the copper/nickel deposits at Selebi-Pikwe has begun. Production at the diamond mines at Letlhakane and Orapa, which contains the second largest pipe discovered outside the U.S.S.R., is projected by De Beers. Much is hoped for from the Shashe complex, based on copper deposits, and envisaging the development of reserves of coal, salt and soda ash, and the extension of irrigation farming. The National Development Plan for 1970–75, towards which the World Bank, the International Development Association and Britain are providing the most aid, expects a 15 per cent annual growth rate. Mining revenues are expected to supplement this considerably. Frequent droughts, the unequal distribution of wealth, reliance on expatriates in managerial positions and the landlocked position of the country are serious obstacles to economic development.

Transport and Communications

Communications are largely undeveloped, with only about 1,500 miles of main roads, and the lifeline of the country is the railway between South Africa and Rhodesia. There are several airfields served by government and private charter companies. In the north the Okavango River represents the only major source of water, one which it has not yet proved possible to exploit, either for irrigation or transport. A large road development plan is under way. In June 1973 the Botswana Government announced that an American firm will build the Botswana-Zambia highway from Nata to Kazungula. It is scheduled to be completed in early 1976 with an American loan of $16.6 million.

Social Welfare

Health services are being developed, and at the end of 1971 there were 13 general hospitals, one mental hospital, 10 health centres, 58 dispensaries and 31 clinics.

Education

In 1973 there were 95,511 pupils in primary schools, mostly financed by district councils, assisted by Government grants in aid. In addition, 8,763 students received secondary education, and some students receive higher education abroad or at the University of Botswana, Lesotho and Swaziland in Lesotho. Literacy in Tswana is about 25 per cent, and in English just over 15 per cent.

Tourism

There is an attractive game reserve at Chobe, only a short drive from Victoria Falls by first-class roads. Most of the main centres of population have hotels, and photographic and big-game safaris can be organized.

Public Holidays

1974: August 5th (Bank Holiday), September 30th (Botswana Day), October 24th (United Nations Day), December 25th (Christmas Day), December 26th (Boxing Day).

1975: January 1st (New Year's Day), March 28th–31st (Easter), May 8th (Ascension), May 19th (Whit Monday), May 26th (President's Day), June 2nd (Commonwealth Day).

Weights and Measures

The imperial system of weights and measures is used.

Currency and Exchange Rates

South African currency: 100 cents = 1 rand.
Exchange rates (April 1974):
£1 sterling = 1.581 rand;
U.S. $1 = 67.11 South African cents.

STATISTICAL SURVEY

AREA AND POPULATION

AREA (sq. miles)	POPULATION							
	Census of Aug. 31st, 1971		Tribes (1964 Census)					
	Total	Non-citizens	Bakgatla	Bakwena	Bamalete	Bamangwato	Bangwaketse	Batawana
231,805	630,379*	11,261	32,118	73,088	13,861	199,782	71,289	42,347

* In addition, there were estimated to be 10,550 nomads.

POPULATION BY CENSUS DISTRICT (1971 Census)

Barolong	12,158	Kweneng	72,093
Central	234,828	Lobatse	12,920
Chobe	5,411	Ngamiland	53,870
Francistown	19,903	Ngwaketse	79,152
Gaborone	18,436	North-East	28,524
Ghanzi	17,352	Orapa	1,209
Kgalagadi	17,289	Selebi-Pikwe	4,940
Kgatleng	35,752	South-East	22,691

Principal Towns and Villages (1971 Census): Selebi-Pikwe (1973 est.) 27,000; Francistown 19,903; Gaborone (capital) 18,436; Serowe 15,723; Lobatse 12,920; Mahalapye 12,056; Kanye 10,664; Maun 9,614; Molepolole 9,448; Ramotswa 7,991; Mochudi 6,945.

ECONOMICALLY ACTIVE POPULATION*

	1964	1972
Agriculture, Forestry, Hunting and Fishing	227,649	237,000
Services	9,798	16,863
Construction	2,704	6,500
Commerce and Finance	2,468	6,300
Manufacturing	2,420	2,600
Transport, etc.	2,315	1,100
Mining	1,940	1,700
Electricity, Gas, Water	120	200
Domestic Service	—	8,000

* The total of economically active persons in 1971 was 293,850, of whom 135,500 were male and 158,350 female.

The number of Batswana recruited for South African mines in 1972 was 23,700. The income for Botswana in deferred payment and remittances was 931,000 rand in 1972.

AGRICULTURE

LAND USE (1971)
('ooo hectares)

Arable land	428
Permanent crops	1
Meadows and pastures . . .	39,508
Forest land	958
Other land	13,546
Inland water	5,596
Total . . .	**60,037**

Source: FAO, *Production Yearbook 1971.*

PRINCIPAL CROPS

	Area ('ooo hectares)			Production ('ooo metric tons)			Yield (100 kg. per hectare)		
	1971	1972	1973	1971	1972	1973	1971	1972	1973
Maize	38	26	22	17	10	6	4.3	3.9	2.8
Millet	29	24	15	3	6	1	1.1	2.5	0.9
Sorghum . . .	161	180	92	73	68	7	4.6	3.8	1.8
Cow Peas . . .	25*	20	18	15*	n.a.	n.a.	6.0*	n.a.	n.a.
Groundnuts . .	6	1	1	6	n.a.	0.1	10.5	n.a.	1.4

* FAO estimate.

LIVESTOCK
('ooo)

	1970/71	1971/72	1972/73
Cattle . . .	1,693	2,218	2,300
Horses . . .	13	8	1
Donkeys . . .	64	38	54
Mules . . .	1	1	1
Sheep . . .	392	402	306
Goats . . .	1,033	983	664
Pigs . . .	16	15	6
Poultry . . .	238	492	470

MEAT AND DAIRY PRODUCE
('ooo metric tons)

	1969	1970	1971*
Beef . . .	21	26.6	33.0
Offal . . .	3*	1.4	1.5
Cows' Milk . .	28*	29*	30
Hen Eggs . .	0.2*	0.2*	0.3

1972 ('ooo metric tons): Beef 32.5; Offal 1.8.
1973 ('ooo metric tons): Beef 34.1; Offal 1.6.

* FAO estimate.

HIDES AND SKINS
(metric tons)

	1968	1969	1970*
Cattle Hides (raw) . . .	2,384	2,500*	2,700
Cattle Hides (salted) . . .	312	320*	320
Calf Skins (,,) . . .	68*	38	50
Sheep Skins (,,) . . .	32*	41*	32
Goat Skins (,,) . . .	80*	116*	104

* FAO estimate.

FORESTRY
ROUNDWOOD PRODUCTION
('ooo cubic metres)

1968	.	.	915
1969	.	.	922
1970	.	.	930

MINING

	Unit	1970	1971	1972
Manganese	metric tons	48,300	35,600	688
Semi-precious Stones . .	,, ,,	120.6	104.6	100.3
Diamonds* . . .	carats	463,595	871,800	2,446,426

* The Orapa diamond mine went into production in July 1971.

FINANCE
South African currency: 100 cents = 1 rand (R).
Coins: ½, 1, 2, 5, 10, 20 and 50 cents.
Notes: 1. 5, 10 and 20 rand.
Exchange rates (April 1974): £1 sterling = 1.581 rand; U.S. $1 = 67.11 S.A. cents.
100 rand = £63.27 = $149.00.

BUDGET
Twelve months ending March 31st.
(R)

Revenue	1972/73	1973/74*	Expenditure	1972/73	1973/74*
Customs and Excise, Sales Duty . . .	12,469,000	20,941,000	Parliament	93,809	102,390
Taxes and Duties . .	3,525,500	4,697,000	State President . .	2,601,221	3,576,090
Licences . . .	512,680	564,400	Ministry of Finance and Development Planning .	2,084,161	3,226,660
Receipts in respect of Departmental Services . .	847,180	1,123,555	Ministry of Health, Labour and Home Affairs . .	1,984,425	2,841,890
Posts and Telegraphs .	1,335,500	1,636,000	Ministry of Agriculture .	2,810,008	3,239,570
Revenue from Government Property . . .	2,480,100	4,440,315	Ministry of Education .	2,145,617	2,383,040
Fines . . .	58,000	43,200	Ministry of Commerce and Industry . . .	2,225,538	783,730
Reimbursements . .	511,810	1,245,100	Ministry of Local Government and Lands . .	1,650,350	2,241,720
Loan Repayments .	1,035,760	1,125,139	Ministry of Works and Communications . .	3,438,940	4,815,730
Interest . . .	100,000	255,000	Administration of Justice .	79,120	129,860
Miscellaneous . .	48,000	179,400	Attorney-General . .	1,032,067	1,286,370
Sales of State Land .	—	—	Auditor-General . .	69,801	80,570
			Recurrent Expenditure Arising from Development Expenditure	100,000	—
Total Ordinary Revenue	22,923,530	36,250,109	Public Debt Service Fund .	950,000	—
			Statutory Expenditure Public Debt . .	1,297,823	1,386,480
Grants and Loans from United Kingdom . .	602,750	600,100	Pensions, Gratuities and Compensation . .	666,600	724,600
Grant-in-Aid, United Kingdom	—	—	Salaries and Allowances, Specified Officers .	27,000	38,020
			Overseas Services Aid Scheme	249,800	193,600
Total Grants and Loans	602,750	600,100	Miscellaneous . .	20,000	30,000
			Ministry of Mineral Resources and Water Affairs. .	—	1,818,780
			Appropriations from Revenue	—	7,921,210
Total Revenue . .	23,526,280	36,850,209	Total Expenditure	23,526,280	36,820,310

* Estimates.

BOTSWANA—(STATISTICAL SURVEY)

NATIONAL DEVELOPMENT PLAN 1970–75 (R '000)

REVENUE (in sight)	TOTAL 1970–75	MAIN EXPENDITURE BY DEPARTMENTS	TOTAL 1970–75
U.K. Government	7,660	Agriculture	4,407
Netherlands Government . . .	88	Education	4,664
Danish Government	340	Shashe Complex	35,540
Swedish Government	734	Interdepartmental Projects . .	1,323
IBRD and IDA	39,928	Public Works	22,366
Others	322	Water Branch	4,814
		Others (incl. unallocated expenditure) .	26,612
		TOTAL	99,726
TOTAL	49,072	Shortfall	50,654

NATIONAL ACCOUNTS
(million rand, July 1st to June 30th)

	1968/69	1971/72
GROSS DOMESTIC PRODUCT (at Factor Cost) of which:	45.8	89.4
Agriculture, hunting, forestry and fishing	21.6	27.4
Mining and quarrying . . .	−1.2 }	18.9
Manufacturing . . .	2.8	
Electricity and water supply . .	0.3	1.4
Construction	1.9	10.0
Transport, storage and communication	3.4	4.5
Retail and wholesale trade, hotels and restaurants	3.0	6.8
Financing, insurance, real estate and business services . . .	0.5	3.1
Ownership of dwellings . .	3.0	3.0
Domestic services . . .	0.4	1.5
Other community, social and personal services . . .	0.9	1.5
Government services . . .	9.5	12.2
Unallocated	−0.2	−0.8
Indirect Taxes less subsidies . .	2.1	11.0
GROSS DOMESTIC PRODUCT (at Market Prices) . . .	47.9	100.4
Less consumption of fixed capital . .	−3.0	−5.2
NET DOMESTIC PRODUCT . .	44.9	85.2
EXPENDITURE ON GROSS DOMESTIC PRODUCT	47.9	100.4
of which:		
Government final consumption .	11.3	16.3
Private final consumption .	42.7	60.0
Increase in stocks . .	5.7	3.8
Gross fixed capital formation .	9.9	55.2
Export of goods and services .	10.3	39.8
Less Import of goods and services .	−32.0	−74.7

EXTERNAL TRADE
(R'000)

	1968	1969	1970/71*	1971/72	1972/73	1973/74†
Imports . . .	23,231	30,833	44,772	62,700	86,900	102,000
Exports . . .	7,491	13,060	20,000	31,000	41,000	58,000
Balance . . .	−15,740	−17,773	−24,772	−31,700	−45,900	−44,000

* From April 1st, 1970, the financial year is used, ending on March 31st.
† Preliminary figures.

PRINCIPAL COMMODITIES
(R'000)

IMPORTS	1972	1973*	EXPORTS	1972	1973*
Food and Live Animals . .	7,940	5,153	Meat and Meat Products .	18,628	16,743
Beverages and Tobacco . .	3,156	3,527	Hides and Skins . . .	835	953
Crude Materials, Inedible,			Other Animal Products . .	84	111
except Fuels . .	995	1,636	Mineral Products . .	19,513	7,863
Mineral Fuels, Lubricants and			Other Commodities . .	5,750	3,119
Related Materials . .	3,854	2,538			
Animal and Vegetable Oils and					
Fats	166	64			
Chemicals	2,894	3,071			
Manufactured Goods Classified					
Chiefly by Material . .	21,104	10,562			
Machinery and Transport					
Equipment . . .	33,626	20,292			
Miscellaneous Manufactured					
Articles	8,467	4,583			
Commodities and Transactions					
Not Classified According to					
Kind	1,787	2,237			
TOTAL. . .	83,989	53,663	TOTAL . .	44,810	28,789

* January to June only (provisional figures).

Of Botswana's exports of animal products in 1966 18 per cent in value (31.6 per cent in 1965) went to South Africa and 18.2 per cent to other African countries. Of the 1966 imports 65.4 per cent in value came from South Africa, and a substantial part of the remainder from Rhodesia.

TRANSPORT
RAILWAYS
(1972)

Passengers Carried*	694,445
Freight Traffic (metric tons)† . . .	1,749,636

* Internal traffic only.

† Including 1,229,641 metric tons in transit.

ROAD TRAFFIC

	1970	1971	1972	1973
Vehicles registered* .	6,215	6,462	7,900	8,357

* Excludes government vehicles (1970: 1,337; 1971: 1,582).

CIVIL AVIATION
(scheduled services)

	1971	1972	1973
Passenger-km. (million) .	9.0	10.0	14.9
Freight ('000 tonne-km.) .	80.0	76.0	90.0
Mail ('000 tonne-km.) .	16.0	11.5	10.0

COMMUNICATIONS MEDIA

	1970	1971	1972	1973
Telephones . .	3,680	4,032	5,244	6,170
Radio Licences .	9,000	n.a.	11,602	n.a.
Daily Newspapers .	1	1	1	1
Periodicals . . .	6	6	7	7

EDUCATION
(1973

	INSTITU-TIONS	STUDENTS
Primary . . .	308	95,511
Secondary . . .	25	8,763
Teacher Training . .	3	392
Vocational Training . .	25	1,521
University* . . .	1	132

* In addition, 211 students were enrolled in third-level institutions abroad.

THE CONSTITUTION

The new Constitution of Botswana came into operation on September 30th, 1966. The principal change from the 1965 Bechuanaland Constitution concerns the creation of the position of President, the holder of which took over the powers and responsibilities formerly exercised by the Prime Minister.

Executive power lies with the President of Botswana, who is also Commander-in-Chief of the armed forces. Election for the office of President is linked with the General Election of members of the National Assembly. Presidential candidates must receive at least 1,000 nominations. If there is more than one candidate for the Presidency, each candidate for office in the Assembly must declare which presidential candidate he supports. The candidate for President who commands the votes of more than half the elected members of the Assembly will be declared President. If the Presidency falls vacant the members of the National Assembly will themselves elect a new President. The President will hold office for the duration of Parliament. After the 1974 elections the President will be an ex-officio member of the assembly.

There is also a Vice-President, whose office is Ministerial. The Vice-President is appointed by the President, and acts as his deputy in the absence of the President. The Cabinet consists of the President, the Vice-President, and nine other Ministers appointed by the President. Every member of the Cabinet accepts responsibility before the National Assembly for the policies of the Government.

The legislative power is vested in Parliament, consisting of the President and the National Assembly, acting after consultation in certain cases with the House of Chiefs. The President may withhold his assent to a Bill passed by the National Assembly, but if it is again presented to him after six months, he is required to assent to it unless he dissolves Parliament within 21 days.

The House of Chiefs has the Chiefs of the eight principal tribes of Botswana as *ex officio* members, 4 members elected by sub-chiefs from their own number, and 3 members elected by the other 12 members of the House. Bills and motions relating to chieftaincy matters and alterations of the Constitution must be referred to the House, which may also deliberate and make representations on any matter, including Bills affecting tribal interests.

The National Assembly consists of the Speaker, the Attorney-General, who does not have a vote, 31 elected members, to be increased to 32 after the next elections, and 4 specially elected members. There is universal adult suffrage. The life of the Assembly is five years.

The Constitution also contains a code of human rights, enforceable by the High Court.

THE GOVERNMENT

President: Dr. Sir SERETSE KHAMA, K.B.E., LL.D.

CABINET

(March 1974)

President: Dr. Sir SERETSE KHAMA, K.B.E., LL.D.

Vice-President and Minister of Finance and Development Planning: Dr. QUET K. J. MASIRE, J.P.

Minister of Agriculture: E. S. MASISI.

Minister of Education: B. C. THEMA, M.B.E.

Minister of Local Government and Lands: K. P. MORAKE.

Minister of Commerce and Industry: D. K. KWELAGOBE.

Minister of Mineral Resources and Water Affairs: M. K. SEGOKGO.

Minister of Information and Broadcasting: E. M. K. KGABO.

Minister of Works and Communications: J. G. HASKINS, O.B.E., J.P.

Minister of Health, Labour and Home Affairs: M. P. K. NWAKO.

Minister of State: B. K. KGARI.

Assistant Minister for Finance and Development Planning: L. MAKGEKGENENE.

DIPLOMATIC REPRESENTATION

HIGH COMMISSIONS AND EMBASSIES ACCREDITED TO BOTSWANA

(In Gaborone, unless otherwise stated)
(HC) High Commission; (E) Embassy.

Austria: Pretoria, South Africa (E).

Belgium: Pretoria, South Africa (E).

Canada: Pretoria, South Africa (HC).

China (Taiwan): P.O.B. 284 (E); *Ambassador:* HSIN-YU LIU.

Czechoslovakia: Lusaka, Zambia (E).

Denmark: Lusaka, Zambia (E).

France: Lusaka, Zambia (E).

Germany, Federal Republic: Lusaka, Zambia (E).

Japan: Lusaka, Zambia (E).

Korea, Republic: Nairobi, Kenya (E).

Netherlands: Lusaka, Zambia (E).

Nigeria: P.O.B. 274 (HC); *High Commissioner:* ALFRED BABALOLA AYODELE.

Romania: Lusaka, Zambia (E).

Sweden: P.O.B. 17 (E); *Chargé d'Affaires:* ETHEL RINGBORG.

Switzerland: Dar es Salaam, Tanzania (E).

Tanzania: Lusaka, Zambia (HC).

U.S.S.R.: Lusaka, Zambia (E).

United Kingdom: P.B. 23 (HC); *High Commissioner:* Miss E. J. EMERY.

U.S.A.: P.O.B. 90 (E); *Ambassador:* CHARLES J. NELSON.

Yugoslavia: Lusaka, Zambia (E).

Zambia: P.O.B. 362 (HC); *High Commissioner:* GILBERT ILUTE YETA.

PARLIAMENT

NATIONAL ASSEMBLY

Speaker: Rev. ALBERT LOCK, C.B.E.
Attorney-General: M. D. MOKAMA.

(General Election of October 1969)

PARTY	VOTES	SEATS
Botswana Democratic Party .	52,859	24
Botswana People's Party . .	9,239	3
Botswana National Front . .	10,362	3
Botswana Independence Party .	4,601	1

HOUSE OF CHIEFS

Chairman: Chief SEEPAPITSO IV.

POLITICAL PARTIES

Botswana Democratic Party: P.O.B. 28, Gaborone; Pres. Sir SERETSE KHAMA; Vice-Pres. A. M. TSOEBEBE; Sec. Q. K. J. MASIRE; 24 seats in National Assembly.

Botswana People's Party: P.O. Francistown; Pres. P. L. MATANTE; 3 seats in National Assembly.

Botswana Independence Party: P.O. Box 37, Palapye; Pres. M. K. MPHO; Sec.-Gen. E. R. MOKOBI; Vice-Pres. J. G. GUGUSHE; one seat in National Assembly.

Botswana National Front: P.O.B. 11, Mahalapye; Parl. Leader ex-Chief BATHOEN II; Vice-Pres. G. F. KGAKGE; Sec.-Gen. M. H. MHOIWA; 3 seats in National Assembly.

JUDICIAL SYSTEM

There is a High Court at Lobatse and Magistrates' Courts in each district. Appeals lie to the Court of Appeal for Botswana.

Chief Justice: Hon. T. AKINOLA AGUDA.

Puisne Judge: Hon. F. X. ROONEY.

Registrar and Master of the High Court: T. ADEWALE ODUNOWO.

President of Court of Appeal: Hon. O. D. SCHREINER, M.C.

Justices of Appeal: Hon. A. MILNE, Hon. J. A. SMIT, Hon. I. A. MAISELS.

Chief Magistrate: A. A. OSIBOGUN.

Senior Magistrate: P. T. W. POWELL.

RELIGION

Most Christians are members of the United Congregational Church of Southern Africa. There are a large number of "Zionist" or Evangelical Christians. In 1970 there were 16,879 Roman Catholics in Botswana.

United Congregational Church of Southern Africa: P.O. Molepolole; brs. throughout Botswana.

United Methodist Church.

Methodist Church in Southern Africa.

Christian Council of Botswana: P.O.B. 355, Gaborone; Gen. Sec. Rev. BRIAN H. BAILEY.

Roman Catholic Bishop of Gaborone: Rt. Rev. U. C. J. MURPHY.

Anglican Bishop of Botswana: Rt. Rev. C. S. MALLORY.

THE PRESS

Daily News: Gaborone; Government-sponsored; circ. 9,000 in English, 5,000 in Setswana.

Kutlwano: Gaborone; monthly; Government-sponsored; in Setswana and English; circ. 10,000.

Mafeking Mail and Botswana Guardian: Mafeking; bilingual weekly; caters specially for the Mafeking district and Botswana.

Masa (*Dawn*): P.O. Francistown; a monthly publication of the Botswana People's Party.

Puisanyo: Selebi-Pikwe; f. 1972.

Puo Pha (*Straight Talk*): P.O.B. 11, Mahalapye; a monthly publication of the Botswana National Front.

Therisanyo (*Consultation*): P.O.B. 28, Gaborone; monthly publication of the Botswana Democratic Party.

RADIO

Radio Botswana: P.O.B. 52, Gaborone; broadcasts 119 hours a week in Setswana and English; f. 1965.

There were about 100,000 radio sets in 1972; Officer-in-Charge P. MOLEFHE.

FINANCE

Barclays Bank International Ltd.: Head Office: London; chief Botswana office: P.O.B. 478, Gaborone; brs. at Gaborone, Lobatse, Francistown, Mahalapye, Selebi-Pikwe and 17 agencies; Botswana Manager L. ATKINSON.

Standard Bank Ltd.: Head Office: London; brs. at Francistown, Lobatse, Mahalapye, Selebi-Pikwe, Orapa, Maun, Serowe and Gaborone and 10 agencies; Botswana Manager, Gaborone.

National Development Bank: P.O.B. 225, Gaborone; f. 1964; priority given to agricultural credit for Batswana farmers, and co-operative credit and loans for local business ventures.

TRADE AND INDUSTRY

Northern Botswana Chamber of Commerce: P.O.B. 2, Palapye; f. 1903; 28 mems.; Chair. C. W. FREEMAN; Sec. T. C. P. SHAW.

There are other Chambers of Commerce at Francistown, Serowe, Selebi-Pikwe and Mahalapye.

Botswana Meat Commission: Private Bag 4, Lobatse; f. 1966; cap. R1,588,325.

Slaughter of livestock, export of hides and carcases, boneless beef, production of by-products, canning.

Chair. R. WHYTE; Gen. Man. A. J. ROBERTS, O.B.E.; 1,100 employees (seasonal).

Botswana Game Industries (Pty.) Ltd.: Private Bag 30, Francistown; f. 1966; paid up cap. R368,000

Tanners and dressers of game skins; taxidermists, ivory buyers, manufacturers of game skin products.

Man. Dir. PETER BECKER; Technical Dir. BODO MUCHE; 210 employees.

DEVELOPMENT ORGANIZATION

Botswana Development Corporation: Development House, P.O.B. 438, Gaborone.

Botswana Trade Union Education Centre: P.O.B. 440, Gaborone.

Botswana General Workers' Organization: Francistown.

Botswana Workers' Union: Francistown.

Botswana Trade Union Congress: Francistown.

Francistown African Employees' Union: P.O.B. 74, Francistown; f. 1949; Chair. P. M. TLHALERWA; Gen. Sec. G. M. K. MMUSI; 400 mems.

Department of Co-operative Development: P.O.B. 86, Gaborone; f. 1964; by December 1971, 78 co-operative societies were registered, of which 32 were marketing co-operatives, 13 consumer co-operatives, 29 thrift and loan societies, 1 co-operative union with membership of 13 marketing and 10 consumer societies and 2 others.

TRANSPORT

RAILWAYS

The main railway line from Cape Town to Rhodesia passes through the country entering at Ramatlabama and leaving at Ramaquabane (394 miles) reaching Rhodesia at Bakaranga. Two new railway lines to serve the Selebi-Pikwe mining complex and the Morupula colliery were completed in June 1973.

Rhodesia Railways: Bulawayo, Rhodesia; operate the railway system in Botswana.

ROADS

In 1970 there were 4,984 miles of gravelled or earth road: 1,565 miles of trunk roads, 1,478 miles of main roads and 1,941 miles of district roads. There are two short lengths of bitumen surface in Lobatse and Francistown and the road between Gaborone and Lobatse is being bitumenized. An American financed 400-mile road from Nata near Francistown to Kazungula is expected to be completed by March 1976. Zambia has installed a new 50-ton ferry at Kazungula which will improve the ferry service between this politically vital area, the meeting place of the borders of Rhodesia, Botswana, Zambia and South West Africa (Namibia), and Livingstone in Zambia.

CIVIL AVIATION

The principal airports are at Francistown and Gaborone.

Botswana Airways Corporation: P.O.B. 92, Gaborone; f. 1969; owned by Botswana Government and the Burton Construction Company; service to Lusaka from Francistown linking with London and daily services operated with South African Airways between Gaborone and Johannesburg; Chair. D. E. G. VIELER; Gen. Man. C. G. KENYON; fleet of 2 Britten-Norman Islanders, 1 DC-3.

Botswana is served by South African Airways and Zambia Airways.

TOURISM

Controller of Tourism, Department of Wildlife and National Parks: Private Bag 47, Gaborone.

UNIVERSITY

University of Botswana, Lesotho and Swaziland: P.O. Roma, Lesotho; 90 teachers, 560 students.

BRAZIL

INTRODUCTORY SURVEY

Location, Climate, Language, Religion, Flag, Capital

Brazil occupies 8,511,965 square kilometres in central and north-eastern South America. To the north are Venezuela, Colombia, Guyana, Surinam and French Guiana, to the west Peru and Bolivia, with Paraguay, Argentina and Uruguay to the south. Climatic conditions vary from the tropical rain forest of the Amazon basin to the savannah grasslands of the central and southern uplands. The language is Portuguese. Over 95 per cent of the population is Roman Catholic. The national flag (proportions 10 by 7) is green with a yellow diamond in the centre charged with a blue celestial globe. The capital is Brasília, though most administrative offices still remain in Rio de Janeiro.

Recent History

From 1930 to 1945, Brazil was ruled by the benevolent dictatorship of Dr. Getúlio Vargas. Under him, stability was maintained, despite strong undercurrents of both Fascist and Communist opposition, and his corporative state made steady economic progress. Vargas resigned in 1945 and in 1946 Eurico Dutra was elected President. However, he was unable to stem the chronic inflation that had beset Brazil, and Vargas was re-elected President in 1951, but failed to create the necessary stability and committed suicide in 1955. The next President was Dr. Juscelino Kubitschek. His most conspicuous achievement was the building of the new capital, Brasília, on a jungle plateau 600 miles inland north-west of Rio. President Kubitschek was succeeded briefly by Dr. Jânio Quadros and then by the left-wing President João Goulart, who was overthrown by a military *coup* led by Gen. Humberto Castelo Branco in April 1964. Marshal Artur da Costa e Silva, who was elected President in October 1966, took office for a four-year term in March 1967. In December 1968 President da Costa e Silva promulgated an Institutional Act giving himself the power to govern the country by decree.

In early 1969 the Brazilian Government extended the security laws in order to combat opposition groups. The death sentence was also reintroduced in answer to the growing number of attacks on government property and the kidnapping of important public figures. President da Costa e Silva stood down from the presidency, following a stroke, and the government was taken over by the three heads of the armed forces in September 1969.

In October 1969 Lt.-Gen. Emílio Garrastazú Médici took office as President, having been elected by Congress under the new Constitution passed by the government junta. Throughout 1970, urban guerrilla activity was widespread: three ambassadors and a consul-general were kidnapped and held to ransom for the release of political prisoners. By means of very stern security measures subversive activity by opposition groups has been largely eliminated, although a renewed conflict between Church and State was heralded in 1973 by a series of trials and house arrests imposed on certain religious authorities for allegedly subversive activities. Gen. Ernesto Geisel was elected by an electoral college as the new President and took office in March 1974.

Government

The Federative Republic of Brazil comprises 22 States, four Territories and one Federal District. The Federal Government consists of the President and the National Security Council, and an independent judiciary. Each State has its own Governor, elected legislature and judiciary.

Defence

Military service is compulsory for one year between the ages of eighteen and forty-five. The armed forces consist of about 208,000 men—army 130,000, navy 43,000 and air force 35,000. Federal para-military forces amount to about 150,000 men. In addition, there are state militias.

Economic Affairs

Agricultural production accounts for a large percentage of Brazilian exports. The country is the world's leading coffee producer and in 1973 it was estimated that Brazil was the world's largest exporter of coffee and sugar. Manufactured goods account for about 30 per cent of exports and include shoes, orange juice, cars and buses, instant coffee, electrical appliances, computers and textiles. In 1973 exports increased by 53 per cent over the previous year. A three-year commercial treaty signed by Brazil and the EEC guarantees Brazilian exports, including beef, better access to Common Market countries. The EEC at present accounts for 33 per cent of Brazil's export trade.

Industry is expanding, particularly in the São Paulo area whose output accounts for over 50 per cent of the national total, and steel and engineering works have been established under the development plans. A second National Development Plan was drawn up at the beginning of 1974. Since 1969 a ship-building and repair industry has been created with government support. Dutch and Japanese shipbuilders have formed partnerships with local interests. Brazil's largest shipyard, which can handle ships of up to 650,000 tons, was opened in Guanabara in January 1974. About half the nation's oil requirements are produced domestically. Copper deposits estimated at 150 million tons have been discovered in Bahia State. The Central Southern area is one of the fastest expanding industrial and agricultural areas in the world. Motor car production totalled 516,000 units in 1971; the Brazilian market is at present dominated by Volkswagen but Ford, General Motors, Fiat and Toyota are currently expanding their output. Important hydro-electric projects are under way; with the vast Urubupungá project (4,600,000 kW capacity) nearing completion, Brazil signed an agreement with Paraguay in July 1973 for the construction of the world's largest hydro-electric project at Itaipu on the Paraná river. The project envisages a final capacity of 10,700,000 kW. Since the late 1960s Brazil has experienced boom conditions in her industrial sector. Inflation, traditionally the country's most pressing problem, has been progressively reduced, and in 1973, at 15 per cent, was at its lowest rate for a decade. The national economic growth rate was between 10 and 11 per cent in 1972; 4 per cent in agriculture and 15 per cent in industry. Tax reduction incentives encourage investment in certain geographic areas or specified industries, and while Brazil is able to call on her immense untapped natural resources, a large and relatively cheap work force, and an attractive investment climate, the boom is likely to continue for a number of years. However, the country's foreign debt is expected to rise rapidly in the near future, and a large proportion of foreign exchange reserves will have to be spent to meet the increased oil bill for 1974. The new administration is expected to be less liberal towards foreign capital. And, despite the boom, the disparity between rich and poor continues to be large. Brazil is a member of LAFTA and the Inter-American Development Bank.

Transport and Communications

Transport services are limited by jungles, rivers and mountains. Over large areas the aeroplane is the only practicable means of transport and Brazil has a large domestic network of internal air services. Modernization of ports, roads and railways is in progress, the most important project being the Trans-Brazilian Highway, running from Recife and Cabedelo to the Peruvian border. Ultimately its length will be about 5,000 km. The second section of the Highway (Itaituba-Humaita) was opened in January 1974. Work has begun on a complementary highway, the Perimetral Norte, due for completion in 1977; this will be 4,138 km. long and will connect Brazil with Caracas in Venezuela and Bogotá in Colombia. There are long-distance express bus services which play an important part in the scheme of public transport. Rivers are very important as a means of transport and 42,720 km. are navigable. The Amazon is navigable for 3,680 km. as far as Iquitos in Peru, and ocean-going ships can reach Manaus, 1,600 km. upstream.

Social Welfare

The trade unions and employers' organizations provide welfare services financed by joint contributions. According to the constitution, employers must fulfil certain obligations, including compulsory accident insurance.

Education

Pre-elementary schooling is provided in urban areas for children up to seven years old. Education is free in official primary schools and compulsory between the ages of seven and fourteen, although the tendency in rural districts for children to start school late brings the average enrolment age to over nine years. Secondary education is divided into a four-year basic course and an advanced course of three years; where necessary it is free, but a system of repayable grants is being encouraged, and the majority of secondary schools are private. The Federal Government is responsible for higher education and there are 64 universities and 555 other institutions of higher education, with a total of over 560,000 students.

Although the high drop-out rate of children at elementary level is still a serious problem, illiteracy has steadily been reduced. A literacy drive (*Movimento Brasileiro de Alfabetização—Mobral*) was launched in 1971, aiming to reach 16 million illiterates by 1980. In 1973 some five per cent of the Federal Budget was to be directly invested in education.

Tourism

Rio de Janeiro, with its famous beaches, is the centre of the tourist trade. Like Salvador, Recife and other towns, it has excellent examples of Portuguese colonial and modern architecture. The new capital, Brasília, incorporates a new concept of city planning and is the nation's showpiece. Other attractions are the Iguaçu Falls, seventh largest (by volume) in the world, and the tropical forests of the Amazon basin.

Visas are not required to visit Brazil by nationals of the following countries: Canada, EEC countries (except Ireland), Greece, Liechtenstein, Morocco, Norway, Portugal, Spain, Sweden, Switzerland, U.S.A. and Latin American countries except Cuba.

Sport

Football is by far the most popular sport; Brazil won the World Cup in 1958, 1962 and 1970. Basketball is the second great national sport, and tennis, water sports, golf, horse racing and recently underwater fishing are also popular.

Public Holidays

1974: September 7th (Independence Day), November 2nd (All Souls' Day), November 15th (Proclamation of the Republic), December 25th (Christmas Day).

1975: January 1st (New Year's Day), February 26th, 27th (Carnival), March 28th (Good Friday), April 21st (National Holiday), May 1st (Labour Day), May 29th (Corpus Christi). All important religious and local festivals.

Weights and Measures

The metric system is in force.

Currency and Exchange Rates

100 centavos = 1 cruzeiro.

Exchange rates (April 1974):
£1 sterling = 15.18 cruzeiros;
U.S. $1 = 6.43 cruzeiros.

STATISTICAL SURVEY

AREA AND POPULATION

	CENSUS POPULATION†				
AREA	September 1st, 1950	September 1st, 1960	September 1st, 1970		
			Total	Males	Females
8,511,965 sq. km.*	51,976,357	70,119,071	93,139,037	46,331,343	46,807,694

Estimated Mid-Year Population: 96,082,000 in 1971; 98,854,000 in 1972; 101,707,000 in 1973.

* 3,286,488 square miles.　　　　† Excluding Indian jungle population, numbering 45,429 in 1950.

ADMINISTRATIVE DIVISIONS
(1970 census)

STATE	POPULATION	CAPITAL	STATE	POPULATION	CAPITAL
Acre . . .	215,299	Rio Branco	Piauí . . .	1,680,573	Teresina
Alagôas . . .	1,588,109	Maceió	Rio de Janeiro . .	4,742,884	Niterói
Amazonas . .	955,235	Manaus	Rio Grande do Norte	1,550,244	Natal
Bahia . . .	7,493,470	Salvador	Rio Grande do Sul .	6,664,891	Pôrto Alegre
Ceará . . .	4,361,603	Fortaleza	Santa Catarina .	2,901,734	Florianópolis
Espírito Santo .	1,599,333	Vitória	São Paulo . .	17,771,948	São Paulo
Goiás . . .	2,938,677	Goiânia	Sergipe . . .	900,744	Aracajú
Guanabara . .	4,251,918	Rio de Janeiro	DISTRITO FEDERAL .	537,492	Brasília
Maranhão . .	2,992,686	São Luís	FEDERAL TERRITORY:		
Mato Grosso . .	1,597,090	Cuiabá	Amapá . . .	114,359	Macapá
Minas Gerais . .	11,487,415	Belo Horizonte	Roraima . .	40,885	Boa Vista
Pará . . .	2,167,018	Belém	Rondônia . .	111,064	Pôrto Velho
Paraíba . . .	2,382,617	João Pessôa	Fernando de		
Paraná . . .	6,929,868	Curitiba	Noronha . .	1,241	
Pernambuco . .	5,160,640	Recife			

PRINCIPAL TOWNS
(1970 census)

Brasília (capital)	.	271,570	Curitiba . . .	609,026	Natal . . .	264,379
São Paulo .	.	5,924,615	Duque de Caxias .	431,397	Maceió . . .	263,670
Rio de Janeiro .	.	4,251,918	Santo André . .	418,826	Juiz de Fora . .	238,510
Belo Horizonte .	.	1,235,030	Goiânia . . .	380,773	Guarulhos . .	236,811
Recife (Pernambuco) .		1,060,701	Campinas . .	375,864	João Pessôa . .	221,546
Salvador (Bahia) .	.	1,007,195	Santos . . .	345,630	Teresina . .	220,487
Pôrto Alegre .	.	885,545	Niterói . . .	324,246	Ribeirão Prêto . .	212,879
Fortaleza . .	.	857,980	Manaus . . .	311,622	São Bernardo do Campo	201,662
Nova Iguaçu .	.	727,140	Osasco . . .	283,073	Olinda . . .	196,342
Belém (Pará) .	.	633,374	São Luís . . .	265,486	Aracajú . . .	183,670

Births and Deaths (1965–70): Average annual birth rate 37.8 per 1,000; death rate 9.5 per 1,000 (United Nations estimates).

ECONOMICALLY ACTIVE POPULATION*
(1970 census)

	Males	Females	Total
Agriculture, Hunting, Forestry and Fishing .	11,832,699	1,257,659	13,090,358
Mining, Manufacturing, Construction, Utilities .	4,659,535	635,892	5,295,427
Commerce	1,893,152	370,387	2,263,539
Transport, Storage and Communications . .	1,182,660	61,735	1,244,395
Services	2,712,065	3,537,391	6,249,456
Others (incl. activities not adequately described) .	937,954	257,338	1,195,292
TOTAL ECONOMICALLY ACTIVE . .	23,218,065	6,120,402	29,338,467

* Excluding persons seeking work for the first time, numbering 218,757 (males 173,712, females 45,045) at the time of the census.

AGRICULTURE
('ooo tons)

	1967	1968	1969	1970*
Coffee	3,015	2,115	2,567	1,726
Cotton (Ginned) . . .	1,692	1,999	2,111	2,173
Maize	12,825	12,814	12,693	15,381
Beans (Feijão)	2,547	2,420	2,200	2,305
Rice	6,792	6,652	6,394	7,482
Manioc	27,268	29,203	30,074	31,181
Wheat . . .	629	856	1,374	1,657
Potatoes (incl. Sweet Potatoes) .	3,692	3,727	3,682	3,717
Sugar Cane . . .	77,087	76,611	75,247	91,113
Cocoa	195	149	211	226
Oranges	2,505	2,717	2,897	3,339
Tobacco Leaf . . .	243	258	250	244
Bananas (million) . . .	8,056	8,437	9,266	9,871
Ground Nuts . . .	751	754	754	928

* Provisional figures.

COFFEE PRODUCTION

STATES	QUANTITY (tons)			VALUE ('ooo cruzeiros)		
	1968	1969	1970*	1968	1969	1970*
Pará	542	547	568	163	166	226
Ceará	10,278	10,082	9,697	3,190	5,005	7,345
Paraíba	1,105	1,183	1,272	221	395	424
Pernambuco . . .	15,808	14,152	14,547	5,508	6,647	10,168
Alagôas	1,012	626	508	369	316	382
Bahia	42,684	43,282	41,966	12,496	18,211	28,333
Minas Gerais . .	240,000	164,000	392,000	107,502	118,941	377,398
Espírito Santo . .	196,000	68,000	228,000	94,968	36,822	157,890
Rio de Janeiro . .	13,971	9,919	7,152	3,207	2,791	2,656
São Paulo . . .	552,000	732,000	588,000	320,528	663,192	644,448
Paraná . . .	1,004,000	1,492,000	196,000	607,809	1,173,458	230,790
Santa Catarina . .	3,283	3,127	3,068	764	980	1,402
Mato Grosso . .	12,633	12,425	13,025	4,286	6,813	9,122
Goiás . . .	21,727	15,356	13,442	6,277	5,459	6,478
TOTAL BRAZIL .	2,115,404	2,567,014	1,509,520	1,167,387	2,039,314	1,477,219

* Provisional figures.

LIVESTOCK
('ooo)

YEAR	CATTLE	HORSES	DONKEYS AND MULES	PIGS	SHEEP	GOATS
1965 . .	90,505	9,344	7,707	63,534	22,312	14,258
1966 . .	89,969	9,155	7,603	62,080	22,170	13,927
1967 . .	89,896	9,238	7,775	63,406	23,065	14,332
1968 . .	92,739	9,146	7,826	64,924	24,606	14,815
1969 . .	95,150	9,100	7,754	65,867	24,449	14,637
1970 . .	97,864	9,114	7,745	66,374	24,727	14,609

FISHING
(metric tons)

1966	1967	1968	1969	1970	1971
435,787	429,422	500,387	501,197	526,292	591,543

MINING

		1966	1967	1968	1969	1970	1971
Bauxite	('ooo metric tons)	250	303	314	362	510	585
Coal	(,, ,, ,,)	3,666	4,339	4,828	5,127	5,172	5,666
Iron Ore	(,, ,, ,,)	23,254	22,298	25,123	27,157	36,381	37,676
Manganese Ore	(,, ,, ,,)	1,455	1,358	2,097	2,011	2,732	2,377
Lead	(,, ,, ,,)	332	296	321	341	354	352
Dolomite	(,, ,, ,,)	201	225	353	707	608	461
Sea Salt	(,, ,, ,,)	1,433	1,087	1,248	1,630	1,826	1,477
Gold	(kilos)	5,224	5,368	5,325	5,354	5,830	5,116
Silver	(,,)	6,916	14,888	14,049	12,170	11,108	19,408

Source: *Anuário Mineral Brasileiro*, Ministério das Minas e Energia.

INDUSTRY

	Unit	1970	1971	1972
Crude Petroleum	('ooo cu. metres)	9,686*	10,114†	9,950‡
Asphalt	(tons)	702,295	575,559	704,156
Electrical Power	(million kWh.)	45,460	50,988	53,767
Steel Ingots	('ooo metric tons)	5,390	5,997	6,518
Rolled Steel	(,,)	257	335	299
Shaped and Steel Bars	(,,)	772	855	896
Steel Plates	(,,)	1,633	1,968	2,313
Cement	(,,)	9,002	9,803	11,381
Pig Iron	(,,)	4,205	4,686	5,300
Sugar	(,,)	5,070	5,081	5,926
Paper	(tons)	1,098,910	1,237,012	1,344,960
Fertilizers	(,,)	941,069	1,303,494	n.a.
Tyres	('ooo)	8,456	9,383	10,800
Motor Vehicles	(,,)	416	516	611

* Including 151,720 cubic metres of natural gas liquids.
† Including 218,299 cubic metres of natural gas liquids.
‡ Including 238,415 cubic metres of natural gas liquids.

FINANCE
100 centavos = 1 cruzeiro.

Coins: 1, 2, 5, 10, 20 and 50 centavos; 1 cruzeiro.

Notes: 1, 5, 10, 50, 100 and 500 cruzeiros.

Exchange rates (April 1974): £1 sterling = 15.18 cruzeiros; U.S. $1 = 6.43 cruzeiros.
100 cruzeiros = £6.59 = $15.55.

BUDGET
(million cruzeiros)

REVENUE	1972	1973	EXPENDITURE	1972	1973
Taxes	29,051	40,551	Legislative and Auxiliary . .	250	315
Patrimonial Revenue . .	25	69	Judiciary	324	436
Industrial Revenue . .	70	50	Executive	31,602	43,083
Other Revenue . . .	380	655	Presidency	148	211
Extraordinary . . .	761	481	Air	1,654	2,063
			Agriculture . . .	477	546
			Communications . .	395	478
			Education and Culture . .	1,811	2,284
			Army	3,256	3,870
			Finance	614	629
			Industry and Commerce .	40	48
			Interior	686	836
			Justice	163	209
			Marine	1,607	1,939
			Mines and Power . .	1,163	1,405
			Foreign Affairs . .	230	270
			Health	400	476
			Work and Social Welfare .	271	310
			Transport . . .	4,346	5,496
			Planning and General Co-ordination . .	156	200
			Unspecified Items . .	14,179	21,815
TOTAL (including others)	32,177	43,834	TOTAL (including others)	32,177	43,834

NATIONAL ACCOUNTS
(million cruzeiros)

	1966	1967	1968	1969
NET DOMESTIC PRODUCT . . .	42,906	57,972	78,281	103,682
Income paid abroad . . .	508	787	922	1,234
NET NATIONAL INCOME . .	42,398	57,185	77,359	102,449
Indirect taxes *less* subsidies .	8,159	9,981	16,654	22,844
NET NATIONAL PRODUCT . .	50,557	67,166	94,013	125,292
Depreciation allowances . . .	2,659	3,533	4,945	6,591
AVAILABLE RESOURCES (GROSS NATIONAL PRODUCT)	53,216	70,699	98,958	131,883
Private	45,384	61,833	84,356	115,233
Governmental	7,892	8,865	14,602	16,650
CONSUMPTION EXPENDITURE AND GROSS FIXED CAPITAL FORMATION	53,275	71,534	100,563	133,023
Private consumption expenditure .	38,837	52,200	71,788	95,606
Government consumption expenditure	6,251	8,486	11,423	15,468
Gross fixed capital formation . .	8,199	10,324	16,635	21,949
Increase in stocks . . .	— 12	524	712	n.a.
Balance of exports and imports of goods and services . . .	449	— 48	—684	94
GROSS NATIONAL EXPENDITURE . .	53,724	71,486	99,879	133,117
Less Income paid abroad . .	508	787	922	1,234
NATIONAL EXPENDITURE . . .	53,216	70,699	98,957	131,883

CURRENCY IN CIRCULATION AND GOLD RESERVES

	1969	1970	1971	1972
Currency in Circulation (million cruzeiros) .	5,387	6,720	8,555	11,547
Gold Reserves (kilos)	40,154	40,154	40,154	41,168

BALANCE OF PAYMENTS
(U.S. $ million)

	1970			1971		
	Credit	Debit	Balance	Credit	Debit	Balance
Goods and Services:						
Merchandise trade f.o.b. . . .	2,739	2,507	232	2,876	3,250	− 374
Freight on merchandise . . .	87	135	− 42	} 94	163	− 69
Insurance on merchandise . .	8	5	3			
Port disbursements . . .	56	63	− 7	} 73	276	− 203
Other transportation . . .	16	146	−130			
Travel	30	160	−130	36	171	− 135
Investment income . . .	49	402	−353	45	465	− 420
Other government services . .	36	105	− 69	42	128	− 86
Non-merchandise insurance . .	3	18	− 15	} 156	221	− 65
Other private services . . .	93	158	− 65			
Total Goods and Services . .	3,117	3,699	−582	3,322	4,674	−1,352
Unrequited Transfers:						
Private	74	61	13	84	77	7
Government	13	5	8	10	6	4
Total Current Account . .	3,204	3,765	−561	3,416	4,757	−1,341
Capital Flows:						
Direct investment . . .	121	14	107	} 679		679
Other private long-term . .	454	229	225			
Other private short-term . .	336	—	336	518		518
Local government . . .	11	—	11	82	(net)	82
Central government . . .	452	248	204	299		299
Total Non-monetary Sectors .	1,374	491	883	1,578		1,578
Private monetary institutions .	260	28	232	436	153	283
Central bank	13	90	− 77	—	80*	− 80*
Total Capital Account . .	1,647	609	1,038	—	—	1,781*
Allocation of Special Drawing Rights .	59	—	59	47	—	47
Net Errors and Omissions . .	38	—	38	72	—	72
Balance (net monetary movements)	574	—	574	559	—	559
of which:						
Increase in reserves, etc. . .	—	574	−574	—	559	− 559

* Net.

OVERSEAS INVESTMENT IN BRAZIL, 1972
(U.S. $'000)

Countries of Origin	Investments	Reinvestments	Total
United States . . .	656,463	615,832	1,272,295
German Federal Republic . .	271,769	100,601	372,370
Canada	236,011	69,337	305,348
United Kingdom . . .	85,380	195,402	280,782
Switzerland	193,058	60,752	253,810
France	43,356	121,755	165,111
Japan	185,645	7,067	192,712
Panama	76,292	22,021	98,313
Netherlands Antilles . .	40,270	36,858	77,128
Netherlands	40,538	29,782	70,320
Sweden	39,338	29,677	69,015
Belgium	45,490	12,769	58,259
Others	167,318	21,322	188,640
Total . . .	2,080,928	1,323,175	3,403,103

EXTERNAL TRADE
(U.S. $ million)

			1968	1969	1970	1971	1972*
Imports	.	.	2,132	2,265	2,849	3,701	4,783
Exports	.	.	1,881	2,311	2,739	2,904	3,991

* Provisional figures.

PRINCIPAL COMMODITIES

IMPORTS	1972* Quantity (tons)	1972* Value (U.S.$ '000)
Special Transactions . .	16,304	46,846
Live Animals . . .	6,214	7,683
Vegetable Products . .	2,315,450	272,102
Animal and Vegetable Fats and Oils . . .	77,423	27,702
Food, Beverages, Vinegar and Tobacco . . .	42,838	23,969
Mineral Products . .	29,058,784	697,395
Products of the Chemical and Allied Industries . .	4,283,895	693,628
Plastic Materials, Resins and Rubber . . .	217,845	116,775
Paper-making Materials, Paper	416,788	127,087
Base Metals and Articles of Base Metal . . .	1,381,304	504,163
Machinery and Mechanical Appliances, Electrical Equipment . . .	352,071	1,493,695
Transport Equipment .	87,967	360,094
Optical, Photographic and Measuring instruments, Clocks and Watches .	10,999	207,613
TOTAL IMPORTS .	**38,487,342**	**4,783,273**

EXPORTS	1972* Quantity (tons)	1972* Value (U.S.$ '000)
Special Transactions . .	263,447	34,119
Live Animals and Animal Products . . .	253,910	252,133
Live Animals . . .	2,867	2,177
Vegetable Products . .	2,649,948	1,214,706
Bananas . . .	114,189	9,584
Brazil Nuts . . .	37,577	20,299
Coffee . . .	1,050,156	989,218
Maté . . .	17,856	3,236
Oranges . . .	66,633	4,741
Rice . . .	1,897	153
Animal and Vegetable Oils and Fats . . .	293,356	111,480
Carnauba Wax . .	12,570	11,222
Castor Oil . . .	127,182	53,817
Food, Beverages, Vinegar and Tobacco . . .	5,487,186	941,437
Cocoa Beans . .	102,254	59,156
Cocoa Butter . .	27,333	33,134
Sugar . . .	2,534,910	403,548
Ethyl Alcohol . .	9,669	838
Tobacco Leaf . .	63,218	46,674
Mineral Products . .	34,122,780	322,262
Haematite . .	30,512,459	231,707
Manganese Ore . .	1,174,682	27,262
Products of Chemical and Allied Industries . .	58,910	63,053
Hides and Skins . .	42,969	76,343
Wood, Charcoal and Cork .	835,882	120,091
Pinewood . .	453,436	63,143
Textiles and Textile Articles	569,024	371,002
Cotton (raw) . .	284,223	188,702
Sisal . . .	152,103	22,489
Machinery and Mechanical Appliances, Electrical Equipment . . .	44,339	139,629
Transport Equipment . .	37,526	54,764
Miscellaneous Manufactured Articles . . .	3,356	6,748
TOTAL EXPORTS .	**45,693,828**	**3,991,219**

1970 Imports: 28,073,605 tons; U.S.$ 2,849,243,000.
1971 Imports: 32,921,952 tons; U.S.$ 3,701,449,000.

1970 Exports: 39,970,000 tons; U.S.$ 2,738,922,000.
1971 Exports: 43,824,286 tons; U.S.$ 2,903,856,000.

* Provisional figures.

PRINCIPAL COUNTRIES
(U.S. $'ooo)

	IMPORTS			EXPORTS		
	1969	1970	1971	1969	1970	1971
Argentina . . .	155,930	170,740	131,684	170,887	185,652	200,581
Belgium-Luxembourg .	36,145	44,400	58,831	64,417	72,642	63,197
Canada	39,211	70,839	99,859	28,634	40,586	42,820
Chile	29,474	35,684	32,559	24,096	23,715	31,645
Denmark . . .	46,977	23,658	26,839	41,121	53,557	37,768
Finland . . .	11,820	14,179	20,443	23,964	20,028	11,262
France	67,148	88,569	145,777	99,048	110,048	95,752
German Federal Republic	286,133	359,461	474,929	220,055	235,506	256,374
Italy	76,073	87,825	123,640	164,404	198,271	202,684
Japan	105,660	177,804	260,421	105,287	144,940	158,387
Netherlands . . .	38,100	49,797	59,975	135,080	154,003	175,759
Norway . . .	23,263	22,327	28,732	27,707	33,385	25,908
Peru	8,364	10,158	14,718	4,874	7,664	11,427
Poland . . .	10,870	11,099	50,090	18,213	23,841	24,056
Saudi Arabia . .	42,376	57,556	131,241	32	19	96
Spain	22,787	32,241	48,818	66,527	107,133	94,356
Sweden . . .	65,575	53,281	75,727	59,706	69,202	53,829
Switzerland . . .	54,992	59,039	72,212	12,462	17,412	17,847
United Kingdom .	90,600	160,870	216,235	99,202	129,804	126,624
U.S.A. . . .	681,971	918,108	1,061,865	609,757	676,058	749,151
U.S.S.R. . . .	16,157	3,491	4,313	43,674	21,237	44,799
Venezuela . . .	60,840	59,012	62,325	4,530	8,203	11,600
Other Countries .	294,190	339,105	500,216	287,492	406,006	467,993
TOTAL . .	2,264,656	2,849,243	3,701,449	2,311,169	2,738,912	2,903,856

TOURISM
(Number of visitors)

1966	1967	1968	1969	1970	1971	1972
133,487	141,426	136,065	162,191	194,186	287,926	333,763

TRANSPORT
RAILWAYS

	PASSENGERS ('ooo)	ANIMALS ('ooo tons)	BAGGAGE AND PARCELS ('ooo metric tons)	FREIGHT ('ooo metric tons)
1968 . .	367,376	992	176	59,471
1969 . .	355,780	783	149	48,073
1970 . .	332,509	568	135	49,747
1971 . .	308,781	413	115	47,404
1972 . .	313,760	448	88	47,918

ROADS
(number of motor vehicles)

YEAR	CARS	LORRIES	BUSES	MOTOR CYCLES (all types)
1966 . .	1,336,952	817,746	81,274	94,714
1967 . .	1,417,895	569,470	53,254	91,772
1968 . .	1,319,890	578,952	46,304	85,822
1969 . .	1,521,884	615,713	50,927	89,326
1970 . .	1,795,846	615,350	50,529	89,209
1971 . .	2,073,049	654,437	57,042	82,708

SHIPPING
(Vessels and Freight entered)

	NUMBER OF VESSELS	FREIGHT ('000 metric tons)
1968 . .	42,202	68,783
1969 . .	41,042	72,591
1970 . .	40,966	81,878
1971* . .	29,654	95,161
1972 . .	31,331	110,347

* Excluding vessels in transit.

CIVIL AVIATION
(Embarked passengers, mail and cargo)

	1969	1970*	1971†
Number of passengers ('000) . .	3,066	2,052	3,832
Freight (metric tons)	39,742	48,265	48,520
Mail (metric tons) .	3,340	3,317	3,307

* Revised.   † Preliminary.

EDUCATION
1971

	INSTITUTIONS	TEACHERS	PUPILS
Primary	148,690*	476,663*	13,640,967*
Secondary . . .	15,641	336,212	4,562,126
Higher . . .	2,473†	58,278†	476,164†

* Preliminary.   † 1972 figures.

Source: Instituto Brasileiro de Estatística, Rio de Janeiro.

THE CONSTITUTION

Brazil is a Republican Federal state made up of the indissoluble Union of the States, the Federal District and the Territories. The Federal District is the capital of the Union.

The Union's competence includes maintaining relations with foreign states and making treaties with them, and taking part in international organizations; declaring war and making peace; decreeing a state of siege; organizing the armed forces, planning and guaranteeing national security, issuing currency; supervising credits, etc.; establishing national services, including communications, development and education services; legislating on the execution of the Constitution and federal services and on civil, commercial, penal, procedural, electoral, agrarian, maritime and labour law. The Union, States, Federal District and Municipalities are forbidden to make any distinction between Brazilians, establish any religious cults or churches against the public interest, and to deny public documents.

The Union may only intervene in state affairs in matters of extreme urgency, such as national security, and then only by Presidential decree. The States are responsible for electing their Governors by universal suffrage by direct secret ballot. The state law will decree the establishment of Municipalities, after due consultation with the local population; it will also decree the division of the States into districts; municipal organization may vary from state to state.

LEGISLATIVE POWER

The legislative power is exercised by the National Congress, which is composed of the Chamber of Deputies and the Federal Senate. Elections for deputies and senators take place simultaneously throughout the country; candidates for Congress must be Brazilian by birth, have full exercise of their political rights and be over twenty-one in the case of deputies and over thirty-five in the case of senators. Congress meets twice a year in ordinary sessions, and extraordinary sessions may be convened on demand of a third of the members of either House or the President. Each Chamber arranges its own internal procedure.

The *Chamber of Deputies* is made up of representatives of the people, elected by direct secret ballot for a period of four years. The number of deputies is fixed at an average of 280 distributed according to the number of electors in each state. There will be a minimum of seven deputies to each State and each Territory will have one deputy.

The *Federal Senate* is composed of representatives of the States, elected by direct secret ballot. Each State will elect three senators with a mandate for eight years, with elections after four years of one-third of the members and after another four years of the remaining two-thirds. Each Senator is elected with his substitute. The Senate approves, by secret ballot, the choice of Magistrates, when required by the Constitution; of the Attorney-General of the Republic, of the Minister of the Accounts Tribunal, of the Prefect of the Federal District, of the Territorial Governors, of the permanent heads of diplomatic missions and other public servants.

The *National Congress* is responsible for legislating on all matters within the competence of the Union; national and regional plans and programmes, the armed forces in times of peace and territorial limits. Voting on the budget is carried out by both houses in joint session. It is also responsible for making definitive resolutions on Presidential treaties, authorizing the President to leave the country; to declare war, to approve boundary changes in the States or Territories. The Executive power must send any bills proposed by the President to the National Congress within fifteen days of signing. Constitutional amendments must be proposed by at least a third of the total number of members of both houses or by the President. Amendments are ratified by a simple majority. No changes may be made to the Constitution during a state of siege. Any Presidential bill must be considered by Congress within forty-five days and the President may oblige Congress to reconsider a rejected bill within ten days. The President is exclusively responsible for legislation concerning finance, creating new public offices, etc., deciding or modifying the armed forces' strength, matters concerning the administration of the Federal District and the Territories.

EXECUTIVE POWER

Executive power is exercised by the President of the Republic, aided by the Ministers of State. Candidates for the Presidency and Vice-Presidency must be Brazilian born, be in full exercise of their political rights and be over thirty-five years of age. The President and Vice-President will be elected by an electoral college in public session by nominal voting. The electoral college will consist of members of National Congress and delegates chosen by the State Legislative Assemblies. The candidates receiving an absolute majority of votes will be considered elected and will serve for a term of five years. If the President violates any of his responsibilities he may be impeached by a two-thirds majority of the Deputies and judged by the Supreme Tribunal or the Senate according to the nature of his crime.

The Ministers of State are chosen by the President and their duties include carrying out the President's decrees, expediting instructions for the enactment of laws, decrees and regulations, presentation to the President of an annual report of their activities.

National security is the responsibility of every citizen. There is a National Security Council, composed of the President and the Vice-President of the Republic and all the Ministers of State.

JUDICIAL POWER

Judicial power in the Union is exercised by the Supreme Federal Tribunal; the Federal Recourse Tribunals and federal judges; Military Tribunals and judges; Electoral Tribunals and judges; Labour Tribunals and judges. Judges are appointed for life; they may not undertake any other employment, receive any percentages from cases tried by them or engage in any party political activity. The Tribunals elect their own presidents and organize their own internal structure.

The *Supreme Federal Tribunal*, situated in the Union capital, has jurisdiction over the whole national territory and is composed of sixteen Ministers. The Ministers are nominated by the President after approval by the Senate, from Brazilian-born citizens, over the age of thirty-five, of proved judicial knowledge and experience.

POLITICAL AND PERSONAL RIGHTS

Registration and voting are compulsory for all Brazilian citizens over the age of eighteen except those who are illiterate or unable to express themselves in the national language or are temporarily or definitively deprived of political rights. The organization of political parties is regulated by federal law, with the guarantee of the fundamental rights of man. Congressional representation is achieved when five per cent of the total electorate votes for one party, with a minimum of seven per cent in each of seven states.

All citizens are equal in the eyes of the law, regardless of sex, race, employment, religion or political convictions; any racialism will be prosecuted; there is no death penalty (except under military legislation in case of external war), no life imprisonment, banishment or confiscation of property. Rights concerning citizens' life, liberty, security and property are inviolable.

The President may declare a state of siege in cases of serious breaches of order or the likelihood of their occurring; or war. Except in cases of war, the state of siege may not last longer than sixty days, with the possibility of extension with the approval of Congress. During a state of siege Congress may suspend constitutional guarantees, and also the immunity of federal deputies and senators.

The Constitution also lays down principles of economic and social order, concerning freedom of enterprise, dignity of human labour, social function of ownership, harmony and solidarity in production, economic development and repression of abuse of economic power. Strikes are not permitted in public services and essential activities, as defined by law. The constitution lays down certain rights for workers, including limited hours of work, paid holidays and social welfare benefits; voting in trade union elections is compulsory.

The law protects family life; education is the right of all, with equal opportunity. Education will be organized by the States and the Federal District and the Union will give technical and financial assistance to develop education.

THE GOVERNMENT

HEAD OF THE STATE

President of the Republic: Gen. ERNESTO GEISEL.
Vice-President: Gen. ADALBERTO PEREIRA DOS SANTOS.

CABINET
(*March* 1974)

Minister of Justice: ARMANDO RIBEIRO FALCÃO.

Minister of Foreign Affairs: ANTÓNIO FRANCISCO AZEREIDO DA SILVEIRA.

Minister of Finance: Prof. MÁRIO HENRIQUE SIMONSEN.

Minister of Planning and General Co-ordination: Prof. JOÃO PAULO DOS REIS VELLOSO.

Minister of the Interior: Prof. MAURÍCIO RANGEL REIS.

Minister of Industry and Commerce: SEVERO FAGUNDES GOMES.

Minister of Mines and Energy: SHIGEAKI UEKI.

Minister of Agriculture: Prof. ALYSSON PAULINELLI.

Minister of Transport: Gen. DIRCEU DE ARAÚJO NOGUEIRA.

Minister of Communications: Capt. EUCLIDES QUANDT DE OLIVEIRA.

Minister of Education and Culture: NEY BRAGA.

Minister of Health: Prof. PAULO DE ALMEIDA MACHADO.

Minister of Labour and Social Welfare: ARNALDO DA COSTA PRIETO.

Minister of the Army: Gen. SILVIO COUTO COELHO DA FROTA.

Minister of the Navy: Adm. GERALDO DE AZEVEDO HENNING.

Minister of Air: Brig. JOELMIR CAMPOS DE ARARIPE MACEDO.

Chief of the President's Military Household: Gen. DILERMANDO DO GOMES MONTEIRO.

Chief of the President's Civil Household: Gen. GOLBERY DO COUTO E SILVA.

Chief of the National Information Agency: Gen. JOÃO BATISTA DE OLIVEIRA FIGUEIREDO.

DIPLOMATIC REPRESENTATION

EMBASSIES AND LEGATIONS ACCREDITED TO BRAZIL

(Brasília, D.F., unless otherwise stated)

(E) Embassy; (L) Legation.

Algeria: SQS 308, Bloco B. Apt. 201 (E); *Ambassador:* ALI LAKHDARI.

Argentina: SDS, Edifício Venâncio VI, 4° andar (E); *Ambassador:* JOSÉ MARÍA ALVAREZ DE TOLEDO.

Australia: SDS, Edifício Venâncio IV, 5° andar, salas 513-514 (E); *Ambassador:* FREDERICK THOMAS HOMER.

Austria: SES, Av. das Nações, Lote 40 (E); *Ambassador:* FRIEDRICH HARTLMAYR.

Bangladesh: Av. W-3 Sul, Quadra 705, Bloco A, Casa 19 (E); *Ambassador:* MUSTAFA KAMAL.

Belgium: Av. das Nações, Lote 32 (E); *Ambassador:* Baron PATERNOTTE DE LA VAILLÉ.

Bolivia: SHIG-Sul, Av. W-3, Quadra 706, Bloco H, Casa 80 (E); *Ambassador:* Col. MARIO ADETT ZAMORA.

Bulgaria: SHIG-Sul, Av. W-3, Quadra 704, Bloco D, Casa 4 (E); *Ambassador:* ATANAS KALBOV.

Canada: SDS, Edifício Venâncio IV, 6° andar (E); *Ambassador:* BARRY C. STEERS.

Chile: SCS, Edifício Mineiro, 5° andar (E); *Ambassador:* HERNÁN CUBILLOS LEIVA.

China (Taiwan): SCS, Edifício Ceará, 5° andar (E); *Ambassador:* CHU FU-SUNG.

Colombia: SQS 113, Edifício Leme, Bloco C, Apt. 105 (E); *Ambassador:* Dr. VÍCTOR G. RICARDO.

Costa Rica: SQS 206, Bloco J, Apt. 503 (E); *Ambassador:* HUMBERTO NIGRO BORBÓN.

Czechoslovakia: Av. das Nações, Lote 21 (E); *Ambassador:* PAVEL BOJAR (also represents Cuba).

Denmark: SQS 105, Bloco F, Apt. 205 (E); *Ambassador:* HANS VON HAFFNER.

Dominican Republic: Av. W-3, Quadra 703, Bloco M, Casa 3 (E); *Ambassador:* FRANZ BAEHR CABRAL.

Ecuador: Av. W-3, Quadra 503, Bloco A, entrada 39, 2° andar (E); *Ambassador:* LUIS VALENCIA RODRÍGUEZ.

Egypt: SQS 106, Bloco J, Apt. 202 (E); *Ambassador:* Dr. HUSSEIN IBRAHIM CHERIF.

El Salvador: SCS, Edifício Casa de São Paulo, Conj. 1307 (E); *Ambassador:* OSCAR RANK ALTAMIRANO.

Finland: SQS 114, Bloco D, Apt. 102 (E); *Ambassador:* HEIKKI LEPPO.

France: SQS 105, Bloco F, Apt. 101–102 (E); *Ambassador:* PAUL FOUCHET.

German Democratic Republic: SHI-Norte, QL 2/8, Casa 19 (E); *Ambassador:* GÜNTHER SEVERIN.

Germany, Federal Republic: Av. das Nações, Lote 25 (E); *Ambassador:* HORST RÖDING.

Ghana: SQS 111, Bloco B, Apt. 603 (E); *Ambassador:* (vacant).

Greece: SCS, Edifício Gilberto Salomão, Bloco M, 2° andar, Conj. 207–211 (E); *Ambassador:* ARISTOTELIS HATZOUDIS (also accred. to Ecuador).

Guatemala: SQS 208, Bloco F, Apt. 102 (E); *Ambassadress:* FRANCISCA FERNÁNDEZ HALL ZUÑIGA.

Guyana: Edifício Venâncio III, salas 410–414; *Chargé d'Affaires:* HAROLDO SAHADEO.

Haiti: SHI-Sul, QI 1/3, Casa 9 (E); *Ambassador:* Dr. GERARD S. BOUCHETTE.

Honduras: SQS 205, Bloco F, Apt. 106 (E); *Ambassador:* GUIDO BACCI DI CAPACI.

Hungary: Av. das Nações, Lote 19 (E); *Ambassador:* Dr. JÁNOS BECK.

India: SCDS, Edifício Venâncio VI, 1° subsolo, Lote E/8 (E); *Ambassador:* PRITHI SINGH (also accred. to Bolivia and Venezuela).

Iran: Av. das Nações, Lote 31 (E); *Ambassador:* DJAMAL HATAM.

Iraq: SCS, Quadra 13, Lotes 13-17, 5° andar (E); *Ambassador:* JIHAD KARAM.

Israel: SCS, Edifício Gilberto Salomão, 2° andar (E); *Ambassador:* MORDEKHAI SHNEERSON.

Italy: SQS 309, Bloco 1, Apts. 23-24 (E); *Ambassador:* CARLO ENRICO GIGLIOLI.

Ivory Coast: SDS, Edifício Venâncio VI, 2° andar (E); *Ambassador:* SEYDOU DIARRA.

Japan: Av. das Nações, Lote 39 (E); *Ambassador:* ATSUSHI UYAMA.

Korea, Republic: SCS, Edifício Central, 4° andar, salas 402-407 (E); *Ambassador:* SONG CHAN HO (also accred. to Colombia).

Lebanon: SDS, Edifício Acropol, Bloco N, Salas 401-407 (E); *Ambassador:* JEAN HADJI-THOMAS.

Malta: Av. L-2 Norte, Quandra 609-D (E); *Ambassador:* Prince JEAN LOUIS DE FAUCIGNY LUCINGE E COLIGNY.

Mexico: SQS 111, Bloco H, Apt. 402 (E); *Ambassador:* JUAN JOSÉ TORRES LANDA.

Morocco: SQS 308, Bloco B, Apt. 402 (E); *Ambassador:* AISSA BENCHEKROUN.

Netherlands: SQS 111, Bloco B, Apt. 13 (E); *Ambassador:* Jonkheer LEOPOLD QUARLES VAN UFFORD.

Nicaragua: SQS 111, Bloco E, Apt. 202 (E); *Ambassador:* JOSÉ SANSOTERÁN.

Nigeria: SDS, Edifício Venâncio II, 4° andar (E); *Chargé d'Affaires:* S. O. OGUNDELE.

Norway: SQS 113, Edifício Gávea, Bloco F, Apt. 605 (E); *Ambassador:* THORLEIF LINTRUP PAUS.

Pakistan: SQS 107, Bloco J, Apt. 502 (E); *Chargé d'Affaires:* AZIZ AHMAD KHAN.

Panama: SQS 205, Bloco F, Apt. 510 (E); *Chargé d'Affaires:* Dr. ALEXANDER CUEVAS.

Paraguay: SQS 307, Bloco H, Apt. 501 (E); *Ambassador:* Admiral J. WENCESLAO BENITES E.

Peru: SHI-Sul, QL 1/4, Casa 8 (E); *Ambassador:* ALBERTO RUIZ-ELDREDGE.

Philippines: SEN, Av. das Nações, Lote 1 (E); *Chargé d'Affaires:* CONSUELO ARRANZ.

Poland: SHIG-Sul, Av. W-3, Quadra 704, Bloco 1, Casa 59 (E); *Ambassador:* EUGENIUSZ CIURUS.

Portugal: Edifício Venâncio III, 3°-4° andares (E); *Ambassador:* JOSÉ HERMANO SARAIVA.

Romania: SHI-Sul, QL 2/2, Casa 6 (E); *Ambassador:* ION MORARU.

Senegal: SHIG-Sul, Av. W-3, Quadra 705, Bloco G, Casa 11 (E); *Ambassador:* ASSANE BASSIROU DIOUF.

South Africa: SCS, Edifício Gilberto Salomão, 12° andar, sala 1204 (E); *Ambassador:* ABRAHAM JACOBUS FRANÇOIS VILJOEN.

Spain: SQS 309, Bloco 1, Apt. 21 (E); *Ambassador:* JOSÉ PÉREZ DEL ARCO Y RODRÍGUEZ.

Sweden: SQS 113, Bloco K, Apt. 404 (E); *Ambassador:* BENGT ODEVALL.

Switzerland: SCS, Edifício das Pioneiras Sociais, 3° andar, sala 318 (E); *Ambassador:* EMIL STADELHOFER.

Syria: CLR Norte, Quadra 703, Bloco F, Lote 22 (E); *Chargé d'Affaires:* RASSEM RASLAN.

Thailand: Av. das Nações Norte, Lote 10 (E); *Ambassador:* Col. ARSH BOONGRAPU.

Trinidad and Tobago: SHIG-Sul, Av. W-3, Quadra 704, Bloco Q, Casa 47 (E); *Ambassador:* ALBERT GERARD MONTANO.

Turkey: SQS 114, Bloco F, Apt. 206 (E); *Ambassador:* VEYSEL VERSAN.

U.S.S.R.: SQS 113, Edifício Tijuca, Bloco K, Apt. 206 (E); *Ambassador:* SERGEI MIKHAILOV.

United Kingdom: Av. das Nações, Lote 8 (E); *Ambassador:* DEREK SHERBORNE LINDSELL DODSON.

U.S.A.: Av. das Nações, Lote 3 (E); *Ambassador:* JOHN HUGH CRIMMINS.

Uruguay: SDS, Edifício Venâncio V, Cobertura (E); *Ambassador:* CARLOS MANINI RÍOS.

Vatican: Av. W-5, Quadra 914, Bloco B (Apostolic Nunciature); *Nuncio:* CARMINE ROCCO.

Viet-Nam, Republic: SHIG-Sul, Av. W-3, Quadra 703, Bloco A, Casa 79 (E); *Chargé d'Affaires:* NGUYEN VAN NGOC.

Yugoslavia: Av. das Nações, Lote 15 (E); *Ambassador:* MIRKO OSTOJIC.

Zaire: Edifício Venâncio III, 2° andar, salas 201-208 (E); *Ambassador:* ASAL BOLUMBA IDZUMBIR.

Brazil also has diplomatic relations with Afghanistan, Albania, Barbados, Cyprus, Dahomey, Iceland, Kuwait, Libya, Malaysia, Mali, Singapore and Zambia.

CONGRESS

President of the Senate: PAULO TORRES.

President of the Chamber of Deputies: FLÁVIO MARCÍLIO.

(*General Election, November* 1970)

PARTY	NUMBER OF SEATS	
	Senate	Chamber of Deputies
ARENA—Aliança Renovadora Nacional	59	223
MDB—Movimento Democrático Brasileiro	7	87

STATE GOVERNORS

Acre: WANDERLEI DANTAS.
Alagôas: AFRÂNIO SALGADO LAGE.
Amazonas: JOÃO WALTER DE ANDRADE.
Bahia: ANTÔNIO CARLOS MAGALHÃES.
Ceará: CÉSAR CALS DE OLIVEIRA.
Espírito Santo: ARTHUR GERHARDT SANTOS.
Goiás: LEONINO DE RAMOS CAIADO.
Guanabara: ANTÔNIO DE PADUA CHAGAS FREITAS.
Maranhão: PEDRO NEIVA DE SANTANA.
Mato Grosso: JOSÉ FONTANILLAS FRAGELLI.
Minas Gerais: RONDON PACHECO.
Pará: FERNANDO JOSÉ DE LEÃO GUILHOM.
Paraiba: ERNANI SÂTIRO E SOUZA.
Paraná: EMÍLIO GOMES.
Pernambuco: ERALDO GUEIROS LEITE.
Piaui: ALBERTO TAVARES DA SILVA.

Rio de Janeiro: RAIMUNDO DELMIRIANO PADILHA.
Rio Grande do Norte: JOSÉ CORTEZ PEREIRA.
Rio Grande do Sul: EUCLIDES TRICHES.
Santa Catarina: COLOMBO MACHADO SALLES.
São Paulo: LAUDO NATEL.
Sergipe: PAULO BARRETO DE MENEZES.

GOVERNORS OF FEDERAL TERRITORIES

Amapá: Capt. ARTHUR AZEVEDO HENNING.
Fernando de Noronha: Lt.-Col. JAYME AUGUSTO DA COSTA E SILVA.
Rio Branco: Gen. CLOVIS NOVA DA COSTA.
Roraima: Dr. FERNANDO RAMOS PEREIRA.
Rondônia: JOÃO CARLOS MARQUES HENRIQUES NETTO.

FEDERAL DISTRICT

Governor of Brasília: Dr. ELMO SEREJO FARIAS.

POLITICAL PARTIES

A new Political Parties Statute, the *Lei Orgánica dos Partidos Políticos*, was signed by the President on July 21st, 1971. It prohibited the establishment of organizations whose programmes were in conflict with the "principles of the democratic régime", or of any party unless it had the support of 5 per cent of the voters who took part in the latest general elections, spread over at least seven states. The following are the only two legal parties:

Aliança Renovadora Nacional (ARENA): Câmara dos Deputados, Palácio do Congresso Nacional, Brasília D.F.; f. 1966; pro-Government party; Leader Sen. PETRÔNIO PORTELLA NUNES; publ. *Carta Mensal*.

Movimento Democrático Brasileiro (MDB): Câmara dos Deputados, Palácio do Congresso Nacional, Brasília D.F.; includes members of former Partido Trabalhista Brasileiro; Leader Sen. ERNANI DO AMARAL PEIXOTO; Presidential and Vice-Presidential candidates in 1973 ULISSES GUIMARÃES and BARBOSA LIMA SOBRINHO.

JUDICIAL SYSTEM

The judiciary powers of the State are held by the following tribunals: the Supreme Federal Tribunal, the Federal Tribunal of Recourses, the State Tribunals of Appeals, the Superior Military, the Electoral, and the Labour Tribunals; and by judges of other courts.

Sixteen ministers, nominated by the President and approved by the Senate, compose the Supreme Federal Tribunal. It judges offences committed by persons exempt from appearing before the normal courts, such as the President, Ministers of State, its own members, judges of other courts, and chiefs of permanent diplomatic missions. It also litigates in disputes between the Union and the states, between the states, or between foreign nations and the Union or the states; disputes as to jurisdiction between justices and/or tribunals of the different states, including those of the federal district and of the territories; in cases involving the extradition of criminals, in certain special cases involving the principle of *habeas corpus*, and in other cases. It is also empowered to judge ordinary appeals in cases in which the Union is interested as plaintiff or defendant.

The Federal Tribunal of Recourses judges the cases in which the Federal Union has interest.

The Tribunals of Appeals, apart from their normal function as a court of appeal, can sit in judgment on their own members. The number of judges varies according to the judiciary organization of each state.

The organs of the Electoral Tribunal (the Superior Tribunal, the Regional Tribunals, and the electoral judges) register the names of political parties, fix the date of elections, supervise the listing of voters, and deal with all infractions of the electoral laws. The seven judges of the Superior Electoral Tribunal are chosen: two from the Supreme Federal Tribunal, two from the Tribunal of Appeals, one from the Tribunal of Justice of the Federal District and two by the President.

The functions of the Military Court are no more than the name implies. The Labour Tribunal deals with labour disputes.

Civil offenders usually come before the courts of the separate states and of the Federal District. Each state organizes its own judiciary system on the principles established in the Constitution, and appoints its own judges from those who have passed the State examination in law.

THE SUPREME FEDERAL TRIBUNAL
Praça dos 3 Podêres, Brasília D.F.

President: ELOY JOSÉ DA ROCHA.

Vice-President: DJACI ALVES FALCÃO.

Justices: LUIZ GALLOTTI, OSWALDO TRIGUEIRO, ALIOMAR BALEEIRO, RAFAEL DE BARROSS MONTEIRO, CARLOS THOMPSON FLORES, BILAC PINTO, ANTÓNIO NEDER, XAVIER DE ALBUQUERQUE, JOSÉ GERALDO RODRIGUES ALCKMIN.

The Supreme Court was founded in 1891; publ. *Revista Trimestral de Jurisprudência* (decisions of the Court).

RELIGION

The majority of the population is Roman Catholic.

ROMAN CATHOLIC CHURCH

Metropolitan Sees:

Aparecida do Norte: His Eminence Cardinal CARLOS CARMELO DE VASCONCELOS MOTTA, Cardinal Primate of Brazil; Praça N. Sra. Aparecida 303, Aparecida, São Paulo S.P.

Pôrto Alegre: His Eminence Cardinal ALFREDO VICENTE SCHERER.

São Paulo: His Eminence Cardinal PAULO EVARISTO ARNS.

São Salvador da Bahia: His Eminence Cardinal AVELAR BRANDÃO VILELA.

São Sebastião de Rio de Janeiro: His Eminence Cardinal EUGENIO DE ARAÚJO SALES.

Most Rev.:

Aracajú	. .	LUCIANO JOSÉ CABRAL DUARTE.
Belém do Pará	.	ALBERTO GAUDÊNCIO RAMOS.
Belo Horizonte	.	JOÃO REZENDE COSTA.
Botucatú	.	VICENTE MARCHETTI ZIONI.
Brasília	.	JOSÉ NEWTON DE ALMEIDA BATISTA.
Campinas	.	ANTÔNIO MARIA ALVES DE SIQUEIRA.
Cuiabá	. .	ORLANDO CHAVES.
Curitiba	.	PEDRO ANTÔNIO FEDALTO.
Diamantina	.	GERALDO DE PROENÇA SIGAUD.
Florianópolis	.	ALFONSO NIEHUES.
Fortaleza	.	ALOISIO LORSCHEIDER.

Most Rev.:

Goiânia	. .	FERNANDO GOMES DOS SANTOS.
Juiz de Fora	.	GERALDO MARIA DE MORAIS PENIDO.
Maceió	.	ADELMO CAVALCANTE MACHADO.
Manaus	.	JOÃO DE SOUSA LIMA.
Mariana	.	OSCAR DE OLIVEIRA.
Natal	.	NIVALDO MONTE.
Niterói	.	ANTÔNIO DE ALMEIDA MORAES.
Olinda and Recife		HELDER PESSÔA CÂMARA.
Paraíba	.	JOSÉ M. PIRES.
Pouso Alegre	.	JOSÉ D'ANGELO NETO.
Ribeirão Prêto	.	BERNARDO JOSÉ BUENO MIELE.
São Luís do Maranhão		JOÃO JOSÉ DA MOTA E ALBUQUERQUE.
Teresina	.	JOSÉ FREIRE FALÇÃO.
Vitória	.	JOÃO BATISTA DA MOTA E ALBUQUERQUE.

PROTESTANT CHURCHES

Igreja Episcopal do Brasil: C.P. 2684, Pôrto Alegre 90,000, R.S.; Primate of the Episcopal Church of Brazil Rt. Rev. A. R. KRATZ.

Igreja Evangélica de Confissão Luterana no Brasil: C.P. 2876, Pôrto Alegre 90,000, R.S.; f. 1949; 800,000 mems.; Pres. Pastor KARL GOTTSCHALD; publs. *Jornal Evangelio, Presença.*

Igreja Metodista do Brasil: Board of Social Action, Rua Germania 175, Campinas, São Paulo; Exec. Sec. Rev. ALMS SAIR DONTOS.

THE PRESS

The first Brazilian newspaper, Hipólito da Costa's *Correio Brasiliense*, was published in London in 1808 and appeared regularly until the end of 1822. During this time, the Brazilian government subsidized several papers to combat da Costa's press, all of which were political. The emergence of the more serious, informative newspapers was very gradual, and it was not until the late nineteenth century that these appeared in the form of regular publications.

The Press of the modern Republic has greatly increased in numbers and circulation, but due to the difficulties of distribution, it is not yet completely national. A new code for newspapers was issued by the Ministry of Justice on September 19th, 1972, prohibiting them from publishing any speculative articles on political issues or unfavourable comments on the financial and economic situation.

DAILY NEWSPAPERS
MORNING
Rio de Janeiro, Guanabara

Brazil Herald: Rua do Resende 65; f. 1946; Managing Partner W. P. WILLIAMSON, Jr.; daily, except Mondays; only English language daily in Brazil; circ. 16,000.

Correio da Manhã: Rua dos Andradas 96; f. 1901; conservative; Dir. PAULO GERMANO DE MAGALHÃES; circ. 102,000.

O Dia: Rua Riachuelo 359; f. 1951; popular labour; Dir. OTHON PAULINO; circ. 201,000 (Sundays 196,000).

Diário Carioca: Av. Rio Branco 9, Sala 146; circ. 60,000.

Diário de Noticias: Rua Riachuelo 114; f. 1930; democratic; Dir. ONDINA PORTELA RIBEIRO DANTAS; circ. 80,000, Sundays 80,000.

O Jornal: Rua do Livramento 189; f. 1919; conservative; Dirs. JOÃO CALMON, THEOPHILO DE ANDRADE, M. GOMES MARANHÃO; circ. 70,000.

Jornal do Brasil: Avda. Rio Branco 110; f. 1891; Catholic, conservative; Dirs. Countess PEREIRA CARNEIRO, MANUEL FRANCISCO DO NASCIMENTO BRITO, BERNARD DA COSTA CAMPOS; circ. 85,000 daily, 149,000 Sundays.

Jornal do Commercio: Rua do Livramento 189; f. 1827; trade; Dirs. RUBENS FURTADO, CARLOS RIZZINI; circ. 30,000.

São Paulo, S.P.

Diário Popular: Rua do Carmo 20; f. 1884; independent; Dir. RODRIGO SOARES Jr.; circ. 30,000.

Diário de São Paulo: Rua 7 de Abril 230; f. 1929; Diários Associados group; Dir. EDMUNDO MONTEIRO; circ. 40,000.

O Estado de São Paulo: Rua Major Quedinho 28, C.P. 8005; f. 1875; independent; Dir. JOSÉ VIEIRA DE CARVALHO MESQUITA; circ. 70,000.

Folha de São Paulo: Alameda Barão de Limeira 401; f. 1920; Dir. OCTÁVIO FRIAS DE OLIVEIRA; circ. 50,000 daily, 60,000 Sundays.

A Gazeta Esportiva: Avda. Paulista 900; f. 1947; Dir. OCTÁVIO FRIAS DE OLIVEIRA; circ. 30,000.

Brasília, D.F.

Correio Brasiliense: Setor das Indústrias Gráficas, Lotes 300/500; f. 1960; Dir. EDILSON VARELA.

Tribuna Brasiliense: Rua Miguel Conto 23; Dir. KARAM JORGE CURY.

AFTERNOON AND EVENING
Rio de Janeiro, Guanabara

O Globo: Rua Irineu Marinho 35; f. 1925; independent conservative; Dir. ROBERTO MARINHO; circ. 120,000.

A Noticia: Rua Riachuelo 359, 4°; f. 1894; popular; Dir. OTHON PAULINO; circ. 80,000.

Tribuna da Imprensa: Rua Lavradio 98; f. 1949; progressive; Dir. ROSA MARIA SERZEDELO MACHADO; circ. 30,000.

Ultima Hora: Avda. Gomes Freire 421; f. 1951; Dir. and Pres. MAURÍCIO NUNES DE ALENCAR; circ. 100,000.

São Paulo, S.P.

Diário Comércio e Industria: Rua Carmelitas 129; f. 1933; Dir. JOSÉ DOS SANTOS; circ. 29,850.

Diário da Noite: Rua 7 de Abril 230; f. 1925; Diários Associados group; Dir. EDMUNDO MONTEIRO; circ. 30,000.

Folha da Tarde: Alameda Barão de Limeira 401; f. 1921; Dir. OCTÁVIO FRIAS DE OLIVEIRA; conservative; circ. 90,000.

A Gazeta: Avda. Paulista 900; f. 1906; independent; Dir. OCTÁVIO FRIAS DE OLIVEIRA; publ. by Fundação Cásper Líbero; circ. 35,000.

PROVINCIAL DAILIES
Belém, Pará

Folha do Norte: Rua Gaspar Viana 253; f. 1896; morning; independent; Dir. AUGUSTO MAGGESSI; circ. 6,000.

Folha Vespertina: Rua Gaspar Viana 253; f. 1896; evening; independent; Dir. AUGUSTO MAGGESSI.

O Liberal: Rua Santo António 433-435; f. 1946; Dir. ROMULO MAIORANA; circ. 2,000.

A Provincia do Pará: Trav. Campos Sales 206-210; f. 1947; Dir. MILTON TRINDADE; circ. 6,000.

Belo Horizonte, Minas Gerais

O Diário: Avda. Francisco Sales 536; f. 1935; morning; Catholic; Pres. SÉRGIO NEVES; circ. 12,000.

Diário do Comércio: Rua Rio de Janeiro 243; f. 1931; economic affairs; Dir. José COSTA; circ. 21,000.

Diário da Tarde: Rua Goiás 36; f. 1936; evening; Dir. PEDRO AGUINALDO FULGÊNCIO; circ. 18,000.

Diário de Minas: Praça Raul Soares; f. 1949; Dirs. JANUÁRIO L. CARNEIRO, LÉO COUTINHO; circ. 15,000.

Estado de Minas: Rua Goiás 36; f. 1927; morning; independent; Dir. PEDRO AGUINALDO FULGÊNCIO; circ. 50,000 (weekdays), 60,000 (Sundays).

Informador Comércial: Rua Rio de Janeiro 243, 4°; f. 1931; commercial information, market studies; Dir. JOSÉ COSTA.

Curitiba, Paraná

Diário do Paraná: Rua José Loureiro 111; f. 1955; Dir. ARMANDO DE OLIVEIRA.

O Estado do Paraná: Rua Barão do Rio Branco 556; f. 1951; Dir. JOÃO FÉDER; circ. 40,000.

Gazeta do Povo: Praça Carlos Gomes 4; f. 1919; Dirs. FRANCISCO DA CUNHA PEREIRA, DILMAR ABILIO ARCHEGAS; circ. 10,000.

Tribuna do Paraná: Rua Barão do Rio Branco 556; Dir. J. B. MORAES; circ. 24,000.

Florianopolis, Santa Catarina

O Estado: Rua Conselheiro Mafra 160; f. 1915; Dir. and Pres. JOSÉ MATUSALÉM COMELLI; circ. 5,000.

A Gazeta: Rua Conselheiro Mafre 51; f. 1933; Dir. MARIA INÁ VAZ; circ. 5,000.

Fortaleza, Ceará

O Povo: Rua Senador Pompeu 1082; f. 1928; evening; Dir. CREUSA DO CARMO ROCHA; circ. 10,000.

Unitário: Rua Senador Pompeu 864; f. 1903; Dir. MANUEL EDUARDO PINHEIRO CAMPOS; circ. 10,000.

Manaus, Amazonas

A Crítica: Rua Lôbo d'Almada 278; f. 1946; Dir. UMBERTO CALDERÃO; circ. 3,000.

O Jornal: Rua Eduardo Ribeiro 556; f. 1930; Dir. MARIA DE LOURDES FREITAS ARCHER PINTO; circ. 2,000.

Natal, Rio Grande do Norte

Diário de Natal: Avda. Rio Branco 325; f. 1939; circ. 4,000.

Tribuna do Norte: Avda. Tavares de Lira 101-105; f. 1950; Dir. GERALDO RAMOS DOS SANTOS; circ. 2,000.

Niterói, Rio de Janeiro

O Fluminense: Rua da Conceição 138; f. 1878; Dir. ALBERT TORRES; circ. 2,000.

Pôrto Alegre, Rio Grande do Sul

Correio do Povo: Rua Caldas Jr. 219; f. 1895; morning; independent; Dir. BRENO CALDAS; circ. 80,000, 100,000 (Sundays).

Diário de Notícias: Rua São Pedro 733; f. 1925; morning; Conservative; Dir. NELSON DIMAS DE OLIVEIRA; circ. 20,000.

Folha da Tarde: Rua Caldas Jr. 219; f. 1936; evening; Dir. BRENO CALDAS; circ. 20,000.

Zero Hora: Avda. Ipiranga 1075; f. 1964; Dir. MAURÍCIO SIROTSKY SOBRINHO.

Recife, Pernambuco

Diário da Noite: Rua do Imperador 346; f. 1946; Dir. F. PESSOA DE QUEIROZ; circ. 23,000.

Diário de Pernambuco: Praça da Independência 12; f. 1825; morning; independent; Dir. ANTIÓGENES FERREIRA DE CASTRO CHAVES; circ. 30,000.

Jornal do Commercio: Rua do Imperador 346; f. 1919; morning; conservative; Dir. F. PESSOA DE QUEIROZ; circ. 20,000.

Salvador, Bahia

Diário de Notícias: Rua Carlos Gomes 57; f. 1875; morning; democratic; Dir. ODORICO TAVARES; circ. 10,000.

Jornal da Bahia: Rua Dr. J. J. Seabra 22; f. 1958; Dir. JOÃO DA COSTA FALCÃO; circ. 20,000.

A Tarde: Praça Castro Alves 5; f. 1912; evening; Dir. RENATO SIMÕES; circ. 40,000.

Santos, São Paulo

A Tribuna: Rua General Camara 90-94; f. 1894; morning; conservative; Dir. GIUSFREDO SANTINI; circ. 36,000.

São Luiz, Maranhão

Jornal do Dia: Rua J. A. Corrêa 199; Dir. ARTHUR CARVALHO; circ. 2,000.

PERIODICALS

Rio de Janeiro, Guanabara

Antenna: Avda. Marechal Floriano 143, C.P. 1131, ZC-00; f. 1926; telecommunications and electronics; monthly; Dir. G. A. PENNA; circ. 18,000.

Conjuntura Econômica: Fundação Getúlio Vargas, Serviço de Publicações, Praia de Botafogo 186; monthly.

O Cruzeiro: Rua do Livramento 179-203; Dir. ACCIOLY NETTO; weekly.

Eletrônica Popular: Avda. Marechal Floriano 143, C.P. 1131, ZC-00; f. 1956; electronics, radio, TV, Hi-Fi; bi-monthly; circ. 19,000.

Informação Brasileira: Rua Buenos Aires 251, 1°; fortnightly; commerce.

Manchete: Rua do Russell 804; f. 1952; weekly; general.

Observador Econômico e Financeiro, O: Avda. Graça Aranha 182, 9°; f. 1936; Dir.-Gen. MARINETTE BOUÇAS; monthly.

Opinião: f. 1972; current affairs; Chief Editor RAIMUNDO RODRIGUES PEREIRA (suspended).

Revista Brasil Ilustrado: Rua da Almirante Gonçalvez 23; fortnightly; illustrated; general interest.

Revista Civilização Brasileira: Rua 7 de Setembro 97; cultural; bi-monthly; circ. 20,000.

Revista do Esporte: Rua São Luiz Gonzaga 601; weekly; sports.

Revista da Semana: Rua Visconde de Maranguape 15; Props. Cia. Editora Americana; Editor REINALDO JARDIM; general; weekly.

Rio Magazine: Rua Senador Dantas 118; f. 1933; monthly; general.

Selecções do Reader's Digest: Editora Ypiranga Avda. Presidente Vargas 62, 7° f. 1933; monthly.

Vida Doméstica: Rua Riachuelo 414; f. 1920; Dir. CARLOS GONÇALVES FIDALGO; monthly; women's interest; also publishes *Vida Infantil*, *Vida Juvenil* and *Coletânea*.

São Paulo, S.P.

Acropóle: Rua Xavier de Toledo 264, 5°, C.P. 3798; f. 1938; architecture; monthly.

Casa e Jardim: Avda. Graça Aranha 182, 6°; f. 1953; homes and gardens; illustrated; monthly.

Claudia: Avda. Octaviano Alves de Lima 800; women's magazine; monthly; circ. 486,000.

Digesto Econômico: Associação Comercial de São Paulo, Rua Boa Vista 51, C.P. 8082; monthly.

Exame: Avda. Octaviano Alves de Lima 800; business; monthly; circ. 55,000.

Iris: Avda. Prestes Maia 220, C.P. 1704; f. 1947; photography, cinema and tape recorder; monthly; Editor Dr. HANS KORANYI.

Máquinas & Metais: Avda. Octaviano Alves de Lima 800; monthly; machine and metal industries; circ. 22,000.

Mundo Elétrico: Rua Xavier de Toledo 264, 5°, C.P. 3798; f. 1959; electricity; monthly.

Quatro Rodas: Avda. Octaviano Alves de Lima 800; motoring; monthly; circ. 95,000.

Realidade: Avda. Octaviano Alves de Lima 800; monthly; illustrated; general interest; circ. 200,000.

Veja: Avda. Octaviano Alves de Lima 800; news weekly; circ. 115,000; Dir. MINO CARTA.

Visão: Rua 7 de Abril 345; f. 1956; business magazine; Editor HERNANE TAVARES DE SÁ; weekly.

NEWS AGENCIES

Agência Nacional: Presidência da República; official; Dir. GERALDO BORGES.

Agência Meridional, Ltda.: Rua Sacadura Cabral 103, Rio de Janeiro; Dir. FRANCISCO BUSTO.

"ANB"—Brastele, Agência Noticiosa Lta.: Avda. Alm. Barroso 72, Rio de Janeiro; f. 1970; Dir. ARLINDO MOREIRA.

FOREIGN BUREAUX

Rio de Janeiro, Guanabara

Agência Nacionale Stampa Associata (ANSA): Largo do Marchado 39, 2°, C.P. 95; Bureau Chief EMILIO MILLUL.

AP: Avda. Rio Branco 25, 13°, C.P. 72-ZC-000; Bureau Chief DENNIS F. REDMONT.

UPI: Avda. Brazil, 6°, C.P. 719; Man. C. HIPPEAU.

The following are also represented: DPA, Jiji Press, Novosti, Reuters, Tass.

ANSA, AP and UPI are represented in Brasília.

ANSA, Jiji Press, Kyodo News Service, Reuters and UPI are represented in São Paulo.

Reuters is represented in Santos.

PRESS ASSOCIATION

Associação Brasileira de Imprensa: Rua Araújo Pôrto Alegre 71, Rio de Janeiro; f. 1908.

PUBLISHERS

Rio de Janeiro, Guanabara

Companhia José Aguilar Editôra: Avda. Rui Barbosa 170, C.P. 302; f. 1958; literature; fiction; Pres. JOSÉ AGUILAR SAMPER; Dir. SILVIA FARRÉ.

Livraria Francisco Alves Editôra, S.A.: Rua Barão de Lucena 43; Dir. and Pres. J. C. DE MACEDO SOARES GUIMARÃES.

Antenna-Emprêsa Jornalistica S.A.: Avda. Marechal Floriano 143, C.P. 1131-ZC-00; br. at Rua Vitória 379-383, São Paulo; f. 1926; technical books and magazines on electronics and radio.

Artes Gráficas Industrias Reunidas, S.A. AGIR: Rua dos Inválidos 198; education, history, philosophy, belles-lettres, fiction; brs. in São Paulo, Belo Horizonte, Brasília.

Editôra Paulo de Azevedo Ltda.: Rua do Ouvidor 166, C.P. 658-ZC-00; f. 1854; text-books, general; Dir. Ivo VIANNA DE AZEVEDO.

Carioca Livraria e Editôra Ltda: Avda. Rio Branco 9, sala 146; general books.

Junta de Educação Religiosa e Publicações da Convenção Batista Brasileira: Rua Paulo Fernandes 24, 1°; f. 1901; Bibles; periodicals; Dir. HORACE VICTOR DAVIS.

Centro Redentor: Rua Jorge Rudge 119; f. 1912; religious works; Pres. ANTÓNIO DO NASCIMENTO COTTAS.

Editôra Civilização Brasileira, S.A.: Rua da Lapa 120, 12°; f. 1932; text-books, general literature, science, national and foreign works; Dirs. ENIO SILVEIRA, JOAQUIM IGNACIO BAPTISTA CARDOSO, MÁRIO DA SILVA BRITO.

Edições O Cruzeiro: Rua Licramente 203; education, history, children's books, science.

Editôra Delta: Avda. Almirante Barroso 63, 26°, salas 2601-9; education, children's books, encyclopaedias and dictionaries.

Editorial Gonzalez Porto: Head Office: Mexico City; Rua Senador Dantas 80, 3°, sala 303; f. 1921; medical, scientific, technical, etc.; Dir. ADOLFO LÓPEZ GUILLÉN; offices in São Paulo and Pôrto Alegre; others throughout South America.

Editôra Guanabara Koogan S.A.: Rua do Ouvidor 132; f. 1930; medical, business and management, children's; Pres. ABRAHÃO KOOGAN.

W. M. Jackson, Inc.: Rua Miguel Couto 35, 5°; f. 1923; encyclopaedias, literary, technical; Dir. ROBERTO CASTRO RIAÑO.

Editôra José Konfino: Avda. Erasmo Braga 227, 1°, C.P. 2746; f. 1937; law only; Dir. JOSÉ KONFINO.

Editorial Labor do Brasil, S.A.: Rua Buenos Aires 104, 1°; f. 1937; art, scientific and technical.

Livraria José Olympio Editôra, S.A.: Rua Marquês de Olinda 12.

Ao Livro Técnico S.A.: Avda. Presidente Vargas 962, 7°, sala 708; technical books.

Livros de Portugal, S.A.: Rua Miguel Couto 40; f. 1941; philology, history, contemporary and classical Portuguese works; Dir. JOÃO FONSECA MARZANO.

Irmãos Pongetti-Editores: Rua Sacadura Cabral 240; f. 1925 as Paulo, Pongetti e Cia., present name 1932; history, general literature; Dirs. RUGGERO and RODOLPHO PONGETTI.

Editôra Tecnoprint, S.A.: Rua Nova Jerusalém 345 (Bonsucesso); f. 1947; education, children's, "Edições de Ouro" paperbacks, crossword puzzle magazines.

Casa Editôra Vecchi, S.A.: Rua do Resende 144; f. 1913; general literature and magazines; Man. AMÁLIA VECCHI.

Editôra Vozes, Ltda.: Rua Senador Dantas 118-A; f. 1901; Catholic publishers; Dir. Dr. MIGUEL GOMES MOURÃO DE CASTRO; publs. *Revista Eclesiástica Brasileira, Revista de Cultura Vozes, Serviço de Documentação (SEDOC), Grande Sinal, Renovação Crista, Centro Informativo Católico (CIC), Studia Entomologica.*

São Paulo

Editôra Abril and **Abril Cultural S.A.:** Avda. Octaviano Alves de Lima 800, C.P. 2372; f. 1950; magazines, textbooks, science, encyclopaedias, guides.

Livraria Freitas Bastos, S.A.: Rua 7 de Setembro 127-129; f. 1918; law books; Pres. LINDA ANTONGINI DE FREITAS BASTOS; Dir. ALBERTO ABULAFIA.

Boa Leitura Editôra, S.A.: Rua General Jardim 359-361, C.P. 738; geography, history, popular sciences.

Editôra do Brasil, S.A.: C.P. 4986; geography, education, physics, literature.

Editôra Brasiliense: Rua Barão de Itapetininga 93, 12°; education, sociology, history, administration, psychology, literature.

Editôra Cultrix: Rua Conselheiro Furtado 648, 6°, sala 61; fine arts, history, popular sciences, fiction, school textbooks.

Difusão Européia do Livro Ltda.: Rua Bento Freitas 362, 6°, C.P. 30,340; f. 1950.

EPU—Editôra Pedagógica e Universitária Ltda.: Praça D. José Gaspar 106, 3° sobreloja No. 15; f. 1952; philosophy, psychology, education, social sciences, economics, anthropology, natural sciences and professional books; Man. Dir. WOLFGANG KNAPP.

Cia. Melhoramentos de São Paulo, Indústrias de Papel: Rua Tito 479, C.P. 8120, 05051; f. 1890; textbooks, science, juvenile, education, history; Pres. MÁRIO TOLEDO DE MORAES.

Companhia Editôra Nacional: Rua dos Gusmões 639, 01212; brs. at Rua Benjamin Constant 30-12, Rio de Janeiro, Recife, Pôrto Alegre, Belém, Brasília and throughout Brazil; f. 1926; textbooks, history, science, social sciences, philosophy, fiction, juvenile; Dir. LINDOLFO MARCONDES FERREIRA.

Editôra Pedagógica Brasileira Ltda: Avda. Viera de Carvalho 141, sobreloja; educational.

Curitiba

Editôra Guaira, Ltda.: Rua D. Julia da Costa 525, C.P. V; f. 1940; law, literature, science; Dir. Supt. Dr. DE PLACIDO E SILVA; Man. ANTÓNIO TEOFILO DE ANDRADE; offices in Rio de Janeiro and São Paulo.

Pôrto Alegre

Editôra Globo: Avda. Getúlio Vargas 1271, C.P. 1520; f. 1883; reference, textbooks, literature, technical works; Dir. HENRIQUE BERTASO; brs. in Bahia, Belo Horizonte, Rio de Janeiro, Salvador and São Paulo.

PUBLISHERS' ASSOCIATION

Sindicato Nacional dos Editôres de Livros: Avda. Rio Branco 37, 15°, salas 1503-1506, 1510-1512, Rio de Janeiro, G.B.; 219 mems.; Pres. GABRIEL ATHOS PEREIRA; Sec. WILSON ELYAS.

RADIO AND TELEVISION

Departmento Nacional de Telecomunicações (Dental) (*National Telecommunications Council*): Rua Miguel Couto 105, Rio de Janeiro.

RADIO

There are 396 commercial broadcasting stations.

The main broadcasting stations in Rio de Janeiro are: Rádio Globo, Rádio Maua, Rádio Nacional, Rádio Tamoio, Rádio Tupi; and in São Paulo: Rádio Cultura, Rádio Difusora de São Paulo, Rádio Gazeta, Rádio Record, Rádio Pan-Americana and Rádio Bandeirantes.

In 1971, there were 5,800,000 radio receivers.

TELEVISION

In 1973 fifty-two commercial television stations were operating, twelve were projected, and about 6,580,000 sets were in use. PAL colour television has been adopted.

BROADCASTING ASSOCIATIONS

Associação Brasileira de Emissoras de Rádio e Televisão, ABERT: Rua Mairink Veiga, 6-12° pav., Rio de Janeiro; f. 1962; mems.: 97 short-wave, 52 FM and 739 medium-wave radio stations and 45 television stations; Pres. JOSÉ DE ALMEIDA CASTRO; Dir.-Gen. RENATO TAVARES.

Diários e Emissoras Associados: Rua Sacadura Cabral 103, Rio de Janeiro; mems.: 23 radio stations, 14 television stations and 33 newspapers; Pres. Dr. JOÃO DE MEDEIROS CALMÓN; Gen. Dir. Dr. PAULO CABRAL DE ARAUJO.

FINANCE

(cap.=capital; p.u.=paid up; dep.=deposits; m.=million; b.=billion; res.=reserves; cr.=cruzeiros; amounts in new cruzeiros, unless otherwise stated.)

BANKING

CENTRAL BANK

Banco Central do Brasil: Avda. Presidente Vargas 84, Rio de Janeiro; f. 1965 as Banco Central da República do Brasil, name changed 1967; issues currency, carries out all gold and exchange transactions, has taken over monetary and credit supervision from SUMOC and functions of Rediscount Department; cap. 34m., res. 2,462m. (Sept. 1972); Pres. PAULO H. PEREIRA LIMA; Dir. PAULO YOKOTA.

FINEX: Fund f. 1966 to finance exports and purchase exportable surpluses.

FUNDEPE—Fundo para Desenvolvimento da Pecuária: f. 1967 to finance development of cattle-raising and wool and milk production; disposable funds 216m., half from an IBRD loan; funds to be allocated mainly in states of Rio Grande do Sul, São Paulo, Paraná, Minas Gerais, Mato Grosso and Goiás.

STATE CONTROLLED BANK

Banco do Brasil, S.A.: Brasília; f. 1808; cap. and res. 4,282.5m., dep. 25,463.8m. (Sept. 1972); Pres. ANGELO CALMON DE SÁ.

DEVELOPMENT AND INVESTMENT BANKS

Banco Bozano Simonsen de Investimento, S.A.: Avda. Rio Branco 138, C.P. 5074-ZC-21, Rio de Janeiro; f. 1967 by Bank of London and South America and Bozano, Simonsen Group; investment bank catering for medium- and long-term capital requirements; cap. and res. 67.2m.; Pres. J. R. DE ARAGÃO BOZANO.

Banco de Desenvolvimiento do Estado do Rio Grande do Sul (Badesul): Pôrto Alegre; initial cap. 300m.; carries out operations in the State of Rio Grande do Sul that were previously reserved to the Banco Regional de Desenvolvimiento do Extremo Sul (BRDE).

Banco Finasa de Investimento S.A.: São Paulo; f. 1965; cap. and res. 184.8m., liabilities 751.8m. (Dec. 1973); medium- and long-term financing for industrial and commercial activities; underwriting of shares and debentures; investment advisers.

Banco Nacional de Crédito Cooperativo: Brasília, D.F.; public financial institution in association with the Ministry of Agriculture, guaranteed by the Federal government; cap. and res. 125.2m.; Pres. PAULO DE O. LEITÃO.

Banco Nacional do Desenvolvimento Econômico: Avda. Rio Branco 53, C.P. ZC-21, Rio de Janeiro; f. 1952 to assist in the financing of development schemes sponsored by the Government, particularly in the fields of railway transport, electric power, basic industries and agriculture and related sectors. Since 1964 more emphasis has been placed on the development of different regions; Pres. MARCOS PEREIRA VIANNA; Exec. Man. ADALMIRO MOURA.

Special funds:

FIPEME—Programa de Financiamento à Pequena e Média Emprêsas: f. 1965; funds made available by the Brazilian Government, IABD and German Kreditanstalt; investment in 1973: 800m.; financing loans to smaller industries, particularly in less developed regions of the country.

FUNTEC—Fundo de Desenvolvimento Técnico-Científico: f. 1964; funds available directly from BNDE; financing technico-scientific research, secondary and higher level technical education and special research programmes in petroleum, siderurgical and paper and cellulose industries.

Total investment in new operations (1973): $U.S. 1,300m.

Banco Nacional de Habitação: Brasília, D.F.; f. 1964; cap. and res. 2,079m. (Sept. 1972); Pres. MAURÍCIO SCHULMAN.

Banco do Nordeste do Brasil, S.A.: Avda. Rio Branco 147, 14°, Rio de Janeiro, G.B.; f. 1952; cap. and res. 940.4m.; dep. 1,763.6m. (Nov. 1973); Pres. ANTÓNIO NÍLSON CRAVEIRO HOLANDA.

Banco Paulista de Desenvolvimento Econômico: São Paulo; f. 1966; provides long-term financing for development and medium- and short-term loans for purchasing machinery and equipment; init. cap. 300,000m. cruzeiros.

Banco Regional de Desenvolvimento do Extremo Sul (BRDE): Pôrto Alegre, Rio Grande do Sul; development bank for the states of Paraná, Rio Grande do Sul and Santa Catarina; f. 1961 in Paraná; acts as agent for numerous federal financing agencies and co-operates with IBRD and Eximbank; finances small- and medium-sized industrial and agricultural enterprises.

Financeira Nacional: Rio de Janeiro; f. 1965 as FINAME, one of the special funds of the Banco Nacional do Desenvolvimento Econômico, present status 1967; financing production of machinery and industrial, agricultural and transport equipment.

Rio de Janeiro, Guanabara

Banco Andrade Arnaud, S.A.: Rua 7 de Setembro 32; f. 1929; cap. and res. 35m., dep. 329m. (Nov. 1970); 76 brs.; Pres. RAUL PINTO DE CARVALHO.

Banco Boavista, S.A.: Praça Pio X 118A, C.P. 1560-ZC-00; f. 1924; cap. and res. 78.2m., dep. 301.7m. (Oct. 1972); Pres. C. GUINLE DE PAULA MACHADO.

Banco do Estado da Guanabara, S.A.: Avda. Nilo Peçanha 175, C.P. 21090 ZC-P; f. 1945; cap. 247.5m., dep. 1,885.8m. (Dec. 1973); Pres. OCTAVIO GOUVEA DE BULHÔES; 49 brs.

Banco Internacional.

União de Bancos Brasileiros.

São Paulo, S.P.

Banco América do Sul, S.A.: Rua Senador Feijé 197-205, C.P. 8075; f. 1940; cap. and res. 63.9m., dep. 513.9m. (Sept. 1972); Pres. APOLONIO JORGE DE FARIA SALLES.

Banco Bandeirantes do Comércio, S.A.: Rua do Tesouro 39, C.P. 30024; f. 1944; cap. and res. 104.2m., dep. 1,012.1m. (Sept. 1973); Pres. Dr. GILBERTO DE ANDRADE FARIA; Dirs. MOACYR DE ARAÚJO SIMÕES, MILTON LOUREIRO, CHRISTOVAM MACHADO BARBOSA.

Banco Brasileiro de Descontos, S.A.: Rua 15 de Novembro 233; f. 1943; cap. and res. 1,047.7m., dep. 6,638.7m. (Dec. 1973); Dir.-Pres. AMADOR AGUIAR.

Banco Cidade de São Paulo.

Banco Comercial Brasul, S.A.: Rua 15 de Novembro 336; f. 1971.

Banco do Comércio e Industria de São Paulo, S.A.: Rua 15 de Novembro 289; f. 1889; cap. and res. 162.1m., dep. 1,111.1m. (Sept. 1972); Pres. ROBERTO F. AMARAL.

Banco do Estado de São Paulo, S.A.: Praça António Prado 6, C.P. 60-B; f. 1926; cap. and res. 961.8m., dep. 6,171.8m. (Nov. 1973); Pres. PEDRO DE MOURA MAIA.

Banco Francês e Brasileiro, S.A.: Rua 15 de Novembro 268; f. 1948; affiliated with Crédit Lyonnais; cap. and res. 102.5m., dep. 409.2m (1972); Pres. J. P. GOUVÊA VIEIRA.

Banco Francês e Italiano para a América do Sul, S.A. Sudameris: Rua Bela Vista 739, Alto da Bôa Vista, Santo Amaro; f. 1949; cap. 41.1m., dep. 483.2m. (Dec. 1972); Chair. ROGERIO GIORGI; Dir.-Supt. MICHEL DONARD.

Banco ITAU, S.A.: Rua Boa Vista 176; f. 1943; cap. and res. 418m., dep. 4,200m. (Dec. 1973); Pres. HERBERT LEVY; Gen. Dir. OLAVO EGYDIO SETUBAL.

Banco Mercantil de São Paulo, S.A.: Head Office: Avda. Paulista 1450; Foreign Exchange Dept.: Rua João Brícola 59; f. 1938; cap. and res. 247.2m., dep. 1,409.4m. (Dec. 1972); Pres. GASTÃO E. DE BUENO VIDIGAL; Vice-Pres. LUIZ DE PAULA FIGUERA.

Banco Nacional do Comércio de São Paulo: Rua Boa Vista 242; f. 1936; cap. and res. 30.3m., dep. 139m. (Sept. 1972); Pres. MAURO PAES DE ALMEIDA.

Banco Real, S.A.: Rua Boa Vista 254, 2°, C.P. 30359; f. 1925; cap. and res. 409.6m., dep. 2,579.4m.; Pres. ALOYSIO DE ANDRADE FARIA.

Banco de São Paulo, S.A.: Rua 15 de Novembro 347; f. 1889; cap. and res. 103.9m., dep. 417.6m. (Sept. 1972); Pres. JOÃO ADHEMAR DE ALMEIDO PRADO.

Fortaleza

Banco do Nordeste do Brasil, S.A.: Rua Major Facundo 500; f. 1955; cap. and res. 940.4m., dep. 1,763.6m. (Nov. 1973); Pres. ANTÓNIO NÍLSON CRAVEIRO HOLANDA.

Belo Horizonte

Banco Mercantil de Minas Gerais, S.A.: Rua Rio de Janeiro 680, C.P. 836; f. 1941; cap. and res. 73.3m., dep. 476.6m. (Sept. 1972); Chair. VICENTE DE ARAÚJO.

Banco de Minas Gerais, S.A.: Rua da Bahia 504; f. 1930; cap. 50m., dep. 750m. (Dec. 1972); Pres. FLÁVIO PENTAGNA GUIMARÃES; Man. JOSÉ GERALDO FURTADO; Exchange Dir. Dr. FRANCISCO DE ASSIS CASTRO.

Juiz de Fora

Banco de Crédito Real de Minas Gerais, S.A.: Rua Halfeld 504; Foreign Exchange Dept.: Avda. Rio Branco 116, 6°, Rio de Janeiro; f. 1889; cap. and res. 121.8m., dep. 710.8m. (Sept. 1972); Pres. BOLIVAR CARVALHO.

Pôrto Alegre

Banco do Estado de Rio Grande do Sul, S.A.: Rua Capitão Montanha 177, C.P. 505; f. 1928; cap. and res. 182.7m., dep. 612.4m. (Sept. 1972); Pres. Dr. ROBERTO BIER DA SILVA.

Banco Sul Brasileiro, S.A.: Rua da Alfândega 2-8, C.P. 290; f. 1973 from merger of Banco Nacional do Comércio, S.A., Banco da Provincia do Rio Grande do Sul, S.A., and Banco Industrial e Comercial do Sul, S.A.; cap. and res. 363.1m., dep. 1,605.9m. (Nov. 1973); Pres. DANIEL MONTEIRO.

Salvador

Banco da Bahia, S.A.: Rua Miguel Calmón 32, 6°, C.P. 118; f. 1858, incorporated **Banco do Povo, S.A.** 1968; cap. and res. 172.3m., dep. 1,163.5m. (Sept. 1972); Pres. Dr. CLEMENTE MARIANI BITTENCOURT.

Banco Econômico da Bahia: Lauro Müller s/n; f. 1834; cap. and res. 139.2m., dep. 726.4m. (Dec. 1972); Pres. Dr. EUGENIO T. LEAL.

FOREIGN BANKS

(Rio de Janeiro, unless otherwise stated)

Banco Holandês Unido (Hollandsche Bank-Unie, N.V.): H.O.: Herengracht 434-440, Amsterdam; Rua Buenos Aires 9-15, C.P. 1242-ZC-00; f. 1917; Man. Dir. F. H. VAN VEENENDAAL.

Banco Internacional S.A.: Rua 15 de Novembro 240, C.P. 8065, São Paulo; affiliated with the Royal Bank of Canada, Montreal, and the Bank of America N.T. and S.A.

Banco Italo-Belga, S.A.: H.O.: 59 rue de l'Association, Brussels 1; Rua Alvares Penteado 195, C.P. 877, São Paulo; f. 1911; 6 brs. in South America; Man. Dir. A. SPEECKAERT.

Bank of London and South America, Ltd.: 40-66 Queen Victoria Street, London, E.C.4; Rua 15 de Novembro 165, São Paulo; Chief Man. H. D. FLOOD; Man. São Paulo Branch F. GOULD; Rio Branch: Rua da Alfândega 29-35; Man. A. LADLEY; 12 other brs. in Brazil.

Chase Manhattan Bank: Avda. Rio Branco 109, C.P. 1576-ZC-00; Rep. W. DE KAY PALMER.

Deutsch-Südamerikanische Bank A.G. (Banco Germánico de la América del Sud) and Dresdner Bank, A.G.: Hamburg and Frankfurt/Main; joint representation Rua da Candelária 60; f. 1906; Gen. Man. KARL SCHMIDT.

The First National Bank of Boston: H.O.: 100 Federal St., Boston; Rua Líbero Badaró 487, São Paulo; Vice-Pres. RICHARD HUBER; 3 other brs.

First National City Bank: H.O.: 399 Park Ave., New York City, U.S.A.; Avda. Rio Branco 85; f. 1812; Vice-Pres. Brazil ANTHONY MORO.

BANKING ASSOCIATIONS

Rio de Janeiro, Guanabara

Sindicato dos Bancos do Estado da Guanabara: Avda. Rio Branco 81.

São Paulo, S.P.

Sindicato dos Bancos no Estado de São Paulo: Rua Líbero Badaró 293, 13° pav.; f. 1924; Pres. LÁZARO DE MELLO BRANDÃO; Sec. OSWALDO MORELLI.

STOCK EXCHANGES

Rio de Janeiro, Guanabara

Bolsa de Valores do Rio de Janeiro: Praça 15 de Novembro 20; 308 stocks quoted; Pres. FERNANDO SOUZA RIBEIRO DE CARVALHO.

São Paulo, S.P.

Bolsa de Valores de São Paulo: Rua Alvares Penteado 165, 7°; c. 400 stocks quoted.

There are commodity exchanges at Pôrto Alegre, Vitória, Recife and Santos.

INSURANCE

Rio de Janeiro, Guanabara

American Motorists Insurance Co.: Rua Debret 79, 10-13°; f. 1955; Gen. Rep. for Brazil H. A. BUFFALO.

Atlântica—Cia. Nacional de Seguros: Rua do Passeio 62; f. 1935; Dir. Pres. ANTÔNIO CARLOS DE ALMEIDA BRAGA.

Colonial—Cia. Nac. de Segs. Gerais: Rua do Rosário 90; f. 1944; Pres. Dr. ANTÓNIO SÁNCHEZ DE LARRAGOITI, Jr.

Columbia—Cia. Nacional de Seguros Gerais: Avda. Almirante Barroso 81, C.P. 334; f. 1943; Pres. CARLOS F. LIMA.

Companhia Boavista de Seguros: Rua do Passeio 62, C.P. 1779; f. 1937; Pres. Dr. ANTÓNIO C. DE A. BRAGA.

Cia. Excélsior de Seguros: Avda. Rio Branco 131, 4°; Pres. Dr. RONALDO XAVIER DE LIMA.

Cia. de Seguros Marítimos e Terrestres Lloyd Sul Americano: Rua Debret 79, 10°-13°, C.P. 580-ZC-00; f. 1919; Dir. H. A. BUFFALO.

Confiança—Cia. de Segs. Marítimos e Terrestres: Rua do Carmo 43, 8°; f. 1872; Pres. OCTAVIO FERREIRA NOVAL.

Continental—Cia. de Seguros: Rua Beneditinos 10, 2°-5°; f. 1924; cap. 2,632m., res. 6m.; Pres. LUÍZ ESTEVES.

Federal de Seguros S.A.: Rua Sta. Luzia 732, 7°; Pres. Gen. ALUIZIO DE ANDRADE FALCÃO.

Fortaleza—Cia. Nac. de Segs.: Avda. Pres. Vargas 409, 14°; f. 1935; Pres. FRANCISCO PINTO, Jr.

Garantia União de Seguros S.A.: Avda. Graça Aranha 416, 5°, C.P. 1259; f. 1866; Pres. ANTÓNIO FERNANDO DE BULHÕES CARVALHO.

Generali do Brasil—Cia. Nac. de Segs.: Avda. Rio Branco 128, 4°; f. 1945; Pres. EDMUNDO P. BARBOSA DA SILVA.

Indenizadora—Cia. de Seguros Marítimos e Terrestres: Avda. Rio Branco 26A, C.P. 914; f. 1888; Pres. Dr. P. BURLAMAQUI DE MELLO.

Independencia—Cia. de Seguros Gerais: Rua México 168, 3°; Pres. V. P. GALLIEZ.

Interamericana—Cia. de Seguros Gerais: Rua Senador Dantas 70-74, 9°; f. 1956; Pres. E. C. DOBBS.

Cia. Internacional de Segs.: Rua Assembleia 104, C.P. 1137; f. 1920; Chair. Dr. CELSO DA ROCHA MIRANDA, K.B.E.

Lloyd Industrial Sul Americano, A.S.: Rua Debret 79, 10-13°, C.P. 530-ZC-00; f. 1920; Dir.-Pres. H. A. BUFFALO.

Nacional—Cia de Segs.: Rua da Quitanda 70, 10°; f. 1946; Pres. EDUARDO CATÃO DE MAGALHÃES PINTO.

Novo Mundo—Cia. Nac. de Seg. Gerais: Rua do Carmo 71; f. 1929; Exec. Dir. GUMERSINDO FERNANDES.

Previdente—Cia. de Seguros: Rua Teófilo Otoni 15, 9°; f. 1872; Pres. P. BRITO BEZERRA DE MELLO.

Riachuelo—Cia de Seguros: Rua Teófilo Otoni 15, 9°; f. 1944; Pres. Dr. O. LYNCH BEZERRA DE MELLO, Jr.

Rio Branco—Cia de Segs.: Rua da Assembleia 104, 2°, C.P. 893-ZC-00; f. 1946; Pres. AGOSTINHO ERMELINO DE LEÃO

Sol—Cia. de Seguros: Rua Ouvidor 108, 10°; f. 1956; Pres. P. TEIXEIRA BOAVISTA.

Solidez—Cia. Nacional de Seguros: Avda. Pres. Vargas 409, 14°, C.P. 2472; f. 1955; Pres. Eng. N. OTTONI DE REZENDE.

Sul América (T.M.A.): Rua Rosária 90 e Rua Buenos Aires 29-37; f. 1895; Pres. Dr. ANTÓNIO SÁNCHEZ DE LARRAGOITI, Jr.

Sul América Terrestres Marítimos e Acidentes—Cia. de Segs.: Rua do Rosário 90, C.P. 1077; f. 1913; Pres. Dr. ANTÓNIO SÁNCHEZ DE LARRAGOITI, Jr.

Ultramer—Cia. Brasileira de Seguros: Rua Passeio 62; Pres. R. R. DE OLIVEIRA REZENDE.

União Brasileira—Cia de Seguros Gerais: Avda. Paulo Frontin 628; Pres. NISSIM PAZUELLO.

Instituto de Resseguros do Brasil (IRB) (*Reinsurance*): Avda. Marechal Câmara 171, C.P. 1440; f. 1939; Pres. JOSÉ LOPES DE OLIVEIRA.

São Paulo, S.P.

Cia. Bandeirante de Seguros Gerais: Praça D. José Gaspar 30, 13°-15°; f. 1943; Pres. DUPRAT FIGUEREIDO.

Brasil—Cia. de Segs. Gerais: Rua Conselheiro Crispiniano 58, C.P. 796; f. 1904; Pres. Dr. EMILIO SORTINO.

Cia. Central de Segs.: Rua Direita 32, 6°; f. 1944; Pres. EMILIO SORTINO.

Cia. de Seguros Cruzeiro do Sul: Avda. S. João 313, 1° e 18°; Pres. L. M. TEIXEIRA PINTO.

Companhia Anglo Americana de Seguros Gerais: Rua Bôa Vista 314, C.P. 1618; f. 1955; Pres. P. KIEHL.

Indiana—Cia. de Segs. Gerais: Rua Bôa Vista 236, C.P. 2581; f. 1945; Pres. D. WILTON PAES DE ALMEIDA.

Ipiranga—Cia. Nacional de Segs.: Rua Barão de Itapetininga 151, 7°, C.P. 1141; f. 1939; Pres. Dr. J. A. DA S. GORDO.

Itaú Seguradora S.A.: Rua Barão de Itapetininga 18; Pres. J. E. DE MORÃES.

A Marítima—Cia. de Segs. Gerais: Rua Xavier de Toledo 114, 9° e 10°, C.P. 5130; f. 1943; Pres. Dr. ALVARO AUGUSTO DE BUENO VIDIGAL.

Cia. Paulista de Seguros: Rua Líbero Badaró 158, 1°-7°; f. 1906; Pres. Dr. NICOLAY MORÃES BARROS.

Companhia Piratininga de Seguros Gerais: Rua Quirino Andrade 215, 11°, C.P. 3648; f. 1938; Pres. ABIBE ISFER.

São Paulo—Companhia Nacional de Seguros de Vida: Rua 15 de Novembro 324, C.P. 1868; f. 1920; Pres. Dr. D. FERRAZ NOVÃES.

Pôrto Alegre

Madepinho Seguradora S.A.: Avda. Julio de Castilhos 360; Dir. Dr. TELEMACO DESIDÉRIO CALEFFI.

Phenix de Pôrto Alegre—Cia. de Seguros Marítimos e Terrestres: Praça 15 de Novembro 16, 2-3°, C.P. 446; f. 1879; Pres. S. S. SARAIVA.

Pôrto Alegrense—Cia. de Seguros: Rua dos Andradas 1234, 20°; f. 1883; Pres. ARGEU ELIZALDE DIEHL.

Previdência do Sul—Cia. de Seguros: Rua dos Andradas 1049, C.P. 76; f. 1906; Dirs. J. C. D'AZEVEDO, W. S. BAUER, V. KERSTING.

Santa Cruz Cia. de Seguros Gerais: Trav. Fco. de Leonardo Truda 98, 6°; Pres. LAURO MIGUEL STURN.

Sul Brasil—de Seguros Terrestres e Marítimos: Rua dos Andradas 1332, C.P. 294; f. 1909; Dir. L. F. KESSLER.

União—Cia. de Seguros Gerais: Avda. Borges de Medeiros 261, 1°, C.P. 400; f. 1891; Pres. Dr. R. BIER DA SILVA.

Principal Provincial Companies

Aliança da Bahia—Cia. de Seguros: Rua Pinto Martins 11, C.P. 351, Salvador; f. 1870; Pres. Dr. P. DE CARVALHO.

Aliança do Pará—Cia. de Seguros: Rua Santo António 316, 12°, Belém, P.A.; f. 1899; Pres. ANTÓNIO NICOLAU VIANNA DA COSTA.

Bamerindus Companhia de Seguros: Rua Mal. Deodoro 314, 5°, C.P. 450, Curitiba; f. 1938; cap. 12m.; Gen. Man. H. PIZZATO.

Companhia de Seguros da Bahia: Rua Miguel Calmon 57, 3-5°, Salvador, Bahia; f. 1929; Pres. F. M. DE GÓES.

Companhia de Seguros Minas Brasil: Rua dos Caetés 745, Belo Horizonte, M.G.; Pres. J. O. ARAUJO.

Novo Hamburgo—Cia. de Seguros Gerais: Rua Julio de Castilhos 462, C.P. 191, Novo Hamburgo; f. 1950; Dir. W. R. KORNDÖRFER.

Pátria—Cia. Brasileira de Seguros Gerais: Rua Pedro Serreira 82-84, Itajai, Santa Catarina; f. 1945; Pres. A. C. DE A. BRAGA.

Seguradora do Estado do Espírito Santo: Rua Gen. Osório 83, Vitório, E.S.; Pres. JOSÉ DE ALMEIDA.

Seguradora Indústria e Comércio, S.A.: Avda. Guararapes 50, C.P. 359, Recife; f. 1935; Pres. L. DIAS LINS.

Seguradora Industrial e Mercantil, S.A.: Avda. Guararapes 50, C.P. 359, Recife; f. 1940; Pres. L. DIAS LINS.

Supervising Authority

Superintendência de Seguros Privados (SUSEP): Ministry of Industry and Commerce, Brasília; f. 1966; replacing the *Departamento Nacional de Seguros Privados;* Superintendent DÉCIO VIEIRA VEIGA.

TRADE AND INDUSTRY

CHAMBERS OF COMMERCE

Rio de Janeiro, Guanabara

Associação Comercial Rio de Janeiro: Rua da Candelaria 9, 11° e 12°; f. 1834; 6,000 members; Pres. RUI GOMES DE ALMEIDA; official Technical Advisory Board for the Federal Govt.; publs. *Revista das Classes Produtoras* (monthly).

Confederação Nacional da Agricultura: Avda. General Justo 171.

Confederação Nacional do Comércio.

São Paulo, S.P.

Associação Comercial de São Paulo: Rua Bôa Vista 51; f. 1894; 11,000 mems.; Pres. BOAVENTURA FARINA; Sec. HERCULANO CARLOS DE ALMEIDA PIRES; publs. *Diário do Comércio, Digesto Econômico, Temas e Problemas.*

Belém

Associação Comercial do Pará: Avda. Presidente Vargas, C.P. 337; f. 1864; 655 mems.; Pres. ANTÓNIO MARTINS, Jr.; Sec. JOSÉ OIAVO IAMARÃO.

Belo Horizonte

Associação Comercial de Minas Gerais: Avda. Afonso Pena 372, 3°, C.P. 1305; f. 1901; Pres. Dr. JOSÉ ROMUALDO CANÇADO BAHIA; 60 Dirs.; publs. *Mensagem Econômica* (monthly), *Boletim da Associação Comercial de Minas* (weekly).

Curitiba

Associação Comercial do Paraná: Rua 15 de Novembro 621, 2°, C.P. 365; f. 1890; 1,141 mems.; Pres. JOÃO CHALBAUD BISCAIA; Sec.-Gen. IVO ZAGONEL; comprises Depts.: Paraguayan Tea (Erva Maté), Coffee, Timber, Trade, Industry, Social, Touring and Publicity; publ. *Fôlha do Comércio.*

Florianópolis

Associação Comercial de Florianópolis: C.P. 377; f. 1915; 242 mems.; Chair. DIETRICH VON WANGENHEIM; publ. *Boletim Comercial e Industrial* (monthly).

João Pessôa

Associação Comercial: Rua Marechal Pinheiro; f. 1887; 204 mems.

Maceió

Associação Comercial de Maceió: Rua da Alfândega 476.

Manaus

Associação Comercial do Amazonas: Rua Guilherme Moreira 281; f. 1871; 400 mems.; publs. *Boletim* (monthly), *Arquivos* (quarterly), *Relatório* (yearly).

Natal

Associação Comercial do Rio Grande do Norte: Avda. Duque de Caxias 191; f. 1892; 370 mems.; Pres. E. DIAS FERNANDES.

Niterói

Associação Comercial de Niterói: Rua da Conceição 95.

Pôrto Alegre

Associação Comercial de Pôrto Alegre: Palácio do Comércio, 6°; f. 1858; 2,150 mems.; Pres. Econ. ENIO AVELINE DA ROCHA; Exec. Dir. JOÃO GOMES MALTEZ; publs. *Boletim Semanal, Boletim Estatístico Mensal.*

Recife

Associação Comercial de Pernambuco: Praça Rio Branco 18; Pres. OSCAR AMORIM.

Associação de Comerciantes Retalhistas de Pernambuco: Rua Duque de Caxias 275; f. 1933; 1,500 mems.

São Luís

Associação Comercial do Maranhão: Palácio do Comércio, Praça Benedito Leite.

Salvador

Associação Comercial da Bahia: Praça Conde dos Arcos 6, C.P. 193; f. 1811; 1,479 mems.; publ. *Casta Informativa.*

Sergipe

Associação Comercial de Sergipe: Rua José do Prado Franco 557, C.P. 239.

Vitória

Associação Comercial de Vitória: Rua Misael Pena 216; f. 1909; 120 mems.

INTERNATIONAL CHAMBERS OF COMMERCE

Rio de Janeiro

Câmara de Comércio Americana (*American*): Avda. Rio Branco 123, 21°; Exec. Vice-Pres. NICOLAU K. BINA MACHADO; publs. *Brazilian Business* (monthly), *Brazilian Newsbriefs* (weekly).

Câmara de Comércio Franco-Brasileira (*Franco-Brazilian*): Avda. Presidente António Carlos 58.

Câmara di Commercio Italiana di Rio de Janeiro (*Italian*): Avda. Pres. A. Carlos 40, 6°; f. 1950; 1,000 mems.

Câmara Teuto Brasileira de Comércio e Industria no Rio de Janeiro (*German-Brazilian*): Avda. Rio Branco 123, Gr. 708-11, C.P. 1790-ZC-00; f. 1916.

Câmara de Comercio Uruguaya del Brasil (*Uruguayan*): Avda. Rio Branco 20, 18°; f. 1934; Exec. Sec. TOBIAS JUCÁ DE CASTRO.

São Paulo

British Chamber of Commerce of São Paulo: Rua Barão de Itapetininga 275, 7°, C.P. 1621.

Câmara de Comércio Holando-Brasileira em São Paulo (*Dutch-Brazilian*): Rua do Riachuelo 201, 8°, São Paulo.

DEVELOPMENT ORGANIZATIONS

Conselho de Desenvolvimento Industrial—CDI (*Industrial Development Council*): Ministry of Industry and Commerce, Brasília; offers incentives for private investment and exemption from import duty on machinery and equipment not available in Brazil.

Conselho Nacional de Comércio Exterior—CONCEX (*Foreign Trade Council*): Ministry of Industry and Commerce, Brasília; f. 1966 to be responsible for foreign exchange and trade policies and for the control of export activities.

Conselho Nacional do Petróleo: Avda. 13 de Maio 13, 26°, Rio de Janeiro; f. 1938; consultative body to the Ministry of Mines and Energy; directs national policy on petroleum; Pres. Gen. ARAKEN DE OLIVEIRA; Vice-Pres. FERNANDO S. FERREIRA COELHO.

Departamento Nacional da Produção Mineral—DNPM: Avda. Pasteur 404, Praia Vermelha, Guanabara ZC-82; f. 1964; responsible for the development of mineral resources; Dir. Dr. YVAN BARRETO DE CARVALHO; publ. *Publicação Especial do D.N.P.M.*

Eletrobrás: Rio de Janeiro; f. 1962; Governmental holding company responsible for planning, financing and managing Brazil's electric energy programme; cap. U.S. $1,450m.; expansion programmes to cost U.S. $1,350m. per year; new generation per year 1,500,000 kW., mostly hydro-electric, including a nuclear power plant with a capacity of 620,000 kW. due for completion by 1975-76; Pres. MÁRIO BHERING.

Empresa Brasileira de Aeronautica (EMBRAER): São José dos Campos, São Paulo; f. 1969, to promote development of the Brazilian aeronautics industry; Pres. ALDO B. FRANCO.

Empresa Telecomunicações Brasileiras—Telebrás: Rio de Janeiro.

Grupo Executivo da Industria Química—GEIQUIM: Praça Mauá 7, sala 1606, Rio de Janeiro; f. 1964 to establish an overall policy for the chemical field and to promote the chemical industry; Exec. Sec. GERALDO GUENNES TAVARES DE LIMA.

Grupo Executivo para o Desenvolvimento Agrícola—Geida: Rio de Janeiro; f. 1968 to supervise the implementation of the National Irrigation Plan, which includes 56 regional projects for which U.S.$120m. has been budgeted till 1974.

Grupo Executivo para a Racionalização da Cafeiculture (GERCA): Instituto Brasileiro do Café, Avda. Rodrigues Alves 129, Rio de Janeiro; to promote coffee production in Brazil; Sec.-Gen. JOSÉ JORGE SEBASTIÃO.

Instituto do Açúcar e do Álcool: Praça 15 de Novembro 42, Rio de Janeiro; C.P. 420-ZC-00, Formiga 21, São Paulo; Government agency for the promotion and development of the Brazilian sugar economy; sole exporter of Brazilian raw sugar; Pres. FRANCISCO OITICICA.

Instituto Brasileiro do Café: Avda. Rodrigues Alves 129, Rio de Janeiro; f. 1952; controls and promotes the production and commerce of coffee and gives technical advice to producers; government agency; Pres. C. A. DE ANDRADE PINTO; Sec.-Gen. G. GOMES DA ROSA.

Instituto Brasileiro do Desenvolvimento Florestal: Rio de Janeiro; f. 1967; independent organization affiliated to the Ministry of Agriculture; responsible for the annual formulation of national and regional forest plans.

Instituto Brasileiro de Reforma Agrária—IBRA: Rio de Janeiro; Govt. body to encourage agrarian reform in specially designated priority areas.

Instituto Nacional de Desenvolvimento Agrário—INDA: Largo de São Francisco 34, 3°, Rio de Janeiro; f. 1964; agricultural development institute under Ministry of Agriculture; encourages all aspects of development to benefit rural communities; Depts. of Colonization, Co-operation and Rural Extension, Rural Development; 21 State offices, 29 regional centres; Pres. Prof. EUDES DE SOUZA LEÃO PINTO; Sec. GENI ARLINDO.

Instituto Nacional de Tecnologia—INT: Avda. Venezuela 82, Rio de Janeiro; f. 1921; co-operates in national industrial development; Dir. Dr. P. M. GUIMARÃES.

Petróleo Brasileiro S.A.—Petrobrás: Praça Pio X 119, C.P. 809, Rio de Janeiro; responsible for development and production of petroleum products; cap. 5,943.7m.; Pres. Rear-Adm. FLORIANO PEIXOTO FARIA LIMA.

Petrobrás Química S.A.—Petroquisa: Avda. Rio Branco 81, 6°, Rio de Janeiro; f. 1968; subsidiary mixed capital company.

Petrobrás Distribuidora S.A.: Praça 22 de Abril 36, Rio de Janeiro; f. 1971; marketing of oil by-products; Pres. (vacant).

Petrobrás Internacional S.A.—Braspetro: Praça Pio X 119, 5°, Rio de Janeiro; f. 1972; foreign operations; Pres. Rear-Adm. FLORIANO PEIXOTO FARIA LIMA.

Companhia de Petróleo da Amazônia—COPAM: Rua México 74, Rio de Janeiro; f. 1972; Pres. LEOPOLDO A. M. DE MELLO.

Superintendência do Desenvolvimento da Amazônia—SUDAM: Belém; f. 1966 to develop the Amazon regions of Brazil; 502 new approved projects with total investment of 6,399.8m. (Jan. 1973), including industrial, cattle breeding and basic services projects; Superintendent Eng. HUGO DE ALMEIDA.

FIDAM: Private investment fund for Amazonia.

Superintendência do Desenvolvimento do Nordeste—SUDENE: Fortaleza, Ceará; f. 1959; assists development of North Eastern parts of the country; Superintendent JOSÉ LINS ALBUQUERQUE.

Grupo Executivo da Grande São Paulo—GEGRAN: São Paulo; f. 1967 to co-ordinate development plans for greater São Paulo.

Superintendência do Desenvolvimento da Região Centro-Oeste—SUDECO: Goiânia; f. 1968 to co-ordinate development projects in the State of Goiás, the Triângulo Mineiro area of Minas Gerais and southern Mato Grosso; replaces Fundação Brasil Central.

Superintendência do Desenvolvimento da Região Sul—SUDESUL: Pôrto Alegre, Rio Grande do Sul; f. 1967 to co-ordinate development in the states of Rio Grande do Sul, Santa Catarina and Paraná, replacing former Superintendência do Desenvolvimento da Fronteira Sudoeste.

EMPLOYERS' ORGANIZATIONS

Confederação Nacional da Indústria (C.N.I.) (*National Confederation of Industry*): Avda. Nilo Peçanha 50, 34°, Rio de Janeiro; f. 1938; set up in 1945 the National Service for Industrial Apprenticeship (SENAI) to provide advanced technical training through its regional training colleges in the Federal District, State capitals and important industrial centres; also administers the Serviço Social da Indústria (SESI), est. 1945, to secure improvements in the general living standards and education of workers; Pres. THOMÁS POMPEU DE SOUZA, BRASIL NETTO.

Federação das Indústrias do Estado de São Paulo (*Federation of Industries of the State of São Paulo*): Viaduto Dona Paulina 80, 6°, São Paulo; f. 1937; 102 member firms; is affiliated to Confederação Nacional da Indústria; promotes periodical exhibitions of industrial products of São Paulo State; Pres. THEOBALDO DE NIGRISS; publs. *Boletim Informativo* (monthly) and legal and economic publications.

TRADE UNIONS

Confederação Nacional dos Trabalhadores na Indústria—CNTI (*National Confederation of Industrial Workers*): Rio de Janeiro; 4 million (est.) mems. including 2 national federations (Workers in the Printing Industry and Public Utility Workers) and 57 state or regional federations; there are also 7 regional councils; Pres. OLAVO PREVIATTI; Gen. Sec. ARGEU EGYDIO DOS SANTOS.

Confederação Nacional dos Trabalhadores no Comércio—CNTC (*National Confederation of Commercial Workers*): Rua Alvaro Alvim 21, 9°, Rio de Janeiro; f. 1947; 2,500,000 (est.) mems.; 22 affiliated federations, including 6 national federations (Hospital Employees, Employees of Resort Centres and Hostels, Hotel Employees, Employees of Commercial Distribution Companies of Minerals and Combustible Minerals, Salesmen and Travelling Salesmen, Warehousemen); Pres. ANTÓNIO ALVES DE ALMEIDA; First Sec. RAYMUNDO NONATO DA COSTA ROCHA; publ. *Boletim Informativo*.

Confederação Nacional dos Trabalhadores em Transportes Terrestres—CNTTT (*National Confederation of Land Transport Workers*): Avda. Rio Branco 20, 17°, Rio de Janeiro; f. 1953; 500,000 mems.; affiliated mems. composed of 3 national federations (Motor Vehicle Operators, Railroad Workers, Trolley Car Workers) and 2 state federations; Pres. MÁRIO LOPES DE OLIVEIRA; Sec. FRANCISCO MURCIA COMPAN; publ. *Boletim de Orientação Sindical* (bi-monthly).

Confederação Nacional dos Trabalhadores nas Empresas de Crédito—CONTEC (*National Confederation of Workers in Credit Institutions*): Avda. Graça Aranha 19, Gr. 904, C.P. 52, Rio de Janeiro; f. 1959; 150,000 (est.) mems.; 10 federations of bank employees are affiliated with 160 Unions and 20 Associations; Pres. RUY BRITO DE OLIVEIRA PEDROZA; Sec.-Gen. LAÉCIO DE FIGUEREIDO PEREIRA.

Major National Unions not affiliated with a National Centre:

Federação Nacional dos Trabalhadores Marítimos—FNTM (*National Federation of Maritime Workers*): Rua Camerino 128, Rio de Janeiro; 180,000 (est.) mems.; Sec. NELSON MENDONÇA.

TRANSPORT

Conselho Nacional de Transportes: Ministério dos Transportes, Brasília; f. 1961 to study, co-ordinate and execute government transport policy and reorganize railway, road and ports and waterways councils; Pres. ARAÚJO NOJUEIRA.

Grupo Executivo para a Integração de Política de Transporte-Geipot: Ministério dos Transportes, Esplanada dos Ministérios, Brasília D.F.; f. 1965; agency for the promotion of an integrated modern transport system and advises the Minister of Transport on transport policy; Dir. Eng. CLORALDINO SOARES SEVERO.

RAILWAYS

Departmento Nacional de Estradas de Ferro (D.N.E.F.) (*National Railways Department*): Rua do Mercado 34, Rio de Janeiro; central authority over all railways open for public service in Brazil; Dir.-Gen. Eng. HORÁCIO MADUREIRA; Gen. Man. Eng. JOÃO CARLOS GURGEL BARBOSA.

Rêde Ferroviaria Federal S.A. (R.F.F.S.A.) (*Federal Railway Corporation*): Praça Duque de Caxias 86, Rio de Janeiro; f. 1957, as a Holding Company for 14 railways owned by the Union; Pres. Gen. ANTÓNIO ADOLFO MANTA.

There are also railways owned by State Governments, administered by the following:

FEPASA—Ferrovia Paulista S.A.: Rua Líbero Badaró 39, São Paulo; 3,671 km. metre gauge (705 km. electrified), 1,656 km. 1.6 m. gauge; Pres. JAUL PIRES DE CASTRO. There are also some five privately owned railways.

Cia Vale do Rio Doce (*Vitória a Minas Railway*): C.P. 155, Vitória, Espírito Santo; 756 km. open; 30m. tons iron ore carried in 1971.

E. F. do Amapa: Porto Santana, Macapa, C.P. 396, Belém; 194 km. open; 1.2m. tons manganese ore carried in 1970.

A total of 10,400m. is to be invested between 1974 and 1978 in the building of new lines, improvements to existing lines and the purchase of rolling stock.

ROADS

Departamento Nacional de Estradas de Rodagem (*National Roads Department*); Dir. ELISEU RESENDE.

In 1973 there were 225,000 km. of roads in Brazil, of which 61,000 km. were Federal, 55,000 being paved.

The Highways section of the National Transport Plan, introduced in 1972, includes the construction or completion of a system of seven radial highways linking the Federal Capital, Brasília, with the state capitals and international border areas. The Plan also provides for the construction of 188 support roads. In all 100,000 km. of new or existing roads are involved in the Plan.

The Plan will be revised every five years by the **Conselho Nacional de Transportes.**

MOTORISTS' ORGANIZATIONS

Automóvel Club do Brasil: Rua do Passeio 90, Rio de Janeiro.

Touring Club of Brazil: Praça Mauá, Rio de Janeiro.

INLAND WATERWAYS

Departamento Nacional de Portos e Vias Navegaveis (*National Ports and Waterways Department*).

Companhia das Docas do Pará: Avda. Presidente Vargas 41, 2°, Belém, Pará; port authority established in 1967 to replace the former **Serviço de Navegação e de Administração do Porto do Pará (SNAPP)** in the administration of the port of Belém; cap. 45m.; Dir.-Pres. Col. RAÚL DA SILVA MOREIRA.

Empresa de Navegação da Amazônia: Avda. Presidente Vargas 41, 1°, Belém, Pará; private navigation company established in 1967 to replace **SNAPP** in the operation of cargo and passenger services on the Amazon river and its principal tributaries, connecting the port of Belém with Santarém, Manaus, Pôrto Velho, Iquitos (Peru) and other river ports.

SHIPPING

The principal ports are Rio de Janeiro, Santos and Vitória. Santos, the largest port in South America, is principally used for export of coffee. In 1966 a new port was opened at Tubarão (Vitória) 175 km. north of Rio, specially equipped to process and handle iron ore shipments, also with ample storage facilities for bulk imports. A 600m. scheme to improve Brazil's iron exports, announced in 1967, includes the building of a new rail terminal and harbour at Sepetiba, just south of Rio de Janeiro. Port improvements are in progress at Recife, Rio de Janeiro, Angra dos Reis, Mucuripe and Santos. Brazil's merchant shipping fleet is the largest in Latin America.

Companhia de Navegação Marítima NETUMAR: Manaus, AM; Rio de Janeiro office: Avda. Pres. Vargas 482, 22-23°; f. 1959; 15 vessels, 125,000 tons d.w.t.; coastal traffic including Amazon region, foreign trade to U.S.A. and Canada, east coast and Great Lakes ports, Argentina and Uruguay.

Companhia de Navegação do Rio São Francisco: Rio de Janeiro; f. 1963; incorporation of four private companies operating on the São Francisco River; 51 per cent government-owned.

Figueiredo Navegação S.A., L.: Avda. Rio Branco 57, 21°, Rio de Janeiro; cargo services between the Amazon and the east coast of the United States and to northern Europe; 6 vessels of 25,970 total gross tonnage; Chair. JOÃO BAPTISTA L. FIGUEIREDO.

Lloyd Brasileiro: Rua do Rosario 1, Rio de Janeiro; partly government-owned; possesses 40 vessels with a total displacement of 350,749 gross tons; has 13 vessels under construction, with a total displacement of 182,100 tons; operates an average of 20 chartered vessels; maintains passenger and cargo services along the coast from the Amazon to Rio Grande do Sul; operates between Brazil, the U.S.A. and Canada, northern Europe, Scandinavia, the Mediterranean, East and West Africa, the Far East, the Arabian Gulf, Japan, Australia and New Zealand, and around the South American coast through the associated company **Lloyd-Libra**. Operates with palletized, containerized and frozen cargoes, as well as with general and bulk cargoes; has recently introduced the roll-on/roll-off system; Pres. JONAS CORREA DA COSTA SOBRINHO.

Navegação Mercantil S.A.: Avda. Rio Branco 103, 3° & 4°, Rio de Janeiro; Brazilian coastal services, Buenos Aires, U.S. Gulf, Mexico, Caribbean; world-wide bulk carrier service; 10 ships totalling 50,940 tons gross; Pres. PAULO FERRAZ.

Petróleo Brasileiro S.A. (Petrobrás) (Frota Nacional de Petroleiros) (Fronape): Rua Carlos Seidl 188, Caju, Rio de Janeiro; transports bulk petroleum products; tanker fleet of 2,059,875 tons d.w.t.; Man. Capt. PAULO TEIXEIRA DE FREITAS.

CIVIL AVIATION

A co-ordinating commission under the leadership of Lt.-Brig. JOELMIR CAMPOS DE ARARIPE MACEDO has been set up by five Brazilian aviation authorities to plan a new international airport at Rio de Janeiro capable of handling new supersonic aircraft.

Santos Dumont Airport, Rio de Janeiro, serves the internal lines. It is serviced by VARIG, Cruzeiro do Sul and VASP.

DOMESTIC LINES

Brasília

Transbrasil S.A. Linhas Aéreas: SQS 305, Bloco C, Lojas 31-33; f. 1955; scheduled passenger and cargo services are operated to points in south-east and north-east Brazil; fleet: 4 BAC 1-11/500, 6 Heralds; on order: 6 EMB-110 Bandeirante; Pres. OMAR FONTANA.

Rio de Janeiro

Serviços Aéreos Cruzeiro do Sul, S.A.: Avda. Rio Branco, 128, C.P. 190, Rio de Janeiro; f. 1927; network routes: Brazil, Argentina, Bolivia, Colombia, French Guiana, Guyana, Peru, Trinidad, Uruguay; fleet: 6 Boeing 727, 6 Caravelle VI-R, 4 YS-11A, 5 DC-3; cap. 50.9m.; Pres. Eng. LEOPOLDINO C. AMORIM, Jr.; Vice-Pres. Flight Capt. MARIO ARAÚJO.

S.A. Empresa de Viação Aérea Rio Grandense (VARIG): Varig Building, Santos Dumont Airport, Rio de Janeiro; f. 1927; international services via São Paulo, Rio de Janeiro, Brasília, Manaus and Belém to New York, Miami, Los Angeles, Tokyo, Johannesburg, Luanda, Asunción, Bogotá, Buenos Aires, Caracas,

Lima, Mexico City, Montevideo, Santiago, Lisbon, Oporto, Frankfurt, Copenhagen, Paris, London, Zurich, Geneva, Madrid and Rome; domestic services to major cities of the country; fleet: 1 DC-8, 15 Boeing 707, 7 Boeing 727, 10 Electra II L-188, 8 Avro HS-748; on order: 4 Douglas DC-10-30, 1 Boeing 707, 2 Boeing 727, 10 Boeing 737; Pres. ERIK DE CARVALHO.

São Paulo

Viação Aérea São Paulo, S.A. (VASP): Edifício VASP, Aeroporto de Congonhas; f. 1933; domestic services covering all Brazil; cargo services to Argentina; fleet: 5 Boeing 737-200, 4 Boeing 737-200 Advanced, 2 BAC 1-11/400, 3 Viscount 827, 3 YS-11A, 3 DC-3, 3 EMB-110 Bandeirante, 4 DC-6C Cargo; on order: 6 Boeing

737-200, 2 EMB-110 Bandeirante; Pres. Dr. LUIZ RODOVIL ROSSI; Vice-Pres. C. W. ARINELLI ESPÍOLA; Exec. Dirs. MÁRIO JORGE JORGE GERMANOS, Col. NATALINO DA S. BRITO.

In addition to the airlines listed above, there are a number of others operating regional services.

FOREIGN SERVICES

The following foreign airlines serve Brazil: Aerolíneas Argentinas, Air France, Alitalia, Avianca (Colombia), Braniff, British Caledonian, Iberia, KLM, LAP, LAN de Chile, Lloyd Aéreo Boliviano, Lufthansa, Pan American, Primeras Líneas Uruguayas de Navegación Aérea, SAS, South African Airways, Swissair, TAP.

TOURISM AND CULTURE

Conselho Nacional de Turismo (CNTUR) (*National Tourism Office*): Ministério da Industria e do Comércio, Esplanada dos Ministérios, Brasília; f. 1966; Exec. Sec. FEDERICO MARAGLIANO CARDOSO.

Divisão de Exposições e Feiras: Departamento Nacional do Registro do Comércio, Ministério da Industria e do Comércio, Esplanada dos Ministérios, Brasília; f. 1967; organizes fairs and exhibitions; Directress WANDA AVELLAR GUIMARÃES; publ. *Calendário de Exposições e Feiras*.

Empresa Brasileira de Turismo—Embratur: Praça Mauá 7, 11°, Rio de Janeiro; f. 1966; studies tourist development projects; investments for the 1969–79 period are estimated at 744m. cruzeiros; Pres. PAULO MANOEL PROTÁSIO.

CULTURAL ORGANIZATION

The cultural heritage of Brazil is rooted in three distinct groups which have fused to make the present population: the European, mainly Portuguese, the African Negro, slaves brought in by the European, and the indigenous Indians. All these elements can be seen in present day cultural manifestations, such as Carnival, where Indian and African influences show clearly in a Christian-based festival. Local legends play an important part in the cultural life, and each State has a department concerned with tourism or culture.

Rio de Janeiro is the venue for the Brazilian Theatre Congress in July, also Folklore Day; there is an international Music Festival in August/September, also the

Brazilian Authors' Festival, Brazilian Popular Music Festival and a bi-annual Piano Competition. At São Paulo there is the famous Biennal, which has received world-wide acclaim and participation, being second only to Venice in importance.

The principal body concerned with the organization of the arts and culture is:

Ministério da Educação e Cultura: Esplanada dos Ministérios, Brasília, D.F.; Minister NEY BRAGA; the Ministry is responsible for a number of cultural organizations, among them:

Comissão Nacional de Belas Artes (*Fine Arts Commission*).

Conselho Federal de Cultura (*Federal Cultural Council*).

Conselho Nacional de Belas Artes (*Fine Arts Council*).

Instituto Nacional do Cinema (*National Cinema Institute*).

Serviço Nacional de Teatro (*National Theatre Service*): f. 1937 to develop and encourage the theatre in Brazil, subsidizing national companies where necessary.

THEATRE

Teatro Municipal do Rio de Janeiro: under Secretaria de Educação do Estado da Guanabara; it accommodates the Rio International Music Festival and many other national and international artistic events.

There are also a number of provincial theatres.

ATOMIC ENERGY

Comissão Nacional de Energia Nuclear: Rua General Severiano, 90 Botafoga ZC-82, 20,000 Rio de Janeiro; f. 1956; Pres. HERVÁSIO GUIMARÃES DE CARVALHO; Dir. Education and Scientific Exchange Prof. WILSON BANDEIRA DE MELLO.

Brazil's first nuclear power station is being built at Angra dos Reis, in the State of Rio de Janeiro. Its initial capacity will be 657 MW. and it is scheduled to come into operation in 1977. Present plans envisage that Brazil will have an installed capacity of 6,000 MW. by 1985.

The 1973 budget of the CNEN amounted to Cr. 210,284,800 (U.S. $33,800,000).

Research reactors: The following research reactors are in operation:

IPR-RI Belo Horizonte, Minas Gerais: capacity 250 kW.

IEA-RI São Paulo: capacity 5 MW.

IEN-RI Rio de Janeiro.

URANIE Belo Horizonte, Minas Gerais.

RESUCO Recife, Pernambuco.

NC-9000 São José dos Campos, São Paulo.

"CAPITU" Belo Horizone, Minas Gerais (under construction).

"SUBLIME" Rio de Janeiro (planned).

COBRA Rio de Janeiro (planned).

A government-owned company, the **Corporação Brasileira de Tecnologia Nuclear (CBTN)**, was formed in December 1971 to act as an executive branch of the CNEN. Its main objectives are to establish a fuel-cycle industry, to promote the progressive assimilation of nuclear technology by private industrial concerns, and to pursue research and development programmes.

Brazil has close co-operation agreements with the nuclear energy authorities of the following countries: Federal Republic of Germany, France, Italy, U.S.A., Israel, Spain, Portugal and India.

Centro Brasileiro de Pesquisas Físicas: Avda. Wenceslau Braz 71, Rio de Janeiro, Guanabara; Dir. ALFREDO MARQUES DE OLIVEIRA.

Centro de Medicina Nuclear: Faculdade de Medicina da Universidade de São Paulo, C.P. 22022, São Paulo; f. 1949; biological and medical uses of radioisotopes; Dir. Dr. TEDE ESTON DE ESTON.

Eletrobrás: Rio de Janeiro; building an atomic power plant with a capacity of 500,000 kW. due for completion by 1975.

Escola Naval: Ilha de Villegagnon, Rio de Janeiro, Guanabara; reactor control courses; Dir. Rear Adml. JOSÉ RODRIGUES DE MATTOSH.

Instituto de Biofísica da Universidade Federal do Rio de Janeiro: Avda. Pasteur 458, Rio de Janeiro ZC-82; f. 1945; medical and biological research using biophysical techniques; Dir. Prof. CARLOS CHAGAS.

Instituto Nacional do Cancer: Praça Vermelha 23, Rio de Janeiro, Guanabara; Dir. Prof. M. SANTOS-SILVA.

Instituto de Energia Atômica: Cidade Universitária, C.P. 11049, Pinheiros, São Paulo; divisions of nuclear physics, reactor physics, reactor operations and maintenance, radio-biology, radio-chemistry, nuclear metallurgy, nuclear engineering, chemical engineering; Dir. Prof. ROMULO R. PIERONI.

Instituto de Mathemática Pura e Aplicada: Rua Luíz de Camões 68, Rio de Janeiro ZC-58, G.B.; f. 1952; Dir. LINDOLPHO DE CARVALHO DIAS; publ. *Monografia*.

Instituto Militar de Engenharia: Praça General Tiburcio, Praia Vermelha, Rio de Janeiro, Guanabara; Dir. Gen. PAULO L. DE REZENDE.

Instituto de Pesquisas da Marinha: Ministério da Marinha, Esplanada dos Ministérios, Brasília; Dir. A. C. AZEVEDE OSORIO.

Instituto de Pesquisas Radioactivas: Cidade Universitária, C.P. 1941, Belo Horizonte, Minas Gerais; f. 1952; Dir. Prof. MÍLTON CAMPOS; Vice-Dir. CARLOS MARCIO MASCARENHAS DALE; publs. technical and scientific reports, bulletin.

Instituto de Pesquisas Tecnológicas: C.P. 7141, Cidade Universitária "Armando de Salles Oliveira", São Paulo; Dir. Eng. ALBERTO PEREIRA DE CASTRO.

Instituto Tecnológico de Aeronáutica: São José dos Campos, São Paulo; f. 1950; Prof. FRANCISCO ANTÓNIO LACAZ NETTO; publ. *ITA Eugenharia*.

Núcleo de Estudos e Pesquisas Científicas (NEPEC): Rua Almirante Alexandrino 1885, Santa Teresa ZC-45, G.B.; f. 1956; research in physics and mathematics; teaching and learning systems in physical sciences; Pres. Prof. ARMANDO DIAS TAVARES; Vice-Pres. Prof. CONSTANTINO MENEZES DE BARROS; Gen. Sec. ADEL DA SILVEIRA; Exec. Dir. Prof. HENRIQUE ALFREDO GALVÃO DE MORÃES.

Universidade do Brasil: Avda. Pasteur 250, Rio de Janeiro, Guanabara; atomic research in medicine, chemistry, engineering and biophysics.

Universidade Católica do Rio de Janeiro: Rua Marques de S. Vicente 263, Rio de Janeiro, Guanabara; nuclear physics; Dir. Dr. ALCEV G. PINHO, Jr.

Universidade Federal da Bahia: Rua Professor Augusto Viana s/n, São Salvador, Bahia; atomic research in chemistry.

Universidade Federal de Minas Gerais: Rua Espírito Santo 1186, Belo Horizonte, Minas Gerais; atomic research in engineering.

Universidade do Recife: Rua do Hospício 619, Recife, Pernambuco; atomic research in chemistry.

Universidade Federal do Rio Grande do Sul: Instituto de Física, 90,000 Pôrto Alegre; f. 1959; research in solid state, nuclear physics, quantum field theory and astronomy; Dir. Prof. WERNER ARTHUR MUNDT.

Universidade do Rio de Janeiro: Rua Marechal Deodoro s/n, Niterói, Rio de Janeiro, Guanabara; nuclear physics, radio-biology.

Universidade de São Paulo: Cidade Universitária, C.P. 8191, São Paulo; atomic research in medicine, physics, agriculture and engineering.

UNIVERSITIES

Universidade Federal de Alagoas: Avda. Orlando Araújo 1914, Maceió, Alagoas; 308 teachers, 2,390 students.

Universidade do Amazonas: C.P. 378, Manáus, Amazonas; c. 160 teachers, c. 1,100 students.

Universidade Federal da Bahia: Rua Augusto Viana s/n, Canela, Salvador, Bahia; 1,155 teachers, 5,538 students.

Universidade de Brasília: Agência Postal 15, Brasília, D.F.; c. 600 teachers, c. 3,400 students.

Universidade Estadual de Campinas: C.P. 1170, Campinas, São Paulo; 691 teachers, 4,000 students.

Universidade de Caxias do Sul: Rua Os 18 do Forte 1771, Caxias do Sul, Rio Grande do Sul.

Universidade Católica de Campinas: Rua Marechal Deodoro 1099, C.P. 317, Campinas, São Paulo; 1,054 teachers, 12,000 students.

Universidade Federal do Ceará: Avda. da Universidade 2853, Fortaleza, Ceará; 568 teachers, 8,493 students.

Universidade Federal do Espírito Santo: Rua Pietrángelo de Biase, Vitória, Espírito Santo; 478 teachers, 3,936 students.

Universidade Federal Fluminense: Rua Miguel de Frias 9, Icaraí, Niterói, Rio de Janeiro; 1,359 teachers, 12,000 students.

Universidade Católica de Goiás: C.P. 86, Goiânia, Goiás; 250 teachers, 3,500 students.

Universidade Federal de Goiás: Avda. Universitária, C.P. 131, Goiânia, Goiás; 736 teachers, 5,000 students.

Universidade do Estado da Guanabara: Avda. Pedro II 293, S. Cristovão, Rio de Janeiro; 601 teachers, 6,760 students.

Universidade Mackenzie: Rua Itambé 45, C.P. 8792, São Paulo; 550 teachers, 8,200 students.

Universidade do Maranhão: Rua 13 de Maio 500, São Luis, Maranhão.

Universidade Federal de Minas Gerais: Cidade Universitária, Pampulha, C.P. 1621, Belo Horizonte, Minas Gerais; 2,194 teachers, 14,892 students.

Universidade Católica de Minas Gerais: C.P. 2686, Belo Horizonte, Minas Gerais; 478 teachers, 5,730 students.

Universidade Federal do Pará: Avda. Governador José Malcher 1192, Belém, Pará; 786 teachers, 8,000 students.

Universidade Federal da Paraíba: Avda. Getúlio Vargas s/n, João Pessoa, Paraíba; 745 teachers, 7,335 students.

Universidade Federal do Paraná: Rua 15 de Novembro s/n, C.P. 441, Curitiba, Paraná; 1,326 teachers, 10,305 students.

Universidade Católica do Paraná: Avda. Imaculada Conceição s/n, C.P. 2293, Curitiba, Paraná; 411 teachers, 5,600 students.

Universidade de Passo Fundo: Avda. Brasil 743, Passo Fundo, Rio Grande do Sul; 286 teachers, 5,500 students.

Universidade Católica de Pelotas: Rua Felix da Cunha 412, Pelotas, Rio Grande do Sul; 350 teachers, 2,951 students.

Universidade Católica de Pernambuco: Rua do Príncipe 526, Recife; 202 teachers, c. 2,000 students.

Universidade Federal de Pernambuco: Avda. Morais Rego s/n, Cidade Universitária, Recife; 1,495 teachers, 11,930 students.

Universidade Federal Rural de Pernambuco: Rua D. Manuel de Medeiros, C.P. 2071, Dois Irmãos, Recife; 190 teachers, 1,979 students.

Universidade Católica de Petrópolis: Avda. Barão do Amazonas 124, Petrópolis; 244 teachers, 2,326 students.

Pontifícia Universidade Católica de Rio de Janeiro: Rua Marquês de São Vicente 209, Rio de Janeiro, Guanabara; 700 teachers, 6,400 students.

Universidade Federal do Rio Grande do Norte: Avda. Hermes da Fonsêca 780, Natal, Rio Grande do Norte; 230 teachers, 3,606 students.

Universidade Federal do Rio Grande do Sul: Avda. Paulo Gama s/n, Pôrto Alegre, Rio Grande do Sul; 1,309 teachers, 33,722 students.

Pontifícia Universidade Católica do Rio Grande do Sul: Avda. Ipiranga 6681, C.P. 1429, Pôrto Alegre; 915 teachers, 10,135 students.

Universidade Federal do Rio de Janeiro: Cidade Universitária, Ilha do Fundão, Rio de Janeiro, G.B.; 2,850 teachers, 21,813 students.

Universidade Federal Rural do Rio de Janeiro: Km. 47 Rodovia Rio-São Paulo, Itaguaí, Rio de Janeiro; 280 teachers, 2,500 students.

Universidade Católica do Salvador: Praça da Sé, Salvador, Bahia.

Universidade Federal de Santa Catarina: Campus Universitário, Trindade, Florianópolis, Santa Catarina; 660 teachers, 5,648 students.

Universidade Federal de Santa Maria: Rua Floriano Peixoto 1184, Santa Maria; 824 teachers, 11,020 students.

Universidade de São Paulo: Cidade Universitária "Armando de Salles Oliveira", C.P. 8191, São Paulo; 3,264 teachers, 28,081 students.

Pontifícia Universidade Católica de São Paulo: Rua Monte Alegre 984, São Paulo; 852 teachers, 9,046 students.

Universidade Federal de Sergipe: Aracajú, Sergipe.

Universidade do Vale do Rio dos Sinos: Praça Tiradentes 35, São Leopoldo, Rio Grande do Sul; 276 teachers, 8,164 students.

BRITISH DEPENDENT TERRITORIES

BELIZE

INTRODUCTORY SURVEY

Location, Climate, Capital

Belize (formerly British Honduras) lies on the Caribbean coast of Central America with Mexico to the north-west and Guatemala to the south-west. The climate is subtropical, tempered by trade winds. Belize City ceased to be the capital in August 1970 when the Government moved to the newly constructed city of Belmopan, about fifty miles inland.

Recent History

A constitution giving full internal self-government came into force on January 1st, 1964. Executive power is in the hands of a Cabinet of Ministers, while the Legislature consists of an eight-man appointed Senate and a house of 18 elected representatives. The Governor retains special powers concerning defence, external affairs and internal security. Guatemalan claims to sovereignty of Belize date back to the mid-eighteenth century and were written into Guatemala's constitution in 1945. Belize has unsuccessfully tried to obtain a defence guarantee to ensure protection against foreign interference, which it wants before independence from Britain. The Guatemalan claim is certain to be an issue in the elections due in 1974.

Economic Affairs

The economy used traditionally to be based on timber exports but the cultivation of sugar and citrus fruit is now more important. Almost half of the annual exports of sugar go to the United States. Rice and bananas are being developed for export with foreign assistance, and cattle-farming and fishing are becoming important industries. Belize is expected to join the Caribbean Community in 1974.

Transport and Communications

There are 850 miles of good roads and 18 airstrips as well as the Belize international airport at Stanley Field. Belize City is the main port; there is a second port at Stann Creek to the south of Belize.

Education

Primary education is principally carried on through subsidized denominational schools under government control. There are also 20 secondary schools, 3 technical colleges, 4 vocational schools and a teacher-training college.

Public Holidays

1974: September 10th (National Day), October 12th (Columbus Day—Northern Districts), November 14th (Prince Charles's Birthday), November 19th (Carib Settlement Day—Southern Districts), December 25th–26th (Christmas).

1975: January 1st (New Year's Day), March 9th (Baron Bliss Day), March 28th–31st (Easter), April 21st (Queen's Birthday), May 1st (Labour Day), May 24th (Commonwealth Day).

Weights and Measures

Imperial weights and measures are used, but petrol and paraffin are sold by the American gallon (231 cu. in.).

Currency

100 cents = 1 Belizean dollar (B$).
Exchange rates (April 1974):
£1 sterling = B$4.00;
U.S. $1 = B$1.694.

STATISTICAL SURVEY

Area and Population: Area (square miles) 8,866; Population (April 1970 census) 130,000; Belize City 43,000, Belmopan *c.* 3,500.

Employment (1967): Agriculture and Forestry 4,225, Transport 589, Manufacturing 2,743, Commerce 1,502.

Forestry (1969 exports): Mahogany Lumber $1,151,000, Cedar Lumber $226,000, Pine Lumber 182,917 board ft. $49,433 (1967).

Agriculture (1969 exports): Grapefruit and Juice $2,895,000, Oranges and Juice $2,712,000, Sugar 52,138 tons. About 1,605,760 acres are available for cultivation, of which 72,173 are under orchards and pasture, 10,000 under maize, 11,549 under rice, 4,383 under sugar, 5,000 under beans, 1,200 under cucumbers and 170 under tomatoes.

Livestock: Cattle 42,165, Pigs 20,000, Horses, Mules and Donkeys 4,987.

FINANCE

100 cents = 1 Belizean dollar (B$).
Coins: 1, 5, 10, 25 and 50 cents.
Notes: 1, 2, 5, 10 and 20 dollars.
Exchange rates (April 1974): £1 sterling = B$4.00; U.S. $1 = B$1.694.
B$100 = £25.00 = U.S. $59.03.

BUDGET (B$)

	1971	1972
Revenue (incl. Overseas Aid Scheme) .	15,932,079	18,162,202
Recurrent Expenditure . . .	16,092,456	16,953,565
Loan Receipts	178,948	100,000
National Revenue . . .	7,936,112	12,892,421

Recurrent Expenditure (1973 est.): B$18.3 million.

EXTERNAL TRADE
(1970)*

Imports: B$56.7m., mainly Food, Machinery and Transport Equipment.

Exports (inc. Re-exports): B$30.9m., mainly Sugar and Raw Materials.

Trade is chiefly with the United Kingdom, the United States, Canada and Jamaica.

* Provisional.

EDUCATION
(1970)

	PRIMARY	SECONDARY	TECHNICAL	TEACHER TRAINING
Schools . . .	182	20	3	1
Pupils . . .	30,591	3,597	267	130

Higher Education Abroad (1972): 224 students, of which 78 are at the University of the West Indies, Jamaica.

THE CONSTITUTION

A constitution providing for internal self-government came into force on January 1st, 1964. It provides for a Governor, a Cabinet of Ministers and a bi-cameral Legislature.

The powers of the Governor are complete only in respect of defence, external affairs and internal security, and for the first two of these there are consultative bodies designed to familiarize Ministers with matters for which they will ultimately have responsibility. There are also advisory commissions for the public service and the subordinate judiciary.

The Legislature consists of (1) A Senate of eight members, five appointed on the advice of the Premier, two on the advice of the Leader of the Opposition, and one after consultation with such persons as the Governor considers appropriate; (2) A House of Representatives consisting of eighteen members elected by universal adult suffrage for a five-year period.

THE GOVERNMENT

Governor and Commander-in-Chief: RICHARD NEIL POSNETT, O.B.E.

CABINET

(April 1974)

Premier and Minister of Finance and Economic Development: GEORGE C. PRICE.

Minister of Trade and Industry: ALEXANDER A. HUNTER.

Minister of Home Affairs and Health: CARL L. B. ROGERS.

Attorney-General and Minister Responsible for Works: V. H. COURTENAY.

Minister of Agriculture, Lands and Co-operatives: SANTIAGO PERDOMO.

Minister of Education, Housing and Labour: LOUIS S. SYLVESTRE.

Minister of Power and Communications: FREDERICK HUNTER.

Minister of Local Government, Community and Social Development: A. E. ARTHURS.

Minister without Portfolio: JOSEPH GRAY.

NATIONAL ASSEMBLY

THE SENATE

Eight members appointed by the Governor; 5 on the advice of the Premier; 2 on the advice of the Leader of the Opposition; 1 after consulting such persons as the Governor considers appropriate.

HOUSE OF REPRESENTATIVES

Eighteen members elected by universal adult suffrage.

(Election, December 5th, 1969)

People's United Party won 17 of the 18 seats.

POLITICAL PARTIES

People's United Party (P.U.P.): Belize; f. 1950; Christian democrat; holds 17 seats (1970); Leader GEORGE PRICE.

National Independence Party: Belize; f. 1958 on a merger of the National Party and the Honduran Independent Party, based on the combined membership of both parties; holds 1 seat (1970); Leader P. W. GOLDSON.

People's Democratic Movement: Belize; f. 1969; breakaway group from the N.I.P.; Leader D. LINDO.

United Black Association for Development (U.B.A.D. Party for Freedom, Justice and Equality): f. 1970; Leader EVAN HYDE.

JUDICIAL SYSTEM

Summary Jurisdiction Courts and District Courts (civil jurisdiction), presided over by magistrates, are established in each of the six judicial districts. Summary Jurisdiction Courts have a wide jurisdiction in indictable and other offences, but in District Courts, which exercise jurisdiction only in civil causes, this jurisdiction is limited to claims not exceeding B $500. Appeals lie to the Supreme Court, which has jurisdiction corresponding to the English High Court of Justice; from the Supreme Court further appeals lie to a Court of Appeal, established in 1968, thence to the Judicial Committee of the Privy Council in England.

Chief Justice: (vacant).

Puisne Judges: G. A. L. STAINE, C. A. B. ROSS.

Magistrates: S. N. NWEKE, G. B. SINGH, L. WAIGHT, G. N. BROWN.

RELIGION

About 65,000 of the population are Roman Catholic, and 28,000 are Anglican or Methodist. There are also a number of Hindus, Muslims and Ba'hais, and a community of 3,500 Mennonites.

CHURCH OF ENGLAND

Bishop of Belize: Rt. Rev. ELDON SYLVESTER.

ROMAN CATHOLIC CHURCH

Bishop of Belize: Most Rev. ROBERT L. HODAPP, S.J., D.D., Bishop's House, North Front Street, Belize City.

METHODIST CHURCH

District Chairman and General Superintendent, Caribbean and the Americas: Rev. JOHN FITZ-ALLEN, Wesley Manse, 88 Albert St., Belize City.

THE PRESS

The Beacon: twice weekly; Editor J. L. R. YOUNG; circ. 5,800.

Belize Newsletter: Government Information Services, Belmopan; official; weekly; Chief Information Officer R. I. CASTILLO.

Belize Times, The: P.O.B. 506, Belize; f. 1956; party political paper of People's United Party; morning daily, Tues. to Sun. inclusive; Editor RAY LIGHTBORN; circ. 4,000.

Government Gazette: Church St., Belize City; official; weekly.

The New Belize: Government Information Services, Belmopan; official; quarterly; available on request.

The Reporter: P.O.B. 707, c/o Industrial Press, 63 Cemetery Rd., Belize City; f. 1968; weekly; independent; Editor PAUL RODRIGUEZ; circ. 6,000.

RADIO

Radio Belize: P.O.B. 89, Belize; f. 1952; government-operated semi-commercial service; transmissions for 17 hours daily; broadcasts in English and Spanish; Chief Broadcasting Officer E. G. WAIGHT.

In 1972 there were 59,931 radio receivers.

FINANCE

Atlantic Bank: Albert St., Belize City; Man. L. A. FISHER.

Bank of Nova Scotia: Offices in Belize City and Corozal Town; Man. H. F. M. BUCKERIDGE.

Barclays Bank International Ltd.: Head Office: 54 Lombard St., London, E.C.3; Belize City Office: Albert St.; Man. N. H. HUNTER; sub-brs. at Barrack Rd., Belize City, Corozal Town, Orange Walk Town and Stann Creek Town; agency at Belmopan.

Royal Bank of Canada: Head Office: Place Ville Marie, Montreal; Office in Belize City; Man. U. I. L. FARIA; brs. at San Ignacio, Orange Walk Town, Corozal Town and Stann Creek Town; sub-br. at Belmopan.

There is also a Government Savings Bank.

FOREIGN INSURANCE COMPANIES IN BELIZE

British American Insurance Co., Caledonian Insurance Co. Ltd., Colonial Insurance Co. Ltd., Commercial Union Assurance Co. Ltd., Guardian Assurance Co. Ltd., Law

Union and Rock Insurance Co. Ltd., Nationals Ltd. (British Honduras), Norwich Union Fire Insurance Society Ltd., Sun Life Insurance Co. of Canada, Yorkshire Insurance Co. Ltd., Belize International Insurance Co.

National Economic Development Council: Belize City; advisory body to government; Financial Sec. R. A. FONSECA, C.M.G.

TRADE AND INDUSTRY

Belize Chamber of Commerce: P.O.B. 291, Belize City; f. 1918; 400 mems.; Pres. KENT McFIELD; Exec. Sec. ALLAN BODDEN.

Belize Reconstruction and Development Corporation: Belize; Chair. Hon. GEORGE C. PRICE, Premier and Minister of Finance and Economic Development; in charge of building new capital; Man. M. HALCROW.

Citrus Growers' Association: P.O.B. 7, Stann Creek; citrus crop farmers' association; Chair. H. T. A. BOWMAN, O.B.E., J.P.

Development Finance Corporation: P.O.B. 279, Belize City; issued cap. B$371,430,000; Chair. HORACE W. YOUNG; Man. RAYMOND FULLER; publs. *Investment Feasibility Studies on Animal Food Pellets, Concrete Tubes and Paints* and annual reports.

Livestock Producers' Association: farmers' association.

Sugar Cane Growers' Association: farmers' association.

EMPLOYERS' ASSOCIATION

Belize Employers' Association: Belize; f. 1961; 21 mems.

TRADE UNIONS

Belize General Workers' Development Union: 24 Craig St., Belize; affiliated to ICFTU; 1,366 mems.; Pres. THOMAS MARTÍNEZ; Gen. Sec. ADOLFOS ROSALES.

There are three branch unions affiliated to the central body.

Belize Public Officers' Union: 6 Regent St., Belize; f. 1922; established public workers; 800 mems.; Pres. EDWIN BELISLE; Sec. PAT BERNARD.

Christian Workers' Union: Regent St., Belize; f. 1962; general; 11,891 mems.; Pres. M. ROSADO.

CO-OPERATIVES

At the end of 1966 there were 41 Credit Unions, 9 Producer Co-operatives, 10 Marketing Co-operatives, 9 Farmers' Co-operatives, and 1 Supplies Co-operative.

There were also 26 junior and 3 senior savings unions and a Credit Union League (39 mems.).

Combined assets totalled B$3,000,000.

TRANSPORT AND TOURISM

ROADS

There are 850 miles of all-weather main and feeder roads, and 180 miles of government-maintained cart roads and bush trails. A number of logging and forest tracks are usable by heavy duty vehicles in the dry season.

SHIPPING

There is a weekly Southern Coastal freight, passenger and mail service and vessels of the Harrison, Royal Netherlands, United Fruit, Buccaneer, Canada, Jamaica, Caribbean and "K" lines call at Belize City.

CIVIL AVIATION

Chief Civil Aviation Officer: P.O.B. 367, Belize; L. C. BALDERAMOS, A.R.AE.S.

Maya Airways Ltd.: P.O.B. 458, Belize City; f. 1961; operates the internal services of the territory; Chair. Hon. W. H. COURTENAY; Dir. GORDON A. ROE.

The following airlines serve Belize: S.A.H.S.A. (Honduras), T.A.C.A. (El Salvador), T.A.N. (Honduras).

Chemicals Ltd.: Air Taxi Service, 15 Princess Margaret Drive, Belize City; f. 1962; runs internal and external charter service; Man. Dir. KURT J. BINDER; Dir. GUSTI H. BINDER.

TOURISM AND CULTURE

Belize Tourist Board: 12 Regent St., Belize City; Chair A. McNAB; Sec. L. CUELLAR.

Festival of Arts Committee: c/o Bliss Institute, Belize City; Chair. Lt.-Col. D. N. A. FAIRWEATHER.

BERMUDA

INTRODUCTORY SURVEY

Location, Climate, Capital

The Bermudas or Somers Islands are an isolated group of small Atlantic islands about 570 miles off the coast of South Carolina, U.S.A. They have a mild climate. The capital is Hamilton.

Government

Bermuda has been a British colony since the seventeenth century, and is now internally self-governing.

Defence

The local defence force is the Bermuda Regiment with a strength of some 425 men.

Recent History

The Parliamentary Election Act, passed in January 1963, enabled those over the age of 25 to vote in the elections to the House of Assembly, and was the first step in the political evolution of Bermuda after the withdrawal of the British garrison in 1953; the Act was extended in 1966 to enfranchise everyone over the age of 21. In 1963 Bermuda's first political party, the Progressive Labour Party, was formed, and in 1964 24 Independent members of the House formed the United Bermuda Party, which is the present majority party. In 1963 a joint select committee was set up to study constitutional changes; its recommendations were forwarded to the British Government in 1966. The Bermuda Constitution Order, which became effective in June 1968, provided for internal self-government, although the British Government retained responsibility in certain areas.

In March 1973 the Governor, Sir Richard Sharples, was assassinated. He was succeeded by Sir Edwin Leather.

Economic Affairs

The chief source of revenue is customs duties, but the tourist business is the most important feature of the economy. Its expansion and its demand for building land reduces the amount of arable acreage available and endangers growth in agriculture. There is no income tax or estate duty, and considerable U.K. capital is invested in Bermudian enterprises.

Transport and Communications

There are good roads and bus and ferry services, while international lines provide regular sea and air services.

Social Welfare

A wide range of welfare work is undertaken by the Department of Health and the Department of Social Services, as well as by a number of voluntary organizations.

In 1960 a State health insurance scheme for government employees was inaugurated. In 1965 the Government Employees' (Health Insurance) Act provided for medical and hospital benefits for all government employees and teachers. The 1967 Contributory Pensions Act enlarged the number of those eligible for pensions, and the 1970 Hospital Insurance Act made hospital insurance available for all. It also provided for free hospital care for children and subsidized rates for the elderly.

Education

There is free compulsory education between the ages of five and sixteen, and a number of scholarships are awarded for higher education and teacher training. The Bermuda College was founded in 1972 and is affiliated to the British Open University.

Tourism

The great attractions of the islands are the climate, scenery, and facilities for outdoor entertainment of all types.

Visas are not required by visitors from non-Communist countries.

Public Holidays

1974: August 1st (Cup Match), August 2nd (Somers' Day), November 11th (Remembrance Day), December 25th and 26th (Christmas and Boxing Day).

1975: January 1st (New Year's Day), March 28th (Good Friday).

Weights and Measures

Imperial and U.S. weights and measures are both used.

Currency

100 cents = 1 Bermuda dollar (B$).

Exchange rates (April 1974):

£1 sterling = B$2.36;

U.S. $1 = B$1.00.

STATISTICAL SURVEY

Area: 20.65 square miles. **Population:** 52,330 (October 29th, 1970); Hamilton (capital) 3,000.

Employment (1970 census): Production and related workers 6,900; Service workers 6,500; Clerical and related workers 4,700; Professional and technical 3,600; Sales workers 2,500; Labourers 1,100; Administrative and managerial 1,000; Farmers and agricultural workers 600.

The total number of non-Bermudians authorized to accept employment in 1971 was 2,868 (1,808 were British, 218 American, 158 Portuguese and 684 others, mostly Europeans).

Agriculture (1971): Principal crops ('000 lb.): Irish Potatoes 2,025, Carrots 400, Bananas 1,245, Tomatoes 216, Sweet Potatoes 150, Other Vegetables 983, Citrus Fruit 96,000 dozen.

Livestock (1971): Pigs 653, Cattle 785, Horses 529, Goats 188.

Fishing (1971): Annual fish landings 1,500,000 lb.; Spiny lobsters 440,000 lb.

Finance: 100 cents = 1 Bermuda dollar (B$). Coins: 1, 5, 10, 25 and 50 cents. Notes: 1, 5, 10, 20 and 50 dollars. Exchange rates (April 1974): £1 sterling = B$2.36; U.S. $1 = B$1.00. *Note:* U.S. and Canadian currencies are also accepted.

Budget (1970/71): Revenue B$28,383,885; Expenditure B$37,441,213.

External Trade (1971): *Imports* $108,478,219; *Domestic Exports* $743,215 (principally consist of concentrated essences, essential oils, beauty preparations, etc.); *Re-exports* $81,061,523.

Transport (1971): *Roads*: Motor and Auxiliary Cycles 24,066, Cars 10,842, Trucks 1,888, Public Service Vehicles 672; miscellaneous 891; *Shipping*: 6,624,300 gross tons handled and 893 vessels entered and cleared; *Civil Aviation*: scheduled aircraft arrivals 4,635, passengers 920,304, air cargo 10,810 kg., air mail 669,944 kg.

Tourism (1971): Number of visitors 412,947, of which 319,310 were arrivals by air, 93,637 cruise passengers. The estimated value of the tourist industry to Bermuda in 1970 was BD $72,800,000. This is an increase of 12 per cent on 1969.

Education (1971): There are six aided schools and 35 maintained schools; also 2 denominational and two non-denominational private schools. Total enrolment through secondary schools in 1971 was 13,242, of whom 6,587 were boys and 6,655 girls. Higher education is available at the Bermuda College, consisting of the Departments of Hotel Technology, Academic Studies and Commerce and Technology. Extra-mural courses are available through Queen's University, Canada, and Maryland University, U.S.A.

THE CONSTITUTION

Under a Constitution introduced on June 8th, 1968, there are provisions relating to the protection of fundamental rights and freedoms of the individual, the powers and duties of the Governor; the composition, powers and procedure of the Legislature; the Executive Council; the Judiciary; the Public Service and Finance.

Her Majesty the Queen appoints the Governor, who retains responsibility for external affairs, defence, internal security and the Police. In other matters the Governor acts on the advice of the Executive Council.

The Legislature consists of Her Majesty, the Legislative Council and the House of Assembly. Five members of the Legislative Council are appointed at the Governor's discretion, four on the advice of the Government leader and two on the advice of the Opposition leader. The Council elects a President and Vice-President. The House of Assembly, consisting of forty members elected under universal adult franchise from twenty constituencies, elects a Speaker and a Deputy Speaker, and sits for a five-year term.

The Executive Council consists of the Government leader and at least six other members of the Legislature. The Governor appoints the majority leader in the House of Assembly as Government leader, who in turn nominates the other members of the Council. They are assigned responsibilities for government departments and other business and, in some cases, are assisted by Parliamentary Secretaries. Meetings of the Executive Council are normally presided over by the Governor. The Secretary to the Executive Council is Head of the Civil Service.

Voters must be British subjects of 21 years or over, and if not possessing Bermudan status, must have been normally resident in the Colony for three years immediately prior to registration. Candidates for election must qualify as electors and in addition must possess Bermudan status.

THE GOVERNMENT

Governor and Commander-in-Chief: Sir EDWIN LEATHER.

EXECUTIVE COUNCIL

Government Leader: The Hon. Sir EDWARD RICHARDS, C.B.E.

Deputy Leader and Member for Finance: The Hon. JOHN H. SHARPE, C.B.E.

Member for Education: The Hon. Mrs. GLORIA McPHEE.

Member for Works and Agriculture: The Hon. J. M. S. PATTON, G.C.

Member for Marine and Air Services: The Hon. F. J. BARRITT.

Member for Organization: The Hon. JOHN R. PLOWMAN, C.B.E.

Member for Labour and Immigration: The Hon. C. V. WOOLRIDGE.

Member for Tourism: The Hon. DE F. W. TRIMINGHAM.

Member for Health and Welfare: The Hon. Q. L. EDNESS.

Member for Planning: The Hon. E. W. P. VESEY.

Member for Transport: The Hon. R. O. MARSHALL.

Member without Portfolio: The Hon. L. I. SWAN.

LEGISLATIVE COUNCIL

President: The Hon. G. O. RATTERAY, C.B.E.

Nominated Members: 11.

HOUSE OF ASSEMBLY

Speaker: A. D. SPURLING, C.B.E., J.P.

Members: 40 (U.B.P. 30, P.L.P. 10).

Government Information Office: GAVIN SHORTO (Director of Public Relations).

GENERAL ELECTION, JUNE 1972

PARTY	SEATS
United Bermuda Party . .	30
Progressive Labour Party .	10

POLITICAL PARTIES

United Bermuda Party (U.B.P.): Central Office, Room 404, Bermudiana Arcade, Queen St., Hamilton; f. 1964; majority party; policy of bi-racial partnership supporting system of free enterprise; won 30 seats in 1968 and 1972 elections; Government Leader Sir EDWARD RICHARDS, C.B.E., M.P.; Chair. Dr. McNEIL WARNER.

Progressive Labour Party (P.L.P.): P.O.B. 1367, Hamilton; f. 1963; stands for rapid progress towards independence inside or outside the Commonwealth; won 10 seats in the 1968 and 1972 elections; Leader L. EUGENE COX, M.P.; Chair. WALTER N. H. ROBINSON.

JUDICIAL SYSTEM

Chief Justice: The Hon. J. C. SUMMERFIELD, C.B.E., Q.C.

Puisne Judge: The Hon. Mr. Justice E. E. SEATON.

Senior Magistrate: R. H. LOWNIE, J.P.

Registrar of Supreme Court and Court of Appeal: J. L. BARRINGTON-JONES, J.P.

There are in Bermuda the Supreme Court, the Court of Appeal and three Magistrates Courts. The Court of Appeal was established in 1964, with powers and jurisdiction of equivalent courts in other parts of the Commonwealth. The Supreme Court was established under the Supreme Court Act of 1905. It has jurisdiction over all serious criminal matters and has unlimited civil jurisdiction. The Court also hears civil and criminal appeals from the Magistrates Courts. The Magistrates Court has jurisdiction over all petty offences, and has a limited civil jurisdiction.

The Race Relations Act was passed in 1970, calling for a Race Relations Council to be appointed by the Governor. Besides advising the Government on race relations, the Council is empowered to investigate complaints of discrimination and, where the settlement of a complaint is sought, to set up a conciliation committee. Where no settlement can be achieved court proceedings under the Race Relations Act, 1969, can be brought by the Council.

Chairman: Rev. GEORGE BUCHANAN, O.B.E.

RELIGION

Most faiths are represented in Bermuda, the major ones being Anglican, African Methodist Episcopal, Roman Catholic, Wesleyan Methodist Presbyterian, Seven Day Adventist, Baptist, Pentacostal.

ANGLICAN

Bishop of Bermuda: Rt. Rev. ERIC JOSEPH TRAPP, D.D., Bishop's Lodge, P.O.B. 769, Hamilton.

There are about 25,000 Anglicans in Bermuda.

ROMAN CATHOLIC

Bishop of Hamilton in Bermuda: Rt. Rev. BERNARD JAMES MURPHY, P.O.B. 1191, Hamilton.

THE PRESS

The Royal Gazette: P.O.B. 1025, Hamilton; f. 1828; morning; circ. 13,396; Editor W. E. HOPWOOD; Gen. Man. R. OATWAY; London Office: 122 Shaftesbury Ave., W.I.

Bermuda Sun, The: P.O.B. 902, Hamilton; f. 1964; Saturday mornings with *T.V. Guide*; Editor ALAN COLES; circ. 12,395.

Bermudian, The: Bermudiana Arcade, Hamilton; f. 1930; monthly; pictorial and resort magazine; circ. 6,500; Editor RONALD JOHN WILLIAMS.

Mid-Ocean News, The: The Bermuda Press Ltd., Reid St., Hamilton; f. 1911; Saturday mornings; circ. 12,000; Editor GORDON ROBINSON; London Reps. Colin Turner (London) Ltd., 122 Shaftesbury Ave., W.I.

Recorder, The: Court St., Hamilton; f. 1938; Independent; Saturday mornings; Editor ALFRED AUGUSTUS.

PUBLISHER

The Royal Gazette Ltd.: Reid St., Hamilton; f. 1828, inc. 1921; Man. RONALD OATWAY.

RADIO AND TELEVISION

RADIO

ZBM: P.O.B. 452, Hamilton; operated by Bermuda Broadcasting Co. Ltd.; f. 1943; operates on three wavelengths, including one FM stereo station; Man. Dir. W. STASKOW; Man. Q. EDNESS.

ZFB: P.O.B. 652, Hamilton; operated by Capital Broadcasting Co. Ltd.; f. 1961; operates on two wavelengths including one FM stereo station; Gen. Man. E. A. C. DAVIS.

Number of radio receivers (1972 est.): 38,000.

TELEVISION

ZBM-TV: owned by the Bermuda Broadcasting Co. Ltd.; commenced transmitting in January, 1958, on Channel 10. It is affiliated with Columbia Broadcasting System, National Broadcasting Co., and Rediffusion International Ltd.; Man. Dir. W. STASKOW; Man. Q. EDNESS.

ZFB-TV: owned by Capital Broadcasting Company Ltd., P.O.B. 652, Hamilton; affiliated with American Broadcasting Company and Thomson Television International; f. 1964; began operations in August 1965; Man. Dir. E. A. C. DAVIS.

Number of television sets (1973 est.): 18,500.

FINANCE

(cap.=capital; dep.=deposits; m.=million; br.=branch)

BANKS

Bank of Bermuda Ltd.: Front St., Hamilton; est. 1889, inc. 1890; cap. $3.6m.; dep. $396m.; Chief Gen. Man. WILLIAM T. WILSON; brs. at Hamilton, St. George's and Somerset.

Bank of N. T. Butterfield and Son Ltd.: Front St., Hamilton; f. 1858; cap. $2.4m.; dep. $299.4m.; Chief Exec. D. L. BAILEY; brs. at St. George's and Somerset.

Bermuda Provident Bank Ltd.: P.O.B. 1748, Hamilton; opened Nov. 1969; cap. $720,000; Man. Dir. P. J. MALLETT; subsidiary trust company (formed in association with Barclays Bank International Ltd., Hambros Bank Ltd., and The Royal Trust Company, Montreal) **International Trust Company of Bermuda Ltd.,** P.O.B. 1255, Hamilton; Gen. Man. R. F. ROBERTSON.

Bermuda National Bank Ltd.: affiliated with the Bank of Nova Scotia, Canada; opened 1969; Head Office: Church St., Hamilton; cap. $1.8m., p.u. $1.56m., res. $1.1m.; Man. Dir. ALEXANDER MCPHEDRAN; brs. in St. George's and Southampton Princess Hotel; wholly owned subsidiary trust company, **Bermuda National Executor and Trustee Company Ltd.**

General insurance is carried on by local companies and British and Canadian companies are represented as well.

TRADE AND INDUSTRY

Bermuda Chamber of Commerce: Hamilton; f. 1905; 485 mems.; Pres. J. G. YOUNG; Exec. Dir. AUDREY BRACKSTONE.

Bermuda Hotel Association: Old Town Hall, Front St., Hamilton; 59 mems.; Chair. Sir BAYARD DILL; Pres. PETER ROSOREA; Exec. Vice-Pres. H. LYNDON D. CLAY.

Bermuda Tourist Board: Old Town Hall, Front St., Hamilton; Chair. and Minister for Tourism Hon. DE FOREST WHEELER TRIMINGHAM, M.P.; Dir. W. JAMES WILLIAMS, O.B.E., M.V.O.

EMPLOYERS' ASSOCIATION

Bermuda Employers' Council: 303 International Centre, Hamilton; f. 1960; 173 mems.; Pres. E. T. SAYER; Exec. Dir. KEITH R. JENSEN.

Construction Association of Bermuda: P.O.B. 238, Hamilton; f. 1968; 18 mems.; Pres. T. D. HUNT; Hon. Sec. N. LISHMAN.

Hotel Employers of Bermuda: c/o Bermuda Hotel Association, Old Town Hall, Front St., Hamilton; f. 1968; 28 mems.; Pres. HARRY SHARPE; Sec. H. LYNDON D. CLAY.

TRADE UNIONS

Amalgamated Bermuda Union of Teachers: P.O.B. 726, Hamilton, f. 1963; 247 mems.; Pres. WINTON WILLIAMS.

Bermuda Cable and Wireless Staff Association: P.O.B. 151, Hamilton; reg. 1970; 75 mems.; Pres. NEVILLE TYRRELL; Sec. MAXWELL ADAMS.

Bermuda Federation of Musicians and Variety Artists: P.O.B. 6, Hamilton; 318 mems.; Sec.-Gen. H. MAXWELL SMITH.

Bermuda Industrial Union: Dundonald St., Hamilton; f. 1946; 5,000 mems.; Pres. OTTIWELL SIMMONS; Sec.-Gen. EUGENE BLAKENEY.

Bermuda Public Service Association: P.O.B. 763, Hamilton; re-formed 1961; 912 mems.; Pres. Mrs. VERBENA DANIELS; Sec. Mrs. VEIDA SMITH.

Union of Government Industrial Employees: P.W.D. Quarry, Hamilton Parish; f. 1967; 120 mems.; Pres. C. C. SNAITH; Sec. CHARLES EDMEAD.

TRANSPORT AND TOURISM

ROADS

There are about 132 miles of well-surfaced roads.

SHIPPING

The chief port of Bermuda is Hamilton with a secondary port at St. George's. Both are used by freight and cruise ships. An administrative Board, the Ports Authority, co-ordinates the capital development of all ports in Bermuda and regulates the berthing, anchoring and mooring of all ships and boats within the ports.

There is a Freeport which is administered by the Public Works Department of the Bermuda Government, but the management of the Freeport commercial docks is conducted on its behalf by the Marine and Ports Services Department. The docks in Hamilton and St. George's are operated by the municipal authorities.

Island Shipping Ltd.: Bank of Bermuda Building, Hamilton; Chair. Sir BAYARD DILL; Sec. FRANK MUTCH; cargo shipping.

Red Rose Navigation Co. Ltd.: Bank of Bermuda Building, Hamilton; Pres. Sir HENRY TUCKER, K.B.E.; Sec. J. A. PEARMAN; investment holdings.

Salient Shipping Co. (Bermuda) Ltd.: P.O.B. 286, Vallis Building, Hamilton; 5 vessels; Dirs. J. A. MARWICK, C. T. COLLIS, Sir H. J. TUCKER, K.B.E.; Sec. J. A. PEARMAN.

Shell Bermuda (Overseas) Ltd.: Shell House, Ferry Reach, St. George's; 34 tankers.

Trader Line Ltd.: c/o Bank of Bermuda, Hamilton; 1 ship; Dir. GRAY ROBINSON.

Principal non-Bermudan lines calling at Bermuda: All America, Atlantic Lines, Bermuda Express Service, Cunard, Flagships Inc., Independent Gulf, Pacific Steam Navigation Co. and Saguenay.

CIVIL AVIATION

Department of Civil Aviation: responsible to the Member of Executive Council for Marine and Air Services for carrying out civil aviation policy. The Director of Civil Aviation is responsible to the Governor on matters concerning the Colonial Air Navigation Order.

The only airfield is the U.S.A.F. base which was completed in 1943 for military purposes. In 1948 this base, known as Kindley Field, was opened to civil aircraft. In 1970 the operation of the base was taken over by the United States Navy, and is now known as the U.S. Naval Air Station, Bermuda. All civil aircraft, after landing, are handled within an area known as the Bermuda Air Terminal, which is under the jurisdiction of the Department of Civil Aviation.

The following airlines operate services to Bermuda; Air Canada, British Airways, Delta Eastern Airlines, Pan American and Qantas.

TOURISM

Department of Tourism: Old Town Hall, Front St., Hamilton; f. 1913; tourism is the principal industry of Bermuda and is government sponsored; in 1973 468,695 tourists, including 82,015 cruise ship passengers, visited Bermuda; Dir. W. JAMES WILLIAMS, O.B.E., M.V.O.; Deputy Dir. D. COLIN SELLEY.

BRITISH ANTARCTIC TERRITORY

The British Antarctic Territory was formally defined by Order in Council in March 1962 and consists of that part of the Falkland Islands Dependencies (q.v.), as formally defined by Letters Patent of 1908 and 1917, lying within the Antarctic Treaty Area (i.e. south of latitude 60° S.). The Territory consists of all lands and islands south of latitude 60° S., between longitudes 20° and 80° W., and includes the South Orkney Islands, the South Shetland Islands and the Antarctic Peninsula (Graham Land).

Area: 666,035 square miles.

Population: There is no permanent population but scientific and support personnel at the six British, seven Argentine, three Chilean, one U.S. and one Soviet scientific stations established within the Territory number about 250 in winter and approximately double in the summer.

High Commissioner: E. G. LEWIS, C.M.G., O.B.E. (Port Stanley, Falkland Islands).

Director of the British Antarctic Survey: Dr. RICHARD M. LAWS (London).

London Office: The British Antarctic Survey, 30 Gillingham St., London, SW1V 1HY.

MAJOR STATIONS

	Latitude	Longitude
Stonington Island . .	68° 11′ S	67° 00′ W
Argentine Islands . .	65° 15′ S	64° 15′ W
Signy Island . .	60° 43′ S	45° 56′ W
Adelaide . .	67° 46′ S	68° 54′ W
Halley Bay . .	75° 31′ S	26° 38′ W
Fossil Bluff . .	71° 20′ S	68° 17′ W
Palmer Station (U.S.A.) .	64° 46′ S	64° 05′ W
Bellingshausen (U.S.S.R.) .	62° 12′ S	58° 56′ W

THE BRITISH VIRGIN ISLANDS

INTRODUCTION

The British Virgin Islands consist of more than 40 islands, of which some 16 are inhabited, lying at the eastern end of the Greater Antilles, 60 miles to the east of Puerto Rico and adjoining the United States Virgin Islands. The capital, Road Town, stands on the island of Tortola.

The bulk of the islands' export trade is in livestock and to a lesser extent fish, fruit and vegetables; agriculture is geared to grass cultivation for the production of livestock. After a late start, the tourist trade is fast becoming a major industry.

Two large-scale development projects are now in progress: a land reclamation scheme involving 70 acres at Wickham's Cay, Road Town, and the complete transformation of the island of Anegada, where the Anegada Development Corporation has already completed a 3,500 ft. airstrip and a deep-water harbour pier and is constructing 30 miles of roads.

STATISTICS

Area and Population: Area 59 square miles. Population 9,672 (April 7th, 1970); Road Town (capital) 2,180.

Finance: United States currency: 100 cents = 1 U.S. dollar ($). Coins: 1, 5, 10, 25 and 50 cents; 1 dollar. Notes: 1, 2, 5, 10, 20, 50 and 100 dollars. Exchange rates (April 1974): £1 sterling = U.S. $2.36; U.S. $1 = 42.35 pence.

Budget (1973 estimates): Revenue $3,846,350; Expenditure $4,776,765.

External Trade (1972): *Imports* U.S. $7,642,230. *Exports* U.S. $71,710, mainly livestock, vegetables, fish, fruit, rum and charcoal.

Tourism: Total number of visitors (1968) 22,793; (1969) 22,010; (1970) 33,167; (1971) 38,000; (1972) 44,800.

Education: 21 primary schools and 1 secondary school, 2,961 pupils in all. Higher education is available at the University of the West Indies at its three campuses in Barbados, Trinidad and Jamaica, but many people go to universities in Canada and the United States.

THE CONSTITUTION

A new constitution came into effect in April 1967. Under its terms, the Governor is responsible for defence and internal security, external affairs, terms and conditions of service of public officers, the administration of the Courts and finance, and possesses reserved legislative powers in respect of legislation necessary in the interests of his special responsibilities; there is an Executive Council with the Governor as Chairman, two ex-officio members (the Attorney-General and the Financial Secretary), the Chief Minister (appointed by the Governor) and two other ministers, appointed by the Governor on the advice of the Chief Minister; and a Legislative Council consisting of a Speaker, chosen from outside the Council, two ex-officio members (the Attorney-General and the Financial Secretary), one nominated member appointed by the Governor on the Chief Minister's advice, and seven elected members to be returned from seven one-member electoral districts.

THE GOVERNMENT

Governor: DEREK GEORGE CUDMORE, C.B.E.

EXECUTIVE COUNCIL

President: The Governor.
Chief Minister: Hon. WILLARD WHEATLEY, M.B.E.
Financial Secretary: Hon. JOHN FROST.
Attorney-General: Hon. PAULA F. BEAUBRUN.
Minister of Natural Resources and Public Health: Hon. CONRAD MADURO.
Minister of Communications, Works and Industry: Hon. OLIVER CILLS.

LEGISLATIVE COUNCIL

Speaker: Hon. H. R. PENN, M.B.E.
Deputy Speaker: Hon. I. DAWSON.
Members: The three ministers; Hon. AUSTIN HENLEY, Hon. H. L. STOUTT (Leader of the Opposition), Hon. Q. W. OSBORNE, Hon. REEIAL GEORGE, Hon. I. DAWSON (nominated), the Attorney General, the Financial Secretary.
Clerk: Mrs. M. BORDE.

JUDICIAL SYSTEM

Justice is administered by the Supreme Court of the West Indies Associated States, which consists of two divisions: The High Court of Justice and The Court of Appeal. There are also a Magistrate's Court, a Juvenile Court and a Court of Summary Jurisdiction.

Chief Justice and President, The Court of Appeal: The Hon. P. C. LEWIS (Acting).
Justices of Appeal: Hon. E. L. ST. BERNARD; Hon. N. PETERKIN (Acting).
Puisne Judge: Hon. E. F. GLASGOW.

THE PRESS

Island Sun, The: P.O.B. 21, Tortola; weekly; Editor CARLOS DOWNING; circ. 1,500.

RADIO

Station Z.B.V.I.: P.O.B. 78, Road Town, Tortola; f. 1965; commercial; 10,000 watts with stand-by transmitting facilities of 1,000 watts; Man. LEOPOLD MILLS.

In 1973 there were over 6,500 radio receivers.

BANKING

Bank of Nova Scotia: Road Town, Tortola; f. 1967; Man. DONALD R. J. H. DORIE.
Barclays Bank International Ltd.: Road Town, Tortola; f. 1965; Man. J. M. DONOVAN.
Chase Manhattan Bank: Road Town, Tortola; f. 1968; Man. W. KLOEPFER.
Virgin Islands National Bank: Head Office: Charlotte Amalie, U.S. Virgin Islands; P.O.B. 67, Road Town, Tortola; f. 1961; Man. A. MADURO.

Two trust companies, the Provident Trust Company (Tortola) and the trust subsidiary of the Bank of Nova Scotia, are in operation. Commercial banking facilities in St. Thomas and St. Croix, United States Virgin Islands, are also available.

TRANSPORT AND TOURISM

Launches maintain a mail and passenger service with St. Thomas, United States Virgin Islands, whence air and sea communications exist to all parts of the world.

There is an automatic telephone system in Tortola and some of the out-islands with direct dialling to St. Thomas and St. Croix.

Work was completed in 1969 on the extension of the runway of Beef Island Airport, which enables prop-jet services to call at the British Virgin Islands.

The following airlines serve the British Virgin Islands: Antilles Air Boats (U.S. Virgin Islands), Leeward Islands Air Transport (LIAT), St. Thomas Tax-air (Puerto Rico) and Prinair (Puerto Rico).

There are over 50 miles of motorable roads and about 2,000 motor vehicles.

There are direct shipping services with the U.S.A. (Atlantic Lines) and with the U.K. and Europe (Booker Line and K.N.S.M.). A monthly freight service to the U.K. is provided by Fyffes Lines.

British Virgin Islands Department of Tourism: Road Town, Tortola; Admin. Sec. E. RHYMER.

British Virgin Islands Tourist Board: Exec. Sec. RICHARD BATHAM.

There are some 24 hotels on the Islands which in 1973 provided a total of about 600 tourist guest nights. Plans are under way for the construction of several new hotels. Facilities for diving and fishing are growing fast. The number of tourists is currently increasing by more than 13 per cent each year.

British Virgin Islands Hotel and Tourist Association: P.O.B. 376, Road Town, Tortola; Pres. ANTHONY MACK; Sec. RICHARD BATHAM; publ. *Welcome*.

CAYMAN ISLANDS

The Cayman Islands lie about 180 miles north-west of Jamaica and consist of three main islands: Grand Cayman, Little Cayman and Cayman Brac.

STATISTICS

Area and Population: Area 100 square miles. Population (1970) 10,652; Grand Cayman 9,309, Cayman Brac 1,334, Little Cayman 9; George Town (capital) 4,106, West Bay 2,786, Bodden Town 1,025, North Side 579, East End 813.

Finance: 100 cents = 1 Cayman Islands dollar (C.I. $). Coins: 1, 5, 10 and 25 cents. Notes: 1, 5, 10 and 25 dollars. Exchange rates (April 1974): £1 sterling = C.I. $2.02; U.S. $1 = 85.55 C.I. cents; C.I. $100 = £49.50 = U.S. $116.89.

Budget (1973 est.): *Revenue*: Recurrent C.I. $4,866,717; Capital C.I. $4,446,316. *Expenditure*: Recurrent C.I. $4,336,404; Capital C.I. $4,470,719.

Development Plan (1971–75): Proposed capital expenditure C.I. $4,470,719 in 1973; projects include comprehensive school, airport, deep water harbour, administration building, roads, etc.

External Trade (1972): *Imports* C.I. $12,799,172 (foodstuffs, textiles, building material); *Exports* C.I. $144,310 (turtle products; meat, soup, leather and shells).

Tourism: (1973) 45,600 visitors.

Education (1972): State primary schools 9; 1,138 pupils; private primary and secondary schools 7; 961 pupils; comprehensive school 973 pupils.

CONSTITUTION AND GOVERNMENT

A new Constitution was introduced in July 1959 under which the islands ceased to be a dependency of Jamaica. The last constitutional ties with that country were severed on August 6th, 1962, and the Islands are now a separate dependent territory of the United Kingdom. Constitutional changes took place in 1972. In the new Executive Council the majority of members are elected and the Legislative Assembly is fully elected. The Governor has reserve powers and Britain retains full control over foreign affairs. There are no political parties in the Caymans and the elections in 1972 were not contested on a party political basis.

Governor: K. R. CROOK.

JUDICIAL SYSTEM

There is a Grand Court of the Islands, a Quarterly Petty Court and a Petty Sessions Court. The Grand Court, which sits six times a year, has jurisdiction in civil matters, bankruptcy, equity, probate and administration, and in felonies and indictable misdemeanours. Appeals lie to the Court of Appeal in Jamaica. The Quarterly Petty Court, presided over by the stipendiary magistrate, deals with civil matters and appeals lie to the Grand Court. The Petty Sessions Court conducts preliminary examinations in indictable offences.

Judge of the Grand Court: Hon. LOXLEY T. MOODY, Q.C.
Attorney-General: Hon. G. E. WADDINGTON, Q.C.

RELIGION

The oldest established Churches are, on Grand Cayman, the United Church of Jamaica and Grand Cayman, and on Cayman Brac the Baptist Church. The chief other churches are the Church of God, Church of God (Full Gospel), Church of Christ, Seventh Day Adventist, Roman Catholic and Pilgrim Holiness.

THE PRESS

The Cayman Compass: P.O.B. 173, Grand Cayman; weekly; circ. 3,000; Editor W. D. BODDEN.

The Caymanian: Grand Cayman; weekly; circ. 3,700; Editor TED LARIMER.

The Gospel of the Kingdom: P.O.B. 829, Grand Cayman; f. 1945; religious, under the auspices of the Church of God; monthly; Editor WILL T. BODDEN; circ. 1,550.

The Northwester Magazine: P.O.B. 243, Grand Cayman; circ. 6,000; monthly; Editor D. SEALES.

FINANCE

Banking facilities are provided by seven commercial and three private banks, and in Grand Cayman and Cayman Brac by the Government Savings Bank. A number of investment and private banks not doing business in the islands maintain their registered offices in Grand Cayman.

Bank of Montreal: P.O.B. 905, Grand Cayman.

Bank of Nova Scotia: P.O.B. 689, Grand Cayman.

Barclays Bank International Ltd.: P.O.B. 68, Grand Cayman; agencies at West Bay and Bodden Town; sub-br. at Stake Bay, Cayman Brac (P.O.B. 48); agencies at Creek and Spot Bay.

Canadian Imperial Bank of Commerce: P.O.B. 695, Grand Cayman.

First National City Bank: P.O.B. 70, Grand Cayman.

The International Bank: Interbank House, George Town.

Mercantile Bank and Trust Co. (Cayman) Ltd.: P.O.B. 609, George Town.

Royal Bank of Canada: P.O.B. 245, Grand Cayman.

Sterling Bank and Trust Co. Ltd.: P.O.B. 692, Grand Cayman.

Arawak Trust Co. (Cayman) Ltd.: P.O.B. 513, Huntlaw Building, Grand Cayman; f. 1968; Chair. Sir FREDERIC BENNETT, M.P.; Man. Dir. R. H. PRINGLE.

Cayman Islands Chamber of Commerce: West Wind Bldg., Grand Cayman; Pres. NORBERG THOMPSON; Sec. P. HARRIS.

In 1973 it was estimated that there were more than 4,400 companies and 600 trusts on the islands. In 1969 there were only 11 financial institutions.

TRANSPORT AND TOURISM

ROADS

There are some 80 miles of motorable road in the Islands, of which 35 are tarmac. The Islands possess approximately 2,600 motor vehicles. In February 1972 an undersea cable with Jamaica was completed.

CIVIL AVIATION

The airport at George Town was enlarged to take jet aircraft in 1966.

Cayman Airways Ltd.: P.O.B. 11, Grand Cayman; operates services between Grand Cayman, Little Cayman, Cayman Brac, Miami (Florida) and Kingston (Jamaica) using DC-3 and BAC 111 aircraft.

Services are also provided by LACSA (Costa Rica).

TOURISM

Tourism is a rapidly expanding industry in the Cayman Islands; in 1973 there were an estimated 45,600 visitors and the total is expected to reach 70,000 by 1975.

Cayman Islands Department of Tourism: P.O.B. 67, Caribbean Bank Bldg., George Town, Grand Cayman; f. 1965; Dir. ERIC BERGSTROM, M.B.E.

FALKLAND ISLANDS

The Falkland Islands lie in the South Atlantic 480 miles north-east of Cape Horn. There are two main islands and about 200 smaller ones, all governed as a single British dependent territory. The islands are claimed by Argentina.

STATISTICS

Area (square miles): 4,700 (approx.), East Falklands 2,610, West Falklands 2,090.

Population (Dec. 1972): 1,957, Port Stanley (capital) 1,081.

Livestock (1972): Sheep 640,000, Cattle 10,063, Horses 3,094.

Finance: 100 new pence (pennies)=1 Falkland Islands pound (F.I.£). Coins: ½, 1, 2, 5 and 10 pence. Notes: 50 pence; 1 and 5 pounds. Exchange rates (April 1974): £1 sterling=F.I.£1.00; U.S. $1=42.35 pence; F.I.£100 =£100.00 sterling=$236.125.

Budget (1973–74 est.): Revenue £559,920, Expenditure £543,008.

Development Plan (1973–74): £100,000.

External Trade (1972): *Imports* £651,579, *Exports* £1,118,379 (nearly all wool). Trade is mainly with the British Commonwealth.

Shipping (1971): Tonnage entered 55,249, total 34 ships; cleared 55,672, total 35 ships.

Education: Education is compulsory. In 1970 there were 2 government schools in Stanley with 199 pupils.

Eight travelling and other teachers with 106 pupils were maintained by the Government in country districts. There is also a boarding school at Darwin, E. Falkland, with 56 pupils.

THE CONSTITUTION

The present Constitution came into force on January 1st, 1949. The Territory is administered by a Governor, assisted by an Executive Council consisting of 2 *ex officio* members, 2 members elected by the Legislature and 2 appointed members; and a Legislative Council composed of 2 *ex officio*, 4 elected and 2 nominated official members. The electoral principle was introduced, on a basis of universal adult suffrage, in 1949.

THE GOVERNMENT

(*April 1974*)

Governor: E. G. LEWIS, C.M.G., O.B.E.

Chief Secretary: T. H. LAYNG.

Executive Council: 6 members.

Legislative Council: The Governor, 2 *ex officio*, 2 nominated and 4 elected members.

JUDICIAL SYSTEM

The judicial system of the Territory and its dependencies is administered by a Supreme Court, with the Governor and Chief Secretary as acting judges, a Magistrates' Court presided over by the Senior Magistrate, and a Court of Summary Jurisdiction, presided over by a bench of magistrates composed of two or more Justices of the Peace. On July 1st, 1965, a Court of Appeal, sitting in England, was established for the Territory.

Acting Judges: E. G. Lewis, C.M.G., O.B.E., T. H. Layng.

Registrar: H. Bennett, J.P.

FALKLAND ISLANDS COURT OF APPEAL

The Court of Appeal sits in London.

President: Sir Alistair Forbes, K.B.

Deputy Registrar: A. C. T. Cochrane.

RELIGION

There are Anglican, Roman Catholic and United Free Church communions.

ANGLICAN

Bishop of the Falkland Islands: Rt. Rev. C. J. Tucker.

Senior Chaplain: Rev. P. Helyer.

ROMAN CATHOLIC

Prefect Apostolic: The Right Reverend Monsignor D. Spraggon, M.B.E.; St. Mary's Presbytery, Stanley.

UNITED FREE CHURCH

Minister: Rev. R. Forrester, Ross Rd., Stanley.

PRESS

There are no newspapers, other than a small monthly publication. The Government publishes *The Gazette*.

RADIO

There is a government-operated broadcasting station at Stanley. The number of licence-holders in 1972 was 705. The Government also operates a wired broadcasting service in Stanley (349 subscribers in 1971) and a wireless station on the West Falkland, to which most of the farms are linked by telephone. The East Falkland has similar telephone facilities. The farm settlements are linked to Stanley by radio telephone. A modern telecommunications link with the United Kingdom was established in 1967.

Falkland Island Broadcasting Service: Broadcasting studios, Stanley; broadcasts in English; Tech. Dir. E. Fuhlendorff; Sec. Mrs. M. J. Kerr.

FINANCE

BANKS

Government Savings Bank: Stanley; dep. £1,198,700 (June 1973).

Lloyds Bank Ltd., and **Hambros Bank** have agencies in Stanley.

INSURANCE

The British Commercial Union, Royal and Sun Insurance companies maintain agencies in Port Stanley.

TRADE AND INDUSTRY

The Falklands Islands Co.: Stanley; f. 1851; is the largest landowner and trading company; Man. A. Sloggie.

TRADE UNION

The General Employees Union: Ross Rd., Stanley; general union; 400 paid-up mems.; Gen. Sec. Richard V. Goss, O.B.E., E.D.

CO-OPERATIVE SOCIETY

Stanley Co-operative Society: Stanley; f. 1952; open to all members of the public; Man. P. R. Short.

TRANSPORT AND TOURISM

ROADS

There are 13 miles of made-up road in and around Stanley. Elsewhere tracks link the settlements which are passable by land rover or motor cycle in all but the worst weather.

SHIPPING AND CIVIL AVIATION

Communication between the Islands and the mainland of South America is by air, following the inauguration of a temporary airstrip in November 1972. A weekly air service is provided with Fokker F-27 aircraft by the Argentine development line L.A.D.E., linking Stanley with Comodoro Rivadavia in southern Argentina. There is a ship on charter to the Falkland Islands Company which makes the round trip to the United Kingdom four or five times a year, carrying mail and cargo.

Falkland Islands Government Air Service: f. 1948; maintains Beaver float-plane services between the settlements and Stanley.

FALKLAND ISLANDS DEPENDENCIES

The Falkland Islands Dependencies were formally defined by Letters Patent of 1908 and 1917 and included an area which, since an Order in Council of 1962 amending the above Letters Patent, has been known as the British Antarctic Territory (*q.v.*). The remaining Falkland Islands Dependencies consist of South Georgia and the South Sandwich Islands.

STATISTICS

Area (Square miles): South Georgia 1,387, South Sandwich 120.

Population: There is no permanent population, but 22 scientists and support personnel man the British Antarctic Survey station at Grytviken, South Georgia. The South Sandwich Islands are uninhabited.

Governor: E. G. Lewis, C.M.G., O.B.E. (Stanley, Falkland Islands).

GILBERT AND ELLICE ISLANDS

The Gilbert and Ellice Islands are in four main groups stretching over a vast area of the Central Pacific Ocean.

Area: Sea 2m. nautical square miles. Land (square miles): Gilbert Islands 102, Ellice Islands 10, Christmas Island 135, other islands about 77. There are 42 islands in all.

Population (Dec. 1968): 55,185, Tarawa (capital) 12,642.

Employment (1972): Phosphate Mining (Ocean Island and the Republic of Nauru) 1,124, Government Service 1,454, Development Authority 1,441.

Finance: Australian currency: 100 cents=1 Australian dollar ($A). Coins: 1, 2, 5, 10, 20 and 50 cents. Notes: 1, 2, 5, 10, 20 and 50 dollars. Exchange rates (April 1974): £1 sterling=$A1.585; U.S. $1=67.23 Australian cents; $A100=£63.10=U.S. $148.75.

Budget (1972): Revenue $A6,424,910; Expenditure $A6,392,610; Development Programme (1972) $A1,743,199.

External Trade (1972): Imports $A5,415,402; Exports $A6,599,472 (including 503,500 tons of phosphate, 5,066 tons of copra).

Trade is mainly with Australia, Fiji, the United Kingdom, Japan and New Zealand.

Transport: *Roads:* There are about 400 miles suitable for motor vehicles. *Shipping:* The Colony Government and the Development Authority maintain a fleet of six passenger/freight vessels for administrative business. During 1972 99 overseas vessels called at the Colony.

ADMINISTRATION

Since January 1st, 1972, the Foreign and Commonwealth Office has been directly responsible for the administration of the Colony. The main change brought about by the transfer of responsibility from the High Commissioner for the Western Pacific was the appointment of a Governor in place of the Resident Commissioner.

There is a House of Assembly comprising 28 elected members, the Deputy Governor, the Attorney-General and the Financial Secretary. The Council of Ministers consists of the Chief Minister, not less than four nor more than six Ministers appointed from among the elected members of the House of Assembly, the Deputy Governor, the Attorney-General and the Financial Secretary.

OFFICIAL

Governor: H.E. John H. Smith, c.b.e.
Deputy Governor: D. M. Freegard, o.b.e.
Attorney-General: J. R. Hobbs.
Financial Secretary: D. W. Reardon, o.b.e.

ELECTED

Chief Minister: Naboua Ratieta.
The Minister of State in the Chief Minister's Office: Ibeata Tonganabeia.
Minister of Commerce and Industry: Sione Tui Kleis.
Minister of Communications, Works and Utilities: Bwebwetake Areieta.
Minister of Education, Training and Culture: Otinuea Tanentoa.
Minister of Health and Welfare: Teweia Uaruta.
Minister of Natural Resources: Isakala Paeniu.

Local Government is by Island Councils elected by universal adult suffrage with a staff of permanent Local Government Officers responsible for education, health, sanitation, local police, bye-laws and local taxation, etc. The Councils are financially assisted by Central Government in specific fields.

JUDICIAL SYSTEM

High Court of the Western Pacific, Senior Magistrates Court, Magistrates Courts and Island Courts: all administer English and Colony law with varying extents of jurisdiction.

Lands Courts: have exclusive jurisdiction in matters connected with land, the administration of estates and certain other powers.

Attorney-General: J. R. Hobbs.
Senior Magistrate: J. J. Fordham.
Registrar and Clerk in Senior Magistrates Court: Karotu Kaeka.

RELIGION

Protestant, Roman Catholic, Seventh-Day Adventist, Baha'i and Church of God Missions.

RADIO

Gilbert and Ellice Islands Broadcasting Service: Broadcasting Office, Tarawa; f. 1954; two transmitters; government run; over 8,000 receivers in use in 1973; programmes in Gilbertese, Ellice and English; Senior Broadcasting Officer M. D. Murray; Programme Man. Kaburoro Tanielu.

FINANCE

BANKING

Bank of New South Wales: Bairiki, Tarawa; f. 1970 (incorporating the *Government Savings Bank*).

TRADE AND INDUSTRY

British Phosphate Commissioners: hold a concession on Ocean Island for phosphate mining.

Copra Board: Betio Tarawa; f. 1955; the sole exporter of copra; 10 mems., appointed by His Excellency the Governor; Chair. P. W. Reardon, o.b.e.; Deputy Chair. M. E. H. Vickers; Sec. D. Brechterfield.

Development Authority: statutory body responsible for carrying out development projects in the Colony. Also concerned with travel, shipping, water supply, power generation, building construction, the hotel trade, civil engineering and vehicle and plant repairs.

CO-OPERATIVE SOCIETIES

In 1972 there were 57 co-operative societies; 40 consumer-marketing societies, 4 secondary societies and 7 others. Total membership 22,026.

TRADE UNIONS

There are four registered trade unions.

TRANSPORT

ROADS

Wherever practicable, roads are built on all atolls and connecting causeways between islets are also being built as funds and labour permit.

SHIPPING

Vessels owned or chartered by the British Phosphate Commissioners visit Ocean Island about six times a month. Australian cargo vessels call at Tarawa every six weeks and United Kingdom cargo ships every four months. Ships call at Tarawa to collect copra every two or three months and at Christmas, Fanning and Washington Islands twice a year. Vessels of the Columbus Line en route from U.S.A. and Australia call at Tarawa at approximately six weekly intervals. There is an irregular service from Tarawa to Suva, Fiji by Colony Government vessels, and a two-monthly service to Fiji and to the Marshall Islands.

Ships owned by the Daiwa Line operate a ten to twelve-weekly service from Japan, and tankers bring fuel from Fiji.

CIVIL AVIATION

Pacific Airways maintain a weekly service from Nadi to Funafuti/Tarawa/Nauru and return. It also operates a twice weekly service between Tarawa and three other islands in the Gilberts. Air Nauru also provides services. There are seven airfields in the colony.

EDUCATION

(1972)

Schools are run by the Government and the Churches; Primary Schools 118; total enrolment 13,962; Secondary Schools 3; total enrolment 781; Teacher Training College 1; Theological Colleges 2; total number of teachers 506 in all establishments.

CENTRAL AND SOUTHERN LINE ISLANDS

The five islands of this Group are all now uninhabited: Flint, Caroline, Vostock, Malden and Starbuck.

HONG KONG

INTRODUCTORY SURVEY

Location, History, Climate, Language, Religion, Capital

The Colony of Hong Kong lies off the south coast of China and consists of the island of Hong Kong, Stonecutters Island, the Kowloon Peninsula and the New Territories, which are partly on the mainland. Hong Kong Island was ceded to Britain under the terms of the Treaty of Nanking in 1842. The Kowloon Peninsula was acquired in 1860. The New Territories were leased by China in 1898 for a period of 99 years. The climate is sunny and dry in winter, and hot and humid in summer. The official language is English, but Cantonese is universally spoken and Mandarin is widely understood. The main religion is Buddhism; Confucianism and Taoism are also practised and there are more than a quarter of a million Christians. The capital is Victoria on Hong Kong island.

Government, Defence

The Colony is administered by the Governor, the Executive Council of five *ex officio* members and eight others (of whom four are Chinese) and the Legislative Council consisting of four of the *ex officio* Executive Council members, ten other official members and fifteen unofficial members (of whom eleven are Chinese). Defence forces in the Colony number 10,100; 9,000 in the army, 600 in the navy and 500 in the air force.

Economic Affairs

Hong Kong is a free trade area and one of the principal entrepôt ports of the world. Industry has expanded rapidly in recent years, and manufactured goods, particularly textiles and electrical goods, now make up three-quarters of total exports. Commerce plays an important part in the economy and Hong Kong banking and mercantile houses have branches all over the Far East. In December 1964 legislation was enacted to limit the activities of unincorporated banks.

Transport

Transport facilities include buses, trams, and ferries and a railway runs north from Kowloon to the Chinese border.

Social Welfare, Education

Social welfare and education are rendered difficult by the heavy influx of refugees from the mainland, estimated at more than a million since the war. Resettlement is undertaken by the Government and many private bodies (Kaifongs). There are about four hospital beds per thousand of population. Since 1965 with the doubling of free places in primary schools and the introduction of a system of subsidized places in primary schools, every child is ensured a primary education. The two universities have a combined enrolment of over six thousand students.

Tourism

Hong Kong is one of the main tourist centres of the Far East.

Visas are not required to visit Hong Kong by nationals of the following countries: Austria, Belgium, Denmark, France, Iceland, Italy, Liechtenstein, Luxembourg, Monaco, Netherlands, Norway, Portugal, San Marino, Spain, Sweden, Switzerland, United Kingdom and U.S.A.

Public Holidays

1974: August 5th (first Monday in August), August 26th (Liberation Day), October 1st (Day following Chinese Mid-Autumn Festival), October 23rd (Chung Yeung Festival), December 25th (Christmas Day), December 26th (first weekday after Christmas Day).

1975: January 1st (first week-day in January), February 11th–13th (Chinese New Year), March 28th, 29th and 31st (Easter), April 5th (Ching Ming), April 21st (The Queen's Birthday), June 14th (Tuen Ng), July 1st (first weekday in July).

Currency and Exchange Rates:

100 cents = 1 Hong Kong dollar (HK $).

Exchange rates (April 1974):

£1 sterling = HK $11.98;

U.S. $1 = HK $5.08.

STATISTICAL SURVEY

AREA AND POPULATION

AREA (sq. miles)				POPULATION (Mid-1973—est.)	
Total	Hong Kong Island	Kowloon and Stonecutters Island	New Territories (leased)	Total	Chinese (approx.)
403.8	29.2	4.1	370.5	4,159,900	98 per cent.

DISTRIBUTION OF POPULATION
(Provisional census figures—March 9th, 1971)

HONG KONG ISLAND	KOWLOON	NEW KOWLOON	MARINE	NEW TERRITORIES
996,183	716,272	1,478,581	79,894	665,700

REGISTERED BIRTHS AND DEATHS
(1972)

BIRTHS		DEATHS	
Number	Rate per '000	Number	Rate per '000
79,053	19.7	21,145	5.4

EMPLOYMENT
(Census figures—March 9th, 1971)

MANUFACTURING	SERVICES	COMMERCE	CONSTRUCTION AND ENGINEERING	AGRICULTURE, FORESTRY AND FISHING	TRANSPORT AND COMMUNICATIONS	PUBLIC UTILITIES	MINING AND QUARRYING	OTHERS	TOTAL
677,498	312,173	208,604	168,773	62,975	114,772	8,870	4,518	24,716	1,582,849

AGRICULTURE
LAND USAGE
(1972)

	AREA (sq. miles)	PERCENTAGE OF WHOLE	REMARKS
Built-up (urban areas) . .	45.8	11.3	Includes roads and railways.
Woodlands . . .	53.3	13.2	Natural and established woodlands.
Grass and Scrub Lands . .	235.2	58.3	Natural grass and scrub, including Prover Cove reservoir.
Badlands	14.7	3.6	Stripped of cover; granite country; capable of regeneration.
Swamp and Mangrove Lands .	5.0	1.2	Capable of reclamation.
Fish Ponds	4.3	1.1	Fresh and brackish water fish farming.
Arable	45.5	11.3	Includes orchards and market gardens.

AGRICULTURAL PRODUCTION*
(HK $'ooo)

	1970/71	1971/72
Crops:		
Flowers . . .	16,434	15,969
Fruit . . .	6,460	6,944
Vegetables . . .	159,106	149,180
Rice (Paddy) . . .	13,831	9,082
Rice Straw . . .	2,680	1,329
Field Crops . . .	6,500	6,462
Livestock:		
Pigs . . .	55,584	64,295
Cattle . . .	3,975	2,855
Milk, Fresh . . .	19,289	22,146
Chickens . . .	119,486	151,382
Hen Eggs . . .	32,234	31,793
Ducks . . .	35,534	46,623
Pigeons . . .	6,078	6,093

* Financial year ending March 31st.

FISHERIES
(HK $'ooo 1971)

Marine Fish (total landings) . .	185,894
Pond Fish	14,128
Oysters (edible)	1,770

LIVESTOCK
(Estimated population 1971–72)

Cattle	14,844
Water Buffaloes	1,079
Pigs	533,890
Chickens	6,370,550
Ducks	564,770
Geese	6,740
Quail	196,900
Pigeons	180,540

MINING
(long tons)

	1971	1972
Iron Ore* . . .	160,168.7	159,719.2
Kaolin . . .	2,486.1	3,111.6
Quartz . . .	5,059.6	3,573.5
Feldspar . . .	1,127.0	1,130.8

* 50–56 per cent iron concentrate.

INDUSTRY
(1972)

	NUMBER OF ESTABLISHMENTS	NUMBER EMPLOYED*
Food Manufacture . . .	755	11,821
Textile Manufacture . . .	3,110	120,900
Footwear and Clothing . . .	3,622	147,680
Printing and Publishing . . .	1,201	18,989
Rubber Products . . .	351	8,398
Fabricated Metal Products . .	3,350	49,690
Manufacture of Machinery . .	844	9,329
Electrical Apparatus . . .	570	62,405
Transport Equipment . . .	82	14,485
Transport, Storage and Communications .	100	21,402
TOTAL (all industries) . .	21,386	619,684

* 1973 (March): 616,609.

BRITISH DEPENDENT TERRITORIES—HONG KONG

FINANCE

100 cents=1 Hong Kong dollar (HK $).
Coins: 5, 10 and 50 cents; 1 dollar.
Notes: 5, 10, 50, 100 and 500 dollars.
Exchange rates (April 1974): £1 sterling=HK $11.98; U.S. $1=HK $5.08.
HK $100=£8.35=U.S. $19.68.

BUDGET*
(HK $ million—Estimates)

REVENUE	1972–73	1973–74	EXPENDITURE	1972–73	1973–74
Duties	457.4	436.2	Education	132.5	152.4
Rates	383.5	335.6	Medical and Health . . .	215.2	267.7
Internal Revenue . .	1,362.2	2,116.8	Police	237.9	263.6
Licences and Franchises .	146.1	247.0	Public Works Department .	192.2	217.8
Fees of Court or Office .	229.6	535.1	Urban Services and Council .	156.7	160.7
Water Revenue . .	166.6	187.4	Public Works (recurrent) .	166.5	207.1
Post Office . . .	167.5	173.8	Public Works (non-recurrent) .	840.6	1,050.0
Land Revenue, Rents, etc. .	393.0	335.7	Defence	122.4	118.3
Land Sales . . .	223.2	322.8	Post Office . . .	106.8	108.6
			Pensions . . .	82.2	99.8
			Subventions—education .	386.9	506.5
			Subventions—medical .	123.0	137.2
TOTAL (incl. others)	3,703.8	4,921.6	TOTAL (incl. others) .	3,656.9	4,408.5

*Financial year ending March 31st.

CURRENCY IN CIRCULATION
(HK $ million)

1970	.	.	2,577.7
1971	.	.	2,932.1
1972	.	.	3,378.2
1973 (July)	.	.	3,483.0

EXTERNAL TRADE
(HK $ million)

	1970	1971	1972	1973*
Imports .	17,607	20,256	21,764	12,364
Exports .	12,347	13,750	15,245	8,177
Re-exports .	2,892	3,414	4,154	2,527

* January-June.

PRINCIPAL COMMODITIES
(HK $ million)

IMPORTS	1971	1972	1973*
Food .	3,474	3,679	1,977
Live Animals .	639	717	363
Meat .	363	378	191
Dairy Products and Eggs .	290	288	149
Fish .	406	470	277
Cereals .	546	583	361
Fruit and Vegetables .	760	818	414
Beverages and Tobacco .	443	474	235
Crude Materials .	1,458	1,417	912
Textile Fibres and Waste .	829	841	506
Other Animal and Vegetable Crude Materials	322	341	266
Mineral Fuels, etc.	653	668	323
Petroleum and Petroleum Products .	626	642	308
Chemicals .	1,517	1,637	938
Chemical Elements and Compounds .	244	279	151
Medicinal and Pharmaceutical Products .	319	317	172
Plastic Materials .	454	478	294
Manufactured Goods .	6,628	7,240	4,211
Textile Yarn, Fabrics, Made-up Articles, etc.	3,450	3,632	2,144
Non-Metallic Mineral Manufactures .	1,437	1,624	953
Iron and Steel .	442	482	307
Paper, Paperboard, etc. .	498	531	275
Machinery and Transport Equipment .	3,467	3,857	2,242
Non-Electric Machinery .	1,225	1,237	699
Electric Machinery .	1,744	2,088	1,195
Transport Equipment .	498	531	348
Other Manufactures .	2,450	2,632	1,447
Clothing .	365	487	239
Scientific Instruments, Photographic and Optical Goods, Watches and Clocks, etc. .	984	1,089	597

* January–June.

EXPORTS	1971	1972	1973*
Food .	239	236	123
Fish .	121	122	63
Cereals .	22	21	12
Fruits and Vegetables .	24	25	14
Sugar, Sugar Preparations and Honey .	22	12	5
Miscellaneous Food Preparations .	41	48	25
Beverages and Tobacco .	49	52	15
Tobacco and Tobacco Manufactures .	45	47	13
Crude Materials .	162	192	96
Textile Fibres and Waste .	14	14	6
Metalliferous Ores and Metal Scrap .	84	103	47
Chemicals .	123	131	69
Dyeing, Tanning and Colouring Materials .	29	31	12
Medicinal and Pharmaceutical Products .	37	37	21
Manufactured Goods .	1,955	2,191	1,205
Textile Yarn, Fabrics, Made-up Articles, etc.	1,398	1,552	850
Non-Metallic Mineral Manufactures .	115	124	76
Iron and Steel .	18	17	10
Manufactures of Metals (others) .	345	415	218
Machinery and Transport Equipment .	1,684	2,125	1,180
Electric Machinery, Apparatus, etc. .	1,541	1,963	1,068
Other Manufactures .	9,490	10,272	5,469
Clothing .	5,464	6,113	3,321
Footwear .	351	304	115
Sanitary, Heating, Lighting Fixtures and Fittings .	187	200	104

* January–June.

PRINCIPAL COMMODITIES—*continued*]

RE-EXPORTS	1971	1972	1973*
Food	335	368	174
Fruits and Vegetables . . .	123	129	58
Coffee, Tea, Spices, etc. . . .	114	83	37
Sugar, Sugar Preparations and Honey .	21	18	44
Cereals	19	66	26
Crude Materials	209	306	220
Oil Seeds, Oil Nuts and Kernels .	12	14	6
Other Animal and Vegetable Crude Materials	154	208	157
Chemicals	571	558	289
Dyeing, Tanning and Colouring Materials .	93	121	74
Medicinal and Pharmaceutical Products .	299	237	99
Manufactured Goods . . .	1,330	1,765	1,072
Textile Yarn, Fabrics, Made-up Articles, etc.	441	587	438
Non-Metallic Mineral Manufactures .	757	1,025	542
Machinery and Transport Equipment .	379	450	280
Machinery other than Electric . .	146	185	110
Electric Machinery, Apparatus, etc. .	191	216	143
Other Manufactures . . .	481	597	431
Clothing	72	103	69
Scientific Instruments, Photographic and Optical Goods, Watches and Clocks, etc. .	271	318	217
Other Manufactured Articles . .	118	148	127

* January–June.

PRINCIPAL TRADING PARTNERS
(HK $ million)

IMPORTS	1971	1972	1973*	EXPORTS	1971	1972	1973*
China . . .	3,330	3,847	2,325	U.S.A. . . .	5,708	6,125	3,056
Japan . . .	4,926	5,045	2,608	United Kingdom . .	1,946	2,195	1,125
U.S.A. . . .	2,535	2,595	1,496	Germany, Federal Republic	1,128	1,525	867
United Kingdom . .	1,593	1,437	771	Canada . . .	484	501	240
France . . .	288	319	180	Australia . .	402	445	267
Thailand . . .	359	465	262	Japan . . .	484	480	377
Germany, Federal Republic	732	748	459	Singapore . . .	332	350	218
Australia . . .	611	557	303	Indonesia . .	78	96	53
Taiwan . . .	991	1,309	756	Sweden . . .	195	254	151
Switzerland . .	541	640	393	Netherlands . .	250	295	182
Singapore . . .	538	668	401	Thailand . . .	77	93	52
Pakistan . . .	366	513	284	New Zealand . .	126	121	66
Belgium and Luxembourg .	276	280	147	Taiwan . . .	213	233	149

* January-June.   * January-June.

RE-EXPORTS	1971	1972	1973*
Indonesia . . .	312	326	173
Japan . . .	644	834	635
Singapore . . .	397	435	276
U.S.A. . . .	303	364	166
Taiwan . . .	200	351	260
South Viet-Nam . .	73	74	33
Belgium and Luxembourg .	95	100	30
Philippines . . .	74	80	40
Nigeria . . .	62	37	15
Macao . . .	123	125	90
Republic of Korea . .	84	142	110
Switzerland . . .	98	108	65
United Kingdom . .	61	98	35

* January-June.

TRANSPORT
(1972)

RAIL TRAFFIC
(Kowloon-Canton railway, British section)

Passengers	12,156,460
Freight (metric tons)	1,164,710

CIVIL AIR TRAFFIC (1971)

PASSENGERS		FREIGHT (metric tons)	
In	Out	In	Out
1,092,137	1,095,191	23,833	51,631

ROAD TRAFFIC

Private Cars	120,725
Goods Vehicles	28,794
Motor Cycles (including scooters) .	19,833
Taxis	3,448
Crown Vehicles (excl. H.M. Forces) .	3,488
Buses	3,248
Public Light Buses . . .	3,828
Private Light Buses . . .	1,684
Public Cars	1,063
TOTAL (incl. others) . .	186,193

MARINE TRAFFIC
(1972)

		OCEAN-GOING	RIVER STEAMERS	JUNKS
Vessels entered	number	7,827	14,861	7,321
Tonnage entered	'000 n.r.t.	28,238	2,816	1,179
Passengers landed	number	11,655	1,930,059	—
Passengers embarked . . .	,,	12,576	1,931,817	—
Cargo tons landed	d.w.t.	10,726,632	4,979	737,673
Cargo tons loaded	,,	3,569,934	5,858	179,349

TOURISM

	1970	1971	1972
Number of Visitors . .	927,256	907,295	1,082,253
Number of Hotel Rooms .	8,670	9,047	10,782

COMMUNICATIONS MEDIA
(1972)

Telephones	651,468
Television Sets . . .	676,000*
Periodicals	187
Daily Newspapers . . .	101

* Estimate.

EDUCATION
(1972)

SCHOOLS	PUPILS
Kindergarten	130,894
Primary	748,291
Secondary	323,090
Post-Secondary . . .	12,593
Adult Education . . .	66,052
Special Education . . .	3,743

Source: Hong Kong Government, *Official Statistics.*

THE CONSTITUTION

The Government of Hong Kong, which consists of the Governor, the Executive Council and the Legislative Council, is constituted under the authority of Letters Patent and Royal Instructions.

The Executive Council is consulted by the Governor on all important administrative questions. In addition to five *ex officio* members, there are eight unofficial members (of whom four are Chinese), and one nominated official member.

The Legislative Council, which advises on and approves the enactment of the Colony's laws and approves all expenditure from public funds, consists of four of the *ex officio* members who sit on the Executive Council, ten other official members and fifteen unofficial members (these include eleven Chinese). It has three Standing Committees, concerned with finance, law and public works respectively; select Committees may be set up on an *ad hoc* basis.

THE GOVERNMENT

Governor: Sir CRAWFORD MURRAY MACLEHOSE, K.C.M.G., M.B.E.

EXECUTIVE COUNCIL
(*January* 1974)

President: The GOVERNOR.

Ex Officio Members: The Commander British Forces (Lt.-Gen. Sir EDWIN BRAMALL, O.B.E., M.C.), The Colonial Secretary (D. T. E. ROBERTS, C.B.E., Q.C., J.P.), The Attorney-General (J. W. D. HOBLEY, Q.C., J.P.), The Secretary for Home Affairs (D. C. BRAY, J.P.), The Financial Secretary (C. P. HADDON-CAVE, C.M.G., J.P.).

Nominated Official Member: Dr. G. H. CHOA, C.B.E., J.P.

Unofficial Members: Sir ALBERT RODRIGUES, C.B.E., E.D., J.P., Sir DOUGLAS CLAGUE, C.B.E., M.C., Q.P.M., T.D., J.P., Sir SIDNEY GORDON, C.B.E., J.P., Sir YUET-KEUNG KAN, C.B.E., J.P., WOO PAK-CHUEN, C.B.E., J.P., G. R. ROSS, C.B.E., J.P., SZETO-WAI, C.B.E., J.P., Dr. CHUNG SZE-YUEN, O.B.E., J.P.

LEGISLATIVE COUNCIL

President: The Governor.

Ex Officio Members: The Colonial Secretary, The Attorney-General, The Secretary for Home Affairs, The Financial Secretary.

Nominated Official Members: D. R. W. ALEXANDER, C.B.E., J.P., J. J. ROBSON, C.B.E., J.P., J. CANNING, J.P., Dr. G. H. CHOA, C.B.E., J.P., D. AKERS-JONES, J.P., M.A., I. M. LIGHTBODY, C.M.G., J.P., D. H. JORDAN, M.B.E., J.P., LI FOOK-KOW, J.P., L. M. DAVIES, C.M.G., O.B.E., D. W. MCDONALD, J.P.

Unofficial Members: WILFRED S. B. WONG, O.B.E., J.P., WILSON T. S. WANG, O.B.E., J.P., LEE QUO-WEI, J.P., OSWALD CHEUNG, O.B.E., Q.C., J.P., ANN TSE-KAI, O.B.E., J.P., Mrs. C. J. SYMONS, O.B.E., J.P., P. G. WILLIAMS, J.P., JAMES WU MAN-HON, J.P., ROGERIO LOBO, O.B.E., J.P., WOO PAK-CHUEN, C.B.E., J.P., SZETO-WAI, C.B.E., J.P., Dr. CHUNG SZE-YUEN, O.B.E., J.P., G. M. SAYER, J.P., HILTON CHEONG-LEEN, O.B.E., J.P., LI FOOK-WO, O.B.E., J.P.

POLITICAL PARTIES

Democratic Self-Government Party: f. 1963; English and Chinese membership; left wing.

Labour Party of Hong Kong: f. 1964 as a breakaway group of the D.S.G.P.

Socialist Democratic Party: f. 1964.

The **Reform Club** and **Civic Association,** which worked in alliance between 1961 and 1964, stand for moderate constitutional changes in Hong Kong's government.

JUDICIAL SYSTEM

The Supreme Court has unlimited jurisdiction in civil and criminal cases, the District Court having limited jurisdiction. Appeals from these courts lie to the Full Court, presided over by the Chief Justice and consisting of two or three Supreme Court judges. Appeals from Magistrates' Courts are heard by a Supreme Court judge.

Supreme Court:

Chief Justice: Sir GEOFFREY G. BRIGGS, Q.C.

Senior Puisne Judge: Hon. Sir ALASTAIR BLAIR-KERR.

Puisne Judges: Hon. Mr. Justice P. F. X. LEONARD, Hon. Mr. Justice J. P. TRAINOR, Hon. Mr. Justice D. CONS, Hon. Mr. Justice M. MORLEY-JOHN, Hon. Mr. Justice SIMON F. S. LI, Hon. Mr. Justice A. A. HUGGINS, Hon. Mr. Justice A. M. MCMULLIN, Hon. Mr. Justice W. F. PICKERING.

District Courts: There are ten District Judges with courts in Victoria, Kowloon and the New Territories.

Magistrates' Courts: There are forty-six Magistrates' Courts.

RELIGION

The Chinese population is predominantly Buddhist, although Confucianism and Taoism are also practised. The three religions are frequently found in the same temple. There are more than 250,000 Chinese Christians and a number of Muslims and Jews.

ANGLICAN

Bishop of Hong Kong: Rt. Rev. J. GILBERT H. BAKER, Bishop's House, 1 Lower Albert Rd.

ROMAN CATHOLIC

Bishop of Hong Kong: Most Rev. FRANCIS XAVIER CHEN PING HSU, Catholic Centre, Grand Bldg., 15/18 Connaught Rd., Central.

THE PRESS

DAILY NEWSPAPERS

English Language

China Mail: P.O.B. 47; f. 1845; evening; tabloid; Editor PETER G. B. ROWLAND; circ. 26,000.

Hongkong Standard: News Building, 635 King's Rd.; f. 1949; Exec. Man. JOSEPH MAK; circ. (weekday and Sunday) 32,000.

South China Morning Post: P.O.B. 47; Editor R. G. HUTCHEON; circ. 55,000.

The Star: 19-21 Pennington St., Causeway Bay; f. 1965; evening; Editor P. OWEN.

English and Chinese

Daily Commodity Quotations: 510 Marina House; f. 1948; morning; commercial news.

Chinese Language

Chi Yin Yat Pao (*Chi Yin Daily News*): 20 Lee Yuen St. East; morning.

Ching Po: 141 Queen's Rd. East, 3rd Floor; f. 1956; Editor CHAN HA TZE; circ. 90,000.

Chiu Yin Po.

Chun Pao (*Truth Daily*): evening.

Chung Ying Daily News.

Fai Po (*Express*): 635 King's Rd., North Point; morning.

Hong Kong Sheung Po (*Hong Kong Commercial Daily*): 28–30 Wing Lok St.; f. 1952; Editor-in-Chief K. CHEUNG; circ. 110,000.

Hong Kong Shih Pao (*Hong Kong Times*): 64–66 Gloucester Rd.; morning; right-wing; expresses the views of the Chinese Nationalist Government in Taiwan (Formosa).

Hsin Sheng Wan Pao (*New Life Evening Post*): 171-173 Hennessy Rd.; f. 1945; independent; Editor and Gen. Man. K. C. CHAN; circ. 30,000.

Hsin Wan Pao (*New Evening Post*): 342 Hennessey Rd.; f. 1951; left-wing; Editor Lo Fu.

Hung Look Yat Po: 37 Gough St.; f. 1939; Prop. YAM Woo FAR; circ. 40,000.

Kung Sheung Man Po (*Industrial and Commercial Evening News*): 18 Fenwick St.; f. 1930; evening; Editor TAM TAT FU; circ. 48,000.

Kung Sheung Yat Po (*Industrial and Commercial Daily News*): 18 Fenwick St.; f. 1925; morning; independent; Editor NELSON LIU; circ. 70,200.

Sing Pao: 101 King's Rd.; morning; circ. 300,000.

Sing Tao Jih Pao: 635 King's Rd., North Point; f. 1938; morning; Editor SEE CHO-YEE; circ. 35,000.

Sing Tao Wan Po: 635 King's Rd.; f. 1938; evening; morning; Editor SEE CHO-YEE; circ. 35,000.

Ta Kung Pao: 342 Hennessey Rd.; f. 1951; morning; left-wing; Editor FEI YEE-MING; circ. 30,000.

Tin Tin Yat Pao: 16 Tong Shui Rd.; f. 1960; Editor C. K. TONG.

Wah Kiu Man Po: 106–116 Hollywood Rd.; f. 1945; evening; Independent; Editor SHUM CHOI-SANG; circ. 49,561.

Wah Kiu Yat Po (*Overseas Chinese Daily News Ltd.*): 106–116 Hollywood Rd.; f. 1925; morning; Independent; Chief Editor Ho KIN CHEUNG; circ. 66,089.

Wen Wei Po: 30 Hollywood Rd.; morning; left-wing; Editor-in-Chief LI TSE-CHUNG.

SUNDAY NEWSPAPERS
English Language

Hong Kong Sunday Post-Herald: P.O.B. 47; Editor ROBIN HUTCHEON; circ. 34,000.

Sunday Examiner: f. 1946; religious (R. Catholic).

Chinese Language

Asia Weekly: 407 Asian House, 1 Hennessy Rd.; f. 1964; Editor WARREN LEE.

PERIODICALS
English Language

Apparel: Connaught Centre, 3/F., Connaught Rd., Hong Kong; f. March 1969; published by the Hong Kong Trade Development Council; concerned with new developments in local manufacturing of garments; bi-annual; circ. 16,000; Editor Ross HAIG.

Asia Magazine: 31 Queen's Rd. Central; f. 1961; general interest; Sunday supplement distributed to English language newspapers; Editor GEORGE LIU.

Asia Pictorial: 82 Yee Wo St., 2nd Floor; f. 1954; independent monthly; general; Editor CHANG KUO-SIN; circ. 20,000.

Asian Building and Construction: c/o Far East Trade Press Ltd., 1908 Prince's Building; f. 1938; monthly; Editor PETER LEUNG.

Asian Business and Industry: c/o Far East Trade Press Ltd., 1908 Prince's Bldg., Des Voeux Rd., Central; monthly; Publisher R. V. PANDIT; Editor T. K. SESHADRI.

Asian Journal of Medicine: 1908 Prince's Building, Des Voeux Rd. Central; f. 1964; published by the Far East Trade Press Ltd.; Editor Dr. W. J. ORAM, F.R.C.S.; Man. Editor R. P. NAYAR; monthly; circ. 20,093.

Asian Manufacturing: c/o Far East Trade Press Ltd., 1908 Prince's Bldg., Des Voeux Rd., Central; monthly; Editor JOHN WOODWARD.

Eastern Horizon: 3rd Floor, 472 Hennessy Rd.; f. 1960; independent monthly, devoted to art and culture; Editor LEE TSUNG-YING; circ. 20,000.

Far Eastern Economic Review: 407 Marina House, P.O.B. 160; f. 1946; weekly; Editor DEREK DAVIES; Gen. Sales Man. F. C. H. WADSWORTH; circ. 20,075 (throughout the world).

Gregg's Medical Directory: c/o Far East Trade Press Ltd., 1908 Prince's Bldg., Des Voeux Rd. Central; annual.

Hong Kong Builder Directory: c/o 704 Lee Hing Bldg., Des Voeux Rd. Central; f. 1935; annual.

Hong Kong Enterprise: Connaught Centre, 3/F., Connaught Rd., Hong Kong; f. Oct. 1967; published by the Hong Kong Trade Development Council; concerned with new developments in local manufacturing; monthly; Editor ELBERT SHEN; circ. 60,000.

Hong Kong Government Gazette: Java Rd., North Point; weekly.

Hong Kong Telegraph: 1–3 Wyndham St.; Editor M. HODGES; weekly.

Modern Asia: P.O.B. 770; f. 1967; business and industry; 9 issues yearly; Editor DAVID J. ROADS; circ. 20,000.

The Reader's Digest (Asian Edn.): Reader's Digest Asia Ltd., 22 Westlands Rd., Quarry Bay; f. 1963; general topics; monthly; sold throughout Asia; Editor Mrs. ELIZABETH G. COOPER; circ. 310,000.

Textile Asia: c/o Business Press Ltd., 501 Yip Fung Bldg., 2-12 D'Aguilar St.; f. 1970; monthly; Editor-in-Chief KAYSER SUNG; circ. 15,000.

Toys: Connaught Centre, Connaught Rd., Hong Kong; f. Dec. 1969; published by the Hong Kong Trade Development Council; concerned with new developments in local manufacturing of toys; annual; circ. 15,000; Editor Ross HAIG.

Travelling Magazine: Room 903, Yat Fat Building, 44 Des Voeux Rd. Central; f. 1965; monthly; Publisher SHAU-FU POK; circ. 50,500.

World Today: 26 Garden Rd.; monthly; circ. 80,000.

Chinese Language

Hong Fook (*Pictorial Happiness*): monthly.

Hsin Kar Ting (*New Home*): monthly.

Kar Ting Sang Wood (*Home Life Journal*): 326 Jaffe Rd. f. 1950; every ten days; Editor TONG BIG CHUEN; circ. 30,000.

Kung Kao Pao: Catholic Press Bureau, Grand Buildings; weekly; f. 1928; religious (R. Catholic).

The Reader's Digest (Chinese Edn.): Reader's Digest Asia Ltd., 22 Westlands Rd., Quarry Bay; f. 1965; general topics; monthly; sold throughout Asia; Chief Editor Miss LIN TAI-YI; circ. 230,000.

Sin Chung Hwa Pictorial: monthly.

Sing Tao Weekly: 179 Wanchai Rd.

Sinwen Tienti (*Newsdom Weekly*): Room 903, Yat Fat Building, 44 Des Voeux Rd. Central; f. 1945; weekly; Publisher SHAU-FU POK; circ. 60,550.

Tien Wen Tai: (*Observatory Review*) 60 Leighten Rd., 6th Floor; f. 1936; alternate days; Editor Gen. CHEN HSIAO-WEI; circ. 20,000.

Travelling Magazine: Room 903, Yat Fat Building, 44 Des Voeux Rd. Central; f. 1966; monthly; Publisher SHAU-FU POK; circ. 50,500.

Tse Yau Chun Hsin (*Freedom Front*): weekly.

Tsing Nin Wen Yu (*Literary Youth*): monthly.

Tung Fung (*East Pictorial*): 141 King's Rd.; weekly.

Tung Sai (*East and West*): fortnightly.

PRESS AGENCIES

Pan-Asia Newspaper Alliance: Printing House, 6 Duddell St. (P.O.B. 836); f. 1949; Editor-in-Chief BRUCE LEE.

New Zealand Press Association: 708 Gloucester Building; Correspondent DEREK ROUND.

FOREIGN BUREAUX

The following agencies have offices in Hong Kong: AFP, Antara, AP, Central News Agency of China, DPA, Jiji Press, Kyodo News Service, Reuters and UPI.

PUBLISHERS

Asia Press Ltd.: 88 Yee Wo St., Causeway Bay; f. 1952; books and magazines; Pres. CHANG KUO-SIN; Gen. Manager CHEN LIU-TO.

Business Press Ltd.: 501 Yip Fung Bldg., 2-12 D'Aguilar St.; f. 1970; textiles periodicals and economics papers; Man. Dir. KAYSER SUNG.

Chung Chi Publications: Chung Chi College, The Chinese University of Hong Kong, Shatin, New Territories; f. 1961; history, philosophy, Asian studies, history of science, *Chung Chi Journal*, etc.

Far East American Publishing Co.: 25A Robinson Rd.; geography, travel, politics, fiction.

Far East Trade Press Ltd.: 1908 Prince's Bldg., Des Voeux Rd. Central; trade magazines and directories; Publisher and Gen. Man. R. V. PANDIT.

Hong Kong University Press: 94 Bonham Rd., University of Hong Kong; f. 1955; scholarly and general; Dir. G. W. BONSALL, M.A., M.L.S.; Editor D. M. JOYCE, M.A.

Longman Group (Far East) Ltd.: Taikoo Sugar Refinery Compound, Quarry Bay; arts, geography, history, education, literature, school books.

Pacific Communications Ltd.: 633 News Bldg., 2/F North Point; f. 1969; art, culture, geography, travel, politics, economics, fashion; Man. Dir. S. DUMLAO, Jr.

PUBLISHERS' ASSOCIATION

Hong Kong Printers' Association: 48–50 Johnston Rd.; f. 1939; 310 mems.; Pres. LEE YAT NGOK; Chair. HO WAI CHUEN.

RADIO AND TELEVISION

RADIO

Radio Hong Kong: Broadcasting House, Broadcast Drive, P.O.B. K200, Kowloon; f. 1928; public service broadcasting department of the Government; services of 20 hours daily in both English and Chinese; television division (RHKTV), producing public affairs programmes in English and Chinese, to be carried by local commercial stations.

Hong Kong Commercial Broadcasting Co. Ltd.: P.O.B. 3000, Hong Kong; f. 1959; broadcasts in English and Chinese; Man. Dir. G. Ho.

Rediffusion (Hong Kong) Ltd.: Television House, 81 Broadcast Drive, Kowloon; subsidiary of Rediffusion Ltd., London; commercial wired television and radio service; two television services (English and Chinese); 110,000 subscribers; two audio channels (numerous Chinese dialects); 40,000 subscribers; Man. Dir. R. J. WARREN; Gen. Man. (Broadcasting) D. P. GALE.

British Forces Broadcasting Service: BFPO 1, Hong Kong; f. 1971; Controller J. M. CAMPBELL, A.M.B.I.M.; Programme Organizer Capt. (QGO) KISHOR KUMAR GURUNG.

In 1973 there were an estimated ten million radio receivers in use.

TELEVISION

Rediffusion Television Ltd.: Television House, 81 Broadcast Drive, Kowloon; f. 1957; commercial wired television service; English and Chinese programmes on separate channels; 110,000 subscribers; Man. Dir. R. J. WARREN; Dep. Man. Dir. D. P. GALE.

Hong Kong Television Broadcasts Ltd.: P.O.B. K100; f. 1967; 2 colour networks; Man. Dir. A. K. W. EU.

In July 1973 there were 727,000 television receivers in use.

FINANCE

Of the Colony's 73 authorized banks, 13 are Communist banks, including the bank of People's Republic of China. Fifty-one of the banks are authorized to deal on the official foreign exchange market. The remainder are non-authorized and deal on the free market.

BANKING

Banking Commission: 1704 Hang Chong Bldg., 5 Queen's Rd. Central; f. 1964; Commissioner J. C. PATERSON; Chief Banking Inspector C. D. W. MARTIN; Senior Banking Officer C. S. LEUNG; publs. monthly banking statistics and other information connected with the banking system.

ISSUING BANKS

Chartered Bank: Head Office: 38 Bishopsgate, London, E.C.2; Principal Hong Kong Office: 4 Des Voeux Rd. Central; brs. (Island): Aberdeen, Causeway Bay, Kennedy Town, North Point, Sai Ying Pun, Shaukiwan, Shek Tong Tsui, Wah Fu Estate, Wan Chai, Wellington St.; (Mainland): Choi Hung Estate, Ferry St., Fung Wong Village, Hung Hom, Kilung St., Kowloon City, Kwun Tong, Lo Fu Ngam, Ma Tau Kok, Mei Foo Sun Chuen, Ngau Tau Kok, Sai Kung, San Po Kong, Shamshuipo, Shek Lei Estate, Shek Yam Estate, Tsim Sha Tsui, Tsuen Wan, Wo Lok Estate, Yaumati.

Mercantile Bank Ltd.: 1 Queen's Rd., Central Hong Kong; cap. p.u. £2.94m.; dep. £37m.; Chair. G. M. SAYER.

Hongkong and Shanghai Banking Corporation, The: 1 Queen's Rd. Central, P.O.B. 64; f. 1865; incorp. in Hong Kong; cap. issued and p.u. HK $560m.; dep. (1972) HK $15,158m.; Chair. G. M. SAYER.

HONG KONG BANKS

Bank of Canton Ltd.: 6 Des Voeux Road Central; Western Branch, 10 Bonham Strand West; Kowloon Branch, 790 Nathan Road, Kowloon; North Point Branch, 382 King's Road; incorp. in Hong Kong in 1912; cap. p.u. HK $7.7m.; total resources (1972) HK $457m.; Chief Man. HUO PAO TSAI.

Bank of East Asia Ltd.: 10 Des Voeux Rd. Central; incorp. in Hong Kong in 1918; cap. p.u. HK $36m.; dep. (1972) HK $968m.; Chair. Hon. Sir Y. K. KAN, C.B.E.

Chekiang First Bank Ltd.: 3 Statue Square; f. 1950; Chair. and Man. TE-CHUAN LI.

China and South Sea Bank Ltd.: 22-26 Bonham Strand East; Man. HUANG CHEN-YING.

Chiyu Banking Corporation Ltd.: 80 Des Voeux Rd. Central; f. 1947.

Dao Heng Bank Ltd.: 17-19 Bonham Strand East, Hong Kong; f. 1921; Chair. TUNG HOK NIN; Man. Dir. TANG PANG YUEN; cap. HK $50m.; resources HK $673m.

Hang Seng Bank Ltd.: 77 Des Voeux Rd., Central; cap. p.u. HK $100m.; dep. HK $3,572m. (1972); Chair. S. H. HO, M.B.E.

Hong Kong Chinese Bank Ltd., The: The Hong Kong Chinese Bank Bldg., 61-65 Des Voeux Rd., Central; f. 1955; dep. HK $125m. (1972); 6 brs.; Chair. and Gen. Man. The Hon. Sir SIK-NIN CHAU, Kt., C.B.E., J.P., LL.D.; Dir. and Deputy Gen. Man. KAI-YIN CHAU; Man. TE-MING TSENG.

Hong Kong Industrial and Commercial Bank: 10 Queen's Rd. Central; f. 1964.

Hong Kong Metropolitan Bank Ltd.: 40-42 Des Voeux Rd. Central, P.O.B. 14612.

Hong Kong and Swatow Commercial Bank Ltd.: 48A Bonham Strand, West.

Kwong On Bank Ltd.: 137-141 Queen's Rd., Central, Hong Kong; f. 1938, inc. 1954; dep. HK $293m. (1972); Chair. and Gen. Man. LEUNG KWAI-YEE; 6 brs.

Nanyang Commercial Bank Ltd.: 1A Des Voeux Rd. Central; f. 1949; cap. p.u. HK $10m.; res. HK $20m.; dep. HK $462.4m. (Dec. 1972); Chair. and Gen. Man. CHUANG SHIH PING; 8 brs.

Overseas Trust Bank Ltd.: 5E Ice House St.; Man. Dir. TSAO YAO.

Shanghai Commercial Bank Ltd.: 12 Queen's Rd., Central; f. 1951; incorp. in Hong Kong; cap. and res. HK $69m.; dep. (1972) HK $720m.; Chair. K. P. CHEN; Gen. Man. K. K. CHEN.

Wing On Bank Ltd.: 22 Des Voeux Rd., Central; incorp. in Hong Kong in 1931; cap. p.u. HK $10.1m.; dep. (Dec. 1972) HK $473,458,949; Chair. LAMBERT KWOK; Dir. WONG HOO CHUEN; Chief Man. LAMSON KWOK; 9 brs.

FOREIGN BANKS

Algemene Bank Nederland N.V.: Holland House, 9 Ice St.; br. in Kowloon; Man. L. J. VAN HELLENBERG HUBAR.

American Express International Banking Corpn.: Union House, 8 Connaught Rd. Central (Head Office: New York); Resident Vice-Pres. T. M. DE'ATH; Man. J. H. GIDWANI.

Bangkok Bank Ltd.: Head Office: 9 Suapa Rd., Bangkok; Hong Kong br.: 26-30 Des Voeux Rd., West; Man. THONGCHAI PHADOEMCHIT, Vice-President; sub-brs.: Shell House, Queens Rd., Central; 556 Nathan Rd., Kowloon; 28 Causeway Rd., Causeway Bay.

Bank of America N.T. and S.A.: San Francisco; Hong Kong G.P.O. Box 472.

Bank of China: Peking; 2A Des Voeux Road C.; Man. LI CHUO-CHIH.

Bank of Communications: Peking; 3A Des Voeux Rd. Central.

Bank of India: Bombay; Dina House, 3-5 Duddell St., P.O.B. 13763; Man. J. N. KARANI.

Bank Negara Indonesia 1946: Head Office: 1 Jalan Lada, Jakarta; f. 1946; Hong Kong br.: 25 Des Voeux Rd. Central.

Bank of Tokyo Ltd.: Sutherland House, Chater Rd., Hong Kong; 691-697 Nathan Rd., Kowloon.

Banque Belge Pour l'Etranger S.A.: Edinburgh House; 8 brs.

Banque de l'Indochine: Paris 8e; 77 Des Voeux Rd. Central.

Banque Nationale de Paris: Central Bldg., 2nd Floor, Queen's Rd., Central; f. 1966.

Chase Manhattan Bank, N.A., The: New York; 15 Queen's Rd., Central, P.O.B. 104; 720 Nathan Rd., Kowloon; Second Vice-Pres. and Man. JOHN C. LINKER.

China State Bank Ltd.: Shanghai; 11B Queen's Rd. Central.

Chung Khiaw Bank Ltd.: 15-18 Connaught Rd. Central.

Thomas Cook and Son (Continental and Overseas) Ltd.: 1236 Union House, Hong Kong and 223 Tung Ying Bldg., 100 Nathan Rd., Kowloon.

Deutsch-Asiatische Bank: Hamburg; Hang Chong Bldg., 5 Queen's Rd., Central; brs.: Jakarta, Karachi, Kuala Lumpur, Singapore.

Equitable Banking Corporation: Manila; Hong Kong Br.: 4 Duddell St.

First National City Bank: New York City 10022; Citibank Tower, 8 Ice House St.; 28 Des Voeux Rd., Central; 12 Pedder St.; 1 Hennessy Rd.; 72 Nathan Rd.; Lee Gardens, 37 Hysan Ave.; Hankow Rd. No. 2; 827 South Bay Rd.; 26-28 Yue Man Square; 421 Castle Peak Rd.; 64-66 Bonham Strand West; 237A To Kwa Wan Rd.; 8c Nassau St.; Mailing address, Hong Kong P.O.B. 14; Vice-Pres. R. A. FREYTAG.

Four Seas Communications Bank Ltd.: Singapore; 36 Bonham Strand West.

Indian Overseas Bank: Madras; 7-9 Duddell St.; Man. J. P. MOSES.

Korea Exchange Bank: Head Office: Seoul, Korea; Hong Kong brs.: 1st floor, Loke Yew Bldg., 50-52 Queen's Rd., Central; Korea Centre Bldg., 119-121 Connaught Rd., Central; Kowloon br.: Alpha House, 27-33 Nathan Rd., Kowloon; overseas brs. in Tokyo, Saigon, New York, Los Angeles, Toronto, Panama, London, Jakarta, Frankfurt, Singapore, Amsterdam, São Paulo, Milan, Vienna, Osaka, Bangkok, Guam.

Malayan Banking Berhad: Hong Kong Office: 1st Floor, Pacific House, 20 Queen's Rd., Central; Kowloon br.: 227 Nathan Rd.

National Bank of Pakistan: Karachi; Hong Kong br.: 129 Central Bldg., Queen's Rd., Central; Kowloon br.: 7 Chatham Rd.

National Commercial Bank Ltd.: Shanghai; Hong Kong Br.: 16-16A Queen's Rd. Central.

Oversea-Chinese Banking Corpn. Ltd.: Head Office: Singapore; Hong Kong Office: Edinburgh House, 13B Queen's Rd. Central; Kowloon Office: Alhambra Bldg., 383 Nathan Rd.

Overseas Union Bank: Singapore; 14-16 Pedder St.

Sanwa Bank Ltd.: Head Office: Fushimimachi 4-chome, Osaka; Hong Kong br.: 20 Des Voeux Rd. Central.

Sin Hua Trust, Savings and Commercial Bank, Ltd.: Peking; Marina House, 17 Queen's Rd. Central; f. 1914; Man. SU TSAN SING.

Sumitomo Bank Ltd.: Osaka; 5 Queen's Rd. Central.

United Commercial Bank: Hong Kong; Prince's Bldg., 5 Statue Square.

United Overseas Bank Ltd.: Incorp. in Singapore; Hong Kong br.: 5 Queen's Rd., Central; Man. H. T. PENG.

BANK ASSOCIATION

The Exchange Banks' Association, Hong Kong: c/o The Hong Kong and Shanghai Banking Corporation, 1 Queen's Rd. Central; f. 1897; an association of major banks with the purpose of representation with official bodies and the co-ordination of the banking services offered by its members; Chair. M. G. R. SANDBERG.

STOCK EXCHANGES

Far East Exchange Ltd.: Room 201, China Building, Queen's Rd. Central, Hong Kong; f. 1969; 344 mems.; Chair. RONALD FOOK-SHIU LI.

Hong Kong Stock Exchange Ltd.: 801 Edinburgh House, Ice House St.; Chair. F. R. ZIMMERN; Vice-Chair. B. K. L. LUI; Sec. R. A. WITTS.

Kam Ngan Exchange: 7th floor, Connaught Centre, Connaught Rd. Central; f. 1970; publs. *Daily Quotation*, *Monthly Bulletin*.

Kowloon Stock Exchange: f. Jan. 1972; 171 mems.; Chair. PETER P. F. CHAN.

TRADE AND INDUSTRY

CHAMBERS OF COMMERCE

Hong Kong General Chamber of Commerce: Union House, 9th Floor, P.O.B. 852; f. 1861; 2,100 mems.; Chair. P. G. WILLIAMS.

Chinese General Chamber of Commerce: 24 Connaught Rd., Central; f. 1900; 6,000 mems.; Chair. WONG KWAN CHENG.

Hong Kong Junior Chamber: 24 Ice House St., 4th Floor; f. 1950; 230 mems.; Pres. ALEX TZANG; Sec.-Gen. IRVING KOO; publ. *Harbour Lights*.

Kowloon Chamber of Commerce: Liberty Ave., Kowloon; Pres. CHEA PAK-CHEONG.

Indian Chamber of Commerce: Dina House, 5A Duddell St., P.O.B. 2742; Chair. K. SITAL; Sec. S. ARUNADRI RAM.

EXTERNAL TRADE ORGANIZATIONS

Hong Kong Trade Development Council: Connaught Centre, Connaught Rd., Hong Kong; f. 1966; a statutory body to promote, assist and develop Hong Kong's overseas trade, with particular reference to exports; and to make such recommendations to the Government as it sees fit in relation to any measures which it considers would achieve an increase in Hong Kong's trade; Exec. Dir. L. DUNNING; publs. *Hong Kong Enterprise* (monthly), *Apparel* (bi-annual), *Toys* (annual).

OVERSEAS OFFICES

Australia: Suite 2311, Level 23, Australia Square Tower, Sydney, N.S.W. 2001.

Austria: Rotenturmstrasse 1-3, 8/F., Apt. 24, 1010 Vienna.

Canada: 347 Bay St., 2/F, Toronto.

Federal Republic of Germany: D-6000 Frankfurt-am-Main, Bockenheimer Landstrasse 51-53; Hansastrasse 1, 2000 Hamburg 13.

Italy: 2 Piazzetta Pattari 2, 20122 Milan.

Japan: Fuji Bldg., 2-3 Marunouchi, 3-chome, Chiyoda-ku, Tokyo.

Netherlands: Frederiksplein 1, Amsterdam.

Sweden: Brahegatan 30, 11437, Stockholm.

United Kingdom: 14–16 Cockspur St., London SW1 5DP; 4 St. James's Sq., Manchester.

U.S.A.: 548 Fifth Ave., New York, N.Y. 10036; 606 South Hill St., Suite 401/402, Los Angeles, Calif. 90014; Suite 1511, 333 North Michigan Ave., Chicago, Ill. 60601.

Hong Kong Exporters' Association: P.O.B. K1864; Office: 626 Star House, Kowloon; f. 1955; 130 mems. consisting of the leading merchants and manufacturing exporters of Hong Kong; Chair. A. M. BLACKSTOCK; Vice-Chair. A. J. MOODY, J. B. M. LITMAATH; Sec. BRIDGET CROSSLEY.

INDUSTRIAL ORGANIZATIONS

Hong Kong Productivity Council, The: Rooms 512–516, Gloucester Bldg., Des Voeux Rd. C.; f. 1967 to promote increased productivity of industry and to encourage more efficient utilization of resources; established by statute and supported by Hong Kong Government, of which the executive body is the *Hong Kong Productivity Centre*; mems.: not more than 21, appointed by the Governor, of which 4 represent management, 4 represent labour, 2 represent academic or professional interests and no more than 10 are public officers; Chair. of Council Dr. the Hon. Sir SIK NIN CHAU, C.B.E., J.P., LL.D.; Chair. of Exec. Cttee. Dr. Hon. S. Y. CHUNG, O.B.E., J.P.; Exec. Dir. W. H. NEWTON; publs. *Hong Kong Productivity News* (monthly, bilingual), industry and survey reports, study mission reports, training brochures, etc.

Federation of Hong Kong Industries, The: Eldex Industrial Bldg., 12th Floor, Unit A, 21 Ma Tau Wei Rd., Hung Hom, Kowloon; f. 1960; about 1,000 individual mems., divided into 21 groups according to type of industry; headquarters of World Packaging Organization; parent organization for Hong Kong Design and Packaging Centres, Hong Kong Designers' Association and Hong Kong Shippers' Council; affiliated mems.: American Chamber of Commerce in Hong Kong, Employers' Federation of Hong Kong, Federation of Hong Kong Garment Manufacturers, Hong Kong Chinese Textile Mills Association, Hong Kong Cotton Made-Up Goods Manufacturers' Association, Hong Kong Cotton Spinners' Association, Hong Kong Garment Manufacturers' Association, Hong Kong General Chamber of Commerce, Hong Kong Japanese Chamber of Commerce, Hong Kong and Kowloon Plastic Products Merchants' United Association Ltd., Hong Kong Plastic Manufacturers' Association, Hong Kong Wool and Synthetic Spinners' Association Ltd., Hong Kong Woollen Knitting Manufacturers' Association Ltd., Indian Chamber of Commerce of Hong Kong, Hong Kong Management Association; Chair. Hon. T. K. ANN, O.B.E., J.P.; Deputy Chair. H. KESWICK; Joint Dirs. A. ISMAIL, CECIL S. O. CHAN; Dir. of Planning and Development Mrs. S. YUEN, J.P.

Chinese Manufacturers' Association of Hong Kong, The: 64–65 Connaught Rd. C.; f. 1934; over 2,000 mems.; Pres. Dr. C. W. CHUANG, LL.D., L.H.D.; Sec.-Gen. J. P. LEE; publs. *Annual Report*, *Directory of Members*.

Federation of Hong Kong Cotton Weavers: Room 1041, Union House Central, Hong Kong; f. 1957; 39 mems.

Hong Kong Cotton Spinners' Association: 1038 Union House; f. 1955; 31 mems.

Hong Kong Jade and Stone Manufacturers' Association: Hang Lung House, 16th Floor, 184-192 Queen's Rd. Central; f. 1965; Pres. R. Y. C. LEE.

Employers' Federation of Hong Kong: P.O.B. 2067; f. 1947; 127 mems.; Chair. J. G. OLIVER; Vice-Chair. J. H. W. SALMON; Sec. and Treas. H. E. AIERS.

TRADE UNIONS

In 1972 there were 385 trade unions in Hong Kong.

Hong Kong and Kowloon Trades Union Council (T.U.C.): Labour Building, 11 Chang Sha St., Kowloon; f. 1949; 85,000 mems. from 104 affiliated unions, mostly covering the catering, building, textiles and craft trades; 35 unions participating in its activities; supports the Chinese Nationalist Govt. in Taiwan; affil. to ICFTU; Gen. Sec. WONG YIU KAM.

Hong Kong Federation of Trade Unions (F.T.U.): 142 Lockhart Road, 3rd Floor; f. 1948; 66 affiliated unions, mostly concentrated in the shipyards, seafaring, textile mills and public utilities, and 16 nominally independent unions which subscribe to the policy and participate in the activities of the F.T.U.; left-wing supporting the Chinese People's Government.

There are a number of independent unions.

CO-OPERATIVES

Registrar of Co-operatives: The Director of Agriculture and Fisheries, 393 Canton Rd., Kowloon; as at March 31st, 1973 there were 421 Co-operatives with a membership of 22,585 and paid-up capital of HK $1,777,727.

CO-OPERATIVE SOCIETIES

(socs.=societies; mems.=membership; cap.=paid-up share capital in HK $; feds.=federations)

Agricultural Credit: socs. 11, mems. 329, cap. $40,930.
Apartment Owners': socs. 2, mems. 156, cap. $10,900.
Better Living: socs. 24, mems. 1,905, cap. $32,180.
Consumers': socs. 10, mems. 2,511, cap. $16,395.
Farmers' Irrigation: socs. 1, mems. 68, cap. $340.
Federation of Fishermen's Societies: feds. 4, member-socs. 56, cap. $5,400.
Federation of Pig Raising Societies: fed. 1, member-socs. 34, cap. $850.
Federation of Vegetable Marketing Societies: fed. 1, member-socs. 29, cap. $5,700.
Fishermen's Credit: socs. 61, mems. 1,337, cap. $31,755.
Fishermen's Credit and Housing: socs. 2, mems. 105, cap. $665.
Housing: socs. 236, mems. 5,042, cap. $1,390,360.
Pig Raising: socs. 30, mems. 1,510, cap. $123,705.
Salaried Workers' Thrift and Loan: socs. 7, mems. 737, cap. $11,161.
Vegetable Marketing: socs. 31, mems. 8,726, cap. $107,386.

MARKETING ORGANIZATIONS

Fish Marketing Organization: f. 1945; statutory organization to control wholesale fish marketing; in 1971 landings marketed through wholesale fish markets totalled 75,463 metric tons valued at HK $141.78m.

Vegetable Marketing Organization: f. 1946; Government agency to collect vegetables and handle wholesale marketing; loan fund to farmers; during 1971 83,222 metric tons of vegetables, valued at HK $65.1m. were sold through the organization.

DEVELOPMENT CORPORATIONS

Hong Kong Housing Authority: 1, Ma Tau Kok Road, Kowloon; Commissioner D. LIAO POON HUAI.

Hong Kong Housing Society: P.O.B. 845; f. 1948 as an offshoot of the Hong Kong Council of Social Service; incorporated by ordinance in 1951; voluntary organization managing 20,288 flats and shops accommodating 127,724 people; Chair. Hon. Sir DOUGLAS CLAGUE, C.B.E.; publ. *Annual Report.*

Kadoorie Agricultural Aid Association: f. 1951; assists farmers in capital construction by technical direction and by donations of livestock, trees, plants, seeds, fertilizers, cement, road and building materials, farming equipment, etc.

Kadoorie Agricultural Aid Association Loan Fund: f. 1954; in conjunction with the Hong Kong Government, provides interest-free loans to assist farmers in the development of projects.

J. E. Joseph Trust Fund: f. 1954; grants credit facilities to farmers; up to 1958 loans amounted to HK $4,465,000.

TRANSPORT AND TOURISM

Transport Commissioner: B. D. WILSON.

RAILWAYS

Kowloon-Canton Railway: the line is 22 miles long and runs from the terminus at Kowloon to the Chinese frontier at Lowu. Through passenger services to China have been in abeyance since 1949; all passengers are obliged to change trains at the frontier. There is a through service in mail and goods traffic, however. Gen. Man. LAM PO-HON, I.S.O., B.SC., D.I.C., C.ENG., F.I.C.E., M.B.I.M., F.C.I.T., J.P.

Work commenced early in 1974 on an underground electric railway system which is eventually expected to cost about HK $9 million. It is expected to be completed in late 1979.

ROADS

There are 618 miles of officially maintained roads, 200 on Hong Kong Island, 188 in Kowloon, and 230 in the New Territories. Almost all of them are concrete or asphalt surfaced. A mile-long cross-harbour tunnel, joining Hong Kong Island to Kowloon, was opened in August 1972.

FERRIES

Four steamers and 11 hydrofoils operate between Hong Kong and Macao.

Star Ferry Company Ltd.: Kowloon; operates passenger ferries between the Kowloon Peninsula and the main business district of Hong Kong; Gen. Man. H. M. G. FORSGATE; Sec. D. T. NOLAN.

Hong Kong and Yaumati Ferry Co. Ltd.: Hong Kong; 13 passenger and two car ferry services within harbour limits and services to outlying districts. Operates a fleet of 67 vessels.

SHIPPING

Regular services are maintained by 20 shipping lines to Europe and 20 lines to North America. Other lines serve Australia, New Zealand, South Africa, South America and the Asian ports.

SHIPPING LINES

Agana Line Ltd.: c/o Jardine, Mathieson & Co. Ltd., P.O.B. 70.

Alfred Shipping & Trading Co. Ltd.: Li Po Chun Chambers, 13th Floor, Des Voeux Rd. Central; agents for American Export Isbrandtsen Lines; Pres. ALFRED HSIEH.

American President Lines Ltd.: St. George's Building.

Australia-West Pacific Line: c/o Everett Steamship Corpn. S/A, 20th floor, Connaught Centre, Connaught Rd., Central.

Barretto Shipping (H.K.) Ltd.: 1202-24 Wing on Life Bldg.

Ben Line Steamers Ltd.: Chartered Bank Bldg.

British India Steam Navigation Co. Ltd. (Calcutta/Japan Service): c/o Jardine, Matheson & Co. Ltd., P.O.B. 70.

Canadian Pacific Steamships Ltd.: 1702 Union House, P.O.B. 17; Overseas Trade Representative C. H. CHAN.

China Navigation Co. Ltd.: Union House, 9 Connaught Rd. Central; f. 1873; Man. Dir. A. D. MOORE.

Chinese Maritime Trust (1941) Ltd.: Room 802, Chartered Bank Bldg.; Man. D. T. YUI.

Clan Line: c/o Jardine, Matheson & Co. Ltd., P.O.B. 70.

Columbia International: c/o Jardine, Matheson & Co. Ltd., P.O.B. 70.

Compagnie Maritime des Chargeurs Réunis (H.K. Branch): 916 Union House, P.O.B. 13364.

Dominion Far East Line: c/o Jardine, Matheson & Co. Ltd., P.O.B. 70.

Dominion Navigation (Bahamas) Ltd.: c/o Jardine, Matheson & Co. Ltd., P.O.B. 70.

Eastern Africa National Shipping Line Ltd.: c/o Jardine, Matheson & Co. Ltd., P.O.B. 70.

East Asiatic Co. Ltd.: 19th floor, Connaught Centre, Connaught Rd., Central.

Eastern Lloyd Ltd.: 206 Shell House.

Everett Steamship Corporation, S/A: Connaught Centre, 20th floor, Connaught Rd., Central; Gen. Man. T. C. LAMB; Asst. Gen. Man. J. STOREY, F.C.I.T., M.I.N.

Gibb Livingston & Co. Ltd.: P.O.B. 55.

Glen Line Ltd.: Agents: John Swire and Sons (Hong Kong) Ltd., P.O.B. 1.

Gold Star Line Ltd.: Head Office: Kobe, Japan; Hong Kong Office: 8th floor, South China Bldg., 1-3 Wyndham St.

Hapag-Lloyd A.G.: c/o Jebsen & Co. Ltd., Prince's Bldg., Ice House St.

Hesco (Hong Kong) Ltd.: Jardine House; f. 1970; Chair. G. B. GODFREY; Man. Dir. H. CHEN.

Indo-China Steam Navigation Co. Ltd., The: c/o Jardine, Matheson & Co. Ltd., P.O.B. 70.

Kuwait Shipping Co. (S.A.K.): c/o Jardine, Matheson & Co. Ltd., P.O.B. 70.

W. R. Loxley & Co. Ltd.: P.O.B. 84.

Lykes Bros. Steamship Co. Inc.: c/o Jardine, Matheson & Co. Ltd., P.O.B. 70.

Cie. des Messageries Maritimes: Union House, 11 Connaught Rd.; P.O.B. 53.

Moller Group: 12th Floor, Union House.

Nedlloyd and Hoegh Lines: c/o Getz Bros., Edinburgh House, Queen's Rd. Central.

Neptune Orient Lines Ltd.: c/o Jardine, Matheson & Co. Ltd., P.O.B. 70.

Norwegian Asia Line: c/o Thoresen & Co., Union House, P.O.B. 6; Man. Dir. T. VINDE.

Paclloyd Shipping Co. Ltd.: Jardine House; f. 1970; Chair. G. B. GODFREY; Man. Dir. H. CHEN.

Pacmarine Agencies Ltd.: 11th floor, P & O Bldg., Des Voeux Rd., P.O.B. 14758, Central.

Paramount Shipping Agency Inc.: c/o Jardine, Matheson & Co. Ltd., P.O.B. 70.

P & O S.N. Co.: c/o Mackinnon Mackenzie & Co. of Hong Kong Ltd., P. & O. Building.

R.I.L. (Hong Kong) Ltd.: 219-232 Prince's Bldg., Ice House St., P.O.B. 45; agents for various Dutch shipping lines and all airline bookings.

Royal Mail Line: c/o Jardine, Matheson & Co. Ltd., P.O.B. 70.

C. F. Sharp & Co., S/A: 30-36 Caxton House, 1 Duddell St.

South African Marine Corp. Ltd. (Safmarine): c/o Jardine, Matheson & Co. Ltd., P.O.B. 70.

States Steamship Co.: Agents: Jardine, Matheson & Co. Ltd., P.O.B. 70.

Sun Hing Shipping Co. Ltd.: 8th & 9th floors, South China Bldg., 1-3 Wyndham St.; Man. Partner SIMON LEE.

Swedish American Line: Agents: Gilman & Co. Ltd., P.O.B. 56; cruise vessels.

Union-Castle Mail Steamship Co. Ltd.: c/o Jardine, Matheson & Co. Ltd., P.O.B. 70.

United States Lines Inc.: 616 Union House.

Wallem & Co. Ltd.: P.O.B. 40, Hong Kong & Shanghai Bank Bldg.; Chair. N. E. WALLEM; Man. Dir. A. J. HARDY.

World-Wide (Shipping) Ltd.: 21st Floor, Prince's Bldg., Hong Kong.

CIVIL AVIATION

Director of Civil Aviation: R. E. DOWNING, J.P.

Cathay Pacific Airways Ltd.: Union House, 9 Connaught Rd.; f. 1946; Parent Company John Swire & Sons Ltd., London; amalgamated with Hong Kong Airways 1959; services to 14 major cities in the Far East and to Perth, Western Australia using a fleet of Convair 880Ms and Boeing 707-320Bs; on order 3 Boeing 707-320B; unduplicated route miles 19,499; Chair. H. J. C. BROWNE; Man. Dir. D. R. Y. BLUCK.

In addition, twenty-three foreign airlines serve Hong Kong.

Note: The airport runway is being expanded and completion is expected by late 1973 when Kai Tak airport will be able to accommodate supersonic aircraft. The helicopter service between the airport and Hong Kong island which was inaugurated in 1970 has expanded rapidly and now runs 36 flights daily.

TOURISM

Hong Kong Tourist Association: 35th floor, Connaught Centre, Connaught Rd. Central, Hong Kong; f. 1957; co-ordinates and promotes the tourist industry; has Government support and financial assistance; 11 mems. of the Board representing Government and the tourist industry; Chair. H. KESWICK, J.P.; Exec. Dir. J. PAINE; Sec. J. R. LAING, A.A.S.A.; Marketing Dir. D. B. DONALDSON; publ. *Hong Kong Travel Bulletin.*

In 1973, more than one million tourists visited Hong Kong.

LEADING ORCHESTRA AND OPERA COMPANIES

The Hong Kong Philharmonic Society Ltd.: City Hall; Chair. Dr. S. M. BARD; Music Dir. LIM KEK-TJIANG; Gen. Man. KLAUS HEYMANN.

Tai Ping Theatre: 421 Queen's Rd. West, Hong Kong; Tai Ping Amusement Co.; Cantonese Opera; Gen. Man. I. H. YUEN.

Chun Chau Chap Chinese Operatic Research Society: 14 Hart Ave., Kowloon; Mandarin Opera; Man. K. Z. LEE.

Oriental Dramatic School: 157 Waterloo Rd., Kowloon; Mandarin Opera; Sec. CHUI CHI FA.

There are also eight choirs active in Hong Kong.

Photography is a most popular pastime and encouragement is given to various cultural activities by the *British Council* (Room 132 Gloucester Building, Hong Kong, Rep. G. A. BRIDGES) and the *City Hall Museum and*

Art Gallery (City Hall High Block, Edinburgh Place, Hong Kong; Curator J. M. WARNER).

UNIVERSITIES

University of Hong Kong: Hong Kong; 390 teachers, 3,607 students.

Chinese University: Shatin, New Territories; 430 teachers, 2,770 students.

MONTSERRAT

Montserrat is one of the Leeward Islands which stretch in an arc south-east from Puerto Rico. It elected not to become part of the West Indies Associated States in January 1967.

STATISTICS

Area (square miles): 39.5.

Population: 12,905 (April 7th, 1972); Plymouth (capital) c. 2,000.

Births and Deaths (1972): 318 live births (birth rate 24.6 per 1,000); 144 deaths (death rate 11.6 per 1,000).

Agriculture: About one-quarter of the land is under cultivation, the principal crops being limes, mangoes, avocadoes, coconuts and vegetables. A further one-half of the island's 25,000 acres is potential agricultural land. The Government is actively pursuing a resettlement programme for small-scale farmers. Though there is only a limited acreage suitable for arable farming, the prospects for livestock are becoming encouraging.

Forestry: An area of 5,000 acres is covered by forests.

FINANCE

100 cents = 1 East Caribbean dollar (EC$).

Coins: 1, 2, 5, 10, 25 and 50 cents.

Notes: 1, 5, 20 and 100 dollars.

Exchange rates (April 1974): £1 sterling = EC $4.80; U.S. $1 = EC $2.03. EC $100 = £20.83 = U.S. $49.19.

BUDGET
(1972—EC$)

Revenue:				
Recurrent Revenue	.	.	.	4,987,038
Capital	.	.	.	3,632,250
TOTAL	.	.	.	8,619,288
Expenditure:				
Recurrent Expenditure	.	.	.	5,120,787
Capital	.	.	.	3,787,150
TOTAL	.	.	.	8,907,937

1972/73 Budget: Estimated Revenue EC $4,505,000, Estimated Expenditure EC $4,384,874.

External Trade (EC $'000—1972): Imports 12,080, Exports 370.

Education (1972): Primary schools 16, pupils 2,853; Secondary school 1, pupils 246.

THE CONSTITUTION

The present Constitution came into force on January 1st, 1960, whereby the territory of Montserrat is governed by a Governor and has its own Executive and Legislative Councils. The Executive Council consists of the Governor as President and two official members and four unofficial members, with two Ministers apart from the Chief Minister. The Legislative Council consists of a President (who is the Governor), seven elected, two official and one nominated member.

Early in 1967, when the other East Caribbean Islands adopted Associated Status *vis-à-vis* the United Kingdom, Montserrat decided to remain a colony until separate arrangements could be worked out, more suitable to her requirements.

THE GOVERNMENT

The Governor: W. H. THOMPSON, O.B.E.

EXECUTIVE COUNCIL
(*March* 1974)

President: The Governor.

Official Members: B. E. DIAS, O.B.E. (Attorney-General), A. COLLINGS (Financial Secretary).

The Chief Minister and Minister of Finance: The Hon. P. A. BRAMBLE.

Minister of Education, Health and Welfare: The Hon. MARY TUITT.

Minister of Agriculture, Trade, Lands and Housing: The Hon. W. H. RYAN.

Minister of Communications and Works: E. A. DYER.

LEGISLATIVE COUNCIL

President: The Governor.

Official Members: The Attorney-General, The Financial Secretary.

Elected Members: 7.

Nominated Members: 1.

Clerk: D. H. BRAMBLE.

At the general election held in September 1973 the Progressive Democratic Party won five of the seven seats in the Council, the other two being taken by independent candidates.

POLITICAL PARTIES

Montserrat Workers' Progressive Party: Leader J. N. EDWARDS.

Progressive Democratic Party: Leader P. A. BRAMBLE.

JUDICIAL SYSTEM

Justice is administered by the West Indies Associated States' Supreme Court, the Court of Summary Jurisdiction and the Magistrate's Court.

Puisne Judge (Montserrat Circuit): Hon. Mr. Justice CORAN LIVERPOOL.

Registrar and Magistrate: J. S. WEEKES.

RELIGION

There are Church of England, Roman Catholic, Methodist, Pentecostal and Seventh-Day Adventist churches and other places of worship on the island.

THE PRESS

The Mirror: P.O.B. 200, Plymouth; weekly.

RADIO AND TELEVISION

Radio Montserrat: P.O.B. 51, Plymouth; f. 1952, first broadcast 1957; government station; Station Man. R. W. WHITE.

Radio Antilles: P.O.B. 35, Montserrat; f. 1965; commercial; broadcasts in English, French, Spanish; Man. G. RIECHER.

Television services can be received from St. Kitts and Puerto Rico, and from Antigua (*Leeward Islands Television Services*) by way of a booster station near Plymouth.

FINANCE

BANKING

Barclays Bank International Ltd.: Church Rd., Plymouth; Man. B. J. DUNLEA.

Chase Manhattan Bank: Plymouth; Man. W. R. HUNT.

Royal Bank of Canada: Head Office: Place Ville Marie, P.O.B. 6001, Montreal; branch in Plymouth; Man. F. R. DE ABREU.

Government Savings Bank: Pymouth; depositors (1972) 2,578.

TRADE AND INDUSTRY

Montserrat Chamber of Commerce: P.O.B. 353, Plymouth; refounded 1971; Pres. H. MERCER; Sec. M. L. KING.

Montserrat Cotton Growers' Association: c/o Department of Agriculture, Plymouth; Chair. J. E. STURGE; Sec. V. C. HENRY.

TRADE UNIONS

Montserrat Allied Workers' Union: Old Chapel St., Plymouth; f. 1973; Pres. Dr. GEORGE IRISH; Sec. Gen. J. D. FENTON.

Montserrat Seamen's and Waterfront Workers' Union: Chapel St., Plymouth; f. 1966; 116 mems.; Pres. MICHAEL DYER.

Montserrat Union of Teachers: Plymouth; f. 1950; 60 mems.; Pres. R. A. LEE.

TRANSPORT AND TOURISM

ROADS

There are 96 miles of good surfaced main roads, 45 miles of secondary unsurfaced roads and 26 miles of rough tracks. There were 1,239 registered vehicles in 1972.

SHIPPING

Steamship services are provided by Harrison Line, the Atlantic and Blue Ribbon Lines and the Royal Netherlands Shipping Service. Inter-island services are provided by West Indies Shipping Service and small vessels.

CIVIL AVIATION

The main airport is at Blackburne. Leeward Islands Air Transport (Antigua) maintains regular inter-island services.

TOURISM

The Montserrat Tourist Board: P.O.B. 7, Plymouth; f. 1961; Chair. ERIC L. KELSICK.

In 1972 there were 12,529 visitors to Montserrat.

PITCAIRN ISLANDS GROUP

The Pitcairn Islands Group comprises four small and widely scattered islands, Pitcairn, Henderson, Ducie and Oeno, of which only Pitcairn Island (situated 20° 04′S and 130° 06′W and about half way between Panama and New Zealand) is inhabited. The island has an area of about 1¾ square miles, and the population at the end of 1972 was 84. The group is administered by the Governor in consultation with an Island Council consisting of four elected, five nominated and one ex officio members.

Governor: Sir DAVID SCOTT, K.C.M.G. (British High Commissioner in New Zealand).

Commissioner: R. J. HICKS.

ISLAND COUNCIL

Island Magistrate: PERVIS YOUNG.

Island Secretary: BEN CHRISTIAN.

Members: IVAN CHRISTIAN, TOM CHRISTIAN, OSCAR CLARK, CAROL CHRISTIAN, THELMA BROWN, STEVE CHRISTIAN, Pastor J. J. DEVER, C. P. B. SHEA.

ST. HELENA

St. Helena lies in the South Atlantic, 1,200 miles from southern Angola in Africa and 1,800 miles from Bahia, Brazil.

STATISTICS

Area: 47 square miles.

Population (1972 est.): 5,056; Jamestown (capital) 1,600; Births 124; Deaths 49.

Livestock (1972): Cattle 853, Sheep 1,425, Goats 1,362; Horses 14, Donkeys 609, Pigs 544, Poultry 11,793.

Forestry (1972): 3 square miles.

Currency: 100 pence=£1 (United Kingdom currency).

Budget (1972/73): *Revenue* £826,956; *Expenditure* £804,868.

External Trade: *Imports* (1971): £403,832 (motor vehicles £27,502, machinery and parts £26,606, fuel oils and motor spirit £24,397, meat £19,755, liquor £18,858, flour £15,972, clothing £10,977, timber £2,591); *Exports* (1968): £14,710. There were no exports in 1969, 1970 or 1971.

Trade is mainly with the United Kingdom and South Africa.

Transport (1972): *Roads:* 717 vehicles; *Shipping:* Tonnage entered and cleared 174,148; ships 42.

Education (1972): Primary Schools 8, Pupils 750; Senior Secondary Schools 4, Pupils 460. There are 68 full-time teachers.

THE CONSTITUTION

An Order in Council and Royal Instructions of November 1966, which came into force on January 1st, 1967, provided for a Legislative Council, consisting of the Governor, 2 *ex officio* members (the Government Secretary and the Treasurer) and 12 elected members; and an Executive Council, consisting of the Government Secretary and the Treasurer as *ex officio* members and the Chairmen of the Council Committees (all of whom must be members of the Legislative Council). The Governor presides at meetings of the Executive Council.

Council Committees, a majority of whose members are members of the Legislative Council, have been appointed by the Governor and charged with executive powers and general oversight of departments of government. General elections were held in February 1968 and in May 1972.

THE GOVERNMENT

Governor: Sir THOMAS OATES, C.M.G., O.B.E.

EXECUTIVE COUNCIL

President: The GOVERNOR.

Ex-Officio Members: The GOVERNMENT SECRETARY, The TREASURER.

Members: THE CHAIRMEN OF THE COUNCIL COMMITTEES.

LEGISLATIVE COUNCIL

President: The GOVERNOR.

Ex-Officio Members: The GOVERNMENT SECRETARY, The TREASURER.

Elected Members: 12.

JUDICIAL SYSTEM

There are four Courts on St. Helena. The Supreme Court, the Magistrate's Court, the Small Debts Court and the Juvenile Court. Provision exists for a St. Helena Court of Appeal which can sit in Jamestown or London.

The Chief Justice: Sir PETER WATKIN WILLIAMS.

Registrar: D. THOMPSON.

Magistrate: Major E. J. MOSS, C.B.E., M.C., J.P.

RELIGION

The majority of the population belongs to the Anglican Communion of the Christian Church.

ANGLICAN

Diocese of St. Helena: The Right Reverend GEORGE KENNETH GIGGALL, O.B.E.; Bishopsholme, St. Helena; the See is in the Church of the Province of South Africa.

ROMAN CATHOLIC

Priest-in-Charge: The Reverend J. KELLY, S.D.B.; Sacred Heart Church, Jamestown; total members 30.

THE PRESS

News Review: Jamestown; f. 1941; Government-sponsored weekly; Editor E. M. GEORGE.

RADIO

Government Broadcasting Station: Information Office, The Castle, Jamestown; 20 hours weekly; Information Officer E. M. GEORGE.

There were 750 radio receivers in 1973.

FINANCE

BANKS

Government Savings Bank: Jamestown; total estimated deposits March 31st, 1972: £458,499.

INSURANCE

Alliance Assurance Co. Ltd.: Agents: Solomon & Co. (St. Helena) Ltd., Jamestown.

TRADE AND INDUSTRY

CHAMBER OF COMMERCE

St. Helena Chamber of Commerce: Jamestown.

TRADE UNION

St. Helena General Workers' Union: Market St., Jamestown; 1,032 mems. (1972); Gen. Sec. E. BENJAMIN.

CO-OPERATIVE

St. Helena Growers' Co-operative Society: for vegetable marketing; 43 mems.; total sales (1972) £5,009.

TRANSPORT

ROADS

There are 48.6 miles of all-weather motorable roads in the island, 39.5 bitumen sealed, and a further 18 miles of earth roads, which can only be used by motor vehicles in dry weather. All roads have steep gradients and sharp curves. There are no railways or airfields.

SHIPPING

Union Castle and **Clan Lines:** to and from the United Kingdom and South Africa; the only service.

ASCENSION
(WIDEAWAKE ISLAND)

Ascension lies in the South Atlantic 700 miles north-west of St. Helena. The island is an important communications centre, being a major relay station for the cables connecting Europe and West Africa with South America and, via St. Helena, South Africa. In addition the United States built an air base—Wideawake Airfield—on the island in 1952; this has recently been re-occupied and is now used as a tracking station for guided missiles. Ascension is otherwise dependent on substantial budgetary aid from the British Government.

Area (square miles): 34.

Population (1972): 1,129 (St. Helenians 660); Births 25, Deaths 5.

Agriculture (1972): Vegetables 35,843 lb., Milk 15,073 gals.; Sheep 2,500, Pigs 277, Cattle 47.

Budget (Jan. 1972—Mar. 1973): Revenue and Expenditure balanced at £77,918.

Government: The Government of St. Helena is represented by an Administrator.

Administrator: G. C. Guy, C.M.G., C.V.O., O.B.E.

Transport: Roads (1972): 511 vehicles; Shipping (1972): tonnage entered and cleared 315,956, ships 52; calls are made by Union Castle or Clan Line ships from St. Helena. Calls are also made by H.M. ships and occasional private yachts.

TRISTAN DA CUNHA

The Island of Tristan da Cunha lies in the South Atlantic 1,500 miles south-west of St. Helena. In 1961 the island was evacuated after volcanic eruptions, but has since been re-settled.

Area (square miles): Tristan da Cunha 38, Inaccessible Island 4, Nightingale Island ¾, Gough Island 35.

Population (1973): 290 on Tristan; there is a small weather station on Gough manned by a team of South Africans.

Constitution: The Administrator, representing the British Government, is aided by a Council of 8 elected and 3 nominated members which has advisory powers in legislative and executive functions. The Council's advisory functions in executive matters are performed through small committees of the Council dealing with the separate branches of administration.

Government: The Administrator: Maj. J. I. H. Fleming.

Legal System: The Administrator is the Magistrate. There is one Justice of the Peace.

Religion: All the islanders are Christian. Their padre is Rev. C. J. Jewell.

SEYCHELLES

A British Crown Colony in the Indian Ocean, consisting of 89 islands and cays. The largest, Mahé, is four degrees south of the Equator, 990 miles east of Mombasa, Kenya, and 934 miles north of the island of Mauritius. The United States has a base on Mahé for satellite tracking and telemetry facilities. After elections held 1974 giving the ruling party a mandate for independence from Britain, the Seychelles are likely to become independent in April 1975.

STATISTICS

Area: 107 square miles (Mahé 57, Praslin 16, Silhouette 6, La Digue 4).

Population (1972 est.): 54,925, Port Victoria (capital) 14,500; Births 1,723; Deaths 520; *Employment:* Agriculture 3,372, Services (incl. domestic) 2,694, Building 4,218, Manufacturing 591, Trade and Transport 2,534, Education and Health 1,422, Public Administration 979.

Agriculture (1972): Copra (excluding copra from British Indian Ocean Territory) 3,477 tons, Cinnamon Bark 1,956 tons, Cinnamon Oil 12 tons (1971).

Livestock (1971): Cattle 1,720, Pigs 7,409, Poultry 65,334.

Fishing (1971 exports): 544 kg. Salted Fish.

Finance: 100 cents=1 Seychelles rupee. Coins: 1, 5, 10, 25 and 50 cents; 1 and 5 rupees. Notes: 5, 10, 20, 50, and 100 rupees. Exchange rates (April 1974): £1 sterling= 13.33 rupees; U.S. $1=5.65 rupees; 100 Seychelles rupees=£7.50=$17.71.

Budget (1973): Est. Revenue Rs. 74,761,725; Est. Expenditure Rs. 77,485,380.

External Trade: Imports (1971) Rs. 84,003,649; Exports (1971) Rs. 7,915,770; Copra Rs. 3,574,021, Cinnamon Bark Rs. 3,322,405, Cinnamon Oil Rs. 288,586, Guano Rs. 331,532.

Transport (1972): *Roads:* 3,207 vehicles. *Shipping:* Cargo landed 106,712 tons; Cargo shipped 15,994 tons; total net registered tonnage of all vessels (excluding warships) entered and cleared with cargo 932,390 tons; number of calls by vessels 311.

Education (1973): Primary: 35 schools, 10,275 pupils; Junior Secondary: 11 schools, 2,054 pupils; 2 Secondary Grammar schools, 727 pupils; 1 Teacher Training College, 104 students; Technical and Vocational courses 432 pupils and adult education classes.

THE CONSTITUTION

Under the new Constitution introduced during 1970 there is a Council of Ministers, consisting of a Chief Minister, up to 4 other Ministers and 3 *ex officio* members, and presided over by the Governor or his Deputy. All the Ministers are elected members of the Legislative Assembly, which comprises 15 elected members and 3 *ex officio* members. Elections are held every five years.

THE GOVERNMENT

Governor: COLIN H. ALLAN, C.M.G., O.B.E.

Deputy Governor: The Hon. J. R. TODD, C.V.O., M.L.C.

Chief Minister: The Hon. JAMES R. M. MANCHAM, F.R.S.A., M.L.C. (elected).

In the 1974 elections the Seychelles Democratic Party won 13 seats and the Seychelles People's United Party won 2 seats.

POLITICAL PARTIES

Seychelles Democratic Party: Victoria; f. 1963; advocates gradual independence from the United Kingdom; 13 seats in Legislative Assembly; Leader J. R. M. MANCHAM, M.L.C.; publ. *Seychelles Weekly*.

Seychelles People's United Party: Victoria; left-wing party urging independence for Seychelles, receives support and aid from the OAU; two seats in Legislative Assembly; Pres. Hon. F. A. RENE; Vice-Pres. Hon. G. SINON, M.L.C.; publ. *The People* (weekly).

JUDICIAL SYSTEM

There are two Courts, the Supreme Court and the Magistrates' Courts. The Supreme Court is also a Court of Appeal from the Magistrates' Courts. Appeals from the Supreme Court in respect of criminal matters go to the Seychelles Court of Appeal in London and thence to the Judicial Department of the Privy Council. Appeals from the Supreme Court in respect of civil matters go to the Court of Civil Appeal of Mauritius and thence to the Judicial Department of the Privy Council.

Chief Justice: The Hon. Sir GEORGE SOUYAVE.

Attorney-General: The Hon. J. A. O'BRIEN QUINN, M.L.A.

RELIGION

Almost all the inhabitants are Christian, 90 per cent of them Roman Catholics and about 8 per cent Anglicans.

ROMAN CATHOLIC

Diocese of Port Victoria: The Right Reverend GERVAIS AEBY, O.F.M., C.A.P., Apostolic Administrator; P.O.B. 43, Port Victoria.

ANGLICAN

Bishop of Seychelles: The Right Reverend GEORGE C. BRIGGS; P.O.B. 44, Victoria.

THE PRESS

Le Seychellois: P.O.B. 32, Victoria; daily except Sunday; f. 1898; publ. in English and French; Conservative; Editor SADEC RASSOOL; Man. GUSTAVE DE CAMARMOND, M.B.E.; publishers: Le Seychellois Press Ltd., Harrison St., Victoria, Mahé; circ. 600.

L'Echo des Iles: P.O.B. 12, Victoria; fortnightly; Roman Catholic mission; Editor Father ALAIN; circ. 2,000.

Le Nouveau Seychellois: Victoria; organ of Le Parti Seychellois; Editor VICTOR WESTERGREEN; circ. 500.

The People: P.O.B. 154, Victoria; organ of the Seychelles People's United Party; weekly; Editor R. JUMEAU; circ. 2,000.

Seychelles Bulletin: Dept. of Broadcasting, Victoria; daily; Editor ANTONIO BEAUDOIN; circ. 2,000.

Seychelles Weekly: P.O.B. 131, Victoria; organ of the Seychelles Democratic Party; Editor F. A. GRAND-COURT; circ. 1,300.

RADIO

Radio Seychelles: P.O.B. 321, Victoria, Mahé; power 10 kWh. on 1331 kHz.; transmissions 8 hours daily; Man. and Chief Engineer Group Captain E. C. PASSMORE, C.B.E.; approx. 10,000 receivers and 40,000 listeners; programmes in English, French and Creole.

Far East Broadcasting Association: P.O.B. 234, Mahé; programmes in Sinhala, Hindi, Urdu, Telegu, English, Tamil, Marathi, Gujarati, Kannada, Malayalam, Farsi, Nepali, Punjabi, Pushto, Turkish, Tibetan, Arabic; Field Dir. L. J. WHEATLEY; Dir. Programmes G. M. COOK.

FINANCE

BANKS

Barclays Bank International Ltd.: P.O.B. 167, Victoria, Mahé.

Government Savings Bank: Port Victoria, Mahé; Grand Anse, Praslin; for deposit accounts.

Post Office Savings Bank: Victoria, Mahé; Grand Anse, Praslin.

The Seychelles Agricultural Loans Board: P.O.B. 54, Victoria; f. 1937, reconstituted 1968; agricultural loans; Chair. The Financial Secretary; Man. The Director of Agriculture.

The Standard Bank Ltd.: P.O.B. 241, Victoria, Mahé.

INSURANCE

There are 7 insurance companies with agencies on the Islands.

TRADE AND INDUSTRY

TRADE UNIONS

There are 15 trade unions including the Teachers' Union; Cable and Wireless Limited Staff Union; Christian Workers' Union; Stevedores', Winchmen and Dock Workers' Union; Transport and General Workers' Union; Civil Servants' Union; Seychelles Building, Construction and Civil Engineering Workers' Union; Artisans', Engineers', Constructors' and Builders' Union; Government Workers' Union; Postal Workers' Union; Praslin Workers' Union; Seamen's Union; Agricultural, Domestic and Shop-workers' Union; Hotels and Allied Employers' Union.

MARKETING ORGANIZATION

Seychelles Copra Association: P.O.B. 32, Victoria, Mahé, Seychelles; f. 1953; an association of planters, producers and dealers who control the export of copra in bulk on behalf of its members; Pres. SULEMAN ADAM; Vice-Pres. SADEC RASSOOL; Sec. GUSTAVE DE COMARMOND, M.B.E.; Treas. HENRY C. GONTIER.

TRANSPORT AND TOURISM

ROADS

There are 67 miles of tarmac road and 9 miles of motorable earth roads on Mahé. Praslin has 4 miles of tarmac road and 20 miles of earth roads. La Digue has 8 miles of earth road.

SHIPPING

The Shipping Corporation of India Ltd.: twice monthly service alternating from Bombay and East Africa; agents Jivan Jetha and Co., P.O.B. 16, Mahé.

The Union Lighterage Company Ltd.: P.O.B. 38, Mahé; f. 1926; agents for Shell Company of the Islands, Royal Interocean, Union Castle, Shaw Savill and Farrell Lines, which run occasional services.

A ferry four times a week between Victoria and the Islands of Praslin and La Digue is operated by the Port and Marine Dept.; capacity 100 persons.

CIVIL AVIATION

The airport at Mahé, financed by the British Government, was completed in 1971. The 9,800 ft. airstrip was constructed on reclaimed land on Mahé's east coast. British Airways run four flights a week from London, two from Tokyo, Hong Kong and Colombo, and one from Johannesburg and Mauritius. Air Malawi has a weekly service from Blantyre. British Caledonian Airways run weekly services from London (Gatwick), and Air Mahé run domestic flights.

TOURISM

Department of Tourism: Kingsgate House, P.O.B. 92, Victoria; Government department; Dir. R. N. LASCELLES.

Tourists (1971): 3'175; estimated expenditure £500,000; (1972): 14,000; estimated expenditure £1.3m.; (1973): 19,484.

BRITISH INDIAN OCEAN TERRITORY

The Colony consists of the Chagos Archipelago, about 1,200 miles north-east of Mauritius and the islands of Aldabra, Farquhar and Desroches in the western Indian Ocean. It was set up in 1965 to provide defence facilities for the British and United States Governments. The Chagos Archipelago, which includes the coral atoll Diego Garcia, was formerly administered by the Government of Mauritius. The other three groups were administered by that of the Seychelles.

It is possible that Diego Garcia could play a key role in Western defence strategy in the Indian Ocean, especially as the alternative policy for Britain, at least, involves closer military co-operation with South Africa. According to the British Ministry of Defence all the islands of the Territory are available for both British and U.S. bases.

In February 1974 it was announced that the U.S.A. was to extend its naval facilities on Diego Garcia in response to the recent expansion of Soviet naval power in the Indian Ocean but this extension now faces delay and possible cancellation. At present, under a 50-year agreement with Britain concluded in 1972, the U.S.A. has a communications station, airstrip and anchorage on the island.

Area: 175 sq. miles approx.

Population (June 1968): 1,019 (Chagos Archipelago 803, Farquhar 50, Desroches 120, Aldabra 42).

Commissioner: The Governor of the Seychelles.

Administrator: J. R. TODD, Queen's Bldg., Port Victoria, Mahé, Seychelles.

TURKS AND CAICOS ISLANDS

The Turks and Caicos Islands consist of more than 30 islands forming the south-eastern part of the Bahamas chain of islands, and lying north of Haiti. Six islands are inhabited: Grand Turk, Salt Cay, South Caicos, Middle Caicos, North Caicos, Providenciales.

STATISTICS

Area: 166 square miles.

Population (1970): 5,675; Cockburn Town (Grand Turk) 2,330, Cockburn Harbour (South Caicos) 1,032. In 1971 birth registrations totalled 190 (birth rate 31.7 per 1,000) and death registrations numbered 59 (death rate 9.8 per 1,000).

Finance: United States currency: 100 cents = 1 U.S. dollar ($). Coins: 1, 5, 10, 25 and 50 cents; 1 dollar. Notes: 1, 2, 5, 10, 20, 50 and 100 dollars. Exchange rates (April 1974): £1 sterling = U.S. $2.36; U.S. $100 = £42.35. *Note*: Until 1973 the islands used Jamaican currency (J $1 = U.S. $1.10 since January 1973).

Budget (1969): Revenue J$1,363,186; Expenditure J$1,367,463.

External Trade (1969): *Imports* J$993,386 (food, drink and manufactured articles); *Exports* J$213,996, of which Crayfish 207,174, Salt 8,150 and Dried Conch 672.

Education (1970): Government Primary Schools 14, pupils 1,615; Private Primary Schools 3, Government Secondary Schools 1, Private Secondary Schools 1.

CONSTITUTION AND GOVERNMENT

The Islands are at present a dependent territory within the Commonwealth and responsibility for the day-to-day administration of the Islands lies with the Governor who is President of the State Council. This council was inaugurated on June 18th, 1969, under a new Constitution which did away with the former Executive Council and Legislative Assembly and vested both executive and legislative power in the State Council which has a majority of elected members.

Governor: A. G. MITCHELL, C.B.E., D.F.M.

JUDICIAL SYSTEM

There is a Resident Magistrate who is also Acting Judge of the Turks and Caicos Islands.

RELIGION
ANGLICAN

Bishop of Nassau and the Bahamas: Rt. Rev. MICHAEL ELDON, Addington House, P.O.B. 107, Nassau, Bahamas.

RADIO

Station VS 18: Cable and Wireless (W.I.) Ltd., Mercury House, Grand Turk; Man. D. R. MATTOCKS.

In 1973 there were approximately 2,900 radio receivers.

FINANCE

Barclays Bank International Ltd: Cockburn Town, Grand Turk; Man. D. BANKS.

Caribbean Bank and Trust Co. Ltd.: Cockburn Harbour, South Caicos.

MARKETING ORGANIZATION

General Trading Company Turks and Caicos Ltd.: P.M.B.I., Cockburn Town, Grand Turk; shipping agents, importers, air freight handlers.

TRADE UNION

St. George's Industrial Trade Union: Cockburn Harbour; 250 mems.; Sec. Mrs. ELIZA BASDEN.

TRANSPORT
ROADS

There are 65 miles of road in the Islands, of which 12 miles are tarmac.

SHIPPING

There are regular services from the Netherlands, Great Britain and Miami, Florida.

K.N.S.M. and Lloyds lines: Agency, Turks Islands Importers Ltd., Grand Turk; Dir. A. BEEN.

CIVIL AVIATION

The two main airfields are located on Grand Turk and South Caicos, and there are landing strips on Middle Caicos, Providenciales, North Caicos and Salt Cay.

Mackay International Inc.: Florida. Twice weekly service to Miami.

Turks and Caicos Airways Ltd.: maintains regular inter-island services and a twice weekly flight to Haiti.

TOURISM

Hotel accommodation is available in Grand Turk, South Caicos and Providenciales. Guest house accommodation is available in Salt Cay. A recent British Government report concluded that the best hope for improving the islands' economy lay in tourism. In 1972 there were 4,670 visitors.

WESTERN PACIFIC HIGH COMMISSION

Headquarters: Honiara, British Solomon Islands.

BRITISH SOLOMON ISLANDS

CIVIL ESTABLISHMENT

High Commissioner: D. C. LUDDINGTON, C.M.G.

Acting Chief Secretary: A. T. CLARK.

Financial Secretary: R. J. WALLACE, O.B.E.

Attorney-General: G. P. NAZARETH.

JUDICIAL SYSTEM

The High Court of the Western Pacific exercises jurisdiction in the British Solomon Islands Protectorate, the Anglo-French Condominium of the New Hebrides and the Gilbert and Ellice Islands Colony. It is constituted by the Western Pacific (Courts) Order in Council, 1961, and consists of a Chief Justice, who is ordinarily resident at Honiara in the Protectorate and a Puisne Judge who is ordinarily resident at Vila in the Condominium. There is resident in the Gilbert and Ellice Islands Colony a qualified Senior Magistrate who exercises an enhanced jurisdiction, supplemented by periodic visits by the Chief Justice or the Puisne Judge.

The High Court is a Superior Court of Record and possesses all of the jurisdiction which is vested in a British High Court of Justice in the United Kingdom subject to the provisions of the Order in Council. Appeals from the decisions of the Court are to the Fiji Court of Appeals. The procedure of the Court is regulated by the High Court (Civil Procedure) Rules, 1964.

The law administered by the High Court consists of local Ordinances, customary native law and certain Imperial Statutes and Orders in Council. Subject to this and in

NEW HEBRIDES

addition, the jurisdiction of the Court is exercised upon the principles of and in conformity with the statutes of general application in force in England on January 1st, 1961, and the substance of English common law and doctrines of equity.

In addition each territory is provided with Magistrates' Courts staffed by lay magistrates exercising limited jurisdiction in both criminal and civil matters. In addition there are also Native Courts staffed by elders of the native communities which have jurisdiction in respect of matters concerning the application and enforcement of established native custom. These courts have a limited jurisdiction in respect of petty crime and the enforcement of Local Government by-laws and regulations applicable to their respective districts.

Appeals from decisions of Native Courts are dealt with administratively by the appropriate District Officers, except in matters relating to native customary land when appeals lie into the High Court as the final tribunal. Appeals from Magistrates' Courts lie to the High Court in the first instance. Appeals from decisions of the High Court in exercise of its original or appellate jurisdiction lie to the Court of Appeal of Fiji from which, in certain cases, a further appeal lies to the Judicial Committee of the Privy Council in England.

High Court of the Western Pacific: Re-constituted 1961; Superior Court of Record. The Chief Justice is appointed by the High Commissioner.

Chief Justice: Sir JOCELYN BODILLY, V.R.D.

Puisne Judge: Hon. Mr. Justice R. DAVIS, O.B.E.

BRITISH SOLOMON ISLANDS PROTECTORATE

The British Solomon Islands, consisting of six major islands and countless smaller ones, extends over 900 miles south-east of Bougainville (Papua New Guinea) in the South Pacific. The capital is Honiara, on the island of Guadalcanal.

STATISTICS

Area: Sea 250,000 nautical square miles; Land 11,500 square miles (Guadalcanal 2,500).

Population (mid-1972 est.): 173,500 (Melanesians 165,700); Honiara (capital) 15,300.

Agriculture (1972): Copra 21,050 tons; Cocoa 88 tons; Rice 1,060 tons; Timber (logs) 7,963,000 cu. ft.; Pigs 25,000 (1969); Cattle 15,721.

Finance: Australian currency: 100 cents = 1 Australian dollar ($A). Coins: 1, 2, 5, 10, 20 and 50 cents. Notes: 1, 2, 5, 10, 20 and 50 dollars. Exchange rates (April 1974): £1 sterling = $A1.585; U.S. $1 = 67.23 Australian cents; A$100 = £63.10 = U.S. $148.75.

Employment (1972): Persons in paid employment 14,454 (est.).

Budget (1973): Estimated at $12,513,260 including $1,878,270 grant-in-aid. In addition, capital expenditure of $4,865,780 mostly from British Development Aid. Sixth Development Plan (1971–73) will invest $16m. in capital expenditure.

External Trade (1973): *Imports:* $14.135m. (mainly machinery and transport, food and manufactured articles); *Exports* $10.628m. (mainly fish, timber, copra, marine shells, scrap metal, manufactured tobacco, cocoa). Imports were mainly from Australia, and exports to Japan and the U.K.

CONSTITUTION

Following the Constitution instituted on April 10th, 1970, by the British Solomon Islands Order 1970, a single-chamber Governing Council was formed with 17 elected members, 6 public service and 3 *ex officio* members. During 1971, the public service members were gradually withdrawn, and, at the general election held in May and June 1973, the number of elected members of the Council was increased to 24. When functioning as a legislature the Council meets in public, but when functioning as an executive, it meets in private, presided over by the High Commissioner.

The Governing Council is aided in its executive functions by 6 executive committees, 5 of which are chaired by elected members. The sixth committee (Finance) is chaired by the Financial Secretary and also includes the chairmen of the other committees. Each elected member must sit on at least one committee. The other committees deal with Communications and Works, Commerce and Industry, Natural Resources, Social Services, and Local Government.

The High Commissioner, as well as being Chairman of the Governing Council and having the power to appoint the chairmen of the executive committees, retains reserve powers on external affairs and security and police, and continues to control the public service.

A new constitution which is likely to replace committees with ministers, and introducing a Chief Minister elected by members, with the High Commissioner redesignated Governor, is expected to come into operation in mid-1974.

GOVERNMENT

CIVIL ESTABLISHMENT

High Commissioner: D. C. LUDDINGTON, C.M.G., C.V.O.

Acting Chief Secretary: A. T. CLARK.

Financial Secretary: R. J. WALLACE, O.B.E.

Attorney-General: G. P. NAZARETH.

GOVERNING COUNCIL

Chairman: D. C. LUDDINGTON, C.M.G.

Ex Officio Members: A. T. CLARK, G. P. NAZARETH, LL.B., R. J. WALLACE, O.B.E.

Elected Members: 24 (elected by universal adult suffrage).

ADMINISTRATION

Government is administered by a number of departments, staffed by 2,033 public servants, 1,661 of whom are Solomon Islanders (1973), with four District Commissioners (Western, Central, Malaita and Eastern) who co-ordinate the departmental activities within their Districts and in particular advise the Local Government Councils.

LOCAL GOVERNMENT COUNCILS

There are 18 Local Councils covering almost the whole area of the country and varying widely in size and wealth. The tendency is towards a Council for the whole of each major island, such as Malaita. Members are elected from the common roll and the Councils are supported financially by rates (varying from $1 to $10 per person), licence fees, local court fees and fines £1, bank interest, fees for services, grants from the Central Government and sundry minor accounts. They operate primary schools and health clinics, and undertake such work as water supplies, wharf, road and airfield construction. Honiara is the only town with a town council. A review of local government which is expected to expand Council powers and finances took place in 1973.

RELIGION

Most of the people are Christian, and the remainder still follow their traditional animism.

Anglican: The Bishop of Melanesia: The Rt. Rev. J. W. CHISHOLM; Assistant Bishops: Rt. Rev. D. TUTI, Buala, Rt. Rev. L. ALUFURAI, O.B.E., TH.L., Auki.

Roman Catholic: Bishop of Honiara, Most Rev. DANIEL STUYVENBERG, S.M., C.B.E.; Bishop of Gizo, Most Rev. EUSEBIUS CRAWFORD, O.P.

PRESS AND RADIO

There is a fortnightly newspaper in the British Solomons, produced by the Government Information Service (circ. 4,000) and each District has a monthly or less frequent Newsletter produced by the District Administration.

The only radio broadcaster is the government-operated Solomon Islands Broadcasting Service (VQO on 1,030 KHz, VQO4 on 3,995 KHz and VQO9 on 9,545 KHz) which accepts commercial advertising and is on the air for 57 hours a week, plus 14 hours for schools. Many of the programmes are in Pidgin English.

In 1972 there were 10,000 receivers.

FINANCE

BANKING

Australia and New Zealand Banking Group Ltd.: P.O.B. 10, Honiara.

Commonwealth Savings Bank of Australia: P.O.B. 37, Honiara.

Commonwealth Trading Bank of Australia: P.O.B. 37, Honiara, P.O. Gizo, Western Solomons.

B.S.I.P. Agricultural and Industrial Loans Board: Honiara.

INSURANCE

About ten of the principal British insurance companies maintain agencies in the Protectorate.

TRADE AND INDUSTRY

The economy of the Protectorate depends on primary production, chief of which is copra ($3.8m. in 1971) with timber (log extraction) a close second. Export of shipjack (tuna) began at the end of 1972 following a joint venture agreement with the Taigo Fishery Co., and export tax is an important addition to revenue. Cocoa and chillies are also exported in small quantities, and after thorough trials a palm oil industry is now being set up. The cattle industry is also growing promisingly, and rice is produced for local consumption. There has been active mineral prospecting in recent years, leading to trial mining of bauxite in 1972 and the possibility of copper and nickel mining in the future.

The building construction industry is fully engaged on buildings for both commerce and government. There is as yet little manufacturing, but a twist tobacco factory supplies local demand and exports. A factory for corrugating iron began in 1972, and there are two ship's biscuit factories providing for both domestic requirements and a small export trade. Furniture, fibre-glass products and soft drinks are also manufactured, and boats are built in several places.

British Solomon Islands Chamber of Commerce: P.O.B. 64, Honiara.

British Solomon Islands Protectorate Copra Board: Honiara; sole exporter of copra; agencies at Yandina and Gizo.

British Solomons Trading Co. Ltd.: P.O.B. 114, Honiara.

CO-OPERATIVE SOCIETIES

In 1973 there were 152 primary co-operative societies working mostly outside the capital.

TRADE UNION

B.S.I.P. General Workers Union: Honiara; f. 1971.

TRANSPORT

ROADS

There are now 211 miles of main road (1972). Road construction and maintenance is difficult because of the nature of the country, and what roads there are serve as feeder roads to the main town of an island. Honiara now has a main road running about 40 miles each side of it along the north coast of Guadalcanal, and Malaita has a road 75 miles long running north from Auki and around the northern end of the island to the Lau Lagoon, where canoe transport takes over.

SHIPPING

Regular shipping services (mainly for freight) exist between the Solomons and Australia (Sydney and Bris-

bane), New Zealand, Bougainville (Kieta), Hong Kong, Japan and U.K./Continent ports. Internal shipping is provided by 37 ships of the government marine fleet and about 100 commercial vessels. Gross tonnage is 3,480. The ports are controlled by the BSIP Ports Authority, Honiara.

British Solomon Islands Ports Authority: Box 307, Honiara.

Services are operated by:

Bank Line: regular monthly service to and from Europe, with some passengers.

China Navigation Co. Ltd.: to and from Hong Kong and Singapore.

Daiwa Navigation Co.: to and from Japan each month via Pacific ports.

Japan South Pacific: regular five-weekly service to Japan.

Karlander New Guinea Line: regular six-weekly cargo services between Papua New Guinea ports, Australia and Honiara.

New Guinea Australia Line: three-weekly services to Australia, Kieta and Honiara.

Shaw Savill Line: cruise ship calls.

Sofrana-Unilines: regular six-weekly service to New Zealand, Papua New Guinea and the New Hebrides.

CIVIL AVIATION

International air services to the Protectorate are provided by Air Pacific (to and from Fiji twice a week, Brisbane and Port Moresby once a week, Air Nauru (twice weekly) and by Trans-Australia Airlines (from Rabaul twice a week). Domestic air services are provided by Solair, operating light aircraft from Honiara with flights to 20 aerodromes in the districts.

Regular services are run by:

Solomon Islands Airways Ltd.: P.O.B. 23, Honiara; internal services and charter. Fleet: Beechcraft Barons and Britten-Norman Islanders.

TOURISM

Guadalcanal Travel Service (Travel Division): G.P.O. Box 114, Honiara.

EDUCATION
(1972)

25,570 children attended 381 registered primary schools, 1,303 attended 6 secondary schools and 400 attended 4 other higher schools.

British Solomons Training College: Box 7, Kukum, Honiara; f. 1958 for training of teachers for Solomon Islands' primary schools; 100 students on two-year courses, up to 25 on six-month courses and up to 15 on three-month in-service courses; controlling authority Dept. of Education, Box 1, Honiara, B.S.I.P.; Principal F. CORE.

Honiara Technical Institute: Kukum; provides courses of between six months and one year's duration in technical and commercial subjects; a variety of short courses, day and evening.

St. Peter's College: Siota, Gela; f. 1912 for training of deacons and priests for the Anglican Diocese of Melanesia (New Hebrides and Solomon Islands); 25 students.

NEW HEBRIDES

The British service in the Anglo-French Condominium of the New Hebrides is controlled by the High Commissioner. For further details *see* the New Hebrides chapter.

BRUNEI

INTRODUCTORY SURVEY

Location, Climate, Language, Religion, Flag, Capital

Brunei, a Sultanate related to Britain by treaty, is on the north-east coast of the island of Borneo. It covers a total area of 2,226 square miles. Brunei has a common border with Sarawak, one of the two eastern states of Malaysia. The climate is tropical, characterized by consistent temperature and humidity. Annual rainfall ranges from about 110 inches in lowland areas to over 150 inches in the interior. Temperatures are high, the annual extreme range being 73°F to 89°F. The principal language is Malay though Chinese is also spoken and English widely used. The Malay population (65 per cent) is Muslim. Most Chinese are Buddhist, Confucian or Taoist. Europeans and Eurasians are largely Christian. The flag comprises two diagonal stripes of black and white on a yellow background, with the state emblem centred in red. The capital is Bandar Seri Begawan, formerly called Brunei Town.

Recent History

In 1888, when North Borneo became a British protectorate, Brunei became a British-protected state. Between 1906 and 1941, a form of government emerged which included a state council. In 1959 a new constitution was adopted. A rebellion broke out in December 1962, prompted by dissatisfaction at the prospect of Brunei's joining the Malaysian Federation. The disorders were suppressed and the Sultan subsequently refused to join Malaysia. A state of emergency has been in force since 1962.

Government

The 1959 constitution provided that Brunei should be a protected state, with defence and external affairs being the exclusive responsibility of the British Government. However, a new agreement amending the constitution was signed in November 1971 which granted full internal self-government. Responsibility for defence and security is now shared between the Sultan and the British Government. The constitution confers supreme executive authority in the State on the Sultan. He is assisted and advised by five Constitutional Councils, the Religious Council, the Privy Council, the Council of Ministers, the Legislative Council and the Council of Succession. The Council of Ministers considers all executive matters including those tabled at the Legislative Council meetings. It normally consists of members and is presided over by the Sultan. The Legislative Council is presided over by the Speaker, appointed by the Sultan, and comprises 22 members, all appointed by the Sultan.

Since the rebellion of 1962 certain provisions of the constitution have been suspended and the Sultan has ruled by decree.

Defence

Under the 1959 Constitution as amended in November 1971, Brunei and Britain share responsibility for the State's defence and security and, in addition to the Royal Brunei Malay Regiment, there are about 1,000 British military personnel.

Economic Affairs

Brunei's agricultural output consists largely of rice (the main crop), while rubber has declined in importance in recent years. Minor crops include coconuts, sago, pepper, vegetables and fruit. By contrast, the production of oil and natural gas assumes particular importance to the economy with crude oil output averaging about 60 million barrels annually. Natural gas production decreased from 221 million cu. ft. in 1971 to 159 million cu. ft. in 1972. Oil constitutes the major part of Brunei's exports, earning over 98 per cent of the State's foreign exchange.

Transport

In 1972 there were 733 miles of motorable roads in Brunei.

Social Welfare

Health facilities are good and serious epidemics are rare. In 1969 there were 3.5 hospital beds per thousand of the population. There is a flying doctor service as well as various clinics, travelling dispensaries and dental clinics.

Education

Schools are classified according to the language of instruction, i.e. Malay, English or Chinese (Mandarin). Total enrolment in primary schools was 29,700 in 1971 while in secondary schools the enrolment was 11,670. There are five technical colleges including a teachers' training college.

Tourism

Tourism is relatively underdeveloped though there are the beginnings of a tourist industry.

Public Holidays

1974: August 17th (*Leilat al Meiraj*, Ascension of Muhammad), October 1st (Constitution Day), October 4th (Nuzul Quaran), October 19th and 21st (Hari Raya Puasa), December 25th and 26th (Christmas Day and Boxing Day), December 27th (Hari Raya Haji).

1975: January 1st (New Year's Day), February 11th (Chinese New Year), March 26th (*Maulud*, Birth of Muhammad), May 31st (Anniversary of the Royal Brunei Malay Regiment), July 15th (Sultan's birthday).

Weights and Measures

The imperial system is in operation but local measures of weight and capacity are used. These include the Gantang (1 gallon), the Tahil ($1\frac{1}{3}$ oz.) and Kati ($1\frac{1}{3}$ lb.).

Currency and Exchange Rate

100 cents = 1 Brunei dollar (B$).
Exchange Rates (April 1974):
£1 sterling = B$5.734;
U.S. $1 = B$2.43.

STATISTICAL SURVEY

Area and Population: Area (sq. miles) 2,226; Population (1973 est.) 145,170 (Malays 65 per cent, Chinese 23 per cent, indigenous 7 per cent, others 5 per cent); Bandar Seri Begawan (capital—1971 Census) 72,481; Birth rate: 40 per thousand (1969); Death rate: 6 per thousand (1969).

Land Use (1971—acres): Forest Reserve 523,460, Forest Licences 84,943, Alienated Land 1,424,640.

Employment (1972): Construction 7,296, Oil Mining 3,084, Agriculture, Forestry and Fishing 913, Total 27,646.

Agriculture (1971): (tons) Paddy 4,312, Rubber 163.09. *Timber* (50 cu. ft.): Heavy Hardwood 234,160; Other Timber 2,422,592; Sawn Timber 26,574 tons.

Livestock: Buffaloes 15,500, Pigs 12,100, Cattle 2,271.

Petroleum: Crude oil production (1972) 67 million barrels.

Natural Gas (1972): 158,906,763 million cu. ft.

FINANCE

100 sen (cents) = 1 Brunei dollar (B$).

Coins: 1, 5, 10, 20 and 50 cents.

Notes: 1, 5, 10, 50 and 100 dollars.

Exchange rates (April 1974): B$1 = 1 Singapore dollar;
£1 sterling = B$5.734; U.S. $1 = B$2.43.
B$100 = £17.44 = U.S. $41.15.

BUDGET 1972
(B$'000—estimates)

REVENUE								EXPENDITURE				
Direct Taxes (from oil)	.	.	.		143,685			Royal Brunei Malay Regiment	.	.		37,310
Royalties (from oil)	.	.	.		60,000			Education				30,752
Interest	.	.	.	.	34,000			Public Works	.	.	.	17,479
Other	.	.	.	.	20			Medical Services	.	.	.	11,253
								Police	.	.	.	11,632
								Other (including Development Fund)	.		43,000
TOTAL	.	.	.		237,705			TOTAL	.	.	.	151,426

DEVELOPMENT BUDGET 1972
(B$'000—estimates)

EXPENDITURE					
Airport Scheme	.	.	.	.	20,000
Electricity generating plant	.	.	.	2,700
Maura Port	.	.	.	.	8,500
Tutong Water Scheme	.	.	.	10,000
Sungei Belait Water Scheme	.	.	.	4,000
Sewerage Works	.	.	.	4,702
Roads	.	.	.	.	4,000
Other*	.	.	.	.	31,200
TOTAL	.	.	.		85,102

* Includes balance of Development Fund carried forward from 1970.

EXTERNAL TRADE
(B$'000)

	1970*	1971†	1972
Imports . .	256,100	456,500	300,206
Exports . .	290,500†	310,650	469,691

* Revised.

† Revised estimate (*UN Monthly Bulletin of Statistics*, April 1973).

Source: Department of Broadcasting and Information.

COMMODITIES
(B$'000)

IMPORTS	1971	1972
Foodstuffs . . .	37,466	43,145
Beverages and Tobacco . .	7,762	7,972
Crude Minerals . . .	6,624	7,646
Refined Petroleum . .	4,603	5,209
Animal and Vegetable Oils .	1,429	1,403
Chemicals . . .	17,667	17,981
Machinery and Transport Equipment . .	214,867	113,108
Manufactures . .	157,546	99,313
Miscellaneous . . .	8,679	4,429

EXPORTS	1971	1972
Crude Oil	304,815	462,054
Natural Gas . . .	536	1,952
Rubber	148	58
Petroleum Products . .	2,519	3,141
Others . . .	470	368
TOTAL . .	308,488	467,573

Source: Department of Broadcasting and Information.

PRINCIPAL COUNTRIES
(B$'000)

	IMPORTS		EXPORTS	
	1971	1972	1971	1972
Sarawak	2,400	2,300	308,300	56,400
Sabah	800	900	2,800	7,400
Australia . . .	9,900	10,200	—	11,000
China, P.R. . . .	7,700	8,800	—	—
Germany, Federal Republic .	11,700	9,900	—	—
Hong Kong . . .	8,300	4,900	1,600	2,000
Japan . . .	136,900	60,200	500	258,800
United States . . .	108,100	57,400	100	41,400
Thailand . . .	5,100	5,600	—	—
Netherlands . .	18,100	17,400	—	—
Singapore . . .	42,300	45,500	4,300	41,500
United Kingdom . .	69,000	42,700	100	200
Others . . .	36,300	34,400	5,900	78,700
TOTAL .	456,600	300,200	323,600	497,400

Source: Department of Broadcasting and Information.

Transport (1972): Cars 15,118, Other Vehicles 499. *Shipping:* Tonnage Entered 1,134,381. *Civil Aviation* (1972): Passengers embarked 45,380.

Education (1971): Number of schools and colleges 171 (Kindergarten 14, Primary 131, Secondary 24, Teacher Training 1, Vocational 1); Number of pupils and students 43,002 (Kindergarten 1,202, Primary 29,692, Secondary 11,670, Vocational 111, Teacher Training 328.

THE CONSTITUTION

A new constitution was promulgated in September 1959. Under it sovereign authority is vested in the Sultan.

The constitution provides for the creation of a Legislative Council, a Council of Ministers and a Privy Council. A Mentri Besar (Chief Minister) appointed by the Sultan is responsible for the exercise of executive power.

The State is divided into four administrative districts, in each of which is a District Officer (Malay) responsible to the Mentri Besar.

A new Agreement replacing that of 1905–06 was concluded with the United Kingdom following the promulgation of the constitution. Under the Agreement, the British Government continued to be responsible for the defence and external affairs of the State and provided for the appointment of a High Commissioner to advise the Sultan on such matters as external affairs, defence, and internal security, and generally on matters other than those affecting the Muslim religion and Malay custom.

An agreement was signed in November 1971 giving Brunei full internal self-government, although Britain still retains responsibility for external affairs.

Note: Parts of the constitution have been in suspense since 1962. *See* below under *The Government.*

THE GOVERNMENT

The Sultan: H.H. Muda Hassanal Bolkiah Mu'izzaddin Waddaulah (succeeded October 5th, 1967; crowned August 1st, 1968).

Mentri Besar: Y.A.M. Pengiran Setia Negara Pengiran Haji Mohd Yusuf bin Pengiran Haji Abdul Rahim.

The constitution provides for a Privy Council, a Council of Ministers and a Legislative Council to advise the Sultan. Since 1962, however, parts of the constitution relating to these councils have been in suspense and the Sultan has ruled by decree.

HIGH COMMISSIONER

The High Commissioner: Dato Peter Gautrey.

POLITICAL PARTY

Brunei People's Independence Front (*Barisan Kemajuan Raya'at*): f. 1966; an amalgamation of all the former parties; Pres. Hafidz Lakasamana; Chair. Pengiran Ali; Sec. Abdul Latif Hamid.

JUDICIAL SYSTEM

The judicial system was created by the Supreme Court Enactment, 1963, under which the Supreme Court consists of the High Court and the Court of Appeal. There are also Magistrates' Courts of First, Second and Third Class.

The Supreme Court: Consists of the Chief Justice and as many Commissioners of the Supreme Court as may from time to time be appointed by the Sultan. The High Court has unlimited original jurisdiction in all civil matters other than the annulment of marriages solemnized between Christians in the United Kingdom or any British Colony, and matters concerning Muslim marriage, religion and divorce. The Court has unlimited criminal jurisdiction.

Courts of Magistrates: The Court of a Magistrate of the First Class has original civil jurisdiction in suits involving not more than $1,000 and original criminal jurisdiction in the case of offences for which the maximum term of imprisonment does not exceed two years and the maximum fine does not exceed $5,000. The Courts of the Second and Third Class Magistrates have civil and criminal jurisdiction in suits involving smaller sums and terms of imprisonment.

Courts of Kadhis: Deal solely with questions concerning Muslim religion, marriage and divorce, and may impose a fine not exceeding $500 or imprisonment not exceeding five years. Appeals lie from these Courts to the Sultan in the Religious Council.

Chief Justice: Geoffrey Gould Briggs.

Chief Kadhi: Begawan Pehin Khatib Dato Seri Utama Haji Metali bin Mat Yassin.

RELIGION

The official religion of Brunei is Islam, and His Highness the Sultan is head of the Islamic population. Muslims number about 60,000, most of them Malays. The Chinese population is either Buddhist, Confucianist or Christian. Large numbers of the indigenous races are animists of various types. The remainder of the population are Roman Catholics, Anglicans or members of the American Methodist Church of Southern Asia.

ANGLICAN

Bishop of Kuching: The Rt. Rev. Datuk Basil Temengong, Bishop's House, Kuching, Sarawak, Malaysia.

ROMAN CATHOLIC

Vicar Apostolic: The Rt. Rev. Anthony Dennis Galvin, o.b.e., Bishop's House, Miri, Sarawak, Malaysia.

THE PRESS

NEWSPAPERS

Borneo Bulletin: P.O.B. 69, Kuala Belait; f. 1953; Independent; English; weekly; Saturday; Man. and Man. Editor J. R. Calver; circ. 25,921.

Pelita Brunei: Dept. of Broadcasting and Information, Brunei; f. 1956; free newspaper in Romanized Malay and Chinese; weekly; circ. 4,500.

Salam: c/o Brunei Shell Petroleum Co. Ltd., Seria; f. 1953; free employee newspaper produced jointly by the Brunei Shell Petroleum Co. Ltd., Sarawak Shell Oilfields Ltd. and the Sabah Shell Petroleum Co. Ltd.; English, Chinese and Romanized Malay in one edition; weekly; Friday; circ. 6,500.

PUBLISHERS

The Brunei Press: P.O.B. 69, Kuala Belait; incorp. 1959; Gen. Man. J. R. Calver.

The Star Press: Bandar Seri Begawan; f. 1963; Man. F. W. Zimmermann.

RADIO

Brunei Broadcasting and Information Service: Brunei; f. 1957; daily broadcasts in Malay, English, Chinese and local dialects. Dir. Dato G. V. DE FREITAS; Deputy Dir. of Broadcasting MOHAMMED SALLEH ABDUL KADIR; publs. *Pelita Brunei* (weekly), *Suara Brunei* (fortnightly).

In 1970 there were 12,000 radio receivers.

FINANCE

Note: Since 1967 the Brunei Currency Board has issued its own notes and coins which were interchangeable with currencies issued by the Malaysian and Singapore Currency Boards until 1973, when the agreement with Malaysia was cancelled. Total currency in circulation (Dec. 1972) was B$54.9 million.

BANKS

Bank of America: Head Office: San Francisco; br. in Bandar Seri Begawan.

Chartered Bank, The: Head Office: 38 Bishopsgate, London, E.C.2; branches in Bandar Seri Begawan, Kuala Belait and Seria.

First National City Bank: Head Office: New York; br. in Bandar Seri Begawan.

Hongkong and Shanghai Banking Corpn., The: Head Office: Hong Kong; brs. in Bandar Seri Begawan, Kuala Belait, Seria and Lumut.

Malayan Banking Bhd.: Head Office: P.O.B. 2010, Kuala Lumpur, Malaysia; branch in Bandar Seri Begawan.

National Bank Ltd.: P.O.B. 321, Bandar Seri Begawan; f. 1965; cap. B$10m., resources B$75m. (1971); Chair. P. H. MEADOWS; Gen. Man. T. P. HEONG; brs. in Seria, Kuala Belait, Tutong and Muara Port.

United Malayan Banking Corpn. Bhd.: Head Office: Kuala Lumpur, Malaysia; br. in Bandar Seri Begawan.

INSURANCE

A number of British insurance companies have agencies in Brunei.

TRADE AND INDUSTRY

Trade in Brunei is largely conducted by the agency houses, European and Chinese, and by Chinese merchants.

Brunei Shell Petroleum Co. Ltd.: Seria; the largest industrial concern in the State and the only oil company at present in production in Brunei; Chief Exec. R. A. B. CLOUGH; output (1973) 250,000 barrels per day.

CHAMBER OF COMMERCE

Brunei State Chamber of Commerce: P.O.B. 2246, Bandar Seri Begawan; br. at Kuala Belait; 36 mems.; Chair. C. R. BEAMES.

TRADE UNIONS

Brunei Oilfield Workers' Union: P.O.B. 175, Seria; f. 1961; 1,168 mems.; Pres. AHMAD TAMIN; Vice-Pres. IBRAHIM METUSSIN; Sec.-Gen. HUSSIN bin ISA; Treas. SANI BASRI.

Contract Officers' Association: 71 mems.

Government Labourers' Union: 679 mems.

Medical and Health Employees' Union: 271 mems.

Permanent Government Officers' Union: 492 mems.

Brunei Shell Employees' Staff Union: 260 mems.

Brunei Government Clerical and Peon Union: 200 mems.

TRANSPORT

RAILWAYS

There are no public railways in Brunei. The Brunei Shell Petroleum Company maintains an eight mile section of light railway between Seria and Badas.

ROADS

In 1972 there were 733 miles of motorable roads in Brunei.

SHIPPING

Straits Steamship Co.: regular passenger and cargo services from Singapore, and non-scheduled services from Labuan and Bangkok.

The Brunei Shell Petroleum Company maintains a considerable fleet of coastal vessels plying between Labuan and Kuala Belait. The State runs a motor launch service connecting with the Labuan steamer service. Numerous native-owned boats and launches carry on coastal trade around Brunei and adjacent Malaysian ports.

A new deepwater port has been completed at Muara and became fully operational in 1973.

CIVIL AVIATION

There is an international airport.

Director of Civil Aviation: Mr. PETER HADFIELD; Department of Civil Aviation, State of Brunei.

Cathay Pacific Airways: Head Office: Union House, 9 Connaught Rd., Hong Kong; Brunei Sales General Agents: The Borneo Company (B) Ltd., 97 Jalan Cator, P.O.B. 2182, Bandar Seri Begawan; twice-weekly flights from Kota Kinabalu to Hong Kong.

Malaysian Airline System Bhd., (M.A.S.): Magnet House, 2-4 Campbell Rd., Kuala Lumpur; operate a mainline daily service connecting Brunei airport with Sabah (North Borneo), Sarawak, Malaya, Thailand and Singapore.

Singapore Airlines (S.I.A.): Head Office: 77 Robinson Rd., Singapore 1, Brunei-Jalan Chevalier; operates a daily service connecting Brunei International Airport with Singapore.

Brunei Shell Petroleum Company: operates a private airfield at Anduki.

TOURISM

Brunei Tourist Association: P.O.B. 701, Bandar Seri Begawan; f. 1968; Chair. Dato R. D. ROSS; Sec. VINCENT PANG.

BURMA

INTRODUCTORY SURVEY

Location, Climate, Language, Religion, Flag, Capital

The Socialist Republic of the Union of Burma lies in the uppermost region of South-East Asia between the Tibetan plateau and the Malayan peninsula. Its principal neighbours are India to the north-west, China to the north-east and Thailand to the south-east. The climate is tropical, with an average temperature of 80°F (27°C) and monsoon rains from May to October. The official language is Burmese and there are also a number of tribal languages. About 75 per cent of the population are Buddhists. There are Christian, Hindu and Muslim minorities, and there is a Chinese community of some 350,000. The national flag (proportions 9 by 5) is red with a blue canton charged with a white star surrounded by five smaller stars. The capital is Rangoon.

Recent History

Burma elected to become an independent State in 1948 after being under British rule. The central government operates from Rangoon, but much power has remained in the Shan and other States. In 1958 the army took over control. Civil rule was restored in 1960, but in March 1962 the army staged another *coup* and set up a Revolutionary Government under General Ne Win. The next decade saw the creation of a more centralized system of government, representing an attempt to win popular support and nationalize the economy. In 1971 it was announced that a new constitution would be drafted with the aim of transforming Burma into a democratic socialist state and a final draft was approved in a national referendum in December 1973. Under this constitution new governmental organizations were created, the Burma Socialist Programme Party (BSPP) became the sole authorized political party and the country's name was changed to the Socialist Republic of the Union of Burma. In March 1974 Ne Win (who, together with other senior army officers, became a civilian in 1972) was elected President by the new Council of State. Despite these developments there have been, in fact, remarkably few changes in the ranks of leading politicians since 1962, while the BSPP, of which the army forms the core, has increased its influence.

Government

Under the new constitution, which came into force in January 1974, the highest organ of state is the 450-member People's Assembly, a legislative body elected by the people. From among its members the Assembly elects a Council of State, which, in turn, elects its own Chairman, who is President of the Republic. The Council is the chief decision-making organ of government and co-ordinates the work of central and local governmental organs. The Assembly also elects the Council of Ministers, which is responsible for the public administration of the state, the Council of People's Justices, the Council of People's Attorneys and the Council of People's Inspectors. As for local government, the state, formerly a federation, is now unitary, and is divided into States or Divisions. These in turn are divided into townships, and townships into wards or village-tracts. People's Councils exist for every sub-division at each of these levels.

Defence

Burma maintains neutrality and has no external defence treaties. The armed forces are largely engaged in internal security duties. In 1973 the armed forces totalled 149,000 men, of whom 135,000 were in the army.

Economic Affairs

Burma is relatively rich in agricultural, fishery, timber, mineral and water resources. In 1973 agriculture produced about 40 per cent of G.N.P. and employed 67 per cent of the labour force. Rice, timber and other agricultural products have traditionally been the main export items, though rice exports have declined drastically since 1964 when they accounted for about 60 per cent of export earnings. In March 1973 they were suspended altogether. Industry accounts for about 50 per cent of the G.N.P. The mining of tin, petroleum and coal is important; the expanding petroleum industry is expected to supply all Burma's requirements for petroleum products by the mid-1970s. There are small deposits of tungsten, lead, zinc, antimony, silver and gold, while a number of other minerals are known to exist. There are about 9,000 industrial establishments, mainly small-scale firms engaged in processing primary products, particularly rice.

Industry, transport, internal and external trade, communications and finance have been nationalized since the 1962 revolution. Economic progress has, however, been very slow, with production rising only slightly faster than the population growth. In 1972–73, the second year of a Four-Year Plan, the economic growth rate actually fell below the population growth rate. In 1973 steps were taken to encourage private enterprise and foreign investment which had previously been banned. A twenty-year plan is scheduled to begin in 1974, aiming to expand state control of industry to 48 per cent by 1994, to double the national income and transform the economy into an industrial one.

Transport and Communications

The chief artery of traffic is the river Irrawaddy, which is navigable as far as Bhamo, 900 miles inland. The Irrawaddy delta has nearly 2,000 miles of navigable waters and some parts of the Salween and the Chindwin are navigable. An agreement was signed with the World Bank in 1973 for a $33 million credit to help rehabilitate the waterways and railways. Railways have been modernized by the introduction of diesel engines and in 1972 comprised 2,623 track miles compared with 2,606 track miles in 1971. The Union of Burma Airways Board provides internal and international air services. All the railways, domestic air services and the other major inland water facilities are owned and operated by the State. All passenger and freight road transport services are to be nationalized. In 1972 there were 8,514 miles of motorable roads.

Social Welfare

Burma has fairly well-developed health facilities but they are not comprehensive. About 500,000 workers are covered by social security insurance.

Education

Education is free, where available. Schools are divided into primary, middle and high schools. There were over 19,000 schools, colleges and professional institutes in 1971–72 with a total enrolment of 4.4 million pupils. Emphasis is placed on vocational and technical training. There are two universities.

Tourism

Tourism is undeveloped. Burma is one of the centres of Buddhism and has many temples and shrines, including the famous Shwe Dagon Pagoda in Rangoon. Mandalay and Pagan also possess outstanding temples and palaces.

Visas are required by all visitors.

Sport

There is little organized sport, but football, basketball, volleyball and tennis are played.

Public Holidays

1974: August 2nd (beginning of Buddhist Lent), October 30th (end of Buddhist Lent), November 28th (Tazaung-daing), December 8th (National Day), December 25th (Christmas Day).

1975: January 4th (Independence Day), February 12th (Union Day), February 24th (Full Moon of Tabaung), March 2nd (Peasants' Day), March 27th (Resistance Day), April 3rd–5th (Thingyan), April 6th (Burmese New Year), April 24th (Full Moon of Kason), May 1st (World Workers' Day), July 19th (Martyrs' Day).

The dates of religious festivals depend on the sighting of the moon and may vary from those given above.

Weights and Measures

The imperial system is in force.

Currency and Exchange Rates

100 pyas=1 kyat.

Exchange rates (April 1974):
£1 sterling=11.37 kyats;
U.S. $1=4.814 kyats.

STATISTICAL SURVEY

AREA AND POPULATION

AREA (square miles)				POPULATION (1970—'000 est.)			
Total	Shan States	Kawthoolei	Kayah State	Total	Shan States	Kawthoolei	Kayah State
261,760	60,155	11,731	4,529	27,584	2,785	813	116

Population (Census of March 31st, 1973): 28,885,867.

PRINCIPAL TOWNS
POPULATION (1970 estimates)

Rangoon (capital)*	. 3,000,000	Henzada . . . 84,898
Mandalay . .	. 401,633	Akyab . . . 82,313
Moulmein . .	. 172,569	Prome . . . 65,392
Bassein . .	. 136,429	Myingyan . . . 64,904
Pegu . .	. 124,643	Tavoy . . . 53,094

* 1972 (Oct.).

EMPLOYMENT
(1970–71)

Total	Central and Local Government	Industry	Agriculture	Other Sectors
11,940,734	1,078,016	762,718	7,300,000	2,900,000

AGRICULTURE
PRINCIPAL CROPS

	PRODUCTION ('ooo tons)			
	1968–69	1969–70	1970–71	1971–72*
Rice (paddy) . . .	7,896	7,859	8,000	8,416
Groundnuts	392	437	521	479
Sesamum .	82	100	130	n.a.
Cotton .	33	33	41	n.a.
Pulses	294	253	271	347
Sugar Cane	1,282	1,291	1,414	1,722
Tobacco .	45	40	40	n.a.
Wheat	25	33	n.a.	n.a.
Jute	21	22	28	n.a.

* Estimate.

Livestock: 6,834,000 oxen, 1,541,000 buffaloes, 1,483,000 goats, 183,000 sheep.

FISHERIES
('ooo tons)

	1967–68	1968–69	1969–70	1970–71
Fresh water .	111	114	119	120
Sea water .	279	294	307	430

TIMBER PRODUCTION
('ooo tons)

	1969–70	1970–71	1971–72
Teak .	340	350	360
Hardwood .	946	920	600

MINING

	UNIT	1968–69	1969–70
Tin Concentrates	tons	506	637
Tin/Tungsten/Scheelite Mixed Concentrates .	,,	123	420
Refined Lead	,,	9,986	8,500
Zinc Concentrates	,,	9,734	7,200
Refined Silver	'ooo oz.	827	740
Coal	tons	7,962	13,000
Limestone	'ooo tons	553	591
Crude Oil	'ooo gall.	208,890	210,000

Source: Report to the People by the Union of Burma Revolutionary Council on the Revolutionary Government's Budget Estimates.

INDUSTRY

		1968–69	1969–70	1970–71
Salt	'ooo tons	174	179	223
Sugar	,, ,,	54	54	66
Cotton Yarn . . .	,, ,,	8	7	7
Bricks and Tiles . .	'ooo	89,000	109,000	122,000
Cement . . .	'ooo tons	180	187	225
Soap	,, ,,	32	29	36
Candles . . .	,, ,,	5	8	8
Matches . . .	'ooo boxes*	294	300	300
Gunny Bags . . .	'ooo	14,942	17,214	20,578
Motor Gasoline . .	'ooo gal.	48,010	59,270	70,210
Kerosene . . .	,, ,,	62,660	73,900	83,670

* One box contains 1,200 packets.

Source: Report to the People by the Union of Burma Revolutionary Council on the Revolutionary Government's Budget Estimates.

FINANCE

100 pyas = 1 kyat.
Coins: 1, 5, 10, 25 and 50 pyas.
Notes: 1, 5, 10 and 20 kyats.
Exchange rates (April 1974): £1 sterling = 11.37 kyats; U.S. $1 = 4.814 kyats.
100 kyats = £8.80 = $20.77.

Note: Between September 1949 and August 1971 the kyat (known as the Burmese rupee before 1952) had a par value of 21 U.S. cents (U.S. $1 = 4.7619 kyats). From December 1971 to February 1973 the central exchange rate was $1 = 5.3487 kyats (1 kyat = 18.696 U.S. cents). In terms of sterling, the value of the kyat between November 1967 and August 1971 was 1s. 9d. (8.75p), the exchange rate being £1 = 11.4286 kyats.

BUDGET
('000 kyats)

	RECEIPTS		EXPENDITURE	
	1969–70	1970–71	1969–70	1970–71
Revenue	—	1,371,100	—	—
Ordinary Account	7,007,661	6,987,000	6,683,472	7,634,300
Capital Account	370,331	—	778,124	989,600
Investment Account	—	—	1,755	15,800
Loans and Interest	663	400	192,103	209,100
Contributions	—	—	56,827	35,900
Loans and Advances	348,848	453,300	337,985	448,500
Public Savings	26,109	28,800	19,441	25,900
TOTAL	7,753,612	8,840,600	8,069,707	9,359,100
Less Expenditure borne out of foreign receipts	—	—	195,622	322,800
NET	7,753,612	8,840,600	7,874,085	9,036,300
Surplus/Deficit	—	—	−120,473	−195,700

BUDGET EXPENDITURE BY SECTOR 1970–71
(million kyats)

Trade	3,090	Transport and Communications . .	480
Economic Affairs	2,110	General Administration and Foreign Affairs	360
Social Welfare	570	Housing and Public Works . . .	310
Defence	480		

Four-Year Development Plan (1971/72–1974/75): aims at (i) maximum production and export of primary products in agriculture, fishery, livestock, forestry and mining, (ii) establishment of consumers goods industries for import substitution, (iii) laying foundation for heavy industries based on minerals.

Foreign exchange reserves: U.S. $80.2 million at December 31st, 1973.

Currency in circulation (million kyats, December): 1,742 in 1970; 2,093 in 1971; 2,389 in May 1972.

BALANCE OF PAYMENTS
(million Kyats)

	1968	1969	1970
Goods and Services:			
Merchandise	−240.2	−293.7	−297.6
Services	− 29.0	− 59.6	− 63.5
Total	−269.2	−353.3	−361.1
Contributions	28.3	69.3	83.7
Loans and Repayments	339.5	85.8	20.5
Investment	− 21.5	− 0.5	—
Foreign Exchange Budget Balance	77.1	−198.7	−256.9
Errors and Omissions	26.0	− 28.9	13.4
Foreign Exchange Reserves Balance	103.1	−227.6	−243.5

EXTERNAL TRADE
(million kyats)

	Imports	Exports
1967–68	757.0	516.1
1968–69	753.3	551.7
1969–70	778.1	538.9
1970–71*	880.0	663.0

PRINCIPAL COMMODITIES
(million kyats)

Imports	1967–68	1968–69	1969–70
Machinery and Transport Equipment	234.4	300.6	243.4
Base Metal Manufactures	93.6	92.6	55.0
Cotton Fabrics	16.7	31.6	76.9
Cotton Yarn	73.3	49.4	87.4
Milk and Milk Products	24.2	25.1	23.0
Pharmaceuticals	15.6	14.3	14.7
Gunny Sacks	1.8	—	—
Paper	35.2	35.3	36.3
Refined Mineral Oil	16.9	13.9	6.2
Chemicals	16.5	17.1	16.1
Coal and Coke	4.2	8.5	13.7

Exports	1967–68	1968–69	1969–70
Rice and Rice Products	238.1	235.3	285.2
Other Agricultural Products	89.7	91.5	89.1
Teak and Hardwood	155.0	159.8	113.9
Metals and Ores	19.2	29.2	25.3
Others	14.1	35.9	25.4

RICE EXPORTS BY COUNTRY
(1969–70—tons)

Ceylon	83,840
Hong Kong	27,873
India	62,612
Mauritius	25,804
Pakistan	6,705
United Kingdom	55,304
Singapore	136,774
U.S.S.R.	748

Rice exports: 1969–70 627,000 tons, 1970–71 749,000 tons, 1971–72 920,000 tons.

PRINCIPAL COUNTRIES
(million Kyats)

IMPORTS	1968–69	1969–70
Australia	14.4	32.7
China, People's Republic	2.4	10.2
Czechoslovakia	49.8	33.6
Germany, Federal Republic	77.2	81.3
India	69.0	120.7
Japan	169.3	176.8
Netherlands	35.0	12.3
Pakistan	11.5	12.3
U.S.S.R.	9.7	17.2
United Kingdom	85.2	69.2
United States	59.7	52.1

EXPORTS	1968–69	1969–70
Denmark	27.9	18.9
Germany, Federal Republic	32.0	23.1
India	140.1	37.1
Indonesia	3.5	61.9
Japan	44.9	46.0
Malaysia	10.7	28.4
Mauritius	13.4	13.1
Pakistan	16.5	11.0
Singapore	25.3	75.8
Sri Lanka	22.8	47.2
U.S.S.R.	17.6	2.7
United Kingdom	42.3	48.3

TOURISM

	1965–66	1966–67	1967–68	1968–69	1969–70
Number of Visitors	2,007	2,682	1,646	2,561	6,853

TRANSPORT

ROAD TRAFFIC

	MOTORCARS	BUSES	LORRIES
1971	24,700	9,300	13,400
1972	22,299	9,140	13,106

RAILWAYS (Burma Railways Board)
(in millions)

	PASSENGERS	PASSENGER MILES	FREIGHT TONS	FREIGHT TON-MILES
1967–68	55.2	1,501.9	2.8	484.9
1968–69	52.8	1,500.6	2.9	512.3
1969–70	52.3	1,466.5	2.7	461.8

INLAND WATER TRANSPORT BOARD
(in millions)

	PASSENGERS	FREIGHT TONS
1967–68	10.4	1.6
1968–69	9.8*	1.6
1969–70	10.5*	1.7*

* Provisional.

SHIPPING
('ooo tons)

	SHIPS		FREIGHT	
	Entered	Cleared	Entered	Cleared
1967–68	1,394	1,435	980	576
1968–69	1,362	1,346	919	645
1969–70	1,513	1,523	913	992

CIVIL AVIATION
(Union of Burma Airways Board)

	PASSENGER MILES	FREIGHT ('000 tons)
1967–68 . . .	63,495	5.7
1968–69 . . .	73,492	6.1
1969–70 . . .	93,362	6.5

EDUCATION
(1969–70)

	INSTITUTIONS	TEACHERS	PUPILS AND STUDENTS
Primary Schools	16,599	65,236	3,328,000
Middle Schools	1,117	14,121	559,012
High Schools	556	7,693	133,278
Vocational Schools	27	618	5,319
Agricultural and Technical Institutes	5	165	2,292
Universities and Colleges . . .	17	3,102	45,876

Source: Report to the People by the Union of Burma Revolutionary Council on the Revolutionary Government's Budget Estimates.

THE CONSTITUTION

The constitution came into force in January 1974, following a national referendum held in December 1973. A summary of the main provisions follows.

Preamble: affirmation of the Burmese Way to Socialism.

Chapter I (*articles* 1–4) The State: definition and designation of Burma.

Chapter II (*articles* 5–27) Basic Principles: Burma a single-party state, power residing in the people; representation of the people; extent of state power.

Chapter III (*articles* 28–40) The State Structure: outline of central and local government.

Chapter IV (*articles* 41–63) The People's Assembly: elected directly by secret ballot; composition, conditions of office and powers.

Chapter V (*articles* 64–81) The Council of State: elected by the Assembly; duties and rights of the Council.

Chapter VI (*articles* 82–94) The Council of Ministers: elected by the Assembly; tasks of the Council; responsibilities of Ministers.

Chapter VII (*articles* 95–110) The Council of People's Justices: elected by the Assembly; system of Bodies of Justices at central and local levels; basis on which justice to be administered; task of supervising all courts and judicial bodies.

Chapter VIII (*articles* 111–117) The Council of People's Attorneys: elected by the Assembly; duty to protect the rights of the people and report on the workings of the judicial system.

Chapter IX (*articles* 118–124) The Council of People's Inspectors: elected by the Assembly to inspect public undertakings.

Chapter X (*articles* 125–144) The People's Councils: Councils to be elected at every level of local and state government, headed by Executive Committees; duties of these.

Chapter XI (*articles* 145–172) Fundamental Rights and Duties of Citizens: qualification for citizenship; right to work, to recreation, to medical treatment and education; rights of women; right to vote, to freedom of expression, to participate in permitted political activity, to assembly, to reside, complain and sue; duty to protect the state, perform military service and pay taxes.

Chapter XII (*articles* 173–186) The Electoral System: aims; principle of direct election; constituency system; eligibility to stand for election; status of the Burma Socialist Programme Party; majority votes to count; conduct of elections.

Chapter XIII (*articles* 187–189) Recall, Resignation and Replacement: conditions under which a representative of the people may be replaced.

Chapter XIV (*articles* 190–193) The State Flag, the State Seal, the National Anthem and the State Capital.

Chapter XV (*article* 194) Amendments.

Chapter XVI (*articles* 195–209) General Provisions.

THE GOVERNMENT

HEAD OF STATE
President: U NE WIN.

COUNCIL OF STATE

Chairman: U NE WIN.

Secretary: Gen. SAN YU.

Members: U KYAW SOE, U KYAW ZAW, Col. KYAW WIN, U KHEN ZA MUNG, U KHIN MAUNG, U SOE HLAING, SAO OHN HNYA, U TIN THEIN, U TUN MYINT, U TUN LIN, U DING RA TANG, U BA NYEIN, Col. MIN THEIN, Dr. MAUNG MAUNG, Dr. MAUNG LWIN, MAHN SAN MYAT SHWE, U HLA TUN PRU, Dr. HLA HAN, U THA DIN, U THAUNG KYI, Cmmdr. THAUNG TIN, Brig. THAUNG DAN, U THAN SEIN, U THAN SEIN (ARAKAN), Dr. THEIN AUNG, THANKIN AUNG MIN, U SEIN WIN.

COUNCIL OF MINISTERS
(*April* 1974)

Prime Minister: U SEIN WIN.

Deputy Prime Minister and Minister for Planning and Finance: U LWIN.

Minister for Home and Religious Affairs: U KO KO.

Minister for Industry: U MAUNG MAUNG KHA.

Minister for Mines: Dr. NYI NYI.

Minister for Transport and Communications: U THA KYAW.

Minister for Construction: U HTIN KYAW.

Minister for Co-operatives: Col. SEIN LWIN.

Minister for Health: Col. KYI MAUNG.

Minister for Education: Dr. KHIN MAUNG WIN.

Minister for Defence: Brig. TIN OO.

Minister for Agriculture and Forests: U YE GOUNG.

Minister for Trade: U SAN WIN.

Minister for Labour: U TUN TIN.

Minister for Information: U CHIT KHIN.

Minister for Social Welfare: U VAN KULH.

Minister for Culture: U AYE MAUNG.

Minister for Foreign Affairs: U HLA PHONE.

DIPLOMATIC REPRESENTATION

EMBASSIES ACCREDITED TO BURMA
(Rangoon unless otherwise indicated)

Afghanistan: New Delhi, India.

Australia: 88 Strand Rd.; *Ambassador:* G. WOODARD.

Austria: Bangkok, Thailand.

Bangladesh: 106–108 Rhyu St.; *Ambassador:* KHWAQA H. KAIZER.

Belgium: Bangkok, Thailand.

Bulgaria: Dacca, Bangladesh.

Canada: Kuala Lumpur, Malaysia.

China, People's Republic: 1 Pyidaungsu Rd.; *Ambassador:* YEH CHENG-CHANG.

Czechoslovakia: 326 Prome Rd.; *Ambassador:* LADISLAV JETMAR.

Denmark: Bangkok, Thailand.

Egypt: 81 Pyidaungsu Yeiktha Rd.; *Ambassador:* B. ABADER.

Finland: New Delhi, India.

France: 102 Halpin Rd.; *Ambassador:* HUBERT YVER DE LA BRUCHOLLERIE.

German Democratic Republic: 17 University Ave.; *Ambassador:* SIEGFRIED KÜHNEL.

Germany, Federal Republic: 32 Natmauk Rd.; *Ambassador:* KLAUS TERFLOTH.

Greece: New Delhi, India.

Hungary: New Delhi, India.

India: 545–547 Merchant St.; *Ambassador:* R. KATHING.

Indonesia: 100 (Ka) Pyidaungsu Yeiktha Rd.; *Ambassador:* Vice-Adml. RADEN SULIYAKTO.

Iran: New Delhi, India.

Iraq: New Delhi, India.

Israel: 49 Prome Rd.; *Ambassador:* DAVID I. HARMOR.

Italy: 343 Prome Rd.; *Ambassador:* Dr. ELIO PASCARELLI.

Japan: 39 Golden Valley; *Ambassador:* TAKASHI SUZUKI.

Khmer Republic: 50 Laris Rd., Golden Valley; *Ambassador:* UM AMRETH (also accred. to Sri Lanka).

Laos: Bangkok, Thailand.

Malaysia: 65 Windsor Rd.; *Ambassador:* ABDUL HAMID bin PAWANCHEE.

Mongolia: New Delhi, India.

Nepal: 16 Nat. Mauk Yeiktha Rd.; *Ambassador:* BHARAT RAZ BHANDARY (also accred. to Malaysia).

Netherlands: New Delhi, India.

Nigeria: New Delhi, India.

Norway: Bangkok, Thailand.

Pakistan: 18 Windsor Rd.; *Ambassador:* RIAZ PIRACHA.

Philippines: 11A Windemere Rd.; *Ambassador:* PABLO A. PENA.

Poland: Dacca, Bangladesh.

Romania: 71 Mission Rd.; *Ambassador:* MIHAIL NICULESCU.

Spain: New Delhi, India.

Sri Lanka: 34 Fraser Rd.; *Ambassador:* (vacant) (also accred. to Laos and Thailand).

Sweden: Bangkok, Thailand.

Switzerland: Bangkok, Thailand.

Thailand: 91 Prome Rd.; *Ambassador:* SRIONG TMAN-GRAKSAT.

Turkey: New Delhi, India.

U.S.S.R.: 52 Prome Rd.; *Ambassador:* ALEXEI I. ELIZA-VETIN.

United Kingdom: 80 Strand Rd.; *Ambassador:* E. G. WILLAN.

U.S.A.: 581 Merchant St.; *Ambassador:* DAVID L. OSBORN.

Yugoslavia: 39 Windsor Rd.; *Ambassador:* AZEM ZULFICARI (also accred. to Thailand).

Burma also has diplomatic relations with Algeria.

PARLIAMENT

PYITHU HLUTTAW

Following national elections early in 1974, the first inaugural session of the Pyithu Hluttaw (People's Assembly) was convened on March 2nd, 1974. Sessions are presided over by the members of a panel of chairmen in rotation.

POLITICAL PARTY

Burma Socialist Programme Party (BSPP) (*Lanzin Party*): Rangoon; f. 1962; the only recognized political party; set up by the Revolutionary Council to implement its policies; consists of cadres as a nucleus for the new National Party; mems. 96,701 (full), 374,724 (candidate); publ. *Lanzin Thadin* (*Party News*) twice a month; Chair. U NE WIN; Gen. Sec. Gen. SAN YU; Joint Gen. Sec. U THAN SEIN.

JUDICIAL SYSTEM

The Chief Court: In April 1962 a new Chief Court was set up combining the functions of both the former Supreme Court and the former High Court. It is the final Court of Appeal.

Chief Justice: Dr. MAUNG MAUNG.

Sessions Courts: Hear serious criminal cases; appeal lies to the Chief Court.

Magistrates' Courts: Magistrates with Special Powers can try any criminal offences, except those punishable with death. Those with First Class Powers can impose sentences up to a limit of two years. Sentences up to a limit of six months and one month can be imposed by magistrates with Second Class Powers.

District Courts: For civil cases; appeals lie to the Chief Court.

RELIGION

Freedom of religious belief and practice is guaranteed for every citizen. About 75 per cent of the population are Buddhists.

Roman Catholic Bishop of Rangoon: Mgr. GABRIEL THOHEY, Archbishop's House, 289 Theinbyu St., Rangoon.

Episcopalian Bishop of Rangoon: Most Rev. FRANCIS AH MYA, Bishopscourt, 140 Pyidaungzu Yeiktha Rd., Rangoon.

THE PRESS

DAILIES

Guardian: 392 Merchant St., Rangoon; f. 1956; nationalized 1964; English; Editor-in-Chief U BA KYAW; circ. 15,000.

Hanthawaddy: 96 Aung San St., Mandalay; f. 1887; Burmese; nationalized 1969; circ. 18,500.

Kyemon (*Mirror*): Rangoon; f. 1951; Burmese; nationalized; Editor U THAUNG; circ. 51,000.

Ludu Pidu Neisin (*Working People's Daily*): 212 Thien Byu St., Rangoon; f. 1963; Burmese and English; official newspaper; Chief Editor U HLA MYIANG; combined circ. 75,000.

Myanma Alim (*New Light of Burma*): 58 Komin Ko-chin Rd., Rangoon; f. 1914; Burmese; nationalized early 1969; circ. 20,000.

Rangoon Daily: 213 Canal St.; f. 1946; Burmese; Editor U AUNG MYINT; circ. 21,000.

Rota Rtaung (*Vanguard Daily*): Rangoon; nationalized; circ. 4,500.

Note: Daily newspaper readership in 1972 was estimated at 780,000.

WEEKLIES AND PERIODICALS

Gita Padetha: Rangoon; journal of Burma Music Council; circ. 10,000.

Guardian Magazine: 392 Merchant St., Rangoon; f. 1953; nationalized 1964; English literary magazine; monthly.

Myawaddy Magazine: 184 32nd St., Rangoon; f. 1952; Burmese; literary magazine; monthly.

Shu Ma Wa Magazine: 146 Western Wing, Bogyoke Market, Rangoon; Burmese; literary; monthly.

Thwe/Thauk Magazine: 185 48th St., Rangoon; f. 1946; Burmese; literary; monthly.

PRESS AGENCY

News Agency of Burma: Theinbyu Rd., Rangoon; f. 1963; Government sponsored.

PUBLISHERS

Hanthawaddy Press: Bo Aung Gyaw St. 157, Rangoon; f. 1889; general publisher of books and journals; Man. Editor U ZAW WIN.

Knowledge Publishing House: 130 Bogyoke St., Rangoon; publishers of travel, fiction, religious and political books and directories.

Kyipwaye Press: 84th St., Letsaigan, Mandalay; arts, travel, religion, fiction and children's books.

Myawaddy Press: 184 32nd St., Rangoon; journals and magazines; Exec. Officer U WINN MAUNG (MIN YU WEI).

Sarpay Beikman Management Board: 529 Merchant St., Rangoon; f. 1947; Burmese encyclopaedia, literature, fine arts and general; also translations; Chair. Brig. THAUNG DAN (Information Minister); Vice-Chair. U SAW AUNG; Sec. U HTIN GYI.

Shumawa Press: 146 West Wing, Bogyoke Market, Rangoon; non-fiction of all kinds.

Shwepyidan Publishing House: 12 Haiaban St., Rangoon; philosophy, politics, law and religion.

Smart and Mookerdum: 221 Sule Pagoda Rd., Rangoon; arts, children's, fiction and non-fiction.

Than Myit Baho Publishing House: Anawyatha Rd., Rangoon; scientific and technical.

Thu Dhama Wadi Press: 55-56 Maung Khine St., P.O.B. 419, Rangoon; f. 1903; Prop. U TIN HTOO; Man. U PAN MAUNG; religious books.

Universities Administration Office: Prome Rd., University Post Office, Rangoon; Chief Editor, Translations and Publications Dept. U WUN; Man. University Press U SOE MYINT.

ASSOCIATION

Burmese Publishers' Association: 146 Bogyoke Market, Rangoon; Pres. U ON PE.

RADIO

Burma Broadcasting Service: Prome Rd., Kamayut P.O., Rangoon; f. 1946; broadcasts are made in Burmese, Shan, Karen, Chin, Kachin, Kayah and English; staff of 411; Dir.-Gen. U Tin Maung Kyi; Dir. U Kyaw Nyein; Technical Dir. U Win Mg.

There were an estimated 627,000 radio receivers in 1972.

There is no television service in Burma.

FINANCE

All banks in Burma have been nationalized and with effect from November 1st, 1969, amalgamated to form the *People's Bank of the Union of Burma*, which in 1973 was renamed the *Union of Burma Bank*. All the financial institutions listed below (Central Bank, State Banks, People's Banks, Union Insurance Board), though integrated into this unified financial structure, continue to function as separate agencies.

BANKING

(cap.=capital; dep.=deposits; p.u.=paid up; m.=million; Ks.=kyats.)

CENTRAL BANK

Union of Burma Bank: 24–26 Sule Pagoda Rd., Rangoon; f. 1969 by amalgamation of all credit institutions in Burma; cap. p.u. Ks. 200m.; brs. and agencies in all towns; Chair. U Kyaw Nyein; Gen. Man. U Tin Tun.

STATE BANKS

Industrial Development Bank: 10 Phayre St., Rangoon; f. 1961; cap. Ks. 50 m.; provides medium and long-term loans; Chair. U Soe Nyun; Gen. Man. U Nyunt We.

Union of Burma Agricultural Bank: Rangoon; f. 1953; cap. Ks. 50m.; 27 brs. and 2,647 village banks.

Union of Burma Bank (Foreign Exchange Division): 80–86 Mahabandoola Garden St., P.O.B. 203, Rangoon; f. 1970; handles all foreign exchange and all international banking transactions; Exec. Dir. U Ki Ko Ko Lay; Asst. Exec. Dirs. U Aung Nyunt Pe, U Sein Min.

PEOPLE'S BANKS

Rangoon

People's Bank No. 1/6: 1 Muang Taulay St.

People's Bank No. 2/10: 27 Phayre St.

People's Bank No. 3/4: 625 Merchant St.

People's Bank No. 5/9: 564 Merchant St.

People's Bank No. 7/8: 1/19 Sule Pagoda Rd.

People's Bank No. 11/12: 312/324 Strand Rd.

People's Bank No. 13/14: 1/7 Latha St.

People's Bank No. 15/16: 26/42 Phayre St.

People's Bank No. 19: 49/53 Phayre St.

People's Bank No. 20: 529–531 Merchant St.

Mandalay

People's Bank No. 26: f. 1963.

INSURANCE

Union Insurance Board: 69 Phayre Street, Rangoon; f. 1952; Principal officers: U Ko Ko Gyi, U San Win, U Than Hla, U Than Pe, U Myint Maung, U Kyaw Myint.

TRADE AND INDUSTRY

GOVERNMENT CORPORATIONS

Agricultural and Rural Development Corporation: Rangoon.

Burma Corporation: Rangoon; nationalized Jan. 1965; development of tin, lead, zinc.

Industrial Development Corporation: 192, Kaba-Aye Pagoda Rd., Rangoon; f. 1952.

Motion Picture Agency: Shwedagon Pagoda Rd., Rangoon; import and distribution of foreign films.

Myanma Export-Import Corporation: Rangoon; Chair. Col. Tan Yu Saing.

Myanma Mineral Development Corporation: Rangoon; Man. Dir. Hkun Naung.

Myanma Oil Corporation: 604 Merchant St., P.O.B. 1049, Rangoon; formerly Burmah Oil Company; nationalized Jan. 1963; Dir. Dr. Aung Khin.

Public Works Corporation: Rangoon.

Trade Corporations: there are 12 Trade Corporations in Rangoon which control exports of commodities.

Socialist Economic Planning Committee: Rangoon; f. 1967; frames plans for a socialist economy; 10 mems.; Chair. U Ne Win; Vice-Chair. Gen. San Yu.

State Timber Board: Rangoon; f. 1948; extraction, processing, and main exporter of Burma teak and other timber.

Union of Burma Agricultural Marketing Board: Rangoon; to control inter-governmental dealings in rice and other agricultural commodities.

CO-OPERATIVES

In 1970–71 the following new co-operatives were formed: 60 township co-operatives, 18 agricultural producers co-operatives, 131 industrial co-operatives, 11 village co-operatives, 1,964 consumers' co-operatives and 703 co-operative credit societies.

WORKERS' AND PEASANTS' COUNCILS

Central People's Workers' Council: Rangoon; f. April 1968 to provide organization for self-government of workers; Chair. U Maung Shwe (Minister of Industries and Labour).

Central People's Peasants' Council: Rangoon; f. Feb. 1969; Chair. U Thaung Kyi (Minister of Agriculture, Forests and Land Nationalization); Sec. Lt.-Col. Kyaw Zaw, B.A.F.

TRANSPORT

RAILWAYS

Burma Railways Board: Head Office: Bogyoke St., Rangoon, P.O.B. 118; government organization which manages State railways; railway mileage (1972) was 2,623 track miles; route mileage in 1971 totalled 1,925; Chair. U Tha Kyaw.

ROADS

The total length of all-weather motorable roads in Burma is over 8,500 miles in 1972, and increase of 200 miles over the previous year.

Road Transport Board: Rangoon; f. 1963 to nationalize gradually all passenger and freight road transport; by 1970–71 operated 18 per cent of trucks and 30 per cent of passenger buses in Burma.

INLAND WATERWAYS

Inland Water Transport Board: 50 Phayre St., Rangoon; Government-sponsored and non-profit-making. Its chief business is the conveyance of rice and rice products from the Irrawaddy Delta Stations, grains and pulses, oil cakes, wax and cotton bales from up-country and Central Burma to Rangoon for export. There is also a passenger steamer service, and fuel oils are carried in tankers; Chair. Lt.-Col. SAW MYA THEIN; Gen. Man. Lt.-Comdr. MAUNG AYE.

SHIPPING

Rangoon is the chief port. Vessels up to 15,000 tons can be accommodated.

Burma Five Star Line Corporation: 132, 134, 136 Theinbyu Rd., Rangoon; f. 1959 by Defence Services Institute; 22 coastal and ocean-going steamers; Chair. U THA GYAW.

Board of Management for the Port of Rangoon: P.O.B. 1, Strand Rd., Rangoon; Chair. U HLA MYINT; services: general port and harbour duties; fleet: 10 vessels totalling 5,400 tons gross and 20 smaller craft.

The following foreign lines call at Rangoon: Hansa Line, Hellenic Lines, Holland-Bengal-Burma Line, Holland-Bombay-Karachi Line, Norwegian Asia Line, Polish Ocean Lines, Union S.S. Co. of New Zealand, Wilhelmsen Lines.

CIVIL AVIATION

Mingaladon Airport, near Rangoon, is equipped to international standards.

Burma Airways Corporation (BAC): 104 Strand Rd., Rangoon; f. 1948; internal network centred on Rangoon; services to 33 stations; external services to Bangkok, Calcutta, Katmandu, Hong Kong, Dacca (currently suspended) and Phnom-Penh (currently suspended); operated by the Government; Gen. Man. Zeya-Kyaw-Htin Lt.-Col. MAUNG MAUNG NYUNT; Operations Man. U KHIN MAUNG LATT; fleet of 1 Boeing 727, 2 Viscount 700, 6 F.27, 6 DC3.

The following foreign airlines are represented in Burma: Aeroflot, Air Cambodge, Air France, Air India, British Airways, CAAC, (General Administration of Civil Aviation of China), Cathay Pacific Airways, Ceskoslovenske Aerolinie, IAC, Japan Air Lines, Lufthansa, Pan American, PIA, Polskie Linie Lotnicze, SAS, Thai Airways International.

ATOMIC ENERGY

Union of Burma Atomic Energy Centre: Kanbe Applied Research Institute, Yankin Post Office, Rangoon; f. 1955; departments of nuclear mineralogical research; nuclear research; radiation protection research; nucleonic instrumentation; Chair. Dr. MEHM THET SAN.

UNIVERSITIES

Arts and Science University, Mandalay: University Estate, Mandalay; 294 teachers, 6,912 students.

Arts and Science University, Rangoon: University Estate, Rangoon, University Post Office; 424 teachers, 7,198 students.

BURUNDI

INTRODUCTORY SURVEY

Location, Climate, Language, Religion, Flag, Capital

The Republic of Burundi lies on Lake Tanganyika in the heart of Africa a little below the Equator. Rwanda is to the north, Tanzania to the south and east and Zaire to the west. The climate is tropical with an irregular rainfall. The official languages are French and Kirundi; and Swahili is used in addition to French in commercial circles. Religious beliefs are African and animistic but missions have converted more than half the population to Roman Catholicism. The national flag (proportions 3 by 2) consists of a white diagonal cross on a background of red and green, with a white circle containing three green-edged red stars in the centre. The capital is Bujumbura.

Recent History

Before independence Burundi formed part of the Belgian-administered UN Trust Territory of Ruanda-Urundi, which was itself formerly part of German East Africa. Internal self-government was granted in January 1962, following elections to a new National Assembly in September 1961, and full independence in July 1962, when the two parts of the Trust Territory became separate states. Burundi continued to be linked to Rwanda in a customs and monetary union, until the agreements were terminated in January 1964. In July 1966 Mwambutsa IV, king since 1915, was deposed by his son Charles, with the help of a group of army officers, and the constitution suspended. In November 1966, Charles, now Mwami (King) Ntare V, was himself deposed by his Prime Minister, Captain (later Lieut.-Gen.) Michel Micombero, who declared Burundi a Republic. Agreement on a settlement of the long dispute with Rwanda, during which armed refugees from both countries had clashed, was reached in March 1967 with the mediation of President Mobutu of Congo-Kinshasa (now Zaire).

During 1969 and 1971 several alleged plots to overthrow the Government were uncovered. In March 1972 the former King Ntare V was arrested on charges of planning an invasion of Burundi. At the end of April there was an abortive *coup*, allegedly led by members of the Hutu tribe, during which Ntare V was killed. This started a series of inter-tribal massacres on the scale of a civil war, which again erupted in May 1973. In April 1972 President Micombero dismissed the Government and temporarily imposed censorship of the press. On June 17th, it was announced that the army was in control of the situation. A new cabinet was appointed on July 15th, 1972, led by a prime minister for the first time since the Republic was established. In June 1973, however, this cabinet resigned, giving way to a seven-member Presidential Bureau headed by Lieut.-Gen. Micombero.

There were several clashes between Burundi and neighbouring Tanzania during 1973. Burundi allegedly violated Tanzanian territory and airspace and a retaliatory advance into Burundi territory was made in July. The troubles continued sporadically until January 1974 when Burundi compensated Tanzania for the damage caused by her troops.

Government

Since November 1966, Burundi has been a Republic, although a new constitution has not yet been promulgated. There are eight provinces, administered by military governors.

Defence

The army was merged with the police force in 1967 and total armed strength is now around 3,000 men. Defence expenditure in 1973 amounted to 21 per cent of the national budget.

Economic Affairs

The economy is based almost entirely on agriculture, the main subsistence crops being manioc and sweet potatoes and the main cash crops coffee and cotton. Coffee accounts for more than 80 per cent of Burundi's total export earnings, the bulk of the crop going to the U.S.A. Cotton is the other main source of revenue abroad, most of it being sold to Belgium. Tea is being developed and the government plans to raise output to around 7,000 tons by 1978, during which time six to eight tea processing factories are to be built.

The mining industry, based on gold and cassiterite, is developing, and exports have been expanding rapidly over the last few years. Manufacturing industry is, however, still in its infancy, accounting for less than one-tenth of Gross Domestic Product, and many industrial and consumer goods have to be imported. Most foreign aid comes from Belgium, with France and Federal Germany also contributing individually and through the EEC. Negotiation of Burundi's application to join the East African Community began in November 1968; and in the same month Burundi and Zambia concluded a trade agreement. Proposals for an economic union between Burundi, Rwanda and Zaire have been shelved for the moment, but three commissions have been set up: Burundi is responsible for the Economic, Financial and Technical Commission, Rwanda for the Social and Cultural Commission and Zaire for the Political and Juridical Commission. In January 1972 a trade and technical co-operation agreement was concluded with the People's Republic of China, which involved a $20 million loan, payable over the period 1972–76. Repayment will be made in the form of exports to China.

Transport and Communications

There are no railways in Burundi. Roads extend for 6,000 kilometres, of which 80 kilometres are asphalted. The main roadway links the capital Bujumbura with Bugarama. The International Development Association has recently made a $5 million loan to Burundi for a four-year road-building project, and a new road from Bujumbura to the Rwandan frontier at Kinyaru is already under construction. There is passenger and freight traffic on Lake Tanganyika with Bujumbura as the main port handling about 250,000 tons of goods yearly, while the port facilities at Kigoma are being extended. There is an international airport at Bujumbura equipped to take large jet aircraft.

Social Welfare

Wage-earners are protected by insurance against accidents and occupational diseases and can draw on a pension fund.

Education

Education is free. French is the language of instruction in the secondary schools and Kirundi in primary schools, with French as a second language. In 1972 there were 179,896 pupils in primary schools, 4,102 in secondary, and 3,384 student teachers. There is a university with three faculties at Bujumbura.

Tourism

Visas are not required to visit Burundi by citizens of Tanzania and Uganda, but, as yet, tourism in Burundi is practically non-existent. There have been recent talks with Uganda, however, on the joint development of a tourist industry.

Sport

Sport is very popular, the chief sport being football.

Public Holidays

1974: August 15th (Assumption), September 18th (Victory of Uprona Party), October 13th (Murder of Hero of the State Rwagasore), November 1st (All Saints'), November 28th (Republic Day), December 25th (Christmas).

1975: January 1st (New Year), March 31st (Easter Monday), May 1st (Labour Day), May 8th (Ascension), May 19th (Whit Monday), July 1st (Independence Day).

Weights and Measures

The metric system is in force.

Currency and Exchange Rates

100 centimes = 1 Burundi franc.
Exchange rates (April 1974):
£1 sterling = 185.95 francs;
U.S. $1 = 78.75 francs.

STATISTICAL SURVEY

AREA AND POPULATION

AREA	Total (1970–71)	POPULATION:					
		Foreigners (1965 est.)			Refugees from Rwanda (1965 est.)	Bujumbura (capital) (1970 est.)	Kitega (1970 est.)
		Africans	Europeans	Asians and Arabs			
27,834 sq. km.*	3,350,000†	24,730	4,190	2,913	160,000	78,810	5,000

* 10,747 square miles.
† Estimate, based on the results of a sample survey covering 25,000 persons.

EMPLOYMENT

(1965)

Traditional agriculture	1,516,350
Fishing	9,200
Craftsmen	4,380
Shopkeepers	11,250
Private sector (modern)	58,130
Public sector	13,980
Professional	1,260
Total active population	1,614,550

AGRICULTURE

PRINCIPAL CROPS
('000 metric tons)

	1969	1970	1971
Wheat . . .	4.4	13.2	7.6
Maize . . .	236.5	287.3	461.0
Finger Millet .	21.4	34.4	35.0
Sorghum . .	50.6	96.0	227.3
Rice . . .	3.4	12.0	8.0
Potatoes . .	41	101	90*
Sweet Potatoes .	874.1	1,074.1	2,817.5
Cassava (Manioc) .	1,024.2	1,576.5	3,558.0
Dry Beans .	312.0	554.0	445.2
Dry Peas . .	19.8	34.4	25.0
Palm Kernels .	0.2*	0.2*	0.2*
Groundnuts (in shell)	19.6	21.6	32.0
Cottonseed .	7.4	8.7	8.7
Cotton (lint) .	2.7	3.3	3.5
Coffee . .	14.6	22.1	25.1
Tobacco . .	1.5*	1.5*	1.5*

* FAO estimate.

Source: Ministry of Agriculture and Livestock; FAO, *Production Yearbook 1971.*

Bananas and Plantains: 1,310,800 metric tons in 1967.

LAND USE, 1972
(hectares)

Arable Land	1,017,632
Land under Permanent Crops . .	170,678
Meadows and Pastures . . .	435,000
Forest	70,222
All other land	871,508
Inland Water	218,360
TOTAL AREA . . .	2,783,400

LIVESTOCK

	1970	1971	1972
Cattle . .	683,000	725,000	756,000
Sheep . .	240,000	278,000	296,000
Goats . .	489,000	560,000	590,000
Pigs . .	27,000	24,000	25,000
Poultry . .	2,200,000	n.a.	n.a.

Source: Ministry of Agriculture and Livestock; FAO, *Production Yearbook 1971.*

FISHING
(metric tons)

	1970	1971	1972
Traditional Fishing .	4,073	5,966	1,846
Small-scale Fishing .	3,759	4,876	1,270
Industrial Fishing .	5,458	5,961	4,327
TOTAL . .	13,290	16,803	7,443

INDUSTRY

	1968	1969	1970	1971	1972
Beer (hectolitres) . . .	197,145	174,557	207,200	239,200	266,400
Lemonade (hectolitres) . .	28,307	31,736	33,700	37,000	38,000
Electricity* ('000 kWh.) . .	17,324	18,033	22,145	24,829	24,517

* Consumption, including purchases from Zaire.

FINANCE

100 centimes = 1 Burundi franc.

Coins: 1, 5 and 10 francs.

Notes: 10, 20, 50, 100, 500, 1,000 and 5,000 francs.

Official exchange rates (April 1974): £1 sterling = 185.95 francs; U.S. $1 = 78.75 francs.

1,000 Burundi francs = £5.38 = $12.70.

BUDGET
(million Burundi francs)

REVENUE	1970	1971	1972
Income Tax	339.4	458.9	550.7
Property Tax .	53.4	54.7	50.5
Other Direct Taxes . . .	248.2	240.1	229.2
Customs Duties . . .	892.0	945.1	1,018.3
Excise Duties . . .	320.9	367.5	402.9
Other Indirect Taxes . .	100.2	105.6	112.0
Administrative Receipts . .	138.8	140.0	165.8
TOTAL	2,092.9	2,311.9	2,529.4

EXPENDITURE	1970	1971	1972
General Administration . . .	827.7	828.5	1,102.1
Social Services . . .	669.1	741.7	702.9
Economic Services . . .	342.0	351.7	398.4
Public Debt . . .	16.5	21.0	34.1
TOTAL	1,855.3	1,942.9	2,237.5

Sources: Ministry of Finance; Bank of the Republic of Burundi.

EXTERNAL TRADE

PRINCIPAL COMMODITIES
(million francs)

IMPORTS	1971*
Foodstuffs	417.4
Wheat Flour	86.1
Fuels and Lubricants . . .	167.8
Fuels	148.4
Raw Materials and Semi-finished Products .	105.8
Mechanical and Electrical Products .	641.0
Iron and Steel Products . .	90.4
Mechanical Engines and Spares . .	133.6
Cars, Jeeps, etc. . . .	90.1
Textiles and Leather Goods . . .	524.1
Rayon Fabrics . . .	156.4
Cotton Fabrics . . .	191.3
Other Industrial Products . .	346.6
All Others	415.1
TOTAL	2,617.8

* Provisional figures. Revised total is 2,618.9 million francs.

1972: Total imports 2,736.4 million francs.

Source: Bank of the Republic of Burundi.

BURUNDI—(Statistical Survey)

EXPORTS	1970	1971	1972
Coffee	1,800	1,293.2	1,927.1
Cotton	184	155.2	113.2
Skins	35	32.2	80.5
Tea	8	17.7	28.9
Minerals	21	21.8	28.3
Other Products	n.a.	101.8	97.2
TOTAL	2,132	1,621.9	2,275.2

Source: Bank of the Republic of Burundi.

PRINCIPAL COUNTRIES
(million francs)

IMPORTS	1970	1971	1972
Belgium-Luxembourg	369.0	528.2	601.7
France	167.9	306.7	188.8
Germany, Federal Republic . . .	190.0	274.9	269.4
Italy	51.1	79.3	103.9
Japan	252.7	259.1	185.3
Kenya	105.0	92.7	74.9
Netherlands	87.4	87.8	108.8
Tanzania	33.3	74.4	76.7
United Kingdom	89.7	134.8	126.3
U.S.A.	97.9	106.9	141.7
Zaire	68.7	81.7	97.9
Others	443.4	592.4	761.0
TOTAL IMPORTS	1,956.1	2,618.9	2,736.4

EXPORTS	1970	1971	1972
Belgium-Luxembourg	84.1	94.2	167.0
France	19.3	18.7	31.5
Germany, Federal Republic . . .	344.0	68.7	142.0
Italy	34.7	21.6	61.8
Netherlands	25.8	59.1	86.2
United Kingdom	163.8	99.3	8.4
U.S.A.	1,214.8	998.5	1,533.8
Others	245.1	261.8	244.5
TOTAL EXPORTS . . .	2,131.6	1,621.9	2,275.2

Source: Bank of the Republic of Burundi.

TRANSPORT

ROAD TRAFFIC

	1970	1971	1972
Passenger Cars .	3,219	3,788	4,164
Vans . . .	923	1,086	1,201
Lorries . . .	555	621	673
All Other Vehicles .	399	421	465
TOTAL .	5,096	5,916	6,503

LAKE TRAFFIC
(Bujumbura—'000 metric tons)

	1970	1971	1972
Goods:			
Arrivals . .	97.0	124.1	127.5
Departures . .	32.5	33.3	39.4

CIVIL AIR TRAFFIC
(Bujumbura Airport)

	1970	1971	1972
Passengers:			
Arrivals . .	17,731	10,654	7,709
Departures . .	22,723	13,315	9,600
Freight (metric tons):			
Arrivals . .	499	219	132.7
Departures . .	391	153	108.2

Sources: Ministry of Telecommunications; Bank of the Republic of Burundi.

EDUCATION
(Number of pupils)

	1968–69	1969–70	1970–71	1971–72
Primary	180,419	182,444	181,758	179,896
Secondary	3,652	3,701	3,969	4,102
Vocational	1,845	1,918	1,814	1,862
Teacher Training	2,522	2,892	3,085	3,384
Ecole Normale Supérieure du Burundi . .	75	86	102	131
Université officielle de Bujumbura . .	286	319	364	355

Source: Ministry of Education and Cultural Affairs.

THE CONSTITUTION

Burundi obtained internal self-government as a kingdom in January 1962 and full independence in July 1962. On July 8th, 1966, the Mwami (King), Mwambutsa IV, was deposed by Prince Charles Ndizeye and the constitution, which provided for a legislative assembly of 33 members and a senate of 16, was suspended. On November 28th, 1966, Captain Micombero, who had been appointed Premier by Charles (as Mwami Ntare V), deposed the King and declared a republic with himself as President, heading a military National Committee of Revolution.

A republican constitution, providing for strong presidential powers and embodying changes in the administration of justice, is being drawn up. Each of the eight provinces is administered by a military governor.

President Micombero inaugurated a Supreme Council of the Republic on October 20th, 1971. The Council, which is composed of 27 army officers, has been set up to advise the President on all problems of national importance.

THE GOVERNMENT

President: Lieut.-Gen. Michel Micombero.

President Micombero decreed a 7-member Presidential Bureau in August 1973.

COUNCIL OF MINISTERS
(*March* 1974)

Minister of National Defence: Lieut.-Gen. Michel Micombero.

Minister of the Interior: Major Joseph Rwuri.

Minister of Foreign Affairs, Co-operation and Planning: Artemon Simbananiye.

Vice-Minister: Gaspard Karenzo.

Minister of Communications and Aviation: Melchior Bwakira.

Minister of Information: Cajetan Nikobamye.

Minister of the Economy: Damien Barakamfitiye.

Minister of Justice: Philippe Minani.

Minister of Civil Service: Gregoire Barakamfitiye.

Minister of Finance: Major Nduwingoma.

Minister of Education and Culture: Gilles Bimazubute.

Minister of Agriculture and Livestock: Pierre Bigayimpunzi.

Minister of Public Health: Dr. Antoine Devenge.

Minister of Social Affairs: Benoit Bihorubusa.

Minister of Public Works, Transport and Equipment: Major Edouard Nzabimana.

DIPLOMATIC REPRESENTATION

EMBASSIES ACCREDITED TO BURUNDI
(In Bujumbura unless otherwise stated)

Austria: Nairobi, Kenya.

Belgium: 9 avenue de l'Industrie, B.P. 1920; *Ambassador:* Claude Ruelle.

Canada: Kinshasa, Zaire.

Chad: *Ambassador:* Alphonse Bainaugam.

China, People's Republic: (E); *Ambassador:* Chen Feng.

Czechoslovakia: Dar es Salaam, Tanzania.

Egypt: 31 ave. de la Liberté, B.P. 1520; *Ambassador.* Salah el Nashar.

Ethiopia: Kinshasa, Zaire.

France: coin avenue de l'Uprona et avenue de l'Angola, B.P. 1740; *Ambassador:* Henri Bernard.

Germany, Federal Republic: 22 rue de la Résidence; *Ambassador:* Thomas Troëmel.

Guinea: Dar es Salaam, Tanzania.

India: Kampala, Uganda.

Italy: Kampala, Uganda.

Japan: Kinshasa, Zaire.

Korea, Democratic People's Republic: Dar es Salaam, Tanzania; *Chargé d'Affaires:* Kim Bong Eun.

Mali: Dar es Salaam, Tanzania.

Netherlands: Kinshasa, Zaire.

Poland: *Ambassador:* Jean Witek.

Romania: *Ambassador:* Alexandru Bujor.

Rwanda: *Ambassador:* Ignace Karuhije.

Somalia: Dar es Salaam, Tanzania.

Spain: Kinshasa, Zaire.

Switzerland: Nairobi, Kenya; *Ambassador:* Richard Pestalozzi.

Syria: Dar es Salaam, Tanzania.

Tanzania: Kinshasa, Zaire.

Uganda: *Ambassador:* Lt. Col. Michaël Edema Ombia.

U.S.S.R.: 9 ave. de l'Uprona, B.P. 1034; *Ambassador:* Mr. Naoumov.

United Kingdom: Kinshasa, Zaire.

U.S.A.: ave. Olsen, B.P. 1720; *Ambassador:* M. Jost.

Vatican: 1 chaussée de Kitega, B.P. 1068; *Chargé d'Affaires:* William Corew.

Viet-Nam, Democratic Republic: Diplomatic relations established at ambassadorial level in April 1973.

Yugoslavia: Kampala, Uganda.

Zaire: 5 avenue Olsen, B.P. 872; *Ambassador:* Col. Ferdinand Maliba.

Zambia: *Ambassador:* Speedwell Makaja.

PARLIAMENT

The Constitution was suspended on July 8th, 1966.

At the last election before the suspension, held on May 10th, 1965, *Uprona* won 21 seats, *Parti du Peuple* 10 and Independents 2 in the Legislative Assembly.

POLITICAL PARTY

Uprona (*Union et progrès national: Unity and National Progress*): declared sole party by royal decree of November 24th, 1966; decree confirmed by republican government; Party's charter accepted by the National Political Bureau on July 30th 1970; Sec.-Gen. Lieut.-Gen. Michel Micombero; Exec. Sec. Bernard Bizindavyi.

Before November 24th, 1966, the main opposition party was the Hutu *Parti du Peuple*.

JUDICIAL SYSTEM

The judicial system is being reorganized and the changes will be incorporated in the new constitution.

Supreme Court: Bujumbura; Pres. Joseph Bukera.

Court of Appeal: Bujumbura; Pres. Charles Mabushi.

Court of First Instance: Bujumbura; Pres. B. Gahungu.

Tribunals of First Instance: Bujumbura: Pres. Michel Ngendankazi; Butare: Pres. Callixte Ndikubwimana. Tribunals to be installed in Kitega, Ngozi and Bururi.

RELIGION

AFRICAN RELIGIONS

Traditional belief is mainly in a God "Imana". Less than 40 per cent of the population are followers of traditional beliefs.

CHRISTIANITY

More than 60 per cent of the population are Christians, mostly Roman Catholics.

Roman Catholics

Archbishop of Kitega: Most Rev. André Makarakiza, B.P. 118, Kitega; Suffragan Sees: Bishop of Ngozi Rt. Rev. Stanislas Kaburungu, Bishop of Bujumbura Rt. Rev. Michel Ntuyahaga, Bishop of Bururi Rt. Rev. Bernard Bududira, Bishop of Muyinga Rt. Rev. Nestor Bihonda, Bishop of Ruyigi Joachim Ruhuna.

Anglicans

Anglicans number about 50,000 and form part of the Province of Uganda.

Archbishop of Uganda: Most Rev. E. Sabiti.

Bishop of Burundi: Rt. Rev. Y. Nkunzumwami, B.P. 58, Ibuye, Ngozi.

Other Protestants

There are about 200,000 other Protestants, some 160,000 of them Pentecostal.

Islam

About 1 per cent of the population is Muslim.

THE PRESS

All publications are strictly controlled by the government.

NEWSPAPERS

Burundi Chrétien: Bujumbura; fortnightly newspaper; French; published by the Archbishopric of Kitega.

Flash-Infor: Ministry of Information, B.P. 1400, Bujumbura; daily; French.

Tribune du Burundi: Bujumbura; weekly newspaper; French; circ. 1,500.

Ubumwe: B.P. 1400, Bujumbura; f. 1972; weekly.

Unité et Révolution: Government Printing Office, B.P. 1400, Bujumbura; f. 1967; an international news service is supplied under special agreement by Tass; weekly.

PERIODICALS

Bulletin Économique et Financier: monthly; Ministry of Economy and Finance, B.P. 482, Bujumbura.

Kindugu: P.O.B. 232, Bujumbura; monthly; Swahili.

Ndongozi: P.O.B. 232, Bujumbura; Catholic; monthly; Kirundi.

RADIO

Voix de la Révolution: B.P. 1900, Bujumbura; Govt. station; broadcasts daily programmes in Kirundi, Swahili and French; Dir. François Maceri.

Radio Cordac: B.P. 1140, Bujumbura; f. 1963; missionary station; broadcasts daily programmes in Kirundi, Swahili, French and English; Dir. J. E. Morris.

There are an estimated 75,000 radio receivers.

FINANCE

(cap. = capital; p.u. = paid up; m. = million; amounts in Burundi francs).

BANKING

Burundi was one of the 19 founding members of the Association of African Central Banks.

Central Bank

Banque de la République du Burundi: B.P. 705, Bujumbura; f. 1964; cap. 30m.; Pres. Bonaventure Kidwingira; Vice-Pres. Patrice Nsababaganwa; Dir. Michel Mbabarempore; Dir.-Gen. Philippe Duvaux.

Banque Belgo-Africaine Burundi: Blvd. de la Liberté, B.P. 585, Bujumbura; f. 1960; cap. 36m.; Chair. Georges Leclerq.

Banque Commerciale du Burundi: B.P. 990, Bujumbura; f. 1960; cap. 75m.; Chair. Daniel Gillet.

Banque de Crédit de Bujumbura: B.P. 300, Bujumbura; f. 1964; cap. and reserves 87m.; Pres. E. Bonvoisin; Man. Dir. Th. de Coster.

Banque Nationale de Développement Economique (BNDE): Bujumbura, B.P. 1620.

Caisse d'Epargne du Burundi: B.P. 615, Bujumbura; f. 1964; Man. L. Nkundwa; Asst. Man. A. Jabon.

INSURANCE

Compagnie d'Assurances d'Outremer: Bujumbura.

TRADE AND INDUSTRY

CHAMBER OF COMMERCE

Chambre de Commerce et de l'Industrie du Rwanda et du Burundi: P.O.B. 313, Bujumbura; f. 1923; Pres. M. R. Leclere; Hon. Sec. M. T. Pojer; 130 mems.

TRADE UNION

Union des Travailleurs du Burundi (UTB): Bujumbura; sole authorized union for Burundi workers; f. 1967 by amalgamation of all previous unions; closely allied with Uprona Party; Sec.-Gen. Pierre-Claver Kayonde.

TRANSPORT

ROADS

The road network is very dense and there are 545 km. of national routes (although only 80 km. are asphalt) and over 5,000 km. of other roads.

INLAND WATERWAYS

Bujumbura is the principal port on Lake Tanganyika and the greater part of Burundi's external trade is dependent on the shipping services between Bujumbura and Tanzania and Zaire.

CIVIL AVIATION

Service des Transports Aériens du Burundi (STAB) (*National Airline Co*): Bujumbura; f. 1970; operates services to Kigali and Kinshasa.

Air Zaire, East African Airways and Sabena operate services to Bujumbura, the airport of which is now being extended.

TOURISM

Office National au Tourisme: Bujumbura; f. 1972; Dir. Libérat Niyondagara.

UNIVERSITY

Université du Burundi: B.P. 1550, Bujumbura; l'Université Officielle de Bujumbura, l'Ecole Normale Supérieure and l'Ecole Nationale d'Administration were amalgamated in September 1973 to form the new university.

CAMEROON

INTRODUCTORY SURVEY

Location, Climate, Language, Religion, Flag, Capital

The United Republic of Cameroon lies on the west coast of Africa with Nigeria to the north, Chad and the Central African Republic to the east and Congo (Brazzaville) and Gabon to the south. The climate is hot and humid with average temperatures of 26°c (80°F). It is hotter and drier inland. The official languages are French and English. In religion roughly half of all Cameroonians follow traditional beliefs. About 35 per cent are Christians, roughly divided between Roman Catholics and Protestants, and about 20 per cent, mostly in the north, are Muslims. The national flag (proportions 3 by 2) consists of a vertical tricolour of green, red and yellow with two gold stars in the green stripe. The capital is Yaoundé.

Recent History

East Cameroon, once a League of Nations Mandate and later a United Nations Trusteeship Territory, was under French administration until it became independent as the Republic of Cameroon on January 1st, 1960. West Cameroon, then the British-administered Trust Territory of Southern Cameroon, opted to join the Republic in February 1961, and a Federal Republic was created on October 1st, 1961. After 1962 the political, economic and social structures became increasingly integrated. In 1966 the governing parties of the two states united in a single party, *Union nationale camerounaise* (UNC). President Ahidjo was re-elected in March 1970. The guerrilla warfare, waged since 1955 by the opposition *Union des populations de Cameroun* (UPC), seemed definitively checked by the capture and execution in 1970 of the last of its leaders. Since 1970 the UNC has grown in significance and now embraces almost all the country's political, cultural, professional and social organizations.

In May 1972, after approval by referendum of a new Constitution, the Federal Republic of Cameroon became the United Republic of Cameroon. A fully centralized political and administrative system was quickly introduced, and in May 1973 a new National Assembly was elected. The United Republic has pursued an independent foreign policy. It withdrew from OCAM in July 1973, and has negotiated a revision of co-operation agreements with France.

Government

Cameroon is governed by a President and a unicameral 120 member National Assembly, each elected for five years by universal adult suffrage. The age of majority is 21. Ministers and Vice-Ministers are appointed by the President who also appoints a Governor to each of the seven provinces.

Defence

Cameroon has an army of 4,000, Gendarmerie of 3,000, National Guard of 2,000 and a civil police of 2,000. The navy numbers 200, and the air force 250.

Cameroon has agreements with France, whereby France will assist her in training and equipping her forces.

Economic Affairs

Cameroon has one of the highest incomes per head in tropical Africa, though the basis of its economy is still essentially agricultural. The most important cash crops are cocoa, coffee, rubber and palm oil. Bananas have declined in importance in export earnings over the last few years, and many plantations have been converted by the Cameroon Development Corporation to more profitable crops.

The industrial sector has grown rapidly since independence, though the Edea Dam and the aluminium smelter which uses 88 per cent of its hydro-electric power have been in operation since 1958. Industry is based on agricultural products, aluminium smelting and chemicals. Douala is the main commercial centre and port.

In 1972 Cameroon's Gross Domestic Product was more than $1,000 million, of which about 40 per cent was derived from agriculture, forestry and fishing, while industry accounted for about 10 per cent. In the preceding decade industrial output grew annually by about 15 per cent, and G.D.P. had a real annual growth rate of 4-5 per cent.

The floating of the French franc in January 1974 led to an equivalent float of the CFA franc.

Cameroon is an associate member of the EEC; and a member of the OAU and UDEAC.

Transport and Communications

Routes in former East Cameroon are linked with those of the ex-French Equatorial states while former West Cameroon is linked to Nigeria. The main rail links are between Douala and Yaoundé, and Yaoundé and Belabo. An extension from Belabo to Ngaoundéré, part of the trans-Cameroon railway project, was opened to traffic in February 1974. It may eventually run into Chad. A major road also links the two regions. British and French shipping lines call at Douala and Victoria. There are internal and international air services.

Social Welfare

The Government and Christian Missions maintain hospitals and medical centres but there are no welfare services covering the whole population.

Education

Education is provided by the Government and missionary societies and is free. In 1974 about 80 per cent of school-age children attended school. The different systems (French and British) used at present should be harmonized by 1976. A Federal University was established in 1962 and in addition some students go to France, U.S.A., U.S.S.R., and the United Kingdom for higher education.

Tourism

Tourists are attracted by the cultural diversity of local customs, and by the national parks, game reserves and sandy beaches. The tourist trade is being expanded and in 1971–72 there were about 10,000 visitors. A visa is required by all foreigners.

Public Holidays

1974: August 15th (Assumption Day), October 1st (to commemorate Reunification), October 19th (Djoulde Soumae, End of Ramadan), November 1st (All Saints' Day), December 10th (Human Rights Day), December 25th (Christmas), December 26th (Festival of Sheep).

1975: January 1st (Independence), February 11th (Youth Day), March 28th (Good Friday), March 31st (Easter Monday), May 1st (Labour Day), May 8th (Ascension), May 19th (Whit Monday), May 20th (National Day).

Weights and Measures

The metric system is in force.

Currency and Exchange Rates

100 centimes=1 franc de la Communauté financière africaine (CFA).

Exchange rates (April 1974):
1 franc CFA=2 French centimes;
£1 sterling=579.75 francs CFA;
U.S. $1=245.625 francs CFA.

STATISTICAL SURVEY

AREA AND POPULATION

AREA	ESTIMATED MID-YEAR POPULATION					
	1965	1966	1967	1968	1969	1970
475,442 sq. km.*	5,309,000	5,415,000	5,522,000	5,631,000	5,736,000	5,836,000

* 183,569 square miles.
Yaoundé (capital) 178,000; Douala 250,000.

EMPLOYMENT
(1971)

	MEN	WOMEN	TOTAL
Agriculture	30,440	1,617	32,057
Extractive Industries . .	156	—	156
Manufactures	10,257	1,089	11,346
Chemical Industries . .	4,895	421	5,316
Public Works . . .	6,863	49	6,912
Electrical Industries . .	1,950	133	2,083
Transport	12,260	171	12,431
Commerce	9,295	1,337	10,632
Public Service . . .	n.a.	n.a.	15,623
Others	2,208	292	2,500

AGRICULTURE
PRINCIPAL CROPS
(metric tons)

	1968	1969	1970
Cocoa*	65,620	73,820	130,000
Cocoa By-products* . .	15,590	19,150	26,600
Coffee*	73,500	68,450	84,000
Bananas*	38,760	46,510	130,000
Cotton	18,840	22,590	38,390
Timber*	364,100	432,480	n.a.
Rubber	12,779	12,977	11,541
Palm Oil	21,588	16,532	23,434
Palm products . . .	23,442	16,912	7,357
Groundnuts	6,122	14,965	23,500
Tea	1,072	980	1,184

* Exports.

LIVESTOCK
(1971–72—'000 head)

Cattle	2,600
Sheep and Goats	3,780
Pigs	330
Poultry (1970)	5,190

Sea Fisheries: (1967) 11,830 tons, (1968) 14,963 tons, (1970) 21,200 tons, (1972) 15,000 tons.

MINING

	1968	1969	1970
Gold, refined (grammes) .	16,370	7,300	15,000
Cassiterite ore, 66% (kg.) .	51,000	41,600	40,000
Aluminium, refined (tons) .	48,324	46,736	52,373

In 1972 46,220 tons of refined aluminium were produced.

FINANCE

100 centimes = 1 franc de la Communauté financière africaine (CFA).
Coins: 1, 2, 5, 10, 25, 50 and 100 francs CFA.
Notes: 100, 500, 1,000, 5,000 and 10,000 francs CFA.
Exchange rates (April 1974): 1 franc CFA = 2 French centimes;
£1 sterling = 579.75 francs CFA; U.S. $1 = 245.625 francs CFA.
1,000 francs CFA = £1.725 = $4.071.

BUDGETS
(million francs CFA)

	1969–70	1970–71	1971–72	1972–73
Revenue . .	36,983	38,500	45,300	52,700
Expenditure . .	33,034	38,500	45,300	52,700

THIRD FIVE–YEAR PLAN
(1971–76—million francs CFA)

Agriculture	20,720
Forestry	5,210
Stockbreeding	3,670
Industry and Mineral Prospecting .	51,500
Power and Oil Refining . . .	18,700
Roads and Bridges	26,400
Railways	15,900
Ports	6,500
Telecommunications . . .	6,300
Civil Aeronautics and Meteorology .	3,500
Education	21,500
Housing	15,000
Town Planning	11,400
Health	6,500
Total (incl. others)	280,000*

* 149,000 million will be publicly financed and 131,000 million privately financed.

BALANCE OF PAYMENTS
('ooo francs CFA)

	1969 Credit	1969 Debit	1969 Balance	1970 Credit	1970 Debit	1970 Balance
Goods and Services:						
Merchandise . . .	50,654,006	46,237,181	4,416,825	60,743,000	55,238,000	5,505,000
Freight on Merchandise .	3,171,312	4,994,903	— 1,823,591	2,935,000	11,763,000	— 8,828,000
Transport . . .	942,954	2,884,718	— 1,941,764	2,651,000	3,365,000	— 714,000
Insurance . . .	1,544,920	2,733,466	— 1,188,546	1,760,000	3,205,000	— 1,445,000
Travel	1,439,657	4,175,076	— 2,735,419	2,384,000	2,496,000	— 112,000
Revenue and Interest .	1,129,456	1,241,780	— 112,324	1,019,000	1,719,000	— 700,000
Salaries . . .	1,601,980	4,798,798	— 3,196,818	2,005,000	4,361,000	— 2,356,000
Other Services . .	6,381,915	7,868,822	— 1,486,907	5,079,000	9,736,000	— 4,657,000
Government Activities .	112,294	3,236,194	— 3,123,900	385,000	3,273,000	— 2,888,000
Gifts	1,234,466	189,248	— 1,045,218	2,518,000	163,000	— 2,355,000
Total . . .	68,212,960	78,360,186	—10,147,226	81,479,000	95,319,000	—13,840,000
Capital Sectors . .	5,403,095	1,204,415	4,199,480	7,584,000	2,008,000	5,576,000
Global Total . .	73,616,055	79,564,601	— 5,947,746	89,063,000	97,327,000	— 8,264,000

EXTERNAL TRADE
(million francs CFA)

	1967	1968	1969	1970	1971	1972
Imports . .	46,419	46,220	53,000	67,241	69,352	76,384
Exports . .	39,100	46,723	58,574	62,777	57,283	55,699

PRINCIPAL COMMODITIES

Imports	1969	1970	1971	Exports	1969	1970	1971
Food, Drink, Tobacco .	5,507	5,771	7,301	Cocoa	12,400	18,643	14,177
Energy, Lubricants .	2,761	2,761	3,621	Coffee (arabica) .	3,869	5,471	5,304
Primary Products .	2,424	2,990	3,217	Coffee (robusta) .	8,601	9,317	9,495
Vegetable or Animal				Bananas . . .	1,324	1,683	763
Origin . . .	1,037	1,291	230*	Rubber . . .	982	1,283	1,463
Mineral Origin . .	1,387	1,759	967*	Groundnuts . .	596	633	526
Semi-manufactured Pro-				Tobacco . . .	1,135	n.a.	n.a.
ducts . . .	5,987	7,000	8,574	Cotton Fibre . .	2,877	3,172	4,216
Machinery Parts . .	10,677	16,274	n.a.	Palm and Palm-cabbage			
Transport Equipment .	5,278	6,505	6,627	Oil . . .	367	452	573
Other Equipment .	5,399	9,769	12,228	Tea . . .	79	136	161
Equipment for Agri-				Cocoa Pulp . .	927	1,300	} 1,693
culture. . .	322	332	323	Cocoa Butter . .	3,324	4,745	
Equipment for Indus-				Logs . . .	3,454	4,316	} 4,147
try . .	5,077	9,437	11,905	Sawn and Rolled Wood .	1,174	1,253	
Consumer Products .	21,916	26,064	27,782	Aluminium Ore .	5,059	5,371	5,173
Domestic Salt . .	8,508	9,423	n.a.	Other Products . .	7,055	7,504	n.a.

* Jan.-June.

COUNTRIES

Imports	1969	1970	1971	Exports	1969	1970	1971
France . . .	26,187	28,992	34,950	France . . .	19,153	20,603	17,162
Other EEC Countries .	11,198	12,098	13,350	Other EEC Countries .	24,174	28,109	24,133
Japan. . . .	1,285	1,569	1,122	Japan. . . .	793	1,172	1,708
UDEAC Countries .	2,719	3,508	3,370	UDEAC Countries .	2,846	3,016	3,348
United Kingdom . .	2,305	2,593	2,684	United Kingdom . .	828	1,003	1,210
U.S.A. . . .	3,211	4,639	6,784	U.S.A. . . .	3,486	5,392	5,199

TRANSPORT
RAILWAYS

	1968	1969	1970
Total receipts (million francs CFA) . .	2,247	2,427	2,918
Passengers carried ('000) . .	1,459	1,589	1,842
Passenger-km. (million) . . .	149	171	209
Freight carried ('000 tons) . .	995	994	1,034
Freight ton-km. (million) . .	208	213	270

Source: Données Statistiques, Institut National de la Statistique et des Etudes Economiques, Paris.

ROADS
Motor Vehicles Registered

	1969	1970	1971
Cars	18,442	20,087	21,569
Buses and Coaches . . .	2,110	2,299	2,468
Goods Vehicles . . .	10,942	11,917	12,797

Source: World Road Statistics 1967–1971, International Road Federation, Geneva.

SHIPPING
(Douala)

	1969	1970	1971
Ships entered . . .	1,769	1,862	1,636
Net tonnage ('000) . . .	3,479	3,820	3,703
Passengers disembarked . .	3,379	429	533
Passengers embarked . .	2,230	241	200
Freight loaded ('000 tons) . .	738	728	732
Freight unloaded ('000 tons) . .	950	1,115	1,164

Source: as Railways.

CIVIL AVIATION
(Douala and Yaoundé)

	1969	1970	1971
Aircraft arrivals and departures . .	15,914	15,439	14,476
Passenger arrivals ('000) . .	136	149	159
Freight loaded (tons) . . .	13,849	14,548	14,328
Freight unloaded (tons) . .	5,478	6,664	5,995
Mail carried (tons) . . .	1,045	1,179	1,124

Source: as Railways.

TOURISM

In 1973 there were about 4,000 tourist beds.

EDUCATION

	1970–71		1971–72	
	Schools	Pupils	Schools	Pupils
Primary (East Cameroon):				
Public	1,888			
Catholic . . .	794			
Protestant	621	n.a.	n.a.	n.a.
Other	75			
Secondary:				
Public	45	19,139	50	23,083
Private	124	36,892	141	42,222
Technical:				
Public	53	5,066	55	5,604
Private	66	14,060	78	15,843
Higher	11	2,690	11	3,559

Primary Pupils (1969): *UN estimate* 888,435.

Sources (unless otherwise stated): Direction de la Statistique et de la Comptabilité Nationale, Yaoundé, Ministry of Education and Ministry of Mines and Energy.

THE CONSTITUTION

(Ratified by referendum May 20th, 1972)

The People of Cameroon

Declares that the human being, without distinction as to race, religion, sex or belief, possesses inalienable and sacred rights.

Affirms its attachment to the fundamental freedoms embodied in the Universal Declaration of Human Rights and the United Nations Charter and in particular to the following principles:

Equal rights and obligations for all, and freedom and security for the individual subject to the rights of others and the higher interests of the State. The home and the privacy of all correspondence are inviolate. Freedom of movement. Freedom within the law. Assurance of a fair hearing and that the law may not act retrospectively.

Freedom of belief. Freedom to practise a religion. The State is secular. Freedom of expression, freedom of the press, freedom of assembly, freedom of association, freedom of trade unions under conditions fixed by law.

Protection of the family as the natural basis of society.

The right to education, the provision and control of which is the duty of the State, the right of ownership unless in violation of public interests, and the right and duty to work. The duty of all to share the burden of public expenditure according to his means.

The State guarantees to all citizens of either sex the rights and freedoms set out in the preamble of the Constitution.

I Sovereignty

1. The Federal Republic of Cameroon, constituted from the State of East Cameroon and the State of West Cameroon, shall become a unitary State to be styled the United Republic of Cameroon with effect from the date of entry into force of this Constitution. The Republic shall be one and indivisible, democratic, secular and dedicated to social service. It shall ensure the equality before the law of all its citizens. Provisions that the official languages be French and English, for the motto, flag, national anthem and seal, that the capital be Yaoundé.

2–3. Sovereignty shall be vested in the people who shall exercise it either through the President of the Republic and the members returned by it to the National Assembly or by means of referendum. Elections are by universal suffrage, direct or indirect, by every citizen aged 21 or over in a secret ballot. Political parties or groups may take part in elections subject to the law and the principles of democracy and of national sovereignty and unity.

4. State authority shall be exercised by the President of the Republic and the National Assembly.

II The President of the Republic

5. The President of the Republic, as Head of State and Head of the Government, shall be responsible for the conduct of the affairs of the Republic.

6–7. Candidates for the office of President must hold civic and political rights and be at least 35 years old, and may not hold any other elective office or professional activity. Election is by a majority of votes cast by the people. The President is elected for five years and may be re-elected. Provisions are made for the continuity of office in the case of the President's resignation and for the President of the National Assembly to act as interim President should the President die or be incapacitated.

8–9. Ministers and Vice-Ministers are appointed by the President to whom they are responsible, and they may hold no other appointment. The President is also head of the armed forces, he negotiates and ratifies treaties, may exercise clemency after consultation with the Higher Judicial Council, promulgates and is responsible for the enforcement of laws, is responsible for internal and external security, makes civil and military appointments, provides for necessary administrative services.

10. The President, by reference to the Supreme Court, ensures that all laws passed are constitutional.

11. Provisions whereby the President may declare a State of Emergency or State of Siege.

III The National Assembly

12. The National Assembly shall be renewed every five years, though it may at the instance of the President of the Republic legislate to extend or shorten its term of office. It shall be composed of 120 members elected by universal suffrage.

13–14. Laws shall normally be passed by a simple majority of those present, but if a bill is read a second time at the request of the President of the Republic a majority of the National Assembly as a whole is required.

15–16. The National Assembly shall meet twice a year, each session to last not more than 30 days; in one session it shall approve the budget. It may be recalled to an extraordinary session of not more than 15 days.

17–18. Elections and suitability of candidates and sitting members shall be governed by law.

IV Relations between the Executive and the Legislature

19. Bills may be introduced either by the President of the Republic or by any member of the National Assembly.

20. Reserved to the legislature are: the fundamental rights and duties of the citizen; the law of persons and property; the political, administrative and judicial system in respect of elections to the National Assembly, general regulation of national defence, authorization of penalties and criminal and civil procedure etc., and the organization of the local authorities; currency, the budget, dues and taxes, legislation on public property; economic and social policy; the education system.

21. The National Assembly may empower the President of the Republic to legislate by way of Ordinance for a limited period and for given purposes.

22–26. Other matters of procedure, including the right of the President of the Republic to address the Assembly and of the Ministers and Vice-Ministers to take part in debates.

27–29. The composition and conduct of the Assembly's programme of business. Provisions whereby the Assembly may inquire into governmental activity. The obligation of the President of the Republic to promulgate laws, which shall be published in both languages of the Republic.

30. Provisions whereby the President of the Republic, after consultation with the National Assembly, may submit to referendum certain reform bills liable to have profound repercussions on the future of the Nation and National Institutions.

V The Judiciary

31. Justice is administered in the name of the people. The President of the Republic shall ensure the independence of the judiciary and shall make appointments with the assistance of the Higher Judicial Council.

VI The Supreme Court

32–33. The Supreme Court has powers to uphold the Constitution in such cases as the death or incapacity of the President and the admissability of laws, to give final judgements on appeals on the Judgement of the Court of Appeal and to decide complaints against administrative acts. It may be assisted by experts appointed by the President of the Republic.

VII Impeachment

34. There shall be a Court of Impeachment with jurisdiction to try the President of the Republic for high treason and the Ministers and Vice-Ministers for conspiracy against the security of the State.

VIII The Economic and Social Council

35. There shall be an Economic and Social Council, regulated by the law.

IX Amendment of the Constitution

36–37. Bills to amend the Constitution may be introduced either by the President of the Republic or the National Assembly. The President may decide to submit any amendment to the people by way of a referendum. No procedure to amend the Constitution may be accepted if it tends to impair the republican character, unity or territorial integrity of the State, or the democratic principles by which the Republic is governed.

THE GOVERNMENT

HEAD OF STATE

President: AHMADOU AHIDJO.

CABINET

(April 1974)

Minister of State, Secretary-General at the Presidency: PAUL BIYA.

Minister of State in charge of the Armed Forces: SADOU DAOUDOU.

Minister, Assistant Secretary-General: FRANÇOIS SENGAT-KUO.

Minister of Finance: CHARLES ONANA AWANA.

Minister of Foreign Affairs: VINCENT EFON.

Minister of Territorial Administration: VICTOR AYISSI MVODO.

Minister of Justice: SIMON ACHU ACHIDI.

Minister of Agriculture: JEAN KEUTCHA.

Minister of National Education: BERNARD BIDIAS À NGON.

Minister of Industrial and Commercial Development: YOUSSOUFA DAOUDA.

Minister of Health and Social Welfare: PAUL FOKAM KAMGA.

Minister of Employment and Social Insurance: ENOCH KWAYEB.

Minister of Public Service: FÉLIX SABAL LECCO.

Minister of Equipment, Housing and Lands: PAUL TESSA.

Minister of Planning and Territorial Development: MAIKANO ABDOULAYE.

Minister of Posts and Telecommunications: EMMANUEL EGBE TABI.

Minister of Information and Cultural Affairs: VROUMSIA TCHINAYE.

Minister of Mines and Power: HENRY NAMATA ELANGWE.

Minister charged with Special Functions at the Presidency: ABDOULAYE YADJI.

Minister of Livestock and Industry: SADJO ANGOKAY.

Minister of Youth and Sport: FÉLIX TONYE MBOG.

Minister of Transport: CHRISTIAN BONGWA SONGWE.

Minister-Delegate to the Presidency, with responsibility for Parliamentary Relations: ZACHÉE MONGO SOO.

Minister-Delegate at the State Inspection: GILBERT ANDZE TCHOUNGUI.

Vice-Minister of Health and Public Assistance: Mrs. DELPHINE TSANGA.

Vice-Minister of National Education: MARTIN NGEHA LUMA.

Vice-Minister of Equipment and Housing: KOUANDI ALIOU.

Vice-Minister of Agriculture: JOSEPH AWOUNTI CHONG-WAIN.

Director of the Civil Cabinet at the Presidency (with ministerial rank): PHILEMON BEB A DON.

PROVINCIAL GOVERNORS

Centre-South Province: GABRIEL MOUAFO.
Eastern Province: STANILAS BIAS.
Coastal Province: MARCEL MENGUÉMÉ.
Northern Province: OUSMANE MEY.
North-Western Province: GUILLAUME NSEKE.
Western Province: MARCEL MEDJO AKONO.
South-Western Province: TANDJONG ENOW.

DIPLOMATIC REPRESENTATION

EMBASSIES ACCREDITED TO CAMEROON

(In Yaoundé unless otherwise indicated)

Algeria: Brazzaville, People's Republic of the Congo.

Austria: Lagos, Nigeria.

Belgium: B.P. 816; *Ambassador:* PIERRE BRANCART.

Canada: B.P. 572; *Ambassador:* PIERRE ASSELIN.

Central African Republic: B.P. 396; *Ambassador:* JEAN-MICHEL BENZOT (also accred. to Gabon and Nigeria).

Chad: Bangui, Central African Republic.

China, People's Republic: *Ambassador:* CHAO HSING-CHIH.

Egypt: B.P. 809; *Ambassador:* MOHAMED MOUSTAPHA OAF EL ASHRI.

Equatorial Guinea: *Ambassador:* GUSTAVO WATSON BUEKO.

Finland: Lagos, Nigeria.

France: B.P. 102; *Ambassador:* JACQUES DUPUY.

Gabon: B.P. 4130; *Ambassador:* JEAN-FÉLICIEN OLOUNA.

Germany, Federal Republic: B.P. 1160; *Ambassador:* HANS-GERO VON HORTSMANN.

Ghana: *Ambassador:* Col. SAMUEL ASANTE.

Greece: *Ambassador:* SATHIS MITSOPOULOS.

Guinea: Lagos, Nigeria.

India: Lagos, Nigeria.

Italy: B.P. 827; *Ambassador:* Guido Natali.

Japan: Kinshasa, Zaire.

Korea, Democratic People's Republic: *Ambassador:* Van Ba Kiem.

Korea, Republic: *Ambassador:* Moon Chulsoon.

Lebanon: Dakar, Senegal.

Lesotho: Nairobi, Kenya.

Liberia: B.P. 1185; *Ambassador:* Peter Thomson.

Mali: Brazzaville, People's Republic of the Congo.

Malta: *Ambassador:* Decase Edouard.

Mauritania: Abidjan, Ivory Coast.

Morocco: Lagos, Nigeria.

Netherlands.

Nigeria: B.P. 448; *Ambassador:* Yusuf Sada.

Norway: Lagos, Nigeria.

Pakistan: Lagos, Nigeria.

Philippines: Lagos, Nigeria.

Saudi Arabia: Lagos, Nigeria.

Spain: B.P. 877; *Ambassador:* Carmelo Matesanz.

Sudan: Lagos, Nigeria.

Sweden: Kinshasa, Zaire.

Switzerland: Lagos, Nigeria.

Tunisia: *Ambassador:* Mohammed Ridha Bach-Baouab.

Turkey: Lagos, Nigeria.

U.S.S.R.: B.P. 488; *Ambassador:* Aleksandr Malychev.

United Kingdom: B.P. 547; *Ambassador:* E. F. Given, c.m.g.

U.S.A.: B.P. 817; *Ambassador:* Robert Moore.

Vatican: *Papal Nuncio:* Mgr. Luciano Storero.

Yugoslavia: Brazzaville, People's Republic of the Congo.

Zaire: P.O.B. 639; *Ambassador:* Tuma-Wahu Dia Baziha.

Cameroon also has diplomatic relations with Bangladesh, Denmark, Ethiopia, German Democratic Republic, Libya, Monaco, Tanzania, Uganda, Democratic Republic of Viet-Nam and the Provisional Revolutionary Government of South Viet-Nam.

NATIONAL ASSEMBLY

President: Solomon Tandeng Muna.

Election, May 18th, 1973

All 120 seats were won by the *Union nationale camerounaise.*

ECONOMIC AND SOCIAL COUNCIL

The Economic and Social Council is a national body set up under the unitary constitution to advise the Government on economic and social problems arising. It replaces the regional organizations which carried out similar functions on a smaller scale. The Council consists of 65 members, who meet several times a year, a permanent secretariat and a president appointed by Presidential decree. The members are nominated for a five-year term, whilst the secretariat is elected annually.

POLITICAL PARTY

Union nationale camerounaise (UNC): Yaoundé; f. 1966 by merger of the governing party of each state of the Federation (*Union camerounaise* and the *Kamerun National Democratic Party*), two opposition parties in East Cameroon (the *Parti démocratique camerounais* and the *Cameroon Socialists*), and the two opposition parties in West Cameroon (the *Cameroon Union Congress* and the *Cameroon People's National Congress*, which had already agreed in August 1965 to co-operate with the ruling KNDP in West Cameroon); its bodies are: Congress which meets every five years, Political Bureau, National Council which includes the Political Bureau, sectional presidents, members of the National Assembly, members of the Government and the President of the Economic Council; Pres. Ahmadou Ahidjo; publ. *l'Unité* (weekly).

The UNC Charter, outlining the party's internal and external policies, was published in April, 1969. It supports efforts towards the liberation and unification of Africa; it supports a democratic system of government within Cameroon; and it lays down that economic and social development should be achieved in Cameroon through encouraging private initiative while reserving for the state a determining and organizing role.

JUDICIAL SYSTEM

Supreme Court: Yaoundé; consists of a President, titular and substitute judges (7 at present), a *Procureur Général*, an *Avocat Général*, deputies to the *Procureur Général*, a Registrar and clerks.

President of the Supreme Court: Marcel Nguini.

Procureur Général: François-Xavier Mbouyom.

Avocat Général: Georges Simon Ekema.

High Court of Justice: Yaoundé; consists of 9 titular judges and 6 substitute judges, all elected by the National Assembly.

RELIGION

It is estimated that 45 per cent of the population follow traditional animist beliefs, 20 per cent are Muslims and 35 per cent Christians, Roman Catholics comprising 21 per cent of the total population.

Roman Catholic Missions: The total number of Roman Catholics is about 1,122,570 (including 26,368 catechumens). The Pères du Sacré-Coeur de Saint-Quentin, the Pères du Saint-Esprit, the Oblats de Marie-Immaculée, the Société de St. Joseph de Mill-Hill and the Petits Frères du Père de Foucauld are the most active missionary orders. There is a seminary for African priests at Nkol-Bisson and a Trappist monastery at Koutaba. The total number of priests (including Africans) is about 870.

Archbishop of Yaoundé: Mgr. Jean Zoa; B.P. 207, Yaoundé.

BISHOPS

Bafia: Mgr. ANDRÉ LOUCHEUR.

Bafoussam: Mgr. DENIS NGANDE.

Bamenda: Mgr. PAUL VERDZEKOV.

Buea: Mgr. JULIUS PEETERS.

Douala: Mgr. SIMON TONYE.

Doumé: Mgr. LAMBERT VAN HEYGEN.

Garoua: Mgr. YVES PLUMEY.

Mbalmayo: Mgr. PAUL ETOGA.

N'Kongsamba: (vacant).

Sangmélima: Mgr. PIERRE-CELESTIN NKOU.

Protestant Churches: There are about 600,000 Protestants, with about 3,000 Church and Mission workers, and four theological schools.

Fédération Évangélique du Cameroun et de l'Afrique Équatoriale: B.P. 491, Yaoundé; Admin. Sec. Pastor MOUBITANG À MEPOUI, includes the following:

Église Presbytérienne Camerounaise: B.P. 519, Yaoundé; Sec.-Gen. Pastor BOKAGNE.

Église Évangélique du Cameroun: B.P. 89, Douala; Sec.-Gen. J. KOTTO.

Union des Églises Baptistes du Cameroun: B.P. 7, New-Bell, Douala; Pres. P. MBENDE.

Mission Protestante Norvégienne: B.P. 6, Ngaoundéré; Pres. ERIK LARSEN.

The Sudan Mission: B.P. 9, Meiganga; Pres. TH. NOSTBAKKEN.

Mission Fraternelle Luthérienne: B.P. 8, Kaélé; Pres. M. STENNES.

Mission Unie du Sudan: Mokolo; Pres. E. EICHEN-BERGER.

Mission Baptiste Européenne: B.P. 82, Maroua; Pres. M. STAÜBLI.

Église Presbytérienne du Cameroun Occidental: P.O.B. 19, Buea; Moderator Rev. KANGSEN.

Église Protestante Africaine: B.P. 26, Lolodorf; Pastor NZHIOU OTTO FRANCK.

Église Evangélique Luthérienne du Cameroun: B.P. 6, Ngaoundéré; Pres. JOSEPH MEDOUKAN.

THE PRESS

DAILY

Cameroon Times: P.O.B. 200, Victoria; f. 1960; circ. 6,000; English; Editor JEROME F. GWELLEM.

La Presse du Cameroun: B.P. 584, Douala; f. 1956; French and English; circ. 12,000; Editor CHRISTIAN DE GASPERIS.

PERIODICALS

Abbia: Yaoundé; f. 1963; cultural; weekly.

Le Bamiléké: B.P. 94, Dschang; every two months.

Bulletin de la Chambre d'Agriculture, de l'Elevage et des Forêts du Cameroun: B.P. 287, Yaoundé; monthly.

Bulletin de la Chambre de Commerce d'Industrie et des Mines du Cameroun: B.P. 4011, Douala; monthly.

Bulletin de Statistique Générale: B.P. 660, Yaoundé.

L'Effort Camerounais: B.P. 345, Yaoundé; f. 1955; Roman Catholic weekly; Dir. J. PAUL BAYEMI; circ. 5,000.

L'Informateur National: B.P. 392, Yaoundé; every two months.; circ. 2,000.

Journal Officiel de la République du Cameroun: Imprimerie du Gouvernement, Yaoundé; weekly.

Mefoe: Elat, Ebolowa; monthly; circ. 3,200.

Miñañ: Elat, Ebolowa; monthly; circ. 1,000.

Le Monde Noir: B.P. 736, Yaoundé.

Mwendi Ma Baptiste: Mondoungue; monthly; circ. 1,000.

Nku-Tam-Tam: Imprimerie Coulouma et Cie., B.P. 134, Yaoundé; bi-monthly; circ. 4,000.

Les Nouvelles du Mungo: B.P. 1, N'Kongsamba; monthly; circ. 3,000.

Le Peuple Camerounais: Yaoundé; weekly; circ. 2,000.

La Semaine Camerounaise: B.P. 1068, Yaoundé; Protestant weekly; circ. 4,000.

L'Unité: Yaoundé; organ of *Union nationale camerounaise*; weekly.

La Voix des Jeunes: Imprimerie St.-Paul-Mvolyé, B.P. 550, Yaoundé; weekly; circ. 2,000.

NEWS AGENCIES

Agence Camerounaise de Presse: B.P. 1170, Yaoundé; Dir. (vacant).

FOREIGN BUREAU

AFP (*France*): B.P. 229, Immeuble le Concorde, Ave. du President J. F. Kennedy, Yaoundé; Corr. PIERRE MENOU.

Tass is also represented in Cameroon.

PUBLISHERS

Editions CLE: B.P. 1501, Yaoundé; f. 1963; Protestant-financed; sociology, African affairs and customs, original fiction and Christian literature.

Librairie Saint Paul: B.P. 763, Yaoundé; education, medicine, philosophy, politics, religion and fiction.

UNESCO Publishing Centre: B.P. 808, Yaoundé; f. 1961; official educational publications and printing training.

RADIO

Radiodiffusion du Cameroun: B.P. 281, Yaoundé; Government service; Dir. EMMANUEL CHOTCHOM MOUDJIH.

Radio Cameroun: B.P. 281, Yaoundé; programmes in French, English and local languages; Dirs. RICHARD EKOKA, SAM EWANDA, M. KANDEM.

Radio Douala: B.P. 986, Douala; programmes in French, English, Douala, Bassa, Ewondo and Bamiléké; Dir. CÉLESTIN-LUCIEN SACK.

Radio Garoua: B.P. 103, Garoua; programmes in French, Hausa and Foulfoudé; Dir. BELLO MAL GANA.

Radio Buéa: P.O.B. 86, Buea; programmes in English, French, Bali, Douala and other local languages; Dir. NGIEWIH ASUNKWAN.

In 1972 there were 214,000 radio receivers.

FINANCE

BANKING

Banque des Etats de l'Afrique Centrale: 29 rue du Colisée, Paris 8, France; B.P. 83, Yaoundé; f. 1973 as the Central Bank of issue of five African states; 4 brs. in Cameroon; cap. 1,250m. francs CFA; Dir. MARCEL YONDO; Gen. Man. CHRISTIAN JOUDIOU; Asst. Gen. Man. J.-E. SATHOUD.

Banque Internationale pour le Commerce et l'Industrie du Cameroun: B.P. 5, Ave. du Président Ahidjo, Yaoundé; f. 1962; affiliated to the Banque Nationale de Paris, Société Financière pour les Pays d'Outre-Mer and Barclays Bank International; 15 brs.; cap. 625m. francs CFA; Pres. T. BOUKAR; Man. Dir. EMMANUEL MOUTERDE.

Cameroon Bank Ltd.: Buéa; 4 brs.; Dir.-Gen. G. M. KWENDE.

Société Camerounaise de Banque: B.P. 145, rue Monseigneur Vogt, Yaoundé; f. 1961; deposit bank; cap. 800m. francs CFA; res. 118m. francs CFA (1972); 18 brs.; Pres. A. FOUDA; Gen. Man. ROBERT PLISSON.

Société Générale de Banques au Cameroun: B.P. 244, rue Monseigneur Vogt, Yaoundé; f. 1963; cap. 400m. francs CFA; res. 331m. francs CFA (1972); 12 brs.; Chair. EL-HADJ AHMADOU HAYATOU; Dir.-Gen. R. DUCHEMIN.

FOREIGN BANKS

Banque Internationale pour l'Afrique Occidentale: 9 ave. de Messine, Paris; ave. de Gaulle, B.P. 4001, Douala; Dir. in Cameroon GUY LECUYER, B.P. 182, Yaoundé.

Standard Bank of West Africa Ltd.: 10 Clements Lane, London, EC4N 7AB; B.P. 5348, rue Joffre, Douala; br. in Victoria.

DEVELOPMENT BANKS

Banque Camerounaise de Développement: B.P. 55, Yaoundé; f. 1951; 75.5 per cent state-owned; gives financial and technical assistance to development projects; cap. 1,500m. francs CFA; Pres. OUSMANE MEY; Dir.-Gen. TITTI GOTTLIEB.

Société Financière pour le Développement du Cameroun: B.P. 5493, Douala.

Société Nationale d'Investissement du Cameroun: B.P. 423, place El Hadj Ahmadou Ahidjo, Yaoundé; f. 1964; invests in and grants loans to new and expanding concerns; cap. 250m. francs CFA; Pres. Dir.-Gen. LAURENT NTAMAG.

INSURANCE

Agence Camerounaise d'Assurances: rue de l'Hippodrome, Yaoundé, B.P. 209; cap. p.u. 8m. f. CFA; Dir. CLAUDE GERMAIN.

Assurances Générales (Chanas et Privat): B.P. 109, Douala; cap. p.u. 3m. f. CFA; 3 agencies.

Les Assureurs-Conseils Camerounais (Faugère, Jutheau et Cie.): B.P. 544, Douala.

Caisse Centrale de Coopération Economique: Yaoundé, B.P. 46; Dir. JOSEPH PAOLINI.

Caisse Nationale de Réassurances: Yaoundé, B.P. 4180; Dir. MARCEL YONDO.

SA E. Casalegno et Cie.: Douala, B.P. 443; Dir. EMILE CASALEGNO; cap. p.u. 5m. f. CFA.

Mutuelle Agricole Camerounaise (MACAM): Yaoundé.

TRADE AND INDUSTRY

CHAMBERS OF COMMERCE

Chambre d'Agriculture, de l'Elevage et des Forêts du Cameroun: B.P. 287, Parc Repiquet, Yaoundé; 44 mems.; Pres. EPHREM MBA; Sec. LOUIS WAMBO; publ. *Bulletin* (monthly).

Chambre de Commerce, d'Industrie et des Mines du Cameroun: B.P. 4011, Douala; f. 1963; 138 mems., 100 in East Cameroon and 38 in West Cameroon; Pres. PAUL MONTHÉ; Sec.-Gen. JEAN MARIE TEDJONG; publ. *Bulletin Mensuel, Commerce Extérieur.*

EMPLOYERS' ASSOCIATIONS

Groupement Interprofessionnel pour l'Etude et la Co-ordination des Intérêts Economiques de Cameroun: B.P. 829, Douala; f. 1957; 101 member associations; Pres. BERNARD CRETIN.

Syndicat des Commerçants Importateurs-Exportateurs du Cameroun: B.P. 562, Douala; Sec.-Gen. P. GIRMA.

Syndicat des Industriels du Cameroun: B.P. 673, Douala; f. 1953; Pres. M. NORGUIN, Mme DE PIERREBOURG.

Syndicat des Producteurs et Exportateurs de Bois: B.P. 1134, Yaoundé; Pres. M. PRION.

Syndicats Professionnels Forestiers et Activités connexes du Cameroun: B.P. 100, Douala.

Union des Syndicats Professionels du Cameroun: B.P. 829, Douala; Pres. MOUKOKO KINGUE.

West Cameroon Employers Association: Tiko.

TRADE UNION

National Union of Cameroon Workers (*Union nationale des travailleurs du Cameroun—UNTC*): Yaoundé; f. 1971; affiliated to *Union nationale camerounaise*; Pres. M. SATOUGLÉ.

DEVELOPMENT ORGANIZATIONS

Cameroons Development Corporation: Bota, Victoria; f. 1947; a statutory authority responsible for the development of 12 plantations of rubber, oil palms, bananas, tea and pepper as a commercial enterprise on 30,643 hectares leased from the Government, due to increase to 33,000 hectares in 1974; negotiations with World Bank and Fond Européen de Développement concluded in 1967 ensure tripled production by 1980; employs 13,000 people; production in metric tons for 1972–73 was: bananas 14,300, palm oil 13,000, palm kernels 3,357, rubber 9,800, tea 796, pepper 49; Chair. NFON V. E. MUKETE; Gen. Man. M. W. F. LEBURN.

Société d'Expansion et de Modernisation de la Riziculture de Yagoury—SEMRY: B.P. 46, Yagoua; expansion of rice-growing in areas where irrigation is possible and commercialization of rice products; Pres. O. MEY; Dir.-Gen. G. MAH DAVI.

West Cameroon Development Agency: f. 1956; makes loans for economic development projects and training schemes; undertakes economic development projects; Gen. Man. T. F. S. KINGA; Chair. V. C. NEHAMI.

PRINCIPAL CO-OPERATIVE ORGANIZATIONS

Bakweri Co-operative Union of Farmers Ltd.: Dibanda, Tiko; produce marketing co-operative for bananas, cocoa and coffee; 14 societies, 2,000 mems.; Pres. Dr. E. M. L. ENDELEY.

Cameroon Co-operative Exporters Ltd.: P.O.B. 19, Kumba; f. 1953; mems. 8 societies; central agency for marketing of members' coffee, cocoa and palm kernels; Man. A. B. ENYONG; Sec. M. M. EYOH (acting).

Coopérative des Planteurs Bamoun du Café Arabica—CPBCA: Foumbot; f. 1942; body for buying, processing and marketing of coffee; Dir. ALAIN CLAVEL.

Coopérative des Planteurs de Café Arabica de Bafoussam—CPCAB: Bafoussam; f. 1958; Dir. CHRISTIAN FENKAM.

Co-operative Union of Western Cameroon Ltd.: policy-making and auditing body for all the societies in the Territory.

Société Africaine de Prévoyance: Yaoundé; a provident society with branches in each region for each particular activity.

West Cameroon Co-operative Association Ltd.: P.O.B. 135, Kumba; founded as central financing body of the Co-operative movement; gives short-term credits to member societies and provides agricultural services for members; policy-making body for the Co-operative Movement in W. Cameroon; 143 member unions and societies with total membership of about 45,000; member of International Co-operative Alliance; Pres. Chief T. E. NJEA.

There are 83 co-operatives for the harvesting and sale of bananas and coffee and for providing mutual credit.

TRANSPORT

RAILWAYS

There are 1,164 km. of one-metre gauge track, the North Line running from Douala to N'Kongsamba (172 km.), with a branch line leading north-east from Mbanga to Kumba (29 km.), and the Centre Line which forms the first stage of the Transcameroon railway and runs from Douala to Belabo (601 km.), with a branch line leading south-west from Otélé to Mbalmayo. The second stage of the Transcameroon railway, from Belabo to Ngaoundéré (325 km.), was opened to traffic in February 1974, and in the future it is to be extended eventually into Chad, to Sahr. In addition an extension of its western branch is projected from Mbalmayo to Bangui, capital of the Central African Republic. Improvements to the line between Douala and Yaoundé will begin in 1974. Narrow gauge railways totalling 147 km. are used in former West Cameroon between the plantations and the ports.

Régie Nationale des Chemins de Fer du Cameroun—REGIFERCAM: B.P. 304, Douala; Dir. A. DESTOPPELEIRE.

Office du Chemin de Fer Transcamerounais: B.P. 625, Yaoundé; supervises the laying of new railway lines and improvements to existing lines and undertakes research in the connection; Dir.-Gen. JEAN BAYON.

ROADS

In 1971, there were 1,050 km. of bitumen-surfaced roads, 5,200 km. of unsurfaced secondary roads and 17,000 km. of unclassified roads. The unclassified roads are maintained by local authorities.

Under the 1971–76 Plan emphasis has been laid on the development of the road network, particularly on the completion of a road linking the north and the south of the country.

SHIPPING

Office National des Ports/National Ports Authority: 5 blvd. Leclerc, B.P. 4020, Douala; Pres. C. BONGWA; Dir.-Gen. S. NGANN YONN.

The port of Douala-Bonaberi has a capacity of 2 million metric tons, traffic in 1972 totalling 1,872,000 tons; it has 1,837 metres of quays and a minimum depth of 5 metres in the channels, 8.5 metres at the quays. There are also ports at Kribi and at Victoria and Tiko, which are to be extended and modernized.

Barber West Africa Line: B.P. 4059, Douala.

Mory et Cie.: rue Joffre, B.P. 572.

SAMOA: blvd. Leclerc, B.P. 1127, Douala; agents for Lloyd Triestino, Black Star Line, Seven Stars Line, Gold Star Line, Europe Africa Line.

Société Africaine de Transit et d'Affrètement (SATA): Blvd. Leclerc, B.P. 546, Douala.

Société Camerounaise de Navigation—SOCANA: B.P. 263, Douala; Dir. PIERRE LAIGO.

Société Navale Chargeurs Delmas-Vieljeux—SNCDV: B.P. 263, rue Kitchener, Douala and B.P. 18, Kribi; Dir. PIERRE LAIGO.

Société Ouest-Africaine d'Entreprises Maritimes (Cameroun)—SOAEM: B.P. 4057, rue du Roi Albert, Douala; f. 1959; Dir. JACQUES FROISSANT.

SOCOPAO (Cameroun): B.P. 215, Douala; agents for Palm/Elder/Hoegh Lines, Bank Line, Dafra Line, Marasia S.A., Splosna Plovba, Greek West Africa Line, Veb Deutsche Seerederei, Polish Ocean Lines, Westwind Africa Line, Nautilus Keller Line, Estonian Shipping Co., A.G.T.I. Paris, K-Line Tokyo, Supermarine A/S.

CIVIL AVIATION

Cameroon's principal airport is at Douala, where a new airport is under construction. Another major airport exists at Yaoundé which is capable of taking Caravelles, and there are about 20 smaller airports.

Cameroon Airlines: B.P. 4092, Douala; f. 1971; owned by the Cameroon Government (70 per cent) and Air France (30 per cent); services to Paris, Marseilles, Rome, Abidjan, Brazzaville, Libreville, Dakar and N'Djamena (Fort-Lamy), and domestic flights; fleet of one Boeing 707, two Boeing 737, two DC-4 and one Convair 440; Pres. Dir.-Gen. SAMUEL EBOUA.

Cameroon is also served by the following foreign airlines: Air Afrique, Air Mali, Air Zaire, Alitalia, Lufthansa, Pan American, Sabena, Swissair and UTA.

TOURISM

In 1973 there were 4,000 tourist beds.

Commissariat-Général au Tourisme: B.P. 266, Yaoundé; f. 1970; provincial offices: B.P. 1310, Douala; B.P.92, Buea; B.P. 50, Garoua; Bafoussam; Commissaire-Général AMINOU OUMAROU.

CULTURAL ORGANIZATIONS

The four important centres for the creation, exhibition and sale of works of art are the handicraft centres of Maroua, Foumban, Bamenda and Douala.

L'Ensemble National: c/o le Ministère de la Jeunesse, de la Culture et de l'Education Nationale; the most famous representatives of Cameroonian traditional art.

UNIVERSITY

Université de Yaoundé: B.P. 337, Yaoundé; f. 1962; 260 teachers, 3,277 students.

CANADA

INTRODUCTORY SURVEY

Location, Climate, Language, Religion, Flag, Capital

The Dominion of Canada occupies the northern part of North America (except Alaska and Greenland) and is the second largest country in the world. The border with the U.S.A. follows the upper St. Lawrence Seaway and the Great Lakes, continuing west along the 49th parallel. The climate is an extreme one, particularly inland. Winter temperatures drop well below freezing with a summer average of about 65°F (18°C). Rainfall varies from moderate to light and there are heavy falls of snow. More than 96 per cent of the population are of European origin, mainly British, French, Irish and German. The two official languages are English and French, the mother tongues of 60.2 per cent and 26.9 per cent, respectively, in 1971. More than 98 per cent of Canadians can speak English or French. In 1971 there were 230,900 Indians and 15,000 Eskimos. Forty-six per cent of the people are Roman Catholics. The largest Protestant churches are the United Church of Canada (17.5 per cent) and the Anglicans (11.8 per cent) but almost every Christian denomination is represented. The national flag (proportions 2 by 1) consists of a red maple leaf on a white field, flanked by red panels. The capital is Ottawa.

Recent History

In 1963, a six-year Conservative government was succeeded by a minority Liberal Government under Lester Pearson. Mr. Pearson retired in April 1968 and his successor, Pierre Trudeau, won an electoral majority for the Liberals in June 1968. Mr. Trudeau's party was returned to power in the 1972 General Election, but with a reduced majority over the Progressive Conservatives. Foreign relations have altered significantly under the Trudeau government, with less emphasis on traditional links with Western Europe and the U.S.A. and a fostering of relations with Far East countries. Canada established diplomatic relations with the People's Republic of China in 1970 and the Prime Minister paid a successful state visit to China in October 1973. Relations with the U.S.S.R. are good and in 1973 Japan ranked as Canada's second largest trading partner. Quebec maintains her own cultural and educational links with France, and there has been pressure from some French-speaking Canadians for the separation of Quebec from the other provinces of the Dominion. The Liberals came into power there with a large majority in 1970 and the Quebec Liberation Front was outlawed after violent terrorist activities.

Trudeau was returned with an overall majority in elections in July.

Government

Queen Elizabeth II, Queen of Canada, is the Head of State and is represented at Ottawa by a Governor-General. Parliament consists of the Queen, the Senate and the House of Commons. Senators are appointed on a regional basis until the age of 75. Members of Parliament are elected by universal suffrage. Executive power lies with the Cabinet selected by the Prime Minister. Each of the ten provinces is headed by a Lieutenant-Governor and governed by a unicameral Legislative Assembly, from which the provincial premiers and cabinets are chosen. Two directly-administered areas, the Yukon Territory and the Northwest Territories, are represented by one member in the Federal House of Commons and locally by a Commissioner.

Defence

Canada co-operates with the U.S.A. in the defence of North America, sends forces to NATO's Atlantic and European sectors, and takes part in UN peace-keeping in the Middle East. Unification of the all-volunteer services as the Canadian Armed Forces was completed in 1968. The total strength of the Canadian Armed Forces has been progressively reduced from 120,000 in 1964 to 82,000 in 1974. The defence budget for 1973–74 was C$2,143 million.

Economic Affairs

The Canadian economy is linked very closely with that of the U.S.A. About 70 per cent of total trade is with the U.S.A. and industry is heavily dependent on foreign investment, 80 per cent of it American. It is estimated that 65 per cent of Canada's largest companies are wholly-owned or effectively controlled by foreign corporations. Efforts to develop other markets, notably Japan, China and the U.S.S.R., and measures such as the Foreign Investments Review Act, which allows for assessment of the benefits to Canada of foreign investors' intentions, are being taken to lessen dependence on the U.S.A. Canada is one of the world's leading industrial countries, although farming still accounts for about 4 per cent of the country's gross domestic product and is the leading primary industry in terms of employment. Canada is the world's fourth largest exporter of agricultural products. The main exports in 1972 were motor vehicles and parts, lumber, newsprint, petroleum and wheat. Canada is the world's largest producer of asbestos, silver, nickel and zinc and is rich in many other minerals, notably iron, copper, uranium, cobalt, elemental sulphur, lead and gold. There are considerable oil and gas resources in Alberta and the Canadian Arctic islands. Although Canada is tenth in world crude oil production, it is Canada's leading mineral in dollar value. Other valuable primary industries are forestry, fishing and fur production. In 1973, for the third successive year, the economy expanded at a rate above its average long-term rate and, while suffering a slightly lower rate of inflation than that of comparable economies, enjoyed one of the highest expansion rates of an industrialized country. Prospects for 1974 are for a less hectic rate of expansion, but a favourable economic position in relation to the major industrial countries.

Transport and Communications

Owing to the size of the country, Canada's economy is particularly dependent upon good communications. Canada's rail, river and canal system is being increasingly supplemented by roads, air services and pipelines. The

St. Lawrence Seaway allows ocean-going ships to reach the Great Lakes; the Trans-Canadian Highway is one of the major features of a network of over half a million miles of roads in Canada. Nearly 600,000 miles of track provide an extensive rail service throughout the country. A railway is being planned to open up north-western British Colombia. Work started in 1970 on a new airport near Montreal and 66,000 miles of gas and oil pipelines have been built since 1950. The North West Passage was negotiated for the first time in 1969, and as a result the Arctic Waters Bill was passed in April 1971 giving Canada effective control of the passage and extending territorial waters from three miles offshore to twelve. Internal air services for freight and passengers play a major role in a country the size of Canada.

Social Welfare

About 25 per cent of the federal budget is devoted to health and welfare. The Federal Government administers family allowances, unemployment insurance and war veterans' and old age pensions. Other services are provided by the provinces, the range varying from province to province. The Canada Pension Plan, introduced in 1966, and its Quebec counterpart provide contributory retirement, disability and survivors' pensions for the majority of workers, based on past earnings. A Federal Medicare nsurance programme in which all ten provinces participate covers all Canadians against medical expenses. The federal-provincial hospital insurance programme covers over 99 per cent of the insurable population of Canada.

Education

Education is a provincial matter and the period of compulsory education varies. French-speaking students are entitled by law to instruction in French. Primary education is from 6–7 years to 13–14, followed by 3–5 years at secondary or high school. There are 72 degree-awarding institutions and 340 affiliated or independent colleges.

Tourism

Canada offers a wide range of outdoor tourist attractions: fishing, hunting, riding, canoeing, etc., in the great National Parks. Winter sports carnivals are held in many centres and Indian and Prairie gatherings are popular, a famous one being the Calgary Stampede. Most visitors are from the U.S.A. (over 38 million in 1971) and tourist spending in 1972 amounted to Canadian $1,283 million.

Visas are not required to visit Canada by nationals of Austria, Belgium, Denmark, Finland, France, German Federal Republic, Greece, Iceland, Ireland, Italy, Japan, Liechtenstein, Luxembourg, Netherlands, Norway, Portugal, South Africa, Spain, Sweden, Switzerland, Turkey, United Kingdom and Commonwealth and U.S.A.

Sport

The national sports are Canadian football and ice hockey. Baseball, tennis, athletics and winter and water sports are all popular and soccer is increasingly played, particularly in southern Ontario. In 1976 the Olympic Games will be held at Montreal.

Public Holidays

1974: September 3rd (Labour Day), October 8th (Thanksgiving Day), November 11th (Remembrance Day), December 25th–26th (Christmas).

1975: January 1st (New Year), March 28th (Good Friday), March 31st (Easter Monday), May 20th (Victoria Day), July 1st (Dominion Day).

Weights and Measures

The imperial system is in general use with the exception of the 2,000 lb. American ton; the introduction of the metric system is under consideration.

Currency and Exchange Rates

100 cents = 1 Canadian dollar (C $).

Exchange rates (April 1974):

£1 sterling = C $2.293;

U.S. $1 = 97.17 Canadian cents.

STATISTICAL SURVEY

Source: Statistics Canada, Ottawa.

AREA AND POPULATION

AREA (sq. miles)			POPULATION	VITAL STATISTICS (1972)		
Total	Land	Water	Estimate (June 1973)	Birth Rate per '000	Marriage Rate per '000	Death Rate per '000
3,851,809	3,560,238	291,571	22,095,000	15.9	8.7	7.4

CHIEF CITIES

(Metropolitan population: 1972 est.)

Ottawa (capital)	613,000	Edmonton	507,000	London	290,000
Montreal	2,761,000	Hamilton	505,000	Windsor	262,000
Toronto	2,672,000	Quebec	487,000	Kitchener	232,000
Vancouver	1,098,000	Calgary	417,000	Halifax	222,637
Winnipeg	550,000	St. Catherines-Niagara	307,000		

CANADA—(Statistical Survey)

PROVINCES AND TERRITORIES

	AREA (sq. miles)	POPULATION (June 1973 est.)	CAPITAL
PROVINCES:			
Alberta	255,285	1,683,000	Edmonton
British Columbia	366,255	2,315,000	Victoria
Manitoba	251,000	998,000	Winnipeg
New Brunswick	28,354	652,000	Fredericton
Newfoundland	156,185	541,000	St. John's
Nova Scotia	21,425	805,000	Halifax
Ontario	412,582	7,939,000	Toronto
Prince Edward Island . . .	2,184	115,000	Charlottetown
Quebec	594,860	6,081,000	Quebec
Saskatchewan	251,700	908,000	Regina
TERRITORIES:			
Yukon Territory	207,076	20,000	Whitehorse
Northwest Territories . . .	1,304,903	38,000	Yellowknife

IMMIGRATION

COUNTRY OF ORIGIN	1969	1970	1971	1972	1973
United Kingdom . . .	31,977	26,497	15,451	18,197	26,973
United States . . .	22,785	24,424	24,366	22,618	25,242
Other	106,769	96,792	82,083	81,251	131,985
TOTAL . .	161,531	147,713	121,900	122,066	184,200

EMPLOYMENT
('000)

	1970 (average)	1971 (average)	1972 (average)
Agriculture	511	510	481
Other Primary Industries .	218	224	217
Manufacturing . . .	1,790	1,795	1,857
Construction . . .	471	495	501
Transport and Utilities .	692	702	730
Trade	1,320	1,330	1,410
Finance, Insurance and Real Estate	365	385	385
Services	2,025	2,118	2,194
Public Administration . .	486	520	
TOTAL (incl. others) .	7,879	8,079	8,329

AGRICULTURE
LAND USE
(sq. miles)

CROPS	PASTURE	FOREST LAND*	FOREST LAND†	OTHER LAND	TOTAL
107,446	15,977	919,208	298,467	2,219,140	3,560,238

* Suitable for regular harvest.   † Unsuitable for regular harvest.

CANADA—(STATISTICAL SURVEY)

CROPS

		AREA ('000 acres)		PRODUCTION ('000)		YIELD PER ACRE	
		1972	1973	1972	1973	1972	1973
Wheat	bushels	21,350	24,761	533,288	628,738	25.0	25.4
Oats	,,	6,104	6,698	300,208	326,880	49.2	48.8
Barley	,,	12,509	11,958	518,316	474,570	41.4	39.7
Rye	,,	635	634	13,524	14,282	21.3	22.5
Corn	,,	1,327	1,286	99,538	108,941	75.0	84.7
Buckwheat . .	,,	103	89	1,711	1,129	16.6	12.7
Beans	,,	134	133	3,233	2,885	24.1	21.7
Flax	,,	1,321	1,450	17,617	19,400	13.3	13.4
Rapeseed . . .	,,	3,270	3,150	57,300	53,200	17.5	16.9
Potatoes . . .	cwt.	244	262	43,886	46,803	179.8	178.5
Tame Hay . .	tons	12,859	13,200	23,929	26,448	1.9	2.0
Sugar Beet . .	tons	78	69	1,070	994	13.8	14.4

LIVESTOCK ('000)

	1968	1969	1970	1971	1972	1973
Horses . . .	359.8	341.0	325.3	354.3	350	342
Milch Cows . .	2,616.4	2,584.0	2,550.6	2,257.5	2,210	2,152
Other Cattle . .	6,513.8	6,572.1	6,864.9	11,020.8	11,446	11,900
Sheep . . .	891.2	883.0	898.0	860.7	845	833
Pigs	5,682.0	5,772.0	7,086.0	8,106.9	6,995	7,022

DAIRY PRODUCE

	MILK ('000 lb.)	BUTTER ('000 lb.)	FACTORY CHEESE ('000 lb.)	ICE CREAM ('000 gallons)	EGGS ('000 doz.)
1969 . . .	18,711,382	355,871	207,137	29,105	464,023
1970 . . .	18,312,599	333,885	215,279	29,839	490,705
1971 . . .	17,774,991	293,618	248,030	29,836	489,663
1972 . . .	17,708,989	298,101	249,421	30,392	467,410

FORESTRY
ESTIMATE OF FORESTED AREA
(sq. miles)

	PRODUCTIVE						NON-PRODUCTIVE	TOTAL
	Softwood Merchantable	Young Softwood	Mixed wood Merchantable	Young Mixed wood	Hardwood Merchantable	Young Hardwood		
Newfoundland .	24,422	5,835	403	269	9	244	53,930	87,792
Prince Edward Is.	78	396	133	145	13	11	122	935
Nova Scotia .	7,270	789	5,250	458	841	45	1,194	16,274
New Brunswick .	6,297	2,889	7,298	2,042	1,939	952	442	24,329
Quebec . .	75,687	40,922	47,500	26,281	14,391	14,344	157,500	378,125
Ontario . .	44,109	35,925	24,533	34,289	6,559	17,961	97,174	261,742
Manitoba . .	14,669	20,366	5,459	6,514	3,403	4,767	64,631	122,820
Saskatchewan .	10,573	3,413	9,011	5,046	9,205	1,773	75,595	117,738
Alberta . .	14,483	14,042	12,636	11,308	5,255	13,728	41,023	157,595
British Columbia	80,330	87,786	—	—	3,945	7,953	59,227	267,638
Northwest Territories and Yukon . .	35,200	10,000	19,800	3,500	4,700	2,500	200,100	275,800
TOTAL . .	313,118	222,363	132,023	89,852	50,260	64,278	750,939	1,710,788

FUR INDUSTRY

NUMBER AND VALUE OF PELTS PRODUCED

PROVINCE	1970–71 SEASON		1971–72 SEASON	
	Number	Value (Canadian $)	Number	Value (Canadian $)
Newfoundland	117,202	946,279	91,848	749,147
Prince Edward Island	10,286	101,767	7,667	107,112
Nova Scotia	147,118	1,275,531	146,378	1,631,329
New Brunswick	35,943	262,311	38,362	407,566
Quebec	476,043	3,237,515	439,273	3,456,742
Ontario	1,161,917	7,807,003	1,023,532	9,688,164
Manitoba	620,915	3,066,438	674,415	3,750,966
Saskatchewan	556,168	1,961,118	644,326	2,631,856
Alberta	672,870	3,213,471	685,985	4,837,851
British Columbia	439,790	3,631,748	314,175	3,537,066
Northwest Territories	176,931	1,112,562	197,489	1,424,444
Yukon	13,891	41,727	21,340	136,007
TOTAL	4,483,486	27,481,493	4,323,948	33,009,928

SEA FISHERIES

	QUANTITY ('000 lb.)		VALUE (Canadian $'000)	
	1971	1972	1971	1972
Atlantic Total	n.a.	n.a.	133,516	143,199
Cod	449,150	396,718	25,127	25,854
Flounders and soles	282,410	257,524	13,910	13,996
Haddock	53,600	31,005	5,981	4,409
Halibut	3,286	2,722	1,578	1,663
Pollock	22,112	33,616	998	1,646
Redfish	248,625	234,229	8,654	9,433
Herring	924,350	649,597	13,158	12,150
Salmon	4,049	3,364	2,266	2,128
Lobsters	38,162	32,794	33,211	36,465
Scallops	11,170	11,980	12,958	19,313
Tuna	6,820	8,728	1,461	2,283
Pacific Total	n.a.	n.a.	58,588	73,356
Halibut	25,294	21,674	8,139	13,489
Herring	22,083	81,780	556	2,534
Salmon	132,376	161,889	44,476	49,280
Canada Total	n.a.	n.a.	192,104	216,555

MINING

	Unit	1972		1973*	
		Quantity ('000)	Value (Canadian $'000)	Quantity ('000)	Value (Canadian $'000)
Metallic					
Bismuth . . .	lb.	275	850	90	444
Cadmium . . .	,,	4,268	10,798	4,285	15,592
Cobalt . . .	,,	3,351	8,321	3,946	11,667
Columbium (Cb_2O_5) .	,,	3,874	3,868	2,867	3,720
Copper . . .	,,	1,586,607	806,427	1,798,950	1,147,629
Gold	troy oz.	2,079	119,742	1,930	186,111
Iron Ore . . .	ton	42,698	489,023	55,107	613,112
Iron, remelt . .	,,	n.a.	41,544	n.a.	41,423
Lead . . .	lb.	738,849	113,990	771,728	124,556
Magnesium . .	,,	11,848	4,537	11,660	4,319
Molybdenum . .	,,	28,493	44,068	27,450	39,188
Nickel . . .	,,	517,975	717,485	537,816	785,213
Platinum group . .	oz.	406	34,657	288	34,274
Solenium . . .	lb.	582	5,186	598	5,430
Silver. . . .	troy oz.	44,792	74,803	48,843	122,107
Uranium (U_3O_8) . .	lb.	9,763	n.a.	9,328	n.a.
Zinc . . .	,,	2,488,284	474,541	2,725,297	652,981
Non-metallic					
Asbestos . . .	ton	1,687	206,089	1,974	241,001
Barite . . .	,,	77	804	98	1,020
Fluorspar . . .	,,	n.a.	5,432	n.a.	5,505
Gypsum . . .	,,	8,099	19,336	8,316	21,998
Magnesitic dolomite, brucite .	,,	n.a.	2,929	n.a.	3,100
Nepheline syenite .	,,	559	5,902	576	7,372
Peat Moss . . .	,,	376	13,612	390	14,855
Potash (K_2O) . .	,,	3,852	135,513	4,432	151,123
Pyrite, pyrrhotite .	,,	126	456	22	147
Quartz . . .	,,	2,664	9,536	2,800	10,250
Salt	,,	5,417	40,144	5,327	45,185
Soapstone and talc† .	,,	81	1,463	110	2,162
Sodium sulphate . .	,,	507	6,201	525	6,930
Sulphur, in smelter gas .	,,	679	5,118	742	9,641
Sulphur, elemental .	,,	3,636	19,588	4,545	22,630
Titanium diozide, etc. .	,,	n.a.	40,828	n.a.	46,318
Fuels					
Coal . . .	ton	20,709	150,600	21,960	176,979
Natural gas . .	m. cu. ft.	2,913,537	397,186	3,152,410	482,155
Natural gas by-products	bbl.	108,587	250,940	118,732	341,127
Petroleum, crude. .	,,	561,977	1,568,828	649,868	2,246,149
Structural materials					
Clay products . .	ton	n.a.	52,348	n.a.	57,995
Cement . . .	,,	9,976	209,221	10,884	228,094
Lime . . .	,,	1,730	26,732	1,826	28,421
Sand and gravel . .	,,	225,194	178,100	228,000	187,500
Stone . . .	,,	80,203	103,326	85,500	107,000

* Preliminary estimate.   † Includes pyrophyllite.

INDUSTRY
VALUE OF SHIPMENTS
(C $'000)

	1969	1970	1971
Motor Vehicle Manufacturers	3,554,131	2,962,528	3,681,719
Pulp and Paper Mills	2,771,276	2,850,836	2,832,267
Slaughtering and Meat Processors . .	1,942,371	2,061,419	2,121,358
Petroleum Refining	1,661,250	1,758,940	2,045,825
Iron and Steel Mills	1,423,256	1,691,662	1,764,037
Motor Vehicle Parts and Accessories Manufacturers	1,340,376	1,272,154	1,660,665
Dairy Products Industry	1,356,453	1,369,206	1,463,218
Sawmills and Planing Mills . . .	1,267,194	1,135,377	1,395,507
Miscellaneous Machinery and Equipment Manufacturers	1,216,164	1,277,801	1,334,704
Smelting and Refining	983,666	1,080,015	1,045,621
Miscellaneous Food Processors . .	714,606	782,492	852,770
Metal Stamping and Pressing Industry .	n.a.	807,569	843,857
Commercial Printing	680,602	711,429	764,189
Communications Equipment Manufacturers .	705,313	712,137	660,190
Publishing and Printing	572,654	588,795	614,935
Feed Industry	543,004	585,843	604,791
Women's Clothing Factories . . .	500,166	512,804	563,112
Men's Clothing Factories . . .	473,724	512,214	550,523
Manufacturers of Electrical Industrial Equipment	466,129	514,134	534,950
Miscellaneous Metal Fabricating Industries .	454,469	478,318	513,675
Bakeries	485,867	502,891	510,123
Plastics Fabricating Industry . . .	432,287	438,310	501,338
Manufacturers of Industrial Chemicals .	n.a.	464,923	484,536
Aircraft and Aircraft Parts Manufacturers .	649,465	543,708	479,286
Wire and Wire Products Manufacturers .	430,520	441,577	478,757

Electric Energy (million kWh.): 204,723 in 1970; 216,472 in 1971; 238,308 in 1972.

FINANCE
100 cents = 1 Canadian dollar (C$).
Coins: 1, 5, 10, 25 and 50 cents; 1 dollar.
Notes: 1, 2, 5, 10, 20, 50, 100, 500 and 1,000 dollars.
Exchange rates (April 1974): £1 sterling = C$2.293; U.S. $1 = 97.17 Canadian cents.
C$100 = £43.61 = U.S. $102.91.

Note: Between May 1962 and May 1970 the par value of the Canadian dollar was 92.5 U.S. cents, giving an exchange rate of U.S. $1 = C$1.081. In terms of sterling, the rate between November 1967 and May 1970 was C$1 = 7s. 8½d. (38.54 new pence) or £1 = C$2.5946.

FEDERAL BUDGET
(C$ million, April 1st to March 31st)

REVENUE	1972/73	EXPENDITURE	1972/73
Income Taxes:		Indian affairs and Northern development . . .	503
Personal	7,188	National Defence . . .	1,981
Corporate	2,654	National Health and Welfare . .	2,909
Non-resident . . .	292	Post Office . . .	464
Estate Taxes	61	Provincial Subsidies . . .	1,304
Customs Duties	1,182	Public Debt Charges . . .	2,147
Sales Taxes	2,289	Secretary of State . . .	955
All other Taxes . . .	1,039	Transport	583
Non-tax Revenues . . .	1,897	Veterans Affairs . . .	445
		Other Expenditure . . .	4,825
TOTAL REVENUE . .	16,602	TOTAL EXPENDITURE .	16,116

Estimates 1973–74: Expenditure C$18,393 million.

NATIONAL ACCOUNTS

(C $ million)

	1969	1970	1971	1972
Wages, Salaries, and Supplementary Labour Income	43,036	46,633	51,260	56,853
Military Pay and Allowances	884	914	908	962
Corporation Profits before Taxes	8,250	7,089	9,050	10,831
Deduct: Dividends paid to Non-residents	−854	−930	−982	−874
Interest, and Miscellaneous Investment Income	3,101	3,411	3,810	4,097
Accrued Net Income of Farm Operators from Farm Production	1,442	1,256	1,549	1,726
Net Income of Non-farm Unincorporated Business Including Rents	5,193	5,325	5,624	6,106
Inventory Valuation Adjustment	−576	−230	−636	−1,008
Net National Income at Factor Cost	60,476	64,188	70,583	78,693
Indirect Taxes *less* Subsidies	10,703	11,232	12,333	13,669
Capital Consumption Allowances and Miscellaneous Valuation Adjustments	9,060	9,878	10,616	11,420
Residual Error of Estimate	−490	151	−438	−847
Gross National Product at Market Prices	79,749	85,449	93,094	102,935

GOLD RESERVES AND CURRENCY IN CIRCULATION

(C $ million)

	1969	1970	1971	1972
Gold Holdings	872.3	790.7	791.8	834.1
U.S. Dollar Holdings	1,743.6	3,022.1	4,060.6	4,355.0
Notes in Circulation	3,446.2	3,632.3	4,103.4	4,806.2

CONSUMER PRICE INDEX

(1961 = 100)

	1968	1969	1970	1971	1972
All Items	120.1	125.5	129.7	133.4	139.8
Food	122.0	127.1	130.0	131.4	141.4
Housing	118.6	124.7	130.9	136.8	143.2
Clothing	121.1	124.5	126.8	128.7	132.0
Transportation	114.7	120.0	124.8	129.9	133.3
Health and Personal Care	127.4	133.6	139.5	142.4	149.2
Recreation and Reading	119.7	126.8	131.2	135.6	139.4
Tobacco and Alcohol	120.4	125.0	126.5	128.6	132.1

BALANCE OF PAYMENTS—ALL FOREIGN COUNTRIES
(C $ million)

	1971			1972		
	Credit	Debit	Balance	Credit	Debit	Balance
Current Account:						
Merchandise	17,830	15,527	2,303	19,937	18,551	1,386
Non-monetary gold	90	—	90	106	—	106
Freight and shipping	1,184	1,176	8	1,260	1,297	— 37
Travel	1,283	1,494	— 211	1,226	1,456	—230
Investment income	557	1,628	—1,071	616	1,553	—937
Transfer payments	828	604	224	858	629	229
Withholding tax	—	278	— 278		285	—285
Other current transactions	1,340	2,008	— 668	1,327	2,140	—813
Total Current Account	23,112	22,715	397	25,330	25,914	—584
Capital Account:						
Direct Investments	885	305	580	680	305	580
Canadian securities	1,162	1,042	120	2,109	605	1,504
Foreign securities	254	63	191	311	57	254
Government loans	36	192	— 156	28	261	—233
Other long-term transactions (net)	—	341	— 341	—	47	— 47
Change in foreign currency holdings	1,123	64	1,059	728	238	490
Other short-term movements (net)*	—	1,073	—1,073	—	1,463	1,463
Capital Balance (exclusive of changes in official holdings)	380	—	380	800	—	800
Allocation of IMF Special Drawing Rights	119	—	119	117	—	117
Net official monetary movements	896	—	896	333	—	333

* Including net errors and omissions.

BALANCE OF PAYMENTS—REGIONAL BREAKDOWN
(Current balances—million C $)

	U.S.A.	United Kingdom	All Other Countries	Total
1967	—1,342	512	331	— 499
1968	— 801	466	228	— 107
1969	— 877	337	—410	— 952
1970	— 169	716	488	1,036
1971	— 161	502	56	397
1972	— 310	301	—575	— 584

EXTERNAL TRADE
(Canadian $ '000)

	1967	1968	1969	1970	1971	1972
Imports	11,075,199	12,357,982	14,130,375	13,951,903	15,607,731	18,551,000
Exports	11,120,674	13,624,013	14,925,871	16,910,098	17,846,924	19,937,000

PRINCIPAL COMMODITIES
(Canadian $'000)

Imports	1971	1972	Exports	1971	1972
Motor Vehicles and Parts	4,104,413	4,986,891	Motor Vehicles and Parts	4,167,734	4,682,412
Non Farm Machinery	1,482,389	1,748,830	Lumber	829,485	1,173,988
Crude Petroleum	541,114	681,519	Newsprint Paper	1,084,478	1,157,509
Communications Equipment	451,821	640,830	Crude Petroleum	787,397	1,007,505
Steel, all types	496,456	528,281	Wheat	887,938	962,677
Electrical Equipment	451,550	461,244	Wood and Similar Pulp	798,141	817,336
Wearing Apparel and Accessories	294,229	383,086	Nickel, Ores and Alloys	726,949	688,930
Tractors and Parts	264,043	324,522	Copper, Ores and Alloys	607,808	663,737
Aircraft and Parts	289,150	293,965	Aircraft and Parts	332,246	467,838
Fruit and Fruit Products	263,672	289,963	Machinery (except farm)	427,284	447,550
Scientific Equipment	261,172	282,500	Aluminium, Ores and Alloys	467,723	403,858
Printed Matter	258,364	277,494	Iron and Steel and Alloys	389,712	392,612
Plastic Materials	218,501	266,028	Iron Ores and Concentrates	413,333	352,681
Chemicals	230,362	262,889	Fish	266,146	309,058
Wood, Lumber Plywood	150,264	224,528	Natural Gas	250,719	306,843
Photographic Products	187,617	221,050	Grains, other than Wheat	259,148	283,830
Electronic Computers	184,161	212,410	Zinc, Ores and Alloys	217,380	256,875
Other Petroleum and Coal Products	213,466	209,603	Fertilizers and Fertilizer Materials	238,442	249,274
Cotton including Yarn, Thread, Fibre, etc.	139,786	179,099	Asbestos Unmanufactured	226,785	229,813
Coal	151,389	178,792	Chemicals	209,138	220,181
Aluminium Ores, Concentrates and Scraps	186,665	177,319	Communications Equipment	216,976	217,871
Medical Products and Supplies	149,305	175,792	Farm Machinery	174,953	216,891
Basic Hardware	165,802	174,047	Whisky	184,961	209,319
Sugar and Sugar Preparations	125,983	166,348	Other Paper	160,629	205,807
Farm Equipment	120,904	166,047	Wood Fabricated Materials	141,558	192,914

PRINCIPAL COUNTRIES
(Canadian $'000)

Country	Imports			Exports		
	1970	1971	1972	1970	1971	1972
Argentina	8,985	7,246	11,662	59,129	50,334	56,982
Australia	146,148	125,671	193,426	197,750	180,188	153,874
Belgium-Luxembourg	51,695	58,981	89,060	189,943	180,544	196,249
Brazil	49,311	50,698	61,698	87,387	93,255	86,227
China, People's Republic	19,028	23,300	48,377	141,995	204,053	258,563
France	158,486	213,093	250,953	154,201	154,292	151,319
German Federal Republic	370,931	429,417	512,498	383,681	317,049	310,762
Hong Kong	78,486	80,187	104,969	20,753	20,028	20,709
India	40,096	44,610	44,404	129,842	142,809	97,906
Italy	144,973	157,472	204,005	183,961	208,191	198,512
Jamaica	27,067	28,551	19,650	46,545	39,259	38,484
Japan	581,715	801,864	1,105,043	810,142	828,789	958,151
Mexico	47,344	50,162	52,945	91,698	78,984	99,060
Netherlands	78,923	76,397	90,808	277,189	234,043	249,181
New Zealand	43,064	40,254	42,696	42,691	34,714	38,226
Norway	49,132	53,195	77,136	178,056	186,106	152,176
South Africa	45,702	54,590	58,942	104,005	63,685	42,933
Spain	34,460	38,546	50,686	64,506	64,249	55,139
Sweden	105,888	114,178	141,008	47,735	43,646	43,912
Switzerland	80,831	86,180	101,667	37,296	35,592	39,732
Taiwan	51,936	80,706	126,155	18,315	13,947	24,444
United Kingdom	738,262	837,258	948,835	1,465,155	1,366,516	1,312,710
United States	9,917,045	10,945,008	12,917,538	10,579,937	11,681,555	13,530,902
U.S.S.R.	9,074	12,647	15,199	101,553	127,638	281,907
Venezuela	339,212	387,664	410,501	111,391	120,072	145,370

TOURISM

	1970		1971	
	NUMBER	EXPENDITURE (Canadian $'000)	NUMBER	EXPENDITURE (Canadian $'000)
Tourists from the United States . . .	37,153,000	1,082,000	38,449,000	1,129,000
Tourists from other countries . . .	536,000	152,000	543,000	154,000

TRANSPORT

RAILWAYS
(millions)

	1971	1972
Passenger-miles . .	2,183	2,042
Net ton-miles . .	116,645	122,399

ROADS
VEHICLES LICENSED
('000)

	1971	1972*
Cars . . .	6,967	7,407
Commercial Vehicles . .	1,856	1,682
Motorcycles . .	199	249

* Preliminary.

INTERNATIONAL SEABORNE SHIPPING

	GOODS ('000 tons)		VESSELS (number)	
	Loaded	Unloaded	Entered	Cleared
1968 . .	86,711	54,130	26,761	27,231
1969 . .	77,638	57,041	25,082	25,479
1970 . .	105,609	58,781	25,384	25,888
1971 . .	105,697	60,257	24,970	25,269

CIVIL AVIATION
CANADIAN CARRIERS—REVENUE TRAFFIC
('000)

	1971	1972
Miles flown . .	217,612	227,557
Passenger-miles . .	11,505,380	13,499,667
Cargo ton-miles . .	382,793	437,231
Mail ton-miles . .	48,702	53,438

INLAND WATER TRAFFIC
('000 cargo tons)

	ST. LAWRENCE SEAWAY	WELLAND CANAL
1967 . . .	44,001	52,850
1968 . . .	47,946	58,105
1969 . . .	41,067	53,573
1970 . . .	51,197	62,966

COMMUNICATIONS MEDIA

	1972	1973
Total Households . .	6,108,000	6,266,000
Homes with Radio . .	5,962,000	6,124,000
Homes with Television . .	5,851,000	6,017,000
Homes with Telephone . .	5,778,000	5,955,000
Daily Newspapers* . .	119	119

* Total circulation 1972 4,780,385.

EDUCATION
(1972–73)

	SCHOOLS	TEACHERS	PUPILS
Primary and Secondary . .	16,710	271,823	5,793,617
Teacher Training* .	14	440	10,848
Universities and Colleges† . .	69	29,947	322,274

* Except in university faculties.
† Degree-granting institutions, full-time teachers and full-time students.

THE CONSTITUTION

Constitutional development has been based mainly upon four important acts of the British Parliament: the Quebec Act of 1774, the Constitutional Act of 1791, the Act of Union of 1840, and the British North America Act of 1867. The first is chiefly important as it established the French civil law throughout the then province of Quebec and guaranteed the free exercise of Roman Catholicism. The second is noteworthy for the division of the province into the French-speaking province of Lower Canada and the English-speaking province of Upper Canada, and for the concession of representative government through an elective Legislative Assembly which, however, had no control over the executive government except in so far as it could refuse to vote taxes (the non-tax revenue of the province was outside of its control). The Act of Union (Section 45) mentions the appointment by Her Majesty of the Executive Council, but does not refer to the responsibility of the Council. It can be stated that responsible government has existed in Canada by constitutional practice and precedent. It was recognized in the instructions which the Colonial Secretary of State transmitted to the Governors.

Responsible government appeared in Canada in 1847, the year when Lord Elgin was appointed Governor-General. On March 11th, 1848, the reorganization of the Baldwin-Lafontaine ministry inaugurated the era of free government in Canada.

The fourth act separated the two Canadas from their existing legislative union to make them provinces, each administering its own local affairs, in a wider confederation, which within a comparatively short period so extended its boundaries as to take in the whole of British North America, except Newfoundland and Labrador.

The British North America Act 1867 provides that the Constitution of the Dominion shall be "similar in principle to that of the United Kingdom"; that the executive authority shall be vested in the Sovereign of Great Britain and Ireland, and carried on in his name by a Governor-General and Privy Council; and that the legislative power shall be exercised by a Parliament of two Houses, called the "Senate", and the "House of Commons".

The present position of Canada in the British Commonwealth of Nations was defined at the Imperial Conference of 1926: "The self-governing Dominions are autonomous Communities within the British Empire, equal in status, though united by a common allegiance to the Crown."

The Statute of Westminster received the Royal Assent in December 1931. In its application to Canada the Statute emancipates the Legislatures of the provinces as well as the Dominion Parliament from the operation of the Colonial Laws Validity Act. A special section was, however, included providing that the Statute should not apply to the repeal, amendment or alteration of the British North America Acts of 1867 to 1930, and also preventing the Dominions and provinces, in the exercise of their enlarged legislative powers, from trenching upon provincial and Dominion fields of legislative power respectively. Numerous attempts to devise amendment procedures within Canada without reference to Westminster have been made without success, and Amendment of the British North America Acts 1867 to 1962 still remains a procedural problem awaiting solution.

The Government

The national government works itself out through three main agencies. There is **Parliament** (consisting of the Queen as represented by the Governor-General, the Senate and the House of Commons) which makes the laws; the **Executive** (the Cabinet or Ministry) which applies the laws; and the **Judiciary** which interprets the laws.

Particular features of the British system of government are the close relation which exists between the Executive and Legislative branches, and the doctrine of Cabinet responsibility which has become crystallised in the course of time. The members of the Cabinet, or executive committee, are chosen from the political party commanding a majority in the House of Commons. Each Minister or member of the Cabinet is usually responsible for the administration of a department, although there may be Ministers without portfolio whose experience and counsel are drawn upon to strengthen the Cabinet, but who are not at the head of departments.

The second characteristic of the British system, the collective responsibility of the Cabinet, is very important. While each Minister is primarily responsible for the administration of his own particular department, that responsibility is shared, before Parliament and the country, by all his colleagues. Thus the Government of the day, not any particular Minister, is answerable for and must continue to exist, or must fall, on the stand taken by a Minister when acting in his official capacity.

Meetings of the Cabinet are presided over by the President of the Privy Council, but all Ministers, including the Prime Minister and the President of the Privy Council, meet as equals and there is no precedence in Council. From the Cabinet signed orders and recommendations go to the Governor-General for his approval, and it is in this way that the Crown acts only on the advice of its responsible Ministers. The Cabinet takes the responsibility for its advice being in accordance with the will of Parliament and is held strictly accountable.

The Federal Parliament

Parliament must meet at least once a year, so that twelve months do not elapse between the last meeting in one session and the first meeting in the next. The duration of Parliament may not be longer than five years. Senators (a maximum of 102 in number) are appointed until age 75 by the Governor-General in Council. They must be at least 30 years of age, British subjects, residents of the province they represent, and in possession of $4,000 over and above their liabilities. Members of the House of Commons are elected by universal adult suffrage for the duration of Parliament.

Under the British North America Act, which is the basis of the Constitution, the Federal Parliament has exclusive legislative authority in all matters relating to public debt and property; regulation of trade and commerce; raising of money by any mode of taxation; borrowing of money on the public credit; postal service; census and statistics; militia, military and naval service and defence; fixing and providing for salaries and allowances of the officers of the Government; beacons, buoys and lighthouses; navigation and shipping; quarantine and the establishment and maintenance of marine hospitals; sea-coast and inland fisheries; ferries on an international or interprovincial frontier; currency and coinage; banking, incorporation of banks, and issue of paper money; savings banks; weights and measures; bills of exchange and promissory notes; interest; legal tender; bankruptcy and insolvency; patents of invention and discovery; copyrights; Indians and lands reserved for Indians; naturalisation and aliens; marriage and divorce; the criminal laws, except the constitution of courts of criminal jurisdiction but including the procedure in criminal matters; the establishment, maintenance and management of penitentiaries; such classes of subjects as are expressly excepted in the enumeration of the classes of subjects exclusively assigned to the Legislatures of the provinces by the Act. Judicial interpretation and later amendment have, in certain cases, modified or clearly defined the respective powers of the Federal and Provincial Governments.

Provincial Government

In each of the ten Provinces (Newfoundland joined with Canada as the tenth province on April 1st, 1949) the Queen is represented by a Lieutenant-Governor, appointed by the Governor-General in Council, and governing with the advice and assistance of the Ministry or Executive Council, which is responsible to the Legislature and resigns office when it ceases to enjoy the confidence of that body. The Legislatures are unicameral, consisting of an elected Legislative Assembly.

The Legislature in each province may exclusively make laws in relation to: amendment of the constitution of the province, except as regards the Lieutenant-Governor; direct taxation within the province; borrowing of money on the credit of the province; establishment and tenure of provincial offices and appointment and payment of provincial officers; the management and sale of public lands belonging to the province and of the timber and wood thereon; the establishment, maintenance and management of public and reformatory prisons in and for the province; the establishment, maintenance and management of hospitals, asylums, charities and charitable institutions in and for the province, other than marine hospitals; municipal institutions in the province; shop, saloon, tavern, auctioneer and other licences issued for the raising of provincial or municipal revenue; local works and undertakings other than interprovincial or international lines of ships, railways, canals, telegraphs, etc., or works which, though wholly situated within one province are declared by the Federal Parliament to be for the general advantage either of Canada or of two or more provinces; the incorporation of companies with provincial objects; the solemnisation of marriage in the province; property and civil rights in the province; the administration of justice in the province, including the constitution, maintenance and organization of provincial courts both of civil and criminal jurisdiction, and including procedure in civil matters in these courts; the imposition of punishment by fine, penalty or imprisonment for enforcing any law of the province relating to any of the aforesaid subjects; generally all matters of a merely local or private nature in the province. Further, provincial Legislatures may exclusively make laws in relation to education, subject to the protection of religious minorities, who are to retain the privileges and rights enjoyed before Confederation.

Municipal Government

Under the British North America Act, the municipalities are the creations of the Provincial Governments. Their bases of organization and the extent of their authority vary in different provinces, but almost everywhere they have very considerable powers of local self-government.

THE GOVERNMENT

Governor-General: JULES LÉGER, C.C.

FEDERAL MINISTRY

(*March* 1974)

Prime Minister: Rt. Hon. PIERRE ELLIOTT TRUDEAU.

Leader of the Government in the Senate: Hon. PAUL MARTIN.

Minister of Transport: Hon. JEAN MARCHAND.

Minister of Labour: Hon. JOHN MUNRO.

Minister of Communications: Hon. GÉRARD PELLETIER.

Minister of Regional Economic Expansion: Hon. DONALD JAMIESON.

Minister of Manpower and Immigration: Hon. ROBERT ANDRAS.

Minister of National Defence: Hon. JAMES RICHARDSON.

Minister of Consumer and Corporate Affairs: Hon. HERB GRAY.

Minister of National Revenue: Hon. ROBERT STANBURY.

Minister of Supply and Services: Hon. JEAN-PIERRE GOYER.

Minister of Industry and Commerce: Hon. ALASTAIR GILLESPIE.

Minister of Agriculture: Hon. EUGÈNE WHELAN.

Postmaster General: Hon. ANDRÉ OUELLET.

Minister of Veterans Affairs: Hon. DANIEL MACDONALD.

Minister of Health and Social Welfare: Hon. MARC LALONDE.

Minister of State for Science and Technology: Hon. JEANNE SAUVÉ.

Solicitor-General: Hon. WARREN ALLMAND.

Secretary of State: Hon. HUGH FAULKNER.

President of the Treasury Board: Hon. CHARLES M. DRURY.

Minister of Finance: Hon. JOHN N. TURNER.

Minister of Justice and Attorney-General: Hon. OTTO EMIL LANG.

Minister of Energy, Mines and Resources: Hon. DONALD S. MACDONALD.

Minister of Indian Affairs and Northern Development: Hon. JEAN CHRÉTIEN.

Minister of the Environment and Minister of Fisheries: Hon. JACK DAVIS.

Secretary of State for External Affairs: Hon. MITCHELL W. SHARP.

Minister of State for Urban Affairs: Hon. RONALD BASFORD.

Minister of State: Hon. STANLEY HAIDASZ.

Minister of Public Works: Hon. JEAN-EUDES DUBÉ.

DIPLOMATIC REPRESENTATION

HIGH COMMISSIONS AND EMBASSIES ACCREDITED TO CANADA

(In Ottawa, unless otherwise stated)

(HC) High Commission; (E) Embassy.

Afghanistan: Washington, D.C. 20008, U.S.A.

Algeria: Suite 402-403, 435 Daly Ave. (E); *Ambassador:* DJAMEL HOUHOU.

Argentina: 10 Driveway (E); *Chargé d'Affaires:* OSCAR C. ATAIDE.

Australia: 90 Sparks St. (HC); *High Commissioner:* JAMES CHARLES INGRAM.

Austria: 445 Wilbrod St. (E); *Ambassador:* Dr. EDUARD SCHILLER.

Bangladesh: 85 Range Rd. (HC); *High Commissioner:* ABDUL MOMIN.

Barbados: Suite 200, 151 Slater St. (HC); *High Commissioner:* OLIVER HAMLET JACKMAN (also accred. to Cuba).

Belgium: Apts. 601-604, 85 Range Rd. (E); *Ambassador:* MARCEL RYMENANS.

Bolivia: Washington, D.C. 20036, U.S.A. (E).

Botswana: Washington, D.C. 20009, U.S.A. (HC).

Brazil: 450 Wilbrod St. (E); *Ambassador:* CARLOS FREDERICO DA ROCHA.

Bulgaria: 325 Stewart St. (E); *Ambassador:* LYUBOMIR ZHELYAZKOV.

Burma: Suite 702, 116 Albert St. (E); *Ambassador:* THAKIN CHAN TUN.

Burundi: New York, N.Y. 10017, U.S.A. (E).

Cameroon: 470 Wilbrod St. (E); *Ambassador:* F. X. TCHOUNGUI.

Central African Republic: Washington, D.C. 20008, U.S.A. (E).

Chile: 56 Sparks St., Suite 204 (E); *Ambassador:* LUCIO PARADA D.

China, People's Republic: 411-415 St. Andrew St. (E); *Ambassador:* CHANG WEN-CHIN.

Colombia: Suite 112, 140 Wellington St. (E); *Ambassador:* Gen. LUIS ERNESTO ORDÓÑEZ CASTILLO.

Congo (Brazzaville): c/o Permanent Mission of the People's Republic of the Congo to the United Nations, New York, U.S.A. (E).

Costa Rica: 1564 Featherston Drive (E); *Ambassador:* V. J. W. FURNISS.

Cuba: 700 Echo Drive (E); *Ambassador:* Dr. JOSÉ FERNÁNDEZ DE COSSIO.

Cyprus: Washington, D.C. 20008, U.S.A. (HC).

Czechoslovakia: 171 Clemow Ave. (E); *Ambassador:* BRETISLAV MATONOHA.

Dahomey: 130 Albert St. Suite 508 (E); *Ambassador:* FAUSTIN A. Y. GBAGUIDI.

Denmark: Suite 702, 85 Range Rd. (E); *Ambassador:* HENNING HJORTH-NIELSEN.

Dominican Republic: Suite 202, 200 Rideau Terrace (E); *Ambassador:* VIRGILIO ALVAREZ SÁNCHEZ.

Egypt: 454 Laurier Ave. (E); *Ambassador:* AHMED SABRI KAMAL.

El Salvador: 100 Bronson Ave. (E); *Ambassador:* RUY CÉSAR MIRANDA.

Fiji: c/o Permanent Mission of Fiji to the United Nations, New York, U.S.A. (HC).

Finland: 85 Range Rd. (E); *Ambassador:* HOLGER SUMELIUS.

France: 42 Sussex Drive (E); *Ambassador:* JACQUES VIOT.

Gabon: 54 Range Rd. (E); *Ambassador:* LUBIN MARTIAL NTOUTOUME OBAME.

Germany, Federal Republic: 1 Waverley St. (E); *Ambassador:* Dr. RUPPRECHT VON KELLER.

Ghana: Suite 810, 85 Range Rd. (HC); *High Commissioner:* SETH K. ANTHONY.

Greece: Suite 110, Château Laurier Hotel (E); *Ambassador:* JOHN YANNAKAKIS.

Guatemala: Washington D.C. 20008, U.S.A. (E).

Guinea: Washington D.C. 20008, U.S.A. (E).

Guyana: 151 Slater St. (HC); *High Commissioner:* Dr. ROBERT MOORE (also accred. to Cuba).

Haiti: 150 Driveway, Apt. 111 (E); *Ambassador:* PHILIPPE CANTAVE.

Honduras: Washington, D.C. 20011, U.S.A. (E).

Hungary: 7 Delaware Ave. (E); *Ambassador:* JÁNOS BARTHA.

Iceland: Washington, D.C. 20008, U.S.A. (E).

India: 200 MacLaren St. (HC); *High Commissioner:* UMA SHANKAR BAJPAI.

Indonesia: Apt. 107-111, 85 Range Rd. (E); *Ambassador:* Lt.-Gen. JAMIN GINTINGS.

Iran: Suite 307-8, 85 Range Rd. (E); *Ambassador:* Dr. PARDIZ ADLE.

Iraq: 377 Stewart St. (E); *Ambassador:* MOHSIN DIZAYEE.

Ireland: 170 Metcalfe St. (E); *Ambassador:* PATRICK F. POWER.

Israel: 45 Powell Ave. (E); *Ambassador:* THEODOR MERON.

Italy: 107 Laurier Ave. W. (E); *Ambassador:* Baron MAURIZIO DE STROBE DI FRATTA E CAMPOCIENO.

Ivory Coast: 381 Wilbrod St. (E); *Ambassador:* DIEUDONNÉ ESSIENE.

Jamaica: 85 Range Rd. (HC); *High Commissioner:* Hon. WILLS OGILVY ISAACS.

Japan: The Fuller Building, 75 Albert St. (E); *Ambassador:* AKIRA NISHIYAMA.

Jordan: Washington, D.C. 20008, U.S.A. (E).

Korea, Republic: Suite 608, 151 Slater St. (E); *Ambassador:* KIM YOUNG-CHO.

Kuwait: Washington D.C. 20008 (E).

Lebanon: 640 Lyon St. (E); *Ambassador:* NABIH NOUSSAIR.

Lesotho: Washington, D.C. 20009, U.S.A. (HC).

Liberia: Washington, D.C. 20011, U.S.A. (E).

Libya: c/o Permanent Mission of the Libyan Arab Republic to the United Nations, New York, U.S.A. (E).

Luxembourg: Washington, D.C. 20008, U.S.A. (E).

Madagascar: New York, N.Y. 10017, U.S.A. (E).

Malaysia: 130 Albert St. (HC); *High Commissioner:* HAJI MOHAMED ZAKARIA.

Mali: Washington, D.C. 20008, U.S.A. (E).

Malta: 1060 Brussels, Belgium (HC).

Mauritania: New York, N.Y. 10018, U.S.A. (E).

Mauritius: Washington, D.C. 20008, U.S.A. (HC).

Mexico: 130 Albert St. (E); *Ambassador:* RAFAEL URDA-NETA DE LA TOUR.

Morocco: 38 Range Rd. (E); *Ambassador:* NOURREDDINE HASNAOUI.

Nepal: Washington, D.C. 20008, U.S.A. (E).

Netherlands: 275 Slater St. (E); *Ambassador:* WADIM THORN LEESON.

New Zealand: Suite 804, 77 Metcalfe St. (HC); *High Commissioner:* Hon. DEAN J. EYRE.

Nicaragua: Washington D.C. 20009, U.S.A. (E).

Niger: 190 Lisgar St. (E); *Ambassador:* MAI ARY TANI-MOUNE.

Nigeria: Place de Ville, Tower A, 320 Queen St. (HC); *High Commissioner:* PETER AYODELE AFOLABI.

Norway: 700 Victoria Building, 140 Wellington St. (E); *Ambassador:* ASBJORN SKARSTEIN.

Pakistan: 505 Wilbrod St. (E); *Ambassador:* IFTIKHAR ALI (also accred. to Cuba).

Peru: 539 Island Park Drive (E); *Ambassador:* Gen. VICTOR ODICIO TAMARIZ.

Philippines: Suite 607, 130 Albert St. (E); *Ambassador:* PRIVADO G. JIMÉNEZ.

Poland: 443 Daly Ave. (E); *Ambassador:* JOSEF CSEZAK.

Portugal: 645 Island Park Drive (E); *Ambassador:* Dr. SALVADOR SAMPAYO GARRIDO.

Romania: 473–475 Wilbrod (E); *Ambassador:* BUCUR SCHIOPU.

Rwanda: 130 Albert St. (E); *Ambassador:* JOSEPH NSEN-GIYUMVA.

Senegal: Washington D.C. 20008, U.S.A. (E).

Sierra Leone: Washington, D.C. 20009, U.S.A. (HC).

Singapore: New York, N.Y. 10017, U.S.A. (HC).

Somalia: New York, N.Y. 10017, U.S.A. (E).

South Africa: 15 Sussex Drive (E); *Ambassador:* NORMAN JOHN BEST.

Spain: Apts. 310–312, 124 Springfield Rd. (E); *Ambassador:* JOSÉ MARÍA MORO.

Sri Lanka: 85 Range Road, Suites 102–104 (HC); *High Commissioner:* P. H. WILLIAM DE SILVA (also accred. to Cuba).

Sudan: Washington, D.C. 20007, U.S.A. (E).

Swaziland: Washington, D.C. 20007, U.S.A. (HC).

Sweden: Suite 604, 140 Wellington St. (E); *Ambassador:* AKE MALMAEUS.

Switzerland: 5 Marlborough Ave. (E); *Ambassador:* ERWIN BERNATH.

Syria: New York, N.Y. 10022, U.S.A. (E).

Tanzania: 50 Range Rd. (HC); *High Commissioner:* ABBAS KLEIST SYKES.

Thailand: 85 Range Rd. (E); *Ambassador:* Col. BANBHOT BHANICH SUPAPOL.

Togo: Washington, D.C. 20008, U.S.A. (E).

Trinidad and Tobago: Suite 508, 75 Albert St. (HC); *High Commissioner:* MATTHEW RAMCHARAM.

Tunisia: 515 O'Connor St. (E); *Ambassador:* BACCAR TOUZANI.

Turkey: 197 Wurtemburg St. (E); *Ambassador:* Gen. IRFAN TANSEL.

Uganda: New York, N.Y. 10017, U.S.A. (HC).

U.S.S.R.: 285 Charlotte St. (E); *Ambassador:* ALEKSANDR NIKOLAYEVICH YAKOVLEV.

United Kingdom: 80 Elgin St. (HC); *High Commissioner:* Sir JOHN JOHNSTON.

U.S.A.: 100 Wellington St. (E); *Ambassador:* Hon. ADOLPH WILLIAM SCHMIDT.

Upper Volta: Washington, D.C. 20008, U.S.A. (E); *Ambassador:* TELESPHORE YAGUIBOU.

Uruguay: Washington, D.C. 20006, U.S.A. (E).

Vatican: 724 Manor Ave., Rockcliffe Park (Apostolic Nunciature); *Pro-nuncio:* Most Rev. GUIDO DEL MESTRI.

Venezuela: 151 Sparks St. (E); *Ambassador:* Vice-Admiral JESÚS CARBONELL-IZQUIERDO.

Yugoslavia: 17 Blackburn Ave. (E); *Ambassador:* PETER BABIC.

Zaire: 18 Range Rd. (E); *Ambassador:* SHALA DIBWE TSHIMBALANGA.

Zambia: 2197 Riverside Drive (HC); *High Commissioner:* DUNSTAN WESTON KAMANA.

DOMINION PARLIAMENT

THE SENATE

Speaker: Hon. MURIEL McQUEEN FERGUSSON.

Liberals	.	73	Ontario . .	24
Progressive Conservatives		17	Quebec . .	24
Independent	.	2	Nova Scotia .	10
Independent Liberal	.	1	New Brunswick .	10
Social Credit	.	1	Prince Edward Is. .	4
Vacant	.	8	British Columbia .	6
			Manitoba .	6
			Saskatchewan .	6
			Alberta .	6
			Newfoundland .	6
		102		102

HOUSE OF COMMONS

Speaker: Hon. LUCIEN LAMOUREUX.

GENERAL ELECTION, OCTOBER 1972

	SEATS
Liberals . . .	109
Progressive Conservatives .	107
New Democratic Party .	31
Social Credit . .	15
Independent . .	2
TOTAL . .	264

PROVINCIAL GOVERNMENTS

ALBERTA

Lieutenant-Governor: Hon. Ralph Steinhauer.
Secretary: Gordon A. Johnston.

MINISTRY
(1973)

Premier, President of the Council: Hon. Peter Lougheed.

Attorney-General and Provincial Secretary: Hon. C. Mervin Leitch.

Minister of Agriculture: Hon. Dr. Hugh M. Horner.

Minister of Federal and Inter-Governmental Affairs: Hon. Donald R. Getty.

Minister of Education: Hon. Louis D. Hyndman.

Provincial Treasurer: Hon. Gordon T. W. Miniely.

Minister of Health and Social Development: Hon. Neil S. Crawford.

Minister of the Environment: Hon. William J. Yurko.

Minister of Municipal Affairs: Hon. David J. Russell.

Minister of Advanced Education: Hon. James L. Foster.

Minister of Manpower and Labour: Hon. Dr. Albert E. Hohol.

Minister of Mines and Minerals: Hon. W. D. Dickie.

Minister of Telephones: Hon. Leonard F. Werry.

Minister of Public Works: Hon. Dr. Winston O. Backus.

Minister of Industry and Commerce: Hon. Frederick H. Peacock.

Minister of Highways and Transport: Hon. Clarence Copithorne.

Minister of Lands and Forests: Hon. Dr. Allan A. Warrack.

Minister of Culture, Youth and Recreation: Hon. Horst A. Schmid.

Minister of Consumer Affairs: Hon. Robert W. Dowling.

Ministers without Portfolio: Hon. George Topolnisky, Hon. J. Allan Adair.

Clerk: W. H. MacDonald.

BRITISH COLUMBIA

Lieutenant-Governor: Hon. Walter Stewart Owen, Q.C., LL.D.

MINISTRY
(1973)

Premier, President of the Council and Minister of Finance: Hon. David Barrett.

Provincial Secretary and Minister of Travel Industry: Hon. Ernest Hall.

Attorney-General: Hon. Alexander Barrett MacDonald, Q.C.

Minister of Land, Forests and Water Resources: Hon. Robert Arthur Williams.

Minister of Agriculture: Hon. David Daniel Stupich.

Minister of Mines and Petroleum Resources: Hon. Leo Thomas Nimsick.

Minister of Transport and Communications: Hon. Robert Martin Strachan.

Minister of Labour: Hon. William Stewart King.

Minister of Education: Hon. Eileen Elizabeth Dailly.

Minister of Municipal Affairs: Hon. James Gibson Lorimer.

Minister of Health Services and Hospital Insurance: Hon. Dennis Geoffrey Cocke.

Minister of Public Works: Hon. William Leonard Hartley.

Minister of Human Resources: Hon. Norman Levi.

Member of Executive Council Without Portfolio: Hon. Frank Arthur Calder.

Minister of Highways: Hon. Graham Richard Lea.

Minister of Recreation and Conservation: Hon. Jack Radford.

Minister of Housing: Hon. Lorne Nicolson.

Minister of Consumer Services: Hon. Phyllis Florence Young.

MANITOBA

Lieutenant-Governor: Hon. William J. McKeag.
Official Secretary: Mrs. M. M. Rutherford.

MINISTRY
(1973)

Premier, President of the Council, and Minister of Dominion-Provincial Relations: Hon. Edward Richard Schreyer.

Minister of Finance: Hon. Saul Cherniak.

Minister of Consumer, Corporate and Internal Services and Minister of Education: Hon. Ian Turnbull.

Minister of Tourism, Recreation and Cultural Affairs: Hon. Laurent L. Desjardins.

Minister of Mines, Natural Resources and Environmental Management: Hon. Sidney Green, Q.C.

Attorney-General and Minister of Municipal Affairs: Hon. Howard Pawley.

Minister of Colleges and Universities Affairs and Minister of Education: Hon. Ben Hanuschak.

Minister of Health and Social Development: Hon. Rene Toupin.

Minister of Public Works: Hon. Russell Doern.

Minister of Labour and Railway Commissioner: Hon. A. R. Paulley.

Minister of Agriculture and Minister of Co-operative Development: Hon. Samuel Uskiw.

Minister of Industry and Commerce: Hon. Leonard Evans.

Minister of Northern Affairs: Hon. Ron McBryde.

Minister of Highways: Hon. Peter Burtniak.

Minister for Urban Affairs: Hon. Saul A. Miller.

NEW BRUNSWICK

Lieutenant-Governor: Hon. H. J. Robichaud.
Official Secretary: Mrs. Marie Hanifan.

MINISTRY
(1973)

Premier: Hon. Richard Hatfield.

Provincial Secretary: Hon. Omer Leger.

Minister of Justice: Hon. John Baxter.

Minister of Finance: Hon. Jean-Maurice Simard.

Minister of Agriculture and Rural Development: Hon. George Horton.

Minister of Economic Growth: Hon. Paul Creaghan.

Minister of Labour: Hon. Rodman Logan.

Minister of Highways: Hon. Wilfred Bishop.

Minister of Supply and Services: Hon. Carl Mooers.

Minister of Natural Resources: Hon. EDISON STAIRS.

Minister of Health: Hon. LAWRENCE GARVIE.

Minister of Municipal Affairs: Hon. HORACE SMITH.

Minister of Fisheries and Environment: Hon. WILLIAM COCKBURN.

Minister of Social Services and Youth: Hon. BRENDA ROBERTSON.

Minister of Education: Hon. LORNE McGUIGAN.

Minister of Tourism: Hon. JEAN-PAUL LeBLANC (acting.)

Minister of Treasury Board: Hon. JEAN-PAUL LeBLANC.

NEWFOUNDLAND AND LABRADOR

Lieutenant-Governor: Hon. E. JOHN A. HARNUM.

Private Secretary: Capt. A. SHEA.

MINISTRY
(1973)

Premier: Hon. FRANK D. MOORES.

Minister of Justice and President of the Council: Hon. ALEX T. HICKMAN.

Minister of Finance and President of the Treasury Board: Hon. J. C. CROSBIE.

Minister of Education: Hon. G. OTTENHEIMER.

Minister of Transport and Communications: Hon. Dr. T. FARRELL.

Minister of Social Assistance: Hon. A. J. MURPHY.

Minister of Health: Hon. A. T. ROWE.

Minister of Industrial Development: Hon. C. W. DOODY.

Minister of Municipal Affairs and Housing: Hon. H. COLLINS.

Minister of Provincial Affairs and Environment: Hon. T. HICKEY.

Minister of Manpower and Industrial Relations: Hon. G. DAWE.

Minister of Agriculture and Forests: Hon. E. MAYNARD.

Minister of Fisheries: Hon. R. CHEESEMAN.

Minister of Public Works and Services: Hon. V. EARLE.

Minister of Tourism: Hon. T. DOYLE.

Minister of Rehabilitation and Recreation: Hon. J. ROUSSEAU.

Minister of Mines and Energy: Hon. L. BARRY.

Minister of Rural Development: Hon. J. REID.

Minister without Portfolio: Hon. WILLIAM MARSHALL.

NOVA SCOTIA

Lieutenant-Governor: Brig. Hon. VICTOR OLAND, E.D

MINISTRY
(1973)

Premier: Hon. GERALD A. REGAN, Q.C.

Minister of Finance: Hon. PETER M. NICHOLSON.

Minister of Highways, Minister of Mines: Hon. LEONARD L. PACE, Q.C.

Provincial Secretary, Minister of Recreation: Hon. A. GARNET BROWN.

Minister of Public Works: Hon. BENOIT COMEAU.

Minister of Education: Hon. J. WILLIAM GILLIS.

Attorney-General, Minister in Charge of the Civil Service Act: ALLAN E. SULLIVAN, Q.C.

Minister of Development: Hon. GEORGE M. MITCHELL, Q.C.

Minister of Public Health, Minister of Labour: Hon. D. SCOTT MacNUTT.

Minister of Municipal Affairs, Minister in Charge of the Liquor Control Act: Hon. J. FRASER MOONEY.

Minister of the Environment, Minister of Tourism: Hon. GLEN M. BAGNELL.

Minister of Lands and Forests: Hon. MAURICE E. DeLORY, M.D.

Minister of Agriculture and Marketing: Hon. JOHN HAWKINS.

Minister of Social Services: Hon. HAROLD M. HUSKILSON.

Minister of Fisheries: Hon. ALEXANDER M. CAMERON.

ONTARIO

Lieutenant-Governor: Hon. PAULINE McGIBBON.

EXECUTIVE COUNCIL
(1974)

Premier and President of the Council: Hon. WILLIAM G. DAVIS, Q.C.

Provincial Secretary for Justice and Attorney General: Hon. ROBERT WELCH, Q.C.

Provincial Secretary for Social Development: Hon. MARGARET BIRCH.

Provincial Secretary for Resources Development: Hon. ALLAN GROSSMAN.

Treasurer of Ontario and Minister of Economics and Inter-governmental Affairs: Hon. J. WHITE.

Chairman, Management Board of Cabinet: Hon. E. WINKLER

Minister of Agriculture and Food: Hon. W. A. STEWART.

Minister of Colleges and Universities: Hon. JAMES AULD.

Minister of Community and Social Services: Hon. R. BRUNELLE.

Minister of Consumer and Commercial Relations: Hon. J. T. CLEMENT.

Minister of Correctional Services: Hon. RICHARD POTTER, M.D.

Minister of Education: Hon. T. L. WELLS.

Minister of the Environment: Hon. WILLIAM NEWMAN.

Minister of Government Services: Hon. J. W. SNOW.

Minister of Health: Hon. F. MILLER.

Minister of Housing: Hon. SIDNEY HANDLEMAN.

Minister of Industry and Tourism: Hon. C. BENNETT.

Minister of Labour: Hon. F. GUINDON.

Minister of Natural Resources: Hon. L. E. BERNIER.

Minister of Revenue: Hon. ARTHUR MEEN.

Solicitor General: Hon. GEORGE KERR, Q.C.

Minister of Transportation and Communications: Hon JOHN RHODES.

Ministers wthout Portfolio: Hon. JACK McNIE, Q.C., Hon. DONALD IRVINE (Special Advisor Municipal Affairs), Hon. DENNIS TIMBRELL (Youth Secretariat).

Secretary of the Cabinet: Hon. C. E. BRANNAN.

Minister of Energy: Hon. W. D. McKEOUGH.

PRINCE EDWARD ISLAND

Lieutenant-Governor: Hon. J. GEORGE MACKAY.

Premier's Secretary: GORDON SAGE.

MINISTRY
(1973)

Premier, Minister of Agriculture and Forestry: Hon. ALEXANDER B. CAMPBELL.

Minister of Public Works and of Highways: Hon. GEORGE FERGUSON.

President of Executive Council, Provincial Secretary, Minister of Justice, and Attorney- and Advocate-General: Hon. GORDON BENNETT.

Minister of Finance: Hon. T. EARLE HICKEY.

Minister of Development and Minister of Industry and Commerce: Hon. JOHN MALONEY.

Minister of Labour, Minister of Health, Minister of Social Services: Hon. BRUCE STEWART.

Minister of Community Services and Minister of the Environment and Tourism: Hon. WILLIAM GALLANT.

Minister without Portfolio, Minister responsible for the P.E.I. Housing Authority: Hon. JEAN CANFIELD.

Minister of Education: Hon. BENNETT CAMPBELL.

Minister of Fisheries: Hon. ROBERT E. CAMPBELL.

QUEBEC

Lieutenant-Governor: Hon. HUGUES LAPOINTE, Q.C.
Official Secretary: Col. GABRIEL TASCHEREAU.

MINISTRY
(1973)

Prime Minister: Hon. ROBERT BOURASSA.

Vice-Prime Minister and Minister of Intergovernmental Affairs: Hon. GÉRARD D. LÉVESQUE.

Minister of Roads, Minister of Transport: Hon. BERNARD PINARD.

Minister of Social Affairs: Hon. CLAUDE FORGET.

Minister of Justice: Hon. JÉRÔME CHOQUETTE.

Minister of Industry and Commerce: Hon. GUY SAINT-PIERRE.

Minister of Finance: Hon. RAYMOND GARNEAU.

Minister of Public Works: Hon. MAURICE TESSIER.

Minister of Financial Institutions, Companies and Co-operatives: Hon. WILLIAM TETLEY.

Minister of Agriculture: Hon. NORMAND TOUPIN.

Minister of Natural Resources: Hon. GILLES MASSÉ.

Minister of Lands and Forests: Hon. KEVIN DRUMMOND.

Minister of Education: Hon. FRANÇOIS CLOUTIER.

Minister of Communications: Hon. JEAN-PAUL L'ALLIER.

Minister of Revenue: Hon. GÉRALD HARVEY.

Minister of Labour and Manpower: Hon. JEAN COURNOYER.

Minister of Immigration: Hon. JEAN BIENVENUE.

Minister of Tourism, Fish and Game: Hon. CLAUDE SIMARD.

Minister of State for Intergovernmental Affaires, Minister of State for Finance and Minister of State for Civil Service: Hon. OSWALD PARENT.

Minister of State responsible for the Environment and Minister for Municipal Affairs: Hon. VICTOR C. GOLDBLOOM.

Minister of State responsible for ODEQ: Hon. ROBERT QUENNEVILLE.

Minister of Transport, Minister of Public Works and Supply: Hon. RAYMOND MAILLOUX.

Minister responsible for Youth, Recreation, Sport: Hon. PAUL PHANEOF.

Minister responsible for Municipal Affairs: Hon. GEORGE VAILLANCOURT.

Minister of Cultural Affairs: Hon. DENIS HARDY.

Minister of State for Social Affairs: Hon. LISE BACON.

Minister of State for Executive Council: Hon. FERNAND LALONDE.

Minister of State responsible for OPDQ: Hon. BERNARD LACHAPELLE.

Minister of State for Transport: Hon. PAUL BERTNIAUME.

SASKATCHEWAN

Lieutenant-Governor: Hon. S. WOROBETZ, M.C., M.D.
Secretary: Mrs. W. A. CHAMP.

MINISTRY
(1973)

Premier and President of the Council: Hon. ALLAN BLAKENEY.

Attorney-General and Deputy Premier: Hon. ROY ROMANOW.

Minister of Agriculture: Hon. J. R. MESSER.

Minister of Public Health: Hon. W. E. SMISHEK.

Minister of Municipal Affairs: Hon. E. I. WOOD.

Minister of Labour: Hon. G. T. SNYDER.

Minister of Natural Resources and Northern Saskatchewan: Hon. G. R. BOWERMAN.

Minister of Education and Continuing Education: Hon. GORDON MACMURCHY.

Minister of Environment, Co-operation and Co-operative Development: Hon. N. E. BYERS.

Minister of Highways and Transportation: Hon. EILING KRAMER.

Minister of Government Services and Telephones: Hon. J. E. BROCKELBANK.

Minister of Industry and Commerce and Minerals: Hon. KIM THORSON.

Minister of Social Services: Hon. ALEX TAYLOR.

Minister of Finance: Hon. E. L. COWLEY.

Minister of Culture and Youth, Consumer Affairs and Provincial Secretary: Hon. E. L. TCHORZEWSKI.

CANADIAN TERRITORIES

NORTHWEST TERRITORIES
(Seat of Government: Yellowknife)

Member of Parliament: R. J. ORANGE.
Commissioner: STUART HODGSON.

YUKON TERRITORY
(Seat of Government: Whitehorse)

Member of Parliament: ERIK NIELSEN.
Commissioner: JAMES SMITH.

POLITICAL PARTIES

The Liberal Party: National Liberal Federation of Canada, 251 Cooper Street, Ottawa; believes in Canadian autonomy, comprehensive social security, freer trade within the North Atlantic Community; Hon. Pres. Rt. Hon. PIERRE ELLIOTT TRUDEAU, M.P.; Pres. Hon. JOHN NICHOL; Exec. Dir. and Organizer A. R. O'BRIEN; Public Relations Dir. IAN HOWARD.

The Progressive Conservative Party of Canada: 178 Queen St., Ottawa 4; f. 1854; the party which was the architect of Canadian Confederation and of Dominion status; believes in individualism and free enterprise wherever feasible and continued participation in NATO and the Commonwealth; Leader Hon. ROBERT L. STANFIELD, P.C., Q.C., M.P., LL.D.; Pres. NATHAN NURGITZ, LL.B., Q.C.; Nat. Dir. LIAM S. O'BRIAN.

The New Democratic Party: 301 Metcalfe Street, Ottawa; f. 1961 by representatives of the Co-operative Commonwealth Federation and Canadian trade union movement; advocates major economic planning, national social security and non-nuclear role for Canada; Leader DAVID LEWIS, M.P.

Social Credit Party: Parliament Bldg., Ottawa, Ont.; advocates monetary reform; governing party of Alberta from 1935 until 1971 and British Columbia 1952 to 1972; Leader RÉAL CAOUETTE, M.P.

The Communist Party: 24 Cecil Street, Toronto, Ontario M5T 1N2; Sec.-Gen. WM. KASHTAN.

L'Union Nationale: Montreal, Quebec; f. 1965; anti-Communist; Leader GABRIEL LOUBIER.

Le Parti Québécois: Montreal, Quebec; f. 1968; provincial separatist; Pres. RENÉ LÉVESQUE; Vice-Pres. CAMILLE LAURIN; 120,000 mems.

JUDICIAL SYSTEM

FEDERAL COURTS

The Supreme Court of Canada has jurisdiction as a Court of Appeal in both civil and criminal cases throughout Canada.

Chief Justice of Canada: BORIA LASKIN.

Puisne Judges: Hon. D. C. ABBOTT, P.C., Hon. RONALD MARTLAND, Hon. WILFRED JUDSON, Hon. R. A. RITCHIE, Hon. EMMETT M. HALL, Hon. W. F. SPENCE, Hon. L. P. PIGEON.

The Federal Court of Canada, Supreme Court of Canada Bldg., Wellington St., Ottawa, Ont. K1A 0H9; the **Trial Division** of the Federal Court has jurisdiction in cases involving the Crown, Crown Officers or servants, relief against Federal Boards, Commissions, and other tribunals, inter-Provincial and Federal-Provincial disputes, industrial or industrial property matters, Admiralty, income tax and estate tax appeals, and other matters where no other court has appropriate jusdiction. As the **Citizenship Appeal Court,** the Trial Division has exclusive jurisdiction to hear all appeals included under the Canadian Citizenship Act. The **Federal Court of Appeal** has jurisdiction on appeals from the Trial Division, Federal Tribunals, and on decisions of Federal Boards and Commissions.

Chief Justice: Hon. WILBUR ROY JACKETT.

Associate Chief Justice: Hon. CAMILIEN NOËL.

Trial Division Judges: Hon. A. ALEX CATTENACH, Hon. HUGH F. GIBSON, Hon. ALLISON M. WALSH, Hon. ROD KERR, Hon. DARREL V. HEALD, Hon. FRANK U. COLLIER.

Court of Appeal Judge: Hon. ARTHUR LOUIS THURLOW.

The Court Martial Appeal Court of Canada

Supreme Court of Canada Bldg., Wellington St., Ottawa, Ont. K1A 0H9.

President: Hon. H. F. GIBSON.

Puisne Judges: Hon. ROD KERR, Hon. W. R. JACKETT, Hon. ARTHUR L. THURLOW, Hon. CAMILIEN NOËL, Hon. A. ALEX CATTANACH, Hon. ALLISON M. WALSH, Hon. Mr. JUSTICE DARREL V. HEALD, Hon. Mr. Justice LOUIS PRATTE, Hon. Mr. Justice FRANK U. COLLIER, Hon. YVES BERNIER, Hon. DAVID M. DICKSON, Hon. GORDON C. HALL, Hon. GORDON L. S. HART, Hon. ARTHUR R. JESSUP, Hon. WILLIAM R. McINTYRE, Hon. WILLIAM R. SINCLAIR, Hon. DAVID R. VERCHERE.

PROVINCIAL COURTS

ALBERTA
Supreme Court—Appellate Division

Chief Justice of Alberta: Hon. S. BRUCE SMITH.

Justices of Appeal: Hons. H. G. JOHNSON (Edmonton), E. W. S. KANE (Edmonton), N. D. McDERMID (Calgary), J. M. CAIRNS (Calgary), G. H. ALLEN (Calgary), C. W. CLEMENT (Edmonton), D. C. PROWSE, W. R. SINCLAIR, A. F. MOIR.

Supreme Court—Trial Division

Chief Justice, Trial Division: Hon. J. V. H. MILVAIN.

Puisne Justices: Hons. NEIL PRIMROSE (Edmonton), P. GRESCHUK (Edmonton), M. E. MANNING (Edmonton), W. J. C. KIRBY (Calgary), A. M. DECHENE (Edmonton), MICHAEL B. O'BYRNE (Edmonton), A. J. CULLEN (Calgary), S. S. LIEBERMAN (Edmonton), H. J. MACDONALD (Calgary), D. H. BOWEN (Edmonton), W. K. MOORE (Calgary), J. C. CAVANAGH, M. E. SHANNON.

BRITISH COLUMBIA
Court of Appeal

Chief Justice of British Columbia: (vacant).

Justices of Appeal: Hons. C. W. TYSOE, H. A. MACLEAN, E. B. BULL, M. M. McFARLANE, A. E. BRANCA, A. B. ROBERTSON, N. T. NEMETZ, J. D TAGGART.

Supreme Court

Chief Justice: Hon. J. O. WILSON.

Puisne Judges: Hons. R. A. B. WOOTTON, J. G. RUTTAN, D. R. VERCHERE, E. E. HINKSON, J. S. AIKINS, V. L. DRYER, W. K. SMITH, G. G. S. RAE, A. B. MACFARLANE, G. F. T. GREGORY, J. G. GOULD, H. C. McKAY, R. P. ANDERSON, T. R. BERGER, J. A. MACDONALD, P. D. SEATON, W. R. McINTYRE, F. C. MUNROE, D. E. ANDREWS.

MANITOBA
Court of Appeal

Chief Justice of Manitoba: S. FREEDMAN.

Puisne Judges: Hons. R. DU VAL GUY, A. MONNIN, G. C. HALL, R. J. MATAS.

CANADA—(Judicial System)

Court of Queen's Bench
Chief Justice: Hon. A. S. Dewar.
Puisne Judges: Hons. I. Nitikman, L. Deniset, J. E. Wilson, J. M. Hunt, J. R. Solomon, A. C. Hamilton, W. S. Wright.

NEW BRUNSWICK
Supreme Court—Appeal Division
Chief Justice of New Brunswick: Hon. Charles J. A. Hughes.
Puisne Judges: Hons. R. V. Limerick, J. N. Bugold, Henry Ryan.

Queen's Bench Division
Chief Justice: Hon. A. J. Cormier.
Puisne Judges: Hons. A. M. Robichaud, J. A. Pichette, D. M. Dickson, J. P. Barry, C. Leger, Ronald Stevenson.

NEWFOUNDLAND
Supreme Court
Chief Justice: Hon. Robert Stafford Furlong.
Puisne Judges: Hons. H. G. Puddester, J. D. Higgins, Arthur S. Mifflin.

NOVA SCOTIA
Supreme Court—Appeal Division
Chief Justice of Nova Scotia: Hon. I. M. McKeigan.
Justices: Hons. T. H. Coffin, A. G. Cooper.

Trial Division
Chief Justice: Hon. G. S. Cowan.
Justices: Hons. F. W. Bissett, J. L. Dubinsky, G. L. S. Hart, V. J. Morrison, M. C. Jones.

ONTARIO
Supreme Court—Court of Appeal
Chief Justice of Ontario: Hon. G. A. Gale.
Justices: Hons. J. B. Aylesworth, F. G. Mackay, W. F. Schroeder, G. A. McGillivray, A. Kelly, G. T. Evans, A. Jessup, J. W. Brooke, J. D. Arnup.

High Court of Justice
Chief Justice: Hon. D. C. Wells.
Justices: Hons. John L. Wilson, J. M. King, C. D. Stewart, E. G. Moorhouse, E. G. Thompson, J. F. Donnelly, J. R. Morand, W. D. Parker, E. A. Richardson, Neil C. Fraser, Campbell Grant, S. H. S. Hughes, E. L. Haines, A. H. Lieff, W. A. Donohue, W. J. Henderson, Alexander Stark, E. P. Hartt, M. N. Lacourciere, D. A. Keith, G. A. Addy, L. T. Pennell, J. H. Osler, L. W.

Houlden, P. Wright, P. T. Galligan, M. Lerner, J. D. Cromarty, T. P. Callon, M. M. Van Camp, J. G. O'Driscoll.

PRINCE EDWARD ISLAND
Supreme Court
Chief Justice: Hon. St. Clair Trainor.
Judges: Hons. George J. Tweedy, R. Reginald Bell, John Nicholson.

Court of Chancery
Master of the Rolls: Hon. R. Reginald Bell.
Vice-Chancellor: Hon. George J. Tweedy.

QUEBEC
Court of Queen's Bench (Appeal Side)
Montreal
Chief Justice: Hon. Lucien Tremblay.
Judges: Hons. P. C. Casey, G-Ed. Rinfret, Georges R. W. Owen, G. H. Montgomery, Roger Brossard, Marcel Crete, Jean Beetz, Fred Kausman, Laurent Bélager.

Quebec City
Judges: Hons. Jean Turgeon, François LaJoie, Antoine Rivard, Claude Gagnon.

SASKATCHEWAN
Court of Appeal
Chief Justice of Saskatchewan: Hon. E. M. Culliton.
Puisne Judges: Hons. Mervyn Woods, R. L. Brownridge, P. H. Maguire, Roy Hall.

Court of Queen's Bench
Chief Justice: Hon. A. H. Bence.
Puisne Judges: Hons. F. W. Johnson, D. C. Disbery, M. A. Macpherson, R. A. MacDonald, W. A. Tucker, A. L. Sirois, E. D. Bayda.

NORTHWEST TERRITORIES
Judge of the Territorial Court: Hon. Mr. Justice W. G. Morrow.

YUKON TERRITORY
Judges of the Territorial Court: Hon. Mr. Justice H. C. B. Maddison (Whitehorse), Hon. W. G. Morrow (Yellowknife).
Clerk of the Territorial Court and Registrar of Appeal Court: J. Worsell, Room 259, Federal Bldg., Whitehorse.

RELIGION

Nearly 80 per cent of the population belongs to the three main churches; in order of size: Roman Catholic, United and Anglican. Numerous other churches and denominations are represented.

THE ROMAN CATHOLIC CHURCH IN CANADA

Roman Catholic population of Canada, 1971 Census: 9,975,000.

Canadian Catholic Conference: 90 Parent Ave., Ottawa, Ont. K1N 7B1; Pres. Most Rev. J. M. FORTIER, Archbishop of Sherbrooke, P.Q.; Vice-Pres. Most Rev. G. E. CARTER, Bishop of London.

Apostolic Pro-Nuncio: Most Rev. GUIDO DEL MESTRI, D.D., Apostolic Nunciature: Manor Ave., Rockcliffe Park, Ottawa, Ont. K1M 0E3.

ARCHBISHOPS

Edmonton: JOSEPH MACNEIL.
Halifax: JAMES M. HAYES.
Kingston: J. L. WILHELM.
St. John's: PATRICK J. SKINNER.
Quebec: Cardinal MAURICE ROY.
Rimouski: GILLES OUELLET.
Regina: CHARLES A. HAPLIN.
Sherbrooke: J. M. FORTIER.
St. Boniface: MAURICE BADOUX.
Toronto: PHILIP POCOCK.
Montreal: PAUL GREGOIRE.
Moncton: DONAT CHIASSON.
Ottawa: J. A. PLOUDRE.
Vancouver: J. CARNEY.
Grouard-McLennan: H. LEGARE.
Keewatin-Le-Pas: P. DUMOUCHEL.
Winnipeg: Cardinal GEORGE FLAHIFF.

THE UNITED CHURCH OF CANADA

2,354 pastoral churches, 2,030 ministers, and 993,190 members (Census figure 3,664,008); United Church House, 85 St. Clair Ave. E. Toronto M4G 1W5.

The United Church of Canada was founded in 1925 with the union of Methodist, Congregational and Presbyterian churches in Canada. Other free churches have since joined and there are proposals for union with the Anglican church.

Moderator: Rt. Rev. N. BRUCE MCLEOD, M.A., B.D.
Secretary: Rev. GEORGE M. MORRISON, D.D., F.C.A.
Treasurer: DOUGLAS BORGAL.

THE ANGLICAN CHURCH OF CANADA

Anglican population of Canada, 1961 Census: 2,409,068 (membership 1,109,221—1971).

Primate of the Anglican Church of Canada: Most Rev. E. W. SCOTT, D.D., D.C.L.

General Sec. of General Synod: Ven. E. S. LIGHT, C.D., B.A., L.TH., D.D., Church House, 600 Jarvis St., Toronto 285.

ARCHBISHOPS

Nova Scotia: W. W. DAVIS.
Qu'Appelle: G. F. C. JACKSON.
Algoma: W. L. WRIGHT.
Caribou: (vacant).

THE PRESBYTERIAN CHURCH IN CANADA

872,330 members (1971 census).
50 Wynford Drive, Don Mills, Ont.

Moderator: Rev. A. H. JOHNSTON, M.A., D.D.
Principal Clerk: Rev. L. H. FOWLER, M.A., B.D., D.D. (Don Mills, Ont.).
Deputy Clerk: Rev. D. C. MACDONALD, B.A., D.D. (Don Mills, Ont.).
Treasurer: R. R. MERIFIELD, Q.C. (Toronto).

Publs. include: *The Presbyterian Record, These Days, Glad Tidings, The Message.*

BAPTIST ORGANIZATION

Baptist Federation of Canada: Box 1298, Brantford Ont.; (1961 census) 519,585; 1,211 churches; membership 140,000; missions: Angola, Kenya, Bolivia, India; Pres. Dr. J. FRANK PATCH; Gen. Sec. Dr. R. F. BULLEN; publs. *The Canadian Baptist, The Atlantic Baptist, Tidings, Link and Visitor, Enterprise.*

THE LUTHERAN CHURCH IN CANADA

Ordained ministers 838, organized congregations 1,014 membership 301,162.

Lutheran Council in Canada: 500-365 Hargrave St., Winnipeg; Gen. Sec. Dr. EARL J. TREUSCH.

Canadian Lutheran World Relief: 1820 Arlington St., Winnipeg; material aid and immigration agency for Lutherans; Exec. Sec. J. G. KEIL.

JEWISH COMMUNITIES

The Jews of Canada number 254,368 (1961 Census).

Canadian Jewish Congress: 1590 McGregor Ave., Montreal 109, Exec. Vice-Pres. S. HAYES.

Jewish Community Council: 151 Chapel St., Ottawa, Ont.; Pres. N. ZAGERMAN; Exec. Dir. HY HOCHBERG.

THE ORTHODOX CHURCH

GREEK ORTHODOX CHURCH

Members (1961 Census), 239,766; 27 Teddington Park Ave., Toronto 12, Titular Bishop of Ancona His Grace THEODOSIOS.

UKRAINIAN GREEK ORTHODOX CHURCH OF CANADA

300 parishes, 150 000 members; 7 St. John's Avenue, Winnipeg 4, Man; f. 1918.

Publ. *Herald* circ. 5,000 (with English supplement).

Metropolitan: Most Rev. ILARION (OHIENKO) Metropolitan of Winnipeg and of all Canada; 332 Bannerman Ave., Winnipeg R2W 0T9.

The Romanian Orthodox and the Syrian Orthodox Churches are also represented in Canada.

UKRAINIAN CATHOLIC CHURCH IN CANADA

228,000 members (1971 Census).

Archeparchy of Winnipeg: Most Rev. MAXIM HERMANIUK, C.S.S.R., D.D., Archbishop Metropolitan of Winnipeg, 235 Scotia St., Winnipeg.

Eparchy of Edmonton: Most Rev. NEIL SAVARYN, O.S.B.M., D.D., 6240 Ada Blvd., Edmonton.

Eparchy of Toronto: Most Rev. ISIDORE BORECKY, D.D.

Eparchy of Saskatoon: Most Rev. Andrew Roborecky, D.D., 866 Saskatchewan Crescent, Saskatoon.

Publs. *Ukrainian News, Our Aim, Progress, The Light, Redeemer's Voice.*

OTHER CHURCHES

Christian Church (Disciples of Christ): 35 churches, 4,700 mems.; 39 Arkell Rd., Guelph, Ontario N1H 6H8; Exec. Minister R. K. Leland; publ. *The Canadian Disciple* (monthly).

Church of Jesus Christ of Latter-Day Saints (Mormons): 60,000 mems.; Ontario Mission: 338 Queen St. East, Brampton, Ontario; Quebec Mission: 1255 Laird Blvd., Suite 150, Montreal 304, Que.; Pres. John K. M. Olsen; Pres. Roy R. Spackman; Alberta-Saskatchewan Mission: 1010-70th Ave., S.W. Calgary Alberta; Pres. H. Clay Gorton; Alaska-British Columbia Mission: 5055 Connaught Drive Vancouver 13 B.C.; Pres. Raymond C. Bowers.

Evangelical United Brethren Church: 10,291 mems.

Pentecostal Assemblies of Canada: 10 Overlea Blvd., Toronto, Ontario M4H 1A5; Gen. Superintendent R. W. Taitinger; Gen. Sec. J. Montgomery; Exec. Dir. Overseas Missions C. W. Lynn; 110,000 mems.; publ. *The Pentecostal Testimony*, circ. 15,000.

Reformed Episcopal Church in Canada: 7,600 mems.; 1654 Renfrew St., Vancouver 6, B.C. V5K 4E1; f. 1873; Bishop Rt. Rev. Gordon Stacey, D.D.; Sec. of the Synod Mrs. J. Gordon.

Religious Society of Friends: 60 Lowther Ave., Toronto 5; Clerk of Canadian Yearly Meeting of Friends Burton S. W. Hill, P.O.B. 33, Rockwood, Ont.; as well as religious activities, the Society is active in peace and social reform; publ. *Canadian Friend.*

Salvation Army in Canada: 20 Albert Street, Toronto, Ont. M5G 1A6; Commissioner Clarence D. Wiseman.

THE PRESS

The vastness of the country hampers distribution and the establishment of a strong national press, so the daily press in Canada is essentially local in coverage, influence and distribution. However, a considerable proportion of the contents of the smaller Canadian papers is from syndicated sources in the U.S.A. or the United Kingdom, and news which is not local has a strong U.S. flavour. There are 117 daily newspapers: 102 in English and 15 in French with a combined circulation of over 4.7 million, representing three-quarters of the country's households and covering the major centres of population.

There is an increasing trend towards group ownership: over a third of daily newspapers are owned by three major groups: Thomson's, Southam and Free Press and twelve groups own over two-thirds of the Canadian dailies. In 1971 14 newspapers accounted for just over half the total daily circulation of newspapers.

About 900 weekly and twice-weekly newspapers with a total circulation of more than 9,000,000 serve the more remote areas of the country and a significant feature of the Canadian press is the publishing of newspapers catering for ethnic groups: there are nearly 90 of these (mainly weekly) publications appearing in over 20 languages, with a total circulation of nearly 3,000,000.

There are numerous periodicals for business, trade, professional, recreational and special interest readership, although periodical publishing, particularly, suffers from substantial competition from publications originating in the U.S.A. Among periodicals, the only one which can claim to be national in its attitudes and readership is the fortnightly *Maclean's Magazine*, which also has a French edition.

DAILY NEWSPAPERS

ALBERTA

Calgary Albertan: 830 10th Avenue, S.W. Calgary; f. 1902; morning; Independent; Publr. Bruce Rudd; Man. Editor Tom Moore; circ. 34,216.

Calgary Herald: 206-7th Ave., Calgary; f. 1885; evening; Independent; Publr. F. G. Swanson; Editor-in-Chief R. L. Sanburn; circ. 111,755.

Journal: 10006-101 St., Edmonton; f. 1903; evening; Independent; Editor A. Snaddon; circ. 168,692.

Lethbridge Herald: 504 7th Street South, Lethbridge; f. 1907; evening; Independent; Editor C. W. Mowers; Man. Editor Don Pilling; circ. 24,000.

Medicine Hat News: 4-6th Ave., Medicine Hat; f. 1910; Independent-Liberal; Publr. Ian C. Macdonald; Editor P. Mossey; circ. 8,674.

Red Deer Advocate: P.O.B. 520, Red Deer; f. 1901; evening, excl. Sun.; Publisher Gordon Grierson; Editor J. E. Bower; circ. 11,443.

BRITISH COLUMBIA

Chinese Times: 1 Pender St. E., Vancouver; f. 1907; morning; Independent; Editor Wayne Lee; circ. 5,000.

Citizen, The: 150 Brunswick St., Prince George; f. 1957; evening; Publr. J. F. Evans; Editor N. A. Skae; circ. 16,603.

Colonist: 2621 Douglas Street, Victoria; f. 1858; morning; daily (ex. Mon.); Independent; Publisher and Editor-in-Chief R. J. Bower; Man. Editor F. Barnes; circ. 41,817 (daily), 47,823 (Sunday).

The Columbian: 329 North Rd., Coquitlam, P.O.B. 730, New Westminster; f. 1861; evening; Independent; Publr. R. D. Taylor; Man. Editor E. A. McLellan; circ. 31,644.

Courier: 492 Doyle Ave., Kelowna; evening; Publr. R. P. Maclean; circ. 10,732.

Free Press: 225 Commercial St., Nanaimo; f. 1874; evening (ex. Sun.); Independent; Publr. C. W. Ramsden; Editor Peter McMullan; circ. 10,118.

News: 266 Baker St., Nelson; f. 1902; morning; Independent; Editor A. W. Gibbon; circ. 8,966.

Province: 2250 Granville Street, Vancouver 9; f. 1898; morning; Independent; Publr. P. Sherman; Man. Editor M. J. Moore; circ. 115,488.

Sentinel: 206 Seymour St. Kamloops; f. 1886; Independent; evening; Publr. R. Laidlaw; Editor T. Loran; circ. 11,533.

Sun: 2250 Granville St., Vancouver; f. 1886; evening; liberal; Editorial Dir. Bruce Hutchison; Publr. J. Stuart Keate; circ. 243,823.

Times: 1163 Cedar Ave., Trail; f. 1895; evening (ex. Sun); Independent; Editor J. Fisher; circ. 5,669.

Vernon Daily News: 3309-31st Ave., f. 1891; evening; Publr. B. M. Rowland; Editor K. W. Bond; circ. 7,565.

Victoria Times: 2621 Douglas Street, Victoria; f. 1884; evening; Ind. Liberal; Publr. H. S. Underhill; Editor Brian A. Tobin; circ. 32,617.

Manitoba

Graphic: 201 Saskatchewan Ave., Portage la Prairie; f. 1895; evening (ex. Sun.); Independent; Editor W. H. Vopni; circ. 3,775.

Reminder: 38 Main St., Flin Flon; f. 1946; Independent; evening, excl. Sun.; Publr. T. W. Dobson; Editor Bruce Keddie; circ. 3,600.

Sun: 501 Rosser Ave., Brandon; f. 1882; evening; Con.; Publr. L. D. Whitehead; circ. 13,955.

Tribune: 257 Smith St., Winnipeg; f. 1890; evening; Independent; Publr. A. R. Williams; Editor Tom Green; circ. 75,909.

Winnipeg Free Press: 300 Carlton St., Winnipeg; f. 1874; Independent; Publr. R. S. Malone; Exec. Editor Peter McLintock; circ. 137,118.

New Brunswick

L'Evangeline: 80 Church St., Moncton; f. 1887; French; morning; Independent; Editor C. Bourque; circ. 9,476.

Gleaner: Phoenix Square, Fredericton; f. 1880; evening; Independent; Dir. R. Wamboldt; circ. 13,366.

Telegraph-Journal and **Evening Times-Globe:** Cnr. Crown and Union Streets, Saint John; Independent; Pres. and Publr. R. Costello; Editor Fred Hazel; circ. 57,808.

Times and Transcript: Moncton Publishing Co. Ltd., 939 Main St., Moncton; morning, evening; Independent; Pres. and Publr. J. K. Grainger; circ. 36,694.

Newfoundland

Evening Telegram: Duckworth St., St. John's; f. 1879; evening; Independent; Thompson Newspapers Ltd.; Publr. S. R. Herder; Editor M. F. Harrington; circ. 29,861, Sat. 48,310.

News: 206 Water St., St. John's; f. 1894; morning; Independent; Publr. and Man. Editor W. R. Callahan; Editor J. R. Thomas; circ. 7,124.

Western Star: Brook St., Corner Brook; f. 1900; evening; Independent; Thompson Newspapers Ltd.; Editor W. McKay; circ. 8,535, Sat. 10,261.

Nova Scotia

Cape Breton Post: Dorchester St., Sydney; f. 1900; evening; Independent; Publr. Roy D. Duchemin; Editor Ian McNeil; circ. 28,608.

Chronicle-Herald: 1650 Argyle St., Halifax; f. 1875; morning; Independent; Editor W. March; Man. Editor A. M. Savage; circ. 67,862.

Daily News: 576 Prince St. Truro; f. 1891; evening (ex. Sun); Independent; Publr. Philip McLeod; Editor Archie MacNeil; circ. 5,066.

Mail-Star: 1650 Argyle St., Halifax; f. 1875; evening; Independent; Man. Editor A. M. Savage; circ. 49,560.

News: Box 280, Amherst; f. 1893; morning; Ind.-Con.; Publr. R. M. van Snick; Editor R. Crowe; circ. 3,882.

News: Provost St., New Glasgow; f. 1910; evening; Conservative; Publr. and Editor J. R. H. Sutherland; circ. 9,940.

Ontario

Beacon-Herald: 108 Ontario St., Stratford; f. 1887; evening; Independent; Editor S. Dingman; circ. 10,415.

Chatham Daily News: 45-7 Fourth St., Chatham; Thompson Newspapers Ltd.; f. 1865; evening; Independent; Publr. and Gen. Man. W. Telfer; Editor D. C. Waite; circ. 14,854.

Citizen: 1101 Baxter Rd., Ottawa; f. 1844; evening; Independent; Editor Christopher Young; Publr. R. W. Southam; Editor C. Young; circ. 91,523.

Corriere Canadese: 1000 Lawrence Ave. Toronto; f. 1954; morning; Italian; Publr. D. Iannuzzi; Man. Editor E. Caprile; circ. 22,317.

Daily Journal Record: 297 Randall St., Oakville; f. 1962; morning; Editor John Strimas; circ. 9,213.

Daily Reporter: 26 Ainstie St., S. Cambridge; f. 1846; evening; Independent; Publr. N. D. Hamilton; Man. Editor M. Mowbray; circ. 13,680.

Daily Times: 33 Queen St. W. Brampton; f. 1885; evening; Publr. E. C. Prince; Man. Editor R. Yaworski; circ. 8,374.

Le Droit: 375 Rideau St., Ottawa; f. 1913; evening; French; Independent; Publr. J.-R. Bélanger; Editor Jean-Guy Bruneau; circ. 43,505.

Examiner: 16 Bayfield St., Barrie; f. 1865; evening; Independent; Publr. J. A. Robb; Man. Editor D. M. Henshaw; circ. 11,115.

Examiner: 400 Water St., Peterborough; f. 1884; evening; Independent; Publr. and Gen. Man. W. J. Garner; Man. Editor: G. F. Toner; circ. 26,069.

Expositor: 53 Dalhousie St., Brantford; f. 1852; evening; Independent; Publr. E. H. Wheatley; Editor K. J. Strachan; circ. 28,063.

Free Press: 369 York St., London; f. 1849; morning and evening; Independent; Publr. Walter J. Blackburn; Editor William C. Heine; circ. 126,797.

Globe and Mail: 444 Front St. W., Toronto; f. 1844; morning; Independent; Pres. and Publr. J. L. Cooper; Editor R. J. Doyle; circ. 265,031.

Intelligencer: 45 Bridge St. E., Belleville; evening; Independent; Publr. G. A. Morton; Man. Editor M. H. Switzer; circ. 17,433.

Mercury: 8 Macdonnell St., Guelph; f. 1854; evening; Independent; Publr. R. L. Hamill; Editor A. Smith; circ. 18,094.

Northern Daily News: 8 Duncan Ave., Kirkland Lake; f. 1922; evening (ex. Sunday); Man. and Editor T. O'Laughlin; circ. 5,813.

Nugget: 259 Worthington St., North Bay; f. 1909; evening; Independent; Man. Editor C. M. Fellman; circ. 21,809.

Observer: 186 Alexander St., Pembroke; f. 1855; evening (ex. Sunday); Publr. R. C. Rooke; Editor W. H. Higginson; circ. 7,623.

Oshawa Times: 44 Richmond St., Oshawa; evening; Independent; Man. Editor Erik Watt; circ. 23,535.

Ottawa Journal: 365 Laurier Avenue W., Ottawa; f. 1885; evening; Independent-Conservative; Man. Editor G. J. Paterson; circ. 83,271.

Packet and Times: 31 Colborne St., Orillia; f. 1867; evening (ex. Sunday); Editor G. Czerny; circ. 8,425.

Record: 225 Fairway, Kitchener; f. 1878; evening; Independent; Publr. and Editor John E. Motz; circ. 45,185.

Recorder and Times: 23 King St., Brockville; f. 1821; evening; Independent; Editor A. C. Runciman; circ. 11,399.

Review: Valley Way and Morrison St., Niagara Falls; f. 1879; evening; Independent; Publr. and Editor W. B. LESLIE; circ. 19,053.

Sarnia Observer: 241 N. Front St., Sarnia; evening; Independent; Publr. and Gen. Man. L. A. DeMARCHI; Man. Editor J. CLARKE; circ. 19,693.

Sault Daily Star: 369 Queen St. E., Sault Ste. Marie; f. 1912; noon and evening; Independent; Man. Dir. R. L. CURRAN; Man. Editor J. A. CURRAN; circ. 23,045.

Sentinel-Review: 16-18 Brock St., Woodstock; f. 1886; evening; Independent; Publr. R. G. DUNDAS; Editor R. MACKENZIE; circ. 9,423.

Shing Wah Daily News: 12 Hagerman St., Toronto; f. 1916; evening (ex. Sun.); Chinese; Editor H. B. GIANG; circ. 4,260.

Spectator: 115 King St. East, Hamilton; f. 1846; evening; Independent; Publr. J. D. MUIR; Exec. Editor G. BULLOCK; circ. 134,749.

Standard: 17-21 Queen St., St. Catherines; f. 1891; evening; Independent; Publr. J. R. BATES; Chief Editor L. N. SMITH; circ. 38,142.

Standard-Freeholder: 44 Pitt St., Cornwall; f. 1846; evening; Independent; Man. Editor RUSS DEWAR; circ. 14,639.

Star: 167 Ferry St., Windsor; f. 1918; evening; Independent; Publr. J. P. O'CALLAGHAN; Editor R. M. PEARSON; circ. 85,249.

Sudbury Star: 33 McKenzie St.; f. 1908; evenings; Publr. and Gen. Man. J. R. MEAKES; circ. 40,294.

Sun-Times: 290 9th St., Owen Sound; Sun f. 1890, Times f. 1853; Independent; Editor ROBERT HULL; Man. Editor JIM MERRIAM; circ. 16,169.

Times-News: 177 Arthur St., Thunder Bay; morning; Publr. G. B. MACGILLIVRAY; circ. 6,735.

Times-Journal: 16 Hincks St., St. Thomas; f. 1881; evening; Independent; Publr. GEORGE M. DINGMAN; Exec. Editor L. J. BEAVIS; Man. Editor HUGH AGNEW; circ. 11,149.

Timmins Daily Press: 125 Cedar South, Timmins; Thomson Newspapers Ltd.; f. 1933; evening; Independent; Publr. J. KOBYLNIK; Editor G. REYNOLDS; circ. 11,816.

Toronto Daily Star: 1 Yonge St.; f. 1892; evening; Independent; Pres. and Publr. BELAND H. HONDERICH; circ. 518,874.

Toronto Sun: 322 King St. West; f. 1971; morning; Independent; Publr. DOUG CREIGHTON; Gen. Man. DON HUNT; Editor PETER WORTHINGTON; circ. 82,870.

Welland-Port Colborne Evening Tribune: 228 E. Main St., Welland; Thompson Newspapers Ltd.; f. 1863; evening; Independent; Gen. Man. A. S. TOPP; Editor P. TISSINGTON; circ. 19,500.

Whig-Standard: 306 King St., Kingston; f. 1810; evening; Independent; Publr. M. L. DAVIES; Editor R. D. OWEN; circ. 33,520.

PRINCE EDWARD ISLAND

Guardian: 165 Prince St., Charlottetown; f. 1887; morning; Independent; Editor D. MACLEOD; circ. 16,740.

Journal-Pioneer: Water St., Summerside; amalgamated 1951; evening (ex. Sat. and Sun.); Editor ELMER MURPHY; circ. 8,025.

Patriot: 165 Prince St., Charlottetown; f. 1851; evening (ex. Sun.); Independent; Editor W. WARD; circ. 5,091.

QUEBEC
F.—Published in French.

A Propos: 3 Place Jean-Talon Quebec; f. 1973; morning; Independent; F.; Publr. J. BELIVEAU; Editor PIERRE LOIGNON; circ. 17,974.

Le Devoir: 211 Rue du St. Sacrement Montreal 125; f. 1910; morning; Independent; F.; Publr. and Editor CLAUDE RYAN; circ. 39,061.

Gazette: 1000 St. Antoine St., Montreal; f. 1778; morning; Independent; Publr. M. FARRELL; Editor R. L. CRYSLER; circ. 138,194.

Le Journal de Montreal: 155 Port Royal W., Montreal 357; f. 1964; morning; F.; Editor JACQUES BEAUCHAMP; circ. 141,596.

Le Journal de Quebec: 450 Bechard St., Ville de Vanier; morning; F.; Chief Editor D. LAMOUREUX; circ. 19,149.

Montreal-Matin: 2580 Blvd. St. Joseph East, Montreal; f. 1930; morning; F.; Independent; Publr. LUC BEAUREGARD; Man. Editor G. CELLIER; circ. 136,815.

Montreal Star: Box 4005, Place D'Armes; f. 1869; evening; Independent; Publr. D. A. PRICE; Editor-in-Chief F. B. WALKER; circ. 190,349.

Le Nouvelliste: 500 St. Georges St., Trois Rivières, P.Q.; f. 1920; morning; F.; Independent; Pres. and Gen. Man. CHARLES D'AMOUR; Man. Editor J. RENE FERRON; Editor S. ST.-AMANT; circ. 49,848.

La Presse: 7 St. James St. West, Montreal; f. 1884; evening; Publr. and Editor ROGER LEMELIN; circ. 183,710.

Le Quotidien: 316 Labrecque Ave., Chicontimi; f. 1973; evening; F.; Editor BERTRAND TREMBLAY; circ. 25,000.

Record: C.P.R. Terrace Sherbrooke; evening; Independent; circ. 6,347.

Le Soleil: 390 St. Vallier St., Quebec; f. 1881; evening; Independent; F.; Editor RAYMOND DUBÉ; circ. 150,346.

Tribune: 221 Dufferin Ave., Sherbrooke; f. 1910; evening; Independent; F.; Pres. YVON DUBÉ; Editor-in-Chief and Man. Editor CHARLES-ANDRÉ BEAUDOIN; circ. 43,425.

La Voix de L'Est: 136 Main St., Granby; f. 1945; evening; F.; Editor ROLAND GAGNE; circ. 11,046.

SASKATCHEWAN

Daily Herald: 30 Tenth St. E., Prince Albert; Thompson Newspapers Ltd.; f. 1971; evening; Independent; Publr. J. P. FRIESEN; Man. Editor D. WRIGHT; circ. 8,371.

Leader-Post: Leader-Post Bldg., Park St. and Victoria Ave., Regina; f. 1883; evening; Independent-Liberal; Editor IVOR WILLIAMS; Exec. Vice-Pres. MAX MACDONALD; circ. 66,063.

Saskatoon Star-Phoenix: 204 5th Ave. W., Saskatoon; f. 1902; evening; Independent; Exec. Vice-Pres. J. STRUTHERS; Exec. Editor S. KING; circ. 44,009.

Times-Herald: 44 Fairford St., West, Moose Jaw; f. 1889; evening; Independent; Publr. J. R. GUAY; Editor L. MEZZAROS; circ. 8,774.

SELECTED PERIODICALS
(W = weekly; F = fortnightly; M = monthly; Q = quarterly.)

ALBERTA

Calgary North Hill News: Box 3160, Stn. B, Calgary; W.; circ. 22,535.

Canadian Author and Bookman/Canadian Poetry: 8128 97th Ave., Edmonton 82; Editor S. W. CHALMERS; circ. 1,600.

Ukrainian News: 10967 97th St., Edmonton 17; f. 1927; Editor Rev. M. SOPULAK; W.; circ. 9,259.

Western Week; 12 Piron St., St. Albert; Publr. W. E. JAMISON; W.

BRITISH COLUMBIA

Country Life in British Columbia: 207 West Hastings St., Vancouver; f. 1915; associated with the B.C. Federation of Agriculture; Editor J. R. ARMSTRONG; M.; circ. 10,969.

Financial Record: Suite 406,198 W. Hastings St., Vancouver 3; Man. Editor S. G. RUSK; W.

Garden Beautiful: Vancouver; f. 1932; Editor S. M. OLIVER; M.

Vancouver Life: 1012 Hornby St., Vancouver 1; f. 1965; Publr. DONALD C. CROMIE; Editor J. LYNDON GROVE; M.

Western Business and Industry: 2000 W. 12th Ave., Vancouver 9; Editor Don JOHNSTON M.

Western Fisheries: 1104 Hornby St., Vancouver 1; f. 1929; commercial fishing industry journal; Pres. E. G. KIDD; Editor HENRY FREW; M.; circ. 2,807.

Western Miner: 1200 West Pender St., Vancouver 1; f. 1928; Editor C. H. MITCHELL; M; circ. 6,408 .

MANITOBA

Beaver: Hudson's Bay Co., Hudson's Bay House, Winnipeg R3C 2R1; f. 1920; travel, exploration, development, ethnology and history of the Canadian North; Editor HELEN BURGESS; Q; circ. 38,000.

Canadian Farmer: 840 Main St., Winnipeg, Man. R2W 3R6; f. 1903; Ukrainian; Independent; Editor-in-Chief MYROSLAW ROMAN SHKAWRYTKO; W; circ. 22,780.

Canadian Register, Manitoba Edition: 504 Scott Building, 272 Main St., Winnipeg; f. 1962; Editor GONTRAN LAVIOLETTE, O.M.I.; circ. 6,800.

Country Guide: 1760 Ellice Ave., Winnipeg R3H 0B6; f. 1882; agriculture; Editor DON BARON; circ. 280,059.

Courier-Nordwesten: 955 Alexander Ave., Winnipeg; f. 1907; German; Independent; Editor-in-Chief B. LAENGIN, W.; circ. 14,378.

Free Press Weekly—Report on Farming: 300 Carlton St., Winnipeg R3C 3C1; f. 1872; Editor BRUCE McDONALD; circ. 261,475.

Israelite Press: 704 Broadway, P.O.B. 741, Winnipeg; f. 1910; Yiddish and English; serving the Jewish community of Western Canada from the Great Lakes to the Pacific; Independent; Editor MELVIN FENSON; W.

Modern Farmer, The: 171 McDermot Ave., Winnipeg; Editor THOMAS PAGE; W.

Motor in Canada: 1077 St. James St., P.O.B. 6900, Winnipeg R3C 3B1; f. 1915; Man. JACK MITCHELL; Editor RALF NEUENDORFF; M.; circ. 13,000.

New Pathway: 184 Alexander Ave., Box 785, Winnipeg R3C 2N4; f. 1930; Ukrainian; Independent; Sat.; Editor A. D. DOBRIANSKY; circ. 12,553.

Nordwesten: 462 Hargrave St., Winnipeg; f. 1888; German; Independent; Editor DIETRICH E. WOLF; W.; circ. 16,909.

Norrona: 8594 Sunbury Place, Delta, B.C.; f. 1910; Norwegian; Editor GUNNAR WAROLIN; twice monthly.

Our Sunday Visitor of Canada: 504 Scott Building, 272 Main St., Winnipeg; f. 1959; Editor GONTRAN LAVIOLETTE, O.M.I.; circ. 41,600.

Trade and Commerce: 1077 St. James St., P.O.B. 6900, Winnipeg 21; f. 1906; Editor R. TYRE; M.; circ. 8,903.

Ukrainian Voice: 210–216 Dufferin Ave.; P.O.B. 3629, Sta. B. Winnipeg R2W 3R4; f. 1910; Independent; Man. Editor M. H. HYKAWY; W.; circ. 13,076.

Western Construction and Industry: 84 Isabel St., Winnipeg R3A 1G1; f. 1949; Editor KING KEARNS; M.; circ. 5,334.

Western Jewish News: 306 Time Building, Winnipeg; Independent; W.; circ. 16,230.

NEW BRUNSWICK

Atlantic Advocate: Gleaner Building, Fredericton; f. 1956; Editor KEN CHISHOLM; M.; circ. 19,516.

NEWFOUNDLAND

Advertiser: Grand Falls; f. 1936; Editor RONALD ENNIS.

Chamber Promoter, The: Box 5309, St. John's; f. 1971; Editor JACK A. BROWN.

Herald: O'Leary Ave., St. John's; f. 1945; Independent; W.; Editor F. WHITEWAY; circ. 21,000.

Newfoundland Herald: O'Leary Ave., St. John's; f. 1946; Editor FRED WHITEWAY; W.

Newfoundland Quarterly: P.O. Box 5874, St. John's; f. 1901; history, the arts and general; Editor L. W. JANES.

Sun: Twillingate; f. 1880; Independent; Editor and Publr. STEWART ROBERTS; W.

NORTH-WEST TERRITORIES

Inuttituut (*The Eskimo Way*): f. 1959; Eskimo and English; Editor HARRIET GORDON RUSTON; circ. 4,000.

NOVA SCOTIA

Casket: Antigonish; f. 1852; Independent; Editor P. A. G. MACKAY; circ. 10,710.

Dalhousie Review: Dalhousie University, Halifax; f. 1921; literary and general; Q.; Editor A. R. BEVAN.

ONTARIO

Agrologist: Suite 907, 151 Slater St., Ottawa K1P 5H4; f. 1934; official organ of the Agricultural Institute of Canada; Editor W. E. HENDERSON; six times yearly; circ. 4,995.

Applied Graphics: Suite 212, Willowdale; f. 1969; Editor PETER PERRY; circ. 7,409.

Arts/Canada: 3 Church St., Toronto, Ontario M5E 1M2; f. 1943; Editor ANNE BRODZKY.

Canada Gazette: Ottawa, K1A O57; f. 1867; official organ of the Government of Canada; Editor Queen's Printer; W.

Canadian Aeronautics and Space Journal: Commonwealth Bldg., 77 Metcalfe St., Ottawa; f. 1954; Man. Editor P. A. COBBETT; M.

Canadian Architect, The: 1450 Don Mills Rd., Don Mills, Ont. M3B 2X7; f. 1955; Publr. CHARLES F. SHEWELL; Editor JAMES A. MURRAY; M.; circ. 5,772.

Canadian Author and Bookman: 8726-116 St., Edmonton, Alberta; f. 1921; organ of the Canadian Authors' Association; literary; Editor MARY E. DAWE; Q.; circ. 2,180.

Canadian Catholic Register: 67 Bond St., Toronto 205; f. 1942; Publr. SHAUN MacGRATH.

Canadian Churchman: 600 Jarvis St., Toronto M4Y 2J6; (newspaper of the Anglican Church of Canada); f. 1871; general and religious; Editor HUGH McCULLUM; M.; circ. 243,293.

Canadian Geographical Journal: 488 Wilbrod St., Ottawa K1N 6M8; f. 1930; organ of the Royal Canadian Geographical Society; Editor DAVID MACLELLAN; M.; circ. 22,702.

Canadian Journal of Public Health: 55 Parkdale Ave., Ottawa K1Y 4G1; journal of the Canadian Public Health Association; f. 1910; Editor JOHN KEAYS, 6 times yearly; circ. 3,301.

Canadian Journal of Surgery/Journal Canadien de Chirurgie: 1867 Alta Vista Dr., Ottawa K1G 0G8; f. 1957; English and French; Editor Dr. J. R. ANDERSON; 6 times yearly; circ. 1,311.

Canadian Labour: 2841 Riverside Drive, Ottawa, Ontario; f. 1956; Labour; Editor K. ROBINSON.

Canadian Nurse: 50 The Driveway, Ottawa K2P 1E2; f. 1905; official organ of the Canadian Nurses' Association; Editor VIRGINIA A. LINDABURY; circ. 102,099; French edition *L'Infirmière Canadienne*; f. 1959; Editor CLAIRE BIGUÉ; circ. 27,515.

Canadian Sportsman: 80 Brock St. E. Tillsonburg; f. 1870; Editor G. CLIFFORD CHAPMAN; W.

Canadian Welfare: 55 Parkdale Ave., Box 3505, Station C, Ottawa K1Y 4G1; f. 1924; publ. by Canadian Council on Social Development; social policy, trends and practices in Canada; Editor NORMAN DAHL; six times a year; circ. 4,570.

Chemistry in Canada: 151 Slater St., Ottawa, Ont. K1P 5H3; f. 1949; Editor D. W. EMMERSON; M.; circ. 9,114.

Cinema Canada: Suite 3, 6 Washington Ave., Toronto 5; Editor and Publ. GEORGE C. KOLLER; 6 times yearly.

Electronics and Communications: 1450 Don Mills Rd., Don Mills, Ont. M3B 2X7; f. 1953; Editor GEOFFREY SPARK; 10 times yearly; circ. 12,562.

Labour Gazette: Canada Department of Labour, Ottawa; f. 1900; English and French editions; labour problems, industrial, economic, statistical; Editor JACK E. NUGENT; M.

Labour Review: Canadian Federation of Labour, Box 64, Terminal "A", Ottawa 2; f. 1936; Editor W. T. BURFORD; M.

Nouvelle Revue Canadienne, La: Case Postale 614, Ottawa; French; literary.

ONTARIO—PUBLISHED IN TORONTO

The following are all published by Maclean-Hunter Publishing Co. Ltd., 481 University Avenue, Toronto M5W 1A7.

Bâtiment: f. 1926; Editor CLAUDE PICHER; M.; circ. 4,568.

Bus and Truck Transport: f. 1925; Editor P. INGRAM; M.; circ. 17,952.

Canadian Automotive Trade: f. 1920; Editor E. BELITSKY; M.; circ. 29,652.

Canadian Aviation: f. 1928; Editor HUGH WHITTINGTON; Publr. CHARLES T. TURNER; circ. 12,000.

Canadian Boating: 4 Collier St., 5; f. 1926; Editor BRUCE PROCTOR. Also published **Annual Cruise Guide;** nine issues yearly.

Canadian Builder: f. 1952; Editor CLIFFORD FOWKE; M.; circ. 17,248.

Canadian Electronics Engineering: f. 1957; Editor C. S. HAND; circ. 10,976.

Canadian Grocer: f. 1886; Editor MAURICE SHORE; F.; circ. 14,726.

Canadian Hotel & Restaurant: f. 1923; Editor ROBERT DICKSON; M.; circ. 22,920.

Canadian Printer and Publisher: Editor and Publr. W. B. FORBES; M.; circ. 6,084.

Chatelaine: f. 1928; women's journal; Editors DORIS ANDERSON, F. MONTPETIT; M.; circ. 1,248,000.

Civic: f. 1949; public works magazine; Editor WALTER JONES; M.; circ. 14,000.

Electrical Contractor and Maintenance Supervisor: Editor GEORGE H. MCNEVIN; M.; circ. 13,200.

Financial Post: f. 1907; Editor and Publr. PAUL S. DEACON; W.; circ. 142,184.

Heavy Construction News: f. 1957; Editor DAVID JUDGE; every second Monday; circ. 17,885.

Home Goods Retailing: f. 1955; Editor HELEN BAMEN; F.; circ. 17,500.

Maclean's Magazine: f. 1905; general interest; Editor BORDEN SPEARS; F.; circ. 769,194.

Mechanical Contracting and Plumbing: f. 1907; Editor TED HEWITT; circ. 17,520.

Modern Power and Engineering: f. 1907; Publr. and Editor W. B. GLASSFORD; circ. 11,044.

Office Equipment and Methods: f. 1955; Editor ARDEN GAYMAN; M.; circ. 16,574.

Style: f. 1888; Editor BRUCE GENDALL; F.; circ. 10,600.

Board of Trade Journal: Board of Trade Building, 11 Adelaide St. W.; f. 1910; Editor D. J. GHENT; circ. 14,456.

CA Magazine: The Canadian Institute of Chartered Accountants, 250 Bloor St. East, Toronto M4W 1G5; f. 1911; Editor L. REESOR; M.; circ. 30,802.

Canadian Bar Review: 2 Tremont Crescent, Don Mills; f. 1923; Editors Dr. J. G. CASTEL, R. C. MERRIAM; Q.; circ. 15,559.

Canadian Broadcaster: 217 Bay St.; f. 1942; trade; Publr. RICHARD G. LEWIS; two-monthly; circ. 2,139.

Canadian Forest Industries: Southam Business Publications Ltd., 1450 Don Mills Rd., Don Mills, Ont.; f. 1880; Editor STEVE TROWER; M.; circ. 11,195.

Canadian Forum: 56 Esplanade St. E., Toronto 1; f. 1920; political, literary and economic; Editor ABRAHAM ROTSTEIN; M.

Canadian Historical Review: University of Toronto Press, Toronto, Ontario M5S 1A6; f. 1920; Editor R. CRAIG BROWN; Q.; circ. 3,835.

Canadian Journal of Economics (Revue canadienne d'Economique): University of Toronto Press, Toronto M5S 1A6; f. 1969; organ of Canadian Economics Association (*Association canadienne d'Economique*); Managing Editors A. ASINAKOPULOS; Q.; circ. 3,505.

Canadian Journal of Mathematics: University of Toronto Press, 5; f. 1949; publ. for the Canadian Mathematical Congress; Editors P. H. H. FANTHAM, P. G. RODNEY; two-monthly; circ. 1,500.

Canadian Journal of Political Science (Revue canadienne de science politique): University of Toronto Press, Toronto, M5S 1A6; f. 1969; organ of the Canadian Political Science Association (*Association canadienne des Sciences politiques*); Co-Editors DAVID HOFFMAN and L. DION; circ. 2,804.

Canadian Journal of Psychology (Revue Canadienne de Psychologie): University of Toronto Press, 5; f. 1947; journal of the Canadian Psychological Assn.; Editor G. J. MOGENSON; Q.

Canadian Motorist: Ontario Motor League, Carlton Tower, 2 Carlton Street; f. 1914; an official publication of the Ontario Motor League; Editor JERRY TUTUNJIAN; six times a year; circ. 111,494.

Canadian Pharmaceutical Journal: 175 College St., Toronto M5T 1P8; f. 1868; Editor ARNOLD V. RAISON; M.; circ. 10,903.

Canadian Poultry Review: 6 Adelaide St., E. M5C 1H6; f. 1876; Editor R. J. BLUHM; M.; circ. 6,295.

Canadian Research and Development: 481 University Ave., Toronto, Ontario M5W 1A7; Editor DOUGLAS DINGELDEIN; two-monthly; circ. 8,200.

Canadian Review of Music and Art: 66 College St.; f. 1942; Editor LOUIS DE B. CORRNEAN; two-monthly.

Canadian School Journal: 51 Eglinton Ave. E., Toronto 12; f. 1921; Editor Mrs. JEAN M. WATSON; circ. 4,712.

Canadian Star Weekly: Southstar Publishers Ltd., 401 Bay St. M5H 2Y8; f. 1965; features and illustrated; Editor MICHAEL HANLON; W; circ. 206,055.

Canadian Travel Press: 150 King St. West, Suite 401, Toronto M5H 1K1; Editor E. BAXTER; fortnightly; circ. 10,271.

Canadian Tribune: 924 King St. West, Toronto 3; f. 1940; Editor JAMES LEECH; W.

Courier: 455 Spadina Ave.; f. 1907; German; Independent; Editors B. LAENGIN, H. BOPP; W.; circ. 9,105.

Design Engineering: 481 University Ave.; Editor J. C. YOUNG; M.; circ. 8,224.

East Toronto Weekly: 1344 Danforth Avenue; f. 1918; Independent; Editor A. L. DEACHMAN; W.

Engineering: 17 Inkerman St.; f. 1957; Editor K. GIBBONS; M.; circ. 55,599.

Engineering and Contract Record: Southam Business Publications Ltd., 1450 Don Mills Road, Don Mills, Ont.; f. 1888; Editor T. BRANDON JONES; circ. 17,100.

Engineering Digest: 46 St. Clair Ave. East, Toronto M4T 1N2; f. 1954; Editor H. W. MEYFARTH; 10 times yearly; circ. 51,518.

Executive (incorporating *Monetary Times*): 1450 Don Mills Rd., Don Mills, Ont.; f. 1958; Editor LOREN J. CHUDDY; M.; circ. 25,000.

Farm and Country: 3rd Floor, 30 Bloor St. W., Suite 305, Toronto M4W 1A2; Editor-in-Chief JOHN PHILLIPS; F.

Farmer's Magazine: 73 Richmond Street West; f. 1909; Editor ROBERT MORJORIBANKS; M.; circ. 137,000.

Fur Trade Journal: Bewdley; f. 1923; trade; Editor CHARLES CLAY; M.; circ. 3,927.

Health: 111 Avenue Rd.; f. 1933; health education; Editor-in-Chief Dr. GORDON BATES; Q.; circ. 25,825.

Holstein-Friesian Journal: 6 Adelaide St. E, Toronto M5C 1H6; f. 1938; official organ of the Holstein-Friesian Association of Canada; Editor H. J. COLSON; M.; circ. 14,219.

Home Building in Canada: 372 Bay St.; f. 1920; building; Editor J. R. WALKER; two-monthly.

In Review: Canadian Books for Children: Provincial Library Service, Ont. Ministry of Colleges and Universities, Mowat Block, Queen's Park, Toronto M7A 1C5; f. 1967; literary; Editor IRMA K. MCDONOUGH; Q.

Independent Forester: 789 Don Mills Rd.; f. 1881; fraternal; Editor FRANCINE FORTIER; circ. 702,903.

Industrial Canada: 67 Yonge St.; Man. A. L. ABBOTT; Editor A. W. HOUSE; M.

Jewish Standard: 53 Yonge St.; f. 1929; Editor JULIUS HAYMAN; two-monthly.

Journal of the Canadian Dental Association: 234 St. George St., Toronto, Ontario M5R 2P2; Editor Dr. R. M. GRANIGER; M.; circ. 9,929.

Kingston Road and Main Street Herald: 73 Adelaide St. West; f. 1928; Conservative; Editor FLORENCE CHARLES; W.

Marketing: 481 University Ave.; f. 1908; Publr. A. L. RODGERS; Editor COLIN MUNCIE; W.; circ. 7,607.

Medical Post: 481 University Ave.; Publr. M. R. MARK; Editor E. DAMUDE; F.; circ. 26,126.

Messenger of the Sacred Heart: 833 Broadview Ave., Toronto, Ontario M4K 2P9; f. 1891; Catholic; Editor Rev. F. J. POWER, S.J.; M.; circ. 20,000.

Metalworking: 297 Old Kingston Rd., West Hill, Ont.; f. 1938; Editor D. QUICK; 10 times yearly; circ. 9,455.

Modern Medicine of Canada—Médecine Moderne du Canada: Southam Business Publs. Ltd., 1450 Don Mills Rd., Don Mills, Ont. M3B 2X7; f. 1946; M.; Editor J. A. KELLEN; Man. T. TUCKER; published in English and French; circ. 23,700 (English), 6,600 (French).

New Equipment News: 46 St. Clair Ave. East; f. 1940; industrial; Editor D. H. GRAHAM; M.; circ. 23,554.

New Review, The: Box 31, Station "E", Toronto 4; East European history; Editors OLEG PIDHAINY, M. MLADENOVIC; Q.; circ. 1,000.

News: 63 Wellesley St., 5; f. 1940; pictorial; Editor JUDITH ROBINSON; W.

Northern Miner: 77 River St., Toronto, M5A 3P2; f. 1915; Editor J. W. CARRINGTON; circ. 22,229. Also publ. **Canadian Mines Handbook** (annually, July); Editor F. M. FIELDER; circ. 20,000.

Ontario Library Review: Provincial Library Service, Ontario Ministry of Colleges and Universities, Mowat Block, Queen's Park, Toronto M7A 1C5; f. 1916; Editor IRMA K. MCDONOUGH.

Ontario Medical Review: 240 St. George St., Toronto 5; f. 1922; Editor GLENN SAWYER, M.D.; M.; circ. 12,468.

Ontario Milk Producer: 50 Maitland St., Toronto M4Y 1C7; f. 1925; Editor D. A. MCGRATH; circ. 29,540.

Oral Health: 1450 Don Mills Rd., Toronto; f. 1911; Editor J. M. KERR, D.D.S.; circ. 9,279.

Phoenix: Univ. of Toronto Press, Trinity College, Toronto 5; journal of the Classical Association of Canada; Editor THOMAS M. ROBINSON; Q.

Physics in Canada/La Physique au Canada: bulletin of the Canadian Association of Physicists, 151 Slater, Suite 903, Ottawa, Ont. K1P 5H3; Editor R. L. CLARKE, Dept. of Physics, Carleton University, Ottawa K1S 5B6, Ont.; 7 times yearly; circ. 2,116.

Quill and Quire: 56 The Esplanade; f. 1935; covers the Canadian book industry; Editor FIONA MEE; 12 a year; circ. 10,970.

Radio and Television Appliance Trade Builder: Hugh C. McLean Publications Ltd., 1450 Don Mills Road; f. 1923; trade; Editor G. B. GILROY; M.

Saturday Night: 52 St. Clair Ave. East, Toronto 7; f. 1887; political, literary and economic; Editor ROBERT FULFORD; M.; circ. 74,007.

Scholarly Publishing: University of Toronto Press, Toronto M5S 1A6; f. 1969; journal for authors and publishers; Editor ELEANOR HARMAN; Q; circ. 1,400.

Sentinel: 94 Sheppard Ave., Willowdale; f. 1875; Protestant; Editor and Business Man. GORDON KEYES; 10 yearly; circ. 5,254.

Studies in Religion/Sciences religieuses: University of Toronto Press, Toronto, M5S 1A6; f. 1971; Man. Editor Prof.. J W. GRANT.

Time (Canada edition): 1155 Dorchester Blvd. W. Montreal H3B 2K2; est. 1943; Pres. and Man. Dir. STEPHEN S. LA RUE; Editor CLELL BRYANT; W.; circ. 482,670.

Toronto Life: 56 The Esplanade; f. 1966; Man. Editor BERNADETTE SULGIT; M.; circ. 20,400.

Trade Builder: 175 Jarvis St., 2; f. 1924; Editor E. F. DAMUDE; M.

University of Toronto Law Journal: University of Toronto Press, Toronto M5S 1A6; f. 1935; Editor R. RISK; Q.

University of Toronto Quarterly: University of Toronto Press, Toronto, M5S 1A6; Canadian Journal of the Humanities; f. 1931; Editors W. F. BLISSETT, D. M. HAYNE; Q.; circ. 1,317.

W. Toronto Weekly: 2995 Dundas St. W. 9; f. 1921; Independent; Editor SAMUEL WILSON; W.

QUEBEC

Canadian Doctor: Gardenvale 800, P.Q.; f. 1935; Publr. A. R. URQUHART; Editor D. ELKINS; M.; circ. 28,656.

Canadian Fisherman and Ocean Science: Muir Publishing Co., Gardenvale, Que. H0A 1B0; f. 1914; Publr. and Editor A. T. MUIR; 6 yearly; circ. 3,743.

Canadian Mining Journal: Gardenvale, f. 1879; Publr. KEVIN McCOLLUM; Editor CHRIS MAMEN; M.; circ. 6,927.

East End News: Verdun; f. 1939; French and English; circ. 25,000.

Lachine Messenger: Verdun, Quebec; f. 1932; French and English; Editor GEORGES LEGAULT; W; circ. 20,500.

Progrès de Rosemount: Verdun; f. 1953; French and English; Gen. Man. D. BLANCHARD; W; circ. 30,000.

La Salle Messenger: La Salle; f. 1954; French and English; Editor ROGER GAGNON; circ. 27,800.

Verdun Messenger: Verdun; f. 1913; French and English; Editor H. J. DUHAMEL; circ. 26,400.

QUEBEC—PUBLISHED IN MONTREAL

L'Actualité Economique: 5255 Ave. Decelles; f. 1925; Editor ROLAND JOUANDET-BERNADAT; Q.; circ. 2,300.

Allo Police: 1117 St. Catherine St., Montreal; f. 1953; Editor ANDRE PARENT; W.; circ. 131,562.

Au Grand Air: 1219 Hotel de Ville; f. 1961; Publr. HARRY A. WILLSIE; 6 yearly.

L'Automobile: 5020 de Salberry; f. 1939; Editor M. DUFRESNE; M.; circ. 10,895.

Building Materials News: 137 Wellington Street W.1; f. 1945; trade; Editor A. CLEMENTS; M.; circ. 19,971.

Bulletin des Agriculteurs: 5670 Chauveau St.; f. 1918; Publr. LUCILLE F. DAVIS; M.; circ. 12,098.

Canadian Business: 1080 Beaver Hall Hill; published by C. B. Media Ltd.; f. 1930; Man. Dir. and Editor ROBIN SCHIELE; M.; circ. 36,992.

Canadian Jewish Chronicle Review: 4781 Van Horne Ave., Montreal, Que. H3W 1J1; f. 1966; Editor and Publr. STANLEY SHENKMAN; M.; circ. 6,232.

Canadian Medical Association Journal: 1867 Alta Vista Dr., Ottawa K1G 0G8; f. 1911; Editor Dr. J. R. ANDERSON; twice-monthly; circ. 27,270.

Canadian Mining and Metallurgical Bulletin: 906-1117 St. Catherine St. West, Montreal H3B 1J3; f. 1898; official publication of Canadian Institute of Mining and Metallurgy; Editor E. G. TAPP.

Canadian Sport Monthly: 1434 St. Catherine Street West, 25; sport; Editor D. H. COLLINS; Publisher H. R. PICKENS, Jnr.; M.

Canadian Textile Journal: 4999 St. Catherine St., W., Montreal; f. 1883; Editor W. DAVIDSON; M.; circ. 3,271.

Chatelaine: 625 President Kennedy Ave.; f. 1960; French edition; women's general; Editor A. MONTPETIT; M.; circ. 300,000.

Commerce: 31 St. James St. W.; Editor MAURICE CHARTRAND; M.

Derniere Heure: 3019 Sherbrooke St. E., Montreal; f. 1965; W.; circ. 44,539.

Dimanche-Matin: 5701 Christophe-Colomb St., Montreal; f. 1954; French; Editor JACQUES FRANCOEUR; W.; circ. 238,928.

Echos Vedettes: 4270 Papineau St., Montreal; f. 1963; W.; circ. 134,714.

Engineering Journal: 2050 Mansfield St., Montreal 110; f. 1918; organ of Engineering Institute of Canada; Editor JAMES G. RIPLEY, M.E.I.C.; M.; circ. 9,136.

Ferme, La: 909 Mount Royal East, Montreal 36; f. 1939; agricultural; Editor ROBERT RAYNAULD; M.; circ. 86,000.

Financial Times of Canada: 10 Arundel St., Place Bonaventure; f. 1912; Editor MICHAEL BARKWAY; W.; circ. 54,640.

Forest and Outdoors and Rod and Gun: 58 Madsen Avenue, Beaconsfield; amalgamated 1959; organ of Canadian Forestry Association; Publr. R. J. COOKE; M.

Front Ouvrier, Le: 4911 Côte des Neiges Road; f. 1944; Independent; Editor LOUIS LAMONTAGNE; W.

Hockey News: 1434 St. Catherine St., f. 1947; Editor CHARLES HAPLIN; W.; circ. 71,256.

L'Ingénieur: a/s Ecole Polytechnique, Casier Postale 6079, succersale A, Montreal, H3C 3A7; f. 1915; Editor MADELEINE G. LAMBERT; M.; circ. 7,490.

Jewish Eagle: 4180 de Courtrai suite 218; f. 1907; Yiddish, Independent; Editor JOSEPH GALLAY; W.; circ. 17,860.

Journal of Canadian Petroleum Technology: 906-1117 St. Catherine St. West, Montreal H3B 1J3; an official publication of Canadian Institute of Mining and Metallurgy, Editor E. G. TAPP; Q.; circ. 1,412.

Journal des Vedettes, Le: 4270 Papineau St.; f. 1954; Editor JACQUES MATTI; W.; circ. 31,711.

Labour World (Le Monde Ouvrier): 177 Sherbrooke Street West, 18; f. 1915; French and English; Labour; Editor GAETEAN DUTOUR; W.; circ. 140,000.

Liberty: 73 Richmond St. West; f. 1947; Editor FRANK RASKY; M; circ. 500,000.

Le Maclean: 235 Avenue du President Kennedy, Montreal H3A 1K5; Publr. LLOYD HODGKINSON; Editor LOUIS MARTIN; M.

Monitor, The: 6525 Somerled, Montreal 265; f. 1925; non-party; Editor LOU MILLER; W; circ. 35,500.

Montrealer, The: 2160 Mountain St., Ste. 706; f. 1926; Editor EILEEN COLLYER; Business Man. JAMES H. COLLYER; circ. 23,964.

Le Nouveau Samedi: 4270 Papineau; f. 1888; Editor ANDRE LECOMPTE; W.; circ. 56,082.

Nouvelle Reléve, La: 60-ouest, rue Saint Jacques; f. 1934; literary; Editors ROBERT CHARBONNEAU, CLAUDE HORTUBISE; M.

Nouvelles Illustrées: 4270 Papineau St.; f. 1954; Editor A. LECOMPE; W.; circ. 106,329.

Patrie, La: 3019 Sherbrooke St.; f. 1878; Pres. JACQUES DION; W.; circ. 79,774.

Perspectives: 231 ouest, St. Jacques; f. 1959; French; Editor PIERRE GASCON; W.; circ. 794,623.

Petit Journal, Le: 3019 Sherbrooke St.; f. 1926; French; Independent; Editor J. C. HARVEY; W.; circ. 132,694.

Le Pharmacien: 625 President Kennedy Avenue, Montreal 111; f. 1929; Editor XAVIER DE LUSIGNY; M.; circ. 2,923.

Photo Age (inc. Canadian Photographer): 970 McEachran Ave.; f. 1954; Editor GUENTER KARKUTT; M.

Photo-Journal: 3019 Sherbrooke St.; f. 1937; Editor PIERRE-PAUL LAFORTUNE; W.; circ. 100,409.

Quebec Industrial, Le: 625 ave. du Président Kennedy; f. 1946; Publr. JEAN M. CHAGNON; Editor ROBERT HENRY; M.; circ. 7,971.

Reader's Digest: 215 Redfern Ave.; f. 1943; Editor CHARLES W. MAGILL; M.; circ. 1,256,209.

Relations: 8100 St. Lawrence Blvd., Montreal, P.Q. H2P 2L9; f. 1941; French; edited by Jesuit Fathers; social, cultural, economic and international affairs; Editor-in-Chief IRÉNÉE DESROCHERS, S.J.; M. circ. 7,570.

Rod and Gun in Canada: 1219 Hotel de Ville; f. 1899; Editor and Publisher HARRY WILLSIE; 6 yearly; circ. 55,500.

Samedi, Le: 4270 Papineau Street,; f. 1889; French; illustrated; Editor ANDRÉ LECOMPTE; W; circ. 78,954.

Sélection du Reader's Digest: 215 Redfern Ave.; Editor DENICE SURPRENANT; M.; circ. 276,120.

Sunday Express: 1229 Mountain St., Montreal; f. 1969; Publr. J. AZARIA; Man. Editor P. CURRAN; W.; circ. 54,259.

Technique pour Tous: 294 carré Saint-Louis; f. 1926; French and English; education; Editor EDDY MACFARLANE; M. (Ex. July and Aug.).

Télé-Radiomonde: 4270 Papineau; f. 1939; Editor PIERRE NADEAU; W.; circ. 72,342.

Terre de Chez Nous: 515 ave. Viger, Montreal 132; f. 1929; agriculture; French; Editor JEAN-MARC KIROUAC; W.; circ. 56,637.

Vers Demain: Rougemont, P.Q.; Social Credit and Roman Catholic; Dir. LOUIS EVEN; Administrator and Editor-in-Chief GILBERTE COTÉ-MERCIER; French edition every two months; circ. 55,000; English edition quarterly, circ. 20,000.

Voix Nationale: 3502 Hutchinson St.; M.

Weekend Magazine: 231 St. James St. W.; f. 1951; Editor FRANK LOWE; W.; circ. 2,017,000.

SASKATCHEWAN

Commonwealth, The: 1630 Quebec St., Regina; f. 1938; N.D.P.; Editor M. JOHNSON; bi-weekly; circ. 18,000.

Fish and Game Sportsman: P.O.B. 1654, Regina; f. 1968; Editor J. B. WILKINSON; Q.; circ. 10,249.

School Trustee: 570 Avord Tower, Regina; f. 1930; Editor L. I. THORSON; 5 a year; circ. 4,458.

Western Producer: P.O.B. 2500, Saskatoon S7K 2C4; f. 1923; world and agricultural news; Editor R. H. PHILLIPS; W.; circ. 153,000.

YUKON TERRITORY

Star: Whitehorse; f. 1900; Independent; Editor GRAEME CONNELL; Publr. BOB ERLAM; twice weekly; circ. 5,200.

NORTHWEST TERRITORY

Drum, The: P.O.B. 1069, Inuvik, N.W.T.; f. 1966; English; Editor THOMAS H. BUTTERS; W.

NEWS AGENCY

Canadian Press, The: 36 King St. E., Toronto, Ont. M5C 2L9; f. 1917; 102 daily newspaper members; national news co-operative; Pres. GABRIEL GILBERT; Sec. and Gen. Man. JOHN DAUPHINEE.

PRESS ASSOCIATIONS

Canadian Community Newspapers' Association: 12 Shuter St., Suite 304, Toronto, Ontario M5B 1A2; f. 1919; 668 mems.; Pres. A. Y. McLEAN; Gen. Man. E. M. WALKER.

Canadian Daily Newspaper Publishers Association: 250 Bloor St. East, Toronto 5; f. 1919; 83 mems.; Pres. JOHN D. MUIR; Gen. Man. JOHN FOY.

Canadian Managing Editors' Conference: 565 Avenue Rd., Toronto 7, Ont.

Canadian Section Commonwealth Press Union: Hon. Sec. P. E. USSHER, 36 King St. E., Toronto, M5C 2L9.

National Press Club of Canada: 150 Wellington, Ottawa 4, Ont.; Pres. C. W. E. MACPHERSON.

Periodical Press Association: 100 University Ave., Ste. 508, Toronto M5J 1V6; Pres. J. L. CRAIG; Man. GEORGE MANSFIELD; constituent associations:

   Agricultural Press Association of Canada: Pres. J. L. DAVIES.

   Canadian Business Press: Pres. R. W. ROBERTSON.

   Magazine Publishers' Association of Canada: Pres. L. M. HODGKINSON.

Toronto Men's Press Club: 119 King St. W., Toronto; Pres. D. K. McKEE.

Winnipeg Press Club: Marlborough Hotel, Smith St., Winnipeg 1, Man.; Pres. IAN SUTHERLAND.

FOREIGN BUREAUX
Montreal

Agence Parisienne de Presse (APP): 664 Grosvenor Ave.

UPI: Place Victoria Suite 432, 800 Victoria Square; Man. Dir. DONALD MACKAY.

The following are also represented: Deutsche Presse-Agentur (DPA), Reuters, Tass.

PUBLISHERS

Addison-Wesley (Canada) Ltd.: 36 Prince Andrew Place, Don Mills, Ont., M3C 2H4; mathematics, science, language, business and social sciences textbooks, trade juveniles.

Editions d'Aigle: 2105, rue Bourdages, Saint-Hyacinthe, P.Q.

Thomas Allen and Son Ltd.: 850 York Mills Rd., Don Mills, Ont. M3B 3A7.

Editions de l'Arbre: 60 St. James West, Montreal, P.Q.

Associated Publishers: 728 Yonge Street, Toronto 5, Ont.

Editions de l'Atelier: 3744 rue Jean-Brillant, Montreal 26; f. 1955; Manager RAYNALD GOUGEON; juvenile, religious books, poetry.

Editions Beauchemin Ltée: 450 ave. Beaumont, Montreal H3N 1T8; f. 1842; Pres. EDMOND FRENETTE; school books and literature.

Bélisle Editeur, Inc.: 35–39 rue Sault-au-Matelot, Quebec, P.Q.; f. 1940; Dir. and Publisher LOUIS-ALEXANDRE BÉLISLE; technical, classical, and literary books; technical, French-English and French-Canadian dictionaries.

Editions Bellarmin: 8100 blvd. Saint-Laurent, Montreal H2P 2L9, P.Q.; f. 1920; Man. Rev. ALBERT PLANTE, s.j.; religious and social.

Bellhaven House Ltd.: 1145 Bellamy Rd. North; Scarborough 707, Ont.; f. 1964; Man. Dir. R. SOUTHGATE; represents foreign educational publishers.

*Book Society of Canada Ltd.: P.O. Box 200, 4386 Sheppard Avenue East, Agincourt, Toronto, Ont.; elementary and secondary school publishers.

Boreal Express: C.P. 418, Station Youville, Montreal H2P 2V6, Quebec; f. 1962; history.

Burns and MacEachern Ltd.: 62 Railside Rd., Don Mills, Ont.; Chair. and Pres. B. D. SANDWELL; art, architecture, general, textbooks.

Canada Law Book Ltd.: 100 Richmond St. East, Toronto 1, Ont.; f. 1855; Pres. W. L. COWING; law reports, law journals, legal textbooks, etc.

Canadian Music Sales Corporation Ltd.: 58 Advance Rd., Toronto, Ont. M8Z 2T8; f. 1937; Pres. T. P. REGAN; music publishers, distributors for music, records.

Centre Educatif et Culturel: 8101 est, boul. Métropolitain, Montreal H1J 1J9, P.Q.; f. 1956; educational books; Pres. EMÉ LACROIX.

Centre Pédagogique: 2299 Versant Nord, Ste-Foy, Quebec, G1N 4C2.

Centre de Psychologie et de Pédagogie (1968) Inc.: 260 ouest, rue Faillon, Montreal 327; f. 1944; Dir.-Gen. GONTRAN TROTTIER.

Le Cercle du Livre de France Ltée.: 3300 blvd. Rosemount, Montreal 36; f. 1947; Pres. PIERRE TISSEYRE; general literature in French.

Clarke, Irwin and Co. Ltd.: 791 St. Clair Ave. West, Toronto M6C 1B8, Ont.; f. 1930; Pres. IRENE I. CLARKE; Exec. Vice-Pres. W. H. CLARKE; educational and general trade publishers.

*William Collins, Sons and Co. (Canada) Ltd.: 100 Lesmill Rd., Don Mills, Ont., M3B 2T5.

Copp Clark Publishing: 517 Wellington St. W., Toronto M5Y 1G1, Ont.; f. 1841; a division of Copp Clark Ltd.; trade books, text and reference material; Pres. M. I. PITMAN.

*J. M. Dent and Sons (Canada), Ltd.: 100, Scarsdale Road, Don Mills, Ont.; Pres. C. SKINNER; text-book and general publishers.

Dodd, Mead and Co. (Canada) Ltd.: 25 Hollinger Rd., Toronto 16, Ont.

Doubleday Canada Ltd.: 105 Bond St., Toronto M5B 1Y3, Ont.

Ecrits du Canada Français: 380 Ouest rue Craig, Montreal H2Y 1J9.

Editeur Officiel du Québec: Ministère des Communications, Cité parlementaire, Quebec, G1A 1G7; f. 1868; French language Govt. publications; Head CHARLES-HENRI DUBÉ.

Encyclopaedia Britannica of Canada Ltd.: 151 Bloor St. West, Toronto 5; f. 1937; Pres. P. B. NORTON; other publs. *Britannica Junior, World Atlas, Britannica Book of the Year, Britannica World Language Dictionary, Great Books of the Western World, Great Ideas Today, F. E. Compton Encylopedia.*

Entreprises Education Nouvelle Inc., Les: 260 ouest, rue Faillon, Montreal 327, P.Q.; f. 1964; Pres., Dir.-Gen. GONTRAN TROTTIER.

Editions de l'Etoile: 325–327 East Mont-Royal, Montreal 151; f. 1939; Dir. JEAN DESGRANGES; history, travel and (in French only) fiction.

Editions Estérel: 6397 rue Saint-Denis, Montreal 10, P.Q.

Evangelical Publishers: 4 Albert St., Toronto 1, Ont., f. 1912; Man. Dir. and Treas. A. J. STEWART.

Les Editions Fides: 245 est, blvd. Dorchester, Montreal 129; f. 1937; Pres. PAUL-A. MARTIN, c.s.c.; Gen. Man. PIERRE CLOUTIER; religious, history, textbooks and literature.

Editions Françaises: 8840 blvd. Saint-Laurent, Montreal 11, P.Q.

Editions France-Quebec Inc.: 3550 est., rue Rachel, Montreal 401, P.Q.

*Samuel French (Canada), Ltd.: 27 Grenville Street, Toronto 5, Ont.; f. in Canada 1933; Manageress Miss M. H. COXWELL; drama.

W. J. Gage Ltd.: 1500 Birchmount Rd., Scarborough, Ont.; f. 1844; Pres. G. H. LOVE.

General Publishing Co. Ltd.: 30 Lesmill Rd., Don Mills, Ont.; f. 1934; Pres. JACK STODDART.

*Ginn and Company, 35 Mobile Drive, Toronto, Ontario, M4A 1H6; f. 1929; Gen. Man. FRANK E. WATSON; textbooks.

Granger Frères Ltd.: 210 Cremazie Blvd. West, Montreal P.Q.; f. 1885; Pres. C. LESLIE ROBERTSON; Man. Dir. ANTONIO LECOMPTE; French textbooks, religious books and prayer books.

*Hamish Hamilton Ltd.: 81 Curlew Dr., Don Mills, Ont. M3A 2R1.

*Hamlyn Publishing Group (Canada) Ltd.: 850 York Mills Rd., Don Mills, Ont. M3B 3A7.

Harvest House Ltd.: 4795 St. Catherine St. W., Montreal, P.Q. H3Z 2B9.

Editions de l'Hexagone: P.O.B. 337, Bureau Postal N, Montreal 129, P.Q.; f. 1953; Dirs. GASTON MIRON, ALAIN HORIC.

* Canadian branches of English Publishers.

*Hodder and Stoughton Ltd., of Canada: 103–107 Vanderhoof Avenue, Toronto 17, Ont.; f. in Canada 1912; Chair. PAUL HODDER-WILLIAMS; Pres. SAM STEWART; Vice-Pres. C. L. WHITESIDE; Treas. A. ECKSTEIN; general.

Holt, Rinehart and Winston of Canada Limited: 55 Horner Ave., Toronto, Ont. M8Z 4X6; f. 1904; general trade, educational, college, reference and children's.

Les Editions de l'Horizon: 6235 rue Deacon, Montreal; f. 1963; Dir. JACQUES DE ROUSSAN; French Canadian history.

Editions Hurtubise HMH, Ltée.: 380 ouest, rue Craig, Montreal 126; f. 1960; Man. CLAUDE HURTUBISE; trade and textbooks.

Information Canada: Ottawa, Ont.; art, business, government, science, social sciences.

Institut de Recherches Psychologiques: 34 ouest, rue Fleury, Montreal H3L 1S9, P.Q.; f. 1959; educational.

Irwin-Dorsey Ltd.: 265 Guelph St., Georgetown, Ont.; a wholly owned subsidiary of Richard D. Irwin, Inc. (U.S.A.); f. 1967; Pres. RICHARD E. WILLIS, Jr.; economics, business and social science.

Editions Jeunesse: 260, ouest, rue Faollon, Montreal 327, P.Q.; f. 1962; Pres. GONTRAN TROTTIER; children's and juvenile books.

Editions du Jour: 3411 rue St.-Denis, Montreal 129; f. 1962; Man. JACQUES HÉRBERT; general.

Editions du Levrier: 5375 ave. Notre-Dame-de-Graces, Montreal, P.Q.; f. 1934; Dir. Rev. PAUL-M. DUPRÉ, O.P.; education, philosophy, psychology, theology, scientific.

Librairie de L'Action: Place Jean-Talon, Quebec, P.Q.; f. 1920; Man. JULES-A. LORTIE; classics, educational, sociology, theology and juvenile.

Librairie DEOM: 1773 rue St.-Denis, Montreal 129; f. 1896; Man. JEAN BODE; poetry and fiction.

Librairie Dussault: 8955 Blvd. St.-Laurent, Montreal, P.Q.; Pres. ANDRÉ DUSSAULT; publishers of general literature in French language and children's books and albums; also wholesale booksellers of all French books published in Europe; branches in Quebec, Ottawa, Sherbrooke, Trois-Rivières and Hull.

Librairie Garneau, Ltd.: 47 Buade, Quebec. P.Q.; f. 1844; Pres. LAVERY SIROIS; Canadian historical publications.

Librairie Générale Canadienne: 5608 Stirling, Montreal, P.Q.; Dir. EUGENE ACHARD; books only.

Librairie Hachette (Canada) Ltée.: 554 Ste. Catherine est., Montreal H2L 2E1; Dir. PASCAL ASSATHIANY.

Librarie Leméac: 371 ouest, ave. Laurier, Montreal H2V 2K6; f. 1952; Pres. GÉRARD LEMÉAC; Dir. Mme. C. VOGLIMACCI; general, specialized and Canadiana.

Librairie St. Viateur: 5199 St. Dominique, Montreal, P.Q.; f. 1886; text and children's books.

Editions Lidec Inc.: 1083 ave. Van Horne, Montreal H2V 1J6, P.Q.

J. B. Lippincott Company of Canada Ltd.: 75 Horner Ave., Toronto 18, Ont.; medical, nursing, dental and pharmaceutical publications.

Little, Brown and Co. (Canada) Ltd.: 25 Hollinger Rd., Toronto 16; trade and educational.

*Longman Canada Ltd.: 55 Barber Greene Rd.. Don Mills, Ont.; f. in Canada 1924; general, medical, educational; Pres. R. KILPATRICK.

Samuel Lowe Company of Canada Ltd.: 184 Front St. East, Toronto 2, Ont.; inc. 1945; Pres. and Gen. Man. R. A. FRY; children's books and games.

McAinsh & Co. Ltd.: 1835 Yonge St., Toronto, Ont., M4S 1L7.

Maclean-Hunter Ltd.: 481 University Ave., Toronto M5W 1A7, Ont.; f. 1887; Chair. DONALD HUNTER; consumer and business periodicals, radio, television, cable television.

McClelland and Stewart, Ltd.: 25 Hollinger Road, Toronto 16, Ont.; f. 1906; Pres. J. G. MCCLELLAND; trade, illustrated and educational.

McGill-Queen's University Press: 3458 Redpath St., Montreal H3G 2G5, P.Q.

McGraw-Hill Ryerson Ltd.: 330 Progress Ave., Scarborough, Ont.; Pres. R. D. BESSE.

George J. McLeod, Ltd.: 73 Bathurst St., Toronto M5V 2P8, Ont.; f. 1898; Pres. H. E. LANGFORD, Q.C.; Vice-Pres. and Gen. Man. DOUGLAS J. MCLEOD; general, fiction, technical, non-fiction.

*Macmillan Company of Canada, Ltd., The: 70 Bond Street, Toronto, M5B 1X3, Ont.; f. 1905; general.

Editions Maristes: 1113 rue Desnoyers, St.-Vincent-de-Paul (Ville Laval), P.Q.; f. 1912; Dir. JEAN POIRIER.

Methuen Publications: 2330 Midland ave., Agincourt, Ont.

Editions Mirabel: 8955 blvd. Saint-Laurent, Montreal H2N 1M6, P.Q.; Pres. ANDRÉ DUSSAULT; trade books in French.

Musson Book Co. Ltd.: 30 Lesmill Rd., Don Mills, Ont.; f. 1894; Pres. JACK STODDART.

National Business Publications Ltd.: Gardenvale, P.Q.: H0A 1B0; Pres. A. W. DANCEY; technical and business journals and directories.

Nelson, Foster and Scott, Ltd.: 299 Yorkland Blvd., Willowdale, Ontario M2J 1S9.

*Thomas Nelson and Sons (Canada) Ltd.: 81 Curlew Drive, Don Mills, Ont.; f. 1913; Pres. J. C. FLEMING; textbooks, trade.

Ontario Publishing Co. Ltd.: 33 Kern Rd., Don Mills, Ont.; f. 1893; Pres. D. W. BEST; Canadian history.

*Oxford University Press (Canadian Branch): 70 Wynford Drive, Don Mills, Toronto, Ont.; f. 1904; Man. L. M. WILKINSON; general, education, religious, juvenile, Canadiana.

Palatine, Ltd.: 1460 ave. Union, Montreal, P.Q.; f. 1947; Pres. MAURICE BOURDEL; Man. Dir. ANDRÉ DUSSAULT; publishers of French books in Canada and distributors in Canada of books in French published in France and Switzerland.

Palm Publishers Press Services Ltd.: 1949 55th Ave., Dorval, Montreal 760; Pres. R. W. KEYSERLINGK.

Editions Parti Pris: C.P. 149—"N", Montreal 18, P.Q.

Editions Pedagogia Inc.: 192 rue Dorchester; f. 1961; Pres. FERNAND BÉRUBÉ; school and library books.

Editions du Pelican: 1432 rue de Villars, Quebec G1K 2C2; f. 1956; Man. RÉAL D'ANJOU; art, history, sport.

Pergamon of Canada Ltd.: Suite 318, 207 Queen's Quay W., Toronto, M5J 1A7, Ont.; f. 1965; Gen. Man. B. H. DUNN; scientific, technical, journals.

*Sir Isaac Pitman (Canada) Ltd.: 495 Wellington St. W., Toronto M5Y 1G1, Ont.; f. 1920; Pres. M. I. PITMAN; general.

Pocket Books of Canada Ltd.: 225 Yonge St., Toronto.

Prentice-Hall of Canada Ltd.: 1870 Birchmount Rd., Scarborough 706, Ont.

Les Presses de l'Université Laval: C.P. 2447, Quebec G1K 7R4; f. 1950; Dir. CLAUDE FRÉMONT; scholarly books and periodicals.

* Canadian branches of English Publishers

Les Presses de L'Université de Montreal: C.P. 6128, Montreal 101, P.Q.

Les Presses de l'Université du Québec: case postale 250, Succursale N, Montréal H2X 3M4.

Progress Books: 487 Adelaide St. West, Toronto, Ont., M5V 1T4.

Random House of Canada Ltd.: 370 Alliance Ave., Toronto M6N 2H8, Ont.; Dir. D. V. BRADSTREET.

Renouf Publishing Co. Ltd.: 2182 St. Catherine St. W., Montreal H3N 1M2, P.Q.

Editions du Renouveau Pédagogique: 8955 blvd. Saint-Laurent, Montreal H2N 1M6, P.Q.; f. 1965; Pres. ANDRÉ DUSSAULT; French textbooks.

Editions du Richelieu: C.P. 216, Saint-Jean-de-Quebec, P.Q.

Riverside Books Ltd.: 47 Green St., Montreal 23.

Saunders of Toronto Ltd.: 1885 Leslie St., Don Mills, Ont.; f. 1935; Dirs. C. R. ALLEN, Ross F. McDONALD, S. W. ALLEN, A. J. RICHARDS.

Smithers and Bonellie Ltd.: 56 Esplanade St., Toronto 1, Ont.; Pres. WILLIAM BONELLIE; Sec. and Treas. JACK T. FINLAY; fiction, non-fiction, children's books.

Group Sogides: Les Editions de l'Homme, de l'Actuelle et des Presse Libres, 955 rue Amherst, Montreal H2L 3K4; comprehensive list.

Southam Business Publications Limited: 1450 Don Mills Rd., Don Mills, Ont.; publish 65 business magazines.

Gordon V. Thompson, Ltd.: 29 Birch Ave., Toronto, M4V 1E2, Ont.; f. 1909; Pres. JOHN C. BIRD; music, educational, sacred, standard and popular.

United Church Publishing House: 47 Coldwater Rd., Don Mills, Ont.

University of Toronto Press: Front Campus, University of Toronto, Toronto, Ont., M5S 1A6; f. 1901; Dir. MARSH JEANNERET; scholarly and university texts and reference books; 17 journals.

Les Editions de l'Université d'Ottawa: 65 Hastey Ave., Ottawa K1N 6N5; f. 1937; Man. Rev. LÉOPOLD LANCTOT, O.M.I.; university books.

Van Nostrand Reinhold Ltd.: 1410 Birchmont Rd., Scarborough, Ont.; f. 1970; technical and educational; Pres. CAMPBELL HUGHES.

G. R. Welch Co. Ltd.: 310 Judson St., Toronto, Ont. M82 1J9; f. 1935; Pres. G. H. WELCH.

Xerox Education Group—Canada: 35 Mobile Drive, Toronto, Ont. M4A 1N6; Pres. F. E. WATSON; textbooks.

ORGANIZATIONS AND ASSOCIATIONS

Canadian Book Publishers' Council: Suite 701, 45 Charles St. East, Toronto, Ont. M4Y 1S2; f. 1910; 53 mems.; trade association of firms who publish and/or represent publishers in the U.K. and the U.S.A.; Pres. W. DARNELL; Exec. Dir. TOIVO ROHT.

Le Conseil Supérieur du Livre: 436 Est. rue Sherbrooke, Montreal H2L 1J6; f. 1961; Pres. PIERRE TISSEYRE; Sec. VICTOR MARTIN; constituent associations:

Association des Editeurs Canadiens: f. 1943; 45 mems.; Pres. JACQÚES HÉRBERT; Dir. Gen. J. Z. LEON PATENAUDE.

Société des Editeurs de Manuels Scolaires: f. 1970; 20 mems.; Pres. ROLAND SASSEVILLE; Sec.-Treas. VICTOR CÔTÉ; Admin. Sec. J. Z. LEON PATENAUDE.

Association des Libraires du Québec: f. 1969; Pres. RAYMOND CARIGNAN; Sec.-Treas. ANDRÉ CONSTANTIN.

* Canadian branches of English Publishers.

RADIO AND TELEVISION

The 1968 Broadcasting Act established broadcasting policy in Canada, reinforcing the Canadian Broadcasting Corporation as the national broadcasting service and creating the Canadian Radio-Television Commission with authority over all aspects of public, private, radio and television broadcasting. The Act stipulates that the Public service should be predominantly Canadian in content; in 1970 new regulations provided for a graduated increase in Canadian television programming to 60 per cent by October 1972, and a minimum of 30 per cent Canadian content in AM radio; in 1971 70 per cent of broadcasting at peak hours was of Canadian origin. Half the population has access to programmes broadcast by networks in the U.S.A.

Canadian broadcasting is a combination of public and private enterprise which provides radio and television services for almost all of the country's population. All stations and networks are subject to the regulations of the Canadian Radio-Television Commission, but are entitled to freedom of expression and enjoy varying degrees of autonomy. Most privately-owned television stations and many of the private radio stations are affiliated with the Canadian Broadcasting Corporation, and help to distribute national broadcasting services over CBC networks. Of the unaffiliated television stations, eleven form the CTV Television Network Ltd., which now reaches over 63 per cent of the population.

In July 1971 the Commission announced policies aimed at integrating cable television into the Canadian broadcasting system.

Canadian Radio-Television Commission: Head Office 100 Metcalfe St., Ottawa, Ont. K1A 0N2; Chair. PIERRE JUNEAU; Sec. Miss MONIQUE COUPAL; Vice-Chair. HARRY J. BOYLE; Full-time mems. Mrs. PAT PEARCE, HAROLD DORNAN, REAL THERRIEN.

Canadian Broadcasting Corporation: 1500 Bronson Ave., P.O.B. 8478, Ottawa K1G 3J5; Pres. LAURENT A. PICARD; Exec. Vice-Pres. LISTER SINCLAIR.

The Corporation is publicly owned and was established by an Act of the Canadian Parliament in 1936 to provide the national broadcasting service in Canada.

The CBC is financed mainly by public funds voted annually by Parliament. Supplementary revenue is obtained from commercial advertising. As a publicly owned corporation, the CBC is responsible to Parliament, and reports on its operations each year through a Cabinet Minister designated in the Broadcasting Act.

The CBC is a member of several international broadcasting organizations and is active in international programme sales and exchanges. With the Canadian International Development Agency and UNESCO, CBC has aided foreign broadcasting organizations and provides broadcasting training for foreign students. CBC maintains offices in London, Paris, New York and Washington and news bureaux in Moscow, Lima and the Far East.

RADIO

The CBC operates two AM networks, in English and in French, an FM network in English, and a multilingual service in the English, French, Indian and Eskimo languages, providing medium and shortwave broadcasting to the Canadian North. There are 436 outlets for the national radio service, 55 CBC-owned originating stations, 278 CBC-owned low-power relay transmitters, and 103 privately-owned affiliated stations. CBC radio service is within reach of 98.7 per cent of the Canadian population. Radio Canada International broadcasts by shortwave in 11 languages to eastern and western Europe, Africa, Australasia, Latin America, the Caribbean and North America. It also distributes programmes to foreign broadcasters. The CBC Armed Forces Service, in co-operation with the Department of National Defence, provides recorded and shortwave programmes and television films for Canadian military bases in Canada and abroad.

TELEVISION

Outlets for the national television service total 385, in-cluding 23 CBC-owned originating stations, 158 CBC-owned network relay and rebroadcasting stations, and 38 privately owned affiliates with their 166 rebroadcasting stations. CBC television services are within reach of 97.4 per cent of the Canadian population. Most evening programming is in colour, and about 32 per cent of households have colour sets.

CTV Television Network: 42 Charles St., E., Toronto M4Y 1T4 and 20 Elmira, Place Bonaventure, Montreal 114; Pres. and Man. Dir. M. CHERCOVER; Exec. Vice-Pres. K. CAMPBELL.

The network is privately-owned and provides a second television service in Halifax, Montreal, Ottawa, Toronto, Winnipeg, Edmonton, Calgary, Kitchener, Moose Jaw, Vancouver, Saskatoon, Sudbury and Moncton.

Global Television Network: 81 Barber Green Rd., Don Mills, Toronto, Ont. M3C 2A3; Chair. P. B. Hill; Pres. and Chief Exec. A. A. BRUNER.

TVA: 1405 Alexandre de Seve, Montreal 133; Admin. Co-ord. G. BELANGER.

FINANCE

(cap. = capital; p.u. = paid up; dep. = deposits; m. = million; $ = Canadian dollar.)

BANKING
CENTRAL BANKS

Bank of Canada: 234 Wellington Street, Ottawa; f. 1934; cap. p.u. $5m. (Dec. 1971); Gov. G. K. BOUEY; Sen. Deputy Gov. R. W. LAWSON.

Industrial Development Bank: Ottawa, Ont.; f. 1944; cap. p.u. $75m. (September 1972); Pres. L. RASMINSKY; Gen. Man. E. R. CLARK.

COMMERCIAL BANKS

Bank of British Columbia: 1725 Two Bentall Centre, Vancouver, B.C.; f. 1968; cap. p.u. $5.1m.; Chair. and Pres. ALBERT E. HALL; Gen. Man. V. DOBB.

Bank of Montreal: 129 James St. West (P.O.B. 6002), Montreal, Que. H3C 3B1; f. 1817; cap. p.u. $68m.; dep. $13,291m. (Oct. 1973); Chair. and Chief Exec. G. ARNOLD HART; Pres. and Chief Oper. Officer F. H. McNEIL.

Bank of Nova Scotia: King and Bay Streets, Toronto, Ont.; f. 1832; cap. p.u. $33.75m.; Chair. T. A. BOYLES; Pres. and Chief Exec. C. E. RITCHIE.

Banque Canadienne Nationale: Place d'Armes, Montreal, Que.; f. 1874; cap. p.u. $14m.; Chair. and Pres. LOUIS HÉRBERT; Vice-Pres. and Chief Gen. Man. GERMAIN PERREAULT.

Canadian Imperial Bank of Commerce: Commerce Court, Toronto, Ont. M5L 1A2; cap. p.u. $69.7m.; Chair. and Chief Exec. Officer J. P. R. WADSWORTH; Vice-Chair. L. G. GREENWOOD; Pres. and Chief Op. Officer R. E. HARRISON; Exec. Vice-Pres. and Chief Gen. Man. R. D. FULLERTON.

Mercantile Bank of Canada, The: 625 Dorchester Blvd. West, Montreal, Que. H3B 1R3; cap. p.u. $10m.; Pres. P. H. AUSTIN.

Provincial Bank of Canada, The: 215 St. James St., Montreal, Que.; f. 1900; cap. p.u. $10.4m.; Pres. and Chief Exec. Officer LÉO LAVOIE; Vice-Pres. and Gen Man. RAYMOND PRIMEAU.

Royal Bank of Canada, The: 1 Place Ville Marie, Montreal, Que.; f. 1869; cap. p.u. $66.5m.; Chair. and Pres. W. E. McLAUGHLIN; Dep. Chair. and Exec. Vice-Pres. J. K. FINLAYSON and W. D. H. GARDINER; Vice Pres. and Chief Gen. Man. R. C. FRAZEE.

Société Financière pour le Commerce et l'Industrie: 800 Place Victoria, Montreal; f. 1961; cap. p.u. $3m.; Pres. R. CHARBONNEAU; Gen. Man. G. LEGRAND.

Toronto-Dominion Bank, The: P.O.B. 1, Toronto Dominion Centre, Toronto 111, Ont.; f. 1856; assets $940m.; Chair. and Chief Exec. A. T. LAMBERT; Pres. R. M. THOMSON; Exec. Vice-Pres. and Chief Gen. Man. J. A. BOYLE.

SAVINGS BANKS WITH FEDERAL CHARTERS

Montreal City and District Savings Bank: 262 St. James St. West, Montreal Que.; cap. p.u. $2m.; Pres. E. DONALD GRAY-DONALD; Vice-Pres. and Gen. Man. F. X. GUÉRARD.

Province of Alberta Treasury Branches: P.O.B. 1440, 9912 107 St., Edmonton, Alta.; f. 1938; Supt. of Branches F. SPARROW.

Province of Ontario Savings Office: Parliament Building, Toronto 2, Ont.; f. 1921; Dir. R. I. NELSON.

TRUST AND LOAN ORGANISATIONS

Caisses Populaires Desjardins: 8175 blvd. St. Laurent, Montreal, P.Q.; Pres. EMILE GIRARDIN; organization operating under the Savings and Credit Unions Act (Quebec).

Canada Permanent Mortgage Corporation and Canada Permanent Trust Company: 320 Bay St., Toronto 1; f. 1855; combined assets $415m.; Pres. DONALD G. NEELANDS.

Canada Trust Co., The Huron & Erie Mortgage Corporation: London, Ont. N6A 4Z2; cap. p.u. $11m.; Chair. J. A. TAYLOR; Pres. and Chief A. H. MINGAY.

Crédit Foncier Franco-Canadien: 612 St. James St., Montreal, Que. H3C 1E1; f. 1880; total assets $415m.; Chair. Exec. BERNARD LECHARTIER; Vice-Chair. Pres and Gen. Man. RAYMOND LAVOIE.

Eastern Canada Savings and Loan Co.: Halifax, N.S.; f. 1888; cap. $2m.; Pres. D. M. SMITH; Gen. Man. D. H. COCHRANE.

Eskimo Loan Fund of the Department of Indian Affairs and Northern Development: a fund set aside for the purpose of making loans to Canadian Eskimos.

Guaranty Trust Co. of Canada: 366 Bay Street, Toronto, Ont.; f. 1925; cap. and reserves $44.975m. (1972); Chair. and Chief Exec. Officer G. R. SHARWOOD; Pres. A. R. MARCHMENT.

Montreal Trust Co.: 1 Place Ville Mari, Montreal, Que.; f. 1889; cap. p.u. $2.6m.; Chair. FRANK E. CASE; Vice-Chair. G. W. HODGSON; Pres. P. BRITTON PAINE, Q.C.; Sec. J. K. REYNOLDS.

National Trust Co. Ltd.: 21 King St. East, Toronto 1, Ont.; f. 1898; cap. and res. $50.2m.; Chair. E. H. HEENEY; Pres. J. L. A. COLHOUN.

Royal Trust Co., The: 630 Dorchester Blvd. West, Montreal, Que.; f. 1892; cap. and reserves $70.4m.; general trust business through 68 offices in Canada, London, Dublin and Channel Islands; Chair. and Chief Exec. Officer CONRAD F. HARRINGTON; Pres. and Chief Operating Officer K. A. WHITE.

Trust Général du Canada: 909 rue Dorchester, Ouest, Montreal, Que.; f. 1928; cap. p.u. $4.5m.; Pres. M. ROBERT JUSSAUME; Dir.-Gen. LOUIS ARCHAMBAULT; Treas. A. COTÉ; Sec. R. PICOTTE.

Victoria and Grey Trust Co.: 85 Kent St., Lindsay, Ont.; f. 1885; cap. p.u. $7.7m.; Chair. H. J. McLAUGHLIN, Q.C.; Pres. Hon. WALTER HARRIS, Q.C.

Western Savings and Loan Association: 280 Smith St., Winnipeg, Man.; cap. p.u. $94.8m.; Chair. C. E. ATCHISON; Pres. A. S. JACKSON.

BANKERS' ORGANIZATION

Canadian Bankers' Association, The: Box 282, Royal Trust Tower, Toronto Dominion Centre, Toronto, Ont. M5K 1K2; f. 1893; Pres. J. A. BOYLE; Exec. Dir. J. H. PERRY; Sec.-Treas. J. F. RIEGERT; 10 mem. banks.

STOCK EXCHANGES

Calgary Stock Exchange: 330 9th Ave. S.W., Calgary 2, Alberta T2P 1K7; f. 1914; 27 mems.; Chair. W. R. FULTON; Vice-Chair. G. H. POWIS; Sec.-Treas. A. S. HAWKINS; Pres. J. R. THOMSON.

Canadian Stock Exchange: 453 St. Francois Xavier St., Montreal, P.Q.; f. 1926; 100 mems.; Pres. C. B. NEAPOLE; Exec. Vice-Pres. GEO. A. CRUIKSHANK.

Montreal Stock Exchange: 453 St. François Xavier Street, Montreal, P.Q.; f. 1874; 80 mems.; Exec. Vice-Pres. GEO. A. CRUIKSHANK.

Toronto Stock Exchange: 234 Bay Street, Toronto, Ont. M5J 1R1; f. 1852; 90 mems.; Pres. J. R. KIMBER, Q.C.

Vancouver Stock Exchange: 536 Howe St., Vancouver 1, B.C.; 52 mems.; Pres. THOMAS A. DOHM.

Winnipeg Stock Exchange: 100-233 Portage Ave., 22 mems. Pres. R. W. RICHARDS; Sec.-Treas. F. W. BUCHANAN.

INSURANCE

PRINCIPAL COMPANIES

⸻ Insurance Company: 1184 St. Catherine St. ⸻treal 110, Que.; f. 1934; Man. Dir. GEORGES ⸻ Pres. J. P. TARDIF.

Antigonish Farmers' Mutual Fire Insurance Co.: P.O. Box 434, Antigonish, N.S.; f. 1910; Man. D. J. CHISHOLM.

Les Artisans, cooperative d'Assurance-vie: 333 est, rue Craig, Montreal, Que. H2X 1R9; f. 1876; Pres. R. PARÉ; Dir.-Gen. L.-P. SAVARD.

Beaver Insurance Co.: 60 Adelaide Street West, Toronto 1, Ont.; f. 1913; Pres. and Man. Dir. D. S. HARLEY, M.C.

British America Assurance Co.: 40 Scott Street, Toronto 1, Ont.; f. 1833; Chair. GRAHAM MORROW, O.B.E.; Pres. D. B. MARTIN, F.I.A.

British Canadian Insurance Co.: 1155 Dorchester Blvd. W., Montreal; f. 1917; Chair. GRAHAM MORROW; Vice-Pres. and Gen. Man. D. B. MARTIN.

British Northwestern Insurance Co.: 217 Bay St., Toronto 1, Ont.; f. 1906; Pres. and Man. Dir. J. F. CAIRD, F.C.I.I., F.I.I.C.

Canada Life Assurance Co.: 330 University Ave., Toronto 100, Ont.; f. 1847; Chair. J. G. HUNGERFORD, Q.C.

Canadian General Insurance Co.: 170 University Ave., Toronto 110, Ont.; f. 1907; Chair. J. W. McCUTCHEON; Pres. R. E. BETHELL.

Canadian Home Assurance Co.: 1075 Beaver Hall Hill, Montreal, P.Q. H2Z 1S6; f. 1928; Pres. H. R. POLLAK.

Canadian Indemnity Company: 333 Main St., Winnipeg, Man.; f. 1912; Chair. C. S. RILEY; Vice-Chair. P. D. CURRY.

Canada Security Assurance Co.: Norwich Union Bldg., 60 Yonge Street, Toronto, Ont. M5E 1H5; f. 1913; Pres. and Gen. Man. J. CAMPBELL.

Canadian Surety Co., The: 8th Floor, 105 Adelaide St. West, Toronto 101, Ont.; f. 1911; Pres. and Gen. Man. DONALD D. McKAY.

Century Insurance Co. of Canada: 1112 West Pender St., Vancouver 1, B.C.; f. 1890; Chair. Hon. W. M. HAMILTON; Pres. G. R. ELLIOTT.

Commerce General Insurance Company, The: 2450 blvd. Girouard, St. Hyacinthe, Que.; f. 1907; Chair. B. BENOIT; Pres. J. R. ST.-GERMAIN; Vice-Pres. and Dir.-Gen. G. ST.-GERMAIN.

Commercial Life Assurance Co. of Canada, The: 1303 Yonge St., Toronto 7, Ont.; f. 1911; Pres. W. L. WILLIAMS; Vice-Pres. H. T. C. TAYLOR; Sec.-Treas. G. JONCKHEER.

Confederation Life Insurance Co.: 321 Bloor St. East, Toronto, Ont. M4W 1H1; f. 1871; Pres. J. CRAIG DAVIDSON.

Les Coopérants Compagnie Mutuelle d'Assurance-Vie: 1259 rue Berri, Montreal 132, Que. H2L 4C7; f. 1936; Pres. PAUL COUTURE; Dir.-Gen. CARMIN GRAVELINE; Sec. PIERRE-EUGÈNE PROULX.

Crown Life Insurance Co.: 120 Bloor St. East, Toronto 5, Ont.; f. 1900; Chair. C. F. W. BURNS; Pres. R. C. DOWSETT.

Dominion Insurance Corpn.: 790 Bay St., Toronto, Ont.; f. 1904; Pres. and Gen. Man. R. H. L. MASSIE.

Dominion Life Assurance Co.: 111 Westmount Road Waterloo, Ont.; f. 1889; Pres. E. G. SCHAFER.

Dominion of Canada General Insurance Co.: 165 University Avenue, Toronto, Ont.; f. 1887; Pres. H. S. GOODERHAM; Gen. Mans. H. N. HANLY, J. M. RUTHERFORD.

Eaton Life Assurance Co: 14 College St., Toronto, Ont.; f. 1920; Chair. G. D. WOTHERSPOON; Pres. A. G. WEAVER.

Excelsior Life Insurance Co.: 20 Toronto St., Toronto, Ont.; f. 1889; Chair. Maj.-Gen. A. BRUCE MATTHEWS, D.S.O.; Pres. J. W. WESTAWAY.

Federation Insurance Co. of Canada: 275 St. James St. W., Montreal, P.Q. H2Y 1M9; f. 1947; Man. Dir. E. E. AHL.

Fidelity Life Assurance Co.: 1112 West Pender St., Vancouver 1, B.C.; f. 1912; Chair. Hon. W. M. HAMILTON; Pres. J. A. BROADBENT; Vice-Pres. J. S. M. CUNNINGHAM.

General Accident Assurance Co. of Canada: 357 Bay St., Toronto 1, Ont.; f. 1906; Pres. JAMES E. BURNS, B.A., A.I.I.C.; Vice-Pres. D. F. SMITH.

Gerling Global General Insurance Co.: 480 University Ave., Toronto, Ont. M5G 1V6; f. 1955; Chair. Dr. H. GERLING; Pres. A. BRANDIN; Snr. Vice-Pres. and Treas. Dr. R. KERN.

Gerling Global Life Insurance Co.: 480 University Ave., Toronto M5G 1V6; f. 1957; Exec. Vice-Pres. K. H. KLAESER.

Gerling Global Reinsurance Co.: 480 University Ave., Toronto, Ont. M5G 1V6; f. 1957; Pres. A. H. BRANDIN.

Globe Indemnity Co. of Canada: 630 Dorchester Blvd. W., Montreal, Que.; f. 1894; Pres. D. B. MARTIN.

Gore Mutual Insurance Co.: Galt, Ont.; f. 1839; Pres. D. MCINTOSH.

Grain Insurance and Guarantee Co.: 574 Grain Exchange Building, Winnipeg, Man.; f. 1919; Pres. W. MCRAIT; Gen. Man. J. TIMMERMAN.

Great-West Life Assurance Co., The: 60 Osborne St. North, Winnipeg; Man. R3C 3A5; f. 1891; Pres. J. W. BURNS.

Guardian Insurance Co. of Canada: 240 St. James St. West; Montreal, Que.; f. 1911; Chair. Col. IRWIN H. EAKIN; Pres. N. H. MANNING; Vice-Pres. and Sec. D. S. HARLEY.

Halifax Insurance Co.: 1303 Yonge St., Toronto 7, Ont., f. 1809; Chair. A. G. S. GRIFFIN; Pres. J. E. MACNELLY.

Hudson Bay Insurance Co.: 630 Dorchester Blvd. W., Montreal, Que.; f. 1905; Pres. J. B. MARTIN.

Imperial Insurance Office: 48 Yonge St., Toronto, Ont.; f. 1907; Pres. and Man. Dir. R. P. SIMPSON.

Imperial Life Assurance Company of Canada: 95 St. Clair Ave. W., Toronto, Ont. M4V 1N7; f. 1896; Chair. A. ROSS POYNTZ, F.C.I.A.; Pres. G. K. FOX, F.C.I.A.

Kings Mutual Fire Insurance Co.: Berwick, N.S.; f. 1904; Pres. M. ELLS; Man. V. L. ROOP.

London and Lancashire Guarantee and Accident Co. of Canada: 61–65 Adelaide Street East, Toronto 1, Ont.; f. 1908; Pres. G. F. BURNE; Man. and Sec. J. HOLDEN.

London Life Insurance Co.: Cnr. Wellington and Dufferin, London, Ont.; f. 1874; Chair. JOSEPH JEFFERY; Pres. A. H. JEFFERY; Exec. Vice-Pres. and Gen. Man. M. C. PRYCE.

Manufacturers' Life Insurance Co.: 200 Bloor Street East, Toronto 5, Ont.; f. 1887; Pres. E. S. JACKSON.

Maritime Life Assurance Co.: 2701 Dutch Village Rd., Halifax, N.S.; f. 1923; Pres. O. M. ERICKSEN; Chair. R. G. SMITH.

Mercantile and General Reinsurance Company of Canada Ltd.: 34 King St. East, Toronto 1, Ont.; f. 1951; Chair. L. W. SKEY; Pres. and Gen. Man. D. M. BATTEN.

Missisquoi and Rouville Insurance Co.: Box 70, Frelighsburg, Que. J0J 1C0; f. 1835; Pres. W. W. FOOT; Vice Pres. and Gen. Man. L. R. BOAST.

Monarch Life Assurance Co.: 333 Broadway Ave., Winnipeg, Man. R3C 0S9; f. 1904; Chair. T. BRUCE ROSS; Pres. HAROLD THOMPSON.

Montreal Life Insurance Co.: 630 Sherbrooke St. West, Montreal, Que. H3A 1E4; f. 1908; Pres. G. ALEXANDER.

Mutual Life Assurance Co. of Canada, The: 227 King Street South, Waterloo, Ont.; f. 1869; Chair. K. R. MACGREGOR, F.S.A.; Pres. J. H. PANABAKER.

National Life Assurance Co. of Canada: 350 Bloor St. East, Toronto, Ont. M4W 1H4; f. 1897; Pres. J. A. RHIND.

North American Life Assurance Co: 105 Adelaide St. West, Toronto, Ont.; f. 1879; Chair. J. H. TAYLOR; Pres. D. W. PRETTY; Vice-Pres. L. S. MACKERSY, J. M. BREEN.

Northern Life Assurance Co. of Canada: 291 Dundas St., London, Ont.; f. 1894; Chair. R. M. IVEY, Q.C.; Vice-Pres. and Gen. Man. G. L. BOWIE.

Portage La Prairie Mutual Insurance Co.: Portage La Prairie, Man.; f. 1884; Pres. J. C. MILLER, Q.C.; Gen. Man. E. M. BROWN.

Provident Assurances Co.: 507 Place d'Armes, P.O. 1270, Place d'Armes, Montreal, Que. H2Y 3K6; f. 1905; Pres. C. A. LANG.

Reliance Insurance Co. of Canada: 759 Victoria Square, Montreal 1, Que.; f. 1920; Pres. P. QUESNOT; Vice-Pres. and Man. Dir. W. G. PEREGO.

The Safeguard Life Insurance Co.: 152 Notre-Dame St. East, Montreal, Que. H2Y 1C4; f. 1901; Pres. and Man. Dir. C. GAUTHIER.

Saskatchewan Government Insurance Office: Government Insurance Building, 2215 11th Ave., Regina, Sask.; f. 1945; Chair. Hon. R. J. ROMANOW; Gen. Man. J. GREEN.

Saskatchewan Guarantee and Fidelity Co. Ltd.: Government Insurance Bldg., 2215 11th Ave., Regina, Sask.; ceased operations 1972.

Scottish Canadian Assurance Corporation: 357 Bay St., Toronto 1, Ont.; f. 1920; Pres. JAMES E. BURNS, A.I.I.C.

Sovereign Life Assurance Co. of Canada, The: 1320 Yonge St., Toronto 7, Ont.; f. 1902; Chair. J. S. LAND; Pres. and Man. Dir. W. R. LIVINGSTON.

Stanstead and Sherbrooke Insurance Co.: 2000 Prospect St., Sherbrooke, P.Q.; f. 1835; Man. Dir. J. P. GAUTIER.

Sun Life Assurance Co. of Canada: P.O.B. 6075, Montreal, Que. H3C 2H6; f. 1865; Chair. A. M. CAMPBELL, F.I.A., F.S.A.; Pres. T. M. GALT, F.S.A.

Toronto Mutual Life Insurance Co.: 175 Bloor St. East, Toronto 5, Ont.; Pres. JOHN T. ENGLISH; Chair. H. W. B. BOYNTON.

United Canadian Shares Ltd.: 333 Main St., Winnipeg 1, Man.; f. 1951; Pres. C. S. RILEY; Vice-Pres. P. D. CURRY.

Waterloo Mutual Insurance Co.: Waterloo, Ont.; f. 1863; Pres. W. J. MCGIBBON; Man. Dir. G. B. KENNEY.

Wawanesa Mutual Insurance Co.: 1 Wawanesa, Man.; f. 1896; Pres. M. C. HOLDEN.

Wellington Fire Insurance Co.: 15 Toronto St., Toronto Ont.; f. 1927; Pres. R. B. MORAN.

Western Assurance Co.: 40 Scott St., Toronto 1, Ont.; f. 1851; Pres. and Gen. Man. D. B. MARTIN.

Western Life Assurance Co.: 105 Main St. East, P.O.B. 67, Hamilton, Ont.; f. 1910; Chair. J. D. MACARTHUR; Pres. and Man. Dir. L. J. LEHANE.

Western Union Insurance Co.: 640–8 Ave. S.W., 811 7th St. S.W., Calgary, Alta.; f. 1840; Man. Dir. D. J. FREEZE.

Zurich Life Insurance Co. of Canada: 188 University Ave. Toronto, Ont. M5H 3C4; Pres. and Chief Exec. Officer, R. N. MACKINTOSH.

International Chemical Workers' Union: Pres. Thomas E. Boyle; Canadian Vice-Pres. and Dir. of Organization in Canada Thomas W. Sloan, Suite 48, Shoreacres House, 1262 Don Mills Rd., Don Mills 404, Ont.; f. 1944; 15,000 mems. in Canada; publ. *Chemical Worker Paper*; circ. 110,000.

International Ladies' Garment Workers' Union: Vice-Pres. in Canada S. Bresner, 405 Concord St., Montreal 2, P.Q.; 25,000 mems.; publ. *La Justice*.

International Union of Electrical, Radio and Machine Workers' AFL.CIO.CLC.: Room 504, 15 Gervais Drive, Don Mills, Ont.; Pres. in Canada George Hutchens; 12,000 mems.

International Woodworkers of America: Rep. in Canada: Joe Miyazawa, Vancouver, B.C.; 41,847 mems.

Labourers International Union of North America: 203, 268 Seymour St., Vancouver, B.C.; Sub-Regional Man. for B.C., Alberta and Saskatchewan W. E. Hart; 43,129 mems.

Oil, Chemical and Atomic Workers International Union: Ste. 100, 9950-107th St., Edmonton, Alberta, T5K 1G5; Canadian Dir. C. Reimer; 14,500 mems.

The Order of Railroad Telegraphers: Vice-Pres. in Canada F. E. Easterbrook, 607-85 Sparks Street, Ottawa 4; 10,268 mems.

Public Service Alliance of Canada: 233 Gilmour St., Ottawa 4; f. 1966; Pres. C. A. Edwards; 120,000 mems.; publs. *Argus-Journal*, M., circ. 110,000, *Civil Service Review*, Q., circ. 11,000.

Retail, Wholesale and Department Store Union: Dir. in Canada G. Barlow, 15 Gervais Drive, Don Mills, Ont.; 26,000 mems.; publ. *The Record*.

Seafarers International Union of Canada: 634 St. James Street West, Montreal; 15,000 mems.

Textile Workers Union of America: Dir. in Canada J. Harold D'Aoust, 137 Bond Street, Toronto; 17,000 mems.

United Automobile, Aerospace and Agricultural Implement Workers of America International Union: Dir. Canadian Region Dennis McDermott 2450 Victoria Park Ave., Willowdale, Ont. M2J 4A1; 120,000 mems.; publ. *Solidarity*.

United Brotherhood of Carpenters and Joiners of America: Official in Canada A. Cooper, 133 Chaplin Crescent, Toronto; 76,501 mems.

United Rubber, Cork, Linoleum and Plastic Workers of America: Dir. in Canada Norman Allison, 33 Cecil Street, Toronto 2B; 13,000 mems.

United Steelworkers of America: National Dir. in Canada W. Mahoney, 55 Eglinton Ave. E., Toronto; 180,000 mems.

United Transportation Union: 1729 Bank St., Ottawa 8, Ont.; Canadian Legislative Rep. W. G. McGregor.

Confederation of National Trade Unions—CNTU: 1001 St.-Denis Street, Montreal, Que. H2X 3J1; f. 1921; Nat. Pres. Marcel Pepin; Sec.-Gen. J. Philbeault; 165,000 mems.; 1,089 unions in Quebec Province, 1 in Newfoundland, and 3 in Ontario; publ. *Le Travail* (monthly).

Affiliated Unions with over 10,000 Members

Fédération canadienne des Employés de Services publics: 429 est Lagauchetière, Montreal, P.Q.; Sec. Francine Xelle; 25,530 mems.

Fédération canadienne des Travailleurs du Textile: 1001 rue St.-Denis, Montreal, P.Q.; Directeur professionnel Yvon Jacques; 11,071 mems.

Fédération du Commerce, Inc. (C.S.N.): 155 blvd. Charest Est, Quebec, P.Q.; Dir. Jacques Archambault.

Fédération nationale des Services, Inc.: 1001 rue St.-Denis, Montreal, P.Q.; Sec. Renaud Flynn; 44,800 mems.

Fédération nationale des Syndicats du Bâtiment et du Bois, Inc.: 155E blvd. Charest, Quebec G1K 3G6; Sec. G. Courtemanche; 25,000 mems.

Federation of Building Workers of Canada: 1231 Demontigny Street East, Montreal; Sec. J. B. Delisle; 20,408 mems.

National Metal Trades' Federation: 2002 St.-Denis St., Montreal, P.Q.; Pres. Adrien Plourde; Sec. Maurice Langevin; 23,800 mems.

Principal Unaffiliated Bodies

L'Union des Producteurs agricoles: 515 Viger Ave., Montreal, Que. H2L 2P2; f. 1924; Sec.-Gen. J.-M. Kirouac; 50,000 mems.; publ. *La Terre de Chez Nous* (weekly), circ. 60,000.

United Electrical, Radio and Machine Workers of America (UE): Canadian Pres. C. S. Jackson, 3 Thorncliffe Square, Toronto 17; 25,740 mems. in Canada.

United Mine Workers of America: Pres. in Canada W. Marsh, McDonnell Building, Glace Bay, N.S.; 21,860 mems. in Canada.

TRANSPORT

RAILWAYS

Algoma Central Railway: 289 Bay St., Sault Ste. Marie, Ont.; passenger service, iron ore, coal grain, forest products and stone transportation; Chair. Sir Denys Lowson; Pres. L. N. Savoie; Vice-Pres. and Gen. Man. J. A. Thompson.

British Columbia Hydro and Power Authority: 970 Burrard St., Vancouver, B.C. V6Z 1Y3; 103 miles, 20 diesel locomotives; Chair. D. Cass-Beggs; Sec. G. G. Woodward.

British Columbia Railway Co.: 1095 West Pender St., Vancouver, B.C. V6E 2N6; f. 1912; owned by British Columbia Govt.; 1,238 miles; 100 diesel locomotives;

Pres. Hon. David Barrett; Exec. Vice-Pres. Hon. W. S. King; Vice-Pres. and Gen. Man. J. S. Broadbent.

Canadian National Railways (Grand Trunk Railway System): Sec. P.O.B. 8100, Montreal, Que. H3C 3N4; Head Office: 935 Lagauchetiere St. W., Montreal; Chair. and Pres. N. J. Macmillan; Vice-Pres. and Sec. R. T. Vaughan.

36,328 miles operated; revenue (Dec. 1972) $1,257,118m.; operating expenses $1,233,250m.

Canadian Pacific Ltd.: Head Office: Windsor Station, Montreal, Que.; f. 1881; Chair. and Chief Exec. Officer I. D. Sinclair, Q.C.; Pres. F. S. Burbridge; Vice-Pres. K. Campbell; Sec. J. A. Ames.

Miles operated (1973): 21,295 including 4,707 for controlled companies; net earnings (1973) $57.6m.

Cartier Railway Co.: Port Cartier, Duplessis County, P.Q.; 279 miles; 28 diesel locomotives; Pres. L. J. PATTERSON.

Northern Alberta Railways: Edmonton, Alta; 923 miles; 17 diesel locomotives; Pres. J. W. G. MacDOUGALL; Sec. R. T. VAUGHAN.

Ontario Northland Railway: North Bay, Ont.; operated by Ontario Govt. Commission; Chair. J. H. JESSIMAN; Gen. Man. F. S. CLIFFORD; rail, highway, boat and communications services.

Quebec North Shore and Labrador Railway Co.: Suite 1150, 1245 Sherbrooke St. West, Montreal, P.Q. H3G 1G8; 358 miles; 80 diesel locomotives; Pres. W. J. BENNETT; Man. D. B. NEUFELD.

Toronto, Hamilton and Buffalo Railway Company: Hamilton, Ont.; 111 miles; 18 diesel locomotives; Pres. J. A. McDONALD, Philadelphia, Pa., U.S.A.

White Pass and Yukon Corporation Ltd.: Standard Bldg., 510 W. Hastings St., Vancouver, B.C.; 111 miles; 18 diesel locomotives; integrated rail-ship-truck transportation system; Pres. R. A. HUBBER-RICHARD.

ROADS

Provincial Governments are responsible for roads within their boundaries. The Federal Government is responsible for the construction of major roads in the Yukon and North-west Territories and in National Parks. At the end of 1971 the mileage of all provincial, federal and municipal roads was 516,783, of which 395,437 miles were surfaced and 121,346 miles were earth roads.

The Trans-Canadian Highway extends from St. John's, Newfoundland, to Victoria, British Columbia.

INLAND WATERWAYS

The St. Lawrence River and the Great Lakes provide Canada and the United States with a system of inland waterways stretching 2,300 miles across the continent. There is a 35 foot navigation channel from Montreal to the sea and a 27 foot channel from Montreal to Lake Erie. The St. Lawrence Seaway project was initiated partly to provide a deep waterway and partly to satisfy the demand for more electric power. Power development has been undertaken by the Provinces of Quebec and Ontario, and by New York State. The navigation facilities and conditions are within the jurisdiction of the federal governments of the United States and Canada.

ST. LAWRENCE RIVER AND GREAT LAKES SHIPPING

Abticosti Shipping Co.: 800 Dorchester Boulevard W., Montreal, P.Q.; cargo, St. Lawrence River ports; Pres. J. D. ANDREW; Man. PIERRE GERMAIN; 4 vessels.

British Columbia Ferries: 816 Wharf St., Victoria, B.C. 1; passenger and car ferries; Gen. Man. C. GALLAGHER; 23 ferries.

Canada Steamship Lines Ltd.: 759 Victoria Sq., Montreal, P.Q. H2Y 2K3 (P.O.B. 100, Station 'A', Montreal, P.Q. H3C 2R7); Chair. and Chief Exec. Officer LOUIS R. DESMARAIS; 30 vessels; 376,100 tons gross.

Hall Corporation (Shipping) Ltd.: 4333 St. Catherine St. W., Montreal, Que. H3Z 1PN; Chair. F. A. AUGSBURY, Jr.; Pres. A. PULLIN; 13 tankers; 8 cargo vessels; 250,000 t.d.w.

Paterson, N. M., and Sons Ltd.: P.O.B. 664, Fort William, Ont.; bulk carriers; Pres. Senator N. M. PATERSON; Vice-Pres. DONALD S. PATERSON, JOHN N. PATERSON; Man. J. N. SUTHERLAND; 16 vessels; 94,862 tons gross.

Scott Misener Steamships Ltd.: 115 Dieppe Rd., P.O.B. 100, St. Catherine's, Ont.; bulk cargo; Chair. RALPH S. MISENER; Pres. S. A. MISENER; 10 vessels; 104,281 tons gross.

Upper Lakes Shipping Ltd.: 49 Jackes Ave., Toronto, Ont. M4T 1E2; Pres. and Dir. J. D. LEITCH; Vice-Pres. and Gen. Man. L. A. KAAKE; bulk carriers; 22 vessels; 480,000 t.d.w.

Westdale Shipping Ltd.: 106 Lakeshire Rd. East., Port Credit, Ont.; bulk cargoes; Pres. K. SMITH; 9 vessels; 92,000 t.d.w.

SHIPPING

Blue Peter Steamships Ltd.: Harbour Drive, St. John's, Newfoundland; refrigerated cargo Canada–U.S.A., Europe; Chair. L. H. M. AYRE; Gen. Man. R. M. CLANCY; 4 vessels.

Branch Lines Ltd.: P.O.B. 200, Sorel, P.Q.; Great Lakes, St. Lawrence River and Gulf, Atlantic Coast, Arctic and N.W.T.; Pres. A. SIMARD; Exec. Vice-Pres. L.-H. TELLIER; Superintendent T. DURAND; 11 tankers, 73,000 t.d.w.; 1 tug.

Canadian Coast Guard: Government of Canada, Ministry of Transport, Tower C, Place de Ville, Ottawa K1A 0N7; fleet of 150 vessels including 15 full ice-breakers; patrol, survey, auxiliary, supply, landing, weather station and various other vessels and 2 hovercraft; 27 helicopters and 1 fixed-wing aircraft; Director Captain W. J. H. STUART.

Canadian City Line: 410 St. Nicholas St., Montreal, P.Q. H2Y 2P5; Canada–India, Pakistan, Bangladesh and Ceylon and South and East Africa; Chair. and Pres. W. R. EAKIN; 5 vessels.

Clarke Transportation Canada Ltd., and Associated Companies: 1155 Dorchester Blvd. West, Montreal, P.Q.; f. 1921; divisions: pool car, domestic steamships, road transport, steamship agency, automobile; Pres. S. D. CLARKE; 5 vessels.

East Coast Marine and Ferry Services: Moncton, N.B. east coast of Canada; Gen. Man. R. J. TINGLEY; 23 ships.

Federal Commerce and Navigation Co. Ltd.: 3800 Stock Exchange Tower, Montreal, P.Q. H4Z 1C4; f. 1944; ship-owners, operators, contractors, Terminal operators; Pres. L. G. PATHY; owned and chartered fleet of 1m. d.w.t.

Imperial Oil Ltd.: Transportation Dept., Marine Division, 111 St. Clair Ave. West, Toronto, Ont. M5W 1K3; coastal, Great Lakes and St. Lawrence River, South American, Caribbean and Gulf ports to Canadian East and U.S. Atlantic ports, Persian Gulf to U.K. and European ports; Pres. J. A. ARMSTRONG; Man. Marine Div. W. G. ABEL; 11 vessels; 200,000 t.d.w.

Saguenay Shipping Ltd.: 1060 University St., Montreal 101, P.Q.; owned by Aluminium Co. of Canada Ltd.; Canada–Caribbean, Central and South America; United Kingdom/North Continent–Caribbean; Pres. JOHN L. EYRE; over 30 vessels chartered.

Seaboard Shipping Co. Ltd.: Seaboard House, Vancouver, B.C.; United Kingdom–Continent, Australia, New Zealand, South Africa, Mediterranean, West Indies, U.S. Atlantic Coast; Pres. C. D. G. ROBERTS; Vice-Pres. R. M. MATHER.

Shell Canadian Tankers (1964) Ltd.: P.O.B. 400, Terminal "A", Toronto; petroleum products in bulk; Pres. and Chief Exec. Officer J. F. BOOKOUT; Man. J. D. FINNIE; 1 ocean tanker, 12,608 g.r.t.; 5 Lake tankers, 15,909 g.r.t.

CIVIL AVIATION

Air Canada: Place Ville Marie, Montreal, P.Q. H3B 3P7; created by Act of Parliament 1937 as a subsidiary of Canadian National Railways; Pres. R. T. VAUGHAN; Chair. and Chief Exec. YVES PRATTE. Operates services throughout Canada to the United States, the British Isles, Paris, Brussels, Prague, Copenhagen, Moscow, Zürich, Vienna, Bermuda and the West Indies; (1972) revenue passengers carried 8.4m.; total revenue ton miles 110m.; fleet of 4 Boeing 747, 6L-1011, 38 DC-8, 50 DC-9, 5 Viscounts.

Canadian Pacific Airlines: 1900 Granville Square, 200 Granville St., Vancouver, B.C. V6C 2R1; Pres. J. C. GILMER; Vice-Pres. and Comptroller C. F. O'BRIEN; Vice-Pres. International and Corporate Services H. D. CAMERON; Vice-Pres. Technical Services I. A. GRAY; Vice-Pres. Customer Service G. E. MANNING; Vice-Pres. Flight Operations R. B. PHILLIPS.

Revenue passenger flight miles (est. 1973) 3,061m.; passengers 1,755,750; revenue cargo ton miles 51m.; revenue mail ton miles 13m.; operates DC-8s, Boeing 737s, 727s, 747s.

Norcanair (*North Canada Air Ltd.*): P.O.B. 850, Prince Albert, Sask.; acquired **Saskair** 1965; Pres. and Gen. Manager J. B. LLOYD; Traffic and Sales Vice-Pres. IAN MACLEOD; Production and Engineering Vice-Pres. J. POOL; unduplicated route mileage 1,650; fleet includes DC-3s, Cansos, F27s, Bristol Freighters and Otters, and other small craft.

Pacific Western Airlines Ltd.: Vancouver Airport, B.C.; Pres. D. WATSON; Vice-Pres. and Gen. Man. W. R. HARRIS; Vice-Pres. Finance and Sec. D. F. GRANGER; operates Boeing 707-138B and 320C, 737-200 and 727-100C, Lockheed L-382 Hercules, Convair 640.

Quebecair: P.O.B. 490, Montreal International Airport, Dorval, P.Q. H4Y 1B5; local and charter services; Pres. Hon. L. CHEVRIER; Vice-Pres. and Gen. Man. A. LIZOTTE; operates 3 BAC 1-11, 4 Fairchild F-27; unduplicated route mileage 6,000.

TransAir-Midwest Limited: Winnipeg International Airport, Winnipeg 21, Manitoba; f. 1969; Pres. A. V. MAURO; Sec. F. C. McKAY; fleet includes YS-11 As; Argosy 200s, 707-320C, F-28's, Twin Otters, Bell 205A, Jet Rangers, Bell 479s.

TOURISM

Canadian Government Office of Tourism: 150 Kent St., Ottawa, Ont. K1A 0H6; Federal Dept. of Industry, Trade and Commerce; Asst. Dep. Minister Tourism T. R. G. FLETCHER.

REGIONAL OFFICES

Eastern United States: 16th Floor, 1251 Avenue of the Americas, New York, N.Y. 10020.

Western United States and Pacific Area: Suite 2300, Crocker Plaza, 600 Market St., San Francisco, Calif. 94104.

Europe: Macdonald House, Room 40, 1 Grosvenor Sq., London W1X 0AB, England.

OVERSEAS OFFICES

Australia: Suite 1900, AMP Bldg., Circular Quay, Sydney, N.S.W. 2000.

France: 4 rue Scribe, Paris 9e.

German Federal Republic: 6 Frankfurt/Main, Biebergasse 6-10.

Japan: AIU Akasaka Bldg., 2nd Floor, No. 1-2, Akasaka 3-chome, Minato-ku, Tokyo.

Mexico: Melchor Ocampo 463, Mexico 5, D.F.

Netherlands: Laan Van Meerdervoort 96, The Hague.

United Kingdom: P.O.B. 9, Canada House, London SW1 Y5DR.

United States: there are offices in Los Angeles, San Francisco, Washington, Atlanta, Chicago, Boston, Detroit, Minneapolis, New York, Cincinnati, Cleveland, Philadelphia, Pittsburgh and Seattle.

Travel Industry Association of Canada: Suite 1016, 130 Albert St., Ottawa, Ont. K1P 5G4; non-profit organization to disseminate travel industry information; publ. *Canadian Tourism* (monthly).

CULTURAL ORGANIZATIONS

Government agencies: **National Film Board, Canadian Broadcasting Corporation, National Arts Centre** and the **National Gallery.** The **Canada Council** also plays an important part in promoting the arts.

Canadian Conference of the Arts: 85 Lombard Street, Toronto, Ont. K1P 5W1; f. 1945; to promote and encourage the arts and culture in Canada; 39 member societies; National Dir. ALAN JARVIS.

Canadian Music Council: 188 Elmwood Ave., Willowdale, Ont. M2N 3M6; f. 1949; mems. 19 national organizations, 29 group mems., CBC and individual musicians; Pres. R. NAPIER; Sec. JOHN COZENS; publ. *The Canada Music Book—Les Cahiers canadiens de musique.*

National Arts Centre: Ottawa; f. 1969; opera house theatre, experimental theatre, salon, resident 46-piece orchestra; Dir.-Gen. GORDON HAMILTON SOUTHAM.

PRINCIPAL THEATRES

Canadian Opera Company: Beardmore Building, 35-39 Front St. E., Toronto, Ont.; f. 1950; Gen. Dir. HERMAN GEIGER-TOREL; publ. *Opera Canada* (quarterly).

Les Feux Follets: Montreal, P.Q.; f. 1952; national folk dance ensemble; Art Dir. ALAN LUND.

Le Grand Theatre: 269 est, St. Cyrille, Quebec 4; f. 1971; arts centre with facilities for dramatic, musical and visual arts; Gen. Man. G. BEAULNE.

National Ballet of Canada: 157 King St. East, Toronto, Ont. M5C 1G9; touring company of 120.

Queen Elizabeth Playhouse: Vancouver, B.C.; f. 1962; home of the Playhouse Theatre Company; 647 seats.

Queen Elizabeth Theatre: Vancouver, B.C.; f. 1959; houses the Vancouver Symphony Orchestra and the Vancouver Opera Asscn.; 2,800 seats.

The Royal Winnipeg Ballet: 289 Portage Ave., Winnipeg, f. 1938; Artistic Dir. ARNOLD SPOHR.

Stratford National Theatre of Canada: Stratford, Ont.; f. 1953; Canada's national English-language theatre company; Dir. JEAN GASCON.

Theatre Department of the National Arts Centre: Box 1534, Station "B", Ottawa, Ont. K1P 5W1; f. 1971; Artistic Dir. JEAN ROBERTS; Assoc. Dir. JEAN HERBIET.

There are theatre centres in Toronto and Manitoba.

PRINCIPAL ORCHESTRAS

Montreal Symphony Orchestra: La Place des Arts, 200 de Maisonneuve Blvd., Montreal 129, P.Q.; f. 1934; Pres. ROBERT J. BRUCK; Gen. Man. JACQUES DRUELLE; Musical Dir. FRANZ-PAUL DECKER.

National Arts Centre Orchestra: resident orchestra of the National Arts Centre, Ottawa, Ont. K1P 5W1; f. 1969; Man. KENNETH MURPHY; Conductor MARIO BERNARDI.

L'Orchestre Symphonique de Quebec: Palais Montcalm, bur. 50, Quebec 4, P.Q.; Musical Dir. PIERRE DERVAUX.

Winnipeg Symphony Orchestra: Room 117, 555 Main St., Winnipeg 2, Manitoba; Gen. Man. L. D. STONE; Conductor and Dir. of Music PIERO GAMBA.

There are also symphony orchestras in a number of cities, including Toronto, Vancouver and Halifax, and youth orchestras in Quebec and Toronto and opera associations in Vancouver and Edmonton.

ATOMIC ENERGY

Atomic Energy of Canada Ltd.: 275 Slater St., Ottawa, Ontario; Pres. J. L. GRAY; federal government agency for nuclear research and development, production of radioactive isotopes and design, development and marketing of power reactors; four research reactors at Chalk River, Ontario, and one at Whiteshell Nuclear Research Establishment, Pinawa, Manitoba; one nuclear power station in operation at Rolphton, Ontario and one at Douglas Point, Ontario (both in conjunction with Ontario Hydro); another reactor, of 250 MW power at Gentilly, P.Q. (in conjunction with Hydro Quebec); nuclear consultant to Ontario Hydro for Pickering (4 540 MW units) and Bruce (4 750 MW units under construction) generating stations, both with AECL designed CANDU reactors.

Atomic Energy Control Board: P.O.B. 1046, Ottawa, Ont.; Pres. Dr. D. G. HURST; responsible for all regulatory matters, makes grants for research.

Eldorado Nuclear Ltd.: Port Hope, Ontario; Pres. W. M. GILCHRIST; produces various forms of uranium.

McMaster University: Hamilton, Ont.; swimming pool reactor, power 5,000 kW., started 1959, and a 20 MeV Tandem Accelerator.

Ontario Hydro: 620 University Ave., Toronto; four 500 M.W. power reactors under construction at Pickering, Ontario; Chair. GEORGE E. GATHERCOLE, LL.D.

University of Toronto: Toronto; sub-critical reactor, started 1958.

UNIVERSITIES

Acadia University: Wolfville, Nova Scotia; 160 teachers, 2,400 students.

University of Alberta: Edmonton and Calgary, Alberta; 2,149 teachers, 22,188 students.

Bishop's University: Lennoxville, Quebec; 92 teachers, 1,380 students.

Brandon University: Brandon, Manitoba; 120 teachers, 2,200 students.

University of British Columbia: Vancouver 8, British Columbia; 1,621 teachers, 20,583 students.

Brock University: St. Catharines, Ontario; 223 teachers, 3,740 students.

University of Calgary: Calgary, Alberta; 810 teachers, 12,227 students.

Carleton University: Rideau River Campus, Colonel By Drive, Ottawa 1, Ontario; 530 teachers, 13,659 students.

Dalhousie University: Halifax, Nova Scotia; 750 teachers, 7,087 students.

University of Guelph: Guelph, Ontario; 841 teachers, 7,942 students.

University of King's College: Halifax, Nova Scotia; 16 professors; 263 students.

Lakehead University: Oliver Rd., Port Arthur, Ontario; 250 teachers, 3,158 students.

Laurentian University of Sudbury: Ramsay Lake Rd., Sudbury, Ontario; 200 teachers, 5,078 students.

Laval University: Cité Universitaire, Quebec, P.Q.; 2,367 teachers, 13,956 students.

University of Lethbridge: Lethbridge, Alberta; 140 teachers, 1,600 students.

McGill University: Montreal 110, Quebec; 3,125 teachers, 17,176 students.

McMaster University: Hamilton 16, Ont.; 882 teachers, 14,601 students.

University of Manitoba: Winnipeg 19, Manitoba; 1,057 teachers, 18,336 students.

Memorial University of Newfoundland: St. John's, Newfoundland; 610 teachers, 10,550 students.

University of Moncton: Moncton, New Brunswick; 425 full-time teachers, 6,050 students.

University of Montreal: C.P. 6128, Montreal, P.Q.; 2,000 professors, 23,055 students.

Mount Allison University: Sackville, New Brunswick; 130 teachers, 1,363 students.

Mount St. Vincent University: Halifax, Nova Scotia; 100 teachers, 1,400 students.

University of New Brunswick: Fredericton, New Brunswick; 387 teachers, 7,031.

Notre Dame University of Nelson: Nelson, B.C.; 50 teachers, 522 students.

University of Ottawa: Ottawa, Ontario; 917 teachers, 12,225 students.

University of Prince Edward Island: Charlottetown, Prince Edward Island; 150 teachers, 2,507 students.

Université du Québec: Sainte Foy, Quebec; 410 teachers; 10,500 students.

Queen's University: Kingston, Ontario; 871 teachers, 11,209 students.

St. Francis Xavier University: Antigonish, Nova Scotia, 209 teachers, 2,899 students.

St. Mary's University: Halifax, Nova Scotia; 150 teachers, 2,864 students.

University of Saskatchewan: Saskatoon, Saskatchewan; 798 teachers, 11,888 students.

Université de Sherbrooke: Cité Universitaire, Sherbrooke, Quebec, P.Q.; 660 teachers, 8,109 students.

Simon Fraser University: Burnaby, British Columbia; 356 teachers, 5,007 students.

Sir George Williams University: 1435 Drummond St., Montreal 25, P.Q.; 682 teachers, 18,121 students.

University of Toronto: Toronto 181, Ontario; 5,141 teachers, 40,131 students.

Trent University: Peterborough, Ontario; 155 teachers, 1,800 students.

University of Victoria: Victoria, B.C.; 146 teachers, 2,458 students.

Waterloo Lutheran University: Waterloo, Ontario; 138 teachers, 2,796 students.

University of Waterloo: Waterloo, Ontario; 796 teachers, 14,826 students.

University of Western Ontario: London, Ontario; 1,500 teachers, 18,000 students.

University of Windsor: 400 Huron Line, Windsor, Ontario; 480 teachers, 8,564 students.

University of Winnipeg: 515 Portage Ave., Winnipeg 2, Manitoba; 223 teachers, 4,674 students.

York University: 700 Keele St., Downsview, Ontario; 888 teachers, 23,316 students.

CENTRAL AFRICAN REPUBLIC

INTRODUCTORY SURVEY

Location, Climate, Language, Religion, Flag, Capital

The Central African Republic lies in the heart of equatorial Africa and is bounded by Chad to the north, the Sudan to the east, the Congo (Brazzaville) and Zaire to the south and Cameroon to the west. Climate is tropical with an average temperature of 26°c (79°F) and heavy rains in the south-western forest areas. The national language is Sangho, but French is the official language. Many of the population hold animist beliefs, but nearly half are Christians. The national flag (proportions 5 by 3) consists of horizontal bands of blue, white, green and yellow, divided vertically by a red band, with a yellow star in the top left-hand corner. The capital is Bangui.

Recent History

Formerly the territory of Oubangui Chari within French Equatorial Africa, the Republic took its present name when it achieved self-government in 1958. Full independence was attained in 1960. The leading figure in the campaign for self-government and the first President, Bartholémy Boganda, died in 1959. His successor, David Dacko, was overthrown by a military *coup d'état* at the end of 1965 which brought to power Colonel (now Gen.) Jean-Bédel Bokassa.

At the beginning of January 1966 Colonel Bokassa formed a new government, rescinded the Constitution and dissolved the National Assembly. An alleged conspiracy against the President in April 1969 led to the arrest and execution of Lt.-Col. Alexandre Banza, the Minister of Health. Bokassa was made Life President in March 1972. In April 1973 a leading Minister, Auguste M'Bongo, was arrested for an alleged attempted *coup d'état*. In January 1974 the leaders of the UGTC, the only trade union in the country, were also arrested for conspiracy.

In 1968 the C.A.R. formed the UEAC with Zaire and Chad, but at the end of the year it withdrew from the organization and rejoined the UDEAC. The C.A.R. is also a member of the United Nations, the French Community, and an associate member of the European Economic Community.

Government

The Constitution was abrogated in January 1966 and the President has full competence to act in all affairs of state.

Defence

The armed forces number about 3,000 men. Military service is compulsory for adult males.

Economic Affairs

The economy is predominantly agricultural, the most important cash crops being cotton and coffee. Forestry is increasing in significance. Diamonds account for over half the country's export earnings. Considerable deposits of uranium have been found, but are not yet being exploited. Bangui has been the headquarters of the UDEAC since 1966.

Transport and Communications

Bangui is about 1,450 km. from the sea but roads (5,000 km. of national roads, 4,000 km. of regional roads and 10,000 km. of rural roads) radiate east, north and west to Sudan, Chad and Cameroon respectively. There are however no railways, and the chief artery of transport is the Oubangui river which flows into the Congo and thereby provides an outlet from Bangui to Brazzaville, from where a railway runs to the port of Pointe-Noire. There are steamer services and considerable freight traffic from Bangui to Brazzaville. There is an international airport at Mpoko, near Bangui, and numerous airfields allow for extensive internal services. Feasibility studies are in progress on the possibility of connecting Bangui, by road or rail, to the trans-Cameroon line to Douala. Under an agreement signed in December 1971, a railway is to be built across the Sudanese-C.A.R. border, assisting the development of the copper industry in both states.

Social Welfare

An Employment Code guarantees a minimum wage for 60,000 employees and provides for employment accident benefits. There are 36 prefectorial hospitals, 36 maternity hospitals, 108 welfare centres and 200 first aid centres.

Education

Schools are divided into primary, secondary and technical categories. A university was founded at Bangui in 1970, and in addition 650 students attend courses of higher education abroad, 250 of them in France.

Tourism

The main tourist attractions are the waterfalls, the forests and many varieties of wild animals. There is excellent hunting and also opportunities for fishing. The 1971-75 Five-year Plan envisages a large expansion of tourism. In 1970 about 8,000 tourists visited the C.A.R.

Public Holidays

1974: August 13th (Independence Day), August 15th (Assumption), November 1st (All Saints'), December 1st (National Day), December 25th (Christmas).

1975: January 1st (New Year), March 29th (Death of Boganda), March 28th–31st (Easter), May 1st (May Day), May 8th (Ascension), May 19th (Whit Monday).

Weights and Measures

The metric system is officially in force.

Currency and Exchange Rate

100 centimes=1 franc de la Communauté financière africaine (CFA).

Exchange rates (April 1974):

£1 sterling=579.75 francs CFA;
U.S. $1=245.625 francs CFA.

STATISTICAL SURVEY

Area: 622,984 sq. km. (240,535 sq. miles).

Population (1971 estimate): 1,637,000, excluding refugees from the Sudan, numbering 28,000 in 1966.

PRÉFECTURES

PRÉFECTURE*	CHIEF TOWN	POPULATION OF CHIEF TOWN (1968)
Ombella-M'Poko .	Boali	238,000
Haute-Sangha .	Berberati	38,000
Ouham . . .	Bossangoa	35,000
Ouaka . . .	Bambari	36,000
Nana-Mambere .	Bouar	48,000
M'Bomou . .	Bangassou	28,000
Haute-Kotto .	Bria	25,000
Lobaye . .	M'Baïki	18,000
Ouham-Pende .	Bozoum	n.a.
Kemo-Gribingui .	Sibut	n.a.
Basse-Kotto . .	Mobaye	n.a.
Bamingui-Bangoran .	N'Délé	n.a.
Haut-M'Bomou .	Obo	n.a.
Vakaga . .	Birao	n.a.

*Bangui (capital, an autonomous commune): population 1968, 298,579.

EMPLOYMENT
('000—1971)

Agriculture, Forestry and Mining . .	475
Manufacturing Industry and Construction .	52
Commerce, Transport and Other Services .	32
Administration	7.5
Unemployed	43.5

AGRICULTURE

LAND USE, 1968
('000 hectares)

Arable Land	5,840
Land under Permanent Crops . .	60
Permanent Meadows and Pastures .	100
Forest Land . . .	7,400
Other areas (including rough grazing)	48,898
TOTAL . . .	62,298

PRINCIPAL CROPS

	AREA ('000 hectares)			PRODUCTION ('000 metric tons)			YIELD (kg. per hectare)		
	1969	1970	1971	1969	1970	1971	1969	1970	1971
Bananas	20*	20	n.a.	170*	170*	n.a.	8,500*	8,500*	n.a.
Cassava (Manioc) . . .	200*	200*	n.a.	1,000*	1,000*	n.a.	5,000*	5,000*	n.a.
Coffee	n.a.	n.a.	n.a.	11.0	9.6	10.5	n.a.	n.a.	n.a.
Cottonseed	134	126	126* {	37	34	31	280	270	240*
Cotton (lint) . . .				22	20	18	160	160	140*
Groundnuts (in shell) . .	90*	105*	105*	75	85	85*	830*	810*	810*
Maize	61	63	58*	47	48	45*	770	770	780*
Millet and Sorghum . .	94	80*	80*	35	50*	50*	370	630*	630*
Oranges and Tangerines . .	n.a.	n.a.	n.a.	11*	11*	11*	n.a.	n.a.	n.a.
Rice (paddy) . . .	15	13	14	12	13	14	820	1,020	1,030
Sesame Seed . . .	52*	52*	52*	16*	16*	16*	310*	310*	310*
Sweet Potatoes and Yams .	16*	16*	18*	47	47*	49*	2,900*	2,900*	2,700*

1972 Production ('000 metric tons): Coffee 12, Cottonseed 36*, Cotton (lint) 18, Groundnuts 85*.

* FAO estimate.

Sources: FAO, *Production Yearbook 1971*; FAO, *Monthly Bulletin of Agricultural Economics and Statistics.*

LIVESTOCK NUMBERS

	1968–69	1969–70*	1970–71*
Cattle . .	463,000	470,000	480,000
Goats . .	515,000*	520,000	530,000
Sheep . .	63,000	64,000	66,000
Pigs . .	52,000*	54,000	56,000
Asses . .	1,000	1,000	1,000
Chickens .	1,050,000*	1,070,000	1,100,000
Ducks . .	5,000*	5,000	5,000

* FAO estimate.

Source: FAO, *Production Yearbook 1971.*

OTHER AGRICULTURAL PRODUCTS
(metric tons)

	1969*	1970*	1971
Meat . . .	13,000	13,000	n.a.
Cows' milk . .	21,000	21,000	22,000*
Honey . . .	4,500	5,000	5,000*
Raw Cattle Hides .	1,670	1,690	n.a.
Hen Eggs . .	700	700	800*

* FAO estimate.

Source: FAO, *Production Yearbook 1971.*

FORESTRY
ROUNDWOOD PRODUCTION
(cubic metres)

1968	1,991,000
1969	2,106,000
1970	2,116,000

Source: FAO, *Yearbook of Forest Products.*

FISHING
(metric tons)

1969	3,000*
1970	3,000*
1971	3,500

* FAO estimate.

Source: FAO, *Yearbook of Fishery Statistics 1971.*

INDUSTRY AND MINING

COTTON MANUFACTURES

	Unit	1969	1970	1971
Loin-cloths	'ooo metres	4,034	3,851	3,146
Cloth	,, ,,	811	1,240	1,237
Unfinished Cloth . . .	,, ,,	3,093	2,955	2,847
Gauze	'ooo sq. metres	750	494	432
Printed Cotton	'ooo metres	5,152	4,684	4,422
Blankets, Rugs, Covers, etc. . .	'ooo	223	140	96
Cotton Wool and Carded Cotton .	'ooo kg.	25	51	31

OTHER INDUSTRIAL AND MINERAL PRODUCTION

	Unit	1969	1970	1971
Beer	hectolitres	97,089	110,231	118,630
Soft Drinks	,,	28,123	31,492	29,646
Sawnwood	cu. metres	55,000	66,617	78,466
Soap	metric tons	2,425	3,279	2,939
Radio Sets	number	9,500	8,804	n.a.
Motor Cycles	,,	5,769	6,375	5,711
Bicycles	,,	7,742	8,852	7,494
Electric Energy . . .	'ooo kWh.	41,200	46,727	47,313
Diamonds	carats	535,317	494,000	468,438

Electric Energy (1971): 47.3 million kWh.

FINANCE

100 centimes=1 franc de la Communauté financière africaine (CFA).
Coins: 1, 2, 5, 10, 25, 50 and 100 francs CFA.
Notes: 100, 500, 1,000, 5,000 and 10,000 francs CFA.
Exchange rates (April 1974): 1 franc CFA=2 French centimes;
£1 sterling=579.75 francs CFA; U.S. $1=245.625 francs CFA;
1,000 francs CFA=£1.725=$4.071.

BUDGET

(million francs CFA)

REVENUE	1970	1971*	1972*	EXPENDITURE	1970	1971*	1972*
Income Taxes	990	1,288	1,288	Transfers to:			
Other Direct Taxes	1,983	2,341	2,341	Households	386	337	333
Import Duties	2,380	2,230	2,170	National Bodies	754	708	496
Export Duties	255	250	250	Foreign Bodies	667	603	385
Taxes on Sales and Turn-over	1,380	1,321	1,320	Gross Fixed Capital Formation	860	1,292	1,234
Other Indirect Taxes	2,030	2,156	2,149	Expenditure on:			
Income from Property	313	403	223	Education	1,652†	1,642	1,808†
Contributions and Sub-sidies	415	550	400	Public Health	656	632	607‡
Reimbursement of Loans and Advances	—	151	42	Agriculture and Cattle Rearing	591	479	725
Other Receipts	1,560	1,849	1,497	Interior	741	838	841
				Defence	1,351	1,468	1,227
				Other Goods and Services	1,681	1,935	1,945
	11,306	12,539	11,680	Other Expenditures	2,745	2,605	2,079
DEFICIT	778	—	—				
TOTAL	12,084	12,539	11,680§	TOTAL	12,084	12,539	11,680§

* Forecasts.
† Including expenditure of the Ministry of Youth and Sports.
‡ Including expenditure of the Ministry of Social Affairs.
§ Revised 1972 revenue and expenditure: 13,800 million francs CFA.

DEVELOPMENT PLAN

(1971–75)

SOURCES OF FINANCING	MILLION FRANCS CFA	PLANNED EXPENDITURE	MILLION FRANCS CFA
Public Sector		Agriculture	14,827
Domestic	28,642	Mining	1,741
Foreign	17,891	Manufacturing and Handicrafts	11,486
Private Sector		Energy	4,698
Domestic	} 12,520	Transport and Communications	13,701
Foreign		Tourism	845
Resources to find	4,726	Commerce	1,204
		Health and Social Affairs	2,160
		Education, etc.	2,839
		Housing and Urban Affairs	4,698
		Other	5,580
TOTAL	63,779	TOTAL	63,779

Planned Growth Rate: 9.2 per cent per annum.

EXTERNAL TRADE*
(million francs CFA)

	1967	1968	1969	1970	1971
Imports	9,895	8,816	9,193	9,491	9,053
Exports	7,166	8,816	9,196	8,492	8,939

* Excluding trade with other countries in the Customs and Economic Union of Central Africa: Cameroon, Congo (Brazzaville), Gabon and, until 1969, Chad.

PRINCIPAL COMMODITIES

IMPORTS	1969	1970	1971
Machinery	1,740	1,830	1,799
Cotton Textiles	1,285	1,230	928
Motor Vehicles	1,363	1,830	1,447
Petroleum Products	691	29	12
Shoes	122	90	69
Paper and Paper Products	257	264	258
Clothing	99	55	74
Tyres	72	99	123

EXPORTS	1969	1970	1971
Diamonds	4,123	3,466	3,367
Coffee	1,404	1,864	2,228
Cotton	2,382	1,896	2,161
Wood	627	517	946
Rubber	93	61	50
Sesame	4	n.a.	n.a.
Palm Products	6	5	n.a.

PRINCIPAL COUNTRIES

IMPORTS	1969	1970	1971
France	5,325	5,484	5,488
U.S.A.	466	529	493
Germany, Federal Republic	696	741	540
United Kingdom	409	265	265
Netherlands	327	293	247

EXPORTS	1969	1970	1971
Belgium/Luxembourg	497	1,029	1,073
Chad	330	457	257
France	4,706	4,225	5,014
Germany, Federal Republic	176	344	382
Israel	1,339	1,265	835
Italy	515	250	109
Japan	152	365	27
South Africa	137	48	21
United Kingdom	248	146	230
U.S.A.	814	20	58

TRANSPORT

ROAD TRAFFIC
Motor vehicles in use

	1969	1970	1971
Passenger Cars	7,308	7,711	8,678
Buses and Coaches	152	195	155
Goods Vehicles	2,369	2,234	1,767
Motor Cycles and Scooters	6,275	n.a.	n.a.

Passenger Cars: (1972): 10,200.

CIVIL AVIATION
Scheduled services*

	1968	1969	1970
Kilometres flown ('000)	1,511	1,688	1,719
Passenger-km. ('000)	55,659	61,867	68,914
Cargo ton-km. ('000)	4,665	5,539	5,811
Mail ton-km. ('00)	464	478	529

* Including one-twelfth of the traffic of Air Afrique, from which the Central African Republic withdrew in August 1971.

INLAND WATERWAYS TRAFFIC
(metric tons)

	1969	1970	1971
Freight loaded at Bangui .	62,308	74,200	62,600
of which:			
Freight from Chad .	34,862	n.a.	n.a.
Freight unloaded at Bangui	154,225	193,000	160,000
of which:			
Freight for Chad .	18,592	n.a.	n.a.

EDUCATION
(1970–71)

	Schools	Pupils
Primary . . .	778	178,550
Secondary . . .	21	9,540
Technical . . .	15	1,420

There are also pre-primary schools which were attended by 6,863 pupils in 1969–70, 4 colleges and a university.

In October 1973 the Ministry of Education announced there were 201,000 pupils in primary schools, 19,000 in secondary, and 1,200 in technical education.

Sources: Direction de la Statistique Générale et des Etudes Economiques, Bangui; FAO, *Production Yearbook 1971* (Rome, 1972).

THE CONSTITUTION

The Constitution of February 16th, 1959, was modified five times up until 1964, and was abrogated on January 4th, 1966, when a constitutional act was adopted giving the President full competence to act in all affairs of state.

THE GOVERNMENT

HEAD OF STATE

Life President of the Republic: Gen. Jean-Bédel Bokassa.

COUNCIL OF MINISTERS
(*March* 1974)

President of the Government, Minister of Justice, National Defence, Information, Civil and Military Aviation, Civil Service and Social Security, Agriculture, Trade, Industry and Mines, Land, River and Air Transport, Commander-in-Chief of the Army: Gen. Jean-Bédel Bokassa.

Minister of Foreign Affairs: Joseph Potolot.

Minister of State Delegate to the Presidency, with Special Duties: Ange Patassé.

Assistant Minister for Defence: François Gon.

Minister of the Interior: Louis Alazoula.

Minister of Finance: Alphonse Koyamba.

Minister of Justice and Labour: Clément Ngai-Voueto.

Minister of the Plan and International Co-operation: Jean-Paul Mokodopo.

Minister of Education: Jean-Louis Psimhis.

Assistant Minister for Agriculture, responsible for Waters, Forests, Hunting and Fishing: Joachim Dama.

Minister of Posts and Telecommunications: Antoine Goala.

Minister Delegate to the Presidency for National Organizations: Jean Amity.

Minister for Ex-Servicemen: Augustin Dallot Befio.

Secretary of State to the Presidency for the Secretariat-General: Alexis Tcheouti.

Secretary of State for Information: Jean-Jacques Saganza.

Secretary of State for Youth and Sports: Louis-Pierre Gamba.

Secretary of State for Transport Improvement: André Zanifé Touambona.

DIPLOMATIC REPRESENTATION

EMBASSIES ACCREDITED TO THE CENTRAL AFRICAN REPUBLIC

(In Bangui unless otherwise stated)

Belgium: Place de la République; *Ambassador:* VICTOR ALLARD.

Cameroon: B.P. 935; *Ambassador:* JEAN BIKANDA (also accred. to Gabon).

Canada: Yaoundé, Cameroon.

Chad: B.P. 461; *Ambassador:* NDJONGA BESSEGALAW.

China (Taiwan): *Ambassador:* KÊ DING-WANG.

Congo (Brazzaville): B.P. 1414; *Ambassador:* ANTOINE MAKOUNAGO.

Egypt: *Ambassador:* AHMED EL SAIS KADEL HAK.

France: blvd. du Général-de-Gaulle, B.P. 934; *Ambassador:* JEAN LE CANNELIER.

Gabon: *Ambassador:* JOSEPH MEGNIER-MBO.

Germany, Federal Republic: rue Lamothe, B.P. 901; *Ambassador:* REINHARD HOLUBEK.

Ghana: Kinshasa, Zaire.

Iraq: *Ambassador:* HIKMAT SALI SOLEIMAN.

Italy: *Ambassador:* BENIAMINO DEL GIUDICE.

Japan: Kinshasa, Zaire.

Korea, Democratic People's Republic: *Ambassador:* RIM MYEUNG MAKOUANGO.

Korea, Republic: *Ambassador:* TAEK KOUN LEE.

Lebanon: *Ambassador:* SAID EL HIBRI.

Liberia: *Ambassador:* JENKINS COOPER.

Mali: Brazzaville, People's Republic of the Congo.

Netherlands: Yaoundé, Cameroon.

Pakistan: *Ambassador:* SHA ANSANI.

Romania: *Ambassador:* GHEORGHE POPESCU.

Senegal: Kinshasa, Zaire.

Spain: Yaoundé, Cameroon.

Sudan: Bangui; *Ambassador:* AMBROSE WOL.

Switzerland: *Ambassador:* JEAN-PIERRE WEBER.

Tunisia: *Ambassador:* (vacant).

U.S.S.R.: B.P. 869; *Ambassador:* YEVGENIY MELNIKOV.

United Kingdom: Yaoundé, Cameroon.

U.S.A.: Place de la République, B.P. 924; *Ambassador:* MELVIN MANFULL.

Vatican: *Nuncio:* Mgr. MARIO TAGLIAFERRI.

Yugoslavia: *Ambassador:* EMILI DJAVID.

Zaire: B.P. 989; *Ambassador:* KABEYA WA MUKEBA.

The Central African Republic also has diplomatic relations with Albania, Cambodia (Government-in-exile), Czechoslovakia, Greece, Hungary and Libya.

PARLIAMENT

The National Assembly was dissolved on January 4th, 1966, and Gen. Bokassa has announced that he has no intention of reinstating it.

POLITICAL PARTY

Mouvement d'évolution sociale de l'Afrique noire (MESAN): Leader Gen. JEAN-BÉDEL BOKASSA; Head of Secretariat GEORGES YAKITÉ.

A government decree passed in November 1968 banned all foreign political parties from the Republic.

JUDICIAL SYSTEM

Supreme Court: Bangui; the highest juridical organ. Acts as a Court of Cassation in civil and penal cases and as Court of Appeal in administrative cases; operates in three sections: judicial, administrative and accounts; President ANTOINE GUIMALI; Vice-Pres. M. LESCUYER.

There are a Criminal Court and 7 Civil Courts, with Justices of the Peace.

RELIGION

It is estimated that 60 per cent of the population follow traditional animist beliefs, 5 per cent are Muslims and 35 per cent Christian; Roman Catholics comprise 20 per cent of the total population.

Roman Catholic Missions: There are 92 parishes and 1,452 mission stations with a personnel of 2,593.

Archdiocese of Bangui: B.P. 798, Bangui; f. 1894; 27 parishes, 55 priests; Archbishop Mgr. JOACHIM N'DAYEN.

Diocese of Bambari: B.P. 80, Bambari; f. 1920; 11 missions, 24 priests; Bishop (vacant); Apostolic Administrator Mgr. J. N'DAYEN.

Diocese of Bangassou: B.P. 84, Bangassou; f. 1929; 21 missions, 39 priests; Bishop Mgr. ANTONIUS MAANICUS.

Diocese of Berberati: B.P. 22, Berberati; f. 1923; 14 missions, 46 priests; Bishop Mgr. ALPHONSE-CELESTIN-BASILE BAUD.

Diocese of Bossangoa: B.P. 7, Bossangoa; f. 1943; 11 missions, 33 priests; Bishop Mgr. TOUSSAINT LÉON CHAMBON.

Episcopal Conference: Secretariat B.P. 1518, Bangui.

Protestant Missions: In the Central African Republic, Chad, Gabon, and Congo (Brazzaville) there are nearly 1,000 mission centres with a total personnel of about 2,000.

Église Protestante de Bangui: Bangui.

PRESS

Bangui La So: Bangui; daily.

Journal officiel de la République Centrafricaine: Secretariat-Général du Gouvernement, Bangui; twice-monthly.

Presse, La: B.P. 373, Bangui; daily.

FOREIGN PRESS BUREAUX

AFP (*France*): B.P. 815, Bangui; Correspondent JEAN-PIERRE GALLOIS.

Tass is also represented in Bangui.

RADIO AND TELEVISION

Radio Bangui: B.P. 940, Bangui; f. 1958 as Radiodiffusion Nationale Centrafricaine; Government station; programmes in French, English and Sango languages; Dir. HENRI KOBA.

There were 46,000 radio receivers in 1970.

Television broadcasting began in January 1974.

FINANCE

BANKS

CENTRAL BANK

Banque des Etats de l'Afrique Centrale: 29 rue du Colisée, Paris; B.P. 851, Bangui; f. 1973 as the Central Bank of issue of five African states; cap. 1,250m. francs CFA; Gen. Man. CHRISTIAN JOUDIOU; C.A.R. Dir. FRANÇOIS PEHOUA.

Banque Nationale Centrafricaine de Dépôts: Place de la République, B.P. 851, Bangui; f. 1971; cap. 150m. francs CFA; Pres. A. TCHEOUTCHI; Dir.-Gen. Mme. BÉATRICE KONGBO.

Banque Nationale de Développement de la République Centrafricaine: B.P. 647, Bangui; f. 1961; cap. 420m. francs CFA; Dir.-Gen. JOSEPH MOUTOU-MONDZIAOU.

Caisse Centrale de Coopération Economique: B.P. 817, Bangui; Dir. P. RAYNAUD.

Union Bancaire en Afrique Centrale: B.P. 59, rue de Brazza, Bangui; f. 1962; cap. 200m. francs CFA; res. 74.8m. francs CFA (1972); Pres. M. MONDZIAOU; Dir.-Gen. JEAN ALBERSSART.

FOREIGN BANKS

Banque Internationale pour l'Afrique Occidentale S.A.: 9 ave. de Messine, Paris 8e, France; B.P. 910, Bangui; f. 1965; Man. in Bangui ANDRÉ BOULIÈRE.

Banque Nationale de Paris S.A.: 16 blvd. des Italiens, 75 Paris 9e, France; f. 1966; brs. in Bangui and Berberati.

INSURANCE

La Paternelle Africaine et Cie. Européenne d'Assurances des Marchandises et de Bagages: c/o S.A.F.C.I., B.P. 821, Bangui.

Société Aéfienne d'Assurances: B.P. 512, Bangui.

Société Jeandreau et Cie. S.A.R.L.: B.P. 140, Bangui; f. 1960; cap. p.u. 500,000 Fr. CFA; Dir. H. JEANDREAU.

Société de Représentation d'Assurances et de Réassurances Africaines (SORAREF): B.P. 852, Bangui; Dir. PIERRE DUROU.

TRADE AND INDUSTRY

Chambre d'Agriculture, d'Élevage, des Eaux et Forêts et des Chasses: B.P. 850, Bangui; Pres. M. SONGOMALI; Sec.-Gen. A. TOMBIDAM.

Chambre de Commerce de Bangui: B.P. 813, Bangui; Pres. JEAN-CHRISTOPHE MACPAYEN; Sec.-Gen. A. MAGBOTIADE.

Chambre des Industries et de l'Artisanat: B.P. 252, Bangui; Pres. JEAN SEBIRO; Sec.-Gen. C. LACROIX.

Chambre des Mines: Bangui.

EMPLOYERS' ORGANIZATION

Association Professionnelle des Banques: Bangui.

TRADE UNION

Union Générale des Travailleurs Centrafricains: B.P. 877, Bangui; became the sole recognized union in 1964; Sec.-Gen. FRED-PATRICE ZEMONIAKO.

TRANSPORT

TRANSPORT

RAILWAYS

There are no railways at present but a 1,100 km. line from Bangui to N'Djamena (Chad) is proposed. The total cost is estimated at 22 million French francs.

A railway is also due to be constructed from Sudan's Darfur province into the C.A.R.'s Vakaga province. An agreement between the two Governments was signed in December 1971.

ROADS

Compagnie Nationale des Transports Routiers: Bangui; f. 1971; Dir.-Gen. I. TINOR; state-controlled.

There are about 19,300 km. of roads, 6,000 km. of which are passable at all seasons by heavy vehicles. The total includes 5,100 km. of *routes nationales*, 3,800 km. of regional roads and 10,400 km. of rural roads. Both the total road length and the condition of the roads is inadequate for the traffic that uses the road system and very few roads have a tarmac surface. Seven main routes leave Bangui, and those that have been surfaced have been toll roads since 1971.

INLAND WATERWAYS

Agence Centrafricaine des Communications Fluviales (ACCF): B.P. 822, Bangui; f. 1969; state-owned; Pres. F. POUNINGUINZA; Dir.-Gen. G. LOUMANDET.

There are two navigable waterways. The first is open all the year and is formed by the Congo and Oubangui rivers; convoys of barges (of up to 800 tons load) ply between Bangui and Brazzaville. The second is the river Sangha, a tributary of the Oubangui, on which traffic is seasonal. There are two ports, at Bangui and Salo, on the rivers Oubangui and Sangha respectively. Efforts are being made to develop the stretch of river upstream from Salo to increase the transportation of timber from this area, and Nola will be developed as a timber port.

CIVIL AVIATION

There is an international airport at Bangui and several small airports for internal services.

Air Centrafrique: B.P. 1432, Rue du Président Boganda, Bangui; f. 1966 as Air Bangui, reorganized in 1971 when the Government planned to withdraw from Air Afrique; extensive internal services; fleet of one DC-3, and one Baron.

Air Afrique: B.P. 875, Bangui; the C.A.R. Government has a 6 per cent share in Air Afrique.

The C.A.R. is also served by the following foreign airlines: Aeroflot, Air Zaire, Cameroon Airlines and UTA.

TOURISM

Direction Générale du Tourisme: P.O.B. 655, Bangui; Dir.-Gen. Mme B. MALENDOMA.

UNIVERSITY

Jean-Bédel Bokassa Université de Bangui: Bangui; f. 1970.

CHAD

INTRODUCTORY SURVEY

Location, Climate, Language, Religion, Flag, Capital

Chad is a landlocked state in north central Africa, stretching south from Libya and the Tropic of Cancer to the Central African Republic. Niger and Cameroon lie to the west and the Sudan to the east. The climate is hot, arid in the desert north and very wet (annual rainfall 196 inches) in the south. The official language is French, but Arabic and various African languages are widely spoken. About half the population are Muslims living in the north; most others follow animistic beliefs. About 5 per cent are Christians. The national flag (proportions 3 by 2) consists of vertical blue, yellow and red stripes. The capital is N'Djamena (formerly Fort-Lamy).

Recent History

Formerly a province of French Equatorial Africa, Chad became independent in 1960. In 1962 a new Constitution providing for a President as Head of State was adopted. Civil disturbances began in 1963 with riots in the capital and a full-scale rebellion broke out in 1965, concentrated mainly in the north, where the nomadic Tuareg-Berbers have traditionally been opposed to their black, southern compatriots. The rebellion spread to the borders with Cameroon and the Central African Republic. The National Liberation Front (FROLINAT), which is officially banned, assumed leadership of the rebellion, which flared up again as civil war in 1969. It was quashed with the help of French military forces, on whom the Government was heavily dependent until 1971.

FROLINAT received Libyan support, but, following the apparent victory of Government forces, Chad's relations with Libya became much more friendly. The Libyan leader, Colonel Muamar al-Gaddafi, visited Chad in March 1974 and promised financial aid for road and water supply projects. During 1973 President Tombalbaye attacked France several times, claiming that the French Government was involved in plots against him, but, early in 1974, despite the President's earlier description of co-operation with France as a new form of colonization, relations improved and Chad accepted French economic aid.

The plots in which France was alleged to be involved showed some opposition to President Tombalbaye within the Chad Progressist Party (PPT). Several ministers were dismissed and the army commander arrested during 1973, and in August Tombalbaye dissolved the PPT. A new party, the National Movement for Cultural and Social Revolution (MNRCS), was formed. The President announced its objectives as the economic revival of Chad, based on independence from foreign influence, total decolonization and a return to African authenticity. All French names for people, streets and places had to be replaced with African names.

Government

Executive power lies with the President assisted by a Council of Ministers. Legislation is carried out by the Legislative Assembly, elected by universal direct suffrage for a five-year term. Chad has officially been a one-party state since 1965. The country is divided for administrative purposes into 13 Prefectures.

Defence

Chad's army numbers about 3,500 men. There are also some 200 men in the air force and 4,000 men in the National Guard and other para-military forces.

Economic Affairs

Chad's economy is essentially one of subsistence, based on agriculture, stock-breeding and fishing, which together employ 89 per cent of the working population. The only significant cash crop is cotton, which provides the basis for Chad's major industry and some two-thirds of all export earnings. Groundnuts are grown, but not in sufficient quantities to meet local demand or to allow Chad's oil-mills to work at full capacity. Animal resources are under-exploited, despite government efforts to improve cattle stock and the construction of modern abattoirs. Lake Chad and the Lagone-Chari basin are well-stocked with fish, producing more than 100,000 tons a year. The drought which has affected the Sahel region in recent years has caused considerable loss of livestock, while fishing and agricultural production in 1973 are likely to show major decreases from previous years.

Industry is almost entirely based on agriculture. Textile production is the most important sector, followed by food and tobacco, particularly sugar refining, brewing, meat-packing and oil and flour milling. Mining is limited to natron, found to the north of Lake Chad, but deposits of tin and tungsten have been found, and concessions have been granted to prospect for petroleum and tungsten. Chad's foreign trade is principally with France and shows a considerable deficit. French financial and technical aid is necessary to meet this deficit. In 1972 only 8.44 per cent of managerial staff in private companies in Chad were Chadians.

Chad is a member of the French Community and the OAU, but has withdrawn from UDEAC and OCAM.

Transport and Communications

There are no railways in Chad but an extension of the Trans-Cameroon railway into Chad is planned, thus connecting Ngaoundéré in Cameroon with Moundou, and eventually Sarh, in Chad. The river Chari is navigable from N'Djamena near to Lake Chad to Sarh in the far south. Roads are inadequate and only short stretches have been surfaced. There is an international airport at N'Djamena and over 40 aerodromes.

Social Welfare

An Employment Code guarantees a minimum wage and other rights for employees. Medical institutions in 1966 comprised 5 hospitals, 38 medical centres and over a hundred infirmaries and dispensaries.

Education

In 1971 about 22 per cent of children between 6 and 14 years old attended school. A National University was opened in 1971 with 300 students and in addition the Republic sends students to foreign universities.

Tourism

Chad provides a variety of scenery from the dense forests of the south to the deserts of the north. Wild animals abound, especially in the two national parks and five game reserves; there is excellent hunting, mainly around Sarh.

Visas are not required to visit Chad by nationals of the following countries: Andorra, Central African Republic, Congo (Brazzaville), Dahomey, France, Gabon, Federal Republic of Germany, Guinea, Ivory Coast, Madagascar, Mali, Mauritania, Mauritius, Monaco, Niger, Rwanda, Senegal, Togo, Upper Volta and Zaire.

Public Holidays

1974: August 11th (Independence Day), August 15th (Assumption), October 18th (Id ul Fitr, end of Ramadan), November 1st (All Saints'), November 28th (Proclamation of the Republic), December 25th (Christmas), December 26th (Id ul Adha, Feast of the Sacrifice).

1975: January 1st (New Year), January 11th (National Holiday), March 26th (Mouloud, Birth of the Prophet), March 31st (Easter Monday), May 1st (Labour Day), May 8th (Ascension), May 19th (Whit Monday), May 25th ("Liberation of Africa").

Weights and Measures

The metric system is officially in force.

Currency and Exchange Rate

100 centimes=1 franc de la Communauté financière africaine (CFA).

Exchange rates (April 1974):

£1 sterling=579.75 francs CFA;

U.S. $1=245.625 francs CFA.

STATISTICAL SURVEY

AREA AND POPULATION

Area: 1,284,000 sq. km. (495,800 sq. miles).   **Population** (1972 estimate): 3,791,000.

PREFECTURES

	AREA (sq. km.)	POPULATION (1972)	DENSITY (per sq. km.)
Batha	88,800	335,000	3.8
Biltine	46,850	146,000	3.1
Borkou-Ennedi-Tibesti (B.E.T.)* .	600,350	82,000	0.1
Chari-Baguirmi . . .	82,910	490,000	5.9
Guéra	58,950	181,000	3.1
Kanem	114,520	193,000	1.7
Lac	22,230	131,000	5.9
Logone Occidental . . .	8,695	252,000	29.0
Logone Oriental . . .	28,035	280,000	10.0
Mayo-Kebbi	30,105	555,000	18.4
Moyen-Chari	45,180	427,000	9.4
Ouadaï	76,240	352,000	5.6
Salamat	63,000	95,000	1.5
Tandjilé	18,045	272,000	15.1
TOTAL	1,284,000	3,791,000	2.95

* The Borkou-Ennedi-Tibesti prefecture was abolished in September 1972 and the three constituent sous-prefectures attached to neighbouring prefectures.

CHIEF TOWNS
(Population—1972 estimate)

N'Djamena (capital)*	179,000	Kélo	16,800
Sarh*	43,700	Bongor	14,300
Moundou	39,600	Doba	13,300
Abéché	28,100	Pala	13,200
Koumra	17,000		

* Fort-Lamy was renamed N'Djamena in November 1973, and Fort-Archambault was renamed Sarh in July 1972.

EMPLOYMENT
(1970—'000)

	MEN	WOMEN	TOTAL
Stock-rearing	90	1	91
Other Agriculture	715	267	982
Fishing	12	1	13
Industry	46	1	47
Transport and Other Services	65	7	72
TOTAL	928	277	1,205

AGRICULTURE
LAND USE, 1968
('000 hectares)

Arable and under Permanent Crops	7,000
Permanent Meadows and Pastures	45,000
Forest Land	16,500
Other Land	58,500
Inland Water	1,400
TOTAL AREA	128,400

Source: FAO, *Production Yearbook 1971.*

PRINCIPAL CROPS

	AREA ('000 hectares)			PRODUCTION ('000 metric tons)			YIELD (kg. per hectare)		
	1968/69	1969/70	1970/71	1968/69	1969/70	1970/71	1968/69	1969/70	1970/71
Cassava (Manioc)	17*	17*	n.a.	55*	55*	n.a.	3,200*	3,200*	n.a.
Cottonseed	} 296	294	300	{ 148	117	95	500	400	315
Cotton (lint)				55	43	35	185	150	115
Dates	n.a.	n.a.	n.a.	22*	22*	22*	n.a.	n.a.	n.a.
Groundnuts (in shell)	145	162	132	110	115	96	760	710	730
Maize	6	12*	12*	12	20*	20*	1,920	1,670*	1,670*
Millet and Sorghum	1,020	921	889	661	681	610	650	740	685
Pulses	185*	185*	185*	90*	90*	95*	490*	490*	510*
Rice	31	36	40	32	36	40	1,030	1,000	1,000
Sesame Seed	40*	40*	40*	12*	12*	12*	300*	300*	300*
Sweet Potatoes and Yams	12*	12*	n.a.	52*	52*	n.a.	4,300*	4,300*	n.a.
Wheat	5	5*	5*	5	8	7	1,000	1,600*	1,400*

* FAO estimate.

Sources: Direction de la Statistique et des Etudes Economiques, N'Djamena, and FAO, *Production Yearbook 1971.*

LIVESTOCK
('000)

	1968–69	1969–70	1970–71
Cattle . .	4,500	4,550	4,690
Goats . .	2,200	2,300*	
Sheep . .	1,800	1,800*	} 5,200
Horses . .	150	150	178
Asses . .	300	285	365
Camels . .	355	370	560
Chickens .	2,800	2,900	2,950*

* FAO estimate.

Sources: Direction de la Statistique et des Etudes Economiques, N'Djamena; and FAO, *Production Yearbook 1971.*

LIVESTOCK PRODUCTS
(metric tons)

	1970	1971	1972
Animal Meat* . .	16,193	16,501	10,122
Beef* . . .	15,382	15,568	9,121
Veal* . . .	192	207	215
Mutton, Lamb and Goats' Meat* .	433	503	542
Pork* . . .	115	129	132
Horse Meat* .	71	94	112
Cows' Milk† .	165,000	167,000	n.a.
Goats' Milk† .	31,000	32,000	n.a.
Sheep's Milk† .	16,000	16,000	n.a.
Cattle Hides† .	5,500	n.a.	n.a.
Hen Eggs† . .	2,500	2,700	n.a.

* Inspected production only, from refrigerated abattoirs at N'Djamena and Sarh.

†FAO estimate.

Sources: Bulletin de Statistique, Sous-Direction de la Statistique, N'Djamena, and United Nations Economic Commission for Africa, *Statistical Yearbook 1972.*

FORESTRY
ROUNDWOOD PRODUCTION
(cubic metres)

1968	2,960,000
1969	2,970,000
1970	2,980,000

Source: FAO, *Yearbook of Forest Products.*

FISHING
FRESH-WATER CATCH
(metric tons)

1969	110,000
1970	120,000
1971	120,000

Source: FAO, *Yearbook of Fishery Statistics.*

INDUSTRY
(1971)

Cotton Fibre ('000 metric tons) .	43
Refined Sugar (" " ") .	15
Beer and Soft Drinks ('000 hl.) .	64
Frozen Meat ('000 metric tons) .	22
Cigarettes (million packets) .	12

1970: Salt production totalled 10,000 metric tons. Cotton textile production totalled 13.5 million metres.

ELECTRIC ENERGY
Production for public use ('000 kWh.)

1970	41,884
1971	48,000
1972	51,340

313

FINANCE

100 centimes = 1 franc de la Communauté financière africaine (CFA).
Coins: 1, 2, 5, 10, 25, 50 and 100 francs CFA.
Notes: 100, 500, 1,000, 5,000 and 10,000 francs CFA.
Exchange rates (April 1974): 1 franc CFA = 2 French centimes;
£1 sterling = 579.75 francs CFA; U.S. $1 = 245.625 francs CFA;
1,000 francs CFA = £1.725 = $4.071.

Budget (1972): Balanced at 13,848 million francs CFA.
Budget (1973): Balanced at 17,018 million francs CFA.
Budget (1974): Balanced at 19,999 million francs CFA.

EXTERNAL TRADE*
(million francs CFA)

	1967	1968	1969	1970	1971	1972
Imports	9,248	8,262	11,914	17,216	17,220	15,476
Exports	6,635	6,824	8,020	8,205	7,787	9,082

* Prior to 1969, figures exclude trade with Cameroon, the Central African Republic, Congo (Brazzaville) and Gabon.

COMMODITIES

IMPORTS	1970	1971	1972
Beverages	375.6	389.2	335.4
Cereal Products	517.9	573.9	550.7
Sugar, Confectionery, Chocolate	1,301.0	1,307.0	1,972.9
Petroleum Products	2,375.4	2,719.0	2,122.6
Textiles, Clothing, etc.	1,135.3	1,002.8	913.1
Pharmaceuticals, Chemicals	697.9	642.2	578.8
Minerals and Metals	1,476.3	1,232.7	959.0
Machinery	949.5	997.7	968.4
Transport Equipment	1,942.9	2,349.4	1,613.5
Electrical Equipment	676.3	810.4	701.0
TOTAL (incl. others)	17,216.2	17,219.6	15,475.7

EXPORTS	1970	1971	1972
Live Cattle	159.6	279.4	374.1
Camels	n.a.	87.7	85.7
Meat	1,451	1,501.6	931.7
Fish	28	32.1	95.6
Natron	n.a.	11.6	90.3
Gums and Resins	34.8	37.3	44.7
Hides and Skins	95	90.9	112.7
Raw Cotton	5,910.4	5,224.6	6,056.1
TOTAL (incl. others)	8,205	7,786.6	9,082.3

COUNTRIES

IMPORTS	1970	1971	1972
Cameroon	458	459	404.7
Central African Republic	309	313	222.5
Congo (Brazzaville)	1,538	697	567.2
France	7,020	7,652	7,472.4
Gabon	418	477	446.9
Germany, Federal Republic	594	549	466.6
Italy	611	380	282.3
Netherlands	504	424	535.2
Netherlands Antilles	399	417	249.7
Nigeria	1,607	1,928	1,690.5
U.S.A.	697	550	492.3
TOTAL (incl. others)	17,216	17,220	15,475.7

EXPORTS	1970	1971	1972
Cameroon	n.a.	n.a.	300.4
Central African Republic	238	213	164.5
Congo (Brazzaville)	374	384	351.6
France	6,005	1,278	145.4
Gabon	162	n.a.	68.3
Germany, Federal Republic	n.a.	n.a.	22.5
Libya	n.a.	n.a.	80.2
Nigeria	256	324	487.4
Sudan	n.a.	n.a.	22.5
United Kingdom	n.a.	n.a.	30.7
Zaire	847	n.a.	n.a.
TOTAL (incl. others)	8,205	7,787	9,082.3

Sources: 1970 and 1971 figures: *L'Economie Africaine en 1973*, Le Moniteur Africain du Commerce et de l'Industrie, Dakar. 1972 figures: *Bulletin de Statistique*, Sous-Direction de la Statistique, N'Djamena.

TRANSPORT

ROAD TRAFFIC
Motor vehicles in use

	1971	1972
Passenger Cars . . .	4,765	5,250
Commercial Vehicles . .	6,048	6,152
TOTAL . . .	10,813	11,402

CIVIL AVIATION
Scheduled services*

	1969	1970	1971
Kilometres flown ('000)	2,243	2,373	2,374
Passenger-km. ('000) .	73,435	78,953	89,000
Cargo ton-km. ('000) .	6,131	6,391	7,783
Mail ton-km. ('000) .	598	651	684

* Including one-twelfth of the traffic of Air Afrique.

Tourism: There are 118 tourist hotel bedrooms in the main towns, and simpler accommodation in outlying places. 3,000 tourists visited Chad in the 1967–68 tourist season (Dec.–July), half of them from France.

EDUCATION
(1970–71)

	SCHOOLS (1970–71/ 1971–72)	PUPILS (1970–71)		
		Boys	Girls	Total
Primary	707	137,059	46,191	183,250
Public	664	129,236	38,681	167,917
Private (Catholic and Protestant) .	43	7,823	7,510	15,333
Secondary	31	8,536	731	9,267
Public	26	8,157	429	8,586
Private	5	379	302	681
Technical	2	473	22	495
TOTAL	740	146,068	46,944	193,012

Source (unless otherwise stated): Direction de la Statistique et des Etudes Economiques, B.P. 453, N'Djamena.

THE CONSTITUTION
(Promulgated June 5th, 1964)

Principles: Defence of the rights of man and public liberties; building of a true democracy founded on the separation of powers. The Republic is indivisible, lay, democratic and social. Sovereignty resides in the people who exercise it by equal, universal and secret suffrage. Equality of race, origin and religion; freedom of belief and opinion, guarantee of education.

Head of State: The Head of State is the President of the Republic, who is nominated by the sole party and elected by universal suffrage for a term of 7 years. He is Head of the Government and President of the Council of Ministers, which he appoints.

Council of Ministers: Appointed by the President, determines policy, law, and public office-holders.

National Assembly: Holds legislative power. Its 105 members are elected from a list presented by the sole party, and serve for five years. In case of a vote of no confidence the President may, after consultation with the President of the Assembly, dissolve Parliament.

Economic and Social Council: Advises the National Assembly on economic and social matters.

Political Party: Chad was officially declared to be a one-party state in November 1965. The party was the Chad Progressist Party (PPT), reformed 1973 as the National Movement for Cultural and Social Revolution (MNRCS).

Judiciary: Independence of the judiciary is guaranteed by the President.

THE GOVERNMENT

HEAD OF STATE

President: N'Garta Tombalbaye (elected June 15th, 1969).

COUNCIL OF MINISTERS

(April 1974)

President of the Council of Ministers: N'Garta Tombalbaye.

Minister of State for the Civil Service and Labour: Djibrine Kheralla.

Minister of State for Agriculture and Stockbreeding: Djidingar Dono N'Gardoum.

Minister of State for the Modern Economy, Planning, Trade and International Co-operation: Abdoulaye Lamana.

Minister to the Presidency for Relations with Parliament and the MNRCS: Mahamat Douba Halifa.

Minister of Foreign Affairs: Djirai Baye Doralta.

Minister of Tourism, Information and Traditional Affairs: Baba Hassane.

Minister of National Defence: Dabai Idabaye.

Minister of Water, Forests, Fishery and Hunting: Desange Togbe.

Minister of Finance: Djengar Mbailemdana.

Minister of Transport and Telecommunications: Ahmann Mahamat.

Minister of National Education: Dikoa Garandi.

Minister of Public Health and Social Affairs: Dr. Jacques Baroum.

Minister of Public Works and Territorial Development: Abdoulaye Djonouma.

Minister of Justice: Brahim Seid.

Secretary of State to the Presidency for Internal Affairs: Yakouma Mahamat.

Secretary of State for the Modern Economy, Trade, Planning and Co-operation: Moundari Ngarhodjina Adoum.

Secretary of State for Public Works and Territorial Development: Golo Toussou.

DIPLOMATIC REPRESENTATION

EMBASSIES ACCREDITED TO CHAD

(In N'Djamena unless otherwise indicated)

Belgium: Yaoundé, Cameroon.

Canada: Yaoundé, Cameroon.

Central African Republic: ave. du Général de Gaulle, B.P. 115; *Ambassador:* D. Wallot.

China, People's Republic: *Ambassador:* Wang Jen-san.

Denmark: Kinshasa, Zaire.

Egypt: *Ambassador:* Mahmoud Hassan Salim.

France: rue du Lieutenant Franjoux, B.P. 350; *Ambassador:* Fernand Wibaux.

Gabon: Yaoundé, Cameroon (E).

German Democratic Republic: ave. du Général Joseph-Désiré Mobutu; *Ambassador:* Gerhard Krausse.

Germany, Federal Republic: 24 rue de Marseille, B.P. 893; *Ambassador:* Werner Seldis.

Ghana: Kinshasa, Zaire.

Italy: Yaoundé, Cameroon.

Japan: Libreville, Gabon.

Korea, Republic: Paris 16e, France.

Lebanon: Accra, Ghana.

Libya: *Ambassador:* Ibrahim Mohamed El Bichary.

Mali: Brazzaville, Congo P.R.

Netherlands: Yaoundé, Cameroon.

Nigeria: 35 ave. Charles de Gaulle, B.P. 752; *Ambassador:* Alhaji Kabir Bayero.

Pakistan: Algiers, Algeria.

Sudan: rue de Havre, B.P. 45; *Ambassador:* Salah El Din Hamid.

Switzerland: Lagos, Nigeria.

Tunisia: Kinshasa, Zaire.

Turkey: Lagos, Nigeria.

U.S.S.R.: ave. Charles de Gaulle extension, B.P. 891; *Ambassador:* Evgeny Nersessov.

United Kingdom: London, England; *Ambassador:* S. V. Dawbarn.

U.S.A.: ave. du Colonel d'Ornano, B.P. 413; *Ambassador:* Edward Mulcamy.

Viet-Nam, Republic: Tunis, Tunisia.

Yugoslavia: Brazzaville, Congo P.R.

Zaire: ave. du 20 août, B.P. 9-10; *Ambassador:* Suminwa K. S. Angazi.

Chad also has diplomatic relations with the Democratic People's Republic of Korea and Oman.

NATIONAL ASSEMBLY

President: ABBO NASSOUR.

Vice-Presidents: LAMIDO SALEH SAIDOU, PAUL RARIKIN-GAR, LÉON MOGOUMBAYE.

ELECTION, DECEMBER 14th, 1969

All 105 seats were won by the *Parti progressiste tchadien* (now held by the *Mouvement national pour la révolution culturelle et sociale*).

ECONOMIC AND SOCIAL COUNCIL

A consultative body set up to advise the President of the Republic; 25 members chosen by the Council of Ministers and divided into three commissions: Finance, Economy, Transport, Tourism and Hunting; Agriculture and Estate Affairs; Social Affairs.

President: MAURICE N'GANGTER.

POLITICAL PARTIES

Mouvement national pour la révolution culturelle et sociale (MNRCS): f. 1973; after dissolution of *Parti progressiste tchadien;* Sec.-Gen. N'GARTA TOMBALBAYE.

There are several opposition groups, chiefly Muslim; all are banned and the leaders are in exile. One, FROLINAT (an acronym from National Liberation Front), claims to lead the revolt; its leaders are Dr. ABBA SIDDICK and HADJ ISSAKA. Another opposition party, *Mouvement Démocratique pour la Rénovation Tchadienne (MDRT),* was formed in Paris in 1973.

JUDICIAL SYSTEM

Supreme Court: N'Djamena; f. 1962; the court for decisions on constitutional matters, it has a President, an Attorney-General and six counsellors in three chambers: judicial, administrative and financial; Pres. PIERRE DJIME.

High Court of Justice: N'Djamena; superior court, empowered to judge the President of the Republic and members of the Government in matters of complicity against the state. The members are elected by the National Assembly.

Court of Appeal: N'Djamena.

A criminal court sits at N'Djamena, Sarh, Moundou and Abéché and wherever else it is necessary, and each of these four major towns has a magistrates' court.

RELIGION

It is estimated that 52 per cent of the population are Muslims, 43 per cent Animists and 5 per cent Christians, mainly Roman Catholics.

Head of the Muslim Community: Imam MOUSSA.

Roman Catholic Church: Metropolitan Archdiocese of N'Djamena and three suffragan dioceses (Moundou, Pala, Sarh), dependent on the Sacred Congregation for the Evangelization of Peoples; 47 educational institutions; 165 resident priests; 178 male and 189 female members of religious institutes; 186,280 Catholics in a total population of 3,275,000 (December 1972 estimate).

Archbishop of N'Djamena: Mgr. PAUL DALMAIS, B.P. 456.

Bishop of Moundou: Mgr. SAMUEL LOUIS GAUMAIN, B.P. 61.

Bishop of Pala: Mgr. GEORGES-HILAIRE DUPONT, B.P. 9.

Bishop of Sarh: Mgr. HENRI VENIAT, B.P. 87.

Protestant Missions: L'Entente Evangélique, B.P. 127, N'Djamena; a fellowship of churches and missions working in Chad: Eglise Baptiste, Eglise Evangélique au Tchad, Assemblées Chrétiennes, Eglise Fraternelle Luthérienne and Eglise Evangélique des Frères.

PRESS

Bulletin Mensuel de Statistiques du Tchad: B.P. 453, N'Djamena; monthly.

Info-Tchad: B.P. 670, N'Djamena; daily news bulletin issued by Chad Press Agency, ATP; in French; circ. 1,500.

Informations Economiques: B.P. 48, N'Djamena; weekly; edited by the Chambre de Commerce de la République du Tchad.

Journal Officiel de la République du Tchad: N'Djamena.

Le Tchad en Marche: Secretariat d'Etat à l'Information, N'Djamena; monthly.

NEWS AGENCIES

Agence Tchadienne de Presse (ATP): B.P. 670, N'Djamena.

FOREIGN BUREAUX

AFP *(France):* B.P. 83, N'Djamena; Corr. JEAN-CLAUDE FIOL.

Reuters (U.K.) is also represented in Chad.

RADIO

Radiodiffusion Nationale Tchadienne: B.P. 892, N'Djamena; government station; programmes in French, Arabic and 7 vernacular languages; a transmitter with a 100 kW circuit for short wave transmissions and a 20 kW circuit for medium wave were put into operation in June 1972; Dir. GRÉGOIRE BICQUET.

There are 70,000 radio licences.

FINANCE

BANKS

CENTRAL BANK

Banque des Etats de l'Afrique Centrale: 29 rue du Colisée, 75008 Paris; B.P. 50, N'Djamena; f. 1973; bank of issue for five central African states; cap. 1,250m. francs CFA; Gen. Man. C. JOUDIOU; Asst. Gen. Man. J.-E. SATHOUD.

Banque de Développement du Tchad: B.P. 19, N'Djamena; f. 1962; cap. 520m. francs CFA; 58.4 per cent state-owned; Dir.-Gen. GEORGES DIGUIMBAYE.

Banque Tchadienne de Crédit et de Dépôts: B.P. 461, 6 rue Robert-Lévy, N'Djamena; f. 1963; cap. 250m. francs CFA; res. 54.8m. francs CFA (May 1972); 51 per cent state-owned; Pres. A. MEAR; Gen. Man. G. PALLAI; br. at Moundou.

Caisse Centrale de Co-opération Economique: B.P. 478, N'Djamena; Dir. R. LOUIS-JOSEPH.

FOREIGN BANKS

Banque Internationale pour l'Afrique Occidentale: 9 ave. de Messine, 75360 Paris; B.P. 87, N.'Djamena and B.P. 204, Sarh; Dir. N'Djamena ANDRÉ BOULIERE.

Banque Nationale de Paris: 16 blvd. des Italiens, Paris; B.P. 38, N'Djamena; Dir. GUY ROMEO.

BANKERS' ORGANIZATIONS

Association Professionelle des Banques au Tchad: N'Djamena.

Conseil National de Credit: N'Djamena; f. 1965 to create a national credit policy and to organize the banking profession.

INSURANCE

Assureurs Conseils Tchadiens Faugère et Jutheau et Cie: B.P. 254, N'Djamena; represents *Groupe des Mutuelles du Mans* and *Cie. d'Assurances Étrangerès*; Dir. J.-C. MEUNIER.

Société de Representation d'Assurances et de Réassurances Africaines (SORARAF): B.P. 481, N'Djamena; Dir. ALAIN ANDRE.

About a dozen leasing French insurance companies are represented in N'Djamena.

TRADE AND INDUSTRY

CHAMBERS OF COMMERCE

Chambre de Commerce, d'Agriculture et d'Industrie de la République du Tchad: B.P. 458, N'Djamena; f. 1938; Pres. GASTON PALLAYE; Sec.-Gen. M. N'GANGBET; publ. *Bulletin des Informations Economiques.*

Chambre de Commerce de Sarh: Sarh.

EMPLOYERS' ORGANIZATION

Union Interprofessionnelle du Tchad (UNITCHA): B.P. 94, N'Djamena; Dir. GILBERT MAILLARD; Vice-Pres. GUY MAHDAVI.

TRADE UNION

Union Nationale des Travailleurs du Tchad (UNATRAT): B.P. 553, N'Djamena; f. 1968; mems. 8,000; Pres. SEMOKO YAMARA; Sec.-Gen. ROBERT GORALLAH.

DEVELOPMENT

Caisse Centrale de Coopération Economique: 110 rue de l'Université, Paris 7e; B.P. 478, N'Djamena.

Mission Permanente d'Aide et de Coopération: B.P. 898, N'Djamena; French technical mission; Head of Mission RENÉ GUILBAUD.

Office National de Développement Rural (ONDR): B.P. 896, N'Djamena; Pres. Dir.-Gen. ADOUM DJONOUMA.

Société Hotelière du Tchad: c/o BDT, B.P. 19, N'Djamena; Pres. BENOÎT PIRCOLOSSOU; Dir.-Gen. GEORGES DIGUIMBAYE.

Société pour le Développement de la Région du Lac (SODELAC): N'Djamena; Pres. Dir.-Gen. MAURICE KOUMADEAU.

TRADE

Société Nationale de Commercialisation du Tchad (SONA-COT): B.P. 630, N'Djamena; f. 1965; 66 per cent state-owned; national marketing, distribution and import-export company; Dir.-Gen. TI-A.

TRANSPORT

Agence Transéquatoriale des Communications: B.P. 110, Sarh; f. 1959; develops common means of transport between the member states of the Scientific and Technical Research Committee of the OAU.

RAILWAYS

In 1962 Chad signed an agreement with Cameroon to extend the Trans-Cameroon railway from N'Gaoundéré to Sarh, a distance of 500 km. The total cost will be about 2,700 million f. CFA, and survey work began in 1964. The section from Belabo to N'Gaoundéré, the last major town in Cameroon before the Chad frontier, was opened to traffic in February 1974. In addition possibilities are being explored to extend Sudanese and Nigerian lines into Chad.

ROADS

Coopérative des Transportateurs Tchadiens(COPORTCHAD); B.P. N'Djamena; road haulage.

In 1972 there were 30,725 km. of roads, of which 2,680 km. were national roads and 3,462 km. were secondary roads. There are also some 20,000 km. of tracks suitable for motor traffic during the dry season from October to July. A 4,840 km. motor track leads from Rouiba, in Algeria, to Chad. In 1968 the International Development Association granted Chad a U.S. $4 million loan for the improvement of its road system, notably in the provision of a direct link between Lake Chad and N'Djamena. Two stretches of road, from N'Djamena to Guelendeng and from N'Djamena to Massaquet, have been asphalted under this scheme. Studies were made in 1971 on a road from the north to the south of the country, linking three main regional centres of N'Djamena, Sarh and Abéché. The cost of the project is estimated at 12,000 million francs CFA.

INLAND WATERWAYS

There is a certain amount of traffic on the Chari and Logone rivers which meet just south of N'Djamena. Both routes, from Sarh to N'Djamena on the Chari and from Bongor and Moundou to N'Djamena on the Logone, are open only during the wet season, August–December, and provide a convenient alternative when roads become impassable.

CIVIL AVIATION

The international airport at N'Djamena has been in use since 1967, and there are over 40 smaller aerodromes.

Compagnie Nationale Air-Tchad: B.P. 168, 27 ave. Charles de Gaulle, N'Djamena; f. 1966; Government majority holding with 36 per cent UTA interest; regular passenger, freight and charter services within Chad; Pres. M. GAMI; Gen. Man. MARCEL DUVERNOIS; fleet of one DC-4, two DC-3 and one Beechcraft Baron.

Chad is also served by the following foreign airlines: Cameroon Air Lines, Air Afrique, Air Zaïre, Sudan Airways and UTA.

POWER

Société Tchadienne d'Energie Electrique: B.P. 44, N'Djamena; f. 1968; cap. 238 million francs CFA; production and distribution of electricity and water; Dir. P. G. PINAULT.

TOURISM

Ministère du Tourisme et de l'Artisanat: B.P. 748, N'Djamena; f. 1962; Dir. (vacant); also at B.P. 62, Sarh.

Agence Tchadienne de Voyages: Tchad-Tourisme, B.P. 894, N'Djamena; Pres. V. N'GAKOUTOU.

UNIVERSITY

Université du Tchad à N'Djamena: B.P. 117, N'Djamena; 25 teachers, 300 students.

CHILE

INTRODUCTORY SURVEY

Location, Climate, Language, Religion, Flag, Capital

Chile is a long, narrow country stretching for 4,480 km. along the Pacific coast of South America from Peru and Bolivia in the north to Cape Horn in the far south. It is separated from Argentina to the east by the high Andes mountains. Both the mountains and the cold Humboldt Current influence the climate; between Arica in the north and Punta Arenas in the extreme south, some 4,000 km., the average maximum temperature varies by no more than 13°C. The language is Spanish. There is no state religion but Roman Catholics represent over 85 per cent of the population. The national flag (proportions 3 by 2) is divided horizontally, the lower half red, the upper half with a white star on a blue square at the hoist and the remainder white. The capital is Santiago.

Recent History

In the elections of September 1970 Dr. Salvador Allende Gossens, the Marxist candidate of Unidad Popular, a coalition of five left-wing parties including the Communist party, was elected President by a narrow majority. Dr. Allende promised to transform Chilean society by constitutional means and among proposed measures designed to bring about "social emancipation" were the nationalization of private banks, the nationalization of the nitrates and copper industries, the intensification of agrarian reforms to give land to the peasants, and the extension of government control over foreign trade. Public opinion approved the nationalization of the copper industry. During 1972 shortages of many basic foodstuffs and consumer goods became more acute. Inflation continued and the combination of these factors caused great discontent, especially among the middle classes. Rumours of further nationalization measures provoked the seven-week long "bosses' strike", which ended in November when General Carlos Prats became Minister of the Interior.

The Government failed to obtain a Congressional majority in the elections of March 1973 and was confronted with a deteriorating economic situation as well as an intensification of violent opposition to its policies. Accelerated inflation led to a run on consumer goods and a consequent shortage of food; demonstrations arising out of the strike of employees at the state-owned copper mines resulted in repeated clashes between pro- and anti-Government activists. President Allende declared his determination to avoid a civil war, and asked his supporters to seek a dialogue with the opposition groups; but a prolonged strike of transport vehicle owners and continuing acts of violence exacerbated the situation to a point where the Government was forcibly overthrown in September by the leaders of the armed forces and President Allende was killed, whether by his own hand or otherwise being unclear. Congress was dissolved, all political activity banned and strict censorship introduced. The new Government stated that the nationalization of the copper mines would not be reversed, but that new negotiations would be initiated regarding compensation for the United States corporations concerned. Other firms legally nationalized are similarly to remain under state control.

Government

Executive power is normally vested in the President, who is elected by popular vote for six years. The legislative organ is the National Congress, consisting of a Senate of 45 members and a Chamber of Deputies of 147 members. All citizens of eighteen or over are eligible to vote. Late in 1969 the Congress approved a reform granting greater independence to the President. Constitutional rule is suspended at present.

Defence

Military service is compulsory for one year at 19 years of age, but exemption is frequent. The army has a strength of 32,000, the air force 10,000 and the navy 18,000. A military assistance pact with the U.S.A. was signed in 1952. Para-military security forces number about 30,000.

Economic Affairs

One third of the population of Chile lives on the land, concentrated particularly in the fertile central region. Although the country has great agricultural potential, inefficient utilization of land resources made it necessary in the 1960s for a third of the nation's food supply to be imported. Agrarian reforms involving the redistribution of land to the peasants under the Allende administration led to a further fall in home production, and the Government was obliged to import large quantities of wheat from Argentina when a transport strike led to the breakdown of bread distribution. Under the military Government, land taken over by the State under President Allende (areas of less than 40 hectares) is being returned to its former owners. The Government is basing its development strategy on the reconstruction of the farming and mining sectors of the economy. Chile is one of the world's largest producers and exporters of copper. As a result of cutbacks in petroleum production, world demand for natural sodium nitrate has increased, and Chilean nitrate mines are preparing to work to full capacity. Inflation remains a major problem. On taking power, the military Government froze wages and granted sharp price rises; a system of bonuses and minimum wage rates was introduced to counter the resultant drastic fall in purchasing power. The currency was devalued by 91 per cent and further devaluations have followed. It is the aim of the Government to reduce the rate of inflation to about 100 per cent in 1974. Partial agreement was reached in Paris in February 1974 regarding the re-financing of Chile's debts. Foreign investment is being encouraged, and banks in Europe and the U.S.A. have re-opened loan facilities for Chile. Chile is a member of the Organization of American States, the Alliance for Progress, LAFTA and the Andean Development Corporation.

Transport and Communications

There are about 9,000 km. of railway track, of which four-fifths are state-owned; 70,701 km. of roads, of which eleven per cent are paved, and 840 km. of navigable rivers. The chief ports are Valparaíso, Talcahuano, Antofagasta, San Antonio and Punta Arenas. Air transport is provided by the state airline Línea Aérea Nacional, Ladeco and several foreign airlines. An international airport is in service at Pudahuel outside Santiago. Plans are going ahead to extend the provincial airport network.

Social Welfare

Employees, including agricultural workers, receive benefits for sickness, unemployment and retirement and there are dependents' allowances. There is a National Health Service which was established in 1952.

Education

Education is free and compulsory between the ages of six and fourteen. Over 90 per cent of the population are literate (95 per cent in the towns). Primary school education has been extended from six to eight years and new academic and technical syllabuses have been drawn up for the secondary school course. There are eight universities with over 80,000 students.

Tourism

The long Andes range of mountains is the chief attraction to tourists. There are good beaches and many lakes, the largest of which is Llanquihue. The special exchange rate for tourists stood at around 1,700 escudos to £1 in April 1974.

Visas are not required to visit Chile for a period of up to 90 days. This applies to all nationalities.

Sport

Football is the most popular sport and ski-ing and fishing are extremely popular.

Public Holidays

1974: August 15th (Assumption), September 18th (Independence Day), September 19th (Army Day), October 12th (Discovery of America), November 1st (All Saints' Day), December 25th (Christmas Day).

1975: January 1st (New Year's Day), March 28th (Good Friday), May 1st (Labour Day), May 8th (Ascension Day), May 21st (Navy Day), May 23rd (Corpus Christi), June 29th (St. Peter and St. Paul).

Weights and Measures

The metric system is officially in force.

Currency and Exchange Rate

1,000 pesos (milésimos) = 100 cóndores (centésimos)
= 1 Chilean escudo.

Exchange rates (April 1974):
£1 sterling = 1,299 escudos;
U.S. $1 = 550 escudos.

STATISTICAL SURVEY

AREA AND POPULATION

AREA	POPULATION	RATE PER '000 (1970)		
(sq. km.)	(1973 estimate)	Births	Marriages	Deaths
756,945	10,228,767	26.96	7.37	8.54

PROVINCES

PROVINCE	AREA (sq. km.)	POPULATION†	CAPITAL	PROVINCE	AREA (sq. km.)	POPULATION†	CAPITAL
Aconcagua	9,873	183,709	San Felipe	Linares	9,414	212,349	Linares
Antofagasta	125,306	286,917	Antofagasta	Llanquihue	18,205	229,943	Puerto Montt
Arauco	5,240	111,391	Lebu	Magallanes*	132,033	103,208	Punta Arenas
Atacama	78,267	178,799	Copiapó	Malleco	14,095	204,575	Angol
Aysén	103,584	56,258	Puerto Aysén	Maule	5,697	92,979	Cauquenes
Bío-Bío	11,135	219,509	Los Angeles	Ñuble	13,951	354,324	Chillán
Cautín	18,377	467,864	Temuco	O'Higgins	7,105	351,051	Rancagua
Chiloé	26,695	125,507	Ancud	Osorno	9,236	181,970	Osorno
Colchagua	8,327	185,345	San Fernando	Santiago	17,686	3,824,014	Santiago
Concepción	5,681	736,574	Concepción	Talca	10,141	260,424	Talca
Coquimbo	39,647	379,999	La Serena	Tarapacá	58,073	211,429	Iquique
Curicó	5,266	127,860	Curicó	Valdivia	18,472	305,329	Valdivia
				Valparaíso	5,118	833,440	Valparaíso

* Excluding Chilean Antarctic Territory.　　　　† 1973 estimates.

CHIEF TOWNS
(1970 estimates)

Santiago (capital) .	2,586,212	Valdivia . . . 92,763
Valparaíso .	292,847	Talca . . . 88,452
Concepción .	196,317	Chillán . . . 85,008
Viña del Mar .	153,085	Osorno . . . 78,187
Antofagasta .	137,968	Rancagua . . . 69,444
Talcahuano .	115,568	Punta Arenas . . 64,456
Temuco . .	104,372	

ECONOMICALLY ACTIVE POPULATION*
(April 1st, 1971)

	MALES	FEMALES	TOTAL
Agriculture, Forestry, Hunting and Fishing .	556,500	18,100	574,600
Mining and Quarrying	56,900	1,700	58,600
Manufacturing	517,700	175,000	692,700
Construction	244,700	1,700	246,400
Electricity, Gas, Water and Sanitary Services .	14,900	400	15,400
Commerce	267,700	139,100	406,800
Transport, Storage and Communication .	245,600	11,700	257,200
Services	285,500	408,400	694,000
Others	3,900	300	4,200
TOTAL	2,193,400	756,500	2,949,900

* Excluding persons seeking work for the first time, numbering 30,800 (males 14,700, females 16,100).

Source: ILO, *Year Book of Labour Statistics 1973.*

AGRICULTURE
PRINCIPAL CROPS

	AREA SOWN ('000 hectares)				PRODUCTION ('000 metric tons)				
	1968–69	1969–70	1970–71	1971–72	1967–68	1968–69	1969–70	1970–71	1971–72
Wheat . . .	743	740	727	712	1,220	1,214	1,307	1,368	1,195
Barley . . .	44	47	53	67	157	80	97	114	139
Oats . . .	81	73	75	84	163	95	111	112	111
Rye . . .	8	8	9	9	8	10	11	12	12
Maize . . .	58	74	77	84	321	154	239	258	283
Beans (Dry) .	47	57	70	79	n.a.	47	66	72	83
Peas (Dry) .	11	11	10	13	12	7	7	9	11
Lentils . .	14	17	18	18	4	8	11	12	11
Chickpeas .	9	11	16	20	8	3	5	7	9
Potatoes . .	76	72	80	79	725	602	684	836	733
Rice . .	16	25	27	26	93	37	76	67	86
Sunflower Seed .	25	20	15	15	43	28	28	20	20
Sugar Beet .	28	42	35	31	1,143	1,066	1,655	1,391	1,202
Rape Seed .	48	54	49	56	48	64	70	82	78

LIVESTOCK
('ooo head)

	1964	1965
Cattle	2,845	2,870
Pigs	959	1,022
Sheep	6,552	6,690
Horses	492	478

Cattle ('ooo head): 3,125 in 1972; 3,150 in 1973.

FISHING
(metric tons)

	1971	1972
Fish	1,396,538	690,407
Shell-fish . . .	97,908	101,572

MINING

		1967	1968	1969	1970	1971	1972
Coal . .	('ooo metric tons	1,496	1,611	1,704	1,510	1,626	1,457
Gold . .	(kilogrammes)	1,808	1,796	1,827	1,623	1,996	2,942
Iodine . .	(tons)	2,217	1,964	2,449	2,223	2,622	2,127
Iron Ore .	('ooo metric tons)	6,853	7,428	7,161	6,940	6,854	5,303
Nitrates .	(,, ,,)	869	679	782	674	829	807
Petroleum .	(cubic metres)	1,966,450	2,177,390	2,122,440	1,976,965	2,048,119	1,992,496
Silver . .	(kilogrammes)	98,158	116,306	95,654	76,205	84,897	45,856

COPPER PRODUCTION
(metric tons)

	1969	1970	1971	1972
Refined copper . . .	574,109	563,820	534,964	n.a.
Minerals, Concentrates, etc.	124,962	146,861	182,368	n.a.
TOTAL . . .	699,071	710,681	717,332	725,720

INDUSTRY

		1970	1971	1972
Sugar	'ooo tons	282	316	324
Paper and Cardboard .	,, ,,	157	159	n.a.
Cement . . .	,, ,,	1,349	1,370	1,408
Liquid Cast Iron . .	,, ,,	466	500	486
Steel Ingots . . .	,, ,,	547	607	580
Beer	million litres	178	279	229
Paraffin . . .	,, ,,	513	655	751
Diesel Oil . . .	,, ,,	731	892	829
Fuel Oil . . .	,, ,,	1,049	1,620	1,611
Tyres . . .	'ooo units	676	791	804
Cigarettes . . .	million units	6,590	8,302	8,514
Matches . . .	'ooo boxes	303	322	413
Glass Sheets . . .	'ooo sq. metres	2,559	2,677	2,355

FINANCE

1,000 pesos (milésimos) = 100 cóndores (centésimos) = 1 Chilean escudo.

Coins: 2, 5 and 10 centésimos.

Notes: 50 centésimos; 1, 5, 10, 50 and 100 escudos.

Exchange rates (April 1974): £1 sterling = 1,299 escudos (trading rate) or 1,747 escudos (non-trade rate);
U.S. $1 = 550 escudos (trading rate) or 740 escudos (non-trade rate).

10,000 Chilean escudos = £7.70 = $18.18 (trading rates).

Note: In recent years the principal rate of exchange for overseas trade transactions fluctuated as follows: U.S. $1 = 12.225 escudos from July 1970 to December 1971; $1 = 15.80 escudos from December 1971 to August 1972; $1 = 25.00 escudos from August 1972 to September 1973. A number of other exchange rates were in force for specific transactions, e.g. imports of non-essential goods, and for non-trade purposes such as tourism. On October 1st, 1973, the new military junta introduced a two-tier system with a single trading rate of $1 = 280 escudos, representing a 91 per cent devaluation from the previous basic rate. Several more devaluations have since occurred. In terms of sterling, the principal trading rate was £1 = 29.34 escudos from July 1970 to August 1971; and £1 = 41.17 escudos from December 1971 to June 1972.

BUDGET, 1969
(million escudos)

REVENUE		EXPENDITURE	
Ordinary Budget:		*Ordinary Budget:*	
Tributary Income	10,332.3	Wages and Salaries	3,887.6
Personal Income	1,274.4	Consumer Goods	631.1
Business Income	1,060.2	Social Security and Family Allowances.	339.7
Property	450.4	Transfers to Public Sector	349.4
Purchases/Sales	3,461.8	Transfers to Private Sector	2,888.5
Production	1,020.0	Interest on Public Debt	405.5
Services	860.6		
Legal Contracts	599.9	TOTAL	8,502.0
Imports	1598.6		
Sundry Taxes	6.4	*Capital Budget:*	
Non-tributary Income	504.9	Direct and Indirect Investment	3,403.6
National Assets	120.7	Debt Payments	739.0
National Services	180.0		
Miscellaneous Revenue	204.2	TOTAL	4,142.6
TOTAL	10,837.2		
Capital Budget:			
Copper Taxes	976.0		
External Loans	896.0		
Internal Loans	145.2		
TOTAL	2,017.2		
GRAND TOTAL	12,854.4	GRAND TOTAL	12,644.6

CONSUMER PRICE INDEX IN SANTIAGO
(December 1969 = 100)

1948	1958	1967	1968	1969	1970	1971	1972
5.2	7.59	56.72	71.83	93.84	124.35	149.29	265.46

Index by Categories
(December 1969 = 100)

	1969	1970	1971	1972
Food	94.65	128.12	158.63	341.45
Housing	94.94	119.41	138.99	177.33
Clothing	91.17	116.45	146.73	233.24
Miscellaneous	92.69	127.63	143.53	230.79
General	93.84	124.35	149.29	265.46

INDEX OF WAGES AND SALARIES
(April 1959 = 100)

	1971	1972	1973
Public Utilities	4,342.7	6,878.6	16,985.7
Mining	4,440.1	5,405.5	15,448.9
Manufacturing Industries . . .	3,117.3	4,927.8	14,853.3
Fiscal Institutions	3,473.6	3,887.3	11,266.0
Semi-fiscal Institutions . . .	2,754.1	3,869.7	9,086.7
Total Wages and Salaries . .	3,253.5	4,563.3	12,602.0
Salaries	3,184.3	4,793.0	13,848.2
Wages	3,318.2	4,348.4	11,408.0

Figures are for April each year.

EXTERNAL TRADE
(U.S. $ million)

	1967	1968	1969	1970	1971	1972
Imports c.i.f. .	722.5	742.7	907.9	930.8	979.9	n.a.
Exports f.o.b. .	907.7	935.9	1,067.9	1,246.9	962.3	855.4

COMMODITIES
(U.S. $'000)

Imports	1970	1971
Livestock and Animal Products . . .	40,666	52,513
Vegetable Products . . .	63,816	70,286
Animal and Vegetable Fats . .	18,578	25,726
Manufactured Foodstuffs, Beverages and Tobacco	15,584	26,956
Mineral Products. . . .	65,356	100,740
Chemicals	98,452	97,208
Synthetic Plastics, Rubber . .	33,144	35,859
Skins and Leather Goods . .	4,325	7,487
Wood, Cork and Basket Products . .	1,972	1,936
Paper and Paper-making Materials .	23,413	22,156
Textiles	46,385	59,156
Plaster, Cement, Ceramics and Glass .	12,221	13,996
Metals and Metal Goods . . .	85,576	67,156
Technical and Electrical Equipment .	257,504	253,554
Transport Equipment . . .	132,110	104,333
Optical and Precision Instruments .	25,620	19,833

COMMODITIES *continued*]

EXPORTS	1968	1969	1970*
Food and Live Animals	46,443	44,580	50,121
Fruit and Vegetables . . .	18,160	16,193	23,490
Meat and Fish Meal Fodder . .	18,382	18,098	15,538
Chemical Wood Pulp	13,277	15,308	16,404
Crude Fertilizers	18,617	17,917	15,082
Natural Sodium Nitrate . . .	15,821	16,791	13,940
Metalliferous Ores and Scrap . .	87,178	98,718	110,627
Iron Ore and Concentrates . .	71,543	71,026	71,374
Copper Ores	15,265	18,676	28,566
Chemicals	5,668	11,516	16,045
Basic Manufactures	736,559	835,038	983,351
Paper and Paperboard . . .	10,201	12,490	15,078
Copper Metal	711,577	811,909	948,642
Copper and Alloys (unwrought) .	702,030	810,418	944,601
Unrefined Copper . . .	252,991	261,728	284,193
Refined Copper . . .	449,039	548,690	660,408
TOTAL (incl. others) . . .	935,864	1,067,883	1,233,611

* Provisional figures. Revised total is $1,246.9 million.

Source: United Nations, *Yearbook of International Trade Statistics.*

PRINCIPAL COUNTRIES
('000 U.S. dollars)

	IMPORTS			EXPORTS		
	1969	1970	1971	1969	1970	1971
Argentina	92,397	93,324	110,664	66,394	78,499	59,529
Belgium and Luxembourg . .	10,352	8,034	12,223	24,964	38,357	17,199
Brazil	31,517	24,795	27,392	23,679	24,400	30,123
Ecuador	12,193	9,032	10,165	2,368	2,619	3,733
France	27,875	31,590	32,340	59,792	68,706	47,088
Germany, Federal Republic .	93,138	115,462	102,521	102,086	134,900	122,900
Italy	28,832	24,757	19,807	87,533	92,439	70,194
Japan	18,167	27,700	44,319	146,017	149,754	183,485
Mexico	21,158	18,664	30,207	7,604	10,495	15,359
Netherlands	12,949	13,033	18,925	119,181	187,764	103,312
Peru	9,633	7,096	6,826	4,603	8,988	8,525
Portugal	1,120	456	504	283	61	15
Spain	16,060	21,346	30,947	33,292	29,727	24,582
Sweden	10,793	10,693	10,728	37,688	39,281	26,903
Switzerland	17,408	16,742	14,178	646	668	784
United Kingdom . . .	48,160	58,103	64,399	154,336	154,155	110,139
U.S.A.	348,983	343,575	267,341	185,885	177,168	76,427

TOURISM

Visitors: 1968: 170,310; 1969: 181,182; 1970: 198,824; 1971: 261,214; 1972: 31,628.

TRANSPORT

PRINCIPAL RAILWAYS
('000)

	1970	1971	1972
Passengers (number) .	21,194	20,746	24,940
Passenger/km. .	2,338,134	2,481,068	3,036,184
Freight . . (tons)	19,069	19,490	16,557

ROADS

	1969	1970	1971
Cars . . .	149,853	176,066	193,914
Buses . . .	13,384	15,956	15,769
Lorries . . .	122,204	133,798	135,692
Motor Cycles . .	19,062	28,336	26,682

SHIPPING
('ooo metric tons)

	1969	1970	1971
Total Tonnage .	29,377	27,228	26,815
Loaded . .	22,563	21,973	20,444
Unloaded . .	6,814	5,255	6,371

CIVIL AVIATION

	1970	1971	1972
Km. Flown ('ooo)	22,694	25,472	24,959
Passengers* (number)	574,880	696,934	708,126
Freight* ('ooo tons/km.)	127,292	156,447	166,411

* Includes foreign airlines.

EDUCATION

	PUPILS		
	1968	1969	1970
Kindergarten	57,518	56,278	60,360
Primary	1,965,331	1,960,815	2,043,032
Secondary. . . .	264,104	265,413	302,461

Source (unless otherwise indicated): Instituto Nacional de Estadísticas, Santiago de Chile.

THE CONSTITUTION

The Constitution of 1925, somewhat amended, remains in force today. It provides for a unitary state and a republican form of government; a bi-cameral legislature and executive power vested in the President, who is elected by direct popular vote. If the presidential candidate with the largest number of votes has not obtained more than half the votes cast—as happened in 1952 and 1958—Congress decides which of the two candidates with the highest number shall be President. The President is ineligible, on retirement, for immediate re-election.

He has wide powers of appointment and dismissal of Cabinet Ministers and some political officials. He is responsible for the maintenance of order and may, in the event of disturbance, declare a state of siege if Congress is not in session. He is also responsible for the conduct of foreign policy.

The President enjoys a modified veto on bills submitted by Congress, his rejections or amendments being over-ruled if a two-thirds majority of both Chambers so votes. Legislation may be initiated by the Chambers or by the President, who is empowered to issue the decrees he may deem necessary for the execution of the laws. Members of his Cabinet, who cannot be members of Parliament, may attend sessions of Congress and speak, but may not vote.

Congress, whose ordinary sessions last from May 21st to September 18th, and whose extraordinary sessions last the rest of the year, consists of a Senate and a Chamber of Deputies. The former has 50 members, elected for eight years by ten provincial groups of departments, each groud electing five Senators. Half of the Senate is renewable every four years. The Chamber of Deputies has 150 members, elected for four years by departments or groups of departments on the basis of proportional representation.

All voting is by ballot. All citizens over the age of 18 are entitled to vote.

The Republic is divided into 25 Provinces (Aconcagua, Antofagasta, Arauco, Atacama, Aysén, Bío-Bío, Cautín, Chiloé, Colchagua, Concepción, Coquimbo, Curicó, Linares, Llanquihue, Magallanes, Malleco, Maule, Ñuble, O'Higgins, Osorno, Santiago, Talca, Tarapacá, Valdivia, Valparaíso).

Note: The Constitution is at present suspended, and objectives for a new Constitution are being considered.

THE GOVERNMENT

JUNTA MILITAR DE GOBIERNO (JMG)

President: Gen. Augusto Pinochet Ugarte (A).

Members: Vice-Adm. José Toribio Merino (N),
Gen. Gustavo Leigh Guzmán (AF),
Gen. César Mendoza Durán (C).

THE CABINET
(*March* 1974)

Minister of the Interior: Gen. Oscar Bonilla (A).

Minister of Foreign Affairs: Rear-Adm. Ismael Huerta Díaz (N).

Minister of Finance: Rear-Adm. Lorenzo Gotuzzo (N).

Minister of Economic Affairs: Fernando Léniz Cerda.

Minister of Education: Adm. Hugo Castro Jiménez (N).

Minister of Justice: Gonzalo Prieto Gandera.

Minister of Defence: Rear-Adm. Patricio Carvajal Prieto (N).

Minister of Public Works and Transport: Gen. Sergio Figueroa Gutiérrez (AF).

Minister of Agriculture: Col. Sergio Crespo Montero (AF).

Minister of Lands and Settlement: Gen. Diego Barba Valdez (C).

Minister of Labour: Gen. Mario McKay Jara Quemada (C).

Minister of Mines: Gen. Arturo Yovane Zúñiga (C).

Minister of Health: Col. Alberto Spoerer Covarrubias (AF).

Minister of Housing: Brig.-Gen. Arturo Viveros Ávila (C).

Secretary-General to the Government: Col. Pedro Ewing Juvens (A).

(A) Army; (AF) Air Force; (N) Navy; (C) Carabineros.

DIPLOMATIC REPRESENTATION

EMBASSIES AND LEGATIONS ACCREDITED TO CHILE
(In Santiago unless otherwise stated)
(E) Embassy; (L) Legation.

Note: The information given below is the most up-to-date available, although it is necessarily incomplete.

Algeria: Buenos Aires, Argentina (E).

Argentina: Avda. Vicuña Mackenna 45 (E); *Ambassador:* Javier Teodoro Gallac.

Australia: Moneda 1123, 9° (E); *Ambassador:* Noel Deschamps.

Austria: Alcántara 142 (E); *Ambassador:* Friedrich Hohenbühel (also accred. to Bolivia and Peru).

Belgium: Capullos 2254 (E); *Ambassador:* Frans Taelemans.

Brazil: Avda. Bernardo O'Higgins 1656 (E); *Ambassador:* Antônio C. da Câmara Canto.

Canada: Ahumada 11, 10° (E); *Ambassador:* Andrew Donald Ross.

China, People's Republic: El Regidor 66, El Golf (E); *Ambassador:* Lin Ping.

Colombia: Isidora Cayenechea 3365 (E); *Ambassador:* Alvaro García Herrera.

Costa Rica: Vitacura 3634 (E); *Ambassador:* Alvaro Bonilla Lara.

Cyprus: (E); *Ambassador:* Zenon Rossidas.

Denmark: (E); *Ambassador:* Bjarne W. Paulson.

Dominican Republic: Dinamarca 2041 (E); *Ambassador:* Franz E. Baehr Cabral.

Ecuador: Merced 280, 6° (E); *Ambassador:* Alfredo Correa E.

Egypt: Triana 865 (E); *Ambassador:* Salah Badr.

El Salvador: Carlos Antunez 2026 (E); *Ambassador:* Armando Peña Q.

Finland: (E); *Ambassador:* Alexander Thesleff.

France: Avda. Condell 65 (E); *Ambassador:* Pierre de Menthon.

Germany, Federal Republic: Agustinas 785 (E); *Ambassador:* Lothar Lahn.

Greece: Agustinas 975, 6° (E); *Ambassador:* Teodoro Baizos.

Guatemala: Avda. Vitacura 2902 (E); *Ambassador:* Mario Juárez Toledo.

Honduras: Bustos 2374 (E); *Chargé d'Affaires:* Carlos Díaz Varela.

Hungary: Los Leones 2279 (E); *Chargé d'Affaires:* Ferenc Császár (relations suspended).

ndia: El Tamarugo 1600, Vitacura (E); *Ambassador:* Gunwantsingh J. Malik (also accred. to Peru).

Indonesia: Buenos Aires, Argentina (E).

Iran: Buenos Aires, Argentina (E).

Israel: Luis Thayer Ojeda 919 (E); *Ambassador:* Moshe Tov.

Italy: Carmen 8, 5° (E); *Ambassador:* Norberto B. dell' Elmo.

Japan: Callao 3796, El Golf (E); *Ambassador:* Sakito Sato.

Jordan: Aurelio González 3600 (L); *Chargé d'Affaires:* Dr. Anton Nabr.

Korea, Democratic People's Republic: (E); *Ambassador:* Kang Chun Hui.

Korea, Republic: (E); *Ambassador:* Hahn Pyong-gi.

Lebanon: Buenos Aires, Argentina (L).

Mexico: Américo Vespucio Norte 846 (E); *Ambassador:* Ismael Moreno Pino.

Morocco: (E); *Ambassador:* Mohammed el Fassi el Halfaoui.

Nepal: Washington, U.S.A. (E).

Netherlands: Apoquindo 5360 (E); *Ambassador:* Izaak C. Debrot.

Nicaragua: Avda. Nueva Los Leones 82 (E); *Ambassador:* Alberto Salinas Muñoz.

Norway: Américo Vespucio Norte 548 (E); *Ambassador:* Ditlef Knudsen.

Pakistan: Buenos Aires, Argentina (E).

Panama: Avda. Irarrázaval 1628, 12°, Of. 123 (E); *Ambassador:* Roger Decerega.

Paraguay: Bombero Salas 1531, Of. 200 (E); *Ambassador:* Pablo González Maya.

Peru: Las Peñas 3280 (E); *Ambassador:* Arturo García.

Philippines: Buenos Aires, Argentina (E).

Poland: Burgos 140 (E); *Ambassador:* Eugeniusz Noworyta.

Portugal: Huérfanos 1175, 6° (E); *Ambassador:* Armando de Castro E. Abreu.

South Africa: Buenos Aires, Argentina (E).

Spain: Avda. República 475 (E); *Ambassador:* (vacant).

Sweden: Pedro de Valdivia 1218 (E); *Ambassador:* (vacant) (also accred. to Bolivia).

Switzerland: Las Hortencias 2322 (E); *Chargé d'Affaires:* Georges Peyraud.

327

Syria: Don Carlos 2941 (E); *Ambassador:* BOURHAN KAYAL.

Thailand: Buenos Aires, Argentina (E).

Turkey: Montolin 150 (E); *Ambassador:* NECDET OZMEN (also accred. to Bolivia and Peru).

United Kingdom: Gertrudis Echerique 96 (E); *Ambassador:* R. L. SECONDÉ.

U.S.A.: Agustinas 1343, 5° (E); *Ambassador:* DAVID POPPER.

Uruguay: El Golf 243 (E); *Ambassador:* MANUEL SÁNCHEZ.

Vatican: Montolin 200 (Apostolic Nunciature); *Nuncio:* Excmo. Rev. Mons. SOTERO SANZ VILLALBA.

Venezuela: Bustos 2021 (E); *Ambassador:* ORLANDO TOVAR TAMAYO.

The military Government has broken diplomatic relations with Bulgaria, Cuba, Czechoslovakia, the German Democratic Republic, Romania, the U.S.S.R. and Yugoslavia.

CONGRESS

Congress was officially dissolved on September 13th, 1973.

POLITICAL PARTIES

All "Marxist" political parties were declared unlawful on September 14th, 1973, and the activities of all political parties, including the **Partido Demócrata Cristiano (PDC)** and the **Partido Nacional** (the leading opposition parties during the administration of President Allende), were suspended on September 27th.

JUDICIAL SYSTEM

The following are the main tribunals:

The Supreme Court, consisting of 13 members, appointed for life by the President of the Republic from a list of five names submitted by the Supreme Court when vacancies arise.

Twelve Courts of Appeal, whose members are appointed for life from a list submitted to the President by the Supreme Court. The number of members of each court varies. Judges of the lower courts are appointed in a similar manner from lists submitted by the Court of Appeal of the district in which the vacancy arises.

Electoral Qualifications Tribunal, consisting of five members, appointed for four years; two of whom must be members of the Supreme Court, one a member of the Santiago Court of Appeal, one an ex-president of the Senate, and one an ex-president of the Chamber of Deputies.

President of the Supreme Court: RAMIRO MÉNDEZ.

Ministers of the Supreme Court: JUAN POMÉS, OCTAVIO RAMÍREZ, EDUARDO VARAS, ARMANDO SILVA, ENRIQUE URRUTIA, JOSÉ M. EYZAGUIRRE, VÍCTOR RIVAS, EDUARDO ORTÍZ SANDOVAL, ISRAEL BÓRQUEZ, RICARDO MARTÍN, RAFAEL RETAMAL, LUIS MALDONADO.

Attorney-General: URBANO MARÍN.

RELIGION

Roman Catholicism is the principal religion.

SANTIAGO

Metropolitan See: Archbishop H.E. Cardinal RAÚL SILVA HENRÍQUEZ, S.D.B., Apostolic Administrator of Santiago and Primate of Chile; La Serena, Casilla 30-D.

Vicar-General: Mgr. SERGIO VALECH.
Five Suffragan Bishops.

ANTOFAGASTA

Metropolitan See: Rt. Rev. FRANCISCO DE BORJA VALENZUELA RÍOS.

Vicar-General: Mgr. ROBERTO BAHAMONDE BARRIENTOS.
Three Suffragan Bishops.

CONCEPCIÓN

Metropolitan See: Most Rev. MANUEL SÁNCHEZ BEGUIRISTAÍN.

Vicar-General: Mgr. RENÉ INOSTROZA ARRIAGADA.
Four Suffragan Bishops.

PUERTO MONTT

Metropolitan See: (vacant).

Vicar-General: Mgr. MANUEL CÓRDOVA.
Three Suffragan Bishops.

LA SERENA

Metropolitan See: Rt. Rev. JUAN FRANCISCO FRESNO LARRAÍN.

Vicar-General: Mgr. MANUEL ALESANDRO CORTÉS ROJAS.
Three Suffragan Bishops.

THE PRESS

As a quarter of the inhabitants of Chile live in Santiago and Valparaíso, the circulation of provincial papers is not large, some appearing only on alternate days or once and twice a week.

El Mercurio and *La Tercera de la Hora* were the only newspapers permitted to continue publication immediately after the assumption of power by the military government; strict censorship is now in force, and many of the newspapers and periodicals listed below have been suspended.

DAILIES
SANTIAGO

Clarín: Galvez 106; f. 1954; daily; Dir. ALBERTO GAMBOA SOTO; circ. 150,000 (morning).

El Diario Ilustrado: Moneda 1162, Casilla 270, 5 Correo; f. 1902; morning; Traditional Conservative, Catholic; Dir. ANDRÉS ABURTO S.; circ. 55,000 (weekdays), 64,000 (Sundays).

El Diario Oficial: Agustinas 1269; Dir. RUBEN ALZOLA BRICEÑO; circ. 15,000.

El Mercurio: Compañía 1214; f. 1900; morning; Rightwing, independent; Santiago Dir. RENÉ SILVA ESPEJO; Propr. Empr. El Mercurio S.A.; circ. 265,000 (weekdays), 310,000 (Sundays).

La Nación: Agustinas 1269; f. 1917; morning; non-party; Propr. Empr. La Nacíon S.A.; Dir. OSCAR WAISS; circ. 45,000.

El Paredón: f. 1961; tabloid; Left-wing; Editor LAUTARO OJEDA.

La Segunda: Compañia 1214, 2°; f. 1931; evening; Dir. MARIO CARNEYRO CASTRO; circ. 45,000, 55,000 (Saturdays) (suspended).

La Tercera de la Hora: Casilla 9-D, Calle V. Mackenna 1870; f. 1950; daily, morning; independent; Dir. RENÉ OLIVARES; circ. 80,000.

Última Hora: Tenderini 171; f. 1943; evening; independent; Dir. FRANCISCO GALDAMES; circ. 180,000.

Las Últimas Noticias: Compañía 1214; f. 1902; midday; tabloid; independent; Dir. NICOLAS VELASCO DEL CAMPO; owned by the Proprs. of *El Mercurio*; circ. 100,000, 125,000 (Saturdays).

VALPARAÍSO

La Estrella: Esmeralda 1002, Casilla 57-V.; f. 1920; evening, except Sundays and holidays; independent; Dir. FRANCISCO LE DANTEC; owned by the Proprs. of *El Mercurio*; circ. 28,000.

El Mercurio: Esmeralda 1002; f. 1827; morning; Dir. FRANCISCO LE DANTEC; owned by the Proprs. of *El Mercurio* in Santiago; circ. 70,000.

La Unión: Casilla 19-V; f. 1885; morning; pro-Catholic; Dir. ALFREDO SILVA CARVALLO; circ. 22,000, 40,000 (Sundays).

ANTOFAGASTA

La Estrella del Norte: f. 1966; morning; Dir. ALFONSO CASTAGNETO; circ. 10,000.

El Mercurio de Antofagasta: Calle Matta 2112; f. 1906; morning; independent; Proprs. Soc. Chilena de Publicaciones; Dir. MARIO CORTEZ FLORES; circ. 22,000.

CHILLÁN

La Discusión: Casilla 14-D; f. 1870; morning; independent; Dir. ALFONSO LAGOS; circ. 8,000.

CONCEPCIÓN

Crónica: Casilla 8-C; f. 1948; evening; tabloid; non-political; Editor A. LAMAS; Dir. IVÁN CIENFUEGOS; circ. 42,000.

La Patria: Huérfanos 1022; f. 1923; morning; independent; Dir. JOSÉ GÓMEZ; publ. by Soc. Periodística del Sur, who also own: *La Prensa*, Osorno; *El Diario Austral*, Temuco; *El Correo de Valdivia*, Valdivia; circ. 32,000.

El Sur: Casilla 8-C; f. 1882; morning; independent; Dir. IVÁN CIENFUEGOS; circ. 42,000.

COQUIMBO

El Norte: Casilla 127; f. 1932; daily.

El Regional: Calle Aldunate 944-54, Casilla 137; daily; non-political; Dir. JUAN R. MARIN M.; circ. 4,000.

CURICÓ

La Prensa: Casilla 17; f. 1898; morning; Right-wing; Man. Dir. OSCAR RAMÍREZ MERINO; circ. 4,500.

IQUIQUE

La Estrella de Iquique: f. 1966; morning; Dir. ENRIQUE RODRÍGUEZ; circ. 4,000.

El Tarapacá: Casilla 557; f. 1894; morning; Right-wing; Dir. MANUEL FERNÁNDEZ; circ. 7,000.

LA LIGUA

La Libertad: Calle Prat 252, Casilla 67; f. 1926; morning, four days a week; independent; Dir. MANUEL J. PÉREZ GONZÁLEZ.

LA SERENA

El Dia: Casilla 13-D; f. 1944; morning; Dir. ANTONIO PUGA R.; circ. 10,800 .

El Serenese: Casilla 357; f. 1948.

LA UNIÓN

La Región: Casilla 360; f. 1958.

Diario La Unión: Prat 1237; f. 1937.

LOS ANDES

Frontera: Casilla 400; f. 1958.

La Nueva Prensa: Santa Rosa 444, Casilla 224; f. 1951; tabloid; Dir. EDUARDO CAMPOS LEIVA; circ. 1,500.

OSORNO

La Prensa: Cochrane 746, Casilla 46-D; f. 1917; morning; Right-wing; Dir. RICARDO GALLARDO; Propr. Soc. Periodística del Sur; circ. 26,000. (*See* under *La Patria*, Concepción.)

OVALLE

La Provincia: Ariztia 258, Casilla 253; f. 1936; morning; Radical; Editor LUIS MÉNDEZ; circ. 4,500.

El Tamaya: Casilla 71; f. 1876; morning; Dir. ARMANDO DIAZ CASTILLO; circ. 1,500.

PUERTO MONTT

El Llanquihue: Antonio Varas 167; f. 1885; morning; independent; Dir. EWALDO HOHMANN J.; circ. 6,000.

PUNTA ARENAS

El Magallanés: Waldo Seguel 636, Casilla 16-D; f. 1894; morning; independent; Dir. JOSÉ BOZIC LABORIC; circ. 9,000.

La Prensa Austral: Waldo Seguel 646, Casilla 9-D; f. 1942; morning; anti-Communist; Dir. OSVALDO WEGMANN HANSEN; circ. 8,000.

RANCAGUA

El Rancaguino: Casilla 50; f. 1915; evening; independent; Dir. HECTOR GONZÁLEZ VALENZUELA; circ. 10,000.

SAN FERNANDO

La Región: Valdivia 753; f. 1952.

La Voz de Colchagua: Casilla 41; f. 1943; circ. 1,700.

TALCA

La Mañana: Casilla 7-D; f. 1906; morning; Right-wing; Editor VICENTE ROJAS; circ. 10,000,

TEMUCO

El Diario Austral: Bulnes esq. de Varas, Casilla 1-D; f. 1916; morning; commercial and agricultural interests, anti-Communist; Dir. RAÚL GALLARDO LARA; Propr. Soc. Periodística del Sur; circ. 26,000. (*See* under *La Patria*, Concepción.)

TOCOPILLA

La Prensa: Casilla 2099; f. 1924; morning; independent; Dir. MARIO CORTES; circ. 8,000.

VALDIVIA

El Correo de Valdivia: Yungay 758, Casilla 15-D; f. 1895; morning; non-party; Dir. and Admin. RAÚL GALLARDO LARA; circ. 12,000.

PERIODICALS

SANTIAGO

El Agrario: monthly; farming interests.

Arquitectura y Construcción: Teatinos 248, 8°; f. 1946; architects' and builders' monthly; Editor Arch. LARGIO ARREDONDO U.

Boletín Banco Central de Chile: Casilla 967; f. 1926; economics; circ. 4,000.

Boletín Minero: Moneda 759; monthly; mining interests.

El Campesino: farming monthly; publ. by the Sociedad Nacional de Agricultura, Tenderini 187, Casilla 40-D; Editor RAFAEL CABRERA M.

Chile Aéreo: Edificio La Nación, Oficina 611, Casilla 913; monthly; official organ of Club Aéreo de Chile.

Chile Filatélico: Huérfanos 972; f. 1889; monthly; Dir. ALVARO BONILLA-LARA.

Chile Textil: Casilla 10172; f. 1944; monthly; textile industry; Editor WALTER LECHNER.

Confidencias: Avda. Santa María 76, Casilla 84-D; weekly; women's magazine; publ. Empresa Editora Zig-Zag; circ. 96,000.

Desfile: Bandera 131; weekly; general interest; illustrated.

Economía y Finanzas: Clasificador 441, Correo Central; f. 1937; financial monthly; Dir. DANIEL ARMANET; Editor CHRISTIAN CASANOVA.

Ercilla: Quebec 497, Casilla 63-D; f. 1934; weekly; general interest; Editor EMILIO FILIPPI M.; Man. GERARDO INFANTE VIAL.

Eva: Casilla 84-D; weekly; women's magazine; publ. Empresa Editora Zig-Zag; circ. 80,000.

La Farmacia Chilena: monthly.

Flash: Avda. Santa María 104, 2°; weekly, general interest; illustrated.

Industria: Sociedad Fomento Fabril, Moneda 759; monthly.

Panorama Económico: Casilla 10220; f. 1947; monthly.

Política y Espíritu: Avda. Colón 3494; f. 1945; monthly; Christian Democrat; Dir. JAIME CASTILLO V.

Punto Final: Unión Central 1010, Oficina 1108; left-wing; fortnightly.

Radiomanía: Huérfanos 979, Oficina 328; monthly; broadcasting and wireless; Dir. LUCHO ARÓN.

Revista Chilena de Ingeniería: engineering bi-monthly.

Revista Médica de Chile: Esmeralda 678, Casilla 23-D; f. 1872; monthly; official organ of the Sociedad Médica de Santiago; circ. 2,000.

Rosita: Avda. Santa María 76, Casilla 84-D; weekly; dressmakers' journal; publ. by Empresa Editora Zig-Zag; circ. 56,000.

Siete Días: Avda. Santa María 188, 2°; weekly; general interest.

Telecran: Avda. Santa María 76; f. 1969; weekly; film and TV magazine; published by Empresa Editora Zig-Zag; circ. 125,000.

El Teniente: Casilla 49-D; f. 1953; magazine of the Sociedad Minera El Teniente; circ. 15,000.

Topaze: Calle Loreto 22, Casilla 2310; f. 1931; weekly; satirical; Dir. LUIS GOYENECHEA.

Vea: Avda. Santa María 188, 1°; f. 1939; weekly; general interest, illustrated; publ. Empresa Editora Zig-Zag; Dir. GENARO MEDINA; circ. 180,000.

En Viaje: Ferrocarriles del Estado, Casilla 1173; general and tourist interest; monthly; also yearly tourist guide with maps and hotel information.

VALPARAÍSO

Mar: Avda. Errázuriz 471, Casilla 117-V; f. 1915; monthly; maritime affairs; organ of the Liga Marítima de Chile; Dir. T. B. SEPULVEDA WHITTLE.

Scientia: Casilla 110-V; f. 1934; quarterly; technical and scientific; edited by Universidad Técnica Federico Santa María; Dir. CARLOS GONZÁLEZ DE LA FUENTE.

PRESS ASSOCIATION

Asociación Nacional de Prensa: Bandera 84, Santiago; Pres. GERMÁN PICÓ CAÑAS.

NEWS AGENCIES

SANTIAGO

ANSA: Agustinas 1269; f. 1954; Bureau Chief GIORGIO BAGONI BETTOLINI.

AP: Calle Compañía 1214; Bureau Chief JOSEPH L. BENHAM.

UPI: Calle Nataniel 47, 9°, Casilla 71-D; Man. MARTIN P. HOUSEMAN.

The following are also represented: Deutsche Press Agentur (DPA), Prensa Latina, Reuters, Tass.

PUBLISHERS

Ediciones Atenea: Universidad de Concepción.

Editorial Andrés Bello: Ahumada 131, 4°, Santiago; medicine, history, economy, sociology.

Empresa Ercilla, S.A.: Avda. Santa María 108, 3°, Santiago; literature, fiction, translations.

Editorial González Porto Ltda.: Miraflores 109, Casilla 165-D, Santiago; juvenile, general non-fiction, textbooks.

Herder Editorial y Librería Ltda.: Bandera 172, Casilla 367, Santiago; philosophy, religion.

Editorial Jurídica de Chile: Ahumada 131, Casilla 4256, Santiago; law, social sciences.

Walter Lechner Ltda.: Casilla 10172, Santiago; handicrafts, fashion, directories.

Librería y Editorial Nascimento: San Antonio 390, Casilla 2298, Santiago.

Editorial del Nuevo Extremo: Ahumada 6, Casilla 10471, Santiago; fiction.

Editorial Orbe: Galería Imperio 256, Santiago; education, children's books, history, fiction.

Editorial Pomaire Ltda.: Avda. Bulnes 80, 5°, Oficina 56, Santiago; fiction.

Editorial Universitaria, S.A.: Dpto. Editorial, María Luisa Santander 0447, Casilla 10220, Santiago; education.

Zamorano y Caperán: Compañía 1015, Casilla 362, Santiago; f. 1909; law, history, bibliography.

Empresa Editora Zig-Zag: Casilla 84-D, Santiago; general publishers of literary works, reference books and magazines; Pres. SERGIO MUJICA L.; Gen. Man. SANTIAGO TORO JORY.

RADIO AND TELEVISION

RADIO

Asociación de Radiodifusoras de Chile (ARCHI): Pasaje Matte 956, Oficina 801, Casilla 10476, Santiago de Chile; f. 1936; 45 broadcasting stations; Pres. Daniel Ramírez Estay; Exec. Dir. Jorge Quinteros Tricot; Admin. Sec. Enrique Prieto Chávez.

Radio Difusoras Australes Soc. Ltda.: Casilla 2871, Santiago; Dirs.-Gen. J. Lavandero E., G. Cortes; four stations.

There are 31 short wave and 144 medium wave stations, most of which are associated with ARCHI.

In 1971 there were about 1,400,000 receiving sets.

TELEVISION

Televisión Nacional de Chile: Plaza de Armas 444, 2°, Santiago; 15 stations; Dir. A. Olivares B.

Universidad Católica de Chile: Casilla 14600, Santiago; non-commercial; Tech. Dir. P. Caraball.

Universidad Católica de Valparaíso: Casilla 3021, Valparaíso; Dir. E. Vargas H.

Universidad de Chile: Casilla 12985, Santiago; f. 1960; educational; Dir. M. Planet.

In 1971 there were about 500,000 receivers.

The first permanent earth station in South America for satellite communications was opened in 1968. It is 70 miles south-west of Santiago and is owned by the Empresa Nacional de Telecommunicaciones, S.A.

FINANCE

(cap.=capital; p.u.=paid up; dep.=deposits; res.= reserves; m.=million; amounts in escudos)

BANKING

Superintendent of Banks: Enrique Marshall.

Central Bank

Banco Central de Chile: Agustinas 1180; f. 1926; issues notes; cap. 10.1m., dep. 15,166m. (May 1972); Pres. Gen. Eduardo Cano; Vice Pres. Vío Valdivieso; Gen. Man. Gen. Molina Orrego.

Santiago

Banco del Estado de Chile: Alameda Bernardo O'Higgins 1111, Casilla 24; f. 1953; cap. p.u. 25m., dep. 20.4m., res. 511m. (Dec. 1971); state bank; incorporates the Caja Nacional de Ahorros, Caja de Crédito Agrario, Caja de Crédito Hipotecario and Instituto de Crédito Industrial; Pres. Gen. Enrique González; Gen. Man. Washington Bertrand Remedy; 208 brs.

Note: Locally-owned banks, nationalized under the Allende régime, are being returned to their former owners.

Banco de Chile: Ahumada 251; f. 1894; cap. and res. 9,457m., dep. 54,460m. (1973); Pres. Manuel Vinagre D.; Gen. Man. Alvaro Valdes T.

Banco de Crédito e Inversiones: Huérfanos 1134, Casilla 136D; f. 1937; Chief Exec. Jorge Yarur Banna; Gen. Man. Guido Giovanetti C.

Banco Español-Chile: f. 1926; cap. 40m., res. 93.3m. (Dec. 1971); Pres. Carlos San Martín Madariaga; Gen. Man. H. Vargas Schneider.

Banco Nacional del Trabajo: Agustinas 828; f. 1955; cap. 18.7m., res. 29.6m. (June 1971); Pres. G. Villablanca Collado; Gen. H. Fuenzalida Labbá.

Banco Sud Americano: Morandé 226; f. 1944; cap. 30m., res. 83.3m. (Dec. 1971); Pres. Eliodoro Matte O.; Gen. Man. G. Morgan Torres.

Valparaíso

Banco Hipotecario de Desarrollo: Esmeralda 978; f. 1883; cap. and res. 58.3m. (Dec. 1973); Pres. Ignacio Cousiño Aragón; Gen. Man. Adriano Simonetti Michieli.

Concepción

Banco de Concepción: O'Higgins 612, Casilla 17-C; f. 1871; cap. 25m., dep. 447.8m. (Dec. 1971); Gen. Man. Otto Bennewitz B.; publ. *Memorias Anuales*.

Osorno

Banco Osorno y La Unión: Casilla 25-O; f. 1908; cap. 23.0m., dep. 1,040m. (June 1971); Pres. Moisés Zeltzer; Gen. Man. Marcelo Ringeling L.

STOCK EXCHANGES

Bolsa de Comercio: Bandera 75, Casilla 123-D, Santiago; f. 1893; 43 mems.; Pres. Eugenio Blanco Ruiz; Man. Carlos Carvallo Stagg; publs. *Cierre y Operaciones Diarias, Indice de Precios y Acciones, Análisis del Mercado Bursatil, Estudios Sobre Empresas, Transacciones, Crías y Dividendos*.

Bolsa de Corredores: Valparaíso.

INSURANCE COMPANIES

Araucania, Compañía de Seguros: Condell 1231, Valparaíso; f. 1944; non-life; Pres. E. Oschwald Chicerio; Man. O. Harlandt Richter.

Caja Reaseguradora Chile: Bandera 84, Carregur; f. 1927; reinsurance in fire, earthquake, marine, hull, life, motor car, aviation, fidelity guarantee, livestock, burglary, glass, miscellaneous; Pres. Hernan Dávila Echaurren; Man. Raúl Undurraga Alemparte.

Consorcio La Chilena Consolidada: Bandera 127, Santiago.

Consorcio Nacional de Seguras: Bandera 236, Santiago.

La Construcción: Bandera 131, Santiago; f. 1954; life; Pres. Luis Cifuentes; Gen. Man. J. Bande Weiss.

La Financiera: Bandera 131, Santiago; f. 1958; non-life; Pres. Guillermo Correa Fuenzalida; Gen. Man. J. Bande Weiss.

La Germania: Condell 1231, Valparaíso; f. 1914; non-life; Pres. E. Oschwald Chicerio; Man. O. Harlandt Richter.

La Independencia: Bandera 236, Santiago; f. 1948; non-life; Pres. A. Fuentes Navarrete; Gen. Man. C. Tomasello Rossl.

Lautaro: Bandera 131, Santiago; f. 1944; non-life, re-insurance; Pres. Víctor Morales Guzmán; Gen. Man. J. Bande.

La Minera: Bandera 131, Santiago; Pres. Salustio Prieto Calvo; Gen. Man. J. Bande Weiss.

Organización Kappés: Agustinas 1137, Santiago.

Philadelphia Consolidada: Bandera 131, Santiago; insurance, reinsurance; Pres. Ernesto Barros Jarpa; Gen. Man. J. Bande Weiss.

La Provincia: Huérfanos 830, Santiago; f. 1942; non-life; Dir.-Gen. D. BARRIOS V.

Sud América de Chile: Bandera 172 esq. Agustinas, Santiago; life, annuities; Pres. GABRIEL GONZÁLEZ VIDELA; Man. RODOLFO BROCH MENGONI.

La Victoria: Bandera 131, Santiago; f. 1919; all classes; Pres. SYDNEY L. SHAW; Gen. Man. J. BANDE WEISS.

TRADE AND INDUSTRY

CHAMBERS OF COMMERCE

Cámara de Comercio de Santiago de Chile: Santa Lucia 302, 3°, Casilla 1297; f. 1919; 2,000 mems.; Pres. FERNANDO SAHLI NATERMANN; Exec. Sec. OSCAR SALAS ELGART; publs. *Boletín Informaciones Comerciales, El Informativo, El Informativo Alalc.*

Cámara Central de Comercio de Chile: Santiago; f. 1858; 120 mems.; Pres. JORGE MARTÍNEZ RODRÍGUEZ; Man. PABLO DE TEZANOS PINTO.

There are Chambers of Commerce in all major towns.

STATE ECONOMIC AND DEVELOPMENT ORGANIZATIONS

Caja Autónoma de Amortización: Bandera 46, Casilla 1627; f. 1932; sinking funds and amortizations; Man. P. ARANDA CODDOU.

Corporación del Cobre: f. 1966 as a result of law providing for the Chileanization of copper to control production and sale of Chilean copper.

Corporación de la Reforma Agraria: Olivares 1229, Casilla 137-D, Santiago; f. 1962; land and crop development; Exec. Vice-Pres. RAFAEL MORENO ROJAS.

CORFO (Corporación de Fomento de la Producción): Ramón Nieto 920, Santiago; investment (1967) 832m. escudos; (1968) 764m. escudos and 75m. U.S.$; Vice-Pres. Gen. SERGIO NUÑO; Gen. Man. CARLOS CROXATTO SILVA; exercises some control over:

Compañia de Acero del Pacífico—CAP: f. 1946; cap. p.u. U.S.$63.5m.; development plans include doubling steel ingot production to 1m. tons.

Empresa Nacional de Petróleo—ENAP: f. 1950; 5,722,000 cubic metres refined 1971; Man. Dir. HÉCTOR DONOSO R.

> **Petroquímica Chilena:** f. 1966 by CORFO and ENAP to supervise the establishment of a petrochemical complex costing U.S. $120m.

Empresa Nacional de Electricidad—ENDESA: Santa Rosa 76, Santiago; f. 1944; cap. p.u. 800m. escudos; installed capacity 1.48m. kW; Gen. Man. ENRIQUE FERNÁNDEZ.

Industria Azucarera Nacional—IANSA: Avda. Bustamante 26, Casilla 6099, Correo 22, Santiago; f. 1953; cap. 1,000m. escudos; average annual production 300,000 tons sugar; factories in Curicó, Linares, Nuble, Bío-Bío, and Llanquihue.

Corporación de la Vivienda (*Housing*): Santiago; government body; encourages and carries out construction work; Vice-Pres. Col. RICARDO MARFULL.

Empresa Nacional de Minería-Enami: Santiago; promotes the development of the small and medium mines.

Instituto de Capacitación e Investigación en Reforma Agraria: Arturo Claro 1468, Casilla 1949, Santiago 11; f. 1964 by agreement with FAO and UN Special Fund; cap. U.S. $1.4m.; to plan and co-ordinate agrarian reform; Dir. ENRIQUE ASTORGA L.; Man. SOLON BARRACLOUGH.

Instituto de Desarrollo Agropecuario—INDAP: Teatinos 40, Santiago; fiscal institution; Pres. Minister of Agriculture; Vice-Pres. Ing. SERGIO HUERTA.

Instituto de Fomento Pesquero: Pedro de Valdivia 2633, Casilla 1287, Santiago; f. 1963 for research in biology, economy and technology to further the fishing industry; library of 4,729 vols.; Dir. Capt. ALFONSO FILIPPI PARADA; publs. *Publicación, Boletín Científico, Circular.*

Oficina de Planificación Nacional: Santiago; f. 1967 to assist the programme of regional development and co-ordinate the national budget with general development plans; Dir. GONZALO MAXTMER GARCÍA.

EMPLOYERS' ORGANIZATION

Sociedad de Fomento Fabril (*Society for Manufacturing Development*): Moneda 759, Casilla 44, Santiago; f. 1883; mems. 2,000; Pres. FERNANDO SMITS; publs. *El Informativo* (weekly), *Industria* and *Hoja Económica* (monthly), *Rol Industrial* (every four years).

TRADE UNIONS

The **Central Única de Trabajadores de Chile (CUTCH)** was outlawed in September 1973 together with all other trade unions. However, former leaders of the principal unions have established a provisional executive council as the first step towards the creation of a new institution, the **Confederación de Trabajadores de Chile,** which will be basically non-political.

TRANSPORT

RAILWAYS

The total length of the railway system in Chile is approximately 9,000 km., four-fifths of which is state-owned. Two lines connect Chile with the Argentine, two with Bolivia and one with Peru.

An extensive programme of renovation, rebuilding and electrification is under way. The electrification of the Santiago-Chillán line was completed in 1967. The Rancagua–Laja line has also been electrified, and work of electrification is to extend as far as Concepción.

STATE RAILWAYS

Empresa de los Ferrocarriles del Estado: Avda. Bernardo O'Higgins 924, Casilla 1173, Santiago; f. 1851; 8,218 km. of track. The State Railways are divided between the *Red Norte* or Northern System, and the *Red Sur* or Southern System and include the former Ferrocarril Transandino por Juncal, Ferrocarril Arica–La Paz (Chilean section) and Ferrocarril Iquique–Pueblo Hundido; Gen. Man. ALFREDO ROJAS CASTAÑEDA. Gauges: South of Calera, 1.676m., and 0.60 m.; north of Calera, 1 m.; Arica 1 m.; Iquique–Pueblo Hundido 1.435 m. and 1 m.

PRIVATE RAILWAYS

Antofagasta (Chili) & Bolivia Railway Co. Ltd.: London Office: 1 Broad Street Place, London, E.C.2; local office in Antofagasta. Chair. Sir DENYS LOWSON, Bt.; Man. Dir. JAMES A. BLAIR. The Chilean part of the system consists of the international railway from Antofagasta to Bolivia, and branches, and the Aguas Blancas Railway; total track length is 723 km. of 1 m. gauge.

Ferrocarril Potrerillos: Potrerillos; H.O.: 25 Broadway, New York City; 100 km. of 1 m. gauge; Man. L. O. FINES.

Ferrocarril Salitrero de Taltal, S.A.: Taltal; owned by Señor Julio Rumio; 183 km. of 1.067 m. gauge; Gen. Man. Julio Gregorio R.

Ferrocarril Rancagua-Teniente: Rancagua; H.O.: Braden Copper Co., 161 East 42nd Street, New York; f. 1909; 69 km. of 0.762 m. gauge; owned by Sociedad Minera El Teniente S.A.; serves El Teniente Mine, Sewell; Supt. Jorge Astorga.

Sociedad Química y Minera de Chile, S.A.: Teatinos 220, Santiago; Tocopilla–Toco nitrate railway; 264 km. of 1.067 m. gauge; Gen. Man. Miguel Labarca.

ROADS

Ministerio de Obras Públicas: Dirección de Vialidad, Morandé 59, 3°, Santiago; the authority responsible for roads; the total length of roads in Chile in 1971, excluding unimproved roads, was 70,701 km., of which 11 per cent were paved. The road system comprises the Pan American or Longitudinal Highway extending 3,500 km. from north to south, completely paved, and about 50,000 km. of transversal roads. Since 1961 the World Bank and the IADB have together granted over $40 million to improve the main road system. International highways are under construction to Salta, Mendoza, San Juan and Bariloche in Argentina. A 4-lane highway from Santiago to Rancagua is completed, and another is being constructed from Padre Hurtado to San Antonio. Other important projects are the building of the Lo Prado tunnel and the bridges over the Maipo and Bío-Bío rivers.

MOTORISTS' ORGANIZATION

Automóvil Club de Chile: San Antonio 220, Casilla 120-D, Santiago; publ. *Revista Rutas* (four issues annually).

SHIPPING

Chile's merchant fleet has a gross registered tonnage of 261,516.

SANTIAGO

Compañía Naviera Santa Fé: Casilla 974; f. 1961 by the Compañía Minera Santa Fé and Compañía Chilena de Navegación Interoceánica to handle iron ore exports, bulk cargo Chile-Argentina; Chair. Alfredo Nenci.

VALPARAÍSO

Compania Chilena de Navegación Interoceánica: Plaza Justicia 59, Casilla 1410; f. 1930; regular sailings from Peruvian and Chilean ports to the River Plate and Brazilian ports via the Magellan Straits; to Japan, Australia and New Zealand via Peru; cargo services; office in Santiago: Ahumada 11, Casilla 4246; Pres. Gabriel Rodríguez García-Huidobro.

Compañía de Muelles de la Población Vergara: Calle Blanco 951, Casilla 131-V; service of cargo vessels between Chile, Peru, Argentina, Brazil, Portugal and Mediterranean ports; Pres. Max Grisar.

Compañía Sud-Americana de Vapores: Blanco 895; office in Santiago: Agustinas 1235, 10°; f. 1872; 12 cargo vessels; regular service between Chile and New York, Gulf Ports and Mexico and North European ports, intermediate ports included; Pres. Luis E. Gubler; Gen. Man. Patricio Falcone S.

Empresa Marítima del Estado: H.O.: Prat 772, 5°, Casilla 105-V; branch offices: Santiago, San Antonio, Puerto Montt, Castro, Antofagasta; 21 vessels; cargo services between Arica and Punta Arenas and overseas; passenger services between Puerto Montt and Puerto Aysén and between Puerto Montt and Punta Arenas; touring trips through the southern channels and archipelagos during the summer season; Dir. Humberto Rivas Burgos.

Naviera Chilena del Pacífico, S.A.: Casilla 370; cargo; associated with Naviera Coronel; Chair. Arturo Fernández Zegers.

Naviera Coronel, S.A.: Casilla 370; cargo; Pres. Arturo Fernández Zegers.

Sociedad Anónima de Navegación Petrolera (SONAP): Errázuriz 471, 3°; f. 1953; tanker services; Pres. Pedro Galarza R.; Man. Iván Souloadre Walker.

There are also several foreign companies with offices in Valparaíso.

PUNTA ARENAS

Compañía Marítima de Punta Arenas, S.A.: Casilla 337; f. 1949; shipping agents and owners operating in the Magellan Straits; Man. Dir. René Venegas Aros.

CIVIL AVIATION

SANTIAGO

Linea Aérea Nacional de Chile (Lan-Chile): Aeropuerto de Los Cerrillos, Casilla 147-D; Government airline; f. 1929; serves 60,000 km. of routes; domestic services: Santiago–Arica, Santiago–Punta Arenas, with intermediate stops; Santiago–Easter Island; regional services based on Puerto Montt and Punta Arenas; international services: Santiago–Lima, Guayaquil, Cali, Panama, Miami, New York; Santiago–Mendoza; Santiago–Buenos Aires, Montevideo, Rio de Janeiro; Antofagasta–Asunción; Santiago–Bariloche; Santiago–Easter Island, Papeete; fleet: 2 Boeing 707, 4 Boeing 727, 3 Caravelle 6R, 9 HS 748, 3 DC-3; Exec. Pres. Gen. Teodoro D. Ruiz.

Linea Aérea del Cobre S.A. (LADECO): Huérfanos 1363; f. 1958; internal services, also cargo flights to Argentina and Brazil; Exec. Vice-Pres. J. Costabal; fleet: 4 Douglas DC-6B, 1 Douglas DC-6A/B, 1 Douglas DC-6A, 1 Douglas DC-3, 1 Beechcraft Baron.

FOREIGN AIRLINES

Chile is served by the following foreign airlines: Aerolíneas Argentinas, Aeroflot, Air France, Alitalia, Avianca (Colombia), Braniff, British United Airways, Canadian Pacific, Ecuatoriana (Ecuador), Empresa Consolidada Cubana de Aviación, Iberia, KLM, Lufthansa, Scandinavian Airlines System, Swissair, Varig (Brazil).

TOURISM

Dirección de Turismo: Calle Catedral 1165, 3°, Santiago; Dir. René Pairoa.

Asociacion Chilena de Agencias de Viajes: Clasificador 897, Santiago; Pres. Carlos K. Stein Curzolo.

CULTURAL ORGANIZATIONS

Instituto de Extensión Musical: Compañía 1264, Santiago; Dir. Carlos Riesco; Administers:

Orquesta Sinfónica de Chile: Compañía 1264; f. 1940; 94 mems.; Conductor David Serendero.

Conservatorio Nacional de Música: Compañía 1264, 3°; Dir. David Serendero.,

Ballet Nacional Chileno: Compañía 1264, 8°; f. 1941; 34 dancers and 6 technicians; Dir. Virginia Roncal; Choreographer Patricio Bunster.

Departamento de Teatro de la Universidad de Chile: Amunátegui 436, 2°; f. 1941; formerly the Teatro Experimental; Dir. Sergio Aguirre G.

ATOMIC ENERGY

Comisión Chilena de Energía Nuclear: Avda. Salvador 943, Casilla 188-D, Santiago; f. 1965; Government body to develop peaceful uses of atomic energy; autonomous organization that concentrates and assesses all research in nuclear energy matters. Pres. Gen. Raúl Contreras Fischer; Exec. Dir. Ing. Marmaduque Abarzúa Astete.

Universidad de Chile: Avda. Bernardo O'Higgins 1058, Casilla 10-D, Santiago; nuclear research in medicine, physics, bio-physics, chemistry and pharmacy; apparatus includes a Cockroft Walton accelerator of 800 kW.

Universidad Católica de Chile: Avda. Bernardo O'Higgins 340, Casilla 114-D, Santiago; atomic research in the fields of engineering, technology, and medicine.

Universidad Técnica "Federico Santa María": Casilla 110-V, Valparaíso; atomic research in chemistry, mathematics and physics, mechanics and electrical engineering.

Universidad de Concepción: Ciudad Universitaria, Casilla 20-C, Concepción; atomic research in engineering, agronomy, medicine, pharmacy, mathematics, chemistry, physics and biology.

Empresa Nacional de Electricidad S.A. (ENDESA): Ramón Nieto 920, Santiago; to study the development of nuclear power for the production of electricity; Gen. Man. Enrique Fernández.

UNIVERSITIES

Note: The military government has reorganized the six principal universities and replaced their rectors by officers of the armed forces, known as delegate-rectors.

Universidad Austral de Chile: Casilla 567, Valdivia; 460 teachers, *c.* 3,400 students.

Universidad de Chile: Avda. Bernardo O'Higgins 1058, Casilla 10-D, Santiago; 9,220 teachers, 50,811 students.

Universidad de Concepción Casilla 20-C, Concepción.

Universidad Católica de Chile: Avda. Bernardo O'Higgins 340, Casilla 114-D, Santiago; 2,091 teachers, 11,884 students.

Universidad del Norte: Casilla 1280, Antofagasta; 336 teachers, 1,900 students.

Universidad Católica de Valparaíso: Casilla 4059, Valparaíso; 161 full-time teachers; 438 part-time teachers; 3,157 students.

Universidad Técnica del Estado: Avda. Ecuador 3469, Correo 2, Santiago; 590 teachers, 9,483 students.

Universidad Técnica "Federico Santa María": Casilla 110-V, Valparaíso; 160 teachers, 1,420 students.

PEOPLE'S REPUBLIC OF CHINA

INTRODUCTORY SURVEY

Location, Climate, Language, Religion, Flag, Capital

The People's Republic of China covers a vast area of eastern Asia, with Mongolia to the north, the Soviet Union to the north and west, Pakistan to the west and India, Nepal and South-East Asia to the south. The climate ranges from sub-tropical in the far south to an annual average temperature of below 50°F (10°C) in the north and from the monsoon climate of East China to the aridity of the north-west. The principal language is Northern Chinese (Mandarin); in the south and south-east local dialects are spoken. The Tibetans, Uighurs, Mongols and other groups have their own languages. The traditional religions and philosophies of life are Confucianism, Buddhism and Taoism. There are also small Muslim and Christian minorities. The national flag (proportions 3 by 2) is plain red with one large and four small gold stars in the top left-hand corner. The capital is Peking.

Recent History

The Allied defeat of Japan in 1945 was followed by civil war in China until 1949 when the Communists under Mao Tse-tung became masters of the country. Between 1949 and 1959 a close relationship was maintained with the Soviet Union but subsequently relations have become embittered. Chinese forces participated on the North Korean side in the Korean War of 1950–53. The People's Republic claims sovereignty over Taiwan (Formosa), now governed by General Chiang Kai-shek, the pre-1949 ruler of China. Late in 1962 Chinese troops were engaged in a short frontier war with India in disputed Himalayan territory in Ladakh and to the north of the Indian province of Assam. Early in 1964 France recognized the People's Republic, which since the breach with the U.S.S.R. has attempted to diversify its foreign associations. China exploded her first nuclear device late in 1964 and by the end of 1968 had successfully completed eight nuclear tests. In November 1965 Chairman Mao Tse-tung launched the "Great Proletarian Cultural Revolution". The motivation and aims of this movement remain obscure, but it proved a prolonged campaign of rectification, bringing about widespread changes in Party and State organs and personnel which were not finally completed until late 1972. Many individuals were publicly criticized, including the Head of State, Liu Shao-chi, who was dismissed from all Party and State posts in October 1968. In April 1969 the long-awaited Ninth Congress of the Chinese Communist Party took place. The personnel changes of the Cultural Revolution were confirmed and Marshal Lin Piao, the Minister of Defence, was officially designated Mao's heir.

However, Lin Piao and several senior military figures disappeared from public life in 1971; it was reported that they had been killed in an air crash while attempting to flee to the Soviet Union. It was not until the Tenth Party Congress, held secretly in August 1973, that this report was confirmed. At the Congress Lin was denounced, the politburo was purged of his associates and his post of Vice-Chairman was split among five persons. A revision of the Party's constitution was also presented at the Con-

gress. The new appointments, together with appearances made by dignitaries at official functions, indicated that many persons dismissed during the Cultural Revolution were being rehabilitated during 1973. The military, moreover, had less influence in the leadership and there was a radical reshuffle of regional military commanders. In the wake of the Tenth Congress came campaigns against Lin, Confucius, western culture and "Soviet revisionism", developments interpreted by observers as signs of further struggle within the Party.

In April 1970, China's first earth satellite was launched successfully. In 1972 diplomatic relations were established with many countries including Japan, while a Sino-U.S. *rapprochement* was brought about, following the visit of President Nixon to Peking in February of the same year. By early 1973 more than 80 countries recognized the Peking Government. On October 25th, 1971, the People's Republic was finally recognized by the United Nations as the representative of China, and simultaneously became one of the five permanent members of the UN Security Council.

Government

China is a unitary state. Directly under the Central Government there are 21 provinces, five autonomous regions (including Tibet) and three municipalities (Peking, Shanghai, Tientsin). The Constitution provides for a National People's Congress, with over 3,000 deputies elected every four years by universal suffrage, with the State Council as its executive organ. Local authorities under the provinces include special districts, counties (*hsien*) and rural districts (*hsiang*). The constitution lays down that each local authority is to have an elected people's congress. The Communist Party, under the chairmanship of Mao Tse-tung, is the controlling authority in the country. In 1961 its membership was said to be 17 million. The Party's directing body is the Politburo.

After November 1965 many new organs were established within the party, the army, and the administration to promote the revolution. By September 1968, Revolutionary Committees (alliances of elements of the Army, the Communist Party and the revolutionary masses) had been established to take over the administration of each of the 29 provinces, autonomous regions and special municipalities. By the end of 1971 Provincial Party Committees, set up in the wake of the Cultural Revolution, had been established in all major administrative regions. Following the rationalization and merging of the functions of the Central Government organs, the number of State Ministries, Commissions and Special Agencies was greatly reduced.

Defence

China is divided into 11 military regions. The People's Liberation Army numbers about 2½ million men. The navy of 180,000 has three fleets totalling 1,300 vessels including submarines some of which are believed to be equipped with missiles. The air force has 3,800 combat aircraft and personnel totalling 220,000. In addition China has 15–20 IRBM and 20-30 MRBM. There are also 300,000 security and border guards. Military service in the army, air force and navy is for 2, 3, and 4 years respectively.

Economic Affairs

Agriculture is China's main industry and agricultural produce is the largest single contributor to the export trade. Approximately two-fifths of total output derives from the agricultural sector, which employs over two-thirds of the working population. Mainly arable crops are grown: rice principally south of the Yangtze, and wheat and millet mainly north of that river. Substantial quantities of wheat are imported from Australia, Canada and South America. The Communist regime aims at achieving self-sufficiency through the internal development of China's natural resources and domestic industries based on this wealth There are large deposits of iron ore, which support the iron and steel industry at Anshan, Shanghai, Paotow and Wuhan. Other important minerals are tin, molybdenum, tungsten and antimony. The traditional location of industry, in the north-east, north and east (particularly Shanghai and Tientsin), remains the major centre but industrial development has been dispersed throughout the country.

The development of the economy since 1949 has been within the framework of four five-year plans to build a socialist economy and to industrialize the country. Ownership of farm lands was transferred to the peasants at an early stage, and from 1955 to 1958 collectives were established over the whole country. The gradual take-over by the state of industry and commerce was speeded up after 1955. During the "Great Leap Forward" of 1958 (a campaign to mobilize fully for economic development the vast population) rural and urban communes were set up as administrative units but the system of producers' collectives was re-introduced during the "three bitter years" between 1959 and 1961, caused by bad harvests, the withdrawal of Soviet aid and internal disorder. Industry was allocated the major share of investment under the first two plans but the development of agriculture was later given prominence. The extent of the disruption caused by the "Great Proletarian Cultural Revolution" is not yet known. Despite delays in the Third Plan (1966-70), the Fourth Plan started in January 1971, but few details have been released. Official reports in 1973 stated that economic progress was good and that plan targets were being fulfilled. A report by the European Economic Community in May 1974 concluded that 1973 had been a relatively successful year for the Chinese economy.

Transport and Communications

Since 1949 an ambitious programme of railway construction has been undertaken, especially in the west and north-west. In 1958 railways were responsible for nearly 80 per cent of the freight turnover by modern means of transport; the total length of railway lines exceeded 31,000 km. Roads are unevenly developed; national and provincial highways total 200,000 km. In 1966 about 40,000 km. of inland waterways were navigable by steamships and civil air routes totalled 33,000 km. Coastal shipping is also important. Since 1964 a number of foreign airlines have been permitted to set up regular services to Peking, Canton and Shanghai.

Social Welfare

Western and traditional Chinese medical attention is available in the cities, and to a lesser degree in rural areas. Since the Cultural Revolution, some 330,000 medical workers have settled in the countryside and an additional 400,000 doctors and nurses have been recruited into mobile teams to tour the villages, according to the New China News Agency. About 1 million "barefoot doctors" or semi-professional peasant physicians assist with simple cures and treatment. Large factories and other enterprises provide social services for their employees. Wage-earners qualify for pensions.

Education

A great expansion has occurred since 1949 in numbers receiving education at all levels, and education is almost universal. Primary schooling covers five years and middle school six years. In 1959 it was claimed that 37 per cent of the adult population was literate. Following the closing of many schools and universities during the Cultural Revolution, PLA-worker teams took over their administration, entrance examinations were abolished and selection for admission was based on political assessment. By 1971 many colleges and universities had re-opened but initial enrolment was reportedly low.

Tourism

Tourism is still of limited extent. Tours are organized for party groups visiting China and the ordinary tourist still requires a visa. Western-style hotels exist in Peking, Shanghai, Canton and other large centres.

Sport

Football and basketball are popular in schools and other institutions. Athletics and swimming are encouraged. Chinese table-tennis players are among the world's best.

Public Holidays

1974: August 1st (Army Day), October 1st (National Day).

1975: February 10th–13th (Lunar New Year), May 1st (Labour Day).

Weights and Measures

1 catty (*jin*) = 0.5 kg. or 1.1023 lb.

1 picul (*dan*) = 0.05 metric ton or 0.0492 long ton.

1 *mou* = 0.0667 hectare or 0.1647 acre.

Currency and Exchange Rates

100 fen = 10 chiao = 1 yüan.

Exchange rates (April 1974):

£1 sterling = 4.69 yüan;

U.S. $1 = 1.986 yüan.

STATISTICAL SURVEY

AREA AND POPULATION

AREA ('ooo sq. km.) 1967	TOTAL POPULATION (million)	
	1953 (Census)	1968 (Est.)
9,561.0	582.60	712.00*

* As announced during the "Great Proletarian Cultural Revolution" (1967–68).

Mid-1972 Population: 786,058,000 (United Nations estimate).

PROVINCES AND AUTONOMOUS REGIONS

PROVINCES	LOCATION	AREA ('ooo sq. km.)	POPULATION (million)		CAPITAL OF PROVINCE OR REGION	POPULATION OF CAPITAL 1958 (Est.)
			1953 (Census)	1968 (Est.)*		
PROVINCES:						
Szechwan . . .	SW.	569.0	65.69	70.00	Chengtu	1.13
Shantung . . .	E.	153.3	48.88	57.00	Tsinan	0.88
Honan . . .	C.	167.0	44.22	50.00	Chengchow	0.78
Kiangsu . . .	E.	102.6	41.25	47.00	Nanking	1.45
Hopei . . .	N.	202.7	38.68	47.00†	Tientsin	3.28
Kwangtung . . .	S.	231.4	34.77	40.00	Canton	2.20
Hunan . . .	C.	210.5	33.23	38.00	Changsha	0.71
Anhwei . . .	E.	139.9	30.34	35.00	Hofei	0.36
Hupeh . . .	C.	187.5	27.79	32.00	Wuhan	2.23
Chekiang . . .	E.	101.8	22.87	31.00	Hangchow	0.79
Liaoning . . .	NE.	151.0	23.70	28.00	Shenyang	2.42
Yunnan . . .	SW.	436.2	17.47	23.00	Kunming	0.90
Kiangsi . . .	C.	164.8	16.77	22.00	Nanchang	0.52
Shensi . . .	NW.	195.8	15.88	21.00	Sian	1.37
Heilungkiang . . .	NE.	463.6	11.90	21.00	Harbin	1.59
Shansi . . .	N.	157.1	14.31	18.00	Taiyuan	1.05
Kweichow . . .	SW.	174.0	15.04	17.00	Kweiyang	0.53
Fukien . . .	S.	123.1	13.14	17.00	Foochow	0.62
Kirin . . .	NE.	187.0	11.29	17.00	Changchun	0.99
Kansu . . .	NW.	366.5	11.23	13.00	Lanchow	0.73
Tsinghai . . .	NW.	721.0	1.68	2.00	Hsining	0.15
AUTONOMOUS REGIONS:						
Kwangsi . . .	S.	220.4	19.56	24.00	Nanning	0.26
Inner Mongolia . .	N.	1,177.5	6.10	13.00	Huhehot	0.32
Sinkiang . . .	NW.	1,646.9	4.87	8.00	Urumchi	0.32
Ninghsia . . .	NW.	66.4	1.70	2.00	Yinchuen	0.09
Tibet . . .	W.	1,221.6	1.27	1.30	Lhasa	0.05
SPECIAL MUNICIPALITIES:						
Peking . . .	NE.	7.1	2.77	7.00	—	4.15
Shanghai . . .	E.	5.8	6.20	10.70	—	6.98
TOTAL . .		9,561.0	582.60	712.00		36.85

* As announced during the "Great Proletarian Cultural Revolution" (1967–68).　　　　† Including Tientsin (4.00).

POPULATION BY RACIAL GROUPS
1953 (Census)—million

Han (Chinese)	547.28
Chuang	6.61
Uighur (Turki)	3.64
Hui	3.56
Yi	3.25
Tibetan	2.77
Miao	2.51
Manchu	2.42
Mongolian	1.46
Puyi	1.25
Korean	1.12
Other	6.72
	582.60

TOWNS OVER 1 MILLION INHABITANTS
1958 (Est.)—million

Shanghai	10.82*
Peking	7.57*
Tientsin	3.28†
Shenyang (Mukden) . .	2.42
Wuhan	2.23
Canton	2.20
Chungking	2.16
Harbin	1.59
Lü-ta	1.59
Nanking	1.45
Sian	1.37
Tsingtao	1.14
Chengtu	1.13
Taiyuan	1.05
Fushun	1.02

* Official 1970 estimates.   † 1968: 4.00.

ECONOMIC INDICATORS

	MILLION				
	1952	1957	1958	1965	1970
POPULATION:					
Joint Economic Committee* . . .	570	642	658	750	836
Far East and Australasia . . .	550	600	615	685	750

	1957＝100				
	1952	1957	1958	1965	1970
AGRICULTURAL AND INDUSTRIAL PRODUCTION: .					
Joint Economic Committee (net)* . . .	72	100	116	119	149
Far East and Australasia . . .	75	100	120	120	150

	U.S. $'000 MILLION				
	1952	1957	1958	1965	1970
NATIONAL INCOME:					
Joint Economic Committee* . . .	59	82	95	97	122
Far East and Australasia . . .	40	55	66	70	90

	U.S. $ PER CAPITA				
	1952	1957	1958	1965	1970
NATIONAL INCOME:					
Joint Economic Committee* . . .	104	128	144	129	146
Far East and Australasia . . .	75	90	105	105	120

* U.S. Congress, Joint Economic Committee, *People's Republic of China: An Economic Assessment*. Washington, 1972.

RATES OF ECONOMIC GROWTH

	PER CENT PER YEAR				
	1952–57	1957–65	1965–70	1957–70	1952–70
POPULATION:					
Joint Economic Committee* . . .	2.5	2.0	2.2	2.0	2.2
Far East and Australasia . . .	1.7	1.8	1.8	1.8	1.8
NATIONAL INCOME:					
Joint Economic Committee* . . .	6.8	2.1	4.7	3.2	4.1
Far East and Australasia . . .	6.4	3.2	4.5	3.7	4.3
NATIONAL INCOME (PER CAPITA):					
Joint Economic Committee* . . .	4.3	0.1	2.5	1.1	2.0
Far East and Australasia . . .	4.7	1.4	2.8	2.0	2.5

* U.S. Congress, Joint Economic Committee, *People's Republic of China: An Economic Assessment*, Washington, 1972.

DOMESTIC PRODUCT AND EXPENDITURE

('ooo million yuan of 1952)

	1952 (Est.)	1957 (Est.)	1958 (Est.)	1965 (Est.)	1970 (Est.)
Gross Domestic Product:					
Agriculture	33.5	40.0	45.0	40.0	46.0
Industry, Mining, Construction, Handicraft .	19.0	30.0	40.0	45.0	60.0
Trade, Public Utilities . . .	22.5	30.0	35.0	45.0	54.0
TOTAL	75.0	100.0	120.0	130.0	160.0
Gross Domestic Expenditure:					
Personal Consumption . . .	52.5	65.0	65.0	78.0	95.0
Government Consumption, Communal Services (Communes)	7.5	10.0	25.0	19.5	25.0
Domestic Gross Investment . . .	15.0	25.0	30.0	32.5	40.0
TOTAL	75.0	100.0	120.0	130.0	160.0

AGRICULTURE
AREA HARVESTED
(million ha.)

	1952 (Actual)	1957 (Actual)	1959 (Claim)	1965 (Est.)	1970 (Est.)
Total Grains	112.3	120.9	121.0	120.0	126.0
Rice	28.4	32.2	n.a.	30.0	32.0
Wheat	24.8	27.5	n.a.	26.0	27.5
Other Grains and Pulses .	50.4	50.6	n.a.	52.0	54.0
Potatoes . . .	8.7	10.5	n.a.	12.0	12.5
Soya Beans . . .	11.5	12.6	12.8	9.0	10.0
Cotton	5.5	5.8	6.0	5.0	6.0

PRODUCTION
(million metric tons)

	1952 (Actual)	1957 (Actual)	1959 (Claim)	1965 (Est.)	1970 (Est.)
Total Grains* . . .	154.5	185.0	270.5	185.0	205.0†
Rice	68.5	86.8	n.a.	85.0	97.0
Wheat . . .	18.1	23.7	n.a.	25.0	31.0
Other Grains and Pulses .	51.5	52.6	n.a.	55.0	52.0
Potatoes* .	16.4	21.9	n.a.	20.0	25.0
Soya Beans . . .	9.5	10.0	11.5	8.0	9.0
Cotton . . .	1.3	1.6	2.4	1.6	2.0
Sugar	0.5	0.9	1.2	1.3	1.7
Vegetable Oils .	1.0	1.5	1.7	1.8	2.4

* Grain equivalent (barn yield).
† Chinese claim: 240; Soviet estimate: 205–210; for 1971: Chinese claim: 246; for 1972: 4 per cent less; for 1973: at or slightly above 1971 level.

YIELD
(tons per hectare)

	1952 (Actual)	1957 (Actual)	1959 (Claim)	1965 (Est.)	1970 (Est.)
Total Grains* . . .	1.38	1.53	2.32	1.54	1.63
Rice	2.41	2.70	n.a.	2.83	3.03
Wheat . . .	0.73	0.86	n.a.	0.96	1.13
Other Grains and Pulses .	1.02	1.04	n.a.	1.06	0.96
Potatoes* .	1.86	2.08	n.a.	1.66	2.00
Soya Beans . . .	0.83	0.80	0.90	0.90	0.90
Cotton . . .	0.24	0.28	0.38	0.30	0.35

* Grain equivalent (barn yield).

LIVESTOCK
(million)

	1952 (Actual)	1957 (Actual)	1959 (Claim)	1965 (Est.)	1970 (Est.)
Horses, Donkeys, Mules .	19.6	19.8	20.0	20.0	20.0
Cattle and Buffaloes .	56.6	65.8	65.4	65.0	70.0
Pigs	89.8	145.9	180.0	180.0	200.0
Sheep and Goats . .	61.8	98.6	112.5	100.0	120.0

MINING AND INDUSTRY

COMMODITIES	UNIT	1952 (Actual)	1957 (Actual)	1965 (Est.)	1970* (Est.)	1972 (Est.)
Coal	million tons	66.5	130.7	230.0	255.0	300.0
Iron Ore . . .	,, ,,	4.3	19.4	33.0	45.0	n.a.
Pig Iron . . .	,, ,,	1.9	5.7	15.0	20.0	n.a.
Crude Steel . .	,, ,,	1.3	5.3	11.0	15.0	21.0
Crude Oil . . .	,, ,,	0.4	1.5	9.0	15.0	25.0
Cement . . .	,, ,,	2.9	6.9	10.5	15.0	18.5
Electricity . . .	'ooo million kWh.	7.3	19.3	45.0	65.0	85.0
Fertilizers . . .	million tons†	0.2	0.8	4.5	7.5	10.5
Machine Tools . .	'ooo units	13.7	28.5	57.5	n.a.	n.a.
Salt	million tons	4.9	8.3	12.5	15.0	17.0
Sugar . . .	,, ,,	0.5	0.9	1.3	1.7	2.0
Vegetable Oils .	,, ,,	1.0	1.5	1.8	2.4	2.8
Cotton Yarn . .	,, ,,	0.7	0.8	0.9	1.4	1.7
Cotton Cloth . .	'ooo million metres	4.2	5.0	5.2	7.5	8.0
Paper . . .	million tons	0.6	1.2	1.8	2.5	3.0

* Chinese claims: Coal 300–350, Steel 21.0, Oil 25.6, Fertilizers 17.0, Cotton Cloth 9.0; Soviet estimates: Steel 15–16 Oil 18–19, Fertilizers 10.0, Cotton Cloth 8.0–8.5.
† In terms of nutrients.

FINANCE

Renminbi (RMB or "People's Currency"):

100 fen (cents)=10 chiao (jiao)=1 Jen Min Piao (People's Bank Dollar), usually called a yüan.

Coins: 1, 2 and 5 fen.

Notes: 10, 20 and 50 fen; 1, 2, 5 and 10 yüan.

Exchange rates (April 1974): £1 sterling=4.69 yüan; U.S. $1=1.986 yüan.

100 yüan=£21.32=$50.35.

BUDGET

(1960—million yüan)

REVENUE		EXPENDITURE	
Taxes on Agriculture . . .	3,300	Economic Development	42,910
Taxes on Industry and Commerce .	19,450	Social Services, Culture and Education .	8,620
Other Taxes	1,610	Defence	5,800
Receipts from State Enterprises .	45,300	Administration	3,170
Other	360	Repayment of Loans	1,200
		Aid to Foreign Countries . . .	500
		Credit Funds allotted to Banks . .	5,800
		General Reserve	1,700
		Other	320
TOTAL	70,020	TOTAL	70,020

FIRST FIVE-YEAR PLAN 1953–57

The First Five-Year Plan aimed at raising basic industrial and agricultural production. The Government claim that most targets were fulfilled.

SECOND FIVE-YEAR PLAN 1958–62

This plan was prematurely terminated and for a number of years, there were only annual, if any, plans in existence.

THIRD FIVE-YEAR PLAN 1966–70

The Third Plan, delayed by economic and political difficulties, was put into operation in January 1966. No details have been issued.

FOURTH FIVE-YEAR PLAN 1971–75

It was announced that a Fourth Five-Year Plan started in January 1971. No details have yet been issued but a few output data were released at the end of 1971.

EXTERNAL TRADE

TRADING AREAS

('ooo million U.S. $)

IMPORTS	1957 (Actual)	1965 (Actual)	1970 (Est.)	1971 (Prel.)	1972 (Prel.)
Communist Bloc . .	0.9	0.5	0.4	0.5	0.5
Developing Countries . .	0.2	0.4	0.3	0.1	0.6
Developed Countries* . .	0.2	0.9	1.5	1.4	1.6
TOTAL . . .	1.3	1.8	2.2	2.3	2.7

EXPORTS	1957 (Actual)	1965 (Actual)	1970 (Est.)	1971 (Prel.)	1972 (Prel.)
Communist Bloc . .	1.1	0.7	0.5	0.6	0.7
Developing Countries . .	0.2	0.5	0.5	0.6	0.6
Developed Countries* . .	0.3	0.9	1.1	1.2	1.6
TOTAL . . .	1.6	2.1	2.1	2.4	2.9

* Including Hong Kong.

COMMODITY COMPOSITION
(per cent)

IMPORTS	1957 (Actual)	1965 (Actual)	1970 (Est.)	1971 (Prel.)
Food, Drink, Tobacco .	5	25	15	10
Raw Materials and Chemicals .	35	30	30	35
Manufactured and Semi-Manufactured Goods .	60	45	55	55
TOTAL	100	100	100	100

EXPORTS	1957 (Actual)	1965 (Actual)	1970 (Est.)	1971 (Prel.)
Food, Drink, Tobacco .	30	30	30	30
Raw Materials and Chemicals .	45	35	25	20
Manufactured and Semi-Manufactured Goods .	25	35	45	50
TOTAL	100	100	100	100

PRINCIPAL TRADING PARTNERS
(million U.S. $—based on partner-country statistics)

EXPORTS TO CHINA	1968	1969	1970	1971	1972
Australia	89.5	117.2	146.5	27.2	71.0
Canada	151.2	113.4	135.3	201.7	261.7
Cuba	n.a.	n.a.	n.a.	65.0	55.0
France	87.8	44.4	81.2	112.7	58.1
German Democratic Republic .	37.2	29.9	42.3	44.0	46.0
Germany, Federal Republic .	174.1	157.9	167.2	138.6	165.2
Hong Kong	7.4	6.2	10.6	10.2	18.2
Italy	61.1	56.3	57.0	59.2	77.1
Japan	325.0	390.8	571.7	578.5	609.5
Malaysia and Singapore .	51.0	59.0	50.3	33.6	47.5
Pakistan	22.2	29.6	36.0	30.2	17.5
Poland	24.6	18.6	26.0	37.0	31.0
Sri Lanka	27.0	29.5	43.9	30.3	27.0
U.S.S.R.	59.3	27.8	24.9	78.0	121.0
United Arab Republic . .	16.3	14.6	18.5	26.6	45.0
United Kingdom . .	68.3	130.8	107.0	69.3	78.1
United States . . .	—	—	—	—	60.2

IMPORTS FROM CHINA	1968	1969	1970	1971	1972
Australia	30.6	35.0	41.5	40.9	51.0
France	53.5	76.7	69.8	71.3	104.9
German Democratic Republic .	27.7	33.1	35.7	39.0	46.0
Germany, Federal Republic .	85.3	88.2	84.4	95.4	106.2
Hong Kong . . .	402.0	445.5	467.1	549.6	685.5
Italy	48.0	64.2	63.1	64.3	84.7
Japan	220.0	234.5	253.8	323.3	491.6
Malaysia and Singapore .	193.0	140.0	204.9	199.9	210.5
Pakistan	27.2	25.5	30.0	35.0	24.0
Poland	31.3	23.4	24.0	21.0	58.0
Sri Lanka	34.6	35.5	44.8	27.1	15.0
U.S.S.R.	36.7	29.0	21.7	76.0	134.0
United Arab Republic . .	10.5	13.0	15.0	18.9	25.0
United Kingdom . .	82.3	90.6	80.9	77.2	89.0
United States . . .	—	—	—	4.9	32.2

TRANSPORT

Railways: Freight carried (1959) 542 million tons.

Roads (1959): Freight carried by lorry 344 million tons.

Merchant Shipping Fleet (1965): 550,000 g.r.t.

Inland and Coastal Shipping (1959): Freight carried 121 million tons.

Civil Aviation: Freight (1959) 1,630,000 ton-kilometres.

COMMUNICATIONS MEDIA

Radio Receivers	7 million
Newspapers (daily circ.)	12 million
Cinema Attendance (per year)	4,000 million

EDUCATION
(1959)

	Pupils
Primary Schools	90,000,000
Middle Schools	10,900,000
Higher Education Establishments	810,000

Number of University Graduates (1962): 220,000.

Estimates by W. Klatt.

THE CONSTITUTION

This Constitution was adopted on 20 September 1954 by the First National People's Congress of the People's Republic of China at its first session.

The preamble speaks of the Chinese people's great victory when, in 1949, the People's Republic of China was founded. This new people's democracy is in a state of transition to socialism; the needs of this phase are reflected in the Constitution. The people's democratic united front, led by the Communist Party of China, is directing the transformation of society. China's different nationalities will become more closely united; their varying needs will, however, be respected. The indestructible friendship of China with the U.S.S.R. and the People's Democracies will be strengthened, and the policy of establishing and extending diplomatic relations with all countries on the principle of equality, mutual benefit and respect for each other's sovereignty and territorial integrity continued, with the aim of furthering the cause of world peace and the progress of humanity.

Chapter I. General Principles

Article 1—The People's Republic of China is a people's democratic state led by the working class and based on the alliance of workers and peasants.

Article 2—All power in the People's Republic of China belongs to the people, who exercise their power through the National People's Congress and the local people's congresses.

These and all other organs of state practise democratic centralism.

Article 3—The People's Republic of China is a unified, multi-national state.

All the nationalities are equal, and have freedom to use their own languages, and to practise their own customs

Discrimination against, or oppression of, any nationality, and acts which undermine the unity of the nationalities are prohibited.

Regional autonomy applies in areas entirely or largely inhabited by national minorities. National autonomous areas are inalienable parts of the People's Republic of China.

Article 4—The People's Republic of China, by relying on the organs of state and the social forces, and by means of socialist industrialization and socialist transformation, ensures the gradual abolition of systems of exploitation and the building of a socialist society.

Article 5—The ownership of the means of production today mainly takes the following forms: state ownership, co-operative ownership, ownership by individual working people, and capitalist ownership.

Article 6—State-owned economy is owned by the whole people; it is the leading force in the national economy and the material basis on which the state carries out socialist transformation. The state ensures priority for its development.

All mineral resources and waters, as well as forests, undeveloped land and other resources which the state owns by law, are the property of the whole people.

Article 7—Co-operative economy is either socialist economy collectively owned by the working masses, or semi-socialist economy in part collectively owned by the working masses. Such partial collective ownership is a transitional form by means of which individual peasants, handicraftsmen and other individual working people organize themselves in their advance towards collective ownership by the working masses.

The state protects the property of the co-operatives, and guides their development. It regards producers' co-operatives as the chief means for the transformation of individual farming and individual handicrafts.

Article 8—The state protects peasant ownership of land and other means of production according to law.

The state encourages individual peasants to increase production and to organize producers', supply and marketing, and credit co-operatives voluntarily.

The policy of the state towards rich-peasant economy is to restrict and gradually eliminate it.

Article 9—The state protects the ownership of the means of production by handicraftsmen and other non-agricultural individual working people according to law, and encourages them to improve the management of their affairs and to organize producers', and supply and marketing co-operatives voluntarily.

Article 10—The state protects the ownership by capitalists of the means of production and other capital according to law.

The policy of the state towards capitalist industry and commerce is to use, restrict and transform them. The state makes use of the positive qualities of capitalist industry and commerce which are beneficial to national welfare and the people's livelihood, restricts their negative qualities and guides their transformation into various forms of state-capitalist economy, by means of control exercised by administrative organs of state, the leadership given by state-owned economy, and supervision by the workers.

The state forbids any kind of illegal activity by capitalists which endangers the public interest, disturbs the social-economic order, or undermines the economic plan of the state.

The state protects the right of citizens to ownership of lawful income, of savings, houses and the means of life (*Article* 11), and to inherit private property according to law (*Article* 12).

Article 13—The state may, in the public interest, buy, requisition or nationalize land and other means of production both in cities and countryside according to provisions of law.

Article 14—The state forbids any person to use his private property to the detriment of the public interest.

Article 15—By economic planning, the state directs the growth and transformation of the national economy to bring about the constant increase of productive forces, in this way enriching the material and cultural life of the people and consolidating the independence and security of the country.

Article 16—Work is a matter of honour for every citizen of the People's Republic of China who is able to work. The state encourages initiative and creative activity of citizens in their work.

Article 17—All organs of state must rely on the masses of the people, constantly maintain close contact with them, heed their opinions and accept their supervision.

Article 18—All persons working in organs of state must be loyal to the people's democratic system, observe the Constitution and the law and strive to serve the people.

Article 19—The People's Republic of China safeguards the people's democratic system, and punishes and suppresses all treasonable and counter-revolutionary activities.

The state deprives feudal landlords and bureaucrat-capitalists of political rights for a specific period of time according to law; at the same time it provides them with a way to live, in order to enable them to reform through work and become citizens who earn their livelihood by their own labour.

Article 20—The armed forces of the People's Republic of China belong to the people; their duty is to safeguard the gains of the people's revolution and of national construction, and to defend the sovereignty, territorial integrity and security of the country.

Chapter II. The State Structure

SECTION 1. THE NATIONAL PEOPLE'S CONGRESS

The National People's Congress of the People's Republic of China is the highest organ of state power (*Article* 21), and the only organ exercising the legislative power of the state (*Article* 22).

Article 23—The National People's Congress is composed of deputies elected by provinces, autonomous regions, municipalities directly under the central authority, the armed forces and Chinese resident abroad.

The number of deputies to the National People's Congress, including those representing national minorities, and the manner of their election, are prescribed by electoral law.

Article 24—The National People's Congress is elected for a term of four years.

Two months before the term of office of the National People's Congress expires, its Standing Committee must carry to completion the election of deputies to the next National People's Congress. Should exceptional circumstances arise preventing such an election, the term of office of the sitting National People's Congress may be prolonged until the first session of the next National People's Congress.

Article 25—The National People's Congress meets once a year, convened by its Standing Committee. It may also be convened whenever its Standing Committee deems this necessary or one-fifth of the deputies so propose.

Article 26—When the National People's Congress meets, it elects a presidium to conduct its session.

Article 27—The National People's Congress exercises the following functions and powers:

(1) to amend the Constitution;

(2) to enact laws;

(3) to supervise the enforcement of the Constitution;

(4) to elect the Chairman and the Vice-Chairman of the People's Republic of China;

(5) to decide on the choice of the Premier of the State Council upon recommendation by the Chairman of the People's Republic of China, and of the component members of the State Council upon recommendation by the Premier;

(6) to decide on the choice of the Vice-Chairmen and members of the Council of National Defence upon recommendation by the Chairman of the People's Republic of China;

(7) to elect the President of the Supreme People's Court;

(8) to elect the Chief Procurator of the Supreme People's Procuratorate;

(9) to decide on the national economic plan;

(10) to examine and approve the state budget and the financial report;

(11) to ratify the status and boundaries of provinces, autonomous regions, and municipalities directly under the central authority;

(12) to decide on general amnesties;

(13) to decide on questions of war and peace; and

(14) to exercise such other functions and powers as the National People's Congress considers necessary.

Article 28—The National People's Congress has power to remove from office:

(1) the Chairman and the Vice-Chairman of the People's Republic of China;

(2) the Premier and Vice-Premiers, Ministers, Heads of Commissions and the Secretary-General of the State Council;

(3) the Vice-Chairmen and members of the Council of National Defence;

(4) the President of the Supreme People's Court;

(5) the Chief Procurator of the Supreme People's Procuratorate.

Article 29—Amendments to the Constitution require a two-thirds majority vote, and laws and other bills a majority vote, of all the deputies.

Article 30—The Standing Committee is the permanent body of the Congress. It is composed of the Chairman, the Vice-Chairmen, the Secretary-General and members, all elected by the Congress.

Article 31—The Standing Committee exercises the following functions and powers:

(1) to conduct the election of deputies to the National People's Congress;

(2) to convene the National People's Congress;

(3) to interpret the laws;

(4) to adopt decrees;

(5) to supervise the work of the State Council, the Supreme People's Court and the Supreme People's Procuratorate;

(6) to annul decisions and orders of the State Council where these contravene the Constitution, laws or decrees;

(7) to revise or annul inappropriate decisions of organs of state power of provinces, autonomous regions, and municipalities directly under the central authority;

(8) to decide on the appointment or removal of any Vice-Premier, Minister, Head of Commission or the Secretary-General of the State Council when the National People's Congress is not in session;

(9) to appoint or remove the Vice-Presidents, judges, and members of the Judicial Committee of the Supreme People's Court;

(10) to appoint or remove the Deputy Chief Procurators, procurators and members of the Procuratorial Committee of the Supreme People's Procuratorate;

(11) to decide on the appointment or recall of plenipotentiary envoys to foreign states;

(12) to decide on the ratification or abrogation of treaties concluded with foreign states;

(13) to institute military, diplomatic and other special titles and ranks;

(14) to institute and decide on the award of state orders, medals and titles of honour;

(15) to decide on the granting of pardons;

(16) to decide, when the National People's Congress is not in session, on the proclamation of a state of war in the event of armed attack against the state or in fulfilment of international treaty obligations concerning common defence against aggression;

(17) to decide on general or partial mobilization;

(18) to decide on the enforcement of martial law throughout the country or in certain areas; and

(19) to exercise such other functions and powers as are vested in it by the National People's Congress.

Article 32—The Standing Committee exercises its functions and powers until the next National People's Congress elects a new Standing Committee.

Article 33—The Standing Committee is responsible to the National People's Congress and reports to it; the Congress has power to recall Committee members.

Article 34—The Congress establishes a Nationalities Committee, a Bills Committee, a Budget Committee, a Credentials Committee and other necessary committees.

The Nationalities and Bills Committees are under the direction of the Standing Committee when the Congress is not in session.

Article 35—Investigation committees may be constituted to enquire into specific questions when the Congress, or its Standing Committee if the Congress is not in session, deems it necessary.

All organs of state, people's organizations and citizens concerned are obliged to supply necessary information to these committees.

Article 36—Deputies to the National People's Congress have the right to address questions to the State Council, or to the Ministries and Commissions of the State Council, which are under obligation to answer.

Article 37—No deputy may be arrested or placed on trial without permission of the Congress or, when it is not in session, of its Standing Committee.

Article 38—Deputies are subject to the supervision of the units which elect them. These electoral units have power to replace at any time the deputies they elect, according to the procedure prescribed by law.

Section 2. The Chairman of the People's Republic of China

Article 39—The Chairman of the People's Republic of China is elected by the National People's Congress. Any citizen of the People's Republic of China who has the right to vote and stand for election and has reached the age of thirty-five is eligible for election as Chairman of the People's Republic of China.

The Chairman's term of office is four years.

Article 40—The Chairman, in accordance with decisions of the National People's Congress or its Standing Committee, promulgates laws and decrees; appoints or removes the Premier, Vice-Premiers, Ministers, Heads of Commissions, the Secretary-General of the State Council, and the Vice-Chairmen and members of the Council of National Defence; confers state orders, medals and titles of honour; proclaims general amnesties and grants pardons; proclaims martial law; proclaims a state of war; and orders mobilization.

Article 41—The Chairman represents the People's Republic of China in its relations with foreign states, receives foreign envoys and, in accordance with decisions of the Standing Committee of the National People's Congress, appoints or recalls plenipotentiary envoys to foreign states and ratifies treaties.

Article 42—The Chairman commands the armed forces of the country, and is Chairman of the Council of National Defence.

Article 43—The Chairman convenes a Supreme State Conference, in which the Vice-Chairman of the Republic, the Chairman of the Standing Committee of the National People's Congress, the Premier of the State Council and other persons concerned take part, whenever necessary and acts as its chairman.

He submits its views to the National People's Congress, its Standing Committee, the State Council, or other bodies concerned for their consideration and decision.

Article 44—The Vice-Chairman of the People's Republic of China exercises such functions and powers of the Chairman as the Chairman may entrust to him.

The provisions governing the election and term of office of the Chairman of the Republic apply also to the Vice-Chairman (*see Article* 39).

Article 45—The Chairman and the Vice-Chairman of the Republic of China exercise their functions and powers until the new Chairman and Vice-Chairman elected by the next National People's Congress take office.

Article 46—Should the Chairman for reasons of health be unable to perform his duties over a long period, the Vice-Chairman exercises the functions and powers of Chairman on his behalf.

Should the office of Chairman fall vacant, the Vice-Chairman succeeds to it.

Section 3. The State Council

Article 47—The State Council of the People's Republic of China, that is, the Central People's Government, is the executive of the highest organ of state power and the highest administrative organ of state.

Article 48—The State Council is composed of the Premier, the Vice-Premiers, the Ministers, the Heads of Commissions and the Secretary-General; its organization is determined by law.

Article 49—The State Council exercises the following functions and powers:

(1) to formulate administrative measures, issue decisions and orders and verify their execution, in accordance with the Constitution, laws and decrees;

(2) to submit bills to the National People's Congress or its Standing Committee;

(3) to co-ordinate and lead the work of Ministries and Commissions;

(4) to co-ordinate and lead the work of local administrative organs of state throughout the country;

(5) to revise or annul inappropriate orders and directives of Ministers or of Heads of Commissions;

(6) to revise or annul inappropriate decisions and orders of local administrative organs of state;

(7) to put into effect the national economic plan and provisions of the state budget;

(8) to control foreign and domestic trade;

(9) to direct cultural, educational and public health work;

(10) to administer affairs concerning the nationalities;

(11) to administer affairs concerning Chinese resident abroad;

(12) to protect the interests of the state, to maintain public order and to safeguard the rights of citizens;

(13) to direct the conduct of external affairs;

(14) to guide the building up of the defence forces;

(15) to ratify the status and boundaries of autonomous *chou*, counties, autonomous counties, and municipalities;

(16) to appoint or remove administrative personnel according to provisions of law; and

(17) to exercise such other functions and powers as are vested in it by the National People's Congress or its Standing Committee.

Article 50—The Premier, assisted by the Vice-Premiers, directs the work of the State Council and presides over its meetings.

Article 51—The Ministers and Heads of Commissions direct the work of their respective departments, and may issue orders and directives within their jurisdiction.

Article 52—The State Council is responsible to the National People's Congress and reports to it, or, when it is out of session, to its Standing Committee.

SECTIONS 4 and 5. THE LOCAL PEOPLE'S CONGRESSES AND LOCAL PEOPLE'S COUNCILS

Article 53—The administrative division of the People's Republic of China is as follows:

(1) the country is divided into provinces, autonomous regions, and municipalities directly under the central authority;

(2) provinces and autonomous regions are divided into autonomous *chou*, counties, autonomous counties, and municipalities;

(3) counties and autonomous counties are divided into *hsiang*, nationality *hsiang*, and towns.

Municipalities directly under the central authority and other large municipalities are divided into districts. Autonomous *chou* are divided into counties, autonomous counties, and municipalities.

Autonomous regions, autonomous *chou* and autonomous counties are all national autonomous areas.

Article 54—People's congresses and people's councils are established in provinces, municipalities directly under the central authority, counties, municipalities, municipal districts, *hsiang*, nationality *hsiang*, and towns. Organs of self-government are established in autonomous regions, autonomous *chou* and autonomous counties.

Articles 55–61 detail the organization and functions of local people's congresses.

Articles 62–66 detail the organization and functions of local people's councils.

Articles 67–70 detail the organization and functions of organs of self-government in autonomous areas.

Article 71—In performing their duties, organs of self-government of all autonomous regions, autonomous *chou* and autonomous counties employ the spoken and written language or languages commonly used by the nationality or nationalities in a given area.

Article 72—The higher organs of state should fully safeguard the right of organs of self-government of all autonomous regions, autonomous *chou* and autonomous counties to exercise autonomy, and should assist the various national minorities in their political, economic and cultural development.

SECTION 6. THE PEOPLE'S COURTS AND THE PEOPLE'S PROCURATORATE

This section, consisting of *Articles* 73–84, is summarized under the heading "Judicial System" (*see below*).

Chapter III. Fundamental Rights and Duties of Citizens

Article 85—Citizens of the People's Republic of China are equal before the law.

Article 86—Citizens who have reached the age of eighteen have the right to vote and stand for election whatever their nationality, race, sex, occupation, social origin, religious belief, education, property status, or length of residence, except insane persons and persons deprived by law of the right to vote and stand for election.

Women have equal rights with men to vote and stand for election.

Article 87—Citizens have freedom of speech, of the press, of assembly, of association, of procession and of demonstration. By providing the necessary material facilities, the state guarantees to citizens enjoyment of these freedoms.

Article 88—Citizens have freedom of religious belief.

Article 89—Freedom of the person of citizens is inviolable. No citizen may be arrested except by decision of a people's court or with the sanction of a people's procuratorate.

Article 90—The homes of citizens are inviolable, and privacy of correspondence is protected by law.

Citizens have freedom of residence and freedom to change their residence.

Article 91—Citizens have the right to work. To guarantee enjoyment of this right, the state, by planned development of the national economy, gradually creates more employment, and better working conditions and wages.

Article 92—Working people in the Republic have the right to rest and leisure. To guarantee enjoyment of this right, the state prescribes working hours and holidays for workers and office employees; at the same time it gradually expands material facilities to enable working people to rest and build up their health.

Article 93—Working people have the right to material assistance in old age, illness or disability. To guarantee enjoyment of this right, the state provides social insurance, social assistance and public health services and gradually expands these facilities.

Article 94—Citizens have the right to education. To guarantee enjoyment of this right, the state establishes and gradually extends the various types of schools and other cultural and educational institutions, paying special attention to the physical and mental development of young people.

Article 95—The People's Republic of China safeguards the freedom of citizens to engage in scientific research, literary and artistic creation and other cultural activity, and encourages those engaged in creative work.

Article 96—Women enjoy equal rights with men in all spheres—political, economic, cultural, social and domestic.

The state protects marriage, the family, and the mother and child.

Article 97—Citizens have the right to bring complaints against any person working in organs of state for transgression of law or neglect of duty by making a written or verbal statement to any organ of state at any level. People suffering loss by reason of infringement by persons working in organs of state of their rights as citizens have the right to compensation.

Article 98—The People's Republic of China protects the proper rights and interests of Chinese resident abroad.

Article 99—The People's Republic of China grants the right of asylum to any foreign national persecuted for supporting a just cause, taking part in the peace movement or engaging in scientific activity.

Article 100—Citizens must abide by the Constitution and the law, uphold discipline at work, keep public order and respect social ethics.

Article 101—The public property of the People's Republic of China is sacred and inviolable. It is the duty of every citizen to respect and protect public property.

Article 102—It is the duty of citizens to pay taxes according to law.

Article 103—It is the sacred duty of every citizen to defend the homeland.

It is the honourable duty of citizens to perform military service according to law.

Chapter IV. National Flag, State Emblem, Capital

Article 104—The national flag of the People's Republic of China is a red flag with five stars.

Article 105—The state emblem is: in the centre, Tien An Men under the light of five stars, framed with ears of grain, and with a cogwheel at the base.

Article 106—The capital of the People's Republic of China is Peking.

THE GOVERNMENT

(*April* 1974)

HEAD OF STATE

Chairman of the People's Republic of China: TUNG PI-WU (Acting Chairman).

Vice-Chairman: SOONG CHING-LING (Mme SUN YAT-SEN).

STATE COUNCIL

Premier: CHOU EN-LAI.

Vice-Premiers: LI FU-CU'UN, LI HSIEN-NIEN, Marshal NIEH JUNG-CHENG, CH'EN YUN, TENG HSIAO-PING.

MINISTRIES OF THE STATE COUNCIL

Ministry of Foreign Affairs: Minister CHI PENG-FEI.

Ministry of National Defence: Acting Minister Marshal YEH CHIEN-YING.

Ministry of Public Security: Minister LI CHEN.

Ministry of Finance: Minister LI HSIEN NIEN.

Ministry of Commerce: Minister FAN TZU-YU.

Ministry of Foreign Trade: Minister LI CH'IANG.

Ministry of Economic Relations with Foreign Countries: Minister FANG YI.

Ministry of Metallurgical Industry: Minister CH'EN SHAO-K'UN.

Ministry of Fuel and Chemical Industries: Minister HSU CHIN-CHIANG.

First Ministry of Machine Building: Minister LI SHUI-CHING.

Second Ministry of Machine Building.*

Ministry of Building Construction: Minister LAI CHI-FA.

Ministry of Light Industry: Minister CH'IEN CHIH-KUANG.

Ministry of Communications: Minister YANG CHIEH.

Ministry of Agriculture and Forestry: Minister SHA FENG.

Ministry of Water Conservancy and Electric Power: Minister CHANG WEN-PI.

Ministry of Public Health: Minister LIU HSIANG-PIN.

* Believed to have been amalgamated with the First Ministry.

COMMISSIONS OF THE STATE COUNCIL

State Planning Commission: Minister YU CHIU-LI.

State Capital Construction Commission: Minister KU MU.

Physical Culture and Sports Commission: Minister WANG MENG.

SPECIAL AGENCIES OF THE STATE COUNCIL

The People's Bank of China: President (vacant).

Central Meteorological Bureau: Director MENG PING.

State Oceanography Bureau: Director CHOU SHAO-T'ANG.

Civil Aviation Administration of China (CAAC): Director KUANG JEN-NUNG.

New China News Agency: Director CHU MU-CHIH.

Central Broadcasting Administration: Director-General MEI YI.

China Travel and Tourism Bureau: Deputy Director LI CH'UAN-CHUNG.

Cultural Group: Head WU TEH.

Foreign Affairs Bureau: Acting Director LI PO-SHIH.

Government Officers' Administration Bureau: Director KAO TENG-PANG.

Publishing Department: Directors LIU MEI, WANG CHI-SHENG.

Scientific and Education Group: Head LIU HSI-YAO.

Supervisory and Guidance Group for Libraries, Museums and Work on Cultural Relics: Acting Director WANG YEH-CHIU.

Staff Office: Acting Director TING CHIANG.

Telecommunications Administration: Director CHUNG FU HSIANG.

FOREIGN ECONOMIC RELATIONS ADMINISTRATION SUBORDINATED TO THE STATE COUNCIL

Staff Office for Finance and Trade

China Committee for the Promotion of International Trade

National Committee for the Promotion of International Trade

Ministry of Foreign Trade

National Corporations (Export and Import)

Diplomatic Missions

Trade Missions

People's Bank of China

Bank of China

Foreign Economic Relations Commission

Foreign Aid and Technical Assistance Missions

DIPLOMATIC REPRESENTATION

EMBASSIES ACCREDITED TO THE PEOPLE'S REPUBLIC OF CHINA
(All in Peking)

Afghanistan: *Ambassador:* MOHAMED ASSAF SOHAIL.

Albania: *Ambassador:* BEHAR SHTYLLA.

Algeria: *Ambassador:* MOHAMED CHERIF SAHLI.

Argentina: *Ambassador:* Dr. EDUARDO BRADLEY.

Australia: *Ambassador:* Dr. STEPHEN FITZGERALD.

Austria: *Ambassador:* FRANZ H. LEITNER.

Belgium: *Ambassador:* JACQUES GROOTHAERT.

Bulgaria: *Chargé d'Affaires a.i.*

Burma: *Chargé d'Affaires a.i.*

Cameroon: *Ambassador:* CLEMENT LANGUE TOOBGNY.

Canada: *Ambassador:* RALPH EDGAR COLLINS.

Chad: *Chargé d'Affaires a.i.*

Congo (Brazzaville): *Ambassador:* CLAUDE-EARNEST NDALLA.

Cuba: *Chargé d'Affaires a.i.*

Cyprus: *Chargé d'Affaires a.i.*

Czechoslovakia: *Ambassador:* STANISLAV KOHOUSEK.

Dahomey: *Chargé d'Affaires a.i.*

Denmark: *Ambassador:* U. S. HANSEN.

Egypt: *Ambassador:* SALAH EL DEN A. EL ABD.

Equatorial Guinea: *Chargé d'Affaires a.i.*

Ethiopia: *Chargé d'Affaires a.i.*

Finland: *Ambassador:* VELI HELENIUS.

France: *Ambassador:* ETIENNE MANAC'H.

German Democratic Republic: *Ambassador:* JOHANN WITTIK.

Germany, Federal Republic: *Ambassador:* ROLF PAULS.

Greece: *Chargé d'Affaires a.i.*

Guinea: *Ambassador:* KAMANA ANSOU.

Guyana: *Ambassador:* (to be appointed).

Hungary: *Ambassador:* JÓZSEF HALASZ.

Iceland: *Chargé d'Affaires a.i.*

India: *Chargé d'Affaires a.i.:* BRAJESH MISHRA.

Iran: *Chargé d'Affairs a.i.*

Iraq: *Chargé d'Affaires a.i.:* OTHMAN HUSSEIN AL-ANI.

Italy: *Ambassador:* FOLCO TRABALZA.

Jamaica: *Chargé d'Affaires a.i.*

Japan: *Ambassador:* HEISHIRO OGAWA.

Korea, Democratic People's Republic: *Ambassador:* HYON CHUN-KUK.

Kuwait: *Chargé d'Affaires a.i.*

Laos: *Chargé d'Affaires a.i.*

Lebanon: *Chargé d'Affaires a.i.*

Madagascar: *Chargé d'Affaires a.i.*

Maldives: *Chargé d'Affaires a.i.*

Mali: *Ambassador:* ASSANE GUINDO.

Malta: *Chargé d'Affaires a.i.*

Mauritius: *Chargé d'Affaires a.i.*

Mauritania: *Ambassador:* MOHAMED A. O. KHARACHY.

Mexico: *Ambassador:* EUGENIO A. ROCH.

Mongolia: *Ambassador:* DONDOGIYN TSEVEGMID.

Morocco: *Ambassador:* ABDELLATIF LAKHMIRI.

Nepal: 27 Kan Mein Hutung; *Ambassador:* CHELTRA BIKRAM RAMA.

Netherlands: 2 San Li Tun; *Ambassador:* J. J. DERKSEN.

New Zealand: *Chargé d'Affaires a.i.*

Nigeria: *Ambassador:* Alhaji MOHAMMAD SANSUI.

Norway: *Ambassador:* OLE AALGAARD.

Pakistan: 16 San Li Tun; *Ambassador:* Khwaja MOHAMMAD KAISER.

Peru: *Chargé d'Affaires a.i.*

Poland: *Ambassador:* WITOLD RODZINSKY.

Qatar: *Chargé d'Affaires a.i.*

Romania: *Ambassador:* AUREL DUMA.

Senegal: *Ambassador:* ALY DIOURI.

Sierra Leone: *Chargé d'Affaires a.i.*

Spain: *Ambassador:* ANGEL SANZ BRIZ.

Sri Lanka: *Ambassador:* D. B. R. GUNAWARDENA.

Sudan: *Ambassador:* FAKREDDINE MOHAMED.

Sweden: *Ambassador:* BERNT ARNE BJÖRNBERG.

Switzerland: *Ambassador:* OSCAR ROSETTI.

Syria: *Ambassador:* YOUSSEF CHAKRA.

Tanzania: *Ambassador:* SALIM AHMED SALIM.

Togo: *Chargé d'Affaires a.i.*

Turkey: *Chargé d'Affaires a.i.*

Uganda: *Chargé d'Affaires a.i.*

U.S.S.R.: *Ambassador:* VASILY TOLSTIKOV.

United Kingdom: *Ambassador:* EDWARD YOUDE.

Viet-Nam, Democratic Republic: *Ambassador:* NGO THUYEN.

Viet-Nam, Provisional Revolutionary Government of the Republic of South: *Chargé d'Affaires:* TRAN BINH.

Yemen Arab Republic: *Ambassador:* ABDOL WAHED AL-KHERBASH.

Yemen, People's Democratic Republic: *Chargé d'Affaires a.i.:* ABDULLA ABODAH HAMAM.

Yugoslavia: *Ambassador:* A. ORESCHANIN.

Zaire: *Ambassador:* ANREA SYLVESTER MASIYE.

Zambia: *Ambassador:* PHILEMON NGOMA.

Relations with the Khmer Republic are suspended. Consular relations have been established with San Marino and Luxembourg. On May 6th, 1973, the U.S. liaison office in Peking was formally opened, headed by DAVID BRUCE, preparatory to the establishment of diplomatic relations.

NATIONAL PEOPLE'S CONGRESS

The highest organ of State power composed of 3,040 deputies elected for a term of four years. The Congress amends the Constitution, enacts laws, and elects the Chairman and Vice-Chairman of the People's Republic. It also decides on the national economic plan and approves the State budget. In 1966 the Standing Committee of the N.P.C. was suspended. In September 1970 it was announced that the N.P.C. was to be reconvened to draft a new state constitution, elect a new Head of State and other prominent party and government officials.

STANDING COMMITTEE

Chairman: CHU TEH.

Vice-Chairmen: KUO MO-JO, KANG SHENG, HSU HSIANG-CH'IEN, NGAPO NGAWANG JIGME, CHOU CHIEN-JEN, SAI SUDIN, LIU PO-CH'ENG.

Secretary-General: LIU NING-YI.

There are 60 members of the Standing Committee.

NATIONALITIES COMMITTEE

Chairman: HSIEH FU-MIN.

Vice-Chairmen: BURHAN, K'UEI PI, CHANG CH'UNG, SANG-CHI-YUEH-HSI, CHU TE-HAI, MA YU-HUAI, SHIH P'ANG-CHIH, T'IEH-MU-ERH-TA-WA-MAI-T'I, T'IEN PAO.

BILLS COMMITTEE

Chairman: CHANG SU.

Vice-Chairmen: WU HSIN-YU, CHOU KENG-SHENG, CHANG YU-YU, CHAO PO-P'ING.

BUDGET COMMITTEE

Chairman: KU MU.

Vice-Chairmen: WANG SHAO-AO, HSUEH MU-CH'IAO.

CREDENTIALS COMMITTEE

Chairman: MA MING-FANG.

Vice-Chairmen: WANG WEI-CHOU, CH'E HSIANG-CH'EN, CHU YUN-SHAN, CH'IEN YING.

CHINESE PEOPLE'S POLITICAL CONSULTATIVE CONFERENCE

Hon. Chairman: MAO TSE-TUNG.

Chairman: CHOU EN-LAI.

Vice-Chairmen: FU TSO-YI, HSU TEH-HENG, TENG TAI-YUAN, LI SZU-KUANG, SHEN YEN-PING, TENG TZU-HUI,

TSAI YING-KAI, WEI KUO-CHING, YEH CHIEN-YING.

The C.P.P.C.C. meets annually to discuss and endorse party policy. It is a united body with consultative functions but no power to legislate.

PROVINCIAL GOVERNMENTS

REVOLUTIONARY COMMITTEES

Revolutionary Committees were established to administer each of the 29 provinces, special municipalities and autonomous regions during the "Great Proletarian Cultural Revolution".

Provinces	Chairman of Committee	Date of Formation
Szechwan	LIU HSING-YUAN.	31 May 1968
Shantung	YANG TEH-CHIH	23 Feb. 1967
Honan	LIU CHIEN-HSUN	27 Jan. 1968
Kiangsu	HSU SHIH-YU	23 March 1968
Hopei	LIU TZU-HOU	3 Feb. 1968
Kwangtung	TING SHENG	21 Feb. 1968
Hunan	HUA KUO-FENG	8 April 1968
Anhwei	LI TE-SHENG	18 April 1968
Hupeh	TSENG SSU-YU	5 Feb. 1968
Chekiang	NAN PING	24 March 1968
Liaoning	CHEN HSI-LIEN	10 May 1968
Yunnan	CHOU HSING	13 Aug. 1968
Kiangsi	CHENG SHIH-CHING	5 Jan. 1968
Shensi	LI JUI-SHAN	1 May 1968
Kweichow	LI TSAI-HAN	13 Feb. 1967
Shansi	HSIEH CH'EN-HUA	18 March 1967
Heilungkiang	WANG CHIA-TAO	31 Jan. 1967
Fukien	HAN HSIEN-CH'U	19 Aug. 1968
Kansu	HSIEN HENG-HAN	24 Jan. 1968
Kirin	WANG HUAI-HSIANG	6 March 1968
Tsinghai	LIU HSIEN-CHUAN	12 Aug. 1967

Special Municipalities		
Peking	WU TE	20 April 1967
Shanghai	CHANG CH'UN-CH'IAO	24 Feb. 1967
Tientsin	HSIEH HSUEH-KUNG	6 Dec. 1967

Autonomous Regions		
Mongolia (Inner)	YU TAI-CHUNG	1 Nov. 1967
Sinkiang	SAIFUDIN	5 Sept. 1968
Ninghsia Hui	K'ANG CHIEN-MIN	10 April 1968
Tibet	JEN JUNG	5 Sept. 1968
Kwangsi	WEI KUO-CH'ING	26 Aug. 1968

COMMUNIST PARTY

Lays down the ideological basis of all nationally-directed activities. The last published membership figure was 17 million in 1961. The Tenth National Congress of the Party was held in August 1973.

TENTH CENTRAL COMMITTEE

Chairman: MAO TSE-TUNG.

Vice-Chairmen: CHOU EN-LAI, WANG HUNG-WEN, KANG SHENG, Marshal YEH CHIEN-YING, Gen. LI TEH-SHENG.

There are 309 Members and Alternate Members of the Tenth Central Committee.

POLITBURO

Members of the Standing Committee: MAO TSE-TUNG, WANG HUNG-WEN, YEH CHIEN-YING, CHU TEH, LI TEH-SHENG, CHANG CHUN-CHIAO, CHOU EN-LAI, KANG SHENG, TUNG PI-WU.

Other Full Members: LIU PO-CHENG, CHIANG CHING, HSU SHIH-YU, HUA KUO-FENG, CHI TENG-KUEI, WU TEH, WANG TUNG-HSING, CHEN YUNG-KUEI, CHEN HSI-LIEN, LI HSIEN-NIEN, YAO WEN-YUAN.

Alternate Members: WU KUEI-HSIEN, SU CHEN-HUA, NI CHI-FU, SAIFUDIN.

Young Communist League: Peking.

OTHER POLITICAL BODIES

Kuomintang Revolutionary Committee: Chair. HO HSIANG-NING.

China Democratic League.

China Democratic National Constructional Association.

China Association for Promoting Democracy: Chair. MA HSU-LUN.

China Peasants and Workers' Democratic Party: Chair. CHI FANG.

China Chih Kung Tang: Chair. CH'EN CH'I-YU.

Chiu San Society: Chair. HSU TE-HENG.

Taiwan Democratic Self-Government League: Vice-Chairman LI CH'UN-CH'ING.

PROVINCIAL PARTY COMMITTEES

Since November 1970, 29 new provincial party committees have been established; the previous party structure was destroyed during the "Great Proletarian Cultural Revolution". The following have been formed:

Province	First Secretary	Date of Formation
Hunan	HUA KUO-FENG	4 Nov. 1970
Kiangsu	HSU SHIH-YU	26 Dec. 1970
Kwangtung	TING SHENG	26 Dec. 1970
Liaoning	CHEN HSI-LIEN	13 Jan. 1971
Anhwei	LI TEH-SHENG	21 Jan. 1971
Chekiang	T'AN CH'I-LUNG	28 Jan. 1971
Kansu	HSIEN HENG-HAN	17 Feb. 1971
Honan	LIU CHIEN-HSUN	3 March 1971
Shensi	LI JUI-SHAN	5 March 1971
Tsinghai	LIU HSIEN-CHUAN	11 March 1971
Kirin	WANG HUAI-HSIANG	24 March 1971
Hupeh	TSENG SSU-YU	28 March 1971
Fukien	HAN HSIEN-CH'U	3 April 1971
Shantung	YANG TEH-CHIH	5 April 1971
Shansi	HSIEH CH'EN-HUA	11 April 1971
Kweichow	LU JUI-LIN	14 May 1971
Hopei	LIU TZU-HOU	20 May 1971
Yunnan	CHOU HSING	3 June 1971
Szechwan	LIU HSING-YUAN	16 Aug. 1971
Heilungkiang (Manchuria)	WANG CHIA-TAO	19 Aug. 1971
Kiangsi	CHENG SHIH-CHING	26 Dec. 1970
Special Municipalities		
Shanghai	CHANG CHUN-CHIAO	10 Jan. 1971
Peking	WU TE	15 March 1971
Tientsin	HSIEH HSUEH-KUNG	26 May 1971
Autonomous Regions		
Sinkiang	SAIFUDIN	11 May 1971
Mongolia (Inner)	YU TAI-CHUNG	18 May 1971
Tibet	JEN JUNG	12 Aug. 1971
Ninghsia Hui	K'ANG CHIEN-MIN	18 Aug. 1971
Kwangsi	WEI KUO-CH'ING	16 Feb. 1971

Note: Of the eighty-six leading members of the newly-established Provincial Party Committees, sixty-three (73 per cent) were members of Revolutionary Committees and sixty-nine (80 per cent) were members of the armed forces.

JUDICIAL SYSTEM

PEOPLE'S COURTS

Supreme People's Court: Peking; f. 1949; the highest judicial organ of the State. Directs and supervises work of lower courts.

President of the Supreme People's Court: YANG HSIU-FENG; term of office four years.

Vice-Presidents: HO LAN-CHIEH, HSING YI-MIN, TSENG HAN-CHOU, WANG-TEH-MAO, CHANG CHIH-JANG, CH'EN CHI-HAN, WANG WEI-KANG, WU TE-FENG, T'AN KUAN-SAN.

Special People's Courts.

Local People's Courts.

PEOPLE'S PROCURATORATES

Supreme People's Procuratorate: Peking; acts for the National People's Congress in examining government departments, civil servants and citizens, to ensure observance of the law; prosecutes in criminal cases.

Chief Procurator: CHANG TING-CHENG elected by N.P.C. for four years.

Deputy Chief Procurators: HUANG HUO-HSING, CHANG SU.

Local People's Procuratorates: undertake the same duties at the local level. Ensure that the judicial activities of the people's courts, the execution of sentences in criminal cases, and the activities of departments in charge of reform through labour, conform to the law; institutes, or intervenes in, important civil cases which affect the interest of the State and the people.

Note: Since the Cultural Revolution, Courts have had their jurisdiction virtually confined to reviewing serious criminal cases. There has been a corresponding tendency to revert to extra-judicial institutions especially at the local level; these are of two main types, "Street Revolutionary Committees" and "Peoples Communes". They settle the vast majority of inter-personal disputes and impose sanctions against people whose misbehaviour is not sufficiently serious to trouble the judicial organs. The advantages offered by these institutions are that they provide an inexpensive and speedy means of resolving disputes by enabling local groups to manage their affairs while also acting as a channel for the inculcation of legal norms and moral values.

RELIGION

ANCESTOR WORSHIP

Ancestor worship is believed to have originated with the deification and worship of all important natural phenomena. The divine and human were not clearly defined; all the dead became gods and were worshipped by their descendants. The practice has no code or dogma and the ritual is limited to sacrifices made during festivals and on birth and death anniversaries.

CONFUCIANISM

Confucianism is a philosophy and a system of ethics, without ritual or priesthood. The respects accorded Confucius are not paid to a prophet or god, but to a great sage whose teachings promote peace and good order in society and whose philosophy encourages moral living.

TAOISM

China Taoist Association: Peking; Chair. Ch'en Ying-ning.

Taoism originated as a philosophy expounded by Lao Tse, born 604 B.C. The establishment of a religion was contrary to his doctrines, but seven centuries after his death his teachings were embodied into a ritual.

BUDDHISM

Chinese Buddhist Association: f. 1953; Pres. Shirob-jaltso; Sec.-Gen. Chao P'u-ch'u.

Buddhism was introduced in China from India in A.D. 61, and now bears little resemblance to the religion in its original form, a number of native Chinese legends, traditions, rites and deities having been added. It is estimated that the present number of Buddhist temples in China is 50,000 with 500,000 monks and nuns.

ISLAM

China Islamic Association: Peking; f. 1953; Chair. Burhan Shahidi.

According to Muslim history, Islam was introduced into China in A.D. 651. Its number of adherents in China is estimated at about 10 million, chiefly among the Uighur and Hui people.

CHRISTIANITY

During the 19th century and the first half of the 20th large numbers of foreign Christian missionaries worked in China. The Chinese People's Republic has steadily discouraged all foreign influences in Chinese religious affairs.

THE PRESS

Only the major newspapers and periodicals are listed below and only a very restricted number are allowed abroad.

PRINCIPAL DAILIES

Kwangming Ribao (*Kwangming Daily*): Peking; f. 1949.

Liberation Army Daily (*Jiefangjun Bao*): Peking; official organ of the P.L.A.

Liberation Daily (*Jiefang Ribao*): Shanghai; f. 1949.

Peking Daily (*Beijing Ribao*): Peking.

People's Daily (*Renmin Ribao*): Peking; f. 1948; organ of the Communist Party of China; 200 staff including 70 foreign affairs specialists; Editor Yao Wen-yuan; circ. 3,400,000.

Wen Hui Pao: Shanghai.

PERIODICALS

China Pictorial: Peking; monthly; published in 16 languages, including English.

China Reconstructs: China Welfare Institute, Peking; monthly; economic, social and cultural affairs; illustrated; English, Spanish, French, Russian and Arabic.

Chinese Literature: Peking; monthly; English translations of contemporary and classical Chinese literature.

Peking Review: Peking; weekly.

Red Flag (*Hung Chi*): monthly; official organ of the Chinese Communist Party; Editor (vacant).

NEWS AGENCY

Hsinhua (New China) News Agency: Peking; f. 1937; offices in all large Chinese towns and some foreign capitals; Dir. Chu Mu-chih.

China News Service: Peking; a subsidiary of Hsinhua News Agency; mainly directed to overseas Chinese newspapers and magazines.

Foreign Bureaux

Bulgarian Telegraph Agency (BTA): Bulgarian Embassy, Peking; Bureau Chief Yordan Bozhilov.

The following are also represented: Agence France-Presse, Czechoslovak News Agency (Četeka), Reuters and Tass.

PUBLISHERS

Publishing is carried on by central and local government departments, universities, scientific and learned societies, trade unions and cultural bodies, as well as by state and private publishing houses. All publishing is controlled by the Propaganda Department of the Party Central Committee.

Publishing Department: Peking; special agency of the State Council; undertakes the major part of book publishing in China.

China Youth Publishing House: Peking; f. 1953; books and periodicals.

Chung Hua Book Co.: Peking; state publishers; specializes in Chinese classics.

Commercial Press: Peking; state publishers; specializes in translation of foreign books on philosophy and social sciences.

Foreign Languages Press: Peking 37; state publishing house; publishes books and periodicals in foreign languages reflecting political, economic and cultural progress in People's Republic of China.

Guozi Shudian (*China Publications Centre*): P.O.B. 399, Peking; publishes periodicals, textbooks, etc. in English; import and export house.

Hsinhua (New China) Book Agency: Peking; since 1951 this agency has functioned as a national enterprise, publishing and distributing books for the State under the auspices of the Ministry of Culture and co-ordinating the activities of all other publishing houses.

National Minorities Publishing House: publishes books in Tibetan, Kazakh, S.E. language group, etc.

People's Educational Publishing House: Shanghai.

People's Literature Publishing House: Peking; Shanghai.

People's Physical Culture Publishing House: Peking, sports books and pictorial magazines.

Popular Press: caters for peasants.

San Lien Publishers: Peking; a state publishing house; general and political.

Workers' Press: Peking; publishing house of All China Federation of Trade Unions.

Writers' Publishing House: Peking; a state enterprise publishing reprints of Chinese literature.

Youth Publishing House: Peking.

RADIO AND TELEVISION

RADIO

In 1972 there were about 10 million radio licences.

Central Broadcasting Administration: Outside Fu Hsing Men, Peking; Dir.-Gen. MEI YI; controls the Central People's Broadcasting Station.

Central People's Broadcasting Station: Hsi Chang An Chieh 3, Peking; has five relay stations broadcasting 1,450 hours per week; also controls 117 local stations; domestic service in Chinese, Cantonese, Tibetan, Tai, Amoy, Hakka, Foochow dialect, Kazakh, Uighur, Mongolian and Korean; foreign service in English, Esperanto, French, German, Indonesian, Italian, Japanese, Portuguese and Spanish.

TELEVISION

There are thirteen television stations at Peking (2), Harbin, Shanghai, Canton, Tientsin, Changchung, Mukden (Shenyang), Sian, Taiyuan, Hofei, Nanking and Wuhan; also twelve experimental stations.

In 1972 there were an estimated 200,000 television receivers.

Note: In September 1971 direct telegraphic links were restored between Shanghai and San Francisco.

FINANCE

BANKING

The People's Bank of China: 22 Hsi Chiao Min Hsiang, Peking; f. 1948; the state bank of the People's Republic of China; more than 34,000 brs.; Pres. (vacant); Vice-Pres. CHIAO PEI-HSIN.

Bank of China: 108 Hsi Chiao Min Hsiang, Peking; f. 1912; handles foreign exchange and international settlements; Gen. Man. KUNG YIN-PING.

Agricultural Bank of China: Peking; f. 1963; functions directly under the State Council and handles State agricultural investments; Pres. HU CHING-YUN.

People's Construction Bank of China: Ministry of Finance, Peking; f. 1954 to make payments for capital construction according to plan and budget approval by the State; issues short-term loans to State contractors.

Bank of Communications: 3 Kung An How Chieh, Peking; f. 1908; operates for the Ministry of Finance; handles State investments in the joint state-private enterprises. Chair. JUNG TZU-HO; Gen. Man. CHANG PIN CHIH.

Chekiang First Bank of Commerce Ltd.: 222 Kiangse Rd., Shanghai; f. 1948; 3 brs.

China and South Sea Bank Ltd.: 110 Hankow Rd., Shanghai; f. 1920; Chair. OEI KIEN SOC.

Kincheng Banking Corporation: Shanghai; f. 1917; Gen. Man. TSE YAO-HWA.

National Commercial Bank Ltd.: Shanghai; f. 1907.

Shanghai Commercial and Savings Bank Ltd.: 50 Ningpo Rd., Shanghai; f. 1915.

FOREIGN BANKS

Chartered Bank: 10 Clements Lane, London, EC4N 7AB; f. 1853; P.O.B. 2135, Yuan Ming Yuan Lu, Shanghai.

Hongkong and Shanghai Banking Corporation: 1 Queen's Road Central, Hong Kong; f. 1865; 185 Yuan Ming Yuan Road, P.O. Box 151, Shanghai.

Oversea-Chinese Banking Corporation Ltd.: China Building, Chulia Street, Singapore; f. 1932; branches in Amoy and Shanghai; Man. Dir. TAN CHIN TUAN.

INSURANCE

China Insurance Company Ltd.: 34 Fa Ti Lu, Peking; f. 1931; freight and transport insurance and reinsurance.

People's Insurance Company of China, The: 34 Fa Ti Lu, Peking; f. 1949; hull, marine cargo, aviation, motor, fire and reinsurance, etc.

Tai Ping Insurance Co. Ltd.: 34 Fa Ti Lu, Peking; general insurance.

TRADE AND INDUSTRY

EXTERNAL TRADE

The structure of the administration of Foreign Economic Relations is given under "Government", *above*.

Ministry of Economic Relations with Foreign Countries: Peking; f. 1972; Minister Fang Yi; Vice-Ministers Han Tsung-cheng, Ch'en Mu Hua, Chung Yu-yi, Hsieh Huai-teh.

China Council for the Promotion of International Trade: Hsi Tan Bldg., Hsi Chang An Chieh, Peking; f. 1952; encourages foreign trade; arranges Chinese exhibitions at home and abroad; Chair. (vacant); Vice-Chair. Li Chuan.

Export and Import Corporations

Subordinate to the Ministry of Foreign Trade.

China National Foreign Trade Transportation Corporation: Erh Li Kou, Hsi Chiao, Peking; arranges customs clearance, deliveries, forwarding and insurance.

China National Animal By-products Import and Export Corporation: 48 Tung An Men Street, Peking.

China National Cereals, Oils and Foodstuffs Import and Export Corporation: 48 Tung An Men Street, Peking.

China National Chemicals Import and Export Corporation: Erh Li Kou, Hsi Chiao, Peking; deals in rubber, petroleum, chemicals and drugs.

China National Complete Plant Export Corporation: Soochow Hutung, Peking.

China National Instruments Import and Export Corporation: Peking; Dep. Dir. Cheng Chi-hsien.

China National Light Industrial Products Import and Export Corporation: 82 Tung An Men Street, Peking.

China National Machinery Import and Export Corporation: Erh Li Kou, Hsi Chiao, Peking.

China National Metals and Minerals Import and Export Corporation: Import Building, Erh-Li-Kou, Peking; f. 1961; incorporating the former China National Metals Import Corporation and China National Minerals Corporation; Dir. Hsieh Shou-tien.

China National Tea and Native Produce Import and Export Corporation: 82 Tung An Men Street, Peking.

China National Technical Import Corporation: Erh Li Kou, Hsi Chiao, Peking; exports and imports; whole-plant projects and equipment.

China National Textiles Import and Export Corporation: 48 Tung An Men St., Peking; Man. Dir. Chen Cheng-chung.

Guozi Shudian: P.O. Box 399, Peking; exporters of books and periodicals.

Sinofracht Ship Chartering and Broking Corporation: Erh Li Kou, Hsi Chiao, Peking.

Waiwen Shudian: P.O. Box 88, Peking; f. 1964; importers of books and periodicals.

INTERNAL TRADE

Central Administration of Industry and Commerce: Peking; under the direct supervision of the State Council; Dir. Hsu Ti-hsin (*position doubtful*).

All-China Federation of Industry and Commerce: Peking; f. 1953; helps industry and traders to execute government policy; Sec.-Gen. Hsiang Shu-hsiang; Members: Provincial Associations of Industry and Commerce; All-China Federation of Co-operatives; Central Organizations of the Joint State-Private Enterprises.

TRADE UNIONS

All-China Federation of Trade Unions: 1 Fu Chien Street, Peking; f. 1948; affiliated to W.F.T.U.; organised on an industrial basis; 22 affiliated national industrial unions; membership is voluntary but some social benefits are open only to trade unionists; trade unions administer state social insurance; mems. about 16 million; Chair. Liu Ning-yi.

TRANSPORT AND TOURISM

RAILWAYS

Ministry of Communications: Peking; controls all railways through regional divisions. The railway network has been extended to all provinces and regions except Tibet, and totalled over 36,000 km. in 1965, in addition to special railways serving factories and mines. Recently-opened lines include those between Lanchow and Urumchi, Tankianghow and Wuhan and Kweiyang and Chiangkow; the Hwa-Foo railway (140 km.) through Anwei Province; a 50-km. line between An-loo and Wei-chia-tien in Hupeh; the Ping-Mei in Northern Kwangtung which will eventually connect with Kanchow in Kiangsi Province. A new road and railway bridge over the Yangtze River at Nanking was opened at the end of 1968.

Note: A new underground system for Peking is under construction which will run for 24 km. One route and 16 stations have been completed.

ROADS

There are about 500,000 km. of paved and unsurfaced roads.

INLAND WATERWAYS

General Inland Navigation Bureau: Controls river and canal traffic. There are 160,000 km. of inland waterways in China, 48,000 of which are open to steam navigation. The main rivers are the Yellow, Yangtze and Pearl. The Yangtze is navigable by vessels of 10,000 tons as far as Wuhan, over 1,000 km. from the coast. Smaller vessels can continue to Chungking. Over one-third of internal freight traffic is carried by water.

SHIPPING

Ministry of Communications: Peking.

The greater part of China's shipping is handled in eight major ports: Dairen (Talien), Chinhuangtao, Tientsin, Tsingtao, Lienyunkang, Shanghai, Canton and Chanchiang (Liuchow). Two-thirds of the handling facilities are mechanical, and harbour improvement schemes are constantly in progress.

China Ocean Shipping Company: Head Office: Peking; br. offices: Shanghai, Canton, Tientsin; the only Chinese line which operates its own shipping outside territorial waters; also operate chartered foreign ships.

FOREIGN LINES SERVING CHINA

Blue Funnel Line: Liverpool; services to Shanghai.

Glen Line: London; services to Chinese ports.

CIVIL AVIATION

Civil Aviation Administration of China (CAAC): 15 Chang-an Street (East), Peking; f. 1950; Dir. KUANG JEN-NUNG; fleet of 6 Viscounts, 9 Ilyushin-18, 58 Ilyushin-14, 5 Ilyushin Il-62, 11 Ilyushin Il-12, 4 Boeing 707, 26 Li-2, 300 An-2, 3 Trident 1E, 8 Trident 2E; 25 Trident 2E, 2 Trident 3B, 2 Boeing 707 and 3 Concordes on order; 10 Boeing 707 transports.

China operates air routes totalling 36,600 km. which link 72 cities. Most of these flights are internal. External flights are operated to the U.S.S.R. (Moscow and Irkutsk), Mongolia, North Korea, Burma, North Viet-Nam and Albania.

FOREIGN AIRLINES

Aeroflot: Moscow; 15 Chang-an St. (East), Peking; twice weekly service Moscow–Irkutsk–Peking.

Air France: Paris; c/o CAAC, Peking; weekly service Paris – Shanghai.

Civil Aviation Administration of the Democratic People's Republic of Korea: Pyongyang; c/o CAAC, Peking; weekly service Shenyang-Peking-Pyongyang.

Ethiopian Airlines: Addis Ababa; c/o CAAC, Peking; weekly service via Bombay to Peking.

Pakistan International Airlines Corporation: Karachi; c/o CAAC, Peking; London–Karachi–Islamabad–Peking–Shanghai, twice weekly.

There are plans for the following airlines to operate flights into China: Alitalia, British Airways, Canadian Pacific Airlines and Japan Airlines.

TOURISM

China International Travel Service (Lüxingshe): Hsitan Building, Peking; makes travel arrangements for foreign parties; brs. in Canton, Shanghai and Hong Kong.

Chinese People's Association for Friendship with Foreign Countries: Peking; Pres. WANG KUO-CHUAN; Sec.-Gen. TING HSEUH-SUNG.

ATOMIC ENERGY

China was believed to have a total of about 40 nuclear reactors in operation at the end of 1966.

Atomic Energy Institute: Academia Sinica, Peking; contains an enriched uranium heavy water reactor and a cyclotron.

Atomic Research Centre: Tarim Basin, Sinkiang; f. 1953; Dir. WANG KAN-CHANG.

Military Scientific Council: Peking; Dir. Dr. CHIEN HSUEH-SRN.

Nuclear Institute of the Academia Sinica: Academia Sinica, 3 Wen Tsin Chen, Peking; Dir. CHEN SAN-CHIANG.

Tsinghua University: Peking; f. 1911; has built its own nuclear reactor; Prof. of Physics CHAO CHUNG-YAO.

UNIVERSITIES

Amoy University: Amoy, Fukien; c. 1,000 teachers, c. 3,000 students.

Anhwei University: Hofei, Anhwei.

Chengchow University: Chengchow, Honan.

People's University of China: Peking; c. 1,000 students.

Chinan University: Canton, Kwangtung; c. 1,900 students.

Chuanchow University: Chuanchow, Fukien.

Chungking University: Chungking, Szechwan.

Futan University: Shanghai, Kiangsu; c. 1,135 students.

Hangchow University: Hangchow, Chekiang.

Hopei Univeristy: Tienstin, Hopei.

Hunan University: Changsha, Hunan.

Hupei University: Wuhan, Hupei.

Inner Mongolia University: Huhehot, Inner Mongolian A.R.

Kirin University: Changchun, Kirin.

Kweichow University: Kweiyang, Kweichow.

Lanchow University: Lanchow, Kansu.

Liaoning University: Shenyang, Liaoning.

Nankai University: Tientsin, Hopei; c. 460 teachers, c. 3,000 students.

Nanking University: Nanking, Kiangsi; c. 1,000 teachers, c. 6,000 students.

Ninghsia University: Yingchwan, Ninghsia; c. 290 teachers, c. 1,000 students.

Northwestern University: Sian, Shensi; c. 300 teachers, c. 3,100 students.

Peking University: Peking; c. 2,000 teachers, c. 10,000 students.

Shantung University: Tsingtao, Shantung.

Sinkiang University: Urumchi, Sinkiang; c. 1,800 students.

Sun Yat-Sen University: Canton, Kwangtung; c. 750 teachers, c. 4,300 students.

Szechwan University: Chengtu, Szechwan; c. 700 teachers, c. 3,700 students.

Wuhan University: Wuchang, Hupei; c. 700 teachers, c. 4,500 students.

Yunnan University: Kunming, Yunnan.

CHINA (TAIWAN)

INTRODUCTORY SURVEY

Location, Climate, Language, Religion, Flag, Capital

The Chinese province of Taiwan comprises the island of Taiwan (Formosa), the nearby Pescadores islets, and the islands of Quemoy and Matsu near the mainland. Taiwan itself lies 200 miles from the coast of south-eastern China. The average temperature is 73°F (23°C) and the average annual rainfall 101 inches. The official language is Mandarin Chinese. The predominant religion is Buddhism and there are Muslims, Catholics and Protestants. Confucianism has a large following. The national flag (proportions 3 by 2) is crimson, with a dark blue rectangular canton containing a white sun. The capital of the province is Taipei.

Recent History

China's Kuomintang government, led by Gen. Chiang Kai-shek, was overthrown by the Communist revolution of 1949. Chiang and many of his supporters left the mainland and established themselves on Taiwan. In 1954 a mutual security pact was signed by which the U.S.A. pledged the protection of Taiwan and the Pescadores; in 1955 the offshore islands of Quemoy and Matsu were included in the protected area. The Taiwan régime, which still claims to be the legal government of all China, was recognized by only 37 countries in 1973, having lost its seat at the United Nations to the Government of the People's Republic of China in October 1971. Elections were held in December 1972 for the first time in 24 years, to increase popular representation in local affairs. In March 1973, the Government rejected a Peking offer to hold secret talks on the reunification of China.

Government

The Head of State is the President, who is elected for terms of six years by the National Assembly. There are five Yuans (governing bodies), the highest legislative organ being the Legislative Yuan, to which the Executive Yuan is responsible. There are also Control, Judicial and Examination Yuans. Elections are by universal adult suffrage, but the great majority of Assembly seats are held by life members who formerly represented mainland constituencies.

Economic Affairs

The economy is progressing towards self-sufficiency, and U.S. aid, which totalled $69 million in 1961, was discontinued in 1965. Trade is chiefly with the U.S.A., Japan and South-East Asia, the most important exports being sugar, bananas, processed foodstuffs, textiles, minerals and metal goods. Cement production is the main industry. Mineral resources include coal, marble and salt. G.N.P. per capita is now amongst the highest in Asia.

Defence

The armed forces total 500,000 men (army 350,000, air force 80,000, navy 35,000 with a marine corps of 35,000). The system of compulsory service for two years was abandoned in 1974. Much of the equipment and some training staff are provided by the U.S.A.

Transport and Communications

There are about 1,000 km. of state railway and over 16,000 km. of roads. The ports of Keelung, Hualien and Kaohsiung handled more than 38 million metric tons of cargo in 1972. The Sungshan airport is used by 11 domestic and international airlines.

Social Welfare

The Labour Security Programme covers more than a fifth of the population and provides benefits for injury, disability, birth, death and old age. Government employees are covered by a special scheme.

Education

Elementary education is free and compulsory between the ages of six and twelve. In 1972–73, there were almost 2.5 million pupils enrolled in state primary schools and about 1.32 million in secondary schools. There are 8 universities and 91 independent colleges and junior colleges.

Tourism

Festivals, ancient art treasures and the island scenery are the principal attractions; 824,393 tourists visited Taiwan in 1973.

Visas are required by all visitors.

Sport

The most popular sports are basketball, baseball and swimming. About 20 national sports associations belong to the China National Amateur Athletic Federation.

Public Holidays

1974: September 28th (Birthday of Confucius), October 10th (Double Tenth Day), November 12th (Birthday of Sun Yat-sen), December 25th (Constitution Day).

1975: January 1st (Founding of the Republic), Chinese New Year.

Weights and Measures

Length: 1 shih chih = 1.084 ft.
1 shih li = 0.311 mile
Area: 1 sq. shih chih = 1.195 sq. ft.
1 shih mow = 0.1647 acre
Weight: 1 shih catty = 1.102 lb.
1 Taiwan catty = 1.333 lb.
1 picul = 110.231 lb.
Volume: 1 cubic shih chih = 1.308 cu. ft.
Capacity: 1 shih sheng = 1 litre

Currency and Exchange Rates

100 cents = 1 New Taiwan dollar (NT $).

Exchange rates (April 1974):

£1 sterling = NT $89.73;
U.S. $1 = NT $38.00.

STATISTICAL SURVEY

AREA AND POPULATION

AREA (sq. miles)	POPULATION (Sept. 1973)*		BIRTHS AND DEATHS (Jan.–Dec. 1972)			
	Total	Taipei	Births	Birth Rate (per 'ooo)	Deaths	Death Rate (per 'ooo)
13,892	15,493,855	1,951,155	365,749	24.2	71,486	4.7

* Excluding armed forces and foreigners.

AGRICULTURE
PRINCIPAL CROPS
(metric tons)

	PRODUCTION			YIELD PER HECTARE (kg.)		
	1970	1971	1972	1970	1971	1972
Rice	2,463,000	2,313,802	2,440,329	3,172	3,071	3,291
Sweet Potatoes . .	3,441,000	3,391,354	2,927,708	15,043	15,053	13,901
Groundnuts . .	122,198	97,579	94,032	1,397	1,130	1,233
Sugar Cane . .	5,991,000	7,881,040	7,091,854	69,460	88,786	78,512

OTHER CROPS
(metric tons)

	1970	1971	1972
Wheat . .	3,664	2,346	1,546
Wheat Flour .	330,414	355,759	419,724
Soya Beans .	65,174	60,990	60,221
Cotton . .	2,715	1,555	1,322
Jute . .	8,198	2,011	1,207
Tea . .	27,648	26,984	26,229
Bananas .	461,829	470,595	366,411
Pineapples .	338,191	358,529	334,384
Citrus Fruit .	209,115	253,149	290,609
Citronella Oil .	1,142	894	833

FORESTRY
(1972)

TOTAL AREA (hectares)	TIMBER PRODUCTION (cubic metres)
2,224,472	1,571,948

FISHERIES
(1972—metric tons)

Deep Sea .	345,086
Inshore .	242,829
Coastal .	25,379
Ponds .	81,336
Total .	694,330

Livestock (1972): Cattle 247,872, Pigs 3,831,293, Goats 177,901.

LIVESTOCK PRODUCTS

	1968	1969	1970	1971
Milk (metric tons) . . .	14,978	14,966	16,123	17,906
Duck Eggs ('ooo) . . .	397,484	432,462	463,518	455,098
Hen Eggs ('ooo) . . .	426,910	527,017	574,961	600,559

INDEX OF AGRICULTURAL PRODUCTION
(1966=100)
Inclusive of more than 60 products and includes forestry, livestock and fishing production.
1970: 117.9; 1971: 120.4; 1972: 122.7.

MINING*

	1971	1972
Coal . . .	4,096,594	3,913,218
Gold (hectograms) .	6,064	5,562
Silver (hectograms) .	22,600	23,020
Electrolytic Copper .	3,670	4,767
Pyrite . . .	45,229	30,871
Crude Petroleum (kilolitres)	125,923	144,611
Natural Gas (cubic metres) .	1,090,773	1,263,857
Salt . . .	668,692	440,079
Gypsum . . .	12,676	3,459
Sulphur . . .	5,191	3,663
Marble . . .	1,510,134	1,772,669
Talc . . .	39,042	24,792
Asbestos . . .	2,327	2,687
Dolomite . . .	90,722	98,246

* Amounts in metric tons unless otherwise specified.

INDUSTRY*

	1971	1972
Refined Sugar† . . .	823,210	732,939
Electric Power (million kWh)	15,171	17,449
Cotton Yarn . .	105,241	91,362
Cotton Fabric ('000 metres)	581,655	498,688
Rayon Filament . .	3,157	3,369
P.V.C. . . .	130,924	171,781
Paper . . .	386,250	453,888
Caustic Soda . .	134,561	151,906
Fertilizer . . .	1,036,783	1,166,954
Plate Glass (case) .	1,772,124	2,187,351
Cement . . .	5,042,947	5,689,503
Steel Bar . . .	642,813	738,804
Aluminium Ingot . .	26,546	32,104
Sewing Machines (sets) .	709,564	916,458
Electric Fans (number) .	468,721	344,166
Fluorescent Lamps (number)	9,321,000	11,565,000
Electric Meters (number) .	624,196	316,798
Shipbuilding (gross tons) .	265,553	292,781

* Amounts in metric tons unless otherwise specified.
† Including brown sugar.

INDEX OF INDUSTRIAL PRODUCTION
(1966=100)
Inclusive of mining, manufacturing, construction, public utilities.
1970: 197.4; 1971: 238.9; 1972: 301.0.

FINANCE
100 cents=1 New Taiwan dollar (NT $).
Coins: 10, 20 and 50 cents; 1 and 5 dollars.
Notes: 1, 5, 10, 50 and 100 dollars.
Exchange rates (April 1974): £1 sterling=NT $89.73; U.S. $1=NT $38.00.
NT $100=£1.114=U.S. $2.632.

BUDGET
(1972–73—NT$ million)

REVENUE		EXPENDITURE	
Taxes	41,034	General Government and Defence .	27,567
Monopoly Profits . . .	6,942	Reconstruction and Communications .	5,480
Non-Tax Revenue from Other Sources .	17,281	Social Development . . .	8,101
		Education	11,046
		Debt Service . . .	3,708
		Enterprise Fund . . .	5,477
		Others	1,564
TOTAL	65,257	TOTAL	62,943

Sixth Four-Year Economic Development Plan (1973–76):
G.N.P. to increase to U.S. $11,600 million by the end of
1976; per capita income to increase by about 80 per
cent to U.S. $550 and a projected annual economic
growth rate of 9.5 per cent. Major projects under the
plan are in the fields of power generation, which is to
increase by 12.1 per cent per year, and traffic volume of
transportation and communications (9.5 per cent per
annum increase). Total investment will amount to
U.S. $12,057 million (at 1972 constant prices).

NATIONAL ACCOUNTS
(NT$ million at current prices)

	1970	1971	1972
GROSS DOMESTIC PRODUCT (AT MARKET PRICE)	218,707	249,398	336,318
NET DOMESTIC PRODUCT	205,763	233,552	273,671
of which:			
Agriculture and Fisheries	34,111	35,210	39,498
Mining	2,652	2,765	2,957
Manufacturing	62,125	74,303	91,754
Electricity	4,514	4,896	5,558
Construction	8,946	10,630	12,179
Transport and communications	10,799	12,414	14,774
Commerce	30,556	34,145	39,682
NET NATIONAL PRODUCT (NATIONAL INCOME)	171,085	196,457	228,406
GROSS NATIONAL PRODUCT	218,428	249,275	292,355
Balance of exports and imports of goods and services	—203	6,510	19,743
AVAILABLE EXTERNAL RESOURCES (end of year)	28,131	35,277	58,341

EXTERNAL TRADE

COMMODITIES
(U.S. $ million)

IMPORTS	1971	1972	EXPORTS	1971	1972
Machinery, Tools	275.7	302.8	Textiles	620.5	814.1
Ores, Metals	239.6	271.9	Metals, Machinery	479.5	717.9
Vehicles, Parts	165.2	67.3	Wood and Products	171.3	244.6
Raw Cotton	91.3	88.8	Bananas	44.2	30.3
Electrical Equipment	291.1	253.3	Chemicals	39.8	40.0
Crude Oils, Fuels	78.8	201.2	Sugar	66.5	84.6
Wheat and Cereals	47.7	157.3	Canned Mushrooms	47.1	55.5
Chemicals	225.9	231.2	Cement and Building Materials	29.8	14.2
Artificial Fibres, Wool	78.2	86.1	Canned Asparagus	35.0	41.5
Beans and Peas	80.7	101.4	Rice	2.9	1.9
Others	415.8	652.2	Others	598.9	871.6
TOTAL	1,990.0	2,413.5	TOTAL	2,135.5	2,916.2

1973: Imports U.S. $3,790.6 million; Exports U.S. $4,473.1 million.

PRINCIPAL TRADING PARTNERS
(U.S. $'000)

	1970		1971		1972	
	IMPORTS	EXPORTS	IMPORTS	EXPORTS	IMPORTS	EXPORTS
United States of America . .	463,424	578,857	594,520	883,173	543,424	1,251,317
Japan	582,051	235,650	767,353	267,029	1,046,002	376,738
Germany, Federal Republic	50,993	73,211	76,181	93,807	91,542	135,281
Thailand . . .	38,256	26,962	26,012	30,560	41,763	45,736
Hong Kong . . .	25,712	138,766	39,433	157,992	59,690	229,105
United Kingdom . .	24,347	16,834	33,822	34,124	37,091	56,478
Australia . . .	49,938	21,646	61,893	35,647	76,202	52,173
Philippines . . .	25,400	17,805	28,231	18,582	36,640	17,964
Singapore and Malaysia .	26,997	56,387	39,165	66,643	62,611	88,526
Viet-Nam, Khmer Republic, Laos	1,010	51,925	2,000*	64,992*	2,718	45,845
TOTAL (incl. others) .	1,527,697	1,561,652	1,990,023	2,135,546	2,513,501	2,916,212

* Excluding Laos.

TRANSPORT

Railways (1972): Passengers 143,000,000, Passenger/km. 7,311,371,000; Freight 33,919,000 metric tons, Ton/km. 2,820,025,000.

Roads (1972): Passengers 714,055,000, Passenger/km. 8,562,593,000; Freight 42,014,000 metric tons, Ton/km. 1,685,049,000.

Shipping (1972): Imports 19,174,905 metric tons, Exports 6,116,037 metric tons.

Civil Aviation (1972): Passengers entered and departed 2,067,068.

Tourism (1972): Total visitors 580,033.

COMMUNICATIONS MEDIA

Radio Receivers (July 1973) 1,469,474; Television Receivers (July 1973) 890,396; Telephones (July 1973) 436,938; Newspaper circulation (1971) 1,100,000.

EDUCATION
(1972–73)

	SCHOOLS	FULL-TIME TEACHERS	PUPILS
Pre-school . .	587	2,649	107,813
Primary . . .	2,337	61,178	2,459,743
Secondary (incl. Vocational) .	951	82,212	1,323,253
Higher . .	99	12,270	251,058
Special . .	6	389	2,749
Supplementary .	231	3,366	124,516
TOTAL (incl. others) .	4,211	132,064	4,269,132

Sources: Directorate-General of Budgets, Accounts and Statistics; Inspectorate-General of Customs; Taipei.

THE CONSTITUTION

The form of government incorporated in the Constitution follows the five-power system envisaged by Dr. Sun Yat-sen, which has the major features of both cabinet and presidential government. The following are the chief organs of government:

National Assembly: Composed of elected delegates; meets to elect or recall the President and Vice-President, to amend the Constitution, or to vote on proposed Constitutional amendments submitted by the Legislative Yuan.

President: Elected by the National Assembly for a term of 6 years, and may be re-elected for a second term (the two-term restriction is at present suspended). Represents country at all state functions, including foreign relations; commands land, sea, and air forces, promulgates laws, issues mandates, concludes treaties, declares war, makes peace, declares martial law, grants amnesties, appoints and removes civil and military officers, and confers honours and decorations. He also convenes the National Assembly, and subject to certain limitations, may issue emergency orders to deal with national calamities and ensure national security.

Executive Yuan: Is the highest administrative organ of the nation and is responsible to the Legislative Yuan; has five categories of subordinate organization:

Executive Yuan Council
Ministries and Commissions
Secretariat
Government Information Office and Personnel Administration Bureau.
Directorate-General of Budgets, Accounts and Statistics.

Legislative Yuan: Is the highest legislative organ of the state, composed of elected members; holds two sessions per year; is empowered to hear administrative reports of the Executive Yuan, and to change Government policy.

Judicial Yuan: Is the highest judicial organ of state and has charge of civil, criminal, and administrative cases, and of cases concerning disciplinary measures against public functionaries (*see* Legal System).

Examination Yuan: Supervises examinations for entry into public offices, and deals with personal questions of the civil service.

Control Yuan: Is a body elected by local councils to impeach or investigate the work of the Executive Yuan and the Ministries and Executives; meets once a month, and has a subordinate body, the Ministry of Audit.

THE GOVERNMENT

THE HEAD OF STATE

President: Generalissimo CHIANG KAI-SHEK.

Vice-President: Dr. YEN CHIA-KAN.

Secretary-General: CHENG YIN-FUN.

THE EXECUTIVE YUAN

(April 1974)

Prime Minister: Gen. CHIANG CHING-KUO.

Deputy Prime Minister: HSU CHING-CHUNG.

Ministers Without Portfolio: GEORGE K. C. YEH, LIEN CHEN-TUNG, YU KUO-HWA, LI LIEN-CHUEN, CHOW SHU-KAI, KUO CHENG, LEE TENG-HUI.

Secretary-General: FEI HUA.

Minister of the Interior: LIN CHIN-SHENG.

Minister of Foreign Affairs: SHEN CHANG-HUAN.

Minister of National Defence: KAO KUEI-YUAN.

Minister of Finance: LI KWOH-TING.

Minister of Education: TSIANG YIEN-SI.

Minister of Justice: WANG JEN-YUAN.

Minister of Economic Affairs: SUN YUN-SUAN.

Minister of Communications: HENRY YU-SHU KAO.

Chairman of the Overseas Chinese Affairs Commission: MO SUNG-NIEN.

Chairman of the Mongolian and Tibetan Affairs Commission: TSUI CHUI-YIEN.

Director of the Government Information Office: FREDRICK F. CHIEN.

OTHER YUAN

President of Legislative Yuan: NIEH WEN-YA.

President of Judicial Yuan: TIEN CHUNG-CHIN.

President of Examination Yuan: YANG LIANG-KUNG.

President of Control Yuan: YU CHUN-HSIEN.

OTHER MINISTERS

Minister of Personnel: SHIH CHUEH.

Minister of Examinations: CHOONG KOW-KWONG.

Auditor-General: CHANG TAO-MING.

Note: President Chiang Kai-shek was elected to his fifth six-year term in March 1972.

DIPLOMATIC REPRESENTATION

EMBASSIES ACCREDITED TO THE REPUBLIC OF CHINA
(In Taipei unless otherwise stated)
(E) Embassy.

Bolivia: Tokyo, Japan (E); *Chargé d'Affaires a.i.:* BERNARDO BAPTISTA GUMUCIO.

Brazil: 15 Jen Ai Rd., Sec. 4 (P.O.B. 10002) (E); *Chargé d'Affaires a.i.:* PAULO DYRCEU PINHEIRO.

Central African Republic: 22, Lane 242, Chien Kuo N. Road; *Ambassador:* SIMON PIERRE KIBANDA.

Colombia: 14, Lane 161, Nan Ya Li Tien Mu; *Chargé d'Affaires a.i.:* HERNANDO RICARDO.

Costa Rica: 11A Lane 23, Rd. 3, Tien Mou (E); *Ambassador:* EDGAR SÁNCHEZ.

Dominican Republic: 54 Nanking E. Rd. (E); *Ambassador:* ADOLFO R. CAMARENA.

El Salvador: Tokyo, Japan; *Ambassador:* Lic WALTER BENEKE MEDINA.

Guatemala: 6, Lane 44, Chien Kuo N. Rd.; *Ambassador:* Col. RAMIRO GEREDA ASTURIAS.

Honduras: Tokyo, Japan (E).

Ivory Coast: Tokyo, Japan (E).

Jordan: 11E Ai Chun Mansion, 120-23 Chung Hsiao E.; *Ambassador:* ANWAR NASHASHIBI.

Korea, Republic: 72 Jen Ai Rd., Sec. 3 (E); *Ambassador:* KIM KAE-WON.

Liberia: Tokyo, Japan (E).

Madagascar: 27 Lane 242, Chien-Kuo N. Rd. (E); *Ambassador:* BENJAMIN RAZAFINTSEHENO.

Nicaragua: Tokyo, Japan (E).

Panama: 3rd Fl., 307 Shih Pai Rd., Sec. 2; *Ambassador:* RICARDO E. CHIARI.

Paraguay: Tokyo, Japan (E).

Philippines: 80 Jen Ai Rd., Sec. 4 (E); *Ambassador:* PELAYO F. LLAMAS.

Saudi Arabia: 7 Alley 8, Lane 27, Jen Ai Rd., Sec. 4 (E); *Chargé d'Affaires a.i.:* FAWZI A. SHOBOKSHI.

U.S.A.: 2 Chung Hsiao West Rd., Sec. 2 (E); *Ambassador:* LEONARD UNGER.

Uruguay: 3 Alley 6, Lane 142, Jen Ai Rd., Sec. 3 (E); *Chargé d'Affaires:* EDISON BOUCHATON.

Vatican: 6 Lane 63, Chin Shan St.; *Papal Nuncio:* Right Rev. Monsignor FRANCESCO COLASUONNO.

Venezuela: Apt. 6A, 66, Lane 189, An Tung St.; *Chargé d'Affaires:* HERNAN CALCURIAN.

Viet-Nam, Republic: 96 Ning Po West St. (E); *Ambassador:* NGUYEN VAN KIEU.

Taiwan also has diplomatic relations with Barbados, The Gambia, Haiti, Lesotho, Libya, Malawi, Niger, Portugal, Swaziland, Thailand, Tonga and Western Samoa.

PARLIAMENT

NATIONAL ASSEMBLY
Following the general election held on December 23rd 1972, the National Assembly now comprises 1,340 life members and 53 new members elected for 6 years. Delegates meet to elect or recall the President and Vice-President, to amend the Constitution or to vote on Constitutional amendments submitted by the Legislative Yuan.

LEGISLATIVE YUAN
The Legislative Yuan is the highest legislative organ of state. In the elections held throughout China in 1948

members elected to the Legislative Yuan totalled 760. Following general elections held on December 23rd, 1972, membership now comprises 418 life members and 36 elected for 3 years.

CONTROL YUAN
The Control Yuan exercises powers of impeachment and censure, and powers of consent in the appointment of the President, Vice-President and the grand justices of the Judicial Yuan, and the president, vice-president and the Members of the Examination Yuan (*see* the Constitution).

POLITICAL PARTIES

Kuomintang (KMT) (*Nationalist Party of China*): 11-A Chung Shan S. Rd., Taipei; f. 1894; aims to overthrow Communist rule in China and promote constitutional government; mems. 1,000,000; Dir.-Gen. (Tsungtsai) President CHIANG KAI-SHEK; Deputy Dir.-Gen. (vacant); Sec.-Gen. CHANG PAO-SHU; Deputy Sec.-Gen. CHIN HSIAO-YI, HSUEH JEN-YANG, LIN CHIN-SHENG.

Young China Party: Taipei; f. 1923; aims: to recover and maintain territorial sovereignty; to safeguard the Constitution, and democracy; to better international understanding between free China and the free world.

China Democratic Socialist Party: Taipei; f. 1932; aims: to promote democracy; to protect fundamental freedoms; to promote public welfare and social security.

JUDICIAL SYSTEM

Judicial Yuan: Pres. TIEN CHUNG-CHIN; Vice-Pres. TAI YEN-HUI; Sec.-Gen. CHENG TEH-SHOW; is the nation's highest Judicial organ, and the interpreter of the Constitution and national laws and ordinances. Its judicial powers are exercised by:

Supreme Court: Pres. CHIEN KUO-CHENG; court of appeal for civil and criminal cases.

Administrative Court: Pres. DAVID DING-YU CHOW; aims at the redress of administrative wrongs.

Committee on the Discipline of Public Functionaries: Chair. KU JU-HSUN; metes out disciplinary measures to persons impeached by the Control Yuan.

The interpretive powers of the Judicial Yuan are exercised by the Council of Grand Justices nominated and appointed for nine years by the President with the consent of the Control Yuan. The President of the Judicial Yuan also presides over the Council of Grand Justices.

The Ministry of Justice of the Executive Yuan has jurisdiction over district and high courts.

RELIGION

BUDDHISM

Buddhists belong to the Mahayana and Theravada schools. Leaders Venerable PAI SHENG, Venerable NAN TING, Venerable YIN SHUNG. The Buddhist Association of Taiwan has 1,900 group members and more than 40,000 individual members.

TAOISM

Leader CHANG EN-PU. There are about 21,000 devotees.

ISLAM

Leader Haji KHALID T. C. SHIH. About 41,000 adherents.

CHRISTIANITY

Roman Catholic: Archbishop of Taipei STANISLAUS LOKUANG, D.S.T., D.PH., D.C.L., Taipei, P.O.B. 7-91; 314,710 adherents.

Episcopal: There are about 2,000 adherents; Bishop of Taiwan (Episcopal Church of America) Rt. Rev. JAMES T. M. PONG, 1-105-7 Hangchow S. Rd., Taipei.

Tai-oan Ki-tok Tiu-Lo Kau-Hoe (Presbyterian Church in Taiwan): 89-5 Chang-Chun Rd., Taipei; f. 1865; Gen. Sec. Rev. C. M. KAO; 70,000 adult mems., constituency 170,000.

THE PRESS

DAILIES

TAIPEI

Central Daily News: 1795 Chung Cheng Rd.; f. 1929; morning; official Kuomintang paper; Dir. TSAO SHENG-FEN; Editor LIN CHIA-CHI; circ. 150,000.

China Daily News (*Northern Edition*): 77 Wuchang St.; morning; f. 1948; Pres. TSU SUNG-CHIU; Editor-in-Chief CHEN CHI-DON.

China News: 277 Hsinyi Rd., Section 2; f. 1949; afternoon; English; Publr. S. LO; Dir. W. T. TING; Deputy Dir. CHRIS YOU; Editor WILLIAM PAN; circ. 20,000.

China Post: P.O.B. 17-18; f. 1952; morning; English; Publr. NANCY YU HUANG; Editor LI WEN-CHE; circ. 42,500.

China Times: 132 Da Li St.; f. 1950; morning; general and financial; Chair. and Publr. CHI-CHUNG YU; circ. 450,000.

Ching Chung Pao: Taipei; every three days; armed forces; Publr. LIANG HSIAO-HUANG.

Economic Daily News: 555 Chung Hsiao E. Rd., Sec. 4; morning; Publr. WANG TIH-WU; Editor WU PU-CHUAN.

Everybody's Daily: 21-2 Cheng-teh Rd.; Publr. CHIEN TEH-FA; Editor LIN CHAO-KAO.

Hua Pao: 100 Wuchang St., Section 2; afternoon; tabloid; Shanghai dialect; Dir. CHU TING-YUN.

Independent Evening News: 11 Pao An St.; afternoon; Publr. WU SAN-LIEM; Editor-in-Chief CHANG SHU BEN.

Independent Evening Post: 11 Pao An St.; afternoon; Publr. WU SAN-LIEM; Editor-in-Chief CHANG SHU BEN.

Mandarin Daily News: 10 Fuchow St.; f. 1948; afternoon; Dir. HUNG YEN-CHIU; Editor YANG RUU DER; circ. 55,000.

Min Tsu Evening News: 235 Kunming St.; f. 1950; afternoon; Publr. WANG CHENG-YUNG; Dir. HO CHU-CHIANG; circ. 120,000.

Shin Sheng Pao: 110 Yenping S. Rd.; f. 1945; morning; Publr. PAI-HUNG LEE; Editor CHEN KAN LIU; circ. 300,000.

Ta Hua (Great China) Evening News: 53 Kwan Chien Rd.; f. 1950; afternoon; Keng Hsiu-yeh Publishers; circ. 50,000 (weekday), 60,000 (Sunday).

United Daily News: 555 Chungsiao East Rd., Section 4; f. 1953; morning; Publr. WANG TIH-WU; Editor C. P. WANG; circ. 450,000.

Young Warrior Daily: 49 Chungking S. Rd.; morning; armed forces; Dir. SHIAO TAO-YING; Editor LO CHENG-MIN.

PROVINCIAL DAILIES

Cheng Chi Chung Hua Pao: Quemoy; morning; Editor CHU KUANG-YA; circ. 6,500.

Cheng Kung Evening News: Tainan; afternoon; Publr. CHU SUNG-CHIU; Editor KAO WEI-LIANG.

Chien Kuo Daily News: Penghu; morning; Publr. MENG CHAO-WEN; Editor SUNG JUI-YUNG.

China Daily News (*Tainan Edition*): Tainan; f. 1946; morning; Publr. HSIAO TZE-CHENG; Editor SU JEN-YU; circ. 115,000.

Chung Hsing Daily News: Changhua; morning; Publr. WU WAN-KUNG.

Chung Kuo Daily News: Taichung; morning; Publr. CHEN SHEN-CHI; Editor LIU SHIH-CHI; circ. 16,000.

Chung Kuo Evening News: Kaohsiung; 243 Hsin Lo St.; f. 1955; afternoon; Publr. YANG NIEN-CHU; circ. 20,000.

Far East Daily News: Taitung; morning; Publr. CHANG PEN-KUAN; Editor GAU-FENG.

Keng Sheng Pao: Hualien; morning; Publr. HSIEH YING-I; Editor CHEN HSING.

Matsu Daily News: Matsu; morning; Publr. SHU KWEI-CHUN; Editor SUN KUANG.

Min Chung Daily News: Keelung; f. 1950; morning; Dir. LI JUI-PIAO.

Min Sheng Daily News: Taichung; morning; Publr. HSU HSIU-LAN.

Shang Kung Daily News: Chiayi; morning; Dir. LIN FU-TI.

Taiwan Daily News: Taichung; morning; f. 1964; Publr. HSIA HSIAO-HUA; circ. 100,000.

Taiwan Hsin Wen Pao: Kaohsiung; f. 1961; morning; Publr. HSIEH JAN-CHI; circ. 85,000.

SELECTED PERIODICALS

Chen Kuang: 6 Lane 6, Lien Yun St., Taipei; f. 1952; monthly arts magazine; Chinese; Publr. WU KA-SHUI; Chief Editor WU KAI-SHUH.

Continent Magazine, The: 13 Chuan Chow Street, Taipei; f. 1950; archaeology, history and literature; fortnightly; Editor Prof. TUNG TSO-PIN; circ. 3,000.

Taiwan Pictorial: 20 Chungking S. Rd., Section 2, Taipei; f. 1951; general illustrated; monthly; Chinese; Publr. CHOW TIEN-KOU; Editor-in-Chief CHANG MING; circ. 70,000.

Taiwan Trade Monthly: P.O.B. 1642, Taipei; f. 1964; Publisher J. F. CHANG; circ. 4,000.

NEWS AGENCIES

Central News Agency: 209 Sungkiang Rd., Taipei; f. 1924; 9 br. offices and 20 overseas offices; 462 mems.; issues daily, morning, evening and financial editions, mimeographed bulletin in English: *Express News*; Dir. MA HSIN-YEH; Editor SHEN CHUNG-LIN.

Chiao Kwang News Photo Service: Taipei.

China Youth News Agency: Taipei.

FOREIGN BUREAUX

UPI: CNA Bldg., 209 Sungkiang Rd., Taipei; Bureau Chief SHULLEN SHAW.

AP and Jiji Press are also represented.

PRESS ASSOCIATION

Taipei Journalists' Association: Taipei; 1,675 mems. representing editorial and business executives of newspapers and broadcasting stations; publ. *Chinese Journalism Yearbook*.

PUBLISHERS

Cheng Chung Book Company: 20 Hengyang Rd., Taipei; humanities, social sciences, natural sciences, medicine, technology, fine arts.

Chung Hwa Book Co.: 94 Chungking S. Rd., Section 1, Taipei; f. 1911; publisher, printers and booksellers for humanities, social sciences, natural sciences, medicine, fine arts, school books; Gen. Man. D. S. HSIUNG.

Commercial Press: 37 Chungking S. Rd., Section 1, Taipei.

Eastern Publishing Co. Ltd.: 121 Chungking S. Rd., Section 1, P.O.B. 75, Taipei; geography, maps, agriculture, gardening, fiction, technology.

The Far East Book Co.: 66-1, 10th Floor, Chungking S. Rd., Section 1, Taipei; art, education, history, physics, mathematics, literature, school books, Chinese/English, English/Chinese dictionaries.

Fu-Hsing Book Co.: 44 Huai Ning St., Taipei; art, arch-aeology, geography, education, history, cookery, technology, economics, school books.

The Great China Book Corporation: 66 Chungking S. Rd., Section 1, Taipei; f. 1952; education, history, agriculture, politics, fiction, technology, economics, textbooks and reference books; Chief Dir. HSIEH CHUNG-LIU; Man. HSEIH YU.

Hua Kuo Publishing Co.: 6 Lane 180, Section 1, Ho-ping East Rd., Taipei; f. 1950; Publr. T. F. WANG.

San Min Book Co.: 77, 1st Sec., Chung Ching So. Rd., Taipei; f. 1953; literature, history, philosophy, social and humanitarian sciences; Man. KO CHUN-CHIN.

Tah Chung Book Co.: 37-1, Chung Shan N. Rd., 2nd Section, Taipei; hygiene, music, physics, technology, economics.

World Book Co.: 99 Chungking S. Rd., Section 1, Taipei.

RADIO AND TELEVISION

RADIO

Broadcasting stations are mostly privately owned, but the Ministry of Communications determines power and frequencies and supervises the operation of all stations, whether private or governmental. In 1972 there were 1.5 million radio receivers. Principal networks:

Broadcasting Corporation of China: 53 Jen Ai Rd., Section 3, Taipei 106; f. 1928; 5 Services: Domestic (3 networks), Mainland and Overseas (all AM); FM, Stereo and TV production; 22 stations, 78 transmitters, 84 frequencies; 18 languages and dialects; total power output 2,607 kW.; Pres. LEE SHIH-FENG; Chair. MAH SOO-LAY.

Cheng Sheng Broadcasting Corporation: 433 Chungking N. Rd., Section 3, Taipei; f. 1950; 14 stations in 10 locations; Pres. LEE LIEN; Gen. Man. LIU I-SHIH.

Fu Hsing Broadcasting Corporation: P.O.B. 799, Taipei; 35 stations in 12 locations; Dir. T. PIN-SUN.

TELEVISION

In 1972 there were over 1 million television sets.

Taiwan Television Enterprise Ltd.: 10 Pa Te Rd., Sec. 3, Taipei; f. 1962; Chair. LIM PECK-SIU; Pres. THOMAS S. CHOU; publ. *TTV* (weekly).

National Educational Television Station: 41 Nan-Hai Rd., Taipei; f. 1962; government; Dir. Prof. C. C. LIU.

FINANCE

(cap.=capital; p.u.=paid up; dep.=deposits; m=million)

BANKING

CENTRAL BANK

Central Bank of China: 21 Paoching Rd., Taipei; f. 1928; issuing bank; Gov. KUO-HWA YU.

NATIONAL BANKS

Bank of Communications: 91 Heng Yang Rd., Taipei; cap. NT $180m.; dep. NT $4,896.1m. (Dec. 1971); Chair. P. C. CHAO; Gen. Man. T. C. PAN.

Bank of Taiwan: 120 Chungking South Rd., Section 1, Taipei; f. 1946; cap. NT $1,000m.; dep. NT $25,522m. (Dec. 1972); Chair. M. S. CHEN; Pres. RONALD H. C. HO; publ. *Bank of Taiwan Quarterly* (Chinese).

Co-operative Bank of Taiwan: 75-1 Kuan Chien Rd., Taipei; f. 1946; primary function: to act as central bank for co-operatives, and as major agricultural credit institution; 44 brs., 41 agents and 255 correspondents; cap. NT $200m.; dep. NT $13,592m. (1971); Chair. LI REN-CHUN; Gen. Man. C. C. WANG.

Farmers' Bank of China: 53 Huai Ning St., Taipei; f. 1933; cap. NT $180m.; dep. NT $4,817m. (Dec. 1972); Chair. TANG TSUNG; Pres. F. M. HSU.

International Commercial Bank of China: 15 Chungshan N. Rd., Section 2, Taipei; f. 1912; cap. NT $720m.; dep. NT $7,717m.; (Dec. 1972); Chair. P. S. LIM; Pres. TSUNG TO WAY; publ. *Economic Review* (bimonthly).

Land Bank of Taiwan: 46 Kuan Chien Rd., Taipei; f. 1946; cap. NT $200m.; dep. NT $7,214m.; Chair. HSIAO TSENG; Gen. Man. CHEN YUN-SHENG; publ. *Quarterly Journal*.

COMMERCIAL BANKS

Central Trust Bank of China: 49 Wu Chang St., section 1, Taipei; f. 1935; cap. NT $196.4m.; dep. NT $6,694.3m. (Dec. 1971); Chair. C. TENG; Pres. Dr. I. SHU AN SUN.

Chang Hwa Commercial Bank Ltd.: 38, Section 2, Tsuyu Rd., Taichung; f. 1905; cap. NT $120m.; dep. NT $20,003m. (Dec. 1972); Chair. P. S. CHANG; Pres. CHIN-CHUAN WU.

First Commercial Bank of Taiwan: 30 Chungking S. Rd., Taipei; f. 1899; cap. NT $128m.; dep. NT $17,102m. (Dec. 1972); Chair. C. C. CHEN; Pres. C. Y. KUO; 93 branch offices.

Hua Nan Commercial Bank Ltd.: Chungking Rd. S., Taipei; f. 1919; cap. NT $120m.; dep. NT $14,213m. (Dec. 1972); Chair. Y. L. LIN; Pres. T. P. KAO.

Overseas Chinese Commercial Banking Corporation: 102 Heng Yang Rd., Taipei; f. 1961; general and foreign exchange banking business; cap. p.u. NT$ 128.4m.; Chair. LAMKO CHUA; Gen. Man. C. Y. WU.

FOREIGN BANKS

American Express International Banking Corpn.: Taipei.

Bangkok Bank Ltd.: 24 Chungshan N. Rd., 2nd Section, Taipei; Asst. Vice-Pres./Man. A. WASANTACHAT.

Bank of America NT and SA: 43 Kuan Chien Rd., Taipei; Man. BREWSTER P. CAMPBELL, Jr.

Dai-Ichi Kangyo Bank: Head Office; Tokyo.

First National City Bank: New York, N.Y., U.S.A.; 53 Nanking East Rd., Section 2, Taipei; Resident Vice-Pres. EARL W. GLAZIER; Gen. Man. W. H. Y. YANG; Man. T. Y. WEI.

DEVELOPMENT CORPORATION

China Development Corporation: 131 Nanking East Rd., Section 5, Taipei 105; f. 1959 as privately owned development finance company to assist in creation, modernization, and expansion of private industrial enterprises in Taiwan, to encourage participation of private capital in such enterprises, and to help to promote and develop a capital market; cap. NT $330m.; Chair. P. S. LIM; Pres. YEN SHEN.

Since the establishment of the C.D.C., industry has become increasingly important in the Taiwan economy, manufactured goods have emerged as significant exchange earners, and the private sector has played an increasing role in industrial development.

STOCK EXCHANGE

Taiwan Stock Exchange Corporation: 9th Floor, City Bldg., 85 Yen-ping South Rd., Taipei; f. 1962; 34 mems.; Pres. T. Y. TSAI; Chair. K. P. CHAO.

INSURANCE

Cathay Insurance Co. Ltd.: 90 Nanyang St., Taipei; Chair. TIN-LI LIN.

China Insurance Co. Ltd.: Head Office: 58 Wu-Chang St., Section 1, Taipei; Chair. H. P. CHEN; Gen. Man. T. L. CHO.

Central Trust of China, Insurance Dept.: 49 Wuchang St., Taipei; fire, marine, casualty, export, life insurance.

China Mariners' Assurance Corporation Ltd.: 4 Kwantsien Road, Taipei.

Tai Ping Insurance Co. Ltd.: 42 Hsu Chang St., Taipei; f. 1929; Chair. TUNG HAN-CHA.

Taiwan Life Insurance Co. Ltd.: 45 Kuan Chien Rd., Taipei; Chair. M. H. CHOU; Gen. Man. P. S. WAN.

TRADE AND INDUSTRY

CHAMBERS OF COMMERCE

General Chamber of Commerce of the Republic of China: 162-28 Hsin Yi Rd., Section 3, Taipei.

Junior Chamber of Commerce: P.O.B. 21014, Taipei; f. 1953; 1,405 mems.; Pres. Y. C. CHEN; Sec.-Gen. FISHER S. W. CHANG.

Taipei American Chamber of Commerce: 903 Traders Bldg., 65 Nanking E. Rd., Section 3, Taipei; Pres. HOWARD R. GIDDENS.

TRADE AND INDUSTRIAL ORGANIZATIONS

China Productivity Centre: 62 Sining South Rd., Taipei; f. 1955; Gen. Man. S. C. KAO.

Chinese National Association of Industry and Commerce: 4 Huai Ning St., Taipei; Pres. KOO CHEN-FU; Sec.-Gen. T. Y. TSAI.

Chinese National Federation of Industries: 162 Shin Yee Rd., Section 3, Rose Bldg., 3rd Floor, Taipei; Chair. Y. S. PAN.

Industrial Development and Investment Centre: Union Bldg., 9 Paoching Rd., Taipei; f. 1959 to assist investment and planning; Dir. M. C. LIU; offices abroad: 515 Madison Ave., New York 22; Exchange Bldg., Rotterdam, Netherlands and in Italy.

Taiwan Handicraft Promotion Centre: 5 Chungshan S. Rd., Taipei; f. 1956; Chair. C. T. CHIEN; Man. PHILLIP P. C. LIU.

Trading Department of Central Trust of China: 49 Wuchang St., Section 1, Taipei; assists the Government in promoting foreign trade and handling exports and domestic sales for public and private enterprises.

TRADE UNIONS

Chinese Federation of Labour: 3-40 Wan Shen Li Road, Ching Mei, Taipei; f. 1948; mems.: 373 industrial unions and 362 craft unions representing 319,065 workers; Chair. CHOU HSUEH-HSIANG; Gen.-Sec. SHUI HSIANG-YUN.

NATIONAL FEDERATIONS

Chinese Federation of Postal Workers: 4th Floor, 99 Kweilin Rd., Taipei; f. 1930; 9,000 mems.; Pres. SHUI HSIANG-YUN.

Chinese National Federation of Railway Workers: 7 Alley 10, Ching Chow Street, Taipei; 23,434 mems.; Chair. CHANG JUI-MING.

Chinese National Federation of Salt Miners: 40-2 Wancheng Road, Chingmei, Taipei; about 6,000 mems.

National Chinese Seamen's Union: 25 Nanking East Rd., Section 3, Taipei; f. 1913; over 30,000 mems.; Pres. HONG DAH-IH; publ. *Chinese Seamen Monthly* (in Chinese).

Taiwan Federation of Textile and Dyeing Workers' Union (TFTDWU): 9 Lane 1530, Chung Cheng Rd., Taipei; f. 1957; 28,000 mems.; Chair. HWANG YUEH-HSIANG.

REGIONAL FEDERATION

Taiwan Federation of Labour: 21 Chengte Rd., Taipei; 304,572 mems. and 35 affiliates; Chair. CHIEN WEN-FA; Man. TSAI FAN-TE.

CO-OPERATIVES

By the end of 1971 there were 2,990 co-operatives with a total membership of 1,838,636 people and total capital of NT$600,996,150. Of the specialized co-operatives, the most important were consumers (2,235 co-ops., 1,054,126 mems., cap. NT$21,288,852), credit (79 co-ops., 390,191 mems., cap. NT$377,889,096), and co-operative farms (173 co-ops., 26,734 mems., cap. NT$11,347,278).

The centre of co-operative financing is the Co-operative Bank of Taiwan, owned jointly by the Taiwan Provincial Government and 674 co-operative units (*see* Finance section). The Co-operative Institute (f. 1928) and the Co-operative League (f. 1940), which has 401 institutional and 4,800 individual members, exist to further the co-operative movement's national and international interests; and departments of co-operative business have been set up at the Taiwan Provincial Chung Hsing University and other colleges.

RURAL RECONSTRUCTION

Joint Commission on Rural Reconstruction (JCRR): 37 Nanhai Rd., Taipei; f. 1948; provides technical and financial assistance to Government in rural reconstruction programmes aiming to improve rural living standards, to increase agricultural production, to develop self-help among the rural population, to strengthen services of agricultural agencies and organizations, and to mobilize volunteers for rural programmes; Chair. Dr. ROBERT C. T. LEE; Commrs. Dr. W. C. CLARK, Dr. Y. S. TSIANG; Sec.-Gen. Dr. WANG; library of 10,605 vols., 9,976 pamphlets; publs. general reports (twice a year), technical papers (irregular), news releases (irregular).

TRANSPORT

RAILWAYS

Taiwan Railway Administration: 2 Yen Ping N. Rd., Section 1, Taipei; a public utility under the provincial government of Taiwan, it operates both the west line and east line systems with a route length of 1,001 km.; there is also a main trunk line from Keelung in the north to Kaohsiung in the south, and another line down the east coast linking Hualien with Taitung; Man. Dir. S. H. CHEN.

There are also 2,838.4 km. of private narrow-gauge railroads operated by the Taiwan Sugar Corporation, the Taiwan Forestry Administration and the Taiwan Metal Mining Corporation. These railroads are mostly used for freight but they also provide public passenger and freight services which connect with those of T.R.A.

ROADS

Taiwan Highway Bureau: 70 Chung Hsiao West Rd., Section 1, Taipei; Dir. HSI-YU LEE.

There are 16,404 km. of highways, most of them asphalt-paved, representing about 50 km. of road per 100 sq. km. of land. There is a national omnibus service operated by the Bureau.

SHIPPING

Kaohsiung is Taiwan's chief port, handling over two-thirds of the country's external commerce. Keelung, near Taipei, is the country's second port.

China Merchants' Steam Navigation Co.: Enterprise Bldg., 9th Floor, 46 Kuan Chien Rd., Taipei; 15 vessels; tanker services worldwide; Chair. C. C. TSAO.

China Union Lines Ltd.: 46 Kwantsien Rd., Taipei; f. 1948; 11 cargo vessels; Chair. C. D. CHOW; Pres. C. CHAO.

Evergreen Marine Corpn.: 24-1 Section 1, Chang An E. Rd., Taipei; f. 1968; 12 cargo vessels; services from

Far East to India, Pakistan, Persian Gulf, Red Sea, Central South America and the Caribbean; Chair. Y. F. CHANG; Gen. Man. C. T. CHIU.

Far Eastern Navigation Corp. Ltd.: 42 Hsu-Chang St. (4th floor), P.O.B. 1120, Taipei; Chair. CHAO CHIN-YANG.

First Steamship Co. Ltd.: 42 Hsu Chang Street, 7th Floor, Taipei; 5 cargo vessels; worldwide service; Chair. H. C. TUNG; Gen. Man. S. C. CHU.

Great Pacific Navigation Co. Ltd.: 79 Chung Shan Rd., North, Section 2, Taipei; 8 vessels; fruit and general cargo services to Japan; Pres. CHA-MOU CHEN.

Taiwan Navigation Co. Ltd.: 6 Chungking S. Rd., Section 1, Taipei; f. 1947; Chair. H. L. HUANG; Pres. T. W. CHEN.

CIVIL AVIATION

China Air Lines Ltd. (CAL): 26 Nanking Rd. East, Section 3, Taipei; f. 1959; has operated since 1965 as the national airline of the Republic of China; scheduled passenger and cargo services are operated from Taipei to Hong Kong, Tokyo, San Francisco, Seoul, Bangkok, Manila, Saigon, Singapore, Kuala Lumpur, Honolulu, Los Angeles and Jakarta; domestic services throughout Taiwan; fleet comprises 6 Boeing 707, 3 727, 2 Caravelles, 1 YS-11A, 4 DC-45, 3 DC-3, 3 C-46; Chair. Gen. H. S. HSU; Pres. Gen. BEN Y. C. CHOW.

Civil Air Transport: 232 Tun Hua North Rd., Taipei; passenger and cargo charter services; fleet one DC-6B, three C-46; Chair. Dr. WANG WEN SUN; Man. Dir. HUGH I. GRUNDY.

Far Eastern Air Transport Corporation: 15 Nanking E. Rd., Section 3, Taipei; f. 1957; domestic services; Chair. K. T. SIAO; Pres. T. C. HWOO.

There is an international airport at Taipei which is served by the following foreign airlines: Air Vietnam, Cathay Pacific, Korean Air Lines, North-west Orient, Singapore Airlines, Thai International, TWA.

TOURISM

Tourism Council, Ministry of Communications: 53, Section 2, P.O.B. 1490, Taipei; f. 1960; Chair. WELLINGTON Y. TSAO.

Taiwan Visitors Information Service: 2 Lane 18, St. 110, Tienmu 1st Rd., Taipei; f. 1966; Dir. Y. C. HSU.

China Tourism Development Corporation: Taipei; f. 1969; state-owned; cap. NT$100 million.

CULTURAL ORGANIZATIONS
PRINCIPAL OPERAS

Foe Hsing Chinese Opera: 68 Wen Chuan Rd., Peitou; f. 1957; Dir. MA CHING-JUI.

Ta Peng Chinese Opera: No. 1 Special, Sungkiang Road, Taipei; f. 1965; Dir. CHANG CHING-CHIU.

PRINCIPAL ORCHESTRA

Taiwan Symphony Orchestra: 162 Hoping E. Road, Section 1, Taipei; f. 1951; Government body under Taiwan Provincial Dept. of Education; Dir. Prof. DAVID C. L. TAI.

ATOMIC ENERGY

Atomic Energy Council: BBC Bldg., 53 Jen Ai Rd., Section 3, Taipei; Chair. CHIEN SHIH-LIANG; Sec. V. CHEN-HWA CHENG; publs. *Nuclear Science Journal* (quarterly), *Chinese AEC Bulletin* (bi-monthly).

National Tsing-Hua University Institute of Nuclear Science: Hsinchu, Taiwan; f. 1956; national research centre with 1,000 kW. reactor, 3 Mev Van de Graaff accelerators; neutron physics, nuclear engineering, isotope production, biological effects of radiation, medical and food preservation uses of radiation, and other studies; staff of over 100.

Biological and Medical Isotope Laboratory: Department of Biochemistry, National Defence Medical Centre, P.O. Box 7432; f. 1957; fall-out and irradiation studies.

National Taiwan University: Taipei; equipped with Cockroft-Walton accelerator and an isotope laboratory.

Note: A 40 MW atomic research reactor built with Canadian assistance in North-west Taiwan for the Institute of Nuclear Energy Research is now in operation.

UNIVERSITIES

PRINCIPAL UNIVERSITIES

National Chengchi University: Mushan, Taipei; 590 teachers, 4,752 students.

National Cheng Kung University: Ta-Hsueh Rd., Tainan; 423 teachers, 3,663 students.

National Chung Hsing University: 250 Kuokuang Rd., Taichung; 433 teachers, 5,014 students.

National Taiwan University: Roosevelt Rd., Taipei; 1,136 teachers, 11,151 students.

National Tsing Hua University: Kuang Fu Rd., Hsinchu; 148 teachers, 807 students.

Soochow University: Wai Shuang Hsi Shihlin; 235 teachers, 2,051 students.

Taiwan Normal University: Taipei; 477 teachers, 6,700 students.

Tunghai (Christian) University: Taichung, Taiwan; 235 teachers, 1,725 students.

COLOMBIA

INTRODUCTORY SURVEY

Location, Climate, Language, Religion, Flag, Capital

The Republic of Colombia lies in the north-west of South America with the Caribbean Sea to the north and the Pacific to the west. Its continental neighbours are Venezuela, Brazil, Peru and Ecuador, while Panama connects it with Central America. The coastal areas have a tropical rain forest climate, the plateaux are temperate and in the Andes there are areas of permanent snow. The language is Spanish. There is freedom of religion; the state religion, to which 90 per cent of the population adhere, is Roman Catholicism. There are small Protestant and Jewish minorities. The national flag (proportions 3 by 2) has horizontal stripes of yellow (half the depth), dark blue and red. The capital is Bogotá.

Recent History

Between 1948 and 1957, Colombia was torn by civil war, known as *La Violencia*, between Conservative and Liberal factions. For the greater part of this period, the country was under the dictatorship of Gen. Gustavo Rojas Pinilla, who was overthrown by a military junta in May 1957. Democratic government was re-established in 1958 with an agreement to form a National Front, by which the two principal parties, Liberal and Conservative, would alternate in power for four-year periods. In 1966 Dr. Carlos Lleras Restrepo was elected Liberal President for a four-year term. Despite much political unrest and continuing guerrilla warfare, Dr. Lleras was able to bring about economic recovery after the crisis left by Gen. Rojas. Presidential elections were held in April 1970 and Dr. Misael Pastrana Borrero of the Conservative Party was elected by a very small majority over Gen. Rojas. Dr. Pastrana's administration was severely hampered during its first two years by the parliamentary alliance between the supporters of Gen. Rojas and a section of the Liberal Party. This alliance threatened to put an end to the National Front government instituted in 1958. However, both the Liberals and Conservatives won back many seats from ANAPO (Rojas Pinilla's party) in the 1972 municipal elections. Later in 1972 two main factions within the Liberal Party agreed to unite their forces. The presidential elections of April 1974 (for which the National Front arrangement was terminated) were won by the Liberal Party, and their candidate, Dr. Alfonso López Michelsen (Minister for Foreign Affairs from 1968 to 1970), is due to take office in August.

Government

The Constitution is that of 1886, which has been revised several times since its promulgation. Executive power is exercised by the President (assisted by a Cabinet) who is elected for a four-year term by universal adult suffrage.

Legislation is carried out by Congress, consisting of the Senate (106 members elected for four years) and the House of Representatives (204 members elected for four years). The country is divided into 23 Departments.

Defence

At the age of 18 every male must present himself as a candidate for military service of at least one year. The strength of the army is 50,000, the navy 7,200 and the air force 6,000. The national police force numbers about 35,000 men.

Economic Affairs

The economy depends principally on coffee, of which Colombia is the world's second largest producer and which accounted for over 40 per cent of export earnings in 1972. Agriculture employs about half the labour force, but efforts have been successfully made to diversify secondary exports, especially bananas, cotton, sugar, textiles, tobacco, timber, hides, meat and livestock, cement, pharmaceuticals and metal products. Colombia produces 90 per cent of the world's emeralds and is the largest gold producer in Latin America; it is one of the few countries where platinum is found. Nearly U.S. $50 million worth of emeralds were exported in 1972. Colombia's oil production is the third largest in South America and substantial deposits are being exploited in the south at Putumayo; three major oil refineries are among the most important industrial projects to be financed in 1974. Steel and cement are the chief industrial products.

To limit the growth of cities resulting from industrial development, the Government has initiated a series of rural development programmes, including projects such as technical education, community development and land reform. The direction of trade is being modified as new markets in western Europe and Latin America open up. The Andean Regional Agreement, which Colombia ratified in 1969, provides a ready market of over 50 million people. Economic progress has meant that Colombia is encountering little difficulty in finding sources of credit; towards the end of 1973 an additional U.S. $2,400 million in foreign credit was granted by the World Bank. Inflation is becoming a serious problem, however, and as a combative measure government expenditure is to be reduced in 1974.

Colombia is a member of the Organization of American States, the Alliance for Progress and the Latin American Free Trade Association.

Transport and Communications

The high mountains make transport difficult. There are 43,400 km. of roads, including three highways, and 3,424 km. of railways. Much freight and cattle as well as passenger traffic is carried on the River Magdalena, which is navigable for 1,440 km. from Barranquilla on the Atlantic coast to Puerto Berrio. A new sea-level canal is planned between Urabá on the Caribbean and Málaga on the Pacific at a cost of $422m. Capable of carrying vessels up to 20,000 tons, the actual canal will be 25 km. long, but the total length, including the Atrato and San Juan rivers, will be 420 km. A new port is to be built at Urabá at a cost of $4.1m. Four national airlines provide internal and international services. There are international airports at Bogotá, Barranquilla and Cali.

Social Welfare

Social welfare is organized by the Institute of Social Security, which provides benefits for sickness, industrial accidents and unemployment. Large firms must provide life insurance for their employees and there is a comprehensive system of pensions.

Education

Education is free but not compulsory, since facilities are inadequate. In 1970 there were 37,257 schools with 3,757,236 pupils. There are 19 public and 16 private universities. There is 60 per cent literacy.

Tourism

The main tourist attractions are the Andes mountains of up to 6,000 metres, the extensive forests and jungles and pre-Colombian relics and monuments of Colonial art.

Visas are not required to visit Colombia by nationals of Austria, EEC countries (except Ireland), Finland, Greece, Japan, Norway, Spain, Sweden and Switzerland.

Sport

The principal sports are football, horse-racing, cycling, baseball and polo. Tejo, a kind of discus-throwing game, is also popular.

Public Holidays

1974: August 7th (Battle of Boyacá), August 15th (Assumption), October 12th (Discovery of America), November 1st (All Saints' Day), November 11th (Independence of Cartagena), December 8th (Immaculate Conception), December 25th (Christmas Day).

1975: January 1st (New Year's Day), January 6th (Epiphany), March 19th (St. Joseph's Day), March 28th, 29th (Easter), May 1st (Labour Day), May 21st (Ascension Day), May 29th (Corpus Christi), June 5th (Thanksgiving), June 29th (SS. Peter and Paul), July 20th (Independence Day).

Note: Both the Church and the Government intend to made radical changes in the holiday calendar. Legislation is pending.

Weights and Measures

The metric system is in force.

Currency and Exchange Rate

100 centavos=1 Colombian peso.

Exchange rates (March 1974):
£1 sterling=61.24 pesos;
U.S. $1=25.58 pesos.

STATISTICAL SURVEY

AREA AND POPULATION

AREA (sq. km.)	ESTIMATED POPULATION (July 15th, 1973)	BIRTHS, MARRIAGES, DEATHS, 1971 (per '000)		
		Births	Marriages	Deaths
1,138,914	23,209,300	36.57	5.24*	9.49

* 1970 figure.

POPULATION OF DEPARTMENTS
(estimates, July 1972)

DEPARTMENTS	POPULATION	CHIEF TOWNS	POPULATION
Antioquia . . .	3,326,700	Bogotá, D.E. . .	2,978,300
Atlántico . . .	999,300	Medellín . . .	1,269,900
Bogotá, D.E. . .	2,978,300	Cali . . .	1,077,000
Bolívar . .	931,200	Barranquilla . .	721,900
Boyacá . .	1,280,200	Bucaramanga . .	364,200
Caldas . . .	871,600	Cartagena . .	362,600
Cauca . . .	750,000	Manizales . .	318,600
Chocó . . .	226,300	Cúcuta . . .	259,400
Córdoba . .	852,500	Pereira . .	258,200
Cundinamarca . .	1,307,800	Ibagué . .	226,500
El César . .	545,800	Armenia . .	196,400
Guajira . .	291,400	Santa Marta . .	174,200
Huila . . .	524,500	Montería . .	173,500
Magdalena . .	667,700	Valledupar . .	161,500
Meta . . .	297,000	Pasto . . .	140,700
Nariño . .	842,300	Neiva . . .	129,700
Quindío . .	370,900		
Risaralda . .	551,500		
Santander del Norte .	663,000		
Santander del Sur .	1,221,000		
Sucre . . .	389,100		
Tolima . . .	957,200		
Valle del Cauca . .	2,316,400		

EMPLOYMENT
(1970)

Agriculture, forestry and fishing . . .	2,349,000
Mining and quarrying . . .	30,000
Manufacturing industries . . .	859,000
Building	221,000
Electricity, gas, water and sanitation .	26,000
Commerce, restaurants and hotels .	754,000
Transport and communications .	229,000
Services	1,208,000
Finance	88,000
TOTAL	5,764,000

AGRICULTURE

PRODUCTION
('ooo metric tons)

	1971	1972*
Rice	864.0	1,000.0
Bananas . . .	351.0	n.a.
Sugar Cane . . .	670.0	n.a.
Maize . . .	915.0	872.0
Potatoes . . .	1,084.0	1,058.0
Wheat . . .	51.0	79.0
Cotton. . . .	323.0	413.0
Tobacco . . .	39.3	n.a.

*Provisional.

Coffee production 1972–73: 480,000 metric tons.

LIVESTOCK
('ooo head)

	1970
Cattle	12,485.2
Pigs	1,542.7
Sheep and Goats . .	n.a.
Horses, Mules and Asses .	197*

*1968.

MINING AND INDUSTRY

		1968	1969	1970	1971	1972
Gold	('ooo troy ounces)	237.5	218.0	202.0	188.0	186.8
Silver	(,, ,, ,,)	98.7	76.1	75.9	67.6	69.9
Platinum (exports) . .	(,, ,, ,,)	n.a.	n.a.	n.a.	n.a.	n.a.
Crude Petroleum (million barrels of 42 U.S. gallons)		63.5	77.3	80.1	78.6	71.6
Natural Gasoline (,, ,, ,, ,, ,,)		13.4	13.9	15.3	16.4	17.5
Cement	('ooo tons)	2,367.2	2,392.9	2,773.9	2,828.4	3,005.6
Salt	(,, ,,)	n.a.	340.3	332.5	337.5	348.7
Sugar	(,, ,,)	663.3	708.7	676.2	744.0	823.7
Electricity (6 Departments) .	(million kWh.)	6,038.2	6,557.9	7,214.4	8,086.7	8,943.8
Steel Ingots . . .	(metric tons)	198,974.0	206,327.0	238,658.0	247,264.0	275,036.0

FINANCE

100 centavos = 1 Colombian peso.

Coins: 1, 5, 10, 20 and 50 centavos.

Notes: 1, 2, 5, 10, 20, 50, 100 and 500 pesos.

Exchange rates (March 1974): £1 sterling = 61.24 pesos (selling rate);

U.S. $1 = 20.38 pesos (coffee export rate) or 25.58 pesos (selling rate).

100 Colombian pesos = £1.633 = = $3.909 (selling rates).

BUDGET
('ooo pesos)

REVENUE	1972	1973	EXPENDITURE	1972	1973
Direct Taxation . .	8,066,662	8,860,000	Finance (incl. debt) . .	3,178,737	6,583,716
Indirect Taxation . .	8,582,843	9,930,516	Defence . . .	1,643,411	2,035,621
Rates and Fines . .	483,756	499,844	Education . . .	2,839,258	4,375,757
Revenue under Contracts .	275,109	276,951	Public Works . .	2,834,685	2,816,281
Credit Resources . .	4,013,675	5,866,106	Police . . .	2,201,001	1,544,583
			Development . .	1,156,737	1,468,076
			Agriculture . .	1,200,352	1,341,963
			Health . . .	1,279,617	2,018,211
			Other Items . .	3,088,247	3,249,209
TOTAL . . .	21,422,045	25,433,417	TOTAL . . .	21,422,045	25,433,417

RESERVES AND CURRENCY

	1968	1969	1970	1971	1972
Gold and Foreign Exchange Reserves at Banco de la República (million U.S.$) . . .	217.6	257.3	257.4	265.2	392.7
Currency in Circulation at end of year (million pesos)	5,897.6	7,014.5	8,356.9	9,137.4	11,399.6

BALANCE OF PAYMENTS
(U.S. $ million)

	1969	1970	1971
CURRENT ACCOUNT:			
Exports (f.o.b.)	608	736	698
Imports (c.i.f.)	−664	−815	−870
Net adjustments	12	− 9	− 29
Non-monetary gold	5	6	2
Other net current account transactions:			
Income from foreign investments . .	−144	−180	−185
Travel	− 14	− 2	− 10
Transfers abroad	38	26	26
Other	− 16	− 55	− 59
BALANCE	−175	−293	−427
CAPITAL ACCOUNT (NET):			
Private sector:			
Long-term	89	57	71
Short-term	− 16	58	83
Government sector . . .	144	169	109
Banco de la República . . .	16	5	25
Private monetary institutions . .	49	57	93
BALANCE	282	346	381
Errors and Omissions	− 46	− 18	47
IMF Special Drawing Rights . . .	—	21	17
Change in Foreign Net Reserves of Banco de la República . . .	61	56	18

Source: Banco de la República.

EXTERNAL TRADE
(U.S.$'000)

	1967	1968	1969	1970	1971
Imports . . .	496,862	643,260	685,273	842,960	929,441
Exports . . .	509,923	558,278	607,510	735,657	690,009

PRINCIPAL COMMODITIES
(U.S. $million)

IMPORTS	1968	1969	1970	1971
Cereals	19.5	20.5	18.3	38.9
Fats and Oils	10.8	10.9	12.0	20.5
Cocoa	5.5	6.3	8.4	8.3
Fuels and Mineral Oils . . .	5.4	8.3	8.7	10.8
Fertilizers	7.9	6.6	7.6	10.7
Plastic Products	14.4	18.8	22.5	28.1
Rubber Products	11.3	14.6	14.1	16.9
Chemicals	60.4	103.1	111.3	121.9
Mechanical Equipment . . .	136.7	134.1	165.8	202.4
Electrical Equipment . . .	50.8	47.4	65.4	70.6
Vehicles	73.8	88.7	108.6	90.0

EXPORTS	1969	1970	1971
Bananas and Plantains . . .	19.7	18.1	14.7
Cattle and Meat	6.0	21.8	28.2
Raw Coffee	343.9	466.7	395.4
Sugar	14.7	14.0	15.7
Raw Cotton	32.6	34.3	29.3
Textiles	7.8	17.4	24.6
Fuel Oil	15.7	12.1	20.5
Crude Petroleum	56.7	58.6	45.7
Leaf Tobacco	7.2	7.2	9.2

COFFEE EXPORTS

	1970		1971	
	Quantity (metric tons)	Value ('000 pesos)	Quantity (metric tons)	Value ('000 pesos)
Argentina	6,572	147,223	4,182	83,913
Belgium and Luxembourg . .	6,648	148,078	8,795	178,386
Canada	3,145	70,854	6,445	130,009
Denmark	4,554	101,700	4,757	96,596
Finland	19,641	441,241	10,354	210,367
German Democratic Republic .	6,392	142,240	5,962	120,557
Germany, Federal Republic .	76,927	1,692,960	81,174	1,645,483
Italy	3,155	70,268	3,023	61,134
Japan	7,599	168,018	3,907	79,344
Spain	25,275	550,659	14,799	298,310
Sweden	16,314	362,680	19,478	394,562
United States . . .	152,667	3,362,927	171,520	3,479,940
Others	61,488	1,366,536	55,381	1,120,219
TOTAL . . .	390,377	8,625,384	389,787	7,898,820

PRINCIPAL COUNTRIES
('ooo pesos)

	1970		1971	
	Imports	Exports	Imports	Exports
Argentina	265,848	212,904	275,906	163,638
Belgium and Luxembourg . .	175,788	162,032	170,243	198,302
Canada	374,032	151,766	421,008	256,074
Ecuador	183,135	232,675	252,771	336,435
Finland	90,880	442,078	122,153	210,610
France	327,227	120,347	513,860	194,234
Germany, Federal Republic .	1,310,285	1,924,380	1,877,563	2,081,928
Italy	389,869	98,502	481,675	99,013
Japan	961,467	378,006	1,256,335	362,864
Netherlands . . .	236,601	728,508	444,739	647,520
Netherlands Antilles . .	12,944	42,711	76,101	76,325
Peru	180,430	463,318	213,462	632,182
Spain	805,102	706,532	698,764	606,126
Sweden	246,050	424,407	334,740	408,358
Switzerland . . .	319,993	49,337	457,746	79,478
United Kingdom . .	622,701	269,689	824,024	211,906
U.S.A. . . .	7,364,784	4,750,636	7,744,968	4,964,561
Others	1,558,266	1,877,435	2,038,220	1,926,178
TOTAL . . .	15,425,402	13,035,263	18,204,278	13,455,732

TRANSPORT
RAILWAYS

	1969	1970	1971	1972
Passengers Carried (number)	2,649,697	2,954,482	3,161,175	4,263,030
Passenger-km.	273,280,702	249,001,744	281,547,332	397,851,197
Freight Carried (metric tons)	3,049,859	2,781,148	2,653,170	2,730,837
Freight ton-km. . .	1,158,740,619	1,172,633,000	1,150,492,073	1,198,486,395

ROADS

	1969	1970	1971
Passenger Vehicles .	219,827	238,499	268,249
Goods Vehicles .	81,107	83,500	86,939
TOTAL .	300,934	321,999	355,188

INLAND WATERWAYS
(River Magdalena)

	1971	1972
Passengers Carried . .	29,421	15,362
Freight Carried (metric tons) .	2,544,488	2,709,585
Cattle Carried* . .	50,803	24,385

* Provisional.

CIVIL AVIATION
(INTERNATIONAL TRAFFIC)

	1971	1972
Passengers Entering ('ooo) .	249	290
Passengers Leaving ('ooo) .	271	307
Cargo Imported (tons) .	10,044	10,052
Cargo Exported (tons) .	14,477	17,899

OCEAN SHIPPING

	1971	1972
Vessels Entered (net registered tonnage) . . .	15,489,690	11,606,005
Goods Unloaded (metric tons) .	1,941,248	1,620,069
Vessels Cleared (net registered tonnage) . . .	15,938,795	11,375,634
Goods Loaded (metric tons) .	1,829,257	1,710,756

EDUCATION
(1970)

	SCHOOLS	TEACHERS	PUPILS
Nursery* . .	3,377	18,565	110,494
Primary . .	29,622	85,009	2,993,153
Secondary (general)	4,258	65,223	653,589
Higher (incl. Universities) . .	62*	8,918*	76,748

Source: Departamento Administrativo Nacional de Estadística, Bogotá.   * 1968 figures.

THE CONSTITUTION

The Constitution now in force was promulgated in 1886 and has been amended from time to time. Following the fall of the Rojas Pinilla régime in May 1957, the Constitution was amended to introduce a sixteen-year period of bi-partisan government. Under this system the Liberal and Conservatives were equally represented in both houses of Congress, in departmental and municipal legislatures and in the national and departmental cabinets. The system came to an end in 1974. Under the 1886 Constitution, the country is governed by a President and a Congress consisting of two Chambers. All citizens over the age of 21 are eligible to vote; women obtained the right to vote in 1955. Liberty of the press, freedom of speech and religious toleration are guaranteed. All male citizens are required to present themselves for possible military service at the age of 18.

THE PRESIDENT

Executive power is vested in the President of the Republic, who is elected by popular suffrage for a four-year term of office.

The President is assisted in the government of the country by a Cabinet which he appoints. A substitute is elected by Congress, subject to bi-annual re-appointment, to act in the event of a Presidential vacancy. The President appoints the governors of the twenty-three Departments, the four Intendencies and the four Commissaries. The Cabinet resigns annually on August 7th to allow the President to replace Ministers if he desires to do so.

CONGRESS

Legislative power is exercised by Congress, which is composed of the Senate and the House of Representatives. Members of both chambers are elected by direct suffrage for a period of four years.

The Presidents in each House are elected for sixty days.

NATIONAL ECONOMIC COUNCIL

Direction of the nation's finances is in the hands of the Controller-General, who is appointed for two years. A National Economic Council including five ministers and also representatives of banking, industrial and agricultural interests, has functioned since 1935.

LOCAL GOVERNMENT

For administrative purposes the country is divided into twenty-three departments, four intendencies and four commissaries. The twenty-three departments of the republic are further divided into municipalities. Governors for the Departments are appointed by the President, but regional legislatures are elected by the local inhabitants and enjoy considerable autonomy, including the management of local finances. Mayors for the municipalities are appointed by the governors.

Various constitutional reforms were promulgated in December 1968, including the following amendments: to increase the membership of the Senate from 106 to 112, and reduce the Chamber of Representatives from 204 to 198; to increase from two to four years the term of office of representatives; to eliminate the two-thirds majority required for matters of importance; to enable the Government to legislate by decree for a maximum period of 90 days in any one year in the event of an economic crisis, though such decrees must relate only to the matters which caused the crisis; from 1970, proportional representation to be allowed in departmental and municipal elections; the same principle to apply to congressional elections after 1974.

THE GOVERNMENT

HEAD OF STATE

President: Dr. MISAEL PASTRANA BORRERO.

CABINET
(*April* 1974)

Minister of the Interior: Dr. ROBERTO ARENAS BONILLA.

Minister of Foreign Affairs: Dr. ALFREDO VÁSQUEZ CARRIZOSA.

Minister of Justice: Dr. JAIME CASTRO.

Minister of Finance: Dr. LUIS FERNANDO ECHEVARRÍA.

Minister of Defence: Gen. HERNANDO CURREA CUBIDES.

Minister of Agriculture: Dr. HERNÁN VALLEJO MEJIÁ.

Minister of Labour: Dr. JOSÉ ANTONIO MURGAS.

Minister of Health: Dr. José María Salazar Bucheli.

Minister of Economic Development: Dr. José Raimundo Sojo Zambrano.

Minister of Mines and Petroleum: Dr. Gerardo Silva Valderrama.

Minister of Education: Dr. Juan Jacobo Muñoz.

Minister of Communications: Dr. Carlos Holguín Sardi.

Minister of Public Works: Dr. Argelino Durán Quintero.

Note: Elections were held in April 1974 and Dr. Alfonso López Michelsen is due to take office as President in August; a new government will be sworn in.

DIPLOMATIC REPRESENTATION

EMBASSIES ACCREDITED TO COLOMBIA

(In Bogotá, unless otherwise stated)

Argentina: Carrera 1, No. 71-65; *Ambassador:* (vacant).

Austria: Carrera 1-A, No. 76-79; *Ambassador:* Herbert Grubmayr.

Belgium: Carrera 4-A, No. 25-B-27; *Ambassador:* Albert Serruys.

Bolivia: Carrera 5, No. 81-26; *Ambassador:* Lt. Col. José Gil Reyes.

Brazil: Avenida Caracas, No. 37-20; *Ambassador:* José Augusto de Macedo Soares.

Bulgaria: Calle 57-B, No. 37-55; *Ambassador:* (vacant).

Canada: Carrera 12, No. 91-24; *Ambassador:* Sidney Freifeld.

Chile: Carrera 5, No. 72-70; *Ambassador:* (vacant).

China (Taiwan): Carrera 3, No. 76-99; *Ambassador:* Sampson C. Shen.

Costa Rica: Calle 59, No. 13-37; *Ambassador:* Alvaro Fernández Escalante.

Czechoslovakia: Calle 92, No. 21-40; *Ambassador:* Ladislav Dvořák.

Denmark: Calle 101, No. 20-28; *Ambassador:* Anthon Christian Karsten.

Dominican Republic: Carrera 30, No. 46-46; *Ambassador:* Eduardo Antonio García Vásquez.

Ecuador: Carrera 14, No. 44-45; *Ambassador:* Gustavo Larrea Córdova.

Egypt: Carrera 19, No. 88-01; *Ambassador:* Saleh Mourad.

El Salvador: Calle 93, No. 10-59; *Ambassador:* Guillermo Rubio Melhado.

Finland: Lima, Peru.

France: Calle 87, No. 8-64; *Ambassador:* René Thibault.

German Democratic Republic: Carrera 7, No. 81-57; *Ambassador:* Walter Weber.

Germany, Federal Republic: Carrera 10-A, No. 70-73; *Ambassador:* Robert von Forster.

Greece: Rio de Janeiro, Brazil.

Guatemala: Calle 70, No. 9-84; *Ambassador:* Alberto Arreaga González.

Haiti: Carrera 4, No. 58-82; *Ambassador:* Gérard Jean Baptiste.

Honduras: Carrera 18, No. 86-A-15; *Ambassador:* Santiago Flores Ochoa.

India: Carrera 7, No. 87-20; *Ambassador:* Madanjeet Singh.

Israel: Calle 92, No. 13-51; *Ambassador:* Victor Eliachar.

Italy: Diagonal 77, No. 6-88; *Ambassador:* Giovanni S. Rocchi.

Japan: Calle 86, No. 9-44; *Ambassador:* (vacant).

Korea, Republic: Avenida 94, No. 9-39; *Ambassador:* Jin Sang An.

Lebanon: Calle 74, No. 12-44; *Ambassador:* J. Goguikian (also accred. to Bolivia, Ecuador and Peru).

Malta: Edificio Bavaria, Carrera 10, No. 27-91; *Ambassador:* Luigi Marengón.

Mexico: Calle 100, No. 24-19; *Ambassador:* Víctor Manuel Barceló Rodríguez.

Netherlands: Calle 87, No. 9-55; *Ambassador:* Jacob Varekamp.

Nicaragua: Calle 77, No. 7-92; *Ambassador:* Reynaldo Navas Barreto.

Norway: Caracas, Venezuela.

Pakistan: Brasília, D.E., Brazil.

Panama: Calle 92, No. 7-66; *Ambassador:* José de la Rosa Castillo.

Paraguay: Carrera 21, No. 58-38; *Ambassador:* Aníbal Mésquita Vera.

Peru: Calle 80-A, No. 6-50; *Ambassador:* Alberto Wagner de Reyna.

Philippines: Mexico, D.F., Mexico.

Poland: Caracas, Venezuela.

Portugal: Calle 70-A, No. 7-51; *Ambassador:* António Eduardo Ressano García.

Romania: Calle 80, No. 12-37; *Ambassador:* Dumitru Moianu.

Spain: Carrera 7, No. 78-01; *Ambassador:* Fernando Olivié González-Pumariega.

Sweden: Carrera 4, No. 72-55; *Ambassador:* Ingvar Grauers.

Switzerland: Calle 75, No. 8-70; *Ambassador:* Etienne H. Serra.

Syria: Caracas, Venezuela.

Trinidad and Tobago: Caracas, Venezuela.

Turkey: Caracas, Venezuela (E).

U.S.S.R.: Carrera 4, No. 75-00; *Ambassador:* Vladimir I. Andreyev.

United Kingdom: Calle 87, No. 10-50; *Ambassador:* Geoffrey Allan Crossley.

U.S.A.: Calle 37, No. 8-40; *Ambassador:* (vacant).

Uruguay: Carrera 2-A, No. 72-77; *Ambassador:* Jorge Justo Boero Brian.

Vatican: Carrera 15, No. 36-33 (Apostolic Nunciature); *Nuncio:* Angelo Palmas.

Venezuela: Carrera 7, No. 85-12; *Ambassador:* Numa Quevedo.

Yugoslavia: Calle 90, No. 9-A-33; *Ambassador:* Miroslav Zotovic.

Colombia also has diplomatic relations with Ethiopia, Hungary and Jamaica.

PRESIDENT AND CONGRESS

PRESIDENTIAL ELECTION

(April 21st, 1974)

Candidates	Votes
Dr. Alfonso López Michelsen (Partido Liberal)	2,535,374
Dr. Alvaro Gómez Hurtado (Partido Conservator).	1,467,845
María Eugenia Rojas (ANAPO) . . .	450,143
Hernando Echeverri Mejía (UNO) . .	123,459

CONGRESS

Congress consists of the Senate (118 members elected for four years) and the House of Representatives (210 members elected for four years).

GENERAL ELECTION

(April 1970)

Party	Seats	
	Senate	House
National Front:		
Liberal . . .	39	58
Conservative . . .	19	31
Opposition:		
Sourdistas (Liberal) . .	5	9
Sourdistas (Conservative) .	5	12
Belisaristas (Liberal) .	3	6
Belisaristas (Conservative) .	9	18
ANAPO (Liberal) . .	12	28
ANAPO (Conservative) . .	26	44
Independent (Liberal) . .	—	4

Early results from the 1974 elections indicate that the Liberals will have a working majority in both the Senate and the House of Representatives.

POLITICAL PARTIES

Partido Liberal: Avda. Jiménez 8–56, Bogotá; divided into two factions in 1958, the party was re-united in 1973; Leader Dr. Julio César Turbay Ayala; Presidential candidate in 1974 Dr. Alfonso López Michelsen.

Partido Conservador: Bogotá; formerly divided into three factions, the party was re-united in 1973; Leader Dr. Humberto González Narvaez; Presidential candidate in 1974 Dr. Alvaro Gómez Hurtado.

Alianza Nacional Popular (ANAPO): Bogotá; f. 1971; Leaders Gen. Gustavo Rojas Pinilla, Guillermo Hernández Rodríguez; Presidential candidate in 1974 María Eugenia Rojas de Moreno Díaz.

Unión Nacional de Oposición (UNO): Bogotá; left-wing coalition comprising the Communist Party, the Movimiento Amplio Colombiano and the Christian Democrat Party; Leader Gilberto Vieira (Communist Party); Presidential candidate in 1974 Hernando Echeverri Mejía.

Ejército Nacional de Liberación (ELN): guerrilla movement; Leader Fabio Vásquez Castaño.

Ejército Popular de Liberación: Maoist guerrilla movement; splinter group from Communist Party.

Fuerzas Armadas Revolucionarios (FARC): military wing of the Communist Party; Leader Manuel Marulanda.

JUDICIAL SYSTEM

The Supreme Court of Justice, which sits in Bogotá, is divided into four subsidiary courts of Civil Cassations, Criminal Cassation, Labour Cassation and Constitutional Procedure. The twenty-four judges of the Supreme Court are elected for life; vacancies are filled by election by the members. For matters of great importance and government business, the three courts of the Supreme Court sit together as a Plenary Court.

The country is divided into judicial districts, each of which has a superior court of three or more judges. There are also other Courts of Justice for each judicial district, and judges for each province and municipality.

President of the Supreme Court: Dr. GUILLERMO GONZÁLEZ CHARRY.

Vice-President: HERNÁN TORO AGUDELO.

SUPREME COURT OF JUSTICE

Liberals	*Conservatives*
HUMBERTO BARRERA DOMÍNGUEZ	JOSÉ ENRIQUE ARBOLEDA VALENCIA
ERNESTO BLANCO CARERA	MARIO ALARIO DI FILIPPO
JORGE GAVIRIA SALAZAR	JUAN BENAVIDES PATRÓN
CESAR GÓMEZ ESTRADA	ERNESTO CEDIEL ANGEL
CROTATAS LONDOÑO C.	JOSÉ GABRIEL DE LA VEGA
JOSÉ MARÍA ESGUERRA SAMPER	JULIO RONCALLO ACOSTA
LUIS EDUARDO MESA VELÁSQUEZ	GERMÁN GIRALDO ZULÚAGA
LUIS ENRIQUE ROMERO SOTO	EDMUNDO HARKER PUYANA
MIGUEL ANGEL GARCÍA	ALVARO LUNA GÓMEZ
LUIS CARLOS PÉREZ	LUIS SARIMENTO BUITRATO
EUSTORGIO SARRIÁ	JOSÉ MARÍA VELASCO GUERRERO

RELIGION

ROMAN CATHOLIC CHURCH

Roman Catholicism is the religion of 90 per cent of the population.

Archbishops:

Primate of Colombia: H.E. Cardinal LUIS CONCHA-CÓRDOBA.

Archbishop of Bogotá, Arzobispado, Carrera 7,n. 10-20; Most Rev. ANÍBAL MUÑOZ DUQUE.

Barranquilla: Most Rev. GERMÁN VILLA GAVIRIA.

Cali: Most Rev. ALBERTO URIBE URDANETA.

Cartagena: Most Rev. JOSÉ IGNACIO LÓPEZ UMAÑA.

Manizales: Most Rev. ARTURO DUQUE VILLEGAS.

Medellín: Most Rev. TULIO BOTERO SALAZAR.

Nueva Pamplona: Most Rev. ALFREDO RUBIO DÍAZ.

Popayán: Most Rev. MIGUEL ANGEL ARCE VIVAS.

Tunja: Most Rev. AUGUSTO TRUJILLO ARANGO.

OTHER RELIGIONS

Episcopalian Bishop of Colombia: Rt. Rev. W. A. K. FRANKLIN; Carrera 1C, 63-39, Apartado Aéreo 52964, Bogotá.

There are about 100,000 adherents with 286 churches; 211 schools with 488 teachers and 11,635 pupils.

Jews: 25,000 strong community with 66 synagogues.

THE PRESS

DAILIES

BOGOTÁ

Diario Oficial: Carrera 15, No. 56 Sur; f. 1864; official Government paper.

El Espacio: circ. 77,098.

El Espectador: Carrera 68, Calle 19; f. 1887; morning; Liberal; Dir. GUILLERMO CANO; Editor LUIS GABRIEL CANO; circ. 211,000.

La República: Calle 16, No. 4-96; f. 1953; morning; Conservative; Dir. SILVIO VILLEGAS; circ. 50,000.

El Siglo: Calle 15, No. 13-26; f. 1925; Conservative; Dir.-Editor ALVARO CAICEDO; circ. 50,000.

El Tiempo: Avda. Jiménez, No. 6-77; f. 1911; morning; Liberal; Editor ROBERTO GARCÍA PEÑA; circ. 200,000 weekdays, 400,000 Sundays.

El Vespertino: evening; circ. 53,038.

BARRANQUILLA

Diario del Caribe: f. 1946; Conservative; Dir. JULIO MARÍA SANTODOMINGO; circ. 24,640.

El Heraldo: Calle 33, No. 40-60; f. 1933; morning; Liberal; Dir. JUAN B. FERNÁNDEZ; circ. 42,000.

El Nacional: Calle 34, No. 36-122; f. 1945; evening; Liberal; Dir. JULIAN DEVIS ECHANDÍA; circ. 24,003.

BUCARAMANGA

El Deber: f. 1923; morning; Conservative; Dir. EFRAIM OREJARENA RUEDA; circ. 21,000.

El Frente: Apdo. Aéreo 665; f. 1942; morning; Conservative; Dirs. Dr. RAFAEL ORTIZ GONZÁLEZ, Dr. CIRO LÓPEZ MENDOZA; Editor CIRO GÓMEZ MEJÍA; circ. 14,000.

Vanguardia Liberal: Calle 34, No. 13-42; f. 1919; morning; Liberal; Sunday illustrated literary supplement and women's supplement; Dir. RODOLFO GONZÁLEZ GARCÍA; Man. ALEJANDRO GALVIS RAMÍREZ; London representatives: S. S. Koppe & Co. Ltd., 69 Fleet St., E.C.4; circ. 28,000.

CALI

El Crisol: f. 1930; morning; Liberal; Dir. RAFAEL I. RODRÍGUEZ; circ. 15,000.

El País: Carrera 2A, No. 24-46; f. 1950; morning; Conservative; Dir. RODRIGO LLOREDA; circ. 100,102.

Occidente: Calle 12, No. 5-22; f. 1961; morning; Conservative; Dir. ALVARO CAICEDO; circ. 76,000.

CARTAGENA

Diario de la Costa: Centro Calle 35A, No. 8-59, Avda. Escallón, Apdo. Aéreo 103; f. 1915; morning; Conservative; Dir. RAFAEL ESCALÓN VILLA; circ. 20,000.

El Universal: Centro Calle 31, No. 3-81, Calle San Juan de Dios; f. 1948; Liberal; Dir. D. LÓPEZ ESCAURIAZA; circ. 5,000.

CÚCUTA

Diario de la Frontera: f. 1950; morning; Conservative; Dir. LUIS PARRA BOLÍVAR; circ. 15,000.

La Opinión: circ. 8,000.

IBAGUÉ

El Cronista: daily except Monday.

MANIZALES

La Patria: Carrera 20, No. 21-51, Apdo. Aéreo 70; f. 1921; morning; Conservative; Dir. GONZALO JARAMILLO J.; circ. 38,000.

MEDELLÍN

El Colombiano: Calle 54, No. 51-22 Apdo. Aéreo 782; f. 1912; morning; Conservative; Editor JUAN ZULETA FERRER; Pub. JULIO C. HERNÁNDEZ; circ. 100,000.

El Correo: Carrera 51A, No. 50-67; f. 1913; Liberal; Dir. ROBERTO DELGADO SAÑUDO; circ. 35,000.

El Diario: Calle 50, No. 64B-52; f. 1930; evening; Liberal Independent; Dir. JOHN GÓMEZ RESTREPO; circ. 28,000.

PASTO

El Derecho: Plaza de Cristo Rey, Apdo. 74; f. 1928; Dir. E. FIGUEROA CORAL; circ. 5,000.

La Radio: Calle 15, No. 28-30; f. 1933; morning; Liberal; Dir. CARLOS CÉSAR PUYANA; circ. 4,200.

PEREIRA

Diario de Risaralda.

El Diario: Calle 18, No. 6-48, Apdo. Aéreo 20; f. 1929; evening; Liberal; Dir. EDUARDO CORREA URIBE; circ. 13,000.

El Imparcial: f. 1948; evening; Dir. RAFAEL CANO GIRALDO; circ. 15,000.

POPAYÁN

El Liberal: Apdo. Aéreo 538, Nacional 43; f. 1938; Dir. GERARDO FERNANDE C.; Chief Editor CARLOS VALENCIA MOSQUERA; circ. 25,000.

SANTA MARTA

La Época.

El Informador: f. 1921; Liberal; Dir. GABRIEL ECHEVERRÍA; circ. 9,000.

PRESS ASSOCIATION

Asociación de Diarios Colombianos: Bogotá.

PERIODICALS

BOGOTÁ

Boletín Informativo: Apdo. 1310; fortnightly; Zionist organ; Dir. AZRIEL CELNIK.

El Campesino: Carrera 39A, No. 15-11; f. 1958; weekly; Catholic; Dir. LUIS ZORNOSA FALLA; circ. 105,486.

El Catolicismo: Apdo. Aéreo 12333; f. 1889; weekly; Catholic cultural; circ. 15,000.

Cenicafé: Chinchiná, Caldas; publ. by National Centre for Coffee Research; f. 1949; quarterly; circ. 3,000; Dir. SILVIO ECHEVERRI.

Colombia Filatélica: monthly.

Correo Universitario: Apdo. 2509; f. 1944; monthly; university gazette; Dir. JAIME IBAÑEZ.

Cromos Magazine: Calle 20, No. 4-55, Apdo. Aéreo 14860, Nacional 5653; f. 1916; weekly; illustrated; general news; Dir. FERNANDO RESTREPO; circ. 85,000.

Estampa: Apdo. Aéreo 4160; f. 1938; weekly; Independent; Dir. FERNANDO MARTÍNEZ DORRIEN; circ. 17,740.

El Gráfico: Calle 14, No. 8-74.

Ingeniería y Arquitectura: every two months.

Lecturas, Libros e Ideas: literary periodical.

El Mes Financiero y Económico: monthly; financial news.

Menorah: Apdo. Aéreo 9081; f. 1950; Independent monthly review for the Jewish community; Dir. ELIÉCER CELNIK; circ. 10,000.

Mujer de América (*Women of America*): Apdo. 10634; f. 1960; Editor-Pres. FLOR ROMERO DE NOHRA: women's periodical; circ. 50,000.

Nuestra Senda: Calle 20, No. 4-81, Apdo. 1627; f. 1940; weekly; organ of Jewish colony; Dir. Dr. JOSEPH GRUTZENDLER.

Proa: Calle 13, No. 9-20; f. 1946; monthly architectural and artistic review; Propr. CARLOS MARTÍNEZ; circ. 2,500.

Revista del Banco de la República: financial and economic review.

Revista Cafetera de Colombia: Avda. Jiménez, No. 40-50; organ of the National Federation of Coffee Growers.

Revista Colombiana del Trabajo: industrial and labour news.

Revista Comercial: Carrera 6, No. 11-57.

Revista del Ejército: Ministerio de Defensa; f. 1961; military review; twice monthly; circ. 8,000; Editor Major RAMIRO ZAMBRANO C.

Revista Javeriana: Catholic monthly; Dir. P. ANGEL VALTIERRA.

Revista Nacional de Agricultura: Carrera 10A, No. 14-56, 3° piso, Apdo. 3638; f. 1906; publ. by The Agricultural Society of Colombia; monthly; Dir. CARLOS JOSÉ GONZALES M.; circ. 6,000.

Rutas: Carrera 6, No. 11-57.

SETT: f. 1962; literary and political; monthly of MRL.

Sucesos: f. 1956; magazine.

UNIOS: Labour monthly.

Vanguardia: f. 1962; weekly of MRL.

Viajes.

La Vida Rural: monthly.

Voz Proletaria: Apdo. Aéreo 19857/8886; f. 1963; weekly; Communist; Dir. M. CEPEDA VARGAS; circ. 24,000.

PRESS AGENCIES

Bogotá

ANSA: Carrera 30, Calle 26, No. 39-21; Bureau Chief URIEL OSPINA.

AP: Bureau Chief DANIEL HARKER.

Novosti: Bureau Chief JOSÉ ARIZALA.

Cali

UPI: Edif. Ulpiano Lloreda, Plaza de Caicedo, Of. 201; Bureau Chief LUIS JORGE MAHECHA.

Tass is also represented in Colombia.

PRESS ASSOCIATION

Asociación Colombiana de Periodistas: Bogotá.

PUBLISHERS

Alvaro Marin: Avenida Jiménez, No. 9-47, Bogotá.

Bibliográfica Colombiana Ltda.: Carrera 7A, No. 24-72, Bogotá; education, journalism.

Cromos Editores e Impresores Ltda.: Avda. 22, No. 19A-55, Bogotá; f. 1916; Dir. Jaime Restrepo.

Cultural Colombiana Ltda.: Carrera 9, No. 16-72, Apdo. Aéreo 6307, Bogotá; f. 1951; textbooks; booksellers.

Ediciones Tercer Mundo: Carrera 7, No. 16-19, Apdo. Aéreo 4817, Bogotá; politics, psychology, sociology, fiction.

Editorial Albon: Calle 53, No. 73-126, Apdo. Aéreo 1943, Medellín.

Editorial Andes: Carrera 39A, No. 15-21, Apdo. Aéreo 20037, Bogotá; Gen. Man. Léon Morales Arenas.

Editorial Antares: Calle 13, No. 6-82, 10° piso, Bogotá; commerce, industry.

Editorial Bedout: Avenida Jiménez, No. 9-47, Apdo. Aéreo 12050, Bogotá.

Editorial Bolívar: Apdo. Aéreo 4160, Bogotá; f. 1938; Dir. and Prop. Fernando Martínez Dorrien; publ. periodicals incl. *Estampa, Bachue* (monthly), *Laboratorio* (quarterly).

Editorial "El Diario": Calle 18, No. 17-30, Pereira.

Editorial Kapelusz Colombiana: Carrera 12, No. 15-99, Bogotá.

Ediciones Lerner: Avenida Jiménez, No. 4-33, Apdo. Aéreo 12050, Bogotá.

Editorial Librería Voluntad, Ltda.: Carrera 7, No. 38-99, Apdo. Aéreo 4692, Bogotá; f. 1928; textbooks; Man. Dir. Dr. Samuel de Bedout T.

Editorial Lumen Christi, S.A.: Calle 12, No. 3-12, Bogotá; religion, belles lettres, fiction.

Editorial Norma: Calle 19, No. 6-68, 2° piso, Apdo. Aéreo 4344, Bogotá; f. 1960; Gen. Man. A. J. Carvajal; educational.

Editorial Temis Ltda.: Calle 13, No. 6-45, Apdo. Aéreo 5941, Bogotá; law, sociology, politics.

E. Ospina-Racines: Edificio Tejada 602, Apdo. P.29-71; Bogotá; f. 1940; weekly publications on petroleum; Dir. E. Ospina-Racines.

Empresa Editorial "La Patria": Carrera 20, No. 21-51, Apdo. Nacional 236, Apdo. Aéreo 70, Manizales; f. 1921; Pres. José Restrepo R.; Man. Luis Fernando Botero R.

Herder Editorial y Librería Ltda.: Apdo. Aéreo 6855, Bogotá; social services.

Instituto Caro y Cuervo: Apdo. Aéreo 20002, Bogotá; f. 1942; philology and general linguistics; Dir. J. M. Rivas Sacconi; publs. *Thesaurus, Noticias Culturales, Anuario Bibliográfico Colombiano* and others.

Legislación Económica: Avda. Las Américas, No. 58-51, Apdo. Aéreo 8646, Bogotá; f. 1952; 19 periodicals covering law, economics and management; Dir. Tito-Livio Caldas.

Minerva Editorial: Carrera 9, No. 7-72, Bogotá.

Universidad Nacional: Ciudad Universitaria, Bogotá.

Universidad Externada de Colombia: Carrera 12, No. 1-17 Este, Bogotá.

Universidad Industrial de Santander: Apdo. Aéreo 678, Bucaramanga.

PUBLISHING ASSOCIATION

Acoeditores: Avenida Jiménez 10-34, Bogotá.

RADIO AND TELEVISION

In 1971 there were 2,250,000 radio licences.

Ministerio de Comunicaciones, División de Telecomunicaciones: Apdo Aéreo 14515, Bogotá; broadcasting authority in Colombia; Dir.-Gen. A. Tapias Rocha.

RADIO

Radiodifusora Nacional: Centro Administrativo Nacional (CAN), Avda. El Dorado, Bogotá; official broadcasting station; f. 1940; Dir.-Gen. Germán Vargas.

Principal Commercial Stations

Radio Cadena Nacional, S.A.: Apdo. Aéreo 1244, Medellín; Pres. Roberto Jairo Arango Mejía.

Caracol-Primera Cadena Radial Colombiana: Calle 19, No. 8-48, Bogotá; Pres. F. Londoño; Dir.-Gen. A. Toro.

Circuito Radial ABC, S.A.: Apdo. Aéreo 1771, Apdo. 206, Cartagena; Propr. R. Fuentes; Man. Nelson Fuentes Martínez.

There are 217 commercial stations and 15 cultural stations.

Commercial Radio Federation

Federación Nacional de Estaciones Radiofónicas: Bogotá; all commercial stations belong to the federation.

In 1970 there were 2,217,000 radio sets in use.

TELEVISION

Instituto Nacional de Radio y Televisión: Centro Administrativo Nacional (CAN), Vía del Aeropuerto El Dorado, Bogotá; f. 1954; Dir.-Gen. Dr. Carlos Delgado Pereira; government-run TV and radio broadcasting network; educational and commercial broadcasting.

Telebogotá: Calle 22, No. 6-27, 6° piso, Bogotá; Dir.-Gen. Consuelo de Montejo.

In 1973, there were 1,300,000 television sets in use.

FINANCE

(cap.=capital; p.u.=paid up; dep.=deposits; m.=million; res.=reserves; amounts are given in pesos.)

BANKING

Superintendencia Bancaria: Calle 16, No. 5-13, Apdo. Aéreo 3460, Bogotá; Banking Superintendent Dr. ABEL FRANCISCO CARBONELL; First Superintendent Dr. MARIO ALBERTO RUBIO CAICEDO.

CENTRAL BANK

Banco de la República: Carrera 7A, No. 14-78, Apdo. Postal 402, Aéreo 3531, Bogotá; f. 1923; cap. p.u. 153.9m., res. 126.9m. (June 1972); Gen. Man. Dr. GERMÁN BOTERO DE LOS RÍOS.

Fondo para Inversiones Privadas: f. 1963 as a special account of the Banco de la República; loans and grants, projects supported must relate directly to increased agricultural or industrial productivity.

Fondo Financiero Agrario: agricultural finance fund.

Fondo Financiero de Desarrollo Urbano: urban development finance fund.

Fondo Financiero Industrial: industrial finance fund.

BOGOTÁ

Banco de América Latina: Carrera 8A, No. 15-73, Apdo. Aéreo 7406; cap. p.u. 15m., res. 4.2m. (June 1972); Gen. Man. ALVARO DUGAND DONADO.

Banco de Bogotá: Carrera 10, No. 14-33, Apdo. Aéreo 3436; f. 1870; cap. p.u. 223.8m., res. 244.4m. (June 1972); Gen. Man. JORGE MEJÍA SALAZAR.

Banco Cafetero: Avda. Jiménez, No. 7-65, Apdo. Aéreo 6824; f. 1953; cap. p.u. 400m., legal reserve 145m., dep. 2,196m. (June 1972); Pres. RODRIGO MUNERA Z.

Banco Central Hipotecario: Carrera 6A, No. 15-32/48; f. 1932; cap. p.u. 166m., liabilities 1,036m. (Dec. 1973); Man. Dr. JORGE CORTÉS BOSHELL.

Banco de Colombia: Carrera 8A, No. 13-25/27, Apdo. Aéreo 6836; f. 1875; cap. p.u. 116.9m., res. 253.5m. (June 1972); Pres. JAIME MICHELSEN URIBE.

Banco del Comercio: Calle 13, No. 8-52, Apdo Aéreo 4749; f. 1949; cap. p.u. 174.7m., res. 76.8m. (June 1972); Pres. CAMILO HERRERA PRADO.

Banco de Construcción y Desarrollo: Carrera 10, No. 16-37, Apdo. Aéreo 6454; f. 1963; cap. p.u. 10m., res. 20m. (Dec. 1973); Pres. A. J. HEEB.

Banco Ganadero: Carrera 8A, No. 13-42, Apdo. Aéreo 7290; cattle finance and credits; cap. p.u. 423.8m., res. 40.1m. (June 1972); Gen. Man. JOSÉ MEJÍA SALAZAR.

Banco Grancolombiano: Carrera 7A, No. 13-41; f. 1961; cap. p.u. 44.8m., res. 14.1m. (June 1972); Man. JAVIER MEJÍA RAMÍREZ.

Banco Industrial Colombiano: Carrera 4, No. 49-72; f. 1945; cap. p.u. 120.9m., res. 61.8m. (1972); Man. IVAN CORREA ARANGO.

Banco Nacional: Carrera 7A, No. 13-88; cap. p.u. 25m., res. 5.9m. (June 1972); Pres. PEDRO ROJAS GUTIÉRREZ.

Banco Panamericano: Avda. Jiménez, No. 8-65; cap. p.u. 7.6m., res. 2.8m. (June 1972); Man. JORGE MONCALEANO R.

Banco Popular S.A.: Calle 17, No. 7-43, Apdo Aéreo 8656; cap. p.u. 90.5m., res. 364.2m. (June 1972); Pres. EDUARDO NIETO CALDERÓN.

Caja de Crédito Agrario, Industrial y Minero: Carrera 8, No. 15-43; f. 1931; cap. 543.3m., res. 74.7m. (June 1972); Gen. Man. Dr. JOSÉ VICENTE DAVILA-SUAREZ.

BARRANQUILLA

Banco de la Costa: Apdo. Aéreo 7938; cap. p.u. 25.9m., res. 2.3m. (June 1972); Man. Dir. JOSÉ ROMÁN FERNÁNDEZ.

BUCARAMANGA

Banco Santander: Calle 35, No. 16-56; cap. p.u. 47.2m., res. 4.5m. (June 1972); Man. JAIME RODRÍGUEZ SILVA.

CALI

Banco de Occidente: Apdo. Aéreo 4409; cap. p.u. 67m., res. 15m. (Dec. 1973); Pres. Dr. GUILLERMO SARMIENTO A.

MANIZALES

Banco de Caldas: Edificio Beneficencia 3, Apdo. Aéreo 617; f. 1965; cap. p.u. 25.8m., res. 4m. (June 1972); Pres. Dr. SILVIO BOTERO DE LOS RÍOS.

MEDELLÍN

Banco Comercial Antioqueño: Calle Colombia, Apdo. Aéreo 750; f. 1912; cap. p.u. 196.1m., res. 211.3m. (June 1972); Pres. VICENTE URIBE RENDÓN; Rep. in Bogotá Dr. J. VALLEJO ARBELÁEZ.

POPAYÁN

Banco del Estado: Calle 4A, Carrera 7A esq.; f. 1884; cap. and res. 49.2m. (Dec. 1973); Pres. JULIO ARBOLEDA VALENCIA.

FOREIGN BANKS

Banco Francés e Italiano para la América del Sud: Carrera 8A, No. 15-42, Apdo. Aéreo 3440, Bogotá; Man. Dr. ALFREDO MIANI.

Bank of America National Trust and Savings Association N.T. and S.A.: Carrera 7, No. 16-36, Apdo. Aéreo 12327, Bogotá; Vice-Pres. and Man. F. CARL REINHARDT; brs. in Cali, Medellín, Barranquilla.

Bank of London and South America Ltd.: Carrera 8A, No. 15-46/60, Apdo. Aéreo 3532, Bogotá; 7 brs. and 9 agencies.

Banco Franco-Colombiano: Carrera 7, No. 14-23, Bogotá; f. 1954; subsidiary of the Banque Nationale de Paris; Man. PIERRE LAMON; brs. in Bogotá (4), Cali (2), Barranquilla, Medellín, Buenaventura.

First National City Bank: New York; Avenida Jiménez, No. 8-89, Bogotá; brs. in Barranquilla, Bogotá, Cali, Cartagena, Cúcuta, Medellín, Pereira; Man. EDWIN HOFFMAN.

Royal Bank of Canada: Montreal; Apdo. Aéreo 3438, Carrera 8A, No. 14-45, Bogotá; brs. in principal towns; District Man. J. F. STECH.

DEVELOPMENT

Corporación Financiera de Caldas: Edificio Banco del Comercio, 11° piso, Apdo. Aéreo 460, Manizales; f. 1961; private development company; Pres. EDUARDO ARANGO R.

Corporación Financiera del Caribe: Calle 13, No. 8-38, Apdo. Aéreo 6836, Bogotá; f. 1967 under auspices of Banco de Colombia; initial cap. 10m.; Pres. ERNESTO B. ENGEL.

Corporación Financiera Central: Carrera 7, No. 14-27, Bogotá.

Corporación Financiera Colombiana: Carrera 13, No. 26-45, pisos 7/8, Apdo. Aéreo 11843, Bogotá; f. 1959; private development bank; cap. 200m.; Pres. IGNACIO COPETE LIZARRALDE.

Corporación Financiera Grancolombiana S.A.: Carrera 7A, No. 14-23, Bogotá; f. 1966; cap. and reserves $12.5m.; dep. $51.8m.; Pres. JAIME URIBE.

Corporación Financiera Nacional: Apdo. Aéreo 1039, Medellín; f. 1959; private development company; Pres. JOSÉ GUTIÉRREZ GÓMEZ; Vice-Pres. CARLOS RESTREPO DUMIT.

Corporación Financiera del Norte: Carrera 44, No. 34-31A, Barranquilla; cap. $46m.; Pres. ALVARO JARAMILLO V.

Corporación Financiera de Occidente: Apdo. Postal 441, Pereira; f. 1966; provides credit and effects investment in the development of industry, agriculture, cattle farming and mining and offers technical assistance; cap. U.S. $1.8m., assets total U.S. $12.6m.; Pres. GERMÁN GAVIRIA VELEZ.

Corporación Financiera Popular: Calle 17, No. 7-43, 5°, Apdo. Aéreo 5179, Bogotá; f. 1967; an affiliate of the Banco Popular; cap. 200m.; provides loans and technical assistance to medium-sized and small industries; Pres. RAUL EDUARDO ARBELAEZ B.

Corporación Financiera de Santander: Calle 35, No. 16-52, 4°, Bucaramanga; f. 1966; cap. 27.8m., to be raised to 60m.; Pres. GUSTAVO LIÉVANO.

Corporación Financiera del Transporte: Carrera 7, No. 16-36, Bogotá; Pres. LUIS AUGUSTO MURCIA.

Corporación Financiera del Valle: Apdo. Aéreo 4902, Cali.

"Cofiagro" Corporacion Financiera de Fomento Agropecuario y de Exportación: Calle 12, No. 7-32, 11° Apdo. Aéreo 16857, Bogotá; Pres. AURELIO CORREA.

Instituto de Fomento Industrial: Adpo. Aéreo 4222, Bogotá 1; state finance corporation; Man. A. LÓPEZ TORO.

BANKING ASSOCIATION

Asociación Bancaria: Apdo. Aéreo 13994, Calle 13, No. 8-39, 2° piso, Bogotá; f. 1936; 26 mem. banks; Pres. JORGE MEJÍA PALACIO; Man. Dr. SERGIO RODRÍGUEZ AZUERO; publs. *Información Financiera, Boletín Jurídico, Boletín Bibliográfico, Manual de Créditos.*

STOCK EXCHANGES

Bolsa de Bogotá: Carrera 8A, No. 13-82, Apdo. Aéreo 3584, Bogotá; f. 1928; Pres. EDUARDO GOEZ; Sec. JORGE RESTREPO.

Bolsa de Medellín: Apdo. Aéreo 3535, Medellín.

INSURANCE

PRINCIPAL NATIONAL COMPANIES

Aseguradora Mercantil S.A.: Carrera 7A, No. 26-20, Apdos. Aéreos 7988 and 6774, Nacionales 412 and 2368, Bogotá; f. 1951; Sec. Gen. GERMÁN ESPINOSA RESTREPO; Man. ALVARO AZCUÉNAGA M.

Aseguradora Grancolombiana S.A.: Carrera 7A, No. 14-23, pisos 3 y 4, Apdo. Aéreo 10454; Pres. J. MICHELSEN URIBE.

Compañía Agricola de Seguros S.A.: Calle 14, No. 7-36, 21°, Apdo. Aéreo 7212, Bogotá; Pres. ARIEL JARAMILLO A.

Compañías Aliadas de Seguros S.A.: Carrera 8A, No. 15-46, 5°, Apdo. Aéreo 6810, Bogotá; Pres. B. PELAEZ E.

Compañía de Seguros, La Andina: Edificio Camacol, Carrera 10, No. 19-65, 5°, Apdo. Aéreo 3838, Bogotá; f. 1937; Man. COLIN G. MARLOW.

Compañía de Seguros Antorcha de Colombia S.A.: Carrera 7A, No. 37-25, 4°, Bogotá; Man. ANDREW M. WILLIAMSON.

Compañía de Seguros Generales, Aurora S.A.: Carrera 10, No. 19-65, 3°; Man. PEDRO ALVEAR RAMOS.

Compañía de Seguros, Bolívar: Edificio Bolívar, Carrera 10A, No. 16-39, Apdo. Aéreo 597, Bogotá; f. 1939; Man. ENRIQUE CORTÉS R.

Compañía Central de Seguros S.A.: Edificio Banco Ganadero, Carrera 5, No. 15-80, 21°, Apdo. Aéreo 57641 Bogotá; f. 1956; cap. 30m.; Man. EFREN OSSA G.

Compañía Colombiana de Seguros: Carrera 7A, No. 17-01, Apdo. Aéreo 3537, Bogotá; f. 1874; Pres. JAVIER RAMIREZ SOTO.

Compañía de Seguros La Fénix de Colombia S.A.: Carrera 8A, No. 15-46, 3°, Bogotá; Man. PHILIP M. TIBBLE.

Compañía Granadina de Seguros S.A.: Avenida Jiménez, No. 8-29, Apdo. Aéreo 6889, Bogotá; f. 1945; separate life office; Man. Dir. FRANCISCO DE RUGGIERO.

Compañía de Seguros, La Continental: Edificio Internacional K13, No. 26-45, 9°, Bogotá; Man. EDWARD McELGUNN.

Compañía de Seguros del Pacífico: Carrera 5A, No. 12-42, 6°, Apdo. Aéreo 8154, Cali; Man. RAFAEL NAVIA GONZÁLEZ.

Compañía Suramericana de Seguros: Centro Suramericana, Carrera 64B, No. 49A-30, Apdos. Aéreos 780 y 2030, Medellín; f. 1944; Pres. JORGE MOLINA M.

Compañía Internacional de Seguros S.A.: Calle 15, No. 9-18, Bogotá; Man. MARIO LASERNA HOYOS.

Grupo Grancolombiana S.A.: Carrera 7A, No. 14-23, Bogotá; Pres. JAIME MICHELSON URIBE.

Inmobiliaria de Seguros S.A.: Calle 16, No. 9-64, 3°; Man. RAFAEL GÓMEZ R.

La Nacional, Compañía de Seguros Generales de Colombia S.A.: Calle 16, No. 6-34, Apdo. Aéreo 5672, Bogotá; f. 1952; Pres. BERNARDO SAIZ DE CASTRO; Man. PIERRE LAMAT.

La Libertad, Compañía de Seguros Generales y de Vida S.A.: Avenida Jiménez, No. 7-25, 3°, Bogotá; Pres. GERARDO HERNÁNDEZ FERIA; Man. LUIS ARTURO RODRÍGUEZ CAMACHO.

La Previsora: Carrera 7, No. 13-52, Bogotá; Man. DANIEL JARAMILLO FERRO.

Reaseguradora de Colombia S.A.: Carrera 10A, No. 16-39, 12°, Apdo. Aéreo 7460, Bogotá; Man. RODRIGO VÁSQUEZ.

Seguros Colombia S.A.: Carrera 13, No. 26-45, 3°, Apdo. Aéreo 9228, Bogotá; Mans. IGNACIO UMAÑA DE BRIGARD, JAIME VARÓN MOJICA.

Seguros La Unión S.A.: Calle 14, No. 16-A-23, 8°, Apdo. Aéreo 12525, Bogotá; Man. FRANCISCO PÉREZ P.

Seguros Médicos Voluntarios: Carrera 10A, No. 19-65, 2°, Apdo. 11777, Bogotá; Man. FERNANDO GÓMEZ B.

Seguros Patria S.A.: Carrera 10A, No. 15-22, Apdo. 7762, Bogotá; Man. CARLOS PACHECO D.

Seguros Tequendama: Carrera 7A, No. 26-20, 26°, Apdo. 7988, Bogotá; Pres. JAIME CABALLERO U.

Seguros Universal S.A.: Avda. Jiménez, No. 8-77, 10°, Apdo. Aéreo 11634, Bogotá; Man. CARLOS MEDINA ZÁRATE.

FOREIGN COMPANIES

Fireman's Insurance Co.: Carrera 7A, No. 26-20, 26°, Apdo. Aéreo 4036, Bogotá; Man. D. GOETZ.

Insurance Company of North America: Carrera 7A, No. 37-69, Apdo. Aéreo 8687, Bogotá; Man. FERNANDO MAYORAL.

Royal Insurance Company Ltd.: Carrera 10A, No. 19-65, 5°, Apdo. Aéreo 3536, Bogotá; Man. C. MARLOW.

INSURANCE ASSOCIATION

Asociación Colombiana de Compañías de Seguros: Calle 19, No. 6-68, 12°, Apdo. Aéreo 5233, Bogotá; 44 mems.; Pres. Dr. JAIME BUSTAMANTE FERRER; Dir. Gen. Dr. RAFAEL H. MARTÍNEZ.

TRADE AND INDUSTRY

CHAMBERS OF COMMERCE

Confederación Colombiana de Cámaras de Comercio "Confecámaras": Carrera 9, No. 16-21, Bogotá; f. 1969; 40 member organizations; Exec.-Pres. GASTÓN E. ABELLO; publ. *Síntesis Mensual*.

Cámara de Comercio de Bogotá: Carrera 9, No. 16-21, Bogotá; f. 1878; 1,285 mem. organizations; Pres. JOSÉ MEJÍA SALAZAR; Sec.-Gen. Dr. FERNANDO SANTOS SILVA; Dir. Centro de Informática Económica (CIEB) Dr. HERNANDO OSPINA; publs. *Revista de la Cámara de Comercio de Bogotá, Boletín Mensual, Servicio Informativo Quincenal, Indicadores Económicos* and others.

There are also local Chambers of Commerce in the capital towns of all the Departments and in many of the other trading centres. Among these are:

Cámara de Comercio de Armenia: Apdo. 595, Armenia, Quindío; f. 1934; Pres. ARTURO ALVAREZ MAYA; Sec. Dr. JOSUÉ MORENO JARAMILLO; publ. *Quindío Comercial*.

Cámara de Comercio de Barranquilla: Apdo. Aéreo 12, Barranquilla; f. 1916; 500 mems.; Pres. LUIS E. POCHET; Sec. JAIRO PEYNADO; publ. *Boletín Semanal CCC*.

Cámara de Comercio de Bucaramanga: Carrera 19, No. 36-20, Apdo. Nac. 221, Aéreo 973, Bucaramanga, Santander; f. 1915; 300 mems.; Pres. GUSTAVO LIÉVANO FONSECA; Sec. ERNESTO SUÁREZ RUEDA; publs. *Noticiero Mercantil* (monthly review), *Bucaramanga en Cifras, Indicadores Económicos Trimestral*.

Cámara de Comercio de Cali: Afiliados 571, Apdo. 140, Aéreo 1565, Cali, Valle de Cauca; f. 1910; 209 mems.; Pres. LUIS EDUARDO LOURIDO; Sec. ALFONSO DE FRANCISCO B.; publ. *Noticiario Comercial, Noticiario Comercial-Suplemento, Boletín Informativo*.

Cámara de Comercio de Cartagena: Apdo. Aéreo 16, Cartagena; f. 1917; 250 mems.; Pres. R. OTERO; publ. *Revista*.

Cámara de Comercio de Honda: Edificio Nacional, Honda, Tolima; f. 1924; Pres. CARLOS CORREA MACHADO; Sec. LUIS MARÍA ARTEAGA.

Cámara de Comercio de Ibagué: Carrera 4A, No. 13-34, Apdo. 34, Ibagué, Tolima; f. 1928; 18 mems.; Pres. CARLOS J. MARTÍNEZ G.; publ. monthly review.

Cámara de Comercio de Manizales: Calle 22, No. 21-48, Apdo. Aéreo 117, Manizales, Caldas; f. 1913; 650 mems.; Pres. GUSTAVO URIBE DUQUE; Sec. A. C. MARULANDA; publ. *Boletín Mensual*.

Cámara de Comercio de Medellín: Calle 51, No. 53-24, Medellín, Antioquía; f. 1904; 500 mems.; Pres. ALBERTO ALVAREZ S.; Sec. Dr. JAIRO MACHADO P.; publs. *Boletín* (weekly), *Carta* (monthly), *Indicadores Económicos* (monthly).

Cámara de Comercio de Pasto: Calle 18, No. 25-31, Pasto, Nariño; 9 mems.; Pres. J. ANTONIO RODRÍGUEZ ROSERO; Sec. VICENTE APRÁEZ APRÁEZ; publ. *Boletín*.

Cámara de Comercio Colombo-Americana (*Colombian-American Chamber of Commerce*): Apdo. Aéreo 8008, Bogotá; publs. *Boletín Semanal de Información Económica, Comercio Colombo-Americano, Directorio Anual*.

Cámara de Comercio Colombo-Alemana (*Colombian-German Chamber of Commerce*): Carrera 9, No. 16-21, Bogotá; publs. *Boletín Semanal de la Actualidad Comercial* (weekly), *Revista Trimestral* (quarterly).

DEVELOPMENT ORGANIZATIONS

Consejo Nacional de Energía: Bogotá; f. 1973 to formulate a short- and medium-term programme for meeting the country's energy requirements.

Departamento Administrativo Nacional de Planeación: Carrera 10, No. 27-27, Bogotá; supervises and administers development projects; investments by government, state enterprises and local authorities (1968): 7,900m. pesos.

Empresa Colombiana de Minas: Carrera 7, No. 14-23, Bogotá; administers state resources of emerald and other minerals.

Empresa Colombiana de Petróleos "Ecopetrol": Carrera 13, No. 36-24, Apdo. Aéreo 5938, Bogotá; participates with private enterprise in refining, transport and export of petroleum; Pres. MARIO GALÁN GÓMEZ.

Fondo de Promoción de Exportaciones: Apdo. Aéreo 17966, Bogotá; f. 1967; aims to diversify exports, strengthen the balance of payments and augment the volume of trade, by granting financial aid for export operations and acting as consultant to export firms, also undertaking market studies.

Fondo Nacional de Proyectos de Desarrollo—Fonade: Bogotá; f. 1968; responsible for channelling loans towards economic development projects; administered by a committee under the head of the *Departamento Administrativo de Planeación*; Fonade works in close association with other official planning organizations.

Instituto de Aprovechamiento de Aguas y Fomento Eléctrico—Electraguas: Edificio Bochica, Carrera 13, No. 27-00, 3°, Bogotá; semi-official undertaking operating on a nation-wide scale through 14 subsidiary companies; concerned in the generation and distribution of electric power.

Instituto Colombiano de Comercio Exterior-Incomex: Carrera 10, No. 15-39, Bogotá; promotes and sets quotas for exports; Dir. ALFONSO SUÁREZ FAJARDO.

Instituto de Desarrollo de los Recursos Naturales Renovables "Inderena": Carrera 10, No. 20-30, 7°, Bogotá; f. 1968; agency regulating the development of natural resources; Dir. JULIO UMAÑA CARRIZOSA.

Instituto de Fomento Algonodero: Carrera 8, No. 11-39, 5°, Bogotá; official government cotton and oil development office.

Instituto Colombiano de Energía Eléctrica (ICEL): Apdo. Aéreo 16243, Bogotá; formulates policy in the field of electrical energy.

Instituto de Fomento Industrial: Carrera 6, No. 14-88, 3°, Bogotá; official government cotton and oil development agency; Dir. ALBERTO LÓPEZ TORO.

Instituto Colombiano de Reforma Agraria—INCORA: Apdo. Aéreo 8691, Bogotá; f. 1962; a public institution which, on behalf of the Government, administers public lands and those it acquires; reclaims land by irrigation and drainage facilities, roads, etc. to increase productivity in agriculture and stock-breeding; provides technical assistance and loans; supervises the redistribution of land throughout the country with the aim of equality of ownership.

EMPLOYERS' AND PRODUCERS' ORGANIZATIONS

Asociación Colombiana Popular de Industriales (ACOPI): Carrera 6, No. 11-87, Of. 806, Apdo. Aéreo 16451, Bogotá; f. 1951; association of small industrialists;

Pres. Dario Monsalve Uribe; Man. Dr. Gustavo Alfonzo V.; publ. *Carta Industrial*.

Asociación Nacional de Cultivadores de Caña de Azúcar—Asocaña: Carrera 5, No. 12-16, Apdo. Aéreo 44-48, Cali; f. 1959; sugar planters association; Pres. Jaime Lozano.

Asociación Nacional de Exportadores de Café: Carrera 8, No. 11-39, Bogotá; private association of coffee exporters; publ. *Boletín Semanal* (weekly).

Asociación Nacional de Industriales (*National Association of Manufacturers*): Carrera 10, No. 14-33, 16°, Bogotá; f. 1944; 526 mems.; Pres. Dr. Luis Prieto Ocampo; 7 brs.; publs. *Boletín Económico, Boletín Comercio Exterior, Boletín Parlamentario, Boletín Social y Laboral, Noticiero, Revista Trimestral*.

Federación Colombiana de Ganaderos—FEDEGAN: Avda. Caracas, No. 36-35, Apdo. Aéreo 9709, Bogotá; f. 1963; cattle raisers' association; about 130,000 affiliates; Gen. Man. Miguel Santamaría Dávila; publs. *Boletín Fedegán* (weekly), *Revista Nacional de Ganadería, Carta Mensual de Ganadería*.

Federación Nacional de Algodoneros: Apdo. Aéreo 8632, Bogotá; federation of cotton growers; Man. Rafael Pardo Buelvas.

Federación Nacional de Cacaoteros: Apdo. Aéreo 5891, Bogotá; cocoa farmers' association.

Federación Nacional de Cafeteros de Colombia (*National Federation of Coffee Growers*): Avda. Jiménez de Quesada, No. 7-65, pisos 4 y 5, Apdo. Aéreo 3938, Bogotá; f. 1927; 203,000 mems.; Man. Arturo Gómez Jaramillo; publs. *Boletín, Revista* (quarterly).

Federación Nacional de Comerciantes (FENALCO) (*National Federation of Tradesmen*): Apdo. Aéreo 4405, Bogotá; f. 1945; Pres. Germán Gaviria Vélez; publ. *Boletín "Fenalco"*.

Sociedad de Agricultores de Colombia (SAC) (*Colombian Agricultural Society*): Apdo. Aéreo 3638, Bogotá.

TRADE UNIONS

Unión de Trabajadores de Colombia—UTC (*National Union of Colombian Workers*): Carrera 10, No. 7-31/32, Bogotá; f. 1946; 800,000 mems.; incorporates 14 area organizations and 37 national and local organizations among its 600 affiliates; admitted to ICFTU; Pres. Tulio E. Cuevas R.; Gen. Sec. Jorge Carrillo; publ. *Justicia Social* (fortnightly).

Affiliated to the UTC are:

Federación Agraria Nacional (FANAL): Carrera 7, No. 4-25, Ciudad; Pres. Gastón A. Jiménez L.; Gen. Sec. Alejandro Jaimes Z.

Federación Colombiana de Trabajadores (FECOLTRACOM): Carrera 10, No. 7-33, Oficina 411, Bogotá; Pres. Héctor Niño Molina; Gen. Sec. José J. Romero.

Federación Nacional de Ferrovías: Carrera 14, No. 15-72, Oficina 205, Bogotá; Pres. Efraín López M.; Gen. Sec. Gustavo Díaz R.

Federación Nacional de Sindicatos Bancarios Colombianos (FENASIBANCOL): Calle 14, No. 12-50, Oficina 615, Apdo. 23370, Bogotá; Pres. Reynaldo Ardila Sanmiguel; Gen. Sec. Pedro Ignacio Rubio Romero.

Federación Nacional de Trabajadores de la Industria Química (FEQUINAL): Calle 13, No. 9-63, Bogotá; Pres. Gustavo Monzón Quintero; Gen. Sec. Rafael Díaz Cardozo.

Unión Nacional de Trabajadores del Transporte: Carrera 36, No. 35-34, Apdo. 2553, Barranquilla; Pres. Gerardo Castro S.

Unión de Trabajadores de la Industria Gastronómica Hotelera y Similares de Colombia (FENALTHYS): Bogotá; Pres. Luis E. Martín; Gen. Sec. Rafael González.

Unión de Trabajadores Metalúrgicos y Mineros de Colombia (UTRAMMICOL): Carrera 10, No. 7-33, 3°, Bogotá; Pres. Teódulo Cabrera; Gen. Sec. José Gregorio Pinto.

Unión de Trabajadores Textiles de Colombia (UTRATEXCO): Carrera 46, No. 46-63, Medellín; Pres. Alberto Gómez Villa; Gen. Sec. Carlos Bedoya T.

Local trade unions for the following towns and provinces are also affiliated: Boyacá, Bolívar, Dulce, Caldas, Cauca, Córdoba, Cundinamarca, Guajira, Huila y Caqueta, Atlántico, Antioquía, Llano, Magdalena, Nariño, Santander del Norte, Quindio, Risaralda, Santander, Sucre, Tolima, Valle.

Confederación de Trabajadores de Colombia—CTC (*Colombian Confederation of Workers*): Carrera 15, No. 12-73, Bogotá; f. 1934; 400,000 mems; 600 affiliates, including 6 national organizations and 20 regional federations; admitted to ICFTU; Pres. José R. Mercado; Sec.-Gen. Tomás Herazo Ríos; publ. *CTC Revista* (monthly).

There are a few independent unions.

TRANSPORT AND TOURISM

TRANSPORT
RAILWAYS

Ferrocarriles Nacionales de Colombia (*National Railways of Colombia*): Calle 13, No. 18-24, Bogotá; Pres. of the Administrative Board The Minister of Public Works; Gen. Man. Alfonso Orduz-Duarte.

The policy of the gradual nationalization of the railways by the Government was begun in 1922, when the Central Northern Railway was taken over, and completed in 1962. The Administrative Council for the National Railways now operates 3,424 km. of track of 0.914-metre gauge. The system is divided into five divisions, each with its own management: Central, Pacific, Antioquía, Santander and Magdalena. A railway modernization programme was carried out between 1966–72, involving expenditure of some 373m. pesos and U.S.$62.5m.

ROADS

There are estimated to be 48,200 km. of roads suitable for motor vehicles. One of the country's most important road projects is the 1,000 km. Caribbean Trunk Highway, intended to link the ports of Cartagena, Barranquilla and Santa Marta with the Venezuelan highway system.

Motoring Organization

Automobile Club: Avda. Caracas, No. 46-64, Bogotá; brs. at Barranquilla, Cali, Cartagena, Manizales and Medellín.

INLAND WATERWAYS

Instituto Nacional del Transporte: Centro Administrativo Nacional (CAN), Bogotá; in charge of all river operations. The waterways system is divided into three sectors: Atlantic, Pacific and Eastern.

Traffic plies regularly on the Magdalena, Cauca, Atrato, Orinoco, Meta, Putumayo and Amazon rivers.

SHIPPING

Empresa Puertos de Colombia "Colpuertos" (*Colombian Port Authority*): Carrera 10, No. 15-22, Apdo. Aéreo 13037, Bogotá; Man. Roberto Mejía Caicedo.

Flota Mercante Grancolombiana: Carrera 13, No. 27-75, Apdo. Aéreo 4482, Bogotá; owned by the Colombian Coffee Growers' Federation (80 per cent) and Ecuador Development Bank (20 per cent); f. 1946; services from Colombia and Ecuador to Canada, Atlantic and Gulf ports of the U.S.A., Central American and Northern European ports, Peru, Chile and Japan; Mans. Alvaro Díaz S., José V. Dávila Tello; Sec.-Gen. Dr. Policarpo Gutiérrez E.

COASTAL SHIPPING COMPANIES

Colombia Railways and Navigation Co., Ltd.: Barranquilla; services between Barranquilla and Cartagena and on the Magdalena River.

Compañías Unidas de Transportes, S.A.: Calle 18, Teatro Alcázar; transport to all parts of the country.

Empresa de Vapores, Julio Montes, Ltda.: Apdo. Aéreo 56, Barranquilla; f. 1937; 6 mems.; Man. Antonio Luis Montes P.

Cooperativa Nariñense de Transportadores Ltda.: Calle 18, No. 18-98, Edificio Pasto Nariño, Apdo. Aéreo 242, Bogotá; transport of passengers and cargo; Man. Arturo Alvarado.

Grace y Cia. (Colombia), S.A.: Calle 12, No.1-16 Norte, Cali.

Naviera Colombiana: Carrera 6, No. 14-53, Bogotá.

Transportes al Norte & Cia. Ltda.: Carrera 25 con Calle 20, Pasto; passengers and freight; agency in Popayán.

Transportes del Pacífico Ltda.: Calle 18, No. 19-02, Pasto.

CIVIL AVIATION

AIRPORTS AUTHORITY

Empresa Colombiana de Aeródromos (ECA): Aeropuerto El Dorado, Bogotá.

NATIONAL AIRLINES

Aerovías Condor de Colombia S.A. (Aerocondor): Carrera 45, No. 34-02, Apdo. 2299, Barranquilla; Carrera 8, No. 17-60, Bogotá; f. 1955; internal services, and to Miami, Fla., Aruba and Curaçao, Netherlands Antilles,

Santo Domingo, Dominican Republic; Gen. Man. Saul Pertuz Jimeno; 5 Lockheed Jet-prop. Electras, 1 Boeing 720B, 4 C-46 cargo.

Aerovías Nacionales de Colombia, S.A. (Avianca): Carrera 7, No. 16-84, Bogotá; operates domestic services to all cities in Colombia and international services to Europe, the United States, Argentina, Chile, Ecuador, Panama, Puerto Rico, Mexico, Venezuela and Peru; fleet: 2 Boeing 707-720B, 7 Boeing 720B, 7 Boeing 727, 1 Avro Jet-Prop, 4 DC-4, 2 DC-3, 4 C-54.

Servicio de Aeronavegación a Territorios Nacionales—Satena: Calle 20, No. 12-44, Bogotá; internal services.

Sociedad Aeronáutica de Medellín Consolidada, S.A. (SAM): Calle 52, No. 52-11, Apdo. Aéreo 1085, Medellín; Avda. Jiménez, No. 5-14, Bogotá; offices in Barranquilla, Cali, Cartagena, Cúcuta, Managua (Nicaragua), Pereira, San José (Costa Rica), San Salvador (El Salvador), Santa Marta, San Andrés; f. 1962; international and internal services; fleet: 8 Lockheed Electra L188A and 3 Douglas DC-4; Gen. Man. Ricardo Hoyos Campuzano.

Colombia is served by the following foreign airlines: Air France, Alitalia, ALM (Netherlands Antilles), Braniff, British Airways, CEA (Ecuador), COPA (Panama), Cruzeiro do Sul (Brazil), Iberia, Lufthansa, Lacsa (Costa Rica), L.A.N. de Chile, Sahsa (Honduras), Varig (Brazil), and Viasa (Venezuela).

TOURISM

Corporación Nacional de Turismo de Colombia: Calle 19, No. 6-68, 7°, Apdo. Aéreo 8400, Bogotá; Gen. Man. Nicolás del Castillo Mathieu.

Asociación Colombiana de Agencias de Turismo—ANATO: Calle 19, No. 4-20, Suite 402, Apdo. Aéreo 7088, Bogotá; Pres. Guillermo Riaño S.

CULTURAL ORGANIZATIONS

Bogotá

Departamento de Bellas Artes: Universidad Nacional de Colombia, Ciudad Universitaria, Bogotá.

Instituto Colombiano de Cultura Hispánica: Calle 12, No. 2-41, Bogotá.

Secretaría de Extensión Cultural.

ATOMIC ENERGY

Instituto de Asuntos Nucleares—IAN: Avda. Aeropuerto El Dorado, Carrera 50, Apdo. Aéreo 8595, Bogotá; f. 1959; experimental facilities; Pres. of Board of Dirs. Jaime Tovar Herrera; Dir. Hernán Ramírez Yusti; publ. *Boletín Bibliográfico de Información*.

UNIVERSITIES

STATE

Universidad de Antioquia: Apdo. Postal 229, Medellín; 1,104 teachers, 12,000 students.

Universidad del Atlántico: Carrera 43, No. 50-53, Apdo. Aéreo 1890, Barranquilla; 150 teachers, 2,100 students.

Universidad de Caldas: Apdo. Aéreo 275, Manizales; 260 teachers, 2,400 students.

Universidad de Cartagena: Apdo. Aéreo 1382, Cartagena; 1,642 students.

Universidad del Cauca: Calle 5A, No. 4-70, Apdo. Nacional 113, Popayán; 240 teachers, 2,930 students.

Universidad Francisco de Paula Santander: Calle 13, No. 5-65, Apdo. Aéreo 1055; 84 teachers, 1,014 students.

Fundación Universidad Central: Calle 21, No. 9-18, Apdo. Aéreo 5896, Bogotá.

Universidad Nacional de Colombia: Ciudad Universitaria, Bogotá; 1,959 teachers, 13,038 students.

Universidad Distrital "Francisco José de Caldas": Carrera 8, No. 40-78, Bogotá; 110 teachers; 1,043 students.

Universidad Pedagógica Nacional: Calle 72, No. 11-60, Bogotá; 182 teachers, 2,056 students.

Universidad Industrial de Santander: Apdo. Aéreo 678, Bucaramanga; 195 teachers, 2,710 students.

Universidad de Nariño Carrera 22, No. 18-109, Pasto, Nariño; 181 teachers, 2,197 students.

Universidad de Pamplona: Apdo. Aéreo 1046, Pamplona; 60 teachers, 900 students.

Universidad del Tolima: Apdo. Aéreo 546, Ibagué; 166 teachers, 2,200 students.

Universidad del Valle: Ciudad Universitaria, Meléndez, Apdo. Aéreo 2188, Cali; 550 teachers, 4,193 students.

Universidad Pedagógica y Tecnológica de Colombia: Tunja, Boyacá; 219 teachers, 2,348 students.

Universidad Tecnológica de Pereira: Carrera 13, No. 18-56, Apdo. Aéreo 97, Pereira; 170 teachers, 1,700 students.

PRIVATE UNIVERSITIES

Fundación Universidad de Bogotá "Jorge Tadeo Lozano": Calle 23, No. 4-47, Bogotá; 360 teachers, 3,584 students.

Universidad Autónoma Latinoamericana: Carrera 55, No. 49-51, Medellín; 170 teachers, 1,800 students.

Universidad Pontificia Bolivariana: Apdo. Postal 109, Medellín; 560 teachers, 9,867 students.

Universidad Externado de Colombia: Carrera 1A Este, Calle 12, Bogotá; 171 teachers, 1,526 students.

Universidad de la Gran Colombia: Carrera 6, No. 13-92, Bogotá.

Universidad de Córdoba: Apdo. Aéreo 354, Montería.

Pontificia Universidad Javeriana: Carrera 7A, No. 40-62, Apdo. Aéreo 5315, Bogotá; 895 teachers, 8,000 students.

Universidad Libre: Carrera 6A, No. 8-06, Bogotá; 220 teachers, 2,000 students.

Universidad de los Andes: Carrera 1E, Calle 18A, Apdo. Aéreo 4976, Bogotá; 300 teachers, 2,587 students.

Universidad de Medellín: Apdo. Aéreo 1983, Medellín; 224 teachers, 3,567 students.

Universidad del Quindio: Carrera 16, No. 20-15, Armenia.

Universidad Santiago de Cali: Apdo. Aéreo 4102, Cali.

Universidad de San Buenaventura: Calle 73, No. 10-45, Bogotá; 110 teachers, 1,600 students.

Universidad de Santo Tomás de Aquino: Carrera 9A, No. 51-23, Bogotá.

Universidad Social Católica de La Salle: Bogotá.

Universidad Tecnológica del Magdalena: Carrera 2A, No. 16-44, Santa Marta.

CONGO (BRAZZAVILLE)

INTRODUCTORY SURVEY

Location, Climate, Language, Religion, Flag, Capital

The People's Republic of the Congo runs north from the Atlantic to Cameroon and the Central African Republic. To the east, across the Congo River (renamed the Zaire by the Kinshasa Government), is the Republic of Zaire. Gabon lies to the west. The climate is tropical with temperatures averaging 21°c–27°c (70°F–80°F) throughout the year with an annual rainfall of about 120 cm. The official language is French. Just over half the people follow traditional beliefs, with Roman Catholic, Protestant and Muslim minorities. The national flag, adopted in January 1970, is plain red with the state emblem (two green palms enclosing a crossed hammer and hoe, surmounted by a gold star) in the upper left. The capital is Brazzaville.

Recent History

Formerly part of French Equatorial Africa, the Republic of the Congo became autonomous within the French Community in 1958 and fully independent in August 1960. The country's first President, the Abbé Fulbert Youlou, was deposed in 1963, and replaced by Alphonse Massemba-Débat. Political unrest culminated in the intervention of the army in 1968; the National Assembly was replaced by the National Council of the Revolution, and in September 1968 Capt. (later Major) Alfred Raoul became head of state. Major Marien Ngouabi, chairman of the Council of the Revolution, took power as President in January 1969.

The Ngouabi government set up a single political party, the Congolese Labour Party, and in January 1970 produced a new constitution, Marxist in inspiration, and changed the country's name. Despite the adoption of the panoply of Marxism, Ngouabi faced considerable opposition from left-wing elements within the Party, the army and the students. He was criticized for allowing foreign economic domination to continue, and receiving massive French financial and technical aid. There were several attempted *coups*, and the Party and Council of Ministers were frequently purged. The left-wing rebellion of Lieut. Ange Diawara, a former Vice-President, was ended when its leaders were killed in April 1973. Strengthened by this success, Ngouabi produced a new Constitution, including the establishment of a National Assembly, adopted by referendum in June 1973. The dismissal of the right-wing Chief of Staff of the army, in October 1973, and measures taken against foreign traders, oil distributors and insurance companies have been taken as signs of a move towards socialism on the part of the Government.

The People's Republic is a member of the French Community, UDEAC, the OAU and the UN, but has withdrawn from OCAM.

Government

There is only one political party, the Congolese Labour Party (*Parti congolais du travail—P.C.T.*).

The Constitution, which came into force following a referendum in June 1973, established a National Assembly of 115 members as the legislature. Executive power rests with the Council of State, which includes both the President and the Prime Minister, who appoints ministers and is responsible to the Party. The President is elected by the Party, and is Chairman of its Central Committee.

Defence

The army, which took over the duties of the police in February 1973, numbers 2,000. There are small naval and air forces, and 4,800 men in para-military forces.

Economic Affairs

The most important economic activity is forestry. The major cash crops are sugar, palm oil, cocoa and tobacco, the processing of which is the basis of industry. Cement, flour and textiles are also produced. The Congo has large reserves of potash, and offshore petroleum deposits are exploited by the French-backed Elf-Congo company. Government receipts from oil production are expected to represent three-quarters of the national budget in 1974. An oil refinery is under construction at Pointe-Noire.

External trade is dominated by France, but the Government hopes both to expand and diversify exports and to find new sources of imports.

Transport and Communications

The River Congo and its tributary the Oubangui are the principal means of transport and Brazzaville is an important port on the River Congo. The rivers and the railway line, from Pointe-Noire on the Atlantic to Brazzaville with a branch to the iron ore mines at Franceville in Gabon, are important links between Chad, the Central African Republic and the coast. Roads are few with 11,000 km. usable throughout the year. The Government plans to improve the poor communications system, which inhibits economic development. The Congo has its own internal air service and the Government has a share in Air Afrique.

Social Welfare

In January 1963 a pension scheme was started by the National Social Security Board, which is also responsible for family allowances and workmen's compensation schemes. The Government also runs hospitals and health centres.

Education

There are not enough primary schools but there is a relatively high literacy rate—education will soon be compulsory from 6 to 16. In 1965 all private schools were taken over by the State. A number of students go to France for technical instruction, but the National University at Brazzaville was founded in 1971 and now caters for over 1,400 students.

Tourism

There are no special facilities for tourism.

Visas: Citizens of all states, with the exception of France, require visas to visit the People's Republic of the Congo.

Sport

Football, volleyball, basketball and athletics are the principal sports. The Congo competes with neighbouring states and within the French Community. The first African Games were held in Brazzaville in July 1965.

Public Holidays

1974: August 15th (Independence Day), December 25th (Christmas).

1975: January 1st (New Year's Day), March 28th–31st (Easter), May 1st (Labour Day).

Weights and Measures

The metric system is in force.

Currency and Exchange Rates

100 centimes=1 franc de la Communauté financière africaine (CFA).

Exchange rates (April 1974):
1 franc CFA=2 French centimes;
£1 sterling=579.75 francs CFA;
U.S. $1=245.625 francs CFA.

STATISTICAL SURVEY

Area: 342,000 sq. km. (132,000 sq. miles).

Population (July 1st, 1972): 1,150,000. Principal towns (1971): Brazzaville 200,000; Pointe-Noire 100,000, Dolisie 20,000, Jacob 15,000. Main ethnic groups: Kongo 350,000, Téké 150,000, M'Bochi 95,000.

AGRICULTURE
PRINCIPAL CROPS
('000 metric tons)

	1969	1970	1971	1972
Cassava	450	450	460	460
Groundnuts (unshelled) .	20	20	20	20
Palm Kernels . . .	3	2	3	3
Palm Oil	6	6	6	6
Refined Sugar . . .	95	98	122	125
Cocoa	1	2	2	2
Coffee	2	2	2	2

Source: United Nations Economic Commission for Africa, *Statistical Yearbook 1972.*

Livestock (1971): Cattle 42,000, Sheep and Goats 116,000, Pigs 28,000.

OTHER PRODUCTION
(metric tons)

	1968	1969	1970	1971
Fisheries:				
Various Fish . .	10,000	1,720	3,418	6,891
Tunny . . .	21,600	9,109	11,521	13,351
Forestry:				
Okoumé . .	n.a.	250,836	258,573	269,386
Mining:				
Gold (kg.) . .	157	121	83	95
Lead and Zinc .	4,100	12,380	n.a.	195
Copper . .	2,610	198	1,000	2,070
Crude Oil . .	43,000	24,215	18,943	14,433
Potassium . .	n.a.	70,000	200,000	430,000
Industry:				
Palm Oil . .	2,765	308	406	n.a.
Cane Sugar . .	102,000	51,800	53,362	16,252
Beer ('000 hectolitres) .	n.a.	76	66	96
Soap . . .	n.a.	4,184	4,522	4,746
Tobacco . . .	n.a.	974	989	904

In 1972 135,522 metric tons of *okoumé* and 473,000 tons of potassium were produced.

CONGO (BRAZZAVILLE)—(STATISTICAL SURVEY)

FINANCE

100 centimes=1 franc de la Communauté financière africaine (CFA).

Coins: 1, 2, 5, 10, 25, 50 and 100 francs CFA.

Notes: 100, 500, 1,000, 5,000 and 10,000 francs CFA.

Exchange rates (April 1974): 1 franc CFA=2 French centimes;

£1 sterling=579.75 francs CFA; U.S. $1=245.625 francs CFA;

1,000 francs CFA=£1.725=$4.071.

BUDGET

1972: Balanced at 21,853m. francs CFA.

1973: Balanced at 24,073m. francs CFA.

1974: Balanced at 27,475m. francs CFA.

EXTERNAL TRADE*

(million francs CFA)

	1968	1969	1970	1971	1972
Imports . . .	20,605	20,291	15,910	21,910	23,081
Exports† . . .	12,189	11,384	8,564	11,759	11,581

* Excluding trade with other countries in UDEAC and, prior to 1969, Chad.

† Including re-exports of industrial diamonds (worth 807 million francs CFA in 1970) originating in Zaire, but not included under imports.

COMMODITIES

IMPORTS	1968	1969	1970	EXPORTS	1968	1969	1970
Wheat and Meslin, un-milled . .	354	181	11	Coffee, raw . . .	143	165	156
Wheat Meal and Flour .	9	298	429	Cocoa Beans . .	205	240	282
Alcoholic Beverages .	503	603	508	Palm Kernels . .	151	93	51
Petroleum Products .	595	636	319	Sugar, raw . .	280	857	710
Medicines and Pharma-ceuticals . .	498	587	513	Wood . . .	5,130	5,908	4,398
Paper and Pulp . .	353	331	314	Veneer and Plywood .	1,157	1,286	726
Cotton Fabrics, woven .	863	968	585	Zinc Ore . . .	19	35	—
Other Textiles . .	369	353	303	Petroleum, crude .	152	99	61
Iron and Steel (bars, plates, sheet, pipes, fittings) . . .	643	494	665	Diamonds* . .	3,834	1,682	807
Finished Structural Parts	1,017	49	45	Copper . . .	104	17	—
Machinery . .	2,186	1,492	1,091				
Telecommunications Apparatus . .	235	354	501				
Road Motor Vehicles .	1,685	1,837	1,610				
Clothing . . .	580	610	441				
Footwear . . .	107	130	128				
TOTAL (incl. others) .	20,605	20,291	15,910	TOTAL (incl. others) .	12,189	11,384	8,564

* Re-exports of stones imported clandestinely and not included in import statistics.

PRINCIPAL COUNTRIES

Imports	1967	1968	1969	Exports	1967	1968	1969
Belgium and Luxembourg . . .	395	521	437	Belgium and Luxembourg . . .	466	1,452	960
China (People's Republic)	622	422	393	France . . .	1,731	1,286	1,576
France . . .	10,927	11,946	11,573	Federal Germany .	2,163	2,641	1,981
Federal Germany .	2,533	1,987	1,701	Israel . . .	601	588	611
Italy . . .	683	459	621	Italy . . .	246	372	555
Japan . . .	243	357	434	Ivory Coast . .	46	180	262
Mauritania . .	455	507	524	Netherlands . .	2,410	1,997	1,646
Netherlands . .	714	727	765	South Africa . .	379	592	698
Netherlands Antilles .	242	64	61	Spain . . .	46	64	381
United Kingdom . .	417	632	433	United Kingdom . .	1,926	1,507	684
U.S.S.R. . .	551	306	90	U.S.A. . . .	208	294	213
U.S.A. . . .	830	1,073	1,375	Zaire . . .	577	171	28

TRANSPORT
(freight in metric tons)

	1969	1970	1971
Railways:			
Passengers	1,221,600	1,256,400	1,007,300
Freight	1,483,200	1,608,000	1,507,200
Sea Transport:			
Ships (arrived and departed) .	2,256	2,052	2,139
Passengers arrived . . .	1,610	239	311
Freight loaded . . .	1,323,200	2,354,400	2,757,200
Freight unloaded . . .	506,400	518,400	581,500
River Transport:			
Freight loaded . . .	177,737	223,034	217,103
Freight unloaded . . .	185,639	214,480	224,444
Air Transport:			
Planes (arrived and departed) .	7,400	8,955	9,867
Passengers (arrived and departed)	99,880	131,008	110,537
Freight loaded . . .	3,246	3,407 }	10,693
Freight unloaded . . .	5,887	6,825 }	
Road Traffic:			
Private Vehicles . . .	1,983	1,677	1,293
Trade Vehicles . . .	514	398	461

EDUCATION
(1971–72)

	Schools	Pupils	Teachers
Primary . . .	922	260,534	3,800
Secondary . . .	55	33,000	672
Technical . . .	34	2,600	n.a.

A National University was opened in 1972 with 1,436 students.

Source: Direction du Service National de la Statistique, B.P. 2031, Brazzaville.

THE CONSTITUTION

(Approved by referendum June 24th, 1973)

Fundamental Principles: The People's Republic of the Congo is a sovereign independent state, in which all power springs from the people and belongs to the people. Treason against the people is the greatest crime. All nationals are guaranteed freedom of conscience and religion, and religious communities are free to practise their faith, but political organizations based on religion are banned. The land is the property of the people, and as necessary the state shall regulate its use. The state directs the economic life and development of the country according to the general plan. The right to own and inherit private property is guaranteed, and expropriation is governed by law.

Head of State: The Chairman of the Central Committee of the *Parti congolais du travail* (*PCT*) is the President of the Republic and Head of State. He is elected for a five-year term by the party congress.

The Executive: Executive power is vested in the Council of State under the Chairmanship of the President of the Republic. It directs and orientates the action of the Government. It consists of the five members of the PCT's political bureau, the executive of the National Assembly, and the Prime Minister. Ministers are appointed by the Prime Minister, who is responsible to the party.

The Legislature: Most legislative powers are vested in the People's National Assembly. It has 115 members, elected by all adults over the age of 18 from a list put out by the PCT. It is responsible to the Prime Minister and undertakes tasks entrusted to him by the party. The President of the National Assembly is second in rank only to the President of the Republic.

The Party: The sole political party is the *Parti congolais du travail* (*PCT*). Its Political Bureau of five members takes part in government. Its Central Committee consists of 40 members, including the Political Bureau, most of the Ministers and the Chief of Staff of the army, chaired by the President of the Republic and Head of State. The Central Committee's powers include the initiation of revisions to the constitution, which revisions are put to the party congress and the people and become final when approved by the Central Committee, and the appointment of judges to the Revolutionary Court of Justice.

THE GOVERNMENT

(*April* 1974)

HEAD OF STATE

President: Commandant MARIEN NGOUABI (appointed January 1969).

COUNCIL OF MINISTERS

Chairman and Minister of Defence: Commandant MARIEN NGOUABI.

Prime Minister and Minister of Planning: HENRI LOPES.

Minister of Agriculture and Stock-Breeding: CHARLES NGOUOTO.

Minister of Foreign Affairs: DAVID CHARLES GANAO.

Minister of Finance: SATURNIN OABE.

Minister of Trade: BONIFACE HATINGOU.

Minister of Town Planning, Housing and Tourism: ROBERT BIKINDOU.

Minister of Industry and Mines: ANDRÉ GEORGES MOUYABI.

Minister of Transport, Public Works and Civil Aviation: LOUIS SYLVAIN GOMA.

Minister of Justice and Labour: ALEXANDRE DENGUET.

Minister of Technical, Professional and Higher Education: JEAN-PIERRE TSHISTER TCHIKAYA.

Minister of the Interior and of Posts and Telecommunications: CHARLES MAURICE SIANARD.

Minister of Health and Social Affairs: ALPHONSE EMPANA.

Minister of Primary and Secondary Education: AUGUSTE BATINA.

Minister of Power: ANTOINE KAINE.

Minister of Culture, Art and Sport: ANDRÉ MOUELE.

Minister of Water and Forest Resources: XAVIER KATALI.

Minister of Information: LAURENT MANE.

POLITICAL BUREAU OF THE CONGOLESE LABOUR PARTY (PARTI CONGOLAIS DU TRAVAIL—PCT)

Chairman: Commandant MARIEN NGOUABI.

Commissioner for Planning: ANGE-EDOUARD POUNGUI.

Commissioner for the Press: PIERRE NZÉ.

Commissioner for Organization: CHARLES NGOUOTO.

Commissioner for Education: HENRI LOPES.

DIPLOMATIC REPRESENTATION

EMBASSIES ACCREDITED TO THE PEOPLE'S REPUBLIC OF THE CONGO
(In Brazzaville unless otherwise indicated)

Algeria: B.P. 2100; *Ambassador:* (vacant).

Belgium: B.P. 225; *Ambassador:* RENÉ MÉRENNE.

Bulgaria: *Ambassador:* IVANOV YANKO.

Cameroon: Bangui, Central African Republic.

Canada: Kinshasa, Zaire.

Central African Republic: B.P. 10; *Ambassador:* AUGUSTE MBOYE.

Chad: B.P. 461; *Ambassador:* (vacant).

China, People's Republic: *Ambassador:* LIEU TCHE-HSIEN.

Cuba: *Ambassador:* MANUEL AGRAMONTE.

Czechoslovakia: *Chargé d'Affaires:* VLADIMIR ZIAK.

Denmark: *Ambassador:* (vacant).

Egypt: *Ambassador:* HASSAN AHMED FAWZI.

Equatorial Guinea: *Ambassador:* CLEMENTE ATEBA.

Ethiopia: *Ambassador:* JACOB GUEBRE LIOULL.

France: rue Alfassa, B.P. 2089; *Ambassador:* PIERRE HUNT.

Gabon: *Ambassador:* (vacant).

German Democratic Republic: B.P. 2244; *Ambassador:* WERNER DORDAN.

Germany, Federal Republic: B.P. 2022; *Ambassador:* ANDREAS MEYER LANDRUT.

Guinea: *Ambassador:* (vacant).

Hungary: Conakry, Guinea.

India: Kinshasa, Zaire.

Italy: *Ambassador:* GALEAZZO PINI.

Korea, Democratic People's Republic: *Ambassador:* LI IN GYU.

Lebanon: Dakar, Senegal.

Mali: *Ambassador:* HALIDOU TOURÉ.

Mauritania: Lagos, Nigeria.

Mongolia: *Ambassador:* BAT OTCHYRIN GOTOV.

Netherlands: Kinshasa, Zaire.

Romania: Kinshasa, Zaire.

Senegal: *Ambassador:* PASCAL ANTOINE SANÉ.

Spain: Kinshasa, Zaire.

Sudan: Kinshasa, Zaire.

Sweden: Kinshasa, Zaire.

Switzerland: Kinshasa, Zaire.

Tunisia: Kinshasa, Zaire.

U.S.S.R.: *Ambassador:* ARKADI BOUDAKOV.

United Kingdom: Kinshasa, Zaire.

Viet-Nam, Democratic Republic: *Chargé d'Affaires:* NGUYEN THAN VAN.

Viet-Nam, Provisional Revolutionary Government of the Republic of South: NGUYEN VAN THANG.

Yugoslavia: *Ambassador:* NIKOLA STEFANOVSKI.

Zaire: B.P. 2457; *Ambassador:* KAPELA KINDUELA.

Zambia: Kinshasa, Zaire.

The People's Republic of the Congo also has diplomatic relations with Libya and with the Royal Government of Khmer National Union (the Cambodian Government-in-Exile).

NATIONAL ASSEMBLY

President: MIAKASSIBA DIEUDONNÉ.

ELECTION, JUNE 24TH, 1973
All 115 seats were won by the *Parti congolais du travail*.

POLITICAL PARTY

Parti congolais du travail—PCT (*Congolese Labour Party*): f. 1969 to replace the *Mouvement national de la révolution*. The Central Committee of the Party has 40 members including all five members of the Political Bureau, most of the Ministers and the Chief of Staff of the Army; **President of the Central Committee:** Commandant MARIEN NGOUABI.

DEFENCE

There is an army of 2,000 men, a gendarmerie of 1,500, a navy of 50 and an air force of 150.

Commander in Chief: Commandant MARIEN NGOUABI.

Chief of Staff of the Armed Forces: Captain VICTOR NTZIKA KABALA.

Chief of Staff of the Army: Captain HENRI ODRIEL.

Commander of the People's Militia: Senior Adjutant ALEXANDRE MOLITON.

JUDICIAL SYSTEM

Revolutionary Court of Justice: created January 1969; competent in cases involving the security of the state; has nine judges selected from list of 50 by Central Committee of PCT.

Supreme Court: Pres. CHARLES ASSEMEKANG.

There is also a court of appeal, a criminal court, *tribunaux de grande instance* (County courts), *tribunaux d'instance* (Magistrate's courts), labour courts, and *tribunaux coutumiers* (courts of common law), the latter to be replaced by *tribunaux d'instance*.

RELIGION

It is estimated that about half the population follow traditional Animist beliefs. Just under half are Christians (Roman Catholics 437,867, Protestants 134,650). Muslims number about 4,540. Church activities are limited by the state and church schools no longer exist.

Roman Catholic Church: Metropolitan Archdiocese of Brazzaville and two suffragan dioceses (Fort-Rousset, Point-Noire), dependent on the Sacred Congregation for the Evangelization of Peoples; 150 resident priests; 128 male and 84 female members of religious institutes; 437,867 Catholics in a total population of 1,153,371 (December 1972 estimate by Catholic Church).

Archbishop of Brazzaville: Cardinal EMILE BIAYENDA, B.P. 2301.

Bishop of Fort-Rousset: Mgr. GEORGES SINGHA, B.P. 6.

Bishop of Pointe-Noire: Mgr. JEAN-BAPTISTE FAURET, B.P. 659.

Protestant Missions: In all four Equatorial states (the Congo, the Central African Republic, Chad and Gabon) there are nearly 1,000 mission centres with a total personnel of about 2,000.

Eglise Evangélique du Congo: B.P. 3205, Brazzaville; Pres. Rev. R. BUANA KIBONGI.

THE PRESS

A censorship committee for all the media was established in 1972.

DAILIES
(Brazzaville unless stated)

Congo Matin: B.P. 495; f. 1965; circ. 500; Publisher F. BOUDZANGA.

Le Courrier d'Afrique: B.P. 2027; circ. 45,000.

L'Eveil de Pointe-Noire: B.P. 660, Pointe-Noire; Editor S. B. PACI; circ. 500.

Le Journal de Brazzaville: B.P. 132; Publisher M. J. DEVOUE.

Journal Officiel de la République du Congo: B.P. 58.

Le Petit Journal de Brazzaville: B.P. 2027; f. 1958; Dir. M. ADAM.

PERIODICALS
(Brazzaville)

Bulletin Mensuel de la Chambre de Commerce de Brazzaville: monthly.

Bulletin Mensuel de Statistique: B.P. 2031; monthly.

Effort: B.P. 64; monthly.

L'Envoi: B.P. 601; monthly.

Etumba: B.P. 23; weekly journal of PCT.

Information-Jeunesse: B.P. 2066.

Nouvelle Congolaise: weekly newspaper.

La Semaine: B.P. 192; f. 1952; published by Archdiocese of Brazzaville; weekly; circulates in Congo, Gabon, Chad and the Central African Republic; Dir. A. DUCRY; circ. 7,000.

PRESS AGENCIES

Agence Congolaise d'Information (A.C.I.): B.P. 2144, Brazzaville; f. 1961; autonomous, but associated with A.F.P. and D.P.A.; Dir. A. B. SAMBA; daily bulletin.

FOREIGN BUREAUX

AFP (*France*): B.P. 2042, Ave. Lumumba, Brazzaville; Corr. FRANÇOIS GALLIENI; also represented in Pointe-Noire.

APN (*U.S.S.R.*): B.P. 170, Brazzaville; Bureau Chief G. KUSHCHIN.

TASS is also represented in Brazzaville.

RADIO AND TELEVISION

Radiodiffusion-Télévision Nationale Congolaise: B.P. 2241, Brazzaville; Dir. DANIEL DJIO.

Television began transmission in 1963 and now transmits for 25 hours a week, of which 8 hours are educational programmes. Dir. S. BEMBA; Tech. Dir. A. L. MALONGA.

La Voix de la Révolution Congolaise: B.P. 2241, Brazzaville; national broadcasting station; programmes in French, Lingala and Kikongo; transmitters at Brazzaville and Pointe-Noire; foreign service to Angola in Portuguese and vernaculars; Dir. F. ITOUA.

In 1973 there were 75,000 radios and 2,600 televisions.

FINANCE

BANKS
CENTRAL BANK

Banque des Etats de l'Afrique Centrale: 29 rue du Colisée, 75008 Paris, France; B.P. 126, Brazzaville; f. 1973 as the Central Bank of issue of five African states; cap. 1,250m. francs CFA; res. 711m. francs CFA; Gen. Man. CHRISTIAN JOUDIOU; Asst. Gen. Man. J. E. SATHOUD.

COMMERCIAL BANKS

Banque Commerciale Congolaise: B.P. 79, avenue Amilcar Cabral, Brazzaville; f. 1963; cap. 300m. francs CFA; res. 64m. francs CFA (Dec. 1972); brs. in Dolisie, Jacob, Loudima, Brazzaville airport and Pointe-Noire; Pres. JUSTIN LEKOUNDZOU; Dir.-Gen. BERNARD BANZA BOUTI.

Banque Internationale pour le Commerce et l'Industrie du Congo: B.P. 147, avenue Amilcar Cabral, Brazzaville; f. 1963; affiliated to Banque Nationale de Paris and Société Financière pour les Pays d'Outre Mer; cap. 150m. francs CFA; res. 19m. francs CFA (Dec. 1972). brs. in Dolisie and Pointe-Noire; Pres. and Gen. Man; E. MOUTERDE; Man. A. COPPEX; publ. *Rapport annuel.*

Banque Nationale de Développement du Congo (BNDC): B.P. 2085, Brazzaville; f. 1961; cap. 462m. francs CFA; gives financial and technical help to all development projects; Dir.-Gen. DANIEL OBELA.

Caisse Centrale de Coopération Economique: B.P. 96, Brazzaville; Dir. MICHEL LANGLOIS.

Crédit Foncier de l'Ouest Africain: B.P. 116, Brazzaville.

Société Générale de Banques au Congo: B.P. 122, 14 Place de la Poste, Brazzaville; f. 1963; cap. 200m. francs CFA; res. 7m. francs CFA (Dec. 1971); 51 per cent owned by Société Générale, Paris, France; br. in Pointe-Noire; Chair. R. DUCHEMIN; Man. G. BROS.

FOREIGN BANKS

Bank of America N.T. and S.A.: Bank of America Center, San Francisco, Calif. 94120, U.S.A.; br. in Brazzaville.

Banque Internationale pour l'Afrique Occidentale: 9 ave. de Messine, 75360 Paris; B.P. 33, Brazzaville; Dir. ROLAND BOITELLE; Point-Noire, B.P. 695, Dir. YVES DURAND.

Union Zaïroise de Banques S.Z.A.R.L.: B.P. 197, Kinshasa, Zaire; f. 1949; brs. in Brazzaville and Pointe-Noire.

INSURANCE

A National Insurance Company was set up by the Government in November 1973, to take over the business of all insurance companies operating in the Congo.

TRADE AND INDUSTRY

CHAMBERS OF COMMERCE

Chambre de Commerce, d'Agriculture et d'Industrie de Brazzaville: B.P. 92, Brazzaville; Pres. CHRISTIAN DIALLO-DRAMEY.

Chambre de Commerce, d'Agriculture et d'Industrie du Kouilou-Niari: B.P. 665, Pointe-Noire; branch in Dolisie; Pres. E. EBOUKA-BABACKAS.

Chambre des Mines de l'Afrique Equatoriale: B.P. 26, Brazzaville; Pres. M. DE LAVALEYE.

TRADE ORGANIZATIONS

Office National du Commerce (OFNACOM): B.P. 2305, Brazzaville.

Office National de Commercialisation des Produits Agricoles (ONCPA): B.P. 144, Brazzaville; marketing of agricultural products from northern Congo and promotion of rural co-operatives; Dir. P.-F. NKOUA.

Office Congolais de l'Okoumé: B.P. 739 Pointe-Noire; marketing of Congolese wood; Dir. E. BRAEKEVELT.

Syndicat des Commerçants, Importateurs et Exportateurs de l'Afrique Equatoriale (SYCOMIMPEX): B.P. 84, Brazzaville; Pres. M. AGOSTINI; Sec.-Gen. M. FULCHIRON.

Syndicat des Industries de l'Afrique Equatoriale (SYNDUSTREF): B.P. 84, Brazzaville; Pres. M. JEANBRAU; Sec.-Gen. M. FULCHIRON.

PROFESSIONAL ORGANIZATION

Union Patronale et Inter-professionnelle du Congo (UNI-CONGO): B.P. 42, Brazzaville; Pres. P. SIGNORET; Sec.-Gen. G. FULCHIRON.

TRADE UNION

Confédération Syndicale Congolaise: Brazzaville; f. 1964; Gen.-Sec. ANATOLE KONDO.

INDUSTRIAL ORGANIZATION

Bureau pour la Création, le Controle et l'Orientation des Entreprises et Exploitations de l'Etat (BCCO): B.P. 211, Brazzaville; f. 1965; supervises nationalized industries; Sec.-Gen. B. MABOUEKI.

DEVELOPMENT

Bureau pour le Développement de la Production Agricole (BDPA): B.P. 2222, Brazzaville; Dir. M. UBAGHS.

Société de Développement Régional de la Vallée de Niari et de Jacob: Jacob; f. 1966; Dir. JEAN-MICHEL MOUMBOUNOU.

Société Nationale d'Élevage (SONEL): Jacob; f. 1967; state-owned; development of semi-intensive cattle-rearing; Dir.-Gen. J. WILFRID.

Société pour le Développement de l'Afrique Equatoriale: B.P. 909, Pointe-Noire; B.P. 56, Brazzaville.

TRANSPORT

Agence Transcongolaise des Communications (ATC): B.P. 670, Pointe-Noire; f. 1969 to control nationalization of transport; has three sections: Congo-Océan railway, inland waterways, and port of Pointe-Noire; is the most important state enterprise with an annual budget of 6,400 m.francs CFA; Pres. L. SYLVAIN GOMA; Dir.-Gen. E. EBOUKA BABACKAS.

RAILWAY

Chemin de Fer Congo-Océan: Pointe-Noire, B.P. 651; a section of *ATC*; Dir. S. TCHICHELLE; there are 515 km. of track from Brazzaville to Pointe-Noire. Only diesel trains are used. A 286 km. section of line linking the manganese mines at Moanda (in Gabon), via a cableway to the Congo border with the main line to Pointe-Noire was opened in 1962. A programme of modernization of both track and rolling stock is under way, helped by $6.3m. loan from the IDA in April 1972.

ROADS

There are 11,000 km. of roads usable throughout the year, of which 310 km. are bitumened. The network consists of 3,768 km. main roads and 7,232 km. secondary roads, with the principal routes linking Pointe-Noire with Brazzaville and Ouesso, and Dolisie with Cameroon, via Gabon.

INLAND WATERWAYS

ATC-Section Voies Navigables, Ports et Transports Fluviaux: B.P. 2048; Brazzaville; waterways authority.

Cie. Congolaise de Navigation (CONGO-NA): B.P. 795; f. 1962; Pres. V. TAMBA TAMBA.

Cie. Maritime d'Expertise (COMEX): B.P. 250.

Cie. Générale de Transports en Afrique Equatoriale: B.P. 76, Brazzaville; f. 1962; cap. 800m. francs CFA; Pres. Dir.-Gen. J.-C.THOREL.

Société Ouest-Africaine d'Entreprises Maritimes: B.P. 674, Pointe-Noire; f. 1959; cap. 115m. francs CFA; Dir. JEAN ROZIE.

Société Equatoriale de Navigation: B.P. 35, Brazzaville; f. 1963; cap. 20m. francs CFA; Dir. JEAN ANSLERT.

Transit Congo Oubangui Tchad: B.P. 2052, Brazzaville; f. 1963; cap. 5m. francs CFA; Dir. M. LANCOMBE.

SHIPPING
Pointe-Noire

ATC-Section Port de Pointe-Noire: B.P. 651; port authority; Dir. I. MBOUNGOU-NGOMA.

Cie. Maritime des Chargeurs Réunis: B.P. 656; agents for Cie. Fabre S.G.T.M., Congona, Elder Dempster Lines, Palm Lines, Cie. Maritime Belge, Nautilus, Shell International Marine Ltd., Gaz Océan, Nigerian Lines, Delta Lines, Navigen Co., Unicorn; Dir. GUY JAQUEMIN.

SOAEM (Congo): B.P. 674; agents for Société Navale de l'Ouest, Lloyd Triestino, Lloyd Brasileiro, Dafra Line, Scandinavian West Africa Line, East Asiatic Co., General Steam Navigation Co., Compagnie Navale des Pétroles, Texaco Inc., Compania Colonial de Navigaçao, Compania National de Navigaçao, Sociedade Geral de Comercio Industria e Transportes, Société Agret, Cobrecaf, Cie. française d'armement maritime, Gold Star Line, A. Halcoussis, Denis Frères, Purfina, Somara, Société Navale Caennaise, Scandinavian East Africa Line, Zim Cargo Line, Saga.

UMARCO: B.P. 723; agents for Farrell Line, Holland West Africa Line, Royal Interocean Lines, Scindia Line, Mobil Shipping Co., Sabline, Panatrans.

Brazzaville

Société Navale Chargeurs Delmas-Vieljeux (SNCDV): B.P. 2345, Brazzaville.

CIVIL AVIATION

The important international airports are at Brazzaville—Maya-Maya, which has the longest runway of French-speaking Africa (3,300 metres), and Pointe-Noire; a third is to be built at Impfondo. There are also 22 smaller aerodromes.

Air Afrique: The Government of the Congo has a 6 per cent share; *see* under Ivory Coast; B.P. 127, Brazzaville.

Lina Congo (Lignes Nationales Aériennes Congolaises): ave. du 28 Août 1940, B.P. 2203, Brazzaville; f. 1966; two-thirds government-owned; operates an extensive internal network; fleet of two AN-24, one F27, one DC-6, one DC-4, two DC-3; Dir.-Gen. AIME PORTELLA; Tech. Dir. TCHICAYA BOUMBAS.

The Congo is also served by the following foreign airlines: Aeroflot, Air Afrique, Air Mali, KLM and UTA.

TOURISM

Office National Congolaise du Tourisme: B.P. 456, Brazzaville; Dir. FÉLIX MALEKAT.

UNIVERSITY

Université Nationale du Congo: B.P. 69, Brazzaville; 1,436 students.

COSTA RICA

INTRODUCTORY SURVEY

Location, Climate, Language, Religion, Flag, Capital

Costa Rica forms a part of the Central American isthmus with the Caribbean to the east and a longer Pacific coastline to the west. The climate is warm and damp in the lowlands—average temperature 27°C (81°F)—and cooler on the Central Plateau—average temperature 22°C (72°F)—where two-thirds of the population live. Eighty per cent of Costa Ricans are of European descent and the country has one of the highest birth-rates in Central America. The language is Spanish. The state religion is Roman Catholicism. The national flag (proportions 3 by 2) consists of horizontal bands of blue, white, red, white and blue, the red band being twice the width of the others. The state flag, in addition, has on the red stripe (to the left of centre) a white disc enclosing the national coat of arms. The capital is San José.

Recent History

After 1948, the predominant figure in Costa Rican politics was José Figueres Ferrer. Leader of the socialist Partido de Liberación Nacional (PLN), which seized power in 1948, he was President three times (1948–49, 1953–58 and 1970–74). Under him, Costa Rica became one of the most democratic countries in Latin America. In 1948 the armed forces were abolished and banks were nationalized, and since then great social improvements have been made. The presidential election in February 1974 resulted in victory for Daniel Oduber Quirós, the candidate of the PLN, who took office in May. He outlined his Government's policy as including the improvement of the wages and living standards of the underprivileged, the creation of new jobs to fight unemployment, and the eradication of the discrepancies of regional development. President Oduber also re-affirmed the Government's intention to continue with the establishment of friendly relations with the socialist states, a policy initiated under President Figueres.

Government

Under the Constitution of 1949 executive power is vested in the President assisted by two Vice-Presidents and a Cabinet. The President is elected for a four-year term and must receive 40 per cent of the votes. The legislative organ is the unicameral Legislative Assembly of 57 members elected for four years. Parliamentary and presidential elections are held by compulsory adult suffrage.

Defence

There have been no armed forces since 1948. Paramilitary forces number about 5,000 men.

Economic Affairs

The economy depends mainly on agriculture. Coffee was, until recently, the most important export commodity, but great diversification has taken place and in 1971 and 1972 bananas were the most important single export item. Cocoa, honey and, more recently, sugar are the other important exports. The increased production and export of meat (mainly beef) have made this commodity an important new source of foreign exchange earnings. Rice, maize and beans are produced mainly for home consumption. Forests cover large areas of the country. Mineral deposits are chiefly of limestone and a little gold. Substantial sulphur deposits were discovered in 1966 and prospecting for bauxite is under way. Industry is on a small scale, the main products being textiles, chemicals, leather goods and furniture. Hydro-electric power is being developed in the highlands. By far the largest of Costa Rica's trading partners is the U.S.A. The German Federal Republic is Costa Rica's second largest trading partner. In recent years inflation has become a serious problem; retail prices rose by 30 per cent in 1973.

Transport and Communications

There are some 4,800 km. of all-weather roads, including 600 km. of the Pan-American Highway. Three railway companies operate 800 km. of track. The main ports handling external trade are Limón on the Caribbean coast and Puntarenas and Golfito on the Pacific coast, and there are local shipping services to Panama. The main towns are connected by internal air services and international air transport is provided by the national airline Líneas Aéreas Costarricenses and six foreign companies.

Social Welfare

A Labour Code provides benefits for employees and there are insurance schemes covering sickness, old age and death. There is no centralized health service, but there are various independent organizations, some of them state-subsidized, governing hospitals, clinics and all medical services.

Education

All education is free and elementary education is compulsory between the ages of six and twelve. Official secondary education is free and consists of two stages: a three-year basic course followed by a more highly specialized course of two years. Escuelas Normales and Escuelas Normales Superiores provide training courses for primary and secondary school teachers respectively. At 80 per cent Costa Rica has the highest literacy rate in Central America. There are about 3,000 primary schools and about 160 secondary schools, with a total of nearly 480,000 pupils. There is a university at San José and a second university, the National University, has been founded in Heredia.

Tourism

The main tourist features are the Irazú and Poas volcanoes, the Orosi waterfalls and relics of Spanish colonial civilization. Tourists also visit San José, the capital, and the Pacific beaches of Puntarenas.

Visas are required by all visitors.

Sport

Football is the national sport and basketball, boxing, baseball, golf, tennis and swimming are also popular.

Public Holidays

1974: August 2nd (Our Lady of the Angels), August 15th (Assumption), September 15th (Independence Day), October 12th (Columbus Day), December 8th (Immaculate Conception), December 25th (Christmas Day), December 28th–31st (Bank Holidays in San José).

1975: January 1st (New Year's Day), March 19th (Feast of St. Joseph), March 28th (Good Friday), April 11th (Anniversary of the Battle of Rivas), May 1st (Anniversary of the Second Battle of Rivas and Labour Day), May 23rd (Corpus Christi), June 29th (St. Peter and St. Paul), July 25th (Anniversary of the Annexation of Guanacaste Province).

Weights and Measures

The metric system is in force.

Currency and Exchange Rates

100 céntimos = 1 Costa Rican colón.

Exchange rates (April 1974):

£1 sterling = 20.31 colones;
U.S. $1 = 8.60 colones.

STATISTICAL SURVEY

AREA AND POPULATION

AREA (sq. km.)	POPULATION (1972)			
	Total	BIRTHS, MARRIAGES, DEATHS (rate per '000)		
		Births	Marriages	Deaths
50,900	1,867,045	31.2	5.8*	5.9

* 1969.

PROVINCES, CAPITALS AND POPULATIONS (1972)

PROVINCE	POPULATION	CAPITAL	POPULATION
Alajuela . .	335,879	Alajuela . .	31,212
Cartago . .	214,415	Cartago . .	24,018
Guanacaste . .	207,441	Liberia . .	9,780
Heredia .	116,434	Heredia . .	25,806
Limón . .	97,316	Limón . .	25,168
Puntarenas . .	230,595	Puntarenas . .	25,426
San José . .	664,965	San José . .	221,425

AGRICULTURE
(1970–71)

Coffee (quintals)	1,606,788
Cotton (quintals)	30,828*
Sugar Cane (quintals) . . .	3,421,495
Cocoa (quintals) . . .	1,032,829*
Bananas (bunches of 56 lbs.) . .	35,801,747

*1969–70.

LIVESTOCK
(1970)

Cattle	1,513,399
Pigs	197,770

Cattle (1971): 1,653,876.

Forestry: Annual output of over 100 million board feet from about 200 sawmills.

Fishing: Tuna, lobster and shrimps are caught in quantity.

Mining: Lime and limestone, gold, calcium carbonate and diatonite are mined, in that order of importance.

Industry: Manufacturing output in 1971 was 1,328 million colones, chief products being furniture, footwear, leather, canned food, textiles and chemicals.

FINANCE

100 céntimos = 1 Costa Rican colón.
Coins: 5, 10, 25 and 50 céntimos; 1 and 2 colones.
Notes: 5, 10, 20, 50, 100, 500 and 1,000 colones.
Exchange rates (April 1974): £1 sterling = 15.77 colones (official selling rate) or 20.31 colones (free rate);
U.S. $1 = 6.68 colones (official selling rate) or 8.60 colones (free rate).
100 Costa Rican colones = £4.92 = $11.63 (free rates).

Note: The Central American peso, used for transactions within the Central American Common Market, is at par with the U.S. dollar.

BUDGET
(million Central American pesos)

	1971	1972
REVENUE:		
Direct Taxes . . .	28.7	34.4
Indirect Taxes . . .	96.0	108.3
Other	13.4	14.8
TOTAL . . .	138.1	157.5
EXPENDITURE:		
Current Expenditure . .	137.5	155.2
Capital Expenditure . .	44.1	52.5
TOTAL . . .	181.6	207.7

Source: Consejo Monetario Centroamericano, *Boletín Estadístico.*

BALANCE OF PAYMENTS
(million Central American pesos)

	1971			1972*		
	Credit	Debit	Balance	Credit	Debit	Balance
Goods and Services:						
Goods	224.6	316.3	− 91.7	271.4	338.2	− 66.8
Services	60.0	89.8	− 29.8	66.6	106.1	− 39.5
Total	284.6	406.1	−121.5	338.0	444.3	−106.3
Transfer Payments . .	12.2	4.8	7.4	8.1	—	8.1
Capital Operations . .	165.4	59.9	105.5	73.6	—	73.6
Net Errors and Omissions . .	20.1	—	20.1	30.4	—	30.4
Changes in Reserves . . .			− 11.5			− 5.8

* Preliminary.

Source: Consejo Monetario Centroamericano, *Boletín Estadístico.*

RESERVES AND CURRENCY
('000 Central American pesos)

	1970	1971	1972
Reserves at Banco Central . . .	17,860	32,214	40,372
of which Gold and Foreign Exchange .	11,641	31,866	36,102
Currency in Circulation (December) . .	57,335	65,495	78,521

SDRs ('000 Central American pesos): 1970 195; 1971 63; 1972 3,989.

EXTERNAL TRADE
('000 U.S. $)

Imports: (1969) 245,137; (1970) 316,687; (1971) 349,743; (1972) 372,775.

Exports: (1969) 189,707; (1970) 231,163; (1971) 225,363; (1972) 280,877.

COSTA RICA—(Statistical Survey)

COMMODITIES
(U.S. $ million)

IMPORTS	1971	1972	EXPORTS	1971	1972
Consumer Durables .	37.6	32.6	Coffee	59.3	77.8
Consumer Non-durables .	74.1	71.8	Bananas	63.9	82.8
Oil and Fuel . . .	6.9	7.5	Sugar	13.0	13.1
Primary Commodities .	120.4	128.3	Cattle and Meat . .	20.8	30.5
Building Material .	16.8	15.2	Others . . .	68.4	76.7
Machinery and Equipment .	78.2	87.3			
Others . . .	15.7	20.5			

COUNTRIES
('000 U.S.$)

	IMPORTS			EXPORTS		
	1970	1971	1972	1970	1971	1972
El Salvador	20,072	21,530	22,808	10,485	11,477	12,659
Germany, Federal Republic . .	26,438	26,875	27,010	19,007	20,993	31,610
Guatemala	21,547	27,063	28,249	11,072	15,407	16,702
Japan	28,542	39,333	40,031	11,060	6,997	5,347
Netherlands . . .	5,508	5,220	3,972	12,223	10,722	10,873
United Kingdom . . .	15,530	16,909	19,507	750	628	650
United States . . .	109,789	113,973	122,841	97,314	91,135	110,965

PRINCIPAL COFFEE EXPORTS (1972)

	METRIC TONS	U.S. $'000
Belgium-Luxembourg .	4,329.3	4,382.6
Finland	6,085.6	6,233.5
France . . .	3,435.2	3,321.3
German Democratic Rep. .	2,586.4	1,513.0
Germany, Federal Rep. .	15,570.0	14,663.3
Italy . . .	1,870.0	1,900.3
Netherlands . .	10,311.0	9,695.2
Sweden . . .	5,110.9	5,204.8
U.S.A. . . .	18,016.5	17,606.4
U.S.S.R. . . .	4,542.0	3,201.2
Yugoslavia . . .	2,826.5	2,077.2

TOURISM

	VISITORS	ESTIMATED REVENUE
1969 . .	121,939	U.S. $18,972,500
1970 . .	154,867	U.S. $20,931,505
1971 . .	170,396	U.S. $23,327,422

TRANSPORT

RAILWAYS

	PASSENGERS	FREIGHT (tons)
1969	2,310,287	1,795,145
1970	2,308,073	2,140,343
1971	2,362,440	2,113,466

SHIPPING
(1971)

PASSENGERS	FREIGHT (tons)
42	2,379,455

ROADS

Motor Vehicles	1969	1970	1971
Cars . . .	21,518	24,501	26,820
Lorries . . .	17,391	20,413	23,448
Buses . . .	2,517	2,736	3,001
Others . . .	13,316	14,759	16,619

CIVIL AVIATION

	Passengers		Freight (metric tons)	
	Arrivals	Departures	Loaded	Unloaded
1969 . .	96,576	100,448	1,678	4,778
1970 . .	112,359	117,046	2,174	6,644
1971 . .	n.a.	n.a.	3,080	6,489

EDUCATION

	Schools		Teachers		Pupils	
	1971	1972	1971	1972	1971	1972
Primary	2,574	2,706	11,541	11,968	356,152	374,269
Secondary	140	159	4,764	3,148	85,381	98,048
Higher	1	7	n.a.	n.a.	15,700	20,914

Source: Dirección General de Estadística y Censos, San José.

THE CONSTITUTION

The present Constitution of Costa Rica was promulgated in November 1949. A committee of lawyers was set up in mid-1967 to study the possibility of reforming the Constitution.

The government is unitary: provincial and local bodies derive their authority from the national government. The country is divided into seven provinces administered by a governor who is appointed by the President. The provinces are divided into cantons, and each canton into districts. There is an elected municipal council in the chief city of each canton, the number of its members being related to the population of the canton. The municipal council supervises the affairs of the canton. Municipal government is closely regulated by national law, particularly in matters of finance.

The government consists of three branches: legislative, executive and judicial. Legislative power is vested in a single chamber, the Legislative Assembly, which meets in regular session twice a year—from May 1st to July 31st, and from September 1st to November 30th. Special sessions may be convoked by the President to consider specified business. The Assembly is composed of 57 deputies elected for four years. The chief powers of the Assembly are to enact laws, levy taxes, authorize declarations of war and, by a two-thirds vote, suspend, in cases of civil disorder, certain civil liberties guaranteed in the Constitution.

Bills may be initiated by the Assembly or by the Executive and must have three readings, in at least two different legislative periods, before they become law. The Assembly may override the presidential vote by a two-thirds vote.

The Executive branch is headed by the President, who is assisted by his Cabinet. The President may not serve two successive periods of office, but may be re-elected after eight years. If he should resign or be incapacitated, the executive power is entrusted to the First Vice-President, and from him to the Second Vice-President, and finally to the President of the Legislative Assembly.

The President sees that the laws and the provisions of the Constitution are carried out, and maintains order. He has power to appoint and remove his ministers and diplomatic representatives; and to negotiate treaties with foreign nations (which are, however, subject to ratification by the Legislative Assembly). He is assisted in his duties by a Cabinet, each member of which is head of an executive department.

A novel feature of the Costa Rican Constitution is the clause outlawing a national army. Only by a continental convention or for the purpose of national defence may a military force be organized.

Suffrage is universal, compulsory and secret for persons over the age of 20; or, if they are completely independent, for persons over 18 years of age.

THE GOVERNMENT

HEAD OF STATE

President: Daniel Oduber Quirós.

THE CABINET

(*May* 1974)

Minister of the Presidency: Dr. Carlos Manuel Castillo Morales.

Minister of Foreign Affairs: Lic. Gonzalo J. Facio Segreda.

Minister of Public Security: Mario Charpentier Gamboa.

Minister of the Interior: Lic. Edgar Arroyo Cordero.

Minister of Finance: Porfirio Morera.

Minister of Labour and Social Security: Francisco Morales Hernández.

Minister of Public Health: Hermann Weinstock.

Minister of Transport: Ing. Álvaro Jenkins Morales.

Minister of Agriculture and Livestock: Hernán Garrón Salazar.

Minister of Education: Lic. Fernando Volio Jiménez.

Minister of Economy, Industry and Commerce: Lic. Jorge Sánchez Méndez.

Minister of Youth, Culture and Sport: Lic. Carmen Naranjo Coto.

DIPLOMATIC REPRESENTATION

EMBASSIES AND LEGATION ACCREDITED TO COSTA RICA

(In San José unless otherwise stated)

(E) Embassy; (L) Legation.

Argentina: Calle 27, Av. Central (E); *Ambassador:* Fernando Requena.

Austria: Mexico City, Mexico.

Belgium: Calle 4A, entrada Los Yoses (E); *Ambassador:* Georges Tilkin.

Bolivia: (E); *Ambassador:* Jerjes Baca Diez.

Brazil: Calle 4A, Av. FG-1a (E); *Ambassador:* Maria Lourdes de Vincenz.

Canada: Ed. Amalia Dent, 5° (E); *Ambassador:* Gilbert Craig Langille.

Chile: Primavera, Calles 5A–7A, Av. Central (E); *Ambassador:* Prof. José Novarro Tobar.

China (Taiwan): Ed. Mendiola, 3°, Av. Central (E); *Ambassador:* Dr. Wen-hui Wu.

Colombia: Calle 5A, Av. 5A (E); *Ambassador:* Jaime Durán Pombo.

Czechoslovakia: Mexico City, Mexico.

Denmark: Bogotá, Colombia.

Dominican Republic: Barrio la Granja (E); *Ambassador:* Alfredo Fernández Simo.

Ecuador: Calles 25–27, Av. 9B (E); *Ambassador:* (vacant).

Egypt: San Salvador, El Salvador.

El Salvador: Calle 5A Norte, Av. Central (E); *Ambassador:* Dr. Ernesto Trigueros Alcaine.

Finland: Mexico City, Mexico.

France: Calle 5A, entrada Los Yoses (E); *Ambassador:* Charles de Geis de Guyon de Pampelonne.

Germany, Federal Republic: Calle 36, Av. 3A (E); *Ambassador:* Wilfried von Eichborn.

Greece: Mexico City, Mexico.

Guatemala: Calle 3A, entrada Los Yoses (E); *Ambassador:* Dr. Jaime Barrios Peña.

Honduras: Calle 2A, Avs. 0 y 2A (E); *Ambassador:* A. Alvarado Puerto.

India: Panama City, Panama.

Israel: Calle 2, Avs. 2 y 4 (E); *Ambassador:* Eli Neuo.

Italy: Ed. Keith & Ramírez, Calle 9A, Avs. Central y Primera (E); *Ambassador:* Dr. Pietro Migone.

Jamaica: Port of Spain, Trinidad.

Japan: Calle 42, Av. 4 No. 274 (E); *Ambassador:* Tetsuaburo Hitomi.

Khmer Republic: Ranch Luna (E); *Ambassador:* Srey Saman.

Korea, Republic: Mexico City, Mexico.

Lebanon: Mexico City, Mexico.

Mexico: Calles 13–15, Av. 7A (L); Lic. Rogelio Martínez.

Netherlands: Calle 21, Av. 10 (E); *Ambassador:* Michiel Petrus Gorsira.

Nicaragua: Ed. Trianón, Calle 5A, Av. Central (E); *Ambassador:* Dr. Juan B. Lacayo.

Norway: Mexico City, Mexico.

Panama: Barrio Roosevelt, San Pedro de Montes de Oca (E); *Ambassador:* David S. Pere.

Paraguay: San Salvador, El Salvador.

Peru: Av. FG-14 (E); *Ambassador:* Dr. José Alvarado.

Poland: Mexico, City Mexico.

Portugal: San Rafael de Escuzú (E); *Ambassador:* António Augusto Coelho Bartolo.

Romania: Calles 29–33, Av. 1A No. 2980 (E); *Ambassador:* Constantin Stanescu.

Spain: Paseo Colón No. 3072 (E); *Ambassador:* Ernesto la Orden Miracle.

Sweden: Guatemala City, Guatemala.

Switzerland: Calle 5A, Avs. 3–5 (E); *Ambassador:* (vacant).

Turkey: Mexico City, Mexico.

U.S.S.R.: (E); *Ambassador:* Vladimir N. Kazimirov.

United Kingdom: Calle 32, Paseo Colón (E); *Ambassador:* John Kenneth Blackwell, c.b.e.

U.S.A.: Calle 1A, Av. 3A (E); *Ambassador:* Viron P. Valky.

Uruguay: Ed. Patterson (E); *Ambassador:* Aldo L. Ciasullo.

Vatican: Urbanización Rohrmoser, Sabana Oeste; *Apostolic Nuncio:* S.E.R. Mgr. Angelo Pedroni.

Venezuela: Paseo Colón No. 2490 (E); *Ambassador:* Dr. Ambrosio Perera Meléndez.

Yugoslavia: Mexico City, Mexico.

Costa Rica also has diplomatic relations with the Democratic People's Republic of Korea and the German Democratic Republic.

PRESIDENT

ELECTION
(*February 3rd*, 1974)

CANDIDATES	PERCENTAGE OF VOTES
Daniel Oduber Quirós (PLN) . . .	42.58
Dr. Fernando Trejos Escalante (PUN) .	30.20
Jorge González Marten (PNI) . . .	11.03
Rodrigo Carazo Odio (RD) . . .	9.73

PLN=Partido de Liberación Nacional; PUN=Partido Unificación Nacional; PNI=Partido Nacional Independiente; RD=Renovación Democrática.

CONGRESS

President of Congress: Luis Alberto Monge Alvarez.

ELECTIONS
(*February* 1974)

PARTY	SEATS
Partido de Liberación Nacional (PLN) . .	27
Partido Unificación Nacional (PUN) . .	16
Partido Nacional Independiente (PNI) . .	6
Others	8

POLITICAL PARTIES

Acción Socialista: San José; left wing, supported by banned Communists; Leader Dr. Licimaço Leiva.

Partido Demócrata Cristiano: San José; Christian Democrat; Leaders Prof. Luis Barahona, Fernando Quiros.

Partido Frente Nacional (PFN): San José; f. 1969; Leader Virgilio Calvo Sánchez.

Partido de Liberación Nacional: Apdo. 2244, San José; f. 1951; socialist party, affiliated to the Socialist International; Leader José Figueres Ferrer; Pres. Daniel Oduber Quirós; Sec.-Gen. Luis Alberto Monge Alvarez.

Partido Unificación Nacional: Presidential candidate for 1974 Dr. Fernando Trejos Escalante; Union of the following parties:

Partido Republicano: San José; moderate radical, Leader (vacant).

Partido Unión Cívico Revolucionaria: San José; Leader Frank Marshall Jiménez.

Partido Unión Nacional: San José; conservative; Leader Otilio Ulate Blanco.

Partido Unión Republicana Auténtica: San José; splinter group from P.U.N.; Leader Mario Echandi Jiménez.

JUDICIAL SYSTEM

Supreme Court: Ultimate judicial power is invested in the Supreme Court, the seventeen justices of which are elected by the Assembly for a term of eight years, and are automatically re-elected for an equal period, unless the Assembly decides to the contrary by a two-thirds vote. Judges of the lower courts are appointed by the Supreme Court in plenary session. The Supreme Court may also meet as:

Corte Plena, with power to declare laws and decrees unconstitutional.

Court of Appeals (*Sala de Casación*).

Civil Court (*Sala Civil*).

Criminal Court (*Sala Penal*).

President of the Supreme Court: Fernando Baudrit Solera.

RELIGION

Roman Catholicism is the official religion of the country, but under the Constitution all forms of worship are tolerated.

ROMAN CATHOLIC CHURCH

Metropolitan See:

San José, Arzobispado, Apdo. 497: Mgr. Dr. Carlos Humberto Rodríguez-Quirós, Archbishop of Costa Rica.

Suffragan Sees:

Alajuela: Mgr. Enrique Bolaños Quesada.

Limón: Mgr. Alfonso Hoefer Hombach, c.m.

San Isidro de El General: Mgr. Delfín Quesada Castro.

Tilarán: Mgr. Román Arrieta Villalobos.

THE PRESS

DAILIES
San José

Boletín Judicial: La Uruca; f. 1904; journal of the Judiciary; published by Imprenta Nacional; circ. 3,000.

El Diario de Costa Rica: f. 1919; morning; Publisher Joaquín Vargas Gene; circ. 12,000.

La Gaceta: Imprenta Nacional, Apdo. 5024; f. 1844; official gazette; Dir. Abel Castillo Solano; circ. 5,000.

La Hora: f. 1946; independent; Dir. Julio Suñol; circ. 13,000.

La Nación: Calle 3, Avda. 1, Apdo. 10138; f. 1946; conservative; Dir. Guido Fernández; circ. 68,642.

La Prensa Libre: Calle 4, Avdas. 4–6, Apdo. 1533; f. 1889; independent; evening; Editor Andrés Borrasé; circ. 38,500.

La República: Urbanización Tournón Norte; f. 1950, reorganized 1967; independent; Dir. Rodrigo Madrigal Nieto; Chief Editor Julio Rodríguez Bolaños; circ. 35,000.

PERIODICALS
San José

Abanico: Calle 4, esq. Avda. 4, Apdo. 1533; Sunday supplement for women; Editor Mercedes Borrase; circ. 32,000.

El Acta Médica: three-monthly; Editor Rodolfo Céspedes.

Eco Católico: Calle 1, Avdas. 2–4, Apdo. 1064; f. 1931; Catholic weekly; Editor Javier Solís; circ. 15,000.

La Epoca Católica: Catholic news; Editor GUILLERMO ANGULO MARÍN.

Fátima: monthly; edited by the Dominican Order.

La Semana Cómica: Calle 3, Avdas. 5-7, Casa 569; f. 1935; weekly; Democratic-Liberal; Dir. JULIO C. SUÑOL; circ. 10,000.

Mujer y Hogar: Apdo. 89; f. 1943; women's journal; weekly; Editor and Gen. Man. CARMEN CORNEJO; circ. 14,600.

Mundo Femenino: Apdo. 4343; weekly women's magazine; circ. 32,000.

Noticiero del Café: Apdo. 37; f. 1964; coffee journal; monthly; owned by the Oficina del Café.

Repertorio Centroamericano: Apdo. 37, Ciudad Universitaria "Rodrigo Facio"; every two months; Central American culture; Dirs. SERGIO RAMÍREZ and ITALO LÓPEZ VALLECILLOS.

Revista de la Academia Costarricense de Ciencias Genealógicas: Apdo. 101; f. 1953; a review of genealogical, heraldic and historical studies; Sec. JORGE A. LINES.

Revista de Agricultura: Apdo. 783; f. 1929; agricultural monthly; Dir. LUIS CRUZ BOLAÑOS.

Revista del Archivo Nacional de Costa Rica: Calle 7, Avda. 4; f. 1936; twice yearly; historical and cultural review; Dir. JOSÉ LUIS COTO CONDE; circ. 2,100.

Revista Costarricense: Catholic weekly; Editors SARA CASAL, VIUDA DE QUIRÓS.

Revista Médica de Costa Rica: Apdo. 978; f. 1933; bi-monthly medical journal; Dir. Dr. MANUEL ZELEDÓN.

Temas Sociales: Apdo. 2041; f. 1954; published by the Ministerio de Trabajo y Previsión Social; quarterly.

Tribuna Libre: weekly.

PRESS AGENCY

Tass is the only press agency in Costa Rica.

PUBLISHERS

Alfalit Ltda.: Apdo. 292, Diagonal a los Tribunales de Justicia, Alajuela; educational; Man. Dir. G. PARAJÓN.

Editorial Universitaria Centroamericana (EDUCA): Apdo. 37, Ciudad Universitaria "Rodrigo Facio", San José; f. 1969; Central American politics, economics, etc.; Dir. ITALO LÓPEZ VALLECILLOS.

Instituto Centroamericano de Administración Pública (ICAP): Apdo. 10025, San José; f. 1954; technical; Dir. CARLOS ENRIQUE GUTIÉRREZ LUNA.

Librería Imprenta y Fotolitografía Universal (Carlos Federspiel & Co., S.A.): Avda. Fernández Güell, Apdo. 1532, San José; f. 1926; Man. HUBERT FEDERSPIEL.

Trejos Hermanos Sucs. S.A.: Avda. Fernández Güell, Calles 13 y 136, Apdo. 1313, San José; f. 1912; general and reference; Man. R. BAUDRIT T.

RADIO AND TELEVISION

Departamento Control Nacional de Radio: Apdo. 3483, San José; governmental supervisory department; Dir. L. H. ANDRÉS.

RADIO

NON-COMMERCIAL

Faro del Caribe: Apdo. 2710, San José; f. 1948; call letters TIFC; religious programmes in Spanish and English; Man. FEDERICO PICADO O.

Radio Fides: Apdo. 5079, San José; Roman Catholic station; Dir. J. JIMÉNEZ.

Radio Universitaria: San Pedro; classical music; Dir. I. BONILLA.

Radio Sinaí: San Isidro de El General; Dir. A. COTO.

COMMERCIAL

Radio Eco: Apdo. 512, San José; Dir. J. F. LAFUENTE.

Radio Musical: Apdo. 854, San José; Dir. J. CASTRO C.

Radio Reloj: Apdo. 341, San José; Dir. R. BARAHONA G.

Radio Titania: Apdo. 512, San José; Dir. M. SOTELA P.

There are 15 other commercial stations.

In 1971 there were 130,000 radio sets.

RADIO ASSOCIATION

Empresarios Radiodifusores Asociados (ERA): Apdo. 2208, San José; Pres. O. SOTELA.

TELEVISION

All stations are commercial.

Corporación Costarricense de Televisión: Apdo. 2860, San José; Pres. MARIO SOTELA PACHECO.

R. Televisión Tic-Tac: Apdo. 4666, San José; operates Radio Tic-Tac (f. 1956), Channel 9 (f. 1962) and Channel 4 (f. 1964); Gen. Man. ARNOLDO VARGAS.

Tele Once S.A.: Apdo. 5542, San José; Gen. Man. JESÚS VILLARAUS GALLO.

Telesistema Nacional: Apdo. 2860, San José; Pres. M. SOTELA PACHECO; Gen. Man. JOSÉ J. ORTIZ.

Televisora de Costa Rica, S.A.: Apdo. 3876, San José; programmes began in May 1960; Pres. OLGA DE PICADO; Gen. Man. AUGUSTO CARBALLO.

In 1973 there were 150,000 television licences.

FINANCE

(cap.=capital; p.u.=paid up; dep.=deposits; m.=million; amounts in colones.)

BANKING

All banks were nationalized in June 1948.

CENTRAL BANK

Banco Central de Costa Rica: Casilla 10058, San José; f. 1950; cap. 5m., dep. 698m. (Dec. 1971); Exec. Pres. CLAUDIO ALPÍZAR VARGAS; Gen. Man. CLAUDIO A. VOLIO GUARDIA.

Banco Anglo-Costarricense: Apdo. 2038, San José; f. 1863; cap. 18m., dep. 344m. (Dec. 1971); Chair. LUIS BONILLA CASTRO.

Banco de Costa Rica: Avda. Fernández Güell y Calle 4, Apdo. 10035, San José; f. 1877; cap. 40m., dep. 520.7m. (June 1973); Pres. JOSÉ J. ECHEVERRÍA; Gen. Man. BORIS MÉNDEZ P.

Banco Crédito Agrícola de Cartago: Apdo. 297, Cartago; f. 1918; cap. 20m., dep. 108.9m. (June 1973); Pres. HERIBERTO PEREIRA C.; Gen. Man. HERNÁN LEIVA Q.

Banco Lyon, S.A.: Calle 2, Apdo. 10184, San José; f. 1871; private company, working solely on capital; Chair. GEORGE A. LYON; Gen. Man. H. WILLFRED BROWN.

Banco Nacional de Costa Rica: Avda. 1A, Calles 2–4, Apdo. 10015, San José; f. 1914; cap. and res. 169m. (Dec. 1970); Gen. Man. ELÍAS QUIRÓS S.

DEVELOPMENT CORPORATION

Corporación Costarricense de Desarrollo: establishment approved by the Legislative Assembly in December 1972; initial cap. 100m. of which the Government subscribed 67m.

CREDIT CO-OPERATIVES

Federación Nacional de Cooperativas de Ahorro y Crédito—Fedecrédito: Apdo. 4748, San José; f. 1964; 80 co-operatives, with 23,000 mems.; combined cap. U.S. $6m.

INSURANCE

Instituto Nacional de Seguros: Apdo. 10061, San José; f. 1924; administers the state monopoly of insurance; services of foreign insurance companies may be used only by authorization of the Ministry of Economy and after the Instituto has certified it will not accept the risk; cap. $15m.; Man. FIDEL TRISTÁN CASTRO.

COMMODITY EXCHANGE

Bolsa de Café: Calle 2, 8°, San José.

TRADE AND INDUSTRY

CHAMBERS OF COMMERCE

SAN JOSÉ

Cámara de Comercio de Costa Rica: Calles 1–3, Avda. Fernández Güell, Apdo. 1114; f. 1915; 500 mems.; Pres. FERNANDO GOICOECHEA Q.; Exec. Sec. JULIO UGARTE.

Cámara de Agricultura: Calle 1, Avda. Fernández Güell; Sec. Lic. JOSÉ ANTONIO FREER JIMÉNEZ.

Cámara de Azucareros: Calle 3, Avda. Fernández Güell, Apdo. 1577; Pres. Lic. MANUEL JIMÉNEZ DE LA GUARDIA.

Cámara de Ganaderos Asociados de Costa Rica: Calle 2, Avda. 2.

Cámara de Ganaderos de Guanacaste: Calle 2, Avda. 2.

Cámara de Industrias de Costa Rica: Calles 13–15, Avda. 6, Apdo. 10003.

Cámara Nacional de Cafetaleros: Calle 2A, Avda. 7A, Apdo. 1310, San José; f. 1948; 300 mems.; Dir. Lic. ARNOLDO LÓPEZ ECHANDI.

Cámara Nacional de Comerciantes Detallistas: Calles 10–12, Avda. 6.

Cámara Nacional de Transportes: Calle 16, Avda. 1–3, Apdo. 2958; 500 mems.; Pres. ARNOLDO ACOSTA.

Cámara Oficial Española de Comercio: Calle 16, Avda. 1–3.

Cámara Productores de Caña del Pacífico y del Atlántico: Apdo. 5315.

DEVELOPMENT ORGANIZATION

Centro de Promoción de Exportaciones e Inversiones: Apdo. 5418, San José; Exec. Dir. Lic. ENRIQUE GONZÁLEZ C.

Oficina Nacional de Planificación de la Presidencia: Calle 15, Avda. 3, San José; f. 1963 to encourage economic and social development in Costa Rica.

EMPLOYERS' ASSOCIATIONS

There are in all some 50 employers' associations and organizations in the Republic.

TRADE UNIONS

Confederación Costarricense de Trabajadores Democráticos: (formerly Confederación Costarricense del Trabajo "Rerum Novarum"); Calle Central, Avda. 5–7, Apdo. 2167, San José; f. 1943; 10,000 mems.; admitted to ICFTU and ORIT; Sec. Gen. CARLOS MANUEL ACUÑA CASTRO.

Confederación General de Trabajadores Costarricenses—CGTC (*General Confederation of Workers of Costa Rica*): Calles 10–12, Avda. 20, Apdo. 1039, San José; admitted to WFTU/CTAL; 10,000 mems.; 3 federated and 32 non-federated unions in affiliation; Sec.-Gen. Lic. ALVARO MONTERO VEGA.

Confederación de Obreros y Campesinos Cristianos (COCC): Calle 6, Avda. 4–6; Sec. Gen. CLAUDIO GAMBOA VALVERDE.

TRANSPORT AND TOURISM

TRANSPORT

RAILWAYS

There are 799 km. of standard gauge railways.

Northern Railway Company: San José; London office: 1–5 Broad Street Place, Blomfield St., EC2M 7HE; 560 km. of track; nationalized in 1972; Chair. Sir ROBERT P. W. ADEANE, O.B.E.

United Fruit Company: 48 km. of two 914 mm. gauge railways.

Ferrocarril Eléctrico al Pacífico (*Pacific Electric Railroad*): Apdo. 543, San José; f. 1897; 124 km. of track open; main line, San José to Puntarenas; branches, Ciruelas to Alajuela; electric (1.067 m. gauge); Gen. Man. RAFAEL PARÍS S.; Man. Railway Division Ing. STANLEY PERALTA A.; Exec. Sec. JULIETA CASAL B.

ROADS

There are about 4,800 km. of all-weather roads, 2,080 km. of them national and regional roads; 650 km. form part of the Inter-American Highway. There are also some 12,800 km. of dry-weather roads.

SHIPPING

Local services operate between the Costa Rican ports of Puntarenas and Limón and those of Colón and Cristóbal in Panama.

Services with America and Europe are:

Limón: Tica Line, Interlines, Buccaneer Line, Flota Mercante Gran Colombiana (to U.S.A.); Hamburg Amerika Linie, Horn Linie, Royal Netherlands Steamship Co. (to Europe).

Puntarenas: Hamburg Amerika Linie, French Line, Royal Netherlands Steamship Co., K Line (to Europe); Chilean Lines, Flota Mercante Gran Colombiana, Mamenic Line (to Europe and South America).

CIVIL AVIATION

Costa Rica's main international airport is the Juan Santamaría Airport (formerly El Coco). An additional airport, capable of accommodating modern jet aircraft, is under construction at Puntarenas.

Líneas Aéreas Costarricenses, S.A.—LACSA (*Costa Rican Airlines*): Apdo. 1531, San José; f. 1945; operates internal services and services to Colombia, North America, Mexico, El Salvador, Panama, Venezuela and British West Indies; Pres. Dr. ANTONIO PEÑA CHAVARRÍA; Chief Exec. Capt. OTTO ESCALANTE W.; fleet: 3 BAC 1-11, 2 DC-6A/B, 2 C-46, 2 CV-440, 1 DC-3.

There are a number of small private airlines.

FOREIGN AIRLINES

The following foreign airlines serve Costa Rica: Compañía Panameña, Iberia, Pan American, SAHSA (Honduras), SAM (Colombia) and TACA (El Salvador).

TOURISM AND CULTURE

Asociación Costarricense de Agencias de Viajes: Apdo. 1864, San José; Pres. GUIDO CASTRO.

Instituto Costarricense de Turismo: Apdo. 777, San José; Man. RICARDO CASTRO CANAS.

CULTURE

Departamento de Extensión Cultural: Ministerio de Educación Pública, San José.

Teatro Nacional: Apdo. 5015, San José; f. 1897; dependent on Ministry of Education; Exec. Dir. MANUEL RODÓ PARÉS; Pres. Doña LOTTIE DE GONZÁLEZ LAHMANN; Sec. Lic. ALBERTO RAVEN.

Orquesta Sinfónica Nacional: Apdo. 5015, San José; f. 1938; Dir. CARLOS ENRIQUE VARGAS MÉNDEZ; Pres. Lic. CARLOS MANUEL BRENES MÉNDEZ.

ATOMIC ENERGY

Comisión Nacional de Energía Atómica: San José; Pres. Dr. OTTO JIMÉNEZ Q.; Sec. Ing. HERNÁN FONSECA Z.

Universidad de Costa Rica: Ciudad Universitaria, San José; atomic research in medicine, microbiology, pharmacy, agronomy and engineering.

Instituto Interamericano de Ciencias Agrícolas de la OEA: San José; Tropical Research and Graduate Training Centre at Turrialba; Dir.-Gen. Dr. J. EMILIO G. ARAUJO; Dir. of Research and Training Ing. MANUEL ELGUETA; publs. *Turrialba, Desarrollo Rural en las Américas.*

UNIVERSITY

Universidad de Costa Rica: Ciudad Universitaria, San José; 1,039 teachers, 14,942 students.

CUBA

INTRODUCTORY SURVEY

Location, Climate, Language, Religion, Flag, Capital

Cuba is the largest island in the Caribbean, lying 90 miles south of Florida, U.S.A. Its other neighbours are Mexico, Jamaica and Haiti. The climate is tropical with the annual rainy season from May to October. The average annual temperature is 25°C (77°F) and hurricanes are frequent. The language is Spanish. The population is predominantly Roman Catholic. The national flag (proprotions 2 by 1) has five horizontal bands, alternating blue, white, blue, white, blue, with a red triangle close to the staff, charged with a silver star. Havana (La Habana) is the capital.

Recent History

In 1959 the dictatorship of Gen. Fulgencio Batista was overthrown, after years of guerrilla war, by Dr. Fidel Castro, who gradually established a Communist system of government. In 1961 Cuban exiles, with some United States support, attempted unsuccessfully to invade the island. The installation of Soviet rockets in Cuba precipitated a crisis with the United States in the early 1960s; Cuba was subsequently suspended from the OAS and since that time has been under an economic blockade by the United States. Economic and social progress have been made, however, with aid chiefly from the U.S.S.R. During 1973 Cuba announced its wish to establish relations with the United States, on condition that the economic blockade be lifted. It seems unlikely, however, that agreement will be reached in the near future. Dr. Castro also spoke in favour of the establishment of a Latin American regional organization that would exclude the United States. A system whereby the people will participate in state administration is to be introduced initially in the province of Matanzas in 1974. The first Congress of the Cuban Communist Party is due to take place in 1975.

Government

Since the 1959 Revolution, Government has been administered under the Fundamental Law of the Republic. A President is appointed by the Prime Minister, who governs the country with the help of an Executive Committee and twenty Ministers. The country is divided into six provinces. There have been no elections since the Revolution.

Defence

Cuba receives considerable aid from Communist countries. The army numbers 90,000, the navy 6,500 and the air force 12,000. Army reserves number a further 90,000. Most fit men and women belong to the militia. Defence is the third largest item in the budget. Conscription was introduced at the end of 1963. Service is for a three-year period at 17 years of age. Conscripts work on the land in addition to their military duties.

Economic Affairs

Cuba's economy is basically agricultural and is closely organized by the state. In 1968 retailing and other forms of private business were nationalized. There has been some progress in building up local industries. Food rationing has been in force since March 1962, and clothes rationing was introduced in February 1963. The island depends to a large extent on economic aid from the U.S.S.R. and most of Cuba's trade is with the Communist bloc, though relations with China have deteriorated. Sugar production occupies half the cultivated land in Cuba and accounts for about 6 to 8 per cent of world output. It was Cuba's aim to produce 10 million tons of sugar annually by 1970. Since 1969, however, crops have been consistently low, and labour and resources have had to be diverted from other production. Mechanization of sugar-harvesting is in progress; the Cuban authorities plan to mechanize 80 per cent of cane-cutting by 1980. The Soviet Union is to build a plant for the assembly of 600 harvesters under an agreement signed in December 1972. Sugar accounts for some 85 per cent of Cuban exports. Tobacco is the second largest crop, and meat production and fishing are also important. Official figures state that 150,229 tons of fish and shellfish were caught in 1973. Cuba is rich in nickel deposits, and copper, chromite and manganese are also found. Cuban mining is being developed with Soviet assistance, and current plans include the construction of a plant capable of producing 30,000 metric tons of nickel sinter and oxide annually. An agreement on economic, scientific and technical co-operation with Peru was signed in October 1973.

Transport and Communications

Railways and roads connect towns and important villages and further roads are being built. There are 14,494 km. of railways, of which 3,179 km. are narrow gauge. There are 18,932 km. of roads, of which 8,115 km. are surfaced. Geographically Cuba is a focal point for shipping and air services, but latterly traffic has been much reduced. A new airport was opened in 1966 at Holguín, and another is nearly completed at Bayano.

Social Welfare

A social security system provides for the unemployed and gives pensions to the old. Hospitals are free. Health care is the second largest item in the budget. Sick pay and retirement pensions equivalent to the full rate of earnings were introduced for selected categories of workers in 1968. Following intensive campaigns no cases of malaria have been reported since 1967.

Education

Education is a very large item in the budget and in recent years illiteracy has been greatly reduced. Education is universal and free up to university level. At the primary stage, between the ages of six and twelve, it is compulsory. Pre-school national schools are run by the State for children of five years of age, and day nurseries are available for all children after their forty-fifth day. University students rely on the national scholarship plans, and those with family responsibilities are assisted by the Students Loans Plan. Workers undergoing university courses receive a state subsidy to provide for their dependants. Barracks and large residential houses have been converted to supply

405

the urgent need for new school buildings, but the acute shortage of teachers is probably the major problem. Courses at intermediate and higher levels are created in accordance with the needs of the country, with emphasis on technology, agriculture and teacher training. Adult education centres have given basic education to over 350,000 people since 1962. 102 new schools were inaugurated in 1973.

Tourism

Cuba has much to attract the tourist—forests, mountains, and a coastline with many bays and inlets and excellent bathing. There are the relics of the Spanish colonial days. There have been fewer tourists since the change of régime.

Visas: Tourists from the following countries do not require a visa for visists of up to thirty days: Bahamas, Belgium, Bermuda, Canada, France, Denmark, German Democratic Republic, Gibraltar, Italy, Norway, Sweden, and Yugoslavia.

All travellers require permission to leave Cuba.

Sport

Sports and recreations are organized at national level by the National Institute of Sports, Physical Education and Recreation (INDER). The national sport is baseball.

Public Holidays

1974: October 10th (Wars of Independence Day).

1975: January 1st (Liberation Day), May 1st (Labour Day), July 26th (Revolution Day).

Weights and Measures

Officially the metric system is in force but the U.S. system is still widely used.

Currency and Exchange Rates

100 centavos=1 Cuban peso.

Exchange rates (April 1974):

£1 sterling=1.955 pesos;

U.S. $1=82.895 centavos.

STATISTICAL SURVEY

AREA AND POPULATION

AREA	POPULATION (Census of September 6th, 1970)				
sq. km.	Total	Havana (capital)	Births	Marriages	Deaths
110,921	8,553,395	1,755,360	226,329	110,982	52,620

Mid-1971 Population: 8,657,160 (official estimate).

POPULATION BY PROVINCES

(1970)

Havana (capital)	.	2,305,241	Matanzas . .	501,273
Camagüey	.	813,204	Oriente . .	2,998,972
Isla de Pinos	.	30,103	Pinar del Río .	542,432
Las Villas	.	1,362,179		

AGRICULTURE

('000 metric tons)

		1965	1966
Sugar Cane	. .	50,695	36,846
Root Vegetables	.	281	431
Fruit	. .	388	388
Tobacco	. .	43	51
Tomatoes	. .	120	133

Fishing: tons landed: (1967) 62,881; (1969) 80,900; (1970) 90,525.

LIVESTOCK

			1964	1967
Cattle	. .	.	3,380,000	7,172,000
Pigs	. .	.	467,100	331,400
Horses	. .	.	n.a.	697,700
Sheep	. .	.	52,500	331,300
Goats	. .	.	n.a.	468,100

MINING
(Exports—metric tons)

	1965	1966	1967
Nickel and Cobalt Sulphur . .	9,544	11,932	11,472
Nickel and Cobalt Oxide* . .	9,633	7,918	10,891
Manganese . .	2,309	1,881	539
Manganese Nodules .	78,281	81,633	59,775

* Short tons.

INDUSTRY

Product		1965	1966	Product		1965	1966
Raw Sugar . .	('ooo tons)	6,051	4,455	Sulphuric Acid Base .	('ooo tons)	202	230
Refined Sugar .	(,,)	1,022	748	Fertilizers . . .	(,,)	473	514
Ethyl Alcohol . .	('ooo hl.)	2,257	2,095	Asbestos and Cement .	('ooo m²)	2,461	2,778
Beverages . . .	(,,)	212	193				
Cigars . .	(millions)	657	623				
Cigarettes . .	(,,)	16,462	18,455				
Matches . .	(million boxes)	278	323				

Raw sugar production: (1967) 6,236,000 tons; (1968) 5,315,197 tons; (1969) 4,459,000 tons; (1970) 8,537,600 tons; (1971) 5,924,000 tons; (1972) 4,388,000 tons.

FINANCE
100 centavos=1 Cuban peso.

Coins: 1, 2, 5, 20 and 40 centavos.

Notes: 1, 5, 10, 20, 50 and 100 pesos.

Exchange rates (April 1974): £1 sterling=1.955 pesos; U.S. $1=82.895 centavos.

100 Cuban pesos=£51.16=$120.635.

Note: Prior to August 1971 the Cuban peso was at par with the U.S. dollar. Between December 1971 and February 1973 the exchange rate was $1=92.105 centavos (1 peso=$1.086). In terms of sterling, the rate between November 1967 and June 1972 was £1=2.40 pesos.

BUDGET EXPENDITURE
(1966—million pesos)

Education . . .	272
Health and Welfare . .	400
Culture, Scientific Research . .	89
Sport and Recreation . .	28
Total (incl. others) . .	2,718

EXTERNAL TRADE
(million pesos)

	1968	1969	1970	1971	1972
Imports . .	1,089.2	1,167.7	1,311	1,385	1,189
Exports . .	650.6	663.5	1,046	859	739

PRINCIPAL COUNTRIES
('ooo pesos)

	1968		1969		1970	
	Imports	Exports	Imports	Exports	Imports	Exports
Belgium	553.0	2,633.4	2,118.6	3,662.8	3,002.7	1,506.0
Canada	8,977.8	4,277.9	18,954.9	6,849.5	27,968.3	8,835.5
Czechoslovakia . . .	38,793.9	41,154.0	28,833.9	43,071.4	30,248.7	49,230.8
France	67,428.0	15,385.1	48,506.6	12,940.5	58,539.6	13,739.6
Federal Republic of Germany .	10,538.7	2,120.2	30,573.8	1,388.5	31,400.0	928.0
Italy	39,714.1	8,549.8	38,971.6	10,788.2	54,616.9	12,506.7
Japan	3,366.3	22,689.9	9,623.6	265,266.3	31,496.4	105,983.4
Poland	4,420.5	6,995.6	3,827.9	6,527.6	3,356.0	5,428.0
Romania	8,515.3	7,978.4	24,931.8	9,557.1	12,973.1	12,819.0
Spain	19,636.9	41,325.4	48,080.0	41,286.0	36,048.7	41,033.4
U.S.S.R.	666,500.0	289,648.6	659,886.5	233,050.1	686,852.6	529,110.7
United Kingdom . . .	29,778.9	13,555.3	40,140.8	14,243.9	58,548.4	19,439.4
Others	190,931.1	194,288.0	218,217.9	214,311.2	265,407.6	292,274.4

SUGAR EXPORTS TO PRINCIPAL COUNTRIES
(metric tons)

	1966	1967	1968
Albania	10,490	4,235	17,098
Algeria	618	42,713	43,494
Bulgaria	158,051	194,671	186,431
Czechoslovakia	262,098	214,884	193,490
German Democratic Republic .	207,192	249,623	243,656
Japan	359,961	542,127	555,422
Democratic People's Republic of Korea .	21,335	83,346	74,910
Spain	145,343	158,581	175,678
Sweden	44,741	22,223	40,893
U.S.S.R.	1,814,930	2,473,305	1,831,727
Yugoslavia	97,912	64,678	75,685
Total Exports (incl. others) .	4,434,639	5,682,872	4,612,923

TRANSPORT

Railways: There are 5,053 km. of track in service. In addition there are 9,441 km. of railways serving the sugar plantations. In 1970 13,005,400 passengers and 11,734,500 tons of freight were carried.

Roads: There are 18,932 km. of roads including 8,115 km. of public roads.

Shipping (1970): Ocean Trade 1,880,600 metric tons, Coasting Trade 884,500 metric tons; *Shipping Fleet* (1970): 49 ships of 412,174 d.w.t.

Civil Aviation: In 1970 876,800 passengers travelled by air on domestic and international flights.

EDUCATION
(1968)

	Schools	Teachers	Students
Primary	43,097	48,994	1,460,754
Secondary	574	15,444	254,411
Higher	3	4,500	35,490

Source: Junta Central de Planificación, La Habana, Cuba.

THE CONSTITUTION

Following the assumption of power of the Castro régime on January 1st, 1959, the Constitution was suspended, and a Fundamental Law of the Republic was instituted with effect from February 7th, 1959. Certain laws are also considered as part of the Fundamental Law; these are the Agrarian Reform Law of May 17th, 1959, the Urban Reform Law of October 14th, 1960, the Nationalization of Education Law of June 6th, 1961, and the Second Agrarian Reform Law of October 3rd, 1963.

The following is a summary of the Fundamental Law of the Republic:

1. The Nation, its Territory and Form of Government (*Articles* 1–7).

Definition of the Republic of Cuba.

2. Nationality (*Articles* 8–18).

Definition of Cuban Nationality.

3. Foreign Residents (*Article* 19).

Rights and duties of foreign residents in Cuba.

4. Individual Rights (*Articles* 20–42).

Definition of the basic rights and freedoms of the individual: principle of political freedom, inviolability of the home, freedom of religion and of assembly.

20. All confiscation of goods is prohibited, except that of the goods of the Tyrant (*Gen. Batista*) after December 31st, 1958, and of his collaborators, those persons responsible for crimes against the national economy or treasury, those who enrich themselves or become enriched illicitly under the protection of Public Power, and those named as counter-revolutionary by the criminal commission, or who having left the national territory, conspire abroad against the Revolutionary Government.

25. The death penalty shall not be imposed, except in the cases of the Armed Forces, repressive Agents of the Tyranny, auxiliary groups organized by the latter, armed groups privately organized to defend it, and informers, for crimes committed on behalf of the restoration or defence of the Tyranny destroyed on December 31st, 1958. Also excepted are those persons guilty of treason or subversion of institutional order or espionage on behalf of the enemy in time of war; and those guilty of counter-revolutionary crimes as defined by the Law and those who injure the National Economy or Public Treasury.

33. Censorship shall only be applied to such books, leaflets, records, films, newspapers or publications of any kind, as commit an offence against the honour of persons, social order or public peace.

5. Family and Culture (*Articles* 43–59).

Recognition of the family unit. The right to free education for children and adults. The importance of culture and education to the Nation.

52. The budget of the Ministry of Education shall not be smaller than that of any other ministry, except in the case of a declared emergency.

6. Work and Property (*Articles* 60–96).

Work as the inalienable right of the individual. The provision of a minimum salary, maximum working hours, social security benefits, public holidays, equal rights for women, the right to strike, collective contracts, formation of co-operative enterprises, provision of housing. Private property as a basic social function.

90. The *latifundio* is prohibited and to bring about its disappearance the Law shall indicate the maximum extent of property which each person or entity can possess for each kind of use to which the land is put. The Law shall restrict the acquisition and possession of land by foreign persons and companies and shall adopt measures to revert the land to the Cuban people.

7. Suffrage and Public Offices (*Articles* 97–117).

Voting is the compulsory right of every Cuban citizen. Eligibility and conditions of public office.

8. Organs of the State (*Article* 118).

The State exercises its authority through the Legislative, Executive and Judicial powers.

9. Legislative Power (*Articles* 119–124).

The legislative rights and duties of the Council of Ministers.

10. Executive Power (*Articles* 125–134).

Eligibility and duties of the President, including the appointment of ministers.

11. Council of Ministers (*Articles* 135–147).

Eligibility and duties of the Council of Ministers.

146. It shall be the duty of the Prime Minister to direct the general policy of the Government, to execute administrative matters with the President of the Republic, together with the Ministers of the appropriate departments.

12. Judicial Power (*Articles* 148–186).

The organization and power of the judicial system.

13. Municipal Government (*Articles* 187–199).

The organization and jurisdiction of municipal government.

14. Provincial Government (*Articles* 200–201).

The organization and jurisdiction of provincial government.

15. State Finance (*Articles* 202–231).

Financial organization of the State.

16. Reform of the Fundamental Law (*Articles* 232–233).

Procedure for alteration to the Fundamental Law.

In 1961, a one-party state was set up and all elections were abolished.

THE GOVERNMENT

HEAD OF THE STATE

President: Dr. Osvaldo Dorticós Torrado.

In November 1972 a special executive committee was constituted in order to facilitate government administration.

EXECUTIVE COMMITTEE

Major (Dr.) Fidel Castro Ruz, Prime Minister, Armed Forces, Interior, National Institute of Land Reform, Public Health and Secretariat to the Government.

Major Raúl Castro Ruz, First Deputy Premier.

Dr. Carlos Rafael Rodríguez, Foreign Affairs.

Major Ramiro Valdés, Construction.

Major Guillermo García, Transport and Communications.

Major Pedro Miret, Basic Industries.

Major Flavio Bravo, Consumer Goods.

Major Belarmino Castillo Mas, Education, Culture and Science.

Major Dioclés Torralba, Sugar Industry.

MINISTERS
(March 1974)

Prime Minister: Major (Dr.) Fidel Castro Ruz.
Deputy Prime Minister, Minister of the Armed Forces: Major Raúl Castro Ruz.
Minister of the Interior: Major Sergio del Valle Jiménez.
Minister of Foreign Affairs: Dr. Raúl Roa García.
Minister of Justice: Dr. Armando Torres.
Minister of Public Health: Dr. José A. Gutiérrez.
Minister of Interior Commerce: Capt. Serafín Fernández Rodríguez.
Minister of Foreign Trade: Marcelo Fernández Font.
Minister of Education: Major José R. Fernández.
Minister of Transport: Major Antonio Lussón Battle.
Minister of Basic Industry: Joel Domenech Benítez.
Minister of Light Industry: Nora Frómeta Silva.

Minister of Mining, Fuel and Metallurgy: Major Manuel Céspedes.
Minister of Communications: Major Pedro Guelmes.
Minister of Sugar Industry: Marcos Lage Cuello.
Minister of Food Industry: José Naranjo Morales.
Minister of Labour: Oscar Fernández Padilla.
Minister for the Merchant Marine and Ports: Capt. Angel Chaveco.
Minister, President of the National Bank of Cuba: Raúl León Torras.
Minister, President of the Central Planning Board: Dr. Osvaldo Dorticós Torrado.
Minister, President of the Committee for Economic and Scientific-Technical Collaboration: Dr. Carlos Rafael Rodríguez.

DIPLOMATIC REPRESENTATION

EMBASSIES ACCREDITED TO CUBA
(Havana unless otherwise stated)

Albania: Calle 13 No. 851 esq. a 4, Vedado; *Chargé d'Affaires a.i.:* Niko Misha.
Algeria: Calle 13 No. 760 esq. a 2, Vedado; *Ambassador:* Abdelkrim Souici.
Austria: Mexico 5, D.F., Mexico.
Barbados: Ottawa, Canada.
Belgium: Avda. 5 No. 2206, Marianao; *Ambassador:* Jean Sommerhausen.
Bulgaria: Calle B No. 252 esq. a 11, Vedado; *Ambassador:* Anguel Budev.
Canada: Calle 30 No. 518, Marianao; *Ambassador:* Malcolm N. Bow.
China, People's Republic: Calle 13 No. 551 entre C y D, Vedado; *Ambassador:* Chang Te-chun.
Congo (Brazzaville): Avda. 5 No. 1003, Marianao; *Chargé d'Affaires a.i.:* Anatole Moyascko.

Czechoslovakia: Avda. Kohly No. 259, Nuevo Vedado; *Ambassador:* Stanislaw Svoboda.
Denmark: Mexico 5, D.F., Mexico.
Egypt: Avda. 5 No. 1801, Marianao; *Ambassador:* M. Fahmy Hamad.
Finland: Mexico D.F., Mexico.
France: Calle 15 No. 607, Vedado; *Ambassador:* Pierre Anthonioz.
German Democratic Republic: Calle 13 No. 652, Vedado; *Ambassador:* H. Bauermeister.
Greece: Mexico D.F., Mexico.
Guinea: Calle 20 No. 504, Marianao; *Ambassador:* M. Sakoo.
Guyana: Ottawa, Canada.
Hungary: Calle G No. 452, Vedado; *Ambassador:* Vilmos Meruk.

Iceland: Washington, D.C., U.S.A.

India: Calle 21 No. 202, Vedado; *Chargé d'Affaires:* Rudolf Gyan D'Mello.

Italy: Paseo No. 606 (altos), Vedado; *Ambassador:* Carlo Albertario.

Japan: Calle 17 No. 552, Vedado; *Ambassador:* Osamu Kataoka.

Korea, Democratic People's Republic: Calle 17 No. 752, Vedado; *Ambassador:* Kim Guk Jun.

Lebanon: Calle 174 No. 1707, Marianao; *Chargé d'Affaires:* Dr. Michel Salameh.

Mali: New York, U.S.A.

Mexico: Avda. 47 No. 1413, Marianao; *Ambassador:* Víctor Alfonso Maldonado.

Mongolia: Calle 66 No. 505, Marianao; *Ambassador:* Damdinerenguin Bataa.

Morocco: Malecón esq. a J, Vedado; *Chargé d'Affaires:* Ben Aouda.

Netherlands: Calle 2 No. 411, Vedado; *Ambassador:* J. B. S. Lamkamp.

Norway: Mexico, D.F., Mexico.

Pakistan: Ottawa, Canada.

Peru: Calle 72 y Avda. 5, Marianao; *Ambassador:* Joaquín Heredia Cabieses.

Poland: Avda. 5 No. 4405, Marianao; *Ambassador:* Marian Henke.

Portugal: Capdevila No. 101, Apto. 5B; (vacant).

Romania: Calle 21 No. 307, Vedado; *Ambassador:* Petre Ionescu.

Sierra Leone: Avda. 47 No. 3417, Marianao; *Ambassador:* Sorsoh Ibrahim Conteh.

Spain: Oficios No. 420; *Chargé d'Affaires:* Francisco Javier Oyarzun Iñarra.

Sri Lanka: Ottawa 2, Canada.

Sweden: Mexico D.F., Mexico.

Switzerland: Avda. 5 No. 2005, Marianao; *Ambassador:* Silvio Masnata.

Syria: Avda. 5 No. 7804, Marianao; *Ambassador:* Hicham Hallaj.

Trinidad and Tobago: c/o Permanent Mission to the UN, New York, U.S.A.

Turkey: Mexico D.F., Mexico.

U.S.S.R.: Calle 13 No. 651, Vedado; *Ambassador:* Nikita P. Tolubeev.

United Kingdom: Edificio Bolívar, 9, Capdevila No. 101; *Ambassador:* Stanley James Gunn Fingland, C.M.G.

Vatican: Calle 12 No. 514, Marianao (Apostolic Internunciature); *Apostolic Nuncio:* Mgr. Dr. Cesar Zacchi.

Viet-Nam, Democratic Republic: Calle N No. 62 esq. a 15, Vedado; *Ambassador:* Nguyen Ngoc Son.

Yemen, People's Democratic Republic: Avda. 5 No. 1808, Marianao; *Ambassador:* Abdullah Abbodan Hunan.

Yugoslavia: Calle 42 No. 115, Marianao; *Ambassador:* Vojin Dakovic.

Cuba also has diplomatic relations with Argentina and Equatorial Guinea.

In 1973 relations were broken with Chile and Israel.

POLITICAL PARTIES

Partido Comunista: Havana; f. 1961 by Organizaciones Revolucionarias Integradas (ORI) from the fusion of the Partido Socialista Popular (Communist), Fidel Castro's Movimiento 26 de Julio and Directorio Revolucionario 13 de Marzo; 100-member Central Committee, Political Bureau, Secretariat and 5 Commissions; 6,000 local party organizations, 45,000 mems. and 5,000 candidate mems.

Political Bureau: mems. Fidel Castro, Raúl Castro, Osvaldo Dorticós, Juan Almeida, Ramiro Valdés, Armando Hart Dávalos, Guillermo García, Sergio del Valle.

Secretariat: Fidel Castro (Gen. Sec.), Raúl Castro, Osvaldo Dorticós, Blas Roca, Faure Chomón, Carlos Rafael Rodríguez, Armando Hart Dávalos (Sec. for Organization).

There are no other political parties. On May 1st, 1961, Fidel Castro stated that there would be no further elections and that public opinion would be sought by mass rallies.

M.I.R.R. (*Revolutionary Insurrectional Recovery Movement*): in exile in Miami, U.S.A.

Alpha 66: in exile in Miami, U.S.A.

JUDICIAL SYSTEM

Justice in Cuba is administered through an independent power called the Judicial Power, in which the Supreme Court acts as the ultimate legal body in the nation.

Supreme Court: is composed of nine members and exercises disciplinary authority over all the members of the judiciary. They are elected by the Ministers' Council on recommendation of the President of the Republic.

Judges of the Supreme Court: Enrique Hart Ramírez (*President*), Juan B. Moré Benítez, José F. Fer-

nández Piloto, José A. García Alvarez, Antonio M. Viera Machado, Rafael Cisneros Ponteau, Nicasio Hernández Armas, Luis M. Buch Rodríguez, Fernando Alvarez Tabío.

Audiencias: maximum legal body within each province.

There are also Judges of First Instance, Judges of Instruction, Judges of Correction and Municipal Judges. Magistrates of Audiencias and Judges are elected by the Supreme Court.

RELIGION

There is no established Church, and all religions are permitted, though Roman Catholicism predominates.

ROMAN CATHOLIC CHURCH

Metropolitan See:
San Cristóbal de la Habana; Mgr. FRANCESCO R. OVES FERNÁNDEZ, Calle Habana 152, Apdo. 594.

Suffragan Sees:
Matanzas: JOSÉ MAXIMINO EUSEBIO DOMÍNGUEZ Y RODRÍGUEZ.
Pinar del Río: Mgr. MANUEL ANTONIO RODRÍGUEZ ROZAS.

Metropolitan See:
Santiago de Cuba: Mgr. PEDRO MEURICE ESTIU.

Suffragan Sees:
Camagüey: Mgr. ADOLFO RODRÍGUEZ HERRERA.
Cienfuegos-Santa Clara: Mgr. FERNANDO PREGO CASAL.

PROTESTANT CHURCH

Convención Bautista de Cuba Oriental: Apdo. 27, Cristo, Oriente; f. 1905; 6,565 mems.; Gen. Missionary Dr. OSCAR RODRÍGUEZ; Pres. Rev. AUGUSTO ABELLA; Sec. Rev. MARIO CASANELLA; publ. *El Mensajero* (monthly).

Consejo de Iglesias Evangélicas (*Council of Evangelical Churches*): Neptuno 629, Havana; Sec. Rev. OSCAR RODRÍGUEZ.

THE PRESS

DAILIES

HAVANA

Granma: Avda. General Suárez y Calle Territorial, Plaza de la Revolución "José Martí", Apdo. 6260; f. 1965 to replace *Hoy* and *Revolución*; official Communist Party organ; morning and weekly editions; also weekly editions in Spanish, English and French; Editor JORGE ENRIQUE MENDOZA; circ. 510,000.

Juventud Rebelde: Prado y Teniente Rey; f. 1965; organ of Communist Youth; evening; Editor MIGUEL RODRÍGUEZ; circ. 68,000.

La Tarde: evening; Editor ERNESTO VERBA; circ. 40,000.

CAMAGÜEY

Adelante: f. 1959; morning, except Mondays; Publisher JUAN MERODIO PÉREZ; circ. 12,500.

HOLGUÍN

Norte.

MATANZAS

Girón: f. 1962; except Mondays; circ. 8,000.

LAS VILLAS

Vanguardia: f. 1962; except Mondays; circ. 28,000.

PINAR DEL RÍO

El Socialista.

SANTIAGO DE CUBA

Sierra Maestra: f. 1959; circ. 40,000.

PERIODICALS

HAVANA

ANAP: for small farmers; monthly; circ. 90,000.

Bohemia: Avda. de Rancho Boyeros y San Pedro, Apdo. 6000; weekly, illustrated; Dir. ENRIQUE DE LA OSA; circ. 220,000.

Boletín del Tribunal Supremo: San Rafael 3; f. 1966; every two months; law journal; Dirs. ENRIQUE HART, JOSÉ FERNÁNDEZ PILOTO, ANTONIO VIERA.

Casa de las Américas: Calle 3 y G, Vedado; f. 1959; monthly; Dir. HAYDÉE SANTAMARÍA; circ. 13,500.

Cine Cubano: Calle 23 No. 1155, Apdo. 55; f. 1961; monthly; Dir. ALFREDO GUEVARA; circ. 30,000.

Comercio Exterior: Ministerio de Comercio Exterior, Infanta 16; monthly.

Con la Guardia en Alto: Salvador Allende No. 601, esq. Marquez González; Committee for Defence of the Revolution; f. 1961; monthly; Editor AURELIO ALVAREZ GONZÁLEZ; circ. 60,000.

Cuadernos de la Casa de Las Américas: f. 1967; politics, literature, history; irregular.

Cuba Internacional: Reina 352; f. 1962; monthly; Spanish and Russian; Editor HUGO CHINEA; circ. 35,000 Spanish, 80,000 Russian.

Cuba-Comercio Exterior: Ministerio de Comercio Exterior, Infanta 16, Apdo. 2549; quarterly.

Gaceta de Cuba: Union of Writers (UNEAC), Calle 17 y H, Vedado; literary; monthly; circ. 8,000.

Hasta la Victoria Siempre: Isla de Pinos; f. 1967.

Ingeniería Civil: f. 1949; monthly.

Islas: Universidad Central de Las Villas; f. 1958; four times a year; Dirs. AIMÉE GONZÁLEZ, CARIDAD REGINA GARCÍA, FRANCISCO RODRÍGUEZ ALEMÁN, ESTHEL GARCÍA DOMÍNGUEZ.

LPV: weekly; sports; circ. 10,000.

Mujeres: Infanta y Peñalver; government-controlled; women's magazine; monthly; Dir. HORTENSIA GÓMEZ; circ. 150,000.

Obra Revolucionaria: irregular; official speeches and documents.

Palante: Calle 23 No. 358; f. 1961; satirical weekly; Dir. RENÉ DE LA NUEZ; circ. 150,000.

Panorama Económico Latinamericano: Calle 23 No. 201, 5° (Prensa Latina), Vedado; f. 1960; monthly; Editor M. FERNÁNDEZ COLINO; total circ. 15,100.

Política Internacional: Ministerio de Asuntos Exteriores; f. 1962; quarterly.

Revista de Agricultura: Academia de Ciencias, Apdo. 6122; f. 1967.

Revista Tecnológica: Ministry of Basic Industry, Salvador Allende No. 666, 7°; f. 1962; every two months.

Revolución y Cultura: Consejo Nacional de Cultura, O'Reilly No. 126; cultural and political; every two months; Dir. LISANDRO OTERO; circ. 15,000.

Tricontinental: OSPAAL, Apdo. 4224; f. 1965; every two months; third-world politics; editions in Spanish, English and French.

Unión: UNEAC (*Writers' and Artists' Union*), Calle 17 y H, Vedado; quarterly.

Universidad de la Habana: every two months.

Universidad de Oriente: every two months.

Verde Olivo: Avda. de Rancho Boyeros y San Pedro, Apdo. 6000; weekly illustrated; organ of the armed forces; Dir. LUIS PAVÓN.

Vida Universitaria: Centro de Información Científica y Técnica de la Universidad de la Habana; f. 1949; every two months; Dir. LEONARDO CUESTA ALVÁREZ.

Voluntad Hidráulica: Humboldt No. 106 esq. P, Vedado; f. 1963; quarterly; circ. 3,000.

PRESS ASSOCIATIONS

Unión de Periodistas de Cuba: Calle 23 No. 452, esq. a I, Havana; f. 1963; Pres. ERNESTO VERA.

Union of Writers and Artists (UNEAC): Calle 17 y H Vedado, Havana; Pres. NICOLÁS GUILLÉN; publ· *Gaceta* (fortnightly).

NEWS AGENCIES

Prensa Latina (Agencia Informativa Latinoamericana, S.A.): Calle 23 No. 201, Vedado, Havana; f. 1959; government-controlled; Dir. MANUEL YEPE M.

FOREIGN BUREAUX

Bulgarian Telegraph Agency: Apdo. 22E, Havana; Chief TODOR STOYANOV.

Czechoslovak News Agency (*Ceskoslovenská Tiskovp Kanceldr*): Edificio Focsa 3A, Vedado, Havana.

Novosti Press Agency (A.P.N.): Calle 9, Vedado, Havana; Correspondent I. PAPOROV.

Tass also has a bureau in Havana.

PUBLISHERS

Cuba's publishing houses have been completely re-organized since 1959. *Casa de las Américas* and the *Instituto del Libro* are Cuba's largest publishers.

HAVANA

Casa de las Américas: Calle G y Avda. 3, Vedado; f. 1960; Latin American literature; Dir. ROBERTO FERNÁNDEZ RETAMAR.

Consejo Nacional de Cultura: O'Reilly No. 126; art books, literary, periodicals, etc.; Pres. EDUARDO MUZIO.

Ediciones C.O.R.: Revolutionary Orientation Commission of the Communist Party; speeches and documentation.

Ediciones Revolución: Plaza Cívica; art and cultural.

Ediciones Uneac: Calle 17 No. 351, Vedado; Cuban literature.

Ediciones Unión: Calle 17 y H, Vedado; literary.

Editora del Consejo Nacional de Universidades: Bernaza No. 5, Havana.

Editora del Ministerio de Educación: Ciudad Libertad, Marianao.

Editora Científica: National Academy of Sciences, Capitolio Nacional, Havana.

Editorial Nacional de Cuba: San Rafael 467, Havana.

Instituto Cubano del Libro: Belascoaín 864, esq. a Desagüe, Apdo. 6540; f. 1967; government publishing company for works of all types; 288 titles published in 1972; exports and imports publications; Dir. ROLANDO RODRÍGUEZ.

RADIO AND TELEVISION

Ministerio de Comunicaciones: Plaza de la Revolución "José Marti", Havana.

Instituto Cubano de Radiodifusión: Edif. Radiocentro, Calle 23 y L, Havana 4; f. 1962; Dir.-Gen. Major JORGE SERGUERA.

RADIO

Radio Habana Cuba: Apdo. 7026, Havana; shortwave station; broadcasts in Arabic, Creole, English, French, Guaraní, Quechua, Portuguese and Spanish; Foreign Dir. MARÍA MONTERO TRIANA.

There are 41 other stations.

In 1970 there were 1,326,000 radio receivers.

TELEVISION

Televisión Nacional: Edif. Radiocentro, Havana; operates 19 stations throughout the country.

In 1972 the total number of television receivers was 365,000.

FINANCE

(cap.=capital; p.u.=paid up; dep.=deposits; m.=million; amounts in pesos)

BANKING

All banks were nationalized in October 1960.

CENTRAL BANK

Banco Nacional de Cuba (*National Bank of Cuba*): Cuba 402, esq. Lamparilla, Apdo. Aéreo 736, Havana; f. 1948; reorganized 1961; cap. p.u. 100m.; Pres. RAÚL LEÓN TORRAS.

The National Bank of Cuba is the sole bank of Cuba. It issues currency, arranges short- and long-term credits, finances investments and operations with other countries, and acts as the clearing and payments centre. There are 5 provincial offices, 44 regional offices and 108 agencies throughout the country. The Banco Nacional de Cuba also has representations in England at 104 Leadenhall St., London, E.C.3; in Switzerland at Lowenstrasse 11, 8022 Zurich.

INSURANCE COMPANIES

STATE ORGANIZATION

Empresa de Seguros Internacionales de Cuba: Obispo 257, Havana; f. 1963; Man. Dir. ANDRÉS GONZÁLEZ HERRERA.

TRADE AND INDUSTRY

IMPORT-EXPORT BOARDS
Havana

Alimport: Calle 23 No. 55, Vedado, Apdo. 7006; controls import of foodstuffs and liquors.

Aviaimport: Calle 23 No. 74, Vedado; import of aircraft and components; Man. Dir. Eddy Martínez Valdés.

Consumimport: Calle 23 No. 55, Vedado, Apdo. 6427; controls import of consumer goods.

Cuba Industrial: Aguiar No. 361, Apdo. 6401; controls import of complete industrial plants.

Cubacontrol: Calle 23 and P, Vedado, Apdo. 35; supervisory work on imports and exports on behalf of foreign clients.

Cubaexport: Calle 23 No. 55, Vedado, Apdo. 6719; general exports.

Cubametales: Infanta No. 16, 4°, Vedado, Apdo. 6917; controls import of metals, fuels and lubricants.

Cubapesca: Instituto Nacional de la Pesca; import of fishing equipment.

Cubatabaco: Aguiar No. 360, Apdo. 6557; f. 1962; controls production and export of leaf tobacco, cigars and cigarettes; Man. (Export Division) Jaime Mas Manzanares.

Cubatex: Calle 23 No. 55, Vedado, Apdo. 7115; controls import of fibres, textiles, hides and by-products.

Cubazucar: Calle 23, Apdo 6647; f. 1962; controls export of sugar, molasses and alcohol; Man. Dir. Emiliano Lezcano Viqueira.

Cuflet: Calle Infanta No. 16, 8°, Vedado, Apdo. 6755; f. 1961; Cuban freight enterprise; Gen. Man. Fernando Hernández.

Distribuidora Internacional de Películas (I.C.A.I.C.): Calle 23 No. 1155, Vedado; enterprise for the export and import of films.

Expedicuba: Aguiar No. 411, Apdo. 6053; enterprise for the dispatch of import and export goods.

Ferrimport: Calle 23, Vedado; import of ironware.

Maprimter: Infanta 16, Apdo. 2110; controls import of raw materials and intermediate products.

Maquimport: Calle 23 No. 55, Vedado, Apdo. 6052; controls import of machinery and equipment.

Medicuba: Central 26 entre Tulipán y Conill, Apdo. 6772; enterprise for the export and import of medical and pharmaceutical products.

Quimimport: Calle 23 No. 55, Vedado, Apdo. 6088; controls import of chemical products.

Tractoimport: Avda. Rancho Boyeros y Calle 100, Apdo. 7007; f. 1963 for the import of tractors and agricultural equipment.

Transimport: Avda. Rancho Boyeros y Tulipán, Apdo. 6665; controls import of land vehicles and transportation equipment; Man. Dir. R. Narbona.

CHAMBER OF COMMERCE

Cámara de Comercio de la República de Cuba: Calle 21 No. 661, Apdo. 370, Vedado, Havana; f. 1963; mems. include all Cuban foreign trade enterprises and the most important agricultural and industrial enterprises; Pres. Amadeo Blanco Valdés-Fauly; Vice-Pres. José M. Díaz Mirabal; publs. *Cuba-Comercio Exterior* (Spanish and English), *Boletín Sumario* (Spanish), *Cuba Economic News* (Spanish and English), *Técnica Comercial* (Spanish).

AGRICULTURAL ORGANIZATIONS

Agency for Agricultural Development: Havana; f. 1968; undertaking extensive projects of irrigation and water conservation.

Instituto Nacional de la Reforma Agraria—INRA (*National Institute for Agrarian Reform*): Havana; f. 1961; government organization in charge of State lands, farms, granaries and rural co-operatives; Minister-Pres. Fidel Castro; Vice-Pres. Raúl Curbelo.

National Association of Small Farmers: Pres. José Ramírez Cruz; Organizational Sec. Antero Regalado.

TRADE UNIONS

Central de Trabajadores de Cuba—CTC (*Workers' Central Union of Cuba*): Palacio de los Trabajadores, Peñalver y San Carlos, Havana; f. 1939; 1,800,000 mems. (est.); affiliated to FSM and CPUSTAL; 33 federated unions affiliated; publ. *Vanguardia Obrera* (weekly).

In 1961 a new decree laid down that all employees were to become members of an industrial union, and that each industry would have its own national union.

Sindicato Nacional de Trabajadores de la Industria Azucarera (S.N.T.-I.A.): Havana; the sugar workers' union.

The following industries also have their own unions: Agriculture, Arts and Entertainment, Aviation, Banks and Insurance, Catering, Commerce, Communications, Construction, Dockers, Education, Electric Power, Food, Health, Leather, Lumber, Metallurgy, Mining, Petrochemical, Printing, Public Administration, Railways, Tobacco, Textiles, Transport.

TRANSPORT

RAILWAYS

The total length of railways in Cuba is 14,494 km., of which 9,441 km. were laid down by the sugar companies primarily to transport cane from the fields to the *centrales* or grinding mills. The remaining 5,053 km. are public service railways. All railways were nationalized in 1960.

Ferrocarriles de Cuba: Egido y Arsenal, Apdo. 450, Havana; f. 1960 when all railways were nationalized by the Government; operates public services; Dir. Manuel E. Escalona. Divided into two Administrative Divisions: Eastern and Western.

Unidad Habana (*Havana Unit*): serves the western part of Las Villas Province, Matanzas, Havana and Pinar del Río (formerly served by Ferrocarriles Occidentales de Cuba, S.A.).

Unidad Camagüey (*Camagüey Unit*): serves the eastern part of Las Villas Province, Camagüey and most of Oriente (formerly served by Ferrocarriles Consolidados de Cuba, Compañía del Ferrocarril del Cuba and Ferrocarriles del Norte de Cuba).

ROADS

The Central Highway runs from Pinar del Río in the west to Santiago in Oriente Province, for a length of 1,144 km. In addition to this paved highway, there are a number of secondary and "farm-to-market" roads. A small proportion of these secondary roads is paved, but the majority are unsurfaced earth roads. There are in addition many hundred kilometres of tracks and paths, some of which can be used by motor vehicles during the dry season.

SHIPPING

Instituto Cubano del Petróleo: Edif. R. Cepero Bonilla, Calle 23 No. 105, entre O y P, Vedado, Havana; Dir. Luis Karakadze.

The only scheduled service to Cuba is by D.S.R. Lines from the German Democratic Republic (East Germany). Some of these cargo vessels carry passengers.

CIVIL AVIATION

Cubana—Empresa Consolidada Cubana de Aviación: Calle 23 No. 64, La Rampa, Vedado, Havana; f. 1961; International Services: Havana to Prague, Mexico, Spain, Santiago de Chile and chartered routes; Internal Services: Havana to Camagüey and Santiago, calling at 12 other cities; fleet: 4 Bristol Britannia, 5 Ilyushin 18, 10 Ilyushin 14, 7 Antonov AN-24B; Dir. Capt. Agustín Venero.

Cuba is also served by the following airlines: Aeroflot, ČSA (Czechoslovakia), Iberia and LAN (Chile).

TOURISM

Instituto Nacional de la Industria Turística (I.N.I.T.): Malecón y G, Vedado, Havana; f. 1959; Dir. Vivián Colls.

Tourism, once of great importance to the economy, declined very rapidly during and since the revolution; most tourists formerly came from the U.S.A., but from 1962 U.S. citizens were forbidden to visit Cuba without special permission from Washington. Many tourist facilities have fallen into disrepair or been converted for other purposes.

CULTURAL ORGANIZATIONS

Consejo Nacional de Cultura: Palacio del Segundo Cabo, Calles O'Reilly y Tacón, Plaza de Armas, Havana; a division of the Ministry of Education; Pres. Dr. Eduardo Muzio Gutiérrez.

Instituto Cubano del Arte e Industria Cinematográficos (ICAIC): Havana; production, distribution and study of films; Dir. Alfredo Guevara.

Unión de Escritores y Artistas de Cuba: Calle 17 No. 351, Vedado, Havana; f. 1961; 605 mems.; contact of Cuban writers and artists with those of other countries; runs two annual literary competitions; Pres. Nicolás Guillén; Admin. Sec. Bienvenido Suárez; publs. *La Gaceta de Cuba* (monthly), *Unión* (quarterly).

NATIONAL COMPANIES

Conjunto Folklórico Nacional: Calle E No. 102, Vedado; Dir. Gilberto González.

Sinfónica Nacional y Orquesta de Cámara: Teatro Amadeo Roldán, Calzado y D, Havana; Dir. Manuel Duchesne Cuzán.

Teatro Nacional Ópera y Ballet: Teatro García Lorca, San Rafael y Prado, Havana.

ATOMIC ENERGY

Instituto de Física Nuclear de Cuba: Academia de Ciencias, Apdo. 6122, Havana; Dir. Capt. Eliodoro Medina Medina.

Instituto de Oncología y Radiobiología: Calle 29 y F, Vedado, Havana; f. 1930; Pres. Dr. Zoilo Marinello.

UNIVERSITIES

Universidad de la Habana: San Lazaro y L, Vedado, Havana; 3,145 teachers, 23,996 students.

Universidad de Oriente: Avda. Patricio Lumumba s/n, Santiago de Cuba; 741 teachers, 6,157 students.

Universidad Central de las Villas: Carretera de Camajuan, Km. 10, Santa Clara L.V.; 337 teachers, 3,457 students.

DAHOMEY

INTRODUCTORY SURVEY

Location, Climate, Language, Religion, Flag, Capital

Dahomey is a narrow stretch of territory in West Africa, flanked by Nigeria and Togo. The climate is tropical, with average temperatures of 20°–34°C (68°–93°F) and heavy rainfall. It is hotter and drier in the north. French is the official language but each tribe has its own tongue. The majority of the people follow traditional beliefs and customs. Christians, mainly Roman Catholics, make up 15 per cent of the population and Muslims 13 per cent. The national flag (proportions 6 by 5) has a broad green vertical stripe in the hoist and two horizontal bands of yellow and red in the fly. The capital is Porto-Novo.

Recent History

Formerly one of the provinces of French West Africa, Dahomey became a self-governing republic within the French Community in December 1958, and an independent state in August 1960. In 1963, after trade union and student riots, President Hubert Maga's government was overthrown and the army, under Col. (later Gen.) Christophe Soglo, brought to power a coalition of Justin Ahomadegbé and Sourou Migan Apithy. In November and December 1965 the army intervened in government twice more, and the second time Soglo became President. In December 1967 a group of younger officers overthrew Soglo and installed Lt.-Col. Alphonse Alley as head of state in preparation for a return to civilian rule. A strong presidential constitution was approved by referendum in March 1968, and presidential elections were held in May. These were annulled after widespread abstentions, and Dr. Emile Derlin Zinsou was appointed President. The army intervened again at the end of 1969 and more elections were held in 1970. These were suspended because of violence and irregularities. A Presidential Council was formed consisting of the three candidates, MM. Maga, Apithy and Ahomadegbé, with the post of President rotating. In October 1972 the army, led by Major Mathieu Kerekou, overthrew the Presidential Council and established a military Government. In April 1973 there was allegedly a plot against the Government led by Alphonse Alley, and in January 1974 open opposition to the régime was manifested in several lycées. Kerekou is introducing a new system of administration and government to replace those inherited from the French.

Government

Dahomey is at present ruled by a military Government of twelve young army officers drawn equally from the three main regions of Cotonou, Porto-Novo and the north. A 100-member Advisory Committee helps define government policy through three sub-committees dealing with general policy, finance and economy, and social and cultural affairs.

Defence

Citizens of both sexes are liable for military service between the ages of eighteen and fifty-one years. The army strength is 2,100, the air force 150 and in addition there are paramilitary forces numbering 1,200 men. France provides technical assistance and equipment.

Economic Affairs

About 80 per cent of Dahomey's population work on the land, but farming is generally at subsistence level, and exportable surpluses are limited. France provides most capital outlay, and also subsidizes the current budget. Dahomey is an Associate Member of the EEC and a member of the West African Monetary Union. Major Kerekou's régime is particularly keen to foster good economic relations with Nigeria. It is also attempting to assert the state's authority over key sectors of the economy.

Transport and Communications

Transport services are few; three short sections of railway run inland from Cotonou, and the coast road links Togo in the west and Nigeria in the east. The new port at Cotonou was officially inaugurated in August 1965.

Education

Education is provided by both the Government and the Christian missions, but many more schools are needed as only 31 per cent of school age children attended school in 1970–71. The University of Dahomey was founded in 1970 and in 1973 had over 1,000 students. Other students go either to France or Senegal.

Tourism

Dahomey made great efforts under the last Five-Year Plan to encourage tourism. Safaris can be arranged to the two National Parks and the numerous hunting reserves. *Visas* are not required by French nationals.

Sport

There is little organized sport but football is generally popular. Big game hunting is possible for tourists.

Public Holidays

1974: August 1st (National Day), August 15th (Assumption), October 19th (Id ul Fitr), November 1st (All Saints'), December 25th (Christmas).

1975: January 1st (New Year), March 31st (Easter Monday), May 8th (Ascension), May 19th (Whit Monday).

Weights and Measures

The metric system is in force.

Currency and Exchange Rates

100 centimes=1 franc de la Communauté financière africaine (CFA).

Exchange rates (April 1974):

1 franc CFA=2 French centimes;

£1 sterling=579.75 francs CFA;

U.S. $1=245.625 francs CFA.

STATISTICAL SURVEY

Area (sq. km.)	Total Population (1972 est.)	Population of Tribes (1969 estimates)								
		Fon	Adja	Bariba	Yoruba	Aizo	Somba	Fulani	Coto-Coli	Dendi
113,048*	2,869,000	850,000	220,000	175,000	160,000	92,000	90,000	68,000	45,000	30,000

* 43,480 sq. miles.

Département	Chief Town	Population of Chief Town (1969 est.)
Ouémé	Porto-Novo (capital)	74,000
Atlantique	Cotonou	120,000
Borgou	Parakou	16,000
Zou	Abomey	29,000
Atacora	Natitingou	n.a.
Mono	Lakossa	n.a.

Employment: Small farmers 750,000; Commerce 3,600; Public Works 6,000; Railways 2,850.

Agriculture (1971—metric tons): Cassava (manioc) 1,192,000, Sweet potatoes and yams 655,000, Maize 216,000, Palm kernels 65,000, Millet and sorghum 68,000, Groundnuts (1970—in shell) 57,000, Dry beans (1970) 25,000, Cotton (1971–72) 47,750, Cocoa (1971–72) 8,000.

Livestock (1971): Cattle 590,000, Sheep 555,000, Goats 650,000, Pigs 345,000.

Fishing (1970): 4,220 metric tons.

Industry (1971): Palm oil 77,000 metric tons, Palmetto oil 28,000 metric tons; (1970–71): Beer 104,000 hl., Carbonated soft drinks 43,000 hl.

Currency: 100 centimes = 1 franc de la Communauté financière africaine.
Coins: 1, 2, 5, 10, 25, 50 and 100 francs CFA.

Notes: 100, 500, 1,000, 5,000 and 10,000 francs CFA. Exchange rates (April 1974): 1 franc CFA = 2 French centimes; £1 sterling = 579.75 francs CFA; U.S. $1 = 245.625 francs CFA; 1,000 francs CFA = £1.725 = $4.071.

Budget: (1972) Revenue 10,429.4m., Expenditure 11,829.4m. francs CFA; (1973) Revenue 12,391m. francs CFA., Expenditure 13,192m. francs CFA; (1974) Revenue 12,485m. francs CFA, Expenditure 13,572m. francs CFA.

Five-Year Plan (1966–70—m. francs CFA): Total investment 35,128 (Foreign Public Aid 20,300); Rural Development 12,065; Communications and Power 10,250; Industrial and Commercial Development 9,934; Social and Administrative Development 2,870.

An interim plan covered the years 1971–72, to complete projects not fully executed by the end of the 1966–70 plan. A new plan will be drawn up for the period 1973–76.

EXTERNAL TRADE
(million francs CFA)

	1965	1966	1967	1968	1969	1970	1971
Imports	8,491	8,264	10,745	12,208	14,129	17,660	21,202
Exports	3,367	2,585	3,750	5,508	7,067	9,062	11,648

COMMODITIES

IMPORTS	1967	1968	1969	EXPORTS	1967	1968	1969
Food and live animals	1,686.3	1,626.5	1,744.1	Coffee (green and roasted) . .	142.0	66.1	334.7
Tobacco and products	391.3	679.3	613.8	Other food . .	425.8	603.4	1,500.0
Petroleum products	453.2	559.4	480.6	Tobacco and products	118.4	184.9	315.2
Chemicals . .	776.1	1,012.3	1,352.5	Groundnuts (green) .	229.6	274.2	264.3
Woven cotton fabrics	1,658.1	1,930.1	2,427.3	Palm nuts and kernels . .	140.0	331.0	273.3
Iron and Steel	404.1	311.0	492.2	Other oilseeds, nuts and kernels .	267.0	353.8	418.2
Machinery (non-electric . .	1,222.0	1,118.5	1,145.5	Raw cotton (excluding linters) . .	331.5	680.3	807.1
Electrical machinery	412.0	545.6	561.9	Palm oil . .	263.6	431.7	431.3
Road Motor Vehicles	728.2	1,002.0	887.6	Palm kernel oil .	895.3	1,778.3	1,500.7
				Machinery and transport equipment .	136.0	282.9	94.2
* TOTAL (incl. others)	10,704.5	12,202.9	14,124.4	* TOTAL (incl. others)	3,751.7	5,504.1	6,937.3

Exports (1971–72): (metric tons) Coffee 2,694, Palm Oil 27,000, Palmetto Oil 9,599, Tobacco 987.

COUNTRIES

IMPORTS	1967	1968	1969	EXPORTS	1967	1968	1969
Belgium/Luxembourg .	371	404	538	Belgium/Luxembourg .	171	156	83
China, People's Republic	243	317	332	France . .	1,300	2,014	2,491
France . .	5,327	5,114	5,475	Germany, Federal Republic . .	243	439	557
Germany, Federal Republic . .	493	505	700	Italy . . .	53	33	145
Italy . .	1,014	1,051	568	Japan . . .	155	206	375
Ivory Coast . .	192	224	415	Netherlands . .	558	332	900
Japan . .	72	219	313	Nigeria . .	169	304	913
Netherlands . .	301	962	1,039	Senegal . .	45	101	188
Nigeria . . .	178	249	302	Togo . . .	205	327	135
Senegal . .	364	415	429	United Kingdom . .	6	157	93
Togo . .	247	316	452	U.S.A. . .	529	1,192	669
United Kingdom . .	251	471	610				
U.S.A. . .	460	479	802				
* TOTAL (incl. others) .	10,705	12,203	14,124	*TOTAL (incl. others)	3,752	5,504	6,937

1970: France 7,455, United Kingdom 952, U.S.A. 948.

1970: France 3,574, Nigeria 847, United Kingdom 381, U.S.A. 444.

* In some cases, totals differ slightly from the figures given in the summary table for trade, which are those published by the national statistical authority.

Source: Mainly *Overseas Associates, Foreign Trade* (Statistical Office of the European Communities, Luxembourg).

TRANSPORT

RAILWAYS

	1970	1971
Passengers Carried ('000) .	1,137	1,404
Passenger–km. (million) .	71.7	83.8
Freight carried ('000 tons) .	252	260
Freight ton–km. (million) .	95.5	94.2

Source: Railway Directory and Yearbook, 1973 and 1974.

ROADS
VEHICLES IN USE (December 31st)

	1968	1969	1970
Private Cars . .	9,856	11,077	12,481
Buses and Coaches .	103	111	113
Goods Vehicles .	5,998	6,474	7,195

Source: World Road Statistics 1968–72 (International Road Federation, Geneva).

SHIPPING
(Cotonou)

	1969	1970	1971
Ships Entered	621	596	755
Net Tonnage of Ships Entered ('ooo metric tons)	1,884	1,699	2,076
Freight Loaded ('ooo metric tons) . . .	170	172	195
Freight Unloaded ('ooo metric tons) . .	375	388	433

CIVIL AVIATION
(Cotonou)

	1969	1970	1971*
Aircraft Arrivals and Departures . . .	2,331	2,416	1,628
Passenger Arrivals	19,078	18,594	15,697
Freight Loaded (metric tons) . .	614	687	703
Freight Unloaded (metric tons) . .	802	941	799
Mail Loaded and Unloaded (metric tons) .	194	160	129

* January–September.

Source (for Shipping and Civil Aviation): *Données Statistiques* (Institut National de la Statistique et des Etudes Economiques).

EDUCATION
(1971–72)

	SCHOOLS	PUPILS
Primary . . .	852	186,000
Secondary . . .	60*	27,000
Technical . . .	7*	2,000
Teacher Training, etc. .	4	2,553
University . . .	1	600

* 1970 figures.

THE CONSTITUTION

The Constitution of May 1970 was invalidated by the military *coup d'état* of October 26th, 1972. After forming a new government on October 27th, President Kerekou set up a Military Council of the Revolution, composed of 14 members, on November 25th; he later stated that he wants Dahomey to follow its own Dahomeyan system. On September 1st, 1973, the creation of institutions associating civilians with the military regime at all levels was announced. The highest of these is the National Council of the Revolution, under the Chairmanship of the Head of State, with 67 members including 30 civilians. In February 1974 it was decided to reorganize the country into six provinces, each divided into districts. The rural and urban communes are to be administered by revolutionary committees and the villages and urban *quartiers* by local revolutionary committees.

419

THE GOVERNMENT

(*March* 1974)

HEAD OF STATE
President: Lieut.-Col. MATHIEU KEREKOU.

CABINET

President and Minister of Defence and Planning: Lieut.-Col. MATHIEU KEREKOU.

Minister of Foreign Affairs: Major MICHEL ALADAYE.

Minister of Finance and the Economy: Captain JANVIER ASSOGBA.

Minister for Justice and Legislation: Major BARTHELEMY OHOUENS.

Minister of Information and Tourism: Captain AUGUSTIN HONVO.

Minister of Rural Development and Co-operation: Captain DJIBRIL MORIBA.

Minister for the Civil Service and Labour: Major PIERRE KOFFI.

Minister of Public Works, Mines and Power: Captain ANDRÉ ACHADE.

Minister of Health and Social Affairs: Captain ISSIFOU BOURAIMA.

Minister of Transport, Posts and Telecommunications: Captain CHARLES BEBADA.

Minister of the Interior and of Security: Captain MICHEL AIKPE.

Minister of Education, Culture, Youth and Sport: Captain VINCENT GUEZODJE.

DIPLOMATIC REPRESENTATION

EMBASSIES AND LEGATION ACCREDITED TO DAHOMEY

(E) Embassy; (L) Legation.

Algeria: Accra, Ghana (E).

Belgium: Abidjan, Ivory Coast (E).

Bulgaria: Lagos, Nigeria.

Canada: Accra, Ghana (E).

China, People's Republic: *Ambassador:* KU HSIAO-PO.

Czechoslovakia: Accra, Ghana (E).

Ethiopia: Lagos, Nigeria (E).

France: B.P. 766, Cotonou (E); *Ambassador:* MICHEL VAN GREVENYNGHE.

Gabon: Abidjan, Ivory Coast (E).

German Democratic Republic: *Chargé d'Affaires:* GERHARD SCHRAMM.

Germany, Federal Republic: blvd. de France, B.P. 504, Cotonou (E); *Ambassador:* Dr. KARL WAND.

Ghana: B.P. 488, Cotonou (E); *Ambassador:* W. L. TSITSIWU.

Guinea: Lagos, Nigeria (E).

Haiti: rue Bellamy, Porto-Novo (E); *Ambassador:* (vacant).

Hungary: Accra, Ghana (E).

India: Lagos, Nigeria (E).

Italy: Abidjan, Ivory Coast (E).

Japan: Abidjan, Ivory Coast (E).

Korea, Republic: Abidjan, Ivory Coast (E).

Lebanon: Abidjan, Ivory Coast (E).

Mali: Accra, Ghana (E).

Mauritania: Dakar, Senegal (E).

Netherlands: Abidjan, Ivory Coast (E).

Niger: Cotonou (L); *Consul:* EL HADJ HAMA BEIDARI YATTARA.

Nigeria: Cotonou (E); *Chargé d'Affaires:* OLAYINKA SIHOYAN.

Norway: Lagos, Nigeria (E).

Pakistan: Lagos, Nigeria (E).

Poland: Accra, Ghana (E).

Spain: Abidjan, Ivory Coast (E).

Sudan: Lagos, Nigeria (E).

Sweden: Lagos, Nigeria (E).

Switzerland: Abidjan, Ivory Coast (E).

Tunisia: Abidjan, Ivory Coast (E).

Turkey: Lagos, Nigeria.

U.S.S.R: B.P. 881, Cotonou (E); *Ambassador:* IGOR SOUKOUSKY.

United Kingdom: Lomé, Togo (E).

U.S.A.: B.P. 119, Cotonou (E); *Ambassador:* ROBERT ANDERSON.

Vatican: *Apostolic Pro-Nuncio:* Mgr. GIOVANNI MARIANI (also accredited to Senegal and Niger).

Viet-Nam, Republic: Abidjan, Ivory Coast (E).

Yugoslavia: Accra, Ghana (E).

Zambia: Lagos, Nigeria (E).

Dahomey also has diplomatic relations with Cambodia (Government-in-exile), the Central African Republic, the Democratic People's Republic of Korea, Libya, Romania and Zaire.

NATIONAL COUNCIL OF THE REVOLUTION

The creation of a National Council of the Revolution was announced on September 1st, 1973. It consists of 67 members, including 30 civilians, under the Chairmanship of the Head of State.

POLITICAL PARTY

The Presidential Council had hoped to establish national unity by the creation of a single party, but no such party was set up.

DEFENCE

Dahomey has an army of 2,100 men, and an air force of 150; paramilitary forces number 1,200 men.

Chief of Staff: Lieut.-Col. Mathieu Kerekou.

Director of State Security: Lieut. François Foulin.

JUDICIAL SYSTEM

THE SUPREME COURT: Cotonou
President of the Supreme Court: Ignacio Pinto.

The work of the Supreme Court is divided into Constitutional, Administrative, Judicial and Accountancy Chambers and has been carried out since 1970.

There is a *tribunal de conciliation* in each of the 31 subprefectures and in main centres and a *tribunal de première instance de deuxième classe* (Magistrate's Court) at Porto-Novo, Cotonou, Ouidah, Abomey, Parakou, Natitingou and Kandi. The Court of Appeal, which has jurisdiction over the Assize Court, sits at Cotonou.

RELIGION

According to the 1961 census 65 per cent of the population hold animist beliefs, 15 per cent are Christians (12 per cent Catholics, 3 per cent Protestants) and 13 per cent Muslims. There are 257 Protestant mission centres with a personnel of about 120. In the Roman Catholic archdiocese of Cotonou, which extends over Dahomey and Niger, there are 470 mission centres with a total personnel of some 2,500.

Archbishop of Cotonou: Mgr. Christophe Adimou; B.P. 491, Cotonou.

Bishop of Abomey: Mgr. Lucien Agboka; B.P. 18, Abomey.

Bishop of Lokossa: Mgr. Robert Sastre; B.P.1, Lokossa.

Bishop of Natitingou: Mgr. Patient Redois; B.P. 102, Natitingou.

Bishop of Parakou: Mgr. Andrew van den Bronk; B.P. 75, Parakou.

Bishop of Porto-Novo: Mgr. Vincent Mensah; B.P. 380, Porto-Novo.

PRESS AND PUBLISHERS

Etablissement National d'Edition et de Presse (E.N.E.P.): Cotonou.

L'Action Populaire: rue de Ouidah, Carré 405, B.P. 650, Cotonou; f. 1964; daily; Dir. Julien Aza.

L'Aube Nouvelle: B.P. 80, Porto Novo; daily.

La Croix du Dahomey: B.P. 32, Cotonou; fortnightly.

Daho-Express: B.P. 1210, Cotonou; government daily; circ. 1,000.

Daho Matin: Carré 96, Cotonou; political; quarterly.

Le Démocrat: Dahomey Press Agency, B.P. 72, Cotonou; daily.

L'Etendard: Pavilion 29, Akpapa, Cotonou; quarterly.

Journal Officiel de la République du Dahomey: Porto-Novo; published by the Government Information Service; fortnightly.

La Patrie Dahoméenne: Porto-Novo; fortnightly.

La Voix du Peuple: Dahomey Press Agency, B.P. 72, Cotonou; daily.

Walloguede (Journal du Parti): Dahomey Press Agency, B.P. 72, Cotonou; fortnightly.

Agence Dahoméenne de Presse: B.P. 72, Cotonou; f. 1961; national news agency; section of the Ministry of Information; Dir. M. Damala.

Deutsche Presse-Agentur and Tass also have offices in Dahomey.

RADIO AND TELEVISION

Voix de la Révolution Dahoméenne: Cotonou, B.P. 366; Government station broadcasting in French, Fon, Yoruba, Bariba, Mina, Peuhl and Dendi; Dir.- Gen. Lieut. Didier Dassi.

There were 85,000 receivers in use at December 31st, 1970.

Following an agreement signed with France in May 1972 television is being installed.

FINANCE

BANKS

Central Bank

Banque Centrale des Etats de l'Afrique de l'Ouest: 29 rue du Colisée, Paris; Cotonou, B.P. 325; Man. M. B. N'Diaye.

Banque Dahoméenne de Développement: rue des Cheminots, Cotonou, B.P. 300; f. 1961; cap. 300m. francs CFA; Pres. Baba Moussa; publ. *Rapports d'activité* (annual).

Caisse Centrale de Coopération Economique: ave. Giram, B.P. 38, Cotonou; Dir. Pierre Canot.

Crédit Agricole: Cotonou; Govt. Commr. Col. Paul Emile de Souza.

Société Dahoméenne de Banque: rue de Révérend Père Colineau, B.P. 85, Cotonou and B.P. 262, Porto Novo; f. 1962; cap. 300m. francs CFA; associated with Crédit Lyonnais; Pres. Bruno Amoussou; Gen. Man. I. W. Lemon.

Foreign Banks

Banque Internationale pour l'Afrique Occidentale: 9 ave. de Messine, Paris; Cotonou, B.P. 47; f. 1961.

Banque Nationale de Paris: 16 blvd. des Italiens, Paris; Cotonou, Avenue du Gouverneur-Général Clozel, B.P. 75; br. at Porto-Novo; Dir. Cotonou: Paul Gilloux.

INSURANCE
Cotonou

L'Union: B.P. 739.

L'Union-Vie: B.P. 80.

TRADE AND INDUSTRY

CHAMBER OF COMMERCE

Chambre de Commerce, d'Agriculture, et d'Industrie du Dahomey: ave. Général de Gaulle, Cotonou, B.P. 31; Pres. PIERRE FOURN; Sec. MICHEL LABELLE.

PROFESSIONAL ORGANIZATIONS

Association des Syndicats du Dahomey (Asynda): Cotonou; Pres. PIERRE FOURN.

Groupement Interprofessionnel des Entreprises du Dahomey (GIDA): B.P. 6, Cotonou; Pres. M. BASTIAN.

Jeune Chambre Economique: Pres. JEAN-BONIFACE AKANNI.

Syndicat des Commerçants Africains du Dahomey (Syncad): Cotonou.

Syndicat des Commerçants Importateurs et Exportateurs: B.P. 6, Cotonou; Pres. M. THOMAS.

Syndicat Interprofessionel des Entreprises Industrielles du Dahomey: Cotonou; Pres. M. DOUCET.

Syndicat des Transporteurs Routiers du Dahomey: Cotonou; Pres. PASCAL ZENON.

TRADE UNIONS

Confédération Dahoméenne des Travailleurs Croyants (CDTC): Bourse du Travail, Cotonou; f. 1952; affiliated to IFCTU; 1,000 mems.; Gen. Sec. GABRIEL AHOUE.

Confédération Nationale des Syndicats Libres (CNSL): Bourse du Travail, Cotonou; f. 1964; 2,250 mems.; Gen. Sec. ETIENNE AHOUANGBE.

Union Générale des Syndicats du Dahomey (UGSD): Bourse du Travail, Cotonou; f. 1964; 8,000 mems.; Sec.-Gen. HONORAT OGOUBIYI-AKILOTAN.

Union Générale des Travailleurs du Dahomey (UGTD): B.P. 69, Cotonou; f. 1961; 10,000 mems.; Sec.-Gen. JACOB PADONOU; publ. *Le Patriote*.

TRANSPORT AND TOURISM

TRANSPORT
RAILWAYS

Organisation Commune Dahomey-Niger des Chemins de Fer et des Transports (OCDN): P.O.B. 16, Cotonou; f. 1959; Dahomey has a 63 per cent share, Niger 37 per cent. The main line runs for 438 km. from Cotonou to Parakou in the interior; a branch runs westwards via Ouidah to Segboroué (34 km.). There is also a line of 107 km. from Cotonou via Porto-Novo to Pobé near the Nigerian border. Total length of railways: 579 km. Dir. M. BOITTIAUX.

The planned extension of the line from Parakou to Dosso (Niger) will be 520 km. long, cost 9,329m. francs CFA and should be completed by 1975.

ROADS

The system is well developed. There are a total of 6,400 km. of classified roads and a further 1,200 km. of tracks suitable for motor traffic in the dry season. The roads along the coast and those from Cotonou to Allada and from Parakou to Malanville, a total of 700 km., are bitumen-surfaced.

SHIPPING

An extensive programme of expansion, at Cotonou, involving a deep water port with one jetty 1,700 metres long and another 800 metres long was completed in 1964 and officially inaugurated in 1965. Further expansion is in progress. 681,619 tons of goods was handled in 1972.

SAMOA: B.P. 694, Cotonou; agents for Hugo Stinnes Transozean Schiffahrt G.m.b.H.

Société Navale Delmas et Vieljeux: ave. Mgr.-Steinmetz, B.P. 213, Cotonou; agents for Cie. Maritimes des Chargeurs Réunis, Compagnie Fabre, Deutsche Afrika Linien and Woermann Linie, Nouvelle Compagnie des Paquebots.

Société Ouest-Africaine d'Entreprises Maritimes (Dahomey) —SOAEM: B.P.74, Cotonou; agents for Lloyd Triestino, Société Navale de l'Ouest.

SOCOPAO: B.P. 253, Cotonou; agents for Acomar, Elder Dempster, Palm Line, Splošna Plovba, United West Africa Service.

Union Maritime et Commerciale: B.P. 128, Cotonou; agents for Holland West Afrika Lijn.

CIVIL AVIATION

The main airport at Cotonou has a 2.4 km. runway and there are secondary airports at Parakou, Natitingou, Kandi and Abomey.

Air Afrique: Cotonou, avenue du Gouverneur Ballot, B.P. 200; the Dahomey Government has a 6 per cent share in Air Afrique (*see* under Ivory Coast).

Cotonou is also served by Cameroon Air Lines, Pan American and UTA.

TOURISM

Direction Générale du Tourisme: Ministry of Labour and Tourism, B.P. 89, Cotonou; Dir. PIERRE COMPLAN.

UNIVERSITY

Université du Dahomey: Abomey–Calavy, B.P. 526, Cotonou; 52 teachers, 1,097 students.

DOMINICAN REPUBLIC

INTRODUCTORY SURVEY

Location, Climate, Language, Religion, Flag, Capital

The Dominican Republic occupies the eastern 48,442 sq. km. of the island of Hispaniola (76,192 sq. km.) which lies between Cuba and Puerto Rico in the Caribbean Sea. Its only border is with Haiti. The climate is sub-tropical with an average temperature of 80°F (27°C). The island lies in the path of tropical cyclones. The official language is Spanish. Over 60 per cent of the population are Roman Catholics. There are small Protestant and Jewish communities. The national flag (proportions 23 by 15) is red and blue, quartered by a white cross, at the centre of which is the coat of arms. The capital is Santo Domingo.

Recent History

The Dominican Republic was ruled from 1930 to 1961 by Generalissimo Rafael Trujillo. After his assassination, a transitional government composed of a seven-man Council of State was set up. Elections were held in December 1962 and Prof. Juan Bosch of the Partido Revolucionario Dominicano (PRD) was elected President. This administration was overthrown by a military *coup* in September 1963. Six right-wing parties endorsed the appointment of a civilian triumvirate led by Emilio de los Santos. After a further *coup* in April 1965 forces of the Organization of American States, including 23,000 U.S. troops, were called in to restore order. Dr. Héctor García Godoy became provisional President; elections were held in June 1966 and resulted in victory for Dr. Joaquín Balaguer. In May 1970, Dr. Balaguer was re-elected for a further four years. Since the elections prominent opposition figures have joined the Government and Dominican politics have been marked by violent in-fighting amongst the divided opposition groups. In February 1973 a state of emergency was declared when it was announced that guerrilla forces had landed on the coast. It was later revealed that Captain Francisco Caamaño Deño, the leader of the 1965 revolt, had been killed, along with his followers. Prof. Bosch and other opposition figures went into hiding; Prof. Bosch later resigned as leader of the PRD, thereby undermining hopes of a united opposition in the May 1974 elections, when Dr. Balaguer was returned with a large majority.

Government

Following the elections in May 1970, 27 senators and 74 representatives were elected for 4-year terms.

Defence

The Republic is a member of the Inter-American Defence Board. Armed forces total about 15,800 men: army 9,000, air force 3,000 and navy 3,800.

Economic Affairs

Seventy per cent of the population live on the land and most exports are agricultural. The main cash crops are sugar, coffee, cocoa and tobacco. Only two-fifths of the cultivable land is in use. Although there has been a heavy influx of population into the towns, unemployment and under-employment remain high in both rural and urban areas. Manufacturing on a small scale covers a wide range of consumer goods. Mineral resources are being developed, the most important product being bauxite, although a Canadian nickel extraction and refining plant, which started production in 1972, is now the leading mineral exporter. Foreign oil companies have undertaken extensive prospecting and the oil refinery jointly owned by the Government and Shell, the Refinería Dominicana de Petróleo, began supplying the home market in 1973. The production of ferro-nickel began in 1972. In 1973 the first stage of the Tavera hydro-electric project came into operation. When completed its capacity will be 80,000 kW. Under a land reform programme initiated in 1972 the Government is empowered by law to expropriate estates of over 70 acres which are suitable for rice growing. It is also empowered to expropriate uncultivated land. In 1973 the Banco Agrícola made available 20 million pesos for land settlement.

Transport and Communications

Transport facilities are limited and about 80 per cent of the railways are used solely to carry sugar from the plantations. Roads are the main means of communication and the network includes some modern motorways. There is no inland waterway system and very little coastal shipping. A number of shipping lines link the island with the United States and other Caribbean islands. There are internal and international air services, the international airport being at Punta Caucedo. A second international airport is to be built on the island of Saona.

Social Welfare

There is no comprehensive system of state welfare but the Government provides some medical and health services.

Education

Primary education is free and, where possible, compulsory from the ages of seven to fourteen. In 1969–70 primary school enrolment totalled 726,306 and an estimated 112,286 pupils received secondary education. There are three universities.

Tourism

Efforts are now being made to develop the tourist industry. Hotels, casinos and seaside resorts are being built and tours have been organized to the old Spanish colonial settlements. In 1972 an estimated 133,036 tourists visited the Republic, spending U.S. $27.9 million.

Visas are not required to visit the Dominican Republic by nationals of Belgium, Colombia, Denmark, France, German Federal Republic, Japan, Luxembourg, Netherlands, Switzerland and the United Kingdom. A tourist card is available for visits of up to 15 days.

Sport

The favourite sport is baseball but swimming and water sports are also popular.

Public Holidays

1974: August 16th (Restoration Day), September 24th (Mercedes), December 25th (Christmas Day).

1975: January 1st (New Year's Day), January 6th (Epiphany), January 21st (Altagracia), January 26th (Duarte), February 27th (Independence Day), March 28th (Good Friday), May 1st (Labour Day), May 29th (Corpus Christi).

Weights and Measures

The metric system is officially in force but the imperial system is often used.

Currency and Exchange Rate

100 centavos = 1 Dominican Republic peso.

Exchange rates (April 1974):

£1 sterling = 2.36 pesos;
U.S. $1 = 1.00 peso.

STATISTICAL SURVEY

AREA AND POPULATION

Area sq. km.	Population (mid-1971)	Births, Marriages, Deaths (1969—per '000)		
	Total	Births	Marriages	Deaths
48,442	4,188,000	39.2	4.1	6.9

CHIEF TOWNS

Population (1970 census)

Santo Domingo (capital)	671,402	San Juan	32,248
Santiago de los Caballeros	155,151	San Felipe de Puerto Plata	32,181
San Francisco de Macorís	43,941	Concepción de la Vega	31,085
San Pedro de Macorís	42,473	Valverde	27,111
Barahona	37,889	San Cristóbal	25,829
La Romana	36,772	Baní	23,716

AGRICULTURE

		1968	1969	1970	1971
Rice	'000 tons	181.4	195.0	210.0	212.0
Maize	,, ,,	40.0	43.0	45.0	50.0
Sugar Cane	,, ,,	6,310.4	7,909.7	8,654.8	9,979.2
Coffee	,, ,,	88.9	87.1	84.9	90.7
Peanuts	,, ,,	47.3	72.6	74.8	79.3
Sweet Potatoes	,, ,,	78.0	84.0	87.0	91.0
Yucca	,, ,,	155.0	165.0	170.0	184.0
Sweet Oranges	million	173.2	174.8	176.4	178.0
Bitter Oranges	,,	107.1	109.3	111.5	113.7
Avocado Pears	,,	357.0	361.8	366.2	370.7
Mangos	,,	555.0	555.5	556.0	556.5
Bananas	'000 tons	1,186.1	1,553.3	n.a.	n.a.
Palm Fruits	,,	67.2	67.2	67.2	67.2

Livestock: (1967 est.) Cattle 810,000, Pigs 508,000, Goats 109,000, Horses 201,000, Asses 85,000; (1971 est). Cattle 1,388,962.

Fisheries (1967) 3,214,228 kg.; (1968) 4,737,865 kg.; (1969) 5,001,708 kg.; (1970) 5,197,215 kg.

Mining: (1968) Bauxite 1,027,000 tons, Gypsum 100,000 tons, Salt 16,000 tons (including sea salt and rock salt); Bauxite ('000 metric tons): 1,103 in 1969; 1,086 in 1970; 1,032 in 1971.

SUGAR PRODUCTION AND UTILIZATION
('ooo tons)

	1970	1971	1972
Sugar Cane	8,654.8	9,979.2	9,831.4
Refined Sugar	55.7	48.2	71.3
Exports	769.5	981.5	1,079.9
Local Consumption	120.7	132.3	141.4
Molasses ('ooo U.S. gals.) . . .	63,603.4	60,131.1	58,969.1

INDUSTRIAL PRODUCTION

		1970	1971	1972
Husked Rice	'ooo tons	128.3	132.0	130.8
Husked Coffee	,, ,,	42.5	45.0	45.3
Wheat Flour	,, ,,	55.0	60.6	64.7
Fertilizers	,, ,,	99.3	117.8	159.6
Cement	,, ,,	492.6	592.9	678.5
Beer	million litre	37.4	43.0	48.8
Spirits	,, ,,	10.1	10.2	10.8
Cigars	million	11.7	11.2	10.8
Cigarettes	,,	2,124.9	2,174.8	2,170.1
Cotton and Rayon Textiles . .	'ooo metres	6,641.7	6,289.9	6,556.0
Electricity	million kWh	927.1	1,068.0	1,273.0
Cardboard Boxes . . .	million units	69.5	117.8	151.3

FINANCE

100 centavos = 1 Dominican Republic peso (RD $ or peso oro).
Coins: 1, 5, 10, 25 and 50 centavos; 1 peso.
Notes: 1, 5, 10, 20, 50, 100, 500 and 1,000 pesos.
Exchange rates (April 1974): £1 sterling = 2.36 pesos; U.S. $1 = 1.00 peso.
100 Dominican Republic pesos = £42.35 = U.S. $100.00.

BUDGET
(1972—RD $ million)

INCOME		EXPENDITURE	
Direct taxes	74.4	Presidency	31.9
Indirect taxes	175.5	Interior and Police	17.5
Other Income	25.7	Armed Forces	33.3
		Education	53.9
		Health	40.3
		Others	124.0
TOTAL	275.6	TOTAL	300.9

COST OF LIVING INDEX
SANTO DOMINGO
(Base: 1969 = 100)

	GENERAL	FOOD	HOUSING	CLOTHING
1969 . .	100.0	100.0	100.0	100.0
1970 . .	105.2	105.5	101.5	96.8
1971 . .	108.3*	110.9	109.0*	98.5
1972 . .	116.8	117.6	120.8	114.9

* Revised.

RESERVES AND CURRENCY IN CIRCULATION
(million pesos)

	1969 (Dec.)	1970 (Dec.)	1971 (Dec.)	1972 (Dec.)
Net Reserves	28.3	23.2	34.3	45.4
of which gold . . .	3.0	3.0	3.0	3.3
Currency in circulation: Notes .	88.0	96.5	97.2	114.2
Coins	7.6	7.5	8.0	8.6

Source: Banco Central de la República Dominicana.

BALANCE OF PAYMENTS
(million pesos)

	1970			1971		
	Credit	Debit	Balance	Credit	Debit	Balance
Goods, Services and Transfers:						
Merchandise	213.2	266.8	− 53.6	243.0	311.1	−68.1
Tourism	15.8	39.0	− 23.2	21.4	36.5	−15.1
Freight and insurance . .	4.9	33.4	− 28.5	5.5	42.0	−36.5
Government and other services .	5.0	1.8	3.2	22.3	20.3	2.0
Interest payments . .	1.5	27.4	− 25.9	1.5	30.3	−28.8
Net private transfers . .	8.5	—	8.5	21.1	—	21.1
Net government transfers .	0.8	—	0.8	1.3	—	1.3
CURRENT BALANCE . .	—	—	−115.3	—	—	−124.1
Monetary and Capital Movements:						
Private capital (net) . .	108.6	—	108.6	109.1	—	109.1
Government capital (net) .	9.2	—	9.2	14.9	—	14.9
Monetary transactions (net) .	—	2.5	− 2.5	0.7	—	0.7
CAPITAL BALANCE . .	—	—	115.3	—	—	129.3
Net Errors and Omissions .	—	—	—	—	5.2	− 5.2

Allocation of IMF Special Drawing Rights (1971): 4.6 million pesos.

EXTERNAL TRADE
(in pesos)

	1967	1968	1969	1970	1971	1972*
Imports . .	174,711,147	196,850,149	217,242,992	278,034,417	309,726,472	337,700,000
Exports . .	156,195,781	163,544,515	183,417,894	211,194,100	240,738,489	347,600,000

* Provisional.

PRINCIPAL COMMODITIES
('000 pesos)

IMPORTS	1968	1969	1970	1971
Cars and Other Vehicles (incl. Spares) . . .	15,193	20,433	27,098	33,795
Chemical and Pharmaceutical Products . .	22,217	22,211	26,335	39,531
Cotton and Manufactures	7,969	8,907	9,251	8,625
Foodstuffs	40,264	31,279	32,975	37,934
Fuels	13,384	18,011	19,229	24,863
Iron and Steel and Manufactures (excl. Building Mats).	12,974	12,735	19,562	21,396
Machinery (incl. Spares)	27,037	33,411	45,905	50,190

PRINCIPAL COMMODITIES—*continued*]

(volume in 'ooo tons; value in 'ooo pesos)

EXPORTS	1970		1971		1972	
	Volume	Value	Volume	Value	Volume	Value
Coffee . . .	25.0	24,931	25.7	22,647	26.5	25,148
Cocoa Beans . .	34.4	19,148	29.1	12,555	32.2	16,042
Chocolate . .	0.1	336	1.2	426	2.5	767
Sugar (raw) . .	763.8	102,915	994.2	131,977	1,098.5	158,982
Tobacco Leaf .	19.5	13,945	25.8	19,825	32.9	31,519
Molasses . . .	85.1	1,830	73.6	2,110	58.8	1,535
Bauxite. . .	1,293.1	15,133	1,311.3	15,983	1,226.8	14,264
Bananas . .	3.8	348	1.3	98	16.0	1,040

PRINCIPAL COUNTRIES

('ooo pesos)

	IMPORTS			EXPORTS		
	1969	1970	1971	1969	1970	1971
Belgium	3,174	4,556	432	5,756	7,626	8,554
France	1,970	2,592	4,498	446	562	2,968
Germany, Federal Republic . .	15,765	18,307	31	2,099	1,457	1,258
Italy	5,620	9,829	10,717	1,145	1,272	999
Netherlands . . .	5,362	10,059	7,232	1,798	1,783	1,483
Norway	2,418	2,791	3,143	759	989	—
Puerto Rico . . .	6,206	7,667	9,826	7,901	10,721	12,891
Spain	4,024	4,493	5,032	5,935	8,371	12,320
United States . .	108,498	123,953	136,227	152,470	162,332	163,937

TRANSPORT

ROADS

	1971	1972
Cars . . .	43,089	48,906
Trucks and Lorries .	22,567	22,807
Motorcycles .	27,296	26,559

SHIPPING

1971	Ships	TONNAGE	
		Gross	Net
Ships Entering	2,127	18,196,863	9,832,720
Ships Leaving	1,823	9,599,340	5,276,281

CIVIL AVIATION

1969	FLIGHTS	PASSENGER/ KILOMETRES	TON/ KILOMETRES
Internal:			
Entering .	86	536,355	—
Leaving .	86	536,355	—
International:			
Entering .	8,420*	16,611,088,972	328,348,013
Leaving .	8,444*	16,865,903,494	1,507,864,291

* 1971 figures.

TOURISM

	TOURISTS	TOTAL VISITORS
1967 . .	45,486	147,682
1968 . .	60,224	171,508
1969 . .	74,163	196,103
1970 . .	67,566	199,119

EDUCATION

In 1969–70 there were 726,306 children in primary schools, 112,286 in intermediate and secondary schools, and 15,377 students in universities.

Source (unless otherwise stated): Dirección General de Estadística y Censos, Santo Domingo.

THE CONSTITUTION

The present constitution of the Dominican Republic was promulgated on November 28th, 1966. Its main points are:

The Dominican Republic is a sovereign, free, independent State; no organizations set up by the State can bring about any act which might cause direct or indirect intervention in the internal or foreign affairs of the State or which might threaten the integrity of the State. The Dominican Republic recognizes and applies the norms of general and American international law and is in favour of and will support any initiative towards economic integration for the countries of America. The civil, republican, democratic, representative Government is divided into three independent powers: legislative, executive and judicial.

The territory of the Dominican Republic is as laid down in the Frontier Treaty of 1929 and its Protocol of Revision of 1936.

The life and property of the individual citizen are inviolable; there can be no sentence of death, torture or any sentence which might cause physical harm to the individual. There is freedom of thought, of conscience, of religion, freedom to publish, freedom of unarmed association, provided that there is no subversion against public order, national security or decency. There is freedom of labour and trade unions; freedom to strike, except in the case of public services, according to the dispositions of the law.

The State will set about agrarian reform, dedicating the land to useful interests and gradually eliminating the *latifundios*. The State will do all in its power to support all aspects of family life. Primary education is compulsory and all education is free. Social security services will be developed. Every Dominican has the duty to give what civil and military service the State may require of him. Every legally entitled citizen must exercise his right to vote. Citizens are all persons over the age of eighteen and all who are or have been married even if they are not yet eighteen.

Legislative Power is exercised by Congress which is made up of the Senate and Chamber of Deputies, elected by direct vote. *Senators*, one for each province and one for the *Distrito Nacional*, are elected for four years; they must be Dominicans in full exercise of their citizen's rights, over 25. Their duties are to elect judges, the President and other members of the Electoral and Accounts Councils, and to approve the nomination of diplomats. *Deputies*, one for every 50,000 inhabitants or fraction over 25,000 in each province and the *Distrito Nacional*, are elected for four years and must fulfil the same conditions for election as Senators.

Decisions of Congress are taken by absolute majority of at least half the members of each house; urgent matters require a two-thirds majority. Both houses normally meet on February 27th and August 16th each year for sessions of 90 days, which can be extended for a further 60 days.

Executive Power is exercised by the President of the Republic, who is elected by direct vote for a four-year term. He and the Vice-President must be Dominican citizens by birth or origin, over 30 years of age and in full exercise of their citizen's rights; they must not have engaged in any active military or police service for at least a year prior to their election. They take office on August 16th following their election. The *President of the Republic* is Head of the Public Administration and Supreme Chief of the armed forces and police forces. His duties include nominating Secretaries and Assistant Secretaries of State and other public officials, promulgating and publishing laws and resolutions of Congress and seeing to their faithful execution, watching over the collection and just investment of national income, nominating, with the approval of the Senate, members of the Diplomatic Corps, receiving foreign Heads of State, presiding at national functions, decreeing a State of Siege or Emergency or any other measures necessary during a public crisis. The President may not leave the country for more than 15 days without authorization from Congress. In the absence of the President, the Vice-President will assume power, or failing him the President of the Supreme Court of Justice.

Judicial Power is exercised by the Supreme Court of Justice and the other Tribunals; no judicial official may hold another public office or employment, other than honorary or teaching. The Supreme Court is made up of at least nine judges, who must be Dominican citizens by birth or origin, at least 35 years old, in full exercise of their citizen's rights, graduates in law and have practised professionally for at least 12 years. There are also five Courts of Appeal, a Lands Tribunal and a Court of the First Instance in each judicial district; in each Municipality and in the Distrito Nacional there are also Justices of the Peace.

Government in the *Distrito Nacional* and the Municipalities is in the hands of local councils, with members elected proportionally to the number of inhabitants, but numbering at least five. Each Province has a civil Governor, designated by the Executive.

All citizens must exercise their suffrage. Elections are directed by the Central Electoral Council. The armed forces are essentially obedient and apolitical, created for the defence of national independence and the maintenance of public order and the Constitution and Laws.

The artistic and historical riches of the country, whoever owns them, are part of the cultural heritage of the country and are under the safekeeping of the State. Mineral deposits belong to the State. There is freedom to form political parties, provided they conform to the principles laid down in the Constitution. Justice is administered without charge throughout the Republic.

This Constitution can be reformed if the proposal for reform is supported in Congress by one third of the members of either house or by the Executive. A special session of Congress must be called and any resolutions must have a two-thirds majority. There can be no reform of the method of government, which must always be civil, republican, democratic and representative.

THE GOVERNMENT

HEAD OF STATE

President: Dr. Joaquín Balaguer.

Vice-President: Lic. Carlos Rafael Goico Morales.

CABINET

(May 1974)

Secretary of State for the Armed Forces: Rear-Adm. Ramón Emilio Jiménez.

Secretary of State for the Interior and Police: Gen. Rafael de Jesús Checo.

Secretary of State for Foreign Affairs: Dr. Víctor Gómez Bergés.

Secretary of State for the Treasury: Carlos Séliman.

Secretary of State for Health and Social Security: Dr. Hector Pereyra Ariza.

Secretary of State for Education and Culture: Dra. Altagracia Bautista de Suárez.

Secretary of State for Labour: Dr. César Estrella Sadhalá.

Secretary of State for Agriculture: Ing. Carlos E. Aquino.

Secretary of State for Public Works & Communications: Ing. Manuel Alsina Puello.

Secretary of State for Industry & Commerce: Federico Antún.

DIPLOMATIC REPRESENTATION

EMBASSIES ACCREDITED TO DOMINICAN REPUBLIC

(In Santo Domingo unless otherwise stated)

Argentina: Máximo Gómez No. 10; *Ambassador:* Fernando L. M. Ricciardi.

Brazil: Anacaona esq. Calle "C"; *Ambassador:* (vacant).

Chile: Bolívar No. 100; *Ambassador:* (vacant).

China (Taiwan): Santiago No. 107; *Ambassador:* P. W. Seng.

Colombia: 27 de Febrero esq. Lincoln; *Ambassador:* Eliseo Arango.

Costa Rica: J. M. Roman No. 2; *Ambassador:* Col. Julio L. Calleja T.

Ecuador: Santiago No. 107; *Ambassador:* Lic. Juan Salazar Sandoval.

El Salvador: Núñez y Domínguez No. 7; *Ambassador:* Dr. José R. Jovel Pineda.

France: César Nicolás Penson No. 53; *Ambassador:* Paul H. le Mire.

Germany, Federal Republic: G. Washington No. 92; *Ambassador:* Hans Peter Hoppe.

Guatemala: Madame Curie No. 19; *Ambassador:* Col. Agustín Donis-Kestler.

Haiti: Máximo Gómez No. 68; *Ambassador:* Lic. Clément Vincent.

Israel: Cd. Sarasota No. 38; *Ambassador:* Johanan Bein.

Italy: Rodríguez Objío No. 4; *Ambassador:* (vacant).

Jamaica: Socorro Sánchez No. 17; *Ambassador:* Adolph A. Thompson.

Japan: Bolívar No. 202-A; *Ambassador:* Hiroshi Nagasaki.

Mexico: Bolívar No. 15; *Ambassador:* Lic. Francisco E. García.

Nicaragua: Anacoana esq. Baoruco; *Ambassador:* Mayor Alfredo López Ramírez.

Panama: José Contreras No. 75; *Ambassador:* Lic. Alejandro Cuéllar Arosemena.

Peru: Edificio La Cumbre, Av. Tiradentes; *Ambassador:* Mariano Pagador.

Spain: Independencia No. 229; *Ambassador:* Lic. Aurelio Valls Carreras.

United Kingdom: Independencia No. 84, Apdo. 1352; *Ambassador:* Paul V. St. John Killick, o.b.e.

U.S.A.: Pedro Enríquez Ureña; *Ambassador:* Robert A. Hurwitch.

Uruguay: Edificio La Cumbre, Av. Tiradentes; *Ambassador:* Edmundo Novoa García.

Vatican: Máximo Gómez No. 27; *Apostolic Nuncio:* Rev. Mgr. Iovanni Gravelli.

Venezuela: Abraham Lincoln No. 103; *Ambassador:* Gloria Stolk.

CONGRESS

President of Assembly: Pedro Váldez.

Elections, May 1966.

	Senate	House
Partido Reformista . . .	22	48
Partido Revolucionario Dominicano . . .	5	26

Presidential Election
(*May 16th*, 1974)

		Votes
Dr. Joaquín Balaguer (PR) . . .		924,779
Adm. Luis Homero Lajara Burgos (PDP) .		105,320

PR=Partido Reformista; PDP=Popular Democratic Party.

Note: The Opposition coalition withdrew from the election on May 14th.

POLITICAL PARTIES

Partido Reformista: ruling party; Leader and Presidential candidate Dr. Joaquín Balaguer.

Partido Revolucionario Dominicano: left-wing; 1970 Presidential candidate Dr. Francisco Peña Gómez.

Partido Revolucionario Social Cristiano: left-wing; supported Bosch in 1966; Pres. Mario Read Vittini.

Partido de Integración Democrática: 1970 Presidential candidate Dr. Augusto Lora.

Partido Quisqueyano Dominicano (PQD): right-wing; 1970 Presidential candidate Gen. Elías Wessín y Wessín.

Movimiento de Conciliación Nacional (MCN): 1970 Presidential candidate Dr. Jaime M. Fernández.

There are also a number of smaller political parties.

JUDICIAL SYSTEM

The Judicial Power resides in the Supreme Court of Justice, the Courts of Appeal, the Tribunals of the First Instance, the municipal courts and the other judicial authorities provided by law. The Supreme Court is composed of nine judges and the Attorney-General and exercises disciplinary authority over all the members of the judiciary. The Attorney-General of the Republic is the Chief of Judicial Police and of the Public Ministry which he represents before the Supreme Court of Justice. All judges are elected by the Senate.

President of the Supreme Court: Manuel Ramón Ruiz Tejada.

RELIGION

The majority of the inhabitants belong to the Roman Catholic Church, but freedom of worship exists for all denominations. There are approximately 30,000 Protestants and a small Jewish community.

Santo Domingo
Metropolitan See: Arzobispado, Apdo. 186; Mgr. Octavio A. Beras Rojas.

Suffragan Sees:
La Vega: Mgr. Juan Antonio Flores Santana.
Nuestra Señora de la Altagracia en Higüey: Mgr. Juan Félix Pepén y Solimán.
San Juan de la Maguana: Mgr. Tomás F. Reilly.
Santiago de los Caballeros: Mgr. Roque Adames Rodríguez.

THE PRESS

DAILIES
Santo Domingo

El Cáribe: El Conde 1, Apdo. 416; f. 1948; morning; Dir. Germán Ornes; circ. 46,000.

Listín Diario: 19 de Marzo 58; f. 1889; morning; Dir. Rafael Herrera; circ. 40,000.

El Nacional: Avda. San Martín 236; f. 1966; evening and Sunday; circ. 20,000.

Ultima Hora: Calle 19 de Marzo 43; evening.

Santiago de los Caballeros
La Información: M. Gómez 16; f. 1915; morning; Editor Luis E. Franco; circ. 15,000.

Puerto Plata
El Porvenir: f. 1872; Dir. Alonso Rodríguez.

San Pedro de Macoris
Diario de Macoris: f. 1922; daily; Dir. Néstor Febles; circ. 3,500.

El Universal: daily.

PERIODICALS AND REVIEWS
Santo Domingo

Agricultura: organ of the State Secretariat of Agriculture and Colonization; f. 1905; monthly; Dir. Miguel Rodríguez, Jr.

Ahora: San Martín 236, Apdo. 1402; f. 1962; weekly; Dir. Rafael Molina Morillo.

La Campiña: San Martín 236, Apdo. 1402; f. 1967; Dir. Ing. Juan Ulises García B.

Cuadernos Dominicanos de Cultura: review of cultural affairs.

Deportes: San Martín 236, Apdo. 1402; f. 1967; Dir. L. R. Cordero; circ. 5,000.

Eva: San Martín 236, Apdo. 1402; f. 1967; Dir. Socorro de Pumarol.

Finanzas: financial review.

El Nacional: San Martín 236, Apdo. 1402; f. 1966; Dir. Dr. Freddy Gatón Arce.

PUBLISHERS

Santo Domingo

Arte y Cine, C. por A.: Isabel la Católica 42.

Editora y Distribuidora Nacional: Arzobispo Nouel 80; f. 1964; general; Man. F. Franco.

Editora "El Cáribe", C. por A.: El Conde 1, Apdo. 416; Dir. Federico A. Mella Villanueva.

Editorial Montalvo: José Reyes 44; Proprietor Virgilio Montalvo.

Julio D. Postigo e Hijos: José Reyes 50; f. 1949; fiction; Man. J. D. Postigo.

RADIO AND TELEVISION

Dirrección General de Telecomunicaciones: Santo Domingo; government supervisory body; Dir.-Gen. J. R. Santa-maría.

RADIO

There were 90 commercial stations and 165,000 radio receivers in 1971.

TELEVISION

Televisión Dominicana: Dr. Tejada Florentino 8, Apdo. 969, Santo Domingo; commercial station; two channels, two relay stations; Dir.-Gen. R. A. Font Bernard.

Rahintel Televisión: Centro de los Héroes de Constanza, Apdo. 1220, Santo Domingo; Gen. Man. P. P. Bonilla.

Color-Visión: Hotel Matum, Santiago; commercial station; two channels; Dir.-Gen. M. Quiroz.

There were 150,000 television sets in 1973.

FINANCE

(cap.=capital; dep.=deposits; m.=million; res.=reserves; amounts in pesos).

BANKING

Central Bank

Banco Central de la República Dominicana: Avda. Dr. Pedro Henríquez Ureña, Santo Domingo; f. 1947; cap. 0.7m.; notes issued 79.4m.; res. 30.7m. (Dec. 1971); Governor Dr. Diógenes H. Fernández.

Banco Agrícola de la República Dominicana: Avda. George Washington, Apdo. 1057, Santo Domingo; f. 1945; government agricultural bank; 20 brs.; Gen. Man. Manuel V. Ramos.

Banco de Crédito y Ahorros, C. por A.: Mercedes 14, Santo Domingo; f. 1949; private institution; 3 brs.; cap. 350,000; total resources 5.3m. (Dec. 1971); Pres. and Man. Dr. Antonio Ibarra-Fort.

Banco Nacional de la Vivienda (BNV): Santo Domingo; housing development bank.

Banco Popular Dominicano: Isabel la Católica 70, Santo Domingo; f. 1963; 4 brs.; cap. 5m.

Banco de Reservas de la República Dominicana: Isabel la Católica 71, Santo Domingo; f. 1941; cap. 20m., res. 2.6m. (Dec. 1971); Gen. Admin. José A. Petit F.

Compañía Financiera Dominicana, S.A.: Socorro Sánchez 11, Apdo. 201-2, Santo Domingo; f. 1968; 187 mems.; financial institution and investment bankers; official intermediary institution of the Central Bank; auth. cap. U.S. $3m.; Pres. Tomás A. Pastoriza.

Instituto Nacional de la Vivienda: Santo Domingo.

FOREIGN BANKS

Bank of America: Head Office: New York; Santo Domingo office: El Conde 13.

Bank of Nova Scotia: Head Office: Halifax, Nova Scotia; Santo Domingo office: Isabel la Católica 52.

Chase Manhattan Bank: Head Office: New York; Santo Domingo office: Isabel la Católica 65; Man. Frank G. Brennan; br. in Santiago de los Caballeros.

First National City Bank: New York; Santo Domingo office: Avda. J. F. Kennedy 1; 2 brs. in Santo Domingo, 1 br. in Santiago de los Caballeros.

Royal Bank of Canada: Head Office: Montreal, Canada; Santo Domingo office: Isabel la Católica 50-a; brs. Santiago de los Caballeros, Mao, Puerto Plata, San Francisco de Macorís, Azua, San Pedro de Macorís and La Romana.

INSURANCE

(Santo Domingo)

National Company

San Rafael, C. por A.: Avda. Tiradentes esq. Papito Sánchez, Ensanche Naco, Apdo. 1018; f. 1932; Gen.-Man. Lic. Miguel A. Rodríguez Pereyra.

TRADE AND INDUSTRY

CHAMBERS OF COMMERCE

Cámara Oficial de Comercio, Agricultura e Industria del Distrito Nacional: Arz. Nouel 52 (altos), Santo Domingo; f. 1910; 800 active mems.; Pres. Dr. Juan Gassó Pereyra; publ. *Comercio y Producción* (monthly).

There are official Chambers of Commerce in the larger towns.

American Chamber of Commerce of the Dominican Republic: Apdo. 95-2, Hotel El Embajador, Santo Domingo; f. 1923; 205 mems.; Exec. Dir. Máximo E. Velázquez.

TRADE AND DEVELOPMENT ORGANIZATIONS

Asociación Dominicana de Hacendados y Agricultores Inc.: Avda. Sarasota 4, Santo Domingo; farming and agricultural organization; Pres. Lic. Silvestre Alba de Moya.

Asociación de Industrias de la República Dominicana: Avda. Sarasota 4, Santo Domingo; industrial organization; Pres. Antonio Najri.

Centro Dominicano de Promoción de Exportaciones (CEDOPEX): Calle Modesto Díaz esq. Huáscar Tejeda, Santo Domingo; organization for the promotion of exports; Exec. Dir. Ing. Fernando Periche.

Comisión de Fomento: Secretaría de Estado de Industria y Comercio, Santo Domingo; consists of president, vice-president and 25 members appointed by the Executive; f. 1951 for the purpose of carrying out investigations into proposed schemes, developing new industries, and granting technical and financial aid to selected private enterprises; Pres. Rafael Paino Pichardo.

Confederación Patronal de la República Dominicana: Isabel la Católica 23, Santo Domingo; Pr s. Ing. HERIBERTO DE CASTRO.

Consejo Estatal del Azúcar (CEA) (*State Sugar Council*): Santo Domingo; f. 1966 to replace Corporación Azucarera Dominicana; autonomous administration for each of the 12 state sugar mills; Exec. Dir. Lic. FERNANDO ALVAREZ BOGAERT.

Consejo Nacional de Hombres de Empresa: Arz. Nouel No. 52 (altos), Santo Domingo; Pres. Dr. ROGELIO A. PELLERANO.

Corporación Dominicana de Empresas Estatales (CORDE) (*Dominican State Enterprise Corporation*): Avda. General Antonio Duvergé, Apdo. 1378, Santo Domingo; f. 1966 to administer, direct and develop state enterprises; auth. cap. RD$ 50m.; Dir. Dr. JOSÉ A. QUEZADA T.

Corporación de Fomento Industrial (C.F.I.): Apdo. 1472, Santo Domingo; f. 1962 to promote industrial development; cap. and res. RD$ 13.3m.

Fondo de Inversión para el Desarrollo Económico (*Economic Development Investment Fund*): c/o Banco Central de la República Dominicana, Avda. Dr. Pedro Henríquez Ureña, Santo Domingo; f. 1965; associated with AID, IADB; resources RD$ 10m.; to encourage economic development in productive sectors of economy, excluding sugar; will authorize complementary financing to private sector for establishing new industrial and agricultural enterprises and develop existing ones.

Fundación Dominicana de Desarrollo (*Dominican Development Foundation*): Apdo. 857, Santo Domingo; f. 1962 to mobilize private resources for collaboration in financing small-scale development programmes; 215 mems.; assets U.S. $2.5m.; Pres. ROBERTO BONETTI; Exec. Dir. BOLÍVAR BÁEZ; publ. *Desarrollo, Directory of Dominican Voluntary Agencies.*

Instituto Azucarero: sugar institute; f. 1965; Chair. Sec. of State for Finance.

Dominican Republic Settlement Association: Sosua, Puerto Plata.

TRADE UNIONS

Confederación de Trabajadores Dominicanos—CTD (*Confederation of Dominican Workers*): Caracas-José Martí, Benito González 81, Santo Domingo; f. 1920; mems. 188,000 (est.); 11 provincial federations totalling 150 unions are affiliated; Sec.-Gen. JUAN A. PARDILLA, Jr.; publ. *Boletín* (quarterly).

Frente Obrero Unido Pro Sindicatos Autónomos—FOUPSA (*United Workers' Front for Autonomous Trade Unions*): Santo Domingo; f. 1961; brought about the rapid termination of the single union system; Pres. MIGUEL SOTO; Sec.-Gen. SÁNCHEZ CÓRDOVA.

TRANSPORT AND TOURISM

RAILWAYS

There are approximately 100 km. of state-owned railway lines and 1,600 km. of private railways used mainly for sugar transport.

Ferrocarriles Unidos Dominicanos: Santo Domingo; government railway.

Sánchez–La Vega Section: Sánchez; 100 km. open, 1,067mm. gauge; Admin. Dir. LOWENSKI FELIZ ACOSTA.

ROADS

There are over 2,560 km. of first-class roads and 3,200 km. of second-class roads. There is a direct route from Santo Domingo to Port-au-Prince in Haiti. In 1966 an emergency plan was introduced to improve local roads at a cost of RD$ 4m. financed by AID funds.

SHIPPING

PRINCIPAL COMPANIES

Flota Mercante Dominicana (*Merchant Fleet*): Isabel la Católica 70, Apdo. 204, Santo Domingo; privately owned; 7,630 g.r.t.; regular cargo and limited passenger services between New York, Halifax, Hamilton, Kingston and the Dominican Republic.

Alcoa Steamship Company Inc.: Apdo. 748, Santo Domingo; regular service from Mobile, Alabama, New Orleans, Houston, U.S.A., and Italy, Spain and Canary Islands; agents for Cía. Transatlántica Española S.A.

Several ships of the European lines call at Santo Domingo.

CIVIL AVIATION

CDA—Compañía Dominicana de Aviación: Head Office: Conde 83, Apdo 322, Santo Domingo; operates on international routes connecting Santo Domingo with San Juan (Puerto Rico), Miami, New York, Curaçao (Netherlands Antilles) and Caracas (Venezuela); Gen. Man. LUIS MAURICIO BOGAERT; fleet: 2 Boeing 727, 1 DC-6B, 1 DC-4, 1 DC-3, 1 C-46.

The Dominican Republic is also served by the following foreign airlines: A.L.M. (Netherlands Antilles), Caribair (Puerto Rico), Iberia, Pan American and Viasa (Venezuela).

TOURISM

Dirección General de Turismo: Calle César Nicolás Penson y Rosa Duarte, Santo Domingo; Dir. ANGEL MIOLÁN

Asociación Dominicana de Agencias de Viajes: Avda. Bolívar 7, Santo Domingo; Pres. MARIANO RAMÍREZ.

CULTURAL ORGANIZATION

Dirección General de Bellas Artes: Santo Domingo; responsible for :

Coro Nacional: f. 1955; Dir. JOSÉ E. DELMONTE PEGUERO.

Coro de Santiago.

Orquesta Sinfónica Nacional: f. 1941.

Teatro de Bellas Artes.

UNIVERSITIES

Universidad Autónoma de Santo Domingo: Ciudad Universitaria, Apdo. 1355, Santo Domingo; 1,039 teachers, 23,028 students.

Universidad Católica "Madre y Maestra": Santiago de los Caballeros; 135 teachers, 1,265 students.

Universidad Nacional "Pedro Henríquez Ureña": Santo Domingo; 301 teachers, 5,500 students.

ECUADOR

INTRODUCTORY SURVEY

Location, Climate, Language, Religion, Flag, Capital

The Republic of Ecuador lies on the west coast of South America. Its neighbours are Colombia to the north and Peru to the east and south. The Galápagos Islands, 800 km. out in the Pacific, belong to Ecuador. The climate is affected by the Andes mountains and the topography ranges from the tropical rain forest on the coast and in the eastern region to the tropical grasslands of the central valley and the permanent snowfields of the highlands. The official language is Spanish but Indian languages are very common. About 90 per cent of the population is Roman Catholic and there are Protestant and Jewish minorities. The national flag (proportions 2 by 1) is a horizontal tricolour of yellow, blue and red, the yellow stripe being twice the depth of the other two. The state flag has, in addition, the national emblem in the centre. The capital is Quito.

Recent History

In November 1961 labour groups, left-wing parties and the armed forces overthrew the President, Dr. José María Velasco Ibarra, who was forced into exile. His successor, Dr. Carlos Julio Arosemena Monroy, formerly Vice-President, was deposed after an army coup in July 1963. A military junta was set up, headed by Rear-Admiral Ramón Castro Jijón, and martial law was proclaimed. This junta was forced to resign in March 1966, and Clemente Yerovi Indaburu was installed as acting President. Following the elections of October 16th, 1966, Dr. Otto Arosemena Gómez became provisional President. Former President Velasco was elected as President in June 1968 and took office in September. In June 1970, with the aid of the army, he declared himself dictator, suspended the constitution and dissolved Congress. But in February 1972 President Velasco was deposed by the armed forces and Brig.-Gen. Guillermo Rodríguez Lara, C.-in-C. of the army, became President.

Government

In February 1972 the new President, Gen. Rodríguez, announced that the Constitution of 1945 would be enforced and a return to civilian government would be achieved in due course. The country is divided into 19 Provinces and the National Territory of the Galápagos Islands. Each Province has a Governor appointed by the President.

Defence

Military service is compulsory for two years at the age of twenty. Defence expenditure is the second largest item in the budget. The armed forces consist of about 22,000 men: army 15,000, navy 3,700 and air force 3,500. Paramilitary forces number 5,800 men.

Economic Affairs

The economy is dominated by three commodities: bananas, coffee and cocoa. Ecuador is the world's largest exporter of bananas. The extensive forests yield valuable hardwoods. Ecuador is also the world's largest producer of balsawood. Minerals include gold, silver, lead and petroleum. The major industries are oil-refining, sugar-refining and cement. With the completion of the trans-Andean

pipeline linking the oilfields of Oriente Province with the tanker-loading port of Esmeraldas in 1972, Ecuador is destined to become an important oil-exporting nation, and the largest oil producer in Latin America after Venezuela. Cepe, the state oil concern, is considering bids from foreign companies for the construction of a major refinery at Esmeraldas. Oil sales in 1972 reached U.S. $60 million and helped to increase total exports by 40 per cent; the 1973 figure is expected to reach $200 million. However, regulations calling for increased investment from oil companies prospecting in the country have resulted in the abandonment by several foreign companies of a large percentage of their holdings. In August 1972 the Government announced a five-year development plan. Revenue from the new oil exports is expected to finance much of the plan's aims. It is proposed to create 560,000 new jobs and to raise the growth rate to 8.4 per cent per year. Total investment is calculated at 63,700 million sucres. In 1973 the Agrarian Reform Law was passed. The law states that the right of private ownership over farmland is to be conditioned by fulfilment of social responsibilities and efficient production. Rural property suitable for agriculture, unexploited for more than two and less than five years, will be liable to expropriation. The law is designed to correct injustices of tenure and exploitation. The extension of the country's electricity resources is one of the Government's priorities; it is hoped that the entire population will benefit from electricity by 1990. The total cost of current extension plans is more than 6,000 million sucres.

Ecuador claims exclusive fishing rights within a limit of 320 km. from the coastline. This claim has been the source of continuing friction with the U.S.A. for some years. Ecuador is a member of the Andean Group, OPEC, the UN, the Organization of American States, the Alliance for Progress and the Latin American Free Trade Association.

Transport and Communications

Communications are rendered difficult by mountains and forests. There are 1,070 km. of railway track, the main railway extending from the coast to Quito and beyond. The Pan-American Highway runs for 1,392 km. through the country with branch roads to the coast. Near the coast the lower reaches of the rivers Guayas, Mira and Esmeraldas are navigable for about 190 km. There are a number of seaports of which Guayaquil and Manta are the most important. Three main Ecuadorean companies and some foreign lines operate internal and international air services.

Social Welfare

Social insurance is compulsory for certain groups of both public and private employees. Benefits are available for sickness, industrial accidents, disability, maternity, old age, widowhood and orphanhood. Hospitals and welfare institutions are run by Central Public Assistance Boards.

Education

Education is compulsory where school places are available. All public schools are free, and considerable co-operation exists between them and the private religious schools which continue to play a vital role in the educational system. Primary education covers the ages of six to twelve and secondary education twelve to eighteen. University courses extend for up to six years and include programmes for teacher training. About 50 per cent of primary school pupils proceed to secondary education, of which only 6 per cent reach university. As part of the current literacy Campaign a number of adult schools and literacy centres have been built. There are seven universities.

Tourism
The main tourist attractions are the magnificent mountain and forest scenery of the highlands, the tropical jungles of the Upper Amazon and the relics of Indian and Colonial Spanish cultures. There are a number of coastal resorts from which deep-sea fishing is possible. Scientific expeditions visit the Galápagos Islands.

Visas are not required to visit Ecuador by nationals of Colombia, EEC countries (except Ireland), Portugal, Spain, Sweden, Switzerland and Uruguay.

Sport
Football and basketball are the most popular sports.

Public Holidays
1974: August 10th (Independence—Quito), October 9th (Independence—Guayaquil), October 12th (Discovery of America—Guayaquil), November 1st (All Saints')*, November 2nd (All Souls'), November 3rd (Cuenca's Day), December 6th (Foundation of Quito), December 25th (Christmas).

1975: January 1st (New Year's Day), February 9th–11th (Carnival), March 27th, 28th (Easter), May 1st (Labour Day), May 24th (Battle of Pichincha), July 24th (Birth of Simón Bolívar).

* Not an official holiday, but almost universally observed.

Weights and Measures
The metric system is in force.

Currency and Exchange Rates
100 centavos = 1 sucre.

Exchange rates (April 1974):
£1 sterling = 59.03 sucres;
U.S. $1 = 25.00 sucres.

STATISTICAL SURVEY

AREA AND POPULATION

AREA (sq. km.)		POPULATION (1971)			
Ecuador*	Galápagos Islands	Total	Births	Marriages	Deaths†
283,561	8,006	6,384,200	243,506	37,329	63,885

Total Population (1973): 6,819,500.

* Excludes eastern provinces, for which no figures are available.
† Provisional figure.

PROVINCES
(1973)

PROVINCE	POPULATION	CAPITAL	PROVINCE	POPULATION	CAPITAL
Azuay . . .	362,972	Cuenca	Los Ríos . . .	401,909	Babahoyo
Bolívar . . .	193,573	Guaranda	Manabí . . .	905,335	Portoviejo
Cañar . . .	142,843	Azogues	Morona Santiago .	46,767	Macas
Carchi . . .	128,948	Tulcán	Napo . . .	44,486	Tena
Cotopaxi . . .	250,609	Latacunga	Pastaza . . .	25,115	Puyo
Chimborazo . .	406,263	Riobamba	Pichincha . . .	946,066	Quito
El Oro . .	275,190	Machala	Tungurahua . .	271,690	Ambato
Esmeraldas . .	200,216	Esmeraldas	Zamora Chinchipe .	21,020	Zamora
Guayas . . .	1,589,288	Guayaquil	Archipiélago de Colón		
Imbabura . .	226,647	Ibarra	(Galápagos) .	4,205	Puerto Baquerizo
Loja . . .	412,358	Loja			(Isla San Cristóbal)

CHIEF TOWNS

Quito (capital) .	.	551,163	Machala . .	63,327
Guayaquil .	.	835,812	Esmeraldas . .	62,912
Cuenca . .	.	79,140	Riobamba . .	55,173
Ambato . .	.	78,006	Portoviejo . .	49,745

AGRICULTURE
(metric tons)

	1969	1970	1971	1972
Potatoes	456,686	541,794	680,740	473,348
Rice	288,016	187,464	131,750	167,422
Barley . . .	77,659	109,990	68,691	73,387
Wheat . . .	94,099	81,000	68,493	50,640
Maize . . .	222,486	269,506	260,913	271,390
Cocoa . . .	47,993	53,584	48,737	66,820
Coffee . . .	55,893	60,427	59,325	58,425
Bananas . . .	5,833,562	4,136,710	3,951,859	3,731,454
Cotton . . .	23,557	7,552	10,714	11,556

Livestock (1972): Cattle 2,358,420, Sheep 2,474,100, Pigs 2,545,000.

Source: Ministerio de Agricultura, Dirección de Ganadería.

DESTINATION OF BANANA EXPORTS
('000 U.S. $)

	1970	1971	1972
Belgium and Luxembourg . .	4,969	7,718	7,556
Chile	4,625	6,206	4,846
Germany, Federal Republic	10,983	16,406	14,744
Japan . . .	34,910	33,549	37,385
United States . . .	25,512	24,316	22,660
Others . . .	13,278	12,959	21,818
Total . . .	94,277	101,154	109,009

DESTINATION OF COFFEE EXPORTS
('000 U.S. $)

	1969	1970	1971	1972
Africa (total) . .	—	13	12	102
France . . .	1,373	1,083	904	1,244
Germany, Federal Republic .	3,023	7,540	3,211	7,285
Hungary . . .	1,289	2,475	3,074	4,382
Italy . . .	588	1,082	491	673
Netherlands . .	138	1,036	489	816
Poland . . .	17	—	2,787	257
Spain . . .	897	920	266	208
Sweden . . .	129	378	439	268
U.S.A. . . .	95,878	33,723	21,785	24,892
Others . . .	3,307	2,279	3,036	2,473
Total . . .	26,639	50,516	36,494	42,600

DESTINATION OF COCOA EXPORTS
('000 U.S. $)

	1970	1971	1972
Belgium and Luxembourg .	731	778	1,013
Colombia	3,426	3,206	4,960
Germany, Federal Republic.	1,167	1,682	1,873
Italy	1,959	1,251	1,487
Japan . . .	1,790	2,116	1,940
Netherlands . .	1,332	1,155	1,624
U.S.A. . . .	7,921	8,639	6,796
U.S.S.R. . . .	81	2,334	—
Others . . .	3,662	4,215	3,626
Total .	22,069	25,376	23,319

MINING

	Unit	1967	1968	1969	1970
Gold	troy ozs.	6,738	8,164	7,354	8,521
Silver	,,	79,657	136,204	124,253	69,761
Copper . . .	kgs.	415,444	558,483	534,576	511,209
Lead . . .	,,	n.a.	n.a.	n.a.	n.a.
Petroleum . . .	'000 galls.	92,300	74,000	65,800	60,700

Petroleum Production: (1971) 55,700,000 gallons; (1972) 1,201,700,000 gallons.

INDUSTRY

	Unit	1969	1970	1971	1972
Refined Petroleum . .	'000 galls.	324,800	366,200	406,800	424,900
Diesel Oil . . .	,,	64,100	77,400	84,400	93,900
Kerosene . . .	,,	26,200	20,600	15,700	16,800
Sugar	metric tons	208,000	248,000	255,000	252,685*
Cement	,,	456,000	458,000	462,000	482,000
Beer	'000 bottles	98,234	107,972	106,872	127,743
Cigars	'000	607	481	681	844
Cigarettes . . .	'000 packets	61,335	63,338	66,872	65,192

* Provisional.

FINANCE
100 centavos=1 sucre.
Coins: 5, 10, 20 and 50 centavos; 1 sucre.
Notes: 5, 10, 20, 50, 100, 500 and 1,000 sucres.
Exchange rates (April 1974): £1 sterling=59.03 sucres; U.S. $1=25.00 sucres.
100 sucres=£1.694=$4.00.

ORDINARY BUDGET
(million sucres)

1972: Revenue 3,800; Expenditure 4,113.

Principal Items of Expenditure

	1969	1970	1971	1972*
Education . . .	598	690	787	1,041
Defence . . .	545	620	742	933
Interior . . .	160	200	223	249
Social Welfare .	21	22	24	29
Public Debt Interest .	355	440	590	578
State Offices and Pensions . . .	74	69	78	110
Public Works . .	2	2	2	2

* Provisional. Includes the period January–March 1973.

DEVELOPMENT BUDGET
(million sucres)

Revenue	1971	1972*	Expenditure	1971	1972*
Taxation . . .	1,290	1,951	Education . . .	371	492
Non-Tax Revenue .	91	93	Public Works . .	832	679
Foreign Loans . .	92	1,000	Natural Resources and Tourism .	106	44
Internal Loans . .	1,083	499	Health . . .	157	143
			Public Debt (Amortization) .	657	625
Total . .	2,556	3,543	Total . .	3,191	3,245

* Provisional.

Source: Ministerio de Finanzas, Estados Financieros de la Tesorería General de la Nación.

NATIONAL ACCOUNTS
(million sucres)

	1970	1971*	1972*
Gross Domestic Product . . .	34,017	40,109	47,910
of which:			
Agriculture	10,372	11,466	12,569
Manufacturing industries . .	5,713	6,757	8,015
Trade, retail and wholesale .	3,505	4,719	5,408
Other services, government, and rent	8,351	9,503	11,225
Net factor income from abroad . .	−1,141	−1,284	−1,210
Gross National Income . .	32,876	38,825	46,700
Less depreciation allowance . .	−1,305	−1,760	−2,375
Net National Income . .	31,571	37,065	44,325
Indirect taxes, less subsidies . .	3,047	3,416	4,155
Net National Product . .	34,618	40,481	48,480
Depreciation allowance . .	1,305	1,760	2,375
Gross National Product . .	35,923	42,241	50,855
Balance of exports and imports . .	2,039	4,517	2,745
Net factor income from abroad . .	1,141	1,284	1,210
Available Resources . . .	39,103	48,042	54,810
of which:			
Private consumption expenditure .	25,581	30,906	36,420
Government consumption expenditure .	5,348	6,644	7,480
Fixed capital formation . . .	7,463	9,666	9,770
Increase in stocks . . .	711	826	1,140

* Provisional.

ECUADOR—(Statistical Survey)

COST OF LIVING INDICES

QUITO (Base: 1965=100)	1971	1972		GUAYAQUIL (Base: 1967=100)	1971	1972
Food and Drink . .	143.6	159.5		Food	123.5	135.3
Housing . . .	127.7	134.9		Housing . . .	125.5	134.0
Clothing . . .	134.9	143.5		Clothing . . .	135.3	144.8
Miscellaneous . .	132.2	138.0		Miscellaneous . .	118.1	120.8
GENERAL INDEX . .	136.6	147.4		GENERAL INDEX . .	124.0	133.2

Index based on low and medium income families. | Index based on a working class family.

CURRENCY AND RESERVES

	1969	1970	1971	1972
Total Currency in Circulation (million sucres) .	4,389.2	5,465.1	6,118.0	7,423.3
of which:				
Banknotes and coins . . .	1,702.5	2,271.9	2,341.6	2,817.6
Monetary deposits . . .	2,686.7	3,193.2	3,776.4	4,605.7
Total International Monetary Reserve (million U.S.$)	39.0	49.0	17.4	119.7
of which:				
Gold reserves	28.4	27.3	26.9	20.7
Currency reserves	10.6	21.7	—9.5	99.0

FOREIGN AID, INCLUDING PRIVATE LOANS
('000 U.S. dollars)

	1970	1971	1972
English Bond Holders	2,901	2,538	2,175
Eximbank	16,423	15,279	15,845
U.S. Government (AID) . . .	71,515	74,859	75,404
International Bank (IBRD) . . .	40,434	31,952	34,294
Interamerican Bank (IDB) . . .	45,103	52,680	58,787
Gregg d'Europe	140	—	—
Dutch Bank Consortium . . .	—	—	—
Coffee Federation of Colombia . .	180	135	90
Ciave	77	77	54
Telenorma	—	—	—
First National City Bank . . .	593	368	602
Ericsson	8,112	8,811	10,707
Pont-à-Mousson	1,117	644	—
Ferrostal	69	7	—
Miscellaneous Sources . . .	54,827	73,409	145,982
TOTAL	241,491	260,759	343,940

EXTERNAL TRADE
('000 U.S. dollars)

	1969	1970	1971	1972
Imports . . .	261,885	247,578	303,920	328,840
Exports . . .	151,886	201,477	217,023	301,489

PRINCIPAL COMMODITIES
('000 U.S. dollars)

IMPORTS	1970	1971	1972
Perishable Consumer Goods	22,027	30,745	36,202
Durable Consumer Goods	12,635	12,174	12,404
Fuels and Lubricants	18,785	23,070	23,152
Raw Materials and Agricultural Products	5,872	5,087	7,140
Raw Materials and Products for Industry	82,248	112,458	118,638
Building Materials	13,703	11,396	14,228
Capital Goods for Agriculture	5,024	4,687	5,280
Capital Goods for Industry	49,034	64,847	70,698
Transport Equipment	37,646	39,409	40,161
Miscellaneous	604	47	937

EXPORTS	1970	1971	1972
Balsa	2,920	3,318	3,787
Bananas	94,092	100,748	108,108
Cocoa	22,069	25,376	23,319
Coffee	50,516	36,494	42,600
Oilseeds	1,750	1,847	4,066
Pharmaceutical Products and Chemicals	1,423	1,748	2,490
Straw Hats	528	2,007	1,989
Molasses	740	699	299
Sugar	9,398	13,474	17,075
Fish Products	6,807	14,625	16,731
Others	11,234	16,687	81,025
TOTAL	201,477	217,023	301,489

PRINCIPAL COUNTRIES
('000 U.S. dollars)

	IMPORTS			EXPORTS		
	1970	1971	1972	1970	1971	1972
Argentina	1,947	1,494	3,011	3,421	4,183	3,145
Brazil	895	1,949	5,839	1,429	1,165	2,733
Canada	3,956	6,994	7,407	1,263	1,099	9,184
Chile	3,929	4,920	1,580	5,600	9,196	10,809
Colombia	18,471	22,487	20,696	4,978	7,173	10,504
Mexico	2,045	3,659	5,094	570	1,091	877
Peru	2,578	3,003	3,676	1,010	5,032	6,146
United States	80,791	103,558	99,152	87,541	85,610	113,097
Uruguay	66	124	92	9	50	26
Venezuela	5,584	8,551	15,149	76	107	80
Belgium and Luxembourg	3,589	4,672	3,452	6,678	8,793	8,626
France	8,381	4,370	6,661	3,401	2,294	3,395
Germany, Federal Republic	30,915	41,118	38,850	20,335	22,151	25,328
Italy	8,540	8,503	8,744	6,600	5,190	5,721
Netherlands	4,127	4,488	868	4,262	5,045	40
Spain	4,621	4,246	3,256	1,004	563	717
Sweden	5,950	7,304	8,114	581	653	545
Switzerland	3,483	5,679	7,863	347	299	413
United Kingdom	11,542	11,641	18,305	953	1,018	1,318
Japan	26,237	36,104	47,396	37,317	36,619	41,249

TRANSPORT

RAILWAYS

	PASSENGERS CARRIED	PASSENGER/ KILOMETRES	FREIGHT/ KILOMETRES
1969	3,439,620	60,090,110	53,135,381
1970	4,413,351	54,046,459	48,296,879
1971	1,704,987	34,118,146	46,671,407

ROADS

	1968	1969	1970
Cars	18,728	20,663	22,650
Pick-ups	14,465	16,088	20,779
Buses	4,900	5,109	5,298
Trucks	8,616	8,793	9,032
Jeeps	3,663	3,992	4,340
Others	280	1,183	1,333

SHIPPING

	1970	1971
Tonnage Entered . . .	1,521,204	1,840,864
Tonnage Cleared . . .	1,768,405	1,745,788

CIVIL AVIATION

PASSENGER MOVEMENT	1969	1970
Internal	278,312	347,157
International . . .	179,262	184,622

TOURISM

NUMBER OF VISITORS	
1967 . . .	41,117
1968 . . .	52,308
1969 . . .	54,960
1970 . . .	57,548

EDUCATION
(1970–71*)

TYPE	ESTABLISHMENTS	PUPILS	TEACHERS
Kindergarten . .	172	14,251	395
Primary . . .	7,779	1,023,690	26,496
Secondary . .	820	216,727	15,699
Higher inc. Universities	15	42,394	n.a.

* Provisional figures.

Source (unless otherwise stated): Banco Central del Ecuador.

THE CONSTITUTION

The Constitution of 1945 states that legislative power is vested in Congress, which is composed of two chambers. They assemble twice a year for a period of sixty days. Members of the Senate are elected for a four-year term, and may be re-elected. There are two senators for each province and one for the Archipelago of Colón. In addition, fifteen "functional" senators are designated by bodies representative of educational institutions, learned societies, the Press, the armed forces; and by labour, industry, agriculture and commerce, in the *sierra* and in the *litoral*.

The Chamber of Deputies has seventy-two members elected for a two-year term. Members are eligible for re-election.

In addition to its law-making duties, Congress supervises the administration and expenditure of the national revenues; ratifies treaties; elects members of the Supreme and Superior Courts; and, from panels presented by the President, the Comptroller-General, the Attorney-General and the Superintendent of Banks. It is also able to over-rule the President's amendment or rejection of a bill which it has submitted to him for his approval, and may grant or refuse the allocation of extraordinary powers to the President.

The presidential term is four years. An ex-President may be re-elected only after four years have elapsed from the date of his terminating office. The President appoints his own cabinet, the governors of provinces, diplomatic representatives and certain administrative employees, and is responsible for the direction of international relations. In the event of foreign invasion or internal disturbance, extraordinary powers may be given him by Congress, or by the Council of State if Congress is not in session.

The Constitution also provides for a Legislative Committee, consisting of nine members, to draw up bills (with the exception of those dealing with economic questions), and codify and edit laws.

As in other post-war Latin-American Constitutions, particular emphasis is laid on the functions and duties of the State, which is given wide responsibilities with regard to the protection of labour; assisting in the expansion of production; protecting the Indian and peasant communities; and organizing the distribution and development of uncultivated lands, by expropriation where necessary.

Every Ecuadorean citizen, male or female, who is literate and over 18 years of age, may vote. Voting is compulsory for all citizens. The Constitution guarantees liberty of conscience in all its manifestations, and states that the law shall not make any discrimination for religious reasons.

THE GOVERNMENT

HEAD OF STATE

President: Gen. GUILLERMO RODRÍGUEZ LARA.

THE CABINET
(*March* 1974)

Minister of the Interior: Rear-Adm. ALFREDO POVEDA BURBANO.

Minister of Foreign Affairs: Dr. ANTONIO LUCIO PAREDES.

Minister of Education: Col. LUIS GUILLERMO DURÁN ARCENTALES.

Minister of Defence: Gen. MARCO ALMEIDA JÁTIVA.

Minister of Public Works: Col. RAFAEL RODRÍGUEZ PALACIOS.

Minister of Natural Resources and Energy: Naval Capt. GUSTAVO JARRÍN AMPUDIA.

Minister of Labour and Social Welfare: Dr. RAMIRO LARREA SANTOS.

Minister of Finance: Econ. JAIME MONCAYO GARCÍA.

Minister of Health: Col. Dr. RAÚL MALDONADO MEJÍA.

Minister of Production: Dr. GUILLERMO MALDONADO LINCE.

Secretary-General of the Administration: Col. CARLOS AGUIRRE AZANZA.

DIPLOMATIC REPRESENTATION

EMBASSIES AND LEGATION ACCREDITED TO ECUADOR
(In Quito unless otherwise stated)

(E) Embassy; (L) Legation.

Argentina: Avda. Colón 716 (E); *Chargé d'Affaires a.i.:* ALBERTO FRAVEGA ROYGT.

Austria: Bogotá, Colombia (E).

Belgium: La Gasca y Carvajal (E); *Ambassador:* EMILE LEEMANS.

Bolivia: Avda. 12 de Octubre 186, 3° piso (E); *Ambassador:* Dr. RAÚL LEMA PELAEZ.

Brazil: Caamaño 130 (E); *Ambassador:* VASCO MARIZ.

Bulgaria: Santiago, Chile (E).

Canada: Calle 58 No. 10-42 (E); *Ambassador:* SIDNEY ALLAN FREIFIELD.

Chile: Avda. 18 de Septiembre 413 y Avda. Amazonas, 3° piso (E); *Ambassador:* Gen. PABLO SCHAFFHAUSER.

Colombia: Calle Tarqui 319 (E); *Ambassador:* DARÍO ARANGO TAMAYO.

Costa Rica: Avda. Orellana 571 (E); *Chargé d'Affaires:* LUZ CALDERÓN DE AGUILAR.

Czechoslovakia: Calle General Salazar 958 y Avda. 12 de Octubre (E); *Ambassador:* BEDŘICH PISTORA.

Denmark: Bogotá, Colombia (E).

Dominican Republic: San Javier 412 (E); *Ambassador:* RODOLFO LEYBA POLANCO.

Egypt: Avda. Orellana 380 (E); *Chargé d'Affaires:* ADEL IBRAHIM KHEIR ELDINE.

El Salvador: San Ignacio 418 y Coruña (E); *Ambassador:* HÉCTOR PALOMO SALAZAR.

Finland: Lima, Peru (E).

France: Plaza 107, esq. Patria (E); *Ambassador:* PIERRE BARBUSSE.

German Democratic Republic: (E); *Chargé d'Affaires:* PETER GLEINIG.

Germany, Federal Republic: Avda. Patria y 9 de Octubre (E); *Ambassador:* WALTER WEBER.

Greece: Rio de Janeiro, Brazil (E).

Guatemala: Calle Ayarza 494 (E); *Ambassador:* RAFAEL AGUILAR SPÍNOLA.

Honduras: Calle Murgeón 518 (E); *Ambassador:* Dr. EFRAIN PONCE TEJADA.

Hungary: Brasília, Brazil.

India: Santiago, Chile (E).

Israel: James Orton 257 (E); *Ambassador:* ITZHAK SHEFI.

Italy: Calle La Isla 111 (E); *Ambassador:* GASTONE ADORNI BRACESSI.

Japan: Calle Checoslovaquia 136 y Avda. Eloy Alfaro (E); *Ambassador:* HIROSHI YOKOTA.

Korea, Republic: Santiago, Chile (E).

Lebanon: Bogotá, Colombia (L).

Malta: Apdo. 211 (E); *Ambassador:* JOSÉ MANUEL JIJÓN-CAAMAÑO Y FLORES.

Mexico: Avda. 6 de Diciembre 2101 (E); *Ambassador:* PLUTARCO ALBARRÁN LÓPEZ.

Netherlands: Avda. 10 de Agosto 1855, 4° piso, Apto. 1 (E); *Ambassador:* JACOB VAREKAMP.

Nicaragua: Isabel la Católica 331 (E); *Ambassador:* Dr. ALFONSO ORTEGA URBINA.

Norway: Caracas, Venezuela (E).

Panama: Calle San Javier 185 (E); *Chargé d'Affaires a.i.:* ROBERTO SAMUEL FÁBREGA COYTIA.

Paraguay: Pasaje Urrutia 181 (E); *Ambassador:* JULIO PEÑA DEL MOLINO TORRE.

Peru: Avda. Colón 951 (E); *Ambassador:* Dr. JORGE MORELLI PANDO.

Poland: Avda. 6 de Diciembre 1625 (E); *Ambassador:* ZDZISLAW SZEWCZYK.

Portugal: Calle Tamayo 1376 (E); *Ambassador:* Dr. JULIO MENINO SALCEDAS.

Romania: Avda. República del Salvador 482 (E); *Ambassador:* DIMITRY MOIANO.

Spain: Veintimilla 1074 (E); *Ambassador:* Dr. JORGE TABERNA LATASA.

Sweden: Avda. 10 de Agosto 1865 (E); *Ambassador:* INGVAR ANDERS HARALD GRAUERS.

Switzerland: Río de Janeiro 130, 10° (E); *Ambassador:* ETIENNE SERRA.

Syria: Rio de Janeiro, Brazil (E).

Turkey: Caracas, Venezuela (E).

U.S.S.R.: Reina Victoria 462 y Roca (E); *Ambassador:* IVAN IVANOVICH MARTCHOUK.

United Kingdom: González Suárez 111 (E); *Ambassador:* PETER MENNELL.

U.S.A.: Avda. Patria 120 (E); *Ambassador:* ROBERT C. BREWSTER.

Uruguay: Avda. 12 de Octubre 1962 (E); *Ambassador:* FERNANDO RIVERA DEVOTO.

Vatican: Avda. América 1830 (Apostolic Nunciature); *Nuncio:* Mgr. LUIS ACCOGLI.

Venezuela: Plaza 1067 y Baquerizo (E); *Ambassador:* SANTIAGO OCHOA BRICEÑO.

Yugoslavia: Caracas, Venezuela (L).

Ecuador also has diplomatic relations with Algeria, Ethiopia, Luxembourg, Morocco, the Philippines and Trinidad and Tobago.

CONGRESS

Congress was dissolved in June, 1970.

POLITICAL PARTIES

Federación Nacional Velasquista (FNV): the Independent Party which won the 1968 elections, led by former President Dr. JOSÉ MARÍA VELASCO IBARRA (in exile).

Acción Revolucionaria Nacional Ecuatoriana (ARNE): Nationalist-Rightist Party, supports the Roman Catholic Church; Leader JORGE CRESPO TORAL.

Partido Radical Liberal: held office from 1895 to 1944 as the Liberal Party which subsequently divided into various factions. The Liberal-Radical Party carries on the traditions of the old party.

Movimiento Social Cristiano: Conservative Party; Leader ex-President Dr. CAMILO PONCE ENRÍQUEZ.

Partido Socialista Ecuatoriano: Edif. Bolívar, Apdo. 103, Quito; f. 1933; 55,000 mems.; Sec. Dr. GONZALO OLEAS ZAMBRANO.

Partido Conservador: Traditional Rightist party; Dir. FRANCISCO SALAZAR-ALVARADO.

Coalición Institucionalista Democrática: Founder and Pres. Dr. OTTO AROSEMENA GÓMEZ.

JUDICIAL SYSTEM

Supreme Court of Justice: Quito; Pres. Dr. BENJAMÍN CEVALLOS A.; 15 Judges and 2 Fiscals.

Higher of Divisional Courts: Ambato, Cuenca, Guayaquil, Ibarra, Loja, Portoviejo, Quito, Riobamba, El Oro, Latacunga and Esmeraldas; 44 judges.

Provincial Courts: in 15 towns; 35 Criminal, 42 Provincial, 87 Cantonal, 445 Parochial Judges.

Special Courts: for juveniles and for labour disputes.

RELIGION

There is no state religion. Roman Catholicism is accepted by the majority and strongly supported by the Conservative Party.

Metropolitan Sees:

Quito: Cardinal PAULO MUÑOZ VEGA, Arzobispado, Apdo. 106, Quito.

Suffragan Sees: Riobamba, Ibarra, Ambato, Guaranda, Latacunga, Tulcan.

Guayaquil: Mgr. BERNARDINO ECHEVERRÍA RUIZ, Ballén 501 y Chimborazo, Casilla 254, Guayaquil.

Suffragan See: Portoviejo; *Prelature:* Los Ríos.

Cuenca: Mgr. ERNESTO ALVAREZ.

Suffragan See: Loja; *Prelature:* El Oro.

Vicariates Apostolic: Méndez, Napo, Zamora, Esmeraldas, Canelos.

Prefectures Apostolic: San Miguel de Sucumbíos, Aguarico, Galápagos.

THE PRESS

PRINCIPAL DAILIES

QUITO

El Comercio: Apdo. 57; f. 1906; morning; commercial; independent; Dir. CARLOS MANTILLA ORTEGA; Proprs. Compañía Anónima El Comercio; circ. 60,000.

Gaceta Judicial: f. 1895; organ of the Supreme Court of Justice; Dir. ARTURO GARCÍA.

Registro Oficial: f. 1830; official gazette; announcements of laws and decrees; Dir. (vacant).

El Tiempo: Calle Gareig Moreno 626; f. 1965; morning; Dir. CARLOS DE LA TORRE R.; circ. 25,000.

Ultimas Noticias: Apdo. 57; f. 1937; evening; independent; commercial; Proprs. Compañía Anónima El Comercio; Dir. CARLOS MANTILLA O.; circ. 35,000.

GUAYAQUIL

La Prensa: Boyacá y 9 de Octubre, Apdo. 78; f. 1923; evening; Liberal; commercial; Dir. MIGUEL ULLOA FIGUEROA; circ. 10,000.

La Razón: Apdo. 5832; evening; liberal; Dir. JORGE PÉREZ CONCHA.

El Telégrafo: Avda. 10 de Agosto 601; f. 1884; morning; liberal; commercial; Proprs. El Telégrafo C.A.; Dir. Gen. EDUARDO AROSEMENA G.; circ. 25,000 (weekdays), 33,500 (Sundays).

El Universo: Apdo. 531; f. 1921; morning; independent; Dir. SUCRE PÉREZ CASTRO; circ. 90,000 (weekdays), 105,000 (Sundays).

AMBATO

El Heraldo: Propr. Obispado de Ambato; Dir. Dr. TANQUINO TORO NAVAS.

BAHÍA DE CARAQUEZ

El Globo: f. 1911; Propr. Empresa El Globo; morning; Dir. Dr. ALBERTO PALAU J.; circ. 8,000.

CUENCA

El Mercurio: Paguirre 161; f. 1924; morning; commercial, independent; Dir. Ing. MIGUEL MERCHÁN; circ. 7,000 (weekdays), 9,000 (Sundays).

El Tiempo: Casilla 4909; f. 1956; Dir. HUMBERTO TORAL.

MACHALA

El Nacional: f. 1964; Dir. RODOLFO VEINTIMILLA.

PORTOVIEJO

Diario Manabita: f. 1934; morning; Dir. PEDRO E. ZAMBRANO; circ. 5,000.

PERIODICALS

QUITO

América: Casilla 75; f. 1925; Indo-American culture; quarterly; Dirs. HUGO MONCAYO, DARÍO GUEVARA.

Boletín Cultural del Ministerio de Relaciones Exteriores: f. 1945; monthly.

La Calle: weekly; Editor ALEJANDRO CARRIÓN.

Comercio Ecuatoriano: Calle Guayaquil 1242, Apdo. 202; commerce.

El Ecuador Comercial: Bolívar 25; f. 1923; commerce, agriculture, industry, finance; monthly.

Ecuador Guía Turística: Edif. Brauer, Meja 438, Of. 43;. f. 1969; tourist information in Spanish and English; Dir. JORGE VACA O.; Propr. Prensa Informativa Turística; circ. 30,000.

La Industria: f. 1952; Dir. FERNANDO MERA.

Letras del Ecuador: Casa de la Cultural Ecuatoriana, Parque de Mayo, Casilla 67; f. 1944; literature and art; non-political; monthly; Dir. EDMUNDO RIBADENEIRA.

El Profesional: Calle Oriente 725; f. 1972; monthly; university and professional interest; independent; Dir. WILSON ALMEIDA MUÑOZ; Man. JULIO ALMEIDA; circ. 3,000.

Sábado: f. 1963; weekly; Dir. J. J. PAZ Y MIÑO.

GUAYAQUIL

Boletín del Sindicato Médico: f. 1911; scientific, literary; independent; monthly.

Ecuador Ilustrado: f. 1924; literary; illustrated; monthly.

Estadio: Apdo. 1239; fortnightly; sport; Dir. GUILLERMO VALENCÍA LEÓN; circ. 40,000.

Hogar: monthly; Dir. ROSA AMELIA ALVARADO R.; circ. 25,000.

Letras y Números: 9 de Octubre 218; f. 1921; literary; independent; monthly.

El Libertador: f. 1928; literary, political; weekly.

Nuevo Suceso: f. 1961; monthly; Dir. EDUARDO CARRIÓN.

Revista de las Fuerzas Armadas: f. 1939; monthly; Dir. Lt.-Col. JOSÉ M. FRECHON S.

Siete Días: bi-weekly.

Vistazo: Aguirre 730, Apdo. 1239; f. 1957; monthly; Dir. XAVIER ALVARADO ROCA; circ. 70,000.

CUENCA

La Alianza Obrera: Apdo. 128; f. 1905; political, informative; bi-weekly.

En Marcha: Apdo. 66; monthly.

ESMERALDAS

El Clarín: f. 1961; Dir. PEDRO MALDONADO.

El Correo: Bolívar 3; f. 1928; commercial, literary; independent; bi-weekly.

El Independiente: f. 1964; Dir. HUMBERTO ORTIZ.

LOJA

Bloque: Apdo. 4; f. 1935; leftist; quarterly.

La Verdad: f. 1963; Dir. Col. GILBERTO ABARCA S.

MANABI

El Demócrata: f. 1962; Dir. GONZALO ZABALA R.

El Globo: f. 1911; Dir. ALBERTO PALAU J.

El Oriente: Sucre y Chile; f. 1914; commercial; independent; bi-weekly.

PRESS AGENCIES

FOREIGN BUREAUX

Agenzia Nazionale Stampa Associata (ANSA): Casilla 2748, Quito; Chief SANTIAGO JERVIS.

Tass also has a bureau in Ecuador.

PUBLISHERS

Artes Gráficas Ltda.: Apdo. 533, Quito.

Editorial Ecuatoriana de la Prensa Católica: Benalcazar 478 (Plaza San Francisco), Quito.

Editorial de la Casa de la Cultura Ecuatoriana: Avda. 6 de Diciembre 332, Apdo. 67, Quito; general, art, law, sociology, fiction, medicine; Man. Dir. JOSÉ FELIX SILVA.

Universidad de Guayaquil: Departamento de Publicaciones, Apdo. 3834, Guayaquil; f. 1930; general literature; Dir. C. VINUEZA.

RADIO AND TELEVISION

Asociación Ecuatoriana de Radiodifusión: Luis Felipe Borja 505, Apdo. 2246, Quito; independent non-governmental association of radio stations; Pres. E. CEVALLOS C.

Instituto Ecuatoriano de Telecomunicaciones: Casilla 3066, Quito; Gen. Man. HERNÁN CASTAÑEDA.

RADIO

There are 229 commercial stations, two cultural stations and one religious (La Voz de los Andes). The following are the most important commercial stations:

Emisoras Gran Colombia: Casilla 2246, Quito; f. 1943; Dir. E. CEVALLOS C.

Radio Casa de la Cultura: Latacunga; Dir. L. BARRIGA L.

Radio Tropicana: Avda. Boyacá 1616, Apdo. 4144, Guayaquil; Dir. R. GUERRERO.

Radiodifusora del Ecuador: Avda. Boyacá 1616, Apdo. 4144, Guayaquil; Dir. R. GUERRERO.

La Voz de la Democracia: Guayaquil 1524, Apdo. 288, Quito; Dir. EDUARDO CEVALLOS CASTAÑEDA.

La Voz de los Andes: HCJB, Casilla 691, Quito; f. 1931; programmes in thirteen languages including Spanish, English and Quechua; Pres. ABE C. VAN DER PUY; Dir. of Broadcasting THOMAS D. FULGHUM.

There were 225,000 receivers in 1971.

TELEVISION

Corporación Ecuatoriana de Televisión: Casilla 1239, Guayaquil; commercial; Man. XAVIER ALVARADO.

Telecuador: Casilla 5902, Guayaquil; Casilla 70, Quito; the country's first commercial station began operations in 1960; Dir.-Gen. P. NORTON.

Telesistema del Ecuador: Casilla 6534, Guayaquil; commercial; Dir.-Gen. P. NORTON.

La Ventana de los Andes: Casilla 691, Quito; private, non-commercial, cultural; Dir. D. C. PETERS.

There were 115,000 television sets in 1973.

FINANCE

(cap.=capital; p.u.=paid up; dep.=deposits; m.=million, amounts in sucres.)

BANKING

Banks came under government control in June, 1970.

Superintendent of Banks: Dr. Gonzalo Córdova Galarza

Central Bank

Banco Central del Ecuador: Avda. 10 de Agosto, Plaza Bolívar, Quito; f. 1927; cap. 47.6m., dep. 3,472.4m. (Dec. 1972); Pres. Ing. Jaime Morillo Battle; Gen. Man. Germánico Espinosa Zambrano.

Commercial Banks

Quito

Banco de Co-operativas del Ecuador: Avda. 10 de Agosto 937; f. 1964; cap. and dep. 20m.; Gen. Man. J. Campuzano.

Banco Nacional de Fomento: Calle Ante 107 y Avda. 10 de Agosto 321, Apdo. 685; f. 1944; Gen. Man. Dr. Carlos Camacho Saá; 48 brs.

Banco del Pichincha S.A.: Casilla 261; f. 1906; Pres. Gonzalo Mantilla M.; Gen. Man. Jaime Acosta V.

Banco de Préstamos, S.A.: Venezuela 659; f. 1909; cap. 24m., dep. 151.2m. (Dec. 1971); Pres. Col. Carlos Flores Guerra; Gen. Man. Dr. Alfredo Albornoz Sánchez.

Cuenca

Banco de Azuay, C.A.: Casilla 33; f. 1913; cap. p.u. 10m., dep. 121.9m. (Dec. 1970); Man. Hernán Borrero V.

Guayaquil

Banco de Descuento: esq. Pichincha y Aguirre, Apdo. 414; f. 1920; cap. 14m., res. 67m. (Dec. 1973); Pres. Antonio Pino Ycaza; Gen. Man. Gonzalo Ycaza Cornejo.

Banco la Filantrópica: Luque 119-21; f. 1908; cap. and res. 106m., dep. 1,200m. (Dec. 1973); Gen. Man. Nahim A. Isaias.

Banco de Guayaquil: Apdo. 1300; f. 1923; cap. 116m., dep. 109m. (Dec. 1970); Pres. Rafael Dillon V.; Gen. Man. Carlos Baquerizo Sotomayor.

La Previsora Banco Nacional de Crédito: Avda. 9 de Octubre 110, Apdo. 44; f. 1920; cap. and res. 160m., dep. 1,900m.; Gen. Man. Rodrigo Ycaza.

Foreign Banks

Bank of America: New York; Quito Office: Calle Guayaquil y Elizalde.

Bank of London and Montreal Ltd.: Nassau, Bahamas; Guayaquil: Calle Pichincha 108-110; Quito: Calle Chile esq. Guayaquil; Man. R. A. Fairhurst.

First National City Bank: New York; Guayaquil: Pichincha 412, Apdo. 5885; Quito: Venezuela 1000 y Mejía, Apdo. 1393.

Hollandsche Bank-Unie N.V.: Amsterdam; Guayaquil office (Banco Holandés Unido): Casilla 5830; Quito office: Avda. 10 de Agosto 911, Casilla 42; Man. C. Groen.

Development Bank

Ecuatoriana de Desarrollo S.A., COFIEC: Quito; f. 1965; authorized cap. 72m., subscribed 65m. (Dec. 1971).

Finance Corporation

Corporación Financiera Ecuatoriana: Avda. 10 de Agosto 1564, Quito; private finance corporation; office in Guayaquil.

INSURANCE

National Companies

Instituto Ecuatoriano de Seguridad Social: Apdo. 2640, Quito; f. 1936; various forms of State insurance provided. The Institute directs the Ecuadorean social insurance system through the Insurance Board (Caja Nacional del Seguro Social) and the Medical Department (Departamento Médico).

Anglo Ecuatoriana de Guayaquil C. Ltda.: Apdo. 57, Guayaquil; f. 1966; cap. p.u. 2m.

Anglo Equatoriana de Quito C. Ltda.: Apdo. 2, Quito; f. 1966; cap. and res. 4,498,600; Pres. John P. Wynne; Gen. Man. Augusto Cordovez.

"Bolívar", Compañía de Seguros del Ecuador, S.A.: Edificio Sud América, Malecón y Simón Bolívar 1401, Apdo. 1047, Guayaquil; f. 1958; Man. Luis A. Carbo Arosemena.

S.A. Comercial Anglo-Ecuatoriana: Apdo. 410, Guayaquil; f. 1916; cap. p.u. 15m.; subsidiary of Lloyds Bank International.

Compañía Ecuatoriana de Seguros, S.A.: Pedro Carbo 632 y Aguirre, Apdo. 3660, Guayaquil; f. 1942; Exec. Pres. Dr. Otto Arosemena Gómez; Gen. Man. Rodrigo Ycaza Candel.

Compañía de Seguros Ecuatoriana-Suiza, S.A.: Calle Fco. de P. Ycaza 203, Apdo. 397, Guayaquil; f. 1954; cap. and res. 9m.; Apdo. 2318, Quito; Man. Econ. Enrique Salas; Sub-Man. Fritz Gfeller.

Huancavilca, Compañía Nacional de Seguros: Avda. 9 de Octubre y Pichincha, Guayaquil; f. 1961; Mans. G. Santos Alcivar, C. Donoso Varas.

"La Nacional", Compañía de Seguros Generales, S.A.: Panamá 809 y V.M. Rendón, Guayaquil; f. 1942; cap. p.u. 5.5m.; Man. Enrique Novás Argudin.

Panamericana, Compañía de Seguros: Apdo. 214, Quito; Man. A. Fabara F.

Sucre, Compañía Nacional de Seguros, S.A.: Pichincha 108, 2° piso, Apdo. 410, Guayaquil; Man. Luis F. Cornejo.

"La Unión", Compañía Nacional de Seguros: Calle Malecón y General Franco, Apdo. 1294, Guayaquil; Man. F. L. Goldbaum.

TRADE AND INDUSTRY

CHAMBERS OF COMMERCE

Quito

Cámara de Comercio de Quito (*Quito Chamber of Commerce*): Guayaquil 1242, Apdo. 202; f. 1923; 1,900 mems.; Pres. Jaime Ponce Yepes.

Guayaquil

Cámara de Comercio de Guayaquil (*Guayaquil Chamber of Commerce*): Avda. Olmedo 414, Casilla de Correo Y; f. 1889; 3,363 mems.; Pres. Benjamín Rosales Aspiazu; First Vice-Pres. José Plaza Luque; Second Vice-Pres. Holbach Pérez Febres Cordero; Sec. Antonio Arosemena Gómez-Lince.

Chambers of Commerce are also established in: Cuenca, Tulcán, Ibarra, Santa Rosa, Latacunga, Ambato, Guaranda, Riobamba, Azogues, Loja, Babahoyo, Machala, Zaruma, Portoviejo, Manta, Bahía de Caraquez, Jipijapa, Esmeraldas, Chone and Milagro.

TRADE UNIONS

Confederación Ecuatoriana de Organizaciones Clasistas— CEDOC: Calle Flores 846, Quito; f. 1938; affiliated to CMT; 80,000 mems. (est.) organized in 15 area organizations; Pres. JACINTO FIGUEROA VERA; Sec.-Gen. CARLOS AROCA.

Confederación Ecuatoriana de Organizaciones Sindicales Libres (C.E.O.S.L.): García Moreno 1244, Quito; f. 1962. affiliated with CIOSL and Organización Regional Interamericana de Trabajadores; Pres. A. CONTRERAS ZÚÑIGA; Sec.-Gen. JAIME HIDALGO FLORES.

Confederación Obrera del Guayas—COG (*Labour Confederation of Guayas*): Calle Quito 710, Apdo. 5501, Guayaquil; f. 1904; admitted to ICFTU/ORIT; 1,000 mems. (est.) in 4 affiliated unions; Pres. LUIS ENRIQUE PÉREZ JURADO; Sec.-Gen. MARCO ALEJANDRO MONTES DE OCA DÍAZ.

Confederación de Trabajadores del Ecuador—CTE (*Confederation of Ecuadorian Workers*): Casa del Obrero, Plaza del Teatro, Manabí 267, Quito; f. 1944; admitted to WFTU and CTAL; 55,000 mems. (est.) in 200 affiliated unions; Pres. LEONIDAS CÓRDOVA.

A number of trade unions are not affiliated to the above groups. These include the Federación Nacional de Trabajadores Marítimos y Portuarios del Ecuador—FNTMPE (*National Federation of Maritime and Port Workers of Ecuador*) and both railway trade unions.

DEVELOPMENT ORGANIZATIONS

Corporación Estatal Petrolera Ecuatoriana (Cepe) (*Ecuadorian State Petroleum Corporation*): Avda. Orellana y Puerto de Palos, Casillas 5007/8, Quito; f. 1972; aims to promote exploration for and exploitation of petrol and natural gas deposits by initiating joint ventures with foreign and national companies; to promote the transport and processing of oil, gas and allied products; to act as the agency controlling the concession of on- and off-shore exploration rights; 1973 budget 94m.; Gen. Man. Col. RENÉ VARGAS PAZOS; Dir. of Refining Dr. LEONARD ESTUPIÑÁN; Dir. of Production Ing. ENRIQUE PÉREZ; Dir. of Commerce and Transport Ing. RAÚL TERÁN KING; Dir. of Finance Econ. RAÚL SAGASTI; Dir. of Industrial Relations ARTURO PEÑAHERRERA; Gen. Sec. Lic. RAÚL DE LA TORRE.

Corporación de Fomento del Norte Ecuatoriano— CORFONOR: Bolívar 62-4, Ibarra; f. 1967; semi-state organization responsible for co-ordinating regional development plans with the General Social Development Plan and the Programmes of Frontier Integration with Colombia; 40 mems.; cap. 8.4m.; Pres. and Gen. Man. Lic. RODRIGO SUÁREZ MORALES.

Instituto Ecuatoriano de Electrificación (INECEL): f. 1961; state enterprise for the generation, transmission and distribution of electrical energy; current plans (until 1980) involve investment of U.S. $825m.; Dir. Ing. NICOLÁS ROMERO SANGSTER.

Instituto Ecuatoriano de Recursos Hidráulicos: undertakes irrigation and hydroelectric projects.

Instituto Ecuatoriano de Reforma Agraria y Colonización (IERAC): f. 1973 to supervise the Agrarian Reform Law under the auspices and co-ordination of the Ministry of Agriculture.

Junta Nacional de Planificación y Coordinación: Quito; aims to formulate a general plan of economic and social development and supervise its execution; also to integrate local plans into the national.

TRANSPORT AND TOURISM

TRANSPORT

RAILWAYS

All railways are government-controlled. Extensive construction work is being undertaken.

Empresa de los Ferrocarriles del Estado Ecuatoriano: Carrera Bolívar 443, Quito. Total length 1,071 km.

Divisional Boards:

Guayaquil-Quito Railway: Apdo. 159, Quito; f. 1871, came into operation 1908; 425 km. of 1,067 mm. gauge; Gen. Man. Ing. MARCELO SAA CHACÓN.

Quito-San Lorenzo Railway: 373 km. of 1,067 mm. gauge; administered by Junta Autónoma del Ferrocarril del Norte.

Sibambe-Cuenca Railway: 116 km. of 1,067 mm. gauge; Superintendent WILSON IBARRA.

El Oro Railway: 100 km. of 750 mm. and 1,067 mm. gauge; Gen. Man. JULIO CUSTODE.

ROADS

The Pan-American Highway runs north from Ambato to Quito and to the Colombian border at Tulcán and south to Cuenca and Loja. Highways in Ecuador total 18,345 km.

Fondo Nacional de Carreteras: Quito; f. 1964; Government agency to co-ordinate highway reconstruction.

SHIPPING

Anglo-Ecuadorian Oilfields Ltd.: Casilla 634, Quito; Chair. N. J. D. WILLIAMS; Gen. Man. (Trading Div.) J. E. COLOMA; Gen. Man. (Oriente Div.) E. TRAFFORD; coastal transport (tankers).

Flota Mercante Grancolombiana, S.A.: Apdo. 3714, Guayaquil; f. 1946 with Colombia and Venezuela. On Venezuela's withdrawal in 1953, Ecuador's 10 per cent interest was increased to 20 per cent. The fleet consists of 35 vessels (27 owned by it and 8 chartered) of a total gross tonnage of 250,000. It operates services from Colombia and Ecuador to European ports, U.S. Gulf ports and New York, Mexican Atlantic ports and East Canada; Man. Naval Capt. J. ALBERTO SÁNCHEZ; offices in Quito, Cuenca, Bahía, Manta and Esmeraldas.

Flota Bananera Ecuatoriana, S.A.: Edif. Gran Pasaje, 6° piso, Of. 602, Apdo. 6883, Guayaquil; f. 1967; 2 vessels; owned by Government of Ecuador and private stockholders; Gen. Man. HÉCTOR ESPINEL; Sub.-Man. ROBERTO SERRANO.

Flota Bananera Franco-Ecuatoriana: f. 1966; purchases and ships bananas to Europe; 6 ships; capital provided by Swiss Conficomex 50 per cent, Federación de Bananeros 35 per cent, Government 15 per cent.

Transnave: controlled by the navy; will eventually transport the bulk of Ecuador's crude oil destined for export markets.

Small shipping firms in Ecuador operate coastal services to Panama and Peru.

CIVIL AVIATION

DOMESTIC AIRLINES

Aerolíneas Nacionales del Ecuador, S.A.—ANDES: Aeropuerto Simón Bolívar, Apdo. 4113, Guayaquil; regular cargo services Miami–Panama–Quito, Guayaquil; Pres. CÉSAR ENDARA; fleet: 4 DC-6A, 1 DC-3, 1 C-46.

Compañia Ecuatoriana de Aviación S.A.—CEA: Calle Guayaquil esq. Chile, Apdo. 505, Quito; scheduled passenger and cargo service to Miami, Mexico, Panama, Cali, Guayaquil, Lima and Santiago; fleet: 3 Electras L-188, 4 DC-6, 1 DC-4, 1 B-23; Pres. Marco T. González; Gen. Man. Col. Gonzalo Fernández.

Transportes Aéreos Militares Ecuatorianos—TAME: Avda. 10 de Agosto 239, Apdo. 2665, Quito; br. in Guayaquil; f. 1962; domestic scheduled services for passengers and freight; Gen. Man. Lt.-Col. Iván Puyol M.; fleet: 4 DC-6B, 2 HS748, 4 DC-3.

Foreign Airlines

Ecuador is also served by the following foreign airlines: Air France, Air Panama, Avianca (Colombia), Braniff, Iberia, KLM, LAN de Chile, Lufthansa.

TOURISM

Asociación Ecuatoriana de Agencias de Viaje y Turismo—ASECUT: Apdo. 1210, Quito; Apdo. 510, Guayaquil; Pres. Armando Espinel Elizalde.

Dirección Nacional de Turismo: Ministerio de Industrias, Comercio e Integración, Apdo. 2454, Quito; f. 1964; Dir. Jorge Gortaire.

CULTURAL ORGANIZATION

Casa de la Cultura Ecuatoriana: Avda. 6 de Diciembre, Apdo. 67, Quito; permanent exhibitions; Dir. Dr. Eduardo Mora Moreno; Sec.-Gen. Lic. Carlos Manuel Arizaga.

ATOMIC ENERGY

Comisión Ecuatoriana de Energía Atómica: Escuela Politécnica Nacional, Apdo. 2759, Quito; Dir. Ing. J. Ruben Orellana R.; research in nuclear physics, radio-isotopes, radio-biology, chemistry and medicine.

UNIVERSITIES

Pontificia Universidad Católica del Ecuador: Avda. 12 de Octubre 1076 y Carrión, Apdo. 2184, Quito; 150 teachers, 3,500 students.

Universidad Central del Ecuador: Ciudadela Universitaria, Quito; 920 teachers, 25,000 students.

Universidad de Cuenca: Apdo. 168, Cuenca; 182 teachers, 2,025 students.

Universidad de Guayaquil: Calle Chile 900, Apdo. 471, Guayaquil; 447 teachers, 4,539 students.

Universidad Nacional de Loja: Casilla Letra "S", Loja; 115 teachers, 1,103 students.

Universidad Católica de Santiago de Guayaquil: Casilla 4671, Guayaquil; 250 teachers, 2,000 students.

Universidad Técnica de Manabí: Casilla 82, Portoviejo, Manabí; 63 teachers, 393 students.

EGYPT

INTRODUCTORY SURVEY

Location, Climate, Language, Religion, Flag, Capital

The Arab Republic of Egypt occupies the north-eastern corner of Africa, with an extension across the Gulf of Suez into the Sinai region which is usually regarded as lying in Asia. It is bounded to the north by the Mediterranean, to the north-east by Israel, to the east by the Red Sea, to the south by the Sudan, and to the west by Libya. (From June 1967 until October 1973 the *de facto* frontier with Israel was the Suez Canal. After the October 1973 war with Israel, agreement was reached that Israeli forces should hold a line about 13 miles east of the canal, separated from Egyptian forces by a UN buffer zone approximately 6 miles wide. Israel continues to occupy the Sinai peninsula, which she has held since June 1967.) The River Nile runs through the country from south to north into the Mediterranean Sea. The climate is arid, with a maximum annual rainfall of only eight inches around Alexandria. More than ninety per cent of the country is desert. Summer temperatures reach a maximum of 43°C (110°F) and winters are mild. Arabic is the official language. Many educated Egyptians speak English or French. Over 90 per cent of the population are Muslims. The remainder are mainly Christians, over a million of whom are Copts. The national flag (proportions 3 by 2) is a horizontal tricolour of red, white, and black; the white stripe is charged with two five-pointed green stars. The capital is Cairo.

Recent History

In July 1952 a group of young army officers, the "Free Officers", seized power in Cairo. King Farouk was forced to abdicate and Gen. Muhammed Neguib installed as head of the military junta. Egypt was declared a republic the following June, when Neguib became President and Prime Minister, and Col. Gamal Abdel Nasser, who was leader of the Free Officers, Deputy Prime Minister. In November 1954 Neguib was relieved of his posts, and Nasser took over as acting head of state.

In October 1954 Britain and Egypt reached agreement on the Suez Canal, when provision was made for the withdrawal of British troops. In June 1956 a new constitution was approved by the people and Nasser elected President. The following month, after Britain and the U.S.A. had withdrawn their offers of finance for the Aswan High Dam, Nasser announced the nationalization of the Suez Canal Company, so that Canal revenues could be used to finance the Dam. This was a cause of great concern to Israel, Britain and France, and Israel invaded Sinai on October 29th while Britain and France began operations against Egypt two days later. Strong UN and American pressure resulted in a ceasefire on November 6th and supervision by the UN of the invaders' withdrawal.

Egypt and Syria formed the United Arab Republic in February 1958, and ties with the Soviet and East European bloc strengthened. Syria withdrew from the union after the army had seized power there in September 1961, but Egypt retained the title "United Arab Republic". Further attempts at federating Egypt, Syria and Iraq also came to nothing during the early 1960s.

The "Six-day War" in June 1967 between the Arabs and Israel left Israel in control of a large area of Arab territory, including all of Sinai, and the Suez Canal was blocked. Soviet military assistance soon made good the Egyptian losses of the war. An uneasy ceasefire, with other powers unsuccessfully trying to achieve a reconciliation, lasted until October 6th, 1973, when Col. Anwar Sadat, who had become President after Nasser's death in September 1970, sent his troops across the Suez Canal in an attempt to recover the territory lost in 1967. After 18 days of fighting a ceasefire proposed by the UN Security Council was accepted by Egypt, Israel and Syria (which was also involved). The U.S. Secretary of State, Dr. Henry Kissinger, was instrumental in arranging peace talks which took place in Geneva in December and January, and for securing acceptance of an agreement for the disengagement of forces, by which Israeli forces withdrew to a line about 13 miles east of the Suez Canal and were separated from Egyptian forces by a UN buffer zone approximately 6 miles wide. Further peace talks were delayed by the difficulty of achieving disengagement on the Syrian front.

In September 1971 a proposed tripartite Federation of Arab Republics, consisting of Egypt, Libya and Syria was approved by a referendum in all three states. The United Arab Republic then became known as the Arab Republic of Egypt. The Federation came into being in 1972, but has had little practical effect. Plans to achieve a union between Egypt and Libya on a much more extensive scale have also made little practical progress. In February 1974 President Sadat concluded an agreement with President Nemery of Sudan on joint political action and economic integration.

Government

The highest authority is the President, elected for a six-year term and he appoints a Council consisting of a Prime Minister, Deputy Prime Ministers and Ministers. The People's Assembly consists of 360 members, half of whom must be workers or peasants. The Assembly has a five-year term.

Since January 1972 Egypt has been a member of the Federation of Arab Republics (*see* Vol. I, Part I), and in September 1972 Egypt and Libya agreed on a future union of the two countries. In August 1973 it was agreed that this union would take place in stages.

Defence

Egypt has total armed forces of 298,000 men, with 534,000 reserves. There is a compulsory three-year period of National Service. The defence budget for 1973–74 is £E700 million.

Economic Affairs

Most of the population are engaged in agriculture. The chief crops are cotton, onions, wheat, maize, millet, rice and sugar-cane. The country depends very largely on the waters of the Nile for its fertility, and the completion of the Aswan High Dam in 1970 increased the fertile land of Egypt by one third. The planned creation of a huge artificial lake in the Qattara depression would make further substantial increases in Egypt's hydro-electric power resources. A programme of socialism has been substantially accomplished. All banks and insurance companies and most industrial and trading concerns have been nationalized, and steps have been taken to re-distribute land to the poorer peasants. In 1966 Suez Canal dues amounted to £95 million. Since the war with Israel in October 1973 Egypt has embarked on a programme of economic and social development aimed at producing a growth rate of 6.5 per cent in 1974. Much of the investment is to come from other Arab countries.

Transport and Communications

The area of the Nile Delta is well served by railways. Lines also run from Cairo southward along the Nile to Aswan, and westward along the coast to Sollum. Roads link the towns. The chief ports are Alexandria and Port Said. Over 21,000 vessels used the Suez Canal, linking the Mediterranean and the Red Sea, in 1966. The Suez Canal was closed by the June 1967 war, but Egypt now has plans to clear and re-open the canal as soon as possible. The River Nile carries much domestic freight and there are long-distance passenger services. Cairo is an important air centre and EgyptAir has branches all over the world. In December 1973 a contract for the building of an oil pipeline from Suez to the Mediterranean was signed.

Social Welfare

Great progress has been made in social welfare services in recent years. There are comprehensive state schemes for sickness benefits, pensions, health insurance and training. An extensive birth control campaign, in 2,400 health centres throughout the country, has been launched with the aim of slowing the rapid population growth. There is a maximum seven-hour working day.

Education

Primary education is extended to all children between the ages of six and twelve, and is compulsory. More than 5.6 million people were receiving state education in the 1972/73 school year. There are eight universities. Education is free at all levels.

Tourism

Egypt has always been a considerable tourist centre. Historical remains of ancient civilisations include the Pyramids and the temples at Abu Simbel. The River Nile is popular for cruises. Over 540,000 people visited Egypt in 1972. Tourists are entitled to a special exchange rate, about £E1.40 to £1 sterling in 1974.

Visas are not required for visits to Egypt by nationals of Algeria, Iraq, Jordan, Kuwait, Lebanon and Syria.

Sport

The chief recreations are football, athletics, basketball, horse-racing, tennis and swimming.

Public Holidays

1974: September 1st (Libyan Revolution Day), October 15th-18th (Ramadan Bairam—Id ul Fitr), December 23rd (Victory Day), December 26th (Kurban Bairam—Id ul Adha).

1975: January 1st (New Year's Day), January 14th (Muslim New Year), March 26th (Birth of the Prophet), April 22nd (Sham El Nessim), June 18th (Evacuation Day), July 23rd (Revolution Day).

Christian holidays include: Eastern Christmas (January), Palm Sunday and Easter Sunday (March–April).

Weights and Measures

The metric system is in force.

Currency and Exchange Rates

1,000 millièmes = 100 piastres = 1 Egyptian pound (£E).

Exchange rates (April 1974):

£1 sterling = 938.8 millièmes;

U.S. $1 = 390.6 millièmes.

STATISTICAL SURVEY

AREA AND POPULATION

AREA (sq. km.)		POPULATION (Census of May 30th, 1966)					
Total	Inhabited	Total	Cairo	Alexandria	Giza	Port Said	Suez
1,001,449	55,039	30,075,858	4,219,853	1,801,056	650,381	282,977	264,098

Total Population (estimated): 35,619,000 (mid-1973).

Population of Cairo (estimated): 5,517,000 (mid-1973).

Population of Alexandria (estimated): 2,201,000 (mid-1973).

GOVERNORATES*

(1965)

GOVERNORATE	AREA (sq. km.)	CAPITAL	GOVERNORATE	AREA (sq. km.)	CAPITAL
Cairo . . .	214.2	Cairo	Munufia . . .	1,532.1	Shibin el-Kom
Alexandria . .	2,679.4	Alexandria	Behera . . .	4,589.5	Damanhur
Port Said . .	72.1	Port Said	Giza . . .	1,009.6	Giza
Ismailia . . .	1,441.6	Ismailia	Beni Suef . . .	1,321.7	Beni Suef
Suez . . .	17,840.4	Suez	Fayum . . .	1,827.2	Fayum
Damietta . . .	589.2	Damietta	Menia . . .	2,261.7	Menia
Dakahlia . . .	3,470.9	Mansura	Asyut . . .	1,553.0	Asyut
Sharkia . . .	4,179.6	Zagazig	Suhag . . .	1,547.2	Suhag
Kalyubia . . .	1,001.1	Benha	Kena . . .	1,850.7	Kena
Kafr el-Sheikh . .	3,437.1	Kafr el-Sheikh	Aswan . . .	678.5	Aswan
Gharbia . . .	1,942.2	Tanta			

* Excluding the four sparsely-populated "frontier districts".

AGRICULTURE
PRINCIPAL CROPS

	AREA ('000 feddans*)				PRODUCTION ('000 metric tons)			
	1968/69	1969/70	1970/71	1971/72	1968/69	1969/70	1970/71	1971/72
Wheat	1,265	1,312	1,356	1,246	1,277	1,519	1,732	1,618
Maize	1,491	1,508	1,526	1,538	2,368	2,397	2,344	2,421
Millet	476	500	494	483	814	874	854	831
Barley	148	88	76	97	117	84	77	109
Rice	1,196	1,142	1,137	1,146	2,561	2,605	2,534	2,507
Clover	2,732	2,748	2,770	2,819	44,300	45,177	46,327	n.a.
Beans† . . .	340	302	262	317	299	278	257	362
Lentils . . .	46	47	65	67	24	33	50	54
Onions† . . .	65	47	56	49	568	451	583	490
Sugar Cane . .	170	186	193	202	6,867	6,934	7,486	7,701

* 1 feddan = 1.038 acres.   † Dry crop and the production of onions includes interplanted crop.

Livestock: (1972 estimates—'000) Cattle 2,129, Buffaloes 2,098, Camels 117, Goats, 1,234, Sheep 2,013, Horses 30, Donkeys 1,430.

Eggs: (1972) 1,498 million

Honey: Production (1972) 7,276 tons.

AREA AND PRODUCTION OF RAW COTTON

	1969–70		1970–71		1971–72	
	'000 feddans*	'000 kantars†	'000 feddans*	'000 kantars†	'000 feddans*	'000 kantars†
Menoufi . . .	376	2,050	363	1,916	305	1,742
Dandara . . .	130	546	117	723	102	722
Ashmouni . . .	176	795	137	838	104	672
Others . . .	945	5,523	908	5,527	1,041	5,892
TOTAL . .	1,627	8,914	1,525	9,004	1,552	9,028

* 1 feddan = 1.038 acres.   † 1 metric kantar = 157.5 kg.

MINING AND INDUSTRY
('ooo tons)

COMMODITY	1969	1970	1971	1972
Crude oil ('ooo cu. metres) .	14,295	16,388	17,010	12,233
Benzine ('ooo cu. metres)	455	360	695	960
Kerosene ('ooo cu. metres) .	428	490	740	970
Mazout ('ooo cu. metres) .	1,479	1,624	2,572	3,217
Asphalt . . .	38	58	73	113
Phosphate . .	660	582	574	572
Manganese . .	4	4	4	3
Common salt . .	385	376	398	341
Iron ore . . .	460	453	n.a.	n.a.
Refined sugar . .	487	286	296	293
Cottonseed oil . .	125	126	118	145
Super phosphate . .	344	411	487	518
Caustic soda . .	20	20	18	16
Cement . . .	3,613	3,259	3,921	3,807
Woollen fabrics . .	3	3	3	9*
Cotton yarn . .	162	164	779*	179
Cotton cloth . .	117	110	110	744*
Electricity (million kWh.) .	7,134	7,592	7,595†	7,720†

* Million metres.   † Fiscal years 1970/71, 1971/72.

PRODUCTION CO-OPERATIVES

	1969	1970	1971*
Agriculture . .	4,955	4,978	4,997
Sea Food . .	54	57	58

* Preliminary.

FINANCE

1,000 millièmes = 100 piastres = 1 Egyptian pound (£E).
Coins: 1, 2, and 5 millièmes; 1, 2, 5 and 10 piastres.
Notes: 5, 10, 25 and 50 piastres; 1, 5 and 10 pounds.
Exchange rates (April 1974): £1 sterling = 938.8 millièmes; U.S. $1 = 390.6 millièmes.
£E100 = £106.52 sterling = $256.00.

Note: Between May 1962 and February 1973 the Egyptian pound was valued at U.S. $2.30. From November 1967 to August 1971 the exchange rate was £1 sterling = £E1.0435.

BUDGET ESTIMATES
(£E million)
EXPENDITURE
(Twelve months ending June 30th)

	CURRENT EXPENDITURE		%		INVESTMENT EXPENDITURE		%	
	1970–71	1971–72	1970–71	1971–72	1970–71	1971–72	1970–71	1971–72
Agriculture and Irrigation . . .	122.9	146.5	6.5	7.3	42.2	55.9	14.1	16.0
Electricity and High Dam . . .	45.1	54.7	2.4	2.7	27.2	25.1	9.1	7.2
Industry, Petroleum and Mineral Wealth .	306.8	302.3	16.3	15.1	109.6	122.0	36.5	34.9
Transport and Communications .	170.1	175.7	9.0	8.8	42.7	54.2	14.2	15.5
Trade and Supply . . .	265.1	275.0	14.1	13.8	7.3	7.8	2.4	2.2
Housing and Public Utilities . .	25.9	28.2	1.4	1.4	18.1	21.6	6.0	6.2
Health, Social and Religious Services. .	93.4	106.5	4.9	5.3	3.2	4.4	1.1	1.3
Education, Culture and National Guidance .	162.2	170.4	8.6	8.5	12.0	14.1	4.0	4.0
Defence, Security and Justice . .	299.6	312.6	15.9	15.6	1.9	1.9	0.6	0.5
Local Administration . . .	43.8	47.3	2.3	2.4	5.5	5.4	1.8	1.5
Non-distributed Investments . . .	—	—	—	—	28.6	33.0	9.6	9.4
Others*	351.9	381.6	18.6	19.1	1.7	4.6	0.6	1.3
TOTAL	1,886.8	2,000.8	100.0	100.0	300.0	350.0	100.0	100.0

Current Revenues: (1970–71) £E1,782.3 million; (1971–72) £E1,922.0 million.
* Includes tours, presidency services and finance.
1974 Budget: Total expenditure £E4,187 million.

PLANNING

A ten-year Development Plan began on January 1st, 1973. The Plan calls for total investments of £E 8,400 million, of which 38 per cent will be invested in the first five years. It aims at doubling G.N.P. by 1982 at an annual growth rate of 7.2 per cent.

RESERVES AND CURRENCY IN CIRCULATION

(million £E at year end)

	1968	1969	1970
Gold Reserves	40.6	40.6	36.0
Currency in Circulation	489.0	517.0	546.0

BALANCE OF PAYMENTS ESTIMATES

(million U.S.$)

	1965	1966	1967	1968	1969	1970
Balance of Goods and Services:						
Trade balance	−392	−356	−360	−185	−227	−374
Transportation (incl. Suez Canal) . . .	205	217	106	− 3	− 5	− 9
Government	− 74	− 69	− 45	− 51	− 50	− 58
Other	− 1	23	1	− 9	− 22	− 22
	−262	−185	−298	−248	−304	−463
Transfers and Capital Movements:						
Transfers: Private	10	6	12	3	8	4
Government . . .	10	6	122	251	288	304
Capital movements: Private . . .	− 16	− 13	− 14	− 17	− 15	− 10
Government . . .	147	128	108	19	− 66	15
	151	127	228	256	215	313
Changes in Assets and Liabilities:						
Commercial banks	12	60	− 12	− 4	34	32
Monetary gold	7	46	—	—	—	8
IMF accounts	− 14	− 25	4	− 2	− 21	24
Other assets and liabilities . . .	100	− 24	81	− 14	80	104
Net errors and omissions . . .	6	− 1	− 3	12	4	− 18
	111	58	70	− 8	89	150

Source: International Monetary Fund.

EXTERNAL TRADE

(£E million)

	1967	1968	1969	1970	1971	1972
Total Imports . . .	344.4	289.6	277.3	341.1	400.0	390.8
Total Exports . . .	246.2	270.3	323.9	331.2	343.2	358.8

PRINCIPAL COMMODITIES

IMPORTS	£E MILLION			
	1969	1970	1971	1972
Cereals and Milling Products . .	39.8	30.5	70.7	51.8
Animal and Vegetable Oils . .	12.4	16.9	23.2	31.0
General Grocery . . .	3.3	11.1	6.2	6.2
Tobacco	7.4	7.5	8.1	9.7
Textiles and Textile Articles .	16.7	19.2	16.1	16.6
Paper and Paper Products . .	10.8	12.2	13.8	10.1
Pottery and Glassware . .	3.5	3.4	3.9	4.0
Clocks, Watches, Scientific Apparatus	2.7	2.8	2.7	2.5
Mineral Products . . .	27.1	35.4	36.4	28.7
Chemical Products . . .	41.5	41.9	47.4	52.4
Wood, Hides and Rubber . .	12.5	23.9	24.6	37.0
Machinery and Electrical Apparatus	40.9	57.1	55.1	53.5
Transport Equipment . . .	25.6	32.6	40.5	30.9
Crude Petroleum . . .	6.7	7.2	13.0	11.1
Iron and Steel . . .	15.6	24.9	28.2	30.9

EXPORTS	1970		1971		1972	
	'ooo tons	£E million	'ooo tons	£E million	'ooo tons	£E million
Cotton, raw . . .	285	147.9	333	175.0	295	162.0
Cotton Yarn . . .	43	35.6	42	35.6	47	46.6
Cotton Piece Goods . .	23	18.1	22	17.5	21	17.5
Rice	654	34.2	515	24.5	456	22.1
Potatoes . . .	90	3.7	61	2.0	77	3.2
Onions . . .	97	7.3	92	5.8	107	5.0
Edible Fruits . . .	110	7.2	145	9.4	90	5.4
Manganese and Phosphates .	319	1.4	282	1.2	212	1.0
Crude Oil	3,579	15.3	529	1.9	5,225	20.3
Benzine, Kerosene and Mazout .	52	0.5	41	0.3	314	1.8
Cement . . .	345	1.7	1,362	5.9	799	3.7

EXPORTS OF COTTON
(kantars; one kantar=99.05 lb.)

PRINCIPAL COUNTRIES	EXPORTS FOR WHOLE SEASON		VARIETIES	EXPORTS FOR WHOLE SEASON	
	1970–71	1971–72		1970–71	1971–72
China, People's Republic .	295,615	337,731	Giza 45 . . .	495,519	525,720
Czechoslovakia . . .	427,083	425,545	Menoufi . . .	1,924,263	1,761,509
France . . .	169,020	198,259	Giza 68 . . .	1,249,173	1,185,506
Fed. Repub. of Germany .	254,353	295,640	Giza 69 . . .	860,081	504,738
India . . .	646,666	494,506	Giza 67 . . .	1,259,165	1,416,621
Italy . . .	288,780	237,240	Dandara . . .	n.a.	156,719
Japan . . .	577,632	489,424	Giza 66 . . .	133,987	218,502
Poland . . .	223,873	164,726	Others . . .	150,916	137,149
Romania . . .	245,249	334,308			
U.S.S.R. . . .	1,945,009	1,773,333	TOTAL . . .	6,073,104	5,906,464

PRINCIPAL COUNTRIES
(£E million)

IMPORTS	1969	1970†	1971	1972
Saudi Arabia	0.1	0.6	0.5	0.4
U.S.S.R.	37.6	34.9	54.0	51.9
Czechoslovakia . . .	8.9	13.6	17.7	13.0
German Democratic Republic	12.8	8.4	15.8	16.5
Yugoslavia	6.2	8.9	6.2	4.7
United Kingdom . . .	12.1	13.5	14.1	15.4
Germany, Federal Republic .	19.3	26.6	28.1	25.8
Italy	16.3	22.6	22.3	13.9
Japan	2.5	5.2	5.1	4.8
India	16.1	27.2	19.2	12.8
U.S.A.	19.6	20.9	22.2	33.9
Poland	6.0	9.9	8.6	6.6
Romania	5.5	11.3	9.9	12.9
France	28.5	25.3	20.7	28.5
China, People's Republic .	5.6	6.7	7.7	11.2

† Excludes crude petroleum.

EXPORTS	1969	1970	1971	1972
U.S.S.R.	107.0	122.4	136.2	126.0
Czechoslovakia . . .	15.3	15.8	17.7	21.0
German Democratic Republic	14.6	19.7	11.2	15.4
Yugoslavia	9.8	8.2	4.1	3.7
United Kingdom . . .	6.7	6.2	7.1	8.0
Germany, Federal Republic .	13.3	8.9	9.6	10.7
Italy	12.7	11.0	9.7	11.2
Japan	12.2	10.6	13.3	15.3
India	16.7	18.0	20.9	18.9
U.S.A.	4.8	2.7	2.9	5.2
Saudi Arabia . . .	2.2	1.6	1.6	1.9
Poland	12.3	7.5	12.4	17.4
Romania	6.0	8.1	7.6	9.4
France	7.5	6.5	5.6	7.9
China, People's Republic .	6.1	7.7	11.5	11.0

TRANSPORT

RAILWAYS

	1970–71	1971–72
Total Freight (million ton km.) .	3,340	2,976
Total Passengers (million passenger km.)	6,772	7,306
Track Length (km.) . . .	4,233	4,385

ROADS
(Licences issued at end of each year)

	1970	1971	1972
Buses	6,888	7,358	8,081
Lorries	23,178	27,351	3,111
Cars	135,670	148,022	158,644
Motor Cycles . . .	25,025	27,494	32,215

SHIPPING
SUEZ CANAL TRAFFIC

	VESSELS	NET TONNAGE ('000)	PASSENGERS ('000)	RECEIPTS (£E '000)
1964 . .	19,943	227,991	270	77,697
1965 . .	20,289	246,817	291	85,792
1966 . .	21,250	274,250	300	95,187
1967: Jan.–May .	9,652	127,825	157	44,000

CIVIL AVIATION
(tons)

	1968	1969	1970	1971	1972
Cargo . . .	12,185	14,512	15,269	17,433	21,766
Mail . . .	1,266	1,379	1,151	1,201	1,301

TOURISM

	TOTAL VISITORS	ARABS	EUROPEANS	AMERICANS	OTHERS	TOTAL (guest-nights) ('000)
1969 . .	345,343	193,977	85,463	32,769	33,134	4,396
1970 . .	357,661	230,803	65,985	25,427	35,446	4,574
1971 . .	428,062	260,169	94,540	30,051	43,302	5,988
1972 . .	540,880	313,960	132,012	44,062	50,846	6,626

Tourist Accommodation (1972): 19,742 hotel beds in 215 hotels under the supervision of the Ministry of Tourism. Other tourist accommodation (1972): 24,331 hotel beds in 720 hotels.

EDUCATION
(1971-72)

	CLASSES	TEACHERS	PUPILS
Primary	90,022	99,351	3,873,297
General and Technical Preparatory .	23,216	27,888	927,703
General Secondary . . .	8,135	14,137	312,489
Technical Secondary . . .	8,502	14,300	289,812
Teacher Training	782	2,172	27,247
Higher Education	n.a.	5,378	241,690

Sources: Central Agency for Public Mobilization and Statistics, Cairo; Research Department, National Bank of Egypt, Cairo; International Monetary Fund.

THE CONSTITUTION

The Permanent Constitution of the Arab Republic of Egypt was approved by referendum on September 11th, 1971. There are six chapters with 193 articles, many of them based on the 1964 Interim Constitution, but chapters 3 and 4 show a considerable degree of liberalization of the former statutes.

CHAPTER I
The State

Egypt is an Arab Republic with a democratic, socialist system based on the alliance of the working people and derived from the country's historical heritage and the spirit of Islam.

The Egyptian people are part of the Arab nation, who work towards total Arab unity.

Islam is the religion of the State; Arabic is its official language and the Islamic code is a principal source of legislation. The State safeguards the freedom of worship and of performing rites for all religions.

Sovereignty is of the people alone which is the source of all powers.

The protection, consolidation and preservation of the socialist gains is a national duty: the sovereignty of law is the basis of the country's rule, and the independence of immunity of the judiciary are basic guarantees for the protection of rights and liberties.

The Arab Socialist Union is the political organization of the State which represents the alliance of the working forces of the people; the farmers, workers, soldiers, the intelligentsia and national capitalism.

CHAPTER 2
The Fundamental Elements of Society

Social solidarity is the basis of Egyptian society, and the family is its nucleus.

The State ensures the equality of men and women in both political and social rights in line with the provisions of Moslem legislation.

Work is a right, an honour and a duty which the State guarantees together with the services of social and health insurance, pensions for incapacity and unemployment.

The economic basis of the Republic is the socialist based on sufficiency and justice. It is calculated to prevent exploitation and to level up differences between classes.

The people control all means of production and regulate the national economy according to a comprehensive development plan which determines the role of Arab and foreign capital.

Property is subject to the people's control.

Property shall be expropriated only by law and against fair compensation. Nationalization shall also be by law for public interest considerations or socialist objectives.

Agricultural holding may be limited by law.

The State follows a comprehensive central planning and compulsory planning approach based on quinquennial socio-economic and cultural development plans whereby the society's resources are mobilized and put to the best use.

The public Sector assumes the leading role in the development of the national economy. The State provides absolute protection of this Sector as well as the property of co-operative societies and trade unions against all attempts to tamper with them.

CHAPTER 3
Public Liberties, Rights and Duties

All citizens are equal before the law. Personal liberty is a natural right and no one may be arrested, searched, imprisoned or restricted in any way without a court order.

Houses have sanctity, and shall not be placed under serveillance or searched without a court order with reasons given for such action.

The law safeguards the sanctities of the private lives of all citizens; so have all postal, telegraphic telephonic and other means of communication which may not therefore be confiscated, or perused except by a court order giving the reasons, and only for a specified period.

Public rights and freedoms are also inviolate and all calls for atheism and anything that reflects adversely on divine religions is prohibited.

The freedom of opinion, the press, printing and publications and all information media are safeguarded.

Press censorship is forbidden, so are warnings, suspensions or cancellations through administrative channels. Under exceptional circumstances as in cases of emergency or in war time, censorship may be imposed on information media for a definite period.

Egyptians have the right to permanent or provisional emigration and no Egyptian may be deported or prevented from returning to the country.

Citizens have the right to private meetings in peace provided they bear no arms. Egyptians also have the right to form societies which have no secret activities or are hostile to the government. Public meetings are also allowed within the limits of the law.

CHAPTER 4
Sovereignty of the Law

All acts of crime should be specified together with the penalties for the acts.

Recourse to justice, it says, is a right of all citizens, and those who are financially unable, will be assured of means to defend their rights.

Arrested persons may protest against their detention and their protests should be decided upon within a prescribed period otherwise they should be released.

CHAPTER 5
System of Government

The President, who must be at least 40 years old, is nominated by at least one-third of the members of the People's Assembly, approved by at least two-thirds, and elected by popular referendum. His term is for six years and he 'may be re-elected for another subsequent term.' He may take emergency measures in the interests of the state but these measures must be approved by referendum within 60 days.

The People's Assembly, elected for five years, is the legislative body and approves general policy, the budget and the development plan. It shall have 'not less than 350' elected members, at least half of whom shall be workers or farmers, and the President may appoint up to ten additional members. In exceptional circumstances the Assembly, by a two-thirds vote, may authorize the President to rule by decree for a specified period but these decrees must be approved by the Assembly at its next meeting.

The Assembly may pass a vote of no confidence in a Deputy Prime Minister, a Minister or a Deputy Minister, provided three days' notice of the vote is given, and the minister must then resign. In the case of the Prime Minister, the Assembly may "prescribe" his responsibility and submit a report to the President: if the President disagrees with the report but the Assembly persists, then the matter is put to a referendum: if the people support the President the Assembly is dissolved; if they support the Assembly the President must accept the resignation of the government. The President may dissolve the Assembly prematurely, but his action must be approved by a referendum and elections must be held within 60 days.

Executive Authority is vested in the President, who may appoint one or more vice-presidents and appoints all ministers. He may also dismiss the vice-presidents and ministers. The President has 'the right to refer to the people in connection with important matters related to the country's higher interests.' The Government is described as 'the supreme executive and administrative organ of the state'. Its members, whether full ministers or deputy ministers, must be at least 35 years old. Further sections define the roles of Local Government, Specialized National Councils, the Judiciary, the Higher Constitutional Court, the Socialist Prosecutor General, the Armed Forces and National Defence Council and the Police.

CHAPTER 6
General and Transitional Provisions

No law shall normally have retroactive effect, but this may be changed, except in criminal matters, with the approval of a majority of the Assembly. Articles of the constitution may be revised, at the suggestion of the President or one-third of the Assembly, but the revision must be submitted for approval by a public referendum. The term of the present President shall date from his election as President of the United Arab Republic.

THE GOVERNMENT

THE PRESIDENCY

President: Col. Muhammad Anwar Sadat.
Vice-Presidents: Husain Shafei, Mahmoud Fawzi.

COUNCIL OF MINISTERS
(*May* 1974)

Prime Minister: Col. Muhammad Anwar Sadat.

First Deputy Premier: Dr. Abdel-Aziz Higazi.

Deputy Premier and Minister of Interior: Gen. Mamdouh Salem.

Deputy Premier and Minister of Waqfs: Dr. Abdel-Aziz Kamel.

Deputy Premier and Minister of Defence: Field-Marshal Ahmad Ismail Ali.

Minister of Foreign Affairs: Ismail Fahmi.

Minister of Communications: Dr. Mahmoud Riyad.

Minister of Planning: Dr. Ismail Sabri Abdulla.

Minister of Tourism and Civil Aviation: Ibrahim Naguib Ibrahim.

Minister of Power: Ahmad Sultan.

Minister of Information: Dr. Ahmad Kamal Abul-Magd.

Minister of Social Affairs: Dr. Aisha Rateb.

Minister of Education: Dr. Mustafa Kamel Hilmi.

Minister of Irrigation: Ahmad Ali Kamel.

Minister of Health: Dr. Mahmoud Muhammad Mahfouz.

Minister of Manpower and Works: Salahuddin Muhammad Gharib.

Minister of War Production: Lieut.-Gen. Ahmad Kamel Badri.

Minister of Culture: Youssef El Sebai.

Minister of Justice: Dr. Mustafa Abu-Zaid.

Minister of Agriculture and Agrarian Reform: Dr. Muhammad Muhib Muhammad Zaki.

Minister of Petroleum: Ahmad Izzedin Hasan Hilal.

Ministry of Industry and Mining: Ibrahim Salem Muhammadin.

Minister of Insurance: Dr. Hasan Sharif.

Minister of Supplies and Home Trade: Hadi Maghrebi.

Minister of Al Azhar Affairs: Sheikh Abdel-Aziz Isa.

Minister of Higher Education and Scientific Research: Dr. Ismail Ghanem.

Minister of Shipping: Gen. Abdel-Mouti Ahmad Fahmi Arabi.

Minister of Reconstruction and Housing: Othman Ahmad Othman.

Minister of Finance: Muhammad Abdel-Fattah Ibrahim.

Minister of Foreign Trade: Fathi Ahmed Madbouli.

Minister of State for Presidential Affairs: Gen. Abdel-Fattah Abdulla.

Minister of State for Cabinet Affairs: Dr. Yahya Abdel-Aziz Gamal.

Minister of State for People's Assembly Affairs: Albert Barsum Salama.

Minister of State for Local Government and Popular Organization: Dr. Ahmad Fuad Muhieddin.

Minister of State for Sudanese Affairs: Dr. Othman Ali Badran.

Deputy Minister for Youth: Dr. Abdel-Hamid Hasan.

DIPLOMATIC REPRESENTATION

EMBASSIES AND LEGATION ACCREDITED TO EGYPT
(In Cairo, unless otherwise stated)
(E) Embassy; (L) Legation.

Afghanistan: 59 Sh. Oroba (Heliopolis) (E); *Ambassador:* Dr. Wahed Karim.

Albania: 29 Sh. Ismail Muhammad (Zamalek) (E); *Ambassador:* Ajet Simixhiu.

Algeria: 14 Sh. Brézil (Zamalek) (E); *Ambassador:* Mezhoudi Ibrahim.

Argentina: 8 Sh. As-Saleh Ayoub (Zamalek) (E); *Ambassador:* Paulino Musacchio.

Australia: 1097 Corniche el Nil (Garden City) (E); *Ambassador:* K. R. Douglas-Scott.

Austria: 21 Sh. Sadd El-Aaly (Dokki) (E); *Ambassador:* Heinz Standenat.

Belgium: 8 Rue Abdel Khalek Saroit (E); *Ambassador:* Pierre Ancieux Henri de Faveaux.

Bolivia: 6 Rue Nawal (Dokki) (E); *Ambassador:* (vacant).

Brazil: 27 Rue El Guézira El Wosta (Zamalek) (E); *Ambassador:* Luiz Bastian Pinto.

Bulgaria: 141 Rue El Tahrir (Dokki) (E); *Ambassador:* Gueorgui Tanev.

Burma: 24 Rue Muhammad Mazhar (Zamalek) (E); *Ambassador:* Zahre Lian.

Burundi: 9 Rue Mahmoud Hassan (Heliopolis) (E); *Ambassador:* Protais Mangona.

Cameroon: 14 Sh. Wodi El Nil (Dokki) (E); *Ambassador:* William Forcho Lima.

Canada: 6 Sh. Muhammad Fahmy El Sayed (Garden City) (E); *Ambassador:* David Stansfield.

Chile: 5 Sh. Chagaret El-Dorr (Zamalek) (E); *Ambassador:* Mario Prieto Serviere.

China, People's Republic: 14 Sh. Bahgat Aly (Zamalek) (E); *Ambassador:* Chai Tse-min.

Colombia: 15 Sh. Aboul Feda (Zamalek) (E); *Ambassador:* Alberto Venecas Tamayo.

Congo (Brazzaville): 16 Sh. Téba, Cité des Ingénieurs (Dokki) (E); *Ambassador:* Jean-Baptiste Lounda.

Cuba: Villa No. 1, Sh. Sennan (Dokki) (E); *Ambassador:* Dr. Carlos Varela.

Cyprus: 3 Sh. Nabil El-Wakkad (Dokki) (E); *Ambassador:* Antis G. Soteriades.

Czechoslovakia: 43 Sh. Muhammad Mazhar (Zamalek) (E); *Ambassador:* Lumir Hanak.

Denmark: 12 Sh. Hassan Sabri (Zamalek) (E); *Ambassador:* Kjeld V. Mortensen.

Dominican Republic: Maison Jacques, Midan Mustafa Kamel (L).

Ecuador: 15 Sh. Aboul Feda (Zamalek) (E); *Chargé d'affaires:* Vicente Aguirre Gonzales.

El Salvador: *Ambassador:* Hugo Lino.

Ethiopia: 12 Midan Bahlawi (Dokki) (E); *Ambassador:* Ato Mallas Mikael Andom.

Finland: 2 El-Malek El-Afdal (Zamalek) (E); *Ambassador:* Babba Malinen.

France: 29 Sh. Guizeh (E); *Ambassador:* Bruno de Leusse de Syon.

German Democratic Republic: 13 Sh. Hussein Wassef (Dokki) (E); *Ambassador:* Hans-Joachim Radde.

Germany, Federal Republic: (E); *Ambassador:* Hans-Georg Steltzer.

Ghana: Villa 24, Sh. 22 (Dokki) (E); *Ambassador:* Maj.-Gen. Clenland Cofie Bruce.

Greece: 18 Sh. Aïcha El-Taïmouria (Garden City) (E); *Ambassador:* Antoine Korantis.

Guatemala: *Ambassador:* Angelo Astura Rivera.

Guinea: 46 Sh. Muhammad Mazhar (Zamalek) (E); *Ambassador:* M'tempa Bangoura.

Hungary: 29 Sh. Muhammad Mazhar (Zamalek) (E); *Ambassador:* Jenö Rande.

India: 5 Mahad El Swissri (Zamalek) (E); *Ambassador:* Ashok Balkrishna Bhadkamkar.

Indonesia: 13 Sh. Aïcha El-Taïmouria (Garden City) (E); *Ambassador:* Mohamed Sharif Padmadisastra.

Iran: 11 Sh. Okhab (Dokki) (E); *Ambassador:* Khosrov Khosrovani.

Iraq: 9 Sh. Muhammad Mazhar (Zamalek) (E); *Ambassador:* Samir Abdul Aziz al-Najm.

Italy: Sh. El Salamlik (Garden City) (E); *Ambassador:* (vacant).

Japan: 10 Sh. Ibrahim Naguib (Garden City) (E); *Ambassador:* Tsutomu Wada.

Jordan: 6 Sh. El-Gohainy (Dokki) (E); *Ambassador:* Abdul Munim al-Rifai.

Kenya: 7 Ahmed El Meleky St. (Dokki) (E); *Ambassador:* (vacant).

Khmer Republic: 2 Sh. Tahawia (Giza) (E); *Ambassador:* Sarin Chhak.

Korea, Democratic People's Republic: (E); *Ambassador:* Kim Byong Ho.

Kuwait: 12 Sh. Nabil El-Wakkad (Dokki) (E); *Ambassador:* Hamad Issa El-Rujaib.

Lebanon: 5 Sh. Ahmed Nessim (Guizeh) (E); *Ambassador:* Mohamed Sabra.

Liberia: 2 Sh. 22, Cité Awkaf (Dokki) (E); *Ambassador:* John W. Grigsby.

Libya: 7 Sh. Saleh Ayoub (Zamalek) (E); *Ambassador:* Saad El Din Bushweirab.

Malaysia: 34 Sh. El Messaha (Dokki) (E); *Ambassador:* Tuan Haji Abdul Khalid.

Mali: 4 Sh. Margil (Zamalek) (E); *Ambassador:* Boubacar Diallo.

Mauritania: 37 Sh. Ismail Muhammad (Zamalek) (E); *Ambassador:* Ahmed Ould Menneya.

Mexico: 5 Sh. Dar El Shifa (Garden City) (E); *Ambassador:* Celso Humberto Delgado Ramírez.

Mongolia: 46 Sh. Gameat El Dowal El Arabia (Dokki) (E); *Ambassador:* Demiddagva.

Morocco: 10 Sh. Saleh El Dine (Zamalek) (E); *Ambassador:* Abdellatif Laraki.

Nepal: 24 Sh. Syria (Dokki) (E); *Ambassador:* Jharendra Narayan Singh.

Netherlands: 18 Sh. Hassan Sabri (Zamalek) (E); *Ambassador:* Franz von Oven.

Nigeria: 13 Sh. Gabalaya (Zamalek) (E); *Ambassador:* H. Musa.

Norway: 2 Sh. Chafik Mansour (Zamalek) (E); *Ambassador:* Tancred Ibsen (also accred. to Ethiopia, Jordan, Lebanon and Sudan).

Pakistan: 22 Sh. Mansour Muhammad (Zamalek) (E); *Ambassador:* Mohamed Islam Malik.

Panama: Villa No. 20 Sh. 75 (Maadi) (E); *Ambassador:* M. Herrera.

Peru: 9 Sh. El Kamel Muhammad (Zamalek) (E); *Ambassador:* Felipe Valivieso Belaúnde.

Philippines: 5 Sh. Ibn El-Walid (Dokki) (E); *Ambassador:* Yusup Abubakar.

Poland: 5 Sh. Aziz Osman (Zamalek) (E); *Ambassador:* Janusz Lewandowski.

Romania: 6 Sh. El Kamel Muhammad (Zamalek) (E); *Ambassador:* Petru Burlacu.

Saudi Arabia: Villa 12, Sh. El Kamel Mohamed (Zamalek) (E); *Ambassador:* Shaikh Fuad Ahmad Nazir.

Senegal: 2 Sh. Ahmed Ragheb (Garden City) (E); *Ambassador:* Mustafa Cisse.

Sierra Leone: 56 Sh. Amman (Dokki) (E); *Ambassador:* (vacant).

Singapore: 6 Sh. Nawal (Dokki) (E); *Ambassador:* (vacant).

Somalia: 9 Sh. Rawakeh (Engineer's City) (E); *Ambassador:* Abdullahi Adan Ahmed.

Spain: 28 Ahmed Hechmat St. (Zamalek) (E); *Ambassador:* Manuel Alabarat.

Sri Lanka: 8 Sh. Yehia Ibrahim (Zamalek) (E); *Ambassador:* Ranawaka Aratchie Perera.

Sudan: 3 Sh. El Ibrahimi (Garden City) (E); *Ambassador:* Muhammad Mirghani Mubarak.

Sweden: 4 Sh. Sadd El Aali (Dokki) (E); *Ambassador:* Lars Petrus Folke von Celsine.

Switzerland: 10 Sh. Abdel Khalek Saroit (E); *Ambassador:* Hans Carl Frey.

Syria: 17 Sh. Ahmad Sabry (Zamalek) (E); *Ambassador:* Ezzedine Neisee.

Tanzania: 18 Sh. Ahmed Hechmat (Zamalek) (E); *Ambassador:* Christopher P. Nguiza.

Thailand: 2 Sh. El Malek El Afdal (Zamalek) (E); *Ambassador:* Nibhon Wilairai.

Trinidad and Tobago: Addis Ababa, Ethiopia (E).

Tunisia: 26 Sh. El Guezira (Zamalek) (E); *Chargé d'Affaires:* Muhammad Ibn Fadl.

Turkey: Avenue El Nil (Giza) (E); *Ambassador:* Fahir Alacam.

Uganda: 9 Midan El Missaha (Dokki) (E); *Ambassador:* Capt. Younis Khamis Wenn.

U.S.S.R.: 95 Sh. El Giza (Giza) (E); *Ambassador:* Vladimir Bolyakov.

United Arab Emirates: (address not available) (E); *Ambassador:* Tarim Omran Tarim.

United Kingdom: Kasrah El Dubara (Garden City) (E); *Ambassador:* Sir Philip Adams.

U.S.A. (E); Ambassador to present credentials; *Ambassador designate:* Hermann Eilts.

Uruguay: 6 Sh. Loutfallah (Zamalek) (E); *Ambassador:* Silvio A. Corradi Irisarri.

Vatican City: 5 Sh. Muhammad Mazhar (Zamalek) (Apostolic Nunciature); *Nuncio:* Mgr. Achille Glorieux.

Venezuela: 5 Sh. Mansour Muhammad (Zamalek) (E); *Ambassador:* (vacant).

Viet-Nam, Democratic Republic: 21 Sh. Giza (Giza) (E); *Ambassador:* Nguyen Xuan.

Viet-Nam, Republic: *Ambassador:* Tran Van Hoa.

Yemen Arab Republic: 28 Sh. Amin El Rafei (Dokki) (E); *Ambassador:* Yehia Mohamed el Moutawakel.

Yemen, People's Democratic Republic: Sh. Hassanein Higazi (Dokki) (E); *Ambassador:* Abdel-malik Ismail Muhammad Hassan.

Yugoslavia: 33 Sh. El Mansour Muhammad (Zamalek) (E); *Ambassador:* Augustin Papic.

Zaire: 23 Sh. Mecca El-Mokarrama (Dokki) (E); *Ambassador:* Giano Biano Te Wapimda.

Zambia: 30 Sh. Montazah (Zamalek) (E); *Ambassador:* Matiya Nealande.

Egypt also recognizes Bangladesh, the Central African Republic, Chad, Madagascar, Mauritius, Rwanda and Swaziland.

PEOPLE'S ASSEMBLY

ELECTIONS

Elections October 27th and November 3rd, 1971

Of the 360 seats (10 appointed and 350 elected), 53 per cent were won by farmers and workers.

Speaker: Hafez Badawi.

POLITICAL PARTY

Arab Socialist Union (ASU): Cairo; f. 1961 as the alliance of all working people's forces; Chair. President Sadat; Sec.-Gen. Muhammad Hafez Ghanem; the Higher Exec. Cttee. has 10 mems.; the Central Cttee. has 230 mems., 200 elected from ASU Governorates' Conferences, and 30 appointed members (2 to represent the police, 2 the students and 4 the armed forces). The National Congress is the largest representative body of the ASU.

JUDICIAL SYSTEM

The Courts of Law in Egypt are basically divided into four categories as follows:

1. *The Supreme Court* (called *The Court of Cassation*)
2. *The Courts of Appeal*
3. *The Primary Tribunals*
4. *The Summary Tribunals*

Each Court contains criminal and civil chambers.

1. The Supreme Court

The highest Court of Law in Egypt. Its sessions are held at Cairo and its jurisdiction covers the whole Egyptian territory.

Final judgements rendered in criminal and civil matters may be referred to the Supreme Court—by the accused or the Public Prosecution in criminal matters, and by any of the litigants in civil matters—in cases of misapplications or misinterpretations of the law as applied by the competent court in final judgement, as well as in cases of irregularity in the form of the judgement or the procedures having effect on that judgement.

The Supreme Court is composed of the Chief Justice, four Deputy-Chief Justices and thirty-six Justices.

2. Courts of Appeal

There are six Courts of Appeal situated in the more important Governorates of Egypt: Cairo, Alexandria, Asyut, Mansura, Tanta, and Beni Suef. Each of these courts contains a criminal chamber, *The Assize Court*, to try cases of felonies, and a civil chamber to hear appeals filed by any of the litigants in civil matters against a judgement rendered by the primary tribunal, where the law so permits.

President in Cairo: M. Mahmoud Abd-el-Latif.

3. Primary Tribunals

In each Governorate, there is a Primary Tribunal, each of which contains several chambers. Each chamber is composed of three Judges. Some of these chambers try criminal cases, whilst others hear civil litigations.

Primary Tribunals sit as Courts of Appeal in certain cases, according to circumstances.

4. Summary Tribunals

Summary Tribunals are branches of the Primary Tribunals and are situated in the different districts of Egypt. Each of these tribunals is composed of a single Judge.

Summary Tribunals hear civil and criminal matters of minor importance according to certain details.

The *Sharia Courts* or courts of Islamic Law, and the religious courts maintained by non-Muslim minorities have been abolished since 1955.

The Public Prosecution

The Public Prosecution is headed by the Attorney-General and consists of a large number of Attorneys, Chief Prosecutors and Prosecutors, who are distributed among the various districts of Egypt. The Public Prosecution is represented at all criminal Courts and also at litigation in certain civil matters. Furthermore, the enforcement of judgement rendered in criminal cases is controlled and supervised by the Public Prosecution.

Attorney-General: Ahmad Musa.

The Supreme Judicial Council

This Council exists to guarantee the independence of the judicial system from outside interference. Under the presidency of the Chief Justice, the Supreme Judicial

Council contains the following members:
 the Chief Justice
 two Deputy Chief Justices
 the Under-Secretary of State for the Ministry of Justice
 the Attorney-General
 the President of the Court of Appeal in Cairo
 the President of the Primary Tribunal in Cairo.

All matters concerning the promotion, discipline or otherwise of the members of the judicial system are referred to this Council.

An Arbitration Bureau was set up in 1966 to investigate cases between state and public sector organizations.

RELIGION

Over 90 per cent of Egyptians are Muslims, and almost all of these follow Sunni tenets. The four tenets are represented in Egypt and all follow the Holy Koran and the Sunna. Villagers adhere strictly to Islamic rites and teachings. Since the Fatimide dynasty Egyptians have attached great importance to the decoration of their mosques. St. Mark is considered to be the first founder of the Coptic Church after Jesus. The Coptic Church is known historically as the Church of Alexandria or the Egyptian Coptic Orthodox Church, and is still considered the main Eastern church. There are over a million Copts in Egypt forming the largest religious minority, there is no discrimination of any kind against them, and they have contributed greatly to the cultural life of Egypt. Besides the Copts there are other Christian minorities numbering about a quarter of a million and consisting of Greek Orthodox, Roman Catholics, Armenians and Protestants. There is also a small Jewish minority.

Grand Sheikh of Al Azhar: Dr. ABDEL-HALIM MAHMOUD.

Grand Mufti of Egypt: Sheikh KHATIR MUHAM MUHAMMAD.

Coptic Orthodox Church: Azbakia, Cairo; f. 61 A.D.; Leader SHENOUDA III.

Coptic Catholic Church: Patriarch Cardinal STEPHANOS I. SIDAROUSS, 34 Sh. Ibn Sandar, Koubbeh Bridge, Cairo; 4 dioceses; 120,000 mems.; publ. Al Salah.

Greek Catholic Patriarchate: P.O.B. 50076 Beirut, Lebanon; 16 rue Daher, Cairo; Patriarch of Antioch, of Alexandria and of Jerusalem His Beatitude MAXIMOS V HAKIM; 750,000 mems. in the Middle East.

Greek Orthodox Church: Patriarch NIKOLAUS VI.

Armenian Apostolic Church: 179 Ramses Ave., Cairo, P.O.B. 48-Faggala; Archbishop MAMPRE SIROUNIAN.

Armenian Catholic Patriarchate: 36 Mohammed Sabri Abou Alam Street, Cairo; Archbishop RAPHAEL BAYAN.

Maronite Church: 15 Hamdi Street, Daher, Cairo; Archbishop JOSEPH MERHI.

Jewish Community: Office of the Chief Rabbi, Rabbi HAIM DOUEK; 13 Sebil-el-Khazindar St., Abbassia, Cairo.

THE PRESS

Despite a high illiteracy rate the Egyptian press is well developed. Cairo is the biggest publishing centre in the Middle East.

Newspapers were placed under the control of the National Union (later reformed as the Arab Socialist Union) by a decree issued by President Nasser in May 1960. Journalists were obliged to obtain licences from the National Union and publishing houses, hitherto free, were placed under its control. All the important newspapers and magazines are now owned by the Government, although the four big publishing houses of al-Ahram, Dar al-Hilal, Dar Akhbar al-Yom and Dar al-Gomhouriya, operate as separate entities and compete with each other commercially. Dar al-Hilal is concerned only with magazines and publishes al-Mussawar, Hawa'u and al-Kawakeb. Dar Akhbar al-Yom publishes the daily newspaper al-Akhbar, the weekly newspaper Akhbar al-Yom and the weekly magazines Akher Saa and Al Guil el Gedid.

Dar al Gomhouriya publishes the daily al-Gomhouriya, the daily English language paper Egyptian Gazette, the daily French newspaper Le Progrès Egyptien and the afternoon paper al-Misaa.

The most authoritative daily newspaper is the very old established al-Ahram. Other popular large circulation magazines are Rose al-Youssef, Sabah al-Kheir and al Izaa w'al Television. Minority language groups are catered for by the Greek language papers Tachydromos and Phos and the Armenian language papers Arev and Houssaper.

In February 1974 President Sadat ended press censorship, except on military matters, and foreign correspondents in Cairo were relieved of the duty of submitting their reports, except those on military matters, for censorship.

DAILIES

ALEXANDRIA

Barid al-Charikat: P.O.B. 813; f. 1952; Arabic; evening; commerce, finance, insurance and marine affairs, etc.; Editor S. BENEDUCCI; circ. 15,000.

al-Ittihad al-Misri: 13 Sharia Sidi Abdel Razzak; f. 1871; Arabic; evening; Propr. ANWAR MAHER FARAG; Dir. HASSAN MAHER FARAG.

Journal d'Alexandrie, Le: 1 Sharia Rolo; French; evening; Editor CHARLES ARCACHE.

Phare Egyptien, Le: 26 Avenue Hourriya; f. 1926; Greek-owned, French language; morning; independent; Editor ANTOINE GERONIMO.

Réforme, La: 8 Passage Sherif; f. 1895; French; noon; Propr. Comte AZIZ DE SAAB; circ. 7,000.

al-Safeer: 4 El-Sahafa St.; f. 1924; Arabic; evening; Editor MOSTAFA SHARAF.

Tachydromos-Egyptos: 4 Sharia Zangarol; f. 1882; Greek; morning; liberal; Publisher PENY COUTSOUMIS; Editor DINOS COUTSOUMIS; circ. 11,000.

CAIRO

al-Ahram (The Pyramids): Gallaa St.; f. 1875; Arabic; morning; independent; Editor AHMED BAHAA EDDINE; circ. 400,000.

al-Akhbar: Dar Akhbar al-Yom, Sharia al-Sahafa; f. 1952; Arabic; independent; Editor MUSTAFA AMIN; circ. 695,000.

Arev: 3 Sharia Soliman Halaby; Armenian; evening; Editor AVEDIS YAPOUDJIAN.

Egyptian Gazette: 24 Sharia Galal; f. 1880; the only English daily; morning; Editor Dr. AMIN MOHAMED ABOUL-ENEIN; circ. 10,000.

al-Gomhouriya (*The Republic*): 24 Sharia Zakaria Ahmed; f. 1953; Arabic; morning; official organ of the Arab Socialist Union; Chief Editor M. B. BADAWI; circ. 250,000.

Houssaper: Armenian; circ. 1,500.

Journal d'Egypte, Le: 1 Borsa Guédida St.; f. 1950; French; morning; Propr. and Editor EDGARD GALLAD; circ. 13,000.

al-Misaa: 24 Sharia Zakaria Ahmed; Arabic; evening; Editor N. MESTIKAOUI; circ. 40,000.

Phos: 14 Zakaria Ahmed St.; f. 1896; Greek; morning; Editor S. PATERAS; Man. BASILE A. PATERAS; circ. 20,000.

Progrès Egyptien, Le: 24 Sharia Zakaria Ahmed; f. 1890; French; morning including Sundays; Editor MAURICE YACCARINI; circ. 14,500.

PERIODICALS

ALEXANDRIA

al Ahad Al Gedid: 88 al-Tatwig Street; Editor-in-Chief MAHMUD ABDEL MALAK KORITAM; General Manager MUHAMMAD KORITAM.

Alexandria Medical Journal: 4 G. Carducci; English, French and Arabic; quarterly; publ. by Alexandria Medical Asscn.; Editor G. E. HANNO; circ. 1,500.

Amitié Internationale: 59 Avenue Hourriya; f. 1957; publ. by Asscn. Egypt. d'Amitié Inter.; Arabic and French; quarterly; Editor Dr. ZAKI BADAOUI.

L'Annuaire des Sociétés Egyptiennes par Actions: 23 Midan Tahrir; f. 1930; annually in December; French; Propr. ELIE I. POLITI; Editor OMAR EL-SAYED MOURSI.

L'Echo Sportif: 7 rue de l'Archevêché; French; weekly; Propr. MICHEL BITTAR.

L'Economiste Egyptien: 11 rue de la Poste, Alexandria; P.O. Box 847; f. 1901; weekly; Propr. MARGUERITE HOSNY.

Egypte-Sports-Cinéma: 7 Avenue Hourriya; French; weekly; Editor EMILE ASSAAD.

Egyptian Cotton Gazette: P.O.B. 433; organ of the Alexandria Cotton Exporters Association; English; twice yearly; Chief Editor Dr. FOUAD A. TAWFIK.

Egyptian Cotton Statistics: English; weekly.

Gazette d'Orient, La: 5 rue de l'Ancienne Bourse; Propr. MAURICE BETITO.

Guide des Industries: 2 Sharia Adib; French; annual; Editor SIMON A. BARANIS.

Informateur des Assurances: 1 Sharia Adib; f. 1936; French; monthly; Propr. ELIE I. POLITI; Editor SIMON A. BARANIS.

Journal Suisse d'Egypte, Le: 18 Sharia Saleh El-Dine; Editor M. MAURICE FIECHTER.

Médecine d'Egypte: 298 rue Port Said, Cléopatra; Editor HUBERT DE LEUSSE; French.

Réforme Illustrée, La: 8 Passage Sherif; f. 1925; French; weekly; Propr. Comte AZIZ DE SAAB; circ. 20,000.

Répertoire Permanent de Législation Egyptienne: 27 Ave. El Guesch, Chatby-les-Bains; f. 1932; French and Arabic; Editor V. SISTO.

Revue des Questions Douanières: 2 Sharia Sinan; Arabic; monthly; economics and agriculture; Propr. ALY MUHAMMAD ALY.

Revue Economique Trimestrielle: c/o Banque de Port-Said, 18 Talaat Harb St., Alexandria; French (f. 1929) and Arabic (f. 1961) editions; quarterly; Editor: MAHMOUD SAMY EL ADAWAY.

Sanaet El-Nassig (*L'Industrie Textile*): 5 rue de l'Archevêché; Arabic and French; monthly; Editor PHILIPPE COIAS.

L'Universitaire—Science et Techniques: 298 Sharia Port Said, Cléopatra; French; scientific and technical; quarterly; Editor HUBERT DE LEUSSE.

Voce d'Italia: 90 Sharia Farahde; Italian; fortnightly; Editor R. AVELLINO.

CAIRO

Actualité: 28 Sharia Sherif Pasha; French; weekly; Dir. and Propr. GEORGES TASSO.

Akhbar al-Yom: 6 Sharia al-Sahafa; f. 1944; Arabic; weekly (Saturday); Editor-in-Chief IHSAN ABDEL KODDOUS; Editing Man. SAID SONBOL; circ. 1,102,000.

Akher Saa: Dar Akhbar al-Yom, Sharia al-Sahafa; f. 1932; Arabic; weekly (Wednesday); independent; Editor-in-Chief ANIS MANSOUR; circ. 184,500.

al-Ahd al-Goumhouri: 132 Sharia Kalaa; Editor ABDEL-KHALEK TAKIA.

al Ahram Al Iqtisadi: United Arab Press, Gallaa St.; economic and political affairs; owned by *Al Ahram*; circ. 12,000.

al-Azhar: Sharia al-Azhar; Arabic; Dir MUHAMMAD FARID WAGDI.

al-Doctor: 8 Hoda Shaarawy St.; f. 1947; Arabic; monthly; Editor Dr. AHMAD M. KAMAL; circ. 30,000.

al-Fussoul: 17 Sharia Sherif Pasha; Arabic; monthly; Propr. and Chief Editor MUHAMMAD ZAKI ABDEL KADER.

al-Garida al-Togaria al-Misriya: 25 Sharia Nubar Pasha; f. 1921; Arabic; weekly; circ. 7,000.

al-Hilal: Dar al-Hilal, 16 Sharia Muhammad Ezz El-Arab; f. 1895; Arabic; monthly; Editor EMILE ZEIDAN.

al-Izaa wal-Television: 13 Sharia Muhammad Ezz El-Arab; f. 1935; Arabic; weekly; Editor RAGA EL AZABI; circ. 120,000.

al-Kawakeb (*The Stars*): Dar al-Hilal, 16 Sharia Muhammad Ezz El-Arab; f. 1952; Arabic; film magazine; Editor FAHIM NAGIB; circ. 38,500.

al-Mukhtar: Dar Akhbar al-Yom, Sharia al-Sahafa; f. 1956; Arabic edition of *Readers' Digest*; Editor MOHAMED ZAKI ABDEL KADER; circ. 50,000.

al-Mussawar: Dar al-Hilal, 16 Sharia Muhammad Ezz El-Arab; f. 1924; Arabic weekly; Editor FIKRY ABAZA; circ. 162,000.

al-Sabah: 4 Sharia Muhammad Said Pasha; f. 1922; Arabic; weekly; Editor MOSTAFA EL-KACHACHI.

al-Tahrir: 5 Sharia Naguib-Rihani; Arabic; weekly; Editor ABDEL-AZIZ SADEK.

al-Talia (*Vanguard*): f. 1965; left wing; monthly.

Ana Wa Inta: Sharia Central; Arabic; monthly; Editor MOHAMED HASSAN.

Arab Observer: published by the Middle East News Agency, 11 Sh. Sahafa; f. 1960; weekly international news magazine; English; has now incorporated *The Scribe*; Editor-in-Chief Dr. ABDEL HAMID EL-BATRIK.

Contemporary Thought: University of Cairo; quarterly; Editor Dr. Z. N. MAHMOUD.

Echos: 15 Sharia Mahmoud Bassiouni; f. 1947; French; weekly; Dir. and Propr. GEORGES ORFALI.

Egyptian Chamber of Commerce Bulletin: 4 Midan Falaki.

Egyptian Directory, The: 19 Sharia Abdel Khalek Sarwat, B.P. 500; f. 1887; French and English; annual; Man. and Editor TAWHID KAMAL.

Egyptian Mail: 24 Sharia Zakaria Ahmed; f. 1910; English; weekly; Editor Dr. AMIN ABOUL-ENEIN.

Egypt's Medical Digest: 56 Sharia Abdel Khalek Sarwat, monthly; English; Editor Dr. KAMEL MIRZA.

Femme Nouvelle, La: 48 Sharia Kasr-el-Nil; French; twice yearly; Editor DORIA SHAFIK.

Gazette of the Faculty of Medicine: Sharia Kasr El-Aini; Kasr El-Aini Clinical Society; English; quarterly.

German-Arab Trade: 2 Sharia Sherif Pasha; German, English, Arabic; Editor KLAUS BALZER; circ. 6,000.

al Guil el Gedid: Dar Akhbar al-Yom, Sharia al-Sahafa; f. 1945; Arabic; weekly; Editor MOUSSA SABRI; circ. 50,000.

Ghorfet al-Kahira (*Journal of Cairo Chamber of Commerce*): 4 Midan Falaky; Arabic; monthly.

Hawa'a (*Eve*): Dar al-Hilal, 16 Sharia Muhammad Ezz El-Arab; women's magazine; Arabic; weekly.

Images: Dar Al-Hilal, 16 Sharia Muhammad Ezz El-Arab; French; illustrated; weekly; Editors EMILE and CHOUCRI ZEIDAN.

Industrial Egypt: P.O.B. 251, 26A Sharia Sherif Pasha, Cairo; f. 1924; Bulletin of the Federation of Egyptian Industries; English and Arabic; quarterly; Editor Eng. GAMIL EL-SABBAN.

Industry and Trade Information: 13 Sharia Abdel Hamid Said; English; weekly; commercial and industrial bulletin; Dir. and Propr. NICOLAS STAVRI; Editor N. GHANEM.

Informateur Financier et Commercial: 24 Sharia Soliman Pasha; f. 1929; weekly; Dir. HENRI POLITI; circ. 15,000.

Kitab al-Hilal: 16 Sharia Muhammad Ezz El-Arab; monthly; Proprs. EMILE and CHOUKRI ZEIDAN.

Lewa al-Islam: 11 Sharia Sherif Pasha; Arabic; monthly; Propr. AHMED HAMZA; Editor MUHAMMAD ALY SHETA.

Lotus Magazine (*Afro-Asian Writings*): 104 Kasr El Eini St.; f. 1968; quarterly; English, French and Arabic; Editor YOUSSEF EL SEBAI.

Magalet al-Mohandeseen: 28 Avenue Ramses; f. 1945; published by The Engineers' Syndicate; Arabic and English; ten times a year; Editor and Sec. MAHMOUD SAMI ABDEL KAWI.

Megakkah al-Zerayia: monthly; Arabic; agriculture; circ. 30,000.

The Middle East Observer: 8 Shawarby St.; f. 1955; weekly; English; specializing in economics of Middle East and African markets; Man. Owner AHMED FODA; Chief Editors A. W. MORSI, AHMED SABRI; circ. 30,000.

Phos-Chronos: 14 Sharia Galal; Greek; Editors B. PATÈRAS, S. PATÈRAS.

Progrès Dimanche: 24 Sharia Galal; French; weekly; Editor M. YACCARINI.

Riwayat al-Hilal: 16 Sharia Muhammad Ezz El-Arab; Arabic; monthly; Proprs. EMILE and CHOUKRI ZEIDAN.

Rose el Youssef: 89A Kasr el Ainei St.; f. 1925; Arabic; weekly; political; circulates throughout all Arab countries, includes monthly English section, Chair. KAMEL ZOHEIRY; Editor ABDUL RAHMAN AL-SHARQAWI; Editor English section IBRAHIM EZZAT; Man. ABDEL GHANI ABDEL-FATTAH; circ. 35,000.

Sabah al-Kheir: 18 Sharia Mohamed Said; Arabic; weekly; light entertainment.

Tchehreh Nema: 14 Sharia Hassan El-Akbar (Abdine); f. 1904; Iranian; monthly; political, literary and general; Editor MANUCHEHR TCHEHREH NEMA MOADEB ZADEH.

Up-to-Date International Industry: 10 Sharia Galal; Arabic and English; foreign trade journal.

NEWS AGENCIES

Middle East News Agency: 4 Sharia Sherrifin, Cairo; f. 1955; regular service in Arabic, English and French; Chair. MOHAMED ABDEL GAWAD.

Misr Egyptian News Agency: 43 Sharia Ramses, Cairo.

FOREIGN BUREAUX

Agence France Presse: 33 Kasr El Nil St., Cairo; Chief JEAN-PIERRE JOULIN.

ANSA: 19 Sh. Abdel Khalek Sarwat, Cairo; Chief GIOVANNI CAMPANA.

AP: 33 Kasr El Nil, Cairo; Chief CHRISTOPHER C. MINICLIER.

Bulgarian Telegraph Agency: 13 Sh. Muhammad Kamel Morsi, Aguza, Cairo; Chief DIMITER MASLAROV.

Četeka (Czechoslovak News Agency): 7 Sh. Hasan Asem, Zamalek, Cairo.

Deutsche Presse Agentur (dpa): 33 Kasr el Nil St., Apt. 13/4, Cairo.

Kyodo News Service: Flat 12, 33 Abdel Khalek Tharawta, Cairo; Chief HIDEO YAMASHITA.

Reuters: Apt. 43, Immobilia Bldgs., 26 Sh. Sherif Pasha, Cairo, P.O.B. 2040.

UPI: 4 Sh. Eloui, P.O.B. 872, Cairo; Chief RAY N. MOSELEY.

Antara and DPA also have bureaux in Cairo.

PUBLISHERS

Egyptian General Organization for Publishing and Printing: 117 Corniche el Nil St., Cairo; affiliated to the Ministry of Culture.

ALEXANDRIA

Alexandria University Press: Shatby.

Artec: 10 Sharia Stamboul.

Dar Nashr ath-Thagata.

Egyptian Book Centre: A. D. Christodoulou and Co., 5 Sharia Adib; f. 1950.

Egyptian Printing and Publishing House: Ahmed El Sayed Marouf, 59, Safia Zaghoul; f. 1947.

Maison Egyptienne d'Editions: Ahmed El Sayed Marouf, Sharia Adib; f. 1950.

Maktab al-Misri al-Hadith li-t-Tiba wan-Nashr: 7 Nobar St.; Man. AHMAD YEHIA.

CAIRO

Akhbar El Yom Publishing House: 6 Sharia al-Sahafa; f. 1944; publishes *al-Akhbar* (daily), *Akhbar al-Yom* (weekly), and magazine *Akher Saa*; Man. Dir. Dr. KASSEM FARAHAT.

Al-Hilal Publishing House: 16 Sharia Muhammad Ezz El-Arab; f. 1895; publishes *Al-Hilal, Riwayat Al-Hilal, Kitab Al-Hilal* (monthlies); *Al Mussawar, Al Kawakeb, Hawa* (weeklies).

Dar al-Gomhouriya: 24 Sharia Galal; publications include the dailies, *al-Gomhouriya, al-Misaa, Egyptian Gazette* and *Le Progrès Egyptien*; Pres. KAMEL EL HENNAWI.

Dar al-Hilal: Al Hilal Bldg., 16 Sharia Mohammed Ezz El-Arab; f. 1892; publishes magazines only, including *al-Mussawar, Hawa'a* and *al-Kawakeb*; Dir. EMILE and CHOUKRI ZEIDAN.

Dar al Kitab al Arabi: Misr Printing House, Sharia Noubar, Bab al Louk, Cairo; f. 1968; Man. Dir. Dr. SAHAIR AL KALAMAWI.

Dar al Maaref Egypt: 1119 Cornich El-Nil St.; f. 1890; Arabic books in all fields; distributor of books in English, French and German; Man. Dir. Dr. SAYED ABUL NAGA.

Documentation and Research Centre for Education (Ministry of Education): 33 Falaky St.; f. 1956; Dir. Mrs. ZEINAB M. MEHREZ; bibliographies, directories, information and education bulletins.

Editions Horus: 1 Midan Soliman Pasha.

Editions le Progrès: 6 Sharia Sherif Pasha; Propr. WADI CHOUKRI.

Editions et Publications des Pères Jésuites: 1 rue Boustan al Maksi, Faggala; scientific and religious publications; Dir. H. DE LEUSSE.

Editions Universitaires d'Egypte, Les: Alla El-Dine El-Chiati and Co.; 41 Sharia Sherif Pasha.

Higher University Council for Arts, Letters and Sciences: University of Cairo.

Imprimerie Argus: 10 Sharia Galal; Propr. SOCRATE SARRAFIAN.

Lagnat al Taalif Wal Targama Wal Nashr (*Committee for Writing, Translating and Publishing Books*): 9 Sharia El-Kerdassi (Abdine).

Librairie La Renaissance D'Egypte (Hassan Muhammad & Sons): 9 Adly St., P.O.B. 2172; f. 1930; Man. HASSAN MUHAMMAD; religion, history, geography, medicine, architecture, economics, politics, law, children's books, atlases, dictionaries.

Maktabet Misr: P.O.B. 16, Faggalah, Cairo; f. 1932; publ. wide variety of fiction, biographies and textbooks for schools and universities; Man. AMIR SAID GOUDA A SAHHAR.

Middle East Publishing Co.: 29 Rue Abdel Khalek Sarwat.

Mohamed Abbas Sid Ahmed: 55 Sharia Nubar.

National Library Press (*Dar al Kutub*): Midan Ahmed Maher; bibliographic works.

New Publications: J. Meshaka and Co., 5 Sharia Maspero.

The Public Organization for Books and Scientific Appliances: Cairo University, Orman, Ghiza; f. 1965; state organization publishing academic books for universities, higher institutes, etc.; also imports books, periodicals and scientific appliances; Chair. KAMIL SEDDIK; Vice-Chair. FATTHY LABIB.

Senouhy Publishers: 54 Sharia Abdel-Khalek Sarwat; f. 1956; Dirs. LEILA A. FADEL, OMAR RASHAD.

Other Cairo publishers include: *Dar al-Fikr al-Arabi, Dar al-Fikr al-Hadith Li-t-Tab wan-Nashr, Dar wa Matabi, Dar al-Nahda al-Arabiya, Dar al-Misriya Li-t-Talif wat-Tardjma, Dar al-Qalam, Dar ath-Thagapa, Majlis al-Ala Li-Riyyat al-Funun, Maktaba Ain Shams, Maktaba al-Andshilu al-Misriya, Maktabat al-Chandshi, Maktabat al-Nahira al-Hadith, Markaz Tasjil al-Athar al-Misriya, Matbaat ar-Risala, al-Qaumiya li-t-Tibaa wan-Nashr Wizarat az-Ziraa Maslahat al-Basatin.*

RADIO AND TELEVISION

Egyptian Radio and Television Corporation: Cairo; f. 1971; supervised by Dep. Prime Minister and affil. to Ministry of Culture and Information.

Société Egyptienne de Publicité: 24-26 Sharia Zakaria Ahmed, Cairo; f. 1906; handles all advertising media in Egypt, including radio and television; affil. to Al Tahrir Printing and Publishing House; Dep. Dir. Gen. KHEDR MOHAMED ABDEL SALAM.

RADIO

Egyptian Broadcasting Corporation: Corniche el Nil, Cairo; f. 1928; 169 hours daily; Chair. MOHAMED MAHMOUD SHAABAN; Dir.-Gen. Arabic Programmes SAFIA EL MOHANDES; Dir.-Gen. Foreign Programmes MOHAMED ISMAIL MOHAMED.

Home service programmes in Arabic, English, French, Armenian, German, Greek and Italian; foreign services in Hebrew, Persian, Spanish, Bengali, Turkish, Folani, Malawi, Shona, Lingala, Yoruba, Dankali, English, Swahili, Urdu, Indonesian, Hindi, Somali, Russian, Sosotho, Sindebek, Amharic, Wolof, French, Hausa, German, Siami, Pushtu, Portuguese, Italian, Zulu, Nianja, Thai, Bambra, Arabic. *Broadcasting and TV* (weekly), *Broadcasting Art* (quarterly).

Middle East Radio: Société Egyptienne de Publicité, 24-26 Sharia Zakaria Ahmed, Cairo; f. 1964; commercial service with 500-kW. transmitter; U.K. Agents: Radio and Television Services (Middle East) Ltd., 21 Hertford St., London, W.1.

In 1973 there were 30 million radio receivers and 1.5 million television sets.

TELEVISION

Egyptian Television Organization: Corniche el Nil, Cairo; f. 1960; 150 hours weekly (two channels); Chair. ABDEL HAMID YOUNES; Dir.-Gen. Programmes Mrs. SAMIHA AB EL-RAHMAN.

FINANCE

BANKING

(cap. = capital; p.u. = paid up; dep. = deposits; m. = million; amounts in £ Egyptian)

The whole banking system was nationalized in 1961.

CENTRAL BANK

Central Bank of Egypt: 31 Sharia Kasr-el-Nil, Cairo; f. 1961; cap. 3.0m., dep. 383m. (June 1973); Governor AHMED ZANDO.

COMMERCIAL BANKS

Arabic Real Estate Bank: Cairo; Vice-Pres. HANAFY LABIB HUSEIN.

Egyptian Real Estate Bank: Cairo; Gov. MOHAMED KAMEL ABASS.

Bank of Alexandria, S.A.E.; 6 Salah Salem St., Alexandria; f. 1864; p.u. cap. 3m., dep. 240m. (December 1972); 80 brs.; incorporated Industrial Bank 1971; Pres. AHMED ABDEL GHAFFAR.

Banque du Caire: 22 Sharia Adly Pasha, P.O.B. 1495, Cairo; f. 1952; cap. and reserves 2.5m., dep. 182m. (Dec. 1972); Chair. HASSAN ZAKI AHMED; Man. Dir. ABDEL LATIF DAHABA.

Banque Misr, S.A.E.: 151 Sharia Mohamed Farid, Cairo; f. 1920; nationalized 1960; incorporated Bank of Suez and Banque Collectivité Financière 1964; absorbed Banque de Port Said 1971; 197 brs.; cap. 2m., res. 27.4m. (June 1970); Chair. and Man. Dir. AHMED FOUAD; publ. *Economic Bulletin*.

National Bank of Egypt, S.A.E.: 24 Sharia Sherif Pasha, Cairo; f. 1898; nationalized 1960; handles all Egyptian import and export operations; cap. and reserves 13.9m., dep. 268m. (December 1972); 90 brs.; Chair. Dr. HAMED A. EL SAYEH; publ. *Quarterly Economic Bulletin*.

DEVELOPMENT BANKS

Arab African Bank: 44 Abdel-Khalek Sarwat St., Cairo; f. 1964; cap. 10m.; undertakes all types of foreign trade finance, investment in development projects in Arab and African countries; Chair. and Man. Dir. SULAIMAN AHMED EL HADDAD (Kuwait); Dep. Chair. and Man. Dir. MAHMOUD BAHIR ONSY (Egypt); branches in Beirut and Dubai, and to be opened in Muscat.

Arab International Bank: Cairo; f. 1971 as Egyptian International Bank; aims to promote trade and investment in Egypt, Libya and other Arab states; Chair. ABDUL-MONEIM KAISSOUNI.

Egyptian General Agricultural and Co-operative Organisation: 110 El-Kasr El-Eini St., Cairo; f. 1964; formerly *Agricultural Credits and Co-operative Bank*.

OTHER BANK

Nasser Social Bank: 35 Kasr El Nil St., Cairo; f. 1971.

STOCK EXCHANGES

Cairo Stock Exchange: 4A Cherifein St., Cairo; f. 1883; Pres. SHOUHDI AZER.

Alexandria Stock Exchange: Pres. M. HASSAN HAGGAG.

INSURANCE

Misr Insurance Company: 7 Sharia Talaat Harb, Cairo; Chair. FATHI MOHAMED IBRAHIM.

Al Chark Insurance Company, S.A.E.: Cairo; 15 Sharia Kasr-el-Nil; f. 1931; Chair. AHMED ZAKI HELMI; general and life; incorporates *Nile Insurance Co.*, *Al Mottahida Insurance Co.*, and *Africa Insurance Co.*

Commercial Insurance Company of Egypt, S.A.E.: 7 Midan E. Tahrir, Cairo; f. 1947; life, fire, marine, accident; Managing Dir. AHMED ZAKY HELMY.

The Egyptian Reinsurance Company, S.A.E.: 28 Talaat Harb St., P.O.B. 950, Cairo; f. 1957; Chair. MOHAMED SAID ELEZABY.

L'Epargne, S.A.E.: Immeuble Chemla Sharia 26 July, P.O.B. 548, Cairo; all types of insurance.

Al Iktisad el Shabee, S.A.E.; 11 Sharia Emad El Dine, P.O.B. 1635, Cairo; f. 1948; Man. Dir. and Gen. Man. W. KHAYAT.

Al Mottahida: 9 Sharia Soliman Pasha, P.O.B. 804, Cairo; f. 1957.

National Insurance Company of Egypt, S.A.E.: 33 Sharia Nabi Danial, P.O.B. 446, Alexandria; f. 1900; cap. 750,000; Chair. MOSTAFA EL-SAYED EL-ESNAWY.

Provident Association of Egypt, S.A.E.: 9 Sharia Sherif Pasha, P.O.B. 390, Alexandria; f. 1936; Man. Dir. C. G. VORLOOU.

TRADE AND INDUSTRY

CHAMBERS OF COMMERCE

ALEXANDRIA

Egyptian Chamber of Commerce, Alexandria: El-Ghorfa Eltegareia St.; Pres. ABDEL HAMIED SERRY; Vice-Pres. ABDEL SATTAR ARAFAH, MOSTAFA KAMAL BARAKAT; Treas. ALY ALY EL KATA, TAWFIC EL MELEIGY; Sec. AHMED EL ALFI MUHAMMAD; Gen. Dir. MUHAMMED FATHY MAHMOUD.

Camera di Commercio Italiana di Alessandria: P.O.B. 1763; f. 1885; 173 mems.; Pres. Cav. LUIGI F. POLVARA; Vice-Pres. Ing. ROBERT MITROVICH, Sig. EMILIO LINDI; Sec. of Council Ing. CARLO SCARPOCCHI; Treas. PIER LUCA CAPPIEILO; Sec.-Gen. PIERO FAZZI; publ. *Rivista degli Scambi Italo-Egiziani*.

Chambre de Commerce Hellénique: 19 Sharia Sherif Pasha; f. 1901; Pres. YANKO CHRYSSOVERGHI; Vice-Pres. C. GEORGIAFENDIS, C. NANOPOULOS; Treas. CHR. KOKKINOS; Hon. Sec. ALEX M. CASULLI.

Chambre de Commerce Turque: 9 Sharia Sherif Pasha; Hon. Pres. TAHA CARIM; Pres. ILHAMI CAKIN; Vice-Pres. IZZET LEVENDER and KASSIM KUTAY; Treas. HABIB ALEX. DIAB; Sec.-Gen. ZIYA SÖNMEZ.

CAIRO

Cairo Chamber of Commerce: 4 Midan El Falaki St.; f. 1913; Pres. MUHAMMAD ALI SHETA; Vice-Pres. ABDEL-AZIZ EL-TOKHI, KAMAL HAFEZ RAMADAN; Treas. ABDEL MENEM MOHMOUD EL-SHERIF; Sec.-Gen. MOSTAFA EL-BELIDY; publ. *Monthly Bulletin*.

Camera di Commercio Italiana per l'Egitto: 33 Sharia Abdel Khalek Sarwat, P.O. Box 19; 1947; Pres. GIUSEPPE SCHIRALLI; Vice-Pres. Ing. GIOVANNI LANFRANCHI; Gen. Sec. Dr. ERNESTO RAVIDÀ; 120 mems.; publs. *Rivista degli Scambi Italo-Egiziani* (every four months).

Chambre de Commerce Hellénique du Caire: 17 Sharia Soliman El Halabi; f. 1923; Pres. P. ARSLANOGLOU; Vice-Pres. C. B. STAVROU; Sec. A. VLASSOPOULOS.

German-Arab Chamber of Commerce: 2 Sharia Sherif Pasha, Cairo; f. 1951; Pres. RUDI STAERKER; Sec.-Gen. Assessor KLAUS BALZER; publ. *German Arab Trade*.

Representation of Federal Chamber of Foreign Trade of Yugoslavia: 47 Sharia Ramses, P.O.B. 448, Cairo; f. 1954; Sec.-Gen. D. STANKOVIĆ.

OTHER TOWNS

Egyptian Chamber of Commerce for Aswan Governorate: Abtal El-Tahrir St., Aswan.

Egyptian Chamber of Commerce for Asyut Governorate: Asyut.

Egyptian Chamber of Commerce for Behera Governorate: Gomhouriya St., Damanhoru.

Egyptian Chamber of Commerce for Beni-Suef Governorate: Mamdouh St., Moqbel El-Guedid, Beni-Suef.

Egyptian Chamber of Commerce for Dakahlia Governorate, Mansura: El-Saleh Ayoub Square, Mansura.

Egyptian Chamber of Commerce for Damietta Governorate: Damietta.

Egyptian Chamber of Commerce for Fayum Governorate: Fayum.

Egyptian Chamber of Commerce for Gharbia Governorate: Tanta.

Egyptian Chamber of Commerce for Giza Governorate: El-Saa Square, Giza.

Egyptian Chamber of Commerce for Ismailia Governorate: Ismailia.

Egyptian Chamber of Commerce for Kafr-el-Sheika Governorate: Kafr-el-Sheikh.

Egyptian Chamber of Commerce for Kena Governorate: El-Gamil Street, Kena.

Egyptian Chamber of Commerce for Menia Governorate: Menia.

Egyptian Chamber of Commerce for Manufia Governorate: Sidi Fayed Street, Shibín-El-Kom.

Egyptian Chamber of Commerce for Port Said Governorate: Port Said.

Egyptian Chamber of Commerce for Kalyubia Governorate: Benha.

Egyptian Chamber of Commerce for Sharkia Governorate: Zagazig.

Egyptian Chamber of Commerce for Suez Governorate: Suez.

Egyptian Chamber of Commerce for Suhag Governorate: Suhag.

NATIONALIZED ORGANIZATIONS

General Organization under the Ministry of War:

Armed Forces: 90 Sh. Al-Azhar, Cairo.

General Organizations under the Ministry of Industry, Petroleum and Mineral Wealth:

Egyptian General Organization for Food Industries: 6 Salem Salem St., Agouza, Cairo; 26 companies; products include most basic foodstuffs, tobacco, sugar, soft and alcoholic drinks, confectionary, essential oils, essences, soap, perfumery, cosmetics, etc.; 90,000 workers; Dir. Prof. Dr. HASSAN ASHMAWI.

Spinning and Weaving: 5 Tolombat St., Garden City, Cairo; 28 companies.

Egyptian General Organization for Engineering, Electric and Electronic Industries: 28 Talaat Harb St., Cairo; 22 companies.

Chemical Industries: 49 Kasr El Nil St., Cairo; 29 companies.

Building Materials and Ceramics: 49 Kasr El Nil St., Cairo; 13 companies.

Metal Industries: 5 July 26th St., Cairo; 9 companies.

Egyptian Organization for Geological Researches and Mining: Pres. RUSHDY SAYED FARAG; Dir. Gen. GALAL EL DIN MOSTAFA.

General Organization under the Ministry of Military Production:

Egyptian General Organization for Military Factories and Industries of Aviation: 8 Gemaee St., Garden City, Cairo.

General Organizations under the Ministry of Marine Transport:

Maritime Transport: 8 Nasser St., Alexandria; 7 affiliated companies.

General Organization under the Minister of Treasury:

Social Insurance General Organization: 126 July St., Cairo.

General Organizations under Ministry of Economy and Foreign Trade:

Egyptian General Organization of Foreign Trade: 2 companies for exporting agricultural products, 2 for engineering and one for cars.

Egyptian General Organization of Cotton: 19 El Gomhouria St., Cairo; 25 El Horria Ave., Alexandria.

General Organization under Ministry of Health:

Egyptian General Organization for Drugs, Chemicals and Medical Equipment: 11 companies.

General Organizations under Ministry of Housing and Construction:

Egyptian General Organization of Housing and Rehabitation: 4 Latin America Street, Garden City, Cairo; 10 companies.

General Organization of Co-operative Housing and Construction: Nasr City, Cairo.

Civil Contracting Company: 14 Talaat Harb, Cairo.

General Organizations under Ministry of Culture and Information:

Egyptian General Organization for Tourism and Hotels: 4 Latin America St., Garden City, Cairo.

Egyptian Broadcasting and T.V. Corporation: Corniche el Nil, Cairo.

General Organizations under the Ministry of Land Reclamation:

General Egyptian Organization of Land Reclamation: Dokki; 6 companies.

Executive Council of Desert Projects.

General Organizations under Ministry of Agriculture:

Co-operative Agriculture: Misr Insurance Bldg., Giza; Dir.-Gen. ABDUL MAKSOUD EZZAT MOHAMED EZZAT.

Poultry: Misr Insurance Bldg., Giza.

Meat: 14 El Gamhouria Sq., Abdin, Cairo.

Maritime Wealth.

General Organization under Ministry of Aviation:

Misr Organization for Aviation.

General Organizations under the Suez Canal Authority:

7 affiliated companies.

OIL

Egyptian General Organization of Petroleum: Cairo; state supervisory authority for the development of the national oil resources; has entered into 50:50 partnership agreements with a number of foreign companies; Pres. Eng. MOHAMED RAMZY EL-LETHY; Gen. Man. MOHAMED HASSAN EL DAWI.

Egyptian Marine Petroleum: Cairo; f. 1970; partnership between EGPC and North Sumatra Oil Development Corporation (an amalgam of Japanese interests, the largest being the Japanese Petroleum Development Corp.); has concession in the Ras Gharib area in the Gulf of Suez.

Compagnie Orientale des Pétroles: Cairo; partnership between EGPC and International Egyptian Oil Company (owned principally by ENI of Italy); developed the Sinai oilfields now occupied by Israel.

Suez Gulf Petroleum Company: Cairo; partnership between EGPC and Pan American Oil (a subsidiary of Standard Oil of Indiana); developed the Morgan oilfield on the western side of the Red Sea; also holds exploration concessions for territory in the Western Desert and the Nile delta.

Western Desert Operating Petroleum Company: Alexandria; f. 1967 as partnership between EGPC and Phillips Petroleum; developed Alamein and later, Yidma fields in the Western Desert, producing approx. 15,000 barrels per day in early 1974; Chair. Dr. Mahmoud Amin.

EMPLOYERS' ORGANIZATIONS

Federation of Egyptian Industries: P.O.B. 251, 26A Sharia Sherif Pasha, Cairo, and P.O.B. 1658, 65 Horia Rd., Alexandria; f. 1922; Pres. Dr. Eng. Mahmoud Aly Hassan; represents the industrial community in Egypt.

Affiliated Organizations

Chamber of Food Industries: Pres. Dr. Hassan Ashmawi.

Chamber of Building Materials and Construction: Pres. Eng. Hassan Muhammad Hassan.

Chamber of Cereals and Related Products Industry: Pres. Dr. Fawzi Youssef Refai.

Chamber of Chemical Industries: Pres. Dr. Hassan Ibrahim Badawi.

Chamber of Engineering Industries: Pres. Eng. Muhammad Abdel Baki El-Kosheiry.

Chamber of Leather Industry: Pres. Dr. Hassan Ibrahim El-Sissy.

Chamber of Metallurgical Industries: Pres. Eng. Ali Morsi.

Chamber of Petroleum and Mining: Pres. Dr. Ahmed Tewfik.

Chamber of Printing, Binding and Paper Products: Pres. Eng. Youssef Moustafa Bahgat.

Chamber of Spinning and Weaving Industry: Pres. Hamed el-Maamoun Habib.

Chamber of Woodworking Industry: Pres. Hassan Soliman Muhammad.

TRADE UNIONS

Egyptian Federation of Labour (EFL): 90 El Galaa St., Cairo; f. 1957; 16 affiliated unions; 2.5 million mems.; affiliated to the International Confederation of Arab Trade Unions and to the All-African Trade Union Federation; Pres. Salah Gharib; Sec. Saeed Gomaa; publ. El Omal (weekly, Arabic).

Arab Federation of Food Workers (AFFW): P.O.B. 877, Cairo; 500,000 mems.; Gen. Sec. Saad Muhammad Ahmed.

Federation of Arab Engineers: 28 Ramses St., Cairo; Sec. Muhammad Saka.

General Trade Union of Agriculture: 31 Mansour St., Bab al-Louk, Cairo; 350,000 mems.; Pres. Salah Al Din Abu Al-Magi; Gen. Sec. Nasr Al Din Mustapha.

General Trade Union of Banking and Insurance: 2 Al Qadi al Fadl St., Cairo; 32,000 mems.; Pres. Muhammad Fathi Fouda; Gen. Sec. Munir Habash.

General Trade Union of Building Industries: 9 Emad el Din St., Cairo; 46,000 mems.; Pres. Abd al Mutale Salem; Gen. Sec. Hamed Hussain Barakat.

General Trade Union of Business and Management Services: 387 Port Said St., Bab al Khalk, Cairo; 46,000 mems.; Pres. Awad Abd Al Qader; Gen. Sec. Abl Al Rahman Khedr.

General Trade Union of the Chemical Industries: 76 Gomhouria St., Cairo; 60,000 mems.; Pres. Muhammad Asaad Rageh; Gen. Sec. Hamya Ali Mahjoub.

General Trade Union of Engineering, Electrical and Metal Industries: 90 El Galaa St., Cairo; 80,000 mems.; Pres. Saeed Gomaa Ali; Gen. Sec. Gamal Tarabishi.

General Trade Union of Nutritional Industries: 3 Hosni St., Qubba al Hadaek, P.O.B. 2230, Cairo; 125,000 mems.; Pres. Mohamed Abdou Gomaa; Vice-Pres. Mahmoud el Askhri.

General Trade Union of Railways: 47 Al Tera al Boulaquiya St., Cairo; 46,000 mems.; Pres. Muhammad Atito; Gen. Sec. Ahmad Fawzi Ali.

General Trade Union of Textiles: 327 Shoubra St., Cairo; f. 1960; 250,000 mems.; Pres. Salah Gharid.

TRANSPORT

RAILWAYS

Egyptian Railways: Cairo; f. 1852; length and gauge 4,510 km., 1,435 mm.; 2,598 km., 1,435 mm. auxiliary lines; 25 km. electrified; Chair. Eng. Mahmoud Kamel Mortagy.

Alexandria Passenger Transport Authority: 21 Saad Zaghloul Square, P.O.B. 466, Alexandria; controls City Tramways (28 km.), Ramleh Electric Railway (16 km.), suburban buses (201 km.); Chair. Eng. Aly Hosny Mahmoud; Tech. Dir. Eng. Mohamed Abdel-Latif Nassef.

Heliopolis Company for Housing and Inhabiting: 28 Ibrahim El Lakkany St., Heliopolis, Cairo; 50 km., 148 railcars; Gen. Man. Abdel Moneim Seif.

A 6¼-mile underground railway is under consideration in Cairo, and a 430 km. line to carry iron ore from the Bahariya mines to the Helwan iron and steel works was opened in August 1973.

ROADS

Egyptian General Organization of Inland Transport for Provinces Passengers: Sharia Kasr-el-Aini, Cairo; Pres. Hasan Mourad Kotb.

There are good metalled main roads as follows: Cairo-Alexandria (desert road); Cairo-Benna-Tanta-Damanhur-Alexandria; Cairo-Suez (desert road); Cairo-Ismailia-Port Said or Suez; Cairo-Fayum (desert road); in 1970 there were over 13,000 miles of good metalled roads.

Automobile et Touring Club D'Egypte: 10 rue Kasr-el-Nil, Cairo; f. 1924; 476 mems.; Hon. Pres. Ing. Hassan Nagi; Pres. Maj.-Gen. Dr. Mohammed Abdel Hamid Mortaghi.

SHIPPING

Egyptian Maritime Co.: 3 rue de l'Ancienne Bourse, Alexandria; f. 1930; services Alexandria/Europe, Canada, Black Sea, Adriatic Sea and Africa; fleet of 39 vessels; Chair. M. Y. Ramadan.

American Eastern Trading and Shipping Co., S.A.E.: 17 Sharia Sesostris, Alexandria; Pres. M. E. WAGNER; Manager, Egypt, AHMED LABIB TAHIO.

Egyptian Stevedoring and Shipping Co., S.A.E.: 17 Sharia Sesostris, Alexandria; f. 1946; Pres. J. H. CHALHOUB; Manager MUHAMMAD FAHMY TAHIO.

Thebes Shipping Agency: P.O. Box 45, 41 Sharia Nebi Daniel, Alexandria; maritime transport.

THE SUEZ CANAL

Suez Canal Authority (*Hay'at Canal Al Suess*): 6 Lazokhli St., Garden City, Cairo; Pres. Eng. MASHHOUR AHMED MASSHHOUR.

Length of Canal: 162.5 km.; maximum permissible draught: 38 ft.; maximum width (at water level): 660 ft.; minimum width (at depth of 36 ft.): 295 ft. The Canal has been closed since the war in June 1967. Work on clearing the canal of mines and obstructions before re-opening it to shipping was well under way by the middle of 1974.

CIVIL AVIATION

EgyptAir: Head Office: Cairo International Airport, Heliopolis, Cairo; f. 1932 as Misr Airwork; operates internal services in Egypt and external services throughout the Middle East, Far East, Africa and Europe; Pres. Gen. MOSSALEM NOFAL; fleet of seven Boeing 707, eight Tu-154, four Comet 4C, three AN-24.

The following foreign airlines serve Egypt: Aeroflot, Air France, Air India, Alia, Alitalia, AUA, British Airways, British Caledonian, ČSA, Cyprus Airways, Ethiopian Air Lines, Garuda, Ghana Airways, Interflug, Iraqi Airways, JAL, JAT, Libyan Arab Airlines, KLM, Kuwait Airways, LOT, Lufthansa, MALÉV, MEA, Olympic Airways, Pan Am, PIA, Qantas, Sabena, SAS, Saudia, Sudan Airways, Swissair, TAROM, TWA and UTA.

TOURISM

Ministry of Tourism: 110 Sh. Kasr-el-Aini, Cairo; f. 1965; branches at Alexandria, Port Said, Suez, Luxor and Aswan; Minister of Tourism ISMAIL FAHMI.

General Organization for Tourism and Hotels: 4 Latin America St., Garden City, Cairo; f. 1961; affiliated to the Ministry of Tourism.

Authorized foreign exchange dealers for tourists include the principal banks and the following:

American Express of Egypt Ltd.: 15 Kasr-el-Nil St., Cairo; f. 1919.

Thomas Cook and Son: 4 Sharia Champollion, Cairo.

CULTURAL ORGANIZATION

Ministry of Culture: Cairo; Minister YOUSSEF EL SEBAI.

PRINCIPAL THEATRES AND ORCHESTRA

Pocket Theatre: Cairo; f. 1961.

Egyptian General Organization of Cinema, Theatre and Music: Ministry of Culture and Information.

Departments include the following: **Opera Lyric Troupe, Opera Ballet, Opera Chorale, Cairo Symphony Orchestra.**

Members frequently take part in performances with visiting opera companies.

National Puppet Theatre: Cairo.

NATIONAL DANCE TROUPES

National Folklore Dance Troupe: Cairo; frequently performs on tours abroad.

Reda Folklore Dance Troupe: 50 Kasr-el-Nil St., Cairo; f. 1959; frequently performs on tours abroad; Dirs. MAHMOUD REDA, ALI REDA; Principal Dancers FARIDA FAHMY, MAHMOUD REDA; Composer and Conductor ALI ISMAIL.

ATOMIC ENERGY

Atomic Energy Organization: Dokki, Cairo; f. 1955; Dir. Dr. SALAH HEDAYET. First reactor with 2,000 kW. power, opened at Inchass in 1961.

Regional Radioisotope Centre: Cairo; f. 1957; eleven laboratories for research and development in scientific, medical, agricultural and industrial fields; in 1963 the Centre was transformed into a Regional Centre for the Arab countries of the Middle East, in co-operation with UN I.A.E.A.

The Institute of Nuclear Engineering at Alexandria University is to use a loan of £E 250,000 from Kuwait to purchase an atomic reactor and laboratory facilities.

UNIVERSITIES

Ain Shams University: Kasr el Zaafran, Abbasiyah, Cairo; 1,025 teachers, 38,200 students.

Alexandria University: Shatby, Alexandria; 2,350 teachers, 49,284 students.

Al-Azhar University: Cairo 1,354 teachers, 31,867 students.

American University in Cairo: 113 Sh. Kasr el Aini, Cairo; 175 teachers, 1,500 students.

East of the Delta University: Mansoura.

Mid-Delta University: Tanta.

University of Assiut: Assiut; 13,177 students.

University of Cairo: Orman, Ghiza; 2,892 teachers, 64,606 students.

EL SALVADOR

INTRODUCTORY SURVEY

Location, Climate, Language, Religion, Flag, Capital

El Salvador occupies 21,393 sq. km. on the Pacific coast of the isthmus of Central America. It is bounded by Guatemala to the west and Honduras to the north and east. The climate varies from the tropical coastal plain to the temperate uplands. The language is Spanish. Eighty-eight per cent of the population are Roman Catholic. The national flag (proportions 3 by 2) consists of three horizontal stripes, blue, white and blue, the central stripe bearing the national coat of arms. The capital is San Salvador.

Recent History

In 1966 General Fidel Sánchez Hernández, leader of the conservative Partido de Conciliación Nacional, a former Minister of the Interior, was elected president. Long-standing animosity between El Salvador and Honduras developed into armed conflict after a Salvadorian victory in the eliminating rounds of the World Cup in 1969. Although El Salvador was largely successful in the so-called "football war" which followed, the war caused her internal difficulties as Honduras expelled 50,000 illegal Salvadorian immigrants from her territory and closed her border to Salvadorian imports and exports in transit. These measures, which threaten the existence of the Central American Common Market, have been circumvented by El Salvador and contacts have reopened with Honduras to seek a way of re-activating CACM. As the Market's most industrialized country and largest exporter, this is of great importance to El Salvador's long-term economic prospects. However, talks held during 1973 involving the Foreign Ministers of the two countries failed to reach agreement on the frontier and other problems preventing the restoration of full relations.

In March 1970 the ruling Partido de Conciliación Nacional gained heavily in congressional and municipal elections. In the presidential elections of 1972 Col. Arturo Armando Molina Barraza, the candidate favoured by President Sánchez Hernández, emerged as the victor over his closest rival, José Napoleón Duarte, the leader of the left-wing coalition party Unión Nacional de Oposición. Col. Molina took office for a five-year period on July 1st, 1972. An attempted *coup d'état* in March 1972 by supporters of Napoleón Duarte was crushed by forces loyal to the outgoing President Sánchez. El Salvador is a member of the UN, the Organization of American States, the Alliance for Progress and the Organization of Central American States.

Government

Executive power is vested in the President, elected by popular vote for five years, assisted by the Cabinet. The legislative organ is the unicameral Legislative Assembly consisting of 52 deputies elected by proportional representation. The country is divided into 14 departments.

Defence

A period of national service is compulsory between the ages of eighteen and thirty. The total strength of the army, navy and air force is fixed annually by the Legislative Assembly and is never less than 3,000 men. In 1972 it totalled 4,500. There is a small navy and an air force of 1,000 men. Para-military forces number 3,000 men. El Salvador has a military bloc alliance with Guatemala and Nicaragua.

Economic Affairs

The economy is agricultural and about 60 per cent of the population work on the land. The principal crop is coffee, which furnishes half of exports. Other products are cotton, maize, rice and sugar. Commercial fisheries have been established in recent years, and fish and shellfish are the third biggest export earner. Industry is being developed and a steel works has been erected. Electric power has been substantially increased by building a dam across the Lempa river. With an annual population growth rate of 3.6 per cent, one of El Salvador's most intractable problems is to provide employment for the labour force. The country's trade has been seriously affected by the dispute with Honduras and the latter's withdrawal from the Central American Common Market, of which El Salvador is a member.

Transport and Communications

The transport network is well developed. Railways are operated by two companies and there are 720 km. of track. The Pan American Highway bisects the country and a parallel coastal highway with interconnecting roads is under construction. The chief port is Acajutla, where improvements costing 12m. colones are under way. La Unión and La Libertad also provide good port facilities. Two domestic airlines and five foreign ones provide international services from the airport at Ilopango, which is equipped for jet aircraft.

Social Welfare

The social welfare system provides for medical services and benefits for industrial injuries, sickness, maternity and old age.

Education

There are about 3,500 public and private schools with over 600,000 pupils, a national university with some 4,000 students, and a private university.

Tourism

El Salvador was one of the centres of the ancient Mayan civilization and the ruined temples and cities are of great interest. The volcanoes and lakes of the uplands provide magnificent scenery and there are fine beaches along the Pacific coast.

Visas are not required to visit El Salvador by nationals of Costa Rica, Guatemala, Honduras, Nicaragua or any West European country (except Italy and Portugal).

Sport

El Salvador has a number of stadiums for national and international fixtures. Football, basketball, baseball and athletics are the most popular sports, and numerous lakes and beaches are used for water sports.

Public Holidays

1974: August 1st–7th (Festival*), September 15th (Independence Day), October 12th (Discovery of America), November 2nd (All Souls' Day), November 5th (First Call of Independence), December 24th–31st (Christmas).

1975: January 1st (New Year's Day), March 25th–31st (Holy Week), May 1st (Labour Day), May 29th (Corpus Christi).

* Not all enterprises are closed during this period.

Weights and Measures

The metric system is in force.

Currency and Exchange Rates

100 centavos = 1 Salvadorian colón.

Exchange rates (April 1974):
£1 sterling = 5.90 colones;
U.S. $1 = 2.50 colones.

STATISTICAL SURVEY

AREA AND POPULATION

AREA	POPULATION			
sq. km.	TOTAL	SAN SALVADOR (capital)	1972 BIRTHS (per '000)	1972 DEATHS (per '000)
21,393	3,760,437*	378,827*	40.7	8.6

* Estimate at July 1st, 1972.

AGRICULTURE
('000 quintals)

	1969–70	1970–71	1971–72
Coffee	3,130	2,815	3,473
Cotton	2,782	3,326	4,088
Maize	6,065	7,893	8,200
Beans	571	650	750
Rice	504	625	775
Sugar	2,536	3,455	4,075

Livestock: Cattle 1,000,950; pigs 307,800; horses 89,589; mules 36,614; goats 14,165; sheep 5,253.

INDUSTRY
('000 colones)

	1968	1969	1970
Beer	16,884	19,136	23,200
Non-alcoholic drinks	10,111	8,569	12,504
Spirits	11,916	13,704	10,845
Vegetable Oils	26,069	35,442	40,140
Cigarettes	18,868	20,189	21,060
Yarns and Textiles	71,688	84,685	100,609
Asbestos and cement	18,842	18,443	19,195
Fertilizers	10,389	21,095	16,177

FINANCE

100 centavos=1 Salvadorian colón.

Coins: 1, 5, 10, 25 and 50 centavos.

Notes: 1, 2, 5, 10, 25 and 100 colones.

Exchange rates (April 1974): £1 sterling=5.90 colones; U.S. $1=2.50 colones.

100 Salvadorian colones=£16.94=$40.00.

BUDGET

(million Central American pesos)

	1971	1972*
Revenue:		
Direct Taxation	28.4	31.0
Indirect Taxation	83.6	91.7
Other	8.0	8.3
TOTAL	120.0	131.0
Expenditure		
Current Expenditure	102.6	112.0
Capital Expenditure	24.5	35.4
TOTAL	127.1	147.4

* Preliminary.

NATIONAL ACCOUNTS

('000 colones)

	1969	1970	1971	1972*
GROSS DOMESTIC PRODUCT (at market prices)	2,381,819	2,564,570	2,697,564	2,890,417
of which:				
Agriculture	607,119	724,845	723,531	740,500
Manufacturing industries	466,239	484,624	519,247	550,228
Finance and commerce	592,981	600,746	649,163	717,951
Public administration	190,560	200,217	218,994	238,281
Income paid abroad	20,130	21,024	25,209	27,580
GROSS NATIONAL INCOME (at market prices)	2,361,689	2,543,546	2,672,355	2,862,837
Less depreciation allowances	119,864	125,039	133,682	173,245
NET NATIONAL INCOME (at market prices)	2,241,825	2,418,507	2,538,673	2,689,592
Indirect taxes less subsidies	161,745	186,290	198,865	229,243
NET NATIONAL PRODUCT (at factor cost)	2,080,080	2,222,217	2,339,807	2,460,349
Depreciation allowances	119,864	125,039	133,682	173,245
GROSS NATIONAL PRODUCT	2,199,944	2,347,256	2,473,489	2,633,594

* Provisional figures.

RESERVES AND CURRENCY

('000 Central American pesos)

	1970	1971	1972
Reserves at Banco Central	62,756	63,179	82,780
of which Gold and Foreign Exchange	62,747	61,003	78,215
Currency in Circulation (Dec.)	54,439	58,077	69,945
Special Drawing Rights	9	2,176	4,065

BALANCE OF PAYMENTS
(ʼooo colones)

	1971			1972*		
	Credit	Debit	Balance	Credit	Debit	Balance
Goods and Services:						
Merchandise	571,046	562,276	8,770	764,754	619,554	145,200
Non-monetary gold	—	1,114	— 1,114	—	1,308	— 1,308
Freight and insurance . . .	—	56,275	— 56,275	—	71,864	—71,864
Transport	4,517	17,501	— 12,984	13,129	14,204	— 1,075
International travel . . .	25,147	50,920	— 25,773	27,197	50,993	—23,796
Insurance (excl. merchandise) . .	8,203	11,817	— 3,614	8,680	13,948	— 5,268
International investment . .	7,703	33,344	— 25,641	6,713	34,586	—27,873
Government operations n.e.s. . .	11,561	7,375	4,186	11,767	8,126	3,641
Other services . . .	11,324	14,629	— 3,305	11,294	14,839	— 3,545
Total . . .	639,501	755,251	—115,750	834,534	829,422	14,112
Donations (Transfer payments) . .	50,355	7,191	43,164	35,817	7,199	28,618
CURRENT BALANCE . . .	689,856	762,442	— 72,586	870,351	836,621	42,730
Private Capital Transactions:						
Assets, long-term . . .	—	1,372	— 1,372	—	895	— 895
Assets, short-term . . .	—	1,612	— 1,612	—	13,683	—13,683
Liabilities, long-term . . .	39,081	22,813	16,268	46,909	31,591	15,318
Liabilities, short-term . . .	44,926	—	44,926	6,546	39,704	—33,158
Total . . .	84,007	25,797	58,210	53,455	85,873	—32,418
Government and Official Transactions:						
Assets, long-term . . .	—	4,804	— 4,804	—	5,708	— 5,708
Liabilities, long-term . . .	13,052	2,808	10,244	39,345	3,979	35,366
Total . . .		14,692	— 14,692		1,005	— 1,005
Net Errors and Omissions . .			48,958			
CAPITAL BALANCE . . .						— 3,765
Changes in Foreign Assets and Liabilities:	13,373	13,272	101	7,188	58,597	—51,409
Net international reserves . .	14,164	—	14,164	2,710	2,038	672
Other foreign liabilities (net) . .	36,900	13,272	23,628	21,670	60,635	—38,965
Total						

* Provisional.

EXTERNAL TRADE
IMPORTS AND EXPORTS
(ʼooo colones)

	IMPORTS	EXPORTS
1968 . .	533,789	531,261
1969 . .	522,600	506,200
1970 . .	533,895	572,695
1971 . .	619,500	571,046
1972 . .	691,418	692,950*

* Preliminary.

COMMODITIES
('ooo colones)

Imports	1969	1970	1971	1972*
Foodstuffs	66,672	61,262	64,398	63,276
Beverages and Tobacco	4,435	4,523	4,482	3,601
Raw Materials, inedible . . .	37,751	26,338	14,972	49,491
Crude Petroleum	16,450	6,599	27,193	24,898
Animal and Vegetable Fats and Oils .	8,215	7,857	9,132	7,014
Chemical Products	114,736	116,724	135,309	143,932
Medicinal and Pharmaceutical Products .	25,082	29,877	32,762	33,491
Manufactured Fertilizers . . .	23,826	25,717	25,754	30,278
Basic Manufactures	189,044	197,823	223,988	234,807
Machinery and Transport Equipment .	101,697	119,160	133,868	188,691
Mining, Building and Industrial Machinery .	36,753	39,421	58,389	64,273
Electrical Machinery and Apparatus .	21,686	28,290	27,035	38,642
Motor Vehicles	29,371	35,825	43,603	52,641
Live Animals, Special Transactions . .	14	207	199	606
Total	522,563	533,895	618,551	691,418

Exports	1969	1970	1971	1972*
Foodstuffs	278,952	337,504	299,452	371,620
Coffee	223,364	284,374	228,551	267,559
Raw Materials, inedible . . .	52,631	61,785	76,667	101,118
Cotton	48,716	57,976	72,537	96,596
Animal and Vegetable Oils and Fats .	2,632	2,013	3,414	2,918
Chemical Products	35,049	34,331	37,411	43,596
Miscellaneous Manufactures . . .	113,122	119,271	136,527	153,644
Other Products (incl. Beverages and Tobacco, Fuels, Machinery)	23,258	17,792	17,531	20,053
Total	505,646	572,695	571,046	692,950

* Preliminary.

PRINCIPAL COUNTRIES
('ooo colones)

	1970		1971		1972*	
	Imports	Exports	Imports	Exports	Imports	Exports
Central American Common Market . .	151,504	184,421	158,968	202,395	185,168	233,205
Costa Rica.	28,010	48,840	27,783	52,326	31,733	54,080
Guatemala.	101,593	99,465	104,789	111,013	119,226	138,780
Honduras	—	—	—	—	—	—
Nicaragua	21,902	36,116	26,397	39,055	34,209	40,345
Germany, Federal Republic . .	42,129	141,375	51,010	113,462	53,878	161,192
Japan	55,431	62,673	73,200	73,475	76,604	96,603
Netherlands	24,750	15,401	23,793	13,995	25,026	15,348
United Kingdom	15,777	749	18,104	1,068	22,051	4,954
United States	157,407	121,866	174,985	130,156	190,176	109,457

* Preliminary.

COFFEE EXPORTS
(bags of 69 kilos)

	1970	1971	1972
United States	484,042	557,257	331,397
Germany, Federal Republic .	778,006	660,263	865,628
Netherlands	77,495	69,285	68,818
Belgium	23,265	16,480	15,230
Italy	5,855	5,643	188,007
Switzerland	13,270	7,606	4,910
Canada	22,700	43,909	23,358
Japan	22,999	3,800	21,950
Others	157,772	38,519	118,244
TOTAL . . .	1,585,404	1,402,762	1,637,542

TRANSPORT

RAILWAYS
('000)

	1968	1969	1970
Passengers Carried .	1,500,349	1,471,625	1,572,402
Freight (tons) . .	447,377	430,575	766,092

ROADS

	1967	1968	1969
Cars and Jeeps .	24,506	26,904	27,887
Trucks and Lorries .	17,027	17,189	14,437
Buses . . .	2,266	3,114	2,398

SHIPPING
('000)

	1972	
	LOADED	UNLOADED
Tonnage . . .	930	1,463
Freight (tons) . .	320	1,091

CIVIL AVIATION
(freight in tons)

	1967	1968
Freight: Loaded . .	1,165	1,554
Unloaded . .	3,570	3,188
Passengers: Entering .	58,672	71,183
Leaving . .	67,964	74,090

EDUCATION
(1972)

	ESTABLISHMENTS	TEACHERS	STUDENTS
Primary . . .	2,618	14,591*	541,931
Secondary . .	1,020	3,140	103,722
University† . .	2	136	1,856

* 1971 figure. † Figures refer solely to the Universidad Católica.

Sources: Dirección General de Estadística y Censos; Banco Central de Reserva de El Salvador; Consejo Monetario Centroamericano, *Boletín Estadístico.*

THE CONSTITUTION

The Constitution of January 1962 provides for a republican, democratic and representative form of government, composed of three Powers—Legislative, Executive, and Judicial—which are to operate independently. Voting is a right and duty of all citizens over eighteen years of age. Presidential and congressional elections may not be held simultaneously.

The Constitution binds the country, as part of the Central American Nation, to favour the total or partial reconstruction of the Republic of Central America. The Executive may, with the approval of the Legislature, endeavour to bring this about in a federal or unitary form, without seeking the approval of a constituent assembly, provided that republican and democratic principles are respected and the basic rights of individuals and of groups fully guaranteed in the new State.

The Legislative Power is vested in a single Chamber, the Legislative Assembly, whose members are elected every two years and are eligible for re-election. The Assembly meets in ordinary session on June 1st and December 1st. Extraordinary sessions may be convened by the Executive or by the Permanent Commission. The Assembly's duties include the choosing of the President and Vice-President of the Republic from the two citizens who shall have gained the largest number of votes for each of these offices, if no candidate obtains an absolute majority in the election. It also selects the members of the Supreme and subsidiary courts; of the Elections Council; and the Accounts Court of the Republic. It fixes taxes; gives power to the Executive to negotiate internal and external loans; sanctions the Budget; regulates the monetary system of the country; determines the conditions under which foreign currencies may circulate; and suspends and re-imposes constitutional guarantees. The right to initiate legislation may be exercised by the Assembly (as well as by the President through his ministers and by the Supreme Court). The Assembly may over-ride by a two-thirds majority the President's objections to a Bill which it has sent to him for approval.

The President is elected for five years, his term beginning and expiring on July 1st. The principle of alternation in the presidential office is established in the Constitution, which states the action to be taken should this principle be violated. The Executive is responsible for the preparation of the Budget and its presentation to the Assembly; the direction of foreign affairs; the organization of the armed and security forces; and the convening of extraordinary sessions of the Assembly. In the event of his death or incapacity, the Vice-President takes his place for the rest of the presidential term; and in case of necessity, the Vice-President may be replaced by one of the three Designates elected by the Legislative Assembly for a period of two years.

The Judicial Power is exercised by a Supreme Court and by other competent tribunals. The Supreme Court is composed of ten members elected by the Legislature. It alone is competent to decide whether laws, decrees and regulations are constitutional or not.

THE GOVERNMENT

President: Col. Arturo Armando Molina Barraza.
Vice-President: Dr. Enrique Mayorga Rivas.

CABINET
(*March* 1974)

Minister for Foreign Affairs: Ing. Mauricio Borgonovo Pohl.

Minister of the Interior: Col. Juan Antonio Martínez Varela.

Minister of Justice: Dr. Enrique Silva.

Minister of Finance: Dr. Vicente Amado Gavidia Hidalgo.

Minister of Economy: Dr. Guillermo Hidalgo Qüehl.

Minister of Education: Dr. Rogelio Sánchez.

Minister of Defence: Col. Carlos Humberto Romero.

Minister of Labour and Social Insurance: Dr. Rogelio Chávez.

Minister of Agriculture and Livestock: Mauricio Eladio Castillo.

Minister of Public Health and Social Welfare: Dr. Julio Astacio.

Minister of Public Works: Ing. Jorge Antonio Seaman.

Minister of the Presidency: Dr. Enrique Mayorga Rivas.

Under-Secretary of Finance: Rigoberto A. Martínez.

Under-Secretary of Economic Integration and International Commerce: Lic. Carlos Valencia Valladares.

Under-Secretary of Economy: Lic Raúl Humberto Ramos.

Under-Secretary of Culture, Youth and Sport: Arq. Alberto Zúniga Wager.

Under-Secretary of Education: Prof. Gilberto Aguilar Avilés.

DIPLOMATIC REPRESENTATION

EMBASSIES ACCREDITED TO EL SALVADOR

(In San Salvador unless otherwise stated)

Argentina: Avda. España y 17a, Calle Poniente 115; *Ambassador:* SANTOS GOÑY DEMAREN.

Austria: Mexico City 5, Mexico.

Belgium: Guatemala City, Guatemala; also represents the interests of Luxembourg and Liechtenstein.

Bolivia: Guatemala City, Guatemala.

Brazil: Avda. Roosevelt, Edificio La Centroamericana; *Ambassador:* MANUEL MARÍA FERNÁNDEZ ALCÁZAR.

Canada: San José, Costa Rica.

Chile: 4a, Calle Oriente 224, Edificio Comercial, 4° piso; *Ambassador:* JUAN FARIAS VIDAL.

China (Taiwan): Alameda Roosevelt 3107, Edificio La Centroamericana; *Ambassador:* MILTON JAN-TZE SHIEH.

Colombia: Alameda Roosevelt 3107; *Ambassador:* Dr. JUAN JOSÉ RINCÓN GALVIS.

Costa Rica: Alameda Roosevelt 1913, Edificio Novoa Paine; *Ambassador:* JULIO BRENES DÍAZ-GRANADOS.

Denmark: Mexico City 10, Mexico.

Dominican Republic: 9a, Calle Poniente 3975, Colonia Escalón; *Ambassador:* Dr. MANUEL GUERRERO POU.

Ecuador: Mexico City, Mexico.

Egypt: 9a, Calle Poniente y 93, Avda. Norte, Colonia Escalón; *Ambassador:* MAHMOUD ANWAR ZAKY; also represents the interests of Iraq.

Finland: Mexico City, Mexico.

France: Calle Loma Linda 278, Colonia San Benito; *Ambassador:* RENÉ LALOUETTE.

Germany, Federal Republic: 3a, Calle Poniente 3831, Colonia Escalón; *Ambassador:* ADAM ERICH HUESCH.

Guatemala: 15a, Avda. Norte 135; *Ambassador:* Gen. FELIPE DOROTEO MONTERROSO MIRANDA.

Israel: Guatemala City, Guatemala.

Italy: 1a, Calle Poniente y 71, Avda. Norte 204; *Ambassador:* (vacant); also represents the interests of Somalia.

Japan: Alameda Roosevelt 3107, Edificio La Centroamericana; *Ambassador:* MASAYUKI HARIGAI.

Korea, Republic: Lomas, Mexico.

Lebanon: Mexico City, Mexico.

Mexico: 7a, Calle Poniente 3804, Colonia Escalón; *Ambassador:* (vacant).

Netherlands: Guatemala City, Guatemala.

Nicaragua: Avda. Las Palmas 131, Colonia San Benito; *Ambassador:* Dr. ARMANDO LUNA SILVA.

Norway: Mexico City, Mexico.

Panama: 1a, Calle Poniente 2506 y 47a, Avda. Norte; *Ambassadress:* IRENE ESKILDSEN ARIAS.

Paraguay: 9a, Calle Poniente 3934; *Ambassador:* Dr. ENRIQUE VOLTA GOANA.

Peru: Alameda Roosevelt 3107; *Ambassador:* Dr. ADELMO RISI FERREYROS.

Philippines: Mexico City, Mexico.

South Africa: *Ambassador:* ARCHIBALD GARDUER DREUN.

Spain: 51a, Avda. Norte 138; *Ambassador:* JOSÉ MARÍA TRIAS DE BES Y BORRÁS.

Sweden: Guatemala City, Guatemala.

Switzerland: Guatemala City, Guatemala.

Turkey: Lomas, Mexico.

United Kingdom: Continuación de la 13, Avda. Norte 611; *Ambassador:* DONOVAN HAROLD CLIBBORN.

U.S.A.: 25, Avda. Norte 1230; *Ambassador:* (vacant).

Uruguay: 9a, Calle Poniente 4612; *Chargé d'Affaires:* APARICIO DAMBOLENA VILLALBA.

Vatican: 87a, Avenida Norte y 7a, Calle Poniente, Colonia Escalón (Apostolic Nunciature); *Nuncio:* EMANUELE GERADA.

Venezuela: 1a, Calle Poniente 3883; *Ambassador:* Dr. RAFAEL SOLÓRZANO BRUCE.

PARLIAMENT

LEGISLATIVE ASSEMBLY

Chairman: Dr. BENJAMÍN ITERIANO.

ELECTION *March* 1970

PARTY	SEATS
PCN . . .	37
PDC . . .	15

POLITICAL PARTIES

Partido de Conciliación Nacional (PCN): 17, Avda. Sur 437, San Salvador; ruling party; Presidential candidate 1972: Col. ARTURO ARMANDO MOLINA BARRAZA.

Partido Demócrata Cristiano (PDC): 17, Avda. Norte 131, San Salvador; f. 1960; 150,000 registered mems.; anti-imperialist, anti-colonialist, advocates self-determination of peoples and Latin American integration; Sec.-Gen. Dr. JUAN RICARDO RAMÍREZ RAUDA; publ. *Revolución Cristiana*.

Partido Movimiento Nacional Revolucionario: 25, Calle Poniente 116, San Salvador.

Partido Popular Salvadoreño (PPS): c/o Consejo Central de Elecciones, 1, Calle Poniente 2723, San Salvador.

Unión Nacional de Oposición (UNO): c/o Consejo Central de Elecciones, 1, Calle Poniente 2723, San Salvador; a coalition party formed to contest the 1972 presidential election; candidate JOSÉ NAPOLEÓN DUARTE (now in exile).

JUDICIAL SYSTEM

Supreme Court of Justice: Palacio Nacional, San Salvador; composed of ten Magistrates, one of whom is the President. The Court is divided into three chambers: Legal Aid, Civil Law, Penal Law.

President: Dr. ALFREDO MARTÍNEZ MORENO.

Chambers of 2nd Instance: composed of two Magistrates.

Courts of 1st Instance: in all chief towns and districts.

RELIGION

ROMAN CATHOLIC

Metropolitan See:
Arzobispado, 1a, Calle Poniente 3412, San Salvador: Most Rev. LUIS CHÁVEZ Y GONZÁLEZ.

Suffragan Sees (Bishoprics):

San Miguel: JOSÉ EDUARDO ALVAREZ RAMÍREZ.

San Vicente: Rt. Rev. PEDRO ARNOLDO APARICIO Y QUINTANILLA.

Santiago de María: Rt. Rev. FRANCISCO JOSÉ CASTRO Y RAMÍREZ.

Santa Ana: Rt. Rev. BENJAMÍN BARRERA Y REYES.

THE PRESS

DAILY NEWSPAPERS

SAN SALVADOR

El Diario de Hoy: 8a, Calle Poniente 215; f. 1936; Dir. N. VIERA ALTAMIRANO; Man. E. ALTAMIRANO MADRIZ; independent; circ. 65,000 daily, 96,273 Sundays.

Diario Latino: 23a, Avda. Sur 225, Apdo. 96; f. 1890; Editor MIGUEL PINTO; circ. 95,000.

Diario Oficial: 4a, Calle Poniente 829; f. 1875; Dir. RICARDO MARTELL CAMINOS; circ. 2,310.

El Mundo: 2a, Avda. Norte 211; evening; circ. 42,000.

La Prensa Gráfica: 3a, Calle Poniente 132; f. 1915; general information; Conservative; Proprietors Dutriz Hermanos; circ. 68,962 daily, 109,261 Sundays.

Tribuna Libre: 1, Calle Oriente 127; f. 1933; general information; Editor ALVARO L. SÁNCHEZ; circ. 20,000.

SAN MIGUEL

Diario de Oriente: Dir. CÉSAR A. OSEGUEDA.

SANTA ANA

Diario de Occidente: 4a, Calle Oriente 5; f. 1910; Dir. ALFREDO PARADA; circ. 2,500.

SONSONATE

El Heraldo: daily; Propr. FERNANDO GARZONA.

USULUTÁN

La Tribuna: daily.

PERIODICALS

Anaqueles: Review of the National Library; Editor ARTURO BENJAMÍN SÁNCHEZ.

Cultura: Ministerio de Educación, Pasaje Contreras 145, San Salvador; educational; quarterly; Dir. CLAUDIA LARS.

El Economista: San Salvador; finance and economics monthly.

El Salvador Filatélico: San Salvador; f. 1940; publ. quarterly by the Philatelic Society of El Salvador.

Mundo: Edificio Darío, San Salvador; general interest; monthly.

Revista del Anteneo de El Salvador: San Salvador; official organ of Salvadorean Athenaeum; three numbers per annum.

Revista Judicial: Palacio Nacional San Salvador; organ of the Supreme Court; Dir. Dr. MIGUEL RAFAEL VRAVIA.

Revolución Cristiana: PDC, Avda. España 602, San Salvador; organ of the Partido Demócrata Cristiano; weekly; circ. 10,000.

PRESS ASSOCIATION

Asociación de Periodistas de El Salvador (*Press Association of El Salvador*): 4, Avda. Sur 135, San Salvador.

PUBLISHERS

Editorial Universitaria: Universidad Nacional, San Salvador; Dir. ITALO LÓPEZ VALLECILLO.

Dirección de Publicaciones: Ministerio de Educación, Pasaje Contreras 145, San Salvador; f. 1948; educational and general; Man. R. HUEZO.

Rodezno & Cia.: 4a, Calle Delgado 2, San Salvador; f. 1927; publishers of *El Diario de Hoy*, *La Prensa*, and *Diario Latino*; Dirs. JOAQUÍN RODEZNO, Jr., ANA VILMA MUNGUÍA DE RODEZNO.

Librería Universal: San Salvador; brs. in San Miguel and Santa Ana.

RADIO AND TELEVISION

RADIO

Government Broadcasting Department: Ministerio del Interior, Palacio Nacional, San Salvador; Dir. Minister of the Interior.

Asociación Salvadoreña de Empresarios de Radiodifusión: Apdo. 210, San Salvador; Pres. M. Flores.

YSS Radio Nacional de El Salvador: 2a, Avda. Sur 113, San Salvador; non-commercial cultural station; Dir.-Gen. L. Heredia.

There are 41 other radio stations, all commercial.

In 1971 there were 500,000 radio licences.

TELEVISION

Canal Dos, S.A.: Apdo. 720, San Salvador; commercial; also operate Channel 4; Gen. Man. B. Eserski.

Canal 6: frente Ministerio de Relaciones Exteriores, San Salvador; commercial; Gen. Man. Salvador Ira Heta.

In 1973 there were 107,950 television sets.

FINANCE

(cap. = capital; p.u. = paid up; dep. = deposits; m. = million; amounts in colones.)

BANKING

San Salvador

Central Bank

Banco Central de Reserva de El Salvador: 1a, Calle Poniente y 7a, Avda. Norte; f. 1934; nationalized April 1961; sole right of note issue; cap. p.u. 2.5m., dep. 319.6m. (Dec. 1973); Chair. Ing. Edgardo Suárez Contreras; Gen. Man. Lic. Julio César Serrano.

Banco Agrícola Comercial de El Salvador: 5a, Avda. Sur 124; f. 1955; cap. and reserves 11.6m., dep. 142.6m. (Dec. 1973); Chair. and Pres. Luis Escalante Arce; Gen. Man. Juan José Miranda.

Banco Capitalizador: f. 1955; cap. 3m., dep. 65.3m. (Sept. 1972); Pres. Enrique Alvarez D.; Gen. Man. José Julio Bolaños.

Banco de Comercio de El Salvador: 4a, Calle Oriente 224, Apdo. 237; f. 1949; cap. 3m.; total resources 112m. (Dec. 1970); Pres. Miguel Dueñas Palomo; Gen. Man. Roberto Imberton.

Banco de Crédito Popular: 2a, Calle Oriente 221; Pres. Francisco Calleja Malaina; Man. Jorge Alfredo Cea.

Banco Hipotecario de El Salvador: Avda. Cuscatlán 317; f. 1935; Pres. Dr. Alvaro Magaña; Man. J. H. Girón.

Banco Salvadoreño: 2, Avda. Norte 129; f. 1885; cap. 6m., dep. 91.6m. (Dec. 1971); Pres. Carlos A. Guirola; Gen. Man. Eric C. Field.

Development Banks

Asociación de Ahorro y Préstamo Atlacatl, S.A.: Boulevard de Los Héroes y Calle Poniente 25; savings and loan association; Pres. Roberto Freund.

Construcción y Ahorro S.A.-CASA: 1a, Calle Poniente 7 9a, Avda. Norte; saving and building finance; Pres. M. G. Novoa.

Crédito Inmobiliario, S.A.: Calle Rubén Darío y 9a, Avda. Sur 606; Pres. Frank P. Townson.

Financiera de Desarrollo e Inversión, S.A.: Alameda Roosevelt y 41, Avda. Sur, Edif. Bustamante; f. 1965; cap. 4m.; long-term finance for development; Pres. Julio Salaverría.

Financiera Nacional de la Vivienda (FNV): 9a, Avda. Sur 106, Edif. Argueta; national housing finance agency f. 1963 to improve housing facilities through loan savings and investments.

Foreign Banks

Bank of London and Montreal: Head Office: P.O.B. 1262, Nassau, Bahamas; San Salvador: 2a, Calle Oriente 215, Apdo. 197; Man. H. M. Halliday; agencies in San Miguel, Santa Ana.

First National City Bank: New York; Apdo. 1324, San Salvador; opened 1964; Man. B. Vidas Dánake.

Stock Exchange

Bolsa de El Salvador: 1a, Calle Poniente, San Salvador; f. 1964.

Insurance

San Salvador

Aseguradora Suiza Salvadoreña S.A.: 6a, Calle Poniente y 23, Avda. Sur; Pres. and Man. Roberto Schild.

La Auxiliadora, S.A.

La Centro Americana, S.A., Cia. Salvadoreña de Seguros: Alameda Roosevelt 31-07, Apdo. 527; f. 1915; Gen. Man. F. A. Mejía.

Compañía General de Seguros, S.A.: Edif. General de Seguros, 2a, Avda. Sur 302; f. 1955; Gen. Man. José Domingo Menéndez.

Inversiones Comerciales, S.A.

Seguros e Inversions, S.A.-SISA: Edif. SISA, Calle a Santa Tecla; f. 1962; Pres. Prudencio Llach.

TRADE AND INDUSTRY

CHAMBER OF COMMERCE

Cámara de Comercio e Industria de El Salvador: Edif. Dueñas, 2a, Avda. Sur 223 (altos), Apdo. 1640, San Salvador; f. 1927; 432 mems.; Pres. Esteban Laínez Rubio; Sec. Antonio Perla B.; Man. Roberto Ortiz Avalos; publ. *Boletín* (2 a month).

TRADE ORGANIZATIONS

Asociación Salvadoreña de Industriales: 11, Avda. Norte 240, San Salvador; f. 1958; 246 mems.; Pres. Joaquín Christ; Man. Dr. Ricardo González Camacho; publ. *Revista Industria.*

Compañía Salvadoreña de Café, S.A.: 6a, Avda. Sur 133, San Salvador; f. 1942; 304 mems.; Pres. Roberto Llach Hill; Man. Dr. Ricardo Falla Cáceres; Asst. Man. Miguel Angel Aguilar, Jr.

Co-operativa Algodonera Salvadoreña Ltda.: 7a, Avda. Norte 418, Apdo. 616, San Salvador; f. 1940; 8,522 mems.; cotton growers' association; Man. Armando Jiménez González.

Federación Cafetera de América (FEDECAME): (*Central American Coffee Growers' Federation*): Apdo. 739, San Salvador; f. 1945; publishes daily and weekly bulletins on coffee production and marketing; number of mems.: 14 Latin American countries.

DEVELOPMENT ASSOCIATIONS

Administración de Bienestar Campesino—ABC: San Salvador; rural welfare; includes agricultural development credit department with an initial cap. of 28m. colones.

Consejo Nacional de Planifcación y Coordinación Económica (CONAPLAN): San Salvador; f. 1959; reorganized 1962; planning and co-ordination council; Exec. Sec. Lic. Atilio Viéytez.

Fondo de Garantía para la Pequeña Industria: Edificio Panamericano, 3° piso, 25, Calle Poniente y Avda. Norte 27, San Salvador.

Instituto de Colonización Rural ICR: Apdo. 119, Troncales, San Salvador; Government body to promote rural development; Dir. Antonio Aguirre.

Instituto Salvadoreño de Fomento Industrial (INSAFI): Calle Rubén Darío 628, San Salvador; f. 1955; 210 mems.; aims to promote the economic well-being and production of El Salvador; provides contracts for joint ventures; Pres. Lic. M. E. Martinez; Gen. Man. Lic. G. A. Roeder; publ. *Memoria Anual*.

Instituto de Vivienda Urbana: Centro Urbano Libertad, San Salvador; Government housing agency; Dir. E. Cromeyer Pérez.

TRADE UNIONS

Confederación General de Sindicatos—CGS (*General Confederation of Unions*): 3a, Calle Oriente 226, San Salvador; f. 1958; admitted to ICFTU/ORIT; 27,000 mems.; publ. *El Sindicalista*.

Confederación General de Trabajadores Salvadoreños—CGTS (*General Confederation of Salvadorian Workers*): San Salvador; f. 1957; 3,500 mems. from 10 affiliated unions; Sec.-Gen. José Alberto López; Asst. Sec.-Gen. Rafael Antonio Rodríguez; publ. *Voz Obrera*.

Federación Unitaria Sindical de El Salvador: 18, Avda. Norte y 11, Calle Oriente, San Salvador.

There are also a number of small unions without a national centre.

TRANSPORT AND TOURISM

TRANSPORT
RAILWAYS

There are about 720 km. of railway track in the country. The International Railways of Central America run from Anguiatú on the El Salvador-Guatemala border to Cutuco on the Gulf of Fonseca, and connect the Republic of El Salvador with Guatemala City and Puerto Barrios on the Atlantic coast.

Principal Railway Company

Ferrocarriles Internacionales de Centro América (*International Railways of Central America*): Head Office: 20 Exchange Place, Jersey City, N.J. 07302; Apdo. 06-91, San Salvador; 456 km. open—1 m. gauge (in El Salvador); Pres. Abraham K. Weber.

ROADS

The country's highway system is well integrated with its railway services. There are some 8,394 km. (including 625 km. of the Pan-American Highway) of roads as follows: paved highways: 982 km., improved roads: 3,197 km., dry-weather roads: 4,215 km.

SHIPPING

Comisión Ejecutiva Portuaria Autónoma—CEPA: Avda. Cuscatlán 317, San Salvador; f. 1961; operates the government-owned ports of Acajutla and La Libertad; Pres. Atilio Viéytez; Gen. Man. Jorge Rochac.

Acajutla has been extensively enlarged and since 1961 has become one of the most important ports of Central America. Other ports include La Unión and La Libertad. Services are provided by a number of foreign lines: Prudential Grace Lines, Flota Mercante Grancolombiana S.A., Central American Services (K.N.S.M.), Elma Line, Lloyd Brasília, Royal Mail Line, Hapag Lloyd, "K" Line, Mitsui O.S.K. Lines, Japan Line, Nippon Yusen Kaisha, States Marine Lines, Mamenic Line, Azta Line, Italian, Línea Mexicana del Pacífico, Naviera Salvadoreña S.A., etc.

CIVIL AVIATION
Domestic Airlines

AESA Aerolíneas de El Salvador, S.A.: Apdo. 513, Colón, Panama City, Panama; cargo and mail service between San Salvador and Miami; Gen. Man. E. Cornejo López.

TACA International Airlines: Head Office: Edif. Caribe, San Salvador; fleet: 3 BAC One-Eleven, 2 Viscount 700, 3 DC-6; Gen. Man. Jaime Quesada.

El Salvador is also served by the following foreign airlines: Aviateca (Guatemala), Copa (Panama), LACSA (Costa Rica), Lanica (Nicaragua) and Pan American.

TOURISM

Instituto Salvadoreño de Turismo ISTU: Calle Rubén Daro 619, San Salvador; Pres. Enrique Aberle.

Asociación Salvadoreña de Agencias de Viajes: Apdo. 1376, San Salvador; Pres. Luis Alonso Rendón.

ATOMIC ENERGY

Universidad de El Salvador: Ciudad Universitaria, Final 25a. Avda, Norte, San Salvador; researches in physiology, radioisotopes and nuclear theory.

UNIVERSITIES

Universidad de El Salvador: Ciudad Universitaria, 7a, Avda. Sur 15, San Salvador; 314 teachers, 3,900 students.

Universidad Centroamericana "José Simeón Cañas": Jardines de Guadalupe, Apdo. 1989, San Salvador; 142 teachers, 2,582 students.

EQUATORIAL GUINEA

INTRODUCTORY SURVEY

Location, Climate, Language, Religion, Flag, Capital

Equatorial Guinea, formerly Spanish Guinea, consists of the islands of Fernando Póo (re-named Macías Nguema Byogo in 1973), Corisco, Great Elobey and Small Elobey, and Annobón, and the mainland territory of Río Muni, on the west coast of Africa. Cameroon lies to the north and Gabon to the east and south of Río Muni, while Fernando Póo lies offshore from Cameroon and Nigeria. The small island of Annobón lies far to the south, beyond the Portuguese islands of São Tomé and Príncipe. The climate is hot and humid with average temperatures over 26°c (80°F). The official language is Spanish. In Río Muni the Fang language is spoken, as well as those of coastal tribes such as the Combe, Bujeba, etc., while in Fernando Póo the principal local language is Bubi, though pidgin English and Ibo are also widely understood. The main religion is Catholicism. The national flag (proportions 3 by 2) has green, white and red horizontal stripes, with a light blue triangle at the hoist. The state flag has, in addition, the national coat of arms on the white stripe. The capital is Santa Isabel (re-named Malabo), on Fernando Póo.

Recent History

After 190 years of Spanish rule independence was declared in October 1968, following a referendum on the proposed constitution. In presidential elections held in September 1968 the Prime Minister of the autonomous government, Sr. Bonifacio Ondo Edu, was defeated by Sr. Francisco Macías Nguema. Sr. Macías formed a coalition government from all the parties represented in the new National Assembly. Relations with Spain became strained early in 1969 after a series of anti-European incidents and an attempted *coup d'état* by the Foreign Minister, Atanasio Ndongo Miyone, who was killed. The President announced in July 1972 that he had been appointed Life President. Relations with Gabon deteriorated when the latter extended her territorial waters to 270 km. in August 1972. After armed incidents off Corisco Island, said to be a training camp for dissidents of Cameroon, Gabon and the Central African Republic, Gabon and Equatorial Guinea agreed to accept OAU mediation in their dispute, and a reconciliation between the two countries was effected in 1973. A new constitution, abolishing the provincial autonomy previously enjoyed by Fernando Póo, was adopted in July 1973. Equatorial Guinea is a member of the OAU and the UN.

Government

Under the independent constitution, Equatorial Guinea is a democratic republic with a presidential system of government. The executive is directly responsible to the President, while there is an elected legislature of 35 deputies. A Council of the Republic has the function of resolving conflicts between the executive and legislative bodies. Justice is independent of the executive; the highest court is the Supreme Tribunal.

Defence

There is a small army. Spain withdrew her forces following the crisis of March 1969.

Economy

The economy is almost entirely based on agriculture, the principal products being cocoa, coffee, palm oil, bananas and okoumé timber. About 90 per cent of the total cocoa production comes from Fernando Póo, where there are 1,000 plantations (800 African-owned) covering more than 41,000 hectares. In Río Muni 10,200 hectares are devoted to cocoa. Coffee and timber are mainly produced in Río Muni, which is heavily forested. The main markets for timber exports are Spain and Federal Germany. Since the end of the Civil War in Nigeria large numbers of plantation workers have sought work in Nigeria. Industry is in Spanish hands, except for a few Fernandino entrepreneurs. Exploration for oil, both onshore and offshore, has begun. Spain covered the budget deficit with a subsidy of about 426 million pesetas in 1969–70, and she also advanced the gold quota necessary for the admission of Equatorial Guinea to the IMF. In addition Spain assisted in the creation of a national bank and ensured the convertibility of the Guinean peseta. Spanish aid has been formalized by the conclusion of an agreement on economic co-operation.

The per capita annual income on Fernando Póo is about $330, while in Río Muni, where the bulk of the population lives, it is about $130.

Transport and Communications

Main roads link the principal centres in the two provinces with about 160 km. of road on Fernando Póo and about 1,015 km. in Río Muni. The principal communications between the provinces are by air. There are no railways.

Social Welfare

There is a fairly adequate health service with 5 hospitals and a leprosy centre. In 1966 there were 1,635 beds. With the exception of 5 or 6 Africans all the doctors were Spanish at independence, and their departure after the March 1969 crisis has created serious problems which are still unresolved, despite international assistance.

Education

Elementary schools provide compulsory education until the age of 12, and primary schools continue it until 14. Secondary education is provided by one centre in Santa Isabel, another at Bata and a third in the Río Muni frontier outpost of Ebebiyin. Bata has a technical secondary school. Santa Isabel also has an Escuela Superior. Bata and Santa Isabel each have a teacher-training school. There is no university and about 100 students study abroad, mainly in Spain.

Tourism

Tourism is not encouraged. Entry of Spanish nationals is subject to an authorization from the Ministry of Foreign Affairs in Santa Isabel.

Public Holidays

1974: August 15th (Assumption), October 12th (Independence), November 1st (All Saints'), December 25th (Christmas).

1975: January 1st (New Year), January 6th (Epiphany), March 28th–31st (Easter), May 1st (St. Joseph the Worker), May 8th (Ascension), May 29th (Corpus Christi).

Weights and Measures

The metric system is in force.

Currency and Exchange Rates

100 céntimos = 1 Guinea peseta.

Exchange rate (April 1974):

    1 Guinea peseta = 1 Spanish peseta;

    £1 sterling = 138.50 pesetas;

      U.S. \$1 = 58.725 pesetas.

STATISTICAL SURVEY

Area: 28,051 sq. km. (Río Muni 26,000 sq. km.).

Population: (1960) Río Muni 183,377 (2,864 Europeans), Fernando Póo 61,557 (4,170 Europeans), Annobón 1,403, Santa Isabel (capital, on Fernando Póo) 37,185, Bata (in Río Muni) 27,024. Total estimated population 286,000 (June 30th, 1969).

The European population has decreased considerably since the March 1969 crisis, and there are now probably less than 100 Spaniards left in Río Muni and about 1,000 on Fernando Póo.

Agriculture (1970—metric tons): Cassava (manioc) 42,000*, Sweet potatoes and Yams 27,000*, Bananas 12,000*, Coffee 7,200, Palm oil 4,000*, Palm Kernels (export only) 2,000, Abaca 100*; (1970–71): Cocoa beans 30,000. (* F.A.O. estimates).

Livestock (1964): 3,000 cattle, 24,100 sheep, 28,150 goats.

Fishing (1966): over 1,000 tons.

Forestry (1967): 337,438 tons of timber.

Electricity Production (1967): Fernando Póo 9,470,000 kWh, Río Muni 5,700,000 kWh.

Currency: 100 céntimos = 1 Guinea peseta; under the July 1973 Constitution the peseta is to become the ekpwele. Coins: 5, 10 and 50 céntimos; 1, 2½, 5, 25, 50 and 100 pesetas.
Notes: 1, 5, 25, 50, 100, 500 and 1,000 pesetas.
Exchange rates (April 1974); 1 Guinea peseta = 1 Spanish peseta; £1 sterling = 138.50 pesetas; U.S. \$1 = 58.725 pesetas.
1,000 Guinea pesetas = £7.22 = \$17.03.

Budget (1969–70): Revenue 712,470,000 pesetas, Expenditure 1,139,045,701 pesetas.

External Trade (1971, first half): (million pesetas) Imports from Spain 454.8; Exports to Spain 867.2.

Transport (1967): *Shipping:* ships entering 663, ships leaving 663; *Civil Aviation:* passengers arriving Santa Isabel 13,863, passengers leaving Santa Isabel 14,166; passengers arriving Bata 7,350, passengers leaving Bata 7,681.

Education: (1966) 147 elementary schools with 21,421 pupils, 32 primary schools with 1,565 pupils, and 271 teachers; (1966–67) 2,095 (310 white) secondary students; about 100 students study abroad, mostly in Spain.

THE CONSTITUTION

On July 14th, 1972 President Macías Nguema was appointed Life President by the Assembly and the Council of the Republic.

Under the provisions of the July 1973 constitution which replaced the independence constitution, no further distinction will be made between the mainland province of the former Spanish colony, Río Muni, the chief island, of Fernando Póo to the north, and various other islands which make up the state of Equatorial Guinea. This move follows certain separatist tendencies voiced on Fernando Póo which were unanimously deplored by the Congress. It was also decided to reshuffle the administration on the island, posting more mainland officials there, and more islanders to the continent, to counteract the divisions.

THE GOVERNMENT

HEAD OF STATE

Life President: Francisco Macías Nguema.

(*Elected September 29th, 1968; proclaimed Life President July 14th, 1972.*)

CABINET

(*March* 1974)

President, Minister of Defence and Minister of Foreign Affairs: Francisco Macías Nguema.

Vice-President, Minister of Trade: Edmundo Bosio Dioco.

Minister of Labour: Román Toichoa.

Minister of Industry and Mines: Rafael Obian Gonsogo.

Minister of Agriculture: Cristobal Ondo Aliogo.

Minister of Education: Agustín Daniel Grange Molay.

Minister of Health: Dr. Pedro Econg Andeme.

Minister of the Interior: Angel Masie Natutumde.

Minister of Public Works: Jesús Alfonso Oyono.

Minister of Finance: Andrés Nko Ivasa.

Minister of Justice: Expedito Rafael Momo.

DIPLOMATIC REPRESENTATION

EMBASSIES ACCREDITED TO EQUATORIAL GUINEA

The following countries have established diplomatic relations with Equatorial Guinea: Cameroon, China, People's Republic (*Ambassador:* CHEN TAN), Cuba, Czechoslovakia, France (*Ambassador:* HENRI BERNARD), Gabon,* German Democratic Republic, Ghana, Democratic People's Republic of Korea, Nigeria (*Ambassador:* Brig. W. BASSEY), Romania, Spain, U.S.S.R., United Kingdom*, U.S.A.*, Yugoslavia.

* Ambassador resident in Cameroon.

NATIONAL ASSEMBLY

ELECTIONS, *September 22nd,* 1968

PARTY	SEATS
Monalige	10
Munge	10
IPGE	8
Unión Bubi . . .	7
TOTAL . . .	35

POLITICAL PARTIES

Following the abortive coup of March 1969, led by the Minister of Foreign Affairs, ATANASIO NDONGO, who was killed, all parties were merged in February 1970 into a Partido Unico Nacional under the President of the Republic, who has assumed most of the powers of the former rival leaders. The party was later renamed the Partido Unico Nacional de los Trabajadores.

JUDICIAL SYSTEM

An independent and secure judiciary is guaranteed by the constitution. The Supreme Tribunal at Santa Isabel is the highest court of appeal.

RELIGION

Some Africans retain traditional forms of worship. There are Spanish Catholic and American Presbyterian and English Methodist missions. Europeans are nearly all Catholics.

Bishop of Sta. Isabel: Mgr. FRANCISCO GÓMEZ MARIJUÁN.

Bishop of Bata: RAPHAEL NZE ABUY.

THE PRESS

Boletín Oficial: Santa Isabel; fortnightly legal review; circ. 1,300.

Ebano: Santa Isabel; daily and Sunday; Spanish; circ. 1,000.

La Guinea Española: Catholic Mission, Santa Isabel; f. 1903; Spanish monthly; literary and scientific; circ. 1,050.

Hoja Parroquial: Santa Isabel; weekly news; circ. 1,500.

Potopoto (*Diario de Río Muni*): Apdo. 236, Bata; Publisher FRANCISCO DE ANTA FRANCO; general news; circ. 550.

RADIO AND TELEVISION

There are two radio stations, both operated by the Government.

Radio Bata: Apdo. 57, Bata, Río Muni; commercial station; Dir. E. E. NAVARRO MAÑEZ.

Radio Santa Isabel: Apdo. 195, Santa Isabel, Fernando Póo; services in Spanish, Fang, Pamue, Bubi, Annobonés, Combe and English; Dir.-Gen. JIMÉNEZ MARHUENDA.

There are 71,500 radio receivers in the country. In 1968 the Spanish Government inaugurated a television transmitter above Santa Isabel in Fernando Póo.

FINANCE

BANKING

Banco Central de Guinea Equatorial: Santa Isabel; f. 1969; central bank.

Banco Español de Credito: Santa Isabel, San Carlos, Bata.

Banco Exterior de España: Léon 1, Apdo. 39, Santa Isabel; branch in San Carlos.

TRADE AND INDUSTRY

Comité Sindical del Cacao: Fernando Póo; grouping of cocoa planters (mainly Spanish owners or leasers and some Portuguese) which buys, stocks and sells the product; used to have paramount role on Fernando Póo.

Cámaras Oficiales Agrícolas de Guinea: Fernando Póo and Río Muni; buys cocoa and coffee from African planters, who are partially grouped in co-operatives.

TRANSPORT AND TOURISM

ROADS

Fernando Póo: a semi-circular tarred road serves the northern part of the island from Santa Isabel down to Batete in the west and from Santa Isabel to Bacake Grande in the east, with a feeder road from San Carlos to Moka and Bahía de la Concepcíon; total length about 160 km.

Río Muni: a tarred road links Bata with Río Benito in the west; another road, partly tarred, links Bata with the frontier post of Ebebiyin in the east and then continues into Gabon; other earth roads join Acurenam, Mongomo de Guadalupe and Nsork; total road network about 1,015 km.

SHIPPING

The main ports are Santa Isabel (general cargo), San Carlos (bananas), Bata (general cargo), Río Benito and Puerto Iradier (timber).

Compañía Transmediterránea: serves Barcelona–Cadiz–Santa Isabel–San Carlos–Bata route and the Bilbao–Cadiz–Equatorial Guinea route, sailing alternately from Barcelona and Bilbao, usually once a month; in 1968 there were six ships for the transatlantic service and two more for internal traffic between Fernando Póo, Río Muni and Annobón (via São Tomé).

Arrivals and repatriation of Nigerian workers takes place through the Santa Isabel–Calabar service.

Of the 663 ships entering and leaving Guinea in 1967 534 were Spanish, 31 German (of the Woermann Linie), 27 British and 10 Norwegian.

CIVIL AVIATION

There are international airports at Bata and Santa Isabel.

Lineas Aéreas Guinea Ecuatorial (LAGE): Bata Airport; f. 1970 as a subsidiary of Iberia (the Spanish airline); scheduled services from Santa Isabel to Bata and Douala (Cameroon), formerly flown by Iberia; fleet of two Convair CV-440.

Air Cameroun also links Bata with Douala, and Iberia also serves Equatorial Guinea.

ETHIOPIA

INTRODUCTORY SURVEY

Location, Climate, Language, Religion, Flag, Capital

The Empire of Ethiopia extends inland from the Red Sea coast. It has a long frontier with Somalia near to the Horn of north-east Africa. The Sudan lies to the west and Kenya to the south. The climate is mainly temperate because of the high plateau terrain, with an average annual temperature of 13°c (55°F), abundant rainfall and low humidity. The lower country and valley gorges are very hot. The official language is Amharic but English is widely used, and Arabic is spoken in the Eritrea province. The Ethiopian Coptic Church has a wide following in the north and on the southern plateau. In much of the south and east there are Muslims and followers of animist beliefs. The national flag (proportions 3 by 2) has three horizontal stripes of green, yellow and red. The state flag has, in addition, a crowned lion in the centre. The capital is Addis Ababa.

Recent History

Since the liberation of Ethiopia from Italian occupation in May 1941, the Emperor Haile Sellassie I has ruled the country. In 1952 Eritrea, formerly a UN Trust Territory administered by Italy, was federated to Ethiopia. This federal arrangement was ended in 1962, when Eritrea was fully incorporated in Ethiopia, though a banned Eritrean separatist movement (Eritrean Liberation Front—ELF) is still active. In 1960 an attempted *coup d'état* during the Emperor's absence was crushed by loyal forces. In December 1970, most of Eritrea was placed under military rule following guerrilla action and sabotage by ELF elements in the province. There has recently been an increase in guerrilla activity and an escalation in the fighting, and 10,000 Ethiopian troops are permanently stationed in Eritrea.

In 1971–72 the Ethiopian Chamber of Deputies again blocked land reform bills. Bitterness between Ethiopia and Somalia over the disputed Ogaden District was renewed in 1973. In the same year drought and famine claimed an estimated 100,000 lives and the Government was strongly criticized for its handling of the crisis.

In February 1974 unrest throughout the armed forces and riots over unemployment and inflation caused the collapse of the Government. The armed forces pledged loyalty to the Emperor, but students riots and a general strike for pay reforms and a minimum wage led to Haile Sellassie's promising sweeping political and social reforms and modification of his own powers. A commission to reform the constitution has been set up but unrest continues.

Government

Government is vested in a Council of Ministers responsible to the Emperor, and a parliament consisting of a Senate and a Chamber of Deputies. A Constitutional Commission to reform the political system is expected to report during 1974 and recommend wide changes. The Senators are nominees of the Emperor, Deputies are elected by universal suffrage. Ethiopia is divided into 14 Provinces, each under a Governor-General. Each Province is divided into sub-provinces.

Defence

Ethiopia maintains a regular army of 41,000 men, an air force of 2,250 and a navy of 1,400. There is also a paramilitary force of 20,400. The U.S.A. operates a strategic military centre at Asmara, and also has a number of military advisers in the country.

Economic Affairs

Agriculture is the mainstay of the economy and coffee is the most valuable crop and export. Fruit and vegetables, oilseeds and hides and skins are also exported. There is scope to develop forestry and industry, growth depending on better transport and the exploitation of hydro-electric power. The Fincha hydro-electric power dam, the largest in Ethiopia, was opened in November 1973. Over 80 per cent of the population still works on the land and there is much poverty, per capita income being amongst the lowest in Africa. Rapid population growth has tended to cancel out recent gains in agricultural production, which is greatly hampered by the system of land tenure and archaic methods of cultivation. Ethiopia's Third Five-Year Plan for the economy (1968–73) was like its predecessors, idealistic rather than practical. Further handicaps are the almost total reliance on foreign loans for industrial progress and the minuscule amounts allotted to agriculture, which was granted only 3 per cent of government expenditure in 1970–71. During 1973 Ethiopia was hit by a catastrophic drought and famine which in some provinces continued into 1974. Despite government and international aid, the situation remains extremely serious.

Transport and Communications

There is a railway from Addis Ababa to Djibouti, capital of the French Territory of the Afars and the Issas, and a narrow-gauge track from Massawa to Akordat near the Sudan border. There are plans to extend the railway in the south to provide a service between Nazareth and Sidamo. There are 8,928 km. of all-weather roads out of a total system of 23,400 km. of roads. Bus services link provincial centres to the capital. There are 33 airfields. The port of Assab can handle up to a million tons of goods a year, and attracts some of the trade which formerly went to French-governed Djibouti.

Social Welfare

The scope of modern health services has been greatly extended since 1960, but they still reach only a small part of the population. With foreign assistance, health centres and clinics are steadily expanding into the rural areas, but in the recent famine Ethiopian health services were grievously inadequate.

Education

Education in Ethiopia is free. However, only about 10 per cent of eligible children attend schools, of which there are few in rural areas and still fewer outside the Amharic areas. Thus little progress has been made in reducing the illiteracy rate of about 90 per cent, and the shortage of educated personnel is a serious brake on economic development. There are universities at Addis Ababa and Asmara and in 1969–70 some 2,000 students were enrolled abroad.

Tourism

The chief tourist attractions are big game hunting, the early Christian monuments and churches and the ancient capitals of Gondar and Axum. The tourist trade is expanding rapidly. The 1970 total of 53,187 visitors rose to an estimated 80,000 in 1972.

Visas are required by all visitors.

Sport

Football, athletics, cycling, basketball, swimming, boxing, horse-riding and tennis are all popular sports.

Public Holidays

1974: August 22nd (Assumption), September 11th (New Year's Day), September 27th (Feast of Maskal), November 2nd (Coronation Day).

1975: January 7th (Christmas), January 19th (Feast of Tuiket), January 20th (Feast of St. Michael), February 19th (Martyrs' Day), March 2nd (Battle of Adowa), March 28th–March 31st (Easter), May 5th (Liberation Day), July 23rd (Emperor's Birthday).

(Note: Ethiopia uses its own solar calendar; the Ethiopian year 1966 began on September 11th, 1973).

Weights and Measures

The metric system is officially in use. There are many local weights and measures.

Currency and Exchange Rates

100 cents=1 Ethiopian dollar (E$).

Exchange rates (April 1974):

£1 sterling=E$4.893;
U.S. $1=E$2.072.

STATISTICAL SURVEY

AREA AND POPULATION

Area: 1,221,900 sq. km. (471,778 sq. miles), including Eritrea (117,600 sq. km.).

Population: 25,933,000 (July 1st, 1972). Average annual birth rate 45.6 per 1,000, death rate 25.0 per 1,000 (UN estimates for 1965–70).

PROVINCES
(1971 estimates)

PROVINCE	POPULATION ('000)	CAPITAL	PROVINCE	POPULATION ('000)	CAPITAL
Arussi	833.5	Asella	Illubabor	674.1	Matu
Bale	692.6	Goba	Kaffa	1,656.7	Jimma
Begemder	1,325.1	Gondar	Shoa	5,209.7	Addis Ababa
Eritrea	1,889.7	Asmara	Sidamo	2,425.0	Awasa
Gemu-Goffa	683.5	Arba Minch	Tigre	1,787.5	Makale
Gojjam	1,712.3	Debra Markos	Wollega	1,241.7	Lekemti
Hararje	3,286.9	Harar	Wollo	2,407.2	Dessye

PRINCIPAL TOWNS
(1971 population)

Addis Ababa (capital)	851,610	Harar	. . .	45,840
Asmara .	232,550	Jimma	. . .	44,780
Dire Dawa	63,670	Nazret	. . .	42,860
Dessie .	47,150	Gondar	. . .	36,570

Employment (1970 estimates): Total economically active population 11,428,000, including 9,668,000 in agriculture.

AGRICULTURE
LAND USE, 1971
('000 sq. km.)

Arable and under Permanent Crops .	98.4
Permanent Meadows and Pastures . .	654.1
Forest Land	88.2
Other Land	260.3
Inland Water	120.9
TOTAL	1,221.9

PRINCIPAL CROPS

	AREA ('000 hectares)			PRODUCTION ('000 metric tons)			YIELD (kg. per hectare)		
	1969	1970	1971*	1969	1970	1971	1969	1970	1971*
Bananas	2.2*	2.2*	n.a.	50*	50*	n.a.	22,700*	22,700*	n.a.
Barley	1,735	1,755*	1,770	1,496	1,525*	1,550*	860	870*	880
Chick-peas . . .	290	294	298	181	185	189*	620	630	630
Coffee (green beans) . .	618	n.a.	n.a.	170	205	215	275	n.a.	n.a.
Dry Beans . . .	94	95*	96	72	72*	74*	770	760*	770
Dry Broad Beans . .	144	148*	152	138	138*	143*	960	930*	940
Dry Peas . . .	135	137*	139	126	127*	130*	940	930*	940
Flax for Seed . . .	120	122*	125	62	60	66*	520	490*	530
Lentils	174	178*	180	106	107*	109*	610	600*	610
Maize	847	860*	870	909	950*	971	1,070	1,100*	1,115
Millet, Sorghum and Teff	3,703	4,420*	4,450	2,539	2,630	2,680*	690	595*	600
Potatoes . . .	30	30*	31	161	162*	163*	5,300	5,400*	5,300
Sesame Seed . . .	141	150*	150	69.4	70*	70*	490	470*	470
Sweet Potatoes and Yams	58	59	59	248	253	254*	4,300	4,300	4,300
Wheat	1,070	1,090*	1,100	808	840*	876	760	770*	795
Other Pulses . . .	96*	97*	98	58*	59*	60*	600*	610*	610

* FAO estimate.

LIVESTOCK*

	1968–69	1969–70	1970–71
Cattle	26,108,300	26,231,500	26,309,700
Sheep	12,509,200	12,678,900	12,841,800
Goats	11,206,800	11,262,500	11,335,300
Asses	3,821,700	3,837,400	3,853,100
Horses	1,381,800	1,392,900	1,404,100
Mules	1,387,100	1,399,600	1,412,200
Camels	974,800	980,600	986,500
Pigs	13,900	14,500	15,200
Poultry	46,300,000	47,200,000	48,100,000

* Estimate.

LIVESTOCK PRODUCE
(metric tons)

	1968	1969	1970
Beef and Veal . .	248,000	248,000*	248,000*
Mutton, Lamb, Goats' Meat .	91,000	92,000*	94,000*
Poultry Meat . . .	50,000*	51,000*	52,000*
Offal	74,000*	76,000*	76,000*
Other Meat . . .	14,000*	14,000*	14,000*
Tallow	9,000*	10,000*	10,000*
Cows' Milk . . .	488,000	502,000	516,000
Goats' Milk . . .	90,000*	92,000*	94,000*
Sheep's Milk . . .	5,000*	5,000*	5,000*
Butter	37,000*	38,000*	39,000*
Hen Eggs . . .	61,300*	61,400*	61,500*
Cattle Hides . . .	63,546*	64,701*	95,025*
Sheep Skins . . .	8,730*	6,973*	8,795*
Goat Skins . . .	7,556*	7,819*	5,680*
Camel Hides . . .	2,520*	2,520*	2,600*

* FAO estimate.

Source: FAO, *Production Yearbook 1971.*

FORESTRY

ROUNDWOOD PRODUCTION
(cubic metres)

1968 . .	22,038,000
1969 . .	22,575,000
1970 . .	23,105,000

Source: FAO, *Yearbook of Forest Products.*

SAWNWOOD
(cubic metres)

1967 . . .	58,000
1968 . . .	59,000
1969 . . .	60,000
1970 . . .	63,000

Source: United Nations *Statistical Yearbook 1972.*

FISHING*
(metric tons)

1968 . . .	6,900
1969 . . .	5,800
1970 . . .	7,000
1971 . . .	7,500

* FAO estimate.

Source: FAO, *Yearbook of Fishery Statistics 1971.*

MINING

Gold (kg.)

1967–68 . . .	956.8
1968–69 . . .	1,222.7
1969–70 . . .	848.6

Salt (metric tons)

1967 . . .	212,000
1968 . . .	215,000
1969 . . .	234,000
1970 . . .	260,000

INDUSTRY

PRINCIPAL PRODUCTS
(Twelve months ending September 10th)

	Unit	1968–69	1969–70
Tinned Meat	metric tons	5,474	5,226
Vegetable Oils (edible) . . .	,, ,,	8,157	10,026
Wheat Flour	,, ,,	41,536	40,019
Macaroni	,, ,,	5,542	5,355
Refined Sugar	,, ,,	66,199	96,967
Liqueurs	hectolitres	42,618	42,140
Wine	,,	50,237	50,950
Beer	,,	238,737	280,239
Lemonade	,,	195,000	213,915
Mineral Waters	,,	114,455	120,169
Cigarettes	'000	764,991	870,393
Cotton Yarn	metric tons	10,027	10,543
Woven Cotton Fabrics . . .	'000 sq. metres	68,164	69,706
Woollen Blankets . . .	number	230,822	133,626
Woollen Carpets . . .	sq. metres	10,557	4,365
Nylon Fabrics	'000 sq. metres	3,287	3,217
Leather Footwear . . .	pairs	868,174	822,235
Canvas and Rubber Footwear . .	,,	430,994	671,121
Plastic Footwear	'000 pairs	1,272	1,287
Plywood	cubic metres	2,253	2,540

[continued on next page

Principal Products—*continued*]

	Unit	1968–69	1969–70
Particle Board	cubic metres	3,472	3,631
Soap	metric tons	4,967	6,700
Ethyl Alcohol	hectolitres	9,664	10,019
Liquefied Petroleum Gas . .	metric tons	2,438	2,387
Motor Spirit (Petrol) . . .	,, ,,	65,287	68,599
Kerosene	,, ,,	2,000	n.a.
Jet Fuels	,, ,,	26,000	31,000
Distillate Fuel Oils . . .	,, ,,	140,000	165,000
Residual Fuel Oils . . .	,, ,,	272,000	311,000
Petroleum Bitumen (Asphalt) .	,, ,,	7,000	16,000
Clay Building Bricks . . .	'000	29,476	35,966
Quicklime	metric tons	21,384	19,937
Cement	,, ,,	173,594	175,405
Nails	,, ,,	4,032	3,865
Electric Energy	'000 kWh.	340,765	367,639

Sources: Annual Industrial Survey; United Nations, *Statistical Yearbook.*

FINANCE

100 cents = 1 Ethiopian dollar (E$).

Coins: 1, 5, 10, 25 and 50 cents.

Notes: 1, 5, 10, 20, 50, 100 and 500 dollars.

Exchange rates (April 1974): £1 sterling = E$4.893; U.S. $1 = E$2.072.

E$100 = £20.44 = U.S. $48.25.

Note: Between January 1964 and August 1971 the par value of the Ethiopian dollar was 40 U.S. cents (U.S. $1 = E$2.50). From December 1971 to February 1973 the rate was U.S. $1 = E$2.303. In terms of sterling, the exchange rate between November 1967 and June 1972 was £1 = E$6.00.

BUDGET
(E$ million, 12 months ending July 7th)

Revenue	1969–70	1970–71	Expenditure	1969–70	1970–71
Direct Taxes . . .	102.3	121.8	Current Expenditure:		
Indirect Taxes . . .	121.8	131.5	General Services . .	213.8	217.4
Taxes on Foreign Trade .	152.7	155.1	Economic Services . .	44.1	47.1
Revenue from State Property	19.6	9.2	Social Services . .	94.2	106.0
External Assistance . .	88.0	93.4	Pension Fund . .	13.8	20.6
Capital Receipts . . .	48.6	61.9	Unallocated Funds . .	107.7	116.0
Pensions Revenue . .	5.3	6.0	Capital Expenditure:		
Other Revenue . . .	27.1	41.2	Social Development .	30.1	18.9
			Economic Development .	75.3	103.9
	565.4	620.1	Public Buildings . .	0.8	1.4
Deficit	14.3	11.2			
Total . .	579.7	631.3	Total . .	579.7	631.3

Currency in Circulation (October 31st, 1973): E$348.5 million.

NATIONAL ACCOUNTS
(E$ million at current prices)

ECONOMIC ACTIVITY	1967	1968	1969
Agriculture and Livestock . . .	1,811.2	1,911.7	2,022.6
Hunting	1.5	1.3	1.2
Forestry and Logging	85.7	88.9	92.7
Fishing	4.2	3.0	3.0
Mining and Quarrying	12.1	11.2	9.1
Manufacturing*	298.1	333.9	388.7
Electricity and Water Supply . .	17.9	20.5	21.7
Construction	217.6	208.5	214.3
Wholesale and Retail Trade . . .	246.2	286.0	319.8
Transport, Storage and Communications	125.7	139.8	142.8
Owner-occupied Dwellings . . .	131.5	138.6	147.4
Finance, Insurance, Property Services .	40.0	43.7	49.5
Educational Services . . .	60.4	64.7	70.0
Medical and Health Services . .	23.3	24.5	24.8
Domestic Service by Households . .	56.6	57.6	58.6
Other Private Services† . . .	64.5	80.9	90.6
Public Administration and Defence .	178.8	191.2	203.9
GROSS DOMESTIC PRODUCT (G.D.P.) AT FACTOR COST . . .	3,375.3	3,606.0	3,860.7
Indirect Taxes, less Subsidies . .	229.5	235.5	237.3
G.D.P. in PURCHASERS' VALUES .	3,604.8	3,841.5	4,098.0
Net Income from Abroad . . .	−16.5	−22.5	−20.2
GROSS NATIONAL PRODUCT AT MARKET PRICES	3,588.3	3,819.0	4,077.8

* Including handicrafts and small-scale industry.
† Including business services, restaurants and hotels.

Source: Central Statistical Office, *Statistical Abstract* 1971.

G.D.P. in purchasers' values (revised estimate, E$ million): 4,071 in 1969; 4,489 in 1970; 4,731 in 1971.

BALANCE OF PAYMENTS
(E$ million)

	1970	1971
Goods and Services . . .	−99.1	−134.1
Merchandise f.o.b. . . .	−54.9	−80.7
Non-monetary gold . . .	1.5	1.1
Freight and insurance . . .	−64.7	−71.0
Other transportation . . .	35.9	33.1
Travel	−3.0	1.4
Investment income . . .	−19.4	−29.2
Other government . . .	16.3	24.1
Other services . . .	−10.8	−12.9
Transfer Payments . . .	20.0	22.5
Private	−6.6	−4.4
Government	26.6	26.9
Capital Movements . . .	45.0	100.0
Private long-term . . .	13.3	19.7
Private short-term . . .	14.8	16.9
Central Government . . .	16.9	63.4
Monetary Institutions:		
Central monetary institutions . .	2.2	16.9
Other monetary institutions . .	40.1	−0.2
Net change on Capital Account . .	87.3	116.7
Net Errors and Omissions . .	−8.4	−5.1

EXTERNAL TRADE
(E$ million)

	1966	1967	1968	1969	1970	1971	1972
Imports . .	404.3	357.4	432.5	388.3	429.2	469.5	435.6
Exports* . .	277.0	252.7	266.0	298.1	305.9	314.1	384.2

* Including re-exports.

PRINCIPAL COMMODITIES
IMPORTS
(E$'000)

	1969	1970	1971
Food and Live Animals	19,687.8	31,446.5	28,525.5
Cereals and Cereal Preparations . . .	6,282.0	16,380.9	13,263.3
Textile Fibres and Waste . . .	14,765.4	8,989.3	12,404.5
Mineral Fuels, Lubricants, etc. . .	28,184.9	33,576.5	44,297.5
Crude Petroleum	16,241.5	18,471.8	20,052.5
Petroleum Products	11,453.3	14,849.0	23,465.0
Chemicals	43,507.7	50,066.7	55,732.4
Medicinal and Pharmaceutical Products	11,058.7	13,506.6	13,763.7
Rubber Manufactures	12,720.1	18,206.4	21,038.3
Tyres and Tubes	11,303.0	n.a.	n.a.
Textile Yarn and Thread . . .	11,382.3	12,127.2	13,034.7
Textile Fabrics, etc. . . .	11,444.6	12,922.4	15,350.6
Iron and Steel	17,345.2	27,813.7	27,664.1
Machinery (non-electric) . . .	55,215.6	67,162.0	71,263.1
Agricultural Machinery and Implements	9,063.3	9,984.7	14,359.9
Textile and Leather Machinery . .	11,726.3	9,653.2	14,036.9
Electrical Machinery, Appliances, etc. .	25,523.5	25,547.0	30,400.2
Telecommunications Apparatus . .	10,319.5	8,508.6	9,528.7
Transport Equipment . . .	52,709.1	54,266.3	62,553.3
Road Motor Vehicles and Parts . .	38,527.9	43,845.7	51,672.4
Aircraft	11,404.2	6,437.5	7,151.6
Clothing	12,854.6	12,190.6	7,908.6
TOTAL (incl. others) . . .	388,302.4	429,167.5	469,542.8

EXPORTS, EXCLUDING RE-EXPORTS
(E$'000)

	1969	1970	1971
Food and Live Animals . . .	221,283.1	223,081.6	229,825.7
Meat and Meat Preparations . .	4,346.3	5,969.1	8,907.8
Fruit and Vegetables . . .	28,684.2	21,338.1	28,378.2
Coffee (green or roasted) . . .	173,946.6	181,268.4	175,210.0
Hides and Skins (undressed) . . .	29,159.0	24,464.9	25,727.6
Oilseeds, Oil Nuts and Oil Kernels .	23,183.2	28,352.6	32,063.6
Sesame Seed	15,607.0	n.a.	n.a.
TOTAL (incl. others) . . .	292,605.4	295,604.4	309,588.0

ETHIOPIA—(Statistical Survey)

PRINCIPAL COUNTRIES
(E$'000)

Imports	1969	1970*	1971*	Exports	1969	1970	1971
Czechoslovakia .	5,363	9,093	6,995	France . . .	8,919	6,618	7,817
France . . .	19,817	12,267	14,842	French Terr. Afars			
Germany, Fed. Rep.	55,635	58,885	51,906	and Issas .	19,153	15,589	19,685
India . . .	8,272	7,552	7,294	Germany, Fed. Rep.	28,791	22,257	24,807
Iran . . .	19,674	25,950	30,811	Italy . . .	21,114	18,991	16,560
Israel . . .	11,071	8,144	8,864	Japan . . .	14,120	16,614	18,713
Italy . . .	59,826	72,627	75,755	Netherlands . .	4,617	3,950	8,594
Japan . . .	42,142	63,610	69,243	Saudi Arabia . .	17,219	16,665	20,172
Netherlands .	10,530	10,901	12,318	Sri Lanka ..	5,292	4,837	6,253
Sweden .	5,315	10,273	8,004	U.S.S.R. .	4,188	1,023	6,823
Switzerland .	4,828	6,050	11,336	United Kingdom .	9,566	5,817	6,905
United Kingdom .	39,027	32,035	44,031	U.S.A. . . .	125,600	149,019	137,906
U.S.A. . . .	39,975	35,885	43,430				
Total (incl. others)	388,302	429,068	469,500	Total (incl. others) .	298,125	305,889	314,014

* Provisional figures.

COFFEE EXPORTS
(E$ '000)

	1969	1970	1971
U.S.A.	119,937	142,319	131,141
Germany, Federal Republic . .	17,291	8,036	10,171
Italy	5,604	2,448	2,889
Saudi Arabia	4,444	5,943	8,631
Japan	4,069	2,850	2,373
France	3,456	2,133	3,493
U.S.S.R.	2,308	—	3,823
Norway	1,700	1,176	730
Total (incl. others) . .	173,947	181,264	175,163

TRANSPORT

RAILWAYS*

	1968–69	1969–70	1970–71
Addis Ababa—Djibouti:			
Passenger-km. ('000) .	83,000	92,000	80,100
Freight ('000 net ton-km.) .	190,000	220,000	243,100

* Excluding Eritrea but including traffic on the portion of the Djibouti–Addis Ababa line which runs through the French Territory of the Afars and the Issas.

ROADS
(Number of vehicles in use)

	1968	1969	1970
Passenger Cars . . .	29,500	33,000	47,200
Commercial Vehicles . .	9,700	10,800	12,300

SHIPPING

INTERNATIONAL SEA-BORNE TRAFFIC

	1969	1970	1971
Vessels Entered ('ooo net reg. tons)	3,146	3,223	3,341
Goods Loaded ('ooo metric tons) .	693	729	362
Goods Unloaded ('ooo metric tons)	834	1,005	1,094

CIVIL AVIATION

	1969	1970	1971
Kilometres flown ('ooo) . .	10,396	10,738	10,836
Passenger-km. ('ooo) . .	300,380	314,325	368,000
Cargo ton-km. ('ooo) . .	15,751	15,143	14,732
Mail ton-km. ('ooo) . .	1,621	1,612	1,976

Tourist arrivals: (1969) 46,521 (incl. 10,272 from the U.S.A.); (1970) 53,187 (incl. 11,289 from the U.S.A.); (1972 est.) 80,000.

EDUCATION

(Number of pupils)

	1968–69	1969–70	1970–71
Primary . . .	513,981	590,445	655,427
Junior Secondary . .	56,918	63,215	73,121
Senior Secondary . .	31,943	42,487	53,236
Specialized Schools . .	9,559	8,968	9,389
University . . .	3,870	4,636	4,543
TOTAL . .	616,271	709,751	795,716

Source: Central Statistical Office, Addis Ababa.

THE CONSTITUTION

The 1931 constitution was revised in 1955 and divides political power between the Emperor and a bi-cameral parliament.

THE EMPEROR

The Emperor appoints Ministers, determines the powers of Ministries and controls officials. With the advice and consent of Parliament he may declare war. As Commander-in-Chief he appoints officers and may determine the size of the armed forces. He may declare a state of siege, martial law or national emergency. The Emperor directs Foreign Affairs. He alone has the right to settle disputes with foreign powers and to ratify treaties and other international agreements. All treaties requiring territorial adjustment or financial expenditure require the approval of both Houses of Parliament. The Emperor has the right to originate legislation and other resolutions in Parliament and to proclaim laws when they have been passed by Parliament. He convenes annual and extra-ordinary sessions of Parliament and has the right to dissolve the same by an order providing at the same time for the appointment of a new Senate and/or election of a new Chamber of Deputies, within four months from the date of the order. He appoints the members of the Senate but the members of the Chamber of Deputies are elected.

In April 1966 a Cabinet of Ministers selected by the Prime Minister was approved by the Emperor. This was the first occasion on which such a procedure was adopted.

MINISTERS

The Prime Minister is appointed by the Emperor to whom he submits the proposed Cabinet Ministers. The Cabinet is responsible to the Prime Minister. The Prime Minister and Cabinet are collectively responsible for legislative proposals to the Emperor and to Parliament. The Prime Minister presents to Parliament proposals of legislation made by the Council of Ministers and approved by the Emperor and presents to the Emperor the proposals of legislation approved by Parliament and decrees proposed by the Council of Ministers. All Ministers have the right to attend any meeting of either Chamber of Parliament and to speak there. They may be obliged to attend, either in person or by deputy, in either Chamber on the request of a majority vote and to answer verbally or in writing questions concerning their office.

PARLIAMENT

Parliament is composed of the Chamber of Deputies and the Senate. The Chamber has 250 members elected by universal adult suffrage every four years. The Senate is composed of a maximum of 125 members appointed by the Emperor for a term of six years with one-third of its members reaching the end of their term every two years. Senators may be reappointed for more than one term. The Chambers may meet in joint session or separately. The date of their regular sessions is fixed by the Constitution. Laws may be proposed to either or both Chambers either by the Emperor or by ten members of either Chamber. Proposals for legislation approved by both Chambers are sent to the Emperor who may return them for further consideration. In case of emergency during a Parliamentary recess decrees may be promulgated by the Emperor having the force of law but such decrees must subsequently be ratified by Parliament. No taxation may

be imposed except by law and all financial legislation must originate in the Chamber of Deputies.

CONSTITUTIONAL CHANGES

Following considerable military and civil unrest in February 1974 the Emperor announced on March 5th, 1974, that a conference would be called within six months to propose revision of the constitution. In a policy statement issued on April 8th, 1974, the Government promised far-reaching reforms of administrative and judicial processes. Both statements proposed the establishment of a constitutional monarchy and implied the transfer of much of the authority vested in the Emperor by the present constitution to Parliament.

ERITREA

In 1950 a UN resolution provided for the federation of Ethiopia and Eritrea. The new constitution came into force in September 1952.

Late in 1962 Eritrea was incorporated as a Province of Ethiopia and the separate Assembly was dissolved. (There are now fourteen Provinces in Ethiopia.)

THE GOVERNMENT

HEAD OF STATE

Emperor of Ethiopia: His Imperial Majesty HAILE SELLASSIE I.

In February 1974 the Emperor announced the formation of an interim administration headed by Lij ENDALKATCHEW MAKONNEN as Prime Minister, and committed to a programme of reform. However in July 1974 the Ethiopian Armed Forces took power from the civilian government and Lij MIKAEL IMRU was appointed Prime Minister by the Armed Forces Committee which at the end of July had almost total political control over Ethiopia.

DIPLOMATIC REPRESENTATION
EMBASSIES ACCREDITED TO ETHIOPIA
(In Addis Ababa)

Austria: P.O.B. 137; *Ambassador:* Dr. EGON LIBSCH.

Belgium: P.O.B. 1239; *Ambassador:* JACQUES DHONT.

Bulgaria: P.O.B. 987; *Ambassador:* ANGEL ZANKOV.

Burundi: P.O.B. 3641; *Ambassador:* Dr. JOSEPH NINDORERA.

Cameroon: P.O.B. 1026; *Ambassador:* EL HADJ MAHMOUDOU HAMAN DEKO.

Canada: P.O.B. 1130; *Ambassador:* RALPH E. REYNOLDS.

China, People's Republic: P.O.B. 5643; *Ambassador:* YU PEI-WEN.

Colombia: P.O.B. 1102; *Ambassador:* Dr. GUILLERMO NANNETTI CONCHA.

Czechoslovakia: P.O.B. 3108; *Ambassador:* ZDENĚK HÁJEK.

Egypt: P.O.B. 1611; *Ambassador:* KHAIRG RAGHEB IL AYUTY.

Equatorial Guinea: P.O.B. 246; *Ambassador:* (vacant).

Finland: P.O.B. 1017; *Ambassador:* VEIKKO LAURI HIETANEN (also accred. to Kenya).

France: P.O.B. 1464; *Ambassador:* ALBERT TRECA.

German Democratic Republic: P.O.B. 5507; *Ambassador:* HELMUT GÜRKE.

Germany, Federal Republic: P.O.B. 660; *Ambassador:* Dr. HERBERT Baron VON STACKELBERG.

Ghana: P.O.B. 3173; *Ambassador:* Y. B. TURKSON.

Greece: P.O.B. 1168; *Ambassador:* NICOLUS PHILOPOULOS.

Guinea: P.O.B. 1190; *Ambassador:* FACINE BANGOURA.

Hungary: P.O.B. 1213; *Ambassador:* ZOLTÁN GYENGE.

India: P.O.B. 528; *Ambassador:* (vacant).

Indonesia: P.O.B. 1004; *Ambassador:* H. M. AMIN AZEHARIE.

Iran: P.O.B. 1144; *Ambassador:* KAZEM NIAMIR.

Italy: P.O.B. 1105; *Ambassador:* LUIGI SABETTA.

Ivory Coast: P.O.B. 3668; *Ambassador:* LOUIS GUIRANDOU-N'DIAYE.

Jamaica: P.O.B. 5633; *Ambassador:* (vacant).

Japan: P.O.B. 1499; *Ambassador:* KENJI NAKAO.

Kenya: P.O.B. 3301; *Ambassador:* N. M. MUGO.

Korea, Republic: P.O.B. 2047; *Ambassador:* CHANG JAE YONG.

Liberia: P.O.B. 3116; *Ambassador:* CHARLES T. O. KING II.

Malawi: P.O.B. 2316; *Ambassador:* B. K. KATENGA.

Malaysia: P.O.B. 3656; *Chargé d'Affaires:* ABDUL MAJID BIN MOHAMMED.

Mexico: P.O.B. 2962; *Ambassador:* Dr. ROBERTO MOLINA PASQUEL.

Morocco: P.O.B. 337; *Ambassador:* ABDURAHIM HARKETT (also accred. to Kenya, Tanzania and Uganda).

Netherlands: P.O.B. 1241; *Ambassador:* JEO VAN SUCHTELEN.

Nigeria: P.O.B. 1019; *Ambassador:* VICTOR ADEGORAYE.

Pakistan: P.O.B. 5663; *Ambassador:* KAMALUDDIN AHMED.

Poland: P.O.B. 1123; *Ambassador:* WLADYSLAW ROLSKI.

Romania: P.O.B. 62; *Ambassador:* TITUS SINU.

Rwanda: P.O.B. 5618; *Ambassador:* MATHIEU NGIRUMPATSE.

Saudi Arabia: P.O.B. 1104; *Chargé d'Affaires:* HOSSAIN BAFAKIH.

Senegal: P.O.B. 2581; *Ambassador:* LATYR KAMARA.

Sierra Leone: P.O.B. 5619; *Ambassador:* Mrs. SHIRLEY Y. GBIYAMA.

Somalia: P.O.B. 1006; *Ambassador:* ABDURRAHMAN A. ALI.

Spain: P.O.B. 2312; *Ambassador:* JOSÉ LUIS DE LA PANAY AZNAR.

Sudan: P.O.B. 1110; *Ambassador:* MUSTAFA MEDANI ABBASHAR.

Sweden: P.O.B. 1029; *Ambassador:* LARS HEDSTRÖM.

Switzerland: P.O.B. 1106; *Ambassador:* HEINZ LANGENBACHER.

Tanzania: P.O.B. 1077; *Ambassador:* G. S. MAGOMBE.

Thailand: P.O.B. 2764; *Ambassador:* BULAM KANGVANTOT.

Trinidad and Tobago: P.O.B. 330; *Ambassador:* J. R. P. DUMAS (also accred. to Ghana and Senegal).

Tunisia: P.O.B. 1333; *Ambassador:* TOUFIK SMIDA.

Turkey: P.O.B. 1506; *Ambassador:* CELAL CALISLAR (also accred. to Tanzania).

Uganda: P.O.B. 5644; *Ambassador:* K. L. LUBEGA.

U.S.S.R.: P.O.B. 1500; *Ambassador:* A. P. RATANOV.

United Kingdom: P.O.B. 858; *Ambassador:* WILLIE MORRIS.

U.S.A.: P.O.B. 1014; *Ambassador:* T. McELHINEY.

Vatican: P.O.B. 588; *Apostolic Nunciate:* (vacant).

Venezuela: P.O.B. 5584; *Ambassador:* G. N. CARILLO.

Yemen Arab Republic: P.O.B. 664; *Ambassador:* AHMED A. AL MOALLEMI.

Yugoslavia: P.O.B. 1341; *Ambassador:* (vacant).

Zaire: P.O.B. 2723; *Ambassador:* BAGBENI ADEITO NZENGEYA.

Zambia: P.O.B. 1909; *Ambassador:* PETTGHO M. NGONDA.

Ethiopia also has diplomatic relations with Albania, Algeria, Argentina, Australia, Botswana, Brazil, Central African Republic, Chad, Congo (Brazzaville), Denmark, Iceland, Iraq, Jordan, Lebanon, Libya, Mali, Mauritania, Mongolia, Norway, Panama, Qatar, Singapore and Swaziland (non-resident representatives not accredited in all cases).

PARLIAMENT

SENATE
President: Bitwoded ZAUDE GEBRE HIWOT.

A maximum of 125 members appointed by H.I.M. The Emperor for a term of six years.

CHAMBER OF DEPUTIES
(General Election, June-July 1973)
President: Hon. Ato ABEBE WONDIMEH.

It contains 250 members elected by universal adult suffrage every four years.

POLITICAL PARTIES

The 1955 Constitution and legislation on associations effectively prevented the formation of political parties. It remains to be seen whether the revision of the Constitution will provide for their formation.

SEPARATIST GROUPS

A number of organizations exist whose aims are to obtain the independence of certain areas populated by religious and/or ethnic minorities. Some, such as the West Somalia Liberation Front, also known as (or associated with) the Ethiopian National Liberation Front, probably exist in name only or ineffectively in exile. However, one movement, the Eritrean Liberation Front (ELF), has established itself as a considerable force. From a modest start in the early 1960s as a reaction to the absorbtion of Eritrea into Ethiopia, and despite factional difficulties, it has attracted support from Arab countries, such as Libya, Iraq, Syria and the People's Democratic Republic of Yemen, and Palestinian organizations such as Al Fatah. After some spectacular guerrilla successes in 1969/70, followed by a period of inactivity, the ELF stepped up activities in September 1973. In March 1974 a guerrilla unit put the new copper mine at Debarwa, near Asmara, out of action.

DEFENCE

The army numbers about 41,000, the air force 2,250 and the navy 1,400. There is also an equivalent total of men in a para-military force.

Chief of Staff of the Armed Forces: Lt.-Gen. WOLDE SELASSIE BEREKE.

Commander of Air Force: Brig.-Gen. ASSEFA GEBRE-EGZY.

Deputy Commander of Navy: Commodore TASEN DESTA.

Governor of Eritrea: H.E. Lt.-Gen. DEBEBE HAILE MARIAM.

JUDICIAL SYSTEM

The Supreme Court: Addis Ababa.

President: Afe Negus TESHOME HAILE MARIAM.

The President sits with two other judges. The Court has eight divisions each presided over by a Vice Afe Negus. The Supreme Court has jurisdiction only to hear appeals from the High Court. Appeals can go from the Supreme Court to the Emperor sitting in Chilot (*Court*) in accordance with Ethiopian custom.

The High Court: Addis Ababa; sits in 12 Divisions each of 3 Judges: 1. Appeals; 2. Criminal; 3. Civil; 4. Land; 5. Government.

Taqlai Ghizat High Courts (*Provincial High Courts*): each Court has a presiding judge and two other judges. There are no foreign judges. The Governor-General of a province may sit as the presiding judge, criminal and civil.

Awraja Ghizat Courts (*Provincial Courts*): composed of three judges, criminal and civil.

Warada Ghizat Courts (*Regional Courts*): criminal cases and limited civil actions.

Meketel Warada Courts (*Sub-Regional Courts*): one judge sits alone with very limited jurisdiction, criminal only

RELIGION

CHRISTIANS

Imperial Ethiopian Orthodox Union Church: official Church of the Emperor and State; founded in the fourth century A.D. There are about 10 million members.

His Holiness the Patriarch ABUNA TEWOFLOS, P.O.B. 1283, Patriarchate, King George IV St., Addis Ababa.

Roman Catholic Church

Alexandrine-Ethiopian Rite:

Metropolitan See: Addis Ababa; Archbishop Mgr. ASRATE MARIAM YEMMERU, Archbishop's House, P.O. Box 1903, Addis Ababa; Eparchy of Adigrat, Adigrat; Eparchy of Asmara, Asmara.

Latin Rite:

Vicar Apostolic of Asmara: Mgr. LUCA MILASI, P.O.B. 224, Asmara; there are also Vicarates Apostolic at Harar and Jimma.

Ethiopian Evangelical Church (Mekane Yesus): Pres. H.E. Ato EMANUEL ABRAHAM, P.O.B. 2087, Addis Ababa; f. 1958; 200,000 mems.

Seventh Day Adventist Church: Pastor TEBEGE GUDDAYE, P.O.B. 145, Addis Ababa; 20,000 mems.

Greek Orthodox Church: Archbishop of Aksum: Most Rev. Dr. METHODIOS FOUYAS, P.O.B. 571, Addis Ababa.

Armenian Orthodox Church: Father ZAVIEN ARMOUNIAN; St. George's Armenian Church, Addis Ababa.

Anglican Church (Diocese of Egypt): The Rev. PHILIP J. COUSINS, P.O.B. 109, Queen Elizabeth St., Addis Ababa; f. 1926; 175 mems.; publ. *Roar* (fortnightly).

American Presbyterian Church: P.O.B. 3507, Addis Ababa.

Lutheran Church: found in urban and rural areas and is responsible for Radio Voice of the Gospel (RVOG), P.O.B. 654, Addis Ababa.

The Lutheran Church is found in both urban and rural areas and there are also Hindu and Sikh religious institutions. The Pentecostal Church and the Sudan Interior Mission also do mission work in Ethiopia.

MUSLIMS

Approximately 50 per cent of the population are Muslims.

TRADITIONAL BELIEFS

It is estimated that between 5 and 15 per cent of the population follow animist rites and ceremonies.

THE PRESS

DAILIES

Addis Soir: P.O.B. 3280, Addis Ababa; publ. by the Ministry of Information; French; Editor Ato MESFIN BERHANU; circ. 1,300.

Addis Zemen: P.O.B. 30145, Addis Ababa; publ. by the Ministry of Information; Amharic; Editor Ato BAALU GIRMA; circ. 18,000 (weekday), c. 20,000 (Sunday).

Ethiopian Herald: P.O.B. 1074, Addis Ababa; publ. by the Ministry of Information; English; Editor Ato TESFAYE-HAPTE-YIMER; circ. 8,000 (weekday), 12,000 (Sunday).

Giornale dell'Eritrea: P.O.B. 1206, Asmara; Italian; Editors Ato ABDELMEGID KADI SAEED IMNAI, ANGELO BARBIERI; circ. 3,000.

Hebret/Al Wahda: P.O.B. 247, Asmara; publ. by the Dept. of Information; Tigrinya, Arabic; Editor GRAZMATCH TESFAI ABRAHA; circ. 6,000.

Quotidiano Eritreo: P.O.B. 247, Asmara; publ. by the Dept. of Information; Italian; Editor Dr. ENRICO MANIA; circ. 4,000.

PERIODICALS

Al-Alem: weekly; P.O.B. 30232, Addis Ababa; publ. by the Ministry of Information; Arabic; Editor Ato MENIR CHEMIR; circ. 1,200.

Ethiopia: weekly; P.O.B. 247, Asmara; publ. by Dept. of Information; Amharic, Arabic; Editor Ato MAMMO WODNEH; circ. 2,000.

Ethiopia Mirror: quarterly; P.O.B. 3732, Addis Ababa; publ. by Alem Publications; English; Editor Ato YE-WANDWASSEN T. MARCOS; circ. 12,000.

Ethiopia Observer: quarterly; f. 1936; publ. in Ethiopia and Britain; P.O.B. 1895, Addis Ababa and 57 Carter Lane, London, E.C.4; English; Editor Dr. RICHARD PANKHURST.

Ethiopia Tourist News: P.O.B. 2183, Addis Ababa; publ. by the Ministry of Commerce, Industry and Tourism; Amharic, English, French, Italian; circ. 10,000.

Matino del Lunedi: weekly; P.O.B. 500, Asmara; Editor ANGELO GRANARA; circ. 2,000.

Menen: monthly; P.O.B. 3732, Addis Ababa; publ. by Alem Publications; Amharic; illustrated; Editor AZARIAH KIROS (acting); circ. 10,000.

Misikire Birhan: monthly; P.O.B. 2248, Addis Ababa; publ. by Bible Churchman's Missionary Society; Amharic; religious; Editor RHENA TAYLOR KEBEDE WOLDE MARIAM; circ. 5,000.

Policina Ermijaw: weekly; P.O.B. 40046, Addis Ababa; Police Journal; Amharic; Editor Lt. GETACHEW MENGISTIE; circ. 85,000.

Trade and Development Buletin: irregular; P.O.B. 856, Asmara; publ. by the Chamber of Commerce, Industry and Agriculture of Eritrea; Amharic, English, Tigrinya, Italian, Arabic; Editor Ato KEBEDE TEDLA.

Tsedei: monthly; P.O.B. 30199, Addis Ababa; Amharic; Editor GETACHEW TAKALYN; circ. 8,000.

Wotaderina Alamaw: fortnightly; P.O.B. 1901, Addis Ababa; publ. by the Ministry of Defence; Editor Capt. NADEW ZEKARIAS; circ. 5,000 (suspended).

Wotaderina Gizew: fortnightly; P.O.B. 663, Addis Ababa; publ. by the Imperial Ethiopian Body-guard; Amharic; Editor Major ASTATIKE TSEGAYE; circ. c. 25,000.

PRESS AGENCIES
FOREIGN BUREAUX

Agence France-Presse: P.O.B. 3537; f. 1963; Chief JEAN MARIE BLIN.

New China News Agency: P.O.B. 2508; Chief JUI YING CHIEH.

Reuters: P.O.B. 2150; Chief J. TALBOT.

Tass: P.O.B. 998; Chief A. BALABENOV.

PUBLISHERS

Asfaw Taffera: P.O.B. 2020, Addis Ababa.

Francescana Tipografia: 2 Abune Yaried St., Asmara.

Haile Sellassie I University Press: P.O.B. 1176, Addis Ababa; f. 1968; educational works; Man. Dir. Mrs. INNES MARSHALL.

Oxford University Press: P.O.B. 1024, Addis Ababa; f. in Ethiopia 1965; educational and academic publishing in English and Amharic; Man. Ato TESFAYE DABA.

RADIO AND TELEVISION

RADIO

Radio Ethiopia: P.O.B. 1020, Addis Ababa; f. 1941; Amharic, English, French, Arabic, Afar, Galigniya, Tigrinya, Tigre and Somali; listeners 9.6 million; advertising is accepted; Gen. Man. H.E. NEGUSSAYE HAPTEWOLD; Dir.-Gen. for Radio NEGASH GEBRE-MARIAM.

Radio Voice of the Gospel: P.O.B. 654, Addis Ababa; f. 1961; Lutheran World Federation Broadcasting Service; medium-wave local services; short-wave services in thirteen languages to Asia, the Middle East and Africa and Madagascar; Gen. Dir. Rev. Dr. SIGURD ASKE; Station Dir. Rev. ERNST BAUEROCHSE; publ. *RVOG News.*

It is estimated that there are 250,000 radio receivers in the country.

TELEVISION

Ethiopian Television Service: P.O.B. 1020, Addis Ababa; television services were inaugurated in 1964, under the initial management of Thomson Television International and operated by the government; advertising is accepted; Dir. H.E. NEGUSSAYE HAPTEWOLD; Dir. Gen. for TV SAMUEL FERENJI.

There are an estimated 20,000 sets in the Addis Ababa region. In Asmara, Eritrea, there is a closed circuit service for the United States Armed Forces with about 1,000 receivers the future of which remains uncertain after the closure of the U.S. communications faculty.

FINANCE

(cap.=capital; p.u.=paid up; E$=Ethiopian dollar; dep. = deposits; m. = million)

BANKING

State Banks

In December 1963 the State Bank of Ethiopia was divided into the National Bank of Ethiopia and the Commercial Bank of Ethiopia (S.C.):

Addis Ababa Bank: P.O.B. 751, Addis Ababa; f. 1963; 40 per cent owned by National and Grindlays Bank; brs. in Addis Ababa and provinces (33 in all); cap. p.u. E$5m.; dep. E$68.6m. (Dec. 1972); Chair. Ato ABEBE KEBEDE; Man. Dir. Ato DEBEBE H. YOHANNES; Man. W. L. GASH.

Commercial Bank of Ethiopia: Haile Sellassie I Square, P.O.B. 255, Addis Ababa; f. 1964; cap. p.u. E$35m.; dep. E$557m. (1973); state-owned bank for commercial business; 91 brs.; Man. Dir. Ato TAFFARA DEGUEFE; publs. *Annual Report, Market Monthly* (monthly).

National Bank of Ethiopia: Haile Sellassie I Square, P.O.B. 5550, Addis Ababa; f. 1964; total assets E$517m. (Jan. 1973); issuing bank; Gov. H.E. Ato MENASSE LEMMA; Vice-Gov. Ato YAWAND-WASSEN MANGASHA; publs. *Annual Report, Quarterly Bulletin*.

Other Banks

Agricultural and Industrial Development Bank S.C.: P.O.B. 1900, Addis Ababa; f. 1970 from a merger of the De-velopment Bank of Ethiopia and the Ethiopian Investment Corporation; provides finance for industry and agriculture; auth. cap. E$100m.; cap. p.u. E$80m.; Man. Dir. H.E. Ato ASAFA DEMISSIE; publs. *Newsletter, Annual Report, Policy Papers*.

Banco di Napoli (Ethiopia) S.C.: P.O.B. 228, Ave. Empress Mennen 40, Asmara; f. 1970 to take over the Asmara branch of the Banco di Napoli; cap. E$2m.; dep. E$10.5m. (Dec. 1972); Gen. Man. DONATO SINISCALCO.

Banco di Roma, (Ethiopia) S.C.: Zerai Derres Square, Asmara; f. 1967; 8 brs. in Addis Ababa, brs. in Assab, Modjo, Massawa and four others; cap. p.u. E$4m.; Pres. Bitwoded ASFAHA WOLDE MIKAEL; Gen. Man GIORGIO GIORGETTIO.

INSURANCE

(Addis Ababa)

African Solidarity Insurance Co. S.C.: Afsol House, Haile Sellassie I Square, P.O.B. 2327; f. 1963; Gen. Man. D. G. SGOLOMBIS; Man. B. D. MURPHY.

Blue Nile Insurance S.C.: Papassinos Bldg., Ras Desta Damtew Ave., P.O.B. 2192; Man. Dir. ABATE FANTAYE.

Imperial Insurance Co. of Ethiopia Ltd.: Imperial Insurance Bldg., Meskel Square, P.O.B. 380; f. 1951; cap. p.u. E$1.2m.; Gen. Man. B. D. O'SHAUGHNESSY.

TRADE AND INDUSTRY

CHAMBERS OF COMMERCE

Ethiopian Chamber of Commerce: P.O.B. 517, Addis Ababa; f. 1947; 564 mems.; Pres. Ato TAFFARA DEGUEFE; publs. *Ethiopian Business* and various books and papers dealing with Ethiopian business, commerce and investment.

Chamber of Commerce, Industry, Agriculture and Handicrafts of Eritrea: Ave. Ras Makonnen, P.O.B. 856, Asmara; f. 1947; Pres. Ato SUNABARA M. DAMMANA.

TRADE ORGANIZATION

Ethiopian Coffee Exporters' Association: P.O.B. 1982, Addis Ababa; 32 mems.; Exec. Sec. Capt. ASRAT H. DEFERESU.

EMPLOYERS ORGANIZATION

Federation of Employers of Ethiopia (FEE): P.O.B. 944, Addis Ababa; f. 1963; 112 mems.

TRADE UNIONS

Confederation of Ethiopian Labour Unions (CELU): CELU Bldg., P.O.B. 3653, Addis Ababa; f. 1962; 85,000 mems.; 152 affiliates; affiliated to ICFTU; Sec.-Gen. FISSEHA TSION TEKIE; publ. *Voice of Labour* (fortnightly).

OIL

Companies are at present prospecting for oil along the Red Sea coast. One, Mobil Esso Ethiopia Inc., found natural gas offshore north of Massawa in 1969. Oil and natural gas is also thought to exist in the province of Bale in southern Ethiopia.

TRANSPORT

RAILWAYS

Franco-Ethiopian Railway: P.O.B. 1051, Addis Ababa; f. 1908; 782 km.; runs from Addis Ababa to Djibouti; Dir-Gen. B. PETIT.

Northern Ethiopian Railways Share Company: Massawa, Eritrea; 306 km.; runs from Massawa on the Red Sea through Asmara to Agordat; Gen. Man. GHETATCHEW MEDHANE.

ROADS

Imperial Highway Authority: P.O.B. 1770, Addis Ababa; constructs and maintains roads and bridges throughout Ethiopia. Out of a total system of 23,400 km. of primary, secondary and feeder roads and trails, there are 8,928 km. of all-weather gravel and asphalt roads. A further 4,835 km. are to be built during the Fourth Five-Year Plan by September 1978.

General Ethiopian Transport Share Company: P.O.B. 472, Addis Ababa; runs urban services in Addis Ababa; long distance services connecting all important provincial towns, and limited tourist services.

SHIPPING

Irregular services by foreign vessels to Massawa and Assab (port for Addis Ababa). Since 1960 Assab's facilities have been greatly extended and the port can now handle over a million tons of merchandise annually. It has an oil refinery with an annual capacity of 500,000 tons. Much trade goes through Djibouti (French Territory of the Afars and Issas) to Addis Ababa.

A. Besse and Co. (Ethiopia) S.C.: P.O.B. 1897, Addis Ababa.

Filli Biga and Co. S.C.: Head Office: P.O.B. 1108, Asmara; f. 1965 as a subsidiary of SCAC/SOCOPAO (France); branches at Addis Ababa, Assab, Massawa and Djibouti.

Ethiopian Shipping Lines (The): P.O.B. 2572, Addis Ababa; f. 1966; cargo, tanker services Red Sea-Europe; 7 vessels.

Gellatly, Hankey and Co. (Ethiopia) S.C.: P.O.B. 906, Asmara; brs. at Addis Ababa, Massawa, Assab and Dire Dawa.

Cie. Maritime Auxiliaire d'Outre-Mer: P.O.B. 1230, Addis Ababa.

Mitchell Cotts and Co. (Ethiopia) Ltd.: P.O. Box 527, Addis Ababa; f. 1960; branches at Asmara, Massawa, etc.; Chair. J. K. DICK, F.C.A.; Man. C. O'TOOLE.

Flli. de Nadai: P.O. Box 731, Asmara.

S.A. Navigatana: P.O. Box 1161, Asmara.

Savon and Riès (Ethiopian Shipping) Co.: P.O.B. 215, Asmara.

CIVIL AVIATION

Ethiopian Airlines: Haile Sellassie I Airport, P.O.B. 1755, Addis Ababa; f. 1945; operates regular domestic and international services; fleet of 9 DC-3, 3 Boeing 720B, 2 Boeing 707, 3 DC-6B, 2 Cessna 180, 3 Piper Cub, 1 Bell 47J Helicopter; Chair. H.E. Lij ENDALKACHEW MAKONNEN; Gen. Man. Lt.-Col. SEMRET MEDHANE.

Air Djibouti, Air France, Air India, Alitalia, British Airways, EAAC, EgyptAir, Lufthansa, Sudan Airways and Saudi Arabian Airlines serve Addis Ababa. Saudi and Yemen Airways serve Asmara only.

TOURISM

Ethiopian Tourist Organisation: P.O.B. 2183, Addis Ababa; f. 1961; Administrator H.E. Ato HAPTE SELLASSIE TAFFESSA.

THEATRES

Haile Sellassie I Theatre: P.O.B. 3200, Addis Ababa; Administrator Capt. ATNAFU MAKONNEN.

Hager Fikr Theatre: Administrator Ato IOEL JOHANNES.

Creative Arts Centre: Haile Sellassie I University, Addis Ababa; f. 1963.

UNIVERSITIES

Haile Sellassie 1 University: P.O.B. 1176, Addis Ababa; 650 teachers, 4,978 full-time students.

University of Asmara: P.O.B. 1220, Asmara; 100 teachers, 1,195 students.

FIJI

INTRODUCTORY SURVEY

Location, Climate, Religion, Flag, Capital

Fiji comprises over 800 islands, of which 100 are inhabited, situated about 1,200 miles south of the equator in the Pacific Ocean. The climate is tropical with temperatures ranging from 60° to 90°F (16°–32°C). The population includes Fijians, Indians, Chinese, Europeans and Melanesian and Polynesian peoples from other island groups including Tonga. About 50 per cent of the people are Christians and 40 per cent Hindus. The national flag (proportions 2 by 1) is light blue, with the United Kingdom flag as a canton in the upper hoist. In the fly is Fiji's national shield. The capital and chief port is Suva.

Recent History and Government

A new Constitution was introduced in 1966. It provided for an enlarged franchise and an expanded Legislative Council, almost wholly elected. On independence, in October 1970, Ratu Sir Kamisese Mara became Prime Minister and formed his first Cabinet, seven of whom were the elected and three the official members of the former Council of Ministers.

There were elections in April 1972 for a House of Representatives of 52 members. There are Fijian, Indian and General rolls. On the General roll are electors, mainly Europeans and Chinese, who are not eligible for inclusion on the Fijian and Indian rolls. Twelve Fijians, 12 Indians and 3 General members were elected on communal rolls. Ten Fijians, 10 Indians and 5 General members were elected on national rolls.

At the constitutional conference it was agreed that after these elections were held a Royal Commission would be set up to recommend the most appropriate method of election and representation in the future. The terms of reference were to be agreed by the Prime Minister with the Leader of the Opposition, but no accord had been reached by mid-1974.

In addition to the House of Representatives, there is an Upper House, the Senate. In this, 8 members are appointed by the Great Council of Fijian Chiefs; 7 by the Prime Minister; 6 by the Leader of the Opposition; and 1 by the Council of Rotuma—an island 400 miles distant from Suva.

With independence, the post of Governor, which carried with it the power of veto in certain matters, was abolished. Instead of a Governor there is now a Governor-General, representing the Queen, who continues to be the Head of State in Fiji. Immediately after independence Fiji joined the British Commonwealth and the United Nations.

Economic Affairs

The economy is basically agricultural, with sugar as the main crop, sales of this commodity accounting for two-thirds of export earnings in 1972. Tourism is developing rapidly and was the second largest source of foreign exchange earnings, followed by gold and coconut products. Domestic industry is still in its infancy but, because of the trade deficit, efforts are being made to encourage industries which will replace imports or provide goods for exports. The sixth Five-Year Development Plan (1971–75) aims to expand production and develop the infrastructure. Gross Domestic Product rose by 7 per cent in 1972, slightly above the Plan target.

Transport and Communications

Fiji lies on the main route between Australia and New Zealand and North America, and is the centre of communications in the southwestern Pacific. The international airport is at Nadi, about 130 miles from Suva. Suva Wharf and Lautoka Wharf were reconstructed in 1962 and 1963. There are no main railways but about 450 miles of light tracks carry sugar cane to the mills.

Currency and Exchange Rates

100 cents = 1 Fiji dollar ($F).

Exchange rates (April 1974):
£1 sterling = $F 1.886;
U.S. $1 = 80.0 Fiji cents.

STATISTICAL SURVEY

Area (square miles): 7,055.

Population: (1966 Census) 476,727 (Indians 240,960, Fijians 202,176, Europeans 6,590, Part-Europeans 9,687); Suva (capital) 54,157. Dec. 1971 estimate: 535,375 (Indians 272,040, Fijians 231,042, Part-Europeans 9,497, Rotumans 6,643, Europeans 4,600); Suva (capital) 60,000.

Agriculture: Exports (1971): Sugar 334,620 tons, Coconut Oil 16,547 tons, Bananas 49,231 cases; also melons, ginger, vegetables, molasses, timber, fish, hides and trochus shell.

MINING

(1971)

		PRODUCTION	VALUE IN $F
Gold	fine oz.	89,121	2,718,439
Silver.	fine oz.	19,893	28,471
Manganese ore . . .	tons	7,536	94,592
Limestone	,,	4,548	94,411
Crushed Metal . . .	cu. yds.	206,775	426,815

FINANCE

100 cents = 1 Fiji dollar.

Coins: 1, 2, 5, 10 and 20 cents.

Notes: 1, 2, 5, 10 and 20 dollars.

Exchange rates (April 1974): £1 sterling = $F1.886; U.S. $1 = 80.0 Fiji cents.

$F100 = £53.02 = U.S. $125.00.

BUDGET 1972

($F)

REVENUE		EXPENDITURE	
Customs	28,598,000	Charges on Public Debt. . .	4,142,753
Port and Harbour Dues, etc. .	799,000	Pensions, etc.	1,533,850
Licences and Taxes . . .	18,730,400	Education	9,444,735
Fees of Court or Office, etc. .	2,510,632	Medical	5,258,575
Post Office	3,255,900	Police	1,873,000
Rent of Government Property .	527,500	Posts and Telegraphs . .	1,969,047
Interest	635,839	Works (Establishment) . .	1,561,821
Miscellaneous	1,410,470	Works Annually Recurrent .	4,726,200
		Contribution to Capital Budget .	4,900,000
		Other	18,670,699
TOTAL . . .	56,467,741	TOTAL . . .	54,080,698

FIVE-YEAR DEVELOPMENT PLAN

1971–75—$F75 million. 1972 provision $F20,898,388.

EXTERNAL TRADE

($F)

	1969	1970	1971	1972
Imports .	77,888,146	90,501,755	111,563,868	131,347,000
Exports .	53,226,800	62,306,995	61,769,000	64,601,000

PRINCIPAL COMMODITIES
(1971—$F)

Imports					Exports				
Machinery, other than electrical	.	.	9,685,384		Sugar	.	.	.	32,851,168
Electrical Machinery and Goods	.	.	8,103,575		Coconut Oil	.	.	.	3,944,511
Transport Equipment	.	.	6,933,305		Unrefined Gold	.	.		2,677,939
Fabrics	.	.	5,948,683		Molasses	.	.	.	488,449
Fish	.	.	5,203,190		Coconut Meal	.	.		230,501
Aviation Turbine Fuel	.	.	3,866,175		Manganese Ore and Concentrates	.	.	57,346
Flour and Sharps	.	.	3,420,578		Ginger	.	.	.	161,268
Gas Oil and Diesel Oil	.	.	3,340,229		Lumber	.	.	.	237,095
Clothing	.	.	2,801,869		Bananas	.	.	.	152,063
Tape Recorders	.	.	1,792,424		Cigarettes	.	.	.	203,079
Meat	.	.	1,941,542						
Motor Spirits	.	.	1,542,806						
Radio Receivers	.	.	2,165,601						
Watches	.	.	2,428,580						
Rice	.	.	1,817,701						

Re-Exports				1971—$F
Aviation Turbine Fuel	.	.	.	4,202,201
Other Fuels	.	.	.	2,422,809
Textile Yarns and Fabrics	.	.	1,225,154
Motor Vehicles	.	.	.	320,034
Clothing	.	.	.	397,233
Aviation Spirit	.	.	.	365,495
Metal Manufactures	.	.	.	172,403

PRINCIPAL TRADING COUNTRIES
(1971)

Imports from:				$F		Exports to				$F
Australia	.	.	.	29,251,901		United Kingdom	.	.	.	17,845,719
United Kingdom	.	.	.	19,975,137		U.S.A.	.	.	.	11,085,766
Japan	.	.	.	19,020,572		Australia	.	.	.	4,758,196
New Zealand	.	.	.	n.a.		Canada	.	.	.	6,262,983
U.S.A.	.	.	.	4,436,443		New Zealand	.	.	.	3,711,820
Malaysia and Singapore	.	.	4,751,246		Japan	.	.	.	2,297,217
Hong Kong	.	.	.	3,409,822		Tonga	.	.	.	1,249,389
India	.	.	.	1,993,865		Western Samoa	.	.	.	1,243,606
Canada	.	.	.	863,574		Malaysia and Singapore	.	.	3,006,678
Iran	.	.	.	2,131,718		Germany, Federal Republic	.	.	262,164
Netherlands	.	.	.	992,343						
Germany, Federal Republic	.	.	1,469,596						

Transport (1971): *Shipping:* Entered 578 ships, 2,189,000 tons. *Civil Aviation:* Landed 164,329 passengers; Departed 163,448; Transit passengers 170,131. **Tourism** (1971) 152,151 visitors.

EDUCATION

(1971)

	Schools	Students
Primary	627	126,331
Secondary . . .	73	18,094
Vocational and Technical .	22	1,172
Teacher Training . .	3	358
Medical	1	207*

There are also 69 Fiji Government scholarship holders in higher education abroad (1973).

*1969.

Source: Public Relations Office, Suva.

THE CONSTITUTION

At present the Constitution derives from an Order in Council of September 1966, providing for a Governor, a Council of Ministers and a Legislative Council. After independence, in October 1970, the post of Governor was replaced by that of Governor-General. The Legislative Council was replaced in April 1972 by an elected 52-member House of Representatives.

Virtually all adults are eligible to register as electors. Twenty-seven members of the new House of Representatives (12 Fijians, 12 Indians and 3 others) were elected on the communal roll and 25 members (10 Fijians, 10 Indians and 5 others) on the national roll (a cross-voting system by which all races vote together). After these elections it was agreed that a Royal Commission would be set up to recommend the most appropriate method of election and representation, but progress in this direction was slow.

THE GOVERNMENT

Governor-General: Ratu Sir George Cakobau, o.b.e., j.p.

THE CABINET

(*May* 1974)

Prime Minister: Rt. Hon. Ratu Sir Kamisese Kapaiwai Tuimacilau Mara, k.b.e., m.a.

Deputy Prime Minister and Minister for Communications, Works and Tourism: Ratu Sir Penaia Ganilau, k.b.e., c.m.g., c.v.o., d.s.o., o.b.e.

Attorney-General: J. N. Falvey, o.b.e., k.c.

Minister of Finance: C. A. Stinson.

Minister for Fijian Affairs and Rural Development: Ratu W. B. Toganivalu.

Minister of Labour: J. Mavoa.

Minister for Youth, Sports and Rural Development: J. B. Naisara.

Minister for Commerce, Industry and Co-operatives: M. T. Khan.

Minister for Urban Development, Housing and Social Welfare: M. Ramzan, m.b.e.

Minister for Lands, Mines and Mineral Resources: Ratu J. B. Toganivalu.

Minister of Health: J. S. Singh.

Minister of Agriculture, Fisheries and Forests: P. W. Brown, m.b.e.

GENERAL ELECTION

(April 1972)

Party	Seats
Alliance	33
National Federation	19
	52

PROVINCIAL GOVERNMENT

There are fourteen provinces, each headed by a chairman.

POLITICAL PARTIES

Alliance Party: multi-racial; government party; 33 members of the House of Representatives; Leader Ratu Sir Kamisese K. T. Mara, k.b.e., m.a.; publ. *Nation.*

National Federation Party: G.P.O. Box 228, Suva; f. 1963; fusion of two parties: the Federation, which was mainly Indian but multi-racial, and the National Democratic Party, a purely Fijian party; 19 members in the House of Representatives, comprising official opposition; Leader S. M. Koya; mems.: approx. 40,000.

DIPLOMATIC REPRESENTATION

Australian High Commissioner: H. W. Bullock (Resident in Suva).

Canada High Commissioner: James Joachim McCardle (Resident in Canberra).

Indian High Commissioner: Bhagwan Singh (Resident in Suva).

New Zealand High Commissioner: Sir John Grace (Resident in Suva).

United Kingdom High Commissioner: John Williams, c.b.e. (Resident in Suva).

JUDICIAL SYSTEM

The law in force in Fiji consists of the Constitution of Fiji as set out in the Fiji Independence Order of 1970, the Ordinances in force on 10th October, 1970, the Acts of the Parliament of Fiji enacted after that date, and subject thereto, and to certain qualifications, the Common Law, Rules of Equity and the statutes of general application which were in force in England on January 2nd, 1875.

Supreme Court: Superior Court of Record, Suva.

Court of Appeal: Suva.

Magistrates' Courts.

Chief Justice: Hon. Mr. Justice C. H. GRANT.

Puisne Judges: Hon. G. MISHRA, Hon. T. TUIVAGA, Hon. K. A. STUART, Hon. J. T. WILLIAMS.

Ombudsman: Hon. MOTI TIKARAM.

RELIGION

Most Fijians are Christians, mainly Protestant. The Indians are mostly Hindus.

Anglican: Bishop in Polynesia Rt. Rev. JOHN TRISTRAM HOLLAND; Bishops House, Box 35, G.P.O., Suva.

Methodist Church: G.P.O. Box 357, Suva; Pres/Sec. Rev. S. G. ANDREWS.

Roman Catholic Archbishop: Most Rev. GEORGE PEARCE, Archbishop's House, P.O.B. 393, Suva.

THE PRESS

NEWSPAPERS AND PERIODICALS

Fiji Holiday: publ. by Fiji Times and Herald Ltd., P.O.B. 1167, Suva; f. 1968; monthly; Editor SUE WENDT; circ. 19,000.

Fiji Royal Gazette: Government Printer, P.O.B. 98, Suva; f. 1874; Fridays.

Fiji Samachar: P.O.B. 151, Suva; f. 1923; Hindustani; weekly; Editor S. M. BIDESI, Jr.; Man. N. P. GANDHI; circ. 4,000.

Fiji Sandesh: Patel Arcade, Suva; f. 1965; Hindi; weekly; Editor V. L. MORRIS.

Fiji Times: P.O.B. 1167, Suva; f. 1869; English, daily; Man. Editor JOHN MOSES; circ. 20,000.

Jagriti: Pacific Periodicals Ltd., P.O.B. 9, Nandi; Editor R. K. SHARMA; circ. 5,500.

Jai Fiji: P.O.B. 109, Lautoka; f. 1959; weekly; Thursdays; Editor K. P. MISHRA; circ. 7,800.

Kisan Mitra: P.O.B. 46, Lautoka; f. 1961; Hindi; weekly.

Nai Lalakai: P.O.B. 1167, Suva; f. 1961; publ. by Fiji Times and Herald Ltd.; Fijian; weekly; Editor LUKE VUIDREKETI.

Na Mata: Fijian Affairs Office, Suva; f. 1876; Fijian; monthly.

Pacific Review: Suva; f. 1949; English and Fijian; weekly; Editor P. GOUNDER.

Shanti Dut: P.O.B. 1167, Suva; f. 1935; publ. by Fiji Times and Herald Ltd.; Hindi; weekly; Editor GURUDAYAL SHARMA.

Tovata (*Nation*): published by Alliance Publications, P.O.B. 1373, Suva; English and Fijian (Natovata); fortnightly; Editor ESALA RASOVO.

Volagauna: P.O.B. 597, Suva; f. 1952; Fijian; weekly; Editor JIOJI R. QALILAWA.

PUBLISHERS

Fiji Times and Herald, Ltd.: P.O.B. 1167, Suva; f. 1869; Man. Editor JOHN MOSES; publish *Fiji Times, Nai Lalakai, Shanti Dut, Fiji Holiday, Fiji Sport, Fiji Photonews, This Week in Fiji.*

Indian Printing and Publishing Co.: P.O.B. 151, Suva; f. 1923; Man. Dir. S. M. BIDESI, Jr.; Sec. RAM CHARITRA.

Pacific Daily (Fiji) Ltd.: G.P.O. Box 1360, Suva; f. April 1968; printers and publishers; publish *Pacific Review.*

Sangam Sarada Printing Press: P.O.B. 9, Nadi; commercial printers and printers of Hindi tri-weekly *Jagriti* for Proprietors of Pacific Periodicals Ltd.

RADIO

Fiji Broadcasting Commission (Radio Fiji): P.O.B. 334, Suva; f. 1954; broadcasts from ten stations; two each at Suva, Lautoka, Rakiraki, Sigatoka and Labasa; in English, Fijian and Hindustani; Chair. W. G. J. CRUICKSHANK, O.B.E.; Gen. Man. HUGH LEONARD.

The estimated number of radio sets in 1973 was 150,000.

FINANCE

BANKS

The Government intends to set up a Central Monetary Authority which will form the basis of a central bank.

Savings Bank of Fiji: Head Office: P.O.B. 1166, Suva; 60 brs.

Australia and New Zealand Banking Group Ltd.: Administrative Office: Melbourne; Fiji Office: P.O.B. 179, Suva; Man. J. H. GARLAND.

Bank of Baroda Ltd.: Head Office: Baroda, India; P.O.B. 57, Suva; brs. at Lautoka, Labasa, Nadi and Ba; agencies at Samabula, Sigatoka, Tavua, Nausori and Raki Raki; Man. A. N. DESAI.

Bank of New South Wales: Head Office: Sydney, N.S.W., Australia; Fiji Office: P.O.B. 283, Suva; brs. at Ba, Lautoka, Nadi, Sigatoka and Tavua; agencies at Levuka, Lautoka, Nausori, Rakiraki, Savusavu, Taveuni, Vatukoula and Walu Bay; Chief Man. L. W. ULLMAN.

Bank of New Zealand: Head Office: Wellington, New Zealand; P.O.B. 177, Suva; brs. at Lautoka, Labasa, Nadi and Sigatoka; sub-br. at Ba; agencies at Nausori and Mark St. (Suva), Namaka (Nadi) and Savusavu; Man. R. W. MEAR.

Barclays Bank International: Suva.

First National City Bank of New York: P.O.B. 56, 66 Thomson St., Suva; f. 1970; brs. at Lautoka, Raiwaga, Suva, Ba and Nadi.

INSURANCE

Fiji Insurance Co. Ltd.: Fiji Development Bank Centre, P.O.B. 1080, Victoria Parade, Suva.

Pacific Insurance Co. Ltd.: Honson Bldg., 68 Thomson St., Suva.

TRADE AND INDUSTRY

DEVELOPMENT CORPORATIONS

Commonwealth Development Corpn.: Fiji and Western Pacific Islands Office, P.O.B. 161, Suva.

Fijian Development Fund Board: P.O.B. 122, Suva; f. 1951; the Fund was established at the request of the Fijian Provincial Councils; funds derived from payments of £10 a ton from the sales of copra; deposits credited to the producing group or individual at 2½ per cent interest for use in Fijian development schemes; July 1971, deps. $F701,577; Chair. Ratu Sir George K. CAKOBAU; Sec. P. J. UNDERHILL.

Fiji Development Bank: Suva; f. 1967 as successor to Agricultural and Industrial Loans Board (f. 1952); finances the development of natural resources, transportation and other industries.

Fiji Development Company Ltd.: P.O.B. 161, Suva; f. 1960; subsidiary of the Commonwealth Development Corporation; Man. J. H. SAND.

Land Development Authority: c/o Ministry of Agriculture, Fisheries and Forests, Suva; f. 1961 to coordinate development plans.

MARKETING ORGANIZATIONS

Fiji Sugar Corporation Ltd.: P.O.B. 283, Suva; buyer of sugar cane and raw sugar manufacturer.

CO-OPERATIVES

In 1971 there were about 800 registered co-operatives.

EMPLOYERS' ORGANIZATION

Fiji Employers' Consultative Association: P.O.B. 575, Suva; represents 132 of the principal employers in the Dominion; Pres. C. D. AIDNEY, O.B.E., D.F.C.; Dir. J. GRUNDY.

TRADE UNIONS

Fiji Trades Union Congress: P.O.B. 781, Suva; affiliated to ICFTU; 20 affiliated unions; over 20,000 mems.; Pres. Hon. SAKIASI WAQANIVAVALAGI; Gen. Sec. MOHAMMED RAMZAN, M.B.E.

Largest affiliated unions:

Fiji Dock Workers' and Seamen's Union: 36 Edinburgh Drive, Suva; f. 1947; 1,608 mems.; Pres. SOLOMON KOROI; Sec. T. VEITATA.

Fiji Sugar and General Workers' Union: Lautoka; Gen. Sec. RAM DAYAL; 2,509 mems.

Public Employees' Union: P.O.B. 781, Suva; over 7,000 mems.; Gen. Sec. JOVECI GAVOKA.

At the end of 1972, 37 trade unions were registered.

TRANSPORT

Railways: There are about 450 miles of light railway. *Roads:* 1,470 miles of roads, of which about 1,000 miles are all-weather roads. *Shipping:* Services include a two-weekly service to New Zealand, Tonga and Western Samoa by the Union Steamship Company and a passenger cargo service to Britain, New Zealand, Australia and between islands of the group. *Island Industries Ltd.:* Rodwell Road (P.O. Box 299), Suva; operates inter-island services. *Airways:* Air Pacific Ltd., P.O.B. 112, Suva; inter-island services and services to Tonga, Samoa, New Hebrides, the Solomons and the Gilbert and Ellice Islands, Port Moresby, Nauru and Brisbane; Canadian Pacific, Polynesian Airlines, Air India, Pan American, Qantas, Air New Zealand, UTA, and American Airlines all call at Nadi, Fiji's international airport; fleet of two One-Eleven 475, three HS 748, four Heron. A charter company, Fiji Air Services, commenced operations in Fiji in July 1967.

UNIVERSITY

The University of the South Pacific: G.P.O. Box 1168, Suva; 104 teachers, 1,062 students.

FRENCH OVERSEAS POSSESSIONS

FRENCH OVERSEAS DEPARTMENTS

GUADELOUPE   MARTINIQUE
FRENCH GUIANA   RÉUNION

The Overseas Departments (départements d'outre-mer) are integral parts of the French Republic, each administered by a Prefect, with elected General Councils and with elected representatives in the French National Assembly and Senate of the Republic in Paris. The administrative structure is the same as in other French Departments; however, each of the Overseas Departments has its own Court of Appeal. Educational services for Guadeloupe, Guiana and Martinique are run by the Academy of the Antilles, and for Réunion by the Marseilles district.

Secretariat of State for Overseas Departments and Territories: rue Oudinot 27, 75007 Paris, France.

Secretary of State: JOSEPH COMITI.

Secretary-General: JEAN-EMILE VIE.

GUADELOUPE

Guadeloupe is the most northerly of the Windward Islands in the east Caribbean; Dominica lies to the south, and Antigua and Montserrat to the north-west. Guadeloupe is formed by two large islands, Grande-Terre and Basse-Terre, separated by a narrow sea channel, with a smaller island, Marie-Galante, to the south-east. There are also a number of small dependencies. The capital is the town of Basse-Terre; the other main town and principal commercial centre is Pointe-à-Pitre on Grande-Terre.

Guadeloupe was first occupied by the French in 1635, and has been an integral part of the French Republic since 1815. She gained departmental status in 1946.

The economy is based on sugar cane, which is mainly exported to France, together with its by-products molasses and rum, and smaller amounts of bananas, vanilla and cocoa. As in the other island departments, the population is rising quickly and there is considerable emigration; attempts are being made to create processing industries and to develop the tourist potential of the islands.

STATISTICS

Area: 1,780 sq. km. Dependencies (La Désirade, Petite-Terre, Les Saintes, Marie-Galante, Saint-Barthélémy, Saint Martin) 271 sq. km.

Population: (1972 estimates): 337,900; Basse-Terre (capital) 15,833, Pointe-à-Pitre 29,538.

Agriculture (1972): Sugar 815,883 quintals.

Livestock (1968): Cattle 70,000, Pigs 30,000, Goats 28,000, Horses 3,200.

Industry (1972 exports—metric tons): Sugar Cane 87,828, Bananas 81,827, Molasses 883, Rum 22,746.

Finance: 100 centimes = 1 franc des départements d'outre-mer (Overseas Departments franc, at par with French franc). Coins: 1, 5, 10, 20 and 50 centimes; 1, 5 and 10 francs. Notes: 5, 10, 50 and 100 francs. Exchange rates (April 1974): £1 sterling = 11.595 francs; U.S. $1 = 4.91 francs. 100 francs = £8.624 = $20.356.

External Trade (1972): *Imports:* 747m. francs; *Exports:* 210m. francs. More than two-thirds of the trade is with France, most of the remainder being with the U.S.A.

Transport: *Roads* (1966): Cars 17,470, Buses 808, Lorries 3,933, Vans 3,889, Special Vehicles and Tractors 1,099; *Shipping* (1972) (Basse-Terre): ships entered 210, 47,982 tons unloaded, 137,243 tons loaded; (Pointe-à-Pitre) ships entered 733, 438,064 tons unloaded, 86,591 tons loaded.

Tourism: 836 hotel rooms (1972).

Education (1971–72): Primary schools 37; Secondary 7; technical 8; Number of pupils (1966–67) (primary) 72,284, (secondary) 6,700, (technical) 3,500.

THE GOVERNMENT

(*March* 1974)

Prefect: JACQUES LE CORNEC.

President of the General Council: HENRI RINALDO.

Representatives in the National Assembly: H. IBÉNÉ, F. JALTON, R. GUILLIOD.

Representatives in the Senate: AMÉDÉ VALEAU, MARCEL GARGAR.

POLITICAL PARTIES

Fédération de la Gauche Démocratique et Socialiste (F.G.D.S.).

Parti Communiste Guadeloupéen (P.C.G.).

Progressive Party.

Section Française de l'Internationale Ouvrière (S.F.I.O.).

Union pour la Défense de la République (U.D.R.).

JUDICIAL SYSTEM

Cour d'Appel: Basse-Terre; Pres. M. CHAPPERT; two Tribuaux de Grande Instance, five Tribuaux d'Instance.

RELIGION

The majority of the population is Roman Catholic.

Bishop of Basse-Terre and Pointe-à-Pitre: Mgr. SIMÉON OUALLI, B.P. 50, 97-1 Basse-Terre.

PRESS AND BROADCASTING

Clartés-Progrès Social: Basse-Terre.

L'Etincelle: Pointe-à-Pitre.

France Antilles: Pointe-à-Pitre; daily; Man. HENRI PIERRE; circ. 20,000.

Le Nouvelliste de Guadeloupe: 52 rue Nozieres; f. 1908; Propr. ROBERT HERSANT; circ. 4,200.

Le Ralliement: Pointe-à-Pitre.

Office de Radiodiffusion-Télévision Francaise (O.R.T.F.): Région Antilles-Guyane: B.P. 402, Pointe-à-Pitre; 16 hours radio and 5 hours television broadcasts daily; Dir. EMILE LAFONT.

In 1973 there were 20,985 radio receivers and 11,171 television sets in use.

FINANCE

(frs. = French francs)

BANKS
CENTRAL BANK

Caisse Centrale de Coopération Economique: 233 Blvd Saint-Germain, Paris 7e, France; Faubourg Frébault, B.P. 196, Point-à-Pitre.

COMMERCIAL BANKS

Banque des Antilles Françaises: 8 rue Magellan, Paris, France; place de la Banque, Pointe-à-Pitre; cours Nolivos, Basse-Terre; f. 1853; cap. 10.7m. frs.; Pres. RENÉ ARNAUD; Gen. Mans. YVES GOUYÉ, CLAUDE GARCIN; Man. DANIEL LABBÉ.

Banque Antillaise: 21 rue Gambetta, Pointe-à-Pitre; f. 1915; brs. at Basse-Terre and Marie Galante; cap. 4.25m. frs., res. 1.19m. frs.; Pres. and Gen. Man. F. CHERDIEU D'ALEXIS.

Banque Nationale de Paris: 16 blvd. des Italiens, Paris, France; 22 rue Achille René Boisneur, Pointe-à-Pitre; Dir. HENRY DUBOIS.

Crédit Guadeloupéen: angle des rues Achille René Boisneuf et Nozieres, Pointe-à-Pitre; f. 1926; cap. 6m. frs., dep. 121.4m. frs.; br. in Basse-Terre; Pres. and Gen. Man. G. BEUZELIN.

Royal Bank of Canada (France) S.A.: 3 rue Scribe, Paris 9e, France; 30 rue Frébault, Pointe-à-Pitre.

INSURANCE
Pointe-à-Pitre

Compagnie Antillaise d'Assurances, Société d'Assurance à Forme Mutuelle: 21 rue Gambetta, B.P. 409; f. 1937/1963; Dir.-Gen. F. CHERDIEU D'ALEXIS.

Some thirty of the principal European insurance companies are represented in Pointe-à-Pitre, and another six companies have offices in Basse-Terre.

TRADE AND INDUSTRY

Chambre de Commerce et d'Industrie de Pointe-à-Pitre: B.P. 64, Pointe-à-Pitre; Pres. JOSEPH BARBOTTEAU.

Chambre de Commerce et d'Industrie de Basse-Terre: 45 rue du Docteur Cabre, B.P. 17, Basse-Terre; Pres. PIERRE RENAISON; Sec.-Gen. GERMAIN WILLIAM.

Société d'Intérêt Collectif Agricole (Assobaf): 15 rue l'Herminier, Basse-Terre.

Syndicat des Producteurs-Exportateurs de Sucre et de Rhum de la Guadeloupe: Zone Industrielle de la Pointe Jarry, 97-1 Baie-Mahault, B.P. 175, Pointe-à-Pitre; f. 1937; 7 mems.; Del.-Gen. MAX MARTIN.

Union Départementale des Syndicats C.G.T.-F.O.: Basse-Terre; about 1,500 mems.; Gen. Sec. CLOTAIRE BERNOS.

Union Départementale de la Confédération Française des Travailleurs Chrétiens: 15 rue Victor Hugo, Pointe-à-Pitre; f. 1937; about 3,500 mems.; Sec.-Gen. E. DEMOCRITE.

Confédération Générale du Travail: Pointe-à-Pitre; affiliated to WFTU; about 5,000 mems.; Sec.-Gen. NICOLAS LUDGER.

TRANSPORT AND TOURISM

TRANSPORT

There are no railways on Guadeloupe.

ROADS

There are 1,924 km. of roads in Guadeloupe, of which 323 km. are Routes Nationales.

SHIPPING

Alcoa Steamship Co.: 8 quai Ferdinand de Lesseps, B.P. 171, Pointe-à-Pitre.

Compagnie des Messageries Maritimes: Pointe-à-Pitre; services to France, Martinique and New Caledonia.

Compagnie Fabre des Transports Maritimes: Pointe-à-Pitre and Basse-Terre.

Compagnie Générale Transatlantique: quai Lefèvre, Pointe-à-Pitre; agent at Basse-Terre; services to France, British West Indies and Venezuela.

Régie Départementale du Service Maritime: Sous-Préfecture, Pointe-à-Pitre; f. 1951; Dir. EDOUARD M. E. BOTINO; services between Guadeloupe and dependencies, Dominica and Martinique.

CIVIL AVIATION

Air Antilles: 41 rue Schoelcher, Pointe-à-Pitre; f. 1954; scheduled services link the Aéroport du Raizet, Pointe-à-Pitre, with Marie-Galante, Désirade and Montserrat.

Services are also provided by Air France, Caribair (Puerto Rico), Leeward Islands Air Transport, Pan Am, Viasa and Windward Island Airways (Netherlands Antilles).

TOURISM

Office du Tourisme: place de la Victoire, Pointe-à-Pitre; Dir. ROGER FORTUNE; Asst. Dir. ERICK W. ROTIN.

Bureau du Développement Touristique: Hôtel de la Préfecture, Basse-Terre; Man. P.Y. CROCHET-DAMAIS.

Syndicats d'Initiative: de la Guadeloupe—quai Ferdinand de Lesseps, Pointe-à-Pitre; de la Basse-Terre—Mairie Basse-Terre; de Saint-Martin—Marigot, Saint Martin, F.W.I.

FRENCH GUIANA

French Guiana lies on the coast of South America with Surinam to the west and Brazil to the south and east. Much the largest of the Overseas Departments, it is also the least densely populated. The climate is humid, with a season of heavy rains from April to July and another short rainy season in December and January. The population includes nomadic Indians, Creoles, Africans and Europeans. The capital and main centre of population is Cayenne.

French occupation commenced in the early seventeenth century, and after periods of Dutch and English rule Guiana reverted to France in 1816. She gained departmental status in 1946.

The economy is based on forestry and agriculture; cassava, bananas, maize and other tropical crops are grown for local consumption while sugar cane is the only cash crop of importance. There are vast timber reserves, which are exploited on a small scale, and important mineral resources, particularly of gold, bauxite and tantalite, from which extractive industries are being developed. Fishing has been increasing in importance since 1965 and is mainly for shrimps, most of which are exported to U.S.A. France set up one of her principal space research stations at Kourou, following the closure of her Saharan station in Algeria in 1967, and this is used by France and ELDO.

STATISTICS

Area and Population: *Area* 90,000 sq. km.; *Population* 51,000 (1970), Cayenne (capital) 24,518 (1967).

Professional Employment (1967): 17,012—Agriculture and Forestry 2,641, Industry and Commerce 6,576, Public Services 4,982.

Agriculture and Forestry (1969): Sugar Cane 3,047 metric tons, Timbers 55,983 cubic metres.

Industry (1969): Sawn Timber 13,462 cubic metres, Shrimps 3,099 metric tons (Exports).

Budget (1970): 118,584,131 French francs.

Finance: 100 centimes=1 franc des départements d'outre-mer (Overseas Departments franc, at par with French franc). Coins: 1, 5, 10, 20 and 50 centimes; 1, 5 and 10 francs. Notes: 5, 10, 50 and 100 francs. Exchange rates (April 1974): £1 sterling=11.595 francs; U.S. $1= 4.91 francs. 100 francs=£8.624=$20.356.

External Trade (1972): *Imports:* 228,138,000 frs. (Foodstuffs, Manufactures, Petroleum Products, Cement, Iron and Steel); *Exports* 23,315,000 frs. (Timber, Shrimps). Most exports went to the U.S.A. but France supplied over two-thirds of the imports.

Transport: *Shipping* (1971): Freight unloaded 126,307 metric tons, loaded 13,938 metric tons. *Civil Aviation* (1972): Freight carried 1,154 metric tons; *Passengers carried:* 45,009; *Roads* (1969): 8,468 vehicles.

Education (1969): Public Primary 7,823 pupils; Private Primary 2,177 pupils; Secondary 1,970 pupils; Technical 756 pupils.

GOVERNMENT

(*March* 1974)

Prefect: JACQUES DELAUNAY.

President of the General Council: LÉOPOLD HÉDER.

Representative to the National Assembly: H. RIVIEREZ.

Representative to the Senate: LÉOPOLD HÉDER.

POLITICAL PARTIES

Cayenne

Parti Socialiste Guyanais: 34 rue Voltaire; f. 1956; Leader LÉOPOLD HÉDER.

Union pour la Nouvelle Guyane (U.N.G.): 78 rue Madame Payé; Sec.-Gen. GEORGES GUÉRIL.

Union pour la Défense de la République (U.D.R.): 7 rue Franklin Roosevelt; f. 1946; Sec.-Gen. PAUL RULLIER; publ. *La Guyane républicaine, L'Union.*

Union du Peuple Guyanais (U.P.G.): rue René Barthélemy; Sec.-Gen. GEORGES PATIENT.

Mouvement Populaire Guyanais (M.P.G.): angle rue du 14 Juillet; Sec.-Gen. Senator ROBERT VIGNON.

JUDICIAL SYSTEM

See: Judicial System, Martinique.

RELIGION

Roman Catholics 41,500, Protestants 100, Seventh Day Adventists 400, Animists 2,900, Jews, etc. 100.

Roman Catholicism: 88 per cent of the population are Roman Catholic; Bishop of Cayenne Mgr. ALFRED MARIE.

PRESS AND BROADCASTING

La Radio Presse: daily and Sunday; Man. EDGARD OCTAVIA; circ. 1,500.

Office de Radiodiffusion-Télévision Française (O.R.T.F.): Région Antilles-Guyane: rue du Dr. Devèze, Cayenne; *Radio-Guyane Inter:* 16 hours broadcasting daily; *Téléguyane:* 34 hours weekly.

In 1973 there were 2,682 radio and 3,038 television receivers.

BANKS

Caisse Centrale de Coopération Economique: Paris 7e, France; 8 rue Christophe Colomb, Cayenne; Dir. R. COUSIGNE.

Banque de la Guyane: 2 place Victor Schoelcher, B.P. 35, Cayenne; f. 1855; affiliated to Banque Nationale de Paris; cap. 5m. frs., res. 2.7m. frs.; brs. at Kourou and St. Laurent de Maroni; Pres. and Gen. Man. A. MARTIN; Man. P. FRICKER.

TRADE AND INDUSTRY

Chambre de Commerce de la Guyane: B.P. 49, Cayenne; Pres. RAOUL TANON.

Jeune Chambre Economique: Cayenne; Pres. ANDRÉ BAUDIN.

Syndicat des Commerçants Détaillants: Cayenne; Pres M. THÉBIA.

TRADE UNION

Union des Travailleurs Guyanais (UTG): 16 ave. de Gaulle, B.P. 265, Cayenne; 3,000 mems.; Sec.-Gen. TURENNE RADAMONTHE; publ. *La Voie des Travailleurs.*

TRANSPORT

RAILWAYS

There are no railways in French Guiana.

ROADS

There are about 250 km. of Routes Nationales (212 asphalt) and 250 km. of departmental roads (138 asphalt).

SHIPPING

Compagnie Générale Transatlantique: 1 place de Grenoble, B.P. 81, Cayenne.

Société Générale des Transports Maritimes: 1 place de Grenoble, B.P. 81, Cayenne.

CIVIL AVIATION

Guyane Air Transport (G.A.T.): Rochambeau, Cayenne; Dir. M. MALIDOR.

The following airlines also serve Cayenne: Air France and Cruzeiro do Sul (Brazil).

Rochambeau International Airport is equipped to handle the largest jet aircraft.

MARTINIQUE

Martinique is one of the Windward Islands in the east Caribbean, with Dominica to the north and St. Lucia to the south. The island is dominated by the volcanic peak of Mont Pelée. The population is of mixed origin, including some descendants of immigrants from the former French Indo-China. The capital is Fort-de-France.

Martinique has been in French occupation since 1635, became an integral part of the Republic in 1790 and gained department status in 1946.

The economy is agricultural, based on sugar cane and tropical fruits. There is extensive emigration to France and to a lesser extent to French Guiana, but there are also many Frenchmen from the mainland in service as civil servants. A number of tax exemptions are designed to encourage industrial and commercial development.

STATISTICS

Area and Population: *Area* 1,110 sq. km.; *Population* 343,100 (June 1973), Fort-de-France (capital) 100,000 (1971).

Employment (1970): Agriculture 24,800, Fishing 3,200, Industry 11,000, Commerce and Services 47,000, Construction 9,500, Public Services 13,000, Others 10,000.

AGRICULTURE
(1970)

	AREA (hectares)	PRODUCTION (metric tons)
Sugar	7,800	26,900
Bananas	9,500	157,500
Pineapples, Fresh	1,050	6,400
Pineapple Jam and Juice	—	12,000

Livestock (1969): Cattle 55,000, Pigs 31,000, Sheep 27,000.

Fishing (1969): 4,500 metric tons.

Currency and Exchange Rates: as in Guadeloupe.

Budget (1971): 593m. French francs.

Aid from France (1971): 307m. French francs.

External Trade (1972): *Imports:* 872m. francs (Foodstuffs, Petroleum products, Fertilizers, Machinery, Cars and Electrical apparatus); *Exports:* 404m. francs (Bananas, Sugar, Rum, Pineapples); trade with France accounts for about 80 per cent of the total.

Roads (1970): The total number of motor vehicles was 43,000, of which 26,200 were private cars.

Shipping (1972): Freight entered 893,438 tons; Freight cleared 438,485 tons.

Civil Aviation (1972): Passengers 270,151, Freight 6,555 metric tons.

Education (1970—number of pupils): Primary 89,000, First Cycle 26,000, Long-course Secondary 3,405, Short-course Secondary 900.

GOVERNMENT
(*March* 1974)

Prefect: CHRISTIAN ORSETTI.

President of the General Council: ÉMILE MAURICE.

Representatives to the National Assembly: AIMÉ CÉSAIRE, CAMILLE PETIT, VICTOR SABLÉ.

Representatives to the Senate: FRANÇOIS DUVAL, GEORGES MARIE-ANNE.

POLITICAL PARTIES

Parti Communiste Martiniquais.

Parti Progressiste Martiniquais (PPM): Leader M. CÉSAIRE.

Union pour la Défense de la République (U.D.R.).

JUDICIAL SYSTEM

Cour d'Appel: Fort-de-France; highest court for Martinique and French Guiana.

Two Tribunaux de Grande Instance at Fort-de-France and Cayenne and three Tribunaux d'Instance, two in Fort-de-France and one in Cayenne.

RELIGION

Roman Catholicism: The majority of the population is Roman Catholic; Archbishop of Fort-de-France and St. Pierre Mgr. MAURICE MARIE-SAINTE.

PRESS AND RADIO
Fort-de-France

Aujourd'hui Dimanche: Presbytère de Bellevue; weekly; Dir. Père GAUTHIER.

France-Antilles: place Stalingrad; f. 1964; daily; Dir. PIERRE FEUERSTEIN; circ. 25,000 (Martinique edition).

Le Combat: 25 rue de la République; weekly.

Le Courrier: 26 rue Victor-Hugo; Dir. D. DE GRAND-MAISON; weekly.

L'Information: f. 1935; Propr. M. VICTOR SURENA; circ. 1,700.

Justice: Carénage; Dir. G. THIMOTÉE; weekly.

Le Progressiste: Trenelle; fortnightly; Dir. A. REGIS.

La Vague: weekly; Dir. JEAN CHARLES.

Office de Radiodiffusion-Télévision Française (O.R.T.F.): Région Antilles-Guyane: Paris; Martinique: La Clairière, B.P. 662, Fort-de-France; transmissions three times a day; Representative M. L. M. COHIC (Fort-de-France).

In 1972 there were 39,912 radio sets and 11,839 television sets in use.

FINANCE

(frs. = French Francs.)

BANKS

CENTRAL BANK

Caisse Centrale de Coopération Economique: 233 blvd. Saint-Germain, Paris 7e, France.

Bank of America NT & SA: San Francisco, Ca. 94120, U.S.A.; Fort-de-France; Dir. M. BELHUMEUR.

Banque d'Aide Mutuelle: 69 rue Schoelcher, Fort-de-France.

Banque des Antilles Françaises: 8 rue Magellan, Paris 8e, France; 34 rue Lamartine, Fort-de-France; f. 1853; cap. 10.7m. frs.; Pres. RENÉ ARNAUD; Gen. Man. YVES GOUYÉ; Man. CLAUDE GARCIN.

Banque Nationale de Paris: 16 blvd. des Italiens, Paris 9e, France; 72 ave Duparquet, Fort-de-France.

Crédit Agricole Mutuelle de la Martinique: 106 blvd. Général de Gaulle, Fort-de-France; f. 1950; 9,500 mems.

Crédit Martiniquais: rue de la Liberté, Fort-de-France; f. 1922 (associated with Crédit Lyonnais and Banque de Paris et des Pays Bas, France); cap. 11.4m. frs., dep. 217m. frs.; br. in St. Pierre; Pres. ANDRÉ DORN.

Crédit Ouvrier: 30 rue F. Roosevelt, Fort-de-France.

Crédit Populaire: rue Gabriel Péri, Fort-de-France.

Royal Bank of Canada (France) S.A.: 3 rue Scribe, Paris 9e, France; 12-21 rue de la Liberté, Fort-de-France.

INSURANCE

Principal companies in Fort-de-France.

La Nationale (GAN): Rep. Marcel et Roger Boullanger, blvd. Général de Gaulle, B.P. 185.

La Protectrice: 27 rue Blériac; Rep. RENÉ MAXIMIN.

Le Secours: 74 ave. Duparquet.

L'Union: Paris, France; R. de Reynal et R. Marry, rue de la République, B.P. 105.

L'Urbaine et La Seine S.A. d'Assurances Contre les Accidents: Paris, France; Rep. Société Foncelac, 17 rue Victor Hugo.

TRADE AND INDUSTRY

Fort-de-France

Chambre de Commerce et d'Industrie de la Martinique: 53 rue Victor-Hugo; f. 1907; 18 mems.; Pres. MAX ELIZÉ; Sec.-Gen. C. F. BEAUREGARD; publs. *Bulletin de la Chambre de Commerce et d'Industrie de la Martinique, Lettre d'Information.*

Chambre Départementale d'Agriculture: 55 rue Isambert, B.P. 432; Pres. GÉRARD DESPORTES.

Chambre des Métiers: 8 rue Félix Eboué; Pres. M. REMINY.

Groupement de Producteurs d'Ananas de la Martinique: B.P. 12, Fort-de-France; f. 1967; Pres. C. DE GRYSE.

Service de Développement Industriel et Touristique: Préfecture, 97262 Fort-de-France; f. 1960; Dir. CHRISTIAN VILLETTE; research and documentation on investment in industry and tourism; publs. *Industrial Investment Incentives*, etc.

Société d'Intérêt Collectif Agricole Bananière de la Martinique (Sicabam): 33 rue Lamartine; Pres. M. FABRE; Dir. H. HAYOT.

Syndicat des Distilleries Agricoles: immeuble Clément, vive droite Lavassor.

Syndicat des Planteurs et Manipulateurs de la Canne: 33 rue Lamartine; Pres. JEAN DE LAGUARIGUE.

Syndicat des Producteurs de Rhum Agricole.

Union Départementale des Coopératives Agricoles de la Martinique: Pres. M. URSULET.

Union Départementale des Syndicats—CFDT: blvd. Chevalier Sainte Marthe; Sec.-Gen. M. MONRAPHA.

Union Départementale des Syndicats—F.O.: Maison des Syndicats, Jardin Desclieux, Fort-de-France; affiliated to ICFTU; about 1,500 mems.; Sec.-Gen. FRANTZ AGASTA.

Confédération Générale du Travail: Maison des Syndicats, Jardin Desclieux, Fort-de-France; affiliated to WFTU; about 4,000 mems.; Sec. Gen. VICTOR LAMON.

TRANSPORT AND TOURISM

TRANSPORT

There are no railways on Martinique.

ROADS

There are approximately 1,500 km. of roads in Martinique.

Automobile-Club Martiniquais: 75 rue Ernest Renan, Fort-de-France; f. 1935; Pres. JOSÉ BEUZELIN.

Touring-Club de France: route de la Dillon, Fort-de-France.

SHIPPING

Fort-de-France

Alcoa Steamship Co., Alpine Line, Agdwa Line, Delta Line, Raymond Witcomb Co., Moore MacCormack, Eastern Steamship Co.: c/o Ets. René Cottrell, 48 rue Ernest-Deproge.

Compagnie Générale Transatlanique: P.O.B. 574, route du Lamentin; also represents other passenger and freight lines.

Royal Netherlands Steamship Co., Surinam Navigation Co. Harrison Line: 97206, Fort-de-France.

United States Lines, Cie. Navale Guyanaise, Société Navale Delmas-Vieljeux: c/o Société Martiniquaise de Commerce et de Représentation, 14 rue Ernest-Deproge.

CIVIL AVIATION

Martinique is served by the following airlines: Air France, Caribair (Puerto Rico), L.I.A.T. (Antigua) and Pan American.

TOURISM

Fort-de-France

Bureau de Promotion Touristique—BPT: Préfecture; Dir. CH. EBION.

Office du Tourisme: Pavillon du Tourisme, blvd. Alfassa, B.P. 520.

Syndicat d'Initiative: B.P. 299; Pres. M. R. ROSE-ROSETTE.

RÉUNION

Réunion is an island in the Indian Ocean about 800 km. east of Madagascar. The population is of mixed origin, including some Muslims of Persian and Arab descent. The capital is Saint-Denis.

First occupied by France in 1642, Réunion gained departmental status in 1946 and became administratively independent in 1971.

The economy is based on sugar cane and rum. Tropical fruits and essences are produced in small quantities.

STATISTICS

Area: 2,510 sq. km. **Population:** 474,400 (September 30th, 1973), Saint-Denis (capital) 87,000 (1968).

Employment (1969): Agriculture 32,000, Industry 20,000, Commerce 14,700, Administration and services 22,800, Domestic Service 10,500.

Agriculture (1971–72): Sugar 186,180 metric tons, Vanilla 143 metric tons, Tea 281 metric tons, Maize 10,000 metric tons, Onions 3,000 metric tons.

Livestock (1971): Cattle 45,000, Pigs 75,000, Goats 15,000, Sheep 2,500.

Currency: 100 centimes=1 franc de la Communauté financière africaine. Coins: 5, 10, 20, 50 and 100 francs CFA. Notes: 500, 1,000 and 5,000 francs CFA. Exchange rates (April 1974): 1 franc CFA=2 French centimes; £1 sterling=579.75 francs CFA; U.S. $1= 245.625 francs CFA. 1,000 francs CFA=£1.725= $4.071.

Budget (1973): Revenue 67,250 million francs CFA (local origin 24,600, French origin 42,650); Expenditure 67,250 million francs CFA (Ministries 47,000, Social Security 17,500, other 2,750).

External Trade (1972): *Imports:* 50,024 million francs CFA (Foodstuffs, Machinery, Fertilizers, Vehicles); *Exports:* 12,724 million francs CFA (Sugar, Rum, Molasses, Essences, Vanilla, Fruit). Three-quarters of trade is with France.

Shipping (1972): Vessels entered 408 (total tonnage 1,223,700), Freight entered 645,173 metric tons, Freight cleared 218,617 metric tons, Passenger arrivals and departures 948.

Civil Aviation (1972): Passengers entered 61,886, Passengers cleared 63,986; Freight entered 3,137 metric tons, Freight cleared 678 metric tons; Mail handled 680 metric tons.

Education (1971–72): *Primary:* Teachers 4,507, Pupils 107,754; *Secondary:* Teachers 1,422, Pupils 32,271. There is a teacher training college (500 students) and a university college (625 students).

THE GOVERNMENT
(*March* 1974)

Prefect: CLAUDE VIEILLESCAZES.

President of the General Council: Dr. PIERRE LAGOURGUE.

Representatives to the National Assembly: HENRI SERS, JEAN FONTAINE, MARCEL CERNEAU.

Representatives to the Senate: GEORGES REPIQUET, ALFRED ISAUTIER.

POLITICAL PARTIES

Almost all the French parties are represented.

Association Réunion département français: owes allegiance to the French Union pour la Défense de la République (U.D.R.), is anti-autonomist.

Parti Socialiste Réunionnais: f. 1972; socialist party distinct from the French Socialist Party; wants autonomy for Réunion and independent, democratic government; Sec.-Gen. VIRGILE BERTILE.

Parti Communiste Réunionnais (P.C.R.): favours autonomy; Sec.-Gen. PAUL VERGÈS.

JUDICIAL SYSTEM

Cour d'Appel: Saint-Denis.

There are two Tribunaux de Grande Instance and five Tribunaux d'Instance.

RELIGION

Roman Catholic: A large majority of the population is Roman Catholic; Bishop of Saint-Denis Mgr. GEORGES GUIBERT, 42 rue de Paris, B.P. 55, 97462 Saint-Denis.

THE PRESS
DAILIES

Journal de l'Ile de la Réunion: 42 rue Alexis de Villeneuve, 97400 Saint-Denis; Dir. HENRI CAZAL; circ. 22,500.

Témoignages: 76 rue Maréchal Leclerc, 97400 Saint-Denis; f. 1944; organ of the Réunion Communist Party; Dir. BRUNY PAYET; circ. 5–6,000.

PERIODICALS

Action Réunionnaise: B.P. 1077, 97400 Saint-Denis; weekly; Dir. HENRI GANOWSKI; circ. 2,500.

Citoyen: 5 *bis* ruelle Edouard, 97400 Saint-Denis; monthly; Dir. PIERRE MARTIN; circ. 5,000.

Le Créole: 4 rue Jules Auber, 97400 Saint-Denis; weekly; Dir. JACQUES RIQUEL.

Le Cri du Peuple: 71 rue Roland Garros, 97400 Saint-Denis; weekly; Dir. Mme LILIANE DENAGE.

Croix-Sud: 18 *bis* rue Montreuil, 97400 Saint-Denis; f. 1924; weekly; Editor R. P. AUBRY; circ. 3,800.

Le Démocrate Réunionnais: 73 rue Maréchal Leclerc, 97400 Saint-Denis; monthly; Dir. YVES CAZAL; circ. 5,000.

La Gazette de l'Ile de la Réunion: angle des rues Bouvet et Monthyon, 97400 Saint-Denis; weekly; Dir. Mme PHILIPPE PONIN BALLOM; circ. 4,800.

Hebdo-Bourbon: angle des rues Bouvet et Monthyon; 97400 Saint-Denis; weekly; Dir. PHILIPPE PONIN BALLOM; circ. 4,700.

Le Progressiste: 10 *bis* rue Voltaire, 97400 Saint-Denis; weekly; Dir. LOUIS VIRAPIN-APOU; circ. 2,000.

La Réunion Agricole: Chambre d'Agriculture; 24 rue de la Source, 97400 Saint-Denis; monthly; Dir. HENRI ISAUTIER; circ. 5,500.

Le Réveil: 5 cité des Lauriers "Les Camélias", 97400 Saint-Denis; weekly; Dir. GABRIEL BATOU; circ. 2,000.

Témoignage Chrétien de la Réunion: 38 rue Saint-Anne, 97400 Saint-Denis; fortnightly; Dir. LUCIEN BIEDINGER; circ. 3,000.

RADIO AND TELEVISION

Office de Radiodiffusion-Télévision Française: Place Sarda Garriga, 97400 Saint-Denis; Dir. IRÉNÉE COLONNE.

In 1972 there were 65,000 radio sets and 23,000 television sets.

FINANCE

BANKS

CENTRAL BANK

Caisse Centrale de Coopération Economique: 233 Boulevard Saint-Germain, 75007 Paris, France; Agence de la Réunion, B.P. 223, Saint-Denis.

Banque de la Réunion: 15 rue Jean-Chatel, Saint-Denis; f. 1849; affiliated to Crédit Lyonnais, France; 8 br; cap. 400m. fr. CFA; Pres. TANNEGUY DE F. DE CHAUVIN; Dir.-Gen. A. GOY.

Banque Nationale pour le Commerce et l'Industrie (Ocean Indien): 7 place Vendôme, Paris, France; rue Juliette Dodu, Saint-Denis.

Caisse d'Epargne et de Prévoyance: Rond-Point du Jardin, Saint-Denis; savings bank.

Caisse Régionale de Crédit Agricole Mutuel de la Réunion: Cité des Lauriers "les Camélias", B.P. 84; f. 1949; Pres. HENRY ISAUTIER; Dir. JEAN DE CAMBIAIRE.

INSURANCE

More than twenty major European insurance companies are represented in Saint-Denis.

TRADE AND INDUSTRY

Saint-Denis

Bureau de Promotion Industrielle: Immeuble des Hares, rue A. Lacaze.

Chambre de Commerce et d'Industrie de la Réunion: 25 rue de Paris, B.P. 120; f. 1850; Pres. JACQUES CAILLE; Sec. Gen. CHARLES AUMONT; publ. *Revue Mensuelle*.

Jeune Chambre Economique: B.P. 120; f. 1963; 43 mems.; Pres. M. J. M. DUPUIS.

Société de Développement Economique: 22 rue de Paris.

Syndicat des Fabricants de Sucre de l'Ile de la Réunion: 46 rue Labourdonnais.

Syndicat des Producteurs de Rhum de l'Ile de la Réunion: 46 rue Labourdonnais.

Syndicat des Industries, des Travaux Publics et du Bâtiment: B.P. 108.

TRADE UNIONS

Réunion has its own sections of the major French trade union confederations: *Confédération Générale du Travail* (C.G.T.), *Confédération Française Démocratique du Travail* (C.F.D.T.) and *Force Ouvrière* (F.O.).

TRANSPORT

There are no railways on Réunion.

ROADS

A Route Nationale runs all round the island, generally following the coast and linking all the main towns. Another Route Nationale crosses the island from south-west to north-east linking Saint-Pierre and Saint-Benoit. Routes Nationales 322 km., departmental roads 657 km., other roads 691 km.

SHIPPING

Cie. des Messageries Maritimes: B.P. 10, rue Alexandre de Lasserve, 97420 Le Port, St.-Denis; freight only.

Nouvelle Compagnie Havraise Peninsulaire de Navigation: Résidence du Barachois, P.O.B. 62, St.-Denis; freight only.

Société de Manutention et de Consignation Maritime (SOMACOM): B.P. 7, Le Port; agents for Scandinavian East Africa Line, Bank Line, Clan Line, Union Castle Mail Steamship Co. and States Marine Lines.

CIVIL AVIATION

The following airlines serve Réunion: Air France, Air Madagascar, Air Mauritius.

TOURISM

Syndicat d'Initiative—Office du Tourisme: rue Rontaunay, Saint-Denis; Pres. S. PERSONNÉ.

Alliance Touristique de l'Océan Indien: Préfecture, Saint-Denis.

Six thousand tourists visited Réunion in 1971.

FRENCH OVERSEAS TERRITORIES

FRENCH TERRITORY OF THE AFARS AND THE ISSAS

COMORO ISLANDS   NEW CALEDONIA   FRENCH POLYNESIA

SAINT PIERRE AND MIQUELON   WALLIS AND FUTUNA ISLANDS

FRENCH SOUTHERN AND ANTARCTIC TERRITORIES

The Overseas Territories (territoires d'outre-mer) are integral parts of the French Republic, each administered by a Governor or Superior Administrator appointed by the French Government, who is the *ex-officio* President of the Council of Government. A Territorial Assembly elected by universal suffrage chooses the Vice-President of the Council. Members of the Council are nominated by the Governor after consultation with the Vice-President. Certain members of the Assembly sit in the National Assembly and Senate of the Republic in Paris.

Director of Overseas Territories: DANIEL VIDEAU.

FRENCH TERRITORY OF THE AFARS AND THE ISSAS

The Territory (known formerly as French Somaliland) lies in East Africa at the head of the Gulf of Aden. The land is arid, semi-desert and the population is largely nomadic, herding camels, sheep and goats. France's involvement dates from 1859 and centres on the port of Djibouti. In recent years there has been some pressure for independence, but the Union and Progress Party, committed to continued union with France, won all the seats in the elections of November 1973.

STATISTICAL SURVEY

Area: 21,783 sq. km. **Population** (1973 estimate): 200,000; including Afars 82,000, Issas and other Somali 62,000, Arabs 8,000, Europeans 8,000, other foreigners 40,000. Djibouti (main town) 100,000; other main towns are Dikhil, Ali-Sabieh, Tadjourah and Obock.

Agriculture: There is little cultivated land.

Livestock (1972 estimates): 10,500 cattle, 150,000 sheep, 400,000 goats, 2,000 asses, 2,500 camels.

Fishing: About 700 tons of sea fish annually.

Currency: 100 centimes = 1 Djibouti franc. Coins: 1, 2, 5, 10, 20, 50 and 100 Djibouti francs. Notes: 50, 100, 500, 1,000 and 5,000 Djibouti francs. Exchange rates (April 1974): 1 Djibouti franc = 2.5875 French centimes; £1 sterling = 448.12 Djibouti francs; U.S. $1 = 189.85 Djibouti francs; 1,000 Djibouti francs = £2.23 = $5.27. The Djibouti franc did not follow the French devaluation of August 1969.

Budget (1973): 2,955 million Djibouti francs.

French Aid: This amounted to 28.8 million French francs in the 1961-68 period. In 1972 budgetary aid totalled 16.2 million French francs plus aid from FIDES of 6 million.

External Trade: (1971—million Djibouti francs): *Exports:* 1,132.8; main products skins, leather and shoes (184.5); principal customer France (491.4). *Imports:* 9,248.5; main items machinery and electrical equipment (888.8), vehicles (936.2); principal suppliers France (4,699.2), Ethiopia (1,053.9), U.K. (542.9), Japan (492.9), Benelux (542.6).

Transport: *Shipping:* has fallen heavily since the closing of the Suez Canal. In 1972 1,046 ships entered Djibouti (the only port), displacement 5.5 million registered tons, freight loaded 133,146 metric tons, freight unloaded 782,222 metric tons, passengers arrived 1,027. *Civil Aviation* (Djibouti Airport—1972): 3,036 aircraft arrived, freight loaded 1,217.8 metric tons, freight unloaded 3,196.1 metric tons, passengers arrived 32,187, mail carried 155.5 metric tons.

Education (1970): Primary—6,329 pupils in 21 public schools and 6 private schools; Secondary—857 pupils in 1 public and 2 private schools; Technical—216 pupils in 1 public and 7 private schools.

THE CONSTITUTION

The Territory is administered by a Governmental Council of from six to twelve Ministers, presided over by a President who acts as the Head of State. These Ministers are elected by the Territorial Assembly and have the right to pass legislation affecting the administration of the Territory. The Territorial Assembly consists of 40 members and is elected by direct universal suffrage. One Deputy and one Senator are elected to the National Assembly and the Senate in Paris. The French High Commissioner has responsibility for foreign policy, defence, currency, credit, citizenship and law other than traditional civil law. The Territory is divided into four administrative areas: Djibouti, Dikhil, Ali-Sabieh and Tadjoura (including the sub-district of Obock).

THE GOVERNMENT

High Commissioner: GEORGES THIERCY.
Deputy High Commissioner: ROBERT GAUGER.

COUNCIL OF GOVERNMENT

(*March* 1974)

President, Minister of Public Works and the Port: ALI ARIF BOURHAN (Afar).

Minister of Home Affairs: ALADJI MOHAMED KAMIL (Afar).

Minister of Finance and Planning: JULIEN VETILLARD (Issa).

Minister of Labour: ABDI DEMBIL EGUAL (Issa).

Minister of the Civil Service: MOHAMED DJAMA ELABE (Issa).

Minister of Education, Sport and Youth: OMAR MUHAMMAD KAMIL (Afar).

Minister of Economic Affairs: HASSAN MUHAMMAD MOYALE (Afar).

Minister of Public Health and Social Affairs: CHEHEM DAOUD CHEHEM (Afar).

Minister of Information and Tourism: DJIBRIL HASSAN REALEH (Issa).

CHAMBER OF DEPUTIES

At elections to the 40-seat Chamber of Deputies in November 1973 a party entitled *Union et Progrès dans l'ensemble français*, under the leadership of ALI ARIF BOURHAN, won all 40 seats.

Representative to the French National Assembly: OMAR FARAH ILTIREH.

Representative to the French Senate: HAMADOU BARKAT GOURAT.

POLITICAL PARTIES

Union et Progrès dans l'ensemble français (*Union and Progress Party*): Djibouti; ruling party; Pres. ALI ARIF BOURHAN.

Ligue Populaire Africaine (*African People's League*): Djibouti; Pres. HASSAN GOULED.

Democratic Union Party: Addis Ababa, Ethiopia; exiled Afar Party.

Djibouti Liberation Movement: Dire Dawa, Ethiopia; Afar party; Leader AHMED BOURHAN OMER.

JUDICIAL SYSTEM

There is a *Tribunal Supérieur d'Appel*, and a *Tribunal de Première Instance* in Djibouti. Criminal cases come under the jurisdiction of the *Tribunal Supérieur d'Appel*, which is the only criminal court. Civil matters come under the jurisdiction of the *Tribunal de Première Instance* and the *Tribunal Supérieur d'Appel* in cases affecting Europeans and other French citizens. Cases involving native customary law are heard by a Qadi, who has conciliatory functions, and by Tribunals of the 1st and 2nd degree.

President of the Tribunal Supérieur d'Appel: M. GESLIN.

President of the Tribunal de Première Instance: G. JAMBON.

General Attorney: L. BOCLE.

RELIGION

Islam: almost the entire native population is Muslim; Qadi of Djibouti SAYED ALI ABOUBAKER ASSAKAF.

Roman Catholics: Secretariat of the Bishopric, B.P. 94, Djibouti; there are about 7,500 Roman Catholics; Bishop of Djibouti Mgr. HENRI BERNARDIN HOFFMANN.

Protestants: Église Évangelique Française à l'Extérieure: ave de la République, B.P. 416, Djibouti; f. 1957; 400 mems.; Pasteur ROGER MULLER; publ. *Echos Protestants de la Mer Rouge* (quarterly).

Orthodox: there are about 350 Greek Orthodox; Archimandrite STAVROS GEORGANAS.

PRESS AND RADIO

Carrefour Africain: Djibouti, B.P. 393; twice a month; published by the Roman Catholic mission; circ. 500.

Journal Officiel: Imprimerie Administrative, B.P. 268, Djibouti; twice a month.

Le Réveil de Djibouti: Djibouti, B.P. 268; weekly; published by the Information Service, Ministry of the Interior; circ. 1,850–2,000; Dir. J. MAHAUT.

ORTF-Djibouti: B.P. 97, Djibouti; administered by Office de Radiodiffusion-Télévision Française; daily programmes in French, Afar and Arabic; 23 hours radio and 3 hours television per day, except on Monday; Dir. A. DAUMAS. There were 7,000 radio sets and 2,000 television sets in 1972.

FINANCE

BANKS

CENTRAL BANK

Trésorerie du Territoire Française des Issas: B.P. 19, place Albert Bernard, Djibouti.

Banque de l'Indochine: 96 boulevard Haussmann, Paris 8, France; place Lagarde, B.P. 88, Djibouti.

Banque Nationale pour le Commerce et l'Industrie (Océan Indien): Head office, 7 place Vendôme Paris 1, France; place Lagarde, B.P. 2122, Djibouti; cap. 25m. francs.

Commercial Bank of Ethiopia, S.C.: P.O.B. 255, Haile Sellassie I Squ., Addis Ababa, Ethiopia; P.O.B. 187, Djibouti.

INSURANCE

Some ten European insurance companies maintain agencies in Djibouti.

TRADE AND INDUSTRY

Chambre de Commerce et d'Industrie: B.P. 84, Djibouti; f. 1912; 14 mems.; Pres. SAÏD ALI COUBÈCHE; Sec. MOHAMMED DJAMA ELABE; publ. *Bulletin Mensuel de la Chambre de Commerce et d'Industrie de Djibouti*.

Union Syndicale Interprofessionelle des Entreprises de TFAI: Pres. M. V. DELL'AQUILA.

Association Professionelle des Banques: Banque de l'Indochine, Djibouti; Pres. M. JACQUES RININO.

Syndicat Autochtone des Cheminots: Sec. M. CASSIM.

TRANSPORT

RAILWAY

Compagnie du Chemin de Fer Franco-Ethiopien: P.O.B. 1051, Addis Ababa; B.P. 2116 Djibouti; f. 1908; 782 km. of track, 100 km. in Territory of Afars and Issas, linking Djibouti with Addis Ababa; metre gauge; Dir.-Gen. B. PETIT.

ROADS

There are approximately 1,650 km. of roads, of which 75 km. are bitumen-surfaced, including the 40-km. road from Djibouti to Arta. Of the remainder 800 km. are serviceable throughout the year, the rest only during the dry season. Half the roads are usable only by lorries.

SHIPPING

Djibouti

Air Djibouti: place Lagarde, B.P. 505; agents for Cie des Messageries Maritimes, Cie Maritime Belge, Société Navale Caennaise, Cie Auxiliaire de Navigation, Cie Africaine d'Armement, Cie Générale Translantique, Mitsui OSK Lines; also Agents for Air France and Air Madagascar; Man. Dir. J. DESCOUSIS.

Compagnie Bourbonnaise de Navigation: P.O.B. 99, Djibouti.

Compagnie Maritime de l'Afrique Orientale: rue du Port, B.P. 89; agents for Achille Onorato, Cie. Maritime des Chargeurs Réunis, Ellerman Lines, Kerk Line, Netherlands Lloyd Line, Nouvelle Cie. Havraise Péninsulaire, Rotterdamsche Lloyd, Scandinavian East Africa Line, Stoomvaart Maatschappij Nederland, Svenska Ostasiatiska Kt., Worms et Cie. and Zim Israel Navigation Co.; Gen. Agent M. POUPEAU.

Feronia International Shipping (Djibouti): Djibouti; 12 supply vessels.

Gellatly Hankey et Cie. (Djibouti) S.A.: rue de Genève, B.P. 81; agents for American President Line, Blue Funnel Line, Bibby Line, Hoegh Line, Nippon Yusen Kaisha, P. Henderson, Peninsular and Orient, Yugoslav Line, B.I. Steam Navigation, Maersk Lines, Waterman Lines, National Shipping Corpn.; Dir. G. W. JOHN.

J. J. Kothari & Co. Ltd.: P.O.B. No. 171, place Lagarde; agents for Fratelli d'Amico, Shipping Corporation of India, Mogul Line, Malabar Steamship Co., United Arab Maritime, Sudan Shipping Line, Onofrio Palmieri, Massawa and others; Dir. R. J. KOTHARI, S. J. KOTHARI, J. J. KOTHARI.

Mitchell Cotts and Co. (Ethiopia) Ltd.: blvd. de la République, B.P. 85; agents for Clan Line, Fearnley and Eger, Harrison Line, Iraqi Maritime Transport Co., Maldivian National Trading Corp., and other shipping and trading companies; Dir. FAHMY S. CASSIM.

Société d'Armement et de Manutention de la Mer Rouge (SAMER): B.P. 10; agents for Pacific International Line, Cunard Brocklebank, Glen Line, Wilhelm Wilhelmsen Co., Pakistan Shipping Co., Aktiebolaget Svenska Östasiatiska Kompaniet, Texaco, Chevron Shipping Co., Kie Hock Shipping Co.; Chair. A. E. BESSE; Man. Dir. VINCENT DELL'AQUILLA.

Société Maritime L. Savon et Riès: ave. St. Laurent du Var, B.P. 125; agents for Blue Star Line, Port Line, Svede Line, Concordia Line, Lloyd Triestino, Louis Dreyfus, Polish Ocean Lines, Isthmian Lines and D.D.G. Hansa; Dir. H. A. JONES.

CIVIL AVIATION
Djibouti

Air Djibouti: B.P. 505; f. 1962; internal flights and services to Aden, Ethiopia and Yemen Arab Republic; fleet of one DC-6, two DC-3, one Cherokee 6, one Bell Jet Ranger; Chair. F. LEGREZ; Man. Dir. J. DESCOUSIS.

Air France, Air Madagascar, Democratic Yemen Airlines, Ethiopian Airlines, Somali Airlines and Yemen Airways Corporation also serve Djibouti.

COMORO ISLANDS

The Comoro Islands lie between the east African coast and Madagascar and comprise four small islands (Grande-Comore, Mayotte, Anjouan and Mohéli) and numerous islets and coral reefs. Moroni, the capital, is on Grande-Comore. Volcanic in origin, the islands are mountainous with a tropical climate which varies according to the altitude and wind. Soil conditions are different on the four islands, but allow forestry on a small scale on Grande-Comore and the cultivation of a wide range of tropical crops, of which the most significant are aromatic plants from which essences are distilled for the perfume industry. The economy relies heavily on French aid.

In December 1972 a "union" of political parties standing for independence from France won a resounding victory in elections to the Chamber of Deputies. After negotiations with France it was agreed in June 1973 that the Comoro Islands should gain independence in five years after a referendum and that a measure of self-government should be attained immediately. The High Commissioner was replaced by a Delegate-General. In December 1973 the Chamber of Deputies voted for independence by 1976. The opposition Mahorais Party is seeking the status of a French Department for the island of Mayotte.

STATISTICS

Area: 2,236 sq. km. (863 sq. miles). **Population** (1972 estimates): 286,762 (including 1,500 Europeans); Moroni (capital) 15,241.

Agriculture (1971—metric tons): Cassava (manioc) 90,000, Rice 12,000, Sweet potatoes and yams 10,000, Copra 5,200, Maize 4,000, Vanilla 207, Cloves 268, Ylang-Ylang 64, Coffee 15; also sisal, perfumes, peppers and spices. In 1970 the coconut crop totalled 64 million nuts (FAO estimate).

Livestock (1973): Cattle 45,000, Goats 48,000, Sheep 6,000, Asses 3,000.

Fisheries: Annual catch: 3,000 metric tons approx.

Electric Energy (1972): 3.2 million kWh. for public use.

Currency: 100 centimes=1 franc de la Communauté financière africaine (CFA). Coins: 1, 2, 5, 10 and 20 francs CFA. Notes: 50, 100, 500, 1,000 and 5,000 francs CFA. Exchange rates (April 1974): 1 franc CFA=2 French centimes; £1 sterling=579.75 francs CFA; U.S. $1=245.625 francs CFA; 1,000 francs CFA= £1.725=$4.071.

Budget (Receipts): 1971: 2,008,027,907 francs CFA; 1972: 2,231,706,973 francs CFA.

National Accounts (1968): Gross Domestic Product 7,100 million francs CFA (U.S. $111 per head).

Aid from France (local section of FIDES): (1973) 750m. francs CFA.

External Trade (1971): *Imports:* 2,835m. francs CFA (Rice, Petroleum products, Vehicles); *Exports:* 1,572m. francs CFA (Vanilla, Essences, Copra, Cloves). Most trade is with France, the U.S.A., Federal Germany and Madagascar.

Roads (1972): 750 km. of officially classified roads, 2,953 motor vehicles.

International Shipping (1972): 319 vessels entered, 11,448 metric tons loaded, 62,725 metric tons unloaded.

Tourism (1972): 200 tourist beds.

Education (1972–73): Primary, 113 schools, 19,694 pupils, 470 teachers; Secondary, 2,150 pupils, 90 teachers.

THE GOVERNMENT
(*January* 1974)

Delegate-General: GEORGES POULET.

COUNCIL OF GOVERNMENT

President: AHMED ABDALLAH.

Minister of Economy and Tourism: ALI MROUDJAE.

Minister of Rural Planning: MOHAMED TAKI.

Minister of Finance and Planning: AHMED ABDOU.

Presidential Delegate representing the Comoros in Paris, in charge of External Affairs: MOUZAOIR ABDALLAH.

Minister of Rural Development: OMAR TAMOU.

Presidential Delegate for Internal Affairs, Information and Administrative Reform: SAID ALI YOUSSOUF.

Minister of Health: YOUSSOUF SAID.

Minister of Civil Service and Labour: ALI MIRGHANE.

Minister for Cultural Affairs, Youth and Sport: MOUHIBAKO BAKO.

CHAMBER OF DEPUTIES

President of the Chamber of Deputies: Prince SAID MOHAMMED JAFFAR.

ELECTION DECEMBER 1972

	SEATS
"Union" parties in favour of independence from France	34
Parti du mouvement mahorais	5

POLITICAL PARTIES

Union démocratique des Comores (UDC) (*Comoros Democratic Union*): Moroni; supports independence from France; Leader AHMED ABDALLAH.

Rassemblement démocratique du peuple comorien (RDPC) (*Comorian People's Democratic Rally*): Moroni; supports independence from France; Leader Prince SAID MOHAMMED JAFFAR.

Parti du mouvement mahorais (*Mayotte Movement Party*): Dzaoudzi; advocates the territory's becoming a French *département*; Leader MARCEL HENRY.

Parti du peuple (UMMA) (*People's Party*): Moroni; supports the *status quo* and is not definitely in favour of independence; Leader Prince SAID IBRAHIM.

Parti socialiste comorien (PASOCO) (*Comorian Socialist Party*): Moroni; Leader MOHAMED FAZUL.

MOLINACO (*National Liberation Movement of the Comoros*): based in Dar es Salaam, with a political wing (*Parti de l'Entente Comorienne—PEC*) active in the Comoros; Leader ABDOU BACAR BOINA.

JUDICIAL SYSTEM

Superior Court of Appeal at Moroni; Courts of First Instance at Moroni, Mamoutzou and Mutsamudu; also 16 Qadi Courts (Muslim Law).

RELIGION

The majority of the population is Muslim.

RADIO

Comores-Inter: Office de Radiodiffusion-Télévision Française, B.P. 250, Moroni (Grande-Comore); Dir.-Gen. A. SIRE.

In 1972 there were 22,000 radio receivers.

FINANCE

Banque de Madagascar et des Comores: 23 ave. Matignon, Paris, France; Moroni; f. 1925; ceased to function except in a caretaker capacity 1973, pending the creation of a new Comoro Islands issuing bank.

TRADE

Chambre de Commerce: Moroni (Grande-Comore); Pres. M. FAVETTO.

TRANSPORT

ROADS

There are approximately 750 km. of roads serviceable throughout the year.

SHIPPING

Large vessels anchor off Moroni, Mutsamudu, Dzaoudzi and Fomboni and the port of Mutsamudu can now accommodate ships of medium tonnage alongside the quay. Goods from Europe come via Madagascar, and coasters serve the Comoros from the east coast of Africa.

Société Comorienne de Navigation: Moroni; services to Madagascar.

CIVIL AVIATION

The international airport is on Grande-Comore and each of the three other islands has a small aerodrome. From June 1974 a runway accommodating Boeing 707's is to be in use at the new airport of Hahaya (Grande-Comore).

Air Comores: B.P. 81, Moroni; f. 1963; services to Anjouan, Mayotte, Mohéli, and to Dar es Salaam, Mombasa and Tananarive; fleet of two DC-4; Man. Dir. YVES LE BRET.

The Comoros are also served by Air France and Air Madagascar.

TOURISM

Alliance Touristique de l'Océan Indien: Moroni; Pres. MOHAMMED DAHALANI.

NEW CALEDONIA

New Caledonia lies in the South Pacific east of Queensland, Australia.

STATISTICS

Area: 19,058 sq. km.; **Population** (Dec. 1971): 121,073. Melanesians 47,113, Europeans (mainly French) 50,710, Wallisians 8,270, Polynesians 6,220, Others 5,090; Nouméa (capital) 55,000.

Employment (December 1972): Commerce 4,951, Public and Semi-Public Sector 3,940, Metallurgy 3,593, Building 4,863, Mines 3,204, Transport (regularly employed) 1,696, Domestic Servants 1,825, Other Industries 4,016, Professions 1,457, Agriculture, Forestry and Stock-breeding 634; 2,980 employers.

Agriculture (1971—metric tons): Maize 1,000, Potatoes 1,392, Vegetables 3,500, Fruit 1,500, Copra 950, Coffee 1,000, Sweet Potatoes 2,700, Yams 8,000, Taro 3,000, Manioc 3,800, Dried Vegetables 35.

Livestock (1971 est.): Cattle 120,315, Sheep and Goats 19,556, Pigs 16,708, Horses 10,275, Poultry 172,877.

17

Mining and Metallurgy (1971—metric tons): Nickel Ore 7,722,000 (metal content 148,750), Chrome Ore (Giobertite) 1,099, Jade 0.2, Nickel Matte 16,138, Ferro Nickel 29,881.

Currency: 100 centimes=1 franc de la Communauté française du pacifique (franc CFP or Pacific franc). Coins: 1, 2, 5, 10, 20 and 50 francs CFP. Notes: 100, 500, 1,000 and 5,000 francs CFP. Exchange rates (April 1974): 1 franc CFP=5.5 French centimes; £1 sterling=210.82 francs CFP; U.S. $1=89.32 francs CFP; 1,000 francs CFP=£4.74=$11.20.

Budget (1971): Revenue 9,990,331,000 francs CFP; Expenditure 9,698,606,000 francs CFP.

Aid from France (francs CFP, 1971): State Budget 3,949,416,216; Local section of FIDES 206,360,108; General section of FIDES 185,617,159.

External Trade (1972—million francs CFP): *Imports:* 19,144.3 (incl. 9,992.2 from France); *Exports:* 17,414.8 (Nickel 4,150.1, Nickel Matte 3,732.5, Ferro-Nickel 9,306.3), incl. 9,550.8 to France.

Roads (1969): Motor Vehicles 27,451, Motor Cycles 10,045, Tractors 454.

Shipping (1971): Vessels entered 732, Freight entered 1,355,000 metric tons, Freight cleared 4,010,000 metric tons, Passenger arrivals 2,872, Departures 1,334.

Civil Aviation (1971): Passenger arrivals 58,412, Departures 57,375, Freight entered 3,267 metric tons, Freight cleared 368 metric tons, Postal Traffic 262 tons.

Tourism (1972): 10,000 visitors.

THE GOVERNMENT

(*April* 1974)

High Commissioner: GABRIEL ERIAU.

Secretary-General: MICHEL LEVALLOIS.

COUNCIL OF GOVERNMENT

President: GABRIEL ERIAU.

Members: JACQUES LAFLEUR, FRANÇOIS NEOERE, PHILÉMON PIDJOT, CLAUDE MEYER, CLAUDE PARAZOLS.

Representative to the National Assembly: ROCH PIDJOT.

Representative to the Senate: HENRI LAFLEUR.

Representative to the Social and Economic Council: ROGER LAROQUE.

TERRITORIAL ASSEMBLY

President: YANN CELENE UREGEI.

GENERAL ELECTION
(*September* 1972)

PARTY	SEATS
Union Calédonienne	12
Union Multiraciale	5
Mouvement Populaire Calédonien . .	2
Union Démocratique . . .	4
Entente Démocratique et Sociale . .	7
Mouvement Libéral Calédonien . . .	5

POLITICAL PARTIES

Entente Démocratique et Sociale: Pres. ROGER LAROQUE; Vice-Pres. MICHEL KAUMA, JACQUES LAFLEUR.

Mouvement Libéral Calédonien: Leaders JEAN LEQUES, GEORGES NAGLE.

Mouvement Populaire Calédonien: Leader ALAIN BERNUT.

Union Calédonienne: Leader MAURICE LENORMAND.

Union Démocratique: Leaders GEORGES CHATENAY, RENÉ HENIN.

Union Multiraciale: Leader YANN CELENE UREGUEI.

JUDICIAL SYSTEM

Cour d'Appel: Nouméa; First Pres. B. RAYMOND; Procureur Général M. REMMY.

Tribunal of First Instance: Nouméa; Pres. V. DELMEE; Procureur de la République E. VERILHAC.

RELIGION

The population is Christian, Roman Catholics comprising some 63 per cent.

Roman Catholicism: In the Archdiocese of Nouméa, comprising New Caledonia and the Loyalty Islands, there are approximately 360 religious personnel. Archbishop of Nouméa, Most Rev. EUGENE X. KLEIN.

Protestantism: There are about 150 centres with a total personnel of some 200.

PRESS, RADIO AND TELEVISION

L'Avenir Calédonien: 10 Rue Gambetta, Nouméa.

Le Drapeau: 21 rue Jules Ferry, Nouméa.

La France-Australe: B.P. 25, Nouméa; f. 1889; daily; Dir.-Gen. MICHEL GERARD; circ. 8,500.

Le Journal Calédonien: 32 rue Colnett, B.P. 831, Nouméa.

Le Semeur Calédonien: B.P. 170, Nouméa; f. 1954; fortnightly; circ. 3,000.

Les Nouvelles Calédoniennes: Librairie JPL, 34 ave. de la République, Nouméa.

Le Voix du Cagou: rue Sébastopol, Nouméa.

Nouméa Soir (Le Bulletin du Commerce): 13 rue de la Somme, Nouméa; f. 1899; Dir. ANDRÉ LEGRAS.

Radio Nouméa: Office de Radiodiffusion-Télévision Française, B.P. 327, Nouméa; f. 1942; Government station; daily programmes in French; 30,000 radio sets in 1973; Dir. R. LE LEIZOUR.

Télé Nouméa: ORTF, B.P. 327, Nouméa; 15,000 television sets in 1973.

BANKS

Banque de l'Indochine: 96 Boulevard Haussman, Paris 8, France; rue de l'Alma et ave., Foch, B.P. 32, Nouméa; 6 other brs.

Banque Nationale de Paris: 16 blvd. des Italiens, Paris 9, France; 60 ave. de la Victoire, B.P. K.3, Nouméa.

Banque de Paris et des Pays-Bas: 3 rue Antin, Paris 2, France; rue G. Clémenceau, Nouméa.

Société Générale: 29 blvd. Haussman, Paris 8, France; ave. Foch, B.P. 1635, Nouméa.

TRADE AND INDUSTRY

Chambre de Commerce: B.P. 10, Nouméa; f. 1880; 12 mems.; Pres. JEAN CHEVAL; Vice-Pres. JEAN LANCHON; Sec. Treas. ANDRÉ DE BÉCHADE; publ. *Bulletin* (monthly).

Chambre d'Agriculture: B.P. 111, Nouméa; f. 1909; 18 mems.; Pres. M. ROGER PENE.

TRADE UNIONS

Fédération des Cadres et Collaborateurs de Nouvelle-Calédonie: B.P. 478, Nouméa; Pres. and Sec.-Gen. F. VIANNENC; trade union organization which includes the following:

Syndicat Général des Cadres et Assimiles de Nouvelle-Calédonie: Sec.-Gen. E. OLIVEAU.

Syndicat Général des Cadres du Commerce de Nouvelle-Calédonie: Sec.-Gen. G. JORE.

Fédération Patronale de Nouvelle-Calédonie et Dépendances: 16 rue d'Austerlitz, B.P. 466, Nouméa; f. 1936; groups the leading companies of New Caledonia for the defence of professional interests, co-ordination, documentation and research in socio-economic fields; Pres. RENÉ FAURE; Sec.-Gen. M. DEMENE.

Syndicat des Ouvriers et Employés de Nouvelle-Calédonie: Sec.-Gen. M. DRAYTON.

Union des Syndicats Autonomes: Sec.-Gen. R. JOYEUX.

Syndicat des Fonctionnaires, Agents et Ouvriers des Services Publics: Sec.-Gen. M. KOLHEN.

Fédération des Syndicats des Mines Nouvelle-Calédonie: Sec.-Gen. M. BENETEAU.

Syndicat des Travailleurs d'Outre-Mer: Sec.-Gen. M. BASTIEN.

TOURISM

Association calédonienne pour le développement du tourisme—ASCADETO: Nouméa.

TRANSPORT

Roads: there are a total of 4,600 km. of roads in New Caledonia, of which 300 are bitumen-surfaced, 1,880 stone-surfaced and 2,500 tracks.

Shipping: Services from Sydney to Nouméa are maintained by *Chargeurs Calédoniens* and from Europe to Nouméa by *Hamburg/Sued* and *Messageries Maritimes*; services calling at Nouméa are maintained by *Karlander* (Sydney–New Hebrides), *Polynésie* (Sydney–New Hebrides), *South Pacific United Lines* (Sydney–Tahiti), *Nauru Pacific Line, China Navigation Co.* (Hong Kong–South Pacific), *Nedlloyd* (Europe–South Pacific), *Daiwa Line* (Japan–South Pacific), *Union Steam Ship Co.* (New Zealand), *Sofrana-Unilines* (Sydney) and *Bank Line* (Europe–South Pacific).

Civil Aviation: *Air Calédonie:* 6 rue de Verdun, B.P. 212, Nouméa; f. 1955; services throughout New Caledonia and to the Loyalty Islands; fleet of three Twin Otters, three Islanders, one Cherokee 6; Pres. and Man. Dir. L. P. ESCHEMBRENNER.

Foreign airlines serving New Caledonia are: Air Nauru, Air New Zealand, Qantas and UTA.

FRENCH POLYNESIA

An Overseas Territory since 1958, French Polynesia consists of the following South Pacific Islands: Iles du Vent (the chief of which is Tahiti), Iles Sous le Vent (which with the Iles du Vent constitute the Society Archipelago), Tuamotu-Gambier Archipelago, Austral Islands, Marquesas Archipelago. The islands cover a wide area lying about two-thirds of the way from the Panama Canal to New Zealand.

STATISTICS

Area: 4,200 sq. km. **Population** (Census of February 8th, 1971): 119,168 (Native 86 per cent, Asiatic 10 per cent, European 4 per cent); Papeete (capital) 25,342.

Agriculture (1971): Copra 19,000 metric tons, (other crops 1966) Coffee 172 metric tons, Vanilla 132 metric tons, Citrus Fruits 1,233 metric tons.

Livestock (1972 estimates): Cattle 12,000, Sheep and Goats 5,000 (1966), Horses 3,600 (1966), Pigs 10,000.

Fishing: About 1,600 metric tons of lagoon and sea fish are caught annually.

Industry: annual output of Mother of Pearl is about 100 metric tons, Beer 64,000 hl.

Currency: 100 centimes=1 franc de la Communauté française du pacifique (franc CFP or Pacific franc). Coins: 50 centimes; 1, 2, 5, 10, 20 and 50 francs CFP. Notes: 5, 20, 100, 500 and 1,000 francs CFP. Exchange rates (April 1974): 1 franc CFP=5.5 French centimes; £1 sterling=210.82 francs CFP; U.S. $1=89.32 francs CFP; 1,000 francs CFP=£4.74=$11.20.

Budget (1967): 2,332 million francs CFP; (1968) 3,072 million francs CFP.

Aid from France (FIDES 1966–70): Local section 1,535 million francs CFP, General section 292 million francs CFP.

External Trade (1972—million francs CFP): *Imports:* 14,270.5 (Cereals, Petroleum Products, Metal Manufactures), principal suppliers France 8,349.8, U.S.A. 2,252.4; *Exports:* 1,340.6 (Copra, Vanilla, Mother of Pearl, Coffee, Citrus Fruits), principal client France 1,007.1.

Tourism (1971): 63,222 visitors, excluding cruise passengers and excursionists (35,250).

Shipping (port of Papeete—1970): ships entered 491, net displacement 1,379,000 registered tons, freight loaded 31,966 metric tons, freight unloaded 390,421 metric tons, passenger arrivals 1,519.

Civil Aviation (Faa airport, Papeete—1971): aircraft arrivals and departures 34,389, freight loaded 270.6 metric tons, freight unloaded 3,038 metric tons, passenger arrivals 208,989, mail loaded and unloaded 351.7 metric tons.

THE GOVERNMENT

(*April 1974*)

Governor: DANIEL VIDEAU.

Secrétaire-Générale: MAURICE VALY.

COUNCIL OF GOVERNMENT

Elected by Territory Assembly.

President: The Governor.

Councillors: EMILE LECAILL, CHARLES TAUFA, JACQUES TEUIRA, JACQUES TEHEUIRA, MARCO TEVANE.

TERRITORIAL ASSEMBLY

Elected every five years on the basis of universal suffrage.

President of the Territorial Assembly: GASTON FLOSSE.

ELECTIONS
(*September* 1972)

PARTY	SEATS
U.T.-U.D.R.	11
Te Ea Api	7
Pupu Here Aia	5
Independents	6
Non-Party	1

Representative to the National Assembly: FRANCIS SANFORD.
Representative to the Senate: ALFRED POROÏ.

POLITICAL PARTIES

Union Tahitienne-Union pour la Nouvelle République (U.T.-U.D.R.): 103 Rue Bréa, Papeete; f. 1958; Pres. GASTON FLOSSE.

Pupu Here Aia: Papeete; f. 1965; 7–8,000 mems.; Pres. JOHN TEARIKI.

Te Ea Api: Papeete; Leader FRANCIS SANFORD.

Judicial System: Tribunal Supérieur d'Appel, Tribunal de Première Instance, Justice de Paix, Tribunal Mixte de Commerce, Tribunal du Travail; Section of the Tribunal de Première Instance at Uturoa; Procureur attached to the Tribunal Supérieur d'Appel and Head of Judicial Service R. GIRARD; Pres. Tribunal Supérieur d'Appel Y. PEGOURIER; Procureur attached to the Tribunal de Première Instance G. AMADEO; Pres. Tribunal de Première Instance J. JUPPE.

Religion: 50 per cent of the population are Protestants, 34 per cent Roman Catholics. The Protestant missions comprise 76 societies and about 57,000 adherents (Pres. Conseil Supérieur des Eglises Tahitiennes Pastor SAMUEL RAAPOTO). Roman Catholics number about 25,000 (Archbishop of Tahiti Mgr. PAUL MAZÉ). There are also Sanito, Mormon, Adventist and Jehovah's Witness missions with about 4,000 adherents in all.

PRESS AND RADIO
Papeete

Le Canard Tahitien: rue Clapier; satirical weekly; Dir. Mme LIENARDS.

La Dépêche de Tahiti: Société Polynésienne de Presse, B.P. 50; f. 1964; daily; Dir. PHILIPPE MAZELLIER.

Le Journal de Tahiti: rue des Remparts, B.P. 600; f. 1962; daily; Dir. MICHEL LEFEVRE; largest circulation in French Polynesia.

Les Nouvelles: B.P. 629; f. 1956; daily; Propr. R. BRISSAUD.

Reef: B.P. 966; f. 1966; bi-monthly; English; general and tourist information; circ. 10,000; Editor BOB DIXON.

Sports Tahiti: rue des Ramparts, B.P. 600; f. 1969; twice weekly; Editor HENRY BOUQUET.

Tahiti Bulletin: Immeuble Laguesse, Place Notre Dame, B.P. 912; f. 1967; daily; English; Editor V. K. BOYACK.

Tahiti—Echoes of Polynesia: B.P. 83; monthly; English; Editor BUZZ MILLER.

Radio-Tahiti: 410 rue Dumont d'Urville, Papeete; f. 1951; Office de Radiodiffusion-Télévision Française; daily programmes in French and Tahitian; 60,000 receivers in 1972; Dir. JEAN SUHAS.

Télé Tahiti: B.P. 125, Papeete; programmes started in 1965; 10,000 television sets in 1972.

FINANCE
BANKS

Banque de l'Indochine: 96 blvd. Haussmann, Paris 8, France; 2 place Notre-Dame, Papeete; brs. in Papeete (Quai Galliéni) in Faa, Pirae and Uturoa.

Banque de Tahiti S.A.: B.P. 1602, rue Paul Gauguin, Papeete; f. 1969; affiliated to Bank of Hawaii, Honolulu, and Crédit Lyonnais, Paris; cap. 100m. frs. CFP; dep. 1,733m. frs. CFP (1972); Pres. G. PRADERE-NIQUET; Gen. Man. C. J. GROEN.

Société de Crédit et de Développement de l'Océanie (SOCREDO): B.P. 130, Papeete; f. 1959; cap. 120m. CFP, dep. 1,379m. CFP; Pres. R. QUESNOT; Dir.-Gen. JEAN VERNAUDON.

TRADE AND INDUSTRY
Papeete

Chambre de Commerce et d'Industrie de la Polynésie Française: B.P. 118; f. 1880; 18 mems.; Pres. CHARLES T. POROÏ; Sec.-Gen. RAMON H. DEXTER; publs. *Les Nouveaux Objectifs*, *Revue Mensuelle* (monthly).

Chambre d'Agriculture et d'Elevage: B.P. 626; f. 1886; 10 mems.; Pres. HUGH LAUHLIN.

Union Territoriale des Syndicats de la Confédération Générale du Travail "Force Ouvrière": Sec.-Gen. W. BREDIN.

Centrale des Travailleurs Chrétiens du Pacifique: B.P. 333; f. 1946; Pres. CHRISTIAN BODIN; Sec.-Gen. JEAN-BAPTISTE VERNIER.

Syndicat Autonome des Fonctionnaires Indépendants: f. 1948; Sec.-Gen. Mlle A. LAGARDE.

Syndicat des Eleveurs de Bovins: B.P. 1325; f. 1951; 80 mems.; Pres. SYLVAIN MILLAUD.

Syndicat des Armateurs: Pres. A. BLOUIN.

Union Patronale: B.P. 317; f. 1948.

TRANSPORT
ROADS

There are 215 km. of bitumen-surfaced and 368 km. of stone-surfaced roads.

SHIPPING
Papeete

Agence Tahiti Poroï: B.P. 83; telegraph: Poroï; f. 1958; commission agents, exporters and importers; Dir. ROBERT WAN.

Compagnie des Messageries Maritimes: P.O.B. 96, Papeete-Tahiti; cargo ship services between Europe, the Far East, Madagascar, East Africa, Oceania and Australia; agents for French Line, Farrell Lines, Holland America Line, Lloyd Triestino, Norwegian America Line, Shaw Savill Line, Sitmar Line, Chevron Shipping Corporation, West Cruise Lines, Lauro Lines, Dominion Far East Line, German Atlantic Line.

Matson Line: Pacific tours.

Pacific Islands Transport Line: Agents: Agence Maritime Internationale Tahiti, B.P. 274, Papeete-Tahiti; services every six weeks to Pago Pago, Apia, Los Angeles, San Francisco, Vancouver.

Sitmar Line: represented by Cie. des Messageries Maritimes, P.O.B. 96, Papeete-Tahiti.

Other companies operating services to, or calling at, Papeete are: Chandris Lines, Karlander, South Pacific United Lines, China Navigation Co., Nedlloyd, Union Steam Ship Co., Bank Line and Silk and Boyd.

CIVIL AVIATION

Papeete

Air Polynésie (R.A.I.): B.P. 314; inter-islands services operated from Papeete to Huahine, Raiatea, Bora Bora, Rangiroa, Manihi, Ua-Huka, Moorea, Maupiti, Tubuai,

Ruruta and Hiva-oa; Gen. Man. J. LESNÉ. *Air Tahiti* operates internal services between Tahiti and Moorea Island.

Six international airlines serve Tahiti: Air New Zealand, Pan American Airways Inc., Qantas Airways, Union des Transports Aériens, Air France, Lan-Chile.

TOURISM

Office de développement du Tourisme de la Polynésie Française: B.P. 65, Papeete.

Syndicat d'Initiative de la Polynésie Française: B.P. 326, Papeete.

ST. PIERRE AND MIQUELON

The islands of St. Pierre and Miquelon (Iles Saint-Pierre-et-Miquelon) lie about 25 kilometres from the coast of Newfoundland, Canada.

STATISTICS

Area: 242 sq. km. **Population** (1969): 5,225; Saint-Pierre 4,565 (1967), Miquelon 621 (1967).

Agriculture: Vegetables are grown and some cattle, sheep and pigs are kept, both for local consumption.

Fishing: The total catch in 1972 was 3,689 metric tons Fish processing is the only industry of consequence and fish products are the main exports.

Currency: 100 centimes=1 franc de la Communauté financière africaine (CFA). Coins: 1 and 2 francs CFA. Notes: 5, 10, 20, 50, 100, 500, 1,000 and 5,000 francs CFA. Exchange rates (April 1974): 1 franc CFA=2 French centimes; £1 sterling=579.75 francs CFA; U.S. $1=245.625 francs CFA; 1,000 francs CFA= £1.725=$4.071.

Budget (1968): 629m. frs. CFA, (1969) 659m. frs. CFA.

French Aid: In the 1961–68 period this amounted to 22.6 million French francs.

External Trade (1972—million francs CFA): *Imports:* 3,684 (Fuel, meat, clothing, electrical equipment and machinery); *Exports:* 1,064 (Fish, marine equipment). Most trade is with Canada, France, the EEC, the U.K. and the U.S.A.

Transport: *Roads:* There are about 500 motor vehicles; *Shipping* (1972): Ships entered 1,482, Freight entered 87,357 metric tons, Freight cleared 1,917 metric tons.

Tourism: In 1969 there were 7,219 tourists.

Education: (1968) Primary: 9 schools, 1,155 pupils; Secondary: 3 schools, 235 pupils; Technical: 6 schools, 142 pupils.

THE GOVERNMENT

(March 1974)

Governor: HENRI BEAUX.

The Governor is assisted by a Privy Council consisting of the service chiefs and two members appointed by the Secretary of State for the Overseas Departments and Territories.

President of the General Council: ALBERT PEN.

Vice-Presidents: MM. ANDRÉ TILLY and EUGENE COUEPEL.

The General Council is composed of 14 members, and the President and Vice-Presidents.

Representative to the National Assembly: JACQUES VENDROUX.

Representative to the Senate: ALBERT PEN.

Representative to the Social and Economic Council: (vacant).

———

Judicial System: Tribunal Supérieur d'Appel at Saint-Pierre (Pres. M. GASTINEL); one Tribunal de Première Instance

Religion: The population is Roman Catholic, with 40 religious personnel.

Press: *Journal Officiel* published by the Government Printer; f. 1886; fortnightly.

Radio and Television: ORTF, Saint-Pierre, the Government station, broadcasts 16 hours of radio programmes daily, and 34 hours of television programmes weekly; Dir. YVES HENRY. In 1972 there were 2,000 radios and 1,600 television sets.

Banks: *Banque des Iles Saint-Pierre et Miquelon:* rue Jacques-Cartier, Saint-Pierre; f. 1889; cap. 2m. frs. CFA; Pres. and Gen. Man. GEORGES LANDRY; Man. GUY ROULET. *Credit Saint-Piérrais:* Man. J. BENE.

Insurance: *Assurances Générales de France:* Paris; *Compagnie d'Assurances La Foncière:* Paris; *Comité Central des Assureurs Maritimes de France:* Paris; Rep. Paturel Frères, B.P. 80, Saint-Pierre.

Trade: *Chambre de Commerce:* Saint-Pierre; Pres. L. E. HARDY.

Transport: *Shipping: Compagnie Générale Transatlantique* and *Italian Line.* Packet boats run to Halifax, Sydney and Louisbourg in Canada. *Civil Aviation:* Air St.-Pierre connects the territory with Sydney, Nova Scotia. Saint Pierre is also served by Air France and TCA.

Tourism: Syndicat d'Initiative; f. 1959.

WALLIS AND FUTUNA ISLANDS

Situated in the South Pacific between Fiji and Western Samoa, 2,000 km. north-east of New Caledonia.

A French Protectorate since 1888, the Islands chose by referendum in December 1959 to become an Overseas Territory. In July 1961 they were granted this status.

Area (sq. km.): Wallis Island 159, Futuna Island and Alofi Island 115, total of all islands 274.

Population: 9,900: Wallis Island 7,000 (chief town Mata-Utu), Futuna Island 2,900; Alofi Island uninhabited; more than 8,000 Wallisians and Futunians live on New Caledonia and in the New Hebrides.

Agriculture: the principal export crop is copra. Yams, taros, bananas and arrowroot and other food crops are also cultivated.

Livestock (1972): 300 horses, 350 cattle, 3,000 pigs.

Currency: 100 centimes=1 franc de la Communauté française du pacifique (franc CFP or Pacific franc). Exchange rates (April 1974): 1 franc CFP=5.5 French centimes; £1 sterling=210.82 francs CFP; U.S. $1=89.32 francs CFP; 1,000 francs CFP=£4.74=$11.20.

Budget (1969): 50,081,763 francs CFP.

External Trade (1969): *Imports:* 125 million francs CFP; *Exports:* 2 million francs CFP.

Government: *Administrateur Supérieur* JACQUES DE AGOSTINI; President of Territorial Assembly SOSEFO MAKAPE; Representative to National Assembly BENJAMIN BRIAL; Representative to Senate SOSEFO MAKAPE PAPILLO.

Religion: The entire population is Catholic; Bishop of Wallis and Futuna Mgr. LOLESIO FUAHEA.

Shipping: Services to Nouméa (New Caledonia), Suva (Fiji), Port Vila and Santo (both in the New Hebrides).

Aviation: *Union des Transports Aériens (UTA):* Wallis Island; twice-monthly service to Nouméa, New Caledonia. *Air Fiji:* Charter services to the Wallis and Futuna Islands.

FRENCH SOUTHERN AND ANTARCTIC TERRITORIES

The French Southern and Antarctic Territories (Terres australes et antarctiques françaises) rank as an Overseas Territory but are administered under a special statute. Adélie Land is a narrow segment of the Antarctic mainland. The Kerguelen and Crozet Archipelagos, Saint Paul and New Amsterdam lie in the Southern Indian Ocean.

Area (sq. km.): Kerguelen Archipelago 7,000, Crozet Archipelago 500, New Amsterdam Island 60, St. Paul Island 7, Adélie Land (Antarctica) 500,000.

Population (the population, comprising members of scientific missions, fluctuates according to season, being higher in the summer; the figures given are approximate): Kerguelen Archipelago, Port-aux-Français 80; New Amsterdam Island at La Roche-Godon 35; Adélie Land at Base Dumont d'Urville 27; the Crozet Archipelago at Alfred-Faure 20; St. Paul Island is uninhabited. Total population (July 1st, 1970): 177.

Production: *New Amsterdam:* Société Anonyme de Pêche Malgache et Réunionnaise (SAP-MER) produces small quantities of lobster-tails for export.

Currency: 100 centimes=1 French franc. Exchange rates (April 1974): £1 sterling=11.595 francs; U.S. $1=4.91 francs.

Budget: Balanced at approx. 20m. francs annually.

External Trade (metric tons): *Imports:* 3,200 (including Food 400, Fuel 100, Technical Equipment 900, Scientific Equipment 500), 2,700 from France and 30 from Madagascar; Exports consist mainly of lobster (about 540 tons annually) and other fish going to France and Réunion.

Government: Superior Administrator PIERRE ROLLAND.

Consultative Council: composed of 7 members appointed by the Ministries of National Defence, the Community, Education, Air, Merchant Marine and two scientists. The President and Secretary are elected annually. There is a Central Administration in Paris. Pres. M. VALABREGUE.

Transport: *Shipping:* Charter vessels call at Kerguelen, New Amsterdam, Adélie Land and Crozet.

Research Stations: There are meteorological stations and geophysical research stations on Kerguelen, New Amsterdam, Adélie Land and Crozet.

GABON

INTRODUCTORY SURVEY

Location, Climate, Language, Religion, Flag, Capital

Gabon is an equatorial country on the west coast of Africa with Cameroon to the north and the Congo (Brazzaville) to the south and east. The climate is tropical with an average temperature of 26°C (79°F) and an annual rainfall of 250 cm. The official language is French but Bantu dialects are widely spoken. About 60 per cent of the population are Christians, mainly Roman Catholics. Most of the others follow animist beliefs. The national flag (proportions 4 by 3) consists of horizontal green, gold and blue stripes. The capital is Libreville.

Recent History

Formerly a province of French Equatorial Africa, Gabon gained internal autonomy in 1957. In 1958 it joined the French Community and attained independence in August 1960. In February 1961, Léon M'Ba was elected the Republic's first President. Shortly before elections called for February 1964, a military *coup d'état*, led by Jean-Hilaire Aubame, a long-standing rival, deposed M'Ba. French intervention restored M'Ba to the Presidency, and elections held in April gave M'Ba's *Bloc démocratique gabonaise* (BDG) a large majority in the National Assembly; during the next two years most of the opposition joined the BDG. In 1967, M'Ba created the post of Vice-President, and when he died in November that year he was succeeded by his deputy Albert-Bernard Bongo. In March 1968, the *Parti démocratique gabonais* was set up and one-party government was formally instituted.

President Bongo has taken a hard line against any form of protest or dissent in the country. At the same time, every effort has been made to attract foreign companies and investors to Gabon. Since July 1972, however, the "Gabonization" of the economy has been undertaken. Foreigners have been replaced by Gabonese in positions of authority and the state has taken a share in the capital of foreign companies. In February 1973 the PDG won all 70 seats in the National Assembly and Bongo was re-elected president with 99 per cent of the votes cast.

Bongo has pursued a policy of close co-operation with France in the fields of economic and foreign affairs, and until recently Gabon had no diplomatic relations with Communist states. Bongo supported the call by Félix Houphouët-Boigny, President of the Ivory Coast, for a dialogue with South Africa and has been slow to take part in the activities of the OAU. Gabon's relations with its neighbours have been good, apart from a dispute with Equatorial Guinea over territorial waters in 1972. In October 1973 the President was converted to Islam and changed his name to Omar Bongo. Some observers have seen the influence of the Libyan leader, Col. Muamar al-Gaddafi, in this conversion and have expected Bongo to pursue a more nationalist policy. However, President Bongo asserts that his conversion is a private matter, and the continued "Gabonization" and recent revision of Gabon's co-operation agreements with France may well be only the continuation of a consistently pragmatic policy.

Government

The Constitution of 1967 vests executive power in the President and a Council of Ministers appointed by him. The legislative organ is the unicameral National Assembly of 70 Deputies elected by universal suffrage for a five-year term. The country is divided into 9 administrative regions, each under a Prefect.

Defence

The army consists of one batallion, the air force of one squadron, and there is a small navy. There is also a *gendarmerie nationale*.

Economic Affairs

Well over half of the population of Gabon is engaged in subsistence agriculture, largely untouched by the expansion of the market economy. There is a little commercial agricultural production, the main crops being palm oil, coffee, cocoa and bananas. For many years the economy was largely dependent upon forestry, particularly production of *okoumé*, a wood used in the making of plywood. Despite the expansion of forestry to avail of a favourable world timber market, mineral production has taken over as the leading activity since the late 1960s. Petroleum production, now the fifth highest in Africa, is expected to increase substantially in the future as the result of new discoveries. The manganese deposits at Moanda in the south form one of the world's richest sources. There are also plans for the exploitation of major iron ore deposits at Bélinga in the north-east. Other minerals produced are uranium and gold. The development of both forestry and mining is hampered by a lack of transport facilities. The Trans-Gabon railway, which was held up for several years by lack of financial backing, is now under construction and should solve the country's major transport problems. Gabon's manufacturing sector is relatively restricted, though it is being expanded. There is an oil refinery at Port-Gentil, which serves the four states of the Customs and Economic Union of Central Africa (UDEAC), and there are important timber-processing plants. A second oil refinery is projected.

Gabon has pursued economic growth as its main objective, giving every encouragement to foreign investment. Its average G.D.P. per head is one of the highest in Africa, and the country has a favourable trade balance. Measures have been taken to counter suggestions that Gabon is not benefiting sufficiently from the exploitation of its natural resources. In July 1972 President Bongo announced that the state would take a 10 per cent interest in all foreign companies in Gabon, to increase eventually to 25 per cent. Gabon became an associate member of the Organization of the Petroleum Exporting Countries (OPEC) in 1973, and in 1974 Bongo announced that the price of uranium would be almost doubled.

Gabon is an associate member of the European Economic Community (EEC), and a member of UDEAC and the Afro-Malagasy Joint Organization (OCAM).

Transport and Communications

There is a 76 km. cableway and a 296 km. railroad linking the manganese mines at Moanda with the Congo (Brazzaville) port of Pointe-Noire. Construction of the first stretch of the Trans-Gabon railway, from Owendo to Booué, was begun in January 1974. When completed, the railway should run from Owendo to Bélinga in the north and Moanda in the south, greatly facilitating exploitation of the forests and the iron ore, manganese and uranium deposits of the country. There are over 2,700 km. of national roads and about 1,750 km. of regional roads. The widespread forests make air transport very important and there is an airport capable of handling jets at Libreville. The main rivers are navigable only from about 300 km. inland. There are two Atlantic ports at Libreville and Port-Gentil, and a third is under construction at Owendo, near Libreville.

Social Welfare

There is a national Fund for State Insurance. Gabon now has 11 hospitals and 29 medical centres with an average of one bed for every 207 inhabitants. Maternal and infant health is a major priority.

Education

Education is undertaken by state and mission schools. In 1972 there were 678 primary schools with over 105,000 pupils, representing over 95 per cent of children of school age. In addition there are 59 secondary, technical and teacher training schools, and a university in Libreville. Many students go to France for university and technical training.

Tourism

Tourism is being extensively developed at the moment, with new hotels and several important projects, including a "holiday village" near Libreville opened in 1973, re-organization of Pointe-Denis tourist resort, and the promotion of national parks. Wild animals abound in the forests, and there is excellent hunting.

Public Holidays

1974: August 15th (Assumption), August 17th (Independence Day), November 1st (All Saints'), November 11th (Armistice Day), December 25th (Christmas).

1975: January 1st (New Year's Day), March 31st (Easter Monday), May 1st (Labour Day), May 8th (Ascension), May 19th (Whit Monday).

Weights and Measures

The metric system is in official use.

Currency and Exchange Rates

100 centimes=1 franc de la Communauté financière africaine (CFA).

Exchange rates (April 1974):

1 franc CFA=2 French centimes;

£1 sterling=579.75 francs CFA;

U.S. $1=245.625 francs CFA.

STATISTICAL SURVEY

AREA AND POPULATION

AREA (sq. km.)	POPULATION (1970 census)
267,000	950,009

PRINCIPAL TOWNS
POPULATION (1970)

Libreville (capital)	75,000
Port-Gentil	30,000
Lambaréné	7,000

EMPLOYMENT
(1972)

Agriculture	267,000
Forestry, Mining and Construction . .	60,000
Commerce and Industry . .	8,200
Civil Service	8,000
Other (incl. Military, Clergy, Students) .	38,200

AGRICULTURE

PRINCIPAL CROPS
('000 metric tons)

	1969	1970	1971
Cereals . . .	3*	3*	3*
Cassava (Manioc) .	167*	167*	n.a.
Bananas . .	10*	10*	n.a.
Palm Oil . .	2	2*	2*
Coffee . .	1.2	0.9	0.9

	1969/70	1970/71	1971/72
Cocoa Beans (October to September) . .	4.7	5.0	5.0

* FAO estimates.

Source: FAO, *Production Yearbook 1971.*

Livestock (1970): Horses 3,382, Goats 86,682, Pigs 6,032.

FORESTRY
('ooo metric tons)

	1968	1969	1970	1971	1972
Okoumé . . .	842	928	924	1,024	1,141
Other Woods . .	159	195	189	197	n.a.

FISHING
('ooo metric tons)

	1968	1969	1970	1971
Total Catch . . .	3.0*	3.8	4.0*	4.0*

* FAO estimates.

MINING

		1969	1970	1971	1972
Petroleum . . .	'ooo metric tons	5,030	5,364	5,785	6,304
Manganese . . .	,, ,, ,,	1,377	1,453	1,866	1,936
Uranium* . . .	metric tons	500	400	540	210
Gold	kg.	443	501	421	355
Natural Gas . . .	'ooo cubic metres	n.a.	25,000	30,539	34,460

* Uranium oxide content of ores. *Source: Uranium,* report of AEN, OCDE and AIEA, 1973.

INDUSTRY

		1970
Beer	hectolitres	50,000
Soft Drinks . . .	,,	25,000
Flour	metric tons	7,968
Bran	,, ,,	1,501
Cattle Feed . . .	,, ,,	1,050
Printed Textiles . .	'ooo metres	5,000
Cement . . .	metric tons	23,000
Electricity . . .	'ooo kWh	110,156

FINANCE

100 centimes = 1 franc de la Communauté financière africaine (CFA).

Coins: 1, 2, 5, 10, 25, 50 and 100 francs CFA.

Notes: 100, 500, 1,000, 5,000 and 10,000 francs CFA.

Exchange rates (April 1974): 1 franc CFA = 2 French centimes;
£1 sterling = 579.75 francs CFA; U.S. $1 = 245.625 francs CFA.
1,000 francs CFA = £1.725 = $4.071.

BUDGET
(million francs CFA)

REVENUE	1971	1972	1973	EXPENDITURE	1971	1972	1973
Current Revenue . .	23,800	28,800	34,300	Current Expenditure .	19,000	22,000	26,200
				Development Expenditure .	5,500	4,700	11,500
TOTAL . .	23,800	28,800	34,300	TOTAL . .	24,500	26,700	37,700

Budget (1974): to balance at 47,885m. CFA francs.

SECOND DEVELOPMENT PLAN 1971–75
(million francs CFA)

INVESTMENT		RESOURCES	
Production	92,114	*Internal Public Funds* . . .	28,749
Forestry and Wood Industries .	13,776	State Budget . . .	26,018
Mining	29,182	Public Organizations . .	2,731
Power and Water . .	11,948	*External Public Funds* . . .	36,723
Industry	31,913	*Private Funds* . . .	84,428
Commerce, Transport and Services .	3,500		
Rural Development . . .	1,795		
Infrastructure . . .	53,375		
Railway	16,500		
Roads	11,030		
Airways	4,375		
Ports	2,686		
Posts and Telecommunications .	1,265		
Radio and Television . .	819		
Tourism	4,510		
Urbanization and Administration .	12,190		
Social Services . . .	4,411		
Health	2,430		
Education . . .	1,833		
Social Action . . .	148		
TOTAL	149,900	TOTAL	149,900

EXTERNAL TRADE*
(million francs CFA)

	1965	1966	1967	1968	1969	1970	1971	1972
Imports . . .	15,425	16,209	16,585	15,875	20,127	22,139	26,810	35,001
Exports . . .	23,686	24,669	29,516	30,714	36,663	33,610	51,800	50,297

* Excluding trade in gold and trade with other UDEAC countries: Cameroon (from 1966), the Central African Republic, Congo (Brazzaville) and, prior to 1969, Chad.

Source: UDEAC.

COMMODITIES
(million francs CFA)

IMPORTS	1968	1969	1970	EXPORTS	1969	1970	1971
Food and Live Animals	1,594	1,741	n.a.	Cocoa Beans . .	482	456	n.a.
Alcoholic Beverages .	812	782	604	Saw and Veneer Logs .	11,029	} 11,044	14,978
Petroleum Products .	267	294	n.a.	Railway Sleepers .	280		
Chemicals . . .	1,076	1,403	n.a.	Manganese Ores and Concentrates .	7,429	7,311	9,366
Textile Yarn, Fabrics, etc. . .	804	801	447	Uranium and Thorium Ores and Concentrates	1,788	2,223	1,526
Iron and Steel . .	1,111	1,537	n.a.	Crude Petroleum . .	12,552	13,755	21,807
Machinery (non-electric)	2,658	3,766	2,814	Veneer Sheets . .	38	} 2,689	3,134
Electrical Equipment .	936	1,281	1,643	Plywood . . .	2,083		
Road Motor Vehicles ..	1,711	2,105	4,056				
Aircraft . . .	265	572	n.a.				
Clothing (except furs) .	424	525	n.a.				
TOTAL (incl. others)	15,875	20,109	22,139	TOTAL (incl. others)	36,663	33,610	51,800

Source: mainly *Overseas Associates, Foreign Trade* (Statistical Office of the European Communities, Luxembourg).

COUNTRIES
(million francs CFA)

IMPORTS	1969	1970	1971	EXPORTS	1969	1970	1971
Belgium/Luxembourg .	495	582	512	Curaçao . . .	n.a.	5,193	5,421
France . . .	11,735	12,593	14,422	France . . .	12,923	14,179	18,142
Federal Germany .	1,691	1,980	2,360	Federal Germany .	3,146	2,267	2,911
Italy . . .	467	521	555	Netherlands . .	1,892	n.a.	2,709
Netherlands . .	771	n.a.	663	Senegal . . .	1,258	1,090	2,180
United Kingdom . .	697	n.a.	744	United Kingdom .	1,190	937	n.a.
U.S.A. . . .	2,157	2,497	2,626	U.S.A. . . .	4,015	1,294	4,157
TOTAL (incl. others)	20,109	22,139	26,810	TOTAL (incl. others)	36,663	33,610	51,800

Source: mainly *Overseas Associates, Foreign Trade* (Statistical Office of the European Communities, Luxembourg). The total of 1969 imports differs slightly from that given in the summary total of trade, which includes the latest figures supplied by the UDEAC.

TRANSPORT

ROAD TRAFFIC
(Number of vehicles in use)

	1968	1969	1970
Cars . . .	5,230	5,921	7,100
Buses . . .	134	168	188
Goods Vehicles .	4,490	4,936	5,800

SHIPPING

	1969	1970	1971
Ships Entered ('000 net reg. tons) . .	9,851	10,212	11,250
Freight Loaded ('000 metric tons) . .	5,545	5,750	7,690
Freight Unloaded ('000 metric tons) .	270	300	302

CIVIL AVIATION

Total Scheduled Services
(including one-twelfth of the traffic of Air Afrique)

	1969	1970	1971*
Kilometres Flown ('000) . . .	2,828	2,889	2,904
Passengers Carried . . .	126,711	120,395	126,000
Passenger-kilometres ('000) .	80,717	85,621	96,000
Freight tonne-kilometres ('000) .	5,642	5,931	7,283
Mail tonne-kilometres ('000) . .	478	529	554

* Provisional.

Source: International Civil Aviation Organization.

EDUCATION
(1971–72)

	Schools	Students
Primary	678	105,600
Secondary . .	41	9,387
Technical . .	12	1,733
Teacher Training . .	6	231
University . . .	1	172*

* There were 618 students at universities abroad.

THE CONSTITUTION

(Revised, February 1967)

Preamble: Upholds the Rights of Man, liberty of conscience and of the person, religious freedom and freedom of education. Sovereignty is vested in the people, who exercise it through their representatives or by means of referenda. There is direct, universal and secret suffrage.

Head of State: The President is elected by direct suffrage for a seven-year term and is eligible for re-election. He is Head of State, of the administration and of the Armed Forces. The President may, after consultation with his Ministers and leaders of the National Assembly, order a referendum to be held. There is a Vice-President elected by direct suffrage. He will replace the President in case of his disability for any reason.

Executive Power: Executive power is vested in the President and the Council of Ministers, who are appointed by the President and are responsible to him. The President presides over the Council.

Legislative Power: The National Assembly is elected by direct suffrage for a seven-year term and normally holds two sessions a year. It may be dissolved or prorogued for up to 18 months by the President, after consultation with the Council of Ministers and President of the Assembly. The President may return a Bill to the Assembly for a second reading when it must be passed by a majority of two-thirds of the members. If the President dissolves the Assembly, elections must take place within 40 days.

Judicial Power: The President guarantees the independence of the Judiciary and presides over the Conseil Supérieur de la Magistrature. There is a Supreme Court and a High Court of Justice. The High Court, which is composed of deputies of the National Assembly elected from among themselves, has power to try the President or members of the Government.

THE GOVERNMENT

HEAD OF THE STATE

President: OMAR BONGO.

Vice-President: LÉON MEBIAME.

COUNCIL OF MINISTERS

(April 1974)

President of the Republic, Prime Minister, Minister of Defence, Information, Development, Planning, National Organization and Foreign Affairs: OMAR BONGO.

Vice-President, Minister of Co-ordination, President of the National Consultative Council: LÉON MEBIAME.

Ministers of State:

Deputy Vice-President, Interior and Relations with the Assemblies: JEAN-STANISLAS MIGOLET.

Social Affairs, Environment and Reafforestation: FRANÇOIS NGUEMA-NDONG.

At the Presidency in Charge of Planning, Development and National Organization: AUGUSTIN BOUMAH.

At the Presidency in Charge of Economic Co-ordination, Personal Representative of the President: GEORGES RAWIRI.

Mines, Industry, Power and Water Resources: EDOUARD ALEXIS MBOUY BOUTZIT.

Ministers:

Economy and Finance: PAUL MOUKAMBI.

Delegate to the Presidency for Foreign Affairs and Co-operation: PAUL OKUMBA D'OKWATSEGUE.

Public Works, Transport and Civil Aviation: BENJAMIN NGOUBOU.

Civil Service and Administrative Reform: THEODORE KWAOU.

Labour and Social Security: JEROME OKINDA.

Public Health and Population: Lt.-Col. RAPHAËL MAMIAKA.

Posts and Telecommunications and Ex-Servicemen: PHILIBERT BONGOTHA.

Agriculture, Stockbreeding and Rural Development: BONJEAN FRANÇOIS ONDO.

Education and Scientific Research: MARTIN BONGO.

Trade and Crafts: SIMON ESSIMENGANE.

Environment and Town Planning: EMILE BIBALOU-ABYBUKA.

Water and Forests, and Public Relations: MICHEL ESSONGHE.

Justice: VALENTIN OBAME.

Tourism and National Parks: JACQUES IGOHO.

Secretary-General to the Presidency: RENÉ RADEMBINO-CONIQUET.

Public Establishments and State Companies: PIERRE CLAVER EYEGUET.

Youth and Sports: EMMANUEL MEFANE.

There are also 7 Secretaries of State and 4 High Commissioners.

DIPLOMATIC REPRESENTATION

EMBASSIES ACCREDITED TO GABON

Belgium: Brazzaville, People's Republic of the Congo.

Cameroon: Bangui, Central African Republic.

Canada: Yaoundé, Cameroon.

Central African Republic: B.P. 2096, Libreville; *Ambassador:* ANTOINE M'BARY-DABA.

Chad: Bangui, Central African Republic.

Congo (Brazzaville): B.P. 269, Libreville; *Ambassador:* FRANÇOIS-XAVIER OLASSA.

Equatorial Guinea: B.P. 14.264, Libreville; *Ambassador:* CLEMENTE ATEBE NSOH.

France: B.P. 25, Libreville; *Ambassador:* JEAN RIBO.

Germany, Federal Republic: B.P. 299, Libreville; *Ambassador:* OTTO WALLNER.

India: Kinshasa, Zaire.

Italy: B.P. 2251, Libreville; *Ambassador:* FURIO ZAMPETTI.

Japan: Kinshasa, Zaire.

Korea, Republic: Paris, France.

Malta: B.P. 3048, Libreville; *Ambassador:* GUY LE GOUVELLO.

Mauritania: Lagos, Nigeria.

Netherlands: Yaoundé, Cameroon.

Senegal: Kinshasa, Zaire.

Spain: B.P. 1157, Libreville; *Chargé d'Affaires:* JOSÉ MARÍA CASTROVIEJO-BOLIBAT.

Sudan: Kinshasa, Zaire.

Sweden: Kinshasa, Zaire.

Switzerland: Kinshasa, Zaire.

United Kingdom: Yaoundé, Cameroon.

U.S.A.: B.P. 185, Libreville; *Ambassador:* JOHN McKESSON.

Vatican: Yaoundé, Cameroon.

Zaire: Libreville; *Ambassador:* MWANE KIKANGALA EBULAYA YA BWANA.

Gabon also has diplomatic relations with Algeria, the People's Republic of China, Cuba, Denmark, Egypt, Greece, Egypt, Lebanon, Mali, Morocco, the Niger, Nigeria, Norway, the U.S.S.R., the Republic of Viet-Nam and Yugoslavia.

NATIONAL ASSEMBLY

President: Georges Damas Aleka.

Secretary General: Antoine Abiague-Angoue.

Election, February 1973

All 70 seats were won by the *Parti démocratique gabonaise*.

POLITICAL PARTY

Parti démocratique gabonais (PDG): Libreville; f. 1968 in succession to the *Bloc démocratique gabonais* (*BDG*); made sole political party by presidential decree of March 12th, 1968, which stated that the Party would be the guarantee of national unity and of the abolition of ethnic discrimination; since the reorganization of 1972, the party's political bureau is tightly linked with government decisions and in addition has independent powers; Sec.-Gen. and Founder Omar Bongo; publ. *Dialogue*.

JUDICIAL SYSTEM

Supreme Court: B.P. 1043, Libreville; has four chambers: constitutional, judicial, administrative, and accounts; Pres. Paul Marie Gondjout.

High Court of Justice: Libreville; members appointed by and from the deputies of the National Assembly.

Court of Appeal: Libreville.

Cour de Sureté de l'Etat: Libreville; 12 members; Pres. Omar Bongo.

Conseil Supérieure de la Justice: Libreville; Pres. Omar Bongo; Vice-Pres. Minister of Justice *ex officio*.

There are also *Tribunaux de Grande Instance* (County Courts) at Libreville, Port-Gentil, Lambaréné, Mouila, Oyem, Franceville and Koulamoutou.

RELIGION

Gabon is the most Christian of the states of the French Community in Africa. About 60 per cent of the population are Christians, Roman Catholics comprising 42 per cent of the total population. About 40 per cent are Animists and less than 1 per cent Muslims.

Roman Catholic Missions: Ste. Marie, Libreville, B.P. 2146.

There are 250,000 Roman Catholics with 36 missions, 100 priests, 57 brothers, 130 sisters and 251 schools with 37,494 pupils.

Archbishop of Libreville: Mgr. André Fernand Anguilé; B.P. 2146, Libreville.

Bishop of Mouila: Mgr. Raymond de la Moureyre; B.P. 95 Mouila.

Bishop of Oyem: Mgr. François Ndong; B.P. 100, Oyem.

Protestant Missions:

Eglise Evangélique du Gabon: B.P. 80, Libreville; f. 1842; the Church has 20 pastors, 180 African teachers, 4 colleges, 66 primary schools and 2 hospitals making a Christian community of about 60,000; Pres. Pastor S. Sima Ndone and Pastor S. Nang Essono.

Christian and Missionary Alliance: The Alliance devotes its activities to the south of the country. There is a total Christian community of 16,000, 7 pastors, 29 missionaries, 1 college and several primary schools with 20 teachers.

PRESS

Bulletin Evangélique d'Information et de Presse (BEIP): B.P. 80, Libreville; monthly; religious.

Bulletin mensuel de la Chambre de Commerce, d'Agriculture, d'Industrie et des Mines du Gabon: B.P. 110, Libreville; f. 1935.

Bulletin mensuel statistique de la République gabonaise: B.P. 179, Libreville; monthly bulletin of the National Service of Statistics.

Dialogue: Libreville; f. 1969; organ of the Parti démocratique gabonais; Chief Editor J.-J. Boucavel; monthly; circ. 3,000.

Gabon d'Aujourd'hui: B.P. 750, Libreville; weekly; published by the Ministry of Information.

Gabon-Matin: B.P. 168, Libreville; daily; published by the Agence Gabonaise de Presse; Man. Julien Loubendje; circ. 2,000.

Journal Officiel de la République Gabonaise: twice monthly.

Patrie gabonaise: B.P. 168, Libreville; monthly.

Le Patriote: B.P. 469, Libreville.

News Agencies

Agence Gabonaise de Presse: B.P. 168, Libreville.

Agence France-Presse: B.P. 472, rue Lamothe; correspondent Jean Burfin.

RADIO AND TELEVISION

RADIO

Radiodiffusion Télévision Gabonaise: B.P. 150, Libreville; government broadcasting corporation; Dir. of Radio and Television Capt. Ondias.

"La Voix de la Rénovation" 24 hours a day on short and medium wave bands in French and local languages. A 100kW. short wave transmitter at Libreville covers the whole country, but it is supplemented by relay stations at Franceville and Oyem. In 1971 there were 120,000 radio receivers.

TELEVISION

The 50W. transmitters at Libreville and Port-Gentil were supplemented in 1972 by two 2kW. transmitters, and coverage now extends inland as far as Kango and Lambaréné. In 1971 there were nearly 6,000 television sets.

FINANCE

BANKS

Central Bank

Banque des Etats de l'Afrique Centrale: 29 rue du Colisée, Paris 8e, France; B.P. 112, Libreville; f. 1973; central bank of five African states; cap. 1,250m. francs CFA; Gen. Man. C. Joudiou; Asst. Gen. Man. J.-E. Sathoud.

Banque Gabonaise de Développement: B.P. 5, Libreville; f. 1959; cap. 110m. francs CFA; Pres. of Admin. Council Michel Anchouey; Dir.-Gen. Jean Félix Mamalepot.

Banque Internationale pour l'Afrique Occidentale: 9 ave. de Messine, Paris 8e, France; B.P. 106, Libreville; f. 1965; cap. 66.2m. francs CFA; brs. in Port Gentil and Mouanda; Gabon Dir. Joseph Beyaert.

Banque Nationale de Paris: 16 Blvd. des Italiens, Paris, France; B.P. 41, Libreville; f. 1966; cap. 500m. F.Fr; res. 382m. F.Fr. (1971); br. in Port-Gentil; Gabon Dir. PAUL GILLOUX.

Union Gabonaise de Banque: B.P. 315, Libreville; f. 1962; cap. 450m. francs CFA; brs. in Port-Gentil and Franceville; Pres. P. NGUEMA; Gen. Man. J. P. CHASSANG.

DEVELOPMENT

Société Gabonaise de Financement et d'Expansion (SOGA-FINEX): Libreville; co-ordinates economic development of Gabon; participants include Gabonese, French and other foreign banks; Pres. G. GAVARRY.

Société Gabonaise de Participation et de Développement (SOGAPAR): B.P. 1624, Libreville; f. 1971; studies and promotes projects likely to contribute to Gabon's economic development; Dir.-Gen. O. MICHON.

Société Nationale d'Investissements du Gabon: B.P. 479, Libreville; state-owned investment company; Pres. Dir.-Gen. R. RADEMBINO-CONQUET.

INSURANCE

Agence Gabonaise d'Assurances: B.P. 131, Libreville; f. 1959; represents *Union des Assurances de Paris* and other French companies; Dir. MAURICE CHAILLOU.

Les Assureurs Conseils Gabonais: ave Savorgnan-de-Brazza, B.P. 272, Port-Gentil; B.P. 2138, Libreville; represents *Mutuelle-Générale Française Acc. et Mar.* (France), Commercial Union Co. Ltd. (U.K.), Guardian Assurance Co. Ltd. (U.K.), St. Paul Fire Assurance Co. Ltd. (U.K.)., *Groupe des Mutuelles du Mans* (France) and other foreign insurance companies; Dir. ROBERT PAOLETTI.

Mutuelle Agricole du Gabon: B.P. 2221, ave. du Colonel Parant; Assurance.

Société de Représentation d'Assurances et de Réassurances Africaines (SORARAF): B.P. 1023, Libreville; Dir. MARCEL GAUTIER.

Most of the major French insurers operate agencies in Gabon.

TRADE AND INDUSTRY

CHAMBER OF COMMERCE

Chambre de Commerce, d'Agriculture, d'Industrie et des Mines du Gabon: B.P. 110, Libreville; f 1935; regional offices at Port-Gentil, Oyem, Ndjolé, Tchibango, Lastoursville, Bitam, Makokou, Franceville, Mouila and Moanda; Pres. JEAN RÉMY AYOUNE.

DEVELOPMENT

Société pour le Développement de l'Afrique Equatoriale (SODAFE): B.P. 131, Libreville.

Société Gabonaise d'Elevage: B.P. 665, Libreville; f. 1962; stock-breeding development; Pres. JEAN DENDE.

NATIONAL AGENCIES

Agence Gabonaise de Promotion Industrielle et Artisanale (PROMO-GABON): B.P. 172, Libreville; supervises small light industries and crafts; Dir.-Gen. J.-P. LEMBOUMBA.

Office National des Bois du Gabon (ONBG): B.P. 67, Libreville; marketing of *okoumé* and ozigo woods; Dir. PIERRE BARBAUD.

Office National de Commercialisation Agricole (ONCA): B.P. 1283, Libreville; marketing of coffee, groundnuts and rice; Dir.-Gen. PAUL LOGI.

EMPLOYERS' FEDERATIONS

Syndicat des Commerçants Importateurs et Exportateurs (SIMPEX—Gabon): B.P. 1743, Libreville; Pres. G. CARRIÈRE; Sec.-Gen. M. TYBERGHEIN.

Syndicat des Entreprises Minières du Gabon: B.P. 578, Libreville; f. 1960; Pres. M. PORTAL; Sec.-Gen. C. L. DURAND.

Syndicat Forestier du Gabon: B.P. 84, Libreville; Pres. G. BOUILLOUX; Sec.-Gen. J. KIEFFER.

Syndicat Professionel des Usines de Sciages et Placages du Gabon: Pres. M. POUZIN.

Union Interprofessionnelle, Economique et Sociale du Gabon (UNIGABON): B.P. 84, Libreville; f. 1959; groups together the principal industrial, mining, public works, forestry and shipping concerns; Pres. M. VIALLET; Sec. Gen. J. KIEFFER.

Union des Représentations Automobiles et Industrielles (URAI): B.P. 1743, Libreville; Pres. M. BOREL; Sec. R. TYBERGHEIN.

TRADE UNIONS

Confédération Gabonaise des Travailleurs Croyants: B.P. 361, Libreville; f. 1956; 8,000 mems.; 19 affiliates; affiliated with the International Federation of Christian Trade Unions and the Pan-African Union of Christian Workers; Sec.-Gen. WALKER ANGUILET.

Fédération Générale des Travailleurs du Gabon: B.P. 1046, Libreville; f. 1962; 6,800 mems.; 4 affiliates; affiliated to ICFTU; Sec.-Gen. LAURENT ESSONE-NDONG.

Fédération Syndicale Gabonaise: B.P. 4017, Libreville; f. 1969 by the Government to organize and educate workers without discrimination on ethnic, religious or other grounds, to contribute to social peace and economic development and to protect the rights of trade unions; Pres. G. GOBA WORA; Sec.-Gen. G. INDASSY-GNAMBAULT.

TRANSPORT AND TOURISM

TRANSPORT

RAILWAYS

Office du Chemin de Fer Transgabonais: Ministère chargé de Mission, Libreville; Sec. PAUL MOUKAMBI.

The manganese mine at Moanda is connected with Pointe-Noire (Congo) by a 76-km. cableway and a 296-km. railway. Work was begun in January 1974 on the Trans-Gabon railway. The first stretch to be completed will be from Owendo to Booué (332 km.). The railway will eventually be extended to Bélinga in the north and Mouanan and Moanda in the south.

ROADS

The total network of 6,119 km. (1972) includes 2,792 km. main roads, 1,581 km. secondary roads and 1,746 km. other roads.

Société Africaine de Transit et d'Affrètement Gabon (SATA-GABON): B.P. 498, Libreville; road freight; Dir. J.-J. TARAIN.

SHIPPING AND INLAND WATERWAYS

The most important river is the Ogooué, navigable from Port-Gentil to N'Djolé (320 km.) and serving the towns of Lambaréné, N'Djolé and Sindara. River traffic, mainly timber, exceeded 408,000 metric tons in 1970.

The two principal ports are Port-Gentil (mainly for timber exports) and Libreville. A deep-water commercial port is under construction at Owendo.

Port de Libreville: B.P. 1051, Libreville; Dir. C. DAMAS.

Société Gabonaise de Transports Maritimes (GATRAMAR): Libreville; river and ocean transport.

Société Navale Chargeurs Delmas Vieljeux: B.P. 77, Libreville, and B.P. 522, Port-Gentil; Dirs. M. LAFARGUE (Libreville), M. MIGNOT (Port-Gentil).

Société Ouest Africaine d'Entreprises Maritimes (SOAEM): B.P. 72, Libreville and B.P. 518 Port-Gentil; shipping freight.

CIVIL AVIATION

There are international airports at Libreville, Port-Gentil and Franceville, 30 other public aerodromes and 55 private ones linked mostly with forestry and oil industries.

Air Afrique: B.P. 311, Libreville; Gabon has 6 per cent share in Air Afrique; *see* under Ivory Coast.

Air Gabon: B.P. 240, Port-Gentil; f. 1956; the fleet comprises one Beechcraft 18, one Cessna 150, three Britten-Norman Islanders, one B.-N. Trislander, two Piper Aztec, one Piper Seneca, two Piper Cherokee, one Navajo, one Twin Comanche and eight helicopters. Gen. Man. PIERRE NICAISE; Man. CHARLES GUILLO-TEAU.

Compagnie Gabonaise d'Affrètements Aériens (Affretair): Bld. de la Mer, Libreville; f. 1969; freight transport; fleet of one DC-8, five DC-7; Gen. Man. Cpt. JACK MALLOCH.

Transgabon (Société Nationale Transgabon): B.P. 2206, Libreville, and B.P. 199, Port-Gentil; f. 1951; internal cargo and passenger services; fleet of two DC-6, one DC-4, two HS.748, one DHC Caribou; Pres. PAUL OKUMBA D'OKWATSEGUE; Dir.-Gen. P. COLLET.

Libreville is also served by the following foreign airlines: Air Zaïre, Cameroon Airlines, Pan American, Swissair and UTA.

TOURISM

Office National Gabonais du Tourisme: B.P. 403, Libreville; Dir.-Gen. ATHANASE BOUANGA.

UNIVERSITY

Université Nationale du Gabon: Boulevard Léon M'Ba, Libreville; 50 teachers, 550 students.

THE GAMBIA
INTRODUCTORY SURVEY

Location, Climate, Language, Religion, Flag, Capital

The Gambia is a narrow territory around the River Gambia in West Africa, surrounded on three sides by Senegal. The climate is tropical, and away from the river swamps most of the country is savanna bush. The average annual temperature in the capital, Banjul, is 80°F (27°C). English is the official language; the principal vernacular languages are Mandinka, Fula and Wollof. The main religions are Islam and Christianity, with some adherents of animism. The National flag (proportions 3 by 2) has red, blue and green horizontal bands, with two narrow white stripes bordering the centre blue band. Banjul (previously Bathurst) is the capital.

Recent History

In 1962 a new constitution came into effect, and after a general election, the leader of the People's Progressive Party, Dr. (later Sir) Dawda K. Jawara, took office as Premier. Full internal self-government followed in October 1963 and the country has remained politically stable. In February 1965 The Gambia became an independent country within the Commonwealth and in April 1970 took Republican status. Special agreements with Senegal cover defence, external affairs and development of the Gambia River basin. In 1973 Sir Dawda Jawara visited Senegal for talks on proposed unification and said that he foresaw inevitable integration developing through economic co-operation.

Government

Legislative power is exercised by Parliament; the House of Representatives is made up of an elected Speaker, the Attorney-General, 32 elected members, four elected Head Chiefs, and four nominated members. Executive authority lies with the President, Vice-President and Cabinet.

Defence

There are no armed forces as such, but the police force is over 600 strong and there is a field force of about 300.

Economic Affairs

The economy is based on peasant cultivation of groundnuts which account for over 90 per cent of The Gambia's exports and make it particularly vulnerable to fluctuations in its harvests and world price changes. The acreage under rice is increasing, progress towards self-sufficiency being aided by Taiwan. Textiles and clothing are significant items of The Gambia's imports. The Senegalese-Gambian Inter-Ministerial Committee has been meeting since 1961, and in 1968 announced agreement in principle on a customs union but this has so far failed to materialize. Budgetary aid from the U.K. continued until 1967; the U.K. provides interest-free loans for development expenditure as well as technical assistance. The 1971–74 development plan is concentrating on developing agriculture and expanding transport and education facilities.

Transport and Communications

Roads in and near Banjul are bitumenized and this has now been extended to the provinces; 322 miles of about 800 miles of roads can be used in all seasons, but in outlying parts they may be closed during the rains, from mid-July to early November. There are no railways. However the Gambia River is the best waterway in Africa. The port of Banjul receives about 300 ships annually, and there are intermittent sailings to and from North Africa, the Mediterranean and the Far East. There is an airport of international standard outside Banjul at Yundum which is being further developed.

Social Welfare

There is a well-equipped modern hospital at Banjul, a small hospital at Bansang in the middle river area, and a network of health centres and dispensaries throughout the country. In addition, there is a tuberculosis sanatorium and a leprosy settlement; treatment for leprosy is available also at fifty clinics. Maternity and child welfare clinics are found at 21 centres.

Education

In The Gambia there are over 100 schools with about 25,000 pupils, half of these being at Banjul. Primary education is free but not compulsory. Gambia High School at Banjul provides full secondary courses to University entrance, and the Catholic Mission runs secondary schools. Education is being expanded in rural areas. In 1968 the literacy rate was estimated at around 15 per cent in English and about 20 per cent in Arabic.

Tourism

The Gambia has potential as a winter tourist resort and the industry is expanding rapidly. It is now second only to agriculture in importance. There is a haven for bird watchers, over 400 species of birds having been recorded.

Visas are not required to visit the Gambia by nationals of: Commonwealth countries, Dahomey, EEC countries (except France), Finland, Greece, Guinea, Iceland, Ivory Coast, Mali, Mauritania, Norway, San Marino, Spain, Sweden, Togo, Tunisia, Turkey and Uruguay.

Sport

Wrestling is the national sport, as well as fishing, sailing, shooting, golf, cricket, and association football.

Public Holidays

1974: August 15th (Assumption), October 18th (Id ul Fitr), December 25th (Christmas), December 26th (Id ul Kabir, Boxing Day).

1975: January 1st (New Year's Day), February 17th (Independence Day), March 26th (Birth of the Prophet), March 28th–March 31st (Easter), April 21st (Queen's Birthday), June 2nd (Commonwealth Day).

Weights and Measures

Imperial weights and measures are used. Importers and traders also use the metric system.

Currency and Exchange Rates

100 butut=1 dalasi.
Exchange rates (April 1974):
 £1 sterling=4.00 dalasi;
 U.S. $1=1.694 dalasi.

STATISTICAL SURVEY

Area: 4,261 square miles.

Population (1973 Census): 494,279; Banjul 39,476. Nearly half the inhabitants belong to the Mandinka tribe.

Employment (1973 est.): Government and Quasi-Government bodies 12,616, Commercial and others 4,107.

AGRICULTURE

PRINCIPAL CROPS
(Production—'000 metric tons)

	1969	1970	1971
Millet and Sorghum . .	45*	30*	45*
Rice (Paddy) . . .	66	50	60*
Cassava (Manioc) . .	6*	6*	n.a.
Bananas . . .	80	85	n.a.
Palm Kernels (exports only)	2	2	2*
Groundnuts (unshelled) .	114	117	117

* FAO estimate.

Source: FAO, *Production Yearbook 1971*.

Livestock (1973 est.): Cattle 270,000, Goats 100,000, Sheep 129,000, Pigs 3,000, Poultry 240,000.

FINANCE

100 butut = 1 dalasi.

Coins: 1, 5, 10, 25 and 50 butut.

Notes: 1, 5 and 25 dalasi.

Exchange rates (April 1974): £1 sterling = 4.00 dalasi; U.S. $1 = 1.694 dalasi.
100 dalasi = £25.00 = $59.03.

Note: The dalasi was introduced on July 1st, 1971, replacing the Gambia pound (G£1 = £1 sterling) at the rate of G£1 = 5.00 dalasi. This exchange rate was maintained until March 1973. Some of the figures below are given in G£.

BUDGET
RECURRENT REVENUE AND EXPENDITURE
(dalasi)

	1972–73	1973–74*
Revenue . . .	21,194,744	20,658,330
Expenditure . . .	21,055,330	22,279,290
Balance . . .	139,414	−1,620,960

* Estimates.

Four-Year Plan (1971-74): 21,000,000 dalasi; Communications 10,197,000; Agriculture 4,135,375; Education 1,195,000.

EXTERNAL TRADE
Twelve months ending June 30th
(dalasi '000)

	1968–69	1969–70	1970–71	1971–72	1972–73
Imports . . .	46,644	35,545	42,587	46,216	54,426
Exports . . .	36,886	32,592	30,660	36,039	26,430

COMMODITIES
(dalasi)

IMPORTS	1970–71	1971–72	1972–73
Food and Live Animals . . .	7,824,365	6,700,167	8,119,695
Beverages and Tobacco . . .	3,057,855	2,916,281	3,039,481
Crude Materials (inedible) except Fuels .	1,334,665	1,902,764	2,511,694
Mineral Fuels, Lubricants, etc. . .	1,320,945	1,601,700	2,489,872
Animal and Vegetable Oils and Fats .	17,825	19,161	97,959
Chemicals . . .	2,940,350	3,579,822	4,317,737
Basic Manufactured Goods . .	15,295,560	16,824,056	19,499,388
Textile Yarn and Fabrics . .	10,589,860	12,234,433	n.a.
Machinery and Transport Equipment .	6,294,870	7,721,572	8,405,247
Miscellaneous Manufactured Articles .	3,404,865	3,631,800	4,629,544
Other Commodities . . .	1,095,765	1,319,012	1,318,241
TOTAL . . .	42,587,065	46,216,335	54,425,859

EXPORTS	UNIT	1970–71 Quantity	1970–71 Value (dalasi)	1971–72 Quantity	1971–72 Value (dalasi)
Groundnuts, Shelled . . .	long tons	30,578	14,964,650	45,714	19,994,168
Groundnut Meal and Cake . .	,, ,,	12,800	3,348,290	14,280	3,009,905
Groundnut Oil . . .	,, ,,	14,032	10,495,065	13,871	11,060,614
Palm Kernels and Palm Nuts . .	,, ,,	2,208	737,310	2,100	454,691
Fish and Fish Preparations . .	cwt.	15,404	210,835	22,921	413,554
Hides and Skins . . .	,, ,,	1,469	80,800	1,878	107,457

1972/73 (value in dalasi)· Shelled Groundnuts 6,062,310, Groundnut Meal and Cake 1,907,464, Groundnut Oil 4,150,991.

PRINCIPAL COUNTRIES

(dalasi)

IMPORTS	1969–70	1970–71	1971–72
Burma	1,548,160	1,486,545	1,402,407
China (Taiwan)	2,950,220	3,364,435	4,031,707
France	1,053,975	1,746,970	1,815,798
Germany, Federal Republic	1,221,715	1,179,190	1,616,552
Hong Kong	904,325	1,196,090	750,819
Japan	4,387,370	6,984,490	7,880,084
Netherlands	674,015	1,372,715	1,126,456
Senegal	310,340	469,730	1,467,294
United Kingdom	11,798,590	12,764,515	14,757,766
U.S.A.	900,075	1,080,760	1,007,616
TOTAL (incl. others)	35,544,580	42,587,065	46,216,335

EXPORTS	1969–70	1970–71	1971–72
France	3,092,010	6,253,640	7,591,304
Germany, Federal Republic	2,921,740	26,490	296,019
Italy	1,265,070	2,476,055	5,625,279
Netherlands	4,365,425	5,115,540	1,196,720
Portugal	1,061,360	1,201,985	4,794,938
Senegal	25,530	107,735	117,731
Switzerland	4,020,560	—	280,545
United Kingdom	15,442,760	14,805,130	14,034,660
TOTAL (incl. others)	32,591,825	30,659,740	36,039,070

Source: External Trade Statistics of The Gambia 1969/70–1971/72.

TRANSPORT

Roads (1972–73): Cars and Commercial Vehicles 5,831 (licences issued).

Shipping (1972–73): Principal port Banjul; Ships entered 306, Tonnage entered 668,879.

Civil Aviation (1968): 1,948 planes landed.

EDUCATION

(1972–73)

	SCHOOLS	TEACHERS	PUPILS
Primary	95	414	19,421
Secondary	22	190	5,373
Vocational	2	13	178
Teacher Training	1	16	148

Sources (unless stated): President's Office, Banjul; Standard Bank *Annual Economic Review: Sierra Leone & The Gambia*, August 1971 and November 1973.

THE CONSTITUTION

The present Constitution came into effect on April 24th, 1970, when The Gambia became a Republic.

The President is Head of State and Commander-in-Chief of the armed forces. There is a Vice-President who is leader of government business in the House.

The House of Representatives consists of a Speaker and a Deputy Speaker (elected by the House) and 32 Members (elected by universal adult suffrage), 4 Chiefs (elected by the Chiefs in Assembly), 3 nominated Members, and the Attorney-General. Parliaments have a five-year term.

THE GOVERNMENT
PRESIDENT AND CABINET
(June 1974)

President: Sir Dawda K. Jawara.

Vice-President and Minister of External Affairs: Andrew D. Camara.

Minister of Finance: J. M. Garba-Jahumpa.

Minister of Education: Alhaji M. C. Cham.

Minister of Health and Labour: Alhaji K. Singateh.

Minister of State, President's Office: B. L. K. Sanyang.

Minister of Agriculture: Alhaji Alieu Badara N'Jie.

Minister of Local Government: Alhaji Yaya Ceasay.

Minister of Works and Communications: Alhaji Sir Alieu Suleyman Jack.

Attorney-General: Alhaji M. L. Saho.

DIPLOMATIC REPRESENTATION

HIGH COMMISSIONS AND EMBASSIES
ACCREDITED TO THE GAMBIA
(In Banjul unless otherwise stated)
(HC) High Commission; (E) Embassy.

Algeria: Dakar, Senegal (E).

Austria: Dakar, Senegal (E).

Belgium: Dakar, Senegal (E).

Canada: Dakar, Senegal (HC).

China (Taiwan): (E); *Ambassador:* Dr. Mei-sheng Shu.

Czechoslovakia: Dakar, Senegal (E).

Egypt: Dakar, Senegal (E).

France: Dakar, Senegal (E).

German Democratic Republic: Conakry, Guinea (E).

Germany, Federal Republic: Dakar, Senegal (E).

Ghana: Dakar, Senegal (HC).

India: Dakar, Senegal (HC).

Italy: Dakar, Senegal (E).

Japan: Dakar, Senegal (E).

Korea, Republic: London, England (E).

Lebanon: Dakar, Senegal (E).

Liberia: Freetown, Sierra Leone (E).

Libya: Nouakchott, Mauritania (E).

Mali: Dakar, Senegal (E).

Mauritania: Dakar, Senegal (E).

Morocco: Dakar, Senegal (E).

Netherlands: Dakar, Senegal (E).

Nigeria: Independence Drive (HC); *High Commissioner:* H. A. Bayero (acting).

Pakistan: Dakar, Senegal (E).

Romania: Conakry, Guinea (E).

Senegal: Cameroon St. (E); *Ambassador:* Saher Gaye.

Sierra Leone: Leman St. (HC); *High Commissioner:* Alieu Badra Mansaray.

Spain: Dakar, Senegal (E).

Sweden: Rabat, Morocco (E).

Switzerland: Dakar, Senegal (E).

Tunisia: Dakar, Senegal (E).

Turkey: Dakar, Senegal (E).

U.S.S.R.: Dakar, Senegal (E).

United Kingdom: 78 Wellington St. (HC); *High Commissioner:* J. R. W. Parker.

U.S.A.: Cameroon St. (E); *Ambassador:* Rudolph Aggrey.

Viet-Nam, Republic: Monrovia, Liberia (E).

Zambia: Abidjan, Ivory Coast (HC).

The Gambia also has diplomatic relations with Bangladesh, Guinea, Hungary and the Democratic People's Republic of Korea.

NATIONAL ASSEMBLY
(Election March 1972)

	Seats
People's Progressive Party	27*
United Party	3
Independent	2

* 28 seats in 1972 election.

Speaker: Dr. S. H. O. Jones, c.b.e.

Nominated Members (without vote): Alhaji Sir Alieu Suleyman Jack, M. B. N'Jie, Jallow Sanneh, The Attorney-General.

POLITICAL PARTIES

People's Progressive Party (PPP): f. 1958; Leader Sir Dawda Jawara; advocates economic and cultural links with Senegal; merged with Gambia Congress Party 1968.

United Party (UP): P.O.B. 63, Buckle St., Banjul; f. 1952; approx. 131,000 mems.; Leader J. R. Forster; Gen. Sec. Coun. K. W. Foon.

JUDICIAL SYSTEM

The judicial system of the Gambia is based on English Common Law but includes subsidiary legislative instruments enacted locally, and a Muslim Law Recognition Ordinance by which a Muslim Court exercises jurisdiction in certain cases between, or exclusively affecting, Muslims.

The Supreme Court: Consists of the Chief Justice and the Puisne Judge; has unlimited jurisdiction; appeal lies to the Court of Appeal.

Chief Justice: Sir P. R. Bridges, q.c., c.m.g.

Puisne Judge: A. Nithianandan.

Master and Registrar: O. S. Batchilly.

The Gambia Court of Appeal: Established in 1961. It is the Superior Court of Record and consists of a President, Justices of Appeal and other Judges of the Supreme Court *ex officio*.

President: C. F. DOVE EDWIN (acting).

Justice of Appeal: J. B. MARCUS JONES.

The Banjul Magistrates Court, the Kanifing Magistrates Court and the **Divisional Courts:** the subordinate courts, are all courts of summary jurisdiction presided over by a Magistrate or in his absence by two or more lay Justices of the Peace. They have limited civil and criminal jurisdiction, and appeal lies from these courts to the Supreme Court.

The Muslim Courts have jurisdiction in matters between, or exclusively affecting, Muslim Gambians and relating to civil status, marriage, succession, donations, testaments and guardianship. The Courts administer Muslim Law. A Cadi, or a Cadi and two assessors, preside over and constitute a Muslim Court. Assessors of the Muslim Courts are Justices of the Peace of Muslim faith.

Group Tribunals are established by the Government under the Group Tribunals Ordinance, 1933. Group Tribunals may try criminal cases which can be adequately punished by 12 months' imprisonment or a fine of £25 or both, and civil cases up to a £50 suit value. Their jurisdiction in land matters is unlimited.

RELIGION

ISLAM

Imam of Banjul: Alhaji MOMODU LAMIN BAH.

The vast majority of the people are Muslims.

AFRICAN RELIGIONS

There are a few animists, mostly of the Jola tribe.

ANGLICAN

PROVINCE OF WEST AFRICA

Archbishop of the Province of West Africa and Bishop of Sierra Leone: Most. Rev. M. N. C. O. SCOTT, D.D., DIP.TH., Bishopscourt, P.O.B. 128, Freetown, Sierra Leone.

Bishop of the Gambia and the Rio Pongas: Rt. Rev. JEAN RIGAL ELISEE, M.A., Bishop's House, P.O.B. 51, Banjul.

ROMAN CATHOLIC

Bishop of Banjul: Most Rev. MICHAEL J. MOLONEY, C.B.E., C.S.SP., D.D.

OTHER CHURCHES

Methodist Church: Rev. C. F. H. ALLEYNE, P.O.B. 288, Banjul.

THE PRESS

Gambia Echo: 2 Russell St., Banjul; f. 1934; weekly; circ. 500; Editor J. R. FORSTER.

Gambia News Bulletin: Banjul; Government newspaper issued 3 times weekly; Editor the Dir. of Information and Broadcasting Services, Banjul; circ. 2,000.

Gambia Onward: Banjul; 3 times weekly; duplicated; Editor R. ALLEN.

Gambia Outlook: Banjul; 3 times weekly; Editor M. B. JONES.

The Nation: People's Press Printers, P.O.B. 334, Banjul; fortnightly; Editor W. DIXON-COLLEY.

Progressive: Banjul; 3 times weekly; duplicated; Editor M'BAKE N'JIE.

The Worker: 3 times weekly; Editor PIERRE M. SOCK.

RADIO

Radio Gambia: Banjul; f. 1962; non-commercial government service of information, education and entertainment; English, Wollof and Mandinka; 60,000 receivers in 1973.

Radio Syd: P.O.B. 280, Banjul; commercial station; broadcasts in English, French, Wollof and Mandinka; tourist information in Swedish; Dir. Mrs. B. WADNER.

There is no television service in The Gambia.

FINANCE

BANKING

Banque Internationale pour le Commerce et Industrie du Senegal: Banjul.

Central Bank of the Gambia: 3–4 Buckle St., Banjul; Gov. SHERIFF S. SISAY; Gen. Man. N. D. NANGIA; publs. *Quarterly Bulletin, Annual Report*.

Commercial and Development Bank of The Gambia: 78–79 Leman St., Banjul; f. 1972; Gen. Man. OUSAINOU N'JIE.

Standard Bank of West Africa Ltd.: P.O.B. 259–260, Banjul; f. 1916; Head Office: 37 Gracechurch St., London, E.C.3.

INSURANCE

Banjul

Compagnie Française de L'Afrique Occidentale—C.F.A.O., S.A.: Marseille; Rep. P.O.B. 297.

The Gambia Insurance Co. Ltd.: 78–79 Leman St.

Guardian Royal Exchange Assurance Co. Ltd.: London; Rep. Standard Bank of West Africa Ltd., P.O.B. 259-260.

Motor Union Insurance Co. Ltd.: London; Rep. Maurel et Prom.

Northern Assurance Co. Ltd.: London; Rep. United Africa Co. of Gambia Ltd.

White Cross Insurance Co. Ltd.: London; Rep. Compagnie Française de l'Afrique Occidentale, P.O.B. 297.

TRADE AND INDUSTRY

CHAMBER OF COMMERCE

Gambia Chamber of Commerce: P.O.B. 333, Banjul; f. 1961; affiliated to Commonwealth Chamber of Commerce, London; Pres. R. MADI; Sec. P. W. F. N'JIE.

MARKETING ORGANIZATIONS

Gambia Produce Marketing Board: Marina Foreshore, Banjul; Chair. L. C. CHERY; Gen. Man. A. DRAPER.

Gambia Co-operative Banking and Marketing Union: 4 MacCarthy Square, Banjul; Sec.-Man. M. M. JALLOW.

EMPLOYERS' ASSOCIATION

Gambia Employers' Association: P.O.B. 333, Banjul; f. 1961; affiliated to the Overseas Employers' Federation, London; Chair. J. MADI; Sec. P. W. F. N'JIE.

TRADE UNIONS

Gambia Labour Union: 21 Clarkson St., P.O.B. 508, Banjul; f. 1928; 6,000 mems.; affiliated to the World Confederation of Labour (formerly IFCTU); Pres. B. B. KEBBEH; Gen. Sec. M. S. CEESAY.

Gambia Trades and Dealers' Union: f. 1960.

Gambia Workers' Union: 68 Hagan St., Banjul; f. 1958; Sec. M. E. JALLOW.

Pan-African Workers' Congress: P.O.B. 307, Banjul; affiliated to WCL; Sec. and Vice-Pres. of WCL G. PONGAULT.

CO-OPERATIVE UNION

Gambia Co-operative Union Ltd.: P.O.B. 505, Banjul; Sec.-Man. D. E. K. SANNEH.

TRANSPORT

ROADS

At the beginning of 1965 there were 322 miles of all-season roads in The Gambia, about 130 bitumenized and over 180 all-season laterite surface. There are about 470 miles of local roads available in the dry season (December–July) but closed during the rains. The South Bank trunk road, linking Banjul with the Trans-Gambia highway, was completed during 1963 and is being extended to Basse.

Improvements to the Trans-Gambian Ferry were discussed at the Senegalese-Gambian Inter-Ministerial Committee meeting in February 1969.

SHIPPING

Gambia Ports Authority: runs Banjul port, now undergoing substantial expansion with a World Bank loan and is scheduled for completion in 1974.

Regular shipping services to Banjul are maintained by **Elder Dempster Lines** and **Palm Lines**. Other British and Scandinavian lines run occasional services. The Gambia is also served by **Nigerian National** and **Black Star** Lines.

A weekly river service is maintained between Banjul and Basse.

CIVIL AVIATION

Gambia Airways: P.O.B. 268, Banjul; handling agency only; operated in partnership with British Caledonian Airways, Gambian Government majority shareholding from June 1973; owns no aircraft; Gen. Man. A. G. BATCHILY.

The only airport is at Yundum, 17 miles from Banjul. It is to be modernized with British aid and the project should be completed at the end of 1974.

FOREIGN AIRLINES

Air Senegal: Banjul.
British Caledonian Airways: P.O.B. 268, Banjul.
Ghana Airways.
Nigeria Airways: WAAC (Nigeria) Ltd., 11-12 Buckle St., P.O.B. 272, Banjul; Rep. SHAFI'I A. USUF.

TOURISM

17,000 tourists visited The Gambia in 1972–73 and an estimated 29,000 in 1973–74.

GHANA

INTRODUCTORY SURVEY

Location, Climate, Language, Religion, Flag, Capital

Ghana lies on the west coast of Africa between the Ivory Coast and Togo. The climate is tropical with temperatures of 70°–90°F (21°–32°C) and rainfall of 80 inches a year on the coast, decreasing inland. English is the official language, but there are eight major national languages. Many people follow traditional beliefs and customs. Christians make up 42 per cent of the population. The national flag (proportions 3 by 2) has three horizontal stripes of red, gold and green, the gold stripe being charged with a five-pointed black star. The capital is Accra.

Recent History

Formerly the British Crown Colony of the Gold Coast, Ghana became independent in 1957. Under Dr. Kwame Nkrumah, who attained a unique status as Africa's most charismatic leader, Ghana played a leading part in forming two African Groups, subsequently dissolved: the Union of African States and the Casablanca Group.

In 1966, President Nkrumah was overthrown by a *coup d'état* and a National Liberation Council (NLC) of army and police personnel was established to rule by decree. On August 22nd, 1969, the Constituent Assembly, set up by the NLC, promulgated the constitution of the Second Republic of Ghana, and, after general elections on August 29th, the return to civilian rule took place. Dr. Kofi Busia and the Progress Party formed the first government under a new democratic constitution, headed by a triumvirate-presidency.

In the wake of increasing economic troubles, which resulted in a 44 per cent devaluation of the cedi in December 1971, and moves against opposition to the Progress Party in the army, civil service and trade unions, the army seized power again on January 13th, 1972. Under the leadership of Lt.-Col. Ignatius Acheampong, the army detained ministers and other government officials (Dr. Busia was out of the country at the time), abolished the constitution and all political institutions, and established a National Redemption Council (NRC). The NRC has been mainly involved with Ghana's internal problems and remains firmly in control. A plot to overthrow it was uncovered in its early stages in July 1972. There are no plans to return Ghana to civilian rule, though in January 1974 Col. Acheampong indicated that civilians would be appointed to several bodies with advisory status to the NRC.

Government

The 1969 Constitution provided for a President, elected by an electoral college, a Prime Minister appointed by the President from the majority party in the Assembly and a National Assembly. Safeguards against abuse of power, such as interference with elections, the judiciary, the press etc., were written into the constitution. It was abolished in January 1972 following the army *coup d'état*, and the governing body is the National Redemption Council headed by Col. Acheampong.

Defence

The defence forces consist of units of the army (16,000), air force (1,600) and navy (1,300). There is a police force of about 9,000, a workers' brigade of 3,000 and three Border Guard battalions. The headquarters of the Defence Commission of the Organization of African Unity is in Accra.

Economic Affairs

Ghana is primarily an agricultural country, and cocoa, of which she is the world's largest producer, is by far the largest export. In 1971 Ghana's economy was badly hit by a sharp decline in world cocoa prices on which it largely depended. Other cash crops include copra, palm oil and kernels, coffee and kola nuts. Over 100 farms are state run. Hardwoods, diamonds and gold are also important. Industrial development is mainly concerned with processing food and raw materials for export. A scheme was launched, with international aid, to exploit the water power of the Volta River, and in January 1966 the main dam at Akosombo was inaugurated. The Volta River scheme has since been expanded and in December 1972 Ghana began supplying power to Togo and Dahomey under an agreement signed in 1969. Ghana opened an oil refinery in 1963, and at the end of 1968 signed agreements with two American companies for the exploration and exploitation of oil both inland and off-shore. An aluminium smelting plant, built as part of the Volta River project, began production in 1967. It is also planned to reclaim 75,000 acres of land in the Volta Region for agriculture.

The Busia government's 44 per cent devaluation of the cedi was partially rescinded by the new military régime in February 1972. The régime repudiated most of Ghana's medium-term debt and has embarked on a programme of stringent import controls. In 1972 Ghana had a trade surplus of 173.9 million cedis and reserves of foreign exchange had risen from 18.7 million cedis in 1971 to 142.4 million cedis in 1972. Numerous foreign companies have been nationalized and a selective alien employment tax was introduced in the 1973–74 Budget. A new long-term Development Plan (1974/75–1979/80) is soon to be introduced.

Transport and Communications

The rail network forms a rough triangle linking Accra and Takoradi on the coast with the inland centre of Kumasi. Road traffic is of increasing importance, the Government operating cross-country bus services. Construction began in 1964 on a metalled road link to the Ivory Coast. National air and shipping lines have been formed and a satellite communications station is to be built outside Accra in 1974. A project to rehabilitate several hundred miles of road is being financed by the International Development Association.

Social Welfare

The Government provides hospitals and medical care at nominal rates, and there is a Government pension scheme. The Department of Social Welfare and Community Development deals with both urban and rural problems including the need to improve literacy, child welfare and factory legislation.

Education

Primary, secondary and technical education are free and compulsory. Despite initial cuts in state aid, the educational system in Ghana has been expanded and diversified since the NRC took power in 1972, and major changes in its structure are expected. There are two universities with over 4,000 students and a new university college has been set up at Cape Coast.

Tourism

Ghana is seeking to develop her tourist trade. The attractions include fine beaches, game reserves, and old trading forts and castles.

Visas are not required to visit Ghana by nationals of: Commonwealth countries, Denmark, Federal Republic of Germany, Ivory Coast, Togo and Upper Volta.

Sport

Ghana's national sport is football and the country's team has won the West African Football Competition three times. Horse racing, tennis, boxing and athletics are popular. The Central Organization of Sports was established in 1960 to develop an active participation in sport and athletics.

Public Holidays

1975: August 5th (Bank Holiday), December 25th–26th (Christmas).

1974: January 1st (New Year's Day), January 13th (National Redemption Day), March 6th (Independence Day), March 28th–March 31st (Easter).

Weights and Measures

The imperial system is in use.

Currency and Exchange Rates

100 pesewas = 1 new cedi.

Exchange rates (April 1974):

£1 sterling = 2.715 cedis;
U.S. $1 = 1.15 cedis.

STATISTICAL SURVEY

AREA AND POPULATION

REGION	1970* POPULATION	1960 POPULATION	PER CENT INCREASE (1960–70)	AVERAGE ANNUAL INCREASE (%)	POPULATION DENSITY (per sq. mile)
All Regions . . .	8,545,561	6,726,815	27.04	2.4	93
Western . . .	768,312	626,155	22.70	2.1	83
Central . . .	892,593	751,392	18.79	1.7	234
Greater Accra . . .	848,825	491,817	72.59	5.6	853
Eastern . . .	1,262,882	1,094,196	15.42	1.5	164
Volta . . .	947,012	777,285	21.84	2.0	119
Ashanti . . .	1,477,397	1,109,133	33.20	2.9	157
Brong-Ahafo . . .	762,673	587,920	29.72	2.7	50
Northern . . .	728,572	531,573	37.06	3.2	27
Upper . . .	857,295	757,344	13.20	1.3	81

* Preliminary Census figures. Revised total is 8,559,313.

Estimated Population: 9,087,000 (July 1st, 1972).

Chief Tribal Groups (1960 census) (per cent): Akan 44, Mole-Dagbani 15.9, Ewe 13, Ga-Adangbe 8.3, Guan 3.7, Gurma 3.5.

Area: 92,100 sq. miles (238,537 sq. km.).

PRINCIPAL TOWNS
(1970 Census)

	CITY PROPER	CONURBATION
Accra (Capital) . .	636,067	738,498*
Kumasi . . .	260,286	345,117
Tamala . . .	83,653	—
Tema . . .	60,767	—
Takoradi . . .	58,161	160,868†
Cape Coast . . .	51,653	—
Sekondi . . .	33,713	—

*Accra-Tema Metropolitan Area.
†Sekondi-Takoradi City Council.

EMPLOYMENT
PERSONS ENGAGED IN WAGE-EARNING EMPLOYMENT

	1967	1968	1969	1970
Agriculture, Forestry and Fishing	43,659	47,536	46,516	48,929
Mining and Quarrying	26,299	26,236	25,955	25,248
Manufacturing	41,155	44,849	52,874	52,785
Construction	47,790	54,783	57,467	49,993
Electricity, Water and Sanitary Services	14,381	16,023	17,642	14,780
Commerce	35,628	36,913	35,930	35,929
Transport, Storage and Communications	29,962	36,374	29,571	32,543
Services	122,477	128,547	134,859	137,761
	361,351	391,261	400,814	397,968

AGRICULTURE
PRINCIPAL CROPS
('ooo metric tons)

	1969	1970	1971
Sugar Cane†	284	522	374
Maize	304	442	430*
Millet	88	93	100*
Sorghum	83	86	110*
Rice (paddy)	61	69	70*
Sweet Potatoes and Yams	1,305	1,642	909
Cassava (Manioc)	1,320	1,596	n.a.
Onions	17*	17*	n.a.
Tomatoes	35	37	n.a.
Oranges and Tangerines	63	71	60*
Other Citrus Fruits	26	26	26*
Pineapples	26	30	n.a.
Palm Kernels	34	37	37
Palm Oil	55	60	60
Groundnuts (unshelled)	61	60	70*
Coconuts (million nuts)	168	201	n.a.
Copra and Coconut Oil (exports only)	3	3	3*
Coffee	5.7	4.5	5.1
Cocoa Beans (purchases for export)‡	327.0	414.3	396.2

* FAO estimates.   † Figures relate to crop year ending in year stated.
‡ Figures relate to 12-month period ending September 30th of year stated. 1971/72: 437,000 metric tons (provisional total).

Source: FAO, *Production Yearbook 1971.*

COCOA EXPORTS

	TOTAL		UNITED KINGDOM		REST OF STERLING AREA		UNITED STATES	
	Tons	Value £'ooo	Tons	Value £'ooo	Tons	Value £'ooo	Tons	Value £'ooo
1969	121,335	79,145	40,050	26,225	17,725	12,008	63,560	40,912
1970	154,527	122,219	30,435	26,279	21,580	19,005	102,512	76,935
1971	118,350	75,056	21,999	14,431	12,925	8,466	83,426	52,159
1972	138,096	96,667	43,292	31,389	23,050	16,883	71,754	48,395

LIVESTOCK

	1970	1971
Horses .	4,000*	4,000*
Asses .	23,000*	24,000*
Cattle .	903,000	933,000
Pigs .	268,000	200,000
Sheep .	1,339,900	1,449,000
Goats .	1,412,400	1,694,000
Poultry .	8,874,000	11,279,000

* FAO estimates.

FISHING
('ooo tons)

	1968	1969	1970
Herring .	12.2	30.4	26.9
Trawl Fish .	23.2	38.4	50.0
Line Fish .	5.3	1.8	8.0
Unsorted .	25.2	40.8	24.2
Tuna .	24.6	23.6	—
TOTAL .	90.5	135.0	109.1

FORESTRY
(million cu. ft.)

	1968	1969	1970	1971
Logs .	49	56	55	57
Sawn .	12	13	13	12

MINING

	1968	1969	1970	1971	1972
Gold ('ooo fine oz. troy) .	740	707	704	698	724
Diamonds ('ooo carats) .	2,447	2,391	2,550	2,562	2,659*
African diggers .	16	7	8	118	107
Companies .	2,431	2,384	2,542	2,444	2,552
Manganese ('ooo tons) .	407	328	392	459	501
Bauxite ('ooo tons) .	280	242	337	323	335

* Provisional.

INDUSTRY
(1970—over 10 employees)

	WORKS	EMPLOYEES
Food (except Milling and Bakery) .	14	5,744
Bakery .	20	539
Beverages, Tobacco .	16	2,871
Textiles, Clothes .	10	5,219
Wood (except furniture) .	45	11,677
Furniture, Fixtures .	15	900
Printing, Publishing .	35	3,695
Leather .	5	273
Chemicals .	17	1,459
Non-metallic products .	1	203
Metals, Machinery .	17	3,504
Body Making, Car and Cycle repairs .	46	5,636
Miscellaneous .	13	885

FINANCE

100 pesewas=1 new cedi.

Coins: $\frac{1}{2}$, 1, 2$\frac{1}{2}$, 5, 10 and 20 pesewas.

Notes: 1, 2, 5 and 10 cedis.

Exchange rates (April 1974): £1 sterling=2.715 cedis; U.S. $1=1.15 cedis.

100 cedis=£36.83=$86.96.

(*Note:* Between November 1967 and August 1971 the central exchange rates were £1=2.449 cedis=$2.40.)

BUDGET
(Estimate for year ending June 30th, 1973—cedis '000)

REVENUE		EXPENDITURE	CURRENT	DEVELOPMENT
Export Duty on Cocoa . . .	87,300	Agriculture	30,411	8,905
Taxes, etc.	236,381	Lands and Mineral Resources .	5,752	5,073
Other Items	78,385	Trade, Industry and Tourism .	1,822	383
		Construction	22,083	42,559
		Transport and Communications .	2,728	2,307
TOTAL . . .	402,066	Education	99,595	6,914
		Health	33,356	7,177
		Labour, Social Welfare and Co-operation . . .	6,373	4,254
		Internal Affairs . . .	19,878	1,552
		Local Government . . .	3,578	2,169
		General Administration . .	23,485	5,213
		Administration of Justice .	3,859	237
		Fiscal Administration . .	31,874	6,155
		Foreign Affairs . . .	8,835	149
		Defence	37,953	7,300
		Statutory Expenditure (Finance Services) . . .	171,457	—
		TOTAL . . .	503,040	100,347

NATIONAL ACCOUNTS
(million cedis)

	1967	1968	1969	1970
AVAILABLE RESOURCES:				
Private consumption expenditure .	1,286	1,467	1,626	1,760
General government consumption expenditure .	308	363	412	450
Gross domestic fixed capital formation, including stocks	219	234	259	324
Exports	265	368	425	496
	2,078	2,432	2,722	3,030
USES OF RESOURCES:				
Gross domestic product . . .	1,778	2,074	2,328	2,565
Imports	300	358	394	465
	2,078	2,432	2,722	3,030

CURRENCY AND RESERVES

	1969	1970	1971	1972
Currency in Circulation (cedis '000) . .	163,846	167,047	176,564	255,837
Gold Reserve Holdings (U.S. $'000) . .	5,592	5,595	6,068	6,074

BALANCE OF PAYMENTS
(million cedis)

	1968	1969	1970
Current Account:			
Visible trade:			
Exports	281.5	326.2	409.8
Imports (f.o.b.)	−266.9	−296.0	−387.0
Trade balance	14.6	30.2	22.8
Invisible balance	− 52.6	− 69.7	− 89.8
Transfer payments	− 13.5	− 12.6	− 9.6
Balance on Current Account . .	− 51.5	− 52.1	− 76.6
Capital Account:			
Balance on Capital Account . .	48.5	61.5	75.5
Overall Surplus or Deficit	− 3.0	9.4	− 1.1
Monetary Institutions:			
IMF account	11.2	− 5.5	− 23.7
Special Drawing Rights . . .	—	—	11.8
Central Bank	− 3.4	− 13.2	1.5
Commercial Banks	− 2.6	16.2	− 11.3
Total Monetary Institutions . .	5.2	− 2.5	− 21.7
Net Unrecorded Items	− 2.2	− 6.9	22.8

Source: Standard Bank Review, March 1972.

FOREIGN AID*
(million U.S. $)

Source	Total up to 1964	Total up to 1967	1967	1968	1969	1970
United States Grants	16.0	22.3	3.6†	2.0	2.7	2.7
United States Credits	14.3	44.4	32.5	18.3	26.9	30.1
IBRD Loans	26.0	46.5	—	0.2	—	—
Other International Agency Aid . .	9.0	86.0	25.0	9.9	10.8	—
Other Western Aid	10.0	25.3	20.3	15.9	22.1	18.5
Soviet Aid	104.2	129.4	10.4	—	15.6	—
People's Republic of China . . .	42.0	43.1	—	—	—	—
Czechoslovakia	14.0	34.6	4.2	—	—	—
Other Communist Aid . . .	59.7	69.8	3.9	1.1	0.3	—

* Provisional.   † Financial Year Basis.

EXTERNAL TRADE

	('000 cedis)						
	1967	1968	1969	1970	1971	1972	1973*
Imports	261,523	314,032	354,391	419,047	443,142	393,293	334,487
Exports, incl. re-exports .	245,122	338,782	333,264	467,378	357,484	564,412	494,910

* January–August.

COMMODITIES
('ooo cedis)

IMPORTS	1970	1971	1972	1973*
Food	79,474	62,510	72,221	67,513
Beverages and Tobacco	3,924	4,624	2,342	3,411
Crude Materials	9,420	12,368	13,244	17,821
Mineral Fuels	24,358	27,030	45,297	27,360
Oils and Fats	3,835	5,246	5,217	4,073
Chemicals	66,874	71,607	63,896	62,153
Manufactures	100,847	99,361	68,196	63,052
Machinery	108,132	131,511	104,294	72,771
Miscellaneous Items	16,376	19,201	11,310	9,318
Other Transactions . . .	5,807	9,684	7,276	7,015

EXPORTS	1970	1971	1972	1973*
Cocoa	300,399	195,066	289,058	266,618
Logs	19,875	20,536	42,292	54,139
Sawn Timber	17,096	12,217	21,173	24,463
Bauxite	1,276	2,290	2,682	1,697
Manganese Ore	7,209	9,640	10,075	6,425
Diamonds	14,467	11,752	18,643	9,013
Gold	25,695	28,454	50,436	45,703
Re-exports and Other Items . .	81,361	77,529	130,053	86,852

* January–August.

COUNTRIES
('ooo cedis)

IMPORTS	1970	1971	1972	1973*
United Kingdom	99,068	110,721	61,209	56,627
Canada	4,637	4,297	10,524	6,506
Hong Kong	6,284	4,542	1,759	2,173
Nigeria	2,599	7,982	13,654	8,599
Other Commonwealth . . .	12,074	11,097	18,032	18,102
Germany, Federal Republic . .	44,691	55,659	49,481	39,950
Italy	9,944	11,539	8,323	6,997
France	15,290	18,555	20,415	17,314
Belgium/Luxembourg . . .	4,969	5,331	1,960	5,467
Netherlands	16,604	14,262	13,648	12,034
U.S.A.	75,718	66,910	68,955	56,761
Japan	25,772	41,270	22,474	21,122
Communist Countries . . .	35,529	27,204	29,471	21,539
Other Countries . . .	63,733	60,259	71,018	59,864
Parcel Post	2,135	3,514	2,370	1,432
TOTAL	419,047	443,142	393,293	334,487

* January–August.

EXPORTS	1970	1971*	1972	1973†
United Kingdom	109,430	86,807	104,664	77,590
Canada	5,307	6,378	12,246	5,661
Hong Kong	623	388	1,423	891
Nigeria	1,192	2,895	1,960	1,589
Other Commonwealth . .	21,150	12,152	18,199	12,952
Germany, Federal Republic .	45,614	37,392	59,311	39,820
Italy	14,700	11,560	17,202	20,002
France	2,336	2,215	3,259	3,552
Belgium/Luxembourg . .	5,976	3,989	9,762	7,648
Netherlands	43,710	35,706	48,908	41,758
U.S.A.	83,963	80,968	74,437	66,747
Japan	30,325	29,543	45,248	44,989
Communist Countries . .	75,502	24,249	80,952	81,313
Other Countries . .	27,446	14,611	86,759	90,343
Parcel Post . . .	103	95	82	55
TOTAL . .	467,378	348,948	564,412	494,910

* Excluding re-exports.   † January–August.

Source: Standard Bank Review, March 1974.

TRANSPORT
RAILWAYS

	PASSENGERS CARRIED	FREIGHT TONS CARRIED	PASSENGER-KILOMETRES	NET TON-KILOMETRES
1968 . . .	7,357,605	1,576,882	425,111,184	276,280,622
1969 . . .	7,930,999	1,624,788	474,165,098	302,195,361
1970 . . .	7,956,135	1,645,398	542,635,604	310,724,148
1971 . . .	7,441,410	1,592,270	447,895,760	292,700,640

ROAD TRANSPORT
(licences current)

	TOTAL	CARS (incl. Taxis)	MOTOR CYCLES	PUBLIC CONVEYANCES	GOODS VEHICLES	TRAILERS AND CARAVANS	SPECIAL SERVICE VEHICLES	PUBLIC SERVICE VEHICLES	TRACTORS AND MECHANIZED EQUIPMENT
1968 .	53,601	29,450	3,079	4,942	12,464	466	2,347	177	676
1969 .	61,207	34,222	3,550	6,077	13,137	445	2,808	192	776
1970 .	74,602	42,094	4,544	7,685	15,692	467	3,010	211	869

SHIPPING

	VESSELS ENTERED (number)	VESSELS CLEARED (number)	TONNAGE ENTERED (net reg. tons)	TONNAGE CLEARED (net reg. tons)	CARGO LOADED (tons)	CARGO UNLOADED (tons)
1968 . .	1,538	1,595	5,282,917	5,311,602	1,143,521	2,361,207
1969 . .	1,538	1,532	5,497,667	5,470,969	2,204,622	2,944,863
1970 . .	1,565	1,553	5,464,632	5,464,445	2,154,759	4,164,329
1971 . .	1,789	1,804	6,368,373	6,386,285	2,374,701	3,221,033

CIVIL AVIATION

	1967	1968	1969
Arrivals	110,859	137,223	137,935
Departures	114,492	141,212	142,126
Freight unloaded (kg.) .	1,361,992	1,680,330	2,145,310
Freight loaded (kg.) . .	1,312,704	1,677,145	1,340,642

EDUCATION
(1970–71)

	PUPILS	TEACHERS
Primary Schools . .	1,447,195*	48,026*
Secondary Schools . .	49,182	2,820
Technical and Trade Establishments	7,577	378
Teacher Training Colleges .	18,368	1,270
Higher Education Institutes	4,759	859

* 1972–73 figures.

Source (except where stated): Central Bureau of Statistics, Accra.

THE CONSTITUTION

The Constitution promulgated in August 1969 was abolished in January 1972 following the army *coup d'état*.

THE GOVERNMENT

NATIONAL REDEMPTION COUNCIL
(*June* 1974)

Chairman: Col. Ignatius K. Acheampong.

Members: Lt.-Col. K. B. Agbo, Maj.-Gen. N. Y. R. Ashley-Lassen, Lt.-Col. Kwame Baah, J. H. Cobbina, Lt.-Col. J. Felli, Lt.-Col. D. A. Iddisah, E. N. Moore, Maj. A. H. Selormey.

COMMISSIONERS IN CHARGE OF MINISTRIES
(*June* 1974)

Chairman of the Council and Commissioner for Defence, Finance and Sport: Col. Ignatius K. Acheampong.

Commissioner for Agriculture: Col. F. G. Bernasko.

Commissioner for Education, Youth and Culture: Col. E. O. Nyante.

Commissioner for Foreign Affairs: Lt.-Col. Kwame M. Baah.

Chief of Defence Staff and Commissioner for Special Duties: Maj.-Gen. N. Y. R. Ashley-Lassen.

Commissioner for Information: Col. C. R. Tachie-Menson.

Commissioner for Economic Planning: Lt.-Col. R. J. A. Felli.

Commissioner for Health: Lt.-Col. A. H. Selormey.

Inspector-General of Police and Commissioner for Internal Affairs: J. H. Cobbina.

Attorney-General and Commissioner for Justice: E. N. Moore.

Commissioner for Labour, Social Welfare and Co-operatives: Lt.-Col. K. B. Agbo.

Commissioner for Lands and Mineral Resources: Maj.-Gen. D. C. K. Amenu.

Commissioner for Local Government: Maj.-Gen. Nathan A. Aferi.

Commissioner for Trade and Tourism: Lt.-Col. D. A. Iddisah.

Commissioner for Transport and Communications: Col. P. K. Agyekum.

Commissioner for Industries: Lt.-Col. P. K. Nkegbe.

Commissioner for Works and Housing: Col. Robert Kotei.

Commissioner in Charge of N.R.C. Affairs: Col. L. A. Okai.

REGIONAL COMMISSIONERS

Region	Commissioner
Ashanti . . .	Cmdr. J. K. Amedume.
Brong-Ahafo . .	Col. Victor Coker-Appiah.
Central . . .	Lt.-Col. E. A. Baidoo.
Eastern . . .	Lt.-Col. G. Minyila.
Greater Accra . .	Lt.-Col. P. K. D. Habadah.
Northern . . .	Lt.-Col. F. F. Addae.
Upper . . .	Col. W. C. O. Acquaye-Nortey.
Volta . . .	Col. J. A. Kabore.
Western . . .	Cmdr. J. A. Kyeremah.

DIPLOMATIC REPRESENTATION

EMBASSIES AND HIGH COMMISSIONS ACCREDITED TO GHANA
(In Accra unless otherwise stated)
(E) Embassy; (HC) High Commission.

Afghanistan: Cairo, Egypt (E).

Algeria: House No. F.606/1, Off Cantonments Rd., X'borg, P.O.B. 2747 (E); *Ambassador:* BOUFELDJA AIDI.

Argentina: Lagos, Nigeria (E).

Australia: No. 6/26 Milne Ave., Off Dr. Amilcar Cabral Rd., Airport Residential Area, P.O.B. 2445 (HC); *High Commissioner:* R. J. PERCIVAL.

Austria: Lagos, Nigeria (E).

Belgium: Plot 56 Cantonments, 3rd Close, Off Rangoon Ave., P.O.B. 5060, Accra-North (E); *Chargé d'Affaires:* D. VAN DER STICHELEN.

Brazil: No. 6 Kanda Estate, P.O.B. 2918 (E); *Ambassador:* LYLE AMAURY TARRISSE DA FONTURA.

Bulgaria: House No. 20, North Ridge Residential Area, Dr. Isert Rd., 7th Ave. Extension, P.O.B. 3193 (E); *Ambassador:* D. VALEV.

Canada: E.115/3, Independence Ave., P.O.B. 1639 (HC); *High Commissioner:* NOBLE E. C. POWER (also accred. as Ambassador to Dahomey and Togo).

China, People's Republic: 8 Dempster Rd., Airport Residential Area, P.O.B. 3356 (E); *Ambassador:* KO HUA.

Czechoslovakia: C.260/5, Kanda High Rd. No. 2, P.O.B. 5226, Accra North (E); *Ambassador:* Dr. JAN SNOBL.

Denmark: Plot No. 67, Dr. Isert's Rd., North Ridge (West) Residential Area, P.O.B. 3328 (E); *Ambassador:* Mrs. NONNY WRIGHT.

Egypt: House No. F.805/1, Off Cantonments Rd., P.O.B. 2508 (E); *Ambassador:* HASSAN AMIN SHASH.

Ethiopia: 13 Morocco Rd., Independence Ave., P.O.B. 1646 (E); *Ambassador:* ZEREMARIAN AZZAZI.

France: 12th Rd., Off Liberation Ave., P.O.B. 187 (E); *Ambassador:* JEAN DECIRY.

German Democratic Republic: House No. 40, Liberation Rd., Airport Residential Area, P.O.B. 2348 (E); *Ambassador:* Dr. JOHANNES VOGEL.

Germany, Federal Republic: Valdemasa Lodge, 7th Ave. Extension, North Ridge, P.O.B. 1757 (E); *Ambassador:* HELMUT MULLER.

Hungary: H/No. F.582 A/1, Salem Rd., Christiansborg, P.O.B. 3027 (E); *Ambassador:* Dr. JÁNOS PATAKI.

India: House No. Z.21, Off Dempster Rd., Airport Residential Area, P.O.B. 3040 (HC); *High Commissioner:* S. BIKRAM SHAH.

Indonesia: Lagos, Nigeria (E).

Iraq: Lagos, Nigeria (E).

Italy: Switchback Rd., P.O.B. 140 (E); *Ambassador:* Baron S. PORCARI LI DESTRI.

Ivory Coast: House No. C.1037/3, Off 7th Ave. Extension, North Ridge Area, P.O.B. 3445 (E); *Ambassador:* DENIS COFFI BILE.

Jamaica: Addis Ababa, Ethiopia (HC).

Japan: Rangoon Ave., Off Switchback Rd., P.O.B. 1637 (E); *Ambassador:* YO KAMIKAWA.

Lebanon: 43 Rangoon Ave., P.O.B. 562 (E); *Chargé d'Affaires:* JEAN HAZOU.

Lesotho: Nairobi, Kenya (HC).

Liberia: House No. F.675/1, Off Cantonments Rd., Christiansborg, P.O.B. 895 (E); *Chargé d'Affaires:* J. DENIS.

Libya: Lagos, Nigeria (E).

Malaysia: Lagos, Nigeria (HC).

Mali: Crescent Rd., Block 1, P.O.B. 1121 (E); *Ambassador:* GUORDO SOW.

Mauritania: Abidjan, Ivory Coast (E).

Mexico: Off Dempster Rd., Plot Z.26, Airport Residential Area, P.O.B. 1984 (E); *Chargé d'Affaires:* CARLOS FERRER.

Netherlands: 89 Liberation Rd., Independence Circle, P.O.B. 3248 (E); *Ambassador:* CHRISTIAAN BENJAMIN ARRIËNS.

Niger: E.104/3, Independence Ave., P.O.B. 2685 (E); *Ambassador:* TIECOURA ALZOUMA.

Nigeria: Nigeria House, 65 Farrar Ave., Asylum Down, P.O.B. 1548 (HC); *Ambassador:* G. O. IJEWERE.

Norway: Lagos, Nigeria (E).

Pakistan: Plot 11, Ring Rd. East (E); *Ambassador:* S. A. MOID.

Philippines: Lagos, Nigeria (E).

Poland: House No. F.820/1, Off Cantonments Rd., X'borg, P.O.B. 2552 (E); *Chargé d'Affaires:* ZYGMUNT KROLAK.

Romania: Lagos, Nigeria (E).

Saudi Arabia: House No. F.868/1, Off Cantonments Rd., P.O.B. 670 (E); *Chargé d'Affaires:* FOUAD IBRAHIM EL-ALFY.

Senegal: Fifth Ave. Extension (Behind Police Headquarters), P.O.B. 3208 (E); *Ambassador:* MAHENTA BIRAME FALL.

Sierra Leone: C.135/3, Asylum Down, P.O.B. 6706 (HC); *High Commissioner:* YANKAY-DAUDI SISAY.

Spain: Airport Residential Area, Off Dempster Rd., P.O.B. 1218 (E); *Ambassador:* JUAN JOSÉ CANO Y ABASCAL.

Sudan: Lagos, Nigeria (E).

Sweden: Lagos, Nigeria (E).

Switzerland: Off 7th Ave. Extension, North Ridge Area, P.O.B. 359 (E); *Ambassador:* MARCEL LUY.

Tanzania: (HC); *High Commissioner:* PHILEMON PAUL MURO.

Togo: Togo House near Cantonments Roundabout, P.O.B. 4308 (E); *Ambassador:* N. M. AKOU.

Trinidad and Tobago: Addis Ababa, Ethiopia (HC).

Tunisia: Abidjan, Ivory Coast (E).

Turkey: No. 13 Mankata Ave., Airport Residential Area, P.O.B. 3104 (E); *Ambassador:* SAIT SAHIPOGLU.

Uganda: Plot No. C/35, P.O.B. 4260 (HC); *High Commissioner:* J. OKULLO (acting).

U.S.S.R.: F.856/1, Ring Rd. East, P.O.B. 1634 (E); *Ambassador:* V. I. TCHEREDNIK.

United Kingdom: Barclays Bank Bldg., High St., P.O.B. 296 (HC); *High Commissioner:* HENRY S. H. STANLEY, C.M.G.

U.S.A.: Intersection of Kinubu Rd. and Liberia Rd., P.O.B. 194 (E); *Ambassador:* FRED L. HADSEL.

Upper Volta: House No. 772/3, Asylum Down, Off Farrar Ave., P.O.B. 651 (E); *Ambassador:* PAUL TENSORE ROUAMBA.

Venezuela: Lagos, Nigeria (E).

Yugoslavia: Plot No. B.79, Ring Rd. North Extension, P.O.B. 1629 (E); *Ambassador:* ZORAVKO PECAR.

Zaire: 58 Rangoon Ave., Off Switchback Rd., P.O.B. 5448 (E); *Ambassador:* N. KITSHODI.

Zambia: Abidjan, Ivory Coast (HC).

Ghana also has diplomatic relations with Cuba and Guinea.

NATIONAL ASSEMBLY

The Assembly was dissolved in January 1972, following the army *coup d'état*.

POLITICAL PARTIES

The ban imposed on political parties in February 1966 was lifted on May 1st, 1969, but reimposed in January 1972 after the *coup d'état*. Before that time, the following parties existed:

Progress Party: Accra; f. 1969; Leader Dr. KOFI A. BUSIA.

Justice Party: Accra; f. 1970 after a merger of the National Alliance of Liberals, United Nationalist Party and the All Peoples' Republican Party; Leader E. MADJITEY.

People's Action Party: Accra; f. 1969; Leader IMORU AYARNA.

People's Popular Party: Accra; banned until 1970 as being Nkrumahist.

All political detainees were released in July 1973.

JUDICIAL SYSTEM

The civil law in force in Ghana is based on the Common Law, doctrines of equity and general statutes which were in force in England in 1874, as modified by subsequent Ordinances. Ghanaian customary law is, however, the basis of most personal, domestic and contractual relationships and the Supreme Court has power to enforce it. Criminal law is based on the Criminal Code, enacted at the end of the nineteenth century and dependent on English Criminal Law, and since amended at intervals. In September 1972 the National Redemption Council abolished the Supreme Court, previously the premier court in Ghana. It said that the court had only sat twice since its establishment, and claimed that its continued existence could no longer be justified after the suspension of the 1969 Constitution which set it up. The supreme tribunal in Ghana is now the Court of Appeal.

The Court of Appeal: The Court of Appeal consists of the Chief Justice and not less than five Judges of the Court of Appeal. It has jurisdiction to hear and determine appeals from any judgement, decree or order of the High Court.

The High Court: The High Court of Ghana consists of the Chief Justice and not less than twelve Puisne Judges and has an original jurisdiction in all matters, civil and criminal. Trial by jury is practised in criminal cases in Ghana and the Criminal Procedure Code, 1960, provides that all trials on indictment shall be by a jury or with the aid of Assessors.

The Circuit Court: Circuit Courts were created in 1960, and the jurisdiction of a Circuit Court consists of an original jurisdiction in civil matters where the amount involved does not exceed NC4,000. It has also jurisdiction with regard to the guardianship and custody of infants, and original jurisdiction in criminal matters in case of offences other than those where the maximum punishment is death or life imprisonment. Finally it has appellate jurisdiction from decisions of any District Court situated within its circuit.

District Courts: District Magistrates exercise summary jurisdiction throughout the country. In criminal cases Magistrates have jurisdiction to impose sentences of imprisonment up to one year and fines not exceeding NC500. They also hear civil suits in which the amount involved does not exceed NC1,000.

Juvenile Courts have been set up in Accra, Kumasi, Koforidua, Sekondi, Tamale, Sunyani and Ho. They consist either of three citizens selected from a panel of Juvenile Court Magistrates or of a Stipendiary Magistrate sitting with two of the panel. The public is excluded from proceedings of Juvenile Courts which are empowered to place a child in the care of a relative, Probation Officer or other suitable person, to negotiate with parents to secure the good behaviour of a child.

Local Courts: Local Courts now replace the former Native Courts. They have both civil and criminal jurisdiction. In civil cases they enjoy exclusive jurisdiction in cases where customary law is involved and in personal suits up to £100. They have limited criminal jurisdiction and cannot impose a fine exceeding £25 or a sentence of three months imprisonment. However, they have unlimited jurisdiction as to persons of all races living within their areas of jurisdiction. Control is exercised by the Judges of the Circuit and High Court by way of appeals and reviews in accordance with the Courts Act, 1960. Appeals lie either to the Circuit or High Court, depending on the nature of the suit. Whilst in land causes a person aggrieved by any decision may appeal to the High Court, in succession causes he may appeal to the Circuit Court.

Chief Justice: Mr. Justice S. Asu Crabbe.

Justices of Appeal: A. N. E. Amissah, P. D. Anin, D. F. Annan, F. K. Apaloo, P. E. N. K. Archer, Mrs. A. R. Jiagge, J. Kingsley-Nyinah, G. S. Lassey, E. N. P. Sowah (Accra).

High Court Judges: I. K. Abban, I. R. Aboagye, J. H. Griffiths-Bandodah, F. J. Hayfron-Benjamin, V. Kisseih, J. E. C. Okai, F. P. Sarkodee (Accra); S. Baidoo, L. K. Wiredu (Cape Coast); K. Ata-Bedu, G. R. M. Francois (Ho); A. Quarshie-Sam, P. K. Jones-Mensah (Koforidua); G. Koranteng-Addow, S. Mensah Boison, Mrs. D. Owusu-Addo, J. N. K. Taylor (Kumasi); C. E. H. Coussey, V. C. R. A. C. Crabbe, E. K. Edusei (Sekondi); J. S. A. Anterkyi, P. V. Osei-Hwere (Sunyani); K. Ata-Bedu, J. H. Griffiths-Randolph (Tamale), G. K. Andoh.

Deputy Judicial Secretary: J. A. Wutoh (Accra).

RELIGION

According to the 1960 census, the distribution of religious groups was:

	per cent
Christians	42.8
Traditional Religions	38.2
Muslims	12.0
No Religion	7.0

CHRISTIANITY

The Christian community in Ghana is divided principally into Anglicans, Roman Catholics, Methodists and Presbyterians.

ANGLICAN COMMUNITY
PROVINCE OF WEST AFRICA

Archbishop of the Province of West Africa and Bishop of Sierra Leone: Most Rev. M. N. C. O. Scott, c.b.e., d.d., dip.th., Bishopscourt, P.O.B. 128, Freetown, Sierra Leone.

Bishop of Accra: Right Rev. Ishmael Samuel Mills Lemaire, P.O.B. 8, Accra.

Bishop of Kumasi: Rt. Rev. John Benjamin Arthur, P.O.B. 144, Kumasi.

ROMAN CATHOLIC CHURCH

Archbishop: Most Rev. John Kodwo Amissah, P.O.B. 112, Cape Coast.

Bishops: Tamale (vacant); Rt. Rev. Anthony Konings, P.O.B. 150, Kpanda; Rt. Rev. Dr. Dominic Kodwo Andoh, P.O.B. 247, Accra; Rt. Rev. Joseph Essuah, P.O.B. 236, Takoradi; Rt. Rev. Peter K. Sarpong, P.O.B. 99, Kumasi; Rt. Rev. Peter Dery, P.O.B. 63, Wa; Rt. Rev. Rudolf Akanlu, P.O.B. 4, Navrongo; Rt. Rev. James Owusu, Sunyani.

METHODIST CHURCH

President: Rev. T. Wallace Koomson.

Secretary: Rev. I. K. A. Thompson, b.d.

Methodist Church of Ghana: Liberia Rd., P.O. Box 403, Accra; became fully autonomous July 1961; 238,538 mems.

PRESBYTERIAN CHURCH

Presbyterian Church of Ghana: P.O.B. 1800, Accra; 244,405 mems.; Moderator Rt. Rev. G. K. Sintim Misa.

OTHER CHURCHES

A.M.E. Zion Church: P.O.B. 239, Sekondi.

Christian Council of Ghana: Rev. W. F. Brandful, P.O.B. 919, Accra.

Christian Methodist Episcopal Church: P.O.B. 3906, Accra.

Evangelical-Lutheran Church: P.O.B. 197, Kaneshie; 123 mems.

Evangelical-Presbyterian Church: P.O.B. 18, Ho.

Ghana Baptist Convention: P.O.B. 1, Abuakwa, Ashanti.

Mennonite Church: P.O.B. 5485, Accra; f. 1960; Moderator L. M. Horst; Sec. Ebenezer K. Nimo; 475 mems.

Salvation Army: P.O.B. 320, Accra.

AFRICAN RELIGIONS

A large proportion of people practise various traditional beliefs.

ISLAM

There are a considerable number of Muslims in the Northern Region.

THE PRESS

NEWSPAPERS
DAILY

Daily Graphic: Brewery Rd., P.O.B. 742, Accra; f. 1950; Editor Richard Horsely; circ. 165,000.

Evening Herald: f. 1974; Editor Eric Heymann.

The Ghanaian Times: P.O.B. 2638, Accra; f. 1958; Editor Editor K. Gyewu-Kyem; circ. 100,000.

Pioneer: Box 325, Kumasi and P.O.B. 4256, Accra; f. 1939; Editor Sule Raji; Accra Rep. Gilly Osei.

WEEKLIES

Business Weekly: P.O.B. 2351, Accra; f. 1966; Editor Mark Botsio; circ. 5,000.

Eastern Star: Koforidua; Editor Maj. A. A. Enninful (acting).

Echo: P.O.B. 3460, Accra; independent; Editor S. Kissi-Afare; circ. 30,000.

Express, The: P.O.B. 4276, Accra; Editor Kwame Kesse-Adu.

Ghana News Bulletin: publ. by Ghana Ministry of Information.

Herald, The: Accra; f. 1959.

Mirror, The: Brewery Rd., P.O.B. 742, Accra; f. 1953; publ. by Ghana Graphic Co. Ltd.; circ. 100,000; Editor Nicholas Alando.

Palaver, The: P.O.B. 5018, Accra; Editor Christian Asher.

Spokesman: P.O.B. 7687, Accra; twice weekly; Editor Kofi Badu.

Sporting News: P.O.B. M.235, Accra; Editor Hene Charles.

Sporting Record: P.O.B. 7962, Accra; Editor L. O. Addy.

Standard, The: P.O.B. 60, Gold Coast; f. 1938; National Catholic paper; Editor Rev. Martin Peters; circ. 8,900.

Voice of the People, The: P.O.B. 3460, Accra; Editor E. K. Mickson.

Weekly Advertiser: P.O.B. 6549, Accra; Editor H. K. Mould.

Weekly Spectator: Guinea Press Ltd., P.O.B. 2638, Accra; f. 1963; Suns.; Editor A. Kutin-Mensah.

Weekly Statesman: P.O.B. 3876, Accra; Editor Augustus Bruce.

PERIODICALS
Fortnightly

Legon Observer: P.O.B. 11, Legon; f. 1966; Editor Paul Ansah.

New Ghana: Information Services Dept., P.O.B. 745, Accra; Editor Neils Palm.

News Review: Information Services Dept., P.O.B. 745, Accra; Editor Mrs. K. Ofosu-Appiah.

Monthly

The Ghana Information Services publish the following works:

Akwansosem (Akwapim Twi): P.O.B. 745, Accra; Editor K. S. Odame.

Kakyevole (Nzima): P.O.B. 745, Accra; Editor (vacant); circ. 10,500.

Kasem Labaie (Kasem): P.O.B. 57, Tamale; Editor A. C. Aziiba.

Kwantabisa (Asante Twi, Fante): P.O.B. 745, Accra; Editor D. Y. Kyei (Asante Twi edition).

Lahabili Tsugu (Dagbani): P.O.B. 57, Tamale; Editor T. T. Sulemana.

Mansralo (Ga): P.O.B. 745, Accra; Editor Martin Nii-Moi.

Motabiala (Ewe): P.O.B. 745, Accra; Editor K. Gropone.

Monthly

Christian Messenger: P.O.B. 3075, Accra; f. 1859; English, Fante and Ga editions; Editor G. B. K. Owusu; circ. 20,000.

Drum: Drum Publications (Ghana) Ltd., P.O.B. 1197, Accra; Editor Joseph K. Mensah; circ. 45,000.

Flamingo: P.O.B. 3075, Accra; f. 1960; general family magazine; Editor G. B. K. Owusu; circ. 100,000.

Ghana Confidential: P.O.B. 4246, Accra; Editor Kwame Kesse-Adu.

Ghana Trade Journal: P.O.B. 2351, Accra; f. 1959; Editor Mark Botsio.

Statesman: P.O.B. 3876, Accra; Editor F. Gass-Porsoo.

Twice Monthly

Chit Chat: P.O.B. 7043, Accra; Editor Miss Rosemond Adu.

Ghana Review: Information Services Department, P.O.B. 745, Accra; f. 1961; review of economic, social and cultural affairs; Editor Simon Ikoi-Kwaku.

Ideal Woman: P.O.B. 5737, Accra; Editor Mrs. Kate Abbam.

Quarterly

Insight Publication: P.O.B. 5446, Accra; Editorial Exec. K. O. Amoah.

Transition: P.O.B. 9063, Accra; Editor Wole Soyinka.

Other

Economic Bulletin of Ghana: Economic Society of Ghana, P.O.B. 22, Legon; Editor Prof. John Coleman de Graft-Johnson.

Ghana Journal of Science: Ghana Science Association, P.O. Box 7, Legon.

Ghana Teacher: Ghana Union of Teachers, P.O.B. 209.

West African Pharmacist: Faculty of Pharmacy, University of Science and Technology, Kumasi; f. 1959; six a year.

NEWS AGENCIES

Ghana News Agency: P.O.B. 2118, Accra; f. 1957; Chair. Kwamina Atta Kakra Erskine; Gen. Man. Kow Bondzie Brown; c. 350 employees.

Foreign Bureaux

Agence France-Presse: P.O.B. 3055; Chief Edward Ankrah.

Associated Press: P.O.B. 2118, Accra; Chief P. K. Cobbina Essem.

The following agencies are also represented: Deutsche Presse-Agentur and Tass.

PUBLISHERS

Anowuo Educational Publications: P.O.B. 3918, Accra; f. 1966; educational books, novels and poetry in English and the nine main Ghanaian languages; about 30 titles annually; Publisher Samuel Asare Konadu.

Bureau of Ghana Languages: P.O.B. 1851, Accra; f. 1951; publishes in nine Ghanaian languages; 30–40 titles a year for schools and the public, serves as research and translation agency; Dir. J. Kwasi Brantuo.

Business Publications: P.O.B. 2351, Accra; publishers of *Business Weekly, Ghana Trade Journal, Ghana Business Guide.*

Catholic Mission Press: P.O.B. 60, Cape Coast; publishers of religious works and textbooks.

Ghana State Publishing Corporation (Publishing Division): P.O.B. 4348, Accra; f. 1965; 30 titles annually, chiefly primary school.

Ghana Universities Press: P.O.B. 4219, Accra; f. 1962; publishes academic works for all the universities and institutions of higher education in Ghana; Dir. N. K. Adzakey, b.a., dip.ed., m.ed.

Graphic Corporation: Brewery Rd., P.O.B. 742, Accra; f. 1950 to publish the *Daily Graphic* and *Sunday Mirror*; also publishes *Ghana Year Book.*

Methodist Book Depot Ltd.: P.O.B. 100, Cape Coast; f. 1882; brs. in Accra, Kumasi, Takoradi, etc.; publishers, book-sellers, stationery manufacturers, educational contractors; Man. Dir. Richard Mathieson.

Moxon Paperbacks Ltd.: P.O.B. M160, Accra; f. 1967; publishers of travel and guide books, handbooks, Africana, modern novels and poetry; quarterly catalogue of Ghana books and periodicals in print; Proprietor R. J. Moxon, o.b.e.

Waterville Publishing House: P.O.B. 195, Accra.

RADIO AND TELEVISION

Ghana Broadcasting Corporation: Broadcasting House, P.O.B. 1633, Accra; f. 1935; Dir.-Gen. S. B. Mfodwo, B.A.; Dirs. S. Amarteifio, A. A. Opoku, J. L. Mills.

RADIO

There is a national service with services in English and six Ghanaian languages; also an external service in English, French, Portuguese, Hausa, Swahili and Arabic. There are 40 relay stations and in 1973 there were 1,057,000 radio receivers and 56,055 loudspeaker boxes.

TELEVISION

The television service came into operation in 1965; there are stations at Accra, Kumasi and Sekondi-Takoradi, with a relay station at Tamale.

In 1973 there were an estimated 25,000 television receivers in the country.

FINANCE

BANKING

(cap.=capital; p.u.=paid up)

CENTRAL BANK

Bank of Ghana: P.O.B. 2674, Accra; f. 1957; cap. p.u. C46m.; Gov. Amon Nikoi.

COMMERCIAL BANKS

Agricultural Development Bank: P.O.B. 4191, Accra; f. 1965; cap. C30m.; state-owned; credit facilities for agriculturists; Chair. and Man. Dir. E. N. Afful.

Ghana Commercial Bank: P.O.B. 134, Accra; f. 1953; state-owned; cap. p.u. C10.0m.; dep. C444.6m. (June 1973); Chair. and Man. Dir. T. E. Amin; over 100 branches and agencies; publs. *Monthly Economic Bulletin* and various reports.

Ghana Savings Bank: General Post Office, Accra.

National Investment Bank: Liberty Avenue, P.O.B. 3726, Accra; f. 1963; cap. p.u. C10.8m.; Chair. and Man. Dir. J. S. Addo.

MERCHANT BANK

National Finance and Merchant Bank Ltd.: f. 1972 to assist Ghanaian businesses in trade, commerce and industry.

FOREIGN BANKS

Barclays Bank of Ghana Ltd.: Head Office, 54 Lombard St., London, E.C.3; Head Office in Ghana: High St., Accra, P.O.B. 2949; Ghana Chair. and Gen. Man. G. E. Davy; Dirs. G. E. Davy, Amishadai Larson Adu, A. E. Ambrose, W. Duncan, T. D. Miles, E. N. Omaboe, R. Mensah, E. N. Nortey.

Standard Bank Ghana Ltd.: High St., P.O.B. 768, Accra; cap. C4.3m.; dep. and a/c. C131,169,228 (1973); Chair. Peter Newton Harris.

INSURANCE

GHANAIAN COMPANIES

The State Insurance Corporation of Ghana: Accra; f. 1962 to undertake general insurance particularly in the areas of housing, agriculture and providing investment to support the economy. Investment reached C16m. by December 1971; includes Ghana Reinsurance Corporation.

Social Security and National Insurance Trust: f. 1972; aims to protect and benefit Ghanaian workers and at present covers 775,490 employees; Chief Administrator Col. John M. Ewa.

There are 8 foreign insurance companies in Ghana, 6 British and 2 Indian.

TRADE AND INDUSTRY

PUBLIC BOARDS AND CORPORATIONS

Ghana Industrial Holding Corporation: P.O.B. 2784, Accra; f. 1968; took over the management of the 19 state enterprises, including the steel, paper, bricks, paint, sugar, textile and boat-building factories; aims to run these on a commercial basis; foreign investment in some of these interests is being encouraged.

Capital Investments Board: P.O.B. M193, Accra; central investment promotion agency of the Government; from 1963 to 1973 invested some C210.3m. in 158 projects; Chair. Kwame D. Fordwor; publs. *Investors' Manual, Investment Journal.*

Cocoa Marketing Company (Ghana) Ltd.: P.O.B. M108, Accra; London Office: 64–66 Oxford St., London, W.1.; f. 1961; markets Ghana's cocoa beans, as well as cocoa butter and cocoa cake produced by West African Mills, Takoradi; wholly-owned subsidiary of Ghana Cocoa Marketing Board (*see below*).

Ghana Cocoa Marketing Board: P.O.B. 933, Accra; f. 1947; responsible for purchase and export of cocoa, coffee, palm kernels and palm kernel oil, copra, coconut, shea nuts, shea butter, groundnuts, bananas, kola nuts and other produce, also subsidizes roads to cocoa-growing areas.

Produce Buying Agency: Subsidiary of Ghana Cocoa Marketing Board.

Ghana Food Marketing Corporation: P.O.B. 4245, Accra; f. 1965; buys, stores, preserves, distributes and sells foodstuffs throughout the country, and organizes exports of foodstuffs for which no local market is available; thus ensures increased production by provision of assured markets and guaranteed prices as well as an even flow of foodstuffs throughout the year; 8 regional centres for preservation, storage, distribution and sales: Accra, Kumasi, Sekondi-Takoradi, Cape Coast, Ho, Sunyani, Tamale, Wa.

Ghana National Trading Corporation: P.O.B. 67, Accra; f. 1962; organizes exports and imports of commodities determined by the Corporation; Man. Dir. Col. M. O. Koranteng.

Ghana Shipping Corporation: Accra.

Ghana Standards Board: c/o P.O.B. M245, Accra; f. 1967; establishes and promulgates standards to ensure high quality of goods produced in Ghana; promotes standardization, industrial efficiency and development and industrial welfare, health and safety; Certification and Mark Scheme (introduced January 1971).

Ghana Timber Marketing Board: P.O.B. 515, Takoradi; f. 1960; assists general development and controls exports of timber; 10 mems.; Chair. Lt.-Col. ODARTEY-WELLINGTON.

Ghana Water and Sewerage Corporation: P.O.B. M194, Accra.

Ghana Workers' Brigade: P.O.B. 1853, Accra; f. 1957; agricultural wing 7,284 mems.; voluntary organization to organize youth otherwise unemployed for large-scale agricultural and food production enterprises and other development projects of public value; under Ministries of Agriculture and Youth and Rural Development.

State Construction Corporation: f. 1966; reorganized since January 1973 into 15 divisions to increase administrative efficiency, construction plans are orientated to aid agricultural production.

State Diamond Marketing Corporation: P.O.B. M108, Accra; f. 1965; charged with securing the most favourable terms for sale of diamonds produced in Ghana; controls and fixes prices paid to winners and producers; Man. Dir. E. K. NANTWI.

State Farms Corporation: Accra.

State Fishing Corporation: P.O.B. 211, Tema; f. 1961; Government sponsored deep-sea fishing, distribution and marketing (including exporting) organization; owns about 12 deep-sea fishing trawlers; Chief Exec. Dr. K. E. ADJEI.

State Gold Mining Corporation: P.O.B. 109, Tarkwa; Accra Office, P.O.B. 3634; London Office, Bush House, North-East Wing, Aldwych, London, W.C.2; f. 1961; manages five gold mines; Man. Dir. J. BENTUM-WILLIAMS.

State Hotels Corporation: P.O.B. 7542, Accra North; f. 1965; responsible for all state-owned hotels, restaurants, etc.; charged with providing such establishments of a reasonable standard in all main cities and towns; 13 brs.

State Housing Corporation: P.O.B. 2753, Accra; f. 1955 to increase housing in Ghana; manages over 19,000 properties; Man. Dir. Col. GEORGE HERBERT SLATER.

Tema Development Corporation: P.O.B. 46, Tema; f. 1952; responsible for administration, planning and development of Tema township, by 1974 had housed over 100,000 people; Man. Dir. O. S. ADAMS; publ. *The Tedeco Annual Report* (circ. 6,000).

CHAMBERS OF COMMERCE

Ghana National Chamber of Commerce, The: P.O.B. 2325, Accra; f. 1961; 584 mems.; Pres. G. Y. ODOI; Sec. ISAAC K. ATIOGBE.

Member Chambers:

Accra District Chamber: 352 mems.

Ho District Chamber: 5 mems.

Keta District Chamber: 7 mems.

Koforidua District Chamber: P.O.B. 266, Koforidua; 34 mems.

Kumasi District Chamber: P.O.B. 528, Kumasi; 80 mems.

Sekondi/Takoradi District Chamber: P.O.B. 45, Takoradi; 56 mems.

Sunyani District Chamber: 5 mems.

Tamale District Chamber: 8 mems.

Tarkwa District Chamber: 10 mems.

COMMERCIAL AND INDUSTRIAL ORGANIZATIONS

Export Promotion Council: Ministry of Trade, P.O.B. 47, Accra; f. 1969; chair. and representatives appointed by Ghana Manufacturers' Association, Ghana National Chamber of Commerce, Ghana Timber Federation, Ghana Timber Producers' Association, Ghana Timber Marketing Board, Bank of Ghana, National Investment Bank, Agricultural Development Bank, Cocoa Marketing Company, Ghana Cocoa Marketing Board and the National Standards Board.

Indian Merchants' Association: P.O.B. 2891, Accra; f. 1939; Sec. SADHWANI JAYDEE.

Institute of Chartered Accountants (Ghana), The: P.O.B. 4268, Accra; f. 1963; 183 mems.; Pres. S. I. K. BOAKYE-AGYEMAN; Hon. Sec. J. K. FORSON.

Lebanese and Syrian Traders' Association: P.O.B. 1080, Accra; f. 1956; 38 mems.; Principal Officers E. S. NASSAR, A. F. NASSAR.

EMPLOYERS' ASSOCIATION

Ghana Employers' Association: Kojo Thompson Rd., P.O.B. 2616, Accra; f. 1959; 290 mems.; Chair. ALFRED GAISIE; Vice-Chair. CHRISTOPHER RICHARDS; Chief Exec. F. BANNERMAN-MENSON; publ. *Newsletter* (monthly).

AFFILIATED BODIES

Ghana Booksellers' Association: P.O.B. 899, Accra.

Ghana Chamber of Mines, The: P.O.B. 991, Accra; f. 1928; promotes mining interests in Ghana; Dir. and Sec. J. E. AMPAH, F.R.ECON.S.

Ghana Electrical Contractors' Association: P.O.B. 1858, Accra.

Ghana National Contractors' Association: c/o J. T. Osei and Co., P.O.B. M11, Accra.

Ghana Port Employers' Association, The: P.O.B. 66, Accra.

Ghana Timber Federation, The: P.O.B. 246, Takoradi; f. 1952; aims to promote, protect and develop timber industry of Ghana; Chair. H. WALTERS.

TRADE UNIONS

Ghana Trades Union Congress: Hall of Trade Unions, P.O.B. 701, Accra; f. 1945; governed by an Executive Board comprising the Chairmen and Secretaries of each of the 17 national unions, the Secretary-General and the Chairman of the Executive Board; 7 specialized departments; total membership 342,480 (1970); Chair. DAVID EYGIR; Sec.-Gen. A. NISSIFU; publ. *Ghana Workers' Bulletin* (fortnightly).

The following unions are affiliated to the Congress: Construction and Building Trades Union: 39,103 mems.; General Agricultural Workers' Union: 35,000 mems.; General Transport and Petroleum Workers' Union: 7,600 mems.; Ghana Private Road Transport Union: 20,000 mems.; Health Services Workers' Union: 9,000 mems.; Industrial and Commercial Workers' Union: 80,000 mems.; Local Government Workers' Union: 38,000 mems.; Maritime and Dockworkers' Union: 10,000 mems.; Mine Workers' Union: 23,000 mems.; National Union of Seamen: 3,000 mems.; Posts and Telecommunications Workers' Union: 5,000 mems.; Public Services Workers' Union: 24,000 mems.; Public Utility Workers' Union: 12,518 mems.; Railway Enginemen's Union: 900 mems.; Railway and Port Workers' Union: 7,388 mems.; Teachers' and Educational Workers' Union: 14,000 mems.; Timber and Woodworkers' Union: 14,000 mems.

CO-OPERATIVES

Department of Co-operatives: f. 1944 as the Department of Co-operation; controlling body of co-operative societies.

Ghana Co-operatives Council: Accra; co-ordinates activities of all co-operative societies; over 100,000 members.

The co-operative movement began in Ghana in 1928 among cocoa farmers, and grew into the largest farmers' organization in the country. In 1944 the Department of Co-operatives, known then as the Department of Co-operation, was established as the controlling body of co-operative societies.

The movement was dissolved by the Nkrumah Government in 1960, but was re-established after the *coup d'état* in 1966. It is now under military leadership. There are 1,261 co-operative societies and 43 co-operative produce marketing unions. The structure of the movement in Ghana is co-operative associations at the top, co-operative unions in a secondary position of seniority in the towns, and village co-operative societies at the base.

The co-operative associations (1974) are:

Ghana Co-operative Credit Association: Accra.

Ghana Co-operative Distillers Association: P.O.B. 3640, Accra; f. 1960.

Ghana Co-operative Fisheries Association: Accra; f. 1967; includes over 200 fish marketing societies.

Ghana Co-operative Marketing Association: P.O.B. 832, Accra; f. 1944.

Ghana Co-operative Poultry Farmers' Association: Accra.

Ghana Co-operative Transport Association: Accra; f. 1960; comprises 28 primary societies with seven regional unions; especially involved with cocoa exporting.

TRANSPORT

RAILWAY AND PORTS

Ghana Railway and Ports Authority: Box 251, Takoradi; is responsible for the operation of 592 miles of railway and the deep-water harbour at Takoradi and for the maintenance of 8 lighthouses and the new deep-water harbour at Tema, opened in January 1962; Tema harbour is to be further developed and the dry dock enlarged; Gen. Man. P. O. AGGREY; Chief Harbour Master (Takoradi) Capt. W. G. TODMAN, O.B.E.

ROADS

There are 19,236 miles of roads, of which 4,420 miles (1,912 miles bitumen) are maintained by the Division of Public Construction. Regional Organizations maintain 3,896 miles, Local and Municipal Councils 5,920, and there are about 5,000 miles of private and Chiefs' roads. The International Development Organization is to rehabilitate 340 miles of roads and survey a further 700 for future up-grading.

Automobile Association of Ghana: Fanum Place, Boundary Road, P.O. Box 1985, Accra; f. 1961; mems. 3,000; Chair. E. A. METTLE-NUNOO; Exec. Dir. DELA SESHIE.

Ghana-Upper Volta Road Transport Commission: Ouagadougou, Upper Volta; f. 1968.

SHIPPING

Black Star Line Ltd.: P.O.B. 2760, Accra; f. 1957; Government-owned line; operates passenger and cargo services to northern Europe, the United Kingdom, Canada and the eastern United States, the Gulf of Mexico, the Mediterranean and West Africa. Agents for Gold Star Line Ltd., Woermann Line, Zim West Africa Lines Ltd., Seven Stars Africa Line and Nigerian National Shipping Line: fleet of 18 freighters. Man. Dir. G. K. B. DE GRAFT-JOHNSON.

Barber Line: P.O.B. 210, Takoradi; 3-weekly cargo service to U.S.A., limited passenger service.

Compagnie Fabre Marseille: Liner Agencies (Ghana) Ltd., P.O.B. 214, Tema; and P.O.B. 210, Takoradi; once-monthly sailings to Mediterranean ports.

Compagnie de Navigation Fraissinet et Cyprien Fabre: Palm Line (Agencies) Ltd., P.O. Box 212, Takoradi; coastal services, services to North Africa and Europe.

Guinea Gulf Line, The: Liner Agencies (Ghana) Ltd., P.O.B. 214, Tema; P.O.B. 210, Takoradi; services to United Kingdom and Europe.

Holland West-Afrika Lijn N.V.: P.O.B. 269, Accra; P.O.B. 216, Tema; and P.O.B. 18, Takoradi.

Kawasaki Kisen Kaisha Ltd.: Liner Agencies (Ghana) Ltd., P.O.B. 214, Tema; and P.O.B. 210, Takoradi; monthly sailings to Japan, Hong Kong and Singapore via South Africa.

Liner Agencies (Ghana) Ltd.: P.O.B. 66, Accra; P.O.B. 210, Takoradi; P.O.B. 214, Tema; freight services to and from United Kingdom, Europe, U.S.A., Canada, Japan and Italy; intermediate services between West African ports; freight services from India and Pakistan; Gen. Man. J. R. G. IRVINE.

Mitsui O.S.K. Lines Ltd.: formerly **Osaka Shosen Kaisha:** Liner Agencies (Ghana) Ltd., P.O.B. 214, Tema; and P.O.B. 210, Takoradi; twice-monthly services to Japan, Hong Kong and Singapore via South Africa.

Nautilus Line S.A.: Union Maritime et Commerciale, P.O.B. 2013, Accra; services to Mediterranean ports, Portugal, Spain and West Africa.

Royal Interocean Lines: Agents Holland West-Afrika Lijn N.V., P.O.B. 269, Accra; and P.O.B. 18, Takoradi; cargo express service Japan, China, Hong Kong, Malaysia, South and East Africa, South America, Australia and New Zealand.

CIVIL AVIATION

The main international airport is at Accra and there are also airports at Takoradi, Kumasi, Sunyani and Tamale.

Ghana Airways Corporation: Ghana House, P.O.B. 1636, Accra; f. 1958; Government-owned company operates international, regional and domestic services; fleet of one DC-3, two Viscounts, one VC-10, one HS 748, one F28; Man. Dir. Lt.-Col. K. K. PUMPUNI.

Pioneer Air Charter Services Ltd.: f. 1974; privately-owned air cargo charter company; fleet of one Boeing 720, one DC-7.

Accra is also served by the following foreign airlines: Air Afrique, Alitalia, Air Mali, British Caledonian Airways, EgyptAir, Ethiopian, KLM, Lufthansa, MEA, Nigeria Airways, PAA, Sierra Leone Airways, UTA.

POWER

The Volta River Authority: P.O.B. M77, Accra; operates the Volta hydro-electric power station at Akosombo; with six units installed, has a total maximum generating capacity of 948 MW; electricity used for mining and the industries, smelting aluminium and domestic consumption; inaugurated 1966; official opening of the Akosombo Expansion Project and the Ghana—Togo—Dahomey Transmission Line was in 1972; Chief Exec. Dr. E. L. QUARTEY.

TOURISM

Ghana's tourist industry is still in its infancy. In 1972 42,870 foreigners visited Ghana.

Ghana Tourist Company Ltd.: Fiase Lodge, Ring Road Central, P.O.B. 2923, Accra; affiliated to I.A.T.A. and International Union of Official Travel Organizations, Geneva; Chair. E. K. DADSON; Man. Dir. V. K. AKAKPO.

Ghana Tourist Corporation: P.O.B. 3106, Accra; Man. Dir. Maj. W. A. ODJIDJA.

State Hotels Corporation: P.O.B. 7542, Accra North. (*See* Trade and Industry, Public Boards and Corporations.)

UNIVERSITIES

University of Ghana: P.O.B. 25, Legon, nr. Accra; 490 teachers, 2,556 students.

University of Science and Technology: Kumasi; 275 teachers, 1,765 students.

University of Cape Coast: Cape Coast; 163 teachers, 1,100 students.

GRENADA

INTRODUCTORY SURVEY

Location, Climate, Language, Religion, Flag, Capital

Grenada is the most southerly of the Windward Islands, in the West Indies. The country also includes some of the small islands known as the Grenadines. The climate is semi-tropical with an average temperature of 78°F (23°C); most of the rainfall occurs between June and December. The majority of the population speak English and belong to Christian churches. The national flag, displaying seven stars and a nutmeg, consists of a diagonally-quartered green and yellow rectangle on a red ground. The capital is St. George's.

Recent History

Grenada was initially colonized by the French but was captured by the British in 1762. Full internal self-government and statehood in association with Britain were achieved in 1967. The political life of Grenada has been dominated by Eric Gairy, the present Prime Minister, whose United Labour Party rose to power in the 1950s with the support of the nascent trade union movement. As a firm advocate of total independence, Mr. Gairy made this the central issue in the elections of 1972, in which the United Labour Party won 13 of the 15 seats in the House of Assembly. Following a constitutional conference in London in May 1973, Grenada became an independent nation within the Commonwealth in February 1974, despite strong opposition within the country. In the weeks preceding independence political tension increased, exacerbated by a worsening economic situation, and widespread demonstrations and strikes came close to crippling the economy.

Government

Grenada has dominion status within the Commonwealth. The Queen is represented by a Governor-General. Executive power is held by the Cabinet. Parliament comprises the Senate and the 15-member House of Assembly.

Economic Affairs

The economy of Grenada is essentially agricultural and centres on the traditional production of spices, and in particular nutmeg. Together with bananas, mace and cocoa, nutmeg is the principal export, although sugar, cotton, coffee, coconuts and citrus fruit are also significant. The United Kingdom is the principal trading partner. The development of manufacturing industries has not kept pace with other activities, due mainly to the small size of the local market, but revenue from the expanding tourist industry is playing an increasingly important role in the economy. Grenada is a member of the Caribbean Community (CARIBCOM).

Transport and Communications

There are some 560 miles of good roads in Grenada and a road-building programme is currently under way. Several foreign shipping lines serve the island and there is an airport 18 miles from St. George's, although this is not fully equipped to cope with the demands of the growing tourist traffic.

Education

The standard of education is high and is modelled to a large extent on the British pattern. There are 58 primary and 11 secondary schools. The Extra Mural Department of the University of the West Indies has a branch in St. George's.

Tourism

The colonial architecture of the capital and Grand Anse beach are the major tourist attractions.

Sport

Cricket is the chief sport, although tennis, football, horse-racing and water sports are also popular.

Weights and Measures

The imperial system is in use.

Currency and Exchange Rates

100 cents = 1 East Caribbean dollar (EC $).

Exchange rates (April 1974):
£1 sterling = EC $4.80;
U.S. $1 = EC $2.03.

STATISTICS

Area: 133 sq. miles.

Population (1972): 107,000; St. George's (capital) 22,893 (1970).

AGRICULTURE

PRINCIPAL CROPS
('ooo lb.)

	1969	1970	1971
Cocoa	9,017	6,008	6,438
Nutmeg	4,877	3,200	3,870
Mace	630	434	594
Bananas	50,526	42,177	31,537
Lime Oil (gallons)	1,720	n.a.	n.a.

FINANCE

100 cents = 1 East Caribbean dollar (EC $).
Coins: 1, 2, 5, 10, 25 and 50 cents.
Notes: 1, 5, 20 and 100 dollars.
Exchange rates (April 1974): £1 sterling = EC $4.80; U.S. $1 = EC $2.03.
EC $100 = £20.83 = U.S. $49.19.

Budget (1972 estimate): Expenditure EC $22.4 million.

External Trade (1970): Imports EC $44,080,000, Exports EC $10,497,000.

Tourism (1972): 37,933 visitors.

THE GOVERNMENT

Governor-General: H.E. Sir Leo de Gale, G.C.M.G.

CABINET
(May 1974)

Prime Minister and Minister for External Affairs, Home Affairs, Planning and Development, Lands and Tourism, Information Service, Public Relations and Natural Resources: Hon. Eric M. Gairy.

Minister of Finance, Trade and Industry: Hon. George Frederick Hosten.

Minister of Social Affairs, Co-operatives and Community Development: Hon. Mrs. Cynthia B. Gairy.

Minister of Health, Housing and Local Government: Hon. David T. Sylvester.

Minister of Communications and Works: Hon. Herbert Preudhomme.

Minister of Youth Development, Sport and Labour: Senator The Hon. W. M. Whyte.

Minister Without Portfolio and Leader of the Senate: Senator Derek Knight.

Minister of State, Trade and Industry: Hon. Franklyn Dolland.

Minister of Agriculture, Fisheries and Forestry: Hon. O. A. T. Raeburn.

Attorney-General: Hon. H. M. Squires.

Cabinet Secretary: G. Braithwaite.

SENATE

President: G. B. James, O.B.E.

Nominated Members: J. Thorne, Dr. A. Bierzynski, T. Forrester, D. Knight, Dr. J. A. Watts, W. Whyte, Ben Joseph Jones.

HOUSE OF ASSEMBLY

The Speaker: Hon. R. C. P. Moore, O.B.E.
Elected Members: 15.
Clerk: C. V. Strachan.

ELECTION, FEBRUARY 1972

Party	Seats
United Labour Party	13
Grenada National Party	2

POLITICAL PARTIES

Grenada National Party: St. George's; f. 1956; Leader Herbert Blaize.

Grenada United Labour Party: St. George's; Leader Eric Gairy.

New Jewel Movement (Joint Endeavour for Welfare, Education and Liberation): St. George's; f. 1972; radical opposition group; Leader Maurice Bishop.

RELIGION

Archdeacon of Grenada (Anglican): (vacant), Rectory, Church St., St. George's.

Bishop of St. George's in Grenada (Roman Catholic): Rt. Rev. PATRICK WEBSTER, Bishop's House, St. George's.

THE PRESS

Government Gazette: St. George's; weekly; official.

The Torchlight: P.O.B. 11, Melville St., St. George's; f. 1955; 3 times weekly.

The West Indian: Hillsborough St., St. George's; f. 1915; daily except Mon. and Fri.; Editor R. CLYNE; London Office: 122 Shaftesbury Ave., W1.

RADIO

Radio Grenada: Broadcasting House, St. George's; f. 1955; medium-wave transmissions to Grenada and the Grenadines, and short-wave transmissions to U.K., Europe and the Americas; Man. NEVILLE P. DaBREO.

FINANCE

BANKING

Grenada Agricultural Bank: Government Buildings, St. George's; f. 1965; Man. R. R. BANFIELD.

Grenada Co-operative Bank Ltd.: 8 Church St., St. George's; f. 1932; Man. Dir. and Sec. G. V. STEELE.

Grenada National Bank and Trust Co.: St. George's; f. 1969; cap. p.u. $136,600.

Bank of Nova Scotia: Head Office: 44 King St. West, Toronto 1, Ontario; Halifax St., St. George's; Man. I. W. MEARNS; sub.-br. Grand Anse.

Barclays Bank International Ltd.: Head Office: 54 Lombard St., London, EC3P 3AH; P.O.B. 37, St. George's; Man. L. R. E. JOHNSON; sub-brs. at Grenville and Carriacou; agencies at Gouyave, Grand Anse, Carenage and Sauteurs.

Canadian Imperial Bank of Commerce: Head Office: Commerce Court, Toronto 1, Ontario; Halifax St., St. George's; Man. A. R. SKOVMOSE; Main St., Sauters St. Patrick's; Man. R. S. GABRIEL.

Chase Manhattan Bank: Head Office: Chase Manhattan Plaza, New York; St. George's.

Royal Bank of Canada: Head Office: Place Ville Marie, Montreal; brs. in St. George's and Grenville; Man. (St. George's) R. F. DE SILVA.

INSURANCE

The larger insurance companies have agents in Grenada and the other islands of the group.

TRADE AND INDUSTRY

Grenada Chamber of Commerce, Inc.: P.O.B. 129, St. George's; f. 1921, incorporated 1947; 45 mems.; Pres. LESLIE PIERRE; Sec. Mrs. R. A. SMITH.

Grenada Cocoa Association: St. George's; f. 1964.

Grenada Co-operative Banana Society: St. George's; f. 1955; a statutory body to control production and marketing of bananas; Sec. W. KNIGHT.

Grenada Co-operative Nutmeg Association: Scott St., P.O.B. 160, St. George's; f. 1947; c. 4,200 mems.; processes and markets all the nutmeg and mace grown on the island on behalf of its 6,000 growers; Sec. R. S. RENWICK.

Jaycees of Grenada: P.O.B. 368, St. George's; Sec. D. FLETCHER.

Grenada Trade Union Council: P.O.B. 405, Otway House, St. George's; f. 1955; about 5,000 mems.; seven affiliated unions; affiliated to CCL and ICFTU; Pres. J. D. KNIGHT; Sec. C. B. STUART; the largest affiliates are:

Manual and Mental Workers' Union: Progress House, St. George's; f. 1951; about 2,000 mems.; Pres. ERIC M. GAIRY.

Technical and Allied Workers' Union: Otway House, St. George's; f. 1958; about 800 mems.; Pres. CURTIS B. STUART.

Grenada Union of Teachers: St. George's Government School, St. George's; f. 1913; 700 mems.; Pres. JEROME McBARNETTE.

Seamen and Waterfront Workers' Union: P.O.B. 154, St. George's; f. 1952; 600 mems.; Pres. GEORGE B. W. OTWAY.

Commercial and Industrial Workers' Union: St. George's.

CO-OPERATIVE SOCIETIES

A Co-operative Department was established in 1957. There are 16 Marketing Societies, 20 Credit Unions, one Credit Union League and one Farmers' Co-operative Council.

TRANSPORT

ROADS

There are approximately 566 miles of goods roads, of which about 356 miles have oiled surfaces. There are about 4,200 registered vehicles.

SHIPPING

The chief ports are St. George's and Grenville on Grenada and Hillsborough on Carriacou.

The chief lines are the Harrison, Saguenay Steamship, Royal Netherlands Steamship, Geest, Booth, Grimaldi Siosa, West Indian Shipping, Atlantic, James Nourse Line, Linca C Line, Booker Seaway and Blue Ribbon Line. Several local craft ply regularly between the islands.

CIVIL AVIATION

The airfield at Pearls, 18 miles from St. George's, is served by LIAT (Antigua). Lauriston Airport, on the Island of Carriacou, offers restricted services.

TOURISM

Grenada Tourist Board: St. George's; Exec.-Sec. Mrs. G. PROTAIN. There were 37,933 tourists in 1972.

GUATEMALA

INTRODUCTORY SURVEY

Location, Climate, Language, Religion, Flag, Capital

Guatemala is one of the seven territories of the Central American isthmus and is bounded to the north and west by Mexico with Honduras and El Salvador to the east and south. It has a long Pacific coastline and a narrow outlet on to the Caribbean. The climate is tropical in the lowlands with an average temperature of 28°c (83°F) and more temperate in the central highland area with an average temperature of 20°c (68°F). The official language is Spanish, but Indian dialects are widely spoken. Most of the people are Roman Catholics; there are a few Protestants. The national flag (proportions 3 by 2) consists of vertical stripes of blue, white and blue, the white stripe bearing the national coat of arms. The capital is Guatemala City.

Recent History

In June 1954 the left-wing President, Col. Jacobo Arbenz Guzmán, was overthrown as a result of a *coup* led by Col. Carlos Castillo Armas, who invaded the country with U.S. assistance. Castillo became President but was assassinated in July 1957. The next elected President, Gen. Miguel Ydigoras Fuentes, took office in March 1958 and ruled until he was deposed by a military *coup* in 1963. Dr. Julio César Méndez Montenegro was elected President in 1966. Much terrorist activity broke out during his term and amongst the worst outrages were the murders of the U.S. and West German ambassadors in 1968 and 1970 respectively. In 1970 the candidate of the Movimiento de Liberación Nacional (MLN), Col. (later Gen.) Carlos Araña Osorio, was elected President after a turbulent campaign. Violence continued during 1970, reaching a peak in September 1970 with several concentrated attacks by guerrilla forces on right-wing groups. A state of emergency was imposed in November 1970. This hardly lessened the rate of violent attacks and reprisals by right and left extremists. The state of emergency was lifted in November 1971, and the spate of political murders abated somewhat during 1972 and 1973. Amid charges of fraud, and claims that the main opposition candidate, Gen. Efraín Ríos Montt, had obtained some 53 per cent of the poll, Gen. Kjell Laugerud García of the MLN was declared President after the elections of March 1974. With no candidate officially obtaining an overall majority, the winner was announced by Congress and is due to take office in July 1974. Guatemala remains steadfast in her claim to the neighbouring territory of Belize and has made several attempts to negotiate with the United Kingdom on this question.

Government

Executive and legislative power is vested in the President, assisted by a Cabinet of ten Ministers. A new Constitution was promulgated in September 1965.

Defence

A military bloc alliance exists with El Salvador, Honduras, Nicaragua and Costa Rica.

Economic Affairs

The economy is predominantly agricultural and nearly one-third of the land is cultivable. Cotton, maize and coffee are the principal products, coffee accounting for about a third of all exports. Extensive forests provide timber and chicle. Mineral products include lead, zinc and chrome and there are commercial deposits of copper, uranium ore, sulphur and mercury. Sugar refining and beverages are the main industries and other light consumer goods are produced. Two oil refineries have been constructed. The exploitation of nickel deposits near Lake Izabal at Chalac-El Estor began early in 1973 after an agreement made in February 1971 between the government and International Nickel's Exmibal company. Plans for the first stage of the project provide for expenditure of $120 million and an annual output of 14,000 tons by 1977. Nickel will become Guatemala's second most important export. Foreign trade is largely with the United States. In 1960 a common market was established with El Salvador and Honduras, Nicaragua and Costa Rica joining later to form the Central American Common Market. A National Development Plan (1971–75) was adopted in July 1971 by Gen. Araña Osorio's administration and aims at encouraging the growth of agriculture, expanding tourism to under-developed areas of the country and improving education and health services. Its target is a 7.8 per cent annual growth in gross domestic product.

Transport and Communications

There are 822 km. of railways operated by one state-owned and one private company, and 11,230 km. of roads. The chief ports are Puerto Barrios, San José and Santo Tomás de Castilla. Internal and international flights are provided by one Guatemalan and six foreign lines. A new airport is to be built in the department of Escuintla at a cost of 25 million quetzales.

Social Welfare

Social security is compulsory, all employers with five or more workers being required to enrol with the State Institute of Social Security. Benefits are available to registered workers for industrial accidents, sickness, maternity, disability, widowhood and hospitalization.

Education

Elementary education is free and, in urban areas, compulsory. Primary education lasts for six years and secondary education for five years. The current rate of illiteracy is some 60 per cent. There are two state and two private universities.

Tourism

The main attractions lie in the mountain regions, with their volcanoes, lakes and mountain villages which remain much the same as in the days of the Maya Empire. The old capital, Antigua, retains the ruins of buildings wrecked in the great earthquake of 1773. In the National Development Plan (1971–75) approximately 11.2 million quetzales have been allocated to the development of tourist facilities, in particular in the El Petén region.

Sport

The main sports are football, baseball, swimming and basketball.

Public Holidays

1974: August 15th (Guatemala City only), September 15th (Independence Day), October 12th (Columbus Day), October 20th (Revolution Day), November 1st (All Saints' Day), December 24th, 25th (Christmas).

1975: January 1st (New Year's Day), March 26th–29th (Easter), May 1st (Labour Day), June 30th (Anniversary of the Revolution), July 1st (Bank Employees' Day).

Weights and Measures

The metric system is in official use, but Spanish weights and measures are used in local trade.

1 libra = 1.014 lb.	1 league = 3.46 miles
1 arroba = 25.35 lb.	1 vara = 32.5 in.
1 quintal = 101.4 lb.	1 quarta = 8.224 in.
1 tonelada = 18.10 cwt.	1 caballería = 110 acres

Currency and Exchange Rates

100 centavos = 1 quetzal.

Exchange rates (April 1974):
£1 sterling = 2.36 quetzales;
U.S. $1 = 1.00 quetzal.

STATISTICAL SURVEY

AREA AND POPULATION

AREA (sq. km.)	POPULATION (1972*)			
	Total	Births	Marriages	Deaths
108,889	5,211,929	118,026	11,616	28,464

* Preliminary.

DEPARTMENTS
(1973*)

Alta Verapaz	. .	276,370	Jalapa . .	118,103
Baja Verapaz	. .	106,909	Jutiapa . .	231,005
Chimaltenango	. .	193,557	Quezaltenango .	311,613
Chiquimula	. .	158,146	Retalhuleu . .	133,993
El Petén .	. .	64,503	Sacatepéquez .	99,710
El Progreso	. .	73,176	San Marcos . .	388,100
El Quiché .	. .	300,641	Santa Rosa .	176,198
Escuintla .	. .	300,140	Sololá . .	126,884
Guatemala .	. .	1,127,845	Suchitepéquez .	212,017
Huehuetenango	.	368,807	Totonicapán .	166,622
Izabal ,	. .	170,864	Zacapa . .	106,726

CHIEF TOWNS

Guatemala City (capital)	717,322	Jutiapa	. . .	52,244
Escuintla .	. .	68,573	Jalapa .	. .	45,417
Quezaltenango	. .	65,733	Cobán .	. .	43,538
Totonicapán	. .	52,599			

* Preliminary.

AGRICULTURE
PRINCIPAL CROPS

		1970	1971	1972*
Sugar . . .	'ooo metric tons	2,348	2,467	2,969
Cotton . . .	„ „ „	54	62	84
Maize . . .	„ „ „	772	756	719
Rice . . .	„ „ „	23	59	69
Dry Beans . .	„ „ „	134	134	135
Wheat . . .	„ „ „	33	38	46
Coffee . . .	„ „ „	127	128	138
Bananas . . .	'ooo stems	266	280	306

* Preliminary.

Livestock (1970–71 'ooo head): Horses 145; Mules 48; Asses 5; Cattle 1,450; Pigs 800; Sheep 510; Goats 16; Poultry 9,700.

INDUSTRY

	1970	1971	1972*
Cement ('ooo metric tons)	231	235	259
Beer ('ooo hectolitres) .	299	328	356
Other Alcoholic Beverages ('ooo hectolitres) .	86	93	94
Sugar ('ooo metric tons)	182	197	221
Electricity (million kWh.) . . .	647	687	773
Cigarettes (million) . . .	2,986	3,071	2,893

* Preliminary.

FINANCE

100 centavos=1 quetzal.

Coins: 1, 5, 10 and 25 centavos.

Notes: 50 centavos; 1, 5, 10, 20, 50 and 100 quetzales.

Exchange rates (April 1974): £1 sterling=2.36 quetzales; U.S. $1=1.00 quetzal.

100 quetzales=£42.35=$100.00.

Note: The Central American peso, used for transactions within the Central American Common Market, is also at par with the U.S. dollar.

BUDGET
(1972—million quetzales)

REVENUE		EXPENDITURE	
Taxation	185.1	Education	34.9
Treasury Bills and Foreign Loans .	73.4	Health	22.8
Other Receipts	1.5	Agriculture	19.0
Deficit	1.5	Defence	22.5
		Communications and Public Works . .	41.9
		Transportation	12.7
		Other Items	107.7
TOTAL	261.5	TOTAL	261.5

GUATEMALA—(STATISTICAL SURVEY)

NATIONAL ACCOUNTS
(million quetzales)

	1970	1971	1972*
GROSS NATIONAL PRODUCT	1,862	1,941	2,115
Less balance of exports and imports . .	16	—28	3
Less net factor income from abroad . .	—42	—44	—49
AVAILABLE RESOURCES	1,888	2,013	2,161
of which:			
Private consumption expenditure . .	1,493	1,588	1,733
Government consumption expenditure .	151	139	149
Gross domestic fixed capital investment .	239	263	285
Increase in stocks	6	22	—5

* Preliminary.

RESERVES AND CURRENCY
('ooo Central American pesos on December 31st.)

	1970	1971	1972
Gross Reserves at the Central Bank . .	85,620	100,135	142,524
Gold and Foreign Currency	83,561	89,303	124,466
Gold Deposits with IMF	11	3,023	9,780
SDRs	2,048	7,809	8,278

BALANCE OF PAYMENTS
(million Central American pesos)

	1971			1972*		
	Credit	Debit	Balance	Credit	Debit	Balance
Goods and Services:						
Goods	286.9	289.9	— 3.0	333.2	295.7	37.5
Services	59.6	128.7	—69.1	65.2	155.9	—90.7
Total	346.4	418.6	—72.1	398.4	451.6	—53.2
Transfer Payments (net) . . .	26.2	—	26.2	29.0	—	29.0
Capital Operations (net) . . .	60.3	—	60.3	79.9	—	79.9
Net Errors and Omissions . . .	0.1	—	0.1	—	17.0	—17.0
Changes in Reserves . . .			—14.5			—38.7

* Preliminary.

EXTERNAL TRADE
('ooo quetzales)

	IMPORTS	EXPORTS
1969	262,880	262,511
1970	295,167	297,138
1971	317,118	286,936
1972	329,847	335,875

PRINCIPAL COMMODITIES
('ooo quetzales)

Imports	1970	1971	1972*
Basic Manufactures	85,085	81,732	84,589
Machinery and Transport Equipment	75,517	81,567	87,500
Chemicals and Products	54,711	59,903	65,047
Food Products	25,224	24,124	24,362
Combustible Minerals, Lubricants and Products	6,180	15,294	21,306
Crude Materials, excl. Combustibles	6,288	7,135	7,312
Animal and Vegetable Oil	4,101	4,893	3,704
Beverages and Tobacco	1,553	1,358	1,112

* Preliminary.

Exports	1970	1971	1972
Coffee, incl. Soluble	102,611	98,034	106,556
Cotton	27,168	25,997	40,917
Fresh Meat	12,654	17,373	18,045
Bananas	13,553	14,467	17,216
Sugar	9,153	9,854	16,118
Zinc, Lead and Other Materials	4,448	3,372	3,845
Vegetables	5,553	3,928	3,431
Tyres and Inner Tubes	4,390	4,629	4,913

PRINCIPAL COUNTRIES

	1971		1972*	
	Imports	Exports	Imports	Exports
Costa Rica	13,572	25,729	13,067	26,661
El Salvador	42,533	40,802	45,768	45,273
Germany, Federal Republic	31,302	30,543	29,955	33,930
Honduras	1,766	9,866	1,281	9,367
Italy	4,644	8,622	4,941	8,070
Japan	32,224	19,486	28,242	26,912
Netherlands	5,123	9,743	4,657	13,897
Nicaragua	8,565	16,741	8,667	17,621
United Kingdom	13,997	2,586	13,501	3,222
U.S.A.	97,279	86,707	103,848	95,071
Venezuela	9,487	16	15,977	73

* Preliminary.

Tourism: 1971: 270,000 visitors; 1972: 340,000; Expenditure 1972: U.S. $37m.

TRANSPORT
ROADS

	1966	1967
Four-wheel Vehicles	51,512	59,625
Two-wheel Vehicles	68,701	70,912

EDUCATION

(1967)

	NUMBER	PUPILS	TEACHERS
Primary . .	4,735	474,919	12,594
Secondary	342	60,340	4,919
Technical	18	2,835	86
University . .	4	11,307	834

Sources: Banco de Guatemala; Consejo Monetario Centroamericano.

THE CONSTITUTION

The present constitution of Guatemala was decreed on September 15th, 1965. The main points are as follows:

Guatemala has a republican representative democratic system of government and power is exercised equally by the Legislative, Executive and Judicial Organisms. The official language is Spanish. Suffrage is universal and secret, obligatory for those who can read and write and optional for those who are illiterate. The free formation and growth of political parties whose aims are democratic is guaranteed. To register, parties must have at least 50,000 adherents, of which at least twenty per cent must be literate. There is no discrimination on grounds of race, colour, sex, religion, birth, economic or social position or political opinions.

The State will give protection to capital and private enterprise in order to develop sources of labour and stimulate creative activity.

Monopolies are forbidden and the State will limit any enterprise which might prejudice the development of the community. The right to social security is recognized and it shall be on a national, unitary, obligatory basis.

Constitutional guarantees may be suspended in certain circumstances for up to thirty days (unlimited in the case of war).

Legislative power is in the hands of Congress, which is made up of deputies elected directly by the people through universal suffrage. Congress meets on June 15th each year and ordinary sessions last four months; extraordinary sessions can be called by the Permanent Commission or the Executive. All Congressional decisions must be taken by absolute majority of the members, except in special cases laid down by law. Deputies are elected for four years; they may be re-elected after a lapse of one session, but only once. Congress is responsible for all matters concerning the President and Vice-President and their execution of their offices; for all electoral matters; for all matters concerning the laws of the Republic; for approving the Budget and decreeing taxes; for declaring war; for conferring honours, both civil and military; for fixing the coinage and the system of weights and measures; for approving, by two-thirds majority, any international treaty or agreement affecting the law, sovereignty, financial status or security of the country.

The President is elected by universal suffrage, by absolute majority for a non-extendable period of four years. Re-election or prolongation of the presidential term of office are punishable by law. The President is responsible for national defence and security, fulfilling the Constitution, leading the armed forces, taking any necessary steps in time of national emergency, passing and executing laws, international policy, nominating and removing ministers, officials and diplomats, co-ordinating the actions of Ministers of State. The Vice-President's duties include presiding over Congress and taking part in the discussions of the Council of Ministers.

The *Guatemalan Army* is intended to maintain national independence, sovereignty and honour, territorial integrity and peace within the Republic. It is an indivisible, apolitical, non-deliberating body and is made up of land, sea and air forces. The President of the Republic is General Commander of the Army.

For the purposes of administration the territory of the Republic is divided into departments and these into municipalities, but this division can be modified by Congress to suit the interests and general development of the Nation without loss of municipal autonomy.

Justice is exercised exclusively by the Supreme Court of Justice and other tribunals. Administration of Justice is obligatory, free and independent of the other functions of State. The President of the Judiciary, judges and other officials are elected by Congress for four years. The *Supreme Court of Justice* is made up of at least seven judges. The President of the Judiciary is also President of the Supreme Court. The Supreme Court nominates all other judges. Under the Supreme Court come the Court of Appeal, the Administrative Disputes Tribunal, the Tribunal of Second Instance of Accounts, Jurisdiction Conflicts, First Instance and Military, the Extraordinary Tribunal of Protection. There is a Court of Constitutionality presided over by the President of the Supreme Court.

THE GOVERNMENT

HEAD OF THE STATE

President: Gen. Carlos Manuel Araña Osorio.
Vice-President: Lic. Eduardo Cáceres Lehnhoff.

THE CABINET

(May 1974)

Minister of Foreign Affairs: Jorge Arenales Catalán.
Minister of the Interior: Dr. Roberto Herrera Ibargüen.
Minister of National Defence: Gen. Fausto David Rubio Coronado.
Minister of Economy: Lic. Carlos Molina Mencos.
Minister of Finance: Lic. Jorge Lamport Rodil.
Minister of Public Health and Social Assistance: Dr. José Trinidad Uclés R.

Minister of Communications and Public Works: Ing. Gustavo Anzueto Vielman.
Minister of Agriculture: Ing. Mario Martínez Gutiérrez.
Minister of Education: Lic. Alejandro Maldonado Aguirre.
Minister of Labour and Social Welfare: Lic. Lionel López Rivera.
Secretary-General to the Presidency: Lic. José Arturo Ruano Mejía.

Note: Following the elections of March 1974, Gen. Kjell Eugenio Laugerud García is due to take office as President on July 1st, 1974, with Lic. Mario Sandóval Alarcón as Vice-President.

DIPLOMATIC REPRESENTATION

EMBASSIES AND LEGATION ACCREDITED TO GUATEMALA

(E) Embassy; (L) Legation.

(Guatemala City, unless otherwise stated.)

Argentina: 2A Avda. 11-22, Zona 10 (E); *Ambassador:* Horacio García Fernández.
Australia: Mexico D.F., Mexico (E).
Austria: Hotel Camino Real, Avda. Reforma y 15 Calle (E); *Chargé d'Affaires (a.i.):* Dr. Hans Kaufmann.
Belgium: 11 Calle 8-35, Zona 1 (E); *Ambassador:* Maurice Seynave (also accred. to Honduras and Nicaragua).
Bolivia: (E); *Ambassador:* Dr. Angel Mendizábal Moya.
Brazil: Edificio La Continental, 6° piso, 7A Avda. 10-34, Zona 1 (E); *Ambassador:* Mario Vieira de Mello.
Canada: Edificio Etisa, 7° piso, Plazuela España, Zona 9; *Chargé d'Affaires:* Clive Alexander Carruthers.
Chile: Edificio Etisa, 5° piso, Plazuela España, Zona 9 (E); *Ambassador:* Manuel Tello Troncoso.
China (Taiwan): 13 Calle 6-77, Zona 1, 6° piso (E); *Ambassador:* Chi-hsien Mao.
Colombia: 5A Avda. 16-73, Zona 10 (E); *Ambassador:* Vicente Laverde Aponte.
Costa Rica: 2A Avda. 12-51, Zona 1 (E); *Ambassador:* Ing. Edwin Góngora Arroyo.
Denmark: Mexico D.F., Mexico (E).
Dominican Republic: 6A Avda. "A" 2-74, Zona 10 (E); *Ambassador:* Conrado Licairac.
Ecuador: Edificio Panamericano, 13 Calle 6-79, Zona 1 (E); *Ambassador:* Dr. José María Ponce Yépez.
Egypt: San Salvador, El Salvador (E).
El Salvador: 7A Avda. 13-56, Zona 9 (E); *Ambassador:* Eduardo Casanova Sandóval.
Finland: Mexico D.F., Mexico (E).
France: 14 Calle 5-52, Zona 9 (E); *Ambassador:* Henri Ruffin.
Germany, Federal Republic: Avda. Reforma 13-70, Zona 9 (E); *Ambassador:* Wolfram Hucke.
Greece: Mexico D.F., Mexico (E).
Honduras: 15 Calle "A" 11-08, Zona 10 (E); *Ambassador:* Manuel Luna Mejía.
Israel: 10A Calle 6-47, Zona 1 (E); *Ambassador:* Yair Behar (also accred. to Honduras).

Italy: 16 Calle 0-55, Zona 10 (E); *Ambassador:* Dr. Fabrizio Pediconi.
Japan: 12 Calle 6-41, Zona 9 (E); *Ambassador:* Junzo Mori.
Korea, Republic: Mexico D.F., Mexico (E).
Lebanon: Mexico D.F., Mexico (E).
Malta: 7A Avda. 7-74, Zona 9 (L); *Minister:* Peter J. Vélez de Silva.
Mexico: 4A Calle 6-55, Zona 9 (E); *Ambassador:* Federico Barrera Fuentes.
Netherlands: Galerías España, Plaza España, Zona 9 (E); *Chargé d'Affaires:* Jacobus Arie Kooy.
Nicaragua: 6A Calle 4-45, Zona 9 (E); *Ambassador:* Carlos Manuel Pérez Alonso.
Norway: Mexico D.F., Mexico (E).
Panama: 3A Calle 6-40, Zona 10 (E); *Ambassador:* Dionisio Johnson.
Paraguay: San Salvador, El Salvador (E).
Peru: 14 Calle 9-30, Zona 10 (E); *Ambassador:* Santiago Marcenaro Romero.
Portugal: Mexico D.F., Mexico (E).
Spain: Galerías España, 6° piso, Plazuela España, Zona 9 (E); *Ambassador:* Justo Bermejo y Gómez.
Sweden: 4A Avda. 12-59, Zona 10 (E); *Ambassador:* Klaes König (also accred. to Nicaragua).
Switzerland: 12 Calle 6-51, Zona 1 (E); *Ambassador:* Gottlieb Gut (also accred. to Honduras and Nicaragua).
Turkey: Mexico D.F., Mexico (E).
U.S.A.: 8A Avda. 11-65, Zona 1 (E); *Chargé d'Affaires:* John T. Dreyfuss.
Uruguay: 10A Calle 6-37, Zona 1 (E); *Ambassador:* Román Marquine Garay.
Vatican: 10A Calle 4-47, Zona 9 (Apostolic Nunciature); *Nuncio:* Mgr. Gerolamo Prigione.
Venezuela: 8A Calle 0-56, Zona 9 (E); *Ambassador:* Dr. Hernán González Vale.

PRESIDENTIAL ELECTION

(March 3rd, 1974)

Gen. Kjell Eugenio Laugerud García (MLN/PID)	298,953
Gen. Efraín Ríos Montt (PDC) . . .	228,067
Col. Ernesto Paiz Novales (PR) . .	143,111

Since no candidate achieved an overall majority, the final decision was made by Congress. Gen. Laugerud García was chosen and is due to take office on July 1st, 1974.

NATIONAL CONGRESS

President: Lic. Mario Sandóval Alarcón (M.L.N.).

ELECTION, MARCH 1970

Party	Seats
M.L.N.	29
P.R.	14
P.I.D.	8
D.C.G.	4

Note: At the time of going to press the composition of the new Congress was not known.

POLITICAL PARTIES

Movimiento de Liberación Nacional (MLN): 5A Calle 1–20, Zona 1, Guatemala City; f. 1960; right-wing, member of ruling coalition; Leader Lic. Mario Sandóval Alarcón; Presidential candidate in 1974 Gen. Kjell Laugerud García; 95,000 mems.

Partido Institucional Democrático (PID): 2A Calle 10–73, Zona 1, Guatemala City; f. 1965; member of ruling coalition; Presidential candidate in 1974 Gen. Kjell Laugerud García; 60,000 mems.

Partido Demócrata Cristiano (PDC): Leader René de León Schlotter; Presidential candidate in 1974 Gen. Efraín Ríos Montt.

Partido Revolucionario (PR): 4A Calle 6–09, Zona 1, Guatemala City; f. 1957; democratic party; Leader Carlos Sagastume Pérez; Presidential candidate in 1974 Col. Ernesto Paiz Novales; 100,000 mems.

Frente Demócrata Guatemalteca: Leader Clemente Marroquín Rojas.

Frente Unido Revolucionario Democrático (FURD): Leader Manuel Colom Argueta (Mayor, Guatemala City).

Partido de Acción y Reconstrucción Nacional: Leader Col. Enrique Peralta Azurdia.

JUDICIAL SYSTEM

President of the Supreme Court: Lic. Miguel Ortiz Passarelli.

Civil Courts of Appeal: 9 courts, 4 in Guatemala City, 2 in Quezaltenango, 1 each in Jalapa, Zacapa and Antigua. The two Labour Courts of Appeal are in Guatemala City.

Judges of the First Instance: 6 civil and 6 penal in Guatemala City, 2 civil each in Quezaltenango, Escuintla, Jutiapa and San Marcos, 1 civil in each of the 18 remaining departments of the Republic.

RELIGION

The predominant religion is that of the Roman Catholic Church.

ROMAN CATHOLIC

Metropolitan See: Arzobispado, Apdo. 723, Guatemala City; His Eminence Cardinal Mario Casariego.

Suffragan Sees:
Huehuetenango: Rt. Rev. Hugo Marcos Gerbermann.
Jalapa: Rt. Rev. Miguel Angel García y Aráuz.
Quezaltenango: Rt. Rev. Luis L. Manresa Formosa.
San Marcos: Rt. Rev. Próspero Penados del Barrio.
Solola: Rt. Rev. Angelico Melotto Mazzardo.
Vera Paz: Rt. Rev. Juan Gerardi Conedera.
Zacapa: Rt. Rev. Constantino Cristiano Luna.

PROTESTANT

Presbyterian: 6A Avda. "A" 6-48, Zona 1.

Union: 12 Calle 7-37, Zona 9, Plazuela España.

Episcopal: Apdo. 58-A, Guatemala; diocese founded 1967; Bishop: Rt. Rev. Anselmo Carral; one parish church and four missions in Guatemala City and eight rural missions.

Church of Jesus Christ of Latter Day Saints: 12 Calle 3-37, Zona 9; 10 bishoprics, 7 chapels; Pres. Guillermo Enrique Rittscher.

Synagogue: 7A Avda., Zona 10.

THE PRESS

PRINCIPAL DAILIES

Guatemala City

Diario de Centro América: 9A Avda. 11-34, Zona 1; f. 1880; evening; official; Dir. Benjamín Paniagua S.; circ. 12,000.

Diario Impacto: 9A Calle "A" 1-56, Zona 1; f. 1959; morning; independent; Dir. Oscar Marroquín Rojas; circ. 18,000 (weekdays), 40,000 (Sundays).

El Gráfico: 14 Avda. 4-33, Zona 1; morning; Dir. Jorge Carpio Nicolle; circ. 48,000.

La Hora: 1A Avda. 9-18, Zona 1; f. 1920; evening; independent; Editor-Dir. Clemente Marroquín Rojas; circ. 15,000.

Headlines: English.

El Imparcial: 3A Avda. Sur; f. 1921; evening; independent; Dir. Ramón Blanco; Editor David Vela; circ. 45,000.

Prensa Libre: 13 Calle 9-31, Zona 1; f. 1951; evening; independent; Dir. Pedro Julio García; Man. Salvador Girón Collier; circ. 45,000.

La Tarde: 14 Avda. 4-33, Zona 1; evening; independent; Dir. Jorge Carpio Nicolle; circ. 19,000.

PERIODICALS
Guatemala City

AGA: 9A Calle 3-43, Zona 1; agricultural monthly.

APG—Asociación de Periodistas de Guatemala (*Organ of the Guatemalan Journalist's Association*): 14 Calle 3-29, Zona 1; f. 1949; quarterly; Dir. Luis Edgardo Tejeda; circ. 1,000.

Boletín del Colegio de Abogados de Guatemala: Avda. Elena 14-45, Zona 1; f. 1952; every four months.

Guayacán: 8A Calle 6-69, Zona 4; agricultural monthly; f. 1962; Editor Ing. José Guillermo Pacheco; circ. 5,000.

La Hora Dominical: 9A Calle "A" 1-56, Zona 1; f. 1948; weekly; Editor Oscar Marroquín Rojas; circ. 26,000.

Industria: Ruta 6 9-21, Zona 4; monthly; official organ of the Chamber of Industry.

Revista Cafetalera: Edif. Etisa, Plazuela España; monthly; official organ of the National Coffee Association; circ. 4,000.

Revista de la Economía Nacional: f. 1946; monthly; publ. by Ministerio de Economía, Palacio Nacional.

Revista de la Federación Médica de Guatemala: f. 1947; monthly.

Revista Militar: Ministerio de Defensa Nacional, Palacio Nacional; quarterly; military; publ. by the Army Staff; circ. 1,200.

Revista Oficial de la Cruz Roja Guatemalteca: 3A Calle 8-40, Zona 1; f. 1935; monthly; organ of the Guatemala Red Cross; Editor Rodulfo Figuera Guillén.

PRESS ASSOCIATION

Asociación de Periodistas de Guatemala (APG): 14 Calle 3-29, Zona 1; Pres. Manuel Eduardo Rodríguez.

NEWS AGENCIES
Foreign Bureaux

Agence France-Presse: 4A Calle 14-22, Zona 13, Guatemala City; Chief Joaquín Méndez.

ANSA: Ruta 1 4-36, Zona 4, Guatemala City; Chief Alfonso Anzueto.

PUBLISHERS
Guatemala City

Editorial González Porto: 11 Calle 4-53; arts, science, fiction, education, textbooks; Man. Salvador Marban Santos.

Cía. Editora El Gráfico S.A.: 14 Avda. 4-33, Zona 1; Dir. Jorge Carpio Nicolle; publs. *El Gráfico, La Tarde.*

Imprenta Iberia Gutenberg: 6A Avda. 15-70; Propr. J. M. Ordóñez.

Sánchez y de Guise: 8A Avda. 12-58, Zona 1; Propr. Raúl de la Rosa y Cobar.

Editorial Universitaria: 10A Calle 9-59, Zona 1; fiction, history, reference, social sciences, secondary educational textbooks; Dir. G. Salazar.

RADIO AND TELEVISION
RADIO

Dirección General de Radiodifusión y Televisión Nacional: Calle 18 de Setiembre 6-72, Zona 1, Guatemala City; f. 1931; Government supervisory body; Dir.-Gen. J. Ramón Bonilla.

There are 5 government and 6 educational stations, including:

La Voz de Guatemala: Calle 18 de Setiembre 6-72, Zona 1, Guatemala City; Government station; Dir. R. Bonilla R.

Radio Cultural: 4A Avda. 30-09, Zona 3, Apdo. 601, Guatemala City; religious and cultural station owned by Central American Mission, 8625 La Prada Drive, Dallas, Tex. 75228, U.S.A.; programmes in Spanish and English, Quiche and Cakchiquel; Dir. Lic. Hugo Morales; Gen. Man. Donald Rutledge.

There are 77 commercial stations of which the most important are:

La Voz de las Américas: 2A Avda. 13-39, Zona 1, Guatemala City; Dir. José Flamenco y Cotero.

Radio Cinco Sesenta: 30 Avda. 3-40, Zona 11, Guatemala City; Dir. R. A. Díaz.

Radio Continental: 13 Calle 12-26, Zona 1, Guatemala City; Dir. R. Vizcaino R.

Radio Fabulosa: Apdo. 1466, Zona 4, Guatemala City; Propr. Francisco Maza C.

Radio Nuevo Mundo: 6A Avda. 10-45, Zona 1, Apdo. 281, Guatemala City; Man. H. González J.

Radio Panamericana: Km. 12, Carretera Roosevelt, Guatemala City; Dir. M. V. de Paniagua.

Radio Super Radio: 6A Avda. 15-40, Zona 1, Guatemala City; Dir. M. A. Rodríguez.

In 1971 there were 221,000 radio receivers.

TELEVISION

Radio-Televisión Guatemala, S.A.: 30A Avda. 3-40, Zona 11, Apdo. 1367, Guatemala City; f. 1956; commercial station; Gen. Man. W. G. Campbell.

Tele Once: 20 Calle 5-02, Zona 10, Guatemala City; commercial; Dir. A. Mourra.

Televicentro: 3A Calle 6-24, Zona 9, Apdo. 1242, Guatemala City; f. 1964; commercial station channel 7; Dir. Dr. J. Villanueva P.

In 1971 there were 85,000 TV receivers.

FINANCE

(cap.=capital; p.u.=paid up; dep.=deposits; m.=million; amounts in quetzales)

BANKING

Superintendencia de Bancos: 7A Avda. 22-01, Zona 1, Guatemala City; f. 1946; Superintendent of Banking Tomás Villamar Contreras; publ. *Boletín Anual.*

Central Bank

Banco de Guatemala: 7A Avda. 22-01, Zona 1, Guatemala City; f. 1946; guarantee fund 10.2m. (Dec. 1971); Pres. Augusto Contreras Godoy; Gen. Man. Manuel Méndez Escobar.

Commercial Banks
Guatemala City

Banco Agrícola Mercantil: 7 Avda. 9-11, Zona 1; f. 1926; cap. p.u. 2.5m., dep. 52m. (Dec. 1973); Man. Dir. Manuel Soto Marroquín.

Banco del Agro S.A.: 9A Calle 5-39, Zona 1; f. 1956; cap. 3.6m., reserves 235,930 (1973); Pres. Ricardo Rodríguez Paul; Man. Julio Gándara Valenzuela.

Banco Granai y Townson S.A.: 7A Avda. 1-86, Zona 4; f. 1962; cap. p.u. 1.8m., dep. 30.6m.; 15 brs.; Pres. MARIO GRANAI ANDRINO; Gen. Man. ARTURO SAÁ DEL RÍO.

Banco Inmobilario S.A.: 8A Avda. 10-57, Zona 1; f. 1958; cap. 2.5m., dep. 22.8m. (Dec. 1971); Pres. Dr. JULIO CLUEVEDO; Man. Dir. MARIO MORY.

Banco Nacional de Desarrollo Agrícola (Bandesa): 9A Calle 9-47, Zona 1.

Banco de los Trabajadores: 8 Avda. 9-41, Zona 1; f. 1966; cap. 4.2m.; government owned; deals with loans for establishing and improving small industries as well as normal banking business.

Crédito Hipotecario Nacional: 7A Avda. 22-77, Zona 1; f. 1930; government owned; cap. 3.15m., dep. 75.9m. (Dec. 1973); Pres. CARLOS CLAVERÍE M.; Gen. Man. LUIS M. MONTÚFAR L.

Quezaltenango

Banco de Occidente: 7A Avda. 11-52, Zona 1; f. 1881; cap. and res. 2.6m., dep. 33.7m. (Jan. 1972); Man. HERCULANO AGUIRRE.

DEVELOPMENT BANKS

Banco Industrial, S.A.: f. 1964, operations began June 1968; to promote industrial development; privately owned; cap. and dep. 55.1m.; Pres. RAMIRO CASTILLO LOVE.

Financiera Industrial y Agropecuaria (FIASA): Avda. La Reforma 10-00, Zona 9, Guatemala City; f. 1967; private development bank; medium and long term loans to private industrial enterprises in Central America; cap. 1.2m., liabilities 59m. (Dec. 1971); Gen. Man. JULIO VIELMAN.

FOREIGN BANKS

Bank of America National Trust and Savings Association: Bank of America Center, San Francisco, Calif.; 5A Avda. 10-55, Zona 1, Apdo. 1335, Guatemala City; Man. WILLIAM H. SNODGRASS.

Bank of London and Montreal: 8A Avda. 10-67, Zona 1, Guatemala City; cap. 2.5m. dep. 58m. (Dec. 1973); Man. O. G. CÁCERES; agencies: 3 in Guatemala City, 1 in Escuintla, 1 in Puerto Barrios, 1 in Antigua.

ASSOCIATION

Asociación de Banqueros de Guatemala: 10A Calle 7-70, Zona 9, Guatemala City; f. 1961; represents all state and private banks; Pres. Lic. MANUEL SOTO MARROQUÍN; Sec. Señorita THELMA ZEBADÚA G.

INSURANCE
Guatemala City

Afianzadora Guatemalteca, S.A.: 8A Avda. 10-64, Zona 1; f. 1946; Gen. Man. JOSÉ ERNESTO ANDRADE KELLER.

Aseguradora Quetzal, S.A.: 5A Calle 4-67, Zona 1; f. 1952; Man. J. BONILLA BARNOYA.

Comercial Aseguradora Suizo-Americana, S.A.: 7A Avda. 7-07, Zona 9; Gen. Man. J. J. PENABAD.

Crédito Hipotecario Nacional: 7A Avda. 22-77, Zona 1; f. 1930; fire and other forms of insurance; Pres. CARLOS CLAVERÍE M.

Granai Townson, S.A.: 7A Avda. 1-82, Zona 4.

La Previsora Ltda.: 8A Calle 3-68, Zona 1; f. 1961; Gen. Man. RAMÓN GARCÍA FARGAS.

Seguros Cruz Azul de Guatemala, S.A.: 5A Avda. 8-30, Zona 1; f. 1951; life, marine, fire, auto; Man. Dir. WILLIAM PENNINGTON BUZZINI.

TRADE AND INDUSTRY

CHAMBER OF COMMERCE

Asociación General de Comerciantes Guatemaltecos: 7A Avda. 10-34, Edificio La Continental, Zona 1, Guatemala City.

Cámara de Comercio de Guatemala: 10A Calle 3-80, Zona 1, Guatemala City; f. 1894; Pres. EDMUNDO NANNE ZIRIÓN.

CHAMBERS OF INDUSTRY

Cámara de Industria de Guatemala: 3A Avda. 12-21, Zona 1, Guatemala City; f. 1958; Pres. JOSÉ MARÍA PASSARELLI; Man. Lic. D. VILLATORO DÁVILA.

Cámara Guatemalteca de la Construcción (*Guatemala Chamber of Building*): 7A Avda. y 1A Calle, Zona 9, Edificio Canella, Guatemala City.

DEVELOPMENT ASSOCIATIONS

Centro Nacional de Promoción de las Exportaciones GUATEXPRO: 7A Avda. 7-78, Zona 4, Edificio Centroamericano, 2°, Guatemala City; national agency for the promotion of Guatemalan exports.

Corporación Financiera Nacional (Corfina): f. 1973 as autonomous state agency to provide assistance for the development of industry, mining and the tourist trade.

Instituto de Fomento de la Producción: 9A Calle 9-47, Zona 1, Guatemala City; f. 1948 to promote the national economy, with particular emphasis on industry and agriculture, by means of electrification and irrigation projects, guaranteed prices, experimental stations; cap. p.u. and res. 9,572.4m.; Pres. Lic. LUIS A. CARRILLO; Man. Lic. JULIO GÁNDARA; publs. *Memoria Anual de Labores, Carta Mensual*.

Empresa Nacional de Fomento y Desarrollo Económico de El Petén (FYDEP): 2A Calle 1-00, Zona 10, Guatemala City; attached to the Ministry of Economy; economic development agency for the Department of El Petén; Dir. OLIVIERO CASASOLA.

Instituto de Fomento de Hipotecas Aseguradas (FHA): 6A Avda. 1-27, Zona 4, 4°, Guatemala City; f. 1961; insured mortgage institution for the promotion of house construction; Pres. JORGE EDUARDO GARCÍA SALAS; Gen. Man. Lic. ENRIQUE SANTA CRUZ.

Instituto Nacional de Administración para el Desarrollo (INAD): 6A Avda. 8-92, Zona 9, Apdo. 971, Guatemala City; f. 1965; provides technical experts to assist all branches of the government in administrative reform programmes; provides in-service training for local and central government staff; has research programmes in administration, sociology, politics and economics; provides post-graduate education; Dir. Dr. F. JOSÉ MONSANTO.

Instituto Nacional de Transformación Agraria: 14 Calle 7-14, Zona 1, Guatemala City; f. 1962 to carry out agrarian reform; current programme includes development of Sebol and Chinaja projects.

Oficina Promotora de Negocios: 8A Calle 9-41, Zona 1, Guatemala City; trade promotion.

PRODUCERS' ASSOCIATIONS

Asociación de Azucareros de Guatemala (*Sugar Producers' Association*): 12 Calle "A" 2-41, Zona 1, Guatemala City.

Asociación de Exportadores de Café: 11 Calle 7-35, Zona 1, Edificio Lido, 4°, Guatemala City; coffee exporters' association.

Asociación de Fabricantes de Alcoholes y Licores (ANFAL): Km. 16 1-2, Carretera Roosevelt, Mixco, Guatemala; distillers' association.

Asociación General de Agricultores (*Association of Agriculturalists*): 9A Calle 3-34, Zona 1, Guatemala City.

Asociación Guatemalteca de Productores de Algodón (*Cotton Producers' Association*): 2 Ruta 2-26, Zona 4, Guatemala City; f. 1954; 60 mems.; Pres. FERMÍN COLINA CAMPOLLO; Man. RAÚL GARCÍA GRANADOS; publ. *Boletín Algodonero*.

Asociación Nacional del Café—Anacafé (*Coffee Planters' Association*): Edificio Etisa, Plazuela España, Zona 9, Guatemala City; f. 1960.

Asociación de Productores de Aceites Esenciales (*Essential Oils Producers' Association*): 26 Calle 6-41, Zona 11 (Calzada Aguilar Batres 26-28), Guatemala City; Gen. Man. F. J. IPPISCH.

Asociación de Productores de Hule: 9A Calle 3-43, Zona 1, Guatemala City; rubber producers' association.

Consejo Nacional del Algodón: 3 Ruta, 2-16, Zona 4, Guatemala City; f. 1965; consultative body for cultivation and classification of cotton; mems.: 14 growers; Man. AMILCAR ALVAREZ B.

TRADE UNIONS

Frente Nacional Sindical—FNS (*National Trade Union Front*): Apdo. 959, Guatemala City; f. 1968, to achieve united action in labour matters; affiliated are two confederations and eleven federations, which represent 97 per cent of the country's trade unions and whose General Secretaries form the governing council of the FNS. The affiliated organizations are:

Confederación General de Sindicatos: 18 Calle 5-50, Zona 1, Apdo. 959, Guatemala City.

Confederación Nacional de Trabajadores: 9A Calle 0-41, Zona 1, Guatemala City.

Consejo Sindical de Guatemala: 18c Calle 5-50, Zona 1, Apdo. 959, Guatemala City; f. 1955; admitted to CIOSL and ORIT; 30,000 mems. in 105 affiliated unions; Gen. Sec. JAIME V. MONGE DONIS.

Federación Sindical de Empleados Bancarios (*Bank Workers' Trade Union Federation*): Apdo. 959, Guatemala City.

Federación de Trabajadores de Guatemala (*Guatemalan Workers' Federation*): 5A Calle 4-33, Zona 1, Guatemala City.

Federación Autónoma Sindical Guatemalteca: 2A Avda. 10-52, Zona 1, Guatemala City.

Federación de Obreros Textiles (*Textile Workers' Federation*): Apdo. 959, Guatemala City.

Federación Central de Trabajadores de Guatemala: 9A Calle 0-41, Zona 1, Guatemala City.

Federación Nacional de Obreros del Transporte (*National Federation of Transport Workers*): 9A Calle 0-41, Zona 1, Guatemala City.

Federación Campesina de Guatemala (*Guatemalan Rural Workers' Federation*): 7A Calle 0-50, Zona 1, Guatemala City.

Federación Nacional Sindical Libre: Escuintla.

Federación Regional de Trabajadores: Morales, Izabal.

Federación Regional de Izabal: Izabal.

A number of unions exist without a national centre, including the Union of Chicle and Wood Workers and the Union of Workers of the Enterprise of the United Fruit Company.

Gremial de Ganaderos (*National Cattlemen's Guild*): Guatemala City; f. 1965; represents all beef and dairy cattlemen's interests.

TRANSPORT

RAILWAYS

Ferrocarriles de Guatemala—FEGUA: Guatemala City; f. 1969; government owned; Guatemalan concession of U.S. owned International Railways of Central America cancelled 1968; 776 km. open. The Railway extends from Puerto Barrios and Santo Tomás de Castilla on the Atlantic Coast to Tecún Umán on the Mexican border, via Zacapa, Guatemala City and Santa María. Br. lines: Santa María–San José; Las Cruces–Champerico. From Zacapa another line branches southward to Anguiatú, on the border with El Salvador.

Verapaz Railway: Livingston, Izabal; 46.4 km., Panzos–Pancajche; serves the coffee district. The Company, which is under Government management, owns river steamers connecting the Polochic River and Livingston via Lake Izabal and Río Dulce. Man. Col. MANUEL MALDONADO.

ROADS

There are 11,230 km. of roads. The Guatemala section of the Pan-American highway is 824 km. long, including 552 km. of paved roads. The 115 km. section of the Inter-American Highway between Barberena and San Cristóbal on the Salvadorian frontier was completed in 1966; a 98 km. road linking Río Hondo with Gualán, Esquipulas and the Honduran border was completed in 1968.

SHIPPING

Various port improvements are under way including a $6m. expansion project for the State Port of Matías de Gálvez. Guatemala's merchant fleet has a total tonnage of 3,629 g.r.t.

Flota Mercante Gran Centro-Americana, S.A.: 1A Calle 7-21, Zona 9, 5°, Guatemala City; f. 1959; services from Europe (in association with WITASS), Gulf of Mexico, U.S. Atlantic and East Coast Central American ports and from the Far East to West Coast Central American ports in association with Japanese lines; Gen. Man. JUAN L. MIRÓN.

CIVIL AVIATION

AVIATECA—Empresa Guatemalteca de Aviación: Avda. Hincapié, Aeropuerto "La Aurora", Guatemala City; f. 1944; operate internal services connecting almost all the principal towns with the capital; external services to Merida, Mexico, D.F., Miami, New Orleans, San Pedro Sula and San Salvador; fleet: BAC 111-500, DC6s and DC3s. Pres. JORGE SENN BONILLA.

The following foreign airlines also serve Guatemala: Air Panama, Iberia, Pan American, Sabena, Sahsa (Honduras), Taca (El Salvador).

TOURISM

Junta Asesora de Turismo: 6A Avda. 5-34, Zona 1, Guatemala City; f. 1966; policy and planning council; 16 mems. representing Ministry of Economy, Ministry of Communications and Public Works, Ministry of Foreign Affairs, Ministry of the Interior, Council of National Economic Planning, Guatemalan Chamber of Commerce, Chamber of Industry, Press Association, Guatemalan Travel Agencies Association, Hotel Association, Guatemalan Airlines Association and Guatemala Tourism Association; Pres. JORGE SENN BONILLA; Sec. Srta. DOLORES YURRITA GRIGNARD.

Instituto Guatemalteco de Turismo (INGUAT): 6A Avda. 5-34, Zona 1, Guatemala City; f. 1967; executive body; Dir.-Gen. JORGE SENN BONILLA; publ. *Boletín Informativo* (monthly).

Asociación Guatemalteca de Agentes de Viajes (AGAV): 11 Calle 4-21, Zona 1, Guatemala City; Pres. ENRIQUE GARCÍA DE LEÓN.

Federación de Asociaciones de Agencias de Viajes de Centro América (FAAVCA): 6A Avda. 15-01, Zona 1, Guatemala City; Pres. RONY E. LIANG L.

CULTURAL ORGANIZATION

Dirección General de Bellas Artes y de Extensión Cultural de Guatemala: Ministerio de Educación Pública, Guatemala City; seven branches covering all aspects of Fine Arts.

PRINCIPAL COMPANIES

Orquesta Sinfónica Nacional: f. 1944.

Ballet Guatemala: f. 1947.

Compañía Nacional de Teatro de Bellas Artes: 3A Avda. 7-40, Zona 1, Guatemala; f. 1965; state-aided; three seasons annually: classical, contemporary international, Guatemalan; directors are engaged for each different season.

ATOMIC ENERGY

GUATEMALA CITY
Instituto Nacional de Energía Nuclear: Apdo. 1421; Pres. Dr. ALBERTO VIAV D.

UNIVERSITIES

Universidad de San Carlos de Guatemala: Ciudad Universitaria, Guatemala City; 665 teachers, 9,388 students.

Universidad Rafael Landívar: 17 Calle 8-64, Zona 10, Guatemala City; 204 teachers, 2,230 students.

PRIVATE UNIVERSITIES

Universidad Doctor Mariano Gálvez de Guatemala: Apdo. 1811, Guatemala; 65 teachers, 1,100 students.

Universidad del Valle de Guatemala: Apdo. 82, Guatemala City; 46 teachers, 250 students.

GUINEA

INTRODUCTORY SURVEY

Location, Climate, Language, Religion, Flag, Capital

The Republic of Guinea lies on the west coast of Africa with Sierra Leone and Liberia to the south, Senegal to the north and Mali and the Ivory Coast inland to the east. The coastal strip is hot and moist with temperatures ranging from about 17°c (62°F) in the dry season to about 30°c (86°F) in the wet season. The interior is higher and cooler. The official languages are French and one of the eight national languages, pending the introduction of either Soussou or Manika as the official language. Most of the people are Muslims but some still adhere to traditional animist beliefs. There are a few thousand Roman Catholics. The national flag (proportions 3 by 2) consists of three vertical stripes—red, yellow and green. The capital is Conakry.

Recent History

Formerly a French Colony, Guinea became independent in 1958 and voted to sever all ties with France. Under the leadership of President Ahmed Sekou Touré, the country has followed a policy of nationalization. In 1967 a cultural revolution was begun with the aim of achieving total literacy in at least one of the eight national languages and of eventually eliminating French and other symbols of colonization. Revolutionary Local Governments were set up in 1968 to execute the programme of the cultural revolution. During 1969 and 1970 abortive invasions and attempts at assassinating President Touré were reported. In November 1970 Portuguese soldiers and Guinean exiles invaded Conakry, attacking the headquarters of the main liberation movement for Guinea-Bissau and other targets, and releasing Portuguese and political prisoners. During 1971 many people were tried for alleged involvement in the invasion and some sentenced harshly. The invasion also brought the leaders of Guinea and Sierra Leone closer together. A defence pact was signed in March 1971 after an attempted coup in Freetown when Guinean troops were flown in to assist loyal sections of the Sierra Leone army in protecting Siaka Stevens and restoring law and order. During 1972 Guinea improved her relations with several African countries, notably Nigeria and Senegal. In 1973, however, Sekou Touré accused Senegal and the Ivory Coast of planning to invade Guinea. Despite the mediation of other African states, relations with these countries remained poor.

Government

The Republic is governed by a president elected by universal suffrage, supported by a unicameral legislature. There is only one political party. Tribal chieftaincies have been abolished, and the Government is highly centralized.

Defence

Guinea has an army of 5,000, a navy of 200 and an air force of 800. There is also a People's Militia of about 30,000. The air force is partly equipped by the U.S.S.R.

Economic Affairs

More than 80 per cent of the population are engaged in farming, the principal export crops being bananas, palm nuts, pineapples, and coffee. Iron ore, diamonds and bauxite are mined and exported, and there are important reserves of calcium carbide. Bauxite dominates the export trade and exploitation of the high-grade deposits in the Boké region, among the richest in the world, is going ahead. FRIGUIA, the bauxite and aluminium producing company, provides more than half of Guinea's foreign earnings. A plan has been announced to increase the exploitation of Guinea's iron-ore deposits. Foreign trade is controlled by the National Trade Office. The principal trading partners are the French Community and Eastern European countries. Guinea belongs to a West African Free Trade Area with the Ivory Coast, Liberia and Sierra Leone. In November 1968 all foreigners were barred from conducting business in Guinea. In January 1969 the establishment of a civic service scheme for all Guineans, mainly directed at the development of agriculture, was announced. Very few economic statistics have been published in recent years.

Transport and Communications

There are plans for extending port facilities at Conakry and for the construction of a new port at Kamsar. There is a railway, 662 km. long, to Kankan, which is to be extended to Bamako in Mali with the co-operation of the Mali and Chinese governments. There is a second line linking Conakry and the aluminium factory of FRIGUIA, and two further lines are planned to connect Kamsar with the bauxite mines of Sangaredi and Conakry with the iron deposits of Simandou. There is an international airport at Conakry. There are about 18,000 km. of roads, mostly soft-surfaced. A cross-country road runs 895 km. from Conakry to Bamako, the capital of Mali, and an international road crosses Guinea connecting Dakar, capital of Senegal, with Abidjan, capital of the Ivory Coast.

Social Welfare

All workers must belong to the National Confederation of Guinean Workers, which is affiliated to the General Union of the Workers of Black Africa. Wages are fixed according to the Government Labour Code. The 48-hour week is in force for industrial workers.

Education

Education is free. There were over 300,000 children at school in 1968. There are three grades of school: primary, superior primary, and secondary. There are also vocational training institutes. In 1966, about 1,000 Guinean students were studying abroad. The eight national languages have been taught since April 1968, though French remains in use for the time being.

Tourism

Guinea is noted for the beauty of its scenery, especially in the mountains of the Futa Jallon.

Visas are not required to visit Guinea by nationals of Cameroon, Liberia, Morocco and Togo.

Public Holidays

1974: September 28th (Referendum Day), October 2nd (Republic Day), October 18th (End of Ramadan), November 1st (All Saints'), December 25th (Christmas).

1975: January 1st (New Year), March 26th (Prophet's Birthday), March 31st (Easter Monday), May 1st (Labour Day).

Weights and Measures

The metric system is in force.

Currency and Exchange Rates

100 corilles=1 sily. (The sily replaced the Guinea franc in 1972, at the rate of 1 sily=10 francs.)

Exchange rates (April 1974):

£1 sterling=48.32 silys;
U.S. $1=20.46 silys.

STATISTICAL SURVEY

AREA AND POPULATION

(1963)

REGION	AREA (sq. km.)	POPULATION ('000)	REGION	AREA (sq. km.)	POPULATION ('000)
Beyla	17,452	170	Kindia	8,828	152
Boffa	6,003	90	Kissidougou	8,872	133
Boké	11,053	105	Kouroussa	16,405	93
Conakry	308	172	Labé	7,616	283
Dabola	6,000	54	Macenta	8,710	123
Dalaba	5,750	105	Mali	8,800	152
Dinguiraye	11,000	67	Mamou	6,159	162
Dubréka	5,676	86	N'Zérékoré	10,183	195
Faranah	12,397	94	Pita	4,000	154
Forécariah	4,265	98	Siguiri	23,377	179
Fria	n.a.	27	Télimelé	8,155	147
Gaoual	11,503	81	Tougue	6,200	75
Gueckédou	4,157	130	Youkounkoun	5,500	55
Kankan	27,488	176			
			TOTAL	245,857	3,360

Population (mid-1972 UN estimate): 4,109,000; (Dec. 1972, Government of Guinea): 5,143,284.

Births and Deaths: Annual average birth rate 47.2 per 1,000, death rate 25.1 per 1,000 (UN estimates for 1965–70).

Principal Town: Conakry (capital) 525,671 (Dec. 1972).

Employment (1970): Total economically active population 1,904,000, including 1,589,000 in agriculture (ILO and FAO estimates).

AGRICULTURE

PRINCIPAL CROPS

('000 metric tons)

	1969	1970	1971
Maize	68*	50	68*
Millet and Sorghum	150*	150	150*
Rice (Paddy)	368	400	400*
Yams and Sweet Potatoes	82*	82*	n.a.
Cassava (Manioc)	470	480	n.a.
Citrus Fruits	80*	80*	80*
Bananas	80	85	n.a.
Pineapples	13	13	n.a.
Palm Kernels (exports only)	15	15	15*
Groundnuts (in shell)	25	25	25*
Coffee	12	10.5	10.5
Tobacco	1.3*	1.3*	1.3*

* FAO estimates.

Source: FAO, *Production Yearbook 1971* (Rome, 1972).

LIVESTOCK
(FAO estimates—'ooo)

	1968–69	1969–70	1970–71
Cattle . . .	1,780	1,800	1,830
Sheep . . .	460	470	480
Goats . . .	490	500	500
Pigs . . .	23	24	25
Asses . . .	3	3	3
Chickens . .	3,900	4,000	4,200

LIVESTOCK PRODUCTS
(FAO estimates, metric tons)

	Cows' Milk	Hen Eggs
1969 . .	41,000	4,100
1970 . .	42,000	4,200
1971 . .	43,000	4,400

FORESTRY
ROUNDWOOD PRODUCTION
(cu. metres)

1967 . .	2,188,000
1968 . .	2,213,000
1969 . .	2,240,000
1970 . .	2,245,000

Source: FAO, Yearbook of Forest Products.

Sea fishing (1969–71): Total catch 5,000 metric tons each year (FAO estimate).

MINING
('ooo metric tons)

	1968	1969	1970	1971
Bauxite	2,112	2,460	2,640	2,900
Alumina	531	572	600	661
Iron Ore	935	1,036	1,036	n.a.
Diamonds*	70	72	74	74

* Exports ('ooo carats).

INDUSTRY

	1968	1969	1970	1971
Electricity (million kWh.) . .	202	232	388	450
Palm Oil ('ooo metric tons) . .	15	16	17	18
Sawnwood ('ooo cubic metres) . .	67	67	67	67

Aluminium production was 700,000 tons in 1972.

FINANCE

100 corilles = 1 sily.

Exchange rates (April 1974): £1 sterling = 48.32 silys; U.S. $1 = 20.46 silys.

100 silys = £2.070 = $4.887.

Note: The sily was introduced on October 2nd, 1972, replacing the Guinea franc (FG) at the rate of 1 sily = 10 francs. Some of the figures in this statistical survey are still in terms of Guinea francs.

BUDGET
('000 million FG)

	1966–67	1967–68	1968–69
Outturn:			
Revenue .	14.4	15.6	n.a.
Expenditure .	16.1	19.1	n.a.
Estimates:			
Fiscal, Parafiscal	11.0	14.5	13.3
Other Revenue*	9.6	7.7	10.0
Expenditure:			
Goods and Services .	11.3	11.9	11.7
Salaries and Wages .	4.2	4.6	5.2
Public Debt .	3.8	4.4	5.6
Other Expenditure .	1.3	1.3	1.0

* This figure includes payments into the Equalization Fund, and the depreciation funds of the state enterprises; in 1966–67 it also includes the revenue of the National Railways Board.

1971–72 Budget (ordinary estimates): 27,800 million FG.

1972–73 Budget (ordinary estimates): 4,500 million silys.

EXTERNAL TRADE

BALANCE OF TRADE
('000 million current FG)

	1964–65	1965–66	1966–67	1967–68	1968–69
Exports:					
Agricultural Products .	3.5	4.0	4.1	4.6	5.1
Minerals . .	9.3	8.8	8.5	8.5	9.0
Imports:					
Fria (now FRIGUIA) .	2.9	2.4	1.6	1.8	1.8
Plan . . .	3.2	3.3	2.4	4.7	3.0
Other . .	9.8	9.3	9.2	5.8	11.3
Balance. . .	−3.1	−2.2	−0.6	0.8	−2.1

The Balance of Trade in 1970 was −3,700 million FG.

PRINCIPAL COMMODITIES
(million FG–1970)

IMPORTS		EXPORTS	
Cotton Textiles	2,500	Bauxite and Aluminium . . .	8,600
Rice	1,700	Coffee	1,500
Others, especially Petroleum Products		Bananas	400
and Machinery	12,800	Palmetto	740
TOTAL	17,000	TOTAL (incl. others) . .	13,300

PRINCIPAL COUNTRIES
(million U.S. $)

	IMPORTS			EXPORTS		
	1968	1969	1970	1968	1969	1970
France	9.2	9.2	20.6	1.5	0.9	1.5
Germany, Federal Republic .	3.4	2.9	4.4	4.1	6.9	7.8
Italy	1.0	2.3	7.9	0.1	0.2	1.0
Norway	—	—	—	9.9	14.1	15.4
Switzerland . . .	1.1	1.1	1.5	3.7	1.0	3.7
United Kingdom . . .	1.8	3.3	3.3	—	0.1	2.3
U.S.A.	6.4	10.6	7.3	4.5	5.4	6.8
Yugoslavia	1.7	4.5	2.8	2.4	1.7	1.2
Total (incl. others) .	49.6	65.3	n.a.	52.9	56.8	56.3

TRANSPORT
(1962)

Railways (1967): Passenger-km. 50m., Freight ton-km. 20m.; (1968) Freight ton-km. 21m.

Roads (1968): Cars 7,600, Lorries and Commercial Vehicles 11,500; (1969) Cars 8,000, Commercial Vehicles 12,000.

SHIPPING
('000 metric tons)

	1968	1969	1970
Freight Loaded . .	975	1,015*	1,100*
Freight Unloaded .	435	500*	530*

* Estimates.

CIVIL AVIATION
SCHEDULED SERVICES

	1969	1970	1971
Kilometres Flown ('000)	720	750	750
Passengers Carried ('000)	46	49	49
Passenger-km. ('000) .	16,000	17,000	17,000
Freight ton-km. ('000) .	100	110	110

EDUCATION

	1966–67		1968
	Schools	Pupils	Pupils
Primary	1,605	149,527	167,340
Secondary . . .	252	36,379	33,348
Vocational . . .			5,334
Teacher Training . .	n.a.	n.a.	2,954
Tertiary	n.a.	660	942

Source: Direction de la Statistique Générale et de la Mécanographie, Conakry; IMF, *International Financial Statistics.*

THE CONSTITUTION

(promulgated November 1958; amended October 1963)

The Constitution was altered and enlarged according to Law No. 1 on October 31st, 1963. The principle of the Republic is "Government of the people by the people for the people".

1. The State is a Democratic Republic.

3. Sovereignty rests in the people, and is exercised by their representatives in the National Assembly.

The National Assembly

4–8. Equal and secret elections for the National Assembly on a national list are held every five years.

10. Representatives enjoy the usual parliamentary immunity.

11. A permanent Commission elected from the National Assembly manages the business of the Assembly between sittings (two per year).

9. The first duty of the Assembly is to pass laws.

14. The President and the Representatives are responsible for the initiation and formulation of laws.

17. The Representatives are in control of the Budget and expenditure; limited only in that any proposal for an increase in expenditure must be accompanied by a corresponding increase in revenue.

The President

20. The President is Commander-in-Chief of the Armed Forces.

21. Executive power is practised solely by the President; the Cabinet is nominated by him and subordinate to him.

22. The President is elected for a period of seven years and can stand for re-election as often as he wishes.

24. The President is responsible to the Assembly, but there are no definite curbs upon the executive.

28. If the Presidency is vacant the Cabinet continues to govern until a new President is elected.

The Judiciary

35. The President guarantees the independence of the judiciary; he also has the power to pardon. The Judges are responsible only to the law.

36. The accused has a right to defence.

The Basic Rights and Duties of the Citizen

39. All the inhabitants of the Republic of Guinea have the right to vote.

40–46. The Constitution confers the right of freedom of speech, assembly, coalition, demonstration and conscience upon all citizens; the Press is free, the post is secret, property is inviolable; all citizens have the right to work, go on holiday, to receive social support and education, and to go on strike.

42. It is the duty of all citizens to uphold the Constitution, to defend their country, and to fulfil social responsibilities.

45. Racial discrimination, or regional propaganda is punishable by law.

THE GOVERNMENT

HEAD OF STATE

President: AHMED SEKOU TOURÉ (re-elected January 1968 for a seven-year term by 99.7 per cent of electorate; sole candidate)

CABINET
(March 1974)

Domain of the President:

President and responsible for Ideology: AHMED SEKOU TOURÉ.

Minister of Information and Ideology: LOUIS BEHAZIM.

Domain of the Prime Minister:

Prime Minister: Dr. LOUIS LANSANA BEAVOGUI.

Minister of the People's Army: TOUMANI SANGARE.

Minister of Foreign Affairs: FILY CISSOKO.

Minister of Planning: ALIOUME DRAME.

Minister of Financial Control: FODÉ MAMADOU TOURÉ.

Interior and Security Domain:

Minister: MOUSSA DIAKITÉ.

Minister of Justice: DIALLO TELLI.

Minister of the Interior and Security: KARIM KEYRA.

Minister of Local Development for Middle Guinea: SEKOU CHERIF.

Minister of Local Development for the Forest Region: DAMANTANG CAMARA.

Minister of Local Development for Maritime Guinea: KARAMOKO KAUYATÉ.

Minister of Local Development for Upper Guinea: CHERIF MABANOU.

Culture and Education Domain:

Minister: MAMADI KEITA.

Minister of Advanced Education and Scientific Research: SIKÉ CAMARA.

Minister of Pre-University Education and Literacy: DIALEMA GUELAVOGUI.

Minister of Youth, Sport and Culture: MAMADOU BANGOURA.

Social Domain:

Minister: SALIFOULAYE DIALLO.

Minister of Health: LANSANA DIANE.

Minister of Social Affairs: MAFOURY BAMFOURA.

Minister of the Civil Service and Labour: ABDOULAYE DIALLO.

Trade and Communications Domain:
  Minister: Alpha Oumar Barry.

  Minister of Internal Trade: Bourbacar Diallo.

  Minister of External Trade: Mamad Kaba.

  Minister of Posts and Telecommunications: Mouctar Diallo.

  Minister of Transport: Thierno Saidou Thaim.

Economy and Finance Domain:
  Minister: Ismaël Touré.

  Minister of Industry and Energy: Mamady Kaba.

  Minister of Finance: Mamadou Boumboura Bella.

Minister of Mines and Geology: Mohamed Laminé Touré.

Minister of Public Works, Urban Affairs and the Environment: Alaphaix Kourouma.

  Governor of Banks: N'Faly Sangare.

Rural Development Domain:
  Minister: Nfamara Keita.

Minister of Agriculture and Production Co-operatives: Alpha Bacar Barry.

Minister of Development and of Waters and Forests: Louis Olimé.

Minister of Livestock and Fisheries: Dr. Thiekoura Camara.

DIPLOMATIC REPRESENTATION

EMBASSIES AND LEGATION ACCREDITED TO GUINEA
(In Conakry unless otherwise stated)
(E) Embassy; (L) Legation.

Algeria: B.P. 1004 (E); *Ambassador:* Messaoudi Zitouni (also accred. to Liberia and Sierra Leone).

Belgium: B.P. 871 (L); *Chargé d'Affaires:* Marcel de Moudt.

Bulgaria: B.P. 629 (E); *Ambassador:* Boris Milev (also accred. to Congo (Brazzaville)).

Canada: (E); Dakar, Senegal.

China, People's Republic: B.P. 714 (E); *Ambassador:* Chai Tse-min.

Cuba: B.P. 71 (E); *Ambassador:* Capt. Aoremante.

Czechoslovakia: rue de l'Aviation, B.P. 1009 *bis* (E); *Ambassador:* Miloš Vojta.

Egypt: B.P. 389 (E); *Ambassador:* Osman Aly Assal.

German Democratic Republic: *Ambassador:* Guenther Fritsch.

Ghana: *Ambassador:* Alhaji Yakubu Tali.

Hungary: B.P. 1008 *bis* (E); *Ambassador:* Imze Sztankovice (also accred. to Congo, Mali and Mauritania).

India: B.P. 186 *bis* (E); *Ambassador:* R. R. Sinha (also accred. to Mali).

Indonesia: B.P. 722 (E); *Ambassador:* Mohamed Ali Moersid.

Italy: B.P. 84 (E); *Ambassador:* Mario Ungaro.

Japan: (E); *Ambassador:* Tatsuo Hirose.

Kenya: *Ambassador:* (vacant).

Korea, Democratic People's Republic: B.P. 723 (E); *Ambassador:* Kim Kwan Seup.

Liberia: B.P. 18 (E); *Ambassador:* Christie W. Doe.

Madagascar: (E); Algiers, Algeria.

Mauritania: (E); Dakar, Senegal.

Mongolia: (E); *Ambassador:* Toumbachin Pourevjal (also accred. to Mali).

Morocco: (E); *Ambassador:* Mahfoud El Khatib.

Nigeria: B.P. 54 (E); *Ambassador:* L. J. Dosunmu.

Pakistan: (E); Accra, Ghana.

Poland: B.P. 1063 (E); *Ambassador:* Wlodimierz Migon.

Romania: B.P. 348 (E); *Ambassador:* Niculai Iaan Vancea (also accred. to Mali).

Saudi Arabia: (E); *Ambassador:* Nasser Gouth.

Sierra Leone: B.P. 625 (E); *Ambassador:* Kojo Randall.

Spain: (E); *Ambassador:* Nicolas Martin.

Syria: (E); *Ambassador:* Naim Kadah.

Turkey: *Ambassador:* Ziya Tepedelen.

U.S.S.R.: B.P. 329 (E); *Ambassador:* Alexander Startsev.

United Kingdom: (E); *Ambassador:* John Curle.

U.S.A.: B.P. 503 (E); *Ambassador:* James Loeb.

Venezuela: (E); Lagos, Nigeria.

Viet-Nam, Democratic Republic: B.P. 1551 (E); *Ambassador:* Nguyen-Thuong (also accred. to Congo (Brazzaville)).

Yugoslavia: B.P. 1554 (E); *Ambassador:* Vrlje Cedomil.

Guinea also has diplomatic relations with Albania, Cameroon, Congo (Brazzaville), Ethiopia, Finland, The Gambia, Guyana, Iran, Jordan, Lebanon, Mali, Netherlands, Niger, Norway, Oman, Sweden, Switzerland, Tanzania, Togo, Tunisia and Upper Volta.

NATIONAL ASSEMBLY

President: Léon Maka.

ELECTION, JANUARY 1968

All 75 seats were won by the *Parti démocratique de Guinée*. The term is for five years but overran in 1973.

POLITICAL PARTY

Parti démocratique de Guinée (PDG): Conakry.

The Party is the ultimate source of authority in the country, possessing "sovereign and exclusive control of all sections of national life".

Central Committee: since 1972 is the directing organ of the party responsible for adopting statutes etc.; 25 members elected at congress for 5 years.

Political Bureau: the executive body; 7 members, the secretary General and 6 members of the Central Committee, all Ministers, elected on his nomination.

Secretary-General: President Sekou Touré.

JUDICIAL SYSTEM

There is a High Court whose jurisdiction covers political cases. The Cour d'Appel, the Chambre des Mises en Accusation and the Tribunal Supérieur de Cassation are at Conakry.

Tribuneaux du Ier Degré exist at Conakry and Kankan and have jurisdiction over civil and criminal cases and also act as Industrial Courts. A Justice of the Peace sits at N'Zérékoré.

Procurator-General: Siké Camara.

Président, Cour d'Appel: Fodé Mamadou Touré.

RELIGION

It is estimated that 62 per cent of the population are Muslims, about 35 per cent animists and 1.5 per cent Christians, mostly Roman Catholics.

In May 1967, the President ordered that all priests should be Guinea nationals.

Roman Catholic Missions: L'Archevêché, B.P. 1006 *bis*; in the archdiocese of Conakry there are about 32 mission centres, with a personnel of 41; **Archbishop of Conakry** Mgr. Raymond Tchidimbo (*condemned to hard labour for life January 1971 for plotting against state*).

Bishop of N'Zérékoré: Eugene Maillat, B.P. 45, N'Zérékoré.

Protestant Missions: There are six mission centres, four run by British and two by American societies.

PRESS AND RADIO

Horoya (*Dignity*): Guinea Press Service, Conakry, B.P. 191; twice weekly; organ of the Parti démocratique de Guinée.

Horoya Hebdomadaire: B.P. 191, Conakry; f. 1969; weekly.

Journal officiel de Guinée: Conakry, B.P. 156; fortnightly government publication.

Travailleur de Guinée: Conakry; organ of the Confédération National des Travailleurs Guinéens.

NEWS AGENCIES

Agence Guinéen de Presse: B.P. 191, Conakry; f. 1960; Dir. Alpha Diallo.

FOREIGN BUREAUX

APN—Novosti Press Agency: c/o U.S.S.R. Embassy, Conakry.

Tass is also represented.

RADIO

Radiodiffusion Nationale de Guinée: B.P. 617, Conakry; programmes in French, English, Créole-English, Portuguese, Arabic and local languages; Dir. E. Tompara.

In 1969 there were about 90,000 receiving sets.

FINANCE

BANKING

CENTRAL BANK

Banque Centrale de la République de Guinée: Boulevard du Commerce, B.P. 692, Conakry; f. 1960; cap. 500m. FG; Gov. Moussa Diakite,

Banque Guinéenne du Commerce Extérieur: Conakry; cap. 150m. FG.

Banque Nationale de Crédit: Conakry; loans to craft co-operatives.

Banque Nationale de Développement Agricole: Conakry; Dir. Gnan Félix Mathos.

Crédit National pour le Commerce, l'Industrie et l'Habitat 6e avenue, Conakry; f. 1961.

INSURANCE

Conakry

National Insurance Co.: B.P. 719; f. 1961; State company.

Société Nationale d'Assurances et de Réassurances de la République de Guinée (SNA): B.P. 179, Conakry; Dir.-Gen. Momory Camara.

Ten of the main French insurance companies maintain agencies in Conakry.

TRADE AND INDUSTRY

CHAMBER OF COMMERCE

Chambre Economique de Guinée: B.P. 609, Conakry; f. 1960; replaces the former Chamber of Commerce and Chamber of Agriculture and Industry; Pres. Baidi Gueyge.

TRADE UNION

Confédération National des Travailleurs Guinéens (CNTG): P.O.B. 237, Bourse du Travail, Conakry; Pres. Mamadi Kaba; 100,000 mems.; 19 federations and national unions, 32 local administrative offices; integrated with PDG; publ. *Le Travailleur de Guinée*.

TRADE ORGANIZATIONS

Prodex: Conakry; state organization for export of handicrafts under the auspices of the Minister of Trade; Dir. Roger Soumah.

Unicomer-Guinée: B.P. 11, Conakry; f. 1962; import-export; Pres. Dir.-Gen. Pierre Vigne; Dir. Boris Treschoff.

TRANSPORT

RAILWAY

Office National des Chemins de Fer de Guinée: B.P. 581, Conakry; Dir. PIERRE DIANÉ.

There are 662 km. of 1 metre gauge track from Conakry to Kankan in the east of the country, crossing the Niger at Kouroussa. A second line, 104 km. long, links Conakry and the aluminium works at Fria. A new line from Kankan to Bamako in Mali is being financed by China. Further lines are planned from Kamsar, on the coast, to the bauxite mines of Sangaredi and from Conakry to the iron deposits of Simandou.

ROADS

There are some 18,000 km. of classified roads (325 km. tarred in 1968), and 2,500 km. of seasonal tracks. The main roads are those running along the coast from Sierra Leone to Guinea-Bissau (via Conakry) and from Conakry into the interior, with branches to the frontiers of Senegal, Mali and the Ivory Coast.

SHIPPING

Port de Conakry: B.P. 534, Conakry.

Conakry's 2,450 metres of quays provide 9 alongside berths for ocean-going vessels. There are plans for the construction of a new port at Kamsar and a second deep-water port at Conakry.

E.N.T.R.A.T.: P.O.B. 315, Conakry; state stevedoring and forwarding firm; Dir.-Gen. A. AMADOU BA.

Société Navale Guinéenne: P.O.B. 522, Conakry; f. 1968; state shipping firm; agents for Cie. Maritime des Chargeurs Réunis, Cie. de Navigation Fraissinet et Cyprien Fabre, Delta Steamship Lines Inc., Elder Dempster Line, Hanseatic Africa Line, Leif Hoëgh and Co. A/S, Lloyd Triestino, Nouvelle Compagnie de Paquebots (N.C.P.), Palm Line Ltd., Scandinavian West Africa Line, Société Navale de l'Ouest, United West Africa Service; Dir.-Gen. YAYA KEITA.

CIVIL AVIATION

Air Guinée: Conakry, B.P. 12; f. 1960; internal and regional services; fleet of two Ilyushin Il-18, four Antonov An-24; Dir.-Gen. DIAWARA DAOUDA.

Aeroflot, Air Afrique, Air Algérie, Air Mali, Air Zaire, ČSA (Czechoslovakia), Interflug, Sabena and UTA also serve Conakry.

GUYANA

INTRODUCTORY SURVEY

Location, Climate, Language, Religion, Flag, Capital

The Co-operative Republic of Guyana lies on the north coast of South America between Venezuela to the west and Surinam (Dutch Guiana) to the east, with Brazil to the south. The narrow coastal belt which supports most of the population has a moderate climate with a wet season from April to August and a dry season from September to November; inland there are tropical forests and savannah and the dry season extends into February. The average temperature is 80°F (27°C). The two main ethnic groups are those of African and Indian origin. There are also about 80,000 people of mixed racial origin and 32,000 Amerindians, who live mainly in the interior. English is the official language but Hindi, Urdu and Amerindian dialects are also spoken. The principal religions are Christianity, Hinduism and Islam. The national flag (proportions 5 by 3 when flown on land, but 2 by 1 at sea) is green, with a white-bordered yellow triangle (apex at the right-hand edge) on which is superimposed a black-bordered red triangle (apex in the centre). The capital is Georgetown.

Recent History

Formerly the British colony of British Guiana, Guyana became independent in 1966. A bi-cameral legislature was introduced in 1953, and the present Constitution was established in 1961, with subsequent modifications. A coalition of the People's National Congress and the United Force led the country to independence under Forbes Burnham. The People's National Congress won the general elections held in December 1968 and again in July 1973, although the results of the latter were disputed by the opposition parties; Forbes Burnham continues as Prime Minister. In February 1970 Guyana became a Co-operative Republic, and Arthur Chung was elected President in March. An extensive area in the west of the country is claimed by Venezuela, but in June 1970 both sides signed the Port of Spain Protocol which it is hoped will ease tensions between the countries and lead to the development of common border areas. Guyana hopes eventually to people the disputed area and to develop the rich mineral resources thought to exist there. Guyana's frontier was also disputed with Surinam, but the dispute was resolved in April 1970. Guyana is a member of the UN and sends an official observer to meetings of the OAS.

Government

After the 1970 amendment of the Constitution, the President is Head of State. The executive body is the Cabinet, headed by the Prime Minister and responsible to Parliament. The latter consists of the 53-man National Assembly, elected by proportional representation for five years, together with the non-elected members of the Cabinet. There are independent Commissions for the judicial, police and public services. The country is divided into six regions, each headed by a Minister of State.

Defence

Guyana has an army of 2,200 men. Para-military forces total 2,500.

Economic Affairs

The economy is based on agriculture, chiefly sugar and rice; bananas are increasingly being exported, coconuts are now the third most important agricultural crop and citrus production is increasing. Forestry, potentially an important source of income, is limited by insufficient transport facilities. The 1972–76 Development Plan concentrates on increasing employment in agriculture and establishing cotton plantations capable of satisfying the needs of the textile industry. Fisheries, timber and beef-production are also given high priority in the Plan. In 1971 The Government nationalized the Canadian-owned Demerera Bauxite Company (Demba), now the Guyana Bauxite Company (Guybau). The mining and processing of bauxite is now the most important industry in Guyana and in 1972 accounted for 43 per cent of total export earnings. Guyana has entered into a trade and technical assistance agreement with the People's Republic of China under which $G 30 million worth of goods are to be exchanged annually. China is also to design a large cotton textile mill for construction near Georgetown, with an anticipated capacity of 20 million yards of cotton cloth annually. Guyana is a founder member of the Caribbean Common Market (CARIBCOM).

Transport and Communication

The coastal strip has a well developed road system of approximately 850 miles. In the whole country there are about 409 miles of hard-surfaced road out of a total of 1,810 miles. The bituminous road to link Georgetown and Linden, the centre for bauxite mining, was opened in 1968. Communication with the interior is still chiefly by river, the main rivers being the Mazuruni, the Cuyuni, the Essequibo, the Demerara, and the Berbice. There are airstrips at the more important settlements in the interior and an international airport at Timehri, 23 miles outside Georgetown.

Social Welfare

In 1973 there were 42 health centres, 3 general hospitals, 11 private hospitals, 3 specialized hospitals, 11 cottage hospitals and 112 maternal and child health units in rural areas. The death rate has decreased to a current 6.25 per thousand (excluding Amerindians). In recent years improved water supplies, anti-tuberculosis campaigns and the control of malaria have steadily improved general health. A National Insurance scheme, compulsory for most workers and employers, was established in 1969, and has since been extended to embrace self-employed people. It is the Government's aim to make Guyana self-sufficient in food and clothing by 1976, and to provide adequate housing for all by this date.

Education

Education is free between the ages of 5 and 16, and compulsory between 6 and 14. The estimated literacy rate is 80 to 85 per cent. There are 390 state-aided primary schools and 44 state and state-aided secondary schools. The total number of pupils in all schools was over 192,000 in 1973. There are also 18 domestic science and 3 technical training centres. Proposals for the establishment of multi-lateral schools to remedy the divorce of technical from academic education are at present being put into effect. The University of Guyana is at Turkeyen where there is also a Teacher Training Centre; a College of Education for the training of secondary school teachers is situated in Georgetown.

Tourism

Guyana does little to encourage tourism despite the beautiful scenery in the interior of the country. Tours to the interior, especially to see the famous Kaieteur falls (741 ft.), may be arranged. In 1970 24,887 tourists visited Guyana.

Passports and visas are not required for visits by citizens of the United States and Canada. British subjects and all others require passports.

Sport

Cricket is very popular, as are hockey, basketball, table tennis, lawn tennis, football, boxing, motor-racing and cycling.

Public Holidays

1974: August 5th (Commonwealth Day), October 24th (UN Day), November 13th (Deepavali), December 25th–26th (Christmas).

1975: January 1st (New Year), February 23th (Republic Day), March 28th, 31st (Good Friday, Easter Monday), May 1st (Labour Day). In addition the Muslim festivals of Eid-ul-Ahaz and Youman Naubi (in the first half of the year) are celebrated. These festivals are dependent on sightings of the moon and their precise dates are not known until two months before they take place.

Weights and Measures

Imperial weights and measures are used.

Currency and Exchange Rates

100 cents=1 Guyana dollar ($G).

Exchange rates (April 1974):

£1 sterling=$G5.21;

U.S. $1=$G2.21.

STATISTICS

AREA AND POPULATION

Area (square miles): 83,000.

Population (1970 est.): 721,098 (East Indian 365,515, Africans 222,665, Mixed 82,240, Portuguese 9,522, Chinese 4,581, Europeans 3,992, Amerindians 32,013, Others 570); Georgetown (capital) 195,000.

Employment: Total labour force 210,000 (1970).

Livestock (1972–73, '000 head): Cattle 260, Pigs 88, Sheep 100, Goats 30, Poultry 8,000.

AGRICULTURE

	Unit	1970	1971	1972
Sugar	'000 tons	311	369	315
Rice	" "	142	120	94
Plantains	lb.	51,304	54,650	52,000
Bananas	"	12,700	13,805	14,803
Beef	"	8,681	9,524	9,600
Poultry	"	7,457	8,709	10,843

MINING AND INDUSTRY

	Unit	1970	1971	1972
Rum	'000 proof galls.	3,187	3,781	4,493
Bauxite (dried)	'000 tons	2,291	2,101	1,643
Bauxite (calcinated)	" "	693	710	693
Alumina	" "	312	305	262
Gold	'000 oz.	4.4	1.4	4
Diamonds	metric carats	58	47	47
Timber	'000 cu. feet	6,418	5,761	5,983

FINANCE

100 cents = 1 Guyana dollar ($G).
Coins: 1, 5, 10, 25 and 50 cents.
Notes: 1, 5, 10 and 20 dollars.
Exchange rates (April 1974): £1 sterling = $G5.21; U.S. $1 = $G2.21.
$G100 = £19.19 = U.S. $45.31.

BUDGET
(1972—$G '000)

REVENUE		EXPENDITURE	
Current Revenue	151,041	Education	24,094
Capital Revenue	38,216	Defence	6,992
		Health	12,896
		Transport	5,807
		Public Works	16,217
		Debt Charges	25,125
		Other Current Expenditure . .	61,988
		Capital Expenditure . . .	56,387
Total	189,257	Total	209,503

Budget (1973 est.): *Revenue* $G260,582,505; *Expenditure* $G322,181,825.
Budget (1974 est.): *Revenue* $G364.2 million; *Expenditure* $G395.2 million.

URBAN CONSUMER PRICE INDEX
(1956 = 100)

	All Items	Food	Clothing	Housing	Miscellaneous
1969 . .	127.5	129.3	114.8	118.2	130.5
1970 . .	131.8	135.0	119.1	121.5	132.3
1971 . .	134.5	138.1	123.3	123.9	133.2
1972 . .	140.5	146.4	128.1	126.8	136.2
1973 (Sept.) . .	150.3	162.5	133.9	129.1	140.3

BALANCE OF PAYMENTS
($G million)

	1971	1972
Goods and Services . . .	−13.2	−23.5
Trade balance	24.9	2.0
Transport and merchandise insurance	1.5	1.9
Investment income . . .	−36.0	−23.4
Other services	− 3.7	− 4.0
Transfers.	1.6	1.4
Private	− 0.6	1.8
Government	2.2	− 0.4
Capital and Monetary Goods:		
Non-monetary sector:		
Direct investment. . .	− 3.6	5.2
Other long-term private . .	14.6	12.8
Other short-term private . .	− 4.8	1.0
Central Government . .	21.6	11.9
Allocation of SDRs . .	4.3	5.4
Monetary sector:		
Central Government assets .	− 2.3	—
Commercial bank assets .	− 0.5	2.4
Commercial bank liabilities .	0.6	− 2.1
Central bank assets . .	− 7.5	−16.1
Post Office savings bank .	—	0.3
Change in holdings of SDRs .	− 4.2	− 4.6
Errors and omissions . .	− 6.7	5.8

EXTERNAL TRADE
($G million)

	1969	1970	1971	1972
Imports . . .	235.8	268.2	267.6	297.8
Exports . . .	242.0	266.9	298.4	306.5

COMMODITIES
($G million)

IMPORTS	1971	1972
Consumer Goods . . .	90.2	99.5
Non-Durables . . .	74.4	81.2
Food, beverages and tobacco	34.1	34.2
Other . . .	40.3	47.1
Durables . . .	15.7	18.3
Motor cars . .	4.0	6.2
Electrical appliances .	2.4	2.7
Other . . .	9.3	9.3
Production Goods . .	177.5	198.3
Capital Goods . . .	97.1	107.4
Agricultural . . .	5.2	4.4
Industrial and mining .	43.3	55.6
Other . . .	48.7	47.4
Intermediate Goods and Raw Materials incl. Fuels . .	80.2	90.9

EXPORTS	1971	1972
Sugar	86.0	101.8
Molasses	4.0	3.3
Rum	n.a.	5.6
Rice	21.3	25.2
Other Agricultural Products .	1.8	n.a.
Shrimps	8.7	10.2
Timber	n.a.	3.5*
Other Forestry Products .	0.8	n.a.
Bauxite/Alumina . .	134.0	132.1
Diamonds	2.5	2.2
Re-exports . . .	10.0	6.6

* Includes pre-fabricated housing.

PRINCIPAL COUNTRIES
($G'000)

IMPORTS	1971	1972
United Kingdom . . .	82,826	90,443
U.S.A.	65,012	72,256
Canada	14,603	15,237
Commonwealth Caribbean Countries . . .	40,575	51,395

EXPORTS	1971	1972
Canada	71,805	19,465
United Kingdom . . .	75,697	90,744
U.S.A.	29,817	77,303
Commonwealth Caribbean Countries . . .	48,438	39,978

TRANSPORT
(1972)

Railways: Nineteen miles on the west coast and 80 miles from Linden to Ituni.

Roads ('000 vehicles): Passenger 20.6; Commercial 5.4; long-distance buses link the principal towns, villages and sugar estates.

Shipping: Tonnage entered 3,270,816 net registered tons, cleared 2,611,413 net registered tons.

Civil Aviation (1968): Passenger arrivals 52,331, departures 55,219; Freight picked up 367 tons, set down 7,259 tons.

TOURISM

	1969	1970
Total Arrivals . . .	51,500	54,424
Sea	13,999	16,307
Air	37,501	38,117
Total Visitors . . .	25,765	24,887

EDUCATION
(1972–73)

	Primary	Secondary	Technical	Teacher Training	University
Schools	390	80	3	2	1
Pupils	168,954	23,464*	3,301†	470	1,232
Teachers	5,754	1,070*	70	48	103‡

* Government and aided only. † Includes part-time students. ‡ Includes part-time teachers.

Source: Ministry of Information, Culture and Youth, Georgetown.

THE CONSTITUTION

Guyana is a sovereign democratic state, and became a republic within the Commonwealth on February 23rd, 1970. The President is elected by the National Assembly.

The executive body consists of a Cabinet, presided over by the Prime Minister, which is collectively responsible to the legislature. The National Assembly, which has a term of five years, contains 53 members elected by a system of proportional representation. Adult suffrage is universal.

Impartial commissions exist for the judiciary, the public service and the police service, and incorporated in the constitution are safeguards to protect the rights to equality, personal freedom and property of all individuals and minority groups. An Ombudsman is appointed, after consultation between Prime Minister and leader of the Opposition, to hold office for four years.

THE GOVERNMENT

President: Raymond Arthur Chung.

CABINET
(March 1974)

Prime Minister: Linden Forbes Sampson Burnham, o.e., s.c.

Deputy Prime Minister and Minister of National Development and Agriculture: Dr. Ptolemy A. Reid.

Minister of Works and Communications: H. Desmond Hoyte, s.c.

Minister of Foreign Affairs and Justice: Shridath S. Ramphal, s.c.

Minister of Co-operatives and National Mobilization: Hamilton Green.

Minister of Energy and Natural Resources: Hubert O. Jack.

Minister of Finance: Frank E. Hope.

Minister of Economic Development: Dr. Kenneth F. S. King.

Minister of Housing: S. S. Naraine, a.a.

Minister of Labour: Winslow G. Carrington.

Minister of Information and Culture: Miss Shirley M. Field-Ridley.

Minister of Parliamentary Affairs and Leader of the House: B. Ramsaroop.

Minister of Education: Miss Cecily L. Baird.

Minister of Health: Dr. Oliver M. R. Harper.

Minister of Trade and Consumer Protection: G. King.

Regional Minister for the Corentyne District: Oscar E. Clarke.

Regional Minister for the Mazaruni-Potaro District: William Haynes.

Regional Minister for the East Coast Demerara-West Coast Berbice District: A. Salim.

Regional Minister for the Rupununi District: P. P. Duncan.

Regional Minister for the Pomeroon-Essequibo Coast District: M. Zaheeruddeen.

Regional Minister for the North West District: F. U. A. Carmichael.

Minister of State for Agriculture: M. Kasim, a.a.

Minister of State for Home Affairs: Claude V. Mingo.

Minister of State, Office of the Prime Minister: Christopher A. Nascimento.

DIPLOMATIC REPRESENTATION

EMBASSIES AND HIGH COMMISSIONS ACCREDITED TO GUYANA
(In Georgetown unless otherwise indicated)

(E) Embassy; (HC) High Commission

Australia: Ottawa, Canada (HC).

Belgium: Caracas, Venezuela (E).

Brazil: Regent and Hincks Sts. (E); *Ambassador:* Melillo Moreia de Mello.

Canada: Bank of Guyana Bldg. (HC); *High Commissioner:* Ormond W. Dier.

China, People's Republic: 102 Duke St. (E); *Ambassador:* Wang Chan-yuan.

Colombia: 32 Coralita Ave., Bel Air Park (E); *Ambassador:* Rafael Perdomo.

Cyprus: UN Permanent Representative, New York, U.S.A. (HC).

Dominican Republic: Kingston, Jamaica (E).

France: Port of Spain, Trinidad (E).

Germany, Federal Republic: 33 North St. (E); *Ambassador:* WERNER KLINGEBERG.

Guinea: (E); *Ambassador:* MOHAMED SAKO.

India: Bank of Baroda Bldg., Ave. of the Republic (HC); *High Commissioner:* Dr. GOPAL SINGH.

Italy: Bogotá, Colombia (E).

Jamaica: St. Clair, Port of Spain, Trinidad (HC); *High Commissioner:* VIVIAN COURTNEY SMITH.

Japan: Bogotá, Colombia (E).

Korea, Republic: Caracas, Venezuela (E).

Mexico: (E); *Ambassador:* JOSÉ CABALLERO.

Nigeria: UN Permanent Representative, New York, U.S.A. (HC).

Pakistan: Ottawa, Canada (HC).

Tanzania: UN Permanent Representative, New York, U.S.A. (HC).

Trinidad and Tobago: 91 Middle St. (HC); *High Commissioner:* ISABEL TESHEA.

U.S.S.R.: Brasília, Brazil (E).

United Kingdom: 44 Main St. (HC); *High Commissioner:* WILLIAM STANLEY BATES.

U.S.A.: 31 Main St. (E); *Ambassador:* SPENCER M. KING.

Venezuela: 92 Middle St. (E); *Ambassador:* ANTONIO JOSÉ MALDONADO.

Yugoslavia: UN Permanent Representative, New York, U.S.A. (E).

Zambia: UN Permanent Representative, New York, U.S.A. (HC).

Guyana also has diplomatic relations with Argentina, Austria, Bahamas, Barbados, Chile, Cuba, Egypt, Ethiopia, German Democratic Republic, Haiti, Kenya, Libya, Netherlands, Panama, Peru, Poland, Sierra Leone, Syria, Turkey and Uganda.

PARLIAMENT

HOUSE OF ASSEMBLY

Speaker: Hon. SASE NARAIN.

Elected Members: 53.

Non-Elected Members: 12.

ELECTION, 1973

Party	Seats
People's National Congress	37
People's Progressive Party	14
Liberator Party (incl. United Force)	2

POLITICAL PARTIES

People's National Congress: 201 New Market St., Georgetown; left-wing Socialist; f. 1955 after a split with the PPP; Leader L. F. S. BURNHAM; Chair. BISHWAISHWAR RAMSAROOP; Sec. HAMILTON GREEN; publ. *New Nation* (weekly), *New Nation International* (fortnightly).

United Force: 96 Robb St., Bourda, Georgetown; advocates rapid industrialization through government partnership and private capital; Leader MARCELLUS F. SINGH.

People's Progressive Party: 41 Robb St., Bourda, Georgetown; f. 1950; extreme socialist party, in process of being transformed into Marxist-Leninist party; Gen. Sec. Dr. CHEDDI JAGAN; International Affairs Sec. JANET JAGAN; publs. *Thunder* (quarterly), *Guyana Information Bulletin* (monthly).

Liberator Party: P.O.B. 730, Georgetown; f. 1972; includes former leaders of United Force and is an off-shoot of the Anti-Discrimination Movement; Leader Dr. GANRAJ KUMAR; Chair. Dr. J. K. M. RICHMOND.

JUDICIAL SYSTEM

The Judicature of Guyana comprises the Supreme Court of Judicature, which consists of a Court of Appeal and a High Court (both of which are superior courts of record), and a number of Courts of Summary Jurisdiction.

The Court of Appeal is constituted of the Chancellor as President, the Chief Justice, and such number of Justices of Appeal as may be prescribed by Parliament. This Court came into operation on June 30th, 1966.

The High Court of the Supreme Court consists of the Chief Justice as President of the Court and nine Puisne Judges. Its jurisdiction is both original and appellate. It has criminal jurisdiction in matters brought before it on indictment. A person convicted by the Court has a right of appeal to the Guyana Court of Appeal. The High Court of the Supreme Court has unlimited jurisdiction in civil matters and exclusive jurisdiction in probate, divorce and admiralty and certain other matters. Under certain circumstances, appeal in civil matters lies either to the Full Court of the High Court of the Supreme Court, which is constituted by not less than two judges, or to the Guyana Court of Appeal.

A magistrate has jurisdiction to determine claims where the amount involved does not exceed $250. Appeal lies to the Full Court.

Chancellor: Hon. Sir EDWARD VICTOR LUCKHOO, Q.C.

Chief Justice: Hon. Sir H. B. S. BOLLERS.

Justices of Appeal: Hons. G. L. B. PERSAUD, P. A. CUMMINGS, V. E. CRANE.

RELIGION

The principal Christian religious bodies with places of worship in the state are Anglican (Church of the West Indies), Roman Catholic, Presbytery of Guyana, Guyana Presbyterian, Methodist, Congregational Union, Moravian, Lutheran and Salvation Army. Hindus and Muslims also maintain places of worship.

Archbishop of the West Indies and Bishop of Guyana (Anglican): Most Rev. A. J. KNIGHT, C.M.G., D.D., LL.B., F.C.P., Austin House, Georgetown; Anglicans in Guyana number about 130,000.

Bishop of Georgetown (Roman Catholic): Rt. Rev. Monsignor G. B. SINGH, S.T.D., 27 Brickdam, Georgetown; Roman Catholics number about 100,000.

Hinduism: The Hindu religious centre is Maha Sabha, Lamaha St., Georgetown; Hindus number about 360,000; Leader SASE NARAIN, J.P., C.M.G., M.P.

Islam: Guyana United Sad'r Islamic Anjuman, 157 Alexander St., Kitty, Georgetown; Muslims number about 93,000; Gen. Sec. MUHAMMAD ZAHUR.

THE PRESS

DAILIES

Chronicle: 18–20 Industrial Estate, Ruimveldt; f. 1881; Editor CARL BLACKMAN.

Evening Post: La Penitence, East Bank, Demerara; f. 1957; daily except weekends; Editor C. POLLARD; circ. 9,500.

Guyana Graphic: Bel Air Park, Georgetown; f. 1945; owned by the Thomson Group; Gen. Man. RICARDO SMITH; Editor W. M. SMITH; circ. 33,000.

Mirror: Industrial Estate, Ruimveldt, East Bank, Demerara; owned by the New Guyana Co. Ltd.; Editor JANET JAGAN; circ. daily 16,800, Sun. 24,000.

WEEKLIES AND PERIODICALS

Booker News: Universal Bldg., 22 Church St., Georgetown; f. 1955; monthly; house journal of the Booker Cos.; Editor McDONALD DASH; circ. 11,000.

Catholic Standard, The: Catholic Centre, Brickdam, Georgetown; f. 1905; weekly; Editor Rev. C. MEERABUX, S.J.; circ. 4,000.

Guyana Business: 156 Waterloo St., Georgetown; f. 1889; organ of the Georgetown Chamber of Commerce; quarterly; Editor C. D. KIRTON.

Guyana Sunday Graphic: Bel Air Park, Georgetown; owned by the Thomson Group; Gen. Man. RICARDO SMITH; Editor MONTY SMITH; circ. 53,541.

Guybau News: Linden; organ of the Guyana Bauxite Co.; Editor A. COLLINS.

New Nation: 105 Brickdam, Georgetown; f. 1955; organ of the People's National Congress; weekly; Editor FRANK AUGUST CAMPBELL; circ. 15,000.

News from Guyana: Ministry of Information, 18–20 Brickdam, Georgetown; weekly; circ. 1,000.

The Official Gazette of Guyana: Ministry of Information, 18-20 Brickdam, Georgetown; weekly; circ. 1,000.

Sunday Chronicle: 18–20 Industrial Estate, Ruimveldt; f. 1881; Editor C. CHICHESTER; circ. 16,800.

Thunder: 41 Robb St., Georgetown; f. 1950; organ of the People's Progressive Party; quarterly; Editor RANJI CHANDISINGH; circ. 10,000.

NEWS AGENCY
FOREIGN BUREAU

Agence France-Presse: P.O.B. 725, Georgetown; Correspondent PAUL PERSAUD.

PUBLISHERS

Guyana Graphic Ltd., The: Lama Ave., Bel Air Park, Georgetown; publs. *Guyana Graphic* and *Sunday Graphic*.

Guyana Lithographic Co. Ltd.: 1 Public Rd., La Penitence, East Bank, Demerara.

Guyana Printers Ltd.: 18–20 Industrial Estate, Ruimveldt.

Post Papers Ltd.: La Penitence, East Bank, Demerara.

RADIO

Guyana Broadcasting Co. Ltd. (Radio Demerara): P.O.B. 561, Georgetown; f. 1950; subsidiary of Rediffusion Ltd., London; commercial; one station (Radio Demerara) since 1958, with national coverage; Gen. Man. RAFIQ KHAN.

Guyana Broadcasting Service: 68 Hadfield St., Lodge; f. 1968; Man. Dir. R. SANDERS; publ. *Action Radio Times*.

In 1971 there were approximately 250,000 radios in use in Guyana.

FINANCE

BANKING

Bank of Guyana: Church St. and Ave. of the Republic, P.O.B. 1003, Georgetown; f. 1965; cap. p.u. $G4.3m., res. 6.5m. (Dec. 1972); Central Bank of note issue; Gov. W. P. D'ANDRADE, A.A.

Guyana Agricultural Co-operative Development Bank: Sandbach Parker Bldg., Water St., Georgetown; f. 1973; Man. Dir. J. C. YATES.

Guyana Co-operative Mortgage Finance Bank: Sandbach Parker Bldg., Water St., Georgetown; f. 1973; Man. Dir. R. D. FIELD-RIDLEY.

Guyana National Co-operative Bank: 1 Lombard and Cornhill Sts., P.O.B. 242, Georgetown; f. 1970; 6 brs. and 1 agency; total resources $G29m. (1972); Man. Dir. W. O. BASCOM.

Bank of Baroda: Head Office: Mandvi, Baroda, India; Lot 10, Ave. of the Republic, Georgetown; Man. N. C. BASU.

Bank of Nova Scotia: Head Office: Toronto, Ontario, Canada; Alico Bldg., Regent and Hincks Sts., Georgetown; Man. D. HOWARD.

Barclays Bank International Ltd.: Head Office: 54 Lombard St., London, E.C.3; 10 offices throughout Guyana; main branch Water St., Georgetown; Guyana Man. JOHN R. BASCOM.

Chase Manhattan Bank: Head Office: New York, U.S.A.; Bank of Guyana Bldg., Georgetown; Man. FLAVIO A. TEIXEIRA.

Royal Bank of Canada: Head Office: Place Ville Marie, Montreal; 10 branches including 6 in Georgetown, 1 Bank Mobile; Man. S. J. R. AFFONSO.

INSURANCE

Demerara Mutual Life Assurance Society Ltd.: 61-62 and 91–92 Robb St. and Ave. of the Republic, Georgetown; f. 1891; Chair. B. A. GONSALVES; Sec. and Gen. Man. HUGH K. GEORGE.

Guyana and Trinidad Mutual Life Insurance Co. Ltd.: Lots 27–29, Robb and Hincks Sts., Georgetown; f. 1925; Chair. C. J. BETTENCOURT-GOMES; Sec. R. E. BOLLERS.

Hand-in-Hand Mutual Fire Insurance Co. Ltd., Hand-in-Hand Mutual Life Assurance Co. Ltd.: Lots 1, 2 and 3, Ave. of the Republic, Georgetown; f. 1865; Chair. Maj. A. D. GOMES, M.B.E.; Sec./Man. CECIL P. FITT.

TRADE AND INDUSTRY

ASSOCIATIONS AND CHAMBERS OF COMMERCE

Berbice Chamber of Commerce and Development Association: CMC Bldg., Esplanade Rd., New Amsterdam; f. 1931; Pres. EDWARD BOWMAN; Sec. JOHN TEIXEIRA.

Consultative Association of Guyanese Industry Ltd.: 201 Camp St., P.O.B. 527, Georgetown; f. 1962; 6 mem. asscns., 12 assoc. mems.; Chair. HAROLD B. DAVIS.

Forest Products Association of Guyana: 7 Water St., Werk-en-Rust, Georgetown; f. 1943; 20 mems.; Pres. L. C. WILLEMS; Sec. W. WELSHMAN.

Georgetown Chamber of Commerce: P.O.B. 10, Georgetown; f. 1889; 131 mems.; Pres. NOEL GONSALVES; publ. *Guyana Business*.

Guyana Manufacturers' Association: Bank of Guyana Bldg., Georgetown; Pres. M. G. N. SANKIES; publ. *Guyana Handbook*.

Guyana Marketing Corporation: 1 Lombard St., Georgetown; Chair. Dr. K. F. S. KING; Sec. FRED VIGILANCE.

Guyana Sugar Producers' Association Ltd.: Lot 201, Camp St., Georgetown; f. 1942; 8 mem. companies; Exec. Dir. W. E. V. HARRISON; Sec. Miss DIANE McTURK.

Rice Producers' Association: Lot 1, Water St., Georgetown; f. 1946; c. 45,000 families; Pres. D. RAMLAKHAN; Gen. Sec. LALTA RAMGOPAL; publ. *Rice Review* (quarterly).

Shipping Association of Georgetown: 28 Main and Holmes Sts., Georgetown; f. 1952; 5 mems.; Chair. M. A. MATTHEWS; Sec. and Man. GEORGE H. D. MORGAN.

Upper Corentyne Chamber of Commerce: Corriverton, Berbice; Pres. DAVID SUBNAUTH.

TRADE UNIONS

There are 78 trade unions with a total membership of over 90,000. The **Trades Union Congress (TUC)** is the national trade union body, with 20 affiliates; Gen. Sec. JOSEPH POLLYDORE.

CO-OPERATIVE SOCIETIES

Chief Co-operatives Officer: G. HOYTE.

In 1972 there were 1,177 registered co-operative societies, mainly agricultural credit societies, with a total membership of 100,000.

DEVELOPMENT AGENCIES

Cane Farming Development Corporation Ltd.: 30–31 Hincks and Regent Sts., P.O.B. 404, Georgetown; f. 1965; 4 mems.; grants loans to peasant cane farmers; Chair. C. P. DE SOUZA.

Guyana Agriculture Co-operative Development Bank: Sandbach Parker Bldg., Georgetown; f. 1973 to promote agricultural development by providing financial credit and advisory services; Man. J. C. YATES.

Guyana Co-operative Mortgage Finance Bank: Sandbach Parker Bldg., Georgetown; f. 1973 to promote private house ownership, to guarantee mortgages, and to encourage the development of the construction industry; Man. R. D. FIELD-RIDLEY.

Guyana Forest Industries Corporation: 1 Water St., Georgetown; f. 1973 to promote the usage of Guyanese wood; Chair. Dr. K. F. S. KING; Gen. Man. PERCY G. A. FORBES.

Guyana National Co-operative Bank: 1 Lombard and Cornhill Streets, Georgetown; f. 1970; provides credit and expert advice to co-operative and private enterprises; Man. WILBERT BASCOM.

Guyana Rice Board: 1–2 Water St., Georgetown; f. 1973 to develop the rice industry and promote the expansion of its export trade, and to engage in commercial, industrial and agricultural activities necessary for the development of the rice industry; Chair. GAVIN KENNARD; Gen. Man. NEVILLE E. SUTHERLAND.

Small Industries Development Corporation: 229 South St., Georgetown; f. 1974 to promote and facilitate the establishment of small industries; Chair. Dr. K. F. S. KING; Gen. Man. R. H. THOMPSON.

TRANSPORT AND TOURISM

TRANSPORT

Transport and Harbours Department: Cornhill St., Georgetown; Gen. Man. W. A. GRIFFITH.

ROADS

Roads and vehicular trails total 1,810 miles, of which 409 are all-weather roads; 596 miles are maintained by the Government, 269 miles by five municipalities and 836 miles by local authorities.

SHIPPING

Guyana's principal ports are at Georgetown and New Amsterdam.

Guyana Railways and Shipping Services operate passenger, cargo and ferry services in and across the main rivers, with a fleet of 15 vessels.

Shipping Association of Georgetown: 28 Main and Holmes Sts., Georgetown; Chair. Capt. R. N. KING; members:

Bookers Shipping (Demerara) Ltd.: 5–9 Lombard St., La Penitence, Georgetown; reps. for Alcoa Steamship Co., Inc., Booker, Harrison and Mitsui O.S.K. Lines, Pan American Airways and Lloyds Agencies.

Caribbean Molasses Co. Ltd.: Mud Lots 1–2, Water St., Georgetown; exporters of molasses in bulk.

John Fernandes Ltd.: Water St., Georgetown; containerized and break bulk cargo; reps. for Atlantic Line, Mini Line, West Indies Shipping Corpn. (WISCO) and Carib Shipping Service.

Sandbach, Parker & Co. Ltd.: 45–48 Water St., Georgetown; reps. for Royal Netherlands Steamship Co. and K-Line.

Sprostons (Guyana) Ltd.: 3–9 Lombard St., Charlestown, Georgetown; reps. for Fabre, N.Y.K., Saguenay Steamship, West India Steamship Co., A/S Bulkhandling, H. Bang & Co., and Stolt Nielsen Chartering Inc.

CIVIL AVIATION

The main airport is Timehri International, 23 miles from Georgetown, which is capable of taking jet aircraft.

Guyana Airways Corporation: 32 Main St., P.O.B. 102, Georgetown; state-owned; Chair. K. KING; Gen. Man. R. L. ABRAMS; operates internal scheduled services and to the Caribbean, Brazil and the United States; fleet of 2 DC-3, 1 Twin Otter, 1 Cessna 310, 2 Caribou, 1 DC-6A.

Guyana is also served by the following foreign airlines: Air France, British Airways, BWIA (Trinidad), Cruzeiro do Sul (Brazil), Cubana, KLM and Pan American.

TOURISM

TOURIST AND CULTURAL ORGANIZATIONS

National History and Arts Council: National Park, Thomas Lands, Georgetown; f. 1965 to promote the study of national history and to encourage cultural development in Guyana as a whole; a division of the Ministry of Information, Youth and Culture, run by Government funds; Chair. Miss LYNETTE DOLPHIN, A.A., M.B.E.; Sec. BASIL DE RUSHE.

The Theatre Guild of Guyana Ltd.: P.O.B. 814, Parade St., Kingston, Georgetown; f. 1957 to sponsor and support West Indian and international plays, promote the writing of local plays and encourage the development of all aspects of theatre in Guyana; non-profit organization, Government subsidy since 1966; Pres. PAT MAGALEE; Playhouse Dir. Mrs. PHYLLIS SHEPHERD; Sec. Mrs. ALMA TAITT.

UNIVERSITY

University of Guyana: P.O.B. 841, Georgetown; 113 teachers, 1,334 students.

HAITI

INTRODUCTORY SURVEY

Location, Climate, Language, Religion, Flag, Capital

The Republic of Haiti occupies the west of the island of Hispaniola in the West Indies. (The Dominican Republic occupies the rest of the island.) Cuba, to the west, is less than 80 km. away. The climate is tropical but the mountains and fresh sea winds mitigate the heat. Temperatures move little with the seasons, the average in Port-au-Prince being about 27°c (80°F). May to September is the rainy season. The official language is French but a Creole dialect is generally spoken. Roman Catholicism is the predominant religion, although voodoo is also practised. The national flag (proportions 2 by 1) has equal vertical bands of black and red, with a white rectangular panel, containing the coat of arms, in the centre. The capital is Port-au-Prince.

Recent History

A military *coup* in 1950 led to the present Constitution. There were further risings in 1956 and 1957 when Dr. François Duvalier was elected President. In May 1963 Dr. Duvalier's term of office was extended for a further six years, but in 1964 his tenure was changed to life Presidency. There were several abortive attempts to overthrow the régime until Dr. Duvalier's death. In January 1971 the President's son, Jean-Claude, was appointed as his successor. This was subsequently ratified almost unanimously by referendum, and on his father's death in April Jean-Claude Duvalier became President for life. Significant cabinet changes in November 1972, and again in January and August 1973, have underlined differences within the Government between the supporters of the former President and their opponents. Relations with other countries, which deteriorated seriously under the elder Duvalier, have improved considerably since 1971, leading to a marked increase in foreign aid, particularly from the United States, Canada, France, the Federal Republic of Germany and the international development agencies.

Government

The country is governed by a President, elected for life by direct popular vote, and by a Cabinet of 12. There is a Chamber of Deputies of 67 members elected by direct popular vote for six years. There are nine Départements.

Defence

Haiti is a member of the Organization of American States and has a defence force with a total strength of about 6,500, including a company of commando-type troops known as the Léopards. The army of about 6,000 men serves also as a gendarmerie. The navy has about 400 men, and the air force about 200. There is also a militia, the National Security Volunteers of some 7,000 men, but their strength and importance have been greatly reduced under the existing President.

Economic Affairs

Haiti is a predominantly agricultural country, with over 80 per cent of the working population on the land. The agricultural sector has, however, performed badly since 1972, when virtually the entire rice crop was lost due to drought and the failure of irrigation systems. Coffee, Haiti's principal export, has similarly suffered from poor yields in recent years. A Five-Year Plan (1972–76) aims at increased agricultural productivity through the improvement of power, transportation and irrigation. A hydroelectric plant at Péligre, which became operational in December 1973, now has a capacity of 45,000 kW. Coffee accounts for about 40 per cent of Haiti's export earnings, followed by bauxite, light industrial products, essential oils and sugar. The economic decline suffered under the late Dr. Duvalier now seems to be over. Industrial investment by United States companies, attracted by low taxes and cheap labour, is beginning to grow again. Transformation industries (among them the traditional production of baseballs) are an important part of the economy, and currently include the manufacture of sophisticated electronic equipment. Tourism and the construction industry are also principal areas of growth. Soap, cloth, cement, cigarettes, drinks, flour and shoes are among locally-produced articles. Trade is largely with the United States, although the EEC is now a significant trade partner. Inflation is an acute problem, particularly in food and housing costs.

Transport and Communications

Two main infrastructure projects are in hand (to be financed by the World Bank and the Interamerican Development Bank respectively) to provide all-weather roads from Port-au-Prince to the north (Cap Haïtien) and to the south (Les Cayes). There are no railways and the Artibonite river, though largely navigable, is little used commercially. There are regular shipping services to New York, Panama and Jamaica and freight services to Europe and South America. An internal air service is operated by Turks and Caicos Airways, and foreign lines link Haiti internationally.

Social Welfare

Industrial and commercial workers are provided with free health care.

Education

Education is free and is provided by the State and by the Roman Catholic Church in nursery schools, elementary schools, secondary schools, including 12 *lycées*, and the State University. It is now compulsory between the ages of 6 and 12 years, but a large majority of children understand insufficient French to benefit. Basic education in Creole dialect is being undertaken by a new organization, ONAAC, in rural areas, where a large proportion of the peasants are illiterate.

Tourism

Haiti's bays, beaches, mountains, folklore and bazaars are of interest to tourists. Another attraction is the magnificent 150-year-old citadel and palace of King Henri Christophe. Tourism is Haiti's second source of external income. In 1972 there were 137,200 foreign visitors compared with 81,400 during the previous year. The majority of tourists come from the U.S.A.

Visas are not required to visit Haiti by nationals of the U.S.A., the United Kingdom and most other European countries.

Sport

The most popular games are football and volleyball. There is also some sea-fishing.

Public Holidays

1974: August 15th (Assumption Day), October 24th (UN Day), November 1st (All Saints' Day), November 2nd (All Souls' Day), November 18th (Army Day), December 5th (Discovery Day), December 25th (Christmas Day).

1975: January 1st (Independence), January 2nd

(Founder's Day), February 11th (Shrove Tuesday), March 27th, 28th (Easter), April 14th (Pan American Day), May 1st (Labour Day), May 8th (Ascension), May 18th (Flag Day), May 22nd (National Sovereignty), June 22nd (President's Day).

Weights and Measures

Officially the metric system is used but in practice many United States measures are used.

Currency and Exchange Rates

100 centimes = 1 gourde.

Exchange rates (April 1974):

£1 sterling = 11.81 gourdes;
U.S. $1 = 5.00 gourdes.

STATISTICAL SURVEY

AREA AND POPULATION

AREA (incl. off-shore islands) 27,750 sq. km.	POPULATION (July 1st, 1972*)			
	Total	Males	Females	Port-au-Prince (capital)
	5,073,292	2,533,853	2,539,439	494,000

* The estimates do not take account of the population survey conducted in September–October 1971. This estimated the total population as 4,243,926.

Births and Deaths: Average annual birth rate 43.9 per 1,000; death rate 19.7 per 1,000 (UN estimates for 1965–70).

AGRICULTURE

PRODUCT	UNIT	1968	1969	1970	1971	1972*
Coffee	'000 60-kg. bags	526	503	450	544	540
Sisal	'000 short tons	19	17	17	18	20
Cotton	'000 250-kg. bags	4	5	7	12	12
Bananas	'000 metric tons	174	189	189	190	195
Cocoa	„ „ „	2.5	2.7	2.9	3.1	3.3
Corn	„ „ „	220	242	240	252	265
Rice	„ „ „	77	83	80	81	92
Sugar Cane	„ „ „	4,300	4,600	4,800	4,900	5,047
Sorghum	„ „ „	189	209	210	211	217
Beans	„ „ „	36	40	40	42	43
Tobacco	„ „ „	1.9	2.2	2.2	2.2	2.3
Sweet Potatoes	„ „ „	6.6	7.4	6.6	7.0	7.2
Cassava (Manioc)	„ „ „	111	112	130	134	141

* Provisional.

INDUSTRY

PRODUCT	UNIT	1969	1970	1971	1972*
Sugar	'000 short tons	58.2	63.9	68.6	75.4
Molasses	million gallons	3.3	3.5	3.3	4.0
Cement	'000 metric tons	51.2	62.4	72.5	84.0
Cotton Textiles	million yards	3.5	3.6	5.9	2.9
Cigarettes	million	361.0	420.7	451.4	461.7
Flour	'000 metric tons	10.9	25.9	32.0	44.5
Soap	„ „ „	4.8	4.4	7.6	4.4
Cooking Oil	„ „ „	5.0	4.9	8.1	11.9
Lard	„ „ „	0.6	0.7	1.5	1.2
Shoes	'000 pairs	173.1	221.2	215.1	243.5
Soft Drinks	million bottles	20.5	25.5	27.8	30.1
Essential Oils	metric tons	306.3	206.0	381.6	316.2

* Provisional.

FINANCE

100 centimes = 1 gourde.

Coins: 5, 10, 20 and 50 centimes.

Notes: 1, 2, 5, 10, 50, 100, 250 and 500 gourdes (U.S. currency notes also circulate).

Exchange rates (April 1974): £1 sterling = 11.81 gourdes; U.S. $1 = 5.00 gourdes.

100 gourdes = £8.47 = $20.00.

BUDGET

(gourdes, year ending September 30th, 1973)

REVENUE		EXPENDITURE	
Ordinary Budget:		*Ordinary Budget:*	
Customs Receipts:		Departments:	
Import Duties	61,400,000	Finance & Economic Affairs	9,336,958
Export Duties	20,000,000	Agriculture, Natural Resources &	
Other	1,800,000	Rural Development	12,785,741
Subtotal	83,200,000	Public Works, Transport and Com-	
Internal Receipts:		munications	9,289,120
Sugar Tax	8,000,000	Foreign Affairs	7,760,731
Other	62,361,000	National Education	19,915,930
		Social Affairs	1,793,120
Subtotal	70,361,000	Commerce and Industry	2,272,145
Special Fiscal Account	1,000,000	Worship	1,400,808
Autonomous Agencies' Contribution	2,100,000	Justice	3,822,921
		Co-ordination and Information	3,058,459
		Interior and National Defence	39,888,677
		Public Health and Population	20,773,087
		Subtotal	132,108,696
		Specialized Services:	
		Tax Administration	6,236,100
		Customs Administration	5,456,500
		Subtotal	11,692,600
		Public Dept. Service	12,859,704
TOTAL ORDINARY REVENUE	156,661,000	TOTAL ORDINARY EXPENDITURE	156,661,000
Development Budget:		*Development Budget:*	
National Funds:		Economic Sectors:	
CONADEP Accounts	11,361,000	Power	15,182,500
Other Accounts	15,804,450	Transport and Communications	34,575,000
Departmental and Autonomous		Agriculture	26,237,430
Agency Contributions	31,478,825	Industry and Tourism	5,715,500
Subtotal	58,644,275	Subtotal	81,710,000
Foreign Assistance	87,554,630	Social Sectors:	
		Education and Community Develop-	
		ment	14,385,750
		Health and Environment	27,544,890
		Subtotal	41,930,640
		Preinvestment and Studies	22,857,836
TOTAL DEVELOPMENT REVENUE	146,298,906	TOTAL DEVELOPMENT BUDGET	146,298,906
TOTAL RESOURCES	302,959,905	TOTAL EXPENDITURE	302,959,905

Note: Development Budget total includes a transfer of 6,000,000 gourdes from Ordinary Budget Funds; total resources should be reduced by that amount.

Source: Le Moniteur, September 28th, 1972.

BALANCE OF PAYMENTS
(U.S. $ million, years ending September 30th)

	1967	1968	1969	1970	1971
Goods and Services:	−18.1	−10.5	−15.6	−24.4	−18.9
Trade balance, f.o.b.	− 8.2	− 2.4	− 5.4	−11.4	− 8.3
Exports	(32.2)	(36.3)	(36.7)	(39.6)	(47.1)
Imports	(−40.4)	(−38.7)	(−42.1)	(−52.0)	(−55.4)
Freight and insurance on merchandise	− 4.0	− 4.1	− 5.8	− 9.2	− 9.1
Travel receipts	2.1	4.5	5.4	6.6	8.7
Investment income	− 3.1	− 3.3	− 3.3	− 2.8	− 3.1
Other	− 4.9	− 5.2	− 6.5	− 7.6	− 7.1
Unrequited Transfers	17.2	12.8	15.8	22.0	18.9
Private	13.2	8.9	10.8	15.0	13.1
Public	4.0	3.9	5.0	7.0	5.8
Capital Movements	− 2.5	3.0	2.3	3.8	5.7
Private	− 1.3	3.2	1.7	0.4	6.1
Public agencies	0.2	1.0	2.5	0.5	1.1
Central Government	− 1.4	− 1.2	− 1.9	2.9	− 1.5
Net Errors and Omissions	1.1	− 5.7	− 1.7	2.6	1.4
Overall Balance	− 2.3	− 0.4	0.8	4.0	7.1
Allocation of SDRs	—	—	—	2.5	2.0
Net International Reserves (increase −)	2.3	0.4	− 0.8	− 6.5	− 9.1
National Bank	2.3	0.8	− 1.1	− 6.3	− 8.3
Other banks	—	− 0.4	0.3	− 0.2	− 0.8

EXTERNAL TRADE
(U.S. $ million, years ending September 30th)

	1967–68	1968–69	1969–70	1970–71	1971–72
Imports	42.8	47.8	59.1	59.2	58.2
Exports	36.2	36.6	39.5	48.2	42.3

PRINCIPAL COMMODITIES
(U.S. $ million)

IMPORTS	1969–70
Foodstuffs	11.7
Beverages and Tobacco	2.0
Chemicals and Pharmaceuticals	4.1
Other Consumer Goods	13.6
Fuels and Lubricants	3.3
Raw Materials	1.4
Construction Materials	2.8
Capital Goods	6.9
Other Machinery and Equipment	1.5
Unclassified Goods	11.8

EXPORTS	1969–70	1970–71
Coffee	15.2	18.8
Bauxite	5.6	6.5
Sisal	1.8	0.8
Sugar	2.5	3.4
Essential Oils	2.5	3.1
Copper Ore*	1.2	1.3
Cocoa and Cocoa Products	1.1	1.2
Other	9.6	12.0

* Ceased 1971.

PRINCIPAL COUNTRIES
(U.S. $'000)

IMPORTS	1970–71	EXPORTS	1970–71
Belgium	1,266.2	Belgium	4,611.6
Canada	2,944.1	France	2,755.3
France	2,957.5	Italy	2,337.8
Germany, Federal Republic	2,881.2	Japan	1,323.3
Japan	5,415.7	Netherlands	2,659.0
Netherlands	1,737.4	United Kingdom	118.8
United Kingdom	2,707.3	U.S.A.	29,845.5
U.S.A.	26,323.7		

COFFEE EXPORTS

	1967–68	1968–69	1969–70	1970–71	1971–72
60 kg. sacks	324,982	308,166	274,766	358,333	310,762
Million U.S. $	14.4	13.4	15.2	18.8	14.7*

* million SDRs.

TRANSPORT AND TOURISM
CIVIL AVIATION

	1970	1971
Number of Passengers on Internal Flights	6,627	11,119
Number of Passengers Arriving on International Flights	52,532	70,694
Number of Passengers Departing on International Flights	64,932	75,905

Tourism (1972): 137,200 visitors. Tourism comes second to coffee as a source of external income.

EDUCATION
(1972)

	SCHOOLS	TEACHERS	PUPILS
Urban Primary	368	3,103	170,945
Country	545	1,693	117,935
Professional	16	350	5,621
Secondary*	26	500	20,000

* Provisional.

Source: Institut Haitien de Statistique, Port-au-Prince; Banque Nationale de la République d'Haiti.

THE CONSTITUTION

Haiti acquired its independence from the French in 1804 but was controlled by the U.S.A. from 1915–34. The Constitution was promulgated in 1957 and revised in 1964 and 1971.

President: Has the right to nominate his successor. The President is assisted by a Council of Secretaries of State nominated by him. The President may dismiss the National Assembly and Cabinet, and govern by decree, in cases of grave conflict.

Legislature: In April 1961 the two houses of the legislature were amalgamated into one, with a National Assembly consisting of 58 deputies who are elected for six years. Men and women over 18 have the vote. Deputies may be re-elected for an indefinite period.

Judicature: A Supreme Court called the Court of Cassation, and subordinate courts.

THE GOVERNMENT

HEAD OF THE STATE

Life President of the Republic: Jean-Claude Duvalier.

COUNCIL OF MINISTERS

(April 1974)

Minister of Finance and Economic Affairs: Emmanuel Bros.

Minister of the Interior and National Defence: Paul Blanchet.

Minister of Public Health: Dr. Daniel Beaulieu.

Minister of Co-ordination and Information: Pierre Gousse.

Minister of Foreign Affairs and Worship: Ednèr Brutus.

Minister of Commerce and Industry: Dr. Serge Fourcand.

Minister of Social Affairs: Max A. Antoine.

Minister of Public Works, Transport and Communication: Pierre Petit.

Minister of Agriculture, Natural Resources and Rural Development: Jaurès Lévêque.

Minister of Education: Jean Montes Lefranc.

Minister of Justice: Aurélien Jeanty.

DIPLOMATIC REPRESENTATION

EMBASSIES AND LEGATION ACCREDITED TO HAITI

(E) Embassy; (L) Legation.

Argentina: Maison R. Martelly, impasse Mérovée, Bourdon (E); *Ambassador:* (vacant).

Brazil: Maison Pierre Wiener, Bourdon (E); *Ambassador:* (vacant).

Canada: rue Camille Léon, Bois Verna (E); *Chargé d'Affaires a.i.:* William McKenzie Wood.

Chile: rue Villate, Pétionville (E); *Chargé d'Affaires:* Sergio Morena.

China (Taiwan): Débussy 28, Pétionville (E); *Ambassador:* Si-Ling Kiang.

Colombia: rue Rigaud, Morne Calvaire, Pétionville (E); *Ambassador:* Carlos Arturo Torres Povena.

Dominican Republic: rue Panaméricaine 93, Pétionville (E); *Ambassador:* Rafael Adriano Valdes.

Ecuador: rue Goulard, Pétionville (E); *Chargé d'Affaires a.i.:* Gonzalo Donoso.

France: pl. des Héros de l'Indépendance, 51 Bourdon (E); *Ambassador:* Bernard Dorin.

Germany, Federal Republic: ave. Marie-Jeanne (Rond Point) (E); *Ambassador:* Erich A. Heusch.

Israel: Berthé, Pétionville (E); *Ambassador:* Zev Bashan.

Italy: ave. José de San Martin, Pétionville (E); *Ambassador:* Angelo Macchia.

Liberia: Canapé Vert 23 (E); *Ambassador:* Charles A. Snetter.

Mexico: Maison Roger Esper, route de Delmas (E); *Ambassador:* Mario Armando Amador Durón.

Nicaragua: (E); *Chargé d'Affaires:* Alfredo López Pastora.

Panama: Berthé, Pétionville (E); *Chargé d'Affaires a.i.:* Benjamin Orejuela.

Peru: Débussy 28, Pétionville (E); *Chargé d'Affaires a.i.:* Edgardo Otorola.

Poland: Maison Pierre Louis, Bourdon (L); *Chargé d'Affaires:* Wiktor M. A. Karasinski.

Spain: Maison Mme Janine Flory, Lyles Estate (E); *Ambassador:* Valentín Alejandro Alzina de Boschi.

United Kingdom: Shell Bldg., rue Dantès Destouches 26 (E); *Chargé d'Affaires a.i.:* J. Dalton Murray, c.m.g.

U.S.A.: Port-au-Prince (E); *Ambassador:* (vacant).

Vatican: ave. John Brown (Lalue) (Apostolic Nunciature); *Apostolic Nuncio:* Mgr. Luigi Barbarito.

Venezuela: rue Courbe 22 (E); *Ambassador:* Adolfo R. Taylhardat.

Haiti also has diplomatic relations with Austria, Belgium, Bolivia, Costa Rica, Dahomey, El Salvador, Ethiopia, Finland, Greece, Guatemala, Guyana, Honduras, Ivory Coast, Jamaica, Japan, Republic of Korea, Lebanon, Mali, Netherlands, Norway, Senegal, Sweden, Switzerland, Trinidad and Tobago, Turkey, Uruguay.

CONGRESS

NATIONAL ASSEMBLY

Fifty-eight deputies—all supporters of President Duvalier—were elected February 11th, 1973. According to the Constitution they hold office for six years.

President: Maître Michel Auguste.

POLITICAL PARTY

Parti de l'Unité Nationale: Port-au-Prince; f. 1963, as Parti Unique de l'Action Révolutionnaire et Governementale; the official party; Leader President Duvalier.

There are several unofficial opposition parties, mostly in exile, actively opposed to the régime of President Duvalier, including: *Front National de Résistance, Parti Uni des Démocrates Haïtiens, Parti d'Entente Populaire, Parti Unifié des Communistes Haïtiens.*

JUDICIAL SYSTEM

Law is based on the French Code, substantially modified during the presidency of Dr. François Duvalier.

Court of Cassation: Port-au-Prince.

President of the Court of Cassation: Fournier Fortuné.

Courts of Appeal. Civil Courts. Magistrates' Courts. Judges of the Supreme Courts and Courts of Appeal appointed by the President.

Courts of Appeal and Civil Courts sit at Port-au-Prince and the three provincial capitals: Gonaïves, Cap Haïtien and Port de Paix. In principle each commune has a Magistrates' Court.

RELIGION

Roman Catholicism is the official religion; the folk religion is voodoo.

Archbishop of Haiti: François-Wolff Ligondé.
There are five Suffragan Bishoprics.

The Episcopal (Anglican) Church is strong and its first Haitian bishop was consecrated in 1971. Other sects are well represented, including Methodists, Baptists and many American missionary churches.

THE PRESS

DAILIES

Port-au-Prince

Haiti-Journal: B.P. 866; f. 1930; French; independent; Editor Edouard Charles; circ. 50,000.

Le Jour: French; pro-government; Editor Weber Alexandre; circ. 5,000.

Le Matin: rue Américaine; f. 1908; French; independent; Editor Dumairic Charlier; circ. 9,000.

Le Moniteur: the official gazette; twice weekly; Dir. Simon Desvarieux.

Le Nouveau Monde: major newspaper of Haiti; Dir. René Piquion.

Le Nouvelliste: B.P. 1013; f. 1896; oldest newspaper in the country; French; evening; independent; Editor Lucien Montas; circ. 6,000.

Oedipe: French; circ. 6,000.

Panorama: French; Editor Paul Blanchet; circ. 3,000.

Provinces

Artibonite Journal: Gonaïves.

Le Courier du Sud: Les Cayes.

Le Journal Sud-Ouest: Jacmel; Editor Emile Delince.

Le Septentrion: Cap Haitien; Editor Nelson Bell.

PERIODICALS

Le Messager du Nord-Ouest: Port de Paix; weekly.

News of Haiti: Port-au-Prince; English; monthly.

Optique: B.P. 1316; monthly; magazine of the French Institute; literature and arts; Dir. Lucien Montas.

Revue de la Société Haitienne d'Histoire: Port-au-Prince; f. 1925; quarterly; Editor Henock Trouillot.

RADIO AND TELEVISION

RADIO

Départment des Travaux Publics: Service des Télécommunications, Port-au-Prince.

There are 4 religious stations and 12 commercial stations. Principal stations:

Radio Métropole: rue Pavée, Port-au-Prince.

Radio Nouveau Monde: pl. d'Italie, Port-au-Prince; Dir. Weber W. A. Guerrier.

Others include:

Magloire Broadcasting: Circuit, rue Américaine, Port-au-Prince.

Radio Caraïbes: ruelle Chavannes 23, Port-au-Prince; Dir. A. Brown.

Radiodiffusion Haïtienne: ruelle Jeanty, Bois Verna, Port-au-Prince; Dir. Y. Michel.

Radio Haiti: B.P. 737, Port-au-Prince; Dir. J. L. Dominique.

Radio Lumière: B.P. 1050, Port-au-Prince; Dir. Edwin Walker; non-commercial; cultural, educational, evangelical; French, Creole.

Radio Port-au-Prince: Stade Sylvio Castor, Port-au-Prince.

La Voix Evangélique d'Haïti—Station 4 VEH: B.P. 1, Cap Haïtien; f. 1950; Dir.-Gen. W. Duewel; non-commercial; a total of 200 hours of programming are broadcast each week in French, Creole, Spanish and English.

In 1970 there were 85,000 radios in use in Haiti.

TELEVISION

Télé Haïti: B.P. 1126, Port-au-Prince; f. 1959; private, commercial company, at present holding monopoly rights of transmission; programmes are transmitted by cable; Gen. Man. A. Apaid; 15,000 receivers (1973).

FINANCE

(cap. = capital; m. = million; dep. = deposits.)

BANKING

Banque Nationale de la République d'Haïti: rue Américaine and rue Férou, Port-au-Prince; f. 1911; the central bank and bank of issue; cap. gourdes 20m., dep. gourdes 227.7m. (Sept. 1972); 11 brs.; Pres. and Dir.-Gen. ANTONIO ANDRÉ; Vice-Pres. LEON B. MIRAMBEAU.

Banque Colombo-Haïtienne: rue du Fort Par, Port-au-Prince.

Banque de l'Union Haïtienne: rue du Quai.

Bank of Boston: rue des F. Forts.

Bank of Nova Scotia: blvd. J. J. Desselines.

First National City Bank: rue du Centre, Port-au-Prince.

Institut de Développement Agricole et Industriel: Port-au-Prince; f. 1961; state bank; cap. gourdes 50m.; Dir. J. DELEJ.

Royal Bank of Canada: rue Abraham Lincoln and rue des Miracles, Port-au-Prince.

TRADE AND INDUSTRY

Chambre de Commerce d'Haïti: Port-au-Prince; Pres. C. J. CHARLES; Sec. JULIEN LAUTURE; publ.: *Bulletin d'Information* (quarterly).

DEVELOPMENT ASSOCIATION

Conseil National de Développement et de Planification (CONADEP): Palais des Finances, Port-au-Prince; f. 1963; deals with plans and major government projects, and general co-ordination of technical assistance. Pres. H.E. JEAN-CLAUDE DUVALIER; Exec. Sec. H.E. EMMANUEL BROS; Dir.-Gen. DONASSON ALPHONSE.

TRADE UNIONS

Union Nationale des Ouvriers d'Haïti—UNOH (*National Union of Workers of Haiti*): B.P. 276, Port-au-Prince; f. 1951; admitted to ORIT; 3,000 mems. from 8 affiliated unions; Pres. MARCEL VINCENT; Sec.-Gen. FRITZNER ST. VIL.

Fédération Haïtienne de Syndicats Chrétiens (*Haitian Federation of Christian Unions*): B.P. 416, Port-au-Prince; Pres. LÉONVIL LEBLANC.

A number of unions are non-affiliated and without a national centre, including a number of unions which have been organized for the workers of particular companies.

TRANSPORT AND TOURISM

RAILWAYS

There are no longer any railways in use.

ROADS

There are 3,157 km. of roads; a project to build two major all-weather roads is in hand.

SHIPPING

Vessels of many European and American lines call at Haiti, most of them en route to other ports.

CIVIL AVIATION

The state airline Cohata is at present non-operational pending the re-organization of internal air services with technical assistance from France. Meanwhile, internal air services are operated under contract by Turks and Caicos Airways.

Haiti is also served by the following foreign airlines: Air France, ALM, American, Caribair, Pan American.

TOURISM

Département du Tourisme et des Relations Publiques: Port-au-Prince; Dir. FRITZ JEAN-BAPTISTE.

ATOMIC ENERGY

Commission Nationale à l'Energie Nucléaire: Port-au-Prince.

UNIVERSITY

Université d'Etat d'Haïti: place des Héros de l'Indépendance, Port-au-Prince; 183 teachers, 2,000 students.

HONDURAS

INTRODUCTORY SURVEY

Location, Climate, Language, Religion, Flag, Capital

Honduras lies in the middle of the Central American isthmus linking North and South America. It has a long northern coastline on the Caribbean and a narrow southern outlet to the Pacific. Its neighbours are Guatemala to the west, El Salvador to the south-west and Nicaragua to the south-east. Mountainous areas and high plateau land divide the northern coastal region from the narrow southern area. The coastal areas have more extreme temperatures and a heavier rainfall than the high inland areas. The rainy season is from May to November. The national language is Spanish. Roman Catholicism is the predominant faith. The national flag (proportions 3 by 2) has three horizontal stripes of blue, white and blue, with five blue stars, arranged in a diagonal cross, in the centre of the white band. The capital is Tegucigalpa.

Recent History

In October 1963 the Liberal President, Dr. Ramón Villeda Morales, was deposed after a *coup* led by the armed forces. Colonel (later Gen.) Oswaldo López Arellano became Head of State, and the constitution was suspended. In June 1965 a new constitution was promulgated and Gen. López became constitutional President for 6 years. At the same time the constituent assembly which had been elected in February was transformed into a national congress.

Friction had existed for some time with neighbouring El Salvador, caused by the entry of an increasing number of Salvadorian immigrants into Honduras. Honduras' elimination from the qualifying rounds of the World Cup by El Salvador sparked off armed conflict between the two countries in June 1969. Although the OAS arranged a ceasefire in July, official contacts have remained broken and a number of border incidents have taken place. In November 1971 the United States ceded the Swan Islands in the Caribbean to Honduras.

Presidential elections took place in March 1971, in which Ramón Ernesto Cruz Uclés, the National Party candidate, was elected. After the presidential inauguration, the arrangement by which the two main political parties enjoyed equal representation in the Congress came under increasing strain. Popular discontent over austerity measures taken by the Cruz government, and peasant unrest over delayed land reforms, caused the former President and current commander in chief of the land forces, Gen. López, to accuse the Government of creating "economic chaos". Gen. López then evicted the Government in a bloodless *coup* on December 4th, 1972, and announced that he would remain in power for the next five years.

Government

Under the 1965 constitution there is an elected President and a National Congress of 64 members elected by proportional representation for six years.

Defence

A period of military service is obligatory between the ages of eighteen and fifty-five. Active service lasts eight months, with subsequent reserve training. The total number of men under arms is 5,735. 4,500 of these are in the army. There is a very small navy and the air force numbers about 1,200 men.

Economic Affairs

Honduras is principally an agricultural country. Bananas form nearly half the exports. Coffee, tobacco, coconuts, cotton, beans, maize and sugar are also grown. Timber is an important export, although large proportions of the forested areas are prone to fires. The most valuable mineral is silver and there is some gold, copper, titanium, zirconium, iron and antimony. There has been some attempt to diversify the economy. Industry is still on a small scale but is being developed, particularly in the San Pedro Sula area. Honduras has been a member of the Central American Common Market since it was formed in 1960. It remains the poorest member country, even after substantial growth during the 1960s. Trade with El Salvador was broken off after the war in 1969 and serious disagreement on policy in the CACM led Honduras to suspend its trading pact with all the CACM countries in December 1970. A 15-year development plan is currently being drawn up. Apart from provisions for agrarian reform, the plan will give prominence to the development of forest resources.

Transport and Communications

There are about 1,059 km. of railways, located entirely in the North and used to carry bananas to the ports. There are over 5,700 km. of national roads. There are airports at Tegucigalpa, La Ceiba and San Pedro Sula. There are internal and international air services including daily flights to the United States.

Social Welfare

There is a state social security system in operation; it provides benefits for sickness, maternity, orphans, unemployment, accidents and professional sickness, and also family and old age allowances A Labour Code affords guarantees for employees.

Education

Education is free and compulsory from seven to fifteen. There are 4,151 primary schools and 139 secondary and technical schools. There is a national university in Tegucigalpa.

Tourism

The ruins of Copán, second largest city of the old Mayan Empire, attract tourists and archaeologists. Lake Yojoa, near San Pedro Sula, provides fishing and boating, and there is bathing on the Bay Islands and along the beaches of the Northern coast.

Visas are not required to visit Honduras by nationals of Belgium, Canada, Colombia, Denmark, Guatemala, Panama, the United Kingdom and the U.S.A.

Sport

Football and basketball are the most popular sports in Honduras. although softball and bowling are becoming increasingly popular.

Public Holidays

1974: September 15th (Independence Day), October 3rd (Morazán Day), October 12th (Discovery Day), October 21st (Army Day), December 25th (Christmas).

1975: January 1st (New Year's Day), March 28th–31st (Easter), April 14th (Pan American Day), May 1st (Labour Day).

Weights and Measures

The metric system is in general use. The old Spanish measures are used locally.

1 libra=1.014 lb., 1 arroba=25.35 lb., 1 quintal= 101.4 lb., 1 tonelada=18.10 cwt.

Currency and Exchange Rates

100 centavos=1 lempira (lp.).

Exchange rates (April 1974):

£1 sterling=4.72 lempiras;
U.S. $1=2.00 lempiras.

STATISTICAL SURVEY

AREA AND POPULATION

| AREA (sq. km.) | POPULATION (1973 est.) | | BIRTHS, MARRIAGES, DEATHS (1971) | | |
	Total	Tegucigalpa (capital)	Births	Marriages	Deaths
112,088	2,780,000	274,850	117,430	7,505*	20,405

* 1967 figure.

AGRICULTURE

| | AREA CULTIVATED ('000 hectares) | | PRODUCTION ('000 quintales) | |
	1971	1972	1971	1972
Maize	288	290	7,918	7,979
Rice	11	10	421	421
Bananas . . .	42	38	1,516	1,388
Dry Beans . . .	75	71	1,152	1,097
Coffee . . .	165	168	641	703
Tobacco . . .	12	12	65	67

Forestry: There are many kinds of wood in the Honduran forests, including pine, mahogany, carreto, lignum vitae, grenadino, walnut and rosewood. The African palm is cultivated. The value of total timber exports in 1972 was 54.2 million lempiras.

Livestock (1970–71—'000): Cattle 1,600; Pigs 820; Horses 280; Mules 118; Asses 46; Goats 56; Sheep 9; Poultry 7,000 (FAO estimates).

MINING

Exports (million lempiras—1972): Lead and Zinc 13.7; Silver 8.2; Production (1970): Silver 119 metric tons; Gold 104 kg.

INDUSTRY
('000 units)

	1971	1972
Raw Sugar (quintales) . .	1,283	1,415
Cement (bags of 42.5 kg.) . .	3,808	4,589
Cigarettes (packets of 20) . .	74,523	76,844
Matches (boxes of 40) .	45,159	48,213
Beer (12 oz. bottles) . .	81,895	86,062
Soft Drinks (6 oz. bottles) . .	327,184	357,820

FINANCE

100 centavos = 1 lempira (lp.).

Coins: 1, 2, 5, 10, 20 and 50 centavos.

Notes: 1, 5, 10, 20, 50 and 100 lempiras.

Exchange rates (April 1974): £1 sterling = 4.72 lempiras; U.S. $1 = 2.00 lempiras.

100 lempiras = £21.175 = $50.00.

Note: The Central American peso, used for transactions within the Central American Common Market, is at par with the United States dollar.

BUDGET
(million Central American pesos)

	1971	1972*
REVENUE:		
Direct Taxes	22.1	21.9
Indirect Taxes	58.6	61.9
Other	9.8	10.2
TOTAL	90.5	94.0
EXPENDITURE:		
Current Expenditure	78.9	82.7
Capital Expenditure	34.0	26.0
TOTAL	112.9	108.7

* Preliminary.

RESERVES
('ooo Central American pesos on December 31st)

	1970	1971	1972
Gross Reserves at the Central Bank	21,239	22,942	37,300
Gold and Foreign Exchange	21,048	20,090	31,377
Gold Deposits with IMF	—	2	2
SDRs	191	2,850	5,921

BALANCE OF PAYMENTS
(million Central American pesos)

	1971			1972*		
	Credit	Debit	Balance	Credit	Debit	Balance
Goods and Services:						
Goods	195.9	177.6	18.3	195.3	173.2	22.1
Services	23.1	67.5	−44.4	23.4	67.8	−44.4
Total	219.0	245.1	−26.1	218.7	241.0	−22.3
Transfer Payments (net)	6.7	—	6.7	6.8	—	6.8
Capital Operations (net)	27.2	—	27.2	24.7	—	24.7
Net Errors and Omissions	—	2.2	− 2.2	2.7	—	2.7
Change in Reserves			− 5.6			−11.9

* Preliminary.

EXTERNAL TRADE
(million lempiras)

Total Imports: (1970) 441.3; (1971) 387.8; (1972) 386.6.

Total Exports: (1970) 347.7; (1971) 373.6; (1972) 400.6.

COMMODITIES
(million lempiras)

IMPORTS	1970	1971	1972
Machinery and Transport Equipment . .	127.6	112.6	101.1
Chemicals	57.3	60.4	62.1
Miscellaneous Manufactured Articles .	46.4	26.8	25.1
Food	42.3	31.2	34.9
Mineral Fuel and Lubricants . .	29.5	34.9	38.4
Animal and Vegetable Oils and Fats .	5.7	4.2	3.6

EXPORTS	1970	1971	1972
Bananas	150.6	191.4	176.9
Coffee	51.8	46.5	54.5
Wood	32.4	38.4	54.2
Frozen Meat	19.4	25.1	32.1
Lead and Zinc	9.4	11.2	13.7
Petroleum Products . . .	12.6	6.0	6.9
Tobacco	4.5	4.2	4.4

PRINCIPAL COUNTRIES
('000 lempiras)

IMPORTS	1969	1970	1971
Costa Rica	14,807	24,703	9,884
El Salvador	24,830	—	—
Germany, Federal Republic . .	23,555	24,242	21,362
Guatemala	35,503	57,055	16,243
Japan	24,010	35,832	43,575
Nicaragua	12,806	27,983	6,600
United Kingdom	9,508	11,923	12,763
U.S.A.	159,308	182,509	182,242
Venezuela	14,703	21,182	23,264

EXPORTS	1969	1970	1971
Belgium	12,598	10,300	n.a.
Costa Rica	11,421	14,096	2,700
Dominican Republic . . .	7,207	9,749	8,684
El Salvador	13,975	—	—
Germany, Federal Republic . .	41,371	36,774	45,032
Guatemala	12,303	13,866	4,711
Italy	15,319	18,263	10,787
Japan	18,920	4,882	n.a.
United Kingdom	1,774	1,281	n.a.
U.S.A.	157,347	179,130	229,995

TRANSPORT

Railways: In 1972 there were 1,059 km. of track, of which 239 km. were owned by the Ferrocarril Nacional.

Roads: In 1972 there were 5,746 km. of road, of which 1,228 km. were paved and 3,028 km. were all-weather roads.

Shipping: In 1966 1,082,862 tons were loaded and 503,063 tons unloaded.

CIVIL AVIATION

	1966		1967	
	Domestic	International	Domestic	International
Passengers . . .	98,890	49,103	117,047	67,665
Freight (ton kilometres) .	922,341	4,810,374	995,190	6,776,979
Mail (ton kilometres) . .	30,557	3	37,158	75

EDUCATION
(1972)

Category	Number of Establishments	Number of Teachers	Number of Pupils
Primary	4,151	11,354	412,050
Secondary	139	2,776	42,966
Teachers' Training College .	1	67	1,137
University	1	427	7,824

Sources: Dirección General de Estadística y Censos, Tegucigalpa; Banco Central de Honduras; Consejo Monetario Centroamericano, San José; FAO.

THE CONSTITUTION

A Constitution was passed by the Constituent National Assembly on June 5th, 1965.

The following are some of its main points:

Honduras is constituted as a democratic Republic. All Hondurans over the age of 18 are citizens.

The Suffrage and Political Parties: The vote is direct and secret. Any political party which proclaims or practises doctrines contrary to the democratic spirit is forbidden. A National Electoral Council will be set up at the end of each Presidential term. Its general function will be to supervise all elections and to register political parties. A proportional system of voting will be adopted for the election of Municipal Corporations.

Individual Rights and Guarantees: The right to life is declared inviolable; the death penalty is abolished. The Constitution recognizes the right of Habeas Corpus and arrests may only be made by judicial order. Remand for interrogation may not last for more than six days, and no-one may be held *incomunicado* for more than twenty-four hours. The Constitution recognizes the rights of free expression of thought and opinion, the free circulation of information, of peaceful, unarmed association, of free movement within and out of the country, of political asylum and of religious and educational freedom. Civil marriage and divorce are recognized.

Workers' Welfare: All have a right to work. Day work shall not exceed eight hours a day or forty-four hours a week; night work shall not exceed six hours a night or thirty-six hours a week. Equal pay shall be given for equal work. The legality of trades unions and the right to strike are recognized.

Education: The State is responsible for education, which shall be free, lay, and, in the primary stage, compulsory. Private education is liable to State inspection and regulation.

Legislative Power: Deputies are obliged to vote, for or against, on any measure at the discussion of which they are present. Congress has power to grant amnesties to political prisoners; approve or disapprove of the actions of the Executive; declare part or the whole of the Republic subject to a state of siege; declare war; approve or withhold approval of treaties; withhold approval of the accounts of public expenditure when these exceed the sums fixed in the Budget; decree, interpret, repeal and amend laws, and pass legislation fixing the rate of exchange or stablizing the national currency. Congress may suspend certain guarantees in all or part of the Republic for sixty days in case of grave danger from civil or foreign war, epidemics or any other calamity. Deputies are elected in the proportion of one Deputy and one substitute for every 30,000 inhabitants, or fraction over 15,000. Congress may amend the basis in the light of increasing population.

Executive Power: The Executive Power is exercised by the President of the Republic, who is elected for a period of six years, beginning on June 6th, by a simple majority of the people. No President may serve two terms in succession.

Judicial Power: The Judiciary consists of the Supreme Court, the Courts of Appeal and various lesser tribunals. The seven judges and five substitute judges of the Supreme

Court are elected by Congress for a period of six years. The Supreme Court can declare laws unconstitutional, and can censure the misconduct of ministers or officials when Congress has declared there is a case to answer.

The Armed Forces: The armed forces are declared by the Constitution to be essentially professional and non-political. The President exercises his power through a Commander-in-Chief who is designated for a period of six years by Congress, which alone, by a two-thirds majority, may dismiss him. Military service is obligatory.

Local Administration: The country is divided into eighteen departments for purposes of local administration, and these are subdivided into autonomous municipalities; the functions of local offices shall only be economic and administrative.

Note: The Constitution has been only partly in force since General López took power; government is at present by decree.

THE GOVERNMENT

Head of State: General Oswaldo López Arellano.

CABINET
(March 1974)

Minister of the Interior: Col. Juan A. Melgar.

Minister of Foreign Affairs: César A. Batres.

Minister of Education: Dr. José Napoleón Alcerro Oliva.

Minister of Finance: Manuel Acosta Bonilla.

Minister of Economy: José A. Bennaton Ramos.

Minister of Health: Dr. Enrique Aguilar Paz.

Minister of Natural Resources: Ing. Raúl Edgardo Escoto.

Minister of Labour: Gautama Buda Fonseca.

Minister of Defence: Col. Pedro Fermín Ramírez Landa.

Minister of Communications: Ing. Miguel A. Rivera.

Secretary for Economic Planning: Manlio Martínez.

DIPLOMATIC REPRESENTATION

EMBASSIES ACCREDITED TO HONDURAS

(Tegucigalpa, unless otherwise indicated)

Argentina: Edificio Lázarus, Calle 604, esq. Salvador Mendieta *Ambassador:* Dr. Carlos Adelmar Ferro.

Austria: Mexico D.F., Mexico.

Belgium: Guatemala City, Guatemala.

Bolivia: San José, Costa Rica.

Brazil: Edificio Banco Atlántida, 2°, Ave. Comayaguela 1; *Ambassador:* Fernando Ronald de Carvalho.

Canada: San José, Costa Rica.

Chile: Edificio Bancahsa, No. 203, P.O.B. 222; *Ambassador:* C. Langille.

China (Taiwan): Colonia Reforma, Casa 117, Calle Principal; *Ambassador:* Yu Kuo-ping.

Colombia: Edificio Bancahsa, 4°, No. 403, P.O.B. 486; *Ambassador:* Dr. E. Gartner Nicholls.

Costa Rica: Colonia Palmira, Boulevard Morazán 113; *Ambassador:* Rafael López Garrido.

Denmark: Mexico D.F., Mexico.

Ecuador: Colonia Palmira, 4A Ave., esq. 2A Calle; *Ambassador:* Dr. Alberto Barriga Ledesma.

Egypt: San Salvador, El Salvador.

France: Ave. La Paz, P.O.B. 14-C; *Ambassador:* Henri Langlais.

Germany, Federal Republic: Calle La Fuente, esq. Ave. Lempira; *Ambassador:* Dr. Gottfried Pagenstert.

Greece: Mexico D.F., Mexico.

Guatemala: Altos del Almacén Fléfil, 20 Callejón Los; *Ambassador:* Col. Luis Urrutia de León.

Israel: San José, Costa Rica.

Italy: Ave. Jerez, frente al Parque Finlay, P.O.B. 317; *Ambassador:* (vacant).

Japan: Primera Ave., Colonia Palmira; *Ambassador:* Katsushige Takeuchi.

Korea, Republic: Mexico D.F., Mexico.

Lebanon: Mexico D.F., Mexico.

Mexico: Edificio Larach, 5°, No. 506, P.O.B. 769; *Ambassador:* Dr. Ernesto de Santiago López.

Netherlands: Guatemala City, Guatemala.

Nicaragua: Colonia Matamoros, P.O.B. 392; *Ambassador:* Ricardo García Leclair.

Norway: Mexico City, Mexico.

Panama: Barrio La Leona, P.O.B. 397; *Ambassador:* Víctor M. Chansón.

Paraguay: San Salvador, El Salvador.

Peru: Edificio Fiallos Soto, P.O.B. 64-C; *Ambassador:* Dr. Abraham Padilla Bendezu.

Poland: Mexico D.F., Mexico.

Portugal: Mexico D.F., Mexico.

Spain: Colonia Matamoros 103; *Ambassador:* ALBERTO PASCUAL VILLAR.

Sweden: Guatemala City, Guatemala.

Switzerland: Guatemala City, Guatemala.

Turkey: Mexico D.F., Mexico.

United Kingdom: Ave. La Paz, P.O.B. 290; *Ambassador:* DAVID MORRIS PEARSON, O.B.E.

U.S.A.: Ave. La Paz, P.O.B. 105; *Ambassador:* PHILIP V. SANCHEZ.

Uruguay: Edificio Midence Soto, 4°, P.O.B. 329; *Ambassador:* MANUEL AREOSA.

Vatican: Palacio de la Nunciatura Apostólica, Colonia Palmira, P.O.B. 324; *Apostolic Nunciate:* (vacant).

Venezuela: Ave. La Paz 421; *Ambassador:* MARCIANO UZCÁTEGUI URDANETE.

Yugoslavia: Mexico D.F., Mexico.

PRESIDENT AND CONGRESS

PRESIDENTIAL ELECTION

(*March 28th, 1971*)

CANDIDATES	VOTES
RAMÓN ERNESTO CRUZ UCLÉS (Partido Nacional)	306,028
Dr. JORGE BUESO ARIAS (Partido Liberal) .	276,777

President Cruz was deposed on December 4th, 1972, and replaced as Head of State by General OSWALDO LÓPEZ ARELLANO.

CONGRESS

Since the *coup* which brought General LÓPEZ to power, Congress has been suspended; government is at present by decree.

POLITICAL PARTIES

Partido Nacional (PN): Traditional right-wing party; Leader Lic. RICARDO ZUNIGA AUGUSTINUS.

Partido Liberal de Honduras (PLH): Liberal Party; Chair. Lic. MAX VELÁSQUEZ DÍAZ.

Partido Popular Progresista: not legally recognized; split from Partido Nacional in 1963; Leader Dr. GONZALO CARÍAS CASTILLO.

Partido Inovación Unidad (PINU): not legally recognized; Leader Dr. MIGUEL ANDONIE FERNÁNDEZ.

Partido Demócrata Cristiano: not legally recognized.

Partido Comunista de Honduras: forbidden by law, although active.

JUDICIAL SYSTEM

There is a supreme court with nine magistrates elected by Congress for terms of six years. In addition, there are five courts of appeal, and departmental courts which have their own local jurisdiction.

Tegucigalpa has two Courts of Appeal which have jurisdiction (1) in the department of Francisco Morazán, and (2) in the departments of Choluteca Valle, El Paraíso and Olancho.

The Appeal Court of San Pedro Sula has jurisdiction in the department of Cortés. That of Comayagua has jurisdiction in the departments of Comayagua, La Paz and Intibucá; that of Santa Bárbara in the departments of Santa Barbara, Lempira, Copán.

President of the Supreme Court of Justice: ROBERTO RAMÍREZ.

RELIGION

The majority of the population are Roman Catholics; the 1965 Constitution guarantees toleration to all forms of religious belief.

ROMAN CATHOLIC CHURCH

Metropolitan See: Arzobispado, Apdo. 106, Tegucigalpa; Mgr. HÉCTOR ENRIQUE SANTOS HERNÁNDEZ.

Suffragan Sees:
Santa Rosa de Copán; Mgr. JOSÉ CARRANZA CHÉVEZ.
San Pedro Sula; Mgr. JAIME BRUFAU MACÍA.
Comayagua; Mgr. BERNARDINO MAZZARELLA.

THE PRESS

DAILIES

Correo del Norte: San Pedro Sula; f. 1956; evening; independent; Editor GABRIEL GARCÍA ARDON; circ. 7,500.

El Crisol: Puerto Cortés.

El Cronista: Barrio Casamata, Tegucigalpa; f. 1912; independent; morning; daily; Dir. ALEJANDRO VALLADARES; circ. 29,000; Sunday 25,000.

El Día: Apdo. 185, Tegucigalpa; f. 1948; evening; independent, anti-Communist; Dir. and Gen. Man. JULIO LÓPEZ PINEDA; circ. 25,000.

La Luz: Santa Bárbara; Catholic.

Diario del Norte: San Pedro Sula.

El Faro Porteño: Puerto Cortés.

La Gaceta: Tegucigalpa; morning; official Government paper; Dir. RODOLFO HERIBERTO GÓMEZ; circ. 2,400.

La Noticia: Tegucigalpa; f. 1973; Dir. Amílcar Santa-María.

La Opinión: San Pedro Sula.

La Prensa: San Pedro Sula; f. 1964; Dir. Lic. Oscar A. Flores; circ. 42,000.

El Tiempo: San Pedro Sula; f. 1970; Dir. Lic. Edmond L. Bogran; circ. 18,000.

PERIODICALS

Acción Social: Tegucigalpa; monthly.

El Alfiler: San Pedro Sula; weekly.

Ariel: Tegucigalpa; monthly.

El Atlántico: La Ceiba; weekly.

El Comercio: Cámara de Comercio e Industrias de Tegucigalpa, Edif. Bancahsa 209, Tegucigalpa; f. 1970; monthly; commercial and industrial news; Dir. Lic Miguel R. Ortega.

En Marcha: San Pedro Sula; weekly.

El Espectador: Tegucigalpa.

Extra: Tegucigalpa; monthly.

Guía Oficial de Centro-América: Apdo. 494, Tegucigalpa; f. 1922; irregular; general official, commercial, industrial and agricultural news.

Hacienda y Comercio: Tegucigalpa.

El Heraldo: La Ceiba; weekly.

El Heraldo: San Pedro Sula; weekly.

Honduras Agrícola: Tegucigalpa.

Honduras Rotaria: Apdo. 38, Tegucigalpa; f. 1943; monthly Rotarian review; Dir. Jorge Fidel Durón; Co-Editors Guillermo López Rodezno, José Martínez O., Jorge E. Zepeda; circ. 1,000.

Impacto: Tegucigalpa; weekly; Gen. Man. Raúl Barnica López.

Letras: Tegucigalpa; literary and political; quarterly.

El Mensajero del Maestro: Tegucigalpa; monthly.

Prensa Obrera: Tela; f. 1962; twice a week.

Presente: Tegucigalpa.

Revista del Archivo y Biblioteca Nacionales: Tegucigalpa; f. 1904; Historical Review of the Society of Geography and History of Honduras; Dir. Roberto Gómez Robele; circ. 5,000.

Revista Farmacéutica: Tegucigalpa; scientific review; Dir. José Reina Valenzuela.

Revista Honduras: Tegucigalpa.

Revista Pan-Americana: Tegucigalpa; monthly.

Semáforo: Tegucigalpa; weekly.

Social: El Progreso; weekly.

Sucesos: Tegulcigalpa; monthly.

Tribuna Gráfica: Tegucigalpa; weekly.

El Trópico: Ave. Atlántida, 3A Calle, La Ceiba; f. 1938; weekly; independent; general news; Dir. Rodolfo Zavala.

NEWS AGENCY

Foreign Bureau

Agence France-Presse: Barrio La Hoya, Casa 907, Tegucigalpa; Correspondent Enrique Gómez.

PRESS ASSOCIATION

Asociación de Prensa Hondureña (*Press Asscn. of Honduras*): 6A Calle (altos), Barrio Guanacaste, Tegucigalpa; Pres. Orlando Henríquez.

PUBLISHERS

Tegucigalpa

Biblioteca Nacional: Dpto. de Publicaciones, Avda. Mendicta.

Imprenta López & Cía.: 11A y 12A Calles No. 1112.

Compañía Editora Nacional, S.A.: 5A Calle Oriente No. 410.

Editorial Nuevo Continente: Ave. Cervantes 123; Dir. Leticia Silva de Oyuela.

Litografía e Imprenta Suárez Romero Ltda.: 3A Avda. No. 605.

Universidad Nacional Autónoma de Honduras: Oficina Co-ordinadora de Publicaciones y Relaciones Públicas.

Editorial Paulino Valladares, Carlota Vda. de Valladares: 5A Avda., 5A y 6A Calles.

Comayagüela

Imprenta Héctor A. Bulnes: 6A Avda., 4A y 5A Calles, No. 433.

Imprenta Cultura, Mario Mencia G.: 7A Avda., 8A y 9A Calles, No. 812.

Imprenta Gómez: 6A Avda., 5A Calle.

Talleres Gráficos, S.R.L.: 4A Avda., 11A Calle, No. 1102.

RADIO AND TELEVISION

RADIO

Dirección General de Comunicaciones Eléctricas: Tegucigalpa; Dir. *Radio Nacional:* H. Andino N.

La Voz de Honduras: 8A Calle, No. 410, Tegucigalpa; Man. R. Breve M.

Emisoras Unidas: Paseo Circunvalación, San Pedro Sula.

Radio Católica: Apdo. Postal 480, Tegucigalpa; non-commercial.

Radio América: Apdo. Postal 259, Tegucigalpa.

Radio Centro: Colonia Florencia, Tegucigalpa.

Radio Cultura: Edificio Jiménez, Tegucigalpa.

La Voz de Atlántida: La Ceiba.

La Voz del Junco: Calle Independencia, Sta. Bárbara; f. 1954; Dir. and Proprietor Miguel Hasbun; Press and News Dir. J. Candido Rodríguez.

There are 51 other commercial stations and religious stations. 147,000 receivers (1971).

TELEVISION

Compañía Teledifusora de Honduras, S.A. (Canal 11): Apdo. Postal 848, Tegucigalpa; one station; Dir.-Gen. Dr. Miguel Andonie Fernández.

Compañía Televisora Hondureña, S.A.: Apdo. Postal 734, Tegucigalpa; two stations, four relay stations; transmissions began in 1959; Dir.-Gen. J. R. Ferrari. 60,000 receivers (1973).

FINANCE

(cap.=capital; p.u.=paid up; dep.=deposits; m.=million; amounts in lempiras)

BANKING

Tegucigalpa

Central Bank

Banco Central de Honduras: P.O.B. C-58, 1A Calle; f. 1950; cap. 5.2m., dep. 73.6m. (Dec. 1970); bank of issue; Pres. Lic. Alberto Galeano Madrid; Vice-Pres. Lic. Héctor Callejas Valentine; Gen. Man. Arturo H. Medrano; publs. *Boletín Mensual, Revista Trimestral, Memoria Anual.*

anco Atlántida: 7A Avda. No. 501, esq. 5A Calle, Apdo. 57-C; f. 1913; cap. 4m., dep. 108.4m. (Dec. 1970); 9 brs.; Pres. Dr. JOSÉ MENDOZA; Vice-Pres. and Gen. Man. PAUL VINELLI.

Banco Centroamericano de Integración Económica: Apdo. 772, Tegucigalpa; f. 1961 to finance the economic development of the Central American common market and its member countries; mems. Guatemala, El Salvador, Honduras, Nicaragua, Costa Rica; cap. p.u. U.S. $40m.; Pres. ENRIQUE ORTEZ C.; publ. *Annual Report.*

Banco de Honduras: Plaza Morazán; f. 1889; affiliate of First National City Bank, New York; Pres. EUGENE N. S. GIRARD; Gen. Man. PEDRO OLIVIA, Jr.

Banco de la Propiedad: Apdo. 343; f. 1952; savings bank.

Banco de los Trabajadores: Apdo. Postal 139-C, Tegucigalpa; f. 1967; 6 brs.; cap. U.S. $2.5m.; Chair. HERNÁN CÁRCAMO TERCERO; Man. ROLANDO DEL CID V.

Banco La Capitalizadora Hondureña, S.A.—Bancahsa: 5A Calle, Apdo. Postal 344; f. 1948; Pres. ARMANDO SAN MARTÍN C.; Gen. Man. P. M. POMPILIO CORRALES; brs. San Pedro Sula, La Ceiba, Puerto Cortés, Progreso and 6 others.

Banco Nacional de Fomento: Apdo. 212; f. 1950; government development bank; loans mainly in agricultural sector, some also to industry; Pres. Lic. GUILLERMO MEDINA S.; Man. EDUARDO ESCOTO.

Financiera Hondureña, S.A.: 5A Ave. S.O. No. 4, San Pedro Sula, Cortés (Main Office); f. 1964; cap. U.S. $306,900, dep. $3.6m. (Dec. 1972); Gen. Man. (Tegucigalpa) JUAN C. MARINAKYS; private finance organization but with loans from Alliance for Progress; industrial loans, some for construction industry, medium and long-term loans; Pres. GABRIEL MEJÍA.

FOREIGN BANKS
Tegucigalpa

Bank of America N.T. & S.A.: Apdo. 199.

Bank of London and Montreal Ltd.: Apdo. 29-C, Cruce entre 5A Avenida y 4A Calle, No. 209; Man. B. W. MUSK; brs. at San Pedro Sula, Apdo. 152, and La Ceiba, Apdo. 11; agencies at Comayagüela, D.C., Apdo. 29-C, Puerto Cortés, Apdo. 26, Barrio Abajo, Apdo. 29-C.

Chase Manhattan Bank: Apdo. 57-C.

INSURANCE
Tegucigalpa

El Ahorro Hondureño, S.A., Compañía de Seguros: Calle Colón, No. 711; f. 1917; Gen. Pres. Dr. A. F. SMITH; Vice-Pres. Lic. DANIEL CASCO.

Aseguradora Hondureña, S.A.: 6A Avenida y 6A Calle, No. 613, Apdo. 312; f. 1954; Gen. Man. MARIO BATRES PINEDA.

Compañía de Seguros Interamericana, S.A.: 3A Calle, No. 1016, Apdo. Postal 593; Gen. Man. RUBÉN ALVAREZ H.

TRADE AND INDUSTRY

CHAMBERS OF COMMERCE

Cámara de Comercio e Industrias de Tegucigalpa: Edif. Barjum, 3°, 5A Calle, No. 408, Tegucigalpa; f. 1910; 250 mems.; Pres. Lic. EMÍN BARJUM; Sec. JUAN ANGEL MONCADA; publs. *El Comercio* (monthly), *Informativo Comercial* (fortnightly).

Cámara de Comercio e Industrias de Cortés: San Pedro Sula; f. 1931; 250 mems.; Pres. GABRIEL A. MEJÍA; publ. *Panorama Económico.*

There are also Chambers of Commerce at La Ceiba, Santa Rosa de Copán, Choluteca and Tela.

PRODUCERS' ASSOCIATIONS

Asociación Nacional de Industriales: Apdo. Postal 20-C, Tegucigalpa.

Federación Hondureña de Cooperativas Cafetaleras (Fehcocal): Tegucigalpa; f. 1969.

Federación Nacional de Cooperativas Cañeras (Fenacocal): Tegucigalpa.

DEVELOPMENT ORGANIZATIONS

Consejo Superior de Planificación Económica: Tegucigalpa; planning office.

Instituto Hondureño del Café: coffee development programme; Man. ENRIQUE LÓPEZ A.

Instituto Nacional Agrario: Tegucigalpa; agricultural development programmes; cap. 30m.

TRADE UNIONS

Asociación Nacional de Campesinos de Honduras (ANACH): San Pedro Sula, Cortés; f. 1962; mems. 30,000 (est.); Pres. REYES RODRÍGUEZ.

Confederación de Trabajadores de Honduras (*Honduras Workers Confederation*): Tegucigalpa; f. 1964; affiliated to ORIT and CIOSL; 3 mem. federations; Pres. CELEO GONZÁLEZ; Sec. Gen. ANDRÉS V. ARTILES.

Federación Central de Sindicatos de Trabajadores Libres de Honduras—FECESITLIH (*Central Federation of Unions of Free Workers of Honduras*): Tegucigalpa; f. 1958; 8,000 mems. (est.) from 54 affiliated unions; Sec.-Gen. GUSTAVO ZELAYA.

Federación Sindical de Trabajadores Norteños de Honduras —FESITRANH (*North Coast Federation of Workers' Unions of Honduras*): San Pedro Sula; f. 1957; 20,000 mems. (est.) from 42 affiliated unions; Pres. CÉLEO GONZALES Y GONZALES; Sec. Gen. FAUSTO A. GALDÁMEZ.

There are a number of unions not affiliated to a national centre.

TRANSPORT AND TOURISM

TRANSPORT
RAILWAYS

The greater part of the rail transport is in the hands of the fruit companies with plantations on the north coast. The companies transport chiefly bananas and sugar, although passengers are taken on most of the routes. The Ferrocarril Nacional de Honduras owns the railway which connects the northern terminus of the main highway system at Potrerillos with the largest port on the Atlantic side, Puerto Cortés. Near this port the railway turns east, passing through the port of Tela and, with one change, continues through another Atlantic port, La Ceiba, and terminates in the valley of the Aguan River. No railway goes direct to Tegucigalpa, the connection being made by road transport. The three railways, totalling approximately 1,059 km., are:

Ferrocarril Nacional de Honduras (*National Railway of Honduras*): San Pedro Sula; 239 km. of track open (1.072 m. gauge); owned by the Government, but operated by the Tela Railroad Co.; Gen. Man. HERMÁN PASCUA LEIVA.

Tela Railroad Co.: Local Offices: La Lima; Head Office: Prudential Center, Boston, Mass., U.S.A.; 376 km. of track open (1.072 m. gauge); Pres. ELI BLACK; Gen. Man. H. H. LACOMBE; Railroad Superintendent K. F. KOCH; the railway is a common carrier.

Standard Fruit & Steamship Co. Railway (Vaccaro Line): Local Offices: La Ceiba; Head Office: 50 California St., San Francisco, Calif. 94111, U.S.A.; 471 km. of track (1 m. gauge); routes between La Ceiba and Tela, and La Ceiba and Olanchito; a common carrier on all routes operated; Pres. C. M. WAITE (U.S.A.); Gen. Man. M. M. ROTOLO (La Cieba).

ROADS

Dirección General de Caminos: Tegucigalpa; highways board.

There are over 5,700 km. of roads in Honduras, including 1,228 km. of paved roads. The Pan American Highway section in Honduras has been completed, as has a road connecting it with Tegucigalpa and Puerto Cortés on the northern coast.

SHIPPING

The United Fruit Co. (U.S.A.), sailing from New York and New Orleans, calls at the Atlantic port of Tela and at Puerto Cortés in Honduras. The Standard Fruit Co. (who own one of the country's railways) also calls at La Ceiba. The ports on the Pacific coast may be reached by the Grace Line, sailing between San Francisco and Los Angeles and Amapala. Other shipping lines serving Honduras are: Hapag-Lloyd, KNSM, Mamenic.

Empresa Nacional Portuaria (*National Commission*): f. 1965; has jurisdiction over most ports in Honduras; manages Puerto Cortés on the Atlantic coast; an improvement programme costing 5.5m. is under way to increase the ports' traffic; a paved road connects Puerto Cortés with the port of San Lorenzo on the Pacific coast via San Pedro Sula and Tegucigalpa. Studies for a deep-water Pacific port in the Gulf of Fonseca started in 1971. The estimated cost of the project is U.S. $5m.; Man. ANTONIO JOSÉ COELLO; Asst. Man. JOSÉ FONSECA GALVÁN.

CIVIL AVIATION

Local airlines in Honduras supply the deficiencies of road and rail transport, linking together small towns and inaccessible districts.

SAHSA (Servicio Aéreo de Honduras, S.A.): Apdo. Postal 129, Tegucigalpa; private company; operates internal routes and also to New Orleans, Managua, Guatemala, Belize, San José, San Andrés Island and Panama; Gen. Man. Capt. HECTOR ROLANDO FIGUEROA.

ANHSA (Aerovías Nacionales de Honduras, S.A.): c/o Sahsa; a local airline which serves the north coast and the east of the country; one DC-3.

TAN (Transportes Aéreos Nacionales, S.A.): Edificio Salame, Tegucigalpa; operates passenger and cargo services, internal and international.

Lineas Aéreas Nacionales S. de R.L. (LANSA): Apdo. Postal 35, La Ceiba; scheduled services within Honduras and to Islas de Balía; four DC-3, one Apache and one Cessna 180.

Honduras is also served by the following foreign airlines: Aviateca (Guatemala), Lanica (Nicaragua) and Pan American.

TOURISM

Instituto Hondureño de Turismo: Apdo. Postal 154-C, Tegucigalpa.

ATOMIC ENERGY

Comisión Hondureña de Energía Atómica: Tegucigalpa; Pres. Dr. JESÚS AGUILAR PAZ.

Universidad Nacional Autónoma de Honduras: Tegucigalpa; atomic research in engineering, agronomy, physics, biology, mathematics, medicine, pharmacy and geology.

UNIVERSITY

Universidad Nacional Autónoma de Honduras: 8A Avenida, No. 804, Tegucigalpa; f. 1847; 7,500 students, 427 teachers.

INDIA

INTRODUCTORY SURVEY

Location, Climate, Language, Religion, Flag, Capital

The Union of India forms a natural sub-continent with the Himalayas to the north and is flanked by the Arabian Sea and the Bay of Bengal. Its neighbours are China and Nepal to the north, Pakistan to the north-west and Burma to the east. Bangladesh is surrounded by Indian territory except for a short frontier with Burma in the east. The climate ranges from temperate to tropical with an average summer temperature over the plains of approximately 27°c (85°F). There are heavy monsoons in June and July and rainfall varies widely. The official language is Hindi, and English is used as an associate language for many official purposes. Sixteen regional languages are also recognized in the Constitution, and many others are widely spoken. About 83 per cent of the population are Hindu and 11 per cent Muslim. There are also Christians, Sikhs, Buddhists, Jains and other minorities. The national flag (proportions 3 by 2) consists of horizontal stripes of saffron, white and green with the Dharma Chakra (Wheel of the Law) in blue on the white stripe. The capital is New Delhi.

Recent History

India became independent in August 1947, when Britain's Indian Empire was partitioned on religious lines between India and Pakistan. Sectarian violence, the movement of 12 million refugees, the integration of the former princely states into the Indian federal structure and the dispute over Kashmir presented major problems for the new nation. Their settlement, and the adoption of a republican constitution in January 1950, were followed by a period of some 12 years in which Indian affairs were dominated by the first Prime Minister, Jawaharlal Nehru. He achieved considerable success for his policy of economic development by industrialization, and gained international respect with a foreign policy based on peace and non-alignment.

India's forcible occupation of Goa and other Portuguese enclaves in December 1961 and the disastrous Chinese attack of October 1962 adversely affected Nehru's prestige internationally and in India. He died in May 1964, and was succeeded as Prime Minister by Lal Bahadur Shastri, who died in January 1966 at Tashkent, U.S.S.R., where he had agreed on a peaceful settlement of the Rann of Kutch dispute which had brought about a short war with Pakistan.

Nehru's daughter, Mrs. Indira Gandhi, became Prime Minister, but met with considerable opposition within the ruling Congress Party, which no longer held its former dominant position in Indian politics. The electoral loss of several State governments and personal and ideological conflicts in the party were followed by a split in November 1969. Mrs. Gandhi's more left-wing ruling Congress faction demonstrated its popular support in the March 1971 general election, gaining 350 of the 518 elective seats in the Lok Sabha.

Indian support for Bengali guerrilla forces in East Pakistan led to border incidents and in December 1971 to war between India and Pakistan. The Indian army rapidly occupied East Pakistan, which India recognized as the independent state of Bangladesh. The war lasted only 12 days, but it was not until July 1972 that India and Pakistan reached an agreement on their cease-fire line in Kashmir and the return of prisoners of war.

Famine, food riots and alleged corruption in the Government and the Congress Party have reduced the popular support for Mrs. Gandhi which was shown in the State elections of February and March 1972. In 1973 there were violent disorders in Tamil Nadu, Andhra Pradesh, Maharashtra, Madhya Pradesh, Gujarat, Uttar Pradesh, Mizoram and elsewhere; the causes were diverse, but chiefly involved food shortages, student grievances and the lack of effective State governments. Separatist movements were active in Nagaland, Mizoram and Andhra Pradesh, and political murders by Naxalites (Maoists) continued in West Bengal. In January 1974 student unrest in Gujarat developed into a mass movement of protest against the corruption which was believed to cause high food prices. General strikes and rioting had to be suppressed by the army, but a similar situation arose in Bihar.

The Congress Party lost support in several state elections in the first three months of 1974, and suffered from internal dissent among its leaders. Their differences became apparent when the Government nationalized the wholesale wheat trade. This measure, intended to lower prices and produce a more even distribution of food, failed in its objectives, and was abandoned in March 1974, after less than a year. Other measures designed to give the Government greater control over the economy have been dropped, and private enterprise is once more being encouraged as the best means of bringing about economic growth.

In May 1974 India exploded its first nuclear device.

Government

India is a Union of States governed by an executive consisting of the President, the Vice-President and the Council of Ministers led and nominated by the Prime Minister. The President is elected for a five-year term. Parliament consists of two Houses, the Rajya Sabha and the Lok Sabha. The country is divided into twenty-one self-governing States each having a Governor, appointed by the President of India, a Council of Ministers headed by the Chief Minister and an elected Legislature. Andhra Pradesh, Bihar, Jammu and Kashmir, Maharashtra, Karnataka, Tamil Nadu and Uttar Pradesh have bi-cameral legislatures, the other 14 states being uni-cameral. Each state has its own legislative, executive and judicial machinery corresponding to that of the Union. The Union has power over defence, foreign affairs, transport and communications, currency and coinage, customs and export duties and the higher courts of justice. State powers include the police, public health, education, agriculture and forests. The Union and the States can both legislate on certain topics, such as trade and industry, economic and social planning, social security and prices. In the event of the failure of constitutional government in a State, presidential rule can be imposed by the Union. There are also nine Union Territories, administered by Chief Commissioners, Lieutenant-Governors or Administrators appointed by the President.

Defence

India has an army of 826,000 men, a navy of 30,000 and an air force of 92,000. Military service is voluntary. Defence spending will consume some 22 per cent of the total budget for 1974–75.

Economic Affairs

Of a total working population of some 180 million in 1971, nearly 130 million were employed in agriculture, which accounts for almost half of India's national income. The major part of the sown area is taken up by cereals, the staple crops, but grain production has failed to keep pace with population growth, and harvests have been adversely affected by bad weather. Government plans to promote irrigation, the use of chemical fertilizers and the introduction of high-yield strains of rice and wheat have increased production, but India still depends on imported wheat. Extensive plantations produce tea, rubber and coffee, while cotton, jute, sugar, oilseeds and other cash crops are also grown.

India has large reserves of iron ore in Bihar and Orissa, as well as bauxite, titanium ore, manganese, rare metals and mica. Oil is found, particularly in Assam and Gujarat; Soviet aid for exploration and refining should lessen dependence on imported oil. The principal industries, apart from processing agricultural products, are iron and steel works, heavy electrical and machine tools, chemicals and textiles. Many industrial enterprises are in the public sector, but the Government has been forced to allow greater freedom for private companies in order to meet the industrialization targets of the most recent Plan, and to encourage investment.

The fourth Five-Year Plan (1969–74) suffered from the strains imposed by defence expenditure and crop failures; the overall growth rate was only 3.7 per cent per annum, against the target of 5.7 per cent. The introduction of the fifth Plan, which aims at non-inflationary growth, particularly in agriculture, and the accelerated development of the core sectors of the economy, steel, coal, oil, cement, fertilizers, power and so on, has been delayed for reconsideration following the rapid rise in world oil prices. The failure of Indian agriculture to meet demand, particularly for cereals, and rising commodity prices will tend to worsen the balance of payments deficit. India's foreign exchange needs have produced dependence on foreign aid, which, it is estimated, will have to continue well into the 1980s.

Transport and Communications

There are more than 60,000 km. of railway track and over 8,000 km. of navigable waterways, of which 2,500 km. are open to power-driven craft. There are over 1 million km. of road, including about 30,000 km. of national highways connecting the main towns. The Indian Airlines Corporation provides internal air transport and there are international airports at Calcutta, New Delhi and Bombay.

Social Welfare

Health programmes are primarily the responsibility of the State Governments, but the Union Government provides finance for improvements in public health services (4,350 million rupees under the 1969–74 Plan). In 1970–71 there were 115,700 doctors. 5,112 primary health centres and 266,200 hospital beds (49.4 per 100,000 people); by the end of the Plan in 1974, these figures were expected to rise to 139,900, 5,427 and 281,600 respectively. Family planning is regarded as a vital part of India's socio-economic development, and the Union allocated Rs. 3,150 million under the Plan for education in family planning, the provision of contraceptives and the sterilization programme.

Education

Education is the responsibility of the States. Primary education is theoretically compulsory in all States except Nagaland and Himachal Pradesh, and in many States all school education is free. In 1971 80 per cent of the 6–11 age group and 35 per cent of the 11–14 age group were enrolled. About 29 per cent of the total population are literate. There are 92 universities, 101 medical colleges and over 3,600 other colleges (1970–71).

Tourism

Despite the possible attractions of Indian scenery, ancient monuments and big game hunting, tourism remains relatively underdeveloped. Less than 300,000 foreign visitors were recorded in 1970, but the need for foreign exchange earning has led to public investment in the expansion of the tourism infrastructure.

Visas: Citizens of Commonwealth countries do not require visas to visit India, with the exception of citizens of Sri Lanka, Commonwealth citizens of Chinese origin, and missionaries.

Sport

The most popular sports in India are hockey, cricket, football, tennis and badminton.

Public Holidays

The public holidays observed in India vary locally. As religious feasts depend on astronomical observations, holidays are usually declared at the beginning of the year in which they are to fall. The following holidays are the ones that have been announced for use in Delhi.

1974: August 15th (Independence Day), October 2nd (Mohandas Gandhi's Birthday), October 18th (Id ul Fitr), October 25th (Dussehra), November 13th (Diwali), November 15th (Bhai Duj), November 29th (Guru Nanak's Birthday), December 25th–26th (Christmas).

Weights and Measures

The metric system has been introduced although both imperial and traditional Indian weights and measures continue in use:

1 tola = 11.66 grammes
1 seer = 933.1 grammes
1 maund = 37.32 kg.
1 lakh = (1,00,000) = 100,000
1 crore = (1,00,00,000) = 10,000,000

Currency and Exchange Rates

100 paisa = 1 Indian rupee.
Exchange rates (April 1974):
£1 sterling = 18.97 rupees;
U.S. \$1 = 8.03 rupees.

STATISTICAL SURVEY

AREA AND POPULATION*

Area	Census Population				Estimated Population (mid-year)		Density (per sq. km.)
	March 1st, 1961	April 1st, 1971			1971	1972	1972
		Males	Females	Total			
3,280,483 sq. km.†	439,072,582‡	283,936,614	264,013,195	547,949,809	551,827,000	563,494,000	171.8

* Including the Indian-held part of Jammu and Kashmir.

† 1,266,602 sq. miles.

‡ Including an estimate of 626,667 for the former Portuguese territories of Goa, Daman and Diu, incorporated into India in December 1961.

STATES AND TERRITORIES

States	Capitals	Area (sq. kilometres)	Population (1971 Census)
Andhra Pradesh	Hyderabad	276,754	43,502,708
Assam*	Dispur	78,523	14,957,542
Bihar	Patna	173,876	56,353,369
Gujarat	Gandhinagar	195,984	26,697,475
Haryana	Chandigarh	44,222	10,036,808
Himachal Pradesh	Simla	55,673	3,460,434
Jammu and Kashmir	Srinagar	222,236	4,616,632
Karnataka (Mysore)	Bangalore	191,773	29,299,014
Kerala	Trivandrum	38,864	21,347,375
Madhya Pradesh	Bhopal	442,841	41,654,119
Maharashtra	Bombay	307,762	50,412,235
Manipur	Imphal	22,356	1,072,753
Meghalaya	Shillong	22,489	1,011,699
Nagaland	Kohima	16,527	516,449
Orissa	Bhubaneswar	155,842	21,944,615
Punjab	Chandigarh	50,362	13,551,060
Rajasthan	Jaipur	342,214	25,765,806
Tamil Nadu	Madras	130,069	41,199,168
Tripura	Agartala	10,477	1,556,342
Uttar Pradesh	Lucknow	294,413	88,341,144
West Bengal	Calcutta	87,853	44,312,011
Territories	**Chief Towns**		
Andaman and Nicobar Islands	Port Blair	8,293	115,133
Arunachal Pradesh	Itanagar	83,578	467,511
Chandigarh	Chandigarh	114	257,251
Dadra and Nagar Haveli	Silvassa	491	74,170
Delhi	Delhi	1,485	4,065,698
Goa, Daman and Diu	Panaji	3,813	857,771
Lakshadweep	Kavaratti	32	31,810
Mizoram*	Aizawl	21,087	n.a.
Pondicherry	Pondicherry	480	471,707

* Population figures for Assam include those for Mizoram.

INDIA—(STATISTICAL SURVEY)

PRINCIPAL CITIES AND TOWNS*
POPULATION (1971 Census)

Calcutta‡	7,031,382	Madurai	711,501	Cochin	439,066
Greater Bombay	5,970,575	Jaipur	636,768	Dhanbad	434,031
Delhi	3,647,023†	Agra	634,622	Srinagar	423,253
Madras	3,169,930	Varanasi	606,721	Salem	416,440
Hyderabad	1,769,339	Indore	560,936	Trivandrum	409,627
Ahmedabad	1,741,522	Jabalpur	534,845	Gwalior	406,140
Bangalore	1,653,779	Allahabad	513,036	Ludhiana	401,176
Kanpur	1,275,242	Surat	493,001	Sholapur	398,361
Poona	1,135,034	Patna	491,217	Ulhasnagar	396,384
Nagpur	930,459	Baroda	467,487	Bhopal	384,859
Lucknow	813,982	Tiruchirapalli	464,624	Hubli-Dharwar	379,166
Howrah City‡	737,877	Amritsar	458,029	Meerut	367,754
Coimbatore	736,203	Jamshedpur	456,146	Visakhapatnam	363,467

* Figures refer to urban agglomerations where appropriate.
† Including the capital, New Delhi, with a population of 292,857 in 1971.
‡ Figure for Howrah City is included in figure for Calcutta.

BIRTH AND DEATH RATES

	BIRTH RATE (per 1,000)	DEATH RATE (per 1,000)	LIFE EXPECTANCY AT BIRTH (years)	GROWTH RATE (%)
1951–61	41.7	22.8	41.2	21.64
1961–71	n.a.	14.0	52.6	24.66

EMPLOYMENT
(1971—'000)

Agriculture:		Household Industry	6,351.7
Cultivators	78,176.7	Other Industry	10,715.8
Agricultural Labourers	47,489.4	Construction	2,215.3
Livestock, Forestry, Fisheries and		Trade and Commerce	10,038.2
other agricultural	4,296.8	Transport, Storage and Communications	4,401.2
		Other Services	15,765.5
TOTAL AGRICULTURAL	129,962.9		
Mining and Quarrying	922.8	TOTAL EMPLOYED	180,373.4

Source: Central Statistical Organization, *Census of India 1971 (Economic Characteristics of Population).*

AGRICULTURE

LAND USE*
('000 hectares)

	1968–69	1969–70
Arable Land	160,670	160,870
Under Permanent Crops	3,920	4,040
Permanent Meadows and Pastures	13,330	13,030
Forest Land	64,570	64,730
Other Areas	63,250	63,080
TOTAL	305,740	305,750

* Reported area only. Total area is 328,048,000 hectares, including the Indian-held part of Kashmir-Jammu.

CROPS

	AREA ('000 hectares)			PRODUCTION ('000 metric tons)		
	1969–70	1970–71†	1971–72	1969–70	1970–71†	1971–72
Rice	37,680	37,592	37,334	40,430	42,225	42,734
Sorghum (Jowar)	18,605	17,374	16,802	9,721	8,105	7,753
Cat-tail Millet (Bajra)	12,493	12,913	11,769	5,327	8,029	5,357
Maize	5,862	5,852	5,637	5,674	7,486	5,026
Finger Millet (Ragi)	2,783	2,472	2,400	2,117	2,155	2,167
Small Millets	4,733	4,782	4,513	1,732	1,988	1,582
Wheat	16,626	18,241	19,163	20,093	23,833	26,477
Barley	2,765	2,555	2,432	2,716	2,784	2,501
Total Cereals	101,547	101,782	100,051	87,811	96,604	93,598
Chick-peas (Gram)	7,752	7,839	8,027	5,546	5,199	5,106
Pigeon Peas (Tur)	2,669	2,655	2,311	1,842	1,883	1,574
Dry Beans, Dry Peas, Lentils and Other Pulses	11,603	12,040	11,836	4,303	4,735	4,370
Total Food Grains	123,570	124,316	122,224	99,501	108,422	104,656
Groundnuts	7,125*	7,293‡	7,240*	5,130*	6,065‡	5,712*
Sesame Seed	2,309*	2,449‡	2,408*	448*	568‡	459*
Rapeseed and Mustard	3,173*	3,323*	3,589*	1,564*	1,975*	1,451*
Linseed	1,803*	1,897*	1,944	469*	474*	510*
Castor Beans	402*	439‡	416*	123*	136‡	144*
Total Oil Seeds	14,811*	15,418*	15,597*	7,734*	9,259*	8,276*
Cotton (lint)	7,731*	7,605*	7,784*	946*	810*	1,175*
Jute	768*	750‡	819*	1,018*	883‡	1,028*
Kenaf (Mesta)	322*	327‡	295*	203*	226‡	203*
Tea	353*	354*	357*	394*	422*	433*
Guar	1,090*	1,554‡	1,552*	412*	755‡	492*
Sugar Cane	2,749*	2,857‡	2,418*	13,783*	13,194‡	11,730*
Tobacco	438*	447*	445*	337*	362*	409*
Potatoes	496*	482*	496*	3,913*	4,807*	4,834*
Chillies (dry)	682*	714‡	n.a.	395*	413‡	n.a.

* Provisional.

† Includes fully revised estimates for some States and final estimates for others.

‡ Final figures.

LIVESTOCK

(FAO estimates, '000 head)

	1968–69	1969–70	1970–71
Cattle	176,350	176,450	176,600
Sheep	42,400	42,600	42,800
Goats	67,000	67,500	68,000
Pigs	4,860	4,800	4,780
Horses	1,050	1,000	950
Asses	1,020	1,000	980
Mules	80	85	87
Buffaloes	53,900	54,200	54,500
Camels	1,100	1,120	1,100
Poultry	116,000	116,500	117,000

Source: FAO, *Production Yearbook 1971.*

MILK PRODUCTION, 1969*

(metric tons)

Cows' Milk	7,420,000
Buffaloes' Milk	13,180,000
Goats' Milk	600,000

Source: FAO, *Production Yearbook 1971.*

* Total Production 1971–72: 22.5 million tonnes.

OTHER LIVESTOCK PRODUCTS
(FAO estimates, metric tons)

	1968	1969	1970
Beef, Veal and Buffalo Meat .	169,000	170,000	172,000
Mutton, Lamb and Goats' Meat .	356,000	356,000	357,000
Pig Meat	51,000	52,000	52,000
Poultry Meat . . .	69,000	69,000	70,000
Edible Offal . . .	91,000	91,500	92,000
Edible Pig Fat . . .	4,000	4,000	4,000
Tallow	31,700	32,000	33,000
Butter and Ghee . .	450,000	448,000	455,000
Hen Eggs . . .	75,000	77,000	78,000
Wool: Greasy . .	35,100	35,200	35,400
Clean . .	21,900	22,000	22,100
Cattle and Buffalo Hides .	222,000	224,000	222,000
Sheep Skins (dry) . .	10,500	11,000	10,500
Goat Skins (dry) . .	20,500	21,000	21,300

1971: Hen Eggs 82,000 metric tons.

Source: FAO, *Production Yearbook 1971.*

FORESTRY
('000 cubic metres)

	ROUNDWOOD REMOVALS			SAWNWOOD PRODUCTION		
	1969	1970	1971	1969	1970	1971
Coniferous (soft wood) . . .	4,200	4,400	4,500	625	650	675
Broadleaved (hard wood) . .	106,200	109,000	111,700	1,875	1,950	2,025
TOTAL . . .	110,400	113,400	116,200	2,500	2,600	2,700

Source: United Nations, *Statistical Yearbook 1972.*

FISHERIES
('000 metric tons)

1967	1968	1969	1970	1971
1,400.4	1,525.6	1,605.0	1,745.9	1,845.0

Source: United Nations, *Statistical Yearbook 1972.*

MINING

	Unit	1968	1969	1970	1971
Hard Coal	'ooo metric tons	70,813	75,411	73,698	71,500
Lignite	,, ,, ,,	4,126	4,187.7	3,544.6	3,660
Iron Ore: gross weight . . .	,, ,, ,,	27,961	29,564.1	31,330	34,260
metal content . .	,, ,, ,,	17,474	18,459	19,654	21,246
Bauxite	,, ,, ,,	961	1,085	1,370	1,517
Chalk	,, ,, ,,	49	52.2	48	48
Clay	,, ,, ,,	1,212	1,274	1,307	1,434
Dolomite	,, ,, ,,	n.a.	1,274.8	1,134.9	n.a.
Gypsum	,, ,, ,,	1,336	1,389.5	915	n.a.
Limestone Flux, etc.	,, ,, ,,	21,030	22,517	23,801	25,020
Manganese Ore: gross weight .	,, ,, ,,	1,610	1,485	1,665.2	n.a.
metal content .	,, ,, ,,	622	556	616	670
Crude Petroleum	,, ,, ,,	5,853	6,723	6,809	7,185
Salt (unrefined)	,, ,, ,,	5,044	5,173	5,588	n.a.
Asbestos	metric tons	9,187	9,876	9,834	11,000
Chromium Ore: gross weight .	,, ,,	206,000	226,568	270,879	n.a.
metal content .	,, ,,	101,284	110,266	135,241	137,709
Copper Ore*	,, ,,	10,234	10,378	10,256	12,000
Corundum	,, ,,	} 2,309 {	452	412	n.a.
Garnet (abrasive)	,, ,,		1,637	986	n.a.
Kyanite	,, ,,	64,361	84,172	119,043	n.a.
Lead Concentrates*	,, ,,	2,743	2,467	2,886	3,241
Magnesite (crude)	,, ,,	253,073	297,893	354,291	296,584
Mica (crude)†	,, ,,	22,192	21,056	26,943	23,876
Natural Phosphates: Apatite .	,, ,,	7,000	9,316	15,678	n.a.
Phosphorite	,, ,,	n.a.	69,175	149,544	n.a.
Pyrites (unroasted) . . .	,, ,,	14,000‡	38,686	26,400	41,000
Sillimanite	,, ,,	4,657	3,946	4,562	n.a.
Steatite	,, ,,	n.a.	176,580	157,612	n.a.
Tungsten Concentrates* . . .	,, ,,	25	26	23	19
Zinc Concentrates*	,, ,,	7,147	7,415	8,390	8,562
Gold*	kilogrammes	3,588	3,062	3,241	3,656
Silver*	,,	2,500	3,278	1,540	4,000
Diamonds: industrial . . .	'ooo metric carats	2	2	4	n.a.
gem	,, ,, ,,	7	10	16	7
Emeralds	,, ,, ,,	n.a.	8.5	11.6	n.a.
Natural Gas	million cubic metres	604	729	676	753

* Figures refer to the metal content of ores and concentrates.
† Exports, including scrap and splittings.
‡ For nine months (April to December).

Sources: The Times of India Directory and Yearbook 1972; United Nations, *The Growth of World Industry.*

1972 ('ooo metric tons): Coal 74,770, Lignite 3,070, Iron Ore 35,200 (gross weight), Bauxite 1,692, Crude Petroleum 7,490, Copper 14.6 (metal content), Lead Concentrates 3.6 (metal content), Zinc Concentrates 9.6 (metal content).

INDUSTRY

	Unit	1969	1970	1971
Refined Sugar*	'ooo metric tons	4,284	3,744	3,381
Cotton Cloth	million metres	7,704	7,848	7,356
Jute Manufactures†	'ooo metric tons	894	954	1,087
Paper and Paper Board	,, ,, ,,	707	757	785
Sulphuric Acid	,, ,, ,,	1,181	1,188	1,021
Soda Ash	,, ,, ,,	422	446	479
Fertilizers	,, ,, ,,	552	726	847
Petroleum Products	,, ,, ,,	16,140	17,376	18,104
Cement	,, ,, ,,	13,624	13,956	14,948
Pig Iron	,, ,, ,,	7,318	6,896	6,722
Finished Steel	,, ,, ,,	4,849	4,819	4,676
Aluminium	metric tons	132,552	161,076	176,118
Diesel Engines (stationary)	number	141,900	68,112	83,846
Sewing Machines	,,	406,800	177,600	328,850
Radio Receivers	,,	1,740,000	1,776,000	1,944,000
Electric Fans	,,	1,560,000	1,572,000	1,944,000
Passenger Cars	,,	43,104	45,168	50,292
Passenger Buses and Trucks	,,	32,580	37,032	37,452
Motor Cycles and Scooters	,,	83,844	101,364	106,944
Bicycles	,,	1,921,600	2,094,000	1,929,600

* Figures relate to crop year (beginning November) and are in respect of cane sugar only.

† Figures refer to production by members of the Indian Jute Mills Association and one non-member.

Source: Central Statistical Organization, *Monthly Abstract of Statistics.*

FINANCE

100 paisa (singular, paise) = 1 Indian rupee.

Coins: 1, 2, 3, 5, 10, 25 and 50 paisa.

Notes: 1, 2, 5, 10, 100, 1,000, 5,000 and 10,000 rupees.

Exchange rates (April 1974): £1 sterling = 18.97 rupees; U.S. $1 = 8.03 rupees.

100 Indian rupees = £5.27 = $12.45.

BUDGET
(million rupees)

Revenue	1970–71 (Revised)	1971–72 (Actual)	Expenditure	1970–71 (Revised)	1971–72 (Actual)
Current Account:			*Current Expenditure:*		
Tax Revenue	31,975	34,031	Debt Collection and Services	6,520	6,693
Non-Tax Revenue	9,494	10,095	Administration	2,009	2,366
Gross Revenue	41,469	44,126	Social and Development Services	3,137	3,764
Less States Share of Taxes	−3,654	−4,275	Multi-purpose River Schemes and Public Works	550	631
Total	37,813	39,851	Transport and Communications	216	226
Capital Account:			Currency	269	284
Receipts	25,933	25,737	Miscellaneous	12,667	14,975
			Extraordinary Items	66	66
			Defence Services (net)	10,399	10,792
			Total	35,833	40,097
			Surplus/Deficit on Current Account	1,980	−246
			Total	37,813	39,851
			Capital Expenditure:		
			Capital Disbursements	30,211	29,460
Total	62,746	65,588	Grand Total	68,024	69,311

Currency in circulation: 58,360 million rupees (June 1973).
Foreign Exchange Reserves: U.S. $626 million (April 1973).

ANNUAL PLAN OUTLAY (PUBLIC SECTOR)
1971–72: Rs. 31,580m.; 1972–73: Rs. 39,730m.

FOURTH FIVE-YEAR PLAN, ALL SECTORS
(million rupees)

	1969–74 FINAL FIGURES
Agriculture	43,280
Irrigation and Flood Control . . .	36,300
Industry (including village and small industries) and Minerals . . .	61,910
Transport and Communication . .	41,570
Education and Scientific Research .	10,030
Health and Family Planning . .	7,490
Housing, Urban and Regional Development	24,120
Social Welfare	2,230
Other Programmes . . .	17,920
Total	248,820

FIFTH FIVE-YEAR PLAN, 1974–79
(Provisional Estimates)
(million rupees)

PUBLIC SECTOR	PRIVATE SECTOR	TOTAL
350,000	160,000	510,000

Note: This estimate is based on an overall growth rate of 5.5 per cent.

BALANCE OF PAYMENTS—WORLDWIDE
(million U.S.$)

	1969	1970
Goods and Services:		
Merchandise	−220	−358
Freight and insurance . .	} 49	52
Other transportation . .		
Investment income . .	−292	−299
Other Government services .	19	6
Other services . . .	64	60
TOTAL . . .	−380	−539
Long-Term Loans and Official Grants Received . .	934	751
Capital and Monetary Gold:		
Non-Monetary Sectors:		
Private long-term . . .	−33	−9
Private short-term . . .	3	—
Central government . .	−93	5
TOTAL . . .	−123	−4

	1969	1970
Monetary Sectors:		
Commercial banks; liabilities .	8	—
Commercial banks; assets .	−13	−9
Reserve bank; liabilities . .	−16	−9
TOTAL . . .	−21	−18
Monetization of Gold . . .	—	17
Allocation of Special Drawing Rights . . .	—	126
Net Errors and Omissions . .	−41	−22
TOTAL . . .	369	168
Balance (net monetary movements) *of which:*		
IMF Special Drawing Rights .	—	44
Reserve position in IMF .	—	21
Foreign exchange reserves .	236	16
Use of IMF credit .	133	230

EXTERNAL TRADE
(million rupees)

Imports: (1968–69) 19,086; (1969–70) 15,821; (1970–71) 16,342; (1971–72) 18,245; (1972–73) 17,964.
Exports: (1968–69) 13,542; (1969–70) 14,087; (1970–71) 15,244; (1971–72) 16,032; (1972–73) 19,545.

COMMODITIES

IMPORTS (c.i.f.)	1971–72	1972–73	EXPORTS	1971–72	1972–73
Food	1,969	1,597	Food	4,353	5,217
Cereals	1,312	808	Tea	1,563	1,473
Beverages and Tobacco	3	3	Beverages and Tobacco	451	641
Crude Materials, Inedible	2,129	1,887	Crude Materials, Inedible	2,406	2,543
Textile Fibres	1,382	1,146	Metal Ores and Scrap	1,210	1,260
Minerals, excl. Fuels and Precious Stones	258	262	Cotton Fibres	183	247
Mineral Fuels and Lubricants	1,946	2,043	Mineral Fuels and Lubricants	116	320
Animal and Vegetable Oils and Fats	465	248	Animal and Vegetable Oils and Fats	79	255
Chemicals	2,185	2,478	Chemicals	354	404
Fertilizers, Manufactured	812	899	Basic Manufactures	6,633	8,141
Basic Manufactures	4,404	4,301	Leather and Leather Goods	908	1,745
Iron and Steel	2,376	2,171	Textile Yarns, Fabrics, etc.	4,288	4,571
Copper	512	486	Cotton Manufactures, excl.		
Metal Manufactures	121	171	Yarn, Thread and Clothing	1,000	1,267
Machinery and Transport Equipment	4,706	4,961	Jute Manufactures	2,633	2,472
Non-Electrical Machinery	2,709	2,850	Machinery and Transport Equipment	738	843
Power-generating Machinery, non-electrical	298	327	Miscellaneous Manufactured Articles	848	1,129
Metal-working Machinery	242	285	Other Items	54	54
Industrial Machinery and Parts	1,857	2,023			
Electrical Machinery	1,051	1,240			
Transport Equipment	946	871			
Miscellaneous Manufactured Articles	329	344			
Other Items	110	104			
TOTAL	**18,245**	**17,964**	**TOTAL**	**16,032**	**19,545**

PRINCIPAL TRADING PARTNERS

IMPORTS	1971–72	1972–73	EXPORTS (f.o.b.)	1971–72	1972–73
Australia	294	324	Australia	279	259
Belgium	343	492	Belgium	240	300
Burma	59	18	Burma	107	43
Canada	1,133	1,051	Canada	394	282
Czechoslovakia	102	155	Czechoslovakia	304	460
France	371	369	Egypt	231	317
German Democratic Republic	203	188	France	241	455
Germany, Federal Republic	1,270	1,607	German Democratic Republic	179	151
Iran	1,264	1,215	Germany, Federal Republic	367	620
Italy	245	356	Italy	241	488
Japan	1,616	1,702	Japan	1,817	2,167
Malaysia	39	75	Malaysia	117	93
Netherlands	309	351	Nepal	248	350
Pakistan	—	—	Netherlands	147	353
Poland	505	345	New Zealand	103	82
Sri Lanka	15	9	Pakistan	—	—
Sweden	127	185	Poland	199	442
Switzerland	78	113	Sri Lanka	212	79
Thailand	38	55	Sudan	517	207
U.S.S.R.	873	1,057	U.S.S.R.	2,087	3,048
United Kingdom	2,208	2,255	United Kingdom	1,681	1,719
United States	4,187	2,246	United States	2,628	2,754
Yugoslavia	54	68	Yugoslavia	244	124

TRANSPORT

RAILWAYS

	Unit	1969	1970	1971
Number of Passengers . .	million	2,341.2	2,328.0	2,482.8
Passenger-kilometres . .	,,	111,048	111,996	121,950
Freight (metric tons) . .	,,	202.8	182.4	194.4
Freight tonne-kilometres . .	,,	119,664	120,936	126,264

Source: Monthly Abstract of Statistics.

ROADS
(Motor vehicles registered at March 31st)

	Total	Private Cars and Jeeps	Public Service Vehicles	Motor Cycles and Auto-Rickshaws	Goods Vehicles	Miscel-laneous
1967 . .	1,187,434	442,217	115,704	280,869	268,327	80,317
1968 . .	1,332,352	480,362	124,719	355,826	284,836	95,609
1969 . .	1,458,583	509,489	137,067	412,646	306,802	102,579

Source: Statistical Abstract of India 1970.

INTERNATIONAL SEA-BORNE SHIPPING
(Twelve months ending March 31st)

	1968	1969	1970
Vessels* ('000 net reg. tons):			
Entered	15,890	16,382	16,971
Cleared	15,775	17,533	18,087
Freight† ('000 metric tons):			
Loaded	25,526	27,037	29,973
Unloaded	26,277	22,972	22,364

* Excluding minor and intermediate ports.   † Including bunkers.

Source: United Nations, Statistical Yearbook 1971.

CIVIL AVIATION
('000)

	1969	1970	1971
Kilometres flown . . .	66,552	65,688	59,340
Passenger kilometres . . .	3,235,056	3,555,288	3,609,084
Freight tonne-kilometres . .	96,252	99,384	111,216
Mail tonne-kilometres . .	20,088	18,900	17,556

Source: Monthly Abstract of Statistics.

COMMUNICATIONS MEDIA
(1970)

Radios (number) . . .	11,836,650
Television sets (number) . . .	33,044*
Telephones (number) . . .	1,319,000†
Newspapers (number) . . .	11,036‡

* June 1971, † 1970–71, ‡ Dec. 31st, 1970.

TOURISM
FOREIGN VISITORS

	1969	1970
Australia	10,615	11,901
Canada	4,846	7,026
France	12,094	16,832
Germany*	14,222	16,685
Italy	4,639	5,954
Japan	8,352	9,432
Malaysia	8,823	10,827
Singapore	3,793	4,918
Sri Lanka	19,891	18,004
Switzerland	4,418	5,220
United Kingdom . . .	38,037	43,212
U.S.A.	52,836	58,793
Total (incl. all others) .	244,724	280,821

* Figure includes visitors from both the German Democratic Republic and the Federal Republic of Germany.

Source: International Union of Official Travel Organisations, *International Travel Statistics.*

EDUCATION
(1970–71)*

	Pupils†	Teachers
Primary: lower . .	63,100,000	1,026,152
upper . .	14,900,000	576,363
Secondary . .	8,400,000	523,341
Higher . . .	2,540,000	119,000

* Academic year. † 1971–72.

Source: Central Statistical Organization, New Delhi; Department of Commercial Intelligence and Statistics, Calcutta.

THE CONSTITUTION

The Constitution of India, adopted by the Constituent Assembly in November 1949, was inaugurated on January 26th, 1950, on which date India became a sovereign democratic republic. India's relations with the British Commonwealth of Nations were defined at the London Conference of Dominion Prime Ministers in April 1949, when it was unanimously agreed that the Republic of India should remain a full member of the Commonwealth.

A Constituent Assembly was set up in 1946 in accordance with the Cabinet Mission Plan, and was subject to the final authority of the British Parliament. In consequence of the Indian Independence Act, 1947, it reassembled as a sovereign body to assume power on behalf of the Government of India, thereby superseding the former Indian legislature, consisting of the Council of States and the Legislative Assembly.

The Constitution declares in the preamble that the People of India solemnly resolve to constitute a Sovereign Democratic Republic and to secure to all its citizens justice, liberty, equality and fraternity. There are 397 articles and 9 schedules, which form a comprehensive document. The Constitution is flexible in character, and a simple process of amendment has been adopted.

Union of States. The Union of India comprises 21 states and 9 Union Territories (1974). There are provisions for the formation and admission of new states.

The Constitution confers citizenship on a threefold basis of birth, descent, and residence. Provisions are made for refugees who have migrated from Pakistan and for persons of Indian origin residing abroad.

Fundamental Rights and Directive Principles. The rights of the citizen contained in Part III of the Constitution are declared fundamental and enforceable in law. "Untouchability" is abolished and its practice in any form is a punishable offence. The Directive Principles of State Policy provide a code intended to ensure promotion of the economic, social and educational welfare of the State in future legislation.

The President is the head of the Union, exercising all executive power on the advice of ministers responsible to Parliament. He is elected by an electoral college consisting of elected members of both Houses of Parliament and the Legislatures of the States. The President holds office for a term of five years and is eligible for re-election. He may be impeached for violation of the Constitution. The Vice-President is the *ex-officio* Chairman of the Upper House and is elected by a joint sitting of both Houses of Parliament.

The Parliament of the Union consists of the President of two Houses: the Rajya Sabha (Upper House) and the Lok Sabha (House of the People). The Rajya Sabha consists of not more than 250 members, of whom 12 are nominated by the President. One-third of its members retire every two years. Elections are indirect, each state's legislative quota being elected by the members of the state's legislative assembly. The Lok Sabha consists of not more than 545 members elected by adult franchise; not more than 20 represent the Union Territories.

Government of the States. The governmental machinery of states closely resembles that of the Union. Each of these states has a governor at its head appointed by the President for a term of five years to exercise executive power on the advice of a Council of Ministers. The state's legislatures consist of the Governor and either one house (legislative assembly) or two houses (legislative assembly and legislative council). The term of the assembly is five years, but the council is not subject to dissolution.

Language. The Constitution provides that the official language of the Union shall be Hindi. (The English language will continue to be an associate language for many official purposes.)

Legislation—Federal System. The Constitution provides that bills, other than money bills, can be introduced in either House. To become law, they must be passed by both Houses and receive the assent of the President. In financial affairs the authority of the Lower House is final. The various subjects of legislation are enumerated on three lists in the seventh schedule of the Constitution: the Union List, containing nearly 100 entries, including external affairs, defence, communications, and atomic energy; the State List, containing 65 entries, including local government, police, public health, education; and the Concurrent List, with over 40 entries, including criminal law, marriage and divorce, labour welfare. The Constitution vests residuary authority in the Centre. All matters not enumerated in the Concurrent or State Lists will be deemed to be included in the Union List, and in the event of conflict between Union and State Law on any subject enumerated in the Concurrent List, the Union Law will prevail. In time of emergency Parliament may even exercise powers otherwise exclusively vested in the states. Under Article 356, "If the President on receipt of a report from the Government of a State or otherwise is satisfied that a situation has arisen in which the government of the State cannot be carried on in accordance with the provisions of this Constitution, the President may by Proclamation: (a) assume to himself all or any of the functions of the Government of the State and all or any of the powers of the Governor or any body or authority in the State other than the Legislature of the State; (b) declare that the powers of the Legislature of the State shall be exercisable by or under the authority of Parliament; (c) make such incidental provisions as appear to the President to be necessary": provided that none of the powers of a High Court be assumed by the President or suspended in any way. Unless such a Proclamation is approved by both Houses of Parliament, it ceases to operate after two months. A Proclamation so approved ceases to operate after six months, unless renewed by Parliament. Its renewal cannot be extended beyond a total period of three years. An independent judiciary exists to define and interpret the Constitution and to resolve constitutional disputes arising between states, or between a state and the Government of India.

Other Provisions of the Constitution deal with the administration of tribal areas, relations between the Union and States, inter-state trade and finance.

The Panchayat Raj scheme, which is designed to decentralize the powers of the Central and State Governments, has been extensively introduced. This scheme is based on the Panchayat (Village Council) and the Gram Sabha (Village Parliament) and envisages the gradual transference of local government from State to local authority. Revenue and internal security will remain State responsibilities at present.

THE GOVERNMENT

President: VARAHAGIRI VENKATA GIRI.

Vice-President: GOPAL SWARUP PATHAK.

THE CABINET
(April 1974)

Prime Minister, Minister of Atomic Energy, Minister of Electronics, Minister of Space: Mrs. INDIRA GANDHI.

Minister of Finance: YESHWANTRAO BALWANTRAO CHAVAN.

Minister of Defence: JAGJIVAN RAM.

Minister of Agriculture: FAKHRUDDIN ALI AHMED.

Minister of External Affairs: Sardar SWARAN SINGH.

Minister of Steel and Mines: K. D. MALAVIYA.

Minister of Law, Justice and Company Affairs: H. R. GOKHALE.

Minister of Home Affairs: UMAR SHANKAR DIKSHIT

Minister of Heavy Industry: T. A. PAI.

Minister of Railways: L. N. MISHRA.

Minister of Works and Housing: BHOLA PASWAN SHASTRI.

Minister of Industrial Development, Science and Technology: C. SUBRAMANIAM.

Minister of Parliamentary Affairs: K. RAGHURAMAIAH.

Minister of Shipping and Transport: KAMLAPATI TRIPATHI.

Minister of Petroleum and Chemicals: DEV KANTA BAROOAH.

Minister of Tourism and Civil Aviation: RAJ BAHADUR.

Minister of Planning: DURGA PRASAD DHAR.

Minister of Health and Family Planning: KARAN SINGH.

Minister of Communications: K. BRAHMANANDRA REDDY.

MINISTERS OF STATE

Commerce: D. P. CHATTOPADHYAYA.*

Law, Justice and Company Affairs: NITI RAJ SINGH CHAUDHARY.

Planning: MOHAN DHARIA.

Finance: K. R. GANESH.

Information and Broadcasting: I. K. GUJRAL.*

Supply and Rehabilitation: R. K. KHADILKAR.*

Petroleum and Chemicals: SHAH NAWAZ KHAN.

Tourism and Civil Aviation: SAROJINI MAHISHI.

Agriculture: B. P. MAURYA.

Parliamentary Affairs and Works and Housing: OM MEHTA.

Home Affairs and Personnel: RAM NIWAS MIRDHA.

Education, Social Welfare and Culture: S. NURUL HASAN.*

Irrigation and Power and Parliamentary Assistant to the Prime Minister for the Departments of Atomic Energy, Electronics and Space: K. C. PANT.*

Industrial Development: MANSINHJI BHASAHEB RANA.

Labour: K. V. RAGHUNATHA REDDY.*

Agriculture: ANNASAHEB P. SHINDE.

Defence Production: VIDYA CHARAN SHUKLA.

Communications: SHER SINGH.

External Affairs: SURENDRA PAL SINGH.

* In charge of Ministries or Departments.

There are also 22 Deputy Ministers.

DIPLOMATIC REPRESENTATION

HIGH COMMISSIONS AND EMBASSIES ACCREDITED TO INDIA

(New Delhi, unless otherwise stated.)

(HC) High Commission; (E) Embassy; (L) Legation.

Afghanistan: 9A Ring Rd., Lajpat Nagar III (E); *Ambassador:* ABDUR REHMAN PAZHWAK.

Algeria: 13 Sundar Nagar (E); *Chargé d'Affaires:* MOHAMED NACER ADJALI.

Argentina: C27/28 South Extension Part II (E); *Chargé d'Affaires:* CARLOS E. APARICIO.

Australia: No. 1/50-G Shantipath, Chanakyapuri (HC); *High Commissioner:* BRUCE ALEXANDER GRANT.

Austria: 18 Jor Bagh (Lodi Rd.) (E); *Ambassador:* Dr. ERNA SAILER.

Bangladesh: 56 Ring Rd., Lajpat Nagar (HC); *High Commissioner:* Dr. A. R. MALLICK.

Belgium: 7 Golf Links (E); *Ambassador:* CHARLES KERREMANS.

Bhutan: 1/21 Shantiniketan (L); *Representative:* LYONPO PEMA WANGCHUK.

Brazil: 8 Aurangzeb Rd. (E); *Ambassador:* ROBERTO LUIZ ASSUMPÇÃO DE ARAUJO.

Bulgaria: 198 Golf Links Area (E); *Ambassador:* STOYAN ZAIMOV.

Burma: 3/50-G-F Nyaya Marg, Chanakyapuri (E); *Ambassador:* U BA SHWE (also accred. to Nepal).

Canada: 7/8 Shanti Path, Chanakyapuri (HC); *High Commissioner:* BRUCE M. WILLIAMS.

Chile: 1/13 Shanti Niketan (E); *Ambassador:* AUGUSTO MARAMBIO.

China, People's Republic: 50-D Shantipath (E); *Chargé d'Affaires:* MA MU-MING.

Colombia: 82D Malcha Marg, Chanakyapuri (E); *Ambassador:* F. N. DE BRIGARD.

Cuba: C-290 Defence Colony (E); *Ambassador:* Dr. ANGEL FERRAS MORENO.

Czechoslovakia: 50-A Niti Marg; *Ambassador:* ZDENĚK TRHLIK.

Denmark: 29 Golf Links Area (E); *Ambassador:* HENNING HALCK.

Ecuador: C-76 Paschim Marg, Vasant Vihar (E); *Chargé d'Affaires:* VINCENTE CRESPO ORDOÑEZ.

Egypt: 55-57 Sundar Nagar (E); *Ambassador:* AMIN HILMY.

Ethiopia: 29 Prithviraj Rd. (E); *Ambassador:* G. MEKASHA.

Finland: 42 Golf Links (E); *Ambassador:* WILHELM SCHRECK.

France: 2 Aurangzeb Rd. (E); *Ambassador:* JEAN-DANIEL JURGENSEN.

Gabon: Paris, France (E).

German Democratic Republic: 2 Nyaya Marg, Chanakyapuri (E); *Ambassador:* HERBERT FISCHER (also accred. to Nepal).

Germany, Federal Republic: 6 Block 50G, Shantipath, Chanakyapuri (E); *Ambassador:* GUNTHER DIEHL.

Ghana: 2 Golf Links (HC); *High Commissioner:* PAUL BOAKYE BUAH.

Greece: 188 Jor Bagh (E); *Ambassador:* BASIL VITSAXIS.

Guyana: 180 Jor Bagh (HC); *High Commissioner:* RAHMAN B. GAJRAJ.

Hungary: 15 Jor Bagh (E); *Ambassador:* FERENC TURI.

Indonesia: 50A Chanakyapuri (E); *Ambassador:* Lt.-Gen. S. TJAKRADIPURA.

Iran: 65 Golf Links (E); *Ambassador:* MOHAMMAD GOODARZI.

Iraq: 33 Golf Links (E); *Ambassador:* Dr. ABDULLAH SALLOUM AL-SAMARRAI.

Ireland: 13 Jor Bagh (E); *Ambassador:* DENIS HOLMES.

Italy: 13 Golf Links (E); *Ambassador:* Dr. AMADEO GUILLET.

Japan: Plot Nos. 4 and 5, Block 50G, Chanakyapuri (E); *Ambassador:* KINYA NIISEKI.

Jordan: 35 Malcha Marg, Chanakyapuri (E); *Ambassador:* WAJIH AL KAYLANI.

Kenya: E-27 Defence Colony (HC); *High Commissioner:* S. K. KIMALEL.

Khmer Republic: 25 Golf Links Area (E); *Chargé d'Affaires:* MECH SARY.

Korea, Democratic People's Republic: 11 Barakhamba Rd. (E); *Ambassador:* YU SONG JIN.

Korea, Republic: Korea House, 5 Mansingh Rd. (E); *Ambassador:* CHAN HUYAN PAK.

Kuwait: 19 Friends Colony West (E); *Ambassador:* ESSA A. RAHMAN AL-ESSA.

Laos: 4 Circular Rd., South Western Ext., Chanakyapuri (E); *Ambassador:* T. CHANTHARASY.

Lebanon: 10 Sardar Patel Marg, Chanakyapuri (E); *Ambassador:* MAHMOUD HAFEZ.

Malaysia: 3 Link Rd., Jangpura (HC); *High Commissioner:* Tuan Haji ABDUL KHALID BIN AWANG OSMAN.

Mauritius: 5 Kautilya Marg, Chanakyapuri (HC); *High Commissioner:* RABINDRAH GHURBURRUN.

Mexico: 136 Golf Links (E); *Ambassador:* C. G. MACÍAS.

Mongolia: 34 Golf Links (E); *Ambassador:* BUYANTYN DASHTSEREN.

Morocco: 199 Jor Bagh (E); *Ambassador:* YOUNES NEK-ROUF.

Nepal: Barakhamba Rd. (E); *Ambassador:* KRISHNA BOM MALLA.

Netherlands: 6/50 F, Shantipath (E); *Ambassador:* TJARK ASUEER MEURS.

New Zealand: 39 Golf Links (HC); *High Commissioner:* R. B. CUNNINGHAME.

Nigeria: 169/170 Jor Bagh (HC); *High Commissioner:* SOJI WILLIAMS.

Norway: Kautilya Marg, Chanakyapuri (E); *Ambassador:* T. CHRISTIANSEN.

Oman: 22 Vasant Vihar (E); *Ambassador:* ALI MOHAMMED AL-JAMALI.

Peru: D-290 Defence Colony (E); *Ambassador:* Dr. RENÉ HOOPER-LÓPEZ.

Philippines: 50-N, Nyaya Marg, Chanakyapuri (E); *Ambassador:* R. S. BUSUEGO.

Poland: 22 Golf Links Area (E); *Ambassador:* WIKTOR KINECKI.

Qatar: A-3 West End Colony (E); *Chargé d'Affaires:* MOHAMMED ABDUL RAHMAN ALKHOLAIFI.

Romania: 9 Tees January Marg (E); *Ambassador:* PETRE TANASIE.

Saudi Arabia: 1 Eastern Ave., Maharani Bagh (E); *Ambassador:* Shaikh YUSUF AL-FOZAN.

Singapore: 48 Golf Links (HC); *High Commissioner:* KENNETH MICHAEL BYRNE.

Spain: 12 Prithviraj Rd. (E); *Ambassador:* G. NADAL.

Sri Lanka: 27 Kautilya Marg, Chanakyapuri (HC); *High Commissioner:* JUSTIN SIRIWARDENE.

Sudan: 6 Jor Bagh (E); *Ambassador:* SAYED ALI AHMED SAHLUL.

Sweden: Nyaya Marg, Chanakyapuri (E); *Ambassador:* Count AXEL LEWENHAUPT.

Switzerland: Nyaya Marg, Chanakyapuri (E); *Ambassador:* Dr. FRITZ REAL.

Syria: 63 Sundar Nagar; *Ambassador:* RASLAN ALLOUSH.

Tanzania: E-104 and E-106, Greater Kailash (HC); *High Commissioner:* A. D. HASSAN.

Thailand: 56-N Nyaya Marg, Chanakyapuri (E); *Ambassador:* Dr. OWART SUTHIWART NARUEPUT.

Trinidad and Tobago: 131 Jor Bagh (HC); *High Commissioner:* SOLOMON SATCUMAR LUTCHMAN.

Turkey: 27 Jor Bagh (E); *Ambassador:* GONDOGDU USTUN.

Uganda: 172 Jor Bagh (HC); *High Commissioner:* EMMANUEL L. SENDAULA.

U.S.S.R.: Shantipath, Chanakyapuri (E); *Ambassador:* VIKTOR F. MALTSEV.

United Arab Emirates: 104 Malcha Marg, Chanakyapuri (E); *Ambassador:* MOHAMMED ISSA AL-ALI.

United Kingdom: Shantipath, Chanakyapuri (HC); *High Commissioner:* Sir MICHAEL WALKER.

U.S.A.: Shantipath, Chanakyapuri (E); *Ambassador:* DANIEL MOYNIHAN.

Uruguay: 45 Ring Rd., Lajpat Nagar III (E); *Ambassador:* ALFREDO URIOSTE.

Vatican: Niti Marg, Chanakyapuri (Apostolic Pronuncio); *Nuncio:* Most Rev. JOHN GORDON.

Venezuela: N-114 Panchaheela Park (E); *Ambassador:* RITA DE ARISMENDI.

Viet-Nam, Democratic Republic: 35 Prithvi Raj Rd. (E); *Ambassador:* CHU VAN BIEN.

Yemen, People's Democratic Republic: C-18 Friends Colony East (E); *Chargé d'Affaires:* MAHMOOD MOHAMMED JAFFAR.

Yugoslavia: 3/50G, Niti Marg, Chanakyapuri (E); *Ambassador:* ILIJA TOPALOSKI.

Zaire: 160 Jor Bagh (E); *Ambassador:* ILEKA MBOYO.

Monaco, San Marino and the Republic of Viet-Nam are represented by Consuls-General.

India also has diplomatic relations with Barbados, Bolivia, Burundi, Cameroon, the Congo (Brazzaville), Costa Rica, Cyprus, Dahomey, the Dominican Republic, El Salvador, Fiji, the Gambia, Guinea, Haiti, Honduras, Iceland, the Ivory Coast, Jamaica, Lesotho, Liberia, Libya, Luxembourg, Madagascar, Malawi, Maldives, Mali, Malta, Mauritania, Nicaragua, Paraguay, Rwanda, Senegal, Sierra Leone, Somalia, Swaziland, Togo, Tonga, Tunisia, the Upper Volta, Western Samoa, the Yemen Arab Republic and Zambia.

PARLIAMENT

RAJYA SABHA
(Council of States)
Chairman: GOPAL SWARUP PATHAK
(*April* 1974)

Party	Seats
Congress	133
Dravida Munnetra Kazhagam (DMK) .	12
Communist (CPI)	12
Jana Sangh	11
Congress (Opposition) . . .	9
Samyukta Socialist and Bharatiya Kranti Dal	9
Communist (Marxist-Leninist) . .	7
Muslim League	5
Swatantra	3
Socialist	2
Anna DMK	2
Akali Dal	2
Independent	12
Others	8
Nominated	12
Vacant	4
TOTAL	243

LOK SABHA
(House of the People)
Speaker: GURDIAL SINGH DHILLON
(*General Election, March* 1971; *Distribution of Seats*
following By-Elections, May 28th, 1973.)

Party	Seats
Congress	362
Jana Sangh	20
Congress (Opposition) . . .	11
Swatantra	7
Socialist	5
Communist (Marxist-Leninist) . .	25
Communist (CPI)	23
Dravida Munnetra Kazhagam (DMK) .	19
Muslim League	3
Regional Parties	9
Independent	19
Others	18
Vacant	7
TOTAL	523*

* Excluding the Speaker who has no party affiliation.

STATES

The distribution of seats shown for the State legislatures refers to the situation after the elections held in February 1973, except in Manipur, Nagaland, Orissa and Uttar Pradesh, where elections were held in February 1974.

Congress	Indian National Congress (Ruling)
Congress (O)	Indian National Congress (Opposition)
Communist-CPI	Communist Party of India
Communist-Marxist-Leninist	Communist Party of India (Marxist-Leninist)

ANDHRA PRADESH
(Capital—Hyderabad)

Governor: KHANDUBAI K. DESAI.

Chief Minister: J. VENGAL RAO (Congress Party).

Legislative Assembly: 287 seats (Congress 216, Communist-CPI 8, Communist-Marxist-Leninist 1, independents 18, others 39, vacant 5).

Legislative Council: 90 seats.

ASSAM
(Capital—Dispur)

Governor: L. P. SINGH.

Chief Minister: SARAT CHANDRA SINHA (Congress Party).

Legislative Assembly: 114 seats (Congress 94, Socialist 4, others 15, vacant 1).

BIHAR
(Capital—Patna)

Governor: R. D. BHANDARE.

Chief Minister: ABDUL GAFOOR (Congress Party).

Legislative Assembly: 318 seats (Congress 171, Communist-CPI 35, Congress (O) 27, Jana Sangh 24, Socialist 19, Swatantra 1, independents 15, others 24, vacant 2).

Legislative Council: 96 seats.

GUJARAT
(Capital—Gandhinagar)

Governor: K. K. VISWANATHAN.

The Congress Party ministry resigned and presidential rule was imposed on February 9th, 1974. The State Assembly was dissolved on March 15th, 1974.

HARYANA
(Capital—Chandigarh)

Governor: B. N. CHAKRAVARTY.

Chief Minister: BANSI LAL (Congress Party).

Legislative Assembly: 81 Seats (Congress 52, Congress (O) 6, Jana Sangh 2, independents 11, others 10).

HIMACHAL PRADESH
(Capital—Simla)

Governor: S. CHAKRAVARTI.

Chief Minister: Y. S. PARMAR (Congress Party).

Legislative Assembly: 68 seats (Congress 53, Jana Sangh 5, Communist-Marxist-Leninist 1, independents 7, others 2).

JAMMU AND KASHMIR
(Capitals—Srinagar (Summer), Jammu (Winter)

Governor: L. K. JHA.

Chief Minister: SYED MIR KASIM (Congress Party).
Legislative Assembly: 75 seats (Congress 58, Jana Sangh 3, independents 9, others 5).
Legislative Council: 36 seats.

KARNATAKA
(Capital—Bangalore)
Governor: MOHAN LAL SUKHADIA.
Chief Minister: D. DEVARAJ URS (Congress Party).
Legislative Assembly: 216 seats (Congress 165, Congress (O) 24, Communist-CPI 3, Socialist 2, independents 21, other 1).
Legislative Council: 63 seats.

KERALA
(Capital—Trivandrum)
Governor: N. N. WANCHOO.
Chief Minister: C. ACHUTHA MENON (Coalition Ministry; major partners: Congress Party, Communists-CPI, Muslim League).
Legislative Assembly: 133 seats (Congress 33, Communist-Marxist-Leninist 32, Communist-CPI 16, Kerala Congress 13, Muslim League 10, Socialist 8, Congress (O) 3, independent 1, others 16, vacant 1).

MADHYA PRADESH
(Capital—Bhopal)
Governor: SATYANARAYANA SINHA.
Chief Minister: P. C. SETHI (Congress Party).
Legislative Assembly: 296 seats (Congress 226, Jana Sangh 43, Socialist 7, Communist-CPI 5, independents 12, vacant 3).
Legislative Council: Not yet formed.

MAHARASHTRA
(Capital—Bombay)
Governor: ALI YAWAR JUNG.
Chief Minister: V. P. NAIK (Congress Party).
Legislative Assembly: 270 seats (Congress 222, Jana Sangh 5, Communist-CPI 2, Communist-Marxist-Leninist 11, independents 5, others 33, vacant 2).
Legislative Council: 78 seats.

MANIPUR
(Capital—Imphal)
Governor: L. P. SINGH.
Chief Minister: MOHAMMED ALIMUDDIN (United Legislature Party).
Legislative Assembly: 60 seats (Manipur People's Party 20, Manipur Hills Union 13, Congress 13, Communist-CPI 6, Socialist 2, independents 6; the United Legislature Party was formed by the Manipur People's Party and the Manipur Hills Union).

MEGHALAYA
(Capital—Shillong)
Governor: L. P. SINGH.
Chief Minister: Capt. W. A. SANGMA (All Party Hill Leaders Conference).
Legislative Assembly: 60 seats (All Party Hill Leaders Conference 37, Congress 8, independents 7, others 7, vacant 1).

NAGALAND
(Capital—Kohima)
Governor: L. P. SINGH.
Chief Minister: VIZOL (United Democratic Front).
Legislative Assembly: 60 seats (United Democratic Front of Nagaland 25, Nagaland Nationalist Organization 23, independents 12).

ORISSA
(Capital—Bhubaneswar)
Governor: B. D. JATTI.
Chief Minister: Mrs. NANDINI SATPATHY (Congress Party).
Legislative Assembly: 147 seats (Congress 69, Utkal Congress 35, Swatantra 21, Communist-CPI 7, Communist-Marxist-Leninist 3, Socialist 2, independents 8, other 1, vacant 1).

PUNJAB
(Capital—Chandigarh)
Governor: MAHENDRA MOHAN CHAUDHURY.
Chief Minister: ZAIL SINGH (Congress Party).
Legislative Assembly: 104 seats (Congress 68, Akali 25, Communist-CPI 10, Communist-Marxist-Leninist 1).

RAJASTHAN
(Capital—Jaipur)
Governor: JOGENDRA SINGH.
Chief Minister: HARIDEO JOSHI (Congress Party).
Legislative Assembly: 184 seats, (Congress 144, Swatantra 11, Jana Sangh 7, Socialist 4, Communist-CPI 4, Congress (O) 1, independents 11, vacant 2).

TAMIL NADU
(Capital—Madras)
Governor: K. K. SHAH.
Chief Minister: M. KARUNANIDHI (Dravidra Munnetra Kazhagam Party).
Legislative Assembly: 234 seats (Dravidra Munnetra Kazhagam 175, Congress (O) 12, Anna DMK 10, Forward Block 7, Congress 6, Swatantra 6, Muslim League 6, other 1, vacant 1).
Legislative Council: 63 seats.

TRIPURA
(Capital—Agartala)
Governor: L. P. SINGH.
Chief Minister: S. SENGUPTA (Congress Party).
Legislative Assembly: 60 seats (Congress 41, Communist-Marxist-Leninist 16, Communist-CPI 1, independents 2).

UTTAR PRADESH
(Capital—Lucknow)
Governor: AKBAR ALI KHAN.
Chief Minister: H. N. BAHUGUNA (Congress Party).
Legislative Assembly: 425 seats (Congress 214, Bharatiya Kranti Dal 106, Jana Sangh 61, Communist-CPI 16, Congress (O) 10, Socialist 5, Communist-Marxist-Leninist 2, Swatantra 1, independents 5, others 3, vacant 2).
Legislative Council: 108 seats.

WEST BENGAL

(Capital—Calcutta)

Governor: A. L. Dias.

Chief Minister: Siddhartha Shankar Ray (Congress Party).

Legislative Assembly: 280 seats (Congress 216, Communist-CPI 36, Communist-Marxist-Leninist 13, Congress (O) 2, independents 4, others 8, vacant 1).

UNION TERRITORIES

Andaman and Nicobar Islands (Headquarters—Port Blair): *Chief Commissioner:* Har Mander Singh.

Arunachal Pradesh (Capital—Itanagar): *Chief Commissioner:* M. L. Kampani.

Chandigarh (Headquarters—Chandigarh): *Chief Commissioner:* N. P. Mathur.

Dadra and Nagar Haveli (Headquarters—Silvassa): *Administrator:* S. K. Banerji.

Delhi (Headquarters—Delhi): *Lieut-Governor:* Baleshwar Prasad.

Goa, Daman and Diu (Capital—Panaji): *Lieut-Governor:* S. K. Banerji.

Chief Minister: Shashikala G. Kakodkar (Maharashtravadi Gomantak Party).

Legislature: 30 seats (Maharashtravadi Gomantak 18, United Goans (Sequiera Group) 10, Congress 1, independent 1).

Lakshadweep (Headquarters—Kavaratti): *Administrator:* W. Shaiza.

Mizoram (Headquarters—Aizawl): *Lieut-Governor:* Shanti Priya Mukherjee.

Chief Minister: Chalchhunga (Mizo Union Party).

Assembly: 30 seats (Mizo Union 24, Congress 6).

Pondicherry (Capital—Pondicherry): *Lieut.-Governor:* Cheddi Lal.

The Anna Dravidra Munnetra Kazhagam—Communist coalition Ministry resigned on March 27th, 1974. The Assembly was dissolved on March 28th, 1974.

POLITICAL PARTIES

The principal parties are:

Indian National Congress: 5 Dr. Rajendra Prasad Rd., New Delhi; was founded in 1885 by A. O. Hume, with the main object of creating national consciousness in India, and securing economic advance in the country. In 1907 Congress was split in two—the Extremists and the Moderates. In 1920, Mahatma Gandhi began to take a leading part in its activities and policies, and Congress soon became a mass organization fighting for complete independence. By 1939 Congress held power in six of the eleven provinces and in two others there were Congress-Coalition Governments. At the outbreak of war in 1939 these ministries gave up office. In 1942 the Congress adopted the policy of "quit India" towards the British. The 1946 elections led to Congress ministries in eight provinces, Congress-Coalition ministries in two, and a Muslim League ministry in one. In 1965 the Jammu and Kashmir National Conference was dissolved and its members joined Congress. Before the 1967 elections a number of splinter groups broke away from Congress to form new parties.

Aims: The well-being and advancement of the people and the establishment by peaceful means of a socialist, co-operative Commonwealth based on equality of opportunity and rights, aiming at world peace; the provision of basic needs and opportunities for culture; full employment in 10 years; Government control of large-scale industries and services; co-operative industry and agriculture; a neutral foreign policy.

Membership: about 11 million, active members 208,954.

Note: On November 1st, 1969, the Indian National Congress split into two distinct organizations when Mrs. Indira Gandhi set up a steering committee, composed of her supporters in the party, in opposition to the standing Working Committee of the Party. The standing Congress Working Committee meeting of 12 November, under the presidency of Mr. Nijalingappa, was attended by her party opponents and Mrs. Gandhi was formally expelled from membership of the party. When parliament re-assembled on 17 November, 111 Congress M.P.s in both houses of parliament withdrew their support from Mrs. Gandhi's government, which continues in office with the support of the D.M.K.,

independent M.P.s and left-wing parties. The Congress parliamentary group opposing the government has become India's first recognized opposition party and has been designated the *Indian National Congress—Opposition*. At a conference in late 1969, the official Congress Party elected a new President and Working Committee. President: Shankar Dayal Sharma. Leader: Mrs. Indira Gandhi.

Indian National Congress (Opposition): 7 Jantar Mantar Rd., New Delhi-1;

President: Sadiq Ali.

Chair. Parliamentary Group: Morarji Desai.

Leader in Lok Sabha: Dr. Ram Subhag Singh.

Leader in Rajya Sabha: S. N. Mishra.

Swatantra Party: Sassoon Bldg., 143 Mahatma Gandhi Rd., Bombay 1; f. 1959; aims: maximum individual freedom; peasant proprietorship in agriculture and free competitive enterprise in industry and trade; alignment with Western democracies in foreign policy; anti-communist.

President: Piloo Mody, m.p.

General Secretary: Madhu Mehta.

Bharatiya Jana Sangh (*People's Party of India*): Vithal Bhai Patel Bhavan, Rafi Marg, New Delhi. Believes in Integral Humanism as opposed to both Marxist economic-interpretation of history and to capitalism. Pledged to check the spread of communism, stands for nationalism and democracy. Opposed to discrimination against, or in favour of, any section of the people on the basis of caste or creed. Upholds the right of all citizens to freedom of conscience and faith and the right to work. Against the establishment of a theocratic state and allows full freedom of modes of worship. Stands for co-partnership for labour in management and profits, Indianization of foreign-owned tea, drugs, soap, match, vegetable products, jute and cigarette industries and nationalization of foreign banks. Favours building up of an Indian nuclear deterrent and utilizing atomic power for speedy industrialization. Envisages foreign-aid-free Five-Year Plans and nationalization of foreign trade with communist countries. Stands for an independent foreign policy based on reciprocity.

President: ATAL BIHARI VAJPAYEE, M.P.

General Secretary: S. S. BHANDARI, M.P.

Membership: 1,500,000.

Socialist Party: 16 Vithalbhai Patel House, Rafi Marg, New Delhi; f. 1971 as a result of union between the former Samyukta Socialist Party, Praja Socialist Party, Socialist Party and other socialist groups. Aims: its primary task is the building up of an effective organizational instrument which will lead people's struggle for economic equality, social mobility and meaningful participation of the people in building a socialist economy.

Chairman: KARPURI THAKUR.

General Secretary: MADHU DANDAVATE, M.P.

The Communist Party of India: 7/4 Asaf Ali Rd., New Delhi.

Aims: The establishment of a socialist society led by the working class, and ultimately of a communist society. Its immediate task is the liquidation of feudal and imperialist survivals and the achievement of a national democratic state.

Chairman: S. A. DANGE.

General Secretary: C. RAJESWARA RAO.

Members of the Secretariat: S. A. DANGE, BHUPESH GUPTA, C. RAJESWARA RAO, N. K. KRISHNAN, YOGINDRA SHARMA, INDRAJIT GUPTA, N. RAJSEKHAR REDDY, INDRADEEP SINHA, S. KUMARAN.

Membership: 245,000 approx.

Communist Party of India (Marxist-Leninist): 49 Lake Place, Calcutta-19, West Bengal; f. 1946 as pro-Peking breakaway group of C.P.I., the Party declared its independence of Peking in 1968.

General Secretary: P. SUNDARAYYA.

Membership: 85,000.

Dravida Munnetra Kazhagam (D.M.K.): Arivagam, Royapuram, Madras-13; aims at a sovereign, independent socialist State of Dravidanad, comprising Tamilnad, Andra, Karnatak and Kerala districts; regional languages as State languages. English as official language.

Leader: M. KARUNANIDHI.

Membership: over 200,000.

Shiromani Akali Dal: Amritsar: Sikh nationalist party; aims at the establishment of a Punjabi-speaking state.

President: GIANI BHUPINDER SINGH.
General Secretary: Sardar ATMA SINGH.
There are two rival groups of the party, one led by Master TARA SINGH, the other by SANT FATEH SINGH.

Peasants and Workers Party of India: Mahatma Phule Rd., Naigaum, Bombay 14; to establish a People's Democracy; to nationalize all basic industries; industrialization; unitary state with provincial boundaries drawn on linguistic basis; Marxist.

General Secretary: DAJIBA DESAI.
Membership: about 10,000.

Akhil Bharat Hindu Mahasabha: Hindu Mahasabha Bhawan, Mandir Marg, New Delhi 1; aims: to establish a democratic Hindu state.

President: BRAJ NARAYAN BRAJESH.
General Secretary: H. B. BHIDE.
Membership: about 2 million.

All India Forward Block: 88 North Ave., New Delhi; socialistic principles, including nationalization of key industries, land redistribution; advocates military action against Pakistan over Kashmir.

Chairman: HEMANTA KUMAR BOSE, M.L.A.
General Secretary: R. K. HALDULKAR.

Republican Party of India: Deeksha Bhoomi, Nagpur-3, Maharashtra; main aims and objectives are to realize the aims and objects set out in the preamble to the Indian Constitution.

President: DADASAHEB GAIKWAD.
General Secretary: B. D. KHOBRAGADE.

JUDICIAL SYSTEM

THE SUPREME COURT

Article 124 of the Constitution provides for the establishment of a Supreme Court of India.

The Supreme Court exercises exclusive jurisdiction in any dispute between the Union and the States (although there are certain restrictions where an acceding state is involved). It has appellate jurisdiction over any judgment, decree or order of the High Court where that Court certifies that either a substantial question of law or the interpretation of the Constitution is involved.

Provision is made for the appointment by the Chief Justice of India of judges of High Courts as *ad hoc* judges at sittings of the Supreme Court for specified periods, and for the attendance of retired judges at sittings of the Supreme Court. The Supreme Court has advisory jurisdiction in respect of questions which may be referred to it by the President for opinion. The Supreme Court is also empowered to hear appeals against a sentence of death passed by a State High Court, in reversal of an order of acquittal by a lower court, and in a case in which a High Court has granted a certificate of fitness.

The Supreme Court also hears appeals which are certified by High Courts to be fit for appeal, subject to rules made by the Court. Parliament may, by law, confer on the Supreme Court any further powers of appeal.

HIGH COURTS

The High Courts are the Courts of Appeal from the lower courts, and their decisions are final except in cases where appeal lies to the Supreme Court.

Trial by jury is the rule in original criminal cases before the High Court, but juries are not employed in civil suits.

LOWER COURTS

Provision is made in the Code for Criminal Procedure for the constitution of lower criminal courts called Courts of Session and Courts of Magistrates. The Courts of Session are competent to try all persons duly committed for trial, and inflict any punishment authorized by the law.

Appeals can be made from a single judge's decision in the High Court, sitting as a court of original criminal jurisdiction, to a bench of not less than two judges of the same Court sitting as a Court of Appeal. The President and the local government concerned exercise the prerogative of mercy.

The constitution of inferior civil courts is determined by regulations within each state.

SUPREME COURT

Chief Justice of India: The Hon. Justice A. N. RAY.

Judges of the Supreme Court: Hons. P. JAGAN MOHAN REDDY, D. G. PALEKAR, K. K. MATHEW, H. R. KHANNA, M. H. BEG, S. N. DWIVEDI, A. K. MUKHERJEA, Y. V. CHANDRACHUD, A. ALAGIRISWAMI, P. N. BHAGWATI, V. R. KRISHNA IYER, P. K. GOSWAMI, R. S. SARKARIA.

RELIGION

The following is a brief summary of the origins and number of adherents of the major Indian faiths.

Hinduism, the predominant religion, originated as a simple form of nature worship. It is not a well-defined creed but a way of life, a fellowship of faiths. Hinduism has inspired a vast and poetic literature of which the *Vedas* are the earliest. According to the 1971 census, Hindus form 82.7 per cent of the population (453.3 million).

Islam was introduced in the seventh century by Arab traders, spreading much more widely after the conquest of India by Turko-Afghans in the twelfth century. Among the religions that entered India from abroad, Islam has the largest following. Muslims are divided into two main sects, Shi'as and Sunnis. Most of the Indian Muslims are Sunnis. In 1971 the Muslim population numbered 61.4 million (11.21 per cent).

Buddhism arose in India in the sixth century B.C. as a revolt against Hindu ritual. Gautama Buddha, its founder, was a prince born in the present State of Bihar; he forsook his kingdom and practised austerities. Buddhism has spread to Sri Lanka, Burma, Tibet and Thailand and can claim more followers in these countries than in India. The Buddhists in Ladakh owe allegiance to the Dalai Lama. Head Lama of Ladakh: KAUSHAK SAKULA, Dalgate, Srinagar, Kashmir. In 1971 there were 3.81 million Buddhists in India.

Sikhism, too, is an offshoot of Hinduism. The movement was founded by Guru Nanak, who was born in the Punjab, in 1469. His teachings are contained in the *Adi Granth*, the holy book of the Sikhs. Sikhs are conspicuous for their distinctive symbols such as wearing their hair long, steel bracelets and always carrying a dagger. According to the 1971 census there were 10.3 million Sikhs in India, the majority living in the Punjab.

Jainism numbers 2.6 million adherents (1971 census). Its origins are obscure and it is likely that it existed in India before the arrival of the Indo-Aryans in about 1,500 B.C. The Jains claim that their religion is eternal and is renewed in successive ages by Jinas (conquerors) of whom the last was Mahavira who lived just before Gautama Buddha. Among the holy places of the Jains are Mount Abu, Girnar, Satrunjaya and Pavapuri.

Zuroastrians worship the one God, of whom fire is a symbol. More than 120,000 Parsis practise the Zoroastrian religion, their ancestors having migrated from Persia to the West coast of India in the eighth century.

Christians fall into two historical groups, the Syrian Christians, who trace their descent from converts in the first centuries of the Christian era, and Christians converted in modern times by Western missionaries. There are 14.2 million Christians in India (1971 census), of whom more than half are Roman Catholics, the others being members of the ancient Syrian and the Protestant churches.

CHRISTIAN CHURCHES

THE ROMAN CATHOLIC CHURCH

Apostolic Pro-Nuncio to India: H.E. the Most Rev. JOHN GORDON, Chanakyapuri, New Delhi 110021.

The Church has 15 archdioceses, 60 suffragan dioceses and 2 prefectures apostolic for Catholics of the Latin rite. There are 3 archbishoprics, 7 suffragan bishoprics and 6 exarchates for the Oriental rite. Total number of Roman Catholics, 7,966,286.

Archbishops

Agra: The Most Rev. Dr. DOMINIC ATHAIDE, O.F.M.CAP.

Bangalore: The Most Rev. PACKIAM AROKIASWAMY.

Bhopal: The Most Rev. Dr. EUGENE D'SOUZA, M.S.F.S.

Bombay: H.E. Cardinal VALERIAN GRACIAS.

Calcutta: The Most Rev. LAWRENCE T. PICACHY, S.J.

Delhi: The Most Rev. Dr. ANGELO INNOCENT FERNANDES.

Goa: H.E. the Most Rev. Dom JOSÉ VIEIRA ALVERNAZ, Patriarch of the East Indies.

Hyderabad: The Most Rev. SAMININI ARULAPPA.

Madras and Mylapore: The Most Rev. RAYAPPA ARULAPPA.

Madhurai: The Most Rev. Dr. JUSTIN DIRAVIAM.

Nagpur: The Most Rev. Dr. LEONARD RAYMOND.

Pondicherry and Cuddalore: The Most Rev. V. S. SELVANATHER.

Ranchi: The Most Rev. Dr. PIUS KERKETTA, S.J.

Shillong-Gauhati: The Most Rev. HUBERT D'ROSARIO, S.D.B.

Verapoly: The Most Rev. JOSEPH KELANTHARA.

ORIENTAL RITE

Changanacherry: The Most Rev. Dr. ANTHONY PADIYARA.

Ernakulam: H.E. Cardinal JOSEPH PARECATTIL.

Trivandrum: The Most Rev. GREGORIOS B. VARGHESE THANGALATHIL.

THE CHURCH OF NORTH INDIA

In November 1970, the Church of India was united with seven other Churches, to become The Church of North India.

Total number of Anglican Christians: 2,690,500.

Bishops

Delhi and Ragasthan: Rt. Rev. E. S. NASIR (Moderator); Bishop's House, 1 Church Lane, New Delhi.

Amaritsar: (vacant).

Andamans and Nicobars: Rt Rev. M. D. SRINIVASAN.

Assam and Darjeeling: Rt. Rev. D. PRADHAN.

Barrackpore and Durgapur: Rt. Rev. D. GORAI.

Bombay: (vacant).

Calcutta: Rt. Rev. J. AMRITANAND.

Chota Nagpur: Rt. Rev. S. A. B. DILBAR HANS, D.D.

Cuttack with Sambalpur: Rt. Rev. J. K. MAHANTY.

Gujarat: Rt. Rev. I. L. CHRISTACHARI.

Jabalpur: Rt. Rev. S. K. PATRO.

Kolhapur: Rt. Rev. I P. ANDREWS.

Lucknow: Rt. Rev. DIN DAYAL.
Nasik: Rt. Rev. A. V. JONATHAN.
Nandyal: Rt. Rev. E. JOHN.
Patna: Rt. Rev. R. R. SOREN.

CHURCH OF SOUTH INDIA

The Church of South India was founded in 1947 by the union of the Anglicans, Methodists, Congregationalists and Presbyterians in South India.

Officers of the Synod: Moderator Rt. Rev. I. R. H. GNANADASAN, M.A., B.D.; Deputy Moderator Rt. Rev. Dr. LESLIE NEWBIGIN, M.A.; Hon. Sec. (Acting) Dr. (Mrs.) R. M. SOMASEKHAR, M.A.; Hon. Treas. P. I. CHANDY, B.SC.

Bishops

Coimbatore: (vacant).
Dornakal: Rt. Rev. P. SOLOMON.
Jaffna: Rt. Rev. D. J. AMBALAVANAR.
Kanyakumari: Rt. Rev. I. R. H. GNANADASAN (Moderator); Bishop's House, Nagercoil 1, Kayakumari District, Tamil Nadu.
N. Kerala: Rt. Rev. Dr. T. B. BENJAMIN.
S. Kerala: Rt. Rev. P. W. VACHALAN.
Krishna-Godavari: Rt. Rev. N. D. A. SAMUEL.
Madhya Kerala: Rt. Rev. Dr. M. M. JOHN.
Madras: Rt. Rev. Dr. LESSLIE NEWBIGIN.
Madura-Ramnad: Rt. Rev. GEORGE DEVADOSS.
Medak: Rt. Rev. H. D. L. ABRAHAM.
N. Mysore: Rt. Rev. W. V. KARL.
S. Mysore: Rt. Rev. S. R. FURTADO.
C. Mysore: Rt. Rev. A. D. JOHN.

Rayalaseema: Rt. Rev. C. S. SUNDARESAN.
Tiruchirapalli-Tanjavur: Rt. Rev. S. DORAISAWMY.
Tirunelveli: Rt. Rev. T. S. GARRETT.

Bishops without Diocesan responsibility: Rt. Rev. Dr. A. B. ELLIOTT, Rt. Rev. BUNYAN JOSEPH, Rt. Rev. Dr. A. J. APPASAMY.

There is a total congregation of about 1,376,824; publ. *The South India Churchman*. Office: C.S.I. Synod Secretariat, Cathedral, Madras 6.

National Christian Council of India: Christian Council Lodge, Nagpur-1, Maharashtra; Pres. Rt. Rev. P. MAR CHRYSOSTOM; Vice-Pres. Dr. J. RADHAKRISHAN, E. D. DEVADASON; Gen. Sec. M. A. Z. ROLSTON; publ. *National Christian Council Review*.

The National Christian Council of India represents all the major Christian churches except the Roman Catholic Church and the Syrian Orthodox Church in India. This Council was organized in 1914 and is a constituent body of the Commission on World Mission and Evangelism of the World Council of Churches. It seeks to serve all Churches.

Federation of Evangelical Lutheran Churches in India: Ranchi, Bihar; Pres. Rt. Rev. R. B. MANIKAM; Sec. Dr. M. BAGE.

Mar Thoma Syrian Church of Malabar: Mar Thoma Sabha Office, Tiruvalla P.O., Kerala.

Syrian Orthodox Church of the East: Catholicate Palace, Kottayam-4; Sec. Metropolitan DANIEL MAR PHILOXENUS.

United Church of North India and Pakistan: Church House, Mhow, M.P.; Sec. Rev. KENNETHYOHAN MASIH. Other groups include Baptist and Methodist Churches.

THE PRESS

The Indian Press owes a large part of its development and present form to the traditions established at the time of the British raj. With the coming of independence the National Congress adopted a number of the press controls instituted by the colonial rulers. The right to freedom of speech and expression is guaranteed by Article 19 of the Constitution, which also empowers the central or state governments to impose restrictions through laws relating to libel, contempt of court or to matters liable to offend public morality or weaken the security of the state. This qualification was extended in 1951 to apply to matter likely to incite offence or to prejudice relations with other countries. Conditions for the reporting of political debate in either of the Houses of Parliament were improved by the Parliamentary Proceedings Act of 1956, which gave protection from prosecution to reports which could claim to be "substantially true".

In 1962 the Defence of India Rules were instituted, giving the Government complete control of the Press in times of crisis in order to prevent the publication of matter on specified subjects prejudicial to the interests of the state. As the Government supplies most of the advertisement matter, which provides the main source of press revenue, its power to withhold this constitutes a means of pressure on editors.

The growth of a thriving Press has been made difficult by cultural barriers caused by religious, caste and language differences. Consequently the English Press, with its appeal to the educated middle-class urban readership throughout the state, has retained its dominance. Though there are more papers in Hindi, the total circulation of the English Press is the greater. The main Indian language dailies also appeal to the urban reader but by paying little attention to rural affairs they fail to cater for the increasingly literate provincial population who know no English. Most Indian papers have a relatively small circulation. Provincial papers frequently play upon religious or local sympathies to ensure their circulation.

The art of reporting and probing for news is far less developed in India than in the West. Many papers, particularly the smaller ones, depend for news on government handouts and on the small number of news agencies, which results in a lack of variety in news content. Provincial papers which cannot afford agencies depend entirely on government handouts. All except the largest newspapers, which have their own correspondents, make use of agencies for foreign news.

The daily papers provide a relatively large proportion of domestic and international news particularly on politics; sports and finance receive good coverage. There is little sensationalism. Advertisements constitute on average 50 per cent of the contents of the larger papers. In contrast to the dailies the periodical press offers more articles of human interest, more coverage of local affairs and among periodicals the English sector plays a far less prominent role.

Problems confronting the Press are the shortage of newsprint, allocation of which is controlled by the Government, and, in the case of the smaller papers, the lack of an adequately trained staff and suitable equipment. In

October 1972, the Indian Supreme Court ruled that a government order introduced in April, which limited the number of daily newspapers' pages to ten, was unconstitutional, since it amounted in effect to government control and as such was an infringement of the right of free expression.

There are about 11,000 newspapers and periodicals with a combined circulation of over 29 million, of which 695 are dailies. Some 72.9 per cent of the dailies had circulations of less than 10,000 and constituted 22 per cent of the total circulation; 21.5 per cent had circulations of 10,000–50,000 and constituted 38 per cent; 56 per cent had circulations of over 50,000 and constituted 40 per cent.

In 1970 there were 72 newspaper groups owning 272 newspapers with a total circulation of 7.6 million. The most powerful groups own most of the large English dailies and frequently have considerable private commercial and industrial holdings. Three of the major groups are as follows:

Times of India Group (controlled by the JAIN and DALMIA families): includes the dailies, *Times of India* the *Evening News of India* (Bombay) and the Hindi *Navbharat Times*, weeklies including the *Illustrated Weekly of India* and the Hindi *Dharmayug*, the fortnightly *Femina* and *Filmfare* and the Hindi monthly *Parag*.

Indian Express Group (controlled by the GOENKA family): the dailies, the *Indian Express*, the Marathi *Lokasatta*, the Tamil *Dinamani*, the Telugu *Andhra Prabha*, the Kannada *Kannada Prabha* and the English *Financial Express*, and the English weeklies the *Sunday Standard* and *Screen* and the Telugu *Andhra Prabha Illustrated Weekly*.

Hindustan Times Group (controlled by the BIRLA family): several dailies including the *Hindustan Times* (Delhi), the *Hindustan Times Evening News*, the *Hindustan Times Kanpur Supplement*, the *Leader* (Allahabad), the *Searchlight* (Patna), the Hindi *Hindustan* (Delhi) and *Bharat* (Allahabad), and the weekly *Overseas Hindustan Times*, *Eastern Economist*, the Hindi *Saptahik Hindustan* (Allahabad) and *Pradeep* (Patna).

The widest circulating and most influential newspapers are the metropolitan dailies in English which in 1970 totalled 74 with a combined circulation of 2.1 million, closely followed by 191 Hindi and 53 Bengali papers with circulation of 1.3 and 1.0 million respectively. A few papers are published simultaneously from several centres, notably the *Indian Express* in six cities, and the *Times of India*, the *Statesman* and the *Navbharat Times* at two each.

Among the most highly respected daily papers are the *Times of India* and the Hindi *Navbharat Times* (Bombay), the *Statesman* (Calcutta), the *Hindu* (Madras), and the *Hindustan Times* and the Hindi *Hindustan* (New Delhi).

In order of circulation the most popular dailies are: the *Indian Express*, the Tamil *Thanthi*, *Mathrubhumi*, the *Times of India*, the Bengali *Ananda Bazar Patrika*, the *Statesman*, the Malayalam *Malayala Manorama*, the Hindi *Navbharat Times*, the *Hindu*, the Marathi *Loksatta*, the *Hindustan Times* and the *Dinamani*.

The more popular weekly periodicals range from the cultural Tamil publications *Kumadam*, *Kalki* and *Anandavikatan* to the sensationalist English *Blitz*. *Filmfare*, *Sports and Pastime* and *Women's Own Weekly* are leading magazines, each catering for a particular readership. Among the largest monthly periodicals are the *Reader's Digest* and the Hindi religious publication *Kalyan*.

PRINCIPAL DAILIES
DELHI

Hindustan: P.B. 40, Connaught Circus; f. 1933; morning; Hindi; Editors G. N. SAHI and R. L. JOSHI; circ. 156,164.

Hindustan Times: Connaught Circus; London Office: Hindustan Times House, 2/3 Salisbury Court, Fleet St., E.C.4; f. 1923; morning; English; Nationalist; Editor B. G. VERGHESE; circ. 142,904.

Indian Express: P.O.B. 570, Mathura Rd.; f. 1932; morning; English; published simultaneously in Delhi, Madurai (Tamilnadu), Madras (Tamilnadu), Bangalore (Mysore), Vijayawada (Andhra Pradesh), Bombay (Maharashtra) and Ahmedabad (Gujarat); circ. (national) 440,640, (Delhi) 88,505.

Milap: 8A Bahadur Shah Zafar Marg; f. 1923; Urdu; Nationalist; Editor RANBIR SINGH; Man. T. R. KAPUR; Advt. Man. R. D. CHOPRA; also published from Jullundur and Hyderabad; circ. 55,840.

Motherland: 7E Jhandewala; f. 1971; English; Editor K. R. MALKANI; circ. 17,000.

Navbharat Times: 7 Bahadur Shah Zafar Marg; f. 1947; also published from Bombay; Hindi; Editor A. K. JAIN; circ. 251,030.

Patriot: P.B. 727, Link House, Bahadur Shah Zafar Marg; f. 1963; English; Editor P. VISWANATH; circ. 45,956.

Pratap: Bahadur Shah Zafar Marg; f. 1919; Urdu; Editor K. NARENDRA; circ. 29,937.

Statesman: Chowringhee Square, Calcutta, P.B. 4; English; Editor K. RANGACHARI; circ. 29,114.

Times of India: 7 Bahadurshah Zafar Marg; f. 1838; English; published from Bombay, Delhi and Ahmedabad; Resident Editor GIRILAL JAIN; circ. (Delhi) 82,644.

Vir Arjun: Pratap Bhawan, Bahadur Shah Zafar Marg; f. 1954; Hindi; Editor K. NARENDRA; circ. 38,777.

ANDHRA PRADESH
Hyderabad

Andhra Janata: Lingampally, Hyderabad-27; f. 1955; Telugu; Editor P. N. RAO; circ. 5,300.

Rehnuma-e-Deccan: Afzalgunj; f. 1949; morning; Urdu; Independent; Editor SYED VICARUDDIN; circ. 11,457.

Siasat Daily: f. 1949; morning; Urdu; Editor ABID ALI KHAN; circ. 9,733.

Vijayawada

Andhra Prabha: f. 1959; Telugu; Editor PANDITHA RADHYOLA NAGESWARA RAO; circ. 83,460 (Vijayawada edition), 25,650 (Bangalore edition).

Indian Express: George Oakes Building, Besant Rd., Gandhinagar 3; (*see also* under Delhi); circ. (Vijayawada, Bangalore, Madras and Madurai) 210,420.

ASSAM

Assam Tribune: Tribune Buildings, Gauhati; f. 1938; English; Editor S. C. KAKATI; circ. 25,400.

BIHAR
Patna

Aryavarta: Mazharul Haque Path; f. 1940; Hindi; morning Editor J. K. MISHRA; circ. 64,901.

The Indian Nation: Mazharul Haque Path; f. 1930; morning; Editor DEENA NATH JHA; circ. 46,943.

Sangam Daily: Lalazar Manzil, P.O.B. 26, Patna-4; f. 1953; Urdu; morning; Editor GHULAM SARWAR; circ. 14,287.

Searchlight: Buddha Marg; f. 1918; English; morning; Editor S. C. SARKER; circ. 13,296.

GUJARAT
Ahmedabad

Gujarat Samachar: Gujarat Samachar Bhavan, Kanpur; f. 1932; Gujarati; morning; Editor SHANTILAL A. SHAH; circ. 53,688.

Indian Express: Janasatta Bldg., Mirzapur Rd.; English; *see* under Delhi; circ. (Ahmedabad) 18,000.

Sandesh: Sandesh Building, Cheekanta Road; f. 1923; Gujarati; Editor C. S. PATEL; circ. 70,988.

Western Times: f. 1967; English; Editor RAMU PATEL; circ. 11,963.

KARNATAKA (MYSORE)
Bangalore

Daily Tarjman: Ludhiana; Urdu; circ. 8,000.

Deccan Herald: 16 Mahatma Gandhi Road; f. 1948. morning; English; Editor V. B. MENON; circ. 64,063.

Indian Express: 1 Queen's Rd.; *see* under Delhi; circ. (Bangalore, Madras, Madurai and Vijayawada) 210,420.

Kannada Prabha: 1 Queen's Rd.; Kannada; f. 1967 Editor K. S. RAMAKRISHNA MURTHY; circ. 60,000.

KERALA
Trivandrum

Kerala Kaumudi: P.B. 77, Pettah, Trivandrum; f. 1940; Malayalam and English; Editor K. SUKUMARAN; circ. 108,257.

Navakeralam: f. 1957; Malayalam; independent; Editor S. SEBASTIAN; circ. 18,039.

Thaninram: f. 1964; Malayalam; Editor K. K. NAIR; circ. 28,455.

Other Towns

Malayala Manorama: P.O.B. 26, K. K. Rd., Kottayam; f. 1888; Malayalam; morning; Chief Editor K. M. MATHEW; circ. 300,000.

Mathrubhumi: P.B. No. 46, Robinson Rd., Kozhikode; f. 1923; Malayalam; Editor K. P. KESAVA MENON; also published from Cochin; circ. 218,296.

MAHARASHTRA
Bombay

Bombay Samachar: Red House, Sayed Abdulla Brelvi Rd., Fort; f. 1822; morning and Sunday weekly; Gujarati; political and commercial; Editors MINOO DESAI (daily), SHANTIKUMAR J. BHATT (Sunday); circ. 108,378 (daily), 121,496 (weekly).

Economic Times: The Times of India Press, Dr. Dadabhai Naoroji Rd.; London Office: 3 Albemarle St., W.1; f. 1961; English; Editor D. K. RANGNEKAR; circ. 29,751.

Evening News of India: Dr. Dadabhai Naoroji Rd.; London Office: 3 Albemarle St., W.1; f. 1923; evening; English; Editor SHAM LAL; circ. 15,280.

The Financial Express: Express Tower, Nariman Point, 1; f. 1961; daily; English; Editor V. K. NARASIMHAN circ. 13,000.

Free Press Bulletin: 21 Dalal St., Fort 1; f. 1947; English; Independent Nationalist; Editor A. B. NAIR; circ. 21,904.

Indian Express: Express Tower, Nariman Point, 1; English; *see* under Delhi; circ. (Bombay) 90,813.

Jam-e-Jamshed: Ballard House, Mangalore St.; f. 1832; English and Gujarati; Chair. RUSTOM P. MARZBAN; Editor ADI MARZBAN; circ. 9,000.

Janashakti: 21 Dalal St., Fort, 1; f. 1950; Gujarati and English; Independent Nationalist; Editor C. P. SHUKLA; circ. 27,505.

Janmabhoomi: Janmabhoomi Bhavan, 24 Ghoga St., Fort; f. 1934; Gujarati; Propr. Saurashtra Trust; Editor M. V. MEHTA; circ. 42,107.

Lokasatta: Newspaper House, Sassoon Dock, Colaba, 5; f. 1948; Marathi; Editor R. N. LATE; circ. 133,568.

Maharashtra Times: The Times of India Press, Dr. Dadabhai Naoroji Rd.; London Office: 3 Albemarle St., W.1; f. 1962; Marathi; Editor G. S. TALWALKAR; circ. 123,000.

Maratha: Lovegrove Rd., Worli; f. 1956; Marathi; Editor P. K. ATRE; circ. 77,312.

Navashakti: 21 Dalal St., Fort; f. 1932; Marathi; Editor-in-Chief P. V. GADGIL; circ. 31,982.

Navbharat Times: Dr. Dadabhai Naoroji Rd.; f. 1950; also published from Delhi; Hindi; Editor A. JAIN; circ. (Bombay) 66,124; (Delhi) 185,300.

Prajatantra: 211–219 Frere Rd., Fort, 1; f. 1954; evening; Gujarati; Editor CHAMANLAL V. SHAH; circ. 23,457.

Sakal: Old Prabhadevi Rd.; f. 1970; daily and Sunday; Marathi.

Times of India: Dr. Dadabhai Naoroji Rd.; London Office: 3 Albemarle St., W.1; f. 1838; morning; English; published from Bombay, Delhi and Ahmedabad; Editor SHAM LAL; circ. (Bombay and Ahmedabad) 185,397.

Nagpur

Hitavada: Wardha Rd.; f. 1911; morning; English; Editor A. D. MANI; circ. 9,160.

Maharashtra: Ogale Rd., Mahal; f. 1914; Marathi; Nationalist; Editor D. B. PANDIT; circ. 7,000.

Nagpur Times: 37 Farmland, Ramdaspeth; f. 1933; English; Editor P. V. DESHPANDE; circ. 15,201 (Nagpur).

Nava Prabhat: f. 1957; Hindi; Editor NAND KISHORE; circ. 17,661.

Tarun Bharat: f. 1954; Marathi; Independent; Editor P. C. KARKARE; circ. 34,754.

Poona

Kesari: 568 Narayan Peth 30; Marathi; Editor J. S. TILAK; circ. 43,167.

Sakal: 595 Budhwar Peth, 2; f. 1932; daily and Sunday; Marathi; Acting Editor Shri S. G. MUNAGEKAR; Gen. Man. Lt.-Col. (retd.) V. V. JOSHI; circ. daily 85,792 Sunday 101,079.

PUNJAB

Tribune: Chandigarh; f. 1881; English; Editor R. M. NAIR; circ. 107,610.

RAJASTHAN

Rashtradoot: Jaipur; f. 1951; Hindi; Editor B. L. SHARMA; circ. 19,165.

TAMIL NADU
Madras

Andhra Patrika: 7 Thambu Chetty St.; f. 1914; evening; Telugu; Editor S. SAMBHU PRASAD; circ. 12,530.

Daily Thanthi: 1 Rundalls Rd., Vepery, 600007; f. 1942; Tamil; Editor R. S. RATHNAM; circ. 271,419.

Hindu, The: 201A Mount Rd.; London Office: 2/3 Salisbury Court, Fleet St., E.C.4; f. 1878; morning; English; Independent; Managing Editor G. NARASIMHAN; Editor G. KASTURI; circ. 213,534.

Indian Express: Express Estates, Mount Rd. 2; *see* under Delhi; circ. (Madras, Madurai, Bangalore and Vijayawada) 210,420.

Mail, The: Mail Buildings, Mount Rd.; London Office: 151 Fleet St., E.C.4; f. 1867; evening; English; Independent; Editor T. A. SUBRAMANIAN; circ. 26,965.

Swadesamitran: Victory House, Mount Rd., 2; London Office: 2-3 Salisbury Court, E.C.4; f. 1880; evening; Tamil; Man. Editor C. R. RAMASWAMY; circ. 15,000.

Madurai

Dinamani: 137 Ramnad Rd. 9; f. 1951; morning; Tamil; Editor A. N. SIVRARAMAN; circ. 95,855.

Indian Express: 137 Ramnad Rd. 9; *see* under Delhi; circ. (Madurai, Madras, Bangalore and Vijayawada) **210,420.**

UTTAR PRADESH
Agra

Amar Ujala: City Station Rd., Agra 3, and 19 Cival Lines, Bareilly; f. 1948 and 1969, respectively; Hindi; Editor D. L. AGRAWAL; circ. (Agra) 35,160, (Bareilly) 11,054.

Sainik: Kaserat Bazar; f. 1925; Hindi; Editor SANTI PRASAD PATHAK; circ. 22,075.

Allahabad

Bharat: Leader Rd.; f. 1928; Hindi; Man. Editor Dr. M. D. SHARMA; Editor S. D. SVIVASTAVA; circ. 9,925.

Northern India Patrika: 10 Edmonstone Road; f. 1959; English; Chief Editor TUSHAR KANTI GHOSH; Gen. Man. KALYAN DASBUPTA; Resident Editor S. K. BOSE; circ. 36,450.

Kanpur

Daily Jagran: 2 Sarvodaya Nagar, P.O.B. 214; f. 1947; Hindi; Man. Editor P. C. GUPTA, Editor NARENDRA MOHAN; circ. 50,572.

Paigham: f. 1956; Urdu; Editor WAJIHUDDIN; circ. 10,562.

Pratap: 22/120 Shri Ganesh Shankar Vidyarthi Rd.; f. 1932; Hindi; Editor SURESH CHANDRA BHATTACHARYA; circ. 10,139.

Telegraph: 48/15 Lathimohal, Kanpur; f. 1943; English; Editor K. V. VENKATARUM; circ. 7,420.

Lucknow

National Herald: published by Associated Journals Ltd., P.O.B. 122; f. 1938 Lucknow, 1968 Delhi; English; Editor M. CHALAPATHI RAU; circ. 50,000.

Pioneer, The: 20A Vidhan Sabha Marg; f. 1865; English; Editor S. N. GHOSH; circ. 16,985.

Swantantra Bharat: f. 1947; Editor Y. P. TRIPATHI; circ. 15,330.

Varanasi

AJ: Kabirchaura, P.O.B. 7; f. 1920; Hindi; Editor S. K. GUPTA; circ. 42,032.

WEST BENGAL
Calcutta

Amrita Bazar Patrika: 14 Ananda Chatterji Lane; f. 1868; published at Calcutta; morning; English; Nationalist; Editor TUSHAR KANTI; circ. 121,831.

Ananda Bazar Patrika: 6 Prafulla Sarkar St.; f. 1878; morning; Bengali; Editor A. K. SARKAR; circ. 211,263.

Dainik Basumati: 166 Bepin Behari Ganguly St.; f. 1921; Bengali; independent Nationalist; Editor B. MUKHO-PADYAYA; circ. 112,777.

Hindusthan Standard: 6 Prafulla Sarkar St.; f. 1937; English; Editor SUDHANSHU KUMAR BASU; circ. 75,850.

Jugantar: 12 Ananda Chatterjee Lane; Bengali; f. 1937; Editor SOOKAMAL KANTI GHOSE; circ. 182,982.

Sanmarg: 160c Chittaranjan Avenue; f. 1948; Hindi; Nationalist; Editor P. A. MISHRA; circ. 14,262.

Statesman: Statesman House, 4 Chowringhee Square, also at Statesman House, New Delhi; London Office: Whitehall House, 41-43 Whitehall, S.W.1; f. 1875; morning; English; Independent; Editor K. RANGACHARI; circ. 191,039.

Vishwamitra: 12 Dalhousie Square East; f. 1916; morning; Hindi; commercial; Dir. B. C. AGARWAL; Editor KRISHAN CHANDRA AGRAWAL; circ. 47,731.

SELECTED PERIODICALS
NEW DELHI

Africa Diary: F-15 Bhagat Singh Market; f. 1961; African events, with Index; weekly; circulation in 75 countries; Editor HARI SHARAN CHHABRA.

African Recorder: 2, Gulmohai Park, P.O.B. 595, 1; f. 1962; fortnightly reference work on African affairs; Editor M. S. R. KHEMCHAND.

Akashvani: P.T.I. Bldg., 2nd Floor, Parliament St., Post Bag 12; All India Radio programmes; Sunday; English; Editor G. C. CHUCKERVERTTY; circ. 6,000.

Alochana: 8 Faiz Bazaar, 6; f. 1951; quarterly; literary criticism; Hindi; circ. 2,000.

Asian Recorder: C-1/9 Tilak Marg, P.O.B. 595, 1; f. 1955; weekly reference work on Asian affairs; circ. in 70 countries; Editor M. HENRY SAMUEL.

Astana: 722 Jama Masjid; f. 1950; Urdu; religion and philosophy; Editor M. M. FARUQI; circ. 60,041.

Caravan: Jhandewalan Estate, Rani Jhansi Rd.; f. 1940; fortnightly; English; Editor VISHWA NATH; circ. 25,000.

Careers and Courses: 94 Baird Rd.; f. 1949; monthly; English; Editor A. C. GOYLE; circ. 45,809.

Dinaman: 7 Bahadurshah Zaffar Marg; f. 1965; Hindi news weekly; Editor RAGHUVIR SAHAY; circ. 45,800.

Diplomat's Directory, The: C-1/9 Tilak Marg; f. 1961; half-yearly journal for diplomats; Editor M. HENRY SAMUEL.

Eastern Economist: United Commercial Bank Building, Parliament St., P.O.B. 34; f. 1943; weekly; English; Editor V. BALASUBRAMANIAN; circ. 5,600.

Filmi Duniya: 16 Darya Ganj, Delhi 6; f. 1958; monthly; Hindi; Editor NARENDRA KUMAR; circ. 100,000.

Foreign Affairs Reports: Indian Council of World Affairs, Sapru House, Barak Lamba Rd., New Delhi 1; f. 1952; monthly; Editor P. RATNAM.

Income & Opportunity: 94 Baird Rd.; f. 1968; monthly; English; Editor KULDIP GOYLE; circ. 18,000.

India Quarterly: Indian Council of World Affairs, Sapru House, Barakhamba Rd.; f. 1944; quarterly; Editor P. RATNAM.

Indian and Foreign Review: Shastri Bhavan; f. 1963; fortnightly; review of political, socio-economic and cultural aspects of India and India in relation to the world; Chief Editor R. P. DHAMIJA.

Indian Economic Diary: F-15 Bhagat Singh Market; f. 1970; weekly; Editor HARI SHARAN CHHABRA.

Indian Horizons: Azad Bhavan, Indraprastha Estate; f. 1951; quarterly; published by the Indian Council for Cultural Relations; Editor A. SRINIVASAN.

Indian Horticulture: India Council of Agricultural Research, Queen Victoria Rd.; also publishes *Indian Farming* and *Indian Journal of Agricultural Science*.

Indian Journal of Animal Sciences: c/o Indian Council of Agricultural Research, Dr. Rajendra Prasad Rd., New Delhi 110001.

Indian Journal of Biochemistry and Biophysics: Hillside Rd., New Delhi 12; f. 1964; quarterly; original research papers; Chief Editor A. KRISHNAMURTHI; circ. 1,200.

Indian Journal of Chemistry: Hillside Road, 12; f. 1963; monthly; original research papers; Chief Editor A. KRISHNAMURTHI; circ. 1,400.

Indian Journal of Experimental Biology: Hillside Road, 12; f. 1963; quarterly; original research papers; Chief Editor A. KRISHNAMURTHI; circ. 1,200.

Indian Journal of Medical Research: Indian Council of Medical Research, Medical Enclave, P.O.B. 4508; f. 1913; monthly; English; Editor Lt.-Col. M. L. AHUJA.

Indian Journal of Pure and Applied Physics: Hillside Road, 12; f. 1963; monthly; original research papers; Chief Editor A. KRISHNAMURTHI; circ. 1,200.

Indian Journal of Technology: Hillside Road, 12; f. 1963; monthly; original research papers in applied sciences and technology; Chief Editor A. KRISHNAMURTHI; circ. 1,200.

Indian Observer: 26F Connaught Place; f. 1958; weekly; English; Editor DURLAB SINGH; circ. 66,733.

Indian Railways: P.O.B. 467, Ministry of Railways, Govt. of India; f. 1956; English; monthly; Editor BEJAN MITRA; circ. 12,000.

Intensive Agriculture: Ministry of Food and Agriculture; monthly; English; circ. 45,000.

Jagat: 818 Kunde Walan, Ajmere Gate; f. 1958; monthly; Hindi; literary and cultural; Editor PREM CHAND VERMA; circ. 23,500.

Journal of Industry and Trade: Ministry of Foreign Trade; f. 1952; English; monthly; Dir. of Commercial Publicity V. C. TIWARI; circ. 4,000.

Journal of Scientific and Industrial Research: Hillside Rd., 12; f. 1942; monthly; Chief Editor A. KRISHNAMURTHI; circ. 1,600.

Krishak Samachar: A-1 Nizamuddin West; f. 1957; monthly; English, Hindi, Marathi; agriculture; Editor Dr. D. A. BHOLAY; circ. (English) 4,000, (Hindi) 4,000, (Marathi) 4,900.

Kurukshetra: Patiala House; fortnightly; English; community development and village democracy; Editor P. SRINIVASAN; circ. 12,000.

Lalita: 92 Daryaganj; f. 1959; monthly; Hindi; Editor SULBHA GUPTA; circ. 19,367.

Link Indian News Magazine: Link House, Mathura Rd.; f. 1958; Independent; weekly; Chair. of the Editorial Board EDATATA NARAYANAN.

Nav Chitrapat: 92 Daryaganj; f. 1932; monthly; Hindi; Editor SATYENDRA SHYAM; circ. 27,000.

New Age: 15 Kotla Rd., 1; f. 1953; organ of the Communist Party of India; weekly; English; Editor BHUPESH GUPTA, M.P.; circ. 15,684.

Organiser: 7E Rani Jhansi Marg, 55; f. 1947; weekly; English; Editor S. C. RAJE; circ. 40,000.

Panchjanya: Sanskriti Mandir, Jhan dewala, 55; f. 1947; weekly; Hindi; Gen. Man. JWALA PRASAD CHATURVEDI; Chief Editor K. R. MALKANI; circ. 44,000.

Parag: 10 Dariyaganj, 6; f. 1958; monthly; Hindi; London Office: 3 Albemarle St., W.1; Editor K. L. NANDAN; circ. 90,000.

Picture Parade: 5A/15 Ansari Rd., Darya Ganj; English; film monthly; Editor D. P. BERRY; circ. 10,000.

Picturegoer: 92 Daryaganj; f. 1940; monthly; English; Editor SATYENDRA SHYAM; circ. 5,000.

Prakashan Samachar: 8 Faiz Bazaar, 6; f. 1953; monthly; trade journal; Hindi; Editor Mrs. S. SANDHU; circ. 3,000.

Priya: 92 Daryaganj; f. 1960; monthly; Hindi; Editor SATYENDRA SHYAM; circ. 25,760.

Punjabi Digest: Union Bank Bldg., Ajmalkha Rd., P.O.B. 2549; f. 1971; literary; monthly; Gurmukhi; Chair. S. KAPUR SINGH, M.A., I.C.S.; Gen. Man. Sardar PARVESH BAHADUR SINGH; circ. 20,000.

Radical Humanist: F-8, Hauz Khas Enclave; f. 1937; monthly; English; Editor V. M. TARKUNDE; circ. 2,000.

Rang Bhumi: 5A/15 Ansari Road, Darya Ganj; f. 1941; Hindi; films; Editor D. P. GUPTA; circ. 25,269.

Review: Bombay Life Bldg., Connaught Circus; f. 1928; monthly; English; Editor FRANK ANTHONY; circ. 6,000.

Sainik Samachar: AFO Mess, Dr. Rajendra Prasad Rd.; f. 1909; weekly; English, Hindi, Urdu, Tamil, Punjabi, Telugu, Marathi, Gorkhali, Malayalam editions; for the Indian Defence Forces; Principal Officers Lt.-Col. J. GULERIA and Dr. S. S. SHASHI.

Saptahik Hindustan: N-Block, Connaught Circus; f. 1950; weekly; Hindi; Editor M. S. JOSHI; circ. 98,000.

Sarita: Jhandewala Estate, Rani Jhansi Rd.; f. 1945; fortnightly; Hindi; Editor VISHWA NATH; circ. 105,000.

Shama: 13/14 Asaf Ali Rd., Ajmeri Gate; f. 1939; monthly; Urdu; Editor M. YUSUF DEHLVI; circ. 120,583.

Shankar's Weekly: Odeon Top, Connaught Place; f. 1948; weekly; English; Editor K. S. PILLAI; circ. 10,995.

Sher-i-Punjab: Union Bank Bldg., Ajmalkhan Rd.; P.O.B. 2549; f. 1911; weekly news magazine; Urdu; Chief Editor Sardar JANG BAHADUR SINGH; Man. Editor Shri S. B. SINGH; circ. over 15,000.

Social Action: Indian Social Institute, Lodi Rd., New Delhi 110003; f. 1951; quarterly; Editor A. DE SOUZA.

Spokesman: 34 Theatre Communication Bldg., Connaught Place; f. 1951; weekly; English; Man. Editor GHANIS-HAM SINGH PASRICHA; circ. 10,000.

Sunday Standard: Sassoon Dock, Colaba; f. 1936; weekly; English; published simultaneously in Delhi, Madurai (Tamilnadu), Madras (Tamilnadu), Bangalore (Mysore), Vijayawada (Andhra Pradesh), Bombay (Maharashtra) and Ahmedabad (Gujarat); Editor-in-Chief FRANK MORAES; circ. (national) 600,000.

Sushama: 13/14 Asaf Ali Rd.; f. 1959; monthly; Hindi; Editor M. YUNUS DEHLVI; circ. 62,750.

Traveller in India: P.O.B. 2011, Delhi 6; f. 1957; monthly; English; transport and communication; Editor Director of Publications Division; circ. 17,551.

Vedic Light: Ram Lila Ground, Mahrshi Dayanand Bharvan; f. 1967; monthly; journal for Vedic ideology; Editor ACHARYA VAIDYANATH SHASTRI.

Vigyan Pragati: monthly; Hindi; scientific; circ. 29,500.

Yojana: Planning Commission, Yojana Bhavan; f. 1957; fortnightly; English, Tamil, Bengali and Hindi; Chief Editor S. SANYAL; circ. 15,000.

ANDHRA PRADESH
Hyderabad

Islamic Culture: P.O. Box 171; f. 1927; quarterly; English; Editor Dr. M. A. MUID KHAN.

Vijayawada

Sunday Standard: George Oakes Bldg., Besant Rd., Gandhinagar 3; *see* under Delhi; circ. (Vijayawada, Bangalore, Madras and Madurai) 235,600.

BIHAR
Patna

Balak: P.O.B. 5, Govind Mitra Rd.; f. 1926; monthly; Hindi; for children; Man. Editor M. S. SINGH; circ. 18,614.

Bihar Herald: Kadamkuan, Patna 3; f. 1874; weekly; English; Editor ARUN ROY CHOUDHURY; circ. 11,950.

Chunumunu: Naya Tola; f. 1950; monthly; Hindi; for children; Editor J. N. MISHRA; circ. 20,000.

Spark: Patna-3; f. 1947; weekly; English; Editor G. S. DALMIA; circ. 6,000.

Yogi: Buddha Marg; f. 1934; weekly; Hindi; Editor B. S. VERMA; circ. 16,295.

GUJARAT
Ahmedabad

Akhand Anand: P.O.B. 50, Bhadra; f. 1947; monthly; Gujarati; Editor T. K. THAKKAR; circ. 49,855.

Aram: Sandesh Limited Press Building, Gheekanta Road; f. 1961; monthly; Gujarati; Editor C. S. PATEL; circ. 7,549.

Chitralok: Gujarat Samachar Bhavan, Khanpur, P.O.B. 254, f. 1952; weekly; Gujarati; films; Editor SHREYANS SHAH; circ. 22,551.

Lokjivan: Navajivan Trust, P.O. Navajivan, 14; f. 1948; fortnightly; Gujarati; Editors BALMUKUND DAVE, RAGHUNATHAJI NAIK.

Shrirang: Gujarat Samachar Bhavan, Khanpur; f. 1955; monthly; Gujarati; Editor S. A. SHAH; circ. 4,623.

Sunday Standard: Janasatta Karyalaya, Mirzapur Rd.; circ. (Ahmedabad) 18,000.

Zagmag: Gujarat Samachar Bhavan, Khanpur; f. 1952; weekly; Gujarati; for children; Editor SHREYANS S. SHAH; circ. 29,730.

KARNATAKA (MYSORE)
Bangalore

Hosiery and Textile Journal: Kucba Rd., Mangatrai; monthly; English and Urdu.

Mysindia: 38A Mahatma Gandhi Road; f. 1939; weekly; English; Editor D. N. HOSALI; circ. 10,500.

Prajamata: North Anjaneya Temple Rd., Basavangudi; f. 1931; weekly; Kannada; Editor H. V. NAGARAJA RAO; circ. 85,000.

Sunday Standard: 1 Queen's Rd.; see under Delhi; circ. (Bangalore, Madurai, Madras and Vijayawada) 235,600.

KERALA
Trivandrum

Dakshina Bharathi: Convent Road; f. 1924; weekly; bi-lingual; Editor N. V. NAIR; circ. 2,000.

Janapatham: Government of Kerala; f. 1970; monthly; Malayalam; Editor M. DIVAKARAN; circ. 4,500.

Other Towns

Kerala Law Journal: 46 Robinson Rd., Calicut 1; f. 1956; English; weekly; Editor M. C. SEN.

Malayala Manorama: P.O.B. 26, Kottayam; f. 1956; weekly; Malayalam; Editor K. M. MATHEW; circ. 329,218.

Mathrubhumi Illustrated Weekly: Robinson Rd.; Kozhikode, Calicut; f. 1932; weekly; Malayalam, Chief Editor K. P. K. MENON; circ. 105,372.

MADHYA PRADESH

Krishak Jagat: P.O.B. 3, Bhopal-462-001; f. 1946; weekly; Hindi; also Marathi edition in Bombay; Man. Editor S. C. GANGRADE; Chief Editor M. C. BONDRIYA; circ. 15,513.

MAHARASHTRA
Bombay

Air and Space Age: Mehta House, Apollo St., Bombay 400001; monthly; circ. 3,000.

Aryan Path: 40 New Marine Lines, 400-020; London Office: 62 Queen's Gardens, W.2; f. 1930; monthly (except June and July); comparative religion and philosophy, literature and social problems; English; Editor SOPHIA WADIA.

Asia Bulletin: c/o Asia Publishing House, Calicut St., Ballard Estate; f. 1954; monthly; English; publicity journal; Editor P. S. JAYASINGHE; circ. 22,000.

Automobile News: Arna House, Calabar; monthly; English; circ. 3,580.

Beej: 62 Karwar Street; f. 1952; monthly; Gujarati; Editor Mrs. M. V. KOTAK; circ. 15,200.

Bharat Jyoti: 21 Dalal St., Fort, 1; f. 1938; weekly; English; Editor A. B. NAIR; circ. 69,243.

Bhavan's Journal: Bharatiya Vidya Bhavan, Chowpatty Rd.; f. 1954; fortnightly; English; Man. Editor J. H. DAVE; Editor S. RAMAKRISHNAN; circ. 37,180.

Blitz News Magazine: 17/17-H Cawasji Patel Street, Fort; f. 1941; weekly; English, Hindi, Urdu and Marathi editions; Editor-in-Chief R. K. KARANJIA; circ. 248,246.

Business Digest of India: monthly; mid-year (annual) and special number; circ. 10,000.

Chemical Industry Developments: 126A Dhurawadi, off Dr. Nariman Rd., Bombay 400025; monthly; English; circ. 4,000.

Chitralekha: Star Printery, 62 Karwar St.; f. 1950; weekly; Gujarati; Editor Mrs. M. V. KOTAK; circ. 9,904.

Commerce: Manek Mahal, 90 Veer Nariman Rd., Churchgate, 20; f. 1910; weekly; English; Editor VADILAL DAGLI; circ. 10,000.

Current: 15 Cawasji Patel Street; f. 1949; weekly; English; Editor D. F. KARAKA; circ. 23,128.

Dharmayug: Dadabhai Naoroji Road; London Office: 3 Albemarle Street, W.1; weekly; Hindi; Editor D. V. BHARATI; circ. 214,243.

Examiner: 35 Dalal St., Fort; f. 1850; weekly; English; religion, philosophy and general culture; Editor Rev. B. M. AGUIAR; circ. 8,500.

Illustrated Weekly of India: Dr. Dadabhai Naoroji Road; f. 1929; weekly; English; Editor KHUSHWANT SINGH; circ. 225,000.

Imprint: Surya Mahal, Military Square Lane, 1; f. 1961; monthly; English; Editor R. V. PANDIT; circ. 25,000.

India Quarterly: c/o Asia Publishing House, Calicut St., Ballard Estate, 1; f. 1953; journal of the Indian Council of World Affairs; Editor S. L. POPLAI.

Indian Cotton Growers' Review: monthly.

Indian and Eastern Engineer: Piramal Mansion, 235 Dadabhai Naoroji Rd., Bombay 400001; f. 1858; monthly; English; Dir. and Editor MICK DE SOUZA; Technical Editor S. K. GHASWALA.

Indian Machine Tools Journal: 75 New Stock Exchange Bldg., Apollo St., Fort 1.

Indian P.E.N.: Theosophy Hall, 40 New Marine Lines, Bombay 20; f. 1934; monthly; organ of Indian Centre of the International P.E.N.; Editor SOPHIA WADIA; Asst. Editor URMILA RAO.

Indian Rubber and Plastics Age: Manu Mansion, 3rd Floor, 16 Old Custom House Rd., Bombay 1.

Industrial India: 12 Rampart Row; monthly; English; official organ of the All-India Manufacturers' Asscn.

Janmabhoomi Pravasi: Janmabhoomi Bhavan, Ghoga St., P.O.B. 62, Fort; f. 1939; weekly; Gujarati; Dir. B. K. DOSHI; Editor M. V. MEHTA; circ. 72,519.

Journal of the Indian Institute of Bankers: Apollo Street; f. 1930; quarterly; English; Editor VADILAL DAGLI; circ. 50,000.

Kaiser-i-Hind: Kaiser Chambers, Town Hall Road, Fort; f. 1881; weekly; Anglo-Gujarati; National; Editor J. E. HEERJIBHEDIN; circ. 7,527.

Marg: Army-Navy Bldg., Mahatma Gandhi Rd.; f. 1946; quarterly; arts; Editor Dr. MULK RAJ ANAND.

Mother India: Sumati Publications Ltd.; f. 1960; monthly; English; Editor BABURAO PATEL, M.P.; circ. 12,500.

Onlooker: Seervai Bldg., 20G Sleater Rd., 7; f. 1939; monthly; English; Editor Mrs. FIROZE N. KANGA; circ. 6,000.

People's Raj (*Lokrajya*): Directorate of Publicity, Government of Maharashtra, Sachivalaya; f. 1947; government activities and publicity; fortnightly; edition in Marathi and English; circ. (all editions) 15,500.

Radio Times of India: 29 New Queen's Road; f. 1946; monthly; Editor D. D. LAKHANPAL.

Reader's Digest: Orient House, Mangalore St., Ballard Estate 1; f. 1954; monthly; English; Man. Dir. and Publisher T. PARAMESHWAR; circ. 175,000.

Samarpan: Bhartiya Vidya Bhavan, Chaupatty; f. 1957; fortnightly; Gujarati; circ. 5,966.

Sarika: Times of India Building, Dadabhai Naoroji Rd.; London Office: 3 Albemarle St., W.1; f. 1960; short story monthly; Hindi; Editor KAMLESHWAR; circ. 31,200.

Screen: Express Towers, Nariman Point, Bombay 400001; f. 1951; film weekly; English; Editor S. S. PILLAI; circ. 142,000.

Silk and Rayon Industries of India: monthly; English; circulates to 2,000 mills throughout India.

Star and Style: Bombay Samachar Marg, Bombay 400001; film and fashion fortnightly; English; Editor GULSHAN EWING; circ. 90,000.

Sudha: Janmabhoomi Bhavan, Ghoga St., Fort; f. 1968; Women's weekly; Gujarati; Propr. Saurashtra Trust; Editor D. G. PATEL; circ. 11,562.

Sunday Lokasatta: Newspaper House, Sassoon Dock, Colaba 5; f. 1948; Marathi; Editor R. N. LATE; circ. 28,996.

Sunday Standard: Sassoon Dock, Colaba; f. 1936; *see* under Delhi; circ. (Bombay) 110,700.

Teaching: Oxford University Press, Oxford House, Apollo Bunder, 1; f. 1928; quarterly; Editor MARGARET BENJAMIN; (*suspended*).

Urvashi: Lamington Road; f. 1959; weekly; Hindi; Editor R. R. K. NAHATA; circ. 11,292.

Vyapar: Janmabhoomi Bhavan, P.O.B. 62, Ghoga St., Fort; f. 1949; financial journal; twice weekly; Gujarati; Editor H. Z. GILANI; Gen. Man. RATILAL SHETH; Dir.-in-Charge B. K. DOSHI; circ. 21,141.

Nagpur

All India Reporter: Congress Nagar; f. 1922; monthly; English; Chief Editor S. APPU RAO; circ. 29,795.

Criminal Law Journal: All India Reporter Ltd., Congress Nagar; f. 1904; monthly; Editor S. APPU RAO; circ. 10,500.

Labour and Industrial Cases: Congress Nagar; f. 1968; monthly; English; Editor S. APPURAO; circ. 3,000.

Rekha: Chitar Oli Chowk, P.O.B. 373, Central Ave.; f. 1955; monthly; Hindi; Editor S. RANDIVE; circ. 22,766.

Taxation Law Reports: Congress Nagar; f. 1971; monthly; English; Editor S. APPURAO; circ. 3,000.

Poona

Swaraj: Bombay Papers Ltd., 595 Budhwar Peth; f. 1936; weekly; Marathi; Man. Lt.-Col. V. V. JOSHI (Retd.); circ. 90,000.

RAJASTHAN

Dharti-Ke-Lal: P.O.B. 12, Kota; f. 1953; monthly; Hindi; agricultural; Editor BABU HINDU; circ. 33,927.

Rastravani: Shayam Sunder Bhargava Building, Jaipur Road, Ajmer; f. 1951; weekly; Hindi; Editor K. BARNWALL; circ. 11,132.

TAMIL NADU
Madras

Ambili Ammavan: 2–3 Arcot Rd., Vadapalani; f. 1970; monthly; Malayalam; Editor Sri CHAKRAPANI; circ. 12,000.

Ambulimama: 2–3 Arcot Rd., Vadapalani; f. 1947; monthly; Tamil; Editor Sri CHAKRAPANI; circ. 38,000.

Ananda Vikatan: 151 Mount Rd.; f. 1924; weekly; Tamil; Editor S. BALASUBRA MANIAN; circ. 207,662.

Andhra Prabha Illustrated Weekly: Express Estates, Mount Rd., 600002; f. 1952; weekly; Telugu; Editor VIDVAN VISWM; circ. 124,575.

Andhra Sachitra Varapatrika: 6 and 7 Thambu Chetty St.; f. 1908; weekly; Telugu; Chief Editor S. RADHA-KRISHNA.

Antiseptic: 323/24 Thambu Chetty Street; f. 1904; monthly; English; Editor Dr. U. VASUDEVA RAU; circ. 13,975.

Bharatham: 2 R. K. Mutt Rd., Mylapore; f. 1959; weekly; Tamil; Editor P. S. RAJAGOPALAN; circ. 25,031.

Chandamama: 2-3 Arcot Road, Vadapalani; f. 1947; monthly; editions in Hindi, English, Gujerati, Telegu, Kannada and Bengali; Editor Sri CHAKRAPANI; combined circ. 298,000.

Chandoba: 2-3 Arcot Rd., Vadapalani; f. 1952; monthly; Marathi; Editor Sri CHAKRAPANI; circ. 66,500.

Cinema Rangam: 65/5, Arcot Rd., 24; f. 1954; monthly; Telegu; films; Editor T. V. RAMANATH; circ. 24,290.

Free India: 77 General Patters Road, Mount Road; f. 1939; weekly; English; Editor D. KRISHNAMURTHY; circ. 9,400.

Jahnamamu: 2-3 Arcot Rd., Vadapalani; f. 1972; monthly; Oriya; Editor Sri CHAKRAPANI; circ. 8,000.

Kalai: 193 Mount Rd.; f. 1958; monthly; Tamil; films; Editor A. SEENU; circ. 26,575.

Kalai Magal: P.O.B. 604, Madras 4; f. 1931; monthly; Tamil; Man. Editor K. V. JAGANNATHAN, M.A.; circ. 42,500.

Kalki: 20 Dr. Guruswamy Mudaliar Rd., Chetput, f. 1941; weekly; Tamil; Editor T. SADASIVAM; circ. 106,513.

Kumudam: 83 Purasawalkam High Road; f. 1947; weekly; Tamil; Editor S. A. P. ANNAMALAI; circ. 304,170.

Madras Law Journal: P.O.B. 604, Madras 4; f. 1891; weekly; English; Editor S. VENKATRAMAN; circ. 2,900.

Malai Mani: 50 Edward Elliots Rd.; f. 1958; weekly; Tamil; Editor P. S. ELANGO; circ. 48,000.

My Magazine of India: 11 Barracks Street, Seven Wells; f. 1929; monthly; English; Editor Miss V. SIVAGAMA-SUNDARI; circ. 12,000.

New Leader: 6 Armenian St.; f. 1887; weekly; English; Editor Rev. Fr. JAMES KOTTOOR; circ. 8,692.

Picture Post: 65/5 Arcot Rd., 24; f. 1943; monthly; Hindi; films; Editor T. V. RAMANATH; circ. 78,746.

Puthumai: 101 Purasawalkam High Road; f. 1957; monthly; Tamil; Editor K. T. KOSALRAM; circ. 34,875.

Sunday Standard: Express Estates, Mount Rd. 2; *see* under Delhi; circ. (Vijayawada, Bangalore, Madras and Madurai) 235,600.

Sunday Times: 69 Peters Rd.; f. 1956; weekly; English; Editor S. V. S. VINOD; circ. 45,923.

Swarajya: 20 Dr. Guruswamy Mudaliar Rd., Chetput; f. 1956; English; weekly; Editor PHILIP SPRATT; circ. 12,805.

Tamilnad Times: 105 C. N. Krishnaswamy Road; f. 1953; fortnightly; English; Editor M. RODGERS; circ. 30,341.

Thanga Thirai: 17 Whites Road, Royapettah; f. 1960; fortnightly; Tamil; Editor A. RAMAMURTHI; circ. 28,000.

Thayaga Kural: 2-16 Mount Road; f. 1961; weekly; Tamil; Editor A. MA. SAMY; circ. 48,900.

Vani: f. 1949; fortnightly; Telugu; All India Radio journal; circ. 16,000.

Vanoli: f. 1939; fortnightly; Tamil; All India Radio journal; circ. 54,000.

Other Towns

Dinamani Kadir: 137 Ramnad Rd. 9; Tamil; weekly; circ. 75,660.

Mathajothidam: 3 Arasamaram, Vellore; f. 1949; monthly; astrology; Tamil; Editor V. K. V. SUBRAMANYAM; circ. 25,961.

Sunday Standard: 137 Ramnad Rd., Madurai 9; *see* under Delhi; circ. (Madurai, Madras, Vijayawada and Bangalore) 235,600.

UTTAR PRADESH
Allahabad

Jasoosi Duniya: 5 Kolhan Tola St.; f. 1953; monthly; Hindi; Editor S. ABBAS HUSAINY; circ. 31,500.

Jasoosi Duniya: 5 Kolhan Tola St.; f. 1952; monthly; Urdu; Editor S. ABBAS HUSAINY; circ. 20,000.

Goenda Jagat: 5 Kolhan Tola St.; f. 1967; monthly; Bengali; Editor S. ABBAS HUSAINY; circ. 3,000.

Kahani: 5 Sardar Patel Marg; f. 1954; monthly; Hindi; Editor SRIPAT RAI; circ. 39,380.

Manmohan: Mitra Prakashan Ltd., 166 Muthiganj; f. 1949; monthly; Hindi; Editor S. V. A. MITRA; circ. 17,750.

Manohar Kahaniyan: Mitra Prakashan Ltd., 166 Muthiganj; f. 1940; monthly; Hindi; Editor R. P. SINGH and A. MITRA.

Manorma: Mitra Prakashan Ltd., 166 Muthiganj; f. 1924; monthly; Hindi; Editor H. D. CHATURVEDI; circ. 17,885.

Maya: 166 Muthiganj; f. 1929; monthly; Hindi; Editors R. P. SINGH and A. MITRA; circ. 35,306.

Saraswati: Indian Press (Publs.) Ltd., 36 Pannalal Rd.; f. 1900; monthly; Hindi; Editor S. N. CHATURVEDI.

Kanpur

The Citizen: P.O.B. 188, Bhargova Estate; f. 1940; weekly; English; Editor S. P. MEHRA; circ. 3,780.

Civic Affairs: P.O.B. 188, Bhargova Estate; f. 1953; monthly journal of city government in India; English; Editor S. P. MEHRA; circ. 2,605.

Vyapar Sandesh: 26/104 Birhana Rd.; f. 1950; weekly; Hindi; gives latest market reports and rates of various commodities; Editor HARISHANKAR SHARMA; circ. 19,700.

Lucknow

Gyan Bharati: B.N. Rd.; f. 1959; monthly; Hindi; Editor HARI KRISHNA; circ. 10,263.

Gyan Bhart Bal Pocket Books: B. N. Rd.; f. 1969; every two months; Hindi; Man. RAKESH BE.

Janmat: Bhopal House, Lall Bagh, P.O.B. 123; f. 1954; Sunday; Bengali; Editor NARENDRA PANDE; circ. 6,000.

Jan Yug: 22 Kaiserbagh; f. 1942; weekly; Hindi; Editor RAMESH SINHA; circ. 12,098.

People (The): 10 Bhopal House, Lall Bagh; f. 1959; weekly; English; Editor N. L. GAUTAM; circ. 7,001.

Rashtra Dharma: P.O.B. 207, Dr. Raghubir Nagar; f. 1964; monthly; Hindi; Editor BHANU PRATAP SHUKLA; Man. NAGESWAR SAHAI; circ. 15,000.

Other Towns

Current Events: 15 Rajpur Rd., Dehra Dun; f. 1955; monthly review of national and international affairs; English; Editor DEV DUTT; circ. 10,000.

Dhanwantari: P.O. Bijai Garh, Distt., Aligarh; f. 1924; monthly; Hindi; Editor V. D. S. GARG; circ. 17,756.

Indian Forester: F.R.I. and Colleges, P.O. New Forest, Dehra Dun; monthly; English; a journal of forestry, agriculture, Shikar, and travel; Editor R. C. GHOSH.

Jeevan Shiksha: Sarvodaya Sahitya Prakashan, Chowk, Varanasi; f. 1957; monthly; Hindi; Editor TARUN BHAI; circ. 11,550.

WEST BENGAL
Calcutta

Akashi: Eden Gardens; f. 1958; fortnightly; Assamese; radio journal; Editor Dr. A. B. GANGULY; circ. 500.

Asian Books Newsletter: 55 Gariahat Rd., P.O.B. 10210; record of books in English published in Asia; monthly; Editor Dr. K. K. ROY.

Assam Review and Tea News: 20 Waterloo St.; f. 1928; monthly; tea plantation industry; Editor J. N. BANERJEE.

Betar Jagat: All India Radio, Akashvani Bhawan, Eden Gardens; f. 1929; twice a month; Bengali; radio journal; Editor S. C. BASU; circ. 30,000.

Bulletin of the Institution of Engineers (India): 8 Gokhale Rd.; f. 1920; monthly; Editor Col. B. T. NAGRANI; circ. 25,000.

Calcutta Medical Journal: Calcutta Medical Club, 91-B Chittaranjan Avenue; f. 1906; Editor Dr. K. K. SEN GUPTA.

Capital: 19 R. N. Mookerjee Rd.; f. 1888; weekly; English; leading financial weekly in India; Editor A. K. GANGULY; circ. 3,000.

Chitra Bharati: 3 Bysak Dighi Lane; f. 1955; weekly; Hindi; Editor M. P. PODDAR; circ. 45,000.

Desh: 6 Prafulla Sarkar St.; f. 1933; weekly; Bengali; Editor A. K. SARKAR; circ. 66,243.

Economic Studies: 2 Private Road, Dum Dum.

Fashion: 3 Bysak Dighi Lane, 7; f. 1961; monthly; Hindi; Editor M. P. PODDAR; circ. 20,000.

Finance and Commerce: 4 Synagogue St., 1; monthly; company law, taxation, accountancy, economics, finance and allied matters; Exec. Editor J. K. SINHA.

Herald: 10 Government Place East, P.O. Box 445; f. 1931; weekly; English; Editor H. ROZARIO, S.J.; circ. 11,200.

India Railway Gazette: 13 Ezra Mansions, P.O.B. 2361, 1; London Office: 69 Fleet St., E.C.4; f. 1903; monthly; English; circulates in India, Pakistan, Ceylon, Malaysia, U.K., U.S.A., Japan and other countries; Man. Editor R. L. SARAOGI; Editor L. K. PADMA NABHAN; circ. 7,669.

Indian Medical Gazette: Block F, 105C New Alipore; f. 1961; monthly; English; Editor L. K. PANDEYA; circ. 7,689.

Indian Medical Review: 48B Sankaritola Street; f. 1953; monthly; English; Editor Dr. S. GHOSH; circ. 12,000.

Indian Minerals: Geological Survey of India; 29 Jawaharlal Nehru Rd., 16; f. 1947; Editors M. K. ROY CHOWDHURY, S. N. SEN, S. ROY, M. D. SRINIVASAN, A. BHATTACHARYA; circ. 1,500.

Indian Trade Journal: Ministry of Commerce and Industry; weekly; English; circ. 4,487.

Journal of the Indian Medical Association: 23 Samavaya Mansions, Corporation Place; f. 1930; twice monthly; English; Editor Dr. N. BANERJEE; circ. 32,000.

Journal of the Institution of Engineers (India): 8 Gokhale Rd.; f. 1920; monthly; English; Editor Col. B. T. NAGRANI; published in 8 parts, circ. of each part 15,000.

Journal of the Institution of Engineers (India) (Hindi Section): 8 Gokhale Rd.; f. 1920; 3 a year; Hindi; Editor Col. B. T. NAGRAWI; circ. of each part 10,000.

Modern Review: 77/2/1 Dharmtalla St.; f. 1907; monthly; English; independent; illustrated; socio-political; Editor ASHOKEE CHATTERJEE.

Mohammadi: 49 Gardener Lane; f. 1904; weekly; Bengali; leading organ of the Muslims; Independent; Editor Md. GHOUSUL ANAM KHAN.

Monthly Review: 5 Mission Row; f. 1936; monthly; English; Editor W. A. STUFF; circ. 4,000.

Naba Kallol: 11 Jhamapooker Lane; f. 1960; monthly; Bengali; Editor S. C. MAZUMDAR; circ. 50,000.

Neetee: 4 Sukhlal Johari Lane; f. 1955; weekly; English; Editor M. P. CHOUDHURY; circ. 25,000.

Planters Journal and Agriculturalist, The: 13 Ezra Mansions, P.O.B. 2361, 1; London Office: 69 Fleet St., E.C.4; f. 1924; monthly; English; circulates in India, Bangladesh, Ceylon, Malaysia, U.K., U.S.A., Japan and other countries; Editor L. K. PADMANABHAN; circ. 8,607.

Science and Culture: 93 Acharya Prelulla, Chandra Road.

Screen: 5 Sukhlal Johari Lane, 7; f. 1960; weekly; Hindi; Editor M. P. PODDAR; circ. 20,000.

Soviet Desh: 1/1 Wood St., 16; f. 1960; fortnightly; Bengali, Oriya and Assamese; Editor G. L. KOLOKOLOV circ. 66,000 (Bengali), 10,500 (Oriya), 12,500 (Assamese).

Statesman: Chowringhee Square; f. 1875; overseas weekly; English; Editor N. J. NANPORIA.

Students' Journal of the Institution of Engineers (India): 8 Gokhale Rd.; f. 1920; quarterly; English; Editor Col. B. T. NAGRANI; circ. of each part 40,000.

Suktara: 11 Jhamapooker Lane, 9; f. 1948; monthly; juvenile; Bengali; Editor M. MAJUMDAR; circ. 72,000.

Sunday Statesman: Chowringhee Square; weekly; Editor N. J. NANPORIA.

NEWS AGENCIES

Nafen (Near and Far East News Ltd.): 70 Forbes Street, Bombay, 1; British-owned; distributes news in English and Indian languages.

Press Trust of India: 357 Dr. D. Naoroji Rd., Bombay; obtains world news from Reuters, Agence France Presse, Kyodo, Allgemeiner Deutscher Nachrichtendienst (ADN), and United Press International, as well as from its own foreign correspondents; Gen. Man. K. S. RAMACHANDRAN.

FOREIGN BUREAUX

A.N.S.A.: D-31, South Extension Part 2, New Delhi 16; Chief Rep. Dr. LAMBERTO A. REM PICCI.

A.P.: 19 Narendra Place, Parliament St., New Delhi; Chief MYRON BELKIND.

Middle East News: 1B-120 Laipatnager, New Delhi; Correspondent K. G. GANABATHY.

Reuters Ltd.: 27-A Prithviraj Rd., New Delhi 11.

PRESS COUNCIL

Press Council of India: 10 Janpath, New Delhi 11; f. 1966; a statutory body formed to preserve the freedom of the Press and to maintain and improve the standards of newspapers and news agencies in India, the Council represents the newspaper management, journalistic profession, news agencies, Parliament, science, law and letters, and has power to examine journalists under oath, and may censure objectionable material, even if no law has been infringed, likewise it may condemn interference with Press freedom; Chair. Justice N. RAJAGOPALA AYYANGAR; Sec. B. P. MATHUR; 26 mems., excluding chairman.

PRESS ASSOCIATIONS

All-India Newspaper Editors Conference: 50–51 Theatre Communication Bldg., Connaught Place, New Delhi; Pres. B. N. AZAD.

Indian and Eastern Newspaper Society: I.E.N.S. Bldgs., Rafi Marg, New Delhi 110001; f. 1939; 273 mems.; Pres. K. M. MATHEW; Sec. G. P. C. GANDHI; publs. *IENS Annual Handbook*, monthly journal planned for 1974.

Indian Federation of Working Journalists: Flat No. 29, New Central Mkt., Connaught Circus, New Delhi-1; f. 1950; Pres. S. B. KOLPE; Sec.-Gen. B. R. VATS; publs. *India's Monopoly Press: A Mirror of Distortion*; *The Working Journalist* (monthly).

Indian Journalists Association: 1249-B Bowbazar Street, Calcutta 12; f. 1922; Pres. ADHIRCHANDRA BANJEE.

Indian Languages Newspapers Association: Janmabhoomi Bhavan, Ghoga Street, Fort, Bombay; f. 1941; 220 mems.; Pres. A. R. BHAT; publ. *Language Press Bulletin* (non-political monthly); circ. 450.

Press Institute of India: Sapru House Annexe, Barakhamba Rd., New Delhi 1; f. 1963; publ. *Vidura* (twice monthly) and special surveys; training courses.

Southern India Journalists' Federation: 15 Ritchie Street, Mount Road, Madras; f. 1950; 326 mems.; Pres. S. A. SUBBIAH; Sec. T. VADIVELU; publ. *The South Indian Journalist;* circ. 500.

PUBLISHERS

BOMBAY

George Allen & Unwin (India) Pvt. Ltd.: 103–105 Walchand Hirachand Marg., 1; f. 1970; Man. Dir. D. R. BHAGI.

Allied Publishers Private Ltd.: 15 Graham Rd., Ballard Estate, 1; f. 1934; economics, politics, history, philosophy; Chair. and Man. Dir. R. N. SACHDEV.

Asia Publishing House: Calicut St., Ballard Estate, 1; f. 1942; humanities, social sciences, science and general; English and Indian languages. Branches: Bangalore, Calcutta, New Delhi, Lucknow, Madras; London Office: 41 Short Gardens, W.C.2; New York Office: 420 Lexington Ave., N.Y. 10017.

Blackie and Son (India) Ltd.: Blackie House, 103–105 Walchand Hirachand Marg., P.B. 21, Bombay 1; f. 1901; educational, scientific and technical, general and juvenile; brs. at 285/J Bepin Behari Ganguly St.,

Calcutta 12; 2–18 Mount Rd., Madras 2; and 4/21-22B Asaf Ali Rd., New Delhi 1; Man. Dir. N. KUMARAVEL MUDALIAR.

Bombay Book Depot: Raja Ram Mohan Roy Marg, Girgaum 4; f. 1947; Partners S. BHATKAL, L. BHATKAL, P. N. KUMTNA, S. BHATKAL.

Hind Kitabs Ltd.: 32–34 Veer Nariman Rd., 1.

Jaico Publishing House: 125 Mahatma Gandhi Rd.; f. 1947; general paperbacks also scientific, technical and educational books; Dirs. JAMAN SHAH, ASHWIN SHAH.

Kitab Mahal Publishers (Wholesale Division) Private Ltd.: Zero Rd. 56-A, Allahabad; high-class Hindi general and educational; Propr. S. M. AGARWAL.

Nirmala Sadanand Publishers: 35c Tardeo Rd., Bombay 400 034 WB; f. 1967; Partners NIRMALA BHATKAL, MANMOHAN BHATKAL.

Popular Book Depot, The: Abid House, Dr. Bhadkamkar Rd., 400 007; f. 1924; Partners S. G. and R. G. BHATKAL.

Popular Prakashan Pvt. Ltd.: 35c Tardeo Rd., Bombay 400034; f. 1963; Dirs. S. G. and R. G. BHATKAL.

Prakashan Mandir: Dadysheth Agyary Lane 42; Propr. OMKAR KUMAR; importers and educational publishers.

Taraporevala, D. B., Sons and Co. (Private) Ltd.: 210 Dr. D. Naoroji Rd., Fort; f. 1864; general; Dir. M. J. TARAPOREVALA; Chief Executive R. J. TARAPOREVALA; publ. *Book Bulletin* (monthly); circ. 6,500.

N. M. Tripathi (Private) Ltd.: Samaldas Gandhi Marg, 2; f. 1888; Chair. P. J. PANDYA; publishers and booksellers, specializing in law and rare books: Dir. and Gen. Man. A. S. PANDYA; Commercial Man. Shri C. C. SHAH.

CALCUTTA

All-India Publishing Co. Ltd.: 30 Bidhan Sarani, 6; f. 1920; Man. Dir. K. G. DAS, B.L.

Assam Review Publishing Co.: 29 Waterloo St., 1; general; Man. J. N. BANNERJEE.

J. Banerjee and Co.: 29 Joy Mitter Street, 5; f. 1891; statisticians and market reporters; Propr. B. CHATTERJEE; Manager B. S. BANERJEE.

Book Co. Ltd., The: 53 Harrison Rd., 9; f. 1919; economics, politics, scientific, oriental, general and rare books; Dir. G. N. MITRA.

Britannia Publishers: 201 Harrison Road, 7; rare British, American and Continental publications.

British India Publishing Co.: Stephen House, Dalhousie Square, 1; Manager A. BRIMS; Asst. Manager S. J. HONEYWELL.

Chuckerverty, Chatterjee and Co. Ltd.: 15 College Square, 12; Dir. BINODELAL CHAKRAVARTI.

David Maximillian and Co.: 12B Windsor House, Mission Row Extension, 1; Propr. C. C. DAVID.

Eastern Law House (Private) Ltd.: 54 Ganesh Chunder Ave., Calcutta 13; f. 1918; legal, commercial, accountancy and general; Man. Dir. ASOK DE; Dirs. B. C. DE, A. K. DE, A. DE, ASOK DE.

Essce (Private) Ltd.: 25 Ganesh Chunder Avenue, 13; f. 1940; general; Dirs. G. KIDD, S. H. ELLIOTT, B. SEE.

Firma K. L. Mukhopadhyay: 257B B. B. GANGULY St., f. 1950; Man. Dir. K. L. MUKHOPADHYAY.

Gurudas Chatterjee and Sons: Bidhan Sarani 203, 6; Editor B. P. N. MUKHERJEE; general.

Ideal Publishers: 28/14 Station Road, 31; Propr. Mrs. P. DAS; Manager U. DAS.

Intertrade Publications (India) Private Ltd.: 55 Gariahat Rd., P.O.B. 10210; f. 1954; publs. Nepal *Trade Directory*, technical and general books; Man. Dir. Dr. K. K. ROY.

Khadi Pradisthan: 15 College Square, 12; Manager A. C. DAS GUPTA; Sec. H. P. DEVI.

Macmillan Company of India Pte., Tne: Head Office: 2/10, 4242 Ansari Rd., Daryaganj, Delhi 6; brs. in Calcutta, Bombay and Madras; Man. U. N. BANERJEE; Asst. Man. A. K. ROY.

Market Reports Publishing Co.: 9 Royal Exchange Place, 1; general; Propr. R. D. KHEDIA.

A. Mukherjee & Co. (P) Ltd.: 2 Bankim Chatterjee St., 12; f. 1940; educational and general; Man. Dir. AMIYA RANJAN MUKHERJEE.

New Era Publishing Co.: 31 Gauri Bari Lane, 4; f. 1944; Propr. Dr. P. N. MITRA, M.A., B.L., D.S.C (U.S.A.); Man. S. K. MITRA.

W. Newman and Co. Ltd.: 3 Old Court House St., 1; f. 1854; general; Man. Dir. O. P. BHARGAVA.

Oriental Publishing Co.: 110 Arpuli Lane, 12; f. 1910; Propr. D. N. BOSE; Man. D. P. BOSE.

Oxford and IBH Publishing Co.: Park Hotel Bldg., 17 Park St., 16; Branch Office: 66 Janpath, New Delhi 110001; science and technology; Mans. GULAB PRIMLANI, MOHAN PRIMLANI.

Oxford Book and Stationery Co.: 17 Park St., 16; f. 1921; Man. GULAB PRIMLANI.

Ray, Chaudhury and Co.: 119 Ashutosh Mukherjee Rd., 25; Man. A. C. R. CHAUDHURY.

Renaissance Publishers Private Ltd.: 15 Bankim Chatterjee St., 12; philosophy; founder M. N. ROY.

M. C. Sarkar and Sons (Private) Ltd.: 14 Bankim Chatterjee St., 12; general.

Thacker's Press and Directories Ltd.: 6B Bentinck St., 1; London Agents: Keith & Slater Ltd., 24–27 High Holborn, W.C.1; *Indian Directory and World Trade.*

DELHI

Amerind Publishing Co. (Pvt.) Ltd.: 66 Jampath, 1; offices at Calcutta, Bombay and New York; Dirs. G. PRIMLANI M. PRIMLANI.

Atma Ram and Sons: Kashmere Gate, Delhi-110006; brs. Jaipur, Lucknow, Chandrigarh.

S. Chand and Co. (Pvt.) Ltd.: Ram Nagar, 110055; f. 1917; educational and general books in Hindi and English; brs. in Jullundur, Lucknow, Bombay, Calcutta, Madras, Hyderabad, and Patna.

City Booksellers: Sohanganj St.; f. 1939; general; Propr. H. CHANDRA.

Eurasia Publishing House (Private) Ltd.: Ram Nagar, New Delhi 55; educational books in English and Hindi; Dirs. S. L. GUPTA, RAJ KUMAR SETH, R. K. GUPTA.

George G. Harrap and Co. Ltd.: c/o Oxford University Press, 2/11 Ansari Rd., Daryaganj, 6; educational.

Hind Pocket Books Private Ltd.: G. T. Rd., Shahdara, Delhi, 110032; f. 1958; paperbacks in English, Hindi, Punjabi and Urdu; Man. Dir. DINASATH MALHOTRA; Sec. VISHWA NATH.

Indian University Publishers Ltd.: Kashmere Gate, 6; f. 1950; technical and general in English, Hindi, Urdu and Punjabi; Man. C. B. MENDN.

Khosla Publishing Co.: 3 Netaji Sukhas Marg, Daryaganj, P.O.B. 1389, Delhi 6; f. 1901; directories; Partners K. R. and K. R. KHOSLA.

Neel Kawal Prakashau: Raj Bhawan, 4/C Daryaganj; educational; Propr. S. K. AGGARWAL.

New Book Society of India: 6A, 53 W.E.A. Pusa Rd.

Orient Longmans Ltd.: 3–5 Asaf Ali Rd., 11001; Dir. and Sec. P. H. PATWARDHAN.

Oxford University Press: 2/11 Ansari Rd., Daryaganj, Delhi 6; brs. at Bombay, Calcutta and Madras; Gen. Man. C. H. LEWIS.

People's Publishing House Ltd.: Rani Jhansi Rd.; f. 1943; Gen. Man. N. PISHARODI.

Publications Division, The: Ministry of Information and Broadcasting, Government of India, Patiala House, New Delhi; art, literature, planning and development, general publications.

Rajkamal Prakashan (Private) Ltd.: 8 Faiz Bazar, 6; f. 1946; Hindi; literary books, quarterly journal of literary criticism, monthly trade journal.

Rajpal and Sons: Kashmere Gate, 6; f. 1891; literary criticism, social and general, humanities, text books, juvenile literature; Hindi and English; Partners DINA NATH MOLHOTRA, VISHWA NATH.

Ranjit Printers and Publishers: 4872 Chandni Chowk, 6; f. 1949; historical, economical, political and general in Hindi and English; Managing Dirs. M. C. GUPTA and R. M. SHAHANI.

Roshan Book Depot: Nai Sarak; educational; Propr. G. DASS AGGARWAL.

Sahgal, N. D., and Sons: Dariba Kalan; f. 1917; politics, history, general knowledge, sport, fiction and children's books, in Hindi; Manager G. SAHGAL.

Shiksha Bharati: Madarsa Rd., Kashmere Gate, 6; f. 1955; textbooks, popular science books and children's books in Hindi and English; General Man. SMT. VEENA MALHOTRA.

Technical and Commercial Book Co.: 75 Gokhale Market, Tis Hazari; f. 1913; Propr. B. R. MALHOTRA, B.A.; Man. D. N. MEHRA.

Yadav Prakahsan: Ajmeri Dwar; anatomy books, and charts in Hindi and English; Proprs. Y. N. and S. MITAL.

MADRAS

Higginbothams (Private) Ltd.: 165 Mount Rd., 2; branches at Bangalore, Ootacamund, Trivandrum, Coimbatore, Ernakulam, Mysore, Hyderabad and Madurai.

B. G. Paul and Co.: 4 Francis Joseph St.; f. 1923; general, educational and oriental; Man. K. NILAKANTAN.

Ranga Raju and Bros: Jagannadha Baugh, Saidapet; general; Propr. J. R. RANGA RAJU; Mans. J. P. RAJU, J. K. RAJU.

Srinivasa Varadachari and Co.: 2–16 Mount Rd.; f. 1879; educational; Propr. G. VENKATACHARI.

Thompson and Co. (Private) Ltd.: 33 Broadway, 1; general.

OTHER TOWNS

Balkrishna Book Co.: B-12A Niralanagar, Lucknow 7; f. 1944; general, scientific and Oriental; Propr. BAL-KRISHNA.

Banaras Book Corpn.: University Rd., Banaras; educational; Dir. L. N. AGARWAL; Man. R. K. AGARWAL.

Catholic Press: Ranchi (Bihar); f. 1930; Dir. Rev. W. DELPUTTE, S.J.

Central Book Depot: 44 Johnston-gunj, Allahabad; Man. B. K. CHATTERJI.

P. C. Dwadash Shreni and Co. Ltd.: Barasani Bazaar, Aligarh; f. 1895; Dirs. H. C. and T. C. DWADASH SHRENI.

Garga Bros.: 1 Katra Rd., Allahabad; f. 1949; educational and reference; Partners R. N. GARGA, T. N. Garga, P. N. GARGA, SANJAI GARGA.

Hindi Sahitya Sadan: Jahanabad P.O., Gaya; general; Proprs. R. PATHAK, K. N. SINHA; Man. N. K. PATHAK, M.I.S.A.

Hindusthan Publishing House: Shanti Bhawan, Nayagaon, Lucknow; Propr. A. KUMVR; Man. M. KUMAR.

Kitabistan: 30 Chak, Allahabad 211003.

Law Book Co.: Sardar Patel Marg, P.O.B. 4, Allahabad 1; f. 1929; legal books; Partners R. R. BAGGA, L. R. BAGGA, B. M. BAGGA, D. BAGGA.

Maheshanand and Sons: Bhaskar Bhavan, Ashoknagar, Lucknow; Man. SHIV PRASAD NAUTIYAL.

Narain Publishing House: Ajitmal, Etawah, Uttar Pradesh; f. 1941; publishers of illustrated *Hindi Who's Who*, directories and general; Propr. Mrs. LILA AGRAWAL.

Navajivan Publishing House: P.O. Navajivan, Ahmedabad, 380014; f. 1919; Gandhian literature; Chair. MORARJI DESAI; Sec. JITENDRA DESAI.

Pioneer Publishing Co.: 40 Elgin Rd., Allahabad 1; f. 1972; law books; Partners J. N. BAGGA, Miss R. BAGGA, Mrs. S. BAGGA.

Rabindra Book Depot: Hospital Rd., Agra; educational; Propr. S. S. LALL BUDHIRAJA; Man. R. K. BUDHIRAJA.

Ram Prasad and Sons: Hospital Rd., Agra 3; f. 1905; agricultural, arts, commerce, education, general, science, technical, economics, mathematics, sociology; Dirs. H. N., R. N., B. N. and Y. N. AGARWAL; Mans. S. N. AGARWAL and R. S. TANDON.

S. J. Singh and Co.: 51–52 Gwynne Rd., Lucknow; nature cure, health, general; Man. S. J. SINGH.

Standard Book Depot: Chowk, Kanpur; official agents for Govt. of U.P.; Propr. G. P. GARG; Man. B. N. AGARWAL.

United Publishers: 1 Katra Rd., Allahabad; f. 1964; reference and degree class publishers; Propr. Mrs. SHILA GARGA.

University Book Agency: 15B Elgin Rd., Allahabad; law; Partners S. D. KHANNA, L. KHANNA, N. KHANNA, K. KHANNA.

Upper India Publishing House Pvt. Ltd.: Aminabad, Lucknow; f. 1921; publishers of books in English and Hindi special subjects—Indian philosophy, history, religion, art and science; Man. Dir. S. BHARGAVA.

Uttarakhand Press: Bhaskar Bhavan, Ashoknagar, Lucknow.

RADIO AND TELEVISION

RADIO

All India Radio (AIR): Akashvani Bhavan, Parliament St., New Delhi 1; broadcasting in India is controlled by the Ministry of Information and Broadcasting. The service is financed from grants voted by Parliament annually; Dir.-Gen. SUBHAS KUMAR MUKHERJEE.

A comprehensive development plan has been evolved and there are now seventy-one broadcasting stations in the whole of India. There are at present regional stations operating from the following centres:

North: Delhi, Ajmer, Allahabad, Bhagalpur, Bhopal, Bikaner, Chandigarh, Gwalior, Indore, Jabalpur, Jaipur, Jodhpur, Jullundur, Kanpur, Lucknow, Mathura, Patna, Ranchi, Raipur, Rampur, Simla, Udaipur, Varanasi and Aligarh.

West: Bombay, Nagpur, Ahmedabad, Baroda, Poona, Rajkot, Bhuj, Parbhani, Panaji, Sangli, Rajkot.

South: Madras, Tiruchi, Vijayawada, Trivandrum, Alleppey, Hyderabad, Trichur, Dhawar, Bangalore, Tirunelveli, Calicut, Vishakhapatnam, Cuddapah, Bhadravathi, Pondicherry, Gulbarga, and Coimbatore.

East: Calcutta, Cuttack, Gauhati, Kohima, Sambalpur, Siliguri, Port Blair, Imphal, Kurseong, Agartala, Shillong, Aijal, Tezu, Pasighat and Dibrugarh.

Radio Kashmir broadcasts from Srinagar, Jammu and Leh.

Broadcasting is particularly important in India owing to the difficulty of reaching the vast masses of the people by any medium other than the spoken word. To enable AIR to reach rural areas, listening is arranged by means of community sets installed for public use in a large number of villages.

A I R network is equipped with a total of 138 transmitters (medium and shortwave) and covers all the important linguistic areas in the country.

The News Services Division, centralized in New Delhi, is one of the largest news organizations in the world. In all, it broadcasts 232 daily news bulletins in 37 languages and in as many dialects, from Delhi in Home and External Services and from regional stations. The External Service transmit 55 news bulletins daily in 24 languages.

As on December 31st, 1971, there were 12,772,797 radio licences issued.

TELEVISION

Akashvani Doordarshan (*All India Radio-Television*): Television Centre, Akashwani Bhawan, Parliament St., New Delhi 1; f. 1959; Dir. ROMESH CHANDER; programmes: 25½ hours weekly (15½ hours general service, 10 hours school service).

Bombay: began transmissions in November 1972; comprises TV studio at Worli and relay transmitter at Sinhagarh, near Poona; broadcasts for 2½ hours in the evenings mainly in Hindi and Marathi.

Srinagar: commenced broadcasting three days a week from February 1973 in Urdu and Kashmiri; Dir. SHAILENDRA SHANKAR.

Amritsar: expected to begin transmitting full programmes in late 1973.

Jaipur: Expected to begin broadcasting by 1979.

Madras: Expected to be commissioned in January 1974.

Lucknow: Expected to begin broadcasting from March 1974; a relay transmitter at Kanpur will extend the range of Lucknow's transmissions.

Calcutta: Expected to begin transmitting in March 1974 using relay stations at Durgapur, Asansol, Midnapur and Khargapur.

The Minister of State for Information and Broadcasting in February 1973 indicated that most of the population will be covered by radio and television by 1979.

In 1972 there were about 20,000 domestic TV sets in use.

FINANCE

(cap.=capital; p.u.=paid up; dep.=deposits; m.=million; Rs.=rupees; brs.=branches.)

BANKING
STATE BANKS

Reserve Bank of India: Mint Rd., Bombay 1; f. 1935; nationalized January 1949; has the sole right to issue notes in India; cap. Rs. 50m., dep. Rs. 5,862.9m. (June 1972); Gov. S. JAGANATHAN; Deputy Govs. J. J. ANJARIA, P. N. DAMRY, R. K. HAZARI; 11 brs.

State Bank of India: Apollo St., Fort, Bombay 1; London Office: 14-18 Gresham St., E.C.2; inc. in India under the State Bank of India Act, 1955; cap. Rs. 56.3m., dep. Rs. 22,261.8m. (Dec. 1972); Chair. R. K. TALWAR; Man. Dir. T. R. VARADACHARY; Chief Man. Int. Div. K. K. BANERJI; 2,484 brs.

India's 14 major commercial banks, listed below, were nationalized by special ordinance in July 1969. Though this was declared to be unconstitutional by the Supreme Court in February 1970, subsequent legislation was passed granting compensation while still allowing the banks to operate as independent units. Eventually they are to be managed by fifteen-member Boards of Directors, five of whom will be government appointed. The day-to-day administration of the bank is one of the chief functions of the government *Custodian* or Bank Chairman. The Department of Banking of the Ministry of Finance now controls all banking operations.

Since nationalization, the number of bank branches has grown from 8,262 to 13,620 (June 1972) whilst deposits have increased from 40,000m. to Rs. 75,000 m. (June 1972).

Allahabad Bank Ltd.: 14 India Exchange Place, Calcutta 1; f. 1865; cap. Rs. 10.5m., dep. Rs. 1,600.4 (Dec. 1971); Custodian B. K. MOOKERJEA; Gen. Mans. R. P.SINGH, B. LONGMATE, A. GHOSH; 290 brs.

Bank of Baroda: Head Office: Mandvi, Baroda; London Office: 31-32 King's St., E.C.2; f. 1908; cap. Rs. 25m., dep. Rs. 6,352.2m. (Dec. 1972); Custodian V. D. THAKKAR; 710 brs.

Bank of India: Express Towers, Nariman Point, Bombay 400001; London: Kent House, 11-16 Telegraph St., E.C.2; f. 1906; cap. p.u. Rs. 40.5m., dep. Rs. 7,187.9m. (Dec. 1972); Custodian JAGDISH N. SAXENA; 620 brs.

Bank of Maharashtra Ltd.: 1177 Budhwar Peth, Poona City 2; f. 1935; cap. Rs. 22m., dep. Rs. 1,320m. (June 1972); Custodian C. V. JOAG; 211 brs.

Canara Bank Ltd: Head Office, 112 Jayachamarajendra Rd., Bangalore 560002, P.B. 6648; f. 1906; cap. Rs. 17.5m., dep. Rs. 3,845.8m. (Dec. 1972); Custodian K. P. J. PRABHU; 688 brs. Publ. *Canara Bank Quarterly*.

Central Bank of India: Chander Mukhi, Narinam Point, Bombay 400001; London: 42–45 New Broad St., E.C.2; f. 1911; cap. p.u. Rs. 47.5m., dep. Rs. 8,047.7m. (Dec. 1972); Custodian B. N. ADARKAR; 1,099 brs.

Dena Bank Ltd.: Devkaran Nanjee Bldgs., 17 Horniman Circle, Bombay 1; f. 1938; cap. Rs. 12.5m., dep. Rs. 2,376.9m. (Dec. 1972); Custodian R. A. GULMOHAMED; Gen. Man. H. K. SWALI; 527 brs.

Indian Bank: Indian Bank Bldgs., 17 North Beach Rd., Madras 1; f. 1907; cap. p.u. Rs. 20m., dep. Rs. 1,789.9m. (Dec. 1972); Custodian G. LAKSHMINARAYANAN; Sec. K. VENKATRAMA AIYER; 360 brs.

Indian Overseas Bank: 151 Mount Rd., Madras 2; f. 1937; cap. p.u. Rs. 20m., dep. Rs. 1,640m. (Dec. 1972); Chair. A. M. KADHIRESAN; Gen. Man. S. V. SUNDARAM.

Punjab National Bank Ltd.: 5 Parliament St., New Delhi; f. 1895; cap. p.u. Rs. 20m., dep. Rs. 5,272m. (Dec. 1971); Custodian P. L. TANDON; Gen. Man. SITA RAM MOHINDROO; 910 brs.

Syndicate Bank: Manipal, South Kanara, Karnataka; f. 1925; cap. Rs. 14.2m., dep. Rs. 2,711m. (Dec. 1972); Custodian K. K. PAI; Gen. Man. H. N. RAO; 564 brs.

Union Bank of India: 66–80 Bombay Samachar Marg, Fort, Bombay 400001; f. 1919; cap. p.u. Rs. 12.5m., dep. Rs. 2,986m. (June 1973); Custodian P. F. GUTTA; Gen. Man. S. D. PARDIWALLA; 529 brs.

United Bank of India Ltd.: 16 Old Court House St., Calcutta 1; f. 1950; cap. p.u. Rs. 26.9m., dep. Rs. 2,478.3m. (Dec. 1971); Custodian B. K. DUTT, Gen. Man. M. SEN SARMA; 353 brs.

United Commercial Bank Ltd.: 10 Brabourne Rd., Calcutta 700001; London: 12 Nicholas Lane, E.C.4; f. 1943; cap. p.u. Rs. 28.0m., dep. Rs. 4,178m. (Dec. 1972); Custodian R. DESAI; 610 brs.

OTHER COMMERCIAL BANKS

Andhra Bank Ltd.: 11/666 Rabindranath Tagore Rd., Machilipatnam; f. 1923; cap. Rs. 50.4m., dep. Rs. 650m. (Dec. 1970); Chair. K. GOPAL-RAO; Gen. Man. M. V. SUBBA RAO; 217 brs.

Bank of Cochin Ltd.: Broadway, Ernakulam; f. 1928; cap. p.u. Rs. 475,672.5, res. Rs. 592,715 (Dec. 1972); Chair. K. M. THARIYAN; Asst. Man. E. K. ANDREW, B.A., B.COM.; 31 brs.

Hindusthan Mercantile Bank Ltd.: 10 Clive Row, Calcutta; cap. p.u. Rs. 5m.; Chair. SETH MOHANLAL JALAN.

Mysore State Co-operative Apex Bank Ltd., The: 1 Pampamahakavi Rd., P.B. 654, Chamarajpet, Bangalore 18; f. 1915; cap. Rs. 28.7m., dep. Rs. 126.6m.; Pres. VEERASETHY CUSHANOOR; Man. Dir. H. K. CHINAIDAIAH.

State Bank of Bikaner and Jaipur: S.M.S. Highway, Jaipur; f. 1944; re-formed 1960 as a subsidiary of the State Bank of India; cap. Rs. 8m., dep. Rs. 1,064.9m. (Dec. 1972); Gen. Man. C. P. SAIGAL.

State Bank of Hyderabad: Gunfoundry, Hyderabad; f. 1941; re-constituted 1959 as subsidiary of the State Bank of India; cap. Rs. 5m., edp. Rs. 1,094.3m. (Dec. 1972); Chair. R. K. TALWAR; Gen. Man. S. K. DATTA.

State Bank of Indore: Bombay Agra Rd., Indore; f. 1920; re-formed 1960 as a subsidiary of the State Bank of India; cap. Rs. 3.5m., dep. Rs. 430m. (Dec. 1971); Chair. R. K. TALWAR; Gen. Man. M. V. BHIDE.

State Bank of Mysore: P.O.B. 9727, Kempegowda Rd., Bangalore 56009; f. 1913; re-formed 1960 as a subsidiary of the State Bank of India; cap. Rs. 10m., dep. Rs. 900m. (Dec. 1972); Chair. R. K. TALWAR; Gen. Man. C. VEERARAGHAVAN.

State Bank of Patiala: The Mall, Patiala; f. 1917; in 1960 re-formed as a subsidiary of the State Bank of India; cap. Rs. 3.5m., dep. Rs. 881m. (Dec. 1972); Chair. R. K. TALWAR; Gen. Man. S. D. GANDA.

State Bank of Saurashtra: P.O.B. 51, Bhavnagar; f. 1950; re-formed 1960 as a subsidiary of the State Bank of India; cap. Rs. 10m., dep. Rs. 666.1m. (Dec. 1971); Chair. R. K. TALWAR; Gen. Man. Shri H. S. MAJUMDER.

State Bank of Travancore: P.O.B. 34, "Devaswom Board Building", Trivandrum 1 (Kerala); f. 1945; re-formed 1960 as a subsidiary of the State Bank of India; cap. Rs. 10m., dep. Rs. 864.2m. (Dec. 1972); Chair. R. K. TALWAR; Gen. Man. S. NIYOGI.

FOREIGN BANKS

Algemene Bank Nederland, N.V.: 32 Vijzelstraat, Amsterdam; Bombay; Man. M. W. VAN HULZEN; in Calcutta, Man. C. H. MATHIEU.

American Express Co. Inc.: 65 Broadway, New York, N.Y.; Oriental Building, 364 Dr. Dadabhai Naoroji Road, Bombay; also in Delhi and Calcutta; f. 1919.

Bank of Tokyo Ltd.: 6, 1-chome, Nihombashi Hongoku-cho, Chuo-ku, Tokyo, Japan; Calcutta, Bombay, New Delhi.

Banque Nationale de Paris: 16 blvd. des Italiens, Paris 9; offices in India: Bombay, Calcutta; representative in New Delhi.

British Bank of the Middle East: 20 Abchurch Lane, London, EC4N 7AY; 314 Dr. Dadabhai Naoroji Rd., Fort, Bombay 1.

The Chartered Bank: 38 Bishopsgate, London, EC2N 4AH; Indian branches: Amritsar, Bombay (6 offices), Calcutta (8 offices), Calicut, Cochin, Delhi, Kanpur, Madras (3 offices), New Delhi, Sambhaji.

First National City Bank: 399 Park Avenue, New York 10022, N.Y.; Bombay (3 offices): 293 Dr. Dadabhai Naoroji Rd.; Calcutta (2 offices), Madras (2 offices), New Delhi.

Mercantile Bank Ltd.: 15 Gracechurch St., London, EC3N 0DU; Bombay, Calcutta, Delhi, Madras and Visakhapatnam.

Mitsui Bank Ltd.: 12 Yurakucho 1-chome, Chiyoda-ku, Tokyo; Bombay.

National and Grindlays Bank Ltd.: 23 Fenchurch St., London, EC3M 3DD; Netaji Subhas Rd., Calcutta; Amritsar, Bangalore, Bombay, Cochin, Darjeeling, Delhi, Lahore, Madras, Simla, etc.

BANKING ASSOCIATION

Indian Banks' Association: Stadium House, 81-83 Veer Nariman Rd., Bombay 400-020; founded to promote the interests of Indian Banks; 64 mems.; Chair. B. N. ADARKAR; Sec. S. G. SHAH.

DEVELOPMENT FINANCE ORGANIZATIONS

Agricultural Finance Corpn.: Dhanraj Mahal, Chatrapati Shivaji Maharaj Marg, Bombay 1; finances irrigation schemes and other projects, techno-economic and investment surveys and project analyses; Chair. Prof. M. L. DANTWALA; Man. Dir. B. RUDRAMOORTHY; Sec. V. K. SHETH.

Agricultural Refinance Corporation: Post Box No. 6552, Worli, Bombay 18 WB; f. 1963 to provide medium-term or long-term finance to the various special schemes of agricultural development which cannot be satisfactorily financed by existing credit agencies; Chair. P. N. DAMRY; Man. Dir. K. MADHAVA DAS.

Credit Guarantee Corporation of India: Vidyut Bhavan, 3rd Floor, B.E.S.T. Bldg., Pathakwadi, Bombay 400002; f. 1971; guarantees loans and other credit facilities extended by banks to small borrowers and co-operative societies; Chair. Dr. R. K. HAZARI; Man. M. J. AMBANI; Sec. F. O. Doss.

Industrial Development Bank of India (IDBI): New India Centre, 17 Cooperage, P.O.B. 1241, Bombay 1; f. 1964; wholly owned subsidiary of the Reserve Bank to co-ordinate and supplement other financial organizations and to finance and promote industrial development; regional offices at Calcutta, Madras, New Delhi and brs. in 11 states; auth. cap. Rs. 500m.; Chair. Shri S. JAGANNATHAN; Vice-Chair. Shri V. V. CHARI; Board of Dirs. (*see* Reserve Bank of India); Gen. Man. C. S. VENKAT RAO.

Industrial Finance Corporation of India: Bank of Baroda Bldg., 16 Parliament St., New Delhi 1, brs. at Calcutta, Bombay, Madras, Ahmedabad, Hyderabad, and Ganhati; f. 1948 under the Industrial Finance Corporation Act to provide medium- and long-term finance to private and public limited companies and Co-operative Societies incorporated and registered in India, engaged in manufacture, preservation or processing of goods, shipping, mining, hotels and power generation and distribution. The Corporation promotes industrialization of less developed areas, and provides training in management techniques and development banking. IFC's activities are: (i) Granting of loans in rupees and foreign currencies; (ii) Subscribing to and underwriting of equity, preference and debenture issues of capital; (iii) Guaranteeing deferred payments for machinery imported or purchased within the country; cap. p.u.

Rs. 10,000m.; Chair. C. D. KHANNA; Gen. Man. BALDEV PASRICHA.

The Industrial Credit and Investment Corporation of India Ltd.: 163 Backbay Reclamation, Bombay 20 BR; f. 1955 to assist industrial enterprises in the private sector by providing finance in both rupee and foreign currencies in the form of long- or medium-term loans or equity participations, sponsoring and underwriting new issues of shares and securities, guaranteeing loans from other private investment sources, furnishing managerial, technical and administrative advice to Indian industry; share cap. Rs. 75m.; res. Rs. 82.3m.; Chair. H. T. PAREKH.

In addition, the Life Insurance Corporation of India and the Unit Trust of India provide loans for private development. There are also statutory finance corporations in each State.

STOCK EXCHANGES

Ahmedabad Share and Stock Brokers' Association: Manekchowk, Ahmedabad; f. 1894; 457 mems.; Pres. MAHENDRAKUMAR CHANDULAL SHETH; Sec. J. C. PANDYA.

Bombay Stock Exchange: Dalal St., Bombay; f. 1875; 504 mems.; Pres. LALDAS JAMNADAS; Chair. P. J. JEEJEEBHOY; Sec. A. J. SHAH.

Calcutta Stock Exchange Association Ltd.: 7 Lyons Range, Calcutta; f. 1908; 636 mems.; Pres. S. K. BAGLA; Sec. B. MAJUMDAR.

Delhi Stock Exchange Association Ltd., The: 3 & 4/4B Asaf Ali Rd., New Delhi; f. 1947; 89 active mems.; Pres. DEV SAIGAL; Exec. Dir. Col. H. C. VERMA.

Madras Stock Exchange Ltd.: 16/17 Second Line Beach, Madras 600001; f. 1937; 24 mems.; Pres. M. S. SIVASUBRAMANIAN; Exec. Dir. E. R. KRISHNAMURTI; Sec. Y. SUNDARA BABU.

INSURANCE

In May 1971, 107 Indian and foreign insurance companies were nationalized by government ordinance. Twenty-one Custodians have been appointed for 84 companies based in Calcutta, 7 for 15 companies in Madras and 2 for 3 companies in Delhi.

Life Insurance Corporation of India: Jeevan Bima Marg, Bombay 20; London Office: York House, 6th Floor, Empire Way, Wembley, Middlesex; f. 1956 by an Act of Parliament nationalizing life assurance industry; controls all life insurance business in India; Chair. Shri K. R. PURI.

Advance Insurance Co. Ltd.: 251 Dr. Dadabhai Naoroji Rd., Fort, Bombay; f. 1942; Man. Dir. M. C. KEDIA.

All India General Insurance Co. Ltd.: Podar Chambers, Sayyed Abdulla Brelvi Rd., P.O.B. 435, Fort, Bombay 1; f. 1944; Chair. R. A. PODAR; Gen. Man. R. R. NAIK.

Anand Insurance Co. Ltd.: Yusuf Building, 43 Mahatma Gandhi Road, P.O. Box 344, Fort, Bombay; f. 1942; Chair. Sir CHUNILAL B. MEHTA; Man. Dir. A. C. MEHTA.

Bhandari Crosfields Pvt. Ltd.: Rampurawala Bldg., 27 Mahatma Gandhi Rd., Indore 452004; f. 1946; Chair. S. N. BHANDARI; Dir. R. S. BHANDARI.

Bharat General Reinsurance Ltd.: 65 Regal Bldgs., P.O.B. 92, New Delhi 1; f. 1942; Custodian S. C. CHATTERJEE.

Bombay Fire and General Insurance Co. Ltd.: Henley House, Graham Road, Ballard Estate, P.O. Box 548, Bombay 1; f. 1935; Chair. M. DOONGURSEE; Man. K. K. DASTUR.

British India General Insurance Co. Ltd.: Mehta House, 79-91 Apollo St., Fort, P.O.B. 950, Bombay; f. 1919; Chair. HOMI F. MEHTA; Gen. Man. N. C. SHROFF (acting).

Calcutta Insurance Ltd.: Reg. Office: 24 Chittaranjan Avenue, P.O. Box 7832, Calcutta; f. 1923; Man. Dir. M. R. DAS GUPTA.

Commonwealth Assurance Co. Ltd.: Commonwealth Building, 2-4 Oak Lane, 82 Meadows Street, Fort, Bombay; f. 1928; Chair. R. V. DONGRE.

Concord of India Insurance Co. Ltd.: Himalaya House, 38 Chowringhee Rd., P.O.B. 9118, Calcutta 16; f. 1931.

Co-operative Assurance Co. Ltd.: Hall Bazar, Amritsar; f. 1906; Man. Dir. L. JAG RAJ.

Co-operative General Insurance Society Ltd.: Narayanguda, P.O.B. 212, Hyderabad 29; f. 1947; Custodian T. S. KRISHNAMURTI; Chief Man. RAM BHAT.

Dena Insurance (Devkaran Nanjee Insurance Co. Ltd.): Devkaran Nanjee Bldg., Fort, Bombay; Chair. L. C. D. NANJEE.

General Assurance Society Ltd., The: 5 Mission Row, Calcutta 1; 1907; Gen. Man. A. GOENKA.

Great Pyramid Insurance Co. Ltd., The: National Tobacco Bldgs., 1 and 2 Old Court House Corner, Calcutta 1; f. 1944.

Hercules Insurance Co. Ltd.: "Dare House Extension", 4th Floor, 2/1 North Beach Rd., P.O.B. 242, Madras 1; f. 1935; Custodian P. C. SEKHAR; Man. E. J. PONCHA.

Hindustan General Insurance Society Ltd.: Everest House, 46c Chowringhee Rd., Calcutta 16; f. 1944; Custodian K. P. MODI, J.P.

Hukumchand Insurance Co. Ltd.: 38 Netaji Subhas Road, Calcutta 1; f. 1929; Gen. Manager K. R. V. ACHARYA.

India Reinsurance Corporation Ltd.: Industrial Assurance Building, Churchgate, Bombay 1; f. 1965; Chair. TULSIDAS KILACHAND.

Indian Guarantee and General Insurance Co. Ltd.: Gresham Assurance House, P. Mehta Rd., P.O.B. 165, Bombay 1; f. 1922; Custodian G. V. JANNAH; Gen. Man. K. S. SHENOY; Jt. Gen. Man. F. K. DARUWALLA.

Indian Mercantile Insurance Co.: 14 Nicol Road, Ballard Estate, Bombay 1; f. 1907; Chair. K. M. D. THACKERSEY; Custodian T. S. SWAMINATHEAN.

Indian Mutual General Association Ltd.: 35 Mount Road, P.O. Box 392, Madras; f. 1946; Manager S. K. SIVARAMAN.

Indian Trade and General Insurance Co. Ltd.: Jehangir Building, Mahatma Gandhi Rd., P.O.B. 146, Fort, Bombay 400001; f. 1944; Custodian P. C. SEKHAR; Gen. Man. B. B. SAWHNEY.

Jayabharat Insurance Co. Ltd.: French Bank Bldg., Homji St., Bombay; f. 1943; Chair. CHANDULAL P. PARIKH; Gen. Man. RASIKLAL C. PARIKH.

Jupiter General Insurance Co. Ltd.: State Bank Bldg. Annexe, Fort, Bombay 1; f. 1919; Gen. Man. R. G. BHENDE; Mans. Y. B. KUNDER, K. L. SHAH; Sec. Y. S. RAMAMURTHY.

National Insurance Co. Ltd.: 18 Rabindra Sarani, P.O.B. 2378, Calcutta 1; f. 1906; Custodian K. P. MODI; Gen. Man. R. S. AGRAWAL; Sec. M. N. RAO.

Neptune Assurance Co.: 104 Apollo St., Fort, Bombay; f. 1930; Man. Dir. M. T. MEHTA.

New Great Insurance Co. of India Ltd.: Bank Building, Mandvi, Baroda; Main Office: 7 Jamshedji Tata Road, Churchgate Reclamation, Bombay 20; f. 1943; Chair. TULSIDAS KILACHAND.

New India Assurance Co. Ltd.: Mahatma Gandhi Rd., Fort, P.O.B. 969, Bombay 400001; f. 1919; Custodian G. V. KAPADIA.

Oriental Fire and General Insurance Co., Ltd.: Oriental Buildings, Mahatma Gandhi Rd., Fort, P.O.B. 1989, Bombay 1; f. 1947; Gen. Man. G. V. JANNAH.

Pandyan Insurance Co.: Pandyan Building, West Veli St., P.O.B. 74, Madurai; f. 1933; Chair. T. V. SIVASAMBAN; Man. S. VINAYAKAM.

Ruby General Insurance Co. Ltd.: Ruby House, 8 India Exchange Place, P.O.B. 2573, Calcutta 1; f. 1936; Custodian Shri K. P. MODI, J.P.

Sentinel Assurance Co. Ltd.: Moti Mahal, Jamshedji Tata Rd., Fort, P.O.B. 17, Bombay 1; f. 1934; Chair. RATILAL NATHALAL; Gen. Man. G. K. PAREKH.

South India Insurance Co. Ltd.: Moti Mahal, Jamshedji Tata Rd., Bombay 20; f. 1934; Man. M. R. RAYAKAR.

Sterling General Insurance Co. Ltd.: Scindia House, P.O.B. 12, New Delhi 1; f. 1943; Gen. Man. S. C. CHATTERJEE.

Triton Insurance Co. Ltd.: 4 Clive Row, Calcutta 1; f. 1850; Man. Dir. G. M. MACKINLAY.

United India Fire and General Insurance Co. Ltd.: Indian Overseas Bank Bldg., 151 Mount Rd., P.O.B. 3719, Madras 2; Gen. Man. V. S. KANAGASABAI.

Universal Fire and General Insurance Co. Ltd.: Universal Insurance Building, Sir P. Mehta Road, P.O. Box 1394, Fort, Bombay; f. 1919; Chair. P. U. PATEL.

Vulcan Insurance Co. Ltd.: Vulcan Insurance Bldg., 202 Veer Nariman Rd., Bombay 400020; f. 1919; Deputy Man. H. V. SETALVAD.

Zenith Assurance Co. Ltd.: Mehta House, Apollo St., Fort, Bombay; f. 1916; 85 mems.; Chair. HOMI F. MEHTA; Gen. Man. M. S. DASTUR.

INSURANCE ASSOCIATION

Indian Insurance Companies' Association: Co-operative Insurance Building, Sir P. Mehta Road, Fort, Bombay; f. 1928 to protect the interests of the insurance industry in India; 43 mems.

UNIT TRUST

Unit Trust of India: Bombay Life Bldg., 45 Veer Nariman Rd., Bombay 1; f. 1964; controlled by the Reserve Bank of India; total assets Rs. 1,448m.; branches at New Delhi, Calcutta and Madras; Chair. of Trustees JAMES S. RAJ; Exec. Trustee Shri S. D. DESHMUKH.

TRADE AND INDUSTRY

TRADE ORGANIZATIONS

CHAMBERS OF COMMERCE

Chambers of Commerce have been established in almost all commercial and industrial centres. The following are among the most important.

Associated Chambers of Commerce and Industry of India: Allahabad Bank Bldg., 17 Parliament St., New Delhi; a central organization of Chambers; 12 Chambers of Commerce and Industry representing 1,500 companies throughout India; 180 associate mems.

Federation of Indian Chambers of Commerce and Industry: Federation House, Bazar Marg, New Delhi; 206 asscns. affiliated as ordinary mems, and 395 concerns as associate mems.; Pres. M. MANGALDAS; Sec.-Gen. G. L. BANSAL; publ. *Fortnightly Review*.

Indian National Committee of International Chamber of Commerce: Federation House, New Delhi 1; f. 1928; organization mems. 44, associate mems. 165; Pres. A. K. JAIN; Sec.-Gen. G. L. BANSAL; Joint Sec.-Gen. P. CHENTSAL RAO.

Bengal Chamber of Commerce and Industry: 6 Netaji Subhas Rd., Calcutta; f. 1934; 206 mems.; Pres. A. W. B. HAYWARD; Sec. A. T. ROBERTSON.

Bengal National Chamber of Commerce and Industry: P-11 Mission Row Extension, Calcutta; f. 1887; 265 mems. and 46 industrial and trading associations are affiliated, some having common working arrangements; Pres. S. B. DUTT; Sec. A. R. DUTTA GUPTA, M.A.

Bharat Chamber of Commerce: 195 Mahatma Gandhi Rd., Calcutta; f. 1900; 601 mems.; Pres. G. N. KHAITAN; Sec. L. R. DASGUPTA.

Bombay Chamber of Commerce and Industry: Mackinnon Mackenzie Bldg., Ballard Estate, Bombay 1-BR; P.O.B. 473; f. 1836; 582 mems.; Pres. R. O. JACKSON; Sec. B. P. GUNAJI.

Cocanada Chamber of Commerce: Commercial Rd., Kakinada 1 (Andhra Pradesh); f. 1868; 12 mem. firms; Chair. S. SIBGATHULLAH; Hon. Sec. N. NAGABHUSHANAM.

Gujarat Chamber of Commerce and Industry (*Gujarat Vepari Mahamandal*): Ranchhodlal Rd., P.O.B. 4045, Ahmedabad; f. 1949; 3,301 mems.; Pres. Dr. BIHARILAL KANAIYALAL; Vice-Pres. Shri RASIKLAL V. VASA; Hon. Sec. Shri BABUBHAI M. GANDHI; Sec. Shri L. V. DANI; publs. monthly bulletin, annual report, special issues on petro-chemicals, sales tax, industries, export promotion, Gujarat Businessmen's Convention Souvenir, Seminar on Ahmedabad Metropolitan Planning, etc.

Indian Chamber of Commerce: India Exchange, India Exchange Place, Calcutta 1; f. 1923; 400 mems.; Pres. SANJOY SEN; Sec. Gen. C. S. PANDE.

Indian Merchant's Chamber: 76 Veer Nariman Rd., Bombay 20; f. 1907; Sec. C. L. GHEEWAHA; publ. *Journal* (monthly).

Madras Chamber of Commerce and Industry: Dare House Annexe, 3/4 Moore St., Madras 1; f. 1836; 143 mem. firms, 6 affiliated and 7 honorary; Chair. C. P. FEATHERSTONE; Sec. C. S. KRISHNASWAMI.

Maharashtra Chamber of Commerce: 12 Rampart Row, Fort, Bombay; f. 1927; over 1,500 mems.; Pres. M. L. APTE; Sec. R. G. MOHADIKAR; publ. *Trade, Commerce and Industry Bulletin* (English).

Merchants' Chamber of Uttar Pradesh: 14/38 Civil Lines, Kanpur; f. 1932; 300 mems.; Pres. Dr. G. H. SINGHANIA; Sec. J. V. KRISHNAN.

Northern India Chamber of Commerce: Dehra Dun, Chandigarh, Punjab; f. 1912; 270 mems.; Pres. S. CHARANJIT SINGH; Hon. Sec. H. S. BALHAYA.

Oriental Chamber of Commerce: 6 Clive Row, Calcutta 1; f. 1932; 115 mems.; Pres. RUSI B. GIMI; Sec. M. S. SALEHJEE.

Punjab, Haryana and Delhi Chamber of Commerce and Industry: Phelps Bldg., 9A Connaught Place, P.B. 130, New Delhi 1; f. 1905; 303 mems.; Chair. Shri PREM PANDHI; Deputy Chair. Shri RAUNAQ SINGH; Sec. M. L. NANDRAJOG.

Southern India Chamber of Commerce and Industry: Indian Chamber Bldgs., Esplanade, Madras 1; f. 1909; 1,000 mems.; Pres. Shri S. NARAYANASWAMY; Sec. Shri D. SRINIVASAN, B.A.B.L.

United Chamber of Trade Asscn.: Katra Rathi Nai Sarak, Delhi; Pres. Shri MA'HESHWAR DAYAL.

Upper India Chamber of Commerce: 14/69 Civil Lines, P.O.B. 63, Kanpur; f. 1888; 161 mems.; Pres. P. N. MATHUR.

Uttar Pradesh Chamber of Commerce: 15/197 Civil Lines, Kanpur; f. 1914; 200 mems.; Pres. SARDAR INDERSINGH; Hon. Sec. B. K. SAKSENA.

FOREIGN TRADE CORPORATIONS

Export Credit and Guarantee Corporation Ltd.: Express Towers, 10th Floor, Nariman Point, Bombay; transformed from Export Risks Insurance Corporation Ltd. in 1964; to assist exporters by insuring risks involved in exports on credit terms and to supplement credit facilities by issuing guarantees, etc.; Chair. T. R. VARADACHARY; Sec. P. B. SATAGOPAN.

State Trading Corporation of India Ltd.: Chandralok, 36 Janpath, New Delhi; f. 1956; a Government of India undertaking dealing in exports and imports; brs. in Bombay, Calcutta, Madras, and in 16 overseas countries; Chair. PRAKASH L. TANDON: Sec. HARISH C. NAKRA.

The Minerals and Metals Trading Corporation of India Ltd.: Express Bldg., 9 and 10, Bahadur Shah Zaffar Marg, New Delhi 110001; f. 1963; export of iron and manganese, ore, ferro-manganese mica, coal and other minor minerals; import of steel, non-ferrous metals and other industrial raw materials, fertilizers and fertilizer raw materials, rough diamonds; auth. cap. Rs. 8om.; Chair. S. RAMACHANDRAN; Sec. O. P. GARG.

The Handicrafts and Handlooms Exports Corporation of India Ltd.: Lok Kalyan Bhavan, 11A, Rouse Ave. Lane, New Delhi 1; f. 1958; a subsidiary of State Trading Corpn. of India Ltd.; undertakes export of handicrafts, handloom goods and ready-to-wear clothes while promoting exports and trade development generally; boutiques Sona of India in New Delhi, New York, Boston, Paris, Tokyo and Nairobi and Carpet Warehousing Depot at Hamburg; auth. cap. Rs. 20m.; Chair. Mrs. PUPUL JAYAKAR; Sec. A. S. PARAMESWARAN.

The Indian Motion Pictures Export Corporation Ltd.: 5th Floor, Shivsagar Estate, Dr. Annie Besant Rd., Worli, Bombay 18; Chair. A. M. TARIQ; Man. Dir. A. K. SUD.

The Trade Development Authority: P.O.B. 767, 16 Parliament St., Bank of Baroda Bldg., New Delhi 110001; f. 1971 to assist small- and medium-sized firms in developing and improving products, services and markets in the export field.

INDUSTRIAL AND AGRICULTURAL ORGANIZATIONS

The following are the principal bodies in existence in 1972.

GENERAL

Cotton Corporation of India Ltd.: Air India Bldg., 12th Floor, Nariman Point, Bombay 1; f. 1970 to act as an agency in the public sector for the purchase, sale and distribution of home-produced cotton and controls the import of imported cotton; Chair. R. S. PANJHAZARI; Man. Dir. N. S. KULKARNI.

The Food Corporation of India: 1 Bahadur Shah Zafar Marg, New Delhi; f. January 1965 to undertake trading in foodgrains on a commercial scale but within the framework of an overall government policy; the important task of the Corporation is to implement effectively the policy of ensuring that the primary producer obtains a remunerative price and to protect the consumer from the vagaries of speculative trade; the Corporation purchases, stores, distributes and sells foodgrains and other foodstuffs and is entrusted with the task of arranging for imports (subject to the decision of the Government of India) and handling of foodgrains and fertilizers at the ports. It also distributes sugar throughout the country and has set up rice mills. Chair. SHAH NAWAZ KHAN; Man. Dir. J. A. DAVE.

Housing and Urban Development Corporation Ltd.: 12-A, Jamnagar House Hutments, New Delhi 11; f. 1970; to finance and undertake housing and urban development programmes including the setting-up of satellite towns and building material industries; auth. cap. Rs. 100m., Chair. KESHUB MAHINDRA; Man. Dir. V. V. PAREKH.

Indian Dairy Corporation: Yashkamal Bldg., Lokmanya Tilak Rd., Baroda 5; objects: to increase the capacity of dairies in 4 major cities (Bombay, Calcutta, Delhi and Madras) under "Operation Flood" Project of the UN World Food programme; to facilitate the re-settlement in rural areas of city-kept cattle and to improve productivity; to develop milk farmers' organizations in rural areas and a national grid for milk with basic transport and storage facilities.

Jute Corporation of India: 1 Shakespeare Sarani, Calcutta 16; f. Sept. 1971; Objects (i) to undertake price support operations in respect of raw jute; (ii) to ensure remunerative prices to producers through efficient marketing (iii) to operate a buffer stock to stabilize raw jute prices; (iv) to handle the import and export of raw jute; (v) to promote the export of jute goods; Chair. DWAIPAYAN SEN; Man. Dir. G. UKIL; Sec. C. RADHAKRISHNADAS.

National Coal Development Corporation Ltd.: Darbhange House, Ranchi; operations extend to Bihar, Orissa, Maharashtra and Madhya Pradesh States. The Corporation has at present 29 coal mining projects, 3 coal washeries, 2 workshops and a coke oven plant in operation; 6 colliery projects include 2 deepshaft mines at Sudamdih and Monidih in the Jharia field in Bihar; total production capacity is estimated at 17.3 million tons (1972/73); Chair./Man. Dir. Shri J. G. KUMARA-MANGALAM.

National Commission on Agriculture: Vigyan Bhavan Annexe, New Delhi; f. Aug. 1970 to examine the current progress of agriculture in India and to make recommendations for its improvement and modernization with a view to promoting the welfare and prosperity of the people; Chair. Shri N. R. MIRDHA, M.P.

National Co-operative Development Corporation: 1C-56, South Extn. 11, New Delhi 16; f. 1962 to plan and promote programmes for the production, processing, marketing, storage, export and import of agricultural produce and notified commodities through co-operative societies; Chair. FAKHRUDDIN ALI AHMAD, Minister of Agriculture; Sec. Shri M. GILL; publs. *Bulletin* (every 2 months), *Report* (annual).

The National Industrial Development Corporation Ltd.: Chanakya Bhavan, N.D.M.C. Complex, Vinay Marg, P.O.B. 458, New Delhi; f. 1954; auth. cap. Rs. 10m.; offers consultative engineering services to Central and State Governments, the UN and overseas investors; Chair. K. B. RAO; Man. Dir. R. K. SETHI; Sec. K. C. BHALLA.

National Mineral Development Corporation Ltd.: 109 Surya Kiran Bldg., Kasturba Gandhi Marg, New Delhi 110001; to exploit minerals in the public sector (excluding copper, coal, lignite oil and natural gas) and for this purpose the corporation may buy, take on lease or otherwise acquire mines for prospecting and developing; Chair. G. Ramnathan.

National Productivity Council: 38 Golf Links, New Delhi; f. 1958 to increase productivity and to improve quality by improved techniques which aim at efficient and proper utilization of available resources of man-power, machines, materials, power and capital, raise the standard of living of the people, and improve the working conditions and welfare of labour; autonomous body representing national organizations of employers and labour, government ministries, professional organizations, Local Productivity Councils, small-scale industries and other interests; total mems.: 75.

National Research Development Corporation of India: 61 Ring Rd., Lajpat Nagar III, New Delhi 110024; f. 1953 to stimulate development and commercial exploitation of patents and inventions arising from national research; Chair. M. S. Pathak; Man. Dir. Dr. C. V. S. Ratnam.

National Seeds Corporation Ltd.: 4E Jhandewalan Extension, Rani Jhansi Rd., New Delhi 110055; f. 1963 to improve and develop the seed industry in India; concentrates on the development and introduction of improved varieties of seeds; Chair. Deo. Rao S. Patil; Man. Dir. A. J. S. Sodhi.

National Small Industries Corporation Ltd.: Near Industrial Estate, Okhla, New Delhi; f. 1955; cap. auth. Rs. 35m., issued Rs. 35m.; established to aid, counsel, finance, protect and promote the interests of small industries; all shares held by the Government of India; Chair. K. N. Sapru.

Rehabilitation Industries Corporation Ltd.: 25, Free School St., Calcutta 16; f. 1959 to create employment opportunities through industries for refugees from Pakistan, repatriates from Burma and Sri Lanka, and other persons of Indian extraction who have immigrated to India; Chair. D. K. Bose; Man. Dir. A. K. Ghosh, i.a.s.; Joint Man. Dir. and Sec. M. N. Chaudhuri, i.a.s.

State Farms Corporation of India Ltd.: A-21 West End Colony, Rao Tula Ram Marg, New Delhi 23; f. 1969 to take over the administration of Central State Farms set up originally for the production of foodgrain seeds, oil seeds, fruit and vegetables; activities include the production of quality seeds of high yielding varieties of wheat, paddy, maize, barja and jowar; provides advice regarding soil conservation, repair and servicing of tractors, consultancy services on farm mechanization; cap. Rs. 70m.; Chair. M. R. Krishna; Man. Dir. F. C. Gera.

There are also industrial development corporations in the separate States. Organizations engaged in the financing of agricultural and industrial development are listed under *Finance*.

PRINCIPAL INDUSTRIAL ASSOCIATIONS

Ahmedabad Millowners' Association: Ranchhodlal Marg, Navrangpura, Ahmedabad 9; f. 1891; Pres. Shri Chandrakant Bakubhai; Vice-Pres. Shri Indravadan Pranlal; Asst. Sec. Shri R. G. Acharya.

Bombay Piece-Goods Merchants' Mahajan: Shaikh Memon St., Bombay 2; f. 1881; 1,627 mems.; Pres. H. S. Fadia; Vice-Pres. V. K. Mehta; Sec. N. M. Boradia.

Bombay Presidency Association: 107 M. Gandhi Rd., Fort, Bombay 1; f. 1886; Pres. Naushir Bharucha; Hon. Secs. Dara Vania, E. A. Sethna.

Bombay Textile and Engineering Association: 343 opp. Railway Station, Grand Rd., Bombay; est. 1900; Pres. N. F. Bharucha; Hon. Sec. K. S. Punegar.

Calcutta Baled Jute Association: 6 Netaji Subhas Rd., Calcutta 1; f. 1892; 58 mems.; Chair. S. C. Bothra; Sec. M. Ghosh.

Calcutta Flour Mills Association: 6 Netaji Subhas Rd., Calcutta 1; f. 1932; 25 mems.; Sec. M. Ghose.

Calcutta Hydraulic Press Association: 6 Netaji Subhas Rd., Calcutta; f. 1903; 13 mems.; Chair. H. M. Bengani; Sec. M. Ghosh.

Calcutta Trades Association: 18H Park Street, Stephen Court, Calcutta 16; f. 1830; Hon. Sec. S. K. Maskara; Master N. K. Jalan.

East India Cotton Association Ltd.: Cotton Exchange, Marwari Bazar, Bombay 400002; f. 1921; 368 mems.; Pres. Madanmohan R. Ruia; Sec. D. G. Damle; publ. *Indian Cotton Annual*.

Engineering Association of India: India Exchange, India Exchange Place, Calcutta; f. 1942; 15 affiliated asscns.; Pres. Shri Stya Paul; Sec.-Gen. C. S. Pande; Sec. Dr. R. D. Vidyarthi.

Federation of Gujarat Mills and Industries: Federation Building, R. C. Dutt Rd., Baroda 390005; f. 1918; 250 mems.; Pres. Shri B. M. Patel; Sec. R. D. Munshi.

Grain, Rice and Oilseeds Merchants' Association: Grain-seeds House, 72/80 Yusuf Meheralli Rd., Bombay 3; f. 1899; 700 mems.; Pres. Shri Devji Rattansey; Sec. Shri Rasiklal J. Bhatt, m.a.; publ. *Vanijya* (monthly).

Indian Chemical Manufacturers Association: India Exchange, Calcutta; f. 1938; 157 mems.; Pres. Shri S. J. Shah; Sec.-Gen. C. S. Pande; Sec. R. D. Vidyarthi; publ. *Chemical Industry News* (monthly), and others.

Indian Colliery Owners' Association: I.C.O. Association Rd., P.O.B. 70, Dhanbad (Dt. Dhanbad), Bihar; f. 1933; 131 mems.; Pres. Rasiklal Worah.

Indian Engineering Association: Royal Exchange, 6 Netaji Subhas Rd., Calcutta 1; f. 1895; 555 mems.; Pres. P. K. Nanda; Sec. M. Ghosh.

Indian Jute Mills Association: Royal Exchange, Calcutta 1; sponsors and operates export promotion, research and product development; regulates labour relations.

Indian Mining Association: 6 Netaji Subhas Rd., Calcutta 1; f. 1892; 50 mems.; Sec. K. Mukerjee.

Indian Mining Federation: 135 Biplabi Rashbehari Basu Rd., Calcutta 1; est. 1913; to aid and stimulate mining, particularly coal, and to protect the commercial interests; Chair. Shri H. N. Mookherjee; Sec. Shri M. Das.

Indian National Shipowners' Association: Scindia House, Ballard Estate, Bombay; f. 1930; 19 mems.; Pres. Shri Vasant J. Sheth; Sec. S. K. Aier; publ. *Indian Shipping*.

Indian Paper Mills Association: India Exchange, 8th Floor, India Exchange Place, Calcutta; f. 1939; 31 mems.; Sec. T. R. Krishnaswami.

Indian Sugar Mills Association: India Exchange Bldg., Indian Exchange Place, Calcutta; est. 1932; 151 mems.; affiliated to the Indian Chamber of Commerce, Calcutta; Sec.-Gen. J. S. Mehta.

Indian Tea Association: Royal Exchange, 6 Netaji Subhas Rd., Calcutta 1; f. 1881; 138 mems.; 291 tea estates; Chair. K. M. Kidwai; Sec. J. D'Souza.

Indian Tea Association (Assam Branch): Dikom P.O., Assam; f. 1899; 260 mems.; Sec. E. K. Rawson-Gardiner.

Indian Tea Association (Surma Valley Branch): Silchar, Cachar, Assam; Chair. G. L. AGARWAL; Sec. M. K. CHAUDHURI.

Jute Balers' Association: 12 India Exchange Place, Calcutta 1; f. 1909; ordinary and Exchange mems. number over 500; represents all Indian Jute Balers; Chair. N. C. JHANWAR; Sec. R. N. MOHNOT; publ. *The Jute Trade* (English, fortnightly).

Jute Development Office: 4 K. S. Roy Rd., Calcutta; f. 1966; Dir. Shri H. D. NAITHANI.

Master Stevedores' Association: Royal Exchange, Calcutta; f. 1934; 23 mems.; Pres. K. C. MOOKERJEE; Sec. A. T. ROBERTSON.

Millowners' Association: Elphinstone Bldg., Veer Nariman Rd., Fort, Bombay; f. 1875; 99 mem. companies; Chair. S. R. DAMANI; Sec. R. L. N. VIJAYANAGAR.

Motor Merchants' Associations Ltd.: Sukh Sagar, 3rd Floor, Sandhurst Bridge, Bombay-7.

Silk and Art Silk Mills' Association Ltd.: Resham Bhavan, 78 Veer Nariman Road, Bombay 20; f. 1939; 706 mems.; Chair. MAGANLAL H. DOSHI; Sec. R. K. BHATNAGAR.

Southern India Millowners' Association: Racecourse, Coimbatore 1, Tamil Nadu; f. 1933; 144 mems.; Sec. C. G. REDDI.

EMPLOYERS FEDERATIONS

Council of Indian Employers: Federation House, New Delhi; f. 1956; consists of:

All-India Organization of Employers: Federation House, New Delhi; f. 1932; mems. 38 industrial associations and 140 large industrial concerns; Pres. H. S. SINGHANIA; Secs. Gen. G. L. BANSAL, P. CHENTSAL RAO.

Employers' Federation of India: Army and Navy Building, 148 Mahatma Gandhi Rd., Bombay; f. 1933; 186 mems.; Pres. N. H. TATA.

Employers' Association of Northern India: 14/69 Civil Lines, P.O.B. 344, Kanpur; f. 1937; 160 mems.; Chair. Shri S. M. BASHIR; Sec. D. N. NIGAM.

Employers' Federation of Southern India: Dare House Annexe, 3/4 Moore St., P.O.B. 35, Madras; 143 mem. firms; Chair. K. V. SRINIVASAN; Sec. C. S. KRISHNASWAMI.

Bharat Krishak Samaj (*Farmers' Forum, India*): A-1 Nizamuddin West, New Delhi 110013; f. 1954 by the late Dr. Panjabrao Deshmukh; national organization of farmers; Pres. Ex-Officio Union Minister for Agriculture; Chair. Shri M. S. ANVIKAR; Sec.-Gen. Dr. D. A. BHOLAY.

TRADE UNIONS

Indian National Trade Union Congress—INTUC: 17 Janpath, New Delhi 1; f. 1947; the largest and most representative T.U. organization in India; over 2,416 affiliated unions with a total membership of 2,221,810; affiliated to ICFTU; 20 state branches and 27 national industrial federations; Pres. B. C. BHAGAVATI; Gen. Sec. Shri G. RAMANUJAM; Asst. Secs. Shri R. L. THAKAR, Shri H. D. MUKERJI; Treas. Shri C. M. STEPHEN; publs. *The Indian Worker* (English weekly).

NATIONAL INDUSTRIAL FEDERATIONS

Indian National Cement Workers' Federation: Mazdoor Karyalaya, Congress House, Bombay 4; Pres. H. N. TRIVEDI.

Indian National Chemical Workers' Federation: Gandhi Majoor Sevalaya, Bhadra, Ahmedabad.

Indian National Defence Workers' Federation: 26/104 Birhana Rd., Kanpur; Pres. Dr. G. S. MELKOTE.

Indian National Electricity Workers' Federation: 19 Japling Rd., Lucknow; Pres. Shri I. G. DESAI.

Indian National Iron and Steel Workers' Federation: 17K Rd., Jamshedpur; Pres. Shri MICHAEL JOHN.

Indian National Mineworkers' Federation: 9 Lala Lajpatrai Sarani, Calcutta 20; f. 1949; 200,000 mems. (est.) in 95 affiliated unions; Pres. Shri R. N. SHARMA; Gen. Sec. KANTI MEHTA.

Indian National Paper Mill Workers' Federation: Shram Shivir, Workshop Rd., Yamunanagar, Ambala; Pres. Shri NIRMAL KUMAR SEN.

Indian National Plantation Workers' Federation: P.O.B. 13, Rehakari, Dibrugarh; 261,000 mems. (est.) in 24 affiliated unions; Pres. G. RAMANUJAM; Gen. Sec. G. SARMAH.

Indian National Port and Dock Workers' Federation: Mazdoor Karyalaya, Congress House, Bombay 4; f. 1954; Pres. H. N. TRIVEDI; Gen. Sec. Dr. Mrs. M. BOSE.

Indian National Press Workers' Federation: 19 Japling Rd., Lucknow.

Indian National Sugar Mills Workers' Federation: 19 Japling Rd., Lucknow; 50,000 mems. (est.); Pres. Shri R. P. SINHA; Gen. Sec. Shri KASHINATH PANDEY.

Indian National Textile Workers' Federation: Mazdoor Manzil, G. D. Ambekar Marg, Parel, Bombay 12; f. 1948; 371,084 mems.; Gen. Sec. A. T. BHOSALA.

Indian National Transport Workers' Federation: Gandhi Majoor Sevalaya, Bhadra, Ahmedabad; Gen. Sec. CHANDULAL G. SHAH.

National Federation of Petroleum Workers: Tel-Rasayan Bhanuan, Tilak Rd., Dadar, Bombay 14, f. 1959; 22,000 mems.; Pres. N. K. BHATT; Gen. Sec. RAJA KULKARNI.

All-India Trade Union Congress: 24 Canning Lane, New Delhi-1; f. 1920; admitted to WFTU; 1,872,982 mems., 3,018 affiliated unions; 16 regional branches; Pres. S. S. MIRAJKAR; Vice-Pres. Dr. R. SEN, P. B. MENON, P. KRISHNAN, S. S. YUSUF, Dr. R. B. GUR, K. DAS; Gen. Sec. S. A. DANGE; publ. *Trade Union Record* (English).

MAJOR AFFILIATED UNIONS

Annamalai Plantation Workers' Union: Valparai, Via Pollachi, Tamilnad; mems. over 20,000.

Zilla Cha Bagan Workers' Union: Malabar, Jalpaiguri, West Bengal; 21,000 mems.

United Trades Union Congress—UTUC: 249 Bepin Behari Ganguly St., Calcutta 12; f. 1949; 362,087 mems.; from 457 affiliated unions; Pres. N. SRIKANTAN NAIR; Vice-Pres. T. CHAUDHURY, R. RAMANATHAN, S. V. R. ACHARYA, T. M. S. VAID; Gen.-Sec. Miss SUDHA ROY.

MAJOR AFFILIATED UNIONS

Bengal Provincial Chatkal Mazdoor Union: 64 Chittarajan Avenue, Calcutta 12; textile workers; over 25,000 mems. (est.).

All-India Farm Labour Union: Bharathi Press Buildings, Mithapur, Patna 1, Bihar; over 35,000 mems. (est.).

Hind Mazdoor Sabha—HMS: Nagindas Chambers, 167 P. D.'Mello Rd., Bombay 40001; f. 1948; admitted to ICFTU; mems. 880,405 from 425 affiliated unions; 17 regional branches; Pres. A. Subramaniam, M.L.A.; Gen. Sec. Mahesh Desai; publ. *Hind Mazdoor*.

Major Affiliated Unions

All-India Port and Dock Workers' Federation: Port Shramik Bhawan, 26 Dr. S. Basu Rd., Calcutta 23; f. 1948; 175,000 mems.; 26 affiliated unions; Pres. S. R. Sulkarni; Gen. Sec. Makhan Chatterjee.

Koyla Mazdoor Panchayat—KMP: Jharia, District Manbhum, Bihar; miners' union; 22,000 mems. (est.); Gen. Sec. Mahesh Desai.

Western Railway Employees' Union—WREU: Grant Rd. Station (East), Bombay 7; f. 1920; 65,090 mems.; Pres. Miss Maniben Kara; Gen. Sec. U. M. Purohit; Joint Gen. Sec. Jagdish Ajmera; Sec. K. C. Trivedi; publ. *Railway Sentinel*.

Confederation of Central Government Employees' Unions: New Delhi; 700,000 mems. (est.); Gen. Sec. S. Madhusudan.

Affiliated Union

National Federation of Post, Telephone and Telegraph Employees—NFPTTE: 9 Pusa Road, New Delhi; f. 1954; mems. 170,000 (est.); Gen. Sec. P. S. R. Anjaneyalu.

National Federation of Indian Railwaymen—NFIR: 166/1 Panchkuian Rd., New Delhi; f. 1953; mems. 348,000 (est.); Pres. A. P. Sharma; Gen. Sec. Keshav H. Kulkarni.

Affiliated Union

All-India Railwaymen's Federation—AIRF: 125E Babar Rd., New Delhi 1; f. 1924; 507,235 mems. (1972); Pres. George Fernandes; Gen. Sec. Priya Gupta; publ. *Indian Railwaymen*.

All-India Bank Employees' Federation—AIBEF: 26/104 Birhana Rd., Kanpur 1; Gen. Sec. V. N. Sekhri; publ. *Bank Karamchari*.

All-India Defence Employees' Federation—AIDEF: Kirkee, Poona; 300,000 mems. (est.); Gen. Sec. S. M. Joshi.

TRANSPORT

RAILWAYS

Indian Government Administration (Railway Board): New Delhi; Chair. B. S. D. Baliga.

The Indian Government exercises direct or indirect control over all railways in the Republic of India through the medium of the Railway Board.

State Railways

The railways have been grouped into nine zones as follows:

Northern: Delhi; Gen. Man. C. S. Parameswaran.

Western: Bombay; Gen. Man. A. K. Gupta.

Central: Bombay; Gen. Man. V. P. Sawhney.

Southern: Madras; Gen. Man. V. T. Narayanan.

Eastern: Calcutta; Gen. Man. G. P. Warrier.

South Eastern: Calcutta; Gen. Man. S. S. Mukerjee.

South Central: Secunderabad; Gen. Man. M. T. Lee.

North Eastern: Gorakhpur; Gen. Man. B. D. Gaur.

Northeast Frontier: Pandu; Gen. Man. N. N. Tandon.

The total length of Indian railways in 1972 was 60,041 route kms. The total length of track was 71,669 km.

Note: An underground railway for Calcutta is scheduled for completion by 1978. It is expected to serve more than one million people and to total 17 km. in length.

ROADS

Ministry of Shipping and Transport (Roads Wing): Transport Bhavan No. 1, Parliament St., New Delhi 1; in 1972 surfaced and metalled roads totalled 476,000 km., and other roads 666,000 km. India has a system of National Highways, with an aggregate length of about 28,819 kms. in 1972 running through the length and breadth of the country, connecting the State capitals and major ports and linking with the highway systems of its neighbours. This system includes 55 highways and they constitute the main trunk roads of the country.

Central Road Transport Corporation Ltd.: 4 Fairlie Place, Calcutta 1; f. 1964 to supplement the transport capacity in the eastern sector of the country; operates a fleet of some 289 trucks; Chair. B. B. Ghosh; Man. Dir. K. Srinivasan.

Border Roads Development Board: f. 1960 to accelerate the economic development of the North and Northeastern border areas; improvement of certain existing roads and tracks and construction of some new ones.

INLAND WATERWAYS

About 2,500 km. of rivers are navigable by mechanically propelled country vessels and 5,500 km. by large country boats. Services are mainly on the Ganges and Brahmaputra.

Central Inland Water Transport Corpn.: 4 Fairlie Place, Calcutta; f. 1967; main activities include shipbuilding and repairing; lighterage, river conservancy, bunkering; ship delivery; manning and operation of river craft; provision of ferry services and pleasure cruises; Man. Dir. K. Srinivasan.

East Bengal River Steam Service Ltd.: 87 Sovabazar Street, Calcutta 5; f. 1906; Man. Dirs. K. D. Roy, B. K. Roy.

SHIPPING

Bombay

Africana Company Pr. Ltd.: 289-93 Narshi Natha Street, Masjid Bridge; Chair. G. Padamshi.

American President Lines Ltd.: Forbes Bldg., Home St., Fort; agents for Royal Interocean Lines, Canadian City Line Ltd., Ellerman City Liners.

Bharat Line Ltd.: Bharat House, 104 Apollo Street, Fort, 1; also at Calcutta, Bhavnagar and Madras.

Bombay Steam Navigation Co. (1953) Ltd.: 7 Kurupta St., Bombay 1; Chair. and Man. Dir. Dr. V. Madhavlal.

Gill Amin Steamship Co. (Private) Ltd.: 15 Khorshed Building, Sir P.M. Road 1; services: Bombay-Karachi-Colombo-East and West Coast India-Burma.

Great Eastern Shipping Co. Ltd.: Mercantile Bank Bldg., 60 Mahatma Gandhi Rd.; f. 1948; Chair. A. H. Bhiwandiwalla; Man. Dir. K. M. Sheth.

Lloyd Triestino: Neville House, Ballard Estate, P.O.B. 1080; also agents Anchor Line Ltd.

Mackinnon Mackenzie and Co. (Private) Ltd.: 4 Ballard Rd., Ballard Estate, Bombay; agents for Panocean Shipping and Terminals Ltd.; P. & O. Lines; States

Marine Lines; Isthmian Lines, Inc.; Bank Line Ltd.; Union Steam Ship Co. of New Zealand Ltd.; Global Bulk Transport, Inc.; National Bulk Carriers Inc.; Associated Bulk Carriers Inc.; Damodar Bulk Carriers (Goa) Ltd.; South India Shipping Corpn. Ltd.; Mauritius Steam Navigation Co. Ltd.; Cities Service Tankers Corpn.; Stravelakis Bros. Ltd.; Naess Shipping Co. Inc.; Apollo Shipping Co. Inc.; Netherlands Norness Shipping Co. Ltd.

Malabar Steamship Co. Ltd., The: 4th Floor Express Towers, Nariman Point, 1; f. 1935; Chair. Pratapsinh Shoorji Vallabhdass, J.P.; Man. Dir. Dilip Shoorji; Gen. Man. Rasiklal H. Narechamia.

Merchant Steam Navigation Co. Pr. Ltd.: 283-93 Narsi Natha Street.

Mitsui OSK Lines Ltd.: Marshall's Bldg., 2nd Floor, Ballard Rd. 1.

Mogul Line Ltd.: 16 Bank St.; f. 1877; state-owned; Chair. C. P. Srivastava; Man. Dir. J. G. Saggi.

Nedlloyd and Hoegh Lines: Patel-Volkart Ltd., 19 Graham Rd., Ballard Estate, 1.

NYK Line: c/o Indian Maritime Enterprises Pvt. Ltd., 6th Floor, New Kamani Chambers, Mangalore St., Ballard Estate, 1.

Polish Ocean Lines: Bharat Insurance Bldg., 15a Horniman Circle, Bombay 1; Dir. J. Mondalski.

Scindia Steam Navigation Co. Ltd.: Scindia House, Narottam Morarjee Marg, Ballard Estate, 1; f. 1919; Chair. K. M. D. Thackersey; Dir.-in-Charge Mrs. Sumati Morarjee; Chief Exec. T. M. Goculdas; Joint Chief Exec. R. A. Patel; also at Calcutta, Saurashtra and Mangalore ports.

Shipping Corporation of India Ltd.: Steelcrete House, 4th Floor, Dinshaw Wacha Rd. 20; f. 1961 as a Government undertaking; fleet of 100 vessels, consisting of tankers, freighters, passenger-cum-cargo ships; operates bulk carriers; operates 27 services; Chair. and Man. Dir. C. P. Srivastava.

South-East Asia Shipping Co. Private Ltd.: Himalaya House, Dr. Dadabhai Naoroji Rd., Fort 1; f. 1948; Dirs. N. H. Dhunjibhoy, J. P. Bragg, D. H. Dhunjibhoy, Prof. M. S. Thacker, K. N. Dhunjibhoy.

United Liner Agencies of India (Private) Ltd.: Wavell House, Graham Rd., Ballard Estate, 1.

Yugoslav Line: Alice Building, Dadabhai Naoroji Road.

Calcutta

American President Lines Ltd.: 3 Netaji Subhas Rd., 1.

Anchor Brocklebank Line: Agents Turner, Morrison & Co. Ltd., 6 Lyons Range, 1.

Anchor Line Ltd.: 4/5 Bankshall St., 1.

Asiatic Steam Navigation Co. Ltd.: 16 Strand Rd., 1.

Bharat Line Ltd.: 13 Brabourne Rd.

Brocklebanks' Cunard Services: Agents Turner, Morrison & Co. Ltd., 6 Lyons Range, 1.

Central Gulf Steamship Corporation: 4 Clive Row, Calcutta.

Ellerman City Liners: Gladstone Lyall & Co. Ltd., 4 Fairlie Place.

Great Eastern Shipping Co. Ltd.: 5 Clive Row, P.B. 566.

Great India Steam Navigation Co. Ltd.: 8 Lyons Range.

India Shipping Co. Ltd.: 21 Old Court House Street, P.O.B. 2090.

India Steamship Co. Ltd.: 21 Old Court House St., P.O.B. 2090, Calcutta.

Indo-Burma Petroleum Co. Ltd.: Gillander House, Netaji Subhas Rd.; f. 1909; Man. Dir. S. B. Budhiraja.

The Indo-China Steam Navigation Co. Ltd.: 4 Clive Row.

Jayanti Shipping Co. (Private) Ltd.: 4-5 Bankshall St.

Mackinnon Mackenzie & Co. (P) Ltd.: 16 Strand Rd., P.O.B. 163; agents for Union Steamship Co. (New Zealand) Ltd.

Malabar Steamship Co. Ltd.: 4 Lyons Range; f. 1935; Chair. Pratapsinh Shoorji Vallabhdass, J.P.; Man. Mulji K. Tanna.

Mitsui OSK Lines Ltd.: Agents F. W. Heilgers & Co. (Private) Ltd., Shipping Dept., 1 India Exchange Place, 1, P.O.B. 185.

NYK Line: 2 Netaji Subhas Rd., 1; Agents James Finlay & Co. Ltd.

Patel-Volkart Ltd.: 5-7 Netaji Subhas Rd., P.O.B. 71; Man. S. N. Mirchandani.

Scindia Steam Navigation Co. Ltd.: 33 Netaji Subhas Road.

Madras

American Mail Lines and American President Lines Ltd.: 6 Mysore Bank Building, PB. 37, Madras 600001.

Bharat Line Ltd.: 8 Second Line Beach; also in Bombay, Calcutta and Bhavnagar.

East Asiatic Co. (India) (Private) Ltd.: P.O.B. No. 146, Madras; also in Bombay, New Delhi and Calcutta.

Jugolinija: agents at Kakinda, Visakhapatnam and Tuticori.

Messageries Maritimes Co.: 6-20 North Beach Rd. (P.O.B. 181).

Mitsui OSK Line: P.O.B. No. 63.

Southern Shipping Corporation Pte. Ltd.: 8 Second Line Beach, 1.

(Shipping companies are also represented at Aleppey, Calicut, Cochin, Kakinada, Pondicherry and Tuticorin.)

CIVIL AVIATION

Air India: 218 Backbay Reclamation, Nariman Point, Bombay 1BR; f. 1953; state corporation responsible for international flights; extensive services to New York, London, Europe, the Middle East, Africa, the Far East and Australia; unduplicated route length; 134,633 km.; fleet of four Boing 747 and ten Boeing 707; Chair. J. R. D. Tata; Man. Dir. Air Marshall M. S. Chaturvedi.

Indian Airlines: Airlines House, 113 Gurudwara Rakab Ganj Rd., New Delhi; f. 1953; state corporation responsible for regional and domestic flights; services throughout India and to Burma, Sri Lanka and Nepal; unduplicated route length; 39,171 km.; fleet of six Boeing 737, seven Caravelles, fifteen HS-748, nine F-27, seven DC-3 and six Viscounts; Chair. and Man. Dir. Air Chief Marshal P. C. Lal.

The following airlines also serve India: Aeroflot, Air Ceylon, Air France, Alitalia, Ariana Afghan, British Airways, ČSA, EAA, EgyptAir, Ethiopian Airlines, Garuda, Gulf Aviation, Iran Air, Iraqi Airways, JAL, KLM, Kuwait Airways, Lufthansa, Pan American, Qantas, Royal Nepal, Sabena, Saudia, SAS, Singapore Airlines, Swissair, Syrian Arab, Thai International and TWA.

TOURISM

Department of Tourism of the Government of India: Ministry of Tourism and Civil Aviation, No. 1 Parliament St., Transport Bhawan, New Delhi; responsible for the formulation and administration of government policy for active promotion of tourist traffic to India, and for planning the organization and development of tourist facilities; regional offices at Delhi, Calcutta, Bombay and Madras; sub-offices at Agra, Aurangabad, Cochin, Jaipur, Jammu, Khajur-aho, Varanasi; overseas offices at New York, San Francisco, Chicago, Toronto, London, Geneva, Frankfurt, Paris, Sydney, Brussels, Singapore, Stockholm, Milan, Tokyo and Vienna. Tourist Promotion Officers at Boston, Washington, Dallas, Miami, Seattle and Detroit.

Indian Tourism Development Corporation Ltd.: Jeevan Vihar, 3 Parliament St., New Delhi 1; f. 1966; aims to promote tourism in India; runs hotels, motels, tourist transport services, duty free shops; production of tourist literature; Chair. and Man. Dir. M. S. SUNDARA.

CULTURAL ORGANIZATIONS

Lalit Kala Akademi (*National Academy of Art*): Rabindra Bhavan, New Delhi 110001; f. 1954; autonomous, government financed; sponsors national and international exhibitions; arranges seminars, lectures, films, etc.; Chair. K. J. KHANDALAVALA; Act. Sec. A. K. DUTTA; publs. on ancient and modern Indian art; two journals *Lalit Kala* (ancient Indian art, annual), *Lalit Kala Contemporary* (modern art, half-yearly).

Sangeet Natak Akademi: National Academy of Dance, Drama and Music; Rabindra Bhavan, Feroze Shah Rd., New Delhi 1; f. 1953; autonomous body responsible for promotion and organization of the arts; maintains Asavari, a gallery of musical instruments, Yavanika, a gallery of theatre arts and a listening room for research scholars; Chair. Smt. INDIRA GANDHI; Sec. Dr. SURASH AWASTHI; publs. *Sangeet Natak* (quarterly) and *News Bulletin* (every two months).

Indian Council for Cultural Relations: Rabindra Bhavan, New Delhi 1; f. 1950 to strengthen cultural relations between India and other countries and to promote cultural exchanges.

THEATRE GROUPS

Bharatiya Natya Sangh: 34 New Central Market, New Delhi; Pres. Smt. KAMLADEVI CHATTOPADHYAYA.

Bohurupee: 11-A Nasiruddin Rd., Calcutta 17; Dir. Shri SOMBHU MITRA.

Children's Little Theatre: Aban Mahal, Gariahat Rd., Calcutta 19; f. 1951; Pres. Dr. BIBEK SEN GUPTA; Hon. Gen. Sec. Sri SAMAR CHATTERJEE; publ. *Rhythms & Rhymes*, quarterly.

Little Theatre Group: 6 Beadon St., Calcutta 6; Dir. Shri UPTAL DUTT.

Little Theatre Group: Flat 10, Shankar Market, Connaught Circus, New Delhi; Arts Dir. INDER DASS.

There are fourteen state Academies of music, dance and drama; ten Colleges of Music, sixteen of Dance and Ballet and fourteen other Theatre Institutes, some of which have semi-professional companies.

ATOMIC ENERGY*

Atomic Energy Commission: Chhatrapati Shivaji Maharaj Marg, Bombay 1; Minister in Charge Mrs. INDIRA GANDHI; Chair. and Sec. Dept. of Atomic Energy H. N. SETHNA.

Babha Atomic Research Centre (BARC): Trombay, Bombay 400085; f. 1957; national centre for research in and development of atomic energy for peaceful uses; 4 reactors: APSARA (1 MW, research and isotope production), CIRUS (40 MW, research, isotope production and materials testing), ZERLINA (Zero Energy Reactor for Lattice Investigations and New Assemblies); PURNIMA (Zero Energy Plutonium Oxide Fast Reactor); other facilities include a 5.5 MeV Van der Graaff accelerator, radio-chemistry and isotope laboratories, electronics prototype engineering laboratory, isotope production and processing unit, ISOMED —Sterilization Plant for Medical Products, pilot plants for production of heavy water, zirconium, titanium, etc., a Thorium plant, a Uranium metal plant, a fuel element fabrication facility, a fuel reprocessing plant, Food Irradiation and Processing Laboratory (FIPLY), gamma field and library and information services. Heavy Water Moderated 100 MW thermal research under construction; research laboratories at Guaribidanur and Kashmir, Reactor Research Centre for Fast Reactor Development at Madras, Variable Energy Cyclotron at Calcutta; Dir. Dr. RAJA RAMANNA.

Indian Space Research Organization (ISRO): F-Block, CBAB Complex, District Office Rd., Bangalore 560 009; f. 1969; Chair. Prof. S. DHAWAN; Scientific Sec. Prof. P. D. BHAVSAR.

Indian National Committee for Space Research (INCOSPAR): c/o ISRO; f. 1962; Chair. Prof. S. DHAWAN; Sec. Prof. P. D. BHAVSAR.

Institute of Nuclear Medicine and Allied Sciences: Delhi-7; f. 1963; run by Research and Development Organization of the Ministry of Defence; carries out investigation into anaemia, Parkinson's disease, liver and kidney diseases, thyroid disorders; undertakes research in health physics, clinical biochemistry, radiation entomology and experimental medicine; also trains physicians and technicians in nuclear medicine; Dir. Col. S. K. MAZUMDAR, M.B., B.S., M.R.C.P.

Madras Atomic Power Project: Kalpakkam; will consist of two reactor units each of 200 MW capacity; it is expected to go critical at end of 1974.

Rajasthan Atomic Power Station: Consists of 2 units of 200 MWe each; first unit went critical in August 1972. The second unit will go critical in March 1975.

Rana Pratap Sagar Atomic Power Station: Rajasthan; Consists of 2 units of 200 MWe each; first unit went into operation in 1972 and second is expected in 1976.

Saha Institute of Nuclear Physics: 92 Acharya Prafulla Chandra Rd., Calcutta 700009; f. 1950; Dir. Prof. D. N. KUNDU.

Tarapur Atomic Power Station: Tarapur, Maharashtra; a 400 MW nuclear power station became operational in October 1969.

Tata Institute of Fundamental Research: Homi Bhabha Rd., Bombay 400005; f. 1945; fundamental research in nuclear science computer science, molecular biology, radio astronomy, and in mathematics; national research centre of the Government of India; Dir. Prof. M. G. K. MENON, F.R.S.

* In addition to Tarapur Atomic Power Station, already operating, two stations with two reactors of 200/235 MWe capacity each are under construction at Kota (Rajasthan) and Kalpakkam (Tamil Nadu). Another station at Narora (U.P.) will come into operation in 1980/1.

UNIVERSITIES

Agra University: Agra, U.P.; 45,758 students.

University af Agricultural Sciences: Hebbal, Bangalore 24, Mysore; 150 teachers, 2,000 students.

Aligarh Muslim University: Aligarh, U.P.; 816 teachers, 9,335 students.

University of Allahabad: Allahabad, U.P.; 8,982 students.

Guru Nanak University of Amritsar: Amritsar, Punjab; 8 Constituent Colleges.

Andhra University: Waltair, A.P.; 346 teachers, 54,921 students.

Andhra Pradesh Agricultural University: Rajendranagar, Hyderabad-30, A.P.; 7 Constituent Colleges.

Annamalai University: Annamalainagar, South Arcot, Madras; 339 teachers, 6,250 students.

Assam Agricultural University: Jorhat 4, Assam.

Banaras Hindu University: Varanasi 5, U.P.; 1,068 teachers, 12,326 students.

Bangalore University: Bangalore 1, Mysore; 1,956 teachers, 41,900 students.

The Maharaja Sayajirao University of Baroda: Baroda, Gujarat; 743 teachers, 17,348 students.

Bhagalpur University: Bhagalpur 7, Bihar; 1,569 teachers, 42,667 students.

University of Bihar: Sahnaya Bhavan, Muzaffarpur, Bihar; 50,505 students.

University of Bombay: Bombay 32; 95,609 students.

University of Burdwan: Burdwan, West Bengal; 1,900 teachers, 41,889 students.

University of Calcutta: Calcutta 12; 40 professors, 196,257 students.

University of Delhi: Delhi 7; 43 professors, 51,371 students.

Dibrugarh University: Rajabheta, Dibrugarh, Assam; 1,095 teachers, 25,600 students.

Gauhati University: Gauhati 14, Assam; 2,657 teachers, 50,181 students.

Gorakhpur University: Gorakhpur, U.P.; 206 teachers, 42,524 students.

Gujarat University: Navrangpura, Ahmedabad 9, Gujarat; 74,849 students in affiliated colleges.

South Gujarat University: Surat, Gujarat; 24 teachers, 103 students.

Indira Kala Sangeet University: Khairagarh, M.P.; 112 teachers, 2,466 students.

University of Indore: Indore, M.P.; 776 teachers, 16,370 students.

Jabalpur University: Jabalpur, M.P.; 683 teachers, 14,837 students.

Jadavpur University: Calcutta 32; 398 teachers, 5,130 students.

Jamia Millia Islamia: New Delhi 25; 173 teachers, 2,179 students.

University of Jammu: Canal Rd., Jammu; 9,253 students.

Jawaharlal Nehru Krishi Vishwa Vidyalala (Jawaharlal Nehru Agricultural University): Krishnagar, Jabalpur, M.P.

Jiwaji University: Vdihya Vihar, Gwalior 2, M.P.; 708 teachers, 29,487 students.

University of Jodhpur: Rajasthan; 400 teachers, 7,153 students.

Kalyani University: P.O. Kalyani Dt. Nadia, West Bengal; 1,964 students.

Kameshwara Singh Darbhagha Sanskrit University: Darbhagha, Bihar; over 500 affiliated institutions.

Karnatak University: Dharwar, Mysore; 48,799 students.

University of Kashmir: Hazratbal, Srinagar 6; 957 teachers, 11,332 students.

University of Kerala: Trivandrum, Kerala; 138,695 students.

Kurukshetra University: Kurukshetra, Punjab; 475 teachers, 4,919 students.

University of Lucknow: Badshaw Bagh, Lucknow, U.P.; 597 teachers, 26,186 students.

University of Madras: Chepauk, Triplicane P.O., Madras 5, Tamil Nadu; 136,466 students.

Madurai University: Madurai, Tamil Nadu; 65 teachers, 56,040 students.

Marathwada University: Aurangabad (Deccan), Maharashtra; 1,375 teachers, 36,558 students.

University of Mysore: P.O.B. 14, Mysore; 73,996 students.

University of Nagpur: Nagpur, Maharashtra; 3,494 teachers, 84,061 students.

University of North Bengal: Raja Rammohanpur, Darjeeling, West Bengal; 21,979 students.

Orissa University of Agriculture and Technology: Bhubaneswar 3, District Purri, Orissa; 144 teachers.

Osmania University: Hyderabad, A.P.; 54 professors, 62,061 students.

University of Patna: Patna 5, Bihar; 12,605 students.

University of Poona: Ganeshkhind, Poona 7; 62,176 students.

Punjab University: Chandigarh 14; 133,717 students (incl. affiliated colleges).

Punjab Agricultural University: Ludhiana, Punjab.

Punjabi University: Patiala, Punjab; 30,241 students.

Rabindra Bharati University: Calcutta 7; 185 teachers, 3,914 students.

University of Rajasthan: Gandhi Nagar, Jaipur; 482 teachers, 10,184 students.

Ranchi University: Ranchi-1, Bihar; 1,571 teachers, 36,892 students.

Ravishankar University: Raipur, M.P.; 22,619 students.

University af Roorkee: Roorkee, U.P.; 303 teachers, 1,936 students.

Sadar Patel University: Vallabh Vidyanagar, Gujarat; 592 teachers, 12,045 students.

University of Sagar: Sagar, M.P.; 18,000 students.

Saurashtra University: Rajkot 1, Gujarat.

Shivaji University: Vidyanagar, Kolhapur 3, Maharashtra; 2,391 teachers, 67,607 students.

Shreemati Nathibai Damodar Thackersey Women's University: 1 Nathibal Thackersey Rd., Bombay 20; 532 teachers, 17,693 students.

Sri Venkateswara University: Tirupati, A.P.; 167 teachers, 1,074 students.

University of Udaipur: Udaipur, Rajasthan; 478 teachers, 7,176 students.

Utkal University: Vani Vihar, Bhubaneswar 4; 1,673 teachers, 33,190 students.

Uttar Pradesh Agricultural University: Pantnagar, Nainital, U.P.; 205 teachers, 1,822 students.

Varanaseya-Sanskrit University: Varanasi 2, U.P.; 28,000 students (incl. affiliated colleges).

Vikram University: Ujjain, M.P.; 13,084 students.

Visva-Bharati: P.O. Santiniketan, District of Birbhum, West Bengal; 254 teachers, 1,171 students.

SIKKIM

Sikkim is a small mountainous state in the Himalayas bounded by the Tibetan Autonomous Region of China, India, Nepal and Bhutan. It is closely related to India by Treaty and is of great strategic importance to both India and China.

STATISTICS

AREA AND POPULATION

AREA (sq. miles)		POPULATION (1961 Census)			
Total	Forest	Total	Males	Females	Gangtok (capital)
2,818	748	162,189	85,193	76,996	6,848

1971 Census: 204,760.

The population includes Nepalese, Bhutias, Lepchas and Tsongs. Principal languages: Sikkimese, Nepalese and Lepcha.

PRINCIPAL PRODUCTS

Crops (1971): Maize (110,000 acres), paddy (30,000 acres), millets, wheat and barley, marna, buck-wheat (160,000 acres), cardamom (155,000 acres), potatoes (5,000 acres), other vegetables (300 acres).

Fruits: Bananas, oranges and pineapples, apples (200 acres). There are government orchards at Lachung and Lachen.

Animals: Cattle, yak, sheep, goats, horses, mules, buffalo and pigs.

Minerals: Copper, graphite, gypsum, iron, gold, silver, lead and zinc.

Industry: Cloth, blankets, copper ware, wooden goods, carpets, hand-made paper. Work began on April 2nd, 1972, on a hydro-electric project at Lower Lagyap which when completed will produce about 12,000 kWh.

Forests: Fir, bamboo, walnut, sal, orchids and medicinal plants.

FINANCE

Indian currency: 100 paisa = 1 rupee.

Coins: 1, 2, 3, 5, 10, 25 and 50 paisa.

Notes: 1, 2, 5, 10, 100, 1,000, 5,000 and 10,000 rupees.

Exchange rates (April 1974): £1 sterling = 18.97 rupees; U.S. $1 = 8.03 rupees.

100 Indian rupees = £5.27 = $12.45.

FOURTH FIVE-YEAR PLAN 1971–76
(million Rs.)

	1966–71 ACTUAL	1971–76 PLANNED
Agriculture and Minor Irrigation	6.6	9.9
Animal Husbandry and Dairying	2.03	3.7
Forestry, Fishing and Soil Conservation	6.17	15.8
Co-operation and Fair Price Shops	1.20	0.2
Power	7.20	17.55
Industry	8.70	25.2
Roads and Road Transport	51.6	79.5
Tourism	0.1	8.8
Education	7.8	17.2
Health and Housing	29.2	13.5
Others	3.92	9.6
TOTAL	124.52	200.95

AID

In the financial year 1971–72, India gave more than Rs. 35 million as development aid to Sikkim to cover new schemes as well as those already in hand, in such fields as agriculture, animal husbandry, forestry, cottage industries, road building, education and health.

SOCIAL SERVICES

Medical and hospital care is provided free; there are 5 hospitals providing 290 beds and 24 dispensaries.

EXTERNAL TRADE

Exports

Cardamom, fruit and vegetables are mainly exported to India in small quantities.

Imports

Machinery, cotton piece goods, foodstuffs and consumer goods from India.

EDUCATION

In 1972 there were 164 primary schools, 21 post-primary schools, 6 high schools and 1 teachers' training college. About 250 students were studying at Indian colleges. The number of pupils in primary, secondary, high schools and teachers' training college was 19,000.

CONSTITUTION

Following the disturbances of April 1973, the Indian Foreign Secretary, the Chogyal and the leaders of the three political parties in Sikkim held discussions which resulted in a constitutional agreement, signed on May 8th, 1973, by all the participants in the discussions. A summary of the main provisions follows:

1. The people of Sikkim will enjoy the right of election on the basis of adult suffrage to give effect to the principle of "one man one vote".

2. There shall be an Assembly, elected every four years, the elections being conducted under the supervision of a representative of the Indian Election Commission who shall be appointed for the purpose by the Government of Sikkim.

3. The Assembly shall have the power to propose laws and adopt resolutions on education, public health, excise, the press and publicity, transport, bazaars, forests, public works, agriculture, food supplies, economic and social planning including state enterprises, home and establishment, finance and land revenue; but shall not discuss the Chogyal and members of the ruling family, any matter pending before a court of law, appointment of the Chief Executive and members of the judiciary, or any matter concerning the responsibilities of the Government of India.

4. There shall be an Executive Council composed of elected members of the Assembly appointed by the Chogyal on the advice of the Chief Executive.

5. The Assembly shall adequately represent the population. No single section of the population shall acquire a dominating position.

6. The Chogyal shall perform the functions of his office in accordance with the Constitution as set out in the agreement.

7. To head the administration in Sikkim there shall be a Chief Executive, appointed by the Chogyal on the nomination of the Government of India.

8. The Chief Executive shall have all necessary powers to discharge his functions; he shall act in consultation with a member of the Executive Council on any matter in which administrative functions have been allocated to that member; he shall submit all important matters to the Chogyal unless immediate action is required; he shall have special responsibility for the proper implementation of the constitutional and administrative changes, for the continuation of the enjoyment of basic rights and freedoms by the Sikkimese people and for the optimum use of funds allocated for the economic and social development of Sikkim.

9. There shall be equality before the law in Sikkim. The judiciary shall remain independent.

10. The palace establishment and the Sikkim guards shall remain directly under the Chogyal.

11. The Government of India reaffirms its determination to discharge its duties towards Sikkim in respect of defence and foreign affairs for the benefit of the people of Sikkim.

THE GOVERNMENT

Head of State: The Denzong Chogyal His Highness Palden Thondup Namgyal, P.V., O.B.E.

Chief Administrator of Sikkim: B. S. Das (India).

Following the popular disturbances in 1973 the Chogyal on April 8th, 1973, asked the Indian Political Officer, Mr. Bajpai, to take over the administration of the country and requested the services of an Indian official whom he would appoint as head of the administration. Mr. B. S. Das was accordingly nominated on April 9th. *See* the Constitution (above) for details of the system of government which is to be instituted.

INDIAN REPRESENTATIVE

Indian Political Officer in Sikkim: K. S. Bajpai.

PARLIAMENT

ASSEMBLY
Election April 1974

Party	Seats
Sikkim National Congress	30
Sikkim National Party	1
Buddhist representative*	1
Total	32

* Non-elective seat.

POLITICAL PARTIES

Sikkim National Congress: Gangtok; incorporated the Sikkim Janata Congress in 1973; Pres. The Kazi Lhendup Dorji (Khangsapa of Chakhung).

Sikkim National Party: Gangtok; conservative.

JUDICIAL SYSTEM

The Judicial System in Sikkim is similar to that of India. Magistrates and Judges administer the Judiciary.

High Court Judge: Shiv Kumar Prasad.

Chief Magistrate: Tarachand Hariomal.

There are four District Magistrates besides two Munsif Magistrates.

RELIGION

At the 1961 census the distribution of the population by religions was: Hinduism 66.7 per cent, Buddhism 30.8 per cent, Christianity 1.7 per cent, Islam 0.7 per cent.

Mahayana Buddhism is the State Religion. Most of the Buddhists are Bhutias and Lepchas. There are 67 monasteries and nearly 3,000 lamas. The main monasteries are at Pemiongchi, Tashiding, Phensung, Phodong, Rumtek and Ralong.

The immigrant Nepalese are mainly Hindus, although a number are either Buddhist or animist. Christian Missions: Church of Scotland and Scandinavian Alliance Mission.

PRESS

There is one Sikkimese newspaper and the Government publishes papers and bulletins from time to time. There is a printing press in Gangtok, printing in Tibetan, Nepalese, Hindi and English.

PERIODICAL

Sikkim: Gangtok; fortnightly; Editor Kaiser Bahadur Thapa.

FINANCE

Local banking facilities are provided by private banks.

TRADE AND INDUSTRY

Sikkim Mining Corporation: Rangpo; f. 1960; joint venture of Governments of India and Sikkim. Mines and processes complex base metal ores to produce copper, lead and zinc concentrates in Sikkim; Chair. I. S. Chopra; Gen. Man. and Ex Officio Sec. J. P. Tewari.

TRANSPORT AND TOURISM

TRANSPORT

There is no railway or airport in Sikkim.

Roads: In 1971 there were 261 miles of motorable roads, 75 miles of which are surfaced. In addition there are 230 miles of 'jeepable' roads and 116 miles of bridle paths.

A 72-mile road from Gangtok connects with the railhead at Siliguri in West Bengal (India) and an 80-mile road with the airport at Bagdogra.

Sikkim Nationalized Transport Service: Gangtok; State road haulage company.

Aerial Ropeway: A ropeway, 13 miles long, links Gangtok to the foot of the Nathu La Pass.

Himalayan Passes: The principal passes into Tibet are the Jelep La (14,000 ft.), the Nathu La (14,200 ft.) on the main routes to the Chumbi Valley. The Dongkya Pass (18,400 ft.) and the Chola Pass (14,500 ft.) also lead to Tibet.

TOURISM

There is a growing tourist industry, consisting mainly of European mountaineers and visitors on trekking holidays along the lower passes. Tourists are also attracted by the wide variety of flora—more than 600 varieties of orchid and 40 varieties of rhododendron.

The highest peaks are Kangchenjunga, 28,208 ft., the third highest mountain in the world, and Kabur, Pyramid Peak, Tent Peak, Talung and the Twin Peak, all over 24,000 ft.

EDUCATION

RESEARCH INSTITUTE

Namgyal Institute of Tibetology: Gangtok; f. 1958; research centre for study of Mahayana (Northern) Buddhism; library of Tibetan literature (canonical of all sects and secular) in MSS. and xylographs; museum of icons and art objects; President H.H. Chogyal Palden Thondup Namgyal of Sikkim; Dir. A. M. D'Rozario; publs. in Tibetan, Sanskrit and English, including *Bulletin of Tibetology* (3 times a year).

INDONESIA

INTRODUCTORY SURVEY

Location, Climate, Language, Religion, Flag, Capital

The Republic of Indonesia consists of a group of over 3,000 islands between South-East Asia and Australia and stretching from the Malayan peninsula to New Guinea. The principal islands are Java, Sumatra, Kalimantan (Borneo), Sulawesi (Celebes), Irian Barat (West New Guinea) and the Moluccas. The climate is tropical with an average temperature of 26°c (80°f) and heavy rainfall during most seasons. The official language is Bahasa Indonesian but more than 200 languages and dialects are spoken. About 94 per cent of the population are Muslims, 5 per cent Christian and the remainder are either Hindu or Buddhist. The national flag (proportions 5 by 3) has two horizontal bands of red and white. The capital is Jakarta on the island of Java.

Recent History

Indonesian independence from Netherlands rule was recognized in 1949, after the Dutch had failed to regain control following the defeat of Japan. Dr. Sukarno, the first President of the Republic, established himself as virtual dictator, obtaining mass support with his demagogy and a policy of extreme nationalism. His economic policies were disastrous, and hyper-inflation ensued. An attempted Communist *coup* in 1965 was followed by the massacre of at least 100,000 suspected left-wingers and Chinese immigrants. Inflation, widespread corruption and Sukarno's Marxist tendencies led to opposition from students, the army and Muslim groups, and between 1966 and 1968 his powers were gradually reduced and transferred to General Suharto, who became President in March 1968.

President Suharto retained the semblance of democracy, but real power passed from the parliament and cabinet to a small group of army officers, the *Aspris* (presidential assistants), and to *Kopkamtib*, the chief security organization. Left-wing movements were suppressed, and a liberal economic policy adopted, encouraging the inflow of foreign capital. Resentment of rising prices and the domination of the economy by Japanese capital, Chinese managers and entrepreneurs and an Indonesian élite, particularly the friends and relations of high-ranking army officers, was expressed in the riots that broke out in January 1974. The President announced steps to combat corruption and return power to the constitutional organs of government, dismissing the *Aspris*. At the same time, he took over command of *Kopkamtib* from his chief rival, General Sumitro, thus assuring his personal dominance.

Government

Indonesia is a Republic with executive power resting with the President, who is also the Prime Minister and leader of the Cabinet. The People's Consultative Assembly elects the President and Vice-President and also lays down the outlines of national policy. Legislation is carried out by the House of Representatives in co-operation with the President. The Supreme Advisory Council of which the President is Chairman, advises the Government on important state matters.

Defence

The armed forces were combined as a single force in 1966 and placed under the single administration of the Ministry of Defence and Security in October 1967. In 1973 total strength was 322,000 men: army 250,000, navy 39,000 and air force 33,000. Defence spending for 1971 was U.S. $286.7 million.

Economic Affairs

In terms of population, Indonesia ranks fifth in the world, but this high population is concentrated on the islands of Java and Madura. Smallholders, using labour-intensive methods to grow rice, the staple crop, and cash crops such as rubber, copra, sugar and spices, make up the mass of the population. Rubber, sugar and coffee are also grown on large commercial plantations. Agriculture, employing about 65 per cent of the labour force, contributes about 50 per cent of the national income, but food production is insufficient for the rapidly growing population, and in recent years rice has had to be imported.

Rising world commodity prices have benefited Indonesia, but while the value of exports of lumber, rubber and copra has risen, production has remained static. Oil production has increased rapidly (15 per cent a year between 1960 and 1972 and by a further 50 per cent in 1973), and oil has been the main generator of recovery from the economic mismanagement of the Sukarno era. Industry has been slow to develop, despite a liberal government policy of encouraging the inflow of foreign capital. The manufacturing sector contributed only 10 per cent of the national product in 1971. There is a lack of indigenous managerial expertise, and the public sector has suffered from incompetence and corruption. The hyper-inflation of the Sukarno era was checked by government retrenchment and a credit squeeze, but inflation worsened in 1972 and 1973 as food prices rose.

Transport and Communications

Inter-island shipping is in the hands of state and private shipping lines and there are many small craft. There are railways on Java and Sumatra totalling nearly 8,600 km. In Java there are adequate roads but on most of the other islands traffic is by jungle track and river boat. There are about 85,000 km. of roads of which over one-quarter are surfaced. Domestic air services link the major cities and international services are provided by the state airline P.N. Garuda Indonesia Airways and nineteen foreign lines.

Social Welfare

There is a limited state welfare service providing old-age pensions and medical care for Government workers. Malaria has been brought under control, but many endemic diseases persist. In 1969, there were an estimated 650 hospitals with 62,130 beds. In 1972 there were 6,000 practising doctors.

Education

In 1970, 12.8 million pupils between 6 and 12 were enrolled in primary schools representing some 58.6 per cent of all children of this age group. Literacy levels are high except in Irian Barat. An eight-year compulsory education programme will be extended throughout the whole country by 1980. There are twenty-nine state and several private universities.

Tourism

Tourism is based mainly on the islands of Java and Bali. Java is famous for mountains and volcanoes and for Buddhist and Hindu temples. Bali, the only remaining Hindu area in South-East Asia, is renowned for traditional dancing and religious festivals. In 1973, 309,675 foreign tourists visited Indonesia, an increase of 40 per cent over 1972.

Sport

Organized sports include football, basketball, badminton and athletics. Cock-fighting is popular, particularly in Bali.

Public Holidays

1974: August 16th (Mi'rha Nabi Muhammad), August 17th (Independence Day), August 26th (Late Summer Holiday), October 17th–18th (Id ul Fitr), December 24th (Id ul Ahda), December 25th (Christmas Day), December 26th (Boxing Day).

1975: January 1st (New Year's Day), March 28th (Good Friday), May 8th (Ascension), May 26th (Spring Holiday).

Weights and Measures

The metric system is in force.

Currency and Exchange Rates

100 sen = 1 rupiah.

Exchange rates (April 1974):
Exports: £1 sterling = 883.11 rupiahs; U.S. $1 = 374.00 rupiahs.
Imports: £1 sterling = 979.92 rupiahs; U.S. $1 = 415.00 rupiahs.

STATISTICAL SURVEY

AREA
(sq. km.)

TOTAL	JAVA AND MADURA	SUMATRA	KALIMANTAN (Borneo)	SULAWESI (Celebes)	OTHER ISLANDS*
2,027,087	134,703	541,174	550,848	227,654	572,708

* Comprises Bali, Nusa Tenggara, Maluku and Irian Barat.

POPULATION
(1961 Census—'000)

TOTAL	JAVA AND MADURA	SUMATRA	KALIMANTAN (Borneo)	SULAWESI (Celebes)	BALI	NUSA TENGGARA (Lesser Sunda Is.)	MALUKU (Moluccas)	IRIAN BARAT (West New Guinea)
97,387	63,226	15,803	4,120	7,109	1,790	3,785	793	761

(1971 Census—'000)

TOTAL	JAVA AND MADURA	SUMATRA	KALIMANTAN (Borneo)	SULAWESI (Celebes)	BALI	NUSA TENGGARA (Lesser Sunda Is.)	MALUKU (Moluccas)	IRIAN BARAT (West New Guinea)
119,232	76,103	20,813	5,152	8,535	2,120	4,559	995	955

CHIEF TOWNS
Population ('000)

	1961 Census	1971 Census		1961 Census	1971 Census
Jakarta (capital) . . .	3,694	5,849	Malang	341	429
Surabaja	1,008	1,269	Jogjakarta . . .	313	394
Bandung	973	1,152	Banjarmasin . . .	214	277
Semarang	503	633	Pontianak . . .	150	194
Medan	479	620	Tjirebon . . .	158	187
Palembang . . .	475	614	Padang . . .	144	187
Makasar . . .	384	497	Bogor	154	183

Births and Deaths (excluding Irian Barat): Average annual birth rate 48.3 per 1,000; death rate 19.4 per 1,000 (UN estimates for 1965–70).

Employment: Of the total population in 1970 the economically active numbered about 39,894,000, including 27,926,000 in agriculture (ILO and FAO estimates).

Total employed in industry in 1972 was 3,435,000.

AGRICULTURE
LAND USE, 1969
('000 hectares)

Arable and Under Permanent Crops .		18,000
Forest Land		121,800
Other Land		41,335
Total Land Area .		181,135
Inland Water		9,300
Total Area . .		190,435

PRINCIPAL CROPS

	Area ('000 ha.)				Production ('000 metric tons)			
	1968	1969	1970	1971	1968	1969	1970	1971
Maize . . .	3,220	2,435	3,018	3,000*	3,166	2,293	2,825	2,632
Rice (Paddy) . .	8,013	8,014	8,186	8,466	14,858	15,553	17,529	18,585
Sugar Cane† . .	114	109	134	134*	9,190*	8,260*	9,785*	9,709*
Sweet Potatoes and Yams . .	404	369	358	347	2,364*	2,260	2,175	2,154
Cassava (Manioc) . .	1,503	1,467	1,434	n.a.	11,356*	11,034	10,451	n.a.
Palm Kernels‡ . .	} n.a.	n.a.	n.a.	n.a.	{ 40.3	41.6	48.0	53.0
Palm Oil‡ . .					181.4	200.3	216.8	248.0
Soybeans . . .	677	554	684	559	420	389	488	391
Groundnuts (in shell) .	394	372	402	400*	478	445	488	467
Copra . . .	n.a.	n.a.	n.a.	n.a.	629	665	694	730
Coffee . . .	338	353	n.a.	n.a.	157.3	175.2	186.3	197.0
Cocoa Beans§ . .	n.a.	n.a.	n.a.	n.a.	0.7	1.6	1.5	1.6
Tea‖ . . .	111	119	120*	120*	72.8	63.0	67.0	70.0
Tobacco . . .	152	96	103*	140*	68.9	68.8	72.2	70*
Kenaf . . .	280	322	327	340*	163	203	221	254
Sisal and Cantala .	5	4	2	n.a.	9.2	8.0	5.0	n.a.
Natural Rubber . .	n.a.	n.a.	n.a.	n.a.	729.9	788	780	834

Coconuts (millions): 5,121 in 1968; 5,536 in 1969; 5,807 in 1970.

Potatoes: 41,000 metric tons per year (FAO estimate for 1961–65).

* FAO estimate.
† Crop year ending in year stated.
‡ Estates only.
§ Twelve months ending September of year stated. 1971–72: 1,600 metric tons.
‖ Figures relate to the planted area on farms and estates only. Farm production constitutes nearly half of total production.

Source: FAO, *Production Yearbook 1971.*

LIVESTOCK

	1967–68	1968–69*	1969–70*	1970–71*
Cattle	6,816,200	6,900,000	7,000,000	7,200,000
Sheep	3,704,300	3,720,000	3,740,000	3,750,000
Goats	7,092,700	7,050,000	7,030,000	7,000,000
Pigs	2,667,700	2,700,000	2,650,000	2,630,000
Horses	632,100	630,000	620,000	610,000
Buffaloes . . .	2,731,700	2,740,000	2,735,000	2,700,000
Chickens . . .	65,000,000*	65,500,000	66,000,000	66,500,000
Ducks . . .	15,000,000*	15,500,000	16,000,000	16,300,000

* FAO estimates.
Source: mainly FAO, *Production Yearbook 1971.*

LIVESTOCK PRODUCTS
(FAO estimates, metric tons)

	1968	1969	1970	1971
Beef, Veal and Buffalo Meat* . .	292,000	292,000	295,000	297,000
Mutton, Lamb and Goats' Meat* .	45,000	45,000	46,000	47,000
Pig Meat*	96,000	96,000	98,000	100,000
Horse Meat† . . .	900	900	900	n.a.
Poultry Meat† . . .	61,000	62,000	63,000	n.a.
Edible Offal†	79,000	79,500	80,000	n.a.
Cows' Milk	38,000	36,000‡	43,000‡	45,000
Hen Eggs	126,000	126,400	128,000	130,000

* Meat from indigenous animals only, including the meat equivalent of exported live animals.
† Inspected production only, excluding farm slaughterings.
‡ Official estimate.
Source: FAO, *Production Yearbook 1971.*

FORESTRY
(U.S. $'000)

	1970	1971	1972*
Logs and Sawn Wood ⎫ Firewood . . ⎭	104,311	161,414	217,940

* Preliminary figure.
Source: Central Bureau of Statistics.

FISHING
(tons)

	1970	1971*
Sea Fisheries . . .	802,000	820,447
Inland Fisheries . . .	446,993	424,108

* Preliminary figure.
Source: Central Bureau of Statistics.

INDUSTRIAL PRODUCTION
(Twelve months ending March 31st)

		1970–71	1971–72	1972–73†
Woven Textiles . . .	million metres	598.4	732.0	852.0
Textile Yarn . . .	'000 bales	217.0	239.0	287.0
Fertilizer . . .	'000 tons	103.0	108.4	177.0
Cement	,, ,,	577.0	531.0	652.0
Paper	,, ,,	22.0	29.0	38.0
Glass	,, ,,	11.0	7.4	14.9
Tyres, Tubes . . .	million	0.4	0.5	0.8
Batteries	'000 cases	56.0	72.0	72.0
Radio Sets . . .	'000	393.0	416.0	700.0
Television Sets . . .	,,	4.7	6.5	6.6
Motor Cars* . . .	,,	2.9	16.6	23.0
Motor Cycles* . . .	,,	31.0	50.0	100.0
Cigarettes . . .	million	13.6	14.7	16.8
Matches . . .	million boxes	322.0	348.0	475.0
Toothpaste . . .	million tubes	25.2	26.0	30.0
Soap	'000 tons	132.2	132.4	132.0

* Assembled. † Preliminary figures.
Source: Central Bureau of Statistics.

MINING

	TIN (quintal)	NICKEL (metric tons)	BAUXITE (metric tons)	GOLD (kg.)	SILVER (kg.)	COAL (metric tons)	OIL ('000 barrels)
1968 . . .	169,390	240,726	879,323	185.6	9,613.3	176,214	219,863
1969 . . .	174,130	254,139	765,282	256.6	10,589.9	191,412	270,942
1970 . . .	192,605	400,000	1,299,168	236.6	8,803.0	172,361	311,552
1971 . . .	197,220	900,000	1,237,607	329.7	8,875.7	197,906	325,672
1972 . . .	213,290	935,075	1,276,578	339.0	8,683.9	179,248	394,606

Source: Central Bureau of Statistics.

OIL

TOTAL OIL PRODUCTION
('000 metric tons)
(1 metric ton = 7.3 barrels approx.)

1970 . .	42,400
1971 . .	47,586
1972 . .	57,619

Source: Central Bureau of Statistics.

CRUDE OIL PRODUCTION BY COMPANY
('000 barrels)

	1970	1971	1972
Lemigas . . .	465	544	369
Pertamina . .	35,533	39,273	63,439
Stanvac . .	17,674	22,951	27,172
Caltex . .	257,877	262,846	303,826
TOTAL . .	311,549	325,614	394,806

Source: Central Bureau of Statistics.

CRUDE OIL PRODUCTION BY PRODUCING AREA
('000 barrels)

	1970	1971	1972
Sumatra . .	302,745	312,771	361,848
Java . .	537	4,610	24,532
Kalimantan (Borneo) .	7,771	7,220	7,411
Irian-Jaya . .	496	1,013	1,015
TOTAL .	311,549	325,614	394,806

Source: Central Bureau of Statistics.

CRUDE OIL EXPORTS
('000 barrels)

	1970	1971	1972
Japan . . .	163,259	176,353	207,045
Australia . .	16,883	3,520	386
U.S.A. . .	23,187	36,653	49,083
Philippines .	15,761	13,684	2,771
Hawaii . .	1,776	4,000	9,608
Other Countries .	7,402	5,374	30,197
TOTAL . .	228,268	239,584	299,090

OIL EXPORTS BY VALUE

	'000 U.S. $
1966 . .	217,314
1967 . .	231,728
1968 . .	290,498
1969 . .	370,210
1970 . .	433,249
1971 . .	549,414
1972 . .	1,211,832

Source: P. N. PERTAMINA, Biro Statistik & Perpustakaan.

FINANCE

100 sen=1 rupiah (Rp.).

Coins: 1, 2 and 5 rupiahs.

Notes: 1, 2½, 5, 10, 25, 50, 100, 500, 1,000, 5,000 and 10,000 rupiahs.

Exchange rates (April 1974):

Exports: £1 sterling=883.11 rupiahs; U.S. $1=374.00 rupiahs.

10,000 rupiahs=£11.32=$26.74.

Imports: £1=979.92 rupiahs; U.S. $1=415.00 rupiahs.

10,000 rupiahs=£10.20=$24.10.

THE BUDGET
(million Rp.—Year ending March 31st)

REVENUE	1970–71	1971–72	EXPENDITURE	1970–71	1971–72
Current Receipts . . .	320,583	415,900	*Current Expenditure* . .	283,475	343,000
Direct Taxes . . .	117,120	144,000	On Personnel and Pensioners .	119,439	153,800
Income Tax . . .	13,250	15,700	Rice Allowances . .	30,734	33,000
Corporation Tax . . .	21,250	21,600	Salaries/Wages/Pensions .	51,938	101,600
Foreign Oil Companies Cor-			Salary Increases (50 per cent) .	21,584	—
poration Tax . . .	61,470	87,200	Other Domestic Personnel Ex-		
M.P.O. . . .	20,900	19,100	penditure . . .	10,922	14,200
Others . . .	250	400	Foreign Personnel . .	4,191	5,000
Indirect Taxes . . .	200,810	267,700	*Material Expenditure* . .	69,443	12,100
Sales Tax . . .	19,000	20,700	Subsidies/Financial Balance		
Sales Tax on Imports .	19,500	29,600	Autonomous Regions .	53,219	67,200
Excise Tax . . .	39,460	45,600	Interest/Debt Repayment .	31,374	66,800
Import Duties . .	70,000	18,600	General Elections . .	10,000	37,200
Export Tax . . .	7,000	28,700	Other Current . .	—	1,500
Other Receipts from Oil .	33,600	39,100	*Development Expenditure* .	161,424	241,900
Others . . .	4,250	5,400	Economic Sector . .	81,644	140,500
Non-Tax Receipts . .	2,653	4,200	Social Sector . .	21,612	24,500
Development Receipts . .	124,316	169,300	General Sector . .	12,528	10,700
Foreign Credits . .	78,676	103,100	Project Loans . .	45,640	66,200
Project Loans . .	45,640	66,200			
TOTAL . . .	444,899	585,200	TOTAL . .	444,899	585,200

Source: Department of Finance.

REVENUE	1970–71 (Actual)	1971–72[†] (Actual)	EXPENDITURE	1970–71 (Actual)	1971–72[†] (Actual)
Direct Taxes . . .	121.7	180.9	Personnel Pensioners . .	131.4	163.3
Indirect Taxes . .	209.8	219.5	Food Procurement . .	—	n.a.
Non Tax Receipts . .	13.1	27.5	Material Expenditures . .	62.6	67.2
Development Receipts . .	120.5	131.1	Subsidies, Autonomous Regions	56.2	66.8
			Interest and Debt Repayment .	25.6	46.6
			Other	12.4	5.2
			Development Expenditures .	169.8	191.5
TOTAL . .	465.1	559.1	TOTAL . .	458.0	540.6

† 1972–73—Est.: Rp. 751.6 million.

Money Supply: (end-1965) 2,572m. Rp.; (end-1966) 122,208m. Rp.; (end-1967) 51,372m. Rp.; (end-1968) 112,303m. Rp.; end 1969) 114,245m. Rp.; (March 1970) 127,671m. Rp.; (May 1971) 171,700m. Rp.; (Dec. 1971) 214,832m. Rp.; (March 1972) 229,924m. Rp.; (October 1972) 418,024m. Rp.; (April 1974) 804,712m. Rp.

FIVE-YEAR PLAN 1969–74

The Five-Year Plan (REPELITA) lays stress on the development of agriculture. Projected rice production by 1974 is 15.4 million tons, rendering the country independent of rice imports. A total of 21,000 million Rp. is to be spent on rice production during the Plan, and a further 236,000 million Rp. is allocated to the rehabilitation and construction of irrigation works. The planned increase in domestic production of fertilizers is from the present level of about 100,000 tons to 1.4 million tons, and

the area of land under cultivation is to be increased to 9.3 million hectares. Those industries supporting the agricultural sector will be developed; an increase of 90 per cent of industrial production is estimated during the period of the Plan.

Of a total amount of 1,420,000 million Rp. to be invested under the Plan, state funds will provide 1,059,000 million Rp.

ALLOCATIONS TO PLAN PROJECTS
('000 million Rp.)

	1972–73	1969–70 to 1973–74 PLAN
Economic Sector:		
Agriculture and Irrigation . .	54	395
Industry and Mining . .	27	380
Electric Power . . .	27	100
Communications and Tourism .	78	265
Village sector	56	50
Total	264*	1,190
Social Sector:		
Health and Family Planning .	9	42
Education and Culture . .	17	95
Social and Others . . .	10	35
Total	36	172
General:		
Defence and Security . .	6	28
Others	8	30
Total	14	58
GRAND TOTAL . . .	314	1,420

* Including other investment.

Source: Bank Indonesia, *Indonesian Financial Statistics.*

FOREIGN AID
(1972–73)

	(million U.S. $)
U.S.A.	203.0
Japan	185.0
Germany, Federal Republic . . .	46.9
U.K.	26.1
Australia	24.4
France	20.6
Canada	16.7
World Bank and Asian Development Bank	145.0
TOTAL (incl. others) . .	723.6

EXTERNAL TRADE

COMMODITY GROUPS
(million U.S. $)

Exports	1970	1971	1972*	Imports (c.i.f.)	1970	1971*	1972*
Animals and Animal Products	13.7	25.5	43.3	Consumer Goods	249.5	221.2	232.2
Vegetable Products	567.5	637.5	673.0	of which:			
Mineral Products	565.0	551.2	790.8	Rice	52.2	8.8	44.0
Other Products	14.3	19.1	26.8	Wheat Flour	33.1	16.0	1.9
				Textiles	6.0	31.4	18.3
				Raw Materials and Auxiliary Goods	376.5	454.5	575.6
				of which:			
				Chemicals and Products	38.2	41.0	54.2
				Fertilizers	18.8	28.2	45.3
				Weaving Yarns	32.9	20.1	23.7
				Capital Goods	373.9	498.4	650.3
				of which:			
				Industrial and Commercial Machinery	112.8	155.8	217.3
Total	1,160.6	1,233.6	1,533.9	Total	1,001.5	1,173.9	1,458.1

* Estimates.

Source: Central Bureau of Statistics, *Indikator Ekonomi*.

MAIN EXPORT COMMODITIES
(million U.S. $)

	1970	1971	1972*
Rubber	253.4	221.9	180.1
Copra	30.3	12.4	4.3
Coffee	69.2	55.3	74.3
Tobacco	4.1	15.2	29.3
Palm Oil	35.1	44.7	40.5
Palm Kernels	5.5	5.1	3.8
Pepper	3.2	24.8	20.4
Tin Ore	106.1	51.9	64.2
Tea	18.3	28.9	29.7
Copra Cakes	5.9	11.9	12.9
Lumber	104.3	161.4	217.8
Petroleum and Products	446.3	477.9	718.9

* Estimated.

Source: Central Bureau of Statistics, *Indikator Ekonomi*.

IMPORTS BY COUNTRY
(million U.S. $)

COUNTRY	1971	1972*
Singapore	70.0	84.3
Thailand	8.9	27.7
Hong Kong . . .	17.3	22.3
Japan	360.9	500.5
China	27.6	36.8
United States . .	174.1	217.5
Canada	3.2	7.3
U.K.	46.4	61.9
Netherlands . .	51.1	59.2
Germany, Federal Republic .	105.0	114.4
Belgium/Luxembourg .	5.6	8.7
France	16.1	17.9
U.S.S.R. . . .	11.6	5.6
Others . . .		281.3
TOTAL . .	1,102.8	1,438.1

* Preliminary.

EXPORTS BY COUNTRY
(million U.S. $)

	1969	1970	1971	1972
Europe . . .	159.0	198.3	196.1	235.6
United Kingdom .	11.9	14.3	11.9	17.1
Federal Rep. of Germany	46.9	54.5	62.2	64.0
Netherlands . .	52.2	63.3	71.1	75.1
America . . .	132.8	148.3	198.9	272.0
U.S.A. . . .	128.6	144.3	192.4	236.0
Africa . . .	1.2	0.9	1.4	4.9
Asia . . .	493.7	773.3	813.0	990.8
Singapore . .	147.1	171.9	160.8	125.7
Thailand . .	11.7	0.2	0.4	0.4
Hong Kong . .	7.3	10.9	11.1	12.8
Japan . .	255.9	452.3	550.4	753.2
Philippines .	25.4	25.6	26.0	3.0
Australia . . .	61.6	36.1	15.9	10.4
Others . . .	5.4	7.7	10.3	20.2
TOTAL . .	853.7	1,160.6	1,233.6	1,533.9

Source: Central Bureau of Statistics, *Indikator Ekonomi.*

TRANSPORT

VEHICLES IN USE
(as at December 31st)

	1970	1971
Cars	238,924	259,282
Trucks	102,265	115,082
Buses	23,541	22,797
Motor Cycles . . .	440,005	528,069
TOTAL . .	804,735	925,230

Source: Central Bureau of Statistics, *Statistik Indonesia 1970 & 1971.*

CIVIL AVIATION
(1969)
(Garuda Indonesian Airways only)

	Aircraft Kilo-metres* ('000)	Passen-gers Carried	Freight and Mail (tons)
Scheduled of which:			
International .	5,477	84,881	11,549
Domestic .	9,483	403,236	3,535

* Non-scheduled (1969): International 91,000 km.; Domestic 327,000 km.

Source: ICAO, *Digest of Statistics 1960–70.*

COMMUNICATIONS MEDIA

Radio Sets: (1972) 2,000,000.
TV Sets: (1972) 200,000.
Newspaper Circulation: (1972) 1,500,000.

TOURISM

Visitors (1972): 221,195.
Receipts (1972): U.S. $47 million.

EDUCATION
(1970)

	SCHOOLS	TEACHERS	PUPILS AND STUDENTS
Basic	73,260	362,530	13,789,100
General . . .	5,940	87,810	1,260,900
Teacher Education . .	903	10,945	114,960
Technological . .	1,112	24,685	287,630
Other Vocational . .	1,644	24,095	246,890

Source: Central Bureau of Statistics, *Statistik Indonesia 1970 & 1971.*

THE CONSTITUTION

Indonesia has had three Constitutions, all provisional: August 1945, February 1950 and August 1950. In July 1959, the constitution of 1945 was re-enacted by Presidential decree.

GENERAL PRINCIPLES

The 1945 Constitution consists of 37 articles, 4 transitional clauses and 2 additional provisions, and is preceded by a preamble. The preamble contains an indictment of all forms of colonialism, an account of Indonesia's struggle for independence, the declaration of that independence and a statement of fundamental aims and principles. Indonesia's National Independence, according to the text of the preamble, has the state form of a Republic, with sovereignty residing in the People, and is based upon the *Pantjasila*:

1. Belief in One Supreme God.

2. Just and Civilized Humanity.

3. Nationalism; the Unity of Indonesia.

4. Democracy; guided by the wisdom of unanimity arising from deliberations (*musjawarah*) and mutual assistance (*gotong royong*).

5. Social Justice; equality of political rights, equality of the rights of citizenship, social equality, cultural equality.

THE STATE ORGANS

Madjelis Permusjawaratan Rakjat (*People's Consultative Assembly*)

Sovereignty is in the hands of the People and is exercised in full by the People's Consultative Assembly as the embodiment of the whole Indonesian People. The Consultative Assembly is the highest authority of the State, and is to be distinguished from the legislative body proper (Dewan Perwakilan Rakjat, *see below*) which is incorporated within the Consultative Assembly. The Consultative Assembly is composed of all members of the Dewan, augmented by delegates from the regions and representatives of the functional groups in society (farmers, workers, businessmen, the clergy, intelligentsia, armed forces, students, etc.). The Assembly sits at least once every five years, and its primary competence is to determine the Constitution and the broad lines of the policy of the State and the Government. It also elects the President and Vice-President, who are responsible for implementing that policy. All decisions are taken unanimously in keeping with the traditions of *musjawarah*.

Members are to be chosen by national elections. Following the dissolution of the elected Assembly in 1960 and pending general elections, the People's Consultative Assembly (MPR) exercises the authority laid down in the 1945 Constitution.

The President

The highest executive of the Government, the President, holds office for a term of five years and may be re-elected. As Mandatory of the MPR he must execute the policy of the State according to the Decrees determined by the MPR during its Fourth General and Special Sessions. In conducting the administration of the State, authority and responsibility are concentrated in the President. The Ministers of State are his assistants and are responsible only to him.

Dewan Perwakilan Rakjat—DPR (*House of Representatives*)

The legislative branch of the State, the House of Representatives, sits at least once a year. Every statute requires the approval of the DPR. Members of the House of Representatives have the right to submit draft bills which require ratification by the President, who has the right of veto. In times of emergency the President may enact ordinances which have the force of law, but such Ordinances must be ratified by the House of Representatives during the following session or be revoked.

Dewan Pertimbangan Agung—DPA (*Supreme Advisory Council*)

The DPA is an advisory body assisting the President who chooses its members from political parties, functional groups and groups of prominent persons.

Mahkamah Agung (*Supreme Court*)

The judicial branch of the State, the Supreme Court and the other courts of law are independent of the Executive in exercising their judicial powers.

Badan Pemeriksa Keuangan (*State Comptrolling Body*)

Controls the accountability of public finance, enjoys investigatory powers and is independent of the Executive. Its findings are presented to the DPR.

THE GOVERNMENT

President: Gen. T. N. I. SUHARTO; inaugurated March 27th, 1968. Re-elected March 1973.
Vice-President: Sultan HAMENGKU BUWONO IX.

CABINET

(May 1974)

Minister of Defence and Security: Gen. MARADEN PANG-GABEAN.

Minister of Foreign Affairs: H. ADAM MALIK.

Minister of Home Affairs: Lt.-Gen. AMIR MACHMUD.

Minister of Justice: Dr. M. KUSUMAADMADJA.

Minister of Information: MASHURI.

Minister of Education and Culture: Dr. SJARIF-THAYEB.

Minister of Religious Affairs: Prof. H. A. MUKTI ALI.

Minister of Social Affairs: H. M. S. MINTAREDJA.

Minister of Health: Prof. Dr. G. A. SIWABESSY.

Minister of Manpower, Transmigration and Co-operatives: Prof. SOEBROTO.

Minister of Trade: Drs. RADIUS PRAWIRO.

Minister of Finance: Prof. Dr. ALI WARDHANA.

Minister of Communications: Dr. EMIL SALIM.

Minister of Agriculture: Prof. THOJIB HADIWIDJAJA.

Minister of Industry: Lt.-Gen. MOHAMMAD JUSUF.

Minister of Mining Affairs: Prof. MOHAMMAD SADLI.

Minister of Public Works and Energy: Ir. SUTAMI.

Minister of State for Economic, Financial and Industrial Affairs: Prof. WIDJOJO NITISASTRO.

Minister of State for Public Welfare: Prof. SUNAWAR SUKOWATI.

Minister of State for Administrative Reforms: Dr. J. B. SUMARLIN.

Minister of State for Research: Dr. SOEMITRO DJOJO-HADIKOESOEMO.

Minister of State for Administrative and Financial Affairs and State Secretary: Maj.-Gen. SUDHARMONO.

DIPLOMATIC REPRESENTATION

EMBASSIES ACCREDITED TO INDONESIA

(Djakarta unless otherwise stated)

Afghanistan: 16 Djalan Tosari.

Algeria: 60 Djalan Tjik Ditiro.

Argentina: 1 Djl. Diponegoro.

Australia: 15 Djalan Thamrin, Gambir; *Ambassador:* G. A. JOCKEL.

Austria: 99 Djalan Hos. Tjokroaminoto.

Bangladesh: *Chargé d'Affaires a.i.*

Belgium/Luxembourg: 4 Djl. Tjitjurug.

Brazil: 38 Djalan Salemba Tengah.

Bulgaria: 34 Djalan Imam Bondjol.

Burma: 109 Djalan Hadji Agus Salim.

Canada: 6 Djalan Budi Kemuliaan.

Cuba: 57 Djalan Teuku Umar.

Czechoslovakia: 29 Djalan Prof. Mohd. Yamin.

Denmark: 12 Djalan Taman Tjut Mutiah.

Egypt: 68 Djalan Teuku Umar.

Finland: 72 Djalan Imam Bondjol.

France: 11 Djalan Imam Bondjol; *Ambassador:* PIERRE GORCE.

German Democratic Republic: 74 Djalan Diponegoro.

Germany, Federal Republic: Djl. M. H. Thamrin; *Ambassador:* KURT MUELLER.

Hungary: 36 Djalan Diponegoro.

India: 44 Djalan Kebonsirih.

Iran: 2 Djalan Mangunsarkoro.

Iraq: 38 Djalan Teuku Umar.

Italy: 47 Djalan Diponegoro.

Japan: 24 Djl. Thamrin; *Ambassador:* RYOZO SUNOBE.

Khmer Republic: 6 Djalan Tjitjurug.

Korea, Democratic People's Republic: 72/74 Djalan Teuku Umar; *Ambassador:* MUNSONG SUL.

Korea, Republic: *Ambassador:* LEE CHAE-SOL.

Malaysia: 17 Djl. Imam Bondjol; *Ambassador:* Z. A. bin SULONG.

Mexico: 46 Djalan Imam Bondjol.

Netherlands: 18 Djl. Kebon Sirih; *Ambassador:* HUGO SCHELTEMA.

New Zealand: 60 Djalan Prof. Mohd. Yamin; *Ambassador:* R. D. G. CHALLIS.

Pakistan: 15 Djalan Teuku Umar; *Ambassador:* ALI HASSAN.

Philippines: 8 Djalan Imam Bondjol.

Poland: 65 Djalan Diponegoro.

Romania: 45 Djalan Teuku Umar; *Ambassador:* ALEXIE MARIN (also accred. to Singapore).

Saudi Arabia: 3 Djalan Imam Bondjol (pav).

Singapore: 23 Djl. Proklamasi.

Sri Lanka: 45 Djl. Lembang.

Sweden: 12 Djalan Taman Tjut Mutiah.

Switzerland: 23 Djl. J. Laturharhary, S.H., *Ambassador:* MAX FELLER.

Syria: 78 Djalan H. A. Salim.

Thailand: 23 Djalan Diponegoro.

Trinidad and Tobago: New Delhi, India.

Turkey: 43 Djalan Imam Bondjol.

U.S.S.R.: 60 Djalan Imam Bondjol.

United Kingdom: 75 Djl. Thamrin; *Ambassador:* Sir W. I. COMBS.

U.S.A.: 5 Djalan Merdeka Selatan; *Ambassador:* DAVID D. NEWSON.

Vietnam, Republic: 25 Djalan Teuku Umar.

Yugoslavia: 41 Djalan Diponegoro.

PARLIAMENT

HOUSE OF REPRESENTATIVES
(Dewan Perwakilan Rakyat—DPR)

In March 1960, a Presidential decree prorogued the elected Council of Representatives and replaced it by a nominated House of 283 members (increased to 460 in 1968). Elections were held in July 1971 when 53 million votes were cast representing a 79 per cent poll. Seats have been distributed as shown below:

Speaker: Dr. IDHAM CHALID.

ELECTION
(July 3rd, 1971)

	SEATS
Government Functional Group (Sekber Golkar)	261
Armed Forces Functional Group	75
Partai Persatuan Pembangunan* comprising:	
NU Party (Muslim Scholars)	58
Parmusi Party (Muslim)	24
PSSI Party (Muslim)	10
Perti Party (Muslim)	2
Partai Demokrasi Indonesia* comprising:	
PNI (Nationalist Party)	20
Parkindo (Christian Party)	7
Katholik (Catholic Party)	3
IPKI (Independence Upholders Party)	0
Murba (People's Party)	0
Women	—
Others	—
TOTAL	460

PEOPLE'S CONSULTATIVE ASSEMBLY
(Madjelis Permusjawaratan Rakjat—MPR)

The Assembly, provided for under the 1945 Constitution, was most recently inaugurated in October 1972. It consists of the members of the House of Representatives and delegates of regional territories and of corporations and functional groups. It must meet at least once every five years. It is the highest authority in the State and appointed the President and Vice-President in March 1973, the former being responsible to the Assembly. Sixth session held in March 1973; total membership: 920.

Chairman: Dr. IDHAM CHALID.

Vice-Chairmen: Dr. SOEMISKUN; DOMOPRANOTO; J. NARO, S.H.; MOHD. ISANAENI.

	SEATS
Government Functional Group (Sekber Golkar)	392
Armed Forces Functional Group	230
Partai Persatuan Pembangunan* comprising:	
NU Party (Muslim Scholars)	78
Parmusi Party (Muslim)	27
PSSI Party (Muslim)	13
Perti Party (Muslim)	3
Partai Demokrasi Indonesia* comprising:	
PNI (Nationalist Party)	27
Parkindo (Christian Party)	9
Katholik (Catholic Party)	4
IPKI (Independence Upholders Party)	1
Murba (People's Party)	1
Women	48
Others	87
TOTAL	920

* Formed January 1973.

POLITICAL PARTIES

A Presidential decree of January 1960 enables the President to dissolve any party whose membership does not cover a quarter of Indonesia, or whose policies are at variance with the aims of the State.

The following parties and groups participated in the general elections held in July 1971, though in January 1973 nine of them were involved in mergers from which two new parties, the *Partai Persatuan Pembangunan* and the *Partai Demokrasi Indonesia* were formed.

Partai Persatuan Pembangunan (*Development Unity Party*): f. 1973 as a result of the merger of the four Islamic parties shown below; the parties retain their independence in non-political matters.

Nahdlatul-'Ulama (*Muslim Scholars Party*): Muslim; 78 seats in the MPR; Chair. K. IDHAM CHALID.

Partai Muslimin Indonesia: The formation of this Muslim party, approved during 1967, was announced in February 1968. The party is a merger of sixteen Islamic organizations and aims to fill the gap left by the mass Muslim party *Masjumi* which was banned in 1960; 27 seats in the MPR; Chair. H. M. S. MINTAREDJA.

Partai Sjarikat Islam Indonesia (*Islamic Association Party*): f. 1912; 13 seats in the MPR; mems.

1,500,000; Chair. ANWAR TJOKROAMINOTO; publ. *Nusaputera* (daily).

Peratuan Tarekat Islam Indonesia (*Muslim Party*): 3 seats in the MPR.

Partai Demokrasi Indonesia (*Indonesian Democratic Party*): f. 1973 as a result of the merger of the five parties shown below; Gen. Chair. ACHMAD SUKARMAWIDJAJA.

Partai Nasional Indonesia (*Nationalist Party*): Djl. Salemba Raya 23, Djakarta; f. 1927; 27 seats in the MPR; Leader MH. ISNAENI.

Ikatan Pendukung Kemerdekaan Indonesia (*Independence Upholders Party*): 1 seat in the MPR.

Partai Katolik (*Catholic Party*): 4 seats in the MPR; Leader T. J. KASIMO.

Partai Kristen Indonesia (*Protestant Party*): Matraman Raya 10A, Djakarta; f. 1945; 7 seats in the MPR; mems. about one million; Gen. Chair. MELANCHTHON SIREGAR; Sec.-Gen. SABAM SIRAIT; publs. *Sinar-Harapan Komunikasi* (bi-weekly), *Berita-Parkindo* (monthly).

Murba (*People's Party*): 1 seat in the MPR.

Sekber Golkar (*Secretariat of Functional Groups*): a Government alliance of groups representing farmers, youth, veterans, co-operatives, entrepreneurs, women, labour; 392 seats in the MPR; Chair. Maj.-Gen. AMRI MURTONO.

DEFENCE

Armed Forces (1973): Total strength 322,000; army 250,000, navy 39,000, air force 33,000; military service is selective.

Equipment: The army has some British and Soviet equipment, while the navy and air force has Soviet and U.S. equipment. In July 1972 it was announced that the air force would receive a squadron of T-33 training aircraft from the U.S.A. Australia has a defence co-operation programme with Indonesia, and provided 16 RAAF Avon-Sabre jets in 1972.

Defence Expenditure: Estimated defence spending for 1971 was U.S. $286.7 million.

Commander-in-Chief of the Armed Forces: General MARADEN PANGGABEAN.

CHIEFS OF STAFF

Army: Lt.-Gen. MAKMUN MUROD.

Navy: Admiral R. SUBONO.

Air Force: Air Vice-Marshal S. BASARAN.

JUDICIAL SYSTEM

Supreme Court. The final court of appeal (cassation).

High Courts in Djakarta, Surabaja, Medan, Makassar, Banda Aceh, Bukit–Tinggi, Palembang, Bandung, Semarang, Bandjarmasin, Menado, Den Pasar, Ambon and Djaja Pura deal with appeals from the District Courts.

District Courts deal with marriage, divorce and recon-ciliation.

Chief Justice: Prof. OEMAR-SENOADJI.

There is one codified criminal law for the whole of Indonesia. Europeans are subject to the Code of Civil Law published in the State Gazette in 1847. For Indonesians the civil law is the uncodified customary law (*Hukum Adat*) which varies from region to region. Alien orientals (i.e. Arabs, Indians, etc.) and Chinese are subject to certain parts of the Code of Civil Law and the Code of Commerce. The work of codifying this law has started but in view of the great complexity and diversity of customary law it may be expected to take a considerable time to achieve.

RELIGION

The provisional 1971 Census figures gave the following percentage estimates:

		Per cent
Muslim	. . . .	94
Christian	. . . .	5
Hindu	. . . .	} 1
Others	. . . .	

MUSLIM

Leader: IDHAM CHALID.

ROMAN CATHOLIC

Archbishop of Djakarta: Mgr. LEO SOEKOTO, S.J.

Archbishop of Semarang: H.E. Cardinal JUSTINIUS DARMOJUWONO.

Archbishop of Endeh: Mgr. DONATUS DJAGOM, S.V.D.

Archbishop of Medan: Mgr. Dr. F. A. H. VAN DEN HURK, O.F.M.

Archbishop of Pontianak: Mgr. HERCULANUS J. M. VAN DER BURGT, O.F.M.

Archbishop of Makassar: Mgr. TH. LUMANAUW.

Archbishop of Merauke: Mgr. J. DUIVENVOORDE.

PROTESTANT CHURCHES

Evangelical Christian Church in West Irian: P.O.B. 14, Sukarnapura; f. 1956; 900 local congregations, 225,000 mems.; publs. *Pedoman Rohani, Serikat*.

Geredja Kalimantan Evangelis (*Kalimantan Evangelical Church*): Djalan Djenderal Sudirman, 8 Bandjarmasin, Kalimantan; f. 1935; 94,619 mems.; Pres. Rev. C. A. KITING; Gen. Sec. Rev. HERMOGENES UGANG.

Geredja Kristen Sulawesi Tengah (*Christian Church of Central Celebes*): Poso, Sulawesi, Tengah, Central Celebes; mems. 125,000; Chair. Rev. J. MELAHA.

Geredja Kristen Djawa Wetan (*East Java Christian Church*): Djalan S. Supriadi 18, Malang; mems. 115,000; Chair. Pdt. SARDJONAN; Gen. Sec. SOEHARTO S. H.

Geredja Masehi Indjili Timor (*Christian Evangelical Church of Timor*): Kupang, Timor; Sec. Rev. RADJAHABA.

Geredja Masehi Indjili Minahasa (*Christian Evangelical Church in Manahasa*): Kantor Synode Tomohon, Sulawesi-Utara; f. 1829; Moderator Rev. REIN M. LUNTUNGAN; Gen. Sec. Rev. W. ABSALOM ROEROE; 500,000 mems., 134 pastors; member of National Council of Churches in Indonesia.

Geredja Protestant Maluku (*Protestant Church of Moluccas*): Kantor Pusat G.P.M., Batungantung, Amboina.

Geredja Protestant di Indonesia (*Protestant Church in Indonesia*): Medan Merdeka Timur no. 10, P.O.B. 2057, Djakarta; Principal Officers Rev. R. M. LUNTUNGAN, Rev. P. H. ROMPAS, M.TH.

Gereformeerde Kerken in Indonesia: Kwutang 28, Djakarta.

Huria Kristen Batak Protestant (*Christian Batak Protestant Church*): Pearadja-Tarutung, Sumatra-Utara; f. 1861 by Nommensen, a Missionary from Germany (R.M.G.); 1,618 preaching places; 1,002,555 mems.; Ephorus; Rev. T. S. SIHOMBING; Gen. Sec. Rev. G. H. M. SIAHAAN.

THE PRESS

PRINCIPAL DAILIES

Java

Abadi: Djl. Kramat Raya 45, Djakarta; Muslim; banned January 1974.

Ampera: Kramat V 14, Djakarta; Trade Unionist; Editor Mudjono; circ. 20,000.

Angkatan Bersenjata: Djalan Asemka 29, Djakarta; official armed forces paper; Dir. Brig.-Gen. H. Sugandhi; Editor Col. S. Djojopranoto; circ. 100,000.

Berita Yudha: Djl. Tanah Abang 11/35, Djakarta; official Army paper; Editor Brig. Gen. M. Nawawi Alif; circ. 95,000.

Djakarta Times: 9 Djalan Majapahit, Djakarta; f. 1966; Dir. and Chief Editor Zein Effendi, s.h.; Man. Editor Fahmi Mu'thi; circ. 25,000; banned January 1974.

Express: Djl. Hajam Wurukg; banned January 1974.

Harian Umum Republic: Djl. Kepodangzo, Semarang; f. 1957; Prop. Chandra Nainggolan; circ. 30,000.

Indonesian Daily News: Djalan Jend. Basuki Rachmat 52, Surabaja; f. 1957; English; Editor Hos. Nuryahya; circ. 6,000.

Indonesian Observer: Djalan M. Sangadji 11, Djakarta; English; independent; mornings; Editors Mrs. Herawati Diah, Sutomo Satiman, Tribuana Said, Mrs. D. Hadmoko Soehoed; circ. 16,500.

Indonesia Raya: Djl. Merdeka Utara 11, Djakarta; banned January 1974.

Kami: Kramat VIII 2-4, Djakarta; f. 1966; students' paper; Editor and Publr. Zulharmans; circ. 25,000; banned January 1974.

Kedaulatan Rakjat: Djalan P. Mangkubumi 40-42, Jogjakarta; f. 1945; Indonesian; independent; Dir. Samawi; Editor M. Wonohito; circ. 30,000.

Kompas: 104 Djalan Gadjah Mada, P.O.B. 615 DAK, Djakarta; mornings; Editor Drs. J. Oetama; circ. 84,000; audited June 1971.

Masa Kini: Djalan K.H.A. 121, Jogjakarta; f. 1966; Chief Editor H. Achmad Basuni; circ. 25,000.

Merdeka: Djalan M. Sangaoji 11, Djakarta; f. 1945; Indonesian; independent; Editor-in-Chief B. M. Diah; circ. 120,000.

Nasional: Bedji 33, Jogjakarta; f. 1946; Indonesian; nationalist (PNI); Editor Issuthiar; circ. 17,000.

Nusantara: 31 Djl. K. H. Hanam Ajjam; banned January 1974.

Operasi: 39 Kebon Sirih, Djakarta; f. 1966; independent; Editor-in-Chief and Man. Dir. Bachtiar Djamily; circ. 25,000.

Pedoman (*Guidance*): Gunung Sahari Antjol 13, Djakarta; f. 1948; Editor Masmimar Makah; circ. 25,000.

Perwarta Surabaja: Petjinan Kulon 23, Surabaja, P.O.B. 85; f. 1905; Indonesian; Editors Tjiook See Tjioe Tan, Phoa Tjong Hway, S. Ridwan, B. P. Parwan; circ. 10,000.

Pikiran Rakjat: 133 Djalan Asia-Afrika, Bandung; f. 1950; independent; Editor Sakti Alamsjah; circ. 42,000.

Sinar Harapan: Djl. Pintu Besar Selatan 93, Djakarta; f. 1961; Independent; Editor Soebagyopr; circ. 60,000.

Sipatahoenan: Djalan Dalem Kaum 42-44, Bandung; Sundanese; Editor Hadji Muhammad Kendana; circ. 7,000.

Suara Merdeka: Djl. Nerak 11, Semarang; f. 1950; Indonesian; Editor Mr. Hetami; circ. 60,000.

Suluh Marhaen: Pintu Besi 31, Djakarta; f. 1953; Indonesian; Nationalist (PNI); Editor Sabilal Rasjad; circ. 30,000.

Suluh Marhaen (*People Guide*): Djalan Kepodang 20, Semarang; f. 1957; Indonesian, independent; Proprietor Chandra Nainggolan; circ. 20,000.

Surabaja Post: Surabaja; independent; Prop. and Editor A. Aziz; circ. 14,000.

Utusan Indonesia: Djalan Veteran 111/3, Djakarta; f. 1963; independent; Editor H. Rahardjo; circ. 15,000.

Warta Bandung: Bandung; Indonesian; circ. 5,500.

Warta Harian: Kosgoro, Djakarta; co-operatives' organ; Editor Mas Isman; circ. 25,000.

Kalimantan (Borneo)

Harian Kerakjatan (*Democracy News*): 59 Djalan Tandjungpura, Pontianak; f. 1970; Editor U. A. Hamid; circ. 1,000.

Indonesia Berdjuang: Djalan Pangeran Samudra 71, Bandjarmasin; f. 1946; Indonesian; Editor A. S. Musaffa Sh; circ. 7,500.

Indonesia Merdeka: Djalan Pasar Baru II, Bandjarmasin; Indonesian; Editor Gt. A. Sugian Novr; circ. 5,000.

Masjarakat Baru: Samarinda; Indonesian.

Pembangunan: Pontianak; Indonesian.

Pembina: Samarinda; Indonesian.

Suara Kalimantan: Djalan Kalimantan 41, Bandjarmasin; Indonesian; circ. 5,000.

Sumatra

Api Pantjasila: Palembang; f. 1966; Editor T. S. Lubis; circ. 7,500.

Haluan: Djalandamar 59 D-E, Padang; f. 1948; Editor-in-Chief Chairul Harun.

Harian Mertju Suar: Djl. Let. Kol. Martinus Lubis 48, Medan; f. 1966; Editor Mahjoedanil; circ. 15,000.

Harian Duta: Djalan Pemuda 13A, Medan; f. 1969; Editor T. Jafizham, s.h.; circ. 5,000.

Mahameru: 3 Djl. Rumah Bari, Palembang; f. 1970; Editor M. Ali; circ. 5,000.

Medan Daily News: Djl. Sei Kera 37, Medan; f. 1969; English; Editor/Publisher H. A. Dahlan; circ. 5,000.

Mimbar Umum: Djalan Riau 79, Medan; f. 1947; Indonesian; independent; Editor Arif Lubis; circ. 50,000.

Penerangan: Djalan Sungai Bong 9/13, Padang; Indonesian; Editor M. Ridwan; circ. 6,000.

Suara Rakjat Semesta Palembang-Indonesia: Palembang; Indonesian; Editor Djadil Abdullah; circ. 10,000.

Waspada: Djalan Suprapto/Katamso 1 and Pusat Pasar 126, Medan; Indonesian; f. 1947; Dir. Mrs. Aniidrus Said; Editors Tribuana Said, Ammary Irabi; circ. 35,000 (daily); weekly edition 15,000.

Sulawesi (Celebes)

Pedoman Rakjat: Djl. H. A. Mapanyukki 28, Makassar; independent; Editor M. Basir; circ. 7,000.

Sultara: Djl. Korengkeng 34 Tilp 4563, 37713, Menado; f. 1968; Chief Editor V. R. Montolalu; circ. 6,000.

Bali

Harian Pagi Umum (*Bali Post*): Djl. Bisma 1, Den Pasar; f. 1948; circ. 10,000.

Suara Indonesia: Den Pasar; Indonesian.

Lombok

Lombok Baru: Ampenan; Indonesian.

Timor

Kupang: Indonesian.

PRINCIPAL WEEKLIES
Java

Armed Forces Courier: Medan Merdeka Barat 13, Djakarta; twice a week; Man. Dir. Col. N. J. Sofjan; circ. 8,000.

Berita Minggu: Djalan Pintu Besi 31, Djakarta; Indonesian; Editor Mawardi Rival; circ. 10,000.

Berita Negara: Djalan Pertjetakan Negara 21, Kotakpos 2111, Djakarta; f. 1960; official gazette; three times weekly.

Bina Pantjasila: Djalan Dr. Wahidin 11/2, Djakarta; bi-weekly; Editor Dr. M. Hoetaroeroek; circ. 25,000.

Business News: Djalan H. Abdul Muis 70, Djakarta; f. 1956; Indonesian and English; Chief Editor Sanjoto Sastromihardjo; circ. 10,000.

Djaja: Djakarta; independent; illustrated; Editor S. Hadisumarto; circ. 40,000.

Djakarta Weekly Mail: Djakarta; Indonesian.

Djojobojo: Pasar Besar Wetan 32, Surabaja; Indonesian.

Koran Minggu: Djalan Suari, Purwodinatan Tengah 7, Semarang; Indonesian.

Koran Minggu Pelopor Jogja: Djl. Djen. A. Yani 175A, Jogjakarta; f. 1966; Editor J. Wirosoebroto; circ. 7,500.

Lembaran Minggu: Djalan Asia-Afrika 133, Bandung; Indonesian.

Madjalah Merdeka: Djalan Hajam Wuruk 9; Indonesian.

Mahasiswa Indonesia: Djakarta; youth; Editor Louis Taolin; circ. 20,000.

Mangle: Djl. Lodaya 19, Bandung; f. 1947; Sundanese; circ. 30,000; Chief Editor R. H. Uton Muchtar.

Minggu Warta Bhakti: Djalan Asemka 29-30, Djakarta; Indonesian.

Panjebar Semangat: Djalan Bubutan 87, Surabaya; f. 1933; Javanese; circ. 50,000.

Pesat: Pakuningratan 67, Jogjakarta; Indonesian.

Sapta Marga: Djalan Segara 5, Djakarta; Indonesian.

Selecta: Djakarta; illustrated; Editor Samsudin; circ. 30,000.

Skrikandi: Djakarta; Editor Mrs. Soedjono; circ. 15,000.

Varia: Djakarta; illustrated; Editor R. Arifien; circ. 40,000.

Wanita Nasional: Semarang; f. 1950; Indonesian; Editors Miss Chafsah Amirin, Miss Setiowati Ramelan; circ. 10,000.

Sumatra

Bhayangkara: Djalan Veteran 34, Telukbetung, Lampung; f. 1967; three times weekly; Editor J. Koesri.

PRINCIPAL PERIODICALS

Al-Djami'ah: Institut Agama Islam Negeri, Demangan, Tromelpos 82, Jogjakarta; f. 1962; university journal of Islam; bi-monthly.

Aneka: Djalan Kebon Sirik 71, Djakarta; Indonesian; every ten days.

Angkasa: Djalan Tanah Abang Bukit 36, Djakarta; Indonesian Air Force magazine; Indonesian; monthly.

Bahasa dan Kesusastraan: Djalan Diponegoro 82, Djakarta; f. 1967; linguistics and literature; bi-monthly.

Basis: P.O.B. 20, Jogjakarta; f. 1951; general Indonesian culture; monthly; Editor Th. Geldorp, s.j.; circ. 5,000.

Budaya: Djalan Faridan M. Noto 11, Jogjakarta; f. 1952; Indonesian culture; monthly.

Dunia Wanita: Djalan Pusat Pasar, P. 125, Medan; f. 1949; Indonesian; women; fortnightly; Chief Editor Mrs. Aniidrus Said; circ. 10,000.

Economic Review of Indonesia: Ministry of Economic Affairs, Djalan Gadjah Mada 8, Djakarta; f. 1947; English; quarterly.

Gadjah Mada: Djalan Merapi 16, Jogjakarta; Indonesia; monthly.

Hemera Zoa (*Indonesian Journal of Animal Science*): Djalan Bubulak 32A, Bogor; f. 1886; bi-monthly; English, French, German.

Horison: Djakarta; cultural; independent; Editor Mochtar Lubis; circ. 10,000.

Idea: Fakultas Pertanian, Bogor; f. 1935; quarterly; English, Dutch.

Ilmu, Teknik dan Hidup: Djalan Sukabami 36, Djakarta; f. 1949; natural sciences; monthly; Indonesian.

Indonesia Magazine: Medan Merdeka Barat 28, Djakarta; monthly; Indonesian, English.

Indonesian Perspectives: Asean Publishing House, 128–130 Anson Rd., Singapore 2; trade, industry and tourism; monthly; English.

Insinjur Indonesia (*Indonesian Engineer*): Djl. W. Monginsidi 13, Kebajoran Baru; f. 1954; monthly; Editor Ir. J. B. Soemargo.

Intisari: Pal Merah Selatan 28, Djakarta; monthly digest; Editor Drs. J. Oetama; circ. (Jan. 1974) 117,500.

Japenpa: Medan Merdeka Barat No. 9, Jakarta; Indonesian Overseas Feature Service; twice a month; English; Exec. Man. Drs. T. Atmadi.

Lembaga Penjelidikan Ekonomi dan Masyarakat Fakultas Ekonomi Universitas Indonesia: Djalan Salemba Raya 4, Djakarta; f. 1954; Economic and Social; Dir. S. B. Joedono.

Madjalah GPS Grafika: Djalan Sawah Besar 29, Djakarta; f. 1962; Indonesian; graphic arts; monthly.

Madjalah Kedokteran Indonesia (*Journal of the Indonesian Medical Association*): Djalan Kesehatan 111/29, Djakarta 11/16; f. 1951; monthly; Indonesian, English; Editor Prof. Dr. Bahder Djohan.

Mimbar Kabinet Pembangunan: Merdeka Baratag, Djakarta; f. 1966; monthly; Indonesian; published by Dept. of Information.

Mimbar Pembangunan: Merdeka Barat 9, Djakarta; f. 1968; Indonesian; monthly; published by Dept. of Information.

Mimbar Penerangan: Merdeka Barat 9, Djakarta; f. 1950; Indonesian; quarterly; published by Dept. of Information.

Nasional: Matraman Raja 50, Djakarta; f. 1948; Indonesian; Editor Wienaktoe; circ. 20,000.

Pentja: Djalan Gadjah Mada 25, Djakarta; Indonesian fortnightly.

Pertani: Perusahaan Pertanian Negara, Djalan Pasarminggu, Kalibata, Djakarta; f. 1963; Indonesian; agricultural; monthly; Pres./Dir. S. Wardojo.

Praba: Bintaran Kidul 5, Jogjakarta; Javanese; fort-nightly.

Publisistik: University of Djakarta; Djln. Gondangdia Lama 3, Djakarta; quarterly; Gen. Man. Drs. D. H. ASSEGAF, Man. Editor Drs. ALADDIN.

Purnama: Parapatan 34A, Djakarta; Indonesian; fort-nightly; films.

Radjawali: Djalan Ir. H. Djuanda 15, Djakarta; Indo-nesian; monthly; Civil Air Transport and Tourism; Dir. SALMAN HARDANI; Man. Editor MOERTHIKO.

Suara-Guru: Djalan Tanah-Abang III/24, Djakarta; f. 1958; Indonesian; teachers' magazine.

NEWS AGENCIES

Antara (*Indonesian National News Agency*): 53 Djalan Antara, Djakarta; f. 1937; 56 newspapers subscribe to the Agency (1973); 15 brs. in Indonesia, 3 abroad; connected with 22 foreign agencies; Gen. Mans; HARSANO, RENO UTOMO; Man. Dir. MOH. NAHAR. Editor-in-Chief Ch. R. PAKASI.

FOREIGN BUREAUX

Agence France-Presse (AFP): Djalan Indramaju 18, Djakarta.

D.P.A., Jiji Press, Kyodo News Service, Reuters and Tass also have offices in Djakarta.

PRESS ASSOCIATIONS

Persatuan Wartawan Indonesia (*Journalists' Association of Indonesia*): Djalan Veteran 7-C, Djakarta; f. 1946; 3,000 mems.; Chair. ROSIHAN ANWAR, B. M. DIAH.

Persatuan Wartawan Tionghoa (*Chinese Journalists' Association*): 29 Pantjoran, Djakarta.

PUBLISHERS

Djakarta

Balai Pustaka: Djalan Dr. Wahidin; f. 1908; children's, literary and scientific publications, periodicals; Pres. Brig.-Gen. SOEJATMO.

BPK Gunung Mulia: Kwitang 22, Djakarta; Dir. A. SIMANDJUNTAK.

Bulan Bintang: Kramat Kwitang 1/8, Djakarta; social science, natural and applied sciences, art; Man. AMELZ.

Djambatan: Djl. Ir. H. Djuanda 15 (2nd Floor), Djakarta; f. 1952; textbooks, religion, philosophy, social sciences, natural and applied sciences, art, language and litera-ture; Man. Dir. Miss ROSWITHA PAMOENTJAK.

Gunung Agung: 6 Djalan Kwitang, P.O.B. 145, Djakarta; f. 1953; Pres. MASAGUNG.

Pembangunan: Djl. Gunung Sahari 84; brs. in Jogjakarta, Madiun, Surabaja and Medan; Textbooks; Man. SOEMANTRI.

Pradjna Paramita: 8 Djalan Madiun, Djakarta; f. 1963; educational; Gen. Man. SADONO DIBJOWIROJO, S.H.

Tintamas Indonesia Djakarta-Pusat P.T.: Kramat Raya 60; f. 1947; modern science and culture, especially Islamic works; Editor ALI AUDAH.

Pustaka Jaya: Taman Ismail Marzuki 73, Djalan Cikini Raya; f. 1971; fiction, essays, poetry and children's books; Man. AJIP ROSIDI.

Yasaguna: Gg. Batik 7, Bendungan Hilir; textbooks and general; Man. HILAM MADEWA.

Jogjakarta

Jajasan Kanisius: Pangeran Senopati 24; textbooks, religious, general books.

Kedaulatan Rakjat: Djl. P. Mangkubumi 42; fiction.

Padang Sidempuan

Pustaka Timur: Djl. Marpinggan.

Almahfuz Budhi: Djalan Veteran 394.

Pematang Siantar

Pustaka Gudang Ilmu: Djl. Penguruan 9.

Parda: Djl. Pattimura 100P.

Surabaya

Assegaff: Djalan Panggung 136; f. 1951; religious books, language books, lower school textbooks; Man. HASAN ASSEGAFF.

Joyoboyo: Djalan Penghela 2 atas; f. 1945; textbooks; Man. TADJIB ERMADI.

Madiun

Sriwidjaja: Djalan Kenari 19, textbooks; Man. DASKAR SUKARDI.

Medan

Gedung Pustaka: Djalan Antara 187c; f. 1948; Pres. A. K. LATHIEF; Sec. AMIRSJAH.

PUBLISHERS' ASSOCIATION

IKAPI (*Association of Indonesian Book-Publishers*): Djalan Pengarengan 32, Djakarta; f. 1950; 98 mems.; Pres. AJIP ROSIDI; Sec. Miss ROSWITHA PAMOENTJAK.

RADIO AND TELEVISION

Radio Republik Indonesia: R.R.I., Medan Merdeka Barat 9, Djakarta; f. 1945; 49 stations; Dirs. ABDUL HAMID (Dir.), M. AMINULLAH (Overseas Service), ATMOTO (Domestic Service), Ir. HENDRO SIDHARTO (Engineer-ing), R. HUTAPEA (Administration), Drs. ANWAR RACHMAN (News Service); publ. *Media* (fortnightly).

In addition to national daily broadcasts in Indonesian, which include school and educational programmes, there are daily broadcasts overseas in Arabic, Chinese, English, French, Hindi, Malaya and Urdu.

In 1973 9,000,000 licences were issued.

COMMERCIAL STATION

Jajasan Televisi Republik Indonesia: Senajan, Djakarta; f. Aug. 1972; government controlled; Dir. IR. S. TJITROSIDOJO; publ. *Monitor TVRI*.

In August 1973 there were 255,308 receivers in use.

FINANCE

(cap. = capital; dep. = deposits; p.u. = paid up; m. = million; amounts in Rupiah.)

BANKING

The General Law on Banking, enacted in December 1967, remodelled the banking structure in Indonesia, which now comprises the following five categories of banks: Central Bank; General Banks; Savings Banks; Development Bank; Special Banks. Special Banks may be set up by the Government to provide banking facilities for specific sectors, e.g. agriculture, industry, communications; a Special Bank is planned to grant credit to farmers, retailers and other small businessmen.

In order to develop the country's capital market the Government, in mid-1973, issued licences for three new monetary institutions and seven investment banks. The three monetary institutions are to be: P.T. Merchant Investment Corporation (P.T. Merincorp), P.T. First Indonesian Finance and Investment Corporation (Ficorinvest) and P.T. Indonesian Investments International (Indovest).

The formerly integrated structure of the Central Bank, composed of five units, was replaced in January 1969 by a single Central Bank and six State banks.

CENTRAL BANK

Bank Indonesia: 2 Djalan M.H. Thamrin, Djakarta; f. 1828; nationalized 1951; promulgated the Central Bank in 1968; Gov. RACHMAT SALEH; Man. Dirs. J. A. SEREH, ARIFIN M. SIREGAR, DURMAWEL AHMAD, J. E. ISMAEL, DJOKO SOEDOMO, MARATHON WIRIJA MIHARDJA.

STATE BANKS

Bank Bumi Daya: Head Office; Djl. Kebonsirih 66–70, P.O.B. 106, Djakarta; f. 1959; state-owned commercial foreign exchange bank; cap. p.u. 300m.; dep. 70,177m. (Dec. 1971); Pres. R. A. B. MASSIE, S.H.; Man. Dirs. R. PRASODJO, R. S. NATALEGAWA, R. MARTOJO KOENTO; 53 brs. in Indonesia; Overseas representative offices in Hong Kong and Amsterdam.

Bank Ekspor Impor Indonesia: Head Office: Djl. Lapangan Setasiun 1, P.O.B. 32, Djakarta-Kola; cap. 200m.; dep. 35,416m. (March 1972); Pres. Dr. J. E. ISMAEL; Man. Dirs. C. BUDIMAN, I. S. HADAJAT.

Bank Rakjat Indonesia (*Indonesian People's Bank*); Djalan Veteran 8, Djakarta; cap. 300m.; specializes in credits to co-operatives in agriculture and fisheries, and in rural credit generally.

Bank Negara Indonesia 1946: 1, Djalan Lada, P.O.B. 1412/DAK, Djakarta-Kota; f. 1946; cap. Rp. 500m.; first and largest State-owned commercial bank; specializes in credits to the industrial sector as well as commercial transactions; Pres. E. SOEKASAH SOMAWIDJAJA; Man. Dir. SOEDJIWO, BC. HK., A. M. LOEBIS, CHAIROEL ZAHAR, M. DJOJOMARTONO; 238 domestic brs. and overseas brs. in Singapore, Hong Kong and Tokyo; Representative offices in London and New York; publ. *Tegas*.

Bank Tabungan Negara (*State Savings Bank*): Djakarta; cap. 100m.; specializes in promotion of savings among the general public.

Bank Dagang Negara (*State Commercial Bank*): Djalan M.H. Thamrin 5, P.O.B. 338 DKT, Djakarta; f. 1960; authorized State Foreign Exchange Bank; specializes in credits to the mining sector; cap. 250m.; dep. 60,860m. (Dec. 1971); Pres. OMAR ABDALLA, Drs. Ec..

Man. Dirs. Drs. R. MOHD, S. SURIAWIDJAJA, H. M, WIDARSADIPRADJA.

DEVELOPMENT BANK

Bank Pembangunan Indonesia (*Development Bank of Indonesia*): Gondangdia Lama 2-4, Djakarta; f. 1960; formerly Bank Industri Negara; state bank; financial assistance to Government enterprises as well as to privately-owned industrial and other productive enterprises; helps in development or establishment of new industries and other productive ventures, or expansion and modernization of existing enterprises; conducts feasibility studies of Government projects; auth. cap. 110m. Rupiah; cap. p.u. 60m. Rupiah; total financial resources 34.935m. Rupiah (Sept. 1973); cap. and dep. 11.96m. Rupiah (Sept. 1973); Pres. KUNTOADJI.

NATIONAL PRIVATE BANKS

P.T. Bank Agung: 338 Djalan Overste Slamet, Rijadi, Solo; f. 1965; Pres. and Dir. R. SABARDI; Dirs. A. KARSONO, R. BUCHARI SOEKARDJO.

P.T. Bank Amerta: 18 Djalan Kwitang, Djakarta; formerly Indonesian Banking Corpn.; Pres. SADJITO; Chair. B. P. H. PRABUNINGRAT.

P.T. Bank Bali: 24 Djalan Pasar Pagi, Djakarta; f. 1954; foreign exchange bank; Chair. DJAJA RAMLI; Pres. G. KARJADI; Man. Dir. P. H. SUGIRI.

P.T. Bank Buana Indonesia: 34-5 Djalan Asemka, Djakarta; f. 1956; cap. p.u. 500.1m.; brs. at Medan, Surabaya and Bandung.

P.T. Bank Dagang Nasional Indonesia (*The Indonesian National Commercial Bank Ltd.*): 2 Djalan Balai Kota, Medan; f. 1945; foreign exchange bank.

N.V. Bank Pasifik: 52 Djalan Tiang Bendera, Djakarta-Kota; Man. Dir. R. M. MOERSODO.

P.T. Bank Pembangunan Industrie: 50 Djalan Orpa, Djakarta; private development bank; f. 1962.

P.T. Bank Umum Agraria (*Indonesian General and Agricultural Bank*): 45 Djalan Roa Malaka Selatan, P.O.B. 1032/DAK, Djakarta-Kota; f. 1967; Chair. JUSUF WIBISONO; Man. Dirs. Ir. R. M. SARSITO MANGOENKOESOEMO, PADMO SUMASTO.

Bank Umum Nasional P.T.: 20 Djalan Kali Besar Barat, Djakarta-Kota; f. 1952; foreign exchange bank; cap. 100m.; dep. 970.om.; Principal Officers NJODO HAN SIANG, M. A. GOWI, BASUKI SAJONO.

Several smaller banks in Djakarta and in the provinces decided to merge in October 1972 under the name **P.T. Sejahtera Bank Umum (SBU)** at the government's recommendation.

There is a large number of small private banks operating in Indonesia.

BANKING ORGANIZATION

Indonesian National Private Banks Association (*Perbankan Nasional Swasta—PERBANAS*): Djalan Sindanglaja 1, Djakarta; f. 1952; 127 mems.; Sec.-Gen. O. P. SIMORANGKIR; publ. *Keuangan dan Bank* (*Finance and Banking*) (quarterly).

665

FOREIGN BANKS

The General Law on Banking permits foreign banks to operate in Indonesia under certain conditions. The following eleven foreign banks (*see* below) have been granted permission to resume operations for the first time since 1963.

Algemene Bank Nederland: Djalan Ir. H. Djuanda 23, P.O.B. 2950, Djakarta; Man. C. H. J. VAN VUURDEN.

American Express International Banking Corporation: Djl. Thamrin, Hotel Asoka, P.O.B. 131/DKT, Djakarta.

Bangkok Bank Ltd.: Djalan M. H. Thamrin 3, Djakarta; branch at Jakarta-Kota. Man. and Asst. Vice-Pres. BOONCHARN TAYJASANANT.

Bank of America: Djl. Merdeka Utara, Djakarta.

Bank of Tokyo: Japanese Embassy Bldg., Djl. Thamrin 24, Djakarta.

Chartered Bank Ltd.: Djl. Abdul Muis 40, Djakarta.

The Chase Manhattan Bank, N.A.: New York; Djakarta Branch; Djalan Medan Merdeka Barat 6, P.O.B. 311; sub-br. at Djakarta-Kota; Vice-Pres. and Man. ADRIAN NOE.

Deutsch-Asiatische Bank: 80 Djalan Imam Bondjol, Djakarta.

Development Bank of Indonesia: Djl. Gondangdia Lama 2-4, Djakarta.

First National City Bank: Djalan M.H. Thamrin 55, and Djakarta-Kota branch at Djalan Hayam Wuruk 127; f. 1812; Gen. Man. J. A. FRANSZ; Vice-Pres. T. C. CROUSE.

Hongkong and Shanghai Banking Corpn.: Djalan Gadjah-Mada No. 18, P.O.B. 2307, Djakarta; branch at Djalan Pintu Besar, Selantan 109.

STOCK EXCHANGE

Stock Exchange of Indonesia: c/o Perserikaṭan Perdagangan Uang dan Efek-Efek; P.O.B. 1224/Dak, Djakarta-Kota; f. 1952; 17 mems.; Chair. Drs. SOEKSMONO BESAR MARTOKOESOEMO; Sec. Drs. KHO HAN TIONG.

INSURANCE

ARDJOENO, Assurantie Maatschappij: Kali Besar Timur 10, P.O.B. 1338, Djakarta; f. 1886; Man. Dir. H. F. THENU.

Central Asia Insurance Co. Ltd.: 101 Djl. Pintu Besar Selatan (1st floor), Djakarta-Kota; f. 1958; general insurance; Chair. LIEM SIOE LIONG.

Djasa Rahardja: Perusahaan Negara Asuransi Kerugian, Djalan Kali Besar Timur 10, Djakarta-Kota.

Garuda Insurance Co. Ltd.: Chartered Bank Bldg., 2 Kali Besar Barat, P.O.B. 1316 Dak, Djakarta; f. 1952; Chair. A. RAMEDHAN.

Javasche Zee- en Brandassurantie Maatschappij: Kali Besar Timur 10. P.O.B. 703, Djakarta; Mans. Sluyters and Co.

Lloyd Indonesia Baru P.T. Maskapai Asuransi: Kepodang 12/14, Semarang; f. 1953.

Lloyd Indonesia P.T. Perusaha'an Asuransi Umum: Kepodang 12/14, Semarang; f. 1916; Man. Dir. HAN BING HOO.

Mercurius N.V. Brandverzekering Maatschappij: Kali Besar Timur 8, P.O.B. 582, Djakarta-Kota; f. 1865; Mans. REIJNST and VINJU.

N.V. Maskapai Asuransi Umum Wuwungan: Pintu Besar Utara 32, P.O.B. 1062, Djakarta; f. 1952; general insurance; national company; Dir. R. A. WUWUNGAN.

N.V. Pasti (N.V. Perusahaan Asuransi Timur): Djl. Djendral Basuki Rachmad 16, Malang, Java; f. 1956; Man. Dir. Prof. Dr. W. HARDIMAN SETIASARWANA.

P.N. Asuransi Djiwasraja (*Djiwasraja State Life Insurance Co.*): 34 Djl. Ir. H. Djuanda, Djakarta; f. 1859; Sec. Drs. HADY SOESETO.

P.T. Asuransi Bendasraja (*Bendasraja General Insurance Co. Ltd.*): Djl. Pintu Besar Utara 4, Djakarta-Koya; f. 1966; general insurance; national company; Pres. SULAIMAN M. SUMITAKUSUMA.

P.T. Asuransi Gadjah Mada: 90 Djl. Tiang Bendera, Djakarta; general insurance; national company; Man. Dirs. Dr. R. F. KATIDJAN, W. A. WOWOR.

P.T. Asuransi Republik: Djl. Abd. Muis 86, Djakarta; f. 1957; general insurance; Man. Dirs. B. NASUTION, NOEHAR, SUWITO REKSOATMOJO.

P.T. Bangka Union Insurance Co. Ltd.: Djl. Modjopahit 26 Belakang, Djakarta; Dir. P. SULAIMAN.

P.T. Maskapai Asuransi Ampuh: Djl. Modjopahit 24-26 Belakang, Djakarta; Dir. P. SULAIMAN.

P.T. Maskapai Asuransi Independent: P.T. Bank Buana Indonesia Bldg. (2nd floor), 34/35 Djl. Asemka, Djakarta; f. 1957; general insurance; Dir. I. H. A. WIDJAYA; Man. M. D. WIDODO.

P.T. Maskapai Asuransi Indonesia Baru (*New Indonesia Insurance Co. Ltd.*): 1A Djl. Kopi, Djakarta; f. 1955; general insurance; Pres. F. A. DARMAWAN, B.B.A.; Man. B. DEN DEKKER.

P.T. Maskapai Asuransi Indrapura: Sancta Maria House (1st floor), 29 Djl. Ir. H. Djuanda, Djakarta; f. 1954; general insurance; Chair. J. TAHIJA.

P.T. Maskapai Asuransi Pancha: 27A/B Djl. H. A. Salim; Djakarta; f. 1957; general insurance; Mans. JOHN R. SIBIH, A. SUPRAPTONO.

P.T. Maskapai Asuransi Ramayana: 4 Kalibesar Barat, Djakarta; f. 1956; general insurance; Dir. R. G. DOERIAT.

P.T. Maskapai Kebakaran Dan Umum Suntad (*Suntad Fire and General Insurance Co.*): 95B Djl. Tiang Bendera, Djakarta-Kota; f. 1964; Dir. R. SOEGIONO.

P.T. Maskapai Reasuransi Indonesia (*Reinsurance Company of Indonesia Ltd.*): 7-9 Djl. Veteran III, Djakarta; f. 1953; professional reinsurance; Man. Dir. Dr. T. S. T. GAUTAMA.

P.T. Perusahaan Asuransi Murni: Djl. Tiang Bendera 90, Djakarta; f. 1953; general insurance; Pres. A. HURSEPUNY.

P.T. Umum International Underwriters: 30 Djalan Salemba Raya, Djakarta; f. 1967; general insurance; Pres. WAHJOE, B.B.A.; Dir. Z. NASUTION.

Reasuransi Umum Indonesia P.N.: Djalan Salemba Raya 30, P.O.B. 2635, Djakarta IV/3; f. 1954.

Samarang Sea and Fire Insurance Co. Ltd.: Djl. Ir. H. Djuanda 30, Djakarta; f. 1866; Mans. M. B. MURPHY and T. E. O'KEEFE.

Veritas Insurance Co. Ltd.: Kali Besar Timur 10, P.O.B. 1338, Djakarta; f. 1878; Man. Dir. H. F. THENU.

Waringin Lloyd N.V. Maskapai Asuransi: Kali Besar Timur 26, P.O.B. 606, Djakarta.

TRADE AND INDUSTRY

CENTRAL ORGANIZATION

National Development Planning Agency (BAPPENAS): 2 Taman Suropati, Djakarta; Chair. Prof. WIDJOJO NITISASTRO.

CHAMBER OF COMMERCE

Dewan Perniagaan dan Perusahaan—DPP (*Indonesian Chamber of Commerce and Industry*): 11 Jalan Merdeka Timur, Djakarta; Pres. M. SOEBCHAN Z. E.

TRADE ORGANIZATIONS

CAFI (*Commercial Advisory Foundation in Indonesia*): 9 Djl. Lombok, Djakarta; f. 1958; information services; Chair. Dr. R. Ng. S. SOSROHADIKUSUMO; Man. Dir. B. R. RANTI.

GINSI (*Importers' Association of Indonesia*): Wisma Nusantara Bldg., Djalan Modjapahit No. 1, Djakarta, P.O.B. 2744 Dkt.; f. 1956; mems.: 3,200 importers throughout Indonesia; Chair. B. R. MOTIK; Sec.-Gen. ZAINI NOORDIN.

Organisasi Exportir Hasilbumi Indonesia—OEHI (*Association of Exporters of Indonesian Produce*): Djl. Tjikini Raya 29, P.O.B. 13, Djakarta; f. 1946; 84 mems.; Chair. R. NG. S. SOSROHADIKOESOEMO.

Perkumpulan Koperasi Gabungan Pembelian Importir Indonesia G.A.—GAPINDO (*Indonesian Importers' Co-operative Union*): Kali Besar Timur 5-7, Djakarta.

Persatuan Exportir Indonesia PEKSI (*Indonesian Exporters' Union*): Djalan Modjopahit 2, Djakarta.

Perserikatan Perdagangan Uang Efek-Efek (*Association of Money and Stockbrokers*): 3 Pintu Besar Utara, P.O.B. 1224/Dak, Djakarta-Kota; f. 1951; organizes the Stock Exchange; 37 mems. (15 banks and 3 brokers); Chair. Drs. SOEKSMONO BESAR MARTOKOESOEMO; Sec. Drs. KHO HAN TIONG; publ. *Daftuar Kurs Resmi* (Official List of Prices) (daily).

STATE TRADING ORGANIZATIONS

General Management Board of the State Trading Corporations (BPU-PNN): 94-96 Djalan Kramat Raya, CTC Bldg., Djakarta; f. 1961; Pres. Col. SUHARDIMAN; publ. *Madjalah Perekonomian Nasional*.

P.N. Aneka Niaga: Djl. Kali Besar Timur IV/I, P.O.B. 1213 DAK, Djakarta-Kota; f. 1964; import and distribution of basic goods, bulb articles, sundries, provisions and drinks, and export of Indonesian produce.

P.N. Dharma Niaga Ltd.: Djalan Abdul Muis 6/8/10, Djakarta; P.O.B. 2028; f. 1964; import of technical articles, equipment and plant; factory representatives, repair and after sales service; export.

P.T. Pantja Niaga: C.T.C. Bldg., 94-96 Djl. Kramat Raya, Djakarta; f. 1964; import, export and distribution.

TRADE UNION ORGANIZATIONS

Serikat Organisasi Buruh Seluruh Indonesia (SOBSI): (*All-Indonesia Central Council of Trade Unions*): Kramat V 14, Djakarta; f. 1946; affiliated unions from all branches of labour; 3,277,032 mems.; affiliated to WFTU; Pres. NJONO; publs. *Ampera* (Indonesian), *Indonesian Trade Union News* (English, monthly).

Gabungan Serikat Buruh Indonesia (GSBI) (*Federation of Unions in Java*): Djakarta; about 89,215 mems.; Chair. R. H. KOESNAN.

Hispaunan Serikat Buruh Indonesia (HISSBI) (*Federation of Indonesian Trade Unions*): Mampang 44, Djakarta; about 413,975 mems.; Pres. A. Z. ABIDIN.

Serikat Buruh Islam Indonesia (SBII) (*Central Indonesian Islamic Trade Union*): Djalan Tambora Dalam 62, Djakarta; f. 1947; Pres. S. NARTO; Sec.-Gen. ASEP HALIM; in April 1967 the SBII merged with:

Kongress Buruh Islam Merdeka (KBIM) (*Free Islamic Trade Union Congress*): Djalan Kramat-Raya 45, Djakarta; f. 1956; 295,000 mems.; Chair. Dr. Haji ALI AKBAR; Sec.-Gen. SADIKIN W.

KESPEKRJ (*Indonesian Christian Workers' Union*): 43 Djalan Guntur, Djakarta 3/10; f. 1955, reconstituted 1963; 16 affiliated unions; Pres. DARIUS MARPAUNG; Sec. ROBERT SMK. SILITONGA; publ. *Bachtera* (monthly).

Serikat Buruh Muslimin Indonesia (SERBUMUSI) (*Muslim Workers' Union*): Surabaja, East Java; about 82,000 mems.; Chair. K. H. MASJKUR; Sec. KI BAGUS PRAKTIKTO.

Gabungan Serikat Buruh Islam Indonesia (GASBIINDO) (*Federation of Indonesian Islamic Trade Unions*): Djalan Tanah Abang III/6, Djakarta; f. 1947 in Jogjakarta; affiliated to ICFTU; 17 affiliated unions; 3,244,593 mems.; Pres. AGUS SUDONO; Sec.-Gen. SJOFJAN HAMDANY.

Gabungan Organisasi Buruh Serikat Islam Indonesia (GOBSII) (*Federation of Indonesian Muslim Trade and Labour Unions*): Djalan Ungaran 34, Djakarta III/10; f. 1956; 45,000 mems.; Sec.-Gen. MOCHTAR KARTOWIDJIHARDJO.

Sentral Organisasi Karyawan Sosialis Indonesia (SOKSI) (*Central Organisation of Indonesian Socialist Workers*); Djalal Petjenongan 40, Djakarta; f. 1961; 600,000 mems.; Chair. Dr. SUHARDIMAN; Sec.-Gen. Dr. SOEROWO ABDOELMANAG.

There are also independent local unions throughout Indonesia.

TRANSPORT AND TOURISM

TRANSPORT
RAILWAYS

Perusahaan Negara Kereta Api—P.N.K.A. (*State Railways*): Geredja 1, Bandung; seven regional offices; controls 8,596 km. (1972) of track, mainly on Java; Chief Dir. R. Soemali.

ROADS

Total length of roads is about 85,000 km., of which about 21,000 km. are asphalted.

MOTORISTS' ORGANIZATION

Notary Public: 8 Djl. Musium, Djakarta; Public Notary Tan Thong Kie.

SHIPPING

Indonesian Commercial Shipping Association: Chair. Mohammad Saad.

Pelajaran Nasional Indonesia—Pelni Lines: Djalan Patrice Lumumba, Djakarta; State-owned national shipping company; 83 ships.

Djakarta Lloyd P.N.: 28 Djl. Hadji Angus Salim, Djakarta; f. 1950; services to U.S.A., Europe, Far East and Australia, twelve cargo vessels; Pres. and Dir. M. J. P. Hahijary.

P.N. Pertambangan Minjak Dan Gas Bumi Negara (PERTAMINA): Djl. Medan Merdeka Barat 3, Djakarta; Pres./Man. Dir. Lt.-Gen. Dr. H. Ibnu Sutowo; cargo and tanker service of state oil mining company; nine tankers etc.

P.T. Perusahaan Pelajaran Samudera—SAMUDERA INDONESIA: 43, Djl. Kali Besar Barat, Djakarta Kota; private company.

P.T. Trikora Lloyd: 1 Djl Malaka, Djakarta-Kota, P.O.B. 1076/Dak.; f. 1964; Pres. Dir. S. Boedihardjo.

Sriwijaya Raya Lines: Djalan Tiang Bendera 52, Djakarta-Kota; Pres. A. D. Harris; Man. Dir. Sjahrul G. Bajumi; interinsular cargo and passenger services; fleet of 5 cargo and 6 passenger-cargo vessels.

N.S.M. "Oceaan": 18 Djalan Gajah Mada, P.O.B. 289/JKT, Djakarta; regular services between Europe and Indonesia.

Blue Funnel Line: 18 Djalan Gadah Mada, P.O.B. 289/JKT, Djakarta; regular services between Indonesia, Europe and Australia.

Blue Sea Line: 18 Djalan Gajah Mada, P.O.B. 289/JKT, Djakarta; regular services between the Far East and the U.S.A.

Thai Mercantile Marine Ltd.: agents: P. T. Samudera Indonesia, Kali Besar Barat 43, P.O.B. DAK/1244, Djakarta.

CIVIL AVIATION

P.N. Garuda Indonesian Airways: Djl. Ir. H. Djuanda 15, Djakarta; f. 1950; operates interinsular services and services to Singapore, Kuala Lumpur, Penang, Bangkok, Manila, Hong Kong, Tokyo, Bombay, Karachi, Damascus, Beirut, Athens, Cairo, Frankfurt, Amsterdam; 1972 fleet of 11 F.27, 6 F.28, 5 DC.9, 3 DC-8; Pres. Dr. Wiweko Soepono.

Merpati Nusantara Airlines: Djl. Patrice Lumumba 2, Kemayoram, Djakarta; domestic and regional services.

PRIVATE COMPANIES

Air Indonesia: Sumatra.

P.T. Zamrud Airlines: Nusa Tenggara.

P.T. Briston Masayu: Sumatra.

The following foreign airlines also serve Djakarta: Aeroflot, Air France, Air India, Alitalia, British Airways, Cathay Pacific Airways, Ceskoslovenske Aerolinie, Japan Air Lines (JAL), KLM, Lufthansa, MSA, Pan American, PIA, Qantas Airways, Scandinavian Airlines System (SAS), Swissair, Thai Airways International, EgyptAir, UTA.

TOURISM

Dewan Pariwisata Indonesia (*Indonesian Council for Tourism*): Djalan Diponergoro 25, Djakarta; f. 1957; private body to promote national and international tourism; Chair. (vacant); Vice-Chair. Sri Budoyo.

ATOMIC ENERGY

National Atomic Energy Agency (*Badan Tenaga Atom Nasional*): Djalan Palatehan 1/26, Blok-K.V., Kebajoran Baru, Djakarta; f. 1958; Dir.-Gen. Prof. Dr. A. Baiquini; publ. *Madjalah Batan*.

UNIVERSITIES

STATE

Universitas Airlangga: Surabaja, Java; 7,000 students.

Universitas Andalas: Djalan Djati 77, Padang, West Sumatra; 487 teachers, 4,000 students.

Bambang Moertyoso Institute: Djalan Djendral Achmad Yani; 11/5 Purwokerto, Central Java.

Institut Teknologi Bandung: Djalan Ganeca 10, Bandung, Java; 438 teachers, 5,500 students.

Institut Pertanian Bogor (*Bogor Agricultural University*): Djalan Oto Iskandardinata, Bogor; 427 teachers, 1,439 students.

Universitas Brawidjaja: Djalan Guntur 1, Malang; 497 teachers, 4,255 students.

Universitas Diponegoro: Peleburan, Semarang; 699 teachers, 5,003 students.

Universitas Negeri Djambi: Djalan Merdeka 16, Djambi; 47 teachers, 371 students.

Universitas Negeri Djember: Djalan Moh. Serudji 120, Djember; 704 teachers, 2,484 students.

Universitas Negeri Djendral Soedirman: Dialan Pengadilan 1, Purwokerto; 150 teachers, 800 students.

Universitas Gadjah Mada: Bulaksumur, Jogjakarta; 877 teachers, 14,134 students.

Universitas Hasanuddin: Djalan Mesdjid Raya, Makassar; 825 teachers, 6,506 students.

University of Indonesia: Salemba Raya 4, Djakarta, Java; 1,370 teachers, 6,986 students.

Universitas Lambung Mangkurat: Bandjarmasin, Kalimantan.

Universitas Mulawarman: Samarinda, Kalimantan.

Universitas Negeri Mataram: Taman Majura, Tjakranegara, Lombok, N.T.B.; 68 teachers, 785 students.

Universitas Negeri Padjadjaran: Djalan Dipati Ukur 37, Bandung, Java; 1,919 teachers, 10,360 students.

Universitas Nusa Tjendana: Kupang Timor.

Universitas Palangka Raya: Palangka Raya.

Universitas Pattimura: Djl. Djenderal Acmad Jani Ambon; 508 teachers, 980 students.

Universitas Riau: Pakanbaru, Sumatra; 346 teachers, 1,605 students.

University Sjiah Kuala: Darusalam Banda, Atjeh, S.U.

Universitas Negeri Sriwidjaja: Djalan Bukit Besar, Palembang; 232 teachers, 2,270 students.

Universitas Sam Ratulangi: Djl. W. Monginsidi, Manado.

Universitas Sumatera Utara (*University of North Sumatra*): Djalan Universitas 22, Medan; 153 teachers, 3,659 students.

Universitas Tanjungpura: Djalan Raja 17, Pontianak.

Universitas Tjenderawasin: P.O.B. 120, Abe-Sukarnapura, West Irian; 44 teachers, 665 students.

Institut Teknologi 10 Nopember Surabaja (*Surabaja Institute of Technology*): Djl. Kaliasin 84, Surabaja; 231 teachers, 3,200 students.

Udayana State University: Denpasar, Bali.

PRIVATE

Universitas Bogor: Djalan Bioskop 31, Bogor; 60 teachers, 350 students.

Universitas Djajabaja: Djakarta.

Universitas Ibnu Chaldun Bogor: Djalan Papandajan 25, Bogor.

Universitas Ibnu Chaldun: Senen Rya 45-47, Djakarta; 80 teachers, 1,000 students.

Universitas Islam Djakarta: Djalan Prof. Muh. Yamin 57; 34 teachers, 309 students.

Universitas Islam Indonesia: Djalan Tjik di Tiro (Terban Taman) No. 1, Jogjakarta, Java; 246 teachers, 5,500 students.

Universitas Islam Sjarief Hidajatullah Tjeribon: Djalan Kapten Samadikun, Tjeribon.

Universitas Islam Sumatera Utara (*Islamic University of North Sumatra*): Djalan Singamangaradja, Teladan, Medan; 279 teachers, 1,251 students.

Universitas Katolik Indonesia "Atma Jaya": P.O.B. 2639 Dak, Djakarta; 230 teachers, 1,168 students.

Universitas Katolik Parahyangan: Djalan Merdeka 32, Bandung; 250 teachers, 3,200 students.

Universitas Krisnadwipajana: Djalan Tegal 10, Djakarta; 128 teachers, 2,000 students.

Universitas Kristen Indonesia: P.O.B. 2, Djakarta; 426 teachers, 1,616 students.

Universitas Muhammadijah: Djakarta.

Universitas Nasional (*National University*): Kramat Raya 47, Djakarta.

Universitas H.K.B.P. Nomensen: Medan.

Universitas Kristen Satya Watjana Salatiga: Djalan Diponegoro 54-56, Salatiga, Java; 116 teachers, 1,227 students.

Universitas Sawerigading: Djalan Sembilan 24, Makassar; 158 teachers, 1,372 students.

Universitas Tandjungpura Pontianak: 17 Djalan Tandjungpura Pontianak, Kalimantan Barat; 154 teachers, 934 students.

Universitas Tarnmanegara: Djakarta; 214 teachers, 1,750 students.

Universitas Tjokroaminto Surakarta: Djalan Asrama 22, Surakarta; 100 teachers, 4,000 students.

Universitas Trisakti: Djl. Kiai Tapa-Grogol, Djakarta; 691 teachers, 5,954 students.

Universitas Veteran Republic Indonesia: Makassar.

IRAN

INTRODUCTORY SURVEY

Location, Climate, Language, Religion, Flag, Capital

Iran is situated in western Asia. It is bordered by the Soviet Union to the north, Turkey and Iraq to the west, the Persian Gulf and the Sea of Oman to the south, and Pakistan and Afghanistan to the east. The climate is one of great extremes. In summer temperatures of over 55°c (130°F) have been recorded, while in the winter, the great altitude of much of the country results in temperatures of −18°c (0°F) and below. The official language is Persian (Farsi), but various dialects of Kurdish and Turki are spoken. The great majority of Persians are Shi'i Muslims. The national flag (proportions 3 by 1) has green, white and red horizontal stripes. The Government flag has, in addition, a lion and sun emblem on the central white stripe. The capital is Teheran.

Recent History

After the Second World War British and American occupying forces left Iran, Soviet forces remaining in Azerbaijan until 1946. In 1951 the Prime Minister, Dr. Mussadeq, nationalized the oil industry and in 1954 an agreement was reached with foreign interests whereby oil concessions were granted to a consortium of eight companies. Since 1949 Iran has placed great emphasis on economic planning. Early in 1963 the Shah began an extensive re-distribution of large estates among small farmers. In the same year women were given the vote, despite opposition from traditionalists which culminated in the assassination of the Prime Minister, Mr. Mansur, in January 1965. Iran became a founder member of the Regional Co-operation for Development (RCD) in 1964. In 1966 Iran joined the Colombo Plan. Relations with Iraq are soured by a continuing dispute over rights in Shatt el-Arab, but diplomatic relations with Iraq were restored in October 1973. In the early months of 1974 fighting frequently took place on the border with Iraq, but both Iran and Iraq have agreed to the appointment of a UN mediator. Iranian troops have been aiding the Sultan of Oman in his struggle against the rebels in Dhofar province.

Government

Iran is a constitutional monarchy, with executive power resting with the Shah. Legislative power rests with the Senate and the National Consultative Assembly (*Majlis*). The Senate has 60 members, half of whom are elected, and half are nominated by the Shah. The National Consultative Assembly consists of 268 elected members. Iran is divided into 14 provinces (*Ostan*), administered by Governors-General nominated by the Ministry of the Interior. These provinces are sub-divided into counties (*Shahrestan*), municipalities (*Bakhsh*), and rural districts (*Dihestan*).

Defence

The Iranian armed forces total 211,500 men, with an army of 160,000, a navy of 11,500 and an air force of 40,000. There is a two-year period of military service. Iran planned to spend £1,200 million on defence in 1973, and has equipped herself with sophisticated weapons for the defence of the Persian Gulf area.

Economic Affairs

Iran is one of the world's leading oil producers, and the massive oil revenues have been instrumental in developing the rest of the economy. Although industry now predominates over agriculture in the formation of the gross national product, the majority of the Iranian people are engaged in agriculture. Most types of grain, sugar beet, fruit, nuts and vegetables are grown. Dairy produce, wool, hair and hides are also produced, especially by the nomads. There is a large fishing industry, both in the Caspian Sea, where caviar is obtained, and in the Persian Gulf. Forests, owned chiefly by the State, cover over 20 million hectares. A large deposit of copper was discovered in south eastern Iran in 1967 and large-scale mining is due to begin in 1974. Oil refining is an important source of employment and production from the Abadan and Masjid-i-Sulaiman refineries was estimated at 168.7 million barrels in 1973. The National Iranian Oil Company achieved greater control of the Iranian oil industry in June 1973 (for details see p. 683) and Iran has benefited from the increased prices of oil which oil-producing countries have been obtaining in late 1973 and early 1974. The Shah has undertaken to use part of his country's enormous increase in oil earnings to further international development, and has lent U.S. $200 million to the World Bank for this purpose.

Iran's Fifth Development Plan (1973–78) envisages total expenditure of U.S. $35,0co million, with the emphasis on education, social reform and agriculture. Iran's "White Revolution", by which land, including the Shah's land, was redistributed to peasants, was completed in 1971. Inflation, which in the 1960s had only been at an annual rate of between 2 and 3 per cent, had risen to 13 per cent by early 1974.

Transport and Communications

Communications are made difficult in Iran by the extensive mountain ranges, but there are over 3,500 km. of railways, and extensions are under construction. There are 35,000 km. of national and provincial roads, and, when completed, the CENTO highway will link Turkey, Iran and Pakistan. The principal ports on the Persian Gulf are Bushire, Lingah, Bandar Abbas, Khorramshahr and Bandar Shahpur. Ports on the Caspian Sea are Bandar Shah and Pahlavi. Iran National Airlines Corporation provides internal and international air services.

Social Welfare

The Pahlavi Foundation established in 1958 has received considerable gifts from the Shah for improving the education, health and social welfare of the poorer classes. National service draftees with medical experience have been formed into a Health Corps, bringing medical assistance to outlying areas of the country. In March 1974 the Shah ordered free public health services for all Iranians.

Education

Primary education is free and compulsory for both sexes, but this has not been fully implemented in rural areas. In 1972, 92 per cent of urban children and 55 per cent of rural children were at primary schools. 426,000 pupils received secondary education in 1965, and there were 96 technical schools. There are eight universities. Vital to the campaign for literacy has been the conscription of young secondary school and college graduates as teachers in place of normal military service.

Tourism

Iran's chief attraction for the tourist is its wealth of historical sites—notably Isfahan, Rasht, Tabriz, Susa, Persepolis—and its museums of Persian art and culture. Tourism is under the care of the Iranian National Tourist Organisation, Teheran.

Visas are not required to visit Iran by nationals of Belgium, France, the Federal Republic of Germany, Greece, Luxembourg, Netherlands, Pakistan, Poland, Turkey, the U.S.S.R. and United Kingdom.

Sport

Wrestling is the national sport of Iran. Basketball and polo are also popular. Winter sports are drawing more visitors to the Elburz mountains.

Public Holidays

The Iranian year 1353 corresponds with the Gregorian calendar March 21st 1974 to March 20th 1975, and the year 1354 with March 21st 1975 to March 20th 1976.

There are 15 official holidays in Iran—five national days and 10 religious days. In the Iranian year 1353 these will be as follows: March 21st–25th (Now Ruz, the Iranian New Year), April 2nd (13th day of Now Ruz), August 5th (Constitution Day), August 7th (Ascension of Muhammad)*, October 6th (Birthday of the Twelfth Imam), October 7th (Id ul Fitr)*, October 26th (The Shah's Birthday), November 10th (Death of Imam Ali), December 14th (Death of Imam Jafar Sadeq), December 15th (Id ul Qurban)*, December 30th (Birthday of Imam Reza), January 14th (Id ul Ghadir)*, January 24th (Ashoura)*.

* Indicates that these are religious holidays whose dates are determined by the lunar calendar; the other holidays fall on the same day each year.

Weights and Measures

The metric system is in force, but some traditional units are still in general use.

Currency and Exchange Rates

100 dinars=1 Iranian rial.

Exchange rates (April 1974):
£1 sterling=159.50 rials;
U.S. $1= 67.62 rials.

STATISTICAL SURVEY

(The Iranian year begins in March)

AREA AND POPULATION

AREA	POPULATION			
	Census (November 1st–20th, 1966)			Estimate (mid-1972)
	Males†	Females†	Total	
1,648,000 sq. km.*	12,981,665	12,097,258	25,785,210	30,550,000

Total Population: 30,956,000 (January 31st, 1973).

* 636,300 square miles.
† Excluding nomadic tribes (totalling 462,146) and other unsettled population (244,141).

CHIEF TOWNS
POPULATION (1973 estimates)

Teheran (capital)	.	4,000,000	Ahwaz .	.	260,000	Kerman .	.	90,000
Isfahan .	.	520,000	Kermanshah	.	187,930*	Arak .	.	90,000
Meshed .	.	510,000	Rasht .	.	143,557*	Khoramabad .	.	59,578*
Tabriz .	.	465,000	Hamadan	.	124,167*	Sanandaj	.	54,578*
Shiraz .	.	325,000	Rezaieh .	.	110,749*	Bandar Abbas .	.	45,000
Abadan .	.	300,000						

* 1967.

ECONOMICALLY ACTIVE POPULATION*
(1966 Census)

	MALES	FEMALES	TOTAL
Agriculture, Forestry, Hunting and Fishing .	2,965,287	203,228	3,168,515
Mining and Quarrying	25,911	401	26,312
Manufacturing	758,799	508,801	1,267,600
Construction	507,703	2,075	509,778
Electricity, Gas, Water Supply . . .	52,165	693	52,858
Commerce	543,096	8,927	552,023
Transport, Storage and Communications . .	221,531	2,555	224,086
Services	759,718	169,967	929,685
Others (not adequately described) . . .	114,203	13,336	127,539
TOTAL IN EMPLOYMENT . . .	5,948,413	909,983	6,858,396
Unemployed†	635,844	89,845	725,689
TOTAL	6,584,257	999,828	7,584,085

* Excluding nomadic tribes and other unsettled population.
† Including persons seeking work for the first time.

INDUSTRIAL EMPLOYMENT 1972

	ESTABLISH-MENTS	EMPLOYEES
Food Manufacturing	28,853	159,939
Beverages	89	4,555
Tobacco	3	5,385
Textiles, Carpets, etc. . . .	49,577	239,798
Clothing	47,462	145,207
Wood and Furniture . . .	14,324	32,958
Paper and Cardboard . . .	297	4,612
Printing and Binding . . .	1,239	12,041
Leather and Hides . . .	1,497	12,027
Rubber and Rubber Products . .	1,244	10,088
Chemicals	1,447	21,613
Non-metallic Minerals . . .	6,655	48,153
Petroleum	15	1,440
Base Metals	944	19,634
Metal Products	29,058	111,162
Non-electrical Machinery . . .	1,653	13,652
Electrical Machinery . . .	3,924	30,146
Transport Equipment . . .	13,788	44,888
Miscellaneous	7,077	18,700
TOTAL	209,146	935,998

AGRICULTURE

PRODUCTION
('000 metric tons)

	1969	1970	1971
Wheat . . .	4,030	4,000	4,800
Milled Rice . .	1,020	1,060	1,046
Barley . .	860	880	800
Sugar Beet . .	3,480	3,850	4,000
Cotton . .	520	500	450
Tea . .	19	20	13
Tobacco . .	18	17	16

LIVESTOCK
('000)

	1969–70	1970–71
Sheep	35,000	35,000
Goats	12,600	12,500
Cattle	5,200	5,100
Asses	2,100	2,000

Source: FAO Production Yearbook 1971.

Fishing: Persian Gulf 14,000 tons, Caspian Sea 3,250 tons (incl. 2,000 tons of sturgeon and over 200 tons of caviar)—annually.

MINING
('ooo metric tons)

	1969–70	1970–71	1971–72
Iron Ore . .	10.0	150.0	98.0
Copper Ore . .	2.6	2.8	3.0
Lead . .	89.0	99.0	77.0
Zinc . .	97.0	66.0	89.0
Chromite . .	222.0	152.0	120.0
Barite . .	77.0	79.0	80.0
Coal . .	530.0	600.0	1,000.0

OIL
CRUDE OIL PRODUCTION
('ooo long tons)

	Total	Export
1967	120,900	99,500
1968	127,325	105,329
1969	165,694	139,942
1970	185,630	162,102
1971	222,181	193,831

Crude oil production in 1972 reached 294.1 million cubic metres, an 11 per cent increase over 1971.

INDUSTRY

	Unit	1969	1970	1971
Sugar (refined)	'ooo metric tons	512	567	663
Edible Oils (refined) . . .	„ „ „	150	167	160
Cigarettes	million	12,104	11,898	13,331
Tobacco	metric tons	18,000	17,000	16,000
Ice	'ooo metric tons	1,509	1,651	n.a.
Cement	„ „ „	2,342	2,587	2,819

FINANCE

100 dinars=1 Iranian rial.

Coins: 5, 10, 25 and 50 dinars; 1, 2, 5 and 10 rials.

Notes: 5, 10, 20, 50, 100, 200, 500, 1,000, 5,000 and 10,000 rials.

Exchange rates (April 1974): £1 sterling=159.50 rials (trade rate);

U.S. $1=67.62 rials (trade rate) or 68.175 rials (par value).

1,000 Iranian rials=£6.27=$14.79 (trade rates).

Note: Prior to February 1973 the exchange rate was U.S. $1=75.75 rials (1 rial=1.32 U.S. cents). In terms of sterling the rate between November 1967 and August 1971 was £1=181.80 rials.

BUDGET
(million rials)

Revenue	1970	1971	1972
Direct Taxes	26,838	30,587	36,771
Indirect Taxes	44,988	54,405	60,829
Monopolies, Government Undertakings	95,327	154,873	188,041
Government Service Revenues	13,008	14,870	17,020
Loans, Aids	58,764	61,062	84,255
Profit-making Enterprises	25,362	40,871	50,887
Commercial Agencies	169,755	213,413	249,049
Social Welfare Institutions	6,343	8,088	9,297
Total	440,385	578,170	696,149

(million rials)

EXPENDITURE	1970	1971	1972
General Services .	26,487	32,762	36,539
Defence and Security .	58,349	78,593	100,941
Social Services .	49,477	66,049	83,094
Economic Services .	91,733	117,739	138,140
Debt Repayments .	12,879	20,655	28,202
Profit-making Enterprises .	25,362	40,871	50,887
Commercial Agencies .	169,755	213,413	249,049
Social Welfare Institutions .	6,343	8,088	9,297
TOTAL .	440,385	578,170	696,149

OIL REVENUES

Total oil revenues received by Iran, in U.S. $ million: (1968) 853.5, (1969) 964.6, (1970) 1,143.5, (1971) 2,111.0.

FIFTH DEVELOPMENT PLAN 1973–78
('000 million rials)

	PUBLIC SECTOR			PRIVATE SECTOR
	Development Allocations	Current Allocations	Fifth Plan Total	Projected Investment
Agriculture .	208.0	58.9	266.9	50.0
Water .	108.0	2.7	110.7	4.0
Industry .	183.9	10.6	194.5	326.8
Mining .	46.5	0.9	47.4	5.2
Oil .	130.7	—	130.7	139.7
Gas .	29.0	—	29.0	47.0
Electricity .	53.5	1.0	54.5	—
Communications .	180.0	20.2	200.2	4.0
Telecommunications .	41.2	18.2	59.4	—
Rural Development .	36.0	1.8	37.8	2.5
Urban Development .	33.0	0.8	33.8	—
Government Construction .	90.8	0.4	91.2	—
Housing .	82.8	0.4	83.2	308.8
Education .	230.0	175.0	405.0	2.6
Arts and Culture .	9.4	6.5	15.9	0.4
Tourism .	7.7	1.3	9.0	12.2
Health .	52.0	64.5	116.5	9.2
Public Welfare .	16.0	38.5	54.5	—
Physical Culture .	10.0	20.9	30.9	—
Statistics .	6.2	10.5	16.7	—
Regional Development .	5.3	0.6	5.9	—

EXTERNAL TRADE

IMPORTS AND EXPORTS
(million rials)

	1970–71	1971–72	1972–73
Imports .	128,260	157,058	134,214
Exports (excluding oil) .	21,192	26,270	22,065
Oil Exports .	164,040	196,483	150,659

OIL EXPORTS

('ooo long tons)

	1969	1970	1971	1972
Crude Oil	139,942	162,102	193,831	220,752
Crude Oil Run to Abadan Refinery	19,954	20,549	17,741	15,872
Export of Oil Products	15,190	15,462	14,808	14,546

COMMODITIES

(million rials)

PRINCIPAL IMPORTS	1970–71	1971–72	1972–73
Iron and Steel	23,382	29,402	20,778
Motor Vehicles and Parts . .	10,526	10,362	10,486
Electrical Machinery and Apparatus .	12,608	19,300	14,388
Boilers and other Machinery . .	28,051	33,807	31,885
Chemicals and Pharmaceuticals . .	6,244	6,694	6,217
Textiles	5,672	5,962	6,369
Wool and Animal Hair . .	2,403	2,414	2,867
Animal and Vegetable Fats .	3,244	3,471	2,223
Paper, Paperboard, etc. . .	3,656	3,497	3,155
Rubber and Products . . .	2,390	2,769	2,972
Sugar and Confectionery . .	549	869	1,620
Cereals	344	7,752	4,052

PRINCIPAL EXPORTS (excl. Oil)	1970–71	1971–72	1972–73
Raw cotton	4,313	5,142	2,761
Wool	15	41	38
Hides and leather	1,102	1,311	1,496
Fruit	3,236	2,880	2,338
Gum Tragacanth	291	361	231
Carpets	4,104	5,761	4,785
Mineral ores	1,499	1,259	1,183
Oil-bearing seeds	658	610	700

PRINCIPAL COUNTRIES

(million rials)

	1968–69		1969–70		1971*	
	Imports	Exports (excl. Oil)	Imports	Exports (excl. Oil)	Imports	Exports (excl. Oil)
Czechoslovakia . .	1,035	561	1,258	858	1,486	716
France . . .	6,894	301	6,483	427	4,715	586
Germany, Federal Republic	22,383	2,380	23,288	2,690	21,717	2,958
India	2,018	147	3,167	129	1,651	95
Italy	6,347	289	5,150	421	5,092	471
Japan	10,025	420	12,621	705	14,330	981
U.S.S.R. . . .	3,376	3,013	8,785	4,357	9,302	3,358
United Kingdom . .	13,623	608	14,243	731	11,904	517
United States . .	17,579	1,692	15,904	1,923	14,446	1,655

*(21 Mar.–21 Dec.)

TRANSPORT
RAILWAYS

		1970–71	1971–72
Passengers	('000)	3,502	4,016
Passenger-kilometres .	(millions)	1,774	1,875
Freight tons carried .	('000)	3,008	3,363

ROADS
('000)

	1970	1971
Cars	261.0	285.4
Goods Vehicles (incl. Buses) .	87.6	96.3
Motor Cycles and Scooters .	144.1	203.9

SHIPPING

	1970	1971
Ships entered . . .	3,021	5,034
Freight loaded ('000 m. tons)	1,079	974
Freight unloaded ('000 m. tons)	2,500	4,107

CIVIL AVIATION

		1969–70	1970–71
Passenger-km. . .	('000)	623,321	653,209
Cargo . .	('000 ton-km.)	3,597	4,033

COMMUNICATIONS MEDIA

	1968–69
Radio Receivers	2,933,000
Television Receivers . . .	198,000
Telephones	268,980
Books Published (titles) . . .	1,757
Daily Newspapers	22
Total Circulation . . .	200,000

TOURISM

	1971	1972
Visitors . . .	426,934	453,881
Approximate Money Spent . (million rials)	4,212	4,673

EDUCATION
(1970–71)

	SCHOOLS	PUPILS ('000)
Elementary . . .	15,202	3,003
Education Corps . .	10,556	504
Secondary . . .	2,509	1,013
Technical and Vocational .	189	31
Primary Teacher Training .	79	5
Universities and Colleges .	n.a.	74

Sources (except where otherwise stated): Ministry of Finance, Teheran; General Department of Trade Statistics, Ministry of Economy, Teheran; Ministry of Education, Teheran; Iranian State Railways, Teheran; National Iranian Oil Co., London.

THE CONSTITUTION

On August 15th, 1906, an Imperial Decree was issued to convoke a Constituent Assembly. This Assembly adopted the Constitution of Iran on December 30th of that year.

THE EXECUTIVE POWER

The executive power rests in the Shah. He appoints the Prime Ministers, who must be approved by the *Majlis*. In addition to their individual responsibility for their departments, ministers have a joint responsibility for the affairs of the country.

In 1949 an amendment to the Constitution was made whereby the Shah was granted the right to dissolve the *Majlis* when it was deemed necessary, provided that a new election was ordered to take place soon afterwards.

THE LEGISLATIVE POWER

According to the Constitutional Law the legislative power comprises the Senate and the National Consultative Assembly (the *Majlis*). The latter Assembly consists of over 200 members elected for four years; the number of members rises with the growth of the population and by the July 1971 elections had reached 268. The Senate, which was convened for the first time in February 1950, comprises 60 Senators: 30 elected and 30 nominated by the Shah, 15 representing Teheran, and 15 representing the provinces. Senators must be Muslims. Their term of office is four years.

PROVINCIAL DIVISIONS

Iran is divided into fourteen provinces (*Ostan*). They are administered by Governors-General (*Ostandar*), who are directly responsible to the central Government. These provinces are sub-divided into counties (*Shahrestan*), municipalities (*Bakhsh*), and rural districts (*Dihestan*).

All towns have a municipal administration, the director of which is chosen by the town council. The nomination must be approved by the Ministry of the Interior.

THE GOVERNMENT

THE HEAD OF STATE

H.I.M. MOHAMMAD REZA PAHLAVI ARYAMEHR, SHAHANSHAH OF IRAN
(succeeded to the throne on the abdication of his father, September 16th, 1941).

THE CABINET
(June 1974)

Prime Minister: AMIR ABBAS HOVEYDA.

Minister of Foreign Affairs: ABBAS ALI KHALATBARI.

Minister of War: Gen. REZA AZIMI.

Minister of Interior and Employment: Dr. JAMSHID AMOUZEGAR.

Minister of Economic and Financial Affairs: Dr. HOOSHANG ANSARI.

Minister of Information and Tourism: GHOLAM REZA KIANPOUR.

Minister of Education: AHMAD HOOSHANG SHARIFI.

Minister of Science and Higher Education: ABDOL HOSAIN SAMII.

Minister of Mines and Industries: FARROKH NAJMABADI.

Minister of Co-operatives and Rural Affairs: REZA SADA-GHIANI.

Minister of Posts, Telephones and Telegraphs: KARIM MOTAMEDI.

Minister of Trade: FERREIDOON MAHDAVI.

Minister of Housing and City Planning: HOMAYOUN J. ANSARI.

Minister of Social Affairs: SHEIKHOL-ESLAMZADEH.

Minister of Agriculture and National Resources: MANSUR ROUHANI.

Minister of Energy: IRAJ VAHIDI.

Minister of State and Head of Plan and Budget Organization: ABDUL MAJID MAJIDI.

Minister of Roads: JAVAD SHAHRESTANI.

Minister of Health: ANUSHIRVAN PUYAN.

Minister of Arts and Culture: MEHRDAD PAHLBOD.

Minister of Justice: SADEQ AHMADI.

Minister of Labour: AMIR GHASEM MOINI.

Ministers without Portfolio: EZATOLLAH YAZDANPANAH, MANUCHEHR KALALI.

Minister of State and Executive Assistant to Prime Minister: HADI HEDAYATI.

Minister of State: SAFI ASFIA.

DIPLOMATIC REPRESENTATION

EMBASSIES ACCREDITED TO IRAN
(In Teheran unless otherwise stated)
(E) Embassy.

Afghanistan: Pahlavi Ave. (Yussefabad), 16 Ebn-Sina Ave., Kucheh Rassia (E); *Ambassador:* (vacant).

Algeria: Baghdad, Iraq (E).

Argentina: Pahlavi Ave. (Tajrish), No. 560 (E); *Ambassador:* (vacant) (also accred. to Afghanistan).

Australia: 23 Ave. Arak, P.O.B. 3408 (E); *Ambassador:* H. D. WHITE.

Austria: Takhte Jamshid, Forsat Ave. (E); *Ambassador:* Dr. ALBERT FILZ.

Bahrain: 31 Ave. Vozara (E); *Ambassador:* ABDUL AZIZ ABDULRAHMAN BUALI.

Belgium: Ave. Takht-e-Tavous, 41 Ave. Daryaye Noor (E); *Ambassador:* MARC TAYMANS (also accred. to Kuwait).

Brazil: Pahlavi Ave., Tajrish No. 69 (E); *Ambassador:* PAULO BRAZ PINTO DA SILVA.

Bulgaria: Aramehr Ave. Hijdah Metri Sevon, No. 23 (E); *Ambassador:* VARBAN TSANEV.

Burma: Islamabad, Pakistan.

Canada: Takhte Jamshid Ave. Forsat, P.O.B. 1610 (E); *Ambassador:* JAMES GEORGE (also accred. to Iraq and Kuwait).

Chad: Moscow, U.S.S.R. (E).

Chile: Ankara, Turkey (E).

China (Taiwan): Pahlavi Ave. No. 647 (E); *Ambassador:* CHEN HSIN-JEN.

Czechoslovakia: Sarshar No. 61 (E); *Ambassador:* Dr. JAN STRAKA.

Denmark: Copenhagen Ave. 13 (E); *Ambassador:* OLE BERNHARD OLSEN (also accred. to Afghanistan).

Egypt: 123 Ave. Abassabad, Ave. Park, P.O.B. 22 (E); *Ambassador:* MUHAMMAD SAMIH ANWAR.

Ethiopia: Ankara, Turkey (E).

Finland: Ankara, Turkey (E).

France: France Ave. (E); *Ambassador:* ROBERT DE SOUZA.

German Democratic Republic: (E); *Ambassador:* FERDI-NAND THUN.

Germany, Federal Republic: Ferdowsi Avenue (E); *Ambassador:* Dr. GEORG VON LILIENFELD.

Greece: Kheradmand Ave., Kucheh Salm, No. 43 (E); *Ambassador:* GEORGE PAPADOPOULOS.

Guinea: Cairo, Egypt (E).

Hungary: Television Ave. No. 7, Rue Sizdahom (E); *Ambassador:* BALINT GAL.

Iceland: Bonn, Federal Republic of Germany.

India: N. Saba Ave. No. 166 (E); *Ambassador:* RAM-CHANDRA DATTATRAYA SATHE.

Indonesia: Shah Abbas Kabir Ave., Magndia Ave. No. 1 (E); *Ambassador:* H. A. A. ACHSIEN.

Iraq: address unavailable (E); *Ambassador:* MIDHAT JUMAA.

Italy: France Ave. 81 (E); *Ambassador:* LUIGI COTTAFAVI.

Japan: Northern Saba Ave. 53 (E); *Ambassador:* KEISUKE ARITA.

Jordan: Bukharest Ave. No. 16th Ave. No. 55 (E); *Ambassador:* SALEH AL-KURDI (also accred. to Afghanistan).

Korea, Republic: Kakh Ave., Heshmatoddowleh No. 427 (E); *Ambassador:* CHONG KYU KIM.

Kuwait: Maikadeh Ave., 3-38 Sazman-Ab St. (E); *Ambassador:* Shaikh NASSER MUHAMMAD AHMAD AL-JABER AL-SABAH.

Lebanon: Bukharest Ave. No. 12 (E); *Ambassador:* KHALIL AL-KHALIL.

Malaysia: Bukharest Ave. No. 8 (E); *Ambassador:* MUHAMMAD YUSOFF BIN ZAINAL.

Malta: London, U.K. (E).

Mexico: Ankara, Turkey.

Mongolia: Moscow, U.S.S.R. (E).

Morocco: Dorahiye Yussofabad, Muhammad Reza Shah Ave. (E); *Ambassador:* MUHAMMAD LARBI EL-ALAMI (also accred. to Turkey).

Nepal: Islamabad, Pakistan (E).

Netherlands: Takhte Tavous, Near Pahlavi Ave. Rue Moazami Rue Jahansouz No. 36 (E); *Ambassador:* P. A. E. RENARDEL DE LAVALETTE.

Norway: Aban Ave. 3 (E); *Ambassador:* NILS ANTON JORGENSEN (also accred. to Afghanistan, Bahrain, Kuwait, Qatar and United Arab Emirates).

Oman: Bukharest Ave. No. 17th Ave. No. 10; *Chargé d'Affaires:* ISMAIL KHALIL AL-RASSASI.

Pakistan: 199 Iranshah Ave. (E); *Ambassador:* HAMED NAVAZ KHAN.

Philippines: Islamabad, Pakistan (E).

Poland: 140 Takhte Jamshid Ave. (E); *Ambassador:* BRONISLAW MUSIELAK.

Portugal: Rodsar Ave. No. 41; *Ambassador:* C. H. F. LEMONDE DE MACEDO.

Qatar: Ave. Abbas Abad, Ave. Télévision, Second Ave. 14-16 (E); *Ambassador:* AHMED HAMD AL-ATEYAH.

Romania: Fakhrabad Ave. 12 (E); *Ambassador:* ALEXANDRU BOABĂ (also accred. to Kuwait).

Saudi Arabia: Ave. Aban, P.O.B. 2903 (E); *Ambassador:* ARAB SAID HASHEM.

Senegal: Ave. Vozara, 8th St. No. 4 (E); *Ambassador:* MASSAMBA SARRE.

Spain: Fisherabad Ave., Khoshbin St. 29 (E); *Ambassador:* JOSÉ MANUEL DE ABAROA.

Sri Lanka: Islamabad, Pakistan (E).

Sudan: Doha, Qatar (E).

Sweden: Takhte Jamshid Ave., Forsat Ave. (E); *Ambassador:* Comte GUSTAF BONDE (also accred. to Afghanistan).

Switzerland: Pasteur Ave. (E); *Ambassador:* DANIEL GAGNEBIN (also accred. to Afghanistan).

Syria: Shiraz Ave. Roudsar Ave. No. 69 (E); *Ambassador:* (vacant).

Thailand: Bou Ali Sina Ave. Park Amine-Dowleh No. 4 (E); *Ambassador:* Rear-Admiral CHAREN PLENWIDYA.

Tunisia: Saltanatabad (E); *Ambassador:* TAOUFIK SMIDA.

Turkey: Ferdowsi Ave. No. 314 (E); *Ambassador:* SADI ELDEM.

U.S.S.R.: Churchill Ave. (E); *Ambassador:* V. Y. EROFEEV.

United Arab Emirates: Ave. Vozara, 8th St. (E); *Ambassador:* Sheikh AL-MAKTOUM.

United Kingdom: Ferdowsi Ave. (E); *Ambassador:* (vacant).

U.S.A.: Takhte Jamshid Ave., Roosevelt Ave. (E); *Ambassador:* RICHARD M. HELMS.

Vatican: France Ave. 97 (Apostolic Internunciature); *Ambassador:* Mgr. Dr. ERNESTO GALLINA.

Venezuela: Aban Ave. No. 90 (E); *Ambassador:* (vacant).

Viet-Nam, Republic: Ankara, Turkey (E).

Yugoslavia: Ave. Arak, rue Shahrivar (E); *Ambassador:* LASLO BALA.

Iran also has diplomatic relations with Nigeria.

PARLIAMENT

THE SENATE

President: Eng. JA'AFAR SHARIF-EMAMI.

The Senate consists of 60 members, 30 of which are appointed by the Shah, and 30 are elected (15 from Teheran and 15 from the Provinces). The term of office is four years.

ELECTIONS JULY 1971

	SENATE	MAJLIS
Iran Novin Party . .	26	228
Mardom Party . . .	9	36
Independent . . .	24	2
Vacant	1	2
TOTAL . .	60	268

NATIONAL CONSULTATIVE ASSEMBLY
(The Majlis)

President: Eng. A. RIAZI.

Elections to the 23rd session of the Majlis were held in July 1971.

STATE OF PARTIES—APRIL 1974

	SENATE	MAJLIS
Iran Novin Party . .	27	229
Mardom Party . . .	9	37
Independent . . .	24	1
Iranian Party . . .	—	1
TOTAL . .	60	268

POLITICAL PARTIES

Iran Novin Party (*New Iran Party*): Teheran; governing party since 1960; Sec. MANOUCHEHR KALALI.

Mardom Party (*People's Party*): Teheran; f. 1957; programme includes agrarian reform, limitation of land ownership and labour welfare; Sec.-Gen. NASSER AMERI.

Pan Iranist Party: Teheran; f. 1949; nationalist; Leader MOHSEN PAZESHKPUR.

Iranian Party: Teheran; Leader FAZLOLLAH SADR.

JUDICIAL SYSTEM

Prosecutor-General: Dr. ABDUL HUSSEIN ALIABADI.

Chief Justice of the Supreme Court: EMAD-E-DIN MIRMO-TAHARI.

SUPREME COURT

The jurisdiction of the Supreme Court in Teheran includes disputes about the competence of Government departments in relation to the existing laws, and it also acts as a Court of First Instance when ministers are prosecuted, either for personal offences or in respect of the affairs of their department. It is also the highest court of appeal. In exceptional cases, at the request of the Prosecutor-General, the Supreme Court deals with criminal cases.

PROVINCIAL COURTS

Courts of Appeal and Central Criminal Courts are established in each province.

OTHER COURTS

There are Courts of First Instance in the towns. The Arbitration Council was established in 1966 to examine and rule on all petty offences. The courts of lowest jurisdiction are those of the Justices of the Peace, which are established in most villages and small towns and deal with small civil cases and petty offences. On June 30th, 1966, the Arbitration Council was added to the judicial organs of the state. This Council is competent to deal with all complaints and petitions filed by businessmen and craftsmen, claims for damages and losses sustained in driving accidents, and domestic disputes, up to a claimed amount of ten thousand Rials in all cases. The Arbitration Council also examines and rules on petty offences (misdemeanour and felony) for which punishment does not exceed two months and/or one thousand two hundred Rials fine. Trials and examinations in such cases are undertaken free of charge.

SPECIAL TRIBUNALS

Special tribunals include Ecclesiastical Courts, which have a limited jurisdiction on matters of marriage and personal status; the Civil Servants' Criminal Court, in Teheran; and Permanent and Temporary Military Courts. Permanent Military Courts exist in all provinces and deal with treasonable offences; Temporary Military Courts are established whenever martial law is declared in a region, and are competent to hear certain cases which are normally within the jurisdiction of the ordinary courts.

RELIGION

MUSLIMS

The great majority of the Iranian people are Shi'i Muslims, and Iran with Iraq and the Yemen Arab Republic are notable as the only countries in the world where Shi'i adherents are in a majority. About five per cent of the population are Sunni Muslims, but there is complete religious toleration. Iran is thus in many ways the centre of the Shi'i faith, and pilgrimage to Iranian shrines is an important activity; Qum and Meshed are in particular regarded as holy cities.

ZOROASTRIANS

There are about 21,000 Zoroastrians, a remnant of a once widespread sect. Their religious leader is MOUBAD. Zoroastrianism was the official religion of pre-Islamic Iran. Many adherents were compelled by Arab persecution to emigrate, and the main centre of their faith is now Bombay.

OTHER COMMUNITIES

Communities of Armenians, and somewhat smaller numbers of Jews, Assyrians, Greek Orthodox, Uniates and Latin Christians are also found as officially recognized faiths. The Baha'i faith, which originated in Iran, has about 60,000 adherents.

Baha'i faith: Shirtat-i-Nawnahalan, Manuchehri Avenue, Teheran; 1,854 centres, 1 school.

Roman Catholic Archbishop of Urmia, Bishop of Salmas and Metropolitan of Iran: Khalifagari Kaldani Katoliq, Rezaieh; (vacant); Patriarchal Administrator Most Rev. YOUHANNAN SEMAAN ISSAYI, Archbishop of Teheran.

Anglican Bishop in Iran: Rt. Rev. HASSAN BARNABA DEHQANI-TAFTI, Bishop's House, P.O.B. 12, Isfahan. Diocese founded 1912.

Synod of the Evangelical (Presbyterian) Church in Iran: Assyrian Evangelical Church, Khiaban-i Shapur, Khiaban-i Aramanch, Teheran; Moderator Rev. ADLE NAKHOSTEEN.

THE PRESS

The working of the Iranian Press is set out in the 1955 Press Law as modified in 1963. This legislation defines the qualities of education and character required in persons intending to publish newspapers; and stipulates that no newspaper may be banned without a court order, except for criticism of religion or the monarchy, for disclosing military information or for provoking the people to oppose government troops. With the exception of scientific, cultural and government publications, newspapers with less than 3,000 circulation and magazines with less than 5,000 are illegal.

In 1965 the cabinet approved the Reporters' Code of Journalism which required reporters to be licensed by the Ministry of Information, prevented them accepting government service and prohibited the reporting or photography of specified military areas and closed court sittings, etc. All communist publications are prohibited in Iran.

Teheran dominates the press scene as many of the daily papers are published there and the bi-weekly, weekly and less frequent publications in the provinces generally depend on the major metropolitan dailies as a source of news. In the city are published some 20 daily and 21 weekly newspapers, and 27 weekly and 44 monthly magazines. There are at least 85 registered provincial papers.

With the exception of a small number of political organs and official publications, all newspapers are owned by private individuals. The chief party organs are the dailies *Nedaye Iran Novin* (New Iran Party) and *Mehre Iran* (Mardom Party) and the weekly *Khak-o-Khun* (Pan-Iranist Party).

The major dailies also publish other papers and periodicals thus forming small publishing groups which are still largely family concerns. The *Ettela'at Group* (Prop. ABBAS MASSOUDI) includes *Ettela'at* with two foreign language daily and two weekly newspapers and four popular weekly magazines, including one for women and two for children. The *Kayhan Group* (Prop. Dr. M. MESBAZADEH) includes *Kayhan* with its English daily, a weekly sports paper, two popular weekly magazines and a medical magazine. The *Echo of Iran Group* (Prop. JAHANGIR BEHROUZ) includes the daily, weekly and monthly *Echo of Iran*, the monthly *Iran Trade* and the annual *Almanac*, all in English.

PRINCIPAL DAILIES

Alik: Naderi Ave., Teheran; f. 1931; morning; political and literary; Armenian; Prop. Dr. R. STEPANIAN; circ. 10,000.

Ayandegan: Shah Ave., 322 Guiti Sq., Teheran; morning; political; Prop. Dr. H. AHARI.

Azhang: Roosevelt St., Teheran; f. 1954; airmail edition *Azhang Havaii*; Editor KAZEM MASOUDI; circ. 10,000.

Bourse: Kh. Sevom Esfand, Ku. Mobarshakat, Teheran; f. 1961; financial; Editor Dr. Y. RAHMATI.

Echo of Iran: Ave. Shiraz, Kuche Khalkhali No. 4, P.O.B. 2008, Teheran; f. 1952; English; political and economic; Editor JAHANGIR BEHROUZ; circ. 6,000.

Erfan: Isfahan; f. 1924; literary; Editor Mrs. MALEK ERFAN; circ. 3,000.

Ettela'at: Khayyam Ave., Teheran; f. 1925; evening; political and literary; Editor HASSAN SADR HAJ SAYYED JAVADI; circ. 100,000.

Ettela'ate Hawaei: Air edition of above; Editor HAMID MASHOUR; circ. 6,000.

Farman: 69 Manuchehri Ave., Teheran; political; Editor A. SHAHANDEH; circ. 15,000.

Iran Presse: Ave. Kheradmand, Ku. Tahbaz No. 19, Teheran; French; Editor S. FARZAMI.

Le Journal de Tehran: Kayyam Ave., Teheran; f. 1934; morning; French; Editor AHMAD CHAHIDI; circ. 8,000.

Kayhan Hava: Political and social; Editor M. SEMSAR; circ. 80,000.

Kayhan International: Ferdowsi Ave., Kuche Atabak, Teheran; political; morning; English; circ. 15,000; Editor W. DULLFORCE.

Keyhan: Ferdowsi Ave., Teheran; evening; political; Propr. Dr. M. MESBAHZADEH.

Khovassan: Meshed; f. 1948; Owner and Editor MUHAMMAD SADEGH TEHRANIAN; circ. 15,000.

Koushesh: Forughi Ave., Teheran; morning; political and scientific; Editor SHOKRULLAH SAFAVI.

Mahde Azadi: Tabriz; political and social; Prop. ESMAIL PEYMAN.

Marde Mobarez: Kh. Manouchehri; political and social; Propr. ASSAD RAZMARA.

Mehre Iran: Zhaleh Ave., Teheran; affiliated to Mardom Party; morning; Editor MOHSEN MOVAGHAR.

Nedaye Iran-Novin: Fisherabad Ave. 41, Sepand St., Teheran; affiliated to New Iran Party; Editor M. A. RASHTI.

Peyghame Emrouz: Kh. Qavam Saltaneh, Teheran; evening; political and social; Dr. ABDOLRASUL AZIMI; circ. 23,000.

Poste Teheran: Kh. Shahabad, Teheran; political evening; circ. 8,000; Editor MUHAMMAD ALI MASSOUDI.

Sedaye Mardom: Kh. Hafez, Teheran; political and literary; morning; Publisher MUHAMMAD HUSSEIN FARIPOUR; Editor FEREIDOON FARIPOUR.

Tehran Journal: Kayyam Ave., Teheran; f. 1954; morning; English; Editor VAHE PETROSSIAN; circ. 10,000.

PRINCIPAL PERIODICALS

Aftabe Shargh: Meshed; weekly; political; Prop. Mrs. NARGESS AMOOZEGAR.

Al-Akha: Khayyam Ave., Teheran; f. 1960; Arabic; weekly; Dir. Sen. ABAS MASSOUDI; Editor NAZIR FENZA.

Bourse Monthly: Sevom-Esfand Ave., Kuche Bakht 15, Teheran; f. 1963; economic; Editor Dr. Y. RAHMATI.

Daneshkade Pezeshki: Faculty of Medicine, Teheran University; medical magazine; monthly; Editor Dr. M. BEHESHTI.

Donya: Istanbul Ave., Teheran; weekly; Editor A. K. TABATABA'I.

Donyaye Varzesh: Khayyam Ave., Teheran; f. 1970; weekly sport magazine; Editor BIJAN RAFIEI.

Ettela'at Banovan: Kayyam Ave., Teheran; women's weekly magazine; Editor Mrs. PARI ABASALTI; circ. 40,000.

Ettela'at Javanan: Khayyam Ave., Teheran; f. 1958; youth weekly; Editor R. ETTEMADI.

Ettela'at Kodekan: Khayyam Ave., Teheran; f. 1957; teenage weekly; Editor NADER AKHVAN HEYDARI.

Ferdowsi: Bahar Ave., Teheran; weekly; Editor N. JAHANBANOIE; circ. 26,000.

Film-Va-Honar: Roosevelt Ave., Teheran; weekly; Editor A. RAMAZANI.

Iran Trade and Industry: Echo of Iran, P.O.B. 1228, Shiraz Ave., Teheran; f. 1965; monthly economic periodical; Editor HASSAN SHAIDA; circ. 10,000.

Iran Tribune: P.O.B. 11/1244, Teheran, Iran; monthly; socio-political-business; English.

Javanan: Ave. Sepah, Teheran; weekly magazine for young people; circ. over 10,000.

Kayhan Bacheha: Kh. Ferdowsi, Teheran; children's magazine weekly; Editor DJAAFAR BADII; circ. 75,000.

Kayhan Varzeshi: Kh. Ferdowsi, Teheran; sport weekly; Editor Dr. M. MEZBAZADEH; circ. 60,000.

Khandaniha: Kh. Ferdowsi; f. 1939; weekly; circ. 25,000; Editor A. A. AMIRANI.

Music Iran: 1029 Amiriye Ave., Teheran; f. 1951; monthly; Editor BAHMAN HIRBOD; circ. 7,000.

Navaye-Khorasan: Meshed; political; weekly; Prop. H. MAHBODI.

Pars: Shiraz; twice weekly; circ. 3,500; Editor F. SHARGI.

Rahnejat: Darvazeh Dowlat, Isfahan; political and social weekly; Prop. N. RAHNEJAT.

Sepahan: Baharestan Square, Teheran; literary; weekly.

Sepid va Siyah: Kh. Ferdowsi; popular monthly; Editor Dr. A. BEHZADI; circ. 30,000.

Setareye Cinema: Lalezar-Now Ave., Teheran; film weekly; Editor P. GALUSTIAN.

Setareye Esfahan: Isfahan; political; weekly; Prop. A. MEHANKHAH.

Sobhe Emroug: Ferdowsi Ave., Teheran; Editor Mrs. AMIDI-NURI.

Sokhan: Hafiz Ave., Zomorrod Passage, Teheran; f. 1943; literary monthly; Editor Dr. P. N. KHANLARI; circ. 5,000.

Sport: P.O.B. 342, Ebne Sina St., Park Aminodoleh, Kakhe Markazi Taj; Teheran; sports, weekly.

Teheran Chamber of Commerce Monthly Journal: Teheran; Farsi; circ. 5,000; also **Weekly Bulletin,** circ. 5,000; both distributed mainly to members.

Tehran Economist: 99 Sevom Esfand Ave., Teheran; f. 1953; Persian and English; weekly; Editor Dr. B. SHARIAT; circ. 12,000 Persian, 4,500 English.

Tehran Messavar: Ave. Jaleh, Teheran; popular weekly; Editor ABDULLAH VALA; circ. 35,000.

Towfigh: Istanbul Ave., Teheran; f. 1921; satirical weekly; Publisher HASSAN TOWFIGH, Editor Dr. ABBAS TOWFIGH; circ. 97,000; also **Towfigh Monthly;** f. 1961; humorous; circ. 58,000; Editor HOSSEYN TOWFIGH.

Zan-E-Ruz (*Women Today*): Kh. Ferdowsi, Teheran; women's weekly; circ. 150,000; Editor Mrs. F. MESBAZADEH.

NEWS AGENCIES

International Press Agency of Iran: Teheran Ghvamsaltaneh Square, P.O.B. 1125, Teheran.

Pars News Agency: General Department of Publications and Broadcasting, Maidan Ark, Teheran; f. 1936; Pres. NASSER SHIRZAD.

FOREIGN BUREAUX

A.F.P.: P.O.B. 1535, Teheran; Correspondent JEAN-CLAUD BRARD.

A.N.S.A.: Ave. Hafez, Kuche Hatef 11, Teheran; Chief EMIRA GIULIANA PIZZUTO.

A.P.: 7 Fifth St., Television Ave., Teheran; Correspondent PARVIZ RAEIN.

Reuter: P.O.B. 1607, Teheran; Correspondent ALI MEHRAVARI.

Tass: Kheyaban Hamid, Kouche Masoud 73, Teheran; Correspondent VLADIMIR DIBROVA.

U.P.I.: P.O.B. 529, Teheran; Correspondent YOUSOF MAZANDI.

PRESS UNIONS

Press Club of Iran: Teheran; f. 1961; Chair. ABBAS MASSOUDI; Sec.-Gen. Dr. M. MESDAZADEH.

Writers and Press Reporters Syndicate: Teheran.

PUBLISHERS

Ali Akbar Elmi: Shahabad Ave.; Dir. ALI AKBAR ELMI.

Amirkabir: Avenue Shahabad; Dir. ABDULRAHIM JAFARI.

Boroukhim: Avenue Ferdowsi, Teheran; dictionaries.

Bungah Tarjomeh va Nashr Ketah: Teheran; affiliated to the Pahlavi foundation.

Danesh: 357 Ave. Nasser Khosrow, Teheran; f. 1931 in India, transferred to Iran in 1937; literary and historical (Persian); imports and exports books; Man. Dir. NOOROUAH IRANPARAST.

Ebn-e-Sina: Meydane 25 Shahrivar, Teheran; f. 1957; educational publishers and booksellers; Dir. EBRAHIM RAMAZANI.

Eghbal Publishing Co.: Shahabad Ave., Teheran; Dir. DJAVAD EGHBAL.

Franklin Book Programs Inc.: 2 Alborz Ave., Shahreza Ave., Teheran; f. 1952; a non-profit organization for International Book Publishing Development; main office in New York; Dir. ALI ASGHAR MOHAJER.

Ibn-Sina: Shahabad St. Teheran.

Iran Chap Company: Ave. Khayyam, Teheran; f. 1966; newspapers, books, magazines, colour printing and engraving; Man. Dir. FARHAD MASSOUDI.

Kanoon Marefat: 6 Lalehzar St., Teheran; Dir. HASSAN MAREFAT.

Khayyam: Shahabad Avenue; Dir. MOHAMMAD ALI TARAGHI.

Majlis Press: Avenue Baharistan, Teheran.

Nil Publications: Mokhberoddowleh Sq., Koutcheh Rafahi, Teheran. Dir. A. AZIMI.

Pirouz: Shahabad Avenue; Dir. MIRMOHAMMADI.

Safiali Shah: Baharistan Square; Dir. MANSOUR MOSHFEGH.

Taban Press: Ave. Nassir Khosrow, Teheran; f. 1939; Propr. A. MALEKI.

Teheran Economist: Sevom Esfand Ave. 99, Teheran.

Teheran University Press: Avenue Shah-Reza.

Towfigh: Istanbul Ave., Teheran; publishes humorous Almanac and pocket books; distributes humorous and satirical books; Dir. Dr. FARIDEH TOWFIGH.

Zawar: Shahabad Avenue; Dir. AKBAR ZAWAR.

RADIO AND TELEVISION

RADIO

Radio Iran: Ministry of Information, Meidan Ark, Teheran; f. 1940; Home service programmes broadcast in Persian; foreign service programmes are broadcast in Urdu, Arabic, Turkish, English, Russian, French, Armenian and Assyrian.

There are twelve regional services, at Ahwaz, Gorgan, Isfahan, Kerman, Kermanshah, Meshed, Rasht, Reza'ieh, Sanandeh, Shiraz, Tabriz and Zahedan. The most powerful transmitters are at Ahwaz, Kermanshah and Zahedan; these broadcast in Arabic, in Kurdish, and in Baluchi and Urdu respectively.

Number of radio receivers: 1,900,000.

TELEVISION

National Iranian Television: Ave. Jâm-e-jam, P.O.B. 33-200, Teheran; f. 1967; state-owned network with limited advertising; 30 transmitting stations; broadcasts a total of 104 hours weekly: National Network—58½ hours weekly; second programme—30 hours weekly; educational programme—27 hours weekly; Man. Dir. R. GHOTBI; Publ. *Tamasha* (weekly magazine).

Number of television receivers (1973): 400,000.

American Forces Radio and Television: Teheran; f. 1954; recordings and films of American programmes; 40 hours weekly.

FINANCE

(cap. = capital; p.u. = paid up; dep. = deposits; m. = million; all figures stated in Rials)

BANKING

CENTRAL BANK

Bank Markazi Iran: Ferdowsi Ave., Teheran; f. 1960; central note-issuing bank of Iran; cap. 5,000m., dep. 167,000m. (Oct. 1973); Gov. MOHAMMED YEGANEH; Deputy Gov. JALIL SHORAKA.

Bank Asnaf Iran (*Guilds Bank of Iran*): Baharestan Square, Teheran; f. 1957; cap. p.u. 100m.; Chair. Gen. ALI AKHBAR ZARGHAM; Gen. Man. GHOLAM REZA ZAERIN.

Bank Bazargani Iran: Maidan Sepah, P.O.B. 2258, Teheran; reps. abroad in London, England and Hamburg, German Federal Republic; f. 1950; cap. p.u. 250m., dep. 23,115m. (March 1973); 215 brs.; Man. Dir. Senator MOSTAFA TADJADOD.

Bank Bimeh Bazerganan: Avenue Shah 145, Teheran; f. 1952; cap. 220m.; Man. Dir. M. M. REZVANI.

Bank Bimeh Iran (*Iran Insurance Bank*): Teheran; under auspices of government-sponsored Sherkate Sahami Bimeh Iran (Insurance Company of Iran); cap. p.u. 400m.; 10 brs. in Teheran, 17 brs. in other towns.

Banque Etebarate Iran (*Iran Credit Bank*): 50 Ave. Sevom Esfand, Teheran; f. 1958; cap. p.u. 400m., dep. 6,107m. (March 1972); Chair. and Man. Dir. H.E. AHMED CHAFIK.

Bank Etebarat Sanati (*Industrial Credits Bank*): Khiaban Ateshkadeh, Teheran; f. 1956; stock owned by the Plan Organization and two subsidiary companies; cap. p.u. 3,110m., dep. 1,840.8m. (1971); Chair. H.E. Eng. AHMAD ZANGENEH; Man. Dir. Dr. ALINAGHI FARMAN-FARMAIAN.

Bank Kar: Ave. Hafez, Teheran; f. 1958; cap. 400m., dep. 3,219m.; Man. ARSEN BARKHORDARIAN.

Bank Kargosha'i Iran (*Pawn Bank*): Moulavi Ave., Teheran; cap. provided by Bank Melli Iran; Principal Officer ESMAIEL TAHERI.

Bank Melli Iran (*The National Bank of Iran*): Ferdowsi Ave., Teheran; state-owned bank; brs. abroad in Frankfurt, Sharjah, Paris, Bahrain, Jeddah, Hong Kong, London, Hamburg, New York, Tokyo and Dubai; f. 1928; cap. and res. 5,441m., dep. 144,173m.,

total assets 181,050m. (March 1973); affiliation Bank Tedjarat Kharedji Iran; 1,300 brs. throughout Iran; Pres. YOUSSOF KHOSHKISH.

Bank of Iran and the Middle East: Kucheh Berlin, Ave. Ferdowsi, P.O.B. 1680, Teheran; f. 1959; brs. at Khorrashar, Abadan and Teheran (17); The British Bank of the Middle East owns 40 per cent of the issued capital; 60 per cent is held by Iranian interests; cap. p.u. 400m., dep. 5,510m.; Chair. Dr. G. H. KHOSHBIN; Gen. Man. M. H. VAKILY; Adviser to the Board D. PATTERSON.

Bank of Teheran: 25 Pahlavi Ave., Teheran; f. 1953; cap. p.u. 800m., dep. 14,007.6 (March 1973); Pres. MOSTAFA FATEH; Man. Dir. BAHMAN BEHZADI.

Bank Omran (*Development Bank*): Teheran; f. 1952 to provide technical guidance and financial support to farmers of distributed Crown villages; also acts as a commercial bank; 144 brs.; Pres. HOUSHANG RAM.

Bank Pars: Avenue Takht-Jamshid, Teheran; f. 1952; cap. p.u. 250m.; Chair. and Pres. E. NIKPOUR.

Bank Rahni Iran (*The Mortgage Bank of Iran*): Ferdowsi Street, Teheran; f. 1939; Government bank (affiliate of Ministry of Development and Housing) which grants loans for building houses; cap. p.u. 5,423m., total assets 21,089m. (March 1973); Chair. and Man. Dir. Eng. A. BEHNIA.

Bank Refah Kargaran (*Workers' Welfare Bank*): 125 Roosevelt Ave., Teheran; f. 1960; cap. p.u. 1,000m.; 65 brs.; state-owned bank; Chair. Dr. MEHDI A. ALIABADI.

Bank Russo-Iran: Jonoobe Park Shahr (South), Teheran; cap. 300m., reserves 86m.

Bank Saderat Iran (*The Export Bank of Iran*): 124 Ave. Shah, Teheran; P.O.B. 2751; f. 1951; cap. p.u. 3,000m.; dep. 72,837m. (March 1973); 3,000 brs. in Iran: brs. in Dubai, Abu Dhabi, Fujaireh, Ras Al Khaimah, Ajman, Sharjah (United Arab Emirates), Qatar; offices in London, Hamburg, Paris, Beirut; agency in New York; Man. Dir. Eng. M. A. MOFARAH.

Bank Sepah (*Army Bank*): Ave. Sepah, Teheran; f. 1925; state-owned bank; cap. p.u. 1,500m., dep. 43,855m. (Sept. 1973); 455 brs.; Pres. MANOUTCHEHRE NIKPOUR; Deputy Pres. DJALIL SASSINI.

Bank Taavon Keshavarzi Iran (*Agricultural Cooperative Bank of Iran*): Khiaban Park Shahr (North), Teheran; f. 1933; cap. 19,462m. (Dec. 1973); Government bank; Pres. HASSAN EMAMI.

Bayerische Vereinsbank: Munich, German Federal Republic; Ave. Rudsar 29, P.O.B. 2437, Teheran; Rep. PETER SCHMID-LOSSBERG; Berliner Bank A.G. and Vereinsbank in Hamburg.

Distributors' Co-operative Credit Bank: 37 Ave. Ferdowsi, Teheran; f. 1963; cap. 600m., dep. 4,472 (1973); Chair. SEIFULLAH RASHIDIAN; Pres. ASSADULLAH RASHIDIAN.

Foreign Trade Bank of Iran (*Bank Tedjarat Kharedji Iran*): Avenue Saadi, Teheran; f. 1960; jointly owned by Bank Melli Iran, Bank of America, Banca Comerciale Italiana and Deutsche Bank A.G.; cap. 275m., dep. 2,997m., reserves 208m. (March 1970); Man. Dir. ASHOT SAGHATELIAN.

Industrial and Mining Development Bank of Iran (IMDBI): 133 Hafez Ave., P.O.B. 1801, Teheran; f. 1954; 84 per cent of shares held by more than 3,100 Iranian individuals and institutions, 16 per cent held by France, U.K., Netherlands, Italy, Japan, U.S.A. and Federal Germany; to develop, encourage and stimulate private industrial, mining and transportation enterprises in Iran; cap. 3,150m. (Oct. 1973); Man. Dir. A. GHASSEM KHERADJOU.

International Bank of Iran and Japan: 750 Ave. Saadi, P.O.B. 1837, Teheran; f. 1959; cap. 500m.; 35 per cent Japanese owned; Chair. MOSTAFA MESBAH-ZADEH; Gen. Man. ABDOLLAH TAHERI.

Iranians' Bank: 184 Takht Jamshid Ave., Teheran; f. 1960; cap. 500m., dep. 3,127m. (1973); associated with First National City Bank; Chair. A. H. EBTEHAJ; Pres. C. SAMII.

Irano-British Bank: Avenue Saadi, P.O.B. 1584, Teheran; f. 1959; affiliated with the Chartered Bank and the Eastern Bank; cap. p.u. 400m.; Gen. Man. W. T. WATSON.

Mercantile Bank of Iran and Holland: Ave. Saadi, P.O.B. 1522, Teheran; f. 1959; affiliated with Algemene Bank Nederland N.V., Amsterdam; cap. p.u. 300m., dep. 3,123m.; 11 brs. in Teheran, 1 in Ahwaz, 1 in Isfahan; Chair. SOLEYMAN VAHABZADEH; Man. Dir. AHMAD VAHABZADEH; Resident Dir. W. M. BROUWER.

Bankers' Association of Iran: Teheran; Pres. Gen. FARAJOLLAH AQEVLI.

STOCK EXCHANGE

Teheran Stock Exchange: Teheran; f. 1968.

INSURANCE

Sherkate Sahami Bimeh Iran (*The Insurance Co. of Iran*): Avenue Saadi, Teheran; f. 1935; Government-sponsored insurance company; all types of insurance; cap. p.u. 200m.; Chair. and Man. Dir. Dr. FARHANG MEHR.

Alborz Insurance Co. Ltd.: Alborz Bldg., 250 Sepahbod Zahedi Ave., Teheran; f. 1959; most classes of insurance except livestock insurance; five brs.; p.u. cap. 150m.; Management Habibollah Nahai and Brothers.

Omid Insurance Co. Ltd.: Boulevard Karaimkhan Zand, Ave. Kheradniand Jonaubi 99, Teheran; f. 1960.

Pars, Société Anonyme d'Assurances: Avenue Saadi, Teheran; f. 1955; fire, marine, motor vehicle and personal accident insurance; Gen. Man. MADJID MALEK; Tech. Man. YERVANT MAGARIAN.

Sherkate Sahami Bimeh Arya (*Arya Insurance Co. Ltd.*): 213 Soraya Ave., Teheran; f. 1952; cap. 100m.; Chair. Dr. G. H. JAHANSHAI; Man. Dir. MOHAMMAD ALI HANDJANI.

Sherkate Sahami Bimeh Asia (*Asia Insurance Co. Ltd.*): Hafez Shomali Ave., 37 Esfandiary St., Teheran; f. 1960; Man. Dir. R. SHAMS.

Sherkate Sahami Bimeh Melli (*The National Insurance Co. Ltd.*): Shah Reza/Villa Ave., P.O.B. 1786, Teheran; f. 1956; all classes of insurance; Chair. H. E. AHMED CHAFIK; Managing Dir. EDWARD JOSEPH.

Sherkate Sahami Bimeh Omid: Boulevard Karimkhan Zand, Ave. Kheradniand Jonoubi 99, Teheran; f. 1960.

All insurance companies are members of the Syndicate of Iranian Insurance Companies.

OIL

National Iranian Oil Company (NIOC), Takhte Jamshid Ave. (P.O.B. 1863), Teheran

A state organization controlling all oil and gas operations in Iran.

NIOC

The National Iranian Oil Company (NIOC) was incorporated April 1951 on nationalization of oil industry to engage in all phases of oil operations; auth. cap. 10,000 million rials, in 10,000 shares, 50 per cent paid up; all shares held by Iranian Government and are non-transferable; Chair. of Board and Managing Dir. H.E. Dr. MANOUTCHEHR EGHBAL; Dirs. H.E. M. FOUROUGHI, H.E. A. K. BAKHTIAR, H.E. Dr. R. FALLAH, H. FARKHAN; Alternate Dirs. Dr. P. MINA, LATIF RAMZAN-NIA, T. MOSSADEQI.

In October 1954 an agreement was concluded between the Iranian Government and NIOC on the one hand and eight major oil companies (subsequently increased to fourteen) on the other, to operate the southern oilfields (as defined) on behalf of NIOC. These companies were collectively known as the Consortium, for which *see below*. The agreement was for twenty-five years with provision for three five-year extensions, at the option of the Consortium under specific terms and conditions, NIOC being responsible for non-industrial activities in the agreement area. It directly operates the Naft-i-Shah oilfield, the Kermanshah refinery, the Teheran refineries, the Shiraz refinery and the Abadan refineries; it also carried out exploration and drilling in all parts of the country not subject to special agreements. NIOC is solely responsible for internal distribution of petroleum products and has laid over 4,570 km. of pipeline throughout Iran. The Petroleum Act of 1957 empowered NIOC to divide Iran into 27 petroleum districts, to invite bids for their exploitation, and to sign agreements. NIOC signed a series of agreements: in 1957 with AGIP Mineraria (an Italian company); in 1958 with Pan American Petroleum Corpn.; in 1965 with six groups listed below, for exploration of offshore areas. In all eight of the companies formed, NIOC had 50 per cent participation. In September 1966 agreement was reached with the French state organization Entreprise des Recherches et d'Activités

Pétrolières (ERAP) to operate as a contractor on behalf of NIOC in exploration both on and offshore. At present ERAP is active only in 3,294.5 sq. km. offshore areas.

In December 1966 the Consortium relinquished one-quarter of the Agreement Area, comprising three parcels totalling 25,069 sq. miles, one in the north-west and two in the south-east, to NIOC. NIOC signed a further two contract type agreements in 1969: one with a group of five companies (ERAP, Agip, Hispanoil, Petrofina and O.e.M.V.) and the other with Continental Oil Company of U.S.A. and Phillips Petroleum Company. Also in 1972 three joint venture agreements were signed; with four Japanese and one U.S. oil companies; with Amerada Hess Corpn.; with Mobil Oil Corporation.

A major change took place in 1973, however, when the Consortium was issued with an ultimatum—the oil companies could either remain in the country until the existing 25-year contract expired in 1979 (with the proviso that they doubled production), after which they would get no more preferential treatment than any other foreign company, or alternatively, the Consortium could agree to be taken over immediately and then make preference agreements with the Government on a long-term basis. The latter course was agreed in March, and under a preliminary agreement signed in June 1973 between Iran and the Consortium, the Consortium is guaranteed a supply of oil over a 20-year period. The Iranian Oil Exploration and Producing Company was liquidated and the Oil Service Company of Iran was established, which operates as a contractor to the National Iranian Oil Company. The operation of Abadan refinery has passed to NIOC who will sell the products to the oil companies.

The decision was due partly to the Iran Government's need for greatly increased funds for the Fifth Development Plan, but also to its aim to gain as much control over foreign oil companies as had been achieved by other Arab states such as Kuwait, Qatar and Saudi Arabia in October 1972.

The company has formed two subsidiaries to represent it in two associated fields—The National Iranian Petrochemical Company and The National Iranian Gas Company. The latter has signed an agreement to supply the Soviet Union with large quantities of natural gas.

Société Irano-Italienne des Pétroles (SIRIP): Ave. Abbas Abad 30, P.O.B. 1434, Teheran; f. 1957: owned jointly by NIOC and AGIP S.p.A.; Man. Dir. Dr. A. ANGELUCCI.

Iran-Pan American Oil Co. (IPAC): 315 Takhte Jamshid Avenue, Teheran; f. 1958; owned jointly by NIOC and Amoco Iran Oil Co.; to exploit Persian Gulf offshore deposits in their agreement area; Man. Dir. M. T. RAZAGHNIA.

Iranian Marine International Oil Company (IMINOCO): 128 Roodsar Ave., Teheran; f. 1965; formed with Phillips Petroleum Co., AGIP (a subsidiary of the Italian ENI) and Hydrocarbons India Pvt. Ltd. (a subsidiary of the Oil and Natural Gas Commission of India); Chair. R. KALHOR; Man. Dir. C. TRAMPINI.

Lavan Petroleum Company (LAPCO): 3 Elizabeth II Boulevard, Teheran; f. 1965; formed with Atlantic Richfield, Murphy Oil Corporation, Sun Oil Co., and and Union Oil Co. of California, who own 50 per cent interest, and the National Iranian Oil Co., who own the remaining 50 per cent; Man. Dir. E. H. CHITTICK.

Iranian Offshore Petroleum Company (IROPCO): P.O.B. 3257, Teheran; f. 1965; formed with CEPSA, and Cities Service Co., Kerr-McGee Corpn., Atlantic-Richfield Co., Skelly Oil Co., Superior Oil Co., and Sunray D.X. Oil Co.; Chair. E. SALJOOGHI; Man. Dir. R. E. BUSH.

Phillips Petroleum Company: P.O.B. 3184, Teheran; assumed operations of area previously operated by CONOCO under agreement signed with NIOC in April 1969 for exploration and development of a 5,000 sq. mile area in South Iran; Vice-Pres. and Man. Dir. WILLIAM B. BELKNAP.

Sofiran: P.O.B. 3220, Teheran; French oil interests. A subsidiary of Elf. ERAP.

ERAP: Teheran; holds a 32 per cent share in a consortium exploring a 10,000 square mile area in Fars province; ENI has a 28 per cent share, Hispanoil 20 per cent, Petrofina 15 per cent and OMV of Austria 5 per cent.

Iran Nippon Petroleum Company (INPECO): 130 Ave. Shah Abbas Kabir, Teheran; f. 1971; partnership—50 per cent NIOC, 50 per cent Japanese group; Man. Dir. SH. HIKATA.

Hormuz Petroleum Company (HOPECO): 290 Ave. Villa, IBM Building, Teheran; f. 1971; partnership—50 per cent NIOC, 50 per cent Mobil; Pres. Dr. R. FELLAH.

Bushehr Petroleum Company (BUSHCO): 41 Ave. Daryaye Noor, between Takhte Tavoos and Abbasabad, Teheran; f. 1971; partnership—50 per cent NIOC, 50 per cent Amerada Hess; Man. Dir. M. QADIMI NAWAI.

THE CONSORTIUM

Consortium members, with percentage shareholdings: Gulf Oil Corporation (7%), Mobil Corporation (7%), Exxon (7%), Standard Oil Co. of California (7%), Texaco Inc. (7%), The British Petroleum Co. Ltd. (40%), Bataafse Petroleum Maatschappij N.V. (14%), Compagnie Française des Pétroles (6%), the remaining 5 per cent being divided amongst the following six American companies: The American Independent Oil Co., The Atlantic Richfield Co., Charter Oil Co., Getty Oil Co., The Standard Oil Company (Ohio), and Continental Oil Co.

REFINERIES' THROUGHPUT
(million barrels)

	Abadan	Masjid-i-Sulaiman
1969	149.5	10.0
1970	153.8	9.5
1971	154.2	16.7
1972	152.2	12.2
1973 (estimate)	155.8	12.9

TRADE AND INDUSTRY

CHAMBERS OF COMMERCE

Iran Chamber of Commerce, Industries and Mines: 254 Ave. Takht-Jamshid, Teheran; f. 1970; supervises the affiliated 17 Chambers in the provinces; Pres. Sen. Dr. TAHER ZIAI.

R.C.D. Joint Chamber of Commerce: Teheran; f. 1965 with Pakistan and Turkey under auspices of Regional Co-operation for Development.

EMPLOYERS' ASSOCIATION

Association des Employeurs Industriels de l'Iran: Teheran.

LABOUR ORGANIZATIONS

All Trade Unions were dissolved in 1963, and syndicates of workers must be registered with the Government. In March 1963 there were 67 syndicates representing various trades, of which the largest included the *National Iranian Oil Company Workers' Syndicate* with 6,000 members.

CO-OPERATIVES

Central Organization for Rural Co-operatives of Iran (C.O.R.C.): Teheran; Man. Dir. ZIAEDIN DANESHWARI. Following the implementation of the Land Reform Act, the C.O.R.C. was established by the Government in 1963. The aim of the organization is to offer educational, technical and credit assistance to rural co-operative societies and their unions. The C.O.R.C. will gradually transfer its stocks to rural co-operative unions and become the National body for Rural Co-operatives. By June 1973, 8,362 rural co-operatives societies and 127 unions with a combined total membership of 2,097,723 had availed themselves of the C.O.R.C. facilities. The share capital of the societies is 3,352m. rials.

TRADE FAIR

Iran International Fairs and Exhibitions Corpn.: P.O.B. 22 Tajrish, Teheran; Dir.-Gen. M. SHEE DFAR; publ *Exhibition News*.

TRANSPORT

RAILWAYS

Iranian State Railway: Head Office: Teheran; f. 1938; Pres. Eng. PARVIZ AVINI; Financial Gen. Dir. R. MOSTOFI; Administrative Gen. Dir. H. MALEKI.

The Iranian railway system includes the following main routes:

Trans-Iranian Railway runs 1,440 km. from Gorgan, in the north, through Teheran, and south to Bandar Shahpur on the Persian Gulf.

> **South Line** links Teheran to Khorramshahr via Ghom, Arak, Dorood, Andimeshk and Ahwaz; 937 km.

> **North Line** links Teheran to Gorgan via Garmsar, Firooz Kooh and Sari; 499 km.

Teheran-Tabriz Line linking with the Azarbaijan Railway (736 km.).

Garmsar-Meshed Line connects Teheran with Meshed, via Semnan, Damghan, Shahrud and Nishabur; 812 km.

Ghom-Zahedan Line when completed will be an intercontinental line linking Europe and Turkey, through Iran, with India. Zahedan is situated 91.7 km. west of the Baluchistan frontier, and is the end of the Pakistani broad gauge railway. The section from Ghom to Kashan is open, and that from Kashan to Yazd has been completed. A branch line from the Kashan-Yazd line to a steel mill at Riz was opened in 1971.

Ahwaz-Bandar Shahpur Line connects Bandar Shahpur with the Trans-Iranian railway at Ahwaz (123 km.).

Azarbaizhan Railway extends from Tabriz to Julfa (146.5 km.), meeting the Caucasian railways at the Soviet frontier. A line from Sharaf-Khaneh to the Turkish frontier at Razi was opened in 1971.

The total length of main lines in January 1972 was 4,560 km.

ROADS

Ministry of Roads: Ministry of Roads and Communications, Teheran; Minister Eng. J. SHAHRESTANI.

There are about 45,000 km. of roads, of which some 12,500 km. had asphalt or paved surfaces by 1973. The Asian (CENTO) Highway provides a two-lane asphalt highway from the Turkish border at Bazergan and the Iraq border at Qasr-e-Shirin to the Afghanistan border at Tayebat. The road connecting Teheran to the border with Pakistan is under construction from Kerman to the border. It will be completed in 1974.

MOTORISTS' ORGANIZATIONS

Touring and Automobile Club of Iran: 37 Varzesh Ave., Teheran; f. 1935; Gen. Man. M. R. SAFFARI.

INLAND WATERWAYS

Principal waterways:

Lake Rezaiyeh (Lake Urmia) 50 miles west of Tabriz in North-West Iran; and River Kharun flowing south through the oilfields into the River Shatt al Arab thence to the head of the Persian/Arabian Gulf near Abadan.

Lake Rezaiyeh: From Sharafkhaneh to Golmankhaneh there is a twice-weekly service of tugs and barges for transport of passengers and goods.

River Karun: Regular cargo service is operated by the Mesopotamia-Iran Corpn. Ltd. Iranian firms also operate daily motor-boat services for passengers and goods.

SHIPPING

Persian Gulf: Principal ports are Khorramshahr, Bushire, Bandar Abbas, Bandar Shahpur. Oil exports from the Abadan refinery are now handled by the new Mahshahr installations (opened December 1967) and Kharg Island terminal in the Persian/Arabian Gulf. Bushire is being developed to supplement the facilities at Khorramshahr, while the capacity of Bandar Abbas has recently been increased.

Caspian Sea: Principal port Bandar Pahlavi.

Arya National Shipping Lines: 2 Pahlavi Ave., Khorramshahr; 13 vessels; liner services between the Persian/Arabian Gulf and Europe.

CIVIL AVIATION

Iran National Airlines Corporation (*Iran Air*): Iran Air Building, Mehrabad Airport, Teheran; f. 1962; replaces Iranian Airways Co.; serves Iran, the Middle East and Europe, Karachi, Kabul and Bombay; Chair. Gen. M. KHATAMI; Man. Dir. Lt.-Gen. ALI M. KHADEMI; fleet of three Boeing 707, four Boeing 727, four Boeing 737

and two DC-6; three Concordes, two Boeing 747 and three Boeing 727 are on order.

Teheran is also served by the following foreign lines: Aeroflot, Air France, Air India, Alia, Alitalia, Ariana Afghan Airlines, British Airways, CSA, El Al, Iraqi Airways, JAL, KLM, Kuwait Airways, Lufthansa, MEA, PAA, Qantas, Sabena, SAS, Swissair, Syrian Arab Airlines.

TOURISM

Iran National Tourist Organization (INTO): 174 Elizabeth Blvd., Teheran; f. 1963; Dir. CYRUS FARZANEH. Publications: *Iran Travel News* (monthly), *INTO News Bulletin* (weekly), *Monthly Statistics Bulletin*, brochures, tourist guide books, road maps, posters.

During 1972 372,074 tourists visited Iran, showing an increase of 18,845 (5.3 per cent) over 1971. The estimated income from tourists over this period was U.S. $53 million.

CULTURAL ORGANIZATIONS

Ministry of Culture and Arts: Kh. Kamal-ol-Molk, Teheran; f. 1964 to replace the Fine Arts Administration; depts. of Creation of Arts and Letters, Art Education (Drama, Music, Ballet, Decorative Arts, Plastic Arts, National Arts), Audiovisual, Cultural Relations, Archaeology, Ethnography, Historical Monuments Preservation, Museums; has under its direction Nat. Org. for Ancient Monuments Preservation, Imperial Foundation of Iranian Academies, Celebrations Secretariat, Superior Council of Culture and Arts, Shahnameh Institute, Public Libraries, Rudaki Hall (opera, ballet, concerts), 25th

Shahrivar Theatre, an International Film Festival, etc.; Minister of Culture and Arts MEHRDAD PAHLBOD.

Teheran Symphonic Orchestra: Kh. Kamal-ol-Molk, Teheran; 75 mems.; Leader FARHAD MESHKAT.

Fine Arts Theatre Group: c/o Ministry of Culture, Teheran; produces weekly programmes for television.

Music Council of Radio Iran: Maidan Ark, Teheran; supervises all music programmes, both Persian and Western (popular and classical), broadcasts on two AM stations and one FM station in Teheran; also serves in advisory capacity all provincial stations; Chair. Dr. H. FARHAT.

Shiraz-Persepolis Festival of Arts: Shiraz; f. 1967; plays, films and music representing both Eastern and Western culture; held for a short fortnight at end of Aug. and beginning of Sept.; partly staged in the ruins at Persepolis; Pres. Dr. MEHDI BOUSHEHRI; publs. various books and brochures in Persian on music and drama, festival brochure annually.

ATOMIC ENERGY

National Iranian Atomic Energy Commission: Ministry of Economy, Teheran; co-ordinates nuclear research, and is undertaking construction of a small research reactor; Sec. Eng. A. SEIRAFI.

Teheran University Nuclear Centre: P.O.B. 2989, Teheran; f. 1958; research in nuclear physics, electronics, nuclear

chemistry, radiobiology and health physics; training and advice on nuclear science and the peaceful applications of atomic energy; a 5-MW pool-type research reactor on the new campus of Teheran University went critical in November 1967; a 3-MeV Van de Graaff-type accelerator became operational in 1972; Dir. Dr. H. ROUHANINEJAD.

UNIVERSITIES

University of Isfahan: Isfahan; 315 teachers, 3,400 students.

Jundi-Shapur University: Ahwaz, Khouzestan Province; 161 teachers, 2,370 students.

University of Meshed: Meshed; 272 teachers, 3,723 students.

National University of Iran: Ewin, Teheran; 426 teachers, 6,089 students.

Pahlavi University: Shiraz; 200 teachers, 3,876 students.

University of Tabriz: Tabriz; 475 teachers, 6,806 students.

University of Teheran: Ave. Shah Reza, Teheran; 1,436 teachers, 17,147 students.

Arya Mehr University of Technology: Karadj Rd., Teheran; 162 teachers, 2,005 students.

IRAQ

INTRODUCTORY SURVEY

Location, Climate, Language, Religion, Flag, Capital

Iraq is an almost landlocked state in the Middle East with a narrow outlet on to the Persian Gulf. Its neighbours are Iran, Turkey, Syria, Jordan, Saudi Arabia and Kuwait. The climate is extreme, with hot, dry summers, rising to over 43°C (110°F), and cold winters. Summers are humid near the Persian Gulf. The official language is Arabic, spoken by about 80 per cent of the population. Kurdish, Persian and Turkish are spoken by the tribesmen of the northern and eastern highlands. Ninety per cent of the population is Muslim. The national flag (proportions 3 by 2) is a horizontal tricolour, red, white and black, the white band charged with three five-pointed green stars. The capital is Baghdad.

Recent History

A *coup d'état* by the army in 1958 resulted in the assassination of King Faisal and the establishment of a Republic under General Kassem. Iraq's withdrawal from the Baghdad Pact soon followed. For over four years General Kassem maintained a precarious and increasingly isolated position opposed by Pan-Arabs, Kurds and other groups. In February 1963 the Pan-Arab element in the armed forces staged a *coup d'état* in which General Kassem was assassinated and a new government set up under Colonel Aref, who initiated a policy of closer relations with Egypt. Martial law, in force since 1958, was brought to an end in January 1965, and a purely civilian government was inaugurated in September 1965. In March 1966 President Aref was killed in an air accident, and was succeeded by his brother, Major-General Abdul Rahman Muhammad Aref. The second President Aref was ousted by members of the Baath Party in July 1968. Major-General (later Field-Marshal) Ahmed Hassan al-Bakr, a former Prime Minister, became President and Prime Minister.

Relations with Iran deteriorated after April 1969, following a dispute over the Shatt el Arab waterway, which forms the frontier. Diplomatic relations, broken off in 1971, were resumed in 1973 after the October war between the Arabs and Israel, but frontier fighting again took place during the first three months of 1974.

A settlement was apparently made with the Kurdish rebels in the north-east in March 1970, by which the Kurds would be granted autonomy by March 1974. Autonomy was offered to the Kurds in March 1974, but rejected by a majority of them because, among other things, the Iraqi Government retained control of the oil-rich Kirkuk area. Fighting took place in March and April 1974 between the Kurds, under Mullah Mustafa Barzani, and Iraqi Government troops. A Kurdish Vice-President of Iraq was appointed in April 1974 in an attempt to reach a settlement with the Kurds.

At the end of June 1973 an abortive *coup* took place, led by the Security Chief, Nazzim Kazzar, in which the Minister of Defence, General Shehab, was killed. Soon afterwards the constitution was amended, increasing the powers of President Bakr. In July 1973 a National Front was formed on the basis of a common programme endorsed by the Baath Party and the Iraqi Communist Party, which was legally recognized for the first time.

Government

Power rests with the President and a Revolutionary Command Council, which can contain up to 12 members, while the day-to-day running of the country is carried out by a Council of Ministers. The country is divided into 16 provinces.

Defence

Military service is compulsory for all men at the age of eighteen years and comprises two years active service and eighteen years with the reserve. The Iraq army has a total strength of about 90,000 men; the air force has a strength of 9,800, and the navy 2,000. The naval units operate on the rivers Tigris and Euphrates.

Economic Affairs

Iraq's wealth is based on oil, which earned her approximately I.D. 450 million in 1973. Current oil production (April 1974) is estimated to be at the rate of 115 million metric tons per year, of which 90 million metric tons is handled by the state-owned Iraq National Oil Company. Iraq nationalized the foreign-owned Iraq Petroleum Company (IPC) in June 1972, and a long-term oil agreement was reached in February 1973, ending 12 years of conflict between the Government and IPC. Iraq nationalized the U.S. and Dutch interests in the Basrah Petroleum Company after the October 1973 war between the Arab States and Israel. Iraq has not, however, cut back her oil production.

About half the total land area is cultivable, but major irrigation projects are in hand. Dates form the chief export crop, with exports of between 150,000 and 250,000 tons per year.

Transport and Communication

Iraq has about 1,500 miles of railway track. The main means of travel is road. New trunk roads have been built and the current development plan provides for building and extending the road system. In many desert areas the natural surfaces are passable for vehicles. The lower reaches of the Euphrates and the combined mouth of the Tigris and Euphrates, the Shatt el Arab, are navigable and deep-water oil berths have been built to serve the oil fields. Iraqi Airways operate services to other Middle Eastern countries, Europe and India.

Social Welfare

A limited Social Security Scheme was introduced in 1957. Benefits are given for old age, sickness, unemployment, maternity, marriage and death.

Education

Education is free and primary education lasting six years is compulsory in an effort to reduce illiteracy. In

1972 over one million children were attending 5,600 primary schools. There are six universities. Many Iraqis study abroad.

Tourism

Iraq is the ancient Mesopotamia of early history, and one of the oldest centres of civilization. The ruins of Ur of the Chaldees, Babylon, Nineveh and other relics of the Sumerian, Babylonian, Assyrian and Persian Empires are of interest to the tourist. Hatra and Ctesiphon represent the early mediaeval period.

Visas are not required to visit Iraq by nationals of Egypt, Jordan, Kuwait Lebanon and Syria.

Sport

There is little organized sport. Football is played, while duck shooting, hawking and other field sports are enjoyed.

Public Holidays

1974: October 15th* (Id ul Fitr), December 26th* (Id ul Adha).

1975: January 6th (Army Day), January 14th (Muslim New Year), January 24th* (Ashoura), February 8th (14 Ramadhan Revolution), March 21st (Nowroos Day), March 26th (Mouloud), May 1st (Labour Day), July 14th (Republic Day), July 17th (second Republic Day).

* Approximate only; these are Muslim holidays determined by sightings of the moon, which vary each year.

Weights and Measures

The metric system is in force. Meshara or dunum = 0.62 acre (2,500 sq. metres).

Currency and Exchange Rates

1,000 fils = 20 dirhams = 5 riyals = 1 Iraqi dinar (I.D.).

Exchange rates (April 1974):
£1 sterling = 699.05 fils;
U.S. $1 = 296.05 fils.

STATISTICAL SURVEY

AREA AND POPULATION

TOTAL AREA	ARABLE	POPULATION (1972)	BAGHDAD (capital)	MOSUL	BASRA
438,446 sq. km.	75,364 sq. km.	10,074,000	1,884,151*	343,121*	420,145*

* 1968 estimate.

A neutral zone of 7,000 sq. km. between southern Iraq and northern Saudi Arabia is administered jointly by the two countries Nomads move freely through it, but there are no permanent inhabitants.

POPULATION BY PROVINCE (MUHAFADHA)
(1971)

Naynawa	. .	839,047
Sulaimaniya	.	487,479
Arbil	. .	432,430
Kirkuk	. .	546,480
Diyala	. .	454,729
Anbar	. .	353,213
Baghdad	. .	2,838,330
Wasit	. .	364,813

Babil	. .	531,490
Kerbela	. .	473,007
Qadisiyah	. .	413,141
Maysan	. .	356,007
Dhiqar	. .	529,207
Basra	. .	825,253
Muthanna	. .	145,180
Duhok	. .	159,791

EMPLOYMENT
(1972)

Agriculture	. .	1,446,200
Mining	. .	17,500
Manufacturing	. .	165,000
Electricity, Gas and Water	. .	13,900
Construction	. .	71,000
Commerce	. .	160,000
Transport	. .	158,000
Services	. .	320,000
Others	. .	285,000
Unemployed	. .	181,400
TOTAL LABOUR FORCE	.	2,818,000

AGRICULTURE

AREA AND PRODUCTION OF PRINCIPAL WINTER CROPS

	1968–69		1969–70		1970–71	
	AREA ('000 dunums)	PRODUCTION ('000 tons)	AREA ('000 dunums)	PRODUCTION ('000 tons)	AREA ('000 dunums)	PRODUCTION ('000 tons)
Wheat	6,645.6	1,183.1	7,034.1	1,235.6	3,793.2	822.3
Barley	3,381.0	963.2	2,690.4	682.2	1,584.3	432.4
Linseed	64.9	11.5	68.9	14.2	37.8	6.1
Lentils	39.0	6.5	42.1	4.5	33.5	3.9
Vetch (Hurtman) . . .	3.4	0.8	37.8	0.9	26.9	0.6
Broad Beans	67.2	17.7	71.2	20.1	78.6	18.5

AREA AND PRODUCTION OF PRINCIPAL SUMMER CROPS

	1969		1970		1971	
	AREA ('000 dunums)	PRODUCTION ('000 tons)	AREA ('000 dunums)	PRODUCTION ('000 tons)	AREA ('000 dunums)	PRODUCTION ('000 tons)
Rice	558.7	284.2	298.0	180.1	436.3	306.7
Sesame	68.4	12.0	73.1	13.3	82.1	13.9
Maize	16.1	4.8	19.6	5.9	37.5	16.0
Green grams	57.5	9.0	61.3	12.9	61.0	10.0
Millet	5.7	1.3	11.0	2.8	22.3	4.8
Giant millet	12.5	3.5	17.2	5.4	44.4	13.3

Livestock (1970): Sheep 13,831,000; Goats 2,412,000; Cattle 1,830,000; Donkeys 566,000; Horses 124,000; Buffaloes 288,000; Camels 252,000; Chickens 5,677,000.

DATE CROP
(tons)

1968–69	1969–70	1970–71	1971–72
260,000	480,000	300,000	450,000

AREA AND PRODUCTION OF COTTON

	1970	1971	1972
Area (dunums) .	134,600	135,600	146,800
Production (tons) .	41,500	42,840	50,800

IRRIGATION

	1968–69	1969–70	1970–71	1971–72
Number of Pumps . .	13,066	13,769	14,135	15,484
Total Horse Power . .	357,099	366,751	350,335	368,885

OIL
PRODUCTION OF CRUDE OIL
('ooo long tons)

	1967	1968	1969	1970	1971	1972*
Iraq Petroleum Co. Ltd. . . .	37,625	54,828	55,441	56,893	51,100	} 69,000
Basra Petroleum Co. Ltd. . . .	20,049	16,511	16,587	17,067	30,100	
Mosul Petroleum Co. Ltd. . . .	1,264	1,281	1,281	1,281	1,300	
Total . . .	58,938	72,620	73,309	75,241	82,500	69,000

* Excluding Government exports.

INDUSTRY
('ooo units)

	1965	1966	1967	1968	1969
Leather tanning:					
Upper leather (sq. ft.) .	5,300.6	6,140.0	6,110.9	6,738.6	n.a.
Toilet Soap (tons) . .	4.6	7.2	5.9	7.6	7.3
Vegetable oil (tons) .	46.7	43.1	50.2	52.9	58.0
Woollen textiles:					
Cloth (metres) . .	902.4	937.7	87.9	835.6	n.a.
Blankets (number) .	461.7	510.9	506.8	447.5	611.0
Cotton textiles (metres)	32,541.7	33,131.9	34,046.5	31,805.7	32,447.0
Beer (litres) . .	4,803.1	5,639.8	5,523.2	6,064.1	n.a.
Matches (gross) . .	1,102.5	1,031.0	1,275.3	1,371.0	1,686.4
Cigarettes (million) .	5.1	5.2	4.9	5.1	5.2
Shoes (pairs) . .	5,203.6	5,363.5	5,145.0	5,619.5	n.a.

FINANCE
1,000 fils = 20 dirhams = 5 riyals = 1 Iraqi dinar (I.D.).
Coins: 1, 5, 10, 25, 50 and 100 fils.
Notes: 250 and 500 fils; 1, 5, and 10 dinars.
Exchange rates (April 1974): £1 sterling = 699.05 fils; U.S. $1 = 296.05 fils.
100 Iraqi dinars = £143.05 = $337.78.

Note: From September 1949 to August 1971 the par value of the Iraqi dinar was U.S. $2.80. Between December 1971 and February 1973 the value was $3.04. In terms of sterling, the exchange rate between November 1967 and June 1972 was £1 = 857.14 fils (£7 = 6 dinars).

Ordinary Budget 1970-71: Revenue I.D. 287 million; Expenditure I.D. 264 million.

Development Budget 1970-71: Revenue I.D. 110 million; Expenditure I.D. 202 million.

The new 1970-74 Development Plan calls for total investment of I.D. 953 million, of which I.D. 829 million will accrue from oil revenues. I.D. 336 million will be invested in agriculture, and I.D. 207 million will be devoted to industry.

CENTRAL BANK RESERVES
(U.S. $ million at December 31st)

	1969	1970	1971	1972	1973
Gold . . .	192.7	143.5	155.8	155.8	173.1
IMF Special Drawing Rights .	—	—	12.7	25.2	24.2
Reserve Position in IMF .	20.0	—	—	18.7	32.9
Foreign Exchange . .	263.7	318.7	431.9	581.8	1,252.0
Total . .	476.4	462.2	600.4	781.5	1,482.2

CONSUMER PRICES INDEX (IFS)
(1963=100)

1966	1967	1968	1969	1970	1971	1972
100.3	103.6	105.9	111.9	116.8	121.0	124.3

EXTERNAL TRADE

TOTAL TRADE
('000 I.D.)

YEAR	IMPORTS	EXPORTS*	RE-EXPORTS	TRANSIT
1969. .	157,169	22,002	3,937	20,356
1970. .	181,651	22,566	2,164	27,942
1971. .	247,870	22,780	n.a.	33,801
1972. .	234,680	23,614	2,394	65,485

* Exports of crude oil are not included.

EXPORTS OF CRUDE OIL
('000 I.D.)

1967	1968	1969	1970	1971
273,541	344,154	346,185	368,065	523,191

COMMODITIES
('000 I.D.)

IMPORTS	1969	1970	1971	EXPORTS	1969	1970	1971
Tea . . .	7,061	6,052	6,072	Barley . . .	1,278	538	n.a.
Sugar . .	8,151	7,927	12,278	Dates . .	7,444	9,278	6,905
Pharmaceutical products . .	5,816	5,481	8,805	Straw and fodder .	305	27	94
Clothing. .	1,247	664	422	Raw wool . .	1,591	1,530	1,403
Boilers and engines .	30,194	28,808	35,098	Raw cotton .	1,204	174	74
Automobiles and parts . .	8,143	12,076	12,115	Hides and skins .	1,699	1,694	1,822
Timber . . .	3,024	2,910	3,182	Cement . .	2,142	2,569	2,712

Date exports in 1972 amounted to over 1 million I.D.

EXPORTS OF CRUDE OIL BY COUNTRY
(million long tons)

	1968	1969	1970	1971
United Kingdom	3.1	3.2	2.5	3.4
France	15.7	14.8	11.8	16.1
Italy	17.6	18.0	22.0	18.5
Netherlands . . .	5.1	6.7	5.1	5.0
Germany, Federal Republic . .	2.5	2.1	2.8	2.8
Japan	1.4	0.2	—	—
Belgium	3.2	1.3	1.0	2.0
Brazil	2.9	3.1	3.2	3.0
Greece	1.7	3.0	3.5	4.1
South Africa . . .	1.9	1.9	2.2	2.2
Spain	1.8	2.0	1.8	2.0
Turkey	2.0	2.0	2.8	2.4
TOTAL (incl. others) . .	69.3	69.7	72.2	78.1

COUNTRIES
('ooo I.D.)

Imports	1970	1971	1972
Australia	2,458	15,444	734
Belgium	9,271	6,338	7,598
Bulgaria	3,487	3,631	3,923
Canada	1,700	16,293	890
China, People's Republic . . .	8,174	7,446	6,531
Czechoslovakia	4,710	12,496	16,321
Egypt	3,421	2,789	3,020
France	10,715	15,344	14,658
German Democratic Republic .	2,877	3,665	7,923
Germany, Federal Republic . .	6,459	8,218	11,342
India	5,281	4,184	5,522
Italy	5,461	7,972	11,478
Japan	5,606	7,482	10,581
Lebanon	4,971	5,484	6,333
Malaysia	6,746	7,822	4,956
Netherlands	4,006	3,257	6,037
Pakistan	2,221	4,253	2,510
Poland	5,129	7,044	6,092
Sri Lanka	3,846	4,997	4,937
Sweden	7,410	6,873	7,302
U.S.S.R.	19,263	29,605	17,030
United Kingdom	21,822	22,626	22,735
U.S.A.	6,532	12,096	9,554

Exports (excluding oil)	1970	1971	1972
China, People's Republic . .	1,440	1,070	2,623
India	1,333	1,197	1,514
Kuwait	2,647	3,002	4,113
Lebanon	2,825	2,829	3,386
Syria	1,430	3,809	2,430
U.S.S.R.	2,029	1,194	2,285
U.A.R. (now Egypt) . . .	3,301	3,299	3,166

TRANSPORT

RAILWAYS

	1967–68	1968–69	1969–70
Passenger km. ('ooo)	366,716	366,847	368,743
Freight ton km. ('ooo)	1,123,215	1,032,140	1,193,857

ROADS
Licensed Vehicles ('ooo)

	1968	1969	1970	1971
Cars . . .	61.5	65.0	67.4	71.8
Goods Vehicles .	31.3	32.5	32.7	33.7
Buses . .	9.2	9.3	9.2	10.9
Motor Cycles .	5.9	6.6	6.9	7.5

Source: International Road Federation.

INLAND WATERWAYS

	1968–69	1969–70	1970–71
Total net reg. tonnage . .	135,698	137,911	140,380
Number of Vessels . .	1,271	1,285	1,264

SHIPPING

Movement of Ocean-going Merchant Vessels at the Ports of Basra and Um Qasr.

	No. of PASSENGERS (Arrivals and Departures)*	No. of VESSELS		TONNAGE OF CARGO (excluding Crude Oil)	
		Loaded (Entered and Cleared)	In Ballast (Entered and Cleared)	Imported	Exported
1968 . .	8,127	955	615	870,221	270,420
1969 . .	6,462	793	491	760,990	392,265
1970 . .	5,610	661	395	945,931	279,914
1971 . .	5,396	718	483	2,132,086	230,964

* Port of Basra only.

In 1972 passenger arrivals at Basra were 2,956 and departures 3,257.

SHIPPING OF CRUDE OIL

Export by Tanker from Ports of Abadan and Khor Al-Amaya.

	1969	1970	1971
Number of ships docking . .	602	604	804
Net registered tonnage . .	7,018,061	7,544,388	12,636,205
Tonnage of cargo . .	16,357,918	17,037,667	29,689,601

CIVIL AVIATION

Flights through Baghdad and Basra Airports.

	FLIGHTS		PASSENGERS			CARGO (kg)	
	Iraqi Airways	Total	Disembarked	Embarked	Transit	Off-Loaded	Loaded
1968 . . .	1,892	4,085	111,563	110,542	8,614	2,113,987	465,742
1969 . . .	2,060	4,132	119,772	116,725	9,065	2,442,518	493,956
1970 . . .	1,527	3,198	110,172	111,841	8,071	2,615,722	528,542
1971 . . .	2,346	4,031	127,404	126,760	n.a.	2,463,596	820,156

TOURISM

	1969	1970	1971
Visitors . . .	429,654	359,929	589,857

EDUCATION

(1972–73)

	SCHOOLS	PUPILS
Primary . . .	3,654	1,298,422
Secondary (General) .	1,032	348,648
Vocational . .	60	11,248
Teacher Training . .	5	7,405
Universities . . .	5	48,073*

* 1971–72.

Source: Central Statistical Organization, Ministry of Planning, Baghdad.

PROVISIONAL CONSTITUTION

The following are the principal features of the Provisional Constitution issued on September 22nd, 1968:

The Iraqi Republic is a popular democratic state. Islam is the state religion and the basis of its laws and constitution.

The political economy of the state is founded in socialism.

The state will protect liberty of religion, freedom of speech and opinion. Public meetings are permitted under the law. All discrimination based on race, religion or language is forbidden. There shall be freedom of the Press, and the right to form societies and trade unions in conformity with the law is guaranteed.

The Iraqi people is composed of two main nationalities: Arab and Kurds. The Constitution confirms the nationalistic rights of the Kurdish people and the legitimate rights of all other minorities within the framework of Iraqi unity.

The highest authority in the country is the Council of Command of the Revolution, which will promulgate laws until the election of a National Assembly. The (five) members of the Council of Command of the Revolution are nominated Vice-Presidents of the State.

Two amendments to the constitution were announced in November 1969. The President, already Chief of State and head of the government, also became the official Supreme Commander of the Armed Forces and President of the Command Council of the Revolution. Membership of the latter body was to increase from five to a larger number at the President's discretion.

Earlier, a Presidential decree replaced the 14 local government districts by 16 governates, each headed by a governor with wide powers.

The fifteen-article agreement which aimed to end the Kurdish war was issued on March 12th, 1970. In accordance with this agreement a form of autonomy was offered to the Kurds in March 1974, but the majority of the Kurds rejected the offer and fresh fighting broke out. A new provisional constitution was announced in July 1970 which took account of the March 1970 agreement. It had 67 articles, the most prominent being the article which further defined the Revolutionary Command Council. This now has up to 12 members, selected from among the members of the Regional Leadership of the Arab Baath Socialist Party. The President is elected by a two-thirds majority of the Council; he is responsible to the Council and the Vice-Presidents and Ministers will be responsible to him.

In November 1971 President Bakr announced a National Charter as a first step towards a permanent constitution. A National Assembly and popular councils are features of the Charter.

In July 1973, under amendments to the Constitution, President Bakr was given powers to appoint and dismiss every minister or official from the Vice-President downwards. He can also assume executive power directly or through the Council of Ministers.

THE GOVERNMENT

HEAD OF STATE
President: Field-Marshal Ahmed Hassan al-Bakr.
Vice-President: Taha Moheddin Maruf.

REVOLUTIONARY COMMAND COUNCIL
President: Field-Marshal Ahmed Hassan al-Bakr
Vice-President: Sadam Hussain Takriti

Members: The President, the Vice-President, Gen. Saadoun Ghaidan, Dr. Izzat Mustafa, Izzat al-Douri, Murtadha Abdul Baqi al-Hadithi, Taha al-Jezrawi, Col. Shafiq Hammudi al Daraji (Sec.-Gen.).

COUNCIL OF MINISTERS
(*January* 1974)

Prime Minister and Minister of Defence: Field-Marshal Ahmed Hassan al-Bakr.

Minister of Foreign Affairs: Murtadha Abdul Baqi al-Hadithi.

Minister of the Interior: Gen. Saadoun Ghaidan.

Minister of Health: Dr. Izzat Mustafa.

Minister of Industry: Taha al-Jezrawi.

Minister of Transport: Nihad Fakhri al-Khaffaf.

Minister of Agriculture and Agrarian Reform: Izzat al-Douri.

Minister of Information and Culture: Hamid al-Jibouri.

Minister of Youth: Adnan Ayoub Sabri.

Minister of Irrigation: Mukarram al-Talabani.

Minister of Labour and Social Affairs: Anwar Abdul Qadir al-Hadithi.

Minister of Education: Dr. Ahmed A. S. al-Jawari.

Minister of Higher Education and Scientific Research: Dr. Hisham al-Shawi.

Minister of Planning: Dr. Jewad Hashim.

Minister of the Economy: Hikmat al-Azawi.

Minister of Oil and Minerals: Dr. Saadoun Hummadi.

Minister of Communications: Dr. Rashid al-Rafaie.

Minister of Finance: Amin Abdul Karim.

Minister of Municipal and Rural Affairs: Ihsan Shirzad.

Minister of Public Works and Housing: Muhsin Desayee.

Minister of Northern Development: Muhammad Mahmoud.

Minister of Unity and the North and Acting Minister of Justice: Dr. Abdulla al-Khudairi.

Ministers of State: Salih al-Yousifi, Aziz Sharif, Nazar al-Tabaqchali, Amir Abdulla, Nouri Shawis.

DIPLOMATIC REPRESENTATION

EMBASSIES ACCREDITED TO IRAQ

(In Baghdad unless otherwise stated)

(E) Embassy.

Afghanistan: 27/1/12 Waziriyah; *Ambassador:* Prof. KHALILLULLAH KHALILI.

Algeria: Karradat Mariam (E); *Ambassador:* OTHMANE SAADI.

Austria: Masbah (E); *Ambassador:* NOREBERT LINHART.

Bangladesh: (E); *Ambassador:* RASHID AHMAD.

Belgium: Abu Nawas St., Kard el Pasha; *Chargé d'Affaires:* Comte ALBERT DE BORCHGRAVE D'ALTONA.

Brazil: *Ambassador:* MARIO LOUREIRO DIAS COSTA.

Bulgaria: 35/1 Karradat Mariam (E); *Ambassador:* PENU IVANOV DOKOUZOV.

Canada: Beirut, Lebanon.

China, People's Republic: Karradat Mariam (E); *Ambassador:* HU CHENG-FANG.

Cyprus: Cairo, Egypt.

Czechoslovakia: 1/7 Karradat Mariam (E); *Ambassador:* JÁN GAZIK.

Denmark: Ankara, Turkey.

Egypt: (E); *Ambassador:* ABDEL MONEIM EL-NAGAR.

Ethiopia: Cairo, Egypt (E).

Finland: Masbah 37/7/35 (E); *Chargé d'Affaires:* MARTII LINTULAHTI.

France: Kard el Pasha 9/G/3 (E); *Ambassador:* PIERRE CERLES.

German Democratic Republic: *Ambassador:* GÜNTHER SCHURATH.

Greece: Damascus, Syria.

Hungary: 40/35 Masbah (E); *Ambassador:* JÓZSEF FERRÓ.

India: Taha St., Najib Pasha, Ahmadiya (E); *Ambassador:* K. R. B. SINGH.

Indonesia: 22/9/21 Masbah; *Ambassador:* MALIKSWARI MUKTAR.

Iran: Karradat Mariam (E); *Chargé d'Affaires:* MUHAMMAD KHAKPOOR.

Italy: Karradat Mariam; *Ambassador:* GIAN PIER NUTI.

Japan: 40/7/35 Masbah; *Ambassador:* SEIICHI SHIMA.

Jordan: *Chargé d'Affaires:* DHYAB AL-AWRAN.

Kuwait: Karradat Mariam; *Ambassador:* KHALID A. L. AL-MUSALLAM.

Korea, Democratic People's Republic: KIM QYO NAM.

Lebanon: 11/35 Masbah; *Ambassador:* SUHAIL SHAMMAS.

Libya: Saadoun Park (E); *Ambassador:* SALEH AL-SENUSSI ABDUL SAYED.

Mauritania: Cairo, Egypt.

Mongolia: Prague, Czechoslovakia.

Morocco: 3/1/37 Masbah (E); *Ambassador:* MOHAMED NACIRI.

Nepal: (E); *Ambassador:* JHARENDRAS SINGHA.

Netherlands: *Chargé d'Affaires:* Baron W. J. J. D. THOE SCHWARTZENBERG EN HOHENLANSBERG.

Nigeria: Cairo, Egypt.

Norway: Ankara, Turkey (E).

Poland: Karrada al-Sharkiya, Masbah (E); *Ambassador:* LUCJAN LIK.

Qatar: (E); *Ambassador:* AHMED ALI MAARIFIYA.

Romania: *Ambassador:* VASILE GEORGE.

Saudi Arabia: Waziriyah (E); *Ambassador:* ALI A. EL-SUGAIR.

Somalia: Cairo, Egypt (E).

Spain: Saadoun Park 162/2; *Ambassador:* AMELIO MARTINE.

Sri Lanka: 10 B/6/12 Alwiyah (E); *Chargé d'Affaires a.i.:* A. T. MOORTHY.

Sudan: 51/5/35 Masbah (E); *Chargé d'Affaires:* SAYID SHARIF AHMED.

Sweden: 132/2 Al Nidhal St.; *Ambassador:* OTTO RATHSMAN.

Switzerland: 3/1/2 Saadoun St. (E); *Chargé d'Affaires a.i.:* Dr. M. VOGEL-BACHER.

Syria: 160/2 Saadoun Park; *Ambassador:* MUNIR AL-KHAIR.

Turkey: 2/8 Waziriyah; *Ambassador:* MELIH AKBIL.

U.S.S.R.: 140 Mansour St., Karradat Mariam; *Ambassador:* ANATOLY BARKOVSKY.

United Arab Emirates: (E); *Ambassador:* RASHID SULTAN AL-MUKHAWI.

United Kingdom: Sharia Salah Ud-Din, Karkh (E); *Ambassador:* (vacant).

Vatican: Karrada al-Sharkiya, Saadoun St. (Apostolic Nunciature); *Apostolic Pro-Nuncio:* JEAN RUPP.

Venezuela: Cairo, Egypt (E).

Viet-Nam, Democratic Republic: Damascus, Syria.

Yemen Arab Republic: Karradat Mariam (E); *Ambassador:* AHMED HUSSEIN AL-MURWENI.

Yemen, People's Democratic Republic: *Ambassador:* HAFIDH QAYID FARI.

Yugoslavia: 10/11/1 Asfar Quarter, Battaween; *Ambassador:* DANILO PURIC.

Iraq also has diplomatic relations with Argentina, Cuba, Guinea, Kenya, Malta, Pakistan and Tanzania.

NATIONAL ASSEMBLY

No form of National Assembly has existed in Iraq since the 1958 revolution which overthrew the monarchy. The existing provisional constitution contains provisions for the election of a new 100-member assembly at a date to be determined by the Government.

POLITICAL PARTIES

National Progressive Front: Baghdad; f. July 1973, when Arab Baath Socialist Party and Iraqi Communist Party signed a joint manifesto agreeing to establish a comprehensive progressive national and nationalistic front; Sec.-Gen. NAIM HADDAD (Baath).

Arab Baath Socialist Party: Baghdad; revolutionary Arab socialist movement founded in Damascus in 1947; has ruled Iraq since July 1968, and since July 1973 in alliance with the Iraqi Communist Party in the National Progressive Front; Regional Sec.-Gen. AHMED HASSAN AL-BAKR; Vice-Regional Sec.-Gen. SADAM HUSSAIN TAKRITI.

Iraqi Communist Party: Baghdad; f. 1934; became legally recognized in July 1973 on formation of National Progressive Front; First Sec. AZIZ MOHAMMED.

Kurdistan Democratic Party: represents majority of Kurds in Iraq; rejected autonomy offered in March 1974; Chair. MULLAH MUSTAFA BARZANI; Sec.-Gen. HABIB MUHAMMAD KARIM.

Kurdistan Revolutionary Party: Kurdish party which accepted terms of autonomy offered in March 1974; Leader ABDEL SATTAR SHARIF.

JUDICIAL SYSTEM

Courts in Iraq consist of the following: The Court of Cassation, Courts of Appeal, First Instance Courts, Peace Courts, Courts of Sessions, Shara' Courts and Penal Courts.

The Court of Cassation: This is the highest judicial bench of all the Civil Courts; it sits in Baghdad, and consists of the President and a number of Vice-Presidents and not less than fifteen permanent judges, delegated judges and reporters as necessity requires. There are four bodies in the Court of Cassation, these are: (a) The General body, (b) Civil and Commercial body, (c) Personal Status body, (d) The Penal body.

A Technical Bureau has been established which is related to the Court of Cassation and is carrying out the work of abstracting and classifying the legal principles which are contained in the judgments issued by it.

Courts of Appeal: The country is divided into five Districts of Appeal: Baghdad, Mosul, Basrah, Hilla, and Kirkuk, each with its Court of Appeal consisting of a President, Vice-Presidents and not less than three members, who consider the objections against the decisions issued by the First Instance Courts of first grade.

Courts of First Instance: These courts are of two kinds: Limited and Unlimited in jurisdiction.

Limited Courts deal with Civil and Commercial suits, the value of which is five hundred Dinars and less; and suits, the value of which cannot be defined, and which are subject to fixed fees. Limited Courts consider these suits in the final stage and they are subject to Cassation.

Unlimited Courts consider the Civil and Commercial suits irrespective of their value, and suits the value of which exceeds five hundred Dinars with first grade subject to appeal.

First Instance Courts consist of one judge in the centre of each *Liwa*, some *Qadhas* and *Nahiyas*, as the Minister of Justice judges necessary.

Revolutionary Courts: These deal with major cases that would affect the security of the state in any sphere: political, financial or economic. In December 1968 the death penalty was introduced for espionage; a special three-man court was then set up to try such cases.

Courts of Sessions: There is in every District of Appeal a Court of Sessions which consists of three judges under the presidency of the President of the Court of Appeal or one of his Vice-Presidents. It considers the penal suits prescribed by Penal Proceedings Law and other laws. More than one Court of Sessions may be established in one District of Appeal by notification issued by the Minister of Justice mentioning therein its headquarters, jurisdiction and the manner of its establishment.

Shara' Courts: A Shara' Court is established wherever there is a First Instance Court; the Muslim judge of the First Instance Court may be a *Qadhi* to the Shara' Court if a special *Qadhi* has not been appointed thereto. The Shara' Court considers matters of personal status and religious matters in accordance with the provisions of the law supplement to the Civil and Commercial Proceedings Law.

Penal Courts: A Penal Court of first grade is established in every First Instance Court. The judge of the First Instance Court is considered as penal judge unless a special judge is appointed thereto. More than one Penal Court may be established to consider the suits prescribed by the Penal Proceedings Law and other laws.

One or more Investigation Court may be established in the centre of each *Liwa* and a judge is appointed thereto. They may be established in the centres of *Qadhas* and *Nahiyas* by order of the Minister of Justice. The judge carries out the investigation in accordance with the provisions of Penal Proceedings Law and the other laws.

There is in every First Instance Court a department for the execution of judgments presided over by the Judge of First Instance if a special President is not appointed thereto. It carries out its duties in accordance with the provisions of Execution Law.

RELIGION

ISLAM

Over 90 per cent of the population are Muslims. The Arabs of northern Iraq, the Bedouins, the Kurds, and some of the inhabitants of Baghdad and Basra, are mainly of the Sunni sect, the remaining Arabs south of the Diyala, belong to the Shi'i sect. Leaders: Mr. ALWAIDH (Sunni), Prof. ABDUL QASSEM AL MOUSAWI AL KHOUI (Shi'i).

CHRISTIANITY

There are Christian communities in all the principal towns of Iraq, but their principal villages lie mostly in the Mosul district. The Christians of Iraq fall into three groups: (a) the free Churches, including the Nestorian, Gregorian, and Jacobite; (b) the churches known as Uniate, since they are in union with the Roman Catholic Church including the Armenian Uniates, Jacobite Uniates, and Chaldeans; (c) mixed bodies of Protestant converts, New Chaldeans, and Orthodox Armenians.

Catholic:

Latin Rite: Archbishop of Baghdad: P.O.B. 2090, Baghdad: Most Rev. Ernest Nyary; approx. 2,000 adherents.

Armenian Rite: Archbishop of Baghdad: Most Rev. Jean Kasparian.

Chaldean Rite: Patriarch of Babylon of the Chaldeans: His Beatitude Paul II Cheikho, with 13 Archbishops and Bishops in Iraq, Iran, Syria and Lebanon. Approx. 330,000 adherents.

Syrian Rite: Archbishop of Mosul: Most Rev. Cyril Emanuel Benni; Archbishop of Baghdad: Most Rev. Athanase J. D. Bakose; approx. 32,000 adherents.

Orthodox Syrian Community: 12,000 adherents.

Orthodox (*Gregorian*) **Community:** 12,000 adherents, mainly Armenians; Acting Bishop of Baghdad: Krikor Hagopian.

JUDAISM

The Jewish community numbered some 250,000 in 1939, but most Jews have left the country since the Second World War, particularly during the nineteen-fifties; unofficial estimates put the present size of the community at 2,500, almost all living in Baghdad.

OTHERS

About thirty thousand Yazidis and a smaller number of Turcomans, Sabeans, and Shebeks make up the rest of the population.

Sabean Community: 20,000 adherents; Head Sheikh Dakhil, Nasiriyah; Mandeans, mostly in Nasiriyah.

Yazidis: 30,000 adherents; Tashin Baik, Asifni.

THE PRESS

DAILIES

Baghdad Observer: P.O.B. 257, Karantina, Baghdad; f. 1967; English; Editor-in-Chief Fuad Yousif Qazanchi; circ. 7,000.

al Jumhuriya (*The Republic*): Karantina, Baghdad; f. 1963, re-founded 1967; Editor-in-Chief Sa'ad Qassim Hammoudi; circ. 25,000.

al Riyadhi (*Sportsman*): Baghdad; f. 1971; published by Ministry of Youth.

al Shaab (*People's Path*): Sadoun, Baghdad; f. 1973; organ of Iraqi Communist Party.

al Taakhi (*Brotherhood*): P.O.B. 5717, Baghdad; re-founded 1968; organ of the Kurdistan Democratic Party; Editor-in-Chief Dara Tawfiq; circ. 25,000.

al Thawra (*Revolution*): Aqaba bin Nafi's Square, P.O.B. 2009, Baghdad; f. 1968; organ of Baath Party; Chief Editor Tarik Aziz; circ. 70,000.

WEEKLIES

al-Aswaq al-Tijariya (*The Commercial Markets*): 28/13 Sharia Hassan Ben Thabit, Baghdad; f. 1951; economic and commercial; Propr. and Editor Jamal Dawood; circ. 3,000.

al-Fikr al-Jadid (*New Thought*): f. 1972; weekly; political; Editor Husain Qasim al-Aziz; circ. 30,000.

Alif Da (*Alphabet*): Karantina, Baghdad; Editor-in-Chief Sami Mahdi; circ. 10,000.

al-Iqtisad al-Iraqi (*The Iraq Economy*): Baghdad; economic affairs; weekly; Editor A. B. Mahmud al-Umar.

al-Mutafarrij: Rashid St., Hayderkhana, P.O.B. 409 Baghdad; f. 1965; satirical; Editor Moujib Hassoon.

al-Nahdha: Sulaymaniya; Arabic and Kurdish; general interest.

L'Opinion de Baghdad: L'Etablissement Géneral de la Presse et de l'Imprimerie, B.P. 580, Baghdad; f. 1970; French; Editor-in-Chief Ali Smida.

Saut al Fallah (*Voice of the Peasant*) Baghdad; f. 1968; organ of General Federation of Peasant Societies; Editor-in-Chief Latif al-Dilaimi; circ. 15,000.

Waee Ul-Omal (*The Workers' Consciousness*): Headquarters of General Federation of Trade Unions in Iraq, Abu Nawas St., P.O.B. 2307, Baghdad; Iraq Trades Union organ; Chief Editor Mohmmad Ayesh; circ. 25,000.

al Watan al-Arab: Baghdad.

PERIODICALS

al Adib al-Muasser (*Contemporary Writer*): Baghdad; published by Iraqi Union of Writers.

al Aqlam (*The Pen*): Baghdad; literary; monthly; Ministry of Culture and Information; f. 1964.

Commerce: Chamber of Commerce, Baghdad; f. 1938; quarterly; commercial and economic; circ. 2,000; also a weekly bulletin dealing in commodity prices and market conditions; circ. 2,000.

al-Idaa'h Wal-Television: Iraqi Broadcasting, Television and Cinema Establishment, Salihiya, Baghdad; radio and television programmes and articles; fortnightly.

Iraq Academy Journal: Iraq Academy, Waziriyah, Baghdad; f. 1947; scientific and cultural, deals with Arabic and Islamic civilization.

Iraq Government Gazette, The: Ministry of Information, Baghdad; f. 1922; Arabic edition irregular, English edition weekly; legal and official; circ. Arabic 4,000, English 500.

Journal of the Faculty of Medicine, The: College of Medicine, University of Baghdad, Baghdad; f. 1941; quarterly; Arabic and English; medical and technical; published by the Faculty of Medicine, Baghdad; Edited by Prof. Yousif D. al Naaman, m.d., d.sc.

Majallat al-Ziraa al-Iraqiyah (*Magazine of Iraq Agriculture*): Baghdad; quarterly; agricultural; published by the Ministry of Agriculture.

Majallat-al-Majma al-'Ilmi al-Iraqi: Iraqi Academy, Waziriyah, Baghdad; f. 1947; quarterly; scholarly magazine on Arabic Islamic culture.

al-Mu'allem al-Jadid: Ministry of Education, Baghdad; f. 1935; quarterly; educational, social, and general; owned and published by the Ministry of Education; Editor Khalil al-Samarrai.

al-Muthaqaf al-Arabi (*The Arab Educator*): Baghdad; f. 1968; Editor-in-Chief Amer R. al-Samarra'ie; monthly; circ. 3,000.

Sawt al-Talaba (*The Voice of Students*): Baghdad; f. 1968; organ of Nat. Union of Iraqi Students; bi-monthly; circ. 25,000.

al-Sinai (*The Industrialist*): P.O.B. 5665, Baghdad; publ. by Iraqi Federation of Industries; Arabic and English; quarterly.

Sumer: Directorate-General of Antiquities, Jamal Abdul Nasr Street, Baghdad; f. 1945; archaeological, historical journal; publ. by the Directorate-General of Antiquities; Chair. of Ed. Board Dr. FAISAL EL-WAELY (Dir.-Gen. of Antiquities); twice yearly.

al-Thaqafa (*Culture*): Baghdad; f. 1968; Marxist; Editor-in-Chief SALAH KHALIS; monthly; circ. 2,000.

al-Thaqafa al-Jadida (*The New Culture*): Baghdad; pro-Communist; Editor-in-Chief MUKARRAM AL-TALABANI; monthly; circ. 3,000.

Tourism in Iraq: Tourism and Resorts Administration, Ministry of Information, Baghdad; bi-monthly; Editor FAKHRI KHALIL AZIZ.

NEWS AGENCIES

Iraqi News Agency: Abu Nawwas St., P.O.B. 3084, Baghdad; f. 1959; gathers and circulates news and photographs for use at home and abroad; independent in financial and administrative affairs; has contracts and agreements with various international commercial agencies and government newsagencies; Board of Directors includes Dir.-Gen. of Iraqi News Agency (Chair.), reps. from Ministries of Information, Foreign Affairs, Dir. of Military Intelligence, Dir.-Gen. of Broadcasting and TV, of P.T.T., representative of Revolutionary Command Council, Chair. of Al-Jamahir Press House, two I.N.A. Directors and two workers representatives; offices in Beirut, Cairo and Kuwait and correspondents in Algiers, Tunis, Khartoum, Tripoli, Sana'a, Aden, Abu Dhabi, Ankara, Moscow, Cyprus, New York, New Delhi, etc.; Dir.-Gen. TAHA YASEEN AL-BASRI.

FOREIGN BUREAUX

AFP (*France*): P.O.B. 5699, South Gate, Baghdad; Chief NAGIB FRANGIEH.

MENA (*Egypt*): Rasheed Str., al-Morabaa, Zaki Gamil Building, P.O.B. 2, Baghdad.

D.P.A. and Tass also have offices in Baghdad.

PUBLISHERS

al Ahliya: Mutanabi St., Baghdad.

Dar al Basri: Amin Square, Rashid Street, Baghdad.

Dar al Bayan: Mutanabi Street, Baghdad.

al Irshad: Baghdad; Arab literature.

al Jumhuriyah Printing and Publishing Co.: Waziriya, Baghdad; f. 1963; the principal Iraqi publishers of newspapers and books.

al Ma'arif Ltd.: Mutanabi Street, Baghdad; f. 1929; publishes periodicals and books in Arabic, Kurdishi Turkish, French and English.

al-Muthanna: Mutanabi St., Baghdad; also in Basrah; Man. MOHAMED AR-RAJAB.

al Nahdah: Mutanabi St., Baghdad; politics, Arab affairs.

Dar al Nathir: North Gate, Baghdad.

National House for Publishing, Distribution and Advertisement: Baghdad; f. 1972; attached to Ministry of Information; publishes and distributes books in Arabic and other languages.

RADIO AND TELEVISION

RADIO

Broadcasting Station of the Republic of Iraq: Iraqi Broadcasting and Television Establishment, Salihiya, Baghdad; home service broadcasts in Arabic, Kurdish, Syriac and Turkuman; foreign service in French, German, English, Russian, Persian, Swahili, Turkish and Urdu; there are 4 medium wave and 13 short wave transmitters; Dir.-Gen. M. S. AL-SAHAF.

Idaa'h Baghdad: f. 1936; 22 hours daily.

Idaa'h Sawt Al-Jamahir: f. 1970; 21 hours daily.

Number of radio receivers (1973): 2.7 million.

TELEVISION

Baghdad Television: Ministry of Information, Iraqi Broadcasting and Television Establishment, Salihiya, Karkh, Baghdad; f. 1956; government station operating 7 hours daily; Dir.-Gen. MOHAMMED S. AL-SAHAF.

Kirkuk Television: f. 1967; government station; commercial; 6 hours daily.

Mosul Television: f. 1968; government station; commercial; 6 hours daily.

Basrah Television: f. 1968; government station; commercial; 6 hours daily.

Missan, Muthanna and Um Qasir stations are under construction.

Number of TV receivers (1973): 350,000.

FINANCE

All banks and insurance companies, including all foreign companies, were nationalized in July 1964. The assets of foreign companies were taken over by the state.

(cap.=capital; p.u.=paid up; dep.=deposits; res.= reserves; m.=million; amounts in Iraqi dinars.)

BANKING

CENTRAL BANK

Central Bank of Iraq: Banks St., Baghdad; f. 1947 as National Bank of Iraq; brs. in Mosul and Basra; has the sole right of note issue; cap. p.u. 25m., dep. 80.4 (Dec. 1973); Gov. FAWZI AL-QAYSSI; publs. *Quarterly Bulletin, Annual Report.*

COMMERCIAL BANKS

Commercial Bank of Iraq: New Banks' St., P.O.B. 66, Baghdad; f. 1953; nationalized 1964; 44 brs.; cap. p.u. 3.75m., res. 1.9m., dep. 81.3m. (Dec. 1972); absorbed the Baghdad Bank and the Credit Bank of Iraq in 1970; Chair. and Gen. Man. ADNAN AL TAYYAR; publs. *Al-Masrafi* (The Banker, monthly), *Al-Masrafi* (weekly).

Rafidain Bank: Banks St., Baghdad; f. 1941; cap. 6.6m., res. 5.5m., dep. 155m. (1973); 72 brs. in Iraq, 6 overseas brs.; Chair. and Gen. Man. ATTA AL-DHAHI.

SPECIALIZED BANKS

Agricultural Bank of Iraq: Rashid St., Baghdad; 24 branches; cap. p.u. 6.4m.; Gen. Man. ABDUL RAZZAK AL-HILALI.

Estate Bank of Iraq: Hassan ibn Thanit St., Baghdad; f. 1949; 19 branches; gives loans to assist the building industry; cap. p.u. 25m.; acquired the Co-operative Bank in 1970; Dir.-Gen. LABEED AL-KARAGULLY.

Industrial Bank of Iraq: Industrial Bank Building, Baghdad; 5 branches; f. 1940; cap. p.u. 5.75m.; Gen. Man. KAMEL I. AL-AZZAWI; publ. *Annual Report.*

INSURANCE

Iraqi Life Insurance Co.: Shabander Bldg., New Banks' St., Baghdad; f. 1960; cap. p.u. 325,000; Chair. and Gen. Man. BADI AHMED AL-SAIFI.

Iraq Reinsurance Company: Reinsurance Building, Khullani Square, P.O.B. 297, Baghdad; f. 1961; to transact reinsurance business on the international market; Chair. and Gen. Man. Dr. MUSTAFA RAJAB; London Office: 5 Fenchurch St., E.C.3.

National Insurance Co.: Al-Aman Bldg., Al-Khulani St., P.O.B. 248, Baghdad; f. 1950; cap. p.u. 1m.; state monopoly for all direct non-life insurance; Chair. and Gen. Man. ABDULBAKI REDHA.

OIL AND GAS

Iraq National Oil Company (INOC): P.O.B. 476, Saadoun St., Baghdad; f. in 1964 to operate the oil industry at home and abroad; one of the main objectives of the July 1968 Revolution was to establish an oil industry capable of fostering the national economy, through direct development and exploitation of crude petroleum; it was decided that national oil development should start at Rumaila fields, Basra.

Iraq Company for Oil Operations (ICOO): Arrapha, Kirkuk; f. 1972; ICOO undertook responsibility for operation of nationalized Iraq Petroleum Co. in Iraq. The company's sphere of activities include drilling, production, processing and transportation of crude oil by pipelines to terminals at Banias in Syria and Tripoli in the Lebanon.

In March 1973, a comprehensive settlement was reached with the international oil companies embracing full compensation for the nationalized assets and surrender to the Government of Iraq of the Mosul Petroleum Co. concession. MPC fields are now maintained and operated by ICOO, which became responsible for the operation of the five producing fields, three near its centre of operations in Kirkuk (Kirkuk, Bai Hassan and Jambur), and two (Ain Zalah and Butmah) in Nineva Governorate; Chair. ABDUL SATTAR F. AL-RAWI.

Basrah Petroleum Company Ltd.: Office: 33 Cavendish Square, London, W1M 0AA; Chair. and Man. Dir. G. G. STOCKWELL; Exec. Dir. H. C. GOFF.

The company operates in southern Iraq. Oil is produced from the Zubair and Rumaila fields and exported via a deep-water loading terminal at Khor-al-Amaya, 24 miles from Fao. Production in 1973 was approximately 35 million tons.

Entreprise des Recherches et d'Activités Petrolières (ELF-ERAP): signed a contract with INOC in 1968 under which it acts as contractor to INOC (amended 1973). It operates a 10,800 sq. km. onshore/offshore area.

Gas Distribution Administration (G.D.A.): Baghdad; f. 1964 to supervise all gas projects, and to distribute and market natural and liquid gas all over Iraq. The sulphur recovery plant at Kirkuk utilizes gas supplied by the Kirkuk oilfield. Two gas pipelines are being laid from Kirkuk to Baghdad, and a liquid gas processing plant (12,000 b/d) has been erected at Taji, north of Baghdad.

Government Oil Refinery Administration: Baghdad; operates refineries at Baghdad, Khanaqin, Kirkuk, Hadithah and Qayyarah; capital investment I.D. 30m.; annual turnover I.D. 25m. approx.

Iraq Petroleum Company Ltd.: Office: 33 Cavendish Square, London, W1M 0AA; Chair. and Man. Dir. G. G. STOCKWELL; Exec. Dir. H. C. GOFF.

Until June 1972 the company produced and exported oil from northern Iraq. In June 1972 the Iraq Government took over the company's assets and operations in Iraq. A settlement between the company and the Government relating to this take-over was reached in February 1973.

TRADE AND INDUSTRY

CHAMBERS OF COMMERCE

Federation of Iraqi Chambers of Commerce: Mustansir St., Baghdad; f. 1969; all Iraqi Chambers of Commerce are affiliated to the Federation; Pres. SHABAN J. AL-RAJAB; Sec.-Gen. KADHIM A. AL-MHAIDI; publs. *Bulletin, Monthly News, Annual Report* and brochures.

Amarah Chamber of Commerce: Al-Amarah; f. 1950; Pres. HAJ J. AL-AMMAR; Sec. R. AL-SAFFAR.

Arbil Chamber of Commerce: Arbil; f. 1966; Pres. SHEK-HEEL HAJ HASSAN; Sec. MUHAMMAD DAZAH (*ad interim*).

Baghdad Chamber of Commerce: Mustansir St., Baghdad; f. 1926; 14,296 mems.; Pres. ABDUL WAHAB ALKASAB; Sec. MOHAMMAD NAYEF AL-SHIBLI; Dir.-Gen. MUNIER SAID; publs. *Weekly Bulletin, Commerce* (quarterly magazine), *Trade Directory*.

Basra Chamber of Commerce: Basra; f. 1926; Pres. AMER AL-TIKRITI; Sec.-Gen. HARITH AL-MAKZOMY; publ. *al Tajir* (monthly).

Diwaniya Chamber of Commerce: Diwaniya; f. 1961; Pres. ABDULLAH AL-KHAFAJI; Sec. AMIN AL-ASADI.

Diyala Chamber of Commerce: Diyala; f. 1966; Pres. ADNAN AL-SARAH; Sec. ABDUL SATTAR HILMI.

Hillah Chamber of Commerce: Hillah; f. 1949; Pres. SAMI ALI AL-SULTAN; Sec. SHAHID AL-KHRIBAWI.

Karbala Chamber of Commerce: Karbala; f. 1952; Pres. MUDHIR SAAD QUANDI; Sec. RASHEED ABUDAGAH; Man. SAHIB H. HILME.

Kirkuk Chamber of Commerce: Kirkuk; f. 1957; Pres. HASSANI AL-HADITHI; Sec. SAMI BUNI.

Mosul Chamber of Commerce: Nineveh St., P.O.B. 35, Mosul; f. 1926; 4,000 mems.; Pres. ABDUL GHANI AL ANNAZ; Vice-Pres. ABDUL MAJEED AL NAFOUSSI; Sec. ABDUL JAWAD AL NEAIMI.

Najaf Chamber of Commerce: Najaf; f. 1950; Pres. MUHAMMAD ALI AL-BALAGHI; Sec. ABDUL MAHDI SHLAL.

Nasiriya Chamber of Commerce: Nasiriya; f. 1958; Pres. SHAIL ABID AL-YASIN; Sec. SATTR SALMON.

Sulaimaniya Chamber of Commerce: Sulaimaniya; f. 1967; Pres. SHAFIQ AHMED AL-CHALABI; Sec. AMIN MOLOOD.

EMPLOYERS' ORGANIZATION

Iraqi Federation of Industries: Iraqi Federation of Industries Bldg., Al-Khulani Square, Baghdad; f. 1956;

4,450 mems.; Pres. HATAM ABDUL RASHID; publs. *Al Sinai* (quarterly), Directory of Iraqi Industries and monthly reports.

INDUSTRIAL ORGANIZATIONS

General Establishment for Industry: Baghdad; state organization controlling most of Iraq's industry; organized into 5 departments covering (1) Clothing, Hides and Cigarettes, (2) Construction industries, (3) Weaving and Textiles, (4) Chemicals and Food-stuffs, (5) Engineering.

Iraqi Dates Organization: Baghdad; responsible for date exports; Dir. Dr. BAHA SHUBBAR.

National Iraqi Minerals Co.: P.O.B. 2330, Alwiyah, Baghdad; f. 1969; 1,210 mems.; responsible for exploiting all minerals in Iraq except oil; Pres. Dr. SHAKIR AL-SAMARRAI.

TRADE UNIONS

General Federation of Trade Unions of Iraq: Abu Nawas St., Baghdad; f. 1964; 12 General Unions with a membership of 1,750,000 are affiliated to the General Federation and registered with the Ministry of Labour and Social Security Affairs; Pres. MOHAMMED AYESH; Sec.-Gen. BEDAN FADHIL; publ. *Wai al-Ummal*.

Union of Teachers: Baghdad; Pres. IBRAHIM MARZOUK.

Union of Palestinian Workers in Iraq: Baghdad; Sec.-Gen. SAMI AL SHAWISH.

CO-OPERATIVES

By the end of 1972 there were 1,167 co-operative societies. There were over 120 joint agricultural co-operatives and 60 local co-operatives outside the agrarian reform areas. The total number of peasants affiliated to the co-operatives is 175,000.

PEASANT SOCIETIES

General Federation of Peasant Societies: Baghdad; f. 1959; has 734 affiliated Peasant Societies.

TRADE FAIR

Baghdad International Fair: Damascus St., Al Mansoor, Baghdad; administered by Iraqi Fairs Administration; held annually in October; f. 1964; 232 foreign companies from 23 countries took part in the 1973 Fair.

TRANSPORT

RAILWAYS

Iraqi Republic Railways: Baghdad Central Station Building, Baghdad; total length of track (1971): 2,528 km., consisting of 1,234 km. of standard gauge, 1,294 km. of one-metre gauge; Dir.-Gen. ABDUL JABBAR SA'ADI; Chief of Traffic HAMID ABDUL MAJEED AL-ANI.

A metre-gauge line runs from Basra through Baghdad, Khanaqin and Kirkuk to Erbil. The standard gauge line covers the length of the country from Rabiyah on the Syrian border via Mosul, Baghdad and Basrah to Um-Qasr. From here it is proposed to extend the track through Kuwait to Dhahran in Saudi Arabia,

thus connecting Europe with the Persian Gulf. The standard gauge line between Baghdad and Basra is eventually intended to replace the metre gauge line between the two cities. Most trains are now hauled by diesel-electric locomotives. As well as the internal services there is also a regular express between Baghdad and Istanbul.

ROADS

The most important roads are: Baghdad–Mosul–Tel Kotchuk (Syrian border), 521 km.; Baghdad–Kirkuk–Arbil–Zakho (border with Turkey), 544 km.; Kirkuk–Sulaimaniya, 109 km.; Baghdad–Amara–Basra–Safwan

(Kuwaiti border), 595 km.; Baghdad–Rutba–Syrian border (to Damascus), 555 km.; Baghdad–Babylon–Diwaniya, 181 km.

Under the 1970–75 Development Plan $91 million have been allocated to rebuilding and extending the present road system. The World Bank has made a $19 million loan towards the project. In 1972 a total of 9,240 km. of paved road had been completed and a further 1,368 km. were under construction.

Iraq Automobile and Touring Association: Al Mansoor, Baghdad; f. 1931; 3,500 mems.; Chair. Dr. ALI GHALIB AL-ANI; Sec.-Gen. HASHIM ABDULLA TAHA.

INLAND WATERWAYS

Directorate-General of Navigation: Basra; Dir.-Gen. (vacant); in 1972 there were 1,041 registered river craft, 65 motor vessels and 106 motor boats.

SHIPPING

Iraqi Ports Administration: Basra; Dir.-Gen. ABDUL JABBAR SAADI.

The Ports of Basra and Um Qasr are the commercial gateway of Iraq. They are connected by various ocean routes with all parts of the world, and constitute the natural distributing centre for overseas supplies. The Iraqi Maritime Company maintains a regular service between Basra, the Gulf and north European ports. Other shipping lines operate cargo and passenger services from Basra and Um Qasr to all parts of the world. There are fast mail and passenger services from Basra to Bombay via Khorramshahr, Bushire, and Karachi, connecting at Bombay with the Peninsula and Orient Mail Services to England, Australia, South Africa, and the Far East.

At Basra there is accommodation for 12 vessels at the Maqal Wharves and accommodation for 7 vessels at the buoys. There are 1 silo berth and 2 berths for oil products at Muftia and 1 berth for fertilizer products at Abu Flus. There is room for 3 vessels at Um Qasr.

In 1972–73 the revenue of the Iraq Ports Administration was I.D. 14,973,697 against a general expenditure of I.D. 10,620,226 (including capital works). Expenditure on planning schemes was I.D. 2,528,475. In 1972–73 the port of Basra was visited by 515 cargo ships; the total tonnage exported was 594,350 and imported tonnage totalled 761,378. Um Qasr port handled 59 cargo vessels, imports were 225,010 tons and exports 8,150.

There are deep-water tanker terminals at Fao and Khor Al-Amaya for 4 and 3 vessels respectively. In 1972–73 35,230,027 long tons of crude oil were exported in 680 tankers.

Iraqi Maritime Transport Co.: P.O.B. 3052, Baghdad; f. 1952; 6 cargo vessels; total g.r.t. 47,105.64 (1973); Dir.-Gen. (acting) EDGAR SARKIES.

CIVIL AVIATION

A new international airport, ten miles from Baghdad, was opened in January 1970. Another airport at Bamerni, in the province of Dhok was opened in August 1972. There is also an international airport at Basra. Internal flights connect Baghdad to Basra and Mosul.

Iraqi Airways: Al Kharkh, Baghdad; f. 1945; Dir.-Gen. ABDUL MUHSEN ABUE AL KHAIL; regular services from Baghdad to Amman, Bahrain, Basra, Beirut, Berlin, Cairo, Damascus, Dhahran, Doha, Frankfurt, Geneva, Istanbul, Kuwait, London, Mosul, Paris, Prague, Teheran, Vienna, Copenhagen, Karachi, New Delhi, Dubai, Moscow, Warsaw; fleet: 3 Tridents, 3 Viscounts.

In 1974 the following airlines also operated services to Iraq: Aeroflot, Air France, Ariana Afghan, Balkan, British Airways, ČSA, Egyptair, Interflug, KLM, Kuwait Airways, LOT, Lufthansa, MEA, PIA, Saudia, Swissair, Syrian Arab.

TOURISM AND CULTURE

Ministry of Information, Tourism and Resorts Administration: Khulani Sq., Baghdad; f. 1956; Dir.-Gen. Dr. ALI GHALIB AL-ANI; publs. *Tourism in Iraq* (bi-monthly), guide books, posters, tourist maps and pamphlets.

THEATRE GROUPS
OFFICIALLY SPONSORED

National Ensemble for Folk Arts: Baghdad; folklore group providing dancing and singing concerts.

National Group for Acting: General Establishment for Broadcasting, Television and Cinema, Baghdad.

PRIVATE

Baghdad Theatre Group: Baghdad; f. 1967.
Contemporary Theatre Group: Baghdad; f. 1966.
Folklore Group: Baghdad; f. 1965.
Free Theatre Group: Baghdad; f. 1965.
14 July Theatre Group: Baghdad; f. 1966.
Theatre Arts Group: Baghdad; f. 1967.
United Artists' Group: Baghdad; f. 1967.

ATOMIC ENERGY

Atomic Energy Commission: Baghdad; f. 1957; an atomic reactor, built with Soviet aid at Tuwaitha, south of Baghdad, was inaugurated in 1968. The reactor will provide isotopes for teaching and civilian research.

UNIVERSITIES

University of Baghdad: Baghdad; 1,509 teachers, 19,274 students.

Basra University: Basra; 126 teachers, 3,213 students.

al Hikma University of Baghdad: P.O.B. 2125, Baghdad; 65 teachers, 610 students.

al Mustansiriya University: Baghdad; 450 teachers, 9,716 students.

Mosul University: Mosul; 149 teachers, 3,275 students.

University of Sulaimaniya: Sulaimaniya; 74 teachers, 1,130 students.

ISRAEL

INTRODUCTORY SURVEY

Location, Climate, Language, Religion, Flag, Capital

Israel lies at the eastern end of the Mediterranean Sea. All Israel's frontiers are with Arab countries, the longest frontiers being with Egypt and Jordan. To the north Israel shares short frontiers with Syria and the Lebanon. The climate is Mediterranean, with hot dry summers when the temperature approaches 100°F (38°C) and mild rainy winters. The language is Hebrew. Arabic is spoken by the quarter of a million Arab minority (as well as the population of the "occupied areas") and many European languages are spoken. Judaism is the religion followed by the great majority of the population. The national flag (proportions 250 by 173) consists of a white background, with a blue six-pointed star composed of two equilateral triangles (the "Shield of David") between two blue horizontal stripes near the upper and lower edges. The capital is Jerusalem.

Recent History

Before 1948 Palestine (of which present-day Israel now forms a part) was a Mandated Territory under British colonial administration. Zionists had long sought to establish a National Home in Palestine; the flow of Jewish immigration, and Arab concern over the displacement of the Palestinians and the impending creation of an alien state, finally led to war between Jews and Arabs in 1947. The State of Israel was created following the termination of the Mandate in May 1948. Fighting continued until January 1949. No peace treaty has been signed and no Arab state has diplomatic relations with Israel. A UN Truce Supervisory Organization continues to operate. A six-day war against the neighbouring Arab countries in June 1967 left the country in possession of all Jerusalem, the west bank of the Jordan, the Sinai peninsula, the Gaza Strip and the Golan Heights. East Jerusalem was almost immediately integrated into the state of Israel; the other regions still retain the status of "occupied areas". There is considerable freedom of movement between the occupied areas and restricted access to and from the state of Jordan. On the death of Mr. Levi Eshkol in February 1969 Mrs. Golda Meir was elected Prime Minister by the Labour Party executive, and continued in office following the general election of October 1969. In August 1970, a cease-fire agreement was reached, but hostilities have continued against both neighbouring Arab states and Palestinian guerrilla organizations. The Lod airport massacre, the death in August 1972 of Israeli sportsmen at the Munich Olympic Games, followed by air raids by the Israeli air force into Lebanon and Syria and the Libyan airliner disaster in 1973, placed fresh barriers in the way of peace negotiations. Another war between the Arab States Israel broke out on October 6th, 1973 (Yom Kippur, the Jewish "Day of Atonement"), and ended with a cease-fire agreement signed in November. A peace conference held in Geneva the following month, with the participation of Egypt, Jordan and Israel, and U.S. mediatory efforts, ultimately led to the withdrawal of Israel's forces from the areas it held west of the Suez Canal as well as from the whole of the east bank during January and February 1974. Sporadic fighting continued with Syria until an agreement

for disengagement on the Golan Heights was signed in May 1974. General elections took place in December 1973 and, despite the weakened majority of the Labour Alignment and internal dissensions, a new coalition Government was formed in March 1974, headed by Mrs. Golda Meir. In April, however, she announced her intention to resign and Gen. Yitzhak Rabin became Prime Minister of a new coalition cabinet in June 1974.

Immigration reached 55,888 in 1972 and 54,800 in 1973, compared with an annual average of 19,751 in 1967-70. This increase was due in part to the change of attitude of the Soviet Union's authorities in allowing Jewish emigration. It has accentuated the problems of housing, educating and employing so many people of different cultures, and programmes, particularly in education, have been devised by the Government to deal with this. The future of the inhabitants of the "occupied areas" is another important issue facing Israel. Some 60,000 Arabs of these areas form part of Israel's labour force, and an estimated 2,300 Jews have now settled there. Israel will have to decide in the future whether to annexe these areas totally or whether to encourage Arab settlement and independence there, whilst maintaining military control of the outer borders with its Arab neighbours.

Government

Supreme authority in Israel rests with the *Knesset* (Assembly), which is elected by universal suffrage under proportional representation for four years. The President, who is Head of State, is elected by the *Knesset* for a period of five years. The Cabinet, which is headed by the Prime Minister, is responsible to the *Knesset*. Ministers are usually members of the *Knesset*, but non-members may be appointed. The country is divided into six administrative districts. Local authorities are elected once every four years at the same time as the *Knesset*. There are 29 municipalities (2 Arab), 118 local councils (47 Arab and Druze) and 48 regional councils (one Arab) comprising representatives of 695 villages.

Defence

The Israel Defence Forces consist of a small nucleus of commissioned and non-commissioned regular officers, a contingent called up for national service, and a large reserve. Unmarried women between the ages of eighteen and twenty-six are called up for twenty months of military service, and men between eighteen and twenty-nine are called up for thirty-six months of military service. Total armed forces number 115,000 and full mobilization of 300,000 men can be achieved within 72 hours. The armed forces are divided into an army of 94,500, a navy of 4,500 and an air force of 16,000. The defence budget 1973-74 amounted to I£6,180 million, approximately 30 per cent of total budget expenditure. Following the October war a supplementary budget increased the amount by I£1,250 million.

Economic Affairs

Thirteen per cent of the labour force is employed in agriculture, and 25 per cent in mining and industry.

Continuous immigration and an Arab economic boycott have obliged Israel to develop both agriculture and industry on an intensive scale and to seek far afield for international trade. Particular features of agriculture are the *Kibbutzim* (collective settlements), the irrigation schemes and the reclamation of the Negev desert in the south. Citrus fruit is the main export crop. A wide variety of industrial goods is produced. Israel is second only to Belgium in processing diamonds. Some 15 per cent of industry is controlled by the *Histadrut* (Israel Federation of Labour) which, in addition to its trade union activity, fosters economic development. Israel receives aid from Jews in North America and Europe. In 1970 Israel entered into a five-year trade agreement with the European Common Market, which provides for mutual tariff reductions.

Since the June war of 1967 Israel has undertaken exploration and exploitation of the mineral reserves of the occupied Sinai peninsula, in particular of crude oil. There is one oil refinery at Haifa and another under construction at Ashdod. A 32 km. oil pipeline was opened in 1972 connecting Ashdod with the port of Ashkelon.

Transport and Communications

The Israel Railway Administration runs 789 km. of main line. Ultimately Eilat, the port on the Gulf of Aqaba, will be served by rail. 3,918 km. of roads are metalled and about 296,000 motor vehicles are in service. Communications with the Arab countries are severely limited. Israel has a merchant fleet of 107 vessels with a capacity of 1,619,000 tons. El Al Israel Airline operates international services and Arkia Israel Inland Airlines provide domestic route coverage. Since 1968 El Al has suffered from numerous sabotage or hijacking attempts made by members of Palestinian guerrilla organizations.

Social Welfare

There is a highly advanced system of social welfare. Old age pensions, industrial injury and maternity benefits, and allowances for large families, are provided under the National Insurance Law. The *Histadrut*, to which almost 90 per cent of all Jewish workers belong, provides sickness benefit and medical care. The Ministry of Social Welfare provides for general assistance, relief grants, child care and other social services.

Education

Israel has European standards of literacy and educational services. Free compulsory primary education is provided for all children between the ages of five and fifteen. There is secondary, vocational and agricultural education. There are five universities, one institute of technology and one graduate school of science.

Tourism

Israel's tourist attractions include biblical sites, and collective farms. The Government maintains 20 tourist offices abroad. 661,000 tourists visited Israel in 1973.

Citizens of Austria, Barbados, Belgium, Central African Republic, Colombia, Costa Rica, Denmark, Dominican Republic, Ecuador, Finland, France, Greece, Hong Kong, Iceland, Jamaica, Lesotho, Liechtenstein, Luxembourg, Maldive Islands, Mauritius, Netherlands, Netherlands Antilles, Norway, Paraguay, Philippines, Surinam, Swaziland, Sweden, Switzerland, Trinidad and Tobago, the United Kingdom and Uruguay do not require *visas* for stays of up to three months. *Visas* can be had free on entry by citizens of Argentina, Australia, Brazil, Canada, Chile, New Zealand, South Africa and U.S.A. All other visitors to Israel are required to obtain *visas* before their departure.

Sport

All sport in Israel is amateur. Football, basketball, swimming, athletics, hockey, tennis, rowing, handball, volleyball, gymnastics, boxing, wrestling and fencing all have their followers.

Public Holidays

The Sabbath starts at sunset on Friday and ends at nightfall on Saturday. The Jewish year 5735 begins on September 17th, 1974.

1974: September 17th (New Year), September 26th (Yom Kippur—Day of Atonement), October 1st–7th (Tabernacles*), October 8th (Simhat Torah).

1975: February 28th (Purim), March 27th–April 3rd (Passover*), April 16th (Independence Day), May 16th (Pentecost), July 17th (Tisha B'ab).

*Half-day holidays only.

Muslim holidays are observed by Muslim Arabs and Christian holidays by the Christian Arab Community.

Weights and Measures

The metric system is in force.
1 dunam = 1,000 sq. metres.

Currency and Exchange Rates

100 agorot = 1 Israeli pound (I£).

Exchange rates (April 1974):
£1 sterling = I£9.89;
U.S. $1 = I£4.20.

STATISTICAL SURVEY

AREA AND POPULATION

Area	Population (May 31st, 1973)	Birth Rate (per '000) 1972	Marriage Rate (per '000) 1972	Death Rate (per '000) 1972
20,700 sq. km.*	3,175,000	27.2	9.4	7.2

* 8,000 square miles.

ADMINISTERED TERRITORIES
(1972)

	Area (sq. km.)	Population
Golan . . .	1,150	n.a.
Judea and Samaria .	5,879	639,300
Gaza	378	} 390,700
Sinai	61,181	
Total . .	68,588	1,030,000

POPULATION OF CHIEF TOWNS
(May 1972–Estimates)

Jerusalem (capital)	.	304,500	Holon	98,000
Tel-Aviv—Jaffa	.	362,200	Petach-Tikva . .	92,400
Haifa .	.	217,400	Beersheba . . .	84,100
Ramat Gan	.	120,100	Bene Beraq . .	74,100

GROWTH OF POPULATION AND JEWISH IMMIGRATION, 1959–72

End of Year	Permanent Population	Jews	Others	Immigration
1959 . . .	2,088,685	1,858,841	229,344	23,895
1960 . . .	2,150,400	1,911,200	239,200	24,510
1961 . . .	2,234,200	1,981,700	252,500	47,638
1962 . . .	2,331,800	2,068,900	262,900	61,328
1963 . . .	2,430,100	2,155,500	274,600	64,364
1964 . . .	2,525,600	2,239,000	286,400	54,716
1965 . . .	2,598,400	2,299,100	299,300	30,736
1966 . . .	2,657,400	2,344,900	312,500	15,730
1967* . . .	2,773,900	2,383,600	390,300	14,327
1968* . . .	2,841,100	2,434,800	406,300	20,544
1969* . . .	2,919,200	2,496,600	422,700	23,510
1970* . . .	3,001,400	2,561,400	440,000	20,624
1971* . . .	3,095,100	2,636,600	458,500	41,930
1972* . . .	3,200,500	2,723,600	476,900	55,888

* These figures exclude the population of the areas occupied by Israel since June 1967 and now known in Israel as the "Administered Territories" (see above), but include the population of the Old City of Jerusalem and the surrounding areas, which Israel annexed in 1967 and regards as Israeli territory (the UN Security Council and General Assembly have declared this annexation invalid).

EMPLOYMENT
('000)

	1969	1970	1971	1972
Agriculture, Forestry and Fishing .	91.3	84.8	84.5	83.4
Mining, Quarrying and Manufacturing .	226.1	233.3	239.6	248.3
Electricity, Gas and Water .	10.6	11.3	11.0	8.8
Construction .	75.9	80.1	88.3	99.3
Trade, Restaurants and Hotels .	125.0	125.0	126.4	137.0
Transport, Storage and Communications	74.7	72.2	74.0	76.9
Financing, Insurance and Business Services	48.5	49.7	56.7	60.2
Community, Social and Personal Services .	290.3	303.8	314.1	328.7
Others .	3.4	3.0	2.5	4.4
TOTAL .	945.8	963.2	997.1	1,047.0

AGRICULTURE
AGRICULTURAL LAND USAGE
('ooo dunums or 'oo hectares)

	1969–70	1970–71	1971–72	1972–73
Field Crops .	2,655	2,695	2,650	2,670
Fruit incl. citrus .	855	835	845	860
Vegetables, potatoes, etc.	346	370	396	415
Nurseries, flowers, fish ponds, etc. .	264	240	239	240
TOTAL Cultivated Area	4,120	4,140	4,130	4,185

PRODUCTION
(metric tons)

	1968–69	1969–70	1970–71	1971–72
Wheat .	155,800	125,000	199,500	301,400
Barley .	20,500	13,600	17,600	32,800
Sorghum .	16,400	10,900	20,600	40,400
Hay .	139,900	137,300	141,200	132,500
Groundnuts .	12,400	18,700	21,200	19,800
Cotton Lint .	39,200	35,300	36,700	40,300
Cottonseed .	61,000	58,600	69,000	65,000
Sugar Beet .	214,600	237,000	258,600	248,500
Melons and Pumpkins .	119,900	131,500	132,900	161,700
Vegetables .	443,000	472,300	490,400	502,600
Potatoes .	114,600	137,100	142,000	143,100
Citrus Fruit .	1,178,100	1,261,900	1,513,500	1,552,800
Other Fruit .	304,800	288,800	307,700	359,800
Milk (kl.) (incl. sheep and goat milk) .	456,000	487,700	497,500	519,200

PRODUCTION OF CITRUS FRUIT
(metric tons)

	1969–70	1970–71	1971–72
Grapefruit . . .	284,300	361,300	334,300
Lemons	39,800	46,400	39,900
Oranges: Shamouti . .	677,900	746,500	842,200
Lates . .	207,600	298,100	273,500
Other varieties . . .	52,300	61,200	62,900
TOTAL . . .	1,261,900	1,513,500	1,552,800

LIVESTOCK
(thousands)

	1970	1971	1972
Cattle	251	253	275
Poultry	8,800	9,600	10,150
Sheep	189	184	188
Goats	136	134	135
Work Animals . .	24	23	n.a.

FISHERIES
(tons)

1968–69	1969–70	1970–71	1971–72
21,900	21,800	26,100	27,100

INDUSTRIAL OUTPUT

(I£ million at market prices)
(Establishments employing 5 or more people)

	1968	1969	1970	1971
Non-Metallic Mineral Products . .	362	395	503	638
Foodstuffs, Beverages and Tobacco . .	1,724	1,966	2,257	2,766
Textiles and Clothing . . .	1,116	1,255	1,515	1,854
Metals and Machinery . . .	1,263	1,583	1,863	2,322
Chemicals and Petroleum Products .	537	590	714	901
Diamond Industry . . .	614	563	518	634
Wood and Wood Products . .	315	329	379	484
Transport Equipment . . .	353	441	657	816
Electrical and Electrical Equipment .	399	625	776	960
Rubber and Plastics . . .	356	408	479	605
Printing and Publishing . .	215	246	275	336
Leather and Leather Products . .	90	104	109	123
Mining and Quarrying . . .	181	222	264	323
Paper and Cardboard . . .	201	209	265	351
Miscellaneous . . .	92	106	117	153

FINANCE

100 agorot (singular, agora)=1 Israeli pound (I£).

Coins: 1, 5, 10, 25 and 50 agorot; 1 pound.

Notes: 1, 5, 10, 50 and 100 pounds.

Exchange rates (April 1974): £1 sterling=I£9.89; U.S. $1=I£4.20.

I£100=£10.11 sterling=$23.81.

CENTRAL GOVERNMENT BUDGET

(I£ million, twelve months ending March 31st)

REVENUE		1971–72	1972–73	1973–74*
Ordinary Budget:				
Income Tax and Property Tax	. .	3,075.5	3,851.0	4,493.0
Customs and Excise	. . .	2,645.5	3,455.5	4,067.0
Purchase Tax	. . .	969.8	1,325.0	1,786.0
Other Taxes .	. . .	432.0	596.0	774.0
Interest	. . .	434.9	492.0	553.4
Loans .	. . .	1,129.9	1,145.0	1,399.0
Other Receipts	. . .	614.0	674.6	679.6
TOTAL	. . .	9,301.6	11,539.1	13,752.0
Development Budget:				
Foreign Loans	. . .	2,488.8	2,406.0	3,276.0
Internal Loans	. . .	1,619.8	2,410.0	2,259.5
Other Receipts	. . .	1,071.2	1,460.4	512.5
TOTAL	. . .	5,179.8	6,276.4	6,048.0
TOTAL REVENUE	. . .	14,481.4	17,815.5	19,800.0

EXPENDITURE		1971–72	1972–73	1973–74*
Ordinary Budget:				
Ministry of Finance	. . .	114.9	132.4	166.0
Ministry of Defence	. . .	5,546.6	5,458.0	6,065.4
Ministry of Health	. .	295.6	n.a.	n.a.
Ministry of Foreign Affairs	. .	105.2	115.1	142.0
Ministry of Education and Culture	. .	816.9	995.8	1,433.3
Ministry of Police .	. . .	183.2	205.8	264.0
Ministry of Social Welfare	. .	100.4	107.0	163.5
Other Ministries .	. . .	458.6	572.8	751.9
Interest	. . .	1,151.7	1,740.0	2,000.1
Transfers to Local Authorities	. .	428.1	520.3	671.9
Subsidies .	. . .	1,249.4	1,347.0	1,550.0
Other Expenditures	. . .	453.6	1,798.3	1,921.9
TOTAL .	. . .	10,904.2	12,892.5	15,130.0
Development Budget:				
Industry and Crafts	. . .	209.5	277.8	285.0
Transport .	. . .	174.4	199.3	254.4
Communications .	. . .	240.2	304.8	330.0
Housing .	. . .	1,142.6	969.1	934.8
Public Buildings .	. . .	189.9	241.1	373.6
Debt Repayment .	. . .	1,138.2	2,125.0	2,028.2
Other Expenditures	. . .	339.8	805.9	464.0
TOTAL .	. . .	3,434.6	4,923.0	4,670.0
TOTAL EXPENDITURE	. .	14,338.8	17,815.5	19,800.0

* Forecasts.

GENERAL CONSUMER PRICE INDEX
(1969=100)

1969	1970	1971	1972
100.0	106.1	118.8	134.1

MONEY SUPPLY
(million I£ at year end)

	1969	1970	1971	1972
Currency held by the public	1,128.9	1,281	1,584	1,974
Demand deposit at banks	1,841.2	2,102	2,757	3,613
TOTAL MONEY SUPPLY . . .	2,970.1	3,383	4,341	5,587

EXTERNAL TRADE
('000 U.S.$)

	IMPORTS	EXPORTS	BALANCE
1965 . . .	814,523	406,095	408,428
1966 . . .	817,091	476,926	340,165
1967 * . .	756,935	517,245	239,690
1968 * . .	1,093,192	602,105	491,087
1969 * . .	1,304,376	688,697	615,679
1970 * . .	1,433,497	733,622	699,875
1971 * . .	1,811,605	915,061	896,544
1972 * . .	1,957,538	1,101,892	855,646

* Excluding trade with the administered territories.

COMMODITIES
('000 U.S. $)

IMPORTS	1970	1971	1972
Diamonds, rough . . .	174,785	240,264	336,589
Boilers, machinery and parts .	172,355	197,818	242,198
Electrical machinery . .	88,568	96,342	127,959
Iron and steel . . .	140,705	144,672	151,162
Vehicles . . .	87,569	96,972	133,445
Chemicals . . .	101,040	117,520	134,627
Crude oil . . .	64,568	84,589	97,308
Cereals . . .	81,846	83 908	77,077
Textiles and textile articles .	64,609	74,201	72,980
Ships, boats, etc. . .	58,437	189,850	64,516

EXPORTS	1970	1971	1972
Diamonds, worked . . .	244,586	303,379	426,867
Edible fruits . . .	94,941	124,474	123,372
Textiles and textile articles .	102,278	119,154	121,364
Fruit and vegetable products .	39,447	50,120	62,202
Resins and plastics . .	9,312	9,858	12,163
Fertilizers . . .	25,552	29,801	29,699
Rubber, including synthetic .	16,820	18,772	20,847
Organic chemicals . . .	13,926	12,524	15,379
Mineral products . . .	5,356	3,906	3,402
Plywood . . .	6,673	6,412	6,287

COUNTRIES

('ooo U.S. $)

	1970		1971		1972	
	IMPORTS	EXPORTS	IMPORTS	EXPORTS	IMPORTS	EXPORTS
Australia and New Zealand . .	4,259	5,492	4,018	7,158	7,203	7,839
Austria	14,040	5,270	12,716	7,654	13,124	8,662
Belgium-Luxembourg . . .	62,835	38,420	75,265	43,886	122,351	46,151
Canada	14,455	15,068	21,355	15,885	27,313	18,682
Denmark	9,014	4,389	9,774	4,157	8,822	6,903
Finland	15,061	6,705	17,843	7,643	20,920	8,491
France	61,352	39,663	85,972	42,453	95,155	54,716
Germany, Federal Republic . .	174,928	66,861	237,888	90,585	228,232	103,455
Hong Kong	1,739	37,197	1,881	45,268	2,592	60,982
Iran	2,695	22,291	2,608	32,913	2,258	44,617
Italy	76,204	14,809	85,161	22,734	166,291	28,860
Japan	61,934	32,299	57,949	48,351	47,286	71,608
Netherlands	71,836	45,519	79,598	57,875	82,827	65,064
Romania	26,491	11,023	26,476	10,745	25,304	10,707
South Africa	10,221	10,689	7,973	9,398	11,591	8,819
Sweden	28,515	11,623	28,613	13,113	37,200	13,784
Switzerland	49,033	33,060	62,087	42,770	70,299	62,083
Turkey	3,727	2,624	5,619	2,482	13,683	2,813
United Kingdom	227,741	81,389	277,157	97,515	365,362	112,892
U.S.A.	324,298	149,114	426,568	185,548	373,235	223,892
Yugoslavia	15,784	9,426	11,211	8,261	18,905	7,560

TRANSPORT

RAILWAYS

	1970	1971	1972
Passengers ('ooo) . .	4,117	4,232	4,424
Freight ('ooo metric tons) .	3,419	3,200	3,136

SHIPPING

('ooo tons)

	1970	1971	1972
Cargo Loaded . .	3,336	3,376	3,464
Cargo Unloaded .	4,261	4,635	4,926

TOURISM

TOURIST ARRIVALS

1969 . . .	409,000
1970 . . .	441,294
1971 . . .	656,756
1972 . . .	727,532
1973 . . .	661,000

ROADS 1972

MOTOR VEHICLES ('ooo)

Private Cars	197.4
Trucks, Trailers . . .	79.7
Buses	4.94
Taxis	3.73
Motorcycles, Motorscooters . .	39.3
Other Vehicles	2.80
TOTAL . . .	327.9

CIVIL AVIATION (El Al revenue flights only)

('ooo)

	1970	1971	1972
Kilometres flown .	29,471	31,825	30,362
Passenger-km. .	2,531,248	3,213,940	3,488,457
Cargo ton-km. .	332,000	404,000	419,000
Mail (tons) .	745	745	746

COMMUNICATIONS MEDIA

(1971–72)

Radios licensed . . .	n.a.
Televisions licensed . . .	n.a.
Telephones	586,500
Daily Newspapers . . .	26

EDUCATION
(1971–72)

	SCHOOLS	PUPILS		SCHOOLS	PUPILS
JEWISH:			ARAB:		
Kindergarten . . .	3,560	115,679	Kindergarten . . .	232	14,271
Primary Schools . . .	1,197	366,591	Primary Schools . . .	281	95,130
Secondary Schools . .	200	54,333	Secondary Schools . .	46	7,912
Vocational Schools . .	288	60,039	Vocational	18	1,120
Agricultural Schools . .	29	7,189	Agricultural Schools . .	2	461
Teachers' Training . .	25	5,381	Teachers' Training . .	2	390
Others (Evening, Handicapped)	282	17,996	Others (Evening, Handicapped)	11	296

Source: Central Bureau of Statistics, Jerusalem.

THE CONSTITUTION

There is no written Constitution. In June 1950, the Knesset voted to adopt a State Constitution by evolution over an unspecified period. A number of laws, including the Law of Return (1950), the Nationality Law (1952), the State President (Tenure) Law (1952), the Education Law (1953) and the "Yad-va-Shem" Memorial Law (1953) are considered as incorporated into the State Constitution. Other constitutional laws are: The Law and Administration Ordinance (1948), the Knesset Election Law (1951), the Law of Equal Rights for Women (1951), the Judges Act (1953), the National Service and National Insurance Acts (1953), and the Basic Law (The Knesset) (1958).

The President

The President is elected by the Knesset for five years.

Ten or more Knesset Members may propose a candidate for the Presidency.

Voting will be by secret ballot.

The President may not leave the country without the consent of the Government.

The President may resign by submitting his resignation in writing to the Speaker.

The President may be relieved of his duties by the Knesset for misdemeanour.

The Knesset is entitled to decide by a two-thirds majority that the President is incapacitated owing to ill-health to fulfil his duties permanently.

The Speaker of the Knesset will act for the President when the President leaves the country, or when he cannot perform his duties owing to ill-health.

The Knesset

The Knesset is the parliament of the State. There are 120 members.

It is elected by general, national, direct, equal, secret and proportional elections.

Every Israel national of 18 years or over shall have the right to vote in elections to the Knesset unless a court has deprived him of that right by virtue of any law.

Every Israel national of 21 and over shall have the right to be elected to the Knesset unless a court has deprived him of that right by virtue of any law.

The following shall not be candidates: the President of the State; the two Chief Rabbis; a judge (*shofet*) in office; a judge (*dayan*) of a religious court; the State Comptroller; the Chief of the General Staff of the Defence Army of Israel; rabbis and ministers of other religions in office; senior State employees and senior Army officers of such ranks and in such functions as shall be determined by law.

The term of office of the Knesset shall be four years.

The elections of the Knesset shall take place on the third Tuesday of the month of Cheshven in the year in which the tenure of the outgoing Knesset ends.

Election day shall be a day of rest, but transport and other public services shall function normally.

Results of the elections shall be published within fourteen days.

The Knesset shall elect from among its members a Chairman and Vice-Chairman.

The Knesset shall elect from among its members permanent committees, and may elect committees for specific matters.

The Knesset may appoint commissions of inquiry to investigate matters designated by the Knesset.

The Knesset shall hold two sessions a year; one of them shall open within four weeks after the Feast of the Tabernacles, the other within four weeks after Independence Day; the aggregate duration of the two sessions shall not be less than eight months.

The outgoing Knesset shall continue to hold office until the convening of the incoming Knesset.

The members of the Knesset shall receive a remuneration as provided by law.

The Government

The Government shall tender its resignation to the President immediately after his election, but shall continue with its duties until the formation of a new Government.

After consultation with representatives of the parties in the Knesset, the President shall charge one of the Members with the formation of a Government.

The Government shall be composed of a Prime Minister and a number of Ministers from among the Knesset Members or from outside the Knesset.

After it has been chosen, the Government shall appear before the Knesset and shall be considered as formed after having received a vote of confidence.

Within seven days of receiving a vote of confidence, the Prime Minister and the other Ministers shall swear allegiance to the State of Israel and its Laws and undertake to carry out the decisions of the Knesset.

THE GOVERNMENT

HEAD OF THE STATE

President of the State of Israel: Lt.-Col. Ephraim Katzir.

THE CABINET

(June 1974)

Prime Minister and Minister of Communications: Maj.-Gen. Yitzhak Rabin (Labour).

Deputy Prime Minister and Minister of Foreign Affairs: Brig.-Gen. Yigal Allon (Labour).

Minister of Defence: Shimon Peres (Labour).

Minister of Finance: Yehoshua Rabinowitz (Labour).

Minister of Labour: Moshe Baram (Labour).

Minister of Education and Culture: Aharon Yadlin (Labour).

Minister of Police and Interior: Shlomo Hillel (Labour).

Minister of Tourism: Moshe Kol (Independent Liberal).

Minister of Justice and Religious Affairs: Haim Zadok (Labour).

Minister of Health and Social Welfare: Victor Shemtov (Mapam).

Minister of Immigration and Absorption: Shlomo Rosen (Mapam).

Minister of Commerce and Industry: Haim Bar-Lev (Labour).

Minister of Housing: Avraham Ofer (Labour).

Minister of Transport: Gad Yaakobi (Labour).

Minister of Agriculture: Aharon Uzan (Labour).

Minister of Information: Aharon Yariv (Labour).

Ministers without Portfolio: Israel Galili (Labour), Gideon Hausner (Independent Liberal), Shulamit Aloni (Civil Rights List).

DIPLOMATIC REPRESENTATION

EMBASSIES AND LEGATIONS ACCREDITED TO ISRAEL

(E) Embassy; (L) Legation.

Argentina: 35 Shaul Hamelekh St., Tel-Aviv (E); *Ambassador:* Jorge E. Casal.

Australia: 145 Hayarkon St., Tel-Aviv (E); *Ambassador:* Rawdon Dalrymple.

Austria: 11 Hermann Cohen St., Tel-Aviv (E); *Ambassador:* Dr. Johanna Nestor.

Barbados: London, United Kingdom (E).

Belgium: 76 Ibn Gvirol St., Tel-Aviv (E); *Ambassador:* Frans Willems.

Bolivia: 1 Avizohar St., Jerusalem (E); *Ambassador:* Roberto Pacheco Hertzog.

Brazil: 53 Sderoth Hen, Tel-Aviv (E); *Ambassador:* P. J. M. da Silva Paranhos do Rio Branco.

Burma: 12 Mateh Aharon St., Ramat Gan (E); *Ambassador:* Ba Ni.

Canada: 84 Ha'hashmonaim St., Tel-Aviv (E); *Ambassador:* T. Paul Malone.

Chile: 10 Brenner St., Jerusalem (E); *Ambassador:* (vacant).

Colombia: 22 Jabotinsky St., Jerusalem (E); *Ambassador:* Ramón Martínez Vallejo.

Costa Rica: 4 Mevo Yoram St., Jerusalem (E); *Ambassador:* Mrs. Carmen Naranjo.

Denmark: 23 Bnei Moshe St., Tel-Aviv (E); *Ambassador:* Sven Ebbesen.

Dominican Republic: 3 Bustanay St., Jerusalem (E); *Ambassador:* José Villanueva.

Ecuador: 37 Jabotinsky St., Jerusalem (E); *Ambassador:* (vacant).

El Salvador: Rome, Italy (E).

Finland: 224 Hayarkon St., Tel-Aviv (E); *Ambassador:* A. von Heiroth.

France: 112 Tayeleth Herbert Samuel, Tel-Aviv (E); *Ambassador:* Jean Herly.

Germany, Federal Republic: 16 Soutine St., Tel-Aviv (E); *Ambassador:* Jesco von Puttkamer.

Greece: 31 Rachel Imenu St., Jerusalem (L); *Diplomatic Representative:* Dimitri Petrou.

Guatemala: 3 Azza St., Jerusalem (E); *Ambassador:* Carlos Manuel Pellecer (also accred. to Greece).

Haiti: 31 Ramat Hagolan St., Jerusalem (E); *Ambassador:* Musset Pierre-Jerome.

Honduras: Paris, France (E).

Iceland: Oslo, Norway (E).

Italy: 24 Huberman St., Tel-Aviv (E); *Ambassador:* Vittorio Cordero di Montezemolo.

Japan: 10 Huberman St., Tel-Aviv (E); *Ambassador:* Kazuhide Komuro.

Khmer Republic: 20 Rashba St., Jerusalem (E); *Ambassador:* Keo Kim San.

Korea, Republic: Rome, Italy (E).

Laos: Paris, France (E).

Malawi: Addis Ababa, Ethiopia (E).

Malta: London, United Kingdom (E).

Mexico: 22 Hei Beiyar St., Tel-Aviv (E); *Ambassador:* Mrs. Rosario Castellanos.

Nepal: Paris, France (E).

Netherlands: Beith Yoel, 33 Yaffo St., Jerusalem (E); *Ambassador:* Gerrit Jan Jongejans.

Nicaragua: Rome, Italy (E).

Norway: 21 Hess St., Tel-Aviv (E); *Ambassador:* Peter Graver (also accred. to Cyprus).

Panama: 6 Yeshayahu Press St., Jerusalem (E); *Ambassador:* ELIO V. ORTIZ.

Peru: 19 Weizmann St., Tel-Aviv (E); *Ambassador:* BERNARDO ROCA REY.

Philippines: 14 Hei Beiyar St., Kikar Hamedina, Tel-Aviv (E); *Ambassador:* Mrs. RAFAELITA SORIANO.

Romania: 24 Adam Hacohen St., Tel-Aviv (E); *Ambassador:* IOAN COVACI.

Sweden: 198 Hayarkon St., Tel-Aviv (E); *Ambassador:* STEN SUNDFELDT.

Switzerland: 228 Hayarkon St., Tel-Aviv (E); *Ambassador:* HANSJOERG HESS (also accred. to Cyprus).

Thailand: Rome, Italy (E).

Turkey: 20 Bialik St., Tel-Aviv (L); *Chargé d'Affaires:* AHMET ASIM AKYAMAC.

United Kingdom: 192 Hayarkon St., Tel-Aviv (E); *Ambassador:* BERNARD LEDWIDGE, C.M.G.

U.S.A.: 71 Hayarkon St., Tel-Aviv (E); *Ambassador:* KENNETH KEATING.

Uruguay: 20 Uziya St., Katamon, Jerusalem (E); *Ambassador:* YAMANDÚ LAGUARDA.

Venezuela: 28 Rachel Imenu St., Jerusalem (E); *Ambassador:* NAPOLEÓN GIMÉNEZ.

Israel also has diplomatic relations with Jamaica, Lesotho, Singapore, South Africa, Swaziland and the Republic of Viet-Nam.

PARLIAMENT

Speaker of the Knesset: YISRAEL YESHAYAHU

The state of the parties in the 8th Knesset, following the General Election of December 1973, was as follows:

PARTY	VOTES	SEATS	PARTY	VOTES	SEATS
Labour-Mapam Alignment	621,183	51	Independent Liberals	56,560	4
Likud	473,309	39	New Communist List	53,353	4
National Religious Party	130,349	10	Arab Lists (affiliated to Labour)	48,961	3
Torah Front (Agudat Israel-Poalei			Civil Rights List	35,023	3
Agudat Israel)	60,012	5	Moked Maki	22,147	1

There was a 78 per cent poll from the 2,034,478 people eligible to vote in the 1973 elections. The Knesset is elected by proportional representation by universal suffrage for four years.

POLITICAL PARTIES

Israel Labour Party: P.O.B. 36, Tel-Aviv; formed in 1968 as a merger of the three former Labour groups, Mapai, Rafi and Achdut Ha'avoda; Zionist Social Democratic party, membership 300,000, including most of Kibbutz (collective) and Moshav (co-operative) villages. In 1973 elections, in alignment with another Zionist Socialist party, Mapam, gained 63 per cent in Histadrut (General Federation of Labour) and, together with affiliated Arab and Druze factions, 54 out of 120 Knesset (Parliament) seats. Holds all central cabinet positions and heads almost all important municipalities, though not Tel-Aviv.

Likud: Tel-Aviv; f. September 1973 under an agreement between Gahal (a merger of Herut and the Liberal Party), the State List, the Free Centre and the Labour Movement for the Land of Israel; party with largest membership in Israel Defence Forces; aims: territorial integrity (advocates retention of all territories occupied in the 1967 war as essential to future security of Israel); absorption of new-comers; a social order based on freedom and justice, elimination of poverty and want; development of an economy that will assure a decent standard of living; improvement of the environment and the quality of life; reforms in local government; assurance of democracy through the formation of a strong political force, as an alternative of the ruling party. Appears as a bloc in the Knesset, municipal and local councils, and the Histadrut, but the constituent parties maintain their own autonomous

organization. Joint Chairmen MENACHEM BEGIN (Herut), Dr. E. S. RIMALT (Liberal Party of Israel).

Gahal (the Herut Movement and Liberal Party Bloc): formed in 1965 as the result of an agreement between:

The Herut (*Freedom*) Movement: P.O.B. 23062, Tel-Aviv; was founded in 1948 by the Irgun Zvai Leumi, which played an activist part in the underground struggle against the British in the closing years of the Mandate.

The Herut Party strives to extend the present frontiers of Israel to its historic boundaries extending on both sides of the Jordan. The party stands for private initiative; 61,000 mems.; Founder and Chair. MENACHEM BEGIN, M.K.

The Liberal Party of Israel: 68 Ibn Gvirol St., Tel-Aviv; f. 1961 by merger of the General Zionists' and Progressive Parties; "Includes all strata of Israel's society. Its basic principles are those of the liberal philosophy. It strives for: national unity, political and economic consolidation of the state, safeguarding its security and integrity; unceasing efforts to achieve a durable peace with Israel's neighbours; a community based on democracy and social justice; ensuring freedom of the individual and his liberties; stimulation of private enterprise; reform of the tax system; narrowing the social and educational gap between the various strata of the nation; extensive immigration and complete material and social integration of newcomers;

equal rights and chances for all citizens of the state.'' Party Chair. Dr. E. S. RIMALT; Exec. Chair. S. EHRLICH.

The State List: f. 1969 by former members of Rafi (Labour group); Sec.-Gen. YIGAL HOROWITZ.

Free Centre: f. 1967 by dissidents from Herut; Chair. SHMUEL TAMIR.

National Religious Party: f. 1956; stands for strict adherence to Jewish religion and tradition, and strives to achieve the application of the religious precepts of Judaism in everyday life. It is also endeavouring to establish the constitution of Israel on Jewish religious law.

The United Workers' Party—Mapam (*Mifleget Hapoalim Hameuchedet*): P.O. Box 1777, Tel-Aviv; f. January 1948.

Mapam is a left-wing Socialist-Zionist party, participating in the coalition government; membership: urban workers, professionals, 75 *Kibbutzim;* aims: public-owned enterprise, guaranteed real wages, progressive taxation, independence of labour movement from state control, large-scale Jewish immigration; equal rights for Arabs, neutralist foreign policy, atomic demilitarization of Israel-Arab region, a negotiated Israel-Arab peace; branches in North and South America, Europe and Australia; since January 1969 grouped in an ''alignment'' (*Ma'arach*) with the Israel Labour Party (*see* above).

The Kibbutz Artzi Federation of collective settlements (affiliated with Mapam) maintains *Hashomer Hatzair*, which educates Jewish youth to pioneer life in Israel, and operates *Sifriat Poalim* (*The Workers' Library*) and *Hadfus Hehadash* (*The New Press*).

Daily newspaper *Al Hamishmar*; weeklies in Arabic, Yiddish, Bulgarian, Persian and Romanian.

Gen. Sec. MEIR TALMI; Political Sec. NAPHTALI FEDER; Organizing Sec. ARIE JAFFE; International Sec. JONA GOLAN.

Independent Liberal Party: P.O.B. 23076, Tel-Aviv; f. 1965 by 7 Liberal Party Knesset members after the formation of the Herut Movement and Liberal Party Bloc; 20,000 mems.; Chair. MOSHE KOL; Gen. Sec. ITZHAK

BARKAI; publs. *Temurot* (Hebrew, monthly), *Die Liberale Rundschau* (German, monthly), *Igeret* (Hebrew, quarterly).

Meri: 12 Carlebach St., Tel-Aviv; f. 1973 by Ha'olam Hazeh (New Force), members of Siah (left-wing group) and the Peace group; supports an Israeli-Arab federation, separation of religion and state, civil rights and freedom of speech and the press; Pres. URI AVNERY.

Communist Party of Israel (MAKI): P.O.B. 1843, Tel-Aviv; f. 1919; opposes present Soviet policy; aims include non-alignment of Israel; peace with the Arab States based on mutual recognition of the just national rights of Israeli and Arab peoples; defence of working class interests and formation of Left alignment for social progress; in 1973 formed an electoral bloc, ''Moked—for Peace and Socialist Transformation''; has one seat in the 8th Knesset. Publishes the Hebrew weekly *Kol Haam* and Arabic *Sout el Shaab* (monthly). Other weeklies in Yiddish, Romanian, Bulgarian; monthlies in English and French.

New Communist List of Israel: broke away from the Communist Party of Israel in 1965; draws its main support from the Arab Community; favours full implementation of UN Security Council resolution of 1967.

Civil Rights List: Tel-Aviv; f. 1973; breakaway movement from the Labour Party; aims: women's liberation; greater freedom for the individual from the influence of the religious ''establishment''; electoral reform; Pres. Mrs. SHULAMIT ALONI.

Agudat Israel (f. 1912) and **Poalei Agudat Israel** (f. 1924) are also Orthodox Judaist parties, the membership of the Poalei Agudat Israel being drawn largely from wage-earners; formed the Torah Front for the December 1973 elections; has five seats in the 8th Knesset.

The official organ of Agudat Israel is the daily *Hamodia*; that of the Poalei Agudat Israel is the daily *Shearim*.

Pres. of Poalei Agudat Israel Dr. K. KAHANA.

Co-operation and Fraternity Party: an Arab party associated with the *Mapai* party.

Progress and Development Party: an Arab party associated with the *Mapai* party; has two seats in the 8th Knesset.

THE JEWISH AGENCY FOR ISRAEL

P.O.B. 92, Jerusalem.

Organization:

The governing bodies are the Assembly which determines basic policy, the Board of Governors which manages the Agency between Assembly meetings and the Executive responsible for the day to day running of the Agency.

Chairman, Executive Committee: LEON DULZIN.

Chairman of Board of Governors: MAX M. FISHER.

Director-General: MOSHE RIVLIN.

History:

Article Four of the League of Nations' Mandate provided for the establishment of a Jewish agency to co-operate with the administration in the economic and social development of the Jewish national home. The Zionist Organization served as this agency until 1929, when the Jewish Agency was finally constituted, with the admission of non-Zionists as well as Zionists to its Council. The Zionist Congress of 1925 bound the Agency to the following ''inviolable principles'': a continuous increase in the volume

of Jewish immigration, the recovery of the land as Jewish public property, agricultural colonization based on Jewish labour, and the promotion of the Hebrew language and Hebrew culture.

When the State of Israel was established in 1948, the provisional Government was formed from the members of the Executive of the Va'ad Leumi (the representative organ of Palestinian Jewry) and members of the Jewish Agency Executive resident in Palestine at the time. The division of tasks between the Jewish Agency and the Government was defined in the Status Law of 1952 and in a Covenant entered into in 1954.

During 1967-71 discussions on reconstituting the Jewish Agency were conducted between the World Zionist Organization and the fund raising organizations of World Jewry. In June 1971, an agreement for the re-constitution of the Agency came into force, separating the functions of the World Zionist Organization from those of the Agency.

Functions:

According to the Agreement of 1971, the Jewish Agency undertakes the immigration and absorption of immigrants in Israel, including absorption in agricultural settlement and immigrant housing, social welfare and health services in connection with immigrants, and education, youth care and training.

Revenue and Expenditure:

The Jewish Agency's chief source of revenue are the voluntary fund-raising campaigns throughout the world.

Approximately two-thirds of the campaign income is derived from the U.I.A. Inc. in the United States, and the rest from campaigns conducted under the auspices of or in co-operation with the Foundation Fund (Keren Hayesod). The Agency also received 18 per cent of German Reparations from 1952–66.

Expenditure abroad, apart from debt service, includes transport of immigrants, aid to Jewish education and cultural activities as well as purchases of equipment and stocks for the new settlements established by the Agency.

Budget: (1972–73) I£1,953 million; (1973–74) I£1,974 million.

JUDICIAL SYSTEM

The law of Israel is composed of Ottoman law, British law, Palestine law, applicable in Palestine on May 14th, 1948, when the independence of the State of Israel was declared, the substance of the common law and doctrines of equity in force in England, as modified to suit local conditions, and religious law of the various recognized religious communities as regards matters of personal status, in so far as there is nothing in any of the said laws repugnant to Israeli legislation and subject to such modifications as may have resulted from the establishment of the State of Israel and its authorities, and also of the laws enacted by the Israeli legislature. The pre-1948 law is increasingly being replaced by original local legislation.

CIVIL COURTS

The Supreme Court is the highest judicial instance in the State. It has jurisdiction as an Appellate Court from the District Courts in all matters, both civil and criminal (sitting as a Court of Civil Appeal or as a Court of Criminal Appeal), and as a Court of First Instance (sitting as a High Court of Justice) in matters in which it considers it necessary to grant relief in the interests of justice and which are not within the jurisdiction of any other court or tribunal. This includes applications for orders in the nature of *habeas corpus*, *mandamus*, prohibition and *certiorari*, and enables the court to review the legality of acts of administrative authorities of all kinds.

President of the Supreme Court: S. AGRANAT.

Permanent Deputy President of the Supreme Court: Y. SUSSMAN.

Justices of the Supreme Court: M. LANDAU, Z. BERINSON, A. WITKON, H. COHN, E. M. MANNY, I. KISTER, M. ETZIONI, I. KAHAN.

The District Courts: Jerusalem, Tel-Aviv-Jaffa, Haifa, Beersheba, Nazareth. They have unlimited jurisdiction as Courts of First Instance in all civil and criminal matters not within the jurisdiction of a Magistrates' Court, all matters not within the exclusive jurisdiction of any other tribunal, and matters within the concurrent jurisdiction of any other tribunal so long as such tribunal does not deal with them, and as an Appellate Court in appeals from judgments and decisions of Magistrates' Courts and judgments of Municipal Courts and various administrative tribunals.

Magistrates' Courts: There are 26 Magistrates' Courts, having criminal jurisdiction to try contraventions and misdemeanours, and civil jurisdiction to try actions concerning possession or use of immovable property, or the partition thereof whatever may be the value of the subject matter of the action, and other civil actions where the amount of the claim, or the value of the subject matter, does not exceed I£10,000.

Labour Courts: Established in 1969. Regional Labour Courts in Jerusalem, Tel-Aviv, Haifa and Beersheba, composed of Judges and representatives of the Public. A National Labour Court in Jerusalem, presided over by Judge Z. Bar-Niv. The Courts have jurisdiction over all matters arising out of the relationship between employer and employee; between parties to a collective labour agreement; matters concerning the National Insurance Law and the Labour Law and Rules.

Municipal Courts: There are 5 Municipal Courts, having criminal jurisdiction over any offences against municipal regulations and by-laws and certain other offences, such as town planning offences, committed within the municipal area.

RELIGIOUS COURTS

The Religious Courts are the Courts of the recognized religious communities. They are competent in certain defined matters of personal status concerning members of their community. Where any action of personal status involves persons of different religious communities the President of the Supreme Court will decide which Court shall have jurisdiction. Whenever a question arises as to whether or not a case is one of personal status within the exclusive jurisdiction of a Religious Court, the matter must be referred to a Special Tribunal composed of two Justices of the Supreme Court and the President of the highest court of the religious community concerned in Israel.

The judgments of the Religious Courts are executed by the process and offices of the Civil Courts.

Jewish Rabbinical Courts: These Courts have exclusive jurisdiction in matters of marriage and divorce of Jews in Israel who are Israeli citizens or residents. In all other matters of personal status they have concurrent jurisdiction with the District Courts with the consent of all parties concerned.

Muslim Religious Courts: These Courts have exclusive jurisdiction in matters of marriage and divorce of Muslims who are not foreigners, or who are foreigners subject by their national law to the jurisdiction of Muslim Religious Courts in such matters. In all other matters of personal status they have concurrent jurisdiction with the District Courts with the consent of all parties concerned.

Christian Religious Courts: The Courts of the recognized Christian communities have exclusive jurisdiction in matters of marriage and divorce of members of their communities who are not foreigners. In all other matters of personal status they have concurrent jurisdiction with the District Courts with the consent of all parties concerned. But neither these Courts nor the Civil Courts have jurisdiction to dissolve the marriage of a foreign subject.

Druze Courts: These Courts, established in 1963, have exclusive jurisdiction in matters of marriage and divorce of Druze in Israel, who are Israeli citizens or residents, and concurrent jurisdiction with the District Courts in all other matters of personal status of Druze with the consent of all parties concerned.

MILITARY COURTS

Courts-Martial: A Court-Martial is competent to try a soldier within the meaning of the Military Justice Law, 1955, who has committed an act constituting a military offence, without prejudice to the power of any other Court in the State to try him for that act if it constitutes an offence under any other law. A Court-Martial is also competent to try a soldier for any offence which is not a military offence, but the Attorney General may order that he be tried by another Court if he is of the opinion that the offence was not committed within the framework of the Army or in consequence of the accused's belonging to the Army.

RELIGION

JUDAISM

Judaism, the religion evolved and followed by the Jews, is the faith of the great majority of the population. Its basis is a belief in an ethical monotheism.

There are two main Jewish communities: the Ashkenazim and the Sephardim. The former are the Jews from Eastern, Central, or Northern Europe, while the latter originate from the Balkan countries, North Africa and the Middle East. Although they have separate synagogues, and differ somewhat in their ritual and pronunciation of Hebrew, there is no doctrinal distinction. The prevailing influence is that of the Ashkenazim Jews, who are more modern and westernized, but the recent Hebrew revival has been based on the Sephardi pronunciation of the ancient Hebrew tongue.

The supreme religious authority is vested in the Chief Rabbinate, which consists of the Ashkenazi and Sephardi Chief Rabbis and the Supreme Rabbinical Council. It makes decisions on interpretation of the Jewish law, and supervises the Rabbinal Courts. There are 8 regional Rabbinical Courts, and a Rabbinical Court of Appeal presided over by the two Chief Rabbis.

According to the Rabbinical Courts Jurisdiction Law of 1953, marriage and divorce among Jews in Israel are exclusively within the jurisdiction of the Rabbinical Courts. Provided that all the parties concerned agree, other matters of personal status can also be decided by the Rabbinical Courts.

There are 195 Religious Councils, which maintain religious services and supply religious needs, and about 405 religious committees with similar functions in smaller settlements. Their expenses are borne jointly by the State and the local authorities. The Religious Councils are under the administrative control of the Ministry of Religious Affairs. In all matters of religion, the Religious Councils are subject to the authority of the Chief Rabbinate. There are 365 officially appointed rabbis. The total number of synagogues is about 7,000, most of which are organized within the framework of the Union of Israel Synagogues.

Head of the Ashkenazi Community: H.E. The Chief Rabbi SHLOMO GOREN.

Head of the Sephardic Community: H.E. The Chief Rabbi OVADIA YOSEF.

Two Jewish sects still loyal to their distinctive customs are:

The Karaites, a sect which recognizes only the Jewish written law and not the oral law of the Mishna and Talmud.

The community of about 12,000 many of whom live in or near Ramla, has been augmented by immigration from Egypt.

The Samaritans, an ancient sect mentioned in 2 Kings xvii, 24. They recognize only the Torah and the Book of Joshua. The community in Israel numbers about 500; they live in Holon, where a Samaritan synagogue has been built. Their High Priest lives in Nablus, near Mt. Gerizim, which is sacred to the Samaritans.

ISLAM

The Muslims in Israel are in the main Sunnis, and are divided among the four rites of the Sunni school of Muslim thought: the Shafe'i, the Hanbali, the Hanafi, and the Maliki. Before June 1967 they numbered approximately 175,000; in 1971, approximately 343,900.

CHRISTIAN COMMUNITIES

The Greek Catholic Church, P.O.B. 279, Haifa; numbers about 35,000 and Haifa is the seat of the Archbishop of Acre, Haifa, Nazareth and all Galilee; Archbishop JOSEPH M. RAYA; publ. *Ar-Rabita* (Arabic monthly; circ. 4,000).

The Greek Orthodox Church in Israel has approximately 22,000 members. The Patriarch of Jerusalem is His Beatitude BENEDICTOS.

The Latin (Roman Catholic) Church has about 10,000 native members in Israel plus about 2,000 Polish and Hungarian Catholic refugees. The Latin Patriarch of Jerusalem is His Beatitude JAMES JOSEPH BELTRITTI; Representative in Israel H.E. Bishop HANNA KALDANY.

The Maronite Community, with approximately 4,000 members, has communal centres in Haifa, Nazareth and Jaffa. The Maronite Patriarch resides in the Lebanon.

The Evangelical Episcopal Church in Israel, which belongs to the Anglican Communion, has 1,000 members and was officially recognised by Israel in April 1970; it comes under the jurisdiction of the Archbishop in Jerusalem and is now being reorganized (Temporary Vicar-Gen., the Most Rev. Dr. ROBERT STOPFORD, St. George's Close, Jerusalem).

Other denominations include the *Armenian Church* (900 members), the *Coptic Church* (700 members), the *Russian Orthodox Church*, which maintains an Ecclesiastical Mission, the *Ethiopian Church*, and the *Baptist Lutheran* and *Presbyterian Churches*.

THE PRESS

Tel-Aviv is the main publishing centre, only three dailies being published in Jerusalem. Largely for economic reasons there has developed no local press away from these cities; hence all papers regard themselves as national. Friday editions, Sabbath eve, are increased to up to twice the normal size by special weekend supplements, and experience a considerable rise in circulation. No newspapers appear on Saturday.

Most of the daily papers are in Hebrew, and others appear in Arabic, English, French, Polish, Yiddish, Hungarian and German. The total daily circulation is 500,000–600,000 copies, or twenty-one papers per hundred people, although most citizens read more than one daily paper.

Most Hebrew morning dailies have strong political or religious affiliations. *Lamerhav* is affiliated to Achdut Ha'avoda, *Al Hamishmar* to Mapam, *Hatzofeh* to the National Religious Front—World Mizrahi. *Davar* is the long-established organ of the Histadrut. Mapai publishes the weekly *Ot* but no daily. Although the revenue from advertisements is increasing, very few dailies are economically self-supporting; most depend on subsidies from political parties, religious organizations or public funds. The limiting effect on freedom of commentary entailed by this party press system has provoked repeated criticism.

The Jerusalem Arabic daily *Al Anba* has a small circulation (12,000) but an increasing number of Israeli Arabs are now reading Hebrew dailies. The daily, *Al Quds*, was founded in 1968 for Arabs in Jerusalem and the West Bank; the small indigenous press of occupied Jordan has largely ceased publication or transferred operations to Amman.

There are around 400 other newspapers and magazines including some 50 weekly and 150 fortnightly; over 250 of them are in Hebrew, the remainder in eleven other languages.

The most influential and respected dailies, for both quality of news coverage and commentary, are *Ha'aretz*, characterized by its sober but proudly independent editorials, and the Union paper, *Davar*, which frequently has articles by government figures. These are the widest read of the morning papers, exceeded only by the popular afternoon press, *Ma'ariv* and *Yedioth Aharonoth*. The *Jerusalem Post* gives detailed and sound news coverage in English.

The Israeli Press Council, established in 1963, deals with matters of common interest to the Press such as drafting the recently published code of professional ethics which is binding on all journalists.

The Daily Newspaper Publishers' Association represents publishers in negotiations with official and public bodies, negotiates contracts with employees and purchases and distributes newsprint, of which Israel now manufactures 75 per cent of her needs.

DAILIES

Al-Anba: P.O.B. 428, Hachavazelet St., Jerusalem; f. 1968; published by Jerusalem Publications Ltd.; Editor Isaac Bar-Moshe; circ. 12,000.

Al Hamishmar (*The Guardian*): Hamishmar House, 4 Ben Avigdor St., Tel-Aviv; f. 1943; morning; organ of the United Worker's Party (Mapam); Editor Ya'akov Amit; circ. 25,000.

Al Quds (*Jerusalem*): P.O.B. 19788, Jerusalem; f. 1968; Arabic; Editor Abu Zalaf.

Chadshot Hasport: Tushia St., P.O.B. 20011, Tel-Aviv 61200; f. 1954; Hebrew; sports; independent; circ. 30,000.

Davar (*The Word*): P.O.B. 199, 45 Sheinkin St., Tel-Aviv; f. 1925; morning; official organ of the General Federation of Labour (Histadrut); Editor Hannah Zemer; circ. 50,000.

Ha'aretz (*The Land*): 56 Mazeh St., Tel-Aviv; f. 1918; morning; liberal, independent; Editor Gershom G. Schocken; circ. 50,000 (week-days), 70,000 (weekends).

Hamodia: Kikar Hacheruth, P.O.B. 1306, Jerusalem; organ of Agudat Israel; morning; Editor Yehuda L. Levin; circ. 8,000.

Hatzofeh: 66 Hamasger St., Tel-Aviv; f. 1938; morning; organ of the National Religious Front; Editor S. Daniel; circ. 11,000.

Israelski Far Tribuna: 113 Givat Herzl St., Tel-Aviv; Bulgarian.

Jerusalem Post: P.O.B. 81, Romema, Jerusalem; f. 1932; morning; independent; English; Editor (vacant); circ. 34,000 (weekdays), 45,000 (weekend edition); there is also a weekly overseas edition (*q.v.*).

Le Journal d'Israel: 26 Agra St., P.O.B. 28330, Tel-Aviv; independent; French; Dir.-Chief Editor J. Rabin; circ. 10,000; also overseas weekly selection; circ. 15,000.

Lamerhav: 1 Nahal Avalon St., Tel-Aviv; f. 1954; morning; socialist; Chief Editor David Pedahzur; circ. 18,000.

Letzte Nyess (*Late News*): 52 Harakevet St., Tel-Aviv; f. 1949; Yiddish; morning; Editor M. Tsanin; circ. 23,000.

Ma'ariv: Ma'ariv House, P.O.B. 20010, Tel-Aviv; f. 1948; evening; independent; Editor Arie Dissentshik; circ. daily 160,000, Friday 210,000.

Nowiny i Kurier: 52 Harakevet St., Tel-Aviv; f. 1952; Polish; morning; Editor S. Yedidyah; circ. 10,000.

Omer: 45 Sheinkin St., Tel-Aviv; Histadrut popular vowelled Hebrew paper; f. 1951; Chief Editor Meir Bareli; circ. 10,000.

Sha'ar: 4A Hissin St., Tel-Aviv 64284; economy and finance; Hebrew and English; Editor S. Lari.

Shearim: 64 Frichman St., Tel-Aviv; organ of Poalei Agudat Israel; Editor Yehuda Nahshoni; circ. 5,000.

Uj Kelet: 52 Harakevet St., Tel-Aviv; f. 1918; morning; Hungarian; independent; Editor Dr. G. Marton; circ. 20,000.

Viata Noastra: 52 Harakevet St., Tel-Aviv; f. 1950; Romanian; supports the Israel Labour Party; morning; Editor Meir Zait; circ. 30,000.

Yedioth Aharonoth: 5 Yehuda Mozes St., Tel-Aviv; f. 1939; evening; independent; Editor Dr. H. Rosenblum; circ. 140,000, Friday 195,000.

Yedioth Hadashot: P.O.B. 1585, 66 Harakevet St., Tel-Aviv; f. 1935; morning; German; independent; Editor Dr. I. Lilienfeld; circ. 18,000.

Yom Yom: P.O.B. 1194, Tel-Aviv; f. 1964; morning; economy and finance; Editor P. Mersten.

WEEKLIES AND FORTNIGHTLIES

Al Ta'awun: P.O.B. 303, Tel-Aviv; f. 1961; published by the Arab Worker's Dept. of the Histadrut and the Co-operatives Dept. of the Ministry of Labour; co-operatives quarterly; Editor Tuvia Shamosh.

Adevarul: 21 Hasharon St., Tel-Aviv; f. 1949; Romanian; weekly; Editor IEHUDA MAERSON-SEVERIN.

Al Harriya: 38 King George St., Tel-Aviv; Arabic weekly of the Herut Party.

Al-Ittihad: P.O.B. 104, Haifa; f. 1944; Arabic; journal of the Israeli Communist Party; Chief Editor EMILE HABIBI.

Al Marsad: P.O.B. 736, 4 Ben Avigdor St., Tel-Aviv; Mapam; Arabic.

Bama'alah: P.O.B. 303, Tel-Aviv; journal of the young Histadrut Movement; Editor N. ANAELY.

Bamahane: Military P.O.B. 1013, Tel-Aviv; f. 1948; military, illustrated weekly of the Israel Army; Editor-in-Chief IZHAK LIVNI.

Bitaon Heyl Ha'avir (*Air Force Magazine*): Doar Zwai 2348; f. 1948; Editor M. HADAR; Managing Editor Y. OFFER; circ. 33,000.

Dvar Hashavua: 45 Sheinkin St., Tel-Aviv; f. 1946; popular illustrated; weekly; published by Histadrut, General Federation of Labour; Editor O. ZMORA; circ. 50,000.

Economic Review: 17 Kaplan St., Tel-Aviv; economic and social problems of immigration and absorption; Editors Dr. L. BERGER, CHAYA LAZAR; circ. English edition 3,500, Spanish edition (*Reseña Económica*) 2,000, French edition (*Revue Economique*) 2,000.

Ethgar: 75 Einstein Street, Tel-Aviv; twice weekly; Editor NATHAN YALIN-MOR.

Frei Israel: P.O.B. 8512, Tel-Aviv; Yiddish, progressive weekly, publ. by Asscn. for Popular Culture; Editor I. LIPSKI.

Glasul Populurui: Eilath St., P.O.B. 2675, Tel-Aviv; weekly of the Communist Party of Israel; Romanian; Editor MEÏR SEMO.

Gold and Monetary Issues: 37 Harbour St., Haifa; f. 1969; fortnightly; English; gold, gold shares, finance and investment; Editor G. ALON.

Haolam Hazeh: P.O.B. 136, 8 Glikson St., Tel-Aviv; f. 1937; independent; illustrated news magazine; weekly; Man. Editor URI AVNERY; Editor ELI TAVOR.

Harefuah: 39 Shaul Hamelech Blvd., Tel-Aviv; f. 1920; with English summary; fortnightly journal of the Israeli Medical Association; Editor I. SUM, M.D.; circ. 6,000.

Hed Hahinukh: 8 Ben-Saruk Street, Tel-Aviv; f. 1926; weekly; educational; published by the Israeli Teachers' Union; Editor ZVI ARAD; circ. 26,000.

Illustrirte Weltwoch: P.O.B. 2571, Tel-Aviv; f. 1956; Yiddish; weekly; Editor M. TSANIN.

The Israel Digest: P.O.B. 92, Jerusalem; f. 1957; independent; fortnightly digest of news and views; circ. 20,000; Editor ZVI SOIFER.

Jerusalem Post Overseas Weekly: P.O.B. 81, Romema, Jerusalem; f. 1959; English; Overseas edition of the *Jerusalem Post* (*q.v.*); circ. 35,000 to 95 countries.

Kol Ha'am (*Voice of the People*): 37 Eilath St., P.O.B. 2675, Tel-Aviv; f. 1947; organ of the Communist Party of Israel; Editor B. BALTI.

Laisha: P.O.B. 28122, 7 Fin St., Tel-Aviv; f. 1946; Hebrew; women's magazine; Editor DAVID KARASSIK.

Liawladina: Arabic Publishing House, P.O.B. 28049, Tel-Aviv; f. 1960; children's; fortnightly; Board of Editors ELIAHU AGHASSI, MISHEL HADDAD, WALID HUSSEIN, AIDA SABBAGH.

Maariv Lanoar: 2 Carlebach St., Tel-Aviv; f. 1956; weekly for the youth; Editor YANAI REUBEN; circ. 25,000.

MB (formerly *Mitteilungsblatt*): P.O.B. 1480, Tel-Aviv; f. 1932; German; journal of the Irgun Olei Merkas Europa; Editor Dr. HANS TRAMER.

Min Hayesod: Tel-Aviv; fortnightly; Hebrew; news and political commentary.

Ot: P.O.B. 36, 10 Dov Hoz St., Tel-Aviv; f. 1971; weekly organ of the Israel Labour Party; Editor DAVID SHAHAM.

Reshumot: Israel Government Printer, Jerusalem; f. 1948; Hebrew and Arabic; official Government gazette, edited by the Ministry of Justice.

Sada-A-Tarbia (*The Echo of Education*): published by the Histadrut and Teachers' Association, P.O.B. 303, Tel-Aviv; f. 1952; Arabic; educational; fortnightly; Editor TUVIA SHAMOSH.

El Tiempo: P.O.B. 671, Tel-Aviv; weekly; Ladino.

OTHER PERIODICALS

Al-Bushra: P.O.B. 6088, Haifa; f. 1935; monthly; Arabic; organ of the Ahmadiyya movement; Editor FAZL ILAHI BASHIR.

Al Hamishmar: 20 Yehuda Halevy Street, Tel-Aviv; Bulgarian monthly of United Workers' Party.

Al Jadid: P.O.B. 104, Haifa; Arabic; literary monthly; Editor HANA NAKARA.

Ariel: Cultural and Scientific Relations Division, Ministry for Foreign Affairs, Jerusalem; f. 1962; quarterly review of the arts and letters in Israel; edns. in English, Spanish, French and German; Editor T. CARMI.

Avoda Ubituach Leumi: P.O.B. 915, Jerusalem; f. 1949; monthly review of the Ministry of Labour, and the National Insurance Institute, Jerusalem; Editor Z. HEYN; circ. 3,000.

Business Diary: 37 Harbour St., Haifa; f. 1947; monthly; English; news digest, trade, finance, new firms, computerized stock exchange listings; Editor G. ALON.

Christian News from Israel: 23 Shlomo Hamelech St., Jerusalem; quarterly issued by the Ministry of Religious Affairs; in English, French, Spanish; Acting Editor SHALOM BEN-ZAKKAI; circ. 20,000.

Dapim Refuiim: 101 Arlosoroff St., P.O.B. 16250, Tel-Aviv; f. 1935; eight times a year; medical; Hebrew with English and French summaries; circ. 5,000; Editor Dr. M. DVORJETSKI.

Divrei Haknesset: c/o The Knesset, Jerusalem; f. 1949; records of the proceedings of the Knesset, published by the Government Printer, Jerusalem; Editor D. NIV; circ. 300.

Dvar Hapoelet: P.O.B. 303, Tel-Aviv; f. 1934; monthly journal of the Council of Women Workers of the Histadrut; Hebrew; Founder and Past Editor Mrs. RACHEL SHAZAR; Editor ZIVIA COHEN; circ. 11,000.

Folk un Zion: P.O.B. 92, Jerusalem; f. 1950; monthly; current events relating to Israel and World Jewry; circ. 6,000; Editor MOSHE HORVITZ.

Gazit: 8 Zvi Brook St., P.O.B. 4190, Tel-Aviv; f. 1932; monthly; Hebrew and English; art, literature; Publisher G. TALPHIR.

Goldene Keit, Die: 30 Weizmann St., Tel-Aviv; f. 1949; Yiddish; literary quarterly; published by the Histadrut; Editor A. SUTZKEVER; Co-Editor E. PINES; Man. Editor SHMUEL CHORESH.

Hameshek Hahaklai: 21 Melchett St., Tel-Aviv; f. 1929; agricultural; Editor ISRAEL INBARI.

Hamis'har (*Commerce*): P.O.B. 852, Tel-Aviv; f. 1932; quarterly; Hebrew; economic and commercial; Chamber of Commerce Tel-Aviv-Yafo; Editor Dr. E. W. KLIMOWSKY; circ. 50,000.

Hamizrah Hehadash: (*The New East*): The Hebrew University of Jerusalem; f. 1949; quarterly of the Israel Oriental Society; Hebrew with English summary; Middle Eastern, Asian and African Affairs; Editor YEHOSHUA PORATH.

Hamlonai (*The Hotelier*): 13 Montefiore St., P.O.B. 2032, Tel-Aviv; f. 1962; monthly of the Israel Hotel Association; Hebrew and English; Editor Dr. K. LICHT.

Hapraklit: P.O.B. 788 Tel-Aviv: f. 1943; quarterly; published by the Israel Bar Association; Editors A. POLONSKY, J. GROSS; circ. 6,000.

Hassadeh: 25 Lilienblum St., Tel-Aviv; f. 1920; monthly; review of mixed farming; Editor J. M. MARGALIT; circ. 10,000.

Hataassiya (*Israel Industry*): 13 Montefiore St., P.O.B. 2032, Tel-Aviv; f. 1941; monthly review of the Manufacturers' Asscn. of Israel; Man. Dir. Z. PELTZ.

Hed Hagan: 8 Ben Saruk St., Tel-Aviv; f. 1935; educational; Editor Mrs. ESTHER RABINOWITZ; circ. 3,500.

Israel Annals of Psychiatry: Jerusalem Academic Press, Givat Saul, P.O.B. 2390, Jerusalem; f. 1963; quarterly; Editor-in-Chief Prof. H. Z. WINNIK.

Israel Economist: P.O.B. 7052, 6 Hazanowitz St., Jerusalem; f. 1945; monthly; English; political and economic; independent; Editor J. KOLLEK, M.JUR.; also publishes *The Tel-Aviv Stock Exchange Information Card Service.*

Israel Exploration Journal: P.O.B. 7041, Jerusalem; f. 1950; quarterly; Editor Prof. M. AVI-YONAH; Associate Editor Dr. D. BARAG; circ. 2,000.

Israel Export and Trade Journal, The: 13 Montefiore St., P.O.B. 2032, Tel-Aviv; f. 1949; monthly; English; commercial and economic; published by Israel Periodicals Co. Ltd.; Editor YOANNE YARON; Man. Dirs. F. A. LEWINSON and ZALMAN PELTZ.

Israel Industry and Commerce: P.O.B. 1199, Tel-Aviv; English; monthly; serves Israeli exporters; Editor SH. YEDIDYAH.

Israel Journal of Medical Sciences: P.O.B. 1435, Jerusalem; incorporating *The Israel Journal of Experimental Medicine* and *The Israel Medical Journal*; f. 1965; monthly; Editor-in-Chief Dr. M. PRYWES; circ. 5,500.

Israels Aussenhandel: 13 Montefiore St., Tel-Aviv; f. 1967; monthly; German; commercial; Editor Z. PELTZ.

Iyyun: Jerusalem Philosophical Society, c/o The Hebrew University, Jerusalem; f. 1945; quarterly; Hebrew (English summaries); Editor EDWARD I. J. POZNANSKI.

Kalkalan: 8 Akiva St., P.O.B. 7052, Jerusalem; f. 1952; monthly; Hebrew commercial and economic; independent; Editor J. KOLLEK, M.JUR.

Kirjath Sepher: P.O.B. 503, Jerusalem; bibliographical quarterly of the Jewish National and University Library, Jerusalem; f. 1924.

Labour in Israel: 93 Arlosoroff St., Tel-Aviv; periodic bulletin of the Histadrut; English, Swedish, French, German, Portuguese and Spanish.

Leshonenu: Academy of the Hebrew Language, P.O.B. 3449, Jerusalem; f. 1929; quarterly; for the study of the Hebrew language and cognate subjects; Editor S. ABRAMSON.

Leshonenu La'am: Academy of the Hebrew Language, P.O.B. 3449, Jerusalem; f. 1945; popular Hebrew philology; Editors E. ETAN, M. MEDAN.

Ma'arachot: Ha'Kirya, 1 Rechov Gimmel, Tel-Aviv; f. 1939; military; Editor Col. GERSHON RIVLIN.

Mada: Weizmann Science Press, P.O.B. 801, Jerusalem; f. 1956; popular scientific bi-monthly in Hebrew; Editor-in-Chief KAPAI PINES; circ. 10,000.

Mibifnim: 27 Sutin St., P.O.B. 16040, Tel-Aviv; f. 1924; quarterly of the United Collective Settlements (Hakibbutz Hameuchad); Editor ZERUBAVEL GILEAD; circ. 8,000.

Molad: P.O.B. 1165, Jerusalem; f. 1948; bi-monthly; independent political and literary review; Hebrew; published by Miph'ale Molad Ltd.; Editor EPHRAIM BROIDO.

Monthly Bulletin of Statistics: Israel Central Bureau of Statistics, P.O.B. 13015, Jerusalem; f. 1949.

> **Monthly Statistics of the Administered Territories:** f. 1971; Hebrew and English.
>
> **Foreign Trade Statistical Quarterly:** f. 1969; Hebrew and English.
>
> **Monthly Statistics of Tourism and Hotel Services:** f. 1973; Hebrew and English.
>
> **Monthly Price Statistics:** f. 1949; Hebrew.
>
> **Monthly Foreign Trade Statistics:** f. 1950; Hebrew and English.
>
> **Immigration Statistics:** f. 1970; monthly and quarterly; Hebrew.

Moznayim (*Balance*): P.O.B. 7098, Tel-Aviv; f. 1929; literature and culture; monthly; circ. 2,500; Editors J. MICHALY BENJAMIN, A. B. YOFFE.

Ner: Ihud, P.O.B. 451, Jerusalem; f. 1948; monthly on political and social problems; advocates Arab-Jewish reconciliation; Hebrew, English, Arabic; circ. 1,500.

New Outlook: 8 Karl Netter St., Tel-Aviv; f. 1957; monthly; circ. 10,000; Editor SIMHA FLAPAN.

Proche-Orient Chrétien: B.P. 19079, Jerusalem; f. 1951; quarterly.

Quarterly Review of the Israel Medical Association (*Mif'al Haverut Hutz*—Non-resident Fellowship of the Israel Medical Association): 39 Shaul Hamelekh Blvd., Tel-Aviv; English; also published in French and Spanish; quarterly; Editor Dr. V. RESNEKOV.

Refuah Veterinarit: P.O.B. 18, Beit Dagan, Tel-Aviv; f. 1943; quarterly review of veterinary surgery.

La Revue de l'A.M.I. (Non-resident Fellowship of the Israeli Medical Association): 39 Shaul Hamelekh Blvd., Tel-Aviv; French, English and Spanish; quarterly; Editor Dr. S. ZALUD.

Scopus: Hebrew University of Jerusalem; f. 1946; published by Department of Information and Public Affairs, Hebrew University of Jerusalem; twice yearly; English; Editor D. A. SUSMAN.

Shituf (*Co-operation*): 24 Ha'arba St., Tel-Aviv, P.O.B. 7151; monthly; Hebrew co-operative journal; published by the Central Union of Industrial, Transport and Service Co-operative Societies; Editor L. LOSH.

Sinai: P.O.B. 642, Jerusalem; Torah, science and literature; Editor Dr. YITZCHAK RAPHAEL.

Sindbad: P.O.B. 28049, Tel-Aviv; f. 1969; children's monthly; Editors ELIAHU AGHASSI, WALID HUSSEIN.

Sion: P.O.B. 14001, Jerusalem; f. 1866; bi-monthly of religion, literature and philology; official organ of the Armenian Patriarchate of Jerusalem; circ. 1,200; Editor His Beatitude Patriarch Y. DERDERIAN.

Sulam: 2 Ben Yehuda St., Jerusalem; political; monthly; Editor Y. SHAIB.

Tarbitz: Magnes Press, the Hebrew University, Jerusalem; f. 1929; quarterly; for Jewish studies; Editor E. E. URBACH; circ. 750.

Terra Santa: P.O.B. 186, Jerusalem; f. 1921; monthly; published by the Custody of the Holy Land (the official custodians of the Holy Shrines); Italian, Spanish,

French and Arabic editions published in Jerusalem, by the Franciscan Printing Press, English edition in Washington, German edition in Vienna, Maltese edition in Valletta.

Teva Vaarez: 25 Lilienblum St., P.O.B. 4, Tel-Aviv; f. 1958; monthly; review of agriculture, nature and geography; Editor Dr. DANIEL RIMON.

Tmuroth: 48 Hamelech George St., P.O.B. 23076, Tel-Aviv; f. 1960; organ of the Liberal Labour Movement; monthly; Editor D. SHLOMI.

Urim La-Orim: 93 Arlosoroff St., P.O.B. 303, Tel-Aviv; educational problems in the family; monthly; Editor HAYIM NAGID.

Vilner Pinkas: P.O.B. 28006, Tel-Aviv; f. 1968; periodical review of current affairs for Vilna-Jews the world over, and for the history of Yerushdayim Delito; Yiddish; Editor M. KARPINOVITZ.

WIZO Review: Women's International Zionist Organization, 38 Sderoth David Hamelekh, Tel-Aviv; English, Spanish and German editions; Editor SYLVIA SATTEN BANIN; circ. 20,000.

Yam: Israeli Maritime League, P.O.B. 706, 5 Habankim St., Haifa; f. 1937; review of marine problems; Editor Z. ESHEL; Pres. S. TOLKOWSKY; circ. 4,000.

Zion: P.O.B. 1062, Jerusalem; f. 1935; research in Jewish history; quarterly; Hebrew and English; Editors I. F. BAER, H. H. BEN-SASSON, S. ETTINGER.

Zraim: 7 Dubnov St., P.O.B. 40027, Tel-Aviv; f. 1935; journal of the Bnei Akiva (Youth of Hapoel Hamizrachi) Movement; Editor SHLOMO SAMSON.

Zrakor: 37 Harbour St., Haifa; f. 1947; monthly; Hebrew; news digest, trade, finance, economics, shipping; Editor G. ALON.

The following are all published by Weizmann Science Press Israel, P.O.B. 801, Jerusalem 91000; Exec. Editor L. LESTER.

Israel Journal of Botany: f. 1951; Editor Prof. LEONORA REINHOLD; quarterly.

Israel Journal of Chemistry: f. 1951; Editor Prof. Y. ELIAZER; bi-monthly.

Israel Journal of Earth-Sciences: f. 1951; Editor Y. WEILER; quarterly.

Israel Journal of Mathematics: f. 1951; Editors B. WEISS, A. PAZI; monthly, 3 vols. of 4 issues each per year.

Israel Journal of Technology: f. 1951; Editor Prof. D. ABIR; 6 issues per year.

Israel Journal of Zoology: f. 1951; Editor Y. L. WERNER; quarterly.

PUBLISHERS' ASSOCIATION

Daily Newspaper Publishers' Association of Israel: P.O.B. 2251, 4 Kaplan St., Tel-Aviv; safeguards professional interests and maintains standards, supplies newsprint to dailies; negotiates with trade unions, etc.; mems. all daily papers except *Ha'aretz*; affiliated to International Federation of Newspaper Publishers.

NEWS AGENCIES

Jewish Telegraphic Agency (JTA): Israel Bureau, Jerusalem Post Building, Romema, Jerusalem 94467; Dir. DAVID LANDAU.

ITIM, News Agency of the Associated Israel Press: 10 Tiomkin Street, Tel-Aviv; f. 1950; co-operative news agency; Dir. and Editor HAYIM BALTSAN.

FOREIGN BUREAUX

Agence France-Presse: 7 Schderot Kheu, Tel-Aviv; Chief NATHAN GURDUS.

ANSA: 25 Ibn Gvirol St., Tel-Aviv; Bureau Chief REPHAEL MIGDAL.

Middle East Bureau: Jerusalem Post Bldg., Jerusalem 94 467.

The following are also represented: AP, DPA, North American Newspaper Alliance, Reuters, Tass.

PUBLISHERS

Achiasaf Ltd.: 13 Yosef Hanassi St., Tel-Aviv; f. 1933; general; Man. Dir. SCHACHMA ACHIASAF.

Am Hassefer Ltd.: 9 Bialik St., Tel-Aviv; f. 1955; Man. Dir. DOV LIPETZ.

"Am Oved" Ltd.: 22 Mazah Street, Tel-Aviv; f. 1942; fiction, scientific, sociology; textbooks, children's books; Man. Dir. N. URIELI.

Amichai Publishing House Ltd.: 5 Yosef Hanassi St., Tel-Aviv; f. 1948; Man. Dir. YEHUDA ORLINSKY.

Arabic Publishing House: 17A Hagra St., P.O.B. 28049, Tel-Aviv; f. 1960; established by the Histadrut (trade union) organization; periodicals and books; Dir. and Gen. Editor ELIAHU AGHASSI.

Bialik Institute, The: P.O.B. 92, Jerusalem; f. 1935; classics, encyclopaedias, criticism, history, archaeology, art, reference books, Judaica; Dir. CHAIM MILKOV.

Carta, The Israel Map and Publishing Co. Ltd.: Mazia St., P.O.B. 2500, Jerusalem; f. 1958; the principal cartographic publisher; Man. Dir. EMANUEL HAUSMAN.

Dvir Publishing Co. Ltd., The: 58 Mazah St., Tel-Aviv; literature, science, art, education; Man. Dir. ALEXANDER BROIDO.

Eked Publishing House: 29 Bar-Kochba St., Tel-Aviv; f. 1959; poetry; Dirs. ITAMAR YAOZ-KEST, MARITZA ROSMAN.

Gazit: 8 Zvi Brook St., Tel-Aviv, P.O.B. 4190; art publishers; Editor GABRIEL TALPHIR.

Haifa Publishing Co. Ltd.: P.O.B. 407, Haifa; f. 1960; fiction and non-fiction.

Hakibbutz Hameuchad Publishing House Ltd.: P.O.B. 16040, Pumbadita St., Tel-Aviv; f. 1940; general; Dir. A. AVISHAI.

Hamenorah Publishing House: 24 Zangwill St., Tel-Aviv; f. 1958; books in Hebrew, Yiddish and English; Dir. MORDECHAI SONNSCHEIN.

Israeli Music Publications Ltd.: 105 Ben Yehuda St., P.O.B. 6011, Tel-Aviv; f. 1949; books on music and musical works; Dir. Dr. PETER E. GRADENWITZ.

Izre'el Publishing House Ltd.: 76 Dizengoff St., Tel-Aviv; f. 1933; Man. ALEXANDER IZREEL.

Jerusalem Academic Press: Givat Shaul, P.O.B. 2390, Jerusalem; f. 1959; scientific and technical publications; Gen. Man. ITZHAK LAHAD.

Jerusalem Publishing House: 39 Tchernechovski St., Jerusalem, P.O.B. 7147; f. 1967; history, archaeology, art and other reference books; Dir. SHLOMO S. GAFNI.

Jewish Agency Publishing Department: P.O.B. 704; Jerusalem; f. 1945; Palestinology, Judaism, scientific, classics, and publicity brochures; Dir. M. SPITZER.

Karni Publishers Ltd.: 11 Yehuda Halevi St., Tel-Aviv; f. 1951; children's and educational books; Dir. SAMUEL KATZ.

Keter Publishing House Jerusalem Ltd.: P.O.B. 7145, Givat Shaul B, Jerusalem; f. 1959; original and translated works in all fields of science and humanities, published in English, French, German, other European languages and Hebrew; publishing imprints; Israel Program for Scientific Translations, Israel Universities Press, Keter Books, Encyclopaedia Judaica; Man. Dir. YITZHAK RISCHIN.

Kiryath Sepher: 15 Arlosorov St., Jerusalem; f. 1933; dictionaries, textbooks, maps, scientific books; Dir. SHALOM SIVAN (STEPANSKY).

Koren Publishers Jerusalem Ltd.: P.O.B. 407, Haifa; Zionism, archaeology, art, fiction and non-fiction.

Lewin-Epstein Ltd.: 9 Yavneh St., Tel-Aviv; f. 1930; general fiction, education, science; Man. Dir. ABRAHAM GOTTESMANN.

Magnes Press, The: The Hebrew University, Jerusalem; f. 1929; general studies; Dir. CHAIM TOREN.

Massada Ltd.: 21 Jabotinsky Rd., Ramat Gan; f. 1931; art, encyclopaedias, literature; Chairmen Mrs. BRACHA PELI, ALEXANDER PELI; Man. Dir. YOAV BARASH.

Ministry of Defence Publishing House: Hakiriya, Tel-Aviv; f. 1939; military literature; Dir. AHARON NIV. MA'ARACHOT.

M. Mizrachi Publishers: 19 Y. L. Peretz, Tel-Aviv; f. 1960; children's books; Dir. MEIR MIZRACHI.

Otsar Hamoreh: 8 Ben Saruk, Tel-Aviv; f. 1951; educational; Dir. MENACHEM LEVANON.

Y. L. Peretz: 31 Allenby Rd., Tel-Aviv; f. 1956; mainly books in Yiddish; Man. Dir. MOSHE GERSHONOWITZ.

Rubin Mass: 11 Marcus St., P.O.B. 990, Jerusalem; f. 1927; Hebraica, Judaica; Dir. RUBIN MASS.

Schocken Publishing House Ltd.: P.O.B. 2316, Tel-Aviv; f. 1938; general; Dir. Mrs. RACHELI EDELMAN.

Shikmona Publishing Co. Ltd.: P.O.B. 407, Haifa; Bible, religion and Judaism.

Sifriat-Ma'ariv Ltd.: Ma'ariv House, 2 Carlebach St., Tel-Aviv; f. 1954; general; Man. YAKIR WEINSTEIN.

Sifriat Poalim Ltd.: 73 Allenby St., P.O.B. 526, Tel-Aviv 65-171; f. 1939; textbooks; Gen. Man. YAAKOV ZVIELI.

Sinai Publishing Co.: 72 Allenby Rd., Tel-Aviv; Hebrew books and religious articles; Dir. AKNAH SCHLESINGER.

Tarbut Ve'Hinuch Publishers: 93 Arlozorov St., Tel-Aviv; f. 1956; educational; Man. IZAAK KOTUNSKY.

Tarhish Books: P.O.B. 4130, 91-040 Jerusalem; f. 1940; plays, poetry, bibliophile, classics; Man. Dir. Dr. MOSHE SPITZER.

Weidenfeld and Nicolson Jerusalem Ltd.: 19 Herzog St., P.O.B. 7545, Jerusalem; branch of the London publishing company; established in Israel 1969; Man. Dir. ASHER WEILL.

Weizmann Science Press of Israel: 33 King George Ave., P.O.B. 801, Jerusalem 91000; f. 1951; publishes scientific books and periodicals; Man. Dir. RAMI MICHAELI; Exec. Editor L. LESTER.

Yachdav United Publishers Co. Ltd.: 29 Carlebach St., P.O.B. 1317, Tel-Aviv; f. 1960; educational; Chair. MORDECHAI BERNSTEIN; Dir. BENJAMIN SELLA.

Yavneh Ltd.: 4 Mazeh St., Tel-Aviv; f. 1932; general; Dir. YEHOSHUA ORENSTEIN.

S. Zack and Co.: 2 King George St., Jerusalem; f. c. 1930; reference books; Dirs. DAVID and MICHAEL ZACK.

Israel Book Publishers Association: 29 Carlebach St., P.O.B. 1317, Tel-Aviv; f. 1939; mems.: 74 publishing firms; Chair. MORDECHAI BERNSTEIN; Sec.-Gen. BENJAMIN SELLA.

Jerusalem International Book Fair: P.O.B. 1508, Jerusalem 91000; takes place in alternate years; more than 600 publishing firms from 30 countries were represented in 1973.

RADIO AND TELEVISION

RADIO

Israel Broadcasting Authority (I.B.A.): 21 Heleni Hamalka, Jerusalem; f. 1948; station, Jerusalem with studios in Tel-Aviv and Haifa; Dir.-Gen. S. ALMOG. I.B.A. broadcasts five programmes for local and overseas listeners on medium, shortwave and VHF/FM in twelve languages; Hebrew, Arabic, English, Yiddish, Ladino, Romanian, Hungarian, Moghrabit, Persian, French, Russian and Georgian.

Number of radio receivers: 700,000.

TELEVISION

Programmes for schools started in spring 1966, and programmes for the general public, run by the Israel Broadcasting Authority, began in 1967.

Instructional Television Centre: Ministry of Education and Culture, Tel-Aviv; f. 1963 by Hanadiv (Rothschild Memorial Group) as Instructional Television Centre; began transmissions in 1966; now broadcasts on a national scale to 1,300 schools with 540,000 pupils, 70 per cent of the high school population; the programmes form an integral part of the syllabus in a wide range of subjects.

Number of TV receivers: 440,000.

FINANCE

(cap.=capital; p.u.=paid up; dep.=deposits; m.=million;
I£=Israeli £; brs.=branches.)

BANKING

CENTRAL BANK

Bank of Israel: Mizpeh Building, 29 Jaffa Rd., Jerusalem,
P.O.B. 780; f. 1954 as the Central Bank of the State of
Israel; (Dec. 1973) cap. I£20m., dep. I£15,448m.; Gov.
MOSHE SANBAR; Dir.-Gen. Dr. E. SHEFFER, Mans. M.
HETH, J. SARIG, S. LEVI, Z. SUSSMAN, M. MEIREV, S.
PELED; 2 brs.; publs. *Annual Report, Economic Review,
Banking Statistics* (monthly).

ISRAELI BANKS

Arab Israel Bank Ltd.: 14 Hatishim Veshalosh St., Haifa;
f. 1959 to serve primarily the Arab sector of the
economy; cap. p.u. I£3.5m., dep. I£63.9m. (Dec. 1972);
Chair. B. YEKUTIELI; Gen. Man. S. SHAUL.

Bank Hapoalim B.M.: 50 Rothschild Blvd., Tel-Aviv;
f. 1921; cap. p.u. I£81.9m., dep. I£9,140m. (Dec.
1972); Man. Dirs. J. LEVINSON (Chair.), E. AVNEYON,
A. DICKENSTEIN, E. MARGALIT, B. RABINOW, M.
OLENIK; 202 brs.

Bank Lemelacha Ltd.: 9 Carlebach St., Tel-Aviv; f. 1953;
cap. p.u. I£17.7m., dep. I£117.4m. (Dec. 1973); Chair.
Dov KANTOROWITZ; Man. Dir. A. FEIN; 14 brs.

Bank Leumi le-Israel B.M.: 24–32 Yehuda Halevy St.,
Tel-Aviv; f. 1902; cap. p.u. I£143.1m., dep. I£16,053m.
(1973); Chair. M. H. SACHS; Man. Dir. and Chief Exec.
E. I. JAPHET; 228 brs.; publ. *Review of Economic
Conditions in Israel* (quarterly).

First International Bank of Israel Ltd.: 18/20 Lincoln St.,
P.O.B. 20185, Tel-Aviv; f. 1972 as a result of a merger
between The Foreign Trade Bank Ltd. and Export
Bank Ltd.; Chair. of Board MARK MOSEVICS; Man.
Dir. DAVID GOLAN; 36 brs.

Israel American Industrial Development Bank Ltd.: 50
Rothschild Blvd., Tel-Aviv; f. 1956; cap. p.u. I£12m.;
dep. I£196m. (Dec. 1973); Chair. A. DICKENSTEIN;
Gen. Man. H. DUVSHANI.

Israel Bank of Agriculture Ltd.: 83 Hashmonayim St.,
Tel-Aviv; f. 1951; cap. p.u. I£171.8m., dep. I£500.2m.
(March 1973); Chair. Prof. H. HALPERIN; Man. Dir.
D. CALDERON.

Israel British Bank Ltd.: 20 Rothschild Blvd., Tel-Aviv;
f. 1929; cap. p.u. and reserves I£55m., dep. I£879m.
(Dec. 1972); Chair. HARRY LANDY; Man. Dirs. JOSHUA
BENSION, DAVID HERSHKOVITZ; 8 brs.

Israel Discount Bank Ltd.: 27–29 Yehuda Halevy St., Tel-
Aviv; f. 1935; cap. p.u. I£60m., dep. I£7,998m. (Dec.
1972); Chair. DANIEL RECANATI; Vice-Chair. RAPHAEL
RECANATI; 147 brs.

Israel General Bank Ltd.: 28 Achad Ha'am St., Tel-Aviv;
f. 1964; cap. p.u. I£4.5m., dep. I£197.4m. (Dec. 1972);
Chair. Baron EDMOND DE ROTHSCHILD; Man. Dir.
DAVID SHOHAM; 3 brs.

Israel Industrial Bank Ltd.: 13 Montefiore St., Tel-Aviv;
f. 1933; cap.p.u. I£12.03m., dep. I£205.3m. (Dec. 1973);
Chair. A. FROMCENKO; Man. Dir. A. D. KIMCHI; 9 brs.

Israel Loan and Savings Bank Ltd.: 21 Herzl St., Tel-
Aviv; cap. I£10.3m.; Chair. E. AVEYNON; Man. Dir.
I. GAFNI.

Japhet Bank Ltd.: 11 Rothschild Blvd., Tel-Aviv; f. 1933;
subsidiary of Bank Hapoalim B.M.; cap. p.u. I£7m.,
dep. I£378.1 m.(Dec. 1972); Chair. E. MARGALIT; Man.
Dir. P. ALROY; 13 brs.

Kupat Am Bank Ltd.: 13 Ahad Ha'am St., P.O.B. 352,
Tel-Aviv; f. 1918; cap. p.u. I£2m., dep. I£165.8m (Dec.
1972); Chair. B. YEKUTIELI; Man. Dir. M. GEFEN; 14
brs.

Mercantile Bank of Israel Ltd.: 24 Rothschild Blvd.,
Tel-Aviv; f. 1924; subsidiary of Israel Discount Bank;
cap. p.u. I£2m., dep. I£102m. (Dec. 1972); Chair.
DANIEL RECANATI; Gen. Man. SHLOMO MAGRISO.

Union Bank of Israel Ltd.: 6–8 Ahuzat Bayit St., P.O.B.
2428, Tel-Aviv; f. 1951; subsidiary of Bank Leumi
le-Israel B.M.; cap. p.u. I£13.8m., dep. I£1,260.9m.
(Dec. 1972); Chair. E. I. JAPHET; Gen. Mans. W. HAUCK,
M. MAYER; 15 brs.; publ. *Newsletter* (monthly).

United Mizrahi Bank Ltd.: 48 Lilienblum St., Tel-Aviv; f.
1923; cap. p.u. I£29.6m., dep. I£1,271.5m. (Dec. 1973);
Chair. N. FEINGOLD; Gen. Man. A. MEIR; 44 brs.

MORTGAGE BANKS

General Mortgage Bank Ltd.: 13 Ahad Ha'am St., Tel-Aviv;
f. 1921; subsidiary of Bank Leumi le-Israel B.M.;
cap. p.u. I£18.2m., dep. I£510.5m. (Dec. 1972); Chair.
E. LEHMANN; Gen. Mans. Y. BACH, M. KAHAN.

Housing Mortgage Bank Ltd.: 115 Allenby St., Tel-Aviv; f.
1951; subsidiary of Bank Hapoalim B.M.; cap. p.u.
I£12.0m., dep. I£230.2m. (Dec. 1971); Chair. A. OFFER.

Israel Development and Mortgage Bank Ltd.: 16 Simtat
Beit Hashoeva, Tel-Aviv; f. 1959; subsidiary of Israel
Discount Bank Ltd.; Gen. Mans. K. REICH, A. VREED-
ENBURG.

Tefahot, Israel Mortgage Bank Ltd.: 9 Heleni Hamalka
St., Jerusalem; f. 1945; cap. p.u. I£58m.; Chair.
JOSEPH SHARON; Man. Dir. MOSHE MANN.

Unico Mortgage and Investment Bank Ltd.: Shalom Tower,
9 Ahad Ha'am Street, Tel-Aviv; f. 1961.

FOREIGN BANKS

Barclays Discount Bank Ltd.: 103 Allenby Rd., Tel-Aviv;
f. 1971 in association with Israel Discount Bank Ltd.
incorporating former brs. of Barclays Bank International Ltd.; cap. p.u. I£11m.; Chair. DANIEL
RECANATI; Gen. Man. RAPHAEL MOLHO; 49 brs.
Affiliated bank: **Mercantile Bank of Israel Ltd.,** 24
Rothschild Blvd., Tel-Aviv.

Exchange National Bank of Chicago: 9 Ahad Ha'am St.,
Shalom Tower, Tel-Aviv 65251; f. 1970; Vice-Pres. and
Gen. Man. AVIEZER CHELOUCHE; 1 br.

STOCK EXCHANGE

Tel-Aviv Stock Exchange: 113 Allenby Rd.; Chair. Dr. E.
LEHMANN; Vice-Chair. D. RECANATI; Exec. Dir. D.
OTENSOOSER; publs. *Official Quotations* (daily, monthly,
annually), *Financial Structure and Performance of
Companies Listed on the Tel-Aviv Stock Exchange*
(annual).

INSURANCE

Ararat Insurance Company Ltd.: Ararat House, 32 Yavneh
St., Tel-Aviv; f. 1949; Man. Dir. PHILIP ZUCKERMAN.

Aryeh Insurance Co. Ltd.: Shalom Tower, Tel-Aviv; f.
1948; Chair. AVINOAM M. TOCATLY.

Hassneh Insurance Co. of Israel Ltd.: 115 Allenby St., P.O.B. 805, Tel-Aviv; f. 1929; Chair. MICHAEL NUSSBAUM.

Israel Phoenix Assurance Company Ltd., The: 30 Levontin St., Tel-Aviv; f. 1949; Chair. of Board and Man. Dir. DAVID J. HACKMEY.

Israel Reinsurance Company Ltd., The: 7 Shadal St., P.O.B. 2037, Tel-Aviv; f. 1951; Chair. Board of Dirs. A. SACHAROV; Gen. Man. S. JANNAI.

Maoz Insurance Co. Ltd.: 36 Lilienblum St., Tel-Aviv; f. 1945; formerly Binyan Insurance Co. Ltd.; Chair. Y. GRUENGARD.

Mazada Insurance Service Ltd.: 3 Ahuzat Bait St., Tel-Aviv; f. 1932; Mans. S. SPIGELMAN, A. SPIGELMAN.

Menorah Insurance and Reinsurance Company Ltd.: Menorah House, 73 Rothschild Blvd., Tel-Aviv; f. 1935; Gen. Man. DAVID HIRSCHFELD.

Migdal-Binyan Insurance Co. Ltd.: 53 Rothschild Blvd., Tel-Aviv; f. 1934; Chair. A. LEHMAN; Man. Dir. J. GRUENGARD.

Palglass Palestine Plate Glass Insurance Co. Ltd.: 30 Achad Ha'am St., Tel-Aviv; f. 1934; Gen. Man. AKIVA ZALZMAN.

Sahar Insurance Company Ltd.: Sahar House, 23 Ben-Yehuda St., Tel-Aviv; f. 1949; Chair. and Man. Dir. A. SHAROV.

Samson Insurance Co. Ltd.: 27 Montefiore St., P.O.B. 29277, Tel-Aviv; f. 1933; Chair. M. NUSSBAUM.

Sela Insurance Co. Ltd.: 6 Ahuzat Bait St., Tel-Aviv; f. 1938; Man. Dir. S. P. LUSTIG.

Shiloah Company Ltd.: 2 Pinsker St., Tel-Aviv; f. 1933; Gen. Man. R. S. BAMIRAH; Man. Mme BAMIRAH.

Yardenia Insurance Company Ltd.: 22 Maze Street, Tel-Aviv; f. 1948; Gen. Man. H. LEBANON.

Yuval Insurance Co. Ltd.: 27 Keren Hayesod, Jerusalem; f. 1962; Man. Dir. J. KAPLAN.

Zigug Glass Insurance Co. Ltd.: 34 Sheinkin St., Tel-Aviv; f. 1952; Chair. D. HIRSCHFELD.

Zion Insurance Company Ltd.: 120 Allenby Rd., Tel-Aviv; f. 1935; Chair. HAIM TAIBER.

THE HISTADRUT

Hahistadrut Haklalit shel Haovdim Beeretz Israel, 93 Arlosoroff Street, Tel-Aviv.

(GENERAL FEDERATION OF LABOUR IN ISRAEL)

Secretary-General: YERUHAM MESHEL (acting).

The General Federation of Labour in Israel, usually known as the Histadrut, is the largest voluntary organization in Israel, and the most important economic body in the State. It is open to all workers, including members of co-operatives and of the liberal professions, who join directly as individuals. The Histadrut engages in four main fields of activity: trade union organization; economic development; social insurance based on mutual aid; and educational and cultural activities. Dues—between 2.5 per cent and 4.5 per cent of wages (up to I£1,000) —cover all its trade union, health and social services activities. The Histadrut was founded in 1920.

ORGANIZATION

In 1973 the Histadrut had a membership of 1,230,200, including over 150,000 in collective, co-operative and private villages (*kibbutzim and moshavim*), affiliated through the Agricultural Workers' Union, and 324,777 wives (who have membership status); 87,916 of the members were Arabs. In addition some 100,000 young people under 18 years of age belong to the Organization of Working and Student Youth, a direct affiliate of the Histadrut. The main religious labour organizations, *Histadrut Hapoel Hamizrahi* and *Histadrut Poalei Agudat Israel*, belong to the trade union section and welfare services, which thus extend to 90 per cent of all workers in Israel.

All members take part in elections to the Histadrut Convention (*Veida*), which elects the General Council (*Moetsa*) and the Executive Committee (*Vaad Hapoel*). The latter elects the 19-member Executive Bureau (*Vaada Merakezet*), which is responsible for day-to-day implementation of policy. The Executive Committee also elects the Secretary-General, who acts as its chairman as well as head of the organization as a whole and chairman of the Executive Bureau. Nearly all political parties are represented on the Histadrut Executive Committee. Throughout Israel there are 72 local Labour Councils.

The Executive Committee has the following departments: Trade Union, Arab Affairs, Mutual Aid, Organization, International, Finance, Legal, Employment, Vocational Training, Absorption and Development, Academic Workers, Pensions, Religious Affairs and Higher Education.

TRADE UNION ACTIVITIES

Collective agreements with employers fix wage scales, which are linked with the retail price index; provide for social benefits, including paid sick leave and employers' contributions to sick and pension and provident funds; and regulate dismissals. Dismissal compensation, until recently fixed by collective agreements, is now regulated by law. The Histadrut actively promotes productivity through labour management boards and the National Productivity Institute, and supports incentive pay schemes.

OFFICERS AND PUBLICATIONS

The principal officers engaged in the Histadrut are as follows:

Secretary-General: YERUHAM MESHEL (acting).

Deputy Secretary-General: YERUHAM MESHEL.

Secretary of Labour Economy (Hevrat Odim): ASHER YADLIN.

Chairman of Trade Union Department: URIEL ABRAHAMOVICZ.

Chairman of Mutual Aid and Insurance Department: AHARON EFRAT.

Chairman of Culture and Education Department: RAPHAEL BASH.

Chairman of Sports and Youth Department: ISRAEL KEISAR.

Treasurer: YEHOSHUA LEVI.

Chairman of Organization Department: AHARON HAREL.

The principal newspapers and periodicals published by the Histadrut are as follows:

Davar (*The Word*) (daily), *Omer* (daily), *Dvar Hashavua* (illustrated weekly), *Davar Liyeladim* (children's weekly), *Devar Hapoalet* (women's monthly), *Israel au Travail* (French, monthly), *Labour in Israel* (English, monthly), *Trabajo en Israel* (Spanish, monthly). (*See* also Press section.)

ECONOMIC ACTIVITIES

General Co-operative Association of Labour in Israel (*Hevrat Ovdim*): Every member of the Histadrut is simultaneously a member of Hevrat Ovdim, and therefore a part-owner in its economy, whether or not he works within its framework. This labour economy includes a variety of structural forms, falling into two main types: co-operative societies run by their own members, such as all *kibbutzim* and *moshavim* and the producer, service, transport and consumer co-operatives; and the collectively-owned enterprises which are initiated by Hevrat Ovdim.

EDUCATION AND CULTURE

The Centre for Education and Culture: 93 Arlosoroff Street, Tel-Aviv; initiates, plans and co-ordinates activities on a national scale, among them immigrant education courses, evening courses for adults, a theatre company, and numerous choirs, folk-dance groups and popular art circles; arranges theatrical performances and concerts in rural centres, supplies films weekly to agricultural villages and produces its own documentary films.

Amal: 93 Arlosoroff Street, Tel-Aviv; a special Histadrut department to operate and co-ordinate a network of 32 technical high schools.

The Organization of Working and Student Youth: 91 Hachashmonaim St., Tel-Aviv; for young people under the age of 18 who have commenced work or are still at secondary school; 100,000 mems.

Hapoel: 8 Haarba St., P.O.B. 7170, Tel-Aviv; f. 1926; the Histadrut sports organization; 600 brs. with 92,500 mems.

The Women Workers' Council (*Moetzet Hapoalot*) and **Union of Working Mothers** (*Irgun Imahot Ovdot*): 93 Arlosoroff Street, Tel-Aviv; cover both women workers and women members who do no paid outside work but actively help in the absorption of immigrants, the welfare of children of members, the promotion of education programmes for women, including the eradication of illiteracy, good citizenship courses and consumers' activities, etc.; 518 day-care centres for 16,910 children; vocational and agricultural training for 6,000 boys, girls and women; over 250 club rooms for both Jewish and Arab women.

INTERNATIONAL RELATIONS

The Histadrut is affiliated to the International Confederation of Free Trade Unions, is active in the International Labour Organization and the International Co-operative Alliance, and has active and friendly relations with labour movements all over the world. Most of its national unions are affiliated to their respective International Trade Secretariats.

Afro-Asian Institute for Co-operation and Labour Studies: P.O.B. 16201, Tel-Aviv; f. 1960; has conducted courses for over 4,700 participants from 89 countries.

Centre for Labour and Co-operative Studies for Latin America: f. 1962; has conducted courses for some 1,500 participants from all the countries of Latin America, and from the Caribbean.

TRADE AND INDUSTRY

CHAMBERS OF COMMERCE

Joint Representation of the Israeli Chambers of Commerce: P.O.B. 501, Tel-Aviv; co-ordinates the Tel-Aviv, Jerusalem and Haifa Chambers of Commerce; Sec. F. B. WAHLE.

Jerusalem Chamber of Commerce: P.O.B. 183, 10 Hillel St., Jerusalem; f. 1908; about 300 mems.; Pres. M. H. ELIACHAR; Vice-Pres. A. P. MICHAELIS, A. DASKAL, Y. PEARLMAN, A. ASHBEL, E. BODENKIN; publ. *Bulletin* (Hebrew and English).

Haifa Chamber of Commerce and Industry (*Haifa and District*): P.O.B. 176, 53 Haatzmaut Rd., Haifa; f. 1921; 700 mems.; Pres. JOSEPH ROSH; Gen. Sec. A. MEHOULAL.

Chamber of Commerce, Tel-Aviv-Jaffa: P.O.B. 501, 84 Hachashmonaim St., Tel-Aviv; f. 1919; 1,200 mems.; Pres. A. BENYAKAR; Secs. D. GRAJCAR, F. B. WAHLE; publ. *Hamishar*.

Federation of Bi-National Chambers of Commerce with and in Israel: 82 Allenby Rd., Tel-Aviv; federates: Israel-America Chamber of Commerce and Industry; Anglo-Israel Chamber of Commerce; Australia-Israel Chamber of Commerce; Chamber of Commerce and Industry Israel-Africa and the Malagasy Republic; Chambre de Commerce Israel-Belgique-Luxembourg; Canada-Israel Chamber of Commerce and Industry; Israel-Danish Chamber of Commerce; Chambre de Commerce Israel-France; Chamber of Commerce and Industry Israel-Germany; Camera di Commercio Israel-Italia; Israel-Japan Chamber of Commerce; Israel-Latin America Chamber of Commerce; Netherlands-Israel Chamber of Commerce; Israel-Norway Chamber of Commerce; Handelskammer Israel-Schweiz; Israel-South Africa Chamber of Commerce; Israel-Sweden Chamber of Commerce; Chair. A. CHELOUCHE; Exec. Dir. H. ZUCKERMAN, O.B.E.; and also incorporates Bi-National Chambers of Commerce existing in 20 foreign countries with Israel.

Anglo-Israel Chamber of Commerce (Israel): 82 Allenby Rd., Tel-Aviv, P.O.B. 1127; f. 1951; 400 mems.; Joint Pres. Dr. A. S. ARNON, C.B.E., A. S. COHEN, C.B.E.; Chair. E. IZAKSON.

TRADE AND INDUSTRIAL ORGANIZATIONS

The Agricultural Union: Tchlenov 20, Tel-Aviv; consists of more than 50 agricultural settlements and is connected with marketing and supplying organizations, and Bahan Ltd., controllers and auditors.

Central Union of Artisans and Small Manufacturers: P.O.B. 4041, Tel-Aviv; f. 1907; has a membership of 40,000 divided into 70 groups according to trade; the union is led by a seventeen-man Presidium; Chair. JACOB FRANK; Gen. Sec. PINHAS SCHWARTZ; publ. *Hamlakha;* 30 brs.

Citrus Control and Marketing Boards: 69 Haifa Rd., Tel-Aviv; the government-established institution for the control of the Israel citrus industry; Boards made up of representatives of the Government and the Growers. Functions: Control of plantations, supervision of picking and packing operations; marketing of the crop overseas and on the home markets; shipping: supply of fertilisers, insecticides, equipment for orchards and packing houses and of packing materials, technical research and extension work; long-term financial assistance to growers.

Farmers' Federation: P.O.B. 209, Tel-Aviv; has a membership of 7,000 independent farmers and citrus growers; Pres. ZVI IZACKSON; Dir.-Gen. ITZHAK ZIV-AV; publ. *The Israeli Farmer* (monthly).

General Association of Merchants in Israel: 6 Rothschild Boulevard, Tel-Aviv; the organization of retail traders; has a membership of 30,000 in 60 brs.

Israel Diamond Exchange Ltd.: P.O.B. 3222, Ramat Gan; f. 1937; production, export, import and finance facilities; estimated exports (1974) U.S. $600m.

Israel Journalists' Association Ltd.: 4 Kaplan St., Tel-Aviv; Sec. MOSHE RON.

Manufacturers' Association of Israel: 13 Montefiore St., P.O.B. 29116, Tel-Aviv; Pres. MARK MOSEVICS; Gen. Man. Col. PELEG TAMIR; Gen. Sec. A. Z. CRYSTAL, F.C.C.S.; publ. *News Bulletin* (every two months).

TRADE UNIONS

Histadrut Haovdim Haleumit (*National Labour Federation*): 23 Sprinczak St., Tel-Aviv; f. 1934; 84,000 mems.; publs. *Hazit Ha 'Oved, Lapid.*

Histadrut Hapoel Hamizrahi (*Mizrahi Workers' Organization*): 108 Ahad Haam St., Tel-Aviv; has 55,000 members in 75 settlements.

Histadrut Poalei Agudat Israel (*Agudat Israel Workers' Organization*): Geula Quarter, Corner Yehezkel St., Jerusalem; has 19,000 members in 12 settlements.

TRANSPORT

RAILWAYS

Israel Railways: P.O.B. 44, Haifa; a department of the Ministry of Transport. All its lines are managed and operated from Haifa. The total length of mainline track in operation is 789 km. Traction is wholly diesel.

The main flow of traffic is from Haifa Port and from the oil installations and industrial centres in the vicinity of Haifa and of minerals from Beersheba, Dimona and Oron, to the north. The bulk of freight traffic consists of grain, cement and building materials, heavy bulk imported commodities, minerals, phosphates and potash, and oils. Passenger traffic is operated between the main towns: Jerusalem, Tel-Aviv, Haifa, Beersheba, Dimona and Nahariya.

Gen. Man. Col. Y. RESHEF; Principal Asst. LEA STEINMETZ.

UNDERGROUND RAILWAYS

Haifa Underground Funicular Railway: Haifa; opened 1959; 2 km. in operation; Man. D. SCHARF.

Tel-Aviv Rapid Transit: Municipal Offices, Tel-Aviv-Jaffa Municipality; a feasibility study has been made on the possibility of building a 48 km. rapid transit line (11 km. underground).

ROADS

Ministry of Labour, Public Works Dept., Jerusalem.

There are 3,700 km. of metalled main roads not including roads in towns and settlements. Under a five-year plan ending in 1975 the following works will be completed:

One hundred km. new roads to be built, 25 km. additional two-lanes for existing roads, 400 km. widening and improving existing roads.

In addition, a 150-mile long first-class road was built between Eilat and Sharm el-Sheikh during 1970-71.

Automobile and Touring Club of Israel (ATCI): 19 Petah Tiqva Rd., P.O.B. 36144, Tel-Aviv 66183; f. 1949; over 11,000 mems.; Sec.-Gen. Mrs. C. NAHMIAS; publ. *Memsi* (monthly).

SHIPPING

The Israel Ports Authority: Maya Building, 74 Petah Tiqva Rd., Tel-Aviv; f. 1961; to plan, build, develop, administer, maintain and operate the ports. In 1973–74 investment will amount to I£77m. for the Development Budget in Haifa, Ashdod and Eilat Ports. Cargo traffic in 1972–73 amounted to 8.4m. tons (oil excluded).

ZIM Israel Navigation Co. Ltd.: 209 Hameginim Ave., P.O.B. 1723, Haifa; f. 1945; runs cargo services in the Mediterranean and to N. Europe, N. and S. America, Far East, Africa and Australia; Chair. M. TZUR; Man. Dir. M. KASHTI.

Cargo Ships "El-Yam" Ltd: P.O.B. 182, Haifa; f. 1952; Man. Dir. RAPHAEL RECANATI; a world-wide cargo tramp service.

Maritime Fruit Carriers Co. Ltd.: 53 Shderot Hameginim, P.O.B. 1501, Haifa; refrigerated cargo services; Chair. YAACOV MERIDOR; Man. Dir. MILA BRENER.

Haifa and Ashdod are the main ports in Israel. The former is a natural harbour, enclosed by two main breakwaters and dredged to 37 ft. below mean sea-level. An auxiliary harbour was opened in 1955. In 1965 the new deep water port was completed at Ashdod which has a capacity of about 4 million tons per year. The Tel-Aviv/Jaffa ports were closed down in 1965 as their facilities were no longer adequate for Israel's needs.

Israel has a merchant fleet of 107 ships, with a displacement of over 1,600,000 tons.

The port of Eilat is Israel's gate to the Red Sea. It is a natural harbour, operated from a wharf. A new port, to the south of the original one, started operating in 1965.

CIVIL AVIATION

El Al Israel Airlines Ltd.: P.O.B. 41, Lod Airport, Tel-Aviv; f. 1949; daily services to most capitals of Europe; over twenty flights weekly to New York; services to Johannesburg, Teheran, Nairobi, Addis Ababa,

Nicosia, Istanbul, Bucharest and Montreal; fleet of two Boeing 720B, three Boeing 707-420, three Boeing 707-320B, two Boeing 707-320C, two Boeing 747B; Pres. M. BEN-ARI.

Arkia, Israel Inland Airlines Ltd.: 88 Ha'Hashmonaim St., Tel-Aviv; f. 1950; scheduled services from Tel-Aviv and Jerusalem to Eilat, Rosh Pina, Haifa, Massada, Abu Rodes, Ophira (Sharm-el-Sheikh) and Santa Katarina; fleet of five Viscounts, four Heralds; Man. Dir. L. BIGON.

The following airlines also serve Israel: Air France, Alitalia, AUA, British Airways, Canadian Pacific, Cyprus Airways, KLM, Lufthansa, Olympic Airways, Sabena, SAS, Swissair, Tarom, THY, TWA.

TOURISM

Ministry of Tourism: Hakirya, P.O.B. 1018, Jerusalem; information offices at Jerusalem, Tel-Aviv, Haifa, Nazareth, Safed, Lod International Airport, Beersheba, Tiberias, Ashkelon, Arad, Bethlehem, Acre, Netanya, Nahariya and Eilat; Minister of Tourism MOSHE KOL; Dir.-Gen. H. GIVTON; publs. *Annual Report, Statistical Year-Book.*

There are also offices in the following countries: England (London), France (Paris), German Federal Republic (Frankfurt), Italy (Rome), Netherlands (Amsterdam), Switzerland (Zürich), Sweden (Stockholm), U.S.A. (New York, Chicago, Boston, Beverly Hills, Atlanta), Argentina (Buenos Aires), Canada (Montreal, Toronto), Denmark (Copenhagen), Belgium (Brussels), South Africa (Johannesburg), Brazil (São Paulo), Australia (Sydney).

CULTURAL ORGANIZATIONS

The Israel Festival: 52 Nachlat Benjamin St., Tel-Aviv, P.O.B. 29874; organizes the Israel Festival which takes place in July/August in Caesarea, Jerusalem and Tel-Aviv; Dir. A. Z. PROPES.

Israel Music Institute: P.O.B. 11253, Tel-Aviv; f. 1961; publishes and promotes Israeli music and musicological works abroad; member since 1969 of International Music Information Centre; Chair. URI TOEPLITZ; Man. Dir. WILLIAM ELIAS.

The National Council of Culture and Art: Hadar Daphna Bldg., Shaul Hamelech Blvd., Tel-Aviv.

PRINCIPAL THEATRES

Cameri Theatre: Tel-Aviv; f. 1944; public trusteeship; repertory theatre; tours abroad.

Habimah National Theatre of Israel: P.O.B. 222, Tel-Aviv; f. 1918 in Russia, moved to Palestine 1928; Jewish, classical and modern drama.

Israel National Opera and Israel National Opera Ballet: 1 Allenby St., Tel-Aviv; f. 1947 by Edis de-Philippe (Dir.); classical and modern opera and ballet; open 50 weeks of the year.

PRINCIPAL ORCHESTRAS

Haifa Symphony Orchestra: 50 Pevsner St., Haifa; Music Dir. SAMUEL FRIEDMAN.

Israel Chamber Orchestra: 103 Ibn Gvirol St., Tel-Aviv; f. 1965; 42 mems.; Artistic Dir. GARY BERTINI.

Israel Philharmonic Orchestra: Frederic R. Mann Auditorium, Tel-Aviv; f. 1936 by Bronislaw Huberman; 106 mems.; frequent tours abroad; 35,000 subscribers; Musical Adviser ZUBIN MEHTA; Concertmasters CHAIM TAUB, URI PIANKA.

The Jerusalem Broadcasting Symphony Orchestra: Israel Broadcasting Authority, P.O.B. 1082, Jerusalem; f. 1938; 80 mems.; Dir. YEHUDA FICKLER; Chief Conductor LUKAS FOSS.

DANCE TROUPES

Bat-Dor Dance Company: 30 Ibn Gvirol St., Tel-Aviv; contemporary repertory dance company; owns theatre in Tel-Aviv; frequent tours abroad; operates Bat-Dor Studios of Dance; Producer BATSHEVA DE ROTHSCHILD; Artistic Dir. JEANNETTE ORDMAN.

Batsheva Dance Company: 9 Sderot Hahaskala, Tel-Aviv.

Inbal Dance Theatre: Tel-Aviv; f. 1949; modern Israeli dance theatre specializing in their traditional folk art, with choreographic themes from the Bible; frequent tours abroad; Founder and Artistic Dir. SARA LEVI-TANAI.

FESTIVALS

Israel Festival of Music and Drama: Caesarea; international festival; of music, dance and drama; f. 1961; one month annually July-August; organized by Israeli Festival Association.

Ein Gev Music Festival: Kibbutz Ein Gev, Kinneret; international festival; annually for one week at Passover.

Zimriya: World Assembly of Choirs, comprising Israeli and international choirs; f. 1952; triennial; next assembly 1976.

ATOMIC ENERGY

Israel Atomic Energy Commission: 26 Rehov Ha Universita, Ramat Aviv, Tel-Aviv; and P.O.B. 17120, Tel-Aviv; f. 1952; advises the Government on policies in nuclear research, supervises the implementation of approved policies and represents Israel in its relations with scientific institutions abroad and international organizations engaged in nuclear research and development (Israel is a member of IAEA); Chair. The PRIME MINISTER; Dir.-Gen. SHALHEVETH FREIER.

The Atomic Energy Commission has two research and development centres: the Soreq Nuclear Research Centre and the Negev Nuclear Research Centre near Dimona. The main fields of research are: nuclear physics and chemistry, reactor physics, reactor engineering, radiation research and applications, application of isotopes, metallurgy, eletronics, radiobiology, nuclear medicine, nuclear power and desalination. The centres also provide national services: health physics including film badge service, isotope production and molecule labelling, activation analysis, irradiation, advice to industry and institutions, training of personnel, technical courses, documentation.

Soreq Nuclear Research Centre: Yavne; f. 1952; equipped with a swimming pool type research reactor IRR-1 of 5 MW thermal; Dir. Prof. I. PELAH.

Negev Nuclear Research Centre: Dimona; equipped with a natural uranium fuelled and heavy water moderated reactor IRR-2 of 26 MW thermal; Dir. JOSEPH TULIPMAN.

Weizmann Institute of Science: Rehovot; in the field of atomic energy, the Institute's equipment includes a 15 MeV Van de Graaff accelerator and a product on-scale plant for the separation of O^{17} and O^{18} from O^{16} Dirs. Prof. IGAL TALMI (Nuclear Physics), Prof. FRITZ KLEIN (Isotope Research).

The Hebrew University of Jerusalem: Jerusalem; engages in atomic research and teaching in chemistry, physics biology and medicine.

Technion: Israel Institute of Technology: Haifa; the Dept. of Physics engages in undergraduate teaching in physics and engineering, as well as graduate teaching and research mainly in nuclear physics, high energy physics, foundations of quantum mechanics, atomic physics, relativity and astrophysics and related fields; the Dept. of Nuclear Engineering undertakes teaching and graduate work in applied nuclear science and engineering; research groups work in the fields of theoretical and experimental nuclear reactor physics, neutron physics, nuclear desalination, heat transfer, nuclear radiations; Head, Nuclear Engineering Dept. Prof. N. SHAFRIR; Chair., Dept. of Physics Prof. P. SINGER.

UNIVERSITIES

Bar-Ilan University: Ramat-Gan; 698 teachers, 6,241 students.

Haifa University: Mount Carmel, Haifa; 652 teachers, 5,000 students.

The Hebrew University of Jerusalem: Jerusalem; 1,955 teachers, 16,000 students.

University of the Negev: P.O.B. 2053, Beersheba; 385 teachers, 3,200 students.

Tel-Aviv University: Ramat-Aviv, Tel-Aviv; 2,086 teachers, 16,384 students.

Technion, Israel Institute of Technology: Haifa; 1,445 teachers, 6,260 undergraduate, 3,300 graduate students.

Weizmann Institute of Science, Feinberg Graduate School: Rehovot; 650 students.

IVORY COAST

INTRODUCTORY SURVEY

Location, Climate, Language, Religion, Flag, Capital

The Ivory Coast lies on the west coast of Africa between Ghana and Liberia, with Guinea, Mali and Upper Volta to the north. The climate is hot and wet with temperatures varying from 14° to 39°c (57° to 103°F). The official language is French and a large number of African languages are spoken. The majority of the population follows traditional beliefs; Christians, mainly Roman Catholic, make up 12 per cent of the population, and Muslims about 23 per cent. The national flag (proportions 3 by 2) is a vertical tricolour of orange, white and green. The capital is Abidjan.

Recent History

The Ivory Coast became an independent Republic in August 1960. Formerly a province of French West Africa, in 1958 it was declared to be a self-governing member of the French Community. In 1959 it joined with Dahomey, Niger and Upper Volta to form the Conseil de l'Entente, a regional politico-economic association. Though it did not rejoin the French Community on attaining independence it is closely bound to France. The President, Félix Houphouët-Boigny, is outspokenly anti-Communist, and has proposed the undertaking of a "dialogue" between South Africa and black African states.

President Houphouët-Boigny was re-elected in November 1965 and again in 1970. He has been President and his party, *Parti démocratique de la Côte d'Ivoire*, has been in power without formal opposition since before independence. The only serious attempt at a *coup d'état* was foiled in 1963. In 1968 and 1969 there was unrest among students and workers, and in September 1969 there was a riot in Abidjan directed at resident African foreigners, after which a law restricting immigration from neighbouring African countries was passed in 1970. Regional revolts in 1969 and 1970 were put down by the Government, and the ending of disparities between the regions is a priority of the 1971–75 development plan. In June 1973 it was announced that a plot had been discovered to stage a *coup d'état* in 1974. Twelve young army officers were brought to trial and death sentences were passed on seven of them. The Government is severely pruning bureaucracy after complaints of wastefulness and corruption.

Government

The Ivory Coast is a Republic with executive power vested in the President, who is elected by direct universal suffrage. The Council of Ministers is directly responsible to him. The National Assembly is elected by a single party system. The country is divided into 24 Départements, each with its own elected Council.

Defence

Defence matters are the concern of the Regional Defence Council of the Conseil de l'Entente through which agreements with France have been negotiated. France supplies equipment and training in return for bases in case of need. The Ivory Coast has over 4,000 men in the army, 300 in the air force, 100 in the navy and a gendarmerie of 3,000.

Economic Affairs

The Ivory Coast was little developed before independence, but economic growth since 1960 has been maintained at a high rate, due to a consistent development policy based on the variety of natural resources and the establishment of light industry. Manganese and diamonds are mined and there are large deposits of high quality iron ore at Bangolo. The country's main cash crops are oil palms, coffee, cocoa, coconut palms, rubber, pineapples and bananas, all of which are being expanded, and a reafforestation programme is under way. The processing of such primary products is the basis of the Ivory Coast's industry, and the 1971–75 development plan envisages further development of industries, so that more local produce is processed before export. The Government continues to encourage private enterprise and foreign investment, but is now responding to demands for *ivoirisation* of capital, and the State owns or part-owns several enterprises. Other products include fuel oils, tobacco, cotton fibre and textiles, metal goods, and furniture. In 1971 industrial products accounted for 20 per cent of exports, which totalled 26,610 million francs CFA, and it is aimed to increase this to 35 per cent by 1975. The main exports are coffee and timber, for both of which the Ivory Coast is Africa's leading exporter, and cocoa beans. Nonetheless there is a serious trade deficit each year, and the country relies on foreign aid and loans, mainly from France and other West European countries, Japan and U.S.A. Unemployment is a major problem exacerbated by the population drift to the towns from rural areas and by the large number of immigrants, principally from Upper Volta. In 1973 production of coffee and cocoa was badly affected by the West African drought. World prices for cocoa have also been unreliable in recent years. Attempts are being made to reduce reliance on these products, both by encouraging other crops, such as bananas and pineapples, and by increasing mineral production. Plans are under way for the construction of a railway or pipeline which would link the new port of San Pedro with the massive iron deposits at Bangolo.

The Ivory Coast is a member of the OAU, CEAO and OCAM and an associate member of the EEC, and since 1964 Abidjan has been the headquarters of the African Development Bank.

Transport and Communications

A one-metre gauge railway runs to Upper Volta from Abidjan. The Ivory Coast has an extensive road system of 39,000 km. of roads, of which nearly 7,000 km. are surfaced. The lower courses of the rivers and the coastal lagoons are used for local transport. Abidjan is the most important seaport in French-speaking West Africa, and in addition a new port at San Pedro in the south-west has been operational since 1971. The Ivory Coast is a member of Air Afrique.

Social Welfare

Medical services are organized by the state. Other social services have yet to be developed.

Education

The Government provides education at nominal rates and attendance at primary school is compulsory, but only 55 per cent of children of primary school age do attend school. In 1971–72 there were 515,000 pupils in primary schools and 75,000 in secondary schools. The University of Abidjan was founded in 1964 and in 1972–73 had 2,700 students. In addition a large number of students enrol at French universities.

Tourism

The game reserves, forests and lagoons, and the capital Abidjan, are all of interest to tourists and there were 53,700 visitors in 1971. The 10 km. coastal strip along the Lagune Ebrié to the west of Abidjan is being developed as a tourist riviera.

Visas are not required by French nationals.

Sport

There is little organized sport. Football is popular.

Public Holidays

1974: August 7th (Independence), August 15th (Assumption), October 18th (Id ul Fitr—End of Ramadan), November 1st (All Saints'), December 25th (Christmas), December 26th (Tabaski).

1975: January 1st (New Year), March 31st (Easter Monday), May 1st (Labour Day), May 8th (Ascension), May 19th (Whitsun).

Weights and Measures

The metric system is in force.

Currency and Exchange Rates

100 centimes=1 franc de la Communanté financière africaine (CFA).

Exchange rates (April 1974):
1 franc CFA=2 French centimes;
£1 sterling=579.75 francs CFA;
U.S. $1=245.625 francs CFA.

STATISTICAL SURVEY

AREA AND POPULATION

AREA (sq. km.)	POPULATION (1969 est.)				
	Total	Foreign	Abidjan (capital)	Bouaké	Gagnoa
322,463	4,200,000	1,000,000	500,000	100,000	45,000

Mid-1972 population (UN estimate): 4,526,000.

Births and Deaths: Average annual birth rate 46.0 per 1,000; death rate 22.7 per 1,000 (UN estimates for 1965–70).

EMPLOYMENT
(January 1st, 1964)

Total population: 3,708,000 (male 1,867,000; female 1,841,000).

Economically active: 1,850,000 (male 979,000; female 871,000).

Agriculture, Forestry, Hunting and Fishing	1,600,000
Mining .	3,070
Manufacturing	15,550
Construction .	16,590
Electricity, Gas and Water	6,810
Commerce	125,300
Transport and Communication	41,870
Services	40,810
TOTAL .	1,850,000

Source: Direction de la statistique, Abidjan, *Bulletin mensuel de statistiques.*

AGRICULTURE

LAND USE, 1968
('000 hectares)

Arable Land .	7,809
Under permanent crops .	1,050
Permanent Meadows and Pastures	8,000
Forest .	12,000
Other Land .	2,941
	31,800
Inland Water .	446
TOTAL AREA .	32,246

PRINCIPAL CROPS
('ooo metric tons)

	1969	1970	1971
Maize	260	231	280
Millet }	} 41	{ 30	} 42*
Fonio		7	
Sorghum	14	13	13*
Rice (paddy)	303	316	350
Sweet Potatoes	21	21	} 1,555
Yams	1,520	1,551	
Cassava (Manioc)	532	540	567
Taros	178	182	172
Bananas	172	179	188
Plantains	638	650	670
Pineapples	90	111	175
Palm Kernels	23	20	19
Palm Oil	36.5	50.0	61.4
Groundnuts (unshelled)	43	43	42
Cottonseed	20	18	28
Copra	5.3	6.9	8.5*
Coffee	279.6	240	268
Cocoa Beans (year ending September)	144.5	180.7	179.6
Cotton (lint)	14	13	20
Natural Rubber (dry weight)	7.1	11.0	13.7
Coconuts (million)	50	64	n.a.

1972 ('ooo metric tons): Maize 300, Bananas 155, Palm Kernels 24.0, Palm Oil 81.0, Groundnuts 42, Cottonseed 35, Coffee 270, Cocoa 225.8 (in 1971/72), Cotton Lint 25, Rubber 14.3.

* FAO estimates.

Principal Sources: mainly FAO, *Production Yearbook 1971* and *Monthly Bulletin of Agricultural Economics and Statistics*.

LIVESTOCK
('ooo)

	1968-69	1969-70	1970-71*
Cattle	392	396	400
Pigs	169	167	168
Sheep	799	829	850
Goats	800	778	770
Poultry	7,700*	7,900*	8,000

* FAO estimates.
Source: FAO, *Production Yearbook 1971.*

LIVESTOCK PRODUCTS
(metric tons)

	1969	1970*	1971*
Cows' Milk	9,000*	10,000	10,000
Beef and Veal	29,000	28,000	28,000
Mutton and Lamb	9,000	9,000	9,000
Pork	4,000	4,000	4,000
Hen Eggs	5,100*	5,200	5,400

* FAO estimate.
Source: FAO, *Production Yearbook 1971.*

FORESTRY
ROUNDWOOD PRODUCTION
(cu. metres)

1968	8,939,000
1969	9,700,000
1970	8,888,000

Source: FAO, *Yearbook of Forest Products.*

FISHING*
(metric tons)

	1969	1970	1971
Atlantic Ocean	67,000	52,900	57,100
Inland Water	4,000	5,000	5,500
TOTAL CATCH	71,000	57,900	62,600
Value of Fish Landed (million francs CFA)	3,038	3,326	3,766

*Figures exclude landings made by foreign fishing vessels.
Source: FAO, *Yearbook of Fishery Statistics 1971.*

MINING

	1967	1968	1969	1970
Manganese (metric tons) . . .	64,168	51,543	57,690	10,377
Diamonds ('000 metric carats) . .	176	187	202	213

Diamond production was 326,000 carats in 1971 and 333,541 carats in 1972.

INDUSTRY

SELECTED PRODUCTS

		1968	1969	1970	1971
Sawnwood	'000 cu. metres	290	307	308	n.a.
Liquefied Petroleum Gas . .	'000 metric tons	11	10	10	6
Motor Spirit	,, ,, ,,	155	159	169	151
Kerosene*	,, ,, ,,	53	39	48	50
Jet Fuels*	,, ,, ,,	27	41	41	41
Distillate Fuel Oils . .	,, ,, ,,	199	218	199	242
Residual Fuel Oils . .	,, ,, ,,	233	267	229	297
Electric Energy . . .	million kWh.	372	440	517	588
Thermal . . .	,, ,,	115	186	257	449
Hydro	,, ,,	257	254	260	139
Cigarettes†	million	1,500	1,978	2,000	1,750

Source: UN, Statistical Yearbook 1972, except:

* Source: U.S. Bureau of Mines.   † Source: U.S. Department of Agriculture.

FINANCE

100 centimes = 1 franc de la Communauté financière africaine (CFA).

Coins: 1, 2, 5, 10, 25, 50 and 100 francs CFA.

Notes: 100, 500, 1,000 and 5,000 francs CFA.

Exchange rates (April 1974): 1 franc CFA = 2 French centimes;

£1 sterling = 579.75 francs CFA; U.S. \$1 = 245.625 francs CFA.

1,000 francs CFA = £1.725 = \$4.071.

RECURRENT BUDGET
(million francs CFA)

Revenue	1967	1968
Direct Taxes . . .	6,700	7,235
Indirect Taxes . . .	29,320	32,100
Licence Fees . . .	1,500	1,100
Others . . .	2,280	2,765
Total . . .	39,800	43,200

Expenditure	1967	1968
Education . . .	7,109	8,327
Defence . . .	3,619	3,789
Public Health . . .	4,194	3,789
Local Government Grants .	5,929	6,018
Public Works and Housing .	4,977	5,219
Public Administration .	7,159	7,552
Agriculture . . .	1,430	1,822
Foreign Affairs . . .	955	1,085
Total (incl. others) .	39,800	43,200

1972 Budget: 72,075 million francs CFA. The investment and equipment budget amounts to a further 34,900m. francs CFA.

1973 Budget: 82,782 million francs CFA.

1974 Budget: 97,700 million francs CFA.

FIVE-YEAR PLAN (1971–75)

Public investment will be 252,000m. francs CFA. Half of this is allocated to infrastructure and 20 per cent to agriculture. The growth rate envisaged is 4.1 per cent per annum for agriculture and 12 per cent p.a. for industry.

BALANCE OF PAYMENTS 1963–68
('000 million francs CFA)

REVENUE	1963	1964	1965	1966	1967	1968
Exports	57.4	73.2	68.4	76.7	80.3	104.9
Public Transfers . . .	4.4	4.2	5.4	4.8	3.6	3.8
Capital: Private Sector . .	4.7	4.9	3.0	3.0	3.0	1.8
Public Sector . .	1.2	1.1	3.4	0.7	0.1	4.8

EXPENDITURE	1963	1964	1965	1966	1967	1968
Imports	41.9	58.1	58.3	63.6	65.1	77.6
Investment Income . . .	5.1	7.0	6.6	8.4	8.9	9.5
Miscellaneous Private Transfers .	3.6	5.0	3.7	5.8	6.2	7.5
Savings Transfers . . .	5.4	7.3	7.5	8.7	8.9	9.2

Source: IMF.

EXTERNAL TRADE*

(million francs CFA)

	1966	1967	1968	1969	1970	1971	1972	1973
Imports	63,533	64,872	75,676	86,235	107,704	110,838	113,094	157,500
Exports	76,657	80,262	104,890	118,223	130,190	126,558	139,541	190,800

* Excluding trade in gold.

PRINCIPAL COMMODITIES

IMPORTS	1969	1970	1971
Food, Drink, Tobacco .	12,344	16,425	16,923
Fuels	4,499	5,123	5,353
Raw Materials . .	2,272	2,960	3,664
Semi manufactures . .	14,439	20,626	21,103
Agricultural and Industrial Equipment .	24,556	30,932	31,323
Consumer Goods .	27,183	31,638	32,472

EXPORTS	1969	1970	1971
Green Coffee . .	30,169	43,172	44,007
Cocoa Beans . .	26,350	26,742	} 27,777
Cocoa Pulp . .	1,927	2,304	
Cocoa Butter . .	3,820	2,915	
Timber . . .	35,119	29,335	30,969
Raw and Unprocessed Cotton . .	2,114	2,066	3,179
Cotton Print . .	1,587	1,832	n.a.
Bananas . .	3,005	3,208	2,974
Rubber . .	903	1,192	1,120
Tinned Pineapples .	1,666	2,379	} 4,537
Fresh Pineapples .	596	782	
Pineapple Juice .	450	648	
Diamonds . .	518	412	n.a.
Manganese Ore . .	167	258	n.a.

PRINCIPAL COUNTRIES

IMPORTS	1969	1970	EXPORTS	1969	1970
France	39,966	49,788	France	37,112	42,526
Other Franc Zone	8,806	10,375	Other Franc Zone	8,662	9,062
United Kingdom	2,221	2,684	United Kingdom	4,786	4,373
U.S.A.	7,135	8,527	U.S.A.	16,465	24,323
Germany, Federal Republic	7,463	9,285	Germany, Federal Republic	11,372	12,506
Italy	4,557	6,945	Italy	12,826	11,204
Netherlands	3,994	5,161	Netherlands	10,927	11,792
Belgium and Luxembourg	2,179	2,794	Belgium and Luxembourg	2,667	11,792
Japan	1,389	2,699	Japan	2,316	2,191
Sino-Soviet Bloc	990	1,590	Sino-Soviet Bloc	1,478	1,006
Taiwan	1,212	1,140	Spain	2,643	2,564
Norway	394	669			
Sweden	280	534			
Switzerland	409	552			
Hong Kong	694	630			

TOURISM

Tourist arrivals at hotels: (1970) 44,826; (1971) 48,722.

TRANSPORT

RAILWAYS
(including Upper Volta traffic)

	1970	1971	1972
Passengers ('ooo)	2,565	2,631	2,595
Passenger/km. ('ooo)	626,000	701,000	777,539
Freight ('ooo metric tons)	756	801	872
Freight (million net ton/km.)	424	448	480

ROADS
(Motor vehicles in use—'ooo)

	1969	1970	1971*
Passenger Cars	47.0	56.4	71.8
Commercial Vehicles	33.0	40.1	46.9

* Estimates.

SHIPPING

	ABIDJAN			SASSANDRA		
	1969	1970	1971	1969	1970	1971
Vessels entered (number)	2,847	2,544	2,880	689	523	625
Vessels entered ('ooo net reg. tons)	9,388	9,716	10,886	2,389	2,021	2,259
Passenger arrivals (number)	3,556	412	281	—	—	—
Passenger departures (number)	5,190	953	853	—	—	—
Freight unloaded ('ooo tons)	2,002	2,335	2,616	4.91	1.70	1.40
Freight loaded ('ooo tons)	3,149	2,733	2,726	437	628	n.a.

Source: INSEE, *Données Statistiques* (Paris, 1972).

CIVIL AVIATION
(Scheduled services*)

	1969	1970	1971
Kilometres flown ('ooo)	1,708	1,770	1,774
Passenger-km. ('ooo)	65,820	70,670	80,000
Freight ('ooo ton-km.)	5,571	5,816	7,183
Mail ('ooo ton-km.)	492	540	574

* Including one-twelfth of the traffic of Air Afrique.

COMMUNICATIONS MEDIA

	1969	1970	1971
Telephones . .	27,220	31,000	34,000
Daily Newspapers .	3	3	3
Radio Sets ('000) .	70	75	80
Television Sets ('000)	10	11	n.a.

Source: UN, *Statistical Yearbook 1972.*

EDUCATION
(1969)

	TEACHERS	PUPILS
Pre-primary . . .	n.a.	3,567
Primary . . .	10,094	464,817
General Secondary . .	1,910	53,267
Vocational . .	402	4,794
Teacher Training . .	95	1,615
University . . .	126	2,042

Source: UN, *Statistical Yearbook 1971.*

Source (unless otherwise stated): Ministère des Finances, des Affaires Economiques et du Plan, Abidjan.

THE CONSTITUTION

(Promulgated October 31st, 1960, modified June 1971.)

Preamble: The Republic of the Ivory Coast is one and indivisible. It is secular, democratic and social. Sovereignty belongs to the people who exercise it through their representatives or through referenda. There is universal, equal and secret suffrage. French is the official language.

Head of State: The President is elected for a 5-year term by direct universal suffrage and is eligible for re-election. He is Head of the Administration and the Armed Forces and has power to ask the National Assembly to reconsider a Bill, which must then be passed by two-thirds of the members of the Assembly; he may also have a Bill submitted to a referendum. In case of the death or incapacitation of the President his functions are carried out by a deputy chosen by the National Assembly.

Executive Power: Executive power is vested in the President. He appoints a Council of Ministers, who may not be members of the National Assembly and are responsible only to him.

Legislative Power: Legislative power is vested in a National Assembly of 100 members, elected for a 5-year term of office at the same time as the Presidential elections. Legislation may be introduced either by the President or by a member of the National Assembly.

Judicial Power: The independence of the judiciary is guaranteed by the President, assisted by a High Council of Judiciary.

Economic and Social Council: An advisory commission of 45 members appointed by the President because of their specialist knowledge or experience.

THE GOVERNMENT

HEAD OF STATE

President: Félix Houphouët-Boigny.

COUNCIL OF MINISTERS
(April 1974)

President of the Council of Ministers and Minister of Defence: Félix Houphouët-Boigny.

Ministers of State: Auguste Denise, Dr. Blaise N'dia Koffi, Germain Koffi Gadeau.

Minister of State for Tourism: Matthieu Ekra.

Minister of State in charge of relations with the National Assembly: Loua Diomandé.

Minister of Justice: Camille Alliali.

Minister of the Interior: Nanlo Bamba.

Minister of Foreign Affairs: Arsène Assouan Usher.

Minister of the Armed Forces and Civic Services: Kouadio M'Bahia Blé.

Minister of Economic and Financial Affairs: Henri Konan Bédié.

Minister of Construction and Town Planning: Alexis Thierry-Lebbé.

Minister of Planning: Mohamed Diawara.

Minister of Posts and Telecommunications: Souleymane Cissoko.

Minister of Agriculture: Abdoulaye Sawadogo.

Minister of Scientific Research: Jean Lorougnon Guédé.

Minister of Technical Education and Professional Training: Ange Barry-Battesti.

Minister of Health and Population: Hippolyte Ayé.

Minister of the Civil Service: Joseph Tadjo Ehué.

Minister of Public Works and Transport: Grah Kadji.

Minister of Animal Production: Dico Garbah.

Minister of Labour and Social Affairs: Vanié Bi Tra.

Minister of Youth, People's Education and Sports: Etienne Ahin.

Minister of Information: Edmon Zégbéhi Bouazo.

Minister of National Education: Paul Yao Akoto.

Secretary of State for Primary Education and Educational Television Broadcasting: Pascal Dikiblé N'Guessan

Secretary of State for the Budget: Abdoulaye Koné.

Secretary of State for Mines: Paul Gui Dibo.

Secretary of State for Posts: Mamadou Doukouré.

Secretary of State for National Parks: Koffi Attobra.

Secretary of State for Reafforestation: Jacques Toro.

Secretary of State for Culture: Jules Hié-Néa.

DIPLOMATIC REPRESENTATION

EMBASSIES ACCREDITED TO THE IVORY COAST
(In Abidjan unless otherwise stated)

Algeria: 53 blvd. Clozel, B.P. 1015; *Chargé d'Affaires:* MOHAMED KHOURI.

Argentina: Dakar, Senegal.

Austria: Dakar, Senegal.

Belgium: 21 ave. Chardy, B.P. 1800; *Ambassador:* PIERRE MARCHAL.

Brazil: Immeuble Delafosse, B.P. 20.910; *Ambassador:* FERNANDO C. DE BITTENCOURT BERENGUER.

Canada: Immeuble "Le Général", B.P. 21.194; *Ambassador:* GILLES MATHIEU.

Central African Republic: *Ambassador:* PROSPER LAVO DRAMA.

China (Taiwan): Résidence Crosson-Duplessis, ave. Crosson-Duplessis, B.P. 2688; *Ambassador:* TCHENG KOA JOEI.

Denmark: Accra, Ghana.

Egypt: 40 rue de la Canebière, Coccody, B.P. 2104; *Ambassador:* ABDEL FATTAH HASSAN CHABANA.

Ethiopia: B.P. 20.802; *Ambassador:* ENGEDA ABEBÉ.

Finland: Lagos, Nigeria.

France: 3 blvd. Angoulvant, B.P. 1393; *Ambassador:* JACQUES RAPHAEL-LEYGUES.

Gabon: Immeuble Shell, 46 ave. Lamblin, B.P. 20.855; *Ambassador:* JOSÉ J. AMIAR.

Germany, Federal Republic: 11 ave. Barthe, B.P. 1900; *Ambassador:* Dr. PAUL VERBEEK.

Ghana: Résidence de la Corniche, blvd. du Général de Gaulle, B.P. 1871; *Ambassador:* MICHAEL KWAKU GBAGONAH.

Greece: Immeuble "El Nasr", B.P. 21.046; *Ambassador:* JEAN LEOPOULOS.

India: Dakar, Senegal.

Italy: 16 rue de la Canebière, Coccody, B.P. 1905; *Ambassador:* GIAN FRANCO FARINELLI.

Japan: ave. Chardy, B.P. 1329; *Ambassador:* SHIGUERU INADA.

Korea, Republic: Immeuble "Le Général", B.P. 21.040; *Ambassador:* KANG YONG-KYU (also accred. to Liberia, Sierra Leone and Niger).

Lebanon: 22 ave. Delafosse, B.P. 2227; *Ambassador:* TOUFIC CHATILLA.

Lesotho: Nairobi, Kenya.

Liberia: Immeuble "Le Général", B.P. 2514; *Ambassador:* BENJAMIN G. FREEMAN.

Malta: B.P. 46; *Ambassador:* EDOUARD LOBKOWICZ.

Mauritania: rue Pierre et Marie Curie, B.P. 2275; *Ambassador:* SINDA OULD CHEIKH TALEB BOUYA.

Morocco: 10 blvd. Roume, B.P. 146; *Ambassador:* BOUBEKER BOUMAHDI.

Netherlands: Immeuble Shell, 48 ave. Lamblin, B.P. 1086; *Ambassador:* FRANS J. T. JOHANNIS VAN AGT.

Niger: 23 blvd. Angoulvant, B.P. 2743; *Perm. Rep.:* EL HADJ ALLEBE.

Nigeria: 53 blvd. de la République, B.P. 1906; *Ambassador:* JOHN EDREMODA.

Norway: Immeuble Shell, 48 ave. Lamblin, B.P. 607; *Ambassador:* PER THEE NAEVDAL.

Pakistan: Accra, Ghana.

Sierra Leone: Monrovia, Liberia.

Spain: 29 blvd. Clozel, B.P. 2589; *Ambassador:* TEODOMIRO DE AGUILAR COLOMER.

Sweden: Monrovia, Liberia.

Switzerland: Immeuble Franchet d'Espéray, Angle ave. Franchet d'Espéray et rue Lecoeur, B.P. 1914; *Ambassador:* ETIENNE SUTER.

Thailand: Lagos, Nigeria.

Tunisia: Immeuble Shell, 48 ave. Lamblin, B.P. 20996; *Ambassador:* MOHAMED RIDHA BACH BAOUAB.

United Kingdom: Immeuble Shell, 48 ave. Lamblin, B.P. 2581; *Ambassador:* PAUL C. H. HOLMER.

U.S.A.: 5 rue Jesse Owens, B.P. 1712; *Ambassador:* ROBERT S. SMITH.

Upper Volta: 2 ave. Terrason de Fougères, B.P. 908; *Ambassador:* MICHEL KOMPAORÉ.

Vatican: Dakar, Senegal (Apostolic Nunciature).

Viet-Nam, Republic: Immeuble Nour-al-Hayat, ave. Chardy, B.P. 531; *Ambassador:* NGUYEN VAN LOC.

Yugoslavia: Accra, Ghana.

Zaire: 29 blvd. Clozel, B.P. 21.051; *Ambassador:* TANGALA AMISI.

Zambia: Immeuble "Le Général", B.P. 21.199; *Ambassador:* ALBERT KALYATI.

Ivory Coast also has diplomatic relations with Colombia, Haiti, Mali, Tanzania and Uganda.

NATIONAL ASSEMBLY

President: PHILIPPE YACÉ.

Vice-Presidents: MARIE-BERNARD KOISSY, CLÉMENT ANET BILÉ, GON COULIBALY, MAURICE OULATÉ, BENOÎT TOUSSAGNON.

ELECTION, NOVEMBER 29TH, 1970

All 100 seats were won by the *Parti démocratique de la Côte d'Ivoire.*

POLITICAL PARTY

Parti démocratique de la Côte d'Ivoire: the national part of the West African *Rassemblement démocratique africain;* headed by a political bureau of 35 mems. and a guiding committee of 85; Hon. Pres. FÉLIX HOUPHOUËT-BOIGNY; Sec.-Gen. PHILIPPE YACÉ.

JUDICIAL SYSTEM

Since 1964 all civil, criminal, commercial and administrative cases have come under the jurisdiction of the *tribuneaux de première instance* (Magistrates' courts), the assize courts and the Court of Appeal, with the Supreme Court as supreme court of appeal.

Courts of First Instance: Abidjan, Pres. Lazeni Coulibaly; Bouaké, Pres. Fadika Mamadou; Daba, Pres. Tahar Chérif Hamza; there are a further 25 courts in the principal centres.

Court of Appeal: Abidjan; hears appeals from the Courts of 1st instance; Pres. M. Belfer.

The Supreme Court: B.P. 1534, Abidjan; has four chambers: constitutional, judicial, administrative and auditing; Pres. Alphonse Boni.

The High Court of Justice: composed of Deputies elected from and by the National Assembly. It is competent to impeach the President or other members of the Government. Pres. Philippe Yacé; Vice-Pres. Marcel Laubouet.

State Security Court: composed of a President and six regular judges, all appointed for five years; deals with all offences against the security of the State; Pres. A. Boni.

RELIGION

It is estimated that 65 per cent of the population follow traditional animist beliefs, 23 per cent are Muslims and 12 per cent are Christian, of whom Roman Catholics account for 8.5 per cent of the total population.

ROMAN CATHOLICS

There are about 500,000 Roman Catholics. The Church operates 122 mission stations.

Archbishop of Abidjan: Mgr. Bernard Yago; B.P. 1287, Abidjan.

OTHER CHRISTIAN COMMUNITIES

Union des Eglises Evangéliques du Sud Ouest de la Côte d'Ivoire and **Mission Biblique:** B.P. 8020, Abidjan; f. 1927; approx. 150 places of worship, 5 missions; publ. *L'Appel de la Côte d'Ivoire.*

Christian and Missionary Alliance: B.P. 585, Bouaké; f. 1929; 7 mission stations; Superintendent Jesse Jesperson; publ. *Ivory Coast Today.*

Conservative Baptist Foreign Mission Society: Ferkessedougou, B.P. 111; f. 1947; active in the northern area in evangelism, teaching and medical work.

Eglise Protestante Méthodiste: 41 blvd. de la République, B.P. 1282, Abidjan; *c.* 89,000 mems.; Pres. Pastor Auguste Ackam.

The Bible Society in Francophone West Africa: Abidjan, B.P. 1529; Sec. Rev. Josué Danho; circ. of Scriptures 228,662 (1971).

Gospel Missionary Union: Man; 5 missions.

Mission Evangélique: B.P. 5, Zuénoula; established 1939; 11 mission stations; Field Dir. J. Reider; Eglise Protestante du Centre de la Côte d'Ivoire: M. Tehi Emmanuel, same address.

PRESS

Bulletin mensuel de la Chambre d'agriculture: Abidjan, B.P. 1291.

Bulletin mensuel de la Chambre d'industrie: Abidjan, B.P. 1758.

Bulletin mensuel de statistiques: Direction de la statistique, Abidjan, B.P. 222.

Bulletin Quotidien d'Information: Abidjan; published by Ivory Coast News Agency (*Agence Ivoirienne de Presse*), B.P. 4312, 11 ave. Bir-Hakein; f. 1961; evenings; Dir. Blaise Agui Miezzan; circ. 800.

Champion: c/o Centre de Publications Evangéliques, Abidjan, B.P. 8900; f. 1964; religious; quarterly; Editor D. Gentil; circ. 15,000.

Eburnea: Ministry of Information, Abidjan; monthly.

Entente Africaine: P.O.B. 20991, Abidjan; Editor Justin Vieyra; Publishers Inter Afrique Presse; quarterly review.

l'Exportateur Ivoirien: f. 1973.

Fraternité-Hebdo: Treichville, B.P. 1212; organ of the Parti Démocratique de la Côte d'Ivoire; weekly; Political Dir. Félix Houphouët-Boigny.

Fraternité-Matin: blvd. du Général de Gaulle, Abidjan, B.P. 1807; f. 1964; official Party daily; Dir.-Gen. Mamadou Coulibaly; Asst. Dir.-Gen. Laurent Dona Fologo; circ. 33,000.

Le Journal des Amis du Progrès de l'Afrique Noire: B.P. 694, Abidjan; f. 1957; five issues a week; left-wing political; Editor Doute Gilberg; circ. 10,000.

Journal officiel de la Côte d'Ivoire: Ministry of the Interior, Abidjan; weekly.

Sports Abidjan: B.P. 932, Abidjan; weekly.

NEWS AGENCIES

Agence Ivoirienne de Presse (AIP) (*Ivory Coast News Agency*): 11 ave. Bir-Hakeim, B.P. 4312, Abidjan; f. 1961; Dir. Tao Issiaka; publs. *Bulletin Quotidien* (daily), *Ivory Coast* (English fortnightly bulletin).

Agence France-Presse: 8 rue Paris-Village, B.P. 726, Abidjan; Chief Jean Ageorges.

Société d'Information et de Diffusion Abidjanaise: Abidjan; f. 1963; Man. Dir. Mamadou Coulibaly.

RADIO AND TELEVISION

Radiodiffusion Télévision Ivoirienne: Abidjan, B.P. 2261; government station broadcasting in French and local languages, regional station at Bouaké, Dir. L. Diallo.

In 1971 there were 80,000 receivers.

Télévision Ivoirienne: Abidjan, B.P. 8883; f. 1963; stations at Abidjan, Bouaké, Man and Koun; Man. G. Tanoh.

In 1970 there were 10,550 television receivers.

FINANCE

BANKS

Banque Centrale des Etats de l'Afrique de l'Ouest: 29 rue du Colisée, Paris 8, France; ave. Terrasson de Fougères, B.P. 1769 Abidjan; Bank of Issue and Central Bank for 6 West African Republics, including Ivory Coast; f. 1955; cap. 250m. frs. CFA; Pres. Jean Tévi; Ivory Coast Man. Jean Charpentier.

Banque Internationale pour l'Afrique Occidentale: 9 ave. de Messine, Paris, France; B.P. 1274, Abidjan; Dir. ANDRÉ CHARDON.

Banque Internationale pour le Commerce et l'Industrie de la Côte d'Ivoire S.A.: B.P. 1298, 16 ave. Barthe, Abidjan; f. 1962; affiliated to Banque Nationale de Paris, Société Financière, Barclays Bank International Ltd.; cap. 750m. francs CFA; 6 brs.; Pres. L. KONAN; Gen. Man. JEAN VITTORI.

Banque Ivoirienne de Développement Industriel: B.P. 4470, Abidjan; f. 1965; cap. 700m. francs CFA; Gov. J. B. AMETHIER; Dir.-Gen. ALPHONSE DIBY.

Banque Nationale pour le Développement Agricole (BNDA): 11 avenue Barthe, B.P. 2508, Abidjan; f. 1968; Dir.-Gen. AUGUSTE DAUBREY.

Caisse Autonome d'Amortissement: Immeuble SMGL, avenue Barthe, B.P. 670, Abidjan; Dir. ANDRÉ HOVINE.

Caisse Centrale de Coopération Economique: 13 boulevard Roume, B.P. 1814; Dir. MICHEL PENENT D'IZAIN.

Caisse Nationale des Marchés de l'Etat (CNME): Abidjan.

Compagnie Financière de Côte d'Ivoire (CONFINCI): Abidjan; f. 1974; cap. 300m. francs CFA.

Crédit de la Côte d'Ivoire: 22 avenue Barthe, B.P. 1720, Abidjan; f. 1955; development bank; cap. 800m. CFA, dep. 14,663m.; Dir.-Gen. RENÉ AMICHIA.

Fonds National d'Investissement (FNI): Abidjan.

Société Générale de Banques en Côte d'Ivoire: 5 ave. Barthe, B.P. 1355, Abidjan; f. 1962 to take over branches of Société Générale; cap. 1,500m. francs CFA; 10 brs., 12 sub-brs.; Man. Dir. P. DUCHEMIN; Man. GÉRARD MADELIN.

Société Ivoirienne de Banque: 34 blvd. de la République, B.P. 1300, Abidjan; f. 1962 to take over branches of Crédit Lyonnais; cap. 1,007m. francs CFA; 16 brs.; Pres. A. BAROU; Gen. Man. A. DOUMBIA.

Société Nationale de Financement (SONAFI): 19 ave. Delafosse, B.P. 1591, Abidjan; f. 1962; cap. 300m. francs CFA; Dir.-Gen. CAMILLE KONAN.

Association Professionelle des Banques et Etablissements Financiers: B.P. 20,900, Abidjan; Pres. JEAN VITTORI.

DEVELOPMENT ORGANIZATIONS

Société pour le Développement et l'Exploitation du Palmier à Huile (SODEPALM): B.P. 2049, Abidjan; f. 1963; national development organization for palm oil; Dir. ANDRÉ FRAISSE.

Société pour le Développement minier de la Côte d'Ivoire (SODEMI): B.P. 2816, Abidjan; f. 1962; national organization for mineral research; Pres. EDOUARD EBAGNITCHIE.

INSURANCE

Abidjan

Assureurs Conseils de Côte d'Ivoire: Faugère and Jutheau et Cie., 2 ave. Lamblin, B.P. 1554.

Comité des Assureurs de la Côte d'Ivoire: B.P. 20.963, Abidjan; Pres. G. LECLERC.

Crédit Foncier de l'Ouest-Africain: ave. Lamblin, B.P. 3.

SACRA (Société Africaine de Courtage et de Représentation d'Assurances): B.P. 20995, Abidjan; p.u. cap. 25m. francs CFA; Dir. GÉRARD GAILLARD.

TRADE AND INDUSTRY

CHAMBERS OF COMMERCE

Chambre de Commerce de la République de Côte d'Ivoire: Abidjan, B.P. 1399; Pres. F. MASSIEYE; publ. daily and monthly bulletins.

Chambre d'Agriculture de la République de Côte d'Ivoire: Abidjan, B.P. 1291; Pres. OKA NIANGOIN; Sec.-Gen. DOGOH PIERRE; publ. monthly bulletin.

Chambre d'Industrie de la République de Côte d'Ivoire: Abidjan, B.P. 1758; Pres. ANDRÉ BLOHORN; publ. monthly bulletin.

PRINCIPAL EMPLOYERS' ASSOCIATIONS

Association Interprofessionelle de la Côte d'Ivoire: B.P. 1340, Abidjan; Pres. Sec.-Gen. A. BLOHORN.

Syndicat Agricole Africain: B.P. 2241, Abidjan; Pres. JOSEPH ANOMA.

Syndicat des Commerçants Importateurs et Exportateurs de la Côte d'Ivoire (SCIMPEX): Annexe de la Chambre de Commerce, B.P. 20.882, Abidjan; Pres. M. KELLER.

Syndicat des Entrepreneurs et des Industriels de la Côte d'Ivoire: B.P. 464, Abidjan; Pres. AUGUSTE BASTID.

Syndicat des Industriels de Côte d'Ivoire: 11 bis avenue Lamblin, B.P. 1340, Abidjan; Pres. ANDRÉ BLOHORN; Sec.-Gen. PH. MEYER.

Syndicat des Négociants Importateurs et Agents de Marques de Matériel Automobile ou Agricole de la Côte d'Ivoire: B.P. 1399, Abidjan; f. 1953; 18 mems.; Pres. M. BROSSET.

Syndicat des Producteurs Forestiers: B.P. 318, Abidjan; Pres. A. LEGRAS.

Syndicat pour la Défense des Intérêts Généraux des Planteurs et Cultivateurs de la Côte d'Ivoire: Treichville, B.P. 6085; Pres. ALEXANDER DJABIA.

Union des Employeurs Agricoles et Forestiers: B.P. 2300, Abidjan; f. 1952; Pres. HUGUES DE QUATREBARBES.

CO-OPERATIVE

Coopérative Bananière et Fruitière (COFRUCI): B.P. 1550, Abidjan; f. 1968; Pres. EDOUARD EBAGNITCHIE.

TRADE UNION

Union Générale des Travailleurs de Côte d'Ivoire: B.P. 1749; Abidjan; f. 1962; 200,000 mems.; Sec.-Gen. JOSEPH COFFIE.

TRANSPORT

RAILWAYS

Régie du Chemin de Fer Abidjan-Niger: Abidjan, B.P. 1394; f. 1904; 1,196 km. of track open of which the main line is 1,145 km. of track linking Abidjan with Ouagadougou, the capital of Upper Volta; 625 km. are in the Ivory Coast; Dir. LANCINA KONATE.

ROADS

There are 6,850 km. of bitumen-surfaced roads, 18,000 km. of all-weather earth roads and 14,000 km. of tracks.

Société Ivoirienne de Transports Publics: B.P. 1822, Abidjan; f. 1964; cap. 17,500m. francs CFA; road transport.

SHIPPING
Abidjan

Compagnie Maritime de l'Afrique Noire (COMARAN): B.P. 640.

Cie. Maritime des Chargeurs Réunis: 25 avenue Général de Gaulle, B.P. 1285.

Delta Line: B.P. 894.

Jugolinija: Cie. Foncière et Commerciale de Distribution, km. 1, rue du Port Bouet, B.P. 4308.

SAMOA: B.P. 1611; agents for Gold Star Line, Lloyd Triestino, Seven Star Line.

Société Ivoirienne de Transport Maritime (SITRAM): 4 ave. Général de Gaulle, B.P. 1546; f. 1967; 5 ships.

Société Navale Chargeurs Delmas et Vieljeux: 17 ave. Louis-Barthe, B.P. 1281; Dir. J.-M. BOILEDIEU.

Société Ouest-Africaine d'Entreprises Maritimes (SOAEM): B.P. 1727; agents for Scandinavian West Africa Line, Société Navale de l'Ouest, Union West Africa Line.

SOCOPAO: Km. 1, blvd. de Marseille, B.P. 1297; agents for Italian West Africa Line, K Line, Palm Line, Splošna Plovba.

SOMICOA: B.P. 640; agents for United West Africa Service.

Transcap-Shipping: B.P. 358; Agents for Elder Dempster Lines, Barber Line, Guinea Gulf Line, Marine Chartering Co., Svea Line, Mitsui-OSK Line, Palm Line, Nordana Line, Nautilus Line (Keller), Hoegh Line; Dir. P. GODOC.

Union Maritime et Commerciale: B.P. 1559; agents for Holland West-Afrika Lijn NV, Royal Interocean Lines.

CIVIL AVIATION
Abidjan

Air Afrique (Société Aérienne Africaine Multinationale): ave. L. Barthe, B.P. 21017, Abidjan; f. 1961; fleet of five DC-8, three Caravelles, one DC-10 (one DC-10 on order); Pres. AOUSSOU KOFFI; Dir.-Gen. J. CADEAC D'ARBAUD; Sec.-Gen. GUIBRIL N'DIAYE; Gen. Rep. for Europe JEAN-CLAUDE DELAFOSSE, 53 rue Ampère, Paris 17e, France.

Air Afrique was established by an agreement between Sodetraf (Société pour le Développement du Transport Aérien en Afrique) and 11 states, formerly French colonies, who each had a 6 per cent share; Togo joined later and Cameroon withdrew in 1971; Sodetraf now has a 30 per cent share and the following have 6 per cent: Central African Republic, Chad, Congo, Dahomey, Gabon, Ivory Coast, Mauritania, Niger, Senegal, Togo, Upper Volta.

Air Ivoire: B.P. 1027; f. 1963; owned by Government (60 per cent), Sodetraf (20 per cent) and Air Afrique (20 per cent); internal services; fleet of two YS-11A, one DC-3, one Aztec, one Baron; Chair. V. NIACIDIE; Man. H. PRIÉ.

The following air lines also serve the Ivory Coast: Air Zaire, Air Mali, Alitalia, Cameroon Airlines, EgyptAir, Ghana Airways, KLM, MEA, Nigeria Airways, PAA, Sabena, SAS, Swissair and UTA.

TOURISM

ICTA (Ivory Coast Travel Agency): P.O.B. 2636, Abidjan.

Ministère du Tourisme: B.P. 20.949, Abidjan.

UNIVERSITY

Université d'Abidjan: B.P. 1880, Abidjan; 204 teachers, 2,700 students.

JAMAICA

INTRODUCTORY SURVEY

Location, Climate, Language, Religion, Flag, Capital

Jamaica is an island in the Caribbean ninety miles south of Cuba. Haiti is nearby to the east. The climate varies with altitude, being tropical at sea level and temperate in the mountain areas. Average annual rainfall is 77 inches. The language is English. The majority of the population belong to Christian churches of which the Church of England and the Baptist Church are the strongest. There is a small Jewish minority. The national flag (proportions 2 by 1) consists of a diagonal gold cross on a black and green background. The capital is Kingston.

Recent History

Formerly a British colony, the island achieved internal self-government in 1959 and full independence in 1962. In 1958 Jamaica joined with Trinidad, Barbados, the Leeward Islands and the Windward Islands to form the West Indies Federation. Jamaica seceded in 1961 following a referendum and the Federation broke up. The two dominant political figures after the war were Sir Alexander Bustamante, leader of the Jamaica Labour Party, who retired as Prime Minister in 1966 on account of ill health, and Mr. Norman Manley, Q.C., a former Premier and leader of the People's National Party, who died in September 1969. The Labour Party won the elections of 1962 and 1967 but under the premiership of Mr. Hugh Shearer it lost the elections of February 1972 to the People's National Party, now led by Mr. Michael Manley, the son of Norman Manley. Jamaica is a member of the Organization of American States and the Caribbean Common Market (CARIBCOM).

Government

The legislature consists of a Senate of 21 members and a House of Representatives of 53 members. Thirteen members of the Senate are appointed by the Governor-General on the advice of the Prime Minister and eight on the advice of the Leader of the Opposition. The House of Representatives is elected by universal adult suffrage. Executive power lies with the Prime Minister and a Cabinet of not less than eleven members. A Privy Council of six members advises the Governor-General on the exercise of the Royal Prerogative of Mercy and on Service appeals of a disciplinary nature.

Defence

Jamaica has a total defence force of some 1,300 men.

Economic Affairs

The economy is based on agriculture and mining. The dominant crop is sugar, with molasses and rum as important by-products. Bananas, citrus fruits and coconuts are also cultivated. A plan to restore Jamaican sugar production to 450,000 tons a year was announced in 1973. This improvement in production is vital to Jamaica's negotiations with the European Economic Community (EEC) concerning sugar exports to the enlarged Community. A more general agricultural development plan is to be introduced in 1974, with measures aimed at bringing more land into production and developing a system of land reform; a major programme of rural electrification has been launched. Jamaica is one of the world's largest producers of bauxite and alumina. In January 1974 the Government announced its intention to re-negotiate contracts with the foreign-owned mining companies. Industry is expanding and covers cement, tobacco and a number of consumer goods. An oil refinery with an initial capacity of 250,000 barrels per day, to be jointly owned with an Italian concern, was under construction in 1974 and will provide the source of cheap power needed for further industrial expansion. Trade is chiefly with the U.S.A., Canada and the United Kingdom. Two valuable sources of income are the tourist trade and remittances from migrants working abroad; Jamaica's foreign exchange position, however, is crucial to the country's economic health, and strict monetary measures including exchange control regulations and import restrictions have been announced. Despite a high economic growth rate, Jamaica has an unemployment rate of between 20 and 30 per cent, and this remains the country's most urgent social and economic problem.

Transport and Communications

There are 205 miles of railway, including the 112-mile line running diagonally across the island from Kingston to Montego Bay; 2,688 miles of main roads and 6,516 miles of secondary roads link towns and villages. The principal ports are Kingston and Montego Bay. Jamaica is well served by a number of international air lines.

Social Welfare

Social welfare is undertaken by the Government, chiefly in co-operation with private charitable organizations. The Social Development Commission arranges and co-ordinates social welfare in the villages.

Education

Primary education is compulsory in certain districts and where schools are available; free secondary education is ensured. In 1972 a campaign to eradicate illiteracy in four years was launched. There were estimated to be 500,000 functional illiterates in 1972. Six faculties of the University of the West Indies are in Kingston.

Tourism

Jamaica attracts many tourists, mainly from the U.S.A. In 1972 479,256 tourists visited the island. There are many hotels and proprietors receive tax concessions to encourage development.

Visas are not required to visit Jamaica by nationals of Commonwealth countries, EEC countries (except Ireland), Finland, Iceland, Israel, Liechtenstein, Norway, San Marino, Spain, Sweden, Switzerland and the U.S.A.

Sport

The chief sports are cricket, tennis, swimming and football.

Public Holidays

1974: August 6th (Independence Day), October 15th (National Heroes' Day), December 25th and 26th (Christmas).

1975: January 1st (New Year), February 12th (Ash Wednesday), March 28th, 31st (Easter), May 23rd (National Labour Day).

Weights and Measures

The imperial system is in force in Jamaica.

Currency and Exchange Rates

100 cents = 1 Jamaican dollar (J$).

Exchange rates (April 1974):
£1 sterling = J$2.171;
U.S. $1 = 90.91 Jamaican cents

STATISTICAL SURVEY

Area (square miles): 4,243.6.

Population: (1970 census) 1,813,594; Kingston 111,879; Birth rate (1972) 34.3; Death rate (1972) 7.2.

Employment: (1972) Total labour force 808,300; Agriculture (incl. Sugar), Forestry, Fishing and Mining 210,542.

AGRICULTURAL PRODUCTION

		1970	1971	1972
Sugar, unrefined	'000 tons	4,056	4,041	4,068
Bananas	'000 stems	15,540	19,323	19,506
Citrus	'000 boxes	3,566	3,941	3,964
Coconuts	'000 nuts	120,500	115,700	117,700
Ginger	'000 lb.	832	912	600

MINING AND INDUSTRIAL PRODUCTION

		1970	1971	1972
Bauxite	'000 metric tons	12,010	13,245	12,784
Cement	,, ,, ,,	457	424	424
Cigars	'000	23,000	27,000	21,000
Cigarettes . . .	million	1,261	1,380	1,571
Sugar	'000 tons	370	379	373
Rum	'000 gal.	2,057	2,240	3,206
Soap	'000 lb.	16,084	16,041	15,920

FINANCE

100 cents = 1 Jamaican dollar (J$).
Coins: 1, 5, 10, 20 and 25 cents.
Notes: 50 cents; 1, 2, 5 and 10 dollars.
Exchange rates (April 1974): £1 sterling = J$2.171; U.S. $1 = 90.91 Jamaican cents.
J$100 = £46.06 = U.S. $110.00.

BUDGET
(J$'000, year ending March 31st, 1973)

REVENUE		EXPENDITURE	
Income Tax	127,250	Interest on Public Debt . . .	21,706
Customs Duties . . .	58,000	General Administration . . .	77,585
Excise and Consumption Duties	54,500	Judicial and Legal . . .	2,545
Land and Property Tax . . .	1,600	Agriculture	18,537
Stamp Duties . . .	10,800	Education and Social Welfare . .	66,379
Motor Vehicle Licences . .	6,400	Public Health	30,138
Other Taxes and Duties . .	4,300	Trade and Industry . . .	5,273
Other Current Receipts . .	19,817	Communications . . .	25,626
Capital Receipts . . .	6,102	Other Current Expenditure . .	7,119
		Other Capital Expenditure . .	21,091
TOTAL	288,769	TOTAL . . .	273,499

COST OF LIVING INDEX
(January 1967=100)

	METROPOLITAN KINGSTON		RURAL AREAS	
	1971	1972	1971	1972
Food and Drink . . .	141.8	146.3	142.4	150.5
Fuels	135.1	147.2	140.0	150.2
Housing	124.9	130.7	123.4	132.8
Household Furnishing .	112.9	119.4	119.3	127.8
Clothing	123.9	131.4	126.1	133.4
Personal	134.6	145.5	127.7	134.6
Transportation . . .	138.3	148.7	134.9	137.7
Miscellaneous . . .	142.1	163.1	132.8	145.2
ALL ITEMS . .	136.0	144.0	135.9	144.0

NATIONAL ACCOUNTS
(J$'000)

	1970	1971	1972†
NET NATIONAL INCOME . . .	840,387	904,558	994,105
Taxes *less* subsidies .	94,271	102,166	107,039
NET NATIONAL PRODUCT . .	934,658	1,006,724	1,101,144
Depreciation allowances . . .	81,284	83,102	96,852
GROSS NATIONAL PRODUCT . .	1,015,942	1,089,826	1,197,996
Balance of exports and imports of goods and services	−98,174	−150,617	−158,371
AVAILABLE RESOURCES *of which:*			
Domestic consumption expenditure	714,864	805,745	893,289
Government consumption expenditure .	124,343	140,251	158,420
Gross domestic capital formation . .	273,433	294,111	302,871

† Preliminary.

BALANCE OF PAYMENTS
(million J$)

	1970			1971			1972		
	Credit	Debit	Balance	Credit	Debit	Balance	Credit	Debit	Balance
Merchandise . . .	285.1	374.3	− 89.2	286.1	395.1	−109.0	302.4	423.4	−121.0
Services:									
Freight and transportation .	23.0	68.8	− 45.8	24.1	69.1	− 45.0	27.0	76.5	− 49.5
Travel . . .	79.6	12.9	66.7	90.8	13.6	77.2	107.9	16.5	91.4
Investment income . .	13.6	95.4	− 81.8	12.4	98.1	− 85.7	11.9	112.3	−100.4
Insurance . . .	—	4.3	− 4.3	—	4.6	− 4.6	—	4.9	− 4.9
Government (n.e.s.) . .	10.8	1.3	9.5	11.7	1.2	10.5	11.5	1.6	9.9
Other services . .	36.9	37.4	− 0.5	39.6	43.4	− 3.8	44.5	49.9	− 5.4
Total . . .	163.9	220.1	− 56.2	178.6	230.0	− 51.4	202.8	261.7	− 58.9
Transfer Payments . .	29.6	12.5	17.1	36.8	19.5	27.3	50.4	28.1	22.3
CURRENT BALANCE . .	478.6	606.9	−128.3	501.5	644.6	−143.1	555.6	713.2	−157.6

EXTERNAL TRADE
(J$'000)

	1969	1970	1971	1972
Imports .	368,586	437,839	459,751	493,166
Exports .	240,870	279,115	275,171	293,077

COMMODITIES
(J$'000)

IMPORTS	1970	1971	1972
Food	69,093	76,606	90,206
Beverages and Tobacco . . .	6,052	7,414	8,176
Crude Materials, inedible, except Fuels .	10,247	12,737	14,614
Mineral Fuels, Lubricants and Related Materials	28,059	43,624	44,567
Animal and Vegetable Oils and Fats . .	2,539	2,428	3,555
Chemicals	32,852	38,302	47,535
Manufactured Goods	114,180	108,190	112,709
Machinery and Transport Equipment .	141,240	133,962	128,390
Miscellaneous Manufactured Articles .	32,848	35,832	42,026
Miscellaneous Transactions and Commodities .	729	656	1,387

EXPORTS (Domestic)	1970	1971	1972
Food	57,681	57,397	62,480
Bananas	11,830	n.a.	n.a.
Sugar (Unrefined)	29,361	n.a.	n.a.
Molasses	2,191	n.a.	n.a.
Beverages and Tobacco . . .	5,211	7,897	9,041
Rum	1,509	n.a.	n.a.
Crude Materials, inedible, except Fuels .	190,136	180,179	190,843
Bauxite	76,490	n.a.	n.a.
Alumina	111,107	n.a.	n.a.
Mineral Fuels, Lubricants and Related Products	6,755	7,670	7,879
Animal and Vegetable Oils . . .	22	31	60
Chemicals	5,186	5,510	6,436
Manufactured Goods . . .	3,260	4,912	4,988
Machinery and Transport Equipment .	969	747	1,112
Miscellaneous Manufactured Articles .	8,474	10,825	10,225
Miscellaneous Transactions and Commodities .	17	3	13

COUNTRIES
(J$'000)

	1970		1971†		1972	
	Imports	Exports	Imports	Exports	Imports	Exports
Canada	39,537	22,620	34,364	23,306	35,188	14,173
United Kingdom . . .	83,894	46,589	90,231	55,290	93,799	64,677
U.S.A.	189,905	150,544	181,781	128,765	182,045	128,078
Venezuela	19,143	506	27,294	2,100	25,094	1,474

† Provisional.

TRANSPORT

Railways (1971): Passengers 39m. passenger-miles; Freight 84m. ton-miles.

Roads (1971–72): 119,146 licensed vehicles (including cars, trucks, tractors, buses, motorcycles and trailers).

Shipping (1971): Freight unloaded 7,696,000 tons; Freight loaded 11,140,000 tons.

Civil Aviation (1972): Passengers arriving 660,701; Cargo handled 18,035 tons.

TOURISM

Total number of visitors (1972): 479,256; expenditure $J107.9m.; number of hotel beds (1972): 17,944.

EDUCATION
(1970–71)

	PRIMARY	JUNIOR SECONDARY	SECONDARY	TEACHER TRAINING	UNIVERSITY
Schools . . .	778	50	54†	7	1
Staff . . .	8,406	1,107	2,443	160	287
Students . . .	322,490*	38,708*	30,718*	2,213	2,886

* Incomplete figures.

† Including Secondary High, High Comprehensive, Technical High and Vocational Trade.

Source: Department of Statistics, Jamaica.

THE CONSTITUTION

THE GOVERNOR-GENERAL

The Governor-General is appointed by The Queen and holds office during her pleasure.

THE LEGISLATURE

The Senate or Upper House consists of 21 Senators of whom 13 will be appointed by the Governor-General on the advice of the Prime Minister and 8 by the Governor-General on the advice of the Leader of the Opposition.

The House of Representatives consists of 53 elected members, to be called Members of Parliament, but provision is included to permit the numbers to be increased to up to 60. (There are 53 seats in the house.)

A person is qualified for appointment to the Senate or for election to the House of Representatives if he is a citizen of Jamaica or other Commonwealth country of the age of 21 or more and has been ordinarily resident in Jamaica for the immediately preceding twelve months.

THE PRIVY COUNCIL

The Privy Council consists of six members appointed by the Governor-General after consultation with the Prime Minister, of whom at least two are persons who hold or who have held public office. The functions of the Council are to advise the Governor-General on the exercise of the Royal Prerogative of Mercy and on appeals on disciplinary matters from the three Service Commisions.

THE EXECUTIVE

The Prime Minister

The Governor-General appoints as Prime Minister the person from the House of Representatives who, in his judgment, is best able to command the support of the majority of the members of that House.

Leader of the Opposition

There is a Leader of the Opposition appointed by the Governor-General in his discretion being the member of the House of Representatives who in his judgment is best able to command the support of the majority of those members of the House who do not support the Government.

The Cabinet

The Cabinet consists of the Prime Minister and not less than eleven other Ministers appointed by the Governor-General on the advice of the Prime Minister.

THE JUDICATURE

The Judicature consists of a Supreme Court, a Court of Appeal and minor courts. Judicial matters, notably advice to the Governor-General on appointments, are considered by a Judicial Service Commission, the Chairman of which is the Chief Justice, members being the President of the Court of Appeal, the Chairman of the Public Service Commission and three others.

CITIZENSHIP

All persons born in Jamaica after Independence automatically acquire Jamaican citizenship and there is also provision for the acquisition of citizenship by persons born outside Jamaica of Jamaican parents. Persons born in Jamaica (or persons born outside Jamaica of Jamaican parents) before independence who immediately prior to independence were citizens of the United Kingdom and Colonies also automatically become citizens of Jamaica.

Appropriate provision is made which permits persons who do not automatically become citizens of Jamaica to be registered as such.

FUNDAMENTAL RIGHTS AND FREEDOMS

The Constitution includes provisions safeguarding the fundamental freedoms of the individual, irrespective of race, place of origin, political opinions, colour, creed or sex, subject only to respect for the rights and freedoms of others and for the public interest. The fundamental freedoms include the right of life, liberty, security of the person and protection from arbitrary arrest or restriction of movement, the enjoyment of property and the protection of the law, freedom of conscience, of expression and of peaceful assembly and association, and respect for private and family life.

THE GOVERNMENT

Governor-General: Most Hon. FLORIZEL A. GLASSPOLE, O.N., C.D.

PRIVY COUNCIL OF JAMAICA

Hon. C. H. BROWNE, Hon. G. ARTHUR BROWN, C.M.G., Hon. CLINTON HART, O.B.E., Hon. Dr. VERNON LINDO, Hon. Dr. K. RATTRAY, Hon. G. OWEN.

THE CABINET
(March 1974)

Prime Minister, Minister of Defence, External Affairs and Economic Affairs: MICHAEL MANLEY.

Deputy Prime Minister, Minister of Finance: DAVID COORE.

Minister of Industry, Commerce and Tourism: P. J. PATTERSON.

Minister of Public Utilities, Communications and Transport: ERIC BELL.

Minister of Education: ELI MATALON.

Minister of Home Affairs and Justice: NOEL SILVERA.

Minister of Health and Environmental Control: Dr. KENNETH MCNEILL.

Minister of Local Government: ROSE LEON.

Minister of Pensions and Social Security: HOWARD COOKE.

Minister of Mining and Natural Resources: ALLAN ISAACS.

Minister of Labour and Employment: ERNEST PEART.

Minister of Works: WINSTON JONES.

Minister of Agriculture: KEBLE MUNN.

Minister of Housing: ANTHONY SPALDING.

Minister of Youth and Community Development: Dr. DOUGLAS MANLEY.

Minister of State in the Prime Minister's Office: DUDLEY THOMPSON.

Minister of State for Regional Affairs: SIDNEY PAGON.

Minister of State in the Ministry of Industry, Commerce and Tourism: VIVIAN BLAKE.

DIPLOMATIC REPRESENTATION

HIGH COMMISSIONS AND EMBASSIES ACCREDITED TO JAMAICA.

(HC) High Commission; (E) Embassy.

Argentina: British-American Bldg., Knutsford Blvd., Kingston 5 (E); *Ambassador:* ROBERTO CUSANO.

Canada: The Dominion Life Building, Cnr. Trafalgar Rd. and Knutsford Blvd., Kingston 10 (HC); *High Commissioner:* JOHN MAURICE HARRINGTON.

Colombia: 27 Tobago Ave., Kingston 10 (E); *Ambassador:* Dr. HERMAN ECHAVARRÍA OLOZAGA.

Dominican Republic: 7 Upper Mark Way, Cherry Gardens, Kingston 8 (E); *Ambassador:* CARLOS NOUEL.

France: 13 Hillcrest Ave., Kingston 6 (E); *Ambassador:* JAQUES O'CONNOR.

Germany, Federal Republic: 13 Waterloo Rd., Kingston 10 (E); *Ambassador:* KURT SCHMIDT.

Guyana: 31 Old Hope Rd., P.O.B. 262, Kingston 5 (HC); *High Commissioner:* Mrs. WINIFRED GASKIN.

Mexico: British-American Bldg. (3rd Floor), Knutsford Blvd., Kingston 5 (E); *Ambassador:* JOSÉ CABALLERO BAZÁN.

Netherlands: British-American Bldg., Knutsford Blvd., Kingston 5 (E); *Ambassador:* ANDRÉ M. BRINK.

Panama: 9 Hall Blvd., Kingston 8 (E); *Ambassador:* ERNESTO ENRIQUE ESTENOZ.

Peru: 1 Hall Blvd., Kingston 8 (E); *Ambassador:* (vacant).

Trinidad and Tobago: 31 Old Hope Rd., Kingston 5 (HC); *High Commissioner:* ANTONY K. SABGA-ABOUD.

United Kingdom: 58 Duke St., P.O.B. 628, Kingston (HC); *High Commissioner:* JOHN HENNINGS, C.M.G.

U.S.A.: 43 Duke St., Kingston (E); *Ambassador:* VINCENT DE ROULET.

Venezuela: British-American Bldg. (3rd Floor), Knutsford Blvd., Kingston 5 (E); *Ambassador:* Dr. RAMÓN A. ILLARRAMENDI.

Jamaica also has diplomatic relations with Austria, Belgium, Brazil, Chile, People's Republic of China, Costa Rica, Cyprus, Egypt, Ghana, India, Israel, Italy, Japan, Republic of Korea, Lebanon, Nigeria, Pakistan, Sierra Leone, Spain, Switzerland, Tanzania, Turkey, Yugoslavia and Zambia.

PARLIAMENT

SENATE

President: A. G. R. Byfield.

21 members, 13 nominated by the Prime Minister, 8 by the Leader of the Opposition.

HOUSE OF REPRESENTATIVES

Speaker: Ripton McPherson.

Election, February 1972

	Seats	Votes
People's National Party . .	37	267,655
Jamaica Labour Party . .	15	204,482
Independent	1	1,040

POLITICAL PARTIES

Jamaica Labour Party (J.L.P.): 7 Retirement Road, Kingston 5; f. 1944 by Sir Alexander Bustamante; the Party draws its main support from worker-members of the Bustamante Industrial Trade Union, founded by Sir Alexander in 1938; the Union has representatives on the Central Executive of the Jamaica Labour Party; Leader Sir Alexander Bustamante, g.b.e.; Chair. Senator Hector Wynter; Sec. Stafford Owen.

People's National Party (P.N.P.): Headquarters: 23/25 South Camp Rd., Kingston; f. 1938 on socialist principles with national independence as its goal; is the governing party by a victory in the election of February 1972. The Party advocates social and economic change through the participation of the masses for the achievement of an egalitarian society, and follows a foreign policy of non-alignment although acknowledging a special relationship with third world countries. The Party has an important affiliate in the National Workers' Union. Pres. Hon. Michael Manley, p.m., m.p.; Sec. Ken Chin-Onn.

JUDICIAL SYSTEM

Justice is administered by several Courts—the Supreme Court, Court of Appeal, Resident Magistrates' Courts and Traffic Courts. There are also Courts of Petty Sessions.

The Supreme Court
P.O. Box 491, Kingston.

Chief Justice: Hon. Kenneth G. Smith, o.j.

Senior Puisne Judge: Hon. L. G. Robinson.

Puisne Judges: U. N. Parnell, H. S. Grannum, E. Zacca, V. C. Melville, K. C. Henry, I. D. Rowe, W. B. Willkie, V. L. Lopez, H. V. T. Chambers, L. L. Robotham, O. D. Marsh, W. D. Marsh, C. A. B. Ross.

Master: V. K. G. McCarthy.

Registrar: Mrs. E. B. Allen.

Deputy Registrars: Miss Hazel Johnson, W. Coke.

Court of Appeal

President: The Hon. Sir Cyril Henriques.

Judges: Sir Joseph Luckhoo, L. B. Fox, A. M. Edun, C. H. Graham Perkins, R. M. Hercules, W. H. Swaby.

Registrar: C. Patterson.

Judicial Service Commission

Chairman: Chief Justice.

Members: President of the Court of Appeal, Chairman of The Public Service Commission and three others.

RELIGION

The Anglican Church is the largest religious body, and had 317,600 adherents according to a 1970 estimate. Presbyterians number about 92,000. The Roman Catholic Church has about 157,593 members, and other religious bodies include the Methodist, Baptist and Congregational Churches, the Salvation Army, The Society of Friends and the Seventh Day Adventist Church.

ANGLICAN CHURCH

Bishop of Jamaica: Rt. Rev. John Cyril Emerson Swaby, Church Offices, Kingston 5.

Suffragan Sees:

Bishop of Kingston: Rt. Rev. J. Clark.

Bishop of Mandeville: Rt. Rev. H. D. Edmondson.

Bishop of Montego Bay: Rt. Rev. N. W. de Souza.

ROMAN CATHOLIC CHURCH

Archbishop of Kingston: Most Rev. Samuel E. Carter, s.j., 21 Hopefield Ave., Kingston 6.

Bishop of Montego Bay: Most Rev. Edgerton R. Clarke, Blessed Sacrament Cathedral Rectory, P.O.B. 197, Montego Bay, St. James.

Assembly of God: Evangel Temple, 3 Friendship Park Rd., Kingston 6; 191,200 mems.; Pastor C. M. Darell-Huckerby.

First Church of Christ, Scientist: 13 West Racecourse, Kingston.

Jewish: 92 Duke St., Kingston.

Methodist: Lyndhurst, Kingston.

Salvation Army: Bramwell Booth Memorial Hall, Kingston.

Seventh Day Adventist: North St., Kingston.

United Church of Jamaica and Grand Cayman: 24 Hagley Park Pl., Kingston 10; 16,000 mems.; Gen. Sec. Rev. C. A. Thomas.

THE PRESS

Daily Gleaner: 7 North St., Kingston; f. 1834; morning; Independent; Man. Dir. G. A. SHERMAN; Editor HECTOR WYNTER; U.K. representatives; Colin Turner (London) Ltd., 122 Shaftesbury Ave., W1V 8HA; circ. 666,762.

Jamaica Daily News: f. 1973; Dir. PETER ROSSEAU; Editor J. C. PROUTE; circ. 40,000.

Star: 7 North St., Kingston; evening; circ. 74,167.

Beacon: P.O.B. 559, Montego Bay; 2 per week.

Caribbean Challenge: 55 Church St., Box 186, Kingston; f. 1957; monthly; circ. 30,000.

Catholic Opinion: 11 Duke St., Kingston; f. 1896; weekly; Editor Rev. JOHN L. SULLIVAN, s.j.; Agents: R. H. Humphrey & Co. Ltd., 39 Brockenhurst Rd., Croydon, Surrey, England; circ. 7,500.

Children's Own: 7 North St., Kingston; weekly; distributed during term time; circ. 116,721.

Chinese Public News: 9 North St., Kingston; Chinese; bi-weekly; circ. 3,500.

Chung San News, The: 130 Barry St., Kingston; Chinese; bi-weekly; circ. 3,500.

Farmer's Weekly: 17 North St., Kingston; circ. 65,650.

Government Gazette: P.O.B. 487, Kingston; f. 1868; circ. 4,817; Government Printer R. HINES.

Jamaica Baptist Reporter, The: The Jamaica Baptist Union, 6 Hope Rd., Kingston 10; Editor Rev. AMBROSE A. FINLAY, B.D., S.T.M.; circ. 3,800.

Jamaica Churchman: Church House, Kingston 5; monthly; circ. 6,000.

Jamaica Weekly Gleaner: 7 North St., Kingston; weekly; overseas; Man. Dir. G. A. SHERMAN; circ. 32,004.

New Nation: P.O.B. 91, Kingston 16.

Pagoda: 13 Lissant Rd., Kingston 16; fortnightly.

Public Opinion: 2 Torrington Road, Kingston; f. 1937; supports People's National Party; weekly; Editor L. NEMBHARD; Agents: R. H. Humphrey & Co. Ltd., 39 Brockenhurst Rd., Croydon, Surrey, England; circ. 13,000.

Sports Life: 18 East St., Kingston; f. 1958; circ. 7,000.

Sunday Gleaner: 7 North St., Kingston; circ. 98,400.

Voice of Jamaica: 94 Maxfield Ave., Kingston 13; organ of Jamaica Labour Party; weekly; circ. 20,000.

Weekend Star: 7 North St., Kingston; Fridays; evening; circ. 96,068.

West Indian Medical Journal: University of the West Indies, Kingston 7; quarterly; circ. 2,000.

West Indian Review, The: 46 East St., Kingston; illustrated; quarterly; English address: The Penthouse, Glenwood, Dorking, Surrey.

West Indian Sportsman: 75 Church St., Kingston; monthly; circ. 7,000.

PRESS ASSOCIATION

Press Association of Jamaica: 2–4 Geffrard Place, Kingston; f. 1943; 140 mems.; Pres. J. C. PROUTE; Sec. KEN CHAPLIN; publ. *Press & Radio* (annual).

Reuters is represented in Jamaica.

PUBLISHERS

Arawak Press Ltd.: 20 Osbourne Rd., Kingston 10.

Caribbean Universities Press: P.O.B. 83, Kingston; f. 1970; general, educational and academic books in English and Spanish.

City Printery Ltd.: 2 Torrington Rd., Kingston; f. 1937; Chair. A. H. B. AGUILAR; Man. Dir. V. BENNETT; publ. *Public Opinion* (weekly).

Gleaner Co. Ltd., The: 7 North St., Kingston; publs. newspapers and magazines; Man. Dir. G. A. SHERMAN.

Government Printing Office: 77 Duke St., Kingston; Government Printer R. HINES.

Jamaica Publishing House: 97 Church St., Kingston; f. 1969; partnership between Jamaica Teachers Asscn. and Macmillan Education of Great Britain; Chair. A. W. POWELL.

Jamaica Times Press Ltd., The: 141 East Street, Kingston; f. 1898.

Longman Caribbean Ltd.: Kingston; f. 1970; general; Dir. HECTOR WYNTER.

West Indian Publishing Co. Ltd., The: 44 East St., Kingston.

RADIO AND TELEVISION

Jamaica Broadcasting Corporation: 5 South Odeon Ave., Kingston 10; f. 1959; a publicly-owned Statutory Corporation run on semi-commercial lines and designed to transmit quality programmes both on radio (from 1959) and television (from 1963) with a broad social purpose; Gen. Man. DWIGHT WHYLIE.

Educational Broadcasting Service: Ministry of Education, Kingston; f. 1964; 20-minute telecasts and 15-minute radio broadcasts daily during school term.

Radio Jamaica Ltd.: Broadcasting House, 32 Lyndhurst Rd., Kingston 5; f. 1950; associated company of Rediffusion International Ltd., London; island-wide commercial and public service broadcasting 144 hours per week; also operates the Reditune background music service; Gen. Man. L. W. DE PASS.

Receiving sets (1972): radio 775,000; television 105,000.

FINANCE

(cap. =capital; p.u. =paid up; dep. =deposits; m. =million;
amounts in Jamaican dollars.)

BANKING

CENTRAL BANK

Bank of Jamaica: P.O.B. 621, Kingston; f. 1960; cap. p.u. 0.5m. (Dec. 1971), dep. 489m. (Sept. 1973); Gov. Hon. G. A. BROWN, C.M.G.

OTHER BANKS

The Bank of Nova Scotia Jamaica Ltd.: 5–7 King St., Kingston; f. 1967; Gen. Man. C. HENRIQUES; cap. p.u. 6m., dep. 202.9m. (Oct. 1973); main br. 35 King St., Man. R. J. KAVANAGH; 52 other brs. throughout Jamaica.

Jamaica Citizens Bank: 4 King St., Kingston 1; f. 1967; cap. 4m., dep. 24m.; Gen. Man. ARTHUR CHAI ONN.

Royal Bank of Jamaica: Head Office: 40 Duke St., P.O.B. 621, Kingston; Main Office: 37 Duke St., P.O.B. 96; brs. in Kingston (10), Mandeville, May Pen and Montego Bay; incorporated with Royal Bank of Canada July 1971; authorized cap. 4m., cap. p.u. 3m., dep. 60.2m. (Sept. 1973); Man. Main Office P. E. RACINE; Man. Dir. R. S. SASSO.

Workers' Savings and Loans Bank: 134–140 Tower St., P.O.B. 473, Kingston; f. 1973 in succession to the Government Savings Bank; Man. Dr. PAUL CHEN-YOUNG.

Bank of Montreal Jamaica Ltd.: Head Office: P.O.B. 1262, Nassau, Bahamas; Kingston: 111–115 Harbour St.; Man. ERIC SHMIDT.

Bank of Nova Scotia Jamaica Ltd.: Head Office: King and Bay Sts., Toronto; 35 King St., Kingston.

Barclays Bank International: Head Office: 54 Lombard St., London, E.C.3; West Caribbean Head Office: 77 King St., Kingston, Dirs. D. A. BANKS, F. D. LONGMIRE; Kingston Office: 54 King St., Man. A. J. BRADLEY; 51 brs., sub-brs. and agencies in Jamaica.

Canadian Imperial Bank of Commerce: Head Office: Commerce Court, Toronto 1, Ontario; Jamaica Area Office: P.O.B. 43, Kingston and Harbour Sts.; Man. (Kingston) W. SHURNIAK.

First National City Bank: Head Office: 399 Park Ave., New York 10022; Jamaica Branches: 4½ King St., P.O.B. 362, Kingston, Man. VINCENT CHUNG; 21 Constant Spring Rd., P.O.B. 124, Kingston 10; 6 other brs. in Jamaica.

First National Bank of Chicago: 32½ Duke St., P.O.B. 219, Kingston.

Royal Bank of Canada: Head Office: Place Ville Marie, Montreal; 37 Duke St., Kingston.

DEVELOPMENT BANKS

Jamaica Development Bank: 15 Oxford Rd., Kingston 5; f. 1969; replaced Development Finance Corporation, f. 1959; initial cap. 20m.; Chair./Man. Dir. NOEL CHIN.

Jamaica Mortgage Bank: Kingston; f. 1971; became a statutory organization wholly owned by the Government in June 1973; established by the Government and the United States Agency for International Development to function primarily as a secondary market facility for home mortgages and to mobilize long-term funds for housing developments in Jamaica.

There are also Peoples' Co-operative Banks, which, under the supervision of the Agricultural Loans Societies Boards, make loans to small farmers.

STOCK EXCHANGE

Jamaica Stock Exchange Ltd.: Kingston; f. 1968; Chair. W. B. SAMMS; Gen. Man. V. H. O. MENDEZ.

INSURANCE

Insurance Company of Jamaica Ltd.: 101–103 Harbour St., P.O.B. 249, Kingston; f. 1931; Chair. LESLIE E. ASHENHEIM, M.A.; Gen. Man. ROBERT D. MARLEY.

Jamaica Co-operative Fire and General Insurance Co. Ltd.: 10 Duke St., Kingston; Gen. Man. C. L. CORP.

Jamaica Mutual Life Assurance Society: P.O.B. 204, Kingston; f. 1844; Chair D. J. JUDAH, C.B.E.; Gen. Man. GILBERT C. LIVINGSTON.

Most of the leading British and some U.S. and Canadian companies have offices or agents.

TRADE AND INDUSTRY

CHAMBERS OF COMMERCE

Jamaica Chamber of Commerce: P.O.B. 172, Kingston; Pres. W. E. MEEKS; Gen. Man. S. M. ABRAHAMS; Sec. N. R. MADDEN; publ. *Chamber of Commerce Journal* (quarterly).

Clarendon Chamber of Commerce: f. 1968; Pres. L. H. S. BAUGH.

Manchester Chamber of Commerce: P.O.B. 197, Mandeville; f. 1964; Pres. CLIFF RUSSEL.

Montego Bay Chamber of Commerce Ltd.: P.O.B. 213, Life of Jamaica Bldg., 9 King St., Montego Bay; f. 1932; 200 mems.; Pres. Dr. ARTHUR ELDEMIRE; Sec. K. W. ARMSTRONG.

Ocho Rios Chamber of Commerce: Pineapple Place, Ocho Rios; Pres. J. H. S. YOUNG; Sec. Mrs. J. M. LYON.

Portland Chamber of Commerce Ltd.: Port Antonio, Portland; f. 1935; 135 mems.; Pres. WILSON LEE SANG.

St. Catherine Chamber of Commerce: 25 King St., Spanish Town; f. 1966; Pres. W. SHADEED.

St. Mary Chamber of Commerce: Highgate, St. Mary; f. 1968; Pres. H. N. CLARE.

Trelawny Chamber of Commerce: f. 1948; Pres. PATRICK TENNYSON.

ASSOCIATIONS

All-Island Banana Growers' Association Ltd.: Banana Industry Building, 10 South Avenue, Kingston Gardens, Kingston; f. 1946; 42,051 mems.; Chair. K. S. FRANCIS; Sec. Miss I. CHANG.

All-Island Jamaica Cane Farmers' Association: 4 North Ave., Kingston 4; f. 1941; registered cane farmers 24,925 mems.; Chair. T. G. MIGNOTT; Man. A. D. BELINFANTI.

Citrus Growers' Association Ltd.: 1A North Ave., P.O.B. 159, Kingston; f. 1955; 26,248 mems.; Chair. C. A. BRODERICK; Admin. E. LINDO.

Importers' and Distributors' Association of Jamaica: 11 Duke St., Kingston.

In-Bond Merchants' Association: 18 Church St., P.O.B. 198, Montego Bay; Chair. ALAN HART.

Jamaica Banana Producers' Association Ltd.: P.O.B. 237, Kingston; f. 1927; Chair. Hon. C. H. BROWNE; Man. Dir. H. T. HART.

Jamaica Hotel and Tourist Association: 2 Ardenne Rd., Kingston 10; Pres. JOHN ISSA.

Jamaica Livestock Association: P.O.B. 36, Newport East, Kingston; f. 1941; 6,000 mems.; Chair. H. L. ROPER; Man. H. J. RAINFORD.

Jamaica Manufacturers' Association Ltd.: 85A Duke St., Kingston; f. 1947; 550 mems.; Pres. DOUGLAS C. VAZ; Sec. E. A. HALL.

Jamaican Association of Sugar Technologists: c/o Sugar Industry Research Institute, Mandeville; Pres. A. S. HART; Hon. Sec. M. E. A. SHAW.

Master Printers' Association of Jamaica: c/o Art Printery, 87 Tower St., Kingston; f. 1943; 32 mems.; Pres. D. BURROWES; Sec. S. McDONALD.

Shipping Association of Jamaica: 161 Water Lane, Kingston; f. 1939; 25 mems.; Chair. L. P. SCOTT; Gen. Man. NOEL A. HYLTON.

Sugar Manufacturers' Association (of Jamaica) Ltd.: 5 Trevennion Park Rd., Kingston 5; comprises all the sugar manufacturers in Jamaica; deals with all aspects of the sugar industry and its by-products; provides liaison between the industry, the Government and overseas interests; Man. C. S. ROBERTS.

Note: A new body, the Jamaica Sugar Manufacturing Corporation, is to be set up. The Government will participate with private sugar interests to establish a central body for the effective operation of the industry.

GOVERNMENT ORGANIZATIONS

Agricultural Development Corporation: 83 Hanover St., Kingston; est. 1952; Chair. HUGH MILLER; Sec. Mrs. OUIDA COOKE.

Agricultural Marketing Corporation: 188 Spanish Town Rd., P.O.B. 144, Kingston 11; f. 1963; Chair. W. D. ROBERTS; Gen. Man. G. H. McFARLANE.

Banana Board: P.O.B. 602, Kingston; f. 1953 under the Banana Board Law; is the sole exporter of bananas and has wide powers over the industry; Chair. T. H. DONALDSON; Sec. N. RAE.

Cocoa Industry Board: P.O.B. 68, Kingston 15; f. 1957; has wide statutory powers to regulate and develop the industry; owns and operates four central fermentaries; Chair. D. E. S. WEBB, J.P.; Sec.-Man. L. P. DELISSER.

Coconut Industry Board: 18 Waterloo Rd., P.O.B. 204, Kingston 10; 9 mems.; Chair. R. D. C. HENRIQUES; Man./Sec. R. A. WILLIAMS.

Coffee Industry Board: P.O.B. 508, Kingston; f. 1950; 7 mems.; has wide statutory powers to regulate and develop the industry; is the sole exporter of coffee; Chair. L. R. MITCHELL; Man. F. A. BRISCOE; publ. *Annual Report.*

Jamaica Industrial Development Corporation: 4 Winchester Rd., Kingston; est. 1952; financed by the Government to facilitate and stimulate industrial projects; maintains a staff of research and advisory specialists and trains personnel in labour and management; Chair. WESLEY A. WAINWRIGHT; Sec./Dir. of Projects RANDY A. CAREY; brs. in London and New York.

Jamaica National Export Corporation: P.O.B. 645, Kingston; f. 1970; responsible to Ministry of Industry, Commerce and Tourism for facilitating and encouraging the development of Jamaica's export trade; Chair. S. C. ALEXANDER; Exec. Dir. REGINALD WEBB-HARRIS.

Sugar Industry Authority: 29 Barbican Rd., Kingston; Chair. R. D. FLETCHER; Sec. L. C. GLAZE.

Sugar Industry Labour Welfare Board: 22 Camp Rd., P.O.B. 34, Kingston 5; Chair. E. G. BARRETT; Man. Mrs. I. SEATON.

Urban Development Corporation: Kingston; f. 1968; responsibility for urban renewal within designated areas; Chair. MOSES MATALON.

TRADE UNIONS

Bustamante Industrial Trade Union (BITU): 98 Duke St., Kingston; f. 1938; 100,459 mems; Pres. Sir ALEXANDER BUSTAMANTE; Gen. Sec. Miss EDITH NELSON.

National Workers' Union of Jamaica: 130 East St., Kingston 16; f. 1952; affiliated to ICFTU, ORIT, etc.; 149,569 mems.; Pres. THOSSY A. KELLY; Gen. Sec. L. GOODLEIGH.

Trades Union Congress of Jamaica: P.O.B. 19, 25 Sutton St., Kingston; affiliated to CCL and ICFTU; mems. 20,000; Pres. EDWARD SMITH; Gen. Sec. HOPETON CAVEN.

PRINCIPAL INDEPENDENT UNIONS

Independent Portworkers' Union: 71 North St., Kingston.

Jamaica Federation of Musicians' Union: P.O.B. 24, Kingston 3; f. 1958; about 900 mems.; Pres. CECIL V. BRADSHAW; Sec. LESLIE A. WILSON.

Machado Employees' Union: 130 East St., Kingston.

United Portworkers' and Seamen's Union: 20 West St., Kingston.

Water Utilities and Allied Workers' Union: 130 East St., Kingston; about 520 mems.; Pres. ISAIAH STEWART; Sec. V. BANCROFT EDWARDS.

There are also 17 employers' associations registered as trade unions.

CO-OPERATIVES

The Jamaica Social Welfare Commission promotes Co-operative Societies in the following categories: Consumer, Co-operative Farming, Credit, Credit and Marketing, Fishermen's Irrigation, Land Lease, Land Purchase, Marketing, Supplies Co-ops., Thrift, Transport and Tillage.

TRANSPORT AND TOURISM

RAILWAYS

Jamaica Railway Corporation: P.O.B. 489, Kingston; Chair. D. C. Tretzel; Gen. Man. A. A. Bennett.

There are 205 miles of standard-gauge railway operated by the Jamaica Railway Corporation. The main lines are from Kingston to Montego Bay, May Pen to Frankfield and Spanish Town to Port Antonio. The Railway is subsidized by the Government.

ROADS

Jamaica has a good network of tar-surfaced and metalled motoring roads. There are some 2,675 miles of main roads which are asphalted or macadamized and about 6,500 miles of secondary roads of which over 3,200 are suitable for motor traffic.

MOTORISTS' ORGANIZATION

Jamaica Automobile Association: 17A Duke St., Kingston; Sec.-Man. E. W. Youngman.

SHIPPING

Passenger and cargo services are provided to Jamaica by the following companies: Alcoa, Achille Lauro, Atlantrafic Express, Blue Sea, Booth American, Canada Jamaica, Cia. Transatlántica Española, Dovar, Elders and Fyffes, French, Grace, Hamburg-Amerika, Harrison, Horn, Jamaica Banana Producers', Jamaica Fruit and Shipping, New Zealand Shipping, New Zealand-West Indies, K. Line, Kirk, Montreal-Australia-New Zealand, Royal Mail, Saguenay, United Fruit Jamaica Co.

CIVIL AVIATION

Air Jamaica (1968) Ltd.: 76 Harbour St., Kingston; f. 1968; services to Miami, Chicago, Philadelphia, New York, Detroit, Toronto, Nassau, London; fleet of two DC-9, three DC-8, two DC-8-61, one DC-8-62; Chair. Hon. G. A. Brown; Pres. Charles Eyre.

Jamaica Air Services Ltd.: Tinson Pen Aerodrome, P.O.B. 255, Kingston 11; f. 1962; scheduled domestic and charter flights; fleet of two Twin Otter, one BN-2A Islander; Chair. Capt. L. A. Rerrie.

Jamaica is also served by the following foreign airlines: Air Canada, British Airways, BWIA, Caribair, Cayman Airways, Delta Air Lines, Eastern Airlines, LIAT (Leeward Islands), Lufthansa, Mexicana, Pan American and TACA (El Salvador).

TOURISM

Jamaica Tourist Board: 80 Harbour St., P.O.B. 284, Kingston; Casa Montego Arcade, Montego Bay; f. 1955; 8 members appointed by the Ministry of Industry, Commerce and Tourism headed by a Director of Tourism; a statutory body set up by the Government for the promotion of tourism; Dir. E. A. Abrahams; in 1972 493,488 tourists visited Jamaica.

OVERSEAS OFFICES:

U.S.A.:
Suite 266, Pan American Bldg., New York, N.Y. 10017.
Suite 1210, 36 South Wabash Ave., Chicago, Ill. 60603.
Suite 1200, 1700 Walnut St., Philadelphia, Pa. 19103.
Suite 604, 3075 Wilshire Blvd., Los Angeles, Calif. 90010.
18th Floor, 230 Peachtree St., N.W., Atlanta, Ga. 30303.
Room 606, Northland Towers West, Southfield, Michigan 48075.
Suite 2001, Bryan Tower, Dallas, Tex. 75201.
Suite 608, Ingraham Bldg., 25 S.E. Second Ave., Miami, Fla. 33131.
Suite 1111, K St., N.W., Washington, D.C. 20006.

Canada:
Suite 220, 102 Bloor St., W., Toronto 181, Ont.
Suite 211, 1118 St. Catherine St. W., Montreal.

U.K.:
6-10 Bruton St., London, W.1.

Germany:
Kaiserstrasse 15, 600 Frankfurt/Main 1, W. Germany.

Jamaica Hotel and Tourist Association: 2 Ardenne Rd., Kingston 10; Pres. John Issa; Gen. Man. Russell E. Lewars, o.b.e.

CULTURAL ORGANIZATIONS

The Institute of Jamaica: 12-16 East St., Kingston; f. 1879; Government-sponsored organization; provides cultural activities, maintains and develops national collections and museums; Dir. Neville Dawes, m.a. (acting); publs. *Jamaica Journal* (quarterly), *Bulletins*, *Science Series* (irregular).

Jamaica Amateur Operatic Society: P.O.B. 299, Kingston 10; f. 1960; engages in the production of open and dramatic musicals.

Jamaican National Dance Theatre Company: c/o The Little Theatre, 5 Tom Redcam Drive, Kingston 5; f. 1962; amateur company; productions reflect the variety of sources of Jamaican and Caribbean life; annual seasons and international tours; Artistic Dir. Rex Nettleford; Chair. Maurice Stoppi; Sec. Verona Ashman.

Jamaica Philharmonic Symphony Orchestra: Y.M.C.A. Headquarters, 21 Hope Rd., Kingston 10; f. 1940; Dir.-Conductor Sibthorpe L. Beckett; Exec. Sec. Mrs. Vivienne Murphy.

The Little Theatre Movement of Jamaica: 4 Tom Redcam Drive, Kingston 5; f. 1941; amateur and semi-professional productions; Pres. Greta Fowler, m.b.e., Sec. Doris Duperly.

UNIVERSITY

University of the West Indies: Mona, Kingston 7; 730 teachers, 5,778 students (incl. faculties outside Jamaica).

JAPAN

INTRODUCTORY SURVEY

Location, Climate, Language, Religion, Flag, Capital

Japan forms a curved chain of islands off the coast of east Asia. There are four large islands, named (from north to south) Hokkaido, Honshu, Shikoku and Kyushu, plus the Ryukyu Islands and many smaller islands. Hokkaido lies just to the south of the large Soviet island, Sakhalin, and about 800 miles east of the U.S.S.R.'s mainland port, Vladivostok. Southern Japan is about 100 miles east of Korea. Although summers are everywhere temperate, the climate in winter varies sharply from north to south. Typhoons and heavy rains are common in summer. The language is Japanese. The major religions are Shinto and Buddhism and there is a minority of Christians. The national flag (proportions usually 3 by 2) consists of a red sun without rays on a white background. The capital is Tokyo.

Recent History

Following the Second World War the United States occupied Japan and introduced a policy of democratization. The Emperor was deprived of his former god-like authority and a new Constitution providing for popular elections became operative. In 1952 Japan regained its independence after signing the San Francisco Peace Treaty. Admission to the United Nations followed in 1956, and in 1964 Japan joined the IMF and the OECD. Diplomatic relations with the Republic of Korea were established in 1965. The Bonin Islands, administered by the U.S.A. from 1945, were returned to Japan in June 1968. On May 15th, 1972 the Ryukyu Islands, including Okinawa (site of a former U.S. military base), reverted to Japanese sovereignty. In January 1972 the Japanese and Soviet Governments agreed to negotiate a peace treaty but to date (July 1974) it has not been concluded.

In July 1972 the Prime Minister, Eisaku Sato, having held office for eight years, resigned and was succeeded by Kakuei Tanaka. In September 1972 Mr. Tanaka paid a six-day visit to the People's Republic of China which resulted in the re-establishment of diplomatic relations. Taiwan severed diplomatic relations with Japan as a result. Further links with China were established by a trade pact in December 1973 and an air agreement in April 1974.

The popular interest aroused both by Mr. Tanaka's China policy and by his plans to relocate industry encouraged him to dissolve the House of Representatives in November 1972. The elections resulted in the retention of power by the Liberal Democratic Party but with a reduced majority. The popularity of the Government declined during 1973, largely through its inability to check inflation, and a radical cabinet reshuffle took place in November. Following the economic uncertainties that arose after the Middle East war of 1973, the violent anti-Japanese demonstrations that accompanied Mr. Tanaka's tour of South-East Asia in December 1973 and the emergence of extreme political groups on both the right and the left, observers discerned a mood of disquiet among the Japanese about their identity in a changing international scene.

Government

Under the Constitution of 1946 the Emperor is Head of State but has no governing power. Executive power lies with the Cabinet consisting of the Prime Minister and 11 to 16 Ministers of State. The legislative body is the Diet, consisting of the House of Representatives (491 seats), whose members are elected for a four-year term, and the House of Councillors (252 seats), members of which are elected for six years, one half retiring every three years. There is universal suffrage at the age of twenty. The country is divided into 47 prefectures.

Defence

Although the Constitution renounces war and the use of force, the right of self-defence is not excluded and ground, maritime and air self-defence forces are maintained. Under security treaties, the United States provides equipment and training staff and also maintains bases at Sasebo (Kyushu) and Yokosuka (near Tokyo). There are about 38,000 U.S. navy and air force personnel based in Japan. There are about 3,000 Japanese military personnel deployed on Okinawa. The total strength of the self-defence forces was estimated at 266,000 in 1973. These forces are being strengthened under a five-year programme which began in 1972, and personnel is to be increased to 286,000 by 1976. The defence budget for 1973–74 was U.S. $3,530 million.

Economic Affairs

Japan is not well endowed with natural resources. Some 66 per cent of the total land area is forested and, although almost completely self-sufficient in rice, the country has to import more than 70 per cent of the other cereals and fodder crops consumed. Mineral resources are meagre, except for limestone and sulphur, and Japanese industry is heavily dependent on imported raw materials and fuels. Based on the promotion of manufacturing industries for the export market, Japan achieved and maintained a very high rate of economic growth after the war. Gross national product (GNP) grew at an average annual rate of 10.3 per cent between 1962 and 1972 and in 1971 Japan's GNP became the second largest in the world, ranking behind only the U.S.A. (Soviet bloc countries excluded). The Economic and Social Development Programmes (1970–75) envisaged an average annual growth rate of 10.6 per cent, but this estimate had to be revised drastically after the Middle East war of October 1973, when Arab countries began to raise the price of oil. Japan depends on oil for 74 per cent of its energy requirements and 80 per cent of this amount comes from the Middle East. Official forecasts for the fiscal year 1974 now estimate growth rate at 2.5 per cent in real terms, and figures for January and February 1974 showed that production and shipment in key industrial sectors were falling off.

Since 1969, concessions have been granted for off-shore oil exploration in the Korean Straits, Sea of Japan and off Hokkaido Island. The first oil drilling began in February 1971, 30 miles off Hamada in the Sea of Japan. Japanese and Soviet government representatives met in February 1972 to discuss the construction of a 6,660 km. oil pipeline to cost £1,600 million to carry oil from the Tyumen fields in Siberia and transport it to Nakhodka on the Soviet Pacific. Discussions were still unresolved in April 1974. In January 1974 Japan and South Korea agreed on the joint development of oil resources on the continental shelf south of Cheju island.

The proportion of the labour force employed in agriculture, forestry and fisheries was 19 per cent in 1970, while the contribution of this sector to the gross domestic product was 6.5 per cent, a decline in each case. The principal crops are rice, wheat, barley and potatoes. Japan is a leading fishing nation, both in coastal and deep-sea waters. Mining, construction and manufacturing contributed 35 per cent of the gross domestic product in 1970, employing 44 per cent of the labour force. Heavy and chemical industries predominate in the increasing output of the manufacturing sector (26 per cent of national income), particularly petrochemicals, automobiles, steel, machinery, electrical equipment and chemicals. Commerce, transport, communications and services accounted for 49 per cent of the gross domestic product and 46 per cent of the labour force.

In recent years demands increased, particularly from the U.S.A., for action to be taken to curb the phenomenal rise in the volume of Japanese exports to Western countries, especially in view of the reluctance of the Japanese government to liberalize restrictions on the import of certain foreign manufactured goods into Japan. The yen, which had become undervalued, was revalued by 17 per cent in the Smithsonian re-alignment of December 1971. It was further revalued when allowed to float, following the U.S. dollar devaluation of February 1973. It was devalued, however, after the Middle East war of October 1973, though it recovered slightly in the early part of 1974. A trade deficit was recorded for 1973, the first since 1968, with imports rising by 67 per cent over the 1972 figures and exports by 30 per cent.

Transport and Communications

Despite difficulties of terrain, rail transport is highly developed, and a 54 kilometre-long tunnel linking Hokkaido and Honshu Islands is being built. Work on a 23 kilometre section, the Seikan Tunnel under the Tsugaru Strait, began in late 1971. The whole project estimated to cost £250 million is expected to be completed by March 1979. There were 24,300 km. of track in 1972, about 60 per cent of which was owned by Japanese National Railways. Work began in 1971 on a new super express railway network linking all of Japan's major cities. To be completed by 1985, it will total 9,000 km. in length and is to cost 11,300,000 million yen. Japan's road network extended to a length of 1,022,936 km. in December 1971 and plans have been made to cover the country with a trunk automobile highway network with a total length of 7,600 km. by 1985. Under the Economic and Social Development Plan (1967–71) $18,330 million was invested in the development of roads, and $2,300 million went towards improving harbour facilities. Large and small craft ply between the islands and there is a big fleet of ocean-going vessels. Japan had 34,929,000 gross tons of mercantile marine on June 30th, 1972. The main ports are Yokohama, Nagasaki and Kobe. Japanese Air Lines (JAL) are state-subsidized and there are over 20 other air transport companies. There are two international airports, at Tokyo and Osaka. Construction has begun on a third near Narita City.

Social Welfare

About 90 per cent of the population are insured under schemes covering health, welfare annuities, unemployment and industrial accidents. In 1972 there were 10.75 hospital beds per thousand of the population.

Education

Education is compulsory and free for nine years (6–15) in elementary and secondary schools. In 1971 there were 14,189,000 pupils enrolled. Enrolment at higher education institutions was over 1,700,000. There are both State and private universities.

Tourism

The forests and mountains, pagodas and temples, traditional festivals and the classical Kabuki theatre are some of the many tourist attractions of Japan.

Visas are not required to visit Japan by nationals of Argentina, Austria, Belgium, Canada, Colombia, Denmark, Dominican Republic, Finland, France, German Federal Republic, Greece, Italy, Luxembourg, Netherlands, Norway, Pakistan, Spain, Sweden, Switzerland, Tunisia, Turkey and United Kingdom.

Sport

Traditional sports with a wide following are Judo, Sumo (Japanese wrestling) and Kendo (Japanese fencing). Baseball, swimming, skiing and table-tennis are the principal other sports and golf is becoming increasingly popular. The Olympic Games were magnificently staged in Tokyo in 1964, and the Winter Olympic games were held at Sapporo in February 1972.

Public Holidays

1974: September 15th (Respect for the Aged Day), September 23rd (Autumnal Equinox Day), October 10th (Physical Education Day), November 3rd (Culture Day), November 23rd (Labour Thanksgiving Day).

1975: December 28th–January 3rd (New Year's Holiday), January 15th (Adults' Day), February 11th (National Foundation Day), March 21st (Vernal Equinox Day), April 29th (Emperor's Birthday), May 3rd (Constitution Memorial Day), May 5th (Children's Day).

Weights and Measures

The metric system is in force.

Currency and Exchange Rates

1,000 rin = 100 sen = 1 yen.

Exchange rates (April 1974):

£1 sterling = 653.00 yen;
U.S. $1 = 276.75 yen.

STATISTICAL SURVEY

AREA AND POPULATION

AREA*		POPULATION ('000) at October 1st.†		
		TOTAL	MALE	FEMALE
377,388.55 square kilometres	1968	101,331	49,739	51,592
	1969	102,536	50,334	52,202
	1970‡	103,720	50,918	52,802
	1971	105,014	51,529	53,485
	1972*	107,332	52,639	54,693

*Figures for area and 1972 population include Okinawa Prefecture, formerly the U.S.-occupied Ryukyu Islands (area 2,196 sq. km.), which reverted to Japan on May 15th, 1972.
†Excluding foreign military and civilian personnel and their dependents.
‡ Census.

CHIEF CITIES
POPULATION ('000)
(October 1st, 1970, census)

Tokyo (capital) .	8,841*	Amagasaki . .	554	Gifu . . .	386
Osaka .	2,980	Sendai . .	545	Niigata .	384
Yokohama .	2,238	Hiroshima .	542	Nishinomiya .	377
Nagoya . .	2,036	Higashiosaka .	500	Okayama .	375
Kyoto . .	1,419	Chiba . .	482	Toyonaka .	368
Kobe . .	1,289	Kumamoto .	440	Wakayama .	365
Kita-Kyushu .	1,042	Hamamatsu .	432	Kanazawa .	361
Sapporo .	1,010	Nagasaki .	421	Yokosuka .	348
Kawasaki .	973	Shizuoka .	416	Matsuyama .	323
Fukuoka .	853	Himeji .	408	Sasebo . .	248
Sakai . .	594	Kagoshima .	403		

* This figure refers to the 23 wards (ku) of the old city. The population of Tokyo-to (Tokyo Prefecture) was 11,408,000.

BIRTHS, MARRIAGES AND DEATHS

	BIRTHS	BIRTH RATE (per '000)	MARRIAGES	MARRIAGE RATE (per '000)	DEATHS	DEATH RATE (per '000)
1968 .	1,871,839	18.6	956,312	9.5	686,555	6.8
1969 .	1,889,815	18.5	984,142	9.6	693,787	6.8
1970 .	1,934,239	18.8	1,029,405	10.0	712,962	6.9
1971 .	2,000,981	19.2	1,091,229	10.5	684,532	6.6
1972* .	2,038,678	19.3	1,099,974	10.4	683,760	6.5

* Provisional figures.

EMPLOYMENT
(annual average in '000)

	POPULATION 15 YEARS OLD AND OVER	LABOUR FORCE			NOT IN LABOUR FORCE
		Total	Employed	Unemployed	
1968 .	76,780	50,610	50,020	590	26,090
1969 .	77,820	50,980	50,400	570	26,750
1970 .	78,850	51,530	50,940	590	27,230
1971 .	79,700	51,780	51,140	640	27,790
1972 .	80,510	51,820	51,090	730	28,510

EMPLOYMENT—*continued*

	1969	1970	1971	1972
All Industries ('000)	50,400	50,940	51,140	51,090
Agriculture and Forestry	8,990	8,420	7,680	7,050
Fishery and Aquatic Culture	470	440	460	490
Mining	240	200	190	160
Construction	3,710	3,940	4,130	4,310
Manufacturing	13,450	13,770	13,810	13,780
Wholesaling, Retailing, Finance, Insurance and Real Estate	11,330	11,440	11,780	11,970
Transport, Communications and Public Utility	3,380	3,530	3,610	3,540
Services	7,220	7,510	7,740	7,970
Government Service	1,560	1,610	1,670	1,750

AGRICULTURE
PRINCIPAL AGRICULTURAL PRODUCTS
('000 metric tons)

	1970	1971	1972
Rice (rough)*	12,689	10,887	11,897†
Barley†	418	364	324
Wheat‡	474	440	284
Potatoes, Sweet and Irish	6,175	5,312	5,520
Silk Cocoons	112	108	105
Soybeans	126	122	127
Tobacco	150	149	145

* Twelve months ending October of year stated.
† Includes Okinawa Prefecture.
‡ Twelve months beginning April 1st of year stated.

LIVESTOCK
('000)

	CATTLE	SHEEP	GOATS	HORSES	PIGS
1969	3,458	64	198	190	5,429
1970	3,593	22	165	137	6,335
1971	3,615	26	160	125	6,904
1972	3,568	21	130	97	6,985

FORESTRY
('000 cubic metres)

	SAWN TIMBER	PULP	PIT PROPS	PLYWOOD	OTHERS	TOTAL
1968	31,301	7,401	1,027	751	7,689	48,169
1969	28,890	6,651	874	795	8,852	46,062
1970	27,362	6,566	727	778	9,918	45,351
1971	26,325	6,019	573	855	11,481	45,253

FISHING
('ooo metric tons)

	1969	1970	1971	1972*
Deep-sea Fishing . .	3,165	3,429	3,674	3,840
Off-shore Fishing . .	2,948	3,278	3,540	3,489
Coastal Fishing . .	1,863	1,891	1,935	1,912
Shallow Sea Culture .	473	549	608	606
Inland Water Fisheries .	164	168	151	109
Total . . .	8,613	9,315	9,908	10,012

* Provisional figures.

MINING

		1968	1969	1970	1971	1972
Coal	'ooo metric tons	46,568	44,690	39,694	33,432	28,099
Lignite . . .	,, ,, ,,	335	251	197	133	102
Zinc	,, ,, ,,	264	269	280	294	281
Iron	,, ,, ,,	1,059	955	862	830	799
Iron Pyrites . .	,, ,, ,,	4,472	4,469	4,463	3,792	2,590
Manganese . .	,, ,, ,,	312	301	270	285	261
Quartzite . . .	,, ,, ,,	5,332	6,228	7,103	7,513	n.a.
Limestone . .	,, ,, ,,	91,528	103,204	116,230	124,701	134,258
Titanium . . .	metric tons	5,871	4,066	3,145	2,376	n.a.
Chromite . . .	,, ,,	27,891	29,782	32,980	31,642	24,819
Copper . . .	,, ,,	119,932	121,124	119,513	120,029	111,934
Lead . . .	,, ,,	62,873	63,460	64,407	70,586	63,449
Crude Oil . . .	million litres	869	875	899	879	883
Natural Gas . .	cu. metres	2,015,707	2,156,990	2,359,218	2,433,457	2,475,055

INDUSTRY

		1969	1970	1971	1972
Pig Iron	'ooo metric tons	58,147	68,048	72,745	74,055
Crude Steel . . .	,, ,, ,,	82,166	93,322	88,557	96,900
Hot Rolled Steel . .	,, ,, ,,	67,060	75,933	72,077	82,099
Wood Pulp . . .	,, ,, ,,	7,685	8,801	9,039	9,458
Cement . . .	,, ,, ,,	51,387	57,189	59,434	66,289
Sewing Machines . .	'ooo	4,752	4,281	4,666	4,461
Washing Machines .	,,	4,182	4,349	4,149	4,201
Refrigerators . .	,,	3,139	2,631	3,003	3,455
Radio Receivers . .	,,	34,090	32,618	28,092	26,833
T.V. Receivers . .	,,	12,685	13,782	13,231	14,300
Telephone Sets . .	,,	3,033	3,682	4,156	4,840
Cameras . . .	,,	4,801	5,813	5,342	5,318
Fabrics:					
Cotton . . .	million sq. metres	2,779	2,616	2,482	2,264
Wool . . .	,, ,, ,,	437	426	424	479
Rayon . . .	,, ,, ,,	409	354	313	264
Spun Rayon . .	,, ,, ,,	862	827	788	718
Silk . . .	,, ,, ,,	187	201	197	197
Synthetic Fibre .	,, ,, ,,	2,398	2,746	2,839	2,839
Chemical Machinery .	tons	506,485	566,210	600,390	n.a.
Household Chinaware .	,,	629,963	648,702	638,418	n.a.
Automotive Tyres . .	,,	297,571	339,765	361,975	411,196
Plastic Products . .	,,	2,030,180	2,386,562	2,601,591	3,174,325
Machine Tools . .	Nos.	231,419	256,694	183,649	164,553
Passenger Cars . .	,,	2,611,499	3,178,708	3,717,858	4,022,289
Ships (only steel vessels) .	'ooo G.R.T.	9,374	10,172	10,996	12,768

FINANCE

1,000 rin = 100 sen = 1 yen.
Coins: 1, 5, 10, 50 and 100 yen.
Notes: 100, 500, 1,000, 5,000 and 10,000 yen.
Exchange rates (April 1974): £1 sterling = 653.00 yen; U.S. $1 = 276.75 yen.
1,000 yen = £1.531 = $3.613.

Note: Prior to August 1971 the official exchange rate was U.S. $1 = 360 yen. Between December 1971 and February 1973 the rate was 308 yen per $. Since February 1973 the yen has been allowed to "float", though the exchange rate was maintained at around 265 yen to the $ until November 1973.

GENERAL BUDGET
Twelve months ending March 31st.
(million yen)

REVENUE	1971–72	1972–73	EXPENDITURE	1971–72	1972–73
Taxes and Stamp . .	7,927,246	9,130,500	Social Security . . .	1,328,707	1,682,167
Public Bonds . .	1,187,146	2,310,000	Education and Science .	1,129,794	1,360,740
Monopoly Profits .	291,064	324,385	Defence . . .	689,863	821,401
Others . . .	565,403	354,064	Public Works . .	1,906,014	2,640,986
			Local Finance . .	1,779,863	2,365,995
			Pensions . . .	331,407	367,736
			Miscellaneous . .	2,195,483	2,879,924
TOTAL . .	9,970,859	12,118,949	TOTAL . . .	9,561,131	12,118,949

BUDGET EXPENDITURE
(million Yen)

	1973–74 (forecast)
Government Loans and Investments .	6,924,838
Public Works including Housing . .	2,840,771
Social Welfare	2,114,538
Education	1,570,225
Defence	935,464
Others	6,823,075
TOTAL	21,208,873

NATIONAL ACCOUNTS
('000 million yen—at current market prices)

	1970	1971	1972
Private Consumption Expenditure . .	36,330	41,266	47,150
Food and Beverages	12,450	13,873	n.a.
Clothing and Other Personal Effects .	3,701	4,247	n.a.
Fuel and Light	963	1,099	n.a.
Housing	7,658	8,961	n.a.
Others	11,558	13,086	n.a.
General Government Consumption Expenditure	5,827	6,884	8,069
Gross Domestic Fixed Capital Formation	24,843	27,179	31,524
Private Enterprises	19,045	19,832	22,428
Dwellings	4,715	5,061	6,386
Other Buildings, Machinery and Equipment	14,330	14,771	16,041
Government	5,787	7,347	9,097
Increase in Stocks	3,213	1,624	1,594
Exports of Goods and Services* . .	8,273	9,896	10,389
Less Imports of Goods and Services† .	7,489	7,807	8,237
Expenditures on Gross National Product .	70,997	79,042	90,489

* Including factor income received from abroad.   † Including factor income paid abroad.

CURRENCY IN CIRCULATION
(million yen)

	THE BANK OF JAPAN NOTES	SUBSIDIARY COINS	TOTAL
1970	5,556,091	341,338	5,897,429
1971	6,407,757	396,186	6,803,943
1972	8,310,742	478,602	8,785,344

GOLD AND FOREIGN EXCHANGE RESERVES
(U.S. $ million at end of period)

1968: 2,891; 1969: 3,496; 1970: 4,399; 1971: 15,235;
1972: 18,365.

BALANCE OF PAYMENTS—ALL FOREIGN COUNTRIES
(U.S.$ million)

	1971			1972		
	CREDIT	DEBIT	BALANCE	CREDIT	DEBIT	BALANCE
Goods and Services:						
Merchandise f.o.b.	23,566	15,779	7,787	28,032	19,061	8,971
Freight	1,295	1,265	30	1,506	1,527	− 21
Insurance on merchandise	68	103	− 35	82	125	− 43
Other transportation	847	1,741	− 894	1,066	2,008	− 942
Tourists	117	257	− 140	133	417	− 284
Other travel	55	252	− 197	68	357	− 289
Investment income	980	1,027	− 47	1,622	1,255	367
Military transactions	623	} 58	507	710	} 72	664
Other government services	22			26		
Non-merchandise insurance	222	242	− 20	299	301	− 2
Other private services	611	1,633	−1,022	726	2,059	−1,333
TOTAL	28,406	22,357	6,049	34,270	27,182	7,088
Unrequited Transfers:						
Private transfer payments	123	156	− 33	132	269	− 137
Reparations	—	38	− 38	—	53	− 53
Other government transfers	4	185	− 181	6	280	− 274
TOTAL	127	379	− 252	138	602	− 464
TOTAL CURRENT ACCOUNT	28,533	22,736	5,797	33,412	25,779	6,624
Capital Flows:						
Long-term Capital:						
Direct investments	210	360	− 150	169	723	− 554
Trade credits (net)	8	863	− 855	− 11	324	− 313
Loans (net)	20	594	− 574	−197	1,684	−1,881
Securities (net)	940	195	745	696	1,188	− 492
External bonds	96	88	8	31	136	− 105
Others	—	256	− 256	—	1,142	−1,142
BALANCE			1,082		5,197	−4,487
Short-term Capital:						
Trade credits (net)	2,315		2,315	1,912	—	1,912
Others (net)	120	—	120	54	—	54
BALANCE ON CAPITAL ACCOUNT			1,353			1,966
NET ERRORS AND OMISSIONS	527	—	527	638		638
OVERALL BALANCE (NET MONETARY MOVEMENTS)*			7,677			4,741
of which:						
Gold and foreign exchange reserves*			10,708			2,970
Commercial banks			−2,531			1,979
Other monetary institutions			− 500			− 208

* Excluding the allocation of Special Drawing Rights from the International Monetary Fund: $122 million in 1970; $128 million in 1971; $160 million in 1972.

Source: Bank of Japan.

BALANCE OF PAYMENTS—REGIONAL SUMMARY 1971
(U.S.$ million)

	World	U.S.A.	OECD Countries in Europe*	Communist Countries	Other Territories	International Institutions
Goods and Services:						
Merchandise f.o.b.	7,787†	3,374	1,440	351	2,609	—
Transportation . . .	— 864	— 617	—380	— 8	141	—
Insurance	— 55	1	— 39	0	— 17	—
Travel	— 337	3	—157	— 9	—174	—
Investment income . . .	— 47	— 137	—164	11	234	9
Government services . . .	587	606	— 12	0	— 14	7
Other private services . . .	— 1,022	— 530	—240	— 5	—247	
Total	6,049†	2,700	448	340	2,532	16
Unrequited Transfers:						
Private	— 33	55	9	— 2	— 95	—
Government	— 219	1	1	0	—196	— 25
Total	— 252	56	10	— 2	—291	— 25
Total Current Account . .	5,797†	2,756	458	338	2,241	— 9
Long-term Capital:						
Direct investments . .	— 150	114	— 31	0	—233	—
Trade credits . . .	— 855	— 36	— 38	— 78	—703	—
Loans	— 574	160	—151	—	—292	— 291
Securities	745	266	372	—	199	— 92
External bonds . . .	8	— 48	56	—	—	—
Others	— 256	— 223	—	2	— 7	— 28
Total	— 1,082	233	208	— 76	1,036	— 411
Basic Balance‡ . . .	4,715†	2,989	666	262	1,205	— 420

* Including Turkey.

† Including a trade balance (net credit $13 million) for transactions not allocated by territories.

‡ Excluding short-term capital movements (net credit $2,435 million) and errors and omissions (net credit $527 million)

Source: Bank of Japan.

JAPANESE DEVELOPMENT ASSISTANCE
(U.S. $'000)

	1970	1971	1972
Official:			
Bilateral Grants:			
Donations	121,200	125,400	170,600
Reparations	99,600	97,700	135,000
Technical Assistance	21,600	27,700	35,600
Direct Loans	250,300	306,700	307,200
Total	371,500	432,000	477,800
Capital Subscriptions or Grants to International Agencies	86,500	78,700	133,300
Total	458,000	510,700	611,100
Other Government Capital:			
Export Credits	349,500	271,700	266,300
Direct Investment Capital	143,100	136,300	264,700
Loans to International Agencies	201,100	243,100	325,400
Total	693,600	651,100	856,400
Total Official	1,151,600	1,161,800	1,467,500
Private:			
Export Credits	386,900	494,000	190,600
Direct Investments	265,000	356,200	844,300
Loans to International Agencies	17,500	125,400	217,400
Donations to non-profit Organizations	2,900	3,100	5,600
Total	672,300	978,700	1,257,900
Grand Total	1,824,000	2,140,500	2,725,400

EXTERNAL TRADE*
(U.S. $ million)

	1966	1967	1968	1969	1970	1971	1972	1973
Imports	9,523	11,663	12,987	15,024	18,881	19,712	23,471	38,303
Exports	9,776	10,442	12,972	15,990	19,318	24,019	28,591	36,914

* Excluding the payment of reparations and all trade in gold, silver and goods valued at less than $100.

PRINCIPAL COMMODITIES
(U.S. $ million)

IMPORTS	1970	1971	1972	EXPORTS	1970	1971	1972
Wheat . . .	318	265	361	Raw Silk . .	1.4	0.2	—
Maize . . .	294	244	271	Cotton Fabrics .	188	196	231
Sugar . . .	284	317	445	Silk Fabrics . .	15	14	—
Raw Wool . .	348	276	620	Wool Fabrics . .	76	39	25
Raw Cotton . .	471	516	1,275	Synthetic Fabrics .	626	751	815
Iron ore . .	1,208	1,331	109	Rayon Fabrics .	45	39	41
Iron scrap . .	341	123	1,016	Spun Rayon Fabrics .	46	37	33
Non-ferrous ore .	1,064	1,013	173	Clothing . .	464	468	429
Hide and Leather .	98	88	474	Fertilizer . .	143	156	212
Soya beans . .	366	421	82	Ceramic Products .	138	147	181
Rubber . . .	115	98	1,727	Metal Manufactures .	715	823	997
Lumber . . .	1,572	1,459	1,078	Iron and Steel .	2,847	3,542	3,610
Coal . . .	1,010	1,005	3,928	Textile Machinery .	197	248	233
Oil . . .	2,236	3,047	n.a.	Sewing Machines .	129	164	191
Chemical Products .	999	999	1,148	Radios . .	697	791	1,033
Business Machines .	322	340	362	Motor Vehicles .	1,344	2,373	2,964
Metal Working Machines.	168	162	112	Ships . .	1,414	1,848	2,399
Iron and Steel .	275	112	104	Plywood . .	75	86	89
Passenger Cars .	n.a.	n.a.	n.a.	Optical Instruments	499	n.a.	n.a.
				Toys . . .	138	139	151

Source: Ministry of International Trade and Industry.

PRINCIPAL TRADING PARTNERS
('ooo U.S. dollars)

	IMPORTS			EXPORTS		
	1970	1971	1972	1970	1971	1972
Asia						
Burma . . .	12,569	17,461	23,822	38,722	58,612	44,033
China, P.R. . .	253,769	323,172	491,116	571,708	578,188	600,921
China (Taiwan) .	250,779	286,017	421,864	702,302	932,332	1,090,616
Hong Kong . .	91,798	98,082	119,402	702,333	787,372	909,728
India . . .	390,047	376,558	407,580	103,269	208,883	239,756
Indonesia . .	636,498	854,466	1,197,501	316,534	452,836	615,471
Iran . . .	995,056	1,361,353	1,489,668	178,988	237,546	321,715
Korea (Republic) .	228,865	274,421	425,992	819,435	855,687	978,973
Malaysia . .	418,903	372,566	395,503	166,685	204,022	263,930
Pakistan . .	42,350	58,068	110,301	134,428	113,388	63,430
Philippines . .	532,940	513,812	476,396	455,243	464,787	459,408
Thailand . .	189,655	229,878	252,057	449,904	445,091	522,180
Europe . . .						
France . . .	186,350	198,169	300,650	127,595	191,242	283,374
Germany, Federal Republic	617,894	606,874	681,094	550,806	658,191	930,334
Netherlands . .	103,604	108,974	134,387	277,461	361,267	424,319
United Kingdom .	394,893	417,126	500,823	480,276	574,325	979,353
U.S.S.R. . .	479,290	495,880	593,906	341,654	377,267	504,179
North and South America .						
Argentina . .	153,811	119,709	98,208	95,801	165,293	125,987
Brazil . . .	217,853	223,063	249,403	166,731	235,211	395,337
Chile . . .	212,396	241,121	179,965	31,441	43,923	32,454
Mexico . . .	151,209	170,502	201,821	93,949	102,001	150,663
Peru . . .	210,429	174,042	185,464	52,934	69,250	70,840
Canada . . .	928,287	1,004,338	1,148,853	564,746	876,209	1,103,994
U.S.A. . . .	5,556,392	4,977,882	5,851,634	5,953,698	7,495,250	8,847,678
Africa . .						
Nigeria . . .	12,841	27,131	79,961	63,805	95,989	125,998
South Africa . .	313,676	333,699	398,866	329,823	413,034	364,081
Liberia . . .	31,913	74,258	72,073	591,976	998,830	1,021,982
Australia and Oceania .						
Australia . .	1,506,704	1,752,374	2,205,167	590,244	718,827	728,430
New Zealand . .	157,559	161,596	248,478	114,295	129,355	165,295

Source: Ministry of International Trade and Industry.

TOURISM

	FOREIGN VISITORS	MONEY RECEIVED (U.S. $ million)	JAPANESE TRAVELLERS ABROAD	TOURIST PAYMENTS ABROAD (U.S. $ million)
1970 . . .	854,419	232	936,205	315
1971 . . .	660,715	172	1,268,217	509
1972* . . .	723,744	201	1,532,928†	775

* Provisional figures.   † Excluding visitors to Okinawa Prefecture since May 15th, 1972.

TRANSPORT

NATIONAL RAILWAYS

	PASSENGERS (million persons)	FREIGHT (million ton-km.)
1968 . .	7,008	58,968
1969 . .	6,618	59,549
1970 . .	6,527	62,075
1971 . .	6,607	61,605
1972 . .	6,724	59,334

PRIVATE RAILWAYS

	PASSENGERS (million persons)	FREIGHT (million ton-km.)
1968 . .	9,372	989
1969 . .	9,469	975
1970 . .	9,833	978
1971 . .	9,787	1,018
1972 . .	10,064	931

ROADS
(licensed vehicles—'000)

	CARS	BUSES	LORRIES	SPECIAL PURPOSE VEHICLES	TOTAL
1969 . . .	6,934	170	8,061	298	15,523
1970 . . .	8,779	188	8,541	341	17,849
1971 . . .	10,572	194	8,928	392	20,086
1972 . . .	12,531	203	9,423	447	22,604

SHIPPING
(International Sea-borne Traffic)

	ENTERED	
	Number	'000 tons
1966 . .	24,841	113,797
1967 . .	26,752	138,869
1968 . .	28,234	159,957
1969 . .	30,475	180,646
1970 . .	33,401	208,061
1971 . .	35,557	224,032
1972 . .	36,243	248,362

MERCHANT FLEET
(registered at June 30th)

	VESSELS	DISPLACEMENT ('000 g.t.)
1969 . .	7,665	23,987
1970 . .	8,402	27,004
1971 . .	8,851	30,509
1972 . .	9,433	34,929

CIVIL AVIATION

	PASSENGERS CARRIED ('000)	PASSENGER/ KM. (million)	FREIGHT TON/KM. (million)*
(Domestic Lines Only)			
1969 . .	10,826	6,440	60.7
1970 . .	14,675	8,815	73.1
1971 . .	16,059	9,998	77.6
1972 . .	17,919	11,816	105.5
(International Services)			
1968 . .	1,018	4,449	224.9
1969 . .	1,314	5,799	337.5
1970 . .	1,628	6,638	357.8
1971 . .	1,891	7,471	481.9
1972 . .	2,307	10,115	584.9

* Freight includes mails.

COMMUNICATIONS MEDIA
('000)

	1970	1971	1972
Television Subscribers . . .	22,819	23,520	24,433
Daily Newspaper Circulation* . .	36,304	36,562	38,162

* At October 1st morning or evening edition only.

EDUCATION
(1970-71)

Passengers (million persons)	INSTITUTIONS	TEACHERS	STUDENTS
Primary Schools . . .	24,540	376,701	9,595,021
Secondary Schools . . .	10,839	235,404	4,694,250
High Schools . . .	4,791	235,507	1,178,372
Technical Colleges . . .	63	5,387	46,707
Junior Colleges . . .	486	32,468	275,256
Graduate Schools and Univer-sities	389	122,821	1,468,538

Sources: Research and Statistical Division, Minister's Secretariat, Ministry of Education.

THE CONSTITUTION

(Summary of the Constitution promulgated November 3rd, 1946, in force May 3rd, 1947)

The Emperor: Articles 1–8. The Emperor derives his position from the will of the people. In the performance of any State act as defined in the constitution, he must seek the advice and approval of the Cabinet though he may delegate the exercise of his functions, which include: (i) the appointment of the Prime Minister and the Chief Justice; (ii) promulgation of laws, cabinet orders, treaties and constitutional amendments; (iii) the convocation of the Diet, dissolution of the House of Representatives and proclamation of elections to the Diet; (iv) the appointment and dismissal of Ministers of State and as well as the granting of amnesties, reprieves and pardons and the ratification of treaties, conventions or protocols; (v) the awarding of honours and performance of ceremonial functions.

Renunciation of War: Article 9. Japan renounces for ever the use of war as a means of settling international disputes.

Articles 10–40 refer to the legal and human rights of individuals guaranteed by the constitution.

The Diet: Articles 41–64. The Diet is convened once a year, is the highest organ of State power and has exclusive legislative authority. It comprises of the House of Representatives (486 seats) and the House of Councillors (250 seats). The members of the former are elected for four years whilst those of the latter are elected for six years, one half of whom retire after three years. If the House of Representatives is dissolved, a general election must take place within 40 days and the Diet must be convoked within 30 days of the date of the election. Extraordinary sessions of the Diet may be convened by the Cabinet when one quarter or more of the members of either House request it. Emergency sessions of the House of Councillors may also be held. A quorum of at least one third of the Diet members is needed to carry on Parliamentary business. Any decision arising therefrom must be passed by a majority vote of those present. A bill becomes law having passed both Houses except as provided by the constitution. If the House of Councillors either vetoes or fails to take action within 60 days upon a bill already passed by the House of Representatives, the bill becomes law when passed a second time by the House of Representatives, by at least a two-thirds majority of those members present.

The Budget must first be submitted to the House of Representatives. If, when it is approved by the House of Representatives, the House of Councillors votes against it or fails to take action on it within 30 days, or failing agreement being reached by a joint committee of both Houses, a decision of the House of Representatives shall be the decision of the Diet. The above procedure also applies in respect of the conclusion of treaties.

The Prime Minister and other government Ministers are responsible to the Diet and may be impeached as provided by law.

The Executive: Articles 65–75. Executive power is vested in the cabinet consisting of a Prime Minister and such other Ministers as may be appointed. The Cabinet is collectively responsible to the Diet. Members of the Cabinet are designated from among members of the Diet by a resolution thereof.

If the House of Representatives and the House of Councillors disagree, and if no agreement can be reached even through a joint committee of both Houses, provided for by law, or the House of Councillors fails to make designation within 10 days, exclusive of the period of recess, after the House of Representatives has made designation, the decision of the House of Representatives shall be the decision of the Diet.

The Prime Minister appoints and may remove other Ministers, a majority of whom must be from the Diet. If the House of Representatives passes a no-confidence motion or rejects a confidence motion, the whole Cabinet resigns unless the House of Representatives is dissolved within 10 days. When there is a vacancy in the post of Prime Minister, or upon the first convocation of the Diet after a general election of members of the House of Representatives, the whole Cabinet resigns.

The Prime Minister submits bills, reports on national affairs and foreign relations to the Diet. He exercises control and supervision over various administrative branches of the Government. The Cabinet's primary functions (in addition to administrative ones) are to: (a) administer the law faithfully; (b) conduct State affairs; (c) conclude treaties subject to prior (or subsequent) Diet approval; (d) administer the civil service in accordance with law; (e) prepare and present the budget to the Diet; (f) enact Cabinet orders in order to make effective legal and constitutional provisions; (g) decide on amnesties, reprieves or pardons. All laws and Cabinet orders are signed by the competent Minister of State and countersigned by the Prime Minister. The Ministers of State, during their tenure of office, are not subject to legal action without the consent of the Prime Minister. However, the right to take that action is not impaired.

Articles 76–95. Relate to the Judiciary, Finance and Local Government.

Amendments: Article 96. Amendments to the Constitution are initiated by the Diet, through a concurring vote of two-thirds or more of all the members of each House and are submitted to the people for ratification, which requires the affirmative vote of a majority of all votes cast at a special referendum or at such election as the Diet may specify.

Amendments when so ratified must immediately be promulgated by the Emperor in the name of the people, as an integral part of the Constitution.

Articles 97–99 outline the Supreme Law, while Articles 100–103 consist of Supplementary Provisions.

THE GOVERNMENT

HEAD OF THE STATE

His Imperial Majesty HIROHITO, Emperor of Japan; succeeded to the throne December 25th, 1926.

THE CABINET
(*July* 1974)

Prime Minister: KAKUEI TANAKA.
Deputy Prime Minister: (vacant).
Justice Minister: UMEKICHI NAKAMURA.
Foreign Minister: MASAYOSHI OHIRA.
Finance Minister: TAKEO FUKUDA.
Education Minister: SEISUKE OKUNO.
Health and Welfare Minister: KUNIKICHI SAITO.
Agriculture and Forestry Minister: TADAO KURAISHI.
Minister of International Trade and Industry: YASUHIRO NAKASONE.
Transport Minister: MASATOSHI TOKUNAGA.
Posts and Telecommunications Minister: KEN HARADA.
Labour Minister: TAKASHI HASEGAWA.
Construction Minister: TAKAO KAMEOKA.
Home Affairs Minister, Chairman National Public Safety Commission, Director-General Hokkaido Development Agency: KINGO MACHIMURA.

Minister of State, Chief Cabinet Secretary: SUSUMU NIKAIDO.

Minister of State, Director-General Prime Minister's Office and Okinawa Development Agency: TOKUSABURO KOSAKA.

Minister of State, Director-General Administrative Management Agency: SHIGERU HORI.

Minister of State, Director-General Defence Agency: SADANORI YAMANAKA.

Minister of State, Director-General Economic Planning Agency: TSUNEO UCHIDA.

Minister of State, Director-General Science and Technology Agency, Chairman Atomic Energy Commission: KINJI MORIYAMA.

Director-General Environment Agency: MATSUHEI MORI.

Director Cabinet Legislation Bureau: ICHIRO YOSHIKUNI.

DIPLOMATIC REPRESENTATION

EMBASSIES ACCREDITED TO JAPAN

(In Tokyo unless otherwise stated)

(E) Embassy.

Afghanistan: 31-21, Jingumae 6-chome, Shibuya-ku (E); *Chargé d'Affaires a.i.:* MOHAMMAD SARWAR DAMANI.

Algeria: Shibusawa Bldg., 3-5-4 Shiba-koen, Minato-ku (E); *Ambassador:* BRAHIM GHAFA.

Argentina: Chiyoda House, 17-8 Nagata-cho 2-chome, Chiyoda-ku (E); *Chargé d'Affaires a.i.:* HORACIO A. LÓPEZ COLOMBRES.

Australia: 1-14, Mita 2-chome, Minato-ku (E); *Chargé d'Affaires a.i.:* D. J. HORNE.

Austria: 1-20 Moto-Azabu 1-chome, Minato-ku (E); *Ambassador:* REGINALD THOMAS.

Bangladesh: 15-19, Minami Aoyama 1-chome, Minato-ku (E); *Ambassador:* ABDUL MUNTAQUIM CHAUDHURY.

Belgium: 5, Niban-cho, Chiyoda-ku (E); *Chargé d'Affaires a.i.:* Baron HENRI BEYENS.

Bolivia: 1st Floor, Ambassador Mansion, 18-2 Kami Osaki 1-chome, Shinagawa-ku (E); *Ambassador:* ARMANDO YOSHIDA VACA.

Brazil: 3rd and 4th Floor, Aoyama Daiichi Mansion, 4-14, Akasaka 8-chome, Minato-ku (E); *Ambassador:* PAUL LEAO DE MOURA.

Bulgaria: 33-5, Yoyogi 5-chome, Shibuya-ku (E); *Ambassador:* PARVAN TCHERNEV.

Burma: 8-26, Kita-Shinagawa 4-chome, Shinagawa-ku (E); *Ambassador:* U CHIT KO KO.

Canada: 3-38, Akasaka 8-chome, Minato-ku (E); *Ambassador:* ROSS CAMPBELL.

Central African Republic: 8-11-43, Akasaka, Minato-ku (E); *Ambassador:* NESTOR KOMBOT-NAGUEMON.

Chile: 2-11, Jingumae 4-chome, Shibuya-ku (E); *Chargé d'Affaires a.i.:* Cmdr. FRANCISCO GHISOLFO ARAYAN.

China, People's Republic: 4-5-30 Minami Azabu, Minato-ku (E); *Ambassador:* CHEN CHU.

Colombia: 9-10 Minami-Aoyama 5-chome, Minato-ku (E); *Ambassador:* Dr. LUIS GONZÁLEZ BARROS.

Costa Rica: 6-15, Horinouchi 2-chome, Suginami-ku (E); *Chargé d'Affaires a.i.:* FRANCISCO J. TACSAM.

Cuba: 6-2, Hiroo 2-chome, Shibuya-ku (E); *Chargé d'Affaires a.i.:* JOSÉ A. GUERRA MENCHERO.

Czechoslovakia: 4-6-1 Shiba Koen, Minato-ku; *Ambassador:* Dr. RUDOLF KOZUZNIK.

Denmark: Denmark House, 17-38, Minami-Aoyama, 4-chome, Minato-ku (E); *Ambassador:* TYGE DAHL-GAARD.

Dominican Republic: 2-28, Shiroganeidai 3-chome, Minato-ku (E); *Ambassador:* ARMANDO GERMÁN.

Ecuador: Azabu Sky Mansion, Room 101, 19-13 Minami Azabu 3-chome, Minato-ku (E); *Ambassador:* Dr. FRANCISCO URBINA.

Egypt: 5-4, Aobsdai 1-chome, Meguro-ku (E); *Ambassador:* Dr. MOHSEN ABDEL-KHALEK.

El Salvador: Yurakucho Bldg., Room 1019, 5, Yurakucho 1-chome, Chiyoda-ku (E); *Ambassador:* WALTER BENEKE MEDINA.

Ethiopia: 2-13, Akasaka 8-chome, Minato-ku (E); *Ambassador:* Lij HAILE MARIAM KEBEDE.

Finland: 2-7, Roppongi 3-chome, Minato-ku (E); *Ambassador:* OSMO LAVES.

France: 11-44, Minami-Azabu 4-chome, Minato-ku (E); *Ambassador:* FRANÇOIS LEFEBVRE DE LABOULAYE.

Gabon: 16-2, Hiroo 2-chome, Shibuya-ku (E); *Ambassador:* CHRISTOPHE BOUPANA.

German Democratic Republic: Akasaka Mansion 7-5-16 Akasaka, Minato-ku; *Chargé d'Affaires a.i.:* SIEGFRIED FISCHER.

Germany, Federal Republic: 5-10, Minami-Azabu 4-chome, Minato-ku (E); *Ambassador:* Dr. WILHELM G. GREWE.

Ghana: 15-12, Higashi Gotonda, 5-chome, Shinagawa-ku (E); *Ambassador:* C. O. C. AMATE.

Greece: 4th Floor, Green Fantasia Bldg., 11-11, Jungumae 1-chome, Shibuya-ku (E); *Ambassador:* THEMISTOCLES L. CHRYSANTHOPOULOS.

Guatemala: 17-1, Shoto 1-chome, Shibuya-ku (E); *Ambassador:* FELIPE ANTONIO GANDARA GARCÍA.

Guinea: Hirakawa Bldg., 1-11-28 Nagata-cho, Chiyoda-ku (E); *Ambassador:* MAMADY LAMINE CONDÉ.

Honduras: 2-25, Minami-Azuba 4-chome, Minato-ku (E); *Ambassador:* CÉSAR MOSSI SORTO.

Hungary: 1-29, Nakameguro 1-chome, Meguro-ku (E); *Ambassador:* ERNŐ HORVÁTH.

Iceland: Bonn/Bad Godesberg, German Federal Republic.

India: 2-11, Kudan-Minami 2-chome, Chiyoda-ku (E); *Ambassador:* V. H. COELHO.

Indonesia: 2-9, Higashi Gotanda 5-chome, Shinagawa-ku (E); *Ambassador:* Brig.-Gen. JUSUF RAMLI.

Iran: 10-32, Minami-Azabu 3-chome, Minato-ku (E); *Ambassador:* ABDUL HOSSEIN HAMZAVI.

Iraq: Riviera Mansions, 21-22, Higashiyama 1-chome, Meguro-ku (E); *Ambassador:* MUNDHER TAWFIQ AL-WANDAWI.

Israel: 2, Niban-cho, Chiyoda-ku (E); *Ambassador:* EYTAN RONN.

Italy: 5-4, Mita, 2-chome, Minato-ku (E); *Chargé d'Affaires a.i.:* MARIO CREMA.

Ivory Coast: 2nd Floor, Aoyama Tower Bldg., 2-45-15 Minami Aoyama, Manato-ku (E); *Ambassador:* PIERRE N. COFFI.

Jordan: Taipei, Taiwan, China.

Khmer Republic: 8-6-9 Akasaka, Minato-ku (E); *Ambassador:* SIM VAR.

Korea, Republic: 2-5 Minami Azabu 1-chome, Minato-ku (E); *Chargé d'Affaires a.i.:* HA JONG YOON.

Kuwait: 13-12, Mita 4-chome, Minato-ku (E); *Ambassador:* TALAT YACOUB AL-GHOUSSEIN.

Laos: 3-21, Nishi-Azabu 3-chome, Minato-ku (E); *Ambassador:* H.R.H. TIAO KHAMHING.

Lebanon: Azabu Tokyo Apts. No. 95, 47, Azabu, Mamiana-cho, Minato-ku (E); *Ambassador:* HALIM SHEBEYA.

Liberia: 1, Kioiocho, Chiyoda-ku (E); *Chargé d'Affaires a.i.:* MARCUS M. KOFA.

Libya: 5-36-21 Shimouma, Setagaya-ku (E); *Ambassador:* HASAN ELHADI BUKRES.

Madagascar: 3-25 Moto Azabu 2-chome, Minato-ku (E); *Ambassador:* J.-P. RAVELOMANANTSOA-RATSIMIHAH.

Malaysia: 20-16, Nanpeidaimachi, Shibaya-ku (E); *Ambassador:* RAJA AZNAM BIN RAJA HAJI AHMAD.

Mali: Moscow, U.S.S.R.

Mexico: 15-1, Nagata-cho 2-chome, Chiyoda-ku (E); *Chargé d'Affaires a.i.:* Lic. JAIME SORIANO.

Mongolia: Ginza Daiichi Hotel, 8-1-13 Ginza Chuo-ku; *Ambassador:* SONOMDORJIIN DAMBADARJAA.

Nepal: 17-1, Higashi Gotonda 5-chome, Shinagawa-ku (E); *Chargé d'Affaires a.i.:* NARAYAN DAS SHRESTHA.

Netherlands: 1, Sakae-cho, Shiba, Minato-ku (E); *Ambassador:* Dr. THEODORE P. BERGSMA.

New Zealand: 20-40, Kamiyama-cho, Shibuya-ku (E); *Ambassador:* T. C. LARKIN.

Nicaragua: 2-3, Roppongi 4-chome, Minato-ku (E); *Ambassador:* MIGUEL D'ESCOTO Y MUÑOZ.

Nigeria: 2-19-7 Uehara, Shibuya-ku (E); *Ambassador:* IGNATIUS JULIUS DAWER DURLONG.

Norway: 12-2, Minami-Azabu 5-chome, Minato-ku (E); *Ambassador:* CHRISTIAN BERG-NIELSEN.

Pakistan: National Azabu Appt., 4-5-2 Minami Azabu Minato-ku; *Ambassador:* Sultan MUHAMMAD KHAN.

Panama: 2-9, Akasaka 9-chome, Minato-ku (E); *Chargé d'Affaires a.i.:* FABRICIO MARTIN ALEXIS.

Paraguay: 2-6-29 Hiroo, Shibuya-ku (E); *Ambassador:* DESIDEIRO MELANIO ENCISO.

Peru: Higashi 4-4-27 Shibuya-ku; *Ambassador:* JOSÉ CARLOS MARIATEGUI.

Philippines: 6-15, Roppongi 5-chome, Minato-ku (E); *Ambassador:* ROBERTO S. BENEDICTO.

Poland: 13-5, Mita 2-chome, Meguro-ku (E); *Ambassador;* ZDZISLAW REGULSKI.

Portugal: Olympia Annex Appt. 306, 31-21, Jungamae 6-chome, Shibuya-ku (E); *Ambassador:* Dr. MANUEL RODRIGUES DE ALMEIDA COUTINHO.

Romania: 3-1, Aobadai 2-chome, Minato-ku (E); *Ambassador:* NICOLAE FINANTU.

Saudi Arabia: 4-18, Moto-Azabu 3-chome, Minato-ku (E); *Ambassador:* Sheikh AOUNEY WAFA DEJANY.

Singapore: Room 1518, Kasumigaseki Bldg., 2-5 Kasumigaseki 3-chome, Chiyoda-ku (E); *Ambassador:* WEE MON CHENG.

Spain: 3-29, Roppongi 1-chome, Minato-ku (E); *Chargé d'Affaires a.i.:* ANTONIO SEGURA MORIS.

Sweden: 10-3, Roppongi 1-chome, Minato-ku (E); *Ambassador:* Prof. GUNNAR EDWARD HECKSCHER.

Switzerland: 9-12, Minami-Azabu 5-chome, Minato-ku (E); *Ambassador:* GIOVANNI E. BUCHER.

Tanzania: 21-9, Kamiyoga 4-chome, Setagaya-ku (E); *Chargé d'Affaires a.i.:* F. R. K. ETUTTU.

Thailand: 14-6, Kami-Osaki 3-chome, Shinagawa-ku (E); *Ambassador:* Dr. SOMPONG SUCHARITKUL.

Trinidad and Tobago: New Delhi, India.

Turkey: 33-6, Jingumae 2-chome, Shibuya-ku (E); *Ambassador:* Dr. SUKRU ELEKDAG.

Uganda: Imperial Hotel 1-1-1 Uchisaiwaicho Chiyoda-ku; *Chargé d'Affaires a.i.:* SAMUSONI TWINE BIGOMBE.

U.S.S.R.: 2-1-1 Azabudai, Minato-ku (E); *Ambassador:* OLEG A. TROYANOVSKY.

United Kingdom: 1, Ichiban-cho, Chiyoda-ku (E); *Ambassador:* FREDERICK WARNER.

U.S.A.: Chancery, 10-5, Akasaka 1-chome, Minato-ku (E); *Chargé d'Affaires a.i.:* THOMAS P. SHOESMITH.

Uruguay: 5-26, Akasaka 9-chome, Minato-ku (E); *Chargé d'Affaires a.i.:* RAÚL BENAVIDES.

Vatican City: 9-2, Sanbancho, Chiyoda-ku (Pro-Nunciature); *Pontifical Representative:* (vacant).

Venezuela: 11-23, Minami Azabu 3-chome, Minato-ku (E); *Ambassador:* Dr. FREDDY AROCHA CASTRESANA.

Viet-Nam, Republic: 50, Motoyoyogi-cho, Shibuya-ku (E); *Ambassador:* DO VANG-LY.

Yugoslavia: 7-24, Kitashinagawa 4-chome, Shinagawa-ku (E); *Ambassador:* JOZE SMOLE.

Zaire: Tsurumi Bldg., 1-1 Tomiya, Shibuya-ku (E); *Ambassador:* Brig.-Gen. LEONARD MULAMBA NYNYI WA KADIMA.

Japan also has diplomatic relations with Bahrain, Ireland, Morocco, Oman, Senegal, South Africa, the Sudan, Tunisia, the United Arab Emirates and the Democratic Republic of Viet-Nam.

PARLIAMENT

THE DIET

The Diet consists of two Chambers—the House of Councillors (Upper House)—which replaces the old House of Peers—and the House of Representatives. The 491 members of the House of Representatives are elected for a period of four years. For the House of Councillors, which has 250 members, the term of office is six years, half the members being elected every three years.

HOUSE OF COUNCILLORS

Speaker: YUZO SHIGEMUNI.

(Election, July 1974)

PARTY	SEATS
Liberal Democrat . .	126
Socialist . . .	62
Komeito . . .	24
Communist . . .	20
Democratic Socialist .	10
Independent and others .	10

HOUSE OF REPRESENTATIVES

Speaker: MITSUJIRO ISHII.

(Election, December 10th, 1972)

PARTY	SEATS
Liberal Democrat . . .	271
Socialist . . .	118
Communist . . .	38
Komeito . . .	29
Democratic Socialist .	19
Independent . . .	14
Others	2

POLITICAL PARTIES

The Political Funds Regulation Law is the basis of political organization in Japan. It provides that any organization which wishes to support a candidate for an elective public office must be registered as a political party. There are over 10,000 registered parties in the country, mostly of local or regional significance. National politics are still largely factional in character, but since the introduction of the western pattern of parliamentary democracy in the 1946 Constitution, a restricted number of major parties has formed, grouping the principal pressure groups and personal followings. The conservative Liberal-Democratic Party has the support of big business and the rural population, and holds a majority of seats in the Diet; it is also by far the richest of the political parties. Support for the two socialist parties comes from the intelligentsia, the trades unions, and younger urban voters, and the proportion of votes for these parties combined has increased slowly at each election since 1952. The split between the two parties reflects a longstanding division between supporters of a mass popular party (now represented by the D.S.P.) and those seeking a class party on Marxist lines. The Communist Party of Japan has split since 1964, the official party being independent and supporting neither the U.S.S.R. nor China. In the 1969 elections the militant religious organization Sokagakkai increased its representation in the Diet through its political wing Komeito, although this was reduced in the 1972 elections, which produced gains for the socialists and communists. There are also a number of small extreme right-wing political organizations.

Liberal-Democratic Party (Jiyu-Minshuto): 7, 2-chome, Hirakawacho, Chiyoda-ku, Tokyo; f. 1955; programme includes the establishment of a welfare state, the build-up of industrial development, the levelling up of educational and cultural systems and the revision of the Constitution where necessary; follows a foreign policy of alignment with U.S.A.; Pres. KAKUEI TANAKA; Sec.-Gen. TOMISABURO HASHIMOTO.

Socialist Party of Japan (Nihon Shakaito): 1-8-1, Nagata-cho, Chiyoda-ku, Tokyo; f. 1945; 35,000 mems.; aims at the establishment of collective non-aggression and mutual security system, including Japan, U.S.A., U.S.S.R. and China; Chair. TOMOMI NARITA; Sec.-Gen. MASASHI ISHIBASHI; publ. *Shakai Shimpo* (twice a week).

Komeito (*Clean Government Party*): 17 Minamimotomachi, Shinjuku-ku, Tokyo; f. 1964; based on middle-of-the-road principle and humanitarian socialism, promotes policies in best regard of "dignity of human life"; mems. 120,000; at present the fourth largest party, with 52 seats in the National Diet, 2,542 seats in local assemblies; Founder DAISAKU IKEDA; Chair. YOSHI-KATSU TAKEIRI; Sec.-Gen. JUNYA YANO; publs. *Komei Shimbun* (daily), *The Komei* (monthly), *Komei Graphic* (bi-monthly).

Democratic Socialist Party (Minshu-Shakaito): Shiba Sakuragawa-cho, Minato-ku, Tokyo; f. 1961 by Right-Wing Socialists of the Social Democratic Party of Japan; 52,000 mems.; aims at the pursuit of an independent foreign policy; Leader EIICHI NISHIMURA; Sec.-Gen. KAZUYUKI KASUGA.

Communist Party of Japan: 26, 4-chome, Sendagaya, Shibuya-ku, Tokyo; f. 1922; independent; 320,000 mems.; Chair. (Central Committee) SANZO NOSAKA; Chair. (Presidium) KENJI MIYAMOTO; Chief Sec. TETSUZO FUWA; publs. *Akahata* (daily and weekly), *Zen-ei* (monthly), information Bulletin for abroad (irregular).

Voice of Japan: Tokyo; f. 1964; breakaway group from Communist Party of Japan; pro-Soviet; Chair. YOSHIO SHIGA.

DEFENCE

Armed Forces and Equipment (1973): Total 266,000: army, 180,000; navy, 41,400; air force, 44,600. The army is equipped with U.S. made weapons including medium tanks, AA guns, 3 surface-to-air missiles (SAM) groups. The navy has 11 submarines, a guided missile destroyer as well as a number of frigates, minesweepers, torpedo boats, landing craft and other vessels. There is also a naval air component comprising 200 aircraft. The air force has 406 combat aircraft plus trainers, helicopters and 4 missile battalions. With the reversion of Okinawa to Japan in May 1972, a total of 2,900 Japanese military personnel were deployed there in December. By the end of June 1973 an air control and warning group was stationed there together with 9 Hercules and Hawk air defence missiles. The systems formerly under U.S. control were transferred to Japanese control when it assumed responsibility for Okinawa's air defence on July 1st, 1973.

Military Service: Voluntary.

Defence Expenditure: Defence Budget 1973–74: 935,500 million yen ($3,530 million).

Chairman of the Joint Staff Committee of the National Defence Agency: Gen. H. KINUGASA.

JUDICIAL SYSTEM

The basic principles of the legal system are set forth in the Constitution, which lays down that the whole judicial power is vested in a Supreme Court and in such inferior courts as are established by law, and enunciates the principle that no organ or agency of the Executive shall be given final judicial power. Judges are to be independent in the exercise of their conscience, and may not be removed except by public impeachment, unless judicially declared mentally or physically incompetent to perform official duties. The judges of the Supreme Court are appointed by the Cabinet, the sole exception being the Chief Justice, who is appointed by the Emperor after designation by the Cabinet, similar to the appointment of the Prime Minister.

The Court Organization Law, which came into force on May 3rd, 1947, decreed the constitution of the Supreme Court and the establishment of four types of inferior courts —High District, Family (established January 1st, 1949), and Summary Courts. The constitution and functions of the courts are as follows:

THE SUPREME COURT

This court is the highest legal authority in the land, and consists of a Chief Justice and fourteen associate judges. It has jurisdiction over the following matters:

(1) **Jokoku** (appeals).

(2) **Kokoku** (complaints), prescribed specially in codes of procedure.

It conducts its hearings and renders decisions through a Grand Bench or three Petty Benches. Both are collegiate bodies, the former consisting of all judges of the Court, and the latter of five judges. A Supreme Court Rule exists determining which cases are to be handled by the respective Benches. It is, however, laid down by law that the Petty Bench cannot make decisions as to the constitutionality of a statute, ordinance, regulation, or disposition, or as to cases in which an opinion concerning the interpretation and application of the Constitution or of any laws or ordinances is at variance with a previous decision of the Supreme Court.

Chief Justice: Tomokazu Murakami.

Secretary-General: Kazuo Yasumura.

INFERIOR COURTS

High Court

A High Court conducts its hearings and renders decisions through a collegiate body, consisting of three justices, though for cases of high treason the number of justices must be five. The Court has jurisdiction over the following matters:

(1) **Koso** appeals from judgments in the first instance rendered by District Courts, from judgments rendered by Family Courts, and from judgments concerning criminal cases rendered by Summary Courts.

(2) **Kokoku** complaints against rulings and orders rendered by District Courts and Family Courts, and against rulings and orders concerning criminal cases rendered by Summary Courts, except those coming within the jurisdiction of the Supreme Court.

(3) **Jokoku** appeals from judgments in the second instance rendered by District Courts and from judgments rendered by Summary Courts, except those concerning criminal cases.

(4) Actions in the first instance relating to cases of **high treason**.

District Court

A District Court conducts hearings and renders decisions through a single judge or, for certain types of cases, through a collegiate body of three judges. It has jurisdiction over the following matters:

(1) Actions in the first instance, except offences relating to high treason, claims where the subject matter of the action does not exceed 300,000 yen, and offences liable to a fine or lesser penalty.

(2) **Koso** appeals from judgments rendered by Summary Courts, except those concerning criminal cases.

(3) Complaints against rulings and orders rendered by Summary Courts, except those coming within the jurisdiction of the Supreme Court and High Courts.

Family Court

A Family Court handles cases through a single judge in case of rendering judgments or decisions. However, in accordance with the provisions of other statutes it conducts its hearings and renders decisions through a collegiate body of three judges. A conciliation is effected through a collegiate body consisting of a judge and two or more members of the conciliation committee selected from among civilians.

It has jurisdiction over the following matters:

(1) Judgment and conciliation with regard to cases relating to family as provided by the law for Adjudgment of Domestic Relations.

(2) Judgment with regard to the matters of protection of juveniles as provided by the Juvenile Law.

(3) Actions in the first instance relating to adult criminal cases of violation of the Labour Standard Law, the Law for Prohibiting Liquors to Minors, or other laws especially enacted for protection of juveniles.

Summary Court

A Summary Court handles cases through a single judge, and has jurisdiction in the first instance over the following matters:

(1) Claims where the value of the subject matter does not exceed 300,000 yen (excluding claims for cancellation or change of administrative dispositions).

(2) Actions which relate to offences liable to fine or lighter penalty, offences liable to a fine as an optional penalty, and certain specified offences such as habitual gambling and larceny.

A Summary Court cannot impose imprisonment or a severer penalty. When it deems proper the imposition of a sentence of imprisonment or a graver penalty, it must transfer such cases to a District Court, but it can impose imprisonment with hard labour not exceeding three years for certain specified offences.

A Procurator's Office, with its necessary number of procurators, is established for each of these courts. The procurators conduct searches, institute prosecutions and supervise the execution of judgments in criminal cases, and act as representatives of the public interest in civil cases of public concern.

RELIGION

The traditional religions in Japan are Shintoism and Buddhism. Neither is exclusive, and many Japanese subscribe at least nominally to both. Since the war a number of new religions based on an amalgamation of Shinto, Buddhist, Taoist, Confucian and Christian beliefs have grown up.

SHINTOISM

Shintoism is an indigenous cult of nature and ancestor worship. It is divided into two cults: national Shintoism, which is represented by the shrines; and sectarian Shintoism, which developed towards the end of the Tokugawa Shogunate. In 1868, Shinto was designated a national religion, and all Shinto shrines acquired the privileged status of a national institution. After the adoption of the present constitution in 1947, however, complete freedom of religion was introduced, and state support of Shinto was banned. There are an estimated 80,000 shrines, 200,000 priests and approximately 80,000,000 adherents.

SHRINE SHINTO

The most important of all Japanese shrines is the Isé Grand Shrine at Ujiyamada, Mié Prefecture. A number of subsidiary shrines, a seminary, a library and two museums are attached.

Religious seminaries consist of the Isé Grand Shrine seminary, a middle-grade school attached to it, a department of religious instruction at Kokogakuin College, and about 26 smaller institutes of religious learning.

SECTARIAN SHINTO

There are about 130 sects in Sectarian Shinto.* Principal among these are:

Shinto Sect: called by the general name given to the national cult before its later branches had developed; 3,405 priests; 1,101,868 adherents.

Kurozumi Sect: f. by Munetada Kurozumi (1780-1850); 2,959 priests and teachers; 613,419 adherents.

Shinto-shusei Sect: f. by Kunitmitsu Nitta (1829-1902); 1,679 priests and teachers; 43,101 adherents.

Taisha Sect: preached by Sompuku Sengé (1845-1918).

Fuso Sect: f. by Takekuni Fujiwara (1541-1646); 1,991 priests and teachers; 140,984 adherents.

Taisei Sect: f. by Shosai Hirayama (1815-1890); 5,671 priests and teachers; 226,508 adherents.

Jikko Sect: f. by Hanamori Shibata (1809-1890).

Shinshu Sect: f. by the Ministry of Education of Japan (1964); 33,265 priests and teachers; 13,248,744 adherents.

Ontaké Sect: 7,724 priests and teachers; 357,334 adherents.

Misogi Sect: f. by Masakané Inouyé (1790-1849); 592 priests and teachers; 100,032 adherents.

Shinri Sect: f. by Tsunehiko Sano (1834-1906); 2,240 priests and teachers; 258,157 adherents.

Konko Sect: f. by Bunjiro Kawaté (1814-1883); 3,229 priests and teachers; 693,314 adherents.

Tenrikyo: f. by Miki Nakayama (1798-1887); 118,949 priests and teachers; 1,323,363 adherents.

BUDDHISM

It is estimated that there are 70 million Buddhists in Japan. The number of temples is about 80,000 and the number of priests 140,000. Twelve universities are under Buddhist administration.

There are over 200 sects of which the eleven principal are as follows:*

Hosso Sect: introduced by Dosho (628-700); 195 priests and teachers; 43,499 adherents.

Kegon Sect: chief temple, Todaiji, Nara; introduced by Roben (688-776); 499 priests and teachers; 51,008 adherents.

Ritsu Sect: chief temple, Toshodaiji, Nara; introduced by Ganjin (686-763); 128 priests and teachers; 70,558 adherents.

Tendai Sect: f. by Chisha Daishi (537-579); introduced by Saicho (766-822); three sub-sects: Tendai Branch (chief temple, Yenryakugi, Shiga); Jimon Branch (chief temple, Onjoji, Shiga); Shinsei Branch (chief temple, Saikyoji, Shiga); 7,958 priests and teachers; 3,629,870 adherents.

Shingon Sect: introduced by Kukai (773-835); its eight branches are: Koya, Omuro, Daikakuji, Daigo, Toji, Yamashina, Ono, Senyuji. Three hundred years after its foundation a new school of Shingon was established by Kokyo Daishi (1094-1143); this has two branches: Chizan (chief temple, Chisaku-in, Kyoto) and Buzan (chief temple, Chokokuji, Hasedera); 6,133 priests and teachers; 2,715,609 adherents.

Yuzu-nenbutsu Sect: chief temple, Dainen butsuji, 10 Uemachi-Hirano Higashisumiyoshi-ku, Osaka; f. 1117 by Ryonin (Shoo Daishi); 1,300 priests and teachers; 350,000 adherents; 560 temples; Archbishop JIYU NISHINOTOIN.

Jodo Sect: f. by Genku (1133-1212); Jodo Shu (chief temple, Chion-in, Kyoto); Seizan Jodo Shu, f. by Shoku (1176-1247), has three sub-branches: Zenrinji (chief temple, Zenrinji, Kyoto); Komyoji (chief temple, Komyoji, Kyoto), and Fukakusa (chief temple, Seigwanji, Kyoto); 12,000 priests and teachers; 5,500,000 adherents.

Shin Sect f. by Shinran (1173-1262); the ten branches are: Honpa-Honganji, Otani, Bukkoji, Takada, Kibé, Kosho, Izumoji, Yamamoto, Jyoshoji, Sammonto; 34,054 priests and teachers; 13,910,869 adherents.

Ji Sect: chief temple, Shojokoji, Kanagawa; f. by Ippen (1239-89); 547 priests and teachers; 444,759 adherents.

Zen Sect: (a) Rinzai Sect; f. by Yeisai (1140-1215); 14 branches: Kenninji, Kenchoji, Tofukuji, Engakuji, Nanzenji, Daitokuji, Myoshinji, Tenryuji, Yeigenji, Shokokuji, Hokoji, Buttsuji, Kokutaiji, Kogakuji; (b) Soto Sect; f. by Dogen (1199-1253); chief temples, Yeiheiji, Sojiji; (c) Obaku Sect; f. by Yin-gen (1592-1673); chief temple, Mampukuji, Uji, Kyoto; 9,829 priests and teachers; 219,773 adherents.

Nichiren Sect: f. by Nichiren (1222-1281); the eight branches are: Nichiren-shu (chief temple, Kuonji, Yamanashi); Hommon-shu (chief temple, Hommonji, Ikegami, Tokyo); Hokké-shu (chief temple, Honjiji, Niigata); Kempon-hokké-shu (chief temple, Kochoji, Shizuoka); Homyo-hokké-shu (chief temple, Honryuji, Tokyo); Nichiren-seishu (chief temple, Daisekiji, Shizuoka); Nichiren-fujufusé-ha (chief temple, Myokakuji, Okayama); Nichiren-shu-fujufusé-komon-ha (chief temple, Honkakuji, Okayama); 6,853 priests and teachers; 1,438,990 adherents.

* Accurate statistics for numbers of priests and adherents are not available; the figures given represent returns made by the various sects at different dates.

World Buddhist Fellowship: Rev. Riri Nakayama, Hozenji Buddhist Temple, 1115, 3-chome, Akabane-cho, Kita-ku, Tokyo.

CHRISTIANITY

In 1969 the number of Christians was estimated at 875,000, with 5,000 churches and 20,000 clergy. Twenty-two universities are maintained by Christian communities.

In 1940 the Religious Organization Law was passed, according to which a religious body must possess at least 50 churches and 5,000 adherents in order to be recognized. Many of the numerous Christian sects united in order to obtain recognition. The Law was repealed at the end of the war and certain groups returned to their original status. The following are the largest groups:

Roman Catholic Church: Archdiocese of Tokyo: Sekiguchi, 3-chome, 16-15, Bunkyo-ku, Tokyo 112; suffragan sees at Sapporo, Sendai, Yokohama, Urawa, Niigata; Archbishop of Tokyo Mgr. Peter Seiichi Shirayanagi; Archdiocese of Nagasaki: 1 Otsu Minami-Yamate-cho, Nagasaki; suffragan sees at Kagoshima, Fukuoka, Oita and Naha (Okinawa); Archbishop of Nagasaki Mgr. Joseph A. Satowaki; Archdiocese of Osaka: 1-55, Nishiyama-chô-Koyoen, Nishihomiyashio, Hyogo-ken; suffragan sees at Kyoto, Hiroshima, Takamatsu; Nagoya; Archbishop of Osaka Mgr. Paul Y. Taguchi, 357,478 adherents.

United Church of Christ in Japan: Japan Christian Center, Room 31, 551 Totsuka-machi 1-chome, Shinjuku-ku, Tokyo 160; f. 1941; union of 34 Presbyterian, Methodist, Congregational, Reformed and other denominations; Moderator Rev. Mitsuho Yoshida; Gen. Sec. Rev. George Hanabusa; 200,800 adherents.

Japanese Orthodox Church: Holy Resurrection Cathedral, (Nicolai-Do), 1-3, 4-chome Surugadai Kanda, Tokyo;

Primate H.E. Most Rev. Theodosius, Archbishop of Tokyo and Metropolitan of Japan; 24,640 adherents.

Nippon Sei Ko Kai (*Japan Episcopalian Church*): 4-21, Higashi 1-chome, Shibuya-ku, Tokyo; in Communion with the Church of England; est. as Province of the Anglican Communion 1887; 52,147 mems.; Acting Primate Most Rev. John Naohiko Okubo (Bishop of Kita-Kanto); 10 other diocesan bishops.

OTHER RELIGIONS

There are an estimated 5,000,000 adherents of other religions, with 1,200 shrines and temples and 15,000 priests.

The "New Religions"

Many new cults have grown up in Japan since the end of World War II. Collectively these are known as the New Religions (*Shinko Shukyo*). The most important are as follows:

Soka Gakkai: 32 Shinano-machi, Shinjuku-ku, Tokyo; f. 1930; the lay society of Orthodox Nichiren Buddhism; membership 7½ million households; Buddhist group aiming at individual happiness and world peace; Pres. Daisaku Ikeda; publs. include: *Selected Works of Daisaku Ikeda, The Human Revolution, Vols.* 1-7, *Science and Religion, Essays on Life, Reflections on Civilization, To My Young Friends, Essays for Women, Dialogue with the Juvenile, Seikyo Shimbun* (daily), *Dai-byaku Renge* (monthly), *Seikyo Graphic* (weekly), *Seikyo Times* (English language monthly), *East and West—Dialogue with Richard E. Coudenhove-Kalevgi.*

Rissho Kosei-kai: 11-1, Wada 2-chome, Suginami-ku; Tokyo 166; f. 1938; Buddhist laymen; Pres. Rev. Nikkyo Niwano; 4 million mems. in Japan and U.S.A.

THE PRESS

The total circulation of Japanese dailies is the third highest in the world after the U.S.S.R. and the United States and the circulation per head of population is second highest after Sweden. The three biggest newspapers are the *Asahi Shimbun* (combined circ. 6.1 million), *Mainichi Shimbun* (4.6 million) and *Yomiuri Shimbun* (5.9 million). There are also two influential financial papers, *Nihon Keizai Shimbun* and *Sankei Shimbun*, both with a combined circulation of over two million. These papers together account for 53.8 per cent of the total circulation of Japanese newspapers. A notable feature of the Japanese Press is the number of weekly news journals, most of which have started in the last ten years.

Technically the Japanese Press is very advanced, and all three of the major newspapers are issued in simultaneous editions in the main centres. This is achieved by high-speed wireless photo-facsimile offset printing. Automatic mono-type setting has been adopted since 1959, and teletype-setting was introduced by Kyodo News Agency in 1960, using a Chinese ideographic teleprinter invented in Japan. Colour printing is another advanced feature of the leading presses.

PRINCIPAL DAILIES*

Tokyo

Asahi Evening News: 8-5 Tsukiji 7-chome, Chuo-ku; f. 1954; evening; English language; Editor Y. Kitamura; circ. 48,528.

* Circulation over 45,000, and English-language press.

Asahi Shimbun: 3, 2-chome, Yuraku-cho, Chiyoda-ku; f. 1935; Editor M. Goto; circ. (all editions) morning 6,055,617, evening 4,002,624.

Business Japan: Sankei Bldg., 7-2, 1-chome, Otemachi, Chiyoda-ku; f. 1955; Pres. N. Shikanai; Man. Editor Ken Yanagisawa; circ. 63,000.

Daily Sports: 1-39, 2-chome, Ikenohata, Taito-ku; f. 1955; morning; Chief Editor K. Iwano; circ. 358,665.

Daily Yomiuri, The: 1-2-3, Ginza, Chuo-ku; f. 1955; English; Editor Hideo Ueno; circ. morning 37,000.

Dempa Shimbun: 11-15, Higashi Gotanda, 1-chome, Shinagawa-ku; f. 1950; morning; Editor H. Sasaki; circ. 200,000.

Denki Kikai Kogyo Shinbun: 11-15, 1-chome, Higashi Gotanda, Shinagawa-ku; f. 1958; morning; Editor T. Ajiki; circ. 45,000.

Hochi Shimbun: 29, 2-chome, Hirakawa-cho, Chiyoda-ku; f. 1871; morning; Chair. K. Sugao; Editor K. Urushizaki; circ. 805,601.

Japan Times, The: 5-4, 4-chome, Shibaura, Minato-ku; f. 1897; morning; English; Pres. Y. Higashiuchi; Editor M. Ogawa; circ. 49,200.

Komei Shimbun: 17 Minami-motomachi, Shinjuku-ku, organ of the Komeito political party; circ. 800,000. Sunday edition 1,400,000.

Mainichi Daily News, The: 1-1-1 Hitotsubashi, Chiyoda-ku; f. 1922; English language; morning; Gen. Man. and Editor HITOSHI OHNISHI; circ. 58,210 (*see* also under Osaka).

Mainichi Shimbun: 1-1, 1-chome, Hitotsubashi, Chiyoda-ku; f. 1872; Editor-in-Chief K. TANAKA; circ. (all editions) morning 4,628,733, evening 2,885,000.

Naigai Sports: Keiso Bldg., 12-8, 1-chome, Shiba, Minato-ku; f. 1962; evening; Man. Editor R. HARIGAYA; circ. 329,408.

Naigai Times: 5, 3-chome, Ginza, Chuo-ku; f. 1949; evening; Pres. TSAI CHANG KENG; Man. Editor S. TAMAKI.

Nihon Keizai Shimbun: 1-9-5 Otemachi, Chiyoda-ku, Tokyo; f. 1876; morning, evening and weekly (English edition: The Japan Economic Journal); economic news; Pres. J. ENJOJI; Chief Editor A. ARAI; circ. morning 1,444,525, evening 1,007,828, weekly 31,200.

Nihon Kogyo Shimbun: 7-2, 1-chome, Otemachi, Chiyoda-ku; f. 1933; morning business and financial; Pres. N. SHIKANAI; Man. Editor T. MASAKI; circ. 425,000.

Nihon Kyoiku Shimbun: 9, 2-chome, Kanda-Hitotsubashi, Chiyoda-ku; f. 1946; educational; Man. Editor K. YOSHIOKA; circ. morning 153,000.

Nihon Nogyo Shimbun: 2-3 Akihabara, Taito-ku; f. 1928; agricultural; Man. Editor S. KIMURA; circ. morning 307,963.

Nikkan Kogyo Shimbun (*Industrial Daily News*): 8-10, 1-chome, Kudan-kita, Chiyoda-ku; f. 1945; morning; Man. Editor SHIGEYOSHI IWANAGA; circ. 600,000.

Nikkan Sports: 5-10, 3-chome, Tsukiji, Chuo-ku; f. 1946; Chair. G. KAWADA; Editor H. SUGIMORI; morning; circ. 617,061.

Sankei Shimbun, The: 7-2, 1-chome, Otemachi, Chiyoda-ku; f. 1933; Man. Editor H. ISHIGURO; circ. morning 2,027,000, evening 1,254,005.

Sankei Sports: 3, 1-chome, Otemachi, Chiyoda-ku; f. 1963; Man. Editor I. TOKAWA; circ. morning 317,407.

Shipping and Trade News: Tokyo News Service Ltd., 10 Ginza Nishi, 8-chome, Chuo-ku, Tokyo 104; f. 1949; English language; Man. Editor M. CHIHAYA; circ. 17,536.

Sports Nippon: 1-1, 1-chome, Hitotsubashi, Chiyoda-ku; f. 1950; Dir. Y. MIYAMOTO; Man. Editor Y. MIYAMOTO; morning; circ. 594,310.

Sports Times: 12-7, 1-chome, Shiba, Minato-ku; f. 1961; Man. Editor M. SEKI; circ. evening 268,700.

Tokyo Shimbun: 3-13, 2-chome, Konan, Minato-ku; f. 1942; Pres. S. MIURA; Man. Editor I. HOTTA; circ. morning 569,000, evening 399,000.

Tokyo Sports: 3, 1-chome, Shiba-Hamamatsu-cho, Minato-ku; f. 1959; Pres. M. NAGATA; Man. Editor H. HIROTA; circ. evening 610,850.

Tokyo Times: 1, 1-chome, Higashi-Shimbashi, Minato-ku; f. 1946; Pres. and Man. Editor Y. TUKOMA; circ. 250,000.

Yomiuri Shimbun: 1-2, 3-chome, Ginza, Chuo-ku; f. 1874; Propr. T. SHORIKI; Pres. M. MUTAI; Man. Editor J. SUMI; morning and evening; circ. (all editions) morning 5,884,962, evening 3,536,638, (Tokyo) morning 3,634,348, evening 2,328,713.

OSAKA DISTRICT

Asahi Shimbun: 3, 3-chome, Nakano-shima, Kita-ku; f. 1879; Man. Editor MORIJI MATSUMOTO; circ. morning 1,848,379, evening 1,149,009.

Daily Sports: 18 1-chome, Kitadori, Edobori, Nishi-ku, Osaka; f. 1948; morning; Editor Y. MORISAWA; circ. 526,853.

Hochi Shimbun: 46 Nozaki-machi, Kita-ku; f. 1964; morning; Chief Editor H. UNNO; circ. 213,115.

Kansai Shimbun: 31 Hashizume-cho, Uchihon-cho, Higashi-ku; f. 1950; evening; Editor H. KIMURA; circ. 110,500.

Mainichi Daily News, The: 36, 2-chome, Dojima-kami, Kita-ku, Osaka; Editor Y. SUMINO; circ. 21,560 (*see* also under Tokyo).

Mainichi Shimbun: 36, 2-chome, Dojima-kami, Kita-ku; f. 1882; Man. Editor K. KOBAYASHI; circ. morning 1,445,470, evening 824,500.

Nihon Keizai Shimbun: 1, 1-chome, Komabashi, Higashi-ku; f. 1950; Editor K. SUZUKI; circ. morning 360,085, evening 262,541.

Nikkan Sports: 40 Toyoyima-cho, Kita-ku; f. 1950; Man. Editor M. WATANABE; morning circ. 391,143.

Osaka Nichi-nichi Shimbun: 69, 1-chome, Edobori-kitadori, Nishi-ku; f. 1946; Pres. J. ISHII; Man. Editor K. KISHIDA; circ. 87,500.

Osaka Shimbun: 27, Umeda-cho, Kita-ku; f. 1922; evening; Pres. Y. SAWAMARA; Editor T. MITSUI; circ. 167,289.

Sankei Shimbun: 27, Umeda-cho, Kita-ku; f. 1933; Man. Editor T. NAGATA; circ. morning 1,007,700, evening 555,908.

Sankei Sports: 27 Umeda-machi, Kita-ku; f. 1955; Dir. K. YAMAJI; circ. morning 323,521.

Shin Kansai: 2-3 3-chome, Minami, Oyodo-cho, Oyodo-ku; f. 1946; Rep. Dir. H. MORIGUCHI; Man. Editor K. KITABATAKE; evening; circ. 147,000.

Shin Osaka: 36 Kawaguchi-cho, Nishi-ku; f. 1946; Man. Editor K. HANAMOTO; circ. evening 29,808.

Sports Nippon: 2-3 Minami, 3-chome, Oyodo-cho, Oyodo-ku; f. 1949; Man. Editor A. HONDA; circ. morning 467,000.

Yomiuri Shimbun: 77 Nozaki-cho, Kita-ku; f. 1952; Chair. T. KURIYAMA; Man. Editor G. SAKATA; circ. morning 1,625,951, evening 1,042,957.

KANTO DISTRICT
(Outside Tokyo)

Chiba Nippo (*Chiba Daily News*): 31, 3-chome, Azuma-cho, Chiba City; f. 1957; Pres. I. KUBO; Editor T. ASANO; circ. 82,152.

Ibaragi: 2-15 Kitami-machi, Mito City, Ibaraki; f. 1891; Man. Editor T. MIKURA; circ. 76,000.

Jyomo Shimbun: 90 Furuichi-machi, Maebashi City, Tochigi; f. 1886; Editor T. KANAI; circ. morning 80,000.

Kanagawa Shimbun: 23 2-chome Otomachi, Naka-ku, Yokohama City; f. 1942; morning; Editor S. YAMAGAMI; circ. 158,580.

Shimotsuke Shimbun: 4-11 Hon-cho, Utsunomiya City, Tochigi; f. 1884; morning; Editor-in-Chief K. KAMAKURA; circ. 99,676.

Tochigi Shimbun: 3-6 Hon-cho, Utsunomiya City, Tochigi; f. 1949; Chair. K. SAKAMOTO; Editor M. WAKU; circ. 81,525.

TOHOKU DISTRICT
(Northeast Honshu)

Akita Sakigake Shimpo: 2-6, 1-chome, Omachi, Akita-shi, Akita, f. 1874; Pres. G. KURATA; Man. Editor K. TAKADA; circ. morning 152,167, evening 152,920.

Daily Tohoku: 3 Bancho, Hachinohe, Iwate; f. 1945; morning; Editor K. OTANI; circ. 65,580.

Fukushima Minpo; 21, Sakae-cho, Fukushima; f. 1892; morning and evening; circ. morning 137,156, evening 17,655; Editor Y. SATO.

Iwate Nippo: 3-7, Uchimaru, Morioka, Iwate; f. 1938; Editor D. TADA; circ. morning 139,875, evening 133,587.

Kahoku Shimpo: 2-28, 1-chome, Hsutsubashi, Sendai City, Miyagi; f. 1897; Editor Y. NIKAIDO; circ. morning 323,682, evening 133,587.

Minyu Shimbun: 9-9 Naka-machi, Fukushima City; f. 1895; circ. morning 116,686, evening 13,819; Man. Editor Y. WAKU.

Too Nippo: 2-11, 2-chome, Shin-machi, Aomori; f. 1888; morning and evening; circ. 151,804 and 150,680; Man. Editor T. OZAKI.

Yamagata Shimbun: 5-12, 2-chome Hatago-cho, Yamagata City; f. 1876; Pres. Y. HATTORI; Chief Editor K. KONDO; morning and evening circ. 145,200.

TOKAI DISTRICT
(Central Honshu)

Asahi Shimbun: 3-3, 1-chome, Sakae, Naka-ku, Nagoya; f. 1935; Man. Editor H. UEDA; circ. morning 373,575, evening 314,915.

Chubu Keizai Shimbun: 24-1 Hijie-cho, Nakamura-ku, Nagoya; f. 1946; Editor K. SUZUKI; circ. 141,378.

Chunichi Shimbun: 12-21, 3-chome, Marunouchi, Naka-ku, Nagoya; f. 1942; the paper has the world's leading newspaper colour printing facilities; Exec. Man. K. OSHIMA; Editor N. WAKAMATSU; circ. morning 1,522,843, evening 862,043.

Chunichi Sports: 24, 2-chome, Miyuki Honmachidori, Naka-ku, Nagoya; morning; circ. 200,000; Chief Editor T. ARIUMI.

Gifu Nichi-nichi Shimbun: 9 Imakomachi, Gifu City; f. 1879; morning and evening; Pres. T. YAMADA; Editor K. TAKIGAWA; circ. morning 134,282, evening 75,436.

Mainichi Shimbun: 1, 4-chome, Horinouchi-machi, Nakamura-ku, Nagoya; f. 1935; morning circ. 308,120, evening 236,895; Man. Editor R. HOSOKAWA.

Nagoya Times: 3-10, 1-chome, Maruno-uchi, Naka-ku, Nagoya City; f. 1946; evening; Editor T. MORI; circ. 130,000.

Shinano Mainichi Shimbun: 657 Minamiagata-cho, Nagano; f. 1873; Editor K. SHIOZAWA; circ. morning 144,714, evening 32,191.

Shizuoka Shimbun: 609, Ishida, Shizuoka City; f. 1941; Chief Editor Y. HOSHINO; circ. morning 430,300, evening 430,600.

Yamanashi Nichi-Nichi Shimbun: 6, 2-chome, Kitaguchi, Kofu City; f. 1872; morning; Editor SUSUMI KANAMURU; circ. 110,000.

Yamanashi Nichinichi Shimbun: 6, 2-chome, Kitaguchi, Kofu City, Yamanashi; f. 1872; morning; circ. 105,240; Man. Editor SUSUMU KANAMARU.

HOKURIKU DISTRICT
(North Coastal Honshu)

Fukui Shimbun: 1302 Yamato-machi, Fukui City; f. 1889; Chief Editor M. MAEDA; circ. morning 126,653, evening 15,243.

Hokkoku Shimbun: 5-1, 2-chome, Korinbo, Kanazawa, Ishikawa; f. 1893; circ. morning 211,274, evening 117,389; Pres. Y. MIYASHITA; Editor M. MITSUNO.

Hokuriku Chunichi Shimbun: 7-15, 2-chome, Karimbo, Kanazawa; circ. morning 126,000, evening 32,000; Editor K. NAKAGAWA.

Kita Nihon Shimbun: 2-14 Yasuzumi-cho, Toyama-shi, Toyama; f. 1940; Man. Editor S. FUKUYAMA; circ. morning 153,000, evening 42,000.

Niigata Nippo: 189-3 Ichiban-cho, Higashinaka-dori, Niigata City; f. 1942; Editor K. KAMIMURA; circ. morning 340,500, evening 99,600.

Yomiuri Shimbun: 5/4 Shomozek, Takaoka; f. 1961; Man. Editor U. BANDO; circ. morning 100,310, evening 13,911.

KINKI DISTRICT
(West Central Honshu)

Hyogo Shimbun: 3-25 Minato-machi, Hyogo-ku, Kobe; f. 1946; evening; circ. 94,257; Editor J. IWASA.

Ise Shimbun: 1871 Sendo-machi, Tsu City, Mie; f. 1878; morning; Man. Editor K. SHIBATA; circ. 85,000.

Kobo Shimbun: 4, 7-chome, Kumoidori, Fukiai-ku, Kobe City; f. 1898; circ. morning 428,335, evening 231,900; Man. Editor H. INAMOTO.

Kyoto Shimbun: 239 Shoshoi-machi Ebisugawa-kitairu, Karasuma-dori, Nakakyo-ku, Kyoto; f. 1942; circ. morning 375,796, evening 309,995; Chief Editor T. HIDAKA.

Wakayama Shimpo: 5, 4-chome, Komatsubara-dori, Wakayama; f. 1940; morning; Editor H. AKAI; circ. 65,000.

CHUGOKU DISTRICT
(Western Honshu)

Bocho Shimbun: 3 Kifune-cho, Shimonseki; f. 1941; morning; Pres. Y. FUURA; Man. Editor Y. MIYOSHI; circ. 36,000.

Chugoku Shimbun: 7-1 Dobashi-cho, Hiroshima City, Hiroshima; f. 1892; morning circ. 424,835, evening circ. 118,624; Pres. A. YAMAMOTO; Man. Editor S. MIYAKI.

Sanyo Shimbun: 1-23, 2-chome, Yanagi-cho, Okayama; f. 1879; circ. morning 284,239, evening 95,941; Man. Editor Y. MATSUOKA.

Shimane Shimbun: 14-3 Sodeshi-machi, Matsue, Shimane; f. 1942; morning; Chief Editor T. NAKAMOTO; circ. 65,500.

Yamaguchi Shimbun: 16, Higashiyamamoto-cho, Shimonoseki; f. 1946; Pres. K. OGAWA; Editors T. ABE, T. FUJITA; circ. 34,700.

SHIKOKU ISLAND

Ehime Shimbun: 12-1, 1-chome, Otemachi, Matsuyama, Ehime; f. 1876; Chair. Y. HIRATA; Chief Editor T. SUGIMOTO; circ. morning 179,859, evening 40,256.

Kochi Shimbun: 24 Honcho, Kochi-shi, Kochi; f. 1904; circ. morning 153,189, evening 99,300; Editor H. KOMATSU.

Shikoku Shimbun: 15-1, Nakono-machi, Takamatsu; f. 1889; Chief Editor Y. SAKANE; circ. morning 113,352, evening 24,084.

Tokushima Shimbun: 32-1 Saiwai-cho, Tokushima; f. 1941; circ. morning 143,574, evening 41,738; Man. Editor K. SUGIMOTO.

HOKKAIDO ISLAND

Asahi Shimbun: 1-1, 1-chome, Nishi, Kita Nijo, Sapporo City; f. 1959; Man. Editor M. TERAZAKI; circ. morning 176,918, evening 116,039.

Hokkai Times: 1, 4-chome, Odori-Nishi, Sapporo; f. 1946; evening and morning; circ. morning 192,605, evening 98,968; Man. Editor H. MIYATA.

Hokkaido Nikkan Sports Shimbun: 1, 4-chome, Odori-nishi, Sapporo; f. 1962; morning; circ. 90,919; Pres. U. Chizaki.

Hokkaido Shimbun: 6, 3-chome, Odori-Nishi, Sapporo; f. 1942; Editor K. Watanabe; 3 editions combined circ. 400,000.

Mainichi Shimbun: 2, Nishi, 4-chome, Kita-Nijo, Sapporo; f. 1959; Editor Z. Watanake; circ. morning 151,600, evening 82,900.

Nikkan Sports: 4-1 Odori-nishi, Sapporo; f. 1962; morning; Pres. U. Chizaki; Man. Editor T. Akasaka; circ. 92,000.

Yomiuri Shimbun: 11, Nishi, 1-chome, Minami-Sanjo, Sapporo; f. 1959; Editor K. Takizawa; circ. morning 200,400, evening 97,000.

KYUSHU ISLAND

Asahi Shimbun: 12-1, 1-chome, Sunatsu, Kokura-ku, Kita-Kyushu City; f. 1935; Man. Editor K. Amano; circ. morning 752,609, evening 280,413.

Fukunichi: 2-1, 1-chome, Imaizumi-machi, Fukuoka; f. 1946; Editor K. Kitagawa; circ. 138,000.

Kagoshima Shimpo: 1-15 Matsubara-cho, Kagoshima; f. 1959; Editor K. Hanamure; circ. 65,910.

Kumamoto Nichi-nichi Shimbun: 2-33 Kamidori-cho, Kumamoto-shi, Kumamoto; f. 1942; Editor Y. Inashita; circ. morning 170,872, evening 62,221.

Mainichi Shimbun: 207-1, 1-chome, Konyu-machi, Kokura-ku, Kitakyushu; f. 1935; circ. morning 605,000, evening 226,500; Man. Editor Hideo Morioka.

Minami Nihon Shimbun: 1-2 Yasui-cho, Kagoshima-shi, Kagoshima; f. 1881; morning circ. 212,062; evening circ. 40,687; Man. Editor T. Kubo.

Miyazaki Nichinichi Shimbun: 1-33, 1-chome Takachiho-dori, Miyazaki; f. 1940; Editor Kuroki; circ. 126,000.

Nagasaki Jiji Shimbun: 6-24 Dajima-machi, Nagasaki; f. 1904; Man. Editor S. Iwamura; circ. morning 65,153.

Nagasaki Shimbun: 6-24 Dejima, Nagasaki; f. 1889; Editor T. Nanano; circ. morning 142,463, evening 142,615.

Nishi Nippon Shimbun: 4-20, 1-chome, Tenjin, Fukuoka; f. 1887; Chief Editor K. Kato; circ. morning 731,042, evening 302,897.

Oita Godo Shimbun: 7-15, 3-chome, Funai-cho, Oita f. 1886; Man. Editor N. Kiyohara; circ. morning 136,200, evening 136,200.

Saga Shimbun: 3-8, 1-chome, Matsubara, Saga City; f. 1884; morning; Man. Editor K. Miyahara; circ. 92,242.

Shin Kyushu: 1-3 Kiyotaki-cho, Moji, Fukuoka; f. 1946; morning; circ. 73,164; Man. Editor S. Kitajima.

Sports Nippon: 3, 1-chome, Kiyotaki-cho, Moji-ku, Kita-Kyushu; Rep. Dir. S. Yamashiro; morning; circ. 211,048.

Yomiuri Shimbun: 1-11 Meiwa-machi, Kokura-ku, Kita-Kyushu; Man. Editor M. Sakurai; circ. morning 360,347, evening 177,063.

WEEKLIES

Asahi Graphic: Asahi Shimbun Publishing Co., Yuraku-cho, Chiyoda-ku, Tokyo; f. 1923; pictorial review; Editor Michito Ito; circ. 200,000.

Asahi Journal: Asahi Shimbun Publishing Co., Yuraku-cho, Chiyoda-ku, Tokyo; review.

Economist: 1-1-1 Hitotsubashi; Chiyoda-ku, Tokyo; f. 1923; published by the Mainichi Newspapers; weekly; economics; Editorial Chief Nozomu Sekine; circ. 117,000.

The Gijitsu Journal: 8-10 Kudan kita, 1-chome, Chiyoda-ku, Tokyo; f. 1959; industrial technology.

Japan Company Directory: 1-4 Hongoku-cho Nihonbashi, Chuo-ku, Tokyo; in English, published by *The Oriental Economist.*

Nippon Shogyo: 3 Bakuro-cho, Chuo-ku, Tokyo; f. 1895; circ. 35,000; Exec. Dir. Ko Takeuchi.

Oriental Economist: 1-4, Hongoku-cho, Nihonbashi, Chuo-ku, Tokyo; f. 1934; economics, politics; English edition; Pres. N. Wada.

Screen and Stage: Chuo-ku, Tokyo; f. 1946; Editor J. Tomoda.

Shukan Asahi: Asahi Shimbun Publishing Co., 2-3 Yuraku-cho, Chiyoda-ku, Tokyo; circ. 1,300,000.

Shukan Bunshun: 3 Kioi-cho, Chiyoda-ku, Tokyo; f. 1959; general; circ. 550,000.

Shukan Sankei: 1-3 Otemachi, Chiyoda-ku, Tokyo; general.

Shukan Shincho: 71 Yarai-cho, Shinjuku-ku, Tokyo; general; circ. 1,040,000.

Shukan Yomiuri: 3-3 Ginza Nishi, Chuo-ku, Tokyo; Editor S. Hara; general.

Student Times: Japan Times Inc., 4-5-4 Shibaura, Minato-ku, Tokyo; English language.

Sunday Mainichi: 11-1 Yuraku-cho, Chiyoda-ku, Tokyo; circ. 1,200,000.

Tenji Mainichi: 2-36 Dojima, Kita-ku, Osaka; f. 1922; circ. 11,000; in Japanese braille; Editor Michitoshi Zenimoto.

Toyo Keizai Shimpo: 1-4 Hongkoku-cho, Nihonbashi, Chuo-ku, Tokyo; f. 1895; weekly; economics; Pres. K. Murayama; circ. 100,000.

PERIODICALS

Airview: 601 Kojun Building, 6 Ginza, Tokyo; f. 1946; monthly; Editor E. Sekigawa.

Alpinist: 24 2-chome, Miyukihonmachi, Nakaku, Nagoya; f. 1942; circ. 20,000; Editor T. Suzuki; monthly.

Asahi Camera: Yuraku-cho, Chiyoda-ku, Tokyo 100; f. 1926; photography; monthly; Editor Shigero Kojima; circ. 200,000.

Bijutsu Techô: Bijutsu Shuppan-sha, 15 Ichigaya Hon-mura-cho, Shinjuku-ku, Tokyo; f. 1948; monthly; fine arts.

Bungaku: Iwanami Shoten, 3, 2-chome, Kanda, Hitotsubashi, Tokyo; f. 1933; Editor Yoshiya Tamura.

Bungei-Shunju: 3 Kioi-cho, Chiyoda-ku, Tokyo; f. 1923; popular monthly; general.

Chuo Koron: 2-1 Kyobashi, Chuo-ku, Tokyo; f. 1886; monthly; political, economic, scientific and literary; Chief Editor Kinjiro Sasahara.

Design: Bijutsu Shuppanh-sha, 15 Ichigaya-honmura-cho, Shinjuku-ku, Tokyo; f. 1955; monthly; covers all aspects of design.

Fujin Koron: Chuo Koron-sha, 1, 2-chome, Kyobashi, Chuo-ku, Tokyo; women's literary monthly.

Geijitsu Shincho: 71 Yarai-cho, Shinjuku-ku, Tokyo; f. 1950; monthly; fine arts, music, architecture, drama and design; Editor-in-Chief Ryoichi Sato.

Gekkan Rodo Mondai: 14 Sugumachi, Shinjuku-ku, Tokyo; labour problem monthly.

Gengo-Seikatsu: Chikuma-shobo, Chiyoda-ku, Tokyo; f. 1951; language and life monthly; Editor NAOO HARADA; circ. 10,000.

Horitsu Jiho: 14 Sugamachi, Shinjuku-ku, Tokyo; law journal.

Ie-no-Hikari (*Light of Home*): 11 Funagawara-cho, Ichigaya, Shinjuku-ku, Tokyo; f. 1925; monthly, rural and general interest; Pres. I. MIYABE; Editor YOSHITAKA MIYMAOTO; circ. 1,400,000.

The Japan Architect: 31-2, Yushima 2-chome, Bunkyo-ku, Tokyo 113; f. 1956; monthly; international edition of *Shinkenchiku*; Editor SHOZO BABA; Publisher YASU-GORO YOSHIOKA; circ. 17,000.

Japan Economic Yearbook: Nihonbashi, Tokyo; in English; published by *The Oriental Economist*.

Japan Electric Engineering: 11-15 Higashi Gotanda, 1-chome, Shinagawa-ku; monthly; circ. 60,000.

Japan Electric Industry: 11-15 Higashi Gotanda, 1-chome, Shinagawa-ku; monthly; circ. 65,000.

Japan Quarterly: Asahi Shimbun-sha, Yuraku-cho, Chiyoda-ku, Tokyo; in English; Exec. Editor YOSHI-MASA YUASA.

Jitsugyo No Nihon: Ginza Nishi, Chuo-ku, Tokyo; semi-monthly; economic and business.

Junkan Yomiuri: 3-1 Ginza Nishi, Chuo-ku, Tokyo; f. 1942; three times monthly.

Kagaku: Iwanami Shoten, publishers 2-5-5 Hitotsubashi Chiyoda-ku, Tokyo; f. 1931; Editor YUKO NATORI.

Kagaku Asahi: 2-3 Yuraku-cho, Chiyoda-ku, Tokyo; f. 1941; scientific; Editor SHINYA TAKATSU; monthly.

Kagakushi-Kenkyu: Department of Humanities, Tokyo Institute of Technology, 2-12-1, O-okayama, Meguro-ku, Tokyo; quarterly Journal of the History of Science Society of Japan.

Keizai Hyoron: 14 Sugamachi, Shinjuku, Tokyo; economic review.

Keizaizin (*Home Economics*): Kansai Economics Federation, Shin-Dai-Bldg., Dojima-Hamadori, Kita-ku, Osakao economics; monthly; Editor Y. MIYANO.

Kikanhanga: Bijutsa Shuppan-sha, 15 Ichigaya-honmura-cho, Shinjuku-ku, Tokyo; f. 1968; quarterly; covers all aspects of printing.

Kokka: Asahi Shimbun Publishing Co., 3, 2-chome, Yuraku-cho, Chiyoda-ku, Tokyo; Far Eastern art, monthly.

Mizue: Bijutsu Shuppan-sha, 15 Ichigaya-honmura-cho, Shinjuku-ku, Tokyo; f. 1905; monthly; fine arts.

Museum: Bijutsu Shuppan-sha, 15 Ichigaya-Honmura-cho, Shinjuku-ku, Tokyo; f. 1951; monthly bulletin of Tokyo National Museum.

New Japan: Mainichi Newspapers, Tokyo; f. 1947; pictorial; Ed. YOSHIMASA SUMINO.

Nogyo Asahi: 2-3 Yuraku-cho, Chiyoda-ku, Tokyo; monthly; scientific.

Nosei Hyoron: 11-1 Yuraku-cho, Chiyoda-ku, Tokyo; agricultural; monthly.

Ongaku no Tomo: Kagurazaka 6-30, Shinjuku-ku, Tokyo; music; monthly.

The Pacific Community: Jiji Press Ltd., Central P.O.B. 1007, Tokyo; f. April 1969; political, economic, diplomatic, cultural, military, etc.; quarterly (Jan., April, July, Oct.) in English; Pres. Jiji Press TATSURO SATO; Editor YUJI HAYASHI; circ. 6,000.

Seibutsu-Kagaku (*Biology*): c/o Dept. of Biology, Faculty of Science, Ochanomizu, University, Tokyo; f. 1949; quarterly.

Sekai: Iwanami Shoten 3, 2-chome, Kanda, Hitotsubashi, Tokyo; f. 1946; reviews; monthly; Editor TORU MIDORIKAWA.

Shakaijin: Yamajin Bldg., 1-1 Ogawa Machi, Kanda, Chiyoda-ku, Tokyo; monthly; political.

Shincho: 71 Yarai-cho, Shinjuku-ku, Tokyo; literary; monthly; Editor JUICHI SAITO; circ. 30,000.

Shinkenchiku: 31-2, Yushima 2-chome, Bunkyo-ku, Tokyo 113; f. 1924; monthly architectural journal; Editor SHOZO BABA; Publisher YASUGORO YOSHIOKA; circ. 48,000.

Shiso (*Ideology*): Iwanami Shoten 3, 2-chome, Kanda, Hitotsubashi, Tokyo; f. 1921; Editor TORU MIDORIKAWA; monthly.

Shizen (*Nature*): Chuo Koron Sha, 1, 2-chome, Kyobashi, Chuo-ku, Tokyo; scientific monthly.

Shosetsu Shincho: Shincho-sha, 71 Yarai-cho, Shinjuku-ku, Tokyo; f. 1945; monthly; literature; Chief Editor TOSHIO SATO.

Shufu to Seikatsu: 1-2 Nishi Kanda, Chiyoda-ku, Tokyo; monthly; women's magazine.

Shufunotomo: 6, 1-chome, Surugadai, Kanda, Chiyoda-ku, Tokyo; monthly; women's magazine.

So-en: Bunka Publishing Bureau, 1-22, 3-chome, Yoyogi, Shibuya-ku, Tokyo; fashion monthly; Chief Editor ISAO IMAIDA; circ. 400,000.

Sports Mainichi: 11-1 Yuraku-cho, Chiyoda-ku, Tokyo; monthly.

Statistical Monthly (*Toyo Keizai Tokei Geppo*): published by *The Oriental Economist*, 1-4 Hongoku-cho, Nihonbashi, Chuo-ku, Tokyo; f. 1895.

Sugaku (*Mathematics*): Mathematical Society of Japan, c/o Faculty of Science, University of Tokyo; f. 1947; quarterly.

Tenbo: Chikuma-Shobo, Chiyoda-ku, Tokyo; f. 1964; general; monthly; Editor NADO HARADA; circ. 30,000.

Yama-To-Keikoku (*Mountain and Valley*): 1-1-33 Shiba-Daimon, Minato-ku, Tokyo; monthly; mountain climbing.

Yomiuri Nenkan (*Yomiuri Yearbook*): published by Yomiuri Shimbun, Ootemachi, Chiyoda-ku, Tokyo 100; f. 1946, general year book and almanac; Editor K. YAMADA.

Zosen: Tokyo News Service Ltd., 10 Ginza Nishi, 8-chome, Chuo-ku, Tokyo; monthly; shipbuilding.

NEWS AGENCIES

Jiji Tsushin-Sha (*Jiji Press*): P.O.B. 1007, Tokyo; f. 1945; general news service by facsimile; Man. Dir. TATURO SATO; publ. *Yearbook*.

Kyodo News Service: 2 Akasaka Aoi-cho, Minato-ku, Tokyo; f. 1945; supplies press, radio and television with foreign and domestic news; Pres. SHINTARO FUKU-SHIMA; Man. Editor TAKEJI WATANABE.

Radiopress Inc.: Fuji Television Annex Bldg., Kawado-cho, Ichigaya, Shinjuku-ku, Tokyo; f. 1945; Pres. K. NAKATA; Man. Editor T. NAKADATE.

Soviet News: Tokyo; monitors Radio Moscow broadcasts.

Sun Telephoto: Palaceside Bldg., 1-chome, Hitotsubashi, Chiyoda-ku, Tokyo; f. 1952; Chair. I. FURUNO; Pres. K. MATSUOKA.

BUREAUX OF FOREIGN AGENCIES
Tokyo

ABC: Asahi Bldg., 6-7, Ginza, 6-chome, Chuo-ku; Bureau Chief IRWIN M. CHAPMAN.

Agence France Presse: Asahi Shimbun Shinkan, 2-3 chome Yurakucho, Chiyoda-ku; Bureau Chief PIERRE BRISARD.

ANSA: Kyodo Tsushin Kaikan, 2 Aoi-cho, Akasaka, Minato-ku; Correspondent MARIA ROMILDA GIORGIS.

Antara: Kyodo News Service Bldg., No. 2, Aoicho Akasaka, Minato-ku; Bureau Chief ALADDIN.

AP: Asahi Shimbun Bldg., 2-3, Yuraku-cho, Chiyoda-ku; Bureau Chief H. HARTZENBUSCH.

Central News Agency of China: Shisei-kaikan, Hibiya 2, Chiyoda-ku; Bureau Chief LEE CHIA.

Czechoslovak News Agency: 5-13, Jingumae 4-chome, Shibuya-ku; Bureau Chief IVO STOLC.

Deutsche Presse-Agentur (dpa): Shisei Kaikan, Room 202, Hibiya 2, Chiyoda-ku; Bureau Chief SIEGFRIED NIEBUHR.

Hapdong News Agency: Kyodo Press Bldg., 2 Aoi-cho, Minato-ku; Bureau Chief SANG KWON LEE.

Keystone: 12-3, Koji-machi, Chiyoda-ku; Bureau Chief H. J. ABRAHAMS.

Novosti: 6-191, Gotanda, Shinagawa-ku; Bureau Chief PETR BARAKHTA.

Reuters: Kyodo Tsushin Kaikan, 2 Akasaka, Aoi-cho, Minato-ku; Chief Representative MICHAEL NEALE.

Sisa News Agency: 2425, 5-chome, Kamimeguro, Meguro-ku; Bureau Chief WHA BONG SHINN.

Tass: 1-5, Hon-machi, Shibuya-ku; Bureau Chief VICTOR ZATSEPIN.

UPI: Palaceside Bldg., 1-1 Hitotsubashi 1-chome, Chiyoda-ku; Man., North Asia, ARNOLD B. C. DIBBLE.

PRESS ASSOCIATIONS

Nihon Shimbun Kyokai (*Japan Newspaper Publishers and Editors Association*): Shiseikaikan Building, Hibiya Park, Chiyoda-ku, Tokyo 100; f. 1946; mems. include 167 companies, including 109 daily newspapers, 8 news agencies, 49 radio and TV companies, and 1 non-daily newspaper; Pres. KOKYO SHIRAISHI; Sec.-Gen. SUSUMU EJIRI; publs. *The Japanese Press* (annual), *Shimbun Kenkyu* (monthly), *Shimbun Kyokai Ho* (weekly), *Nihon Shimbun Nenkan* (annual), *Shimbun Insatsu Gijutsu* (quarterly), *Shimbun Keiei* (quarterly).

Foreign Correspondents' Club of Japan: 1-2, Marunouchi 2-chome, Chiyoda-ku, Tokyo, Japan 100.

Japan Magazine Publishers' Association: 7, 1-chome, Kanda Surugadai, Chiyoda-ku, Tokyo.

PUBLISHERS

KYOTO

Jimbun Shoin: Takakura-Nishi-Hairu, Bukkoji-dori, Shimokyoku; f. 1922; literary, philosophy, history, fine art; Pres. MUTSUHISA WATANABE.

TOKYO

Baifukan Co. Ltd.: 4-3-12 Kudan Minami, 4-chome, Chiyoda-ku; f. 1924; mathematics, natural and social science, technology; Pres. K. YAMAMOTO.

Bijutsu Shuppan-Sha: 15 Ichigaya Honmura-cho, Shinjuku-ku; f. 1906; art and architecture; Pres. ATSUSHI OSHITA.

Chijin Shokan 2-112 Totsuka-machi, Shinjuku-ku; Science and technical, agriculture, geography; Pres. ISAMU KAMIJO.

Chuokoron-sha Inc.: 2-1, Kyobashi, Chuo-ku; f. 1886; philosophy, history, sociology, literature; Pres. HOJI SHIMANAKA.

Froebel-Kan Co. Ltd.: 3-1 Kanda Ogawa-machi, Chiyoda-ku; f. 1907; juvenile, educational, music; Pres. KENSUKE SUGANO.

Fukuinkan Shoten: 1-1-9, Misaki-cho, Chiyoda-ku; f. 1950; juvenile, education, religion; Pres. TADASHI MATSUI.

Gakken Co. Ltd.: 4-40-5, Kamiikedai, Ohta-ku, f. 1946; juvenile, education, reference; Pres. HIDETO FURUOKA; Man. Dir. HIROSHI FURUOKA.

Hakusui-Sha: 3-24 Kanda-Ogawa-machi, Chiyoda-ku; f. 1915, general literature, science and languages; Pres. TEISHI KUSANO.

Heibon Sha: 4-1 Yonban-cho, Chiyoda-ku; f. 1914; encyclopaedias, art, science books, atlases, etc.; Pres. KUNIHIKO SHIMONAKA.

Hokuseido Press: 3-12, Kanda-Nishiki-cho, Kanda, Chiyoda-ku; f. 1914; Pres. JUMPEI NAKATSHUCI; regional non-fiction.

Ie-No-Hikari Association: 11 Funagawara-cho, Ichigaya, Shinjuku-ku; f. 1925; agriculture, education; Pres. RYOHEI ADACHI; Man. Dir. YOSHIRO TAKAHASHI.

Iwanami Shoten: 2-5-5, Hitotsubashi; f. 1913; natural and social sciences, literature, history, geography, Pres. YUJIRO IWANAMI.

Kanehara Shuppan Co. Ltd.: 2-31-14, Yushima, Bunkyo-ku; f. 1875; medical, agricultural, engineering and scientific; Pres. SHIRO KANEHARA.

Kodansha Ltd.: 2-12, Otowa 2-chome, Bunkyo-ku; f. 1909; art, education, children's picture books, fiction, cookery, reference books, and various other types of book in English and other languages; weekly, monthly and quarterly magazines; Pres. SHOICHI NOMA.

Kyoritsu Shuppan Co. Ltd.: 4-6-19 Kobinata, Bunkyo-ku; f. 1926; scientific and technical; Pres. MASAO NANJO.

Maruzen Company Ltd.: 6 Tori, 2-chome, Nihonbashi, Chuo-ku; f. 1869; general; Pres. SHINGO IIZUMI; Chair. TADASHI TSUKASA; Man. Dir. MASAO NAKATA.

Misuzu Shobo Publishing Co.: 3-17-15, Hongo, Bunkyo-ku; f. 1947; fine art, science, medicine, politics; Pres. TAMIO KITANO; Man. Dir. TOSHITO OBI.

Nikkan Kogyo Shimbun: 1-8-10 Kudan Kita, 1-chome, Chiyoda-ku, Tokyo 102; f. 1911, revived 1945; technical, business and management, dictionaries; Pres. TOSHIO SHIRAI.

Nippon Hyoron Sha: 14 Suga-machi, Shinjuku-ku; law, economics, sociology, business; Pres. MIOKICHI SUZUKI.

Obunsha Co. Ltd.: 55 Yokodera-cho Shinjuku-ku; f. 1931; textbooks, reference books, general science and fiction; magazines; audio-visual aids; Pres. YOSHIO AKAO.

OHM-Sha Ltd., The: 3-1 chome, Kanda-Nishiki-cho, Chiyoda-ku; f. 1914; engineering, technical and scientific; Pres. F. SUNAGA; Man. Dir. N. TATSUMI.

Ongaku No Tomo Sha Corpn.: 6-30, Kagurazaka, Shinjuku-ku; f. 1941; music books, magazines and scores; Chair. Keizo Horiuchi; Pres. Sansaku Meguro; Man. Dir. Sunao Asaka.

Risosha: 46 Akagashita-machi, Shinjuku-ku; f. 1927; philosophy, religion, social science; Pres. S. Ohe.

Sanseido (*Sanseido Publishing Co.*): 1-1, Kanda-Jinbo-cho, Chiyoda-ku; dictionaries, education, languages, science, sociology; Pres. Masakaze Ogura.

Seibundo-Shinkosha Publishing Co. Ltd.: 1-chome, Kanda Chiyoda-ku; f. 1912; technical and scientific, agriculture, history, geography; Pres. and Man. Dir. Y. Kawasaki.

Shinkenchiku-Sha Ltd.: 31-2, Yushima,, 2-chome, Bunkyo-ku; f. 1925; architectural; Editor and Publisher Y. Yoshioka; Man. Dir. Y. Yoshida.

Shogakukan Publishing Co. Ltd.: 2-3-1, Kanda, Hitotsu-bashi, Chiyoda-ku; f. 1922; juvenile, education, geography; Pres. T. Ohga.

Shokokusha Publishing Co. Inc.: 25 Saka-machi, Shinjuku-ku; f. 1932; architectural, technical and fine art; Chair. G. Shimoide; Pres. K. Shimoide; Man. Dir. K. Komparu.

Shufunotomo Co. Ltd.: 1-6, Kanda, Surugadai, Chiyoda-ku; f. 1916; domestic science, juvenile, fine art; Pres. Kazuo Ishikawa.

Shunju-Sha Co. Ltd.: 2-18-6 Sotokanda, Chiyoda-ku; f. 1918; philosophy, religion, literary, economics, music, etc.; Man. R. Kanda.

Taishukan Shoten: 3-24, Kanda-Nishiki-cho, Chiyoda-ku; f. 1918; reference, language, sport, social science, textbooks, dictionaries; Chair. Katashi Inoue; Pres. Toshio Suzuki.

Tokyo News Tsushiu-Sha: 8-10 Ginza-Nishi, Chuo-ku; f. 1947; sociology, economics, general non-fiction; Pres. I. Okuyama.

University of Tokyo Press: 7-3-1 Hongo, Bunkyo-ku; f. 1951; humanities, history, sociology, economics, politics, science; Man. S. Minowa.

Yama To Keikoku Sha Co. Ltd.: 1-1-33, Shiba-Daimon, Minato-ku;, f. 1930 mountaineering, skiing and travel books; Pres. K. Kawasaki.

Yamakawa Shuppan Sha: 1-13-13, Uchi-kanda, Chiyoda-ku; history, education, dictionaries, textbooks; Pres. Shigeji Nozawa.

Yuhikaku Co.: 17, 2-chome, Kanda Jimbo-cho, Chiyoda-ku; f. 1877; social sciences; Dir. T. Egusa; Man. S. Egusa.

Zeimukeiri Kyokai: 3-53-9, Totsuka-machi, Shinjuku-ku; law, economics, business, sociology, education; Pres. Hango Otsubo.

Zenkoku Kyodo Shuppan: 1-10-32, Wakaba, Shinjuku-ku; agriculture, sociology, economics; Pres. Kinnosuke Onaka.

Japan Book Publishers Association: 6 Fukuro-machi, Shinjuku-ku; Tokyo.

RADIO AND TELEVISION

There were an estimated 23,500,000 radio receiving sets in 1971 and 23,800,000 televisions in 1972.

Nippon Hoso Kyokai, N.H.K. (*Japan Broadcasting Corporation*): Nippon Hoso Kyokai Bldg., 2-2-1 Jinnan, Shikuya-ku, Tokyo; f. 1925; Chair. Board of Govs. S. Ito; Pres. Kichiro Ono.

N.H.K. is a non-commercial public corporation whose Governors are appointed by the government. Five (2 TV and 3 radio) networks and 3,500 stations cover the country, the TV ones equipped for colour broadcasting, equally divided between general and educational networks; central stations at Tokyo, Osaka, Nagoya, Hiroshima, Kumamoto, Sendai, Sapporo and Matsuyama. The International Service broadcasts in 21 languages.

National Association of Commercial Broadcasters in Japan: Bungei Shunju Bldg., 3, Kioicho, Chiyoda-ku, Tokyo; Pres. Junzo Imamichi; Exec. Dir. Kazuo Sugiyama; Sec.-Gen. Nagato Izumi; association of 102 companies (86 TV companies, 16 radio companies. Among 86 TV companies, 50 operate radio and TV) with 161 radio stations and 1,356 TV stations. They include:

Asahi Broadcasting Co.: 2-2 Oyodo-cho, Oyodo-ku, Osaka; Chair. T. Suzuki.

Far East Network (AFRTS): H.Q. A.P.O. San Francisco 96267; serves U.S. forces in Japan; 6 stations (Tokyo, Okinawa, Misawa, Iwakuni, Chitose, Sasebo) operate 24 hours; 3 TV stations (Misawa, Iwakuni and Okinawa); 1 FM station (Okinawa); Commander Lieut.-Col. Frank J. Morris, U.S.A.F.

Nippon Cultural Broadcasting, Inc.: Shinju-ku, Tokyo; Pres. S. Tomoda.

Nippon System, Inc.: 7, 1-chome, Yuraku-cho, Chiyoda-ku, Tokyo; Chair. K. Uemura; Pres. N. Shikanai.

Nihon Short-Wave Broadcasting Co.: 9-15 Akasaka 1-chome, Minato-ku, Tokyo; Pres. M. Nakajima.

Tokyo Broadcasting System, Inc.: Akasaka, Minato-ku, Tokyo; f. 1951; Chair. Junzo Imamichi; Pres. Hiroshi Suwa.

There are also 77 commercial stations operated by Radio Tokyo, Asahi Broadcasting Co., Nippon TV Network Co., Nippon Educational TV Co. and others, including:

NET Television Network Co. Ltd.: 4-10, 6-chome Roppongi, Minato-ku, Tokyo; f. 1957; Chair. Yoshio Akao; Pres. Takeo Yokota.

YTV—Yomiuri Telecasting Corporation: 2-74 Iwaicho, Kita-ku, Osaka; f. 1957; 18 hrs. broadcasting a day, of which 62 hrs. per week in colour; Pres. Y. Mutai; Exec. Dir. T. Okano; Programme Man. U. Tanaka.

Regular colour television transmissions started on September 10th, 1960. By 1967 NHK and 46 commercial companies were engaged in colour broadcasting.

Television News Agencies

NET-Ashi Productions Ltd.: 6-4-10 Roppong, Minato-ku, Tokyo; f. 1958; Pres. T. Fujii.

Kyodo Television News: 7 Kawata-cho, Ichigaya, Shinjuku-ku, Tokyo; f. 1958; Chair. R. Nozawa; Pres. N. Aizawa.

FINANCE

BANKING

(cap. = capital; p.u. = paid up; dep. = deposits; m. = million; amounts in yen)

Japan's central bank and note-issuing body is the Bank of Japan, founded in 1882. More than half the credit business of the country is handled by approximately one hundred commercial banks and three long-term credit institutions, collectively designated "All Banks". The most important of these are the thirteen city banks, many of which have a distinguished history, reaching back to the days of the *zaibatsu*, the private entrepreneurial organizations on which Japan's capital wealth was built up before the Second World War. Although the *zaibatsu* were abolished as integral industrial and commercial enterprises during the Allied Occupation, the several businesses and industries which bear the former *zaibatsu* names, such as Mitsubishi, Mitsui and Sumitomo, continue to flourish and to give each other mutual assistance through their respective banks and trust corporations. Among the commercial banks, one, the Bank of Tokyo, specializes in foreign exchange business, while the Industrial Bank of Japan provides a large proportion of the finance for capital investment by industry. The Japan Long-Term Credit Bank also specializes in industrial finance; the work of these two privately-owned banks is supplemented by the government Japan Development Bank.

The Government has established a number of other specialized organs to supply essential services not performed by the private banks. Thus the Japan Export-Import Bank advances credits for exports of heavy industrial products and imports of raw materials in bulk. A Housing Loan Corporation assists firms building housing for their employees, while the Agriculture, Forestry and Fisheries Finance Corporation gives loans to the named industries for equipment purchases. Similar services are provided for small businesses by the Small Business Finance Corporation.

An important part is played in the financial activity of the country by co-operatives, and by the many small enterprise institutions. Each prefecture has its own federation of co-operatives, with the Central Co-operative Bank of Agriculture and Forestry as the common central financial institution. This Central Co-operative Bank also serves as an agent for the government's Agriculture, Forestry and Fisheries Finance Corporation.

The commonest form of savings is through the government-operated Postal Savings System, which collects petty savings from the public by means of the post office network. The funds thus made available are used as loan funds by the government financial institutions, through the government's Trust Fund Bureau.

Clearing houses operate in each major city of Japan, and total 80 institutions. The largest are those of Tokyo and Osaka.

CENTRAL BANK

Nippon Ginko (*Bank of Japan*): 2-2-1 Hongoku-cho, Nihonbashi, Chuo-ku, Tokyo; f. 1882; cap. 100m., dep. 1,525,630m. (September 1973); Gov. TADASHI SASAKI; Vice-Gov. MICHIKAZU KONO.

PRINCIPAL COMMERCIAL BANKS

Bank of Fukuoka Ltd.: 12-18 Kamikawabata-machi, Fukuoka; f. 1945; cap. 5,000m., dep. 571,180m. (Sept. 1972); Pres. G. ARIKAWA.

Bank of Tokyo Ltd.: 6, 1-chome, Nihombashi Hongoku-cho, Chuo-ku, Tokyo; f. 1946; specializes in foreign exchange business; cap. p.u. 20,000m., dep. 1,300,072m. (March 1972); Pres. SUMIO HARA.

Dai-Ichi Kangyo Bank Ltd.: 6-2 1-chome, Marunouchi, Chiyoda-ku, Tokyo; f. 1971; cap. p.u. 54,000m., dep. 5,063,181m. (Sept. 1972); Chair. KAORU INOUYE; Pres. T. YOKOTA.

Daiwa Bank Ltd.: 21 Bingomachi, 2-chome, Higashi-ku, Osaka; f. 1918; cap. p.u. 24,000m., dep. 1,665,078m. (Mar. 1972); Pres. TAKEO TERAO.

Fuji Bank Ltd.: 1-chome, Otemachi, Chiyoda-ku, Tokyo; f. 1880; cap. p.u. 66,000m., dep. 4,903,662m. (March 1973); Chair. Advisory Cttee. YOSHIZANE IWASA; Chair. of Board and Pres. KUNIHIKO SASAKI.

Hokkaido Takushoku Bank Ltd.: 7 Nishi, 3-chome, Odori, Chuo-ku, Sapporo; f. 1900; cap. 20,000m. dep. 1,212,341m. (Sept. 1972); Chair. KEIICHI HIROSE; Pres. TAKEI TOJO.

Hokuriku Bank Ltd.: 2-26, Tsutsumichodon 1-chome, Toyama; f. 1943; cap. 8,000m., dep. 778,527m. (Sept. 1972); Pres. SEISUKE MASE.

Kyowa Bank Ltd.: 5-1, Marunouchi, 1-chome, Chiyoda-ku, Tokyo; f. 1945; cap. 32,000m., dep. 2,088,534m. (Sept. 1972); Pres. YOSHIAKI IROBE; Chair. SHUICHI SHINOHARA.

Mitsubishi Bank Ltd.: 7-1 Marunouchi, 2-chome, Chiyoda-ku, Tokyo; f. 1880; cap. 50,400m., dep. 4,522,209m. (March 1973); Pres. TOSHIO NAKAMURA.

Mitsui Bank Ltd.: 12 Yurakucho 1-chome, Chiyoda-ku, Tokyo; f. 1876; cap. p.u. 40,000m., dep. 3,324,847m. (March 1973); Chair. KYUBEI TANAKA; Pres. GORO KOYAMA.

Nippon Kogyo Ginko (*The Industrial Bank of Japan Ltd*): 1-1 Yaesu, 5-chome Chuo-ku, Tokyo 104; f. 1902; long-term financing of industrial enterprises in Japan; cap. p.u. 48,000m., debentures and dep. 3,602,371m.; total loans 998,738m. (Sept. 1972); Pres. ISAO MASAMUNE.

Saitama Bank Ltd.: 9-15, Takasago 2-chome, Urawa, Saitama Prefecture; f. 1943; cap. 22,680m., dep. 1,624,353m. (March 1973); Chair. TAIZO ISHIZAKA; Pres. KYOSUKE NAGASHIMA.

Sanwa Bank Ltd.: 10 Fushimimachi, 4-chome, Higashi-ku, Osaka 541; f. 1933; cap. 50,400m., dep. 3,848,824m. (Sept. 1972); Chair. T. WATANABE; Pres. T. MURANO.

Sumitomo Bank Ltd.: 22, 5-chome, Kitahama, Higashi-ku, Osaka; f. 1895; cap. 50,400m., dep. 3,792,832m. (March 1972); Pres. SHOZO HOTTA.

Taiyo Kobe Bank Ltd., The: 56 Naniwa-cho, Ikutaku, Kobe; f. 1973; cap. p.u. 49,000m., dep. 3,491,900m. (Oct. 1973); Chair. KAZUYUKI KOHNO; Pres. SHINICHI ISHINO.

Tokai Bank Ltd.: 21-24, Nishiki, 3-chome, Naka-ku, Nagoya; f. 1941; cap. p.u. 38,000m., dep. 2,660,786m. (Mar. 1972); Chair. and Pres. SHIGEMITSU MIYAKE

GOVERNMENT CREDIT INSTITUTIONS

Agriculture, Forestry and Fisheries Finance Corporation: 9-3, Otemachi 1-chome, Chiyoda-ku, Tokyo; f. 1953; finances plant and equipment investment; cap. 170,000m.; Pres. SEIZO TAKEDA; Vice-Pres. HAJIME IWAO.

Central Bank for Commercial and Industrial Co-operatives (*Shoko Chukin Bank*): Yaesu 6-5, Chuo-ku, Tokyo; f. 1936 to provide normal banking services to facilitate finance for smaller enterprise co-operatives and other organizations formed mainly by small- and medium-scale enterprises; 20,871 affiliated orgs.; cap. p.u. 50,200m., dep. 577,527m. (June 1973); Pres. HAJIME TAKAGI; Vice-Pres. MAKOTO WATANABE; publ. *Shoko Kinyu* (Commerce-Industry Financing, monthly).

Central Co-operative Bank for Agriculture and Forestry (*Norinchukin Bank*): 1-8-3 Ohtemachi, Chiyoda-ku, Tokyo; f. 1923; apex organ of financial system of agricultural, forestry and fisheries co-operatives; receives deposits from individual co-operatives, federations and agricultural enterprises; extends loans to these and to local government authorities and public corporations; adjusts excess and shortage of funds within co-operative system; issues debentures, invests funds and engages in other regular banking business; 13,183 mems.; cap. p.u. 20,000m., dep. and debentures 3,292,246m.; Pres. SHINKICHI KATAYANAGI; Vice-Pres. KANICHI OHSHIMA; publs. *The Central Co-operative Bank Review* (quarterly), *Statistics of Agricultural Finance in Japan* (irregular).

Export-Import Bank of Japan, The: 1-9-1 Otemachi, Chiyoda-ku, Tokyo; f. 1950 to supplement or encourage the financing of exports, imports and overseas investment by ordinary financial institutions; cap. p.u. 639,300m., dep. 2,249,024m. (Sept. 1973); Pres. SATOSHI SUMITA.

Housing Loan Corporation: 10-4, 1-chome, Koraku, Bunkyo-ku, Tokyo; f. 1950 to provide long-term capital for the construction of housing at low interest rates; cap. 97,200m.; funds disbursed 1,783,116m. (end March 1970); Pres. KIYOSHI ASAMURA; Vice-Pres. TOSHIHIDE TAKAHASHI; publs. *Housing Loan Report* (monthly), *Housing Loan Annual Report*, *Business Statistics* (annual), *Guidance of Loans for Housing* (annual), *Table of the Housing Loan Corporation's Business* (annual).

Japan Development Bank, The: 5-5, Otemachi, 1-chome, Chiyoda-ku, Tokyo; f. 1951; provides long-term funds to private industry for the acquisition of new plant and equipment or the improvement of existing plant and equipment; cap. 650m.; loans outstanding (June 1970) $4,483,206; Gov. KANEO ISHIHARA; Vice-Gov. YUTAKA FUKUCHI.

Long-Term Credit Bank of Japan Ltd., The: 2-4, Otemachi 1-chome, Chiyoda-ku, Tokyo; f. 1952; cap. p.u. 34,000m., dep. and debentures 2,829,875m. (Sept. 1972); Pres. BINSUKE SUGIURA; Chair. KAZUO MIYAZAKI.

Medical Care Facilities Finance Corporation: 2 Nibancho, Chiyoda-ku, Tokyo; f. 1960; cap. and dep. 11,500m.; Pres. MASAYOSHI YAMAMOTO.

The Overseas Economic Co-operation Fund: 1-1 Uchisaiwaicho, 2-chome, Chiyoda-ku, Tokyo; f. 1961; cap. U.S. $192.62m. (Sept. 1970); Pres. Dr. SABURO OKITA.

People's Finance Corporation: 1-9-3 Ohtemachi, Chiyoda-ku, Tokyo; f. 1949 to supply business funds particularly to very small enterprises among those sections of the population who are unable to obtain loans from banks and other private financial institutions; cap. p.u. 20,000m.; 4,208 mems.; Pres. YASUSHI SAWADA; Vice-Pres. NOBUKUNI YOSHIDA; publ. *Chosageppo* (monthly research report in Japanese).

Small Business Finance Corporation: 9-3, 1-chome, Ohtemachi, Chiyoda-ku, Tokyo; f. 1953 to lend equipment funds and long-term operating funds (directly or indirectly through agencies) which are necessary for the promotion of small businesses (capital not more than 100m., or not more than 300 employees) but which are not easily secured from other financial institutions; cap. p.u. 25,210m. (March 1973) wholly subscribed by Government; Gov. EIICHI YOSHIOKA; Vice-Gov. SHINICHI ARAI; publs. *Financial Statistics Quarterly*, *Monthly Bulletin of Small Business Finance Corporation*.

PRINCIPAL TRUST BANKS

Mitsubishi Trust and Banking Corporation: 4-5, 1-chome, Marunouchi, Chiyoda-ku, Tokyo; f. 1927; cap. 25,000m., dep. 2,625,789m.; Chair. TERUOMI CHIKAMI; Pres. YOSHIHIRO AKAMA.

Mitsui Trust and Banking Co. Ltd.: 1-1, Nihonbashi-Muromachi, 2-chome, Chuo-ku, Tokyo; f. 1924; cap. 16,000m., dep. 2,068,119m. (Sept. 1972); Pres. SENKICHI SHONO.

Sumitomo Trust and Banking Co. Ltd.: 15, 5-chome, Kirahama, Higashi-ku, Osaka; f. 1925; cap. 25,000m., dep. 2,679,340m. (Sept. 1973); Pres. SEN-ICHI OKUDAIRA.

Yasuda Trust and Banking Co. Ltd., The: 3, 1-chome, Yaesu, Chuo-ku; Tokyo, f. 1925; cap. 10,000m., dep. 814,227m. (Sept. 1969); Pres. TAKEO HISATOMI.

FOREIGN BANKS

Algemene Bank Nederland N.V.: Amsterdam (head office); Fuji Bldg., 3-2-3 Marunouchi, Chiyoda-ku, Tokyo 100, C.P.O. Box 374; brs. in Kobe, Osaka.

American Express International Banking Corpn.: New York, 6th Floor, Chamber of Commerce Bldg., 2-2, Marunouchi, 3-chome, Chiyoda-ku, Tokyo 100.

Bangkok Bank Ltd.: Bangkok; Mitsui Bldg. 6th Annex, 8-11, Nihonbashi Muromachi 2-chome, Chuo-ku, Tokyo; Man. PHAIBUL INGKHAVAT.

Bank of America—National Trust and Savings Association: San Francisco; Shin Marunouchi Bldg., 4, 1-chome Marunouchi, Tokyo; brs. in Yokohama, Osaka and Kobe.

Bank of China: 4-2, 1-chome, Marunouchi, Chiyoda-ku, Tokyo.

Bank of India Ltd.: Bombay; Mitsubishi Denki Bldg., 2-3, Marunouchi 2-chome, Chiyoda-ku, Tokyo; br. also in Osaka.

Bank Indonesia: Head Office: Jakarta; 309–311 Hibiya Park Bldg., 1, 1-chome, Yuraku-cho, Chiyoda-ku, Tokyo.

Bank of Korea: Seoul; Room 611 Hibiya Park Building, 1 Yuraku-cho 1-chome, Chiyoda-ku, Tokyo.

Bank Negara Indonesia: Head Office: 1 Jalan Lada, Jakarta; Kosusai Bldg., Room 1, Marunouchi, Chiyoda-Ku, Tokyo; brs. Hong Kong, Singapore and offices in London and New York.

Banque de l'Indochine: Paris; Tokyo, Central, P.O. Box 314.

Central Trust of China: Taipei, 5th Floor, Togin Bldg., 4-2 Marunouchi, 1-chome, Chiyoda-ku, Tokyo 100; f. 1935; Vice-Pres. and Man. YUAN-LING PEI.

Chartered Bank: London; 2-3, 3-chome, Marunouchi, Tokyo; brs. in Kobe, Osaka, Yokohama.

Chase Manhattan Bank, N.A.: New York; Tokio Kaijo Bldg., 2-1, Marunouchi 1-chome, Chiyoda-ku, Tokyo 100; Itoh Bldg., 47, 4-chome, Minami Honmachi, Higashi-ku, Osaka 541; Vice-Pres. and Gen. Man. A. CUSHMAN MAY.

Continental Illinois National Bank and Trust Company of Chicago: Tokyo Branch: Mitsui Seimei Bldg., 2-3 Ohtemachi, 1-chome Chiyoda-ku; Vice-Pres. J. H.

BRINCKMANN; Man. J. H. LERCH; Osaka branch; 35-11 Hiranomachi, 3-chome Higashi-ku; Man. T. DE HAAN.

First National Bank of Chicago: Chicago; Tokyo Branch, 409 Fuji Bldg., 2-3, 3-chome, Marunouchi, Chiyoda-ku, Tokyo; Vice-Pres. and Gen. Man. KEVIN G. WOELFLEIN.

First National City Bank: New York; 2-1 Ohtemachi 2-chome, Chiyoda-ku, Tokyo 100; brs. in Osaka, Yokohama, Nagoya, Camp Zama.

Hong Kong and Shanghai Banking Corporation: Hong Kong; 1-2, Marunouchi 2-chome, Chiyoda-ku, Tokyo.

Korea Exchange Bank: Seoul; New Kokusai Bldg., 4, 3-chome, Marunouchi, Chiyoda-ku, Tokyo; Second Shinsaibashi Bldg., 23-1, 4-chome, Sueyoshibashidori, Minami-ky, Osaka; f. 1950 (present name adopted 1968); Dir. BONG-EUN KIM; Man. YOON SUP HONG.

Manufacturers Hanover Trust Co.: New York; 21st Floor, Asahi Tokai Bldg., 6-1, Ohtemachi 2-chome, Chiyoda-ku, Tokyo; Vice-Pres. JOHN A. SCHAFFER; Man. SEIMA NAKAZAWA.

Mercantile Bank Ltd.: Hong Kong; P.O.B. Central 86, 450-91 Nagoya; f. 1892; cap. p.u. Stg. £2,940,000; Nagoya Man. J. H. KIELTY.

Morgan Guaranty Trust Co.: New York; New Yurakocho Bldg., 11, 1-chome, Yuraku-cho, Chiyoda-ku, Tokyo 100; Vice-Pres. and Gen. Mans. G. DENHAM, E. CHALONER.

BANKERS' ASSOCIATION

Federation of Bankers' Associations of Japan, The: 1-3-1, Marunouchi, Chiyoda-ku, Tokyo; f. 1945; 73 member associations; Chair. TAKASHI YOKOTA; Vice-Chair. SHIGEO MATSUMOTO; publs. *Zenkoku Ginko Tempo Ichiran* (list of bank offices in Japan), annual; *Zenkoku Ginko Yakuin Meibo* (list of members of Boards of Directors of all banks in Japan), annual; *Tegata Kokan Tokei-Nempo* (annual statistics of Clearing House); *Kinyu* (Finance); *Banking System in Japan* (occasional in English).

Local Bankers' Association: 3-1-2 Uchi-Kanda, Chiyoda-ku, Tokyo.

Tokyo Bankers' Association Inc.: 1-3-1 Marunouchi, Chiyoda-ku, Tokyo; f. 1945; 78 member banks; Chair. TAKASHI YOKOTA.

STOCK EXCHANGES

Tokyo Stock Exchange: 6, 1-chome, Nihonbashi-Kabuto-cho, Chuo-ku, Tokyo; f. 1949; 83 mems.; Pres. TEIICHIRO MORINAGA; publ. *Securities* (monthly), *TSE Monthly Statistics Report*, *Annual Statistics Report*.

Hiroshima Stock Exchange: 14-18, Kanayama-cho, Hiroshima; f. 1949; 15 mems.; Principal Officer SHIGERU AKAGI.

Fukuoka Stock Exchange: 55, Tenjin-cho, Fukuoka.

Nagoya Stock Exchange: 3-17, Sakae-Sanchome, Naka-ku, Nagoya; f. 1949; Pres. TAKUMI YOSHIHASHI; Man. Dir. ISAMU INAGAKI.

Osaka Securities Exchange: 2-chome, Kitahama, Higashi-ku, Osaka 541; f. 1949; 55 regular mems. and Nakadachi mems.; Pres. and Chair. KANAME TAKAHASHI; publ. *Investment* (bi-monthly), *Monthly Statistical Report*, *Annual Statistical Report*, *O.S.E. Official Quotation Daily*.

INSURANCE

The principal companies are as follows:

LIFE

Asahi Mutual Life Insurance Co.: 7-3, 1-chome, Nishi-Shinjuku, Shinjuku-ku, Tokyo; f. 1888; Chair. SADAMU HARUYAMA; Pres. KIYOSHI KAZUNO.

Chiyoda Mutual Life Insurance Co.: 19-18, Kamimeguro 2-chome, Meguro-ku, Tokyo; f. 1904; Pres. YUKICHI KADONO.

Daido Mutual Life Insurance Co.: 1, 1-chome, Tosabori, Nishiku, Osaka; f. 1902; Pres. N. IZUHARA; Senior Man. Dir. A. UEDA.

Daihyaku Mutual Life Insurance Co., The: 4-go, 1-ban, 3-chome, Shibuya, Shibuya-ku, Tokyo; f. 1914; Pres. D. KAWASAKI.

Dai-ichi Mutual Life Insurance Co., The: 9, 1-chome, Yurakucho, Chiyoda-ku, Tokyo; f. 1902; Chair. TSUNEHISA YADA; Pres. RYOICHI TSUKAMOTO.

Fukoku Mutual Life Insurance Co.: 6, 3-chome, Kudan, Chiyoda-ku, Tokyo; f. 1923.

Kyoei Life Insurance Co. Ltd.: 18-8, 1-chome, Shimbashi, Minato-ku, Tokyo; Pres. CHIKI ARIMA.

Meiji Mutual Life Insurance Co.: 1-1, 2-chome, Marunouchi, Chiyoda-ku, Tokyo; f. 1881; Pres. YOSHITOMI SEKI.

Mitsui Mutual Life Insurance Co.: 1-2-3 Ohtemachi, Chiyoda-ku, Tokyo; f. 1927; Pres. TAKAHIRO TAJIMA.

Nippon Dantai Life Insurance Co. Ltd.: 1-2-19, Higashi, Shibuya-ku, Tokyo; f. 1934; Pres. TAKEO HIRAKURA.

Nippon Life Insurance Co.: 7, 4-chome, Imabashi, Higashi-ku, Osaka; f. 1889.

Nissan Mutual Life Insurance Co.: Aobadai 3-6-30, Meguro-ku, Tokyo; f. 1909; Pres. MASAO FUJIMOTO.

Sumitomo Mutual Life Insurance Co.: 16, 2-chome, Nakanoshima, Kita-ku, Osaka; f. 1926; Chair. TAIZO ASHIDA; Pres. MASAAKI ARAI; Senior Man. Dirs. T. YUASA, S. OSHIMA.

Taisho Mutual Life Insurance Co.: 7, 1-chome, Yurakucho, Chiyoda-ku, Tokyo; f. 1913; Pres. SHIGEJI YAMANODA.

Taiyo Mutual Life Insurance Co.: 8, 2-chome, Edobashi, Nihonbashi, Chuo-ku, Tokyo.

Toho Mutual Life Insurance Co.: 3-1, 3-chome, Ginza, Chuo-ku, Tokyo; f. 1898; Chair. SEIZO OHTA; Pres. BENJIRO OHTA.

Tokyo Mutual Life Insurance Co.: No. 5-2, 1-chome, Uchisaiwaicho, Chiyoda-ku, Tokyo; f. 1895; Pres. KIICHI KIMURA.

Yamato Mutual Life Insurance Co.: 1, 1-chome, Uchisaiwaicho, Chiyoda-ku, Tokyo; f. 1911; Pres. KOHEI MAEYAMA.

Yasuda Mutual Life Insurance Co., The: P.O.B. 28, Shinjuku, Tokyo 160-91; f. 1880; Chair. HAJIME YASUDA; Pres. M. MIZUNO.

NON-LIFE

Asahi Fire and Marine Insurance Co. Ltd.: 10, 2-chome, Kanda Kajicho, Chiyoda-ku, Tokyo; f. 1951; Pres. TOMIO VEMATSU.

Chiyoda Fire and Marine Insurance Co. Ltd.: 3-1, 1-chome, Kyobashi, 1-chome, Chuo-ku, Tokyo; f. 1898; incorporating Chitose Fire and Marine, Okura Fire and Marine, Fukoku Fire and Marine, Nippon Kyoritsu Fire companies; Chair. SHOTARO KAMIYA; Pres. TSUNEJIRO TEJIMA.

Daido Fire and Marine Insurance Co. Ltd.: 14-8, 1-chome, Kumoji, Naha-shi, Okinawa; Pres. YUSHO VEZU.

Daiichi Mutual Fire and Marine Insurance Co.: 1-10, 4-chome, Shimbashi, Minato-ku, Tokyo; f. 1949; Pres. N. NISHIHARA; Chair. Y. NARUSE.

Dai-Tokyo Fire and Marine Insurance Co. Ltd., The: 1-6, Nihonbashi, 3-chome, Chuo-ku, Tokyo; f. 1918; incorporating Tokyo Movable Property Fire and Toshin

Fire; Pres. KIN-ICHI AKITA; Vice-Pres. SEI-ICHI SORIMACHI.

Dowa Fire and Marine Insurance Co. Ltd.: 61 Shinmei-cho, Kita-ku, Osaka; f. 1944; incorporating Yokohama Fire, Kobe Marine, Kyodo Fire, Asahi Marine; **Chair.** TAKASHI OTSUKI; Pres. TSUYOSHI HOSOI.

Fuji Fire and Marine Insurance Co. Ltd.: 3, 2-chome, Sueyoshibashi-dori, Minamiku, Osaka; f. 1918; Pres. ISAMU WATANABE.

Japan Earthquake Reinsurance Co. Ltd.: 6-5, 3-chome, Kanda Surugadai, Chiyoda-ku, Tokyo; Pres. H. SEGAMI.

Koa Fire and Marine Insurance Co. Ltd.: 5, 1-chome, Nihonbashi Muromachi, Chuo-ku, Tokyo; f. 1944; incorporating Tatsuma Marine and Fire, Amasaki Marine and Fire, Shinkoku Marine and Fire, and Taihoku Fire and Marine; Pres. S. MAETANI; Chair. KATSUMI YAMAGATA.

Kyoei Mutual Fire and Marine Insurance Co.: 18-8, 1-chome, Shimbashi, Minato-ku, Tokyo; f. 1942; Pres. MORITAKA MAEDA; Vice-Pres. SHUGO TANAKA.

Nichido Fire and Marine Insurance Co. Ltd.: 3-16, 5-chome, Ginza Chuo-ku, Tokyo; f. 1914; incorporating Toho Fire; Pres. T. KUBO.

Nippon Fire and Marine Insurance Co.: 2-10, Nihonbashi, 2-chome, Chuo-ku, Tokyo; f. 1892; Pres. YASUTARO UKON.

Nissan Fire and Marine Insurance Co. Ltd.: 9-5, 2-chome, Kita-Aoyama, Minato-ku, Tokyo; f. 1911; incorporating Taiheiyo Fire and Marine, Showa Fire and Marine; Pres. YOSHITSUGU OISHI.

Nisshin Fire and Marine Insurance Co. Ltd.: 5-1, 1-chome, Otemachi, Chiyoda-ku, Tokyo; f. 1908; incorporating Toyo Marine and Fire, Fukuju Fire, Hokoku Fire; Pres. SEIJI KAJINISHI; Senior Man. Dirs. TEIJIRO INOUE, MASAO NAKAMURA.

Sumitomo Marine and Fire Insurance Co. Ltd.: 3-5, Yaesu 1-chome, Chuo-ku, Tokyo; f. 1944; incorporating Osaka Fire and Marine, Sumitomo Marine and Fire; Pres. Y. MOROKUZU.

Taisei Fire and Marine Insurance Co. Ltd., The: 11 Kanda Nishiki-cho, 2-chome, Chiyoda-ku, Tokyo; f. 1950; Pres. TOKIO NODA.

Taisho Marine and Fire Insurance Co. Ltd.: 5, 1-chome, Kyobashi, Chuo-ku Tokyo; f. 1918; member of Mitsui group of companies; Pres. AKIO HIRATA; Exec. Dir. N. MISAWA; Man. Dirs. T. MATSUBA, H. INOUE, M. YAMAGUCHI, Y. YAMAZAKI, T. ISAKA, S. ASUKABE, S. TANAKA.

Taiyo Fire and Marine Insurance Co.: 5, Tori 3-chome, Nihonbashi, Chuo-ku, Tokyo; f. 1951; Pres. M. KABURAGI; Man. Dir. K. KANEKO.

Toa Fire and Marine Insurance Co.: 6-5, 3-chome, Kanda Surugadai, Chiyoda-ku, Tokyo; f. 1940; Pres. Y. YASUDA.

Tokio Marine and Fire Insurance Co. Ltd. (*Tokio Kaijo*): 1-1, 3-chome, Marunouchi, Chiyoda-ku, Tokyo; f. 1879; incorporating Mitsubishi Marine and Fire, Meiji Fire and Marine insurance companies; cap. 20,000m.; Chair. GENZAETION YAMAMOTO; Pres. MINORU KIKUCHI.

Toyo Fire and Marine Insurance Co.: 2-1, 1-chome, Yurakucho, Chiyoda-ku, Tokyo; f. 1950; Pres. T. KAKEHASHI; Chair. YASUSABURO HARA.

Yasuda Fire and Marine Insurance Co. Ltd.: 5-4, Otemachi Itchome, Chiyoda-ku, Tokyo; f. 1887; incorporating Tokyo Fire and Marine and other companies; overseas offices in New York, Los Angeles, London, Düsseldorf, São Paulo, Rio de Janeiro, Sydney, Hong Kong, Jakarta, Beirut; Pres. T. MIYOSHI.

In addition to the commercial companies, the Post Office runs life insurance and annuity schemes.

INSURANCE ASSOCIATIONS

Life Insurance Association of Japan (*Seimei Hoken Kyokai*): New Kokusai Bldg., 4-1, 3-chome, Marunouchi, Chiyoda-ku, Tokyo; f. 1908; 20 mem. cos.; Chair. K. KAZUNO; Exec. Dir. H. FURUKAWA; Man. Dir. T. NAKAZAWA.

Marine and Fire Insurance Association of Japan: Non-Life Insurance Building, 9, 2-chome, Kanda Awaji-cho, Chiyoda-ku, Tokyo; f. 1907; 22 mems.; Pres. GENZAEMON YAMAMOTO; Vice-Pres. TSUNEJIRO TEJIMA; Exec. Dir. FUMIO IMAI; Man. Dirs. SHIRO YOSHIMI, SADAFUMI NISHIZAWA.

Fire and Marine Insurance Rating Association of Japan: Sonpo Kaikan, 9, 2-chome, Kanda Awajicho, Chiyoda-ku, Tokyo; f. 1948; Pres. YASUTARO UKON; Exec. Dir. TSUTOMU SAITO.

TRADE AND INDUSTRY

TRADE ORGANIZATIONS

CHAMBERS OF COMMERCE AND INDUSTRY

Japan Chamber of Commerce and Industry, The (*Nippon Shoko Kaigi-sho*): 2-2, 3-chome, Marunouchi, Chiyoda-ku, Tokyo; f. 1922; mems. 458 local Chambers of Commerce and Industry; the central organization of all chambers of commerce and industry in Japan.

Principal Officers: Pres. SHIGEO NAGANO, K.B.E. (Pres. Tokyo Chamber of Commerce and Industry, 2-2 3-chome, Marunouchi, Chiyoda-ku, Tokyo); Vice-Pres. ISAMU SAEKI (Pres. Osaka Chamber of Commerce and Industry, 58-7 Hashizume-cho, Uchihonmachi, Higashi-ku, Osaka), MOTOO TSUCHIKAWA (Pres. Nagoya Chamber of Commerce and Industry, 2-10-19 Sakae, Naka-ku, Nagoya), TAKASHI RINOIE (Pres. Yokohama Chamber of Commerce and Industry, 11 Nippon Odori, Naka-ku, Yokohama), HIROM MORISHITA (Pres. Kyoto Chamber of Commerce and Industry, Karasuma-dori, Nakagyo-ku, Kyoto), MASASHI ISANO (Pres. Kobe Chamber of Commerce and Industry, 5-2-1, Hamabe-dori, Fukiai-ku); publs. *Standard Trade Index of Japan* (annual), *Japan Commerce and Industry* (bi-annual).

Kobe Chamber of Commerce and Industry, The: Kobe CIT Center Bldg., 2-1, Hamabe-dori 5-chome, Fukiai-ku, Kobe 651; f. 1878; mems. 4,799; Pres. MASASHI ISANO; Man. Dir. SHIRO HATA; publs. *Kobe Directory* (annual), *Current Economic Survey of Kobe* (annual), *The Trade Bulletin* (weekly).

Kyoto Chamber of Commerce and Industry: Karasuma-dori Ebisugawa agaru, Nakakyo-ku, Kyoto 604; f. 1882; mems. 6,996; Pres. HIROUMA MORISHITA; Man. Dir. KUNIO SHIMAZU; publs. *Kyoto Business Directory*, *Members Report* (monthly in Japanese),

Kyoto Directory of manufacturers, exporters, and importers (annual), *The Trade Opportunities* (twice monthly).

Nagoya Chamber of Commerce and Industry: 10-19, Sakae 2-chome, Naka-ku, Nagoya; f. 1881; mems. 5,631; Pres. MOTOO TSUCHIKAWA; Man. Dir. RYOJIRO KURITA.

Osaka Chamber of Commerce and Industry: 58-7, Uchi-hommachi Hashizume-chome, Higashi-ku, Osaka; f. 1878; mems. 19,324; Pres. ISAMU SAHEKI; Sen. Man. Dir. TAKEHISA IZUCHI; publs. *Chamber* (Japanese, monthly), *Osaka* (English, quarterly), *List of Members* (Japanese), *Daisho Shimbun* (Japanese newspaper), *Osaka Business Directory* (English) ,*List of Overseas Chambers of Commerce and Industry, Economic Organizations* (English), *Guide to Osaka Merchandise* (English), *Yearbook of Osaka Economy* (Japanese) and *White Paper on Wages in Osaka* (Japanese).

Tokyo Chamber of Commerce and Industry, The: 2-2, Marunouchi 3-chome, Chiyoda-ku, Tokyo; f. 1878; mems. 13,700; Pres. SHIGEO NAGANO; Man. Dir. EIJI KAGEYAMA.

Yokohama Chamber of Commerce and Industry, The: 11, Nihon-Odori, Nakaku, Yokohama; f. 1880; mems. 5,200; Pres. TAKASHI IHARA; Dir. and Gen. Sec. MASAO KAWAMURA; publs. *Yokohama Economic Statistics* (Japanese and English, annual), *Monthly Report* (Japanese) and *Chamber's News* (Japanese, monthly).

FOREIGN TRADE ORGANIZATIONS

Association for the Promotion of International Trade, Japan: Nippon Bldg., 5th Floor, No. 2-6-2, Ohtemachi, Chiyoda-ku, Tokyo; for the promotion of private trade with the People's Republic of China, the Democratic Republic of Korea and the Democratic Republic of Viet-Nam; handles 90 per cent of Sino-Japanese trade; Pres. A. FUJIYAMA; Exec. Dir. TEIJI HAGIHARA.

China-Japan Memorandum Trade Office: Ishiba, Kotohira-cho, Minato-ku, Tokyo; responsible for official trade with People's Republic of China; Chair. KAHEITA OKAZAKI.

Council of All-Japan Exporters' Association: Kikai Shinko Kaikan Bldg., 13-5 Tsukiji 1-chome, Chuo-ku, Tokyo.

Japan External Trade Organization—JETRO: 2 Akasaka Aoi-Cho, Minato-ku, Tokyo; est. 1958; information for foreign firms, investigation of foreign markets, exhibition of Japanese commodities abroad, etc.; Pres. KICHIHEI HARA; Vice-Pres. KIMITAKA MURAKAMI; publs. *Trade and Industry of Japan* (monthly), *Japan Trade Bulletin* (every ten days), etc.

Japan Foreign Trade Council, Inc. (*Nippon Boeki-Kai*): 6th Floor, World Trade Center Bldg., 4-1, 2-chome, Hamamatsu-cho, Minato-ku, Tokyo 105; f. 1947; 410 mems.; Pres. TATSUZO MIZUKAMI; Man. Dir. NAOJI HARADA; Exec. Dir. ZENJI KYOMOTO; publ. *Bulletin* (in Japanese).

Society for Trade with the U.S.S.R.: Tokyo; f. 1967; Pres. SHIGEO HORIE.

TRADE ASSOCIATIONS

Fertilizer Traders' Association: Chikusan Kaikan, 4, 4-chome, Ginza Higashi, Chuo-ku, Tokyo.

Foreign Film Importers-Distributors' Association of Japan: Shochi-ku Kaikan, 13-5 Tsukiji, 1-chome, Chuo-ku, Tokyo.

Japan Agricultural Products Exporters' Association: 12-3, 2-chome, Shimbashi, Minato-ku, Tokyo.

Japan Automobile Importers' Association: c/o Friend Bldgs., 2-4-11 Nagata-cho, Chiyoda-ku, Tokyo.

Japan General Merchandise Exporters' Association: 2, 3-chome, Nihonbashi Muro-machi, Chuo-ku, Tokyo, f. 1953, 850 mems., Pres. KYUZABURO JUBA.

Japan Lumber Importers' Association: Yushi Kogyo Bldg., No. 13-11, Nihonbashi 3-chome, Chuo-ku, Tokyo.

Japan Sugar Import and Export Council: Ginza Gas-Hall, 9-15, 7-chome, Ginza, Chuo-ku, Tokyo.

Japan Tea Exporters' Association: 81-1 Kitaban-cho, Shinzuoka, Shinzuoka Prefecture.

Japan Timber Exporters' Association: 18-12, Katsunai-cho, Otaru, Hokkaido.

TRADE FAIR

Tokyo International Trade Fair Commission: 16, 4-chome, Harumi, Chuo-ku, Tokyo (C.P.O. Box 1201, Tokyo).

INDUSTRIAL ORGANIZATIONS

GENERAL

Industry Club of Japan: 4-6, Marunouchi, 1-chome, Chiyoda-ku, Tokyo; f. 1917 to develop closer relations between industrialists at home and abroad and promote expansion of Japanese business activities; ca. 1,600 mems.; Pres. TAIZO ISHIZAKA; Exec. Dir. GINICHI YAMANE; publs. bulletins (6 a year), pamphlets, economic surveys of major countries (2 a year).

Japan Committee for Economic Development (*Keizai Doyukai*): Kogyo Club Bldg., 1-chome, Marunouchi, Chiyoda-ku, Tokyo; an influential group of business interests concerned with aid to foreign nations.

Japan Federation of Economic Organizations—KEIDAN-REN (*Keizaidantai Rengo-kai*): 9-4, Otemachi, 1-chome, Chiyoda-ku, Tokyo, 100; f. 1946; private non-profit association to study domestic and international economic problems; mems. 107 professional organizations,

769 firms (Sept. 1973); Pres. KOGORO UEMURA; Dir.-Gen. TEIZO HORIKOSHI.

Japan Federation of Smaller Enterprises: 2-4 Kayabacho, Nihonbashi, Chuo-ku, Tokyo.

Japan Productivity Centre (*Nihon Seisansei Honbu*): 3-1-1 Shibuya, Shibuya-ku, Tokyo; f. 1955; 9,000 mems.; concerned with management problems; Chair. KOHEI GOSHI; Exec. Dir. TAKEO TAMARUSHIMA; publ. *Japan Productivity News* (weekly).

ARBITRATION

Japan Commercial Arbitration Association: Tokyo Chamber of Commerce and Industry Bldg., 2-2, 3-chome, Marunouchi, Chiyoda-ku, Tokyo; f. 1950; 1,025 mems.; provides facilities for adjustment, conciliation and arbitration in international trade disputes; Pres. SHIGEO NAGANO; Man. Dir. TADATOSHI FUKUSHIMA; publ. monthly and quarterly journals.

PRINCIPAL INDUSTRIAL ORGANIZATIONS

Nihon Keieisha Dantai Renmei—NIKKEIREN (*Japan Federation of Employers' Associations*): 4-6, Marunouchi 1-chome, Chiyoda-ku, Tokyo; f. 1948; covers 95 member organizations, Man. Dirs. MASARU HAYAKAWA, YOSHINOBU MATSUZAKI; Sec.-Gen. ICHIRO MIYAMOTO; publs. *Nikkeiren News* (quarterly, English), *Nikkeiren Times* (weekly, Japanese).

FISHING AND PEARL CULTIVATION

Japan Coastal Trawler Fisheries Association: Showa Kaikan, 1, Sannen-cho, Chiyoda-ku, Tokyo; f. 1948; Pres. KASUKE HOSONO.

Japan Fisheries Association (*Dai-nippon Suisan Kai*): Sankaido Bldg., 9-13, Akasaka 1, Minato-ku, Tokyo.

Japan Pearl Export and Processing Co-operative Association: 7, 3-chome, Kyobashi, Chuo-ko, Tokyo, f. 1951, 130 mems.

Japan Pearl Exporters' Association: 122 Higashi-machi Ikuta-ku, Kobe; Tokyo branch: 7, 3-chome Kyobashi, Chuo-ku, Pres. ATSUSHI KANAI.

Japan Pearl Promoting Society: 7, 3-chome, Kyobashi, Chuo-ku, Tokyo; f. 1956.

National Federation of Fishery Co-operative Associations, The: Sankaido Bldg., 1-9-13 Akasaka, Minato-ku, Tokyo.

TEXTILES

Central Raw Silk Association of Japan, The: 7, 1-chome, Yuraku-cho, Chiyoda-ku, Tokyo.

Japan Chemical Fibres Association: Mitsui Bekkan, 3, Nihonbashi Muromachi, 3-chome, Chuo-ku, Tokyo.

Japan Cotton and Staple Fibre Weavers' Association: 8, 3-chome, Tsukiji, Chuo-ku, Tokyo.

Japan Export Clothing Makers' Association: 4-5, 2-chome, Utsubo, Nishi-ku, Osaka; f. 1956; 698 mems.; promotion and internal policy body for the manufacture of cotton clothing for export; Pres. K. KONDO; publ. *JECMA News* (Japanese), *Directory* (English).

Japan Knitted Goods Manufacturers' Association: Nihon Meriyasu Kaikan Bldg., 6, 1-chome, Nihonbashi, Yoshi-cho, Chuo-ku, Tokyo.

Japan Silk Association, Inc.: Sanshi Kaikan, No. 7, 1-chome Yurakucho, Chiyoda-ku, Tokyo; f. 1959; mems. 14 asscns.; Pres. RISHICHI TAKADA.

Japan Silk and Rayon Weavers' Association: Chuo-ku, Tokyo.

Japan Spinners' Association: Mengyo Kaikan Building, 8, 3-chome, Bingo Machi, Higashi-ku, Osaka; f. 1948; 98 member firms; Chair. NAOICHI SETO; publ. *Monthly Report.*

Japan Staple Yarn Merchants' Federation: 2, 1-chome, Nihonbashi Kobune-cho, Chuo-ku, Tokyo.

Japan Textile Council: Sen-i-Kaikan Bldg., 9, 3-chome, Nihonbashi Honcho, Chuo-ku, Tokyo; f. 1948; mems. 24 asscns.; publs. *Textile Yearbook*, *Textile Statistics* (monthly), *Textile Japan* (annual in English).

The Japanese Textile Machinery Manufacturers' Association: Room No. 310, Kikai Shinko Bldg., 3-5-8 Shiba Koen, Minato-ku, Tokyo; f. 1951; Pres. NOBUYOSHI NOZAKI.

Japan Wool Industry Conference: Sen-i-Kaikan, 9, 3-chome, Nihonbashi Hon-cho, Chuo-ku, Tokyo.

Japan Wool Spinners' Association: Sen-i-Kaikan 9, 3-chome, Nihonbashi Hon-cho, Chuo-ku, Tokyo; f. 1958; Chair. S. ABE; Man. Dir. H. SAKAI; publ. *Statistical Data on the Wool Industry in Japan* (monthly).

Japan Worsted and Woollen Weavers' Association: Sen-i-Kaikan 9, 3-chome, Nihonbashi Hon-cho, Chuo-ku, Tokyo; f. 1948; Chair. S. OGAWA; Man. Dir. K. OHTANI.

PAPER AND PRINTING

Japan Paper Association: Kami-Parupu Kaikan Bldg., Ginza 3-chome, 9-11 Chuo-ku, Tokyo; f. 1946; 112 mems.; Pres. S. KANEKO; Dir.-in-Chief M. MATSUNAGA.

Japan Paper Exporters' Association: 9-11, Ginza, 3-chome, Chuo-ku, Tokyo.

Japan Paper-Products Exporters' Association: 18-2, 1-chome, Higashi-Komagata, Sumida-ku, Tokyo; f. 1959; Exec. Dir. KIYOSHI SATOH.

Japan Paper-Products Manufacturers' Association: 18-2. 1-chome, Higashi-Komagata, Tokyo; f. 1949; Exec, Dir. KIYOSHI SATOH.

Japan Printers' Association: 1-16-8, Shintomi, Chuo-ku, Tokyo; Pres. TAKASHI MUROTANI; Exec. Dir. MORIMASA SADA.

Machine-Made Japanese Paper Industry Association: 9-11, Ginza, 3-chome, Chuo-ku, Tokyo.

CHEMICALS

Federation of Pharmaceutical Manufacturers' Associations of Japan: 9, 2-chome, Nihonbashi Hon-chu, Chuo-ku, Tokyo.

Japan Perfumery and Flavouring Association: Nitta Bldg., 8, 8-chome, Ginza, Chuo-ku, Tokyo.

Japan Chemical Industry Association: Tokyo Club Bldg. 2-6, 3-chome, Kasumigaseki, Chiyoda-ku, Tokyo; f. 1948; 207 mems.; Pres. HIDEO SHINOJIMA.

Japan Cosmetic Makers' and Wholesalers' Association: 3, 3-chome, Nihonbashi Bakuro-cho, Chuo-ku, Tokyo; f. 1895; 365 mems.; publ. *The Nihon Syogyo* (weekly).

Japan Gas Association: 38 Shiba Kotohira-cho, Minato-ku, Tokyo; f. 1912; Pres. HIROSHI ANZAI; Man. Dir. Y. SHIBASAKI; publ. *Monthly Journal.*

Japan Inorganic Chemical Industry Association: Sanko Bldg., 1-13-1 Ginza Chuoku, Tokyo; f. 1948; Pres. KAN-ICHI TANAHASHI.

Japan Pharmaceutical, Medical and Dental Supply Exporters' Association: 3-6, Nihonbashi-Honcho 4-chome, Chuo-ku, Tokyo 103; f. 1953; 181 member firms; Pres. CHOBEI TAKEDA; Man. Dir. MITSUO SASAKI.

Japan Urea and Ammonium Sulphate Industry Association: Hokkai Bldg., 1-3-13 Nihombashi, Chuo-ku, Tokyo.

The Photo-Sensitized Materials Manufacturers' Association: Fukuoka Bldg., 1, 6-chome, Yaesu, Chuo-ku, Tokyo.

Society of Synthetic Organic Chemistry, Japan: Echiso Bldg., 39-7, 2-chome, Hongo, Bunkyo-ku, Tokyo; f. 1942; 4,814 mems.; Pres. Y. IWAKURA; Man. S. NAKAMURA; publ. *Monthly Journal.*

MINING AND PETROLEUM

Asbestos Products Industrial Association: Daiichi Kaikan Bldg., 10-5, 7-chome, Ginza, Chuo-ku, Tokyo; f. 1937; Chair. SHIN-ICHIRO KONDO.

Cement Association of Japan, The: Hattori Bldg., 1, 1-chome, Kyobashi, Chuo-ku, Tokyo; f. 1948; 20 member companies; Chair. C. TAKEYASU; Exec. Man. Dir. H. KUROSAWA; publ. *Cement and Concrete* (monthly, Japanese), *Cement Statistics in Japan* (annual, English), *Semento Gijutsu Nenpo* (annual in Japanese), *Review of General Meeting—Technical Session* (annual, English).

Japan Coal Association: Nikkatsu Kokusai Kaikan, 1, 1-chome, Yuraku-cho, Chiyoda-ku, Tokyo.

Japan Mining Industry Association: Shin-hibiya Bldg., 3-6, 1-chome, Uchisaiwai-cho, Chiyoda-ku, Tokyo 100; f. 1948; 83 member companies; Pres. T. KAWAI; Vice-Pres. G. MORI; Dir.-Gen. T. SAITO.

Petroleum Association of Japan: Keidanren Kaikan, 5, 1-5-7 Ohtemachi, Chiyoda-ku, Tokyo; f. 1955; 22 mems.; Pres. SHINGO FUJIOKA; Man. Dir. KINZABURO IKEDA.

METALS

Japan Brass Makers' Association: 1-12-22, 1-chome, Tsukiji, Chuo-ku, Tokyo; f. 1948; 81 mems.; Pres. K. TOSHIMA; Man. Dir. T. WADA.

Japan Iron and Steel Federation: Keidanren Kaikan, 1-9-4 Ohtemachi, Chiyoda-ku, Tokyo; f. 1948; Chair. Y. INAYAMA; Pres. SHIGEO NAGANO.

Japan Light Metal Association: Nihonbashi Asahiseimei Bldg., 1-3, Nihonbashi 2-chome, Chuo-ku, Tokyo 103.

Japan Stainless Steel Association: Tekko Kaikan Bldg., 16, 3-chome, Nihonbashi Kayaba-cho, Chuo-ku, Tokyo; Pres. SATORU MORI; Exec. Dir. HIROSHI SATO.

The Kozai Club: 3-16 Kayabacho, Chuo-ku, Tokyo; f. 1947; mems. 36 manufacturers, 102 dealers; Chair. YOSHIHIRO INAYAMA.

Steel Castings and Forgings Association of Japan (JSCFA): Tekko Bldg., 8-2, 1-chome, Marunouchi, Chiyoda-ku, Tokyo 100; f. 1972; mems. 98 companies, 110 plants; Exec. Dir. KYOZO IWAMURA.

MACHINERY AND PRECISION EQUIPMENT

Electronic Industries Association of Japan: Tosho Bldg., 2-2, 3-chome ,Marunouchi, Chiyoda-ku, Tokyo; f. 1948; mems. 520 firms; Pres. KOJI KOBAYASHI; publs. *Denshi* (Electronics) (monthly), *Index of Japanese Electronic Manufacturers and Products* (annual, English), *Electronic Industry in Japan* (annual, English).

Japan Camera Industry Association: Mori Building Ninth, 3, 1-chome, Shiba-Atago-cho, Minato-ku, Tokyo; f. 1954; Pres. KAZUO TASHIMA.

Japan Electric Association: 1-3 Yurakucho, Chiyoda-ku, Tokyo 100; f .1921; Pres. MICHIO YOKOYAMA; publs. *Daily Electricity, Journal of the Japan Electric Association, Production and Electricity, Monthly Report on Electric Power Statistics.*

Japan Electrical Manufacturers' Association: 4-15, 2-chome, Nagata-cho, Chiyoda-ku, Tokyo; f. 1948; mems. 152 firms; Pres. S. MAEDA; Exec. Dir. K. IWASAKI; publ. descriptive information on Japanese Electrical Machinery (in English).

Japan Farm Machinery Manufacturers' Association: 5, 1-chome, Ueno-machi, Taito-ku, Tokyo.

The Japan Machinery Federation: Kikai Shinko Bldg., 5-8-3 Shiba Koen, Minato-ku, Tokyo.

Japan Machine Tool Builders' Association: Kikai Shinko Bldg., 5-1-21 Shibakoen, Minato-ku, Tokyo; f. 1951; 105 mems.; Exec. Dir. K. SUGIYAMA.

Japan Measuring Instruments Industrial Federation: Japan Metrology Bldg., 1-25 Nando-cho, Shinjuku-ku, Tokyo.

Japan Microscope Manufacturers' Association: c/o Olympus Optical Co. Ltd., 43-2, Hatagaya, 2-chome, Shibuya-ku, Tokyo; f. 1946; mems. 27 firms; Chair. T. NAITO.

Japan Motion Picture Equipment Industrial Association: Kikai-shinko Bldg., 3-5-8, Shibakoen, Minato-ku, Tokyo.

Japan Optical and Precision Instrument Manufacturers' Association: Kikai-Shinko Kaikan, 5-8 Shiba Park 3, Minato-ku, Tokyo 105; Gen. Man. Y. TSUDA; publ. *Guidebook.*

Japan Photographic Equipment Industrial Association: Shin-Kaede Bldg., 3-3, 2-chome, Uchikanda, Chiyoda-ku, Tokyo.

Japan Power Association: Daido Building, 7-13, 1-chome, Nishi-Shimbashi, Minato-ku, Tokyo; f. 1950; 95 mems., Pres. GORO INOUYE; Sec. SACHIO TANAKA; publ. *Power* (quarterly).

Japan Society of Industrial Machinery Manufacturers: Kikai-Shinko Kaikan, 3-5-8, Shibakoen, Minato-ku, Tokyo; f. 1948; 297 mems.; Chair. KENKICHI TOSHIMA.

TRANSPORTATION MACHINERY

Japan Association of Rolling Stock Manufacturers: Tekko Bldg., 1-1 Marunouchi, Chiyoda-ku, Tokyo.

Japan Auto Parts Industries Association: 1-16-15 Takanawa, Minato-ku, Tokyo; f. 1948; mems. 350 firms; Pres. K. FUJIOKA; Man. Dir. T. KUROME; publ. *Auto Parts* (monthly, Japanese).

Japan Automobile Manufacturers Association, Inc.: Ohtemachi Bldg., 6-1 Otemachi 1-chome, Chiyoda-ku, Tokyo; f. 1967 in succession to the Automotive Industrial Asscn.; mems. 14 firms; Pres. E. TOYODA; Man. Dir. T. NAKAMURA.

Japan Bicycle Industry Association: 7-3 Akasaka Ta-machi, Minato-ku, Tokyo.

Japanese Shipowners' Association: Kaiun Bldg., No. 10, 2-4, Hirakawa-cho, Chiyoda-ku, Tokyo.

Shipbuilders' Association of Japan: 35 Shiba-Kotohiracho, Minatoku, Tokyo; f. 1947; 50 mems.; Pres. RENZO TAGUCHI; Man. Dir. HAJIME YAMADA.

The Ship Machinery Manufacturers' Association of Japan: Sempaku-Shinko Bldg., 35, Shiba Kotohira-cho, Minato-ku, Tokyo; f. 1956; 270 mems.; Pres. MAKOTO ISOGAI.

The Society of Japanese Aircraft Constructors: Chiyoda Bldg., 1-2, 2-chome, Marunouchi, Chiyoda-ku, Tokyo; f. 1952; 130 mems., 17 assoc. mems.; Chair. G. MORIYA; Exec. Dir. KOZO HIRATA; publs. *Monthly Report* (in Japanese), *Directory of the Aerospace Industry in Japan* (English, annual), *The Aircraft Industry Year Book* (Japanese, annual).

MISCELLANEOUS

Association of Tokyo Exporting Toy Manufacturers: 3-16, 4-chome, Higashi-Komagata Sumida-ku, Tokyo; f. 1948; 200 mems.; Pres. EIJIRO TOMIYAMA.

Canners' Association of Japan: Marunouchi Bldg., 18, 2-chome, Marumouchi, Tokyo.

Communication Industries Association of Japan: Sankei Bldg., 1-7-2 Otemachi, Chiyoda-ku, Tokyo; f. 1948; Pres. HIROKICHI YOSHIYAMA; Exec. Dir. SHUZO OHIZUMI; publ. *Tsushin-Kogyo* (monthly in Japanese).

Japan Construction Materials Association: Kenchiku Kaikan Bldg., 19-2, 3-chome, Ginza, Chuo-ku, Tokyo; f. 1947; Pres. KENTARO ITO; publ. *Construction Material Industry* (monthly).

Japan Plywood Manufacturers' Association: Meisan Bldg., 17-18, 1-chome, Nishishimbashi, Minato-ku, Tokyo; f. 1948; 251 mems.; Pres. HIROTADA DANTANI.

Japan Pottery Manufacturers' Federation: 32 Nunoike-cho, Higashi-ku, Nagoya; f. 1931; 50 mem. asscns.; Pres. JUKURO MIZUNO; Man. Dir. K. MITSUI.

Japan Raw Fur Association: 2, 4-chome, Tsukiji, Chuo-ku, Tokyo.

Japan Rubber Manufacturers' Association, The: Tobu Bldg., 1-5-26, Moto Akasaka, Minato-ku, Tokyo; f. 1950; 200 mems.; Pres. YOSHIO SHIMASAKI.

Japan Sewing Machine Association: 13 Sakamachi, Shinjukuku, Tokyo.

Japan Spirits and Liquors Makers' Association: Koura Bldg., 7th Floor, 2 Nihombashi Kayabacho, 1-chome, Chuo-ku, Tokyo 103.

Japan Sugar Refiners' Association: 5-7 Sanbancho, Chiyoda-ku, Tokyo; f. 1949; Man. Dir. ICHIRO FURUNISHI; Man. KIYOHISA NAGAMIYA; publs. *Sato Tokei Nenkan* (Sugar Statistics Year Book), *Kikan Togyoshiho* (Quarterly Sugar Journal).

Japan Watch and Clock Association: Nomura Bldg., 2, 2-chome, Otemachi, Chiyoda-ku, Tokyo.

Motion Picture Producers' Association of Japan: Sankei Kaikan Bldg., 7-2, 1-chome, Otemachi, Chiyoda-ku, Tokyo; Pres. SHIRO KIDO.

TRADE UNIONS

A feature of Japan's trade union movement is that the unions are in general based on single enterprises, embracing workers of different occupations in that enterprise, rather than organizing the workers of the same trade in different enterprises on an industry-wide basis.

PRINCIPAL FEDERATIONS

Nihon Rodo Kumiai Sohyogikai—SOHYO (*General Council of Trade Unions of Japan*): 8-2 Shiba-park, Minato-ku, Tokyo; Pres. TOSHIKATSU HORII; Sec.-Gen. A. IWAI; total mems. 4,208,000.

Major Affiliated Unions

National Council of Local and Municipal Government Workers' Unions (*Jijiro*): approx. 704,000 mems.; Pres. M. KURIYAMA.

Japan Teachers' Union (*Nikkyoso*): 550,000 mems.; Pres. S. MIYANOHARA.

National Railway Workers' Union (*Kokuro*): approx. 218,000 mems.; Pres. YOSHIO KAMBE.

Japan Postal Workers' Union (*Zentei*): approx. 238,000 mems.; Pres. F. TAKARAGI.

General Federation of Private Railway Workers, Unions (*Shitetsuzoren*): approx. 240,000 mems.; Pres. T. HORII.

National Metal and Machine Trade Union (*Zenkoku Kinzoku*): approx. 202,000 mems.; Pres. S. TSUBAKI.

Japan Telecommunication Workers' Union (*Zendentsu*); approx. 184,000 mems.; Pres. T. KASAHARA.

National Federation of Iron and Steel Workers' Unions (*Tekko Roren*): approx. 200,000 mems.; Pres. K. MITO.

Japanese Federation of Synthetic Chemistry Workers' Unions (*Goka Roren*): approx. 122,000 mems.; Pres. K. OTA.

Japan Broadcast Corporation Workers' Union (*Nipporo*): approx. 111,000 mems.; Chair. TETSU UEDA.

Japan Coal Miners' Union (*Tanro*): approx. 68,000 mems.; Pres. T. YAMAMOTO.

All-Japan Free Workers' Union (*Zennichi Jiro*): approx. 221,000 mems.; Pres. FUMIO WADA.

National Forest Labour Union (*Zenriya*): approx. 74,000 mems.; Pres. TAKESHI TAMURA.

Japan Federation of Municipal Transportation Workers' Unions (*Toshikotsu*): approx. 70,000 mems.; Pres. ATSUSHI MIYAHARA.

All-Japan Agriculture and Forestry Ministry's Workers' Union (*Zen Norin*): approx. 57,000 mems.; Pres. T. WATARAI.

Zen Nihon Rodo Sodomei Kaigi—DOMEI (*Japanese Confederation of Labour*): 20-12 Shiba, 2-chome, Minato-ku, Tokyo; f. 1964; 2.1 million mems.; affiliated to ICFTU; Pres. MINORU TAKITA; Vice-Pres. SEIJI AMAIKE; Sec.-Gen. TAKUMI SHIGEEDA.

Affiliated Unions

Japan Federation of Textile Workers' Unions (*Zensendomei*): Pres. MINORU TAKITA; Gen. Sec. TADANOBU USAMI; 516,578 mems.

National Federation of Metal Industry Trade Unions (*Zenkindomei*): Pres. SHIGEO IBORI; Gen. Sec. SEIJI AMAIKE; 220,000 mems.

All Japan Seamen's Union (*Kaiin*): Pres. YUTAKA NABASAMA; 142,900 mems.

Federation of Japan Automobile Workers' Unions (*Jidosharoren*): Pres. ICHIRO SHIOJI; Gen. Sec. SHOZO AKAGI; 129,540 mems.

Federation of Electric Workers' Unions of Japan (*Denroren*): Pres. CHOZUI KAMEYAMA; Gen. Sec. SOOICHI SUZUKI; 127,798 mems.

Japanese Federation of General Trade Unions (*Ippan Domei*): Pres. MISAO MASUHARA; Gen. Sec. TSUTAR SATOH; 105,772 mems.

Japanese Federation of Chemical and General Workers' Unions (*Zenkadomei*): Pres. SHIGEO MURAO; Gen. Sec. KEITARO NAKAJIMA; 72,790 mems.

Japan Federation of Transport Workers' Unions (*Kotsuroren*): Pres. ISAMU YAMAMOTO; Gen. Sec. KENJI NAGASAWA; 67,877 mems.

General Federation of Shipbuilding Workers' Unions (*Zosensoren*): Pres. MASASHICHI MOTOI; Gen. Sec. HARUZO NISHIMOTO; 56,512 mems.

Mitsubishi Heavy Industry Workers' Union Council (*Domei-Mitsubishi*): Pres. AKIRA KINOSHITA; Gen. Sec. KOSHIRO MIKI; 40,800 mems.

National Union of Coal Mine Workers (*Zentanko*): Pres. TAKUMI SHIGEEDA; Gen. Sec. EIJI HAYADATE; 35,137 mems.

National Federation of Food Industry Workers' Unions (*Zenshokuhindomei*): Pres. GENJIRO TSURUTA; Gen. Sec. EIJI OHSEKO; 27,820 mems.

Federation of Japanese Metal Resource Workers' Unions (*Shigenroren*): Pres. TOHRU ENDO; Gen. Sec. KAZUHIRO IIOKA; 12,530 mems.

National Council of Paper and Pulp Workers' Unions "NPU" (*Domeizenkamipa*): Pres. ICHIRO MICHIKAWA; Gen. Sec. HIDEKA HOSOKAWA; 7,937 mems.

National Cinema and Theatre Workers' Union (*Zen-Eien*): Pres. ISAO MASUDA; Gen. Sec. HIROSHI HARIU; 3,220 mems.

Preparatory Council of National Federation of Dockers' Unions (*Kowandomei Jumbikai*): Chair. SADAO HISATSUNE; 800 mems.

Japan Emigration Service Workers' Union (*Kaigai-Ijuroso*): Pres. TADAO IMAMURA; Gen. Sec. MASAJI SAITO; 300 mems.

Japanese Federation of National Railway Workers' Unions (*Shinkokuro*): Pres. EIETSU SUGAWARA; Gen. Sec. KOOICHI TANIMURA; 74,360 mems.

All Japan Special Post Office Labour Union (*Zenyusei*): Pres. TSUTOMU NAKAMURA; Gen. Sec. HIDEMASA FUKUI; 28,840 mems.

National Tax Office Employees' Union (*Kokuzeiroso*): Pres. YASUJI NAKAZAWA; Gen. Sec. MUTSUO SHIMIZU; 10,200 mems.

National Forest Workers' Union of Japan (*Nichirinro*): Pres. KAZUO KUMAI; Gen. Sec. YASUO YAMADA; 10,062 mems.

New Nippon Telephone and Telegram Workers' Union (*Dendenshinro*): Pres. JOTARO TANI; Gen. Sec. TADAO IKEDA; 250 mems.

Domei's Local Federations (*Chihodomei*): 200,000 mems.

Fraternal Organizations

National Council of Government and Public Corporation Workers' Unions (*Zenkanko*): Chair. EIETSU SUGAWARA; 150,000 mems.

National Council of Democratic Unionists (*Zenkoku-minren*): Chair. SHIMPACHI KUDO; 300,000 mems.

Churitsu Rode Kumiai Renraku Kaigi—CHURITSU ROREN (*Liaison Council of Neutral Trade Unions*): 4-9, 1-chome, Shiba, Minato-ku, Tokyo; f. 1964; over 1,400,000 mems.; Gen. Sec. SHIGERU OKAMURA.

Major Affiliated Unions

National Federation of Cement Workers' Unions (*Zenkoku Semento*): 29-2, 5-chome, Shinbashi, Minato-ku, Tokyo; approx. 22,000 mems.; Pres. YORIO ABE; Sec.-Gen. MANJI YAMAMOTO.

National Federation of Electric Machine, Tool and Appliance Workers' Unions (*Denki Roren*): 13-10, 3-chome, Minami-Ohoi, Shingawa-ku, Tokyo; f. 1964; approx. 440,000 mems.; Pres. SHINRYO KIYOTA; Sec.-Gen. TARIKICHI SEKI.

Japanese Federation of Food and Allied Workers' Unions (*Shokuhin Roren*): 4-9, 1-chome, Shiba, Minatoku, Tokyo; approx. 92,000 mems.; Pres. SHIGERU OKAMURA.

National Federation of Life Insurance Employees' Unions (*Zenseiho*): 6 Kabuto-cho, 3-chome, Nihonbashi, Chuo-ku; approx. 82,000 mems.; Pres. JUNNOSUKE TANABE.

All-Japan Shipbuilding and Engineering Union (*Zenzosen*): 60-5, Sendagaya-3, Shibuya, Tokyo; f. 1964; 52,000 mems.; Pres. ISAO HASEGAWA; Sec.-Gen. NABEZO OHODE; publ. *Zenzosenkikai* (3 times monthly).

Zenkoku Sangyobetsu Rodo Kumiai Rengokai—SHIN SAMBETSU (*National Federation of Industrial Trade Unions*): Tokyo; approx. 70,000 mems.

MAJOR NON-AFFILIATED UNIONS
Tokyo

All-Japan Federation of Automobile Workers' Unions (*Zenkoku Jidosha*): f. 1962; approx. 120,000 mems.; Pres. KAZUO ITO; Sec.-Gen. TATSUYA KUBO.

Federation of City Bank Employees' Unions (*Shiginren*): c/o Yaesu, Chuo-ku; approx. 130,000 mems.; Pres. T. FURUKAWA.

Federation of Textile Clothing Workers' Unions of Japan (*Asa Ryokyo*): Katkura Bldg., 3-2 Kyobashi, Chuo-ku; approx. 25,000 mems.; Pres. KENZO OGUCHI.

National Federation of Mutual Bank Employees' Unions (*Zenso Ginren*): 40 Higashi Matsushita-cho; approx. 28,000 mems.; Pres. K. ISHIKAWA; Sec.-Gen. S. SAKAI.

Japan Council of Construction Industry Employees' Unions (*Nikkenkyo*): 5, 3-chome, Kanda-Kaji-cho, Chiyoda-ku; f. 1954; approx. 30,000 mems.; Pres. T. KUROMUSHA; Gen. Sec. N. RIOJA.

Labour Council of Governmental Special Corporations (*Seryokyo*): c/o Nichijuo 14, 1-chome, Kudan, Chiyoda-ku; approx. 19,000 mems.; Pres. K. TAKIZAWA.

All-Japan Damage Insurance Employees' Unions (*Zensonpo*): c/o Morizui Bldg., 3, 2-chome, Kyobashi, Chuo-ku; approx. 38,000 mems.; Pres. T. UEDA.

All-Japan Day Workers' Union (*Zennichijiro*): 3-22-10, Zoshigaya Toshimaku, Tokyo; f. 1947; approx. 153,000 mems.; Pres. FUMIO WADA; publs. *Jikatabi* (weekly), *Gakusku* (monthly).

National Council of Medical Treatment Workers' Unions: approx. 49,000 mems.

Federation of Tokyo Metropolitan Government Workers' Unions (*To Roren*): c/o Tokyo-to Office, Marunouchi, Chiyoda-ku; approx. 120,000 mems.; Pres. U. OKAMOTO; Sec.-Gen. T. NAKAGAWA.

Japan Federation of Teachers (*Zenkyoren*): approx. 47,000 mems.; Pres. MASAO SUZUKI; Sec.-Gen. T. KIRUCHI.

Japan High School Teachers' Union (*Nikkokyo*): c/o Kyoiku Kakika, Hitotsubashi, Kanda, Chiyoda-ku; f. 1950; approx. 48,000 mems.; Pres. K. OGASAWARA.

Japan National Railways Locomotive Workers' Union: 3-2-13 Nishi-Gotanda, Shinagawa-ku, Tokyo; f. 1951; approx. 59,000 mems.; publ. weekly newsletter.

NATIONAL COUNCILS
Co-ordinating bodies for unions whose members are in the same industry or have the same employer.

Zenkoku Shogyo Rodo Kumiai Kyogi-kai—Zen Shokyo (*National Council of Commerce Workers' Unions*): 1-2 Nishi-Ginza, Chuo-ku, Tokyo; approx. 153,652 mems.; Gen.-Sec. TATSUO MATSUDA.

Zenkoku Kinyu Kikan Rode Kumiai Kyogi-kai—Zen Kinyu (*National Council of Finance Industry Workers' Unions*): 1-2 Nishi-Ginza, Chuo-ku, Tokyo; approx. 120,000 mems.; Sec.-Gen. MASAYA OKABE.

Zen Nippon Shokuhin Rodo Kumiai Rengo-kai—Shokuhin Roren (*Japanese Federation of Food and Allied Workers' Unions*): 1-4-9 Shiba, Minato-ku, Tokyo; f. 1954; approx. 94,000 mems.; Chair. SHIGERU OKAMURA.

Nihon Kankocho Rodo Kumiai Kyogi-kai—Kankoro (*Liaison Organization of Public Workers' Unions*): Sohyo Kaikan, Shiba Koen, Minato-ku, Tokyo; approx. 2,500,000 mems. from SOHYO affiliates; Sec.-Gen. REIICHIRO TOYOTA.

Zen Nippon Kotsu Unyu Rodo Kumiai Kyogi-kai—Zenkoun (*All-Japan Council of Traffic and Transport Workers' Unions*): c/o Kokutetsu Rodo Kaikan, 2-1 Marunouchi, Chiyoda-ku, Tokyo; f. 1947; about 800,000 mems.; Pres. TOSHIKATSU HORII; Gen. Sec. ICHIZO SAKAI.

National Council of Government Enterprise Workers' Unions: Tokyo; approx. 1,000,000 mems.

National Liaison Council of Shipping and Harbour Workers' Unions: Tokyo; approx. 200,000 mems.

Kokusai Jiyuroren Kameikumiai Linkai (*Co-ordinating Committee of the I.C.F.T.U. Affiliated Unions in Japan*): c/o Kawate Bldg., 5-8, 1-chome, Nishi-Shimbashi, Minato-ku, Tokyo; about 2,400,000 mems.; Gen. Sec. EIICHI OCHIAI.

CO-OPERATIVE ORGANIZATION

National Federation of Purchasing Associations—ZEN-KOREN: 5-12 Omotemachi, Chiyoda-ku, Tokyo; principal agricultural co-operative federation; collective purchase and sale of agricultural materials and produce.

TRANSPORT

RAILWAYS

Japanese National Railways (J.N.R.): Kokutetsu Building 6-5, 1-chome, Marunouchi, Chiyoda-ku, Tokyo; f. 1949 as a public corporation; underwent reorganization, August 1970; 1.067 gauge; the 1.435 gauge, very high speed, Shinkansen line linking Tokyo with Yokohama, Nagoya, Kyoto and Shin-Osaka was completed in 1964; this line was extended to Okayama in 1972, and further construction to Hakata in Kyushu is due to be opened in December 1974; 20,924 km. of track, 6,685 km. of 1.067 gauge is electrified; Pres. M. FUJII; Exec. Vice-Pres. K. INOUE; Vice-Pres. Engineering M. TAKIYAMA.

PRINCIPAL PRIVATE COMPANIES: 6,593 km. of track of which 5,607 km. are electrified.

Hanshin Electric Railway Co. Ltd.: 8, Umeda-cho, Kita-ku, Osaka; f. 1899; Pres. CHUJIRO NODA.

Keihan Electric Railway Co. Ltd.: 47-5, 1-chome, Kyobashi, Higashi-ku, Osaka; Pres. S. MURAOKA.

Kei-Han-Shin Kyuko Railway Co. Ltd.: 41, Kakutacho, Kita-ku, Osaka; f. 1907; links Osaka, Kyota and Kobe; Dir. and Pres. YONEZO KOBAYASHI.

Keihin Kyuko Electric Railway Co. Ltd.: 17, Takanawa-minami-cho, Shiba, Minato-ku, Tokyo; Pres. HYAPPO TANAKA.

Keio Teito Electric Railway Co. Ltd.: 48, 3-chome, Shinjuku, Shinjuku-ku, Tokyo; Pres. S. INOUE.

Keisei Electric Railway Co. Ltd.: 10-3, 1-chome, Oshiage Sumidaku, Tokyo; f. 1909; Pres. C. KAWASAKI; Man. Dir. IKUJIRO FUKUDA.

Kinki Nippon Railway Co. Ltd.: 1, 6-chome, Uehom-machi, Tennoji-ku, Osaka; f. 1910; Pres. ISAMU SAHEKI.

Nagoya Railroad Co. Ltd.: 223, 1-chome, Sashima-cho, Nakamura-ku, Nagoya-shi; Pres. MOTOO TSUCHIKAWA.

Nankai Railroad Co.: 12, Rokuban-cho, Nanbashinchi, Minami-ku, Osaka; Pres. I. SAHEKI.

Nippon Express Co. Ltd.: 12-9, 3-chome, Sotokanda, Chiyoda-ku. Tokyo; f. 1937; Pres. T. SAWAMURA; Vice-Pres. S. HIROSE, G. HOSOI; cap. 46m.

Nishi Nippon Railroad Co. Ltd.: 12-1 Tenjin-cho, Fukuoka; serves northern Kyushu; Pres. MUNEO KUSUNE.

Odakyu Electric Railway Co. Ltd.: 28, 2-chome, Yoyogi, Shibuya-ku, Tokyo; Pres. N. ANDO.

Seibu Railway Co. Ltd.: 16-15, 1-chome, Minami-Ikebukuro, Toshima-ku, Tokyo; f. 1912; Pres. SHOJIRO KOJIMA; Vice-Pres. YOSHIAKI TSUTSUMI, SEIJI TSUTSUMI; Senior Man. Dir. IWAO NISUGI.

Teito Rapid Transit Authority: 19-6, 3-chome, Higashi Ueno, Taito-ku, Tokyo; f. 1941; underground railway service for Tokyo; Pres. TATSUYA USHIJIMA.

Tobu Railway Co. Ltd.: 2, 1-chome, Oshiage, Sumida-ku, Tokyo; Pres. KAICHIRO NEZU.

Tokyu Corporation: 26-20 Sakuragaoka-cho, Shibuya-ku, Tokyo; f. 1922; Pres. NOBORU GOTOH.

SUBWAYS AND MONORAILS

Subway service is available today in four major cities, Tokyo, Osaka, Kobe and Nagoya, with a combined network of over 200 km. New subway services were inaugurated in Yokohama and Sapporo, the latter in time for the Winter Olympics in 1972. Most new subway lines are directly linked with existing J.N.R. or private railway terminals which connect the cities with suburban areas.

Japan started its first monorail system on a commercial scale in 1964 with straddle-type cars between downtown Tokyo and Tokyo International Airport, a distance of 13 km. In 1969, the total monorail mileage was 24 km. Work started in 1971 on the 34-mile Seikan Tunnel (electric rail only) linking Honshu island with Hokkaido.

Tokyo Underground Railway: Teito Rapid Transit Authority, 19-6 Higashi Ueno, 3-chome, Taito-ku, Tokyo; f. 1941; Pres. M. ARAKI; total length 117.5 km. (April 1971).

ROADS

In December 1971 Japan's road network extended to 1,022,936 km. Plans have been made to cover the country with a trunk automobile highway network with a total length of 7,600 km. expected to be completed by 1985.

A 190 km. stretch of trunk highway between Nagoya and Kobe (Meishin Expressway) was completed in July 1965, and in May 1969 a 346 km. stretch between Nagoya and Tokyo (Tomei Expressway) was also completed.

There is a national omnibus service, 54 publicly operated services and 294 privately operated services.

SHIPPING

Shipping in Japan is not nationalized but is supervized by the Ministry of Transport. On June 30th, 1971 gross registered tonnage totalled 30,509,000.

PRINCIPAL COMPANIES

Daiichi Chuo Kisen Kaisha: 7-3 Nihonbashi-Dori, Chuo-ku, Tokyo; f. 1960; fleet of 24 vessels; bulk ore and oil carriers; Pres. KOTARO TSUCHIKANE.

Japan Line Ltd.: Kokusai Bldg., 1-1, 3-chome, Marunouchi, Chiyoda-ku, Tokyo; f. 1948; container ship, tanker, liner, tramp and specialized carrier services; Pres. H. MATSUNAGA.

Japan Marine Products Co.: 3, 2-chome, Marunouchi, Chiyoda-ku, Tokyo; cargo and tanker services; fleet of 15 vessels; Pres. H. NAKAI; Vice-Pres. T. ITO, O. KAJIYAMA; Man. Dirs. Y. NAGASAWA, T. TSUAKI, T. MURAKAMI.

Kansai Steamship Co. Ltd.: 1 Soze-cho, Kita-ku, Osaka; f. 1942; fleet of 39 vessels; tramp, cargo/passenger services to Far East, Philippines and Australia; Pres. SHIGERU HASEGAWA.

Kawasaki Kisen Kaisha (*K Line*): 8 Kaigan-dori, Ikuta-ku, Kobe; f. 1919; fleet of 91 vessels; cargo, tanker and bulk ore carrying services worldwide; Chair. MOTOZO HATTORI; Pres. M. ADACHI.

Mitsui O.S.K. Lines Ltd.: 3-3, 5-chome, Akasaka, Minato-ku, Tokyo; f. 1964 by merger of Mitsui Steamship Co. and O.S.K.; fleet of 130 vessels; cargo, tanker and ore carrying services world-wide; Pres. JIRO GONDA.

Nippon Yusen Kafushiki Kaisha: 3-2, Marunouchi, 2-chome, Chiyoda-ku, Tokyo; merged with Mitsubishi Steamship Co. 1964; fleet of 160 vessels; world-wide cargo, tanker and bulk carrying services; Chair. Y. ARIYOSHI; Pres. S. KIKUCHI.

Nissho Shipping Co. Ltd.: 2-1, Marunouchi, 2-chome, Chiyoda-ku, Tokyo; fleet of 17 vessels; tanker, lumber and ore carrying services to Arabian Gulf, North America, Philippines, New Caledonia, Chile; Pres. J. MATSUSHIMA; Sen. Man. Dir. K. ISHIMARU.

Sanko Steamship Co. Ltd., The: Shinyuurakucho Bldg., 1-chome, Yuurakucho, Chiyoda-ku, Tokyo; f. 1933; fleet of 45 vessels; overseas tramping (cargo and oil); Pres. TOSHIO KOHMOTO.

Sankyo Kaiun Co. Ltd.: Miki Bldg., No. 5, 3-chome, Nihonbashi Edobashi, Chuo-ku, Tokyo; fleet of 15 vessels; liner and tramp services to the Far East; Pres. H. IKEMURA; Man. Dir. S. SHIRAISHI.

Shinwa Kaiun Kaisha Ltd.: 1-3, Kyobashi, Chuo-ku, Tokyo; f. 1950; fleet of 46 vessels; ore carrying, cargo and tanker services to Pacific, Far East and U.S.; Pres. HIROSHI MIWA.

Showa Shipping Co. Ltd.: 1, 4-chome, Nihonbashi, Muromachi, Chuo-ku, Tokyo; f. 1964 by merger of Nippon Oil Tanker Co. Ltd. and Nissan Steamship Co. Ltd.; cargo, tanker, tramping and container services worldwide; Pres. M. ARAKI; Vice-Pres. T. MATSUE.

Taiheiyo Kaiun Kabushiki Kaisha (*The Pacific Transportation Co. Ltd.*): Room 314, Marunouchi Bldg., 4-1, 2-chome, Chiyoda-ku, Tokyo; fleet of 15 vessels; cargo and tanker services; Pres. S. YAMAJI.

Yamashita-Shinnihon Steamship Co., Ltd.: 1-1, Hitotsubashi, 1-chome, Chiyoda-ku, Tokyo 100; f. 1917, as Yamashita Steamship Co., Ltd., merger with Shinnihon Steamship Co., Ltd. 1964; fleet of 65 vessels; liner and tramp services to U.S. Far East, etc.; Chair. K. YAMAGATA; Pres. S. YAMASHITA.

CIVIL AVIATION

Japan Air Lines—JAL (*Nihon Koku Kabushiki Kaisha*). 7-3, 2-chome, Marunouchi, Chiyoda-ku, Tokyo 100; f. 1951; operates domestic and international services from Tokyo to Honolulu, Los Angeles, San Francisco, Vancouver, New York, Seoul, Pusan, Khabarovsk, Okinawa, Hong Kong, Manila, Bangkok, Jakarta, Kuala Lumpur, Singapore, Sydney, Guam, New Delhi, Teheran, Beirut, Calcutta, Karachi, Cairo, Rome, Frankfurt, Hamburg, Copenhagen, Amsterdam, Moscow, Paris, Mexico City, Athens and London; Pres. SHIZUO ASADA; fleet of 16 Boeing 747, 44 DC-8 and 7 Boeing 727.

Japan Domestic Airlines Co. Ltd.: Tokyo International Airport, Haneda, Tokyo; f. 1964; passenger services throughout Japan; fleet of three Boeing 727, fifteen YS-11; Pres. TATSUHIKO KAWABUCHI.

All Nippon Airways: 2-5, Kasumigaseki 3-chome, Chiyoda-ku, Tokyo; domestic passenger and freight services; Pres. ISAMU MORIMURA; fleet of 32 Boeing 727, 13 Boeing 737, 18 Friendship 27, and 30 YS-11.

Toa Domestic Airline Co.: Tokyo International Airport, 9-1, 1-chome, Haneda-Kuko, O'hta-ku, Tokyo; f. 1970 through a merger of *Japan Domestic Airlines* and *Toa Airways*; began operations June 1971; domestic scheduled services throughout Japan from Tokyo and Osaka; Pres. Gen. TOMINAGA; Vice-Pres. NOBURO KAMEYAMA; Chair. YAICHI SHIMOMURA; fleet of 29 YS-11A, 2 Tawron, 17 Kawasaki.

Tokyo is served by the following foreign airlines: Aeroflot, Air France, Air India, Air Siam, Alitalia, British Airways, Cathay Pacific Airways Ltd., Air Canada, EgyptAir, Garuda Indonesian Airways, KLM, Korean Airlines, Lufthansa, Northwest Orient Airlines, Philippine Airlines, PIA, Sabena, Singapore Airlines, Northwest Orient Airlines, Pan American, Qantas, SAS, Swissair, Thai Airways International, Varig.

TOURISM

Japan National Tourist Organization: Tokyo Kotsu Kaikan Bldg., 2-13 Yuraku-cho, Tokyo; Pres. SABURO OHTA.

OVERSEAS OFFICES

Australia: Bankers and Traders Bldg., 115 Pitt St., Sydney, N.S.W.

Brazil: Av. Paulista 1009, Cj. 2003, São Paulo.

Canada: 165 University Ave., Toronto, Ontario M5H 3B8.

France: 8 rue de Richelieu, Paris 1er.

Germany: 2nd Floor, City Centre Bldg., Biebergasse 6-10, Frankfurt a/M.

Hong Kong: Room 601, Peter Bldg., 58 Queen's Rd., Hong Kong.

Mexico: Reforma 122, 5° piso, B-2 Mexico 6, D.F.

Switzerland: rue de Berne 13, Geneva.

Thailand: 56 Suriwong Rd., Bangkok.

United Kingdom: 167 Regent St., London, W.1.

United States: 45 Rockefeller Plaza, New York, N.Y. 10020; 333 North Michigan Ave., Chicago, Illinois 60601; 1420 Commerce St., Dallas, Texas 75201; One Wiltshire Bldg., 624 South Grand Ave., Suite 2707, Los Angeles, Calif. 90017; 109 Kaiulani Ave., Honolulu, Hawaii

96815; Japanese Cultural and Trade Center, 1737 Post St., San Francisco, Calif. 94115.

Japan Travel Bureau Inc.: 6-4, Marunouchi 1-chome, Chiyoda-ku, Tokyo; f. 1912; approx. 13,000 mems.; Chair. T. NISHIO; Pres. H. TSUDA; Exec. Vice-Pres. M. KANEMATSU, M. HATA; publ. *JTB News* (monthly).

Department of Tourism: 2-1-3 Kasumigaseki, Chiyoda-ku, Tokyo; f. 1946; inner department of the Ministry of Transport; Dir.-Gen. SHUNICHI SUMITA.

THEATRES

Kabukiza Theatre: Ginza-Higashi, Tokyo; national Kabuki theatre centre.

National Theatre of Japan (*Kokuritsu Gekijo*): 13 Hayabusa-cho, Chiyoda-ku, Tokyo 102; f. 1966; Pres. SEIICHIRO TAKAHASHI; Chief. Dir. SAKUO TERANAKA; Dirs. KOSABURO SHIBATA, JIRO OSARAGI, YUKISO MIRSHIMA.

Nissei Theatre: 1-12 Yuraku-cho, Chiyoda-ku, Tokyo; f. 1963; drama, opera and concerts; mems. 300; Gen. Dir. KEITA ASARI.

MUSIC FESTIVAL

Osaka International Festival: Osaka; joined European Asscn. of Music Festivals 1966.

ATOMIC ENERGY

Japan's atomic energy development programme began towards the end of 1955 with the government's enactment of the Basic Law of Atomic Energy, and setting up the Atomic Energy Commission of Japan. In 1956 the first research centre, Japan Atomic Energy Research Institute, was established in Tokai village, Ibaraki prefecture. In 1962 the Nuclear Ship Development Agency was established, and in 1967 the Power Reactor and Nuclear Fuel Corporation was established to develop advance thermal reactors and fast breeder reactors, as well as nuclear fuels.

Four nuclear power stations were in operation by 1971 and nine more are expected to become operational by 1975 with a combined capacity of 3,600 MWe.

Japan is an active member of the IAEA. She also has Co-operation Agreements on Atomic Energy with the U.S., U.K. and Canada. Through these agreements, various collaborations such as the exchange of technological information, supply of nuclear fuel and instruments, etc., have been carried out. The nine regional electricity companies of Japan have engaged foreign firms to undertake prospecting and mining for uranium in North America on their behalf.

Projected Generating Capacity: 1975: 6,000 MW; 1985: 30,000–40,000 MW.

Japan Atomic Energy Commission (JAEC): 2-2-1 Kasumigaseki, Chiyoda-ku, Tokyo; policy board for research, development and peaceful uses of atomic energy; Commissioners: GORO INOUYE, TOSHINOSUKE MUTO, EIICHI TAKEDA, AKIRA MATSUI, EIZO TAZIMA, TASABURO YAMADA.

Atomic Energy Bureau (AEB): Science and Technology Agency, 2-2-1 Kasumigaseki, Chiyoda-ku, Tokyo; central administrative agency; Dir. TOSHIHAM NARITA.

Japan Atomic Energy Research Institute (JAERI): 1-1-13 Shinbashi, Minato-ku, Tokyo; five reactors for training, isotope production and research; f. 1956; Pres. EIJI MUNEKATA; Vice-Pres. HIROSHI MURATA.

Fund for Peaceful Atomic Development of Japan: 1-1-13, Shinbashi, Minato-ku, Tokyo; education of the Japanese people in understanding atomic energy and its applications; Pres. REINOSUKE SUGA.

Japan Atomic Industrial Forum (JAIF): 1-1-13, Shinbashi, Minato-ku, Tokyo; collates the activities of private industry in connection with peaceful uses of atomic energy; Chair. REINOSUKE SUGA.

PRINCIPAL JAERI ESTABLISHMENTS

Radioisotope Centre: The University of Tokyo, Yayoi 2-11-16, Bunkyo-ku, Tokyo.

Tokai Research Establishment: Tokai-mura, Naka-gun, Ibaraki-ken.

Takasaki Radiation Chemistry Research Establishment; 1233 Watanuki-cho, Takasaki-shi, Gumma-ken.

Oharai Establishment: Narita-machi, Oharai-cho, Higahiibaraki-gun, Ibaraki-ken.

CONTRACTORS

The First Atomic Power Industry Group (FAPIG): Nissho-Iwai Bldg., 4-5, Akasaka 2-chome, Minato-ku, Tokyo 107; f. 1957; constructed the Tokai Power Station for JAPCO; member firms mostly belong to the Furukawa, Kawasaki and Suzuki groups; Chair. S. MAEDA.

Mitsubishi Atomic Power Industries, Inc.: Ohtemachi Bldg., 6-1, 1-chome Ohtemachi, Chiyoda-ku, Tokyo 100; set up 1958 to construct nuclear reactors and power plants and to fabricate nuclear fuel; is building the reactor for Japan's first atomic powered ship, Takahama Unit No. 1, No. 2, Ohi Unit No. 1, No. 2 and Mihami Unit No. 3 nuclear power plants of the Kansai Electric Power Co. Inc., Ikata Unit No. 1 nuclear power plant of Shikoku Electric Power Co. Inc., and Genkai Unit No. 1 nuclear power plant of Kyushu Electric Power Co. Inc.; mems. 25 firms, mostly members of the Mitsubishi group; Pres. EITARO ISHIHARA.

Nippon Atomic Industry Group Co. Ltd. (NAIGCO): 2-5 Kasumigaseki, 3-chome, Chiyoda-ku, Tokyo; f. 1958; set up to construct atomic energy facilities; mems. 36 firms, mostly members of the Toshiba and Mitsui group; Chair. TAIZO ISHIZAKA; Pres. DOKO TOSHIO.

Sumitomo Atomic Energy Industries, Ltd.: 22, 5-chome, Kitahama Higashi-ku, Osaka; f. 1958; set up to utilize nuclear materials and build necessary instrumentation; mems. 37 firms, mostly members of Sumitomo group; Pres. MASATOSHI HIRATSUKA.

Tokyo Atomic Industrial Consortium (TAIC): Hitachi Bldg., 4-6 Surugadai Kanda, Chiyoda-ku, Tokyo; set up to utilize nuclear materials and build necessary instrumentation; mems. 26 firms, mostly members of Hitachi group; Chair. KENICHIRO KOMAI.

INDUSTRIAL RESEARCH

Electric Power Development Company (EPDC): 8-2, Marunouchi, 1-chome, Chiyoda-ku, Tokyo; f. 1952; almost entirely government-owned corporation devoted to promoting the development mainly of large-scale hydro-power resources, construction of thermal and nuclear power projects and to wholesaling the generated power to nine privately-owned power companies; also overseas engineering assistance in the development of water resources.

The Japan Atomic Power Company (JAPC): 1-6-1, Otemachi, Chiyoda-ku, Tokyo; private consortium building nuclear power plants; Japan's first commercial nuclear unit of 166,000 kW.; advanced Calder Hall type at Tokai Power Station; Ibaraki Prefecture opened 1966; second unit at Tsuruga Power Station of 357,000 kW. BWR opened in 1970 in Tsuruga City; second unit to Tokai Power Station of 1,100,000 kW. BWR to be opened 1976; Pres. TOMIICHIRO SHIRASAWA.

Japan Nuclear Ship Development Agency (JNSDA): 35 Shiba-Kotohira, Minato-ku, Tokyo; f. 1963; designing, navigating and constructing an 8,300-ton training and special cargo ship, to be completed by 1973; Pres. SHUICHI SASAKI; Gen. Man. TORATARO UCHIKOGA.

Power Reactor and Nuclear Fuel Development Corporation (PNC): 9-13, 1-chome Akasaka, Minato-ku, Tokyo; f. 1967; public corporation for developing advanced thermal reactor and fast breeder reactor, and for prospecting, mining, manufacture and processing of nuclear fuel; Pres. S. KIYONARI.

Chubu Electric Power Co.: 10-1 Toshin-cho, Higashi-ku, Nagoya; one of the nine electric utilities operating in Japan, plans to add 11,850,000 kW. by 1978, including nuclear power; Pres. OTOSABURO KATO.

Hitachi Company Ltd.: Kawasaki-shi, Kanagawa-ken; swimming-pool reactor.

Kansai Electric Power Co.: Fukui, Mihama Unit 1 (340 mW) went into commercial operation in Nov. 1970, Mihama Unit 2 (500 mW) and Takahama Units 1 and 2 (826 mW) will become operational in 1972, 1974 and 1976 respectively; Pres. S. YOSHIMURA.

Mitsubishi Electric Co. Ltd.: Tokai-mura, Naka-gun, Ibaraki-ken; swimming-pool reactor.

Tokyo Electric Power (TODEN): 1-3, 1-chome, Uchisaiwai-cho, Chiyoda-ku, Tokyo; has a nuclear power station at Fukushima which will have 6 generating units in 1976; Chair. K. KIKAWADA; Pres. H. MIZUNO.

Tokyo Shibaura Electric Co. Ltd.: Komukai Toshiba-cho, Kawasaki; 100 kW. swimming-pool reactor; Principal Official T. NISHIJIMA.

ACADEMIC RESEARCH

Kinki University: Fuse-shi Osaka-fu; U.T.R.-type reactor.

Kyoto University: Yoshida Honmachi, Sakyo-ku, Kyoto; swimming-pool type reactor at Osaka, critical 1964.

Musashi Institute of Technology: Ozenji, Kawasaki-shi, Kanagawaken; f. 1963; research reactor of Triga II type.

National Institute of Radiological Sciences (NIRS): 9-1, 4-chome, Anagawa, Chiba-shi; f. 1957; research on effects and medical uses of radiation and training of researchers; Dir. KEISUKE MISONO; publs. *Hosha-Sen Kagaku* (Radiology, monthly), *Annual Report NIRS* (English), *Radioactivity survey data* (English, quarterly).

UNIVERSITIES

NATIONAL UNIVERSITIES

Chiba University: Yayoicho, Chiba City; 845 teachers, 6,270 students.

Gunma University: 3 Showa-Machi, Maebashi-city; 524 teachers, 3,860 students.

Hirosaki University: 1 Bunkyo-cho, Aomori-ken, Hirosaki; 471 teachers, 3,514 students.

Hiroshima University: Higashisenda-machi, Hiroshima; 1,114 teachers; 8,357 students.

Hitotsubashi University: Kitatama-gun, Tokyo; 139 teachers, 2,617 students.

Hokkaido University: Nishi 5, Kita 8, Sapporo; 1,726 teachers, 8,827 students.

Ibaraki University: 2127 Watarimachi, Ibaraki Pref., Mito; 244 teachers, 3,365 students.

Kagawa University: 121 Saiwai-Cho Takamatsu-Chi, Kagawa-Ken; 590 teachers, 2,318 students.

Kagoshima University: Uerata-cho, Kagoshima; 811 teachers, 5,843 students.

Kanazawa University: 1-1 Marunouchi, Kanazawa City; 722 teachers, 5,850 students.

Kobe University: Rokko, Nada-ku, Kobe; 1,002 teachers, 9,530 students.

Kumamoto University: Kurokami-machi, Kumamoto; 697 teachers, 5,500 students.

Kyoto University: Yoshida-hommachi, Sakyo-ku, Kyoto; 558 professors, 14,648 students.

Kyushu University: Hakozaki, Fukuoka City, Fukuoka Prefecture; 855 teachers, 10,101 students.

Nagasaki University: 1-14 Bunkyo-cho, Nagasaki; 621 teachers, 3,900 students.

Nagoya University: Furo-cho, Chikusa-ku, Nagoya; 1,171 teachers, 8,831 students.

Nara Women's University: Kita-Uoya-Nishi-Machi, Nara City; 306 teachers, 1,215 students.

Niigata University: Asahimachidori 1-Bancho, Niigata; 850 teachers, 5,885 students.

Ochanomizu Women's University: 1-1, 2-chome, Otsuka, Bunkyo-ku, Tokyo; 239 teachers, 1,698 students.

Okayama University: Tsushima, Okayama; 885 teachers, 6,117 students.

Osaka University: 36 Joancho, Kita-ku, Osaka; 391 professors, 8,448 students.

Osaka University of Foreign Studies: 8-chome Uehonmachi Tennoji-ku, Osaka; 123 teachers, 1,831 full-time students.

Shimane University: 1060 Nishikawatsu-cho Matsue-chi, Shimane-Ken, 243 teachers, 2,407 students.

Shinshu University: 109 Asahi-machi, Matsumoto; 1,125 teachers, 4,165 students.

Shizuoka University: Oiwa-cho, 2-chome, Shizuoka; 457 teachers, 5,330 students.

Tohuku University: Katahiracho, Sendai; 2,049 teachers, 10,425 students.

University of Tokushima: 6 Shinkura-cho, 2-chome, Tokushima-shi, Tokushima-ken; 569 teachers, 3,240 students.

The University of Tokyo: Hongo, Bunkyo-ku, Tokyo; 3,558 teachers, 15,808 students.

Tokyo Medical and Dental University: 5-47, 1-chome, Yushima, Bunkyo-ku, Tokyo; 587 teachers, 1,249 students.

Tokyo University of Education: 24 Kubomachi Otsuka, Bunkyo-ku, Tokyo; 500 teachers, 5,000 students.

Tokyo University of Foreign Studies: 51 Nishigawara; 4-chome, Kita-ku, Tokyo; 116 teachers, 2,041 students.

Tottori University: 1, 5-chome, Tachikawa-cho, Tottori City; 209 teachers, 1,952 students.

Toyama University: 3,190 Gofuku Toyama City; 339 teachers, 3,825 students.

Wakayama University: 278 Sekido, Wakayamasi; 210 teachers, 2,340 students.

Yamagata University: 1-4-12 Koshirikawa-machi, Yamagata City; 448 teachers, 4,684 students.

Yamaguchi University: Shimmichi, Yamaguchi; 645 teachers, 4,385 students.

Yamanashi University: Kofu City, 4-4-37 Takeda; 278 teachers, 2,391 students.

Yokohama National University: 702 Ohokahachi, Mina-miku, Yokohama; 287 teachers, 5,395 students.

PUBLIC, PREFECTURAL AND MUNICIPAL UNIVERSITIES

Fukushima Medical College: Fukushima City; 209 teachers, 545 students.

Kyoto Prefectural University of Medicine: 465, Kjii-cho Kawaramachi, Hirokoji, Kamikyo-ku, Kyoto; 222 teachers, 583 students.

Mie Prefectural University: Torii-cho, Tsu.

Nagoya City University: 1 Kawasumi, Mizuho-cho, Mizuho-ku, Nagoya; 353 teachers, 1,617 students.

Nara Medical University: 840 Shijo-cho, Kashihara-shi, Nara; 223 teachers, 416 students.

Osaka City University: 459 Sugimotocho, Sumiyoshi-ku, Tokyo; 827 teachers, 6,349 students.

University of Osaka Prefecture: 804 Mozu-Umemachi 4-cho, Sakai, Osaka; 602 teachers, 4,193 students.

Osaka Women's University: Tezukayama 3-chome, Sumiyoshi-ku, Osaka; 76 teachers, 675 students.

Sapporo Medical College: S.1, W.17, Sapporo City; 259 teachers, 549 students.

    Attached Institute: *Cancer Research Institute:* f. 1952; Dir. H. TSUKUDA.

Shizuoka College of Pharmacy: 160 Oshika, Shizuoka-shi; 412 students.

Tokyo Metropolitan University: 1-1-1 Yagumo, Meguro-ku, Tokyo; 556 teachers, 3,604 students.

Wakayama Medical College: 9 Kuban-cho, Wakayama City; 200 teachers, 400 students.

Yokohama Municipal University: 4646 Mutsuura-machi, Kanazawa-ku, Yokohama; 400 teachers, 3,000 students.

PRIVATE UNIVERSITIES

Aoyama-Gakuin University: 4-4-25 Shibuya, Shibuya-ku, Tokyo 150; 300 teachers, 16,602 students.

Azabu Veterinary College: 1-17-71 Fuchinobe, Sagamihara City, Kanagawa; 65 teachers, 1,000 students.

University of Buddhism: 96 Kitahananobo-cho, Murasakino, Kita-ku, Kyoto; 180 teachers, 1,474 students.

Chuo University: 3-9 Kanda-Surugadai, Chiyoda-ku, Tokyo; 1,159 teachers, 36,078 students.

Dai-ichi College of Pharmacy: 93 Tamagawa-cho, Takamiya, Fukuoka City; 85 teachers, 924 students.

Daito Bunka University: 1-9-1 Takashimadaira, Itabashi-ku, Tokyo; 150 teachers.

Doshisha University: Karasuma Imadegawa, Kamikyo-ku, Kyoto; 362 teachers, 19,681 students.

Doshisha Women's College: 602 Genbu-cho, Teramachi-Nishiiru, Imadegawa-dori, Kamikyo-ku, Kyoto; 75 full-time, 107 part-time teachers, 2,564 students.

Fukuoka University: 11 Nanakuma, Fukuoka; 194 teachers, 13,000 students.

Gakushuin University: 1-1057 Mejiro-cho, Toshima-ku, Tokyo; 170 teachers, 5,827 students.

Hanazono University: 1-Hanazono Kitsujikita-cho, Ukyo-ku, Kyoto.

Hannan University: 4-35 5-chome Amami, Higashi, Matsubara City, Osaka; 36 full time, 37 part-time teachers, 1,152 students.

Hiroshima Jogakuin College: 720 Ushita-Machi, Hiroshima City; 50 teachers, 900 students.

Hokkai Gakuen University: 8-60, Asahimachi, Sappro, 062; 226 teachers, 5,992 students.

Hosei University: 17-1 Fujimi 2-chome, Chiyoda-ku, Tokyo; 400 teachers, 29,817 students.

International Christian University: Osawa, Mitaka-shi, Tokyo; 87 teachers, 1,300 students.

Iwate Medical University: 19-1 Uchimaru, Morioka, Iwate; 333 teachers, 1,482 students.

Japan Women's University: Mejirodai, Bunkyo-ku-Tokyo; 178 teachers, 3,519 students.

The Jikei University School of Medicine: 3-25-8 Nishi Shinbashi Minato-ku, Tokyo 105; 989 teachers, 1,118 students.

Kagoshima College of Economics: 8850 Shimofukumoto-cho, Kagoshima; 63 teachers, 2,300 students.

Kanagawa University: 3-chome Rokkaku-Bashi, Kanagawa-ku, Yokohama; 196 teachers, 10,000 students.

Kansai University: 3-35 Yamate-cho 3-chome, Suita-shi, Osaka; 471 teachers, 24,430 students.

Kanto Gakuin University: Muutsuura 4834 Kanzawa-ku, Yokohama; 409 teachers, 7,572 students.

Keio University: Mita, Minato-ku, Tokyo; 1,056 teachers, 25,827 students.

Kinki University: 321 Kowakae, Higashiosaka, Osaka; 441 teachers, 23,683 students.

Kogakuin University: 24 Tsunohazu 2-chome, Shinjuku-ku, Tokyo 160; 241 teachers, 7,654 students.

Kokugakuin University: 10-28 Higashi 4-chome, Shibuya-ku, Tokyo; 480 teachers, 12,974 students.

Komazawa University: Komazawa 1-chome, Fukazawa-machi, Setagaya-ku, Tokyo; 362 teachers, 18,927 students.

Konan University: Okamoto Motoyama-cho, Higashi Nada-ku, Kobe City; 174 teachers, 4,922 students.

Koyasan University: Koyasan, Ito-gun, Wakayama-ken; 31 teachers, 415 students.

Kurume University: 67 Asahi-machi, Kurume-shi, Fukuoka-ken, 334 teachers, 2,717 students.

Kwansei Gakuin University: Uegahara, Nishinomiya-shi, Hyogo-ken; 277 teachers, 13,273 students.

Kyoto Women's University: 17 Kita Hiyoshi-cho, Imakumano, Higashiyama-ku, Kyoto; 115 teachers, 2,187 students.

Kyoto College of Pharmacy: 5-Nakauchi-cho, Misasagi Yamashina Higashiyama-ku Kyoto; 29 teachers, 990 students.

Matsuyama University College of Commerce: Bunkyo-cho, Matsyama 790; 103 teachers, 3,550 students.

Meiji University: Kanda-Surugadai 1-1, Chiyoda-ku, Tokyo-To; 538 teachers, 31,743 students.

Meiji Gakuin University: 1-2-37 Shirokanedai, Minato-ku, Tokyo; 145 full-time, 220 part-time teachers, 8,500 day-time, 3,500 evening-time students.

Meijo University: Yagoto-Urayama, Tenpaku Showa-ku, Nagoya; 470 teachers, 18,000 students.

Miyagi Women's College: 166 Higashi San-Bancho, Sendai-shi, Miyagi-ken; 129 teachers, 1,350 students.

Nanzan University: 18 Yamazato-cho, Showa-ku, Nagoya 466; 140 teachers, 4,108 students.

Nihon University: 2-chome, Nishi-Kanda, Chiyoda-ku, Tokyo City; 3,077 teachers, 71,933 students.

Nippon Dental College: 9-20 1-chome, Fujimi, Chiyoda-ku, Tokyo; 266 teachers, 1,665 students.

Notre Dame Women's College: 1-2 Minami Nonogami-cho, Shimogamo, Sakyo-ku, Kyoto; 25 full-time, 55 part-time, teachers, 719 students.

Rikkyo University: Nishi-Ikebukuro, Toshima-ku, Tokyo; 683 teachers, 11,625 students.

Rissho University: 160 4-chome, Higashi-Osaki, Shinagawa-ku, Tokyo; 98 teachers, 3,536 students.

Ritsumeikan University: Kyoto-shi, Kamikyo-ku, Hirokoji-dori Termachi; 289 teachers, 21,160 students.

Ryukoku University: Nanajo-Omiya, Shimogyo-ku, Kyoto; 200 teachers, 4,298 students.

University of the Sacred Heart: Hiroo 4-chome, 3-1 Shibuya-ku, Tokyo; 160 teachers, 1,367 students.

Saitama University: 255 Shimo Okubo Urawa City; 385 teachers, 4,640 students.

Science University of Tokyo: 1-3 Kagurazaka, Shinjuku-ku, Tokyo; 226 teachers, 8,294 students.

Seijo University: 6-1-20 Seijo, Setagaya-ku, Tokyo; 110 full-time, 120 part-time teachers, 3,222 students.

Seisen Women's College: 3-chome, 16 Ban 21 Go, Higashi-Gotanda Shinagawa-ku, Tokyo; 95 teachers, 1,140 students.

Senshu University: Chiyoda-ku Kanda Jinbo-cho, Tokyo-to; 153 teachers, 11,624 students.

Showa Women's University: 1-chome, Taishido, Setagaya-ku, Tokyo; 110 teachers, 1,981 students.

Sophia University: Chiyoda-ku, Kioicho 7, Tokyo; 757 professors, 8,947 students.

Takachiho College of Commerce: 2-19-1 Ohmiya Suginami-ku, Tokyo; 53 teachers, 1,710 students.

Takushoku University: 14-4-3 Kohinata Bunkyo-ku, Tokyo; 214 teachers, 7,514 students.

Tamagawa University: 6-1-1 Tamagawa Gukuen Machida-shi, Tokyo; 832 teachers, 4,596 full-time students.

Tenri University: 1050 Somanouchi-cho Tenri City, Nara; 244 teachers, 1,795 students.

Tohoku Gakuin University: 1 Minami-Rokken-Cho, Sendai; 193 teachers, 8,761 students.

Tokai University: 2-28 Tomigaya, Shibuya-ku, Tokyo; 244 teachers, 9,458 students.

Tokyo College of Economics: 7-1 chome, Minamicho, Kokubunji, Tokyo 185; 200 teachers, 8,000 students.

Tokyo College of Pharmacy: 600 Kashiwagi 4-chome, Shinjuku-ku, Tokyo; 168 teachers, 3,076 students.

Tokyo Women's Medical College: 10 Kawada-cho Shinjuku-ku, Tokyo; 441 teachers, 594 students.

Toyo University: 17 Haramachi, Bunkyo-ku, Tokyo; 201 full-time teachers, 20,224 students.

Tsuda-Juku Women's College: 11491 Tsuda-Machi, Kodaira City, Tokyo; 60 teachers, 1,400 students.

Waseda University: Totsuka-Machi, Shinjuku-ku, Tokyo; 2,037 teachers, 42,780 students.

TECHNOLOGICAL UNIVERSITIES

Akita University: Tegata Fukada, Akita.

Chubu Institute of Technology: 1200 Matsumoto-cho, Kasugai-shi Aichi Prefecture; 144 teachers, 4,060 students.

Ehime University: 3 Bunkyo-cho, Matsuyama.

Fukui University: Makinoshima-cho, Fukui.

Gifu University: Monzen-cho, Naka-cho, Inaba-gun, Gifu-Ken.

Himeji Institute of Technology: Idei Himeji, Hyogo; 133 full-time, 28 part-time teachers, 1,071 students.

Iwate University: 3-18-8 Ueda, Morioka, Iwate; 291 teachers, 3,366 students.

Kobe University of Mercantile Marine: Fukae, Honjo-cho, Higashimada-ku, Kobe.

Kyoto University of Industrial Arts and Textile Fibres: Matsugasaki-Hashigamicho, Sakyo-ku, Kyoto.

Kyushu Institute of Technology: 752 Nakabaru, Tobata, Kitakyushu; 97 teachers, 1,954 students.

Miyazaki University: 100 Funatsuka-cho, Miyazaki; 299 teachers, 2,311 students.

Muroran Institute of Technology: 17 Mizumoto-cho, Muroran.

Nagoya Institute of Technology: Gokisho-cho, Showa-ku, Nagoya.

Sagami Institute of Technology: 1-1 Nishi Kaigan Tsujido, Fujisawa City; 200 teachers, 1,500 students.

Tokyo Electrical Engineering College: Kanda-Nishikicho, Chiyoda-ku, Tokyo; 500 teachers, 7,000 students.

Tokyo University of Agriculture: 1-1-1 Sakuragaoka, Setagaya-ku, Tokyo; 470 teachers, 7,953 students.

Tokyo University of Agriculture and Technology: 1-8 Harumi-cho, 3-chome, Fucho-shi, Tokyo.

Tokyo Institute of Technology: 1 Ookayama, Meguro-ku, Tokyo; 734 teachers, 4,315 students.

Tokyo University of Fisheries: Konan 4-5-7, Minato-ku; Tokyo.

Tokyo University of Mercantile Marine: Echujima 2-1-6 Fukagawa Koto-ku, Tokyo; 70 full-time teachers, 834 students.

University of Telecommunications: 14 Kojima-cho, Chofu, Tokyo; 104 full-time teachers, 1,950 students.

RYUKYU ISLANDS

The Ryukyu Islands extend in an arc from Kyushu, the southernmost of the four major islands of Japan, towards the northeastern shores of Taiwan.

Following the defeat of Japan in 1945 the Ryukyus south of latitude 30° N. were occupied by the United States. In 1953, the Amami and Tokara groups, which belong to the northern Ryukyus, were returned to Japan and incorporated into Kagoshima prefecture. The United States remained in occupation of Okinawa and the surrounding islands in the southern Ryukyus until May 1972, when the islands reverted to Japan and formed Okinawa prefecture. The United States still had 77 military bases on the prefecture in February 1974, but had agreed to return 32 of these.

STATISTICS

Area (sq. miles): Total 848, Okinawa group 544 (Okinawa Island 454); Miyako group 85, Yaeyama group 219.

Population (October 1970): Total 945,111; Okinawa group 839,787; Miyako group 60,953; Yaeyama group 44,371; Naha (capital—on Okinawa Island) 276,390; Births (1970) 21,038; Deaths (1970) 5,173.

Employment (1970): Agriculture, Forestry and Fishing 104,000; Other Industries 285,000.

Agriculture (1970—metric tons): Rice 10,941; Sugar Cane (1970–71) 1,982,189; Pineapple (1970–71) 66,852; Sweet Potatoes (1970) 114,338; Tea (1970) 194; Tobacco (1970—dried weight measure) 524.

Livestock (December 1970): Beef Cattle 27,572; Dairy Cattle 2,678; Horses 7,609; Hogs 249,811; Goats 27,483; Chickens 2,015,861.

Fisheries (1970—metric tons): Total 36,094 (Tuna 10,286; Skipjack 9,781; Swordfish 2,777; Other 13,250).

Industry (1970–71): Sugar 229,309 metric tons; Pineapple 1,458,581 cases.

Currency: The Japanese yen is now the legal currency.

Budget (1971): *Government of the Ryukyu Islands (GRI): Revenue:* $263,633,584 (Taxes $104,243,200, U.S. Grant-in-Aid $8,850,000;* Japanese Grant-in-Aid $116,380,782;* Other Sources $34,159,602). *Expenditure:* $199,170,000 (Education $57,770,000; Health and Welfare $34,123,000; Economic Development $14,052,000; Public Works and Services $32,746,000; Public Safety $11,209,000; Other Government Operations $44,370,000; Loan Repayment and Interest $4,900,000).

U.S. Civil Administration of the Ryukyu Islands (USCAR): Expenditure: (1971) Administration of the Ryukyu Islands, Army Appropriation $7,146,000; Administrative Activities $3,301,000; Aid to the Ryukyuan Economy $3,845,000; (1970) U.S. Grants to GRI $15,310,000; USCAR-Administered Programmes $2,185,000.

External Trade (1971—$'000): *Total Imports:* 559,459; Beverage and Tobacco Products 8,393; Food 80,286; Raw Materials 90,330; Machinery and Equipment 138,798; Building Materials 77,536; Others 164,116. *Total Exports:* 118,369; Agricultural and Forestry Products 945; Marine Products 4,070; Sugar Products 50,896; Processed Pineapple Products 12,334; Livestock Products 4,338; Other Manufactured Products 14,258; Metal Scrap 3,333; Used Machinery 7,605; Other 20,590.

    * Includes appropriations from the USCAR General Fund.

Roads (December 1970): Total Motor Vehicles 114,112 (not including official or privately owned U.S. Forces vehicles); Registered Passenger Carriers 52,374 (including buses), Registered Cargo Carriers 32,242, Registered Special Purpose Motor Vehicles 1,875, Registered Heavy Equipment 2,087, Registered Light Motor Vehicles 25,514.

Shipping (1970): Total tons of cargo handled 3,303,000, International 3,002,000 tons, Inter-Island 301,000 tons.

Education (April 1971): *Primary:* Schools 244, Teachers 4,907, Pupils 133,495; *Junior High:* Schools 152, Teachers 3,422, Students 71,882; *Senior High:* Schools 43, Teachers 2,905, Students 54,485; *Special:* Schools 6, Teachers 248, Students 946; *Universities and Junior Colleges:* 8, Teachers 347, Students 9,992 (May 1971).

THE GOVERNMENT

Governor of Okinawa Prefecture: Chobyo Yara.

Director-General of Okinawa Development Agency: Tokusaburo Kosaka.

RELIGION

The Ryukyu population is mainly Shinto or Buddhist. There are few Christians.

THE PRESS

Okinawa Times: P.O.B. 293, Naha, Okinawa; f. 1948; Japanese; morning and evening; Pres. Kazafumi Uechi; Man. Editor Seiko Higa; total circ. 132,500.

Ryukyu Shimpo: P.O.B. 15, Naha, Okinawa; f. 1893; Japanese; morning and evening; Pres. Shui Ikemiyagi; Editor S. Hokama; circ. 90,548.

Morning Star: P.O.B. 282, Naha, Okinawa; English; Editor Robert Prosser; circ. 15,000.

Six papers circulate in Miyako and Yaeyama Islands, with a circulation of about 13,000.

NEWS AGENCIES

Foreign Bureaux

The Jiji Press and the Kyodo News Service have offices in Naha.

PUBLISHERS

Okinawa Times: P.O.B. 293, Naha, Okinawa; f. 1948; publishers of Okinawa Year Book (Japanese language) and others related to the Ryukyu Islands.

Ryukyu Shimpo: P.O.B. 15, Naha, Okinawa; books dealing with the Ryukyu Islands.

RADIO AND TELEVISION

RADIO

Ryukyu Broadcasting Corporation: C.P.O. Box 4, Naha, Okinawa; two sound stations: one Japanese-speaking (KSAR), one English-speaking (KSBK); Pres. SEITOKU ZAYASU.

Kyokto Hoso Zaidan Hojin: C.P.O. Box 55, Naha, Okinawa-ken; commercial and religious broadcasts in Japanese (JOTF); Dir. KANZO TOKUYAMA.

Radio Okinawa Co. Ltd.: P.O.B. 405, Naha, Okinawa; broadcasts in Japanese (KSDT); Pres. JUGO TOMA.

Voice of America Station in Okinawa: Okinawa; relays broadcasts in English, Chinese and Korean.

In 1971 there were an estimated 339,000 radio sets.

TELEVISION

Okinawa Hoso Kyokai (*Okinawa Public Broadcasting System*): Service Center 342, Sobe, Naha, Okinawa; televises in Japanese; Pres. CHOSEI KABIRA; Vice-Pres. HISAO TANIGUCHI; Programme Dir. YUKINORI YOSHIDA; Business Man. MASAHARU MINEI; Chief Engineer NOBORU SHIMOJI; Auditor SHIZEN SAKUMOTO.

Okinawa Central Broadcasting Station (*KSGB-TV*): 1019 Takayasu Tomigusuku-Son, Okinawa; transmitter output power 5 kW. (Video) Japan-2ch.

Miyako Broadcasting Station (*KSDY*): Sodeyama, Higashinakasone, Hirara City; transmitter output power 1 kW. (Video) U.S.-9ch.

Yaeyama Broadcasting Station (*KSGA*): Akao, Tonoshiro, Ishigaki City; transmitter output power 1 kW. (Video) U.S.-11ch.

Other relay stations: Kabira Station (500 W.) at Ishigaki City; Sonai Station (100 W.) at Iriomote-shimai Yonaguni Station (10 W.) at Yonaguni-shima.

Okinawa Television Broadcasting Co. Ltd.: 1-chome, Matsuyama-cho, Naha, Okinawa; televises in Japanese (KSDW-TV); Pres. Y. YAMASHIRO; Man. Dir. N. KAMESHIMA.

Ryukyu Broadcasting Corporation Ltd.: P.O.B. 4, Naha, Okinawa; televises in Japanese (KSAR-TV); Pres. SEITOKU ZAYASU.

Far East Network (AFRTS): Okinawa; televises programmes for the U.S. forces and dependent personnel.

In 1971 there were an estimated 250,000 television sets.

FINANCE

(cap.=capital; dep.=deposits; m.=million; amounts in U.S. $)

BANKING

GOVERNMENT BANKS

Central Bank for Agriculture, Forestry and Fisheries Co-operatives: 182-1 Matsuo, Naha, Okinawa; cap. 11.4m.; dep. 20.8m. (June 1969); Pres. GENPEI OSHIRO.

Okinawa Development Finance Corporation: Kokuba Bldg., 21-1, 3-chome, Kumoji, Naha; f. 1972; cap. 24,544m. yen (May 1972); Pres. HIROSHI SATAKE.

COMMERCIAL BANKS

Bank of the Ryukyus Ltd.: 1-13 Kumoji 1-chome, Naha, Okinawa; f. 1948; cap. 1,126m.; dep. 177.2m. (Sept. 1973); Pres. SHUEI SAKIHAMA.

Bank of Okinawa: 1-42 Miebashi, Naha, Okinawa; cap. 1.3m.; dep. 99.5m. (June 1969); Pres. SEIKO KOHAGURA.

MUTUAL LOANS AND SAVINGS BANKS

Chuo Sogo Bank: 2-8 Kumoji, Naha, Okinawa; f. 1964 by merger of *Daiichi Sogo* and *Okinawa Sogo*; cap. 19.3m.; dep. 81.8m. (Dec. 1971); Pres. CHOKO NAKAYOSHI.

Nanyo Sogo Bank: 131-4, 2-chome, Naha, Okinawa; f. 1952; cap. 0.8m.; dep. 39.5m. (September 1970); Pres. KATSUO GIMA.

AMERICAN BANKS

Bank of America National Trust and Savings Association: San Francisco; 2-5-1 Higashimachi, C.P.O. Box 378, Naha, Okinawa; dep. 20.2m. (in Okinawa; Dec. 1972); Man. A. R. CAUDRON; branch in Koza, Okinawa.

American Express International Banking Corpn.: New York; 242 Yamazato, Koza, Okinawa; C.P.O. Box 189, Naha, Okinawa; dep. 33.3m. (in Okinawa; June 1969); Man. W. J. CARR.

INSURANCE

RYUKYUAN COMPANIES
(Naha, Okinawa)

Daido Fire and Marine Insurance Co. Ltd., The: 1-46 Kumoji-cho, Naha; P.O.B. 628; f. 1971; Pres. YUSHO UEZU.

Kyowa Fire and Marine Insurance: 1-46 Banchi, Kumoji-cho, Naha-City; f. 1963; Pres. YOSHO UEZU; Man. Dir. TEL KUDAKA; Exec. Dir. TAKASHI TOKUDA.

Okinawa Mutual Life Insurance Co.: 1-46 Kumoji; Pres. SEIKUN MAEDA.

Ryukyu Mutual Life Insurance Co.: 1-42 Miebashi, Naha; Pres. NOBORU KAKAZU.

There are also nine foreign insurance companies operating in the Ryukyu Islands.

TRADE AND INDUSTRY

CHAMBERS OF COMMERCE

American Chamber of Commerce in Okinawa: P.O.B. 77, Urasoe, Okinawa; Pres. DANIEL A. LOWELL.

Ryukyu Chamber of Commerce and Industry: 1-49 Kume-cho, Naha, Okinawa; Pres. KOTARO KOKUBA.

Okinawa Junior Chamber of Commerce: 468 Asato, Naha, Okinawa; Pres. HIROYOSHI HIGA.

INDUSTRIAL ORGANIZATIONS

Ryukyu Industrial Federation: 468 Asato, Naha, Okinawa; Pres. M. NAKADA.

Ryukyu Agricultural Co-operatives Federation: 284 Kohagura, Naha, Okinawa; 80 member Co-operatives (July 1969); Pres. YUKEN TOME.

Ryukyu Fisheries Co-operatives Federation: 2-211 Maejima-Cho, Naha, Okinawa; 41 member Co-operatives (Aug. 1969); Pres. KOZO TOKASHIKI.

Ryukyu Contractors Association: 1-35 Miebashi, Naha, Okinawa; 223 member contractors (Aug. 1969); Pres. KOTARO KOKUBA.

TRANSPORT

RAILWAYS

There are no railways.

ROADS

Buses and taxis provide the principal means of public transport. There are a number of companies on all the island groups.

SHIPPING

INTERNATIONAL LINES

There are 75 large and small ports in the Ryukyu Islands. The most important commercial ports are Naha Port and Tomari Port, both in Naha City. Naha Port was completed in 1955 and the wharf is 1,600 metres long.

American Mail Line: Local Agency: Everett Steamship Corpn., P.O.B. 91, Naha, Okinawa; Man. JOHN H. HAY.

American President Lines Ltd.: Agent: Connell Bros. & Co., P.O.B. 57, Naha, Okinawa; Man. J. E. KAY.

Everett Orient Line: Local Office: P.O.B. 91, Naha, Okinawa; Man. JOHN H. HAY.

Kansai Steamship Company: Local Agency: Okinawa Koun Co., 1-5, Nishi-Honmachi, Naha, Okinawa; Pres. YOSHIO FUKUZATO.

Osaka Shosen Mitsui Senpaku Kaisha: Local Agency: Daiwa Koun Company, 3-44, Nishi-Shinmachi, Naha, Okinawa; Pres. KOKICHI KOKUBA.

Nihonkai Kisen Kaisha: Local Agency: Okinawa Tsuun Co., 5-7, Nishi-Honmachi, Naha, Okinawa; Pres. KOKICHI KOKUBA.

Nippon Yusen Kaisha: Local Office: P.O.B. 281, 3-70, Nishi-Shinmachi, Naha, Okinawa; Pres. CHORYO ISHIMINE.

Okinawa Kisen Kaisha: Head Office: 2-226, Maejima-Cho, Naha, Okinawa; Pres. KOKICHI KOKUBA.

Pacific Far East Line: Local Agency: Connell Bros., P.O.B. 57, Naha, Okinawa; Man. J. E. KAY.

Ryukyu Kaiun Kaisha: Head Office: 1-5, 1 chome, Nisi Naha, Okinawa; Pres. MASHI AZAMA.

Ryukyu Unyu Company: Head Office: 1-1, Nishi-Honmachi, Naha, Okinawa; f. 1950; Pres. TADAYOSHI MIYARA.

C. F. Sharp and Co.: Local Office: P.O.B. 24, Naha, Okinawa; Man. H. M. FERNANDES.

States Steamship Co.: Local Agency: E. J. Griffith Transportation Dir., C.P.O. Box. 67, Naha, Okinawa; Man. M. S. KINGSBURY.

States Marine Lines: Local Agency: Okinawa Maritime Co., P.O.B. 429, Naha, Okinawa; Pres. CHENG KWAN HWA.

Talai Steamship Company: Local Office: P.O.B. 280, Naha, Okinawa; Man. HUNG CHIN SHING.

Western Pacific Line: Local Agency: Western Pacific Corporation, 173, Makiminato, Urasoe, Okinawa; Rep. DAVID J. O'ROURKE.

CIVIL AVIATION

Southwest Air Lines Co. Ltd.: 306-1 Aza Kagamizu, Naha, Okinawa; Japanese-Ryukyuan Corporation, providing inter-island air carrier service with the Ryukyu Islands; Pres. MASAO MASUMO.

The following foreign airlines serve the Ryukyu Islands: All Nippon Airways, Cathay Pacific Airways Ltd., China Airlines, Continental Airlines (Air Micronesia), Japan Air Lines, Northwest Orient Airlines, Trans World Airlines.

TOURISM

Okinawa Tourism Development Corporation: 117-3, Matsuo, Naha, Okinawa; f. January 1968; Pres. MORISADA TONAKI.

Okinawa Tourism Association: 1-49, Kume-Cho, Naha, Okinawa; f. 1953; Pres. H. TAKARA.

TOURIST SERVICE COMPANIES

Okinawa Tourist Service: 175 Aza-Matsuo, Naha, Okinawa; Pres. MIKE R. HIGASHI; Man. Dir. JOHN S. MIYAZATO.

Okinawa Travel Agency: 259-1 Matsuo, Naha, Okinawa; Pres. S. YAMAMOTO.

International Travel Service Co.: 159 Matsuo, Naha, Okinawa; Pres. YOSHIAKI YOZA.

Johnny Tours: Head Office: Tamaki Bldg., 1-10, Matsuyama-cho, Naha, Okinawa; Kadena Office: 53 Hamakawa, Chathan-son, Okinawa; Pres. J. N. TAKAGI.

UNIVERSITIES

Kokusai University: Yamazato, Koza, Okinawa; 35 teachers, 1,914 students.

Okinawa University: Kokuba, Naha, Okinawa; 27 teachers, 2,835 students.

University of the Ryukyus: 1, 2-chome, Tonokura-cho, Naha, Okinawa; 290 teachers, 3,768 students.

JORDAN

INTRODUCTORY SURVEY

Location, Climate, Language, Religion, Flag, Capital

Jordan is an almost landlocked state in the Middle East, Israel separating it from the Mediterranean with Syria to the north, Iraq to the east and Saudi Arabia to the south. The port of Aqaba in the far south gives Jordan a narrow outlet to the Red Sea. The climate is hot and dry. The average temperature is 15.5°c (60°F) but the winters can be cold. The official language is Arabic. Over 90 per cent of the population are Sunni Muslims and there are small communities of Christians and Shi'ite Muslims. The national flag (proportions 2 by 1) is a horizontal tricolour of black, white and green, with a red triangle, containing a seven-pointed white star, at the hoist. The capital is Amman.

Recent History

After the 1948 Armistice between Israel and the Arab States Jordan gained territory west of the River Jordan and the country changed its name from Trans-Jordan to the Hashemite Kingdom of Jordan. In April 1965, by special decree, King Hussein proclaimed his brother Prince Hassan Crown Prince, passing over his own son. The war with Israel in June 1967 left Israel in possession of all the Jordanian territory on the West Bank of the Jordan. The Old City of Jerusalem has now been incorporated into Israel; the rest of the conquered area has the status of an Israeli "occupied territory". Many refugees are still housed in camps on the East Bank. Jordan used to be a base for several Palestine guerrilla organizations in their raids on the occupied territories. The strength of these organizations frequently constituted a challenge to the government's authority as well as to Israel; the latter responded with frequent attacks on suspected commando camps on the East Bank. The conflict between the Government and the guerrilla groups developed into civil war in 1970, and the Government finally overcame the guerrilla forces in July 1971. Since then King Hussein has resolutely refused to allow guerrilla activity from Jordan, although in September 1973 he issued an amnesty which released over 700 guerrilla prisoners.

In March 1972 King Hussein announced plans for a United Arab Kingdom, in which a Palestinian region (capital Jerusalem) would be federated with the Jordanian region, whose capital, Amman, would also be the federal capital. Israel, Palestinian organizations and Arab governments all reacted unfavourably to the plans, and Egypt broke off diplomatic relations, which were not restored until September 1973, when King Hussein became reconciled with President Sadat of Egypt and President Assad of Syria.

Jordanian troops fought on the Syrian front in the October 1973 war between the Arabs and Israel. In 1974 King Hussein announced his willingness to recognize the Palestinian Liberation Organization as the sole legitimate representative of the Palestinian people at peace talks, and is ready to agree to the eventual establishment of an independent Palestinian State on the West Bank of the Jordan.

Government

Jordan is a constitutional Monarchy. The King is head of the state and appoints the Prime Minister. There is a bi-cameral Legislature. The Senate is appointed by the King. The House of Deputies is elected.

Defence

The total strength of the Jordanian armed forces is 72,850. The army consists of 66,000 men and its equipment includes U.S. and British tanks. There is a large para-military force of 22,000 consisting of a Civil Militia of 15,000 and a Public Security Force of 7,000. The two-year period of military service is now voluntary.

Economic Affairs

The loss of Jerusalem and the West Bank in 1967 completely transformed Jordan's economic position, which had been improving rapidly. Almost half the population lived in areas now occupied by Israel, which also contained the most fertile land (25 per cent of Jordan's cultivable area), the bulk of the small industrial sector and nearly all the historic and biblical places of interest to tourists; the latter had provided most of the country's foreign exchange earnings. Jordan also has more than 700,000 Arab refugees on her territory, and her lack of natural resources forces her to rely heavily on foreign aid, which in recent years has been coming increasingly from oil-rich Arab governments, and from Iran. Phosphates are the country's biggest natural resource, production of which was 560,000 tons in the first six months of 1973.

King Hussein announced a three-year development scheme (costing J.D. 179 million, and to run from 1973 to 1975) in November 1972. 300 projects would be completed in the East Bank, and it was hoped that Arab countries and international agencies would participate.

Transport and Communications

Jordan has one railway but most traffic runs along the excellent roads. Parts of the desert can be traversed safely by vehicles except after heavy rain. The port of Aqaba in the far south is Jordan's only outlet to the sea and civil aviation is of increasing importance. Two oil pipelines cross Jordan, the Trans-Arabian Pipeline (TAPLINE) running from Saudi Arabia to the Lebanon and the Iraq to Israel (Haifa) line, which has not been used since 1947. Pack transport is still used by nomads.

Social Welfare

There is no comprehensive welfare scheme but the Government runs medical and health services. There are now some 700,000 Arab refugees in Jordan. Refugees from the pre-1967 State of Israel are under the care of the United Nations Relief and Works Agency for Palestine Refugees in the Near East (UNRWA); those from East Jerusalem and the occupied West Bank are provided for by the Jordan government.

Education

Primary education is free and, where possible, compulsory. It starts at six to eight and lasts for six years. A further three-year period, known as the preparatory cycle, is also compulsory. UNRWA provides schooling for the Palestinian refugees. Jordan's first university was inaugurated in December 1962.

Tourism

Visas are required by nationals of all countries except Arab countries.

Sport

There is little organized sport. Car racing, horse racing and hawking are popular. Water skiing takes place at Aqaba.

Public Holidays

1974: August 11th (King Hussein's Accession), August 14th (Ascension of the Prophet), October 16th (Id ul Fitr), November 14th (King Hussein's Birthday), December 26th (Id ul Adha).

1975: January 14th (Muslim New Year), January 15th (Arbor Day), March 22nd (Arab League Day), March 26th (Birthday of the Prophet), May 25th (Independence Day).

Weights and Measures

The metric system is in force.
4 dunums = 1 acre (approx.).

Currency and Exchange Rates

1,000 fils = 1 Jordanian dinar (J.D.).
Exchange rates (April 1974):
£1 sterling = 758.97 fils;
U.S. $1 = 321.43 fils.

STATISTICAL SURVEY

AREA AND POPULATION

Total Area	Arable Land	Pastures	Forest	Population (1972 est.)
94,500 sq. km.	10,695 sq. km.	75,000 sq. km.	1,250 sq. km.	2,497,000

Amman (capital) (1972 est.): 560,000.

1972: Births 80,327, Deaths 6,261, Marriages 11,039.

AGRICULTURE
PRINCIPAL CROPS

	Area ('ooo dunums)			Production ('ooo metric tons)		
	1970	1971	1972	1970	1971	1972
Barley	408.5	524.5	605.6	5.3	26.2	34.0
Maize	3.4	2.8	2.5	0.1	0.8	0.3
Sesame	6.4	11.1	12.5	0.2	0.2	0.3
Wheat	2,228.4	2,438.6	2,236.7	54.1	168.2	211.4
Broad Beans	7.3	2.3	2.7	n.a.	0.1	0.1
Chick Peas	12.8	7.1	30.9	0.3	0.6	2.0
Kersenneh	82.8	69.1	71.0	2.5	5.3	6.8
Lentils	205.8	205.3	284.1	5.0	20.8	22.4

FRUIT AND VEGETABLES
('ooo metric tons)

	1970	1971	1972		1970	1971	1972
Almonds . . .	0.5	1.2	1.0	Tomatoes . . .	137.4	147.6	152.7
Apples and Pears .	0.5	0.6	2.9	Eggplants . . .	23.1	50.2	32.5
Apricots . . .	—	0.3	0.4	Onions and Garlic . .	3.3	1.5	0.7
Citrus Fruits . .	3.8	9.3	20.9	Cauliflowers and Cabbages	10.9	5.4	13.2
Figs . . .	3.0	2.9	2.2	Watermelons and Melons.	22.5	28.0	63.0
Bananas . . .	8.2	4.2	6.7	Potatoes . . .	2.1	0.4	0.9
Plums and Peaches .	0.5	0.3	0.1	Broadbeans (green) . .	5.1	4.2	5.1
				Cucumbers . . .	6.8	10.2	17.7

LIVESTOCK
('ooo)

	1970	1971	1972
Camels . . .	9.5	17.3	16.1
Cattle . . .	32.1	38.8	45.9
Sheep and Goats . .	1,013.7	1,051.9	1,128.2

FORESTRY

	1969	1970
Area newly planted ('ooo dunums)	1,936	1,949
Timber production (cu. metres) .	1,666	1,392

FISHING

	1970	1971	1972
Quantity of fish landed at Aqaba and on Jordan and Yarmuk rivers (tons) .	122.5	152.4	134.8

INDUSTRY
('ooo tons)

	1969	1970	1971	1972
Phosphates . . .	1,089.0	912.7	651.1	714.9
Cement . . .	480.6	377.5	418.9	661.6
Alcohol ('ooo litres) .	260.8	228.3	192.6	208.2
Beer ('ooo litres) .	n.a.	n.a.	1,734.7	1,753.4
Tobacco (Kg.) . .	9,634	8,294	8,224.0	7,517.0
Cigarettes (Kg.) . .	1,818,062	1,609,827	1,533,291.0	1,511,336.0
Electricity (million kWh.)	199.8	187.4	210.1	n.a.

FINANCE

1,000 fils=1 Jordanian dinar (J.D.).

Coins: 1, 5, 10, 20, 25, 50, 100 and 250 fils.

Notes: 500 fils; 1, 5 and 10 dinars.

Exchange rates (April 1974): £1 sterling=758.97 fils (central rate); U.S. $1=321.43 fils (central rate) or 329 fils (trade rate).

100 Jordanian dinars=£131.76=$311.11 (central rates).

BUDGET 1970
(J.D. '000)

REVENUE		EXPENDITURE	
Internal Revenue . . .	30,260	Defence and Police . . .	37,860
Foreign Grants	37,481	Administration	14,189
Foreign Borrowing . . .	4,459	Social Services	10,158
Internal Borrowing . . .	4,200	Economic Services. . .	14,578
Loans Repaid	—	Transport and Communications .	4,975
TOTAL	76,400	TOTAL	81,760

1972 Budget: Balanced at J.D. 124.8 million.

1973 Budget: Balanced at J.D. 148.6 million.

1974 Budget: Revenue J.D. 153.1 million; Expenditure J.D. 165.7 million.

NATIONAL ACCOUNTS
(million J.D.)

	1970	1971	1972
GROSS DOMESTIC PRODUCT (at factor cost) .	189.56	202.58	217.00

DEVELOPMENT EXPENDITURE ESTIMATES
1973–75
(million J.D.)

Agriculture	13.020
Irrigation	14.636
Mining and Industry . . .	26.120
Tourism and Antiquities . .	7.170
Electricity	9.781
Transportation	35.812
Communications	6.712
Trade	0.775
Education	10.914
Public Health	1.480
Social Welfare and Labour . .	1.455
Housing and Government Buildings .	34.890
Municipal and Village Affairs . .	14.758
Miscellaneous	1.477
TOTAL	179.000

Source: National Planning Council.

EXTERNAL TRADE

('ooo J.D.)

	1968	1969	1970	1971	1972
IMPORTS	55,048	67,700	65,882	76,627	95,310
EXPORTS	11,327	14,700	12,170	11,440	17,005

COMMODITIES

('ooo J.D.)

IMPORTS	1970	1971	1972	EXPORTS	1970	1971	1972
Animals and Products .	4,538.4	4,139.1	5,574.8	Phosphates . . .	2,236.7	2,238.8	3,497.1
Grains and Legumes .	6,162.0	4,029.5	4,580.6	Tomatoes . . .	1,569.7	1,183.3	724.3
Vegetables . .	1,092.2	914.8	719.5	Lentils . . .	537.0	335.2	918.8
Fruits . . .	1,912.6	2,778.4	2,552.4	Water Melons . .	75.4	28.2	38.5
Spices . . .	1,692.0	2,094.2	1,858.4	Other vegetables and fruit .	1,833.5	1,435.0	2,145.0
Other Agriculture .	55.6	1,798.3	2,248.5	Cigarettes . . .	519.1	367.9	397.7
Forestry Products .	1,344.1	491.2	837.7	Bananas . . .	147.8	78.5	105.9
Mining and Quarrying .	454.8	4,271.8	4,973.9	Raw Hides and Skins .	166.2	66.2	130.1
Food Manufactures .	3,626.5	7,289.3	12,675.2	Electric Accumulators .	303.7	332.6	432.7
Textiles . .	4,864.5	6,186.4	8,081.1	Olive Oil and Prepared			
Clothing . .	2,309.4	1,659.5	1,762.4	Olives . . .	210.9	392.9	376.2
Wood and Cork .	51.0	553.4	564.9				
Paper and Products .	1,227.5	1,070.5	1,902.3				
Printing and Publishing .	175.2	415.4	406.1				
Rubber and Products .	863.4	766.6	1,137.0				
Chemical Products .	2,171.7	3,982.4	6,089.5				
Petroleum (refined) .	1,132.6	719.5	1,193.0				
Non-Metallic Minerals .	595.1	1,292.5	1,401.2				
Metallic Minerals . .	5,807.9	3,741.4	7,300.6				
Non-Electric Machines .	4,264.0	2,891.6	4,988.5				
Electric Machines .	2,186.5	2,181.2	3,989.4				
Transport Equipment .	4,502.9	11,418.6	6,473.7				

COUNTRIES

IMPORTS	1970	1971	1972	EXPORTS	1970	1971	1972
United Kingdom . .	8,815.9	6,783.0	8,645.2	Kuwait . . .	1,318.4	1,334.9	1,685.2
U.S.A. . . .	7,380.5	18,133.0	16,887.3	Iraq . . .	1,312.3	747.0	1,504.9
Germany, Fed. Repub. .	5,911.5	4,524.6	8,693.3	Lebanon . . .	1,433.8	964.4	1,529.8
Lebanon . .	4,409.1	5,319.3	5,045.5	Saudi Arabia . .	1,578.9	1,535.9	2,140.5
Japan . . .	3,868.7	4,190.9	4,598.0	India . . .	252.8	956.5	1,404.9
Syria . . .	3,191.9	2,313.9	4,143.7	Syria . . .	1,477.5	1,496.1	1,611.9
Saudi Arabia . .	2,543.1	4,172.5	3,379.0	Yugoslavia . .	787.6	463.3	201.2
Italy . . .	2,235.4	1,824.0	2,677.6	Turkey . . .	359.6	166.2	247.5
China, People's Repub. .	1,496.7	1,555.6	1,997.2	China . . .	201.4	—	—
France . . .	1,648.0	2,333.3	2,284.3	Czechoslovakia .	193.4	122.6	210.6
U.S.S.R. . .	2,342.1	996.6	1,117.4				
Netherlands . .	1,271.7	1,635.5	2,441.9				
Egypt . . .	2,052.1	3,651.6	2,446.1				
India . . .	1,634.7	1,071.4	1,396.5				
Romania . .	1,386.8	745.2	1,886.5				

TRANSPORT

RAILWAYS

	1970	1971	1972
Passengers carried .	16,757	16,450	n.a.
Freight carried (tons) .	77,547	55,111	56,305

ROADS

	1970	1971	1972
Cars (private) . .	10,059	10,356	11,173
Taxis . . .	3,509	4,391	4,785
Buses . .	501	504	470
Lorries and Vans .	5,110	5,387	5,243
TOTAL (with others) .	22,743	24,220	24,320

SHIPPING
(Aqaba port)

	1970	1971	1972
Number of vessels calling .	220	254	327
Freight loaded ('ooo tons) .	186.3	387.2	704.9
Freight unloaded ('ooo tons)	195.6	278.1	518.6

CIVIL AVIATION
('ooo)

	1969	1970	1971
Passengers . .	121,300	119,400	125,900
Freight (tons) . .	1,164.1	1,132.2	1,622.6

TOURISM

	1970	1971	1972
Visitors to Jordan .	321,657	256,775	292,041

COMMUNICATIONS MEDIA

Number of telephones (1971) . .	19,150
Number of radio sets (1969) . .	150,000
Number of cinemas (1972) . .	32

EDUCATION

	SCHOOLS AND UNIVERSITIES (East Bank)	TEACHERS (East Bank)	PUPILS (East and West Bank)
1970-71 .	1,531	11,947	611,735
1971-72 .	1,712	13,136	630,235

Source: Department of Statistics, Amman.

THE CONSTITUTION

(Revised Constitution approved by King Talal I on January 1st, 1952)

THE Hashemite Kingdom of Jordan is an independent, indivisible sovereign state. Its official religion is Islam; its official language Arabic.

Rights of the Individual. There is to be no discrimination between Jordanians on account of race, religion or language. Work, education and equal opportunities shall be afforded to all as far as is possible. The freedom of the individual is guaranteed, as are his dwelling and property. No Jordanian shall be exiled. Labour shall be made compulsory only in a national emergency, or as a result of a conviction; conditions, hours worked and allowances are under the protection of the State.

The Press, and all opinions, are free, except under martial law. Societies can be formed, within the law. Schools may be established freely, but they must follow a recognized curriculum and educational policy. Elementary education is free and compulsory. All religions are tolerated. Every Jordanian is eligible to public office, and choices are to be made by merit only. Power belongs to the people.

The Legislative Power is vested in the National Assembly and the King. The National Assembly consists of two houses; the Senate and the House of Representatives.

The Senate. The number of Senators is one-half of the number of members of the House of Representatives. Senators must be unrelated to the King, over 40, and are chosen from present and past Prime Ministers and Ministers, past Ambassadors or Ministers Plenipotentiary, past Presidents of the House of Representatives, past Presidents and members of the Court of Cassation and of the Civil and Sharia Courts of Appeal, retired officers of the rank of General and above, former members of the House of Representatives who have been elected twice to that House, etc.... They may not hold public office. Senators are appointed for four years. They may be re-appointed. The President of the Senate is appointed for two years.

The House of Representatives. The members of the House of Representatives are elected by secret ballot in a general direct election and retain their mandate for four years. General elections take place during the four months preceding the end of the term. The President of the House is elected by secret ballot each year by the Representatives. Representatives must be Jordanians of over 30, they must have a clean record, no active business interests, and are debarred from public office. Close relatives of the King are not eligible. If the House of Representatives is dissolved, the new House shall assemble in extraordinary session not more than four months after the date of dissolution. The new House cannot be dissolved for the same reason as the last.

General Provisions for the National Assembly. The King summons the National Assembly to its ordinary session on November 1st each year. This date can be postponed by the King for two months, or he can dissolve the Assembly before the end of its three months' session. Alternatively, he can extend the session up to a total period of six months. Each session is opened by a speech from the throne.

Decisions in the House of Representatives and the Senate are made by a majority vote. The quorum is two-thirds of the total number of members in each House. When the voting concerns the Constitution, or confidence in the Council of Ministers, "the votes shall be taken by calling the members by name in a loud voice". Sessions are public, though secret sessions can be held at the request of the Government or of five members. Complete freedom of speech, within the rules of either House, is allowed.

The Prime Minister places proposals before the House of Representatives; if accepted there, they are referred to the Senate and finally sent to the King for confirmation. If one house rejects a law while the other accepts it, a joint session of the House of Representatives and the Senate is called, and a decision made by a two-thirds majority. If the King withholds his approval from a law, he returns it to the Assembly within six months with the reasons for his dissent; a joint session of the Houses then makes a decision, and if the law is accepted by this decision it is promulgated. The Budget is submitted to the National Assembly one month before the beginning of the financial year.

The King. The throne of the Hashemite Kingdom devolves by male descent in the dynasty of King Abdullah Ibn al Hussein. The King attains his majority on his eighteenth lunar year; if the throne is inherited by a minor, the powers of the King are exercised by a Regent or a Council of Regency. If the King, through illness or absence, cannot perform his duties, his powers are given to a Deputy, or to a Council of the Throne. This Deputy, or Council, may be appointed by *Iradas* (decrees) by the King, or, if he is incapable, by the Council of Ministers.

On his accession, the King takes the oath to respect and observe the provisions of the Constitution and to be loyal to the nation. As head of the State he is immune from all liability or responsibility. He approves laws and promulgates them. He declares war, concludes peace and signs treaties; treaties, however, must be approved by the National Assembly. The King is Commander-in-Chief of the Navy, the Army and the Air Force. He orders the holding of elections; convenes, inaugurates, adjourns and prorogues the House of Representatives. The Prime Minister is appointed by him, as are the President and members of the Senate. Military and civil ranks are also granted, or withdrawn, by the King. No death sentence is carried out until he has confirmed it.

The King exercises his jurisdiction by *Iradas*. These are signed by the Prime Minister and the Minister concerned, and the King places his signature above the others.

Ministers. The Council of Ministers consists of the Prime Minister, President of the Council, and of his Ministers. Ministers are forbidden to become members of any company, to receive a salary from any company, or to participate in any financial act of trade. The Council of Ministers is entrusted with the conduct of all affairs of State, internal and external. Oral or written orders of the King do not release Ministers from their responsibility.

The Council of Ministers is responsible to the House of Representatives for matters of general policy. Ministers may speak in either House, and, if they are members of one House, they may also vote in that House. Votes of confidence in the Council are cast in the House of Representatives, and decided by a two-thirds majority. If a vote of "no confidence" is returned, the Ministers are bound to resign. Every newly-formed Council of Ministers must present its programme to the House of Representatives and ask for a vote of confidence. The House of Representatives can impeach Ministers, as it impeaches its own members.

Titles. By an order of the Regency Council (August 1952) all titles, e.g. those of Pasha and Bey, have been abolished. All subjects are now addressed as Assayed.

In March 1972 King Hussein announced plans for a new federal constitution.

THE GOVERNMENT

HEAD OF STATE

King Hussein ibn Talal; proclaimed King by a decree of the Jordan Parliament on August 11th, 1952; crowned on May 2nd, 1953.

Chief of Royal Cabinet: Bahjat al-Talhouni.

Political Adviser to King: Abdel-Muneim Rifai.

CABINET

(*April* 1974)

Prime Minister, Minister of Foreign Affairs and Defence: Zaid al-Rifai.

Minister of Reconstruction and Development: Dr. Subhi Amin A'amr.

Minister of Culture and Information: Adnan Abu-Odeh.

Minister of Agriculture: Marwan El-homoud.

Minister of Islamic Affairs: Abdul Aziz Khayat.

Minister of Justice: Salim al-Masa'adeh.

Minister of Tourism and Antiquities: Ghaleb Barakat.

Minister of Public Works: Ahmad Shawbaki.

Minister of Supply: Sadeq As-shar.

Minister of Transport: Nadeem al-Zaru.

Minister of Education: Modar Badran.

Minister of Finance: Thuqan Hindawi.

Minister of Health: Fouad Keilani.

Minister of Interior: Ahmad Abdul-Kareem Tarawneh.

Minister of Communication: Muhieddin Husseini.

Minister of National Economy: Omar Nabulsi.

Minister of Social Affairs and Labour: Yusuf Thuhni.

Minister of Interior for Municipalities: Fouad Kakish.

Minister of State for Foreign Affairs: Zuhayr Mufti.

Minister of State for the Occupied Land: Taher Nashat Masri.

Minister of State for Cabinet Affairs: Marwan Doudeen.

ADMINISTRATIVE PROVINCES (LIWAS)

Province	Location
Ajlun . . .	Northern Jordan, between the River Yarmuk and Wadi Zerqa.
Balqa . . .	Between Wadi Zerqa and Wadi Mujib.
Kerak . . .	Between Wadi Mujib and the edge of the desert.
Ma'an . . .	Southern Jordan, including Aqaba on the Red Sea.
Nablus* . . .	Includes the towns of Tulkarm and Jenin.
Jerusalem Governorate* .	Includes Jerusalem, Ramallah, Jericho and Bethlehem.
Hebron* . . .	Central Jordan.
Amman Governorate .	Includes Amman and Zarka.

* Indicates a province which has been occupied by Israel since the war of June 1967.

DIPLOMATIC REPRESENTATION

EMBASSIES AND LEGATIONS ACCREDITED TO JORDAN

(E) Embassy; (L) Legation.

Afghanistan: Jeddah, Saudi Arabia.

Algeria: Amman (E); *Ambassador:* Abu as-Sami.

Argentina: Beirut, Lebanon.

Austria: Beirut, Lebanon.

Belgium: Beirut, Lebanon (E).

Brazil: Beirut Lebanon (E).

Bulgaria: Amman (E); *Ambassador:* (vacant).

Canada: Beirut, Lebanon (E).

Chad: Beirut, Lebanon (E).

Chile: Amman (E).

China (Taiwan): Amman; *Ambassador:* Shu-ming Wang.

Czechoslovakia: Amman; *Ambassador:* Dr. Karel Blazek.

Denmark: Beirut, Lebanon (E).

Egypt: Amman; *Ambassador:* Fathi Qandeel.

Finland: Beirut, Lebanon (E).

France: Amman; *Ambassador:* Le Marquis Jacques de Folin.

Germany, Federal Republic: Amman (E); *Ambassador:* Alois Schegl.

Greece: Damascus, Syria (L).

Guinea: Cairo, Egypt (E).

Haiti: Amman (E); *Ambassador:* Dr. Josef Younis.

Hungary: Damascus, Syria.

India: Amman; *Ambassador:* Dr. Amrik S. Mehta.

Indonesia: Jeddah, Saudi Arabia (E).

Iran: Amman; *Ambassador:* Fereidun Mouassaghi.

Iraq: Amman; *Ambassador:* Hashim Al-A'ni.

Italy: Amman (E); *Ambassador:* Dante Matacotta.

Japan: Beirut, Lebanon (E).

Korea, Republic: Ankara, Turkey.

Kuwait: Amman; *Ambassador:* Ahmed Gheyth Abdul-lah.

Lebanon: Amman (E); *Ambassador:* Abdel Rahman Sami Solh.

Malaysia: Jeddah, Saudi Arabia (E).

Morocco: Amman (E); *Ambassador:* Muhammad Tazi.

Nepal: Cairo, Egypt (E).

Netherlands: Beirut, Lebanon (E).

Nigeria: Jeddah, Saudi Arabia (E).

Norway: Cairo, Egypt (E).

Pakistan: Amman (E); *Ambassador:* Mahdi Masud.

Poland: Amman; *Ambassador:* Dr. Tadeusz Wujek.

Portugal: Beirut, Lebanon.

Qatar: Amman; *Ambassador:* Sheikh Hamad bin Mohammad.

Romania: Beirut, Lebanon (E).

Saudi Arabia: Amman (E); *Ambassador:* Sheikh Ahmed
al-Kuheimy.

Senegal: Cairo, Egypt.

Somalia: Jeddah, Saudi Arabia (E); *Ambassador:* Ahmad
Issa.

Spain: Amman (E); *Ambassador:* Don Juan Duran-
Loriga.

Sri Lanka: Cairo, Egypt (E).

Sweden: Beirut, Lebanon (E).

Switzerland: Amman; *Ambassador:* Pierre Dumont.

Tunisia: Amman; *Ambassador:* Salah Eddine Abdullah.

Turkey: Amman (E); *Ambassador:* Sahin Uzgören.

U.S.S.R.: Amman (E); *Ambassador:* Alexey Voronin.

United Arab Emirates: Amman; *Ambassador:* Dr. Faisal
bin Khalid al-Qasemi.

United Kingdom: Amman (E); *Ambassador:* Hugh
Balfour Paul.

U.S.A.: Amman (E); *Ambassador:* Thomas Pickering.

Venezuela: Beirut, Lebanon (L).

Viet-Nam, Republic: Ankara, Turkey.

Yugoslavia: Damascus, Syria (L).

PARLIAMENT

THE SENATE

(House of Notables)

President: Said al Mufti.

The Senate consists of 30 members, appointed by the King.

HOUSE OF REPRESENTATIVES

Speaker: Kamil Arikat.

Elections to the 60-seat House of Representatives took place in April 1967. There were no political parties.

POLITICAL PARTIES

Political parties were banned before the elections of July 1963. In September 1971 King Hussein announced the formation of a Jordanian National Union. This is the only political organization allowed and represents both East and West Banks. Communists, Marxists and "other advocates of imported ideologies" are ineligible for membership. In March 1972 the organization was renamed the Arab National Union. It is estimated that there are about 100,000 members.

Secretary-General: Jumaa Hamad.

JUDICIAL SYSTEM

With the exception of matters of purely personal nature concerning members of non-Muslim communities, the law of Jordan was based on Islamic Law for both civil and criminal matters. During the days of the Ottoman Empire, certain aspects of Continental law, especially French commercial law and civil and criminal procedure, were introduced. Due to British occupation of Palestine and Trans-Jordan from 1917 to 1948, the Palestine territory has adopted, either by statute or case law, much of the English common law. Since the annexation of the non-occupied part of Palestine and the formation of the Hashemite Kingdom of Jordan, there has been a continuous effort to unify the law. This process of unification is now virtually completed, with the promulgation of new laws to replace older laws on both sides of the River Jordan.

Court of Cassation. The Court of Cassation consists of seven judges, who sit in full panel for exceptionally important cases. In most appeals, however, only five members sit to hear the case. All cases involving amounts of more than J.D. 100 may be reviewed by this Court, as well as cases involving lesser amounts and cases which cannot be monetarily valued. However, for the latter types of cases, review is available only by leave of the

Court of Appeal, or, upon refusal by the Court of Appeal, by leave of the President of the Court of Cassation. In addition to these functions as final and Supreme Court of Appeal, the Court of Cassation also sits as High Court of Justice to hear applications in the nature of habeas corpus, mandamus and certiorari dealing with complaints of a citizen against abuse of governmental authority.

Courts of Appeal. There are two Courts of Appeal, each of which is composed of three judges, whether for hearing of appeals or for dealing with Magistrates' Courts judgments in chambers. Jurisdiction of the two Courts is geographical, with the Court for the Western Region sitting in Jerusalem (which has not sat since June 1967) and the Court for the Eastern Region sitting in Amman. The regions are separated by the River Jordan. Appellate review of the Courts of Appeal extends to judgments rendered in the Courts of First Instance, the Magistrates Courts, and Religious Courts.

Courts of First Instance. The Courts of First Instance are courts of general jurisdiction in all matters civil and criminal except those specifically allocated to the Magistrates' Courts. Three judges sit in all felony trials, while only two judges sit for misdemeanor and civil cases. Each of the seven Courts of First Instance also exercises appellate jurisdiction in cases involving judgments of less than J.D. 20 and fines of less than J.D. 10, rendered by the Magistrates' Courts.

Magistrates' Courts. There are fourteen Magistrates' Courts, which exercise jurisdiction in civil cases involving no more than J.D. 250 and in criminal cases involving maximum fines of J.D. 100 or maximum imprisonment of one year.

Religious Courts. There are two types of Religious Court: The Sharia Courts (Muslims); and the Ecclesiastical Courts (Eastern Orthodox, Greek Melkite, Roman Catholic and Protestant). Jurisdiction extends to personal (family) matters, such as marriage, divorce, alimony, inheritance, guardianship, wills, interdiction and, for the Muslim community, the constitution of Waqfs (Religious Endowments). When a dispute involves persons of different religious communities, the Civil Courts have jurisdiction in the matter unless the parties agree to submit to the jurisdiction of one or the other of the Religious Courts involved.

Each Sharia (Muslim) Court consists of one judge (Qadi), while most of the Ecclesiastical (Christian) Courts are normally composed of three judges, who are usually clerics. Sharia Courts apply the doctrines of Islamic Law, based on the Koran and the Hadith (Precepts of Muhammad), while the Ecclesiastical Courts base their law on various aspects of Canon Law. In the event of conflict between any two Religious Courts or between a Religious Court and a Civil Court, a Special Tribunal of three judges is appointed by the President of the Court of Cassation, to decide which court shall have jurisdiction. Upon the advice of experts on the law of the various communities, this Special Tribunal decides on the venue for the case at hand.

RELIGION

Over 80 per cent of the population are Sunni Muslims, and the king can trace unbroken descent from the Prophet Muhammad. There is a Christian minority, living mainly in the towns, and smaller numbers of non-Sunni Muslims.

Prominent religious leaders in Jordan are:

SHEIKH ABDULLAH GHOSHEH (Chief Justice and President of the Supreme Muslim Secular Council).

SHEIKH MOHAMMED FAL SHANKITI (Director of Sharia Courts).

SHEIKH ABDULLAH QALQILI (Mufti of the Hashemite Kingdom of Jordan).

THE PRESS

DAILIES

Al-Destour (*The Constitution*): P.O.B. 591, Amman; f. 1967; Arabic; publ. by the Jordan Press and Publishing Co.; circ. 14,000.

Al-Rai: Amman; government-controlled.

PERIODICALS

Amman al Masa'a: P.O.B. 522, Amman; f. 1961; Arabic; weekly; political and cultural; circ. 12–15,000; Editor ARAFAT HIGAZI.

Al Aqsa: Amman; armed forces magazine; weekly.

Huda El Islam: Amman; f. 1956; monthly; Islamic; scientific and literary; published by the Department of Islamic Affairs; Editor ABDULLAH KALKELI.

Huna Amman (*Amman Calling*): f. 1961; monthly; published by the Television Corporation; circ. 5,000.

Jordan: P.O.B. 224, Amman; f. 1969; published quarterly by Jordan Tourism Authority; circ. 5,000.

Military Magazine: Army Headquarters, Amman; f. 1955; quarterly; dealing with military and literary subjects; published by Armed Forces.

Official Gazette: Amman; f. 1923; weekly; circ. 8,000; published by the Jordan Government.

Rural Education Magazine: P.O.B. 226, Amman; f. 1958; published by Khadouri Agricultural College, Teachers' Training College at Beit Haninah and Teachers' Training College at Howwarah (jointly).

Sharia: P.O.B. 585, Amman; f. 1959; fortnightly; Islamic affairs; published by Sharia College; circ. 5,000.

Al Usra: Amman; Arabic; monthly; womens' magazine.

NEWS AGENCIES

Jordanian News Agency: Amman; Dir. (vacant).

FOREIGN NEWS BUREAUX

D.P.A. and Tass maintain bureaux in Amman.

PUBLISHERS

Jordan Press and Publishing Co. Ltd.: Amman; f. 1967 by owners of the former *al Manar* and *Falastin*; cap. J.D. 100,000, of which 25 per cent held by govt.; publishes *al-Destour*.

Other publishers in Amman include: *Dairat al-Ihsaat al-Amman, George N. Kawar, al-Matbaat al-Hashmiya* and *The National Press*.

RADIO AND TELEVISION

The Hashemite Jordan Broadcasting Service (H.B.S.): P.O.B. 909, Amman; f. 1959; station at Amman broadcasts daily 19½ hours in Arabic to the Arab World, 7 hours in English to Europe and 1 hour in Arabic to Europe; Dir.-Gen. MARWAN DUNIN.

Jordan Television Corporation: P.O.B. 1041, Amman; f. 1968; government station broadcasting for 48 hours weekly in Arabic and English; advertising accepted; Dir.-Gen. M. KAMAL.

Number of radio receivers: 155,000.
Number of TV receivers: 85,000 (East Bank only).

FINANCE

(cap. = capital; p.u. = paid up; dep. = deposits; m. = million; J.D. = Jordan dinars.)

BANKING

CENTRAL BANK

Central Bank of Jordan: P.O.B. 37, Amman; f. 1964; cap. J.D. 2m.; dep. 20.2m (1972); Gov. Dr. KHALIL SALIM; Deputy Gov. MUHAMMAD TOUKAN.

NATIONAL BANKS

Agricultural Bank: P.O.B. 77, Amman; f. 1970; government-owned credit institution; Dir.-Gen. M. O. QUR'AN.

Arab Bank Ltd.: King Faisal St., Amman, P.O.B. 68; f. 1930; cap. p.u. and reserves J.D. 16m.; dep. 185m.; total assets 280m. (September 1973); branches in several Arab countries, and in U.K.; affiliates and sister institutions in Germany, Switzerland, Luxembourg and Nigeria; Chair. ABDUL HAMEED SHOMAN.

Bank of Jordan Ltd.: P.O.B. 2140, Jabal Amman on 3rd Circle, Amman; f. 1960; cap. p.u. J.D. 533,360; dep. 7.1m. (December 1973); Chair. and Gen. Man. HUSNI SIDO AL-KURDI.

Cairo Amman Bank: P.O.B. 715, Shabsough St., Amman; f. 1960; cap. J.D. 750,000; dep. 14.1m. (1972); 7 brs.; Chair. JAWDAT SHASHA'A; Gen. Man. HAIDAR CHUKRI; associated with Banque du Caire, Cairo, and succeeded their Amman Branch.

Industrial Development Bank: Amman; f. 1965; cap. J.D. 3m. of which J.D. 1m. owned by the government.

Jordan National Bank S.A.: P.O.B. 1578, Amman; f. 1956; cap. p.u. J.D. 1m.; dep. J.D. 12.7m. (Dec. 1972); 7 brs. in Jordan, 3 brs. in Lebanon; Chair. and Gen. Man. H.E. SULEIMAN SUKKAR; Deputy Gen. Man. H.E. ABDUL-KADER TASH.

FOREIGN BANKS

British Bank of the Middle East: 20 Abchurch Lane, London, EC4N 7AY; Amman; f. 1889; Chair. C. E. LOOMBE, C.M.G.; Area Man. F. J. ROBBINS.

National and Grindlays Bank: 23 Fenchurch Street, London EC3M 3DD; Amman; acquired the Ottoman Bank interests in Jordan in 1969; brs. in Amman (7 brs.), Aqaba, Irbid (sub-branch in Northern Shouneh), Zerka (sub-branch in Russeifeh); Gen. Man. in Jordan J. C. HENDRY.

Rafidain Bank: Baghdad; Amman; f. 1941; Chair. and Gen. Man. ATTA AL-DHAHI.

INSURANCE

Al Chark Insurance Co.: P.O.B. 312, Prince Mohamad St., Amman.

Jordan Insurance Co. Ltd.: P.O.B. 279, King Hussein St., Amman; cap. p.u. J.D. 350,000; brs. in five Arab countries and the U.K.

Many of the larger British and American insurance companies have branches or agents in Jordan.

TRADE AND INDUSTRY

CHAMBERS OF COMMERCE

Chamber of Commerce, Amman: P.O.B. 287, Amman; f. 1923; Pres. MUHAMMAD ALI BDEIR; Dir. SAID MATOUK.

Chamber of Commerce, Irbid: P.O.B. 13; f. 1950; Pres. MUFLEH HASSAN GHARAIBEH; Dir. HASSAN M. MURAD.

PUBLIC CORPORATION

East Ghor Canal Natural Resources Authority: P.O.B. 878, Amman; the 50-mile canal is now completed, and work is in progress on the irrigation system; the U.S.A. has provided $12m. towards the cost of the canal; the project provides irrigation for some 20,000–30,000 acres. Israeli attacks on the canal in June and August 1969 seriously damaged the irrigation system, but the canal is now in operation again and most of the irrigation system has been completed. An additional 6 miles of main canal and irrigation system have been completed with an additional irrigated area of 5,000 acres, financed by Kuwait Government grants of $3m.

TRADE UNIONS

The General Federation of Jordanian Trade Unions: Wadi as-Sir Rd., P.O.B. 1065, Amman; f. 1954; 15,000 mems.; member of Arab Trade Unions Confederation; Gen. Sec. MOHAMMAD H. JAWHAR.

There are also a number of independent unions, including:

Drivers' Union: P.O.B. 846, Amman; Sec.-Gen. SAMI MANSOUR.

Union of Petroleum Workers and Employees: P.O.B. 1346, Amman; Sec.-Gen. BRAHIM HADI.

OIL

Oil has yet to be discovered in commercial quantities in Jordan. In April 1969 INA, a Yugoslavian consortium, was granted a 25-year exploration concession on a 16,000 square kilometre area on Jordan's eastern frontier.

TRANSPORT AND TOURISM

TRANSPORT

RAILWAYS

Hedjaz Jordan Railway: (administered by the Ministry of Transport): P.O.B. 582, Amman; f. 1902; length of track 366 km.; Gen. Man. M. R. Qoseini.

This was formerly a section of the Hedjaz railway (Damascus to Medina) for Muslim pilgrims to Medina and Mecca. It crosses the Syrian border and enters Jordanian territory south of Dera'a, and runs for approximately 366 km. to Naqb Ishtar, passing through Zarka, Amman, Qatrana and Ma'an. Some 836 km. of the line, from Ma'an to Medina in Saudi Arabia, have been abandoned for the past fifty years. Reconstruction of the Medina line, begun in 1965, was scheduled to be completed in 1970 at a cost of £15 million, divided equally between Jordan, Saudi Arabia and Syria. However, due to some misunderstanding between the interested Governments, the reconstruction work has been suspended. A new 115 km. extension to Aqaba is to be financed by a J.D. 12 million loan from the German Federal Republic; currently being re-examined, the project is hoped to be completed during the first half of 1975. The extension will mainly be used for transporting phosphates and will connect Aqaba to Beirut.

As at the end of 1972 there were 17 locomotives, 344 goods wagons, 45 oil tank wagons and 8 passenger cars.

ROADS

Ministry of Public Works: Amman.

Amman is linked by road with all parts of the kingdom and with neighbouring countries. In addition, several thousand km. of tracks make all villages in the kingdom accessible by motor transport in summer. At the end of 1973 Jordan had 1,751 km. of main roads, 1,548 km. of secondary roads and 2,582 km. of other roads. 83 per cent of the roads are metalled.

Royal Automobile Club of Jordan: P.O.B. 920, Jebel Lweibdeh, Amman; Head Office: Wadi Seer Cross Roads, Telephone 22467, 44261; f. 1953; affiliated to the F.I.A., A.I.T.; Pres. of Honour H.M. King Hussein; Gen. Man. D. H. Ledger.

SHIPPING

The port of Aqaba is Jordan's only outlet to the sea and has two general berths of 340 metres and 215 metres, with seven main transit sheds, covered storage area of 4,150 sq. metres, an open area of 50,600 sq. metres and a phosphate berth 210 metres long and 10 metres deep.

PIPELINES

Two oil pipelines cross Jordan. The Iraq Petroleum Company pipeline, carrying petroleum from the oilfields in Iraq to Haifa, has not operated since the Arab-Israeli hostilities commenced. The 1,067-mile pipeline, known as the Trans-Arabian Pipeline (Tapline) carries petroleum from the oilfields at Dhahran in Saudi Arabia to Sidon on the Mediterranean seaboard in Lebanon. It traverses Jordan for a distance of 110 miles and Jordan receives about £1½ million per annum in royalties. Tapline has frequently been cut by hostile action.

CIVIL AVIATION

In addition to Jordan's international airport of Amman, a new airport at Aqaba was opened in May 1972.

Alia (The Royal Jordanian Airline): Head Office: P.O.B. 302, Arab Insurance Building, First Circle, Jabal, Amman; f. 1963; government-owned; services to Middle East, Europe and Pakistan; fleet of one Caravelle, one Boeing 707, two Boeing 720; Man. Dir. Ali Ghandour.

The following airlines also serve Jordan: Alitalia, EgyptAir, Iraqi Airways, KLM, Kuwait Airways, MEA, Saudia.

TOURISM

Jordan Tourism Authority: P.O.B. 224, Amman; f. 1952; Chair. Ghaleb Barakat; Dir. Fawaz Abul Ghanam; publ. *Jordan* (quarterly).

CULTURAL ORGANIZATION

The Department of Culture and Arts: Ministry of Culture and Information, P.O.B. 6140, Amman; aims to encourage artistic movements throughout the Kingdom, promote growth of talents and prepare specialists in all fields of culture and fine arts. Consists of six Divisions:

Division of Culture: publishes books, issues literary magazines (*Afkar* and *Resalat al-Urdon*) and collaborates with men of letters in the Kingdom.

Division of Folklore Arts: aims to carry out research into and promote the traditional customs of folkloric arts; organizes folklore festivals in different parts of the Kingdom.

Division of the Dramatic Arts: aims to train actors; produces plays and encourages playwrights.

Division of Painting and Sculpture: aims to encourage painting and sculpture and to offer all assistance to improve and widen talents in these fields; arranges local art exhibitions.

Division of Music: aims to develop musical talents on a sound and educational basis; a teaching institute has been established.

Jordanian Folklore Dancing: This group revives folk dancing in Jordan and organizes festivals in different parts of the world and in neighbouring Arab countries.

UNIVERSITY

University of Jordan: near Jubaiha, P.O.B. 1682, Amman; 218 teachers, c. 3,600 students.

KENYA*

INTRODUCTORY SURVEY

Location, Climate, Language, Religion, Flag, Capital

Kenya lies astride the equator on the east coast of Africa, with Somalia to the north-east, Ethiopia to the north, Uganda to the west and Tanzania to the south. The climate varies with altitude: the coastal zone is hot and humid, temperatures averaging 69°–90°F (20.5°–32°C), while inland, above 5,000 ft., it averages 45°–80°F (7°–27°C). The highlands and western areas receive ample rainfall but most of the northern part is very dry. Swahili is the official language; English, Kikuyu and Luo are also widely spoken. The majority of the African population follows traditional beliefs. Christians make up about 25 per cent of the population, Muslims 6 per cent, many of them Ismaili followers of the Aga Khan. The national flag (proportions 3 by 2) has horizontal stripes of black, red and green, separated by two narrow white stripes. Superimposed is a red shield, with black and white markings, upon crossed white spears. The capital is Nairobi.

Recent History

Following internal self-government in June 1963, Kenya became independent within the Commonwealth in December 1963, and in 1964 it became a Republic. Kenya is a member of the United Nations and the Organization of African Unity, and Nairobi is the headquarters of some services of the East African Community. Since 1966 there have been various measures aimed at the "Kenyanization" of the economy and many Asians, mostly holding British passports, have left the country. In 1973 the number of Asians leaving Kenya was substantially more than in previous years. The Trade Licensing Act came into force at the beginning of 1969, resulting in the withdrawal of the licences of many non-Kenyan traders.

Tom Mboya, the Minister for Economic Planning and Development and Secretary-General of the Kenya African National Union (KANU), was assassinated in July 1969. Following civil unrest, the opposition Kenya People's Union was banned. The 1969 elections for the National Assembly, contested only by KANU, resulted in the defeat of many sitting M.P.s. Jomo Kenyatta, re-elected as President, has since independence symbolized continuity and loyalty in Kenya, and his personal prestige in the country and in Africa is immense though there has been much speculation about his successor. Despite an unsuccessful plot to overthrow the Government in 1971, the political situation in Kenya is stable. With tourism now the country's second most important single industry, stability has acquired an even greater importance.

Government

Executive power is in the hands of a President, Vice-President and Cabinet. The Legislature comprises a single National Assembly, the former Senate and House of Representatives having been merged in 1967, and only one party (KANU) is represented. There are seven Provinces with their own Advisory Councils.

Defence

Of a total armed force of 6,730, the army numbers 6,000, the navy 250 and the air force 480. The army comprises three battalions of the Kenya Rifles, and specialized troops. In 1973 it was announced that a further battalion would be formed. A small navy was inaugurated in 1964. There is also a police force of about 11,500 men, with a light air wing. Since independence Kenya has had some military assistance from Britain and has signed a mutual defence pact with Ethiopia.

Economic Affairs

Kenya's prosperity rests largely on the production and processing of agricultural and pastoral products and over 80 per cent of Kenya's population is dependent on agriculture. Farming is often adversely affected by climatic conditions, as was the case in 1971, though there was a substantial recovery in agriculture during 1972. The principal cash crops are coffee, tea, wheat, maize, sugar, sisal, pyrethrum, pineapple and wattle. African farmers, through their co-operatives, produce a very high proportion of the total. Pastoral farming varies from the traditional herding of the Masai tribes to the pedigree stock-raising of dairy and beef cattle on the Highland farms. Kenya is one of the few African countries with an important dairy industry. In 1973 the Government decided to launch a foreign-financed $51.6 million livestock project.

Manufactures and food processing accounted for about 10 per cent of gross domestic product in 1972, and industry continues to expand. Kenya has close trading links with her partners in the East African Economic Community, Tanzania and Uganda, with whom she participates in a customs union. Kenyan exports within the Community showed a surplus of K£17.9m. in 1971 but inter-community tensions, particularly between Tanzania and Uganda, have caused stagnation in relationships between the three countries. An oil refinery was opened in 1964 and this is to be expanded to increase its production by 50 per cent. Oil prospecting started in 1966 and is continuing, though without results up to 1974. The most important mineral is soda ash, other minerals are salt, gold and limestone. Mineral production is likely to increase considerably with the discovery of two million tons of lead and silver at Kinangoni, and the exploitation of a fluorospar ore deposit in the Kerio valley. Up to 1974, however, mineral output remained minimal.

In 1973 the marketed production of Kenyan agriculture grew by up to 20 per cent, coffee prices rose, foreign reserves reached a record level, and the adverse trade balance narrowed. Despite the effects of soaring oil costs, the Government decided to continue with the ambitious 1974–78 Plan, with a target annual growth rate of 7.4 per cent, compared with the 6.8 per cent average achieved between 1968 and 1972. Government expenditure in the Plan is estimated at K£470 million, with the emphasis on rural development and increasing employment opportunities. The Government accepted with reservations the

*See also East African Community in Vol. I.

ILO Report on the Kenya economy in 1972, which emphasized the need for full employment and progress towards equality of wealth and opportunity. In the first decade since independence, from 1963 to 1973, the Kenya economy achieved remarkable self-sufficiency and growth; Kenya's per capita G.D.P. increased by 27 per cent and the value of smallholders' farm production rose by nearly 50 per cent.

Transport and Communications

Kenya's railways, inland waterways and harbours are administered by the inter-territorial East African Community, through which the transport network extends into Tanzania, Zambia and Uganda. There are international airports at Nairobi and Mombasa. Air services are also run in common with her neighbours. Main roads link the big towns and there is a country-wide bus service. The World Bank has granted Kenya a $44 million loan for expanding its road system. Mombasa is a fully-equipped international seaport which is undergoing expansion, scheduled for completion in 1975, and serves Uganda and some parts of Tanzania, as well as Kenya. Kenya's power supply will be more than doubled when the Kamburu project on the Tana River is completed in 1974.

Social Welfare

There are State pension and welfare schemes and a National Social Security Fund has been set up. The Government runs hospitals and medical services; no fees are charged to out-patients. Free attention is given in case of need. Missions, private charities and commercial firms provide further facilities. A National Council of Social Services co-ordinates the work of voluntary agencies. Major rural health improvements including the construction of numerous health centres, and the launching of a family planning programme with Swedish aid were announced in November 1973.

Education

Education is not compulsory and less than half of the population is literate. The Government provides or assists in the provision of schools. Education is multi-racial at all levels. The National University in Nairobi, which has nearly 4,000 students, was founded originally in 1956 as a college and was part of the University of East Africa between 1963 and 1970. Over 5,000 students a year study overseas.

Tourism

Kenya's attractions as a tourist centre are mainly the wildlife and the good all-year-round climate. There are eight National Parks and one National Reserve open to the public, several of which provide overnight accommodation. Hunting and photographic safaris are arranged and big game hunting licences are available. By September 1974 all tour operations are to be under Kenyan control.

Tourism in Kenya recently enjoyed unprecedented expansion. Several hotels and game lodges are being expanded or are under construction and more overseas tourist offices have been opened. The total 1971 foreign exchange receipts from tourism were estimated to be 30 per cent higher than those for 1970 though in 1973 tourism showed a sharp fall compared with 1972.

Visas are not required to visit Kenya by nationals of Commonwealth countries (except India), Denmark, Ethiopia, the Federal Republic of Germany, Ireland, Italy, Norway, San Marino, Spain, Sweden, Turkey and Uruguay.

Sport

Organized sports include football, tennis, cricket and athletics. Watersports are popular in the coastal areas. Kenya has competed most successfully in Commonwealth and international sporting events and her athletics team was outstanding at the 1968 Olympic Games.

Public Holidays

1974: August 26th (Summer Holiday), October 18th (Id-ul-Fitr), October 21st (Kenyatta Day), December 12th (Independence Day), December 25th–26th (Christmas and Boxing Day).

1975: January 1st (New Year's Day), March 28th–31st (Easter), May 1st (Labour Day), May 27th (Spring Holiday), June 2nd (Madaraka Day).

Weights and Measures

The metric system is in use.

Currency and Exchange Rates

100 cents = 1 Kenya shilling (Ks.).
Exchange rates (April 1974):

$£1$ sterling = 16.85 Ks.;
U.S. $1 = 7.143 Ks.

STATISTICAL SURVEY

AREA
(sq. km.)

Total	Land	Water	Lakes		National Parks		
			Victoria (in Kenya)	Rudolf	Tsavo	Aberdare	Mount Kenya
582,646*	569,250	13,396	3,831	6,405	20,899	572	464

* 224,961 sq. miles.

LAND CLASSIFICATION, 1968
(sq. km.)

	Area
Trust land and private freehold land which was formerly Trust land.	464,259
National Forests	9,753
Urban Area	954
Government reserves (agricultural, veterinary, railway, etc.)	1,160
Alienated government land	26,698
Private freehold land which was not formerly Trust land (incl. settlement schemes)	6,703
National Parks	22,071
Unalienated government land	46,512
Open water	4,603
	582,713*

* Revised figure 582,646.

POPULATION
(1969 Census)
PROVINCES

Total	Central	Coast	Eastern	North-Eastern	Nyanza	Rift Valley	Western
10,942,705	1,676,000	944,000	1,907,000	246,200	2,122,000	2,210,000	1,328,000

The estimated total population for 1972 is 12,067,000 and for 1973 12,504,000.

CHIEF TOWNS (with 1969 population)

Nairobi (capital)	509,286	Eldoret		18,196
Mombasa	247,073	Nanyuki		11,624
Nakuru	47,151	Kitale		11,573
Kisumu	32,431	Kericho		10,757
Thika	18,387	Malindi		10,144

1970 estimates: Nairobi 535,200, Mombasa 255,400.

MAIN TRIBES OF KENYA

(1969 Census)

	MALE	FEMALE	TOTAL
Kikuyu	1,091,413	1,110,219	2,201,632
Luo	763,080	758,515	1,521,595
Luhya	723,071	730,231	1,453,302
Kamba	592,889	604,823	1,197,712
Kalenjin	600,031	590,172	1,190,203
Kisii	356,730	344,949	701,679
Meru	276,325	277,931	554,256
Mijikenda	255,508	265,012	520,520
Somali	136,894	116,146	253,040
Turkana	107,249	95,928	203,177
Masai	77,745	77,161	154,906
Embu	58,223	59,746	117,969
Taita	52,501	55,993	108,494
All Other Tribes . .	249,046	249,548	498,594
TOTAL . .	5,340,705	5,336,374	10,677,079

In addition, non-Kenyan Africans numbered 59,432 and non-Africans numbered 209,503.

Births and Deaths:

Annual average birth rate 47.8 per 1,000, death rate 17.5 per 1,000 (UN estimate for 1965–70).

MIGRATION

	IMMIGRANT ARRIVALS	LONG-TERM EMIGRANTS
1969	19,082	13,526
1970	19,879	14,020
1971	1,421	15,840
1972	555	120,260

EMPLOYMENT

Total labour force (1970): 4,319,000 economically active, including 3,472,000 in agriculture (ILO and FAO estimates).

Total reported employees*

(1971—'000)

	ALL RACES	AFRICAN	ASIAN	EUROPEAN
Agriculture and Forestry . . .	189.6	188.1	0.5	1.0
Private Industry and Commerce . .	234.4	205.6	20.4	8.4
Public Services	255.7	245.1	6.4	4.2
All Employees	679.7	638.8	27.3	13.6

* This table refers only to employment in urban areas and on large farms. Employment in other areas is estimated to be between 300,000 and 500,000.

AGRICULTURE

PRINCIPAL CROPS
('ooo metric tons)

	1969	1970	1971
Wheat	210	205	210*
Maize	1,425	1,500	1,400*
Millet and Sorghum	330*	330*	330*
Sugar Cane†	1,301	1,451	1,750
Potatoes	200*	200*	210*
Sweet Potatoes and Yams	463*	463*	n.a.
Cassava (Manioc)	620*	620*	n.a.
Pulses	280*	280*	280*

1972: Maize 1,665,000 metric tons.

* FAO estimate.   † Crop year ending in year stated.

Fruit and Nuts (FAO estimates): Pineapples: 27,000 metric tons in 1969, 40,000 metric tons in 1970; Coconuts: 65 million per year (annual average, 1961–65).

Source: FAO, *Production Yearbook 1971* and *Monthly Bulletin of Agricultural Economics and Statistics*.

CROP DELIVERIES
(metric tons)

	1970	1971	1972
Sugar Cane	1,451,200	1,378,002	1,062,295
Wheat	221,486	205,743	164,382
Maize*	205,662	256,590	372,985
Rice	28,547	29,983	33,785
Tea	41,077	36,290	53,322
Coffee	58,337	59,459	62,048
Sisal	43,930	44,827	41,210
Seed Cotton	14,017	16,764	16,981
Pyrethrum Extract	95.2	142.8	184.9

*Deliveries to the Marketing Board only.

LIVESTOCK
('ooo)

	1968–69	1969–70	1970–71*
Cattle	7,908	8,600	8,500
Sheep	4,056	3,700*	3,700
Goats	4,334	4,000*	4,000
Pigs	70	72*	75
Camels	312	315*	320
Poultry	10,300*	10,600*	11,900

*FAO estimate.

DAIRY PRODUCE
('ooo metric tons)

	1969*	1970	1971*
Cows' milk	803	820	840
Sheeps' milk	16	15*	15
Goats' milk	43	40*	40

*FAO estimate.

('ooo litres)

	1970	1971
Butter	105,395	79,163
Ghee	18,905	13,397

('ooo litres)*

	1970	1971	1972
Whole milk (sales)	103,011	105,777	119,662
Milk for Butter	105,395	79,163	102,982
Milk for Ghee	18,905	13,397	13,397
Milk for Cheese	4,606	4,716	7,095

*Factory production only.

MEAT PRODUCTION†
('ooo metric tons)

	1969	1970	1971*
Beef and Veal‡	28	30*	32
Pork	4*	5	5

*FAO estimate.

† Meat from indigenous animals, including the meat equivalent of exported live animals.

‡ Commercial production only.

OTHER AGRICULTURAL PRODUCTS
(metric tons)

	1969	1970	1971*
Hen Eggs	14,700*	15,100	16,200
Wool: Greasy	2,100	2,200	2,200
Clean	1,000	1,100	1,100

* FAO estimate.

FORESTRY

ROUNDWOOD PRODUCTION
('000 cubic metres)

1968	.	.	8,174
1969	.	.	8,341
1970	.	.	8,401

Source: FAO, *Yearbook of Forest Products.*

FISHING
(metric tons)

	1969	1970	1971
Inland water . .	25,200	25,800	26,200
Indian Ocean . .	6,700	7,900	8,800
TOTAL CATCH .	31,900	33,700	35,000
Value of fish landed (K£'000)	1,391	1,517	1,533

Source: FAO, *Yearbook of Fishery Statistics 1971.*

MINING

	1967	1968	1969
Gold (kg.) . . .	1,038	994	557
Salt (metric tons) .	27,000	29,000	42,000

1970: Salt 39,000 metric tons.
1971: Salt 43,000 metric tons.

INDUSTRY

	UNIT	1969	1970	1971	1972
Wheat Flour	'000 metric tons	90.2	127.9	120.4	116.6
Soda Ash	,, ,, ,,	102.7	160.1	161.3	164.2
Cement	,, ,, ,,	642.4	792.1	794.0	800.0
Sugar	metric tons	115,052	125,291	123,898	67,186*
Soap	,, ,,	24,003	23,421	27,434	19,784*
Cigarettes	,, ,,	1,814	2,081	2,242	1,721*
Beer	'000 hectolitres	647.6	795.3	935.4	738.6
Mineral Waters . .	,, ,,	278.8	314.3	400	280.1
Oil Refined . . .	million litres	2,510.0	2,508.3	2,966.2	2,926.1
Electricity	million kWh.	459.4	508.6	555.6	661.0

* January–September.

FINANCE

100 cents = 1 Kenya shilling (Ks.).
Coins: 5, 10, 25 and 50 cents; 1 and 2 Ks.
Notes: 5, 10, 20, 50 and 100 Ks.
Exchange rates (April 1974): £1 sterling = 16.85 Ks.; U.S. $1 = 7.14 Ks.
100 Ks. = £5.94 = $14.00.

Note: Between June 1973 and January 1974 the central exchange rate was U.S. $1 = 6.90 Kenya shillings. Prior to June 1973 the value of the shilling in U.S. currency was the same as that adopted in January 1974. In terms of sterling the value of the Kenya shilling between November 1967 and August 1971 was 1s. 2d. (5.83p), the exchange rate being £1 = 17.14 Ks. In this survey the symbol "K£" is used to denote amounts of 20 Ks., equivalent to £1.19 sterling in April 1974.

RECURRENT BUDGET

(K£'000—1972–73*)

REVENUE		EXPENDITURE	
Taxes on Income and Capital	46,620	Social, Economic and General Expenditure	106,331
Taxes on Consumption and Production	62,286	Recurrent Financial Obligations	22,315
Charges for Goods and Services	15,607		
Loan Charges	4,256		
TOTAL (incl. others)	140,532	TOTAL (incl. others)	133,894

Budget (1973–74): Revenue K£166m.; Expenditure K£222m.*

DEVELOPMENT

(K£'000)

EXPENDITURE	1970–71	1971–72	1972–73*
Roads	13,644	16,479	16,663
Agriculture and Forestry	4,288	7,300	7,663
Commerce and Industry	4,815	5,894	7,274
Labour	2,721	3,637	4,766
Transport (excl. roads)	892	1,166	4,244
Education	1,687	2,832	4,216
Health	2,626	2,849	2,488
Defence	336	918	1,623
Tourism and National Parks	614	1,067	1,613
TOTAL (incl. others)	45,489	57,990	68,047

* Provisional.

Development Expenditure: (1973–74) K£68m.*

* Estimates.

Five-Year Development Plan (1970–74): Total Investment K£683m. (Public Sector K£244m., Private Sector K£439m.); Principal fields of Central Government Development Expenditure: Transport 26 per cent, Agriculture (including Land Settlement) 21 per cent, Social Services (including Education) 27 per cent.

EXTERNAL TRADE*

(K£'000)

	1968	1969	1970	1971	1972	1973†
Imports	114,765	116,950	142,026	184,105	177,621	203,286
Exports (incl. re-exports) .	62,941	68,510	77,451	78,342	95,454	127,684

* Excluding inter-trade of local produce and locally manufactured goods between Kenya, Uganda, Tanganyika and, beginning 1968, Zanzibar.

† Provisional.

COMMODITIES

(K£'000)

IMPORTS	1969	1970	1971	1972
Crude Petroleum	10,168	11,023	12,798	14,587
Motor Vehicles and Chassis . . .	9,894	11,473	16,676	13,492
Agricultural Machinery and Tractors . .	1,911	2,420	3,004	3,266
Industrial Machinery (including electrical) .	15,427	22,413	29,972	34,083
Iron and Steel	6,473	9,004	11,311	10,167
Fabrics of Cotton	1,923	1,022	1,174	769
Fabrics of Synthetic Fibres . . .	2,354	3,849	3,776	3,488
Paper and Paper Products . . .	5,697	6,648	8,313	7,702
Pharmaceutical Products . . .	2,459	2,712	3,288	3,586
Fertilizers	2,272	3,041	3,063	3,746

(K£'000)

DOMESTIC EXPORTS*	1969	1970	1971	1972
Coffee (not roasted)	16,837	22,259	19,530	24,769
Sisal (fibre and tow) . . .	1,717	1,865	1,515	2,068
Tea	11,271	12,704	11,876	16,417
Pyrethrum (extract and flowers) . .	2,795	2,163	3,332	4,572
Meat and Meat Products . . .	2,595	2,853	3,661	4,876
Hides and Skins (undressed) . . .	1,871	1,653	2,439	3,777
Manufactured Goods:				
Soda Ash	904	1,673	1,860	1,935
Wattle Extract	1,144	1,141	1,206	1,687
Petroleum Products	7,623	8,176	8,869	8,917
Cement	1,434	1,644	1,566	1,964
Other	4,014	4,467	5,978	5,779

1973: Coffee exports K£33.2 million.

* Excluding re-exports.

COUNTRIES
(K£'000)

	IMPORTS				DOMESTIC EXPORTS*			
	1969	1970	1971	1972	1969	1970	1971	1972
Western Europe:								
United Kingdom .	36,453	41,459	56,249	50,560	14,787	14,847	14,758	19,855
Other EEC .	24,283	28,651	37,807	40,235	12,894	13,295	12,928	20,630
Other .	5,799	7,048	10,288	11,006	4,640	6,823	5,608	8,188
Eastern Europe .	2,605	3,476	5,289	4,103	1,278	1,953	2,367	1,436
North and South America	9,595	12,805	17,492	13,463	6,496	8,299	6,105	7,226
Africa . . .	1,279	1,833	2,674	2,657	8,235	9,158	11,734	12,067
Asia:								
Japan .	9,344	15,196	19,330	17,870	1,287	1,225	2,630	2,090
Other .	21,545	23,697	28,878	29,591	5,392	7,372	7,672	8,670
All Other Countries .	6,046	7,859	6,097	8,134	8,324	8,634	9,383	10,427
TOTAL .	116,951	142,026	184,105	177,621	63,333	71,606	73,185	90,590

* Excluding re-exports.

INTER-COMMUNITY TRADE

	TANZANIA		UGANDA	
	Imports	Exports	Imports	Exports
1969 . .	4,018	12,845	7,803	15,949
1970 . .	5,938	14,752	10,048	16,698
1971 . .	7,932	14,743	8,026	19,150
1972 . .	5,887	16,286	7,583	16,507

TOURISM
ARRIVALS OF VISITORS AND PERSONS IN TRANSIT

	1970	1971	1972
British . . .	100,339	100,328	91,938
Federal German .	23,067	37,780	41,334
Other European .	52,484	67,128	76,663
American and Canadian .	51,511	63,539	72,854
Indian and Pakistani .	17,483	17,937	14,536
Ugandan and Tanzanian .	60,471	69,462	83,432
Other African .	10,638	16,157	17,946
All Others . .	22,780	27,374	29,691
TOTAL .	338,773	399,705	428,394

TRANSPORT

EAST AFRICAN RAILWAYS
Total track mileage (1972) 5,897 km., in Kenya, Uganda
and Tanzania, combined.

ROADS
(New registrations of vehicles)

	Motor Cars	Light Vans etc.	Lorries etc.	Buses and Coaches	Motor Cycles	Other New Vehicles	Second-hand Vehicles	Total
1968 . .	5,631	3,465	1,483	271	1,016	1,186	1,146	14,198
1969 . .	6,389	4,232	1,760	311	1,244	1,045	1,111	16,092
1970 . .	7,680	4,959	2,469	435	1,317	1,427	1,317	19,604
1971 . .	8,072	5,514	2,038	639	1,393	1,157	1,616	20,429
1972 . .	6,337	4,671	1,494	408	1,427	1,419	1,778	17,544

SHIPPING
Entered*

	Vessels	Net Tonnage	Passengers	Cargo† ('ooo tons)
1969 . . .	1,813	7,446,000	41,869	5,092
1970 . . .	1,762	7,214,700	36,948	5,795
1971 . . .	1,859	7,510,000	23,311	5,570
1972 . . .	1,788	7,208,000	19,033	5,483

* Mombasa only.　　　　† Loaded and unloaded.

CIVIL AVIATION
External Air Traffic*

	Passengers		Freight Kg.	
	Arrivals	Departures	Unloaded	Loaded
1970 . .	323,300	334,500	5,970,700	11,008,400
1971 . .	370,900	380,200	7,349,200	12,670,900
1972 . .	396,100	411,500	8,862,300	16,621,800

* Nairobi Airport only.

EDUCATION
(1972*)

	Establishments	Teachers	Pupils
Primary and Intermediate Schools . .	6,657	53,751	1,675,919
Secondary Schools and Secondary Technical Schools . .	846	7,053	157,590
Vocational Schools	9	201	3,389
Teacher Training Colleges	25	651	9,293

* Estimate.

In 1970 there were 10,443 students at university.

Sources (unless otherwise stated): East African Statistical Department, Nairobi; Ministry of Economic Planning and Development, Nairobi; Ministry of Information, Broadcasting and Tourism, Nairobi; *Kenya Statistical Digest*, Ministry of Finance and Planning, Nairobi; *Annual Economic Review*, Standard Bank.

THE CONSTITUTION

The Independence Constitution for Kenya came into force in June, 1963, with the introduction of full internal self-government.

Amendments were made in November, 1964, by which Kenya became a Republic within the Commonwealth. Under the terms of the Constitution, individual rights and liberties are protected, including freedom of expression and assembly, privacy of the home, the right not to be detained without cause, and the right of compensation for compulsory purchase of property.

By a voluntary evolution the Republic of Kenya is now a One-Party State governed by a united Central Government. For administrative purposes, the country is divided into seven Provinces, each of which has a Provincial Council playing a purely advisory role, especially in respect of rural development. The Provincial Councils and County Councils are maintained by grants from the Central Government, but raising of all other taxes and of foreign investment capital is the sole responsibility of the Central Government.

The central legislative authority is the National Assembly consisting of a single elected assembly. There are 158 Representatives elected for four years, and 12 Members nominated by the President.

Executive power is in the hands of the President, Vice-President and Cabinet. The Cabinet shall be formed by the President, who, following constitutional amendments adopted in June 1968, is to be directly elected by popular vote at general elections. In the event of his death or resignation the Vice-President will assume the Presidency, with limited powers, for a maximum period of three months. The Presidency becomes vacant on the dissolution of Parliament.

In October, 1963, certain amendments to the Constitution were introduced. The Police and Public Services are to be centrally controlled. Changes in the Constitution about Human Rights, structure of Regions, Land, the Senate, and amendment procedure can only be made by a 75 per cent majority vote of the National Assembly. Changes concerning other clauses, including those affecting Regional powers, may be made by a 75 per cent vote of the Assembly or failing this by a two-thirds majority in a national referendum.

THE GOVERNMENT

HEAD OF STATE

President of the Republic: Mzee Jomo Kenyatta.

Vice-President: Daniel T. Arap Moi.

CABINET

(June 1974)

President and Commander-in-Chief: Mzee Jomo Kenyatta.

Vice-President and Minister of Home Affairs: Daniel T. Arap Moi.

Minister of State at the President's Office: Mbiyu Koinange.

Minister of Foreign Affairs: Dr. Njoroge Mungai.

Minister of Finance and Economic Planning: Mwai Kibaki.

Minister of Defence: James S. Gichuru.

Minister of Agriculture and Animal Husbandry: Jeremiah J. M. Nyagah.

Minister of Health: Dr. Zachary Onyonka.

Minister of Local Government: Dr. James C. N. Osogo.

Minister of Power and Communications: Isaac E. Omolo Okero.

Minister of Labour: Eliud N. Mwendwa.

Minister of Tourism and Wildlife: Juxon L. M. Shako.

Minister of Lands and Settlement: Jackson H. Angaine.

Minister of Housing: Paul J. Ngei.

Attorney-General: Charles Njonjo.

Minister of Information and Broadcasting: Robert S. Matano.

Minister of Natural Resources: William O. Omamo.

Minister of Co-operatives and Social Services: Masinde Muliro.

Minister of Commerce and Industry: Dr. Julius G. Kiano.

Minister of Education: Taita A. Towett.

Minister of Works: James Nyamweya.

DIPLOMATIC REPRESENTATION

EMBASSIES AND HIGH COMMISSIONS ACCREDITED TO KENYA

(In Nairobi, unless otherwise indicated)

(E) Embassy; (HC) High Commission.

Algeria: Dar es Salaam, Tanzania (E).

Australia: City House, Wabera St. (HC); *High Commissioner:* K. H. ROGERS.

Austria: City House, Wabera St., P.O.B. 30560 (E); *Ambassador:* Dr. GEORG REISCH.

Belgium: Silopark House, Mama Ngina St., P.O.B. 30461 (E); *Ambassador:* M. ARNOLD J. E. DE COEYER.

Botswana: Lusaka, Zambia (HC).

Brazil: Jeevan Bharati Bldg., Harambee Ave., P.O.B. 39754 (E); *Ambassador:* F. T. DE MESQUITA.

Bulgaria: Archer Rd., P.O.B. 30058 (E); *Chargé d'Affaires:* TODOR DIMITROV.

Burundi: Dar es Salaam, Tanzania.

Canada: Kimathi St., IPS Building, P.O.B. 30481 (HC); *High Commissioner:* W. M. OLIVIER (also accred. to Uganda).

China, People's Republic: Woodlands Rd. (off Argwings-Kodhek Rd.), P.O.B. 30508 (E); *Chargé d'Affaires:* LI SHIH.

Czechoslovakia: Crauford Rd., P.O.B. 30204 (E); *Ambassador:* J. UHER.

Denmark: Hughes Bldg., Kenyatta Ave., P.O.B. 40412 (E); *Ambassador:* HANS KUHNE.

Egypt: Total House, Koinange St., P.O.B. 30285 (E); *Ambassador:* MOSTAFA MOHAMED TAWFIK.

Ethiopia: State House Ave., P.O.B. 45198 (E); *Ambassador:* Ato ABATE AGHIDE.

Finland: Addis Ababa, Ethiopia (E).

France: P.O.B. 41784 (E); *Ambassador:* RENÉ MILLET.

Germany, Federal Republic: Embassy House, Harambee Ave., P.O.B. 30180 (E); *Ambassador:* Dr. HARALD HEIMSOETH.

Ghana: International Life House, P.O.B. 48534 (HC); *High Commissioner:* S. M. ADU-AMPOMA.

Greece: IPS Bldg., Kimathi St., P.O.B. 30543 (E); *Ambassador:* MICHAEL MOUZAS.

Guinea: Dar es Salaam, Tanzania (E).

Hungary: Arboretum Rd., P.O.B. 30275 (E); *Ambassador:* JÓZSEF BAJNOK.

India: Jeevan Bharati Bldg., Harambee Ave., P.O.B. 30074 (HC); *High Commissioner:* K. CHANDRASEKHARAN NAIR.

Iran: Bruce House, Standard Street, P.O.B. 49170 (E); *Ambassador:* ANOUSHIRAVAN KAZEMI.

Iraq: International Life House, P.O.B. 49213 (E); *Ambassador:* HASSAN KITTANI.

Italy: Prudential Assurance Bldg., Wabera St., P.O.B. 30107 (E); *Ambassador:* Dr. FRANK MACCAFERI.

Ivory Coast: Addis Ababa, Ethiopia.

Japan: Bank of India Bldg., Kenyatta Ave., P.O.B. 20202 (E); *Ambassador:* MASAME MAKANE.

Korea, Republic: IPS Bldg., Kimathi St., P.O.B. 30455 (E); *Ambassador:* IN HAN PAIK.

Kuwait: IPS Bldg., Kimathi St., P.O.B. 42353 (E); *Ambassador:* SAEED Y. SHAMMAS.

Lesotho: International Life House, Mama Ngina St., P.O.B. 44096 (HC); *High Commissioner:* M. B. MDINISO.

Liberia: Bruce House, P.O.B. 30546 (E); *Ambassador:* R. FRANCIS OKAI.

Malawi: Gateway House, Government Rd., P.O.B. 30453 (HC); *High Commissioner:* B. W. KATENGA.

Mali: Dar es Salaam, Tanzania (E).

Morocco: Addis Ababa, Ethiopia (E).

Netherlands: Uchumi House, City Square, P.O.B. 41537 (E); *Ambassador:* J. POLDERMAN.

Nigeria: Agip House, Haile Sellassie Ave., P.O.B. 30516 (HC); *High Commissioner:* L. S. MOMODU.

Norway: Silopark House, Mama Ngina St., P.O.B. 46363 (E); *Ambassador:* R. F. HANCKE.

Pakistan: Agip House, Haile Sellassie Ave., P.O.B. 30045 (E); *High Commissioner:* MAKHDUMZADA S. HAMID RAZA GILANI.

Poland: Archer Rd., P.O.B. 30086 (E); *Ambassador:* Dr. EMIL HACHULSKI.

Romania: Dar es Salaam, Tanzania.

Rwanda: International Life House, Mama Ngina St., P.O.B. 48579 (E); *Chargé d'Affaires:* REHABIA BANGUKA.

Senegal: Addis Ababa, Ethiopia (E).

Somalia: International Life House, Mama Ngina St., P.O.B. 30769 (E); *Ambassador:* HASHI ABDULLAH FARAH.

Spain: Bruce House, Standard St., P.O.B. 45503 (E); *Ambassador:* MIGUEL VELARDE.

Sri Lanka: International Life House, Mama Ngina St., P.O.B. 49145 (HC); *High Commissioner:* I. B. FONSEKA.

Sudan: Shankardass House, Government Rd., P.O.B. 48784 (E); *Ambassador:* EL AMIN MOHAMED EL AMIN.

Swaziland: Silopark House, P.O.B. 41887 (HC); *High Commissioner:* S. MUSA KUNENE.

Sweden: International Life House, Mama Ngina St., P.O.B. 30600 (E); *Ambassador:* L. B. RYDFORS.

Switzerland: International Life House, Mama Ngina St., P.O.B. 20008 (E); *Ambassador:* Dr. R. PESTALOZZI.

Thailand: Addis Ababa, Ethiopia (E).

Tunisia: Addis Ababa, Ethiopia (E).

Turkey: Silopark House, Mama Ngina St., P.O.B. 30785 (E); *Ambassador:* O. F. TEVS.

U.S.S.R.: Lenana Rd., P.O.B. 30049 (E); *Ambassador:* D. P. MIROSHNETCHENKO.

United Kingdom: Bruce House, Standard St., P.O.B. 30465 (HC); *High Commissioner:* A. A. DUFF.

U.S.A.: Cotts House, Wabera St., P.O.B. 30137 (E); *Ambassador:* ROBINSON MCILVAINE.

Vatican: Churchill Ave., P.O.B. 14326 (Apostolic Nunciature); *Apostolic Nuncio:* Most Rev. Archbishop PIERLUIGI SARTORELLI.

Yemen Arab Republic: Mogadishu, Somalia (E).

Yugoslavia: State House Ave., P.O.B. 30504 (E); *Ambassador:* IVO PELICON.

Zaire: Cearn Chambers, P.O.B. 48106 (E); *Ambassador:* KALUME MWANA KAHAMBWE.

Zambia: International Life House, City Hall Way, P.O.B. 48741 (HC); *High Commissioner:* MATIYA NGALANDE.

Kenya also has diplomatic relations with Colombia, Cyprus, Ireland, Madagascar and Malaysia.

NATIONAL ASSEMBLY

The Senate and House of Representatives were merged in February 1967 to form a single Assembly of 158 elected members, and 12 co-opted members.

Speaker: F. M. G. Mati.

Deputy Speaker: Dr. M. Waiyaki.

ELECTIONS, DECEMBER 1969

Only KANU was represented in the primary elections to the National Assembly, to which 108 new members were elected.

New elections are to be held, probably at the end of 1974.

POLITICAL PARTY

Kenya African National Union (KANU): P.O. Box 12394, Nairobi; f. 1960; a nation-wide African party which led the country to self-government and independence; Pres. Jomo Kenyatta; 8 provincial Vice-Pres.

DEFENCE

Of a total armed force of 6,730, the army numbers 6,000, the navy 250 and the air force 480. The civil police numbers 11,500 and includes some para-military units. Military service is voluntary.

Commander-in-Chief of the Armed Forces: Mzee Jomo Kenyatta.

Deputy Chief of Defence Staff: Brig. Kakenyi.

Commander of the Army: Maj.-Gen. J. Mulinge.

Commander of the Air Force: Col. Dedan Gichuru.

JUDICIAL SYSTEM

The Court of Appeal for East Africa: P.O.B. 30187, Nairobi. It is the Final Court of Appeal from High Courts of Partner States in both Civil and Criminal matters. The jurisdiction of the Court is provided for by the laws in force in each Partner State and exercises any power, authority and jurisdiction in connection with appeals as are provided for by the laws and as are vested in the Court from which the appeal is brought. The Court has its headquarters in Nairobi but holds sessions at Kampala in Uganda, Dar es Salaam, Arusha and Mwanza in Tanzania and Mombasa in Kenya.

The judges of the Court are President, Vice-President and four justices of Appeal:

President: Sir William Duffus.

Vice-President: Mr. Justice Spry.

Registrar: T. T. M. Aswani.

Deputy Registrar: P. K. O. Shayo.

The High Court of Kenya: Nairobi; has unlimited criminal and civil jurisdiction at first instance, and sits as a court of appeal from subordinate courts in both criminal and civil cases. The High Court is a court of admiralty. There is a resident Puisne Judge at Mombasa, Nakuru and Kisumu. Regular sessions in Kisii, Nyeri and Meru.

Chief Justice: Hon. James Wicks.

Puisne Judges: Hons. C. B. Madan, E. Trevelyan, Chanan Singh, C. H. E. Miller, L. G. E. Harris, L. P. Mosdell, A. H. Simpson, K. C. Bennett, A. A. Kneller, J. M. Waiyaki, M. G. Muli, Sir D. J. Sheridan, Z. R. Chesoni.

Registrar: J. O. Nyarangi.

SUBORDINATE COURTS

Resident Magistrates' Courts: have country-wide jurisdiction, with powers of punishment by imprisonment up to five years or by fine up to K£500.

District Magistrates' Courts: of First, Second and Third Class; these have jurisdiction within Districts and powers of punishment by imprisonment up to five years, one year and six months respectively, or by fine up to K£500, K£100 and K£50 respectively.

Kadhi's Courts: have jurisdiction within Districts, to determine questions of Muslim law.

RELIGION

African religions, beliefs and forms of worship show great variety both between races and tribes and from one district to another. The Arab community is Moslem, the Indians are partly Moslem and partly Hindu, and the Europeans and Goans are almost entirely Christian.

Moslems are found mainly along the coastline but the Moslem faith has also established itself among Africans around Nairobi and other towns up-country and among some tribes of the Northern Frontier Province.

Christian missions are active and about 25 per cent of Africans are Christian and East Africa is also an important centre for the Baha'i faith.

CHRISTIANS

All Africa Council of Churches: Africa Headquarters P.O.B. 20301, Nairobi; Gen. Sec. Canon Burgess Carr.

National Christian Council of Kenya: Gen. Sec. J. Kamau, P.O.B. 45009, Nairobi.

ANGLICAN PROVINCE OF KENYA

Archbishop (*and Bishop of Nairobi*): Most Rev. F. H. Olang', P.O.B. 40502, Nairobi.

ROMAN CATHOLIC CHURCH

Archbishop: Most Rev. Maurice Otunga, P.O.B. 14231, Nairobi.

There are some 1,150,000 Roman Catholics in Kenya.

PRESBYTERIAN CHURCH OF EAST AFRICA

Moderator: Rt. Rev. Charles Muhoro Kareri, P.O.B. 8286, Nairobi.

The Salvation Army and the Africa Inland Mission are represented in Kenya.

PRESBYTERIAN CHURCH OF KENYA

Moderator: Rev. Crispus Kiongo, P.O.B. 8268, Nairobi.

METHODIST CHURCH OF KENYA

President: Rev. Lawi Imathiu, P.O.B. 47633, Nairobi.

BAHA'I

Kenya Headquarters: P.O.B. 47562, Nairobi; 2,617 centres, 2 teaching institutes.

THE PRESS

DAILIES

Daily Nation: P.O.B. 49010, Nairobi; f. 1960; Man. Editor J. RODRIGUES; circ. 69,990.

East African Standard: P.O.B. 30080, Nairobi; f. 1902; Editor (vacant); circ. 37,000.

Evening News: Nairobi.

Taifa Leo: P.O.B. 9010, Nairobi; Swahili; f. 1960; daily and weekly edition; Editor A. G. MBUGUA; circ. 27,087.

SELECTED PERIODICALS

WEEKLIES

Africa Samachar: P.O.B. 41237, Nairobi; f. 1954; Gujarati; Editor C. N. BHATT; circ. 18,000.

Baraza: P.O.B. 30080, Nairobi; f. 1939; Swahili; Editor FRANCIS JOSEPH KHAMISI; circ. 64,000.

Kenya Gazette: P.O.B. 30128, Nairobi; f. 1898; government notices of non-commercial nature and amendments to laws; every Friday; edited for Government of Republic of Kenya; circ. 5,000.

Kitale Weekly: P.O.B. 179, Kitale; every Wednesday.

New Era: P.O.B. 46854, Nairobi; f. 1966; for young people; Editor KUL BHUSHAN; circ. 5,000.

Sunday Nation: P.O.B. 49010, Nairobi; English; Editor JOHN GARDNER; circ. 70,076.

Sunday Post: P.O.B. 30127, Nairobi; f. 1936; English; Editor S. LOVE; circ. 27,000.

Taifa Weekly: P.O.B. 9010, Nairobi; f. 1958; Editor A. G. MBUGUA; circ. 66,390.

Trans Nzoia Post: P.O.B. 34, Kitale; f. 1930; local news; every Wednesday; Editor N. G. LAKHANI.

FORTNIGHTLY

Sikio: P.O.B. 30121, Nairobi; English/Swahili; organ of East African Railways; Editor the Public Relations Officer; circ. 18,000.

MONTHLIES

Africa ya Kesho: P.O. Kijabe; Swahili; Editor J. N. SOMBA; circ. 10,000.

Arrow: P.O.B. 4959, Nairobi; English; f. 1956; children's newspaper; Editor BARBARA PHILLIPS; circ. 25,000.

Drum: P.O.B. 3372, Nairobi; f. 1956; East African edition; Editor TABAN-LO-LLYONG.

East Africa Journal: P.O.B. 30571, Nairobi; Editor Dr. B. A. OGOT; political, economic, social and cultural; circ. 3,000.

E. A. Medical Journal: P.O.B. 41632, Nairobi; f. 1924; Editor HILLARY P. OJIAMBO, M.D.; circ. 1,000.

Flamingo: P.O.B. 20223, Nairobi; f. 1961; Kenya edition of African family magazine; non-political; Editor GERALD MALMED.

Kenya Coffee: P.O.B. 30566, Nairobi; f. 1935; English; publ. by Coffee Board of Kenya; Editor S. N. KINYUA.

Kenya Dairy Farmer: University Press of Africa, Bank House, P.O.B. 43981, Nairobi; f. 1956; English and Swahili; Editor Mrs. J. McALLEN; circ. 4,000.

Kenya Farmer (Journal of the Agricultural Society of Kenya): c/o English Press, P.O.B. 30127, Nairobi; f. 1954; English with Swahili articles included; Editor Mrs. I. BAKER; circ. 22,000.

Lengo: P.O.B. 72839, Nairobi; f. 1964; Swahili; Editor ODHIAMBO W. OKITE; circ. 20,000.

Nyota Afrika: P.O.B. 49010, Nairobi; Swahili; Man. Editor ANTHONY GEORGE MBUGUA; circ. 46,452.

Sauti ya Vita: P.O.B. 575, Nairobi; f. 1928; Swahili/English; Salvation Army; Editor Capt. S. OGWENO; circ. 9,100.

Target: P.O.B. 2839, Nairobi; f. 1964; English; Editor ODHIAMBO W. OKITE; circ. 15,000.

Today in Africa: P.O. Kijabe; English; Editor E. H. ARENSEN; circ. 10,000.

Twi ba Meru: P.O.B. 16, Meru; Kimeru; Roman Catholic; Editor Fr. J. BONZANINO; circ. 5,000.

Uchumi wa Kahawa: P.O.B. 2768, Nairobi; f. 1962; Swahili; Editor E. N. KURIA; African coffee growers; circ. 5,000.

Ukulima wa Kisasa: P.O.B. 9010, Nairobi; f. 1961; Swahili; Editor MOHAMED KOOR; circ. 20,000.

OTHER PERIODICALS

African Scientist: P.O.B. 30197, Nairobi; Editor Dr. T. ODHIAMBO; circ. 2,000; three times a year.

Africana: P.O.B. 49010, Nairobi; f. 1962; incorporating the East African Wild Life Society's Review; Editor JOHN EAMES; circ. 20,000; quarterly.

Busara: P.O.B. 30197, Nairobi; Editor Prof. GURR; circ. 2,000; three times a year.

East African Directory: P.O.B. 41237, Nairobi; f. 1960; commercial directory of seven East African countries; Editor G. C. KIMANI; annual.

E.A. Pharmaceutical Journal: Journal of the Pharmaceutical Society, University Press of Africa, Bank House, P.O.B. 43981, Nairobi; f. 1970; English; Editors Mrs. S. NANJI JUMA and P. PATEL; circ. 4,700; quarterly.

Education in Eastern Africa: P.O.B. 45869, Nairobi; Editor JOHN C. B. BIGALA; circ. 2,000; twice yearly.

Inside Kenya Today: P.O.B. 30025, Nairobi; English; Editor W. N. MUNENE; circ. 30,000; quarterly.

Journal of the Language Association of Eastern Africa: P.O.B. 30571, Nairobi; Editor T. P. GORMAN; circ. 2,000; twice yearly.

Kenya Education Journal: P.O.B. 2768, Nairobi; f. 1958; English; Editor W. G. BOWMAN; circ. 5,500; quarterly.

Plan (Architectural Association of Kenya Journal): University Press of Africa, Bank House, P.O.B. 43981, Nairobi; f. 1971; Editor Mrs. E. MANN; circ. 3,000; twice monthly.

Proceedings of the East African Academy: P.O.B. 30756, Nairobi; f. 1963; quarterly.

Spear: P.O.B. 30121, Nairobi; f. 1952; English; published by East African Railways; circ. 6,000; quarterly.

Trans African Journal of History: P.O.B. 30571, Nairobi; Editor J. A. KIERAN; circ. 2,000; twice yearly.

Women in Kenya: P.O.B. 308, Nairobi; English; quarterly.

NEWS AGENCIES

Kenya News Agency: Information House, Nairobi; f. 1964; teleprinter service based on Reuter, A.F.P., U.P.I., Tass and Home Service.

FOREIGN BUREAUX

Agence France-Presse: P.O.B. 8406, Nairobi.

AP: P.O.B. 47590, Nairobi; Correspondent ANDREW TORCHIA.

Ceteka: P.O.B. 8727, Nairobi.

Ghana News Agency: P.O.B. 6977, Nairobi.

Novosti Press Agency: P.O.B. 30383, Nairobi; Chief. V. SAVELYEV.

Reuters: P.O.B. 9331, Nairobi.

UPI: P.O.B. 42249, Nairobi; Correspondent RAYMOND WILKINSON.

Tass also has a bureau in Nairobi.

PUBLISHERS

E.A. Directory Co. Ltd.: P.O.B. 41237, Nairobi; f. 1947; subsidiary: United Africa Press Ltd.; publishes directories; Man. Dir. CHANDU BHATT.

East African Literature Bureau: P.O.B. 30022, Nairobi; f. 1948; part of East African Community; encourages the publication and sale of books; publishes, prints and distributes books, including adult education books; promotes African authorship; Dir. N. G. NGULUKULU.

East African Publishing House Ltd.: P.O.B. 30571, Nairobi; educational, academic and general; also publishes *East Africa Journal* and other periodicals; Dirs. Dr. B. A. OGOT, Dr. I. N. KIMAMBO, Prof. W. B. BANAGE, Dr. D. S. NKUNIKA, H. KALBITZER, J. C. NOTTINGHAM.

Equatorial Publishers: Mercury House, P.O.B. 7973, Nairobi; f. 1967; subsidiary: Equator Press; textbooks and literary works.

Heinemann Educational Books (EA) Ltd.: P.O.B. 45314, Nairobi; f. 1967; subsidiary of Heinemann Educational Books Ltd., 48 Charles St., London W.1; textbooks at university and secondary school level, African creative writing in English and the vernacular, general topical books; Man. Dir. R. C. MARKHAM.

Longman Kenya Ltd.: P.O.B. 45925, Nairobi; f. 1965; textbooks and educational materials; Man. T. J. OPENDA.

Marketing and Publishing Ltd.: P.O.B. 49010, Nairobi; f. 1954; publ. *Africana* magazine.

Njogu Gitene Publishers: Nairobi.

Oxford University Press, Eastern Africa Branch: P.O.B. 72532, Nairobi; educational and general; Gen. Man. R. G. HOUGHTON.

Sir Isaac Pitman and Sons Ltd.: Banda St., P.O.B. 46038, Nairobi; Man. D. J. GUMMER.

United Africa Press Ltd.: P.O.B. 1237, Nairobi; f. 1952; Man. Dir. CHANDU BHATT.

University Press of Africa: Bank House, Government Rd., P.O.B. 3981, Nairobi; educational works.

RADIO AND TELEVISION

RADIO

Ministry of Information and Broadcasting: P.O.B. 30025, Nairobi; responsible for Voice of Kenya, the national broadcasting service.

Voice of Kenya: P.O.B. 30456, Nairobi; Kenya Broadcasting Service; f 1959; Dir. J. R. KANGWANA; Chief Engineer S. N. MACHARIA.

Voice of Kenya operates three services: *National:* Kiswahili; *General:* English; *Vernacular:* Hindustani, Kikuyu, Kikamba, Kimeru, Kimasai, Somali, Borana, Luluyia, Kalenjin, Kisii, Kuria, Rendile, Teso, Turkana, Luo; 341 hours' broadcasting a week in 17 languages.

Number of radio receivers: 1,250,000.

TELEVISION

Voice of Kenya Television: Nairobi; television started in October 1962; revenue from licence fees and commercial advertisements; the first installation was at Nairobi in Band 1 on the 625-line system, and there is a second station at Kisumu. A station is planned at Mazeras and a repeater at Nakuru. A television service started in Mombasa on June 1st, 1970.

Number of TV receivers: 36,000.

FINANCE

BANKING

(cap.=capital; p.u.=paid up; dep.=deposits; res.=reserves).

Central Bank of Kenya: P.O.B. 30463, Nairobi; f. 1966; cap. 26m. Ks.; bank of issue, has assumed the Kenyan responsibilities of the former East African Currency Board; 82 branches; Gov. DUNCAN N. NDEGWA.

COMMERCIAL BANKS

Algemene Bank Nederland N.V.: Head Office: 32 Vijzelstraat, Amsterdam, Netherlands; f. 1824; branches at Nairobi (Man. A. TH. HEERENS) and Mombasa (Man. J. J. TER BURG).

Bank of Baroda: Mandvi, Baroda, India; f. 1908; Kenya Head Office: Nairobi; branches at Mombasa, Kisumu and Thika; cap. Ind. Rs. 250m.; dep. Ind. Rs. 4,210m.

Bank of India: Head Office: Express Towers, Nariman Point, Bombay, India; f. 1906; branches at Nairobi (Man. N. T. BHAVNANI), Kisumu, and Mombasa (Man. N. J. PATEL).

Barclays Bank Ltd.: P.O.B. 30120, Queensway House, Mama Ngina St., Nairobi; brs. throughout Kenya; Chair. B. J. COMLEY.

Commercial Bank of Africa Ltd.: P.O.B. 30437, Commercial Bank Building, Standard St., Nairobi; f. 1967 to take over branches in Kenya and Uganda of Commercial Bank of Africa Ltd., incorporated in Kenya; affiliated to Société Financiére pour les Pays d'Outre-Mer, Geneva; Man. Dir. P. HUIZER; Gen. Man. R. M. STANLEY.

Grindlays Bank International (Kenya) Ltd.: P.O.B. 30550, Nairobi; f. 1970; res. K£520,000; merchant and international bankers; 40 per cent government holding; one main office in Nairobi, one in Mombasa; Gen. Man. R. PLANT.

Habib Bank (Overseas) Ltd.: Nkrumah Rd., Fort Mansion, P.O.B. 83055, Mombasa; f. 1952; cap. p.u. Pak. Rs. 5m.; dep. Pak. Rs. 903,589,780 (June 1972).

Kenya Commercial Bank: P.O.B. 48400, Nairobi; f. 1970; 60 per cent government holding.

National Bank of Kenya Ltd.: P.O.B. 72497, Nairobi; f. 1968; cap. p.u. Ks. 20,000,000; dep. Ks. 400,000,000 (June 1973); Chair. P. NDEGWA; Gen. Man. R. S. ATTWOOD.

Standard Bank Ltd.: P.O.B. 30003, Nairobi; cap. p.u. K£4.6m.; 51 brs., 1 trustee br., 10 sub-brs., 40 agencies; Exec. Dir. D. A. STEWART.

MERCHANT BANK

East African Acceptances: Nairobi; cap. p.u. K£75,000.

CO-OPERATIVE BANK

Co-operative Bank of Kenya: P.O.B. 48231, Nairobi.

STOCK EXCHANGE

Nairobi Stock Exchange: Stanbank House, Government Rd., P.O.B. 43633, Nairobi; f. 1954; Chair. F. M. THUO.

INSURANCE

NATIONAL COMPANIES

Jubilee Insurance Co. Ltd.: P.O.B. 30376, Nairobi; f. 1937; Chair. Sir EBOO PIRBHAI, O.B.E.; Man. Dir. P. I. W. VOLKERS, A.C.I.I.

Kenya National Assurance Co.: Nairobi; f. 1965; cap. Ks. 7,015,000; Government holding 96 per cent.

Pan Africa Insurance Co. Ltd.: Pan Africa Insurance Bldg., Kilindini Rd., P.O.B. 90383, Mombasa; f. 1946; cap. p.u. K. sh. 8,000,000; Chair. CHIMANLAL AMBALAL PATEL; Man. A. A. PATEL; Exec. Dir. M. D. NAVARE.

Pioneer General Assurance Society Ltd.: P.O.B. 20333, Nairobi; f. 1930; Chair. OSMAN ALLU; Man. Dir. NIMJI JAVER KASSAM.

FOREIGN COMPANIES

Some twenty of the main British firms, eight Indian companies, and several other insurance organizations are represented in Kenya.

TRADE AND INDUSTRY

East African Industrial Council: P.O.B. 1003, Arusha, Tanzania; grants licences for the scheduled class of products included under the East African Industrial Licensing Ordinance; Chair. D. MWIRARIA.

CHAMBERS OF COMMERCE

Kenya National Chamber of Commerce and Industry: Embassy House, Harambee Ave., P.O.B. 47024, Nairobi; f. 1965; Pres. Z. K. GAKUNJU; Chief Exec. A. M. MATHU.

Constituent branches:

Bungoma: P.O.B. 186, Bungoma.

Busia: P.O.B. 86, Busia.

Eldoret: P.O.B. 313, Eldoret.

Embu: P.O.B. 172, Embu.

Kakamega: P.O.B. 420, Kakamega.

Kericho: P.O.B. 407, Kericho.

Kisumu: P.O.B. 771, Kisumu.

Machakos: P.O.B. 243, Machakos.

Meru: P.O.B. 136, Meru.

Mombasa: P.O.B. 90271, Mombasa.

Nakuru: P.O.B. 178, Nakuru.

Nyeri: P.O.B. 207, Nyeri.

Thika: P.O.B. 147, Thika.

TRADE ASSOCIATIONS

East African Hides & Skins Exporters' Association: P.O.B. 2384, Mombasa; Secs. Tombooth Ltd.

East African Tanners' Association: c/o Post Office, Limuru.

East African Tea Trade Association: Box 42281, Nairobi; f. 1956; 167 mems.

Hard Coffee Trade Association of Eastern Africa: Box 288, Mombasa; 170 mems.; Pres. H. G. FABIAN.

Kenya Wattle Manufacturers' Association: P.O. Box 190, Eldoret.

Mild Coffee Trade Association of Eastern Africa: P.O.B. 2732, Nairobi; f. 1945; 80 mems.

STATUTORY BOARDS

Central Province Marketing Board: P.O.B. 189, Nyeri.

Coffee Board of Kenya: P.O.B. 30566, Nairobi; f. 1947: Chair. E. N. KURIA; Gen. Man. S. CANYOKO.

Kenya Dairy Board: P.O. Box 30406, Nairobi.

Kenya Sisal Board: Mutual Building, Kimathi St., P.O.B. 1179, Nairobi; Exec. Officer R. WILSON-SMITH.

Maize and Produce Board: P.O.B. 30586, Nairobi; f. 1966; Chair. B. M. KAGGIA; Gen. Man. W. K. MARTIN.

Pyrethrum Board of Kenya: P.O.B. 420, Nakuru; f. 1935; 21 mems.; Chair. I. KURIA.

Pyrethrum Marketing Board: P.O.B. 420, Nakuru; f. 1964; Chair. I. N. KURIA; publ. *Pyrethrum Post* (twice-yearly).

Tea Board of Kenya: P.O.B. 20064, Nairobi; f. 1951; 14 mems.; Chair. P. S. T. MIRIE; Sec. S. M. KAMUYU.

DEVELOPMENT CORPORATIONS

Agricultural Development Corporation: Nairobi; f. 1965 to promote and execute schemes for agricultural development and reconstruction.

Agricultural Finance Corporation: P.O.B. 30367, Nairobi; provides loans to farmers for agricultural purposes including land purchases.

Commonwealth Development Corporation: P.O.B. 43233, Nairobi; the C.D.C. had 52 projects in the East Africa Region in December 1972.

Development Finance Co. of Kenya Ltd.: P.O.B. 30483, Nairobi; f. 1963; private limited company with government participation; cap. £3m.

East African Industrial Research Organization: P.O.B. 30650, Nairobi; f. 1942; research and advisory service in the technical problems of industrial development; Dir. C. L. TARIMU.

Industrial and Commercial Development Corporation: P.O.B. 45519, Nairobi; f. 1954; financed by the Government; facilitates the industrial and commercial development of Kenya; Chair. J. KERAGORI; Exec. Dir. J. E. MATU WAMAE.

Kenya Tea Development Authority: P.O.B. 30213, Nairobi; f. 1960 to develop tea growing, manufacturing and marketing among African smallholders, supported by the Kenya Government, C.D.C., the World Bank and Federal Republic of Germany; 76,000 planted tea acres by 79,000 registered growers (1972–73); Chair. JACKSON KAMAU; Gen. Man. C. K. KARANJA.

Settlement Fund Trustees: c/o Ministry of Lands and Settlements, P.O.B. 30450, Nairobi; administers one of the most ambitious land purchase programmes involving over one million acres for resettlement of African farmers. Over 33,000 plots were allocated to approximately 35,000 families between June 1963 and December 1970.

EMPLOYERS' ASSOCIATIONS

Federation of Kenya Employers: Embassy House, Harambee Ave., P.O.B. 48311, Nairobi; Chair. J. K. GECAU; Exec. Dir. DAVID RICHMOND.

AFFILIATES

Agricultural Employers' Association: P.O.B. 1225, Nakuru; Chair. D. WANGUHU.

Association of Local Government Employers: P.O.B. 48311, Nairobi; Chair. Councillor JOHN KERICH.

Association of Pharmaceutical Industries: P.O.B. 48311, Nairobi; Chair. C. MILLAR.

Distributive and Allied Trades Union: P.O.B. 48311, Nairobi; Chair. D. G. Sevastopulo.

Engineering and Allied Industries Employers' Association: P.O.B. 48311, Nairobi; Chair. T. M. Bell.

Federation of Master Printers: P.O.B. 48311, Nairobi; Chair. C. H. Malavu.

Kenya Association of Building and Civil Engineering Contractors: P.O.B. 48311, Nairobi; Chair. W. Greenhut.

Kenya Association of Hotelkeepers and Caterers: P.O.B. 44365, Nairobi; Chair. E. C. Jessop.

Kenya Bankers' (Employers') Association: P.O.B. 30664, Nairobi; Chair. J. T. Smith.

Kenya Coffee Growers' Association: P.O.B. 72832, Nairobi; Chair. V. E. Kirkland.

Kenya Sugar Employers' Union: P.O.B. 48311, Nairobi; Chair. I. M. Shah.

Kenya Tea Growers' Association: P.O.B. 320, Kericho; Chair. P. Robertson.

Motor Trade and Allied Industries Employers' Association: Chair. P. Shepherd.

Nairobi Petrol Dealers' Association: P.O.B. 48311, Nairobi; Chair. A. H. Somji.

Sisal Employers' Association (Kenya): P.O.B. 47523, Nairobi; Chair. R. Bennett.

Timber Industries Employers' Association: P.O.B. 48311, Nairobi; Chair. F. T. Henson.

TRADE UNIONS

Central Organization of Trade Unions (Kenya): Solidarity Bldg., Digo Rd., P.O.B. 13000, Nairobi; f. 1965 as the only federal body of Trade Unionism in Kenya; Pres. Gen. Council F. E. Omido; Chair. Philip Mwangi, J. Nymbira; Sec.-Gen. J. D. Akumu, m.p.; Treas. J. Ndambuki Munene.

Principal Affiliated Unions

Chemical Workers' Union: P.O.B. 73820, Nairobi; Gen. Sec. Were Ogutu.

Civil Servants' Union: P.O.B. 8083, Nairobi; Gen. Sec. Kimani Wa Nyoike.

Dockworkers' Union: P.O.B. 98207, Mombasa; Gen. Sec. Juma Boy.

Electrical Trades Workers' Union: P.O.B. 20226, Nairobi; Gen. Sec. Augustine Sakwa.

External Telecommunications Workers' Union: P.O.B. 30488, Nairobi; Gen. Sec. Mr. Ndola.

Kenya African Custom Workers' Union: P.O.B. 9178, Mombasa; Gen. Sec. Mr. Ogala.

Kenya Engineering Workers' Union: P.O.B. 90443, Mombasa; Gen. Sec. C. Mboya.

Kenya Game and Hunting Workers' Union: P.O.B. 7509, Nairobi; Gen. Sec. M. Ndolo.

Kenya Management Staff Association: P.O.B. 11856, Nairobi; Gen. Sec. Adel Kitito.

Kenya National Parks Employees' Union: P.O.B. 13195, Nairobi; Gen. Sec. P. P. Ooko.

Kenya Petroleum and Oil Workers' Union: P.O.B. 10376, Nairobi; Gen. Sec. Jacob Ochino.

Motor Engineering and Allied Workers' Union: P.O.B. 73651, Nairobi; Gen. Sec. F. E. Omido.

National Union of Journalists: P.O.B. 47035, Nairobi; Gen. Sec. George Odiko.

National Union of Musicians: P.O.B. 7043, Nairobi; Gen. Sec. James Yongo.

National Union of Seamen: P.O.B. 81123, Mombasa; Gen. Sec. I. S. Abdallah.

Plantation and Agricultural Workers' Union: P.O.B. 1161, Nakuru; Gen. Sec. Philip Mwangi.

Printing and Kindred Workers' Union: P.O.B. 72358, Nairobi; Gen. Sec. C. Lubembe.

Quarry and Mine Workers' Union: P.O.B. 48125, Nairobi; Gen. Sec. Henry Koweru.

Shoe Leather Workers' Union: P.O.B. 9629, Nairobi; Gen. Sec. Joshwa Abongo.

Timber Workers' Union: P.O.B. 13172, Nairobi; Gen. Sec. D. N. Matheru.

Union of Sugar Plantations: P.O.B. 766, Kisumu; Gen. Sec. J. D. Akumu.

Principal Independent Unions

East African Railways and Harbours Asian Union (Kenya): P.O.B. 1270, Mombasa; f. 1947; 1,017 mems.; Pres. L. V. Thakar; Gen. Sec. M. S. Jaswal.

Kenya National Union of Teachers: P.O.B. 30407, Nairobi; f. 1957; Sec.-Gen. A. A. Adongo.

Senior Civil Servants' Association of Kenya: P.O.B. 40107, Nairobi; f. 1959; 2,000 mems.; Pres. F. B. Maiko; Gen. Sec. B. A. Ohanga; publ. *The Senior Civil Servants' Association Magazine.*

TRANSPORT

RAILWAYS

East African Railways Corporation: P.O.B. 30121, Nairobi; self-contained and self-financing organization within the East African Community; Chair. D. Wadada Nabudere; Resident Dirs. J. K. Njoroge (Kenya), J. S. Kasambala (Tanzania), H. R. Berunga (Uganda).

There are 5,860 km. of metre-gauge line in East Africa. The main lines are from Mombasa to Nairobi (Kenya) and Kampala (Uganda) and from Dar es Salaam (Tanzania) to Mwanza (Tanzania).

ROADS

East African Road Services Ltd.: P.O.B. 30475, Nairobi; provide bus services within East Africa from Nairobi to Dar es Salaam, Moshi, Kampala, Mombasa and to all major towns in Kenya.

There were approximately 46,768 km. of roads of varying quality at the end of 1972. A total of £11.9m. was spent on road improvement under the 1966–70 development plan. In August 1968 a 495 km. trunk road from Nairobi to Mombasa was opened to traffic. Road development is continuing and the Kenya section of the Nairobi-Dar es Salaam road was tarmacademized in 1972. Reconstruction to make an all-weather road joining Nairobi to Addis Ababa is well under way in both Kenya and Ethiopia.

SHIPPING

East African Harbours Corporation: P.O.B. 9184, Dar es Salaam, Tanzania; responsible for the harbours and controls Mombasa in Kenya as well as Dar es Salaam, Tanga and Mtwara in Tanzania; Chair. P. K. Kinyanjui.

East African Cargo Handling Services: subsidiary of East African Harbours Corpn.; employs 13,000 workers in Mombasa.

Eastern Africa National Shipping Line: Kilindini; f. 1966 by the co-operation of East and Central African governments and Southern Line Ltd.

Bay of Bengal African Line: Agents: The African Mercantile Co. (Overseas) Ltd., P.O.B. 90110, Mombasa; cargo services between E. African ports and Bangladesh, Burma, India and Sri Lanka.

British India Line: Agents: Mackenzie Dalgety (Kenya) Ltd., P.O.B. 90120, Mombasa; joint service with Union Castle Line to United Kingdom and continental ports.

Christensen Canadian African Lines: P.O.B. 80149, Mombasa; direct service to and from Canada via South and East African ports.

Clan Line: Agents: The African Mercantile Co. (Overseas) Ltd., P.O.B. 90110, Mombasa; cargo services between the United Kingdom and East African ports.

D.O.A.L. (Deutsche Ost Afrika Linie): P.O.B. 90171, Mombasa; services to Europe.

Eastern Africa National Shipping Line Ltd.: P.O.B. 90331, Mombasa; operating liner services between East Africa, Europe and the Far East.

Farrell Lines: Mombasa; monthly services to North Atlantic and U.S.A. East Coast Ports.

Harrison Line: Agents: The African Mercantile Co. (Overseas) Ltd., P.O.B. 90110, Mombasa; services between U.K. and East African ports.

Jadranska Slobodna Plovidba: P.O.B. 84831, Mombasa; services to and from Adriatic and East African Red Sea ports.

Lloyd Triestino Line: c/o Mitchell Cotts & Co. (East Africa) Ltd., Kilindini Rd., P.O.B. 90141, Mombasa; monthly passenger and cargo services to Italy.

Lykes Lines: P.O.B. 90150, Mombasa; services to U.S.A. Gulf ports via South African ports.

Mitsui O.S.K. Lines Ltd.: P.O.B. 49952, Nairobi; services to Japan, Hong Kong and Malaysia.

Nedlloyd (EA) Ltd.: P.O.B. 80149, Mombasa; Africa/Europe services to and from Mediterranean and N.W. Continental ports; Africa/Pacific to U.S.A., Pacific ports and Vancouver.

Oriental African Line: Agents: The African Mercantile Co. (Overseas) Ltd., P.O.B. 90110, Mombasa; cargo services between E. African ports and Malaysia, Singapore, Thailand, Indonesia, Hong Kong and Japan.

Robin Line (*Moore McCormack Lines Inc., Robin Line Service*): c/o Mitchell Cotts and Co. (East Africa) Ltd., Kilindini Rd., P.O.B. 90141, Mombasa; services to U.S.A. Atlantic ports from Kenya and Tanzania, and South and Portuguese East Africa.

Royal Interocean Lines: P.O.B. 90342, Mombasa; services to Singapore/Malaysia, Hong Kong and Japan, Australia, New Zealand and Persian Gulf, with connections to other Far East, Pacific and South American and West African ports.

Scandinavian East Africa Line: Agents: The African Mercantile Co. (Overseas) Ltd., P.O.B. 90110, Mombasa; services between E. African and Scandinavian and Baltic ports.

The Shipping Corporation of India Ltd.: Head Office: Steelcrete House, Dinshaw Wacha Rd., Bombay; Branches: P.O.B. 2653, Calcutta, P.O.B. 82364, Mombasa; services include regular and fast cargo services from India to East Africa.

Southern Line Ltd.: P.O.B. 90102, Mombasa; operating dry cargo and tankship vessels between East African coastal ports, Red Sea Ports and Indian Ocean Islands.

Svedel Line: P.O.B. 84831, Mombasa; to and from North-West Continental and East African Red Sea ports.

Swedish East Africa Line: Mombasa; services to Scandinavian, Baltic and North French ports.

Union-Castle Line: Agents: Mackenzie Dalgety (Kenya) Ltd., P.O.B. 90120, Mombasa; joint service with British India Line offers regular sailings to United Kingdom.

Zim Lines: P.O.B. 90150, Mombasa; services to Eilat via Red Sea ports and from Eliat to Australia via Mombasa, Tanga and Dar es Salaam.

CIVIL AVIATION

Caspair Limited: Head Office: P.O.B. 42890, Nairobi; Chief Pilot Capt. STRETTON; f. 1947; Exec. Chair. H. R. PARKER; scheduled services, charter, sales and maintenance.

East African Airways Corporation: *Headquarters:* Sadler House, Koinange St., P.O.B. 41010, Nairobi, Kenya; f. 1945; owned by the East African States; operates extensive services throughout Kenya, Tanzania and Uganda; also regular scheduled services to Europe, the United Kingdom, Pakistan, India, Zambia, Ethiopia, Somalia, Tanzania, Mauritius and Malawi; passenger and cargo charters are operated by Simbair, a subsidiary of EAA; fleet of four VC 10, three DC-9-30, four Fokker F-27, five DC-3; Chair. ARNOLD KILEWO (Tanzania); Dir.-Gen. Col. GAD WILSON TOKO (Uganda).

The East African Directorate of Civil Aviation: P.O.B. 30163, Nairobi; established under the Air Transport Authority in 1948; to advise on all matters of major policy affecting Civil Aviation within the jurisdiction of the East African Community, on annual estimates and on Civil Aviation legislation; the Area Control Centre and an Area Communications Centre are at East African Community, Nairobi. Air traffic control is operated at Nairobi, Dar es Salaam, Entebbe and Mombasa airports, at Wilson (Nairobi) Aerodrome and aerodromes at Arusha, Kisumu, Mwanza, Malindi, Moshi, Mtwara, Tabora, Tanga and Zanzibar; Dir.-Gen. Z. M. BALIDDAWA.

Safari Air Services Tours Ltd.: Head Office: P.O.B. 41951, Nairobi; f. 1969; Man. Dir. JUDY HOURY; tour operators.

The following international airlines run regular services to and from Kenya: Aeroflot, Air France, Air India, Air Madagascar, Air Malawi, Alitalia, British Airways, British Caledonian, EgyptAir, El Al, Ethiopian Air Lines, KLM, Lufthansa, Olympic, PAA, Sabena, SAS, Sudan Airways, Swissair, TWA and Zambian Airways.

TOURISM

Over 400,000 tourists visited Kenya during 1972 and earnings from tourism rose to K£26.5 million.

Ministry of Tourism and Wildlife: P.O.B. 30027, Nairobi; the national tourist body for Kenya.

Kenya Tourist Development Corporation: P.O.B. 42013, Nairobi; f. 1965; Gen. Man. R. M. MAINA; Deputy Gen. Man. W. A. O. MUTSUNE; Finance Man. A. S. BASSAN.

OVERSEAS OFFICE

United Kingdom: Kenya Tourist Office, 318 Grand Buildings, Trafalgar Square, London, W.C.2; Chief Officer PETER MUIRURI.

UNIVERSITY

University of Nairobi: P.O.B. 30197, Nairobi; 340 teachers, 3,857 full-time students.

KHMER REPUBLIC

(CAMBODIA)

INTRODUCTORY SURVEY

Location, Climate, Language, Religion, Flag, Capital

The Khmer Republic, formerly the Kingdom of Cambodia, occupies part of the Indo-Chinese peninsula in South-East Asia. It is bounded by Thailand and Laos to the north, by the Republic of Viet-Nam to the east and by the Gulf of Siam to the south. The climate is tropical. The heaviest rainfall occurs in September. The temperature ranges from 20° to 36°c (68° to 97°F), the average at Phnom-Penh being 27°c (81°F). The Khmer language is the official language spoken by all except the Vietnamese and Chinese minorities. The official religion is Theravada Buddhism. There are about 10,000 Roman Catholics. The national flag, introduced in 1970, is blue, with three five-pointed white stars, arranged horizontally, in the upper fly. In the upper hoist is a red canton containing a white pagoda. The capital is Phnom-Penh.

Recent History

Formerly a French protectorate, in 1949 Cambodia was recognized by France as an independent state within the French Union. In 1953 Cambodia was granted complete independence under its King, Norodom Sihanouk. He abdicated in 1955 to become a political leader, and was elected Head of State in 1960. Now a Prince, he ruled through a cabinet and parliament, but with frequent direct appeals to the electorate to bolster his personal authority. His Government maintained an official policy of neutrality, but during the 1960s developed good relations with the People's Republic of China and North Viet-Nam, while being highly critical of the United States' role in Asia. From 1964, however, the Prince's Government was faced with a pro-Communist insurgency movement, the *Khmer Rouge*. Also, it became increasingly difficult to isolate Cambodia from the war in Viet-Nam. Large numbers of North Vietnamese and National Liberation Front (NLF) troops were on Cambodian soil, and Cambodian territory was violated by Saigon and U.S. air and ground forces.

In March 1970 a *coup* led by the Prime Minister, Lt.-Gen. (later Marshal) Lon Nol, deposed Sihanouk. The new Government pledged itself to the removal of foreign Communist forces and appealed to the U.S.A. for military aid. Supporters of Sihanouk's Government-in-exile, comprising Royalists and the *Khmer Rouge*, aided by the NLF and North Vietnamese troops, quickly put the new régime in jeopardy. In April 1970 a large-scale incursion of Saigon and U.S. forces into Cambodia was required to defend Phnom-Penh. Two months later U.S. troops withdrew, but bombing raids continued and U.S. military assistance was essential to the survival of Lon Nol's régime.

In October 1970 a republic was proclaimed and in June 1972, after the promulgation of a new constitution, Marshal Lon Nol became the first President of the Khmer Republic. His régime has never controlled more than a small fraction of rural areas and its hold on the towns has been precarious. Phnom-Penh has been virtually encircled

by Sihanoukist troops since the inception of the Republic. In August 1973, when U.S. bombing in Cambodia was halted, there was a widespread expectation that Phnom-Penh would fall, but the Sihanoukists seem incapable of a decisive military victory. Prince Sihanouk has claimed that, unwilling to alienate the U.S. Government, North Viet-Nam and China are supplying insufficient arms to allow a victory.

During 1973 an increasing number of foreign states recognized the Government-in-exile as the rightful government of Cambodia. In September 1973 Prince Sihanouk represented his country at the conference of non-aligned nations in Algiers. However, his attempts to replace the Khmer Republic at the UN have so far failed. In Republican-controlled areas inflation and rice shortages have led to strikes, while failure to pay troops has provoked protests and desertions. Phnom-Penh has to hold over half a million refugees at a time when the war has reduced supplies. Corruption is rife in high ranks of the army and Government. An American-inspired attempt to broaden the base of Lon Nol's Government led to the appointment of opposition politicians to high positions in early 1973, but the experiment collapsed in December when Gen. In Tam, a leading opposition figure, resigned as Prime Minister. Prince Sihanouk has so far refused to negotiate with Lon Nol.

Government

Under the Constitution, parliament comprises an upper house, the Senate, and a lower house, the National Assembly. The President is directly elected for a term of five years and is the head of the armed forces. In a national emergency the President may prorogue parliament for one year.

Defence

The Republican armed forces comprise 187,200 men, including an army of 180,000. Hostilities continue against opposition forces. Estimates of their strength vary between 40,000 and 200,000 men, including about 2,000 North Vietnamese military advisers. The Republic is one of the Protocol States of the South East Asia Treaty Organization (SEATO).

Economic Affairs

The economy is based on agriculture and fishing. Rice is the staple food crop and was until recently the principal export. Rubber, maize and pepper are also exported. Since independence there has been considerable small-scale industrial development. Under French sponsorship an oil refinery was constructed at Kompong-Som. Until 1970, despite some difficulties, the economy was functioning well and the population had a good standard of living by South-East Asian standards. The continuing military conflict has since severely disrupted the economy, both through war-damage and the deliberate economic blockade of the Republic by insurgent forces. The area of rice under cultivation dropped from 2,428,000 hectares in 1969 to 782,000 hectares in 1973. Very little rice or rubber is allowed to pass from rebel-controlled areas to the Government side. The Republic has become a net importer of rice and rubber exports have fallen dramatically.

There is a large balance of payments deficit. The Government's 1973 budget estimates put expenditure at about four times revenue. Disruption of communications has hampered industry, and political uncertainty has reduced investment. The Republic has become almost totally dependent upon U.S. aid, which amounted to $341 million in 1972 and has been rising since.

Transport and Communications

A railway of 385 km. links Phnom-Penh with Thailand's border at Poipet via Battambang. Another (270 km.), links Phnom-Penh with Kompong-Som. The port of Kompong-Som on the Gulf of Siam was opened in 1960. The port is linked by road to Phnom-Penh. The Mekong river and the waters of the Tonlé-Sap (*Great Lake*) provide the main inland waterways and are extensively used.

Social Welfare

Prior to the start of hostilities there were over 600 hospitals and dispensaries but about half of these have since been destroyed. There is a system of unemployment insurance for industrial workers. There are about 1 million refugees and some 20,000 homes have been demolished.

Education

In 1972, 446,537 primary school children and 84,440 secondary students were enrolled. Primary education commences at six years of age and continues for six years. There are five universities.

Tourism

Principal attractions are the many monuments of the great Khmer Empire (9th to 14th century A.D.). The temple complex of Angkor Wat is one of the architectural wonders of the world. Until 1970 tourism was an important section of the economy, but since then has ceased owing to military activity.

Visas are required by all visitors.

Sport

There is little organized sport. Cock-fighting and cricket fighting are popular.

Public Holidays

1974: September 26th–28th (Ceremony of the Dead), October 9th (Republic Day), October 24th (UN Day), November 9th–12th (Ceremony of the Waters), December 10th (Rights of Man).

1975: February 17th (Makhaboja), April 27th (New Year), May 1st (Labour Day), May 12th (Constitution Day), May 17th (Visakhanaboja).

There are also a number of religious holidays dependent on the lunar calendar.

Weights and Measures

The metric system is in force.

Currency and Exchange Rates

100 sen = 1 riel.

Exchange rates (January 1974):

£1 sterling = 687.65 riels;
U.S. $1 = 302.00 reils.

STATISTICAL SURVEY

AREA AND POPULATION

AREA*	POPULATION (1962 Census)					
	Total	Races				Phnom-Penh (capital)
		Khmer	Vietnamese	Chinese	Others	
181,035 sq. km.	5,728,771	5,334,000	218,000	163,000	14,000	393,995

* 2.59 sq. km. = 1 sq. mile.   **Population** (estimate 1972): 6,944,000.

Other Towns: Battambang (38,800 in 1962), Kompong Chhnang, Kompong Cham, Kompong Som.

Births and Deaths: Average annual birth rate 44.6 per 1,000; death rate 15.6 per 1,000 (UN estimates for 1965–70).

Employment (1970): Total economically active population 2,963,000, including 2,264,000 in agriculture (ILO and FAO estimates).

AGRICULTURE

LAND USE, 1967
('000 hectares)

Arable Land	2,832
Under Permanent Crops	152
Permanent Meadows and Pastures . .	580
Forest Land	13,372
Other Land	724
TOTAL LAND AREA .	17,660
Inland Water . . .	444
TOTAL	18,104

Source: FAO, *Production Yearbook.*

PRINCIPAL CROPS
('000 metric tons)

	1967–68	1968–69	1969–70	1970–71
Rice (paddy)*	3,251.0	2,503.0	3,814.0	2,732.0
Rubber	53.7	51.1	46.0	—
Beans	29.0	31.7	34.2	19.5
Maize	154.0	117.2	137.0	121.0
Manioc	40.1	31.0	36.0	14.9
Cane Sugar (raw value) .	49.8	45.0	50.0	29.6
Tobacco	11.8	13.7	14.6	9.7
Peanuts	21.1	25.7	23.6	16.8
Palm Sugar . . .	44.6	47.0	34.2	22.6
Sweet Potatoes . . .	15.8	18.2	19.0	17.3

* 1971–72: 1,927,000 metric tons.

LIVESTOCK
('000)

	1966–67	1967–68	1968–69
Cattle	2,269	2,399	1,918
Buffaloes . . .	856	898	718
Pigs . . .	1,078	1,152	1,151

FORESTRY

	1967–68	1968–69	1969–70
Timber ('000 cu. m.) .	327.7	362.5	89.9
Charcoal (tons) .	14,709.7	16,935.9	6,600

INDUSTRY

		1967	1968	1969
Electricity	million kWh.	95,300	128,300	127,829†
Cement	metric tons	60,000	57,800	59,000
Paper	,, ,,	3,695	4,582	4,164
Plywood . . .	sq. metres	1,600,000	3,300,000	1,920,000
Jute Bags . . .	units	1,700,000*	4,000,000	4,200,000
Refined Sugar . .	metric tons	10,000	12,300	11,500
Textile Fabrics . .	metres	54,000,000	51,000,000	59,500,000
Alcohol . . .	hectolitres	99,000	100,000	100,000
Cigarettes . . .	million	3,500	3,700	3,807†
Car Tyres . . .	units	22,800	35,000	39,000
Fertilizers . . .	metric tons	10,000	11,400	10,000

* Seven months. † Revised.

Cigarettes (million): (1970) 3,853; (1971) 3,338; (1972) 2,700.
Diesel Oil ('000 litres) (1969) 73,200; (1970) 32,700; (1971) 28,200.
Electricity (million kWh.): (1970) 132,700; (1971) 147,900; (1972) 151,200.

KHMER REPUBLIC—(Statistical Survey)

FINANCE

100 sen = 1 riel.

Coins: 10, 20 and 50 sen.

Notes: 1, 5, 10, 20, 50, 100 and 500 riels.

Exchange rates (January 1974): £1 sterling = 687.65 riels; U.S. $1 = 302.00 riels.

1,000 riels = £1.454 = $3.311.

BUDGET*
(million riels)

REVENUE	1970	1971	EXPENDITURE	1970	1971
Customs Duties	3,300	1,315	Defence	3,332	11,031
Income and Business Taxes . .	3,279	2,056	General Administration . .	3,255	3,993
Other Taxes and Administrative			Education	1,992	2,350
Revenue . . .	1,286	811	Health and Welfare . .	461	503
Land Revenue . . .	180	66	Public Works and Communications	445	507
Extraordinary Receipts . .	1,775	14,452	Agriculture. . . .	314	283
			Commerce, Industry and Mines .	21	33
TOTAL . .	9,820	18,700	TOTAL . .	9,820	18,700

* No official budget estimates were made for 1972.

Currency in circulation: Riels 18,429m. (March 1972).

EXTERNAL TRADE
(million riels)

	1966	1967	1968	1969	1970	1971
Imports .	3,888	3,365	4,043	4,234	2,892	4,191
Exoprts .	2,356	2,907	3,098	2,729	2,124	827

COMMODITIES
(million riels)

IMPORTS	1969	1970	EXPORTS	1969	1970
Agricultural and Food Products .	321.4	258.1	Rice	478.5	894.4
Mineral Products . . .	243.9	248.8	Rubber	1,101.1	349.1
Textiles	243.2	107.5	Maize	154.3	107.5
Metals and Metal Manufactures .	2,016.5	1,278.6	Haricot Beans . . .	132.1	99.1
Pharmaceuticals . . .	326.2	213.6	Timber	125.2	68.5
Chemicals . . .	372.5	296.5	Sesamum . . .	36.4	82.4
TOTAL (incl. others) .	4,233.6	2,893.0	TOTAL (incl. others) .	2,729.2	2,124.6

Source: Banque Nationale du Cambodge, *Bulletin Mensuel.*

PRINCIPAL TRADING PARTNERS
(million riels)

	IMPORTS		EXPORTS	
	1969	1970	1969	1970
Bulgaria	2.4	1.1	29.2	n.a.
China, People's Republic . . .	312.0	42.1	54.7	159.1
Czechoslovakia . . .	63.9	29.7	17.3	200.9
France and Franc Zone . .	1,142.4	726.0	718.9	443.2
German Democratic Republic .	37.7	60.8	n.a.	n.a.
Germany, Federal Republic .	185.3	174.6	66.6	40.1
Hong Kong	268.0	275.5	371.3	414.1
India	59.9	1.4	n.a.	n.a.
Indonesia	14.0	1.7	0.3	n.a.
Italy	64.5	48.6	85.2	35.5
Japan	1,002.0	669.4	145.0	124.3
Malaysia	5.4	7.7	n.a.	17.5
Singapore	250.5	294.7	173.9	191.1
Netherlands . . .	54.6	21.8	129.3	37.4
Pakistan	48.5	n.a.	n.a.	n.a.
Poland	2.7	5.8	n.a.	n.a.
U.S.S.R.	37.0	22.4	n.a.	63.5
United Kingdom . . .	143.5	98.9	110.0	52.7
U.S.A.	151.5	135.3	135.1	13.9
Viet-Nam, Democratic Republic .	32.7	22.4	56.7	18.0
Viet-Nam, Republic . . .	28.5	11.0	555.5	275.2
Yugoslavia	12.8	1.0	n.a.	n.a.

Source: Banque Nationale du Cambodge, *Bulletin Mensuel.*

TRANSPORT

Railways (1970): Passenger/km. 100,000,000*, Freight/km. 78,000,000†.

Roads (1970): Cars 1,355, Trucks 9,627, Motor Cycles and Scooters 17,954.

Shipping (1971—Phnom-Penh): Ships arriving 241, ships departing 241; Freight unloaded 307,686 metric tons, loaded 94,932 metric tons; (1970—Kompong-Som-ville): Ships entered and cleared 180; Freight unloaded 449,363 metric tons, loaded 287,564 metric tons.

Civil Aviation (1970): Passenger arrivals 133,376, departures 149,789; Freight (tons) loaded 327.8, unloaded 414.7.

* 1971: 90,528,000.   † 1971: 39,600,000.

EDUCATION
PUBLIC AND PRIVATE
(1970–71)

	SCHOOLS	TEACHING STAFF	STUDENTS*
Primary	1,490	n.a.	446,537
Secondary . . .	95	3,513	84,440
Technical and Professional .	78	280	3,039
Higher	47†	1,603	10,793

* 1971–72.   † 1969–70.

Source: Institut National de la Statistique et des Recherches Economiques, Phnom-Penh.

THE CONSTITUTION*

(promulgated April 30th, 1972)

The preamble states that the Constitution of the Khmer Republic is based on the fundamental principles contained in the Universal Declaration of Human Rights. The Constitution promotes a political and social democracy within a republican framework. Buddhism is the state religion. There is complete freedom of conscience, worship, expression and association subject to the maintenance of public order. The State assures every citizen the freedom to exercise his full political rights, including that of publicly expressing his opposition to the Government, providing that this is done without recourse to violence and in a law-abiding manner. The official language is Khmer. The formation of political parties is free though the State encourages the evolution of a bi-partite form of government. *Habeas Corpus* is guaranteed and capital punishment abolished except in the case of national emergency. All citizens aged 18 and over are entitled to vote.

The President

The President and Vice-President are elected by direct suffrage for a period of five years. The President nominates the Prime Minister and the Council of Ministers of which he is the chairman. The President is Commander-in-Chief of the armed forces. He can declare war or a state of emergency upon a government proposal and after approval by both Chambers sitting jointly.

Parliament

Parliament is composed of the National Assembly and the Senate. The National Assembly comprises 126 seats, Deputies are directly elected for four years. The Senate is made of forty Senators serving for six years, three-fifths of whom are elected indirectly by the people, one-fifth by the civil administration and the remaining fifth by the Council of the Armed Forces. Half of the Senate is re-elected every three years. Parliament is in session twice a year and votes on government bills, bills presented by either Chamber, the budget, state loans, declarations of war and of national emergency. With the advice of the *Conseil d'Etat* it gives its approval to financial matters. In time of war or national emergency, members of Parliament may be elected by direct suffrage. In the event of an election being impossible, the President of the Republic has the power to prorogue the Parliament for a period of one year. In both cases the Constitutional Court must be previously consulted.

The Judiciary

The Supreme Court is composed of nine judges including its president who are elected by both Chambers of Parliament from a list of twenty judges presented by the members of the judiciary. The Supreme Court can initiate legislation affecting the functioning of the judiciary. By a two-thirds majority it can dissolve political parties whose activities are judged to be harmful to the State. The Constitutional Court supervises the election of the President and decides disputes arising from parliamentary elections. It determines the constitutionality of bills presented to Parliament.

Constitutional Amendment

The initiative for amendment of the Constitution may come from the Government or from at least half of the members of one of the two Chambers of Parliament. A majority of three-quarters of each of the Chambers is required before a proposed amendment can be put to the people for their approval.

* Following an abortive *coup* by supporters of Prince Sihanouk on March 17th, 1973, civil rights and freedom of the Press were suspended for six months.

Note: The Constitution was approved in a referendum held on April 30th, 1972. The voting was as follows: 1,608,298 in favour; 41,172 votes against.

THE GOVERNMENT

HEAD OF THE STATE

President: Marshal LON NOL (elected June 4th, 1972).

HIGH EXECUTIVE COUNCIL

Chairman: Marshal LON NOL, *President of the Republic.*
Members: LONG BORET, *Prime Minister*; Gen. SOSTHENE FERNANDEZ, *Chief of Armed Forces*; SIRIK MATAK, *Special Presidential Adviser.*

THE CABINET

(*July* 1974)

Prime Minister: LONG BORET.

First Deputy Prime Minister and Minister of Education and Relations with Parliament: PAN SOTHI.

Second Deputy Prime Minister and Minister of Defence, War Veterans and War Wounded, Public Works and Communications: THAPPANA NGINN.

Minister of the Interior, Religious Affairs, General Mobilization, Pacification and Security: EK PREUNG.

Minister in charge of the Prime Minister's Department and Minister of National Reconciliation: HOU HONG.

Minister of Information CHHANG SONG.

Minister of Foreign Affairs: KEUK KY LIM.

Minister of Finance, Planning and Economy: KHY TAING LIM.

Minister of Commerce and Provisioning: IEU YANG.

Minister of Culture: DUONG SARIN.

Minister of Justice: LY KVANG PAN.

Minister of Public Health: KIM VIEN.

Minister of Agriculture: UNG SU HAI KIM PENG.

Ministry of Industry, Fishing and Natural Resources: CHEAV SEANG LEANG.

Minister of Labour and Social Action: THACH TOAN.

Minister of Refugees and Community Development: KONG ORN.

Minister of Tourism: LOEUNG NAL.

DIPLOMATIC REPRESENTATION

EMBASSIES AND LEGATIONS IN PHNOM-PENH
(E) Embassy.

Australia: 94 Moha Vithei 9 Tola (E).

Belgium: *Ambassador:* M. DE VLEESCHAUWER.

Burma: 70 Moha Vithei 9 Tola (E) (also accred. to Laos).

Czechoslovakia: 100 Moha Vithei 9 Tola (E) (*chargé d'affaires*).

France: 25 Moha Vithei Preah Bat Monivong (E) (*chargé d'affaires*).

German Democratic Republic: (*chargé d'affaires*).

India: 219 Vithei Oknha Men (E) (*chargé d'affaires*).

Indonesia: 18 Vithei Samdech Pann (E) (also accred. to Laos).

Israel: 7 Vithei Oknha Nhiek Tioulong (E).

Japan: 4 Moha Vithei Prates Barang Ses (E).

Laos: 13 Vithei 18 March (E).

Philippines: 65 Vithei Samdech Pann (E).

Poland: 253 Moha Vithei Preah Bat Monivong (E) (*chargé d'affaires*).

Singapore: 16 Vithei Keo Chea (E); *Ambassador:* HARRY CHAN KENG HOWE.

Spain: 6 Vithei Samdech Pann (E).

U.S.S.R.: 45–47 Vithei Botun Soryavong (E).

United Kingdom: 96 Moha Vithei 9 Tola (E); *Ambassador:* JOHN POWELL-JONES.

U.S.A.: 9 Tola (E).

Diplomatic relations have been established with Bangladesh, the Republic of Korea, the Republic of Viet-Nam, Malaysia, Thailand and the Federal Republic of Germany.

PRESIDENT

(Elections held in government-controlled areas, June 4th, 1972)

CANDIDATE	VOTES CAST	PERCENTAGE OF VOTES CAST
Marshal LON NOL	578,203	55.9
General IN TAM	257,320	24.0
KEO AN	217,341	20.1
TOTAL	1,052,864	100.0

PARLIAMENT

NATIONAL ASSEMBLY

Comprises 126 seats (*see* also the Constitution). The first elections for seats to the National Assembly were held on September 3rd, 1972, when the Social Republican Party (*see* under Political Parties) secured all the seats.

SENATE

Comprises forty seats (*see* also the Constitution). On September 17th, 1972, Government candidates won all of the seats contested.

POLITICAL PARTIES

Social Republican Party: Phnom-Penh; f. June 1972 to contest general elections held in September 1972; government party; 126 seats in the National Assembly; Sec.-Gen. HANG THUN HAK.

People's Party (*Pracheachon*): f. June 1972 to contest general elections held in September 1972; socialist of left-wing complexion; Leader Major PEN YUT.

DEFENCE

Armed Forces (1973): Total strength 187,200; army 180,000, navy 3,400, air force 3,800; military service is voluntary though conscription is authorized but not yet in force.

Equipment: The army has French and American tanks, armoured cars and Soviet artillery. The navy is equipped with various gunboats, patrol and torpedo boats of undisclosed origin. The air force has American and some Soviet aircraft and French helicopters.

Defence Expenditure: The Defence Budget for 1973 was 17,800 million riels.

Chief of Staff (Khmer Armed Forces): Gen. SOSTHENE FERNANDEZ.

JUDICIAL SYSTEM

Khmer law is based on the French system, modified to suit local conditions (*see* also under Constitution).

The Supreme Court

The Supreme Court, established by the Constitution, is the highest judicial authority in the country. It is composed of nine judges, including its president, who are elected by both Chambers of Parliament from a list of twenty judges presented by the members of the judiciary.

Magistrates stationed in the interior have preliminary civil and criminal powers. Important cases are referred to the provincial Tribunals which also have power to revise sentences passed by the magistrates. The Supreme Court is the final judicial authority in the country. It has original jurisdiction in matters like treason and constitutional rights and has appellate jurisdiction over all other matters.

Chief Justice: Ly Kvan Pan.

Superior Council of Magistrates

This Council, established by the constitution, ensures conformity with the laws, discipline and independence of the magistrates in the Republic. It is composed of the Minister of Justice (President); four members elected by the National Assembly; and two members elected by the Magistrates.

The Council takes all its decisions by majority vote. In case of a tie the President has a casting vote.

RELIGION

BUDDHISM

The state religion of the Khmer Republic is Theravada Buddhism, (Buddhism of the Little Vehicle), the sacred language of which is Pali. There are more than 2,500 monasteries throughout the land and nearly 20,000 Bonzes (Buddhist priests).

Supreme Authority: The Head of State.

Sangaraja of the Khmer Republic His Eminence Huot Tath, Vat Unnalon, Phnom-Penh.

CHRISTIANITY

There are about 10,000 Roman Catholics (3,000 Khmers, 2,000 Europeans, 4,000 Vietnamese and 1,000 Chinese). Vicar Apostolic of Phnom-Penh Mgr. Yves Ramousse, 69 Boulevard Monivong, Phnom-Penh; Apostolic Prefecture of Battambang Mgr. Tef Im Suthu; Prefecture of Kompong Cham Mgr. Andre Yesouef.

THE PRESS

All Khmer language publications were suspended following an abortive *coup* against the President on March 19th, 1972, by supporters of the exiled Prince Sihanouk.

DAILIES

Le Républicain: 223E Vithei Charles de Gaulle; f. 1967; French; State controlled; Editor-in-Chief P. Littaye Suon.

Koh Santepheap: 678 Vithai Nehru; Khmer; Editor-in-Chief Saing Hell.

Le Courrier Phnompenhois: 31 Vithai Samdech Iem; French; State controlled; Editor-in-Chief Sath Hassavy.

Le Nouvelle Depeche: P.O.B. 647, Phnom-Penh.

Nokor Thom: 377 Vithai Serei Pheap; Khmer; Editor-in-Chief Vath Van.

Prayoch Khmer: 25 Vithai Monireth; Khmer; State controlled; Editor-in-Chief Saloth Chhay.

Sathea Ranak Khmer: 294 Blvd. Monivong; Khmer; Dir. Keam Reth.

Sethkech Khmer: 92 Vithei Prey Nokor; Khmer; Editor-in-Chief (vacant).

Sroch Srang Cheat: 133 Vithei Kampuchea Krom; Chinese and Vietnamese editions; State controlled; Editors-in-Chief Khuon Thay, Lam Bieu.

WEEKLIES

Jeunesse de Sauvetage: c/o Ministry of Youth and Sports; Khmer; Editor-in-Chief Non Neavear.

Réalités Cambodgiennes: 4 Vithei Okhna Oum; French; State controlled; Dir. Chak Sarik.

Revue Economique: 2 Vithei Kanha Diepvanara (B.P. 44), Phnom-Penh; f. 1941; organ of the *Chambre Mixte de Commerce, d'Agriculture et d'Industrie*; published Tuesday and Friday.

FORTNIGHTLY

Fou Nan: Khmer and French; State controlled; Man. Chum Sarun.

MONTHLY

Khmer Nouveau: 98 Vithei Decho Dam Din; French and English; State controlled; Editor-in-Chief Lim Leang Chin.

PERIODICAL

Nokor Khmer: Secretariat General du Sangkum, Phnom Penh; French; monthly; Dir. Sim Var.

PRESS AGENCY

A.K.P. (Agence Khmère de Presse): Vithei Ang Non, Phnom-Penh; f. 1951; Dir. Thong Lim Huong; Editor-in-Chief Chea Van; Admin. Hong Neak.

Agence France-Presse (A.F.P.) and Tass are also represented.

RADIO AND TELEVISION

RADIO

Radiodiffusion Nationale Khmère: 28 Avenue Chuon Nath, Phnom-Penh; controlled by the Ministry of Information; services in Khmer, French, English, Thai, Chinese, Laotian and Vietnamese; Dir.-Gen. Ly Kim Uong.

Number of radio receivers (1972): 105,000.

TELEVISION

Radio Khmère-Television: 28 Avenue Preah Mohaksatryany Nossamak, Phnom-Penh; services started March 1962.

Number of television receivers (1972): 30,000.

FINANCE

BANKS

Central Bank

Banque National du Cambodge: 22-24 Moha Vithei 9 Tola, Phnom-Penh; f. 1955; cap. p.u. 200m. riels; total resources: riels 24,081.4m. (Dec. 31st, 1971); Gov. M. Hing Kunthel; Deputy Gov. Chai Thoul.

State Commercial Banks

Banque Khmère pour le Commerce: 26 Vithei Kramuon Sâr, P.O.B. 627, Phnom-Penh; f. 1964; the most important State Commercial Bank for all banking transactions; cap. 417m. riels; total resources 4,468.7m. riels (Dec. 31st, 1971); eight branches in the Khmer Republic; Pres. and Dir.-Gen. Hing Kunthon.

Banque Inadana Jati: 28 Pau Kambo, Phnom-Penh; principal State Commercial Bank for Industry and Commerce; f. 1964; cap. 100m. riels; total resources 1,977.5m. riels (Dec. 31st, 1971); 13 brs.; Chair. Seng Bun Korn.

Foreign Banks

The *Banque Nationale de Paris*, the *Banque Française Commerciale* and the *Chartered Bank* are authorized to maintain representatives.

INSURANCE

(Nationalized 1964)

Société Nationale d'Assurances-S.N.A.: 174-182 M. V. Prachea Thippatei, Phnom-Penh, P.O.B. 37; f. 1964; cap. 8om. riels; Gen. Man. Ky Beng Chhon, LL.D.

TRADE AND INDUSTRY

Chambre Mixte de Commerce, d'Agriculture et d'Industrie de Phnom-Penh: 2 Kannha Diep Vannara; publ. *Revue Economique.*

Entreprise Nationale des Produits Pharmaceutiques— ENAPHAR: Phnom-Penh; import, processing and distribution of pharmaceutical products.

Société nationale d'importation (SONAPRIM): Phnom-Penh.

TRANSPORT AND TOURISM

Railways (*Chemins de Fer de la République Khmère*): Gare Centrale de Phnom-Penh, Moha Vithei Preah Bat Monivong, Phnom-Penh; Pres. and Dir.-Gen. In Nhel; Asst. Dir.-Gen. Seng Kim Chun; Sec.-Gen. Var Heng. A line, built in 1930–32 and 1939–40 and totalling 385 km. in length, connects Phnom-Penh with the Thai border (at Poipet) via Battambang. Since June 1970, owing to war damage, only the Pursat-Poipet section (225 km.) is open. Construction of a new line, 270 km. in length and linking Phnom-Penh with Kompong-Somville, via Takeo and Kampot, was started in 1960, opened in December 1969, has been closed since April 1970. Total length is about 1,370 km.

Roads: There are nearly 11,000 km. of motorable roads and tracks, of which about 2,000 km. are asphalted.

Waterways: The major routes are along the Mekong River, and up the Tonlé-Sap River into the Tonlé-Sap (Great Lake) covering in all about 1,400 km.

Shipping: The main port is Kompong-Som on the Gulf of Siam, which handles vessels up to 10,000 tons; the total of berths was raised to 10 in 1970 at a cost of U.S. $50m. Phnom-Penh, which lies some distance inland, can take steamers of up to 4,000 tons.

CIVIL AVIATION

National Line

Air Cambodge: AC Bldg., Viethei Chan Nak, B.P. 539, Phnom-Penh; f. 1956; services to Hong Kong, Singapore, Saigon, Bangkok; domestic services to Battambang, Kompong Som; Pres. and Dir.-Gen. Ung Krapum Phka; Comm. Dir. Ke Sath; fleet of one Caravelle, one DC-6, three DC-4, two DC-3, one B.N. Islander.

Foreign Lines

The following foreign air lines are represented: Air France, Air Vietnam, Royal Air Lao, U.T.A.

TOURISM

Commissariat Général au Tourisme: 161–163 Kralahom Kong St., Phnom-Penh. B.P. 392; General Commissioner for Tourism Mrs. Ung Mung.

UNIVERSITIES

Université des Beaux-Arts: Phnom-Penh; *c.* 120 teachers, *c.* 500 students.

Université Bouddhique: Phnom-Penh; *c.* 20 teachers, 180 students (ment).

Université de Phnom-Penh: Phnom-Penh; *c.* 340 teachers, *c.* 5,300 students.

Université des Sciences Agronomiques: Phnom-Penh; 46 teachers, 124 students.

Université Technique: Phnom-Penh; 234 teachers, 928 students.

DEMOCRATIC PEOPLE'S REPUBLIC OF KOREA

INTRODUCTORY SURVEY

Location, Climate, Language, Religion, Flag, Capital

The Korean peninsula juts south from North China, between the Yellow Sea and the Sea of Japan, the Democratic People's Republic occupying the northern part of the peninsula, north of a line which roughly follows the 38th parallel. (The southern part is occupied by the Republic of Korea.) The climate is continental, with cold, dry winters and hot, humid summers; average temperatures range from −6°C (21°F) to 25°C (77°F). The language is Korean. Buddhism, Confucianism, Taoism, Shamanism and Chundo Kyo are the chief religions. The national flag (proportions 65 by 33) is red with blue stripes on the upper and lower edges, each separated from the red by a narrow white stripe. Left of centre is a white disc containing a five-pointed red star. The capital is Pyongyang.

Recent History

The ancient sovereign kingdom of Korea was occupied by Japan from 1910 to 1945, when the northern part of the peninsula was taken by the U.S.S.R. and the southern part by the U.S.A. No agreement could be reached on a unified government and in 1946 the North Korean Provisional People's Committee was set up. The Soviet army withdrew in 1948 and in 1950 the Korean War broke out. The Northern Korean forces were supported by the Chinese People's Republic and Southern Korea by a United Nations Force composed of units from sixteen countries. In 1953 a Military Armistice Agreement was signed at Panmunjom, establishing the present frontier. The well-established government of Marshal Kim Il Sung, in power since 1948, has maintained a militant attitude towards the U.S. and her Asian allies. In August 1971 talks took place for the first time between the Red Cross Societies of both North and South Korea with the aim of fostering greater intercourse between the two parts.

In July 1972 a North-South Korean agreement was announced in which both parties affirmed that reunification should be achieved through peaceful means, that hostile propaganda should cease, and that official contacts between the two countries be encouraged. Reunification talks were, however, suspended in 1973, and prospects for *détente* suffered a serious setback when in February 1974 North Korean gunboats sank a South Korean trawler in disputed waters and took another boat captive, accusing the South Korean government of sending the boats on an espionage mission. In December 1972 the fifth session of the Supreme People's Assembly adopted a new constitution and elected Kim Il Sung as President. The Democratic People's Republic of Korea has observer status at the United Nations and is a member of the World Health Organization.

Government

The Constitution was adopted on December 27th, 1972. Under it the highest organ of government is the Supreme People's Assembly. Its principal functions include the election of the President, Vice-President, members of the Central People's Committee and the Premier of the Administration Council. It also approves the budget and decides on questions of war and peace. The President convenes and presides over the Administration Council, promulgates legislative enactments and other decisions of the Supreme People's Assembly and other state organs and is responsible to the former. The Central People's Committee is responsible for the administration of government both at central and local levels.

Defence

Defence treaties have been signed with the U.S.S.R. and the Chinese People's Republic. Military service is selective: army 3 years, navy and air force 4 years. The total strength of the armed forces is reportedly 470,000 men and an estimated 1.5 million men are in the Workers' and Peasants' Militia. The air force comprises 45,000 men and the navy 17,000. Defence expenditure in 1973 (1,282 million won) represented some 15 per cent of total government expenditure.

Economic Affairs

With the establishment of the Democratic Republic all industry was nationalized and land distributed among the peasants. The Korean War destroyed most of the country's resources and in 1957 the first of two plans was launched to restore production and lay the foundations of future industrial development. Agriculture has been collectivized and production has increased. About half the working population are still employed on the land. A Six-Year Plan (1971–76) aims at doubling the output of coal, electricity, iron and steel by 1976. Industrial development has concentrated on heavy industry: electricity, metallurgy, machine-building and chemicals. The country is rich in minerals. Coal production reportedly totalled 27.5 million metric tons in 1970 (U.S. estimate: 24 million tons). China, the U.S.S.R. and Japan account for the majority of North Korea's trade. Agreements have been signed with Mongolia and the German Democratic Republic. Trade with non-communist countries is growing rapidly.

Transport and Communications

The road and rail network was almost completely destroyed during the Korean War. Part of the new railway system is electrified and there are direct rail links with Moscow and Peking. Roads have been rebuilt to take the increasing traffic. There are regular passenger and freight services along the Aprok, Daidong and Ryesung rivers, but little air traffic exists. International air services connect Pyongyang to Peking and Moscow. A radio broadcasting network covers most villages. A television network is to be introduced within five years.

Social Welfare

The state provides rest homes, sanitoria and free medical services.

Education

Free and compulsory primary education was introduced in 1956. All children between the ages of 5 and 16 receive free education in state schools, including one year of kindergarten. There is one university with more than 16,000 students, and 98 other higher educational institutions.

Tourism

Tourism has yet to be developed although the country has great potential. Mount Keumgang and Songdowon are beauty spots.

Sport

The state encourages athletics, football, wrestling and table tennis.

Public Holidays

1974: August 15th (Anniversary of Liberation), September 9th (Independence Day).

1975: January 1st (New Year), May 1st (May Day).

Weights and Measures

The metric system is in force.

Currency and Exchange Rates

100 jun (jeon)=1 won.

Exchange rates (April 1974):
£1 sterling=2.373 won;
U.S. $1=1.005 won.

STATISTICAL SURVEY

AREA AND POPULATION

AREA*	POPULATION					
	Official Estimates‡		UN Estimates (mid-year)			
	Dec. 31st, 1960	Oct. 1st, 1963	1970	1971	1972	1973
120,538 sq. km.†	10,789,000	11,568,000	13,892,000	14,281,000	14,680,000	15,087,000

* Excluding the demilitarized zone between North and South Korea, with an area of 1,262 square kilometres (487 square miles).

† 46,540 square miles.

‡ *Source:* Institute of Economics of the World Socialist System, Moscow.

ADMINISTRATIVE DISTRICTS
(Population '000—December 1966)

North and South Pyongan	3,474	Kangwon	1,050
North and South Hwanghae	2,294	Chagang	739
North and South Hamgyong	3,032	Yanggand	422
Pyongyang City (including metropolitan area)	1,364	Kaesong	265

PRINCIPAL CITIES
(1960 population)

Pyongyang (capital)*	653,100
Chongjin	184,300
Hungnam	143,600
Kaesong	139,900

* Population 1,364,000 (including metropolitan area) in December 1966.

BIRTHS AND DEATHS

	Births (per '000)	Deaths (per '000)
1960	38.5	10.5
1961	36.7	11.5
1962	41.1	10.8
1963	42.7	12.8

1965–70 (UN estimates): Average annual birth rate 38.8 per 1,000; death rate 11.2 per 1,000.

EMPLOYMENT

	1959 %	1963 %
Factory Workers	37.2	40.2
Office Workers	13.4	15.1
Peasants on Co-operatives	45.7	42.8
Handicraftsmen in Co-operatives	3.3	1.9
Others	0.4	—
	100.0	100.0

Total employment (1964): 2,092,000 (incl. 780,000 women).

Total labour force (mid-1970): In a population of 13,674,000, the economically active numbered 5,898,000, including 3,138,000 in agriculture (FAO and ILO estimates).

AGRICULTURE

LAND USE, 1960
('ooo hectares)

Arable and under permanent crops . .	1,894*
Forest Land	8,970†
Other land and inland water . .	1,190
TOTAL AREA . . .	12,054

* Excluding temporary meadows and pastures.

† Including rough grazing. Data taken from the world forest inventory carried out by the FAO in 1958.

PRINCIPAL CROPS
(FAO estimates)

	AREA HARVESTED ('ooo hectares)				PRODUCTION ('ooo metric tons)			
	1968	1969	1970	1971	1968	1969	1970	1971
Wheat	160	160	160	160	85	85	85	85
Rye	8	8	8	8	7	7	7	7
Barley	220	240	240	240	250	275	275	275
Oats	80	83	83	83	56	60	60	60
Maize	820	860	860	860	1,600	1,800	1,800	1,800
Millet	450	450	450	450	330	350	350	350
Sorghum	65	65	65	65	55	55	55	55
Rice (Paddy) . . .	700	700	700	700	2,450	2,700	2,800	2,800
Potatoes . . .	150	160	160	160	930	1,000	1,000	1,000
Sweet Potatoes and Yams .	35	35	35	n.a.	250	250	275	n.a.
Pulses . . .	700	710	710	700	420	425	430	420
Soybeans . . .	385	385	385	385	215	215	225	225
Cottonseed . . .	} 15	15	15	15	{ 6	6	6	6
Cotton (Lint) . . .					3	3	3	3
Tobacco . . .	33	33	33	33	40	40	40	40
Hemp Fibre . . .	7	7	7	8	2.2	2.2	2.2	2.3

Source: FAO, *Production Yearbook 1971.*

Six-Year Plan 1971-76: 1976 targets include 7.0–7.5 million tons of grain (including 3.5 million tons of rice), and 0.8 to 1 million tons of fruits.

LIVESTOCK
(FAO estimates for December)

	1967	1968	1969	1970
Cattle	700,000	720,000	730,000	740,000
Pigs	1,280,000	1,300,000	1,330,000	1,370,000
Sheep	165,000	170,000	180,000	192,000
Goats	168,000	169,000	170,000	173,000
Horses	25,000	26,000	26,000	27,000
Asses	3,000	3,000	3,000	3,000

Source: FAO, *Production Yearbook 1971.*

Sericulture (1961): Silk Cocoons 7,501 tons.

LIVESTOCK PRODUCTS
(FAO estimates, metric tons)

	1968	1969	1970	1971
Beef and Veal*	18,000	19,000	19,000	20,000
Mutton, Lamb and Goats' Meat* . .	2,000	2,000	2,000	2,000
Pork*	47,000	47,000	47,000	48,000
Poultry Meat	14,000	15,000	15,000	n.a.
Cows' Milk	11,000	15,000	16,000	17,000
Hen Eggs	45,000	45,200	46,000	47,000

* Meat from indigenous animals only, including the meat equivalent of exported live animals.

Source: FAO, *Production Yearbook 1971.*

FORESTRY
ROUNDWOOD REMOVALS
('ooo cubic metres)

	1968	1969	1970
Coniferous (soft wood) .	3,000	3,100	3,100
Broadleaved (hard wood)	1,500	1,500	1,600
Total .	4,500	4,600	4,700

Source: United Nations, *Statistical Yearbook 1971.*

FISHING
(tons)

1962	1963	1964	1967
840,000	640,000	770,000	1,200,000

Fish Caught: Myungtai (cod-like fish), Pollack, Mackerel, Herring, Yellow Tail, Grunt, Mullet, Hair-Tail, Carp, Octopus, Magin Clam, Sea Cucumber, Oyster, etc.

MINING
(estimated production, 'ooo metric tons)

	1967	1968	1969	1970
Hard Coal	17,000	20,400	22,200	24,000
Lignite and Brown Coal . . .	4,400	4,500	4,900	5,700
Iron Ore*	3,252	3,506	3,760	4,014
Copper Ore*	12	12	12	13
Lead Ore*	65	70	70	70
Magnesite	1,250	1,361	1,542	1,633
Tungsten concentrates† . . .	2.7	2.7	2.7	2.7
Zinc Ore*	115	120	125	130
Salt	550	544	544	544
Phosphate Rock	250	300	300	300
Sulphur‡	200	200	200	200

Note: No recent data are available for the production of graphite (62,000 metric tons in 1960), molybdenum ore and asbestos.

* Figures relate to the metal content of ores.
† Figures relate to the tungsten trioxide content of concentrates.
‡ Figures refer to the sulphur content of iron and copper pyrites, including pyrite concentrates obtained from copper, lead and zinc ores.

Source: United Nations, *Statistical Yearbook 1972,* quoting (except for lignite) the Bureau of Mines, U.S. Department of the Interior.

INDUSTRY
(estimated production—'000 metric tons)

	1967	1968	1969	1970
Nitrogenous Fertilizers (a)* . . .	115	117	157	205
Phosphate Fertilizers (b)* . . .	80	75	80	100
Coke Oven Coke	1,800	2,000	2,000	2,200
Cement†	2,590	2,695	3,000	4,010
Pig Iron and Ferro-alloys† . .	1,795	2,050	2,300	2,400
Crude Steel† . . .	1,450	1,750	2,000	2,180
Refined Copper (unwrought)† .	12	12	12	13
Lead (primary metal)† . . .	55	55	55	55
Zinc (primary metal)† . . .	88	80	60	90

* Figures for fertilizer production are unofficial estimates quoted by the FAO. Output is measured in terms of (a) nitrogen or (b) phosphoros pentaoxide.
† *Source:* Bureau of Mines, U.S. Department of the Interior.

SIX-YEAR PLAN 1971–76

	Unit	Reported 1970 Targets	1976 Targets
Electricity	million kWh.	16.5	28–30
Coal	million tons	27.5	50–53
Iron Ore . . .	,, ,,	7.2	n.a.
Pig and Granulated Iron . .	,, ,,	2.3	3.5–3.8
Crude Steel . . .	,, ,,	2.2	3.8–4.0
Rolled Steel . . .	,, ,,	1.7	2.8–3.0
Chemical Fertilizers . . .	,, ,,	1.5	2.8–3.0
Cement	,, ,,	4–4.5	7.5–8.0
Magnesium Clinker . . .	,, ,,	n.a.	1.6
Grain	,, ,,	5–7	7.0–7.5*
Textiles . . .	mill. metres	350–400	500–600
Chemical Fibres . . .	'000 tons	80–100	50
Synthetic Resin . . .	,, ,,	60–70	n.a.
Tractors . . .	numbers	n.a.	21,000
Machine Tools . . .	,,	n.a.	27,000
Refrigerators . . .	,,	n.a.	126,000

* Of which 3.5 is rice.

FINANCE
100 jun (jeon) = 1 won.
Coins: 1, 5 and 10 jun.
Notes: 50 jun; 1, 5, 10, 50 and 100 won.
Exchange rates (April 1974): £1 sterling = 2.373 won; U.S. $1 = 1.005 won.
100 won = £42.15 = $99.52

BUDGET
(million won)

	1968	1969
Revenue . . .	5,038.2	5,995.4
Expenditure . .	4,835.0	5,995.4
of which:		
National Economy .	2,364.3	3,002.7
Defence . .	1,566.5	1,798.7

1971: Revenue 6,357,350,000 won; Expenditure 6,301,680,000 won.

1972 (proposals): Revenue and Expenditure to balance at 7,374 million won (defence spending 17 per cent of the total).

EXTERNAL TRADE

COMMODITIES
(U.S. $'000)

	JAPAN*		OTHER WESTERN COUNTRIES†	
	Exports	Imports	Exports	Imports
	1963–68	1963–68	1965–68	1965–68
Food and Live Animals	10,044	149	261	43,788
Beverages and Tobacco . . .	61	—	33	120
Crude Materials (non-fuels) . . .	46,638	2,840	2,114	884
Mineral Fuels . . .	4,769	311	—	22
Animal and Vegetable Oils and Fats .	—	1,450	—	56
Chemicals	410	12,392	79	2,493
Manufactured Goods . . .	68,604	29,122	23,320	4,905
Machinery and Transport Equipment .	48	15,014	62	24,980
Miscellaneous Manufactured Goods .	183	3,112	203	1,072
Other Goods and Transactions . .	1	829	—	502
TOTAL‡	130,724	65,276	26,211	78,803

* 1970: Exports U.S.$23.3 million; Imports U.S.$34.4 million.

† Western Europe and Canada (but excluding Norway and Sweden). ‡ Including others.

Note: North Korean trade with Japan and other Western Countries represents about 15 per cent of all foreign trade.

TRADING PARTNERS
(1966)
(Compiled from statistics of partner countries)
(U.S. $'000)

	IMPORTS	EXPORTS
U.S.S.R.	85,600	92,300
Poland	5,780	6,400
Czechoslovakia . . .	3,800	10,100
German Democratic Republic .	3,800	3,100
Romania. . . .	3,600	3,100
Hungary . . .	800	3,100
Cuba . . .	2,600	—
Japan . . .	24,000*	32,000*
Hong Kong . . .	153*	3,200*
France . . .	7,800*	15,700*

* 1969.

TRANSPORT
INTERNATIONAL SEA-BORNE SHIPPING
(estimated traffic, '000 metric tons)

	1969	1970
Goods loaded . . .	1,200	1,300
Goods unloaded . .	310	420

Source: United Nations, *Statistical Yearbook 1972.*

EDUCATION
(1966–67)

	SCHOOLS	TEACHERS	PUPILS
Primary . .	4,064	22,132	1,113,000†
Middle . .	3,335	30,031	704,000†
Technical .	1,207	12,144	285,000†
Higher Technical .	500*	5,862	156,000†
University and Colleges .	129*	9,244	200,000*

* 1970. † 1964–65.

Sources (unless otherwise stated): Society for Cultural Relations with Foreign Countries, Pyongyang; *Far Eastern Economic Review,* Hong Kong; *Korea Today,* Pyongyang; The American University *Area Handbook for North Korea* 1969.

THE CONSTITUTION

(adopted December 27th, 1972)

The following is a summary of the main provisions of the Constitution.

Articles 1-6: The Democratic People's Republic is an independent socialist State (Art. 1); the revolutionary traditions of the State are stressed (its ideological basis being the *Juche* idea of the Workers' Party of Korea) as is the desire to achieve national reunification by peaceful means on the basis of national independence.

Articles 7-10: National sovereignty rests with the working people who exercise power through the Supreme People's Assembly and People's Assemblies at lower levels, which are elected by universal, secret and direct suffrage.

Articles 11-17: Defence is emphasised as well as the rights of overseas nationals, the principles of friendly relations between nations based on equality, mutual respect and non-interference, proletarian internationalism, support for national liberation struggles and due observance of law.

Articles 18-48: Culture and education provide the working people with knowledge to advance a socialist way of life. Education is free and there are universal and compulsory one-year pre-school and ten-year senior middle school programmes in being.

Articles 49-72: The basic rights and duties of citizens are laid down and guaranteed. These include the right to vote (for those over the age of 17), to work (the working day being eight hours), to free medical care and material assistance for the old, infirm or disabled, to political asylum. National defence is the supreme duty of citizens.

Articles 73-88: The Supreme People's Assembly is the highest organ of State power, exercises exclusive legislative authority and is elected by direct, equal, universal and secret ballot for a term of four years. Its chief functions are: (i) adopts or amends legal or constitutional enactments; (ii) determines State policy; (iii) elects the President, Vice-President, Secretary and members of the Central People's Committee (on the President's recommendation); (iv) elects members of the Standing Committee of the Supreme People's Assembly, the Premier of the Administration Council (on the President's recommendation), the President of the Central Court and other legal officials; (v) approves the State Plan and Budget; (vi) decides on matters of war and peace. It holds regular and extraordinary sessions, the former being twice a year, the latter as necessary at the request of at least one-third of the deputies. Legislative enactments are adopted when approved by more than half of those deputies present. The Standing Committee is the permanent body of the Supreme People's Assembly. It examines and decides on bills; amends legislation in force when the Supreme People's Assembly is not in session; interprets the law; organizes and conducts the election of Deputies and judicial personnel.

Articles 89-99: The President as Head of State is elected for four years by the Supreme People's Assembly. He convenes and presides over Administrative Council meetings, is the Supreme Commander of the Armed Forces and chairman of the National Defence Commission. The President promulgates laws of the Supreme People's Assembly and decisions of the Central People's Committee and of the Standing Committee. He has the right to issue orders, to grant pardons, to ratify or abrogate treaties and to receive foreign envoys. The President is responsible to the Supreme People's Assembly.

Articles 100-106: The Central People's Committee comprises the President, Vice-President, Secretary and Members. The Committee exercises the following chief functions: (a) directs the work of the Administration Council as well as organs at local level; (b) implements the constitution and legislative enactments; (c) establishes and abolishes Ministries, appoints Vice-Premiers and other members of the Administration Council; (d) appoints and recalls ambassadors and defence personnel; (e) confers titles, decorations, diplomatic appointments; (f) grants general amnesties, makes administrative changes; (g) declares a state of war. It is assisted by a number of Commissions dealing with Internal Policy, Foreign Policy, National Defence, Justice and Security and other matters as may be established. The Central People's Committee is responsible to the Supreme People's Assembly's Standing Committee.

Articles 107-114: The Administration Council is the administrative and executive body of the Supreme People's Assembly. It comprises the Premier, Vice-Premiers and such other Ministers as may be appointed. Its major functions are the following: (i) directs the work of Ministries and other organs responsible to it; (ii) works out the State Plan and takes measures to make it effective; (iii) compiles the State Budget and gives effect to it; (iv) organizes and executes the work of all sectors of the economy as well as transport, education and social welfare; (v) concludes treaties; (vi) develops the armed forces and maintains public security; (vii) may annul decisions and directives of State administrative departments which run counter to those of the Administration Council. The Administration Council is responsible to the President, Central People's Committee and the Supreme People's Assembly.

Articles 115-132: The People's Assemblies of the province (or municipality directly under central authority), city (or district) and county are local organs of power. The People's Assemblies or Committees exercise local budgetary functions, elect local administrative and judicial personnel and carry out the decisions at local level of higher executive and administrative organs.

Articles 133-146: Justice is administered by the Central Court—the highest judicial organ of the State, the local Court, the People's Court and the Special Court. Judges and other legal officials are elected by the Supreme People's Assembly. The Central Court protects State property, Constitutional rights, guarantees that all State bodies and citizens observe State laws and executes judgements. Justice is administered by the court comprising one judge and two people's assessors. The Court is independent and judicially impartial. Judicial affairs are conducted by the Central Procurator's Office which exposes and institutes criminal proceedings against accused persons. The Office of the Central Procurator is responsible to the Supreme People's Assembly, the President, and the Central People's Committee.

Articles 147-149: These articles describe the national emblem, the national flag and designate Pyongyang as the capital.

THE GOVERNMENT

(*April* 1974)

President: Marshal KIM IL SUNG.

Vice-Presidents: CHOE YONG KUN, KANG RYANG UK.

CENTRAL PEOPLE'S COMMITTEE

Members: KIM IL SUNG, CHOE YONG KUN, KANG RYANG UK, KIM IL, PAK SUNG CHUL, CHOE HYON, O JIN U, KIM DONG GYU, KIM YONG JU, KIM CHUNG NIN, HYON MU GWANG, YANG HYON SOP, KIM MAN GUM, LI GUN MO, CHOE JAE U, LI JONG OK, RIM CHUN CHU, YON HYONG MUK, O TAE BONG, NAM IL, HONG WONG GIL, RYU JANG SIK, HO DAM, KIM BYONG HA.

Secretary: RIM CHUN CHU.

ADMINISTRATION COUNCIL

Premier: KIM IL.

Vice-Premiers: PAK SUNG CHUL, KIM MAN GUM, CHOE JAE U, NAM IL, HO DAM, LI GUN MO, CHONG CHUN GI, HONG SONG NAM, KIM YONG JU.

Chairman of the State Planning Commission: HONG SONG NAM.

Chairman of the Heavy Industry Commission: LI JONG OK.

Chairman of the Machine-building Industry Commission: HONG WONG GIL.

Chairman of the Light Industry Commission: NAM IL.

Chairman of the Agricultural Commission: SO KWAN HI.

Chairman of the Transport and Communication Commission: HYONG MU GWANG.

Chairman of the Commission for the Service of the People: PAK SUNG CHUL.

Minister of the People's Armed Forces: CHOE HYON.

Minister of Foreign Affairs: HO DAM.

Minister of Public Security: LI CHIN SU.

Minister of the Ship Machine-building Industry: HAN SONG YONG.

Minister of the Chemical Industry: KIM HWAN.

Minister of Fisheries: KIM YUN SANG.

Minister of the Building Materials Industry: MUN BYONG IL.

Minister of Higher Education: SON SONG PIL.

Minister of Common Education: KIM SU TOK.

Minister of Culture and Art: LI CHANG SON.

Minister of Finance: KIM GYONG PYON.

Minister of Commerce: LI SANG SON.

Minister of Foreign Trade: KYE UNG TAE.

Minister of External Economic Affairs: KONG JIN TAE.

Minister of Construction: PAK IM TAE.

Minister of Labour Administration: CHONG DU HWAN.

Minister of Public Health: LI RAK BIN.

Secretary of the Administration Council: HONG WONG GIL.

DIPLOMATIC REPRESENTATION

EMBASSIES AND LEGATIONS ACCREDITED TO THE
DEMOCRATIC PEOPLE'S REPUBLIC OF KOREA

(In Pyongyang)

Albania, Bulgaria (*Ambassador:* K. KELCHEV), Burundi, Cambodia (Royalist government-in-exile), Cameroon, Central African Republic, Chad, People's Republic of China (*Ambassador:* LI YUN-CHUAN), The People's Republic of the Congo (*Ambassador:* OKYEMBA MORLENDE PASCAL), Cuba, Dahomey, Equatorial Guinea, the Gambia, German Democratic Republic (*Ambassador:* FRANZ EVERHARTZ), Ghana, Guinea (*Ambassador:* KAMANO ANSOU), Guinea-Bissau, Iraq (*Ambassador:* YACOUB K. AL HAMDANI), Madagascar, Maldives, Mali (*Ambassador* resident in Peking), Malta, Mauritania, Mongolia (*Ambassador:* GELEGBARMIDIYN VANDAN), Nepal (*Consul-General:* NIRANJAN BATTARAI), Pakistan, Romania (*Ambassador:* DUMITRU POPA), Somalia (*Ambassador:* AHMED MOHAMMED DARMAD), Sudan, Syria (*Ambassador:* YASSIR FARRA), Tanzania (*Ambassador:* SALIM AHMED SALIM), Togo, Uganda, U.S.S.R. (*Ambassador:* N. G. SUDARIKOV), Upper Volta, Democratic Republic of Viet-Nam (*Ambassador:* LE THIET HUNG), Provisional Revolutionary Government of the Republic of South Viet-Nam (*Ambassador:* NGUYEN VAN HOA), Yemen Arab Republic (*Ambassador:* ABDOU OTHMAN MOHAMED), People's Democratic Republic of Yemen and Zambia.

The Democratic People's Republic of Korea also has diplomatic relations with Argentina, Austria, Bangladesh, Burma, Costa Rica, Czechoslovakia, Denmark, Egypt, Finland, France, Iceland, India, Indonesia, Iran, Kuwait, Lebanon, Liberia, Malaysia, Mauritius, Norway, Poland, Rwanda, Senegal, Sierra Leone, Sweden, Yugoslavia and Zaire.

PARLIAMENT

SUPREME PEOPLE'S ASSEMBLY

(Fifth Session held December 25th–29th, 1972)

Chairman: HWANG JANG YOP.

Vice-Chairmen: HONG GI MUN, HO JONG SUK.

Deputies: The 457 Deputies of the fifth Supreme People's Assembly were elected on December 13th, 1972.

STANDING COMMITTEE

Chairman: HWANG JANG YOP.

Vice-Chairmen: HONG GI MUN, HO JONG SUK.

Secretary: CHON CHANG CHOL.

Members (*December* 1972): SO CHOL, IK SU, CHON CHANG CHOL, PAK SHIN DOK, KIM YONG NAM, CHONG JUN GI, RYOM TAE JUN, KIM SONG AE, KIM I HUN, LI YONG BOK, YUN GI BOK, LI DU CHAN, KANG SONG SAN, O HYON JU, CHON SE BONG, LI MYON SANG.

POLITICAL PARTIES

The Workers' Party of Korea: Pyongyang, f. October 10th, 1945; the ruling party; membership: 1,600,000.

General Secretary of the Central Committee: KIM IL SUNG.

Party Organs:
Rodong Sinmun (newspaper), *Gunroja* (theoretical journal).

The Democratic Front for the Reunification of the Fatherland: Pyongyang; f. 1949; a united national front organization embracing patriotic political parties and social organizations for reunification of North and South Korea.

Members of the Central Committee:
KIM RYO JUNG, KANG RYANG UK, HAN DUK SU, SO CHOL, LI GUK RO, KO JUN TAEK.

North Korean Democratic Party: Pyongyang; f. 1945; Chair. KANG RYANG UK.

Religious Chungu Party: Pyongyang; f. 1946; Chair. PAK SHIN DUK.

JUDICIAL SYSTEM

Central Court: Pyongyang, the Central Court is the highest judicial organ and supervises the findings of all courts.

President: PANG HAK SE.

Central Procurator's Office: supervises work of procurator's offices in provinces, cities and counties.

Procurator-General: CHONG DONG CHOL.

Procurators supervise the ordinances and regulations of all ministries and the decisions and directives of local organs of state power to see that they conform to the Constitution, laws and decrees, as well as to the decisions and orders of the Cabinet. Procurators bring suits against criminals in the name of the state, and participate in civil cases to protect the interests of the state and citizens.

RELIGION

The traditional religions are Buddhism, Confucianism, Shamanism and Chundo Kyo, a religion peculiar to Korea combining elements of Buddhism and Christianity.

BUDDHISM

Korean Buddhist Federation: Pyongyang; Chairman AN SOOK YONG.

THE PRESS

PRINCIPAL NEWSPAPERS

Jokook Tongil: Pyongyang; organ of the Committee for the Peaceful Unification of Korea.

Joson Inmingun (*Korean People's Army*): Pyongyang; f. 1948.

Kyowon Shinmoon: Ministry of General Education.

Minjoo Chosun: Pyongyang; Supreme People's Assembly and the Cabinet.

Nongup Keunroja: Pyongyang; Central Committee of the Korean Agricultural Working People's Union.

Pyongyang Shinmoon: Pyongyang; general news.

Rodong Sinmun (*Labour Daily*): Pyongyang; f. 1945; organ of the Central Committee of the Korea Worker's Party; Editor-in-Chief CHONG JUN GI; circ. 300,000.

Rodongja Shinmoon: Pyongyang; General Federation of Trade Unions of Korea.

Saenal: Pyongyang; Socialist Working Youth League.

Sonyun Shinmoon: Pyongyang; Publishing House of the Socialist Working Youth League.

PERIODICALS
PRINCIPAL PERIODICALS

Children's Literature: Pyongyang.

Chullima: Pyongyang; popular general.

Economic Knowledge: State Publishing House, **Pyongyang**; scientific.

Keunroja: Pyongyang; Korean Workers' Party.

Korean Arts: Pyongyang.

Korean Film: Pyongyang; for amateur artists.

Korean Fine Arts: Pyongyang.

Korean Literature: Pyongyang.

Korean Music: Korean Composers' Union, Pyongyang.

Korean Women: Korean Women's Democratic Union, Pyongyang.

Youth Life: Pyongyang.

FOREIGN LANGUAGE PUBLICATIONS

Information on Korea: Pyongyang; Spanish.

Korea: Pyongyang; pictorial; in Russian, Chinese, English and French.

Korea Today: Pyongyang; English, French, Spanish and Japanese.

Korean Information: Pyongyang; French.

Korean Stamps: Philatelists' Union, Oesong District, Pyongyang; English; bi-monthly.

Korean Trade: Pyongyang; Russian and English.

Korean Trade Union: Pyongyang; Russian and English.

Korean Women: Pyongyang; English.

Korean Youth and Student: French, Russian, English.

New Korea: Pyongyang; Russian and Chinese.

The Pyongyang Times: Pyongyang; English.

NEWS AGENCIES

Korean Central News Agency: Pyongyang; sole distributing agency for news in Korea; publs. *Korean Central News Agency* (daily), *Photo Dispatch*, *Daily Release* (English and Russian), *Korean Year Book*.

FOREIGN BUREAU

Tass is the only foreign agency with a bureau in Pyongyang.

PUBLISHERS

PYONGYANG

Academy of Sciences Publishing House: Central District Nammundong; f. 1953; publs. *Kwahakwon Tongbo* (Journal of the Academy of Sciences of the D.P.R. of Korea) bi-monthly; *Kwahakgwa Kwahakgoneop* (Journal of Chemistry and the Chemical Industry) bi-monthly; also quarterly journals of Geology and Geography; Metals; Biology; Analytic Chemistry; Mathematics and Physics; and Electricity.

Academy of Social Sciences Publishing House.

Agricultural Books Publishing House: Pres. LI HYUN U.

Economic Publishing House.

Educational Books Publishing House.

Foreign Languages Publishing House: Pres. L. RYANG HUN.

Higher Educational Books Publishing House: Acting Pres. SHIN JONG SUNG.

Industry Publishing House.

Korean Workers' Party Publishing House.

Mass Culture Publishing House.

Medical Science Publishing House.

Photo Service.

Publishing House of the General Federation of Literary and Art Unions.

Transportation Publishing House: f. 1952; Acting Editor PAEK JONG HAN.

RADIO

Korean Central Broadcasting Committee: Pyongyang; programmes relayed nationally with local programmes supplied by local radio committees. Loudspeakers are installed in factories and in open spaces in all towns. Home broadcasting hours: 0500 to 0200 hrs. Foreign broadcasts are in Russian, Chinese, English, French, Spanish, Arabic and Japanese.

Note: A national TV network is to be inaugurated within the next five years. Production of TV sets is expected to reach 100,000 by 1976.

FINANCE

BANKING

Korean Central Bank: Pyongyang; f. 1946; res. 500m. won; the issuing and control bank; loans for industrial and rural construction.

Foreign Trade Bank of the Democratic People's Republic of Korea: Namoondong, Central District, Pyongyang; f. 1963; state bank; operates payments with foreign banks and control of foreign currencies.

Korean Industrial Bank: Pyongyang; f. 1964; operates short-term loan, saving, insurance work, guidance and control of financial management of co-operative farms and individual remittance.

INSURANCE

State Insurance Bureau: Pyongyang; handles all life, fire, accident, marine, hull insurance and reinsurance as the national enterprise.

Korea Foreign Insurance Co. (*Chosunbohom*): Dongdaewan District, Pyongyang; handles all foreign insurance.

TRADE AND INDUSTRY

Korean Committee for the Promotion of International Trade: Pyongyang; Sec.-Gen. PAK SE CHAN.

Korean Council of the Central Federation of Consumption Co-operative Trade Union: Pyongyang.

Korean General Merchandise Export and Import Corporation: Pyongyang.

Korea Minerals Export and Import Corporation: Pyongyang.

TRADE UNIONS

General Federation of Trade Unions of Korea: Pyongyang; f. 1945; total membership (1970) 2,200,000; 10 affiliated unions; Chair. RYOM TAE JUN; publs. *Rodongja Shinmoon, Rodongja, Korean Trade Unions.*

General Federation of Literature and Arts of Korea: Pyongyang; f. 1961; Chair. of Central Committee LI KI YONG.

Branch unions:

Korean Painters' Union: Pyongyang; Chair. CHONG KWAN CHUL.

Korean Writers' Union: Pyongyang; Chair. CHUN SE BONG.

Korean Cameramen's Union: Pyongyang; Chair. KO RYONG JIN.

Korean Dancers' Union: Pyongyang; Chair. PAK KYONG JA.

Korean Drama Workers' Union: Pyongyang; Chair. LI JAI DUK.

Korean Film Workers' Union: Pyongyang; Chair. LI JONG SOON.

Korean Musicians' Union: Pyongyang; Chair. LI MYUN SANG.

General Federation of Agricultural and Forestry Technique of Korea: Chung Ku-yuck Nammundong, Pyongyang; f. 1946; publ. *Nong-oup Kisyl* (monthly journal of technical information on agriculture).

General Federation of Industrial Technology of Korea: Pyongyang; f. 1946; 65,368 mems.

Korean Agricultural Working People's Union: Pyongyang; f. 1965 to replace former *Korean Peasants' Union*; 2,400,000 mems.; Chair. LI RIM SU.

Korean Architects' Union: Pyongyang; f. 1954; 500 mems.; Chair. KIM JUNG HI.

Korean Democratic Lawyers' Association: Pyongyang; f. 1954; Pres. KIM HYUNG KUN.

Korean Democratic Scientists' Association: Pyongyang; f. 1956.

Korean Journalists' Union: Pyongyang; f. 1946; Chair. CHONG JUN GI.

TRANSPORT AND TOURISM

TRANSPORT

Railways: 10,500 km. of track; steam, diesel and electric trains, through services to Peking and Moscow. Electrification is 21 per cent. There are two main lines; the Kaesong–Sinuiji (431 km.), and the Najin–Rashin (862 km.), in operation.

Rivers: Yalu and Daidong, Dooman and Ryesung are the most important commercial rivers. Regular passenger and freight services: Manopo-Chosan-Soopoong; Chungsoo-Shinuijoo-Dasado; Nam-po-Jeudo; Pyongyang-Nampo.

Shipping: There is much fishing and coastal traffic. Foreign vessels call at Nampo, Chongjin and Hamheung. There is a joint D.P.R.K.-Polish shipping company (*Korean Polish Maritime Brokers' Agency*) in Pyongyang; operates services between North Korean, Asian and Australian ports.

Civil Aviation: Civil Aviation Administration of the D.P.R. of Korea: Stalin St., Pyongyang; internal and external services; fleet: Il-14, Li-2.

Services are also provided by *C.A.A.C.* and *Aeroflot.*

TOURISM

Korean International Tourist Bureau: "Ryuhaingsa", Pyongyang.

UNIVERSITY

Kim Il Sung University: Pyongyang; f. 1946; 900 teachers, over 16,000 full and part-time students.

REPUBLIC OF KOREA

INTRODUCTORY SURVEY

Location, Climate, Language, Religion, Flag, Capital

The Republic of Korea forms the southern part of the Korean peninsula between North China and Japan. To the north, separated by a frontier which roughly follows the 38th parallel, is the Democratic People's Republic of Korea. The climate is marked by cold, dry winters with an average temperature of –6°C (21°F) and hot, humid summers with an average temperature of 25°C (77°F). The language is Korean. Mahayana Buddhism is the principal religion with over 7 million adherents. Christians number about 4,000,000, of whom about 80 per cent are Protestant. Other religions include Confucianism, Taoism and Chundo Kyo, a religion peculiar to Korea, combining elements of Shaman, Buddhist and Christian doctrines. The national flag (proportions 3 by 2) consists of a disc divided horizontally by an S-shaped line, red above and blue below, on a white field with parallel black bars (broken and unbroken) in each corner. The capital is Seoul.

Recent History

The ancient sovereign kingdom of Korea was held by Japan from 1910 to 1945, when the southern part was occupied by U.S. forces and the northern part by the U.S.S.R. Since no agreement could be reached to form a unified government, elections were held in 1948 in the southern half of the country, under United Nations auspices, and a Republican Government was established. In 1950 a major war broke out between North and South Korea. South Korea was supported by a UN force drawn from 16 nations and led by the U.S.A. North Korea was supported by Chinese forces. In 1953 a Military Armistice Agreement was signed at Panmunjom, establishing the present frontier with a demilitarized zone on either side. Following the fall of President Syngman Rhee in 1960 conditions were unsettled but after a military *coup* in 1961 general elections were held in November 1963, and civilian rule was again established. A Normalization Treaty with Japan was signed in Tokyo in June 1965. The government of President Park Chung Hee lived down the unpopularity of this measure, and in 1967 the President and his government were re-elected with increased majorities. President Park was re-elected for a third term in May 1971.

In July 1972 a joint North-South Korean agreement was announced which included resolutions for peaceful reunification and the fostering of official contacts. Opposition to President Park's régime, and in particular to the activities of the Korean Central Intelligence Agency, led to the imposition of martial law in October 1972. This was lifted for the elections of February 1973, in which the ruling Democratic Republican Party obtained a majority of elected members in the new unicameral National Assembly. However, a growing call for the restoration of democracy led to two emergency measures in January 1974 prohibiting criticisms of the October 1972 constitutional amendments.

Government

Under the Constitution of 1963, the President is elected by popular vote for a four-year term. The unicameral National Assembly, the highest legislative body, consists of 219 seats representing both regional and national constituencies. The Prime Minister and Cabinet are appointed by the President. Under constitutional amendments introduced in October 1972, the President can be elected for life and can exercise extraordinary powers. A National Conference for Unification, having a six-year term, elects the President and one-third of the members of the new National Assembly which, though having reduced powers, can dismiss the Prime Minister and other Ministers.

Defence

Protection of the Korean frontier is a United Nations' responsibility and a United Nations' force, consisting chiefly of about 43,000 American troops (reduced from 63,000 in June 1971), is maintained. Military service in South Korea lasts for thirty-three months in the army and three years in the navy and air force. In 1973 the strength of the Korean Armed Forces amounted to 668,500 men. Defence expenditure for 1973 is estimated at U.S. $476 million.

Economic Affairs

The Republic's economy was completely disrupted by the Korean War, but a complete recovery was achieved by the United Nations Korean Rehabilitation Agency (UNKRA) and the United States. Agriculture is the mainstay of the economy, about 58 per cent of the working population being engaged in farming in 1972. The chief crop is rice. Wheat, barley and sweet potatoes are also important. Fishing is both an export and a food source, and South Korea is now one of the world's leading ocean-fishing nations. A deep-sea fishing base and associated processing plants are being built at Ulsan. There are substantial coal deposits and other minerals include iron ore, tungsten, gold, graphite and fluorite. A five-year natural resources development plan was announced in 1973. New industries are playing an increasingly important role in the economy, especially electronics, cotton textiles and food processing. Internal demand for iron and steel can now be met from domestic sources; and other heavy industries, such as chemicals, have been developed in recent years. A petrochemical plant at Ulsan was completed in 1973. Investment in oil facilities is expected to be of major importance in the future, and shipbuilding is also growing in significance. The trade deficit, which stood at $1,327 million in 1971, has been financed through external borrowing; war earnings in Viet-Nam, U.S. military spending and aid grants. The United States and Japan are the Republic's leading trade partners. The third Five-Year Economic Plan (1972–77) is aimed at improving the living standards of the rural population and raising provincial productivity. Preliminary reports suggest that a record economic growth rate of 16.9 per cent was achieved in 1973.

Transport and Communications

Roads and railways have been rebuilt since the war. There were 5,650 km. of railway track in 1972. In 1971 there were 40,650 km. of roads reaching all parts of the country. The Government hopes to pave all highways by 1980. Coastal shipping is important, the chief ports being Pusan, Inchon and Masan. There are internal and international air services. In June 1970 a satellite communications system became operational at the Kumsan ground station, which relays signals via Intelsat-3. In April 1971, work began on the construction of an underground railway system for Seoul. Costing an estimated U.S. $70 million, it will be 133 km. in length and the first line was scheduled to open early in 1974.

Social Welfare

The Government provides social relief services for the handicapped, wounded veterans and war widows. Special grants or subsidies are also given to the aged, disaster victims and orphans by numerous official and voluntary bodies.

Education

Primary education between the ages of six and twelve is free and compulsory and about 5.8 million children were enrolled in 1971 with nearly 2 million in secondary schools. There are 72 universities and colleges, 34 junior technical colleges and 66 graduate schools. Total student enrolment in 1972 was estimated at 180,000.

Tourism

Korea has much to offer in mountain scenery, and the temples and museums and the Royal Palaces at Seoul contain many examples of the traditional Korean arts. There are excellent hunting and fishing facilities.

Visas are required to visit the Republic of Korea by nationals of all countries except the United Kingdom.

Sport

The most popular sports are football, baseball, basketball and volleyball. Table-tennis, tennis and badminton are also played.

Public Holidays

1974: August 15th (Liberation Day), October 1st (Armed Forces' Day), October 3rd (National Foundation Day), October 9th (Hangul Nal—Anniversary of Proclamation of Korean Alphabet), October 24th (United Nations Day), December 25th (Christmas Day).

1975: January 1st–3rd (New Year), March 1st (Sam Il Chul—Independence Movement Day), April 5th (Arbor Day), June 6th (Memorial Day), July 17th (Constitution Day).

Weights and Measures

The metric system is in force, although a number of traditional measures are also used.

Currency and Exchange Rate

100 chun = 10 hwan = 1 won.
Exchange rates (March 1974):
£1 sterling = 952.81 won;
U.S. $1 = 398.00 won.

STATISTICAL SURVEY

AREA AND POPULATION

AREA*	CENSUS POPULATION				
	December 1st, 1960	October 1st, 1966	October 1st, 1970		
			TOTAL	MALE	FEMALE
98,477 sq. km.†	24,989,241	29,192,726	31,469,132	15,778,923	15,690,209

* Excluding the demilitarized zone between North and South Korea, with an area of 1,262 sq. km. (487 sq. miles).
† 38,022 sq. miles.

Estimated Population: 32,848,000 (April 30th, 1973).

PRINCIPAL TOWNS
(1970 Census)

Seoul (capital) .	5,536,377	Kwangchu (Gwangju)	502,753
Pusan (Busan) .	1,880,710	Taejon (Daejeon) .	414,598
Taegu (Daegu) .	1,082,750	Chonchu (Jeonju) .	262,816
Inchon .	646,013	Masan .	190,992

ECONOMICALLY ACTIVE POPULATION*

(sample survey, 1971)

	MALES	FEMALES	TOTAL
Employed Persons:			
Agriculture, Hunting, Forestry and Fishing .	2,716,000	1,993,000	4,709,000
Mining and Quarrying . . .	77,000	11,000	88,000
Manufacturing	832,000	455,000	1,287,000
Electricity, Gas and Water Supply .	23,000	1,000	24,000
Construction	324,000	9,000	333,000
Trade, Restaurants and Hotels .	842,000	679,000	1,521,000
Transport, Storage and Communications .	329,000	25,000	354,000
Finance, Insurance, Property and Business Services	103,000	23,000	126,000
Community, Social and Personal Services	849,000	417,000	1,266,000
TOTAL IN EMPLOYMENT . . .	6,095,000	3,613,000	9,708,000
Unemployed	336,000	121,000	457,000
TOTAL	6,431,000	3,734,000	10,165,000

* Excluding armed forces.

AGRICULTURE
PRINCIPAL CROPS
('000 metric tons)

	1969	1970	1971
Wheat	365.6	356.8	322
Barley	916.4	819	742
Naked Barley	1,150.1	1,154.9	1,115
Maize	63	68	64
Foxtail (Italian) Millet . .	60.4	43.8	34
Rice (Paddy) . . .	5,688	5,476	3,975
Potatoes	599	605	589
Sweet Potatoes and Yams .	2,123	2,136	1,901
Onions: Green . . .	58	70	72
Dry	99	83	89.1
Tomatoes	50	54	67
Cabbages	846	847	1,035
Cucumbers and Gherkins . .	86	89	97
Melons	91	98	99
Water Melons	117	119	152
Dry Beans	32	31	n.a.
Apples	219	212	221
Pears	46	52	48
Peaches	68	78	66
Grapes	37	34	33
Soybeans	229	232	222
Tobacco	59.2	56.3	63.4

Source: FAO, Agricultural Yearbook 1973.

LIVESTOCK
(recorded numbers at December)

	1968	1969	1970	1971
Cattle	1,207,300	1,220,500	1,293,600	1,280,000
Pigs	1,395,700	1,338,500	1,121,400	1,332,500
Goats	109,300	99,400	98,000*	128,000
Sheep	2,200	2,500	3,000*	3,000
Horses	19,900	17,600	16,000*	12,900
Rabbits	650,600	489,000	n.a.	363,600
Chickens	25,967,800	22,651,400	23,476,900	25,903,100
Ducks	319,200	199,500	170,500*	252,000
Geese	10,000	11,000	10,000*	11,000
Turkeys	1,700	1,700	n.a.	1,900
Beehives	125,000	112,000	n.a.	n.a.

* FAO estimate.

LIVESTOCK PRODUCTS
(metric tons)

	1969	1970	1971
Beef and Veal* . . .	33,000	37,000	39,000
Pork	76,000	82,500	81,000
Poultry Meat . . .	47,900	46,000	50,000
Other Meat . . .	2,064	1,484	1,341
Cows' Milk . . .	35,000	52,000	65,000
Goats' Milk . . .	2,809	2,545	2,330
Hen Eggs . . .	126,400	130,000†	127,000
Honey	1,361	1,217	1,237
Raw Silk . . .	2,561	3,026	3,041
Fresh Cocoons . . .	20,747	21,409	24,692
Cattle Hides . . .	4,557†	3,906†	n.a.

* Inspected production only, i.e. from animals slaughtered under government supervision.
† FAO estimate.

FISHING
('000 metric tons)

	1967	1968	1969	1970	1971
Fish . . .	482.5	512.3	598.0	597.9	726.8
Crustaceans . .	25.1	15.9	9.4	16.3	15.4
Molluscs . . .	140.5	192.4	163.4	188.7	200.3
Sea Plants . .	87.8	119.5	80.6	116.6	117.2
Others . . .	14.2	12.0	11.2	15.7	14.0
TOTAL . .	750.3	852.2	862.7	935.4	1,073.7

1972 ('000 metric tons): Total production 1,344.

MINING
('ooo metric tons)

	1969	1970	1971
Anthracite	10,272.6	12,393.6	12,785.0
Iron Concentrates . . .	709.9	571.0	442.0
Tungsten Concentrates . .	3.6	3.7	4.0
Lead Concentrates . . .	33.0	32.0*	26.5*
Copper Ore	19.2	18.7	14.6
Zinc Concentrates . . .	41.2	48.0	60.0
Manganese Concentrates .	2.3	2.4	2.1
Molybdenum Concentrates .	0.2	0.2	0.2
Graphite, Amorphous . .	73.4	59.3	37.4
Kaolin	52.9	84.6	124.4
Talc	130.9	135.3	104.4
Fluorite	24.1	29.9	50.8
Limestone	7,530.1	9,936.9	11,213.1
Gold ('ooo kg.) . . .	1.4	1.3	0.9
Silver ('ooo kg.) . . .	19.6	51.2	46.8

* Lead Ore.

INDUSTRY

		1969	1970	1968
Wheat Flour . . .	'ooo bags	37,789.0	41,663.0	48,976.0
Sugar, Refined . .	'ooo tons	185.5	211.0	237.0
Newsprint . . .	" "	84.2	104.1	107.5
Soap	" "	47.9	56.2	65.2
Plastics . . .	" "	57.9	109.4	137.7
Cement . . .	" "	4,865.0	5,812.0	6,872.0
Aluminium products .	" "	1.2	1.5	1.3
Car tyres . . .	'ooo	877.0	923.0	1,029.0
Rubber Shoes . .	million pairs	33.3	27.8	27.3
Matches . . .	'ooo boxes	159,618.0	151,088.0	90,662.0
Pottery . . .	million pieces	33.9	33.7	29.1
Motors . . .	'ooo	9.3	9.0	7.5
Cotton Yarn . .	million kg.	64.7	71.9	85.2
Cotton Cloth . .	million sq. metres	191.7	186.4	229.7
Plywood . . .	'ooo cu. metres	978.0	1,126.0	1,375.0
Sewing Machines . .	'ooo	114.2	107.5	124.7
Bicycles . . .	"	197.0	214.0	222.2
Pencils . . .	"	798.2	928.0	10.94
Worsted Yarn . .	1,000 kg.	3,189.0	2,028.0	1,648.0

FINANCE

100 chun (jeon) = 10 hwan = 1 won.
Coins: 1, 5 and 10 won.
Notes: 1, 5, 10, 50, 100 and 500 won.
Exchange rates (March 1974): £1 sterling = 952.81 won; U.S. $1 = 398.00 won.
1,000 won = £1.050 = $2.513.

BUDGET
(million won)

Revenue	1970	1971
Taxes and Customs . .	334,723	407,648
Monopoly Profit .	30,100	
Miscellaneous Revenue .	21,740	
Trust Fund and Interest .	6,996	144,314
Foreign Loan Fund .	28,600	
United States Aid .	22,356	
Total (incl. others) .	445,857	551,962

Expenditure	1970	1971
General Expenditure . .	68,595	168,600
Defence . . .	100,512	82,500
Investment and Loans .	150,982	106,000
Other Items . . .	630	n.a.
Salaries and Pensions .	55,379	n.a.
Local Government .	70,175	n.a.
Total . .	446,273	357,100

THIRD FIVE-YEAR ECONOMIC PLAN, 1972–76

It is planned that G.N.P. will grow by an average of
8.6 per cent per annum and that by 1976 it will have
increased by 66 per cent by value over the total for 1970,
i.e. from 2,562,000 million won to 4,257,000 million won.

GOLD RESERVES AND MONEY SUPPLY
(At year's end)

	1970	1971	1972*
Gold Reserves (U.S.$'000) . . .	3,410	3,459	4,000
Currency in Circulation (million won) . .	133,338	162,761	218,900
Monetary Deposits (million won) . .	173,132	198,086	290,400
Total Money Supply (million won) . .	306,470	360,847	509,400

* 1972 figures supplied by the Asian Development Bank.

BALANCE OF PAYMENTS—WORLDWIDE SUMMARY
(million U.S.$)

	1970			1971		
	Credit	Debit	Balance	Credit	Debit	Balance
Goods and Services .	1,379.0	2,181.7	−802.7	1,616.0	2,634.1	−1,018.1
Transfer Payments .	205.2	25.0	180.2	194.4	23.8	170.6
Capital and Monetary Gold .	722.2	83.5	638.7	844.4	10.0	834.4

EXTERNAL TRADE
(U.S. $ million)

	Imports	Exports
1967	996.2	320.2
1968	1,462.9	455.4
1969	1,823.6	622.5
1970	1,984.0	835.2
1971	2,394.3	1,067.6
1972	2,522.0	1,624.1

PRINCIPAL COMMODITIES
(U.S. $'000)

Imports	1970	1971
Machinery	305,858	350,740
Raw Cotton . . .	62,669	84,188
Rice	145,400	150,200
Wheat	79,528	115,101
Electrical Machinery and Appliances	132,892	167,184
Wood, Lumber . . .	125,413	153,733
Chemicals . . .	163,781	201,006
Raw Sugar . . .	23,479	31,069
Raw Rubber . . .	17,563	20,238
Rayon Yarn . . .	2,217	4,966
Iron and Steel . . .	89,591	128,658
Petroleum Products . .	132,931	187,106
Total (incl. others) .	1,983,974	2,394,320

Exports	1970	1971
Clothing	213,566	304,265
Veneer Sheets . . .	91,746	124,274
Wigs	100,868	69,866
Tungsten	17,209	10,957
Raw Silk	35,821	39,273
Tobacco	13,435	14,076
Fish	40,832	42,236
Laver	13,047	7,259
Electrical Machinery .	43,874	68,486
Total (incl. others) .	835,185	1,067,607

PRINCIPAL TRADING PARTNERS
(U.S. $'000)

	Imports			Exports		
	1969	1970	1971	1969	1970	1971
Japan	753,817	809,283	953,778	133,326	234,329	261,988
Taiwan	23,195	33,998	39,097	13,275	7,210	12,030
U.S.A.	530,179	584,793	678,331	312,175	395,182	531,814
Federal Republic of Germany .	78,971	67,204	73,719	16,415	27,330	31,357
Italy	17,758	19,581	19,277	3,566	7,182	5,570
Philippines . . .	37,377	41,683	44,151	688	1,128	4,325
United Kingdom . .	32,037	32,799	56,186	10,560	13,021	14,110
Netherlands . . .	17,994	23,255	14,798	9,477	13,513	15,931
Hong Kong . . .	19,969	19,738	19,695	24,443	27,574	41,448
France	36,423	52,242	71,753	1,752	1,568	2,560
Singapore . . .	10,097	13,543	16,763	12,046	11,023	10,112

TOURISM

VISITORS	
1967 . .	84,216
1968 . .	102,748
1969 . .	126,686
1970 . .	173,335
1971 . .	232,785

TRANSPORT

RAILWAYS
('000)

	1969	1970	1971
Passengers . .	154,696	131,251	128,159
Freight (metric tons)	29,153	30,298	30,696

ROADS

	1969	1970	1971
Passenger Cars .	50,299	60,677	67,582
Trucks . . .	40,134	48,901	53,405
Buses . . .	14,237	15,831	16,171

SHIPPING
(metric tons)

	1969	1970	1971
Loaded . .	11,054,812	14,132,700	15,453,100
Unloaded . .	25,172,340	29,172,100	32,521,200

CIVIL AVIATION
(Domestic Services only)

	1969	1970	1971
Passengers . .	627,668	909,477	1,105,470
Freight (kg.) .	2,771,207	4,631,840	7,194,173
Mail (kg.) .	23,983	31,176	90,297

EDUCATION
(1971)

	SCHOOLS	TEACHERS	PUPILS
Elementary Schools.	6,085	103,756	5,807,448
Middle Schools .	1,794	35,938	1,921,000*
Academic High Schools . .	398	10,700	337,125
Vocational High Schools .	500	11,615	310,055
Junior Technical Colleges .	34	1,436	27,864
Junior Colleges .	13	167	4,009
Junior Teachers Colleges .	16	773	12,535
Colleges and Universities.	72	8,071	155,369
Graduate Schools .	66	123	7,300

* 1972 estimate.

Source: The Korea Annual 1972.

General Sources: Bureau of Statistics of the Republic of Korea, except where otherwise indicated.

THE CONSTITUTION*

In May 1961, the Government was taken over by a Supreme Council for National Reconstruction. Political parties, Parliament and the Constitution were dissolved.

A new Constitution was approved by national referendum in November 1972. The main provisions are:

Political Parties: A plural-party system is guaranteed with a view to preventing a one-party dictatorship. Parties must, however, organize chapters with at least 50 members in at least 40 cities. An amendment to the law has lifted the long-standing ban on independent parliamentary candidacy. However, independent candidates must deposit a sum of 3 million won in public trust.

The National Assembly: The National Assembly is to be unicameral with a membership of between 150 and 250. The Prime Minister and other Cabinet members are appointed by the President without the necessity of approval from the National Assembly. It has the power to recommend to the President the removal of the Prime Minister or any other Cabinet Minister. The National Assembly may pass a motion for impeachment of the President, which would be tried by an Impeachment Council composed of four Judges of the Supreme Court and five members of the National Assembly.

The President: The President is elected indirectly by a special electoral college called the National Conference for Unification. Should a vacancy occur in the presidency, the Premier or one of the members of the State Council acts as President until an election is held. The office of President may not be combined with that of Prime Minister, member of the Cabinet or other public or private positions as determined by law.

The Judiciary: The Supreme Court has power to decide with finality the constitutionality of laws. It also has final appellate jurisdiction over the military tribunals.

Fundamental Rights: Freedom of speech, press, assembly and association are guaranteed but the standards of newspapers or news agencies may be prescribed by law. Time and place of outdoor assembly may also be determined in accordance with the law.

* The Extraordinary State Council (dissolved following the convening of a new National Assembly on March 12th, 1973), which was set up to perform the functions of the previous National Assembly and presided over by President Park, announced a number of draft amendments to the Constitution on October 27th, 1972, with the aim of achieving peaceful unification (with North Korea), reforming existing political institutions, "maximizing efficiency" and "organizing national strength". These major amendments as embodied in a new draft constitution, and approved in a referendum held on November 21st by 92 per cent of all votes cast are as follows:

1. *Peaceful Unification:* This is declared to be one of the supreme national aspirations and is arrived at through the North-South Co-ordination Committee and the North-South Red Cross Talks. A constitutional organ, the National Conference for Unification has been established to assist in bringing this about (*see* below).

2. *Establishment of the National Conference for Unification:* This is the supreme representative body for national consensus on matters concerning national unification and comprises 2,359 delegates. It is elected by direct ballot, elects the President and one-third of the members of the National Assembly and has authority to discuss and confirm by majority votes of the delegates, proposed constitutional amendments.

3. *Presidential Powers:* Under certain conditions, the President may take extraordinary measures in times of national emergency or when national security is seriously threatened or likely to be so. The President's term of office is extended from four to six years and he may be elected for an unlimited number of such terms and has power to dissolve the National Assembly.

4. *The National Assembly:* Regular sessions are to be held once a year for a maximum period of 90 days with extraordinary sessions being held twice a year for no longer than 30 days, though in exceptional circumstances and at the President's behest, an emergency session may be convened. The Parliamentary term is extended from four to six years. Members elected by the National Conference will have three year terms.

5. *Relations between the Administrative and Legislative Branches:* The National Assembly has the right of concurrence in the appointment of the Prime Minister by the President and the right to adopt a resolution on the removal of the Prime Minister or other Ministers. If the former, then the whole Cabinet must resign.

6. *The National Referendum:* A referendum may be held as deemed necessary by the President on policy matters of major national importance.

7. *Establishment of a Constitutional Commission:* The Constitutional Commission comprising nine members is appointed by the President for six years (three of whom are selected by the National Assembly and a further three upon recommendation of the Chief Justice).

8. *Rights and Duties of Citizens:* Though civil rights are guaranteed and *in general* are subject to legal restrictions in those cases deemed necessary for the maintenance of order and public welfare, legal restrictions are, in addition, to apply to *specific* liberties or rights.

9. *Constitutional Amendments:* Constitutional amendments may be either introduced by the President or by more than half of the members of the National Assembly. The President's proposals are decided by referendum while those of the National Assembly become effective when passed by a two-thirds majority of members thereof having also received confirmation by the National Conference.

10. *Other Provisions:* Besides those proposed Amendments mentioned above, there are no substantial departures from or amendments to the present Constitution with regard to the Executive, the Judiciary, Political Parties, or in other fields such as the National Economy.

THE GOVERNMENT

President: General PARK CHUNG HEE (re-elected December 23rd, 1972.)

THE CABINET
(April 1974)
(Democratic Republican Party)

Prime Minister: KIM CHONG PIL.
Deputy Prime Minister and Chairman of the Economic Planning Board: TAE WAN SON.
Foreign Minister: KIM DONG CHO.
Home Minister: HONG SONG CHOL.
Minister of Finance: NAM DUCK WOO.
Minister of Justice: LEE BONG SONG.
Minister of Defence: SU CHONG CHUL.
Minister of Education: MIN KWAN SHIK.
Minister of Agriculture and Fisheries: CHUNG SO YOUNG.
Minister of Commerce and Industry: CHANG YE CHOON.

Minister of Construction: LEE NAK SON.
Minister of Health and Social Affairs: KO CHAE PIL.
Minister of Transport: KIM SHIN.
Minister of Communications: MUN HYONG TAE.
Minister of Information and Cultural Affairs: YOON CHOO YONG.
Minister of Science and Technology: CHOI HYONG SUP.
Minister of Government Administration: SHIM HEONG SUN.
National Unification Board: KIM YUNG SHIK.
Ministers without Portfolio: LEE BYONG HEE, KU TAE HOE.

DIPLOMATIC REPRESENTATION

EMBASSIES ACCREDITED TO THE REPUBLIC OF KOREA
(Seoul unless otherwise stated)

Argentina: 1-41 Dongbinggo-dong, Yongsan-Ku; *Ambassador:* (vacant).
Australia: 5th Floor Kukdong-Shell House, 58-1 Shinmoon-ro 1-ka, Chongro-ku; *Ambassador:* M. G. M. BOURCHIER.
Austria: Tokyo, Japan.
Belgium: 1-37 Hannam-dong, Yongsan-ku; *Ambassador:* JEAN F. TRINE.
Brazil: 3rd Floor, New Korea Hotel Bldg., 192-11, 1-ka, Ulchiro, Choong-ku; *Ambassador:* MILTON TELLES RIBEIRO.
Canada: 9th Floor, 14 Chunghak-dong, Chongro-ku.
Central African Republic: Tokyo, Japan.
China (Taiwan): 83, 2-ga, Myong-dong, Chung-ku; *Ambassador:* LOH YING-TEH.
Colombia: Tokyo, Japan.
Costa Rica: Tokyo, Japan.
Denmark: Tokyo, Japan.
Dominican Republic: Tokyo, Japan.
Ecuador: Tokyo, Japan.
El Salvador: Tokyo, Japan.
Ethiopia: Tokyo, Japan.
France: 30 Hap-dong, Sudaimum-ku; *Ambassador:* PIERRE LANDY.
Gabon: Taipei, Taiwan, China.
Germany, Federal Republic: 9th Floor, Dae Han Bldg., 75 Susomun-dong, Sudaimun-ku; *Ambassador:* WILFRIED SARRAZIN.
Greece: Tokyo, Japan.
Guatemala: Tokyo, Japan.
Iran: Tokyo, Japan.
Israel: 308-9 Dongbinggo-dong, Yongsan-ku; *Ambassador:* YEHUDA HORAM.
Italy: 1-169, 2-ga, Shinmun-ro, Chongno-ku; *Ambassador:* GIULIANO BERTUCCIOLI.

Ivory Coast: Tokyo, Japan.
Japan: 18-11 Chunghak-dong, Chongno-gu; *Ambassador:* TORAO USHIROKU.
Jordan: Taipei, Taiwan.
Khmer Republic: Garden Tower 98-78, Wooni-dong, Chongro-ku; *Ambassador:* POC THIEUN.
Liberia: Tokyo, Japan.
Madagascar: Washington D.C., U.S.A.
Malaysia: 726 Hannam-dong, Yongsan-gu; *Ambassador:* TOH CHOR KEAT.
Mexico: Tokyo, Japan.
Morocco: Tokyo, Japan.
Netherlands: 1-85 Tongbinggo-dong, Yongsan-gu; *Ambassador:* Dr. TH. P. BERGSMA.
New Zealand: 1-42 Tongbinggo-dong, Yongsan-gu; *Ambassador:* THOMAS CEDRIC LARKIN.
Nicaragua: Tokyo, Japan.
Norway: Tokyo, Japan.
Panama: Tokyo, Japan.
Paraguay: Tokyo, Japan.
Peru: Tokyo, Japan.
Philippines: 258-25 Itaewon-dong, Yongsan-ku; *Ambassador:* BENJAMIN T. TIRONA.
Saudi Arabia: Tokyo, Japan.
Spain: Tokyo, Japan.
Sweden: Tokyo, Japan.
Switzerland: 32-10 Songwol-dong, Sodaemun-gu; *Ambassador:* Dr. GIOVANNI ENRICO BUCHER.
Thailand: House 127, New Itaewon, Yongsan-ku; *Ambassador:* PAYONG CHUTIKUL.
Turkey: 148 Ankuk-dong, Chongro-ku; *Ambassador:* MELIH ERCIN.

United Kingdom: 4 Chung-dong, Sudaimum-ku; *Ambassador:* J. C. PETERSON.

U.S.A.: 82 Sejong-no, Chongno-gu; *Ambassador:* PHILIP C. HABIB.

Uruguay: 260-199 Itaewon-dong, Yongsan-ku; *Ambassador:* JUAN CARLOS PEDEMONTE.

Vatican: 2 Kungjung-dong, Chongno-ku; *Chargé d'Affaires:* Rev. LUIGI BRESSAN.

Venezuela: Tokyo, Japan.

Viet-Nam, Republic: 24-31, 1-ka Chungmu-ro, Chang-gu; *Ambassador:* PHAM XUAN CHIEU.

Zaire: Tokyo, Japan.

The Republic of Korea also maintains diplomatic relations with Bangladesh, Cameroon, Dahomey, Finland, the Gambia, Guyana, Iceland, India, Indonesia, Maldives, Malta, Mauritius, Nepal, Pakistan, Qatar, Rwanda, Senegal, Sierra Leone, Togo, Uganda and the Upper Volta.

NATIONAL ASSEMBLY

(elected February 27th, 1973)

PARTY	SEATS
Democratic Republican Party . . .	144
New Democratic Party	52
Democratic Unification Party . .	2
Independents	21
	219

Speaker of the National Assembly: CHUNG IL KWON.

NATIONAL CONFERENCE FOR UNIFICATION (NCU)

(*see* also under the Constitution)

(Elected December 22nd, 1972)

AREA	ELECTORAL DISTRICTS	DELEGATES
Seoul	67	303
Pusan	24	104
Kyonngi	207	280
Kangwon	111	145
Chungbuk	107	127
Chungnam	185	231
Chonbuk	168	200
Chonnam	242	312
Kyongbuk	268	354
Kyongnam	236	278
Cheju	15	25
TOTAL . . .	1,630	2,359

POLITICAL PARTIES

Democratic Republican Party: 112-3, Sokong-Dong, Chung-ku, C.P. Box 196, Seoul; f. 1963; Government Party; 1,359,863 mems.; President Gen. PARK CHUNG HEE; Chair. RHEE HYO SANG; Sec.-Gen. KIL CHON SHIK; Publs. *The Democratic Republican Forum, The D.R.P. Bulletin, Policy Quarterly.*

Democratic Unification Party: Seoul.

Nationalist Party (*Kungmin Party*): Kong-pyong-dong, Chongno-gu; f. 1971; Leader CHO CHUNGSO.

New Democratic Party: 103 Kwanhun-dong, Chongno-gu, Seoul; opposition coalition formed 1967 by the Sinhan and Minjung Parties; Pres. YU CHIN SAN.

Minjung Dang (*Popular Party*): 94-10, 2-ga, Chongno, Chongno-gu, Seoul; f. 1967; left-wing; Leader SO MIN-HO.

Unified Socialist Party (*Tongsa Dang*): Tongkwang Bldg., 138 Nakwon-dong, Chongro-ku; Leader KIM CHUL.

Taejung Dang (*Masses Party*): 24, 1-ka, Hoehyondong, Chung-gu, Seoul; Leader SONG PO-GYONG.

JUDICIAL SYSTEM

Supreme Court: is the highest Court. It consists of sixteen Justices including the Chief Justice. It has jurisdiction over Civil, Criminal and Special (Administrative and Election) cases, and its power is exercised through a conference attended by two-thirds or more of all the Justices. A case may first be considered and adjudicated by a division of three or more Justices.

Appellate Courts: consist of a Chief Judge and a specified number of Judges; have Civil, Criminal and Special Divisions. The Courts are situated at Seoul, Taegu and Kwangjoo. All cases are heard by a Collegiate Division of three Judges.

District Courts: there are eleven District Courts, with thirty-six branch courts. They consist of a Chief Judge and Judges, and have Civil and Criminal Divisions. Cases may be heard by a single Judge or a Collegiate Division of three Judges as prescribed by law.

Family Court: there is one Family Court, in Seoul, with a Chief Judge and Judges and Probation Officers. This deals with domestic relations and juvenile delinquency.

THE SUPREME COURT

Chief Justice: MIN POK-KI.

Justices: SON TONG UK, KIM CHI GOL, SA KWANG UK, HONG SUN YOP, YANG HOE KYONG, PANG SOON WON, LEE YONG SOP, NA HANG YUN, CHU CHAE HWANG, HONG NAM PYO, U CHAE PANG, KIM YOUNG SAE, HAN BONG SAE, MIN MOON KEE, YANG BYUNG HO.

Director of Court Administration: KIM BYUNG-HWA.

RELIGION

The traditional religions are Buddhism, Confucianism, Taoism and Chundo Kyo, a religion peculiar to Korea combining elements of Buddhism and Christianity.

RELIGIONS
(as of November 1971)

	TEMPLES OR CHURCHES	PRIESTS	BELIEVERS
Buddhism .	3,271	17,236	7,106,018
Confucianism .	231	11,831	4,423,000
Protestantism .	13,037	15,789	3,217,996
Roman Catholicism	393	3,125	779,000
Chundo Kyo .	119	997	636,067
Others . .	900	4,476	1,808,274

Source: Ministry of Information and Cultural Affairs.

Buddhism: Korean Buddhism has 16 denominations. The Chogye-jong is the largest Buddhist order in Korea being introduced from China in 372 A.D. The Chogye Order accounts for some 5 million out of a total of 7,106,018 adherents. It has also more than 200 out of 370 Buddhist temples. Leader The Venerable KANG SOK CHU.

Roman Catholic: Archbishop of Seoul: H.E. Cardinal STEPHEN SOU-HWAN KIM, Archbishop's House, 2-Ga 1, Myong Dong, Chung-gu, Seoul.

Protestant: Anglican Church in Korea: Bishop of Seoul Rt. Rev. PAUL LEE, 3 Chong Dong, Seoul; Bishop of Taejon Rt. Rev. C. R. RUTT, P.O.B. 22, Taejon.

THE PRESS
DAILIES*

Chosun Ilbo: 61, 1-ga, Taepyeong-ro 1, Chung-gu, Seoul; f. 1920; morning, weekly and children's editions; independent; circ. (morning edn.) 405,000; Chair. IL-YOUNG BANG; Pres. WOO-YOUNG BANG; Editor SUNU HWY.

The Daily Sports: 14 Chunghak-dong, Chongno-ku, Seoul.

Dong-A Ilbo (*The Oriental Daily News*): 139 Sechong-ro, Chongno-gu, Seoul; f. 1920; evening; independent; circ. 626,700; Pres. Dr. JAI WOOK KOH; Editor DONG WOOK LEE.

Hankook Ilbo: 14 Chunghak-dong, Chongno-gu, Seoul; f. 1954; morning; independent; circ. 350,000; Publr. CHANG KANG-JAE.

Joong-ang Ilbo: 58-9 Seosomun-dong, Seodaemun-gu, Seoul.

The Korea Herald: 31, 1-ga, Taepyeong-ro, Seoul; English; morning; independent; Pres. WOHN KYUNG-SOO; Editor-in-Chief KAY KWANG GIL.

The Korea Times: 14 Chunghak-dong, Chongno-gu, Seoul; f. 1950; morning; English; independent; circ. 33,500; Pres./Publr. CHANG KANG-JAE; Editor HONG SOON-IL.

Kyunghyang Shinmun: 74 Sogong-dong, Chung-ku, Seoul; f. 1946; evening; independent; circ. 300,000; Publisher KIM KYONG-RAE; Editor CHOI CHI-WHAN.

The Seoul Kyungje: 14 Chunghak-dong, Chongno-ku, Seoul.

Seoul Shinmun: 31, 1-ga, Taepyeong-no, Seoul; evening; independent; circ. 320,000; Pres. SHIN BOM-SHIK; Man. Ed. JAE HEE NAM.

Shin-A Ilbo: 31-1 Seosomun-dong, Seodaemun-gu, Seoul.

Sonyon Dong-A: 139 Sechong-ro, Chongno-ku, Seoul; children's daily; circ. 118,300.

* TOTAL CIRCULATION (1972): 2,700,000 copies.

WEEKLIES
Korean Business Review: 28th Floor, Samilro Bldg., 10 Kwanchul-dong, Chongro-ku, Seoul; organ of the Federation of Korean Industries.

Weekly Chosun: 61 Taepyong-ro 1, Chung-ku, Seoul; circ. (weekly) 170,000 (*see under* Dailies).

The Weekly Hankook: 14 Chunghak-dong, Chongno-ku, Seoul; f. 1964; Editor HONG YOO SUN; circ. 400,000.

The Women's Weekly: 14 Chunghak-dong, Chongno-ku, Seoul.

SELECTED MONTHLIES
Donghwa News Graphic: 43-1, 1-ga, Pildong, Chung-gu, Seoul; f. 1958; Publisher JAE HO CHUNG.

FKTU News: Federation of Korean Trade Unions, 20 Sogong-dong, Chung-gu, Seoul; labour; f. 1958; Publisher LEE CHAN-KYU.

Hyundae Munhak: 136-46 Yunji-dong, Chongno-gu, Seoul; f. 1955; literature; Chief Editor YUN HYUN CHO; circ. 115,000.

Shin Dong-A (*New Far East*): 139 Sejong-ro, Chongno-gu, Seoul; f. 1931; general; Editor SONG-HAN KIM; circ. 56,500.

Wolkan Joong-ang (*Monthly Joong-ang*): 58-9 Seosomun-dong, Seodaemun-gu, Seoul.

The Yosong Dong-A (*Women's Far East*): 139 Sejong-ro, Chong-gu, Seoul; f. 1933; women's magazine; Editor SONG-HAN KIM; circ. 92,000.

NEWS AGENCIES
Hapdong News Agency: 101 Ulchi-ro 1, Chung-ku, Seoul; f. 1945; contracts with AFP, Reuters, Dpa, Kyodo, Editor's Press Services and Overseas Commentary Service; Pres. WON-KYUNG LEE; Editor YOO SEUNG-BUM.

Orient Press: 188 Chongjin-dong, Seoul; Pres. SEUNG-HI HONG; Chair. SUNG-KON KIM; Sen. Man. Dir. IN-BAE KIM.

FOREIGN BUREAUX
Agence France-Press (AFP): 101, 1-ga, Ulchi-ro, Chung-gu, Seoul.

ANSA: 1-17 Chung Dong, Su Dae Mon Ku, Seoul; Chief UGO PUNTIERI.

AP: 108-4 Susong-dong, Chongro-ku, Seoul; Correspondent K. C. HWANG.

Central News Agency of China: (I.P.O. Box 2139) 1-ka, Ulchiro, Seoul; Correspondent LITAI FANG.

Jiji Press: 58-9 Sosomun-dong, Sodaemun-gu, Seoul; Correspondent KIM CHONG-HAN.

Kyodo News Service: Kyodonews Seoul, c/o Hapdong News Agency, 101, 1-ga, Ulchi-ro, Chung-gu, Seoul; Correspondent HISHIKI KAZUYOSHI.

Reuters: 101 Ulchi-ro 1, Chung-gu, Seoul; Correspondent YI SI-HO.

United Press International (UPI): 81-6 Sejong-no, Chongno-gu, Seoul; Correspondent KIM CHUN-HWAN.

PRESS ASSOCIATIONS

The Korean Newspapers Association: Room 205, 206 The Press Centre of Korea, 31, 1-ga, Taepyeong-ro, Jung-gu, Seoul; 36 mems; Pres. Sin Pom-sik.

PUBLISHERS

Dong-A Publishing Co., Ltd.: West Gate, Seoul; f. 1956; Pres. Kim Sang-Moon; Man. Dir. Park Young-Ki; dictionaries, text books, reference books and general.

Ge Mong Sa: 12-23 Kwangchul-dong, Seoul; Dir. Won Dae Kim; juvenile literature and educational books.

Hak Won Sa: 106 Yangpyung-dong-5 ka, Yeongdeungpo-ku, Seoul; f. 1945; Pres. Ick-Tal Kim; encyclopaedia and general.

Hollym Corporation: 11-1 Kwan Chul-dong, Chongro-ku, Seoul; f. 1963; Man. Dir. Yong Won Kim; fiction, literature, biography, history.

Hwimoon Publishing Co.: 30 Kyunji-dong, Chongro-ku, Seoul; f. 1961; Man. Dir. Dong Won Kim; fiction, biography, history, philosophy, religion.

Hyeon-Am Sa: 66-13 Won Nam-dong, Chongro-ku, Seoul; f. 1951; Man. Dir. Cho Sang Won; history, philosophy.

Ilji Sa: 37 Gyueonji-dong, Jongro-gu, Seoul; f. 1956; Seong Jae Gim; fiction, literature, reference, text books.

Jeongeum Sa: 3-2 Hoehyeon-dong, 1-ka, Chung-ku, Seoul; Man. Dir. Yong Hae Choe; fiction, literature, travel.

Minjungseogwan Publishing Co.: 35 Tongui-dong, Chongro-ku, Seoul; Chair. Byung Jun Lee; Pres. Nam-Wonu; textbooks, dictionaries and general.

Mun Ho Sa: 92 2nd Street, Simmun-ro, Seoul; Dir. Chong Tae Lee; primary school books.

Sae Mun Sa: 13 Sam-ka Nam Sang Dong, Chung-ku, Seoul; Pres. Sung Jin Cho; general books.

Se Kwang Publishing Co.: 147 Chongno 3-ka, Chongro-ku, Seoul; f. 1953; Man. Dir. Yoon Min Eun; music.

Tamgu Dang Book Centre: 101-1 Kyung woon-dong, Seoul; Pres. Hong Suk-U; Man. Dir. Yoh Woon-Hak; history; fine arts, reference, text books.

Ul Yu Publishing Co.: 112 Kwanchul-dong, Seoul; Dir. Chin-Sook Choung; textbooks and general.

Yang Mun Sa: 5 Susong-dong, Seoul; Dir. Ho Sung Pyun; textbooks and general books.

Young Ji Publishing Co.: 32 Gyunji-dong, Seoul; Dir. Man Du Paek; textbooks.

PUBLISHERS' ASSOCIATION

Korean Publishers' Association: 3-1, Doyum-dong, Chong-no-ku, Seoul; f. 1947; Pres. Chin Sook Chung; Vice-Pres. Man Nayun Han, Sang Won Cho; Sec.-Gen. Kyung Hoon Lee; Publs. *The Korean Books Journal* (monthly), *Korean Publication Yearbook*.

RADIO AND TELEVISION

There are 45 radio and 12 television stations, of which the following are the more important:

RADIO

Korean Broadcasting System (KBS): Yejangdong 8, Chung-ku, Seoul; government agency with one key and 27 local stations; overseas service in Korean, English,

French, Spanish, Chinese, Japanese, Vietnamese and Russian; Dir.-Gen. C. C. Bong.

Pusan Moonwha Broadcasting Corporation (HLKU): 3-ka, Choong-Ang Dong, Pusan; independent commercial station; programmes in Korean; Pres. S. S. Ahn; Dir.-Gen. A. Sung Soo.

Radio Station HLKX: C.P.O.B. 5255, Seoul; f. 1956; religious, educational station operated by Evangelical Alliance Mission, P.O.B. 969, Wheaton, Ill. 60187, U.S.A.; programmes in Korean, Chinese, Russian, Mongolian and English; Dir. W. S. Winchell.

Christian Broadcasting System (CBS): 136 Yun Chi Dong, Chongno-II, Seoul; independent religious semicommercial station with four network stations in Taegu, Pusan, Kwangju and Iri; programmes in Korean; Pres. Chae Kyung Oh.

Tong-yang Broadcasting Co. Ltd.: 58-9 Seosomun-dong, Seoul; commercial; Man. Dir. Kim Duk-Po; Dir. Park Moo Sung.

Dong-A Broadcasting System (DBS): P.O.B. Kwang Hwa Moon 250, 139 Sejong-no, Chongno-gu, Seoul; f. 1963; commercial; Pres. Jae Uk Koh; Dir.-Gen. Sang Ki Kim.

Hankuk Munhwa Broadcasting Corporation: 22 Jung-dong, Sudaemun-ku, Seoul; commercial; Pres. H. E. Lee; Exec. Dir. H. S. Lee.

American Forces Korea Network: Head Office: Seoul; Mil. Address: A.P.O. San Francisco, 96301, U.S.A.; f. 1950; eight originating stations and twelve relay stations; broadcasts 24 hours a day; Commanding Officer Lt.-Col. Howard A. Myrick; Deputy Richard A. Toothaker; Production Chief Ed Masters; Chief Engineer Gerald McDonald.

There are about 3,335,000 radio receivers (1972).

TELEVISION

Korean Broadcasting System (KBS): Yejangdong 8, Chung-ku, Seoul; government corporation; Dir. Chong Chul Hong.

Tong-yang Broadcasting Co. Ltd. (TV-AM-FM): 58-9 Seosomun-dong, Seoul; commercial; Pres. Kim Duk-Po; Exec. Dir. Park Moo-sung.

American Forces Korea Network: Head Office: Seoul; Mil. Address: A.P.O. San Francisco, 96301, U.S.A.; f. 1957; key station in Seoul; nine rebroadcast transmitters throughout Korea, and four low-wattage translators located strategically; on the air 70 hours weekly (*see above*, Radio).

In 1972 there were 400,000 receiving sets.

FINANCE

(cap.=capital; p.u.=paid up; dep.=deposits; res.= reserves; m.=million; amounts in won)

BANKING
Central Bank

Bank of Korea, The: 110, 3-ka, Namdaemun-ro, Chung-ku, Seoul; f. 1950; res. 2,264m.; 10 domestic brs., 4 overseas offices; Chair. Duk Woo Nam; Gov. Sung Whan Kim; Dep. Gov. Soo Kon Pae; publ. *Annual Report, Review of Korean Economy, Monthly Economic Review*, etc.

NATIONAL BANKS

Bank of Seoul: 116-1 Sokong-Dong, Chung-ku, Seoul; f. 1959; cap. 8,000m., dep. 126,700m. (Sept. 1973); Pres. BYUNG SHIK SHIM; Vice-Pres. YUNG DUCK KIM.

Cho-Heung Bank Ltd.: 14, 1-ka, Namdaemun-ro, Chung-ku, Seoul; f. 1897; Pres. TAI JIN KOH; Exec. Dir. KANG WON LEE.

Citizen's National Bank: 9-1, 2-ga, Namdaemun-ro, Chung-gu, Seoul; f. 1962; credit bank; Pres. SUH CHUNG KOOG; Vice-Pres. BAE SOOK.

Commercial Bank of Korea Ltd., The: 111-1, 2-ka, Namdaemun-ro, Chung-ku, Seoul; f. 1899; cap. 6,600m., dep. 159,309m. (Sept. 1972); Pres. BONG EUN KIM; Exec. Vice-Pres. DONG SOO LEE.

Hanil Bank: 130, 2-ka, Namdaemun-ro, Chung-ku, Seoul (I.P.O. Box 1033); f. 1932; cap. p.u. U.S. $12m., dep. U.S. $312m.; Pres. JIN SOO HA; Snr. Exec. Dir. HONG SOO HAN.

Korea Development Bank: I.P.O.B. 4570, Seoul; f. 1954; cap. $300m.; Gov. WOUN GIE KIM.

Korea Exchange Bank: 10 Kwanchul-dong, Chung-ku, Seoul; f. 1967; 14 overseas brs., cap. p.u. 20,000m.; dep. 268,900.7m. (Dec. 1971); Pres. KIM WOO KEUN.

Korea First Bank: 53-1, 1-ka, Chungmu-ro, Joong-ku, Seoul; f. 1929; cap. 4,000m., dep. 196,083.4m. (March 1973); Pres. YOUNG HOON MIN; Exec. Vice-Pres. NAM JIN LEE.

Korea Housing Bank: 61-1, 1-ga, Taepyung-ro, Choongo-ku, Seoul; f. 1967; Pres. LEE SANG-DUK.

Medium Industry Bank: 36-1, 2-ka, Ulchiro, Choong-ku, Seoul; f. 1961; industrial credit bank; cap. 3,060m., dep. 87,558m. (1972); Pres. WUCHANG CHUNG.

PRIVATE BANK

Bank of Taegu: 20-3 Namil-dong, Jungku, Taegu; f. October 1967; cap 300m., dep. 1,829m. (Jan. 1969); Pres. JUNSUNG KIM; Senior Exec. Dir. OKHYUN NAM.

ASSOCIATION

Bankers' Association of Korea: 4, 1-ka, Myung-Dong, Chung-ku, Seoul; mems. 13 financial institutions; Chair. SUNG WHAN KIM (Gov. Bank of Korea); Sec.-Gen. S. H. KOO.

FOREIGN BANKS

Central Trust of China: Head Office: Taiwan; Seoul Office: C.P.O. 361, Seoul; Rep. T. S. HSU.

Chartered Bank: Head Office: 38 Bishopsgate, London, E.C.2; Samsung Building, 50 1-ka, Ulchiro, Choong-ku, Seoul; P.O. Box Kwangwhamun 259, Seoul; Man. H. H. LILLER.

Chase Manhattan Bank, N.A.: New York; Seoul Branch: 50, 1-ka, Ulchiro, Choong-ku, I.P.O. Box 2249; Second Vice-Pres. and Man. VICTOR J. REIZMAN.

Dai-Ichi Kangyo Bank Ltd.: Kal Bldg., No. 502, 118, 2-ka, Namdaemun-ro, Chung-ku, Seoul.

Bank of Tokyo: 6, 1-chome, Nihombashi Hongokucho, Chuo-ku, Tokyo, Japan; Seoul.

First National City Bank: 28, Sokong-dong, Chung-ku, and 8, 1-ka, Shinchang-dong, Chung-ka, Pusan, Seoul.

Mitsubishi Bank Ltd.: 6, Mukyodong, Chung-ku, Seoul; f. 1967; Man. TAKEO FUNABASHI.

DEVELOPMENT AGENCY

Korea Development Finance Corporation: 12th Floor, The Cho Heung Bank Bldg., 14, Namdaemun-ro 1-ka, Chung-ku, Seoul; f. 1967; assists in the development of private enterprise by medium- and long-term financing including loans, guarantees and purchase of equities; cap. p.u. 1,634m. won; Chair. CHAI SUN HONG; Pres. CHIN HYUNG KIM.

INSURANCE

PRINCIPAL COMPANIES

Ankuk Fire and Marine Insurance Co. Ltd.: 50, 1-ka, Ulchi-ro, Chung-ku, Seoul; P.O.B. 469; f. 1952; Pres. YUNG KI SOHN; Man. Dir. MAN KYU PARK.

Dae Han Fire and Marine Insurance Co. Ltd.: 75 Susomun-dong, Sudaemun-ku, Seoul; f. 1946; premium income (1971-72) 1,070m. won, res. 1,023m. won; (Dec. 1971) Pres. CHI BOK KIM; Vice-Pres. BONG IK LEE.

Dai Han Life Insurance Co.: P.O.B. 290, Seoul; f. 1946; Gen. Man. CHANG HO IM.

Eastern Marine and Fire Insurance Co., The: 8-1 Namdaemun-ro, 2-ka Chung-ku, Seoul; f. 1955; Pres. CHUN KYU CHOI.

First Fire and Marine Insurance Co. Ltd., The: 18, 1-ga, Namdaemoon-ro, Chung-ku, C.P.O. Box 530, Seoul; f. 1949; Pres. YE CHUL LEE.

Haedong Fire and Marine Insurance Co. Ltd.: 199-50, 2-ka, Ulchi-ro, Chung-ku, Seoul; f. 1953; premium income 545m. won, res. 296m. won (1971); Pres. DONG MAN KIM; Dir. HA YONG SUNG.

Korean Reinsurance Corporation: I.P.O. Box 1438, Seoul; f. 1963; auth. cap. 3,000m. won; Pres. YI YANG-HO; Vice-Pres. CHONG CHIN LEE.

Koryo Fire and Marine Insurance Co. Ltd.: 84-8, 2-ka, Chong-ro, Chongro-ku, Seoul; f. 1948; auth. cap. 500m. won; Pres. WOO-POONG LEE; Man. Dir. YOON-BOK LEE.

Oriental Fire and Marine Insurance Co. Ltd.: 19, 1-ka, Tae Pyong-ro, Chung-ku, P.O.B. 230, Kwanghwamoon, Seoul; f. 1922; cap. p.u. 1,000m. won (1972); Chair. CHOONG HOON CHO; Pres. IN WAN CHUNG; Exec. Man. Dir. YOUNG SUH KIM; Man. Dirs. YOUNG DAL KIM, BYOUNG KUN KIM.

Pan Korea Insurance Co.: 77 Sokong-dong, Chung-ku, Seoul; f. 1959; premium income U.S. $7,771,000m., res. U.S. $3,120,000; Pres. BO HYOUNG LEE; Vice-Pres. DOO HWOI KOO.

Shindong-A Fire and Marine Insurance Co. Ltd.: 43, 2-ka, Taepyung-ro, Chung-ku, Seoul; f. 1946; premium income U.S. $3,355,000, res. U.S. $2,356,000 (1971); Chair. SUNG MO CHOI; Pres. WOO JIK CHOI.

TRADE AND INDUSTRY

CHAMBERS OF COMMERCE AND INDUSTRY

Korea Chamber of Commerce and Industry: 111 Sokong-dong, Choong-ku, Seoul; f. 1894; total mems. over 200,000; 37 local chambers; promotes modernization of industry and stimulates regional trade and investment; Pres. SUNG KON KIM; publs. *Korean Business Directory, K.C.C.I. News, Chamber Review.*

Gwangju Chamber of Commerce and Industry: 7, 2-ka, Kumnam-dong, Gwangju, Chunnam Province.

Inchon Chamber of Commerce and Industry: 3, 3-ka, Songhak-dong, Inchon, Kyonggi Province.

Jeonju Chamber of Commerce and Industry: 80, 3-ka, Chungang-dong, Jeonju, Chunbuk Province.

Masan Chamber of Commerce and Industry: 4, 1-ka, Chungang-dong, Masan, Kyoungnam Province.

Pusan Chamber of Commerce and Industry: 36, 2-ka, Daegyo-dong, Jung-gu, Pusan; f. 1888; 1,830 mems.; Pres. SUK-CHIN KANG; Exec. Vice-Pres. BUM-SOO AHN.

Taegu Chamber of Commerce and Industry: 197 Sinchun-Dong, Taegu; f. 1904; about 30,000 mems.; cap p.u. 107,810,000 won; Pres. IL YONG OH; Exec. Vice-Pres. JONG WANG LEE; publs. *Review of Taegu Economy* (monthly), *Bulletin* (monthly).

Taejon Chamber of Commerce and Industry: 142-2 Eun Haeng Dong, Taejon; f. 1933; 8,000 mems.; cap. $250,000; Pres. KWANG PYO HONG; Vice-Pres. BONG SEOK YANG, DEOK YUNG SONG; publ. *Taejeon Sang Gong* (monthly).

FOREIGN TRADE ORGANIZATIONS

Donghae Trading Co. Ltd.: 180, 1-ka, Eulji-ro, Chung-ku, Seoul; f. 1966; Pres. SHIM HYUN-DAE.

Korea Export Industrial Corporation: 188-5 Kuro-dong Youngdungpo-ku, Seoul; f. 1964; encourages industrial exports; Chair. CHOI MYUNG-HUN.

Korean Trade Promotion Corporation (KOTRA): 46, 4-ka, Namdaemun-ro, Chung-gu, Seoul; f. 1962; Pres. AHN KWANG HO; publs. *Korean Trade, Korean Trade and Investment.*

Korea Electronic Products Exporters Association: 37, 1-ka, Eulji-ro, Chung-ku, Seoul; f. 1970; Chair. PARK SUNG-CHAN.

Jedong Industrial Co. Ltd.: 70-3, 2-ka, Taepyung-ro, Chung-ku, Seoul; f. 1951; deep-sea fishery import and export; Pres. SHIM SANG-JOON.

INDUSTRIAL ORGANIZATIONS

Agriculture and Fishery Development Corporation—AFDC: 111 Hap-Dong, Sudaemun-ku, Seoul, I.P.O. Box 3212; f. 1967 to develop principal producing areas for various agricultural and fisheries produce, to develop and encourage processing, preservation and marketing of such products and to cement links among activities relating to the production, processing, preservation, marketing and consumption of such goods; thereby to elevate income levels of farming and fishing communities; cap. 10,000m. won; Pres. DOO YUL CHOI; Exec. Vice-Pres. JUNG OH KIM.

Federation of Korean Industries: 28th Floor, Samilro Bldg., 10 Kwanchul-dong, Chongro-ku, Seoul; f. 1961; conducts research and survey work on domestic and overseas economic conditions and trends; makes recommendations on important economic matters to the government and other interested parties; exchange of economic and trade missions with other countries with a view to exploring markets and fostering economic co-operation; sponsoring of regular business conferences with friendly countries; mems. 178 companies and 48 business asscns.; Pres. YONG WAN KIM; Exec. Vice-Pres. IP SAM KIM; Dir.-Gen. TAI YEOP YOON; Sec.-Gen. NEUNG SUN YOON; publs. *Kyong Hyup* (monthly), *Korean Business Review* (every two months), *Federation of Korean Industries* (annual), *Korean Economic Yearbook, FKI Bulletin* (weekly).

Korea Development Association: 340, 2-ga, Taepyeong-ro Jung-gu, Seoul.

Korea Productivity Centre: 10, 2-ga, Pil-tong, Chung-gu, Seoul; f. 1957; Pres. EUN BOK RHEE; Chair. SUK CHUN LIM; publ. *Journal* (monthly).

Korea Traders' Association: 10-1, 2-ka, Hoehyon-dong, Chung-gu, Seoul; f. 1946; Pres. HWAI LEE; Vice-Pres. JIN HA KIM; publs. *Korean Trade News* (daily), *Korean Trade Directory* (annual).

Construction Association of Korea: 31-23, 1-ka, Taepyung-ro, Chung-ku, Seoul; f. 1959; Pres. CHO JUNG-KOO.

Daehan Coalmines Association: 2-15, Changkyo-dong, Chung-ku, Seoul; f. 1957; Pres. WOO SUNG-WHAN.

The Electric Constructors Association of Korea: 76-9, Pyung-dong, Suhdaemun-ku, Seoul; f. 1960; Pres. KI SANG-DO.

The Korea Electric Association: 11-4, Supyo-dong, Chung-ku, Seoul; f. 1965; Pres. KIM CHONG-JOO.

Korea Petroleum Association: 59-23, 3-ka, Chungmu-ro, Chung-ku, Seoul; f. 1956; Chair. PARK MAN-HI.

Korea Sericulture Association: 15-1, Kwanchul-dong, Chongro-ku, Seoul; Pres. CHANG YUNG-JIN.

Korea Shipowners Association: 10-3, Buckchang-dong, Chung-ku, Seoul; f. 1960; Pres. CHU YO-HAN.

Korea Steelmakers Association: 11th Fl., Ankuk Bldg., 175-87 Ankuk-dong, Chongro-ku, Seoul; f. 1963; Pres. CHUN SUN-HAN.

Mining Association of Korea: 35-24, Tongui-dong, Chongru-ku, Seoul; f. 1918; Pres. HWANG KY-RYONG.

Spinners' and Weavers' Association of Korea: 116-1, 1-ka, Namdaemun-ro, Chung-gu, Seoul; f. 1947; Pres. KIM YONG-JOO.

CO-OPERATIVES

Following legislation on land reform (1950) and rural organization (1957), the Agriculture Bank and Agricultural Co-operatives were established, the latter forming a federation in 1958. In 1961, the two organizations merged to form the National Agricultural Co-operative Federation (N.A.C.F.) which now undertakes a wide range of activities for the member co-operatives—purchase, supply, marketing, utilization and processing, mutual insurance, banking and credit services, education and guidance, research and surveys, international co-operation.

The N.A.C.F. affiliates the following: general co-operatives comprising 2.2 million farmers in over 17,000 village (*Ri* or *Dong*) co-operatives and 139 city or county (*Gun*) co-operatives; 140 special co-operatives comprising about 47,000 farmers engaged in orchard cultivation, livestock rearing, vegetable growing and other crop farming.

National Agricultural Co-operative Federation: 75, 1st-ka, Chunjung-Ro, Sudaemun-gu, Seoul; f. 1961; Pres. YOUN HWAN KIM; Vice-Pres. SANG KYUM KO; cap. 2.8 billion won (Dec. 1971); publs. *Agricultural Year Book, Agricultural Co-operative Monthly Survey, Annual Report, New Farmer* (monthly), *Newspaper, Marketing of Agricultural Products*, surveys and reports (irregular).

Central Federation of Fisheries Co-operatives: 88, Kyeongun-dong, Chongro-ku, Seoul; f. 1962; Pres. KIM DUK-YUP.

Federation of Korea Knitting Industry Co-operatives: 48, 1-ka, Shinmun-ro, Chongro-ku, Seoul; f. 1960; Pres. KI SANG-DO.

Korea Agricultural Chemical Co-operatives Asociation: 45-1, Kwanchul-dong, Chongro-ku, Seoul; f. 1962; Pres. CHUNG KI-YUNG.

National Federation of Medium Industry Co-operatives: 138-1, Kongpyong-dong, Chongro-ku, Seoul; f. 1962; Chair. BONGJAI KIM; Vice-Chair. YONGWOON WON; publ. *Medium Industry News*.

EMPLOYER'S ASSOCIATION

The Korean Employers' Association: 10, Kwanchul-dong, Chongro-ku, Seoul; f. 1970; Pres. KIM YONG-JOO.

TRADE UNIONS

Federation of Korean Trade Unions (F.K.T.U.): 20 Sokong-dong, Chung-ku, Seoul; f. 1946; Pres. Choi Yong Soo; 17 unions are affiliated with a membership of 493,711 (August 1971); affiliated to ICFTU; publ. *FKTU News* (monthly); major affiliated unions are:

National Textile Workers' Union: 60 Myong-dong, Chung-ku, Seoul; Pres. Lee Chun Sun; 58,412 mems.

National Railway Workers' Union: 40, 3-ka, Hangkang-ro, Yongsan-ku, Seoul; Pres. Oh Sang Kyu; 34,796 mems.

National Mine Workers' Union: 15-8, Pildong 2-ka, Chung-ku, Seoul; Pres. Suh Won U; 34,951 mems.

National Auto Workers' Union: 213 Ulchiro 5-ka, Chung-ku, Seoul; Pres. Kim Kee Tae; 77,084 mems.

National Printing Workers' Union: 20 Sokong-dong, Chung-ku, Seoul; Pres. Kim Sang Kon; 4,490 mems.

National Dock Workers' Union: 2-5, Dodong 1-ka, Chung-ku, Seoul; Pres. Park In Kun; 20,725 mems.

National Maritime Workers' Union: 15 Tongkwang-dong 2-ka, Pusan; Pres. Chang Ul Yong; 42,697 mems.

TRANSPORT AND TOURISM

TRANSPORT

RAILWAYS

Korean National Railroad: Head Office: 3, 1-ka, Doding, Chung-gu, Seoul; f. 1963; operates, as a separate entity under the Ministry of Transportation, all railways and railway repair shops in the Republic of Korea; total route mileage of 3,358 standard gauge with 78 miles of narrow gauge (July 1971); Dir.-Gen. Yong Lee; Deputy Dir.-Gen. Jong Hyok Yoon.

ROADS

There are about 25,400 miles of roads of which about 9 per cent are paved. A number of highways are under construction; the most important, the 428 km. (267 miles) long Seoul-Pusan motorway, was formerly opened in July 1970. Other routes—Taejon to Sunchon (180 miles), Seoul to Kangnung (150 miles) and Samchuck to Sokcho—are expected to be completed by 1974. There are about 125,000 non-military vehicles in the Republic.

Korea Highway Corporation: 3-106, 1-ka, Do-dong, Choong-ku, Seoul; f. 1969; responsible for construction and maintenance of toll roads; Pres. Ki Suk Park; Exec. Vice-Pres. Kwang Sup Yim; cap. p.u. U.S. $101,592,500; employees: 1,227.

SHIPPING

Office of Marine Affairs: Seoul; f. 1955; supervises all branches of shipping. Chief ports: Pusan, Inchun, Mookmo, Masan, Yusoo, Goonsan. Ships of U.S., British, Japanese, Dutch and Norwegian lines call at the principal ports.

Far Eastern Marine Transport Co. Ltd.: 180, 1-ka, Ulji-ro, Choong-gu, Seoul; f. 1952; 5 cargo vessels; Pres. Ryun Namkoong.

Korea Shipping Corporation Ltd.: Daihan Ilbo Building, 340, 2-ka Taepyung-ro, Seoul (P.O.B. International 1164); f. 1950; 21 cargo vessels; world-wide transportation service and shipping agency service in Korea; Pres. Chu Yo-Han; Vice-Pres. Seh Hyuck Ryu.

Korea United Lines, Inc.: 50-10, 2-ka, Chungmu-ro, Chung-ku, Seoul; f. 1967; world-wide transportation with bulk carriers; Pres. Lee Chung-Nim.

Pan Ocean Bulk Carriers Ltd.: Daehan Bldg., 75 Seosomun-dong, Seoul; f. 1965; 8 tankers; transportation of petroleum products; Pres. K. S. Park; Man. Dir. Capt. H. H. Park.

Samyang Navigation Co. Ltd.: 32-2, Mukyo-dong, Chung-ku, Seoul; f. 1966; 3 tankers; Chair. Han Byung-Ki.

CIVIL AVIATION

Korean Air Lines: P.O.B. 864 Central, Seoul; KAL Bldg., 2-ka Namdaemun-ro, Chung-ku, Seoul; f. 1962 by the Korean Government; transferred 1969 to the *Hanjin Group*; the only scheduled airline in the Republic of Korea, serves 16 major domestic cities and flies to Tokyo, Fukuoka, Osaka, Taipei, Hong Kong, Bangkok, Honolulu, Los Angeles; Pres. Choong Hoon Cho; Vice-Pres. Choong-Kun Cho, Myung-Sup Chun, Eui Taek Myung; fleet: 5 Fokker F-27, 4 B-707/320C, 2 DC-8, 3 B-727, 7YS-11, 1 B-747F, 2 707-720.

The following foreign airlines also serve Seoul: Cathay Pacific Airways, China Airlines, Japan Air Lines, Northwest Orient Airlines.

TOURISM

Korea Tourist Association: room 502, Hanil Bldg., 132-4, 1-ka, Bongrae-dong, Chung-ku, Seoul; f. 1963; Pres. Cho Choong-Hoon.

Korea Tourist Bureau (KTB): rooms 204,208,212,240, Bando Hotel, Ulchiro 1-ka, Chung-ku, Seoul; f. 1912; Pres. Kukwhan Sul.

ATOMIC ENERGY

In October 1970 the government gained the international credit necessary to finance construction of the Republic's first nuclear power station, which is to be completed near Pusan by 1975 and will be capable of generating 595,000 kWh.

Office of Atomic Energy: 170-2, Kongneung-dong, Sungbook-ku, Seoul; f. 1959; responsible for management, control, development, production and utilization of nuclear energy; Dir.-Gen. Sang Soo Lee; Bureau Dir. Chi Eun Kim. The following three institutes are under the control of this office: Atomic Energy Research Institute (AERI) (*see below*); Radiological Research Institute (Dir. Jang Kyu Lee); Radiation Agriculture Research Institute (Dir. Sang Chil Shim).

Atomic Energy Commission: 21- Chung-dong, Sudaemun-ku, Seoul; under the direct supervision of the Ministry of Science and Technology; 7 members appointed by the President of the Republic; fundamental plans and policies, furtherance of research and training of personnel; Chair. Kee Hyong Kim.

Atomic Energy Research Institute: (AERI): P.O.B. 7, Chungryang-ri, Seoul; Divisions for Reactor Engineering, Electronics, Physics, Chemistry, Biology and Health Physics; Triga Mark II (100 kW.) reactor in operation, Triga Mark III (2 mW.) under construction; Dir. Young Jae Lee.

PRINCIPAL UNIVERSITIES

Chonnam National University: Kwang Joo, Chollanam Do; 321 teachers, 5,800 students.

Chosun University: Kwang Joo; 247 teachers, 4,140 students.

Chungang University: Huksuk Dong, Seoul; 200 teachers, 6,800 students.

Chungnam National University: Taijon; 270 teachers, 1881 students.

Chunpuk National University: Chun-Joo, Cholla Puk Do; 4,020 students.

Dong A University: 13-ka, Dong-Daesin-Dong, Seo-ku, Pusan; 340 teachers, 4,380 students.

Dong-Kook University: Pil Dong, Seoul; 300 teachers, 4,700 students.

Ewha Women's University: Daihyun-Dong, Seoul; 745 teachers, 7,894 students.

Hankuk University of Foreign Studies: 270 Rimoon-Dong, Dongdaemoon-ku, Seoul; 200 teachers, 2,300 students.

Hanyang University: 8-2 Haengdang-Dong, Sung dong-ku, Seoul; 640 teachers, 9,200 students.

Jeon Buk National University: 2-22 Rue 2, Jouk-gm, Jeon Buk.

Kon-Kuk University: Sung-dong ku, Seoul; 112 teachers, 8,000 students.

Korea University: Anam-Dong, Seoul; 283 teachers, 8,477 students.

Kyung Hee University: Hoeki Dong, Seoul; teachers 440, 4,600 students.

Kyungpuk National University: Taegu; 329 teachers, 4,737 students.

Pusan National University: Dong Nae-ku, Pusan; 300 teachers, 3,374 students.

Seoul National University: Dong Soong-Dong, Seoul; 1,200 teachers, 14,000 students.

Sogang University: 1, Siasudong, Mapoku, Seoul; 176 teachers, 1,696 students.

Sookmyung Women's University: Chungpa-Dong, Seoul; 200 teachers, 3,300 students.

Sung Jun University: 135 Sang Do-Dong Seoul; 98 teachers, 1,876 students.

Sung Kyun Kwan University: Myung Ryun Dong, Seoul; 364 teachers, 4,836 students.

Woo Sok University: 42nd St., Myung-Yung-Dong, Chong-No-Koo, Seoul.

Yeungnam University: 317-1 Tae-Myung-Dong, Nam-ku, Taegu; 154 teachers, 7,052 students.

Yonsei University: Sodaemoon-ku, Seoul; 628 teachers, 10,082 students.

KUWAIT

INTRODUCTORY SURVEY

Location, Climate, Language, Religion, Flag, Capital

The State of Kuwait lies at the north-west extreme of the Persian Gulf and is bordered to the north-west by Iraq and to the south by Saudi Arabia. In the extreme south-east lies a Partitioned Zone, the oil wealth of which is shared equally between the two concessionaires of Kuwait and Saudi Arabia. Kuwait is a desert country with a hot and humid climate: temperatures average 24°c (75°F) and can soar very high, with humidity of 60–80 per cent in July and August. The language is Arabic, but English is widely used. In 1970 nearly 95 per cent of the inhabitants were Muslim, with a small minority of Christians. The national flag (proportions 2 by 1) has horizontal green, white and red stripes, with a black trapezoid next to the staff. The capital is Kuwait City.

Recent History

Until 1961, Kuwait accepted British protection and foreign policy was controlled by the British Government. Kuwait became independent in June 1961 and joined the United Nations in 1963. During 1965 agreement was reached with Saudi Arabia over sharing of oil revenues from the Neutral Zone (now called "Partitioned Zone"). In October 1963 Iraq recognized the State of Kuwait. Kuwait has played an important part in stimulating Arab co-operation. In November 1965 Shaikh Abdullah as-Salim as-Sabah, the first ruler of independent Kuwait, died and was succeeded by his brother Shaikh Sabah as-Salim as-Sabah, Individual Kuwaiti residents (many formerly Palestinians) have given much financial assistance to the Palestinian guerrilla organizations, while the Government has been granting substantial financial assistance to Jordan and Egypt since September 1967.

In January 1971 a more representative national assembly was elected, and an extensive cabinet reshuffle took place for the first time since independence. In 1973 and 1974 the National Assembly has asserted itself by refusing to ratify participation agreements signed by the Kuwaiti Government and the Kuwait Oil Company. In March 1973 there were clashes with Iraq on the border between the two countries and the dispute has continued into 1974.

Government

The Ruler of Kuwait and Head of State is the Amir. Under the Constitution of 1962 executive power is exercised by a Prime Minister and a Council of Ministers, both appointed by the Amir. The Legislative organ is the National Assembly of fifty members elected for four years by adult males except for servicemen and policemen. The country is divided into three provincial governorates.

Defence

Kuwait has a small but well trained and equipped army numbering about 8,000 men, an air force of 2,000 men with over 40 aircraft, and a navy of about 200 men manning a dozen vessels.

Economic Affairs

The economy is based on extremely rich deposits of oil, most of which is exploited by the Kuwait Oil Company, owned jointly by the British Petroleum Company and the Gulf Oil Corporation of America. Other companies with interests in Kuwait and the Partitioned Zone are the American Independent Oil Company, the Getty Oil Company, the Japanese-owned Arabian Oil Company, Royal Dutch-Shell and the Kuwait National Petroleum Co. (K.N.P.C.). Oil refining and the production of natural gas are increasingly important industries. Other products include ammonium sulphate and urea. Minor industries make bricks, concrete and beverages. On January 8th, 1973, a participation agreement was signed with British Petroleum and Gulf Oil, under which the Kuwaiti Government would pay £62.5 million for its initial 25 per cent share in the oil companies operations. This agreement was not ratified by the National Assembly. A further agreement, giving the Kuwaiti Government a 60 per cent initial share, was signed in January 1974, but this also was not ratified by the National Assembly, which is in favour of faster progress towards nationalization. Kuwait has been one of the leading Arab States in limiting her oil production and securing higher prices for her oil in 1973 and 1974.

Kuwaitis receive considerable preference in business enterprises. Kuwait rivals the Lebanon as the Middle East's leading financial centre. There is a little agriculture at subsistence level, and the Government has made much progress with the help of an experimental station in improving farming techniques. A Fund for Arab Development set up by Kuwait has given generous grants to member-states of the Arab League.

Transport and Communications

There are no railways, and no internal air flights. The 1,920 km. of roads include the dual carriageway from Kuwait City to the border with Iraq. The port of Kuwait is an important Middle Eastern port of call and has been modernized. Special oil terminals facilitate oil shipments, the chief one being Mina Al-Ahmadi. Kuwait Airways and a number of foreign airlines provide international air services.

Social Welfare

A Labour Law safeguards employment and there are benefits for sickness, and industrial accidents and diseases. Public assistance is provided for the poor, aged, orphans widows and tubercular persons. Medical treatment is free, and medical teams from Kuwait assist other Arab governments.

Education

Education is free. Education is graded into pre-primary (four to six), primary (six to ten), intermediate (ten to fourteen) and secondary (fourteen to eighteen). There is a technical college and a university. Over 2,000 Kuwaiti students are now receiving education abroad.

Tourism

Visas are not required to visit Kuwait by nationals of Algeria, Bahrain, Egypt, Iraq, Jordan, Lebanon, Libya, Morocco, Qatar, Saudi Arabia, Syria, Sudan, Tunisia, the United Arab Emirates and the United Kingdom.

Public Holidays

1974: August 18th (Ascension of the Prophet), October 18th (Id ul Fitr), December 24th–26th (Christmas and Id ul Adha.)

1975: January 14th (Muslim New Year), February 25th (Kuwait National Day), March 26th (Birthday of the Prophet), March 28th–31st (Easter).

Weights and Measures

The metric system is in force.

Currency and Exchange Rates

1,000 fils = 1 Kuwait dinar (KD).

Exchange rates (April 1974):
£1 sterling = 698.5 fils;
U.S. $1 = 296.05 fils.

STATISTICAL SURVEY

AREA AND POPULATION

Area (sq. km.)		Population (Census of April 19th, 1970)†					
Kuwait	Partitioned Zone*	Total	Kuwaitis	Foreigners	Males	Females
16,918	5,700	738,662	347,396	391,266	419,881	318,781

Estimated Population: 883,000 (July 1st, 1973).

* The Partitioned Zone lies south-east of Kuwait and is partitioned between Kuwait and Saudi Arabia.

† Including 754 Kuwaiti nationals abroad.

Principal Towns (1970 Census): Kuwait City (capital) 80,405; Hawalli 106,542; Salmiya 67,346.

ECONOMICALLY ACTIVE POPULATION*
(1970 Census)

	Males	Females	Total
Agriculture, Hunting, Forestry and Fishing .	4,051	9	4,060
Oil and Natural Gas, Mining and Quarrying .	6,455	716	7,171
Manufacturing	31,973	115	32,088
Electricity, Gas and Water Supply .	7,236	16	7,252
Construction	33,606	68	33,674
Trade, Restaurants and Hotels . .	28,954	329	29,283
Transport, Storage and Communications .	11,997	141	12,138
Finance, Insurance, Property and Business Services .	3,506	242	3,748
Community, Social and Personal Services .	89,320	14,816	104,136
Other Activities (not adequately described) .	797	30	827
TOTAL IN EMPLOYMENT .	217,893	16,478	234,371
Unemployed	4,782	118	4,900
TOTAL	222,675	16,596	239,271

* Including Kuwaiti nationals outside the country.

OIL

KUWAIT (Kuwait Oil Co.)	
	PRODUCTION (long tons)
1967 . .	113,355,644
1968 . .	120,162,473
1969 . .	127,502,203
1970 . .	135,494,480
1971 . .	144,468,129
1972 . .	148,711,076

KUWAIT/SAUDI ARABIA PARTITIONED ZONE
(American Independent Oil Co. and Getty Oil Co.)

	PRODUCTION (long tons)
1968 . .	6,636,777
1969 . .	6,493,592
1970 . .	8,940,000
1971 . .	9,910,000
1972 . .	8,190,464

KUWAIT/SAUDI ARABIA PARTITIONED ZONE OFFSHORE
(Arabian Oil Co.)

	PRODUCTION (long tons)
1968 . .	15,316,000
1969 . .	16,150,000
1970 . .	16,960,000
1971 . .	18,690,000
1972 . .	20,000,000*

* Approximate.

OIL EXPORTS
(1972)

DESTINATION	CRUDE OIL*		REFINED PRODUCTS INCLUDING LIQUEFIED PETROLEUM GAS	
	million U.S. barrels	%	million U.S. barrels	%
Western Europe	610.2	57.0	14.7	10.1
Asia and Oceania . . .	407.4	38.1	76.3	52.3
North and South America . .	38.2	3.6	6.9	4.7
Arab and Other Countries . .	14.6	1.3	48.0	32.9
TOTAL . . .	1,070.4	100.0	145.9	100.0

* Excludes American Independent Oil Company production of crude oil, which is included in the refined products figure for the company.

KUWAIT OIL COMPANY CRUDE OIL EXPORTS BY DESTINATION

	1969		1970		1971		1972	
	tons	%	tons	%	tons	%	tons	%
United Kingdom .	19,602,763	17.3	25,236,126	21.2	25,842,332	20.2	24,070,928	17.9
Japan . . .	12,163,417	10.8	15,353,896	12.9	17,783,685	13.9	22,465,540	16.7
Netherlands . .	13,531,653	12.0	10,812,790	9.1	12,015,376	9.4	14,872,166	11.0
Italy . . .	14,758,426	13.0	12,374,513	10.4	11,954,502	9.3	13,526,299	10.0
France . . .	9,367,952	8.3	10,697,850	9.0	11,117,512	8.7	16,599,045	12.3
Ireland . . .	8,194,332	7.2	10,515,043	8.8	10,445,691	8.2	6,668,442	5.0
Singapore . .	4,675,820	4.1	4,377,414	3.7	6,183,626	4.8	7,884,940	5.9
South Korea .	3,207,755	2.8	2,416,540	2.0	5,894,861	4.6	5,380,114	4.0
Federal Germany .	1,308,558	1.2	4,110,392	3.4	4,427,435	3.5	4,360,783	3.2
Taiwan . . .	3,757,194	3.3	2,764,286	2.3	3,166,073	2.5	2,813,214	2.1
Belgium . . .	4,295,911	3.8	2,958,250	2.5	2,555,098	2.0	496,908	0.4
Other Countries .	18,460,741	16.2	17,521,860	14.7	16,671,833	12.9	15,563,501	11.5
TOTAL . .	113,324,522	100.0	119,138,960	100.0	128,058,024	100.0	134,701,880	100.0

Arabian Oil Company
Crude Oil Exports by Destination, 1972
(long tons)

Europe	667,000
Japan	30,800,000
Australia	2,352,000

American Independent Oil Company
Exports of Refined Products
(barrels)

1968 . . .	11,886,830
1969 . . .	12,805,358
1970 . . .	28,640,259
1971 . . .	30,551,116
1972 . . .	29,308,905

Kuwait National Petroleum Company
Production Exports of Refined Oil Products
(barrels)

	1970	1971
Light Distillates . .	13,260,425	11,786,382
Gasoline Premium . .	2,431,377	2,366,210
Gas Oil . . .	18,814,287	18,164,374
Fuel Oil . . .	44,866,491	42,315,787
Aviation Kerosene . .	818,544	810,056
Kerosene . . .	315,565	422,082
Asphalt. . .	186,801	169,416
Light Benzine . .	540,068	608,059
Diesel . . .	1,733,061	1,835,263

NATURAL GAS PRODUCTION
(million cu. ft.)

	Gas Produced	Used by Companies	Used for Injection	Used by State	Total Gas Used
1969 . .	513,690	86,769	49,352	44,868	180,988
1970 . .	570,376	90,000	45,342	52,707	188,048
1971 . .	643,710	93,830	69,469	63,224	226,522
1972 . .	647,808	95,904	65,903	85,741	247,548

INDUSTRY

		1970	1971	1972
Motor Spirit	'ooo metric tons	1,192	506	n.a.
Kerosene .	,, ,, ,,	613	701	n.a.
Distillate Fuel Oils . . .	,, ,, ,,	7,471	7,118	n.a.
Residual Fuel Oil . . .	,, ,, ,,	12,017	11,570	n.a.
Ammonium Sulphate . . .	metric tons	71,198	65,450	92,179
Electricity Generated . . .	million kWh.	2,213	2,636	3,295
Potable Water . . .	million galls.	6,683	7,675	8,584
Brackish Water	,, ,,	5,755	5,507	5,397
Sodium Chloride . . .	tons	4,653	4,731	4,977
Chlorine . . .	,,	1,661	1,674	1,723
Caustic Soda	,,	1,876	1,890	1,944
Hydrochloric Acid . . .	galls.	160,709	126,774	140,786
Lime-Sand Bricks . . .	cubic metres	87,882	196,446	230,451
Milling (Kuwait Flour Mills Co.) .	tons	84,307	95,504	96,480

FINANCE

1,000 fils = 1 Kuwait dinar (KD).
Coins: 1, 5, 10, 20, 50 and 100 fils.
Notes: 250 and 500 fils; 1, 5 and 10 dinars.
Exchange rates (April 1974): £1 sterling = 698.5 fils; U.S. $1 = 296.05 fils.
100 Kuwait dinars = £143.16 = $337.78.

BUDGET
(1972–73)

REVENUE	KD	CURRENT EXPENDITURE	'000 KD
Income Tax	386,906,000	Head of State	8,000
Production and Consumption Taxes and		Information	6,769
Fees	128,699,300	Public Works	14,224
Services Revenues . . .	17,416,944	Posts, Telegraphs and Telephones	7,642
Miscellaneous Revenues and Dues .	1,603,756	Education	47,115
Incidental Revenues . . .	1,600,000	Foreign Affairs . . .	3,600
		Interior	28,568
		Defence	30,694
		Public Health . . .	22,976
		Social Affairs and Labour .	8,161
		Electricity, Water, Power and Water Distillation Plant and Chlorine Plant.	15,340
		Finance and Oil, including Customs and Ports and Housing . . .	14,191
		Unclassified and Transferable .	86,565
		Other Expenditure . . .	16,721
TOTAL . . .	536,226,000	TOTAL . . .	310,566

1973–74: Revenue 568.1m.; Expenditure 470.1m. (est.).

EXTERNAL TRADE
(million KD)

	1968	1969	1970	1971	1972
Imports .	218.3	230.8	223.3	232.3	262.2
Exports* .	20.8	23.1	26.4	34.4	49.6

* Export figures exclude oil.

COMMODITIES
('000 KD)

	IMPORTS			EXPORTS		
	1970	1971	1972	1970	1971	1972
Food and Live Animals . . .	37,804	40,924	46,133	5,481	6,561	6,902
Beverages and Tobacco . . .	5,724	6,094	6,512	1,247	913	1,424
Crude Materials, inedible, except fuels	3,400	4,015	3,956	1,280	748	914
Mineral Fuels, Lubricants and Related Materials . . .	1,588	2,154	2,597	349	339	232
Animal and Vegetable Oils, Fats .	609	1,117	1,040	48	36	46
Chemicals	10,354	10,684	12,736	5,177	6,484	12,333
Manufactured Goods . . .	47,515	51,340	56,316	2,658	4,194	8,949
Machinery and Transport Equipment	80,070	77,501	85,552	7,778	12,537	14,288
Miscellaneous Manufactured Articles	35,823	37,980	46,822	1,772	1,968	3,850
Others	381	497	514	593	602	657

PRINCIPAL COUNTRIES
('ooo KD.)

IMPORTS	1970	1971	1972	EXPORTS*	1970	1971	1972
Australia	5,267	6,475	7,466	Bahrain	603	1,069	1,335
Belgium and Lux'bourg	2,586	3,610	3,238	Egypt	417	800	530
China, People's Republic	7,269	7,629	8,456	India	1,750	654	3,222
France	10,696	14,002	11,016	Iran	3,399	2,501	3,745
Federal Germany	18,690	17,598	21,762	Iraq	2,902	3,814	2,730
India	8,337	7,384	7,595	Jordan	530	1,277	490
Iran	3,795	4,047	3,754	Lebanon	1,498	2,360	2,557
Italy	10,733	9,782	11,258	Pakistan	502	1,131	2,158
Japan	33,946	32,789	41,967	Qatar	900	923	1,597
Lebanon	9,743	10,654	13,545	Saudi Arabia	3,896	6,803	12,252
Netherlands	5,523	5,649	6,678	United Arab Emirates	2,798	2,491	3,833
Switzerland	3,541	3,429	3,537	United Kingdom	1,214	2,523	3,716
United Kingdom	26,411	26,841	26,613	U.S.A.	862	1,159	725
U.S.A.	29,595	33,622	34,328				

* Excludes oil exports (*see* OIL *above*).

TRANSPORT

Shipping (1972): *Arrivals:* 1,160 ships; passenger arrivals 20,739; passenger departures 20,884.

Vehicles: Total (1969) 136,622; (1970) 149,150; (1971) 157,876; (1972) 175,087.

Civil Aviation: Kuwait Airport, total aircraft movements (1969) 13,379; (1970) 14,088; (1971) 13,998; (1972) 13,549.

EDUCATION*
(1972–73)

	SCHOOLS	TEACHERS	STUDENTS
Kindergarten	49	882	12,786
Primary	96	3,753	69,241
Intermediate	78	3,677	52,399
Secondary	28	2,261	21,278
Commercial	3	192	1,173
Industrial College	1	212	739
Religious Institute	1	38	270
Special Training Institutes	11	271	1,385
Teacher Training Colleges	4	219	960

* Data for government schools only; in 1972–73 there were 1,707 teachers, 36,691 pupils at private schools.

Sources: Central Statistical Office, Planning Board, Kuwait; Ministry of Finance and Oil, Kuwait; Ministry of Education, Kuwait; National Bank of Kuwait, S.A.K.; Kuwait Oil Co. Ltd., Ahmadi, Kuwait.

THE CONSTITUTION

(Promulgated November 16th, 1962)

The principal provisions of the Constitution are as follows:

SOVEREIGNTY

Kuwait is an independent sovereign Arab State; her sovereignty may not be surrendered, and no part of her territory may be relinquished. Offensive war is prohibited by the Constitution.

Succession as Amir is restricted to heirs of the late MUBARAK AL-SABAH, and an Heir Apparent must be appointed within one year of the accession of a new Amir.

EXECUTIVE AUTHORITY

Executive power is vested in the Amir, who exercises it through a Council of Ministers. The Amir will appoint the Prime Minister "after the traditional consultations", and will appoint and dismiss Ministers on the recommendation of the Prime Minister. Ministers need not be members of the National Assembly, though all ministers who are not Assembly members assume membership *ex-officio* in the Assembly for the duration of office. The Amir also lays down laws, which shall not be effective unless published in the *Official Gazette*, The Amir sets up public institutions. All decrees issued in these respects shall be conveyed to the Assembly. No law is issued unless it is approved by the Assembly.

LEGISLATURE

A National Assembly of 50 members will be elected for a four-year term by all natural-born literate Kuwait males over the age of 21, except servicemen and police, who may not vote. Candidates for election must possess the franchise and be over 30 years of age. The Assembly will sit for at least eight months in any year, and new elections shall be held within two months of the last dissolution of the outgoing Assembly.

Restrictions on the commercial activities of Ministers include an injunction forbidding them to sell property to the Government.

The Amir may ask for reconsideration of a Bill passed by the Assembly and sent to him for ratification, but the Bill would automatically become law if it were subsequently passed by a two-thirds majority at the next sitting, or by a simple majority at a subsequent sitting. The Amir may declare Martial Law, but only with the approval of the Assembly.

The Assembly may pass a vote of no confidence in a Minister, in which case the Minister must resign. Such a vote is not permissible in the case of the Prime Minister, but the Assembly may approach the Amir on the matter, and the Amir shall then either dismiss the Prime Minister or dissolve the Assembly.

An annual budget shall be presented, and there shall be an independent finance control commission.

CIVIL SERVICE

Entry to the Civil Service is confined to Kuwait citizens.

PUBLIC LIBERTIES

Kuwaitis are equal before the law in prestige, rights and duties. Individual freedom is guaranteed. No one should be seized, arrested or exiled except within the rules of law.

No punishment shall be administered except for an act or abstaining from an act considered a crime in accordance with a law applicable at the time of committing it, and no penalty shall be imposed more severe than that which could have been imposed at the time of committing the crime.

Freedom of opinion is guaranteed to everyone, and each has the right to express himself through speech, writing or other means within the limits of the law.

The Press is free within the limits of the law, and it should not be suppressed except in accordance with the dictates of law.

Freedom of performing religious rites is protected by the State according to prevailing customs, provided it does not violate the public order and morality.

Trade unions will be permitted and property must be respected. An owner is not banned from managing his property except within the boundaries of law. No property should be taken from anyone, except within the prerogatives of law, unless a just compensation be given.

Houses may not be entered, except in cases provided by law. Every Kuwaiti has freedom of movement and choice of place of residence within the state. This right shall not be controlled except in cases stipulated by law.

Every person has the right to education and freedom to choose his type of work. Freedom to form peaceful societies is guaranteed within the limits of law.

THE GOVERNMENT

HEAD OF STATE

Amir of Kuwait: His Highness Sheikh SABAH AS-SALIM AS-SABAH (succeeded on the death of his brother, November 24, 1965).

COUNCIL OF MINISTERS

(May 1974)

Prime Minister: Sheikh JABIR AL-AHMAD AL-JABIR.

Minister of Education: JASIM KHALID AL-MARZOUQ.

Minister of Public Works: HUMMOUD YOUSUF AL-NUSUF.

Minister of Social Affairs and Labour: HAMAD MUBARAK AL-AYYAR.

Minister of Interior and Defence: Sheikh SA'AD AL-ABDULLAH AL-SALEM AL-SABAH.

Minister of Foreign Affairs and Acting Minister of Information: Sheikh SABAH AL-AHMAD AL-JABIR.

Minister of Trade and Industry: KHALID SULAIMAN AL-ADSANI.

Minister of Awqaf and Islamic Affairs: RASHID ABDULLAH AL-FARHAN.

Minister of Finance and Oil: ABDURRAHMAN SALEM AL-ATIQI.

Minister of Public Health: Dr. ABDURRAZAQ MISHARI AL-ADWANI.

Minister of Posts, Telephones and Telegraphs: ABDUL AZIZ AS-SARAWI.

Minister of Electricity and Water: ABDULLAH YOUSUF AL-GHANIM.

Minister of Justice: MUHAMMAD AHMAD AL-HAMID.

Minister of State for Cabinet Affairs: ABDUL AZIZ HUSAIN.

Special Adviser to the Amir: Sheikh ABDULLAH AL-JABIR AL-SABAH.

PROVINCIAL GOVERNORATES

Ahmadi: Sheikh JABIR ABDULLAH JABIR AL-SABAH.

Hawalli: Sheikh NAWAF AL-AHMAD AL-JABIR.

Kuwait: Sheikh NASSER SABAH AL-NASSER AL-SABAH.

DIPLOMATIC REPRESENTATION

EMBASSIES ACCREDITED TO KUWAIT

(In Kuwait City unless otherwise indicated)

(E) Embassy.

Afghanistan: (E); *Ambassador:* KHALILALLAH KHALILI.

Algeria: Istiqlal St. (E); *Ambassador:* MUHAMMAD Y. AL-GHASSIRI.

Argentina: Beirut, Lebanon.

Austria: Beirut, Lebanon (E).

Belgium: Beirut, Lebanon.

Brazil: Beirut, Lebanon (E).

Bulgaria: (E); *Ambassador:* ZDRAVKO ZELENOGRADSKI.

Canada: Teheran, Iran (E).

China, People's Republic: (E); *Ambassador:* SUN CHIENG-WEI.

Colombia: Beirut, Lebanon (E).

Costa Rica: Beirut, Lebanon (E).

Cyprus: *Ambassador:* (vacant).

Czechoslovakia: No. 14, Diyya Quarter (E); *Ambassador:* LADISLAV TISLIAR.

Denmark: Beirut, Lebanon (E).

Egypt: Mussa'ed al Saleh Bldg., Istiqlal St., (E); *Ambassador:* IZZ-AL ARAB AMIN IBRAHIM.

Finland: Beirut, Lebanon (E).

France: Kuwait Bldg. 4th Floor No. 202, Fahad al-Salem St. (E); *Ambassador:* PAUL CARTON.

German Democratic Republic: *Ambassador:* GÜNTER SCHURATH.

Germany, Federal Republic: (E); *Ambassador:* HANS FREUNDT.

Greece: Beirut, Lebanon (E).

Guinea: Cairo, Egypt (E).

Hungary: Baghdad, Iraq (E).

India: Ring Rd. No. 1 (E); *Ambassador:* R. AXEL-KHAN.

Indonesia: Baghdad, Iraq (E).

Iran: Haj Abdulla Dashti Bldg., Istiqlal St. (E); *Ambassador:* Dr. FEREYDUN ZAND-FARD.

Iraq: 37 Istiqlal St. (E); *Ambassador:* MUHAMMAD SABRI AL-HADEETHI.

Italy: (E); *Ambassador:* ROMANO ROSSETTI.

Japan: Al-Khalid Bldg., Fahad-al-Salem St. (E); *Ambassador:* RYOKO ISHIKAWA.

Jordan: Mansour Qabazard Bldg., Istiqlal St.; *Chargé d'Affaires:* AWAD ABU-OBEID.

Kenya: Cairo, Egypt (E).

Lebanon: (E); *Ambassador:* SAMIH AL-BABA.

Libya: (E); represented by Egypt's ambassador.

Malaysia: Jeddah, Saudi Arabia (E).

Mali: Cairo, Egypt. (E).

Malta: (E); *Ambassador:* (vacant).

Mauritania: Jeddah, Saudi Arabia (E).

Morocco: Ville No. 7, Rd. 14, Shuwaikh (E); *Ambassador:* AHMAD BEN LAMIH.

Nepal: Cairo, Egypt (E).

Netherlands: Baghdad, Iraq (E).

Nigeria: Jeddah, Saudi Arabia (E).

Norway: Ankara, Turkey (E).

Oman: (E); *Ambassador:* AHMAD M. AL-NABUANI.

Pakistan: Salah Jamal Bldg., No. 7, Nuzha St. (E); *Ambassador:* SHAHRYAR KHAN.

Poland: 48 Istiqlal St. (E); *Ambassador:* ZDZISLAW TADEUSZ WOJCIK.

Qatar: (E); *Ambassador:* MUHAMMAD M. AL-KHELAIFI.

Romania: Beirut, Lebanon (E).

Saudi Arabia: Sheikh Fahad al-Salem Bldg., al-Hilali St., Sharq (E); *Ambassador:* HUMOID FAHAD AL-ZAID.

Senegal: Jeddah, Saudi Arabia (E).

Somalia: *Ambassador:* MUSA ISLAM FAREH.

Spain: (E); *Ambassador:* RAMÓN ARMENGOD.

Sudan: Badr al-Mulla Bldg., Fahad al-Salem St. (E); *Ambassador:* IBRAHIM M. ALI.

Sweden: Baghdad, Iraq (E).

Switzerland: Amman Jordan (E).

Syria: Thounayan al-Ghanim Bldg., Fahad al-Salem St. (E); *Ambassador:* HAJJ ABDULLAH RAZOUQ.

Tunisia: Ghanim al-Shaheen al-Ghanim Bldg., Istiqlal St. (E); *Ambassador:* HABIB NOUIRA.

Turkey: Beirut, Lebanon (E).

U.S.S.R.: Sheikh Ahmad al-Jaber al-Sabah Bldg., No. 5 Dasman District (E); *Ambassador:* NIKOLAI TUPITSYN.

United Arab Emirates: (E); *Ambassador:* RASHID A. A. AL-MAKHAWI.

United Kingdom: Arabian Gulf St. (E); *Ambassador:* ARTHUR JOHN WILTON.

U.S.A.: Bnaid Al-Gar (E).

Venezuela: Beirut, Lebanon (E).

Yemen Arab Republic: (E); *Ambassador:* ABDULLAH ALI AL-DHABI.

Yugoslavia: Baghdad, Iraq (E).

Kuwait also has diplomatic relations with Guyana, Madagascar, Tanzania, Trinidad and Tobago, Uganda and Upper Volta.

NATIONAL ASSEMBLY

In elections held for the third time under the new Constitution on January 23rd, 1971, 184 candidates were nominated for the 50 seats (5 seats in each of 10 districts). There are no official political parties, the candidates standing as individuals. In the 1971 elections, however, five members of the radical Arab Nationalist Movement were returned. The vote is limited to natural-born Kuwaiti males over 21 who are able to read and write (about 40,000 voters).

Secretary: Ibrahim Al-Khreibit.

Speaker: Khalid Salih Al-Ghunaim.

Deputy-Speaker: Yousuf Al-Mukhlid.

JUDICIAL SYSTEM

There is a codified system of law based largely upon the Egyptian system. In criminal matters, minor contraventions are dealt with by Magistrates Courts, felonies by Criminal Assize Courts. Appeal in the case of misdemeanours is to a Misdemeanours Court of Appeal.

Civil cases are heard by a General Court within which are separate chambers dealing with commercial cases, other civil cases and matters of personal status. Appeal is to a High Court of Appeal. Matters of personal status may go beyond the High Court of Appeal to a Court of Cassation.

In criminal cases, investigation of misdemeanours is the responsibility of the police, while responsibility for the investigation of felonies lies with the Attorney-General's Office.

RELIGION

MUSLIMS

The inhabitants are mainly Muslims of the Sunni and Shiite sects.

CHRISTIANS

Anglican Chaplain in Kuwait: Rev. John Pragnell, c/o Kuwait Oil Co. Ltd., 3 Ninth Avenue, Ahmadi 6, Kuwait.

Roman Catholic: Right Rev. Mgr. V. San Miguel, o.c.d., Administrator Apostolic of Kuwait, Bishop's House, P.O.B. 266, Kuwait.

National Evangelical Church in Kuwait: Rev. Yusef Abdul Noor, Box 80, Kuwait; a United Protestant Church founded by the Reformed Church in America; services in Arabic, English and Malayalam.

There are also Armenian, Greek, Coptic and Syrian Orthodox Churches in Kuwait.

THE PRESS

DAILIES

Akhbar al-Kuwait (*Kuwait News*): P.O.B. 1747, Shuwaikh, Kuwait; f. 1961; Arabic; independent; Editor Abdul-Aziz Fahad Al-Fulaij; circ. 4,000.

Al-Qabas: P.O.B. 21,800, Ahmad al Jabir St., Kuwait; f. 1972; Arabic; Editor Jassim Ahmad al-Nusuf; circ. 5,000.

Al-Siyasa: P.O.B. 2270, Kuwait; f. 1965; Arabic; political; Editor Ahmed Al-Jarallah; circ. 19,000.

Ar Rai al-Amm (*Public Opinion*): P.O.B. 695, International Airport Road, Shuwaikh Industrial Area, Kuwait; f. 1961; Arabic; political, social and cultural; Editor Fahad al-Massa'id; circ. 15,000.

Daily News: P.O.B. 695, International Airport Rd., Shuwaikh Industrial Area, Kuwait; f. 1963; English; political, independent; Editor-in-Chief Fahad al Massa'id; circ. 10,000.

Kuwait Times: P.O.B. 1301, Fahed Al Salem Ave., Kuwait; f. 1961; English; political; Owner and Editor-in-Chief Yousuf Alyan; circ. 5,000.

WEEKLIES AND PERIODICALS

Kuwait Al-Youm (*Kuwait Today*): P.O.B. 193, Kuwait; f. 1954; Sunday; the "Official Gazette"; Amiri Decrees, Laws, Govt. announcements, decisions, invitations for tenders, etc.; published by the Ministry of Information; circ. 5,000.

Adhwa al-Kuwait: P.O.B. 1977, Kuwait; f. 1962; literature and arts; Arabic; weekly; free advertising magazine; Editor Myrin Al Hamad; circ. 5,000.

Al-Arabi: P.O.B. 748, Kuwait; f. 1958; Arabic; science, history, arts; monthly; published by the Ministry of Information; Editor Dr. Ahmed Zaki; circ. 125,000.

Al-Balagh: Kuwait; weekly.

Al-Hadaf (*The Aim*): P.O.B. 1142, Al Sur St., Kuwait; weekly; f. 1961; Arabic; political and cultural; Editor-in-Chief M. M. Saleh; Proprietor D. M. Saleh; circ. 8,000 (also monthly supplement: *Economic Review*).

Al-Ittihad: P.O.B. 13189, Kuwait; monthly organ of the National Association of Kuwait Students.

Al Kuwaiti: Ahmadi; fortnightly journal of the Kuwait Oil Co. Ltd. (also in English edition: *The Kuwaiti*).

Al-Mujtama'a: P.O.B. 4850, Kuwait; f. 1969; Arabic weekly issued by the Social Reform Society.

Al Nahdha (*The Renaissance*): P.O.B. 695, International Airport Road, Shuivaikh Industrial Area, Kuwait; f. 1967; weekly; Arabic; Editor Youssuf Al-Massaeed; circ. 8,000.

Ar Ressaleh (*The Message*): P.O.B. 2490, Shuwaikh, Kuwait; f. 1961; weekly; Arabic; political, social and cultural; Editor Jassim Mubarak.

Ar-Raid (*The Pioneer*): P.O.B. 11259, Cairo Rd., Kuwait; f. 1969; weekly; issued by Kuwaiti Teachers' Association; circ. 4,000.

At-Tali'a: P.O.B. 1082, Mubarak al-Kabir St., Kuwait; f. 1962; weekly; Arabic; Editor Sami Ahmed Al-Munais; circ. 10,000.

Al-Watan (*The Homeland*): P.O.B. 1774, Kuwait; f. 1964; political weekly circ. 1,000.

Al-Yaqza (*The Awakening*): P.O.B. 1617, Kuwait; f. 1966; political weekly; circ. 1,000.

Hayatuna (*Our Life*): P.O.B. 1708, Kuwait; f. 1968; medicine and hygiene; Arabic; fortnightly; published by Al-Awadi Press Corporation; Editor Dr. Abdul Rahman Al-Awadi; circ. 6,000.

Journal of the Kuwait Medical Association: P.O.B. 1202, Kuwait; f. 1967; English; quarterly; published by Medical Assoc.; Editor Dr. Abdul Razzak Al Yusuf; circ. 1,500.

Kuwait Chamber of Commerce and Industry Magazine: P.O.B. 775, Kuwait; f. 1960; monthly; circ. 5,200.

Mejallat al-Kuwait (*Kuwait Magazine*): P.O.B. 193, Kuwait; news and literary articles; Arabic; fortnightly illustrated magazine; published by Ministry of Information.

Saut al-Khaleej (*Voice of the Gulf*): P.O.B. 659, Kuwait; f. 1962; political weekly; Editor BAQER KHRAIBITT; circ. 9,000.

Usrati (*My Family*): P.O.B. 2995, Kuwait; women's magazine; Arabic; fortnightly; Editor Mrs. GHANIMA AL-MARZOOG; circ. 10,000.

NEWS AGENCIES
FOREIGN BUREAUX

AFP: Sayyid Nabeel Shami, P.O.B. 193, Kuwait.

Hsinhua: P.O.B. 22168, nr. Dasman Palace, Kuwait.

Middle East News Agency: P.O.B. 1927, Fahd El-Salem St.

Reuters: P.O.B. 5616, Kuwait.

Tass: P.O.B. 1455, Kuwait.

RADIO AND TELEVISION

RADIO

Kuwait Broadcasting Station: P.O.B. 397, Kuwait; f. 1951; broadcasts in Arabic and English; short wave (250 kW.), medium wave (750 kW.) and F.M. stereo transmitters; Asst. Under-Sec. for Broadcasting Affairs ABDUL AZIZ MOHAMED JA'FFER; Asst. Under-Sec. for Engineering Affairs ABDUL-RAHMAN IBRAHIM AL-HUTY.

Number of radio receivers (1971): 110,000.

TELEVISION

Television of Kuwait, Ministry of Information: P.O.B. 621, Kuwait; f. 1961; broadcasts in Arabic; three transmitters are used, and broadcasts reach Saudi Arabia, southern Iraq, and other Gulf States; advertising is accepted, and colour television is planned for 1974; Asst. Under-Sec. of TV Affairs MUHAMMAD SANOUSSI; Programme Controller IBRAHIM AL-YUSUF.

Number of television receivers (1971): 120,000.

FINANCE

(cap.=capital; p.u.=paid up; dep.=deposits; m.=million; amounts in Kuwait Dinars)

BANKING
NATIONAL BANKS

Central Bank of Kuwait: P.O.B. 526, Kuwait; f. 1969; replaced Currency Board in administering currency and credit policies; cap. 2m., reserves 3m.; Governor HAMZAH ABBAS HUSSAIN; publ. *Annual Report*.

National Bank of Kuwait, S.A.K.: Abdullah Al-Salim St., P.O.B. 95, Kuwait; f. 1952; cap. and res. 23.8m., total assets 348.8m. (Dec. 1973); 28 brs.; Chair. YACOUB YOUSUF AL HAMAD; Gen. Man. C. D. FEARS.

Alahli Bank of Kuwait K.S.C.: Commercial Centre 5, P.O.B. 1387, Kuwait; 10 brs.; cap. p.u. 2m.; Gen. Man. P. DUJARDIN.

Bank of Kuwait and the Middle East K.S.C.: P.O.B. Safat 71, Kuwait; 49 per cent owned by the Government; began operations in Dec. 1971 when it took over former branches of the British Bank of the Middle East; cap. p.u. 2m.; Chair. FAHAD AL BAHAR; Gen. Man. L. J. McLEAY.

Commercial Bank of Kuwait, S.A.K.: Mubarak Al Kabir St., P.O.B. 2861, Kuwait; cap. and res. 8.2m., dep. 158m. (Dec. 1973); 19 brs.; Chair. ABDUL AZIZ AL AHMAD AL BAHAR; Gen. Man. H. T. GRIEVE.

Gulf Bank K.S.C.: P.O.B. Safat 3200 Abdullah Al-Salim St., Kuwait; f. 1961; cap. p.u. 3,267m.; 14 brs.; Chair. KHALID YUSUF AL-MUTAWA; Gen. Man. R. SINCLAIR.

Savings and Credit Bank: Arabian Gulf St., P.O.B. 1454, Kuwait; f. 1960; cap. p.u. 31m., dep. 29.1m. (March 1973); 11 brs. throughout Kuwait; Chair. AHMED Z. AL-SERHAN; Dir.-Gen. YOUSEF M. SHAIJI.

INSURANCE
NATIONAL COMPANIES

Al Ahleia Insurance Co., S.A.K.: P.O.B. 1602, Ali Al-Salim St., Kuwait; f. 1962; covers all classes of insurance; cap. K.D. 1m.; Chair. MUHAMMAD Y. AL-NISF; Man. Dir. ABDULLA A. AL-RIFAI; Gen. Man. Dr. RAOUF H. MAKAR.

Gulf Insurance Co. K.S.C.: P.O.B. 1040, Kuwait; f. 1962; cap. 900,000; Gen. Man. ELIAS N. BEDEWI.

Kuwait Insurance Co.: Abdullah Al-Salim St., P.O.B. 769, Kuwait; f. 1960; cap. p.u. 750,000; Gen. Man. SHAKIB S. SHAKHSHIR; Deputy Gen. Man. FOUAD A. AL-BAHAR.

FOREIGN COMPANIES

Some 20 Arab and other foreign insurance companies are active in Kuwait.

OIL

Kuwait National Petroleum Co., K.S.C.: P.O.B. 70, Kuwait; f. 1960; 60 per cent state-owned; refining, exploring and marketing company; a large new refinery at Shuaiba opened in May 1968; p.u. cap. 15m.; Chair. AHMED ABDUL MOSHIN AL MUTAIR.

Kuwait Oil Co.: Ahmadi, Kuwait; f. 1934 and jointly owned by BP Exploration Company (Associated Holdings) Ltd. and Gulf Kuwait Company. It had 692 wells producing at end of 1972; oil production in 1972 was 148.7 million long tons. The original concession area covered all of Kuwait, including territorial waters to a six-mile limit. In May 1962 exploratory rights to 9,262 square kilometres, roughly 50 per cent of the original concession area, were voluntarily relinquished to the state. Further offshore areas were relinquished in 1967 and 1971; in 1973, as a result of the Participation agreement of October 1972, the Kuwaiti Government took a 25 per cent share of KOC with an option to raise its shareholding by 5 per cent in 1979, 1980, 1981 and 1982, and by 6 per cent in 1983—giving a majority interest of 51 per cent. As of end 1973 the agreement had been signed by the Government but not yet ratified by the National Assembly; a further agreement is also awaiting ratification by the National Assembly; Man. Dir. J. A. STRAND.

Kuwait Shell Petroleum Development Co. (*Royal Dutch Shell*): Fahad al-Salim St., Kuwait; has concession, signed January 1961, of 5,595 sq. km. offshore from Kuwait; operations suspended pending clarification of the offshore boundary disputes with Iraq, Iran and Saudi Arabia.

Kuwait Spanish Petroleum Co.: P.O.B. 20467, Kuwait; f. 1968; 51 per cent owned by Kuwait National Petroleum Co., 49 per cent by Hispanoil of Spain; holds concessions of 910,000 hectares (about half the land area of Kuwait) for a period of 35 years from 1968; drilling began in 1970.

American Independent Oil Co.: Main Office 50 Rockefeller Plaza, New York, N.Y.; Kuwait Office P.O.B. 69, Kuwait: shares with Getty Oil Co. (from Saudi Arabia) concessions in Kuwait/Saudi Arabia Partitioned Zone onshore; combined oil production in 1972 was 8,190,464 long tons.

Arabian Oil Co.: Head Office Tokyo; Kuwait Office P.O.B. 1641, Kuwait; Field Office Ras Al-Khafji, Kuwait Partitioned Zone; a Japanese company which has concessions offshore of the Partitioned Zone; there are 56 producing wells as well as four flow stations in operation; in 1971 crude oil production reached 18,690,000 long tons.

TRADE AND INDUSTRY

CHAMBER OF COMMERCE

Kuwait Chamber of Commerce and Industry: P.O.B. 775, Chamber's Bldg., Ali Salem St., Kuwait State; f. 1959; 3,500 mems.; Pres. ABDUL AZIZ AL-SAGER; Vice-Pres. YOUSEF AL-FULEIJ and MOHAMAD A. AL-KHARAFI; Gen. Sec. HAYTHAM MALLUHI; publs. *Monthly Magazine* (circ. 4,900) and annual economic and administrative reports.

DEVELOPMENT

Kuwait Chemical Fertilizer Co. K.S.C.: P.O.B. 3964, Kuwait; f. 1964; government enterprise (with British Petroleum and Gulf Oil Co. holding minority interests) for manufacture of liquid ammonia, sulphuric acid, urea and ammonium sulphate.

Kuwait Foreign Trading, Contracting and Investment Co.: P.O.B. 5665, Kuwait; f. 1965; overseas investment company; 80 per cent government holding; total assets KD 27.4m. (1972); Man. Dir. ABDULAZIZ AL-BAHAR.

Kuwait Fund for Arab Economic Development: Mubarak Al-Kabir, P.O.B. 2921, Kuwait; cap. KD 200m.; wholly Government owned; assists other Arab governments with development loans; Chair. ABDULREHMAN SALEM AL-ATEEQY; Dir. Gen. ABDLATIF Y. AL-HAMAD.

Kuwait Investment Co. S.A.K.: P.O.B. 1005, Kuwait; f. 1961; cap. KD 8.3m.; investment banking institution owned 50 per cent by the Government and 50 per cent by Kuwaiti nationals; international banking and investment; Man. Dir. BADER ALI AL-DAWOOD.

Kuwait National Industries Company: Kuwait; f. 1960; 51 per cent Government owned company with controlling interest in various construction enterprises.

Kuwait Planning Board: Kuwait City; f. 1962; supervises the 1967–68/1971–72 Five-Year Plan; through its Central Statistical Office publishes information on Kuwait's economic activity; Dir.-Gen. AHMED ALI AL DUAIJ.

Shuaiba Area Authority: P.O.B. 4690, Kuwait; f. 1964; an independent public body developing a new town with dockyard and industrial estate.

TRANSPORT

ROADS

Roads in the towns are metalled and the most important are dual carriageway. There are metalled roads to Ahmadi, Mina Al-Ahmadi and other centres of population in Kuwait, and to the Iraqi and Saudi Arabian borders.

Automobile Association of Kuwait and the Gulf: P.O.B. Safat 2100, Kuwait; f. 1964; Pres. H. E. Sheikh NASSER ATHBI AL-SABAH.

Gulf Automobile Association: P.O.B. 827, Fahad al Salem St., Kuwait.

Kuwait Automobile and Touring Club: Airport Rd., Khaldiah, P.O.B. Safat 2100, Kuwait; f. 1956; Pres. H. E. Sheikh NASSER AL ATHBI AL SABAH.

Kuwait International Touring and Automobile Club: P.O.B. Safat 2100, Kuwait; f. 1966; Sec.-Gen. A. W. MONAYES.

Kuwait Transport Co. S.A.K.: Kuwait; provides internal bus service; regular service to Iran inaugurated December 1968.

SHIPPING

A modern port has been built at Shuwaikh, two miles west of Kuwait Town, which is capable of handling simultaneously up to eight large cargo ships and several smaller ships. Ships of British and other lines make regular calls.

A second port is under construction at Shuaiba to the south of Kuwait.

The oil port at Mina al-Ahmadi, 40 km. south of Kuwait Town is capable of handling the largest oil tankers afloat, and oil exports of over 2 million barrels per day.

Kuwait Oil Tanker Co. S.A.K.: P.O.B. 810, Kuwait; f. 1957; 1,500 shareholders; cap. KD 11.5m.; owns 6 vessels totalling 800,000 deadweight tons; tankers on order 1,344,000 deadweight tons; sole tanker agents for Mina al-Ahmadi and agents for other ports.

Kuwait Shipping Co. S.A.K.: P.O.B. Safat 3636, Kuwait; f. 1965; 76.9 per cent government owned; services to Europe, the Far East and America; 27 vessels totalling 367,625 tons; fully paid cap. KD 18m.; Man. Dir. NOURI MUSAED AL SALEH; Gen. Man. D. H. TOD.

CIVIL AVIATION

Kuwait Airways Corporation: Al-Hilali St., P.O.B. 394, Kuwait; f. 1954; services to Abadan, Abu Dhabi, Aden, Athens, Baghdad, Bahrain, Beirut, Bombay, Cairo, Damascus, Delhi, Dahran, Doha, Dubai, Frankfurt, Geneva, Jeddah, Karachi, London, Muscat, Paris, Rome, Sana'a, Teheran; fleet of 5 Boeing 707; Chair. and Gen. Man. FAISAL SAOUD AL-FULAIJ; Man. Dir. JASSIM YOUSEF AL-MARZOOK; publs. *Al-Boraq* (Magazine), *KAC News*.

Kuwait is also served by the following airlines: Air France, Air India, Alia, British Airways, CSA (Czechoslovakia), Democratic Yemen Airlines, EgyptAir, Gulf Aviation, Iranair, Iraq Airways, KLM, Lufthansa, MEA, PIA (Pakistan), Saudia, Syrian Arab Airlines and Yemen Airways.

UNIVERSITY

Kuwait University: P.O.B. 5969, Kuwait; f. 1966; 3,292 students (1973); 73 professors.

LAOS

INTRODUCTORY SURVEY

Location, Climate, Language, Religion, Flag, Capital

The Kingdom of Laos is a small landlocked country in South-East Asia bordered by the People's Republic of China to the north, North and South Viet-Nam to the east, the Khmer Republic to the south, Thailand to the west and Burma to the north-west. The climate is tropical, with a rainy monsoon season lasting from May to October. The official language, Lao or Laotian, is spoken by about two-thirds of the population. French is used widely and there are a number of tribal languages including Meo. The state religion, adhered to by most Laotians, is Buddhism. There are also some Christians and followers of animist beliefs. The national flag (proportions 3 by 2) is red, charged with a traditional emblem (in white): a three-headed elephant under a nine-pointed parasol. The Royal capital is Luang Prabang and the administrative capital Vientiane.

Recent History

Formerly a part of French Indo-China, Laos attained independence in 1949. In 1953 the country was invaded by Communist Viet-Minh troops aided within Laos by members of the Pathet Lao movement. Despite the Geneva cease-fire agreement of 1954 and the Vientiane Agreement of 1957, guerrilla warfare continued and in 1960 a rival government was established at Khang Khay headed by Prince Souvanna Phouma and supported by the Pathet Lao. In 1961 a fourteen-nation conference gathered at Geneva to work out a Laotian settlement. The three princely leaders of the Communist, neutral and right-wing parties finally agreed to form a coalition government under Prince Souvanna Phouma. This was set up in 1962. Early in 1963 further fighting took place in the Plain of Jars and continued sporadically for 10 years, with a new and serious offensive by Pathet Lao and North Vietnamese troops in early 1969. Fierce fighting continued into 1970. Prince Souvanna Phouma's neutralist Government was handicapped by the refusal of the Pathet Lao to co-operate in the administration. Communist military activity continued from 1970 onwards, with only one third of the country under the effective control of the Vientiane Government. In January 1973 the Government put forward ceasefire proposals and an agreement was signed in February. A protocol to the agreement was signed in September to the effect that a provisional coalition government (comprising two neutral ministers and eleven members each from the Pathet Lao and the Vientiane government) and a Joint National Political Council be set up. The provisional Government under Prince Souvanna Phouma took office in April 1974, together with the Political Council under Prince Souphannouvong. The two main towns of Vientiane and Luang Prabang were neutralized and put under the jurisdiction of joint police and defence forces in order to create secure working conditions for the new Government. The strength of Pathet Lao influence in the coalition was felt early in its administration when the Government ruled that the traditional opening of the National Assembly should not take place.

Government

Laos is a constitutional monarchy with the King as Head of State and C.-in-C. of the Army. The King appoints a Prime Minister who is responsible for forming the Government, which must be approved by the 59-member legislative body, the National Assembly. The Assembly is elected by universal suffrage every five years. A provisional coalition government came into being in April 1974 together with a Joint National Political Council that is independent of and equal to the Government and co-operates closely with it in managing state affairs. The country is divided into 18 Khouengs or provinces, each administered by a Governor appointed by the Minister of the Interior. The tribal population is represented in the National Assembly but is virtually independent in local affairs.

Defence

According to official U.S. reports Royal Lao forces numbered 68,000 at the time of the 1973 ceasefire. The strength of the Pathet Lao was estimated at 30,000 troops, together with a number of foreign forces including 55,000 North Vietnamese. Under the terms of the ceasefire agreement, all foreign troops were to be withdrawn within 60 days of the formation of the provisional Government.

Economic Affairs

Nearly 80 per cent of the population is engaged in subsistence farming. Agricultural techniques are primitive and periodic droughts and floods greatly affect the harvest. Wet rice is cultivated in the Mekong valley and other valleys in north and north-east Laos. About 70,000 tons of rice have to be imported annually. Fish is a principal source of protein, and the rice and fish diet of the Lao farmer is supplemented by domestic fowls, eggs, pork, vegetables and fruit. The cultivation of dry rice, involving the periodical clearing of forest lands, is practised in the hill regions. The Meo peoples also grow maize.

Tin, extracted at the Phon Tiou mines, and timber are the principal exports, the former representing 55 per cent and the latter 41 per cent of total exports in 1971, and there are also exploitable deposits of copper, lead, iron, coal and other minerals. Industry is at the earliest stages of development: tobacco products, matches and rubber shoes are manufactured, while there are also saw mills and a bottling plant, and a cement factory is to be constructed. Hydro-electric power is supplied by the Nam Ngum with an initial capacity of 30,000 kW. (but scheduled to rise to 110,000 kW. by 1977) and smaller dams constructed within the Mekong River Development Project.

As well as rice, essential imports include textiles, pharmaceuticals, petroleum products, and transportation and electrical equipment. Major exports are tin, timber, benzoin, green coffee, cardamom and other food and medicinal oil plants. An import-export trade in gold has grown up and the 4 per cent import duty levied is a major source of budgetary revenue. The balance of trade is unfavourable and essential imports are supported by foreign aid, notably from the U.S.A. Economic assistance is also received from France, German Federal Republic, Netherlands, UN agencies and member countries of the Colombo Plan. The Foreign Exchange Operations Fund, maintained by contributions from Australia, France, Japan, the U.K. and the U.S.A., was set up in 1964 to attempt to control inflation. The Fund pledged U.S. $27.6 million for 1974.

Transport and Communications

The Mekong and its left-bank tributaries form the principal artery of transport, although the size of craft is limited by rapids and traffic is seasonal. There are no railways in Laos. A road/rail project, linking Vientiane with Bangkok and sponsored by the Mekong River Development Project, is under survey. It is hoped that if peace returns to Indo-China it will be possible to develop new outlets to Vinh and Quang Tri in North and South Viet-Nam. In 1971 there were about 6,500 km. of roads, of which about 12 per cent were sealed. A new road from Vientiane to Luang Prabang has been built. Five airfields are used for internal and international air services by the state airline, Royal Air Lao, and seven foreign companies.

Social Welfare

There are no state social services. In 1970 there were 24 hospitals and 126 dispensaries in Laos.

Education

Education was largely disrupted by the civil war, causing a high illiteracy rate. Educational facilities have since greatly improved, and education is compulsory for three years. Total enrolment at all educational institutions was 262,000 in 1971. College-level schooling is now available in Laos and there are six teacher-training institutes. The University of Sisavangvong has more than 1,600 students.

Tourism

The main attractions of Laos are the ancient temples, the traditional dancing and the forest and mountain scenery.

Visas are required by all visitors.

Public Holidays

1974: four religious feast days at the beginning, in the middle and at the end of the Buddhist fast, July–October, October 13th (Canoe Festival), November 13th (King's birthday), December 8th, 9th, 11th (Feast of That Luang).

1975: March 23rd (Army Day), mid-April (Buddhist New Year), May 11th (National Day), May 16th–17th (Rocket Festival), July 19th (Independence Day).

Weights and Measures

The metric system is in force.

Currency and Exchange Rate

100 at=10 bi=1 kip.

Exchange rates (April 1974):
£1 sterling=1,417 kips;
U.S. $1=600 kips.

STATISTICAL SURVEY

AREA AND POPULATION

Area: 236,800 sq. km. (91,400 sq. miles). **Population:** 3,106,000 (estimate for July 1st, 1972).

PROVINCES

Luang Prabang	Sayaboury	Attopeu	Borikhane	Wapikhamthong
Xieng Khouang	Saravane	Houa Phan (Sam Neua)	Sithandone	Champone*
Savannakhet	Phong Saly	Khammouane	Sedone	Vanvieng*
Houa Khong (Nam Tha)	Vientiane	Champassak		

* New provinces established in November 1973.

PRINCIPAL TOWNS

Population (estimated 1970)

Vientiane (capital) 150,000; Savannakhet 40,000; Pakse 36,000; Luang Prabang (royal seat) 25,000; Khammouane 13,000.

Births and Deaths: Average annual birth rate 42.1 per 1,000; death rate 17.2 per 1,000 (UN estimates for 1965–70).

Employment (1970): Total economically active population 1,556,000, including 1,218,000 in agriculture (ILO and FAO estimates).

AGRICULTURE

LAND USE, 1970
('000 hectares)

Arable and Under Permanent Crops	950
Permanent Meadows and Pastures .	800
Forest Land .	15,000
Other Areas .	6,930
Total .	23,680

Source: FAO, *Production Yearbook 1971.*

PRINCIPAL CROPS

	AREA (hectares)			PRODUCTION (metric tons)		
	1969	1970	1971	1969	1970	1971
Maize	38,000	40,000	40,000*	23,000	25,000	25,000*
Rice (Paddy)	665,000	670,000	665,000*	894,850	916,000	900,000*
Potatoes	2,500*	2,500*	2,500*	13,000	14,000*	14,000*
Sweet Potatoes and Yams . .	2,200*	2,200*	n.a.	15,000*	15,000*	n.a.
Cassava (Manioc) . . .	1,200*	1,200*	n.a.	12,000*	12,000*	n.a.
Cottonseed	7,000*	6,000*	6,000*	6,000	4,000*	4,000*
Cotton (Lint) . . .				3,000	3,000*	3,000*
Coffee	6,000	6,000	n.a.	3,400	3,200	2,800
Tobacco	6,000	6,000	7,000	3,800	3,800	4,000

* FAO estimate.

Source: mainly FAO, *Production Yearbook 1971.*

LIVESTOCK
('000)

	1966–67	1967–68*	1968–69*	1969–70*	1970–71*
Cattle	380	390	400	420	435
Pigs	995	1,000	1,050	1,100	1,150
Goats	31*	32	33	34	35
Buffaloes . . .	865	900	920	935	940
Horses . . .	24	25	26	27	28
Chickens . . .	11,573	12,000	11,600	11,500	12,000
Ducks . . .	200*	201	200	198	190
Geese . . .	51	51	51	49	50

Domestic elephants: 892 recorded in 1971.

* FAO estimates.

Source: mainly FAO, *Production Yearbook 1971.*

LIVESTOCK PRODUCTS
(FAO estimates)

		1968	1969	1970	1971
Cows' Milk	metric tons	27,000	28,000	29,000	30,000
Hen Eggs	" "	8,000	8,100	7,500	8,000
Cattle and Buffalo Hides (dry) . . .	number	12,000	10,000	9,000	n.a.

Source: FAO, *Production Yearbook 1971.*

FORESTRY

		1969	1970	1971	1972
Timber	cu. metres	114,541	73,349	76,732	98,635
Firewood . . .	" "	25,272	36,409	43,085	29,214
Charcoal . . .	tons	13,467	10,540	10,828	6,524
Cardamom . . .	"	2	1,980	33	15

INDUSTRY

		1968	1969	1970	1971	1972
Electricity* . . .	million kWh.	28.0	20.8	12.4	16.1	64.0
Tin (50% concentrate) .	tons	978.6	1,262.0	1,380.0	1,572.6	1,885.8
Matches . . .	million packets	1	3.6	3.6	3.6	14.8

* Excludes Laotian consumption of energy generated in Thailand. This totalled (in million kWh.): 16.8 in 1969; 38.3 in 1970.

FINANCE

100 at (cents) = 10 bi = 1 kip.

Coins: 10, 20 and 50 at.

Notes: 1, 5, 10, 20, 50, 100, 200, 500 and 1,000 kips.

Exchange rates (April 1974): £1 sterling = 1,417 kips; U.S. $1 = 600 kips.

10,000 kips = £7.057 = $16.667.

BUDGET

Twelve months ending June 30th

(million kips)

REVENUE	1969–70	1970–71	1971–72†	1972–73†
Direct Taxes	697	804	790	895
Import and Customs Duties . .	5,746	3,862	5,425	3,700
Registration Tax	184	180	211	250
Other Indirect Taxes . . .	913	1,345	1,875	2,105
Revenue from Services . . .	552	553	764	857
Other receipts	86	67	35	201
TOTAL . . .	8,178	6,811	9,100	8,008

EXPENDITURE	1969–70	1970–71	1971–72†	1972–73†
Education and Culture . .	1,532.6	1,764.3	1,949.5	2,323.2
Social Security and Health .	536.9	607.0	635.3	711.4
Public Works	386.5	391.8	400.5	454.4
Defence	8,850.3	9,411.7	9,337.8	11,321.9
State Administration . .	2,890.0	2,935.9	3,046.7	3,666.6
National Economy . . .	236.9	254.5	286.3	305.0
Debt Services	215.0	176.0	325.0	405.0
Transfers	94.2	142.5	156.3	372.9
Other Expenditure . .	2,601.1	2,589.2	3,062.7	3,247.1
TOTAL . . .	17,343.6	18,272.9	19,200.1	22,807.5

† Voted estimates.

FOREIGN EXCHANGE OPERATIONS FUND

(million U.S. $)

Contributor	1966	1967	1968	1969	1970	1971	1972
United States . . .	13.7	13.8	16.1	16.6	16.1	20.1	16.1
France	1.7	1.7	1.7	1.7	1.7	1.7	1.7
Japan	1.7	1.7	1.7	1.7	2.0	2.3	2.6
United Kingdom . .	1.7	1.7	1.7	1.7	1.7	1.7	1.8
Australia	0.8	0.6	0.8	0.7	0.7	0.7	0.7
Total . .	19.6	19.5	22.0	22.4	22.2	26.5	22.9

Note: The Foreign Exchange Operations Fund was set up in 1964 to attempt to control inflation; the total for 1964 was U.S. $7.8 million, and the total for 1965 was U.S. $11.9 million.

MONEY SUPPLY

(million kips at December 31st)

	1966	1967	1968	1969	1970	1971	1972
Bank Deposits . .	1,118	1,000	1,068	1,327	1,141	1,231	1,731
Money in Circulation .	9,624	10,260	11,294	12,497	14,215	17,723	21,743

COST OF LIVING

Consumer Price Index, Vientiane.

(base: 1963=100).

	1961	1962	1964	1965	1966	1967	1968	1969	1970	1971	1972
All Items .	45	52	198	223	254	274	288	297	298	302	377.7
Food Only .	36	45	183	197	233	247	262	266	248	249	336.4

September 1973: All Items 553; Food 560.

EXTERNAL TRADE*

(million kips)

	1965	1966	1967	1968	1969	1970	1971	1972
Imports . .	7,893.2	10,017.2	11,796.4	12,878.6	19,854.5	27,329.1	19,739.7	26,205.4
Exports . .	240.2	357.7	1,064.4	1,448.1	1,032.9	1,726.7	1,485.4	1,752.8

* Trade, excluding gold, valued at the rate of 240 kips per U.S. $ until November 1971, when the official free rate was fixed at 600 kips per $.

COMMODITIES

Imports (Excluding gold)	1970	1971	1972*
Animals and Meat. . . .	1,196	697	1,089
Vegetables	2,449	2,405	3,294
Fats and Oils	47	67	146
Industrial Food Products . .	2,864	1,867	1,644
Mineral Products . . .	7,754	5,178	5,725
Chemical Products . . .	1,968	973	872
Leather Products . . .	14	13	6
Wood and Wood Products . .	195	77	53
Paper and Paper Products .	549	396	481
Textiles	1,507	1,264	510
Clothing	52	49	24
Ceramic Products . . .	182	180	207
Precious Metals . . .	13	18	259
Metal Products . . .	2,201	1,238	1,343
Machinery	2,597	2,275	1,488
Transport Vehicles . . .	2,322	1,997	1,392
Scientific Instruments . .	681	489	341
Others.	738	557	479
Total . . .	27,329	19,740	19,353

* For 9 months only.

Exports	1970	1971	1972†
Tin	616.4	762.5	916.9
Timber	402.5	604.4	572.7
Green Coffee. . . .	88.7	13.1	—
Cardamom	2.0	3.9	3.1
Benzoin	—	—	—
Sticklac	—	—	—
Leather and Hides. . .	16.1	14.3	16.0
Others	601.0	87.2	31.4
Total . . .	1,726.7	1,485.4	1,540.1

† Provisional.

PRINCIPAL TRADING PARTNERS

(million kips)

Imports	1970	1971	1972*
France	2,194.9	1,377.4	823
Germany, Federal Republic . .	177.6	341.6	178
Hong Kong	398.4	363.6	315
Indonesia	4,173.0	2,113.3	2,033
Japan	3,925.8	3,843.5	1,487
Singapore	1,529.0	1,823.2	789
China (Taiwan) . . .	266.1	269.0	238
Thailand	5,622.8	5,086.0	8,741
United Kingdom . . .	675.0	366.2	249
U.S.A.	6,647.9	3,143.0	3,529
Others	1,718.6	1,012.9	971
Total . . .	27,329.1	19,739.7	19,353

* For 9 months only.

PRINCIPAL TRADING PARTNERS—*continued*]

EXPORTS	1970	1971	1972*
Singapore and Malaysia . .	689.2	773.7	1,027.2
Thailand	472.6	634.6	457.0
Hong Kong . . .	44.0	25.5	19.7
Viet-Nam, Republic . .	18.6	0.2	—
TOTAL (incl. others) . .	1,726.7	1,485.4	1,540.1

* Provisional.

TRANSPORT

VEHICLES IN USE
(1971)

Cars 12,054; Trucks 2,060; Motor Cycles 5,630.*
* 1966.

CIVIL AVIATION

TOTAL SCHEDULED SERVICES

	1968	1969	1970
Aircraft Departures . . .	2,935	2,675	3,124
Kilometres Flown . . .	1,145,000	1,066,000	938,000
Passengers Carried . . .	64,940	48,306	55,928
Passenger-km.	24,191,000	22,810,000	26,190,000
Freight Carried (metric tons) . .	n.a.	n.a.	2,856*
Freight tonne-km. . . .	767,000	699,000	700,000
Mail tonne-km.	29,000	31,000	28,000

* 1971: 1,719.

Source: International Civil Aviation Organization.

Tourism (1971): 7,332 visitors.

EDUCATION
(1971–72)

	SCHOOLS	TEACHERS AND ADMINISTRATORS	PUPILS
State Primary	3,239	6,723	238,167
State Secondary . . .	22	370	7,917
Private Primary and Secondary.	108	1,024	35,511
State Technical . . .	3	144	1,124
Teacher Training . . .	9	236	3,784
Higher Education . . .	3	101	523
Fine Arts	2	77	277

Sources (unless otherwise indicated): Service National de la Statistique, Vientiane; and *Far Eastern Economic Review* Hong Kong.

THE CONSTITUTION

The future of Laos rests upon unity and independence within all her provinces. The people affirm their loyalty to the King of Laos and declare their wish to be governed democratically. The Constitution recognizes the principle of equality and protection at law, freedom of conscience and other democratic freedoms as legally defined. It imposes National Service, the fulfilment of family obligations and the observation of the law.

GOVERNMENT

HEAD OF STATE

His Majesty Boroma-setha Khatya Sourya-vongsa Phra Maha Sri Savang Vathana.

PROVISIONAL GOVERNMENT OF NATIONAL UNION

(The letters V, P and N in the lists below indicate whether a member of the Government or the Political Council was chosen as a representative of the former Vientiane Government or the Pathet Lao or as a "neutralist".)

Prime Minister and President of the Council of Ministers: Prince Souvanna Phouma (N).

Vice-President of the Council of Ministers and Minister of Foreign Affairs: Phoumi Vongvichit (P).

Vice-President of the Council of Ministers and Minister of National Education, Youth, Sports and Fine Arts: Leuam Insisienmay (V).

Minister of the Interior and of Social Security: Pheng Phongsavan (V).

Minister of Finance: Ngon Sananikone (V).

Minister of Information and Tourism: Tiao Souk Vongsak (P).

Minister of National Defence and War Veterans: Chao Sisouk Na Champassak (V).

Minister of Public Works and Transport: Singkapo Sikotchounnamaly (P).

Minister of Justice: Khamking Souvanlasy (N).

Minister of Economy and Planning: Sot Phethrasy (P).

Minister of Posts and Telecommunications: Kampheng Boupha.

Minister of Religion: Maha Kou Souvannamethi (P).

Minister of Health: Khamphai Abhay (V).

Secretary of State for National Defence and War Veterans: Kham Ouane Boupha (P).

Secretary of State for Religion: Soukan Vilaysarn (V).

Secretary of State for the Interior: Deuane Sounnarath (P).

Secretary of State for Information and Tourism: Ouday Souvannavong (V).

Secretary of State for Finance: Boussabong Souvannavong (P).

Secretary of State for Public Works and Transport: Houmphanh Saignasith (V).

Secretary of State for Justice: Somvang Sensathit (N).

Secretary of State for Posts and Telecommunications: Touby Lyfoung (N).

Secretary of State for National Education, Youth, Sports and Fine Arts: Oun Neua Phimmasone (P).

Secretary of State for Foreign Affairs: Tianethone Chantharasy (V).

Secretary of State for Public Health: Dr. Khamlieng Pholsena (P).

Secretary of State for Planning and Economy: Dr. Somphou Oudomvilay (V).

JOINT NATIONAL POLITICAL COUNCIL

Chairman: Prince Souphannouvong (P).

Vice-Chairmen: Khamsouk Keola (P), Prince Sisoumang Sisaleumsak (V).

Members: Ouane Rathikoun, Sanane Southichak, Chau Sinh, Phao Phimphachanh, Houmpanh Norasingh, Maha Khamphan Vilachit, Khamla Kingsada, Mme. Chansouk Vongvichit, Vannavong Rajakoun, Lofoung, Bounthanh Heuangpaseuth, Thammasing, Khafan Nouansavan, Y. Bottiphanit, Bounteng Insisiengmay, Visit Southivong, Souvan Sananikhom, Pao Vanthanouvong, Phom Bounlutay, Souvandy, Heng Saythavy, Maha Boudi Soulignasak, Salath Rasasak, Mme. Phayboun Pholsena, Prince Siharaj Phasouc, Thiep Litthideth, Dr. Yang Dao, La Soukan, Viboun Abhay, Pha Vongsay, Bounnak Souvannavong, Khamleck Saignasith, Khamta, Houmpheng Soukhaseum, Khampheng Saignasith, Sisavang Chanthepha, Khamphanh Simalavong, Vongsavanh Boutsavath, Dr. Tane Paphatsarang.

DIPLOMATIC REPRESENTATION

EMBASSIES AND LEGATIONS ACCREDITED TO LAOS

(In Vientiane unless otherwise indicated)

(E) Embassy; (L) Legation.

Australia: Quartier Phone Xay (E); *Ambassador:* A. H. Borthwick.

Austria: Bangkok, Thailand (E).

Belgium: Bangkok, Thailand (E).

Bulgaria: Hanoi, Democratic Republic of Viet-Nam (E).

Burma: Phnom-Penh, Khmer Republic (E).

China, People's Republic: (E); *Chargé d'Affaires:* Kuo Ying.

Czechoslovakia: Phnom-Penh, Khmer Republic (E).

Denmark: Bangkok, Thailand (L).

France: (E); *Ambassador:* GEORGES CARDI.

Germany, Federal Republic: Bangkok, Thailand (E).

Hungary: Hanoi, Democratic Republic of Viet-Nam (E).

India: (E); *Ambassador:* ALFRED S. GONSALVES.

Indonesia: Phnom-Penh, Khmer Republic (E).

Iran: Bangkok, Thailand (E).

Italy: Bangkok, Thailand (E).

Japan: (E); *Ambassador:* MORIKI TANI.

Khmer Republic: *Ambassador:* IAT BOUNTHENG.

Malaysia: Bangkok, Thailand (E).

Mongolia: Hanoi, Democratic Republic of Viet-Nam (E).

Nepal: Rangoon, Burma (E).

Netherlands: Bangkok, Thailand (E).

New Zealand: Bangkok, Thailand (E).

Pakistan: Bangkok, Thailand (E).

Philippines: 4 Thadena Rd. (E); *Ambassador:* FELIPE MABILANGAN.

Poland: Phnom-Penh, Khmer Republic (E).

Romania: Hanoi, Democratic Republic of Viet-Nam (E).

Sri Lanka: Rangoon, Burma (E).

Sweden: Bangkok, Thailand (E).

Switzerland: Bangkok, Thailand (E).

Thailand: (E); *Chargé d'Affaires a.i.*

Turkey: Bangkok, Thailand (L).

U.S.S.R.: (E); *Ambassador:* V. I. MININE.

United Kingdom: (E); *Ambassador:* ALAN DAVIDSON.

U.S.A.: (E); *Ambassador:* G. WHITEHOUSE.

Viet-Nam, Democratic Republic: (E); *Ambassador:* LE VAN HIEN.

Viet-Nam, Republic: (E); *Ambassador:* HOANG CO THUY.

Yugoslavia: Phnom-Penh, Khmer Republic (E).

PARLIAMENT

KING'S COUNCIL

Twelve members—six appointed by the King and six by the National Assembly.

President: H.R.H. Prince KHAMMAO.

NATIONAL ASSEMBLY

President: PHOUI SANANIKONE.

There is a total of 59 members, elected as individuals. The majority of those elected in January 1967 support the government of Prince SOUVANNA PHOUMA.

POLITICAL ORGANIZATIONS

There are no well-defined political parties, but the following organizations have been active in recent years; *Rassemblement du Peuple Lao* and *Les Forces Neutralistes Véritables du Laos* (neutralist groupings); *Social Democratic Party, Lao Luam Lao* and *Lao Noum* (right-wing groupings); and *Santhiphap* (Peace Party; left wing).

The *Neo Lao Haksat* does not yet participate in the National Assembly.

Pathet Lao: Pro-communist; Leader H.H. Prince SOUPHA-NOUVONG.

    Neo Lao Haksat: Vientiane; political section of Pathet Lao; Leader PHOUMI VONGVICHIT.

JUDICIAL SYSTEM

Supreme Court: Vientiane; exercises supervisory jurisdiction over all lower courts; Pres. OULOM SOUVANNA-VONG.

Court of Appeal: Vientiane; hears civil and criminal appeals from the Criminal Courts and other Courts of First Instance.

Criminal Courts: Vientiane, Pakse and Luang Prabang; appeals can be made from the decisions of these courts to the Courts of Appeal and Supreme Court.

There is also a Provincial Tribunal in each of the provincial capitals (14 in all). There are 37 District Justices of the Peace.

The King's Council: also performs important judicial functions in addition to its legislative duties. The Council can pass judgement on the constitutionality of laws passed by the National Assembly. It may also be constituted as a High Court of Justice to try government officials charged with grave felonies.

RELIGION

The State religion of Laos is Buddhism (Hinayana). Vientiane and Luang Prabang are known as the "Cities of a Thousand Temples" and Buddhist temples are seen in every village. The life of the Laotian peasant is organized around religion and the Buddhist calendar commands most of his activities.

BUDDHISM

His Eminence The Sangharaja, WAT MAI SUWANNA-BHUMARAMA, Luang Prabang.

CHRISTIANITY

Roman Catholic: Vicars Apostolic: Mgt. ETIENNE LOOS-DREGT, Mission Catholique, Vientiane, Mgr. PIERRE BACH, Khammouane, Mgr. PIERRE URKIA, Paksé, Mgr. ALESSANDRO STACCIOLI, Luang Prabang.

PRESS

PRINCIPAL NEWSPAPERS AND PERIODICALS

Anakhot: Vientiane; Editor KHABOUANKANE NEOTHAN-GNOUM.

Bulletin Quotidien Lao Presse: B.P. 122; daily; published by the Ministry of Information.

L'Indépendent: 268 rue san sene Thai, P.B. 182, Vientiane; Dir. PHOUI SANANIKONE.

Lao Rouam Samphan: Vientiane; Editor H.E. BONG SOUVANNAVONG.

Pheuan Lao (*Friend of the Lao*): fortnightly; Editor INPENG SOURYADHAY.

Sieng-Mahason (*Voice of the People*): Vientiane; Editor SOPHON BOUPHASIRI.

La Voix du Peuple: Pakse; French; weekly; Editor BOUNLAP NHOUYVANISVONG.

Xatlao (*Lao Nation*): Rue Luang Prabang, Vientiane; national daily; Editor and Gen. Man. PHONE CHAN-THARAJ; circ. 5,000.

PRESS AGENCIES

Lao Presse: Vientiane; f. 1953; organ of the Ministry of Information.

FOREIGN BUREAU

UPI: Constellation Hotel, Vientiane; Correspondent PHONE CHANTHARAJ (Editor, *Xatlao*).

PUBLISHERS

Lao-Phanit: Vientiane.

Ministère de l'Education Nationale, Comité Littéraire, Bureau des Manuels Scolaires: Vientiane; arts, geography, education, history, cookery, music, physics, fiction, sociology, economics.

Vieng Krung: Vientiane.

RADIO

Radiodiffusion Nationale Lao: B.P. 310, Vientiane; f. 1951; government-owned; programmes in Lao, French and Vietnamese (news only) G.M.T. 23.00–02.30 (03.00 Sat./Sun.), 05.00–14.30 (15.00 Sat./Sun.); two regional stations Luang Prabang and Paksé; Dir.-Gen. SAMLITH RATSAPHONG; number of radio sets (1973 est.) 150,000. A television service is scheduled to start in 1974–75.

FINANCE

(cap.=capital; p.u.=paid up; dep.=deposit; m.=million)

BANKING

CENTRAL BANK

Banque Nationale du Laos: Rue Yonnet, Vientiane; f. 1955; central bank; cap. p.u. 260m. Kips; dep. 15,593.4m. Kips (Dec. 1970); Governor OUDONG SOUVANNAVONG; Gen. Sec. KHAM-OUANE RATANAVONG.

FOREIGN BANKS

Bank of Tokyo, Ltd.: Tokyo; Vientiane.

Banque de l'Indochine: 1 rue Pangkham, Vientiane, B.P. 84.

INSURANCE

Optorg: rue du Boun, Vientiane; national company.

Sisavan Pakan Phai: Vientiane.

TRADE AND INDUSTRY

Chambre Nationale de Commerce et d'Agriculture: Vientiane.

Chambre Interprovinciale de Commerce et d'Agriculture du Centre: Vientiane.

Chambre Interprovinciale de Commerce et d'Agriculture du Sud: Pakse.

Chambre Mixte de Commerce et d'Agriculture: Vientiane.

DEVELOPMENT ORGANIZATION

Agriculture Development Organization: Vientiane; sponsored by the Laotian and U.S. Governments; receives commodity donations from the Governments of the U.K., Japan and Australia; sells, and provides credit for, rice seeds, fertilizers, pumps and implements, which can be paid for when rice is harvested, in cash or in kind; also conducts national rice marketing programme.

TRANSPORT AND TOURISM

TRANSPORT

There are no railways in Laos.

ROADS

There are about 6,500 km. of roads of which 765 km. are sealed. Private operators run local bus services and long-distance services linking Vientiane and Luang Prabang with Saigon (South Vietnam) and Phnom-Penh (Khmer Republic). There are also usable roads linking Vientiane with Savannakhet, Phong Saly to the Chinese border, and Vientiane with Luang Prabang. A rail and road project, linking Vientiane with Bangkok and sponsored by the Mekong Development Committee, is under survey.

INLAND WATERWAYS

The River Mekong is Laos' greatest traffic artery. Ferry services are run by government and private operators. The river is interrupted by rapids and is navigable between the following points only (traffic fluctuating seasonally):

Vientiane—Savannakhet (458 km.) ships of 200 gross tons, drawing 1.75 metres at 7 knots.

Savannakhet—Paksé (257 km.) ships of 200 gross tons, drawing 1.75 metres at 12 knots.

Pakse—Khone—Saigon, ships of 500 gross tons, drawing 2.5 metres at 7 knots.

MEKONG RIVER DEVELOPMENT PROJECT

Co-ordination Committee: Bangkok; f. 1957; set up by Economic Commission for Asia and the Far East (ECAFE), to develop the resources of the Mekong River.

Members: PHLEK CHHAT (Khmer Republic), OUKEO SOUVANNAVONG (Laos), Dr. BOONROD BINSON (Thailand), BUI HUU VINH (Republic of Viet-Nam).

Executive Agent: W. J. VAN DER OORD.

Australia, Canada, France, India, Iran, Japan, New Zealand, the United Kingdom, and the U.S.A. are giving assistance.

CIVIL AVIATION

Royal Air Lao: Head Office: 2 rue Pangkham, B.P. 181, Vientiane; f. 1961; national airline, of which the Government owns 90 per cent; domestic services and international routes to Bangkok, Saigon and Hong Kong; Pres. PHAGNA NGON SANANIKONE; Dir.-Gen. NIKORN PHANKONGSY. Fleet: two DC-4, two DC-3, one DHC Beaver.

Lao Airlines: 17-19 Luang-Prabang Highway, B.P. 829, Vientiane.

FOREIGN AIRLINES

The following foreign airlines are represented in Vientiane: Air France, Air Vietnam, Cathay Pacific Airways, Air Khmer, Swissair, Thai Airways and Union des Transports Aériens.

TOURISM

Direction du Tourisme: Avenue Lane Xang, Vientiane.

UNIVERSITY

Université Sisavangvong: Vientiane; 130 teachers, 1,620 students.

LEBANON

INTRODUCTORY SURVEY

Location, Climate, Language, Religion, Flag, Capital

Lebanon lies at the eastern end of the Mediterranean Sea. Its neighbour to the north and east is Syria, and to the south Israel. The climate varies widely, coastal lowlands being hot and humid in summer and mild in winter but in the hills there is a heavy winter snowfall. Rainfall is on the whole abundant. Arabic is spoken everywhere and French and English are widely understood. The population of the Lebanon is almost equally divided between Christians and Muslims. The Christians are mainly Maronites, but many other sects flourish. The national flag (proportions 3 by 2) has horizontal stripes of red, white (half the depth) and red. In the centre of the white stripe is a cedar tree. The capital is Beirut.

Recent History

Before the Second World War Lebanon was a French mandated territory. Independence was proclaimed in 1941 and French forces left the country in 1946. The Lebanon has been a member of the Arab League since 1945 and has tried to follow a policy of neutrality in the disputes between Arab states, although accepting the Arab policy of boycotting Israel. Israeli commandos raided Beirut airport in December 1968, destroying or damaging aircraft worth £15 million belonging to Arab airlines. The raid, said to be a reprisal for Palestinian guerrilla forces' use of Lebanon as a base, caused the fall of the coalition government in January 1969. A new ministry led by Rashid Karami resigned in April but continued as a caretaker government until November 1969. Sulaiman Franjiya was elected President in August 1970, and Saeb Salam formed a new Cabinet in October 1970. Palestinian guerrilla raids into Israel from bases on Lebanese territory have frequently provoked reprisals from Israeli forces, encouraging the Lebanese Government to restrain the guerrilla groups. An Israeli raid on Beirut in April 1973 resulted in the resignation of Saeb Salam's Government. Under the new Government of Dr. Amin Hafez fierce fighting broke out between the Lebanese army and the guerrillas. An agreement was eventually reached with the guerrillas, but in June Dr. Hafez resigned and was replaced in July by Takieddin Solh as Prime Minister. Lebanon offered its assistance to the Arab cause in the war of October 1973 between the Arabs and Israel.

Government

Legislative power is exercised by the Chamber of Deputies, which has 99 members elected by universal adult suffrage. The electoral law maintains a ratio of 6 Christians to 5 Muslims in the Chamber of Deputies. The President of the Republic is elected for a term of six years. He chooses the Prime Minister and Council of Ministers, who carry out laws passed by the Chamber of Deputies.

Defence

The total strength of the Lebanese armed forces is 15,250 men, with an army of 14,000, a navy of 250 and an air force of 1,000. The defence budget for 1972 was £L225 million.

Economic Affairs

Lebanon has traditionally favoured a private enterprise economy. Many people are employed in service industries, relatively few in agriculture. The principal crops are grain, olives and citrus fruits. Lebanon is a free market and about two-thirds of trade is transit traffic, Beirut being the principal commercial and financial centre of the Middle East. In October 1966 a national crisis was feared as a result of the failure of Intra Bank, the biggest of Beirut's international finance houses. The repercussions of the closure were widespread and the economy declined for four years. From September 1970, however, the economy has shown an upward trend, and is now booming, although inflation is presenting a problem. The chief Lebanese industries are oil-refining, food processing and cement. Tourism is a valuable source of income, but was depressed by the internal situation in 1973.

Transport and Communications

There are over 400 kilometres of railway, some of it narrow gauge. Towns are connected by good roads and there is heavy traffic between Beirut and Damascus, the capital of Syria, Beirut is the principal port of call for the main shipping lines covering the eastern Mediterranean. The port of Tripoli is the terminus of an oil pipeline from Iraq, and Sidon of the pipeline from Saudi Arabia. Beirut is an important international air junction and some 40,000 aircraft use the airport annually.

Social Welfare

A scale of compensation for loss of employment was introduced by the State in 1963. Medical services are largely in private hands but there is a Social Security Fund which covers the medical expenses of workers. Under a national agreement, wages are paid by employers for up to 26 weeks during sickness.

Education

There is state primary and secondary education but private institutions provide the main facilities for secondary and higher education. The literacy rate is over 80 per cent, the highest in the Arab world.

Tourism

Lebanon is a tourist centre for the Middle East. Scenic beauty, sunshine and historical sites, notably Baalbek and Byblos, are the main attractions. There are many modern hotels, and more than a million tourists visit the country annually.

Visas are not required to visit Lebanon by nationals of Arab League member-states.

Sport

Football, basketball, tennis, swimming, skiing, water-skiing and golf are the most popular sports.

Public Holidays

1974: August 15th (Feast of the Assumption), October 16th–17th (Id ul Fitr), November 1st (All Saints' Day), November 22nd (Independence Day), December 25th (Christmas Day), December 31st (Evacuation Day).

1975: January 1st (New Year's Day), January 14th (Muslim New Year), January 24th (Ashoura), February 9th (Feast of St. Maron), March 22nd (Arab League Anniversary), March 26th (Mouloud), March 28th (Good Friday—Western Church), March 31st (Easter Monday—Western Church), May 1st (May Day), May 2nd (Good Friday—Eastern Church), May 5th (Easter Monday—Eastern Church), May 6th (Martyrs' Day), June 5th (Ascension Day—Eastern Church).

Weights and Measures

The metric system is in force.

Currency and Exchange Rates

100 piastres = 1 Lebanese pound (£L).
Exchange rates (April 1974):

£1 sterling = £L5.30;
U.S. $1 = £L2.25.

STATISTICAL SURVEY

AREA AND POPULATION

AREA
(hectares)

TOTAL	CULTIVATED	IRRIGATED	MARGINAL AND GRAZING	FOREST	WASTE
1,040,000	270,000	72,000	128,800	73,200	549,200

POPULATION (1972)

TOTAL*	BEIRUT* (capital)	TRIPOLI*	BIRTHS	MARRIAGES	DEATHS
2,600,000	800,000	150,000	74,980	17,359	30,718†

* Estimate.

† Large increase due to registration of hitherto unregistered deaths prior to 1972 parliamentary elections.

AGRICULTURE

PRINCIPAL CROPS

	AREA ('000 hectares)			PRODUCTION ('000 tons)			YIELD (tons per hectare)
	1969	1970*	1971*	1969	1970*	1971*	1971*
Wheat	43.2	60.0	60.0	33.0	50.0	50.0	0.8
Barley	8.3	9.0	10.0	7.8	8.0	10.0	1.0
Sugar Beet	2.2	2.0	2.5	94.0	94.0	120.0	48.0
Potatoes	9.0	8.0	9.0	86.6	75.0	85.0	9.4
Onions	1.9	2.0	n.a.	30.0	30.0	n.a.	n.a.
Tobacco	6.6	7.0	7.0	6.7	7.3	7.3	1.0
Citrus Fruit	11.3	n.a.	n.a.	208.5	270.0	285.0	n.a.
Apples	14.1	n.a.	n.a.	66.5	90.0	100.0	n.a.
Grapes	16.6	17.0	n.a.	76.6	80.0	n.a.	n.a.
Olives	27.7	n.a.	n.a.	46.3	20.0	n.a.	n.a.
Tomatoes	5.7	6.0	n.a.	70.0	75.0	n.a.	n.a.

* FAO estimates.

LIVESTOCK
('ooo)

	1968	1969	1970	1971
Goats . . .	357	348	330	318
Sheep . . .	200	213	214	218
Cattle . . .	86	86	85	84
Donkeys . . .	28	28	26	25
Poultry . . .	16,538	17,463	17,800	n.a.

INDUSTRY

		1969	1970	1971	1972
Tobacco Manufactures . .	tons	2,650	2,281	3,122	3,250
Refined Sugar . . .	,,	31,613	—	—	—
Fertilizers . . .	,,	52,870	—	—	—
Timber . . .	cu. metres	46,342	46,545	48,793	57,748
Cement . . .	'ooo tons	1,252	1,339	1,499	1,626
Electricity . . .	million kWh.	1,139	1,230	1,375	1,548

OIL REFINING
('ooo tons)

	1966	1967	1968	1969	1970	1971	1972
Crude Oil intake .	1,652	1,730	1,803	1,849	1,992	2,001	2,039
Petrol . .	310	303	347	347	374	397	446
Paraffin . .	154	180	190	207	212	218	155
Gas Oil . .	232	269	281	318	338	343	329
Fuel Oil . .	883	891	897	884	958	947	1,082
Butane . .	23	21	24	23	22	24	26

FINANCE

100 piastres = 1 Lebanese pound (£L).

Coins: 1, 2½, 5, 10, 25 and 50 piastres.

Notes: 1, 5, 10, 25, 50 and 100 pounds.

Exchange rates (April 1974): £1 sterling = £L5.30; U.S. $1 = £L2.25.

£L100 = £18.87 sterling = $44.44.

ORDINARY BUDGET ESTIMATES
(Expenditure 1972—million £L)

Defence	212.7
Education	172.0
Public Works and Transport . .	144.9
Ministry of the Interior . .	n.a.
Debt Servicing . . .	n.a.
Hydro-electric Resources . .	n.a.
Total (including others) .	980.0

1973 Budget: £L1,077 million.

1974 Budget: £L1,385 million.

EXTERNAL TRADE*
(£L'000)

	1967	1968	1969	1970	1971	1972
Imports	1,769,992	1,865,087	2,006,431	2,252,177	2,451,922	2,819,932
Exports . . .	453,347	510,261	554,301	650,619	815,619	1,168,195
Transit Trade† . . .	957,715	1,532,938	1,348,894	1,272,105	2,429,687	1,350,430

* Based on the rate of free market prices of the U.S. dollar.
† Through the free port of Beirut; includes crude oil pumped through the Lebanon.

PRINCIPAL COMMODITIES
(£L '000)

IMPORTS	1971	1972	EXPORTS*	1971	1972
Precious Metals, Stones, Jewellery and Coins . .	304,584	238,113	Vegetable Products . .	121,598	145,834
Vegetable Products . .	237,959	243,223	Precious Metals, Stones, Jewellery and Coins .	51,413	125,062
Machinery and Electrical Apparatus . .	282,274	384,865	Animals and Animal Products .	55,050	57,874
Textiles and Products .	284,802	342,035	Machinery and Electrical Apparatus . .	98,702	141,681
Non-precious Metals and Products	202,642	244,329	Non-precious Metals and Products	80,230	99,994
Transport Vehicles . .	170,396	236,711	Textiles and Products . .	79,527	131,027
Animals and Animal Products .	122,916	124,287	Beverages and Tobacco .	49,445	99,280
Industrial Chemical Products .	182,041	227,856	Transport Vehicles . .	57,997	160,345
Mineral Products . .	139,487	169,650			
Beverages and Tobacco .	142,273	155,491			

* Including re-exports.

PRINCIPAL COUNTRIES
(£L '000)

IMPORTS	1970	1971	1972	EXPORTS	1970	1971	1972
Belgium . .	44,216	54,773	63,347	France . . .	12,673	13,896	52,750
Czechoslovakia .	37,971	41,384	56,096	German Federal Rep.	9,413	13,496	12,039
France . . .	211,030	266,549	282,352	Greece . . .	2,593	2,083	1,793
German Federal Rep.	197,630	264,295	287,527	Iraq . . .	36,974	68,641	69,440
Iraq . . .	91,923	98,017	122,308	Italy . . .	13,000	14,855	16,875
Italy . . .	149,663	187,269	236,046	Jordan . . .	37,022	37,843	23,513
Japan . . .	87,618	103,370	120,246	Kuwait . . .	79,528	88,690	110,620
Jordan . . .	19,560	13,895	16,835	Saudi Arabia . .	125,157	125,387	190,284
Netherlands . .	42,495	56,897	53,749	Spain . . .	1,007	1,207	3,023
Saudi Arabia . .	22,473	32,983	51,762	Syria . . .	43,432	75,654	83,366
Switzerland . .	273,223	228,307	176,415	U.S.S.R. . .	11,159	9,404	8,192
Syria . . .	66,907	35,312	80,287	United Kingdom .	14,533	26,508	44,962
Turkey . . .	33,787	56,574	38,958	U.S.A. . .	24,261	23,164	71,636
United Kingdom .	258,168	198,054	232,279				
U.S.A. . . .	223,990	250,408	324,550				

TRANSPORT
RAILWAYS

	PASSENGERS ('000)		GOODS ('000)		REVENUE ('000 £L)		
	Journeys	Passenger-Kms.	Tons	Ton-kms.	Passengers	Goods	Total
1968 .	88	6,691	489	37,036	148	3,067	3,215
1969 .	78	7,278	313	24,455	178	2,018	2,196
1970 .	76	7,430	258	20,082	187	1,916	2,103
1971 .	71	7,187	325	26,789	184	2,236	2,420
1972 .	55	5,004	417	33,116	134	2,313	2,447

ROADS

	1968	1969	1970	1971	1972
Motor cars (taxis and private) .	123,891	129,674	136,016	146,270	164,790
Buses	1,645	1,763	1,794	1,905	2,067
Lorries	13,404	14,473	14,795	15,656	17,130
Motor cycles	11,291	12,004	9,800	9,731	10,734

SHIPPING IN BEIRUT

	SHIPS ENTERED		MERCHANDISE (Metric Tons)	
	Number	Tonnage	Entered	Cleared
1968 .	2,879	4,146,000	1,916,000	654,000
1969 .	3,126	4,361,512	1,995,000	700,000
1970 .	3,128	4,428,491	2,289,321	728,144
1971 .	3,320	4,837,003	2,456,517	626,384
1972 .	3,586	6,197,000	2,665,000	678,000

TRAFFIC THROUGH THE INTERNATIONAL AIRPORT IN BEIRUT

	AIRCRAFT USING AIRPORT	PASSENGERS USING AIRPORT	FREIGHT THROUGH AIRPORT (metric tons)
1968 .	41,082	1,512,599	51,238
1969 .	42,733	1,571,667	53,594
1970 .	41,553	1,558,246	57,691
1971 .	39,643	1,832,514	69,742
1972 .	38,735	2,090,634	87,991

TOURISM

	1969	1970	1971	1972
Total Foreign Visitors (except Syrians) .	777,135	822,347	1,015,772	1,048,163
of which:				
Visitors from Arab countries .	459,858	534,250	619,171	577,186
Visitors from Europe . .	172,462	149,518	213,698	250,914
Visitors from the Americas .	76,964	67,190	94,076	116,153
Syrian Visitors	810,050	863,833	1,241,633	1,232,903
TOTAL . . .	1,587,185	1,686,180	2,257,405	2,281,066

EDUCATION

(1971–72)

	SCHOOLS	PUPILS	TEACHERS
Public:			
Primary, Kindergarten and Upper Primary	1,278	273,092	14,763
Secondary	39	10,531	1,618
Private:			
Primary and Kindergarten .	} 1,501	{ 406,789	} 21,083
Upper Primary and Secondary .		{ 90,032	

Source: Direction Centrale de la Statistique, Ministère du Plan, and Direction Générale des Douanes, Beirut.

THE CONSTITUTION

(Promulgated May 23rd, 1926; amended October 27th, 1927, May 8th, 1929, November 9th and December 7th, 1943.)

According to the Constitution, the Republic of the Lebanon is an independent and sovereign State, and no part of the territory may be alienated or ceded. Lebanon has no State religion. Arabic is the official language. Beirut is the capital.

All Lebanese are equal in the eyes of the law. Personal freedom and freedom of the Press are guaranteed and protected. The religious communities are entitled to maintain their own schools, provided they conform to the general requirements relating to public instruction as laid down by the State. Dwellings are inviolable; rights of ownership are protected by law. Every Lebanese citizen who has completed his twenty-first year is an elector and qualifies for the franchise.

Legislative Power

Legislative power is exercised by one house, the Chamber of Deputies, with 99 seats, 54 of which are allocated to Christians and 45 to Muslims (for full details of allocation, *see* Parliament, p. 886). Its members must be over 25 years of age, in possession of their full political and civil rights, and literate. They are considered representatives of the whole nation, and are not bound to follow directives from their constituencies. They can only be suspended by a two-thirds majority of their fellow-members. Secret ballot was introduced in a new election law of April 1960.

The Chamber holds two sessions yearly, from the first Tuesday after March 15th to the end of May, and from the first Tuesday after October 15th to the end of the year. The normal term of the Chamber of Deputies is four years; general elections take place within sixty days before the end of this period. If the Chamber is dissolved before the end of its term, elections are held within three months of dissolution.

Voting in the Chamber is public—by acclamation, or by standing and sitting. A quorum of two-thirds and a majority vote is required for constitutional issues. The only exceptions to this occur when the Chamber becomes an electoral college, and chooses the President of the Republic, or Secretaries to the Chamber, or when the President is accused of treason or of violating the Constitution. In such cases voting is secret, and a two-thirds majority is needed.

Executive Power

The President of the Republic is elected for a term of six years, and is not immediately re-eligible. He and his ministers deal with the promulgation and execution of laws passed by the Chamber of Deputies. The Ministers and the Prime Minister are chosen by the President of the Republic. They are not necessarily members of the Chamber of Deputies, although they are responsible to it and have access to its debates. The President of the Republic must be a Maronite Christian and the Prime Minister a Sunni Muslim; and the choice of the other Ministers has to reflect the division between the communities in the Chamber.

The President himself can initiate laws. Alternatively, the President may demand an additional debate on laws already passed by the Chamber. He can adjourn the Chamber for up to a month, but not more than once in each session. In exceptional circumstances he can dissolve the Chamber and force an election. Ministers can be made to resign by a vote of no confidence.

THE GOVERNMENT

HEAD OF STATE

President of the Republic: SULAIMAN FRANJIYA (took office September 23rd, 1970).

THE CABINET

(*May* 1974)

Prime Minister and Minister of Finance: TAKIEDDIN SOLH.

Minister of Foreign Affairs: FUAD NAFAA.

Deputy Prime Minister, Minister of Public Works and Transport: FUAD GHUSN.

Minister of Interior: BAHIJ TAKIEDDIN.

Minister of Defence: NASRI MAALOUF.

Minister of Economy and Trade: Dr. NAZIH BIZRI.

Minister of Health: OTHMAN DANA.

Minister of Information: FAHMI SHAHIN.

Minister of Social Affairs and Labour: EMILE ROUHANA SAQR.

Minister of Education: EDMOND RIZQ.

Minister of Posts and Communications: TONY FRANJIYA.

Minister of Agriculture: SABRI HAMADA.

Minister of Justice: KAZEM KHALIL.

Minister of Co-operatives and Housing: MICHEL SASSIN.

Minister of Tourism: SOUREN KHANAMERIAN.

Minister of Power and Hydroelectric Resources: JOSEPH SKAFF.

Minister of Oil and Industry: TAUFIQ ASSAF.

Minister of Planning: Dr. HASSAN RIFAI.

Ministers of State: MAJID ARSLAN, Dr. ALI KHALIL, JOSEPH SHADER, Dr. ALBERT MUKHAIBER.

DIPLOMATIC REPRESENTATION

EMBASSIES AND LEGATION ACCREDITED TO LEBANON (Beirut unless otherwise indicated)
(E) Embassy; (L) Legation.

Afghanistan: Rue Verdun, Imm. Belle-Vue (E).

Algeria: Jnah (opposite Coral Beach) (E); *Ambassador:* MUHAMMAD YAZID.

Argentina: 149 Ave. Fouad 1er (E); *Ambassador:* RAÚL A. MEDINA MUÑOZ.

Australia: SFAH Bldg., Rue Kantari; *Ambassador:* PIERRE HUTTON.

Austria: Quartier Sursock, Rue Négib Trad, Villa Nocolas Cattan (E); *Ambassador:* Dr. WALTER R. BACKES.

Bahrain: address unavailable; *Ambassador:* ALI IBRAHIM MAHROUS.

Bangladesh: address unavailable; *Ambassador:* KHONDKER GOLAM MUSTAFA.

Belgium: 15th Floor, Centre Verdun, Rue Dunant (E); *Ambassador:* HUBERT BEDUWE.

Bolivia: Place de l'Etoile, Imm. Naffah (E).

Brazil: Rue Verdun, Imm. Mahmassani (E); *Ambassador:* CARLOS DA PONTE RIBEIRO EIRAS.

Bulgaria: Boulevard Chish-Hedoth, Imm. Lati (E); *Ambassador:* GEORGI HRISTOV TANEV.

Cameroon: Cairo, Egypt (E).

Canada: Rue Hamra, Centre Sabbagh (E); *Ambassador:* JACQUES GIGNAC.

Chad: Bid Solh, Forêt Kfoury, Imm. Kalot Frères (E); *Ambassador:* MAROUN HAIMARI.

Chile: Rue Maamari, Imm. Lion's (E); *Ambassador:* GUILLERMO OVALLE BLANCHET.

China, People's Republic: Rue 62, Nicolas Ibrahim Sursock, Ramlet El-Baida (E); *Ambassador:* HSU MING.

Colombia: Chouran, Imm. Jaber al-Ahmad al-Sabbah (E); *Ambassador:* ALBERTO LOSADA LARRA.

Congo (Brazzaville): Cairo, Egypt (E).

Costa Rica: Rue Hamra (E); *Chargé d'Affaires:* RIAD ABDEL-BAKI.

Cuba: Rue Jnah, Imm. Sélim Abboud (E); *Ambassador:* Dr. CARLOS E. ALFARAS VARELA.

Cyprus: Cairo, Egypt (E).

Czechoslovakia: Rue Fouad 1er, Imm. Kayssi (E); *Ambassador:* Dr. KAREL BLAZEK.

Denmark: Rue Clemenceau, Imm. Minkara (E); *Ambassador:* MOGENS WARBERG.

Egypt: Rue Ramlat el Baida (E); *Ambassador:* AHMAD LOUTFI MOUTAWALLI.

Ethiopia: Cairo, Egypt (E).

Finland: Centre Gefinor, Rue Clemenceau (E); *Ambassador:* CAROLUS LASSILA.

France: Rue Clemenceau (E); *Ambassador:* MICHEL RAUL GUILLAUME FONTAINE.

German Democratic Republic: (E); *Ambassador:* GERHARD HERDER.

Germany, Federal Republic: Rue Hamra, Imm. Arida; *Ambassador:* HANS CHRISTIAN LANKES.

Ghana: Jnah, Imm. Cheikh Sabah Ahmad Al-Sabah (E); *Chargé d'Affaires a.i.:* JOSEPH KODJO ARTHUR.

Greece: Rue de France (E); *Chargé d'Affaires:* SPYRIDON ADAMOPOULOS.

Guinea: Cairo, Egypt (E).

Haiti: Rue du Fleuve, Imm. Sarkis (E); *Ambassador:* PIERRE SARKIS.

Hungary: Jnah, Imm. Cheikh Salem Al-Sabah (E); *Ambassador:* JÁNOS VERES.

India: Rue Kantari, Imm. Samharini (E); *Ambassador:* S. K. SINGH.

Indonesia: Corniche Mazraa, Imm. Khaouam (E); *Ambassador:* MUHAMMAD SHARIF PADMADISASTRA.

Iran: Jnah, Imm. Sakina Mattar (E); *Ambassador:* MANSOUR QADR.

Iraq: Ramlat al-Baida, Imm. Ali Arab (E); *Ambassador:* YOUNES HASSAN AL-MOSLEH.

Italy: Rue Makdissi, Imm. Cosmidis (E); *Ambassador:* CESARE REGARD.

Ivory Coast: Avenue Sami Solh, Imm. Georges Tazbek (E); *Ambassador:* AMADOU BOCOUM.

Japan: Corniche Chouran, Imm. Olfat Nagib Salha (E); *Ambassador:* JIRO INAGAWA.

Jordan: Rue Verdun, Imm. Belle-Vue (E); *Ambassador:* AKRAM ZOAITER.

Kenya: Cairo, Egypt (E).

Kuwait: Bir Hassan, The Stadium Roundabout (E); *Ambassador:* MUHAMMAD YOUSSEF AL-ADASSANI.

Liberia: Rome, Italy (E).

Libya: Jnah, Imm. Cheikh Abdallah Khalifé Al-Sabbah; *Ambassador:* MUHAMMAD ABDEL-QADER GHOUQA.

Malaysia: Cairo, Egypt (E).

Mali: Cairo, Egypt (E).

Malta: Achrafié, Rue Marian Geahchan, Imm. Varkés Sarafian (L); *Minister:* UMBERTO TURATI.

Mauritania: Cairo, Egypt (E).

Mexico: Rue Hamra, Imm. Arida (E); *Ambassador:* Dr. FRANCISCO APODACA.

Morocco: Corniche Masraa, Imm. Chamat (E); *Ambassador:* ABDEL-QADER SAHRAWI.

Nepal: Cairo, Egypt (E).

Netherlands: Rue Kantari, Imm. Sahmarani (E); *Ambassador:* ADRIANUS CORNELIS VROON.

Nigeria: Cairo, Egypt (E).

Norway: Cairo, Egypt (E).

Pakistan: 2699 Rue de Lyon (E); *Ambassador:* Dr. S. M. KORESHI.

Panama: address unavailable (L).

Peru: Cairo, Egypt (E).

Poland: Furn el-Chebbak, Rue Asile des Veillards, Imm. Haddad Frères (E); *Ambassador:* Dr. TADEUSZ WUJEK.

Qatar: Dibs Building, Chouran Street (E); *Ambassador:* MUHAMMAD BEN HAMAD AL THANI.

Romania: Avenue Sami el-Solh, 215 Forêt Kfouri, Imm. Boutros et Chammah (E); *Ambassador:* Dr. MIHAIL LEVENTE.

Saudi Arabia: Rue Bliss, Manara (E); *Ambassador:* Sheikh Muhammad al-Mansour al-Rumaih.

Senegal: Corniche Mazraa, Rue Ibn el-Assir, Imm. Kholy el-Kataby (E); *Ambassador:* Alphonse N'Diaye.

Singapore: Cairo, Egypt (E).

Spain: Ramlet el Baida, Imm. White Sands (E); *Ambassador:* José Luis Florez-Estrada.

Sri Lanka: Cairo, Egypt (E).

Sudan: Rue Verdun, Imm. Mahmassani (E); *Ambassador:* Salah Ahmed.

Sweden: Rue Clemenceau, Imm. Moukarzel et Rubeiz (E); *Ambassador:* Åke A. Jonsson.

Switzerland: Avenue Perthuis, Imm. Achou (E); *Ambassador:* Charles-Albert Dubois.

Thailand: Cairo, Egypt (E).

Tunisia: Ramlet el-Baida, Imm. Rock and Marble (E); *Ambassador:* Muhammad Amamou.

Turkey: Rue Bliss, Imm. Dr. Nassif (E); *Ambassador:* Necmettin Tunal.

U.S.S.R.: Rue Mar Elias el-Tina (E); *Ambassador:* Sarvar Azimov.

United Arab Emirates: Massabili & Serhal Bldg., Cairo Street (E); *Ambassador:* Said Ahmad el-Ghabbash.

United Kingdom: Avenue de Paris, Ain el-Mreissé (E); *Ambassador:* P. H. G. Wright, C.M.G., O.B.E.

U.S.A.: Avenue de Paris (Corniche), Imm. Ali Reza; *Ambassador:* McMurtrie Godley.

Uruguay: Rue John Kennedy (E); *Ambassador:* Rodolfo Comas Amaro.

Vatican: Rue Georges Picot; Apostolic Nuncio: Mgr. Alfredo Bruniera.

Venezuela: Rue Kantari, Imm. Sahmarani (E); *Ambassador:* Col. Jesús Manuel Pérez Morale.

Viet-Nam, Republic: (information unavailable).

Yemen Arab Republic: Bld. Khaldé-Quzai, Imm. Ingénieur Ryad Amaiche (E); *Ambassador:* Ahmed Basha.

Yemen, People's Democratic Republic: Corniche Mazra, Imm. Najij (E); *Chargé d'Affaires a.i.:* Muhammad Nasser Muhammad.

Yugoslavia: Rue Chouran, Sakiet el-Janzir, Imm. Hindi (E); *Ambassador:* Milic Bugarcic.

Zaire: Cairo, Egypt (E).

Zambia: Cairo, Egypt (E).

Lebanon also has diplomatic relations with Central African Republic, Dahomey, Dominican Republic, Ecuador, El Salvador, Gabon, Guatemala, Honduras, Ireland, Khmer Republic, Luxembourg, Madagascar, Monaco, Nicaragua, Niger, Paraguay, Philippines, Sierra Leone, Togo, Upper Volta.

Diplomatic relations with Portugal were broken off in February 1974.

PARLIAMENT

CHAMBER OF DEPUTIES

The electoral reform bill of April 1960 maintained the existing ratio of 6 Christians to 5 Muslims in the Chamber of Deputies. It is the custom for the President of the Chamber of Deputies to be a Shi'i Muslim.

President of Chamber: Kamal Asaad.

Deputy President of Chamber: Nasim Majdalani.

RELIGIOUS GROUPS

Maronite Christians	30
Sunni Muslims	20
Shi'i Muslims	19
Greek Orthodox	11
Greek Catholics	6
Druses	6
Armenian Orthodox	4
Armenian Catholics	1
Protestants	1
Others	1
Total	**99**

There was a General Election in May 1972, but the diversity of allegiance in the Chamber makes a strict analysis by party groupings impossible. The distribution of seats among religious groups is laid down by law.

POLITICAL PARTIES AND GROUPS

Baath Party: Beirut; Lebanese branch of Arab reformist party.

Constitutional Party (Destour): Leader Sheikh Michel el Khoury.

Democratic Socialist Party: southern Muslims; Leader Kamel al Assad.

Lebanese Communist Party: Beirut; legalized August 1970; Sec.-Gen. Nicolas Chaoui.

Mouvement de l'Action Nationale: f. 1965; Leader Uthman Dana.

National Bloc: Leader Raymond Eddé.

National Liberal Party: Leader Camille Chamoun.

Organization of Communist Action in Lebanon: f. 1971.

Phalangist (Kata'eb) Party: Place Charles Hélou, P.O.B. 992, Beirut; f. 1936; democratic social party; 70,260 mems.; Leader Pierre Gemayel; Vice-Pres. Joseph Chader; Gen. Sec. Joseph Saade; publs. *Al-Amal* (Arabic daily), *Action—Proche Orient* (French political and scientific monthly).

Progressive Socialist Party: Zkak-el-Blat, P.O.B. 2893, Beirut; f. 1949; over 16,000 mems.; Principal Officer: Kamal Jumblatt; publ. *Al-Anba'* (weekly).

Social Nationalist Party (Partie Populaire Syrienne): resumed operations in 1969; advocates a "Greater Syria"; Leader Yousef Ashkar.

Tachnag Party: right-wing Armenian party.

JUDICIAL SYSTEM

Law and justice in the Lebanon are administered in accordance with the following codes, which are based upon modern theories of civil and criminal legislation:

(1) Code de la Propriété (1930).

(2) Code des Obligations et des Contrats (1932).

(3) Code de Procédure Civile (1933).

(4) Code de Commerce (1942).

(5) Code Maritime (1947).

(6) Code de Procédure Pénale (Code Ottoman Modifié).

(7) Code Pénal (1943).

(8) Code Pénal Militaire (1946).

(9) Code d'Instruction Criminelle.

The following courts are now established:

(*a*) Fifty-six "Single-Judge Courts", each consisting of a single judge, and dealing in the first instance with both civil and criminal cases; there are seventeen such courts at Beirut and seven at Tripoli.

(*b*) Eleven Courts of Appeal, each consisting of three judges, including a President and a Public Prosecutor, and dealing with civil and criminal cases; there are five such courts at Beirut.

(*c*) Four Courts of Cassation, three dealing with civil and commercial cases and the fourth with criminal cases. A Court of Cassation, to be properly constituted, must have at least three judges, one being the President and the other two Councillors. The First Court consists of the First President of the Court of Cassation, a President and two Councillors. The other two civil courts each consist of a President and three Councillors. If the Court of Cassation reverses the judgment of a lower court it does not refer the case back but retries it itself.

First President of the Court of Cassation: BADRI MEOUCHI.

(*d*) The Council of State, which deals with administrative cases. It consists of a President, Vice-President and four Councillors. A Commissioner represents the Government.

President of the Court of the Council of State: ABOU KHAIR.

(*e*) The Court of Justice, which is a special court consisting of a President and eight judges, deals with matters affecting the security of the State.

In addition to the above, Islamic, Christian and Jewish religious courts deal with affairs of personal status (marriages, deaths, inheritances, etc.).

There is also a Press Tribunal.

RELIGION

PRINCIPAL COMMUNITIES

Maronites	424,000
Greek Orthodox	149,000
Greek Catholic	91,000
Sunni Muslim	286,000
Shi'i Muslim	250,000
Druzes	88,000

It will be seen that the largest single community in the Lebanon is the Maronite, a Uniate sect of the Roman Church. The Maronites inhabited the old territory of Mount Lebanon, i.e. immediately east of Beirut. In the south, towards the Israeli frontier, Shi'i villages are most common whilst between the Shi'i and the Maronites live the Druzes (divided between the Yazbakis and the Jumblatis). The Bekaa has many Greek Christians, whilst the Tripoli area is mainly Sunni Muslim. Altogether, of all the regions of the Middle East, the Lebanon probably presents the closest juxtaposition of sects and peoples within a small territory. As Lebanese political life is organized on a sectarian basis, the Maronites also enjoy much political influence, including a predominant voice in the nomination of the President of the Republic.

Patriarch of Antioch of the Maronites: H.E. Cardinal PAUL PIERRE MEOUCHI.

Patriarch of Cilicia of the Armenians: Rt. Rev. Mgr. IGNACE PIERRE XVI BATANIAN.

Patriarch of Antioch and all the East, of Alexandria and of Jerusalem (*Melkite-Greek Catholic*): P.O.B. 50076, Beirut; MAXIMOS V. HAKIM.

Union of the Armenian Evangelical Churches in the Near East: P.O. Box 377, Beirut; Moderator Prof. HOV P. AHARONIAN; the Union includes some thirty Armenian Evangelical Churches in Syria, Lebanon, Egypt, Cyprus, Greece, Iran and Turkey.

THE PRESS

With 96 newspapers, some 40 of them dailies, serving a readership drawn from a population of only two and a half million, the Lebanese Press is highly competitive. It is also relatively free from external controls, compared with most of the other Middle East countries. Freedom of the press, along with freedom of expression and association, is guaranteed, within the limits of the law, by article 13 of the Constitution. However, the legal limitations on the expression of opinion are somewhat restrictive. The basic press law is that of 1948, under which all papers and periodicals have to be licensed by the Ministry of the Interior. The licence can be withdrawn if a paper ceases publication temporarily within six months of its inception, or if circulation drops below 1,500 for thirty days. The editor must have a university qualification, and must deposit a security. The 1948 law also made journalists subject to the judgements of a tribunal of discipline. After a period of conflict between the Government and the Press, the existing law was revised by the press law of 1958, which abolished the procedure for detaining journalists pending investigations, and, with certain exceptions, made it possible for persons convicted of infringement of press regulations to lodge an appeal.

The most important dailies are *Al-Hayat* and *An-Nahar*, which have the highest circulations, *The Daily Star*, *Al-Jaryda* and *L'Orient-Le Jour*, the foremost French paper. The latter two are owned by Georges Naccache, former Lebanese ambassador to France, and tend to take a pro-government line. In a country where most of the élite speak French the other French daily, *Le Soir*, is also influential, and, for the same reason, the twice-weekly publication *Le Commerce du Levant* occupies an important place in the periodical press.

The Lebanese Press has benefited indirectly from Beirut's status as by far the most important base for foreign correspondents covering the Middle East. Long-distance communications have consequently been developed to a high standard.

DAILIES

al-Amal: Place Charles Hélou, P.O.B. 992, Beirut; f. 1939 as a weekly, 1946 as a daily; Phalangist Party; Arabic; circ. 14,000; Editor GEORGES OMEIRA.

al-Anwar: Dar Assayad, P.O.B. 1038, Beirut; f. 1959; independent; Arabic; published by Dar Assayad S.A.L.; Propr. SAID FREIHA; Editor ISSAM FREIHA; circ. 75,200.

al-Bairaq: Rue Sursock, Beirut; National Bloc; Arabic; Editors ASSAD and FADEL AKL; circ. 3,000.

Beirut al-Masa: Place des Capucins, P.O.B. 1203, Beirut; Arabic; Editor ABDALLAH MASHNUQ; circ. 6,000.

al Dastour: Beirut; Editor MUHYEDDINE MIDANI; circ. 3,000.

al Dunia: P.O.B. 4599, Beirut; f. 1953; Arabic; political; also publishes books; Chief Editor SULIMAN ABOU ZAID.

al-Dyar: Place Tabaris, P.O.B. 959, Beirut; f. 1941; independent; Arabic; Editor G. W. SKAFF; circ. 22,300.

al Hadaf: Rue Béchir, Immeuble Esseilé, P.O.B. 39, Beirut; Arabic; Editor ZOUHAIR OSSEIRAN.

al-Hayat: Rue Al-Hayat, P.O.B. 987, Beirut; f. 1946; independent; Arabic; circ. 25,000.

al-Jaryda: Place Tabaris, P.O.B. 220, Beirut; f. 1953; independent; Arabic; circ. 22,600; Editor GEORGES SKAFF.

al-Kifah: Rue Mère Gelas, P.O.B. 1462, Beirut; f. 1950; Arabic; Editor RIAD TAHA; circ. 21,000.

Lissan-ul-Hal: Rue Chateaubriand, P.O.B. 4619, Beirut; f. 1877; Arabic; Editor GEBRAN HAYEK; circ. 32,000

al Moharrer: P.O.B. 5366, Beirut; Arabic; nationalist; Propr. and Editor HISHAM ABU DAHR; circ. 4,000.

an-Nahar: Rue Banque du Liban, Hamra; Press Cooperative Building, P.O.B. 226, Beirut; f. 1933; Arabic; independent; circ. 74,538; Publisher and Editor-in-Chief GHASSAN TUENI.

Nida: P.O.B. 4744, Beirut; Arabic; Communist; Editor SUHEIL YAMOUT; circ. 1,500.

an-Nidal: Rue Mère Yilas, Beirut, P.O.B. 1354; f. 1939; independent; Arabic; Editor MUSTAPHA MOQADDAM; circ. 25,000.

Rakib al-Ahwal: Rue Patriarche Hoyek, P.C.B. 467, Beirut; Arabic; Editor SIMA'N FARAH SEIF.

ar-Rawwad: Rue Mokhalsieh, P.O.B. 2696, Beirut; Arabic; Editor BESHARA MAROUN.

as Safa: P.O.B. 9192, Beirut; French; published by Soc. Nat. de Presse et d'Edition S.A.L.; Editor RENÉ AGGIOURI; circ. 15,000.

Saout Al Ourouba: P.O.B. 3537, Beirut; Arabic.

al Shaab: P.O.B. 5140, Beirut; Arabic; nationalist; Propr. and Editor MUHAMMAD AMIN DUGHAN; circ. 7,000.

al-Sharq: Rue de la Marseillaise, P.O.B. 838, Beirut; f. 1945; Arabic; Editor KHAIRY AL-KA'KI.

Telegraph-Beirut: Rue Béehara el Khoury, P.O.B. 1061, Beirut; f. 1930; Arabic; political, economic and social; Editor TEWFIQ EL METNI; circ. 15,500 (5,000 outside Lebanon).

al Yaum: P.O.B. 1908; Beirut; Arabic; Editor AFIF TIBI.

az-Zaman: Rue Boutros Karameh, Beirut; Arabic; Editor ROBERT ABELA.

Ararat: Nor Hagin, Beirut; Hunchag Party; Armenian; Editor KRIKOR JABULIANO.

Aztag: Rue Zokak El-Blatt, P.O.B. 587, Beirut; Tachnak Party; Armenian; Editor HAIK BALYAN.

Daily Star, The: Rue Al-Hayat, P.O. Box 987, Beirut; f. 1952; independent; English; circ. 8,250; Editor GEORGE S. HISHMEH.

Le Orient-Le Jour: Rue Banque du Liban, P.O.B. 2488, Beirut; f. 1924; independent; French; circ. 20,000.

Le Soir: Rue de Syrie, P.O.B. 1470, Beirut; f. 1947; political independent daily; French; circ. 16,500; Gen. Man. and Editor DIKRAN TOSBATH.

Zartonk: Rue de l'Hôpital-Français, P.O. Box 617, Beirut; f. 1937; official organ of Armenian Liberal Democratic Party; Armenian; Editor P. TOUMASSIAN.

WEEKLIES

Achabaka: Dar Assayad, P.O. Box 1038, Beirut; f. 1956; society and features; Arabic; Prop. SAID FREIHA; Editor GEORGE IBRAHIM EL-KHOURY; circ. 121,575.

al-Ahad: Rue Mère Gelas, P.O.B. 1462, Beirut; Arabic; RIAD TAHA; circ. 32,000.

al-Anba': Rue Maroun Naccache, P.O.B. 2893, Beirut; Progressive Socialist Party; Arabic; Editor KAMAL JUMBLATT.

al-Anwar Supplement: P.O.B. 1038, Beirut; cultural-social; every Sunday; supplement to daily *al-Anwar*; Editor ISSAM FREIHA; circ. 66,900.

al-Ash-Shir': 144 Rue Gouraud, Beirut; f. 1948; Catholic; Arabic; Editor Father ANTOINE CORTBAWI.

al Awassef: Homs Bldg., P.O.B. 2492, Beirut; f. 1953; Arabic; Trade union news; Dir. DAHER KHALIL ZEIDAN; circ. 8,000.

al Hawadess: P.O.B. 1281, Beirut; f. 1911; Arabic political; Chair. and Gen Man. SALIM LOZI; circ. 90,000.

al-Hurriya: P.O.B. 857, Beirut; f. 1960; voice of Arab Nationalist Movement; Arabic; Chief Editor MUHSIN IBRAHIM; circ. 12,000.

al-Iza'a: Rue Selim Jazaerly, P.O.B. 462, Beirut; f. 1938; politics, art, literature and broadcasting; Arabic; circ. 11,000; Editor FAYEK KHOURY.

al-Liwa: Rue Abdel Kaim Khalil, P.O.B. 2402, Beirut; Arabic; Propr. ABDEL GHANI SALAAM.

al-Jamhour: Mustapha Naja St., Mussaïtbeh, P.O.B. 1834, Beirut; f. 1936; Arabic; illustrated weekly news magazine; Editor FARID ABU SHAHLA; circ. 45,000, of which over 30,000 outside Lebanon.

al Rassed: P.O.B. 2808, Beirut; Arabic; Editor GEORGE RAJJI.

al-Usbua al-Arabi: P.O.B. 1404, Beirut; f. 1959; Arabic; Publishers Les Editions Orientales, S.A.L.; Editor ASSAD MOKADDEM; circ. 147,500 (circulates throughout the Arab world).

Argus: Bureau des Documentations Libanaises et Arabes, P.O.B. 3000, Beirut; circ. 1,000.

Assayad: Dar Assayad, P.O.B. 1038, Beirut; f. 1943; Prop. SAID FREIHA; Editor RAFIQUE KHOURY; circ. 81,225.

Combat: Beirut; French; Editor GEORGES CORBAN.

Commerce du Levant, Le: P.O.B. 687, Kantari St., SFAH Bldg., Beirut; f. 1929; twice weekly; also publishes monthly edition; commercial; French; circ. 15,000; Editor: Société de la Presse Economique; Pres. E. S. SHOUCAIR.

Dabbour: Museum Square, Beirut; f. 1922; Arabic; Editors MICHEL RICHARD and FUAD MUKARZEL; circ. 12,000.

Kul Shay': Rue Béehara el Khoury, P.O.B. 3250, Beirut; Arabic.

Magazine: P.O.B. 1404, Beirut; in French; Publ. Les Editions Orientales S.A.L.; Editor MILAD SALAME; circ. 8,345.

Massis: Place Debbas, Beirut; f. 1949; Armenian; Catholic; Editor F. VARTAN TEKEYAN; circ. 2,000.

an-Nahda: Abdul Aziz St., P.O.B. 3736, Beirut; Arabic; independent; Man. Editor NADIM ABOU-ISMIL.

Middle East Economic Survey: Middle East Research and Publishing Centre, P.O.B. 1224, Beirut; f. 1957; oil topics; Editor and Publr. FUAD W. ITAYIM.

Revue du Liban: Rue Allenby, Beirut; f. 1928; French; Editor IBRAHIM MAKHLOUF; circ. 15,000.

OTHER SELECTED PERIODICALS

Note: published monthly unless otherwise stated.

al-Adib: P.O.B. 878, Beirut; f. 1942; Arabic, artistic, literary, scientific and political; Editor ALBERT ADIB.

al-Afkar: Rue Mère Gelas, Beirut; international; French; Editor RIAD TAHA.

Arab Oil & Gas Journal: Arab Petroleum Research Centre, P.O.B. 7167, Beirut; Arabic, English and French; Dir. Dr. NICOLAS SARKIS.

al-Intilak: c/o Michel Nehme, al-Intilak Printing and Publishing House, P.O.B. 4958, Beirut; f. 1960; literary; Arabic; Chief Editor MICHEL NEHME.

al-'Ulum: Dar al Ilm Lil Malayeen, rue de Syrie, P.O.B. 1085, Beirut; scientific review.

Alam Attijarat (*Business World*): Strand Bldg., Hamra St., Beirut; f. 1965 in association with Johnston International Publishing Corpn., New York; bi-monthly; commercial; Editor NADIM MAKDISI; international circ. 13,600.

Lebanese and Arab Economy: Allenby Street, P.O. Box 1801, Beirut; f. 1951; fortnightly; Arabic, English and French; publisher Beirut Chamber of Commerce and Industry and SAMI N. ATIYEH; Editor and Dir. ABDEL-WAHAB RIFA'I.

L'Economie des Pays Arabes: B.P. 6068, Beirut; f. 1969; French; published by Centre d'Etudes et de Documentation Economiques Financières et Sociales S.A.L.; Dir. Dr. CHAFIC AKHRAS; circ. 5,000.

Majallat al Izaat al Loubnaniat: Lebanese Broadcasting Corporation, Beirut; Arabic; broadcasting affairs.

Naft al Arab: Beirut; f. 1965; monthly; Arabic; oil; Publisher ABDULLAH AL TARIQI.

Nous Ouvriers du Pays: 144 Rue Gouraud, Beirut; Catholic; English-French; social welfare; Editor Father ANTOINE CORTBAWI.

Rijal al Amal (*Businessmen*): P.O.B. 220, Cornishe Square, Beirut; business magazine; Arabic, with special issues in English and French; Editor G. W. SKAFF; circ. 12,000.

Sawt al-Mar'ah: Dar al-Kitab, P.O.B. 1284, Beirut; Lebanese Women's League; Arabic Editor: Mrs. J. SHEIBOUB.

Tabibok: P.O.B. 4887, Beirut; f. 1956; medical, social, scientific; Arabic; Editor Dr. SAMI KABANI; circ. 78,000.

Welcome to Lebanon and the Middle East: Tourist Information and Advertising Bureau: Starco Centre, North Block 711, P.O.B. 4204, Beirut; f. 1959; on entertainment, touring and travel; English; Editor SOUHAIL TOUFIK ABOU-JAMRA; circ. 6,000.

NEWS AGENCIES

FOREIGN BUREAUX

AP: Antoine Massoud Building, Rue Mgr. Chebli, No. 12, Beirut; Chief of Middle East Services ROY ESSOYAN.

Četeka (Czechoslovak News Agency): P.O.B. 5069, Beirut; Chief Middle East Correspondent VLADIMIR OTRUBA.

Middle East News Agency: 72 Al Geish St., P.O.B. 2268, Beirut.

North American Newspapers Alliance: Palm-Beach Hotel, Beirut; Chief ANDREW J. NASH.

UPI: Press Co-operative Building, Rue Hamra, Beirut; Bureau Man. GERARD LOUGHRAN.

DPA, Iraq News Agency and Reuters also have offices in Beirut.

PRESS ASSOCIATION

Lebanese Press Syndicate: P.O.B. 3084, Beirut; f. 1911; 12 mems.; Pres. RIAD TAHA; Vice-Pres. FARID ABOU SHAHLA; Sec. MOHAMMAD BADIH SERBEY.

PUBLISHERS

Dar al Adab: Beirut; literary and general.

Dar al Iim Lil Malayeen: Rue de Syria, P.O.B. 1085, Beirut; f. 1945; dictionaries, textbooks, Islamic cultural books; owners: Munir Ba'albaky and Bahij Osman.

Dar-Alkashaf: P.O.B. 112091, A. Malhamee St., Beirut; f. 1930; publishers of *Alkashaf* (Arab Youth Magazine), maps and atlases; printers and distributors; Propr. M. A. Fathallah.

Dar al-Kitab al-Jadid: Hamra St., Hindi Building, P.O.B. 1284, Beirut; political studies; owner: Fuad Badr.

Dar al-Makshouf: Rue Amir Beshir, Beirut; scientific, cultural and school books; owner: Sheikh Fuad Hobeish.

Dar Al-Maaref Liban S.A.L.: P.O.B. 2320, Esseily Bldg., Riad Al-Solh Square, Beirut; f. 1959; textbooks in Arabic, English and French; Gen. Man. Joseph Nashou.

Dar Al Mashreq (Imprimerie Catholique): P.O.B. 946, Beirut; f. 1853; religion, art, literature, history, languages, science, philosophy, school books, dictionaries and periodicals; Dir. Paul Brouwers, sj.

Dar An-Nahar S.A.L.: B.P. 226, Beirut; f. 1967; publishes *Kadaya Moua'ssira* (quarterly), circ. 7,000; Gen. Man. Charles Raad.

Dar Assayad S.A.L.: P.O.B. 1038, Beirut; f. 1943; publishes *Al-Anwar* (daily), circ. 75,000, *Assayad* (weekly), circ. 81,225, *Al-Tayar* (monthly), circ. 75,000, *Achabaka* (weekly), circ. 121,500; *Samar* (weekly), circ. 50,000; has offices and correspondents in Arab countries and most parts of the world; Chair. Said Freiha; Man. Dir. Bassam Freiha.

Dar Beirut: Librairie Beyrouth, Immeuble Lazarieh, rue Amir Bechir, Beirut; f. 1936; Prop. M. Safieddine.

Institute for Palestine Studies, Publishing and Research Department: Ashqar Bldg., Clémenceau St., P.O.B. 7164, Beirut; f. 1963; private non-profit making research organization; to promote better understanding of the Palestine problem; publishes research papers, documentary material, yearbook (in Arabic), *Bulletin* (fortnightly, Arabic), *Journal of Palestine Studies* (quarterly, English); library: 6,000 vols.; Chair. Constantine Zurayk; Exec. Sec. Walid Khalidi.

The International Documentary Center of Arab Manuscripts: Syria St., Salha and Samadi Bldg., P.O.B. 2668, Beirut; f. 1965; publishes and reproduces ancient and rare Arabic texts; Propr. Zouhair Baalbaki.

Khayat Book and Publishing Co. S.A.L.: 90-94 rue Bliss, Beirut; history, literature, economy, language, Arabic reprints; Man. Dir. Paul Khayat.

Librairie du Liban: Sq. Riad Solh, Beirut; languages and general books.

Middle East Publishing Co.: Beirut, Rue George Picot, Imm. El Kaissi; f. 1954; publishes *Medical Index* and *Revue Immobilière* (Real Estate); Man. Editor Elie Sawaf.

New Book Publishing House: Beirut.

Rihani Printing and Publishing House: Jibb En Nakhl St., Beirut; f. 1963; Propr. Albert Rihani; Man. Daoud Stephan.

Other publishing houses in Beirut include: *Dar al-Andalus, Dar Majalaat Shiir, Imprimerie Catholique, Imprimerie Universelle, Al Jamiya al Arabi, Al Kitab al Arabi, Librairie Orientale, Al Maktab al-Tijari, Middle East Stamps Inc., Mu'assasat al-Marif, Nofal and Bait at Hikmat, Saidar.*

RADIO AND TELEVISION

RADIO

Lebanese Broadcasting Station: rue Arts et Métiers, Beirut; is a part of the Ministry of Information; f. 1937; Dir.-Gen. K. Hage Ali; Technical Dir. J. Rouhayem; Dir. of Programmes N. Mikati; Head of Administration A. Aoun.

The Home Service broadcasts in Arabic on short wave, the Foreign Service broadcasts in Portuguese, Arabic, Spanish, French and English.

Number of radio receivers: 605,000.

TELEVISION

Compagnie Libanaise de Télévision (C.L.T.): P.O.B. 4848, Beirut; f. 1959; commercial service; programmes in Arabic, French and English on four channels; Pres. Dir.-Gen. General S. Nofal; Technical Man. M. S. Karimeh; Programme Dir. Paul Tannous.

Télé Orient: P.O.B. 5054, Beirut; f. 1960; Compagnie de Télévision du Liban et du Proche-Orient (S.A.L.); commercial service; programmes in Arabic, French and English on two channels (11 and 5); Acting Gen. Man. Claude Sawaya.

Number of TV receivers: 325,000.

FINANCE

(cap. = capital; p.u. = paid up; dep. = deposits; m. = million; L£ = Lebanese £; res. = reserves.)

Beirut has for long been the leading financial and commercial centre in the Middle East, as can be seen from the extensive list of banking organizations given below. However, public confidence in the banking system was strained by the closing of the Intra Bank, the largest domestic bank, late in 1966 when its liquid funds proved insufficient to cope with a run of withdrawals. The bank obtained enough guarantees to re-open in January 1968, though it is now an investment bank managed by a New York company. Before this crisis the government had passed a law stipulating a minimum capital of £L 3 million for all banks. This was followed in 1967 by a new law authorising a government take-over of a private bank facing difficulties threatening the interests and deposits of its clients; all depositors are to be paid in full by the State. This law was invoked in June 1968 when the Banque al-Ahli was taken over. The new Bank Control Commission has taken over a number of small banks and assisted in the liquidation of several others. The major foreign-owned banks now have a much larger proportion of deposits than before the Intra crisis, and a number of the major American banks have acquired interests in Beirut.

CENTRAL BANK

Banque du Liban: rue Masraf Loubnane, Beirut; P.O.B. 5544, Beirut; f. 1964; central bank; cap. L£15m.; total resources L£1,792m.

DEVELOPMENT BANK

National Bank for Industrial and Tourist Development: Beirut; f. 1973; 51 per cent government-owned.

PRINCIPAL LEBANESE BANKS

Arab Libyan Tunisian Bank S.A.L.: P.O.B. 9575, Chaker & Owen Bldg., Riad al Solh Square, Beirut; cap. p.u. L£10m.; Pres. and Gen. Man. MOHAMED ABDEL JAWAD.

Bank Almashrek S.A.L.: Bank Almashrek Bldg., Riad El Solh St. 52, Beirut; Affil. with Morgan Guaranty Trust; cap. L£15m., dep. L£64.4m. (1973); Chair. FAHD ALBAHAR; Man. Dir. RODNEY B. WAGNER.

Bank of Beirut and the Arab Countries S.A.L.: Allenby Street, P.O.B. 1536, Beirut; f. 1957; cap. L£5m., dep. L£108.3m. (1972); Chair. TOUFIC S. ASSAF; Vice-Chair. and Gen. Man. NASHAT SHEIKH EL-ARD; Joint Gen. Man. AMIN M. ALAMEH.

Banque al-Ahli (Banque Nationale) Foncière, Commerciale et Industrielle S.A.L.: Rue Foch, Beirut, P.O.B. 2868; f. 1953; cap. L£10m.; res. L£3.16m.; Pres. and Gen. Man. BOUTROS EL KHOURY (*see note above*).

Banque Audi S.A.L.: rue Al Arz, Imm. Beydoun, P.O.B. 2560; f. 1928; cap. p.u. L£10m.; dep. L£173.2m. (1972); Gen. Man. GEORGES OIDIH AUDI.

Banque de Crédit Agricole, Industriel et Foncier: Beirut; f. 1954; Dir.-Gen. Sheikh BOUTROS EL KHOURY; took over several banks in 1967–68, including Banque de l'Economie Arabe, Banque d'Epargne and Union National Bank.

Banque de Crédit National S.A.L.: rue Allenby, Beirut, P.O.B. 204; f. 1959; cap. and reserves L£4.1m.; dep. L£20.7m. (Dec. 1972); Pres. and Gen. Man. EDMOND J. SAFRA; Deputy Gen. Man. HENRI KRAYEM.

Banque de l'Industrie et du Travail, S.A.L.: B.P. 3948, rue Riad Solh, Beirut; f. 1961; cap. L£10m.; dep. L£103m. (1973); Chair. LAURA E. BUSTANI; Gen. Man. W. F. GOSLING, O.B.E.

Banque du Liban et d'Outre-Mer (S.A.): ave. Foch, P.O.B. 1912, Beirut; f. 1951; cap. p.u. L£8m., dep. L£245.4m. (Dec. 1972); Chair., Gen. Man. Dr. NAAMAN AZHARI.

Banque de la Méditerranée S.A.L.: P.O.B. 348, Beirut; f 1944; cap. L£5m.; dep. L£74m. (1972); Pres. JOSEPH S. NAGGEAR; Gen. Man. JOSEPH A. EL-KHOURY.

Banque Française pour le Moyen-Orient S.A.L.: P.O.B. 393, Imm. Starco, Rue Omar Daouk, Beirut; f. 1971 to take over branches in Lebanon of Société Centrale de Banque; affil. to Banque de l'Indochine; cap. L£5m.; total resources L£212.7m. (Dec. 1971); Pres. and Gen. Man. RENÉ BOUSQUET.

Banque Libanaise pour le Commerce S.A.L.: P.O.B. 1126, rue Riad El-Solh, Beirut; f. 1950; cap. L£5m.; res. L£12.3m. (Dec. 1972); Man. JEAN FARES SAAD ABI-JOUADE.

Banque Libano-Bresilienne S.A.L.: P.O.B. 3310, Maarad St., Beirut; f. 1962; cap. L£5m.; res. L£1.3m. (Dec. 1973); Gen. Man. J. A. GHOSN.

Banque Libano-Française S.A.L.: P.O.B. 808, Sehnaoui Building, Riad el Solh St., Beirut; f. 1968; took over Lebanese branches of Compagnie Française de Credit de Banque; cap. L£5m., dep. L£354.8m. (Dec. 1972); Chair. JEAN GILBERT; Gen. Man. FARID RAPHAEL.

Banque Sabbag S.A.L.: P.O.B. 144, Sabbag Centre, Hamra, Beirut; f. 1880 as H. Sabbag et Fils, since 1950 a joint stock company with Banque de L'Indochine and Banca Commerciale Italiana; cap. L£6m., dep. L£132m. (1973); Chair. PAUL-MARIE CRONIER.

Banque Saradar S.A.L.: Kassatly Bldg., Fakhry Bey St., Beirut, P.O.B. 1121; f. 1948; cap. p.u. L£3m.; dep. L£73.8m. (1973); Pres.-Gen. Man. JOE MARIUS SARADAR; Asst. Gen. Man. ABDO I. JEFFI.

Banque G. Trad (Crédit Lyonnais) S.A.L.: Weygand St., Beirut; f. 1951; cap. L£3m.; dep. L£228.4m. (Dec. 1972); Pres. G. A. TRAD.

Beirut-Riyad Bank S.A.L.: Beirut-Riyad Bank Bldg., Riad Solh St., P.O.B. 4668, Beirut; f. 1959; cap. p.u. L£12.5m.; dep. L£175m. (Dec. 1973); Pres. and Gen. Man. HUSSEIN MANSOUR.

Continental Development Bank, S.A.L.: Beydoun Bldg., Arz St., Beirut, P.O.B. 3270; f. 1961; cap. L£8m.; Chair. and Gen. Man. RICHARD K. O. CAREY.

Federal Bank of Lebanon S.A.L.: Parliament Square, P.O.B. 2209, Beirut; f. 1952; cap. L£10m.; Pres. M. SAAB; Vice-Pres. A. FARID M. SAAB; Mans. G. A. KHOURY, A. B. ATAMIAN.

MEBCO BANK—Middle East Banking Co. S.A.L.: B.P. 3540, Beydoun Bldg., Beirut; f. 1959; cap. p.u. L£6.25m.; dep. L£48m. (1973); Chair. M. J. BEYDOUN.

Rifbank S.A.L.: Head Office: P.O.B. 5727, rue Kantari Beirut; f. 1965; in association with Commerzbank A.G., The National Bank of Kuwait S.A.K., The Commercial Bank of Kuwait S.A.K.; cap. p.u. L£4m.; dep. L£117m. (1973); Chair. A. A. BASSAM; Man. G. H. CLAYTON, F.I.B.

Société Bancaire du Liban S.A.L.: rue Allenby, Beirut; P.O.B. 435; f. 1899; cap. p.u. and reserves L£4m.; dep. L£70.57m. (Dec. 1973); Chair. S. LAWI (LEVY).

Société Générale Libano-Européenne de Banque S.A.L.: P.O.B. 2955, Beirut; f. 1953; cap. p.u. L£5m., dep. L£185m. (1972); Chair. A. M. SEHNAOUI; Gen. Man. GÉRARD GLORIEUX.

Société Nouvelle de la Banque de Syrie et du Liban S.A.L.: P.O.B. 957, Beirut; f. 1963; cap. p.u. L£10.4m.; Pres. GUY TRANCART.

Trans Orient: Beirut; f. 1966; cap. p.u. L£3m.; joint venture with the International Bank of Washington and Lebanese private investors.

PRINCIPAL FOREIGN BANKS

Algemene Bank Nederland N.V. (*General Bank of the Netherlands*): Amsterdam; P.O.B. 3012, Beirut; brs. in 35 countries outside the Netherlands.

Arab Bank Ltd.: Amman; Beirut Main Branch: Riad Solh St., Beirut; f. 1930.

Banco del Atlántico: Barcelona 8, Spain; Arab Bank Bldg., Riad Solh St., Beirut.

Banco di Roma: Rome, Italy; Beirut.

Bank of America (National Trust and Savings Assen.): San Francisco; f. 1904; P.O.B. 3965, Beirut; Man. C. HOLLANDER.

Bank of Nova Scotia: Toronto, Ont.; Riad el Solh St., P.O.B. 4446, Beirut.

Bank of Tokyo: Tokyo; Arab Bank Bldg., P.O.B. 1187, Beirut; Reps. Y. MORIMOTO, K. KATO.

Bank Saderat Iran: Teheran, Iran; Beirut Branch, P.O.B. 5126, Beirut.

Bankers Trust Co.: New York, U.S.A.; Shaker Oueini Bldg., Place Riad Solh, P.O.B. 6239, Beirut; f. 1903; Vice-Pres. Resident Rep. MUHAMMAD SALEEM.

Banque Libano-Française-Beyrouth: 1 Rue Riad El Solh; f. 1968; cap. p.u. L£5m.; dep. L£305m. (Dec. 1972); Pres. and Chair. JEAN GIBERT; Dir. and Gen. Man. FARID RAPHAEL.

Banque pour le Développement Commercial: Geneva, Switzerland; Beirut.

Bayerische Vereinsbank: Munich; K.L.M. Bldg., rue de l'Armee, Beirut; Rep. PETER SCHMID-LOSSBERG; also representing Berliner Bank A.G., Frankfurter Bank, Norddeutsche Kreditbank A.G., Westfalenbank A.G.

Berliner Bank: Berlin; Beirut (see Bayerische Vereinsbank).

British Bank of the Lebanon: rue Trablos, P.O.B. 7048, Beirut; f. 1971; dep. L£26.6m. (1972); subsidiary of British Bank of the Middle East; Chair. J. C. KELLY, O.B.E.; Man. Z. N. AUDEH.

British Bank of the Middle East: London; Beirut; brs. at Ras Beirut, St. George's Bay, Mazra'a and Tripoli.

Chase Manhattan Bank, N.A.: New York; P.O.B. 3684, Beirut; Vice-Pres. ADOLF KNUL; Rep. CHARLES L. WIDNEY.

Chemical Bank: 20 Pine St., New York 10015; P.O.B. 7286, Riad el Solh St., Beirut; Rep. MICHAEL DAVIS.

Commercial Bank of Czechoslovakia Ltd.: Prague, Czechoslovakia; Middle East Office: B.P. 5928, Beirut.

Commerzbank A.G.: Düsseldorf, Frankfurt, Hamburg, Berlin, German Federal Republic; P.O. Box 3246, Beirut; Rep. KLAUS TJADEN.

Dresdner Bank A.G.: Frankfurt/Main, Federal Republic of Germany; Imm. Starco, B.P. 4831, Beirut; Reps. M. S. HADDAD and REINER AURICH.

First National City Bank: New York, N.Y. 10022; P.O.B. 3648, Beirut; Gen. Man. MICHAEL A. CALLEN.

Frankfurter Bank: Frankfurt, German Federal Republic; P.O.B. 3247, Beirut (see Bayerische Vereinsbank).

Habib Bank (Overseas) Ltd.: Karachi, Pakistan; Beirut.

Jordan National Bank, S.A.: Amman, Jordan; Beirut, Tripoli and Saida.

Manufacturers Hanover Trust Co.: New York; B.I.T. Bldg., Riad el-Solh St., Beirut; Rep. HASSAN HUSSEINI.

Morgan Guaranty Trust Co.: New York, U.S.A.; P.O.B. 5752, Beirut-Riyad Bank Bldg., rue Riyad Solh, Beirut; Rep. in Middle East P. J. DE ROOS.

Moscow Narodny Bank Ltd.: Head Office: London, E.C.4; Beirut Branch: P.O.B. 5481, Beirut; Man. in Beirut T. ALIBEKOV.

National Bank of China: the Government of the People's Republic of China announced in January 1972 that a branch was to be opened in Beirut.

Norddeutsche Kreditbank: Bremen, German Federal Republic; Beirut (see Bayerische Vereinsbank).

Rafidain Bank: Head Office: Baghdad, Iraq; Beirut Branch: Bazirkan Souk, Beirut, P.O.B. 1891; f. 1941.

Royal Bank of Canada (Middle East) S.A.L.: Lebanon; P.O.B. 2520, SFAH Bldg., Kantari, Beirut.

Saudi National Commercial Bank: Jeddah, Saudi Arabia; P.O.B. 2355, Beirut; f. 1938.

The Chartered Bank: London; P.O.B. 3996, Riad el Solh St., Beirut; Man. in Beirut G. R. LOVELL.

Westfalenbank: Bochum, German Federal Republic; Beirut (see Bayerische Vereinsbank).

Association of Banks in Lebanon: Army St., P.O.B. 967, Beirut; f. 1959; 87 mems.; Pres. JOSEPH GEAGEA; Gen. Sec. Dr. PIERRE NASRALLAM.

INSURANCE

NATIONAL COMPANIES

"La Phenicienne" (S.A.L.) (formerly al Ahli): Centre Géfinor, rue Clemenceau, P.O.B. 5652, Beirut; f. 1964; Chair., Gen. Man. ANTOINE K. FEGALY; Dep. Gen. Man. NICOLAS MAASSAB.

al-Ittihad al-Watani: Head Office: Immeuble Fattal, P.O.B. 1270, Beirut; Chair. JOE I. KAIROUZ.

Arabia Insurance Co. Ltd. S.A.L.: Arabia House, Phoenicia St., P.O.B. 2172, Beirut; Gen. Man. BADR S. FAHOUM.

Commercial Insurance Co., S.A.L.: Starco Centre, P.O. Box 4351, Beirut; f. 1962; Chair. J. SABET; Gen. Man. R. M. ZACCAR.

Compagnie Libanaise d'Assurances (S.A.L.): Riad El Solh Street, P.O. Box 3685, Beirut; f. 1951; Managing Dir. JEAN F. S. ABIJAOUDÉ; Man. PEDRO J. S. ABIJAOUDÉ.

Some twenty of the major European companies are also represented in Beirut.

TRADE AND INDUSTRY

CHAMBERS OF COMMERCE AND INDUSTRY

Beirut Chamber of Commerce and Industry: Ayass Bldg., Allenby St., P.O.B. 1801, Beirut; f. 1898; 7,000 mems.; Pres. KAMAL JABRE; Gen. Dir. WALID AHDAB; publ. The Lebanese and Arab Economy (twenty issues per annum).

Tripoli Chamber of Commerce and Industry: Tripoli.

Sidon Chamber of Commerce and Industry: Sidon.

Zahlé Chamber of Commerce and Industry: Zahlé; f. 1939; 497 mems.; Pres. ALFRED SKAFF.

Association des Industriels du Liban: Beirut.

EMPLOYERS' ASSOCIATIONS

Association of Lebanese Industrialists: Chamber of Commerce and Industry Bldg., Justinian St., P.O.B. 1520, Beirut.

Conseil National du Patronat: Beirut; f. 1965.

TRADE UNION FEDERATIONS

Confédération Générale des Travailleurs du Liban (C.G.T.L.): Beirut; confederation of the following four federations; Pres. GABRIEL KHOURY.

Federation of Independent Trade Unions: Central Bldg., rue Mère Galace, Beirut; f. 1954; estimated 6,000 mems. in 7 trade unions; affiliated to Confed. of Arab

T.U.'s; Pres. Mohamed el-Assir; Sec.-Gen. Ali Hourani; publ. *Sawt al 'Amel.*

Federation of Unions of Workers and Employees of North Lebanon: Al-Ahram Building, Abu-Wadi Square, Tripoli; f. 1954; affiliated to Confed. of Arab T.U.'s; 3,700 mems. in 14 trade unions; Pres. Moustafa Hamzi; Sec.-Gen. Khaled Baradi; publ. *Al A'mel.*

Ligue des Syndicats des Employés et des Ouvriers dans la République Libanaise (*League of Trade Unions of Employees and Workers in the Lebanese Republic*): Immeuble Rivoli Place des Canons, Beirut; f. 1946; estimated 6,000 mems. in 21 trade unions; affiliated to ICFTU; Pres. Hussein Ali Hussein; Vice-Pres. Halim

Mattar; Sec.-Gen. Fouad Kharanouh; Foreign Sec. Antoine Chiha; Del. to ICFTU and mem. ot Exec. Cttee. Antoine Chiha; publ. *Al-Awassef.*

United Unions for Employees and Workers: Imm. Waqf Bzoummar, rue Béchara el Khoury, Beirut, B.P. 3636; f. 1952; affiliated to ICFTU; 16,000 mems. in 21 trade unions; Pres. Gabriel Khoury; Sec.-Gen. Antoine Aoun; publ. *La Gazette.*

RESEARCH CENTRE

ICFTU Trade Union Research Centre: P.O.B. 3180, Beirut; f. 1964.

TRANSPORT

RAILWAYS

Office des Chemins de Fer de l'Etat Libanais et du Transport en Commun de Beyrouth et de sa Banlieue: Head Office: P.O.B. 109, Beirut; since 1960, all railways in Lebanon have been state-owned. There are 335 km. of standard-gauge railway and 82 km. of narrow-gauge local lines; Chair. Afif Salman; Interim Dir.-Gen. Antoine Barouki.

ROADS

Lebanon has 7,100 km. of roads, of which 1,990 km. are main roads. Most are generally good by Middle Eastern standards. The two international motorways are the north-south coastal road and the road connecting Beirut with Damascus in Syria. Among the major roads are that crossing the Bekaa and continuing South to Bent-Jbail and the Chtaura-Baalbek road. Hard-surfaced roads connect Jezzine with Moukhtara, Bzebdine with Metn, Meyroub with Afka and Tannourine.

Automobile et Touring Club du Liban: Immeuble Fattal, rue du Port, P.O.B. 3545, Beirut.

SHIPPING

Beirut is the principal port of call for the main shipping and forwarding business of the Levant. Tripoli, the northern Mediterranean terminus of the oil pipeline from Iraq (the other is Haifa), is also a busy port, with good equipment and facilities. Saida is still relatively unimportant as a port.

There are many shipping companies and agents in Beirut. The following are some of the largest:

"Adriatica" S.p.A.N.: Rue Riad E. Solh, Immeuble Gellad, Beirut, P.O.B. 1472; Dir. Aldo Silli.

American Lebanese Shipping Co. S.A.L.: P.O.B. 215, Imm. Fattal, rue du Port, Beirut; f. 1951; Pres. P. Paratore.

American Levant Shipping & Distributing Co.: P.O.B. 1429, Rue Patriarch Hoyek, Immeuble Anwar Dassouki & Co.; agents for: Holland America Line, Lykes Bros. Steamship Co., Prudential Steamship Corpn., Chevron Shipping Co., Ciro Pellegrino & Figlio, Bermare—Marittima di Navigazione; branches and correspondents throughout Middle East; Man. Dir. Samir Ishak.

Arab Shipping and Chartering Co.: P.O.B. 1084; agents for China National Chartering Corpn., China Ocean Shipping Co., Kiu Lee Shipping Co. Ltd., Chinese-Tanzanian Joint Shipping Co.

Ets. René Balgis: Port St., P.O.B. 806; agents for: Hellenic Mediterranean Lines Ltd. (Piraeus), Linea "C" (Genoa), Home Lines (Genoa), Sun Lines (Athens), Uiterwyk Shipping Ltd. (Tampa, Florida), Charles Thorburn (Udwalla, Sweden), S. Livanos Shipbrokers Ltd. (London) and many other companies.

Catoni & Co. S.A.L.: P.O.B. 800, rue du Port; f. 1960; Chair. H. J. Beard; agents for: British Maritime Agencies (Levant) Ltd., Royal Netherlands Steamship Co., Lloyd's.

Ets. Derviche Y. Haddad: rue Derviche Haddad, P.O.B. 42; agents for: Armement Deppe, Antwerp and Compagnie Maritime Belge, Antwerp.

Daher & Cie. S.A.L.: Byblos Bldg., Place des Martyrs, P.O.B. 254; agents for: Cie. de Navigation Daher, Concordia Line, Navale et Commerciale Havraise Peninsulaire, Société Maritime des Petroles B.P., Cie Navale des Petroles, Cie. Générale Transatlantique, Nouvelle Cie. de Paquebots, Sudcargos.

O. D. Debbas & Sons: Head Office: Sahmarani Bldg., Kantary St., P.O.B. 3, Beirut; Man. Dir. Elie O. Debbas.

British Maritime Agencies (Levant) Ltd.: rue du Port, agents for: Ellerman and Papayanni Line Ltd., Ellerman's Wilson Line Ltd., Prince Line Ltd., etc.

Fauzi Jemil Ghandour: P.O.B. 1084; agents for: Denizçilik Bankası T.A.O. (Denizyolları), D.B. Deniz Nakliyatı T.A.Ş. (Dbcargo), Iraqi Maritime Transport Co.

T. Gargour & Fils: rue Foch, P.O.B. 371; f. 1928; agents for: Assoc. Levant Lines S.A.L.; Dirs. Nicolas T. Gargour, Habib T. Gargour.

Henry Heald & Co. S.A.L.: Im. Fattal, Rue du Port, P.O.B. 64; f. 1837; agents for: Canadian Pacific Lines, Nippon Yusen Kaisha, P. & O. Group, Royal Mail Lines, Scandinavian Near East Agency, Vanderzee Shipping Agency, Worms and Co.; Chair. J. L. Joly; Dirs. G. Hani, M. J. H. Moffett.

Hitti Frères: Rue de Phenicie, P.O.B. 511; airlines and shipping agents.

Khedivial Mail Line: Rue du Port.

Raymond A. Makzoumé: rue de la Marseillaise, P.O.B. 1357; agents for: Jugoslav Lines, Italian Lines, Hellenic Lines Ltd. (New York), Fenton Steamship Co. Ltd. (London).

Mena Shipping and Tourist Agency: El Arz St., Modern Bldg., P.O.B. 884, Beirut.

Messageries Maritimes: Rue Allenby, P.O. Box 880.

Rudolphe Saadé & Co., S.A.L.; Freight Office: P.O.B. 2279, Rue de la Marseillaise; Travel Office: Ave. des Français; agents for American Export Lines, Rosade Lines and Syrian Arab Airlines; f. 1964; Pres. Jacques R. Saade.

Union Shipping & Chartering Co. S.A.L.: P.O.B. 2856; agents for Yugoslav vessels.

CIVIL AVIATION

MEA (*Middle East Airlines, Air Liban*): MEA Bldgs., Airport Blvd., Beirut, P.O.B. 206; f. 1945; regular services throughout Europe, the Middle East and Africa; fleet of 3 Boeing 707, 16 Boeing 720, 1 Caravelle 6N; Pres. and Chair. Sheikh Najib Alamuddin; Gen. Man. Asad Nasr.

Trans-Mediterranean Airways (TMA): Beirut International Airport, P.O.B. 3018, Beirut; f. 1953; world-wide cargo services between Europe, Middle East, S.-E. Asia, the Far East and U.S.A., including a round-the-world cargo service; Pres. and Chair. Munir Abu-Haidar; Exec. Vice-Pres. M. V. Richmond.

The following foreign companies also operate services to Lebanon: Aeroflot, Air Algérie, Air France, Air India, Alia, Alitalia, Ariana Afghan Airlines, AUA, British Airways, CSA, EgyptAir, Ethiopian, Garuda, Ghana Airways, Iberia, Interflug, Iranair, Iraqi Airways, JAL, JAT, KLM, Kuwait Airways, Libyan Arab Airlines, LOT, Lufthansa, Malev, Olympic Airways, Pan American, PIA, Sabena, SAS, Saudia, Sudan Airways, Swissair, Syrian Arab Airlines, Tarom (Romania), THY (Turkey), TWA, UTA, Varig, Viasa and Yemen Republic Airlines.

TOURISM

Ministry of Tourism: P.O.B. 5344, Beirut, f. 1966; official organization; Dir.-Gen. Dr. Hassan El Hassan.

National Council of Tourism: P.O.B. 3544, rue de la Banque du Liban, Beirut; government-sponsored autonomous organization; overseas offices in New York, Paris, Frankfurt, Stockholm, Brussels and Cairo; Pres. Cheikh Habib Kayrouz; Vice-Pres. Selim Salam.

THEATRES

Baalbek Festival Modern Theatre Group: Baalbek; Dir. Mounir Abu-Debs.

National Theatre: Beirut; Dir. Nizar Mikati.

UNIVERSITIES

American University of Beirut: Beirut; 500 teachers, 4,250 students.

Beirut Arab University: Tarik El-Jadidé, P.O.B. 5020, Beirut; 163 teachers, 23,000 students.

Université Libanaise (*Lebanese University*): Bir Hassan, Beirut; 698 teachers, 14,018 students.

Université Saint Joseph: B.P. 293, Beirut; 65 teachers, 3,500 students.

Université Saint-Esprit De Kaslik: Jounieh; 117 teachers, 403 students.

LESOTHO

INTRODUCTORY SURVEY

Location, Climate, Language, Religion, Flag, Capital

The Kingdom of Lesotho, formerly the British High Commission Territory of Basutoland, is completely surrounded by the Republic of South Africa, with the Orange Free State to the north and west, Natal and Griqualand East to the east, and Cape Province to the south. Rainfall averages about 28 in. per year, mostly falling between October and April. There are two main geographic regions: the Lowlands (about 5,000–6,000 feet above sea level, in the west, and the Highlands (rising to over 11,000 feet), in the east. The official languages are English and Sesotho, the language of the Basotho people. Eighty per cent of the people of Lesotho are Basotho; and about 75 per cent are Christians, mainly Roman Catholic, Lesotho Evangelical and Anglican. The national flag (proportions 3 by 2) is blue with green and red vertical stripes at the hoist, and a white Basotho hat in the centre. The capital is Maseru.

Recent History

Basutoland's progress to independence as the Kingdom of Lesotho was initiated by the Constitution of 1959 which established representative government. On April 30th, 1965, Basutoland became self-governing under a new constitution, with a bi-cameral parliament and a ministerial council. Lesotho achieved independence within the Commonwealth on October 4th, 1966. Following the general election of January 27th, 1970, in which the opposition Congress Party claimed to have won a majority, Chief Leabua Jonathan, the Prime Minister at the time, declared a state of emergency, suspended the Constitution and arrested Mr. Ntsu Mokhehle and other leaders of the Congress Party. King Moshoeshoe II, who had previously been detained in December 1966, was also placed under house arrest and later exiled, though he returned to Lesotho in December 1970, after accepting a government order prohibiting the monarchy from participating in politics in any way. Most of those detained in January 1970 had been released by January 1972, during Chief Jonathan's declared "holiday from politics", and during 1973 there was hope of a gradual return to democracy. Political instability has recently returned with the failure of an attempted *coup*, reportedly backed by the Congress Party, and the arrest or escape of prominent Congress leaders. Strict new security laws were introduced in February 1974.

Government

The Independence Constitution was suspended in January 1970. Fresh elections are promised after the drawing up of a new constitution. In 1973 Chief Jonathan created an interim National Assembly in which his own National Party has an inbuilt majority. This remains in force but strong opposition protests followed the arbitrary manner in which it was set up. Serious unrest in early 1974 made the constitutional position extremely uncertain. Lesotho is divided into nine Districts.

Defence

Lesotho has no armed forces, but the police force of 1,500 includes some para-military units.

Economic Affairs

The economy is primarily agricultural, R20 million of the Gross Domestic Product of R58.4 million in 1971–72 being accounted for by agriculture. Development in this sphere is greatly hampered by a complicated and archaic system of land tenure. Lesotho's main exports are diamonds, wool, mohair and livestock, but the economy suffers from huge balance of payments problems, lack of natural resources, a shortage of job opportunities outside government employment, eroded land with low yields and overwhelming dependence on South Africa, where more than 100,000 of the population work as migrant labourers on five-year contracts in the mines. A hydro-electric scheme, the Malibamatso River Project, using the waters of the Oxbow Gorge, has been studied, and it has potential in the long term but the first stage of its development would cost an estimated $115 million.

Until recently half of Lesotho's revenue was made up of grants from Britain. Together with South West Africa (Namibia), Botswana and Swaziland, Lesotho forms part of the customs and monetary area of South Africa, with which Lesotho's government signed a new customs union agreement in December 1969. This replaced the principle of fixed proportions of the total revenue of the union for each member with a more complicated method of calculating the division of the revenue. It makes provision for consultation, and for some protection for infant industries in the former High Commission territories, by levying additional duties on imports. Lesotho's earnings from this agreement rose from R1.9 million in 1968–69 to R6 million in 1972–73. They now account for over 50 per cent of the country's total national revenue. The United Kingdom is still the largest aid donor. Lesotho's trade gap widened to R37.1 million in 1972.

Transport and Communications

There is no railway apart from one mile of South African Railway line at Maseru. The main road from Butha-Buthe to Quthing is 191 miles long, 90 miles, from Leribe to Tsoaing, being tarred. There are 367 miles of minor roads. The first airport, Leabua, was opened in December 1968, and there are 32 airstrips throughout the country. No international airlines serve Lesotho but there is now a scheduled twice-weekly air service to Johannesburg in South Africa.

Education

All primary education is free, and is largely in the hands of the three main missions (Lesotho Evangelical, Roman Catholic and Church of England) under the direction of the Ministry of Education. There are 1,149 schools and institutions in the country which has one of the highest literacy rates in Africa. Post-secondary education is provided by the University of Botswana, Lesotho and Swaziland, which has 724 students at the Roma branch.

Tourism

The tourist trade in Lesotho is rapidly expanding. In 1971–72 there were 60,000 visitors, and the Lesotho

National Development Corporation is planning new hotels, a national park near Maseru and a ski resort in the Maluti Mountains. The magnificent scenery and a casino are the main tourist attractions.

Visas are not required to visit Lesotho by nationals of Belgium, Commonwealth countries, Denmark, Finland, Greece, Iceland, Ireland, Israel, Italy, Japan, the Republic of Korea, Luxembourg, the Netherlands, Norway, San Marino, South Africa and Sweden.

Sport

Football is the national sport and tennis, athletics and netball are also popular.

Public Holidays

1974: August 5th (National Tree Planting Day), October 1st (National Sports Day), October 4th (National Independence Day), December 25th–26th (Christmas and Boxing Day).

1975: January 1st (New Year's Day), March 12th (Moshoeshoe's Day), March 28th–31st (Easter), May 2nd (King's Birthday), May 8th (Ascension Day), June 2nd (Commonwealth Day).

Weights and Measures

The imperial system of weights and measures is in force.

Currency

South African currency: 100 cents = 1 rand (R).

Exchange rates (April 1974):

£1 sterling = 1.581 rand;

U.S. $1 = 67.11 S.A. cents.

STATISTICAL SURVEY

AREA

11,716 square miles.

POPULATION

(1966 Census)

	MEN	WOMEN	TOTAL
African . . .	367,087	482,926	850,013
European . .	801	781	1,582
Asian . . .	367	399	766
TOTAL . .	368,255	484,106	852,361
Absentee* . .	97,529	19,744	117,273
GRAND TOTAL .	465,784	503,850	969,634

* Citizens working in South Africa.

Mid-1972 estimate: 972,000, excluding absentee workers.

Births and Deaths: Birth rate 36.7 per 1,000, death rate 14.5 per 1,000 (1973 estimates).

DISTRICTS

(1973 est.)

Each District has the same name as its chief town.

	POPULATION*
Maseru	237,800
Berea	135,600
Butha-Buthe	73,800
Leribe	187,600
Mafeteng	134,600
Mohale's Hoek	132,200
Mokhotlong	70,000
Quacha's Nek	72,300
Quthing	86,600
TOTAL	1,130,500

* Including absentee workers in South Africa.

Capital: Maseru, population 14,000 in 1966.

EMPLOYMENT

There were about 21,000 people employed in non-agricultural activities in Lesotho in 1971. During 1973, 112,989 Basotho were recruited to the gold mines and collieries in the Republic of South Africa.

Lesotho's labour force was estimated at about 535,650 persons in 1973. About 45% of the male labour force of 263,220 and 6–10% of the female labour force sought employment in South Africa. In 1966 of the resident African population of 850,013, an estimated 743,000 were dependent on agriculture.

RECRUITMENT AND REMITTANCES OF BASOTHO IN SOUTH AFRICA

	1971	1972	1973*
Numbers Recruited . .	88,012	101,515	112,989
Voluntary Deferred Pay . .	R2,689,940	R3,425,301	R4,611,224
Remittance Payments . .	R2,648,110	R2,392,874	R3,910,726

* Provisional.

AGRICULTURE

LAND USE, 1970
('000 hectares)

Arable Land	368
Permanent Meadows and Pastures . .	2,479
Other Areas	189
Total	3,036

LIVESTOCK

	1973
Sheep	1,556,900
Goats	961,900
Cattle	465,500
Pigs	75,600
Horses	114,000
Asses	97,400
Mules	2,500

PRINCIPAL CROPS
('000 metric tons)

	1969	1970	1971*
Wheat	59	58	70
Barley	3*	1	3
Maize	95	67	80
Sorghum	42	57	60
Dry Peas	15*	5	16

* Estimate.

LIVESTOCK PRODUCTS
(metric tons)

	1969	1970	1971*
Cows' Milk . .	28,000*	29,000*	30,000
Beef and Veal† .	12,000*	13,000*	13,000
Mutton and Lamb† .	10,000*	11,000*	11,000
Wool: Greasy . .	4,500	4,500	4,500
Clean . .	2,200	2,200	2,200

* FAO estimate.

† Meat from indigenous animals only, including the meat equivalent of exported live animals. Figures for mutton and lamb include goats' meat.

AGRICULTURAL EXPORTS
(1972)

Wool	kilogrammes	3,708,314
Mohair	,,	767,065
Wheat	tons	1,835
Sorghum	,,	1,240
Peas	,,	1,571
Beans	,,	2,889
Hides	number	9,478
Skins	,,	44,482

Maize Imports (bags): (1967–68) 176,200; (1968–69) 370,000; (1969–70) 360,000.

MINING
DIAMONDS
(carats)

1971 . . .	6,815
1972 . . .	9,019
1973 . . .	8,588

FINANCE

South African currency: 100 cents=1 rand (R).
Coins: ½, 1, 2, 5, 10, 20 and 50 cents.
Notes: 1, 2, 5, 10 and 20 rand.
Exchange rates (April 1974): £1 sterling=1.581 rand; U.S. $1=67.11 S.A. cents.
100 rand=£63.27=$149.00.

BUDGET
('000 rand, years ending March 31st)

Revenue	1970–71	1971–72	Expenditure	1970–71	1971–72
Taxes	1,908	2,358	Education	2,971†	2,228
Customs and Excise*	6,317	5,932	Agriculture	1,083	1,237
Posts and Telecommunications	534	737	Health and Social Welfare	n.a.	1,028
Licences and Duties	448	472	Police	1,558	1,525
Fees of Court or Office	144	145	Public Works	982	1,107
Judicial Fines	74	87	Interior	495	457
Earnings of Departments	647	676	Justice	415	430
Interest	78	66	Finance	1,299	1,088
Rents from Government Property	171	181	Prisons	385	367
Miscellaneous	376	442	Posts and Telecommunications	411	514
Reimbursements	24	37	Prime Minister's Office	831	988
			Foreign Affairs	387	462
Total	10,721	11,133	Other Departments	169	143
Grant in Aid	395	1,206			
Overseas Service Aid Scheme	122	71	Total Controllable Expenditure	10,986	11,574
British Exchequer Loan	171	—	All Other Items	1,266	867
Total Revenue	11,409	12,410	Total Expenditure	12,252	12,441

* Lesotho is a member of the South African Customs Union, and receives a percentage of the total revenue collected.

† Including Health and Social Welfare.

BALANCE OF PAYMENTS—GLOBAL SUMMARY
(Rand '000)

	1971–72		
	Credit	Debit	Balance
Goods and Services	13,931	35,941	−22,010
Transfer Payments	12,550	134	12,416

EXTERNAL TRADE
(Rand million)

	1968	1969	1970	1971	1972
Imports	23.9	23.9	22.8	27.9	43.3
Exports	3.4	4.0	3.7	2.1	6.2

COMMODITIES
(Rand '000)

IMPORTS		1970	1971
Foodstuffs and Livestock	.	5,982	5,640
Beverages and Tobacco	.	1,116	1,256
Crude Materials	.	314	579
Mineral Fuels and Lubricants	.	1,476	1,723
Animal and Vegetable Oils	.	198	277
Chemicals	.	1,273	1,845
Manufactured Goods	.	3,983	5,912
Machinery and Transport Equipment	.	3,058	4,114
Miscellaneous Manufactured Goods	.	4,816	5,989
Commodities n.e.s.	.	590	662
TOTAL . . .	.	22,806	27,997

EXPORTS		1970	1971
Livestock and Foodstuffs:			
Cattle	.	684	606
Sheep	.	104	87
Other Live Animals	.	33	7
Wheat	.	927	140
Peas and Beans	.	127	187
Other Foodstuffs	.	11	12
TOTAL .	.	1,886	1,039
Crude Materials:			
Wool	.	547	322
Mohair	.	416	325
Hides and Skins	.	24	22
Diamonds	.	652	241
Other	.	11	3
TOTAL .	.	3,536	1,952
TOTAL OTHER EXPORTS	.	180	245
TOTAL EXPORTS	.	3,716	2,197

Most trade is with the Republic of South Africa, detailed figures for trade by countries are not available.

TRANSPORT

MOTOR VEHICLE REGISTRATION
(1972)

Total 5,972; Private Cars 1,956, Vans 1,439, Landrovers 591, Trucks 547, Buses 135, Tractors 818, Motor Cycles 145, Trailers 341.

EDUCATION
(1972)

	SCHOOLS	ENROLMENT
Primary . . .	1,085	176,404
Secondary . .	40	8,873
Teachers Training Colleges .	7	510
Technical and Vocational Schools . . .	16	623
Universities . . .	1	169

Source: Bureau of Statistics, Maseru (except where otherwise stated).

THE CONSTITUTION

(The Constitution was suspended in January 1970 and a new one is being drawn up.)

The King, Motlotlehi Moshoeshoe II, is Head of State and constitutional monarch. The executive body is the Cabinet consisting of the Prime Minister and not fewer than 7 other Ministers. There are two houses in the Parliament. The Senate contains the 22 principal chiefs and 11 other persons nominated by the King.

The National Assembly has 60 members elected by universal adult suffrage in 60 single member constituencies. The Prime Minister must be able to command majority support in the National Assembly. If challenged, the government must establish in the courts, that where there are several ways of achieving its objective, the means least restrictive of civil liberties has been chosen.

In March 1973 Chief Jonathan said that Lesotho would return to parliamentary rule with an interim national assembly of nominated members. The Assembly was inaugurated on April 27th, and incorporates the Senate making provision for 93 members. The State of Emergency was lifted in July 1973, but stringent new security measures, such as the Internal Security Bill of February 1974, were subsequently introduced.

THE GOVERNMENT

Head of State: His Majesty King Moshoeshoe II (christened Constantine Bereng Seeiso).

COUNCIL OF MINISTERS

(*July* 1974)

Prime Minister, Defence and Internal Security, Chief of Electoral Affairs: Chief J. Leabua Jonathan.

Deputy Prime Minister and Minister of Works, Posts and Telecommunications: Chief Sekhonyana N. 'Maseribane.

Minister of Foreign Affairs: J. R. Kotsokoane.

Minister of the Interior: J. Monaleli.

Minister of Finance: Rets 'Ilisitsoe Sekhonyana.

Minister of Commerce and Industry: J. Moitse.

Minister of Justice: C. D. Molapo.

Minister of Health: Chief Patrick Mota.

Minister of Education: A. F. Ralebitso.

Minister of Agriculture: Chief Peete N. Peete.

Minister to the Prime Minister: Gabriel C. Manyeli.

Ministers of State: Chief Tlohang Lerotholi, J. Khasoane.

Minister of State attached to Minister of Health: J. Mothepu.

DIPLOMATIC REPRESENTATION

EMBASSIES AND HIGH COMMISSIONS ACCREDITED TO LESOTHO
(E) Embassy; (HC) High Commission.

Austria: Pretoria, South Africa (E).
Belgium: Pretoria, South Africa (E).
Canada: Pretoria, South Africa (HC).

China (Taiwan): Maseru (E); *Ambassador:* Ta-jen Livo.
France: Lusaka, Zambia (E).
Germany, Federal Republic: Blantyre, Malawi (E).
Ghana: Nairobi, Kenya (HC).
India: Blantyre, Malawi (HC).
Iran: Johannesburg, South Africa (E).
Israel: Mbabane, Swaziland (E).
Italy: Pretoria, South Africa (E).
Japan: Nairobi, Kenya (E).
Kenya: Lusaka, Zambia (HC).
Korea, Republic: Nairobi, Kenya (E).
Netherlands: Pretoria, South Africa (E).
Nigeria: Nairobi, Kenya (HC).
Sweden: Pretoria, South Africa (E).
Switzerland: Pretoria, South Africa (E).
United Kingdom: Maseru (HC); *High Commissioner:* M. J. Moynihan, c.m.g., m.c.
U.S.A.: Maseru (E); *Chargé d'Affaires:* N. H. Frisbie.
Vatican City: Pretoria, South Africa.
Zambia: Gaborone, Botswana (HC).

PARLIAMENT

NATIONAL ASSEMBLY

Election, January 27th, 1970

Only 46 seats had been declared before a state of emergency was declared and the election results invalidated. At that time the National Party had reportedly won half the 46 seats and the Congress Party the other half.

INTERIM NATIONAL ASSEMBLY

The interim National Assembly consists of the 22 principal chiefs and 11 nominees previously in the Senate, and 60 nominated members. Seven members of the Congress Party including its leader who were nominated as members have boycotted the Assembly.

Party	Seats
Basotho National Party	34*
Opposition Parties	19†
Principal Chiefs	22
Nominees for "distinguished services" .	11
	86

* Includes 9 ministers and 3 ministers of state.
† Excludes 7 who boycotted the Assembly from the Congress Party.

There is also a College of Chiefs which has the power under traditional law to depose the king by a vote of the majority.

POLITICAL PARTIES

Basotho National Party: P.O.B. 124, Maseru; f. 1959; 80,500 mems.; Leader Chief Leabua Jonathan; Gen. Sec. Dr. K. T. Maphathe; publ. *Mareng-A-Meso*.

Congress Party: P.O.B. 111, Maseru; f. 1952; 75,000 mems.; Leader Ntsu Mokhehle; Sec.-Gen. K. Chakela; Treas.-Gen. S. R. Mokhehle; Nat. Chair. G. Khasu; publs. *Makatolle, The Range, Commentator*.

Marema Tlou Freedom Party: P.O.B. 475, Maseru; f. 1962; 50,000 mems.; Pres. (vacant); Vice-Pres. EDWIN LEANYA; Sec.-Gen. B. M. KHAKETLA.

Lesotho United Democratic Party: Nqechane, P.O. Leribe; Leader CHARLES MOFELI.

Communist Party: P.O.B. 330, Maseru; f. 1961; about 500 mems.; Sec. JOHN MOTLOHELOA; publ. *Tokoloho*.

DEFENCE

There is a small police mobile unit.

Commander: Maj. McFALL.

JUDICIAL SYSTEM

The Judicial department of the territory is the responsibility of the Minister of Justice.

Chief Justice of Lesotho: Hon. J. T. MAPETELA.

Court of Appeal. A Lesotho Court of Appeal was established after independence in 1966 to replace the previous Court of Appeal which served all three former High Commission Territories. Members of the Court of Appeal are: Justice O. D. SCHREINER (President), Justice I. A. MAISELS and Justice A. MILNE.

The High Court. This is a Superior Court of Record, and in addition to any other jurisdiction conferred by local law, possesses and exercises all the jurisdiction, power and authorities vested in a Divisional Court of the Supreme Court of South Africa. Appeals may be made to the Court of Appeal.

District Courts. Each of the nine districts possesses the following subordinate courts: Resident Magistrate Courts, or First Class, Second Class and Third Class.

Judicial Commissioners' Courts. These deal with civil and criminal appeals from Central and Local Courts. Further appeal may be made to the High Court.

Central and Local Courts. There are 71 of these courts, of which 58 are Local Courts and 13 are Central Courts which also serve as courts of appeal from the Local Courts. They have limited jurisdiction on civil and criminal cases.

RELIGION

About 75 per cent of the people are Christians.

Christian Council of Lesotho: Gen. Sec. P.O.B. 260, Maseru.

ANGLICAN

CHURCH OF THE PROVINCE OF SOUTH AFRICA

Bishop of Lesotho: P.O.B. 87, Maseru; Rt. Rev. J. J. A. ARROWSMITH MAUND, M.C., B.A

ROMAN CATHOLIC

Archdiocese of Maseru: P.O.B. 267, Maseru; 275,247 adherents; Archbishop: Most Rev. ALPHONSO LIQUORI MORAPELI.

Diocese of Leribe: P.O.B. 1, St. Monica; 87,090 adherents; Bishop: Rt. Rev. PAUL KHOARAI.

Diocese of Qacha's Nek: P.O.B. 5, Qacha's Nek; 79,149 adherents; Bishop: Rt. Rev. JOSEPH DELPHIS DE ROSIERS.

LESOTHO EVANGELICAL

President: Rev. J. M. DIAHO, P.O.B. 27, Mafeteng.

THE PRESS

Koena News: P.O.B. 358, Maseru; publ. by Dept. of Information.

Leselinyana la Lesotho: P.O.B. 7, Morija; f. 1863; Lesotho Evangelical Church; fortnightly; Sesotho, with occasional articles in English; Editor E. M. MOTUBA; circ. 22,000.

Lesotho News: P.O.B. 111, Ficksburg, Orange Free State, South Africa; f. 1927; weekly; English; Editor G. BOSCH; circ. 800.

Mareng-A-Meso: P.O.B. 557, Maseru; f. 1965; organ of the Basotho National Party; weekly; Sesotho and English; Editor Chief N. J. MOLAPO.

Moeletsi oa Basotho (*The Counsellor of Basotho*): P.O. Mazenod; f. 1933; Catholic weekly; Sesotho and English; Editor Rev. Father F. MAIROT, O.M.I.; circ. 13,500.

Mohlabani (*The Warrior*): Mohlabani Printers and Publishers, P.O.B. 65, Maseru; f. 1954; fortnightly; Sesotho and English; Editor B. M. KHAKETLA; circ. 10,000.

Molia: P.O.B. 353, Maseru; publ. by Dept. of Information; thrice weekly; circ. 15,000.

PUBLISHERS

Mazenod Institute: P.O.B. 18, Mazenod, Lesotho; f. 1931; educational and religious books; Sotho literature and dictionary; *Moeletsi oa Basotho*; Man. Father M. GAREAU, O.M.I.

Morija Sesuto Book Depot: P.O.B. 4, Morija; f. 1861; run by the Lesotho Evangelical Church; publishers and booksellers of religious works, school books, linguistic and historical books and novels mainly in Southern Sotho and English.

RADIO

Radio Lesotho: P.O.B. 552, Maseru; programmes in Sesotho and English; two medium wave transmitters and one short wave transmitter; Dir. of Broadcasting V. M. MALEBO.

Radio Station 7PA22: Catholic School Secretariat, P.O.B. 80, Maseru; one short-wave station; educational programmes in Sesotho, English and French; Dir.-Gen. M. GAREAU, O.M.I.; Mgr. F. MARIOT; Dir. Tec. B. CHABOT.

Number of radio receivers: 10,500.

FINANCE

BANKING

Barclays Bank International Ltd.: P.O.B. 115, Maseru; Man. J. A. BAMBER, Maseru; 1 sub-branch and 2 agencies; Leribe Branch, P.O.B. 121, Leribe; Man. J. R. PHELPS.

Lesotho National Development Bank: P.O.B. 999, Maseru; Man. Dir. K. H. BECHTEL.

Standard Bank Ltd.: P.O.B. 1001, Maseru; Chief Lesotho Man. G. M. TABOR; branches at Maseru, Mohale's Hoek and Maputsoe and 9 agencies.

Post Office Savings Bank: Maseru; f. 1966; dep. R2,000,000.

TRADE AND INDUSTRY

DEVELOPMENT ORGANIZATION

Lesotho National Development Corporation: P.O.B. 666, Maseru; f. 1967; first national factory, Kolonyama candle factory, opened under its auspices in September 1968; carpet and tyre-retreading factories opened early 1969; other operations include a furniture factory, potteries, two diamond prospecting operations, a fertilizer factory, a clothing factory, a diamond cutting and polishing works, a jewellery factory, a housing company, an international hotel with a gambling casino, Lesotho Airways Corporation and a training centre for motor mechanics; Chair. Prime Minister Chief LEABUA JONATHAN; Man. Dir. K. H. BECHTEL (acting).

MARKETING ORGANIZATION

Lesotho Farmers' Produce Marketing Corporation: P.O.B. 800, Maseru; f. 1971; sole organization for marketing livestock from Lesotho; agents appointed by it give farmers advance payments of up to one-half the estimated slaughter value of their stock and pay out the balance later after the animals have been resold in South Africa; the agents operate under the rules of the South African Meat Control Board; Man. Dir. THOMAS T. MAKASE.

TRADE UNIONS

Lesotho General Workers' Union: P.O.B. 322, Maseru; f. 1954; Chair. L. RAMATSOSO; Sec. A. MOFAMMERE.

Lesotho Industrial Commercial and Allied Workers' Union: P.O.B. 144, Maseru; f. 1952; Chair. R. MONESE; Sec. T. MOKHEHLE.

Lesotho Labour Organization: P.O.B. 26, Mohale's Hoek; f. 1962; Chair. J. MOHAPI; Sec. A. MOTSEKO.

Lesotho Transport and Telecommunication Workers' Union: P.O.B. 266, Maseru; f. 1959; Pres. S. RAFUTO; Sec. S. MOREKE.

Lesotho Union of Printing, Bookbinding and Allied Workers: P.O. Mazenot, Maseru; f. 1963; Pres. G. MOTEBANG; Sec. P. K. MONESE.

National Union of Construction and Allied Workers: P.O.B. 327, Maseru; f. 1967; Pres. L. PUTSOANE; Sec. T. TLALE.

Union of Employers in Lesotho: P.O.B. 79, Maseru; f. 1961; Chair. E. R. CLIFFORD; Sec. P. S. HOGGE.

Union of Shop Distributive and Allied Workers: P.O.B. 327, Maseru; f. 1966; Pres. P. BERENG; Sec. J. MOLAPO.

CO-OPERATIVE SOCIETIES

Registrar of Co-operatives: J. MOLLO (acting), P.O.B. 89, Maseru.

By the end of 1960, there were 193 co-operative societies with a total membership of about 21,000 and a turnover of roughly R204,700. The development of these societies is a Government responsibility, and the first Registrar of Co-operative Societies was appointed in 1968.

Co-op Lesotho Ltd.: Maseru.

Lesotho Co-operative Savings Society: P.O.B. 167, Maseru; Sec. J. NTBELE.

TRANSPORT

RAILWAYS

The territory is linked with the railway system of the Republic of South Africa by a short line from Maseru to Marseilles on the Bloemfontein/Natal main line.

ROADS

The main road system, 560 miles, is principally confined to the western lowlands. A 90-mile stretch of the main lowland road, from Leribe in the north to Tsoaing, past Maseru, has been bitumenized and is now all-weather. Other parts of this road are being improved to an all-weather gravel surface. Many other new roads, principally in the mountains, are being constructed under self-help campaigns, and the government has given top priority to road construction. There are 367 miles of minor roads serving trading stations and Basotho villages; these are maintained by the traders and subsidized by the government. There are about 1,600 miles of bridle paths which are constructed and maintained by the Basotho Administration.

CIVIL AVIATION

Lesotho Airways Corporation: P.O.B. 861, Maseru; f. 1971; successor to Lesotho Airways (Pty.) Ltd.; fleet of one Cessna 337, two Cessna 206, one Cessna 205 and two Cessna 180; Chair. H. M. NTS'ABA; Gen. Man. M. S. PIKE.

There are 32 air strips in Lesotho, with scheduled charter, tourist, government communications and mail services between Maseru and all the main centres. There is also a scheduled passenger service (thrice weekly), using HS 748 pressurized aircraft, between Maseru and Jan Smuts Airport, near Johannesburg, operated jointly by Lesotho National Airways and South African Airways.

UNIVERSITY

The University of Botswana, Lesotho and Swaziland: P.O. Roma, Lesotho; f. 1964; 127 teachers, 724 students (1973).

LIBERIA

INTRODUCTORY SURVEY

Location, Climate, Language, Religion, Flag, Capital

The Republic of Liberia lies on the west coast of Africa with Sierra Leone and Guinea to the north and the Ivory Coast to the east. The climate is tropical with temperatures ranging from 65°F (18°C) to 120°F (49°C). English is the official language but the 28 tribes speak their own languages and dialects. Liberia is officially a Christian state, though some Liberians hold traditional beliefs. There are about 200,000 Muslims. The national flag (proportions 19 by 10) has 11 horizontal stripes, alternately of red and white, with a navy blue square canton, containing a five-pointed white star, in the top left-hand corner. The capital is Monrovia.

Recent History

Liberia has played a leading part in African affairs and in 1961 initiated the meeting of twenty African nations in Monrovia which founded the Inter-African and Malagasy States Organization (the Monrovia Group), subsequently re-formed as Organisation Commune Africaine et Malgache—(OCAM). President Tubman, in office since 1944, died in July 1971, and was succeeded by his Vice-President, William R. Tolbert. There have been no major changes of policy since he took office. The "open door" policy of the late President, William Tubman, remains in force and, although President Tolbert constantly emphasizes Liberia's African identity, the country continues its close alliance with the U.S.A.

Government

The Constitution is based on that of the United States. Executive power lies with the President, assisted by a Vice-President and Cabinet. The bi-cameral legislature consists of the Senate of 18 members and the House of Representatives of 52 members. The President is elected for an initial eight-year term and may stand for re-election every four years. The country is divided into the Coastal Region of five Counties and the Hinterland of four Counties. Each County is headed by a Superintendent appointed by the President.

Defence

The armed forces of Liberia consist of a National Guard of about 5,000 men, a para-military force of 1,300 men and a Coastguard Service. Military service commences at the age of sixteen. The United States provides technical assistance. In 1967 the number of regiments was increased to seventeen.

Economic Affairs

The economy is predominantly agricultural, about 90 per cent of the population living on the land. Much farming is at subsistence level, but there are plantations producing chiefly rubber. Other crops include cassava, maize, rice, cocoa, coffee and palm oil. Timber resources are vast and since 1967 timber production has increased tenfold. The country is rich in iron ore, which as an export far exceeds the value of rubber, Liberia's traditional export. In 1970 73.2 per cent of Liberia's total export earnings came from iron ore and diamonds. A free zone embracing Liberia, Guinea, Ivory Coast and Sierra Leone came into being in March 1965, though these countries receive only one per cent of Liberia's exports. Liberia's economy has expanded very fast as a result of her "open door" policy to foreign investors. The Liberian-American-Swedish Minerals Company (LAMCO) has exploited the biggest iron ore deposits, constructed Africa's first pelletizing plant at Buchanan, a new port at Buchanan and a 170-mile railway as part of the Nimba project. Foreign investment in Liberia, particularly in mining, is vast, totalling some $800 million. This has led to a difficult budgetary situation and much inequality of wealth, in spite of excellent trade returns. In 1972 exports, at $224 million, far exceeded imports, which totalled $179 million. Liberia receives large quantities of aid, mostly from the United States.

Transport and Communications

The railways are used to carry iron ore to the coast and a passenger service was introduced in 1964. New roads are being constructed and a highway crossing the country from west to east was completed late in 1963. Most roads, however, are poor in quality. There are nine ports including the deep-water berths at Monrovia. A large number of vessels based on many countries are registered as belonging to the Liberian merchant fleet. In 1967 this became the world's largest merchant fleet, and in 1970 it totalled more than 33 million gross tons. Liberian National Airways and foreign lines operate internal and international air services.

Social Welfare

The only state social welfare service is the free care of children until the age of two. Initiating this in October 1972, President Tolbert said this was the first step towards the formation of a state welfare system. The state runs a number of hospitals and others are operated by U.S. Missionary Societies.

Education

Liberia still spends a lower proportion of her total expenditure on education than most other African countries do, but the education programme is being expanded. Literacy is estimated at 15 per cent. Enrolment in government schools in 1973 was about 128,000, an increase of 30 per cent over 1971, and tuition is free. Secondary education is mostly subsidized also, and there is a university with about 1,000 students.

Tourism

Tourism is slowly being developed, though communications outside Monrovia are poor and this is a major hindrance to expansion as is the scarcity of funds for tourist facilities.

Visas are required by all nationalities.

Sport

Football and athletics are the most popular sports.

Public Holidays

1974: August 24th (National Flag Day), November 7th (Thanksgiving Day), December 1st (Matilda Newport Day), December 25th (Christmas).

1975: January 1st (New Year's Day), January 7th (Pioneers' Day), February 11th (Armed Forces Day), March 12th (Decoration Day), March 15th (J. J. Roberts' Day), March 28th–31st (Easter), April 11th (Fast and Prayer Day), May 14th (National Unification Day), May 25th (African Liberation Day), July 26th (Independence Day).

Weights and Measures

Imperial weights and measures, modified by United States usage, are in force.

Currency and Exchange Rates

100 cents=1 Liberian dollar (L$).

Exchange rates (April 1974):

£1 sterling=L$2.36;
U.S. $1=L$ 1.00.

STATISTICAL SURVEY

AREA AND POPULATION

AREA	POPULATION (February 1974)	
sq. miles	Total	MONROVIA (capital)
43,000	1,496,000	180,000

Foreign Population (1964): 30,818.

Births and Deaths (1969–70): Annual birth rate 51 per 1,000, death rate 16 per 1,000.

EMPLOYMENT

ECONOMICALLY ACTIVE POPULATION (1962 census)*

	MALE	FEMALE	TOTAL
Agriculture, Forestry, Hunting and Fishing .	194,581	138,536	333,117
Mining	14,071	370	14,441
Manufacturing	7,730	742	8,472
Construction	11,852	180	12,032
Electricity, Gas and Water . . .	366	9	375
Commerce	7,604	3,936	11,540
Transport and Communications . .	3,683	94	3,777
Services	21,230	3,708	24,938
Others	2,443	659	3,102
TOTAL	263,560	148,234	411,794

* Excluding armed forces.

Source: Bureau of Statistics, National Planning Agency, *Statistical Newsletter.*

AGRICULTURE

LAND USE, 1964

('000 hectares)

Arable and Under Permanent Crops .	3,850
Permanent Meadows and Pastures . .	240
Forest	3,622
Other Land	1,919
Inland Water . . .	1,506
TOTAL . . .	11,137

Source: FAO, *Production Yearbook.*

LIBERIA—(Statistical Survey)

PRINCIPAL CROPS
(metric tons)

	1970	1971	1972
Cassava (Manioc)	370,000*	n.a.	n.a.
Rice (Paddy)	138,000	91,000	n.a.
Maize	33,000*	33,000*	n.a.
Natural Rubber (dry weight)† . .	83,400	74,200	82,972
Palm Kernels†	14,100	16,600	4,496
Coffee	5,100	4,500	5,594
Cocoa Beans	1,800‡	1,800‡	3,184†

Palm oil production (1963): 41,200 metric tons.

* FAO estimate.   † Exports only.   ‡ Twelve months ending September.

Source: mainly FAO, *Production Yearbook 1971.*

ACREAGE AND PRODUCTION OF RUBBER CONCESSIONS AND PRIVATE RUBBER FARMS
(lb. dry rubber content—1972)

ENTERPRISE	LOCATION	ACREAGE UNDER RUBBER	ACREAGE IN PRODUCTION	PRODUCTION
Firestone Plantations Company . . .	Harbel and Cavalla	92,068	60,920	92,939,113
The Liberia Company	Cocopa	5,569	3,709	4,782,416
B. F. Goodrich Liberia Inc. . . .	Clay (Kle)	14,013	11,639	14,702,294
African Fruit Company Laeisz & Co. .	Greenville	5,376	4,658	3,547,204
Uniroyal Liberian Agricultural Company .	Buchanan	18,201	11,709	11,109,770
Salala Rubber Corporation . . .	Salala	5,133	4,424	5,910,248
Other Companies	Liberia	150,900	88,000	48,100,000
GRAND TOTAL	Liberia	291,260	185,059	181,091,045

LIVESTOCK
(1971 Census estimates)

Sheep	28,202
Goats	58,895
Pigs	17,491
Cattle	25,862
Chickens	346,457
Ducks	22,568
Turkeys	1,333

Production of hen eggs (FAO estimates, metric tons):
1,500 in 1969; 1,600 in 1970; 1,700 in 1971.

FORESTRY
ROUNDWOOD PRODUCTION
('ooo cubic metres)

1967 . . .	1,146
1968 . . .	1,303
1969 . . .	1,500
1970 . . .	1,580
1972 . . .	1,200

Source: FAO, *Yearbook of Forest Products.*

FISHING
(metric tons)

	1968	1969	1972
Atlantic Ocean . .	15,600	18,500	13,223
Inland Water* . .	4,000	4,000	4,000
TOTAL CATCH . .	19,600	22,500	17,223
Value of Fish Landed (U.S. $'ooo) . .	5,157	6,116	4,881

* FAO estimate.

1970-71: 23,000 metric tons each year (FAO estimate).

MINING

	1969	1970	1971	1972
Iron Ore ('000 metric tons)*	14,786	15,388	16,728	22,030‡
Gold (kg.)	35	n.a.	n.a.	50
Diamonds ('000 carats)†	836	826	739	890

* Metal content.   † Exports only.   ‡ Gross weight.

PRODUCTION OF IRON ORE CONCESSIONS
(gross weight, million long tons—1972)

Concession	Location	Production
Liberian American Swedish Minerals Company (LAMCO)	Nimba Mountains	8.29
Libeth American Swedish Mineral Company	Nimba Mountains	2.46
The Liberia Mining Company (LMC)	Bomi Hills	2.65
The National Iron Ore Company (NIOC)	Mano River	3.62
German-Liberian Mining Company (DELIMCO)	Bong Range	5.36
Total	Liberia	22.38

Source: Information from the iron ore concessions.

INDUSTRY

	Unit	1968	1969	1970
Beer	'000 hectolitres	25	32	33
Cement	'000 metric tons	59	73	88
Motor Spirit (Petrol)*	,, ,, ,,	2	44	55
Kerosene*	,, ,, ,,	—	23	22
Distillate Fuel Oils*	,, ,, ,,	6	91	127
Residual Fuel Oils*	,, ,, ,,	17	105	181
Electric Energy	million kWh.	573	632	502

Source: U.S. Bureau of Mines.

FINANCE

100 cents = 1 Liberian dollar (L$).
Coins: 1, 2, 5, 10, 25 and 50 cents; 1 Liberian dollar (U.S. coins are also legal tender).
Notes: 1, 5, 10 and 20 U.S. dollars.
Exchange rates (April 1974): £1 sterling = L$2.36; U.S. $1 = L$1.00.
L$100 = £42.35 = U.S. $100.00.

BUDGET
(U.S. $'000)

Revenue	1971	1972	Expenditure	1971	1972
Income Tax	7,600	7,611	Recurrent Expenditure	42,034	44,888
Iron Ore Profit Sharing	14,000	13,612	Debt Servicing	20,479	20,786
Other Direct Taxes	8,100	11,886	Development Expenditures	8,686	7,374
Import Duties	19,000	20,817			
Export Duties	825	868			
Consular Fees, etc.	1,500	1,722			
Vessel Registration and Tonnage Tax	6,200	7,232			
Other Revenues	11,520	10,843	Total	71,200	73,048
IMF Drawings (net)	2,100	3,520			
			Development Financed from Abroad	n.a.	n.a.
Total	70,845	78,111			

Budget (1973): Estimated Revenue $83 million; Estimated Expenditure $83 million.
Budget (1974): Estimated Expenditure $98 million.

EXTERNAL TRADE

Imports: (1969) $114.7 million; (1970) $149.7 million; (1971) $162.4 million; (1972) $178.7 million.
Exports: (1969) $195.9 million; (1970) $213.7 million; (1971) $224.0 million; (1972) $244.4 million.

COMMODITIES
($'000)

IMPORTS*	1971	1972
Food	24,376	25,487
Beverages and Tobacco . .	4,522	3,832
Crude Materials (excl. fuels) .	1,657	1,646
Mineral Fuels and Lubricants .	11,841	12,030
Oils and Fats . . .	889	1,140
Basic Manufactures . .	35,231	40,566
Machinery and Transport Equipment	54,176	63,397
Miscellaneous . . .	18,179	20,670
TOTAL . . .	162,420	178,683

EXPORTS	1971	1972
Rubber	32,498	29,144
Iron Ore	160,617	182,709
Palm Kernels . . .	2,168	447
Cocoa	1,255	1,466
Coffee	4,013	4,556
Diamonds	5,650	6,315
Other Commodities . .	17,797	19,757
TOTAL . . .	223,998	244,394

* Excluding live animals.

COUNTRIES
($'000)

IMPORTS	1971	1972
United States . . .	51,918	54,152
Germany, Federal Republic .	15,622	20,658
United Kingdom . . .	14,512	16,401
Netherlands . . .	13,013	9,560
France	4,212	4,493
Belgium	2,315	2,698
Japan	13,143	13,895
Italy	3,419	4,142
Sweden	5,203	7,629
Others	39,063	45,055
TOTAL . . .	162,420	178,683

EXPORTS	1971	1972
United States . . .	49,830	50,416
Germany, Federal Republic .	41,367	42,032
United Kingdom . . .	7,583	5,650
Netherlands . . .	33,635	35,366
France	12,208	13,333
Belgium	11,737	15,824
Japan	24,681	43,802
Italy	28,675	437
Sweden	242	18,733
Others	14,040	18,801
TOTAL . . .	223,998	244,394

TRANSPORT

SEA TRAFFIC: MONROVIA
(long tons)

	1971	1972
General Cargo Landed and Loaded . .	553,565	524,190
Iron Ore Loaded . .	10,658,376	11,145,165
Petroleum Landed . .	510,497	478,502
TOTAL CARGO HANDLED	11,722,438	12,147,857

ROADS
(Number of registered vehicles)

1969	.	.	21,136
1970	.	.	23,210
1971	.	.	21,033
1972	.	.	22,179

EDUCATION

	No. of Schools	No. of Students	No. of Teachers
1969 . .	n.a.	147,187	4,200
1970 . .	1,087	138,125	4,265
1971 . .	1,121	146,571	4,316
1972 . .	1,118	146,306	3,596

Source: Ministry of Planning and Economic Affairs, Monrovia.

THE CONSTITUTION

Liberia was founded by the American Colonisation Society in 1821, and constituted a free and independent Republic on July 26th, 1847. The Constitution of the Republic is modelled on that of the United States of America. Authority is divided into the Legislative, the Executive and the Judicial.

Legislative authority is vested in a Legislature consisting of two Houses: the Senate, with 18 members, elected for a six-year term; and the House of Representatives elected for four years, consisting of 52 members.

Electors must either pay a hut tax, or own property in fee simple, or own land. They must be citizens of Liberia.

The Executive power rests with the President, who, with the Vice-President, is elected for an eight-year term. They may be re-elected for periods of four years.

THE GOVERNMENT

President: WILLIAM R. TOLBERT, Jnr.
Vice-President: JAMES EDWARD GREENE.

THE CABINET
(*June* 1974)

Minister of Foreign Affairs: CECIL C. DENNIS.
Minister of Finance: STEPHEN TOLBERT.
Attorney-General: CLARENCE SIMPSON, Jnr.
Postmaster-General: MCKINLEY A. DE SHIELD.
Minister of National Defence: ALLEN H. WILLIAMS.
Minister of Local Government, Rural Development and Urban Reconstruction: EVERETT J. GOODRIDGE.
Minister of Education: JACKSON DOE.
Minister of Public Works: GABRIEL J. TUCKER.

Minister of Agriculture: JAMES T. PHILIPS, Jnr.
Minister of Commerce, Industry and Transportation: WILLIAM E. DENNIS, Jnr.
Minister of National Planning and Economic Affairs: D. FRANKLIN NEAL.
Minister of Information, Cultural Affairs and Tourism: Dr. EDWARD B. KESSELLY.
Minister of Health and Welfare: OLIVER BRIGHT.
Minister of State for Presidential Affairs: E. REGINALD TOWNSEND.
Minister of Public Utilities Authority: TAYLOR E. MAJOR.
Minister of Lands and Mines: NYEMA JONES.
Minister of Youth and Labour: J. JENKINS PEAL.

DIPLOMATIC REPRESENTATION

EMBASSIES ACCREDITED TO LIBERIA
(In Monrovia unless otherwise indicated)
(E) Embassy.

Cameroon: P.O.B. 616 (E); *Ambassador:* MARTIN EPIE.
Central African Republic: P.O.B. 545 (E); *Ambassador:* JEAN PIERRE BOUBA.
China (Taiwan): P.O.B. 27; *Ambassador:* WEILIANG YIN.
Czechoslovakia: Accra, Ghana.
Egypt: P.O.B. 462; *Ambassador:* HASSAN A. ELSINBAWI.
Ethiopia: P.O.B. 640 (E); *Ambassador:* GETANEH HAILE MARIAM.
France: P.O.B. 279 (E); *Ambassador:* ROGER VINCENOT.
Germany, Federal Republic: P.O.B. 34; *Ambassador:* (vacant).

Ghana: P.O.B. 471 (E); *Ambassador:* Commodore PHILEMON F. QUAYE.
Guinea: P.O.B. 416 (E); *Ambassador:* TOURÉ SOULEYMANE BEN DAOUDA.
Haiti: P.O.B. 41 (E); *Ambassador:* ARSÈNE POMPÉE.
Italy: P.O.B. 225; *Ambassador:* (vacant).
Ivory Coast: P.O.B. 126 (E); *Ambassador:* GEORGES ANOMA.
Japan: P.O.B. 2053; *Chargé d'Affaires:* K. KIKUCHI.
Korea, Republic: P.O.B. 7760; *Chargé d'Affaires:* HI CHUL MOON.
Lebanon: P.O.B. 134 (E); *Ambassador:* FOUAD KHOURY.

Malta: Mamba Point (E); *Chargé d'Affaires:* Umberto Dente Degli Scrovegni (acting).

Netherlands: P.O.B. 284 (E); *Ambassador:* Dr. F. van Raalte.

Nigeria: P.O.B. 366 (E); *Ambassador:* C. O. Hollist.

Sierra Leone: P.O.B. 575 (E); *Ambassador:* Hector R. S. Bultman.

Spain: P.O.B. 275 (E); *Chargé d'Affaires:* Manuel Cabrera García.

Sweden: P.O.B. 335 (E); *Ambassador:* Bengt Friedman.

Switzerland: P.O.B. 283; *Chargé d'Affaires:* Theodor Schopfer.

U.S.S.R.: (E); *Ambassador:* Dmitri Safonov.

United Kingdom: P.O.B. 120 (E); *Ambassador:* John Reiss.

U.S.A.: P.O.B. 98; *Ambassador:* Melvin A. Manfull.

Vatican City: P.O.B. 298; *Apostolic Pronuncio:* Archbishop Francis J. Carroll.

Zaire: P.O.B. 1038 (E); *Ambassador:* Panza Nawozi Wa Mutshitu.

Liberia also has diplomatic relations with Austria, Canada, German Democratic Republic, Greece, Republic of Guinea-Bissau, India, Indonesia, Jordan, Mauritania, Norway, Panama, the Philippines, Romania, Senegal, Yugoslavia and Zambia.

CONGRESS

SENATE
Eighteen members.
President: F. Tolbert.

HOUSE OF REPRESENTATIVES
Fifty-two members.
Speaker: R.A. Henries.

POLITICAL PARTY

True Whig Party: in power for more than fifty years; progressive democratic.

JUDICIAL SYSTEM

The judicial authority in the Republic of Liberia is vested in the Supreme Court, the Circuit Courts, and the Lower Courts. There are ten Circuit Courts, two established at Monrovia and the others throughout the country. One Territorial Court is established in the Marshall Territory, and one in River Cess Territory. Lower Courts function in the Districts and Settlements.

Chief Justice: James A. A. Pierre.

Associate Justices: A. H. Roberts, W. E. Wordsworth, Lawrence Mitchell, C. L. Simpson, Jnr.

RELIGION

Liberia is officially a Christian state though complete religious freedom is guaranteed throughout the Republic. Christianity and Islam are the two main religions. There are a large number of sects and some Liberians hold traditional beliefs.

Christian Churches represented in Liberia include the following:

Providence Baptist Church: Corner of Broad and Center Sts., Monrovia; f. 1822; its history is closely bound up with the history of Liberia; Pastor Rev. Dr. John B. Falconer; Chair. of Board of Trustees Deacon William E. Dennis; Sec. Deacon Samuel Hill. Associated with: **The Liberia Baptist Missionary and Educational Convention, Inc.:** f. 1880; Pres. Rev. Dr. William R. Tolbert, Jnr.; National Vice-Pres. Rev. T. I. B. Findley; Gen. Sec. Nathaniel R. Richardson.

Methodist Church in Liberia: P.O.B. 1010, Monrovia; f. 1822; 24,000 adherents, 244 congregations, 245 ministers, 13 schools; Resident Bishop Bennie D. Warner; Sec. Rev. Isaac M. Davis; Educational Sec. Rev. Arthur F. Kulah.

Roman Catholic Church: Catholic Mission, P.O.B. 297, Monrovia; f. 1907; approx. 20,000 mems., 7,000 pupils in elementary schools, 5,000 in high schools and colleges.

Vicar-Apostolic of Monrovia: His Grace, Archbishop P. Francis Carroll, s.m.a., Apostolic Nunciature, Monrovia.

Vicar-Apostolic of Cape Palmas: (vacant).

Education Secretary: F. van Vyfeyken, s.m.a.

Assemblies of God in Liberia: P.O.B. 40, Monrovia; 235 churches; approx. 9,000 adherents.

American Protestant Episcopal Church: Monrovia; f. 1836; approx. 12,612 mems.; 40 elementary schools, 5 high schools and 1 college; approx. 12,600 mems.; Bishop: Rt. Rev. George D. Browne.

Other denominations are: African Methodist Episcopal Church, African Methodist Episcopal Zion Church, Evangelical Lutheran Church, National Baptist Mission, Presbyterian Church in Liberia, Jehovah's Witnesses, Prayer Band, Church of the Lord Aladura.

Islam: divided into two denominations, Ahmadyya and Mohammedanism. The total community is about 200,000.

THE PRESS

NEWSPAPERS

Daily Listener, The: P.O.B. 35, Monrovia; f. 1950; Editor-in-Chief and Publisher Charles C. Dennis Sr.; circ. 3,500 (temporarily closed).

Diplomatist & News Digest, The: Johnson St., Monrovia; f. 1961; weekly; Editor and Publisher Kingspride Ugboma; circ. 500.

Liberian Age, The: P.O.B. 286, Monrovia; f. 1946; twice weekly; organ of the True Whig Party; circ. 10,000.

Liberian Star, The: P.O.B. 691, United Nations Drive, Monrovia; f. 1964; five times a week; independent; Publisher Liberia Publishing Co. Inc.; Editorial Dir. James L. Marshall; circ. 7,000.

PERIODICALS

Journal of Commerce, Industry and Transportation: Bank of Liberia Bldg., Monrovia; twice-yearly; publ. by Palm Publs. for Ministry of Commerce, Industry and Transportation.

Kpelle Messenger, The: Kpelle; Kpelle-English monthly newspaper; Kpelle Literary Center, Lutheran Church, P.O.B. 1046, Monrovia.

Liberian Churchman, The: Robertsport Cape, Mount Country; journal of the Protestant Episcopal Church; every two months; Editor Rt. Rev. D. H. Brown; circ. 1,000.

Liberia Journal of Commerce and Industry: Palm Publications Co., Bank of Liberia Bldg., Monrovia; quarterly; Man. Editor James C. Dennis.

Liberian Review, The: P.O.B. 268, Monrovia; illustrated quarterly; Editor Henry B. Cole; circ. 5,000.

Liberian Trade and Industry Handbook: P.O.B. 286, Monrovia; annual; Editors Henry B. Cole and Arthur B. Cassell, Sr.; circ. 10,000.

Liberian Year Book, The: P.O.B. 268, Monrovia; f. 1956; Editor Henry B. Cole; circ. 15,000.

Loma Weekly Paper, The: P.O.B. 1046, Monrovia; bilingual weekly in Loma and English.

New Day: Fundamental & Mass Education Department of Public Instruction, Monrovia; illustrated monthly for new literates; Editor Mrs. Margaret Traub; circ. 500.

Palm: Monrovia; news magazine; monthly.

Saturday Chronicle: P.O.B. 35, Monrovia; f. 1969; weekly; Publisher and Editor-in-Chief Charles C. Dennis, Sr.; circ. 8,000 (temporarily closed).

Sunday Digest: P.O.B. 35, Monrovia; f. 1967; weekly; Publisher and Editor-in-Chief Charles C. Dennis, Sr.; circ. 4,500 (temporarily closed).

PRESS AGENCIES

Ministry of Information, Cultural Affairs and Tourism: Monrovia; receives world news from centres, UPI, AP, AFP, and Tass.

FOREIGN BUREAUX

Reuters and UPI have offices in Monrovia; Tass has a correspondent.

RADIO AND TELEVISION

Liberian Broadcasting Corporation: P.O.B. 594, Monrovia; controls all forms of broadcasting; Chief Exec. Officer Chauncey Cooper; Radio Man. Jonathan Reffell; Television Man. J. Eustace Smith.

RADIO

E.L.B.C.: P.O.B. 594, Monrovia; f. 1960; commercial station sponsored by Liberian Government.

ELWA: P.O.B. 192, Monrovia; Station of the Sudan Interior Mission; religious, cultural and educational broadcasts in English, French, Arabic and 35 West African Languages; Broadcasting Dir. Barton Bliss.

Lamco Broadcasting Station (ELNR): Nimba; owned by Lamco J. V. (see Transport); relays BBC World News, E.L.B.C. programmes and broadcasts its own programmes in English and African languages for Lamco workers; Gen. Man. R. Morris.

Voice of America: Washington, D.C. 20547, U.S.A.; Monrovia; a short-wave relay station, the biggest in Africa, came into operation in 1964; broadcasts in English, French and Swahili.

Number of radio receivers: 250,000 (1973).

TELEVISION

ELTV: Liberian Broadcasting Corporation, P.O.B. 594, Monrovia; f. 1964; commercial station sponsored by the Liberian Government.

Number of TV receivers: 10,000 (1973).

FINANCE

BANKING

Bank of Liberia Inc.: P.O.B. 2031, Carey and Warren Streets, Monrovia; f. 1955; affiliate of Chemical Bank, New York; full service commercial bank; Man. Tom Duffy.

Bank of Monrovia: P.O.B. 280, Ashmun St., Monrovia; f. 1955 as fully owned affiliate of the First National City Bank, New York; 4 brs.; Pres. H. Hugh Mitchell.

Chase Manhattan Bank N.A.: Corner of Randall and Ashmun Streets, P.O.B. 181, Monrovia; f. 1961; one sub-branch; f. 1970; Gen. Man. Peter G. Bates.

Commercial Bank of Liberia: P.O.B. 262, Monrovia.

International Trust Co. of Liberia: P.O.B. 292, 80 Broad St., Monrovia; f. 1948; br. at Nimba; Pres. Henry N. Conway, Jnr.

Liberian Bank for Industrial Development and Investment (LBIDI): 100 Broad St., P.O.B. 547, Monrovia; f. 1965 by IFC, Liberian, European and U.S. investors; development bank; cap. $1m.

Liberian Trading and Development Bank Ltd. (TRADEVCO): P.O.B. 293, 80 Ashmun St., Monrovia; f. 1955; cap. $200,000, dep. (1971) $5,167,008; Chair. Massimo Spada; Man. F. Bernandini.

Union National Bank (Liberia) Inc.: Water-Randall Streets, P.O.B. 655, Monrovia; f. 1962; Lebanon-owned with a 20 per cent holding by Liberians; cap. $1m.

INSURANCE

American Life Insurance Co.: Union National Bank Bldg., P.O.B. 60, Monrovia.

Insurance Co. of Africa: 80 Broad St., P.O.B. 292, Monrovia; Pres. Henry N. Conway, Jnr.

Lone Star Insurances Inc.: P.O.B. 1142, Monrovia; represents St. Paul Fire and Marine Insurance Co., Minnesota, U.S.A.; Gen. Man. Reinhard F. Ricater.

TRADE AND INDUSTRY

LIBERIA-U.S. COMMISSION

Joint Liberia-U.S. Commission for Economic Development: Ashmun St., P.O.B. 141, Monrovia; f. 1950; Exec. Sec. Emmett Harmon.

CHAMBER OF COMMERCE

Liberia Chamber of Commerce: P.O.B. 92, Monrovia; f. 1951; Pres. Hon. P. Clarence Parker; Sec.-Gen. David N. Howell.

DEVELOPMENT ORGANIZATION

Liberian Development Corporation: Department of Commerce and Industry Bldg., Monrovia; f. 1961; independent agency of the Government; to stimulate industrial development and foster existing industries; Gen. Man. Mrs. Louise Summerville; Exec. Sec. E. Momolou Freeman; publs. *Feasibility and prefeasibility studies*, other technical documents (reports).

EMPLOYERS' ASSOCIATION

National Business Association of Liberia: P.O.B. 518, Monrovia; Pres. Emmanuel Shaw, Sr.

TRADE UNIONS

Congress of Industrial Organizations: 29 Ashmun St., P.O.B. 415, Monrovia; Pres. W. V. S. Tubman, Jnr.; Sec. Tom Sawyer; 5 affiliated unions.

Labour Congress of Liberia: 71 Gurley St., Monrovia; Sec.-Gen. P. C. T. Sonpon; 8 affiliated unions.

TRANSPORT AND TOURISM

TRANSPORT

RAILWAYS

Bong Mining Co. Ltd.: P.O.B. 538, Monrovia; 45 miles of track to transport iron ore concentrates and pellets from Bong Mine to Monrovia; Gen. Man. K. A. Hedderich.

Liberia Mining Co.: P.O.B. 251-2, Monrovia; 91 miles of track, Bomi to Monrovia, for transport of iron ore; Vice-Pres. and Gen. Man. J. L. Pervola.

Lamco J.V. Operating Co.: P.O.B. 69, Monrovia; 170 miles of standard track extending from Buchanan to the iron ore mine at Nimba; opened 1963; Gen. Man. O. Wijkstroem; Man. Operation Buchanan Olle Goransson; Man. Operation Nimba Bo Stenberg.

ROADS

The mileage of public and private roads is 6,375. The main trunk road is the Monrovia-Sanniquellie Motor Road extending north-east from the capital to the country's border with Guinea, near Ganta, and eastward through the hinterland. A trunk road has been completed to Tappita, headquarters of District 3, Central Province, and has been extended through Eastern Province. The entire route from Monrovia to Cape Palmas was finished in 1963. In October 1972 the government, with the assistance of the World Bank, embarked on a $38 million five-year highway maintenance and development plan.

SHIPPING

In 1967 the National Port Authority was created to develop and manage all Liberian ports (Exec. Officer Board of Dirs. George E. Tubman). The Free Port, covering 550 acres, and largest of Monrovia's nine ports, is directed by the Monrovia Port Management Company Ltd., P.O.B. 14, Monrovia. It comprises the Republic of Liberia and seven American firms: Farrell Lines Inc., Firestone Plantations Co., Liberia Co., Liberia Mining Co. Ltd., Mississippi Shipping Co. (Delta Line), Socony-Vacuum Oil Co. and Texas Co.; Pres. of the Board Admiral Wavehope; Commissioner for Maritime Affairs Fulton Yancy.

There are about 150 shipping companies registered at Monrovia. In 1972 2,331 vessels of which 863 were tankers were registered with Liberia which has the largest merchant navy in the world.

The principal lines calling at Monrovia are: Chargeurs Réunis, Delta Lines, Elder Dempster Lines, Farrell Lines, Hanseatischer Afrika-Dienst, Holland-West Africa Line, Jugolinija, Lloyd Triestino, Palm Line, Royal Interocean Lines, Scandinavian West Africa Line, United West Africa Service.

CIVIL AVIATION

Liberia's chief airport is at Robertsfield Airport, 50 miles east of Monrovia. A five-year development plan for this airport was financed by a $4,500,000 loan agreement between the U.S. and Liberian Governments for a new Control Tower, landing system and taxiway. Spriggs Payne Airfield, Sinkor, Monrovia, handles chiefly internal traffic. There are numerous other airfields and airstrips, some linking Spriggs Payne Airfield with Robertsfield.

NATIONAL LINES

Air Liberia: Roberts International Airport; f. 1949 as Liberian National Airways, reorganized 1974 with participation of Hughes Air West; services from Roberts International Airport and Monrovia to Sinoe, Cape Palmas and Tchien; fleet includes two DC-3, two Fokker F-27; Chair. William E. Dennis, Jr.

Air Taxi Company of Liberia: P.O.B. 183, Monrovia; operates internal services; Pres. Hon. Samuel D. George; Bus. Man. J. Caesar Greene.

FOREIGN AIRLINES

Monrovia is also served by the following foreign airlines: Air Afrique (Ivory Coast), Air Guinée, Air Mali, British Caledonian, Ghana Airways, KLM, MEA, Nigeria Airways, Pan American, Sabena, SAS, Sierra Leone Airways, Swissair, UTA.

TOURISM

Tourism in Liberia is still in its infancy. The number of tourists in 1971 was 250 and this rose to 1,004 in 1972.

Bureau of Tourism: Office in the Ministry of Information, Cultural Affairs and Tourism; Minister Dr. the Hon. Edward B. Kesselly; Assistant Minister for Tourism Miss Valerie Morris; Dir. Louis A. Wah.

UNIVERSITY

University of Liberia: Monrovia; f. 1862; 110 teachers, 1,000 students.

LIBYA

INTRODUCTORY SURVEY

Location, Climate, Language, Religion, Flag, Capital

The Libyan Arab Republic stretches along the Mediterranean from Tunisia to Egypt. Even at the coast the climate is dry and desert conditions prevail over most of the territory with average temperatures between 55° and 100°F (13° and 38°C). Arabic is the official language but English and Italian are used in trade. The great majority of the population are Muslims. The national flag (proportions 2 by 1) has three equal horizontal stripes of red, white and black, with an eagle emblem in gold at the centre of the white stripe. The capital is Tripoli.

Recent History

Formerly an Italian colony, Libya was conquered in 1942 by British and French troops, Cyrenaica and Tripolitania being subsequently governed by the British and Fezzan by the French. In 1949 the United Nations General Assembly resolved that Libya should become an independent state and the United Kingdom of Libya was duly formed in 1951. Libya then drew upon British and American aid in return for the uses of Libyan bases by Allied troops, but since the discovery of oil this has not been necessary. Libya enjoyed internal political stability and good relations with both the Arab world and the West, though oil supplies to the latter were restricted immediately after the "Six-Day War" between Israel and the Arab states in June 1967. The bloodless revolution of September 1st, 1969, brought a group of young nationalist army officers to power and deposed the aged King, then convalescing abroad.

Since the *coup* Libya has assumed a much more active role in the Arab world. In January 1972 various schemes for Arab unity at last came to fruition with the formation of the Federation of Arab Republics, comprising Libya, Egypt and Syria. In August 1972 Libya concluded an agreement with Egypt to merge the two countries in September 1973. Neither of these unions has proved effective in practice and in January 1974 the Chairman of the Revolution Command Council, Col. Gaddafi, announced impending union with Tunisia, which also proved abortive.

In April 1973 Col. Gaddafi introduced a "cultural revolution", which involved the formation of people's committees and an attempt to run the country on a wholly Islamic basis. Relations with Egypt, strained when the Libya-Egypt union took place in principle rather than in fact, further deteriorated when President Sadat embarked on the October 1973 war with Israel without consulting Col. Gaddafi. In April 1974 Col. Gaddafi announced that, while remaining Chairman of the Revolution Command Council, he would concentrate more on matters of ideology and organization.

Government

All power is now centred in the Revolution Command Council, which announced a provisional constitution in December 1969. The Council appoints the Cabinet, the judiciary and the local governors. In July 1970 the country was officially divided into ten provinces. There is no National Assembly and the Arab Socialist Union is the only political party.

Defence

Libya's armed forces total 25,000 men. Military service is voluntary. The army is equipped with British and Soviet tanks, while France has supplied jet fighters for the air force. Libya's defence budget for 1973 amounted to LD 43 million.

Economic Affairs

Until several years after independence Libya had to rely on U.S., U.K. and UN aid to supplement a primarily subsistence agriculture with some export of livestock, hides and skins, nuts and seeds. From 1955 to 1970 prospecting for petroleum yielded increasing returns and Libya is now one of the largest oil producers in the world. Expansion was particularly rapid owing to political stability, nearness to the Western European markets, and to the oil's freedom from sulphur which makes it especially suitable for refining. Libya now has the highest gross national product per head in Africa. Oil now accounts for some 98 per cent of Libya's export earnings, although it provides employment for only about 5 per cent of the total labour force.

Libya also exports liquefied natural gas. In common with other oil-producing countries Libya has been entering into participation agreements with some of the foreign oil companies operating on her soil and in some cases has nationalized their assets. She has been in the forefront of moves to limit oil production and secure higher prices for crude oil in late 1973 and early 1974. Libya has also used some of her wealth from oil in sending aid to some of the drought-stricken countries of Africa and in providing finance for revolutionary movements throughout the world.

Transport and Communications

Good main roads run along the coast, and inland from Tripoli to Sebha, chief city of the Fezzan area. The Tripoli-Benghazi highway has been improved. A 149-km. railway line linking Libya and Egypt is under construction. The port of Tripoli is a natural deep-water harbour and those of Benghazi and Tobruk are being improved. Tripoli and Benina (for Benghazi) are international airports and Tripoli provides internal links with Benghazi and Sebha.

Social Welfare

The Government runs medical services including two big hospitals in Benghazi and Tripoli. There is a scheme of national insurance and Government servants contribute to a pension scheme.

Education

Primary education is compulsory and there are secondary schools and institutes for agricultural, technical and vocational training. There are a number of foreign schools in Tripoli and Benghazi. The University of Libya, which was founded in 1956, has faculties in Tripoli and Benghazi. According to the 1964 census, the literacy rate was then just over 25 per cent.

Tourism

Tripoli with its beaches and clubs and its annual International Fair, attracts numerous visitors, while three Roman provincial cities, Sabratha, Leptis Magna and Cyrene, have been well excavated and are of considerable interest. Inland are the historic Oases of Ghadames and Mizda.

Sport

Football is the most popular sport.

Public Holidays

1974: September 1st (Revolution Day), October 7th (Evacuation Day), October 16th–18th (Id ul Fitr), December 26th (Id ul Adha).

1975: January 14th (Muslim New Year), January 24th (Ashoura), March 26th (Birthday of the Prophet), May 25th (Sudanese National Day), June 11th (Evacuation Day), July 23rd (National Day—Egypt).

Weights and Measures

The metric system is in force.

Currency and Exchange Rates

1,000 dirhams = 1 Libyan dinar (LD).

Exchange rates (April 1974):

£1 sterling = 699.05 dirhams;
U.S. $1 = 296.05 dirhams.

STATISTICAL SURVEY

AREA AND POPULATION

AREA (sq. km.)	POPULATION	
	1964 Census	1973 Census
1,759,540	1,564,369	2,257,037

About 30 per cent of the population are nomadic or semi-nomadic according to 1964 census.

POPULATION BY DISTRICT
(1964 Census)

Tripoli	379,925	Khoms		136,679
Benghazi	278,826	Jebel Akhdar		88,016
Zavia	190,708	Darna		84,112
Jebel Gharbi	180,883	Sebha		47,436
Misurata	145,894	Ubari		31,890

AGRICULTURE

DISTRIBUTION OF LAND
(1960 census—'000 hectares)

	TRIPOLITANIA	CYRENAICA	FEZZAN
Arable	1,605	742	28
Pasture	1,121	15	—
Permanent Crops, Forests	154	37	7

LIVESTOCK
(Estimates—'000)

	1970	1971
Sheep	2,163	2,284
Goats	1,234	1,141
Cattle	108	101
Camels	163	120

PRINCIPAL CROPS
(tons)

	1970	1971	1972
Barley	52,808	32,127	116,395
Wheat	21,112	17,726	41,585
Olives	71,154	5,000	94,533
Citrus Fruits	20,050	24,918	27,138
Groundnuts	10,685	11,075	13,692
Almonds	3,787	3,560	4,515
Tomatoes	136,413	130,816	170,038
Dates	49,111	66,190	59,544
Potatoes	9,982	22,813	49,046

Tobacco leaf production (1970) 2 million kilos, manufactured tobacco production 170,000 kilos. Grapes are also grown in quantity (about 7,000 metric tons in 1970).

INDUSTRY
(Value of Output in LD'000—Large establishments only)

	1970	1971
Food Manufacturing	8,258	10,221
Beverage Industries	2,174	2,252
Tobacco Manufactures	9,219	11,286
Chemicals and Products	5,060	4,916
Textiles	1,743	2,011
Cement and Products	2,371	2,786
Fabricated Metal Products	1,828	1,747
Total (incl. others)	30,653	38,323

OIL
CRUDE OIL PRODUCTION
(metric tons)

1966	72,645,000
1967	83,477,000
1968	125,539,000
1969	149,728,000
1970	161,708,000
1971	132,396,000
1972	106,400,000
1973	105,200,000

FINANCE

1,000 dirhams=1 Libyan dinar (LD).
Coins: 1, 5, 10, 20, 50 and 100 dirhams.
Notes: 250 and 500 dirhams; 1, 5 and 10 dinars.
Exchange rates (April 1974): £1 sterling=699.05 dirhams; U.S. $1=296.05 dirhams.
100 Libyan dinars=£143.05=$337.78.
Note: The dinar is equivalent to the former Libyan pound, which it replaced in 1971.

DEVELOPMENT BUDGET
(1971–72: LD'000)

Agriculture and agrarian reform	50,400
Industry	32,000
Education and National Guidance	27,150
Information and Culture	27,000
Public Health	17,000
Transport and Communications	39,800
Municipalities	29,150
Housing	40,000
Public Works	21,500
Total (including others)	300,000

Development Budget 1972–73: LD 367 million.

ORDINARY BUDGET
(1971–72: LD million)

Education and National Guidance	46.3
Defence	n.a.
Police and Public Security	n.a.
Total (including others)	201.0

DEVELOPMENT COUNCIL THREE-YEAR PLAN

In March 1972 a three-year development budget was published, to run until the end of March 1975. In the Spring of 1973 this budget was revised to bring the three-year total expenditure to LD 1,965 million.

EXTERNAL TRADE
(LD'000)

	1968	1969	1970	1971	1972
Imports	230,200	241,301	198,002	250,352	343,204
Exports	669,800	772,765	841,829	959,918	966,307

SELECTED COMMODITIES
(LD'000)

IMPORTS	1970	1971	1972	EXPORTS	1970	1971	1972
Food and Live Animals	39,326	47,574	53,128	Crude Petroleum .	841,134	959,392	948,230
Beverages and Tobacco	2,532	2,484	1,201	Groundnuts . .	—	235	408
Mineral Fuel .	3,618	5,770	7,393	Hides and Skins .	202	284	1,247
Animal and Vegetable Oils and Fats . .	2,777	5,539	2,786	Castor Oil Seed . .	5	3	16
Inedible Crude Materials excluding Fuel .	6,300	8,307	9,980	Wool and other Animal Hair . . .	488	—	311
Chemicals . .	11,415	15,123	16,646				
Manufactures .	42,384	52,025	81,220				
Machinery . .	58,708	72,963	117 780				
Miscellaneous . .	30,942	40,557	53,069				

PRINCIPAL COUNTRIES
(LD'000)

IMPORTS	1969	1970	1971	1972
Italy	54,788	42,712	57,712	88,352
U.S.A. . . .	45,152	27,307	17,323	21,635
U.K. . . .	29,768	18,579	24,866	29,911
Germany, Federal Republic .	21,426	17,950	23,167	32,825
Netherlands . .	8,871	6,190	7,600	10,135
France . . .	12,015	12,724	21,402	24,206
Belgium . . .	3,318	2,212	—	
Japan . . .	11,747	11,116	15,193	19,930
China, People's Republic	5,388	3,781	6,444	8,433
Lebanon . . .	3,726	5,628	7,335	11,149
Other Countries . .	n.a.	50,003	53,847	96,628

EXPORTS OF CRUDE OIL
(LD'000)

COUNTRY	1969	1970	1971	1972
U.K.	106,405	127,697	157,230	129,620
Germany, Federal Republic .	167,732	147,305	168,260	238,332
Italy . . .	178,618	218,090	230,526	185,714
France . . .	89,871	113,344	119,492	84,619
Netherlands . .	78,457	79,627	56,928	44,063
U.S.A. . . .	39,548	22,251	57,746	74,867
Belgium . . .	30,327	32,634	23,550	11,132
Spain . . .	38,503	38,363	39,060	24,107
TOTAL (incl. others) .	771,857	841,134	956,867	948,231

TRANSPORT
ROADS

	1969	1970	1971
Private Cars . .	86,814	95,762	110,312
Lorries . .	39,947	44,582	50,435
Buses . .	727	820	877
Taxis . .	3,884	4,367	4,703

SHIPPING

| | SHIPS ('ooo N.R.T.) | | CARGO ('ooo metric tons) | |
	Entered	Cleared	Loaded	Unloaded
1969 .	4,908	4,886	27	3,099
1970 .	4,381	4,357	39	2,600
1971 .	4,559	4,487	18	3,004
1972 .	4,792	4,801	22	5,649

CIVIL AVIATION

	1970	1971	1972
Number of Passengers			
Entering . .	165,369	128,005	274,243
Leaving . .	170,854	124,356	237,548
Cargo Unloaded (tons) .	8,835	12,111	13,808
Cargo Loaded (tons) .	2,459	2,412	2,763

EDUCATION
(1971–72)

STATE SCHOOLS	SCHOOLS	STUDENTS	TEACHERS
Primary . .	1,413	407,805	14,421
Preparatory . .	203	43,790	3,039
Secondary . .	39	9,642	1,007
Teacher-Training .	20	5,984	518
Technical . .	9	3,202	376

Source: Census and Statistical Dept., Ministry of Economy and Trade, Tripoli.

THE CONSTITUTION

A new provisional constitution of 37 articles was proclaimed in December 1969. The following is a summary of its principal features:

Libya is a democratic and free Arab Republic with sovereignty of the people who constitute part of the Arab nation and whose objective is comprehensive Arab unity.

The official religion of the state is Islam but the state guarantees religious freedom.

Supreme authority is vested in the Revolution Command Council which has power to appoint the Council of Ministers, to sign and modify treaties and to declare war. It retains power over the armed forces and the diplomatic corps.

All citizens are equal and the foundations of the country are built on family unity.

The state will aim to achieve socialism by means of social justice which forbids all forms of exploitation. It will work towards the liberation of the national economy from every foreign influence, guiding it towards productivity and stability.

The property of the state is also the property of the public. Private property cannot be exploited and is guaranteed by the state. It can only be expropriated as laid down by law.

Freedom of speech is guaranteed as long as it does not transgress the principles of the revolution.

The extradition of political prisoners is forbidden.

All titles, including those granted by the previous government, have been revoked.

Medical care is a guaranteed right for all citizens; education will be compulsory until the end of primary stage (now at the age of nine).

THE GOVERNMENT

REVOLUTION COMMAND COUNCIL

Chairman: Col. MUAMMAR AL-GADDAFI.

Members: Lt.-Col. ABU BAKAR YUNIS JABER, Maj. ABDUL SALAM JALLOUD, Maj. BASHIR AL SAGHIER HAWADY, Maj. ABDUL MONIEUM AL TAHER AL HUNY, Maj. AL KHOWEILDY AL HAMIDY, Maj. MUSTAFA AL KHARROBY, Maj. MUKHTAR ABDULLAH AL GERWY, Maj. MUHAMMED NAJIM, Maj. AWAD ALI HAMZA, Maj. OMAR AL-MAHIDI.

CABINET

(May 1974)

Prime Minister: Maj. ABDUL SALAM JALLOUD.

Minister of Defence: (vacant).

Minister of Education: MOHAMED AHMED AL CHERIF.

Minister of Housing and Public Services: MUHAMMAD AHMAD MANQOUSH.

Minister of Communications and Electricity: TAHA SHARIF BIN AMIR.

Minister of Justice: MUHAMMAD ALY AL JADY.

Minister of Health: Dr. MEFTAH AL USTA OMAR.

Minister of Agriculture and Agrarian Reform: MUHAMMAD ALI TABOU.

Minister of Petroleum: EZZEDIN MABROUK.

Minister of Labour: ABDUL ATY AL ABEIDY.

Minister of the Interior: Maj. AL KHUWAILDI AL HUMAIDI.

Minister of Information and Culture: ABOU ZEID OMAR DOURDA.

Minister of the Economy: ABU BAKR AL CHERIF.

Minister of the Treasury: MOHAMED AL ZARROUK RAGAB.

Minister of Industry and Mineral Resources: GABALLAH AZOUZ TALHI.

Minister of Youth and Social Affairs: ABDEL HAMID AL ZINATI.

Minister of Planning: ABDUL KARIM BALLO.

Minister of the Civil Service: MOHAMED ABU BAKR BEN YOUNIS.

Minister of Agricultural Development: ABDUL MAJED AL QAOWD.

DIPLOMATIC REPRESENTATION

EMBASSIES ACCREDITED TO LIBYA

(Tripoli unless otherwise stated)

(E) Embassy.

Afghanistan: Cairo, Egypt (E).

Algeria: Sharia Qayrouan 12 (E); *Ambassador:* 'ALI KAAFI.

Argentina: Algiers, Algeria (E).

Austria: Tunis, Tunisia (E).

Belgium: Sharia Sidi 'Isa (E); *Ambassador:* CHARLES LOODTS.

Brazil: Tunis, Tunisia (E).

Bulgaria: Sharia Murad Agha (E); *Ambassador:* STYKO NEDELCHEV.

Canada: Cairo, Egypt (E).

Chad: Sharia Bin 'Ashur; *Ambassador:* KAHLIL OTHMAN.

Chile: Cairo, Egypt.

China (Taiwan): Sharia al-Hadi Ka'bar (E); *Ambassador:* TSAI PA.

Czechoslovakia: Sharia Mahmud Shaltut (E); *Chargé d'Affaires:* VLADIMIR STOKL.

Denmark: Cairo, Egypt (E).

Egypt: Sharia Bin 'Ashur (Relations Office); *Acting Head:* MUHSIN FAHMI.

Finland: Sharia Mustafa Kamel (E); *Chargé d'Affaires:* ANTON RATIA.

France: Sharia Huper (E); *Ambassador:* GUY GEORGY.

German Democratic Republic: (E); *Ambassador:* RONALD BÖTTCHER.

Germany, Federal Republic: Sharia Hassan al-Masha (E); *Ambassador:* Dr. GUNTHER F. WERNER.

Greece: Sharia Jalal Bayar, 18; *Ambassador:* DIMITRI A. PAPADAKIS.

Guinea: Cairo, Egypt (E).

Hungary: Cairo, Egypt (E).

India: Sharia Mahmud Shaltut (E); *Ambassador:* HOMI J. H. TALEYARKHAN.

Iran: Tunis, Tunisia (E).

Iraq: Sharia Nasser (E); *Ambassador:* FA'IQ MAKKI AL TAKRITI.

Italy: Sharia 'Oran 1 (E); *Ambassador:* ALDO CONTE MAROTTA.

Japan: Collina Verde (E); *Chargé d'Affaires:* KAZU WANIBUCHI.

Kuwait: Sharia Bin Yassir (E); *Ambassador:* YUSIF AL-MENAISI.

Lebanon: Sharia Bin Yassir (E); *Ambassador:* MUHAMMAD MALEK.

Mali: Cairo, Egypt (E).

Malta: Sharia Bin Ka'ab, 13 (E); *Chargé d'Affaires:* EVARIST SALIBA.

Mauritania: Sharia Bin Ka'ab (E); *Ambassador:* YAATHA OULD SIDI AHMED.

Morocco: Sharia Bashir al-Ibrahimi (E); *Ambassador:* (vacant).

Netherlands: Sharia Celal Bayar 20 (E); *Chargé d'Affaires:* Dr. J. J. DE ROOS.

Niger: Sharia Bin 'Ubaydallah (E); *Ambassador:* OUMAROU AMADOU.

Nigeria: Sharia Ammar Ben Yaser (E); *Ambassador:* OSMAN AHMADU SUKA.

Norway: Rabat, Morocco (E).

Pakistan: Sharia al-Khitabi (E); *Ambassador:* Lt.-Gen. RAHMAN GUL.

Poland: Cairo, Egypt (E).

Saudi Arabia: Sharia al-Qayrouan 2 (E); *Ambassador:* ABD AL-MUSHIN AL-ZAYD.

Senegal: Cairo, Egypt (E).

Somalia: (address unavailable); *Ambassador:* MUHAMMAD HASHI ABDI.

Spain: Sharia al-Jazayri (E); *Ambassador:* CARLOS ROBLES.

Sri Lanka: Cairo, Egypt (E).

Sudan: Sharia Donato Suma (E); *Ambassador:* Abdul Aal Sanada.

Sweden: Tunis, Tunisia (E).

Switzerland: Tunis, Tunisia (E).

Syria: Sharia Muhamed Rashid Rida, 4 (Relations Office); *Head:* 'Adam Kilani.

Tunisia: Sharia Bashir al-Ibrahimia (E); *General Commissioner:* Amor Fezzani.

Turkey: Sharia al-Fatah 36 (E); *Ambassador:* (vacant).

Uganda: (address unavailable); *Ambassador:* Jack Bunyenyezi.

U.S.S.R.: Sharia Solaroli (E); *Ambassador:* Ivan N. Yakushin.

United Arab Emirates: (address unavailable) (E); *Chargé d'Affaires:* Saif Aly al Jarwan.

U.K.: Tariq al-Fatah (E); *Ambassador:* D. F. Murray.

U.S.A.: Sharia al-Nasr (E); *Chargé d'Affaires:* Robert Stein.

Venezuela: Sharia Abdulrahman Kwakby (E); *Ambassador:* Dr. Pedro Barradas.

Yemen Arab Republic: Sharia Ubai Ibn Kaa'b 36 (E); *Ambassador:* Abdul Malik al Tayyib.

Yemen, People's Democratic Republic: Sharia Bin 'Ashur (E); *Ambassador:* Ali Ahmed al-Sulami.

Yugoslavia: Sharia Bashir al-Ibrahimi (E); *Ambassador:* Boris Rafajlovski.

PARLIAMENT

The Senate and House of Representatives were dissolved after the *coup d'état* of September 1969, and the provisional constitution issued in December 1969 made no mention of elections or a return to Parliamentary procedure. However, in January 1971 Col. Gaddafi announced that a new Parliament would be appointed, not elected; no date was mentioned. All political parties other than the Arab Socialist Union are banned.

POLITICAL PARTY

Arab Socialist Union: f. 1971; the only legal party; there are 366 basic units; elections to them began in November 1971; Sec.-Gen. Major Bashir Hawady.

JUDICIAL SYSTEM

President of the Supreme Court: Muhammad Abdulkareem Azzuz.

The law of the Judicial System of 1954 established the following courts: the Federal Supreme Court, the Courts of Appeal, the Courts of First Instance and the Summary Courts. Sittings are in public, unless the court decides to hold them *in camera* in the interests of decency or public order. Judgment is in all cases given in public. The language of the courts is Arabic, but there is a translation office attached to each Court to help non-Arabic speaking parties, judges or lawyers.

In October 1971 the Revolution Command Council decreed that all legislation should conform with the basic principles of Islamic Law and set up committees to carry this out.

The **Supreme Court** consists of a Chief Justice and ten justices appointed by the Revolution Command Council.

Courts of Appeal exist in Tripoli, Benghazi and Missurata, consisting of a President, Vice-President and three judges; judgments must be given by three judges. Each Court of Appeal includes a Court of Assize consisting of three judges.

Courts of First Instance are set up in the provinces, consisting of a President, Vice-President and a number of judges; judgment in these courts is given by one judge.

Summary Courts, composed of one judge, exist within the territorial jurisdiction of every Court of First Instance.

The People's Court is a special court set up by decree in October 1969. It deals with any crimes the Revolution Command Council sees fit to refer to it, but is particularly concerned with cases of political or administrative corruption.

RELIGION

Muslims: The Libyan Arabs practically without exception follow Sunni Muslim rites.

Chief Mufti of Libya: Sheikh Taher Ahmed al Zawi.

Christians: The Christian community numbered about 35,000, mostly Italian Roman Catholics, before the 1969 revolution; its numbers have been greatly reduced by the departure of the Italians during 1970. The Roman Catholic Cathedral in Tripoli was transformed into a mosque in November 1970.

THE PRESS

DAILIES

Tripoli

Al-Fajr al-Jadid: Sharia Tariq; f. 1969; official journal; Editor Omar al Hamdi.

Al Balagh.

Benghazi

Al Kifah (also Tripoli).

As Shura: f. 1973.

PERIODICALS

Tripoli

Al Jundi: Libyan Army Publication, weekly.

The Libyan Arab Republic Gazette: published by the Ministry of Justice; legal; weekly.

Al Wahdah: monthly.

NEWS AGENCIES

Arab Revolution News Agency: Tripoli; f. 1965; attached to Ministry of Information and Culture. Serves the Libyan radio network, newspapers and Government departments (name changed from Libyan News Agency, June 1973).

Foreign Bureaux

DPA, Reuters and Tass have offices in Tripoli.

PUBLISHER

Dar Libya Publishing House: P.O.B. 2487, Benghazi; f. 1966; general books.

RADIO AND TELEVISION

General Organization of People's Revolution Broadcasting: P.O.B. 333, Tripoli; P.O.B. 274, Benghazi; f. 1957 (TV 1968); broadcasts in Arabic and English from Tripoli and Benghazi; from September 1971 special daily broadcasts to Gaza and other Israeli-occupied territory were begun; under the direction of the Minister of Information and Culture; Dir.-Gen. IBRAHIM EL BISHARY.

Number of radio receivers: 100,000 (1973).

A national television service was inaugurated in December 1968. Number of TV receivers: 15,000 (1973).

FINANCE

BANKING

(cap. = capital; p.u. = paid up; dep. = deposits; LD = Libyan Dinar; m. = million)

CENTRAL BANK

Central Bank of Libya: Fatah St., P.O.B. 1103, Tripoli; br. at Benghazi; f. 1955; central bank with facilities for commercial business; cap. p.u. LD 1m.; dep. LD 868.6m.; Gov. K. M. SHERLALA.

Wahda Bank: P.O.B. 452, Jamal Abdul Naser St., Benghazi; f. 1970 to take over Bank of North Africa, Commercial Bank, S.A.L., Nadha Arabia Bank, Kafila Ahly Bank and Soc. Africaine de Banque; cap. and res. L.D. 4m.; dep. L.D. 43m. (Dec. 1972); Chair. and Gen. Man. MOHAMED S. KHLEIF.

Masraf al Gumhouria: Giaddat Emhamed El Megarief St., P.O.B. 3224, Tripoli; f. Nov. 1969 as successor to Barclays Bank D.C.O. in Libya; government owned; brs. throughout Libya; cap. L.D. 1.5m.; dep. L.D. 74.4m. (Sept. 73); Chair. NURI A. BARYUN.

Masraf al Sahara: P.O.B. 270, 1st September St., Tripoli; f. 1964; Chair. and Gen. Man. FARAG A. GAMRA.

Umma Bank S.A.L.: P.O.B. 685, 1 Giaddet Omar Mukhtar, Tripoli; brs. in Benghazi, Sebha, Kufra, Hoon, Nalut Gasr Ben Gashir; f. 1969; cap. L.D. 500,000; dep. L.D. 69m.; Chair. and Gen. Man. YOUSEF I. AGHIL.

OIL

Petroleum affairs in Libya are dealt with entirely by the Ministry of Petroleum which is charged, in accordance with Article 2 of Law 170 of 1970, with organization, control, follow-up and supervision of petroleum resources within the limits of the State's general policy, development plan and regulations in force concerning petroleum matters. In 1973 and 1974 Libya has been entering into participation agreements with some of the foreign oil companies, and nationalizing others.

Ministry of Petroleum: P.O.B. 256, Tripoli.

Libyan National Oil Corporation (LINOCO): P.O.B. 2655, Tripoli; f. 1970 as successor to the Libyan General Petroleum Corporation, to undertake joint ventures with foreign companies; to build and operate refineries, storage tanks, petrochemical facilities, pipelines and tankers; to take part in arranging specifications for local and imported petroleum products; to participate in general planning of oil installations in Libya; to market

crude oil and to establish and operate oil terminals; Chair. OMAR MUNTASAR.

The following are some of the most important oil companies operating in Libya.

Amoco Libya Oil Co.: P.O.B. 982, Tripoli; Pres. and Resident Man. R. E. MOYAR.

Aquitaine Libye: P.O.B. 282, Tripoli; subsidiary of Société Nationale des Pétroles d'Aquitaine; operates for Hispanoil, Murco Libya Oil, Elf Libye and Aquitaine Libye on concessions 104–105; operates for Elf Libye and Aquitaine Libye on concession 137; operates for National Oil Corporation, Elf Libye and Aquitaine Libye on blocs LP1, LP2, and LP3.

Arabian Gulf Exploration Co.: P.O.B. 263, Benghazi; f. 1971 after nationalization of BP interests; Chair. and Gen. Man. ABDULLATIF YUSEF ZARROUQ.

Esso Sirte Inc.: P.O.B. 565, Tripoli; Pres. and Board Chair. H. H. GOERNER.

Esso Standard Libya Inc.: P.O.B. 385, Tripoli; exploration, production, transportation, refining, marketing of crude oil and other hydrocarbons; transportation and marketing of petroleum products and related specialities; Pres. and Board Chair. H. H. GOERNER.

Gelsenberg Libyan Branch: P.O.B. 2537, Tripoli; Gen. Man. FRIEDRICH R. EDTINGER.

Mobil Oil Libya Ltd.: P.O.B. 690, Tripoli; Gen. Man. D. F. PENDLEY.

Nelson Bunker Hunt: P.O.B. 20, Benghazi.

Oasis Oil Company of Libya Inc.: P.O.B. 395, Tripoli; operator for Continental, Marathon, Amerada and Shell companies; Chair. and Chief Exec. W. E. SWALES.

Occidental of Libya Inc.: P.O.B. 2134, Tripoli; runs a pipeline from the Intisar field to a terminal at Zuetina; present production 600,000 BPD; Pres. and Dir. R. H. ESPEY.

Umm Al-Jawaby Petroleum Company S.A.L.: P.O.B. 693, Tripoli; 100 per cent owned by Libyan National Oil Corporation; Chair. and Gen. Man. H. S. BELAZI.

Agip, a subsidiary of the Italian state company ENI, has formed a company to participate with the Libyan National Oil Corporation (LINOCO).

TRADE AND INDUSTRY

CHAMBERS OF COMMERCE

Tripolitania Chamber of Commerce and Industry: Sharia Al Jumhouria, Tripoli; f.1952; Pres. ABDUL LATIF KEKHIA; Sec.-Gen. KAMAL ARAB; 40,000 mems.; publs. *Quarterly Bulletin*, *Commercial Directory* (annual, English and Arabic).

Benghazi Chamber of Commerce, Industry and Agriculture: P.O.B. 208-1286, Benghazi; f. 1953; Pres. HASAN H. MATAR; Sec.-Gen. MUHAMMAD H. ALGAZERI; 5,400 mems.

DEVELOPMENT

Industrial and Real Estate Bank of Libya: Tripoli and Benghazi; f. 1965; state industrial development and house-building finance agency, cap. LD 10m.; Dir. MOHAMED RABEI.

Kufrah and Sevir Authority: Council of Agricultural Development, Benghazi; f. 1972 to develop the Kufrah Oasis and Sevir area in south-east Libya.

National General Organization for Industrialization: P.O.B. 4388, Tripoli; f. March 1970; Chair. ABDEL SALAM JALOOD; Deputy Chair. ABU-BAKR SHERIF.

NATIONALIZED INDUSTRIES

General Tobacco Monopoly: P.O.B. 696, Tripoli; develops the production and curing of tobacco; leaf production (1971) 1.35 million kilos, manufactured tobacco production 2.4 million kilos per year.

TRADE UNIONS

National Trade Unions' Federation: (affiliated to ICFTU); P.O.B. 734, 2 Sharia Istanbul, Tripoli; f. 1952; Sec.-Gen. SALEM SHITA; 30,000 mems.; Publ. *Attalia* (weekly).

Engineering Union: Tripoli; f. 1971; membership open to foreign engineers working in Libya, as well as Libyans.

Union of Petroleum Workers of Libya: Tripoli; also branch in Benghazi.

TRADE FAIR

Tripoli International Fair: P.O.B. 891, Tripoli; under control of General Board of Tourism and Fairs; annual fair March 1st–20th; Chair. and Dir.-Gen. SALEH F. AZZABI.

TRANSPORT

ROADS

The most important road in Libya is the national coast road, 1,822 km. in length, which runs the whole way from the Tunisian to the Egyptian border, passing through Tripoli and Benghazi. This road has recently been widened and re-surfaced. It has a second link between Barce and Lamluda, which is 141 km. long. The other federal road completed (in 1962) runs from a point on the coastal road 120 km. south of Misurata through Sebha (capital of Fezzan) to Ghat near the Algerian border (total length of 1,250 km.). There is a branch 260 km. long running from Vaddan to Sirte. There is a new road crossing the desert from Sebha to the frontiers of Chad and Niger.

In addition to the national highways, the west of Libya has about 1,200 km. of black-top and macadamized roads and the east about 500 km. Practically all the towns and villages of Libya, including the desert oases, are accessible by motor vehicle, but the going is sometimes rough.

General Corporation for Public Transport (GCPT): Tripoli; f. 1971 to manage public transport utilities throughout the country.

SHIPPING

Principal ports are Tripoli, Benghazi, Port Brega and the Oasis Marine Terminal at Es-Sider. Port Brega was opened to oil tankers in 1961. A 30-inch crude oil pipeline connects the Zelten oilfields with Marsa El Brega. Another pipeline joins the Sarir oilfield with Marsa Hariga, the port of Tobruk, and a pipeline from the Sarir field to Zuetina was opened in 1968. There is another oil port at Ras Lunuf.

Maritime Transport Corporation: Tripoli; f. 1970 to handle all projects dealing with maritime trade.

The following shipping companies are among those operating services through Libyan ports:

Abdurrahman R. Kikhia and Co. (Shipping Division): f. 1968; offices in Tripoli: P.O.B. 401; Benghazi: P.O.B. 157; Tobruk: P.O.B. 16.

The Libyan Transport Co.: Benghazi; Sharia Omar El Mukhtar, P.O.B. 94; f. 1949; brs. at Beida, Tobruk, Marsa Brega and Cairo; Dirs. A. S. FERGIANI, A. T. BUZER, A. F. JIAFAR.

Giaber Agency: f. 1946; membership 25; Head Office: Tripoli, 12-16 Jebba St.

National Navigation Co. of Libya: Tripoli: 67 Bagdad St., P.O.B. 2437; Benghazi: P.O.B. 139; f. 1964; regular services from Tunisian, French, Spanish, Moroccan, Algerian, Turkish and Italian ports to Tripoli and Benghazi; Man. L. TAKTAK.

Tirrenia, Società per Azioni di Navigazione: Tripoli: c/o Libyan Shipping and Travel Agency, Sharia Istiklal, Badri Bldg., P.O.B. 985; Benghazi: G. Gabriel, c/o Libyan Transport Co., Sharia Omar El Mukhtar 19.

CIVIL AVIATION

There are four civil airports:

The International Airport, situated at Ben Gashir, 21 miles from Tripoli.

Benina Airport, 12 miles from Benghazi.

Sebha Airport.

Misurata Airport (domestic flights only).

Libyan Arab Airlines: P.O.B. 2555, Tripoli; f. 1965; services to Benghazi, Tripoli, Athens, Cairo, Rome, Tunis, Malta, Paris, Beirut, Belgrade, London, Khartoum, Damascas, Algiers, Casablanca; domestic services throughout Libya; fleet includes two Boeing 727, three Caravelle 6R aircraft and four Fokker F-27; Chair. ABDULGADER GEBANI; Vice-Chair. and Gen. Man. HASSAN KUNIALI.

Libyan Aviation Ltd.: Benghazi; Domestic services.

Linair (*Libyan National Airways*): P.O.B. 3583, Tripoli; f. 1962; domestic services; Pres. Z. Y. LENGHI, Gen. Man. P. W. BAKKER.

Libya is also served by the following foreign airlines: Aeroflot, Air Algérie, Alitalia, British Caledonian, ČSA, EgyptAir, JAT, KLM, Lufthansa, Malta Airlines, Saudia, Sudan Airways. Swissair, Syrian Arab, Tunis Air, UTA.

TOURISM

General Board of Tourism and Fairs: Tripoli; f. 1964.

Tourism is being developed in Libya, but major potential attractions include the superb Roman remains at Leptis Magna, Sabratha and Cyrene, the fine climate, mountains and hundreds of miles of unspoilt beaches.

UNIVERSITY

University of Libya: Benghazi; f. 1955; 950 teachers, 16,320 students (1973–74).

MADAGASCAR

INTRODUCTORY SURVEY

Location, Climate, Language, Religion, Flag, Capital

The Malagasy Republic occupies the island of Madagascar (by which name it is generally known), and lies 300 miles off the coast of Mozambique (Portuguese East Africa). The climate is tropical. The northern parts of the island receive monsoon rains from December to April but the rest of the country is fairly dry. The official languages are Malagasy and French. Hova and other dialects are widely spoken. About half the population follow animist beliefs, Christians constitute about 40 per cent and the remainder are Muslims. The national flag (proportions 3 by 2) has a vertical white stripe (one-third of the length) at the hoist and horizontal stripes of red and green. The capital is Tananarive.

Recent History

Formerly a French colony, Madagascar became a self-governing member of the French Community in 1958 and attained full independence in 1960. In 1961 the country played a leading role in the formation of the Union Africaine et Malgache. The first President was Philibert Tsiranana, founder of the *Parti social démocrate* (PSD). He was re-elected in 1965, and his party maintained a strong majority. After 1967 the economy declined, the Government became more conservative and authoritarian, and by 1969 opposition was considerable. Other parties were too small or localized to challenge the Government, but in April 1971 discontent surfaced in an armed uprising in the poor Tuléar region, involving the *Mouvement national pour l'indépendence de Madagascar* (MONIMA). This uprising was quickly suppressed by the Government, who attributed it to a Communist plot; MONIMA was outlawed but its membership grew. In January 1972 Tsiranana presented himself again as the sole candidate for the Presidency and was re-elected by 99.9 per cent of votes cast. However, on May 13th, 1972, riots broke out in the capital between security forces and a group combining students, teachers, labourers and the *zoam* (urban unemployed), who with others formed the May 13th Movement (KIM). After three days of violence and 34 deaths, the President handed over full powers to his Chief-of-Staff, Major-Gen. Gabriel Ramanantsoa, who followed a policy of appeasing the Government's critics. Gen. Ramanantsoa permitted a KIM congress in September and agreed to act on some of its recommendations, if given a mandate by the people to govern for five years without the institutions of the 1959 Constitution, and to restore order and economic stability. In the referendum held on October 8th, 1972, 96 per cent of votes cast were in Ramanantsoa's favour, and he took office as Head of Government on November 7th. His policy is one of conciliation and national independence. His Government has disavowed agreements with South Africa and entered into diplomatic relations with several Communist states, released political prisoners and has begun to "Malagasize" education. In 1973 it renegotiated all co-operation agreements with France, obtaining the closing of French military bases on the island. In the same year Madagascar withdrew from the Franc Zone and OCAM. The Government has faced some internal political difficulties. In early 1973 there was violent rioting between the Merina, a tribal group with whom the Government is identified, and the more affluent *cotiers*, their traditional rivals. There has been widespread discontent over high prices, rising unemployment and food shortages. Several opposition leaders have been imprisoned for short periods. However, the elections to the People's National Development Council in October 1973 were a great victory for pro-Government parties.

Government

The Presidential form of Government adopted under the 1959 Constitution was put into abeyance in May 1972 and officially suspended for five years on November 7th, 1972, when Major-Gen. Gabriel Ramanantsoa was granted full powers for five years. His 16-man cabinet is drawn from both military and civilian life and includes the six newly-appointed Heads of Provinces. Two new representative advisory bodies have been set up to replace the suspended bi-cameral legislature. Rural communes have been replaced by the traditional community units, *fokonola*, which form the basis of the four-storey pyramid structure of Government. As Head of Government, Gen. Ramanantsoa rules by ordinance. In 1972 the age of majority was lowered to 18 years.

Defence

In 1973 total armed forces numbered 4,250 men; army, 3,700; navy, 250; and air force, 300. There is a para-military gendarmerie of 4,000. Under an agreement signed in 1973 all French land troops have been withdrawn from the island and the French naval base at Diégo-Suarez is to be closed.

Economic Affairs

The economy is principally agricultural with the great majority of the population living on the land. Agricultural produce is mainly for subsistence but also forms the bulk of exports, the most important of which is coffee, followed by cloves and clove oil, vanilla, rice and sugar. Tobacco, pepper and bananas are also grown for export. Large herds of cattle are maintained but contribute little to the economy. There are extensive mineral deposits including graphite, mica, nickel and copper, but only limited commercial exploitation. Since 1969 chromite deposits at Andriamena have been mined, and in 1971 over 62,000 tons of chromium ore were extracted. In 1971 bauxite was found in the south and a company set up to mine it. The oil refinery at Tamatave, which is based on imported petroleum, has contributed significantly to exports since 1967. Industry is confined largely to processing agricultural produce. The present Government is pursuing a policy of "Malagasization" of the economy. Essential sectors of the economy are being nationalized, Europeans are being replaced by Malagasy in top posts, and efforts are being made to ensure that the profits of enterprises in Madagascar benefit the local people. These measures have led to a drop in foreign investment. Madagascar withdrew from the Franc Zone in 1973. There is a chronic balance of payments deficit, and the solvency of the Government is seriously in question. The rate of inflation in 1973 was very high and there have been serious shortages, especially of rice, the basic food on the island.

Transport and Communications

The terrain is difficult and transport is not well developed. There are 884 km. of railway, mainly single track and narrow gauge. Of the 38,000 km. of roads and tracks, most can be used only in dry weather. Most of the west coast rivers are navigable for about 160 km., and on the east coast the Pangalanes canal follows the coast from Tamatave to Farafungana. The chief ports are Tamatave, Majunga and Diégo-Suarez. The international airport is at Ivato, near Tananarive, and there is an extensive internal airways network which provides the main means of travel, especially in the wet season.

Social Welfare

All medical services are free and there are family allowances as well as benefits for industrial accidents and occupational diseases. Much welfare is offered by Christian missions. France and Madagascar signed an agreement, granting reciprocal benefits to expatriate workers in each other's country, in 1967.

Education

Madagascar has both public and private schools. Efforts are being made to increase the number of schools and the primary schools can now accommodate over half the children. There is one university. The education system is closely modelled on that of France, and many of the teachers are French nationals, but changes are being introduced to "Malagasize" it.

Tourism

Plans have been prepared to develop tourism and it was hoped to increase the number of tourists from 6,000 in 1968 to 20,000 in 1973, but this has proved over-optimistic.

Visas are not required to visit the Malagasy Republic by nationals of France.

Sport

The most popular sports are football, rugby, basketball and swimming. Athletics, tennis, golf and volleyball also have their following.

Public Holidays

1974: August 15th (Assumption), October 16th (Madagascar National Day), November 1st (All Saints' Day), December 25th (Christmas).

1975: January 1st, 2nd (New Year), March 29th (Commemoration of 1947 Rebellion), March 31st (Easter Monday), May 1st (Labour Day), May 8th (Ascension Day), May 19th (Whitsun), May 28th (African Liberation Day), June 26th (Independence Day).

Weights and Measures

The metric system is in force.

Currency and Exchange Rates

100 centimes=1 franc Malgache (MG).

Exchange rates (April 1974):

1 franc MG =2 French centimes;

£1 sterling=579.75 francs MG;

U.S. $1=245.625 francs MG.

STATISTICAL SURVEY

AREA AND POPULATION

AREA (sq. km.)	POPULATION (1971)						
	Total	Malagasy	French	Comorians	Indians	Chinese	Others
587,041	7,655,134	7,550,508	30,788	40,698	17,992	9,881	5,267

PRINCIPAL ETHNIC GROUPS
(1972)

Merina (Hova)	.	2,066,994	Sakalava . .	470,156
Betsimisaraka	.	1,165,592	Antandroy . .	428,350
Betsileo .	.	953,968	Antaisaka . .	406,468
Tsimihety .	.	572,847		

MAIN TOWNS
(estimated population, 1972)

Tananarive (capital)	. 366,530	Diégo-Suarez . .	45,487
Majunga . .	. 67,458	Tuléar . .	38,978
Tamatave . .	. 59,503	Antsirabé . .	33,287
Fianarantsoa .	. 58,818		

REGISTERED BIRTHS AND DEATHS, 1972

Births	Birth Rate	Deaths	Death Rate
280,131	35.3 per 1,000	81,760	10.3 per 1,000

Birth registration is estimated to be 80 per cent complete and death registration 60 per cent complete. Rates for 1966 (based on a sample survey) were: Births 46 per 1,000, deaths 25 per 1,000.

AGRICULTURE

LAND USE, 1969
('000 hectares)

Arable and Under Permanent Crops . .	2,856
Permanent Meadows and Pastures . .	34,000
Forest	12,470
Other Land	8,828
Inland Water	550
Total	58,704

Source: FAO, Production Yearbook.

PRINCIPAL CROPS
('000 metric tons)

	1969	1970	1971
Maize	143	109	118
Rice (Paddy)	1,858	1,865	1,873
Sugar Cane*	949	1,113	1,239
Potatoes	97	94	108
Sweet Potatoes and Yams .	367	350	344
Cassava (Manioc) . . .	1,253	1,218	n.a.
Dry Beans	56	49	52†
Oranges and Tangerines .	47	57	62
Bananas	257	262	344
Pineapples	35	35	n.a.
Groundnuts (in shell) . .	44	41	40
Cottonseed	17	7	23
Cotton (Lint)	6	7	9
Tung Nuts	5	5†	n.a.
Coffee	63.9	66.6	57.7
Cocoa Beans‡ . . .	0.8	0.9	1.1
Tobacco	5.6	4.9	5.7
Sisal	29.5	26.3	25
Cape Peas	17	20.5	n.a.
Cloves	2.5	12	n.a.
Vanilla	1.2	1.2	n.a.
Pepper	2	n.a.	n.a.

1972 ('000 metric tons): Rice (Paddy) 1,685, Sugar Cane 969, Groundnuts 49, Cottonseed 24, Coffee 55, Tobacco 6.4, Sisal 21, Cape Peas 23, Cloves 5, Vanilla 1.5, Pepper 2.5.

* Crop year ending in year stated.   † FAO estimate.
‡ Twelve months ending in September of year stated.
Source: FAO, Production Yearbook 1971.

LIVESTOCK
('000)

	1968–69	1969–70	1970–71
Cattle . . .	10,422	9,881	10,000*
Pigs . . .	522	525	530*
Sheep† . .	605	492	500*
Goats . . .	773	876	900*
Chickens . .	10,900*	11,000	11,200
Ducks . . .	1,900*	2,000	2,050*
Geese . . .	1,900*	2,000	2,100*
Turkeys . .	900*	1,000*	1,050*

* FAO estimate.
† Figures relate to animals registered for taxation.
Source: FAO, Production Yearbook 1971.

LIVESTOCK PRODUCTS
(metric tons)

	1969	1970	1971*
Cows' Milk . . .	37,000*	38,000*	40,000
Beef	114,000*	118,000*	112,000
Hen Eggs . . .	9,200	9,200	9,500
Honey	13,000	13,500*	14,000

* FAO estimate.
Source: FAO, Production Yearbook 1971.

FORESTRY

ROUNDWOOD PRODUCTION
('ooo cubic metres)

1967 . . .	4,500
1968 . . .	4,781
1969 . . .	4,862
1970 . . .	5,236

Sawnwood: 100,000 cubic metres in 1971.

Source: FAO, *Yearbook of Forest Products.*

FISHING
(metric tons)

	1969	1970	1971
Inland Water . .	33,900	35,100	36,900
Indian Ocean . .	9,100	10,400	11,100
TOTAL CATCH .	43,000	45,500	48,000

Source: FAO, *Yearbook of Fishery Statistics 1971.*

MINING

	UNIT	1968	1969	1971
Graphite	metric tons	16,430	16,888	20,051
Salt	,, ,,	17,000	22,000	28,000
Mica	,, ,,	906	829	588
Industrial Beryls . . .	,, ,,	65.10	75	60
Industrial Garnets . .	,, ,,	1.35	n.a.	n.a.
Quartz	,, ,,	1.35	n.a.	n.a.
Gold	kg.	15	20	13

1969: Chromium ore 18,582 metric tons.

1970: Chromium ore 43,444 metric tons; Gold 16 kg.

1971: Chromium ore 62,200 metric tons.

INDUSTRY

	UNIT	1969	1970	1971‡	1972‡
Raw Sugar	metric tons	98,000	102,000	93,310	103,806
Tapioca	,, ,,	5,620‡	3,695‡	3,754	2,001
Vegetable Oils	,, ,,	6,236‡	7,159‡	5,898	6,137
Beer	hectolitres	80,199‡	92,764‡	112,440	120,770
Cigarettes	metric tons	790	951	944	1,092
Chewing Tobacco . . .	,, ,,	1,270‡	1,551‡	1,755	1,869
Cotton Yarn	,, ,,	4,600	4,900	6,200	n.a.
Woven Cotton Fabrics . .	,, ,,	3,700	4,700	5,500	n.a.
Cement	,, ,,	76,000	76,000	76,930	64,177
Liquefied Petroleum Gas . .	,, ,,	6,000	8,000	8,000	n.a.
Motor Spirit (Petrol) . .	,, ,,	95,000	125,000	114,000	n.a.
Kerosene	,, ,,	60,091‡	75,935‡	70,372	17,910
Jet Fuels	,, ,,	12,000	n.a.	n.a.	n.a.
Distillate Fuel Oils . . .	,, ,,	126,000	157,000	149,000	n.a.
Residual Fuel Oils . . .	,, ,,	158,000	210,000	212,561	201,208
Lubricating Oils . . .	,, ,,	7,000	n.a.	n.a.	n.a.
Petroleum Bitumen (Asphalt) .	,, ,,	7,000	n.a.	n.a.	n.a.
Paints	,, ,,	2,018‡	2,561‡	n.a.	2,611
Soap	,, ,,	4,079	6,444	9,802	12,343
Electric Energy	million kWh.	150‡	172‡	195	213

Sources: United Nations, *Statistical Yearbook 1971* and *The Growth of World Industry*, except:

    * *Source:* U.S. Department of Agriculture.

    † *Source:* U.S. Bureau of Mines.

    ‡ *Source:* Institut National de la Statistique et de la Recherche Economique, Tananarive.

FINANCE

100 centimes = 1 franc Malgache.
Coins: 1, 2, 5, 10 and 20 francs MG.
Notes: 50, 100, 500, 1,000 and 5,000 francs MG.
Exchange rates (April 1974): 1 franc MG = 2 French centimes; £1 sterling = 579.75 francs MG;
U.S. $1 = 245.625 francs MG.
1,000 francs MG = £1.725 = $4.071.

Note: In 1973 the Government announced plans to create a new national currency, the ariary, equivalent to 5 francs MG

Budget (1972): balanced at 81,000 million FMG.

Budget (1973): balanced at 89,084 million FMG.

Five-Year Plan (1970–74): Minimum sum for investment 120,000 million FMG; the main emphasis of the plan will be on agricultural development.

Currency in Circulation (May 1973): 24,940 million francs MG.

EXTERNAL TRADE
(million FMG)*

	1965	1966	1967	1968	1969	1970	1971	1972
Imports . . .	34,089	35,004	35,847	41,937	47,198	47,346	59,220	51,753
Exports . . .	22,632	24,132	25,711	28,608	29,154	40,222	40,807	41,864

* Excluding trade in gold and military goods.

PRINCIPAL COMMODITIES
(million FMG)

IMPORTS	1970	1971	1972	EXPORTS	1970	1971	1972
Chemical Products . .	6,496	6,511	5,453	Coffee (Green) . . .	10,935	10,811	11,643
Mineral Products . .	4,148	4,750	5,085	Rice	3,072	2,050	1,651
of which Crude Petroleum	2,406	2,428	3,089	Vanilla	3,610	3,566	3,819
Cotton Textiles . .	3,021	3,329	3,002	Sugar	1,547	1,099	1,475
Metal Products . .	6,343	6,692	5,509	Tobacco	n.a.	684	922
Machinery . . .	5,534	7,028	7,012	Cloves and Clove Oil .	4,697	6,501	4,962
Electrical Equipment .	2,965	4,396	4,018	Raffia	n.a.	420	473
Vehicles and Parts .	5,637	7,953	6,545	Groundnuts . . .	n.a.	n.a.	328
				Petroleum Products . .	1,555	1,470	1,671

PRINCIPAL COUNTRIES
(million FMG)

IMPORTS	1970	1971	1972	EXPORTS	1970	1971	1972
Belgium/Luxembourg .	1,545	1,152	560	France	13,756	13,937	16,051
France	25,982	33,397	28,645	Germany, Federal Republic	1,651	1,335	1,448
Germany, Federal Republic	4,287	5,179	4,922	Italy	n.a.	832	801
Iran	222	503	479	Japan	1,267	1,828	1,936
Italy	2,800	2,373	2,002	Malaysia	2,355	2,822	1,763
Japan	1,295	1,325	2,302	Netherlands . . .	433	541	735
Netherlands . . .	1,171	1,843	1,225	Réunion	4,612	3,403	3,184
United Kingdom . .	839	1,215	895	United Kingdom . .	777	641	691
U.S.A.	2,688	2,881	2,024	U.S.A.	9,117	9,094	8,573

MADAGASCAR—(Statistical Survey)

TRANSPORT

RAILWAYS

	1970	1971	1972
Passengers ('000) . .	2,365	2,595	2,587
Passenger/km. (millions) .	182	200	192
Freight ('000 metric tons) .	703	751	648
Ton/km. (millions) . .	224	246	205

ROADS
Vehicles in Use

	1968	1969	1970
Cars . .	40,544	43,096	45,992
Lorries . .	27,538	29,220	31,147
Buses . .	2,446	2,866	3,149
Other Commercial Vehicles . .	2,381	2,684	2,882

SHIPPING

	MAJUNGA			TAMATAVE		
	1970	1971	1972	1970	1971	1972
Vessels Entered . . .	1,584	1,620	1,603	933	945	721
Passengers Arrived . . .	3,522	2,530	1,802	1,125	2,227	556
Passengers Departed . . .	3,761	3,248	2,763	1,729	2,511	588
Freight Entered ('000 tons) . .	178	222	194	341	365	274
Freight Cleared ('000 tons) . .	134	120	108	318	287	259

CIVIL AVIATION

	PASSENGERS		FREIGHT (metric tons)	
	Arrived	Departed	Unloaded	Loaded
1969 . .	80,425	77,231	1,863	3,679
1970 . .	83,284	84,929	2,033	4,672
1971 . .	92,359	93,456	2,154	5,031

Source (for Railways, Shipping and Civil Aviation): I.N.S.E.E., *Données Statistiques*, Paris, 1972.

COMMUNICATIONS
TELEPHONES IN USE

1968 . .	23,993
1969 . .	25,258
1970 . .	27,000

EDUCATION

	1971			1972		
	Schools	Teachers	Pupils	Schools	Teachers	Pupils
Primary*	5,706	14,424	938,015	6,054	15,553	1,004,447
Secondary†	514	n.a.	101,412	526	n.a.	105,320
Technical†	128	665	9,006	128	684	10,177
Higher (University) . .	1	n.a.	5,293	1	n.a.	5,874

* Figures refer to both public and private schools.
† Figures refer to public schools only; in addition approximately 70,000 pupils attended private secondary schools.

Source (unless otherwise stated): Institut National de la Statistique et de la Recherche Economique, Tananarive.

THE CONSTITUTION

The constitutional law adopted after the referendum of October 8th, 1972, grants Major-Gen. Gabriel Ramanantsoa full powers for five years as Head of Government, and in December 1972 it was announced that "until the adoption of the new Constitution and the establishment of new institutions, the attributes, powers and prerogatives conferred on the President of the Republic by the former Constitution of April 29th, 1959, and the legislation in force will be exercised by the Head of Government". The Senate and the National Assembly have been suspended for the five-year term of Gen. Ramanantsoa's Government, which has, however, established two representative advisory bodies, a Higher Institutional Council and a People's National Development Council. Local government has been reorganized on traditional lines with *fokonola* (small communities) replacing communes within the Provinces. A Constitutional Committee is to be set up, and the Government is pledged to draw up a new Constitution to come into effect at the end of the five-year period.

THE GOVERNMENT

HEAD OF GOVERNMENT

Maj.-Gen. Gabriel Ramanantsoa (*appointment ratified by referendum October* 1972).

CABINET
(*May* 1974)

Head of Government, in charge of the Ministry of Defence and the Armed Forces: Maj.-Gen. Gabriel Ramanantsoa.

Minister of Territorial Planning: Brig. Gilles Andriamahazo.

Minister of Justice: Jacques Andrianada Vahazabe.

Minister of Cultural Affairs and National Education: Prof. Justin Manambelona.

Minister of Economy, Trade and Finance: Albert-Marie Ramaroson.

Minister of Social Affairs: Dr. Albert Zafy.

Minister of Home Affairs and Commander of the National Gendarmerie: Lt.-Col. Richard Ratsimandrava.

Minister of Information: Lieut.-Col. Joël Rakotomalala.

Minister of Foreign Affairs: Capt. Didier Ratsiraka.

Minister of Rural Development: Dr. Emmanuel Rakotovahiny.

Minister of Civil Service and Labour: Daniel Rajakoba.

Head of the Province of Tuléar: Capt. Soja.

Head of the Province of Majunga: Cmdr. Mampila.

Head of the Province of Tananarive: Cmdr. Raymond Razafintsalama.

Head of the Province of Tamatave: Capt. Raveloson Mahasampo.

Head of the Province of Fianarantsoa: Lt.-Col. Lucien Rakotonirainy.

Head of the Province of Diégo-Suarez: Capt. Guy Albert Sibon.

DIPLOMATIC REPRESENTATION

EMBASSIES ACCREDITED TO MADAGASCAR
(In Tananarive unless otherwise stated)

Algeria: Dar es Salaam, Tanzania.
Austria: Addis Ababa, Ethiopia.
Belgium: Nairobi, Kenya.
Canada: Addis Ababa, Ethiopia.
China, People's Republic: Dar es Salaam, Tanzania.
France: Maison de France, Antaninarenina; *Ambassador:* Maurice Delauney.
Germany, Federal Republic: 101 route circulaire, Ambodirotra; *Ambassador:* Alfred B. Vestring.
Ghana: Kinshasa, Zaire.
Greece: Addis Ababa, Ethiopia.
Guinea: Dar es Salaam, Tanzania.
India: 77 ave. Maréchal Foch; *Ambassador:* Nugahalli Kesavan.
Italy: 22 rue Docteur Besson, Ankadivato; *Ambassador:* Lionello Cozzi.
Japan: 20 rue Clémenceau; *Ambassador:* Shiro Shimizi.
Korea, Democratic People's Republic: Dar es Salaam, Tanzania.
Korea, Republic: Paris, France.

Netherlands: Addis Ababa, Ethiopia.
Nigeria: *Ambassador:* Mr. Osobase.
Norway: Nairobi, Kenya.
Pakistan: Dar es Salaam, Tanzania.
Spain: Nairobi, Kenya.
Sweden: Addis Ababa, Ethiopia.
Switzerland: 17 rue Cavayon; *Ambassador:* Heinz Langenbacher.
Turkey: Addis Ababa, Ethiopia.
U.S.S.R.: Paris, France.
United Kingdom: rue Choiseul, Parc d'Ambohijatovo; *Ambassador:* Timothy Crosthwait.
U.S.A.: 14 rue Rainitovo, Antsahavola; *Ambassador:* Joseph A. Mendenhall.
Vatican: Carrefour d'Ivandry, Amboniloha (Apostolic Nunciature); *Apostolic Nuncio:* Michel Cecchini.
Viet-Nam, Democratic Republic: *Ambassador:* (to be appointed).
Yugoslavia: Nairobi, Kenya.

Madagascar also has diplomatic relations with Argentina, Finland, Luxembourg, Philippines, Romania and Tunisia.

HIGHER INSTITUTIONAL COUNCIL

The *Conseil supérieur des institutions* is to have control over the Government's legislative power and advise it in its executive functions. It is also the upholder of the temporary five-year constitution and must ensure that the people are periodically consulted.

PEOPLE'S NATIONAL DEVELOPMENT COUNCIL

The *Conseil national populaire de développement* is the consultative body which replaces Parliament for five years under the temporary constitution. It has 162 members of whom all but 18 government appointees are elected by universal suffrage. Elections were held on October 21st, 1973.

POLITICAL PARTIES

Elan populaire pour l'unité nationale (VONJY): Tananarive; f. 1973; nationalist; Leader Dr. Jérôme Razanabahiny Marojama.

Mouvement national pour l'indépendance de Madagascar (MONIMA): left wing, nationalist party; supports Gen. Ramanantsoa's Government; Leader Monja Jaona.

MFM (Mouvement pour le pouvoir prolétarien or "pouvoir aux petits"): extreme left-wing party; Leader Manandafy Rakotonirina.

Parti du congrès de l'indépendance de Madagascar (PCIM or AKFM): 43 Lalana Rakotomalala Ratsimba, Andravoahangy, Tananarive; f. 1958; 450 member sections; left wing; supports Gen. Ramanantsoa's Government; Pres. Richard Andriamanjato; Sec.-Gen. Gisèle Rabesahala.

Parti démocratique chrétien malgasy: Tananarive; merged with Manjakavahoaka 1968; Leader Alexis Bezaka.

Parti socialiste malgache (PSM): Tananarive; f. 1974 by merging of *Parti social démocrate* and *Union socialiste malgache*; favours closer links with France; Sec.-Gen. André Resampa.

No party is represented in the Government.

JUDICIAL SYSTEM

Supreme Court: 8 Anosy, Tananarive; Pres. Edilbert Razafindralambo.

Attorney-General: Rafamantanantsoa.
Chamber Presidents: Raharinaivo, Rakotobe, Marmot.
Advocates-General: Ratsisalotafy, Rousseau.

Court of Appeal: Tananarive; Pres. Armand Rafalihery.
Attorney-General: Victor Ramanitra.
Chamber Presidents: Rabemalanto, Keromes.

Courts of First Instance: at Tananarive, Tamative, Majunga, Fianarantsoa, Diégo-Suarez and Tuléar; for civil and commercial matters; also Courts of Petty Sessions.

Criminal Courts: at the Court of Appeal; presided over by a Counsellor. Justices of the Peace sit in the main centres.

RELIGION

It is estimated that 57 per cent of the population follow traditional animist beliefs, 38 per cent are Christians (with Roman Catholics comprising 20 per cent of the total population) and 5 per cent are Muslims.

Roman Catholic Church: Three archdioceses:
Archbishop of Tananarive: Cardinal Jérôme Rakotomalala, Ando-halo, Tananarive; there are five dioceses (Ambatondrazaka, Antsirabé, Minrinarivo, Tamatave and Tsiroanomandidy) and about 541 mission centres with a total personnel of 1,800.
Archbishop of Diégo Suarez: B.P. 415, Diégo-Suarez; Mgr. Albert Joseph Tsiahoana; two dioceses (Ambanja and Majunga).
Archbishop of Fianarantsoa: Mgr. Gilbert Ramanantoanina; B.P. 1170; seven dioceses (Farafangana, Fort-Dauphin, Ihosy, Mananjari, Morombe, Morondava and Tuléar).

Eglise Episcopale de Madagascar: 24 rue Jean Laborde, Tananarive; f. 1874; about 35,000 mems.; Anglican; Bishop in Madagascar Mgr. Jean Marcel.

Eglise de Jésus-Christ à Madagascar: 19 rue Fourcadier B.P. 623, Tananarive; f. 1968; Pres. Rev. Joseph Ramambasoa; Gen. Sec. Rev. Richard Rakotondraibe; publ. *Vaovao F.J.K.M.* (French information bulletin).

Christian Council of Madagascar: Theological College, Fianarantsoa; f. 1963; Pres. Prof. Dr. Rakoto Andrianarijaona.

Lutheran Church: Fianarantsoa; Pres. Dr. R. Andrianarijaona.

Church of the Lord's Disciples: Soatanana; Pres. Benjamin Randrianaivo.

Adventist Church: Mandrosoa, Tananarive; Pres. M. Rajoelison.

Independent Church of Antranobiriky: rue Admiral Peter, Tananarive; Pres. M. Z. Randrianaivo.

THE PRESS

PRINCIPAL DAILIES

Imongo Vaovao: 11-k 4 bis Andravoahangy, Tananarive; opposition paper; Dir. Ramamonjisoa Clement; circ. 1,000.

Madagascar-Matin: Imprimerie Centrale, 1 ave de Lattre de Tassigny, Tananarive; in French and Malagasy; Editor Robert Hantzberg; circ. 30,300.

Madagasikara Mahaleotena: Imprimerie Centrale, Analakely, Tananarive; official; Editor E. Rabarison; circ. 5,000.

Maresaka: 12 ave. Rigault-Isotry, Tananarive; f. 1954; independent; Editors S. Rakotoarimah, M. Ralaiarijaona; Malagasy circ. 5,500.

Ny Gazetintsika: Imprimerie Masoandro, Ampasanisadoda, Tananarive; Dir. Edouard Ratsimandisa.

Vaovao: B.P. 271, Tananarive; f. 1894; Government paper; Editor Xavier Ranaivo; circ. 17,000.

PRINCIPAL PERIODICALS

L'Aurore: Majunga; French weekly; circ. 5,000.

Bulletin de Madagascar: Direction de la Presse (Ministère d l'Information), Place de l'Indépendance, B.P. 271, Tananarive; f. 1950; economics, society, culture, linguistics, education; monthly; Editor M. Randriamarozaka; circ. 1,400.

Bulletin de la Société du Corps Médical Malgache: Imprimerie Volamahitsy, Tananarive; monthly; Dir. Dr. RAKOTOMALALALA.

L'Ecole Publique de Madagascar: Direction des Services Académiques de la République Malgache; f. 1951; teaching administration; monthly.

Fanasina (*Salt*): B.P. 1574, Analakely-Tananarive; f. 1957; independent; politics, economics, literature; weekly; Dir. PAUL RAKOTOVOLOLONA; circ. 10,000.

Fanilo: Imprimerie Catholique Fianarantsoa; weekly; Dir. J. RAJAOBELINA.

Hehy: B.P. 1648, Tananarive; f. 1949; fortnightly; humorous; Editor C. ANDRIAMANANTENA; circ. 15,000.

Info-Madagascar: Service de la Presse, Direction de l'Information, B.P. 271, Tananarive; f. 1966; weekly; in French; Editor G. RAMAMONJISOA; circ. 1,000.

L'Information Economique Juridique de Madagascar: Tananarive; every two months.

Journal Officiel de la République Malgache: B.P. 38, Tananarive; f. 1883; official publication; French; weekly; Dir. LUCIEN REJO.

Lakroan'i Madagasikara: Imprimerie Catholique Ambatomena, Fianarantsoa; weekly; Editors F. RÉMY RALIBERA, F. XAVIER TABAO; circ. 8,000.

Lumière: Fianarantsoa; French Catholic weekly; Dir. CHARLES R. RAKOTONIRINA; circ. 10,500.

La République: Tananarive; organ of the Parti Social Démocrate; Dir. VINCENT RABOTOVAVY; Editor A. ANDRIATSIAFAJATO; circ. 8,000.

Revue de Madagascar: Service de Presse du Ministère de l'Information, B.P. 271, Tananarive; f. 1933; annual; Dir. DÉSIRÉ RAZANAMAHOLY; circ. 1,600.

Revue Médicale de Madagascar: B.P. 1655, Tananarive; monthly; Dir. Dr. GOULESQUE.

PRESS AGENCY

Agence Madagascar-Presse: 8 rue du R. P. Callet, Behoririka, B.P. 386, Tananarive; f. 1962; Dir. EMILE RAKOTONIRAINY; publ. *Bulletin Quotidien d'Information.*

PUBLISHERS

Fanontam-Boky Malagasy: Tananarive.

Imprimerie des Arts Graphiques: B.P. 194, rue Dupré, Tananarive; f. 1931.

Imprimerie Centrale: P.O.B. 1414, Tananarive; f. 1959; university and school books, daily newspaper *Madagascar-Matin*; Man. M. HANTZBERG.

Imprimerie Industrielle Catholique: Fianarantsoa.

Imprimerie Nationale: B.P. 38, Tananarive; all official publications; Dir. PARFAIT RAVALOSON.

Librairie-Imprimerie Protestante: Imarivolanitra, Tananarive; f. 1865; religious and school books; Man. GEORGES ANDRIAMANANTENA.

Société Malgache d'Edition: Ankorondrano, B.P. 659, Tananarive; f. 1943; Gen. Man. ANDRÉ IZOUARD.

Trano Printy Loterana: B.P. 538 ave. Grandidier, Antsahamanitra, Tananarive; f. 1968; religious, educational and fiction; Man. Rev. LAUREL O. JOHNSON.

RADIO AND TELEVISION

Radiodiffusion Nationale Malgache: Tananarive, B.P. 442; Government station; fourteen transmitters; programmes in French and Malagasy; foreign service in French and English; Dir. ROGER RABESAHALA.

There is also a Rediffusion station at Fenoarivo, with eight transmitters.

Number of radio receivers: 540,000 in 1970.

Télévision Malgasy: Tananarive, B.P. 442; f. 1967 by Government decree to install and operate a national television service; started operations in Tananarive district 1967; reception in Tananarive area only; programmes in French and Malagasy; Dir. JOCELYN RAFIDINARIVO.

Number of television receivers: 7,000 in 1973.

FINANCE

BANKS

NATIONAL BANKS

Institut d'Emission Malgache: ave. Le-Myre-de-Vilers, BP 550, Tananarive; f. 1962; administrative council of eight; Pres. VICTOR MIADANA; Dir. Gen. JEAN KIENTZ.

(To be replaced by a Central Bank under entirely Malagasy administration).

Banque Malgache d'Escompte et de Crédit (BAMES): Place de l'Indépendance, B.P. 183, Tananarive; f. 1964; cap. FMG 750m.; Pres. LÉON RAJAOBELINA; Gen. Man. JEAN MARIE SÉGUR.

Banque Nationale Malgache de Développement (BNP): ave. Le-Myre-de-Vilers, B.P. 365, Tananarive; f. 1961; administrative council of twelve; cap. FMG 2,000m.; Pres. EMILE RAMAROSAONA; Dir. Gen. CHRISTOPHE ANDRIANARIVO.

FOREIGN BANKS

Banque Française Commerciale S.A.: 74 rue St. Lazare, Paris 9e, France; rue de Liège, B.P. 440, Tananarive.

Banque Nationale pour le Commerce et l'Industrie (Océan Indien): 7 place Vendôme, Paris 1e, France; 74 ave. du 18 Juin, B.P. 174, Tananarive; f. 1919; cap. 25m. French frs.; dep. 995m. French frs.; Pres. and Gen. Man. A. BERONIE (Paris); 15 brs. in Madagascar.

INSURANCE

Syndicat Professionnel des Agents Généraux d'Assurances: Tananarive, 3 rue Benyowski, B.P. 487; f. 1949; Pres. RICHARD MAYER; Sec. YVES DENIER.

The principal French insurance companies, and a few British and Swiss companies, have offices in Tananarive.

TRADE AND INDUSTRY

CHAMBER OF COMMERCE

Fédération des Chambres de Commerce, d'Industrie et d'Agriculture de Madagascar: B.P. 166, 20 rue Colbert, Tananarive; Pres. JEAN RAMAROMISA; Sec.-Gen. H. RATSIANDAVANA.

There are Chambers of Commerce, Agriculture and Industry at Antalaha (Pres. C. TSIHOMANKARY), Antsirabé (Pres. RAJAOFERSON), Diégo-Suarez (Pres. BLAISE RANTOANINA), Fianarantsoa (Pres. JUSTIN MAHALANONA), Fort-Dauphin (Pres. D. N. RAJOELINA), Majunga (Pres. J. RAZAFINDRABE), Mananjary (Pres.

Michel Ratsimbazafy), Morondava (Pres. M. Babilasy), Nossi-Bé (Pres. M. Bleusez), Tamatave (Pres. J. Ramorasata), Tananarive (Pres. H. Razanatseheno) and Tuléar (Pres. J. Etono).

TRADE ORGANIZATION

Société Nationale de Commercialisation Extérieure (SONACO): f. 1973; cap. 120 million FMG; will replace or take a majority share in existing private companies engaged in export.

DEVELOPMENT ORGANIZATIONS

Bureau de Développement et de Promotion Industriels (BDPI): 43 SIAG, ave. Marcel Olivier, B.P. 31, Tananarive.

Société Nationale d'Investissement (SNI): B.P. 222, Tananarive; f. 1962; by the end of 1972 SNI had nearly 2,000m. FMG invested in 50 industrial projects; Dir. Gen. David Rakotopare.

PRINCIPAL EMPLOYERS' ORGANIZATIONS

Groupement des Entreprises Privées de Madagascar: Place Roland Garros, B.P. 1338, Tananarive; f. 1973; 18 syndicates and 14 firms; Sec.-Gen. Mme C. Vabois-Andriamady.

Syndicat des Entrepreneurs: Tananarive, 407 route Circulaire, B.P. 522.

Syndicat des Exportateurs de Vanille de Madagascar: Antalaha; 23 mems.; Pres. Monsieur Bourdillon.

Syndicat des Importateurs et Exportateurs de Madagascar: 2 rue Georges Mandel, B.P. 188, Tananarive; Pres. Monsieur Fontana.

Syndicat des Industries de Madagascar: 41 rue de Choiseul, B.P. 1695, Tananarive; Pres. Léopold Rajoély.

Syndicat des Planteurs de Café: Tananarive, rue de Liège, B.P. 173.

Syndicat des Riziers et Producteurs de Riz de Madagascar: 2 rue Georges Mandel, B.P. 1329, Tananarive.

TRADE UNIONS

Confédération des Travailleurs Malgaches (*Fivomdronam-Ben'ny Mpiasa Malagasy—FMM*): 3 ave. Maréchal Joffre, Ambatomitsanga, B.P. 1558, Tananarive; f. 1957; Sec.-Gen. C. Randrianatoro; 30,000 mems.

Confédération Malgache des Syndicats Libres (Force Ouvrière): Tananarive.

Fédération de l'Education Nationale (FEN): Tananarive; Sec.-Gen. Jean Faugerolle.

Fivondrononam Ben'ny Sendika Kristianina Malagasy—SEKRIMA (*Christian Confederation of Malagasy Trade Unions*): Soarano, route de Majunga, B.P. 1035, Tananarive; f. 1937; Pres. Charles Ralainaorina; Gen. Sec. Hubert Blaise Robel; 158 affiliated unions, 41,670 mems.

Union des Syndicats Autonomes de Madagascar (USAM): Ampasadratsarahoby, Lot II-H-67, Faravohitra, B.P. 1038, Tananarive; Pres. Norbert Rakotomanana; Sec.-Gen. Victor Rahaga; 46 affiliated unions; 29,445 mems.

Union des Syndicats des Travailleurs de Madagascar (*Firaisan'ny Sendika eran'i Madagaskara—FISEMA*): f. 1956; Cimelta, Tananarive; 30,000 mems.

TRANSPORT

RAILWAYS

There are 884 km. of one metre gauge track. One line links Tamatave on the east coast with Antsirabe in the interior via Brichaville, Moramanga and Tananarive, with a branch line from Moramanga to Vohidiala which divides to Lake Alaontra and Morarano to collect chromium ore. The other links Manahara on the south-east coast and Fianarantsoa, and it is proposed to join the lines between Fianarantsoa and Antsirabe.

Réseau National des Chemins de Fer: B.P. 259, Tananarive; f. 1909; Gen. Man. Raymond Ranaivoarivelo.

ROADS

Madagascar has 8,400 km. of national highways of which 3,370 are bitumen-surfaced. There are also 17,600 km. of provincial roads and 12,000 km. of local roads. In each category large parts of roads are not servicable throughout the year.

Automobile Club de Madagascar: route des Hydrocarbures, B.P. 571, Tananarive; f. 1949; Pres. Charles Rakotondralambo; Dir. Pierre Hyais; publ. *Guide Routier et Touristique* (includes Madagascar, Réunion, Mauritius, Comores, Seychelles).

INLAND WATERWAYS

The Pangalanes Canal runs for 700 km. near the east coast from Tamatave to Farafangana. In the west the rivers are navigable.

SHIPPING

There are 18 ports, the largest being at Tamatave and Majunaga. A new port is planned in the Bay of Narinda, 140 km. north of Majunga.

Compagnie Malgache de Navigation: rue Rabearivelo, B.P. 1021, Antsahavola, Tananarive; coasters; Pres. J. Barnaud; Dir. F. Monty.

Cie. Maritime des Chargeurs Réunis: Tamatave, rue du Commerce.

Ets. A. Stefani: B.P. 25, Diégo-Suarez; agents for Svedel Line, Cie. des Transports et Remorquages.

La Ligne Scandinave Agence Maritime: 1 *bis* rue Clémenceau, B.P. 679, Tananarive; agents for Scandinavian-East Africa Line.

S. A. M. Darrieux et Cie.: rue du Commerce, Tamatave; agents for Royal Inter-Ocean Lines.

Société Industrielle et Commerciale de l'Emyrne: B.P. 61, rue Sylvain Roux, Tamatave; agents for B.P. Tanker Co., Shell International Marine Ltd.

Société Malgache des Transports Maritimes: B.P. 4077, 6 rue de Nice, Tananarive; f. 1963; services to Europe; Pres. Jean Bemananjara; Dir. Hubert Rajaobelina.

Société Maritime de Madagascar: ave. Grandidier, Tananarive; f. 1956; tankers; Pres. Dir.-Gen. Pierre Segond.

CIVIL AVIATION

The international airport is at Tananarive. In all there are 199 aerodromes of which 86 are private and many are small, but in addition to Tananarive both Tamatave and Majunga have facilities for jets.

Société Nationale Malgache des Transports Aériens (*Air Madagascar*): B.P. 437, 31 ave. de l'Indépendance, Tananarive; f. 1962; internal service between all the principal towns and weekly external services; 51 per cent owned by the state, 40 per cent by Air France; fleet comprises one Boeing 707, two Boeing 737, three DC-4, one DC-3, one Nord, nine Pipers, five Twin Otter; Pres. D. Andriantsitohaina; Dir.-Gen. Jaques Alexandre.

Madagascar is also served by Air France, Alitalia and East African Airways.

TOURISM

Alliance Touristique de L'Océan Indien: B.P. 3835, Tananarive.

Office National du Tourisme de Madagascar: Place d'Ambohij-atovo, B.P. 610, Tananarive.

CULTURAL ORGANIZATIONS

Ministère de l'Information, du Tourisme et des Arts traditionnels: Ave. de France, Tananarive.

Département des Arts du Ministère des Affaires Culturelles: Place Goulette, Tananarive; concerned in promoting all the arts.

Imadefolk—Institut Malgache des Arts dramatiques et folkloriques: Centre Culturel Albert Camus, ave. de l'Indépendence, Tananarive; f. 1964; theatre tours at home and abroad; traditional songs and dances; Dir. Odéam Rakoto.

Ny Antsaly: Anatihazo-Isotry, Tananarive; f. 1960; traditional music and dancing; Dir. Sylvestre Randafison.

UNIVERSITY

Université de Tananarive: Campus Universitaire Ambohitsaina, B.P. 566, Tananarive; 260 teachers, 7,000 students.

MALAWI

INTRODUCTORY SURVEY

Location, Climate, Language, Religion, Flag, Capital

Malawi, formerly the British Protectorate of Nyasaland, is an inland state in southern central Africa, with Zambia to the west, Mozambique to the south and east, and Tanzania to the north. Lake Malawi (formerly Lake Nyasa) forms most of the eastern boundary. The climate is tropical, but much of the country is high enough to modify the heat. The official language is English, though Chichewa is being promoted as the basis for a "Malawi Language". Most Africans follow traditional beliefs. There are about 10 per cent Protestants and 10 per cent Roman Catholics, and there is a Muslim community among the Asians, as well as a Hindu minority. The national flag (proportions 3 by 2) has black, red and green horizontal stripes, with a rising sun in red on the black stripe. The capital is Zomba, but a new capital is being built at Lilongwe.

Recent History

The Federation of Rhodesia and Nyasaland, set up in 1953, was dissolved at the end of 1963 and Nyasaland, under the name of Malawi, became independent in July 1964. The country became a Republic and one-party state in July 1966, with Dr. Hastings Kamuzu Banda as President. In 1967 the country created a major controversy amongst African states by officially recognizing the Republic of South Africa and this recognition has continued to draw much criticism from leaders of other African states. In 1971 Dr. Banda became Life President of Malawi. In August 1971 he became the first African head of state to visit South Africa, and in September he paid an official visit to Mozambique. Relations with Tanzania remain strained, and Malawi, both economically and militarily, lies in the South African sphere of influence. Malawi has an extradition agreement with South Africa, which has also supplied Malawi with arms. At the end of 1972 some 20,000 Jehovah's Witnesses fled from Malawi to neighbouring Zambia, claiming persecution by the ruling Congress Party.

Government

Malawi is an independent Republic within the Commonwealth, with an elected President whose term of office is normally five years, though Dr. Banda is now President for life. Executive power is vested in the President and there is a National Assembly of 75 members, 60 elected and 15 nominated. The country is divided into three Regions and 24 Districts.

Defence

Malawi's defence forces include a battalion of regular infantry, and territorial and reserve forces. A second battalion is being formed. There are also national police forces totalling about 3,000 men.

Economic Affairs

Malawi has small resources. Most of her population are farmers, and there are few European settlers. The principal crops are cotton, groundnuts, tobacco, maize and tea. Production of both tea and tobacco has risen appreciably over the last few years, the latter crop being helped by the difficulties of the industry in Rhodesia. In 1971 agricultural products still accounted for 94 per cent of domestic export receipts and supported 90 per cent of the population. Malawi's economy is hampered by a consistently adverse balance of trade, although the variety in her agricultural exports is some protection against fluctuations in domestic production and world prices. The lack of mineral wealth is a seriously limiting factor. Trade is mainly with Britain, Rhodesia and South Africa, with the latter country becoming steadily more important. The 1965-69 development plan has been extended yearly and the 1972-73 programme provided for the expenditure of K31.3 million with priority being given to agriculture, transport, power, education and construction of the new capital, Lilongwe. In November 1973 Malawi broke the links between the kwacha and sterling.

Transport and Communications

Malawi railways operate 289 miles of the 515-mile rail link from Salima to the Mozambique Port of Beira. The system also has a link with Nacala in Mozambique to serve the new capital of Lilongwe. There are about 2,000 miles of trunk roads; and as well as Air Malawi there are air charter firms. Since the Rhodesian Government's declaration of independence, Blantyre has become a focal point for regional air services in southern Africa. Lake Malawi carries an important traffic with Mozambique and Tanzania, though it operates at a loss.

Social Welfare

A social development agency, now part of the Ministry of Labour, was set up in 1958. Its work includes care and protection of young people, the destitute, and the physically handicapped, probation work, sport, community centres and women's clubs. The Ministry of Community Development and of Social Welfare, created in 1972, initiates and expands welfare projects. Hospitals and health facilities are to be extended under the 1973-74 development plan.

Education

Malawi has high literacy and in 1972-73 there were nearly 500,000 African children receiving primary education. Secondary education is provided in government and government-aided schools. The University of Malawi opened in October 1965 and now has more than 1,000 students. The Malawi Correspondence College had enrolled nearly 28,000 students by the end of 1972. Many students go to the United Kingdom and the U.S.A.

Tourism

The country has a small but growing tourist industry. Big game, fine scenery and an excellent climate form the basis of the country's tourist potential.

Visas are not required to visit Malawi by nationals of

EEC countries (except France), Finland, Iceland, Israel (diplomatic and military only), Madagascar, Norway, Portugal, Rhodesia, San Marino, South Africa, Sweden, Commonwealth countries and United States of America (for duration of a year).

Public Holidays

1974: August 5th (Bank Holiday), October 17th (Mother's Day), December 25th–26th (Christmas and Boxing Day).

1975: January 1st (New Year's Day), March 3rd (Martyrs' Day), March 28th–31st (Easter), May 14th (Kamuzu Day).

Weights and Measures

The imperial system is in use.

Currency and Exchange Rates

100 tambala = 1 kwacha (K).

Exchange rates (April 1974):

£1 sterling = 1.978 kwacha;

U.S. $1 = 83.78 tambala.

STATISTICAL SURVEY

AREA AND POPULATION

(Census of August 9th, 1966)

AREA (sq. miles)	POPULATION	AFRICANS	EUROPEANS	ASIANS AND OTHERS
45,747*	4,039,583	4,020,724	7,395	11,464

Total Population (estimate): 4,666,000 (July 1st, 1972).

* Includes 9,422 sq. miles of inland water.

REGIONS

REGIONS	POPULATION	CHIEF TOWNS	POPULATION
Southern	2,067,140	Zomba (capital)	19,666
		Blantyre	104,461
Central	1,474,952	Lilongwe	19,425
Northern	497,491	Mzuzu	8,490

LAND DISTRIBUTION

(1968—'000 acres)

Unalienated African Trustland . . .	19,500
Unalienated Government Land . . .	3,200
Freehold	400
Leasehold	200
TOTAL	23,300

EMPLOYMENT

	1970		1971		1972	
	Number Employed*	Percentage of Total Employment	Number Employed*	Percentage of Total Employment	Number Employed†	Percentage of Total Employment
Agriculture, Forestry and Fishing .	53,695	33.7	57,380	33.3	64,782	34.1
Manufacturing and Mining . .	20,139	12.6	22,521	13.1	23,944	12.6
Construction . . .	18,355	11.5	17,610	10.2	18,438	9.7
Transport, Power, etc.‡ . .	10,227	6.4	11,309	6.6	12,045	6.3
Distribution and Finance§ .	13,478	8.5	15,192	8.8	17,120	9.0
Other Services n.e.s.‖ . .	43,448	27.3	48,269	28.0	53,738	28.3
TOTALS: Private . . .	110,091	69.1	119,451	69.3	131,217	69.0
Government . . .	49,251	30.9	52,830	30.7	58,850	31.0
GRAND TOTAL . .	159,342	100.0	172,281	100.0	190,067	100.0

* Averages of four quarters.

† Estimated from first three quarters.

‡ Includes transport and communications, storage, electricity, water and sanitation.

§ Includes wholesale and retail trade, hotels, restaurants, banks, insurance and business services.

‖ Community, personal and social services.

AGRICULTURE

MARKETED PRODUCTION OF MAIN CROPS

	1967	1968	1969	1970	1971	1972
Tea (production of made tea—million lb.) . . .	37.1	34.8	37.3	41.3	41.0	45.6
Tobacco (million lb.) . .	35.6	33.5	28.8	48.9	57.9	67.6
Flue Cured (auction sales) . .	4.0	6.1	6.1	10.3	14.1	19.1
Burley (auction sales) . .	5.9	6.7	7.6	12.5	12.5	12.4*
Fire Cured (auction sales) . .	23.2	18.4	13.0	22.0	26.2	29.7
Sun/Air (auction sales) .	2.5	2.3	2.1	4.1	5.1	6.4
Groundnuts (ADMARC's purchases—'ooo short tons) . .	47.3	25.1	40.9	29.8	40.5	43.3
Seed Cotton (ADMARC's purchases—'ooo short tons) .	13.2	12.8	20.2	23.5	24.5	24.3
Maize (ADMARC's purchases—'ooo short tons) . .	100.0	92.2	58.1	9.1	38.2	67.5
Pulses (ADMARC's purchases—'ooo short tons) .	23.3	3.8	18.1	8.9	19.0	17.6
Raw and Refined Sugar (production—'ooo short tons) .	18.1	21.9	29.6	36.1	35.7	37.1
Paddy (ADMARC's purchases—'ooo short tons) . .	5.1	2.3	9.3	9.9	20.0	21.7

* Includes carry over of 500,000 lb. from 1971 crop.

TEA PRODUCTION AND EXPORTS 1969-72

	1969	1970	1971	1972
Tea Acreage ('ooo acres) . . .	37.1	37.6*	n.a.	n.a.
Production (million lb.) . . .	37.3	41.3*	n.a.	45.6
Exports (million lb.) . . .	38.0	39.0	40.0	43.9
Exports f.o.b. (K million) . .	9.5	11.0	11.9	12.2
Average Price c.i.f. (d/lb.)† . .	28.1	43.4*	n.a.	n.a.

* Estimate.   † Weighted average London auction price.

LIVESTOCK

('ooo)

	1967	1968	1969
Cattle . . .	464	480	491
Sheep . . .	81	90	81
Goats . . .	668	617	599
Pigs	149	180	150

FOREST INDUSTRY DIVISION SALES BY CATEGORIES

	1969	1970	1971	1972*
Sawn Timber (K) . . .	318,000	388,300	532,422	655,000
Volume (cu. ft.) . . .	244,647	277,360	354,950	437,000
Creosoted Products (K) . . .	112,700	83,496	82,436	72,000
Other Products (K) . . .	95,100	156,274	183,352	193,000

* Estimate.

FISH IMPORTS, EXPORTS AND ESTIMATED LANDINGS

					1970	1971	1972*
Landings (short tons)	.	.	.	.	37,000	43,100	44,000
(K)	.	.	.	.	2,812,000	2,758,000	2,904,000
Imports (short tons)	.	.	.	.	700,500	304,800	400,000
(K)	.	.	.	.	218,100	172,400	220,000
Exports (short tons)	.	.	.	.	1,800,900	1,361,600	1,894,600
(K)	.	.	.	.	272,600	277,700	355,800
Aquarium Fish Exports (K)	.	.	.		39,100	55,000	65,300

* Estimate.

FINANCE

100 tambala = 1 Malawi kwacha (K).

Coins: 1, 2, 5, 10 and 20 tambala.

Notes: 50 tambala; 1, 5 and 10 kwacha.

Exchange rates (April 1974): £1 sterling = 1.978 kwacha; U.S. $1 = 83.78 tambala.

100 Malawi kwacha = £50.55 = $119.37.

BUDGET
(K'000)

					TOTAL RECEIPTS	TOTAL EXPENDITURE
1969	.	.	.	.	59,926	60,504
1970–71	.	.	.		85,498	82,115
1971–72	.	.	.		83,774	81,628
1973–74	.	.	.		51,690*	84,120

* Excludes aid, borrowings, etc.

MONEY SUPPLY
(K'000)

1968 (Dec.)	1969 (Dec.)	1970 (Dec.)	1971 (Dec.)
15,113	28,481	32,681	38,810

FOREIGN EXCHANGE RESERVES
(K'000—at December 31st)

RESERVES				1967	1968	1969	1970	1971	1972
Reserve Bank	.	.	.	15,054	14,410	14,146	21,050	22,276	23,892
Commercial Banks	.	.	.	−5,112	−3,494	−2,542	−2,536	−1,745	−1,318
Banking System	.	.	.	9,942	10,916	11,604	18,514	20,531	22,574
Other Official*	.	.	.	3,701	4,350	3,357	3,285	2,226	3,922
TOTAL	.	.	.	13,643	15,266	14,961	21,799	22,757	26,496

* Other official reserves consist of the Reserve position with IMF, Treasury balances with the Crown Agents and a balance account of the proceeds from the sale of the Zambezi Bridge.

EXTERNAL TRADE

(K million)

	1969	1970	1971	1972
Imports	61.5	71.5	89.9	104.3
Exports (incl. re-exports) . .	36.6	40.6	59.3	64.5

COMMODITIES

(K'ooo)

IMPORTS	1970	1971	1972‖	EXPORTS	1970	1971	1972‖
Goods Mainly for Final Consumption:				**Smallholder Crops:**			
Motor Cars and Bicycles . . .	3,054	2,794	2,340	Tobacco* . . .	8,413	11,671	13,155
Piece Goods . .	3,506	3,906	4,480	Groundnuts . .	4,241	5,883	6,880
Motor Spirit . .	1,892	2,283	2,450	Cotton . .	2,777	2,547	2,600
Other . . .	14,545	15,497	17,470	Beans, Peas, etc.	1,038	1,227	1,100
				Maize . . .	—	411	1,220
TOTAL .	22,997 (28%)	24,480 (27%)	26,740 (26%)	Cassava . .	724	545	1,110
				Sunflower Seed .	46	317	375
Capital Equipment:				Rice . . .	556	956	1,680
Transport Equipment n.e.s. . .	8,923	9,696	16,260	Coffee . .	102	161	70
Other . . .	9,807	10,378	12,470	TOTAL . .	17,943	23,718	28,190
TOTAL .	18,730 (23%)	20,074 (22%)	28,730 (28%)	**Estate Crops:**			
				Tobacco† . .	8,179	10,395	11,375
				Tea . . .	10,916	11,905	12,200
Materials for Building Construction . .	6,128 (7%)	7,423 (8%)	10,715 (10%)	Tung Oil . .	411	239	175
				Sisal . . .	—	—	—
				Sugar . .	158	314	360
Goods Mainly for Intermediate Consumption:				TOTAL . .	19,664	22,853	24,110
Petroleum Products n.e.s. . .	4,479	5,325	5,470	**Main Manufactures:**			
Parts, Tools and Miscellaneous appliances . . .	3,365	4,040	2,960	Cattle Cake . .	343	360	460
				Cement . .	—	—	1
Other . . .	25,316	27,037	28,230	Wooden Boxes . .	84	76	100
				Clothing and Footwear . .	524	388	275
TOTAL .	33,160 (40%)	36,402 (41%)	36,660 (35%)	Other‡ . .	260	273	185
				TOTAL . .	1,211	1,097	1,021
Other	1,465 (2%)	1,371 (2%)	1,360 (1%)	TOTAL DOMESTIC EXPORTS (incl. other)§ . .	40,577	49,577	55,145
TOTAL .	82,480 (100%)	89,750 (100%)	104,205 (100%)				

* Dark-fired, fire-cured, sun/air-cured and oriental tobacco.

† Flue-cured and burley tobacco.

‡ Glycerol, paper products, holloware, fishing nets.

§ Mainly: fish, hides and skins, precious stones and migrants' effects.

‖ Estimate.

COUNTRIES
(K'000)

Imports	1970	1971	1972*	Exports	1970	1971	1972*
United Kingdom . .	18,998	25,224	31,045	United Kingdom . .	19,536	21,625	23,384
Rhodesia . . .	15,505	13,247	16,714	Rhodesia . . .	3,130	3,437	3,437
South Africa . .	8,968	9,421	13,502	South Africa . .	1,708	2,390	2,932
Japan . . .	3,752	6,504	7,520	U.S.A. . . .	1,197	2,343	2,847
U.S.A. . . .	3,719	3,649	2,141	Netherlands . .	1,847	2,379	2,788
Germany, Federal Republic . . .	2,697	3,655	3,072	Ireland . . .	1,136	2,304	—
Zambia . . .	2,498	3,134	2,802	Germany, Federal Republic . . .	1,242	964	1,348
Australia . . .	1,321	2,573	2,184	Zambia . . .	1,305	2,278	1,824
All Other Countries .	13,909	22,343	25,334	All Other Countries .	9,239	11,857	16,436
Total . .	71,367	89,750	104,314	Total .	40,340	49,577	54,996

* Estimate.

Source: Standard Bank Review, September 1973.

TOURISM

	1971	1972
Arrivals	10,221	14,422
Total Expenditure (K'000) .	578	876

TRANSPORT

RAILWAYS

	1970	1971	1972*
Passengers (number)	840,600	862,200	967,500
Freight (short ton miles) . .	117,700	127,800	131,700

* Estimated.

ROADS
(Number of licensed motor vehicles)

	1971	1972
Cars . . .	9,862	11,231
Goods vehicles . . .	8,367	9,673
Tractors . . .	1,124	1,280
Motor cycles . . .	2,693	3,253

TRAFFIC AT CHILEKA AIRPORT (BLANTYRE)

	Passengers	Freight ('000 kg.)	Mail ('000 kg.)
1968 . .	104,117	970.9	159.1
1969 . .	131,423	1,094.1	161.7
1970 . .	163,879	1,134.1	188.2
1971 . .	193,209	1,499.9	194.6
1972 . .	224,171	1,792.9	210.0

EDUCATION
AFRICAN EDUCATION
Government, Local Authority, Aided and Unaided Schools

	PUPILS	TEACHERS
	1972–73	1972–73
Primary . . .	484,676	9,590
Secondary . . .	13,451	604
Teacher Training . .	1,321	96
Technical and Vocational .	1,600	84

The University of Malawi at Blantyre had 1,027 full-time students in 1973.

Source: Malawi Statistics 1973.

Sources: National Statistical Office, Zomba; *Budget Document No.* 4, Malawi Government Annual Economic Report.

THE CONSTITUTION

A new Constitution was introduced in 1966. Malawi is a one-party state with a Presidential form of government. There is a unicameral parliament of 73 members.

Fundamental Rights

The following rights are guaranteed by the Constitution: life, personal liberty, protection from slavery and forced labour, from inhuman treatment, from deprivation of property, privacy of the home, security under the law, freedom of conscience, of expression, of assembly and association, of movement, protection from racial discrimination.

The President

Malawi is a Republic with a President. By an amendment of November 1970, provision was made for a Life President limited to the present presidency only. Dr. Banda accepted the position in 1971.

Parliament

There is a Parliament, consisting of the President and the National Assembly. The National Assembly has 73 members, 60 elected and 13 nominated. The number is soon to be increased to 76. A Speaker is elected from among the ordinary members of the Assembly. The Assembly may change the Constitution by a two-thirds majority on the second and third readings. All members must belong to the Malawi Congress Party. The Parliamentary term is normally five years. The President has power to prorogue or dissolve Parliament.

Executive Powers

Executive power is exercised by the President acting as Prime Minister. Ministers are responsible to the President.

Judicature

The Judicature is a separate organ of the Government. There is a High Court, consisting of the Chief Justice and not less than two Puisne Judges, a Supreme Court of Appeal, and subordinate courts. The Local Courts were renamed Traditional Courts and given greater powers in November 1969. There is also a Judicial Service Commission with power to appoint judicial officers. During 1970, three new Traditional Courts were set up having jurisdiction in each of Malawi's three regions, and a National Traditional Court of Appeal was set up for the whole of Malawi.

THE GOVERNMENT

Life President: Ngwazi Dr. HASTINGS KAMUZU BANDA, LL.D., PH.B., M.D., L.R.C.P., L.R.C.S., L.R.F.P.S., Minister of Defence, External Affairs, Works and Supplies, Agriculture and Natural Resources.

CABINET
(*June* 1974)

Minister of Finance, and of Trade, Industry and Tourism: D. T. MATENJE.

Minister of Health: P. L. MAKHUMULA NKHOMA.

Minister of Education: R. T. C. MUNYENYEMBE.

Minister of Justice, of Local Government and Attorney-General: RICHARD BANDA.

Minister of Labour: M. M. LUNGU.

Minister for Community Development and Social Welfare: D. D. KAINJA-NTHARA.

Minister of Transport and Communications: W. B. DELEZA.

Minister of State in the President's Office: A. MUWALO NQUMAYO.

Minister of Youth and Culture: G. C. CHAKUAMBA PHIRI.

Regional Ministers:
Northern Region: M. Q. Y. CHIBAMBO.
Central Region: J. R. KUMBWEZA BANDA.
Southern Region: A. CHIWANDA GAMA.

Minister for O.A.V. Affairs: R. B. CHIDZANJA NKHOMA.

Minister without Portfolio: A. E. GADAMA.

DIPLOMATIC REPRESENTATION

EMBASSIES AND HIGH COMMISSIONS ACCREDITED TO MALAWI

(E) Embassy; (HC) High Commission.

Austria: Nairobi, Kenya (E).

Belgium: Bujumbura, Burundi (E).

Botswana: Lusaka, Zambia (HC).

Canada: Lusaka, Zambia (HC).

China (Taiwan): Glyn Jones Rd., Blantyre, P.O.B. 929 (E); *Ambassador:* Dr. Chin Yung Chao.

Denmark: Nairobi, Kenya (E).

France: Kamuzu Highway, Blantyre, P.O.B. 90 and 920 (E); *Ambassador:* René de Crouy-Chanel.

Germany, Federal Republic: Kamuzu Highway, Limbe, P.O.B. 5695 (E); *Ambassador:* Herr von Wartenburg.

Greece: Pretoria, South Africa.

India: Hotel Rd., P.O.B. 681, Lilongwe (HC); *Chargé d'Affaires:* P. Balakrishnan.

Iran: Addis Ababa, Ethiopia (E).

Israel: 3rd Floor, Development House, Henderson St., P.O.B. 689, Blantyre (E); *Ambassador:* Jacob Monbaz.

Italy: Lusaka, Zambia (E).

Japan: Nairobi, Kenya (E).

Korea, Republic: Nairobi, Kenya (E).

Netherlands: Lusaka, Zambia (E).

Nigeria: Kampala, Uganda (HC).

Norway: Nairobi, Kenya (E).

Portugal: Claim Bldg., Glyn Jones Rd., P.O.B. 1297, Blantyre (E); *Ambassador:* Dr. V. F. Pereira.

South Africa: 6th Floor, Delamere House, Victoria Ave., Blantyre, P.O.B. 1072 (E); *Ambassador:* Louis Voster.

Sweden: Lusaka, Zambia (E).

Switzerland: Nairobi, Kenya (E).

Turkey: Nairobi, Kenya.

United Kingdom: Victoria Ave., P.O.B. 479, Blantyre (HC); *High Commissioner:* K. G. Ritchie, c.m.g.

U.S.A.: 4th Floor, Unit House, Victoria Ave., Blantyre, P.O.B. 380 (E); *Ambassador:* William C. Burdett.

Vatican: Lusaka, Zambia.

Zambia: Kanabar Bldg., Victoria Ave., P.O.B. 556, Blantyre (HC); *High Commissioner:* R. K. Chinambu.

Malawi also has diplomatic relations with Spain.

NATIONAL ASSEMBLY

Speaker: Alec Nuyasulu.

The Malawi Congress Party holds all seats. The last election was held in April 1971.

POLITICAL PARTY

Malawi Congress Party: P.O.B. 5250, Limbe; f. 1959; succeeded the Nyasaland African Congress; Life Pres. Dr. Hastings Kamuzu Banda; Sec.-Gen. A. Muwalo Nqumayo.

JUDICIAL SYSTEM

The Courts administering justice are the Supreme Court of Appeal, High Court, Magistrates' Courts and Traditional Courts.

The High Court consists of the Chief Justice and three Puisne Judges. The High Court has unlimited jurisdiction in civil and criminal matters. It hears appeals from the Magistrates' Courts. The Minister of Justice has the power to restrict appeals from Traditional Courts where the majority of civil cases are heard and determined to Traditional Appeals Courts. Appeals from the High Court go to the Supreme Court of Appeal in Blantyre.

Chief Justice: The Hon. Sir J. Skinner.

Registrar: M. R. Truwa, P.O.B. 954, Blantyre.

RELIGION

AFRICAN RELIGIONS

Most of the Africans follow their traditional religions.

CHRISTIANS

Anglican Community: Bishop of Lake Malawi: Rt. Rev. Josiah Mtekateka, P.O.B. 24, Nkhotakota; f. 1882; 50,000 mems.; Bishop of Southern Malawi: Most Rev. Donald S. Arden (Archbishop of Central Africa), P.O. Kasupe; f. 1888; 30,000 mems.; publ. *Ecclesia* (monthly); circ. 2,250.

Roman Catholic Church: Archbishop of Blantyre: Most Rev. James Chiona, Archbishop's House, P.O.B. 385, Blantyre; Catholic Secretariat, P.O.B. 5368, Limbe; Major Seminary, P.O.B. 23, Mchinji; the Roman Catholic Church has 821,738 baptized members and 117,068 catechumens, and runs 629 primary schools and 26 post-primary institutions in Malawi.

Church of Central Africa (Presbyterian): Blantyre Synod: P.O.B. 413, Blantyre; Gen. Sec. Rev. J. D. Sangaya; Livingstonia Synod: P.O. Livingstonia; Gen. Sec. Rev. P. C. Mzembe; Mkhoma Synod: Gen. Sec. Rev. K. Mgawi; total membership 711,000.

The Catholic Secretariat: P.O.B. 5368, Limbe; Sec.-Gen. Rev. Fr. G. v.d. Asdonk, s.m.m.

Christian Council of Malawi: P.O.B. 5368, Blantyre; Chair. Rev. K. J. Mgawi; Sec. Rev. S. P. Kamanga.

Evangelical Association: Chair. W. S. Saukila, P.O.B. 13, Thyolo; Sec. Rev. M. E. Udd, P.O.B. 5436, Limbe.

Bible Society: P.O.B. 740, Blantyre.

OTHER RELIGIONS

Of the Asians in Malawi over 50 per cent are Muslims and about 25 per cent are Hindus. There are also a small number of African Muslims.

THE PRESS

African, The: P.O.B. 133, Lilongwe; f. 1950; fortnightly; Catholic periodical; English, Chichewa; Editor A. MBEDE; circ. 14,000.

Boma Lathu: f. 1973; publ. by the Ministry of Information and Broadcasting; Chichewa.

Kuunika: Presbyterian Church of Central Africa, P.O. Mkhoma; f. 1909; Chichewa; Editor J. J. MBUKA BANDA.

Malawi Government Gazette: Government Printer, Box 53, Zomba; f. 1894; weekly.

Malawi News: P.M.B. 39, Blantyre; f. 1959; English and Chichewa; organ of Malawi Congress Party; once a week; Editor HARVEY MLANGA; circ. 20,000.

Moni: P.O.B. 5592, Limbe; f. 1964; Chichewa, English; monthly; Editors Montfort Press; circ. 22,000.

The Times: P.O.B. 458, Ginnery Corner, Blantyre; f. 1895; English; weekdays only; Editor AL. S. OSMAN; circ. 14,000.

Vision of Malawi: Published by the Ministry of Information and Broadcasting, P.O.B. 494, Blantyre; f. 1964; quarterly; Government publication in English, *This is Malawi*, monthly; *Malawi Mwezi Uno*, monthly, in Chichewa.

PUBLISHERS

Blantyre Printing and Publishing Co. Ltd.: P.M.B. 39, Blantyre; f. 1895; Man. Dir. G. P. BARRETTA; Asst. Man. J. E. MARSHMENT.

The White Fathers: Likuni Parish, P.O.B. 133, Lilongwe; Treas.-Gen. H. ROSARY PARISH.

RADIO

Malawi Broadcasting Corporation: P.O.B. 30133, Chichiri, Blantyre 3; f. 1964; Dir.-Gen. S. D. KALIYOMA; Dir. of Programmes P. T. KANDIERO; statutory body; semi-commercial, semi-state financed; domestic services in English and Chichewa, 0300-2115 (G.M.T.) daily, incl. *"International Service"* 1600-1800 hrs. (G.M.T.) in the 90 metre band.

There are 112,000 radio sets in use in Malawi (1974).

FINANCE

BANKING

(cap. = capital; m. = million; dep. = deposits)

Reserve Bank of Malawi: P.O.B. 565, Blantyre; f. 1964; Bank of Issue; Gov. J. Z. U. TEMBO.

Commercial Bank of Malawi: Head Office: P.O.B. 1111, Blantyre; London Office: Halton House, 20–23 Holborn, E.C.1; f. 1970; jointly owned by Malawi Development Corporation and Portuguese interests; encourages greater Malawian participation in business; Chair. J. P. JARDIM; Deputy Chair. J. POMBEIRO DE SOUSA; Gen. Man. R. D. MANSELL; cap. K1,150,000; dep. K19,000,000; 9 brs.

Investment and Development Bank of Malawi Ltd.: P.O.B. 1358, Blantyre; f. 1972; cap. K2.5m.; to provide loans to private enterprises in the agricultural, industrial and commercial sectors, on a joint-financing basis.

National Bank of Malawi: Head Office, P.O.B. 945, Henderson St., Blantyre; cap. K1m.; Chair. J. G. KAMWENDO; Man. Dir. O. A. STEPHENSON; brs. at Blantyre (3), Lilongwe (2), Limbe (2), Mzuzu, Zomba; agency representation throughout Malawi.

INSURANCE

The National Insurance Co. Ltd.: P.O.B. 501, Blantyre; f. 1971; cap. K200,000; agencies throughout Malawi.

TRADE AND INDUSTRY

Malawi Buying and Trade Agents: 32–34 St. John's Wood Rd., London, NW8 8RA; official buying agents to the Malawi Government, the Malawi Railways and all Statutory Corporations in Malawi; promotion of Trade, Tourism and Investment in Malawi; recruitment of Professional and Technical staff for service in Malawi; registered office Malawi Railways Ltd.

CHAMBER OF COMMERCE

The Chamber of Commerce and Industry of Malawi: P.O.B. 258, Blantyre; f. 1892; 350 mems.; Chair. R. A. S. STURGESS; Sec./Man. Mrs. M. PEARSON.

INDUSTRIAL AND COMMERCIAL ORGANIZATIONS

Tea Association (Central Africa) Ltd.: P.O.B. 950, Blantyre; f. 1936; 29 mems.; Chair. J. S. SANDERSON; Sec. Business Services Ltd.

Tobacco Association: P.O.B. 15, Blantyre; f. 1928; 159 mems.; Chair. J. A. A. HENDERSON, M.P.; Sec. G. D. M. HENDERSON.

Tobacco Exporters' Association of Malawi: P.O.B. 5653, Limbe; f. 1931; 16 mems.; Chair. J. E. BISHOP.

Agricultural Development and Marketing Corporation (ADMARC): P.O.B. 5052, Limbe; purchases and exports groundnuts, cotton, cottonseed, cottonseed products, tobacco, maize, coffee, rice, cassava, beans, peas, oilseeds, canned fruits and vegetables, etc.; assists generally in the development and improvement of agriculture; Exec. Chair. Chair. L. W. MASIKU.

GOVERNMENT DEVELOPMENT CORPORATION

Malawi Development Corporation: P.O.B. 566, Blantyre; f. 1964; to assist agriculture, commerce and industry by way of equity, loans and management advice; Chair. S. B. SOMANJE; Gen. Man. S. E. HELMORE.

EMPLOYERS' ASSOCIATIONS

Employers' Consultative Association of Malawi: P.O.B. 950, Blantyre; f. 1963; 31 mems.; Chair. J. BROOKFIELD; Sec. Business Services Ltd.

Agricultural Employers' Association: P.O.B. 950, Blantyre; f. 1960; 46 mems.; Chair. A. SCHWARZ; Sec. Business Services Ltd.

Master Builders', Civil Engineering Contractors' and Allied Trades' Association: P.O.B. 950, Blantyre; registered 1955; Chair. W. E. ANSTEAD; Sec. Business Services Ltd.

Master Printers' Association: P.O.B. 6, Blantyre; f. 1962; 9 mems.; Chair. G. P. Barretta; Sec. D. Burnett.

Motor Traders' Association of Malawi: P.O.B. 311, Blantyre; registered 1954; paid-up membership 35; Chair. J. Cottingham; Sec. Business Services Ltd.

Road Transport Operators' Association: P.O.B. 950, Blantyre; registered 1956; paid-up membership 9; Chair. J. Brookfield; Sec. Business Services Ltd.

TRADE UNIONS

Trades Union Congress of Malawi: P.O.B. 355, Blantyre; f. 1964; 6,500 mems.; Chair. J. D. Liabunya; Gen. Sec. L. Y. Mvula; Treas. A. Nancuele.

Principal Affiliated Unions

Building Construction, Civil Engineering and Allied Workers' Union: P.O.B. 110, Limbe; f. 1961; 1,300 mems.; Pres. D. J. Chanache; Gen. Sec. G. Sitima.

Malawi Railway Workers' Union: P.O.B. 393, Limbe; f. 1954; 2,100 mems.; Pres. F. L. Matenje.

Organizations not affiliated to T.U.C.M.:

Malawi National Teachers' Association: P.O.B. 252, Limbe; f. 1964; 3,000 mems.; Pres. M. M. Mkandawire; Sec.-Gen. R. J. Mehta.

Malawi Government Employees' Association, The: P.O.B. 64, Blantyre; 300 mems.; Pres. M. Mughogho; Gen. Sec. G. M. Namate.

Overseas Officers' Association: P.O.B. 207, Zomba; 224 mems.; Sec. Mrs. B. M. Evans.

TRANSPORT

RAILWAYS

Malawi Railways Ltd.: Regd. Offices: Abbey House, 6 Victoria St., London, S.W.1; P.O.B. 5144, Limbe; Exec. Chair. D. R. Katengeza; Gen. Man. A. Baker.

Malawi Railways Ltd. and the Central Africa Railway Co. Ltd., its wholly-owned subsidiary, operate between Border Station on the southern border with Mozambique and Salima in the north, and between Nkaya, from a point ten miles south of Balaka, and Nayuci on the eastern border with Mozambique, a total route mileage of 352 miles. The two railways, together with the Trans-Zambesia Railway Co. Ltd. and Mozambique Railways form the links from the Mozambique ports of Beira and Nacala to Malawi and countries to the west. The most spectacular engineering feature is the Lower Zambezi Bridge across the River Zambezi at Sena, with its thirty-three main spans and a length of 12,064 ft., the largest single track railway bridge in the world.

The line has a rail/lake interchange station at Chipoka on Lake Malawi from where steamer services are operated by the railways to other lake ports in Malawi.

Malawi Railways also operate a local collection and delivery road service in Blantyre and co-ordinated trunk road haulage arrangements are carried out by Road Motor Services Ltd., a subsidiary of Malawi Railways Ltd., in all regions of the country.

ROADS

The total road mileage in the country is approximately 6,700 miles, of which 1,830 miles are main roads. The spinal column of the road system runs from the Salisbury-Blantyre road east and then north through Blantyre, Lilongwe and Mzimba to join Tanzania and Zambia at Tunduma. Other important roads link this north-south route with the railway and Lake Malawi in the east, and Zambia and Portuguese East Africa in the west. A 300-mile highway along the edge of Lake Malawi, the "Kamuzu Highway", is under construction. All main, and most secondary roads, are all-weather roads. A further 140 miles from Liwonde to the new capital at Lilongwe has been completed and bitumenized. Most of the lakeshore road from Balaka to Salima is now tarred as is a large part of the Nkhotakota-Nkhata Bay Road.

CIVIL AVIATION

The country's main airport is at Chileka, 11 miles from Blantyre.

Air Malawi Ltd.: P.O.B. 84, Blantyre, also in Johannesburg, Salisbury and Nairobi; f. 1967; services to Salisbury, Zomba, Beira, Johannesburg, Lusaka, Ndola, Nairobi, Seychelles, Lilongwe, Mzuzu, Karonga, Salima and Mangoche; a new weekly service to London is operated; Chair. P. Howard; Gen. Man. John Bryne; fleet of one BAC One-Eleven 475, two HS 748, two Viscount 700, two Britten-Norman Islander.

Leopard Air Ltd.: P.O.B. 70, Thyolo, Blantyre Airport; private air charter company; Cessna Dealer, P.O. Chileka.

Capital Air Services Ltd.: P.O.B. 14, Zomba.

Malawi is also served by the following foreign airlines: British Airways, British Caledonian, DETA, EAA, SAA, Air Rhodesia and Zambia Airways.

TOURISM

Department of Tourism: Ministry of Trade, Industry and Tourism, Kanabar House, P.O.B. 402, Blantyre; responsible for Malawi tourist policy, administers government rest houses, sponsors training of hotel staff; publs. tourist literature; in 1972 foreign exchange receipts from tourism totalled K1,335,610; Dir. J. T. X. Muwamba.

Hotels and Tourism Ltd.: established by the Government to promote tourist enterprises.

UNIVERSITY

University of Malawi: P.O.B. 278, Zomba; f. 1964; 162 teachers, 1,027 students (1973).

MALAYSIA

INTRODUCTORY SURVEY

Location, Climate, Language, Religion, Flag, Capital

The Federation of Malaysia is divided into two parts. Peninsular Malaysia (known until 1973 as West Malaysia) consists of the eleven States of the former Federation of Malaya, which make up the southern part of the Kra peninsula, with Thailand to the north and the island of Singapore to the south. Peninsular Malaysia is separated by several hundred miles of open sea from Sabah and Sarawak (formerly known as East Malaysia) in northern Borneo, bordering Indonesia. The climate is tropical, with uniformly high temperatures and rain in all seasons. The indigenous population of Peninsular Malaysia, apart from some 50,000 primitive animists, consists of Muslim Malays, who make up about 53 per cent of the total population; a further 35 per cent are Chinese and 10 per cent Indian or Pakistani in origin. In Sabah and Sarawak the animists of the interior outnumber the Malays and the large Chinese community on the coast. The official language is *Bahasa Malaysia*, based on Malay, but English is widely used. Malaysia's national flag (proportions 2 by 1) has 14 horizontal stripes, alternating red and white, with a blue canton containing a yellow crescent and star. The capital is Kuala Lumpur. Each of Malaysia's thirteen states has its own flag and its own capital. In some states there is in addition a Royal capital.

Recent History

In 1948 the Federation of Malaya was created under British protection. In the same year an armed Communist revolt broke out and was not completely suppressed until 1960. In August 1957 Malaya became a sovereign, independent nation.

Malaysia was established on September 16th, 1963, through the union of the independent Federation of Malaya, the internally self-governing state of Singapore, and the former British colonies of Sarawak and North Borneo (Sabah). Singapore left the federation in August 1965 and later became an independent Republic. Malaysia (as Malaya) joined the UN in 1957, and is also a member of the Colombo Plan and the Association of South-East Asian Nations (ASEAN), which incorporates the former Association of South-East Asia (ASA).

Indonesia opposed the establishment of Malaysia and maintained an economic blockade against the new state. This policy of "confrontation" was brought to an end in August 1966 with the signing of a joint agreement at Bangkok. Diplomatic relations were established with Indonesia in August 1967. In March 1970 a Treaty of Friendship between the two countries was signed.

In September 1970 Tunku Adbul Rahman, Prime Minister of Malaya since independence and the politician chiefly responsible for the creation of Malaysia, resigned and was succeeded as Prime Minister by Tun Abdul Razak. His Alliance Party was successful in broadening its support by creating a coalition with local and ethnic parties, particularly the Partai Islam, which gave the Government an overwhelming majority in Parliament. Outside Parliament it met with growing opposition; there was a resurgence of Communist guerrilla activity in the Peninsula and in Sarawak, and the racial tension between Malays and Chinese, which led to severe rioting in 1969, remains unresolved. The economic and managerial dominance of the Chinese community still causes considerable resentment among Malays, and the Government's policy of encouraging Malay participation in business has offended the Chinese. Under Tun Abdul Razak Malaysia has tended to move away from its previous pro-Western, anti-Communist stance in international affairs, taking a more neutral line and recognizing Communist states. Diplomatic relations with the People's Republic of China were established in June 1974.

The Government

Malaysia is a federation of the following 13 states: Johore, Kedah, Kelantan, Malacca, Negri Sembilan, Pahang, Penang, Perak, Perlis, Sabah, Sarawak, Selangor, Trengganu. The capital, Kuala Lumpur, became a separate Federal Territory in February 1974. The Supreme Head of Malaysia is an elected monarch. The monarch acts on the advice of Parliament and a Cabinet. Parliament consists of the Dewan Negara (Senate) and the Dewan Ra'ayat (House of Representatives). The Senate has 58 members. 26 elected and 32 appointed. The House of Representatives consists of 144 elected members, 104 from Malaya, 26 from Sarawak and 14 from Sabah.

Defence

Malaysia is responsible for its own defence and has an army, navy and air force, with an estimated total strength of 56,000. The Five-Power Defence Arrangement for joint consultations between Malaysia, New Zealand, Australia and the United Kingdom in the event of actual or potential aggression established a token Commonwealth force in Malaysia. In April 1972 a mutual defence agreement was signed with Indonesia to counter Communist terrorism on the Sarawak-Kalimantan border. Estimated spending for 1973 totalled M$680 million (U.S. $287m.)

Economic Affairs

The bulk of the Federation's rapidly growing population is found in Peninsular Malaysia, which has always been the more economically advanced region. The primary sector of the economy (subsistence farming, cultivation of export crops and mining), employs about 60 per cent of the working population, while about 10 per cent and 30 per cent are engaged in the secondary and tertiary sectors respectively.

The economy is based on the export earnings of a narrow range of products, in which rubber, tin, palm oil and timber predominate. Malaysia is the world's leading producer of natural rubber. The main growing areas are on the west coast of Peninsular Malaysia and rubber is grown both in plantations, which are mostly owned by Europeans and Chinese, and on smallholdings. Rubber provides about one-third of total export earnings, and exports have benefited from price rises and the world oil crisis, which made synthetic rubber more expensive. Palm oil and timber are increasing in importance as export items, and other plantation crops, such as pineapples, tea and pepper, are grown. The peasant sector of the economy is mainly involved in rice-growing, although hunting remains a significant activity in Sarawak and Sabah.

Malaysia is also the world's major producer of tin, providing about 40 per cent of the total output in non-Communist countries. Mined exclusively in Peninsular Malaysia, tin ores and concentrates provide about one-quarter of total export earnings and are sold mainly to the U.S.A. Iron ore (shipped mostly to Japan), gold, ilmenite and bauxite are also valuable resources. Minor deposits of coal are found in East Malaysia. Oil production is becoming increasingly important. At present oil is produced in commercial quantities only in the offshore fields of Sarawak, but oil and gas have been found off Sabah and the east coast of the Peninsula. Esso and Shell have refineries at Port Dickson in the Peninsula, and much of the Sarawak production goes to the refinery at Lutong. Long-established industries process plantation crops and minerals for export, and private foreign investment is developing manufacturing industries. Local industry is small-scale and predominantly owned by Chinese. A wide range of consumer goods is produced. Both thermal and hydro-electric power are generated; the potential for hydro-electricity is great and a major project is under way in the Cameron Highlands.

Transport and Communications

Communications within Malaya are excellent and there are frequent services by sea and air between the Malayan peninsula and Sarawak and Sabah. In Peninsular Malaysia there are over 4,000 miles of Federal roads and 10,000 miles of State roads. The state-owned Malayan Railway has a total length of 1,659 km.; the system connects with the State Railway of Thailand. The country has a network of airfields and four major international airports at Kuala Lumpur, Penang, Kuching and Kotah Kinabalu. The major ports, which have undergone considerable extension, are Penang, Port Klang, Dungun, Telok Auson, Malacca and Port Dickson.

A major port expansion programme, costing M$120 million, was launched at the end of 1971. It includes the reconstruction of the two main ports of Sabah—Kotah Kinabalu and Sandakan—and of Kuching and Sibu ports in Sarawak. It is expected to be completed by 1975.

A second satellite station costing M$9 million is to be set up in late 1973. The first, at Kuantan in Pahang, was commissioned in April 1970 and provides satellite communications with 51 countries.

Social Welfare

Social welfare comes under the two Malaysian Ministries of Health and of Welfare Services. Employers and employees contribute to the Employees' Provident Fund for retirement benefits. The independent Social Welfare Lotteries Board contributes large sums to welfare schemes. Government-sponsored social work among the aged and disabled is supported by many voluntary societies. Under the Second Five-Year Plan (1971–75), M$1,105 million is to be spent on social services.

Education

Total school enrolment in 1972 was estimated at more than 2.4 million. In 1973, 92 per cent of the 6 to 11 age group in Peninsular Malaysia were enrolled at primary schools. Some 70 per cent of the total population are literate. Education between the ages of 6 and 15 is free and compulsory in Peninsular Malaysia. Sabah and Sarawak, although under the Federal Ministry of Education, enjoy some local autonomy over education. There are three universities.

Tourism

Malaysia has a fast-growing tourist industry, the cultures of the many ethnic groups present being a particular attraction. Tourists totalled 157,000 in 1972.

Visas are not required to visit Malaysia by nationals of Belgium, Denmark, Finland, France, German Federal Republic, Iceland, Ireland, Italy, Liechtenstein, Luxembourg, Netherlands, Norway, San Marino, Sweden, Switzerland, United Kingdom and Commonwealth and U.S.A.

Sport

The national sport is football but badminton, cricket, tennis, golf, basketball, table tennis and bowling are also played. There is some sea-fishing and jungle exploration.

Public Holidays

Each State has its own public holidays, and the following federal holidays are also observed:

1974: August 31st (National Day), October 17th–18th (Hari Raya Puasa), November 13th (Deepavali), December 24th (Hari Raya Haji), December 25th (Christmas).

1975: February 10th (Chinese New Year), March 26th (Birth of Muhammad), May 1st (Labour Day), May 6th (Wesak), June 4th (Birthday of H.M. the Yang di-Pertuan Agong).

Weights and Measures

Since 1971, the metric system has been in use in addition to the imperial system. There is also a local system of weights and measures:

	1 chupak	= 1 quart
	1 gantang	= 1 gallon
	1 tahil	= $1\frac{1}{3}$ ounces
16 tahils	= 1 kati	= $1\frac{1}{3}$ lb.
100 katis	= 1 picul	= $133\frac{1}{3}$ lb.
40 piculs	= 1 koyan	= $5,333\frac{1}{3}$ lb.

Currency and Exchange Rates

100 cents = 1 Malaysian dollar (M$).

Exchange rates (April 1974):

£1 sterling = M$ 5.656;
U.S. $1 = M$ 2.395.

STATISTICAL SURVEY

AREA AND POPULATION

	AREA (sq. miles)	POPULATION (Census, August 24th–25th, 1970)*			ESTIMATED POPULATION (Dec. 31st, 1971)	1971 DENSITY (per sq. mile)
		Males	Females	Total		
West Malaysia . .	50,806	4,431,311	4,370,088	8,801,399	9,604,692	189.0
Sabah . . .	28,460	339,727	315,895	655,622	711,306	25.0
Sarawak . . .	48,050	492,009	485,004	977,013	1,016,004	21.1
TOTAL . .	127,316†	5,263,047	5,170,987	10,434,034	11,332,002	89.0

* Excluding transients afloat.   † 329,747 square kilometres.

PRINCIPAL RACES
(Estimated as at December 31st, 1971)

	WEST MALAYSIA	SABAH	SARAWAK
Chinese . .	3,470,150	146,481	340,017
Malays . .	4,886,863	—	190,498*
Indians and Pakistanis .	1,050,193	—	—
Land Dyak . .	—	—	87,696
Malanau . .	—	—	56,395
Kadazan . .	—	203,833	—
Bajau . .	—	80,841	—
Murut . .	—	29,582	—
Ibans . .	—	—	280,163
Other Indigenous .	—	129,516	—
Other . .	197,486	121,053	61,235

* Excludes Indonesians.

STATES

	AREA sq. miles	POPULATION* 1970 Census	CAPITAL	POPULATION* 1970 Census
Johore . . .	7,330	1,276,969	Johore Bahru	136,229
Kedah . . .	3,639	954,749	Alor Star	66,260
Kelantan . . .	5,765	686,266	Kota Bharu	55,124
Malacca . . .	637	404,135	Malacca Town	87,160
Negri Sembilan . .	2,565	481,491	Seremban	80,921
Pahang . . .	13,886	504,900	Kuantan	43,358
Penang and Province Wellesley . .	399	775,440	George Town	269,247
Perak . . .	8,110	1,569,161	Ipoh	247,969
Perlis . . .	307	120,991	Kangar	8,758
Sabah . . .	28,460	654,043	Kota Kinabalu	40,939
Sarawak . . .	48,050	977,438	Kuching	63,535
Selangor . . .	3,166	1,630,707	Kuala Lumpur†	451,810
Trengganu . . .	5,002	405,539	Kuala Trengganu	53,320

* 1970 Population and Housing Census of Malaysia (Community Groups).

† Capital of Malaysia.

MALAYSIA—(STATISTICAL SURVEY)

MIGRATION*
(West Malaysia—'000)

	IMMIGRATION			EMIGRATION		
	1968	1969	1970	1968	1969	1970
Malays	135.1	133.3	162.7	168.0	143.0	168.5
Chinese	100.4	109.3	146.1	110.4	114.9	148.6
Indians and Pakistanis . . .	45.7	43.6	44.7	38.3	39.6	40.2
Others	127.7	142.5	184.8	112.3	128.8	180.8
TOTAL	408.9	428.7	538.3	429.0	426.3	538.1

* The table does not include movements between West Malaysia and Singapore.

EMPLOYMENT
NUMBERS EMPLOYED IN PRINCIPAL OCCUPATIONS
(estimate)

	PLANTATIONS	MINING	MANUFACTURING	TRANSPORT	GOVERNMENT AND PUBLIC SERVICES
W. Malaysia (1972).	252,000	45,300	120,304*	32,500†	n.a.
Sarawak (1969) .	3,957‡	1,168	8,933	2,075	17,500
Sabah (1972) .	10,301	—	17,366	—	14,636

* Survey of 76 industries accounting for 89 per cent Value Added and 82 per cent of total paid employment.
† Includes road haulage, bus companies and railways.　　　　　‡ Agriculture and logging only.

AGRICULTURE
LAND USE
(West Malaysia—'000 acres)

	RUBBER PLANTATIONS	FOREST*	RICE	OIL PALM (estates only†)
1968 . .	4,291	31,900	1,183	496
1969 . .	4,264	31,030	1,234	597
1970 . .	4,275	30,940	1,318	675
1971 . .	4,246	30,400	1,365	769
1972 . .	n.a.	n.a.	1,414	n.a.

* Square miles.

† An oil palm estate is defined as having an average of one acre or more.

West Malaysia
PRODUCTION

	RUBBER (tons)	RICE (tons)	PALM OIL (tons)	PALM KERNEL (tons)	COPRA (tons)	COCONUT OIL (tons)	COPRA CAKE (tons)	TEA (lb.)
1970 . .	1,196,535	914,550	395,952	85,808	28,710	100,340	73,898	7,454,000
1971 . .	1,250,371	989,530	542,145	117,091	23,307	93,964	74,276	7,321,000
1972 . .	1,258,489*	1,001,930	648,913*	134,755*	22,888*	91,462	74,303	7,418,000*

* Provisional.

Sabah (1972—tons): Rubber n.a., Copra n.a., Sawlogs 5,244,456,† Sawn Timber 3,005,195 cu. ft.

Sarawak‡ (1972—tons): Rubber 19,623, Sago Flour 18,127, Pepper 25,764, Sawlogs 1,107,408,† Sawn Timber 214,090.

† Tons of 50 cu. ft.　　　　　‡ Export figures only.

LIVESTOCK
West Malaysia
('ooo)

	1969	1970	1971
Oxen	300	305	317
Buffalo . . .	225	233	215
Goats . . .	320	333	322
Sheep . . .	39	38	37
Pigs	678	724	742

TIMBER
West Malaysia
PRODUCTION

	'ooo solid cu. ft.				'ooo tons of 50 cu. ft.
	ROUND TIMBER	POLES	CHARCOAL	FIREWOOD	SAWN TIMBER
1969 . . .	189,444	2,838	17,647	5,481	1,454.3
1970 . . .	231,055	2,886	16,394	4,733	1,641.0
1971 . . .	252,974	3,247	21,114	4,810	1,742.3
1972 . . .	308,331	3,439	18,921	3,854	2,210.4

Sarawak (1971—tons of 50 cu. ft.): 2,169,281 of Logs.

FISHING
West Malaysia

	NUMBER OF VESSELS		LANDINGS OF FISH (tons)
	Powered	Non-powered	
1969 . . .	13,575	5,609	296,911
1970 . . .	15,029	5,277	293,436
1971 . . .	16,320	4,821	317,148
1972 . . .	16,954	4,665	306,209

MINING
West Malaysia
PRODUCTION

	TIN-IN-CONCENTRATES Tons	IRON ORE Tons	GOLD (RAW) Troy Ozs.	ILMENITE* CONCENTRATE Tons	BAUXITE Tons
1967 .	72,121	5,349,780	1,290	89,372	885,389
1968 .	75,069	5,085,342	1,454	123,838	786,042
1969 .	72,167	5,151,022	3,152	130,533	1,056,068
1970 .	72,630	4,420,143	3,912	219,095	1,121,318
1971 .	74,253	934,982†	4,491	153,489	962,497
1972 .	75,619	520,018	3,853	149,777‡	1,059,382

* Exports.
† Two large mines closed down towards the end of 1970.
‡ Provisional.

Sarawak (1972): Crude Oil 4,362,455 long tons, Gold 1,663 troy oz.

INDUSTRY

West Malaysia

PRODUCTION OF FACTORY REMILLED RUBBER AND SMOKED SHEETS (R.S.S.)

(Excludes production in Estate Factories)

(tons)

	R.S.S.	THIN REMILLED CREPE	THICK REMILLED CREPE	THIN LIGHT BROWN CREPE	FLAT BARK CREPE	TOTAL CREPE
1968	102,349	4,018	14,677	146,121	882	165,698
1969	141,111	7,722	16,063	125,113	1,558	150,456
1970	167,417	n.a.	17,387	135,174	n.a.	159,330
1971	134,213	—	—	—	—	141,581
1972	123,968	—	—	—	—	114,311

MANUFACTURED GOODS

		1970	1971	1972
Rubber:				
Foam Rubber (excl. mattresses)	'ooo lb.	4,286	4,308	4,421
Rubber Compound	,, ,,	9,972	12,016	12,482
Tubing and Hoses	,, ,,	73	48	40
Tubing and Hoses, part rubber	,, ,,	1,362	1,704	1,432
Inner Tubes	'ooo pieces	4,018	4,372	4,581
Footwear	doz. pairs	1,956,792	1,920,089	1,973,525
Foam Rubber Mattresses	number	226,936	166,018	5,372
Cement	tons	1,013,262	1,078,221	1,142,021
Cigars, Cigarettes, Cheroots and other Manufactured Tobacco	'ooo lb.	19,813	20,296	21,330
Aerated Waters and Cordials	'ooo gallons	19,725	17,100	20,579

FINANCE

100 cents (sen) = 1 Malaysian dollar (M$) or ringgit.

Coins: 1, 5, 10, 20 and 50 cents; 1 dollar.

Notes: 1, 5, 10, 50, 100 and 1,000 dollars.

Exchange rates (April 1974): £1 sterling = M$5.656; U.S. $1 = M$2.395.

M$100 = £17.68 = U.S. $41.75.

ORDINARY BUDGET

(million M$)

REVENUE	1971 (Actual)	1972 (Revised)	1973 (Est.)	EXPENDITURE	1971 (Actual)	1972 (Revised)	1973 (Est.)
Duties, Taxes and Licences	2,085	2,304	2,522	Defence and Internal Security	592	627	833
Government Services	82	89	96	Health	209	211	244
Commercial Undertakings	176	195	212	Social Welfare	17	8	10
Rent and Interest	68	75	109	Education	536	607	701
Miscellaneous Receipts	126	262	146	Posts and Telecommunications	141	162	176
				Administration	879	1,100	1,102
				Allocations to States	147	163	168
TOTAL	2,537	2,925	3,085	TOTAL	2,521	2,878	3,234

DEVELOPMENT BUDGET
(million M$)

EXPENDITURE	WEST MALAYSIA	SABAH	SARAWAK	TOTAL
1971 (Actual) . . .	1,044	39	59	1,142
1972 (Revised) . . .	1,280	82	83	1,445
1973 (Estimates) . .	1,339	112	125	1,576

SECOND MALAYSIA PLAN 1971–75

PUBLIC SECTOR	million M$ (Revised)
Agriculture and Rural Development .	2,073.7
Other Economic Services . .	3,355.9
Social Services	1,105.1
Defence and Security . . .	1,050.9
General Administration . .	262.5
TOTAL . . .	7,848.1
PRIVATE SECTOR	6,175.0
GRAND TOTAL . . .	14,023.1

RESERVES AND CURRENCY IN CIRCULATION
(At 30 June—million M$)

	1971	1972	1973
Official Reserves including Gold . . .	2,818	2,805	3,224
Commercial Banks (Net) . . .	85	27	—70
Currency in Circulation (Gross) . .	1,078.1	1,194.5	1,653.4

EXTERNAL TRADE
(million M$)

	1969	1970	1971	1972*
Imports . .	3,593	4,265	4,422.1	4,512.7
Exports . .	5,042	5,151	5,016.9	4,844.2

* Provisional.

COMMODITY GROUPS
(million M$—1972)

IMPORTS*	WEST MALAYSIA	SABAH	SARAWAK	TOTAL MALAYSIA
Food	678.9	64.0	64.6	807.5
Beverages and Tobacco . . .	52.1	24.8	3.8	80.7
Crude Materials, inedible, excluding fuels .	278.1	1.1	19.5	308.7
Mineral Fuels, Lubricants and Related Materials	246.0	26.0	88.0	360.0
Animal and Vegetable Oils and Fats . .	18.4	3.2	0.7	22.3
Chemicals	347.2	16.5	14.9	378.6
Basic Manufactures	725.0	71.1	44.9	841.0
Machinery and Transport Equipment . .	1,221.5	170.2	69.6	1,461.3
Miscellaneous Manufactured Articles .	163.5	20.4	11.9	195.8
Miscellaneous Transactions and Commodities .	42.9	6.0	7.9	56.8
TOTAL	3,773.6	413.3	325.8	4,512.7

EXPORTS*	WEST MALAYSIA	SABAH	SARAWAK	TOTAL MALAYSIA
Food	272.7	19.4	67.1	359.2
Beverages and Tobacco . . .	8.5	19.1	0.1	27.2
Crude Materials, inedible, excluding fuels .	1,649.3	447.8	148.8	2,245.9
Mineral Fuels, Lubricants and Related Materials	20.1	3.3	295.5	318.9
Animal and Vegetable Oils and Fats .	374.8	37.6	1.5	413.9
Chemicals and Products . . .	45.2	0.3	0.1	45.6
Basic Manufactures	1,152.8†	19.5	41.1	1,213.4†
Machinery and Transport Equipment .	64.0	19.0	7.1	90.1
Miscellaneous Manufactured Articles .	69.9	1.1	0.4	71.4
Miscellaneous Transactions n.e.s. .	40.8	13.7	3.6	58.1
TOTAL . . .	3,698.1	580.8	565.3	4,844.2

* Provisional figures.   † Includes exports of tin blocks: M$924.1 million.

PRINCIPAL TRADING PARTNERS
(million M$—1972)

IMPORTS*	WEST MALAYSIA	SABAH	SARAWAK	TOTAL MALAYSIA
Australia	315.4	10.6	12.2	338.2
China, People's Republic . . .	141.0	22.8	30.8	194.6
German Federal Republic . . .	186.5	10.5	7.6	204.6
Indonesia	132.7	2.9	17.5	153.1
Japan	778.0	105.5	48.4	931.9
Singapore	251.2	62.9	42.4	356.5
Thailand	160.3	18.4	14.2	192.9
United Kingdom	501.2	47.8	32.8	581.8
U.S.A.	336.2	56.4	14.7	407.3
TOTAL (incl. others) . .	3,773.6	413.3	325.8	4,512.7

EXPORTS*	WEST MALAYSIA	SABAH	SARAWAK	TOTAL MALAYSIA
Australia	78.7	5.4	4.6	88.7
Canada	88.8	0.2	0.9	89.9
France	94.2	1.5	0.6	96.3
German Federal Republic . .	130.4	1.8	20.4	152.6
Italy	133.9	0.6	9.6	144.1
Japan	421.0	298.9	111.2	831.1
Netherlands	244.0	1.5	3.5	249.0
Singapore	815.0	47.8	264.0	1,126.8
U.S.S.R.	102.5	—	—	102.5
United Kingdom	303.4	26.2	12.8	342.4
U.S.A.	628.0	10.9	31.5	670.4
TOTAL (incl. others) . .	3,698.1	580.8	565.3	4,844.2

* Provisional figures.

TRANSPORT
RAILWAYS
West Malaysia

	Total Railway Revenue	Total Railway Expenditure	Paying Coach Mileage	Paying Goods Mileage	Freight Tons	Net Ton Mileage Freight	Passengers	Passenger Miles	Track Mileage
	'ooo Malaysian dollars		'ooo miles		'ooo tons	'ooo ton-miles	'ooo	'ooo miles	miles
1969 .	65,665	75,886	2,621	3,453	3,687	744,293	5,103	333,718	1,342
1970	69,190	82,239	2,687	3,652	3,633	735,012	5,181	386,389	1,342
1971	68,730	82,179	2,731	3,400	3,328	673,719	5,272	401,851	1,343
1972 .	76,284	84,276	2,734	3,291	3,401	718,852	5,645	451,479	1,343

Sabah

	Passenger-Miles	Freight Ton-Miles
	'ooo	'ooo
1966 . .	12,190	2,850
1967	13,650	3,151
1968	14,346	3,750
1969	16,085	3,949

ROADS
West Malaysia
REGISTRATION OF VEHICLES

	Private Motor Cycles	Private Motor Cars	Buses	Lorries and Vans	Taxis
1969	312,686	213,247	5,347	51,375	5,955
1970	350,049	231,539	5,932	55,823	6,715
1971	389,133	253,491	6,447	60,543	7,179
1972	435,334	279,300	6,839	64,979	7,256

Sabah: Licensed motor vehicles: (1967) 24,960; (1968) 26,728; (1969) 31,265; (1970) 34,992; (1971) 40,342; (1972) 44,701.

Sarawak: Licensed vehicles: (1967) 24,680; (1968) 28,927; (1969) 33,538; (1970) 39,512; (1971) 46,139; (1972) 52,271.

SHIPPING
West Malaysia
FOREIGN TRADE
(vessels over 75 n.r.t.)

	Entered		Cleared	
	No. of vessels	'ooo net registered tons	No. of vessels	'ooo net registered tons
1969 . .	5,169	21,244	5,171	21,281
1970 . .	5,206	20,557	5,190	20,704
1971 . .	5,059	18,861	5,057	18,842
1972 . .	5,242	20,791	5,236	20,765

Sabah (1972): Passengers entered and departed 111,849; Freight loaded and unloaded 5,486,066 tons.

Sarawak (1972)*: Tonnage entered 5,203,598; tonnage cleared 5,209,790.

* Vessels below 75 tons n.r.t. included.

COASTAL TRADE
West Malaysia
(vessels over 75 tons n.r.t.)

	ENTERED		CLEARED	
	No. of vessels	'000 net registered tons	No. of vessels	'000 net registered tons
1969 . .	3,059	868,334	3,024	862,229
1970 . .	3,066	974,222	3,042	970,870
1971 . .	3,169	1,004,889	3,159	1,008,634
1972 . .	3,263	1,050,230	3,244	1,043,067

CIVIL AVIATION
West Malaysia

	AIRCRAFT LANDINGS		PASSENGERS LANDED		TOTAL FREIGHT HANDLED		TOTAL MAIL HANDLED	
					'000 kilos			
	Internal Flights*	International Flights†	Internal Flights*	International Flights†	Landed	Despatched	Landed	Despatched
1968	10,296	7,814	124,242	163,872	1,888	1,472	517	482
1969	10,625	8,386	138,787	179,298	1,722	1,372	547	514
1970	11,880	9,407	160,846	243,337	2,028	1,445	514	539
1971	12,770	10,876	196,096	306,489	2,266	1,662	491	751
1972	12,354	14,865	239,837	352,659	2,990	1,832	516	865

* Includes Singapore flights.   † Excludes Singapore flights.

Sabah (1972): Total passengers embarked 379,622; total passengers disembarked 377,975.

Sarawak (1972 estimates): Total passengers embarked 235,035; passengers disembarked 229,617.

West Malaysia
COMMUNICATIONS MEDIA
(1972)

Television sets in use	261,636*
Radio receivers in use	343,228*
Total daily newspaper readership . .	585,557

* September.

TOURISM

	TOURISTS
1966 . . .	45,914
1967 . . .	42,602
1968 . . .	50,588
1969 . . .	53,071
1970 . . .	76,374
1971 . . .	165,232
1972 (estimated) .	157,000

EDUCATION
West Malaysia
(1972)

	ESTABLISHMENTS	TEACHERS	STUDENTS
SCHOOLS:			
Malay Medium . . .	2,666	27,686	987,214
English Medium . . .	963	24,448	562,383
Chinese Medium . . .	1,058	13,423	458,671
Tamil Medium . . .	639	3,301	78,914
Vocational and Professional .	89	2,284	38,317
TOTAL . . .	5,415	71,142	2,125,499

Sabah (1972): *Primary:* schools 726, pupils 117,831; *Secondary:* schools 100, pupils 39,035; *Technical and Vocational:* schools 2.

Sarawak (1972): Total schools 1,329; primary pupils 151,313 (provisional); secondary students 38,015 (provisional).

Source: Department of Statistics, Kuala Lumpur, Kuching and Kota Kinabalu.

THE CONSTITUTION

Supreme Head of State

(YANG DI-PERTUAN AGONG)

His Royal Highness the Yang di-Pertuan Agong (King or Supreme Sovereign) is the Supreme Head of Malaysia. Every act of government flows from his authority although he acts on the advice of Parliament and the Cabinet. The appointment of a Prime Minister lies within his discretion, and he has the right to refuse to dissolve Parliament even against the advice of the Prime Minister. He appoints the Judges of the Federal Court and the High Courts on the advice of the Prime Minister. He is the Supreme Commander of the Armed Forces. The Yang di-Pertuan Agong is elected by the Conference of Rulers, and to qualify for election he must be one of the nine Rulers. He holds office for five years or until his earlier resignation or death. Election is by secret ballot on each Ruler in turn, starting with the Ruler next in precedence after the late or former Yang di-Pertuan Agong. The first Ruler to obtain not less than five votes is declared elected. A Deputy Supreme Head of State (the Timbalan Yang di-Pertuan Agong) is elected by a similar process. On election the Yang di-Pertuan Agong relinquishes, for his tenure of office, all his functions as Ruler of his own State and may appoint a Regent. The Timbalan Yang di-Pertuan Agong exercises no powers in the ordinary course, but is immediately available to fill the post of Yang di-Pertuan Agong and carry out his functions in the latter's absence or disability. In the event of the Yang di-Pertuan Agong's death or resignation he takes over the exercise of sovereignty until the Conference of Rulers has elected a successor.

Conference of Rulers

The Conference of Rulers consists of the Rulers and Governors. Its prime duty is the election by the Rulers only of the Yang di-Pertuan Agong and his deputy. The Conference must be consulted in the appointment of Judges, the Attorney-General, the Elections Commission and the Public Services Commission. The Conference must likewise be consulted and concur in the alteration of State boundaries, the extension to the Federation as a whole of Muslim religious acts and observances, and in any bill to amend the Constitution. Consultation is mandatory in matters affecting public policy or the special position of the Malays and natives of the Borneo States. The Conference also considers matters affecting the rights, prerogatives and privileges of the Rulers themselves.

Federal Parliament*

Parliament has two Houses—the Dewan Negara (Senate) and the Dewan Ra'ayat (House of Representatives). The Senate has a membership of 58, made up of 26 elected and 32 appointed members. Each State Legislature, acting as an electoral college, elects two Senators; these may be members of the State Legislative Assembly or otherwise. The Yang di-Pertuan Agong appoints the other 32 members of the Senate. Members of the Senate must be at least 30 years old. The Senate elects a President and a Deputy President from among its members. It may initiate legislation, but all money bills must be introduced in the first instance in the House of Representatives. All bills must be passed by both Houses of Parliament before being presented to the Yang di-Pertuan Agong for the Royal Assent in order to become law. A bill originating in the Senate cannot receive Royal Assent until it has been agreed to by the House of Representatives, but the Senate has only delaying powers over a bill originating from and approved by the House of Representatives. Senators serve for a period of six years, but the Senate is not subject to dissolution. Parliament can by statute increase the number of Senators elected from each State to three. The House of Representatives consists of 144 elected members. Of these, 104 are from the 11 States of Malaya, 26 from Sarawak and 14 from Sabah. In the case of the 11 States of Malaya, members are returned from single-member constituencies on the basis of universal adult franchise. The present members of the House of Representatives from Sabah and Sarawak are elected by their respective State Legislative Assemblies. Direct elections to the Federal Parliament and to the State Legislative Assemblies in Sabah and Sarawak will be held after the fifth anniversary of Malaysia Day or earlier if agreed. The life of the House of Representatives is limited to five years, after which time a fresh general election must be held. The Yang di-Pertuan Agong may dissolve Parliament before then if the Prime Minister so advises.

The Cabinet

The Yang di-Pertuan Agong appoints a Cabinet to advise him in the exercise of his functions, consisting of the Prime Minister and an unspecified number of Ministers who must all be members of Parliament. The Prime Minister must be a citizen born in Malaysia and a member of the House of Representatives who, in the opinion of the Yang di-Pertuan Agong, commands the confidence of that House. Ministers are appointed on the advice of the Prime Minister. A number of Assistant Ministers (who are not members of the Cabinet) are also appointed from among Members of Parliament. The Cabinet meets regularly under the chairmanship of the Prime Minister to formulate policy.

Public Services

The Public Services, civilian and military, are non-political and owe their loyalty not to the party in power but to the Yang di-Pertuan Agong and the Rulers. They serve whichever governments may be in power, irrespective of the latter's political affiliation. To ensure the impartiality of the service, and to protect it from political interference, a number of Services Commissions are established under the Constitution to select and appoint officers, to place them on the pensionable establishment, to decide as to promotion, and to maintain discipline.

The States *

With the exception of Malacca, Penang, Sabah and Sarawak, each of the States has a Ruler. The Ruler of Perlis has the title of Raja and that of Negri Sembilan, Yang di-Pertuan Besar. The rest of Their Highnesses are Sultans. The heads of the States of Malacca, Penang and Sarawak are Governors. The Head of State of Sabah is designated Yang di-Pertuan Negara. Each of the 13 States has its own written Constitution, and a single Legislative Assembly. Every State Legislature has powers to legislate on matters not reserved for the Federal Parliament. Each State Legislative Assembly has the right to order its own procedure, and the members enjoy parliamentary privilege. All members of the Legislative Assemblies of the 11 States of Malaya are directly elected from single-member constituencies, except that in the case of Malaya both the Legislative Assemblies and Executive Councils include three non-elected official experts. In the case of Sabah, the elected local authorities, functioning as electoral colleges, elect 18 members to the Legislative Assembly which may

* *See also* the Amendment to the Constitution.

not have more than six other nominated members. Sarawak has a three-tier system, with the elected District Councils forming themselves into electoral colleges to elect members to the Divisional Advisory Councils which, in turn, as electoral colleges, elect 36 members to the Council Negri. There may be up to three nominated members in addition to a "standing member" under a previously existing arrangement.

In the case of Sabah and Sarawak, the State Secretary, the State Attorney-General and the State Financial Officer are *ex-officio* members of the State Legislature as well as the State Executive Council. The Ruler or Governor acts on the advice of the State Government, which advice is tendered by the State Executive Council or Cabinet in precisely the same manner as the Federal Cabinet tenders advice to His Majesty the Yang di-Pertuan Agong.

The Legislative authority of the State is vested in the Ruler or Governor in the State Legislative Assembly. The executive authority of the State is vested in the Ruler or Governor but executive functions may be conferred on other persons by law. Every State has an Executive Council or Cabinet to advise the Ruler or Governor, headed by a Chief Minister (in Malacca, Penang, Sabah and Sarawak) or Mentri Besar (in other States), and collectively responsible to the State legislature. Every State has its own State Civil Service. Each State in Malaya is divided into administrative districts under a District Officer drawn from the Malayan Civil Service or the appropriate State Civil Service. Sabah is divided into four residencies: West Coast, Interior, Sandakan and Tawau with headquarters at Kota Kinabalu (formerly Jesselton), Keningua, Sandakan and Tawau respectively. The Island of Labuan is administered by a District Officer responsible direct to the State Secretary in Kota Kinabalu. Sarawak is divided into five Divisions, each in charge of a Resident—the First Division, with headquarters at Kuching; the Second Division, with headquarters at Simanggang; the Third Division, with headquarters at Sibu; the Fourth Division, with headquarters at Miri; the Fifth Division, with headquarters at Limbang.

Amendment

From February 1st, 1974, the city of Kuala Lumpur, formerly the seat of the Federal Government and capital of Selangor State, is designated the Federal Territory of Kuala Lumpur. It is administered directly by the Federal Government. The status of existing Members of Parliament and of members of the Selangor State Legislative Assembly is not affected until the next dissolution of both bodies. At the next General Election after February 1st, 1974, the membership of the Dewan Ra'ayat is reconstituted; its total membership is increased to 154, the new Federal Territory of Kuala Lumpur returns five members and adjustments are made to the number of members returned by other States. Sabah returns 16 and Sarawak 24 members.

THE GOVERNMENT

THE SUPREME HEAD OF STATE
(His Majesty the Yang di-Pertuan Agong)
His Majesty Sultan ABDUL HALIM MU'AZZAM SHAH ibni AL-MARHUM Sultan BADLISHAH (Sultan of Kedah).

DEPUTY SUPREME HEAD OF STATE
(Timbalan Yang di-Pertuan Agong)
H.R.H. Tuanku YAHYA PETRA ibni AL-MARHUM Sultan IBRAHIM (Sultan of Kelantan).

THE CABINET
(*April* 1974)

Prime Minister and Minister of Foreign Affairs: Tun Haji ABDUL RAZAK bin HUSSEIN.

Deputy Prime Minister and Minister of Trade and Industry: Datuk HUSSEIN bin Datu ONN.

Minister of Finance and Chairman of the National Financial Council: (vacant).

Minister of National Unity: Tun V. T. SAMBANTHAN.

Minister of Communications: Tan Sri Haji SARDON bin Haji JUBIR.

Minister without Portfolio and Ambassador to the U.S.A.: Enche MOHAMED KHIR JOHARI.

Minister of Sarawak Affairs: Tan Sri TEMENGGON JUGAH Anak BARIENG.

Minister of Labour and Manpower: Tan Sri V. MANICKAVASAGAM.

Minister of Agriculture and Fisheries: Tan Sri Haji MOHAMED GHAZALI bin Haji JAWI.

Minister of Rural Economic Development: Enche ABDUL GHAFAR bin BABA.

Minister of Works and Power: Datuk ABDUL GHANI GILONG.

Minister of Health: Tan Sri LEE SIOK YEW.

Minister of Land Development and Special Functions: Datuk Haji MUHAMMAD ASRI.

Minister of Defence: Datuk HAMZAH bin Datuk ABU SAMAH.

Attorney-General: Tan Sri ABDUL KADIR bin YUSOF.

Minister of Home Affairs: Tan Sri MUHAMMAD GAZALI bin SHAFIE.

Minister of Local Government and Housing: ONG KEE HUI.

Minister of Primary Industries: Datuk Haji ABDUL TAIB bin MAHMUD.

Minister of Welfare Services: Puan Hajjah AISHAH binti Haji ABDUL GHANI.

Minister of Technology, Research and Co-ordination of New Villages: Enche LEE FAN CHOON.

Minister of Culture, Youth and Sport: Enche ALI bin Haji ACHMAD.

Minister of Education: Tuan Haji MUHAMMAD bin YAACOB.

Minister of Information and Special Functions: Tunku ACHMAD RITHAUDDEEN Al Haj bin Tunku ISMAIL.

Minister with Special Functions: Enche MICHAEL CHEN WING SUM.

DIPLOMATIC REPRESENTATION

HIGH COMMISSIONS AND EMBASSIES ACCREDITED TO MALAYSIA

(In Kuala Lumpur unless otherwise stated)

(HC) High Commission; (E) Embassy.

Algeria: 13 Sundar Nagar, New Delhi, India (E).

Argentina: 116/1 Silom Road, Bangkok, Thailand (E).

Australia: 44 Jalan Ampang (HC); *High Commissioner:* A. R. PARSONS.

Austria: 518/2 Ploenchit Rd., Bangkok, Thailand (E).

Belgium: 2 Jalan Ampang (E); *Ambassador:* P. Y. DE VLEESCHAUWER.

Brazil: 518/2 Ploenchit Rd., Bangkok, Thailand (E).

Bulgaria: Chartered Bank Bldg., Jalan Ampang (E); *Ambassador:* N. PAPAZOV.

Burma: 7 Jalan Taman Freeman (E); *Ambassador:* U HLA MAW.

Canada: AIA Bldg., Jalan Ampang (HC); *High Commissioner:* E. R. RETTIE.

Denmark: 86 Jalan Ampang (E); *Ambassador:* KARL RAAVAD.

Egypt: 118 Jalan Berhala Brickfields (E); *Ambassador:* MOHD. KHAIR EL-DIN NASSER.

France: 210 Jalan Bukit Bintang (E); *Ambassador:* FRANCOIS SIMON DE QUIRIELLE.

Germany, Federal Republic: Bangunan UMBC, 17th Floor, Jalan Suleiman, P.O.B. 23 (E); *Ambassador:* GERHARD FISCHER, K.M.N.

Ghana: Canberra, Australia (HC).

Greece: P.O.B. 3058, New Delhi, India (E).

Hungary: Jakarta, Indonesia (E).

India: 19 Malacca St. (HC); *High Commissioner:* Shri A. K. DAR.

Indonesia: 91 Jalan Campbell (E); *Ambassador:* Brig.-Gen. SUPERDJO.

Iran: Bangkok, Thailand (E).

Iraq: Jakarta, Indonesia (E).

Italy: Jalan Ampang (E); *Ambassador:* Dr. PIER MARCELLO MASOTTI.

Japan: AIA Bldg., Jalan Ampang (E); *Ambassador:* SHIGERU HIROTA.

Jordan: New Delhi, India (E).

Khmer Republic: 69 Jalan Ampang, Hilir (E); *Ambassador:* NONG KIMNY.

Korea, Republic: 422 Circular Rd. (E); *Ambassador:* Dr. SUNG YONG KIM.

Kuwait: Tokyo, Japan (E).

Laos: Bangkok, Thailand (E).

Morocco: Islamabad, Pakistan (E).

Nepal: 16 Natmauk Yeiktha, Rangoon, Burma (E).

Netherlands: 86 Ampang Rd. (E); *Ambassador:* G. J. DE GRAAG.

New Zealand: 6th Floor, Bangunan Sharikat Polis, Jalan Suleiman (HC); *High Commissioner:* R. L. HUTCHENS, D.S.O.

Norway: Bangkok, Thailand (E).

Pakistan: 132 Ampang Rd. (E); *Ambassador:* S. IRTIZA HUSSAIN.

Philippines: 1 Changkat Kia Peng (E); *Ambassador:* ROMEO S. BUSUEGO, P.M.N.

Poland: 65 Jalan Diponegoro, Jakarta, Indonesia (E).

Romania: Jakarta, Indonesia (E).

Saudi Arabia: 5th Floor, Bangunan Sharikat Polis, Jalan Suleiman (E); *Ambassador:* Tan Sri HUSSEIN FATANY.

Singapore: Straits Trading Bldg., Leboh Pasar Besar (HC); *Ambassador:* Dr. CHIANG HAI DING.

Spain: Bangkok, Thailand (E).

Sri Lanka: AIA Bldg., Jalan Ampang, P.O.B. 990 (HC); *High Commissioner:* A. K. DAVID.

Sudan: New Delhi, India (E).

Sweden: AIA Bldg., Jalan Ampang (E).

Switzerland: 16 Pesianan Madge (E); *Ambassador:* Dr. THEO SCHMIDLIN.

Thailand: 206 Ampang Road (E); *Ambassador:* M. R. SANGKADIS DISKUL.

Turkey: Bangkok, Thailand (E).

U.S.S.R.: 263 Jalan Ampang (E); *Ambassador:* V. N. KUZNETSOV.

United Kingdom: Wisman Damansara, Jalan Samantan (HC); *High Commissioner:* Sir ERIC NORRIS.

U.S.A.: AIA Bldg., Jalan Ampang Rd. (E); *Ambassador:* JACK WILSON LYDMAN.

Viet-Nam, Republic: 8th Floor, Bangunan Sharikat Polis, Jalan Suleiman (E); *Ambassador:* NGUYEN DUY QUANG.

Yugoslavia: Jakarta, Indonesia (E).

Diplomatic relations are also maintained with Bangladesh, the People's Republic of China, the German Democratic Republic, Ireland, Lebanon and the Democratic Republic of Viet-Nam.

THE STATES

JOHORE
(Capital: Johore Bahru)

The Sultan of Johore: His Royal Highness Sultan ISMAIL Ibni AL-MARHUM Sultan IBRAHIM, D.K., D.M.N., S.M.N., S.P.M.J., S.P.M.K., D.K. (Brunei), K.B.E., C.M.G., D.K. (Pahang).

Chief Minister (The Mentri Besar): Datuk Haji OTHMAN bin Haji SA'AD.

STATE ASSEMBLY
(Elected May 1969)

PARTY	SEATS
Alliance	30
Democratic Action Party	1
Independent	1
TOTAL	32

KEDAH
(Capital: Alor Star)

The Regent of Kedah: His Royal Highness Tenghu ABDUL MALEK Ibni AL-MARHUM Sultan BADLISHAH, D.K., S.P.M.K.

Chief Minister (The Mentri Besar): Datuk SYED AHMAD bin SYED MAHMUD SHAHBUDDIN, S.P.M.K., J.M.N., J.P.

STATE ASSEMBLY
(Elected May 1969)

PARTY	SEATS
Alliance	14
Partai Islam	8
PGRM (Malaysian People's Movement) .	2
TOTAL	24

KELANTAN
(Capital: Kota Bahru)

The Sultan of Kelantan: His Royal Highness Tuanku YAHAYA PETRA Ibni AL-MARHUM Sultan IBRAHIM, D.K., D.M.N., S.P.M.K., S.J.M.K., S.M.N., D.K. (Trengganu). D.K. (Selangor), D.K. (Brunei), D.K. (Kedah).

Chief Minister: (vacant).

STATE ASSEMBLY
(Elected May 1969)

PARTY	SEATS
Partai Islam	19
Alliance	11
TOTAL	30

MALACCA
(Capital: Malacca)

The Governor of Malacca: His Excellency Tan Sri ABDUL AZIZ bin Haji ABDUL MAJID, P.M.N., D.P.M.K., P.J.K.

Chief Minister: Tuan Haji ABDUL GHANI bin ALI.

STATE ASSEMBLY
(Elected May 1969)

PARTY	SEATS
Alliance	15
Democratic Action Party	2
Independent	3
TOTAL	20

NEGRI SEMBILAN
(Capital: Seremban)

The Yang di-Pertuan Besar: His Royal Highness Tuanku JAAFAR Al-Haj Ibni AL-MARHUM Tuanku ABDUL RAHMAN, D.M.N., D.K. (Brunei).

Chief Minister (The Mentri Besar): Datuk MANSOR bin OSMAN, K.M.N., P.J.K.

STATE ASSEMBLY
(Elected May 1969)

PARTY	SEATS
Alliance	16
Democratic Action Party	6
Independent	2
TOTAL	24

PAHANG
(Capital: Kuantan)

The Sultan of Pahang: His Royal Highness Sultan ABU BAKAR RI'AYATUD'DIN ALMUADZAM SHAH Ibni AL-MARHUM AL-MU'TA-SIM BILLAH Al-Sultan ABDULLAH, D.M.N., D.K. (Brunei), D.K. (Johore), D.K. (Kedah), D.K. (Perak), S.J.M.P., G.C.M.G.

Chief Minister (The Mentri Besar): Tan Sri Haji YAHYA bin Haji MOHAMED SEH, S.J.M.P., P.S.N., P.J.K., J.P.

STATE ASSEMBLY
(Elected May 1969)

PARTY	SEATS
Alliance	20
PSRM (People's Socialist Party) . .	2
PGRM (Malaysian People's Movement) .	2
TOTAL	24

PENANG
(Capital: George Town)

The Governor of Penang: His Excellency Tun SYED SHEH bin SYED HASSAN BARAKBAH, S.S.N., S.M.N., S.P.M.K., P.S.B. (Kedah).

Chief Minister: Dr. LIM CHONG EU.

MALAYSIA—(THE STATES)

STATE ASSEMBLY
(Elected May 1969)

PARTY	SEATS
PGRM (Malaysian People's Movement) ⎫	
Alliance . . . . . ⎬	17
Democratic Action Party . . .	3
PKM (Social Justice Party) . . .	3
Partai Socialist Rakyat . . .	1
TOTAL	24

PERAK
(Capital: Ipoh)

The Sultan of Perak: His Royal Highness Sultan IDRIS AL-MUTAWAKIL ALLALLAH SHAH Ibni AL-MARHUM Sultan ISKANDAR SHAH KADDASALLAH, D.K., D.M.N., S.P.M.P., D.K. (Johore), P.J.K., C.M.G.

Chief Minister (The Mentri Besar): Datuk Haji KAMARUD-DIN bin MAT ISA, D.P.M.P., K.M.N., J.P.

STATE ASSEMBLY
(Elected May 1969)

PARTY	SEATS
Alliance	22
People's Progressive Party . . .	9
Democratic Action Party . . .	5
PGRM (Malaysian People's Movement) .	1
Partai Islam	2
Independent	1
TOTAL	40

PERLIS
(Capital: Kangar)

The Raja of Perlis: His Royal Highness Tunku SYED PUTRA Ibni AL-MARHUM SYED HASSAN JAMALULLIL, D.K., D.M.N., S.M.N., S.P.M.P.

Chief Minister (The Mentri Besar): Encik JA'AFAR bin HASSAN.

STATE ASSEMBLY
(Elected May 1969)

PARTY	SEATS
Alliance	11
Partai Islam	1
TOTAL	12

SABAH
(Capital: Kota Kinabalu)

Yang di-Pertuan Negara (Head of State): His Excellency Tun Pengiran Haji AHMAD RAFFAE bin Orang Kaya Pengiran Haji OMAR, S.M.N., P.J.K., O.B.E.

Chief Minister: Tun Datuk MUSTAPHA bin Datuk HARUN S.M.N., P.N.B.S., S.P., D.K., S.P.M.J., K.V.O., O.B.E.

STATE ASSEMBLY
(Elected October 1971)

PARTY	SEATS
Alliance	32
TOTAL	32

SARAWAK
(Capital: Kuching)

Governor: His Excellency Tun Tuanku Haji BUJANG bin Tuanku Haji OTHMAN, S.M.N., P.S.N., O.B.E.

Chief Minister: Datuk Haji ABDUL RAHMAN YA'AKUB, S.P.D.K., P.N.B.S., B.M. (Indonesia), O.S.E.(G.S.), O.S.M.

STATE ASSEMBLY
(Elected June 1970)

PARTY	SEATS
Alliance . . . . ⎫	
Sarawak United People's Party ⎬ . .	38
Sarawak National Party . . .	10
TOTAL	48

SELANGOR
(Capital: Kuala Lumpur*)

The Sultan of Selangor: His Royal Highness Sultan SALAHUDDIN ABDUL AZIZ SHAH Ibni AL-MARHUM Sultan HISAMUDDIN HALIM SHAH, D.K., D.M.N., S.P.M.J., D.K. (Brunei), D.K. (Trengganu).

Chief Minister (The Mentri Besar): Datuk HARUN bin HAJI IDRIS, S.P.M.S.

STATE ASSEMBLY
(Elected May 1969)

PARTY	SEATS
Alliance	17
Democratic Action Party . . .	8
PGRM (Malaysian People's Movement) .	1
PKM (Social Justice Party) . . .	2
TOTAL	28

* Following the amendment to the Constitution (q.v.) in which Kuala Lumpur is redesignated as the Federal Territory of Kuala Lumpur, a new Selangor State capital is to be established at Shah Alam in 1976 or 1977.

TRENGGANU
(Capital: Kuala Trengganu)

The Sultan of Trengganu: His Royal Highness Sultan ISMAIL NASIRUDDIN SHAH Ibni AL-MARHUM Sultan ZAINAL ABIDIN, D.K., D.M.N., S.P.M.T., D.K. (Kelantan), D.K. (Selangor), K.C.M.G.

Chief Minister (The Mentri Besar): Datuk NIK HASSAN bin Haji NIK ABDUL RAHMAN, D.P.M.T., K.M.N.

STATE ASSEMBLY
(Elected May 1969)

PARTY	SEATS
Alliance	15
Partai Islam	9
Total	24

PARLIAMENT
DEWAN NEGARA
(Senate)

58 members, 26 elected, 32 appointed. Each State Assembly elects two members. The Monarch appoints the other 32 members.

President: Tan Sri Ong Yoke Lin.

DEWAN RA'AYAT
(House of Representatives)

144 elected members, 104 from Malaya, 16 from Sabah and 24 from Sarawak.

(*April* 1973)

PARTY	SEATS
Alliance* }	
Partai Islam* }	112
DAP	8
SNAP	5
Social Justice	4
Independents and Others . . .	15

* Formed Government Coalition in January 1973.

Opposition Leader: Lim Kit Siang.

Speaker: Datuk C. M. Yusuf.

POLITICAL PARTIES
WEST MALAYSIA

The Alliance Party, Malaysia: U.M.N.O. Bldg., 399 Jalan Tunku Abdul Rahman, P.O.B. 249, Kuala Lumpur; a coalition party, formed by the United Malays National Organization, the Malaysian Chinese Association, the Malaysian Indian Congress, the Sabah Alliance and the Sarawak Alliance; Chair. Tun Haji Abdul Razak bin Datuk Haji Hussein, s.m.n.; Sec.-Gen. Michael Chen, m.p.

United Malays National Organization: U.M.N.O. Bldg., 399 Jalan Tunku Abdul Rahman, Kuala Lumpur; f. 1946; a Malay organization; one of the three component parties of the ruling Alliance Party; nationalist policy, i.e. subscribing to the ideal that all Malaysians irrespective of racial origin have a place and a future in the country, but at the same time the Party believes that the nation should be better consolidated by having a common national language while safeguarding the status of other languages and cultures; 500,000 mems.; Pres. Tun Abdul Razak; Sec.-Gen. Senu Abdul Rahman.

Malaysian Chinese Association: M.C.A. Bldg., Jalan Ampang, P.O.B. 626, Kuala Lumpur; f. 1949; aims at promoting inter-racial goodwill and harmony, and at safeguarding and advancing the interests of its members; 225,000 mems.; Acting Pres. Datuk Lee San Choon; Sec.-Gen. Chan Siang Sun.

Malaysian Indian Congress: 1 Jalan Pasar Borong, off Jalan Maxwell, Kuala Lumpur; f. 1946; represents the Indian community in Malaysia; 80,000 mems.; Pres. Rt. Hon. Tan Sri Dato V. Manickavasagam, s.p.m.s., p.s.m., p.j.k.; Sec.-Gen. S. Subramaniam.

Democratic Action Party: f. 1966; Opposition; advocates multi-racial Malaysia based on democratic socialism; Chair. Dr. Chen Man Hin; Sec.-Gen. Lim Kit Siang; 8 seats in House of Representatives.

Partai Islam: 300-6B Jalan Pekeliling, Kuala Lumpur; f. 1951; aims to achieve a government based on Islamic principles; principal coalition partner with Alliance Party (q.v.); 2 in Senate; Pres. Datuk Haji Muhammad Asri; Dep. Pres. Haji Hassan Adli; Sec.-Gen. Haji Hassan Shukri; Treas. Baharuddin Latif.

Party Ra'ayat (People's Party): Kuala Lumpur; f. 1955; Chair. Kassim Ahmad; Sec.-Gen. S. Husin Ali.

Labour Party of Malaya: Penang; f. 1952; aims to establish democratic socialism; Sec.-Gen. Dr. Wee Lee Fong.

People's Progressive Party of Malaya: 7 Hale St., Ipoh; f. 1955; left wing; Pres. S. P. Seenivasagam; 4 seats (opposition) in the House of Representatives; 9 seats in the Perak State Assembly.

Gerakan Rakyat Malaysia (*Malaysian People's Movement*): 4320 Jalan Tuanku Abdul Rahman, Kuala Lumpur; f. 1968; democratic socialist; 7 seats in House of Representatives; Sec.-Gen. (acting) Ong Boon Seong; Acting Chair. Dr. Lim Chong Eu.

Partai Keadilan Masharakat (*Social Justice Party*): f. 1971; aims to strive for a true Malaysian nationalism on the basis of the Constitution; 4 seats in the House of Representatives; Sec.-Gen. Dr. Tan Chee Khoon.

SABAH

Sabah Alliance Party: P.O.B. 1014, Kota Kinabalu; Chair. Tun Datuk Haji Mustapha bin Datuk Harun, s.m.n., p.d.k., k.v.o., o.b.e.; Sec.-Gen. Enche Abdul Momen bin Haji Kalakhan, a.d.k. The ruling party, composed of the following parties:

United Sabah National Organization (USNO): P.O.B. 927, Kota Kinabalu; f. 1962; Pres. Tun Datuk Haji Mustapha bin Datuk Harun, s.m.n., p.d.k., k.v.o., o.b.e.; Sec.-Gen. Datuk Aliuddin bin Datuk Harun, s.p.d.k.

Sabah Chinese Association (S.C.A.): P.O.B. 704, Kota Kinabalu; Pres. Enche Peter Lo Su Yin; Sec.-Gen. Enche Wong Lok Kiam.

Sabah Indian Congress (S.I.C.): P.O.B. 238, Kota Kinabalu; f. 1962; Chair. Enche Udam Singh; Sec.-Gen. Enche Paul Benjamin.

United Sabah Action Party: P.O.B. 1411, Sabah; f. 1971; multi-racial and non-denominational; Leader Richard E. Yap.

SARAWAK

Sarawak United People's Party (S.U.P.P.): Central Rd., Kuching; f. 1959; 51,906 (claimed) mems., mainly Chinese with a few Malays; Pres. Ong Kee Hui; Sec.-Gen. Stephen K. T. Yong.

Sarawak National Party (S.N.A.P.): 115 Green Rd., Kuching; f. 1961; mems. (registered) 104,795 mainly Dayaks (Sea, Land and Ulu Dayaks), Malays, Chinese and others; Pres. Datuk Stephen Kalong Ningkan; Sec.-Gen. Tuan Edmund Langgu Saga, m.p.

Sarawak Alliance Party: 54 Jalan Muhibbah, Kuching, P.O.B. 881; Exec. Sec. Sidi Munan; is composed of the following political parties:

Pasaka: f. 1962; 90,000 (claimed) mems., mainly Dayaks with a few Malays; Pres. Tan Sri Temenggong Jugah ak. Barieng; Sec.-Gen. Thomas Kana.

Sarawak Chinese Association: f. 1963; 50,000 mems.; Pres. Datuk Ling Beng Siew; Sec.-Gen. Chen Ko Ming.

Bumiputera: f. 1967 by the amalgamation of the *Party Barjasa* and the *Party Negara*; mems. (claimed): 120,000 Malays, Melanaus, some Land Dyaks and Ibans; Chair. Abang Ikhwan bin Haji Zainie; Sec.-Gen. Abdul Taib bin Mahmud.

DEFENCE

Armed Forces (1973): Total strength 56,000; army 46,500, navy 4,800, air force 4,700; military service is voluntary. Paramilitary forces number 54,000.

Equipment: The army and navy have mainly British equipment while the air force has Australian fighter-bombers and French helicopters. Under a recently concluded contract the Royal Malaysian Air Force will receive a squadron of supersonic F-5E fighter aircraft which will raise its total strength to over 190 aircraft.

Defence Expenditure: The estimated expenditure on defence for 1973 is M$680 million (U.S. $287 million).

CHIEFS OF STAFF

Chief of the Armed Forces Staff: Gen. Datuk Ibrahim bin Ismail, D.P.M.J., P.D.K., J.M.N., P.I.S.

Army: Gen. Ungku Nazaruddin bin Ungku Mohamed, J.M.N., P.J.K.

Navy: Commodore Datuk K. Thanabalasingam, D.P.M.J., G.M.N., S.M.J.

Air Force: Air Commodore Datuk Sulaiman bin Sujak, D.P.M.S., J.M.N.

JUDICIAL SYSTEM

The two High Courts, in Malaya and Borneo, have original, appellate and revisional jurisdiction as the federal law provides. Above these two High Courts is a Federal Court which has, to the exclusion of any other court, jurisdiction in any dispute between States or between the Federation and any State; and has special jurisdiction as to the interpretation of the Constitution. There is also unlimited right of appeal from the High Courts to the Federal Court and limited right of appeal from the Federal Court to the Yang di-Pertuan Agong who refers such appeals to Her Britannic Majesty's Privy Council. The High Courts each consist of the Chief Justice and a number of Puisne Judges. The Federal Court consists of the Lord President together with the two Chief Justices of the High Courts and four Federal Judges. The Lord President and Judges of the Federal Court, and the Chief Justices and Judges of the High Courts, are appointed by the Yang di-Pertuan Agong on the advice of the Prime Minister, after consulting the Conference of Rulers.

The Sessions Courts, which are situated in the principal urban and rural centres, are presided over by a President, who is a member of the Federation Legal Service and is a qualified barrister. Their criminal jurisdiction covers the less serious indictable offences, excluding those which carry penalties of death or life imprisonment. Civil cases

are usually heard without a jury. Civil jurisdiction of a President Sessions Court is up to $5,000 and Special President's Sessions Courts can hear cases of up to $10,000. The Presidents are appointed by the Yang di-Pertuan Agong.

The Magistrates' Courts are also found in the main urban and rural centres and have both civil and criminal jurisdiction, although of a more restricted nature than that of the Sessions Courts. The Magistrates consist of officers from either the Federation Legal Service or are seconded from the administration to the Judicial Department for varying periods up to three years. They are appointed by the Rulers of the States in which they officiate on the recommendation of the Chief Justice.

Lord President of the Federal Court of Malaysia: Hon. Tun Azmi bin Haji Mohamed, S.S.N., P.M.N., D.P.M.K., P.J.K.

Chief Justice of the High Court in Peninsular Malaysia: Hon. Tan Sri Mohamed Suffian bin Hashim, P.S.M., D.I.M.P., S.M.B. (Brunei), J.M.N., P.J.K., Hon. LL.D. (Singapore), Hon. D.LITT. (Malaya), M.A. (Cantab.), LL.B. (Cantab), Bar.-at-Law.

Chief Justice of the High Court in Sabah and Sarawak: Hon. Tan Sri Ismail Khan, P.M.N.

RELIGION

Islam is the religion of Malaysia, but every person has the right to practise his own religion. All Malays are Muslims. A small minority of Chinese are Christians but most Chinese follow Buddhism, Confucianism and Taoism. Of the Indian community, about 70 per cent are Hindu, 20 per cent Muslim, 5 per cent Christian and 2 per cent Sikh. In Sabah and Sarawak there are many animists.

ISLAM

President of the Majlis Islam: Al-Ustaz Mohammed Mortaza bin Haji Daud.

CHRISTIANITY
Anglican Communion

Bishop of Peninsular Malaysia: The Rt. Rev. J. G. Savarimuthu, B.D., 14 Pesiaran Stonor, Kuala Lumpur.

Bishop of Sabah: Rt. Rev. Luke Chhoa Heng Sze; Bishop's House, P.O.B. 811, Kota Kinabalu, Sabah.

Bishop of Kuching: Rt. Rev. Basil Temengong, Bishop's House, P.O.B. 347, Kuching, Sarawak.

Roman Catholic Communion

Archbishop of Singapore: The Rt. Rev. M. Olçomendy; 31 Victoria St., Singapore 7.

Archbishop of Kuala Lumpur: Rt. Rev. Dominic Vendargon; 528 Jalan Bukit Nanas, Kuala Lumpur.

Bishop of Penang: Rt. Rev. Gregory Yong, Sooinghean, 1 Bell Rd., Penang.

Bishop of Kuching: Rt. Rev. Charles Reiterer.

Bishop of Miri: Rt. Rev. A. D. Galvin, Catholic Mission, P.O.B. 108, Sarawak.

Vicar Delegate: The Very Rev. H. van Erp, Catholic Mission, Kuching; about 66,615 adherents.

Methodist Church

Bishop for Malaysia and Singapore: Rev. Yap Kim Hao; P.O.B. 483, Singapore 6; the Church has 40,000 members.

THE PRESS

PENINSULAR MALAYSIA

DAILIES

ENGLISH LANGUAGE

Malay Mail: 31 Jalan Riong, P.O.B. 250, Kuala Lumpur; f. 1896; afternoon; Editor P. J. JOSHUA; circ. 25,000.

Straits Echo: 216 Penang Rd., Penang; f. 1903; morning; Editor WILSON DE SOUZA; circ. 10,000.

Straits Times: 31 Jalan Riong, P.O.B. 250, Kuala Lumpur; also published in Singapore; Editor-in-Chief LEE SIEW YEE; circ. Malaysia 135,000, Singapore 134,000.

CHINESE LANGUAGE

Chung Kuo Pao (*China Press*): 2 Market St., Kuala Lumpur; f. 1946; morning; Editor S. H. WONG; circ. 36,700.

Kin Kwok Daily News: 21 Panglima St., Ipoh; f. 1940; morning; Editor CHONG YOUN HING; circ. 12,000.

Kwong Wah Yit Poh: 2 and 4 Chulia St., Ghuat Penang; f. 1910; morning; Editor WEN TZE-CHUAN; circ. 36,000.

Malayan Thung Pau: 40 Jalan Lima off Jalan Chan Sow Lin, Kuala Lumpur; Editor CHIEW POH CHIN; circ. 34,600.

Nanyang Siang Pau: 80 Jalan Riong, Kuala Lumpur; f. 1923; Editor CHU CHEE CHUAN; circ. 85,000 (daily), 110,000 (Sunday).

Shin Min Daily News: 82-B Jalan Rodger, Kuala Lumpur; Editor PAUL CHIN.

Sin Chew Jit Poh (Malaysia): 83 Jalan Sultan, Kuala Lumpur; Chief News Editor CHAN KEN SIN.

Sing Pin Jih Pao: 8 Leith St., Penang; f. 1939; morning; Gen. Man. FOO YEE FONG; circ. 45,000.

TAMIL LANGUAGE

Tamil Malar: Jalan Bersatu, Petaling Jaya; f. 1963; Editor S. MOHIDEEN; circ. 13,150.

Tamil Murasu: 3 Jalan 201, Petaling Jaya; Editor G. SARANGAPANY.

Tamil Nesan: 37 Ampang Rd., Kuala Lumpur; f. 1924; morning; Independent Malaysia; Propr. N. M. NAGAPPAN; Man. M. SETHURAMAN; Editor MURUGU SUBRAMANIAN; circ. 20,000 (daily), 30,000 (Sunday).

Sevika: 3A Mount Erskine Rd., Penang; f. 1945; afternoon; Editor T. S. KANAGASUNDRUM; circ. 2,000.

MALAY LANGUAGE

Berita Harian: 31 Jalan Riong, P.O.B. 250, Kuala Lumpur; morning; Editor SAMAD bin ISMAIL; circ. Malaysia 36,000, Singapore 20,000.

Majlis: 157 Batu Rd., Kuala Lumpur; f. 1930; afternoon; Editor A. SAMAD HAMAD; circ. 3,000.

Mingguan Malaysia: 31 Jalan Rd., Kuala Lumpur; Sunday; Editor Enche MELAN ABDULLAH; circ. 72,000.

Utusan Malaysia: 46M Chan Chow Lin Rd., Kuala Lumpur; f. 1965; Editor Enche ZAINUDDIN MYDIN; circ. 34,000.

Utusan Melayu: 46M Jalan Chan Sow Lin, Kuala Lumpur; morning; Editor MELAN bin ABDULLAH; circ. 50,000.

Warta Negara: P.O.B. 471, 34 Argyll Rd., Penang; f. 1945; morning; Editor MISBAH TAHIR; circ. 10,000.

PUNJABI LANGUAGE

Malaya Samachar: 256 Jalan Bricklands, Kuala Lumpur; Editor TIRLOCHAN SINGH.

Navjiwan: 52 Jalan 8/18, Petaling Jaya; Asst. Editor TARA SINGH.

SUNDAY PAPERS

ENGLISH LANGUAGE

Sunday Gazette: 216 Penang Rd., Penang; f. 1930; morning; Editor CHEAH CHEONG LIN; circ. 16,000 (*see* Straits Echo, Penang).

Sunday Mail: 31 Jalan Riong, P.O.B. 250, Kuala Lumpur; Editor P. J. JOSHUA; circ. Malaysia 35,000, Singapore 18,000.

Sunday Times: 31 Jalan Riong, P.O.B. 250, Kuala Lumpur; f. 1931; Editor P. C. SHIVADAS; circ. Malaysia 172,000, Singapore 146,000.

MALAY LANGUAGE

Berita Minggu: 31 Jalan Riong, P.O.B. 250, Kuala Lumpur; Editor SAMAD bin ISMAIL; circ. Malaysia 55,000, Singapore 20,000.

Utusan Zaman: 46M Jalan Chan Sow Lin, Kuala Lumpur; Editor MELAN bin ABDULLAH; circ. 69,000.

Warta Mingguan: P.O.B. 471, 34 Argyll Rd., Penang; Sunday Edition of *Warta Negara*; Editor MISBAH TAHIR.

PERIODICALS

ENGLISH LANGUAGE

Malayan Forester, The: Malayan Forest Department, Kuala Lumpur; f. 1931; Business Editor ISMAIL bin Haji ALI.

Malayan Nature Journal, The: P.O.B. 750, Kuala Lumpur; f. 1940 by the Malayan Nature Society; Pres. Encik MOHD. KHAN bin MOMIN KHAN; Hon. Editor Dr. H. S. YONG; Hon. Sec. P. J. VERGHESE; circ. 900.

Malaysia Warta Kerajaan Seri Paduka Baginda (H.M. Government Gazette): Kuala Lumpur; fortnightly.

Malaysian Agricultural Journal: Ministry of Agriculture and Fisheries, Kuala Lumpur; f. 1901; twice yearly.

Malaysian Digest: Ministry of Foreign Affairs, Jalan Wisma Patra, Kuala Lumpur; English; twice monthly; publishes airmail edition.

Planter, The: No. 1, Pesiaran Lidcol, off Jalan Yap Kwan Seng, P.O.B. 262, Kuala Lumpur; f. 1919; Incorporated Society of Planters' monthly; Editor D. A. EARP; circ. 1,700.

CHINESE LANGUAGE

Sin Lu Pao (*New Path News*): P.O.B. 513, Kuala Lumpur; produced by the Psychological Warfare Section; monthly; circ. 50,000 (Chinese), 3,200 (English).

MALAY LANGUAGE

Balai Muhibbah: National Goodwill Council, Kuala Lumpur; Editor ABU BAKAR bin KAMAT.

Dewan Masharakat: c/o Dewan Bahasa dan Pustaka, Kuala Lumpur; Editor KAMARUDDIN bin MUHAMMAD.

Dewan Pelajar: c/o Dewan Bahasa dan Pustaka, Kuala Lumpur; monthly; Editor KAMARUDDIN bin MUHAMMAD.

Filem dan Feshen: Utusan Melayu, Kuala Lumpur; fortnightly; Editor OSMAN ABADI.

Guru: Malay School, Jelutong, Penang; f. 1924 by Federation of Malay Teachers' Union of the Federation of Malaya (*Kesatuan Persakutuan Guru Melayu Persakutuan Tanah Melagu*); educational magazine; monthly; Pres. and Editor MOHAMED NOOR BIN AHMED; circ. 10,000.

Mastika: 46M Jalan Chan Sow Lin, Kuala Lumpur; Malayan illustrated magazine; monthly; Editor MELAN bin ABDULLAH; circ. 12,000.

Panduan Raayat: Brockman Rd., Kuala Lumpur; produced by the Information Services, Kuala Lumpur; monthly; Editor CHE RAMLY bin HAJI TAHIR; circ. 65,000.

Pengasoh: Majlis Ugama Islam, Kota Bahru, Kelantan; f. 1925; monthly; Editor HASAN HAJI MUHAMMAD; circ. 12,000.

Suara Umno: Johore Bahru; Editor SYED JA'AFFER bin HASSAN ALBAR; circ. 1,500.

Utusan Film and Sports: 46M Jalan Lima, Chan Sow Lin Rd., Kuala Lumpur; weekly.

Utusan Pelajar: Utusan Melayu, Kuala Lumpur; fortnightly; Editor OSMAN ABADI.

Utusan Radio dan TV: Utusan Melayu, Kuala Lumpur; weekly; Editor OSMAN ABADI.

Wanita: Utusan Melayu, Kuala Lumpur; monthly; Editor OSMAN ABADI.

TAMIL LANGUAGE

Janobahari: Brockman Rd., Kuala Lumpur; f. 1946; monthly; produced by Information Services; Editor C. V. KUPPUSAMY; circ. 25,000.

Solai: Messrs. Solai & Co., Kuala Lumpur; monthly; Editor K. L. RAMANATHAN; circ. 2,000.

SABAH
DAILIES

Api Siang Pau (*Kota Kinabalu Commercial Press*): P.O.B. 170, 24 Australian Place, Kota Kinabalu; f. 1954; Chinese; Editor LO KWOCK CHUEN; circ. 12,000.

Borneo Times: Tamah Merah, P.O.B. 455, Sandakan; f. 1956; Chinese; Editor CHAN KIAN TIAN; circ. 11,500.

Daily Express: P.O.B. 139, Kota Kinabalu; f. 1963; English and Malay; Editor LEONG C. SANG; circ. 25,795.

Hua Chiau Jit Pao (*Overseas Chinese Daily News*): P.O.B. 139, Kota Kinabalu; Chinese; f. 1936; Editor YEH PAO TZU, A.M.N.; circ. 27,925.

Kinabalu Daily News: P.O.B. 700, Sandakan; f. 1968; Chinese; circ. 2,000.

Kinabalu Sabah Times: P.O.B. 970, 67 Gaya St., Kota Kinabalu; f. 1947; English; Editor IGNATIUS P. DAIM; circ. 2,096.

Kinabalu Sabah Times: P.O.B. 970, 67 Gaya St., Kota Kinabalu; f. 1963; Chinese; Editor HALIM LOY CHEE FATT; circ. 12,000.

Malaysia Daily News: 7 Island Rd., Sandakan; f. 1968; Editor WONG CHING CHIONG.

Merdeka Daily News: P.O.B. 332, Sandakan; f. 1968; Chinese; Editor YAM YUE TUNG.

Overseas Chinese Daily News: P.O.B. 139, 9 Gaya St., Kota Kinabalu; f. 1936; Chinese; Editor HII YUK SEN; circ. 22,670.

Sandakan Jih Pao: P.O.B. 337, Sandakan; f. 1960; Chinese; Editor CHAN CHONG FOON; circ. 8,789.

SARAWAK
DAILIES

Chinese Daily News: Abell Rd., Kuching; f. 1945; Chinese; Editor SIA SWEE WANG; circ. 2,400.

Daily Herald: 8 North Yu Seng Rd., Miri; f. 1973; Editor GEORGE RASIAH; circ. 12,000.

International Times: Abell Rd., Kuching; f. 1965; Chinese; Editor WEE TIN FATT; circ. 5,000.

Malaysia Daily News: 7 Island Rd., Sibu; f. 1968; Chinese; Editor WONG YEW MING.

Miri Daily News: 8 North Yu Seng Rd., Miri; f. 1957; Chinese; Editor CHAI SZE-VOON; circ. 15,420.

Sarawak Siang Pau: P.O.B. 370, Sibu; f. 1966; Chinese; daily; Editor CHEE GUAN HOCK; circ. 5,000.

Sarawak Tribune and Sunday Tribune: 19 Jalan Tun Haji Openg, Kuching; f. 1945; English; Editor DENNIS LAW; circ. 4,350.

Sarawak Vanguard: 9 Temple St., Kuching; f. 1952; Chinese; Editor DESMOND LEONG KOK SHIN; circ. 19,500.

See Hua Daily News: 11 Island Rd., Sibu; f. 1952; Chinese; daily; Editor CHEE GUAN HOCK; circ. 9,500.

Utusan Sarawak: Abell Rd., Kuching; f. 1949; Malay; Editor MOHAMMED GOL SAFAR; circ. 5,000.

The Vanguard: 9 Temple St., Kuching; f. 1963; English; Editor DESMOND LEONG KOK SHIN; circ. 6,000.

PERIODICALS

Dolphin: Borneo Literature Bureau, P.O.B. 1390, Kuching, Sarawak; English; f. 1960 (circ. 6,000); Chinese: f. 1961 (circ. 11,000); Nendak (Iban): f. 1967 (circ. 1,000) Perintis (Bahasa Malaysia): f. 1970 (circ. 5,000).

Nendak: Borneo Literature Bureau, P.O.B. 1390, Kuching; f. 1967; Iban; monthly; Editor CHARLES SAONG; circ. 1,385.

Pedoman Ra'ayat: Malaysian Information Service, Kuching; f. 1956; Malay; monthly; Editor AFFANDI bin TARIKH; circ. 6,000.

Pemberita: Malaysian Information Office, Kuching; f. 1956; Iban and Chinese; monthly; Editor FREDERICK AUGUST anak ENCHANA; circ. 6,000.

Sarawak Dalam Sa-Minggu: State Information Office, Kuching; weekly; Editor AFFANDI bin TARIKH.

Sarawak Gazette: Govt. Printing Office, Kuching; f. 1870; English; monthly; Editors SAFRI AWANG ZAIDELL, LOH CHEE YIN; circ. 500.

Sarawak Karang Sa-Minggu: State Information Office, Kuching; Editor FREDERICK AUGUST.

Sarawak Museum Journal: Sarawak Museum, Kuching; f. 1911; English; twice yearly; Editor BENEDICT SANDIN; circ. 2,000.

Sarawak by the Week: Malaysian Information Services, Mosque Rd., Kuching; f. 1961; weekly; Malay and Iban; circ. 2,700.

NEWS AGENCY

Bernama (*National News Agency of Malaysia*): Bernama, Wisma Belia, Jalan Lornie, P.O.B. 24, Kuala Lumpur; f. 1967; general news service, economic service, photo service and feature service; teleprinter network between Head Office and regional bureaux and newspaper offices throughout the country; daily output in Bahasa Malaysia and English; Gen. Man. MOHAMED SOPIEE.

PRESS AGENCIES
FOREIGN BUREAUX

Agence France-Presse: 73 Jalan Ampang, Kuala Lumpur; Correspondent N. G. NAIR.

Antara News Agency: 36 Jalan Jugra, off Jalan Klang, Kuala Lumpur; Correspondent KAHARUDDIN.

Associated Press: China Insurance Bldg., 174 Jalan Tuanku Abdul Rahman, Kuala Lumpur; Correspondent H. SUBRAMANIAM.

Cathay Information Service: 239 Jalan Pekeliling, Kuala Lumpur; Dir. Senyung Chow.

Central News Agency: G-4 Sam Mansion, Jalan Tuba, Kuala Lumpur; Representative Jack C. Wang.

Reuter and Visnews: Asia Insurance Bldg., 2 Jalan Weld, Kuala Lumpur; Correspondent Allan Reditt.

TASS Soviet National News Agency: 6 Jalan Tebu, off Ulu Klang, Kuala Lumpur; Representative Sergei Frolkin.

Thai News Agency: 124-f Burmah Rd., Penang; Kuala Lumpur Representative Sook Buranakul.

United Press International: 95 Jalan Travers, Kuala Lumpur; Man. Max B. Vanzi.

PUBLISHERS

Penang

Georgetown Printers Ltd.: 5 China St., Ghaut, Penang; f. 1939; Man. Dir. Tan Chin Boon; Dirs. Tan Chiew Seng, Ooi Siew Kee.

Kwong Wah Yit Poh Press Bhd.: 2 and 4 Chulia St., Ghaut, P.O.B. 31; f. 1910; Man. Dir. Chew Meng Tow; Man. Lau Hong Chong.

National Press, The: 46–48 Prangin Lane; Man. Dir. Tan Cheng Tit; Gen. Man. Tan Chong Heng.

Phoenix Press Limited: 6–8 Church St.; Man. Dir. Tan Chin Boon; Dir. Ooi Siew Kee; Man. Tan Chiew Seng.

Perak

Al-Zainiyah: 66a Assam Kumbang, Taiping; religious books and periodicals.

Caxton Press, The (Ipoh): 130 Belfield St., P.O.B. 140, Ipoh; Man. Cyril R. LaBrooy.

Charles Grenier Sdn. Bhd.: Head Office: 37/39 Station Rd., P.O.B. 130, Ipoh; br. at 8 Medan Pasar, P.O.B. 183, Kuala Lumpur; Man. Dir. H. D. G. Jansz.

Peter Chong Printers Sdn. Bhd.: 120 Belfield St., Ipoh; f. 1921; publishers, offset/letterpress; printers and stationers; Man. Dir. J. Kong.

Kuala Lumpur

Commercial Press Sdn. Bhd.: 99 Jalan Bandar, Kuala Lumpur; Man. Dir. Yuen Sze Kin.

Economy Printers, Ltd.: 12 Jalan Mountbatten, Kuala Lumpur.

Federal Publications Sdn. Bhd.: Balai Berita, 170 Jalan Sungei Besi, Kuala Lumpur and River Valley Rd., Singapore 9; educational books; Gen. Man. P. Mowe.

Longman Malaysia Sdn. Bhd.: 2nd Floor, Wisma Damansara, Jalan Semantan, Damansara Heights, Kuala Lumpur; textbooks, educational materials.

Loyal Press, The: 16 Jalan Mountbatten, P.O.B. 162, Kuala Lumpur; f. 1933; Man. Ooi Phee Cheng.

Malaysia Publishing House Ltd.: 279 Jalan Tuanku Abdul Rahman, Kuala Lumpur; br. of *M.P.H. Ltd.* of Singapore.

Marican and Sons (Malaysia) Sdn. Bhd.: 321 Jalan Tuanku Abdul Rahman, Kuala Lumpur; publishers and booksellers.

Oxford University Press: Bangunan Loke Yew, Jalan Belanda, Kuala Lumpur; Gen. Man. R. E. Brammah; history, reference, geography and education.

Peter Chong and Co.: 31 Ampang St., Kuala Lumpur; educational books; Propr. Peter Chong.

Shang-Wu Press, K.L., The: 41 Petaling St., Kuala Lumpur; sub-branch of *Commercial Press Ltd.*, Singapore; Man. Soon Kah Kee.

University of Malaysia Press Ltd.: c/o University of Malaysia, Pantai Valley, Kuala Lumpur; history, philosophy, medicine, politics, social science.

Negri Sembilan

Bharathi Press: 23–24 Jalan Tuan Sheikh, Seremban; P.O.B. 74; f. 1939; Proprs. Rama Sinniah, C. Ramasamy; Man. M. R. N. Muthurengam.

Malay Press, The: 198 Tong Yen Rd., Kuala Pilah; Malay story books.

Peter Chong and Co.: 68 Birch Rd., Seremban; Propr. Peter Chong.

Association of Southeast Asian Publishers (ASEAP): Kuala Lumpur; f. 1972; comprises 16 publishers from Indonesia, Khmer Republic, Singapore, Thailand, Philippines and Malaysia; Pres. Encik Ghazali Yunus; Sec. Gen. Encik R. Narayana Menon.

Sarawak

Borneo Literature Bureau: P.O.B. 1390, Kuching; sponsored by the State Governments of Sabah and Sarawak; educational, general and children's books in English, Iban, Malay, Chinese and other languages spoken in Sabah and Sarawak; also monthly magazines *Dolphin* (English and Chinese), *Perintis* (Bahasa Malaysia) and *Nendak* (Iban); Dir. Edward Enggu.

RADIO AND TELEVISION

RADIO

Peninsular Malaysia

Department of Broadcasting: P.O.B. 1074, Federal House, Kuala Lumpur; stations of "Radio Malaysia" are operating at Kuala Lumpur, Penang, Malacca, Ipoh, Kota Bahru, Johore Bahru, Kuantan and Kuala Trengganu; broadcasts 419 hours 20 minutes weekly in Malay, English, Tamil and Chinese (four dialects); Dir.-Gen. Dol Ramli.

Rediffusion (Malaya) Ltd.: subsidiary of Rediffusion Ltd., London; P.O.B. 570, Kuala Lumpur; f. 1949; 2 programmes; Gen. Man. M. J. Bleeck; 18,584 subscribers in Kuala Lumpur; 8,881 subscribers in Penang; 5,996 subscribers in Ipoh.

Sabah

Dept. of Broadcasting (Sabah): P.O.B. 1016, Kota Kinabalu; inaugurated in 1955 and broadcasts programmes 126 hours a week in Malay, English, Chinese (3 dialects), Kadazan, Murut, Indonesian and Bajau; Dir. of Broadcasting, Sabah, Suhaimi Haji Amin.

Note: A television service began in December 1971 for 5 hours daily.

Sarawak

Radio Malaysia (Sarawak): Broadcasting House, Kuching; f. 1954, incorporated as a department of Radio Malaysia 1963; broadcasts $267\frac{1}{2}$ hours in Malay, English, Land Dayak, Chinese, Iban, Bidayuh, Melanau and Kayan/Kenyah; Schools Broadcasting Service started 1959; branch station at Limbang opened April 1971; Dir. of Broadcasting, Sarawak, Mohamed Salleh bin Askor, P.B.S.

In September 1972 there were 343,228 licensed radio receivers.

TELEVISION

Radio Telivision Malaysia: Dept. of Broadcasting, Angkasa puri, Kuala Lumpur; f. 1963; Dir.-Gen. Dol Ramli, Dir. of Programmes Raja Iskandar.

In September 1972 there were 261,636 licensed television receivers. Colour television is expected to be introduced by the end of 1975.

FINANCE

(cap.=capital; p.u.=paid up; dep.=deposits; m.=million; brs.=branches; M$=Malaysian dollars.)

BANKING

Central Bank of Malaysia

Bank Negara Malaysia: Jalan Kuching, P.O.B. 922, Kuala Lumpur; brs. at Kuala Lumpur, Penang, Kota Kinabalu, Johor Bahru, Kuching; f. 1959; from June 1967 the Bank assumed function of currency issue in succession to Board of Commissioners of Currency, Malaya and British Borneo; cap. p.u. M$40m., dep. M$1,512m. (Sept. 15th, 1973); Gov. and Chair. Tan Sri Ismail bin Mohamed Ali, p.m.n.; Deputy Gov. Rastam bin Abdul Hadi, k.m.n.; Advisers Syed Adam Al-Ja'fri, Abdul Aziz bin Haji Taha, k.m.n.; publs. *Annual Report and Statement of Accounts, Quarterly Economic Bulletin, Monthly Statistical Supplement, Malaysia in Figures.*

PENINSULAR MALAYSIA

Commercial Banks

Bank Bumiputra Malaysia Bhd.: P.O.B. 407, 21 Jalan Melaka, Kuala Lumpur; f. 1965; Commercial Bank established by the Government to facilitate capital formation, and provide banking and financial services to all sectors of the economy; 24 brs. including East Malaysia; wide network of corresponding banks throughout the world; cap. $20m.; cap. p.u. $16.5m.

Co-operative Bank of Malaysia Ltd.: 140 Jalan Ipoh, Kuala Lumpur; f. 1954; cap. p.u. M$2m.; dep. M$11m.; Man. Dir. Inche Abu Mansor Basir, a.c.a.; Sec.-Gen. Man. Inche Ismail Din.

Kwong Yik Bank Bhd.: 75 Jalan Bandar, P.O.B. 135, Kuala Lumpur; f. 1913; Chair. Inche Azman Bin Hashim; Man. Dir. Lim Khin Seong; Man. Peter M. C. Kwan.

Malayan Banking Bhd.: 92 Jalan Bandar, P.O.B. 2010, Kuala Lumpur; f. 1960; cap. M$45m.; dep. M$724.6m. (June 1971); Chair. Tan Sri Taib bin Haji Andak, p.m.n., d.p.m.j.; Vice-Chair. Hew Kiang Main, f.a.s.a., c.p.a. (Malaysia).

Oriental Bank Bhd.: P.O.B. 243, 16 Jalan Silang, Kuala Lumpur; Dirs. Tan Sri Haji Hussain bin Haji Mohd. Sidek, p.s.m., j.m.n., s.m.p., p.k.t., p.j.k., Cho Jock Kim, Edwin T. Nicholas, Datuk Foo See Moi, d.p.m.k., j.p.; Gen. Man. James L. P. Leow; Sec. Mohamed Yusoff bin Abdul Latif.

Pacific Bank Berhad: 145 Jalan Bandar, Kuala Lumpur; branch at Batu Pahat, Johore; f. 1963.

United Malayan Banking Corporation Bhd.: Bangunan UMBC, Jalan Suleiman, Kuala Lumpur; f. 1960; cap. p.u. M$30m.; dep. M$635.4m. (1973); Chair. Saw Choo Theng; Man. Dir. Kang Kock Seng.

Foreign Banks

Algemene Bank Nederland N.V.: 32 Vijzelstraat, Amsterdam; 15 Jalan Gereja, Kuala Lumpur and 9 Beach St., Penang; Man. (Kuala Lumpur) G. A. Coronel; Man. (Penang) A. Oortman Gerlings.

Bangkok Bank Ltd.: 9 Suapa Rd., Bangkok; 105 Jalan Bandar, Kuala Lumpur; Chair. Gen. Prapas Charusathiara; Pres. Chin Sophonpanich.

Bank of America N.T. and S.A.: Bank of America Center, San Francisco, California 94120; G.P.O.B. 950, 2 Weld Rd., Kuala Lumpur.

Bank of Canton Ltd., The: 6 Des Voeux Rd. Central, Hong Kong; 18 Pudu St., Kuala Lumpur; f. 1912.

Bank of Tokyo Ltd.: 6, 1-chome, Nihombashi Hongokucho, Chuo-ku, Tokyo; 22 Medan Pasar, Kuala Lumpur.

Banque de l'Indochine: 96 blvd. Haussman, Paris; 44 Jalan Pudu, Kuala Lumpur; sub-branch at 488 Jalan Tuanku Abdul Rahman, Kuala Lumpur.

Chartered Bank, The: 38 Bishopsgate, London, E.C.2; 2 Jalan Ampang, Kuala Lumpur, and 34 brs. in E. and W. Malaysia; Chief Man. C. Little (Malaysia).

Chase Manhattan Bank, N.A.: 1 Chase Manhattan Plaza, New York ,N.Y. 10015, U.S.A.; 9 Jalan Gereja, P.O.B. 1090, Kuala Lumpur; Man. Daniel A. Reid.

Chung Khiaw Bank Ltd.: Head Office: 59 Robinson Rd., Singapore; 11 Leboh Pasar Besar, Kuala Lumpur; 33 brs.; f. 1950; Man. Dir. Wee Cho Yaw.

Europaeisch Asiatische Bank AG (*European Asian Bank*): P.O.B. 944, 7 Rathausstrasse, Hamburg 1, Federal Republic of Germany; brs. at Jakarta, Hong Kong, Karachi, Singapore and Kuala Lumpur.

First National City Bank: 399 Park Ave., New York; 99 Jalan Ampang, Kuala Lumpur; f. 1812.

Habib Bank Ltd.: Habib Square, Karachi, Pakistan; 17 Jalan Gereja, Kuala Lumpur.

Hong Kong and Shanghai Banking Corporation, The: 1 Queen's Rd., Central, Hong Kong; 2 Lepoh Ampang, Kuala Lumpur, and 22 other brs.; Man. I. N. MacLeod.

Lee Wah Bank Ltd., 18 South Canal Rd., Singapore; 10-14 Medan Pasar, Kuala Lumpur; Man. W. F. Chen.

Mercantile Bank Ltd.: 15 Gracechurch St., London, E.C.3; 19-21 Leboh Pasar Besar, P.O.B. 41, Kuala Lumpur and 13 brs.

Oversea-Chinese Banking Corpn. Ltd.: Block 3, Upper Pickering St., Singapore; 30 Jalan Mountbatten, Kuala Lumpur; f. 1932; Chair. Tan Sri Tan Chin Tuan; Dir. and Gen. Man. Lin Jo Yan.

Overseas Union Bank Ltd.: Head Office: Singapore; Sarawak branch: P.O.B. 653, 1 Main Bazaar, Kuching; Man. C. H. Sia.

BANKERS' ASSOCIATION

Association of Banks in Malaysia-Singapore, The: c/o Oversea-Chinese Banking Corpn. Ltd., 30 Jalan Mountbatten, Kuala Lumpur; f. 1965; Chair. Tan Chin Tuan (Oversea Chinese Banking Corpn. Ltd.); Sec. for Malaysia Teh Thean Choo.

INSURANCE

Malaysian National Insurance Bhd.: 91 Jalan Campbell (3rd Floor), P.O.B. 799, Kuala Lumpur; state-run company handling non-life and general insurance; auth. cap. M$10m.; Chair. Y. M. Tengku Razaleigh Hamzah; Man. Dir. A. Rahman Hamidon; Dirs. Y. B. Datuk Kurnia Jasa Haji Osman bin Talib, Y. B. Datuk Abdullah bin Ayub, Tahir bin Abdul Rahim.

STOCK EXCHANGE

Stock Exchange of Malaysia and Singapore: 7th Floor, Bangkok Bank Bldg., Jalan Bandar, Kuala Lumpur.

SABAH

COMMERCIAL BANKS

Bank Negara Malaysia: Head Office: Kuala Lumpur; br. in Kota Kinabalu.

Chartered Bank, The: Head Office: London; Sabah: P.O.B. 99, Kota Kinabalu; brs. at Kudat, Labuan, Lahad Datu, Sandakan, Tenom and Tawau; Man. A. A. NORRIE.

Chung Khiaw Bank Ltd.: Head Office: Singapore; brs. in Sabah: P.O.B. 539, Kota Kinabalu; P.O.B. 902, Sandakan; P.O.B. 111, Tuaran; Man. for Sabah CHOW SHEE SENG, P.G.D.K., O.ST.J.

Hongkong and Shanghai Banking Corpn., The: Head Office: Hong Kong; brs. at Kota Kinabalu, Labuan, Beaufort, Sandakan, Papar and Tawau; Man. P. S. INGHAM.

Malayan Banking Bhd.: Head Office: Kuala Lumpur; Sabah: 55 Jalan Dua, P.O.B. 374, Sandakan.

United Overseas Bank Ltd.: Head Office: 175-179 Cecil St., Singapore; Regional Office: 22 Neil Malcolm St., Kota Kinabalu, Sabah; Man. CHOU CHUNG CHING.

SARAWAK

COMMERCIAL BANKS

Bank Negara Malaysia: Head Office: Kuala Lumpur; Kuching.

Chartered Bank, The: Head Office, London; Sarawak: Jalan Tun Haji Openg, Kuching; brs. at Sibu, Miri, Sarikei, Bintulu and Simanggang.

Hock Hua Bank Bhd: Head Office: Central Rd., Sibu: f. 1952; cap. M$5m.; res. M$0.5m.; Chair. Datuk LING BENG SIEW, P.N.B.S.; Vice-Chair. Datuk LING BENG SIONG, P.N.B.S.; Man. Dir. Datuk TING LIK HUNG, O.B.E., P.B.S.; Exec. Dir. TING MING HUI; brs. in Kuala Lumpur, Kuching and Miri; Associated Co. in Sandakan (Sabah).

Hongkong and Shanghai Banking Corporation: Head Office: Hong Kong; Sarawak: brs. in Kuching and Sibu.

Malayan Bank: Kuala Lumpur; brs. at Miri, Limbang and Kuching.

Oversea-Chinese Banking Corporation, Ltd.: Head Office: Singapore; Sarawak: P.O.B. 60, Kuching.

Overseas Union Bank Ltd: Head Office: Singapore; Sarawak Branch: P.O.B. 653, 1 Main Bazaar, Kuching; Man. CHAN WAN CHEONG.

Post Office Savings Bank: Kuching; dep. M$7.3m. (1972).

Sarawak Co-operative Central Bank: 46 Ban Hock Rd., Kuching; f. 1953; the Bank receives and invests funds from member societies and acts as agent to supply goods and make loans; 142 member societies.

Wah Tat Bank Bhd.: 12 Old St., Sibu; br. in Kuching; Man. Dir. CHEW CHOO SING.

TRADE AND INDUSTRY

PENINSULAR MALAYSIA

CHAMBERS OF COMMERCE

The National Chambers of Commerce of Malaysia: P.O.B. 2529, Kuala Lumpur; f. 1962; 4 mems., namely Associated Malay, Chinese, Indian Chambers of Commerce of Malaysia and the Malaysian International Chamber of Commerce; Chair. Tengku RAZALEIGH HAMZAH, S.P.M.K.; Sec. JUNUS SUDIN, J.S.M.

Associated Chinese Chambers of Commerce of Malaysia: Chinese Assembly Hall, Ground Floor, 1 Jalan Birch, Kuala Lumpur 08-02.

Associated Indian Chambers of Commerce of Malaya: 18 Jalan Mountbatten, P.O.B. 675, Kuala Lumpur; Pres. Sen. Tan Sri S. O. K. UBAIDULLA; Sec. G. S. GILL.

Associated Malay Chambers of Commerce: Room 201 MARA Bldg., Jalan Tunku Abdul Rahman, Kuala Lumpur.

Malacca Chamber of Commerce: 89 Wolferstan Rd., Malacca; f. 1948; Pres. GOH KENG HOW; Sec. C. F. GOMES & Co.; publ. *Bulletin* (quarterly)

The Malaysian International Chamber of Commerce (MICC): Chartered Bank Chambers, P.O.B. 192, Kuala Lumpur; f. 1916 as Federated Malay States (F.M.S.) Chamber of Commerce; 173 mem. companies; Pres. A. KEOW; Exec. Sec. D. C. L. WILSON; publ. *Annual Year Book.*

Penang Branch: Chartered Bank Chambers, P.O.B. 331, Penang, Peninsular Malaysia; f. 1795; Chair. J. McKEOWN; Secs. Evatt & Co.

Perak Branch: Chartered Bank Chambers, P.O.B. 136, Ipoh; f. 1906; Chair. E. J. HUGHES; Secs. Evatt & Co.

Selangor Branch: Chartered Bank Chambers; P.O.B. 192, Kuala Lumpur; f. 1906; Chair. A. KEOW; Secs. Evatt & Co.

Penang Chinese Chamber of Commerce: 2 Penang St., Penang; f. 1903; Pres. CHOONG HAN LEONG, J.P.; Sec. CHOY MENG FOOK, P.B., A.M.N.; 800 mems. (1973).

Perak Chinese Chamber of Commerce: 35–37 Hale St., Ipoh; f. 1908; Pres. YEOH KIM TIAN, J.P.; Vice-Pres. Datuk CHONG KOK LIM, CHONG WAI WENG; Hon. Gen. Sec. LOO WENG CHOON, J.P.; 1,500 mems.

Selangor Chinese Chamber of Commerce: Chinese Assembly Hall, 1st Floor, Birch Rd., Kuala Lumpur; Pres. The Hon. Senator Tan Sri T. H. PAN, P.M.N., J.M.N., C.W.E., M.P.; Exec. Sec. YEANG KIM SIEW.

Selangor Indian Chamber of Commerce: 116 (1st Floor), Jalan Tuanku Abdul Rahman, Kuala Lumpur; Pres. G. S. GILL; Hon. Sec. JASWANT SINGH GILL.

Chinese, Indian and Malay Chambers of Commerce are also represented in most of the important towns of Peninsular Malaysia.

DEVELOPMENT ORGANIZATIONS

Commonwealth Development Corporation: Head Office: London; Malaysia Office: P.O.B. 494, Kuala Lumpur; Resident Man. E. J. NEAL, O.B.E.

Federal Land Development Authority: Jalan Maktab, Kuala Lumpur; f. 1957; to raise the productivity of low income groups and so their earned income and to open up new land for development; Chair. Enche MUSA HITAM; Gen. Man. Y. M. R. M. ALIAS; publ. *Annual Report.*

Maylis Amanah Ra'ayat (*Council of Trust for Indigenous People*): 232 Jalan Tuanku Abdul Rahman, Kuala Lumpur; f. 1965 to carry on the manufacture, assembly, processing and marketing of products; to undertake research in industry and joint ventures; Dir.-Gen. Encik Ahmad bin Haji Abdul Rahim; Sec. Encik Mohamed Zahudi bin Abdul Jalil.

PUBLIC CORPORATIONS*

Federal Industrial Development Authority: 5th and 6th Floor, Wisma Damansara, P.O.B. 618, Kuala Lumpur; Dir. Encik Mohd. Zain bin Haji Abdul Majid.

National Land Co-operative Society Ltd.: 6th Floor, M.I.C. Bldg., Maxwell Rd., Kuala Lumpur; f. 1960; to mobilize capital from rubber industry workers and others to purchase rubber estates; 60,300 mems.; owns 19 rubber, tea, oil-palm and coconut plantations; cap. p.u. M$13.1m.; Pres. Y. A. B. Tun V. T. Sambanthan; Chair. Enche S. S. Govindasamy; Vice-Chair. Enche S. Murugesu; Hon. Sec. Enche V. J. Bala Sundaram.

Malaysian Industrial Development Finance Bhd.: 117 Jalan Ampang, P.O.B. 2110, Kuala Lumpur; f. 1960 by the Government, Banks, Insurance Companies; shareholders include International Finance Corporation, Commonwealth Development Finance Co.; provides capital for industry; marketing services and builds factories; Chair. Tan Sri Ismail Mohamed Ali; Gen. Man. H. F. G. Leembruggen.

Perbadanan Nasional Bhd. (PERNAS): 9th Floor, Bank Bumiputra Bldg., 21 Jalan Melaka, P.O.B. 493, Kuala Lumpur; f. 1969, incorporated 1971; a government sponsored company established to promote trade, property development, construction, mineral exploration, inland container transportation, mining, insurance, industrial development; Auth. cap. M$50m.; cap. p.u. M$11.25m.; has seven wholly owned subsidiary companies; Chair. Tengku Razaleigh Hamzah; Man. Dir. A. Rahman Hamidon.

INDUSTRIAL AND TRADE ASSOCIATIONS

Export Promotion Council: c/o Export Promotion Division, Ministry of Trade and Industry, Kuala Lumpur; f. 1971; Chair. Tengku Ahmad bin Tengku Yahya.

Federal Agricultural Marketing Authority: Tingkat 4 dan 5, Bangunan Bangkok Bank, 105 Jalan Bandar, Kuala Lumpur; f. 1965 to supervise, co-ordinate, improve existing markets and methods of marketing of agricultural produce and seek and promote new markets and outlets for agricultural produce; Chair. Y. B. Datuk Haji Abdullah bin Mahmood, s.j.m.k., d.p.m.k., j.m.n.

Three Agricultural Marketing Boards have been established under Section 6(1) of the Federal Agricultural Marketing Authority's Act to manage and control the marketing of fish, pepper, coffee and other minor agricultural crops. The three Boards are:

The Fish Marketing Board: f. 1971; Chair. Encik Abdul Rahman bin Haji Yusof, a.m.n.

The Pepper Marketing Board: f. 1972; Chair. Y. B. Encik Simon bin Dembab Maja.

The Agricultural Produce Marketing Board: f. 1972; Chair. Encik Abdul Rahman bin Haji Yusof.

The Federation of Malaya Timber Exporters Association: 81 Ampang Rd., Kuala Lumpur; Pres. Tan Sri Nik Ahmad Kamil; 17 mems.

Federation of Malaysian Manufacturers: 4th Floor, Oriental Plaza, Jalan Parry, Kuala Lumpur.

Federation of Rubber Trade Associations of Malaysia: 138 Jalan Bandar, Kuala Lumpur.

* It was announced in February 1972 that a National Oil Corporation would be established.

Malayan Agricultural Producers' Association: Bangunan Getah Asli, Jalan Ampang, P.O.B. 1063, Kuala Lumpur; f. 1966; 467 member estates and 16 factories; Pres. Senator Tan Sri Gan Teck Yeow, p.s.m., j.m.n., m.p.; Dir. and Sec. W. Fernando, k.m.n.

The Malayan Pineapple Industry Board: P.O.B. 35, Batu 5, Jalan Scudai, Johore Bahru; Room 7, 2nd Floor, Malayan Bank Chambers, Battery Rd., Singapore 1; 25 Victoria St., London.

Malayan Rubber Fund Board: Head Office: Kuala Lumpur; U.K. Office: 19 Buckingham St., London, WC2N 6EJ; undertakes research into rubber production and classification; cost-benefit analysis; packaging, shipping and handling; Overseas Offices in U.S.A., Australia, Federal Republic of Germany, Austria, Spain, Italy, India, Japan and New Zealand; Dir. Dr. L. Bateman; publ. *Rubber Developments* (quarterly); published for the Natural Rubber Research Asscn.

The Malayan Rubber Goods Manufacturers' Association: c/o Messrs. Low and Co., 63 Klyne St., Kuala Lumpur.

Malaysia Timber Industry Board: 5th Floor, Wisma Bunga Raya, Jalan Ampang, P.O.B. 887, Kuala Lumpur; to promote, regulate and control the export of timber and timber products from peninsular Malaysia; f. 1968; Chair. Tuan Haji Abdul Majid bin Haji Mohamed Shahid; Sec. Ahmad Naziree bin Mohamed Yusoff; publs. *Timber Trade Review, Maskayu.*

Rubber Trade Association: 296 Brewster Rd., Ipoh.

Rubber Trade Association: 128A Wolferston Rd., Malacca.

Rubber Trade Association of Penang: 16 Anson Rd., Penang; f. 1919; 170 mems.; Pres. Saw Choo Theng; Sec. Koh Pen Ting; Treas. Tan Hoay Eam.

Rubber Trade Association of Selangor and Pahang: 138 Jalan Bandar, Kuala Lumpur.

States of Malay Chamber of Mines: 1 Post Office Rd., P.O.B. 127, Ipoh; f. 1914; Pres. D. H. Davidson, o.b.e.; Vice-Pres. P. A. W. Thuell; Sec. M. S. Olver; No. of mems.: 51 companies, 165 individuals, 2 associations.

Timber Trade Federation of the Federation of Malaya: No. 336-A, Lorong Haji Taib Satu, Batu Rd., Kuala Lumpur.

TRADE UNIONS

Malaysian Trades Union Congress: 19 Jalan Barat (First Floor), Petaling Jaya; P.O.B. 457, Kuala Lumpur; f. 1949; 103 affiliated unions, 500,000 mems.; Pres. Yeoh Teck Chye; Sec.-Gen. S. J. H. Zaidi; publ. *Suara Buroh* (monthly).

Affiliated Unions with membership over 10,000:

National Mining Workers' Union of Malaya: 282A Brickfields Road, Kuala Lumpur; f. 1955; about 14,000 mems.; Gen. Sec. Mohammad bin Takim.

National Union of Plantation Workers in Malaya: Plantation House, Petaling Jaya, Kuala Lumpur; f. 1954; about 165,000 mems.; Gen. Sec. P. P. Narayanan.

Railwaymen's Union of Malaya: 258A Brickfields Road, Kuala Lumpur; f. 1960; about 14,000 mems.; Pres. Yahaya bin Mohd. Ali; Gen. Sec. Lim Lye Huat.

INDEPENDENT FEDERATIONS

Malayan Federation of Clerical and Administrative Staff Unions: Chan Wing Bldg., Mountbatten Rd., Kuala Lumpur; f. 1949; 4 affiliates.

Amalgamated Union of Employees in Government Clerical and Allied Services: 1362 Kandang Kerbau Rd., Brickfields, Kuala Lumpur; about 6,000 mems.

All Malayan Federation of Government Medical Employees Trade Unions: District Hospital, Ipoh; f. 1947; 9 affiliates.

Federation of Government Medical Services Unions: General Hospital, Pakang Rd., Kuala Lumpur; 9 affiliates.

Federation of Indian School Teachers' Unions: 5 affiliates.

SABAH
CHAMBERS OF COMMERCE

Chinese Chamber of Commerce: P.O.B. 100, Beaufort; P.O.B. 63, Kota Kinabalu; P.O.B. 14, Keningau; P.O.B. 31, Labuan; P.O.B. 32, Lahad Datu; P.O.B. 28, Papar; P.O.B. 161, Sandakan; P.O.B. 12, Semporna; P.O.B. 164, Tawau; P.O.B. 6, Tenom; P.O.B. 37, Tuaran.

North Borneo United Chinese Chamber of Commerce: P.O.B. 156, Sandakan.

Sabah Chamber of Commerce: P.O.B. 1204, Sandakan; Pres. R. J. A. LEE.

TRADE UNIONS AND ASSOCIATIONS

Chinese School Teachers' Association: P.O. Box 10, Tenom; f. 1956; 74 mems.; Sec. VUN CHAU CHOI.

Employees' Trade Union: P.O. Box 295, Sandakan; f. 1955; 40 mems.; Sec. LOUIS L. QUYN.

Kota Kinabalu Teachers' Association: P.O.B. 282, Kota Kinabalu; f. 1962; 258 mems.; Sec. K. J. JOSEPH.

Sabah Civil Service Union: P.O.B. 175, Kota Kinabalu; f. 1952; 1,356 mems.; Pres. J. K. K. VOON; Sec. STEPHEN WONG; publ. *Union News Letter*.

Sabah Commercial Employees' Union: P.O.B. 357, Kota Kinabalu; f. 1957; 1,200 mems.; Sec. KOK FUNG CHONG.

Sandakan Tong Kang Association: 120 Mile ½, Leila Rd., Sandakan; f. 1952; 86 mems.; Sec. LAI KEN MIN.

The Incorporated Society of Planters, (North-East) Sabah Branch: P.O.B. 203, Sandakan; f. 1962; 44 mems.; Chair. A. J. WONG.

CO-OPERATIVES

Co-operatives include general purpose village stores for consumer needs and sale of produce; milling of rice and coffee; paddy storage; rubber curing and sale; buffalo rearing and grazing; sale of meat, vegetables and fish; transport; tractor ploughing; labour contracting; timber extraction; thrift and loan schemes; land purchase and land development.

SARAWAK
CHAMBERS OF COMMERCE

Chinese Chamber of Commerce: 68 Queen's Sq., Marudi, Baram, Fourth Division; 21 Court Rd., Binatang, Third Division; Daro, Third Division; 31 Limbang Bazaar, Limbang, Fifth Division; Matu, Third Division; 28 High St., Miri, Fourth Division; Sarikei, Third Division; Theatre Rd., Mukah, Third Division; 12 Old Rd., Sibu, Third Division; 32 River Rd., Sibuti; Song, Third Division; Marudi Bazaar, Baram, Fourth Division.

Kuching Chinese General Chamber of Commerce: Main Bazaar, Kuching, First Division.

South Indian Chamber of Commerce of Sarawak: 37-c India St., Kuching, First Division.

Sarawak Chamber of Commerce: c/o Turquand Youngs and Co., Lanka Bldg., Khoo Hun Yeang St., Kuching, First Division; f. 1953; Chair. C. J. E. GURR; Vice-Chair. J. K. CLIFFORD.

DEVELOPMENT ORGANIZATIONS

Borneo Development Corporation Sdn. Bhd.: shareholders; Governments of Sarawak and Sabah; Commonwealth Development Corporation, London; Head office and Sarawak Office: Electra House, P.O.B. 342, Power St., Kuching; Sabah Office: P.O.B. 721, 1st Floor, Jalan Haji Jacob, Kota Kinabalu.

Sarawak Economic Development Corporation: Electra House, P.O.B. 400; f. 1958; a statutory organization responsible for economic development in Sarawak; provides agricultural, commercial and industrial credit as well as participating in trading and industrial activities either on its own or jointly with foreign and local entrepreneurs; Chair. Encik MOHD. AMIN bin Haji SATEM; Deputy Chair. Encik SUFIAN bin SAUFI.

Borneo Housing Mortgage Finance Bhd.: Registered and br. office: Electra House, Power St., Kuching; Head Office: 9 Jalan Pantai, Kota Kinabalu, Sabah; jointly owned by State Governments of Sabah and Sarawak and the Commonwealth Development Corpn.; provides long-term loans for housing; auth. cap. M$50m.; loans and dep. M$52.3m. (Sept. 1973); Mortgage Securities M$90.5m. (Sept. 1973); Chair. W. A. BELSHAM; Gen. Man. YAP HYUN PHEN, B.A. (Hons.); Sec./Accountant STEPHEN CHAN KIN WING, B.COM., A.C.I.S., A.C.A. (N.Z.).

TRADE UNIONS

Many of the unions are small, catering for wharf labourers working in up-river areas. The largest is:

Sarawak Government Asian Officers' Union: Batu Lintang Rd., P.O.B. 626, Kuching; f. 1946; largest civil service union in Sarawak; Pres. Encik SARJIT SINGH KHAIRA; Vice-Pres. Encik JOSEPH YONG KIM KWEE; Gen. Sec. Encik SIM TECK CHAI; publ. *Voice*, circ. 3,000.

TRANSPORT

RAILWAYS
PENINSULAR MALAYSIA

Malayan Railway Administration: P.O.B. No. 1, Kuala Lumpur; Gen. Man. Datuk SHARIFF bin HASSAN, D.P.C.M.

The main line, 787 km. long, follows the west coast and extends from Singapore in the south to Butterworth (opposite Penang Island) to the north. The new Butterworth station is adjacent to the Penang Port Commission's pier from where ferry services to Penang are operated. The rail link also serves the proposed new wharves for ocean-going ships at Bagan Luar.

From Bukit Mertajam, close to Butterworth, the line branches off to the Thai border at Padang Besar where connection is made with the State Railway of Thailand. Three through international passenger train services are operated thrice-weekly between Butterworth and Bungkok, and a through coach ("the ASA coach"), which runs from Kuala Lumpur to Bangkok, is attached to one of the international expresses. Though there is no express service from Bangkok to Tumpat on the East Coast, there are daily passenger train services from the border station of Sungei Golok to stations on the East Coast. There is also a through rail car service between Butterworth and Haadyai in Thailand.

The East Coast Line, 526 km. long, runs from Gemas to Tumpat (near Kota Bharu). A 21-km. branch line from Pasir Mas, which is 27 km. miles south of Tumpat, connects with the State Railway of Thailand at the border station of Sungei Golok.

Branch lines serve railway-operated ports at Port Dickson, Teluk Anson and Port Weld as well as Port Klang and Jurong (Singapore).

Diesel rail car services are operated between Ipoh and Butterworth, Butterworth and Kuala Lumpur and Ipoh, Sultan Street and Ampang. In addition to the normal express services between Kuala Lumpur and Singapore, there is a rapid diesel rail car service. Total distance (1971): 1,659 km.

SABAH

Sabah State Railways: Kota Kinabalu; the total length of the railway is 155 km. The line is of metre gauge and runs from Kota Kinabalu to Melalap serving part of the west coast and the interior; diesel and steam trains are used; Gen. Man. WONG LEN HIN, D.I.P.C.E., GRAD.I.E.

ROADS

There are 15,236 miles of roads in Peninsular Malaysia, of which 4,428 miles are maintained by Federal authorities and 10,808 miles by the States. Of this total there are about 12,000 miles of metalled roads. Construction began in 1971 of the East-West Highway, between Kota Baru and Butterworth, which will be 233 miles long when completed in 1976.

Automobile Association of Malaysia: P.O.B. 34, Pataling Jaya, Selangor; f. 1932; mems. 12,500 (1973); Chair. Y. A. M. TUNKU SHAHABUDDIN, D.K.; Vice-Chair. W. G. PILLAY; Sec.-Gen. Mrs. K. S. LIM; publs. *A.A.M. News* (monthly), *Handbook* (every 18 months).

SABAH

The Public Works Department has constructed and maintained a network of trunk, district and local roads comprising 299 miles of bitumen, 922 miles of metal (gravel) and 371 miles of earth surface making a total of 1,592 miles up to 1968.

SARAWAK

The State government maintains about 140 miles of hard-surfaced roads, 370 miles of gravelled and 50 miles of earth roads. In addition local authorities maintained some 340 miles of roads.

SHIPPING

PENINSULAR MALAYSIA

The principal ports in the peninsula are Port Klang (formerly Port Swettenham), Penang and Prai; Malacca is an occasional port of call for ocean vessels. Under the Second Five-Year Plan, a major port development programme has begun, costing over M$20m.; it involves the construction of 2,800 ft. of wharves at Port Klang for conventional and containerized cargo, the building of new ports at Kuantan and Jahore Bahru and the expansion of existing port facilities.

Malaysian International Shipping Corporation Berhad (*National Shipping Line of Malaysia*): 30E Jalan Ampang, P.O.B. 371, Kuala Lumpur; Europe Office: Parklaan 34, Rotterdam 3002, Netherlands; London agent Lambert Bros. (Shipping) Ltd., 193–207 High Rd., Ilford, Essex; f. 1968; fleet of 12 vessels; 7 bulk carriers and coastal vessels on order; regular sailings between Far East and Europe; Chair. KUOK HOCK NIEN; Gen. Man. LESLIE EU; Sec. MAH HON CHOON.

Sharikat Perkapalan Kris Sdn. Bhd. (*The Kris Shipping Company of Malaysia*): Straits Trading Bldg., Kuala Lumpur; fleet of 10 tankers and cargo vessels; services from Malaysia to Thailand; Dirs. R. E. L. WINGATE, M.B.E.; GAN TECK YEOW, H. W. LADE, G. H. POSTLETHWAITE; Sec. ABDUL RAHIM ISMAIL.

SABAH

The chief ports are Labuan, Sandakan, Kota Kinabalu, Kudat, Tawau, Sempoma and Lahad Datu. The operation of all ports, except Labuan, is carried out by the Sabah Ports Authority. The Authority also controls the minor port of Kunak which has facilities for loading palm oil in bulk to ocean carriers and a small landing jetty for general cargo from local craft. A three year M$78 million port development programme began in July 1972 covering the ports of Kota Kinabalu and Sandakan.

There are many shipping lines using the ports and the main lines listed below run regular services to and from the State. Local services are maintained by a fleet of coastal steamers and numerous small craft to all ports in Sabah, Brunei and Sarawak.

Director of Marine: Capt. H. M. STANFIELD, Labuan.

Australian West Pacific Line: From Japanese and Australian ports.

Ben Line: Monthly services to United Kingdom and Europe.

Blue Funnel Line: Monthly services to United Kingdom and Europe.

Iino Line: Monthly service between Japan and West Australia.

Indo-China Steam Navigation Co.: Frequent sailings from East Coast ports to Japan and from Hong Kong.

Kinabalangan/Man Tung Shipping Co.: From Japan, Taiwan and Hong Kong to Sabah ports.

Netherlands Royal Dutch Mail: From United Kingdom and other European ports.

Nissho Line: Service between Sabah, Brunei and Japan.

Norwegian Asia Line: A fortnightly service to Sabah ports from Hong Kong, Japan and Shanghai; also a three-weekly service from Bangkok.

Pacific International Line: From Singapore and West Malaysian ports.

Royal Inter-Ocean Line: From Australian, Indonesian and Thai ports.

Royal Rotterdam Lloyd: From United Kingdom and other European ports.

Shell Tankers Ltd.: West Malaysia, Singapore, Sarawak and Sabah ports with bulk petroleum.

Straits Steamship Co.: Weekly cargo, passenger and mail service from Singapore; agents Harrisons and Crosfield (Sabah) Ltd., Prince Philip Drive, P.O.B. 22, Kota Kinabalu.

SARAWAK

Under the Second Five-Year Plan, work has started on a new port of Pending Point, near Kuching. The M$23 million project will be completed in 1974. Port facilities at Sibu will be extended by 1,000 feet.

Ben Line: Sarawak Agents: C.T.C. Shipping Agencies Sdn. Bhd., Sibu and Sarikei; direct sailings U.K./Tanjong Mani, Sarawak.

Blue Funnel and Glen Line: Sarawak Agent: The Borneo Co. (Malaysia), Sendirian Berhad., Kuching and Sibu; direct sailings from Rejang, Sarawak to U.K.

"K" Line: Sarawak Agent: Guthrie Boustead Shipping Agencies Ltd.; regular cargo service: Western Australia/Tanjong Mani, Sarawak.

Norwegian Asia Line: Agents Harper Gilfillan (Borneo) Sdn. Bhd.; direct service Japan–Hong Kong–Sabah–Sarawak, carrying cargo.

Sarawak Steamship Co. Bhd.: 14 Carpenter St., P.O.B. 131, Kuching, Sarawak; operates weekly services to and from Singapore to Kuching and from Port Klang to

Kuching; local shipping company, shipping agents and travel agents.

Polish Ocean Lines: Sarawak Agent: Borneo United Sawmills Sdn. Bhd.; Sibu and Kuching; Australian services: Sydney, Melbourne, Adelaide and Brisbane.

Straits Steamship Co. Ltd.: 14 Carpenter St., P.O.B. 131, Kuching, Sarawak; operates weekly services to and from Singapore to East Malaysian and Brunei ports, and to and from Port Klang/Singapore to East Malaysian ports.

Note: A direct ferry service linking Malaysia with North Sumatra (Indonesia) is expected to be operational by the end of 1974.

CIVIL AVIATION

Under the Second Five-Year Plan, $250 million has been allocated for airport improvements.

PENINSULAR MALAYSIA

Malaysian Airline System (MAS) Bhd.: UMBC Bldg., 4 Jalan Sulaiman, Kuala Lumpur; commenced operations in October 1972 as the Malaysian successor to the Malaysia Singapore Airlines (MSA); Chair. Raja Tan Sri MOHAR bin Raja BADIOZAMAN; Gen. Man. SAW HUAT LYE; operates a fleet of 7 Boeing 737, 10 F.27 and 4 BN-2 to more than 45 international and domestic destinations. Its regional network consists of Boeing flights from Kuala Lumpur to Hong Kong and Taipei, Brunei, Bangkok, Medan, Jakarta and Singapore. In 1974 MAS will be opening up services to Tokyo. Malaysia has three other international airports at Penang, Kota Kinabalu and Kuching. A M$15 million international airport at Senai, 15 miles from Johore Bahru, is expected to be open to traffic in September 1974.

FOREIGN AIRLINES

The following foreign airlines serve Malaysia: Aeroflot, Air Ceylon, Air India, Alitalia, Air Vietnam, British Airways, Cathay Pacific Airways, China Airlines, ČSA, Garuda Indonesia Airways, JAL, KLM, PIA, Qantas, Singapore Airlines, SAS, Thai International.

SABAH

There is an international airport at Kota Kinabalu. A runway extension programme is in operation to enable it to take Boeing 707s. There are civil airports at Sandakan, Kudat, Lahad Datu, Tawau, Keningau, Ranau, Telupid and Sepulot.

Regional Director of Civil Aviation: T. ARULAMPALAM, Dept. of Civil Aviation, Kota Kinabalu.

SARAWAK

There are two airports, at Kuching and Sibu, and many airstrips.

Malaysian Airline System (MAS) Bhd.: Electra House, Power St., Kuching; services to Singapore, Kuala Lumpur, Brunei and Sabah and scheduled internal and international services.

Southern Cross Malaysia Airline Bhd.: f. 1971; international charter services initially to London.

TOURISM

PENINSULAR MALAYSIA

Tourist Development Corporation of Malaysia: Ministry of Commerce and Industry, P.O.B. 328, Kuala Lumpur; f. Aug. 1972; 29 mems.; responsible for the co-ordination of activities relating to tourism; formulating recommendations thereon and for promoting tourism overseas; Chair. BURHANUDDIN b. MOHD. SAMAN RAIS.

SABAH

Sabah Tourist Association: P.O.B. 946, Kota Kinabalu; f. 1962; 100 mems.; semi-governmental promotion organization; Chair. SYED KECHIK; Exec. Sec. ABDUL RASIP LATIFF; publs. *Sabah Tourist Guide* and others.

CULTURAL ORGANIZATIONS

Arts Council of Malaysia: P.O.B. 630, Kuala Lumpur; promotes the accessibility, improvement and utilization of the arts in Malaysia; Pres. Tan Sri M. GHAZALI bin SHAFIE; Chair. KINGTON LOO.

Liberal Arts Society of Malaysia: 10th Floor, Kwong Yik Bank Bldg., Jalan Bandar, Kuala Lumpur; non-profit cultural society for music, drama, etc.; Pres. VINCENT YONG; Sec. ABRAHAM SAMUEL.

ATOMIC ENERGY

In early 1973, the Minister for Technology, Research and Local Government, Datuk ONG KEE HUI announced a M$2 million scheme to finance a nuclear reactor project. The reactor will be used solely for medical, industrial and agricultural research. Several overseas countries have promised assistance.

UNIVERSITIES

Kebangsaan National University: P.O.B. 1124, Jalan Pantai Baru, Kuala Lumpur; f. 1970; 99 teachers, 1,003 students.

University of Malaya: Pantai Valley, Kuala Lumpur; f. 1959; 8,000 students.

Universiti Sains Malaysia (University of Penang): Gelugor, Penang; f. 1969; 105 teachers, 1,358 students.

MALDIVES

INTRODUCTION

The Republic of Maldives, lying about 420 miles south-west of Sri Lanka, is an independent state consisting of some 2,000 islands in the Indian Ocean. A Sultanate until 1968, they achieved independence on July 26th, 1965, after being under British protection since 1887, when the Sultan signed an agreement with the Government of Ceylon; further agreements were signed in 1948 and 1960.

In 1956 the Maldivian and United Kingdom Governments agreed to the establishment of a Royal Air Force staging post on Gan, an island in the southernmost atoll, Addu. The Maldivian Government accorded free and unrestricted use by the United Kingdom Government of Gan Island and of 110 acres of Hittadu Island (for a radio station). Under the 1960 Agreement, the Maldivian Government entrusted Gan and the demarcated area on Hittadu as a free gift to the United Kingdom, together with the free use of Addu Lagoon and the territorial waters adjacent thereto, for a period of 30 years—this period to be extendable by agreement. Since the granting of independence the British Government still retains the facilities in Addu Atoll accorded to them by the 1960 agreement for purposes of Commonwealth defence. The United Kingdom Government undertook to pay the Maldivian Government £100,000, with a further £750,000 spread over five years or more, for economic development.

Maldives has been a member of the Colombo Plan since 1963 and of the United Nations since December 1965.

STATISTICAL SURVEY

Area: the archipelago consists of 19 atolls, comprising nearly 2,000 islands, of which 192 are inhabited; the total area is 20,000 square miles, including lagoons. The land area is 115 square miles (298 square km.).

Population (1972): 122,673. The population of the capital, Malé, was 15,740.

Births and Deaths (1972): 5,589 registered births; 2,395 registered deaths.

Employment: Fishing, copra-production, and making coir yarn; about 500 are employed at the Royal Air Force staging post on Gan Island.

Agriculture: Coconut palms, papaya, screwpine, pomegranates, pineapples, some citrus fruit, plantains, breadfruit, sweet potatoes, millet, cassava, sorghum, maize, onions, chillies and yams.

Fishing: Total catch (metric tons): 17,161 in 1970; 16,088 in 1971; 13,177 in 1972.

Currency: 100 larees=1 Maldivian rupee. Exchange rates (April 1974): £1 sterling=11.65 rupees; U.S. $1=4.934 rupees; 100 Maldivian rupees=£8.58=$20.27.

Budget: Government Expenditure (1972) 22,599,740 rupees.

Exports (1972–metric tons): dried fish 3,843; fresh fish 2,039; other fish and fish-products 64.196; shells 14.255; copra 16.036.

The entire output of Maldive fish is sold to the Sri Lanka Government and to the Marubeni fishing corporation of Japan.

Transport: International shipping (metric tons): 1971–72 (two years) loaded 13,703; unloaded 27,587.

Communications (1972): radio licences issued 2,335.

Education (1970): Primary: 29 teachers, 648 pupils; Secondary: 26 teachers, 327 pupils.

THE CONSTITUTION

A referendum was held throughout Maldives in March 1968 to ascertain what form of government was desired by the Maldivians. Over 80 per cent of those who voted approved a proposal to establish a republic in place of the constitution of the Sultanate, which was introduced in 1954 and amended in June 1964 and July 1967. The Republic of Maldives was proclaimed on November 11th, 1968. The main provisions of the republican constitution are:

1. The Head of State is the President and he is vested with certain executive powers.
2. The President is elected by a popular vote every five years.
3. The President appoints a Prime Minister and a Cabinet.
4. The members of the Cabinet are individually responsible to the *Majlis*, or the elected legislature.
5. The powers of the President, the Cabinet and the legislature are laid down in the Constitution.
6. The *Majlis* or legislative body, consisting of 54 members representing the population of just over 119,000, is elected every five years.
7. The basic rights of the people, guaranteeing their freedom of life, movement, speech and development, without contravening the provisions of Islam, are laid down in the Constitution.

THE GOVERNMENT

(*April* 1974)

HEAD OF STATE

President: AMIR IBRAHIM NASIR, N.G.I.V., R.B.K.

THE CABINET

Prime Minister and Minister of External Affairs: AHMED ZAKI.

Minister of Justice: SHEIKH MOOSA FATHHY.

Minister of Health: IBRAHIM RASHEED.

Minister of Education: ADNAN HUSSAIN.

Minister of Finance: ABDULL SATTAR MOOSA DIDI.

Minister of Public Safety: ABDULL HANNAN HALEEM.

Minister of Agriculture: FAROUK ISMAIL.

Minister of Fisheries: AHMED HILMY DIDI.

Minister of Trade and Development: HASSAN ZAREER.

Attorney-General: IBRAHIM SHIHAB.

LEGISLATURE

MAJLIS

Comprises 54 members, of whom 8 are nominated by the President, 8 elected by the people of Malé and 2 elected from every atoll.

Speaker: AHMED SHATHIR.

DIPLOMATIC REPRESENTATION

There are no resident diplomatic missions in Maldives. The following countries maintain diplomatic relations with the Republic of Maldives. In most cases the missions are in Sri Lanka: Burma, People's Republic of China, Egypt, France, German Democratic Republic, German Federal Republic, India, Republic of Iraq, Israel, Italy, Japan, Democratic People's Republic of Korea, Republic of Korea, Malaysia, Pakistan, Sri Lanka, U.S.S.R., United Kingdom, U.S.A.

LAW AND RELIGION

The administration of justice is based on the Islamic Law of Shariat.

Islam is the State religion. The Maldivians are Sunni Muslims.

TRANSPORT

SHIPPING

Powered vessels operate between Maldives and Sri Lanka at frequent intervals.

CIVIL AVIATION

An airport is under construction on the island of Hululé, about a mile from the capital island, Malé.

There are no regular flights but the government arranges flights by Air Ceylon mostly under charter.

MALI

INTRODUCTORY SURVEY

Location, Climate, Language, Religion, Flag, Capital

Mali is a land-locked state in West Africa, bounded by Algeria to the north, Mauritania and Senegal to the west, Guinea and Ivory Coast to the south and Upper Volta and Niger to the east. The climate is hot and dry with average temperatures ranging from 24°–32°C (75°–90°F) and increasing northward into the Sahara Desert. The official language is French but a number of other languages including Bambara and Sonrai are widely spoken. About 65 per cent of the population are Muslims and more than 30 per cent follow animist beliefs, the remainder being Christians. The national flag (proportions 3 by 2) is a vertical tricolour of green, gold and red. The capital is Bamako.

Recent History

The Republic of Mali, formerly the French colony of Soudan, was proclaimed in September 1960. The first President, Modibo Keita, adopted authoritarian socialist policies and broke away from the French political and financial bloc. Despite Communist aid, rapid inflation forced Keita to return to the Franc Zone in 1967, at the price of a 50 per cent devaluation. His socialist management of the economy necessitated heavy taxes to pay for a large, inefficient bureaucracy which intervened in all aspects of economic life, causing unrest among the peasants who were denied access to a free market for their crops. Keita was overthrown in November 1968 by a group of junior army officers, who ruled as the Military Committee of National Liberation (CMLN).

Lt. (later Col.) Moussa Traoré emerged as the dominant figure in the new régime, with the posts of Head of State and President of the CMLN, and in September 1969 replaced Yoro Diakité as President of the Government. His Government's main concerns have been budgetary retrenchment and the encouragement of both public and private investment, and the problem of the famine caused by the Sahel drought.

Government

Since the *coup* of 1968, the Military Committee of National Liberation has ruled by decree. A new constitution was approved by referendum in June 1974, but the CMLN will remain in power for a further 5 years.

Defence

The army numbers 3,500, including a paratroop company. There are also three patrol boats on the Niger, and 150 men in the Soviet-equipped air force.

Economic Affairs

Mali is poor in natural resources. A large part of the country lies in the Sahara Desert and is capable of supporting only a sparse nomadic population dependent on its flocks and herds. By 1973 the Sahel drought had killed as much as 80 per cent of the livestock in the north. Only about 20 per cent of the land is suitable for cultivation, the principal crops being rice, cotton, millet and groundnuts. There is extensive river fishing and dried and smoked fish are exported. Industry still occupies a minor position in the economy and is based on the processing of food, cotton, hides, skins and wool. Exports are growing slowly but the trade gap is widening, due mainly to imports of cereals and consumer goods.

Mali is non-aligned, receiving aid from all sources, particularly the People's Republic of China, the U.S.S.R. and France. Mali is a member of the Organization of African Unity (OAU), the Economic Community of West Africa (CEAO) and the Organization for the Development of the Senegal River (OMVS), and an associate of the European Economic Community (EEC).

Transport and Communications

The river Senegal and the river Niger, which is navigable for its total length in Mali of 1,782 kilometres, form the chief arteries of transport. The only railway runs from Koulikoro via Bamako to the Senegal border (640 km.) and then to Dakar (Senegal). Roads are being improved, and almost half the 12,000 km. of classified roads are open all the year. Domestic and international air services are provided by Air Mali and several foreign airlines.

Social Welfare

The Government maintains anti-smallpox and yellow fever services and there are a number of state hospitals and medical centres.

Education

Education is free and, in theory, compulsory for all children between the ages of 6 and 15. In 1971 only 20 per cent of children eligible for primary education and 2 per cent of those eligible for secondary education were enrolled at schools. The army has set up a mass literacy programme, teaching peasants to read and write. Over 500 Malian students receive higher education abroad, mainly in France and Senegal.

Tourism

Tourism is being developed, based on hunting and fishing and the celebrated city of Timbuktu.

Visas are required to visit Mali by citizens of all countries except France.

Public Holidays

1974: September 22nd (Independence Day), October 18th (Id ul Fitr), December 25th (Christmas), December 26th (Id ul Adha).

1975: January 14th (Muslim New Year), March 26th (Mouloud, Birth of the Prophet), May 1st (Labour Day), July 14th (National Day).

Weights and Measures

The metric system is in force.

Currency and Exchange Rate

100 centimes = 1 franc malien (Mali franc).
Exchange rates (April 1974).

    1 Mali franc = 1 French centime;
    £1 sterling = 1,159.50 Mali francs;
    U.S.$ 1 = 491.25 Mali francs.

STATISTICAL SURVEY

AREA AND POPULATION

AREA (sq. km.)	POPULATION (July 1st, 1972)
1,240,000*	5,257,000

* 478,767 sq. miles.

MAIN TRIBES
(1963 estimates)

BAMBARA	FULANI	MARKA	SONGHAI	MALINKÉ	TOUAREG	SÉNOUFO	DOGON
1,000,000	450,000	280,000	230,000	200,000	240,000	375,000	130,000

Chief Towns (1971): Bamako (capital) 200,000, Mopti 32,000, Ségou 27,000, Kayes 24,000, Sikasso, San, Tombouctou (Timbuktu).

Births and Deaths: Average annual birth rate 49.8 per 1,000, death rate 26.6 per 1,000 (UN estimates for 1965–70).

Employment (1970): Total economically active population 2,756,000, including 2,511,000 in agriculture (ILO and FAO estimates).

AGRICULTURE

LAND USE, 1970
('000 hectares)

Arable and Under Permanent Crops . .	11,600
Permanent Meadows and Pastures . .	30,000
Forest	4,457
Other Land	75,943
Inland Water	2,000
TOTAL	124,000

PRINCIPAL CROPS
('000 metric tons)

	1970	1971	1972†
Millet, Sorghum and Fonio . .	600	900	916
Rice (Paddy) . .	138	150	174
Maize . . .	80*	80*	96
Sugar Cane† . .	55	61	57
Sweet Potatoes and Yams . .	67*	71*	n.a.
Cassava (Manioc) . .	155	160	n.a.
Pulses . . .	9*	9*	n.a.
Groundnuts (in shell) .	158	143*	152
Cottonseed . .	37	42	68
Cotton (Lint) . .	22	25	26

* FAO estimate.

† Crop year ending in year stated.

Source: mainly FAO, *Production Yearbook 1971.*

LIVESTOCK
('000)

	1968–69	1969–70	1970–71
Cattle . . .	5,350	5,350	5,500*
Sheep . . .	5,750	5,750	5,900*
Goats . . .	5,500	5,500	5,650*
Pigs . . .	32	32	33
Horses . . .	170	170	174*
Asses . . .	476	476	460*
Camels . . .	218	218	215*
Poultry . . .	13,400*	13,500*	14,000*

* FAO estimate.

Source: FAO, Production Yearbook 1971.

1971–72 ('000): 5,350 Cattle; 11,250 Sheep and Goats; 619 Horses and Asses; 217 Camels. It is estimated that 40 per cent of these have since died during the drought.

LIVESTOCK PRODUCTS
(metric tons)

	1969	1970	1971*
Cows' Milk . .	102,000*	103,000*	104,000
Sheep's Milk .	32,000*	32,000*	33,000
Goats' Milk . .	63,000*	62,000*	61,000
Butter . .	2,000	2,000	n.a.
Beef and Veal†	48,000*	50,000*	50,000
Mutton and Lamb† .	32,000*	33,000*	34,000
Hen Eggs . .	7,000*	7,000*	7,100
Cattle Hides . .	6,800*	7,000*	6,600
Sheep Skins . .	3,335*	3,480*	3,625
Goat Skins . .	2,450*	2,500*	2,520

* FAO estimate.

† Meat from indigenous animals only, including the meat equivalent of exported live animals.

Source: FAO, Production Yearbook 1971.

FORESTRY

ROUNDWOOD PRODUCTION
('000 cubic metres)

1968 . . .	2,560
1969 . . .	2,590
1970 . . .	2,615

Source: FAO, Yearbook of Forest Products.

Fishing: Total catch 90,000 metric tons in 1971. In 1966 about 30 per cent of the catch was dried and smoked.

Mining (1967–70): About 4,000 metric tons of unrefined salt produced each year.

INDUSTRY

	Unit	1968	1969	1970
Vegetable Oils . . .	metric tons	3,000	4,000	n.a.
Refined Sugar . . .	,, ,,	5,000	5,000	5,000
Sugar Confectionery . .	,, ,,	280	480	980
Beer . . .	'000 hectolitres	n.a.	n.a.	960
Soft Drinks . .	,, ,,	44	46	50
Cement . . .	metric tons	n.a.	n.a.	40,000
Soap . . .	,, ,,	6,220	2,641	2,645
Electric Energy . .	million kWh.	35	37	40

Source: United Nations, The Growth of World Industry.

Other industries include cotton ginning, hardware and brickmaking.

FINANCE

100 centimes = 1 franc malien (Mali franc).

Coins: 5, 10 and 25 Mali francs.

Notes: 50, 100, 500, 1,000, 5,000 and 10,000 Mali francs.

Exchange rates (April 1974): 1 Mali franc = 1 French centime = 50 centimes CFA;

£1 sterling = 1,159.50 Mali francs; U.S. $1 = 491.25 Mali francs.

10,000 Mali francs = £8.624 = $20.356.

Note: In recent years the central exchange rates for the Mali franc have fluctuated as follows:

Sterling: July 1962 to May 1967, £1 = 691.19 Mali francs; May to November 1967, £1 = 1,382.38 Mali francs; November 1967 to August 1969, £1 = 1,184.89 Mali francs; August 1969 to June 1972, £1 = 1,333.01 Mali francs.

Dollars: July 1962 to May 1967, $1 = 246.853 Mali francs; May 1967 to August 1969, $1 = 493.706 Mali francs; August 1969 to August 1971, $1 = 555.419 Mali francs; December 1971 to February 1973, $1 = 511.570 Mali francs.

Budget (1973): Balanced at 28,125 million Mali francs.

Budget (1974): Balanced at 29,000 million Mali francs.

Three-Year Plan (1970–1973): Organized by the Council of Planning to replace the first five-year plan which failed to reach its target. Twenty new factories were created, and industrial production expanded. Agriculture suffered from drought, but 81 per cent of the Plan's objectives were achieved.

Currency in Circulation (April 1973): 21,950 million Mali francs.

FOREIGN PUBLIC DEBT, 1968
('000 million Mali francs)

U.S.S.R.	32.6
France	26.9
China, People's Republic	23.5
Egypt	7.3
Ghana	6.5
Other Countries	5.2
IMF and IBRD	9.0
TOTAL*	110.0

*U.S. $236.6 million at January 1st, 1971.

NATIONAL ACCOUNTS
(million Mali francs at current prices)

ECONOMIC ACTIVITY	1969	1970	1971
Agriculture	58,700	66,300	66,900
Manufacturing	11,300	12,500	
Electricity, Gas and Water Supply	1,400	1,500	22,200
Construction	6,200	7,000	
Commerce	32,600	35,000	
Transport and Communications	5,400	6,000	
Public Administration and Defence	16,000	17,000	64,900
Other Services	3,900	3,200	
GROSS DOMESTIC PRODUCT	135,500	148,500	154,000

Source: UN Economic Commission for Africa, *Statistical Yearbook 1972.*

EXTERNAL TRADE
(million Mali francs)

	1968	1969	1970	1971	1972
Imports	16,937	20,100	26,200	30,500	35,680
Exports	5,300	8,760	18,240	19,630	17,230

PRINCIPAL COMMODITIES
(million Mali francs)

IMPORTS	1968	1969
Sugar and Honey . .	1,903	1,143
Other Food . .	1,157	1,715
Petroleum Products .	1,301	1,759
Animal and Vegetable Oils and Fats . . .	544	29
Chemicals . .	1,459	2,044
Woven Cotton Fabrics .	1,307	1,374
Other Textile Fabrics, Yarn, etc.	930	843
Lime, Cement, etc. . .	561	368
Iron and Steel . .	954	501
Machinery (non-electric) .	787	1,281
Electrical Equipment .	660	1,036
Road Motor Vehicles. .	1,271	1,934
Other Transport Equipment .	210	1,903
TOTAL (incl. others) .	16,937	20,099

EXPORTS	1968	1969
Live Cattle . . .	664	3,624
Live Sheep, Lambs and Goats .	40	625
Fish (salted, dried or smoked) .	691	1,259
Oil-Seed Cake and Meal, etc. .	82	237
Other Food . .	170	245
Groundnuts (green) .	562	253
Other Oil-Seeds, Nuts and Kernels .	382	547
Raw Cotton (excl. linters) .	2,099	895
Fixed Vegetable Oils . .	163	603
TOTAL (incl. others) .	5,300	8,941

1970 (million Mali francs): Cattle 2,932; Fish 667; Groundnuts 1,634; Cotton 4,061; total 18,240.

Source: mainly *Overseas Associates, Foreign Trade* (Statistical Office of the European Communities, Luxembourg). Totals for 1969 differ slightly from the figures given in the summary table for trade, which are those of the national statistical authority.

PRINCIPAL COUNTRIES
(million Mali francs)

IMPORTS	1968	1969
Belgium/Luxembourg . .	128	339
China, People's Republic .	2,236	1,706
Egypt	347	610
France . . .	5,345	7,790
Germany, Federal Republic .	422	572
Italy	38	486
Ivory Coast . .	1,498	1,725
Japan	315	131
Netherlands . .	309	303
Poland . . .	282	14
Senegal . . .	1,218	1,685
Switzerland . .	54	674
U.S.S.R. . .	3,116	1,976
United Kingdom . .	267	240
U.S.A. . . .	163	530
TOTAL (incl. others) .	16,937	20,099

EXPORTS	1968	1969
China, People's Republic .	280	0
France . . .	866	1,434
Germany, Federal Republic .	147	10
Ghana . . .	507	1,877
Ivory Coast . .	1,337	3,509
Japan . . .	327	411
Netherlands . .	446	1
Senegal . . .	816	425
U.S.S.R. . .	0	212
Upper Volta . .	106	230
TOTAL (incl. others) .	5,300	8,941

1970 (million Mali francs): France 3,373; Ghana 1,733; Ivory Coast 6,350; Senegal 2,985.

1970 (million Mali francs): China 1,794; France 9,086; Ivory Coast 2,393; Senegal 1,605; U.S.S.R. 2,788.

Source: mainly *Overseas Associates, Foreign Trade* (Statistical Office of the European Communities, Luxembourg). Totals for 1969 differ slightly from the figures given in the summary table for trade, which are those of the national statistical authority.

TRANSPORT

Railways (1967–68): Passengers 702,700, Passenger/km. 77.6m.; Freight 225,633 tons, Freight ton/km. 103.6m.

Roads (1969): 4,500 passenger cars; 5,700 commercial vehicles; 1971: total of 16,000 vehicles.

River Traffic (1967–68): Passengers 71,939; Freight 62,001 metric tons; Passenger/km. 22m.; Freight ton/km. 36.3m.

Civil Aviation (1971): Aircraft (arrivals and departures) 2,025; Passenger arrivals 29,486; Passenger departures 26,036; Freight unloaded 986 metric tons; Freight loaded 501 metric tons.

COMMUNICATIONS

Radio sets: 75,000 in 1973

Telephones: 7,800 in 1968.

EDUCATION

(1970–71)

	SCHOOLS	TEACHERS	TOTAL PUPILS	FEMALE PUPILS
Pre-Primary (1969–70) . . .	25	135	4,735	2,345
Primary . . .	956	6,614	229,879	78,925
Secondary: General . . .	n.a.	290	3,507	422
Vocational . . .	n.a.	332	3,386	666
Teacher Training . .	n.a.	92	1,551	269
Literacy Courses . . .	n.a.	3,308	61,665	n.a.
Tertiary . . .	n.a.	151	731	77

Source: UNESCO *Statistical Yearbook 1972.*

Source (unless otherwise stated): Direction Générale de la Statistique, Bamako.

THE CONSTITUTION

The 1960 Constitution was abrogated by the Military Committee of National Liberation (CMLN), which in November 1968 replaced it by a "Fundamental Law". Under this, the CMLN and the Supreme Court rule by decree. A constitutional referendum was held in June 1974; the new constitution provides for a return to electoral government, but allows the CMLN to remain in power for five more years. The President of the CMLN acts as Head of State, and is Commander-in-Chief of the Armed Forces.

THE GOVERNMENT

HEAD OF STATE

President: Col. Moussa Traoré.

MILITARY COMMITTEE OF NATIONAL LIBERATION (CMLN)

President: Col. Moussa Traoré.

Vice-President: Capt. Baba Diarra.

Commissioner: Capt. Youssouf Traoré.

Permanent Secretary: Capt. Filifing Sissoko.

Members: Captains J. Mara, K. Doukara, T. Bagayoko, M. Sanogo, C. S. Sissoko, M. Koné and K. Dembélé.

GOVERNMENT

(October 1973)

President of the Government and Head of State: Col. Moussa Traoré.

Minister Delegate to the CMLN for Labour and the Civil Service: Sori Coulibaly.

Minister of Foreign Affairs and Co-operation: Capt. Charles Samba Sissoko.

Minister of Defence, Interior and Security: Capt. Kissima Doukara.

Minister of Information: Capt. Youssouf Traoré.

Minister of Finance: Tiéoulé Konaté.

Minister of Trade: Hassim Diawara.

Minister of Justice: Capt. Joseph Mara.

Minister of Health and Social Affairs: Aly Cisse.

Minister of Industrial Development and Public Works: Mamadou Keita.

Minister of Production: Sidi Coulibaly.

Minister of Transport, Tourism and Telecommunications: Capt. Karim Dembélé.

Minister of Higher and Secondary Education and Scientific Research: Yaya Bagayoko.

Minister for State Enterprises: Sekou Sangaré.

Minister of Basic Education, Youth and Sport: Moustapha Soumaré.

DIPLOMATIC REPRESENTATION

EMBASSIES ACCREDITED TO MALI

(In Bamako unless otherwise stated)

Albania: Accra, Ghana.

Algeria: *Ambassador:* Aidi Boufeldja.

Argentina: *Ambassador:* Mario Raúl Pico.

Belgium: Abidjan, Ivory Coast.

Brazil: *Ambassador:* Cabral de Melo.

Canada: Dakar, Senegal.

China, People's Republic: B.P. 112; *Ambassador:* Meng Yueh.

Cuba: *Ambassador:* Oscar Oramas Oliva.

Czechoslovakia: *Chargé d'Affaires:* Jaroslav Kozak.

Egypt: *Ambassador:* Moustapha Mohammed Tewfik.

France: B.P. 17; *Ambassador:* Louis Dallier.

German Democratic Republic: *Ambassador:* Johanne Schoeche.

Germany, Federal Republic: *Ambassador:* Joachim Von Stülpnagel.

Ghana: *Ambassador:* Abu Wemah.

Guinea: *Ambassador:* Mamadou Diakité.

Hungary: Conakry, Guinea.

India: *Ambassador:* R. R. Sinha.

Indonesia: Conakry, Guinea.

Italy: Abidjan, Ivory Coast.

Japan: Dakar, Senegal.

Korea, Democratic People's Republic: *Ambassador:* (vacant).

Lebanon: Dakar, Senegal.

Liberia: Dakar, Senegal.

Libya: *Ambassador:* Mohamed Hamed El Mograhi.

Mauritania: Dakar, Senegal.

Mongolia: Conakry, Guinea.

Morocco: B.P. 78; *Ambassador:* (vacant).

Netherlands: Dakar, Senegal.

Pakistan: Dakar, Senegal.

Poland: *Ambassador:* Eugeniusz Kulaga.

Romania: Conakry, Guinea.

Saudi Arabia: B.P. 81 (also accred. to Niger).

Senegal: *Ambassador:* Moustafa Cissé (also accred. to Niger).

Sierra Leone: *Ambassador:* Lloyd Kojo Randall.

Spain: Nouakchott, Mauritania.

Sweden: Algiers, Algeria.

Switzerland: Dakar, Senegal.

Tunisia: Dakar, Senegal.

Turkey: Dakar, Senegal.

U.S.S.R.: *Ambassador:* Leonid Moussatov.

United Kingdom: Dakar, Senegal.

U.S.A.: B.P. 34; *Ambassador:* Ralph McQuire.

Upper Volta: *Ambassador:* Henri Ouattara.

Viet-Nam, Democratic Republic: B.P. 48; *Ambassador:* Vu Hac Bong (also accred. to Mauritania).

Yugoslavia: B.P. 207; *Chargé d'Affaires:* M. Radenkovic.

Mali also has diplomatic relations with the Royal Government of Khmer National Union (the Cambodian Government-in-Exile).

PARLIAMENT

The National Assembly was abolished in January 1968. The President and, since November 1968, the Military Committee of National Liberation rule by decree.

POLITICAL PARTIES

The "Fundamental Law" proclaimed in November 1968 guaranteed freedom of political activity within the law. No political parties appear to be active.

DEFENCE

The army numbers 3,500 and the air force 150. There are also three patrol boats on the Niger. There is a gendarmerie of 1,500 and a civil police of 1,000 men.

Chief of Staff of the Army: Major BOUGOURY SOUGARÉ.

JUDICIAL SYSTEM

Supreme Court: Bamako; established September 1969; 19 members; judicial section comprising three civil chambers and one criminal chamber; administrative section dealing with appeals and fundamental rulings; members are nominated for five years and may not be members of the Government nor practice law privately during that time; Pres. ASSANE SEYE.

Court of Appeal: Bamako.
There are two Tribunaux de Première Instance (Magistrate's Courts) and also courts for labour disputes.

RELIGION

It is estimated that 65 per cent of the population are Muslims, about 30 per cent Animists and 5 per cent Christians, with Roman Catholics comprising 1 per cent of the total population.

Chief Mosque: Bagadadji, Place de la République.

Roman Catholic Church: Metropolitan Archdiocese of Bamako and five suffragen dioceses (Kayes, Mopti, San, Ségou, Sikasso), dependent on the Sacred Congregation for the Evangelization of Peoples; 65 educational institutions; 160 resident priests; 163 male and 176 female members of religious institutes; 43,245 Catholics in a total population of 5,136,500 (December 1972 estimate by Catholic Church).

Archbishop of Bamako: Mgr. Luc AUGUSTE SANGARÉ, B.P. 298.

Bishop of Kayes: Mgr. ÉTIENNE COURTOIS, B.P. 91.

Bishop of Mopti: Mgr. GEORGES BIARD, B.P. 45.

Bishop of San: Mgr. JOSEPH PERROT, B.P. 48.

Bishop of Ségou: Mgr. PIERRE LOUIS LECLERC, B.P. 109.

Bishop of Sikasso: Mgr. DIDIER PÉROUSE DE MONTCLOS, B.P. 74.

Protestant Missions: There are many mission centres with a total personnel of about 370, run by American societies.

PRESS

Barakela (*Worker*): mimeographed daily bulletin.

Bulletin d'information: Bamako; published daily by the Agence Nationale d'Information.

Bulletin de Liaison: Office du Niger, Ségou.

Bulletin de Statistiques: Ministry of Planning, Bamako; monthly.

L'Essor (*Progress*): B.P. 1463, Bamako; organ of the Military Committee for National Liberation; daily.

L'Informateur: Ministry of Information, Bamako; f. 1956; monthly.

Kibaru: monthly; in Bambara; first periodical for rural areas; circ. 5,000.

Journal Officiel de la République du Mali: B.P. 1463 Bamako; published by the government printers at Koulouba.

NEWS AGENCIES
FOREIGN BUREAUX

Agence France-Presse: B.P. 778, Bamako; Correspondent LAURENT CHENARD.

Četeka, Novosti and Tass maintain bureaux in Mali.

PUBLISHER

Editions Populaires: Bamako; school books, history, sociology, folk-tales.

RADIO

Radio Mali: B.P. 171, Bamako; f. 1957; government station; programmes in French, English, Bambara, Peulh, Sarakolé, Tamachek, Sonrai, Moorish, Ouolof; Dir.-Gen. MOUSSA KEITA.

In 1973 there were 75,000 receiving sets.

FINANCE
BANKS
CENTRAL BANK

Banque Centrale du Mali: B.P. 206, Bamako; f. 1968; Central Bank of Issue; cap. 1,000m. Mali francs; Pres. SÉKOU SANGARE; Dir.-Gen. GEORGES DUSSINE.

NATIONAL BANKS

Banque de Développement du Mali: B.P. 94, Bamako; f. 1968; cap. 3,000m. Mali francs; Pres. Dir.-Gen. TIÉOULÉ KONATÉ; Joint Dir.-Gen. MAMADOU HAÏDARA; regional brs. at Gao, Mopti, Ségou, Sikasso and Kayes.

Banque Malienne de Crédit et de Dépôts: ave. Modibo Keita, B.P. 45, Bamako; f. 1961 to take over branches of Crédit Lyonnais; cap. 150m. Mali francs; res. 64m. Mali francs (Dec. 1972); Pres. and Gen. Man. D. DIAKITE.

FRENCH BANKS

Banque Internationale pour l'Afrique Occidentale: 9 ave. de Messine, 75360 Paris 8e, France; ave. Mohammed 5, B.P. 15, Bamako.

Caisse Centrale de Coopération Economique: B.P. 32, rue Festard, Bamako; Dir. LOUIS VIELH.

INSURANCE

Several French companies maintain agencies in Bamako.

TRADE AND INDUSTRY

Chambre de Commerce, d'Agriculture et d'Industrie de Bamako: B.P. 46, Bamako; f. 1908; 46 mems.; Pres. El Haj DOSSOLO TRAORÉ; Sec. Gen. BONOTA TOURÉ; publs. *Bulletin quotidien, Circulaire mensuelle d'information.*

Chambre de Commerce de Kayes; B.P. 81, Kayes; Pres. DEMBA SISSOKO; Sec.-Gen. BAKARY DIAWARA.

Société Malienne d'Importation et d'Exportation (SOMIEX): B.P. 182, Bamako; state-owned company for the export of groundnuts and the import of primary products; Dir. OUMAR COULIBALY.

SOMIEY: Bamako; employers' federation.

Syndicat des Transporteurs Soudanais: Bamako.

DEVELOPMENT ORGANIZATIONS

Bureau pour le Développement de la Production Agricole: B.P. 72, Bamako; Dir. M. GIORDANO.

Office du Niger: Ségou; f. 1932; taken over from the French Government in 1958; the French project involved a major dam, begun in 1935, 45 miles above Ségou, to direct water into extensive irrigation networks covering one million hectares to be devoted to rice and cotton on the left bank of the Niger. By 1958 a mere 48,000 hectares had been irrigated. Since independence the irrigated area has been extended by 4,000 hectares per year. The office also operates a number of research stations, a cotton-ginning factory and a sugar refinery and distillery. Dir. Gen. Lieut. ISSA ONGOIBA.

TRADE UNIONS

All trade unions were dissolved in November 1968. They were allowed to resume activities in December 1969, but in October 1970 the CMLN dissolved the provisional consultative committee of the *Union nationale des travailleurs du Mali* (UNTM) and in January 1971 most of the members of the committee were arrested.

TRANSPORT

RAILWAY

Régie du Chemin de Fer du Mali: B.P. 260, Bamako; Dir. D. DIALLO. 1,287 km. of track linking Dakar (Senegal) with Bamako and Koulikoro, of which 642 km. are in Mali; metre gauge. Passenger services twice weekly Bamako–Dakar, freight services daily, and one petrol train weekly.

Plans have been drawn up, with Soviet help, for a new line via Siguiri and Kouroussa, linking Bamako with the existing Guinean railway which runs to Conakry. This line would give Mali a second outlet to the Atlantic.

ROADS

There are about 13,000 km. of classified roads, of which only about 7,500 km. are practical for motor traffic throughout the year. The roads between Bamako and Bougouni (160 km.) and between Bamako and Ségou (240 km.) are asphalted. The length of asphalt roads totalled 1,600 km. in 1972. A new asphalt road from Mopti is planned to run via Ouagadougou (Upper Volta) to the coast at Tema (Ghana).

Cie. Malienne de Transports Routiers: rue du Commandant-Riault, Bamako; f. 1968; Man. Mme. COLETTE DURRIEU.

INLAND WATERWAYS

The Niger is navigable throughout its course through Mali (1,782 km.) from July to March. The Senegal is navigable from Kayes to Saint-Louis (Senegal).

Compagnie Malienne de Navigation: B.P. 150, Bamako; Dir.-Gen. SALIF KONATE.

CIVIL AVIATION

The principal airport is at Bamako, but the facilities there are not suitable for large jet aircraft. A new airport is being built at Senou, 14 km. outside Bamako, with French aid and should be ready for use in 1974. There are six other aerodromes.

Air Mali: B.P. 27, Bamako; state airline; cap. 50m. Mali francs; daily services to West Africa, weekly services to Paris; local services; fleet: one Boeing 727, three DC-3, one Ilyushin 18, one Antonov 24B, two AN 2; 529 employees; Gen. Man. A. G. MAIGI.

Mali is also served by the following foreign airlines: Air Afrique, Air Algérie, Air Guinée, Aeroflot, Interflug and UTA.

TOURISM

Commissariat au Tourisme: B.P. 222, Place de la République, Bamako; f. 1966; Dir. MAMADOU SY.

Touring-Club: B.P. 104, Grand Hotel, Bamako; Delegate A. CHAZAL.

POWER

Energie du Mali: B.P. 69, ave. Lyautey, Bamako; f. 1961; cap. 100 million Mali francs.

Production and distribution of electricity and water. Dir.-Gen. BOCAR THIAM; 681 employees.

MAURITANIA

INTRODUCTORY SURVEY

Location, Climate, Language, Religion, Flag, Capital

The Islamic Republic of Mauritania extends east and north from the west coast of Africa, with Spanish Sahara and Algeria to the north, Mali to the east and south and Senegal due south. The north of the country is mainly desert, but the south is more fertile and suitable for cultivation. The climate is hot and dry. The official languages are French and Arabic, although most people speak Arabic or Hassaniya. The population is almost entirely Muslim. The national flag (proportions 3 by 2) is emerald green with a five-pointed gold star and a horizontal gold crescent moon in the centre. The capital is Nouakchott.

Recent History

Mauritania, a former French colony, became independent in November 1960. President Moktar Ould Daddah has held power since then, meeting opposition from the non-Arab minority who objected to the use of Arabic as an official language, and from the small proletariat. Miners' strikes led to the integration of the trade union into the sole political party.

Mauritania has moved away from the French sphere of inuflence, leaving OCAM in 1965, ending French military assistance and setting up a national currency outside the Franc Zone in 1973. President Daddah has stressed Islamic links, considering joining a Maghreb union, attending the Lahore Islamic conference and joining the Arab League.

Government

The single political party, the *Parti du peuple mauritanien*, nominates the President, who exercises executive power and appoints ministers. Legislative power belongs to the National Assembly, elected by universal suffrage for five years.

Defence

There is an army of 1,400 men, a gendarmerie of 500, and a small navy and air force. Military service for two years is compulsory.

Economic Affairs

Nomadic Moors, many of whom are slaves, living by herding cattle and sheep, make up some 80 per cent of the population. Agriculture is restricted to the African peasants of the Senegal valley, who grow millet and rice. The rich offshore fishing grounds are exploited by Spanish and Japanese vessels. The freezing and processing of their catch at Nouadhibou is the only significant industry.

Iron ore from F'Derik and copper from Akjoujt provide some 80 per cent of export earnings, and give Mauritania a trade surplus. These mineral reserves, which are expected to last less than 20 years, are exploited by foreign companies; their profits are exported and they make little contribution to economic development. SNIM, a state corporation, has plans for a copper and steel industry at Nouakchott, gypsum mining and sugar and oil refineries, to end dependence on iron and copper mining.

Transport and Communications

The Senegal river is an important artery of transport. A 652-km. railway has been built from F'Derik (Fort-Gouraud) to Nouadhibou (Port Etienne) for the transport of iron ore. The port of Nouadhibou has been extended to handle mineral exports and accommodate the fishing industry. The main international airport is at Nouakchott, with a second at Nouadhibou, while 14 small airfields provide for internal services, which are run by Air Mauritanie. Mauritania is a member of Air Afrique. There are about 6,200 km. of roads and tracks, of which large stretches have recently been improved.

Social Welfare

The National Social Insurance Fund administers family allowances, industrial accident benefits, insurance against occupational diseases, and old-age benefits. Nouakchott has a 600-bed hospital and there are a few regional dispensaries.

Education

Despite expansion in education facilities since 1960, including provisions for nomadic families, only 12 per cent of children attend school. Arabic has been compulsory since 1967, in addition to French, and a bi-lingual teacher-training college was opened in 1971.

Tourism

Owing to the hot climate, the best months for visiting Mauritania are from November to May. There are hotels in the principal towns. Hunting, visiting the oases, and touring the Berber villages are the chief attractions.

Visas are not required to visit Mauritania by the nationals of Andorra, Central African Republic, Chad, Congo (Brazzaville), Dahomey, France, Gabon, Guinea, Ivory Coast, Libya, Mali, Monaco, Niger, Senegal, Togo, Tunisia and Upper Volta.

Sport

There is little organized sport, although football is sometimes played. Hunting and fishing are popular.

Public Holidays

1974: August 5th (Leilat al Meiraj—Ascension of Muhammed), October 18th (Korité—Id ul Fitr), November 28th (National Day), December 26th (Tabaski—Id ul Adha).

1975: January 1st (New Year's Day), January 14th (Muslim New Year), March 26th (Mouloud—Birth of Muhammad), May 1st (Labour Day), May 25th (African Liberation Day).

Weights and Measures

The metric system is in force.

Currency and Exchange Rates

5 khoums = 1 ouguiya.

Exchange rates (April 1974):

£1 sterling = 108.715 ouguiya.
U.S. $1 = 46.04 ouguiya

STATISTICAL SURVEY

AREA AND POPULATION

The eight regions are known only by a number; the capital comprises a separate District.

Regions	Chief Town	Area (sq. km.)	Population (July 1972 estimate)
I	Néma . .	166,000	190,000
II	Aïoun El Alrouss	57,000	99,000
III	Kiffa . .	46,800	190,000
IV	Kaédi . .	14,100	95,000
V	Aleg . .	131,200	210,000
VI	Rosso . .	112,400	220,000
VII	Atar . .	471,200	89,000
VIII	Nouadhibou .	31,000	29,000
District	Nouakchott .	1,000	48,000
	Total .	1,030,700*	1,180,000

* 397,950 square miles.

PRINCIPAL TOWNS
POPULATION (July 1972 estimates)

Nouakchott (capital)	48,000*	Kaédi	13,000
Nouadhibou (Port-Etienne)	20,000	Rosso	13,000
F'Derik (Fort-Gouraud) .	18,000	Atar	10,000

* The population of Nouakchott was estimated to be 130,000 in June 1973.

Births and Deaths: Average annual birth rate 44.4 per 1,000, death rate 22.7 per 1,000 (UN estimate for 1965–70).

EMPLOYMENT
(1972)

Agriculture	360,000
Wage and Salary Earners:	
Public Sector . . .	11,000
Private Sector . . .	19,000

AGRICULTURE
LAND USE, 1964
('000 hectares)

Arable Land	258
Land Under Permanent Crops .	5
Permanent Meadows and Pastures .	39,250
Forest	15,134
Other Areas	48,423
Total . . .	103,070

Source: FAO, *Production Yearbook 1971.*

PRINCIPAL CROPS
(metric tons)

	1970	1971*	1972
Millet and Sorghum . .	81,000	80,000	n.a.
Maize	4,000	3,000	5,700
Rice	1,365	n.a.	25,000
Wheat	240	n.a.	200
Sweet Potatoes and Yams .	3,000*	n.a.	n.a.
Cow Peas . . .	10,000	10,000	15,000
Dates	15,000	15,000	13,000
Groundnuts . . .	3,000	n.a.	3,000

* FAO estimate.

Source: mainly FAO, *Production Yearbook 1971.*

MAURITANIA—(STATISTICAL SURVEY)

LIVESTOCK
('000)

	1968–69*	1969–70	1970–71
Cattle . . .	2,600	2,660*	2,700*
Sheep . . .	2,700	2,800*	2,900*
Goats . . .	2,300	2,400*	2,450*
Asses . . .	220	225*	230*
Horses . . .	21	23*	24*
Camels . . .	685	690*	700
Poultry . . .	2,400	2,500	2,600

* FAO estimate.

Source: FAO, *Production Yearbook 1971.*

LIVESTOCK PRODUCTS
(FAO estimates, metric tons)

	1969	1970	1971
Cows' Milk . .	84,000	85,000	86,000
Sheep's Milk . .	41,000	42,000	43,000
Goats' Milk . .	81,000	82,000	84,000
Hen Eggs . .	2,100	2,200	2,300
Beef . .	26,000	27,000	27,000
Mutton and Lamb .	15,000	15,000	15,000
Poultry and Other Meat . . .	10,000	10,000	10,000

Source: FAO, *Production Yearbook 1971.*

FORESTRY
ROUNDWOOD PRODUCTION
(cubic metres)

1968 . . .	521,000
1969 . . .	531,000
1970 . . .	541,000

Source: FAO, *Yearbook of Forest Products.*

Fishing: Total catch in 1967 was 30,700 metric tons (sea 17,700, inland water 13,000). Exports of fish: 31,500 metric tons in 1970; 22,600 metric tons in 1971.

MINING
IRON ORE PRODUCTION
(gross weight, metric tons)*

1968 . . .	7,704,000
1969 . . .	8,457,000
1970 . . .	9,118,000
1971 . . .	8,600,000
1972 . . .	8,628,000

* The metal content is approximately 66 per cent.

Copper ore (1971): 5,340 metric tons; Salt (1969): 500 metric tons.

There are also plans for exploiting gypsum and titanium deposits.

Industry: Date packing, frozen meat, dried and frozen fish, matches, carpets, a national printing office and other light industrial enterprises.

Electricity Production (million kWh.): 43.8 in 1968; 56.2 in 1969; 73.6 in 1972.

FINANCE

5 khoums = 1 ouguiya.

Coins: 1 khoum; 1, 5, 10 and 20 ouguiya.

Notes: 100, 200 and 1,000 ouguiya.

Exchange rates (April 1974): £1 sterling = 108.715 ouguiya; U.S. $1 = 46.04 ouguiya.
1,000 ouguiya = £9.20 = $21.72.

Note: The ouguiya was introduced on June 29th, 1973, replacing the franc CFA at the rate of 1 ouguiya = 5 francs CFA. Many of the figures in the tables below are expressed in francs CFA.

Budget (1972 estimates): Balanced at 10,413.5 million francs CFA.

(1973 estimates): Balanced at 12,453 million francs CFA.

(1974 estimates): Balanced at 3,105 million ouguiya (15,525 million francs CFA).

Development Budget (1972 estimate): 1,400 million francs CFA.

Currency in Circulation (February 28th, 1973): 619 million ouguiya.

EXTERNAL TRADE*
(million francs CFA)

	1964	1965	1966	1967	1968	1969	1970	1971
Imports . . .	3,879	5,864	5,523	9,105	8,713	11,764	13,138	15,780
Exports . . .	11,307	14,219	17,089	17,779	17,714	20,015	25,023	25,129

* Recorded transactions only. Trade crossing land frontiers is understated.

PRINCIPAL COMMODITIES

IMPORTS	1969	1970	1971
Cereals and Preparations	669	n.a.	n.a.
Rice	n.a.	284	511
Sugar and Honey	819	n.a.	1,342
Tea and Maté	n.a.	142	258
Petroleum Products	n.a.	930	1,089
Manufactured Fertilizer . . .	n.a.	65	87
Lime and Cement . . .	n.a.	167	161
Iron and Steel . . .	1,008	n.a.	n.a.
Iron bars and rods . .	n.a.	75	64
Machinery (non-electric) . . .	2,808	n.a.	n.a.
Electrical Equipment . . .	552	n.a.	n.a.
Railway Vehicles . . .	282	872	525
Road Motor Vehicles . . .	1,029	593	1,021
Aircraft	n.a.	25	149
Ships and Boats	n.a.	38	217
TOTAL (incl. others) . .	11,764	13,138	15,780

EXPORTS	1970	1971	1972
Iron Ore	20,924	20,847	19,894
Fish	2,029	2,137	2,842
of which: Salted and dried . .	805	693	744
Fresh and frozen .	856	481	353
Natural Gums . . .	492	434	700
Copper Concentrates . . .	—	1,035	2,715
TOTAL (incl. others) . .	25,023	25,129	n.a.

Sources: Direction de la Statistique et des Etudes Economiques, Nouakchott; Europe Outremer *L'Afrique d'Expression Française et Madagascar 1973*; UN Economic Commission for Africa *Statistical Yearbook 1972*.

COUNTRIES

IMPORTS	1969	1970	1971	EXPORTS	1969	1970	1971
Belgium/Luxembourg .	462	506	235	Belgium/Luxembourg .	2,424	3,464	3,286
China, People's				Congo (Brazzaville) .	566	446	432
Republic . . .	1,040	160	278	France . . .	3,935	4,857	5,362
Congo (Brazzaville) .	324	321	—	Germany, Federal			
France . . .	4,435	5,261	6,147	Republic . . .	2,829	2,886	2,908
Germany, Federal				Italy	2,654	3,607	2,882
Republic . .	568	465	811	Japan . . .	495	1,634	1,623
Italy	98	390	178	Netherlands . .	559	n.a.	n.a.
Spain	377	229	290	Senegal . . .	470	584	510
United Kingdom .	1,160	1,035	1,131	Spain . . .	766	2,246	2,168
U.S.A. . . .	1,686	2,081	1,664	United Kingdom .	4,720	4,082	4,132
TOTAL (incl. others)	11,764	13,138	15,780	TOTAL (incl. others)	20,015	25,023	25,129

TRANSPORT

Road Traffic (January 1st, 1973): 11,753 motor vehicles in use, including: 5,654 passenger cars, 5,590 vans and trucks.

Shipping (1972): goods handled at Point-Central: 8,625,600 metric tons; Nouadhibou 192,100 metric tons; Nouakchott (wharf) 122,300 metric tons.

Civil Aviation (1972, Nouadhibou-Nouakchott): 91,067 passenger arrivals and departures; 2,544 tons of freight received and dispatched.

Tourist Accommodation: Nouakchott had 97 tourist hotel bedrooms in August 1972.

Education (1972–73): Primary Education 38,900 pupils; Secondary Education 4,073; Technical Education and Lycée 247; 491 university students at institutes abroad.

Source (unless otherwise stated): Direction de la Statistique et des Etudes Economiques, Ministère de la Planification et du Développement Industriel, Nouakchott.

THE CONSTITUTION

(Promulgated May 20th, 1961. Revised February 12th, 1965, July 12th, 1966, and February 1968.)

Sovereignty: The State is republican, indivisible, democratic and social. Islam is the religion, and there is freedom of conscience and of religious practice. Government resides in the Mauritanian people who exercise it through representatives and by referenda. Suffrage is universal, equal and secret. It is open to all Mauritanian citizens of both sexes who are of age, and who hold civil and political rights.

Government: The President decides and conducts the policy of the country. The sole candidate for the Presidency is appointed by the *Parti du peuple mauritanien* (*PPM*) and the President is elected by direct and universal suffrage for five years. The President orders the administration and the internal security forces, exercises power according to law, executes the laws, appoints state officials, and negotiates and concludes settlements with the Community and its member states. He nominates and dismisses the members of the government. The members of the government take the oath in front of the bureau of the National Assembly.

National Assembly: Legislative power belongs to the Assembly, which is elected for five years. All citizens of the Republic over 25 years of age, holding civil and political rights, are eligible for seats. The PPM is the only official party and institutionalized as such. The Assembly holds two ordinary sessions a year. The Assembly can hold a special session at the request of the President or of the majority of members.

The Supreme Court: Its organization and functions are determined by the Constitution.

Justice: The judiciary is independent of any other authorities. Judges may under certain circumstances be removed from office. Justice is administered in the name of the people of Mauritania. The President of the Republic is guarantor of the independence of the magistrature.

Local Government: The organs of local government are the region and the commune, administered by the local councils.

Revision: The power to revise the Constitution is in the hands of the Prime Minister and the members of the Assembly.

THE GOVERNMENT

HEAD OF STATE

President: Moktar Ould Daddah (re-elected August 1966 and 1971).

CABINET

(*April* 1974)

President: Moktar Ould Daddah.

Minister of Foreign Affairs: Hamdi Ould Mouknass.

Minister of National Defence: Sidi Mohamed Diagana.

Guardian of the Seals and Minister of Justice: Abdallahi Ould Boye.

Minister of the Interior: Ahmed Ould Mohamed Sallah.

Minister of Industrial Development, Planning and Economic Affairs: Sidi Ould Cheikh Abdallahi.

Minister of Finance: Soumaré Diaramouna.

Minister of Rural Development: Diop Mamadou Amadou.

Minister of Handicrafts and Tourism: Maloum Ould Braham.

Minister of Trade and Transport: Abdallahi Ould Cheikh.

Minister of Equipment: Abdallahi Ould Daddah.

Minister of Culture and Information: Ahmed Ould Sidi Baba.

Minister of National Education: Mohameden Babah.

Minister of Youth and Sports: Ba Mamadou Alassane.

Minister of Primary Education and Religious Affairs: Ahmed Ben Amar.

Minister of Civil Service and Labour: Baro Abdoulaye.

Minister of Health and Social Affairs: Abdallahi Ould Bah.

DIPLOMATIC REPRESENTATION

EMBASSIES ACCREDITED TO MAURITANIA

(In Nouakchott unless otherwise stated)

Albania: Algiers, Algeria.

Algeria: Dakar, Senegal.

Austria: Dakar, Senegal.

Belgium: Dakar, Senegal.

Brazil: *Ambassador:* João Cabral de Neto.

Bulgaria: Bamako, Mali.

Canada: Dakar, Senegal.

China, People's Republic: B.P. 196; *Ambassador:* Wang Peng.

Egypt: B.P. 176; *Ambassador:* Ahmed Mohamed Tohamy.

France: B.P. 189; *Ambassador:* (vacant).

Gabon: *Ambassador:* José Amiar.

Germany, Federal Republic: *Ambassador:* Wolf von Arnim.

Ghana: Conakry, Guinea.

Guinea: *Ambassador:* Mamadou Tounkara.

Hungary: Conakry, Guinea.

India: Dakar, Senegal.

Italy: Dakar, Senegal.

Japan: Dakar, Senegal.

Korea, Democratic People's Republic: *Ambassador:* Kim Seung-Hyeuk.

Kuwait: *Ambassador:* Nouri Abdessalam Chouaïb.

Libya: *Ambassador:* Mohamed Ahmed Almagrahi.

Mali: Dakar, Senegal.

Mongolia: Algiers, Algeria.

Morocco: *Ambassador:* Mohamed Mesfioui.

Netherlands: Dakar, Senegal.

Romania: *Ambassador:* Ion Moanga.

Saudi Arabia: *Ambassador:* Mohamed Al Fadh El Issa.

Senegal: B.P. 611; *Ambassador:* Alioune Cisse.

Spain: B.P. 232; *Ambassador:* Juan Bautista Andrada Vanderwilde.

Sweden: Rabat, Morocco.

Switzerland: Dakar, Senegal.

Tunisia: Dakar, Senegal.

U.S.S.R.: B.P. 258; *Ambassador:* Mikhailovich Lavroj.

United Kingdom: Dakar, Senegal.

U.S.A.: *Chargé d'Affaires a.i.:* Robert Stein.

Viet-Nam, Democratic Republic: Bamako, Mali.

Yugoslavia: Dakar, Senegal.

Zaire: *Ambassador:* Kayukua Kimotu.

Mauritania also has diplomatic relations with Cameroon, German Democratic Republic, Ivory Coast, Jordan, Lebanon, Sudan, the Royal Government of Khmer National Union (Cambodia) and the Provisional Revolutionary Government of the Republic of South Viet-Nam.

PARLIAMENT

NATIONAL ASSEMBLY

(*General Election of August* 1971)

President: Da Ould Sidi Haïba.

Composition: all 50 members belong to the *Parti du peuple mauritanien.*

POLITICAL PARTY

Parti du peuple mauritanien (PPM): B.P. 61, Nouakchott; f. 1961 by coalition of the *Parti du regroupement mauritanien, Union nationale mauritanienne, Nahda* and *Union des socialistes musulmans mauritaniens*; the only recognized party; National Political Bureau of 41 mems.; Sec.-Gen. Moktar Ould Daddah; Perm. Sec. Abdoul Aziz Sall.

DEFENCE

The total armed forces number 1,530 of which the Army numbers 1,400, the Navy 30 and the air force 100. There is a gendarmerie of 500 and a civil police of 1,000. Compulsory military service was introduced in 1962.

Chief of Staff of the Army: Capt. Maustapha Ould Mohamed Saleck.

JUDICIAL SYSTEM

Supreme Court: Nouakchott; f. 1961; intended to ensure the independence of the judiciary; the Supreme Court is competent in electoral matters; Pres. Ahmed Ould Mohamed Salah; Vice-Pres. Abdullah Ould Boyé.

High Court of Justice: consists of a President, who is a stipendiary magistrate, and eleven other judges, six of whom are elected by the National Assembly from amongst its members, and five of whom are elected by the Assembly from a list of Islamic lawyers.

The Code of Law was founded in 1961 and subsequently modified to integrate modern law with Muslim institutions and practices. Seventy-five per cent of the Magistrature and all clerks of the court are now Mauritanian nationals. The main courts are: a *tribunal de première instance* (Magistrate's court) with six regional sections, 42 *tribunaux de cadis* (departmental civil courts), labour courts, military courts and the Court of State Security.

RELIGION

Islam is the official religion of Mauritania. The population is almost entirely Muslim of the Malekite sect, less than 1 per cent being Christian. The most important of the religious groups is that of the Qadiriya (Leader M. Ould Sheikh Sidya). Chinguetti, in the district of Adrar, is the seventh Holy Place in Islam. The 6,500 Roman Catholics who are mainly aliens, come under the jurisdiction of the Diocese of Nouakchott; Bishop of Nouakchott Mgr. Michel Bernard, B.P. 353.

PRESS

Journal Officiel: Ministry of Justice, Nouakchott; twice monthly.

Nouakchott Information: Direction de l'Information Nouakchott; daily.

Le Peuple: P.P.M., Nouakchott; bi-monthly in French and Arabic.

NEWS AGENCY

Agence France-Presse: B.P. 217, Nouakchott; Correspondent JEAN-MARIE BLIN.

RADIO

Radiodiffusion Nationale de Mauritanie: B.P. 200, Nouakchott; four transmitters, two of 100 kW.; broadcasts in French, Arabic, Wolof, Toucouleur and Sarakolé; advertising is accepted; Dir. MOHAMED OULD WEDADY; Sec.-Gen. YAHYA OULD ABDI.

Number of radio receivers: 75,000.

There is no television.

FINANCE

BANKING

CENTRAL BANK

Banque Centrale de Mauritanie: Nouakchott; f. 1973; cap. 200 million ouguiyas; Gov. AHMED OULD DADDAH; Deputy Gov. MOUSTAPHA OULD CHEIKH MOHAMEDOU.

Banque Arabe Libyenne Mauritanienne pour le Commerce Extérieur et le Développement: Nouakchott; f. 1972; cap. 25om. francs CFA (51 per cent Libya, 49 per cent Mauritania).

Banque Internationale pour l'Afrique Occidentale: 9 ave. de Messine, 75360 Paris 8e, France; Nouakchott; offices also at Nouadhibou, Rosso, Zouérate and Akjoujt.

Banque Mauritanienne de Développement: B.P. 219, Nouakchott; f. 1962; cap. francs CFA 200m. of which 58 per cent state-owned.

Société Mauritanienne de Banque: B.P. 614, ave. Gamal Abdel Nasser, Nouakchott; f. 1967; affiliated to Société Générale, Paris, France; cap. 150m. frs. CFA; Chair. ROGER DUCHEMIN; Man. G. RAYNAUD.

DEVELOPMENT

Société d'équipement de la Mauritanie: B.P. 28, Nouakchott; f. 1964; the state holds a majority interest; Pres. and Dir.-Gen. MAMADOU CISSOKO.

INSURANCE

Cie. d'Assurances Générales: Nouadhibou.

Société Africaine d'Assurances: c/o Société Commerciale de Transports Transatlantiques, Nouadhibou.

TRADE AND INDUSTRY

CHAMBER OF COMMERCE

Chambre de Commerce, d'Agriculture, d'Industrie et de Mines de la Mauritanie: Nouakchott, B.P. 215; f. 1954; Pres. AHMED OULD DADDAH; Sec.-Gen. ELIMANE ABOU KANE; publ. *Bulletin* (twice monthly).

INDUSTRIAL ORGANIZATIONS

Société Nationale d'Importation et d'Exportation (SONIMEX): B.P. 290, Nouakchott; f. 1966; holds a monopoly of imports of consumer goods such as rice, tea, sugar, and exports of gum-arabic; cap. 250m. francs CFA; Dir.-Gen. AHMED OULD DADDAH.

Union Nationale des Industriels, Commerçants et Entrepreneurs de Mauritanie (UNICEMA): B.P. 383, Nouakchott; f. 1958; Pres. G. ESQUILAT, Sec.-Gen. J. MALVAES.

TRADE UNIONS

A National Commission of Trade Union Reconciliation was set up at the end of 1970 to resolve the split in the *Union des Travailleurs de Mauritanie* caused by the opposition of some unions to affiliation to the ruling PPM. In June 1972 the PPM reiterated its demand that all unions must integrate with the party, and by April 1973, when the UTM held its congress, this integration had taken place.

Union des Travailleurs de Mauritanie: B.P. 63, Bourse du Travail, Nouakchott; f. 1961 by merger of *Union Nationale des Travailleurs de Mauritanie;* and *Union Générale des Travailleurs de Mauritanie;* 10,000 mems.; affiliated to ICFTU; Sec.-Gen. MALIK FALL.

Unions affiliated to the Union des Travailleurs de Mauritanie:

Fédération du Commerce et de l'Alimentation: f. 1963.

Fédération de la Construction: f. 1963.

Fédération de l'Education Nationale: f. 1963.

Fédération de la Santé: f. 1963.

Fédération des Mines et des Industries Extractives: f. 1963.

Fédération de l'Administration Intérieure: f. 1963.

Fédération des Activités Rurales: f. 1963.

Fédération des Transports et Télécommunications: 1963.

MINERALS

DEVELOPMENT

Société Nationale Industrielle et Minière (SNIM): B.P. 1260, Nouakchott-ksar; f. 1972; national company for state intervention in research, exploitation and transformation of minerals; manages public holdings in MIFERMA and SOMIMA; cap. 2,153 million francs CFA; Dir.-Gen. ISMAEL OULD AMAR.

IRON ORE

Société Anonyme des Mines de fer de Mauritanie (MIFERMA): 87 rue la Boétie, Paris 8e; B.P. 42, Nouadhibou; F'Derik; 200 millions tons of iron ore are known to be available for immediate exploitation, of comparable quality to Swedish ores, yielding 66 per cent pure iron; capital 13,300m. francs CFA; Hon. Pres. LEROY BEAULIEU; Pres. Delegate JEAN AUDIBERT.

Ownership:	Per cent
Mauritanian Government	5.00
French Bureau of Geological and Mining Research	23.89
French Steel Concerns	9.49
French Financial Concerns	22.42
British Steel Corporation	19.00
Italian FINSIDER Group	15.20
German THYSSEN Group	5.00

COPPER ORE

Société Minière de Mauritanie (SOMIMA): B.P. 275, Nouakchott; f. 1967; exploitable reserves are estimated at 7.7m. tons; a total investment of U.S.$60m. is anticipated; cap. 2,000m. francs CFA; initial production was expected to be at an annual rate of 28,000 tons of copper-in-concentrates; Pres. Mohamed Ba.

Ownership:		Per cent
Mauritanian Government .	.	22.00
Charter Consolidated Ltd.	.	44.60
S.F.I.	.	15.00
Société Min. et Mét. de Penar-		
roya . . .	.	6.57
B.R.G.M. . . .	.	6.13
Cie. Fin de Paris et des Pays-Bays		3.77
Cofimer . . .	.	1.93

OIL

Prospecting is being undertaken by the Planet Oil and Mineral Corpn., Texas, U.S.A.

TITANIUM

Syndicat de Recherches d'Ilménite: Paris; Nouakchott; joint venture of the French Bureau of Geological and Mining Research and Etablissements Kuhlmann; proved deposits of 4m. tons of mineral sands.

TRANSPORT

RAILWAYS

A railway connecting Nouadhibou with Tazadit and the new iron ore fields at F'Derik was opened in 1963 and is 650 km. long. Known as the Miferma railway, it is used primarily for transporting iron ore to the coast.

S.A. des Mines de Fer de Mauritanie: 87 rue de la Boétie, Paris 8e, France; owns the railway

ROADS

There are about 6,200 km. of roads and tracks including 560 km. of tarred road. Two important routes have recently been completed (Nouakchott–Rosso, Nouakchott–Akjoujt) and another is under construction (Kaédi–Kiffa).

Etablissements Lacombe et Cie.: B.P. 204, Nouakchott; road transport.

INLAND WATERWAYS

Messageries du Sénégal: Saint Louis (Senegal); the river Senegal is navigable by small coastal vessels as far as Kayes (Mali) and by river vessels as far as Kaédi in the wet season; in the dry season as far as Rosso and Boghe, respectively.

SHIPPING

Société Ouest Africaine d'Entreprises Maritimes (Mauritanie): B.P. 351, Nouakchott; Dir. (Nouakchott) Jean-Pierre Giromagny.

Several shipping companies serve Nouadhibou and Nouakchott, the most important being La Compagnie Paquet and La Compagnie Maurel-Prom.

The Nouadhibou development programme, which will make the port one of the most important in Africa, is estimated to cost £50 million. More than 8.6 million tons of goods were handled at Nouadhibou in 1972. The port of Nouakchott is also being developed, to handle the copper from Akjoujt.

CIVIL AVIATION

There are two airfields, at Nouadhibou and Nouakchott, and a number of smaller airstrips.

Air Mauritanie: B.P. 41, Nouakchott; f. 1962; scheduled domestic services from Nouakchott and Nouadhibou and international services to Dakar, Las Palmas and Casablanca; 170 employees; fleet of two DC-4, one DC-3 and one Navajo; Dir.-Gen. Ahmed Ould Bah.

Air Afrique: Mauritania has a six per cent share in Air Afrique; *see* under Ivory Coast.

Mauritania is also served by the following airlines: Air Algérie, Iberia, Royal Air Maroc and Union des Transports Aériens (UTA).

TOURISM

The Ministry of Crafts and Tourism is responsible for the development of tourism in Mauritania.

Ministère de l'Artisanat et du Tourisme: B.P. 246, Nouakchott; f. 1972; Sec.-Gen. Ahmed Ould Die.

MAURITIUS

INTRODUCTORY SURVEY

Location, Climate, Language, Religion, Flag, Capital

Mauritius covers less than 800 square miles in the Indian Ocean. The principal island, from which the country takes its name, lies about 885 km. east of Madagascar. The other main islands are: Rodrigues, 585 km. east of Mauritius; the Agalega Islands, 935 km. north; and the Cargados Carajos Shoals (St. Brandon Islands), 370 km. north. The climate is sub-tropical, and cyclones can be severe, causing much damage to crops and buildings. History and the racial mixture are reflected in the languages in use; English, French, Creole (derived from French), Hindi, Urdu and Chinese are all spoken by the various communities, though the first two are normally used for official purposes. Europeans and Creoles are mostly Roman Catholics; 75 per cent of the Indian population are Hindus, the rest being Muslims. The national flag (proportions 3 by 2) has four equal horizontal stripes: red, blue, gold and green. The capital is Port Louis.

Recent History

The island was a French colony from 1715 to 1810, when it was taken by Britain. Immigration, however, came mainly from East Africa and India (Mauritius had no indigenous human inhabitants) and the European population is largely French-speaking. Racial strife led to serious riots in January 1968. Following the victory of the pro-independence Labour Party in the August 1967 general election, Mauritius attained independence within the Commonwealth in March 1968, with Dr. Sir Seewoosagur Ramgoolam as Prime Minister. A new government of national unity was formed in December 1969 between the Labour Party and the Parti Mauricien Social Démocrate (PMSD), and general elections were postponed to 1976. Strong opposition to the government came from the radical Movement Militant Mauricienne (MMM). A state of emergency had been in force from just before independence but was revoked at the end of 1970. It was reimposed in December 1971, when a general strike started, and several trade unions were suspended. Many leading members of the MMM were arrested during 1971 and 1972 though most were subsequently released. The state of emergency was renewed again on November 16th, 1972. The coalition of the Labour Party and the PMSD broke up in December 1973. Increases in taxation, Labour's policy of closer links with Communist states and the PMSD leader's desire for closer relations with South Africa and for a French military base on the island were the main issues which finally split an uneasy partnership.

Government

Mauritius remains a member of the Commonwealth and Queen Elizabeth II is the head of state, being represented by a Governor-General. The legislative assembly has 62 elected members and eight additional members, in addition to the Speaker. The Cabinet comprises the Prime Minister and 14 other ministers. In November 1969 the Constitution was amended to provide for 21 ministers instead of 15 and 10 parliamentary secretaries instead of 5.

Defence

The country has no standing defence forces, but the government has signed a six-year defence agreement with Britain.

Economic Affairs

The island is an extreme example of a one-crop economy, being dependent on sugar for over 90 per cent of its export earnings. Sugar is the crop best suited to local conditions (there was a record crop in 1973) but production is unlikely to rise fast enough to support the rapidly expanding population. Of the total sugar exports, ranging from 530,000 to 600,000 tons each year, about two-thirds is sold to Britain. Substantial British aid continues, notably in the form of a preferential sugar price, more than twice the world price, as well as considerable loans for development. Molasses and other sugar by-products are also produced and exported, as are small quantities of tea and tobacco.

There is a serious lack of employment opportunities on the island, and this factor is thought to be partly responsible for the racial tension. The 1971–75 Development Plan is specifically designed to alleviate this major problem and the Government hopes to provide full employment by 1980. Mauritius is a member of OCAM which it joined in 1971. In May 1972 it became a full associate member of the European Economic Community, under the terms of the Yaoundé Convention, and exports to the Community will benefit from a reduction in tariffs, though sugar is excluded. The Commonwealth Sugar Agreement is due to be renewed in 1974 and the Yaoundé Convention in 1975. The decisions taken will be vital for the economic future of the island.

Transport and Communications

Port Louis is served by several shipping lines crossing the Indian Ocean, and there is an international airport at Plaisance on the far side of the island. In 1974 the harbour at Port Louis was being modernized and a new airport at Plaines des Roches was being planned. The road network is good considering the mountainous terrain, and there are also coastal shipping services.

Social Welfare

The social infrastructure includes a well developed health service and several hospitals: about a seventh of the total budget is devoted to other welfare services.

Education

Standards are high, most of the population being literate, though education is not compulsory. There are 689 primary and pre-primary schools, 130 secondary schools, ten vocational and technical colleges, a teacher training college and a university. In 1972 there were 155,624 pupils in primary schools, over 90 per cent of the relevant age group, and 52,378 in secondary schools.

Tourism

Major attractions include the superb beaches, fine mountain scenery, the ideal climate and the blend of cultures.

Distance from major centres of population has so far limited the industry's development to the luxury trade but income from tourism now amounts to some Rs. 16 million annually. There is major expansion of tourist facilities. over 68,000 tourists visited Mauritius in 1973.

Visas are not required to visit Mauritius by nationals of the United Kingdom and Commonwealth; nationals of Belgium, Denmark, Finland, the Federal Republic of Germany, Greece, Iceland, Israel, the Netherlands, Norway, Spain, Sweden and Tunisia require no visas for a visit of six months or less, and nationals of France, Italy and South Africa for a visit of three months or less.

Sport

Fishing, swimming, hunting, rugby and golf are popular sports.

Public Holidays

The different communities all observe their particular holidays; national holidays are:

1974: October 24th (United Nations Day), November 1st (All Saints' Day), December 25th–26th (Christmas).

1975: January 1st and 2nd (New Year), March 12th (Independence Day), May 1st (Labour Day).

Weights and Measures

The metric system is in standard use.

Currency and Exchange Rates

100 cents=1 Mauritian rupee.
Exchange rates (April 1974):

£1 sterling=13.33 rupees;
U.S. $1=5.65 rupees.

STATISTICAL SURVEY

Area (sq. km.): Mauritius 1,865; Rodrigues 109; others 71; Total 2,045.

Population: Island of Mauritius (1972 Census) 825,690; *Towns* (1971): Port Louis (capital) 142,000, Beau Bassin/Rose-Hill 73,000, Curepipe 53,000; *Ethnic groups* (1971 estimates): 575,123 Indo-Mauritians (437,365 Hindus, 137,758 Muslims), 230,487 general population (including Creole and Franco-Mauritian communities) and 24,996 Chinese.

Employment (Sept. 1972): Agriculture, etc. 61,900, Services 37,000, Manufacturing 11,600, Construction 3,000, Commerce 5,300, Total 146,800.

Agriculture (1972): Sugar cane 6,314,762 metric tons, Tea 23,519 metric tons, Tobacco 614 metric tons.

Forestry (1970): Timber 370,000 cu. ft., Firewood 2,261,000 cu. ft.

Industry (1972): Sugar 686,366 metric tons, Molasses 176,489 metric tons, Tea (manufactured) 4,578 metric tons, Aloe Fibre 1,556 metric tons, Alcohol 16,920 hectolitres, Rum 17,996 hectolitres; (1973) Sugar 718,000 tons.

FINANCE

100 cents=1 Mauritian rupee.
Coins: 1, 2, 5, 10, 25 and 50 cents; 1 rupee.
Notes: 5, 10, 25 and 50 rupees.
Exchange rates (April 1974): £1 sterling=13.33 rupees; U.S. $1=5.65 rupees.
100 Mauritian rupees=£7.50=$17.71.

BUDGET 1971–72
(Rupees)

Revenue		Expenditure	
Direct Taxes	74,230,890	Administration, Police, etc. . . .	32,647,860
Indirect Taxes	161,886,880	Financial Services . . .	84,156,993
Receipts from Public Utilities .	24,555,353	Agricultural Services . . .	8,621,199
Receipts from Public Services .	9,085,567	Public Works	19,051,550
Rent of Government Property .	2,316,729	Commerce and Industry . .	1,562,629
Interest and Royalties . .	14,825,899	Education and Cultural Affairs .	41,137,878
U.K. Reimbursements . .	553,000	Health	30,580,702
Admiralty Reimbursements .	165,163	Labour	1,216,736
Other Reimbursements . .	6,461,010	Local Government and Co-operative Development	9,269,746
Redemption of Loans . .		Housing, Lands and Town and Country Planning	2,122,455
		Information and Broadcasting . .	1,497,519
		Social Security	33,343,191
		Communications . . .	12,362,834
		External Affairs, Tourism and Emigration	5,614,197
Total . . .	294,080,491	Total	283,185,489

EXTERNAL TRADE
(Rs. million)

	1968	1969	1970	1971	1972
Imports . . .	421.1	376.0	419.9	461.6	635.8
Exports . . .	354.0	365.2	384.5	360.8	573.8

PRINCIPAL COMMODITIES
(Rs. million)

Imports	1970	1971	1972
Rice	38.2	31.3	42.6
Wheat Flour	22.8	23.5	29.0
Alcoholic Beverages	3.8	4.7	6.0
Petroleum Products	29.3	28.9	49.9
Edible Vegetable Oils	15.3	21.4	16.7
Fertilizers (manufactured) . . .	18.2	16.8	28.5
Cotton Fabrics	9.5	11.2	12.2
Other Textile Fabrics	14.3	15.1	29.1
Cement	7.1	9.1	10.1
Iron and Steel	21.3	17.8	22.7
Manufactures of Metals . . .	11.2	13.3	17.6
Non-electric Machinery . . .	22.6	41.6	44.9
Electric Machinery	15.9	18.2	41.4
Vehicles and Parts	15.0	16.7	23.6
Total (incl. others) . . .	419.9	461.6	635.8

Exports	1970	1971	1972
Sugar	341.2	313.4	507.6
Molasses	10.6	8.3	14.2
Tea	14.1	17.0	20.8
Total (incl. others) . . .	384.5	360.8	573.8

PRINCIPAL COUNTRIES
(Rs. million)

Imports	1970	1971	1972
Australia . . .	30.4	30.2	44.9
Burma . . .	23.1	17.3	34.4
France . . .	29.5	32.6	43.3
Germany, Federal Republic . .	20.5	22.3	36.6
Hong Kong . .	10.2	9.9	17.6
India . . .	12.8	12.9	16.8
Iran . . .	14.9	22.4	42.1
Japan . . .	21.8	30.5	49.3
South Africa . .	37.8	36.0	50.4
Thailand . .	12.8	12.9	2.9
United Kingdom . .	88.0	100.9	131.0
U.S.A. . . .	23.9	31.8	21.6
Total (incl. others)	419.9	461.6	635.8

Exports	1970	1971	1972
Canada . . .	77.6	101.1	107.7
Italy . . .	0.2	—	0.1
Madagascar . .	2.6	2.5	2.2
Netherlands . .	—	1.4	3.9
New Zealand . .	0.3	0.3	0.6
Réunion . .	3.9	5.3	7.7
South Africa . .	12.1	15.8	18.9
United Kingdom . .	260.4	198.4	339.5
U.S.A. . . .	21.1	21.9	36.2
Total (incl. others)	384.5	360.8	573.8

TRANSPORT

Roads (Dec. 1972): Private Cars 12,079, Taxis 1,397, Buses 831, Commercial Vehicles 4,649, Government Vehicles 1,201, Motor Cycles 3,265, Auto Cycles 3,261.

Shipping (1972): Entered: Ships 1,100, Passengers 3,208, Freight 718,426 tons; Cleared: Ships 1,092, Passengers 3,417, Freight 798,335 tons.

Civil Aviation (1972): Landed: Planes 1,333, Passengers 75,078, Freight 526,520 kg.; Departed: Planes 1,333, Passengers 78,993, Freight 1,054,261 kg.

EDUCATION
(1972)

	Schools	Pupils
Pre-Primary . . .	329	9,198
Primary	360	155,624
Secondary . . .	130	52,378
Teacher Training . .	1	639
Vocational and Technical .	10	688
University . . .	1	1,353

Students Overseas (1972): 1,697 (excluding nursing students).

Source: Central Statistical Office, Rose Hill.

THE CONSTITUTION

The Mauritius Independence Order, 1968, as amended by the Constitution of Mauritius (Amendment) Act No. 39 of 1969, provides for a Cabinet consisting of the Prime Minister and not more than twenty other Ministers. The Prime Minister, appointed by the Governor-General, is the member of the Legislative Assembly who appears to the Governor-General best able to command the support of the majority of members of the Assembly. Other Ministers are appointed by the Governor-General acting in accordance with the advice of the Prime Minister.

The Legislative Assembly consists of the following:

(i) The Speaker.
(ii) Sixty-two elected members.
(iii) Eight additional members.

(iv) The Attorney-General if not an elected member.

For the purpose of electing members of the Legislative Assembly, the island of Mauritius is divided into twenty-three member constituencies. Rodrigues returns two members. The official language of the Legislative Assembly is English but any member may address the Chair in French.

The State of Emergency, which has been in force since just before independence in 1968, was revoked at the end of 1970. At the same time a Public Order Act, giving the Government wide-ranging powers in certain situations, came into force. A State of Emergency was reimposed in December 1971 and is still in force.

THE GOVERNMENT

Governor-General: Sir Abdul Raman Osman.

COUNCIL OF MINISTERS

(*June* 1974)

Prime Minister and Minister of Defence, Internal Security, External Affairs, Tourism and Immigration, and Information and Broadcasting: The Rt. Hon. Sir Seewoosagur Ramgoolam.

Minister of Finance: The Hon. Veerasamy Ringadoo.

Minister of Health: The Hon. Sir Harold H. Walter.

Minister of Education and Cultural Affairs: Dr. The Hon. R. Chaperon, c.m.g.

Minister of Labour and Industrial Relations: Dr. The Hon. Beergoonath Ghurburrun.

Minister of Social Security: The Hon. K. Tirvengadum.

Minister of Agriculture, Natural Resources and the Environment: The Hon. Satcam Boolell.

Minister of Energy, Fuel and Power: The Hon. R. Devienne.

Minister of Works: The Hon. Abdul Hak Mohammed Osman.

Minister of Industry and Commerce: The Hon. Rajmohun-singh Jomadar.

Minister of Local Government: The Hon. Jean E. M. Lin Ah Chuen.

Minister of Justice and Attorney-General: The Hon. E. Bussier.

Minister of Communications: The Hon. P. G. Raymond Rault.

Minister of Economic Planning and Development: The Hon. Keharsingh Jagatsingh.

Minister of Housing, Lands and Town and Country Planning: The Hon. Sir Abdul Razak Mohammed.

Minister of Youth and Sports: The Hon. Basant Rai.

Minister of Employment: The Hon. A. Rima.

Minister of Co-operatives and Co-operative Development: The Hon. H. Ramnarain.

Minister of Fisheries: The Hon. R. Modun.

Minister of Reform Institutions: The Hon. R. Jaypal.

DIPLOMATIC REPRESENTATION

EMBASSIES AND HIGH COMMISSIONS ACCREDITED TO MAURITIUS
(In Port Louis unless otherwise stated)
(E) Embassy; (HC) High Commission.

Australia: Dar es Salaam, Tanzania (HC).

Belgium: Nairobi, Kenya (E).

Canada: Dar es Salaam, Tanzania (HC).

Central African Republic: P.O.B. 688 (E); *Ambassador:* A. MBOE.

China, People's Republic: Royal Rd., Belle Rose, Quatre Bornes (E); *Ambassador:* WANG TSE.

Egypt: Dar es Salaam, Tanzania (E).

France: rue St. Georges (E); *Ambassador:* RAPHÄEL TOUZE.

Germany, Federal Republic: Tananarive, Madagascar (E).

India: Fifth floor, Bank of Baroda Bldg., Sir William Newton Street (HC); *High Commissioner:* KRISHNA DAYAL SHARMA.

Italy: Tananarive, Madagascar (E).

Japan: Tananarive, Madagascar (E).

Madagascar: Sir William Newton Street (E); *Chargé d'Affaires:* J. J. MAURICE.

Netherlands: Nairobi, Kenya (E).

Pakistan: Anglo-Mauritius House, Intendance St. (E); *Chargé d'Affaires:* M. S. MAGSUD.

Switzerland: Addis Ababa, Ethiopia (E).

U.S.S.R.: Floreal (E); *Ambassador:* N. BANDOURA.

United Kingdom: Cerné House, La Chaussée (HC); *High Commissioner:* A. HENRY BRIND.

U.S.A.: Anglo-Mauritius House (E); *Chargé d'Affaires:* J. P. SULLIVAN.

Vatican: Tananarive, Madagascar.

Mauritius also has diplomatic relations with Denmark, Finland, Israel, Norway, Portugal, Sweden, Syria and Yugoslavia.

LEGISLATIVE ASSEMBLY

Speaker: The Hon. Sir HARILAL R. VAGHJEE.

Deputy Speaker: The Hon. R. GUJADHUR.

The results of the election of August, 1967, were as follows:

PARTY	SEATS*
Independence Party	43
P.M.S.D.	27

* Includes the eight additional members (the most successful losing candidates of each community).

The membership of the various parties in the Assembly in 1974 is:

PARTY	SEATS*
Labour Party	38
P.M.S.D.	13
C.A.M.	5
I.F.B.	6
U.D.M.	5
MMM(SP)	1
Independents	2

POLITICAL PARTIES

Parti Mauricien Social Démocrate (PMSD): Port Louis; national party representing all communities; campaigned against independence in the 1967 election; left governing coalition in Dec. 1973; Pres. Hon. J. H. YTHIER, M.L.A.; Parl. Leader Hon. C. GAËTAN DUVAL, M.L.A.

Parti Travailliste (Labour Party): Port Louis; Pres. Hon. Dr. R. CHAPERON, M.L.A.; Parl. Leader Hon. Sir SEEWOOSAGUR RAMGOOLAM, M.L.A.

Independent Forward Bloc (IFB): 14 Vallonville St., Port Louis; f. 1958; democratic party; 6 seats; Pres. Hon. G. GANGARAM, M.L.A.; Leader SOOKDEO BISSOONDOYAL.

Comité d'Action Musulman (CAM): Port Louis; supports the interests of the Indo-Mauritian Muslims; in governing coalition; Pres. Hon. A. M. OSMAN, M.L.A.; Parl. Leader Hon. Sir ABDUL RAZAK MOHAMMED, M.L.A.

Mauritius People's Progressive Party: 38 Sir William Nowton St., Port Louis; affiliated member of Afro-Asian People's Solidarity Organization since 1963; Sec. Gen. T. SIBSURUN.

Parti du Centre: Bahemia Bldg., P. Hennessy St., Port Louis; Leader FRANCE VALLET.

Union Démocratique Mauricienne (UDM): opposition party formed from Parti Mauricien Social Démocrate; Leader MAURICE LESAGE.

Mauritian Militant Movement (MMM): Port Louis; Leader PAUL BÉRENGER (arrested Aug. 1971, later released); publ. *Le Militant* (suspended).

Mauritian Militant Mauricien Socialist Party (MMM(SP)): opposition party formed from MMM; Leader DER VERASWAMY.

JUDICIAL SYSTEM

The laws of Mauritius are derived partly from the old French Codes suitably amended and partly from English Law. The Judicial Department consists of the Supreme Court, presided over by the Chief Justice and four other Judges who are also Judges of the Court of Criminal Appeal, the Intermediate Court, the Court of Civil Appeal, the Industrial Court and 10 District Courts. The Master and Registrar is the executive officer of the Judicial Department and is also Judge in Bankruptcy.

Supreme Court: Superior Court of Record.

Court of Criminal Appeal.

Court of Civil Appeal.

Intermediate Court.

District Courts: presided over by Magistrates.

Industrial Court: jurisdiction over labour disputes.

Chief Justice: Hon. Sir M. Latour-Adrien.

Senior Puisne Judge: Hon. H. Garrioch.

Puisne Judges: Hon. C. Moollan, Hon. D. Ramphul and Hon. M. Rault.

RELIGION

Hindus 51 per cent, Christians 30 per cent, Muslims 16 per cent, Buddhists 3 per cent (1974 estimates).

The main religion of those of European and African descent is Roman Catholic (approximately 265,000 adherents); Bishop Jean Margéot, Port Louis. In 1962 there were 6,700 members of the Church of England and 3,980 other Protestants. The Anglican Archbishop of Mauritius and the Indian Ocean is the Rt. Rev. Ernest Edward Curtis, M.A., Phoenix, whose diocese includes the Seychelles. The Minister for the Presbyterian Church of Scotland is the Rev. T. Robinson, H.C.F.

PRESS AND PUBLISHERS

DAILIES

Advance: 5 Dumat St., Port Louis; f. 1939; English and French; Editor G. Ramloll; circ. 8,500.

L'Aube: Félicien Malfille St., Port Louis; f. 1972; English and French; Dir. J. Marcel Mason; circ. 3,000.

Le Cernéen: 8 St. Georges St., Port Louis; f. 1832; English and French; circ. 10,600; Editor J. P. Lenior.

China Times: Joseph Rivière St., Port Louis; f. 1953; Chinese; Editor L. S. Ah-Keng; circ. 200.

Chinese Daily News: 32 Remy Ollier St., Port Louis; f. 1932; Chinese; Editor Tu Wai Man; circ. 100.

L'Express: 3 Brown Sequard St., Port Louis; f. 1963; English and French; circ. 13,000; Editor Dr. P. Forget.

Le Mauricien: 8 St. Georges St., Port Louis; f. 1908; English and French; circ. 12,000; Editor L. Riviere.

The Nation: Port Louis; circ. 6,000; Publisher Independent Publications; Dir. Prakash Ramlallah.

New Chinese Commercial Paper: 19 Joseph Rivière St., Port Louis; f. 1956; Chinese; circ. 100; Editor Yeung Lam Ko.

Le Populaire: St. Georges St., Port Louis; f. 1973; English and French; Editor B. Gowrisunkur; circ. 3,000.

Star: 3 President John Kennedy St., Port Louis; f. 1963; English and French; circ. 4,000; Editor Dr. H. Fakim.

WEEKLIES

Aryoday: 16 Frère Felix de Valois Street, Port Louis; f. 1949; English and Hindi; Editors M. Mohit (Hindi) D. N. Beegun (English); circ. 1,000.

Le Dimanche: 3 Vieux Conseil St., Port Louis; f. 1961; English and French; Editor Regis Nauvel; circ. 18,000.

Janata: 5 Dumat St., Port Louis; f. 1947; Hindi; twice weekly; Editor L. Badry.

Mauritius Times: 23 Bourbon St., Port Louis; f. 1954; weekly; English and French; circ. 2,000; Editor D. Bheenuck.

Le Progrès: 3 Vieux Conseil St., Port Louis; f. 1973; English and French; Editor Sylvio Michel.

La Vie Catholique: 42 Pope Henessy St., Port Louis; f. 1930; French; circ. 10,000; Editor Louis Espitalier-Noël.

Week-End: St. Georges St., Port Louis; f. 1966; French and English; Editor J. Rivet; circ. 22,000.

FORTNIGHTLIES

Le Message: Dar es Salaam; P.O.B. 6, Rose Hill; f. 1961; English and French; Editor M. A. Qureshi; circ. 1,000.

Tamil Voice: 12 Farquhar St., Port Louis; f. 1964; English, French and Tamil; Editor C. Narayanan.

La Voix de L'Islam: Mesnil, Phoenix; f. 1951; English and French; Editor A. A. Peeroo; circ. 1,000.

Zamana: 14 Vallonville St., Port Louis; f. 1948; Hindi, French, English and Sanskrit; Editor B. Bucktowar-singh.

PERIODICALS

Indian Cultural Review: Port Louis; f. 1936; English and French; Editor Sir Seewoosagur Ramgoolam.

Le Progrès Islamique: 51 Solferino St., Rose Hill; f. 1948; English and French; monthly; Editor Mrs. A. N. Sookia; circ. 500.

Revue Agricole et Sucrière de l'Ile Maurice: University of Mauritius, Reduit; French and English; Editor Prof. E. Limfat.

Trait d'Union: P.O. Box 278, Port Louis; f. 1959; English and French; monthly; Editor Edwin de Robillard M.B.E.

PUBLISHERS

Editions Croix du Sud: 1 Barracks St., Port Louis; general.

Editions Nassau: Rue Barclay, Rose-Hill; f. 1970; publishes magazines; Pres. Dir.-Gen. R. A. Y. Vilmont; Sec.-Gen. E. H. Dennemont.

RADIO AND TELEVISION

Mauritius Broadcasting Corporation: Forest Side; f. 1964; national radio and television station; has a monopoly over broadcasting in the island; Dir.-Gen. J. R. Delaître; Sales Man. Jacques Cantin.

There are 82,497 radio sets in use.

Television services started in February 1965. There are 25,336 licences.

FINANCE

BANKS

Bank of Mauritius: P.O.B. 29, Port Louis; f. 1967 as central bank; cap. p.u. Rs. 10m.; Gov. G. Bunwaree; Man. Dir. I. Ramphul.

Development Bank of Mauritius: f. 1936; cap. Rs. 10m.

Mauritius Co-operative Central Bank: Port Louis; f. 1948; 211 mem. societies; Chair. P. R. Madiah; Gen. Man. M. Sidambaram, F.C.C.S., F.B.S.C.

———

Barclays Bank International Ltd.: Sir William Newton St., Port Louis; 6 brs., 2 sub-brs. and 6 agencies in Mauritius; Manager J. M. Lawson.

Bank of Baroda: Head Office: Baroda, India; Sir William Newton St., Port Louis; cap. Rs. 80m.; Man. C. J. Shah.

Banque National pour le Commerce et l'Industrie (BNCIOI): Queen St., Port Louis; Man. R. Bach.

Habib Bank (Overseas) Ltd.: Port Louis; f. 1952; Pakistani Bank; cap. Rs. 11.5m.; Man. Sheikh Ehsanuddin.

Mauritius Commercial Bank Ltd.: 11 Sir William Newton St., Port Louis; f. 1838; cap. Rs. 7m.; 12 brs.; Gen. Man. P. L. Eynaud.

Mercantile Bank Ltd.: Head Office: Hong Kong; Place d'Armes, Port Louis; 7 brs.; Man. J. C. Wright.

INSURANCE

Anglo-Mauritius Assurance Society Ltd.: Anglo-Mauritius House, Intendance St., Port Louis; incorp. 1951; Chair. Raymond Hein, Q.C.; Man. Dir. A. René Adam.

Birger & Co. (Insurance) Ltd.: 18 Jules Koenig St., Port Louis; incorp. 1954; Man. Isia Birger.

L & H Vigier de La Tour: Place Foch, Port Louis; Man. M. de Robinard.

Mauritius Eagle Insurance Co. Ltd.: Queen St., Port Louis; Man. R. Hepburn.

Mauritius Union Assurance Society Ltd.: 13 Sir William Newton St., Port Louis; incorp. 1948; Man. Dir. A. Noel Coignet.

Swan Insurance Co. Ltd.: 6–10 Intendance St., Port Louis; incorp. 1955; Chair. Raymond Hein, Q.C.

Forty-eight British companies and 33 other companies have branches in Mauritius.

TRADE AND INDUSTRY

CHAMBERS OF COMMERCE

Mauritius Chamber of Commerce and Industry: Anglo-Mauritius House, Port Louis; f. 1850, inc. 1892; 168 mems.; Pres. J. de Gersigny; Vice-Pres. M. Yayid.

Chinese Chamber of Commerce: 5 Joseph Rivière St., Port Louis; f. 1908, inc. 1914; to protect the interests of Chinese traders and to see to the welfare of Chinese immigrants; Pres. Philippe L. Man Hin; Sec. Louis Roger Chan.

TRADE UNIONS

Mauritius Federation of Labour: Port Louis; affiliated to WFTU; Pres. L. Badry; Gen. Sec. L. Lubidineuse.

Mauritius Trade Union Congress: 7 Guy Rozemont Square, Port Louis; 12,562 mems.; 17 affiliated unions; Gen. Sec. Cyril Canabady.

Principal Unions

Agricultural and Other Workers' Union: 6 Edith Cavell St., Port Louis; 12,000 mems.; Pres. L. Badry; Sec. P. I. K. Bhatoo.

General Workers' Federation (GWF): Moka St., Port Louis; Negotiator Paul Berenger.

Government and Other Manual Workers' Union: 6 Edith Cavell St., Port Louis; 1,163 mems.; Pres. I. Allybokus; Sec. L. Lubidineuse.

Government Servants and Other Employees' Association: 194 Royal Rd., Beau-Bassin; f. 1945; 4,342 mems.; Pres. A. H. Malleck H. Amode; Sec. R. Sumputh.

Government Labour Power Union: 7 Guy Rozemont Square, Port Louis; 950 mems.; Pres. L. L'Aimable; Sec. P. Kerpal.

Government Teachers' Union: 10 Canal Street, Beau-Bassin; 848 mems.; Pres. B. Dabee; Sec. H. Ernest.

Mauritius Labour Congress: Little Pump St., Port Louis; Pres. S. Jugdambi; Sec. C. Canabady.

Plantation Workers' Union (Amalgamated Labourers' Association): 8 Little Pump St., Port Louis; 19,896 mems.; Pres. H. Ranarain, m.l.c.; Sec. M. C. Bhagirutty.

CO-OPERATIVE SOCIETIES

There are 335 Co-operative Societies in Mauritius and Rodrigues.

The Mauritius Co-operative Union Ltd.: Co-operation House, Dumat St., Port Louis; f. 1952; 211 member societies; Sec. P. Maureemootoo.

The Mauritius Co-operative Agricultural Federation: Port Louis; f. 1950; 153 mem. societies; Chair. P. Kistnah; Sec. J. Chundunsing.

Mauritius Co-operative Wholesale Ltd.: Port Louis; f. 1949; 53 mem. societies; 32 brs.; Sec. P. T. Barosee.

TRANSPORT AND TOURISM

TRANSPORT

ROADS

Mauritius has approximately 15 km. of motorway, 547 km. of main roads, 622 km. of secondary roads and 588 km. of other roads, totalling 1,772 km. Ninety-three per cent of the roads have been asphalted. There are no railways.

SHIPPING

Regular services to Europe are provided by the British and Commonwealth Shipping Line, Scandinavian East Africa Line, Messageries Maritimes Ltd. and Nouvelle Cie. Havraise Péninsulaire and Hansa Line. Royal Interocean Lines provides a Far East-South Africa, South America, Australia, Africa service.

Other services are provided by Bank Line, Zim Israel, Compagnie Malgache de Navigation, Société Mauritienne de Navigation and Colonial Steamships Co. Ltd.

Director of Marine: Capt. V. C. Nicolin.

CIVIL AVIATION

Director of Civil Aviation: P. Soobarah.

Air Mauritius: 1 Sir William Newton St., P.O.B. 60, Port Louis; joint services with British Airways to London via Nairobi, with Air France to Paris and Réunion and to South Africa in partnership with South African Airways; Chair. A. A. Maingard; Chief Exec. Officer L. J. Ribet.

Mauritius is linked by air with Europe, Africa, India and Australia by the following airlines: Air France, Air India, Alitalia, British Airways, East African Airways, Lufthansa, Qantas, SAA and Zambia Airways. In 1972 a thrice-weekly air service to Rodrigues was inaugurated, using initially one Piper Navajo. A regular air cargo service between France and Mauritius was also begun. In 1974 an airlink to Moscow was established with the Soviet airline Aeroflot.

TOURISM

Alliance Touristique de L'Ocean Indien (ATOI): Galerie Rémy Ollier, Place Foch, Port Louis; Gen. Sec. Jaques Caradec.

Mauritius Government Tourist Office: Cerné House, La Chaussée, Port Louis; Gen. Man. Régis Fanchette.

UNIVERSITY

University of Mauritius: Reduit; f. 1965; 55 teachers, 923 full-time, 1,268 part-time students.

OTHER ISLANDS

RODRIGUES

Area 109 sq. km. Population (1968) 22,400. Administered by a Magistrate and Civil Commissioner who is advised by a committee composed of the Agricultural Officer, the Senior Medical Officer, the Roman Catholic and Anglican parish priests, the Manager of Cable and Wireless Station and 11 Rodriguans appointed by the Governor. Fishing and farming are the principal activities, there is no deep water harbour and the only links with Mauritius are thrice-weekly flights and a sea voyage every four to five weeks. The inhabitants, mostly Creoles, strongly opposed independence. Rodrigues is represented in the Legislative Assembly by two members.

THE LESSER DEPENDENCIES

The Lesser Dependencies are the islands of Agalega, lying about 935 km. north of Mauritius, and Cargados Carajos, about 400 km. to the north-east. (In 1965 the Chagos Archipelago, formerly administered by Mauritius, became part of the new British Indian Ocean Territory—*see* under Seychelles.)

MEXICO

INTRODUCTORY SURVEY

Location, Climate, Language, Religion, Flag, Capital

Mexico links North America to the Central American isthmus. Guatemala lies to the south and Cuba is 160 km. east in the Caribbean Sea. The climate varies with altitude. The lowlands are hot and wet with an average temperature of 18°c (64°F) while the highlands are temperate. Much of the north and west is desert. The principal language is Spanish, the mother tongue of 90 per cent in 1970, while about 8 per cent speak indigenous languages. About 96 per cent of the population are Roman Catholics and there are about 900,000 Protestants. The national flag (proportions 7 by 4) consists of vertical green, white and red stripes, the central white stripe being charged with the state emblem. The capital is Mexico City.

Recent History

Since 1927 the country has been governed by a nominally left wing one-party system, while maintaining a democratic form of election. In 1940 the President, Gen. Manuel Avila Camacho, embarked on a programme of industrialization which was accelerated when Mexico entered the World War in 1942. His successor, President Miguel Alemán Valdés, concentrated on expanding Mexico's educational services. Women were granted the franchise in 1953. President Adolfo López Mateos, who held office from 1958 to 1964, opposed the expulsion of Cuba from the Organization of American States in 1962. In 1963 agreement was reached with the United States over the disputed Chamizal zone, which forms part of El Paso, Texas. Under the agreement 437 acres of land were transferred to Mexico. In July 1964 Lic. Gustavo Díaz Ordaz was elected President and took office in December. The 1968 Olympic Games were held in Mexico City in October and were accompanied by violent worker and student demonstrations against the Government. Lic. Luis Echeverría Alvarez won the presidential elections of 1970 and pledged that his government would extend the benefits of Mexico's prosperity to all sectors of the population. During 1972 the Mexican government strengthened its diplomatic links with other Central and South American countries, notably Chile, Cuba and Peru. Diplomatic relations were also established with the People's Republic of China. Mexico is a member of LAFTA and the UN.

Government

The United Mexican States form a federal republic with a Constitution similar to that of the U.S.A. Mexico's executive is led by the President, elected for six years, who appoints the Cabinet. The Legislature or Congress consists of two houses, the Senate of sixty members elected for six years and the Chamber of Deputies of 194 members elected for three years. Both Presidential and Congressional elections are by direct popular vote. The federation is made up of twenty-nine states, each with its own Constitution, Governor and Chamber of Deputies, two Territories and a Federal District (Mexico City), seat of the Federal Government.

Defence

Military service is voluntary but there is a part-time conscript militia. The regular army numbers 54,000 men. The navy, including air services and marines, numbers 13,200 men. The air force numbers 6,000 men. In 1971 military expenditure amounted to 1,722 million pesos.

Economic Affairs

Agriculture accounts for about a quarter of the national income, although only 15 per cent of Mexico's land is cultivable and over 40 per cent of arable land requires artificial irrigation. Reduced farm production, due to adverse weather conditions, led to serious repercussions on the food supply in 1973. The principal crops are maize, wheat, cotton (Mexico is the world's second largest exporter), sugar cane and alfalfa. The forests provide a variety of hard and soft woods. Mexico is one of the world's leading producers of silver and sulphur, and other minerals include coal, zinc, lead and manganese. Mexico is nearly self-sufficient in oil; with the opening of new refining plant, the country's refining capacity increased from 592,000 barrels per day in 1972 to 780,000 in 1973. There has been considerable expansion of industry in recent years and 80 per cent of consumer goods are now made in Mexico. Decentralization of industry away from Mexico City is being encouraged. A law regulating foreign investment, passed in 1973, confirmed state ownership of the following industries and activities: petroleum, basic petrochemicals, electricity, railways, telegraph and wireless communications. The following activities are reserved for Mexicans or Mexican companies: radio and television, transport on federal highways, gas distribution and forestry. The law also specified the proportions of foreign holdings allowable in companies operating in other spheres of economic activity. In late 1973 the Government adopted a number of measures to curb inflation; these range from changes in the allocation of public spending to strict control of basic commodity prices.

Transport and Communications

Road transport accounts for some 70 per cent of all public passenger traffic and 60 per cent of freight traffic. Uneconomic railway lines have been replaced by highways, narrow-gauge sections by broad-gauge, and a network of feeder roads serves the main-line railways. There are 24,700 km. of railways and 160,000 km. of all-weather roads, including two sections of the Pan American Highway. About 60 per cent of the road network is paved. The difficult terrain encourages air transport and there are nearly 900 airports and landing fields. A new international airport at Manzanillo (Colima) was opened in 1973. International air transport is provided by a large number of national and foreign airlines. The chief ports are Veracruz, Tampico and Acapulco and regular shipping services are maintained by Mexican, European and American lines.

Social Welfare

Social welfare is administered by the Mexican Social Security Institute and financed by contributions from employers, employees and the Government. In May 1970 a new Labour Law was instituted to replace the existing law of 1931. It provided for longer holidays, overtime rates and restrictions, increased bonuses, sexual equality, and trade union surveillance of company tax returns. Of particular note was the innovation of compulsory profit-sharing, and the law's demand that employers provide housing for their employees. A Population Law is to be promulgated, aimed at stabilizing population growth without violating religious beliefs.

Education

State education is free and compulsory and covers two years of pre-primary and six years of primary schooling followed by three years at secondary school or a specialized institute. Much is being done in the field of adult education and the illiteracy rate dropped from 52 per cent in 1946 to 24 per cent in 1971; about a sixth of the national budget is allocated to education. About 250,000 students receive higher education. There are 38 universities.

Tourism

Mexico is much visited by Americans. The country is famous for volcanoes, coastal scenery and the great Sierra Nevada (Sierra Madre) and Rocky Mountain ranges. The relics of the Mayan and Aztec civilizations and of Spanish Colonial Mexico are of historic and artistic interest. There are many festivals. Special residence facilities are offered to foreigners wishing to retire to Mexico. Tourist facilities were improved for the Olympiad in 1968, including work on 5 airports and provision for some 20,000 more hotel beds in the main centres. Zihuatanejo on the Pacific coast and Cancún on the Caribbean are being developed as tourist resorts by the Government with funds supplied by the World Bank and the Inter-American Development Bank.

Visas are not required to visit Mexico by nationals of the following countries: Austria, Belgium, Canada, Denmark, Finland, France, the Federal Republic of Germany, Italy, Luxembourg, Netherlands, Norway, Sweden, Switzerland, the United Kingdom and the U.S.A.

Sport

Football and baseball are the chief sports and cycling, boxing, tennis, basketball, horseracing, polo, golf and climbing have a considerable following; bullfighting, rodeos and jai-alai (pelota) retain their popularity. Facilities for swimming and sea-fishing are excellent.

Public Holidays

1974: September 1st (Presidential Message), September 15th (Anniversary of *El Grito*), September 16th (Independence Day), October 12th (Discovery of America), November 1st (All Saints' Day), November 2nd (All Souls' Day), November 20th (Anniversary of the Revolution), December 12th (Our Lady of Guadalupe), December 25th (Christmas).

1975: January 1st (New Year's Day), February 5th (Constitution Day), March 21st (Birthday of Benito Juárez), March 27th–28th (Easter), May 1st (Labour Day), May 5th (Anniversary of the Battle of Puebla).

Weights and Measures

The metric system is in force.

Currency and Exchange Rates

100 centavos=1 Mexican peso.
Exchange rates (April 1974):
£1 sterling=29.49 pesos;
U.S. $1=12.50 pesos.

STATISTICAL SURVEY

AREA AND POPULATION

Area (sq. km.)	Population (June 30th, 1971)		
	Total	Federal District (including Mexico City)	Mexico City (Capital)
1,972,547	50,829,474	7,232,229	2,902,969*

Mid-1972 Estimate: Total population 52,641,000.

* Population at Census of January 28th, 1970.

1970: Births 2,132,630; Marriages 356,658; Deaths 485,656.
1971: Births 2,221,999; Marriages 373,777; Deaths 258,323.

ADMINISTRATIVE DIVISIONS
(Estimates at June 30th, 1974)

STATES	AREA (sq. km.)	POPULATION	CAPITAL
Aguascalientes . . .	5,589	393,187	Aguascalientes
Baja California . . .	70,113	1,102,250	Mexicali
Baja California, T.* . .	73,677	157,390	La Paz
Campeche	51,833	302,543	Campeche
Coahuila	151,571	1,225,210	Saltillo
Colima	5,455	287,449	Colima
Chiapas	73,887	1,767,063	Tuxtla Gutiérrez
Chihuahua	247,087	1,827,840	Chihuahua
Distrito Federal† . .	1,499	8,050,642	Mexico City
Durango	119,648	1,034,439	Durango
Guanajuato . . .	30,589	2,568,006	Guanajuato
Guerrero	63,794	1,830,590	Chilpancingo
Hidalgo	20,987	1,298,101	Pachuca
Jalisco	80,137	3,782,071	Guadalajara
México	21,461	5,292,003	Toluca
Michoacán . . .	59,864	2,572,655	Morelia
Morelos	4,941	763,247	Cuernavaca
Nayarit	27,621	633,814	Tepic
Nuevo León . . .	64,555	2,084,599	Monterrey
Oaxaca	95,364	2,164,103	Oaxaca
Puebla	33,919	2,799,511	Puebla
Querétaro . . .	11,769	560,475	Querétaro
Quintana Roo, T.* . .	50,350	114,158	Chetumal
San Luis Potosí . .	62,848	1,405,903	San Luis Potosí
Sinaloa	58,092	1,530,366	Culiacán
Sonora	184,934	1,283,127	Hermosillo
Tabasco	24,661	938,800	Villahermosa
Tamaulipas . . .	79,829	1,712,362	Ciudad Victoria
Tlaxcala	3,914	459,638	Tlaxcala
Veracruz	72,815	4,450,148	Jalapa
Yucatán	39,340	835,427	Mérida
Zacatecas	75,040	1,019,821	Zacatecas
TOTAL . . .	1,972,547	56,246,938	—

* Territory   † Federal District

PRINCIPAL TOWNS
(1970 census)

Mexico City (capital) .	2,902,969	Torreón . . .	223,104	Nuevo Laredo . .	148,867
Guadalajara .	1,194,626	Veracruz Llave . .	214,072	Matamoros . .	137,749
Monterrey . .	858,107	Mérida . . .	212,097	Reynosa . .	137,383
Ciudad Netzahualcóyotl	580,436	Aguascalientes .	181,277	Cuernavaca . .	137,117
Ciudad Juárez .	407,370	Tampico . .	179,584	Jalapa . .	122,377
Puebla de Zaragoza .	401,603	Hermosillo .	176,596	Poza Rica de Hidalgo	120,462
León . .	364,990	Acapulco de Juárez .	174,378	Mazatlán . .	119,553
Tijuana . .	277,306	Culiacán Rosales .	167,956	Irapuato . .	116,651
Mexicali .	267,356	Saltillo . .	161,114	Ciudad Obregón .	115,262
Chihuahua .	257,027	Morelia . .	161,040	Toluca de Lerdo .	114,079
San Luis Potosí .	230,039	Victoria de Durango .	150,541	Querétaro . .	112,993

ECONOMICALLY ACTIVE POPULATION

	1970*
Agriculture, Livestock, Forestry and Fishing	5,103,519
Petroleum	85,106
Mining	95,069
Manufacturing	2,169,074
Construction	571,006
Electrical Energy	53,285
Commerce	1,196,878
Transport	368,813
Services	2,158,175
Government	406,607
Others	747,525
Total	12,955,057

* Census returns.

AGRICULTURAL PRODUCTION
('ooo metric tons)

	1970–71	1971–72
Maize	9,850	8,926
Wheat	1,861	1,789
Beans	979	739
Sorghum	2,630	2,584
Sugar Cane	25,524	26,254
Cotton ('ooo bales)	1,421	1,691
Coffee ('ooo bags)	3,200	3,200

Timber (1972—provisional): Area forested 18m. hectares (1970); Production (cu. m.): Sawn timber 3,115,127, Prepared 66,439.

Livestock (1970—'ooo head): Cattle 34,696, Sheep 5,321, Goats 8,468, Horses 5,026, Pigs 11,721, Asses 3,199, Mules 2,603.

Fisheries (1972—metric tons): Total catch 301,055; Marketed 240,928; Processed 60,127.

MINING
(metric tons)

	1970	1971	1972
Antimony	4,468	3,361	2,976
Arsenic	6,922	8,717	4,481
Bismuth	571	570	629
Cadmium	1,967	1,662	1,757
Coal	188,099	167,450	143,191
Copper	61,012	63,150	78,720
Crude Petroleum ('ooo cu. m.)	28,235	29,216	31,441
Gold (kgs.)	6,166	4,694	4,543
Graphite	55,648	50,916	55,110
Iron	2,612,376	2,818,678	3,053,360
Lead	176,597	156,852	161,358
Manganese	98,609	96,081	106,424
Mercury	1,043	1,220	776
Molybdenum	141	79	78
Silenium	126	52	44
Silver	1,332	1,140	1,166
Sulphur	1,380,812	1,178,454	944,190
Tin	533	479	354
Tungsten	288	408	362
Zinc	266,400	264,972	271,844

INDUSTRY
(metric tons)

	1971
Beer ('ooo litres)	1,265,612
Cement	7,521
Cigars and Cigarettes ('ooo Packets)	2,156,158
Fertilizers	2,981,056
Paper and Cellulose	1,178,814
Pig-iron	2,353,000
Steel Ingots	3,774,000
Synthetic Fibres	110,782
Yeasts, Malt products	522,307
Tinned Foods	1,701,235
Animal Food products	474,653
Tyre and Inner Tubes ('ooo units)	16,263
Vegetable Oils and Fats	1,057,982
Vehicles (units)	212,565

FINANCE

100 centavos = 1 Mexican peso.

Coins: 1, 5, 10, 20, 25 and 50 centavos; 1 and 5 pesos.

Notes: 1, 5, 10, 20, 50, 100, 500 and 1,000 pesos.

xchange rates (April 1974): £1 sterling = 29.49 pesos; U.S. $1 = 12.50 pesos.

100 Mexican pesos = £3.39 = $8.00.

BUDGET ESTIMATES 1974
(Total public sector, million pesos)

REVENUE		EXPENDITURE	
Income Tax	31,682	Legislature	121
Tax on the Exploitation of Natural Re-		Executive	398
sources	1,100	Judiciary	173
Tax on Industry, on Production and Com-		Interior	438
merce, and on the Possession or Use of		Foreign Affairs	448
Goods and Industrial Services	14,946	Finance and Public Credit	2,829
Sales Tax (Mercantile Income)	12,692	Defence	3,121
Stamp Tax	951	Agriculture and Livestock	2,006
Import Duties	6,809	Communications and Transportation	3,348
Export Duties	765	Industry and Commerce	514
Tax on Expenses for Payment of Personal		Public Education	19,113
Labour rendered under the Management		Health and Welfare	3,706
of and Dependence on an Employer	1,041	Navy	2 019
Other Taxes	638	Labour and Social Security	198
Social Security Quotas paid by Employers		Agrarian Affairs and Settlement	705
and Workers	15,260	Water Resources	7,865
Fees for Public Services	2,659	Attorney General	145
Proceeds	1,463	National Properties	993
Other non-Tax Income	1,165	Defence Industry	152
Income derived from the sale of Goods and		Public Works	5,704
Securities	50	Tourism	218
Capital Recuperation	750	Investments	8,358
Income derived from Borrowings	37,418	Public Debt	23,746
Other Income:		Additional Expenditures	27,810
From autonomous agencies	64,355		
From state-participation enterprises	17,267	Sub-total	114,128
Borrowings of state-participation agen-		Autonomous Agencies and Federal Govern-	
cies and enterprises	19,950	ment Enterprises	116,832
TOTAL	230,961	TOTAL	230,960

Estimated Public Sector Expenditure (million pesos): 123,381 in 1972; 173,879 in 1973.

COST OF LIVING INDEX—MEXICO CITY
(1939 = 100)

	1969	1970	1971
General	897.6	951.0	981.5
Food	886.8	946.7	965.2
Domestic Services	852.9	895.5	986.7
Clothing	1,005.6	1,028.8	1,077.9

NATIONAL ACCOUNTS
(million pesos at 1960 prices)

	1969	1970
GROSS DOMESTIC PRODUCT	277,400	298,700
of which:		
Agriculture, forestry, fishing	32,912	34,730
Mining	2,777	2,818
Petroleum	11,525	12,638
Food, drink and tobacco	18,473	19,832
Textiles and leather	10,374	11,276
Wood, furniture, paper	4,774	5,138
Chemicals and plastics	8,388	9,279
Non-metallic mineral products	2,811	2,972
Basic metal industries	4,286	4,635
Metal manufactured goods	13,181	14,902
Construction	12,961	13,559
Electricity	4,812	5,341
Commerce	88,724	96,266
Transport and communications	8,714	9,406
Services	56,031	59,540
Government	15,585	16,411
Others	40,446	43,129
Banking services	3,343	3,632

CURRENCY IN CIRCULATION
(million pesos)

	1969	1970	1971	1972*
Total Currency in Circulation	44,340	49,013	53,060	64,302
of which:				
Notes	16,777	18,487	19,795	24,001
Coins	1,764	1,657	2,029	2,786
Cheques	26,095	28,869	31,236	37,514

* Provisional.

BALANCE OF PAYMENTS
(U.S. $ million)

	1971	1972*
Balance of Goods and Services . . .	−714.2	−853.3
Exports of Goods and Services . . .	3,390.7	3,973.4
Merchandise	1,473.7	1,813.7
Silver production	46.9	47.7
Tourism	616.3	726.0
Border transactions	966.9	1,061.1
Others	286.9	324.9
Imports of Goods and Services . . .	4,104.9	4,826.7
Merchandise	2,407.3	2,936.8
Tourism	172.2	220.4
Border transactions	612.5	669.0
Remittances abroad of direct foreign investments	376.3	411.0
Interest on official debts . . .	238.1	266.2
Nafinsa and others . . .	220.6	247.7
Government	17.5	18.5
Others	298.5	323.3
Net Errors, Omissions and Short-Term Capital Movements	374.9	377.5
Net Long-Term Capital Movements . .	499.7	690.6
Direct foreign investment . . .	196.1	179.0
Net share operations . . .	52.0	6.2
Credits	281.2	496.1
Placings	758.1	996.0
Redemptions	−476.9	−499.9
Net government debt . . .	− 28.9	35.6
Net credit abroad . . .	− 0.7	− 16.3
IMF Special Drawing Rights . .	39.6	49.9
Changes in the Reserve of the Bank of Mexico .	200.0	264.7

* Provisional.

EXTERNAL TRADE*
(million Mexican pesos)

	1966	1967	1968	1969	1970	1971	1972
Imports c.i.f. . . .	20,064	21,824	24,527	25,974	30,760	30,091	36,689
Exports f.o.b. . . .	14,988	14,316	15 720	17 875	17,523	18,388	22,811

* Excluding transactions in gold.

PRINCIPAL COMMODITIES

(million U.S. $)

IMPORTS	1970	1971*	EXPORTS	1970	1971*
Consumer Goods . . .	528.1	536.1	Agricultural Products . . .	410.1	423.3
Food and Beverages . .	115.4	85.2	Raw Cotton . . .	123.7	117.6
Motor Vehicles and Parts .	184.0	202.6	Coffee . . .	86.1	81.1
Other Consumer Goods . .	228.7	248.3	Tomatoes . . .	107.7	91.0
Producer Goods . . .	1,932.7	1,871.2	Melons, Oranges and Water-		
Raw and Semi-finished Materials	797.9	816.4	melon . . .	17.7	20.7
Textile Fibres . . .	13.7	12.7	Maize, Wheat and Beans .	4.1	28.1
Chemicals and Chemical Pro-			Other . . .	70.8	84.8
ducts . . .	131.1	174.4	Livestock and Meat . .	125.6	120.9
Fertilizers . . .	6.7	11.6	Livestock . . .	79.2	74.6
Pulp and Newsprint . .	35.9	22.0	Fresh Meat . . .	42.4	42.3
Iron and Steel Products .	56.4	38.6	Other . . .	4.0	4.0
Petroleum Products . .	53.9	57.3	Apiculture . . .	5.7	4.8
Other Raw and Semi-finished			Fish . . .	68.0	75.2
Materials . .	500.2	499.8	Shrimp . . .	63.0	69.1
Capital Goods . . .	1,134.8	1,054.8	Other . . .	5.0	6.1
Railway Materials . . .	17.4	7.6	Minerals . . .	219.0	195.9
Electrical Equipment . .	112.9	98.9	Zinc (ore and metal) . .	57.4	48.9
Trucks, Tractors, Earth-moving			Lead (metal) . . .	26.0	19.1
Equipment and Parts .	99.9	86.4	Fluorite . . .	23.9	29.0
Machinery and Parts . .	294.7	322.5	Sulphur . . .	16.4	15.8
Aircraft and Parts . .	55.8	22.4	Petroleum and Natural Gas .	37.9	31.1
Other Capital Goods . .	554.1	517.0	Other . . .	57.4	52.0
			Manufactured Goods . .	544.6	654.4
			Sugar and Syrup . .	97.4	102.4
			Henequen Yarn and Other		
			Textiles . . .	23.5	32.5
			Iron and Steel Products .	39.0	63.1
			Processed Fruits and vegetables	35.9	34.1
			Automobiles and Parts .	26.4	37.5
			Chemicals . . .	49.6	54.9
			Radios and TV Sets . .	16.9	18.8
			Other . . .	255.9	311.1
TOTAL . . .	2,460.8	2,407.3	TOTAL . . .	1,373.0	1,474.5

* Provisional.

PRINCIPAL COUNTRIES
(1972—'000 pesos)

	IMPORTS	EXPORTS
LAFTA	1,497,653	1,838,091
Argentina	279,671	184,698
Brazil	381,310	424,075
Chile	95,281	291,947
Colombia	31,939	223,102
Peru	157,142	150,830
Venezuela	485,152	484,702
CACM	58,745	443,331
Guatemala	19,420	162,822
Latin America (remainder)	182,910	341,540
Panama	182,447	128,138
CARIFTA	1,585	22,874
Canada	932,384	259,262
U.S.A.	22,180,901	16,103,772
America (remainder)	339,401	38,376
Netherlands Antilles	280,401	7,737
Eastern Europe	84,529	46,997
EEC	5,920,129	1,102,032
Germany, Federal Republic	3,295,260	476,620
France	1,045,029	121,209
Italy	583,128	283,402
Netherlands	553,143	169,290
EFTA	2,719,989	414,947
Norway	26,611	4,509
United Kingdom	1,160,982	176,942
Sweden	591,737	36,846
Switzerland	829,003	161,234
Western Europe (remainder)	879,179	355,623
Spain	731,937	193,487
China, People's Republic	32,019	217,843
Asia (excluding China, P. R.)	1,623,624	1,517,985
Japan	1,442,887	1,390,709
Middle East	7,569	26,689
Africa	78,854	54,355
Oceania	149,320	27,040
Australia	102,073	25,168

TOURISM

	1968	1969	1970	1971
Tourists	2,063,127	2,290,095	2,496,646	2,769,987
Total Expenditure ('000 dollars)	1,095,000	1,203,500	1,370,000	1,576,000

TRANSPORT

RAILWAYS
('ooo)

	1971	1972*
Passengers carried . .	33,500	34,288
Passenger-kilometres . .	4,361,729	4,466,647
Freight (tons) . . .	48,399	50,473
Ton-kilometres . . .	22,373,996	24,134,999

* Provisional.

ROADS

	1971	1972
Cars.	1,342,231	1,520,144
Buses	34,953	35,723
Lorries	560,262	592,772
Motor Cycles . . .	159,891	168,312

SHIPPING

	1970	1971
Registered Tonnage entered	25,628,188	29,167,390
Registered Tonnage leaving	26,012,333	29,209,016
Cargo loaded (tons) . .	19,349,958	20,041,025
Cargo unloaded (tons) .	13,021,543	15,461,644

CIVIL AVIATION

	1971	1972*
Kilometres flown (millions) .	163	183
Number of Passengers ('ooo) .	5,163	5,782
Cargo carried (tons) . .	131,373	144,459

* Provisional.

EDUCATION
(1971)

	Schools	Students	Teachers
Nursery*	3,312	468,909	13,280
Primary*	47,634	9,860,933	219,565
Secondary	2,981	871,043	67,445
Vocational	78	44,687	4,031
Preparatory	402	115,999	11,245
Commercial	759	82,821	6,712
Normal	224	62,913	5,648
Professional	282	112,793	11,702
Specialized	517	52,660	3,531

* 1972 figures.

Source: Dirección General de Estadística, Mexico D.F.; Banco Nacional de Comercio Exterior, Mexico D.F.

THE CONSTITUTION

The present Mexican Constitution was proclaimed on February 5th, 1917, at the end of the revolution which began in 1910 against the régime of Porfirio Díaz. Its provisions regarding religion, education and the ownership and exploitation of mineral wealth reflect the long revolutionary struggle against the concentration of power in the hands of the Church and the large landowners, and the struggle which culminated in the 'thirties in the expropriation of the properties of the foreign oil companies. It has been amended from time to time; the most recent amendment converted the Territory of Northern Lower California into a State.

According to the Constitution, the providing of educational facilities is the joint responsibility of the federation, the states and the municipalities. Education shall be democratic, and shall be directed to developing all the faculties of the individual, at the same time imbuing him with a love of his country and a consciousness of international solidarity and justice. Religious bodies may not provide education, except training for the priesthood. Private educational institutions must conform to the requirements of the Constitution with regard to the nature of the teaching given. The education provided by the states shall be free of charge.

Religious bodies of whatever denomination shall not have the capacity to possess or administer real estate or capital invested therein. Churches are the property of the nation; the headquarters of bishops, seminaries, convents and other property used for the propagation of a religious creed shall pass into the hands of the State, to be dedicated to the public service of the federation or of the respective state. Institutions of charity, provided they are not connected with a religious body, may hold real property. The establishment of monastic orders is prohibited. Ministers of religion must be Mexican; they may not criticize the fundamental laws of the country in a public or private meeting; they may not vote or form associations for political purposes. Political meetings may not be held in places of worship.

Article 27 of the Constitution vests direct ownership of minerals and other products of the subsoil, including petroleum and water, in the nation, and reserves to the federal government alone the right to grant concessions in accordance with the laws to individuals and companies, on the condition that they establish regular work for the exploitation of the materials. At the same time, the right to acquire ownership of lands and waters belonging to the nation, or concessions for their exploitation, is limited to Mexican individuals and companies, although the State may concede similar rights to foreigners who agree not to invoke the protection of their governments to enforce such rights. No alien may acquire direct ownership over lands and waters within an area 100 kilometres wide along the frontiers or 50 kilometres along the coast.

The same article declares null all alienations of lands, waters and forests belonging to towns or communities made by political chiefs or other local authorities in violation of the provisions of the law of June 25th, 1856,* and all concessions or sales of communally-held lands, waters and forests made by the federal authorities after December 1st, 1876. The population settlements which lack *ejidos*, or cannot obtain restitution of lands previously held, shall be granted lands in proportion to the needs of the population.

* The Lerdo Law **against ecclesiastical privilege**, which became the basis of the Liberal Constitution of 1857.

The area of land granted to the individual may not be less than 10 hectares of irrigated or watered land, or the equivalent in other kinds of land.

The owners affected by decisions to divide and redistribute land (with the exception of the owners of farming or cattle-rearing properties) shall not have any right of redress, nor may they invoke the right of *amparo* in protection of their interests. They may, however, apply to the Government for indemnification. Small properties, the areas of which are defined in the Constitution, will not be subject to expropriation. The Constitution leaves to Congress the duty of determining the maximum size of rural properties.

Monopolies and measures to restrict competition in industry, commerce or public services are prohibited.

The President and Congress. The President of the Republic, in agreement with the Council of Ministers and with the approval of Congress or of the Permanent Committee when Congress is not in session, may suspend constitutional guarantees in case of foreign invasion, serious disturbance, or any other emergency endangering the people.

Congress is composed of a Chamber of Deputies elected every three years, and a Senate whose members hold office for six years. One deputy is elected for every 200,000 inhabitants or for a fraction exceeding 100,000. The Senate is composed of two members for each state and two for the federal district. Regular sessions of Congress begin on September 1st and may not continue beyond December 31st of the same year. Extraordinary sessions may be convened by the Permanent Committee.

The powers of Congress include the right to pass laws and regulations; impose taxes; specify the bases on which the Executive may negotiate loans; declare war; raise, maintain and regulate the organization of the armed forces; establish and maintain schools of various types throughout the country; approve or reject the budget; sanction appointments submitted by the President of ministers of the Supreme Court and magistrates of the superior courts of the Federal District and the territories; approve or reject treaties and conventions made with foreign powers; and ratify diplomatic appointments.

The Permanent Committee, consisting of 29 members of Congress (15 of whom are deputies and 14 senators), officiates when Congress is in recess, and is responsible for the convening of extraordinary sessions of Congress.

The exercise of supreme executive authority is vested in the President, who is elected for six years and enters upon his office on December 1st of the year of his election. The presidential powers include the right to appoint and remove members of his cabinet, the Attorney-General, the governors of the Federal District and the territories; to appoint, with the approval of the Senate, diplomatic officials, the higher officers of the army, and ministers of the Supreme and higher courts of justice. He is also empowered to dispose of the armed forces for the internal and external security of the Federation.

In common with the constitutions of Guatemala, El Salvador, Nicaragua and Honduras, the Mexican Constitution provides for the procedure known as *juicio de amparo*—a wider form of *habeas corpus*—which the individual may invoke in protection of his constitutional rights.

A section of the Constitution deals with work and social security.

Voting rights are exercised by all Mexicans who are 18 years old.

The States. Governors are elected by popular vote in a general election every six years. The local legislature is formed by deputies, who are changed every three years. The judicature is specially appointed under the Constitution by the competent authority (it is never subject to the popular vote).

Each state is a separate unit, with the right to levy taxes and to legislate in certain matters. The states are not allowed to levy inter-state customs duties.

The Federal District consists of Mexico City and several neighbouring small towns and villages. The Governor is appointed by the President.

THE GOVERNMENT

HEAD OF THE STATE
President: Lic. LUIS ECHEVERRÍA ALVAREZ.

THE CABINET
(*March* 1974)

Secretary of the Interior: Lic. MARIO MOYA PALENCIA.

Secretary for Foreign Affairs: Lic. EMILIO O. RABASA.

Secretary for Defence: Gen. HERMENEGILDO CUENCA DÍAZ.

Secretary for the Navy: Adm. LUIS MARIO BRAVO CARRERA.

Secretary for Finance and Public Credit: Lic. JOSÉ LÓPEZ PORTILLO.

Secretary for National Property: Lic. HORACIO FLORES DE LA PEÑA.

Secretary for Industry and Commerce: Lic. JOSÉ CAMPILLO SAINZ.

Secretary for Agriculture and Livestock: Dr. OSCAR BRAUER HERRERA.

Secretary for Communications and Transport: Ing. EUGENIO MÉNDEZ DOCURRO.

Secretary for Public Works: Ing. LUIS ENRIQUE BRACAMONTES.

Secretary for Water Resources: Ing. LEANDRO ROVIROSA WADE.

Secretary for Education: Ing. VÍCTOR BRAVO AHUJA.

Secretary for Health and Public Assistance: Dr. JORGE JIMÉNEZ CANTÚ.

Secretary for Labour and Social Security: Lic. PORFIRIO MUÑOZ LEDO.

Secretary of the Presidency: Lic. HUGO CERVANTES DEL RÍO.

Chief of Agrarian Department: Lic. AUGUSTO GÓMEZ VILLANUEVA.

Chief of Tourism Department: JULIO HIRSCHFELD ALMADA.

Commissioner for Federal District: Lic. OCTAVIO SENTÍES GÓMEZ.

Attorney-General: Lic. PEDRO OJEDA PAULLADA.

DIPLOMATIC REPRESENTATION

EMBASSIES AND LEGATION ACCREDITED TO MEXICO
(In Mexico City, unless otherwise stated)

(E) Embassy; (L) Legation.

Afghanistan: Washington, D.C., U.S.A. (E).

Algeria: Ottawa, Canada (E).

Argentina: Reforma 350 (Lomas) (E); *Ambassador:* (vacant).

Australia: Paseo de la Reforma 195, 5° piso (E); *Ambassador:* O. L. DAVIS, O.B.E. (also accred. to Guatemala).

Austria: Campos Elíseos 305 (Polanco) (E); *Ambassador:* EUGEN BURESCH (also accred. to Honduras, Nicaragua, Panama).

Belgium: Dante 36, 11° piso (Anzures) (E); *Ambassador:* Baron PIERRE DE GAIFFIER D'HESTROY.

Bolivia: Avda. Mariano Escobedo 724, 6° piso (E); *Ambassador:* Dr. MARIO FRANCO FRANCO.

Brazil: Paseo de la Reforma 455 (Cuauhtémoc) (E); *Ambassador:* GERALDO DE C. SILOS.

Canada: Melchor Ocampo 463, 7° piso (Anzures) (E); *Ambassador:* MAURICE SCHWARZMANN.

Chile: Reforma 379, 5° piso (E); *Ambassador:* HUGO VIGORENA RAMÍREZ.

China, People's Republic: Campos Elíseos 69 (Chapultepec-Morales) (E); *Chargé d'Affaires a.i.:* LI SHAN-YI.

Colombia: Génova 2 (E); *Chargé d'Affaires a.i.:* Dr. CARLOS ARTURO CAPARROSO.

Costa Rica: Salamanca 102 (Roma) (E); *Ambassador:* Sra. MARIAELENA ORTIZ DE TERÁN.

Cuba: Francisco Márquez 160 (Col. Condesa) (E); *Ambassador:* Dr. FERNANDO L. LÓPEZ MUIÑO.

Czechoslovakia: Paseo de las Palmas 720 (Lomas) (E); *Ambassador:* Dr. JOSEF RUTTA.

Denmark: Campos Elíseos 170-5 (Polanco) (E); *Ambassador:* VAGN HOELGAARD (also accred. to Honduras, Panama).

Dominican Republic: Nuevo León 78-202 (Condesa) (E); *Ambassador:* Dr. GUSTAVO E. GÓMEZ CEARÁ.

Ecuador: Río Nazas 23 (Cuauhtémoc) (E); *Ambassador:* Dr. JOSÉ RICARDO MARTÍNEZ COBO.

Egypt: Avda. Rubén Darío 30 (Polanco) (E); *Ambassador:* Dr. ADEL ABDEL HAMID FADEL.

El Salvador: Galileo 17 (Polanco) (E); *Ambassador:* Gen. FIDEL TORRES.

Ethiopia: Miguel de Cervantes Saavedra 455-602 (Irrigacíon) (E); *Ambassador:* CHANYALEW TESHOME (also accred. to Venezuela).

Finland: Homero 136, 4° piso (Polanco) (E); *Ambassador:* ERIK OLOF TORNQVIST.

France: Havre 15 (Juárez) (E); *Ambassador:* JEAN BELIARD.

German Democratic Republic: Moliere 118 (Polanco) (E); *Ambassador:* GERHARD KORTH.

Germany, Federal Republic: Lord Byron 737 (Polanco) (E); *Ambassador:* Dr. HANS SCHWARZMANN.

Ghana: Washington, D.C., U.S.A. (E).

Greece: Paseo de la Reforma 284 (E); *Ambassador:* Dr. CLEON CATSAMBIS (also accred. to Nicaragua).

Guatemala: Vallarta 1, 5° piso (E); *Ambassador:* MANUEL VILLACORTA VIELMAN.

Guinea: Havana, Cuba (E).

Haiti: Humboldt 56 (E); *Ambassador:* GEORGES SALOMON.

Honduras: Avda. Juárez 64 (E); *Ambassador:* Dr. TITO H. CARCAMO TERCERO.

Iceland: Washington, D.C., U.S.A. (E).

India: Comte 44 (Anzures) (E); *Ambassador:* S. K. ROY.

Indonesia: Julio Verne 27 (Polanco) (E); *Ambassador:* HIDAYAT MUKMIN.

Israel: Río Rhin 57 (Cuauhtémoc) (E); *Ambassador:* SHLOMO ARGOV.

Italy: Liverpool 88 (Juárez) (E); *Ambassador:* Dr. RAFFAELE MARRAS.

Jamaica: Eucken 32 (Anzures) (E); *Ambassador:* Sir EGERTON R. RICHARDSON, K.T., C.M.G.

Japan: Córdoba 127, esq. Guanajuato (Roma) (E); *Ambassador:* TADAO KATO.

Korea, Republic: Paseo de Las Palmas 755, 2° piso (E); *Ambassador:* CHANG HEE LEE.

Lebanon: Julio Verne 8, esq. Campos Elíseos (Polanco) (E); *Ambassador:* Lic. JOSEPH NAFFAH (also accred. to Honduras, Nicaragua, Panama).

Luxembourg: Washington, D.C., U.S.A. (E).

Morocco: Washington, D.C., U.S.A. (E).

Netherlands: Mariano Escobedo 752, 11° y 12° pisos (E); *Ambassador:* Lic. BEREND JAN SLINGENBERG.

Nicaragua: Paseo de la Reforma 400-702 (E); *Ambassador:* Lic. EDGAR ESCOBAR FORNOS.

Norway: Virreyes 1460 (Lomas) (E); *Ambassador:* Lic. SVEN BRUN EBBELL (also accred. to Honduras, Nicaragua, Panama).

Pakistan: Washington, D.C., U.S.A. (E).

Panama: Reforma 403 (E); *Ambassador:* EMILIA AROSEMENA VALLARINO.

Paraguay: Citlaltépetl 25 (Condesa) (E); *Ambassador:* Dr. MANUEL GILL MORLIS.

Peru: Paseo de la Reforma 35 (E); *Ambassador:* Dr. ALFONSO BENAVIDES CORREA.

Philippines: Sierra Torrecillas 125 (Lomas) (E); *Ambassador:* LÉON MARÍA GUERRERO.

Poland: Cracovia 40 (San Angel) (E); *Ambassador:* Dr. MIECZYSLAW GRAD (also accred. to Honduras, Nicaragua, Panama).

Portugal: Palmas 765-202 (Lomas) (E); *Ambassador:* JOÃO MARCAL DE ALMEIDA (also accred. to Honduras).

Saudi Arabia: Washington, D.C., U.S.A. (E).

Senegal: Washington, D.C., U.S.A. (E).

Spain: Londres 7 (Juárez) (L); *Chargé d'Affaires:* MANUEL MARTÍNEZ FEDUCHY; represents the Spanish Republican Government in exile.

Sri Lanka: Washington, D.C., U.S.A. (E).

Sweden: Homero 136, 10° piso (E); *Ambassador:* CARL SWARTZ.

Switzerland: Hamburgo 66, 5° y 6° pisos (Juárez) (E). *Ambassador:* ALFRED FISCHLI (also accred. to Jamaica).

Syria: New York, U.S.A. (E).

Trinidad and Tobago: Washington, D.C., U.S.A. (E).

Tunisia: Washington, D.C., U.S.A. (E).

Turkey: Avda. de las Palmas 1525 (Lomas) (E); *Ambassador:* DOGAN TURKMEN (also accred. to Honduras, Nicaragua, Panama).

U.S.S.R.: Calzada de Tacubaya 204 (Condesa) (E); *Ambassador:* NIKOLAI KONSTANTINOVICH TARASOV.

United Kingdom: Lerma 71 (Cuauhtémoc) (E); *Ambassador:* JOHN EDGAR GALSWORTHY, C.M.G.

U.S.A.: Reforma 305 (E); *Ambassador:* JOSEPH JOHN JOVA.

Uruguay: Hegel 149, 1° piso (Polanco) (E); *Ambassador:* JUAN BAUTISTA OCHOTECO.

Venezuela: Edif. Simón Bolívar, Londres 167 (Juárez) (E); *Ambassador:* ROBERTO MOREAN SOTO.

Yugoslavia: Prado Sur 225 (Lomas) (E); *Ambassador:* VOJISLAV COLOVIC (also accred. to Honduras, Panama).

STATES AND TERRITORIES

Federal District: Octavio Sentíes Gómez.

STATE GOVERNORS

Aguascalientes: Prof. Enrique Olivares Santana.
Baja California Norte: Milton Castellanos.
Campeche: Rafael Rodríguez Barrera.
Coahuila: Eulalio Gutiérrez Treviño.
Colima: Prof. Pablo Silva García.
Chiapas: Dr. Manuel Velasco Suárez.
Chihuahua: Oscar Flores.
Durango: Alejandro Paez Urquidi.
Guanajuato: Luis Humberto Ducoing.
Guerrero: Israel Nogueda Otero.
Hidalgo: Lic. Carlos Ramírez Guerrero.
Jalisco: Alberto Orozco Romero.
México: Prof. Carlos Hank González.
Michoacán: Carlos Torres Manzo.
Morelos: Ing. Felipe Riva Palacio.

Nayarit: Lic. Roberto Gómez Reyes.
Nuevo León: Lic. Pedro G. Zorrilla Martínez.
Oaxaca: Lic. Fernando Gómez Sandoval.
Puebla: Guillermo Morales Blumenkron.
Querétaro: Antonio Calzada Urquiza.
San Luis Potosí: Lic. Antonio Rocha.
Sinaloa: Lic. Alfredo Valdez Montoya.
Sonora: Faustino Felix.
Tabasco: Mario Trujillo García.
Tamaulipas: Manuel Ravizé.
Tlaxcala: Gen. Ignacio Bonilla.
Veracruz: Lic. Rafael Murillo Vidal.
Yucatán: Carlos Loret de Mola.
Zacatecas: Ing. Pedro Ruíz Gonzlez.

TERRITORIAL GOVERNORS

Baja California Sur: Félix Agramont Cota.

Quintana Roo: Lic. David Gustavo Gutiérrez Ruiz.

PRESIDENT

PRESIDENTIAL ELECTION
(July 5th, 1970)

Luis Echevarría Alvarez: Partido Revolucionario Institucional; 11,923,755.
Efraín González Morfín: Partido Acción Nacional;
1,945,391.
Other Candidates: 158,670.

CONGRESS

SENATE
(*Elections*, July 1970)
President: Prof. Enrique Olivares Santana.
The Partido Revolucionario Institucional won all 60
seats.

FEDERAL CHAMBER OF DEPUTIES
(*Elections*, July 1973)
President: Luis Dantón Rodríguez.

Party	Seats
Partido Revolucionario Institucional . .	180
Partido Acción Nacional . . .	25
Partido Popular Socialista . . .	10
Partido Auténtico de la Revolución Mexicana	7
Total	222

POLITICAL PARTIES

Partido Revolucionario Institucional (PRI): f. 1928 as the *Partido Nacional Revolucionario*, but is regarded as the natural successor to the victorious parties of the revolutionary period; broadly based and moderately left-wing Government party; Pres. JESÚS REYES HEROLES; Gen. Sec. ENRIQUE GONZÁLEZ PEDRERO; Presidential candidate (1970) LUIS ECHEVERRÍA ALVAREZ; publ. *La República*.

Partido Acción Nacional (PAN): Serapio Rendón 8, 4° piso, Mexico 4, D.F.; f. 1939; Radical opposition party; Presidential candidate (1970) EFRAÍN GONZÁLEZ MORFÍN; Gen. Sec. G. MEDINA VALDEZ; publ. *La Nación*.

Partido Popular Socialista (PPS): left-wing party; demands the liquidation of large land holdings (*latifundios*) and the nationalization of many sectors of the economy; Pres. JORGE CRUIKSHANK GARCÍA.

Partido Auténtico de la Revolución Mexicana (PARM): to sustain the ideology of the Mexican Social Revolution, as embodied in the Mexican Political Constitution of 1917; 191,546 mems.; Pres. Gen. JUAN BARRAGÁN; publ. *El Auténtico*.

The following parties are not legally recognized:

Partido Comunista Mexicano: Frontera 100-304, Mexico 7, D.F.; f. 1919; Sec. ARNOLDO MARTÍNEZ VERDUGO; publs. *Oposición, La Voz de México*.

Movimiento de Liberación Nacional (MLN): f. 1961; Leader Prof. HERBERTO CASTILLO.

Central Campesina Independiente (CCI): left-wing; f. 1963; Leaders ARTURO CORONA, RAMÓN DANZOS PALOMINO, ALFONSO GARZÓN SANTIBÁÑEZ.

JUDICIAL SYSTEM

The Mexican legal system follows strictly the principle of written law. Accordingly, the definition of rights and duties, and their scope, and the procedure to ensure and enforce them are fixed in codes, such as the civil code, criminal procedure code, etc. The penal code of January 1st, 1930, abolished the death penalty, except for the army.

The courts include the Supreme Court with twenty-one ministers; five Circuit Collegiate Tribunals (*Tribunales Colegiados de Circuito*), each with three magistrates; six Circuit Unitary Tribunals (*Tribunales Unitarios de Circuito*), each with six magistrates; and forty-six District Courts with forty-six judges. The system of trial by jury also exists. Ministers of the Supreme Court, circuit magistrates and district judges, once appointed, may only be removed on the ground of misconduct.

SUPREME COURT
President: Lic. ALFONSO GUZMÁN NEYRA.

FIRST CHAMBER—PENAL AFFAIRS
President: Lic. MARIO G. REBOLLEDO FERNÁNDEZ.

SECOND CHAMBER—ADMINISTRATIVE AFFAIRS
President: Lic. JORGE SARACHO ALVAREZ.

THIRD CHAMBER—CIVIL AFFAIRS
President: Lic. RAFAEL ROJINA VILLEGAS.

FOURTH CHAMBER—LABOUR AFFAIRS
President: Lic. SALVADOR MONDRAGÓN.

AUXILIARY CHAMBER
President: Lic. ANTONIO CAPPONI GUERRERO.

RELIGION

RELIGIOUS AFFILIATION
(1970 Census)

Roman Catholic	.	46,380,401	Others	. .	150,329
Protestant	.	876,879	None	. .	768,448
Jewish	. .	49,181	Not indicated		—

ROMAN CATHOLIC

The prevailing religion is Roman Catholicism, but the Church, disestablished in 1857, is, under the Constitution of 1917, subject to State control.

METROPOLITAN SEES:

Chihuahua . . Most Rev. ADALBERTO ALMEIDA MERINO.
Suffragan See: Ciudad Juárez.

Durango . . Most Rev. ANTONIO LÓPEZ AVIÑA.
Suffragan Sees: Culiacán, Mazatlán, Torreón.

Guadalajara . . His Eminence Cardinal JOSÉ SALAZAR LÓPEZ.
Suffragan Sees: Aguascalientes, Autlán, Colima, Tepic, Zacatecas.

Hermosillo/Sonora Most Rev. CARLOS QUINTERO ARCE.
Suffragan Sees: Ciudad Obregón, Mexicali, Tijuana.

Jalapa . . Most Rev. EMILIO ABASCAL SALMERÓN.
Suffragan Sees: Papantla, San Andreas Tuxtla, Tuxpan, Vera Cruz.

Mexico City . . His Eminence Cardinal MIGUEL DARÍO MIRANDA Y GÓMEZ.
Suffragan Sees: Acapulco, Chilapa, Cuernavaca, Texcoco, Tlalnepantla, Tula, Tulancingo.

Monterrey . . Most Rev. ALFONSO ESPINO Y SILVA.

Monterrey—*cont.* . . **Suffragan Sees:** Saltillo, San Luís Potosí, Tampico, Matamoros, Ciudad Valles, Linares, Ciudad Victoria.

Morelia . . Most Rev. Estanislao Alcaraz Figueroa.
Suffragan Sees: León, Querétaro, Tacámbaro, Zamora, Apatzingán, Ciudad Altamirano.

Oaxaca/Antequera Most Rev. Ernesto Corripio Ahumada.
Suffragan Sees: Chiapas, Tapachula, Tehuantepec, Tuxtla Gutierrez.

Puebla de los Angeles . . Most Rev. Octaviano Márquez y Tóriz.
Suffragan Sees: Huejutla, Huajuápan de León, Tehuacan, Tlaxcala.

Yucatán . . Most Rev. Manuel Castro Ruiz.
Suffragan Sees: Campeche, Tabasco.

PROTESTANT

Episcopalian Church: La Otra Banda 40, Mexico 20, D.F.; Bishop: Rt. Rev. José Guadalupe Saucedo; suffragan bishops in Monterrey and Guadalajara.

Iglesia Metodista de México: Calzada México Coyoacán 349, Mexico 13, D.F.; Bishop: Rt. Rev. Alejandro Ruíz M.

Federación Evangélica de México: Apdo. 1830, Mexico, D.F.

Most of the main protestant denominations have churches in the larger cities; there are also Jewish synagogues in Mexico City, Monterrey and other centres.

THE PRESS

DAILY NEWSPAPERS

Mexico City

ABC: Avda. Morelos 58; f. 1953; morning; Publisher Federico Barrera Fuentes; circ. 48,000.

La Afición: Ignacio Mariscal 23, Apdo. 64 *bis*; f. 1930; sport, entertainment; Dir. Antonio Andere; Gen. Man. Rafael Ruano Uribe; circ. 92,500.

Avance: Iturbide 36b; f. 1967; Dir. Fernando Alcalá Bates; circ. 25,000.

Cine Mundial: Bucareli 20, 4° piso, Apdo. 21099; f. 1953; morning; entertainments; Dir. Octavio Alva; circ. 50,000.

El Día: Avda. Insurgentes Centro 123, Apdo. 10528; f. 1962; morning; Nationalist, loyal to the National Revolution; Dir.-Gen. Enrique Ramírez y Ramírez; circ. 20,000.

Diario de Mexico: Chimalpopoca 34; f. 1951; Dir. Federico Bracamontes; circ. 47,000.

Diario de la Tarde: Balderas 87; f. 1957; evening edition of *Novedades*; Dir. Rómulo O'Farrill, Sr.; circ. 82,000.

Esto: Guillermo Prieto 7; f. 1941; morning; sports appeal; Dir. José García Valseca; circ. 145,000.

Excélsior: Paseo Reforma 18, Apdo. 120 *bis*; f. 1917; morning; independent; Dir. Julio Scherer García; circ. 175,000.

El Heraldo de México: Dr. Carmona y Valle 150; f. 1965; morning; publ. by Editora Alarcón S.A.; Dir. Gabriel Alarcón; circ. 175,000.

Monitor Comercial: Versalles 38, Col. Juárez; f. 1918; morning; business news; Dir. and Editor Alejandro Hernández Romo; circ. 6,000.

El Nacional: Ignacio Mariscal 25, Apdo. 446; f. 1929; morning; official government organ; Dir. Agostín Arroyo; circ. 60,000.

The News: Balderas y Morelos; f. 1950; morning; English; publ. by Publicaciones Herrerías; Pres. Rómulo O'Farrill; Editor Jaime Plenn; circ. 24,000.

Novedades: Balderas 87; f. 1936; morning; independent; publ. by Publicaciones Herrerías; Pres. Rómulo O'Farrill, Sr.; Vice-Pres. and Editor Rómulo O'Farrill, Jr.; circ. 140,000.

Ovaciones: Lago Zirahuen 279; f. 1947; morning and evening editions; Dir. Lic. Fernando González D.L.; circ. 220,000.

La Prensa: Basilio Vadillo 40; f. 1928; independent pictorial tabloid; publ. by Editora de Periódicos, S.C.L.; Dir. Mario Santaella; circ. 185,361.

El Sol de México: Guillermo Prieto 7; f. 1965; morning and evening editions; Dir. José García Valseca; circ. 157,000.

Ultimas Noticias de Excélsior: Paseo Reforma 18, Apdo. 120 *bis*; f. 1936; afternoon and evening editions; independent; Dir. Manuel Becerra Acosta; circ. 47,000.

El Universal: Bucareli 8; f. 1916; morning; independent; Conservative; Editor R. Alcántara Pastor; circ. 165,000.

El Universal Gráfico: Bucareli 8; f. 1927; evening; independent pictorial tabloid; Editor Alfonso Argudín; circ. 74,228.

Aguascalientes

El Heraldo: José María Chávez 114; f. 1945; morning; Dir. Leandro Martínez Bernal; circ. 17,000.

El Sol del Centro: Avda. Madero 460, Apdo. 88; f. 1945; morning; Dir. José García Valseca; circ. 20,000.

Chihuahua

El Fronterizo: f. 1943; morning; Editor Oscar W. Ching Vega; circ. 33,596.

El Heraldo: Avda. Universidad 2507, Apdo. 1515; f. 1927; morning and evening; Dir. José García Valseca; circ. 45,000.

Norte: Juárez 1105, Apdo. 477; f. 1954; morning; Dir. Luis Fuentes Saucedo; circ. 16,000.

Ciudad Juárez

El Fronterizo: Ramón Corona y Galeana; f. 1943; morning; Prop. Cadena de Periódicos García Valseca; circ. 34,000.

El Mexicano: Ramón Corona y Galeana; f. 1947; evening; Prop. Cadena de Periódicos García Valseca; circ. 23,000.

Ciudad Obregón

Diario del Yaqui: Sinaloa 418 Sur, Apdo. 196; f. 1942; morning; Dir. Jesús Corral Ruiz; circ. 15,000.

CULIACÁN

El Sol de Culiacán: f. 1956; evening; Dir. José García Valseca; circ. 15,000.

El Sol de Sinaloa: f. 1956; morning; Dir. José García Valseca; circ. 16,000.

DURANGO

El Sol de Durango: Zaragosa 202 Sur, Apdo. 184; f. 1947; morning; Prop. Cadena de Periódicos García Valseca; Dir. Bertha Isaac Ahumada; circ. 15,000.

GUADALAJARA

El Informador: Unión Editorial S.A., Independencia 300, Apdo. 3 bis; f. 1917; morning; independent, conservative; Dir. Jorge Alvarez del Castillo; circ. 45,000.

El Occidental: Independencia 324 Sur, Apdo. 699; f. 1942; morning; conservative; Propr. Cadena de Periódicos García Valseca; Dir. Ernesto Corona Ruesga; circ. 85,000.

El Sol de Guadalajara: f. 1948; evening; Propr. Cadena de Periódicos García Valseca; Dir. Ernesto Corona Ruesga; circ. 60,000.

HERMOSILLO

El Imparcial: Mina y Sufragio Efectivo 71; f. 1937; evening; independent; Dir. José A. Healy; circ. 12,000.

El Sonorense: Veracruz y 12 de Octubre; f. 1963; morning; independent; Editor José Luis Argelles; circ. 18,500.

IRAPUATO

El Sol de Irapuato: f. 1954; morning; Propr. Cadena de Periódicos García Valseca; circ. 25,000.

LEÓN

El Heraldo: Hermanos Aldama 222, Apdo. 299; f. 1957; morning; independent; Editor Miguel Barragán T; circ. 35,000.

El Sol de León: Francisco I. Madero 312; f. 1946; morning; general appeal; Propr. Cadena de Peródicos García Valseca; Man. Luis Bernal Santos; circ. 44,000.

MATAMOROS

El Gráfico: Calle 6a 200; f. 1964; midday; independent; Dir. Juan Villarreal de los Santos; circ. 15,000.

El Regional: Dir. Camilio Fuentes; circ. 10,000.

MAZATLÁN

El Sol del Pacífico: Aquiles Serdán y H. Galeana; f. 1947; morning; Dir. Ernesto Centeno Carreón; circ. 17,000.

Noticias de El Sol: Aquiles Serdán y H. Galeana; f. 1964; evening; Dir. Ernesto Centeno Carreón; circ. 15,000.

MÉRIDA

Diario del Sureste: Calle 60 532, Apdo. 35; f. 1931; morning; organ of state government; Dir. Pedro Pacheco Herrera; circulates in States of Yucatán, Campeche, Tabasco and Territory of Quintana Roo; circ. 24,000.

Diario de Yucatán: Calle 60 521, Apdo. 64; f. 1925; morning; independent; Editor Abel Menéndez; circulates in States of Yucatán, Campeche, Chiapas, Tabasco and Veracruz and Territory of Quintana Roo; circ. 50,000, Sunday 52,000.

Novedades de Yucatán: Calle 62 514; f. 1965; morning; independent; Man. Andrés García Lavín; circulates in Yucatán and other states; circ. 46,000, Sunday 47,000.

MEXICALI

La Voz de la Frontera: Avda. Francisco I. Madero 1545; morning; independent; Dir. and Editor Jorge Davo Lozano; circulates in State of Baja California; circ. 34,000.

MICHOACÁN

La Voz de Michoacán: Quintana Roo 186, Apdo. 121; f. 1948; morning; independent; Dir. José Tocavén; circ. 21,000.

MONTERREY

El Norte: Washington 629, Apdo. 186; f. 1938; morning; independent; magazine supplement; Editor Alejandro Junco de la Vega; circulates in States of Nuevo León, Tamaulipas, Coahuila, San Luis Potosí; circ. 72,000, Sunday 78,000.

El Porvenir: Galeana Sur 344, Apdo. 218; f. 1919; morning; Catholic; Dir. Rogelio Cantú; circ. 44,000, Sunday 48,000.

El Sol: Washington 629, Apdo. 186; f. 1922; evening; independent; Editor Alejandro Junco de la Vega; circ. 46,000.

Tribuna de Monterrey: f. 1968; morning; Propr. Cadena de Periódicos García Valseca; circ. 65,000.

NUEVO LAREDO

El Diario de Nuevo Laredo: González 2411, Apdo. 101; f. 1948; morning; independent; Dir. Ruperto Villarreal; circ. 15,000.

OAXACA

El Imparcial: Armanta y López 312, Apdo. 322; f. 1951; morning; independent; Dir. Manuel G. Pichardo; circ. 3,200.

PUEBLA DE ZARAGOZA

El Sol de Puebla: Avda. 3 Oriente 201, Apdo. 190; f. 1944; morning; Propr. Cadena de Periódicos García Valseca; Man. Salvador Borrego Escalante; circ. 43,000.

La Voz de Puebla: Avda. 3 Oriente 201, Apdo. 190; f. 1953; evening; Propr. Cadena de Periódicos García Valseca; Man. Salvador Borrego Escalante; circ. 35,000.

REYNOSA

El Mañana: Río Guayalejo 103, Apdo. 14; f. 1932; morning; independent; special sections for principal towns in State of Tamaulipas; Dir. Heriberto Deánder Amador; circ. 45,000.

SALTILLO

El Heraldo: Bravo Norte 395, Apdo. 451; f. 1963; morning; independent; Editor Ing. Javier de la Peña; circ. 7,000.

El Sol del Norte: Cuauhtémoc 349 Sur; f. 1963; morning; Propr. Cadena de Periódicos García Valseca; Man. Roberto Escamilla González; circ. 19,000.

SAN LUIS POTOSÍ

El Heraldo: Villerías y Guerrero, Apdo. 304; f. 1942; morning; independent; Gen. Man. Mauricio Bercún; circ. 24,000, Sunday 27,000.

El Sol de San Luis: Avda Universidad 565, Apdo. 342; f. 1952; morning; independent; Dir. Ignacio Rosillo; circ. 29,000.

TAMPICO

El Mundo: Ejército Nacional 201, Col. Guadalupe, Apdo. 379; f. 1918; morning; independent; Man. Germán Sigrist López; circ. 66,014, Sunday 67,044.

El Sol de Tampico: Altamira 311 Pte., Apdo. 434; f. 1950; morning (evening edition *El Sol de la Tarde*); Propr. Cadena de Periódicos García Valseca; Man. RUBÉN DÍAZ DE LA GARZA; circ. 75,000.

TIJUANA

El Mexicano: Avda. México 120; f. 1959; morning; independent; special editions for Mexicali and Ensenada; Dir. Lic. ENRIQUE GALVÁN; circ. 42,000.

TORREÓN

La Opinión: Matamoros y Falcón, Apdo. 86; f. 1917; morning; independent; Dir. EDMUNDO GUERRERO ALVAREZ; circ. 32,000, Sunday 36,500; evening edition *La Opinión de la Tarde*, circ. 10,000.

El Siglo de Torreón: Avda. Matamoros 1056 Pte., Apdo. 19; f. 1922; morning; independent; Conservative; Dir. ANTONIO DE JUAMBELZ; circ. 29,000.

VERACRUZ LLAVE

El Dictamen: Miguel Lerdo 87, Apdo. 232; f. 1898; morning; independent; Dir. JUAN MALPICA MIMENDI; circ. 23,000, Sunday 30,000; evening edition *La Tarde*, circ. 21,000.

La Nación: Pino Suárez 260, Apdo. 272; f. 1963; morning; independent; Dir. Ing. FERNANDO DE LA MIYAR B.; circ. 19,000.

PERIODICALS

MEXICO CITY

Alarma: Manuel Ma. Contreras 30; f. 1963; weekly; publ. by Publicaciones Llergo S.A.; Dir.-Gen. MARIO SOJO ACOSTA; circ. 800,000.

Artes de México: Amores 262; monthly; art history and anthropology; Spanish and English editions; Dir. JOSÉ LOZADA TOMÉ; circ. 20,000.

Automundo: Editorial Mex-Abril S.A., Morelos 16, 4° piso; f. 1970; monthly; motoring and tourism; Pres. RÓMULO O'FARRILL; Editor LUIS ARENAS ROSAS; circ. 40,000.

El Campo: Mar Negro 147, Apdo. 17-506; f. 1924; monthly; agricultural; Dir. ARMANDO PALAFOX FLORES; circ. 27,000.

Casos de Alarma: Manuel Ma. Contreras 30; f. 1971; weekly; Dir.-Gen. BENJAMÍN ESCAMILLA; circ. 1,050,000.

Cine Avance: 5 de Febrero 246, 2° piso; f. 1962; weekly; cinema; publ. by Editorial Ferro S.A.; Dir. LINCOLN SALAZAR GRIS; circ. 76,000.

Cine Universal: Arteaga 33; weekly; cinema; Dir. FRANCISCO CABRAL RÍOS; circ. 48,000.

Claudia: Morelos 16, 4° piso; f. 1965; monthly; women's magazine with accent on fashion; publ. by Editorial Mex-Abril, S.A.; Dir. ANNA I. FUSONI; circ. 119,000.

Comercio: Reforma 42, Apdo. 32005; f. 1960; monthly; organ of the Cámara Nacional de Comercio de la Ciudad de México; Dir. PORFIRIO REYES LAMADRID; circ. 40,000.

Confidencias: Plaza de la República 48, 5° piso; weekly; popular appeal; Dir. Prof. JULIO ALAIZ DEL VALLE; circ. 108,000.

Contenido: Liverpool 10-201; f. 1963; monthly; popular appeal; Dir. ARMANDO AYALA A.; circ. 130,000.

El Correo Económico: Mirto 25; f. 1963; fortnightly; commercial and economic; Dir. GREGORIO ROSAS HERRERA; circ. 25,000.

Diversión: Manuel Ma. Contreras 30; f. 1967; weekly; Dir. MARIO SOJO ACOSTA; circ. 150,000.

Escuela: México-Coyoacán 321; f. 1954; monthly; education; Dir. Luís FERNÁNDEZ G.; circ. 45,000.

La Familia: Tacubaya 103; f. 1927; fortnightly women's magazine; Dir. LUCILA RUIZ; circ. 130,000.

La Familia Cristiana: Taxqueña 1792, Apdo. 19082: f. 1953; monthly; Dir. JUÁN MANUEL GALAVIZ H.; circ. 75,000.

Feminidades: Tenayuca 55, 5° piso; f. 1946; monthly; women's magazine; publ. by Prensa Especializada S.A.; Dir. ARTURO TORRES YÁNEZ; circ. 75,000.

El Figaro: Morelos 45-406; f. 1952; weekly; general interest; Dir. J. SALVADOR ACEVEDO L.; circ. 55,000.

Fotomundo: Editorial Mex-Abril S.A., Morelos 16, 4° piso; f. 1969; monthly; photography; Editor JULIO PERALES GAY; circ. 30,000.

Hoy: Sinaloa 20-402; f. 1937; weekly; political, literary; Dir.-Gen. RAYMUNDO AMPUDIA; circ. 30,000.

Impacto: Manuel Ma. Contreras 30; f. 1949; weekly; general interest; Dir.-Gen. REGINO HERNÁNDEZ LLERGO; circ. 37,000.

Intercambio: Tiber 103, 6° piso; monthly; organ of the British Chamber of Commerce; Editor N. PELHAM WRIGHT; circ. 3,000.

Ja-Já: Reforma 18, 4° piso; f. 1940; weekly; humorous; Dir. FRANCISCO PATIÑO; circ. 58,000.

Jueves de Excélsior: Reforma 18; weekly; publ. by Excélsior y Cía; general information; Dir. MANUEL HORTA; circ. 27,000.

Kena: 5 de Febrero 246, 2° piso; f. 1963; fortnightly; women's magazine; publ. by Editorial Ferro, S.A.; Dir. MARÍA EUGENIA MORENO; circ. 170,000.

El Libro y el Pueblo: Subsecretaría de Asuntos Culturales, esq. Argentina y Luis González Obregón; monthly; organ of the Secretaría de Educación Pública; Dir. PEDRO GUILLÉN; bibliographical and cultural.

El Médico: Hamburgo 31, 4° piso; f. 1950; monthly; medical; Dir. CYRUS COOPER; circ. 20,000.

Mexican American Review: Lucerna 78, Apdo. 82 *bis*; monthly; organ of the American Chamber of Commerce of Mexico; Editor STUART J. BARNES; circ. 3,000.

México al Día: Río Tíber 103; f. 1926; fortnightly; general interest; publ. by Impresora y Editora Mexicana, S.A. de C.V.; Dir. LUIS GABRIEL TORRES; circ. 30,000.

Mexico This Month: Atenas 42-201; f. 1955; monthly; English; Dir. ANITA BRENNER; circ. 30,000.

Mujer de Hoy: Avena 23; f. 1960; fortnightly; women's magazine; Dir. RAIMUNDO AMPUDIA; circ. 105,000.

Negocios y Bancos: Bolívar 8-601, Apdo. 1907; f. 1951; monthly; business; Dir. ALFREDO FARRUGIA REED; circ. 60,000.

Nocturno: Morelos 16, 4° piso; f. 1964; fortnightly; women's magazine; publ. by Editorial Mex-Abril, S.A.; Man. JORGE DE ANGELI; circ. 119,000.

Notitas Musicales: Illinois 55, Col. Napolés; f. 1956; monthly; music; popular appeal; Dir. ENRIQUE ORTIZ REYES SPÍNDOLA; circ. 120,000.

Panorama: Miguel Schultz 140; f. 1906; monthly; organ of the Asociación Nacional Automovilística; Dir. PEDRO MARTÍN PUENTE; circ. 30,000.

El Redondel: Avda. Juárez 104-25, Apdo. 2349; f. 1928; weekly; bullfighting; Editor ALBERTO DE ICAZA; circ. 45,000.

Tiempo: Gen. Prim 38, Apdo. 1122; f. 1942; weekly; general interest; Dir. A. DIEZ DE LA CRUZ; circ. 22,000.

Tierra: Díaz Mirón 58; f. 1945; monthly; agricultural; Dir. Ing. GABRIEL ITIE; circ. 42,000.

Todo: Hamburgo 36, Apdo. 2517; f. 1933; general, literary and political; Man. Dir. ENRIQUE SALCEDO LEDESMA; circ. 38,000.

Visión: Hamburgo 20; fortnightly; Latin America news and general; Dir. JULIO G. SMITH FOVO.

ASSOCIATIONS

Agrupación Nacional Periodística: Avda. Juárez 76-609, Mexico 1, D.F.; Pres. DOMINGO SALAYANDÍA.

Asociación Mexicana de Periodistas A.C.: Filomeno Mata 8, 3° piso, Mexico, D.F.

PRESS AGENCIES

A.P.: Paseo de Reforma 46, Mexico, D.F.; Exec. Rep. for Central America CHARLES H. GREEN.

Četeka: Avda. Morelos 58, Mexico 1, D.F.; Man. HORYMÍR JUNEK.

Kyodo News Service: Avda. San Juan de Letran 100-401, Mexico 1, D.F.

U.P.I.: Avda. Morelos 110, Mexico 10, D.F.; Man. H. DENNY DAVIS.

D.P.A., Prensa Latina, Reuters and Tass also have offices in Mexico.

PUBLISHERS

MEXICO CITY

Editorial Abeja, S.A.: Londres 35, Coyoacán; Dir. ROBERTO M. GILBERT.

Editorial Acrópolis: Palma Norte 518, Apdo. 1718; f. 1944; Propr. JOSÉ GONZÁLEZ PORTO; Man. Dir. LUIS ALVAREZ PASTOR; publs. *Enciclopedia UTEHA para la Juventud, Enciclopedia Cultural, Libro de Oro de los Niños, Libro de Nuestros Hijos, Sagrada Biblia,* etc.

Aguilar Editor S.A.: Avda. Universidad 757; fine and applied art, history, geography, medicine, children's books, fiction.

Ediciones Alonso: Regina 84-15; f. 1929; Propr. JOSÉ E. M. ALONSO; publs. *Boletín Particular Técnico-Fiscal* (circ. 7,000) as well as fiscal law books.

Ediciones Andrade, S.A.: Colima 213; Dir. MANUEL ANDRADE D.

Ediciones Andrea: Edison 62; Dir. P. F. DE ANDREA.

Ediciones Ateneo: Guerrero 62; Dir. MODESTO VÁZQUEZ GARCÍA.

Editorial Avante: Luis González Obregón 9 (altos); Dir. ALBERTO CASTRO FLORES.

Editorial Azteca S.A.: Calle de la Luna 225-7, Mexico 3, D.F.; f. 1956; literature and technical; Man. Dir. A. ALEMÓN JALOMO.

Librería y Ediciones Botas, S.A.: Justo Sierra 52, Apdo. 941; f. 1905; Dir. ANDRÉS BOTAS ARREDONDO; history, law, philosophy, poetry, fiction.

Editorial Casa de América: Motolinia 2.

Casa Unida de Publicaciones: Héroes 83, Col. Guerrero, Apdo. 97 *bis*; f. 1921; Man. Prof. JUAN DÍAZ GALINDO; philosophy, history, religion.

Central de Publicaciones, S.A.: Juárez 4; f. 1933; art; Dir. ALBERTO J. MISRACHI.

Compañía Editorial Continental, S.A.: Calzada de Tlalpan 4620, Mexico 22, D.F.; science, technology, general, textbooks; Man. Dir. J. NORIEGA MILERA.

Editorial Cumbre, S.A.: Guanajuato 215, 2° piso, Mexico 7, D.F.

Editorial Esfinge, S.A.: Colima 220-503; geography, history, philosophy, law, literature and mathematics.

Editorial Diana S.A.: Roberto Gayol 1219, Mexico 14, D.F.; f. 1946; Man. Dir. J. L. RAMÍREZ COTO; general fiction and technical books.

Ediciones Era S.A.: Avena 102, Mexico 13, D.F.; f. 1960; Man. Dir. Mrs. NIEVES ESPRESATE; general and social science.

Fondo de Cultura Económica: Avda. Universidad 975, Mexico 12, D.F.; f. 1934; Dir. F. J. ALEJO L.; economics, history, philosophy, science, politics, psychology, sociology.

Editorial González Porto: Avda. Independencia 10, Apdo. 140 *bis*; f. 1922; Dir. JOSÉ GONZÁLEZ PORTO; literary, scientific and technical works; brs. throughout Latin America.

Editorial Grijalbo S.A.: Avda. Granjas 82, Mexico 17, D.F.; f. 1954; Man. Dir. A. L. QUINTANAR.

Nueva Editorial Interamericana S.A. de C.V.: Cedro 512, Apdo. 26370, Mexico 4, D.F.

W. M. Jackson Inc.: Avda. Insurgentes Sur 993, 6° piso, Mexico 12, D.F.

Ediciones Larousse, S.A.: Marsella 53; Dir. PIERRE SADORGE.

Editora Latino Americana, S.A.: Guatemala 10-220; Dir. ROGER ORELLANA GALLARDO.

Ediciones Lerner Mexicana: Newton 186; f. 1966; Dir. LUIS M. REGALADO L.; publ. *Tribuna Médica* (circ. 20,000).

Publicaciones Llergo, S.A.: Manuel Ma. Contreras 30, Apdo. 2986; f. 1949; Dir. REGINO HERNÁNDEZ LLERGO; Gen. Man. MARIO SOJO ACOSTA; publs. *Impacto, Alarma, Diversión, Casos de Alarma.*

Editorial Limusa, S.A.: Calle Arcos de Belén 75, Mexico 1, D.F.; f. 1962; science, general, textbooks; Pres. CARLOS NORIEGA MILERA.

Impresora y Editora Mexicana, S.A. de C.V.: Río Tíber 103, Mexico 5, D.F.; f. 1926; Dir. LUIS GABRIEL TORRES; general and fiction; publ. *México al Día* (fortnightly).

Editorial Joaquin Mortiz, S.A.: Tabasco 106, Mexico 7, D.F.; fiction, history, psychology; Man. Dir. J. DIEZ CANEDO.

Organización Editorial Novaro S.A.: Apdo. 10500; f. 1950; adult books, children's magazines, books and games; Dir. RICHARD SMALL.

Ediciones Oasis, S.A.: Oaxaca 28; f. 1958; Dir. JOSÉ GIMÉNEZ GÓMEZ; literary, sociological, technical.

Editorial Orion: Sierra Mojada 325; archaeology, philosophy, psychology, Spanish literature, fiction; Dir. Sra. SILVIA H. VDA. DE CÁRDENAS.

Editorial Patria, S.A.: Uruguay 25, Apdo. 784; f. 1933; Dir. GUILLERMO DE LA MORA; publs. books on the traditions and history of Mexico, and school textbooks.

Editorial Porrúa S.A.: Argentina 15, 5° piso, Mexico 1, D.F.; f. 1944; general literature; Man. J. A. PÉREZ PORRÚA.

Promotora Hispano-Americana de Música, S.A.: Calzada Mariano Escobedo 166, 2° piso, Mexico 17, D.F.; f. 1939; Man. Ramón Paz López; publishers and distributors of music throughout Mexico; affiliations throughout the world in association with the Southern Music Publishing Co. and Peer International Corpn.

Editorial Reverté Mexicana, S.A.: Río Pánuco 141-a; Dir. Ing. Cándido Rancaño.

Editorial Roble: Hamburgo 20, Mexico 6, D.F.; f. 1960; economics, business; Man. Dir. A. Ben Candland.

Salvat Editores Mexicana, S.A.: Madrid 21-a, Mexico 4, D.F.

Editorial Siglo XXI: Avda. Cerro de Agua 248, Villa Alvaro Obregón, Mexico 20, D.F.; fiction, history, social science; f. 1966; Dir. Dr. Arnaldo Orfila Reynal.

Editorial F. Trillas S.A.: Avda. 5 de Mayo 43-105; f. 1954; social science, educational textbooks; Man. Dir. F. Trillas Mercader.

Unión Tipográfica Editorial Hispano Americana (UTEHA): Avda. Universidad 767, Mexico 12, D.F.; Apdo. 1168, Mexico 1, D.F.; f. 1937; scientific, literary, economical, historical and technical; Propr. José González Porto.

Universidad Nacional Autónoma de México, Dirección General de Publicaciones: Ciudad Universitaria, Mexico 20, D.F.; publications in all fields; Dir.-Gen. Jorge Gurría Lacroix.

ASSOCIATIONS

Cámara Nacional de la Industria Editorial: Vallarba 21, 3° piso, Mexico 4, D.F.

Instituto Mexicano del Libro: Paseo de la Reforma 95, Mexico, D.F.

RADIO AND TELEVISION

Subsecretaría de Radiodifusión: Torre de Comunicaciones, Mexico, D.F.; government regulatory and supervisory body; Dir.-Gen. Julio C. Contreras Camacho; publ. *Comunicaciones y Transportes*.

Cámara Nacional de la Industria de Radio y Televisión: Paseo de la Reforma 445, 9° piso, Mexico, D.F.; Pres. Carlos Flores Alvarez.

RADIO
COMMERCIAL STATIONS

There are 34 commercial stations, of which the most important are:

Radio Cadena Nacional: Vallarta 1, 6° piso, Mexico, D.F.; affiliated stations; Dir.-Gen. A. Jiménez P.

Radio Mil: Insurgentes Sur 1870, Mexico, D.F.; Dir.-Gen. E. G. Salas.

Radio Programas de México: Reforma 322, 4° piso, Mexico D.F.; 73 affiliated stations; Pres. C. Serna Martínez.

Radio 6.20 (XENK): Balderas 32, 4° piso, Mexico 1, D.F.; Dir.-Gen. V. Blanco R.

CULTURAL STATIONS

There are ten cultural stations, including:

Radio Universidad de Chihuahua: Domicilio Conocido, Chihuahua; Dir. A. Varona T.

Radio Universitaria: Ciudad Universitaria, Mexico 20, D.F.; f. 1937; Dir. S. Armando Zayas.

Number of radio sets (1971): 4,032,614.

TELEVISION
COMMERCIAL STATIONS

There are 82 commercial television companies, of which the most important is:

Televisa, S.A.: Edificio Televicentro, Chapultepec 18, Mexico, D.F.; 79 affiliated stations; Dir.-Gen. E. Azcárranga M.

Other companies operate from Tijuana, Ciudad Juárez, Mexicali, Nuevo Laredo, Torreón, Chihuahua, Hermosillo, Guadalajara, Mexico City, Monterrey, Mordia, Colima, Merida, Nogales, Veracruz, Ciudad Obregón and Ensenada.

CULTURAL STATIONS

IP-TV: Instituto Politécnico Nacional, Carpio 475, Casco de Santo Tomás, Mexico 17, D.F.; Dir.-Gen. Ing. R. Porras B.

Televisión Cultural de México: Comisión de Radiodifusión, Torre de Comunicaciones, Insurgentes Sur, Mexico, D.F.

Number of TV receivers (1971): 2,500,000.

Some colour television equipment has been in use since mid-1967.

FINANCE

(cap.=capital; p.u.=paid up; dep.=deposits; m.=million; res.=reserves; amounts in pesos)

CENTRAL BANK

Banco de México, S.A.: Avda. 5 de Mayo 2, Apdo. 98 *bis*, Mexico 1, D.F.; f. 1925; currency issuing authority; cap. 500m., res. 1,560.5m. (1972); Gen. Man. Ernesto Fernández Hurtado; International Organizations Man. Alfredo Phillips; Foreign Division Man. José Alvarez; 8 brs., 3 agencies.

STATE BANKS
MEXICO CITY

Nacional Financiera, S.A.: Isabel la Católica 51, Mexico 1, D.F.; f. 1934; Government industrial development bank; provides loans, guarantees and investments; contracts and handles development loans from abroad; cap. p.u. 1,849m., res. 523m.; Gen. Dir. Lic. Gustavo Romero Kolbeck; publ. *Mercado de Valores*.

Banco Nacional de Comercio Exterior, S.A.: V. Carranza 32; f. 1937; cap. 33.5m., dep. 773.9m. (Dec. 1971); Dir.-Gen. Francisco Alcalá Quintero.

Banco Nacional de Crédito Agrícola, S.A.: Motolinía 11; cap. 842m.; Man. Dir. NATALIO VÁZQUEZ PALLARES.

Banco Nacional de Crédito Ejidal, S.A.: Avda. Uruguay 56; f. 1935; cap. 60m.; Man. Dir. Prof. FRANCISCO HERNÁNDEZ Y H.

Banco Nacional de Fomento Cooperativo, S.A.: Versalles 15, esq. con Atenas; f. 1944; cap. p.u. 70m.; Pres. Lic. CARLOS TORRES MANZO; Gen. Dir. Lic. JORGE MARTÍNEZ GÓMEZ DEL CAMPO; 9 brs.

Banco Nacional de Obras y Servicios Públicos, S.A.: Insurgentes Norte 423, 22° piso; f. 1933; cap. p.u. 200m.; Dir.-Gen. Ing. JESÚS ROBLES MARTÍNEZ.

Financiera Nacional Azucarera, S.A.: Balderas 36; f. 1953; cap. p.u. 60m.; Dir.-Gen. Lic. CARLOS GIRÓN PELTIER.

COMMERCIAL BANKS
MEXICO CITY

Banco Aboumrad, S.A.: Avda. Isabel la Católica 33, Apdo. 21 bis; f. 1932; cap. 17.5m.; Dir. ALFREDO ABOUMRAD.

Banco del Atlántico, S.A.: Venustiano Carranza 48; f. 1949; cap. p.u. and res. 98m. (July 1971); Pres. Lic. CARLOS ABEDROP DÁVILA; Dir.-Gen. JUAN DE MARCE.

Banco Comercial Mexicano, S.A.: Isabel la Católica 43; res. 65m., dep. 3,247m. (Dec. 1971); Dir.-Gen. ANIBAL DE ITURBIDE; 123 brs.

Banco de Comercio, S.A.: Venustiano Carranza 44, Apdo. 9 bis; f. 1932; cap. p.u. and res. 663.0m. (Dec. 1972); Chair. and Man. Dir. MANUEL ESPINOSA YGLESIAS; Banco de Comercio system comprises 35 deposit and savings banks throughout Mexico as well as Financiera Bancomer (development bank) and Hipotecaria Bancomer (mortgage bank); London representation: 85 Gracechurch St., EC3V 0DY.

Banco Continental, S.A.: Ajusco 105, esq. Reforma (Lomas); f. 1941; cap. p.u. 12.5m.; Pres. IGNACIO BETETA, Jr.; Gen. Man. FRANCISCO SCHWARTAU.

Banco de Industria y Comercio, S.A.: Balderas 36, Apdo. 121 bis; f. 1932; cap. p.u. 50m., dep. 625m. (Dec. 1973); Chair. Lic. AARÓN SÁENZ; Pres. ROLANDO VEGA; Man. International Division ROLANDO VEGA S.; 23 brs.

Banco Internacional, S.A.: Paseo de la Reforma 156; f. 1941; cap. p.u. 79.8m., res. 43.4m., dep. 1,585m. (Dec. 1973); Pres. ALFREDO A. LUENGAS.

Banco de Londres y México, S.A.: Avda. 16 de Septiembre y Bolívar; f. 1864; cap. 250m., dep. 4,304.9m. (Dec. 1971); Chair. MAXIMINO MICHEL; Gen. Dir. JOSÉ ANTONIO CÉSAR; 104 brs.

Banco Mexicano, S.A.: Gante 20, Apdo. 53 bis; f. 1932; cap. p.u. and res. 123m. (Dec. 1973); Dir. Lic. JOSÉ GÓMEZ GORDOA; Sub.-Dir. HÉCTOR BOTELLO R.

Banco Nacional de México, S.A.: Isabel la Católica 44; f. 1884; cap. p.u. and dep. 944.8m. (Jan. 1973); Dir.-Gen. (vacant); 366 brs.

Banco del País, S.A.: Avda. Madero 1, Apdo. 498-2747; f. 1942; Man. Dir. RODRIGO VÁZQUEZ A.

INVESTMENT BANKS
MEXICO CITY

Banco Nacional Cinematográfico, S.A.: Avda. División del Norte 2462, 2° piso, Mexico 13, D.F.; f. 1947; cap. 10m.; Dir.-Gen. Lic. EMILIO O. RABASA.

Crédito Algodonero de México, S.A.: Isabel la Católica 44, Mezzanine; f. 1944; cap. p.u. 10m.; Gen. Man. MANUEL G. VARELA.

Crédito Minero y Mercantil, S.A.: Paseo de la Reforma 144, Apdo. 6-608; f. 1934; cap. p.u. 50m. (Dec. 1970); Pres. ALBERTO BAILLERES; Dir.-Gen. HÉCTOR FLORES E.

Financiera Colón, S.A.: Reforma 185, 2° piso; f. 1941; cap. p.u. 11m.; Chair. ALEJANDRO C. DENNISTON; Man. ROBERTO VALES.

Financiera Sofimex, S.A.: Bolívar 18, esq. 5 de Mayo; f. 1937; cap. p.u. 16m.; Chair. Lic. J. MANUEL GÓMEZ MORÍN; Dir. and Vice-Pres. ARMANDO RODRÍGUEZ TORRES.

Impulsora Comercial e Industrial, S.A.: Mariano Escobedo 510, Apdo. 5-1839; f. 1942; cap. p.u. 27.5m.; Dir.-Gen. JACK KALB.

Sociedad Financiera de Industria y Descuento, S.A.: Avda. Madero 42; f. 1943; cap. p.u. 20m.; Dir.-Gen. MANUEL G. VARELA.

Sociedad Mexicana de Crédito Industrial, S.A.: Paseo de la Reforma 213, Mexico 5, D.F.; f. 1941; cap. p.u. 300m.; Dir.-Gen. JULIO SÁNCHEZ VARGAS.

MORTGAGE, CAPITALIZATION AND TRUSTEE BANKS
MEXICO CITY

Asociación Hipotecaria Mexicana, S.A.: Paseo de la Reforma 96, Mexico 1, D.F.; f. 1933; cap. p.u. and res. 25.8m.; Dir.-Gen. and Trustee Del. Lic. ANTONIO ESPERÓN UNZUETA.

Banco Capitalizador de Ahorros, S.A.: Paseo de la Reforma 133, Apdo. 62 bis; f. 1933; cap. 14m.; Pres. ANTONIO CUÉ LOIZAGA; Gen. Man. JOSÉ MA. DE IZAURIETA.

Banco de Cédulas Hipotecarias, S.A.: Paseo de la Reforma 364; f. 1941; cap. 150m. (April 1973); Pres. ELÍAS SOURASKY; Dir. Dr. JAIME P. CONSTANTINER.

Banco Hipotecario, Fiduciario y de Ahorros: Humboldt 59; f. 1942; cap. 10m.; Dir.-Gen. and Trustee Del. JAIME ACEVEDO MICHAUS.

Crédito Hipotecario, S.A.: Paseo de la Reforma 144, 1° piso; f. 1936; cap. 180.2m., dep. 3,957.5m. (Dec. 1973); Dir. JOAQUÍN GALLO S.

FOREIGN BANKS

Banco de Santander: Santander, Spain; Mexico, D.F.

Bank of America National Trust and Savings Association: San Francisco, U.S.A.; Avda. Juárez, Apdo. 14-811, Mexico 1, D.F.

Bank of Tokyo: Tokyo, Japan; Mexico, D.F.

Chase Manhattan Bank: New York City, U.S.A.; Calle Condesa 6, Mexico, D.F.

Deutsch-Südamerikanische Bank A.G./Dresdner Bank A.G.: Joint representation: Avda. Juárez 64, Mexico, D.F.

Deutsche Bank AG: Düsseldorf and Frankfurt am Main, German Federal Republic; Apdo. M-2920, Mexico, D.F.; Representative NORBERTO S. NECKELMANN.

The First National City Bank: New York City, U.S.A.; Isabel la Católica 54, Apdo. 87 bis, Mexico, D.F.; Vice-Pres. GEORGE N. FUGELSANG; Resident Vice-Pres. RAFAEL MORENO VALLE; Man. (Operations) CAMILO CASTROAGUDÍN L.

NATIONAL COMMISSIONS

Comisión Nacional Bancaria y de Seguros (*National Banking and Insurance Commission*): República de El Salvador 47, Mexico 1, D.F.; f. 1924; government control commission; 6 mems.; Pres. Lic. JOSÉ SÁENZ ARROYO; Sec. MANUEL LÓPEZ; publs. *Boletín Mensual Estadístico, Anuario Estadístico de Seguros,* etc.

Comisión Nacional de Valores (*National Securities Commission*): Reforma 77, 12° piso, Mexico 4, D.F.; f. 1946;

Board composed of reps. of Secretariats of Finance and Public Credit and Industry and Commerce, Nacional Financiera, S.A., Banco de México, S.A., Comisión Nacional Bancaria y de Seguros, Banco Nacional de Obras y Servicios Públicos, S.A., Asociación de Banqueros de México, Asociación Mexicana de Instituciones de Seguros, and Bolsas de Valores; a Federal organization; Pres. JULIÁN BERNAL MOLINA; Dir. of Studies and Operations Lic. RAMÓN ESQUIVEL AVILA; publs. *Boletín Bimestral, Memoria Anual*.

BANKERS' ASSOCIATION

Asociación de Banqueros de México (*Bankers' Association*): San Juan de Letrán 2, 9° piso, Mexico I, D.F.; f. 1928; Hon. Chair. Dir. of Banco de México, S.A.; Chair. AGUSTÍN F. LEGORRETA; Dir. Lic. ALFONSO CERVERA DEL CASTILLO; 275 mems.; publs. *Anuario Financiero de México, Revista Bancaria* and various bulletins.

STOCK EXCHANGES

Bolsa de Valores de México S.A. de C.V.: Uruguay 68, Mexico, D.F.; Pres. ARTURO ALONSO CASSANI.

Bolsa de Valores de Monterrey: Escobedo Sur 733, Monterrey; f. 1950; Dir. AUGUSTO TRIGOS J.; Man. FERNANDO A. SÁNCHEZ H.; publ. *Monterrey Financiero*.

Bolsa de Valores de Guadalajara, S.A.: Miguel Blanco 865; Man. JUAN MANUEL RIZO TORRES.

INSURANCE

a=accidents, ea=earthquakes, f (at end of entry)=fire, fa=farm stock, l=life, m=motor car, ma=marine, pg= plate glass, r=reinsurance, t=transport, th=theft.

MEXICO CITY

El Agente Viajero, Sociedad Mutualista de Seguros sobre la Vida: Independencia 59, 7° piso; f. 1940; Gen. Man. J. ORTIZ HARO; l.

Anglo-Mexicana de Seguros, S.A.: Avda. Chapultepec 246, 3° piso; f. 1897; Pres. Ing. JOSÉ LUIS LLANO DE LA VEGA; Man. Dr. CARLOS CASALI.

Aseguradora Aztlán, S.A.: Paseo de la Reforma 445, 8° piso; f. 1958; Gen. Man. Lic. MIGUEL MACEDO.

Aseguradora Cuauhtémoc, S.A.: Liverpool 88, Col. Juárez; f. 1944; Dir.-Gen. Dr. GAETANO ZOCCHI BALBIANI; general.

Aseguradora Hidalgo, S.A.: Puente de Alvarado 75; f. 1931; Gen. Man. Lic. RAFAEL LEBRIJA; l.

Aseguradora Mexicana, S.A.: Plaza de los Ferrocarriles 9, Apdo. 1458; f. 1937; Dir. GUILLERMO CHAVEZ; general, except life.

Aseguradora Universal, S.A., Compañía de Seguros y Reaseguros: Plaza de la República 17; f. 1956; Gen. Man. MOISÉS COSÍO ARIÑO; f, m, ma.

La Atlántida, S.A.: Independencia 37, Apdo. 152; f. 1941; Pres. ENRIQUE MADERO; general, except life.

Compañía Mexicana de Seguros La Equitativa, S.A.: Paseo de la Reforma 364, Apdo. 58; f. 1936; Pres. Lic. RICARDO J. ZEVADA; Dir.-Gen. ELÍAS SOURASKY; f, t, ma, th, pg, ea, etc.

La Continental Seguros, S.A.: San Juan de Letrán 2, 10° piso; f. 1936; Pres. Ing. TEODORO AMERLINCK; Gen. Man. ADOLFO MONROY; f, m, ma, t, etc.

El Fénix de México, Compañía de Seguros Generales, S.A.: Liverpool 143, Apdo. 1919; f. 1937; Pres. MARCOS ORTIZ; f, m.

General de Seguros, S.A.: Patriotismo 266; f. 1945; Pres. FERNANDO CACHO V.

La Ibero Mexicana, S.A., Seguros de Vida: Durango 175, Apdo. 24390; f. 1952; Gen. Man. JORGE CARBONELL A.; l.

La Latino Americana, Seguros de Vida, S.A.: San Juan de Letrán 2, Apdo. 131 *bis*; f. 1906; Chair. Ing. RODRIGO AMERLINCK Y ASSERETO; a, l.

La Libertad, Compañía General de Seguros, S.A.: Liverpool 54; f. 1945; Chair. ADOLFO AUTREY D.; Dir. GERARDO DAMM PENSKI; general.

La Nacional, Compañía de Seguros, S.A.: Avda. Juárez 4; f. 1901; Pres. GREGORIO GUTIÉRREZ PARDO; Dir. JUAN B. RIVEROLL; a, l.

Pan American de México, Compañía de Seguros, S.A.: Paseo de la Reforma 355, Apdo. 139 *bis*: f. 1940; Dir.-Gen. GILBERTO ESCOBEDA PAZ; l, a.

Previsión Obrera, Sociedad Mutualista de Seguros sobre la Vida: Calz. Nonoalco 216, 1° piso; f. 1934; Man. JERÓNIMO QUERO CARDONA; l.

La Provincial, S.A.: Avda. Miguel Angel de Quevedo 915; f. 1936; Dir.-Gen. JUAN B. RIVEROLL; general.

Reaseguros Alianza, S.A.: Dinamarca 51; f. 1940; Man. HANS H. ZOLLINGER; a, f, fa, m.

Reaseguradora Patria, S.A.: Tonalá 63; f. 1953; Gen. Man. F. UREÑA CORIA; general.

La República, S.A., Compañía Mexicana de Seguros Generales: Paseo de la Reforma 134; f. 1966; Gen. Man. JUAN ANTONIO DE ARRIETA; general.

Seguros América Banamex, S.A.: Avda. Juárez 42, Edificio "B"; f. 1933; Pres. JAVIER BUSTOS BARRENA; Dir.-Gen. PATRICIO DE PREVOISIN; general.

Seguros Atlas, S.A.: Balderas 36, 7° piso; f. 1941; Pres. Lic. AARÓN SÁENZ; Vice-Pres. FÉLIX DÍAZ GARZA; general, including life.

Seguros Azteca, S.A.: Avda. Insurgentes 102; f. 1933; Pres. JUAN CAMPO RODRÍGUEZ; a, f, fa, m.

Seguros Bancomer, S.A.: V. Carranza 42, 5° piso, Apdo. 7817; f. 1967; Dir.-Gen. GUILLERMO A. JENKINS; general.

Seguros Chapultepec, S.A.: Miguel Schultz 140, Apdo. 1720; Pres. Lic. PEDRO VIYAO DE LA PRIDA; m.

Seguros La Comercial, S.A.: Avda. Insurgentes Sur 3900; f. 1936; Pres. MANUEL SENDEROS I.; Dir. GILDARDO TORRES SCOTT; f, m, t, a, l, ma.

Seguros Independencia, S.A.: Paseo de la Reforma 243; f. 1954; Dir.-Gen. JUAN J. SAMPSON; f, l, ma.

Seguros Océanica Internacional, S.A.: Paseo de la Reforma 156; f. 1945; Pres. ALFONSO DÍAZ GARZA; general.

Seguros Progreso, S.A.: Avda. Francisco I. Madero 69; f. 1944; Gen. Man. ANTONIO ISLAS DÍAZ; general.

Seguros Protección Mutua, S.A.: Puebla 162; f. 1933; Gen. Man. G. GONZÁLEZ NOGUÉS; general.

Seguros Tepeyac, S.A.: Avda. Insurgentes Sur 102, 6° piso; f. 1944; Pres. A. LÓPEZ SILANES; general.

Seguros "La Territorial", S.A.: Avda. Revolución 1586; f. 1937; Pres. J. BUSTOS; general.

Unión de Seguros, S.A.: Plaza de la República 55, 4° piso, Apdo. 1582; Pres. JOSÉ MENDOZA FERNÁNDEZ; Dir.-Gen. TOMÁS LOYOLA BARRENECHE; a, f, m, t.

CIUDAD JUÁREZ, CHIHUAHUA

Alianza Hispano Americana, S.A.: Avda. Lerdo Norte 118, Apdo. 208; f. 1936; Man. J. CARBONELL; m.

CIUDAD OBREGÓN

Cajeme, Sociedad Mutualista de Seguros Agrícolas y de Incendio: Sonora 254 Sur, Edif. Laborín; f. 1955; Man. H. NAVARRETE DONDÉ; f.

Seguros La Comercial del Noroeste, S.A.: No Reelección 925; f. 1949; Man. E. MAYORAL L.; f, ma.

GUADALAJARA, JALISCO

Nueva Galicia, Compañía de Seguros Generales, S.A.: Avda. Juárez 520, Apdo. 410; f. 1946; Pres. S. VEYTIA Y VEYTIA; f.

Seguros La Comercial de Occidente, S.A.: Avda. Juárez 685, Apdo. 1-585.

HERMOSILLO, SONORA

Seguros del Pacífico, S.A.: Avda. Serdán 20 Poniente, 3° piso; f. 1940; Gen. Man. JULIO ARAIZA M.; f.

LEÓN, GUANAJUATO

Compañía Mexicana de Seguros del Centro, S.A.: Avda. Emiliano Zapata 118; f. 1943; Gen. Man. PEDRO FÉLIX HERNÁNDEZ; f.

MÉRIDA, YUCATÁN

La Peninsular, Compañía General de Seguros, S.A.: Apdo. 378; f. 1940; Gen. Dir. MANUEL VEGA IBARRA; f, ma, m.

MONTERREY, NUEVO LEÓN

Monterrey, S.A.: Edif. Monterrey, Parás 850 Sur; f. 1940; Pres. ROBERTO G. SADA, IGNACIO A. SANTOS; l, f, m, a.

Seguros La Comercial del Norte, S.A.: Escobedo Sur 740, Apdo. 944; f. 1939; Pres. MANUEL L. BARRAGÁN; Dir.-Gen. EDUARDO MAIZ MIER; general.

Seguros Monterrey del Círculo Mercantil, S.A., Sociedad General de Seguros: Zaragosa Sur 1202; f. 1937; Man. SALVADOR D. GARCÍA; l.

PUEBLA, PUEBLA

Oriente de México, Compañía Mexicana de Seguros, S.A.: Avda. 5 Sur 101-A, Apdo. 194; f. 1942; Gen. Man. R. WHITE ROCA; f.

Seguros La Comercial de Puebla, S.A.: Avda. 3 Poniente 106; f. 1942; Man. RAFAEL ESPEJEL GONZÁLEZ; f.

TORREÓN, COAHUILA

Mutualidad de Seguros Agrícolas "La Laguna": Calzada Manuel Avila Camacho 3900; f. 1945; Man. COSME ARROYO MARTÍNEZ; f, fa, m.

Torreón, Sociedad Mutualista de Seguros: J. A. de la Fuente 180 Sur; f. 1952; Dir. CARLOS GONZÁLEZ TABOADA; f, fa.

VERACRUZ

Compañía de Seguros Veracruzana, S.A.: Independencia 835; f. 1908; Man. ROBERTO LAGOS L.; f, m, t.

ASSOCIATION

Asociación Mexicana de Instituciones de Seguros, A.C.: Avda. Insurgentes Sur 102, 1° piso, Mexico 6, D.F.; Man. Lic. FRANCISCO PARRA MARTÍNEZ NEGRETE.

TRADE AND INDUSTRY

CHAMBERS OF COMMERCE

Confederación de Cámaras Nacionales de Comercio—CONCANACO (*Confed. of Nat. Chambers of Commerce*): Balderas 144, 2° y 3° pisos, Apdo. 113 *bis*, Mexico 1, D.F.; f. 1917; Pres. MIGUEL M. BLÁSQUEZ; Gen. Man. ENRIQUE MORENO DE TAGLE; comprises 263 regional Chambers, with members divided into the Special Sections of *Comercio Interior* (Internal Trade), *Comercio y Relaciones Internacionales* (Foreign Trade and Relations), *Industrias Varias* (Various Industries), *Crédito, Seguros y Fianzas* (Banking and Insurance), *Comercio en Pequeño* (Retail Trade), *Turismo y Transportes* (Tourism and Transport), *Relaciones y Promoción* (Trade Relations and Development), and *Trabajo y Previsión Social* (Labour and Social Welfare). In 1936 it was combined with CONCAMIN, but the organizations separated again in 1941. Both are officially recognized consultative bodies; publ. *Carta Semanal* (weekly).

Cámara Nacional de Comercio de la Ciudad de México (*National Chamber of Commerce of Mexico City*): Paseo de la Reforma 42, Apdo. 20905, Mexico 1, D.F.; f. 1874; Pres. L. L. MORTON; Man. Lic. PORFIRIO REYES LAMADRID; publ. *México* (monthly).

Chambers of Commerce exist in the chief town of each State as well as in the larger centres.

American Chamber of Commerce of Mexico: Lucerna 78, Mexico 6, D.F.; f. 1917; 2,200 mems.; Pres. GEORGE B. BLAKE.

Cámara de Comercio Mexicano-Estadounidense: Mexico, D.F.; f. 1973.

RETAIL TRADE

Cámara de Comercio e Industria en Pequeño (*Chamber of Retail Trade and Industry*): Avda. Madero 61-101 y 102, Mexico 1, D.F.; Pres. R. CASTILLO; Dir. JUAN RODRÍGUEZ SALAZAR.

CHAMBERS OF INDUSTRY

The 59 Industrial Chambers and 16 Associations, many of which are located in the Federal District, are representative of the major industries of the country.

CENTRAL CONFEDERATION

Confederación do Cámaras Industriales de los Estados Unidos Mexicanos—CONCAMIN (*Confed. of Industrial Chambers*): Manuel María Contreras 133, 8° piso, Mexico 5, D.F.; f. 1917; Pres. CARLOS YARZA OCHOA; Dir. HUMBERTO ESCOTO O.; Deputy Dir. FRANCISCO R. CALDERÓN; publ. *Confederacón* (fortnightly).

DEVELOPMENT

Asociación Nacional de Importadores y Exportadores (*National Association of Importers and Exporters*): Paseo de la Reforma 122, Mexico 6, D.F.; f. 1944; Pres. ERNESTO AMTMANN.

Comisión Nacional Consultiva para la Pesca (*National Advisory Commission on Fishing*): Mexico, D.F.; f. 1961; established to study the industry, promote its development and advise the Government on its management; Vice-Pres. Lic. JORGE ECHANIZ R.

Comisión Nacional de Ganadería (*National Livestock Commission*): Mexico, D.F.; f. 1966; a federal government consultative body; Pres. Minister of Agriculture and Livestock.

Compañía Nacional de Subsistencias Populares (CONASUPO): Mexico, D.F.; f. 1972 to protect the income of small farmers, improve the marketing of basic farm commodities and supervise the operation of rural co-operative stores; cap. 500m.; Dir.-Gen. JORGE DE LA VEGA DOMÍNGUEZ.

Instituto Mexicano del Café: Mexico, D.F.; controls areas under cultivation and sets production targets for coffee; Dir. Lic. FAUSTO CANTÚ PEÑA.

Instituto Mexicano de Comercio Exterior (*Institute for Foreign Trade*): Insurgentes Sur 1443, Mexico 19, D.F.; f. 1971; Dir. JULIO FAESLER C.

Instituto Mexicano del Petróleo: Mexico, D.F.; f. 1965 to further petroleum and petrochemical industries through research and development, technical training and exchange abroad; cap. $10m.; directed by PEMEX; Dir.-Gen. BRUNO MASCANZONI FABRI.

Instituto Nacional de Investigaciones Agrícolas (*National Agricultural Research Institute*): Apdo 6-882, Mexico 6, D.F.; f. 1960; contributes to Government agricultural policy and provides training schemes; operates under auspices of the Secretariat of Agriculture and Livestock; Dir. Gen. Dr. NICOLÁS SÁNCHEZ DURÓN; publ. *Agricultura Técnica en México* (bi-annual).

Instituto Nacional de Pesca (*National Fishery Institute*): Avda. Cuauhtémoc 80, 6° piso, Mexico 7, D.F.

Petróleos Mexicanos—PEMEX: Marina Nacional 329, Mexico 17, D.F.; f. 1938; Government-controlled company for the exploitation of Mexico's oil resources; budget for 1974: 31,354m. pesos; Dir.-Gen. ANTONIO DOVALÍ JAIME.

EMPLOYERS' ORGANIZATION

Confederación Patronal de la República Mexicana (COPARMEX) (*Employers' Federation*): Liverpool 48, 4° piso, Apdo. 6959, Mexico, D.F.; f. 1929; Pres. Lic. JORGE ORVAÑANOS Z.; Gen. Man. Lic. ISAAC GUZMÁN VALDIVIA; 10,000 mems.; publs. *Labor-Lex, Boletin de Seguro Social*. The Confederation is a national syndicate of free affiliated businessmen organized to promote the economic development of Mexico. It studies questions concerning the relations between employers and workers with a view to the adoption by employers of common policies. It plays no formal part in the negotiation of wages and conditions of employment.

TRADE UNIONS

Confederación de Trabajadores de México—CTM (*Confederation of Mexican Workers*): Calle Vallarta 8, Mexico, D.F.; f. 1936; admitted to ICFTU; 2,120,000 mems.; 29 national unions, 32 state and territorial federations, 65 regional federations and 81 municipal federations; Sec.-Gen. FIDEL VELÁZQUEZ SÁNCHEZ.

Federación Obrera de Organizaciones Femeniles—FOOF (*Workers' Federation of Women's Organizations*): Vallarta 8, Mexico, D.F.; f. 1950; a women workers' union within CTM (*see* above); 400,000 mems.; Sec.-Gen. HILDA ANDERSON NEVAREZ.

Congreso del Trabajo: Mexico, D.F.; Pres. ANTONIO J. HERNÁNDEZ.

Confederación Regional Obrera Mexicana—CROM (*Regional Confederation of Mexican Workers*): República de Cuba 60, Mexico, D.F.; f. 1918; 120,000 mems., 900 affiliated syndicates; Sec.-Gen. AGUSTIN PÉREZ CABALLERO.

Confederación Revolucionaria de Obreros y Campesinos—CROC (*Revolutionary Confederation of Mexican Workers and Farmers*): San Juan de Letrán 80, 6° piso, Mexico, D.F.; 120,000 mems. in 22 state federations and 8 national unions; Gen. Sec. MANUEL RIVERA A.

Confederación Revolucionaria de Trabajadores—CRT (*Revolutionary Confederation of Workers*): Niño Perdido 16-3, Mexico, D.F.; f. 1954; 10,000 mems., 10 federations and 192 syndicates; Sec.-Gen. MARIO FORASTIERI.

Federación de Sindicatos Independientes de Nuevo León (*Federation of Independent Trade Unions of Nuevo León*): Isaac Garza 311, Oriente, Monterrey, Nuevo León; f. 1936; 70,000 mems., 650 syndicates; Sec.-Gen ISAAC TREVIÑO FRÍAS.

Federación de Sindicatos de Trabajadores al Servicio del Estado—FSTSE (*Federation of Unions of Government Workers*): Lucerna 55, Mexico 6 ,D.F.; f. 1938; 350,000 mems.; 30 affiliated unions; Sec.-Gen. GILBERTO ACEVES ALCOCER.

Unión General de Obreros y Campesinos de México—UGOCM (*General Union of Workers and Farmers of Mexico*): Humboldt 8, Mexico, D.F.; f. 1949; admitted to WFTU/CTAL; 7,500 mems., over 2,500 syndicates; Sec.-Gen. JACINTO LÓPEZ.

A number of major unions are non-affiliated; they include:

Sindicato Industrial de Trabajadores Mineros, Metalúrgicos y Similares de la República Mexicana (*Industrial Union of Mine, Metallurgical and Related Workers of the Republic of Mexico*): Dr. Vertiz 668, Col. Narvaete, Mexico 12, D.F.; f. 1933; 86,000 mems.; Sec.-Gen. Senator NAPOLEÓN GÓMEZ SADA.

Sindicato de Trabajadores Ferrocarrileros de la República Mexicana (*Union of Railroad Workers of the Republic of Mexico*): Calz. Nonoalco 206, Mexico 3, D.F.; f. 1933; 100,000 mems.; Sec.-Gen. MARIANO VILLANUEVA MOLINA.

Sindicato Unico de Trabajadores Electricistas de la República Mexicana: Mexico, D.F.; Sec.-Gen. Senator FRANCISCO PÉREZ RÍOS.

TRANSPORT

Secretaria de Comunicaciones y Transportes: Avda. Universidad y Xola, Mexico, D.F.

RAILWAYS

Ferrocarriles Nacionales de México (*Nat. Railways of Mexico*): Centro Administrativo, Avda. Central 140, Mexico 3, D.F.; f. 1882; 13,752 km. open; system extends from United States border at Ciudad Juárez (El Paso), Piedras Negras (Eagle Pass), Nuevo Laredo (Laredo), and Matamoros (Brownsville) to Guatemalan frontier; Gen. Man. Lic. LUIS GÓMEZ ZEPEDA; Government-owned since 1937.

Ferrocarril de Coahuila y Zacatecas, A.G.: Apdo. 116, Saltillo, Coahuila; f. 1889; 166 km. open (914 mm. gauge); Gen. Man. Ing. ALFREDO MAGALLANES RÍOS.

Ferrocarril de Chihuahua al Pacífico, S.A. (*Chihuahua-Pacific Railway*): Méndez y 24A, Chihuahua, Chihuahua; 1,515 km. open (1.435 m. gauge); Ojinaga (Chih.)-Topolobampo (Sin.) and Ciudad Juárez-La Junta (Chih.); Pres. Ing. EUGENIO MENDEZ DOCURRO; Gen. Man. Eng. LUIS KAT TOLEDO.

Ferrocarril de Nacozari S.C.T.: Estación de Ferrocarril, Agua Prieta, Sonora; f. 1899; 124 km. open (1.435 m. gauge); copper-lead-zinc mining district in N.E. Sonora; Man. RAFAEL ESQUIVEL CALDERÓN.

Ferrocarril del Pacífico, S.A. de C.V.: Avda. Tolsa 336, Guadalajara; f. 1909; 2,156 km. open, Nogales–Guadalajara, with branches in Sonora and Sinaloa, connects with Southern Pacific of the U.S.A. at Nogales, Naco and Agua Prieta, with the Sonora–Baja California Railway at San Blas, with the National Railways of Mexico at Guadalajara; Gen. Man. Lic. LUIS GÓMEZ ZEPEDA; Asst. Gen. Man. ALFREDO SUÁREZ R.; principally Government-owned since 1951.

Ferrocarril Sonora-Baja California: Apdo. 182, Mexicali, Baja California; 521 km. open (1.435 m. gauge); Gen. Dir. R. IBARA HERNÁNDEZ.

Ferrocarriles Unidos del Sureste, S.A. de C.V.: Calles 55 y 48, Apdo. 117, Mérida, Yucatán; 927 km. open (1.435 m. gauge); Pres. Ing. EUGENIO MÉNDEZ DOCURRO; Gen. Man. Ing. GELASIO LUNA Y LUNA.

The first stage of a combined underground and surface railway system in Mexico City was opened in 1969. Further lines are under construction.

ROADS

In 1973 there were 160,000 km. of all weather road, of which some 60 per cent were paved. It is estimated that there were 2.1 million motor vehicles on Mexican roads in 1972.

Long-distance buses form one of the principal methods of transport in Mexico, and there are some 20 lines operating services throughout the country.

Asociación Nacional Automovilística (ANA): Miguel Schultz 140, Mexico, D.F.

Pemex Travel Club: Calle Bucarelli 35, Mexico 1, D.F.; special services to motorists; offices in Laredo, Texas, Nogales, Arizona and El Paso, Texas.

SHIPPING

Mexico's merchant navy has a total deadweight tonnage of about 600,000. The Government operates the facilities of the 36 seaports.

Linea Mexicana del Pacífico, S.A.: Insurgentes Sur 432, 4° piso, Mexico, D.F.; f. 1966 as general agents for **Servicios Marítimos Mexicanos, S.A.** and **Marítima Mexicana, S.A.,** to render a joint general cargo service between Mexican, U.S., Central and South American ports on the Pacific.

Petróleos Mexicanos: Avda. Marina Nacional 329, Edificio 1917, 2° piso, Mexico 17, D.F.; 21 tankers and 20 seagoing and river tugs and other small craft; Dir.-Gen. A. D. JAIME.

Transportación Marítima Mexicana, S.A.: Insurgentes Sur 432, 3° piso, Mexico 7, D.F.; f. 1960; services to United States, Far East and European ports; affiliates provide services to Central and West Coast South American ports.

The following foreign shipping lines call at Mexican ports:

Acapulco: *Chandris, Grace Lines, Orient Overseas, P. & O., Shaw Savill, Westfal-Larsen.*

Tampico: *Hamburg-Amerika Linie, Holland-Amerika Lijn, North German Lloyd, Ozean/Stinnes Lines, Sidarma Line.*

Vera Cruz: *Armement Deppe S.A., Farrell, Hamburg-Amerika Linie, Holland-Amerika Lijn, Nedlloyd Line, North German Lloyd, Ozean/Stinnes Lines, Sidarma Line, Spanish Line, Wilhelmsen Lines.*

CIVIL AVIATION

Aeroméxico S.A.: Blvd. Aeropuerto Central 161, Mexico 9, D.F.; f. 1934; services between most principal cities of Mexico and to U.S.A. (Houston, Los Angeles, Miami, New York, Phoenix, Tucson and Detroit), Canada (Montreal, Toronto), Madrid, Paris, Panama and Caracas; Pres. Ing. EUGENIO MÉNDEZ DOCURRO; Gen. Dir. Ing. RAYMOND CANO PEREIRA; fleet: 2 DC-8-63CF, 5 DC-8-50, 1 DC-9-30, 10 DC-9-10.

Compañía Mexicana de Aviación, S.A. (Mexicana): Balderas 36, Apdo. 901, Mexico 1, D.F.; f. 1924; international services between Mexico City and Chicago, Dallas, Denver, Kingston, Los Angeles, Miami, San Antonio, San Juan (Puerto Rico); domestic services between Mexico City and Acapulco, Cancún, Cozumel, Guadalajara, Hermosillo, Mazatlán, Mérida, Mexicali, Minatitlán, Monterrey, Nuevo Laredo, Oaxaca, Puerto Vallarta, Tampico, Tuxtla Gutiérrez, Veracruz and Villahermosa; Chair. Ing. CRESCENCIO BALLESTEROS; Pres. and Chief Exec. MANUEL SOSA DE LA VEGA; publ. *Caminos del Aire* (monthly); fleet: 9 Boeing 727-100, 7 Boeing 727-200, 3 Douglas DC-6.

Servicios Aéreos Especiales, S.A. (Saesa): Blvd. Aeropuerto Central 273, Apdo. 1715, Mexico 9, D.F.; f. 1960; services between Mexico City, Poza Rica, Tampico, Reynosa, Monterrey and Mérida; Pres. FERNANDO ONGAY MÉNDEZ; Gen. Man. JUAN TILGHMAN; fleet: 3 HS-748, 2 Twin Otter.

In addition, lines with head offices in provincial cities operate local services.

Mexico is also served by the following foreign airlines: American Airlines, Aerolíneas Argentinas, Air France, Air Panama, Air West (U.S.A.), Avianca (Colombia), Aviateca (Guatemala), Braniff (U.S.A.), British Airways, Canadian Pacific, Cubana, Eastern (U.S.A.), Ecuatoriana,

Iberia, KLM, Lacsa (Costa Rica), Lanica (Nicaragua), Lufthansa, Pan American, Qantas, Sabena, TACA (El Salvador), TAN (Honduras), Texas International, Varig (Brazil), Viasa (Venezuela) and Western Air Lines (U.S.A.).

TOURISM

Departamento de Turismo (*Mexican Government Tourist Department*): Avda. Juárez 92, Mexico, D.F.; Minister Julio Hirschfeld Almada; Sec.-Gen. Adolfo de la Huerta; offices in all State capitals and Montreal, Toronto, New York, Washington, Chicago, Los Angeles, San Francisco, Dallas, New Orleans, Miami, San Antonio, Houston, San Diego, Phoenix, Tucson and Buenos Aires.

Asociación Mexicana de Agencias de Viajes (AMAV): Lerma 143-502, Mexico, D.F.; Pres. Raul García Vidal.

Consejo Nacional de Turismo: Mariano Escobedo 726, Mexico 5, D.F.; Pres. Lic. Miguel Alemán; European

office: 65 Faubourg St. Honoré, 75008 Paris, France; brs. in Brussels, Frankfurt, London, Madrid, Rome.

CULTURAL ORGANIZATIONS

Instituto Nacional de Bellas Artes: Palacio de Bellas Artes, Lado Oriente, Alameda Central, Mexico, D.F.; f. 1947; dependent on Secretariat of Public Education; departments comprise: Literature, Plastic Arts, Administration, Theatre, Dance, Co-ordination, Architecture and Music; Dir.-Gen. José Luis Martínez; publs. *Revista de Bellas Artes*, *Boletín Mensual*, catalogues, programmes and cultural books.

PRINCIPAL ORCHESTRA

Orquestra Sinfónica de México.

BALLET COMPANY

Ballet Folklórico de México: national and internationa tours; Dir. and Choreographer Amalia Fernández.

ATOMIC ENERGY

Instituto Nacional de Energía Nuclear: Insurgentes Sur 1079, 3° piso, Mexico, D.F.; f. 1955; exercises control over prospecting for, exploitation, export, import and use of uranium, thorium and other radio-active materials. A U.S.$10m. reactor came into operation in 1967; it is estimated it will supply all Mexico's requirements for radio-active isotopes; a contract for the building of Mexico's first nuclear power plant was awarded in spring 1970, to be completed by 1976; Dir.-Gen. Dr. Fernando Alba Andrade; Deputy Dir.-Gen. Luis Gálvez Cruz; Gen. Sec. Jorge González Durán.

Departmento de Proyectos Especiales: Instituto Tecnológico y de Estudios Superiores de Monterrey, Avda. Tecnológico, Monterrey, Nuevo León; f. 1951; technology development, x-rays, materials research, etc.; Dir. Ing. Raúl Reyna; publ. bi-monthly bulletin.

Instituto Politécnico Nacional: Unidad de Zacatenco, Mexico 14, D.F.; atomic facilities include nuclear physics and radioisotope laboratories.

Instituto Tecnológico y de Estudios Superiores de Monterrey: Sucursal de Correos "J", Monterrey, Nuevo León; atomic research in engineering, agronomy, physics and chemistry.

Universidad Autónoma de Guadalajara: Apdo. 1-440, Guadalajara, Jalisco; atomic research in engineering, medicine and pharmacy.

Universidad Autónoma de Puebla: Avda. 4 Sur 104, Puebla; atomic research in engineering, chemistry, biology and medicine.

Universidad de Chihuahua: Chihuahua; atomic research in engineering, chemistry, biology and medicine.

Universidad de Coahuila: Edificio "Ateneo Fuente", 2° piso, Saltillo, Coahuila; application of atomic research to engineering, agronomy, chemistry, biology, mathematics, medicine and pharmacy.

Universidad Juárez Autónoma de Tabasco: Zona de la Cultura, Villahermosa, Tabasco; atomic research in petroleum engineering, veterinary medicine, civil engineering.

Universidad de Morelos: Avda. Morelos 107, Cuernavaca, Morelos; atomic research in chemical engineering.

Universidad Nacional Autónoma de México: Ciudad Universitaria, Mexico 20, D.F.; atomic research undertaken by the Centre for Nuclear Studies, the Faculty of Sciences and the Institute of Physics; the university has laboratories of nuclear and atomic physics, electronic microscopes, spectrographs, etc.

UNIVERSITIES

Universidad Nacional Autónoma de México: Ciudad Universitaria, Villa Obregón Mexico 20, D.F.; 13,182 teachers, 170,463 students.

Universidad Autónoma del Estado de México: Avda. de los Constituyentes 100, Oriente, Toluca, Mexico.

Universidad Femenina de México: Avda. de los Constituyentes 151, Tacubaya, Mexico 18, D.F.; 160 teachers, 1,900 students.

University of the Americas: Cholula, Puebla; 100 teachers, 1,500 students.

Universidad Anáhuac: Lomas Anáhuac, Mexico 10, D.F.; 137 teachers, 710 students.

Universidad Autónoma del Estado de Baja California: Obregón 910 (altos), Mexicali, Baja California.

Universidad de Chihuahua: Ciudad Universitaria, Chihuahua; 365 teachers, c. 5,000 students.

Universidad de Coahuila: Blvd. Constitución y Durango, Apdo. 308, Saltillo, Coahuila; 477 teachers, 10,127 students.

Universidad de Colima: Niños Héroes y 27 de Setiembre, Colima; 150 teachers, 1,850 students.

Universidad "Juárez" de Durango: Constitución 404 Sur, Durango.

Universidad de Guadalajara: Juárez 975, Guadalajara, Jalisco; 2,000 teachers, 39,000 students.

Universidad Autónoma de Guadalajara: Pavo 209, Guadalajara, Jalisco; 452 teachers, 7,215 students.

Universidad de Guanajuato: L. de Retana 5, Guanajuato; 1,153 teachers, 7,179 students.

Universidad Autónoma de Guerrero: Avda. Juárez 14, Chilpancingo, Guerrero.

Universidad Autónoma de Hidalgo: Abasolo 600, Pachuca, Hidalgo; 3,116 students.

Universidad Iberoamericana: Avda. Cerro de las Torres 395, Mexico 21, D.F.; 718 teachers, 5,202 students.

Universidad Interamericana, A.C.: General Francisco Murgía 453 Norte, Saltillo, Coahuila.

Universidad La Salle: Avda. Franklin 47, Mexico 18, D.F.; 500 teachers, 5,000 students.

Universidad Michoacana de San Nicolás de Hidalgo: Santiago Tapia 403, Morelia, Michoacán; 510 teachers, 8,558 students.

Universidad Motolinia: Ameyalco, Obregón y Magdalena, Mexico 12, D.F.

Universidad de Nayarit: Ciudad de la Cultura, Amado Nervo, Nayarit; 230 teachers, 2,480 students.

Universidad de Nuevo León: Ciudad Universitaria, Monterrey, Nuevo León; 1,380 teachers, 18,363 students.

Universidad "Benito Juárez" de Oaxaca: Apdo. 76, Oaxaca; 265 teachers, 2,810 students.

Universidad Autónoma de Puebla: Avda. 4 Sur 104, Puebla; 620 teachers, 10,000 students.

Universidad Autónoma de Querétaro: Avda. 16 de Setiembre 65, Querétaro; 135 teachers, 2,077 students.

Universidad Jaime Balmes de Saltillo: Apdo. 477, Saltillo, Coahuila; 50 teachers, 500 students.

Universidad Autónoma de San Luis Potosí: Avda. Obregón 64, San Luis Potosí; 671 teachers, 7,825 students.

Universidad Autónoma de Sinaloa: Gral. Angel Flores s/n, Culiacán, Sinaloa; 400 teachers, 6,500 students.

Universidad de Sonora: Hermosillo, Sonora; c. 300 teachers, 6,000 students.

Universidad del Sudeste: Ciudad Universitaria, Campeche; 139 teachers, 700 students.

Universidad "Juárez" Autónoma de Tabasco: Villahermosa, Tabasco; 171 teachers, 2,070 students.

Universidad Autónoma de Tamaulipas: Matamoros y 8, Ciudad Victoria, Tamaulipas; 9,718 students.

Universidad del Valle de México: Sadi Carnot 57, Mexico 4, D.F.; 250 teachers, 4,200 students.

Universidad Veracruzana: Jalapa, Veracruz; 1,823 teachers, 12,000 students.

Universidad de Yucatán: Calle 60 y 57, Mérida, Yucatán; 224 teachers, 4,829 students.

Universidad Autónoma de Zacatecas: Galeana 1, Zacatecas; 190 teachers, 2,500 students.

MONGOLIA

INTRODUCTORY SURVEY

Location, Climate, Language, Religion, Flag, Capital

The Mongolian People's Republic lies in Central Asia with the Soviet Union to the north and China to the south, east and west. The climate is dry and extreme with winter temperatures well below freezing. The language is Mongolian. Kazakh is spoken in the province of Bayan Ulgy. There is no State religion but traces of Buddhist Lamaism still survive. The national flag (proportions 2 by 1) has red, blue and red vertical stripes with a golden star and the soyonbo emblem on the left-hand stripe. The capital is Ulan Bator.

Recent History

Mongolia proclaimed its independence of China in 1911. A revolutionary government came to power in 1921 with Soviet assistance and a People's Republic was proclaimed in 1924. Mongolia has maintained close relations with the Soviet Union. Its party and state structure and cultural life imitate the Soviet model, and the various changes in Soviet political life have been faithfully reflected in Mongolia. Since 1960 relations between Mongolia and China have deteriorated. Mongolia accuses China of ill-treating the large Mongol population in China and of wishing to expand at Mongolia's expense. There have been border incidents and the forces on the frontier have been increased.

Government

Legislative power is vested in the People's Great Hural, which meets annually and is elected for a three-year term. In the period between sessions the highest organ of state power is the Presidium of the People's Great Hural. The highest executive organ is the Council of Ministers, responsible to the People's Great Hural. Mongolia is divided into 18 provinces (*Aymag*) for administrative purposes. Elections are by universal suffrage of citizens over 18.

Defence

Defence forces comprise an army of 28,000 men with about 1,000 air force personnel and some Soviet technical advisers.

Economic Affairs

Animal herding is the main economic activity and is practised throughout the country. Horses, oxen, sheep, goats and camels are raised. The herdsmen are organized in collectives, along Soviet lines. State farms, of which there were 32 in 1970, practise agriculture on a large scale. The principal crops produced are cereals, potatoes and vegetables. Also organized into a co-operative and state sector, industry contributes less to GNP (20 per cent in 1969) than agriculture (21.5 per cent in 1969). The output of co-operative industry is limited to items of domestic use and is on a much smaller scale than state industry. The country's industrialization has been greatly assisted by foreign aid, initially from China and subsequently from the U.S.S.R. and Eastern Europe. The major industrial centres are at Choibalsan and Darkhan, near supplies of coal. Other minerals include tin, lead, copper and some gold. The deterioration of relations with China led to the loss of Chinese labour and consumer goods and of income from freight traffic between China and the Soviet Union. There have been frequent complaints of inefficiency and poor workmanship in industry. As in the U.S.S.R., a new management system is being introduced, involving greater flexibility in planning and the use of economic incentives.

Mongolia is a member of the Council for Mutual Economic Assistance (CMEA) and about 60 per cent of trade is conducted with the Soviet Union and 35 per cent with the other members of CMEA.

Under the Fifth Five-Year Plan (1971–75), national income is expected to increase by about one third, industrial production (based on existing capacity) by about three fifths, and the volume of foreign trade and gross grain production by almost one third each.

Transport and Communications

The Mongolian railway system has a total length of about 1,397 km. There are over 1,500 km. of motorable roads but much traffic is along the caravan routes by camel, yak, ox and horse. Steamer services operate on the Selenga and Orkhon rivers. Air transport operates to Irkutsk, Moscow and Peking, and throughout the country.

Social Welfare

There were over 100 hospitals with 12,400 beds in 1971. There are also a number of clinics and medical stations.

Education

Elementary education is compulsory. The curriculum varies between four, seven and ten years. In 1971 enrolment in general schools was 260,800 and in secondary specialized schools 11,100. Students receiving higher education in 1971 totalled 8,500 with about 700 teachers. There is one university and six other institutions of higher education.

Sport

Wrestling and horse-riding are the chief sports. Winter sports, athletics and weight lifting are also popular.

Public Holidays

1974: July 11th (National Day), November 7th (Russia's October Revolution).

1975: January 1st (New Year), May 1st (Labour Day).

Weights and Measures

The metric system is in force.

Currency and Exchange Rates

100 möngö=1 tögrög (tughrik).

Exchange rates (April 1974):
£1 sterling=7.91 tögrög;
U.S. $1=3.35 tögrög.

STATISTICAL SURVEY

Revised by **A. J. K. Sanders**

AREA AND POPULATION

AREA (sq. km.)	POPULATION	
	Total (1974)	Ulan Bator (1973)
1,565,000	1,377,900	300,000

Average expectation of life (1964–65): Males 64 years, Females 66 years.

ADMINISTRATIVE REGIONS

PROVINCE (AYMAG)	AREA ('000 sq. km.)	PROVINCIAL DISTRICTS (sum)*	POPULATION ('000)†	PROVINCIAL CENTRE
Arhangay	55	17	72.3	Tsetserleg
Bayanhongor	116	19	52.4	Bayanhongor
Bayan-ölgiy	46	12	58.1	Ölgiy
Bulgan	49	14	37.4	Bulgan
Dornod (Eastern) . .	122	13	42.9	Choybalsan
Dornogov' (East Gobi) .	111	14	30.9	Saynshand
Dundgov' (Central Gobi) .	78	15	30.7	Mandalgov'
Dzavhan	82	22	70.8	Uliastay
Gov'-altay	142	17	47.4	Altay
Hentiy	82	20	40.1	Öndörhaan
Hovd	76	15	54.0	Hovd
Hövsgöl	101	23	74.8	Mörön
Ömnögov' (South Gobi) .	165	15	26.4	Dalandzadgad
Övörhangay	63	18	66.8	Arvayheer
Selenge	43	12	42.7	Sühbaatar
Sühbaatar	82	13	35.3	Baruun urt
Töv (Central) . . .	81	24	63.6	Dzuun mod
Uvs	69	19	60.3	Ulaangom

* January 1st, 1970. † 1969 census.

EMPLOYMENT
('000—1969)

TOTAL	INDUSTRY	AGRICULTURE	CONSTRUCTION	TRANSPORT AND COMMUNICATIONS	TRADE
197.0	45.8	19.3	16.6	20.4	25.1

AGRICULTURE

	Crops 1971 ('ooo tonnes)	Sown Area 1971 ('ooo ha.)	Crops 1972 ('ooo tonnes)	Sown Area 1972 ('ooo ha.)
Cereals . . .	414.0	411.0	232.0	
Vegetables . .	n.a.	n.a.	n.a.	
Potatoes . .	n.a.	3.0	n.a.	475.3
Fodder Crops . .	n.a.	n.a.	n.a.	
Hay . . .	688.0	n.a.	600.0	n.a.

FARM MACHINERY
('ooo)

	1960	1965	1970
Tractors	1.7	4.3	4.6
Tractor-drawn Ploughs . .	1.6	2.3	2.0
Tractor-drawn Cultivators .	0.4	0.6	0.7
Tractor-drawn Seed Drills .	1.7	3.6	2.7
Combine Harvesters . .	1.1	2.1	1.6
Lorries	1.7	2.4	2.8

LIVESTOCK
('ooo)

	1960	1965	1970
Sheep . . .	12,101.9	13,838.0	13,311.7
Goats . . .	5,631.3	4,786.3	4,204.0
Horses . . .	2,502.7	2,432.6	2,317.9
Cattle . . .	1,905.5	2,093.0	2,107.8
Camels . . .	859.1	684.7	633.5
TOTAL	23,000.5	23,834.6	22,574.9
Pigs . . .	10.9*	19.6	10.7
Poultry . . .	104.4*	179.0	132.6

* 1961.

Total livestock: 22,674,900 in 1971; 23,083,000 in 1972; 23,546,700 in 1973.

PROCUREMENT

		1960	1965	1970
Cattle	'ooo tons live weight	48.3	41.7	42.3
Sheep	,, ,, ,, ,,	69.0	79.0	77.4
Goats	,, ,, ,, ,,	18.3	22.4	16.3
Horses	'ooo head	38.8	86.7	88.8
Milk	million litres	94.6	89.7	63.2
Wool	'ooo tons	14.8	18.6	18.5
Camel Hair . . .	,, ,,	3.8	3.4	3.2
Cattle Hides . . .	'ooo	196.1	248.6	291.0
Sheep Skins . . .	,,	1,277.3	1,839.4	2,232.5
Marmot Pelts . . .	,,	1,034.2	1,208.8	1,201.0
Squirrel Skins . . .	,,	140.3	112.8	35.6
Fox Skins	,,	34.3	49.5	41.4

INDUSTRY

INDUSTRIAL PRODUCTION

		1960	1965	1970
Electricity	million kWh.	106.4	242.0	493.0
Coal	ʼooo tons	618.8	989.5	1,997.4
Fluorspar	„ „	40.3	49.6	76.9
Bricks	million	77.5	43.6	61.7
Lime	ʼooo tons	17.3	15.3	28.4
Sawn Timber	ʼooo cu. metres	151.7	187.0	382.6
Felt	ʼooo metres	295.2	445.8	550.1
Leather Footwear . . .	ʼooo pairs	904.3	1,403.0	1,618.8
Matches . . .	million boxes	32.7	4.5	35.0
Woollen Fabric . . .	ʼooo metres	229.1	514.1	623.7
Flour	ʼooo tons	26.3	77.1	83.3
Meat	„ „	13.1	19.6	34.9
Fish	tons	815.0	357.3	337.5
Butter	ʼooo tons	4.8	4.1	2.9
Vodka	ʼooo litres	909.3	978.6	2,691.4
Beer	„ „	1,129.4	1,712.0	1,801.1

EMPLOYEES IN INDUSTRY
(ʼooo)

	1960	1965	1970
Power	0.6	1.5	2.6
Coal	2.3	2.6	2.6
Petroleum	0.4	0.4	0.4
Non-ferrous Metallurgy and Ore Mining .	0.4	0.6	0.5
Engineering and Metal-working . .	0.8	1.5	2.3
Chemicals	0.7	0.8	0.9
Building Materials . . .	3.7	3.5	5.9
Timber and Wood-working . .	3.9	6.2	6.2
Glass and Porcelain . . .	0.2	0.2	0.4
Textiles	1.1	2.2	2.2
Tanning, Furs and Shoes . .	3.5	4.6	5.0
Printing and Publishing . .	1.2	1.7	1.8
Food Industry	5.0	9.2	8.8
Total . . .	35.3	39.9	45.8

ELECTRICITY CONSUMPTION
(ʼooo kWh.—1968)

Gross Generation	381,701.6
Industry	157,523.6
Agriculture	17,232.3
Forestry	37.8
Construction	8,027.6
Transport	13,914.1
Communications	8,622.0
Trade, Procurement and Supply .	10,136.5
Housing and Utilities . . .	86,265.0
Science, Education, Culture . .	13,909.1
Health, Welfare, Sport . . .	6,395.5
Other	7,120.5
Own Use	28,063.5
Loss in Circuit	24,454.1

BUILDING MACHINERY

	1960	1965	1970
Excavators . . .	71	103	181
Scrapers	20	35	25
Bulldozers . . .	68	118	165
Cranes	17	233	391

HOUSING CONSTRUCTION

	1960	1965	1970
Completed (ʼooo sq. m.) .	91.0	80.2	85.8

FINANCE

100 möngö = 1 tögrög (tughrik).
Coins: 1, 2, 10, 15, 20 and 50 möngö; 1 tögrög.
Notes: 1, 3, 10, 25, 50 and 100 tögrög.
Exchange rates (April 1974): 1 tögrög = 22.5 Soviet kopeks; £1 sterling = 7.91 tögrög; U.S. $1 = 3.35 tögrög.
100 tögrög = £12.64 = $29.86.

BUDGET 1974
(million tögrög)

Revenue		Expenditure	
Turnover Tax	1,683.0	National Economy	1,043.7
Deductions from Profits . .	736.2	Social and Cultural Services . . .	1,082.6
Revenue from Forestry and Hunting .	63.2	Administration	121.7
Income Tax from Rural Co-operatives .	7.8	Defence	362.0
Social Insurance	96.7		
Other Taxes	33.1		
Total	2,620.0	Total	2,610.0

EXTERNAL TRADE

IMPORTS AND EXPORTS BY COMMODITY
(%—1970)

	Export	Import
Machinery and Equipment .	0.3	26.5
Fuels, Minerals, Metals .	5.2	14.2
Chemicals, Fertilizers, Rubber .	—	5.4
Building Materials . .	0.9	1.8
Raw Materials of Plant and Animal Origin, excl. Foodstuffs .	58.2	2.1
Raw Materials for Production of Foodstuffs . . .	19.7	0.3
Foodstuffs . . .	9.7	13.5
Industrial Consumer Goods .	6.0	32.9
Total . . .	100.0	100.0

IMPORTS AND EXPORTS BY GROUPS OF COUNTRIES
(%)

	1960	1965	1970
Exports	100.0	100.0	100.0
to Socialist Countries .	99.7	99.2	99.1
including:			
CMEA . . .	94.0	92.7	94.4
Others . . .	5.7	6.5	4.7
to Capitalist Countries .	0.3	0.8	0.9
Imports	100.0	100.0	100.0
from Socialist Countries .	99.8	99.2	99.1
including:			
CMEA . . .	75.9	94.4	97.3
Others . . .	23.9	4.8	1.8
from Capitalist Countries	0.2	0.8	0.9

Mongolia's Trade Within CMEA
Approximately 95 per cent of Mongolia's trade is with CMEA countries.

	Exports			Imports		
	1967	1968	1969	1967	1968	1969
U.S.S.R. (million roubles)	n.a.	47.8	47.5	n.a.	174.5	176.6
Bulgaria (million leva)	2.6	1.9	n.a.	2.9	2.5	n.a.
Czechoslovakia (million Czech crowns) . .	49.0	46.0	n.a.	66.0	57.0	n.a.
German Democratic Republic (million marks) .	n.a.	12.2	16.7	n.a.	26.4	22.1
Hungary (million foreign exchange forints) .	n.a.	24.5	23.7	n.a.	71.0	49.5
Poland (million złotys)	n.a.	17.1	17.0	n.a.	14.5	14.1
Romania (million lei)	n.a.	9.1	10.9	n.a.	11.3	12.6

Note: Trade between Mongolia and China in 1970 and 1971 has been estimated at U.S. $1,000,000 each way in both years.

In 1971, trade with the U.S.S.R. was worth 240 million roubles both ways, and with Poland 6 million roubles both ways. In 1972, foreign trade turnover rose by 8.5 per cent, exports by 12 per cent. A 15 per cent increase in trade turnover with the U.S.S.R. is planned for 1973. Foreign trade turnover as a whole in 1973 is planned to rise by 6.8 per cent, including exports by 9.5 per cent and imports by 4.8 per cent. In the first six months of 1973, compared with the period January–June 1972, foreign trade turnover rose by 32.1 per cent, including exports by 36.7 per cent and imports by 30.6 per cent.

TRANSPORT
FREIGHT TURNOVER
(million ton/km.)

	1960	1965	1970	Growth 1971–75* (%)
Rail	3,036.3	900.3	1,527.6	25.0
Road	201.4	417.8	610.5	20.0
Water	2.6	3.1	3.7	n.a.
Air	0.8	1.2	1.5	n.a.
Total . . .	3,241.1	1,322.4	2,143.3	24.4

FREIGHT CARRIAGE
(million tons)

	1960	1965	1970
Rail	3.9	2.4	4.7
Road	3.4	8.9	9.7
Water	0.02	0.02	0.03
Total . . .	7.3	11.3	14.4

PASSENGER TURNOVER
(million passenger/km.)

	1960	1965	1970	Growth 1971–75* (%)
Rail	0.4	0.4	0.7	13.0
Road	17.6	28.5	51.4	28.0†
Air	0.05	0.1	0.2	10.0
Total . .	18.0	29.0	52.3	21.8

Note: Air route length in 1969: 31,000 km.
* Five-Year Plan. † Urban transport.

COMMUNICATIONS MEDIA

	1960	1965	1970
Post Offices	230	376	401
Telephone Exchanges . . .	36	67	93
Telephones ('000)	5.6	11.8	19.5
Radio Relay Stations . . .	44	134	141
Radio Sets ('000) . . .	19	82.7	99.8
Television Sets ('000) . . .	—	—	20
Telephone and Telegraph Lines ('000 km.) .	13.8	14.1	16.8

	Growth 1971–75* (%)
Length of Telephone and Telegraph Lines	51.1
Capacity of Telephone Exchanges .	21.7
Number of Television Sets . .	100.0

* Five-Year Plan.

EDUCATION

	INSTITUTIONS			STUDENTS ('000)			TEACHERS ('000)		
	1960	1965	1970	1960	1965	1970	1960	1965	1970
General Schools .	468	557	593	115.3	164.4	239.6	5.7	6.9	8.7
Secondary Specialized .	15	18	19	8.8	9.2	11.1	0.6	0.6	0.7
Higher . . .	7	7	5	6.9	10.7	8.4	0.6	0.6	0.7

Students (1971): General schools 260,800, Secondary specialized 11,100, Higher 8,500.

(1972): General schools 261,200, Secondary specialized 11,100, Higher 8,900.

(1973) General schools 274,500, Technical 11,600, Secondary specialized 11,300, Higher 10,100.

Source: 50 years of the MPR, Central Statistical Board, Ulan Bator, 1971.

THE CONSTITUTION

The Mongolian People's Republic is a sovereign democratic state of working people. All land, natural resources, factories, transport and banking organizations are state property. In addition to state ownership the people have co-operative ownership of public enterprises, especially in livestock herding. A limited degree of private ownership is also permitted.

The supreme state power is the People's Great Hural (Assembly), which is elected every four years by universal, direct and secret suffrage of all citizens over the age of 18; the last elections took place in June 1973. It has the power of amending the Constitution (by a two-thirds majority), adopting laws, formulating the basic principles of policy and approving the budget and economic plans. Its Presidium consists of a Chairman (who is Head of State), First Vice-Chairman, a Vice-Chairman, a Secretary and seven members. The functions of the Presidium are to interpret legislation and issue decrees, ratify treaties and appoint or dismiss (with the approval of the People's Great Hural) the members of the Council of Ministers.

The Council of Ministers is the highest executive power and consists of the Chairman, First Vice-Chairmen, Vice-Chairmen, Ministers and Chairmen of State Commissions.

Local government is exercised by Hurals and their executive committees at Aymag (Province) and Somon (County) levels.

THE GOVERNMENT

HEAD OF STATE

Chairman of the Presidium of the People's Great Hural: Marshal YUMJAAGIYN TSEDENBAL.

First Vice-Chairman of the Presidium of the People's Great Hural: SONOMYN LUVSAN.

THE COUNCIL OF MINISTERS

(June 1974)

Chairman: JAMBYN BATMONH.

First Deputy Chairmen: DAMDINJAVYN MAYDAR (Chairman, State Committee for Science and Technology), TÜMENBAYARYN RAGCHAA.

Vice-Chairmen: BAMDARIYN DÜGERSÜREN, DAMDINY GOMBOJAV (Chairman, Commission for CMEA Affairs), SONOMYN LUVSANGOMBO (Chairman, Commission for Construction and Architecture), DONDOGIYN TSEVEGMID (Chairman, Committee for Higher and Special Secondary Education).

Chairman, State Planning Commission: DUMAAGIYN SODNOM.

Minister of Agriculture: MANGALJAVYN DASH.

Minister of Fuel, Power and Geology: MYATAVYN PELJEE.

Minister of Light and Food Industries: PAAVANGIYN DAMDIN.

Minister of Construction and Building Materials Industry: ORONY TLEYHAN.

Minister of Forestry and Woodworking Industry: KATUUGIYN CHIMID.

Minister of Transport: BATMÖNHIYN ENEBISH.

Minister of Water Economy: BAVUUDORJIYN BARS.

Minister of Communications: DAHYN GOTOV.

Minister of Trade and Procurement: DUNJMAAGIYN DORJGOTOV.

Minister of Foreign Trade: YONDONGIYN OCHIR.

Minister of Finance: TSENDIYN MOLOM.

Minister of Foreign Affairs: LODONGIYN RINCHIN.

Minister of Defence: Army Gen. BATYN DORJ.

Minister of Public Security: Lt.-Gen. BUGYN DEJID.

Minister of Education: DENDZENGIYN ISHTSEREN.

Minister of Health: DAR'SÜRENGIYN NYAM-OSOR.

Minister of Communal Economy and Services: ORSOOGIYN NYAMAA.

Minister of Justice: Donoyn Pürev.

Chairman, People's Control Committee: Legdengiyn Damdinjav.

Head, Central Statistical Directorate: Damiranjavyn Dzagasbaldan.

Chairman, Board of State Bank: Püreviyn Tömör.

President, Academy of Sciences: Badzaryn Shirendev.

Chairman, State Committee for Labour and Wages: Myatavyn Lhamsüren.

Chairman, State Committee for Information, Radio and Television: Sereeteriyn Pürevjav.

Head, Civil Defence Directorate: Jambyn Jam'yan.

Director of Administration, Council of Ministers: Baldangiyn Badarch.

First Deputy Chairman, State Planning Commission (Minister): Byambyn Rinchinpeljee.

Deputy Head, Mongolian Side of Mongol-Soviet Commission for Economic Co-operation (Minister): Magsaryn Chimiddorj.

Note: The acting Minister of Culture, S. Luvsanvandan, is not a member of the Council of Ministers.

DIPLOMATIC REPRESENTATION
AMBASSADORS ACCREDITED TO MONGOLIA
(Res.) Resident in Ulan Bator.

Afghanistan: Mohammad Aref (Moscow).

Algeria: Abd Ar-Rahman Khiwan (Peking).

Australia: Lawrence John Lawrey.

Austria: Heinrich Heimerle (Moscow).

Bangladesh: *Chargé d'Affaires a.i.*

Belgium: André Forthomme.

Bulgaria: Khristo Ivanov (Res.).

Burma: U Thein Maung (Peking).

China, People's Republic: (vacant).

Congo (Brazzaville): Pierre Nguonimba Nkzari.

Cuba: Ricardo A. Dansa Sigas.

Czechoslovakia: Vladimir Bartos (Res.).

Denmark: Anker Svart (Moscow).

Egypt: Yahya Abdel Kader (Moscow).

Finland: B. O. G. Alholm (Moscow).

France: Georges Perruche.

German Democratic Republic: B. Handwerker (Res.).

Guinea: Fasy Matias Moribo.

Hungary: István Kadas (Res.).

India: Sonam Narbu (Res.).

Indonesia: Suryono Darusman (Moscow).

Iran: Mohammed Reza Amirteimur.

Italy: Franco Bounous.

Japan: Itaru Tsuge (Moscow).

Korea, Democratic People's Republic: Choe Chong-Kon (Res.).

Laos: Phagna La Norindr (Moscow).

Mali: Guisse Tidiani (Moscow).

Mauritania: Abdallahi Ould Sidya.

Nepal: Balachandra Sharma (Moscow).

Netherlands: A. R. Tammenoms Bakker.

Norway: Frithjof H. Jacobsen (Moscow).

Pakistan: S. K. Dehlavi.

Philippines: (vacant).

Poland: Franciszek Nowak (Res.).

Romania: Traian Girba (Res.).

Sri Lanka: R. L. A. I. Karannagoda (Peking).

Switzerland: Jean de Stoutz (Moscow).

Syria: (vacant).

Tanzania: (vacant).

Turkey: Ilter Turkmen.

*U.S.S.R.: A. I. Smirnov (Res.).

United Kingdom: John Colvin (Res.).

Viet-Nam, Democratic Republic: Do Quoc Cuong (Res.).

Viet-Nam, Provisional Revolutionary Government of the Republic of South: Nguyen Van Thang.

Yugoslavia: (vacant).

Diplomatic relations have also been established with Argentina, Canada, Central African Republic, Cyprus, Ethiopia, Federal Republic of Germany, Ghana, Greece, Iraq, Liberia, Malaysia, Morocco, Nigeria, Senegal, Singapore, Somalia, the Sudan and the People's Democratic Republic of Yemen. Relations have been broken off with Albania and Chile and the position with regard to the Khmer Republic is uncertain.

* The U.S.S.R. has a Consulate-General in Choybalsan and a Consulate in Darhan; Mongolia has a Consulate in Irkutsk.

PARLIAMENT

PEOPLE'S GREAT HURAL

Presidium

Chairman: Yumjaagiyn Tsedenbal.

First Vice-Chairman: Sonomyn Luvsan.

Vice-Chairman: Tsagaanlamyn Dügersüren.

Secretary: Tsedendambyn Gotov.

Members: Namsrayň Luvsanravdan, Sanjiyn Bataa, Dondoviyn Yondondüychir, Gombojavyn Ochirbat, Choyjilyn Pürevjav, Sonomyn Udval, Dovchingiyn Yadamsüren.

Chairman of the People's Great Hural: N. Luvsanchültem.

Chairman of the Executive Committee of the Parliamentary Group: D. Tsevegmid.

POLITICAL PARTY

Mongolian People's Revolutionary Party: Ulan Bator; f. 1921 as the Mongolian People's Party, name changed 1924; total membership 58,048 (April 1st, 1971).

The Central Committee elected at the XVIth Congress in June 1971 had 83 members and 55 candidate members.

First Secretary of the Central Committee: Yumjaagiyn Tsedenbal.

Members of the Political Bureau and Secretaries of the Central Committee: Nyamyn Jagvaral, Demchigiyn Molomjamts, Sampilyn Jalan-aajav.

Members of the Political Bureau: Sonomyn Luvsan, Damdinjavyn Maydar, Namsrayn Luvsanravdan (also Chairman of the Party Control Committee).

Candidate Members of the Political Bureau: Tümenbayaryn Ragchaa, Bat-chiryn Altangerel.

Secretary of the Central Committee: Dejidiyn Chimeddorj.

Director of the Institute of Party History: Badamtaryn Baldoo.

Director of the Higher Party School: Baytatsyn Hurmyetbyek.

DEFENCE

Armed Forces and Equipment (1973): Total strength 29,000; army 28,000, air force 1,000. There are also about 18,000 security police. Military service is for 2 years. Both branches of the armed forces have Soviet equipment comprising in the case of the army medium tanks, armoured personnel carriers, heavy artillery including howitzers and AA guns. The air force has no combat aircraft but uses transports, trainers and helicopters in support of the army. It also has some surface-to-air missiles.

Defence Expenditure: Estimated defence spending for 1973 was 212 million tögrög ($64.2 million).

Chief of Staff of the Mongolian People's Army: Gen. J. Yondon.

JUDICIAL SYSTEM

Justice is administered by the Supreme Court, the City Court of Ulan Bator, 18 aymag (provincial) courts and local somon (county) courts. The Chairman and members of the Supreme Court are elected by the People's Great Hural for a term of four years; other judges are elected by local Hurals for terms of three years. The Procurator of the Republic is also appointed by the People's Great Hural for a term of four years. A Ministry was set up in 1972.

Chairman of the Supreme Court: Ravdangiyn Günsen.

Procurator of the Republic: Jarantayn Avhia.

RELIGION

Religious freedom is guaranteed by the Constitution. Traces survive of Buddhism (of the Tibetan variety).

Hamba Lama: Head of the Gandandegchilen Monastery (the only active temple of Mongolia): S. Gombojav.

PRESS AND PUBLISHING

The following are the most important newspapers and periodicals:

NEWSPAPERS

Ünen (*Truth*): Nayramdlyn Gudamj 24, Ulan Bator; f. 1920; organ of the Central Committee of the Mongolian People's Revolutionary Party and M.P.R. Council of Ministers; daily except Mondays; circ. (Jan. 1970) 110,000; Editor-in-Chief Tsendiyn Namsray.

Hödölmör (*Labour*): Ulan Bator; f. 1947; organ of the Central Council of Trade Unions; 144 issues a year.

Pionyeriyn Ünen (*Pioneers' Truth*): Ulan Bator; f. 1943; organ of the Central Council of the D. Sühbaatar Pioneers' Organization of the Central Committee of the Revolutionary Youth League; 48 issues a year; Responsible Editor Ts. Dashdondov.

Sotsialist Hödöö Aj Ahuy (*Socialist Agriculture*): Nayramdlyn Gudamj 24, Ulan Bator; f. 1961; weekly; circ. 14,000.

Ulaan Od (*Red Star*): Ulan Bator; f. 1930; paper of the Ministries of Defence and Public Security; 104 issues a year; Responsible Editor Col. J. Yadmaa.

Utga Dzohiol Urlag (*Literature and Art*): Ulan Bator; f. 1954; organ of the Writers' Union and Ministry of Culture; weekly; Editor S. Erdene.

Dzaluuchuudyn Ünen (*Young People's Truth*): Ulan Bator; f. 1924; organ of the Central Committee of the Revolutionary Youth League; 144 issues a year; Editor S. Bataa.

Shine Hödöö (*New Countryside*): Ulan Bator; f. 1970; weekly.

There are also 18 provincial newspapers, published bi-weekly by provincial Party and executive committees, including one in Kazakh (**Jana Ömir** (*New Life*) in Bayan-ölgiy Aymag). Ulan Bator, Nalayh and Darhan cities and the Ulan Bator Railway also have their own newspapers. **Ulaanbaataryn Medee** (*Ulan Bator News*) was founded in 1954 and has 208 issues a year. Its editor is G. Dugar.

PERIODICALS

Ajilchin (*Worker*): Ulan Bator.

Akadyemiyn Medee (*Academy News*): Lenin St., Ulan Bator; f. 1933; journal of the Mongolian Academy of Sciences.

Ardyn Tör (*People's Government*): Ulan Bator; f. 1949; organ of the Presidium of the People's Great Hural; 6 issues a year; Editor Ts. GOTOV.

Barilgachin (*Builder*): Ulan Bator; 4 issues a year.

Dzalgamjlagch (*Successor*): Ulan Bator; 6 issues a year.

Dzaluu Üye (*Young Generation*): Ulan Bator; 6 issues a year; Editor H. BATAA.

Dzuragt Huudsan Sonin (*Illustrated News*): Ulan Bator.

Ediyn Dzasgiyn Asuudal (*Economic Questions*): Ulan Bator; 6 issues a year; Editor-in-Chief Ts. GÜRBADAM.

Erüül Mend (*Health*): Ulan Bator; 4 issues a year.

Holboochin (*Communications Worker*): Ulan Bator; organ of the Ministry of Communications.

Hödöö Aj Ahuy (*Agriculture*): Ulan Bator; 4 issues a year.

Hödöö Aj Ahuynhand Dzövlölgöö (*Advice to Agricultural Workers*): Ulan Bator; 16 issues a year.

Hudaldaaniy Medeelel (*Trade Information*): Ulan Bator; 4 issues a year.

Hüühdiyn Hümüüjil (*Children's Education*): Ulan Bator; published by Ministry of Education; 6 issues a year.

Kino Medee (*Cinema News*): Ulan Bator; organ of Mongol Kino.

Mongol Uls (*Mongolia*): Ulan Bator; f. 1956; 12 issues a year; Editor-in-Chief CH. CHIMID.

Mongolyn Anagaah Uhaan (*Mongolian Medicine*): Ulan Bator.

Mongolyn Emegteychüüd (*Mongolian Women*): Ulan Bator; 4 issues a year.

Mongolyn Hudaldaa (*Mongolian Trade*): Ulan Bator; 4 issues a year.

Mongolyn Üyldverchniy Evlel (*Mongolian Trade Union*): Ulan Bator; 4 issues a year.

Namyn Am'dral (*Party Life*): Ulan Bator; f. 1923; organ of the Central Committee of the Mongolian People's Revolutionary Party; 12 issues a year; Editor-in-Chief GOMBO-OCHIRYN CHIMID.

Nayramdal (*Friendship*): Ulan Bator; organ of the Mongolian-Soviet Friendship Society.

Oyuun Tülhüür (*Key to Knowledge*): Ulan Bator; 4 issues a year.

Shinjleh Uhaan Am'dral (*Science and Life*): Mongolian Academy of Sciences, Ulan Bator; f. 1935; magazine published by the Society for the Dissemination of Scientific Knowledge; 6 issues a year; Editor-in-Chief M. JAMSRAN.

Sotsialist Huul' Yos (*Socialist Law*): Ulan Bator; journal of the Procurator's Office, Supreme Court and Ministry of Justice; 4 issues a year.

Sportyn Medee (*Sports News*): Ulan Bator; 54 issues a year; Editor G. TSENDDORJ.

Soyol (*Culture*): Ulan Bator; 4 issues a year.

Surgan Hümüüjüülegch (*Educator*): Ulan Bator; 6 issues a year; Editor N. TSEVGEE.

Teevriyn Medeelel (*Transport Information*): Ulan Bator; published by Ministry of Transport; quarterly.

Tonshuul (*Woodpecker*): Nayramdlyn Gudamj 24, Ulan Bator; f. 1935; humorous magazine published by the editorial office of *Ünen*; 24 issues a year; Editor O. PUNTSAG; circ. 35,000.

Tsog (*Spark*): Ulan Bator; f. 1944; political and literary magazine of the Union of Writers; 6 issues a year; Responsible Editor D. TARVA.

Tyehnik, Tyehnologiyn Medee (*News of Techniques and Technology*): Ulan Bator; 4 issues a year.

Uhuulagch (*Agitator*): Ulan Bator; f. 1931; 18 issues a year; Editor P. PERENLEI.

FOREIGN LANGUAGE PUBLICATIONS

Foreign Trade of Mongolia: Nayramdlyn Gudamj 24, Ulan Bator; annual, published by the Ministry of Foreign Trade; English and Russian; Editor-in-Chief D. NATSAGSAMBUU.

Novosti Mongolii (*News of Mongolia*): Sühbaataryn Talbay 15, Ulan Bator; f. 1946; newspaper published by Montsame in Russian; 104 issues a year; Editor-in-Chief E. TÜMENJARGAL.

Mongolia: Moscow; English edition of *Mongol Uls*; 6 issues a year.

Mongoliya (*Mongolia*): Ulan Bator; Russian edition of *Mongol Uls*; 12 issues a year; Editor-in-Chief CH. CHIMID.

Menggu Xiaozibao (*News of Mongolia*): Ulan Bator; newspaper published by Montsame in Chinese; 52 issues a year.

News from Mongolia: Ulan Bator; information bulletin published by Montsame's Foreign Service, Sühbaataryn Talbay 9; 52 issues a year.

Les Nouvelles de Mongolie: Ulan Bator; French edition of *News from Mongolia*.

PRESS AGENCY

Montsame (Mongol Tsahilgaan Medeeniy Agentlag): Mongolian Telegraph Agency, Sühbaataryn Talbay 9, Ulan Bator; f. 1957; government owned; publs. (*see* above). Tass maintains a representative in Ulan Bator.

PUBLISHING

State Publishing Committee: Ulan Bator; f. 1921; in overall charge of all publishing; Editor-in-Chief T. SODNOMDARJAA.

There are also publishing committees in each province, and a Department for Supervision of the Press and Literature in Ulan Bator.

RADIO AND TELEVISION

RADIO

Ulan Bator Radio: State Committee for Information, Radio and Television, P.O.B. 365, Ulan Bator; programmes in Mongolian (two), Russian, Chinese, English, French and Kazakh; Chair. of the State Committee SEREETERIYN PÜREVJAV; Head of Foreign Service L. GÜNSEN.

Loudspeakers 78,800, sets 112,700 (1972).

TELEVISION

A television centre has been built by the U.S.S.R. at Ulan Bator, and a television service was opened in November 1967. Daily transmissions (for Ulan Bator and Darhan areas only), comprising locally-originated material and/or relays of Moscow programmes via the Molniya satellite and the Orbita ground station. Dir. of Television MAGSARYN CHOYJIL.

Television sets 34,000 (1973).

FINANCE

State Bank of the Mongolian People's Republic: Oktyabriyn Gudamj 6, Ulan Bator; f. 1924; 65 brs.; Chair. of Board PÜREVIYN TÖMÖR.

Insurance is covered by a non-contributory scheme administered by the State Directorate for Insurance of the Ministry of Finance; Head J. PÜREVDORJ.

TRADE AND INDUSTRY

All trade and industry is concentrated in the hands of the state, either through direct state ownership or through co-operatives.

Ministry of Trade and Procurement: Ulan Bator; Minister Dunjmaagiyn Dorjgotov.

Central Council of Mongolian Trade Unions: Ulan Bator; branches throughout the country; Chair. Gombojavyn Ochirbat; Head of Foreign Department G. Jigjid-süren; 220,000 mems. (1971); affiliated to WFTU.

CO-OPERATIVES

Federation of Agricultural Production Associations (Co-operatives): Ulan Bator; body administering the 268 agricultural co-operatives throughout the country; Chair. of Council Mangaljavyn Dash (Minister of Agriculture); Secretary D. Rinchinsangi.

Industrial co-operatives have now been absorbed into the state industrial structure. Industrial production associations are gradually being established under various ministries; they are not co-operatives but groupings of allied enterprises (flourmilling, leather processing, etc.)

FOREIGN TRADE

The Mongolian People's Republic has trading relations with over 20 countries. The Ministry of Foreign Trade is responsible for the foreign trade monopoly and controls the operations of several importing and exporting companies.

Minister of Foreign Trade: Yondongiyn Ochir.

There are four specialized import and export organizations dealing in trade with foreign countries.

Mongoleksport: Export of Mongolian goods.

Mongolraznoimport: Import of consumer goods.

Mongoltekhnoimport: Import of machinery and equipment, other than motor vehicles, fuels and lubricants.

Avtonefteimport: Import of motor vehicles, fuels and lubricants.

Mongolbook: Export of Mongolian publications.

Chamber of Commerce of the Mongolian People's Republic: Nayramdlyn Gudamj 24, Ulan Bator; f. 1960; is responsible for establishing economic and trading relations, contacts between trade and industrial organizations both at home and abroad and assists foreign countries; organizes commodity inspection, press information and international exhibitions and fairs at home and abroad; Pres. D. Hishge; Gen. Sec. Yondon.

TRANSPORT AND TOURISM

TRANSPORT

RAILWAYS

Ulan Bator Railway: Ulan Bator; Dir. V. Sukachev; Deputy Dir. N. Tserennorov.

External Lines: from the Soviet frontier at Naushki/Sühbaatar (connecting with the Trans-Siberian Railway) to Ulan Bator (opened 1950), on to the Chinese frontier at Dzamyn-üüd/Erhlien (opened 1955) and connecting with Peking (total length 1,115 km.); broad gauge, single track.

Branch: from Darhan to Sharyn Gol coalfield (length 68 km.); broad gauge, single track; branch planned from near Darhan westwards to Erdenetiyn-ovoo opencast ore mine in Bulgan Province (length about 170 km.).

A narrow-gauge line, 42 km. long, was built between Ulan Bator and Nalayh coalfield in 1938.

Eastern Railway: Choybalsan; from the Soviet frontier at Borzya/Ereentsav to Choybalsan (length 237 km.); broad gauge, single track; narrow-gauge lines from Choybalsan to Jargalant and Tamsagbulag; built in 1939.

A narrow-gauge line from Choybalsan to Onon (Öldziy), marked on maps after 1947, may have been broadened and extended to the Soviet frontier.

There are two international train services a week, Moscow–Ulan Bator and Moscow–Ulan Bator–Peking, and return. There is a twice-weekly service between Ulan Bator and Choybalsan and return, via the Trans-Siberian Railway.

ROADS

Main roads link Ulan Bator with the Chinese frontier at Dzamyn üüd/Erhlien and with the Soviet frontier at Altanbulag/Kyakhta. A road from Chita in the U.S.S.R. crosses the frontier in the east at Mangut/Onon (Öldziy) and branches for Choybalsan and Öndörhaan. In the west and north-west, roads from Biysk and Irkutsk in the U.S.S.R. go to Tsagaannuur, Bayan-ölgiy Aymag, and Hanh, on Lake Hövsgöl, respectively. The total length of these and other main roads is about 8,600 km. The length of asphalted roads is now approaching 1,600 km., almost entirely in towns.

There are bus services in Ulan Bator and other large towns, and lorry services throughout the country on the basis of 25 motor transport depots, mostly situated in provincial centres.

INLAND WATERWAYS

Water transport plies Lake Hövsgöl and the River Selenge (474 km. navigable) in the northern part of the country. Tugs and barges on Lake Hövsgöl transport goods brought in by road to Hanh from the U.S.S.R. to Hatgal on the southern shore.

CIVIL AVIATION

Mongolian Civil Air Transport (MIAT): Ulan Bator; f. 1956; internal services to most provincial centres and many county centres; thrice-weekly service from Ulan Bator (Buyant-Uhaa) to Irkutsk; equipment includes An-24, Il-14, An-2, Mi-4, Ka-26; Chair. of Civil Air Transport Board Maj.-Gen. Dugaryn Gungaa.

Aeroflot: Moscow and Ulan Bator; thrice-weekly service from Ulan Bator to Moscow and return by Il-18.

TOURISM

Juulchin: Ulan Bator; the official foreign tourist service bureau; Dir. (vacant).

UNIVERSITY

Mongolian State University: Ulan Bator; Rector Porf. N. Sodnom; 300 teachers, 3,300 students.

MOROCCO
INTRODUCTORY SURVEY

Location, Climate, Language, Religion, Flag, Capital

The Kingdom of Morocco is situated in the extreme north-west of Africa and is washed by the Atlantic to the west and the Mediterranean to the north. It is bordered by Algeria to the east and by Spanish Sahara to the south. The climate is warm and sunny on the coast, while the plains of the interior are intensely hot in summer. Average temperatures are 27°C (81°F) in summer and 7°C (45°F) in winter for Rabat, and 38°C (101°F) and 4°C (40°F) respectively for Marrakesh. The rainy season in the north is from November to April. The official language is Arabic, but a large minority speak Berber. Spanish is widely spoken in the northern regions and French in the rest of Morocco. The established religion is Islam, to which most people belong, and there are Christian and Jewish minorities. The national flag (proportions 3 by 2) is red with a five-pointed green star in the centre. The capital is Rabat.

Recent History

From 1912 to 1956 Morocco was divided into French and Spanish Protectorates and the International Zone of Tangier (created in 1923). In 1956 the country became independent and Tangier's special status was ended in 1960. Previously a Sultanate, Morocco became a Kingdom in 1957 and acquired the northern strip of Spanish Sahara in 1958. In 1960 King Mohammed V took charge as Prime Minister but died the following year and was succeeded by his son, the present King Hassan II. A new constitution was drawn up in 1962 to provide for a more widely-based government. Following disturbances in Casablanca, a "state of exception" was declared in June 1965, and Parliament was suspended until 1970, when an amended constitution, approved in July, set up a unicameral Parliament and strengthened the power of the King.

In July 1971 a section of the army attempted to overthrow the monarchy, but the revolt was suppressed by loyal troops led by Gen. Mohammed Oufkir. There were many arrests and executions and a purge of government officials was carried out. At the same time numerous members of the left-wing *Union Nationale des Forces Populaires* (UNFP) were put on trial for allegedly plotting to overthrow the Government, and in September five were sentenced to death. Another new constitution was approved by referendum in March 1972.

An unsuccessful attempt to assassinate King Hassan was made in August 1972, apparently instigated by the Minister of Defence and Army Chief of Staff, Gen. Oufkir, who committed suicide immediately afterwards. The King took personal command of the army and offered government participation to the opposition parties, Istiqlal and UNFP. However, he refused to allow the fundamental reforms which they demanded as a pre-condition of acceptance. Terrorist activities in early 1973 were officially interpreted as the beginnings of a guerrilla movement, backed by the military régime in Libya. The Rabat section of the UNFP was outlawed and several hundred people, including UNFP leaders, were arrested. Sixteen people were subsequently sentenced to death and a large number received long prison sentences. The King retains full power, and the promised elections have still not taken place. Nationalist reforms introduced by the King in March 1973 included recouping lands from French and Spanish owners to form state farms, the "Moroccanization" of certain economic sectors and the extension of fishing limits from 12 to 70 miles. The last measure led to incidents involving Moroccan and Spanish fishing vessels, but the dispute was settled by an agreement between the two countries in January 1974. Morocco gave economic and diplomatic support to the Arab cause during the October War in 1973, and a small Moroccan force was engaged in the fighting.

Morocco is a member of the OAU and the Arab League and an associate member of the EEC, and was a founder member of the Maghreb Permanent Consultative Committee.

Government

Under the Constitution of 1972 the King appoints the Prime Minister and Cabinet, approves legislation and has the right to dismiss parliament. Legislation is carried out by a single Chamber of Representatives, two-thirds of whom are elected by direct universal suffrage and a third of whom are indirectly elected. The country is divided into nineteen provinces and two prefectures.

Defence

Until independence in 1956 defence was the responsibility of the protecting Powers. Since then Morocco has built up its own army of about 52,000 men and established a navy of 2,000 and an air force of 4,000 men. An eighteen-month period of compulsory military service has been in force since 1966.

Economic Affairs

Agriculture and mining are the mainstays of the economy. The chief crops are wheat, barley and maize. Livestock-raising is important and fishing is well developed. The most important minerals extracted are phosphates, of which Morocco is a leading producer and exporter, and other deposits include iron ore, coal, lead and manganese. Industry is still on a small scale but has been developed under a series of Five-Year Plans since 1960. A number of important dam projects have been completed providing both power and irrigation. Oil deposits have been discovered recently but their importance has still to be assessed. King Hassan has wished to combine aspects of socialism and capitalism. A policy of agrarian reform has been pursued since 1966, involving the redistribution of foreign-held land among the peasantry. In March 1973 the transformation of 200,000 hectares of such land into State farms was begun. The "Moroccanization" of certain sectors of industry is also under way. An experiment in worker-participation is being made in the running of State farms and some industrial enterprises. Foreign investment and private enterprise are still encouraged, however. There is a serious unemployment problem and emigration of workers is encouraged, the money they earn abroad being an important source of income for the country. Tourism is also a valuable developing sector of the economy. During the 1968–72 development plan an average growth rate of 5.5 per cent per annum was achieved, and the 1973–77 plan envisages an annual growth rate of 6.5 per cent.

Transport and Communications

There are 1,770 km. of railway of which 708 km. are electrified. Paved roads extend for 21,580 km., of a total road length of 52,000 km. The chief ports are Casablanca, Safi and Mohammedia. There are five international airports and about 50 airfields.

Social Welfare

All employees are required to contribute to a Social Welfare Fund which provides against illness, occupational accidents and old age. There were 22,570 hospital beds in 1970.

Education

There are state primary, secondary and technical schools and also private schools. All primary school teachers are Moroccan, but about 7,000 secondary school teachers come from France, although teacher-training is expanding. Over half the children of school age attend school. Education for both sexes between 7 and 13 years old has been compulsory since 1963. Girls generally leave school younger than boys and make up only 28 per cent of secondary school pupils and 13 per cent of students in higher education. There are two universities and several other institutions for higher education.

Tourism

Morocco is famous for a hot and sunny climate, its ancient, walled towns, the modern capital Rabat and the modern port Casablanca, for desert and mountains and Atlantic and Mediterranean resorts. Tourists from all over the world visit Fez and Marrakesh.

Visas are not required to visit Morocco by nationals of Arab League states (except Sudan), Argentina, Australia, Brazil, Canada, Chile, Ghana, Guinea, Indonesia, Ivory Coast, Japan, Liberia, Madagascar, Mali, Mexico, New Zealand, Nigeria, Peru, Philippines, Puerto Rico, Turkey, U.S.A., Venezuela, Zaire, or any West European country (except Portugal and Spain).

Sport

Football is the most important sport and tennis and skiing are also popular.

Public Holidays

1974: September 19th (Beginning of Ramadan), October 18th (Eid el Seghir-Id ul Fitr), November 18th (Independence Day), December 26th (Eid el Kebir-Id ul Adha).

1975: January 14th (Muslim New Year), January 23rd (Ashoura), March 3rd (Festival of the Throne), March 26th (Mouloud—Birth of the Prophet), May 1st (Labour Day).

Weights and Measures

The metric system is in force.

Currency and Exchange Rates

100 Moroccan francs (centimes) = 1 Moroccan dirham.
Exchange rates (April 1974):

£1 sterling = 10.15 dirhams;
U.S. $1 = 4.195 dirhams.

STATISTICAL SURVEY

AREA AND POPULATION

AREA (sq. km.)	POPULATION (Census of July 20th, 1971)		
	Total	Moroccans	Aliens
446,550	15,379,259	15,267,000	112,000

Estimated Population: 15,825,000 (July 1st, 1972).

CHIEF TOWNS

POPULATION (1971 Census)

Casablanca	1,506,373	Oujda	175,532
Rabat (capital)	367,620	Salé	155,557
Marrakesh	332,741	Kénitra	139,206
Fez	325,327	Tétuan	139,105
Meknès	248,369	Safi	129,113
Tangier	187,894		

AGRICULTURE

('ooo tons)

	1969–70	1970–71	1971–72
Wheat	1,800	2,188	2,162
Barley	1,953	2,572	2,466
Maize	320	390	368
Olives	160	506	n.a.
Dates	90†	90†	n.a.
Pulses	392	354	414
Tomatoes . . .	250†	250†	112*
Potatoes . . .	300†	300†	81*
Citrus Fruit . .	887	832	852
Sugar Beet . .	1,114	1,584	1,677
Cotton . . .	19	19	27
Wine ('ooo hectolitres) .	1,253	1,150	1,500‡

* Amount exported.   † FAO estimate.   ‡ Official estimate.

Livestock (1971): Cattle 3,630,000; Sheep 17,500,000; Goats 8,850,000; Camels 230,000; Horses 400,000; Pigs 14,000; Poultry 15,800,000.

Fishing (1971): The total catch was 228,700 metric tons, of which sardines comprised 183,000 tons.

MINING

('ooo tons)

	1970	1971	1972
Phosphates . . .	11,424	12,030	15,105
Iron Ore . . .	872	623	234
Coal . . .	433	475	547
Manganese . . .	112	160	96
Lead . . .	121	124	146
Petroleum . .	46	23	28
Zinc . . .	32	22	36
Cobalt . . .	6	10	11

INDUSTRY*

	Unit	1968	1969	1970	1971
Cement	'ooo tons	1,011	1,165	1,405	1,481
Processed Lead . .	,, ,,	24	27	20	18
Refined Sugar . . .	,, ,,	425	409	399	424
Soap	tons	29,472	27,593	28,771	n.a.
Paint	,,	8,252	9,714	11,219	n.a.
Textiles	,,	31,690	37,153	40,446	n.a.
Electricity (hydraulic and thermal) .	'ooo kWh.	1,538	1,693	1,830	1,962
Cars†	number	12,162	18,210	20,009	n.a.
Tyres (tubes)	,,	308,000	363,000	411,000	n.a.
Shoes	'ooo pairs	5,127	5,537	4,494	n.a.
Flour	tons	667,218	625,426	818,000	817,700
Refined Petroleum . . .	'ooo tons	1,322	1,470	1,506	1,473
Superphosphate . . .	,, ,,	253	281	180	n.a.

* Major industrial establishments only.   † Assembly only.

FINANCE

100 Moroccan francs (centimes) = 1 Moroccan dirham.

Coins: 1, 2, 5, 10, 20 and 50 francs; 1 and 5 dirhams.

Notes: 5, 10, 50 and 100 dirhams.

Exchange rates (April 1974): £1 sterling = 10.15 dirhams (selling rate); U.S. $1 = 4.195 dirhams (par value).

100 Moroccan dirhams = £9.85 = $23.84.

ORDINARY BUDGET
(million dirhams)

Revenue: (1971) 4,432; (1972) 5,799; (1973) 6,175.   **Expenditure:** (1971) 4,432; (1972) 6,197; (1973) 6,632.

FIVE-YEAR DEVELOPMENT PLAN 1973-77
INVESTMENT*

	million dirhams
Agriculture	2,300
Industry	1,120
Mining	1,000
Energy	1,000
Transport	1,000
Housing	600
Tourism	600
Posts and Telecommunications	500
Education	450
Administration	310
Hospitals	225
Youth and Sports	85
TOTAL (incl. others)	26,000

* Provisional figures.

Currency in Circulation (Note issue at year end): (1969) 2,123m. dirhams; (1970) 2,262m. dirhams; (1971) 2,473m. dirhams.

BALANCE OF PAYMENTS—ALL FOREIGN COUNTRIES
(million dirhams)

	1971			1972		
	Credit	Debit	Balance	Credit	Debit	Balance
Goods and Services:						
Merchandise f.o.b.	2,518.4	3,207.1	−688.7	2,946.7	3,241.6	−294.9
Gold for Industry	—	4.3	− 4.3	—	11.5	− 11.5
Transport and Insurance	174.0	403.6	−229.6	221.3	431.5	−210.2
Travel	760.0	300.0	460.0	893.3	388.2	505.1
Income from Investments	69.8	310.4	−240.6	59.9	323.7	−263.8
Government n.e.s.	195.9	312.7	−116.8	194.4	309.9	−115.5
Other services	81.7	112.2	− 30.5	80.4	104.9	− 24.5
Transfer Payments	842.6	293.3	549.3	980.7	349.1	631.6
CURRENT BALANCE	4,642.4	4,943.6	−301.2	4,396.0	4,811.3	−415.3
Capital and Monetary Gold:						
Public Sector:						
Commercial Credits	432.1	155.1	277.0	284.6	242.7	41.9
Foreign Exchange Loans	311.9	140.9	171.3	217.6	90.3	127.3
Loans in Dirhams	4.2	18.2	− 14.0	0.7	18.4	− 17.7
Others	7.6	1.0	6.6	6.1	1.3	4.8
Private Sector:						
Commercial Credits	165.9	76.8	89.1	24.9	65.9	− 41.0
Loans and Investments	168.8	49.7	119.1	160.7	94.1	66.6
Others	13.9	63.4	− 49.5	78.8	197.2	−118.3
CAPITAL BALANCE	1,104.4	504.8	599.6	773.4	719.2	54.2
Special Drawing Rights	—	—	—	61.0	—	61.0
TOTAL	5,746.8	5,448.4	298.4	6,211.1	5,879.6	331.5

EXTERNAL TRADE
(million dirhams)

	1966	1967	1968	1969	1970	1971	1972
Imports	2,418	2,620	2,790	2,844	3,471	3,532	3,577
Exports	2,168	2,146	2,278	2,455	2,469	2,526	2,953

PRINCIPAL COMMODITIES
(million dirhams)

IMPORTS	1970	1971	1972
Milk, Butter and Cheese	71	73	71
Coffee	49	32	35
Tea	90	84	86
Wheat	130	243	137
Sugar	138	149	170
Petroleum	114	145	172
Timber (raw and prepared)	102	105	102
Paper and Products	48	47	71
Cotton Textiles	108	86	43
Motor Vehicles and Parts	182	193	212

EXPORTS	1970	1971	1972
Tomatoes	180	163	179
Fresh Vegetables and Potatoes	87	81	122
Cotton	28	23	40
Citrus Fruits	357	389	429
Preserved Fish	127	148	134
Wine	43	19	35
Phosphates	572	588	673
Iron Ore	29	23	11
Lead Ore	71	69	90
Zinc Ore	14	7	10
Cork and Cork Products	21	15	25

PRINCIPAL COUNTRIES
(million dirhams)

IMPORTS	1970	1971	1972
China, People's Republic	n.a.	60	86
Cuba	n.a.	74	45
France	1,074	1,083	1,111
Germany, Federal Republic	304	267	268
Italy	187	210	200
Netherlands	n.a.	102	111
U.S.S.R.	166	142	142
United Kingdom	161	144	160
U.S.A.	392	301	270

EXPORTS	1970	1971	1972
Belgium/Luxembourg	n.a.	100	121
France	904	918	964
Germany, Federal Republic	227	214	265
Italy	163	139	265
Netherlands	116	80	110
Poland	n.a.	51	66
Spain	n.a.	107	164
U.S.S.R.	n.a.	89	113
United Kingdom	138	126	136

TRANSPORT

ROADS

	1970	1971
Tonnage Transported . .	6,619,000	7,168,000
Cars	222,460	242,086
Lorries and Vans . .	83,899	90,495
Motor Cycles . .	14,670	14,849

SHIPPING

FREIGHT	UNIT	1971	1972
Tonnage Loaded . .	'000 tons	13,354	16,367
Tonnage Unloaded . .	,, ,,	5,198	4,871

Source: Institut National de la Statistique et des Etudes Economiques, Paris, *Données Statistiques.*

CIVIL AVIATION

	1971	1972
Total passengers . .	1,124,140	1,191,033
Freight (metric tons) . .	11,142	14,461

TOURISM

COUNTRY OF ORIGIN	1970	1971	1972
Algeria . . .	60,238	66,632	91,578
Belgium . .	21,585	21,775	25,906
France . . .	174,050	188,175	210,625
Federal Germany	55,405	70,702	95,272
Italy . . .	18,462	17,904	125,147
Scandinavia . .	12,105	8,621	9,454*
Spain . . .	41,969	42,789	76,107
Switzerland . .	10,116	12,591	19,091
U.K. . . .	84,411	80,882	107,733
U.S.A. . .	117,820	136,677	194,071
Others . .	150,692	176,168	208,469
TOTAL .	746,860	822,916	1,063,453
Cruise Passengers .	105,505	91,376	127,580
GRAND TOTAL .	852,365	914,292	1,191,033

* Denmark only.

Hotel Capacity (1972): 52,000 beds.

EDUCATION

	PRIMARY SCHOOL PUPILS	SECONDARY SCHOOL PUPILS	STUDENTS ENGAGED IN HIGHER EDUCATION
1970–71 . .	1,175,277	298,880	13,572
1971–72 . .	1,231,436	313,424	15,148
1972–73 . .	1,277,660	334,959	n.a.

Sources (unless otherwise stated): Direction de la Statistique, Rabat; Banque Marocaine du Commerce Extérieur.

THE CONSTITUTION

(Promulgated March 10th, 1972, after having been approved by national referendum.)*

Preamble: The Kingdom of Morocco, a sovereign Moslem State, shall be a part of the Great Maghreb. As an African State one of its aims shall be the realization of African unity. It will adhere to the principles, rights and obligations of those international organizations of which it is a member and will work for the preservation of peace and security in the world.

General Principles: Morocco shall be a constitutional, democratic and social monarchy. Sovereignty shall pertain to the nation and be exercised directly by means of the referendum and indirectly by the constitutional institutions. All Moroccans shall be equal before the law, and all adults shall enjoy equal political rights including the franchise. Freedoms of movement, opinion and speech and the right of assembly shall be guaranteed. Islam shall be the state religion.

The Monarchy: The Crown of Morocco and its attendant constitutional rights shall be hereditary in the line of H.M. King Hassan II, and shall be transmitted to the oldest son, unless during his lifetime the King has appointed as his successor another of his sons. The King is the symbol of unity, guarantees the continuity of the state, and safeguards respect for Islam and the Constitution. The King shall have the power to appoint and dismiss the Prime Minister and Cabinet Ministers and shall preside over the Cabinet. He shall promulgate legislation passed by parliament and have the power to dissolve the House of Representatives; is empowered to declare a state of emergency and to initiate revisions to the Constitution. The Sovereign is the Commander-in-Chief of the Armed Forces; makes appointments to civil and military posts; appoints Ambassadors; signs and ratifies treaties; presides over the Council for National Development Planning and the Supreme Judiciary Council; and exercises the right of pardon.

Parliament: Parliament shall consist of a single assembly, the House of Representatives, which shall comprise 240 members elected for a four-year term. Two thirds of the members shall be elected by direct universal suffrage, and one third by an electoral college composed of councillors in local government and employers' and employees' representatives. Parliament shall pass legislation, which may be initiated by its members or by the Prime Minister; authorize any declaration of war; and approve any extension beyond thirty days of a state of emergency.

Government: The Government shall be responsible to the King and the House of Representatives and shall ensure the execution of laws. The Prime Minister shall be empowered to initiate legislation and to exercise statutory powers except where these are reserved to the King. He shall put before parliament the Government's intended programme and shall be responsible for co-ordinating ministerial work.

Relations between the Authorities: The King may request further consideration of legislation by parliament before giving his assent; submit proposed legislation to a referendum by decree; and dissolve the House of Representatives if a Bill rejected by parliament is approved by referendum. He may also dissolve the House of Representatives by decree, but the succeeding House may not be dissolved within a year of its election. The House of Representatives may defeat the Government either by refusing a vote of confidence moved by the Prime Minister or by passing a censure motion; either eventuality shall involve the Government's collective resignation.

Judiciary: The Judiciary shall be independent. Judges shall be appointed on the recommendation of the Supreme Council of the Judiciary presided over by the King.

* For the most part the Constitution is unchanged from the one drawn up by King Hassan II and promulgated in 1962. This provided for two houses of parliament, one elected by universal suffrage and one by electoral colleges, and was superseded by that of June 1970, which introduced a unicameral parliament, of which one-quarter of the members were to be elected by universal suffrage, and it increased the powers of the monarch.

THE GOVERNMENT

HEAD OF THE STATE

H.M. King Hassan II (accession February 26th, 1961).

CABINET

(May 1974)

Prime Minister and Minister of National Defence: Ahmed Osman.

Minister of State for Culture: Hadj M'Hamed Bahnini.

Minister of State for Information: Ahmed Taïbi Benhima.

Minister of State for Foreign Affairs: Dr. Ahmed Laraki.

Minister of State for Co-operation and Professional Training: Dr. Mohamed Benhima.

Minister of the Interior: Mohamed Haddou Echiguer.

Minister of Posts, Telegraphs and Telecommunications: Gen. Driss Ben Aomar El Alami.

Minister of Administrative Affairs: M'Hamed Benyakhlef.

Minister of Health: Dr. Ahmed Ramzi.

Minister of Justice: Abbes Kaissi.

Minister of Waqfs and Islamic Affairs: Ould Sidi Baba.

Minister of Finance: Abdelkader Benslimane.

Minister of Agriculture and Agrarian Reform: Salah M'Zili.

Minister of Tourism, Housing, Town Planning and the Environment: Hassan Zemouri.

Minister of Trade, Industry, Mines and Merchant Shipping: Abdellatif Ghissassi.

Minister of Public Works: Ahmed Tazi.

Minister of Higher Education: Ben Abdeljalid.

Minister of Primary and Secondary Education: Mohamed Bouamoud.

Minister of Labour and Social Affairs: Mohamed Larbi El Khattabi.

Secretaries of State: *Responsible to the Prime Minister:* Abdallah Gharnit, Abdeslem Znined, Mohamed

Belhayat, Tayeb Bencheik; *Finance:* Kamal Regheghaye; *Trade, Industry, Mines and Merchant Shipping:* Oussa Saadi; *Housing, Tourism, Town Planning and the Environment:* Jalas As-Saïd; *Interior:* Driss Basri; *Information:* Mohamed Mahjoubi; *Waqfs and Islamic Affairs:* Hassab Loukach; *Youth and Sport:* Mohamed Tahiri Jotti.

DIPLOMATIC REPRESENTATION

EMBASSIES ACCREDITED TO MOROCCO

(In Rabat unless otherwise stated)

Algeria: 46 blvd. Front l'Oued; *Ambassador:* Ferhat Tayeb Hamida.

Argentina: 4 blvd. Moulay Hassan; *Ambassador:* Florencio Méndez Gazariego.

Austria: 2 rue de Tedders; *Ambassador:* Ernst Hessenberger.

Belgium: 6 avenue de Marrakech; *Ambassador:* Baron Roland D'Anethans.

Brazil: 34 rue Lamartine; *Ambassador:* Jose Jobim.

Bulgaria: 6 rue Blaise Pascal; *Ambassador:* Arsène Petrov Tarkov.

Cameroon: (address not available); *Ambassador:* Ferdinand Leopold Oyono.

Canada: Madrid, Spain.

Chile: rue Docteur Laraki, Quartier Souissi; *Chargé d'Affaires:* José Mario.

China, People's Republic: 6 rue Joachim du Bellay; *Ambassador:* Yang Chi-liang.

Cuba: 4 rue El Jabarti; *Ambassador:* Juan Antonio García.

Czechoslovakia: 4 rue Normand; *Ambassador:* Dr. Joseph Soltesz.

Denmark: 5 ave. de Marrakech; *Ambassador:* Arne Boegh Andersen (also accred. to Libya and Senegal).

Egypt: 31 rue d'Alger; *Ambassador:* Izz-al-din Ramzi.

Ethiopia: Hotel Rex; *Ambassador:* Gen. Makonnen Deneke.

Finland: *Ambassador:* Hanikainen Heikki Juhani.

France: ave. Mohammed V; *Ambassador:* Jean-Bernard Raimond.

Gabon: *Ambassador:* Léon N'Dony.

German Democratic Republic: *Ambassador:* Walfred Kitler.

Germany, Federal Republic: 2 blvd. Front d'Oued; *Ambassador:* Heinrich Kendus.

Ghana: Abidjan, Ivory Coast.

Greece: 9 rue de Kairouan; *Ambassador:* G. Warsamy.

Guatemala: Madrid, Spain.

Guinea: *Ambassador:* Camara Nabiyaya.

Hungary: 12 rue de Talda; *Ambassador:* László Guyaros.

India: 11 rue Descartes; *Ambassador:* Valliath Madhavan-Nair.

Indonesia: 29 rue Zankat Al Jaseir; *Ambassador:* Ahmed Janus Mokiginta.

Iran: 7 rue Montaigne; *Ambassador:* Abbes Nayeri Iram.

Iraq: 17 ave. de la Victoire; *Ambassador:* Dr. Hamad Dali al-Arbouli.

Italy: 9 ave. Franklin Roosevelt; *Ambassador:* Giovanni Ludovico Borromeo.

Ivory Coast: 21 rue de Tedders; *Ambassador:* Amadou Thiam.

Japan: 7 rue de Midelt; *Ambassador:* (vacant).

Jordan: 1 rue de Kairouan; *Ambassador:* Hachim Abou Amara.

Korea, Republic: 9 ave. de Meknès; *Ambassador:* Shi Hak Hyun.

Kuwait: 48 ave. Pasteur; *Ambassador:* Muhallal Al-Mudif.

Lebanon: 5 rue de Tedders; *Ambassador:* Abdul Rahman Adra.

Libya: 1 ave. A.-Derraq; *Ambassador:* Mohammed Tlissi.

Luxembourg: (*see* Netherlands).

Malaysia: *Ambassador:* Tan Sri Abd-Al-Latif.

Mali: *Ambassador:* Amadou Diababa.

Mauritania: *Ambassador:* Sidna Ould Shaikh Taleb Bouya.

Mexico: *Ambassador:* Ernesto Madeno.

Netherlands: 38 rue de Tunis; *Ambassador:* Jonkheer Jan-Derck van Karnebeek (also represents Luxembourg).

Norway: 20 ave. Yarmouk; *Ambassador:* Olav Moltke-Hausen.

Pakistan: route des Zaërs; *Ambassador:* Maqbul Abid.

Peru: Algiers, Algeria.

Poland: rue Omar Slaoui; *Ambassador:* Zdziz Ian Pacowski.

Portugal: 45 rue Maurice Pascouet; *Ambassador:* (vacant).

Qatar: *Ambassador:* Abdullah Youssef Al-Jida.

Romania: 10 rue d'Ouezzane; *Ambassador:* Coronel Purtica.

Saudi Arabia: 45 place Ibn Said; *Ambassador:* Fakhry Sheikh El Adhr.

Senegal: 3 rue Descartes; *Ambassador:* Lamine Diakhate.

Spain: 1 ave de Marrakech; *Ambassador:* Adolfo Martín Gamero y Gonza.

Sudan: Cairo, Egypt.

Sweden: 6 rue Slaouane; *Ambassador:* Bo Siegbahn (also accred. to Libya and Senegal).

Switzerland: square Condo de Sabriano; *Ambassador:* Jean Strohlin.

Syria: *Ambassador:* GHALEB HAMDI ABDOUN.

Tunisia: 5 rue Montaigne; *Ambassador:* BASHIR MEHEDEBI.

Turkey: 6 rue El Yarmouk; *Ambassador:* KAMURAN ACET.

U.S.S.R.: 18 ave. Abderrahmane Aneggai; *Ambassador:* LOUCA BALAMARTCHOUK.

United Arab Emirates: *Ambassador:* MOHAMED ALI TAJIR.

United Kingdom: 28 ave. Allal Ben Abdullah; *Ambassador:* RONALD BAILEY.

U.S.A.: 45 ave. Allal Ben Abdullah; *Ambassador:* ROBERT NEUMANN.

Uruguay: 18 rue Descartes; *Ambassador:* JULIO PONS.

Venezuela: *Ambassador:* PEDRO BARRADAS.

Viet-Nam, Republic: 5 ave. de Meknès; *Chargé d'Affaires:* BUU-KINH.

Yugoslavia: 10 rue de Djebli; *Ambassador:* LJUPCE TAVCIOVSKI.

Zaire: *Ambassador:* (vacant).

Zambia: *Ambassador:* MATIVA N'GALANTE.

Morocco also has diplomatic relations with Afghanistan, Albania, Chad, Costa Rica, the Republic of Guinea-Bissau, Mongolia, Niger, Nigeria, Oman and the Vatican.

NATIONAL ASSEMBLY

Although the constitution of March 1972 provides for a
new form of Assembly, a date has not yet been set for
elections, and parliament remains dissolved.

POLITICAL PARTIES

Mouvement Populaire: Leader MAHJOUBI AHERDAN; had 60 seats in Chamber of Representatives.

Progrès Social: represents salaried workers' groups; 10 seats in former Chamber of Representatives.

Istiqlal: f. 1944; aims to raise living standards, to confer equal rights on all, stresses the Moroccan claim to Mauritania and the Spanish Sahara; formed a National Front with UNFP July 1970; 9 seats in former Chamber of Representatives; Sec.-Gen. MOHAMED BOUCETTA; publs. *Al Alam* (daily) and *L'Opinion* (daily).

Union National des Forces Populaires—UNFP (*National Union of Popular Forces*): B.P. 747, Casablanca; f. 1959 by MEHDI BEN BARKA from a group within Istiqlal; left wing; opposition party; formed National Front with Istiqlal July 1970; 2 seats in former Chamber of Representatives; in July 1972 the national administrative committee suspended the 10-man secretariat general and rejected the 3-man political bureau for failing to arrange a third congress and acting autocratically; five permanent committees have replaced them.

Union National des Forces Populaires—UNFP (**Rabat section**): Rabat; f. 1972 by the political bureau of the UNFP when the party split in July; Leader ABDERRAHIM BOUABID.

Parti Démocratique Constitutionnel: Leader MOHAMMED HASSAN WAZZANI; 1 seat in former Chamber of Representatives.

Mouvement Populaire Constitutionnel et Démocratique—MPCD: breakaway party from *Mouvement Populaire*; Leader ABDELKRIM KHATIB.

JUDICIAL SYSTEM

The **Supreme Court** (*Majlis el Aala*), created on September 27th, 1957, is responsible for the interpretation of the law and regulates the jurisprudence of the courts and tribunals of the Kingdom. The Supreme Court sits at Rabat and is divided into four Chambers:

1 Civil Chamber (the First Chamber).
1 Criminal Chamber.
1 Administrative Chamber.
1 Social Chamber.

First President and Attorney-General: BRAHIM KEDDARA.

There are 20 Counsellors and 4 General Advocates.

Three Courts of Appeal. The Fez Court covers all the former Southern Zone and comprises:

8 Regional Tribunals.
11 Sadad Tribunals and branch chambers.

The Court of Appeal at Marrakesh comprises:

4 Regional Tribunals.
7 Sadad Tribunals and branch chambers.

The Court of Appeal at Casablanca comprises:

4 Regional Tribunals.
9 Sadad Tribunals and branch chambers.

The **Sadad Tribunals** pass judgment, without possibility of appeal, in personal, civil and commercial cases involving up to 300 dirhams. These tribunals also pass judgment, subject to appeal before the Regional Tribunals, in the same cases up to 900 dirhams, in disputes related to the personal and successional statutes of Moroccan Muslims and Jews, and in penal cases involving misdemeanours or infringements of the law.

The **Regional Tribunals** deal with appeals against judgments made by the Sadad Tribunals; and pass judgment in the first and last resort in cases of personal property of 900 to 1,200 dirhams or property producing a yield of up to 80 dirhams. The Regional Tribunals also pass judgment, subject to appeal before the Court of Appeal, in actions brought against public administrations in administrative affairs, and in cases of minor offences in penal matters.

Labour Tribunals settle, by means of conciliation, disputes arising from rental contracts or services between employers and employees engaged in private industry. There are 14 labour tribunals in the Kingdom.

A special court was created in 1965 in Rabat to deal with corruption among public officials.

RELIGION

MUSLIMS

Most Moroccans are Muslims.

CHRISTIANS

There are about 400,000 Christians, mostly Roman Catholics.

Archbishop of Rabat: Jean Marcel Chabbert, 1 rue de l'Evêché, B.P. 258, Rabat.

Archbishop of Tangier: Francisco Aldegunde Dorrego; 55 S. Francisco, B.P. 2116, Tangier.

JEWS

There are between 60,000 and 80,000 Jews.

Grand Rabbi of Casablanca: 167 blvd. Ziraoui, Casablanca; Chalom Messas, President of the Rabbinical Court of Casablanca, Palais de Justice, Place des Nations Unies.

THE PRESS

DAILIES
Casablanca

Maghreb Informations: 16 rue de Foucauld; f. 1966; organ of U.M.T.; suspended by government 1968–71; Dir Boubker Monkachi.

Maroc Soir: 34 rue Mohammed Smiha; f. Nov. 1971 to replace *La Vigie Marocaine*, closed down by the Government; French; Dir. Moulay Ahmad Alawi; circ. 30,000.

Le Matin: rue Mohammed Smiha; f. Nov. 1971 to replace *Le Petit Marocain*, closed down by the Government; French; Dir. Ahmed Benkirane; circ. 45,000.

Rabat

Al Alam (*The Flag*): ave. Allal Ben Abdullah 11; organ of the Istiqlal Party; f. 1946; Arabic; Dir. M. A. Ghallab; circ. 30,000; also *Al Alam Book*.

Al Anba'a (*Information*): rue Hamdani, B.P. 65; Arabic; Dir. Ali Alaoui; circ. 5,000.

L'Opinion: ave. Allal Ben Abdullah 11; f. 1965; Istiqlal party newspaper; French; Dir. Abdelhamid Aouad; circ. 60,000.

Tangier

Diario España: Calle Cervantes; f. 1938; Spanish; independent; Pres. Luis Zarraluqui; Dir. Manuel Cruz.

PERIODICALS
Casablanca

Al Ahdaffe: left-wing weekly; Dir. Ahmed Al Kharrass.

Akbar Al-Dounia: Arabic; weekly; independent; satirical.

At Talia: Arabic; organ of U.M.T.; weekly; Editor Mahjub Ben el Seddiq.

L'Avant Garde: 222 ave. de l'Armée Royale; French and Arabic; trade union affairs; weekly; Dir. Mohammed Tibary; circ. 10,000.

Al Bayane: 32 rue Ledru-Rollin, B.P. 152, Casablanca; Arabic and French; weekly; Dir. Ali Yata.

Al Fallah: 49 rue Tizi Ougli, Ain Sebâa; agricultural; fortnightly; Dir. Ahmed Nejjai.

Index Analytique de la Production Marocaine: 61 blvd. de Bordeaux; industrial directory; French, English and German; Editor J. Axelrod.

Lamalif: French; monthly; non-political features and cultural magazine.

Maroc-Médical: Immeuble Liberté, 287 Bd. de la Liberté; f. 1920; French; monthly medical journal; Dir. E. Lepinay; Editor Prof. Agr. J. Chenebault.

Al Mohirrin (*The Liberator*): 46 rue de la Garonne; organ of UNFP (Rabat section); Dir. Omar Benjelloun (arrested March 1973).

L'Opinion: published by the Istiqlal Party; f. 1962; circ. 50,000.

Al Oummal (*The Workers*): 10 ave. de l'Armée Royale; trade union affairs (U.G.T.M.); Arabic; weekly.

Tahrir: 13 rue Soldat Roche; Arabic.

La Vie Economique: 5 ave. Abdallah Ben Yacine; f. 1921; French; weekly; Editor Marcel Herzog.

Fez

Al-Siassa (*Politics*): 10 rue de l'Angleterre; Arabic; f. 1967; weekly; Man. Dir. Mohammed Hassan Quazzani.

Rabat

Achaab (*The People*): 2 rue Parmentier, B.P. 364; independent; twice weekly; Arabic; Founder and Editor M. Mekki Naciri; Dir. Mustapha Belhaj; circ. 25,000.

Action Africaine: 10 place Mohammed V; popular; circ. 3,000.

Atlas: ave. Mohammed V; Arabic; fortnightly; illustrated; political and general information.

Chenguit: Arabic; weekly.

Al Fellah: Chamber of Agriculture; on agricultural affairs; weekly; Arabic.

Al Idaa al Watania: Arabic; monthly.

Al Janoub: Ministry of State for Mauritanian and Saharan Affairs, 6 ave. Moulay Hafid; southern affairs; Dir. Khalifa Mahfoud; circ. 30,000.

Al Maghreb al Arabi: 8 place Mohammed V; weekly.

Al Manarat: 281 ave. Mohammed V; F.D.I.C. weekly; Arabic.

Maroc-65: Ministry Representative of H.M. the King; f. 1965.

Al Nidal (*The Fight*): ave. Allal Ben Abdullah 18; political; weekly; Arabic; liberal; independent.

Sahraouna: 6 rue Moulay Hafid; Arabic; weekly.

Sawt al Maghreb (*Voice of the Maghreb*): 1 rue Pierre Parent; organ of the R.T.M.; Arabic; monthly.

La Voix des Communautés: 12 Sh. el Amir Moulay Abdullah; monthly organ of the Jewish Community; French; Dir. DAVID AMAR.

Tangier

Al Mitak: Kasba 39; f. 1962; religious; fortnightly; Dir. Prof. ABDALLAH GUNNOUN.

Journal de Tanger: B.P. 420; French; weekly; Dir. R. DELAUNAY.

Tanjah: 8 place de France, B.P. 1055; f. 1956; French and Arabic; weekly; Dir. MOHAMMED MEHDI ZAHDI.

NEWS AGENCIES

Maghreb Arabe Presse: 10 rue Al-Yamama, Rabat; f. 1959; Arabic, French and English; independent; Casablanca, Tangier; Man. Dir. MEHDI BENNOUNA.

Moroccan National News Agency: Rabat; became Government-owned 1973.

FOREIGN BUREAUX

AFP (*France*): place Mohammed V, B.P. 118, Rabat; f. 1920; French; Dir. DAVID DAURE; Sec. and Editor MANOUBI MEKNASSY.

ANSA (*Italy*): c/o "MAP", 10 rue Al-Yamama, Rabat; Chief (vacant).

DPA, Reuters and Tass also have bureaux in Rabat.

PUBLISHERS

Dar El Kitab: Place de la Mosquée, B.P. 4018, Casablanca; philosophy, law, etc.; Arabic and French; Dir. BOUTA-LEB ABDELHAY.

Imprimerie Artistique: 31 avenue Es-Sellaoui, Fez.

Imprimerie de Fedala: rue Ibn Zaidoun, Mohammedia; f. 1949; education, history, theology.

RADIO AND TELEVISION

RADIO

Radiodiffusion Télévision Marocaine: 1 Zenkat Al Brihi, Rabat; Government station; Network 1 in Arabic, Network 2 in French, Network 3 in Berber, Spanish and English; Foreign Service in Arabic, French and English; Dir. Radio and TV TAIEB BELLARBI; publ. *Sawt al Maghreb*.

Number of radios (1972): 2,000,000.

Voice of America Radio Station in Tangier: Voice of America, Washington, D.C. 20547, U.S.A.

TELEVISION

Radiodiffusion Télévision Marocaine: 11 rue Al Brihl, Rabat; f. 1962; 60½ hours weekly; French and Arabic; linked with Eurovision in 1964; carries commercial advertising; Dir.-Gen. TAIEB BELLARBI.

Number of television sets (1973): 319,278.

FINANCE

(amounts in dirhams unless otherwise indicated.)

BANKING

CENTRAL BANK

Banque du Maroc: 277 ave. Mohammed V, Rabat; f. 1959; cap. 20m.; dep. 486m. (Dec. 1971); Gov. Prince MOULAY HASSAN BEN MEHDI; Vice-Gov. AHMED BENNANI.

MOROCCAN BANKS

Algemene Bank Nederland (Maroc) S.A.: Place du 16 Novembre, Casablanca; branch in Tangier; f. 1948; wholly owned subsidiary of Algemene Bank Nederland N.V., Amsterdam, Netherlands; cap. 5m.; Man. B. HANSEN.

Banco Español en Marruecos, S.A.M.: blvd. Mohammed V, Casablanca; f. 1964; affil. to Banco Exterior de España, Madrid; cap. 2.5m.; dep. 70.4m. (Dec. 1972); Chair. MANUEL ARBURÚA DE LA MIYAR; Gen. Man. JOSÉ-MARIA BRAVO IBÁÑEZ.

Banque Americano Franco-Suisse pour le Maroc: 26 avo. de l'Armée Royale, B.P. 972, Casablanca; f. 1951; affil. to Swiss Bank Corporation, Crédit Commercial de France and Continental Illinois National Bank & Trust Co. of Chicago; cap. 4.5m.; Man. ROLAND FREY.

Banque Commerciale du Maroc S.A.: 81 ave. de l'Armée Royale, Casablanca; f. 1911; affiliated to Crédit Industriel et Commercial, Paris, France; cap. 10m., dep. 538m. (Dec. 1972); Pres. R. BELIN; Gen. Man. A. ALAMI; 5 brs.

Banque Marocaine du Commerce Extérieur: 241 boulevard Mohammed V, Casablanca; f. 1959; took over Société de Banque du Maghreb, oldest-established foreign bank, 1971; partly state-owned; cap. 20m., res. 29m. (Dec. 1972); Chair. and Chief Exec. HADJ ABDEL MAJID BENGELLOUN; Man. Dir. DRISS GUEDDARI; 50 brs. in Morocco, one in Paris, one in Tangiers Free Zone.

Banque Marocaine pour le Commerce et l'Industrie: 26 place Mohammed V, Casablanca, P.O.B. 573; f. 1964; cap. 12m., res. 19m. (Dec. 1972); Pres. HADJ AHMED BARGACH; Gen. Man. MOHAMED BENKIRANE; 23 brs.

Banque A Mas: 51 ave. Hassan-Seghir, Casablanca.

Banque Nationale pour le Développement Economique: B.P. 407, place des Alaouites, Rabat; f. 1959; cap. p.u. 3.2m.; Pres. and Gen. Man. MUSTAPHA FARES; publ. *Rapport annuel.*

Banque de Paris et des Pays-Bas (Maroc): 79 avenue Hassan II, Casablanca; f. 1968; cap. 5m.; Gen. Man. F. JOURDAN.

British Bank of the Middle East (Morocco): 80 ave. Lalla Yacout, P.O.B. 880, Casablanca; f. 1948; 3 brs. in Casablanca, one in Tangier; Chair. C. E. LOOMBE, C.M.G.

Compagnie Marocaine de Crédit et de Banque S.A.: 1 ave. Hassan II, Casablanca; f. 1964; affiliated to Compagnie Française de Crédit et de Banque, Paris, France; cap. 14.5m., res. 5.4m.; Pres. ALI KETTANI; 46 brs.

Credit du Maroc S.A.: B.P. 579, 48–58 blvd. Mohammed V, Casablanca; f. 1963; cap. 8m., res. 15m. (Dec. 1971); Pres. M. KARIM-LAMRANI; Dir.-Gen. JAWAD BEN BRAHIM.

Société Générale Marocaine de Banques: 84 blvd. Mohammed V, B.P. 90, Casablanca; f. 1962; cap. 11m., res. 7m. (Dec. 1971); Chair. HAMED BARGACH; Man. Dir. YVES BONDIL; 18 brs.

Unión Bancaria Hispano Marroquí: 69 rue du Prince Moulay Abdullah, Casablanca; f. 1958; cap. 16m., dep. 229m. (Dec. 1971); Pres. ANTONIO SAEZ DE MONTAGUT; Gen. Man. PEDRO LANDRA VELON; 15 brs.

Worms et Cie. (Maroc): 81 rue Colbert, Casablanca, B.P. 602; f. 1960; cap. 6,048,000; brs. in Rabat and Casablanca; Pres. ROBERT DUBOST; Gen. Man. JEAN PINEILL.

FOREIGN BANKS

Arab Bank Limited: Amman, Jordan; Casablanca and Rabat.

Several Spanish banks have branches in Ceuta.

BANK ORGANIZATIONS

Groupement Professionnel des Banques du Maroc: 27 ave. Hassan II, B.P. 577, Casablanca; f. 1967; groups all commercial banks for organization, studies, inquiries of general interest, and connection with official authorities; Pres. Hadj ABDELMAJID BENGELLOUN.

Association Professionelle des Intermédiaires de Bourse: 27 ave Hassan II, B.P. 577, Casablanca; f. 1970; groups all banks and brokers in the stock exchange of Casablanca, for organization, studies, inquiries of general interest and connection with official authorities; Pres. Hadj ABDELMAJID BENGELLOUN.

STOCK EXCHANGE

Bourse des Valeurs de Casablanca: Chamber of Commerce Building, 98 boulevard Mohammed V, Casablanca; f. 1929; Dir. ABDERRAZAK LARAQUI; publ. *Bulletin de la Cote.*

INSURANCE

Atlanta: 243 blvd. Mohammed V, Casablanca; f. 1947; Dir. M. POIRRIER.

Atlas: 44 rue Mohammed Smiha, Casablanca; Dir. M. POIRRIER.

Cie. Africaine d'Assurances: 123 blvd. Rahal el Meskini, Casablanca; Dir. M. ROUTHIER.

Cie. Nordafricaine et Intercontinentale d'Assurances (C.N.I.A.): 157 ave. Hassan II, Casablanca; cap. 1.8m.; Pres. ABDELKAMEL RERHRHAYE.

Cia. Marroqui de Seguros: 62 rue de la Liberté, Tangier; Dir. M. BUISAN.

COMAR Paternelle-Prévoyance: 42 avenue de l'Armée Royale, Casablanca; cap. 3.1m.; Gen. Man. BERNARD PAGEZY.

L'Empire: 45 rue du Cdt. Lamy, Casablanca; Dir. M. LÓPEZ.

L'Entente: 2 rue Mohammed Smiha, Casablanca; f. 1960; Pres. PIERRE ESTEVA; Man. Dir. MAURICE FLEUREAU.

Mutuelle Agricole Marocaine d'Assurances: 14 rue Abou Faras El Marini, Rabat; Dir. Gen. YACOUBI SOUSSANE.

La Providence Marocaine: 1 rond-point St. Exupéry, Casablanca; Dir. M. DE ROQUEFEUIL.

La Royale Marocaine d'Assurance: 67 ave. de l'Armée Royale, Casablanca; cap. 1.1m.; Dir.-Gen. MAHOMED BEN JILALI BENNANI.

Es Saada, Cie. Générale d' Assurances et de Réassurances: 123 ave. Hassan II, Casablanca.

Société Centrale de Réassurance: P.O.B. 435, 31 boulevard des Alaouites, Rabat; f. 1961; Dir. MOHAMED AIMARAH.

Société Marocaine d'Assurances: 1 rond-point Saint Exupéry, Casablanca; Dir. M. GIUSTINIANI.

Fédération Marocaine des Sociétés d'Assurances et de Réassurances: 300 rue Mustafa el Maani, Casablanca; f. 1958; Pres. M'HAMED BEN JILALI BENNANI; Dir. SEBTI ABDELHAQ.

TRADE AND INDUSTRY

CHAMBERS OF COMMERCE

Chambre de Commerce et d'Industrie de Casablanca: 98 blvd. Mohammed V, B.P. 423, Casablanca; Pres. ABDELLAH SOUIRA.

Chambre Française de Commerce et d'Industrie du Maroc (CFCI): 15 avenue Mers Sultan, B.P. 73, Casablanca; Pres. J. F. BRANDENBURG; Dir. PIERRE ROUSSELOT.

La Fédération des Chambres de Commerce et d'Industrie du Maroc: B.P. 218, 11 ave. Allal Ben Abdullah, Rabat; f. 1962; groups the 15 Chambers of Commerce and Industry; Pres. ABDELLAH SOUIRA; publ. *Revue Trimestrielle.*

DEVELOPMENT ORGANIZATIONS

Bureau d'Etudes et de Participations Industrielles (BEPI): 8 rue Michaux-Bellaire, Rabat; f. 1958; a state agency to develop industry.

Bureau de Recherches et de Participations Minières (BRPM): 27 Charia Moulay Hassan, Rabat; f. 1928; a state agency to develop the mining industry; Dir.-Gen. ABDELAZIZ BENJELLOUN.

Caisse Marocaine des Marchés (*Marketing Fund*): Casablanca.

Caisse Nationale de Crédit Agricole (*Agricultural Credit Fund*): B.P. 49, Rabat.

Crédit Immobilier et Hôtelier: 159 ave. Hassan II, Casablanca; f. 1920; cap. 20m.; Dir. Gen. MOHAMED BENCHEKROUN.

Office de Commercialisation et d'Exportation (OCE): 45 ave des F.A.R., Casablanca; f. 1965; turnover (1970–71) 1,300m. Dirhams; takes part in productivity planning, industrialization and overseas trade; Dir. SBIHI ABDELHADI.

STATE ENTERPRISES

Complexe Textile de Fes (COTEF): B.P. 267, Fez; f. 1967; 90 per cent state participation; a plant for weaving up to 45 million sq. metres of cloth per annum, started full activity in Jan 1972.

Mines du Rif de Nador (SEFERIF): Nador; nationalized 1967; two iron mines produce 1,380,000 tons of ore per annum for the Nador iron and steel complex.

Office Chérifien des Phosphates (OCP): Rabat; f. 1921; a state company to produce and market rock phosphates and derivatives; Dir.-Gen. MOHAMMED KARIM LAMRANI.

Office National de l'Electricité: B.P. 498, Casablanca; state electrical authority.

EMPLOYERS' ORGANIZATIONS

Association Marocaine des Industries Textiles: 58 rue Lugherim, Casablanca; f. 1958; mems. 300 textile factories; Pres. MOHAMED DRISSI; publ. *Bulletin* (weekly).

Association des Producteurs d'Agrumes du Maroc (ASPAM): 44 rue Mohamed Smiha, Casablanca; links Moroccan citrus growers; has its own processing plants.

Confédération Générale Economique Marocaine (C.G.E.M.): 23 blvd. Mohammed Abdouh, Casablanca; Pres. MOHAMED AMOR; Sec.-Gen. M. FAYÇAL CHRAÏBI.

Office Chérifien Interprofessionelle des Céréales: Casablanca; Dir. MOHAMED BRICK.

Union Marocaine de l'Agriculture (U.M.A.): rue Michaux-Bellaire, Rabat; Pres. M. NEJJAI.

TRADE UNIONS

Union Générale des Travailleurs du Maroc (U.G.T.M.): 9 rue du Rif, angle Route de Médiouna, Casablanca; associated with Istiqlal; supported by unions not affiliated to U.M.T.; Sec.-Gen. ABDERRAZZAQ AFILAL.

Union Marocaine du Travail (U.M.T.): Bourse du Travail, 222 avenue de l'Armée Royale, Casablanca; left wing and associated with UNFP (Rabat); most unions are affiliated; 700,000 mems.; Sec. MAHJOUB BEN SEDDIQ; publs. *Maghreb Informations* (daily), *L'Avant Garde* (French weekly), *At Talia* (Arabic weekly).

Union Syndicate Agricole (U.S.A.): agricultural section of U.M.T.

Syndicat National Libre: blvd. Hansali (prolongé), Casablanca; f. 1958; 69,000 mems.; Sec.-Gen. MEEKI IBRAHIMY.

Union Agricole pour le Progrès Rural: Agricultural union; associated with *Mouvement populaire*.

Union Marocaine de l'Agriculture (U.M.A.): Pres. M. NEJJAI.

TRADE FAIR

Foire Internationale de Casablanca: 11 rue Jules Mauran, Casablanca; international trade fair; alternate years usually for two weeks in April–May; next fair will be 1975.

TRANSPORT

RAILWAYS

Railways cover 1,756 km. of which 161 km. are double track; 708 km. of lines are electrified and diesel locomotives are used on the rest. All services are nationalized.

Office National des Chemins de Fer du Maroc (ONCFM): 19 ave. Allal Ben Abdallah, Rabat; f. 1963; runs all Morocco's railways; Pres. SALAH M'ZILY; Dir. MOUSSA MOUSSAOUI.

ROADS

There are about 52,000 km. of roads of which 42 per cent are surfaced. In 1972 there were 14 km. of modern motorway and 7,620 km. of main roads. Road length increases by about 300 km. a year. Most public transport is by road.

Compagnie Auxiliaire de Transports au Maroc (C.T.M.): 303 blvd. Brahim Roudani, Casablanca; Agencies in Tangier, Rabat, Meknès, Oujda, Marrakesh, Agadir, El Jadida, Safi, Essouira, Ksar-Es-Souk and Ouarzazate.

MOTORISTS' ORGANIZATIONS

The Royal Moroccan Automobile Club: place des Nations Unies, P.O.B. 94, Casablanca; f. 1913; 10,000 mems.; offices at Kenitra, Meknès, Fez, Oujda, Tangier, El Jadida, Safi, Marrakesh, Agadir, Taza, Khouribga, Youssoufia and Tétuan; Pres. MOHAMMED M'JID.

Touring Club du Maroc: 3 ave. de l'Armée Royale, Casablanca; 645 mems., 10,021 associate mems.; Pres. LARBI LAMRANI.

SHIPPING

The chief ports of Morocco are Tangier, Casablanca, Safi, Mohammedia, Kenitra and Agadir. In January 1962 the port of Tangier became an International Free Zone. Tangier is the principal port for passenger services. Casablanca is the principal freight port, handling 70 per cent of Morocco's trade.

Agence Gibmar S.A.: 3 rue Henri Regnault, Tangier; also at Casablanca; regular sea services from Tangier to Gibraltar.

Compagnie Chérifienne d'Armement: 5 ave. de l'Armée Royale, Casablanca; f. 1929; Pres. BENNANI-SMIRES; regular lines to North France and Europe.

Compagnie Maritime des Chargeurs Réunis: Agence Paquet, 65 ave. de l'Armée Royale, B.P. 60, Casablanca.

Compagnie Marocaine de Navigation: 28 rue de Lille, Casablanca; f. 1946; Pres., Dir.-Gen. A. BOUAYAD.

Limadet-ferry: 3 rue Henri Regnault, Tangier; operates between Malaga and Tangier.

Normandy Ferry Co.: Casablanca; regular car ferry service to Lisbon and Southampton.

Transmediterranea S.A., Cia: 39 rue du Mexique, Tangier, and at Casablanca; daily services Algeciras to Tangier.

Voyages Paquet: 65 ave. de l'Armée Royale, Casablanca; 21 ave. d'Espagne, Tangier.

CIVIL AVIATION

There are international airports at Casablanca, Rabat, Tangier, Marrakesh and Agadir.

NATIONAL AIRLINES

Royal Air Maroc: Aéroport International Casablanca, Nouasseur; f. 1953; 67.7 per cent owned by the Government; domestic flights and services to Algeria, Austria, Belgium, Canada, France, Federal Germany, Italy, Mauritania, Netherlands, Senegal, Spain, Switzerland, Tunisia, United Kingdom and U.S.A.; fleet of three Boeing 727, four Caravelles; Chair. AHMED LASKY; Gen. Man. SAID BEN ALI.

Royal Air Inter: Aéroport Casablanca-Anfa; f. 1970; operates domestic services from Casablanca to Agadir, Al Hoceima, Fez, Ksar-es-Souk, Marrakesh, Ouarzazate, Oujda, Rabat, Tangier and Tetouan; fleet of two F-27; Dir. Gen. HASSAN YACOUBI SOUSSANE.

Casablanca is served by the following foreign airlines: Aeroflot, Air Afrique, Air Algérie, Air France, Air Mali, Alitalia, Balkan, British Caledonian, Iberia, KLM, Lufthansa, Pan American, Sabena, Saudia, Swissair and Tunis Air. In addition, ČSA fly to Rabat, British Airways to Marrakesh and Agadir, and Gibair to Tangier.

TOURISM

Office National Marocain de Tourisme: B.P. 19, 22 ave. d'Alger, Rabat; f. 1946; Dir. ABDELLATIF AMOR; publ. *Maroc-Tourisme* (quarterly).

CULTURAL ORGANIZATIONS

Direction des Affaires Culturelles: Ministry of Education and Fine Arts, Jardin de la Mamounia, Rabat; consists of three departments: Cultural Activities, Fine Arts and Folklore, Historical Monuments and Antiquities, which together administer all national cultural activities; Publs. *Bulletin d'Archéologie Marocaine, Etudes et Travaux d'Archéologie Marocaine.*

Association des Amateurs de la Musique Andalouse: Casablanca; directed and subsidized by the Ministry of Education and Fine Arts; Dir. Hadj DRISS BENJELLOUN.

PRINCIPAL THEATRES

Théâtre National Mohammed V: Rabat; Morocco's national theatre with its own troupe, subsidized by the state; Dir. M. A. SEGHROUCHNI.

Théâtre Municipal de Casablanca: blvd. de Paris, Casablanca; f. 1922, reorganized 1934 and 1949; presents a large number of foreign and national productions; maintained by the Casablanca Municipality; Dir. TAIB SADDIKI; Gen. Administrator ALI KADIRI.

PRINCIPAL ORCHESTRAS

Orchestre Symphonique du Conservatoire National de Musique: Rabat; European classical music and Andalusian (Arabic) music; chamber orchestra.

Orchestre du Conservatoire de Tétouan: Tetuan; specializes in Andalusian (Arabic) music; Dir. M. TEMSEMANI.

Orchestre du Conservatoire Dar Adyel: Fez; specializing in traditional music; Dir. Hadj ABDELKRIM RAIS.

FESTIVAL

Folklore Festival: Marrakesh; national festival of folk dancing; annually April–May; organized by the Ministry of Tourism under the direction of the Ministry of Education and Fine Arts.

UNIVERSITIES

Al Quarawiyin University: 27 rue St. Pierre et Miquelon, Rabat; f. A.D. 859; 866 students.

Université Mohammed V: ave. Moulay Chérif, Rabat; f. 1957; 15,893 students.

NAURU

INTRODUCTORY SURVEY

Location, Climate, Religion, Flag

The Republic of Nauru is a small island in the Central Pacific, lying about 1,300 miles north-east of Australia. Nauru has a warm and pleasant climate. About half the population are Nauruans, most of them belonging to the Nauruan Protestant Church. The national flag (proportions 2 by 1) is blue, divided by a horizontal gold bar, with a 12-pointed white star at the lower left.

Recent History

A former German colony, the island was occupied by Australia during the 1914–18 war. The island continued under the administration of Australia under a League of Nations mandate which also named the United Kingdom and New Zealand as co-trustees. Between 1942 and 1945 Nauru was occupied by the Japanese. In 1947 the island was placed under United Nations Trusteeship, with Australia as the administering power on behalf of the Governments of Australia, New Zealand and the United Kingdom. The UN Trusteeship Council proposed in 1964 that the indigenous people of Nauru be resettled on Curtis Island, off the Queensland coast. This offer was made in anticipation of the progressive exhaustion of the island's phosphate deposits. The Nauruans elected to remain on the island, and studies were put in train in 1966 for the shipping of soil to the island to replace the phosphate rock. Nauru received a considerable measure of self-government in January 1966, with the establishment of Legislative and Executive Councils, and proceeded to independence on January 31st, 1968.

Government

The Head of State is the President who governs the Republic, assisted by a Cabinet; legislative power is vested in an elected parliament.

Nauru is a special member of the Commonwealth. The status of "Special Membership", announced in November 1968, gives Nauru the right to participate in all functional activities of the Commonwealth and to receive appropriate documentation in relation to them as well as the right to participate in non-governmental Commonwealth organizations. Nauru is not represented at Meetings of Commonwealth Heads of Government, but attends Commonwealth Meetings at ministerial or official level in such fields as education, medical co-operation, finance, and other functional and technical areas. Nauru is eligible for Commonwealth technical assistance.

Economic Affairs

The island's only industry is phosphate mining, which is manned largely by indentured labour. About four-fifths of the area is phosphate-bearing rock, but deposits are expected to be exhausted by 1992.

Education

In 1971 the island had 10 primary schools, with 65 teachers and 1,118 pupils, and two secondary schools with 29 teachers and 364 pupils.

STATISTICAL SURVEY

Area: 8.2 square miles.

Population (June 30th, 1972): Total 6,768 (Nauruan 3,471, Other Pacific Islanders 1,787, Chinese 883, European 627).

Employment: Total 2,473 (Administration 845, Phosphate Mining 1,408, Other activities 220).

Finance: Australian currency: 100 cents=1 Australian dollar ($A). Coins: 1, 2, 5, 10, 20 and 50 cents. Notes: 1, 2, 5, 10, 20 and 50 dollars. Exchange rates (April 1974): £1 sterling=$A1.585; U.S. $1=67.23 Australian cents. $A100=£63.10= U.S. $148.75.

Budget (1971–72—$A): Revenue: Total $7,503,943. Expenditure: Total $7,721,890 (Health $389,738, Education $649,194).

Imports (1970–71) ($A): Total $4,502,123 (from Australia $4,148,435).

Exports (1968–69): Phosphate only, 2,186,000 tons. Exports to Australia 1,424,050 tons, United Kingdom 73,800 tons, New Zealand 526,950 tons, Japan 161,200 tons.

THE CONSTITUTION

Protects the fundamental rights and freedoms and provides for a Cabinet responsible to a popularly elected Parliament. The President of the Republic is elected by Parliament from among its members. The Cabinet is composed of five members including the President who presides. There are eighteen members of Parliament including the Cabinet. Voting is compulsory for those over 20 years of age, except in certain specified instances.

The highest judicial organ is the Supreme Court and there is provision for the setting up of subordinate courts with designated jurisdiction.

There is a Treasury Fund from which moneys may be taken by Appropriation Acts.

A Public Service is provided for with the person designated as the Chief Secretary being the Commissioner of the Public Service.

THE GOVERNMENT

President: HAMMER DeROBURT, O.B.E., M.P. (elected May 1968; re-elected January 26th, 1971, and December 18th, 1973).

CABINET

Minister of External Affairs, Minister of Internal Affairs, Minister of Island Development and Industry and Minister of Civil Aviation: HAMMER DeROBURT, O.B.E., M.P.

Minister of Health and Education: The Hon. AUSTIN BERNICKE, M.P.

Minister of Works and Community Services and Minister Assistant to the President: The Hon. R. BURARO DETUDAMO, M.P.

Minister of Finance: The Hon. James Ategan Bop, M.P.

Minister of Justice: The Hon. Joseph Detsimea Audoa, M.P.

PARLIAMENT

Elected December 15th, 1973.
18 members.

Speaker: The Hon. K. Aroi, M.P.

DIPLOMATIC REPRESENTATION

Nauru Representative in Australia and New Zealand: A. E. Holmes, Nauru Government Office, 227 Collins St., Melbourne, Vic. 3000.

Nauru Representative in the United Kingdom: Q. V. L. Weston, Nauru Government Office, 11 Carteret St., London, SW1H 9DJ.

Nauruan Consul in Japan: T. Moses, New Shinsaka Bldg. 10, 28 Chome Aleasaka, Minato-ku, Tokyo.

Honorary Consul General in U.S.A.: Carlton Skinner, 110 Sutter St., Suite 1003, San Francisco, Calif. 94194.

Australia (High Commissioner): L. G. Sellars.

JUDICIAL SYSTEM

SUPREME COURT

Chief Justice: His Honour Mr. Justice Ian Roy Thompson.

DISTRICT COURT

Acting Resident Magistrate: Richard Da Silva.

Magistrates: J. A. Doguape, R. K. H. Grundler, V. Eoaeo.

RELIGION

About 43 per cent of Nauruans are adherents of the Nauruan Protestant Church. The Sacred Heart of Jesus Mission (Roman Catholic) is also represented.

PRESS AND RADIO

Bulletin: Local news; fortnightly; Editor Des Telfer; circ. 950.

Radio Nauru: Opened August 1968; Man. David Agir; Broadcasts Officer Rantag Harris.

FINANCE

BANKING

There is one bank:

Bank of New South Wales: 341 George St., Sydney, N.S.W., Australia; br. in Nauru.

INSURANCE

Union Assurance Society Ltd.: maintains an agent in Nauru.

TRADE AND INDUSTRY

Nauru Phosphate Corporation: Nauru, Central Pacific, f. 1970; Chair. and Man. Dir. T. A. Adams; Dirs. R. S. Leydin, c.b.e., P. Cook, T. W. Star. The Corporation operates the phosphate industry of the Republic of Nauru on behalf of the Nauruan people. It is responsible for the mining and marketing of phosphate.

TRANSPORT

There are 3¼ miles of 3 ft. gauge railway to serve the phosphate workings. A sealed road 12 miles long circles the island, and another connects with Buada District.

Registered Vehicles (June 30th, 1972): 1,534.

Shipping (1971–72): Ships calling 89; g.r.t. 1,479,600.
Nauru has its own ships, M.V. *Eigamoiya*, M.V. *Rosie D*, M.V. *Cenpac Rounder*, M.V. *Enna G* and M.V. *Kolle D*, owned by Nauru Local Government Council. Ships ply between Australia and Islands of the Pacific, including Japan, Philippines, Guam, U.S. Trust Territory and Tarawa.

Air Transport: *Air Nauru* operates a twice weekly service linking Nauru with Majuro and Melbourne (the latter via Brisbane, Nouméa and Honiara), a weekly service to Kagoshima (Japan), and a fortnightly service to Tarawa, in the Gilbert Islands. Fleet: one Fokker F.28. *Air Pacific:* operates a fortnightly service via Tarawa (Gilbert and Ellis Islands) from Fiji.

NEPAL

INTRODUCTORY SURVEY

Location, Climate, Language, Religion, Flag, Capital

Nepal is a landlocked kingdom in the Central Himalayas between India and the Tibetan Autonomous Region of the Chinese People's Republic. The climate varies sharply with altitude. The central Valley of Kathmandu is warm and sunny in summer with an average annual temperature of about 62°F (11°c). Winter temperatures fall below zero at times in January. The official language is Nepali, spoken in varying dialects. Over 50 per cent of the population are Hindus and the remainder mainly Buddhists. The national flag (proportions 3 by 4) is comprised of two crimson pennants, each with a blue border. The upper section is charged with a white crescent moon and the lower section with a white sun in splendour. The capital is Kathmandu.

Recent History and Government

Nepal promulgated her first Constitution in 1959 but considerable opposition to the elected government developed, and in 1960 the King took over the administration, dissolved Parliament and suspended parts of the Constitution. A new Constitution based on the Village Councils or *Panchayats* was introduced in 1962. Under this system the National Assembly consists partly of elected members and partly of nominated members.

A Sino-Nepalese friendship treaty was concluded in 1956, and in 1961 Nepal signed a border agreement with China defining the Himalayas. Good relations with China, the Soviet Union and the U.S.A. have been successfully maintained in recent years. Relations with India have improved, following the settlement in August 1972 of terms for a renewal of the 10-year trade and transit agreement (*see* under Economic Affairs *below*) which expired in October 1970. In January 1972, King Mahendra died and was succeeded by his son, Prince Birendra.

Following food shortages and demands in the *Rashtriya Panchayat* (National Assembly) for greater democratization, a grave parliamentary crisis arose in June 1972.

In response to a wave of student strikes and vociferous protests in the Assembly, King Birendra announced in October the appointment of Dr. Tulsi Giri as a political aide, with Cabinet rank, who would advise on ways of strengthening democracy. In November Kirti Nidhi Bista, the Prime Minister, paid a ten-day visit to the People's Republic of China, where he signed an economic and technical co-operation agreement. In June 1973 the theft of bank funds from a hijacked aircraft led to a claim by exiled members of the disbanded Congress that the money was in their possession and would be used to finance a revolution. In July the Prime Minister resigned following an unpopular announcement that the trade in marijuana and opium would henceforth be forbidden. He was succeeded by Nagendra Prasad Rijal. In October the King visited India, and this was followed by a visit to China in December.

Defence

Nepal has a great fighting tradition and many Nepalis have served with British Gurkha regiments. Nepal has its own army of about 10,000 men. In August 1970 India withdrew the last of her Military Liaison Group.

Economic Affairs

Much of the country is heavily forested and too steep for cultivation, yet 92 per cent of the population depend on agriculture. The agricultural settlements are confined to the Kathmandu Valley and wider sections of the river valleys and there is a small exportable surplus of foodstuffs. Steps are being taken to develop agriculture with particular emphasis on irrigation. The only mineral so far discovered in significant quantities is mica, mined east of Kathmandu; there are also small deposits of lignite, copper, cobalt and iron ore. Nepal has received considerable sums in aid from India, China and the U.S.A. Many transport, industrial, irrigation, flood control and hydroelectric projects are under way, including a scheme to harness the Karnali river in western Nepal with a series of hydro-electric stations; the first phase (costing more than $100 million) would supply all the energy requirements of northern India. A fourth Five-Year Plan (1970–75) envisages the expenditure of 3,540 million Nepalese rupees. Seventy-five per cent of expenditure in the 1973–74 budget was allocated for development.

In August 1972 the Trade and Transit Treaty with India was renewed. India agreed to increase Nepal's transit routes to thirteen for trade with third countries, i.e. Bangladesh, and to nineteen for bilateral trade with India. Under the terms of a technical and economic co-operation agreement, China has agreed to assist Nepal in building the Noranghat Gorkha road, a Kathmandu-Makhwanpur trolley bus service, a cotton textile factory and the expansion of a brick and tile factory. Nepal is a member of the Colombo Plan.

Transport and Communications

There are short sections of motorable roads around Kathmandu and a mountain road links the capital with the Indian railhead at Raxaul. Heavy goods on this route are transported by a 26-mile ropeway from Hetaura to Kathmandu. A number of important new roads have been built, notably that linking Kathmandu and the Tibetan border at Kodari, and others are under construction, including the 640-mile East-West (Mahendra) Highway. There are two sections of railway totalling 63 miles. Coolies, however, are still the principal means of transport, supplemented by ponies, mules and yaks in the more open upper valleys. A national shipping corporation was set up in 1971. Regular air services link India, Thailand and the larger towns in Nepal. Nepal has telegraph links with both India and Pakistan.

Social Welfare and Education

In 1972 there was one hospital bed for every 5,000 of the population and one physician for every 30,000. In 1971–72 primary school pupils totalled some 479,000, and there were more than 1,100 secondary and higher educational establishments. A national education plan with a vocational emphasis was introduced in 1971 to ensure greater manpower utilization. There is one university.

Tourism and Sport

Tourism is being developed by the construction of new tourist centres in the Kathmandu valley and regular air services link Kathmandu with Pokhara Lake. Mountaineering requires large-scale organization and Sherpa porters may be engaged. Big game hunting can be found in the "Terai" of southern Nepal. Major tourist attractions include Lumbini, the birthplace of Buddha, and Mount Everest.

Visas are not required to visit Nepal by nationals of India.

Public Holidays

Prithvi Javanti, Ba Sant Panchami, Shivarati, Holi, Ram Nawam, New Year's Day (mid-April), Buddha Jayanti, December 28th (King Birendra's Birthday), July 1st (King Tribhuvan's Birthday), Janai Purnima, Krishna Jayanti, Ghatasthapana, Dashain, Thihar, December 16th (Constitution Day).

Weights and Measures

Nepal uses the Indian system of weights but has other measures of its own. Steps have been taken to introduce the metric system.

Currency and Exchange Rates

100 paisa (pice) = 1 Nepalese rupee (NR).

Exchange rates (April 1974):

£1 sterling = 24.93 NR;

U.S. $1 = 10.56 NR.

STATISTICAL SURVEY

AREA AND POPULATION

AREA (sq. km.)	POPULATION (1971 census)	
	Total	Kathmandu (capital)
141,577	11,555,983	150,402

Employment (1972): Agriculture 92 per cent.

AGRICULTURE

LAND USE
(sq. km.)

TOTAL	FOREST	PERPETUAL SNOW	CULTIVATED	RECLAIMABLE WASTE	UNRECLAIMABLE WASTE	RIVERS, ROADS, TOWNS
141,577	44,750	21,121	19,800	18,600	26,441	10,865

CROP AREA
(estimates—'000 hectares)

	PADDY RICE	MAIZE AND MILLET	WHEAT	OIL SEEDS	TOBACCO	JUTE	SUGAR CANE
1971–72	1,205	550	239	111	9	60	15
1972–73	1,103	554	226	117	9	55	15

PRODUCTION
('ooo metric tons)

	1970–71	1971–72	1972–73
Paddy Rice . . .	2,305	2,354	2,010
Maize	833	761	815
Millet	130	130	134
Wheat	193	223	248
Oil Seeds . . .	55	57	69
Sugar Cane . . .	236	245	245
Tobacco . . .	7	7	7
Jute	53	58	55

MEAT PRODUCTION
('ooo metric tons)

	1967–68	1968–69	1969–70
Buffalo	18.3	18.7	19.0
Sheep	2.6	2.6	2.7
Goats	2.5	2.7	2.9
Pigs	3.8	4.0	4.2
Poultry	16.3	16.9	17.5

DAIRY FARMING

	MILK (litres)	BUTTER (kg.)	CHEESE (kg.)
1970–71 .	1,766,999	18,761	19,000
1971–72 .	1,632,748	18,761	19,000
1972–73 .	2,482,825	44,619	30,224

INDUSTRY

	1970–71	1971–72*	1972–73†
Jute (metric tons) . . .	13,502	12,938	7,430
Sugar (metric tons) . .	14,534	7,559	3,643
Cigarettes ('ooo sticks) . .	2,083,200	2,235,000	1,045,000
Matches (gross) . .	491,000	527,000	202
Cotton (metres) . .	984,000‡	48,000	n.a.
Shoes (pairs) . . .	65,757	69,983	3,725
Stainless Steel Utensils (metric tons) .	356	132	81

* Nine months.　　† Six months.　　‡ Synthetics included.

FINANCE

100 paisa (pice) = 1 Nepalese rupee (NR).
Coins: 1, 2, 5, 10, 20, 25 and 50 paisa; 1 rupee.
Notes: 1, 5, 10, 100, 500 and 1,000 rupees.
Exchange rates (April 1974): 1 Indian rupee = 1.391 NR;
£1 sterling = 24.93 NR; U.S. $1 = 10.56 NR.
100 Nepalese rupees = £4.01 = $9.47.

Note: Between December 1967 and February 1973 the exchange rate was U.S.$1 = 10.125 NR.

BUDGET ESTIMATES

(million NRs—Twelve months ending July 15th, 1974)

REVENUE		EXPENDITURE	
Land	90.0	REGULAR:	
Customs	281.3	Administration	116.9
Interest and Dividends . . .	37.7	Defence	83.2
Excise	76.9	Other	305.6
Income Tax	27.5		
Other	202.3	TOTAL	505.7
TOTAL	715.7		
		DEVELOPMENT:	
Foreign Aid	255.3	Industry and Commerce . . .	122.7
Deficit	576.5	Education	82.2
External Loan	237.9	Agriculture	107.3
Internal Loan	200.0	Health	39.4
Carry Balance (Surplus) . . .	138.7	Other	690.1
TOTAL	1,408.4	TOTAL	1,041.7
GRAND TOTAL . . .	2,124.1	GRAND TOTAL . . .	1,547.4

FOREIGN AID

('000 NRs)

	1972–73	1973–74*
India	94,800	113,400
China	34,200	43,900
United States . . .	38,600	43,700
U.K.	16,100	24,900
U.S.S.R.	2,500	n.a.
Others	18,100	29,400
TOTAL . . .	204,300	255,300

* Estimates.

FOURTH FIVE-YEAR PLAN

(1970–75)

('000 NRs)

Transport and Communication . . .	1,252,000
Agriculture, Irrigation, etc. . .	1,171,800
Industry, Commerce, Power, etc. . .	720,000
Education, Social Services, etc. .	381,500
Statistics	14,700
TOTAL	3,540,000

EXTERNAL TRADE

(Value in million NRs)

Imports: (1966–67) 499.3; (1967–68) 478.6; (1968–69) 747.7; (1969–70) 884.6.*

Exports: (1966–67) 426.3; (1967–68) 392.9; (1968–69) 572.0; (1969–70) 489.2.*

* Latest available figures.

COMMODITIES

(1969–70—million NRs)

	IMPORTS	EXPORTS
Food and Live Animals	157.2	296.3
Beverages and Tobacco	11.0	2.2
Raw Materials	62.4	120.5
Minerals and Fuels	87.9	—
Animal Fats, Vegetable Oils and Chemicals	8.1	1.6
TOTAL	326.6	420.6
Machinery and Transport Equipment	78.8	0.2
Other Manufactured Goods	366.9	47.9
Miscellaneous	112.3	20.5
TOTAL	558.0	68.6
GRAND TOTAL	884.6	489.2

TRANSPORT

ROAD TRAFFIC
(1972)

MOTOR CARS	COMMERCIAL PASSENGER VEHICLES	OTHER COMMERCIAL VEHICLES
11,131	396	1,546

TOURISM*

1966	.	.	12,567
1967	.	.	18,093
1968	.	.	24,209
1969	.	.	34,886
1970	.	.	45,970
1971	.	.	49,414

* Tourist arrivals.

CIVIL AVIATION
ROYAL NEPAL AIRLINES CORPORATION (1969–70)*

Passengers	182,538
Freight (kg.)	2,302,371

* Latest figures available.

EDUCATION
(1971–72)

	ESTABLISH-MENTS	TEACHERS	PUPILS
Primary	7,331	11,490	478,743
Secondary	1,094	3,334	257,245
Higher	49	1,070	25,000

Source: Research and Publicity Division, National Planning Commission Secretariat, HMG/Nepal.

THE CONSTITUTION

(Promulgated December 1962)

The Constitution of Nepal comprises a constitutional monarchy with executive power vested in the King but ordinarily exercised on the recommendation of a Cabinet consisting of a Prime Minister, selected by the King from among the membership of the National Panchayat or Assembly, and not more than 14 Ministers appointed on the recommendation of the Prime Minister. The Cabinet is responsible to the Panchayat but the King has power to grant or withhold assent to Bills at his discretion.

The Constitution also provides for a State Council which will declare upon the succession or appoint a Regency Council, besides giving advice to the King in times of emergency.

The Rashtriya (National) Panchayat, which is at the apex of the party-less Panchayat system of democracy, is the supreme national unicameral legislature, comprising 125 members, 90 of them are elected from among the members of the Anchal Sabhas (Zonal Councils), who in turn are elected from among the members of Zilla Sabhas (District Councils) who, again in turn, are elected from the Gaon Sabhas (Village Councils). In other words, membership of the Rashtriya Panchayat is based on the popular election of Local Panchayat (which is the basic unit of the four-tiered Panchayat System), from each of which members choose from among themselves representatives for District Panchayat. They may advance by similar stages to the zonal and then to the Rashtriya Panchayat. Of the remaining 35 members, 15 members are elected from various Class Organizations, 4 from the peasants' organization, 2 from the labour organization, 4 from the youth organization, 3 from the women's organization and 2 from the ex-servicemen's organization. Four members are elected from nation-wide Graduate Constituencies and the remaining 16 members (i.e. 15 per cent of the total elective members) are nominated by the Crown according to the Constitution.

The Rashtriya Panchayat is a perpetual body, one-third of its members elected from Zonal Councils retiring every two years. Other members serve for a fixed term of four years. Proceedings of the House are open to the following: members of the Royal Family; members of the Raj Sabha; any person who in the opinion of the Chairman of the House is concerned with the business of the House; any member of a Local Panchayat or of the Executive Committee of various levels of the Class Organizations and Professional Organization, if the Chairman gives permission after consultations with the Steering Committee. It is open to the public on such occasions as the address to the House by His Majesty or by any distinguished invitee. A summary record of the proceedings of every meeting of the House or its committees is published.

The members have full authority to move, reject, or pass with or without amendment any bill except those relating to the Royal Family and the armed forces. It can adopt motions and pass resolutions. Any member may introduce legislation except that on financial and military affairs, for which the prior approval of His Majesty the King is essential. The annual budget is submitted to the House for consideration, deliberation and adoption. And in order that these legislative tasks be conducted with becoming dignity and efficiency, the members of the House fully enjoy the privilege of freedom from arrest for anything spoken in the House or the manner in which voting is exercised.

The Rashtriya Panchayat was formed on April 14th, 1963 (New Year's Day); and, constituted into the National Group, has been a member of the Inter-Parliamentary Union since September 1967.

Besides enumerating a number of fundamental rights, including the right against exile, the Constitution lays down a series of fundamental duties of the citizen.

Amendments to the 1962 Constitution, adopted in 1967, include the following provisions: Prime Minister to be appointed by the King who may, if he wishes, consult the National Panchayat; Ministers to be collectively and individually responsible to the King; King to appoint directly the Zonal Commissioners who are to enjoy greater powers than the Chairmen of Zonal Panchayat Assemblies; Associations for non-political purposes allowed but political parties continue to be banned, provision for appointment of an independent Election Commission.

LAND REFORM

Under the Act, the Land Reform Programme has been implemented in phases. It was introduced for the first time in sixteen districts in 1964, in twenty-five districts in 1965, and it became applicable to all districts in 1966. Its basic objective is to develop the agricultural sector which may eventually foster the industrialization programme in the country. The important features of the programme are: fixation of a ceiling on land holdings; guarantee of tenancy rights; fixed rate of rent; provision of loans to peasants for agricultural purposes. The loan fund has been partly created by the compulsory saving scheme, which forms part of the land reform programme; compulsory saving is collected from both landowners and peasants at the ward level in each Village Panchayat.

THE GOVERNMENT

Head of State and Supreme Commander of the Armed Forces: H.M. King BIRENDRA BIR BIKRAM SHAH DEVA.

ADVISER

Adviser to H.M. the King: TULSI GIRI.

COUNCIL OF MINISTERS

(*May* 1974)

Prime Minister, Minister of Defence and Palace Affairs: NAGENDRA PRASAD RIJAL.

Minister of Finance and Foreign Affairs: GYANENDRA BAHADUR KARKI.

Minister for Home, Law and Justice: HOM BAHADUR SHRESTRA.

Minister of Food, Agriculture and Land Reforms: LAL BAHADUR KHADAYAT.

Minister of Health and Education: KRISHNA RAJ ARYAL.

Minister for Panchayat Affairs: DAMODAR SHUMSHER J. B. RANA.

State Minister for Power, Water Resources and Forests: NARAYAN DUTTA BHATTA.

State Minister for Commerce and Industry: BHUBAN MAN SINGH.

State Minister for Communications and General Administration: RADHA PRASAD GHIMIRE.

State Minister for Finance: BHEKH BAHADUR THAPA.

DIPLOMATIC REPRESENTATION

EMBASSIES IN KATHMANDU

China, People's Republic: Toran Bhawan, Naksal; *Ambassador:* WANG TSE.

France: Lazimpat; *Ambassador:* FRANÇOIS TOUSSAINT.

German Democratic Republic: *Ambassador:* HERBERT FISCHER.

Germany, Federal Republic: Kanti Path.

India: Lain Chaur; *Ambassador:* MAHARAJKRISHNA RASGOTRA.

Israel: *Ambassador:* M. CASBI.

Italy: *Ambassador:* FOLCO ALOISI DE LARDEREL DI ALLUMIERE.

Japan: Hotel de l'Annapurna.

Pakistan: Thapathali.

Romania: *Ambassador:* PETRE TANASIE.

U.S.S.R.: Dilli Bazar; *Ambassador:* G. N. DZYUBENKO.

United Kingdom: Lain Chaur; *Ambassador:* MICHAEL SCOTT.

U.S.A.: Kanti Path; *Ambassador:* WILLIAM I. CARGO.

Nepal also has diplomatic relations with Afghanistan, Algeria, Argentina, Australia, Austria, Bangladesh, Belgium, Bulgaria, Burma, Canada, Chile, Czechoslovakia, Denmark, Egypt, Greece, Hungary, Iran, Iraq, Jordan, Democratic People's Republic of Korea, Republic of Korea, Kuwait, Laos, Lebanon, Malaysia, Mongolia, Netherlands, New Zealand, Poland, Singapore, Spain, Sri Lanka, Sweden, Switzerland, Thailand, Turkey and Yugoslavia.

PARLIAMENT

In December 1960 Parliament was dissolved. Political parties are banned under the Panchayat People's Council system, presided over by the King.

Chairman of the National Panchayat: RAM HARI SHARMA.

POLITICAL PARTIES

(All political parties were banned in December 1960).

Nepali National Congress: New Delhi, India; nationalist organization, Leader Gen. SUBARNA SHUMSHERE JANG BAHADUR RANA.

Nepal Communist Party: G.P.O. Kathmandu; pro-Peking, Leader PUSHPA LAL.

JUDICIAL SYSTEM

There is one Supreme Court, 15 Zonal and 75 Distric Courts. These have both civil and criminal jurisdiction.

The Supreme Court: The Constitution of Nepal provides for a Supreme Court which shall have a Chief Justice and not more than six other Justices unless otherwise specified by law. The Supreme Court is to hold appellate as well as original jurisdiction, and may function as a court of review. The Supreme Court protects the fundamental rights of the people and guarantees the Rule of Law.

Chief Justice: Hon. RATNA BAHADUR BISTA.

RELIGION

Over half the population are Hindus, which is the religion of the Royal Family. Most others are Buddhists. One per cent are Muslims.

BUDDHISM

Nepal Buddhist Association: Rev. AMRITANANDA, Ananda Kuti, Kathmandu.

Young Buddhist Council of Nepal: Rev. AMRITANANDA.

THE PRESS

Commoner: Naradevi, Kathmandu; English daily; Editor Gopal Das; circ. 7,000.

Dainik Nepal: Kathmandu; Nepali daily; Editor I. K. Mishra; circ. 900.

Gorkha Patra: Dharma Path, Kathmandu; Nepali daily; Editor Gopal Prasad Bhattarai; circ. 25,000.

The Motherland: Kathmandu; English daily; Editor M. R. Shrestha; circ. 1,200.

Naya Samaj: Kathmandu; f. 1957; Nepali daily; Editor P. D. Pandey; circ. 3,000.

Naya Sandesh: Kathmandu; Nepali and English; daily; Editor Ramesh Nath Pandey; circ. 2,200.

Nepal Bhasa Patrika: Bheda Singh, Kathmandu; Newari daily; Editor F. B. Singh; circ. 800.

Nepal Samachar: Nepal Today Press, Kathmandu; Nepali daily; Editor S. N. Sharma; circ. 900.

Nepal Times.

Nepali: Kathmandu; Hindi daily; Editor Uma Kant Das; circ. 9,500.

Perspective: New Rd., Kathmandu; English weekly.

The Rising Nepal: Dharma Path, Kathmandu; English daily; Editor Barun Shamsher Rana; circ. 8,000.

Royal Nepal Economist: 41/44 Tripureswar, Kathmandu; monthly in English and Nepali; Editor Bhesh Raj Sharma; circ. 500.

Samaj: Dhobidhara, Kathmandu; Editor Mani Raj Upadhyaya.

Samaya: Wotu Tole, Kathmandu; Nepali daily; Editor Manik Lall Shrestha; circ. 18,000.

Sameeksha: Nepali weekly; Editor M. M. Dikshit; circ. over 4,000.

NEWS AGENCIES

Rastriya Samachar Samiti (R.S.A.): P.O.B. 220, Kathmandu; f. 1962; Chair. and Gen. Man. Govinda Prasad Pradhan.

FOREIGN BUREAUX

Agence France-Presse (France): G.P. Box 402, 6/126 Puranobhansor, Kathmandu; Man. Kedar Man Singh.

Deutsche Presse-Agentur (*Federal Republic of Germany*): Balwatar, Kathmandu.

Tass (U.S.S.R.) is also represented.

Nepal Journalists Association (NJA): Kathmandu.

PUBLISHERS

Department of Publicity: Ministry of Communications, Kathmandu.

La Kaul Press: Palpa Tanben.

Mahabir Singh Chiniya Main: Makhan Tola, Kathmandu.

Mandas Sugatdas: Kamabachi, Kathmandu.

Ratna Pustak Bhandar: Bhotahitit Tola, Kathmandu.

Sajha Prakhashan: Kathmandu; f. 1966; educational and general; Chair. Shri Kamal Mani Dixit.

RADIO

Radio Nepal: Singha Durdar Compound, Kathmandu; f. 1951; broadcasts on short and medium wave in Nepali, Hindi, Newari and English. In 1971 there were about 60,000 receiving sets. Dir. Bhogya Prasad Shaha. There is no television.

FINANCE

(cap.=capital; p.u.=paid up; dep.=deposits; m.=millions; N.Rs=Nepali Rupees)

BANKING

Nepal Rashtra Bank: Lalita Niwas, Baluwatar, Kathmandu; f. 1956; state bank of issue; cap. N.Rs. 10m.; dep. N.Rs. 459.5m. (July 1972); Gov. Kul Shekhar Sharma

Nepal Bank Ltd.: H.O. Dharma Path, Kathmandu; f. 1937; cap. p.u. N.Rs. 5m.; dep. N.Rs. 540m. (Dec. 1973); Chair. Shri Kalyan Bikram Adhikari; Gen. Man. Shri Ananda Bhakta Rajbhandary; publ. *Nepal Bank Patrika* (ten a year).

Rastriya Banijya Bank (*National Commercial Bank*): Kathmandu; f. 1965; cap. p.u. N.Rs. 3m.; dep. N.Rs. 80m.; Gen. Man. B. M. Singh.

Agricultural Development Bank: Dharmapath, Kathmandu; f. 1963; only statutory financial body providing credit to co-operatives, individuals and associations in agricultural development; receives deposits from individuals, co-operatives and other associations to generate savings in the agricultural sector; cap. p.u. N.Rs. 49m.; dep. N.Rs. 34m.; Chair. Kulshekhar Sharma; Gen. Man. Basudev Pekurel; publs. annual report, booklets.

Agricultural Co-operative Societies also advance credit to members.

Land Reform Savings Corporation: Nepal Bank Bldg. No. 2, P.O.B. 378, Dharmapath, Kathmandu; f. 1970; accepts deposits from and advances loans to more than 3,700 village committees; provides technical assistance to agriculture, industry and agro-trade, and to Department of Land Reform in the administration of Compulsory Savings Schemes; promotes and participates in agriculture and industrial enterprises; auth. cap. N.Rs. 100m.; dep. N.Rs. 30.6m.; Gen. Man. P. K. Shrestha; publs. pamphlets, booklets.

INSURANCE

There is one insurance company:

Rastriya Beema Sansthan (*National Insurance Corporation*): P.O.B. 527, Kathmandu, Nepal; f. December 1967; government undertaking; underwriting of life and general insurance business within and outside Nepal; cap. p.u. N.Rs. 2.4m.; Chair. N. K. Adhikary; Gen. Man. L. B. Bista.

TRADE AND INDUSTRY

National Planning Commission: Kathmandu, Chair. The Prime Minister Rt. Hon. Sri K. N. Bista; Vice-Chair. Hon. Dr. H. B. Gurung; Sec. G. B. N. Pradhan.

Federation of Nepalese Chambers of Commerce and Industry: Meera Home, Khichapokhari, P.O.B. 269, Kathmandu; f. January 1966; independent federation comprising 66 industrial and business organizations; represents members' interests and provides a variety of services; Pres. Pashupati Giri; Vice-Pres. Raj Bahadur Chipalu; Secs. Yogendra Purush, P. G. Amatya; publ. *Udyog Banijya Patrika* (fortnightly).

Nepal Chamber of Commerce: Nepal Bank Bldg. No. 2, P.O.B. 198, Kathmandu; f. 1952; non-profit making organization devoted to cause of industrial and commercial development in Nepal and to the service of its members; about 450 mems.; publs. *Chamber Patrika* (monthly, Nepalese), *Nepal Trade Directory*.

Agricultural Marketing Corporation: Teku, Kuleswar, P.O.B. 195, Kathmandu; f. June 1972; Functions: to procure and distribute inputs needed for agricultural development, namely chemical fertilizers, improved seeds, improved agricultural tools and implements, plant protection materials, etc.; all inputs are imported except improved seeds and small tools; cap. p.u. Rs. 10m.; mems. 262 retail dealers; Chair. SURENDRA RAJ SHARMA; Gen. Man. SAGAR BAHADUR PRADHAN.

National Trading Ltd.: Teku, Kathmandu; f. 1962; government undertaking; imports and distributes construction materials, machinery, vehicles, consumer and luxury goods; handles clearing and forwarding of government consignments; exports Nepalese products, mainly timber, medicinal herbs, raw wool, hessian sacking, raw jute, handicrafts and curios; Exec. Chair. and Gen. Man. NAYAN RAJ PANDEY; Deputy Gen. Man. RAMESWAR PRASAD SHAH; publ. *Vyapar Patrika* (monthly trade journal) and other trade directories.

Nepal Industrial Development Corporation (NIDC): NIDC Bldg., P.B. No. 10, Kathmandu; f. 1959; state-owned, has shares in 15 industrial enterprises, offers financial and technical assistance to the private sector; cap. N.Rs. 99m.; Chair. K. S. SHARMA; publs. *Industrial Digest* (annual), *Annual Report, Prospects of Industrial Investment in Nepal* and various brochures.

Salt Trading Corporation Ltd.: Kalimati, Kathmandu; f. Sept. 1963 as a joint venture of the public and private sectors (30 and 70 per cent respectively) to manage the import and distribution of salt in Nepal; now also deals in sugar, edible oils and wheat flour throughout Nepal; Chair. A. M. SHERCHAN; Gen. Man. H. B. MALLA.

TRADE UNION

Nepal Mazdoor Sangathan (*Nepal Labour Organization*): c/o Ministry of Home and Panchayat Affairs, Singha Durbar, Kathmandu; f. 1963; 14,000 mems.; Chair. M. K. POKHERAL.

TRANSPORT

Ministry of Public Works, Transport and Health: Sec. BHARAT BAHADUR PRADHAN.

ROADS

There are over 2,700 kilometres of roads, of which about 1,700 are metalled. About 2,000 kilometres were constructed during the last Three-Year and the Third Five-Year Plan periods. There are short sections of motorable roads around Kathmandu and a mountain road, Tribhuwana Rajpath, links the capital with the Indian railhead at Raxual. Mahendra Highway, formerly known as the East-West Highway, is under construction sector by sector. Its total length is estimated at 992 km. The Siddhartha Highway constructed with Indian assistance was formally opened on May 8th, 1972. It connects the Pokhara Valley in mid-west Nepal with Sonauli on the Indian border in Uttar Pradesh. A British-built section linking Butwal with Barghat and totalling 40 km. was opened on November 20th, 1972.

RAILWAYS, ROPEWAYS AND CONTAINER TRANSPORT

Nepal Yatayat Samsthan (*The Transport Corporation of Nepal*): Responsible for the operation of road transport facilities, railways and ropeways; Chair. DEVENDRA RAJ UPADHYA.

A 3-mile section of narrow-gauge railway links Raxaul (India) with Birgunj, an industrial town in the Terai. Another section, 33 miles long, links Jaya Nagar (India) with Janakpurdham and Bijalpura. A 26-mile ropeway links Hetauda and Kathmandu and can carry 25 tons of freight per hour throughout the year. Food grains, construction goods and heavy goods on this route are transported by this ropeway. A fleet of container trucks is being operated between Calcutta and Raxaul and other points in Nepal for transporting exports to, and imports from, third countries.

SHIPPING

Royal Nepal Shipping Corpn.: Kalimati, Kathmandu; f. 1971; became operational in May 1972; Man. Dir. Brig. Gen. R. S. RANA.

Royal Nepal Shipping Line: f. 1971; became operational in May 1972; Man. Dir. Dr. J. JHA.

CIVIL AVIATION

There are regular Boeing services to New Delhi, Calcutta and Bangkok (non-stop). Helicopter and charter services have been provided to the remote and higher mountain regions and larger towns.

Royal Nepal Airlines Corporation: RNAC Bldg., Kantipath, Kathmandu; f. 1958; fleet of one Boeing 727, two Avro HS-748, four DC-3, four Twin Otters, two Pilatus Porters; Chair. R. C. MALHOTRA; Deputy Gen. Man. D. B. RANA.

The following foreign airlines operate services to Nepal: Burma Airways, Indian Airlines Corporation, Thai International.

TOURISM

Department of Tourism: Ministry of Industry and Commerce, Basantpur, Kathmandu; Dir. T. R. TULADHAR.

Department of Information: Ministry of Communications, Singha Durbar, Kathmandu; Dir. B. P. SHAH.

UNIVERSITY

Tribhuvan University: Tripureswor, Kathmandu; *c.* 120 teachers, *c.* 13,000 students.

NETHERLANDS ANTILLES AND SURINAM
NETHERLANDS ANTILLES
INTRODUCTORY SURVEY

Location, Climate, Language, Religion, Flag, Capital

The Netherlands Antilles consist of two groups of islands in the Caribbean, some 800 km. apart. The main group, lying off the coast of Venezuela, consists of Aruba, Bonaire and Curaçao; to the north, forming part of the Leeward Islands, lie the small volcanic islands of St. Eustatius, Saba and St. Maarten (the northern half of the latter island being part of the French dependency of Guadeloupe). The climate is tropical, moderated by the sea, with temperatures averaging 28°C (82°F), and little rainfall. Dutch is the official language, though in the southern group English and Spanish are also widely spoken; there is also a local dialect, Papiamento, a mixture of Dutch, Spanish, Portuguese, English and African dialect. In the Leeward Islands English is generally spoken. The population is almost all Christian, and 80 per cent are Roman Catholics. The state flag (proportions 3 by 2) has a red vertical stripe on a white background, crossed by a horizontal blue stripe charged with six white stars arranged in an oval. The capital is Willemstad in Curaçao.

Recent History

Although first discovered by Spanish explorers in 1499, the Netherlands Antilles have been in Dutch possession since the seventeenth century. In 1954 a Charter gave the islands full autonomy in domestic affairs. In May 1969, severe workers' riots, in which over half of Willemstad was destroyed, brought about the resignation of the Prime Minister; elections were held in October. In February 1970, the socialist government of C. D. Kroon resigned over the nomination of a new governor and in 1971 the government of E. Petronia resigned over the defeat in the *Staten* of new financial measures. Elections were held in August 1973, and J. M. G. Evertsz became Prime Minister.

Government

Executive power in internal affairs is vested in the Council of Ministers who are responsible to the legislature (*Staten*). The Governor is responsible for external affairs and is assisted by an Advisory Council.

Economic Affairs

Agriculture is comparatively unimportant, due to the light rainfall, although efforts are being made by the Government to promote farming, cattle raising and horticulture in Bonaire and the Leeward Islands. The chief products are aloes (Bonaire is a major exporter), sorghum, divi-divi, groundnuts and beans, fresh vegetables and tropical fruit. The chief industry is oil refining; Curaçao and Aruba have become increasingly important with the development of the Venezuelan oil industry. The Shell refinery at Curaçao (capacity 350,000 bbl./day) and that of Lago Oil in Aruba (capacity 400,000 bbl./day) are among the largest in the world. Oil refining accounts for 95 per cent of total exports by value. A further 2 per cent of exports consist of chemicals, including phosphate, nitric acid and fertilizers. One of the largest commercial drydocks in the Western Hemisphere, capable of handling ships of 120,000 tons, is in operation in Curaçao.

Public Holidays

1974: August 15th (Assumption Day), November 1st (All Saints' Day), December 15th (Statute Day), December 25th–26th (Christmas).

1975: January 1st (New Year's Day), March 28th–31st (Easter), April 30th (Queen's Birthday), May 1st (Labour Day), May 8th (Ascension Day), May 19th (Whit Monday).

Weights and Measures

The metric system is in force.

Currency

100 cents = 1 Netherlands Antilles gulden (guilder) or florin (N.A.Fl.).

Exchange rates (April 1974):
£1 sterling = 4.227 N.A.Fl.;
U.S. $1 = 1.790 N.A.Fl.

STATISTICAL SURVEY
AREA AND POPULATION
AREA
(sq. km.)

TOTAL AREA	CURAÇAO	ARUBA	BONAIRE	ST. MAARTEN (Dutch side)	ST. EUSTATIUS	SABA
996	444	193	288	37	21	13

POPULATION
(Dec. 31st, 1972)

TOTAL	CURAÇAO	ARUBA	BONAIRE	ST. MAARTEN (Dutch side)	ST. EUSTATIUS	SABA	BIRTHS*	MARRIAGES*	DEATHS*
230,824	150,008	61,293	8,181	8,970	1,401	971	4,928	1,481	1,110

Willemstad, Curaçao (capital) 50,000*.

* 1970.

Agriculture: There is little cultivation. *Livestock:* (1970-71) 7,000 cattle, 7,000 pigs, 1,000 goats and 26,000 sheep.

Oil: Curaçao and Aruba are bases for the transhipment and refining of Venezuelan oil. *Exports* (value): (1971) 1,291m. N.A.Fl.; (1972) 1,243m. N.A.Fl.

Mining: *Exports* ('000 metric tons) Phosphate (1970) 92; (1971) 61.

FINANCE
100 cents = 1 Netherlands Antilles gulden (guilder) or florin (N.A.Fl.).
Coins: 1, 2½, 5, 10 and 25 cents; 1 and 2½ N.A.Fl.
Notes: 1, 2½, 5, 10, 25, 50, 100, 250 and 500 N.A.Fl.
Exchange rates (April 1974) £1 sterling = 4.227 N.A.Fl.; U.S. $1 = 1.790 N.A.Fl.
100 N.A.Fl. = £23.66 = $55.87.

Budget (1966—'000 N.A.Fl.): Central Revenue 66,609; Central Expenditure 66,593.

COST OF LIVING INDICES
(1970 = 100)

	1971	1972
Food	107.6	114.2
Housing	102.8	104.6
Clothing	101.4	103.6
Other	103.3	105.6
General Index	104.4	108.1

CURRENCY IN CIRCULATION
('000 N.A.Fl.)

	1970	1971	1972
Notes in circulation	60,900	64,719	72,287
Gold owned by the Bank of the Netherlands Antilles	36,515	37,252	37,252

BALANCE OF PAYMENTS
(million N.A.Fl.)

	1970 Credit	1970 Debit	1971 Credit	1971 Debit	1972 Credit	1972 Debit
Merchandise	230.2	430.4	184.8	434.7	38.1	448.1
Tourism	46.9	14.9	105.6	16.5	232.6	50.3
Government Transfers n.e.s.	28.3	13.8	35.5	11.0	41.2	8.2
Investment Income	17.3	13.3	16.8	13.4	22.5	22.2
Private Transfers	8.6	36.2	13.9	49.6	16.6	50.2
Receipts by Foreign-owned Companies	160.5	—	182.1	—	171.4	1.4
Other Services and Income*	72.8	68.6	56.7	44.3	10.8	8.2
Unrequited Transfers	17.4	—	26.5	—	24.4	
Private Capital Transfers	9.8	26.4	8.0	37.3	15.4	37.8
Government Capital Transfers	30.6	4.3	38.8	30.2	35.0	6.8
Net Errors and Omissions		11.9		0.2		—
Balance (net monetary movements)†		2.6		31.5		8.1

* Including *net* receipts of oil companies and mining company. The appropriate items are thus excluded from merchandise. For complete figures of merchandise transactions, *see* tables on External Trade below.

† Net change in reserves.

EXTERNAL TRADE
('000 N.A.Fl.)

	1969	1970	1971
Imports	1,302,770	1,493,000	1,651,000
Exports	1,177,810	1,274,000	1,365,000

COMMODITIES
('000 N.A.Fl.)

IMPORTS	1970	1971	EXPORTS	1970	1971
Food and Live Animals	66,954	82,924	Food and Live Animals	1,096	1,056
Beverages and Tobacco	10,127	10,841	Beverages and Tobacco		
Crude Materials	3,796	5,735	Animal and Vegetable Oils and Fats		
Mineral Fuels and Related Materials	1,052,428	1,141,365	Crude Materials	6,420	5,209
Animal and Vegetable Oils and Fats	1,311	2,591	Mineral Fuels and Related Materials	1,196,277	1,301,808
Chemicals	45,215	48,820	Chemicals	32,779	28,911
Manufactured Goods	95,214	97,753	Manufactured Goods	2,398	1,764
Machinery and Transport Equipment	123,523	158,378	Machinery and Transport Equipment	32,038	23,204
Miscellaneous	93,775	103,802	Miscellaneous	2,959	2,981

COUNTRIES
('000 N.A.Fl.)

IMPORTS	1969	1970	EXPORTS	1969	1970
Colombia	11,810	7,442	Argentina	11,940	12,826
Gabon	30,760	33,616	Brazil	20,960	125,957
Netherlands	54,110	71,494	Canada	84,340	110,054
Trinidad	12,000	13,295	Japan	19,470	23,856
United Kingdom	17,890	33,547	Netherlands	26,970	27,858
U.S.A.	149,780	176,360	United Kingdom	47,540	52,591
Venezuela	893,620	916,591	U.S.A.	651,670	662,814
Others	132,800	240,000			

TOURISM
(1971)

	Curaçao	Aruba	Bonaire	St. Maarten
Number of visitors . .	108 443	85 755	5,573	44,265
Number of days . .	552,047	530,850	17,133	221,227

1972: (Curaçao) 108,192 visitors, 519,369 days; (Aruba) 88,652 visitors, 598,196 days.

TRANSPORT
ROADS

	1969		1970		1971	
	Curaçao	Aruba	Curaçao	Aruba	Curaçao	Aruba
Cars	20,184	} 10,547	23,618	} 11,230	23,115	} 11,739
Lorries . . .	3,013		3,411		3,161	
Buses . . .	445	112	405	105	422	112
Taxis . . .	126	51	155	63	184	66
Other Cars . .	88	22	74	23	64	23
Motor Cycles . .	893	267	640	256	370	182
Total	24,749	10,999	28,303	11,677	27,316	12,122

SHIPPING

ARUBA

Vessels	1971		1972	
	No. of Vessels	Tonnage ('000 G.R.T.)	No. of Vessels	Tonnage ('000 G.R.T.)
Tankers . .	1,430	27,489	1,465	29,002
Steamers and Motor Vessels	1,039	5,745	929	5,835
Sailing Vessels .	—	—	—	—
Total .	2,469	33,234	2,394	34,974

CURAÇAO

Vessels	1971		1972	
	No. of Vessels	Tonnage ('000 G.R.T.)	No. of Vessels	Tonnage ('000 G.R.T.)
Tankers . .	1,867	31,848	1,731	29,820
Steamers and Motor Vessels	3,704	13,072	3,601	12,182
Sailing Vessels .	19	1	1	—
Total .	5,590	44,921	5,333	42,002

PASSENGER TRAFFIC
(Curaçao and Aruba)
By Sea

	NUMBER TO EMBARK	NUMBER TO DISEMBARK	NUMBER IN TRANSIT
1972	12,938	11,570	193,312

By Air

	NUMBER TO EMBARK	NUMBER TO DISEMBARK	NUMBER IN TRANSIT
1972	432,088	428,966	204,640

EDUCATION

	1969–70			1971–72		
	Schools	Pupils	Teachers	Schools	Pupils	Teachers
Primary . . .	121	43,628	1,215	119	37,884	1,245
Junior High . . .	33	8,430	322	31	8,917	354
Senior High . . .	5	2,660	132	4	2,653	175
Senior Technical . . .	2	499	12	2	476	13

Sources: Bureau voor de Statistiek; Bank van de Nederlandse Antillen.

THE CONSTITUTION

The latest constitutional changes for Surinam and the Netherlands Antilles are embodied in the Charter of the Kingdom of the Netherlands, which came into force on December 29th, 1954. Under the Charter the Netherlands, Surinam and the Netherlands Antilles (and Netherlands New Guinea) were constituted as a single realm under the House of Orange.

The Netherlands, Surinam and the Netherlands Antilles each enjoy full autonomy in domestic and internal affairs and are united on a footing of equality for the protection of their common interests and the granting of mutual assistance.

Whenever the Netherlands Council of Ministers is dealing with matters coming under the heading of joint affairs of the realm (in practice mainly foreign affairs and defence) the Council assumes the status of Council of Ministers of the Kingdom. In that event the two Ministers Plenipotentiary appointed by the Government of Surinam and the Netherlands Antilles respectively take part with full voting powers in the deliberations.

A legislative proposal regarding affairs of the realm and applying to Surinam and the Netherlands Antilles as well as to the metropolitan Netherlands is sent, simultaneously with its submission to the Netherlands Parliament, the States-General, and to the parliamentary bodies of Surinam and the Netherlands Antilles. The latter bodies can report in writing to the States-General on the draft Kingdom Statute and designate one or more special delegates to attend the debates and furnish information in the meetings of the Chambers of the States-General. Before the final vote on a draft the Ministers Plenipotentiary have the right to express their opinion thereupon. If they state their disapproval of the draft, and if in the Second Chamber a three-fifths majority of the votes cast is not obtained, the discussions on the draft are suspended and further deliberations take place in the Council of Ministers of the Kingdom. When special delegates attend the meetings of the Chambers this right devolves upon the delegates of the parliamentary body designated for this purpose.

Executive power in internal affairs is vested in a nominated Council of Ministers, who are responsible to the legislature (Staten). The Netherlands Antilles Staten consists of twenty-two members elected by general adult suffrage. The Governor is responsible for external affairs and is aided by an Advisory Council.

THE GOVERNMENT

Governor: B. M. Leito.

Advisory Council: Dr. W. R. Boom (Vice-Pres.), W. F. Craane, G. de Veer, Jr., Dr. S. W. van der Meer, Mrs. L. C. van der Linde-Helmijr, E. Voges, R. Moreno, J. C. Paap (Sec.).

MINISTERS
(*April* 1974)

Prime Minister and Minister of General Affairs: J. M. G. Evertsz.

Deputy Prime Minister and Minister of Justice: E. J. Vos.

Minister of Education and Islands' Political Structure: H. Croes.

Minister of Social Affairs and Labour: Dr. R. F. McWilliam.

Minister of Economic Affairs, Sport, Culture and Recreation: C. D. Kroon.

Minister of Economic Development: M. A. Pourier.

Minister of Health: Mrs. L. E. da Costa Gomez-Matheeuws.

Minister of Traffic and Transport: E. Voges.

Minister Plenipotentiary for the Netherlands Antilles at The Hague: Dr. R. Pieternella.

PARLIAMENT

Staten of the Netherlands Antilles: Speaker R. ELHAGE.

POLITICAL PARTIES

Nationale Volkspartij (*National People's Party*): Willemstad; government party; Pres. and Parliamentary Leader J. M. G. EVERTSZ.

Democratische Partij van Curaçao (*Curaçao Democratic Party*): Willemstad; opposition party; Leader S. G. M. ROZENDAL.

Movimiento Electoral di Pueblo: Aruba.

Partido Democrático Bonairiano (*Democratic Party of Bonaire*): Kralendijk; opposition party; Pres. L. A. ABRAHAM.

RELIGION

Roman Catholics form the largest religious community numbering more than 80 per cent of the population. The Anglican, Methodist, Dutch Reformed and other Protestant Churches have memberships of about 15,000. There are approximately 1,000 Jews.

Roman Catholic Bishop: Brionplein 2, Willemstad; Mgr. WILLEM MICHEL ELLIS, Bishop of Willemstad.

JUDICIAL SYSTEM

The administration of justice is entrusted to a Supreme Court of Justice, the members of which are nominated by the Crown, and a Court of First Instance. Appeals from the Supreme Court lie with the High Court of the Netherlands.

President of the Supreme Court: Dr. J. C. A. ENGEL.

Attorney-General: Dr. J. R. BOUWER.

THE PRESS

Amigoe di Aruba: P.O.B. 323, Oranjestad; f. 1883; daily; Dutch; Editor/Man. J. A. VAN DER SCHOOT; circ. 11,000.

Amigoe di Curaçao: Consciëntiesteeg 29, P.O.B. 577, Willemstad; f. 1883; Catholic; daily; Dutch; Editor C. MAAS; circ. 10,000.

Arubaanse Courant: Bachstraat 6, Oranjestad, Aruba; f. 1938; liberal; Papiamento; daily; Editor THOMAS PIETERSZ; circ. 13,000.

Beurs- en Nieuwsberichten: W.I. Compagniestraat 41, P.O.B. 215, Willemstad; f. 1935; liberal; Dutch; daily; Chief Editor H. M. VAN DELDEN; circ. 8,000.

La Cruz: Consciëntiesteeg 29, P.O.B. 577, Willemstad; f. 1894; weekly; Papiamento; Editor A. E. PANNEFLEK; circ. 4,500.

Culturele Kroniek: P.O.B. 31, Willemstad, Curaçao; published by Radio Curom and several other cultural organizations.

Curaçaosche Courant: P.O.B. 15, Curaçao; f. 1812; weekly; Dutch; Editor P. C. GORSIRA.

Democraat: Willemstad; Dutch and Papiamento; fortnightly.

The Local: San Nicolás, Oranjestad, Aruba; English; weekly; Editor F. L. HODGE.

El Mensajero: Breedestraat 29 OB, Willemstad; Dutch, Spanish and Papiamento; weekly.

Monthly Publication for Trade and Industry of Curaçao: Columbusstraat 19F, Willemstad, Curaçao; f. 1944; economic and industrial paper; English and Dutch; monthly; Editor H. J. JANSSEN.

The News: San Nicolás, Aruba; daily; English; Editor B. BLANCHARD; circ. 3,000.

Nobo: Curaçao; daily; Papiamento.

La Prensa: Breedestraat 138, Willemstad; f. 1929; daily; Spanish and Papiamento; Editor AGUSTÍN DÍAZ; circ. 12,500.

NEWS AGENCIES

Algemeen Nederlands Presbureau (Dutch News Agency, A.N.P.): P.O.B. 439, Willemstad; Representative H. S. PIETERSZ.

U.P.I.: Willemstad; Representative M. HEERING.

A.F.P.: Andromedaweg 4, Willemstad; Representative Mrs. E. GORSIRA.

A.P.: Willemstad; Representative M. JEUKEN-OLSON.

I.P.I.: Willemstad; Representative Dr. G. SWART.

PUBLISHERS

Curaçao Drukkerij en Uitgevers Maatschappij: Pietermaaiweg, Willemstad, Curaçao.

De Wit Stores N.V.: VAD Bldg., L. G. Smith Blvd. 110, Oranjestad, Aruba; f. 1948; Man. Dir. F. OLMTAK.

Ediciones Populares: Willemstad, Curaçao; f. 1929; Dir. A. A. JONCKHEER.

Van Dorp Aruba N.V.: Nassaustraat 77, P.O.B. 596, Oranjestad, Aruba.

Van Dorp Caribbean Inc.: Breedestraat 42, Willemstad, Curaçao.

Drukkerij de Stad, N.V.: Van Swietenstraat 8, Curaçao.

Tipografía Nacional: Bitterstraat 3, Curaçao.

Volksdrukkerij N.V.: Van Swietenstraat 8, Curaçao.

RADIO AND TELEVISION

RADIO

Curaçaose Radio Vereeniging (*Radio Curom*): P.O.B. 31, Willemstad, Curaçao; f. 1933; broadcasts in Dutch, Papiamento, English and Spanish; Pres. C. G. GROOTENS.

Radio Antiliana: P.O.B. 28, Bernardstraat 61, St. Nicolaas, Aruba; commercial station; programmes in Dutch, English, Spanish and Papiamento; Dir.-Gen. H. BOOY.

Radio Caribe: Nieuwestraat 22B, Willemstad, Curaçao; f. 1955; commercial station; programmes in Dutch, English, Spanish and Papiamento; Dir.-Gen. C. R. HEILLEGGER.

Radio Hoyer: Julianaplein 21, Willemstad, Curaçao; commercial; three stations; Radio Hoyer I & II in Curaçao and Voice of Bonaire in Bonaire; programmes in Dutch, English, Spanish and Papiamento; Dir.-Gen. H. E. Hoyer.

Radio Kelkboom: P.O.B. 146, Oranjestad, Aruba; f. 1954; commercial radio station; programmes in Dutch, English, Spanish and Papiamento; Owner and Dir. Carlos A. Kelkboom.

Radio Victoria: P.O.B. 410, Oranjestad; f. 1958; religious and cultural station owned by the Evangelical Alliance Mission; programmes in Dutch, English, Spanish and Papiamento; Man. Rev. Paul Pietsch, Jr.

Trans World Radio: Kralendijk, Bonaire; religious and cultural station; programmes to South, Central and North America, Middle East and Europe in 15 languages; Man. T. J. Lowell.

Voice of Aruba: P.O.B. 219, Oranjestad, Aruba; commercial radio station; programmes in Dutch, English, Spanish and Papiamento; Man. A. Arends.

Windward Islands Broadcasting: commercial; programmes in English; Man. Vance W. James.

Number of radio receivers (1973): 150,000.

TELEVISION

Tele-Curaçao: P.O.B. 415, Curaçao; f. 1960; run by the Netherlands Antilles Television Company Ltd.; commercial; Gen. Man. C. S. Corsen.

Tele-Aruba: Pos Chiquito 1A, Aruba; f. 1963; run by the Antilliaanse Televisie Maatschappij; commercial; Man. S. L. Salas.

Number of television sets (1971): 32,000.

FINANCE

(cap.=capital; p.u.=paid up; dep.=deposits; m.=million; res.=reserves; amounts in Netherlands Antilles florins)

BANKING

CENTRAL BANK

Bank van de Nederlandse Antillen (*Bank of the Netherlands Antilles*): Fort Amsterdam 4, Willemstad, Curaçao; f. 1828; cap. and res. 19m. (June 1973); Man. Dir. Dr. V. A. Servage; Sec. J. G. J. van Delden; publs. annual reports, statistical bulletins (quarterly).

Algemene Bank Nederland N.V.: Kralendijk, Bonaire; f. 1962; Man. J. Domacasse.

Algemene Bank Nederland N.V.: P.O.B. 469, Willemstad, Curaçao; f. 1856; res. 1.9m. (1970); 1 br.; Mans. J. J. van Thiel, A. R. Vinck, R. A. Plantinga, E. J. van Scherpenseel.

Algemene Bank Nederland N.V.: P.O.B. 391, Oranjestad, Aruba; f. 1949; Man. J. Jacobs.

Algemene Bank Nederland N.V.: P.O.B. 295, Philipsburg, St. Maarten; Man. C. Blankenstijn.

Aruba Bank N.V.: P.O.B. 192, Oranjestad, Aruba; f. 1936; cap. p.u. 1m., dep. 14.7m. (1970); Man. Dir. E. E. Croes.

Banco di Caribe N.V.: Handelskad 4, Willemstad, Curaçao; Man. E. de Kort.

Banco Industrial de Venezuela: Heerenstraat 19, Willemstad, Curaçao; f. 1973; Man. E. A. Alvarez.

Banco Popular Antiliano N.V.: Nassaustraat, P.O.B. 385, Oranjestad, Aruba; f. 1960; cap. 1.8m., dep. 27.2m. (Dec. 1973); 4 brs.; Mans. T. C. M. Schouten, J. M. Crawford.

Banco Popular Antiliano N.V.: Gaito Bldg., Curaçao; Man. R. de Rooy.

Caribbean Mercantile Bank N.V.: Nassaustraat 53, P.O.B. 28, Oranjestad, Aruba; f. 1962; affiliated with Maduro and Curiel's Bank N.V., the Bank of Nova Scotia and Bank Mees and Hope N.V.; cap. p.u. 2m., dep. 25m.; Man. G. J. Montgomery.

Maduro & Curiel's Bank (Bonaire), N.V.: Kralendijk, Bonaire; f. 1963 (*see below*); Man. G. Curiel.

Maduro & Curiel's Bank N.V.: de Ruyterplein 2-4, Willemstad, Curaçao; f. 1916; affiliated with Bank of Nova Scotia, Toronto, and Bank Mees & Hope N.V., Amsterdam; Man. Dirs. L. Capriles, J. S. Roberts.

The Windward Islands Bank Ltd.: P.O.B. 220, Philipsburg, St. Maarten; affiliated to Maduro and Curiel's Bank, N.V.; f. 1960; Man. Dir. J. Jansen; Man. E. W. West.

International Bank & Trust Corporation: P.O.B. 640, Willemstad, Curaçao; f. 1958; "off-shore" bank with no permit to operate locally; cap. $50,000; Dirs. M. Solis, D. da Silva Solis.

Pierson, Heldring & Pierson Curaçao: Fuikstraat 6, P.O.B. 889, Willemstad; f. 1952; "off-shore" bank with no permit to operate locally.

Bank of America N.T. & S.A.: P.O.B. 763, Willemstad; Man. Ulf S. Holmberg.

Bank of Nova Scotia N.V.: P.O.B. 303, Philipsburg, St. Maarten; Man. W. Boyko.

Chase Manhatten Bank N.A.: P.O.B. 200, Philipsburg, St. Maarten; Man. J. F. Lanz.

First National City Bank: Nassaustraat 67, P.O.B. 709, Oranjestad, Aruba; Madurostraat, P.O.B. 736, Willemstad, Curaçao; Man. Netherlands Antilles Raymond Minioni.

INSURANCE

A number of foreign companies have offices in Curaçao and Aruba, mainly British, Canadian, Dutch and North American.

TRADE AND INDUSTRY

CHAMBERS OF COMMERCE AND INDUSTRY

Aruba Chamber of Commerce and Industry: Wilhelminastraat 22, P.O.B. 140, Oranjestad; Chair. Albert H. Raven; Sec. A. Polvliet.

Curaçao Chamber of Commerce and Industry: Willemstad; Chair. H. H. van Grieken; Sec. Dr. L. C. Kolff.

TRADE ASSOCIATIONS

Aruba Trade and Industry Association: P.O.B. 562, Oranjestad, Aruba; Pres. A. B. Kuiperi, Jr.

Vereniging Bedrijfsleven Curaçao (*Curaçao Trade and Industry Association*): Pietermaai 21, P.O.B. 49, Curaçao.

TRADE UNIONS

Algemeen Verbond van Vrije Vak Verenigingen (*Antillean Confederation of Free Trade Unions*): Amsterdam 1, Willemstad, Curaçao; f. 1965; Pres. H. L. Spencer; Sec. K. van den Bosch.

Curaçaosche Federatie van Werknemers (*Curaçao Federation of Workers*): Schouwburgweg 44, Curaçao; f. 1964; about 6,000 mems.; Pres. E. W. Ong-a-Kwie; Sec.-Gen. H. J. van Sichem; 132 affiliated unions.

Curaçaosche Verbond van Vakvereenigingen—CVV (*Christian Confederation of Trade Unions in the Netherlands Antilles*): Bargestraat 1, P.O.B. 562, Willemstad, Curaçao, f. 1950; about 3,990 mems.; 9 affiliated unions; Pres. H. A. Rojer, Sec. O. I. Semerel.

De Algemene Nederlands Antilliaanse Ambtenaren Federatie (*General Union of Netherlands Antillean Civil Servants*): P.O.B. 604, Willemstad, Curaçao; 5,000 mems.; Pres. R. J. Sammy; Sec. Dr. H. Arends.

Independent Oil Workers' Federation: Grensweg 7, San Nicolas; f. 1961; 2,600 mems.; Pres. F. L. Maduro; Sec.-Gen. L. Albus; publ. *Iowua News*.

Petroleum Workers' Federation of Curaçao: affiliated to Int. Petroleum and Chemical Workers' Fed.; f. 1955; about 3,000 mems.; Pres. H. L. Spencer; Sec.-Gen. L. Janzen; publ. *Petrolero*.

TRANSPORT AND TOURISM

There are no railways.

Roads: All islands have a good system of all-weather roads.

Shipping: Curaçao and Aruba are important centres for the refining and transhipment of Venezuelan oil. A dry dock at Curaçao capable of servicing ships of 120,000 tons was completed in 1972.

Besides tankers, which comprise about 85 per cent of the tonnage calling at Curaçao, ships of the following companies call regularly: Royal Netherlands Steamship Co., Holland American Line, North German Lloyd, Hamburg America Line, Germanischer Lloyd, Cunard, Delta Line, Italian Line, French Line, Johnson Line, Grace Line, Mitsui O.S.K., Fred Olson Line and Alcoa.

CIVIL AVIATION

There are airports at Curaçao (Dr. A. Plesman, also known as Hato), Aruba (Princess Beatrix), Bonaire (Flamingo Field), St. Maarten, St. Eustatius and Saba.

A.L.M.—Dutch Antillean Airlines: Dr. A. Plesman Airport, Curaçao; f. 1964; internal services between Aruba, Bonaire, Curaçao and St. Maarten; external services to North, Central and South America and the West Indies; fleet: 3 DC 9/15, 1 Beechcraft A80, 1 DC 6 A/B freighter; Pres. C. O. Yrausquin.

Caraibische Lucht Transport Maatschappij (*Caribbean Air Transport*): Zeelandia 3, Willemstad, Curaçao; f. 1962; operates throughout the Caribbean and Central America; non-scheduled flights to Miami; Dirs. A. J. P. Kusters, J. V. Kusters, H. Venekatte; fleet: 1 DC-6A, 2 C-46.

Windward Islands Airways International: P.O.B. 288, St. Maarten; charter flights and scheduled flights throughout the Caribbean; Gen. Man. Georges Greaux; fleet: 2 Fairchild F-27J, 2 Twin Otter, 1 BN-2A Islander, 2 Twin Bonanza.

The Netherlands Antilles are also served by the following foreign airlines: *Curaçao*—American Airlines, Caribair (Puerto Rico), Dominicana, KLM, LAV (Venezuela), Surinam Airlines, Trans Caribbean (U.S.A.), Viasa (Venezuela). *Aruba*—American Airlines, Aerovías Condor (Colombia), Caribair (Puerto Rico), KLM, LAV (Venezuela), Sabena, Trans Caribbean (U.S.A.), Viasa (Venezuela). *St. Maarten*—Air France, Caribair (Puerto Rico), LIAT (Antigua).

TOURISM

Aruba Tourist Bureau: A. Shüttestraat 2, Oranjestad; branches in New York, Miami and Caracas; Dir. O. B. Arends. There were 2,170 hotel beds in Aruba in 1973.

Curaçao Government Tourist Bureau: Plaza Piar, Willemstad; branches in New York and Miami; Dir. E. A. V. Jesurun (acting).

SURINAM
(NETHERLANDS GUIANA)

INTRODUCTORY SURVEY

Location, Climate, Language, Religion, Flag, Capital

Surinam (formerly Dutch Guiana) lies on the north-east of the South American continent between the Republic of Guyana and French Guiana, with a 560 km. Caribbean seaboard. Inland, the frontier to the south is with Brazil. The country has a subtropical climate with fairly heavy rainfall, and temperatures varying between 21°–30°C (73°–88°F). The population of Surinam is made up of 31 per cent Creoles (Surinam-born with mixed European/African and other descent), 37 per cent Indians (Hindus), 15 per cent Indonesians, 13 per cent Bush Negroes and Amerindians and small groups of Europeans, Chinese and Syrians. Dutch is the official and commercial language, but English, Spanish, French, Chinese, Javanese and Hindi are also used; a pidgin English (*Taki-taki*) is the native dialect. The state flag (proportions 3 by 2) is white, with five five-pointed stars (white, black, brown, red and yellow) arranged in an oval. Paramaribo, the capital and chief port, stands on the Surinam river, about 32 km. from the sea.

Recent History

Under the 1954 Charter, Surinam, a Dutch possession since 1816, became an equal partner with Holland in the Kingdom of the Netherlands (together with the Netherlands Antilles) with full autonomy in domestic affairs. Elections for the *Staten* (Legislative Assembly), held in November 1973, resulted in a victory for an alliance of parties favouring complete independence from the Netherlands. The ruling Progressive National Party retained no seats. A Government refusal to grant wage increases had led earlier in the year to a wave of strikes and violence; peace was gradually restored with the resignation of the Prime Minister in February. Draft proposals formulated by the Dutch Government recommend independence for the Netherlands Antilles and Surinam with a transitional period beginning in 1975.

Government

(*See* Netherlands Antilles).

Economic Affairs

The economy of Surinam is based primarily on the bauxite industry, supported by agriculture, timber and manufacturing. Rice is the staple food crop and the main agricultural export; sugar and bananas are also important. Other exports include prawns, coffee, cocoa and citrus fruit. Bauxite is mined near the Cottica and Para rivers. In 1971 the Government entered into agreements with Reynolds Surinam Mines Ltd. and the Grasshopper Aluminium Company for the joint exploitation of the bauxite deposits in the Bakhuys-Coppename region in western Surinam.

Education

Compulsory education for children between the ages of 7 and 12 has existed since 1876 and is given in government and denominational schools.

Public Holidays

1974: October 18th* (Idul Fitri), December 25th–26th (Christmas).

1975: January 1st (New Year's Day), February* (Phagwah), March 28th (Good Friday), April 30th (Queen's Birthday), May 1st (Labour Day), July 1st (Labour Day).

* Exact date dependent upon sightings of the moon.

Weights and Measures

The metric system is in force.

Currency

100 cents = 1 Surinam gulden (guilder) or florin.

Exchange rates (April 1974):
£1 sterling = 4.224 guilders;
U.S. $1 = 1.789 guilders.

STATISTICAL SURVEY

AREA AND POPULATION

AREA (sq. km.)	POPULATION (1971 Provisional census figures)								
	Total	Creoles	Hindus	Indonesians	Europeans	Chinese	Amerindians	Bush Negroes	Others
12,000	384,900	118,500	142,300	58,900	4,000	6,400	10,200	39,500	5,200

Paramaribo (capital): Estimated population 151,500.

AGRICULTURE
('ooo metric tons)

	1969	1970	1971
Rice	113	122	122*
Maize . . .	1	1	1
Cocoa . . .	0.3	0.3	0.3
Coffee . . .	0.4	0.3	0.4
Bananas . . .	25	25	n.a.
Sugar Cane . .	220	190	210
Grapefruit . .	5	6	6
Oranges . . .	12	12	12
Coconuts (millions)* .	7	7	7

* FAO estimate.

Livestock (1970-71—'ooo): Cattle 45, Goats 5, Sheep 3, Pigs 11, Poultry 467.

Fishing (1966—'ooo kg.): Fish 3,857, Shrimp 3,077.

MINING
('ooo metric tons)

	1968	1969	1970
Bauxite:			
Production . . .	5,660	6,236	6,011
Exports . . .	3,800	3,700	3,400
Alumina:			
Production . .	813	949	1,014
Exports . .	702	857	893
Aluminium:			
Production . .	43	53	55
Exports . .	43	53	53

Gold: 146 kg. in 1968; 74 kg. in 1969.

INDUSTRY

	1970	1971	1972
Raw Sugar ('ooo metric tons)	13	11	12
Beer ('ooo hectolitres) .	86	79	88
Cigarettes (million) .	187	208	244
Aluminium, unwrought ('ooo metric tons) .	55.0	55.0	n.a.
Electricity (million kWh) .	1,322	1,362	n.a.
Gas (million cu. metres) .	5	4	4

FINANCE

100 cents = 1 Surinam gulden (guilder) or florin.

Coins: 1, 5, 10 and 25 cents; 1 guilder.

Notes: 1, 2½, 5, 10, 25, 100 and 1,000 guilders.

Exchange rates (April 1974): £1 sterling = 4.224 guilders; U.S. $1 = 1.789 guilders.

100 Surinam guilders = £23.68 = $55.905.

Budget (1971 estimate—million Surinam guilders): Total Revenue 132.4; Total Expenditure 143.6.

Development Plans: Ten-Year Plan (1966–75). Envisages an outlay of 1,657.2m. Surinam guilders (Mining 807.6m., Agriculture and Fishing 178.7m., Hydro-electric energy 170m., Communications 112m., Industry and Tourism 82m., Education 44m., Public Works 43.5m., Forestry 30.4m.)

BALANCE OF PAYMENTS
(million Surinam guilders)

	1968	1969*	1970*
Current Account	−42.0	−44.0	−44.5
Goods	33.5	43.2	41.3
Services	−75.6	−87.1	−85.3
Private transfers . . .	0.1	−0.1	−0.5
Private Capital	19.1	2.9	−9.0
Public Capital and Transfers .	18.8	34.7	44.8
Errors and Omissions . . .	10.5	14.4	20.6
Overall Balance . . .	6.4	8.0	11.9
Commercial banks . . .	−4.9	1.3	−3.8
Central Bank . . .	−1.5	−9.1	−8.1

* Provisional.

EXTERNAL TRADE
(million Surinam guilders)

	1964	1965	1966	1967	1968	1969	1970	1971
Imports c.i.f. . . .	152.0	179.5	168.8	194.0	188.9	207.7	217.7	237.8
Exports f.o.b.* . . .	88.8	109.0	171.2	198.2	216.5	247.0	252.4	293.9

* Excluding re-exports.

PRINCIPAL COMMODITIES
('000 Surinam guilders)

IMPORTS	1970	1971
Food	25,142	26,354
Beverages and Tobacco . .	4,296	4,391
Crude Materials . .	3,399	6,464
Mineral Fuels and Related Materials .	26,901	31,789
Animal and Vegetable Oils .	1,409	3,467
Chemicals . . .	26,828	42,497
Basic Manufactures . .	48,663	44,191
Machinery and Transport Equipment . .	62,166	60,026
Miscellaneous Manufactured Articles . .	18,703	18,449
Other Transactions . .	148	187
TOTAL . . .	217,654	237,815

EXPORTS	1970	1971
Food	11,468	16,252
Beverages . . .	261	334
Crude Materials* . .	185,653	225,946
Chemicals . . .	287	23
Basic Manufactures† .	54,203	50,892
Machinery and Transport Equipment . .	123	160
Miscellaneous Manufactured Articles . .	376	280
Other Transactions . .	25	9
TOTAL . . .	252,393	293,907

* Mainly bauxite and alumina.
† Mainly aluminium metal.

COUNTRIES

IMPORTS	1970	1971
Netherlands . . .	48,430	53,841
U.S.A. . . .	76,812	79,460
Germany, Federal Republic .	12,921	13,173
Trinidad . . .	22,113	27,505
United Kingdom . .	13,493	13,255
Japan . . .	13,760	15,619
Other Countries . .	30,125	34,962

EXPORTS	1970	1971
Netherlands . . .	33,723	44,886
U.S.A. . . .	98,637	131,859
Canada . . .	5,914	8,123
Germany, Federal Republic .	37,067	22,489
Other Countries . .	77,052	86,550

TOURISM
10,421 tourists visited Surinam in 1966.

TRANSPORT
ROADS
(1972)

Passenger Cars . .	90,609
Lorries . . .	2,122*
Buses . . .	255*
Motorcycles and Powered Bicycles .	31,939

* 1966 figures.

CIVIL AVIATION
(1971)

Landings . . .	916*
Passengers in . .	17,351
Passengers out . .	28,554

* 1966 figure.

Shipping (1969—'000 metric tons): Goods loaded 4,650; Goods unloaded 850.

Source: Algemeen Bureau voor de Statistiek, Paramaribo; FAO; United Nations, *The Growth of World Industry.*

THE CONSTITUTION

(*See* Netherlands Antilles).

THE GOVERNMENT

The Governor is the representative of the Queen and the constitutional Head of the Government. He appoints the Cabinet Ministers and the Advisory Council of at least 7 members.

The Legislative Council, the Staten, is a representative body of 36 members elected by general adult suffrage for a four-year period.

Governor: Dr. J. H. E. FERRIER.

Advisory Council: E. M. L. ENSBERG (Pres.), A. D. FERNANDES, Dr. J. P. KAULESAR-SUKUL, W. H. C. MONKAU, A. E. G. ZAAL.

MINISTERS

(*April* 1974)

Prime Minister and Minister of Finance: HENK ARRON.

Vice-Prime Minister and Minister for Local Administration: O. VAN GENDEREN.

Minister of Justice and Police: EDDY HOOST.

Minister of Development: Dr. MICHEL CAMBRIDGE.

Minister of Home Affairs: Dr. COEN OOFT.

Minister of Education and People's Development: Dr. R. VENETIAAN.

Minister of Economic Affairs: EDDY BRUMA.

Minister of Agriculture and Fisheries: W. SOEMITA.

Minister for Social Welfare: A. SOEPERMAN.

Minister for Buildings, Traffic and Waterways: A. KARAMAT ALI.

Minister of Health: Dr. M. BRAHIM.

Minister of Labour and Housing: F. FRIJMERSUM.

Minister Plenipotentiary of Surinam at The Hague: (vacant).

PARLIAMENT

COMPOSITION OF STATEN

(*November* 1973)

PARTY	SEATS
Nationale Partij Kombinatie . . .	22
Vooruitstrevende Hervormings Partij . .	17

POLITICAL PARTIES

Nationale Partij Surinam: f. 1946; member of Government alliance; Leader H. ARRON.

Vooruitstrevende Hervormings Partij: f. 1949; Leader J. LACHMON.

Kaum-Tani Persatuan Indonesia: f. 1947; Leader I. SOEMITA.

Partij Nationalistische Republiek: member of Government alliance; Leader EDDY BRUMA.

Progressieve Nationale Partij: Leader Dr. J. SEDNEY.

Progressieve Surinaamse Volkspartij: Keizerstraat 122, Paramaribo; f. 1946; Chair. J. A. DE MIRANDA; Leader E. L. WIJNTUIN.

Surinaamse Democratische Partij: Leader D. G. A. FINDLAY.

Surinaamse Volkspartij: P.O.B. 573, Paramaribo; f. 1958; 3,500 mems.; Pres. C. R. BISWAMITRE; Sec. C. A. SLUER.

JUDICIAL SYSTEM

The administration of justice is entrusted to a Court of Justice, the 7 members of which are nominated for life by the Crown, and three Cantonal Courts.

President of the Court of Justice: Dr. S. GELD.

Attorney-General: Dr. M. G. DE MIRANDA.

RELIGION

(1964)

Hindu	.	.	.	87,580
Roman Catholic	.	.	.	71,170
Muslim	.	.	.	63,810
Moravian Brethren	.	.	.	54,390
Dutch Reformed	.	.	.	11,910
Lutheran	.	.	.	4,760
Confucian	.	.	.	150
Other	.	.	.	30,000

Roman Catholic Bishop of Paramaribo: Mgr. ALOYS F. ZICHEM; Gravenstraat 12, P.O.B. 1230, Paramaribo.

THE PRESS

Gouvernements-Advertentieblad: Paramaribo; f. 1871; biweekly; Dutch; Editor P. WIJNGAARDE.

Nieuw Suriname: Wanicastraat 147B, Paramaribo; f. 1954; daily; Editor P. H. AUGUSTUSZOON; circ. 3,500.

Omhoog: Gravenstraat 21, P.O.B. 1802, Paramaribo; f. 1955; Roman Catholic; weekly; Dutch; Publisher Diocese Paramaribo Suriname S.A.; circ. 2,350.

Onze Tijd: Wagenwegstraat 60, Paramaribo; f. 1955; weekly; Dutch; Editor N. M. I. HAAGSTAM.

Suriname: Jodenbreestraat 61, P.O.B. 56, Paramaribo; f. 1859; daily; Dutch; Editor P. WIJNGAARDE; circ. 3,000.

De Vrije Stem: Dr. J. F. Nassylaan 107–109, Paramaribo; daily; Dutch; Editor W. H. LIONARONS; circ. 3,000.

De Vrijheid: Keizerstraat 42, Paramaribo; Chinese; daily.

De Ware Tijd: Malebalirumstraat 13, P.O.B. 1200, Paramaribo; f. 1957; daily; Dutch; Editor L. E. M. MORPURGO; circ. 10,000.

De West: Dr. Mirandastraat 4, Paramaribo; f. 1909; daily; Dutch; Editor D. G. A. FINDLAY; circ. 7,000.

PRESS AGENCIES

Algemeen Nederlands Presbureau (*Netherlands News Service*): Gravenstraat 7, Paramaribo; 3 daily bulletins in Dutch and English; Bureau Chief A. J. M. JUDELL.

Informa (*Surinam News Service*): Herenstraat 11; Bureau Chief J. SLAGVEER.

PUBLISHERS

Lionarons Drukkerij N.V.: Dr. J. F. Nassylaan 107–109, Paramaribo.

Varekamp and Co., N.V.: Dominéstraat 26, P.O.B. 1841, Paramaribo.

Leo Victor: Gemenlandsweg 4, Paramaribo.

RADIO AND TELEVISION

RADIO

Stichting Radio-omroep Suriname: Roode Kruislaan, P.O.B. 271, Paramaribo; f. 1965; commercial; all local languages; Dir. R. Rens.

Radio Apintie: Dominéstraat 11, P.O.B. 1838, Paramaribo; f. 1958; commercial; home service in local languages, foreign service in English and Spanish; Dir. E. Vervuurt.

Radio Paramaribo: Gravenstraat 118, P.O.B. 9751, Paramaribo; f. 1957; commercial; home service in all local languages, foreign service in English and Spanish; Dir. W. H. Lionarons.

Radinka: Waterloostraat, Nieuw Nickerie; f. 1962; commercial; Dutch and Hindi.

Number of radio sets (1973): 120,000.

TELEVISION

Surinaamse Televisie Stichting (S.T.V.S.): Cultuurtuinlaan, P.O.B. 271, Paramaribo; f. 1965; local languages and English; Dir. F. J. Pengel.

Number of television sets (1971): 31,000.

FINANCE

(cap.=capital; p.u.=paid up; dep.=deposits; m.=million; res.=reserves; amounts in Surinam guilders)

BANKING

CENTRAL BANK

Centrale Bank van Suriname: Waterkant 20, P.O.B. 1801, Paramaribo; f. 1956; cap. 3m., dep. 12.8m. (Dec. 1969); Pres. V. M. de Miranda; Man. H. L. Crisson.

Hakrinbank N.V.: Dr. Sophie Redmondstraat 13, P.O.B. 1813, Paramaribo; cap. 7.5m.; Mans. J. R. van Dommelen, J. H. J. de Groot.

Nationale Ontwikkelingsbank, N.V.: A Postraat 34, P.O.B. 677, Paramaribo; f. 1963; government-supported development bank; Man. Dir. E. S. Sewbarath Misser.

De Surinaamsche Bank, N.V.: Gravenstraat 26, P.O.B. 1806, Paramaribo; f. 1865; cap. 5m., res. 4.2m. (Dec. 1973); Dirs. A. J. Brahim, W. J. A. Wijnhoven.

Surinaamse Hypotheekbank, N.V.: Noorderkerkstraat 5, Paramaribo.

Surinaamse Postspaarbank: Knuffelsgracht 11, Paramaribo; f. 1879.

Surinaamse Volkscredietbank: Steenbakkerijstraat 2, hoek Waterkant, Paramaribo; Man. Dir. Dr. T. H. van Philips.

Algemene Bank Nederland N.V.: Vijzelstraat 32, Amsterdam; Kerkplein 1, Paramaribo; Man. Dr. H. W. Bunschoten; 2 agencies.

Landboubank N.V.: Paramaribo; f. 1972; Man. J. J. A. Nagel.

INSURANCE

American Life Insurance Company: Wagenwegstraat 59, Paramaribo.

British American Insurance Company: Gravenstraat 32, Paramaribo.

Eerste Nederlandsche Verzekeringmaatschappij Invaliditeit N.V.: A Postraat 30-32, Paramaribo.

Eerste Surinaams-Nederlandse Levensverzekering Maatschappij: P.O.B. 454, Paramaribo.

N.V. Eerste Sur. Verzekeringsmaatschappij De Nationale: Gravenstraat 3, Paramaribo.

First Federation Life Insurance Company: A Postraat 26, Paramaribo.

The Manufacturers Life Insurance Company: P.O.B. 1392, Paramaribo.

De Nederlanden van 1845: P.O.B. 1845, Paramaribo.

S.G.A. Verzekeringen: Gravenstraat 23-25, Paramaribo.

TRADE AND INDUSTRY

CHAMBER OF COMMERCE

Surinam Chamber of Commerce and Industries: Dr. J. C. de Mirandastraat 10, P.O.B. 149, Paramaribo; f. 1910; 4,500 mems.; Chair. H. W. Mohamed Radja; Sec. J. Ch. Heave; publ. *Bulletin* (fortnightly, Dutch).

DEVELOPMENT ORGANIZATIONS

Stichtung Planbureau Suriname (*Planning Bureau*): Gravenstraat 5, Paramaribo; responsible for programming the Ten-Year Plans and implementing two- and four-year intermediate programmes.

Stichtung Industriele Ontwikkelung Suriname (*Industrial Development Commission*): conducts economic and marketing surveys to determine the feasibility of establishing or expanding industries and provides technical assistance and personnel training; also responsible for stimulating foreign investment in Surinam.

EMPLOYERS' ASSOCIATION

Vereniging Surinaams Bedrijfsleven (*Surinam Trade and Industry Association*): c/o Krasnapolsky, 6th floor, Dominéstraat, P.O.B. 111, Paramaribo; f. 1973; 106 mems.; Chair. Dr. J. Michels; publ. *Weekbericht*.

TRADE UNIONS

Surinaamse Mijnwerkers Unie (*Surinam Mine Workers' Union*): Paramaribo; about 80 mems.; Pres. L. E. Eliazer; Sec. F. R. L. Keteldijk; 3,360 miners in three unions: Paranam Miners' Union, Moengo Miners' Union, and Billiton Miners' Union.

Surinaamse Werknemers Moeder Bond (*Surinam Workers Parent Union*): Surinamestraat 37, Paramaribo; about 5,000 mems.; Sec. F. E. Zwakke.

Progressieve Werknemers Organisatie (*Progressive Workers' Organization*): Gravenstraat 21, Paramaribo; f. 1948; about 2,000 mems., 10 affiliated unions; Pres. L. J. Weidman; Sec. E. Ment.

De Samen Werkende Organisatie van Landsdienaren (*Co-operative Organization of Civil Service Employees*): Cornelis Jongbouwstraat 8, Paramaribo; f. 1957; about 2,000 mems.; Sec. S. P. Ammersingh.

TRANSPORT AND TOURISM

TRANSPORT

RAILWAYS

Paramaribo Government Railway: Onverwacht, Paramaribo; 86 km. open (1 m. gauge), from Onverwacht to Brownsweg; Dir. M. Nahor.

ROADS

There are 1,560 km. of main roads. The main east-west road, 390 km. in length, links Albina on the eastern border with Nieuw Nickerie on the west.

SHIPPING

The following shipping lines maintain services:

Alcoa Steamship Co. Inc.: van 't Hoogerhuysstraat 55, P.O.B. 1842, Paramaribo; agents for Mitsui OSK and Ivaran Lines; fortnightly sailings between Houston, New Orleans, Mobile and Paramaribo; regular passenger service between Trinidad and Paramaribo.

Compagnie Générale Transatlantique: Waterkant 12, Paramaribo; passenger services to Europe.

Royal Netherlands Steamship Co.: Waterkant 84, P.O.B. 1805, Paramaribo; regular services between Amsterdam, Rotterdam, Antwerp, Bremen, Hamburg and Paramaribo, and Mobile, Houston and New Orleans, New York, Baltimore and Paramaribo; sailings to Georgetown and Caribbean ports.

Surinam Navigation Co. Ltd.: Waterkant 44, P.O.B. 1824, Paramaribo; services to Puerto Rico, U.S. Gulf ports, Haiti and Dominican Republic; regular cargo and passenger services on Surinam coast and in the interior.

Other shipping lines: Bookers, Harrison Line.

CIVIL AVIATION

The main airport is Zanderij airport, 45 km. from Paramaribo. In January 1973 improvements to the runways were completed.

Surinam Airways Ltd.: Zorg en Hoop Airfield, P.O.B. 2029, Paramaribo; f. 1955; services to the Guianas, the Caribbean and an extensive network of domestic services; Gen. Man. Bert Maes; fleet 2 Twin Otter.

The following foreign airlines also serve Surinam: Air France, ALM, KLM, Pan American.

TOURISM

Surinam Tourist Development Board: P.O.B. 656, Paramaribo; f. 1953; Chair. O. R. G. Vervuurt; Dir. F. L. de Rooy; publ. *Surinam Sun* (twice a month).

NEW HEBRIDES

The New Hebrides, an Anglo-French condominium, lie in the South Pacific between New Caledonia and Fiji.

STATISTICAL SURVEY

Area: 5,700 square miles (12 large and 60 small islands between 13°–21° S. and 166°–170° E., forming a double chain of islands about 440 miles long).

Population (1967 Census): 77,982 (73,937 indigenes), Vila (capital) 7,738, Santo 2,564. Est. population mid-1973: 90,250.

Employment: The native population is mainly engaged in peasant agriculture, producing both subsistence and cash crops. Most Europeans are employed in commerce and government service.

Agriculture: 200,000 acres are cultivated; there are 750,000 acres of forests. Production (1972): 18,282 metric tons of copra; 10,836 cubic metres of timber; small quantities of cocoa and coffee.

Livestock (1972): 84,000 cattle. Pigs (mainly native owned) and small number of goats, sheep and horses.

Mining: 36,965 tons of manganese were exported in 1972. Surveys have so far failed to discover worthwhile deposits of other minerals.

Finance: Australian and local currency are both legal tender.

100 cents = 1 Australian dollar ($A). Coins: 1, 2, 5, 10, 20 and 50 cents. Notes: 1, 2, 5, 10, 20 and 50 dollars. Exchange rates (April 1974): £1 sterling = $A1.585; U.S. $1 = 67.23 Australian cents; $A100 = £63.10 = U.S. $148.75.

100 centimes = 1 New Hebrides franc (franc néo-hébridais). Exchange rates (April 1974): 1 NH franc = 6.1875 French centimes; £1 sterling = 187.39 NH francs; U.S. $1 = 79.39 NH francs; 1,000 NH francs = £5.34 = U.S. $12.60.

The currencies are locally interchangeable at the rate of $A1 = 100 NH francs.

Condominium Budget (1973 est., $A): Recurrent Revenue and Expenditure 6,071,775. Capital Expenditure under the Development Plan 1971–75: 3,080,000.

British Budget (1973–74 est., $A): Revenue and Expenditure 6,158,000.

French Budget (1973 est., $A): Expenditure 7,524,000.

External Trade (1972): *Imports:* $A23,725,000 (chief items rice, canned foods, beer and wines, building materials, petrol and fuel oils, clothing, textiles, machinery, vehicles and spares). *Exports:* $A12,062,000 (chief items frozen fish, copra; others: timber, manganese, cocoa, frozen and canned beef). Principal trading partners are Australia, France, Japan and U.S.A.

Transport (1972): *Roads:* 3,100 vehicles. *Shipping:* 386 ships called at New Hebrides ports, 362 passengers landed, 337 departed. *Aviation:* 608 aircraft landed, 19,009 passengers arrived and 18,358 departed.

THE CONSTITUTION

In 1902, Joint Deputy Commissioners were appointed by Britain and France and in 1906 an Anglo-French Convention established the Condominium as a Joint Administration. Citizens of the two Powers enjoy equal rights of residence, personal protection and trade. Each Power retains sovereignty over its nationals and business corporations. There is no Territorial sovereignty and natives bear no allegiance to either Power.

There are three elements in the structure of administration: the British National Secretariat, the French National Secretariat and the Condominium (Joint) Departments. An Advisory Council established in 1957, is presided over by the Resident Commissioners.

More than half the islands have local authorities and preparations for the establishment of municipal authorities in Vila and Santo have been made.

THE GOVERNMENT

British High Commissioner: E. N. LARNOUR, C.M.G. (resident in London).

French High Commissioner: GABRIEL ERIAU (resident in Nouméa, New Caledonia).

The High Commissioners are joint and equal heads of the Administration acting locally through British and French Resident Commissioners. The Joint Administration consists of the British National Service, the French National Service and certain Condominium services, including Treasury, Customs and Inland Revenue, Public Works and Transport, Posts and Telephones, Radio, Lands, Survey, Ports and Harbours, Civil Aviation, Agriculture and Meteorology. A rough balance is kept between nationalities in numbers appointed.

BRITISH NATIONAL ADMINISTRATION
Resident Commissioner: R. W. H. DU BOULAY, C.V.O.

FRENCH NATIONAL ADMINISTRATION
Resident Commissioner: R. LANGLOIS.

ADVISORY COUNCIL

Presided over by the two resident commissioners and composed of 4 official and 24 private members.

Private members:

14 elected, of which 6 are Europeans (3 British and 3 French) and 8 are New Hebridean.

10 nominated, of which 3 are British, 3 French, 4 New Hebridean.

JUDICIAL SYSTEM

CONDOMINIUM COURTS

The Joint Court: comprises a neutral President, a British Judge and a French Judge assisted by a neutral Public Prosecutor, a Registrar and a Native Advocate.

President: (vacant).

British Judge: D. R. DAVIS, O.B.E.

French Judge: L. CAZENDRES.

Courts of First Instance: In each District. Composed of British and French District Agents sitting with one assessor.

NATIONAL COURTS

For all suits between non-natives, except for certain land claims.

NATIVE COURTS

Composed of one of the two Agents of the District sitting with two native assessors. Their jurisdiction covers all offences peculiar to natives under the police and administrative regulations and by the code of native laws.

RELIGION

Most of the inhabitants are Christian. A number of missions are established in the Group including Presbyterian, Anglican (Melanesian Mission) and Roman Catholic.

Anglican: Assistant Bishop: The Rt. Rev. D. A. RAWCLIFFE; Lolowai, Longana.

Roman Catholic: Bishop of Port Vila: The Rt. Rev. LOUIS JULLIARD, S.M., C.B.E.; B.P. 59, Port Vila.

Press: There are no newspapers. *Nakamel*, monthly journal published by Sté-PEN, Vila. *New Hebridean Viewpoints*, bi-monthly journal published by New Hebrides National Party, Aoba. *Newsletter:* British Residency; f. 1955; fortnightly; circ. 2,550. *Bulletin d'Information:* French Residency; f. 1961; weekly; circ. 1,200.

Radio: Radio Vila; f. 1966. In 1972 there were 9,000 receivers.

Finance: Banque de l'Indochine, Barclays DCO, Commercial Banking Company of Sydney, Bank of New South Wales, Commonwealth Savings Bank of Australia (agency), National Bank of Australasia, Hong Kong and Shanghai Bank, Australia and New Zealand Bank.

Shipping: Messageries Maritimes: regular service to France, French Oceania, Australia and New Caledonia at three-to four-week intervals. Burns Philp (New Hebrides) Ltd.: regular services linking the New Hebrides with Australia, British Solomon Islands and New Guinea.

Civil Aviation: *Union des Transports Aériens:* five services per week to and from New Caledonia. *Air Pacific:* service thrice weekly to Fiji and Solomon Islands, one of these going to Australia, another to Papua New Guinea. *Air Melanesia:* P.O.B. 72, Hotel Vate Bldg., Rue Higginson, Port Vila; f. 1966; joint regular and charter service throughout the group of islands by New Hebrides Airways and Société Français Air Hebride, a subsidiary of Union de Transport Aeriens.

EDUCATION

There are no joint services. A Teacher Training College, Secondary School and three multi-racial primary schools at Vila, Santo and Tanna are run by the British Administration, together with four junior primary schools. About twenty senior primary schools and two hundred junior primary schools are operated by missions and voluntary agencies. An increasing share of the cost of running English-medium mission schools is being borne by the British Administration. The French Administration run two lycées at Vila and Santo and 47 primary schools, two with secondary facilities.

NEW ZEALAND

INTRODUCTORY SURVEY

Location, Climate, Language, Religion, Flag, Capital

New Zealand lies in the South Pacific Ocean, 1,100 miles south-east of Australia. It consists of North Island and South Island, separated by the narrow Cook Strait, and several smaller islands, including Stewart Island in the south. New Zealand also administers a number of Pacific islands. The climate is moderate with an average temperature of 52°F (12°C) except in the far north where higher temperatures are reached. The language is English and the Maori population also uses its own tongue. About 34 per cent of the population are Anglicans, 22 per cent Presbyterian and 16 per cent Roman Catholics, with the remainder belonging to other Christian denominations. The national flag (proportions 2 by 1) is blue, with a United Kingdom flag as a canton in the upper hoist. In the fly are four five-pointed red stars, edged in white, in the form of the Southern Cross. The capital is Wellington, on North Island.

Recent History

Since the war New Zealand has taken an increasing part in world affairs. It has contributed to Asian development through the Colombo Plan. It is a member of the Anzus Pact (Australia, U.S.A. and New Zealand), the Asian and Pacific Council (ASPAC), and the South East Asia Treaty Organization (SEATO). In 1965 New Zealand and Australia established a free trade agreement (NAFTA), under which duties on selected commodities have been progressively eliminated. In 1962 Western Samoa, formerly administered by New Zealand as a United Nations Trusteeship Territory, attained independence, and in 1965 the Cook Islands attained full internal self-government, but retained many links, including common citizenship, with New Zealand. In November 1969 the National Party government of Sir Keith Holyoake was re-elected for a further three-year term. Sir Keith retired from the Premiership in February 1972, when John Marshall succeeded him as Prime Minister. In December 1972 the first Labour government for over 12 years came to power under the premiership of Norman Kirk.

Government

New Zealand is a self-governing member of the Commonwealth and Queen Elizabeth II is Queen of New Zealand and Head of State. She is represented by a Governor-General who is aided by an Executive Council. The Legislature is unicameral; it consists of a House of Representatives of 84 members (including four Maoris), elected for a term of three years. Voting is by universal adult suffrage, only Maoris being entitled to vote at elections for the four Maori members of Parliament.

Defence

The total strength of regular forces in 1973, was 12,789—army 5,498, navy 2,972, air force 4,319. Defence spending for 1973–74 amounts to $NZ132 million.

Economic Affairs

The external economy is heavily dependent on the pastoral and agricultural industries; wool, meat and dairy produce account for 80 per cent of total exports. In 1971 the United Kingdom imported about 35 per cent of New Zealand's meat and dairy exports. The effect of the United Kingdom's entry in January 1973 into the EEC has been to diminish trade, but better terms than were expected, especially for New Zealand's dairy produce, have been negotiated. New Zealand's second largest overseas market in 1971 was the U.S.A., which took 17.8 per cent of its total exports, followed by the EEC (10.7 per cent), Japan (9.1 per cent), Australia (8.5 per cent) and Canada (2.8 per cent). Markets are being extended in the Pacific region, Latin America and South-East Asia.

Industrial production now makes up almost two-thirds of total production and accounts for 29 per cent of G.N.P. Exotic forests, under controlled management, provide a continuing supply of timber for the growing pulp and paper industry. Coal production is sufficient for all local needs and an oil refinery, using imported crude oil, supplies most of the country's petroleum and related products. Light industry continues to expand, the principal branches being food-processing and canning, car-assembly, transport equipment, wood and cork products, textiles and footwear, apparel and made-up textile goods. Hydro-electric power resources have been further developed. A government-sponsored steel industry, based on the smelting of local iron sands, is in operation on the west coast of the North Island, and a large aluminium smelter has been built at Bluff to process Australian bauxite and produces about 80,000 tons annually. High quality silica sand has also been found in South Canterbury (South Island). In addition to the oil refinery at Marsden Point, Whangarei, and an inland natural gas field at Kapuni, North Island, off-shore oil and natural gas deposits have recently been discovered at Maui off the Taranaki Coast and oil prospecting is in progress off the east coast of South Island.

Price controls were found to be necessary in the first half of 1973 but, despite these, inflation was running at an annual rate of 11 per cent by the middle of the year. However, when links with the U.S. dollar were severed in July, and the New Zealand dollar was allowed to float, it effectively appreciated by 3 per cent. Further price controls and a 10-month wage freeze following an immediate 8.5 per cent increase were introduced in August. In addition to these measures a further upward revaluation of the dollar, this time by 10 per cent, was decided upon in September.

Transport and Communications

There are almost 5,000 km. of railways and about 90,000 km. of roads. There are forty ports, the chief of which are Auckland, Wellington, Lyttelton (the port of Christchurch) and Dunedin. Much traffic between North and South Island is by air; there are also roll-on roll-off ferry services linking Wellington with Picton and Lyttelton. The main centres are joined by an air service network and New Zealand is linked to most major Pacific countries by international airlines. In July 1971 the earth satellite station at Warkworth (north of Auckland) was opened and is linked to the INTELSAT III communications system over the Pacific.

Social Welfare

New Zealand has a comprehensive social welfare system administered by the Department of Social Security. A tax is levied on all incomes to finance the services, which provide medical care and benefits for old age, blindness, widowhood, orphanhood, unemployment and sickness, as well as superannuation and family benefits. There are reciprocal agreements with Australia and the U.K.

Education

State education is free and, between the ages of six and fifteen, compulsory. Primary education lasts from five to twelve or thirteen after which children pass on to secondary schools until the age of eighteen. In 1972 more than 520,000 pupils were enrolled in primary schools and almost 200,000 in secondary schools. Special educational services cater for children in remote areas and for the physically handicapped. There are six universities.

Tourism

New Zealand's tourist attractions are chiefly natural: high mountains, lakes, hot springs and beaches. There are abundant opportunities for outdoor recreation and New Zealand is particularly well-known for its fishing.

Visas are not required to visit New Zealand by nationals of Belgium, Denmark, France, Liechtenstein, Luxembourg, Monaco, the Netherlands, Norway, Sweden, Switzerland and the United Kingdom.

Public Holidays

1974: October 22nd (Labour Day), December 25th (Christmas Day), December 26th (Boxing Day).

1975: January 1st (New Year's Day), February 6th (New Zealand Day), March 28th–31st (Easter), April 25th (Anzac Day), Queen's Official Birthday.

In addition to the above there is in each provincial district a holiday for the provincial anniversary.

Weights and Measures

Imperial weights and measures are in use. The metric system was introduced into the schools in 1971; the whole country is expected to go metric by 1976.

Currency and Exchange Rates

100 cents = 1 New Zealand dollar ($NZ).

Exchange rates (April 1974):
£1 sterling = $NZ 1.631;
U.S. $1 = 69.09 NZ cents.

STATISTICAL SURVEY

AREA AND POPULATION

AREA (sq. miles)			POPULATION (April 1973)		
Total*	North Island	South Island	Total	North Island, etc.	South Island, etc.
103,736	44,281	58,093	2,974,659	2,145,139	829,520

Maoris (June 30th, 1972): 236,066.

* Includes Stewart Island (670 sq. miles), Chatham Islands (372 sq. miles) and other minor islands.

Total Population (July 1st, 1973): 2,963,844.

CHIEF TOWNS
(April 1973)

Wellington (capital) . 337,680	Christchurch . . 313,210
Auckland . . . 747,339	Hamilton . . 136,006*
Dunedin . . . 118,970	

* 1971 census.

Immigration: (1970–71) 39,377; (1971–72) 45,099; (1972–73) 54,651.

Emigration: (1970–71) 31,958; (1971–72) 37,546; (1972–73) 35,483.

Births: (1972) 63,482. **Deaths:** (1972) 24,801. **Marriages:** (1972) 26,868.

EMPLOYMENT

(April 1973)

	Males ('000)	Females ('000)	Total ('000)
Agriculture and Other Primary	125.2	16.7	141.9
Manufacturing Industry	213.5	73.1	286.6
Electricity, Gas and Water	13.2	1.3	14.5
Construction	86.1	2.7	88.8
Wholesale and Retail Trade	111.7	78.4	190.1
Transport, Storage and Communications	86.6	17.9	104.5
Finance, Insurance, Real Estate, etc.	41.0	30.2	71.2
Community, Social and Personal Services	125.2	113.7	238.9
Total in Industry	802.5	334.0	1,136.5
Armed Forces in New Zealand	10.6	0.6	11.2
Registered Unemployed	1.6	0.9	2.5
Total Labour Force	814.7	335.5	1,150.2

AGRICULTURE

CROPS

	Area ('000 acres)			Production† ('000 bushels)		
	1969–70	1970–71	1971–72	1969–70	1970–71	1971–72
Wheat	268	241	263	10,553	11,965	14,337
Oats	52	55	40	3,181	3,293	2,731
Barley	139	201	238	7,692	11,400	14,792
Maize	20	23.2	n.a.	2,308	n.a.	n.a.
Peas	61	n.a.	n.a.	1,822	1,905	n.a.
Potatoes	24.5	18.9	n.a.	249	207	n.a.

† Bushel weights: wheat 60 lb., oats 40 lb., barley 50 lb., maize 56 lb., peas 60 lb.

LIVESTOCK

('000 at January 31st)

	1969	1970	1971	1972
Dairy cows in milk	2,304	2,321	2,239	2,200
Total cattle	8,605	8,777	8,819	8,774
Breeding ewes	43,385	42,912	43,017	44,152
Total sheep	59,937	60,276	58,913	60,883
Total pigs	553	578	617	580

ANIMAL PRODUCTS

		1970–71	1971–72	1972–73
Butter (Creamery) . . ('ooo tons)		227.6	241.5	218.5
Cheese . . . . ,, ,,		106.1	102.7	97.4
Preserved milk* . . . ,, ,,		166.7	253.8	242.9
Casein . . . . ,, ,,		54.8	39.6	45.5
Meat—total . . . ,, ,,		1,040.0	1,066.0†	1,072.0†
Mutton and lamb . . ,, ,,		555.0	560.0†	545.0†
Wool, greasy basis ('ooo metric tons)		334.0	322.0	309.0

* Skim-milk powder, condensed and powdered whole-milk, butter-milk powder.

† Estimate.

FORESTRY

(Rough sawn timber production—'ooo board feet)

SPECIES	1967–68	1968–69	1969–70	1970–71	1971–72	1972–73
Rimu and Miro . . .	153,600	135,900	137,900	137,900	128,500	119,100
Matai	17,000	15,400	15,300	11,400	7,500	7,700
Totara	6,500	6,500	5,600	5,000	4,300	3,900
Kahikatea	17,700	16,600	14,800	12,700	13,000	12,000
Beech	10,000	10,600	10,900	11,300	9,700	10,400
Exotic Pines . . .	421,300	475,600	504,100	536,000	495,000	523,100
TOTAL (incl. others) .	674,900	732,600	765,000	784,300	740,500	756,600

FISHERIES

	UNIT	QUANTITY			VALUE ($NZ 'ooo)		
		1970	1971	1972	1970	1971	1972
Wet Fish	cwt. ('ooo)	800	866	790	6,425	7,153	6,819
Oysters	sacks ('ooo)	120	122	164	1,437	1,776	1,628
Rock Lobster	cwt. ('ooo)	127	112	90	8,052	9,432	8,145
Other.	,,	48	92	103	351	782	717

MINING

	UNIT	1969	1970	1971	1972
Coal and Lignite . . .	'ooo tons	2,327	2,348	2,091	2,147
Gold	'ooo oz.	11	11	9	14
Silver	,, ,,	22	16	66	31
Petroleum (crude) . . .	'ooo gals.	106	16,334	28,125	39,130
Natural Gas	million cu. ft.	2,336	3,769	10,627	12,484
Iron Sands	'ooo tons	19	141	567	1,359
Silica Sand	,, ,,	106	133	123	108
Limestone	,, ,,	2,593	2,762	2,887	2,971
Salt	,, ,,	49	52	43	59

INDUSTRY
SELECTED COMMODITIES

	Unit	1970	1971	1972
Canned Meat	'ooo lb.	8,949	11,118	9,303
Flour	short tons	216,978	223,132	225,256
Refined Sugar	tons	139,868	141,943	144,539
Biscuits	,,	23,361	23,912	24,527
Jam*	,,	5,291	3,791	5,855
Canned Fruit*	,,	22,610	21,187	18,471
Canned Vegetables* . . .	,,	17,618	17,893	14,521
Soap Flakes and Powder . .	,,	11,533	11,487	10,075
Beer and Stout	'ooo gallons	73,765	78,007	79,509
Wool Yarn	'ooo lb.	30,884	32,016	33,984
Woollen and Worsted Piece Goods .	'ooo sq. yds.	5,865	4,068	2,913
Refrigerators	number	134,674	159,100	167,722
Washing Machines . . .	,,	55,383	63,590	71,327
Lawn Mowers	,,	69,324	61,974	69,394
Radios	,,	119,471	137,653	141,241
Tobacco	'ooo lb.	2,390	2,305	2,281
Cigarettes	million	5,364	5,107	5,620
Chemical Fertilisers . . .	'ooo tons	1,880	1,823	2,173
Cement	,,	816	810	885
Passenger Cars	number	55,282	59,395	68,546
Trucks, Vans, Buses . . .	,,	16,545	20,883	14,464

* Year ended June.

FINANCE

100 cents = 1 New Zealand dollar ($NZ).

Coins: 1, 2, 5, 10, 20 and 50 cents.

Notes: 1, 2, 5, 10, 20 and 100 dollars.

Exchange rates (April 1974): £1 sterling = $NZ1.631; U.S. $1 = 69.09 NZ cents.

$NZ100 = £61.30 = U.S. $144.74.

BUDGET (1973–74)
($NZ million)

Income		Expenditure	
Income Tax	1,610	Administration	249
Estate and Gift Duty . . .	30	Defence	130
Land Tax	4	Foreign Affairs	38
		Development of Industry . . .	171
Total Direct Taxation . .	1,644	Education	407
		Social Services	609
Customs Duty	194	Health	388
Beer Duty	44	Transport and Communications . .	180
Sales Tax	195	Debt Services and Miscellaneous Invest-	
Payroll Tax	30	ment Transactions . . .	313
Racing Duty	18		
Other Stamp Duties . . .	24	Total Net Expenditure . . .	2,485
Other	21	Supplementary	120
Total Indirect Taxation . .	526		
Total Taxation Receipts, Consolidated Revenue Account . .	2,170		
Highways Tax	101		
Total Taxation . . .	2,271		
Interest, Profit and Miscellaneous Receipts	102		
Borrowing	232		
Total	2,605	Total	2,605

WORKS AND CAPITAL EXPENDITURE
($NZ million)

	1971–72	1972–73	1973–74 (est.)
Electricity	79.8	103.9	100.0
Forest Development . . .	3.3	4.2	5.5
Land Utilization . . .	4.0	2.7	4.2
Housing	11.0	10.6	16.0
Public Buildings . . .	10.9	21.9	28.0
Railways	9.2	11.1	13.3
Air Transport	6.0	8.1	8.9
Roads	90.5	104.1	104.4
Education	59.1	70.9	82.9
Post Office	27.2	33.0	36.8
Health and Hospital Building .	4.7	4.4	4.3
Defence	5.2	6.2	7.8
TOTAL (incl. others) .	328.3	400.4	437.8

NATIONAL INCOME AND EXPENDITURE
($NZ million)

	1969–70	1970–71	1971–72
NATIONAL INCOME AT FACTOR COST . .	4,031	4,634	5,392
Indirect taxation	377	459	538
Subsidies	−24	−46	−89
NATIONAL INCOME AT MARKET PRICES .	4,384	5,047	5,840
Depreciation	357	385	420
GROSS NATIONAL PRODUCT . . .	4,741	5,432	6,260
EXPENDITURE ON G.N.P.:			
Personal expenditure on consumer goods and services	2,829	3,351	3,642
Public authority current expenditure . .	723	884	1,001
Gross domestic capital formation in N.Z. .	1,019	1,204	1,427
Change in stocks . . .	130	188	190
Exports of goods and services . .	1,277	1,295	1,547
Imports of goods and services . .	−1,140	1,413	−1,472
EXPENDITURE ON GROSS DOMESTIC PRODUCT .	4,838	5,509	6,335
Net factor payments to rest of world . .	−97	−77	−75
EXPENDITURE ON GROSS NATIONAL PRODUCT .	4,741	5,432	6,260

Currency in Circulation: $NZ204,500,000 (November 30th, 1972).

OVERSEAS RESERVES
($NZ million)

END OF MARCH	ASSETS OF N.Z. BANKING SYSTEM	OVERSEAS SECURITIES		GOLD	IMF RESERVE POSITION	IMF SPECIAL DRAWING RIGHTS	TOTAL RESERVES
		Treasury-held	Other Government-held				
1969 . .	183.2	80.5	15.3	1.2	—	—	280.1
1970 . .	204.8	87.5	16.1	0.8	—	23.6	332.7
1971 . .	172.4	117.3	17.4	0.7	45.1	19.6	372.5
1972 . .	331.4	186.3	18.9	0.7	45.1	47.5	629.9
1973 . .	561.9	235.0	22.3	0.7	45.1	52.1	917.2

BALANCE OF PAYMENTS
($NZ million)

SUMMARY OF CURRENT ACCOUNT	1970–71*			1971–72†		
	Credit	Debit	Balance	Credit	Debit	Balance
Merchandise transactions f.o.b. . .	1,102.7	1,042.0	60.7	1,311.0	1,074.7	236.3
Non-monetary gold . . .	—	—	—	—	—	—
Transport	88.9	171.9	− 83.0	112.2	185.2	−73.0
Travel	33.6	61.9	− 28.3	45.1	75.5	−30.4
Insurance	0.9	4.2	− 3.3	0.2	4.6	− 4.4
International investment income .	42.8	117.9	− 75.1	47.0	122.2	−75.2
Government transactions . .	15.8	29.9	− 14.1	17.8	40.1	−22.3
Miscellaneous receipts and payments	35.2	88.4	− 53.2	37.2	91.1	−53.9
Transfers	47.8	61.8	− 14.0	69.2	65.1	4.1
						−18.8
BALANCE ON CURRENT ACCOUNT .	1,367.7	1,578.0	−210.3	1,639.7	1,658.5	

* Revised. † Provisional.

SUMMARY OF CAPITAL ACCOUNT	1970–71*		1971–72†	
	Increase in		Increase in	
	Assets	Liabilities	Assets	Liabilities
Long-term Capital (Private):				
Overseas direct investment in New Zealand .	—	130.0	—	100.9
New Zealand direct investment overseas .	7.8	—	10.5	—
Other long-term capital movements . .	—	8.7	—	90.5
Long-term Capital (Government):				
Government investments . . .	31.4	—	12.2	—
Public debt	—	50.6	—	72.2
Local Authority debt . . .	—	− 1.3	—	−1.4
Asian Development Bank:				
Holdings of N.Z. securities . .	—	1.0	—	—
N.Z. subscription . . .	2.0	—	—	—
International Bank for Reconstruction and Development (World Bank):				
Holdings of N.Z. securities . .	—	—	—	0.4
N.Z. subscription and security .	—	—	0.4	—
Other	—	−11.5	—	1.3
Monetary Institutions:				
Reserve Bank of New Zealand:				
IMF drawings and repurchases .	—	−35.0	—	—
N.Z. subscription . . .	—	—	—	—
Allocation of Special Drawing Rights	—	19.3‡	—	19.1‡
Increase in Quota . . .	40.2	—	—	—
Holdings in N.Z. Currency .	—	30.1	—	—
Other borrowing and lending .	—	− 5.1	—	−5.4
Monetary gold . . .	− 0.1	—	—	—
Reserve Bank of New Zealand and Other Banks:				
Assets of N.Z. banking system . .	−32.4	—	159.0	—
Special Drawing Rights of IMF addition to official reserves . . .	− 4.0	—	27.9	—
Official Export Credits . . .	5.7	—	4.3	—
Short-term Capital (Government):				
Government cash balances . .	—	—	—	—
Other	− 0.3	—	57.6	—
Other Short-term Capital Movements including Errors and Omissions . . .	—	73.8	—	13.1
BALANCE ON CAPITAL ACCOUNT . .	−210.3		−18.8	

* Revised. † Provisional.

‡ Allocation of Special Drawing Rights is not an increase in liabilities but is entered here as a contra entry to their addition to official reserves to maintain the correct balance of the capital account.

REGIONAL BALANCES ON CURRENT ACCOUNT*
(1970–71—$NZ million)

	United Kingdom	Other Sterling Countries	United States and Canada	EEC Countries	Other Countries	International Organizations	Total All Countries
Merchandise . . .	78.4	−148.5	40.9	53.0	38.1	—	61.9
Transport	−44.5	2.1	− 7.6	−15.3	−21.5	—	− 86.9
Travel	−11.5	− 14.9	− 1.5	− 1.5	− 2.2	—	− 28.3
Insurance . . .	− 1.5	− 0.6	− 1.4	0.1	—	—	− 3.5
International investment income . . .	−38.7	− 6.6	−21.5	− 3.5	− 6.6	—	− 76.9
Government transactions .	− 6.4	− 6.6	− 0.3	− 1.7	0.9	0.5	− 13.6
Miscellaneous . .	−18.4	− 17.4	−13.0	− 1.9	− 2.6	—	− 53.2
Transfers . . .	6.6	− 13.0	2.9	− 1.3	− 2.2	−7.0	− 14.0
Balance on Current Account . . .	−36.0	−205.6	1.8	28.0	3.9	−6.5	−214.4†

* Provisional.

† This $214.4m. balance on current account differs from the more recent $210.3m. shown in the previous table because the above Regional Balances on Current Account table is the latest to be released to date.

EXTERNAL TRADE
($NZ '000)
Twelve months ending June 30th.

	1970–71	1971–72
Imports (f.o.b.) . .	1,070,567	1,149,572
Exports (f.o.b.) . .	1,131,719	1,369,837

COMMODITIES

	Imports (c.d. value)			Exports* (f.o.b.) (re-exports omitted)		
	1969–70†	1970–71†	1971–72‡	1969–70†	1970–71†	1971–72‡
Food and Live Animals . .	45,212	55,312	56,258	614,617	651,805	797,141
Beverages and Tobacco . .	8,666	12,237	12,868	1,121	1,503	1,578
Crude Materials . . .	51,396	47,354	45,171	324,290	315,003	377,385
Mineral Fuels . . .	59,094	60,625	66,591	5,742	7,257	8,153
Animal and Vegetable Oils .	1,709	2,586	2,744	10,035	10,967	9,804
Chemicals	116,345	134,804	142,782	33,552	40,285	34,171
Manufactures . . .	271,612	296,296	285,961	49,953	54,259	77,894
Machinery and Transport Equipment	319,713	370,811	443,216	15,598	16,669	23,249
Miscellaneous . . .	66,552	77,228	84,099	9,218	10,281	12,367
Other Transactions . .	4,027	13,314	9,882	341	62	66
Total . . .	944,326	1,070,567	1,149,572	1,064,467	1,108,091	1,341,808

* Main exports during year ended June 1972 were: Meat and meat preparations ($NZ399.3 million), Dairy products ($NZ326.8 million), Wool ($NZ229.3 million), Hides, skins and pelts ($NZ62.3 million).

† Revised.   ‡ Provisional.

PRINCIPAL TRADING PARTNERS

	IMPORTS		EXPORTS*	
	1969–70	1970–71‡	1969–70	1970–71‡
Australia	197,872	225,467	87,311	96,133
Fiji	959	3,072	8,848	12,449
Hong Kong	17,867	18,655	4,597	6,747
Malaysia	6,440	5,535	7,269	7,959
South Africa . . .	3,941	3,287	3,197	8,953
United Kingdom . . .	279,090	309,946	386,017	384,660
Belgium and Luxembourg .	4,442	6,767	21,292	25,529
France and Monaco . .	7,529	11,001	28,682	27,648
Germany, Federal Republic .	36,776	49,184	29,682	30,297
Italy and San Marino . .	11,913	14,361	23,724	19,228
Netherlands . . .	9,664	14,179	16,113	17,014
Canada	37,489	38,378	45,343	32,186
U.S.A.	123,105	129,857	166,493	192,754
Japan	78,096	110,272	105,557	102,684
TOTAL (incl. others) .	944,324	1,070,567	1,075,212	1,117,713

* Excluding ship's stores, specie and gold. ‡ Revised.

1971-72: Total exports NZ$1,352.6 million, including NZ$418.4 million to the United Kingdom.

TOURISM

(1971–72)

FROM	VISITORS ('000)
Australia	87.5
U.S.A.	43.9
United Kingdom . . .	10.1
Canada	7.1
Japan	3.6
Fiji	3.6
New Caledonia . . .	2.1
Other Countries . . .	18.7
TOTAL .	176.6

TRANSPORT

RAILWAYS

YEAR ENDING MARCH 31st	PASSENGER JOURNEYS ('000)		GOODS CARRIED ('000 tons)				NET TON MILES (million)
	RAILWAY	MOTOR*	TIMBER	LIVESTOCK	AGRICULTURAL LIME	TOTAL (incl. others)	
1971	21,008	22,599	2,164	198	146	11,699	1,745.4
1972	20,668	21,524	2,013	135	148	11,336	1,698.2
1973	18,565	20,866	2,103	103	201	12,127	1,874.4

* Railway Department's motor services only.

ROADS: MOTOR VEHICLES LICENSED

(as at March 31st)

	1971	1972	1973
Private cars	918,700	966,566	1,032,228
Lorries	181,762	190,625	194,654
Buses and service cars	3,113	3,102	3,100
Trailers	224,667	238,798	256,281
Motor cycles and power cycles . . .	53,206	63,112	72,648
Other vehicles	87,889	87,974	94,047
TOTAL . . .	1,469,337	1,550,177	1,652,958

SHIPPING

	ENTERED				CLEARED			
	OVERSEAS		COASTAL		OVERSEAS		COASTAL	
	VESSELS	NET TONNAGE ('000)	VESSELS	NET TONNAGE ('000)	VESSELS	NET TONNAGE ('000)	VESSELS	NET TONNAGE ('000)
1970	3,757	17,258	7,671	8,322	3,749	17,272	7,662	8,320
1971	3,551	16,740	7,753	8,503	3,556	16,699	7,744	8,548
1972	3,770	18,947	7,980	9,779	3,751	18,831	7,991	9,827

AIR TRANSPORT

('000)

YEAR ENDING MARCH 31st	INTERNAL SERVICES			OVERSEAS SERVICES		
	Miles Flown	Passenger-Miles	Cargo Ton-Miles	Passengers Carried	Freight Carried (single tons)	Mail Carried (single tons)
1971	11,910	413,435	10,509.3	566.9	11,332.7	1,337.0
1972	12,357	423,735	10,797.8	667.2	13,418.7	1,574.7
1973	13,175	468,758	12,411.9	770.1	16,338.3	1,649.6

COMMUNICATIONS MEDIA

	March 1973
TV Sets Licensed	732,000
Daily Newspapers	41
Telephones per 100 people . . .	44

EDUCATION

(1972)

	INSTITUTIONS	PUPILS	TEACHERS‡
Pre-School . .	973	46,170	690
Primary (State and Private) .	2,853	520,668	19,499
Secondary (State and Private) .	393	197,381	10,915
Technical . .	12	94,937*	1,111
Teacher Training†	13	8,495	640
University .	7	39,019	2,259

* Including part-time or correspondence students.
† Including 4 Kindergarten Training Centres.
‡ Full-time teaching staff.

Source: Department of Statistics, Wellington, 1.

THE CONSTITUTION

Executive Council

The powers, duties and responsibilities of the Governor-General and the Executive Council under the present system of responsible government are set out in Royal Letters Patent and Instructions thereunder of May 11th, 1917. In the execution of the powers and authorities vested in him the Governor-General must be guided by the advice of the Executive Council; but if in any case he sees sufficient cause to dissent from the opinion of the Council, he may act in the exercise of his powers and authorities in opposition to the opinion of the Council, reporting the matter to Her Majesty without delay, with the reasons for his so acting.

In addition to the Governor-General, the Executive Council consists of all the ministers of the Crown. Two members, exclusive of His Excellency or the presiding member, constitute a quorum. Authority is given in the Civil Lists for the appointment of one or two Maoris or half-castes as members of the Executive Council representing the Maori race.

House of Representatives

The number of members constituting the House of Representatives is eighty-seven—eighty-three Europeans and four Maoris. They are designated "Members of Parliament".

Quinquennial Parliaments, instituted under the Constitution Act, were abolished by the Triennial Parliaments Act, 1879, which fixed the term at three years. General elections have been held at three-yearly intervals since 1881, with a few exceptions.

Since the abolition of plural voting in 1889 and the introduction of women's suffrage in 1893 every person of twenty-one years of age or over (reduced to twenty in 1969) has had the right to exercise a vote in the election of members for the House of Representatives. Since 1957 to be registered as an elector a person must be a British subject or Irish citizen, ordinarily resident in New Zealand at some period, having resided continuously in New Zealand for at least a year and who has resided continuously for three months or more in the electoral district for which he claims to vote. A system of compulsory registration of all electors except Maoris was introduced at the end of 1924; it was introduced for Maoris in 1956.

There are 80 European electoral districts and four Maori electoral districts. Only Maoris may vote in Maori district elections. A Maori half-caste is entitled to be registered as an elector of a Maori or a European electoral district.

By the Electoral Amendment Act, 1937, which made provision for a secret ballot in Maori elections, Maori electors were granted the same privileges, in the exercise of their vote, as European electors.

For the system of local government administration a modified form of franchise exists, a ratepaying qualification being necessary for the exercise of votes on financial issues.

THE GOVERNMENT

Head of State: H.M. QUEEN ELIZABETH II.

Governor-General and Commander-in-Chief: Sir EDWARD DENIS BLUNDELL, G.C.M.G., K.B.E., G.C.V.O.

THE MINISTRY
(*April* 1974)

Prime Minister, Minister of Foreign Affairs, Minister in Charge of the Audit Department, Minister in Charge of the Legislative Department, Minister in Charge of the New Zealand Security Intelligence Service: Rt. Hon. NORMAN E. KIRK.

Deputy Prime Minister, Minister of Labour, Minister of Works and Development, Minister in Charge of Publicity: Hon. HUGH WATT.

Minister of Trade and Industry, Minister of Energy Resources: Hon. WARREN W. FREER.

Minister of Finance, Minister in Charge of the Department of Statistics, Minister in Charge of Friendly Societies: Hon. WILLIAM E. ROWLING.

Minister of Justice, Attorney-General, Minister in Charge of Civil Aviation: Hon. Dr. A. MARTYN FINLAY.

Minister of Maori Affairs, Minister of Lands: Hon. MATIU RATA.

Minister of Police, Minister of Customs, Associate Minister of Finance: Hon. MICHAEL A. CONNELLY.

Minister of Defence, Minister in Charge of War Pensions, Minister in Charge of Rehabilitation: Hon. ARTHUR J. FAULKNER.

Minister of Social Welfare, Minister in Charge of the Government Printing Office: Hon. NORMAN J. KING.

Minister of State Services, Minister of Health, Minister in Charge of State Advances Corporation: Hon. ROBERT J. TIZARD.

Minister of Agriculture and Fisheries, Minister of Forests, Minister of Science: Hon. COLIN J. MOYLE.

Minister of Housing, Minister in Charge of the Earthquake and War Damage Commission, Minister in Charge of the Public Trust Office: Hon. WILLIAM A. FRASER.

Minister of Local Government, Minister of Internal Affairs, Minister in Charge of the Valuation Department: Hon. HENRY L. J. MAY.

Minister of Transport, Minister in Charge of the State Insurance Office: Hon. Sir BASIL ARTHUR.

Minister of Education, Minister of Island Affairs: Hon. PHILIP A. AMOS.

Minister of Tourism, Associate Minister of Social Welfare: Hon. T. WHETU M. TIRIKATENE-SULLIVAN.

Minister of Overseas Trade, Minister for the Environment, Minister of Recreation and Sport, Associate Minister of Foreign Affairs: Hon. JOSEPH A. WALDING.

Minister of Immigration, Minister of Mines, Associate Minister of Labour, Associate Minister of Works and Development: Hon. FRASER M. COLMAN.

Minister of Railways, Minister of Electricity, Minister of Civil Defence: Hon. THOMAS M. McGUIGAN.

Postmaster-General, Minister of Broadcasting, Minister in Charge of the Government Life Insurance Office: Hon. ROGER DOUGLAS.

COMMISSIONERS OF TERRITORIES

Cook Islands: G. J. BROCKLEHURST (High Commissioner).

Niue Island: C. A. ROBERTS (Resident Commissioner).

Tokelau: W. G. THORP (High Commissioner in Western Samoa).

DIPLOMATIC REPRESENTATION

HIGH COMMISSIONS, EMBASSIES AND LEGATION ACCREDITED TO NEW ZEALAND
(In Wellington, unless otherwise indicated)
(E) Embassy; (HC) High Commission; (L) Legation.

Argentina: Canberra, Australia (E).

Australia: I.C.I. House, Molesworth St., I, P.O.B. 12145 (HC); *High Commissioner:* Dame ANNABELLE RANKIN.

Austria: Canberra, Australia (E).

Bangladesh: Canberra, Australia (HC).

Belgium: Dominion Farmers' Institute Bldg., Featherston St., I, P.O.B. 3841 (E); *Ambassador:* HERMAN J. MATSAERT.

Brazil: Canberra, Australia (E).

Burma: Canberra, Australia (E).

Canada: I.C.I. House, Molesworth St., I, P.O.B. 12049 (HC); *High Commissioner:* J. A. DOUGAN.

Chile: Canberra, Australia (E).

China, People's Republic: 2–6 Glenmore St. (E); *Ambassador:* PEI TSIEN-CHANG.

Czechoslovakia: 12 Anne St., Wadestown, P.O.B. 2843 (L); *Chargé d'Affaires:* MIROSLAV PRAVDA.

Denmark: Government Life Insurance Bldg., Customhouse Quay, I., P.O.B. 111 (E); *Ambassador:* P. A. VON DER HUDE.

Egypt: Canberra, Australia (E).

Finland: Canberra, Australia (E).

France: Government Life Insurance Bldg., Customhouse Quay, I., P.O.B. 1695 (E); *Ambassador:* CHRISTIAN DE NICOLAY.

Germany, Federal Republic: 3 Claremont Grove, I., P.O.B. 1687 (E); *Ambassador:* ECKART BRIEST.

Greece: Canberra, Australia (E).

India: 49 Willis St., I. (HC); *High Commissioner:* L. N. RAY.

Indonesia: 11 Fitzherbert Terrace (E); *Ambassador:* SOETIKNO LOEKITODISATRO.

Ireland: Canberra, Australia (E).

Israel: Canberra, Australia (E).

Italy: 24 Grant Rd., Thorndon, I., P.O.B. 463 (E); *Ambassador:* BENEDETTO FENZI.

Japan: 298 Oriental Parade (E); *Ambassador:* TOSHIO MITSUDO.

Khmer Republic: Canberra, Australia (E).

Korea, Republic: Canberra, Australia (E).

Laos: Canberra, Australia (E).

Malaysia: 200 Oriental Parade (HC); *High Commissioner:* J. D. DE SILVA.

Nepal: Tokyo, Japan (E).

Netherlands: Fifth Floor, Shell House, The Terrace, C.1, P.O.B. 840 (E); *Ambassador:* H. C. JORISSEN.

Norway: Canberra, Australia (E).

Pakistan: Canberra, Australia (E).

Peru: Canberra, Australia (E).

Philippines: Canberra, Australia (E).

Singapore: 1st Floor, Molesworth House, 101 Molesworth St., I. (HC); *High Commissioner:* CHAN KENG HOWE.

Spain: Canberra, Australia (E).

Sri Lanka: Canberra, Australia (HC).

Sweden: 17th Floor, Aurora House, 48–64 The Terrace, P.O.B. 1800 (E); *Ambassador:* OLAF G. BJURSTROM.

Switzerland: Panama House, 22–24 Panama St., P.O.B. 386 (E); *Ambassador:* MAX CORTI.

Thailand: 2 Burnell Avenue, I., P.O.B. 2530 (E); *Ambassador:* SOMCHAI ANUMAN-RAJADHON.

U.S.S.R.: 57 Messines Rd., 5 (E); *Ambassador:* A. I. IVANTSOV.

United Kingdom: Reserve Bank Bldg., 2 The Terrace, P.O.B. 1812 (HC); *High Commissioner:* Sir DAVID SCOTT, K.C.M.G.

U.S.A.: I.B.M. Centre, 151–165 The Terrace, P.O.B. 1190 (E); *Ambassador:* I. ARMISTEAD SELDEN, Jnr.

Viet-Nam, Republic: Fourth Floor, D.I.C. Bldg., 40 Panama St., P.O.B. 2833 (E); *Ambassador:* DOAN BA CANG.

Yugoslavia: 49 Hobson St., Wellington 1 (E); *Ambassador:* IVAN TOSEVSKI.

New Zealand also has diplomatic relations at consular level with Costa Rica, Ecuador, El Salvador, the German Democratic Republic, Mexico, Poland, Portugal, Romania, South Africa, Turkey and Venezuela.

PARLIAMENT

THE HOUSE OF REPRESENTATIVES

OFFICERS

Speaker: STANLEY WHITEHEAD.

Chairman of Committees: RONALD BAILEY.

Clerk of the House: F. A. ROUSSELL.

Leader of the Opposition: Rt. Hon. J. R. MARSHALL.

GENERAL ELECTION, 25th November 1972

PARTY	VOTES	VOTES (per cent)	SEATS
Labour .	677,475	48.0	55
National .	581,422	41.2	32
Social Credit .	93,197	6.6	—
Others . .	40,830	4.2	—

POLITICAL PARTIES

Labour Party, The: P.O.B. 6373, Te Aro, Wellington; f. 1916; The policy of the Party is the maximum utilization of the Dominion's resources for organizing an internal economy to distribute goods and services so as to guarantee to every person able and willing to work an adequate standard of living.

New Zealand Pres.: C. M. BENNETT.

Gen. Sec.: J. F. WYBROW.

New Democratic Party: P.O.B. 143, Nelson; f. May 1972; aims to dismantle the centralized government and restore maximum freedom for each individual to control his environment.

Leader: J. B. O'BRIEN.

New Zealand National Party: Corner Customhouse Quay and Hunter St., Wellington 1; f. 1936; The National Party represents the Conservative and Liberal elements in New Zealand politics. In office 1949–57 and 1960–72, the Party stands for maintenance of democratic government, and the encouragement of private enterprise and competitive business, coupled with maximum personal freedom.

Leaders: G. A. CHAPMAN (President), Rt. Hon. JOHN R. MARSHALL, M.P., (Parliamentary Leader).

Gen. Dir. and Sec.: B. P. LEAY.

Communist Party of New Zealand: Auckland; pro-Chinese; 300 mems.; Gen. Sec. VICTOR WILCOX; publ. *People's Voice* (weekly).

Social Credit League: 170 Cuba St., Wellington 1; f. 1954; aims to cut taxes and increase social security benefits through the "use and ownership of the people's own credit" under a national credit authority; 10,000 mems.; publ. *New Guardian* (monthly).

Leader: B. C. BEETHAM.

Socialist Unity Party: Box 1987, Auckland; f. 1966; Marxist socialist; Pres. G. H. ANDERSEN; Sec. GEORGE JACKSON; publ. *New Zealand Tribune* and *Socialist Politics.*

Values Party: P.O.B. 137, Wellington; f. May 1972; humanist party; represented by regional spokesmen with no centralized leadership.

DEFENCE

Armed Forces (1973): Total strength 12,789; army 5,498 (excluding a territorial reserve of 11,405), navy 2,972, air force 4,319. Military service is voluntary though this is supplemented with three months selective national service in the army.

Equipment: The army has scout cars of British manufacture; medium tanks, armoured personnel carriers, and artillery. The navy has a small number of frigates armed with surface-to-air missiles; other craft include minesweepers and patrol boats. The air force has 29 combat aircraft and some helicopters.

Defence Expenditure: Defence spending for 1973–74 totals $NZ132 million (U.S. $175 million).

Chief of the Defence Staff: Maj.-Gen. L. A. PEARCE, O.B.E.

Chief of Staff (Army): Lieut.-Gen. R. J. H. WEBB, C.B., C.B.E.

Chief of Staff (Navy): Rear-Adml. E. C. THORNE, C.B.E.

Chief of Staff (Air Force): Air Vice-Marshal D. F. ST. GEORGE, D.F.C., A.F.C.

JUDICIAL SYSTEM

The Judicial System of New Zealand comprises a Court of Appeal, a Supreme Court, a Court of Arbitration and a Compensation Court. There are also Magistrates' Courts, having both civil and criminal jurisdiction and Wardens' Courts dealing with Mining proceedings.

Chief Justice: Rt. Hon. Sir RICHARD WILD, K.C.M.G.

THE COURT OF APPEAL

President: Rt. Hon. Sir THADDEUS McCARTHY.

Judges: Rt. Hon. C. P. RICHMOND, Rt. Hon. Sir RICHARD WILD, K.C.M.G. (ex officio), Hon. A. O. WOODHOUSE.

Registrar: D. V. JENKIN.

THE SUPREME COURT

Judges: Hon. A. L. HASLAM, Hon. I. H. MACARTHUR, Rt. Hon. Sir RICHARD WILD, K.C.M.G., Hon. A. O. WOODHOUSE, Hon. A. C. PERRY, Hon. J. N. WILSON,

Hon. L. F. MOLLER, Hon. G. D. SPEIGHT, Hon. C. M. ROPER, Hon. J. C. WHITE, Hon. D. S. BEATTIE, Hon. J. P. QUILLAM, Hon. D. W. McMULLIN, Hon. P. T. MAHON, Hon. R. B. COOKE, Hon. J. B. O'REGAN, Hon. M. F. CHILWELL.

Registrar: D. V. JENKIN.

COMPENSATION COURT

Judges: Hon. A. P. BLAIR, Hon. K. C. ARCHER.

COURT OF ARBITRATION

The Court of Arbitration consists of one Judge, an Employers' representative and a Workers' representative.

Judge: Hon. A. P. BLAIR.

Employers' Representative: W. N. HEWITT.

Worker's Representative: W. C. McDONNELL.

Registrar: R. D. LUMSDEN.

RELIGION

There is no established church in New Zealand.

CHURCH OF ENGLAND
(Province of New Zealand)

Archbishop: Most Rev. A. H. JOHNSTON, LL.D., L.TH.; Bishop's House, 322 Cobham Drive, Hamilton.

Provincial Secretary: J. C. COTTRELL, J.P., P.O.B. 800, Christchurch.

Bishops

Auckland	Rt. Rev. ERIC AUSTIN GOWING, M.A.
Christchurch	Rt. Rev. WILLIAM ALLAN PYATT, M.A.
Dunedin	Rt. Rev. W. W. ROBINSON, M.A.
Melanesia	Rt. Rev. J. W. CHISHOLM, B.A.
Nelson	Rt. Rev. P. E. SUTTON, M.A.
Polynesia	Rt. Rev. JOHN TRISTRAM HOLLAND, M.A.
Waiapu	Rt. Rev. P. A. REEVES, M.A.
Waikato	Rt. Rev. A. H. JOHNSTON, LL.D., L.TH.
Wellington	Rt. Rev. E. K. NORMAN, D.S.O., M.C., B.A.

Suffragan Bishop

Waiapu	Rt. Rev. M. A. BENNETT, D.D.

Comprises 133 parishes; 225 parochial districts; 24 native pastorates; 707 clergy; 819 lay readers; 938 churches; 923,278 adherents.

ROMAN CATHOLIC CHURCH
Archbishop

Wellington	His Eminence Cardinal PETER McKEEFRY, D.D., P.O.B. 198, Wellington.

Bishops

Auckland	The Most Rev. REGINALD J. DELARGEY.
Christchurch	The Most Rev. BRIAN P. ASHBY, D.D.
Dunedin	The Most Rev. J. P. KAVANAGH, J.C.D., D.D.

There are also Bishops in the following centres: Alexishaven, N.G.; Tahiti; Rarotonga, Cook Islands; Aitape; N.G.; Ulewak, N.G.; Rabaul, N.G.; Kavieng, N.G.; Port Moresby, Papua; Gilbert Islands; Samarai, Papua; Wallis and Futuna; Samoa and Tokelau; Fiji; Tonga; Northern Solomons; Southern Solomons; New Caledonia-New Hebrides. There are over 450,000 adherents to the Roman Catholic faith in New Zealand.

OTHER DENOMINATIONS

Baptist Church (*Baptist Union of New Zealand*): 185–187 Willis St., Wellington 1 (P.O.B. 27–390); f. 1882; Pres.

of Union Rev. E. F. SHERBURD; Gen. Sec. Rev. HUGH NEES; Treas. Rev. P. G. BUCHANAN, L.TH.; Principal of College Rev. Dr. R. J. THOMPSON, M.A., B.D., TH.M., DR.THEOL.; Dir. of Christian Education Rev. J. ROBERTS-THOMSON, B.SC., B.D., M.TH.; 17,458 mems.

Churches of Christ in New Zealand (Associated): P.O.B. 30516, Lower Hutt; 12,500 mems.; Gen. Sec. H. C. BISCHOFF; publs. *N.Z. Christian, Moment* (youth magazine).

Congregational Churches (*The Congregational Union of New Zealand*): f. 1883; Chair. Rev. J. B. CHAMBERS, M.A.; Treas. A. I. LAM, B.COMM.; Sec. Mrs. J. B. CHAMBERS (28 Wright St., Wellington 2); 478 mems.

Methodist Church of New Zealand: Connexional Headquarters: Box 931, Christchurch; approx. 140,000 mems; General Sec. Rev. W. R. LAWS, M.A., B.D.; Gen. Sec. Overseas Division Rev. G. G. CARTER, M.A. (Auckland); Principal of Theological College Rev. J. J. LEWIS, M.A., B.D., PH.D. (Auckland); Gen. Supt. Development Division Rev. B. E. JONES, B.A. (Auckland).

Presbyterian Church of New Zealand: P.O.B. 10-000, Wellington; Moderator Rt. Rev. G. F. McKENZIE; Assembly Exec. Sec. Rev. W. A. BEST; Gen. Treas. D. A. LARSEN, A.C.A.; Sec. of Overseas Missions Rev. D. E. DUNCAN, B.A.; Dir. of Ministry Rev. W. B. WATT, B.A.; Moderator of Maori Synod Rev. T. HAWEA; Convenor of Christian Education Rev. D. I. KEALL, B.A.; 86,131 communicant mems.; 576,293 under pastoral care; publ. *The Outlook* (monthly).

Salvation Army: Territorial Headquarters: 204–206 Cuba St., Wellington (P.O.B. 6015); approx. 19,000 mems.; Territorial Commander: Lieut.-Commissioner Dr. HARRY WILLIAMS, O.B.E.; Chief Sec. Colonel ERNEST R. ELLIOT.

Maori Denominations: numbers in brackets denote numbers of officiating ministers.

Ratana Church of New Zealand	(145)
Ringatu Church	(73)
Church of Te Kooti Rikirangi	(12)
Absolute Maori Established Church	(15)
United Maori Mission	(4)

Total membership: 31,592.

THE PRESS

Note: Total daily newspaper readership in 1972 was 1,558,866.

NEWSPAPERS AND PERIODICALS

DAILIES

Dominion, The: Dominion Building, Mercer St., Wellington; f. 1907; morning; Editor J. A. KELLEHER; circulation 78,550.

Ashburton Guardian: 117 Burnett St., Ashburton; f. 1880; Dunedin; Independent; evening; Editor G. CONNELL.

Auckland Star: P.O.B. 3697, Auckland; f. 1870; evening; Editor Ross SAYERS; circ. 136,000.

Bay of Plenty Times: P.O.B. 648, Tauranga; f. 1872; Independent; evening; Editor E. F. T. BEER; circ. 14,111.

Central Hawke's Bay Press: P.O.B. 21, Waipukurau; f. 1905; evening; Editor M. R. GOEBEL.

Christchurch Star: Kilmore Street, P.O.B. 2651, Christchurch; f. 1868; Independent; evening; Editor B. A. MAIR.

The Chronicle: P.O.B. 352, Levin; f. 1893; evening; Editor: G. H. KERSLAKE; circ. 4,546.

The Daily News: P.O.B. 444, New Plymouth; f. 1857; morning; Editor R. J. AVERY; circ. 21,000.

Daily Post, The: P.O.B. 1442, Rotorua; f. 1886; evening; Editor I. F. Thompson; circ. 15,000.

Daily Telegraph: P.O.B. 173, Napier; f. 1871; evening; Man. Dir. B. S. Geddis; cir. 17,500.

Evening News Dannevirke: P.O.B. 92, Dannevirke; f. 1909; evening; Editor L. J. Appleton; circ. 2,904.

Evening Post: Willis St., P.O.B. 1398, Wellington; f. 1865; Independent; Editor T. K. Rowe; circ. 100,000.

Evening Standard: P.O.B. 3, Palmerston North; f. 1880; evening; Editor R. D. Watson; circ. 25,000.

Evening Star: P.O.B. 517, Dunedin; f. 1863; Editor W. J. Noble; circ. 30,000.

Gisborne Herald: 64 Gladstone Rd., P.O.B. 573, Gisborne; f. 1874; Independent; evening; Editor E. W. Dumbleton.

Greymouth Evening Star: P.O.B. 182, Greymouth; f. 1866; Liberal; evening; Editor R. W. Nelson.

Hauraki Plains Gazette: P.O.B. 130, Paeroa; Editor R. L. Darley.

Hawera Star: P.O.B. 428, Hawera; f. 1880; Liberal; evening; Editor D. W. Hetherington; circ. 3,180.

Hawke's Bay Herald-Tribune, The: Karama Rd. North, P.O.B. 180, Hastings; f. 1937; Independent Conservative; evening; Editor E. G. Webber.

Hokitika Guardian and Times: P.O. Box 122, Hokitika; f. 1875; evening; Editor K. Sherman.

King Country Chronicle: P.O.B. 269, Te Kuiti; f. 1906; twice weekly; Editor R. S. Craig; circ. 2,600.

Marlborough Express: 64 High St., Blenheim; f. 1866; evening; Editor J. G. Furness; circ. 8,279.

Morrinsville Star: P.O.B. 26, Morrinsville.

Nelson Evening Mail: P.O. Box 244, Nelson; f. 1866; evening; Editor G. D. Spencer.

New Zealand Herald: P.O.B. 32, Auckland; f. 1863; the only daily morning paper in Auckland; Editor J. F. W. Hardingham; circ. over 227,000.

Northern Advocate: Water St., P.O.B. 210, Whangarei; f. 1875; evening; Man. Dir. B. W. Crawford; circ. 16,290.

Northern News: Box 1, Kaikohe.

Northland Age: P.O.B. 45, Kaitaia; twice weekly; Editor B. Berry.

Northland Times: P.O.B. 96, Dargaville; f. 1904; evening; Editor A. McG. Membery.

Oamaru Mail: 9 Tyne St., P.O.B. 303, Oamaru; f. 1876; evening; Editor John H. F. Whyte.

Otago Daily Times: Lower High St., P.O.B. 181, Dunedin; f. 1861; the only morning paper in Otago province; Editor E. Allan Aubin; circ. 42,000.

Press, The: Cathedral Square, Christchurch; f. 1861; morning; Editor N. L. Macbeth; circ. 72,000.

Southland Times: P.O.B. 805, 67 Esk St., Invercargill; f. 1862; morning and afternoon; Editor P. M. Muller; circ. 32,000.

Taranaki Herald: Currie St., New Plymouth; f. 1852; evening; Editor G. K. Koea; circ. 12,414.

Thames and Peninsula Gazette: Belmont Rd., P.O.B. 130, Paeroa.

Thames Star and Hauraki Daily News: Sealey St., P.O.B. 48, Thames; f. 1868; evening; Man. R. E. Tyack; Editor F. L. Trott.

Timaru Herald: Sophia St., Timaru, P.O.B. 46; f. 1864; morning; Editor G. J. Gaffaney; Man. Dir. J. M. Kerr; circ. 16,082.

The Times: Victoria Street, Hamilton, P.O.B. 444; f. 1872; Independent; evening; Editor and Man. Dir. P. V. Harkness; circ. 35,000.

Wairarapa Times-Age: Chapel St., Masterton; f. 1938; evening; Editor J. J. L. Sulzberger.

Wanganui Chronicle: 20 Wicksteed Place, P.O.B. 433, Wanganui; f. 1856; Independent; morning; Editor J. A. Colway; circ. 11,957.

Wanganui Herald: 20 Wicksteed Place, P.O.B. 435, Wanganui; f. 1867; evening; Editor H. F. Low; circ. 10,500.

Westport News: Palmerston St., P.O.B. 249, Westport; f. 1873; evening; Editor Reg Spowart; circ. 2,200.

WEEKLIES

Christchurch Star Sports Edition: Box 2651, Christchurch; Saturday evening; circ. 37,000.

Economic News: Universe Press Agency, 201 Lambton Quay, Hamilton Chambers, P.O.B. 1026, Wellington; f. 1954; Editor Miss S. H. Elliott.

8 O'Clock: P.O.B. 3697, Auckland; sports results and features, weekend news, etc.; Saturday evening; Editor Neil Anderson; circ. 112,000.

Mercantile Gazette of New Zealand: 271 Madras St., P.O.B. 13-027, Armagh, Christchurch; f. 1876; economics, finance, management, stock market, politics; publs. *Mercantile Gazette*, fortnightly, circ. 24,000; *Tenders Gazette*, weekly, circ. 3,000; *New Zealand Company Director and Executive*, monthly, circ. 3,500; *New Zealand Shipping Gazette*, weekly, circ. 2,800; Man. W. R. Dalley; Editor J. D. Watson.

New Zealand Gazette: Dept. of Internal Affairs, Wellington; f. 1840; Thursday; Clerk T. Cousins.

New Zealand Listener: P.O.B. 3140, Bowen State Building, Wellington; f. 1939; Monday; official radio and television programmes; feature articles on letters and life; short stories; verse; music notes; book reviews; film criticisms; Editor Ian Cross; circ. over 223,000.

New Zealand Tablet: 24 Filleul St., Dunedin; f. 1873; Wednesday; Roman Catholic; Editor J. P. Kennedy; circ. 12,149.

New Zealand Truth: 23-27 Garrett St., P.O.B. 1122, Wellington; f. 1904; Tuesday; international and local news and comment; sports; finance; women's interests; Independent; Editor R. N. Edlin; circ. 242,700.

New Zealand Woman's Weekly: P.O.B. 1409, Auckland; f. 1934; Monday; family magazine, general interests; Editor Jean Wishart; circ. over 223,000

North Shore Times Advertiser: P.O.B. 33-235, Takapuna, Auckland 9; twice weekly; Editor Mrs. P. M. Gundry; circ. 41,000.

South Auckland News Advertiser: P.O.B. 174, Papakura; Gen. Man. Editor D. J. Galvin; circ. 18,000.

South Waikato News: P.O.B. 89, Tokoroa; f. 1951; bi-weekly; Man. Editor B. D. Burmester; circ. 4,500.

Sports Post: Box 1398, Wellington; Saturday evening; circ. 104,000.

Star 7 O'Clock: Box 517, Dunedin; Saturday evening.

Sunday Herald: P.O.B. 32, Auckland; Sunday; f. 1971; Editor J. W. F. Hardingham.

Sunday Times, The: Dominion Bldg., Mercer St., Wellington; f. 1965; Editor F. A. HADEN; circ. 143,000.

Taieri Herald: P.O.B. 105, Mosgiel; Editor J. F. Fox; circ. 3,950.

Te Aroha News: P.O.B. 131, Te Aroha; f. 1883; bi-weekly; Editor P. J. REILLY.

Waihi Gazette: P.O.B. 130, Waihi; Editor R. L. DARLEY.

Wairoa Star: P.O.B. 39, Wairoa; f. 1877; tri-weekly; Editor R. C. WILSON; circ. 2,250.

Wairarapa News: P.O.B. 18, Carterton; f. 1869; Editor R. W. ROYDHOUSE.

Waitara Times: West Quay, Waitara; f. 1960; Editor B. L. OLDFIELD.

Zealandia: 2 St. Patrick's Square, Auckland; f. 1934; Thursday; Roman Catholic; Editor Rev. D. J. HORTON; circ. 20,000.

OTHER PERIODICALS

Accountants' Journal: 99 The Terrace, Wellington.

Better Business: P.O.B. 793, Auckland; f. 1938; monthly.

Board and Council: P.O.B. 807, Auckland; f. 1921; Local Authorities Review; monthly.

Building Materials News: Private Bag, Glen Innes, Auckland; f. 1963; monthly; Editor P. D. REAVES.

Church and People: P.O.B. 10345, Wellington North; monthly; Editor S. G. DINNISS; circ. 10,000.

Comment: P.O. Box 1746, Wellington; f. 1959; quarterly; Independent; Editors S. ZAVOS and P. J. DOWNEY.

Engineering Management: Private Bag, Glen Innes, Auckland; Editor L. J. SMITH.

"Eve": P.O.B. 3697, Auckland; circ. 52,000.

Home and Country: Kerslake, Billens and Humphrey Ltd., P.O.B. 352, Levin; monthly; official journal of N.Z. Country Women's Institutes; Editor Mrs. E. J. TENQUIST.

Journal of the Polynesian Society: P.O.B. 10323, The Terrace, Wellington; f. 1892; the anthropology, ethnology, philology, history and antiquities of the Polynesians and other related peoples; Editor Dr. M. McLEAN; circ. 1,500.

Landfall: Caxton Press, 119 Victoria St., P.O.B. 25-088, Christchurch, C.1; quarterly; Editor LEO BENSEMANN.

Live Lines: P.O.B. 1097, Wellington; official journal of the Electrical Supply Authorities of New Zealand; monthly; Editor A. H. HEIR, A.C.I.S., A.I.A.O., J.P.

Management: P.O.B. 3159, Auckland; f. 1954; business; 1st of month; Editor SHANE C. NIBLOCK, circ. 6,700.

Monthly Abstract of Statistics: Dept. of Statistics, Private Bag, Wellington; f. 1914; monthly; official; Editor E. A. HARRIS, Acting Govt. Statistician.

Motorman: Fourman Holdings Ltd., P.O.B. 1343, Wellington; f. 1957; motoring monthly; Editor DAVID HALL.

Nation: P.O.B. 1564, Wellington; f. 1911; monthly; current topics; Editor M. W. LEAMAN.

New Zealand Concrete Construction: Concrete Publications Ltd., Securities House, 126 The Terrace, G.P.O. Box 3644, Wellington; f. 1957; Man. Editor M. A. CRAVEN, Man. R. M. LITTLE; circ. 1,800.

New Zealand Dairy Exporter: P.O.B. 1001, Wellington; Editor J. D. McGILVARY; circ. 21,000.

New Zealand Economist: P.O.B. 11-137, Wellington; business and investment; Editor DAVID YEREX; circ. 3,860.

New Zealand Electrical Journal: Technical Publications Ltd., P.O.B. 3047, 127 Molesworth St., Wellington; f. 1928; monthly; Managing Editor F. N. STACE; circ. 1,800.

New Zealand Engineering: Technical Publications Ltd.; P.O.B. 3047, 127 Molesworth St., Wellington; f. 1946; monthly; Man. Editor F. N. STACE; circ. 5,150.

New Zealand Farmer, The: P.O.B. 1409, Auckland, C.1; f. 1885; twice monthly; Editor RONALD VINE; circ. 26,500.

New Zealand Financial Times: P.O.B. 1367, Wellington; f. 1930; finance, investment, business; Man. Editor E. C. MARRIS.

New Zealand Gardener: P.O.B. 32, Auckland; f. 1944; monthly; Editor D. WHITE; circ. 18,000.

New Zealand Gazette: c/o Dept. of Internal Affairs, Private Bag, Wellington; Editor T. COUSINS; circ. 1,600.

New Zealand Holiday: P.O.B. 1209, Auckland; f. 1956; quarterly; Editor W. PYE; circ. 12,000.

New Zealand Home Journal: P.O.B. 3697, Auckland; f. 1934; monthly; Editor Miss Jo NOBLE; circ. 90,000.

New Zealand Jewish Chronicle: P.O.B. 9384, Wellington; f. 1944; official organ of the Zionist Council of New Zealand; bi-monthly; Editor Mrs. C. DURDEN.

New Zealand Journal of Agricultural Research: Department of Scientific and Industrial Research, Private Bag, Wellington 1; f. 1958; science and technology related to agricultural and pastoral production; quarterly; Editor G. J. NEALE; circ. 1,450.

New Zealand Journal of Agriculture: P.O.B. 32, Auckland; f. 1910; monthly; Editor D. WHITE; circ. 32,000.

New Zealand Journal of Botany: Department of Scientific and Industrial Research, Private Bag, Wellington; f. 1963; quarterly; Editor GWENDA M. HARRIS; circ. 750.

New Zealand Journal of Experimental Agriculture: Department of Scientific and Industrial Research, Private Bag, Wellington; f. 1973; agricultural science of particular interest to extension and advisory workers; quarterly; Editor G. J. NEALE; circ. 1,350.

New Zealand Journal of Geology and Geophysics: Department of Scientific and Industrial Research, Private Bag, Wellington 1; f. 1958; quarterly; Editor I. W. MACKENZIE.

New Zealand Journal of Marine and Freshwater Research: Department of Scientific and Industrial Research, Private Bag, Wellington 1; f. 1967; quarterly; Editor E. K. SAUL; circ. 750.

New Zealand Journal of Science: Department of Scientific and Industrial Research, Private Bag, Wellington 1; f. 1958; chemistry, engineering, mathematics, meteorology, physics; quarterly; Editor J. G. GREGORY.

New Zealand Journal of Zoology: Department of Scientific and Industrial Research, Private Bag, Wellington; f. 1974; quarterly; Editor J. G. GREGORY.

New Zealand Law Journal: Butterworths of New Zealand Ltd., 26–28 Waring Taylor St., Wellington; fortnightly.

New Zealand Manufacturer: Private Bag, Glen Innes, Auckland; monthly; circ. 3,700.

New Zealand Medical Journal: P.O.B. 181, Dunedin; f. 1887; twice monthly; Editor R. G. ROBINSON, G.M., CH.M., F.R.C.S.

New Zealand Methodist: P.O.B. 2986, Auckland; f. 1871; fortnightly; Editor Rev. JOHN BLUCK, M.A., B.D.; circ. 52,000.

New Zealand Motor World: P.O.B. 1, Wellington; f. 1936; bi-monthly; official organ of 14 automobile associations, 9 caravan clubs; Man. Editor R. A. Hocking; circ. 94,000.

New Zealand Poultry World: N.Z. Poultry Board, P.O.B. 9567, C.P. Wellington; monthly; circ. 3,000; Editor J. F. Ewan.

New Zealand Science Review: P.O.B. 1874, Wellington; f. 1942; every 2 months; Editor R. F. Benseman.

New Zealand Sports Digest: I.N.L. Print Ltd., Eastern Hutt Rd., Taita, Wellington; f. 1949; monthly; Editor B. F. O'Brien.

New Zealand Woman: P.O.B. 957, Dunedin; circ. 32,500.

New Zealand Wood Industries: Private Bag, Glen Innes, Auckland; f. 1954; monthly; Editor P. D. Reaves.

N.Z. Engineering News: Technical Publications Ltd., P.O.B. 3047, 127 Molesworth St., Wellington; f. 1970; monthly; Editor B. A. Lovett; Man. Editor F. N. Stace; circ. 8,200.

NZIA Journal: New Zealand Institute of Architects, P.O.B. 438, Wellington; f. 1905; monthly; Man. Ed. C. J. G. McFarlane.

Otago Farmer: P.O.B. 105, Mosgiel; fortnightly; Editor J. F. Fox; circ. 5,000.

Outlook: P.O.B. 320, Christchurch; f. 1894; official journal of the Presbyterian Church; monthly; circ. 10,000; Editor Rev. C. L. Gosling, b.a., b.d.

Pacific Viewpoint: P.O.B. 196, Wellington; Editors Prof. S. H. Franklin, Prof. R. F. Watters; circ. 1,050.

Pharmaceutical Journal of New Zealand: P.O.B. 26-141, Epsom, Auckland; Editor G. Gunn; circ. 2,900.

Road Transport and Contracting: Private Bag, Glen Innes, Auckland; official journal of the N.Z. Contractors Federation (Inc.); monthly; circ. 4,000.

Sea Spray: Universal Business Directories Ltd., Box 793, Auckland; f. 1945; boating (power and sail) monthly; Editor David Pardon; circ. 14,000.

Straight Furrow: P.O.B. 1654, Wellington; f. 1933; fortnightly; Editor O. K. G. Riddell; circ. over 44,000.

Te Ao Hou (*The New World*): Box 2390, Wellington; f. 1952; Maori and English; quarterly; Editor Joy Stevenson; circ. 7,200.

Thursday Magazine (inc. N.Z. Family Doctor): P.O.B. 32, Auckland; fortnightly; circ. 62,500.

Wings: Aeronautical Press, P.O.B. 173, Wellington; f. 1932; monthly; Editor R. S. Dunlop.

World Affairs: UN Asscn. of N.Z., Box 1011, Wellington; f. 1945; quarterly; Editor W. E. Rose.

Young Country: Agricultural Promotion Associates, P.O.B. 11-137, Wellington; official magazine of New Zealand Federation of Young Farmers' Clubs and Country Girls' Club Federations; monthly; Editor Tony Cronin; circ. 9,500.

NEWS AGENCIES

New Zealand Press Association: Box 1599, Wellington; f. 1879; non-political; Chair. H. N. Blundell; Man. Editor H. L. Verry.

South Pacific News Service (SPNS): P.O.B. 5026, Lambton Quay, Wellington; f. 1948; Man. Dir. E. W. Benton.

FOREIGN BUREAU
Reuters is the only foreign bureau in New Zealand.

PRESS COUNCIL

New Zealand Press Council: f. September 1972; Chair. Sir Alfred North.

PRESS ASSOCIATIONS

Newspaper Publishers' Association of New Zealand (Inc.): Newspaper House, P.O.B. 1066, 93 Boulcott St., Wellington; f. 1898; 45 mems.; Pres. E. N. Wilkinson; Sec. M. J. Thompson.

New Zealand Section Commonwealth Press Union: P.O.B. 180, Hastings; Chair. E. G. Webber, m.b.e.; Sec. M. C. Muir (P.O.B. 573, Gisborne).

PUBLISHERS

Blundell Bros. Ltd.: 82–88 Willis St., Wellington.

Board and Council Publishing Co. Ltd.: Tingey's Building, P.O.B. 807, Auckland; f. 1921; Editor-Man. E. D. Bennett.

Bullivant, H. W. and Co. Ltd.: 163 Armagh St., Christchurch.

Butterworths of New Zealand Ltd.: 26–28 Waring Taylor St., Wellington.

Cassell & Co. Ltd.: P.O.B. 1388, Christchurch; Man. Dir. B. Palmer.

Christchurch Caxton Press: P.O.B. 25-088, 119 Victoria St., Christchurch 1; f. 1936; poetry, prose; Dirs. D. Donovan L. Bensemann.

Collins Bros. & Co. Ltd.: P.O.B. 1, Auckland; Man. Dir. D. Bateman.

Commercial Print Ltd.: 127–131 Park Rd., Miramar, Wellington; f. 1911; Chair. I. Jackson.

Coulls, Somerville, Wilkie Ltd.: 360 Cumberland St., Dunedin; f. 1922; Gen. Man. T. R. Coull.

Heinemann Educational Books Ltd.: P.O.B. 36-064, Auckland; f. 1969; educational, technical, academic; Man. Dir. D. Heap.

Hodder and Stoughton Ltd.: 52 Cook St., Auckland; Man. Dir. R. J. Coombes.

Hutcheson, Bowman and Stewart Ltd.: P.O.B. 9032, 15–19 Tory St., Wellington.

Hutchinson Publishing Group: P.O.B. 2881, Auckland; Man. Dir. C. Hanna.

Independent Newspapers Ltd. (Holding Company): Dominion Building, 27–35 Mercer St., Wellington; f. 1907; Subsidiaries: Wellington Publishing Co. (1972) Ltd., publishers of *The Dominion* (daily); Sunday Times (N.Z.) Ltd., publishers of *The Sunday Times*; Truth (N.Z.) Ltd., publisher of *Truth* (weekly); C. M. Banks Ltd., A. B. D. Clark Ltd., Fanfold Business Forms Ltd., New Media Ownership Ltd., News Media (Auckland) Ltd. (publishers of *The Sunday News*), Electronic Data Systems Ltd., Kapiti Observer (1971) Ltd., N.Z. Carbon Products Ltd., Upper Hutt Leader Ltd.; Independent

Publishers Ltd., publishers of *The Waikato Times* (daily); Blundell Bros. Ltd., publishers of *The Evening Post;* INL Print Ltd., The Hutt Printing and Publishing Works Ltd., publishers of *Hutt News;* Kapi-Mani News Ltd., publishers of *Kapi-Mani News;* Waikato & King Country Press Ltd., East Waikato Publishers Ltd., Periodical Press Ltd., Taupo Times Ltd., Thames Star Co. Ltd., Tokoroa Publishing Co. Ltd.

Longman Paul Limited: c/o Penguin Books (N.Z.) Ltd., C.P.O. Box 4019, Auckland 1; Dirs. W. P. KERR, W. A. H. BECKETT, J. H. ADAM, L. V. GODFREY, P. C. MEIKLE.

New Zealand Council for Educational Research: P.O.B. 3237, Wellington; f. 1934; scholarly books, research monographs, bulletins, educational tests, research summaries, academic journal; Chair. Prof. F. W. HOLMES; Dir. J. E. WATSON.

Otago University Press: P.O.B. 56, Dunedin; f. 1958.

Oxford University Press: P.O.B. 11-344, Wellington; Man. Dir. R. GOODERIDGE.

Pegasus Press Ltd.: 14 Oxford Terrace, P.O.B. 2224, Christchurch; f. 1948; publishers and printers; fiction, poetry, history, art and education; Man. Dir. ALBION WRIGHT; Editor ROBIN MUIR.

Pelorus Press Ltd.: MK Bldg., 21 Great South Rd., Newmarket, Auckland (P.O.B. 26-065 Epsom); f. 1947; Dirs. G. M. TRIGG, L. I. TAYLOR, R. L. G. DENNIS.

Reed, A. H. and A. W. Ltd.: 182 Wakefield St., Wellington (head office), and at Auckland, Christchurch, Sydney, Melbourne and London; f. 1907; general books, educational books, gramophone recordings relating to Australia, New Zealand and the South Pacific; Chair. M. J. MASON; Deputy Chair. J. H. RAY RICHARDS.

Sporting Publications (A. H. Carman): 7 Kowhai St., Linden, Tawa; sports annuals.

Sweet and Maxwell (N.Z.) Ltd.: P.O.B. 5043, Wellington; Dir. F. KANE.

Whitcoulls Ltd.: 111 Cashes St., Private Bag, Christchurch; publishers and printers of N.Z. books of all descriptions, general and educational; brs. throughout New Zealand, Australia, and in London.

Wise, H., and Co. (New Zealand) Ltd.: 27 St. Andrew St., Dunedin; f. 1865; publishers of maps and street directories, N.Z. Guide and N.Z. Post Office Directories; Man. J. A. DeCOURCY.

RADIO AND TELEVISION

New Zealand Broadcasting Authority: P.O.B. 10129, Wellington; set up in 1968 by Act of Parliament in 1968.

New Zealand Broadcasting Corporation (NZBC): P.O.B. 98, Wellington; f. 1962; Chair. Maj.-Gen. W. S. McKINNON; Deputy Chair. J. COLLINS; Mems. Dr. E. R. BLACK, B. G. CATHIE, J. CLARKE, P. J. DOWNEY, Rev. K. M. IHAKA, M. L. TRONSON; Dir.-Gen. of Broadcasting L. R. SCEATS; publ. *N.Z. Listener.*

Legislation is currently being enacted to effect a completely new broadcasting structure for New Zealand, under which both the New Zealand Broadcasting Authority and the NZBC would be abolished and replaced by three separate and independent public corporations with smaller boards.

One corporation would run the present television network, which changed to colour in October 1973, another, the projected second channel network, to begin also in colour, by about October 1974; and the third, radio. The Broadcasting Authority would be replaced by a body responsible for common services, including news, and for

broadcasting standards and other matters outside the proposed scope of the three corporations.

RADIO

The Corporation operates 51 medium-wave stations throughout the country broadcasting commercial, part-commercial and non-commercial programmes. Two short-wave transmitters broadcast non-commercial programmes mainly to the Pacific Islands, the Ross Dependency and Australia (Radio New Zealand).

In October 1971 the radio licence fee was abolished. At that time there were 712,794 licensed radio sets.

TELEVISION

A national network through four metropolitan television stations is operated by the New Zealand Broadcasting Corporation. Broadcasts 65 hours weekly, with commercial programmes on Tuesdays, Wednesdays, Thursdays and Saturdays. A system of relay stations operates throughout the country.

There were 732,000 television sets in use in 1973.

FINANCE

(**cap.**=capital; **p.u.**=paid up; **dep.**=deposits; **m.**=million; **$NZ**=$ New Zealand)

BANKING

CENTRAL BANK

Reserve Bank of New Zealand: P.O.B. 2498, 2 The Terrace, Wellington; f. 1934; became State-owned institution 1936; Bank of Issue; dep., demand $NZ250.7m., term $NZ219.5m. (1973); Gov. A. R. LOW; Deputy Gov. R. W. R. WHITE.

COMMERCIAL BANKS

ANZ Savings Bank (New Zealand) Ltd.: 196 Featherston St., Wellington; Gen. Man. N. T. CARADUS.

Bank of New Zealand: Lambton Quay, Wellington (P.O.B. 2392); f. 1861; Cap. subs. and p.u. $NZ16.5m; dep. $NZ886.6m. (March 1973); Chair. D. O. WHYTE, C.B.E.; Gen. Man. B. H. SMITH.

Bank of New Zealand Savings Bank Ltd.: Lambton Quay, P.O.B. 2392, Wellington; f. 1964; cap. subs. and p.u. $NZ1m; dep. $NZ138.0m. (March 1973); Chair. D. O. WHYTE, C.B.E.; Gen. Man. B. H. SMITH.

National Bank of New Zealand Ltd.: 8 Moorgate, London, EC2R 6DB; 170–186 Featherston St., Wellington; cap. p.u. £3.5m. sterling; dep. £275.5m. sterling (Oct. 1972); Gen. Man. in New Zealand J. MOWBRAY.

National Bank of New Zealand Savings Bank Ltd.: 170–186 Featherston St,. Wellington; f. 1964; auth. cap. $NZ2m.; dep. $NZ76.0m. (Oct. 1973); Man. A. A. K. GRANT.

Australia and New Zealand Banking Group Ltd.: 71 Cornhill, London, E.C.3; 196 Featherston St., Wellington; New Zealand Gen. Man. K. R. PORTER.

Commercial Bank of Australia: 335–339 Collins Street, Melbourne, Victoria; 328–330 Lambton Quay, Wellington.

Bank of New South Wales: Sydney, N.S.W.; Chief Office for New Zealand; 306-308 Lambton Quay, Wellington; f. 1817; Chief Man. for New Zealand J. P. ANDREWS.

STOCK EXCHANGES

Auckland Stock Exchange: 82–84 Albert St., Auckland; Chair. GARTH S. GRIFFITHS; Sec. D. S. WRIGHT.

Christchurch Stock Exchange Ltd., The: P.O.B. 639, Christchurch; Chair. J. B. HINDIN; Sec. P. F. MAPLES.

Dunedin Stock Exchange: P.O.B. 483, Dunedin; Chair. H. R. WILSON; Sec. K. R. SELLAR.

Wellington Stock Exchange: P.O.B. 767, Corner Grey and Featherston Sts., 1; Chair. W. R. HOCKING; Sec. T. D. McTAGGART.

INSURANCE

Government Life Insurance Office: P.O. Box 590, Wellington, C.1; f. 1869; Commissioner A. C. PAINE; Sec. E. D. SINCLAIR; Actuary O. D. GOOD, B.A., F.I.A.

State Insurance Office: Lambton Quay, Wellington, C.1; fire branch f. 1905, accident branch f. 1925; Gen. Man. N. R. AINSWORTH.

A.A. Mutual Insurance Company: P.O.B. 1348, Wellington; f. 1928; name changed from N.I.M.U. Insurance Co. in 1972; Chair. J. C. BATES; Gen. Man. L. A. RANDERSON; Asst. Gen. Man. and Sec. M. A. DUDDRIDGE.

A.M.P. Fire and General Insurance Company (N.Z.) Limited: 86/90 Customhouse Quay, Wellington; f. 1958; Chair. Sir CLIFFORD PLIMMER, K.B.E.; Man. N. B. WILCOX; fire, accident, marine, general.

Colonial Mutual Life Assurance Society Ltd.: Customhouse Quay, P.O.B. 191, Wellington; Man. R. P. MARTELL; life, accident, sickness, staff superannuation.

Commercial Union Assurance: 142 Featherston St., P.O.B. 2797, Wellington; Gen. Man. B. V. McHUGH; fire, accident, marine, life.

Dominion Life Assurance Office of New Zealand Ltd.: P.O.B. 2797, Wellington, C.1; f. 1928; a member of the Commercial Union Group of Companies; Chair. P. H. SCOTT.

Export Guarantee Office: EXGO State Insurance Bldg., Lambton Quay, Wellington 1; f. 1964; Gen. Man. N. R. AINSWORTH.

Farmers' Mutual Insurance Association: Harvest Court, George St., Dunedin; f. 1904; Chair. T. G. McNAB; Gen. Man. J. D. WILDE; fire and accident.

Mercantile and General Insurance Company Ltd.: Wellington; f. 1923; Chair. D. McGRATH.

Metropolitan Life Assurance Company of N.Z. Ltd.: 22/24 Kitchener Street, Auckland; f. 1962; Chair. D. ST. CLAIR BROWN; life.

National Insurance Company of New Zealand Ltd., The: 300 Princes St., Dunedin; f. 1873; Chair. J. M. RITCHIE; Gen. Man. B. M. SIMPSON; Sec. P. R. JACOMBS, A.C.A. (N.Z.).

National Mutual Group of Companies: National Mutual Centre, 153–161 Featherston St., P.O.B. 1692, Wellington; Man. S. R. ELLIS; life, fire, accident, marine, personal accident, sickness.

New Zealand Counties' Co-operative Insurance Company Limited: Local Government Bldg., Lambton Quay, Wellington, C.1; f. 1942; Chair. R. A. HUTCHINSON; fire, accident, fidelity guarantee, motor car, employer's liability.

New Zealand Insurance Company Ltd., The: Auckland; f. 1859; Chair. D. H. STEEN; Gen. Man. D. G. HARE.

New Zealand Municipalities Co-operative Insurance Company Limited, The: Local Government Bldg., 114-118 Lambton Quay, Wellington; f. 1960; Chair. C. L. BISHOP, O.B.E.; Man. L. J. SULLIVAN; Sec. K. F. J. BRYANT, B.COM., A.C.A.; cap. $NZ2m.; fire, motor vehicle, employer's liability, accident.

Phoenix Group of Companies: 125–127 Featherston St., P.O.B. 894, Wellington; Gen. Man. W. DORAN, A.A.I.I.; fire, accident, marine, life.

Primary Industries Insurance Company Ltd., The: 70 Queen St., P.O.B. 616, Palmerston North; f. 1957; Chief Exec. Officer J. HACKETT; fire, accident, motor car, workmen's compensation, marine, life.

Provident Life Assurance Company Ltd.: 125-127 Featherston St., P.O.B. 894, Wellington, C.1; f. 1904; Chair. R. C. B. GREENSLADE; Man. W. DORAN.

Prudential Assurance Co. Ltd.: 332–340 Lambton Quay, P.O.B. 291, Wellington; Man. J. SNELL; life, fire, accident, marine.

S.I.M.U. Mutual Insurance Association: 29–35 Latimer Square, Christchurch; f. 1926; Chair. E. J. BRADSHAW.

South British Insurance Company Ltd. (New Zealand): South British Building, Shortland Street, Auckland; f. 1872; Chair. K. B. MYERS; Gen. Manager D. L. BULLOCK.

Transport, Fire and General Insurance Company Ltd.: 126 The Terrace (P.O.B. 1080), Wellington; f. 1960; Chair. E. J. ALEXANDER; Sec. R. J. PINCOTT; fire, accident.

TRADE AND INDUSTRY

CHAMBERS OF COMMERCE

Associated Chambers of Commerce of New Zealand: P.O.B. 1071, Wellington; Pres. B. N. VICKERMAN; Dir. G. L. HAWTHORNE; publ. *New Zealand Commerce* (monthly).

Chambers of Commerce are organized in fifty-four towns, including the following:

Ashburton Chamber of Commerce (Inc.): P.O.B. 271, Ashburton; f. 1924; Pres. D. G. ROTHERHAM; Sec. N. A. CALDER; 96 mems.

Canterbury Chamber of Commerce: Cnr. Oxford Terrace and Worcester St., Christchurch 1; f. 1859; Pres. J. G. GRIGOR; Sec. P. L. BUSH; 1,920 mems.; publ. *Economic Bulletin* (monthly).

Hastings Chamber of Commerce: P.O.B. 144, Hastings; f. 1907; 241 mems.; Pres. L. PATMORE; Sec. H. G. HUGHES; publ. *Newsletter* (monthly).

Invercargill Chamber of Commerce (Inc.): P.O.B. 311, Invercargill; Pres. R. D. ALLAN; Sec. A. S. ALSWEILER; 200 mems.; publ. *Annual Report and Statement of Accounts.*

Kawerau Chamber of Commerce Inc.: P.O.B. 19, Kawerau, Bay of Plenty; Pres. M. G. DIPPIE; Sec.-Treas. Mrs. J. MARKLAND; 57 mems.; publ. *Newsletter* (quarterly).

Napier Chamber of Commerce Inc.: P.O.B. 259, Napier; f. 1882; Pres. E. A. MILLER; Sec. H. M. SWINBURN; 151 mems.; publ. *Newsletter* (monthly).

Otago Chamber of Commerce Inc.: 123 Princes St., P.O.B. 908, Dunedin; f. 1861; Pres. G. W. T. CHRISTIE; Sec. Miss E. M. WAIGTH; 515 mems.; publs. *Newsletter* (monthly), *Annual Report.*

Palmerston North Chamber of Commerce Inc.: Construction House, 275 Broadway Ave., P.O.B. 1791, Palmerston North; f. 1898; Pres. B. K. PLIMMER; Sec. W. L. MAY; 320 mems.; publ. *Newsletter* (bi-monthly).

Rotorua Chamber of Commerce Inc.: P.O.B. 1049, Rotorua; f. 1924; Pres. R. W. C. WEARNE; Sec. J. A. W. DE VOS; 150 mems.; publ. *Newsletter* (irregular).

Wanganui Chamber of Commerce and Industry Inc.: P.O.B. 88, Wanganui; f. 1885; Pres. B. T. IRETON; Sec. B. SUTCLIFFE; 129 mems.; publs. *Newsletter, Annual Report and Statement of Accounts.*

Wellington Chamber of Commerce: Commerce House, 126 Wakefield St., Wellington; f. 1856; Pres. D. A. GRAHAM; Dir. G. W. ANNAND; Sec. R. J. F. AIREY; 900 mems.; publs. *Voice of Business* and *Information and Trade Enquiry Bulletin* (every two months), *Register of Members* (yearly), *Annual Report.*

MANUFACTURERS' ORGANIZATIONS

Auckland Manufacturers' Association, The: P.O.B. 28-090, Remuera, Auckland 5; f. 1886; Pres. A. L. LAIDLAW; Dir. J. WHATNALL; 1,150 mems.

Canterbury Manufacturers' Association: P.O.B. 13-152, Armagh, Christchurch; f. 1879; Dir. I. D. HOWELL; 675 mems.

N.Z. Industries Fair: P.O.B. 13-152, Armagh, Christchurch; f. 1936; Dir. I. D. HOWELL.

Otago-Southland Manufacturers' Association Inc.: P.O.B. 5118, Moray Place, Dunedin; Pres. M. R. ELLIS; Dir. J. G. CRAWFORD; 240 mems.

Wellington Manufacturers' Association: P.O.B. 9234, Wellington; f. 1895; Pres. L. G. BROWN; Dir. W. L. GARDNER; 700 mems.

DEVELOPMENT ORGANIZATIONS

Development Finance Corporation: f. 1964 to provide medium- and long-term finance for the establishment of new, and the expansion of existing, industries especially in development regions; cap. p.u. $NZ4m.

Export-Import Corporation: f. 1973; undertakes trade promotion and marketing, and provides advisory services; acts as a selling and buying agent for the Government; the export of wood products, pulp, dairy produce and canned foods to Asia and the Middle East.

PRODUCERS' ORGANIZATIONS

Federated Farmers of New Zealand: 7th Floor, Commercial Union House, Featherston Street, P.O.B. 715, Wellington, C.1; f. 1945; Pres. W. N. DUNLOP; Sec. J. G. PRYDE; 39,000 mems.; publ. *Straight Furrow* (fortnightly).

Meat Producers' Board: P.O.B. 121, Wellington, C.1; f. 1922; Chair. C. HILGENDORF; Deputy Chair. BRUCE RYAN; Gen. Man. G. ANDERSON; Sec. W. L. KEEN; 9 mems.; publ. *Meat Producer* (monthly).

National Beekeepers' Association of New Zealand Inc.: f. 1913; Pres. I. J. DICKINSON; Sec. E. R. NEAL, A.C.A.; P.O.B. 1879, Wellington, 1; 1,100 mems.; publ. *N.Z. Beekeeper.*

New Zealand Berryfruit Growers' Federation (Inc.): Securities House, P.O.B. 1784, Wellington; Pres. J. G. WEEDON, Jnr.; Sec. D. W. GOBLE; 426 mems.

New Zealand Dairy Board: (Statutory Board—13 members); Massey House, Lambton Quay, Wellington, C.1; f. 1961; Chair. A. L. FRIIS, C.M.G.; Gen. Man. S. T. MURPHY; Gen. Sec. P. S. GREEN; publs. *Annual Report*, various industry information booklets, reports, etc.

New Zealand Fruitgrowers' Federation Ltd.: Huddart Parker Bldg., Wellington, C.1; f. 1915; Gen. Man. A. C. GREER; publ. *The Orchardist of New Zealand.*

New Zealand Poultry Board: P.O.B. 379, Wellington, C.1; f. 1933; Chair. L. G. BEDFORD; Gen. Man. M. R. K. COWDREY; Sec. B. J. WAYMOUTH; 7 mems. (2 Government and 5 producer); publ. *N.Z. Poultry World* (monthly).

New Zealand Vegetable and Produce Growers' Federation (Inc.): Securities House, P.O.B. 1784, Wellington; Pres. T. H. WARBURTON; Gen. Sec. D. W. GOBLE; 4,250 mems.

New Zealand Wool Board: 138–141 Featherston St., P.O.B. 3248, Wellington; f. 1944; 9 mems.; Chair. J. CLARKE; Gen. Man. A. F. COSSIE; Deputy Gen. Man. and Sec. G. H. DREES.

New Zealand Wool Marketing Corpn.: P.O.B. 3849, Wellington C.1; f. 1972; operates a support scheme for wool growers; Chair. W. M. D. BREMNER; Man. Dir. WILSON J. WHINERAY.

Pork Industry Council: P.O.B. 417, Wellington; Chair. R. A. OLIVER; Sec. G. A. BEARD; publ. *Pork Industry Gazette*; circ. 3,500.

EMPLOYERS' ASSOCIATIONS

New Zealand Employers' Federation (Inc.): 95-99 Molesworth St., Wellington; f. 1902; links district employers' associations and other national industrial organizations; Pres. J. E. S. HAMMOND; Vice-Pres. D. G. R. SUTCLIFFE, E. J. BRENAN; Exec. Dir. P. J. LUXFORD.

PRINCIPAL UNIONS OF EMPLOYERS

Auckland Fruit and Vegetable Retail Asscn. Inc.: P.O.B. 2081, Auckland; f. 1936; 325 mems.; Sec. W. FONG.

Auckland Hotel Association: Suite 5, Eden Hall, Eden Crescent, Auckland (P.O.B. 746); Sec. E. F. YOUNG.

Auckland Master Bakers and Pastrycooks: Corner Shortland and Queen Streets, Auckland; 117 mems.; Sec. R. S. HARROP.

Auckland Master Builders' Association: 22-24 Hobson St., P.O.B. 2856, Auckland, C.1; f. 1898; 440 mems.; Pres. S. E. SUTTON; Man. G. F. KNOWLES.

Auckland Master Plumbers' Association (Inc.): 26 Albert St., Auckland; 330 mems.; Sec. J. W. VEALE, A.C.A.

Auckland Retail Grocers: P.O.B. 1514, Auckland; f. 1899; 600 mems.; Sec. B. C. TURLEY.

Auckland Vegetable and Produce Growers' Society Ltd.: 17 Overton Rd., Papatoetoe, Auckland; 660 mems.; Pres. K. BARNETT; Sec. A. McDELL.

Canterbury Master Builders' and Joiners' Association (Inc.): Shaw Savill Bldg., 220 High St., P.O.B. 359, Christchurch; 230 mems.; Sec. N. M. WEST.

New Zealand Animal By-Products Exporters' Association: 95-99 Molesworth St., Wellington; 23 mems.; Sec. G. A. TURNER.

New Zealand Dental Employers: 95-9 Molesworth St., Wellington; 741 mems.; Sec. G. A. TURNER.

New Zealand Engineering Employers Federation: 95-9 Molesworth St., Wellington; 316 mems.; Sec. P. J. LUXFORD.

New Zealand Fibrous Plaster Manufacturers: 95-9 Molesworth St., Wellington; 75 mems.; Sec. G. A. TURNER.

New Zealand Fruitgrowers I.U. of Employers: 95-9 Molesworth St., Wellington; 550 mems.; Sec. P. J. LUXFORD.

New Zealand Motion Picture and General Theatrical Industrial Union of Employers: P.O.B. 363, Wellington; 110 mems.; Sec. A. B. CUNNINGHAM.

New Zealand Motor Body Builders Assn. Inc.: 95-9 Molesworth St., Wellington; 666 mems.; Sec. G. A. TURNER.

New Zealand Retailers' Federation (Inc.): P.O.B. 12086, 101-103 Molesworth St., Wellington; 9 mem. asscns.; Exec. Dir. BARRY I. PURDY.

New Zealand Sheepowners: Commercial Union House, 140-144 Featherston St., Wellington; 350 mems.; Pres. M. O'B. LOUGHNAN; Sec. R. B. McLUSKIE.

New Zealand Timber Industry (New Zealand Sawmillers' Federation Inc.): P.O.B. 12017, 95-99 Molesworth St., Wellington; 250 mems.; Man. W. F. COADY.

Painting Contractors' Association of Auckland (Inc.): 26 Albert St., P.O.B. 3999, Auckland; 140 mems.; Sec. J. W. VEALE, A.C.A.

Wellington and Hutt Valley Master Builders' and Joiners' Association (Inc.): 77 Abel Smith St., P.O.B. 6048, Wellington; 300 mems.; Sec. R. A. KREBS.

TRADE UNIONS

The New Zealand Federation of Labour: 25 Trades Hall, Wellington, C2; f. 1937; Pres. T. E. SKINNER; Sec.-Treas. W. J. KNOX; affiliated to ICFTU.

AFFILIATED UNIONS WITH A MEMBERSHIP OF OVER 3,000

National Union of Railwaymen: P.O.B. 858, Wellington; f. 1886; 16,000 mems.; Pres. R. J. DOHERTY; Gen. Sec. N. A. COLLINS; publ. *N.Z. Railway Review* (monthly).

New Zealand Carpenters and Related Trades Industrial Union of Workers: 6 St. Martin's Lane, P.O.B. 3868, Auckland; 4,000 mems.; Pres. J. GILLIES; Sec. P. PURDUE; publ. *Level*, circ. 4,200.

New Zealand Clerical Employees' Association: Cnr. Marion and Vivian Streets, Wellington; f. 1938; Pres. E. E. BELL; Vice-Pres. T. BRASS; Sec. Chief Exec. D. JACOBS; publ. *Clerical News*; circ. 40,000.

New Zealand Dairy Factories and Related Trades Union: 333 Great South Rd., Beerescourt, Hamilton, Auckland; f. 1937; 4,590 mems.; Sec. S. I. WHEATLEY.

New Zealand Engineering, Coachbuilding, Aircraft, Motor and Related Trades Industrial Union of Workers: 123 Abel Smith St., Wellington; 40,000 mems.; Nat. Sec. J. A. BOOMER.

New Zealand Hotel, Hospital and Restaurant Industrial Association of Workers: 151 Newton Road, Auckland; f. 1908; 29,118 mems.; Sec. G. ARMSTRONG.

New Zealand Meat Workers and Related Trades Union: Room 11, Trades Hall, Gloucester St., Christchurch; 20,000 mems.; Sec. F. E. McNULTY.

New Zealand Printing and Related Trades Industrial Union of Workers: Labour Party Building, 101 Vivian St., Wellington, P.O.B. 6413, Te Aro, Wellington; f. 1862; 11,500 mems.; Pres. W. H. CLEMENT; Sec. G. C. DITCHFIELD; publ. *Imprint*.

New Zealand Shop Employees Federation: P.O.B. 1914, Christchurch; 16,000 mems.; Nat. Sec. B. ALDERDIC.

New Zealand Waterside Workers' Federation: P.O.B. 1073, Wellington; Sec. J. E. NAPIER.

New Zealand Workers' Union: 79 Manchester St., Feilding; 16,000 mems.; Gen. Sec. D. J. DUGGAN; publ. *Bulletin* (quarterly).

North Island Electrical Workers' Union: Wellington; 7,500 mems.; Pres. C. T. LYNCH; Sec. A. J. NEARY.

Northern Drivers' Union: P.O.B. 8169, Newton, Auckland; 7,000 mems.; Sec. G. H. ANDERSON; publ. *Road Transport Worker*.

United Mineworkers of New Zealand: Taylorville, West Coast, S.I.; Pres. A. V. PRENDIVILLE; Sec. J. WHITE.

Wellington Clothing Trades Union: Wellington; 4,202 mems.

TRANSPORT

RAILWAYS

New Zealand Government Railways: Wellington, C.I; are under the jurisdiction of the Minister of Railways; kilometres open (at March 31st, 1973) 4,799; gauge 1,062 mm.; Minister of Railways T. M. McGuigan; Gen. Man. T. M. Small; Deputy Gen. Man. J. W. Dempsey.

ROADS

National Roads Board: P.O.B. 12-041, Wellington; est. 1953; Chair. Hon. H. Watt, Minister of Works; Deputy Chair. T. E. V. Turpin; Sec. D. J. Chapman.

The Board consists of ten members nominated to represent various interests; it is advised by District Roads Councils. New Zealand is divided into 22 geographical Roads Districts, each of which is administered by a Roads Council. The Board and Councils are responsible for the Administration of State Highways. Maintenance and construction expenditure of these highways is met from the National Roads Fund.

Rural roads and Borough streets are the full responsibility of County, Borough and City Councils, which are assisted in meeting expenditure by the National Roads Board.

There were 91,474 kilometres of roads in 1973.

SHIPPING

New Zealand Ports Authority: Wellington; f. 1968; to foster an integrated and efficient ports system for New Zealand and to keep under review a national ports plan for the development of ports and harbours. Chair. Hon. J. K. McAlpine; Mems. A. T. Gandell, Capt. J. B. McGowan, F. R. Askin, F. A. Reeves.

PRINCIPAL COMPANIES

Anchor Shipping and Foundry Co. Ltd.: Wakefield Quay, P.O. Box 1007, Port Nelson; f. 1862; services Wellington – Picton, Nelson-Westport-Greymouth; New Plymouth, Wanganui, Raglan, Portland, Onehunga, Motueka, Tarakohe, Napier, Gisborne; 4 vessels in service; Chair. H. G. West; Gen. Man. A. K. Gellatly.

Holm Shipping Co. Ltd.: Huddart Parker Bldg., Wellington; fleet of 11 cargo vessels; coaster and Pacific Islands services; Chair./Man. Dir. Capt. J. H. Holm, D.F.C.; Gen. Man. Capt. I. A. McKay; brs. in Auckland, Onehunga, Lyttleton and Christchurch.

P. and O. (NZ) Ltd.: Maritime Bldg., Custom-house Quay, Wellington; f. 1873; services New Zealand–United Kingdom via Panama Canal; 28 vessels in service; Man. Dir. G. Hunter.

Northern S.S. Co. Ltd.: 22–24 Quay St., Auckland; f. 1881; coastal services; 4 vessels in service; Chair. D. R. Richards; Mans. J. Ellis, I. C. Skudder.

Shaw Savill Line: P.O.B. 592, Wellington; f. 1858; cargo services New Zealand–United Kingdom via Panama Canal, Mediterranean and Europe, South America and West Indies. Passenger services United Kingdom–New Zealand via Panama, New Zealand–United Kingdom via South Africa, Panama, Caribbean; Gen. Man. for New Zealand M. J. Smith.

Union Steam Ship Company of N.Z. Ltd.: P.O.B. 1799, Wellington; f. 1875, reconstructed 1913; branches and agencies at all New Zealand and major Australian ports and throughout the Pacific Islands and South East Asia; London Representative c/o McIlwraith McEacharn Ltd., Stevinson House, 154-156 Fenchurch St., London, EC3M 6AU; cargo services between New Zealand, the Pacific Islands and South East Asia; also passenger and cargo services on New Zealand coast; cargo services between New Zealand and Australia and on Australian coast; Booking Agents for all other principal sea, air and land services; vessels in service: 2 passenger, 34 conventional cargo vessels, 1 tug, 8 roll-on roll-off cargo vessels; Chair. Sir Peter Abeles.

CIVIL AVIATION

The main international airports are at Auckland and Christchurch.

Air New Zealand Ltd.: Air New Zealand Hse., 1 Queen St., Auckland; f. 1940; network: Auckland–Sydney, Auckland–Melbourne, Auckland–Brisbane, Wellington–Sydney, Wellington–Melbourne, Wellington-Brisbane, Christchurch–Sydney, Christchurch—Melbourne, Nandi-Rarotonga, Auckland–Nandi (Fiji), Nandi-Pago Pago (American Samoa), Auckland–Rarotonga, Pago Pago-Rarotonga, Rarotonga–Papeete, Auckland–Norfolk Island, Auckland–Noumea, Auckland–Los Angeles (via Honolulu), Auckland–Los Angeles (via Tahiti), Auckland–Hong Kong (via Sydney northbound, and via Brisbane and Sydney southbound), Auckland–Singapore (via Sydney); Chair. of Dirs. Sir Geoffrey Roberts, c.b.e., a.f.c.; Gen. Man./Chief Exec. C. J. Keppel; Sec. and Dir. of Finance A. A. Watson, d.f.c.; fleet of 6 DC-8, 3 DC-10-30s.

Mount Cook Airlines: 47 Riccarton Rd., Christchurch; f. 1920; domestic services throughout New Zealand; Gen. Man. A. K. Rollinson; Asst. Gen. Man. M. L. Corner; fleet of 3 HS-748, one DC-3, one Turin Otter, 2 BN-2A Islanders, 17 Cessna, 4 Widgeon, one FU-24.

New Zealand National Airways Corporation: P.O.B. 96, Wellington; f. 1947; Technical Headquarters, International Airport, Christchurch, N.Z.; operates regular daily services to all parts of New Zealand; Chair. A. F. Gilkison; Chief Exec. and Gen. Man. D. A. Patterson; Deputy Gen. Man. L. L. Ford; Flight Operations Man. Capt. A. C. Kenning; operates 4 Boeing 737, 5 Vickers Viscounts V807, 15 Friendship F27; publs. *Airline Review* (circ. 63,000), *Skylines* (circ. 3,000).

Safe Air Ltd.: Huddart Parker Bldg., Post Office Square, P.O.B. 751, Wellington; f. 1951; Chair. L. G. Hucks, o.b.e.; Gen. Man. D. P. Lynskey; is the chief air freight carrier; operates Bristol Freighters.

The following foreign Airlines serve New Zealand: American Airlines, British Airways, Pan Am, Qantas, U.T.A.

TOURISM

New Zealand Tourist and Publicity Department: P.O.B. 95, Wellington; f. 1901; National Tourist Office; Gen. Man. J. E. HARTSTONGE; offices in Auckland, Wellington, Christchurch, Dunedin, Invercargill and Rotorua; overseas offices in London, New York, San Francisco, Los Angeles, Sydney, Melbourne and Brisbane, Tokyo and Frankfurt.

OVERSEAS OFFICE

Australia: 115 Pitt St., Sydney; 93–95 Elizabeth St., Melbourne; MLC Bldg., Adelaide St., Brisbane.

Germany: Rathenauplatz 1A, 6-Frankfurt-am-Main.

Japan: 20-40 Kamiyama-cho, Shibuya-ku, 150, Tokyo.

United Kingdom: N.Z. House, Haymarket, London, SW1 Y4TQ.

U.S.A.: 153 Kearney St., San Francisco; 510 W. 6th St., Los Angeles; Suite 530, 630 5th Ave., New York.

New Zealand National Travel Association Inc.: Hume House, 152 The Terrace, Wellington; represents tourist industry interests; Chief Executive A. C. STANIFORD; publ. *New Zealand Holiday* (quarterly).

CULTURAL ORGANIZATION

Queen Elizabeth II Arts Council: P.O.B. 10342, Wellington; f. 1964 in succession to the Arts Advisory Council; a statutory body which administers state aid to the arts; Chair. Dr. W. B. SUTCH; Acting Dir. JOAN KERR.

MUSIC

Association of Ballet and Opera Trust Boards of New Zealand: P.O.B. 17058, Wellington; Administrator G. H. STRINGER; Gen. Man. P. J. HOLLAND.

Music Federation of New Zealand (Inc.): P.O.B. 3391, Wellington; f. 1950; arranges about 25 concerts a year, about one third by overseas groups, for its 20 member societies (which include Fiji), 25 associated regional organizations and in schools; active educational work includes organization of a nation-wide school chamber music contest, master classes, etc.; mems. over 8,000; Pres. A. HILTON; Administrator Miss E. AIREY; Sec. B. E. J. McELWAIN; publ. *Theme* (annually).

The New Zealand Ballet: Box 2442, Wellington.

New Zealand Broadcasting Corporation: P.O.B. 98, Wellington; symphony orchestra; comprises about 90 players; presents Prom and main season concerts; school and lunch-time performances, etc.

ATOMIC ENERGY

New Zealand Atomic Energy Committee: c/o D.S.I.R., Private Bag, Lower Hutt; responsible to the Minister of Science for advising Government on the development of peaceful uses of atomic energy in New Zealand; Chair. A. G. ROBB; Exec. Sec. J. T. O'LEARY.

New Zealand Institute of Nuclear Sciences: Gracefield Rd., Lower Hutt; administered by the Department of Scientific and Industrial Research and incorporates the Department's former Division of Nuclear Sciences; facilities available to other government departments and to the universities; Dir. T. A. RAFTER, M.SC., D.SC.

Department of Health: P.O. Box 5013, Wellington; radiation protection; advised by the Radiological Advisory Council.

National Radiation Laboratory: P.O.B. 25-099, Christchurch; branch of the Department of Health; radiation protection, licensing, measurement standards, practical services and research; Dir. H. J. YEABSLEY.

University of Auckland: Private Bag, Auckland; research and training.

University of Canterbury: Christchurch; research and training.

University of Otago: Dunedin; research and training.

Victoria University of Wellington: P.O.B. 196, Wellington; research and training.

UNIVERSITIES

University of Auckland: Princes St., Auckland; 503 teachers, 9,538 students.

University of Canterbury: P.O.B. 1471, Christchurch; 429 teachers, 7,101 students.

Massey University: P.O. Palmerston North; 310 teachers, 5,900 students.

University of Otago: Dunedin; 450 teachers, 6,001 students.

Victoria University of Wellington: Wellington; 405 teachers, 6,379 students.

University of Waikato: Waikato; 120 teachers, 2,000 students.

NEW ZEALAND'S ISLAND TERRITORIES AND THE COOK ISLANDS

COOK ISLANDS (Self-Governing Territory)   NIUE (Dependent Territory)
TOKELAU ISLANDS (Dependent Territory)

COOK ISLANDS
The Cook Islands lie in the South Pacific 2,000 miles north-east of New Zealand.

STATISTICS

AREA
(acres)

Rarotonga 16,602, Mangaia 12,800, Atiu 6,654, Mitiaro 5,500, Mauke 4,552, Aitutaki 4,461, Penrhyn 2,432, Manuae 1,524, Manihiki 1,344, Pukapuka 1,250, Palmerston 500.

There are fifteen main islands scattered throughout an area of 850,000 sq. miles of the South Pacific Ocean. The largest Southern islands are elevated and fertile; the Northern group are sea-level coral atolls.

POPULATION

At the Census taken on December 1st, 1971, the population totalled 21,227: 10,840 males and 10,387 females.

Rarotonga (Capital)	11,388	Mauke . .	763
Aitutaki . .	2,854	Pukapuka .	728
Mangaia . .	2,071	Penrhyn . .	612
Atiu . .	1,455	Rakahanga .	339
Manihiki .	452	Other Islands .	565

AGRICULTURE
AREA OF CROPS
(acres)

Coconuts .	. 28,250	Tomatoes .	.	200
Citrus .	1,200	Pineapples	.	250
Maniota (Cassava)	360	Taro .	.	420
Coffee .	140	Kumara .	.	215
Bananas .	200	Yams .	.	10
	Pepper	. .	15	

Livestock: Horses 1,539, Cattle 159, Pigs 9,678, Goats 2,000.

EMPLOYMENT

Most of the working population are engaged in agriculture, copra-making and fruit packing. There are two clothing factories, a fruit canning factory and a paua shell factory in Rarotonga. A tourist industry is in the early stages of formation and will before long provide significant employment opportunities as well as a stimulus to the economy. Employment prospects are at present limited.

CO-OPERATIVES
There are over 70 co-operatives, covering such activities as village and school savings, credit, processing and marketing, supply, audit, and development.

FINANCE
BUDGET
($NZ'000)

	REVENUE	EXPENDITURE	NEW ZEALAND SUBSIDY
1966–67	1,684	3,460	1,869
1967–68	1,817	3,686	1,869
1968–69	1,559	3,619	2,062
1969–70	779*	3,006*	2,375
1970	1,917	4,618	2,375†

* Nine months to December 1970.

† Year to March 1971.

Principal sources of revenue: Import and export duties, stamp sales, income tax.

Primary items of expenditure: Education, public health, public works.

EXTERNAL TRADE
(1971)

Total Imports: $5,766,000, principal items are foodstuffs, drapery and piece goods, oils and petrol, timber, cement, vehicles and parts.

Total Exports: $2,691,635, principal items are tomatoes, mother-of-pearl, copra, citrus fruit, fruit juices and canned fruit preparations, clothing, handicrafts.

Trade is chiefly with New Zealand, the enlarged EEC, Japan, U.S.A., Hong Kong and Australia. Imports from New Zealand represented 76.25 per cent of total imports in 1970.

TRANSPORT

Ships from New Zealand, the United Kingdom and U.S.A. call at Rarotonga. The New Zealand Government's vessel *Moana Roa* calls monthly. There is at present no civil airline service but an international jet airport has been built at Rarotonga. Passenger flights to and from New Zealand are made by Air N.Z. Ltd. twice a week, once direct and once via Fiji.

GOVERNMENT

The Cook Islands were proclaimed a British Protectorate in 1888 and a part of New Zealand in 1901. On August 4th, 1965 they became a self-governing territory in free association with New Zealand. The people are British subjects and New Zealand citizens. Executive authority is vested in Her Majesty the Queen in right of New Zealand. The High Commissioner of the Cook Islands represents Her Majesty the Queen as well as the New Zealand Government, and resides in Rarotonga.

Executive Government is carried out by a Cabinet consisting of a Premier and five other ministers who are collectively responsible to the Legislative Assembly.

High Commissioner: G. J. BROCKLEHURST.

THE CABINET

(April 1974)

Premier, Minister of Civil Aviation, External Affairs, Police and Tourism: Sir ALBERT R. HENRY, K.B.E.

Minister of Social Services: TUPUI ARIKI HENRY.

Minister of Economic Services: WILLIAM ESTALL.

Minister for Financial Services: GEOFFREY ARAMA HENRY.

Minister for Supportive Services: ANATIO AKARURU.

Minister of Justice and Land Development: APENERA PRA SHORT.

Minister of Outer Island Affairs: TIAKANA ANNANGA.

LEGISLATIVE ASSEMBLY

The Legislative Assembly consists of 22 members elected by universal suffrage every four years from a common roll for both Maoris and Europeans and is presided over by a Speaker.

Speaker: Mrs. MARGUERITE STOREY.

President of the House of Arikis: MAKAE NIU TEREMOANA ARIKI, O.B.E.

Each of the main islands has an Island Council.

POLITICAL PARTIES

Cook Islands Party: Rarotonga; the government party; 15 representatives in the Legislative Assembly; Leader Sir ALBERT HENRY.

Democratic Party: Rarotonga; opposition party; Leader Dr. TOM DAVIS.

JUDICIAL SYSTEM

High Court; Land Court; Land Appellate Court.

The High Court exercises civil and criminal jurisdiction throughout the Cook Islands. The Land Court is concerned with litigation over land and titles. The Land Appellate Court hears appeals over decisions of the Land Court.

Chief Judge of Land Court: J. A. FRAZER.

RELIGION

Main groups are Cook Islands Christian Church (Congregational), Roman Catholic, Latter Day Saints and Seventh Day Adventists.

EDUCATION

(1969)

Government schools: 6,839 pupils; Mission schools: 376 pupils.

Free secular education is compulsory for all children between the ages of six and fifteen.

Secondary education is provided at Tereora College in Rarotonga and junior high schools on Aitutaki, Mangaia and Atiu. Under the New Zealand Training Scheme, the New Zealand Government offers education and training in New Zealand, Fiji and W. Samoa for secondary and tertiary education, career training and short-term in-service training. At 31 March 1970 there were 88 long-term students under this scheme.

NIUE

STATISTICS

(sq. miles) (approx.)	POPULATION (1971)		
	Male	Female	Total
100	2,507	2,483	4,990

The birth rate in 1971 was 31.8 per 1,000 and the crude death rate, 5.71. The infant mortality rate per 1,000 live births was 38.4.

AGRICULTURE
AREA OF CROPS
(acres)

Coconuts . .	5,000	Cassava (Manioc) .	25
Taro . .	350	Kumara . .	35
Yams . .	25	Passion Fruit .	35
Limes . .	42		

50,900 of the island's 64,900 acres are used for agriculture and 13,600 acres are merchantable forest. The main livestock are beef cattle, pigs and poultry.

EMPLOYMENT

Under a three-year programme the Government of Niue and the Niue Development Board are aiming to rehabilitate the coconut industry as well as to develop grass land, cattle and other farming operations. The Niue Public Service has 305 permanent employees, including 43 expatriate New Zealand staff, and 339 casual employees who are employed by the following departments: The Treasury, Post Office, Justice, Education, Health, Administrative, Police, Works, Radio and Agriculture. The figures include teachers and nurses.

FINANCE

	REVENUE $NZ	EXPENDITURE $NZ	NEW ZEALAND SUBSIDY $NZ
1969–70	834,852	1,766,909	941,300
1970–71	1,036,827	2,102,720	972,365
1971–72	980,219	2,023,781	1,139,760

Revenue is raised mainly from import and export duties, sale of postage stamps, court fines and income tax.

EXTERNAL TRADE
(1971)

IMPORTS	EXPORTS	TOTAL
$NZ 810,682	$NZ 178,969	$NZ 989,651

Export items include copra, plaited ware, kumaras, honey and passion fruit.

New Zealand takes most of Niue's export (nearly 90 per cent in 1971) and provides a large part of the island's imports (nearly 79 per cent in 1971). The main imports are foodstuffs, vehicles and spares, building materials, and oil and petrol.

TRANSPORT

There are 77 miles of all-weather roads and 66 miles of access and plantation roads. At March 31st, 1972, there were 689 registered motor vehicles, of which 410 were motor cycles. The best anchorage is an open roadstead at Alofi, the largest of Niue's 13 villages. A shipping service is maintained with New Zealand via Tonga, Fiji and Samoa on a regular four-weekly basis.

An airstrip of 5,400 ft., capable of taking most types of aircraft except modern jet aircraft, and a weekly air service from New Zealand, via Fiji and Tonga, is operated by Air N.Z. Ltd.

GOVERNMENT

An Executive Committee, comprising a Leader of Government Business and three other members, is elected by the Niue Island Assembly, the Resident Commissioner being Chairman. A full member system of government was introduced on 1 November 1968, by which the Resident Commissioner delegated certain powers and functions to the Executive Committee, including responsibility for portfolios controlling all government departments.

A Legislative Assembly of 14 members is elected by universal suffrage every three years, the Resident Commissioner being President. It has budgetary control of internal revenue and New Zealand grants and may make laws for the peace, order, and good government of Niue.

Resident Commissioner: C. A. ROBERTS.

Leader of Government and Minister of Finance and Government Administration: ROBERT R. REX.

Minister of Agriculture, Economic Development, Tourism and Education: M. Y. VIVIAN.

Minister of Health, Justice, Radio and Post Office: Dr. E. LIPITOA.

Minister of Works and Police: F. F. LUI.

JUDICIAL SYSTEM

The High Court: exercises civil and criminal jurisdiction in Niue.

The Land Court: is concerned with litigation over land and titles.

The Resident Commissioner acts as Judge of both courts.

Land Appellate Court: hears appeals over decisions of the Land Court.

EDUCATION

There are 8 primary schools and 1 secondary, and 1 Teacher Training Centre. Education is free and compulsory between the ages of six and fourteen. In March 1972 there were 1,325 primary and 293 High School pupils. There were also 45 students undertaking long-term education or training in New Zealand under the auspices of the New Zealand Training Scheme, and 13 students at the teacher-training centre in Niue.

TOKELAU ISLANDS

STATISTICS

AREA (acres)

ATAFU	NUKUNONU	FAKAOFO	TOTAL
500	1,350	650	2,500

POPULATION

Total (1971): 1,655 (Atafu 632, Nukunonu 398, Fakaofo 625). Because of the limited economic and social future of the group, about 100 persons are being voluntarily resettled in New Zealand every year.

BUDGET
($NZ)

1969–70: Revenue 31,497; Expenditure 181,719; New Zealand subsidy 197,000.

1970–71: Revenue 54,068; Expenditure 215,447; New Zealand subsidy 177,000.

Revenue during 1971–72 totalled $24,860 and expenditure $259,504. Financial aid from New Zealand totalling $541,000 for the three years 1971–72 to 1973–74 was announced in July 1971.

Revenue is derived mainly from copra export duty, import duty, and sale of postage stamps. Expenditure is devoted mainly to the provision of social services, particularly health, education, and agriculture.

EXTERNAL TRADE

The main export is copra which during 1971–72 earned $NZ12,961. The main imports are foodstuffs, building materials, and kerosene.

TRANSPORT

The Group is visited five times a year by a ship from Western Samoa. In 1971 the Shaw Savill liner *Ocean Monarch* became the first passenger liner to visit the Tokelaus.

GOVERNMENT

In 1925, the Government of the United Kingdom transferred administrative control of the Group to the Governor-General of New Zealand. In 1946, the Group was officially designated the Tokelau Islands and by an act of 1948, under which formal sovereignty was transferred to New Zealand, they were included within the territorial boundaries of New Zealand. From 1962 until the end of 1971 the High Commissioner for New Zealand in Western Samoa was also the Administrator of the Tokelau Islands. From January 1st, 1972, the office of Administrator was transferred to the New Zealand Secretary for Maori and Island Affairs. Provision was made for certain powers to be delegated to the District Officer of the Tokelau Islands Administration in Apia, Western Samoa.

LOCAL GOVERNMENT

There is a *Faipule* (who is also the magistrate) on each island who is democratically elected by the people triennially. He is responsible to the Administrator and presides over the Council of Elders (*Fono*).

RELIGION

On Atafu and Fakaofo most inhabitants are members of the London Missionary Society; on Nukunonu all are Roman Catholic.

EDUCATION

The Administration and Churches co-operate in this field. There are three schools, one on each atoll. At the beginning of 1969, an expatriate teaching couple took up their position on each of the three atolls to improve the general standard of education. In addition there are 28 trained Tokelauan teachers and 6 teacher-aides. The Administration offers scholarships for study in Western Samoa and Fiji in the fields of agriculture and medicine. On March 31st, 1970, there were 34 students undertaking long-term study in New Zealand under the New Zealand Training Scheme.

ROSS DEPENDENCY
(ANTARCTICA)

Administered by New Zealand since 1923.

AREA
(sq. miles)

TOTAL	LAND AREA	ICE SHELF
290,000	160,000	130,000

Scott Base on Ross Island established in 1957. Cape Hallett, joint New Zealand-United States base. Both bases are permanently occupied.

Ross Dependency Research Committee: Wellington; responsible for co-ordinating and supervising all activity in the Dependency.

NICARAGUA

INTRODUCTORY SURVEY

Location, Climate, Language, Religion, Flag, Capital

With an area of 130,000 sq. km., Nicaragua is the largest country of the Central American isthmus and is the most sparsely populated, having a population density of 15 inhabitants per square kilometre. However, nine-tenths of the population is concentrated in the south-west of the country between Lake Nicaragua and the Pacific coast. Bounded by the Pacific Ocean to the west and the Caribbean to the east, the country is bisected by a mountain range, with swampy marshland near to the Caribbean. Nicaragua's neighbours are Honduras to the north and Costa Rica to the south. The climate is tropical, with a mean average temperature of 25.5°C (78°F). The rainy season extends from May to October. The national language is Spanish, although English is widely understood. There is no state church but Roman Catholicism is dominant. The national flag (proportions 2 by 1) has three horizontal stripes of blue, white, and blue, with the state emblem in the centre. Managua is the capital.

Recent History

Since 1936 the Somoza family has dominated Nicaraguan politics. In that year Gen. Anastasio "Tacho" Somoza, commander of the National Guard, seized power by *coup d'état*. On his death by assassination in 1956, his son Luis became president and another son, Anastasio "Tachito", assumed the command of the National Guard. On the retirement of Luis Somoza in 1963, René Schick Gutiérrez became president until his death in 1966. After a violent electoral campaign, he was succeeded in 1967 by Gen. Anastasio Somoza Debayle, who retained his command over the National Guard. Gen. Somoza's term as President ended on April 30th, 1972.

Following a pact between the opposition Conservatives and the Liberal Party, which supports Gen. Somoza, both houses of Congress voted their dissolution in August 1971 in order that elections be held to form a constituent assembly which would amend the Constitution to allow Gen. Somoza to be re-elected as President in December 1974. In the meantime a triumvirate composed of members of the Liberal and Conservative parties is ruling the country.

On December 23rd, 1972, an earthquake destroyed about three-quarters of the buildings in Managua, making some half a million people homeless and killing about 6,000 others. In January 1973 Gen. Somoza announced plans to rebuild the city. The commercial sector of the city is to be built about six miles from its former site. It is estimated that reconstruction will take at least three years. Nicaragua is a founder member of the United Nations and the Central American Common Market.

Government

Since May 1972 Nicaragua has been ruled by a transitional National Governing Council composed of two Liberals and one Conservative. The new Constitution which will govern the presidential elections to be held in December 1974 has not yet been published.

Defence

A member of the Organization of American States and the Organization of Central American States, Nicaragua has armed forces totalling 7,100 men. Of these 5,400 are in the army. Both the navy and the air force are small. Paramilitary forces number 4,000 men.

Economic Affairs

Nicaragua is primarily an agricultural country. Cotton and coffee dominate the export list, with cotton accounting for 40 per cent of annual exports; sugar, cattle, timber and gold are also important. The National Development Institute lends state money to exploit the mineral resources (silver, copper, iron as well as gold). Urban industry is on a relatively modest scale, but increasing; it includes a petroleum refinery, textile mills, tobacco, cement and soluble coffee plants, dairies and a fairly wide range of processing plants. Workable deposits of gold, silver, lead and zinc were discovered in 1968 in northern Nicaragua. As a result of the earthquake of December 1972 Nicaragua's industrial production capacity is reported to have fallen by ten per cent. The Minister of the Economy estimated that one thousand million U.S. dollars were required to restore the economy. Nicaragua is a member of the Central American Common Market.

Transport and Communications

There are some good main roads, the most important being the 485 km. north-south stretch of the Pan American Highway. State railways (317 km.) join important towns and private lines serve the banana plantations. Several rivers are navigable to small craft and steamers serve towns on Lake Nicaragua. LANICA, the state airline, operates internal and international services.

Social Welfare

There is a compulsory national health insurance scheme for wage-earners in Managua, and health expenditure ranks high in the budget. A campaign against malaria has been successful.

Education

Primary education is free and compulsory for children between the ages of 6 and 13. In 1971 there were 2,382 primary and secondary schools. The literacy rate is about 50 per cent. There are many commercial schools and two universities.

Tourism

The mountainous region with its occasionally active volcanoes, the Huellas de Acahualinca outside Managua which show ancient footprints of men fleeing from volcanic lava, the mineral baths of Tipitapa and the abundant sea, lake and river fishing are the principal tourist attractions of Nicaragua.

Visas are not required to visit Nicaragua by nationals of Costa Rica, El Salvador, Guatemala and Honduras.

Sport

Baseball and basketball are widely played. Swimming and fishing are popular.

Public Holidays

1974: August 10th (Managua local holiday), September 14th (Battle of San Jacinto), September 15th (Independence Day), October 12th (Columbus Day), November 1st (All Saints' Day), December 8th (Immaculate Conception), December 24th–25th (Christmas).

1975: January 1st (New Year's Day), March 25th–31st (Holy Week), May 1st (Labour Day), May 27th.

A considerable number of local holidays are also observed.

Weights and Measures

The metric system is officially used, although the following Spanish and local units are also in general use:

Length: cuarta = 8.13 inches
vara = 2.76 feet
cuadra = 91.9 yards
legua = 2.6 or 3 miles

Weight: libra = 1.014 lb.
arroba = 25.362 lb.
quintal = 101.44 lb.

Volume: liquid galon = 0.888 gallon

Area: manzana = 1.74 acres
caballería = 27.9 acres
legua cuadrada = 12 sq. miles

Capacity: medio = 500 cu. inches
= 1 peck.
fanega = 24 medios

Currency and Exchange Rates

100 centavos = 1 córdoba.

Exchange rates (April 1974):
£1 sterling = 16.62 córdobas;
U.S. $1 = 7.00 córdobas.

STATISTICAL SURVEY

AREA AND POPULATION

AREA (sq. km.)	POPULATION (December 1971)				
	Total	Managua (capital)	Births (1971)	Marriages (1971)	Deaths (1971)
130,000	1,961,268	479,511	86,553	8,616	25,820

AGRICULTURE
PRINCIPAL CROPS

	AREA (manzanas)*		PRODUCTION ('000 quintals)†	
	1971–72	1972–73	1971–72	1972–73
Beans . . .	88,939	87,030	1,236.3	939.9
Coffee . . .	118,450	118,452	912.0	871.8
Cotton . . .	156,079	n.a.	2,231.4	2,293.2
Maize . . .	379,677	301,578	5,277.5	2,865.0
Rice . . .	37,364	37,364	1,111.2	1,009.0
Sorghum . .	79,432	53,950	1,127.0	871.0
Sugar Cane .	49,500	51,530	42,872.0	44,321.0

* 1 manzana = 1.74 acres.　　　† 1 quintal = 46 kg.

Livestock: (1969 estimate) Cattle 2,473,000.

Forestry: cedar, mahogany, rose-wood, etc.; sawn timber production averages about 60m. board feet a year.

MINING AND INDUSTRY

		1971	1972
Gold	troy oz.	108,000	82,000
Silver	,, ,,	161,000	126,000
Copper	tons	22,000	11,000
Matches	boxes	42,380,000	n.a.
Vegetable Oils	lb.	n.a.	n.a.
Sugar	quintals	3,438,300	4,149,200
Cement	sacks of 94 lb.	3,276,300	n.a.
Beer	litres	14,380,000	15,200,000
Cigarettes	'000 packets	7,006,600	n.a.
Timber	tons	84,000	185,000
Cotton Cloth	yards	22,339,000	n.a.

FINANCE

100 centavos = 1 córdoba.

Coins: 5, 10, 25 and 50 centavos.

Notes: 1, 5, 10, 20, 50, 100, 500 and 1,000 córdobas.

Exchange rates (April 1974): £1 sterling = 16.62 córdobas; U.S. $1 = 7.00 córdobas.

100 córdobas = £6.02 = $14.29.

Note: The Central American peso (C.A.$), used for transactions within the Central American Common Market, is at par with the United States dollar.

BUDGET EXPENDITURE
(million C.A. $)

	1970	1971	1972
REVENUE:			
Direct taxation	15.2	16.7	18.9
Indirect taxation	56.7	61.7	65.1
Other	8.1	8.6	6.0
TOTAL	80.0	87.0	90.0
EXPENDITURE:			
Current expenditure	68.6	72.7	71.1
Capital expenditure	23.5	39.8	48.7
TOTAL	92.1	112.5	122.8

NATIONAL ACCOUNTS
(million C.A.$)

	1970	1971	1972
GROSS NATIONAL PRODUCT	819.4	876.8	951.9
Income paid abroad	25.2	29.3	38.0
GROSS DOMESTIC PRODUCT	844.6	906.1	989.9
Balance of exports and imports of goods and services	19.1	18.5	−30.0
AVAILABLE RESOURCES	863.7	924.6	959.9
of which:			
Private consumption expenditure	646.3	696.3	723.4
Government consumption expenditure	71.0	75.0	76.0
Private fixed capital formation	146.4	153.3	160.5

INTERNATIONAL RESERVES
('000 C.A.$)

	1970	1971	1972
Gross Reserves at the Central Bank .	48,701	57,801	77,945
Gold and Foreign Exchange . .	47,749	54,125	71,187
IMF Special Drawing Rights . .	952	3,676	6,758

BALANCE OF PAYMENTS
(million C.A.$)

	1971			1972		
	Credit	Debit	Balance	Credit	Debit	Balance
Goods and Services:						
Merchandise . . .	186.5	189.5	— 3.0	248.9	195.2	53.7
Services	40.3	82.2	—41.9	41.3	103.3	—62.0
Total	226.8	271.7	—44.9	290.2	298.5	— 8.3
Transfer Payments . . .	7.0	2.0	5.0	6.0	2.0	4.0
Capital Operations . .	80.1	24.1	56.0	81.9	35.2	46.7
Net Errors and Omissions . .	—	2.8	— 2.8	—	7.3	— 7.3

EXTERNAL TRADE

Imports: (1971) U.S. $165,685,000, (1972) U.S. $147,588,000. **Exports:** (1971) U.S. $119,436,000, (1972) U.S. $160,306,170.

COMMODITIES

IMPORTS
('000 U.S. dollars)

	1971	1972
Foodstuffs	18,577	18,554
Iron and Steel Manufactures .	21,800	17,439
Machinery . . .	56,746	40,557
Pharmaceutical and Chemical Products . . .	40,694	41,040
Petrol	11,068	11,945
Motor Vehicles and Spares .	16,800	18,053

EXPORTS
('000 U.S. dollars)

	1971	1972
Bananas . . .	3	3,402
Cattle . . .	78	647
Coffee . . .	29,251	32,877
Cotton (raw) . .	41,320	62,868
Cottonseed . .	792	1,611
Gold . . .	3,845	3,173
Meat . . .	28,672	38,277
Sugar (refined) . .	11,631	15,207
Timber . . .	3,836	5,414

COUNTRIES
('000 U.S. dollars)

	1970		1971		1972	
	Imports	Exports	Imports	Exports	Imports	Exports
Belgium	3,613	4,314	4,304	4,045	1,156	5,177
Canada . . .	2,762	2,733	2,769	3,780	3,081	4,082
El Salvador . .	15,426	7,811	16,061	9,149	16,612	11,110
Germany, Federal Republic .	11,477	20,824	15,151	14,837	16,241	18,054
Japan	12,724	24,683	17,227	32,801	18,133	44,918
Netherlands . .	5,824	5,747	6,175	3,981	2,734	6,110
Netherlands West Indies .	2,801	65	2,714	73	1,764	95
Panama . . .	4,478	871	1,163	1,135	3,547	1,787
United Kingdom . .	6,869	1,691	6,539	1,133	7,339	778
United States of America .	71,967	56,008	69,589	62,405	69,033	82,046
Others . . .	60,809	53,689	68,750	54,353	78,846	75,922

Inter-Central American trade totals: (1970) U.S. $96,071,000, (1971) U.S. $100,944,000.

TRANSPORT

RAILWAYS

	Passengers	Passenger/ Kilometres	Ton/ Kilometres
1970	759,674	30,392,097	16,367,026
1971	760,984	31,294,164	14,538,217
1972	669,427	28,041,486	13,926,572

ROADS

		1968	1969	1970
Cars	. .	13,366	14,419	15,586
Buses	. .	1,919	2,120	1,858
Vans	. .	10,914	12,195	11,150
Lorries	. .	4,331	5,390	5,215
Jeeps	. .	5,750	6,062	6,340
Motor-cycles and others.	.	6,717	7,525	7,790

SHIPPING

		1970	1971	1972
Cargo Tonnage				
Unloaded	.	2,376,204	2,317,618	2,901,765
Loaded	.	2,355,380	2,336,647	2,877,836

CIVIL AVIATION

		1970	1971	1972
Passengers				
Entering	.	72,321	77,631	83,286
Leaving	.	75,845	80,222	86,404
Cargo (kg.)				
Entering	.	6,891,321	6,219,660	6,054,918
Leaving	.	4,374,331	5,116,935	5,546,778

EDUCATION
(1971)

*Schools	Teachers	Pupils
2,382	10,161	364,603

* Primary and Secondary.

Source: Banco Central de Nicaragua, Managua.

THE CONSTITUTION

On August 30th, 1971, the Nicaraguan Congress voted its dissolution in order that the Constitution could be reformed by a constitutional assembly.

NATIONAL GOVERNING COUNCIL

From May 1st, 1972, until elections are held in December 1974, Nicaragua is being ruled by a triumvirate:

Dr. Edmundo Paguaga Irías (*Partido Conservador Nicaragüense*).
Gen. Roberto Martínez Lacayo (*Partido Liberal Nacionalista*).
Dr. Alfonso Lovo Cordero (*Partido Liberal Nacionalista*).

MINISTERS
(April 1974)

Minister of the Interior: Dr. Leandro Marín Abaunza.
Minister for Foreign Affairs: Dr. Alejandro Montiel Arguello.
Minister of Economics, Industry and Commerce: Juan José Martínez L.
Minister of Finance and Public Credit: Gen. Gustavo Montiel.
Minister of Education: José Antonio Mora.
Minister of Public Works: Cristóbal Rugama Núñez.
Minister of Defence: Col. Heberto Sánchez.

Minister of Agriculture and Livestock: Ing. Noel Somarriba Barreto.
Minister of Public Health: Dr. Fernando Valle López.
Minister of Labour: Ernesto Navarro Richardson.
Minister for the National District and Secretary to the Cabinet: Dr. Luis Valle Olivares.
Secretary of State for Information and Press: Iván Osorio Peters.

Commander of the National Guard: Gen. Anastasio Somoza Debayle.

DIPLOMATIC REPRESENTATION

EMBASSIES AND LEGATIONS ACCREDITED TO NICARAGUA
(In Managua unless otherwise stated)
(E) Embassy; (L) Legation.

Argentina: Reparto Las Colinas, Pasaje Los Cerros III, Apdo. Postal 703 (E); *Ambassador:* CÉSAR RUIZ MORENO.

Austria: Mexico 5, D.F. (L).

Belgium: San José, Costa Rica (E).

Bolivia: Guatemala City, Guatemala (E).

Brazil: Kilómetro 13½, Carretera Sur, Apdo. Postal 264 (E); *Ambassador:* MILTON FARIA.

Canada: San José, Costa Rica (E).

Chile: Optica Santa Lucía, 2° piso, frente al Colegio Americano, Carretera a Masaya, Apdo. Postal 1704 (E); *Chargé d'Affaires a.i.:* JORGE DEL PULGAR BARRUETO.

China (Taiwan): Kilómetro 7½, Carretera Sur, Barrio Sevilla Sacasa, Apdo. Postal 187 (E); *Ambassador:* FANG CHIN-YEN.

Colombia: Reparto Las Colinas, Kilómetro 14½, Carretera vieja a León, Apdo. Postal 1062 (E); *Ambassador:* JULIO BARON ORTEGA.

Costa Rica: Apdo. Postal 932 (E); *Ambassador:* NOEL HERNÁNDEZ MADRIGAL.

Denmark: Bogotá, Colombia (E).

Dominican Republic: Apdo. Postal 614 (E); *Ambassador:* JOSÉ ANGEL SAVIÑÓN.

Ecuador: Hotel Intercontinental, Apdo. Postal 1323 (E); *Ambassador:* LUIS YÉPEZ CALISTO.

Egypt: San Salvador, El Salvador (E).

El Salvador: Apdo. Postal 149 (E); *Ambassador:* MARIO MODESTO CHACÓN AREVALO.

France: esq. Avda. del Ejército, Apdo. Postal 1227 (E); *Ambassador:* PAUL ROUHIER.

Germany, Federal Republic: Kilómetro 11¾, Carretera Sur (E); *Ambassador:* Baron GOETZ VON HOUWALD.

Greece: Mexico 6, D.F. (E).

Guatemala: Kilómetro 13, Carretera a Masaya, Apdo. Postal 695 (E); *Ambassador:* ENRIQUE PELLECER LÓPEZ.

Honduras: Apdo. Postal 321 (E); *Ambassador:* MOISES LÓPEZ MALDONADO.

India: Mexico, D.F. (E).

Israel: San José, Costa Rica (E).

Italy: (E); *Chargé d'Affaires a.i.:* LUIGI NUNZIANTE.

Japan: Hospital El Retiro, Apdo. Postal 1789 (E); *Ambassador:* TOMIHIKO KAMBARA.

Korea, Republic: Mexico 10, D.F. (E).

Lebanon: Mexico, D.F. (E).

Mexico: Reparto Las Colinas, Apdo. Postal 834 (E); *Ambassador:* ANTONIO DE ICAZA.

Netherlands: San José, Costa Rica (E) (also represents Luxembourg).

Norway: Mexico 10, D.F. (E).

Panama: Apdo. Postal 1 (E); *Chargé d'Affaires a.i.:* RUBÉN DARÍO MASCUÑANA.

Paraguay: San Salvador, El Salvador (E).

Peru: Kilómetro 10½, Carretera Sur, Apdo. Postal 884 (E); *Ambassador:* RAÚL GARREAUD FERNÁNDEZ.

Poland: Mexico 20, D.F. (L).

Spain: Reparto Las Palmas, frente al Templo Mormón, Apdo. Postal 284 (E); *Ambassador:* JOSÉ GARCÍA BAÑÓN.

Sweden: Guatemala City, Guatemala (E).

Switzerland: Guatemala City, Guatemala (E).

Turkey: Mexico 10, D.F. (E).

United Kingdom: Reparto Las Colinas, Avda. Las Colinas, Lote 100, Apdo. Postal 13 (E); *Ambassador:* DAVID FRANCIS DUNCAN.

U.S.A.: Kilómetro 4½, Carretera Sur (E); *Ambassador:* TURNER B. SHELTON.

Uruguay: Reparto Las Colinas, Paseo El Club 80, Apdo. Postal 3843 (E); *Ambassador:* (vacant).

Vatican: Las Piedracitas, Apdo. Postal 506 (Apostolic Nunciature); *Nuncio:* Mgr. JANUSZ BOLONEK (acting).

Venezuela: Apdo. Postal 406 (E); *Ambassador:* MANUEL ANGARITA SOULES.

Nicaragua also has diplomatic relations with Haiti, the Philippines and Portugal.

POLITICAL PARTIES

Partido Liberal Nacionalista de Nicaragua (PLN): Casa del Partido Liberal; f. 1876; Government party; Leader Gen. ANASTASIO SOMOZA.

Partido Conservador Nicaragüense: official Opposition party; Leaders Dr. EDMUNDO PAGUAGA IRÍAS, JOSÉ JOAQUÍN QUADRA.

Movilización Republicana (MR): forms part of the National Opposition Front with PLI and PCN.

Partido Liberal Independiente (PLI): f. 1946; Pres. EDUARDO RIVAS G.

Partido Salvación Nacional: Leaders PEDRO JOAQUÍN CHAMORRO, RAMIRO SACAZA, LUIS PASOS ARGUELLO, ROBERTO ARGUELLO HURTADO, CARLOS TUNNERMANN B.

Partido Social Cristiano Nicaragüense (PSCN): Apdo. 1715, Managua; f. 1957; Pres. Dr. MANOLO MORALES P.; Sec.-Gen. Dr. ROBERTO FERREY ECHAVERRY.

JUDICIAL SYSTEM

The Supreme Court: Ciudad Jardín, Managua; deals with both civil and criminal cases, acts as a Court of Cassation, appoints Judges of First Instance, and generally supervises the legal administration of the country. It is composed of five magistrates and two alternates, who hold office for six years.

President: Salvador Mayorga Orozco.

There are five **Courts of Appeal,** or of **Second Instance**—at León, Masaya, Granada, Matagalpa and Bluefields. Each consists of a criminal court and a civil court.

Each district or department has its **Judges of First Instance** who deal with civil, criminal and commercial matters. Minor cases come before the **Local Tribunals,** of which there are about 150 in the Republic.

Magistrates of the Supreme Court: Dr. Adán Sequeira Arellano, Dr. Gonzalo Barberena Romero, Dr. Rodolfo Sandino Arguello, Dr. Juan Huembes y Huembes, Dr. Rafael Antonio Díaz, Dr. Alejandro Barberena Pérez.

RELIGION

Most of the people of Nicaragua are Roman Catholics, but all religions are tolerated.

THE ROMAN CATHOLIC CHURCH

Metropolitan See:

Managua: Arzobispado, Apdo. 2008, Managua; Most Rev. Miguel Obando Bravo.

Suffragan Sees:

Estelí: Most Rev. Clemente Carranza López.

Granada: Rt. Rev. Rafael García y García de Castro.

León: Rt. Rev. Manuel Zalazar Espinosa.

Matagalpa: Rt. Rev. Julián Luis Barni.

EPISCOPAL CHURCH

Bishop of Nicaragua and El Salvador: Apdo. 1207, Managua.

THE PRESS

Bluefields Información: León; weekly.

El Centroamericano: Calle 4A, León; f. 1917; morning; liberal; Dir. R. Abaunza Salinas; circ. 4,000.

Diario de Granada: Granada; daily.

Educación: Ministerio de Educación Pública, Managua.

La Gaceta: Avda. Central Sur 604, Managua; f. 1912; morning; official.

La Nación: 5A Calle N.O. 304, Apdo. 2245, Managua; daily; conservative; circ. 3,000.

La Noticia: Costado Norte de la Catedral, Apdo. 441, Managua; f. 1915; morning; independent liberal; Dir. Pedro Rafael Gutiérrez; circ. 9,800.

Novedades: Avda. Roosevelt 503, Apdo. 576; f. 1937; morning; liberal; Dir. Luis H. Pallais D.; circ. 22,000 daily, 29,000 Sundays.

El Observador: Apdo. 1482, Managua; weekly; Catholic.

El Pez y la Serpiente: Apdo. 192, Managua; f. 1964; monthly; cultural.

La Prensa: Calle de Triunfo, Apdo. 192, Managua; f. 1926; evening; independent; Editor Pedro Joaquín Chamorro Cardenal; circ. 45,000 daily, 50,000 Sundays.

La Prensa Gráfica: Calle del Banco Central 75, Varas Abajo 110, Managua; daily; liberal; Dir. Rafael Rojas Jarquín; circ. 20,000.

Revista Comercial de Nicaragua: Editorial Atlántida, Managua; monthly.

Revista del Pensamiento Centroamericano: Apdo. 2108, Managua; cultural and historical journal; quarterly; Editor Xavier Zavala Cuadra; circ. 3,000.

El Universal: León; evening; liberal; Propr. Silvio Arguello Cardenal.

PUBLISHERS

Academia Nicaragüense de la Lengua: Biblioteca Nacional, Managua.

Editorial Alemana: 2A Calle S.O. 108, Managua.

Editorial Chile: 8 Avda., Calle S.E. 604, Managua.

Club del Libro Nicaragüense: Librería Siglo XX, Managua; Dir. Dr. Fernando Centeno Zapata.

Editorial Lacayo: 2A Avda. S.E. 507, Managua; religion.

Editorial Nicaragüense: Calle del Triunfo, Managua; Dir. Mario Cajina Vega.

Editorial Nuevos Horizontes: Calle de Candelaria, Managua; Dir. María Teresa Sánchez.

Editorial San José: Calle Central Este 607, Managua.

Editorial Unión: Avda. Central Norte, Managua; travel.

Librería y Editorial Universidad Nacional de Nicaragua: León; education, history, sciences, law, literature, politics.

RADIO AND TELEVISION

Dirección Nacional de Radio y Televisión: Apdo. 209, Managua; government supervisory body; Dir. Alberto Luna S.

RADIO

Radiodifusora Nacional: Apdo. 1731, Managua; government station; Dir.-Gen. S. Cisneros Leiva.

Radio Ondas de Luz: Apdo. 607, Managua; religious station; Dir. F. M. Doña.

Radio Mundial: 5A Avda. N.O. 703, Managua; commercial; Gen. Man. M. Araña.

There are 50 other radio stations.

In 1970 there were 110,000 receiving sets.

TELEVISION

Televisión de Nicaragua, S.A.: Apdo. 1505, Managua; f. 1956; call sign YNSA-TV; commercial station; Gen. Man. R. O. Caño.

Televicentro de Nicaragua: Las Nubes, El Crucero; Managua; commercial; Dir. O. Sacasa S.

In 1972 there were 60,000 T.V. sets.

FINANCE

(cap.=capital; p.u.=paid up; dep.=deposits; m.=million; amounts in córdobas)

BANKING

Superintendent of Banks: Dr. Julio Linares.

Central Bank

Banco Central de Nicaragua: Apdos. 2252/3, Managua; f. 1961; 237 mems.; bank of issue and Government fiscal agent; cap. 20m., res. 24.9m., dep. 144.4m. (Dec. 1971); Pres. Dr. Roberto Incer Barquero; Gen. Man. Carlos Múñiz Bermúdez.

Other Banks

Banco Nacional de Nicaragua: Apdo. 328, Managua; f. 1912; state-owned bank; cap. 174m., res. 44.4m., dep. 434.6m. (Dec. 1973); Pres. Dr. Karl Hueck.

Banco de Crédito Popular de Nicaragua: Apdo. 3904, Managua; f. 1972 as autonomous state institution to promote savings and make available bank loans to lower income groups; total assets U.S. $4.3m.; Pres. and Gen. Man. Gustavo Gómez Casco; 2 brs.

Banco de América: Avda. Roosevelt y 4A Calle Sur Este, Apdo. 285, Managua; f. 1952; cap. 26.5m., dep. 438.6m. (Dec. 1973); Pres. F. A. Pellas; Exec. Dir. Ernesto Fernández; Gen. Man. J. C. Quadra.

Banco Caley-Dagnall, S.A.: Apdo. 554, Managua; cap. and res. 6,235,517 (Dec. 1972); Pres. K. I. Matheson.

Banco Nicaragüense: Avda. Roosevelt, Apdo. 549, Managua; f. 1953; cap. p.u. 31.7m., dep. 281.9m. (Dec. 1972); Pres. Carlos Reyes M.; Gen. Man. Eduardo Montealegre M.

Banco Obrero y Campesino: Managua; f. 1966; initial cap. 5m.

Banco de la Vivienda de Nicaragua: Kilómetro 4½, Carretera Sur, Apdo. 553, Managua; f. 1966; Pres. Fausto Zelaya Centeno.

Foreign Banks

Bank of America National Trust and Savings Association: Head Office: San Francisco, Calif.; Avda. Roosevelt, Managua; Man. J. Zavala.

Bank of London and South America Ltd.: Head Office: London, England; Plaza de Compras, Colonia Centroamérica, Apdo. 91, Managua; agencies in Managua, Matagalpa, León and Chinandega; Man. P. V. Coggins.

First National City Bank: Head Office: New York, U.S.A.; Kilómetro 4, Carrera Norte, Apdo. 3102, Managua; f. 1967; Man. C. R. Ortiz.

BANKING ASSOCIATION

Asociación de Instituciones Bancarias de Nicaragua (AIBANIC): f. 1966; member banks work to promote the development of Nicaragua and economic integration within the CACM.

INSURANCE

Managua

Compañía de Seguros "La Protectora", S.A.: Apdo. 1147; f. 1954; Pres. P. J. Frawley.

Compañía Nacional de Seguros de Nicaragua: Kilómetro 4, Carretera Sur, Apdo. 129; f. 1940; Gen. Man. Dr. Leonel Arguello.

Compañía Nicaragüense de Seguros, S.A.: Apdo. 3262; f. 1962; Pres. Carlos Bermúdez Vanegas.

TRADE AND INDUSTRY

CHAMBER OF COMMERCE

Cámara Nacional de Comercio de Managua: Apdo. 135, Managua; 294 mems.; Pres. Dennis Gallo; publ. *Boletín* (monthly).

INDUSTRY AND DEVELOPMENT

Cámara de Industrias de Nicaragua: Apdo. 1436, Managua; f. 1958; 383 mems.; Pres. Alfonso Robelo C.; Sec. Dr. Roberto Solórzano Marín; publ. *Socio*.

Comisión Nacional del Algodón: Managua; official government cotton development office.

Corporación Nicaragüense de Inversiones: Managua; f. 1964 to channel foreign and national financial resources towards national industrial investment; cap. p.u. 9.4m.; Gen. Man. Jorge A. Montealegre C.

Instituto Agrario de Nicaragua: La Borgoña, Ticuantepe, Managua; Pres. Dr. Rodolfo Mejía Ubilla.

Instituto Nacional de Comercio Exterior e Interior (INCEI): Salida Autopista Norte, Apdo. 1041, Managua; f. 1960 to regulate prices and trade balances; Gen. Man. Lic. Rodolfo Bojorge.

Instituto de Fomento Nacional (INFONAC): Kilómetro 12, Carretera Norte, Managua; f. 1954 to develop industry and agriculture; cap. $100m.; Dir. Ing. Noel Pallais D.

Instituto Nicaragüense del Café: Reparto Serrano, Managua; f. 1964 as autonomous government agency to implement the International Coffee Agreement; controls quality and exports; advises producers; Pres. Lic. Juan José Martínez; Man. Francisco Chavarría Valenzuela.

CO-OPERATIVES

Cooperativa de Algodoneros: Managua; Pres. Lic. Andrés Largaespada; Sec. Daniel Pallais Sacasa.

Cooperativa de Fomento: Managua; Pres. José Dolores Maltez; Sec. Joaquín Ruiz Aguilar.

Cooperativa Nacional de Agricultura, S.A.: Managua; Pres. Lic. Andrés Largaespada; Sec. Daniel Pallais Sacasa.

Cooperativa Nacional de Cafetaleros: Managua; Pres. Jaime Cuadra Somarriba; Exec. Sec. Ramón Gutiérrez Castrillo; Sec. Fabio Gallo Garrido.

TRADE UNIONS

Confederación Nacional de Trabajadores de Nicaragua—CNT (*National Confederation of Workers of Nicaragua*): Calle 11 de Julio, Managua; f. 1953; mems. 4,843 (est.) from 6 federations with 40 local unions, and 6 non-federated local unions; Sec.-Gen. Domingo Vargas M.

Confederación General del Trabajo—CGT (*General Confederation of Labour*): Managua; f. 1949; mems. 4,050 (est.) from 6 federations and 8 non-federated unions; Sec.-Gen. Andrés Ruiz Escorcia.

Federación de Transportadores Unidos Nicaragüense—FTUN (*United Transport Workers' Federation of Nicaragua*): Apdo. 945, Managua; f. 1952; mems. 2,880 (est.) from 21 affiliated associations; Pres. Carlos Navarrete.

Federación Sindical de Maestros de Nicaragua—FSMN (*Nicaraguan Teachers' Trade Union Federation*): Casa del Maestro, Apdo. 413, Managua; f. 1947; mems. 2,000 (est.) from 20 affiliated associations; Pres. Nicolás Morales Amador.

Movimiento Sindical Autónomo de Nicaragua (MOSAN) (*Autonomous Trade Union Movement*): Managua; f. 1962; mems. 2,500 (est.) from 9 affiliated associations; Sec.-Gen. Edgardo Herrera.

TRANSPORT AND TOURISM

TRANSPORT

RAILWAYS

Ferrocarril del Pacífico de Nicaragua: Antigua Escuela de Artes, Managua; f. 1881; government-owned; main line from Managua to the Pacific port of Corinto via León and Chinandega, and from Managua to Granada on Lake Nicaragua; 317 km. open (1.067m. guage); Dir.-Gen. A. Somoza D.; Admin. Capt. Noel González Gutiérrez.

ROADS

In 1971 there were some 13,147 km. of roads and tracks. Of these 1,335 km. were paved and 5,040 km. were classed as all-weather. The rest can be used only in the summer. The Pan American Highway runs for 485 km. in Nicaragua and links Managua with the Honduran and Costa Rican frontiers and the Atlantic and Pacific Highways connecting Managua with the coastal regions.

SHIPPING

Corinto, Puerto Somoza and San Juan del Sur, on the Pacific, and Puerto Cabezas and El Bluff, on the Atlantic, are the principal ports. Corinto deals with about 60 per cent of trade.

Marina Mercante Nicaragüense (Mamenic): Managua; regular services between Central America, New York, New Orleans and Europe.

Regular steamship services are provided by Grace, Holland-America, Mamenic, Pacific, Royal Mail, Royal Netherlands, Standard Fruit and United Fruit and the following lines also call at Nicaraguan ports: Azta, Cia. de Navegación Chilena, Gran Colombiana, Hamburg America, Mexicana, Mitsui O.S.K., P.S.N.C., and State Marine Lines.

CIVIL AVIATION

DOMESTIC AIRLINE

Líneas Aéreas de Nicaragua S.A. (LANICA): Apdo. 753, Managua; f. 1945; international services Managua—San Salvador—Mexico, Managua—San Pedro Sula—Miami; internal services linking Managua with all main towns; Pres. Eugene S. Dudkiewicz; Gen. Man. Capt. Miguel Murciano, Jr.; fleet: 2 CV-880, 4 DC-6, 3 C-46.

Nicaragua is also served by Compañía Panameña, Pan American, SAHSA (Honduras) and TACA (El Salvador).

TOURISM

Dirección Nacional de Turismo: Apdo. 122, Managua; Dir. Lic. Alfredo Bequillard, Jr.

Asociación Nicaragüense de Agencias de Viajes: Apdo. 765, Managua; Pres. Claudio Fonseca S.

THEATRICAL COMPANY

Comedia Nacional de Nicaragua: Managua; f. 1965; Dir. César Sobrevallos.

ATOMIC ENERGY

Universidad Nacional Autónoma de Nicaragua: León; atomic research in science and technology, civil engineering, medicine and pharmacy.

Universidad Centro-Americana: Apdo. 69, Managua; atomic research in engineering.

UNIVERSITIES

Universidad Nacional Autónoma de Nicaragua: León; 391 teachers, 8,505 students.

Universidad Centro-Americana (Sección de Nicaragua): Apdo. 69, Managua; 135 teachers, 2,125 students.

NIGER

INTRODUCTORY SURVEY

Location, Climate, Language, Religion, Flag, Capital

The Republic of Niger is a landlocked state in West Africa, stretching from Algeria and the Tropic of Cancer in the north to Nigeria in the south. Mali and Upper Volta lie to the west and Chad to the east. The climate is hot and dry with an average temperature of 28°C (84°F). The official language is French but numerous indigenous languages are used, including Hausa, spoken by half the population, Tuareg, Djerma and Fulani. About 85 per cent of the population are Muslims. Most of the remainder follow animist beliefs and there is a small Christian minority. The national flag (proportions 8 by 7) is a horizontal tricolour of orange, white and green, the central white stripe being charged with an orange disc. The capital is Niamey.

Recent History

Formerly a part of French West Africa, Niger was granted independence in 1960. Hamani Diori was elected President, and re-elected in 1965 and 1970, when he received the support of 98 per cent of the electorate. His one-party government, having repressed an attempted rebellion in 1963–64, seemed one of the most secure in Africa, and President Diori himself gained considerable international prestige as a spokesman for francophone Africa. He maintained very close links with France, and received aid from Nigeria and Libya. The discovery of uranium in Niger, and its exploitation by France, provided an opportunity for the economic development of the country, previously limited to simple agriculture and nomadic stock-raising.

In recent years the Sahel drought has affected Niger very severely, and the administration of famine relief and the refugee camps was widely considered to be both corrupt and inefficient. The grievances of civil servants and students, denied any legal form of expression by the one-party system, resulted in a strike in schools and colleges, lasting from October 1973 to January 1974, and a number of violent demonstrations. In April 1974, the army staged a brief and almost bloodless *coup*. Diori was arrested, and Lieut.-Col. Seyni Kountché, the Chief of Staff of the Armed Forces, became President. The new military Government announced that its main objectives were the elimination of corruption and greater efficiency in dealing with the famine.

Government

Since the military *coup* of April 1974, Niger has been ruled by a Supreme Military Council of army officers. Twelve officers have been appointed as ministers to direct the executive organs of the Government.

Defence

Niger's armed forces are on a very small scale. There is an army of 2,000 men, a gendarmerie of 500 and a republican guard of 120. The army includes a company of parachutists and a tank squadron. Arms and equipment come mainly from France. The air force consists of 100 men and a few transport planes.

Economic Affairs

The economy is agricultural and 90 per cent of the people are dependent on agriculture and the raising of livestock. Livestock is at present the main source of wealth. The herds of cattle, sheep and goats are large but often of poor quality. Much of the land is desert. The chief crops are millet, sorghum, cassava and groundnuts. A ten-year development plan for 1973–82 emphasizes the importance of rural development. Priority will be given to growing millet, both for food and for export after processing. Groundnut production is increasing and contributes to economic growth. Persistent drought is a major problem.

Large uranium deposits at Arlit, in the north-west, were discovered in 1966 by the French Atomic Energy Commissariat, which has been granted mining rights for 75 years. Production from the first mine began in 1971. Further deposits have been discovered, to be exploited at a later date. Cassiterite and gold are mined, and other minerals have been found. Several permits have been granted for oil exploration. Industry is on a small scale and manufacturing accounted for only 6.4 per cent of Gross Domestic Product in 1969. The industrial sector is to be expanded under the current ten-year plan, mainly to replace imports.

Transport and Communications

There are no railways. Two highways cross the country from east to west and from north to south giving access to neighbouring countries. French and Czech experts have drawn up a plan for financing the Trans-Saharan Highway which will link Algiers with Gao in Mali and Tahoua in Niger. Roads and tracks total about 12,500 km. With a Canadian government loan, the first stage (459 km.) of the "Unity Highway", which will link Gouré in the west with N'Guigma on Lake Chad, was opened in 1973. The River Niger is navigable for 300 km. In January 1973 a river route between Gaya, in the south of Niger, and Port Harcourt was opened, giving access to the sea. The internal airways system is operated by Air Niger. The main international airport is at Niamey.

Social Welfare

There are 22 departmental medical centres, 92 dispensaries and a number of mobile clinics.

Education

Education is free but there are insufficient schools; in 1970 only 14 per cent of children of school age received primary education, and 0.9 per cent received secondary education. A university is planned, centred on the Centre d'Enseignement Supérieur at Niamey, which opened in 1971. Scholarships are provided for higher education in France and Senegal.

Tourism

There is an abundance of wild life and hunting is the chief tourist attraction. Lake Chad also provides game fishing.

Visas for visits to Niger are not required by subjects of the following countries: Andorra, Central African Republic, Chad, Congo (Brazzaville), Dahomey, France, Gabon, Guinea, Ivory Coast, Mali, Mauritania, Monaco, Senegal, Togo, Upper Volta.

Sport

There is very little organised sport but football is popular.

Public Holidays

1974: August 3rd (Independence Day), October 18th (Id ul Fitr), December 18th (Republic Day), December 26th (Id ul Adha).

1975: January 1st (New Year's Day), January 14th (Muslim New Year), March 26th (Mouloud—Birth of the Prophet).

(*Note:* the Christian community in Niger also observes Easter, Whitsun, Ascension Day, Assumption, All Saints' Day and Christmas.)

Weights and Measures

The metric system is in force.

Currency and Exchange Rates

100 centimes=1 franc de la Communauté financière africaine (CFA).

Exchange rates (April 1974):

1 franc CFA=2 French centimes;
£1 sterling=579.75 francs CFA;
U.S. $1=245.625 francs CFA.

STATISTICAL SURVEY

AREA AND POPULATION

AREA sq. km.	ESTIMATED POPULATION (July 1st, 1972)					
	Total	Hausa	Djerma-Songhai	Fulani (Peulh)	Tuareg, etc.	Beriberi-Manga
1,267,000*	4,239,000†	2,276,343	1,000,404	449,334	127,170	385,749

* 489,190 sq. miles.   † Revised total 4,243,000. Mid-1973 estimate: 4,356,000.

CHIEF TOWNS
(1972 est.)

Niamey (capital)	.	102,000	Maradi . . .	37,079
Zinder . .		39,427	Tahoua . .	30,577

AGRICULTURE
PRINCIPAL CROPS
('000 metric tons)

	1969	1970	1971
Maize	2	2	2*
Millet	1,095	901	800
Sorghum	289	337	300
Rice	39	37	40
Sugar Cane (crop year ending in year stated)	25	25	25*
Sweet Potatoes and Yams . . .	9	10*	n.a.
Cassava (Manioc) . . .	199	200*	191
Onions	27	30*	32
Cow Peas	160	150*	150*
Dates	5*	5*	5*
Groundnuts (unshelled) . . .	207	205	256
Cottonseed	8	6	7*
Cotton Lint	4	3	4*

* FAO estimates.

1972: Groundnuts 270,000 metric tons.

Source: mainly FAO, *Production Yearbook 1971.*

LIVESTOCK
('000—FAO estimates)

	1969–70	1970–71	1971–72
Horses . . .	180	180	200
Donkeys . . .	360	370	370
Cattle . . .	4,300	4,400	4,200
Pigs . . .	23	26	n.a.
Sheep . . .	2,750	2,800	2,850
Goats . . .	6,000	6,200	6,300
Camels . . .	400	410	345
Poultry . . .	6,750	7,000	n.a.

Source: FAO, Production Yearbook 1971.

By the end of 1973 pastureland had been halved because of the severe drought and livestock numbers reduced by up to 80 per cent.

LIVESTOCK PRODUCTS
(FAO estimates)

	1969	1970	1971
Hides and Skins ('000) .			
Cattle . . .	180	233	n.a.
Sheep . . .	408	233	n.a.
Goat . . .	1,046	1,316	n.a.
Milk ('000 metric tons) .			
Cow . . .	105	108	110
Sheep . . .	14	14	15
Goat . . .	118	119	120
Hen Eggs (metric tons) .	4,400	4,500	4,500

Source: FAO, Production Yearbook 1971.

Fishing: About 12,000 metric tons of fish are caught annually in the River Niger and Lake Chad.

MINING

	Unit	1969	1970	1971	1972
Cassiterite	metric tons	124	106	125	136
of which: Tin . . .	,, ,,	35	67	68	n.a.
Gypsum . . .	,, ,,	1,300	n.a.	n.a.	n.a.
Uranium* . . .	,, ,,	—	54	508	867†
Gold	kilogrammes	5	7.4	n.a.	n.a.

* Uranium oxide content of ores.   † Smelter production of metal.

INDUSTRY

	1970	1971	1972
Beer and Soft Drinks ('000 hl.) . . .	n.a.	47	n.a.
Electricity (million kWh.) .	39	42	49

FINANCE

100 centimes=1 franc de la Communauté financière africaine (CFA).
Coins: 1, 2, 5, 10, 25, 50 and 100 francs CFA.
Notes: 100, 500, 1,000 and 5,000 francs CFA.
Exchange rates (April 1974): 1 franc CFA=2 French centimes;
£1 sterling=579.75 francs CFA; U.S. $1=245.625 francs CFA.
1,000 francs CFA=£1.725=$4.071.

Budget 1972: balanced at 11,886 million francs CFA.

Budget 1973: balanced at 15,668.6 million francs CFA.

GROSS DOMESTIC PRODUCT
(million francs CFA at current prices)

ECONOMIC ACTIVITY	1967	1968	1969	1970
Agriculture, Hunting, Forestry and Fishing .	53,725	50,959	50,101	59,900
Mining and Quarrying	34	119	105	
Manufacturing	6,169	6,489	6,282	11,800
Electricity, Gas and Water Supply .	405	436	604	
Construction	2,175	2,364	3,144	
Trade, Restaurants and Hotels . .	13,788	13,301	14,421	
Transport, Storage and Communications .	2,768	2,639	3,131	29,200*
Other Producers and Services . .	18,525	19,211	20,020	
TOTAL (in purchasers' values) .	97,592	95,518	97,808	100,900

* Including 5,900 million francs CFA for public administration and defence.

Sources: United Nations, *Yearbook of National Accounts Statistics*; UN Economic Commission for Africa, *Statistical Yearbook*.

Development Plans: The three-year plan (1970–73) is a part of the overall ten-year plan (1965–74), and is based on an investment of 44,731m. francs CFA.

The principal investors are the IBRD, providing 29.2 per cent, the European Development Fund, providing 24 per cent, and the Fonds d'Aide et Coopération, providing 23.3 per cent. The greatest expenditure will be on the improvement of industrial production, and the expansion of communications.

The policies of the new ten-year plan (1973–1982) have been set out but without details of finance and investment.

EXTERNAL TRADE
(million francs CFA)

The figures below are taken from the records of the Customs Posts at the frontiers. These records are not fully representative of external trade for much smuggling occurs, particularly between Niger and Nigeria.

	1966	1967	1968	1969	1970	1971	1972
Imports .	11,115	11,352	10,237	12,570	16,213	14,721	16,500
Exports .	8,574	8,226	7,125	6,250	8,795	10,652	13,700

PRINCIPAL COMMODITIES

IMPORTS	1970	1971	1972	EXPORTS	1970	1971	1972
Cotton Fabrics . . .	3,077	2,416	2,570	Live Cattle . . .	1,232	1,703	2,209
Road Vehicles . . .	1,208	2,181	1,896	Live Sheep and Goats .	157	270	302
Petroleum Products . .	624	1,120	1,467	Leather and Hides . .	232	397	435
Machinery . . .	1,434	1,377	1,408	Raw Cotton . . .	160	594	194
Sugar and Confectionery .	515	448	836	Onions . . .	n.a.	192	181
Cereals . . .	445	125	319	Groundnuts, Shelled .	4,934	3,413	
Pharmaceuticals . .	347	n.a.	301	Groundnut Oil . .	566	967	}6,478
Tobacco . . .	222	228	247	Groundnuts, Cake .	193	265	
Electrical Equipment .	797	624	232	Uranium . . .	n.a.	1,737	2,369
Beverages . . .	175	141	186				
Iron, Cast Iron, Steel .	464	427	913				
Metal Products. . .	1,194	788	n.a.				
TOTAL (incl. others) .	16,213	14,721	16,500	TOTAL (incl. others) .	8,795	10,652	13,700

Sources: Service de la Statistique et de la Mécanographie, Niamey; Institut National de la Statistique et des Etudes Economiques, Paris, *Données Statistiques Africaines et Malgaches*; *Africa Research Bulletin.*

PRINCIPAL COUNTRIES

IMPORTS	1970	1971	1972	EXPORTS	1970	1971	1972
China, People's Republic .	478	391	293	Dahomey. . . .	n.a.	478	145
France . . .	7,428	6,466	7,721	France . . .	4,110	5,509	5,260
Germany, Federal Republic	1,259	1,154	1,325	Germany, Federal Republic	47	0.5	924
Italy . . .	232	454	402	Ghana . . .	233	120	n.a.
Ivory Coast . .	836	807	1,259	Italy . . .	1,312	363	710
Netherlands . .	784	797	739	Ivory Coast . .	n.a.	264	300
Nigeria . . .	234	348	463	Nigeria . . .	1,738	2,726	3,772
Senegal . . .	870	295	312	United Kingdom . .	39	199	n.a.
United Kingdom . .	365	565	423				
U.S.A. . . .	862	1,172	810				
Venezuela . . .	—	341	420				

TRANSPORT
ROADS
VEHICLES IN USE

	1969	1970	1971
Cars	4,742	5,427	6,118
Buses and Coaches . . .	104	140	167
Goods Vehicles . . .	1,811	1,965	2,073
Tractors	351	420	457
Motor Cycles and Scooters . .	544	582	n.a.

CIVIL AVIATION

	1969	1970	1971
Aircraft Arrivals and Departures . . .	2,955	2,930	3,084
Passenger Arrivals and Departures . .	36,849	37,554	39,927
Freight Loaded (metric tons) . .	1,620	1,709	1,679
Freight Unloaded (metric tons) . .	2,394	2,238	2,583
Mail Handled (metric tons) . . .	168	165	174

Source: Institut Nationale de la Statistique et des Etudes Economiques, Paris, *Données Statistiques.*

EDUCATION
(1970–71)

	Schools	Teachers	Pupils
Primary	699	2,275	88,594
Secondary	23	187	4,946
Technical	1	80	328
Teacher Training (1969–70) .	5	37	548

Source: UNESCO *Statistical Yearbook 1972.*

In addition 222 students studied abroad on government grants for higher and technical education.

Source (unless otherwise stated): Service de la Statistique et de la Mécanographie, Commissariat Général au Développement, Présidence, Niamey, Niger.

THE CONSTITUTION

The 1960 Constitution was suspended following the military *coup* of April 1974. Niger is ruled by a Supreme Military Council of army officers, who have taken over the direction of the executive.

THE GOVERNMENT

HEAD OF STATE

President: Lt.-Col. Seyni Kountché (*took power April 15th,* 1974).

PROVISIONAL GOVERNMENT

(*Appointed April 22nd,* 1974; *re-formed June 8th,* 1974.)

President of the Supreme Military Council, Minister of the Interior and of National Defence: Lieut.-Col. Seyni Kountché.

Minister of National Education, Youth and Sports: Col. Dupuis Henry Yacouba.

Minister of Development, Mines and Water Resources: Commandant Sani Souna Sido.

Minister of the Civil Service and Labour: Commandant Idrissa Arouna.

Minister of Justice: Commandant Sory Mamadou Diallo.

Minister of Finance: Intendant Moussa Tondi.

Minister of Foreign Affairs and Co-operation: Capt. Moumouni Djermakoye Adamou.

Minister of the Rural Economy and Aid to the Population: Capt. Ali Seybou.

Minister of Public Health and Social Affairs: Capt. Moussa Sala.

Minister of Public Works, Transport and Town Planning: Capt. Bayere Moussa.

Minister of Economic Affairs, Trade and Industry: Capt. Boulama Manga.

Minister of Posts and Telecommunication and of Information: Lieut. Gabriel Cyrille.

Secretary of State for the Interior: Alou Harouna.

Secretary of State for the Rural Economy: Annou Mahaman.

Secretary of State for Development: Mounkeila Arouna.

Secretary of State for Co-operation: Alfidja Abder-rahmane.

DIPLOMATIC REPRESENTATION

EMBASSIES ACCREDITED TO NIGER

(In Niamey unless otherwise stated)

Algeria: *Ambassador:* Abderrahmane Nekli.

Belgium: Abidjan, Ivory Coast.

Canada: Abidjan, Ivory Coast.

China (Taiwan): B.P. 732, Niamey; *Ambassador:* Lee Nan-hsing.

Egypt: El Nasr Building; *Chargé d'Affaires:* Gamal Abal-Oyun.

Ethiopia: Lagos, Nigeria.

France: B.P. 240; *Ambassador:* Paul Gaschignard.

Gabon: Abidjan, Ivory Coast.

Germany, Federal Republic: B.P. 629, Niamey; *Ambassador:* Günter Joetze.

Ghana: Abidjan, Ivory Coast.

Italy: Abidjan, Ivory Coast.

Japan: Abidjan, Ivory Coast.

Korea, Republic: Abidjan, Ivory Coast.

Lebanon: Abidjan, Ivory Coast.

Libya: B.P. 633; *Permanent Chargé d'Affaires:* Mohamed A. Shennib.

Mauritania: Tripoli, Libya.

Morocco: Abidjan, Ivory Coast.
Netherlands: Abidjan, Ivory Coast.
Nigeria: B.P. 617, Niamey; *Ambassador:* Sani Kontagora.
Norway: Abidjan, Ivory Coast.
Pakistan: Lagos, Nigeria.
Peru: Abidjan, Ivory Coast.
Poland: Lagos, Nigeria.
Romania: Lagos, Nigeria.
Saudi Arabia: Bamako, Mali.
Senegal: Bamako, Mali.
Sierra Leone: Lagos, Nigeria.
Spain: Abidjan, Ivory Coast.
Sudan: Lagos, Nigeria.

Sweden: Lagos, Nigeria.
Switzerland: Abidjan, Ivory Coast.
Tunisia: Abidjan, Ivory Coast.
Turkey: Lagos, Nigeria.
U.S.S.R.: El Nasr Building; *Ambassador:* Gennadiy D. Sokolov.
United Kingdom: Abidjan, Ivory Coast.
U.S.A.: B.P. 201; *Ambassador:* Roswell D. McClelland.
Vatican: Dakar, Senegal (Apostolic Nunciature).
Viet-Nam, Republic: Abidjan, Ivory Coast.
Yugoslavia: Lagos, Nigeria.
Zaire: Abidjan, Ivory Coast.

Niger also has diplomatic relations with Bahrain, Dahomey, Guinea, Hungary, the Ivory Coast, the Democratic People's Republic of Korea, Kuwait, Liberia and Luxembourg.

NATIONAL ASSEMBLY

The National Assembly was dissolved following the military *coup* of April 15th, 1974.

POLITICAL PARTIES

The military Government installed by the *coup* of April 1974 ordered the suppression of all political organizations. The *Parti progressiste nigérien* was previously the only legal party.

JUDICIAL SYSTEM

Supreme Court: suspended following the *coup* of April 1974.
Court of Appeal: Niamey: Pres. Viaud-Murat.
Tribunaux de premiere instance (*District Magistrate's Courts*): at Niamey, Maradi and Zinder; with sections at Tahoua, Birni-N'Konni, Agadez, Diffa and Dosso.
Justices of Peace: at Tillabéri, Ouallam, Dosso, Madaoua, Tessaoua, Gouré, N'Guigmi, Bilma and Birni-N'Gaoure.
Labour Courts: are set up at Niamey, Zinder, Maradi, Tahoua, Birni-N'Konni, Agadez, Dosso and Diffa.
Court of State Security: Martial court for criminal offences.

RELIGION

It is estimated that 85 per cent of the population are Muslims, 14.5 per cent Animists and 0.5 per cent Christians. The most influential Muslim groups are the Tijaniyya, the Senoussi and the Hamallists.

Roman Catholic Missions: Diocese of Niamey, B.P. 208, Niamey; f. 1961; 19 schools, 25 priests, 12,300 Catholics; Bishop of Niamey Mgr. Hippolyte Berlier.

Protestant Missions: 13 mission centres are maintained, with a personnel of 90.

PRESS AND RADIO

Le Niger: B.P. 368, Niamey; f. 1961; edited by the Service de l'Information; weekly; circ. 800.

Le Sahel: B.P. 368, Niamey; f. 1960; mimeographed daily news bulletin of the Service de l'Information; circ. 1,300; Dir. Sidikou Garba.

Journal Officiel de la République du Niger: B.P. 211, Niamey; monthly.

Office de Radiodiffusion-Télévision du Niger (ORTN): Niamey, B.P. 361; Government station; programmes in French, Hausa, Zerma, Tamachek, Kanuri, Fulfuldé, English (twice a week) and Arabic; Dir.-Gen. Sani Issaka.

In 1972 there were 100,000 radio sets.

FINANCE

(amounts in francs CFA)

BANKS
Central Bank

Banque Centrale des Etats de l'Afrique de l'Ouest: 29, rue du Colisée, 75008 Paris, France; B.P. 487, Rond-Point de la Poste, Niamey; bank of issue and central bank for 7 West African states including Niger; f. 1955; cap. and res. 3,923m.; br. at Zinder; Man. in Niamey Charles Godefroy.

Commercial Banks

Banque de Développement de la République du Niger: B.P. 227, Niamey; f. 1962; cap. 450m.; res. 923m. (Sept. 1971); 55 per cent state-owned; Pres. and Man. Dir. Boubou Hama; brs. at Maradi and Zinder.

Caisse Centrale de Coopération Economique: B.P. 212, Niamey; Man. Hervé Bizien.

Crédit du Niger: B.P. 213, Niamey; f. 1958; cap. 220m. of which 50 per cent state-owned; Pres. Dir.-Gen. Boubou Hama; Dir. Oumarou Moussa.

Union Nigérienne de Crédit et de Co-opération: B.P. 296, Niamey; f. 1962; cap. 245m.; Government-owned; Pres. Boubou Hama; Dir. Ahmed Mouddour.

Caisse Nationale de Crédit Agricole (CNCA): B.P. 295, Niamey; f. 1967; cap. 67m.; Pres. Boubou Hama; Dir. Oumarou Moussa.

Banque Internationale pour l'Afrique Occidentale: 9 ave. de Messine, 75360 Paris, France; B.P. 628, Niamey; brs. in Arlit, Zinder and Maradi.

United Bank for Africa Ltd. (USA): Niamey.

INSURANCE

Several French insurance companies are represented in Niger.

TRADE AND INDUSTRY

CHAMBERS OF COMMERCE

Chambre de Commerce, d'Agriculture et d'Industrie du Niger: B.P. 209, Niamey; f. 1954; 40 elected mems., 20 official mems.; Pres. J. NIGNON; Sec.-Gen. PIERRE DE VENEL; publ. *Weekly Bulletin*.

Chambre de Commerce et d'Agriculture de Maradi: B.P. 79, Maradi.

Chambre de Commerce et d'Agriculture de Zinder: B.P. 83, Zinder.

EMPLOYERS' ORGANIZATIONS

Syndicat des Transportateurs et Routiers du Niger: Niamey.

Syndicat des Commerçants Importateurs et Exportateurs du Niger: Niamey, B.P. 137; Pres. M. LAMBERT; Sec. JEAN MERIC.

Syndicat Patronal des Entreprises et Industries du Niger: Niamey, B.P. 95; Pres. EL HADJ CISSÉ BOUBAKAR; Sec. MICHEL GORGEARD.

Syndicat des Ingénieurs, Cadres, Agents de Maîtrise, Techniciens et Assimilés du Niger: Niamey.

TRADE UNIONS

Union Nationale des Travailleurs du Niger—U.N.T.N.: Niamey; f. 1960; divided into three sections for Maradi, Niamey and Zinder; affiliated to the African Trade Union Confederation; 31 affiliates; 15,000 mems.; Sec.-Gen. RENÉ DELANNE.

DEVELOPMENT

Caisse de Stabilisation des Prix des Produits du Niger (CSPPN): B.P. 480, Niamey; price control office for Niger goods.

Centre Technique Forestier Tropical (CTFT): P.O.B. 225, Niamey; Dir. J.-C. DELWAULLE IGREF.

Compagnie Française pour le Développement des Fibres Textiles: B.P. 717, Niamey.

Fonds National d'investissement (FNI): Niamey; f. 1969 by the Government; finances development projects with revenues from tax on uranium and French aid.

Fonds National pour le Développement Economique et Social: Niamey.

Ministère du Développement et de la Coopération: Niamey; f. 1972.

TRADE ORGANIZATION

Société Nationale de Commerce et de Production du Niger (COPRO-Niger): B.P. 615, Niamey; f. 1962; 47 per cent state-owned; export marketing; Pres. Dir.-Gen. JACQUES NIGNON.

TRANSPORT

ROADS

There are 554 km. of bitumenized roads, 2,469 km. of earth roads, and a total road and track network of 7,468 km.

Société Nationale des Transports Nigériens: B.P. 135, Niamey; f. 1961; 51 per cent state-owned; national road hauliers; Dir. JACQUES COLOMBANI.

RAILWAYS

Organisation Commune Dahomey-Niger des Chemins de Fer et du Transport (OCDN): Niamey; B.P. 16, Cotonou, Dahomey; f. 1959; manages the Benin-Niger railway in which Niger has a share.

A railway is proposed between Niamey and Tillabéri.

CIVIL AVIATION

The international airports are at Niamey, Maradi and Zinder, the former being most important, and there are 99 other aerodromes and airstrips 20 of which are public.

Air Afrique: Niger Delegation, B.P.84, Imm. Petrocokino, Niamey; Niger has a 6 per cent share in Air Afrique; *see* under Ivory Coast.

Air Niger: Immeuble Sempastous, B.P. 205, Niamey; services from Niamey to Tahoua, Maradi Zinder, Arlit and Agadez; fleet of one DC-4, two DC-3; Dir.-Gen. P. GABRIELLI.

Niamey is also served by the following airlines: Air Algérie, Air Mali, Nigerian Airways, Sabena and UTA.

TOURISM

Office du Tourisme du Niger: B.P. 612, Niamey; Dir. ISSOUFOU SEYFOU.

NIGERIA

INTRODUCTORY SURVEY

Location, Climate, Language, Religion, Flag, Capital

The Federal Republic of Nigeria is a West African coastal state within the Gulf of Guinea, with Niger to the north and flanked by Dahomey and Cameroon. The climate is tropical in the south with an average temperature of 90°F (32°C) and high humidity. It is drier and semi-tropical in the north. Rainfall reaches more than 150 inches in parts of the south-east. The official language is English. Hausa, Ibo and Yoruba are spoken in the north, east and west respectively. Islam is the main religion in Northern and part of Western Nigeria. Some of the population follow animist beliefs and about a quarter are Christians. The national flag (proportions 2 by 1) has vertical bands of green, white and green. The capital is Lagos.

Recent History

The Nigerian people, previously organized in the Yoruba, Hausa, Bornu, Fulani, Ibo and other states, obtained their independence from Britain on October 1st, 1960, as a federation of four regions. In 1961 the northern part of the British-administered Trust Territory of Cameroon was incorporated into the Northern Region. In October 1963 Nigeria became a Republic within the Commonwealth. In January 1966 civil Government was brought to an end by the overthrow and death of two Regional Premiers and of the Federal Prime Minister, Alhaji Sir Abubakar Tafawa Balewa. A Supreme Military Council was set up by the Army Commander, Maj.-Gen. Johnson Aguiyi-Ironsi, who proposed to abolish the federal structure and establish a unitary state. Inter-communal violence, in which many Ibos living outside their homeland in the Eastern Region were killed or forced to leave, resulted in dislocation of the country and the breakdown of central authority. Gen. Aguiyi-Ironsi was killed in July 1966 and his successor, Lt.-Col. (later Gen.) Yakubu Gowon, revived the Federation.

Early in 1967 relations between the Federal Government and the Military Governor of the Eastern Region, Lt.-Col. Chukwuemeka Odumegwu-Ojukwu, rapidly grew worse as the various military and civilian leaders failed to agree on proposals for a new constitution. On May 28th Col. Gowon proclaimed a state of emergency and promulgated a decree for the creation of 12 states to replace the four Regions. Two days later, on May 30th, Col. Ojukwu announced the secession of the Eastern Region and its independence as the Republic of Biafra. War between the Federal Government and Biafra broke out on July 7th, 1967, and continued until January 1970. After Ojukwu's departure to the Ivory Coast, Biafra surrendered. Meanwhile, the Federal Government's 12-state structure came into effect on April 1st, 1968.

Since the end of the war, Gen. Gowon's policy of re-conciliation with the former Eastern Region has been a remarkable success, particularly in the reconstruction of devastated areas and the return of many Ibos to their pre-war employment.

In 1970 Gen. Gowon gave 1976 as the target date for a return to civilian rule. A national census, the first since the controversial enumeration of 1963, took place in November 1973.

In September 1973 Gen. Gowon announced that political activities would be allowed to resume at the end of 1974. The army has been re-organized and the Federal Government is attempting to unify the trade union movement. Nigeria's present internal peace and stability has enabled it to play a dominant role in African affairs, both at the Organization of African Unity (OAU), where Gen. Gowon is Chairman of the Assembly of Heads of State for 1973–74. and at the UN, where Nigerian spokesmen have strongly criticized the white minority régimes in southern Africa. Nigeria has strengthened its ties with both Western and Communist countries while maintaining its policy of non-alignment, and playing a leading role in the negotiations between the EEC and African and Caribbean States.

Government

The constitutional decree of March 1967 vests executive and legislative power in the Supreme Military Council, composed of the Military Governors of the 12 states, the heads of services and the Inspector-General of Police under the chairmanship of the Commander-in-Chief, General Gowon. The Military Governors exercise executive and legislative powers in their own states.

Defence

Estimates put the current strength of the army at 150,000 men. Naval strength is 3,000 and the air force has 4,000 men. There is a civil police force of 40,000. There is a national service scheme for graduates. A re-organization programme for the army began in February 1973. At present reserves total over 100,000 and Nigeria has the largest defence force in Africa.

Economic Affairs

Agriculture used to be the mainstay of the economy and in 1960 provided 80 per cent of total export earnings. By 1972, because of the vast growth in petroleum exports, agriculture's share had dropped to 17 per cent though it still employs over two-thirds of the working population. The main commercial crops are cocoa, palm oil and kernels, groundnuts, cotton and rubber. There is extensive exploitation of forests for various timbers. Nigeria's fish resources are to be developed. Fishing provides a living for an estimated 1.5 million people. There are also plans to expand and modernize the livestock industry. Minerals include tin, columbite (of which Nigeria supplies 95 per cent of the world's industrial requirements), coal, iron ore and crude petroleum, all of which are processed in Nigeria.

The huge rise in the price of oil after the 1973 Middle East War has given an extra impetus to the Nigerian economy. As a member of OPEC and the world's eighth largest producer of oil (1974), the benefits for Nigeria from the oil boom have been enormous. The foreign exchange position has been strengthened, reserves have increased, dependence on foreign aid has been reduced and large numbers of jobs created. In 1973 crude petroleum exports provided 83 per cent of the total value of exports, and

Nigeria's trade balance, which has consistently remained in surplus since 1965 despite the civil war, more than doubled from 1972 to 1973. Output is increasing; already known reserves could support an estimated 25 years of exploitation, and new fields are regularly being discovered, though the cost of prospecting is high. It is estimated that by late 1975 production may double to between three and four million barrels per day. A natural gas plant, to be operable by 1976, is planned at Port Harcourt. In 1974 negotiations led to a Nigerian Government majority shareholding in Shell/BP, Agip, Mobil and Texaco.

Under the 1972 Nigerian Enterprises Promotion Decree, "indigenization" has been energetically pursued, alien participation in many small businesses has been barred, and Nigerian shareholding in numerous larger firms made compulsory.

Industry is diversified, and there has been rapid expansion of manufacturing industries. Brewing, aluminium products, textiles, cigarettes and cement are important. The First National Development Plan (1962–68) was succeeded by the National Reconstruction and Development Plan (1970–74). The main priorities are to deal with the problems of economic management and unemployment. In August 1973 the Government issued guidelines for the 1975–80 Development Plan which will lay emphasis on development of agriculture and increased Federal aid for education and health. The Government is seeking a trade agreement with the European Economic Community and is actively urging the formation of a West African Economic Community.

Transport and Communications

There are 2,190 miles of railways and over 55,000 miles of roads. The Nigerian Government has embarked on a major road construction programme to which it has allocated N368 million for the 1970–74 development plan.

The Niger and other rivers are navigable for over 4,000 miles. The chief ports are Lagos and Port Harcourt. An internal air network links the principal towns, and international services are provided by Nigerian Airways and foreign lines. Eighteen airports in Nigeria are to be redeveloped by the Government and Nigerian Airways, fleet is to be expanded. Each of the state capitals is to have a modern airport.

Social Welfare

The National Provident Fund provides against sickness, retirement and old age. A scheme of retirement pensions and other benefits covers Government employees. During 1974 the Federal Government is to introduce legislation to give protection to the welfare of workers as a supplement to the Factories Act, and a National Emergency Relief Agency to provide help in any part of Nigeria is to be established.

Education

In January 1974 the Government announced that free and compulsory primary education would be introduced in 1975. Education in the States is primarily the responsibility of the State Governments though in 1972 the Federal Government extended its control over the universities of Ife, Nigeria, Benin and Ahmadu Bello. The Federal Government is responsible for education in Lagos and the Universities of Ibadan and Lagos. In 1970, there were 101,366 teachers and 3,396,000 pupils. There are six universities. A seventh university is planned at Port Harcourt and it is estimated that N50 million will have been spent on universities out of the 1970–74 Development Plan. A vast new programme to improve the literacy rate, establish new schools and train more teachers has been launched. Its estimated cost is N2,000 million over some five years from 1975.

Tourism

Tourism is being developed and the Nigeria Tourist Association was set up in 1963, but it is hampered by lack of funds at present. It has future potential and the modernization of hotels has been given priority at present. The country has fine coastal scenery, thick forests and a stimulating climate on the northern plateau. Nigerian traditional art has exceptional richness and diversity. In 1972 the All Nigerian Festival of Arts and Culture was held at Kaduna and a Black Arts Festival is scheduled for 1974.

Visas are not required to visit Nigeria by nationals of Cameroon, Chad, Dahomey, Ireland, Ivory Coast, Morocco, Niger, Togo, United Kingdom and Commonwealth countries.

Sport

Football, boxing, wrestling, athletics, tennis and swimming are the most popular sports. Two Nigerian boxers have been world champions. The Second All-Africa games were held in Nigeria during 1972 and Nigerian athletes were second only to those of Egypt. The Government has allocated N7 million for expenditure on sports projects in 1975.

Public Holidays

1974: October 1st (National Day), October 16th and 17th (Id-ul-Fitr), December 23rd and 24th (Id-al-Kabir), December 25th–26th (Christmas and Boxing Day).

1975: January 1st (New Year's Day), March 26th (Mouloud), March 28th–31st (Easter).

Weights and Measures

Imperial weights and measures are officially in force and a variety of native weights and measures are used in local commerce.

Currency and Exchange Rates

100 kobo = 1 naira.

Exchange rates (April 1974):

£1 sterling = 1.546 naira;
U.S. $1 = 65.79 kobo.

Note: This decimal currency replaced the Nigerian pound (£N) on January 1st, 1973, at the rate of £N1 = 2 naira.

STATISTICAL SURVEY

AREA AND POPULATION

(Census, November 1963)

State	Area (sq. miles)	Population	Persons per sq. mile	State Capital (with population)
North-Western . . .	65,143	5,733,296	88	Sokoto (89,817)
North-Central . . .	27,108	4,098,305	151	Kaduna (149,910)
Kano	16,630	5,774,842	347	Kano (295,432)
North-Eastern . . .	103,639	7,793,443	75	Maiduguri (139,965)
Benue-Plateau . . .	40,590	4,009,408	99	Jos (90,402)
Kwara	28,672	2,399,365	84	Ilorin (208,546)
Lagos	1,381	1,443,567	1,045	Lagos (665,246)
Western	29,100	9,487,525	326	Ibadan (627,379)
Mid-Western . . .	14,922	2,535,839	170	Benin City (100,694)
East-Central . . .	11,310	7,227,559	639	Enugu (138,457)
South-Eastern . . .	11,166	3,622,589	324	Calabar (76,418)
Rivers	7,008	1,544,314	220	Port Harcourt (179,563)
Total . . .	356,669	55,670,052	156	

It is generally believed that the 1963 enumeration overstated the number of inhabitants, but the reported total provided the basis for subsequent official estimates of the country's population. Listed below are two sets of mid-year estimates, one official and the other prepared by the Population Division of the United Nations:

	Total Population ('000)	
	Official Estimates	UN Estimates
1963 . . .	n.a.	46,324
1964 . . .	57,062	47,491
1965 . . .	58,489	48,676
1966 . . .	59,951	49,882
1967 . . .	61,449	51,116
1968 . . .	62,986	52,386
1969 . . .	64,560	53,702
1970 . . .	66,174	55,074
1971 . . .	n.a.	56,511
1972 . . .	69,524	58,020
1973 . . .	71,262	59,607

Note: Both sets of estimates assume a steady growth of population and take no account of the military activities and economic blockade which followed the attempted secession of the former Eastern Region ("Biafra") in 1967–70.

Census (November 25th–30th, 1973): Total population 79,758,969 (provisional figure).

CHIEF TOWNS

POPULATION (1970 estimates)

Lagos (Federal capital)	875,417	Zaria . . .	197,524	Enugu . . .	164,582
Ibadan . . .	745,756	Ilesha . . .	197,111	Ede . . .	159,938
Ogbomosho . .	380,239	Onitsha . . .	193,793	Aba . . .	155,720
Kano . .	351,175	Iwo . . .	188,506	Ife . . .	154,589
Oshogbo . .	248,394	Ado-Ekiti . . .	187,239	Ila . . .	136,328
Ilorin . . .	247,896	Kaduna . . .	178,208	Oyo . . .	133,548
Abeokuta . . .	222,630	Mushin . . .	173,520	Ikere-Ekiti . .	127,447
Port Harcourt .	213,443	Maiduguri . . .	166,374	Benin City . .	119,692

Births and Deaths: Average annual birth rate 49.6 per 1,000; death rate 24.9 per 1,000 (UN estimates for 1965–70).

EMPLOYMENT
ECONOMICALLY ACTIVE POPULATION
(1963 Census)

Agriculture, Fishing, etc. . . .	10,201,328
Sales	2,806,071
Crafts, Production Process, Labouring .	2,190,073
Services, Sports, Recreation . .	870,884
Professional, Technical, etc. . .	440,613
Transport, Communications . .	279,255
Clerical	228,018
Mining, Quarrying, etc. . . .	13,856
Unspecified	891,415
Unemployed	344,921

AGRICULTURE
LAND USE, 1961
('000 hectares)

Arable and Under Permanent Crops . .	21,795
Permanent Meadows and Pastures . .	25,800
Forest Land	31,592*
Other Areas	13,190
Total	92,377

* Data from the world forest inventory carried out by the FAO in 1963.

PRINCIPAL CROPS
('000 metric tons)

	1969	1970	1971
Maize	1,219*	1,220*	1,220*
Millet	2,800*	2,800*	2,800*
Sorghum (Guinea Corn) . . .	3,500*	3,500*	3,500*
Rice (paddy)	563	550	550*
Sugar Cane[1]	240*	240*	240*
Sweet Potatoes and Yams . .	12,500*	13,500*	13,600*
Cassava (Manioc) . . .	6,800*	7,300*	7,330*
Cow Peas and Other Pulses . .	700*	710*	700*
Palm Kernels	261	295	307
Palm Oil	425	488	500
Soybeans[2]	34	25	33*
Groundnuts (in shell) . . .	1,365	780	850
Cottonseed	110	184	78
Cotton (Lint)	55	92	39
Sesame Seed[3]	25	20	10
Copra[4]	2.1	2.1*	2.1*
Coffee	3.0	5.4	3.9
Cocoa Beans[5]	191.8	222.9	304.8
Tobacco	10.3	12.0	17.5
Natural Rubber[6]	56.8	59.3	50.2

Coconuts (1968–70): 200 million nuts each year (FAO estimate).

1972 ('000 metric tons): Maize 1,350*, Palm Kernels 280*, Palm Oil 450*, Groundnuts 1,100, Cottonseed 76, Cotton Lint 38, Natural Rubber 51*.

* FAO estimate.
[1] Crop year ending in year stated.
[2] Purchases for export.
[3] Commercial production only.
[4] Exports of copra and coconut oil in copra equivalent.
[5] Twelve months ending in September of year stated. 1971–72: 256,600 metric tons.
[6] Exports only.

Source: mainly FAO, *Production Yearbook 1971*.

LIVESTOCK
('000—FAO estimates)

	1968–69	1969–70	1970–71
Cattle . . .	11,500	11,550	11,600
Sheep . . .	7,900	8,000	8,100
Goats . . .	23,300	23,400	23,500
Pigs . . .	800	820	840
Horses* . .	340	335	300
Asses* . .	860	840	820
Camels . .	18	19	20
Poultry . .	80,000	82,000	83,000

* Figures relate to the former Northern Region only.

Source: FAO, *Production Yearbook 1971.*

LIVESTOCK PRODUCTS
(FAO estimates, metric tons)

	1969	1970	1971
Cows' Milk .	403,000	405,000	407,000
Beef and Veal* .	173,000	174,000	175,000
Mutton and Lamb .	108,000	111,000	112,000
Hen Eggs .	78,400	80,400	82,500
Cattle Hides .	21,800	21,800	21,900

* Including goats' meat.

Source: FAO, *Production Yearbook 1971.*

Butter production (official estimates): 23 metric tons in 1967; 112 metric tons in 1968.

FORESTRY

ROUNDWOOD PRODUCTION
(cubic metres)

1968 . .		53,492,000
1969 . .		55,235,000
1970 . .		57,060,000
1971 . .		58,810,000

Source: FAO, *Yearbook of Forest Products.*

EXPORTS
('000 cu. metres)

	1970*	1971	1972
Logs . .	6,062	37.38	16.49
Sawn Timber .	1,674	35.74	15.64

* '000 cu. ft.

EXPORTS OF LOGS AND SAWN TIMBER
BY MAIN SPECIES
(cu. ft.)

	1970	1971
Obeche . . .	3,598,955	3,438,611
Abura . . .	704,297	916,346
Agba . . .	980,492	758,242
Masonia . . .	354,798	180,493
African Mahogany . .	189,093	126,837

FISHING
(metric tons)

	1967	1969	1970
Atlantic Ocean . .	66,800	48,400	62,300
Inland water . .	52,500	66,700	93,500
TOTAL .	119,300	115,100	155,800

Source: FAO, *Yearbook of Fishery Statistics 1971.*

MINING

	Unit	1968	1969	1970	1971	1972
Coal . . .	'ooo metric tons	—	16	58	194	307
Gold . . .	kilogrammes	7	9	38	26	n.a.
Lead Ore . . .	metric tons	—	—	—	n.a.	n.a.
Tin Concentrates . .	,, ,,	9,804	8,741	7,959	7,320	9,103
Columbite . . .	,, ,,	1,129	1,491	1,616	1,381	1,361
Kaolin . . .	,, ,,	n.a.	n.a.	300	n.a.	n.a.
Natural Gas . . .	million cubic metres	147	64	81	112	14,121
Crude Petroleum . .	'ooo metric tons	7,127	27,001	54,095	76,374	88,800

INDUSTRY

OUTPUT AND EMPLOYMENT, 1972
(Establishments with 10 or more employees)

	Establish- ments	Persons Engaged*	Gross Output in Producers' Values (£N'000)
Food Products	219	21,073	77,546
Beverages	16	4,338	46,721
Tobacco	5	4,263	28,342
Textiles	61	32,942	83,874
Clothing (except footwear) . . .	45	7,478	14,805
Leather Products	10	1,647	4,240
Footwear	15	2,900	7,666
Wood Products (except furniture) . .	106	10,054	9,450
Furniture and fixtures (non-metal) . .	66	5,937	3,418
Paper and Paper Products . . .	12	2,910	10,367
Printing and Publishing . . .	65	7,965	13,873
Industrial Chemicals . . .	5	513	3,768
Other Chemical Products . . .	36	6,650	32,751
Miscellaneous Petroleum Products . .	3	423	29,214
Rubber Products	27	6,031	14,981
Other Plastic Products . . .	19	2,991	8,576
Pottery and Glass	6	1,659	1,866
Other Non-metallic Mineral Products . .	29	5,760	14,410
Metals and Metal Products . . .	76	17,468	58,169
Machinery (non-electric) . . .	8	631	1,157
Electrical Machinery, Apparatus, etc. . .	4	844	2,769
Transport Equipment	7	9,371	903
Scientific Equipment . . .	8	723	4,457
Other Manufactured Products† . . .	22	2,431	3,760
Total Manufacturing Industries† .	870	148,568	477,082
Metal Ore Mining	95	50,560	9,474
Electric Light and Power . . .	58	7,897	22,636

* Including homeworkers.
† Excludes sales and repair of vehicles and transport equipment.

Source: Annual Industrial Survey.

PRODUCTION

	Unit	1969	1970	1971	1972
Tinned Meat	metric tons	1,151	n.a.	1,025	899
Margarine	,, ,,	2,809	3,712	4,812	5,147
Vegetable Oils	,, ,,	174,000	n.a.	191,196	102,400
Wheat Flour	,, ,,	126,567	191,000	n.a.	n.a.
Biscuits	,, ,,	6,722	11,855	12,919	10,789
Raw Sugar	,, ,,	12,000	12,000	48,964	43,674
Sugar Confectionery	,, ,,	11,110	14,142	22,121	13,095
Prepared Animal Feeds	,, ,,	n.a.	n.a.	36,588	45,661
Beer (including stout)	hectolitres	878,122	1,065,000	1,313,502	1,649,392
Soft Drinks	,,	248,000	336,000	501,979	569,596
Cigarettes	metric tons	6,269	8,502	4,247	7,703
Cotton Yarn, Pure	,, ,,	3,005	4,033	4,225	n.a.
Woven Cotton Fabrics	million sq. metres	236	224	375	n.a.
Knitted Fabrics	metric tons	2,053	1,686	1,730	1,400
Leather Footwear	'ooo pairs	3,576	n.a.	5,593	5,317
Other Non-rubber Footwear	,, ,,	7,529	n.a.	11,724	12,171
Sawnwood	cubic metres	494,000	n.a.	n.a.	n.a.
Plywood	,, ,,	28,000	n.a.	n.a.	n.a.
Paints	metric tons	8,006	12,000	11,256†	13,127†
Soap	,, ,,	28,073	29,558	36,495	44,320
Motor Spirit (Petrol)	,, ,,	—	184,000	472,000	516,000
Kerosene	,, ,,	—	125,000	272,000	304,000
Distillate Fuel Oils	,, ,,	—	204,000	473,000	n.a.
Residual Fuel Oils	,, ,,	—	297,000	698,000	747,000
Liquefied Petroleum Gas	,, ,,	19,000	n.a.	n.a.	n.a.
Bicycle and Motor Cycle Tyres	'ooo	1,123	n.a.	1,839	1,906
Other Road Vehicle Tyres	,,	240	n.a.	315	222
Rubber Footwear	'ooo pairs	3,270	4,312	1,906	1,733
Cement*	metric tons	566,400	596,000	664,000	1,135,057
Tin Metal, Unwrought	,, ,,	8,981	8,069	7,350	n.a.
Nails, Screws, Nuts, Bolts, etc.	,, ,,	5,939	n.a.	n.a.	n.a.
Radio Receivers	number	133,495	207,000	161,394	122,943
Television Receivers	,,	2,714	5,983	3,170	3,496
Lorries Assembled	,,	6,213	7,502	6,897	6,119
Electric Energy	million kWh.	1,248	1,550	1,820	n.a.

* Incomplete coverage.   † Thousand litres.

Source: mainly United Nations, *The Growth of World Industry.*

FINANCE

100 kobo = 1 naira.

Coins: ½, 1, 5, 10 and 25 kobo.

Notes: 50 kobo; 1, 5, and 10 naira.

Exchange rates (April 1974): £1 sterling = 1.546 naira; U.S. $1 = 65.79 kobo.

100 naira = £64.69 = $152.00.

Note: This decimal currency was introduced on January 1st, 1973, replacing the Nigerian pound (£N) of 20 shillings (240 pence) at the rate of £N1 = 2 naira. Some tables in this survey contain figures in the old currency. Between September 1949 and August 1971 the Nigerian pound was valued at U.S. $2.80. In December 1971 the value was revised to $3.04. The value of the naira was consequently fixed at $1.52. The Nigerian pound was at par with the pound sterling until November 1967, after which the exchange rate was £N1 = 1.167 sterling until June 1972.

FEDERAL BUDGET 1974-75*

(Twelve months ending March 31st—N'ooo)

REVENUE		EXPENDITURE	
Gross Revenue	3,122	Capital Expenditure	1,639
		Defence	336
Less: Statutory Appropriations to State Governments†	626	Land Transport	226
		Education	213
		Town and Country Planning	200
		Electricity and Fuel	196
		Recurrent Expenditure	995
TOTAL	2,496	TOTAL	2,634

* Estimates.

† Total revenues granted to the States during 1974/75 estimated at N1,126 million including development loans.

(£N million)

	1969–70	1970–71	1971–72*
Recurrent Revenue . . .	191.7	326	475
Less: Statutory Appropriation to State Governments	92.0	109	126
Revenue Retained by Federal Government	99.7	217	349
Recurrent Expenditure . . .	109.9	186	219
Contribution to Development Fund .	—	10	120
Overall Surplus/Deficit . . .	—10.2	21	10

* Estimated.

STATE BUDGETS
(£N million)

	1971–72	1972–73
Benue-Plateau . . .	18.8	26.9
East-Central . . .	25.9	n.a.
Kano	22.5	26.6
Kwara	16.0	21.9
Lagos	16.1	21.1
Mid-Western . . .	29.3	34.9
North-Central . . .	23.0	31.0
North-Eastern . . .	27.0	32.1
North-Western . . .	26.9	29.7
Rivers	29.2	38.8
South-Eastern . . .	13.6	15.5
Western	38.9	43.9

SECOND NATIONAL DEVELOPMENT PLAN 1970–74
INVESTMENT AND FINANCING
(£N million)

Public Sector Capital Investment:

Economic	580.8
Social	286.4
Administration	148.7
Financial Obligations . . .	9.5
Nominal Total . . .	1,025.4
Less: Transfers . . .	37.2
Gross Public Investment . .	988.2
Less: Probable Spill-over . .	208.2
Net Public Investment . . .	780.0

Private Sector Investment:

Incorporated Business: Oil . .	267.5
Incorporated Business: Non-Oil .	425.3
Households	123.0
	815.8
TOTAL INVESTMENT . .	1,595.8

Public Sector Financing:

Federal and State Budget Surpluses .	450.2
Public Corporation and Marketing Board Surpluses	106.5
Central Bank and Other Domestic Borrowing	72.3
External Finance . . .	151.0
	780.0

Private Sector Financing:

Capital Inflow	412.5
Net Corporate Capital Reserves .	307.5
Personal Saving . . .	95.8
	815.8
TOTAL FINANCE . .	1,595.8

GROSS DOMESTIC PRODUCT
(£N million—at 1962–63 factor cost)

	1969–70*	1970–71	1971–72
Agriculture, Livestock, etc. . .	767.3	894.4	935.0
Mining and Quarrying	150.5	296.2	412.4
Manufacturing and Crafts	142.5	164.5	189.1
Electricity and Water . . .	10.0	11.3	13.4
Building and Construction . .	61.0	96.0	110.0
Distribution	198.0	235.0	256.0
Transport and Communications .	63.0	74.5	83.8
General Government . . .	111.4	114.4	117.5
Education	51.0	54.0	57.0
Health	11.1	13.6	14.7
Other Services . . .	39.0	42.0	46.0
TOTAL	1,604.8	1,995.9	2,234.9

* Excluding the three States of the former Eastern Region.

MONEY SUPPLY*
(N million)

	1969	1970	1971	1972
Currency with Non-Bank Public .	273.2	370.4	354.5	385.2
Demand Deposits . . .	185.6	289.6	274.4	315.0
TOTAL MONEY SUPPLY .	458.8	660.0	628.9	700.2
Savings and Time Deposits . .	215.4	336.8	371.8	456.9

* December of each year.

Currency in Circulation (April 30th, 1973): 361.1 million naira.

BALANCE OF PAYMENTS
(£N million)

	1967		1968		1969†		1970‡	
	Oil	Non-Oil*	Oil	Non-Oil	Oil	Non-Oil	Oil	Non-Oil
Current Account:								
Visible Trade:								
Exports (f.o.b.) .	72.0	166.8	37.0	171.4	131.0	182.3	263.0	180.0
Imports (c.i.f.) .	−17.5	−200.9	− 9.9	−181.2	−11.1	−217.8	10.0	349.0
Trade Balance . .	54.5	− 34.1	27.1	− 9.8	119.9	− 35.5	253.0	−169.0
Transport, Freight and								
Insurance . .	—	0.8	—	2.2	—	4.2		
Investment Income .	−19.8	− 20.6	—	− 53.9	—	− 55.0		
Other Services . .	−31.5	− 40.0	−28.2	− 38.7	−44.8	− 49.2		
Transfer Payments:								
Private . . .	—	− 4.5	—	3.5	—	2.0		
Official . . .	—	12.2	—	13.7	—	8.4		
Balance on Current Account . .	3.2	− 86.2	− 1.1	− 83.0	75.1	−125.1		
Capital Account:								
Private Capital . .	45.5	6.0	29.9	49.3	−19.2	55.6		
Government Capital .	—	9.9	—	0.8	—	1.4	n.a.	n.a.
Balance on Capital Account . .	45.5	15.9	29.9	50.1	−19.2	57.0		
Overall Surplus or Deficit	48.7	− 70.3	28.8	− 32.9	55.9	− 68.1		
Monetary Sectors:								
Commercial Banks .	—	2.6	—	2.0	—	− 1.9		
Federal Institutions .	—	31.1	—	− 5.0	—	− 5.7		
Total Monetary Sectors . . .	—	33.7	—	− 3.0	—	− 7.6		
Net‖ Unrecorded Items .	−12.1		7.1		19.8			

* All sectors except for oil prospecting and mining companies.   † Provisional.   ‡ Estimate.

EXTERNAL TRADE
(N million)

	1969	1970	1971	1972*	1973*
Imports . .	497.4	756.4	1,078.9	990.6	1,234.0
Exports . .	629.3	877.1	1,280.8	1,421.6	2,226.6

* Estimates.

PRINCIPAL COMMODITIES
(£N'000)

Imports	1970	1971	1972
Cereals and Preparations . . .	10,960	16,567	16,500
Petroleum Products . .	21,116	4,127	2,500
Medicaments . . .	12,757	20,639	15,900
Paper and Paperboard . .	10,904	13,965	11,800
Textile Yarn, Fabrics, etc. .	26,419	40,034	38,700
Iron and Steel . . .	38,040	43,746	35,600
Machinery (non-electric) . .	62,725	101,047	76,000
Electrical Equipment . .	26,029	33,598	28,900
Road Motor Vehicles . . .	34,463	45,552	72,800
Total (incl. others) .	378,200	539,450	495,300

Principal Commodities—*continued*]

EXPORTS			1971	1972*
Crude Petroleum	.	.	476,520	588,100
Cocoa	.	.	71,560	50,600
Groundnuts	.	.	12,150	9,600
Palm Kernels	.	.	12,960	7,800
Palm Oil	.	.	1,690	100
Rubber	.	.	6,200	3,700
Raw Cotton	.	.	5,550	1,300
Timber, Logs and Sawn	.	.	2,640	3,150
Tin Metal	.	.	12,410	9,600
Other	.	.	38,740	27,050
Re-exports	.	.	6,290	6,300
TOTAL	.	.	646,710	707,300

* Provisional figures. The revised total (in £N'ooo) is 717,100.

COUNTRIES
('ooo naira)

IMPORTS		1971	1972	EXPORTS†		1971	1972
Belgium and Luxembourg	.	18,200	19,000	Belgium and Luxembourg	.	6,200	7,200
China, People's Republic	.	20,200	17,400	Eastern Europe*	.	36,800	21,400
Eastern Europe*	.	33,600	21,000	France	.	190,400	208,200
France	.	44,000	58,400	Germany, Federal Republic	.	70,600	65,000
Germany, Federal Republic	.	131,400	134,800	Ghana	.	8,400	4,600
Hong Kong	.	17,400	17,800	Italy	.	56,600	64,600
India	.	13,600	10,800	Netherlands	.	176,000	194,000
Japan	.	91,000	98,200	Norway	.	17,800	6,800
Netherlands	.	37,200	45,200	United Kingdom	.	280,600	299,800
Norway	.	6,600	5,200	U.S.A.	.	225,600	298,400
United Kingdom	.	344,200	292,000				
U.S.A.	.	151,400	103,200				
TOTAL (incl. others)	.	1,078,900	990,600	TOTAL (incl. others)	.	1,280,800	1,421,600

* Czechoslovakia, German Democratic Republic, Finland, Hungary, Poland, U.S.S.R.
† Excluding re-exports.

TOURISM
ARRIVALS BY COUNTRY OF ORIGIN

		1966	1967	1968	1969	1970
United Kingdom	.	2,939	5,869	5,828	4,338	3,113
U.S.A.	.	3,106	4,069	3,654	1,556	1,480
Others and Unspecified*	.	10,833	11,891	13,891	7,873	8,501
TOTAL*	.	16,878	21,829	23,373	13,767	13,094

* Including arrivals of Nigerian nationals resident abroad: 2,695 in 1966; 1,383 in 1967; 1,775 in 1968; an unspecified number in 1969; and 2,263 in 1970.

Source: United Nations, *Statistical Yearbook.*

TRANSPORT

RAILWAYS
(Twelve months ending March 31st)

	1967–68	1968–69	1969–70	1970–71
Passenger-km. (million) . . .	397	586	728	987
Net ton-km. (million)* . . .	1,613	1,788	1,615	1,595

* Including the railways' own service traffic.

ROADS
MOTOR VEHICLES IN USE

	1967	1968	1969
Passenger Cars	70,300	42,800	39,300
Commercial Vehicles . .	31,900	22,500	23,700
TOTAL	102,200	65,300	63,000

Source: United Nations, *Statistical Yearbook 1971.*

MERCHANT SHIPPING FLEET
(registered at June 30th each year)

	DISPLACEMENT (gross tons)
1968 . .	71,000
1969 . .	98,000
1970 . .	99,000
1971 . .	96,000

INTERNATIONAL SEA-BORNE SHIPPING

	1968	1969	1970	1971
Vessels Entered ('000 net tons) . .	4,794	1,945	5,343	n.a.
Goods Loaded ('000 metric tons) .	9,181	28,903	53,551	73,212
Goods Unloaded ('000 metric tons) . .	2,832	3,279	3,693	4,692

CIVIL AVIATION
Scheduled Services

	1967	1968	1969	1970
Kilometres Flown ('000) . . .	4,584	3,905	5,524	5,381
Passenger-km. ('000) . . .	152,921	154,336	190,542	213,623
Cargo ton-km. ('000) . . .	4,717	4,671	5,396	5,835
Mail ton-km. ('000) . . .	1,148	1,010	1,060	1,098

COMMUNICATIONS

RADIO AND TELEVISION
(Receivers in use at December 31st)

	Radio	Television
1963 . .	400,000	10,000
1964 . .	600,000	15,000
1965 . .	n.a.	30,000
1966 . .	n.a.	40,000
1967 . .	n.a.	42,000*
1968 . .	1,260,000	n.a.
1969 . .	1,265,000	53,000
1970 . .	1,275,000	75,000

* September.

TELEPHONES
(Number in use at January 1st)

1967 . .	73,000
1968 . .	77,883
1969 . .	75,900
1970 . .	81,440
1971 . .	80,000

Source: American Telephone and Telegraph Company.

EDUCATION
(1966)

	Establishments	Teachers	Students
Primary	14,907	91,049	3,025,981
Secondary	1,350	11,644	211,305
Technical	73	789	15,059
Teacher Training . . .	193	1,837	30,493
Universities (1971) . . .	6	2,628	17,495

1970: Primary Schools had 101,366 teachers and 3,696,000 students.

Sources (except where otherwise stated): Federal Office of Statistics, Lagos; *Nigeria Trade Journal*; Standard Bank *Annual Economic Review: Nigeria*, June 1972; *Barclays Overseas Survey 1971*; *Nigeria Year Book 1971*; *Nigeria Handbook 1973*; United Nations, *Statistical Yearbook 1971*; Nigeria High Commission, London.

THE CONSTITUTION

A new Constitutional Decree was published in Lagos on March 17th, 1967, to replace all earlier Decrees. The following are its principal provisions:

1. Legislative and executive power is vested in the Supreme Military Council. The Chairman of the Council is the head of the Military Government. The Supreme Military Council is composed of the Regional Military Governors and the Military Administrator of the Federal Territory; the Heads of the Nigerian Army, Navy and Air Force, the Chief of Staff of the Armed Forces and the Inspector-General of Police or his Deputy.

2. The Supreme Military Council can delegate powers to a Federal Executive Council, which is predominantly composed of civilian Commissioners drawn from all the States of the Federation, with representatives of the armed forces. The Federal Attorney-General and the Secretaries to Federal and State Governors, as well as other appropriate officials, may attend the meetings of either Council in an advisory capacity.

3. On certain matters of legislation, the concurrence of all the Military Governors is required. These matters in-

clude any decrees affecting or relating to the territorial integrity of a State, or altering entrenched clauses of the 1963 Constitution, or affecting the Federation in respect of trade, commerce, transport, industry, communications, labour, the public service or public finance (including approval of new capital projects in Federal estimates), or affecting external or security affairs, or affecting the professions and higher education.

4. Special powers are given to the Supreme Military Council to override State legislation, with the concurrence of a majority of Military Governors, if that legislation impedes the exercise of Federal authority or constitutes a danger to the continuance of Federal Government in Nigeria.

5. The creation of new States will be treated as an entrenched clause of the Constitution.

6. Certain additional matters covered by the Decree include: the revived power to appoint local authority police; one Federal Supreme Court judge will be appointed by each State; decrees made since January 1966 may be repealed or amended by individual Military Governors; the new Decree cannot be challenged in a court of law; power of appointment to higher Civil Service posts is in the hands of the Supreme Military Council, acting on the advice of the Public Service Commission.

On May 27th, 1967 the Supreme Military Council issued a decree creating 12 states out of the four existing Regions.

Northern Region was divided into six States and Eastern Region into three. Lagos State was created by the merger of the Colony Province of Western Region with the Federal Territory of Lagos. The rest of Western Region became Western State. The Mid-Western Region retained the same boundaries as Mid-Western State.

FEDERAL GOVERNMENT

SUPREME MILITARY COUNCIL
Chairman: Gen. YAKUBU GOWON.

Members: Admiral JOSEPH E. A. WEY (Chief of Staff, Supreme Headquarters), Brig. E. E. IKWUE (Commandant of the Nigeria Air Force), Maj.-Gen. DAVID A. EJOOR (Chief of Staff, Army), Rear-Admiral NELSON SOROH (Chief of Staff, Nigeria Navy), Alhaji KAM SELEM (Inspector-General of Police). The Military Governors of the twelve states in the Federation are *ex-officio* members of the committee.

FEDERAL EXECUTIVE COUNCIL
(June 1974)
Chairman and Commander-in-Chief of Armed Forces: Gen. YAKUBU GOWON.

Commissioner for Finance: Alhaji SHEHU SHAGARI.

Commissioner for Establishments: Maj.-Gen. HASSAN U. KATSINA.

Commissioner for External Affairs: Dr. OKOI ARIKPO.

Commissioner for Communications: JOSEPH S. TARKA.

Commissioner for Agriculture and Natural Resources: Dr. J. O. J. OKEZIE.

Commissioner for Education: Chief ABDUL YUSSUF EKE.

Commissioner for Health: Alhaji AMINU KANO.

Commissioner for Economic Development and Reconstruction: Dr. A. ADEDEJI.

Commissioner for Labour and Information: Chief ANTHONY ENAHORO.

Commissioner for Internal Affairs and Inspector-General of Police: Alhaji KAM SELEM.

Commissioner for Justice and Attorney-General: Dr. W. GRAHAM-DOUGLAS.

Commissioner for Mines and Power: SHETTIMA ALI MONGUNO.

Commissioner for Industries: Dr. JOSEPH E. ADETORO.

Commissioner for Transport: Dr. RUSSELL A. B. DIKKO.

Commissioner for Works and Housing: FEMI OKUNNU.

Commissioner for Trade: WENIKE O. BRIGGS.

STATE GOVERNMENTS

There are between eight and twelve Ministries in each State, each headed by a Commissioner and together presided over by the Governor.

NAME	CAPITAL	GOVERNOR
North-Western	Sokoto	Alhaji USMAN FARUK
North-Central	Kaduna	Brig. ABBA KYARI
Kano State	Kano	Alhaji ABDU BAKO
North-Eastern	Maiduguri	Brig. MUSA USMAN
Benue-Plateau	Jos	JOSEPH D. GOMWALK
Kwara	Ilorin	Col. DAVID L. BAMIGBOYE
Lagos State	Lagos	Brig. MOBOLAJI O. JOHNSON
South-Eastern	Calabar	Brig. UDOAKAHA J. ESUENE
Rivers State	Port Harcourt	Lt.-Cmdr. ALFRED P. DIETE-SPIFF
East-Central	Enugu	UKBABI ASIKA
Mid-Western	Benin	Col. SAMUEL O. OGBEMUDIA
Western	Ibadan	Brig. C. O. ROTIMI

DIPLOMATIC REPRESENTATION

HIGH COMMISSIONS AND EMBASSIES ACCREDITED TO NIGERIA

(In Lagos unless otherwise stated)

(HC) High Commission; (E) Embassy.

Algeria: 26 Maitama Sule St., S.W. Ikoyi, P.O.B. 7228 (E); *Ambassador:* NOUREDDINE DJOUDI.

Argentina: 93 Awolowo Rd., Ikoyi, P.O.B. 2456 (E); *Ambassador:* FRANCISCO BENGOLEA.

Australia: 21-25 Yakubu Gowon St., P.O.B. 2427 (HC); *High Commissioner:* W. H. BRAY.

Austria: 8-10 Yakubu Gowon St., P.O.B. 1914 (E); *Ambassador:* ELMAR GAMPER.

Belgium: 8-10 Yakubu Gowon St., P.O.B. 149 (E); *Ambassador:* M. DE BRUYNE.

Brazil: 21-25 Yakubu Gowon St., P.O.B. 1931 (E); *Chargé d'Affaires:* PAULO DIAS PEREIRA.

Bulgaria: 25 Norman Williams St., S.W. Ikoyi, P.M.B. 4441 (E); *Ambassador:* ILIA IGNATOV.

Cameroon: 26 Moloney St. (E); *Ambassador:* El Hadji HAMMADOU ALIM.

Canada: New Niger House, Tinubu St., P.O.B. 851 (HC); *High Commissioner:* W. K. WARDROPER.

Chad: 2 Goriola St., Victoria Island, P.M.B. 2801 (E); *Chargé d'Affaires:* ABAKAR ABOUA ABDELKERIM.

China, People's Republic: 19A Taslim Elias Close, Victoria Island, P.O.B. 5653 (E); *Ambassador:* YANG CHI-LIANG.

Czechoslovakia: 2 Alhaji Masha Close, Ikoyi, P.O.B. 1009 (E); *Ambassador:* JAROMÍR VRLA.

Dahomey: 36 Breadfruit St., P.O.B. 5705 (E); *Ambassador:* J. ADANDE.

Denmark: 4 Eleke Crescent, Victoria Island, P.O.B. 2390 (E); *Ambassador:* F. AASBERG PETERSON.

Egypt: 81 Awolowo Rd., Ikoyi, P.O.B. 538 (E); *Ambassador:* KAMAL MOHAMED ABDUL-KHEIR.

Equatorial Guinea: 6 Alhaji Bashorun St., S.W. Ikoyi, P.O.B. 4162 (E); *Ambassador:* JOSÉ W. OKORI-DOUGAN.

Ethiopia: Ademola St., Ikoyi, P.M.B. 2488 (E); *Ambassador:* Ato BELETE GABRE TSADIK.

Finland: 8-10 Yakubu Gowon St., P.O.B. 4433 (E); *Chargé d'Affaires:* ORA MERES-WUORI.

France: 161 Taslim Elias Close, Victoria Island, P.O.B. 567 (E); *Ambassador:* ANDRÉ ROGER.

German Democratic Republic: Federal Palace Hotel, Victoria Island, P.O.B. 1106 (E); *Ambassador:* GERHARD KÜNZEL.

Germany, Federal Republic: 15 Eleke Crescent, Victoria Island, P.O.B. 728 (E); *Ambassador:* Dr. ERNST JUNG.

Ghana: King George V Rd. (HC); *High Commissioner:* Col. S. M. ASANTE.

Greece: 150 Yakubu Gowon St., P.O.B. 1199 (E); *Ambassador:* PANAYOTIS RELLAS.

Guinea: 8 Abudu Smith St., Victoria Island, P.O.B. 2826 (E); *Ambassador:* LAYE KOUROUMA.

Hungary: 9 Louis Solomon Close, Victoria Island, P.O.B. 3168 (E); *Ambassador:* MARTON SZABÓ.

India: 40 Marina, P.M.B. 2322 (HC); *High Commissioner:* A. N. MEHTA.

Indonesia: 5 Anifowoshe St., Victoria Island, P.O.B. 3473 (E); *Ambassador:* Maj.-Gen. ALIBASJAH SATARI.

Iran: c/o Ikoyi Hotel (E); *Ambassador:* DJAMCHID MEFTAH.

Iraq: 7 Keffi St., Ikoyi, P.O.B. 2859 (E); *Ambassador:* TAKA M. AL-QAISI.

Ireland: 31 Marina, P.O.B. 2421 (E); *Ambassador:* TADHG O'SULLIVAN.

Italy: Elere Crescent, Victoria Island, P.O.B. 2161 (E); *Ambassador:* Dr. LUIGI GASBARRI.

Japan: 24-25 Apese St., Victoria Island, P.M.B. 2111 (E); *Ambassador:* AKIRA SHIGEMITSU.

Kenya: 53 Queen's Drive, Ikoyi, P.O.B. 6464 (HC); *High Commissioner:* J. K. KIMANI (acting).

Lebanon: 57 Raymond Njoku Rd., S.W. Ikoyi, P.O.B. 651 (E); *Ambassador:* HUSSEIN AL-ABDULLAH.

Liberia: 19 Alhaji Bashorun St., P.O.B. 3007 (E); *Ambassador:* LAFAYETTE DIGGS.

Libya: 46 Raymond Njoku Rd., Ikoyi, P.O.B. 2860 (E); *Chargé d'Affaires:* SULEIMAN M. ELFEITORY.

Malaysia: Kofo Abayomi/Anifowoshe St., Victoria Island, P.O.B. 3729 (E); *High Commissioner:* ABDUL MANAF MOHAMED (acting).

Netherlands: 24 Ozumba Mbadiwe Ave., Victoria Island, P.O.B. 2426 (E); *Ambassador:* P. W. VAN HEUSDE.

Niger: 15 Adeola Odeku St., Victoria Island, P.M.B. 2736 (E); *Ambassador:* IBRAHIM LOUTOU.

Norway: 8-10 Yakubu Gowon St., P.M.B. 2431 (E); *Ambassador:* P. M. MOTZFELDT.

Pakistan: 20 Keffi St., Ikoyi, P.O.B. 2450 (E); *Ambassador:* SYED ZAFAURI ISLAM.

Philippines: 19 Alhaji Ribadu Rd., Ikoyi, P.O.B. 2948 (E); *Ambassador:* PEDRO ANGARA-ARAGON.

Poland: 32 Gerrard Rd., Old Ikoyi, P.O.B. 410 (E); *Ambassador:* JÓZEF FILIPOWICZ.

Romania: 30 Raymond Njoku Rd., Ikoyi, P.O.B. 595 (E); *Ambassador:* GHEORGHE IASON.

Saudi Arabia: 182 Awolowo Rd., Ikoyi, P.O.B. 2836 (E); *Ambassador:* MANSOUR AREF.

Senegal: 8 Kofo Abayomi Rd., Victoria Island, P.M.B. 2197 (E); *Ambassador:* LAMINE DIAKHATE.

Sierra Leone: 192 Awolowo Rd., Ikoyi, P.O.B. 2821 (HC); *High Commissioner:* Dr. WILLIAM FITZJOHN.

Spain: 9 Queen's Drive, P.M.B. 2738 (E); *Ambassador:* EDUARDO S. DE ERICE.

Sudan: 40 Awolowo Rd., Okoyi, P.O.B. 2428 (E); *Ambassador-Designate:* OMAN ABDALLA HAMID.

Sweden: 8-10 Yakubu Gowon St., P.O.B. 1097 (E); *Ambassador:* PIERRE BOTHEN.

Switzerland: 11 Anifowoshe St., Victoria Island, P.O.B. 536 (E); *Ambassador:* FRIEDER H. ANDRES.

Syria: 4 Raymond Njoku Rd., Ikoyi, P.O.B. 3088 (E); *Chargé d'Affaires:* Dr. ZAKARIA SIBAHI.

Tanzania: 45 Ademola St., Ikoyi, P.O.B. 6417 (HC); *High Commissioner:* PHILEMON P. MURO.

Thailand: 1 Ruxton Rd., Old Ikoyi, P.O.B. 3095 (E); *Ambassador:* ARI BUPHAVESA.

Togo: 96 Awolowo Rd., Ikoyi, P.O.B. 1435 (E); *Ambassador:* GEORGES APEDO-AMAH.

Turkey: 3 Okunola Martins Close, Ikoyi, P.O.B. 1758 (E); *Ambassador:* TALAT BENLER.

U.S.S.R.: 5 Eleke Crescent, Victoria Island, P.O.B. 2723 (E); *Ambassador:* B. S. VOROBYOV.

United Kingdom: 62-64 Campbell St., P.M.B. 12136 (HC); *High Commissioner:* MARTIN LE QUESNE.

U.S.A.: 1 King's College Rd. (E); *Ambassador:* JOHN E. REINHARDT.

Venezuela: 10 Ikoyi Crescent, Ikoyi, P.O.B. 3727 (E); *Chargé d'Affaires:* HECTOR GRIFFIN.

Yugoslavia: 7 Maitama Sule St., Ikoyi, P.M.B. 978 (E); *Ambassador:* A. Božović.

Zaire: 23A Kofo Abayomi Rd., Victoria Island, P.O.B. 1216 (E); *Ambassador:* OFUNGA W'AYOKO.

Zambia: 11 Keffi St., S.W. Ikoyi (HC); *High Commissioner:* A. S. MASIYE.

Nigeria also has diplomatic relations with Albania, Botswana, the Central African Republic, Chile, Gabon, Iceland, Jamaica, Jordan, Malawi, Mali, Malta, Mauritania, Trinidad and Tobago, Uganda, the Upper Volta and Uruguay.

POLITICAL PARTIES

All political parties were banned in May 1966 after the military *coup d'état*. General Gowon has announced that Nigeria is to return to civilian rule by 1976.

DEFENCE

Of a total armed force of 157,000, the army numbers 150,000 men, the navy 3,000 and the air force 4,000. There is also a civil police of 40,000. Military service was voluntary until 1973 when a national service scheme for graduates was established. Reserve forces total 103,000 (1973). In the 1974–75 budget N336 million was allotted for defence expenditure.

Chief of Staff: Admiral JOSEPH E. A. WEY.

Chief of Army Staff: Maj.-Gen. DAVID A. EJOOR.

Commandant of Air Force: Brig. E. E. IKWUE.

Chief of Naval Staff: Rear-Admiral NELSON B. SOROH.

Director of National Youth Service Corps: Lt.-Col. A. A. ALI.

Inspector-Gen. of Police: Alhaji KAM SELEM.

JUDICIAL SYSTEM

The High Courts of Justice are superior Courts of Record and have unlimited jurisdiction in the first instance except in certain cases which are reserved to the Federal Supreme Court, for example, disputes between any of the component parts of the Federation involving any question as to the existence or extent of any legal right, and matters arising under any Treaty or affecting Consular Officers or any international organization outside Nigeria. The High Courts also have jurisdiction to hear appeals from Magistrates' and Native Courts.

The Magistrates' Courts have original jurisdiction in a large variety of civil and criminal cases, some also have jurisdiction to hear appeals from Native Courts. The offices of Chief Magistrate have been retained in all areas.

Native Courts have been retained throughout the Federation. The law administered in those Courts is, generally speaking, the Native Law and Custom prevailing in the area of their jurisdiction. In the Islamic districts of

the Northern States Muslim law is administered and the Sharia Courts act as the courts of appeal.

The Federal Supreme Court is the final Court of Appeal in Nigeria, consisting of the Chief Justice and eight Justices of the Supreme Court.

The Judges of the Federal Supreme Court and of the High Courts of Justice are appointed by the President. Judges of the High Courts of the States are appointed by the Governor of each State.

FEDERAL SUPREME COURT

Chief Justice of the Federation: Dr. TASLIM O. ELIAS.

Federal Justices: Mr. Justice G. B. A. COKER, Sir IAN LEWIS, Sir UDO UDOMA, Mr. Justice C. O. MADARIKAN, Mr. Justice A. FATAYI-WILLIAMS, Mr. Justice G. S. SOWEMIMO, Mr. Justice DANIEL ONWURA IBEKWE, Mr. Justice AYO IRIKEFE.

RELIGION

AFRICAN RELIGIONS

The beliefs, rites and practices of the people of Nigeria are very diverse, varying from tribe to tribe and family to family. About 10,000,000 persons profess local beliefs.

MUSLIMS

There are large numbers of Muslims in Northern and Western Nigeria, and over 26 million were enumerated in the whole of Nigeria in the 1963 Census.

Spiritual Head: The Sardauna of Sokoto.

CHRISTIANS

The 1963 Census recorded over 19 million Christians in Nigeria.

ANGLICAN
PROVINCE OF WEST AFRICA

Archbishop of the Province of West Africa and Bishop of Sierra Leone: Most Rev. M. N. C. O. SCOTT, C.B.E., D.D., DIP.TH, Bishopscourt, P.O.B. 128, Freetown, Sierra Leone.

ROMAN CATHOLIC

National Episcopal Conference of Nigeria: *Secretariat:* P.O.B. 951, Lagos; Pres. Most Rev. Dr. DOMINIC I. EKADEM, Bishop of Ikot-Ekpene; Sec. Rt. Rev. Dr. A. O. MAKOZI, Bishop of Lokoja.

Catholic Secretariat of Nigeria: P.O.B. 951, Lagos; Sec.-Gen. Rt. Rev. Dr. G. G. GANAKA, Auxiliary Bishop of Jos.

Archbishop of Kaduna: Most Rev. JOHN MACCARTHY Archbishop's House, P.O.B. 14, Kaduna.

Archdiocese of Lagos: the Vicar Capitular, P.O.B. 8, Lagos.

Archbishop of Onitsha: Most Rev. FRANCIS ARINZE, Archbishop's House, P.O.B. 411, Onitsha.

THE PRESS

DAILIES

Daily Express: Commercial Amalgamated Printers, 5–11 Apongbon St., P.O.B. 163, Lagos; Editor EDWARD ADERINOKUN.

Daily Sketch: Sketch Bldgs., Ijebu By-Pass, P.M.B. 5067, Ibadan; f. 1964; Western State of Nigeria Government-owned company; Chair. A. A. K. DEGUN; Gen. Man. SIMEON LABANJI BOLAJI; Editor J. AYO ADEDUN; circ. 19,140.

Daily Times: The Daily Times of Nigeria Ltd., 3–5 Kakawa St., P.O.B. 139, Lagos; f. 1925; Chief Alhaji BABA-TUNDE JOSE; Editor AREOYO OYEBOLA; circ. 205,857.

Morning Post: Nigerian National Press, Malu Rd., Apapa, P.M.B. 2099, Lagos; f. 1961; Editor MAGNUS BARA-HART; circ. 56,000 (suspended).

New Nigerian: New Nigerian Newspapers Ltd., Ahmadu Bello Way, Kaduna; has opened an office in Lagos in 1973; f. 1965; Editor RASAK AREMU; circ. 45,000.

Nigerian Observer: The Mid-West Newspapers Corporation, 18 Airport Rd., Benin City; f. 1968; Editor SAM EGUAUDEN; circ. 40,000.

Nigerian Tribune: 98 Shittu St., P.O.B. 78, Ibadan; f. 1949; Action Group of Nigeria; circ. 30,000; Editor AYO OJEWUNMI.

Renaissance: 9 Works Rd., Enugu; also Sundays; Editor A. OZUMBA.

West African Pilot: 34 Commercial Ave., Yaba; Main organ of Zik Enterprises Ltd.; circ. 47,323; Editor AINA JACOB (acting).

SUNDAY PAPERS

Sunday Observer: Mid-west Newspapers Corporation, 18 Airport Rd., Benin City; f. 1968; Editor T. O. BORHA; circ. 60,000.

Sunday Post: Nigerian National Press Ltd., P.M.B. 1154, Malu Rd., Apapa, Lagos; f. 1961; Editor A. SOGUNLE; circ. 70,000 (suspended).

Sunday Punch (Nigeria) Ltd.: P.M.B. 1240, Ikeja; Man. Editor SAM AMUKAPENN.

Sunday Sketch: Sketch Bldgs., Ijebu By-Pass, P.M.G. 5067, Ibadan; f. 1964; Western State of Nigeria Government-owned company; Editor OLAJIDE ADELEYE; circ. 22,900.

Sunday Star: People's Star Press, Yemetu Aladorin, Ibadan; f. 1966.

Sunday Times: The Daily Times of Nigeria Ltd., 3–7 Kakawa St., P.O.B. 139, Lagos; f. 1953; Editor GBOLABO OGUNSANWO; circ. 368,000.

WEEKLIES

African Impact: Ethiope Publishing Corpn., 34 Muritala Mohammed Rd., Benin.

Champion: Calabar Advertising Co., 31 Eyo Edem St., Calabar; twice-weekly.

Eleti-Ofe: 28 Kosoko St., Lagos, P.O.B. 467; f. 1923; English and Yoruba; Editor OLA ONATA DE; circ. 30,000.

Gaskiya ta fi Kwabo: New Nigerian Newspapers Co. Ltd., Kaduna; f. 1939; Hausa; Editor Alhaji UTHMAN MAIRIGA; (twice weekly).

Gbohungbohun: Western State Government publication; Editor OLU OLOFIN.

Imole Owuro: People's Star Press, Yemetu Aladorin, Ibadan; f. 1962; Editor LAWUYI OGUNNIRAN.

Independent (The): P.M.B. 5109, Ibadan; f. 1960; English; Editor Rev. F. B. CRONIN-COLTSMAN; circ. 13,000; national Catholic weekly.

Irohin Imole: 15 Bamgbose St., Lagos; f. 1957; Yoruba; Editor: TUNJI ADEOSUN.

Irohin Yoruba: 212 Yakubu Gowon St., P.M.B. 2416, Lagos; f. 1945; Yoruba; Editor S. A. AIIBADE; circ. 70,000.

Lagos This Week: 5 Williams St., Lagos; Editor YEM MARTINS.

Lagos Weekend: 3-5-7 Kakawa St., P.O.B. 139, Lagos; f. 1965; news and pictures; Fri.; published by Daily Times group; Editor SOZA ODUNFA; circ. 181,553.

Mid-West This Week: Arin Associates 50B New Lagos Rd., Benin City; Editors TONY OKODUWA, Prince A. R. NWOKO.

Nigerian Catholic Herald: Ondo St., P.O.B. 19, Lagos; English; St. Paul's Press Catholic Mission.

Nigerian Chronicle: South-Eastern State Newspaper Corpn., Calabar; Editor MOSES EKPO.

Nigerian Radio Times: Broadcasting House, Lagos; Editor A. Y. S. TINUBU.

Nigerian Standard: Benue State Printing and Publishing Corpn., 5 Zaria By-Pass; Editor ILIYA AUDU.

Nigerian Statesman: 7 Kester Lane, Lagos; f. 1947; Socialist; circ. 14,165; Editor O. DAVIES.

Nigerian Tide: Rivers State Newspaper Corpn., 4 Ikwerre Rd., P.M.G. 5072, Port Harcourt; Editor R. H. AMAEWHULE.

Ribway News: Benin City; Editor DICKSON O. UWAGBOE.

Sporting Record: 3 Kakawa St., P.O.B. 139, Lagos; f. 1961; publ. by Daily Times of Nigeria Ltd.; Editor CYRIL KAPPO; circ. 114,140.

Truth (The Weekly Muslim): 45 Idumagbo Ave., P.O.B. 418, Lagos; f. 1951; Editor M. A. SHAHID.

ENGLISH PERIODICALS

African Journal of Pharmacy and Pharmaceutical Sciences: Development House, 21 Wharf Rd., P.O.B. 399, Apapa; f. 1970; incorporated "West African Pharmacist" in 1971; monthly; circ. 6,000; Editor BODE LADEJOBI.

Amber: 122 Investment House, P.O.B. 2592, Lagos; monthly.

Construction in Nigeria: P.O.B. 282, Lagos; journal of the Federation of Building and Civil Engineering Contractors in Nigeria; monthly; Editor M. M. Norton; circ. 3,500.

Drum: P.M.G. 2128, Lagos; f. 1954; picture monthly; circ. 172,000; Editor Olu Adetule.

Federal Nigerian: Ministry of Information, Yakubu Gowon St., Lagos; f. 1958; official monthly; Editor A. G. Y. S. Momodu.

Film: Drum Publications Nigeria Ltd., P.M.G. 2128, Lagos; f. 1967; photo weekly; circ. 55,000; Editor Olu Adetule.

Flamingo: P.O.B. 237, Lagos; f. 1960; monthly; Editor Gerald Malmed; circ. 100,000.

Happy Home: P.M.G. 1049, Ebute Metta; family magazine; Editor Sam Amuka.

Home Studies: P.O.B. 139, Lagos; f. 1964; monthly; Editor Mrs. Yetunde Makanju; circ. 18,000.

Insight: P.O.B. 139, 3 Kakawa St., Lagos; features about contemporary problems in Nigeria, Africa and the world; quarterly; Editor Sam Amuka; circ. 5,000.

Journal of the Historical Society of Nigeria: university publication.

Journal of the Nigerian Medical Association: Times Press Ltd., Apapa; quarterly; Editor Prof. A. O. Adesola.

Kano Studies: Ahmadu Bello University, Kano Campus; journal of Saharan and Sudanic research; Editor John Lavers.

Management in Nigeria: P.O.B. 139, Lagos; twice-monthly; journal of Nigerian Institute of Management.

Modern Woman: P.O.B. 2583, Lagos; f. 1969; Editor Toyin Onibuwe-Johnson.

New World: publ. by Novosty Press Agency; monthly; Editor Goke Ajiboye.

Nigeria: Exhibition Centre, Marina, Lagos; f. 1932; travel, cultural, historical and general; quarterly.

Nigeria Magazine: P.O.B. 2099, Lagos; f. 1932; travel, cultural, historical and general; quarterly; circ. 14,000; Editor T. O. A. Adebanjo.

Nigeria Trade Journal: Federal Ministry of Information, Commercial Publications Section, Lagos; quarterly; London Agents: Africa and Overseas Press Agency Ltd.; 122 Shaftesbury Ave., London, W.1.

Nigerian Businessman's Magazine: 39 Mabo St., Surv-Lere-Lagos; monthly; Nigerian and overseas commerce.

Nigerian Field: university publication.

Nigerian Grower and Producer: P.N.B. 12002, Lagos; quarterly.

Nigerian Journal of Economic and Social Studies: published March, July and November by the Nigerian Economic Society, c/o Dept. of Economics, University of Ibadan; Editor Dr. O. Teriba.

Nigerian Journal of Science: publication of the Science Association of Nigeria; f. 1966; twice-yearly.

Nigerian Opinion: Nigerian Current Affairs Society, Faculty of the Social Sciences, University of Ibadan; f. 1965; quarterly; economic and political commentary; Chief Editor Billy Dudley.

The Nigerian Sportsman: P.O.B. 2146, Kaduna; quarterly; published for the National Sports Commission; Editor Mrs. M. Segum; circ. 10,000.

Nigerian Teacher: 3 Kakawa St., P.O.B. 139, Lagos; quarterly.

Nigerian Worker: United Labour Congress, 97 Herbert Macaulay St., Lagos; Editor Lawrence Borha.

Radio-Vision Times: Western Nigerian Radio-Vision Service, Television House, P.O.B. 1460, Ibadan; monthly; Editor Alton A. Adedeji.

Sadness and Joy: Drum Publications Nigeria Ltd., P.M.B. 2128, Lagos; f. 1968; photo weekly; circ. 55,000; Editor Olu Adetule.

Savanna: Ahmadu Bello University, Zaria; environmental and social science studies; Editor Michael Mortimore.

Spear: 3-5-7 Kakawa St., P.O.B. 139, Lagos; f. 1962; publ. by Daily Times of Nigeria Ltd.; family magazine; Editor Tony Momoh; circ. 110,000.

Teacher's Monthly: General Publications Section, Ministry of Education, P.M.B. 5052, Ibadan.

Teen and Twenty: monthly; youth magazine; Editor Labake Paul.

Today's Challenge: P.M.B. 12067, Lagos; f. 1974, formerly African Challenge; publ. by Evangelical Churches of West Africa Publications Division; monthly; religious and educational; English; Editor J. K. Bolarin; circ. 20,000.

Trust: Drum Publications Nigeria Ltd., P.M.G. 2128, Lagos; f. 1971; mid-month pictorial; circ. 100,000; Editor Nelson Ottah.

West Africa Link: Mainland Press, Block 2, Unit 8; Industrial Estate, Yaba, P.O.B. 2965, Lagos; f. 1964; monthly; bi-lingual French and English; Editor Alexander Chia.

West African Chartered Engineer: P.O.B. 2363, Lagos; twice yearly.

West African Journal of Biological Chemistry: University of Ibadan; f. 1957; quarterly; Editor C. Bassir.

West African Journal of Education: Institute of Education, University of Ibadan; f. 1957; three a year; circ. 1,600; Editors Prof. J. A. Majasan, Dr. E. A. Yoloye.

West African Medical Journal: P.M.B. 12002, Lagos; six a year; Editor Prof. H. Orismejolomi Thomas, C.B.E.

West African Pharmacist: P.O.B. 2, University College, Ibadan; f. 1959; two-monthly.

Western Nigerian Illustrated: Ministry of Information, Western Nigerian Government, Ibadan; quarterly.

Women's World: P.O.B. 139, Lagos; Editor Adaora Lily Ulasi; circ. 23,000.

VERNACULAR PERIODICALS

Futila: North-Central State Ministry of Information; Hausa; monthly.

Harsunan Nijeriya: linguistic journal.

PRESS AGENCIES
Foreign Bureaux

Ghana News Agency: P.O.B. 2844, Lagos.

Novosti: 6 Akanbi Damola St., South-West Ikoli, Lagos; Chief E. Korshunov.

Reuters: Kajola House (5th floor), 62/64 Campbell St., Lagos.

AP, DPA, The Jiji Press and Tass also have offices in Lagos.

PUBLISHERS

African Universities Press: P.O.B. 3560, Lagos; educational and general; 10–15 titles annually.

Commercial Amalgamated Printers Ltd.: P.O.B. 163, 5/11 Apongbon St., Lagos.

Daily Times of Nigeria Ltd.: 3-5 Kakawa St., P.O.B. 139, Lagos; publishers of *Daily Times, Sunday Times, Lagos Weekend, Sporting Record, Spear Magazine, Woman's World, Home Studies, Insight* and *Nigerian Year Book*; Chair. and Man. Dir. Alhaji BABATUNDE JOSE.

Ethiope Publishing Corporation: P.M.B. 1192, Benin; f. 1970; books and periodicals; Chair. J. P. CLARK.

Evans Brothers (Nigeria Publishers) Ltd.: P.O.B. 5164, Ibadan; f. 1966; br. of Evans Brothers Ltd., United Kingdom; educational; Man. Dir. J. BERKHOUT.

Gaskiya Corporation: Zaria; printing and publishing corporation wholly owned by the six states of Northern Nigeria; Gen. Man. CLAUDE SCOTT.

Government Press: Federal Ministry of Information, Printing Division, Lagos.

Heinemann Educational Books (Nigeria) Ltd.: P.O.B. 5205, Ibadan; f. 1960; general, schoolbooks; Man. Dir. AIGBOJE HIGO.

Ibadan University Press: Ibadan; f. 1952; scholarly and educational; Man. Editor N. J. UDOEYOP.

Longmans (Nigeria) Ltd.: P.M.B. 1036, 52 Oba Akran Ave., Ikeja.

Mbari: P.M.B. 5162, Ibadan; occasional fiction, plays poetry, *Black Orpheus.*

Macmillan and Co. (Nigeria) Ltd.: Publishing Office: P.O.B. 1463, Ibadan; Editor A. O. AMORI; Warehouse: P.O.B. 264, Yaba, Lagos; Man. Dir. OLU ANULOPO; publishers of educational and general books; bankers for United Bank for Africa Ltd.

Nigeria Technical Publications Ltd.: 5 Station Rd., P.M.B. 2146, Kaduna; branches in Kano, Lagos and Enugu; publs. *Construction in Nigeria, Nigerian Sportsman.*

Nigerian National Press: P.M.B. 1154, Apapa; f. 1961; publishers of *Nigerian Sunday Post*; Chair. Alhaji EATARI ALI.

Onibonoje Press and Book Industries (Nigeria) Ltd.: P.O.B. 3109, Ibadan; educational and general publishers and printers.

Oxford University Press (Nigerian Branch): P.M.B. 5095, Oxford House, Iddo Gate, Ibadan; warehouse at Jericho, Ibadan; Chair. T. T. SOLARU; Editorial Man. M. O. AKINLEYE.

Pilgrim Books Ltd.: African Universities Press; P.O.B. 3560, Lagos; f. 1966; educational books for Africa; merged with African Universities Press; Gen. Man. W. T. SHAW.

University of Ife Press: University of Ife, Ile-Ife; scholarly books and periodicals, specializing in African law and local government and administration; Man. Dir. HANS M. ZELL.

RADIO AND TELEVISION

RADIO

Nigerian Broadcasting Corporation: Broadcasting House, Lagos; f. 1957. The Corporation was set up as a public, independent and impartial broadcasting system controlled by a board of Governors. The Federal Parliament gave the Minister responsible for broadcasting control over the Corporation's policy and board appointments in August 1961. Services are operated from Lagos (National Programme), Kaduna, Ibadan, Benin, Enugu, Ilorin, Katsina, Kano, Sokoto, Zaria, Jos, Maiduguri, Calabar, Port Harcourt, Onitsha, Warri, Abeokuta, Ijebu-Ode. Chair. of Central Board Alhaji ABUBAKAR TATARI-ALI; Dir.-Gen. CHRISTOPHER O. KOLADE; Dir. of Programmes SUNDAY YOUNG-HARRY; Sec. O. FASHINA.

Programmes are broadcast in English and the following Nigerian languages:

Hausa	Tiv	Urhobo
Yoruba	Nupe	Edo
Ibo	Idoma	Ijaw
Fulfude	Igalla	Itsekiri
Kanuri	Igbirra	Efik
	Birom	

Northern States Broadcasting Area: Broadcasting House, Kaduna; State Controller Mallan J. H. CINDO.

Western Broadcasting Area: Broadcasting House, Ibadan; State Controller ISOLA FOLORUNSO.

Mid-Western Broadcasting Area: State Controller JOE SNOMI.

East Central Broadcasting Area: Broadcasting House, Enugu; State Controller RAPH OPARA.

North-Eastern Broadcasting Area: Broadcasting House, Maiduguri; Officer-in-Charge BAGUDU BIDA.

North-Western Broadcasting Area: Broadcasting House, Sokoto; Officer-in-Charge 'TUNDE OYELEKE.

South-Eastern Broadcasting Area: Broadcasting House, Calabar; Officer-in-Charge D. A. BASSEY.

Rivers State Broadcasting Area: Broadcasting House, Port-Harcourt; Officer-in-Charge T. S. OGBANGA.

Benue Plateau State Broadcasting Area: service to begin in 1974.

External Service of NBC ("Voice of Nigeria"): International services in English, French, Arabic, Hausa; f. 1962.

Radio-Television Kaduna: P.O.B. 250, Kaduna; f. 1961; operated by 6 Northern States of Nigeria with Nigeria Radio Corporation, EMI Electronics Ltd. and Granada Group Ltd. for sound and television; has one of the biggest transmitters in Africa; Chair. Alhaji IDRIS GANA; Gen. Man. A. ZORU.

Rediffusion (Nigeria) Ltd.: P.O.B. 3156, Ibadan, and Rediffusion House, Lagos; f. 1952; subsidiary of

Rediffusion Ltd., London; wired broadcasting service in Ibadan, Lagos and 90 other towns and villages; distributes the programmes of the Nigerian Broadcasting Corporation; 52,000 subscribers (1969); Dir. and Gen. Man. E. A. D. SAUL.

Western Nigeria Radiovision Service Ltd. (WNTV-WNBS): P.O.B. 1460, Ibadan; f. 1959; commercial radio and television service; educational, public service and commercial broadcasts received in Lagos, Western States, and parts of Republic of Dahomey; Gen. Man. TEJU OYELEYE; Public Relations Officer ALTON A. ADEDEJI.

There are 5 million radio receivers in Nigeria.

TELEVISION

Nigerian Broadcasting Corporation (Television): P.M.B. 12005, Lagos; f. 1962; part of Nigerian Broadcasting Corporation; Dir.-Gen. C. O. COLADE; Dir. of Television M. A. OLUMIDE; Controller of Programmes O. OLUSOLA; Sales Rep. in Britain B. OVBIAGELE; Head of Programme Planning AYO OKESANYA; Controller of News EMMANUEL BIOTER OTERSOPE.

Radio-Television Kaduna (Northern Nigeria): *see* under Radio, above.

Western Nigeria Radiovision Service: *see* under Radio, above.

There were 85,000 television receivers in 1974.

FINANCE

BANKING

(cap. =capital; p.u. =paid up; dep. =deposits; m. =million; res. =reserves; £N=Nigerian pounds; N=naira)

Figures for capital and deposits in Commercial Banks relate to December 1973.

Central Bank of Nigeria: Tinubu Square, P.M.B. 12194, Lagos; f. 1958; issuing bank; cap. p.u. N2.5m.; dep. N86.56m.; general reserves N6.76m.; Gov. Dr. C. N. ISONG.

Federal Savings Bank: operates savings accounts; dep. N4.5m.

African Continental Bank Ltd.: 148 Yakubu Gowon St., P.M.B. 2466, Lagos; f. 1948; cap. p.u. N12m.; dep. N46.7m.; Chair. Dr. P. O. AHIME; Gen. Man. C. K. N. OBITS.

Agricultural Credit Bank: for funds to farmers to improve production techniques; cap. N24.0m.

Bank of the North Ltd.: P.O.B. 211, Kano; f. 1959; cap. p.u. N3.0m.; dep. N59.7m.; Gen. Man. H. M. T. HOLROYD.

Co-operative Bank of Eastern Nigeria Ltd.: Milton Ave., Aba; f. 1961; cap. p.u. N1.3m.; dep. N8.5m.

Co-operative Bank Ltd.: Co-operative Bldgs., New Court Rd., P.M.B. 5137, Ibadan; f. 1953; res. N1.4m.; cap. p.u. N22.9m.; 13 brs.; Pres. Pastor E. T. LATUNDE, O.B.E.; Gen. Man. G. AYODELE ONAGORUWA, LL.B., A.I.B., B.L.

Mercantile Bank Ltd.: 1 Barracks Rd., P.M.B. 1084, Calabar; cap. p.u. N2.0m.; dep. N11.2m.; Chair. E. C. D. ABIA.

National Bank of Nigeria Ltd.: 82-86 Yakubu Gowon St., Lagos; f. 1933; nationalized by the Western State of Nigeria Govt. in 1961; cap. p.u. N6.5m.; dep. N73.6m.; Pres. H. S. A. ADEDEJI; Man. Dir. F. O. SOGUNRO.

New Nigeria Bank Ltd.: Ring Rd., P.M.B. 1193, Benin City; owned by government of Mid-West State; 8 brs.; cap. p.u. N2.4m.; dep. N19.4m.

Nigerian Bank for Commerce and Industry: f. 1973; Government bank to aid indigenization.

Pan African Bank Ltd.: 5 Liberation Drive, John Holt Bldg., Port Harcourt; cap. p.u. N2,640m.; dep. N12.1m.; Chair. G. K. J. AMACHREE.

Wema Bank Ltd.: 52–54 Denton St., Ebute-Metta, P.M.B. 1033; 8 brs.; cap. p.u. N2.8m.; dep. N7.0m.

FOREIGN BANKS

Arab Bank (Nigeria) Ltd.: 36 Balogun Square, P.O.B. 1114, Lagos; f. 1969; cap. N1.5m.; res. N193,216,000; dep. N6.0m.; Chair. A. M. SHOMAN; Man. Dir. H. A. DARWISH; 3 brs.

Bank of America (Nigeria) Ltd.: 138–146 Yakubu Gowon St., P.O.B. 2317, Lagos; br. at Port Harcourt; cap. p.u. N1.5m.; dep. 18.1m.

Bank of India Ltd.: P.O.B. 1252, 47-48 Breadfruit St., Lagos; f. 1962; cap. N1.5m.; dep. N3.1m.; Man. R. M. BOSE.

Barclays Bank of Nigeria Ltd.: P.M.B. 2027, 40 Marina, Lagos; f. 1972; cap. N12m.; dep. N315.8m.; 48.3 per cent government shareholding; Chair. Alhaji MUSA DAGGASH; Man. Dir. G. A. O. THOMSON; 87 brs. and agencies in all the states.

International Bank for West Africa Ltd.: 94 Yakubu Gowon St., P.O.B. 12021, Lagos; brs. at Apapa, Kano and Port Harcourt; cap. p.u. N1.7m.; dep. N18.5m.

Standard Bank Nigeria Ltd.: Head Office, 35 Marina, P.O.B. 5216, Lagos; cap. N9.7m.; dep. 244.6m.; 79 brs. throughout Nigeria; Chair. Mallam AHMADU COOMASSIE; Exec. Vice-Chair. C. P. JOHNSTON; Man. Dir. ROBERT PIERCY.

United Bank for Africa (UBA) Ltd.: 97/105 Yakubu Gowon St., P.O.B. 2406, Lagos; f. 1961; 28 brs.; cap. p.u. N6m.; dep. N145.8m.; Chair. Sir PATRICK REILLY, G.C.M.G., O.B.E.; Gen. Man. LOUIS MICHEL.

DEVELOPMENT BANK

Nigerian Industrial Development Bank Ltd.: P.M.G. 2357, Mandlas House, 96-102 Yakubu Gowon St., Lagos; f. 1964 to finance industry, mining, hotels and tourism generally, to attract foreign capital and personnel, and to encourage investment; cap. p.u. £N3m.; Chair. Mallam AHMADU COOMASSIE; Gen. Man. S. B. DANIYAN.

STOCK EXCHANGE

Lagos Stock Exchange: P.O.B. 2457, 114 Yakubu Gowon St., Lagos; f. 1960; three Dealing Members; Chair. S. B. DANIYAN; Sec. M. A. ODEDINA, F.C.I.S., A.A.I.A.; publ. *Lagos Stock Exchange Daily List*.

INSURANCE

In July 1973 there were 71 insurance companies registered in Nigeria.

African Alliance Insurance Co. Ltd.: 112 Yakubu Gowon St., Lagos; Man. Dir. T. A. BRAITHWAITE.

African Insurance Co. Ltd.: 134 Nnamdi Azikiwe Street, P.O.B. 274, Lagos.

Great Nigeria Insurance Co. Ltd.: 39–41 Martins St., P.O.B. 2314, Lagos; f. 1960; life and property insurance; cap. p.u. £N90,000; Man. Dir. F. O. OGUNLANA.

Guinea Insurance Co. Ltd.: P.O.B. 1136, Lagos; f. 1958; fire, accident, marine; cap. p.u. £N76,000; Man. A. T. CAIN, F.C.I.I.

Gulf Assurance Corporation Ltd.: 17A Nnamdi Azikiwe St., P.O.B. 2799, Lagos.

Law Union and Rock Insurance Co. of Nigeria Ltd.: 88/92 Yakubu Gowon St., P.O.B. 944, Lagos; 4 brs.

Lion of Africa Insurance Co. Ltd.: (Incorporated in Nigeria) P.O.B. 2055, Ebani House, 149/153 Yakubu Gowon St., Lagos; all classes; cap. p.u. £N135,000; Gen. Man. B. LAND, F.INST.D.

National Insurance Corporation of Nigeria: 97/105 Yakubu Gowon St., Lagos; br. in Kaduna.

NEM Insurance Company (Nigeria) Ltd.: 12–14 Yakubu Gowon St., P.O.B. 654, Lagos.

New Africa Insurance Co. Ltd.: Head Office: 31 Marina, Lagos; incorporated 1955; life, fire, accident, marine; cap. p.u. £N200,000; Chair. Alhaji SHEHU AHMED, O.O.N., O.B.E.

New India Assurance Co. (Nigeria) Ltd.: 34 Balogun Sq., Lagos.

New Insurance Co. (Nigeria) Ltd.: 12/14 Yakubu Gowon St., P.O.B. 944, Lagos.

Nigerian General Insurance Co. Ltd.: 1 Nnamdi Azikiwe St., P.O.B. 2210, Lagos; f. 1951; 15 brs.; Gen. Man. J. A. AWOYINKA.

Riv-Bank Insurance Company: owned by the Rivers state government; cap. N400,000.

Royal Exchange Assurance (Nigeria) Group: 31 Marina, P.O.B. 112, Lagos; 8 brs.

United Nigeria Insurance Co. Ltd.: 53 Marina, Lagos; brs. throughout Nigeria; Gen. Man. J. H. DAY.

West African Provincial Insurance Co.: Head Office: Wesley House, 21 Marina, P.O.B. 2103, Lagos.

TRADE AND INDUSTRY

CHAMBERS OF COMMERCE

Association of Chambers of Commerce, Industry & Mines of Nigeria: P.O.B. 109, Lagos; mems. Chambers of Commerce of Lagos, Calabar, Ibadan, Kano, Jos, Warri, Benin, Sapele and Enugu; Pres. Chief S. L. EDU.

African Chamber of Commerce: 73 Oluwole St., P.O.B. 478, Lagos.

Benin Chamber of Commerce: P.O.B. 487, Benin City.

Calabar Chamber of Commerce: P.O.B. 76, Calabar; 16 mems. (trading and shipping companies).

Enugu Chamber of Commerce: P.O.B. 734, Enugu.

Ibadan Chamber of Commerce: Barclays Bank Bldg., Bank Rd., P.M.B. 5168, Ibadan; publ. *Commercial Directory*.

Kano Chamber of Commerce and Industry: P.O.B. 10, Kano; 104 mems.; Pres. A. J. AKLE.

Lagos Chamber of Commerce and Industry: 131 Yakubu Gowon St., P.O.B. 109, Lagos; f. 1888; 380 mems.; Pres. J. ADE TUYO; Chair. Chief HENRY FAJEMIROKUN; Sec. Mrs. J. ADUKE MOORE, B.L.

Nigerian National Chamber of Commerce: f. 1960; Pres. M. A. AJAO.

Ondo Chamber of Commerce: P.O.B. 3, Ondo.

Onitsha Chamber of Commerce: 50 Old Market Rd., P.O.B. 181, Onitsha; f. 1953; Chair. C. T. ONYEKWELY; Sec. ALEXANDER IBEKWE AGWUNA.

Port Harcourt Chamber of Commerce: P.O.B. 71, Port Harcourt.

Sapele Chamber of Commerce: P.O.B. 109, Sapele.

Warri Chamber of Commerce: P.O.B. 302, Warri.

TRADE ASSOCIATIONS

Abeokuta Importers' and Exporters' Association: c/o Akeweje Bros., Lafenwa, Abeokuta.

Ijebu Importers and Exporters' Association: 16 Ishado St., Ijebu-Ode.

Nigerian Association of African Importers and Exporters: 35 Kosoko St., Lagos.

Nigerian Association of Native Cloth Dealers and Exporters: 45 Koesch St., Lagos.

Nigerian Association of Stockfish Importers: 10 Egerton Rd., Lagos.

Union of Importers and Exporters: P.O.B. 115, Ibadan; f. 1949; Chair. E. A. SANDA; Sec. C. A. ADEGBESAN.

OTHER ORGANIZATIONS

Association of African Miners: 32 Lonsdale St., Jos.

Association of Master Bakers, Confectioners and Caterers of Nigeria: 13-15 Custom St., P.O.B. 4, Lagos; f. 1951; 250 mems.; Acting Pres. J. ADE TUYO; Sec. M. A. OKI, F.INST.B.B.

Federation of Building and Civil Engineering Contractors in Nigeria: 34 McCarthy St., P.O.B. 282, Lagos; publ. *Construction in Nigeria* (monthly); circ. 3,500.

Indian Merchants' Association: Inlaks House, 19 Martins St., P.O.B. 2112, Lagos.

Institute of Chartered Accountants of Nigeria: 60 Marina, P.O.B. 1580, Lagos.

Lagos Association of Benin Carvers: 16 Tinubu St., Lagos.

Nigerian Chamber of Mines: P.O.B. 454, Jos; f. 1950; Pres. G. GRIFFIN; Sec. Lt.-Col. H. E. BARLOW.

Nigeria Employers Consultative Association: P.O.B. 2231, 31 Marina, Lagos; f. 1957; 450 mems.; Dir. W. G. TRACY; publ. *NECA News*.

Nigerian Livestock Dealers' Association: P.O.B. 115, Sapele.

Nigerian Recording Association: 9 Breadfruit St., P.O.B. 950, Lagos.

Nigerian Rubber Dealers' Association: Sapele.

Nigerian Society of Engineers: Lagos.

Nigeria Timber Association: 19 Shopeju St., Shogunle, P.M.B. 1185, Ikeja; f. 1957; Pres. S. A. PITAN; Sec. J. H. BEELEY.

Pharmaceutical Society of Nigeria: 4 Tinubu Square, P.O.B. 546, Lagos.

Union of Niger African Traders: 18 Notteridge St., Onitsha.

PUBLIC CORPORATIONS AND DEVELOPMENT ORGANIZATIONS

Agricultural Development Corporation: Ministry of Agriculture, Enugu.

Development Corporation (West Africa) Ltd.: Akuro House, 5 Custom Street, Lagos; subsidiary of the Commonwealth Development Corporation; provides finance and personnel for viable commercial projects; commonly operates through locally registered companies in partnership either with Government or with commercial firms.

Federal Institute of Industrial Research: P.M.B. 1023, Ikeja; f. 1955; plans and directs industrial research and provides technical assistance to Nigerian industry; specializes in foods, minerals, textiles, natural products, industrial intermediates and others; Dir. I. A. AKINRELE.

Gaskiya Corporation: Zaria; f. 1938; owned by Northern State Government; undertakes printing.

Industrial Training Fund: 127/129 Yakubu Gowon St., Lagos; f. 1971; to promote and encourage skilled workers in industry.

Lagos Executive Development Board: P.O.B. 907, Lagos; f. 1928; planning and development of Lagos; 9 mems.; Chair. Dr. G. A. WILLIAMS, Medical Officer of Health, Lagos; Chief Executive Officer S. O. FADAHUNSI.

New Nigeria Development Company Ltd.: 18/19 Ahmadu Bello Way, Development House, P.M.B. 2120, Kaduna; f. 1968; development/investment agency owned by the six state governments of Northern Nigeria; Chair. Mallam AHMED TALIB; Sec. Mallam MUSA BELLO.

New Nigeria Development Company (Properties) Ltd.: P.M.B. 2040, Kaduna; helps to create better living conditions throughout the six Northern States of Nigeria.

Nigerian Enterprises Promotion Board: 15 Keffi St., Obalende, Lagos; f. 1972; to promote indigenization of Nigerian enterprises.

Nigerian Industrial Development Bank: P.M.B. 2357, M. & K. House, 96-102 Yakubu Gowon St., Lagos; f. 1964; to finance industry and mining, to attract foreign capital and personnel and to further the growth of investment; cap. p.u. £N4.5m.; Chair. Mallam AHMADU COOMASSIE; Gen. Man. S. B. DANIYAN.

Nigerian Industrial Products Agencies Co. Ltd. (NIPACO): 11 Martins St., P.O.B. 1035, Lagos; supplies building and agricultural materials.

Nigerian National Oil Corporation: holds the Nigerian Federal Government's share in the oil companies and deals with oil exploration production refining and transportation.

Northern Nigeria Housing Corporation: Bida Rd., P.M.B. 2040, Kaduna; grants loans for housing; has chairman and six members.

Northern Nigeria Investments Ltd.: Yakubu Gowon Way, P.O.B. 138, Kaduna; f. 1959 jointly by the Commonwealth Development Corporation and the New Nigeria Development Co. Ltd. to investigate and promote commercial projects, both industrial and agricultural in the six Northern States of Nigeria; present share capital £N4.4m.; Man. P. D. PARTRIDGE, B.COM., F.C.A.; Sec. JAMES PARRISH, F.C.A.

Price Control Board: f. 1970; under Federal Ministry of Trade; 23 mems.; fixes basic price for controlled commodities.

Rivers State Development Corporation: 35 Yakubu Gowon Drive, Port Harcourt.

South-Eastern State Agricultural Development Corporation: P.M.B. 1042, Calabar.

Western Nigeria Agricultural Credit Corporation: Lebanon St., P.M.B. 5200, Ibadan; f. 1964; controlled by Military Governor; grants loans to farmers; promotes agricultural development by encouraging modern methods of farming; participates in establishment of rubber plantations; Chair. S. A. YEROKUN; Gen. Man. E. O. OTITOJU.

Western Nigeria Development Corporation: P.M.B. 5085, Ibadan; f. 1959; initiates industrial and agricultural schemes; has 10 agricultural projects covering cocoa, rubber, palm products, coffee, pineapple and cashew; industrial projects now number 31, 5 of which are wholly owned and managed by the Corporation; the remaining 26 industries are partly owned with foreign and indigenous investors; also owns 2 modern hotels.

Western Nigeria Finance Corporation: P.M.B. 5119, Ibadan; f. 1955; finances projects which further the economic development of Western Nigeria, particularly industrial enterprises; Chair. Chief TAJUDEEN OKI; Exec. Dir. Chief A. A. AKISANYA; Acting Sec. E. O. AKISANYA; Acting Sec. E. O. OTITOJU.

Western Nigeria Housing Corporation: Ibadan; f. 1958 to develop house building and industrial estates in the Region; grants mortgages and loans for house purchase and operates a savings scheme; Chair. F. A. O. SHOGA; Gen. Man. A. ADESIDA.

Western Nigeria Printing Corporation: Ibadan; f. 1956 to produce all types of exercise book; also prints a wide range of literature and vernacular publications for all grades of education.

MARKETING BOARDS

The competence of the State Marketing Boards includes: fixing the legal minimum buying price of primary produce for the whole season and minimizing price alterations from season to season; maintaining and improving the quality of export produce; aiding economic development and research by grants, loans, investments; supplying produce to industries processing local primary produce.

Benue Plateau Marketing Board: P.M.B. 83, Jos; Gen. Man. S. P. S. GUSAH.

East Central State Marketing Board: Enugu; Gen. Man. H. N. NTEPHE.

Lagos State Marketing Board: Ministry of Finance and Economic Development, City Hall, Lagos; Chair. F. C. O. COKER.

Mid-Western Nigeria Marketing Board: Benin City; Gen. Man. E. U. EWEKA.

Nigerian Produce Marketing Board: Chair. H. A. EJUEYITCHE.

Northern States Marketing Board: Yakubu Gowon Way, P.M.B. 2124, Kaduna; f. 1954; serves all six Northern States; Gen. Man. M. M. ISMA.

Rivers State Marketing Board: Port Harcourt; Gen. Man. G. T. G. TOBY.

South-Eastern State Marketing Board: 2 Edem St., P.M.B. 1039, Calabar; Gen. Man. U. B. UMOH (acting).

Western State Marketing Board: P.M.B. 5032, Ibadan; Chair. A. A. LADEINDE.

TRADE UNIONS

In November 1973 the new Trade Union Decree, replacing the Trade Union Act of 1938 came into force. It stipulates the non-political nature of trade unions and gives the Government the power to regulate the conditions for federating unions and for the banning of unions in certain departments. Strikes are illegal under Decree 53 of 1969 which is still in force and the Government has declared its intention to unify the labour movement in Nigeria as the left-wing NTUF and conservative NWC and ULC are ideologically opposed.

FEDERATIONS

Christian Nigerian Workers' Council (NWC): 7 Montgomery Rd., Yaba, Lagos; affiliated to ICFTU; f. 1962; Sec.-Gen. CHUKWURU NNEMEKA.

Nigerian Trade Union Federation (NTUF): f. Oct. 1973 and composed of the former Nigerian Trade Union Congress (NTUC), former Labour Unity Front and mems. from the United Labour Congress of Nigeria; c. 800 unions claimed as mems.

United Labour Congress of Nigeria (ULC): 97 Herbert Macaulay St., Ebute-Metta, Lagos; affiliated to I.C.F.T.U.; officially recognized by the Government; 600,000 mems.; Pres. Alhaji YUNUSA KALTUNGO; Gen. Sec. EMMANUEL ODEYEMI (Nigeria OATUU Representative).

PRINCIPAL UNIONS

Amalgamated Union of Building and Woodworkers of Nigeria: 46 Osholake St., Ebute-Metta, Lagos; f. 1963; 70,000 mems.; Pres. E. EKAHARTTA; Sec.-Gen. R. O. GBADAMOSI.

Association of Locomotive Drivers, Firemen, Yard Staff and Allied Workers' of Nigeria: 231 Herbert Macaulay St., Yaba; f. 1940; 3,500 mems.; Gen. Sec. DEJI OYEYEMI.

C.F.A.O. and Associated Companies' African Workers' Union: 365 Herbert Macaulay St., Yaba, Lagos; f. 1957; 5,000 mems.; Gen. Sec. O. ESHIETT.

Consolidated Petroleum, Chemical and General Workers' Union of Nigeria: 231 Herbert Macaulay St., P.M.B. 1065, Yaba; Gen. Sec. A. E. OTU; publ. *The News*.

Holts African Workers' Union: 31 Bola St., Ebute-Metta, Lagos; 8,000 mems.; Pres. O. O. ODUYE; Gen. Sec. E. A. OMODARA.

Medical and Health Department Workers' Union: 9 Aje St., Yaba; f. 1941; 5,000 mems.; Gen. Sec. H. I. S. UCHE.

Municipal and Local Authorities Workers' Union: 28 Clifford St., Ebute-Metta, Lagos; f. 1951; 5,000 mems.; Gen. Sec. S. U. BASSEY.

Nigeria Civil Service Union: 23 Tokunboh St., P.O.B. 862, Lagos; f. 1912; 11,520 mems.; Sec. ALABA KALEJAIYE.

Nigerian Coal Miners' Union: 17-19 Udi Ave., Udi Siding, Enugu; f. 1951; 32,300 mems.; Gen. Pres. E. A. BASSEY; Gen. Sec. J. J. MADU.

Nigerian Dockers' Transport and General Workers' Union: 9 Rosamond St., Suru-Lere, Yaba; f. 1950; 3,500 mems.; Gen. Sec. A. E. OKON.

Nigerian Mines Workers' Union: P.O.B. 40, Bukuru; f. 1948; 15,000 mems.; Gen. Sec. Mr. LANIYAN.

Nigerian Union of Local Authority Staff: P.O.B. 3050, Mapo Hill, Ibadan; f. 1942; 15,000 mems.; Pres. J. A. WOYE; Sec. Chief A. A. ADEGBAMIGBE; Treas. S. I. AMOLE.

Nigeria Union of Teachers: 29 Commercial Ave., P.M.B. 1044, Yaba, Lagos; f. 1931; 58,000 mems.; Gen. Sec. A. F. ADE AWOLANA; Pres. R. O. ASENIME; First Vice-Pres. S. B. C. ANYANINU; publ. *Nigerian Schoolmaster*.

Public Utility Technical and General Workers' Union of Nigeria and Cameroons: 48 Coates St., Ebute-Metta; f. 1941; 16,793 mems.; Sec. N. O. ESHIETT.

Railway and Port Transport Staff Union: 97 Herbert Macaulay St., Ebute-Metta, Lagos; f. 1937; 4,600 mems.; Gen. Sec. H. P. ADEBOLA.

U.A.C. and Associated Companies' African Workers' Union of Nigeria: 83A Simpson St., Yaba; f. 1955; 10,510 mems.; Pres. D. O. EHIOGHAE; Gen. Sec. F. N. KANU.

Union of Post and Telecommunications Workers of Nigeria: 16 Bishop St., P.O.B. 1020, Lagos; f. 1942; 3,500 mems.; Pres. S. A. ADESUGBA; Gen. Sec. G. C. NZERIBE.

CO-OPERATIVES

There are over 4,500 Co-operative Societies in Nigeria.

Co-operative Federation of Nigeria: c/o Co-operative Div., Ministry of Labour, P.M.B. 12505, Lagos.

Association of Nigerian Co-operative Exporters Ltd.: New Court Rd., P.O.B. 477, Ibadan; f. 1945; producers/exporters of cocoa and other cash crops.

Co-operative Supply Association Ltd.: 349 Herbert Macaulay St., Yaba, Lagos; importers and dealers in agricultural chemicals and equipment, fertilizers, building materials, general hardware, grocery and provisions.

Co-operative Union of Western Nigeria Ltd.: P.M.B. 5101, New Court Rd., Ibadan; education, publicity.

East Central State Co-operative Produce Marketing Association Ltd.: Ministry of Trade, Enugu; f. 1970; cap. £N2,258; Pres. J. U. AGWU; Vice-Pres. S. O. IHEANACHO.

Kabba Co-operative Credit and Marketing Union Ltd.: P.O.B. 25, Kabba; f. 1953; producers of food and cash crops and dealers in consumer goods; Pres. A. B. PHILLIPS; Man. H. A. SHEM.

Kwara Co-operative Federation Ltd.: Ilorin; operates transport and marketing services in Kwara state; Gen. Man. J. OBARO.

Lagos Co-operative Union Ltd.: c/o Co-operative Div., Ministry of Labour, Lagos; co-operative publicity.

TRANSPORT

RAILWAYS

Nigerian Railway Corporation: Ebute Metta, Lagos; f. 1955; has wide powers to enable it to operate as a commercial undertaking and is responsible for the management and operation of Nigerian railways, including the fixing of rates and fares, subject to an upper limit fixed by the Federal Minister of Transport, who may also intervene on important matters of policy, Chair. Alhaji Ibrahim Dasuki; Acting Gen. Man. T. I. O. Nzegwu; Acting Sec. J. T. D. Duncan; publs. *Nigerail* (House Journal), *Nigerian Railway Annual*.

Length of railways: 2,190 miles. A recent extension to the rail system runs for 400 miles from Kafanchan to Maiduguri.

ROADS

There are about 55,000 miles of motor road, of which over 9,500 miles are bitumen surfaced. A large-scale programme of road development is under way.

In April 1972 Nigeria changed from left-hand to right-hand drive.

INLAND WATERWAYS

Inland Waterways Department: Federal Ministry of Transport, Lagos; responsible for all navigable waterways; publ. *Navigational Bulletin*.

SHIPPING

The principal ports are Lagos (Apapa) and Port Harcourt. The World Bank has granted Nigeria N7m. for expansion of Port Harcourt, which will enable ships of 33,000 tons to come alongside the main wharf.

Nigeria Shipping Federation: P.O.B. 107, N.P.A. Commercial Offices Block "A", Wharf Rd., Apapa; f. 1960; Chair. J. D. Prifti; Gen. Man. D. B. Adekoya.

Nigerian Ports Authority: 26–28 Marina, Private Mail Bag No. 12588, Lagos; f. 1955; is responsible for the general cargo quays in Lagos and Port Harcourt, and harbour facilities in the 11 Nigerian ports; dredging, lighting, survey work and lighthouses; Chair. A. I. Wilson; Gen. Man. M. Tokunboh; publs. *NPA News* (quarterly), *NPA Annual Report*, *NPA Brochure*, *The History of the Ports of Nigeria*.

Nigerian National Shipping Line Ltd.: Development House, 1 Creek Rd., P.O.B. 326, Apapa; f. 1959; government-owned; operates cargo and limited fast passenger services between West Africa, the United Kingdom and the Continent; Chair. (vacant); Gen. Man. Dr. H. Dehmel; Sec. J. O. Itodo.

The following shipping companies run cargo and passenger services to Nigeria:

Acomar: c/o Alraine (Nigeria) Ltd., P.O.B. 2206, Lagos.

Barber Steamship Lines Inc.: 17 Battery Place, New York, N.Y. 10004, U.S.A.

Black Star Line: (*see* State Shipping Corporation).

Chargeurs Line (Compagnie Maritime des Chargeurs Réunis): UMARCO, P.O.B. 94, Apapa.

Delta Line (Delta Steamship Lines Inc.): Union Maritime et Commerciale, P.O.B. 217, Lagos.

Deutsch-Afrika Linie: Woermann Agency (Nigeria) Ltd., 21 Warehouse Rd., Apapa; P.O.B. 593, Lagos.

Elder Dempster Lines Ltd.: P.O.B. 167, Lagos.

Fabre Line (Compagnie Fabre & S.G.T.M.): UMARCO (Nigeria) Ltd., P.O.B. 94, Apapa.

Farrell Lines Inc.: P.M.B. 1151, Apapa; twice-monthly services to North America; Man. (West Africa) Capt. R. H. Ballard.

Gold Star Line: Lagos and Niger Shipping Agencies Ltd., P.M.B. 192, Apapa.

Greek West Africa Line: c/o Alraine (Nigeria) Ltd., P.O.B 2206, Lagos.

Guinea Gulf Line Ltd.: c/o Elder Dempster Agencies Ltd., P.O.B. 167, Lagos.

Holland West Afrika Lijn N.V.: P.O.B. 20, Lagos; North-west Europe to West Africa.

Hugo Stinnes Transozean Schiffahrt G.m.b.H.: Transocean Nigeria Ltd., Development House, 21 Wharf Rd., P.O.B. 1101, Lagos.

John Holt Ltd.: P.O.B. 157, Ebani House, 149–153 Yakubu Gowon St., Lagos.

Kawasaki Kisen Kaisha Ltd.: Palm Line Agencies of Nigeria Ltd., P.O.B. 531, Lagos; monthly direct service to Japan via Hong Kong.

Leif Hoegh & Co.: c/o Alraine (Nigeria) Ltd., P.O.B. 2206, Lagos.

Lloyd Triestino, S.p.A.: UMARCO, P.O.B. 94, Apapa.

Marasia: c/o Alraine (Nigeria) Ltd., P.O.B. 2206, Lagos.

Marconi International Marine Co. Ltd.: 4 Creek Rd., P.O.B. 211, Apapa.

Mitsui Line: Palm Line Agencies of Nigeria Ltd., P.O.B. 531, Lagos.

Nigerian National Shipping Line Ltd.: Development House, 21 Wharf Rd., P.O.B. 326, Apapa.

> **Nigerline (U.K.) Ltd.:** Oriel Chambers, Water St., Liverpool, L2 8TG, England; f. 1972; subsidiary of the Nigerian National Shipping Line Ltd.; Man. Dir. D. A. Okwuraiwe.

Palm Line Ltd.: c/o Palm Line Agencies of Nigeria Ltd., P.O.B. 531, Lagos.

Polish Ocean Line: c/o Alraine (Nigeria) Ltd., P.O.B. 2206, Lagos.

Royal Interocean Lines: P.O.B. 20, Lagos; West Africa to East Africa, Far East, Australia, New Zealand and South America.

Scandinavian West Africa Line: Union Maritime et Commerciale, P.O.B. 94, Apapa.

Seven Stars (Africa) Line (Zim Israel Navigation Co. Ltd.): Lagos and Niger Shipping Agencies Ltd., P.O.B. 192, Apapa.

Splosna Plovba: c/o Alraine (Nigeria) Ltd., P.O.B. 2206, Lagos.

State Shipping Corporation (Black Star Line): 21-23 King George V Rd., P.O.B. 1488, Lagos.

Veb Deutsche Seereederei: c/o Alraine (Nigeria) Ltd., P.O.B. 2206, Lagos.

Woermann Line: c/o Alraine (Nigeria) Ltd., P.O.B. 2206, Lagos.

CIVIL AVIATION

INTERNAL

Nigeria Airways: Airways House, P.O.B. 136, Lagos Airport; f. 1958 as successor to West African Airways Corpn.; operates internal services and links Nigeria with Ghana, Sierra Leone, Gambia, Ivory Coast,

Lebanon, Liberia and Cameroon; VC10 service to the United Kingdom via European airports; pool service with Pan-American Airways to New York and with UTA to Paris; operates two Boeing 707-320C, two 737-200, three Fokker F.28-2000, five Fokker F27, one Aztec; Chair. S. M. C. OBI; Gen. Man. L. L. T. LAWSON (acting).

Aero Contractors Company of Nigeria: P.O.B. 2519, 8–10 Yakubu Gowon St., Western House, Lagos; f. 1959; Man. Dir. A. SLOT; air charter company.

Pan African Airlines (Nigeria): P.M.B. 1054, Ikeja; charter air company.

INTERNATIONAL

The following international airlines also serve Nigeria: Aeroflot, Air Afrique, Air Niger, Air Togo, Air Zaire, Alitalia, British Caledonian, Cameroon Airlines, EAAC, EgyptAir, Ethiopian Airlines, Ghana Airways, KLM, Lufthansa, MEA, PAA, Sabena, Swissair and UTA.

POWER

The National Electric Power Authority: this body now controls:

Electricity Corporation of Nigeria: 24-25 Marina, P.M.B. 2030, Lagos; f. 1950; chief authority for the generation and supply of electricity in Nigeria; Chair. Sir MILES CLIFFORD.

Niger Dams Authority: P.M.B. 12605, Lagos; f. 1962; operating and maintaining Kainji hydroelectric plant and 330 kV. transmission lines and substations in Nigeria; Chair. Alhaji AHMADU DANBABA.

Nigerian Coal Corporation: Enugu; f. 1950; generally controls the coal industry including mining development and the distribution of coal; operates one colliery near Enugu.

TOURISM

Nigeria Tourist Association: P.O.B. 2944, 47 Marina, Lagos; f. 1963; Sec.-Gen. I. A. ATIGBI, B.A.; publs. *Nigeria Tourist Guide, Hotels and Catering in Nigeria,* and a wide range of other information material for tourists.

UNIVERSITIES

Ahmadu Bello University: Zaria; f. 1962; 899 teachers, 4,944 students.

University of Benin: Benin City; f. 1970; 81 teachers, 417 students.

University of Ibadan: Ibadan; f. 1962; 723 teachers, 3,795 students.

University of Ife: Ile-Ife; f. 1961; 370 teachers, 2,753 students.

University of Lagos: Lagos; f. 1962; 328 teachers, 1,973 students.

University of Nigeria: Nsukka; f. 1960; 600 teachers, 3,363 students.

University of Science and Technology: Port Harcourt; under construction.

OMAN

INTRODUCTORY SURVEY

Location, Climate, Language, Religion, Flag, Capital

The Sultanate of Oman lies at the extreme south-east of the Arabian peninsula and is flanked by the United Arab Emirates on the extreme north, by Saudi Arabia on the north and west, and by the People's Democratic Republic of the Yemen on the extreme west. The frontier with Saudi Arabia is very ill-defined. The climate is exceptionally hot and humid in the summer (maximum temperature 42°C (108°F)) and mild in the winter. The official language is Arabic, though English is spoken in business circles. The majority of the population are Ibadhi Muslims; about a quarter are Sunni Muslims. The national flag has horizontal stripes of white, red (one-fifth of the depth) and green, with a red vertical stripe at the hoist. In a canton at the upper left is the state badge, in white. The capital is Muscat.

Recent History

Officially known as Muscat and Oman until 1970, the Sultanate has had a special relationship with Britain since the nineteenth century. The small army and police force still have British officers. Sultan Said bin Taimur succeeded his father in 1932, and maintained a strictly conservative and isolationist rule until July 1970, when he was over-thrown by his son in a bloodless palace *coup*. The new Sultan, Qabus bin Said, then began a cautious liberaliza-tion of the régime, and increased spending on development which is expected to account for nearly three-quarters of government expenditure by 1973–74.

A major problem in recent years has been the continuing conflict with Marxist guerrilla forces in Dhofar Province. These groups united to form the Popular Front for the Liberation of Oman and the Arabian Gulf in 1972. However, government forces have been gaining the upper hand during 1973.

Government

The Sultan rules with the advice of a cabinet of minis-ters. Legislation is by decree.

Defence

The Omani army numbers about 10,000, including 250 British officers and N.C.O.s on secondment or contract. Defence expenditure rose from 12.4 million rials in 1970 to over 30 million in 1972. Defence support for the Dhofar operations has come from Jordan, Saudi Arabia, Iran and the United Arab Emirates.

Economic Affairs

Cereal crops are grown for local consumption, while dates, limes and pomegranates are the chief export crops. Cattle breeding is extensive in Dhofar, and the Oman camel is highly valued throughout Arabia. The most urgent problem is the shortage of water. Production of oil was begun in August 1967 by Petroleum Development (Oman) Ltd., which is 85 per cent owned by Shell, 10 per cent by the Compagnie Française des Pétroles and 5 per cent by the Gulbenkian Foundation; concessions have been awarded to other companies since then (see Oil section).

Public Holidays

1974: August 14th* (Ascension of the Prophet), October 14th–16th* (Id-ul-Fitr), November 18th (National Day), November 19th* (Birthday of the Sultan), December 26th* (Id-ul-Adha).

1975: January 14th* (Muslim New Year), March 26th* (Mouloud).

* Dependent on the Muslim lunar calendar; these dates may vary by one or two days from the dates given.

Weights and Measures

The imperial, metric and local systems are all used.

Currency and Exchange Rates

1,000 baiza = 1 rial Omani.

Exchange rates (April 1974):

£1 sterling = 815.6 baiza;
U.S. $1 = 345.4 baiza.

STATISTICAL SURVEY

Area: 120,000 square miles.

Population: 750,000 (estimate for mid-1973); Muscat (capital) 6,200, Matrah 14,000. Estimated number of gainfully employed 150,000: agriculture 109,000; fisheries 15,000; government 10,000; construction 6,000; oil, banking, services 5,000; others 5,000.

Agriculture: Land utilization 1971 (hectares): Batinah 13,800; Interior 19,920; capital area 1,080; Musandam 400; Dhofar 800. Crops include dates, lucerne, limes, onions, pomegranates, wheat, bananas, mangoes, tobacco, chickpeas and coconuts.

Currency: 1,000 baiza = 1 rial Omani (formerly called the rial Saidi). Coins: 2, 5, 10, 25, 50 and 100 baiza. Notes: 100, 250 and 500 baiza; 1, 5 and 10 rials. Exchange rates (April 1974): £1 sterling = 815.6 baiza; U.S. $1 = 345.4 baiza; 100 rials Omani = £122.61 = $289.52.

Budget: Revenues depend almost entirely on oil royalties and other payments by oil companies; in 1972 these were estimated at over 49 million Omani rials.

External Trade: Exports (1972): 49.7 million Omani rials, of which 49.3 million were oil exports. Imports (1972): 51.4 million Omani rials (estimate).

EXTERNAL TRADE
IMPORTS*
(Omani rials)

	1971	1972
Australia	969,852	1,068,843
Burma	1,095,536	365,862
Germany, Fed. Repub.	352,661	654,437
Japan	847,003	1,949,435
India	971,405	1,124,468
Iran	801,501	429,003
Netherlands	498,337	957,427
U.A.E.	2,457,225	3,920,822
United Kingdom	2,707,558	3,872,289
Others	n.a.	4,342,595
Total	10,699,078	18,713,181

* Total of non-oil and non-government imports.

NON-OIL EXPORTS

Non-oil exports consist mainly of limes, fish and tobacco:
(Omani rials) 1970 388,500; 1971 429,804; 1972 394,100.

OIL PRODUCTION
(million tons)

1968	12.1
1969	16.1
1970	17.2
1971	14.7
1972	13.6

Oil: The main oilfields are at Fahud, Natih and Yibal. Output in 1971 was 14.7 million tons; the Government receives 50 per cent of the net income, plus 12.5 per cent of total oil exports.

EDUCATION

	PRIMARY		SECONDARY	
	Boys	Girls	Boys	Girls
1970–71	3,008	470	—	—
1971–72	13,450	2,351	—	—
1972–73	25,414	4,774	623	128

THE GOVERNMENT

Head of State and Premier:

Sultan Qabus bin Said.

CABINET
(*January* 1974)

Governor of Muscat: Sayyid Thuwaini bin Shihab.

Minister of the Interior and Justice: Sayyid Hilal bin Hamad al-Sammar.

Minister of Health: Dr. Assim Jamali.

Minister of Land Affairs: Sayyid Muhammad bin Ahmed.

Minister of Communications and Public Services: Abd-al-Hafiz Salim Rajab.

Minister of Waqf and Islamic Affairs: Shaikh Alwalid bin Zaher.

Minister of Social Affairs and Labour: Khalfan Nassir al-Wahaibi.

Minister of Information and Tourism: Sayyid Fahad bin Mahmoud al-Said.

Minister of Education: Sayyid Faisal Ali al-Said.

Minister of Development: Karim Ahmed al-Haramy.

Minister of State for Foreign Affairs: Qais Zawawi.

Deputy Minister of Defence: Sayyid Fahar bin Taimur.

Secretary to the Cabinet: Sayyid Hamad Hamoud.

DIPLOMATIC REPRESENTATION

EMBASSIES ACCREDITED TO OMAN
(In Muscat unless otherwise stated)

Egypt: (E); *Ambassador:* Hassan Ali Hassan Salim.

France: Kuwait City, Kuwait (E).

India: (E); *Ambassador:* J. Singh.

Italy: Kuwait City, Kuwait (E).

Japan: Kuwait City, Kuwait (E).

Jordan: (E); *Ambassador:* Dr. Yacoub Abu Ghosh.

Kuwait: *Chargé d'Affaires:* Abdul Latif al Dowaisan.

Morocco: Kuwait City, Kuwait (E).

Netherlands: Baghdad, Iraq (E); *Consul in Muscat:* W. J. Thate.

Pakistan: (E); *Chargé d'Affaires:* G. Rabbani.

Qatar: (E); *Ambassador:* Mohamed Saad Fuhaid.

Saudi Arabia: (E); *Ambassador:* Sheikh Salah Al Suqair.

Spain: Kuwait City, Kuwait (E).

Tunisia: Kuwait City, Kuwait (E).

United Kingdom: (E); *Ambassador:* Donald Hawley.

U.S.A.: Kuwait City, Kuwait (E); *Chargé d'Affaires in Muscat:* C. J. Quinlin.

Oman also has diplomatic relations with Algeria, Australia, Chad, Greece, Lebanon, Syria and Turkey.

JUDICIARY AND RELIGION

Legal System: Jurisdiction is exercised by the Sharia Courts, applying Islamic Law. Local courts are officered by *Qadhis* appointed by the Sultan. The Chief Court is at Muscat. Appeals from the Chief Court go to the Sultan.

Religion: The majority of the population are Ibadhi Muslims; about a quarter are Sunni Muslims.

PRESS

Gulf Weekly Mirror: P.O.B. 455, Manama, Bahrain; weekly English newspaper for the Southern Gulf; Editor Stephen Kemball.

Oman: P.O.B. 600, Muscat; Government weekly newspaper; Arabic; published by the Ministry of Information.

Al-Watan: Muscat; weekly newspaper.

RADIO

Radio Oman: Muscat; f. 1970; transmissions 7 hours daily; Dirs. SALIM AL-FAHID, Shaikh ABDULLAH AL-AMRI.

The British Broadcasting Corporation has built a powerful new medium-wave relay station on the island of Masirah, off the Oman coast. It is used to expand and improve the reception of the B.B.C.'s Arabic, Farsi and Urdu services.

FINANCE
BANKING

British Bank of the Middle East: London; f. 1889; P.O.B. 234, Muscat; handles government finance; branches in Matrah, Mina Al-Fahal, Al Falaj Hotel, Saham, Salalah, Seeb International Airport, Sohar and Nizwa; Man. P. F. H. MASON.

The Chartered Bank: P.O.B. 210, Muscat; Man. A. H. DEVERELL; brs. in Matrah, Ruwi and Sur.

National and Grindlays Bank: London; P.O.B. 91, Muscat; Man. R. MURRAY.

National Bank of Oman: Muscat.

Other banks include: Arab Bank, Habib Bank Overseas, Bank Melli Iran, Bank of Oman, Bahrain and Kuwait, Arab-African Bank.

INSURANCE

Gray, Mackenzie and Co. Ltd.: Muscat; representatives of several British insurance companies.

OIL

Petroleum Development (Oman) Ltd.: P.O.B. 81, Muscat; f. 1937; since 1967 85 per cent owned by Shell, 10 per cent by Compagnie Française de Pétroles and 5 per cent by Gulbenkian interests; exports oil from the Fahud, Yibal and Natih and Al-Huwaisah oilfields via a pipe-line to a terminal at Mina al Fahal, near Muscat; in December 1973 the Government of Oman acquired a 25 per cent interest in the concession on terms similar to those agreed elsewhere in the Gulf area. At the same time, Petroleum Development (Oman) relinquished some 35,000 sq. miles of concession area; exports (1973) 106.8 million barrels.

Wintershall AG: P.O.B. 155, Muscat; holds offshore exploration concession in the Gulf of Oman; drilling since 1968; Wintershall heads consortium with 50 per cent, Shell 24 per cent, Deutsche Schachtbau 10 per cent, and Partex 7 per cent; exploration is at present taking place off the Batinah coast.

In February 1973 an agreement was signed with a group of four companies (two Canadian, one German, one American) to explore an offshore area of 13,000 sq. km. south-west of Masinah Island. Early in December 1973 a concession for some 5,300 sq. km. off the Musandam Peninsula was awarded to the French company ELF-ERAP. The agreement provided for participation by the Sultanate Government.

TRANSPORT

Pack animals, especially camels, remain the favoured means of transport for most of the population, but the number of motor vehicles is rapidly increasing. In 1972 9,771 vehicles were registered as opposed to 5,516 in 1971.

ROADS

On the coastal plain there is a graded motor road from Sohar to Sharjah and to Buraimi through the Wadi Jizzi. The Oil Company and the Development Department also maintain several graded motor roads in the interior linking Muscat with the Sharqiyah to the south-east, with Nizwa to the west, and with Ibri and Buraimi to the north-west, covering approximately 500 miles. The Government is now constructing a macadamized road from Muscat to Sohar on the coast (232 km.), at a cost of £10.5 million. It was due to be completed in 1973, and will serve as the main land link between Oman and the United Arab Emirates.

SHIPPING

The construction of Port Qabus, a new port at Matrah costing £20 million, is due to be completed in the summer of 1974; it will be able to accommodate the largest freighters in the Gulf. About 200 cargo vessels call annually, and regular calls are also made by the Bombay–Gulf passenger vessels. All vessels at present discharge into lighters off Matrah.

Other ports for small craft only are Murbat, Sohar, Kuburah, Sur and Salalah.

Gray, Mackenzie and Co. Ltd.: P.O.B. 70, Muscat; shipping, clearing and forwarding agents and general merchants.

CIVIL AVIATION

All domestic and international flights now operate from Seeb International Airport; the terminal building is still under construction and expected to be completed by early 1974. From Muscat Gulf Aviation operates 16 flights to Bahrain, Dubai, Abu Dhabi, Doha, Bombay, Karachi and London, and a bi-weekly service to Salalah, in Dhofar Province. International flights are also operated by British Airways, MEA, KAC, PIA and Air India. Use of the airfield by unscheduled aircraft is subject to at least 72 hours notice and the permission of the Oman Government.

Gulf Aviation Co. Ltd.: Head Office: P.O.B. 1388, Bahrain; f. 1950; shareholders: Governments of Bahrain, Qatar, Abu Dhabi and the Sultanate of Oman with 19 per cent each, and British Airways Associated Companies Ltd. with 23 per cent; fleet: two VC 10, three BAC 1-11, three Fokker F.27, three Skyvan, one Skyliner, two Queen Air B80, two BN-2A Islander; Chair. G. H. C. LEE; daily services between Muscat and Dubai, Muscat and Abu Dhabi, Muscat and Doha and Muscat and Bahrain. Service twice a week to Bombay and twice a week to Karachi.

PAKISTAN

INTRODUCTORY SURVEY

Location, Climate, Language, Religion, Flag, Capital

The Islamic Republic of Pakistan is bordered by India to the east and Afghanistan and Iran to the west. It has a short frontier with China in the far north-east. The climate is hot and dry with an average temperature of 80°F (27°C) except in the mountains where the winters are cold. The national language is Urdu; English is extensively used. The state religion is Islam, embracing about 97 per cent of the population, the remainder being mainly Hindu or Christian. The national flag (proportions 3 by 2) is dark green, charged with a white crescent moon and a five-pointed white star, with a vertical white stripe at the hoist. The capital is Islamabad (created July 1965).

Recent History

Pakistan was created in August 1947 by the partition of the former British India into the independent states of India and Pakistan. It originally had two parts, East Pakistan and West Pakistan, separated by about 1,000 miles of Indian territory. The new nation was formed in response to demands by Muhammad Ali Jannah's Muslim League for a specifically Islamic state, to free Muslims from domination by the Hindu majority in the sub-continent. Partition led immediately to religious and frontier conflicts in which hundreds of thousands of lives were lost. Pakistan's frontiers with India have never been satisfactorily settled; she maintains a claim to Kashmir which has been a source of armed conflict.

From the time of partition the eastern and western sections of the country were united only by religion, with no geographical, economic or racial coherence. The majority of the population lived in the smaller wing, East Pakistan, but political and military power were concentrated in the West. Pakistan's difficulties were increased by the search for a workable political system. A republic was established in March 1956 but in October 1958 parliamentary government ceased and was replaced by martial law. General (later Field-Marshal) Muhammad Ayub Khan was appointed Martial Law Administrator and in 1960 was elected President by the "basic democracy" system he had established. In 1962 a new constitution was proclaimed, giving the President wide-ranging powers and strengthening the central government at the expense of federalism.

Ayub Khan seemed firmly in control until 1968, when disorders broke out on a large scale, especially in East Pakistan. There were demands for democracy, provincial autonomy and a solution to the economic problems of the country. In March 1969 Ayub Khan was forced to resign. He was replaced by General Agha Muhammad Yahya Khan and martial law was reimposed.

In December 1970 elections were held for an assembly which was to draw up a new constitution. For the first time the East Pakistanis were to be allowed a majority in the assembly. Sheikh Mujibur Rahman's Awami League, standing for extreme autonomy, won with an overwhelming majority in East Pakistan and the Pakistan People's Party (P.P.P.) won most seats in the West. Yahya Khan tried to persuade Sheikh Mujib to form a coalition government with the P.P.P., but negotiations broke down and in March 1971 the army was sent in to settle the matter by force. East Pakistan declared its independence as the People's Republic of Bangladesh and civil war broke out between the martial law authorities and the followers of Sheikh Mujib (the *Mukhti Bahini*).

During October and November Indian support for the Bengalis grew and there were clashes with Pakistani troops. In December full-scale war between the two countries broke out. Within two weeks the Pakistani army in the East was forced to surrender and Bangladesh's independence became a reality. A cease-fire was accepted and Yahya Khan resigned. Zulfiqar Ali Bhutto, head of the P.P.P., became President of the truncated Pakistan.

Bhutto's Government embarked on a series of negotiations to deal with the aftermath of the war. In August 1973 an agreement was reached with India on the repatriation of Pakistani prisoners of war and the return of Bengalis in Pakistan to Bangladesh. In February 1974 Pakistan recognized Bangladesh and by May the repatriation of Pakistani prisoners was completed.

President Bhutto continued the search for a workable constitution and in 1972 one was proposed which seemed to have the support of all parties. In early 1973, however, opposition parties of the right and left formed a United Democratic Front to demand amendments which would create "a truly Islamic, democratic and federal constitution". Their fears that the constitution gave too much power to the Prime Minister and the central government were encouraged by events in Baluchistan where tribal fighting was followed, in February 1973, by the imposition of direct presidential rule and the taking of emergency powers. The governors of Baluchistan and the North West Frontier Province, members of the opposition National Awami Party, were replaced by central government appointees.

In March 1973, faced by an opposition threat to boycott Parliament and rioting in the streets, Bhutto compromised. An amended constitution was passed in April and came into force in August 1973, with Bhutto as Prime Minister. The situation in Baluchistan remained grave with fighting between government forces and tribal guerrilla groups. In August 1973 several leading opposition figures were arrested. In April 1974 the Government announced the ending of army operations in Baluchistan and an amnesty for political opponents, but fighting has continued.

Pakistan's former alignment with the Western bloc, seen in membership of CENTO and SEATO (she withdrew from the latter in 1972), has to a large extent given place to improved relations with China, North Viet-Nam, North Korea, Iran, Turkey and especially the United Arab Emirates.

Government

The new interim Constitution was adopted on April 10th, 1973 (for details *see* page 1156).

Defence

In 1973 the armed forces totalled 402,000 men including 10,000 in the navy and 17,000 in the air force. In the financial year 1972–73 about 50 per cent of the budget was devoted to defence. Pakistan is a member of the Central Treaty Organization (CENTO).

Economic Affairs

Agriculture is the backbone of Pakistan's economy. Wheat, sugar cane, rice and cotton are all important crops. During the 1960s agricultural production increased, but only kept pace with population growth. The average per capita income is still one of the lowest in Asia. Despite recent legislation to limit the size of holdings, land is very unevenly distributed.

Pakistan is poorly endowed with natural resources. Water is a valuable resource and extensive irrigation works have been undertaken. The Indus Basin water harnessing scheme is expected to improve the supply and use of water.

Pakistan has experienced a rapid growth in industrial output, with the former emphasis on consumer goods giving place to the development of export and capital industries. There is a serious balance of payments deficit and heavy dependence on foreign aid. Military expenditure is a burden on the economy. The loss of East Pakistan has deprived the economy of a large internal market and important revenue from jute exports. Bhutto's government has taken over or nationalized most major industries, insurance companies, banks, shipping firms and distributors of petroleum products.

Transport and Communications

Pakistan's rail and road systems, which were developed before Partition, have had to be adjusted to the new frontiers although some rail transit facilities have been negotiated with India. There are nearly 5,400 miles of railways in Pakistan. The principal port of Pakistan is Karachi. International air transport is provided by Pakistan International Airways Corporation (PIA) and twenty-three foreign lines.

Social Welfare

Social welfare services are run mainly through the Development Schemes and Urban Community Projects. The National Council of Social Welfare provides care for children, women, delinquents and the handicapped.

Government support is given to voluntary bodies providing social relief.

Education

Universal free primary education is a constitutional right but less than half Pakistan's children in fact receive it, and only about 10 per cent reach secondary education. Some 15 per cent of the population is literate. There are 7 universities.

Tourism

The Himalayan hill stations of Pakistan provide magnificent scenery, a fine climate and excellent opportunities for field sports, mountaineering and winter sports.

Visas are not required to visit Pakistan by nationals of Austria, Belgium, Denmark, France, Federal Republic of Germany, Greece, Iran, Japan, Luxembourg, Netherlands, Norway, Sweden, Tunisia and Turkey. The period of exemption is three months.

Sport

Pakistan's principal sports are hockey, cricket, football, wrestling and squash rackets. Polo, athletics and swimming are also popular.

Public Holidays

1974: August 14th (Independence Day), September 6th (Defence of Pakistan Day), September 11th (Anniversary of Death of Quaid-i-Azam), October 18th–19th (Eid-ul-Fitr), November 3rd (Jumatul Wida), December 25th (Birthday of Quaid-i-Azam and Christmas), December 26th (Eid-ul-Azha).

1975: January 23rd (Muharram Ashura), March 23rd (Pakistan Day).

Weights and Measures

The imperial system of measures is in force. Local measures of weight include:

1 maund = 82.27 lb.
1 seer = 2.057 lb.
1 tola = 180 grains

Currency and Exchange Rates

100 paisa = 1 Pakistani rupee.

Exchange rates (April 1974):

£1 sterling = 23.38 rupees;
U.S. $1 = 9.90 rupees.

STATISTICAL SURVEY

(figures relate to present-day Pakistan, excluding Bangladesh, except where otherwise stated).

AREA AND POPULATION*

AREA	CENSUS POPULATION				ESTIMATED POPULATION (mid-year)		
	February 1st, 1961	September 1972			1971	1972	1973
		Male	Female	Total			
310,403 sq. miles†	42,978,261‡	34,417,000	30,475,000	64,892,000	62,170,000	64,420,000	66,760,000

* Excludes data for the disputed territory of Jammu and Kashmir. The Pakistan-held part of this region, known as Azad ("Free") Kashmir, has an area of 32,358 sq. miles and an estimated population of more than one million.

† 803,943 sq. kilometres.

‡ Excluding adjustment for underenumeration, estimated by the Pakistan Planning Commission to have been 8.3 per cent for the whole of Pakistan (including what is now Bangladesh).

POPULATION OF PRINCIPAL CITIES

	1961 CENSUS	1972 ESTIMATE†		1961 CENSUS	1972 ESTIMATE†
Islamabad (capital)	50,000*	235,000*	Gujranwala	196,154	335,000
Karachi	1,912,598	3,469,000	Sialkot	164,346	169,000
Lahore	1,296,477	2,148,000	Sargodha	129,291	225,000
Hyderabad	434,537	834,000	Quetta	106,633	140,000
Lyallpur	425,248	1,109,000	Sukkur	103,216	143,000
Multan	358,201	723,000	Jhang	95,000	127,000
Rawalpindi	340,175	508,000	Bahawalpur	84,000	181,000
Peshawar	218,691	331,000			

* Islamabad is a newly-built city, which has been the administrative centre since July 1965. Population (1968): 75,000.

† Estimates are based on the intercensal growth rate.

AGRICULTURE

LAND USE, 1969–70
(million acres)

Cultivated Area	47.5
Not Available for Cultivation	50.4
Other Uncultivated Land	28.3
Forest	4.6
Area Not Reported	65.9
TOTAL	196.7

PRINCIPAL CROPS
(Years July to June)

	Area Sown ('000 acres)			Production ('000 long tons)			Yield (maunds* per acre)		
	1969/70	1970/71	1971/72	1969/70	1970/71	1971/72	1968/69	1969/70	1970/71
Rice . . .	4,008	3,715	3,643	2,363	2,165	2,169	14.2	16.5	15.9
Wheat . . .	15,393	14,771	14,578	7,179	6,374	n.a.	11.6	12.3	11.6
Cat-tail Millet (Bajra) .	1,560	1,852	1,876	297	349	354	4.9	5.2	5.1
Sorghum (Jowar) .	1,212	1,378	1,253	279	324	307	6.0	6.3	6.4
Maize . .	1,600	1,581	1,563	657	706	694	11.0	11.1	12.2
Barley . . .	399	347	327	102	90	101	6.7	7.3	n.a.
Chick-peas (Gram) .	2,314	2,280	2,237	503	492	n.a.	6.0	5.9	n.a.
Sugar Cane . .	1,532	1,572	1,365	25,953	22,801	19,648	442.6	461.1	457.6
Rape and Mustard .	1,184	1,260	1,200	251	265	n.a.	5.8	n.a.	n.a.
Sesame . .	56	76	103	88	10	13	3.2	3.2	3.6
Cotton (lint) . .	4,338	4,284	n.a.	527	534	n.a.	3.3	3.3	3.3
Tobacco . . .	149	150	130	115	111	n.a.	20.5	20.8	n.a.

* 1 maund = 82.27 lb.

Source: *Ministry of Food, Agriculture and Underdeveloped Areas*, Islamabad, 1972.

FISHING
(metric tons)

	1969	1970	1971
Indian Ocean:			
Shads	2,900	9,400	8,500
Redfishes, Basses, etc. . .	56,200	48,100	55,200
Indian Oil-sardine .	9,900	3,400	4,300
Tunas, Bonitos, etc. .	9,300	11,400	10,000
Silver Ribbonfish . .	9,300	12,000	8,800
Sharks, Rays, etc. .	37,700	39,800	41,800
Other Marine Fish .	2,000	4,000	2,500
	127,300	128,100	131,000
Prawns and Shrimps . .	20,700	25,700	19,800
Total Sea Catch .	148,000	153,800	150,900
Freshwater Fish . . .	30,600	19,000	18,400
Total Catch . .	178,600	172,800	169,300
Value of landings ('000 rupees) .	329,538	392,950	350,526

Source: FAO, *Yearbook of Fishery Statistics, 1971.*

MINING

(Years July to June)

	PRODUCTION (tons)			
	1968–69	1969–70	1970–71	1971–72
Chromite	25,621	25,137	27,318	34,169
Limestone	2,172,637	2,871,956	2,707,433	2,587,032
Gypsum	234,404	203,797	163,267	21,469
Fireclay	19,184	28,240	28,016	21,321
Silica Sand . . .	148,156	42,678	33,630	42,898
Celestite	580	507	478	254
Ochres	449	390	2,706	4,998
Iron Ore	425	154	n.a.	n.a.
Rock Salt	365,377	305,239	344,168	352,767
Coal	1,373,000	1,249,000*	n.a.	n.a.
Crude Petroleum ('000 galls.) .	136,872	136,041	n.a.	n.a.
Natural Gas ('000 cu. ft.) . .	100,070,944	127,648,681	n.a.	n.a.

* Estimated.

Source: Central Statistical Office, *Monthly Statistical Bulletin.*

INDUSTRY

(Years July to June)

		1969–70	1970–71	1971–72	1972–73
Cotton Yarn . . .	million lb.	602.4	669.7	740.1	803.8*
Cotton Fabric . . .	million yds.	725.5	787.3	751.3	701.4*
Art Silk and Rayon Cloth .	million sq. yds.	78.6	67.7	10.1	5.7*
Sugar	'000 tons	599.9	510.8	369.1	n.a.
Vegetable Products . .	,, ,,	121.9	133.5	158.9	184.1
Sea Salt . . .	,, ,,	248.0	215.0	236.0	186.0*
Cement	,, ,,	2,614.0	2,659.0	2,564.0	2,697.0*
Urea	,, ,,	203.1	201.5	388.5	524.7
Superphosphate . . .	,, ,,	22.9	25.0	27.0	45.0
Ammonium Sulphate . .	,, ,,	57.4	58.7	65.7	57.5*
Sulphuric Acid . . .	,, ,,	31.0	30.2	31.2	37.9*
Soda Ash	,, ,,	66.7	76.8	75.6	73.1
Caustic Soda . . .	,, ,,	28.0	30.5	30.9	30.4*
Chlorine Gas . . .	,, ,,	2.3	2.4	2.0	1.9
Cigarettes	million	22,369.0	24,166.0	21,772.0	27,623.0

* Provisional.

Source: Central Statistical Office, *Monthly Statistical Bulletin.*

FINANCE

100 paisa = 1 Pakistani rupee.

Coins: 1, 2, 5, 10, 25 and 50 paisa; 1 rupee.

Notes: 1, 5, 10, 50 and 100 rupees.

Exchange rates (April 1974): £1 sterling = 23.38 rupees; U.S. $1 = 9.90 rupees.

100 Pakistani rupees = £4.278 = $10.101.

Note: From July 1955 to May 1972 the par value of the Pakistani rupee was 21 U.S. cents (U.S. $1 = 4.7619 rupees). Between May 1972 and February 1973 the exchange rate was U.S. $1 = 11.00 rupees. In terms of sterling, the exchange rate was £1 = 11.43 rupees from November 1967 to August 1971; and £1 = 12.41 rupees from December 1971 to May 1972.

REVENUE BUDGET

Twelve months ending June 30th

(1972–73 estimates—million Rs.)

REVENUE		EXPENDITURE	
Customs	2,600	Revenue Collecting Departments	53
Central Excise	2,250	Civil Administration	904
Income Tax and Corporation Tax	965	Defence Services	4,230
Sales Tax	700	Civil Works and Central Road Fund	70
Post Office, Telegraphs and Telephones (net)	117	Interest Payments	1,936
Interest Receipts	889	Provincial Governments (Non-Development)	140
Currency and Mint	203	Other Non-Development	151
Defence Services	139	Provincial Governments (Development)	210
Other Revenue	646	Other Development	190
		Less: Development Expenditure met from Foreign Aid and Reserve Funds	−97
		Plus: Revenue Assignments to Provinces	1,083
		Plus: Revenue Surplus	(−)361
TOTAL	8,509	TOTAL	8,509

CAPITAL BUDGET

Twelve months ending June 30th

(1972–73 estimates—million Rs.)

REVENUE		EXPENDITURE	
Revenue Surplus	(−)361	Post Office, Telegraphs and Telephones	
Debt raised in Pakistan (net)	90	Irrigation	
Foreign Loans and Grants	3,128	Industrial Development	
Floating Debt (net)	206	Civil Aviation	
Unfunded Debt (net)	281	Broadcasting	
Recoveries of Loans and Advances	529	Ports	1,455
Accretions to Reserve Funds	1,066	New Federal Capital	
Other Deposits and Remittances (net)	4	Civil Works	
Other Capital Receipts	25	Food Storage and Other Works	
		Miscellaneous Investments	
		Other Expenditure	—
		Loans to Semi-Independent Bodies, etc.	1,055
		Loans and Grants to Provincial Governments	1,287
		Loans to Private Sector	256
		Non-Development Expenditure	1,362
		Contingency Item	—
		Cash Balance Improvement	−447
TOTAL	4,968	TOTAL	4,968

STATE BANK RESERVES*

(U.S.$ million at December 31st)

	1964	1965	1966	1967	1968	1969	1970	1971	1972
Gold	53	53	53	53	54	54	54	60	60
IMF Special Drawing Rights .	—	—	—	—	—	—	10	14	21
IMF Gold Tranche Position .	16	—	—	—	—	—	—	—	—
Foreign Exchange . .	175	167	145	103	185	270	118	107	192
Total . . .	244	220	198	156	239	324	182	181	273

* Beginning December 1971, gold is valued at $38 per troy ounce.

Source: IMF, *International Financial Statistics*.

Note: Figures include the former province of East Pakistan.

COST OF LIVING

Consumer Price Index for Karachi industrial workers

(base: 1963=100)

	1966	1967	1968	1969	1970	1971	1972	1973*
All Items . .	117.9	126.0	126.2	130.2	137.2	143.7	156.4	184.3
Food only . .	123.2	132.3	131.2	135.3	145.3	152.8	171.1	208.7

* Average for the month of June.

Source: United Nations, *Monthly Bulletin of Statistics*.

NATIONAL ACCOUNTS

(million rupees at current factor cost, July to June)

Sectors	1969–70	1970–71	1971–72	1972–73*
Agriculture	15,649	15,870	17,528	19,690
Crops	11,102	11,076	12,475	14,364
Livestock . . .	4,547	4,794	5,053	5,326
Fishing	233	261	295	335
Forestry	82	105	111	130
Mining and Quarrying . . .	229	243	268	355
Manufacturing	6,923	7,450	7,557	8,742
Construction	1,822	1,979	1,763	2,151
Electricity, Gas, Water, Sanitation .	661	782	823	886
Transport, Storage, Communications .	2,928	3,000	3,228	3,759
Wholesale and Retail Trade . .	6,475	6,781	7,085	8,333
Banking and Insurance . .	771	882	968	1,091
Ownership of Dwellings . .	1,614	1,752	1,913	2,143
Public Administration and Defence .	2,778	2,967	3,450	4,238
Other Services	3,134	3,475	3,894	4,454
Gross Domestic Product . .	43,299	45,547	48,883	56,307
Net Factor Income from Abroad . .	3	−82	99	374
Gross National Product . .	43,302	45,465	48,982	56,681

* Provisional.

Source: Ministry of Finance, Planning and Development, *Monthly Statistical Bulletin*.

EXTERNAL TRADE

(million rupees, July 1st to June 30th)

	1968–69	1969–70	1970–71	1971–72	1972–73
Imports . . .	3,046.4	3,285.1	3,602.4	3,495.3	8,398.3
Exports* . . .	1,762.7	1,657.0	2,110.8	3,423.2	8,623.5

* Including re-exports.

Source: Central Statistical Office, *Monthly Statistical Bulletin.*

COMMODITIES

('000 Rs.)

IMPORTS	1969–70	1970–71	1971–72
Food and Live Animals			
Rice	78,157	93,602	20,996
Wheat .	363,528	327,586	269,829
Sugar	5,460	44	26,578
Spices	20,822	17,699	17,053
Crude Materials inedible, excluding Fuels			
Raw and Waste Cotton . . .	11,278	6,312	9,388
Raw Wool	11,922	24,730	23,707
Wood and Timber .	56,244	44,733	58,467
Mineral Fuels, Lubricants and Related Materials			
Coal	34,717	26,491	4,194
Oil (Animal, Vegetable and Mineral). . .	413,458	653,406	385,576
Chemicals and Pharmaceuticals			
Dyes and Colours . . .	87,829	82,167	58,220
Manufactured Goods classified chiefly by material			
Paper, Pasteboard and Stationery . .	47,113	55,794	69,976
Rayon Yarn	3,591	6,267	7,514
Iron, Steel and Manufactures . . .	552,989	605,316	438,953
Cutlery, Hardware and Tools .	33,825	83,068	55,909
Non-ferrous Metals and Manufactures .	85,622	90,565	59,085
Machinery and Transport Equipment			
Electrical goods	338,756	319,554	257,154
Machinery other than electric . . .	1,090,441	862,708	594,254
Vehicles	424,962	563,928	197,197
Miscellaneous Manufactured Articles			
Building and Engineering Material . . .	40,024	32,698	19,814

EXPORTS	1969–70	1970–71	1971–72
Food and Live Animals			
Fish (excl. Canned Fish)	89,835	72,828	96,746
Tea	3	—	—
CrudeMaterials inedible, excluding Fuels			
Raw Jute	762,404	501,151	49
Raw Cotton	210,557	271,476	954,747
Raw Wool	26,642	20,936	24,603
Raw Hides and Skins	15,521	16,799	19,601
Manufactured Goods classified chiefly by material			
Jute Manufactures	788,885	648,789	17,606
Cotton Twist and Yarns . . .	268,390	365,195	605,630
Cotton Textiles	269,750	322,847	387,310

Note: Figures, other than for 1971–72, include the former province of East Pakistan.

TRADING PARTNERS
('000 Rs.)

	IMPORTS			EXPORTS		
	1969–70*	1970–71*	1971–72	1969–70*	1970–71*	1971–72
U.K.	580,010	545,723	353,331	370,768	317,907	259,853
U.S.A.	1,321,410	1,529,905	728,768	373,114	382,217	174,145
Japan	563,818	539,098	349,545	171,961	226,417	540,123
Germany, Federal Republic .	583,235	523,048	343,971	136,318	106,819	105,279
India	191	—	—	62	—	—
Sri Lanka	29,582	33,655	109,432	47,767	63,359	65,298
Malaysia	25,837	25,826	15,635	9,840	11,527	23,826
Belgium and Luxembourg .	51,974	60,883	41,259	90,879	74,210	28,430
France	138,969	73,092	76,260	76,240	54,336	62,152
Bahrain	55	12,549	2,112	31,573	20,362	28,725
Hong Kong	22,084	16,112	24,448	153,904	250,825	505,199
Australia	102,132	59,978	36,490	93,699	66,307	28,476
Italy	205,787	205,711	191,674	104,292	92,098	125,090
China, People's Republic .	94,608	149,857	99,083	138,065	94,269	146,041

* Figures include the former province of East Pakistan.

TRANSPORT

RAILWAYS
(Formerly Pakistan Western Railway)

	1968–69	1969–70	1970–71	1971–72*
Number of Passengers ('000) . .	134,776	128,670	126,037*	124,207
Passenger-miles (million) . . .	6,482	5,944	5,823*	5,914
Freight ('000 tons) . . .	14,540	12,329	12,341	12,599
Net Freight ton-miles (million) .	4,761	4,675	4,581	4,722

* Provisional.

Source: Ministry of Finance, Planning and Development, *Monthly Statistical Bulletin.*

ROADS

	PASSENGER CARS	MOTOR RICKSHAWS	TAXIS	BUSES	TRUCKS	TOTAL
1965 . .	99,478	14,569	7,938	14,025	31,203	167,213
1966 . .	89,213	15,153	7,922	14,393	30,683	157,364
1967 . .	100,316	15,943	8,734	16,210	33,718	174,921
1968 . .	109,566	17,577	9,386	17,903	35,345	189,777
1969 . .	112,833	17,407	10,714	18,808	36,029	195,791
1970 . .	141,263	19,393	12,826	21,426	41,340	236,248

SHIPPING

	VESSELS ('ooo net registered tons)		GOODS ('ooo metric tons)	
	Entered	Cleared	Loaded	Unloaded
1968–69 .	5,680	5,555	2,788	5,515
1969–70 .	6,024	5,813	3,372	5,929
1970–71 .	6,129	6,106	3,157	6,279
1971–72 .	5,872	5,701	3,010	6,296
1972–73 .	6,465	6,452	3,185	7,188

Source: Ministry of Finance, Planning and Development, *Monthly Statistical Bulletin.*

CIVIL AVIATION

(Figures include the former province of East Pakistan)

	1968	1969	1970	1971*
Kilometres flown ('ooo) .	26,601	27,846	28,927	28,798
Passengers ('ooo) .	1,164	1,279	1,336	1,086
Passenger-kilometres (million)	1,459	1,634	1,748	2,084
Freight tonne-kilometres ('ooo)	54,915	62,206	69,630	63,393
Mail tonne-kilometres ('ooo) .	6,689	7,291	8,042	7,738

* Provisional.

Source: United Nations, *Statistical Yearbook 1972.*

TOURISM

FOREIGN VISITORS

(Figures include the former province of East Pakistan)

COUNTRY OF ORIGIN	1970	1971
Afghanistan	10,672	n.a.
Australia . . .	3,576	3,423
Canada . . .	3,033	2,953
France . . .	6,587	6,860
Germany, Federal Republic .	10,239	9,306
Iran	2,885	2,927
Italy . . .	2,786	3,157
Japan . . .	4,068	3,256
Switzerland . .	2,711	2,646
U.K.	23,212	20,090
U.S.A. . . .	21,008	16,579
Others . . .	31,320	42,103
TOTAL . . .	122,097*	113,300

* Excludes 4,669 "Indian nationals" arriving at frontiers.

Source: United Nations, *Statistical Yearbook 1972.*

THE CONSTITUTION

The following proposals were unanimously adopted by leaders of all parliamentary parties, meeting in Islamabad under the Chairmanship of President Bhutto on October 20th, 1972. The new Constitution was adopted by the National Assembly on April 10th, 1973 and came into force on August 14th, 1973.

TWO HOUSES

In the Federal Parliamentary system the Head of the State is to be a constitutional President on whom the advice of the Prime Minister shall be binding in all respects. The Prime Minister, who is to be the chief executive, and his Cabinet shall be answerable to the Federal Legislature.

The Federal Legislature shall comprise two houses—the lower house called the National Assembly of 200 members elected directly on the basis of universal adult suffrage and the upper house called the Senate of 60 members. Each Provincial Assembly is to elect 14 Senators. The tribal areas are to return five and the remaining two are to be elected from the Federal Capital Territory by members of the Provincial Assemblies. For a period of 10 years women are to get 10 seats in the National Assembly raising its strength to 210.

SENATE

The role of the Senate in an overwhelming majority of the subjects, shall be merely advisory. Disagreeing with any legislation of the National Assembly, it shall have the right to send it back only once for reconsideration. In case of disagreement in other subjects, the Senate and National Assembly shall sit in a joint session to decide the matter by a simple majority.

An amendment to the Constitution shall require two-thirds majority in the National Assembly and its endorsement by a simple majority in the Senate. The members of the Senate may be taken in the Federal Cabinet provided their total number does not exceed 25 per cent of the total number of Central Ministers.

The stability of the parliamentary system is sought to be ensured through four main provisions. Firstly the Prime Minister shall be elected by the National Assembly and the President must call on him to form a government. Secondly, any resolution calling for the removal of a Prime Minister shall have to name his successor in the same resolution which shall be adopted by not less than two-thirds of the total number of members of the lower house. The requirement of two-thirds majority is to remain in force for 15 years or three electoral terms whichever is more. Thirdly, the Prime Minister shall have the right to seek dissolution of the legislature at any time even during the pendency of a no-confidence motion. Fourthly, if a no-confidence motion is defeated, such a motion shall not come up before the house for the next six months.

All these provisions for stability shall apply *mutatis mutandis* to the Provincial Assemblies also.

AUTONOMY

In the matter of relations between Federation and Provinces, Parliament shall have the power to make laws, including laws bearing on extra-territorial affairs, for the whole or any part of Pakistan, while a Provincial Assembly shall be empowered to make laws for that Province or any part of it. Matters in the Federal Legislative List shall be subject to the exclusive authority of Parliament, while Parliament and a Provincial Assembly shall have power to legislate with regard to matters referred to in the Concurrent Legislative List. Any matter not referred to in either list may be the subject of laws made by a Provincial Assembly alone, and not by Parliament, although the latter shall have exclusive power to legislate with regard to matters not referred to in either list for those areas in the Federation not included in any Province.

The executive authorities of every Province shall be required to ensure that their actions are in compliance with the Federal laws which apply in that Province. The Federation shall be required to consider the interests of each Province in the exercise of its authority in that Province. The Federation shall further be required to afford every Province protection from external aggression and internal disturbance, and to ensure that every Province is governed in accordance with the provisions of the Constitution.

To further safeguard the rights of the smaller provinces, a Council of Common Interests shall be created. Comprising the Chief Ministers of the four provinces and four Central Ministers to decide upon specified matters of common interest, the Council shall be responsible to the Federal Legislature. The constitutional formula gives the net proceeds of excise duty and royalty on gas to the province concerned. The profits on hydro-electric power generated in each province shall go to that province.

THE GOVERNMENT

HEAD OF THE STATE

(Sworn in August 14th, 1973)

President of the Republic: FAZAL ELAHI CHAUDRY.

THE CABINET

(July 1974)

Prime Minister and Minister of Foreign Affairs, Defence and Atomic Energy: ZULFIQAR ALI BHUTTO.

Minister of Presidential Affairs, Production and Commerce: BAFI RAZA.

Minister of Law and Parliamentary Affairs, Education and Provincial Co-ordination: ABDUL HAFIZ PIRZADA.

Minister of Finance, Planning and Development: Dr. MUBASHIR HASAN.

Minister of Social Welfare and Health: Sheikh MUHAMMAD RASHID.

Minister of Minority Affairs and Tourism: RAJA TRIDIV ROY.

Minister of Interior Affairs, Frontier Regions and Kashmir Affairs: KHAN ABDUL QAYYUM KHAN.

Minister of Labour, Works and Local Bodies: RANA MUHAMMAD HANIF.

Minister of Haj, Auqaf and Broadcasting: MAULANA KASUR NIAZI.

Minister Without Portfolio: KHURSHID HASAN MEER.

DIPLOMATIC REPRESENTATION

EMBASSIES ACCREDITED TO PAKISTAN

Afghanistan: 176, Sector F-7/3, Islamabad; *Ambassador:* Dr. ALI AHMED POPAL (also accred. to Thailand and Sri Lanka).

Albania: Cairo, Egypt.

Algeria: 72, Sector F-6/2, Islamabad.

Argentina: 233 Sector F-6/2, Islamabad; *Ambassador:* CARLOS FEDERICO SILVA GUZMÁN.

Australia: 2nd Floor, National Bank Bldg., Civic Centre G/6, Islamabad; *Ambassador:* A. M. MORRIS.

Austria: 415, F-6/3, Islamabad; *Ambassador:* Dr. ERNST JOSEF PLOIL.

Belgium: 291, Sector F-6/3, Islamabad; *Ambassador:* KAREL COECKX.

Brazil: 486-F, Sector G-6/4, Islamabad; *Ambassador:* QUINTINO S. DESETA.

Bulgaria: 26, Sector F-6/2, Islamabad; *Ambassador:* Prof. IVAN NENOV.

Burma: 386, Sector F-6/3, Islamabad; *Ambassador:* U THA TUN.

Canada: Diplomatic Enclave, Islamabad; *Ambassador:* J. G. HADWEN (also accred. to Afghanistan).

China, People's Republic: 23–24, Sector F-6/4, Islamabad; *Ambassador:* CHANG T'UNG.

Czechoslovakia: 25, Sector F-6/2, Islamabad; *Ambassador:* VLADIMIR LUDVIK.

Denmark: 302-F/6-3, Islamabad.

Egypt: 449-F, Sector G-6/4, Islamabad; *Ambassador:* ABOU EL FADL KASHABA.

Finland: Diplomatic Enclave, Islamabad.

France: 217-C, Sector F-7/4, Islamabad; *Ambassador:* HENRI BAYLE.

German Democratic Republic: Islamabad; *Ambassador:* Dr. HANS MERITZKI.

Germany, Federal Republic: 288 Peshawar Rd., Rawalpindi; *Ambassador:* Dr. ULRICH SCHESKE.

Ghana: 400, Sector F-6/2, Islamabad; *Ambassador:* GORDON C. N. CUDJOE.

Greece: Teheran, Iran.

Hungary: Diplomatic Enclave, Islamabad; *Ambassador:* JÁNOS VERTES.

Indonesia: 223, Sector F-6/3, Islamabad; *Ambassador:* Air Marshal SOETOPO.

Iran: Islamabad; *Ambassador:* MANOUTCHEHR ZELLI (also accred. to Sri Lanka).

Iraq: 178, Sector G-6/3, Islamabad; *Ambassador:* ABDUL-MALIK SALIM AL-ZAIBAK (also accred. to Thailand and Sri Lanka).

Italy: 28 Harlay St., Rawalpindi; *Ambassador:* Dr. OBERTO FABIANI.

Japan: 227, Sector F-6/2, Islamabad; *Ambassador:* TAKESHI KANEMATSU.

Jordan: 435, Sector G-6/4, Islamabad; *Ambassador:* ADEL HUSSEIN KHALIDI.

Khmer Republic: Cairo, Egypt.

Korea, Democratic People's Republic: *Ambassador:* OM GYONG CHOL.

Kuwait: 148, Sector G-6/3, Islamabad; *Ambassador:* Youssef Abdul Latif al-Abdul Razzaq.

Lebanon: 156, Sector F-6/3, Islamabad; *Ambassador:* Abdul Rahman Adra.

Libya: 344, Sector F-6/3, Islamabad; *Ambassador:* Ibrahim Ali El Jerbi.

Malaysia: 346, F-6/3, Islamabad; *Ambassador:* Kamaruddin Mohamed Arif.

Mauritius: *Ambassador:* Ameen Kasenally.

Mexico: Beirut, Lebanon.

Mongolia: Peking, China.

Morocco: 206, Sector G-6/3, Islamabad; *Ambassador:* Dr. Mohamed Saadani (also accred. to Malaysia).

Nepal: 64, Sector G-6/3, Islamabad; *Ambassador:* Khadga Man Singh.

Netherlands: 153, G-6/3, Islamabad; *Ambassador:* H. C. Maclaine Pont.

Nigeria: 440, Sector F-6/3, Islamabad; *Ambassador:* Alhaji Abdulkadir Dafuwa.

Norway: Diplomatic Enclave, Islamabad.

Philippines: 68, Sector F-6/2, Islamabad; *Ambassador:* Juan C. Dionisio (also accred. to Iran and Afghanistan).

Poland: 172, Sector G-6/3, Islamabad; *Ambassador:* Alojzy Bartoszek.

Portugal: 130-H, Sector G-6/3, Islamabad; *Ambassador:* Dr. Albertino dos Santos Matos.

Qatar: *Ambassador:* Mubarak Nassar Al Kuwarit.

Romania: 131, Sector G-6/3, Islamabad; *Ambassador:* Mihai Magheru.

Saudi Arabia: 68 Muslimabad, Dadabhoy Naoroji Rd.; *Ambassador:* Sheikh Riyadh Al-Khatib.

Somalia: Jiddah, Saudi Arabia.

Spain: 69, Sector G-6/3, Islamabad; *Ambassador:* Marcelino Fernandez Diez.

Sri Lanka: 468-F, Sector G-6/4, Islamabad; *Ambassador:* Feisal Junaid (also accred. to Iran).

Sudan: 189, Sector G-6/3, Islamabad; *Ambassador:* El-Baghir Abdel Mutaal (also accred. to Afghanistan).

Sweden: Diplomatic Enclave, Islamabad; *Ambassador:* Rune Nystrom.

Switzerland: 489, Sector G-6/4, Islamabad; *Ambassador:* Jacques Albert Mallet.

Syria: 355 F-6/3, Islamabad; *Ambassador:* Abdul Aziz Allouni.

Thailand: Diplomatic Enclave, Islamabad; *Ambassador:* Wichet Suthayakhom.

Turkey: 200-A Mayo Rd., Rawalpindi; *Ambassador:* Erdem Erner.

U.S.S.R.: 11 Diplomatic Enclave, Islamabad; *Ambassador:* A. A. Rodionov.

United Arab Emirates: *Ambassador:* Abdullah Darwish Ahmed.

United Kingdom: Diplomatic Enclave, Islamabad; *Ambassador:* Sir Laurence Pumphrey.

U.S.A.: Diplomatic Enclave, Islamabad; *Ambassador:* Henry Byroade.

Vatican City: Diplomatic Enclave, Islamabad (Apostolic Nunciature); *Nuncio:* J. Uhac.

Yugoslavia: 555-F Sumbul East Rd., Islamabad; *Ambassador:* Dr. Vido Knezevic.

Pakistan also has relations with the Gambia, Tunisia and the Democratic Republic of Viet-Nam.

PARLIAMENT

Under the 1973 Constitution the Federal Legislature comprises a lower house (The National Assembly) of 200 seats with 10 reserved for women elected on the basis of proportional representation and an upper house (The Senate) which has 60 members elected by the provincial assemblies.

NATIONAL ASSEMBLY

On August 14th, 1973, when the new Constitution came into effect, the Assembly comprised 146 members.

Speaker: Sahibzada Farooq Ali.

SENATE

On August 14th, 1973, when the new Constitution came into effect, the Senate comprised 45 members.

Chairman: Khan Habibullah.

PROVINCES

Pakistan has been divided into the four provinces of Sind, Baluchistan, Punjab and the North-West Frontier Province.

Sind

Governor: Begum Ra'ana Liaquat Ali Khan.

Baluchistan

Governor: Ahmed Yar Khan.

Punjab

Governor: Sadiq Hussain Qureshi.

North-West Frontier Province

Governor: Maj.-Gen. Said Ghawas.

POLITICAL PARTIES

Jamaat-i-Islami: 5-A Zaildar Park, Ichhra, Lahore; f. 1941; aims at the establishment of the Islamic state; Leader MIAN MUHAMMED TUFAIL.

Justice Party: f. early 1969 to work for establishment of federal parliamentary democracy through a lawful process; Pres. MIAN MUNZAR BASHIR.

National Awami Party: f. 1968; leftist; supports pro-Soviet line; Leader/Pres. KHAN ABDUL WALI KHAN.

Pakistan Democratic Party (P.D.P.): f. June 1969; aims to uphold "democratic and Islamic values"; Sec.-Gen. Sheikh NASIM HASAN.

Pakistan Muslim League: Muslim League House, 33 Davis Rd., Lahore; Pres. PEER SAHIB PAGAROO; Sec.-Gen. MALIK MOHAMMAD QASIM.

Pakistan People's Party: f. Dec. 1967; party of the Government; Islamic socialism, democracy and an independent foreign policy; Chair. President ZULFIQAR ALI BHUTTO.

ISLAM

Muslims make up 97.1 per cent of the population.

Chief Mufti: Mufti A-AZAM.

HINDUISM

Hindus make up 1.6 per cent of the population.

CHRISTIANITY

CHURCH OF PAKISTAN

The Church of Pakistan was inaugurated in November 1970 as a result of the organic union of the Anglicans, Methodists, Lutherans and Presbyterians (Church of

JUDICIAL SYSTEM

SUPREME COURT

Chief Justice: Hon. Mr. Justice HAMOODUR RAHMAN.

Puisne Judges: Hons. M. YAQUB ALI, A. SATTAR, S. A. JAN WAHID-UD-DIN-AHMAD.

HIGH COURT OF LAHORE

Chief Justice: Hon. Justice MOHAMMAD IQBAL.

HIGH COURT OF KARACHI

Chief Justice: Hon. Justice TUFAIL ALI ABDUR RAHMAN.

HIGH COURT OF PESHAWAR

Chief Justice: Hon. Justice GHULAM SIFDAR SHAH.

RELIGION

Scotland related) in Pakistan. United membership is approx. 250,000.

Moderator: The Bishop of Lahore: The Rt. Rev. INAYAT MASIH, Bishopsbourne, Cathedral Close, The Mall, Lahore.

ROMAN CATHOLIC CHURCH

The Archbishop of Karachi is H. E. Cardinal JOSEPH CORDEIRO, D.D., Archbishop's House, St. Patrick's Cathedral, Karachi 3.

The Apostolic Pro-Nuncio in Pakistan is His Excellency The Most Rev. Mgr. Joseph UHAC, Vatican Embassy, 317 F-6/3, P.O.B. 1106, Islamabad.

THE PRESS

Pakistan's press today is largely a remnant of the Muslim press that became prominent during the struggle for the national State (1940–47). The first Urdu-language newspaper, the daily *Urdu Akhbar*, was founded in 1836. After 1945, with the introduction of modern equipment, the more influential English newspapers, such as *Dawn* and *Pakistan Times*, were firmly established, while several new Urdu newspapers, for example *Naww-i-Waqt* and *Imroz*, became very popular.

In Pakistan there are 12 English dailies, 62 Urdu dailies and 10 in regional languages. In addition there are 230 weeklies and 16 bi-weeklies. These together with other publications number in all 1,222.

The Urdu press comprises 550 newspapers, with *Imroze*, *Nawa-i-Waqt* and *Mashriq* being the most influential. The largest daily is *Jang* (245,000 circulation). Though the English-language press reaches only 1 per cent of the population and totals 150 publications, it is influential in political, academic and professional circles.

PRINCIPAL DAILIES

RAWALPINDI

Jang: Jang House, P.O.B. 30, Dariabad; Rawalpindi edn. f. 1959; published simultaneously in Rawalpindi, Quetta and Karachi; Urdu; independent national; Editor-in-Chief Mir KHALIL-UR-RAHMAN; circ. (Rawalpindi) 65,000.

Nawa-i-Waqt: *see* Lahore, below.

Pakistan Times: *see* Lahore, below.

Ta'Meer: Saidpur Road; f. 1949; Urdu independent; Organizer S. M. AHSAN; Editor RIAZ HUMAYUN.

KARACHI

Aghaz: Preedy St., 11 Japan Mansion, Saddar; Urdu; Editor M. O. FARUQI.

Business Post: 4 Amil St., off Robson Rd., 1; f. 1963; morning; English; economic and business news; Editor AMEEN K. TAREEN.

Business Recorder: 531 Nazrul Islam Rd., 5; f. 1963; English; Editor M. A. ZUBERI.

Comment: 52 Ratan Talao, off Akhbar Rd.; f. 1952; evening; English; Editor H. M. ABBASI; circ. 2,000.

Daily News: Jang House, McLeod Rd.; f. 1962; evening; English; Editor WAJID SHAMSUL HASAN; circ. 35,000.

Dawn: Dr. Ziauddin Rd.; f. 1948; English, Gujarati; circ. 49,000; Editors AHMAD ALI KHAN (English edn.), M. Sadiq (Gujarati edn.).

Hurriyat: Hurriyat Office; Urdu; Editor F. ZAIDI.

Jang: Jang House, P.O.B. 52, McLeod Rd.; Karachi edn. f. 1937; published simultaneously in Karachi, Rawalpindi, Quetta and London; Urdu; independent national; Editor-in-Chief Mir KHALIL-UR-RAHMAN; circ. (Karachi) 180,000.

Leader: New Challi; English; Editor S. Ahmed.

Millat: 191 South Napier Rd.; f. 1946; Gujarati; Independent; circ. 9,400; Editor S. I. Matri.

Morning News: Saifee House, Dr. Ziauddin Ahmed Rd.; f. 1942; English; Editor-in-Chief Sultan Ahmed.

Nai Roshni: Nicol Rd.; f. 1949; Urdu; Independent; circ. over 20,000; Managing Editor M. Ashraf.

Vatan: Haroon House, Dr. Ziauddin Ahmed Rd.; f. 1942; Gujarati; Editor M. Sadiq; circ. 12,000.

LAHORE

Daily Business Report: 7A Nisbet Rd.; Urdu; Editor Ch. Shah Mohammad Azil.

Daily Rehbar: Urdu; Chief Editor Malik Mohammad Hayat, t.k. See also Daily Rehbar, Bahawalpur.

Imroze: Rattan Chand Rd.; f. 1948; Urdu; circ. Lahore 40,000, Multan 10,000.

Maghribi-Pakistan: 11A Lawrence Rd.; Urdu; Editor M. Shafaat Khaleel Saleh Muhammed Siddiq.

Mashriq: 46 Nisbet Rd.; f. 1963; Urdu; simultaneous editions in Karachi, Quetta and Peshawar; Editor Iqbal Zuberi; circ. 160,000.

Mujahid: 4 McLeod Rd.; f. 1948; Urdu; Editor A'si Nizami.

Nawa-i-Pakistan: Railway Rd.; f. 1948; Independent; Urdu; Editors Mujahidul Husain, Muhammad Rafique.

Nawa-i-Waqt Daily: Shahra-e-Fatima Jinnah, Lahore; f. 1940; Urdu-English; simultaneous edition in Rawalpindi; Editor M. Nizami; circ. 300,000.

Pakistan Times: P.O.B. 223; f. 1947; English; Liberal; Chief Editor K. M. Asaf.

Safeena: 78 Chamberlain Rd.; f. 1947; Urdu; Editor Ali Shamsi; circ. 6,000.

OTHER TOWNS

Aftab: Hyderabad; Editor R. A. Ajmeri.

Alfalah: Chhoti Lal Kurti, P.O.B. 35, Peshawar Cantt.; f. 1939; Urdu and Pashtu; Editor S. Abdullah Shah.

Al-Jamiat-i-Sarhad: Kissa Khani Bazar, Peshawar; f. 1941; Urdu-Pashtu; Editor S. M. Hassan Gilani.

Daily Rehbar: Rehbar Office: Chah Fateh Khan, Bahawalpur; f. 1952; Urdu; Chief Editor Malik Mohammad Hayat, t.k.. See also Daily Rehbar, Lahore (above).

Hilal-e-Pakistan: Haji Aminuddin Rd., P.O.B. 200, Hyderabad; f. 1946; Sindhi; Editor S. A. Mohammad.

Indus Times: Indus Times Office, Hyderabad; Editor A. G. Mirza.

Khyber Mail: 95A Saddar Rd., Peshawar; f. 1932; English; circ. 5,000; Editor Askar Ali Shah.

Shahbaz: Kissa Kahani Bazar, Peshawar; f. 1947; Urdu and Pashtu; Editor Maqbool Elahi Malik; circ. 7,000.

Zamana: Jinnah Rd., Quetta; Urdu; Editor Syed Fasih Iqbal; circ. 85,000.

SELECTED WEEKLIES

Ajkal: Kabuli Gate, Peshawar; f. 1958; Urdu; Editor Jamil Akhtar.

Akhbare Jehan: P.B. 32, McLeod Rd., Karachi; f. 1967; Urdu; independent national; illustrated family magazine; Editor-in-Chief Mir Habib-ur-Rahman; circ. 70,000.

Al-Tahir Weekly: 25 Haroon Chambers, Altaf Hussain Rd., Karachi; f. 1956; Urdu; Editor Syed Tahir Hussain; circ. 10,000.

Al Wahdat: Peshawar; Urdu and Pashtu; Editor Nurul Haq.

Amal: Aiwan-a-Abul Kaif, Abul Kaif Rd., Shah Qabool Colony, Peshawar; f. 1958; Urdu; Editor Aqai Abul Kaif Kaifi Sarhaddi.

Awam: Altaf Husain Row, P.O.B. 5257, Karachi; f. 1958; Urdu; political; Editor Abdur Rauf Siddiqi; circ. 3,000.

Bank Insurance News: 4 Amil St., Karachi; f. 1971; English; Editor Ameen K. Tareen.

Basant: Mutton Market, Rawalpindi; f. 1941; Urdu; Editor Ch. Hukam Chand Anand.

Chatan: 88 McLeod Rd., Lahore; f. 1948; Urdu; Editor Agha Shorish Kashmiri.

Dastkari: 8 McLagan Rd., Shara-e-Quaid-e-Azam, Lahore; Urdu; women's; Editor Begum Shafi Ahmed.

Hilal: Hilal Rd., Rawalpindi; f. 1951; Urdu; Friday; Illustrated Services journal; Editor Ikram Qamar; Business Man. A. Ghafoor Siddiqui; circ. 35,000.

Illustrated Weekly of Pakistan: Haroon Chambers, South Napier Rd., P.O.B. 635, Karachi; f. 1948; Sundays; English; circ. 21,450; Editor Ajmal Husain.

Insaf: P-929, Banni, Rawalpindi; f. 1955; Editor Mir Abdul Aziz.

Insaf: Bahalwalpur; f. 1946; Urdu; circ. 2,500; Editor Nasrullah Khan Tareen.

Investor: 8 Muhamed Bldg., Bunder Rd., Karachi; f. 1955; English; Editor A. R. G. Khan.

Karachi Commerce: P.O.B. No. 7442, 2/5 Akbar Rd., Karachi; f. 1947; circ. 5,500; English; Editor Z. I. Zobairy.

Lahore: Balwant Mansion, Beadon Rd., Lahore; f. 1952; Editor Saqib Ziravee; circ. 10,000.

Light: Ahmadiyya Building, Lahore; English; Editor Mirza Muhammad Hussain.

Memaar-i-Nao: 39 K.M.C. Bldg., Leamarket; Labour magazine; Urdu; Editor M. M. Mubasir.

Naqid: Chughtai Manzil, Padshah Rd., Sadar-3, Karachi; f. 1955; Urdu; Editor Badar Chughtai.

Noor Jehan: 1 Koh-i-Noor Cinema Chambers, Marshal St., Karachi; f. 1948; circ. 16,000; film journal; Urdu; Editor S. A. Chawla.

Pak Kashmir: Pak Kashmir Office, Mesay Gate, Rawalpindi; f. 1951; Urdu; Editor Muhammed Fayyaz Abbazi.

Parsi Sansar and Loke Sevak: Marston Rd., Karachi; f. 1909; English and Gujarati; Wed. and Sat.; Editor P. H. Dastur.

Parwaz: Madina Office, Bahawalpur; Urdu; Editor Mustaq Ahmed.

Pictorial: Jamia Masjid Rd., Rawalpindi; f. 1956; English; Editor Muhammad Safdar.

Qalandar: Peshawar; Urdu; Editor R. U. K. Sherwani.

Qindeel: 3A Shah Din Building, Shara-e-Quaid-e-Azam, Lahore; f. 1948; Urdu; Editor Sher Mohamad Akhtar.

Quetta Times: Albert Press, Jinnah Rd., Quetta, Baluchistan; f. 1924; English; Editor S. Rustomji; circ. 4,000.

Rahbar-e-Sarhad: Peshawar; f. 1956; Urdu; Editor M. Shabir Ahmad.

Shahab e Saqib: Maulana St., Peshawar; f. 1950; Urdu; Editor S. M. Rizvi.

Statesman, The: G.P.O. Box 212, 260-C Commercial Area P.E.C.H.S., Karachi 29; f. 1955; English; Editor Mohammad Owais.

Sunday Post: 4 Amil St., off Robson Rd., Karachi 1; f. 1957; English; social and cultural magazine of general interest; Editor Ameen Tareen.

Tanvir: Bazar Kissa Khani, Peshawar; Independent; Urdu; Editor AMIR SIDDIQI.

Tarjaman-i-Sarhad: Peshawar; Urdu and Pashtu; Editor MALIK AMIR ALAM AWAN.

SELECTED PERIODICALS
(Karachi unless otherwise stated)

Afkar: Robson Rd.; f. 1945; Urdu; art, literature, films; monthly; Editor SAHBA LUCKNAVI.

Ahang: Pakistan Broadcasting Corpn., PBC Publications, Kassam Manzial, Randal Rd.; fortnightly; Urdu; Chief Editor SABIH MOHSIN

Alam-i-Niswan: Peshawar Cantt., Peshawar; f. 1957; Urdu; monthly; Editor DOST MOHAMMAD FAKHRI.

Al-Ma'arif (formerly *Thaqafat*): Institute of Islamic Culture, Club Rd., Lahore; f. 1968; Urdu; monthly; Chief Editor Prof. M. SAEED SHEIKH; Editor S. H. RAZZAQI; Sec. Editorial Board M. ASHRAF DAAR.

Al-Masiha: Al-Masiha Bldg., 47 Abdullah Haroon Rd.; f. 1970; economic journal; monthly; Editor IQBAL HAIDARI; circ. 5,000.

Chaupal: National Development Organization; Block 45, Pakistan Secretariat; f. 1961; English; quarterly; Editor IBNE INSHA; circ. 2,500.

The Criterion (*Journal of the Islamic Research Academy, Karachi*): 10/C/163, Federal "B" Area, Karachi 38; literature, politics, religion; English; monthly; Editor KAUKAB SIDDIQUE.

Director: 42 Commercial Buildings, Shara-e-Quaid-e-Azam-Lahore; f. 1948; Urdu; monthly; films, literature and arts; circ. over 21,000; Editor M. FAZALHAQ.

Eastern Finance: NAZ Chambers, McLeod Rd.; English; fortnightly; Editor S. M. SHAMASUDDIN.

Eastern Message: Pakistan Union Store, Jamia Masjid, Mipur Khas; f. 1959; English; quarterly; Editor Sultan AHMAD ANSARI.

Economic Observer: 827 Mohammadi House, McLeod Rd., P.O.B. 5202; f. 1948; fortnightly; English; circ. 4,000; Editor H. A. RAZI.

Economic Review: Al-Masiha, 3rd Floor, 47 Abdullah Haroon Rd., Karachi 3; f. 1969; monthly; Pakistan's economic development; Editor IQBAL HAIDARI; circ. 10,000.

Enterprise: South Napier Rd.; English; monthly; Editor QAYYUM MALICK; circ. 8,000.

Federal Economic Review: University of Karachi; f. 1954; English; twice yearly; Editor Prof. Q. M. FAREED; circ. 500.

Flyer International: 189-B/2, PECH Society, P.O.B. 8034, Karachi 29; aviation and tourism; Editor ASGHAR AHMAD.

Gul-o-Khar: 83 Shara-e-Quaid-e-Azam, P.O.B. 84, Lahore; f. 1949; films and literature; monthly; Urdu; Editor MUHAMMAD SADIQ.

Hamdard-i-Sehat: Institute of Health and Tibbi Research, Hamdard National Foundation, Hamdard, P.O. Nazimabad, Karachi 18; f. 1933; Urdu; monthly; Editor HAKIM MOHAMMED SAID.

Industry and Trade Review: Inder St., Multan Rd., Lahore; f. 1959; English; monthly; Editor A. HAMID; circ. 6,200.

Iqbal: 2 Narsinghdas Garden, Club Rd., Lahore; f. 1952; critical review of Islamic philosophy, art, history and sociology; English/Urdu; quarterly; Editor Prof. M. M. SHARIF; circ. 1,100.

Izat Pakistan: Radio Pakistan, 71 Garden Rd.; fortnightly; Arabic.

Journal of Hamdard: Institute of Health and Tibbi Research, Hamdard National Foundation, P.O. Hamdard, Nazimabad, Karachi 18; f. 1957; English; Editor HAKIM MOHAMMED SAID.

Journal of the Pakistan Historical Society: 30 New Karachi Housing Society; f. 1950; English; quarterly; Editor Dr. MOINUE HAQUE.

K.P.T. News Bulletin: Karachi Port Trust; f. 1966; English; fortnightly; Editor I. A. QURAISHI; circ. 3,000.

Mah-i-Nau: P.O.B. 183; Pakistan Publications; f. 1948; illustrated, cultural monthly; Urdu; circ. 14,000; Editor MUHAMMED RAFIQ KHAWAR.

Makhzan: 2A Shah Din Bldg., Shara-e-Quaid-e-Azam, Lahore; f. 1906; monthly; Urdu; literary; Editor HAMID NIZAMI.

Medicus: Pakistan Chowk, Dr. Ziauddin Ahmed Rd., 1; f. 1950; English; medical journal; monthly; Editor M. S. QURESHI.

Museums Journal of Pakistan: Victoria Memorial Hall, Peshawar; f. 1954; English; quarterly; Editor M. QURESHI.

Muslim News (International): G.E.M. Chambers, Zaibunnisa St.; f. 1962; current affairs; monthly; circ. 10,000; Editor MEHDI ALI SIDDIQUI.

The Nucleus: Pakistan Atomic Energy Commission, P.O.B. 3112; f. 1963; quarterly; Editor (vacant).

Pak Travel: 7A Nisbet Rd., Lahore; f. 1955; English; monthly; Editor MUZAFFAR ALI QURESHI.

Pakistan Calling: Pakistan Broadcasting Corpn., PBC Publications, Kassam Manzil, Randal Rd.; monthly; English, Urdu, Persian and Arabic; Chief Editor SABIH MOHSIN.

Pakistan Export Directory: Trade and Industry House, 14 West Wharf Rd., P.O.B. 4611; f. 1966; English; annually; Editor-in-Chief GHAZI NASEERUDDIN.

Pakistan Horizon: Pakistan Institute of International Affairs, Strachan Rd.; f. 1948; international affairs; English; quarterly; Editor K. SARWAR HASAN; circ. 1,200.

Pakistan Journal of Forestry, The: P.O. Forest Institute, Peshawar (NWFP); f. 1951; English; quarterly; Editor MAHMOOD IQBAL SHEIKH; circ. 425.

Pakistan Journal of Scientific and Industrial Research: Pakistan Council of Scientific and Industrial Research, 39 Garden Rd., Karachi 3; f. 1958; English; Chief Editor M. A. HALEEM; six times a year.

Pakistan Management Review: Pakistan Institute of Management, P.I.D.C., Shahrah Iran, Clifton, Karachi 6; f. 1960; English; quarterly; Editor HAFEEZ R. KHAN.

Pakistan Medical Forum: 15 Nadir House, I. I. Chundrigar Rd., Karachi 2; f. 1966; monthly; English; Man. Editor M. AHSON.

Pakistan Paediatric Journal: III-D, 27/7 Nazimabad, Karachi 18; f. 1970; English; quarterly; Editor A. J. KHAN, M.B., B.S., M.R.C.P., D.C.H., F.R.F.P.S.

Pakistan Pictorial: P.O.B. 183, Karachi; f. 1948; English; all aspects of Pakistani life; non-political; published in seven languages including English, French, Urdu and Arabic; every two months; Editor S. AMJAD ALI; circ. 50,000.

Pakistan Press Directory: Chronicle Publications, Altaf Husain Rd.; P.O.B. 5257; annual.

Pakistan Review, The: Ferozsons Ltd., 60 Shara-e-Quaid-e-Azam, Lahore; f. 1953; English; monthly, political, cultural, social and economic affairs of Pakistan and the Islamic World; Editor-in-Chief Dr. A. WAHEED; Editor M. A. MAJEED.

Pakistan Textile Journal: 505 Qamar House, Bunder Rd.; f. 1950; monthly; English; Publisher-Editor MAZHAR YUSUF.

Pakistan Trade: Export Promotion Bureau; f. 1950; English; monthly; Editor A. F. MD. SHAMUZZAMAN.

Pasban: Faiz Modh Rd., Quetta; Urdu; fortnightly; Editor MOLVI MOHD. ABDULLAH.

Perspective: P.O.B. 183, Sharah Iraq; f. 1948; English; monthly digest; Editor JALALUDDIN AHMAD; circ. 10,000.

Port of Karachi Magazine: Karachi Port Trust; f. 1954; English; quarterly; Editor AZIZ AHMED; circ. 2,000.

Punjab Educational Journal: University Book Agency, Lahore; f. 1937; English; monthly.

Sadaf: Karachi Port Trust; f. 1961; Urdu; quarterly; circ. 2,000; Editor AZIZ AHMED.

Spem: Hamdard Waqf, Hamdard P.O.; f. 1959; English; quarterly; Editor HAKIM MOHAMMED SAID.

State Bank of Pakistan Bulletin: State Bank of Pakistan, Central Directorate, Chundrigar Rd.; f. 1951; English; monthly; Editor H. U. SHAHAB.

Statistical Bulletin: Statistical Div., I, S.M.C.H. Society; P.O.B. 7766; f. 1952; English; monthly.

Talim-o-Tarbiat: Ferozsons Ltd., 60 Shara-e-Quaid-e-Azam, Lahore; f. 1941; children's monthly; Urdu; Editor Dr. ABDUL WAHEED; circ. 25,000.

This Fortnight in Pakistan: 505 Qamar House, Bunder Rd.; f. 1965; Editor MAZHAR YUSUF and G. M. MEHKRI.

Trade and Industry: Trade and Industry House, 14 West Wharf Rd., P.O.B. 4611; f. 1957; English; monthly; Editor-in-Chief GHAZI NASEERUDDIN.

Trade Chronicle: Altaf Husain Rd.; f. 1953; English; monthly; trade and economics; Editor ABDUL RAUF SIDDIQI; circ. 5,500.

Trade Journal: Aiwan-e-Tijarat, Nicol Rd.; f. 1961; official organ of the Chamber of Commerce and Industry; Editor SYED ALI BAQAR; circ. 3,000.

Ummah: Central Institute of Islamic Research, Ministry of Education, Rawalpindi; English; monthly; Editors Dr. FAZLUR RAHMAN, Dr. S. H. MASUMI.

Venture: Karachi University; f. 1961; review of English language and literature; bi-annual; Editor SYED ALI ASHRAF; circ. 500.

Vision: 1 Victoria Chamber, Victoria Rd.; monthly; English; Editor YUNUS M. SAID.

Voice of Islam: A.M. 20, off Frere Rd., Saddar; monthly; English; Editor MUMTAZ AHMAD; Man. M. W. GAZDAR.

West Pakistan: 21 Abbot Rd., Lahore; f. 1958; English; monthly; Editor SYED A. Z. ZAIN.

Woman's World: 43/4A Pechs, Block 6; f. 1958; English; monthly; Editor Begum MUJEEB M. AKRAM.

Yaqeen International: Shahrah-e-Liaquat, Saddar, Karachi 3; f. 1952; English and Arabic; Islamic organ; Editor MUHAMMED SALEEM AHMAD.

FOREIGN BUREAUX

UPI: Victoria Rd., at Randal Rd. (near Tram Godi); Chief SHIRIN MANZIL.

Antara News Agency, DPA, Reuters and Tass also have offices in Pakistan.

PRESS ASSOCIATIONS

All Pakistan Newspapers Society: 3rd Floor, 32 Farid Chambers, A. Haroon Rd., Karachi-3; f. 1949; 49 mems.; Pres. Sh. AFTAB AHMED; Hon. Gen. Sec. KAZI SAEED AKBAR.

PUBLISHERS

Amalgamated Press: Bazar Kathian, Sialkot City; printers of newspapers.

Barque and Co.: Barque Chambers, Barque Square, Ali Khan, Lahore; f. 1930; trade directories, Who's Who, periodicals; brs. in Karachi; Man. Dir. A. M. BARQUE; Controlling Dir. FAROOQ U. BARQUE.

Crescent Publications: Urdu Bazar, Lahore.

Din Muhammadi Press: McLeod Rd., Karachi; f. 1948; reference books; Man. Dir. KHAWAJA GHULAM HUSSAIN.

Director Magazine Book Depot: 42 Commercial Buildings, Shara-e-Quaid-e-Azam, Lahore.

Economic and Industrial Publications: Al-Masiha, 47 Abdullah Haroon Rd., Karachi 3; f. 1965; books on Pakistan's economic and industrial development and weekly investors' service on corporate companies in Pakistan; monthly journal *Economic Review*; Editor FARZANA KHAN.

Ferozsons Ltd.: Mr. Abdul Qayyum Khan, Peshawar; f. 1894; books, periodicals, maps, charts, stationery, etc.; branches: Lahore, Peshawar, Rawalpindi, Karachi and Hyderabad; Chair. Dr. A. WAHEED; Man. Dir. A. HAMEED KHAN; Dir. A. SALAM KHAN.

Fine Art Printers: 46 Edwards Rd., Rawalpindi; f. 1928; Dirs. NAIEEM, SHAMEEM YAMIN.

Frontier Marketing Federation Ltd.: Sadar Rd., Peshawar Cantt.

Frontier Publishing Co.: Urdu Bazar, Lahore.

Government Publications: Manager of Publications, Central Publications Branch, Government of Pakistan, Block 44, Shahrah Iraq, Karachi.

International Printers: Dyal Singh Mansion, Shara-e-Quaid-e-Azam, Lahore; f. 1960; children's books; Principal Officials ZIA H. MIAN, MUKHTARAHMAD.

Islami Kutub Khana: Sadar Bazar, Mianwali (Punjab).

Islamic Publications Ltd.: 13-E, Shah Alam Market, Lahore; Islamic literature in Urdu and English; Dir. AKHLAQ HUSSAIN.

Kitabistan Ltd.: f. 1950; branches in Karachi (Hotel Metropole, Victoria Rd.), Man. Dir. E. M. ABBASI.

Madni Publications: Darus Salam, Thatta (Sind).

Maktaba-e-Islamia: Chowk Bazar, Bahawalpur.

Mercantile Guardian Press and Publishers: 81–83 Shara-e-Quaid-e-Azam, Lahore; f. 1949; trade directories, etc.; Editor MAHMOOD AHMAD MIR.

Nairoshni: Nicol Road, Karachi 2.

Orientalia Publishers: Lahore; Islamic publications.

Pak Publishers: Urdu Bazar, Lahore.

Pakistan Publications: P.O.B. 183, Shahrah Iraq, Karachi 1; general interest and literary books and magazines about Pakistan in English, Urdu and Arabic, etc.

Pakistan Publishing Co. Ltd.: 56-N, Gulberg Industrial Colony, Lahore; f. 1932; textbooks; government printers; Man. Dir. S. M. SHAH.

Pakistan Publishing House: Victorian Chambers 2, A. Haroon Rd., Karachi; f. 1959; Dir. M. NOORANI, B.COM.

Peco Ltd.: P.O.B. 70, Lahore; f. 1936; Koran and Islamic literature; Man. Dir. JAMEEL MAZHAR.

Pioneer Book House: 1 Avan Lodge, Bunder Rd., P.O.B. 37, Karachi; periodicals, gazettes, maps and reference works in English, Urdu and other regional languages.

Publishers International: Bandukwala Building, 4 McLeod Road, Karachi; f. 1948; reference books, advertising; Man. Dir. KAMALUDDIN AHMAD.

Publishers United Ltd.: 176 Anarkali, Lahore; textbooks, technical, reference and general books.

Punjab Religious Books Society: Anarkali, Lahore 2; educational, religious, law and general; Chair. Rt. Rev. INAYAT MASIH, Bishop of Lahore; Gen. Man. Capt. H. C. RAE.

"Rast Guftar" Press: Bhawana Bazar, Lyallpur; f. 1889; Publishers and Printers; Man. and Propr. SHAMSHAR ALI BASKHSHI.

Shaikh Muhammad Ashraf: Kashmiri Bazar, Lahore; f. 1923; books on all aspects of Islam in English; Man. S. A. HUSAIN SHAH.

Sindhi Adabi Board: Amin Manzil, Garri Khata, Hyderabad (Sind); f. 1951; history, literature, culture of Sind; translations into Sindhi, especially social sciences.

M. Siraj ud Din & Sons: Kashmiri Bazar, Lahore 8; f. 1905; religious books in many languages; Man. M. SIRAJ UD DIN.

Taj Company Ltd.: P.O.B. 530, Karachi; religious books; Man. Agent SH. ENAYET ULLAH.

Times Press: Mansfield St., Sadar, Karachi 3; f. 1948; books and periodicals; Man. Dir. SHUJAUDDIN.

Universal Publishing Co.: Urdu Bazar, Lahore.

University Book Agency: Kutchery Rd., Lahore.

PUBLISHERS' ASSOCIATION

Pakistan Publishers' and Booksellers' Association: Y.M.C.A. Bldg., Shara-e-Quaid-e-Azam, Lahore; Pres. CH. ABDUL HAMID; Sec. S. A. BUKHARI.

RADIO AND TELEVISION

RADIO

Pakistan Broadcasting Corpn.: 81A Satellite Town, Rawalpindi; f. December 1972; Dir.-Gen. SHAID HUSSAIN.

National broadcasting comprising seven stations: Rawalpindi-Islamabad, Karachi, Lahore, Multan, Peshawar, Hyderabad and Quetta. External services in 16 languages.

There were 1,500,000 radio receivers in use in 1972.

TELEVISION

Pakistan Television Corporation Ltd.: 1 Tulsa Rd., Lalazar Colony, P.O.B. 230, Rawalpindi, Punjab; Man. Dir. ASLAM AZHAR; Dir. (Programmes) AGHA NASIR.

Programmes daily 18.00–22.00 hours.

Extended transmissions on Fridays and Saturdays. Stations at:

Lahore-Ch 5: f. 1964; Gen. Man. ZAHEER BHATTI.

Rawalpindi-Islamabad-Ch 8: f. 1969.

Karachi-Ch 4: f. 1967; Gen. Man. K. AFTAB.

FINANCE

(cap. = capital; p.u. = paid up; dep. = deposits; m. = million; Rs. = Rupees)

BANKING

In January 1974, all Pakistani banks were nationalized. Foreign banks were not affected, but were not permitted to open any new branches in Pakistan.

CENTRAL BANK

State Bank of Pakistan: P.O.B. 4456, McLeod Rd., Karachi; f. 1948; controls and regulates currency and foreign exchange and has the sole right of note issue; cap. p.u. Rs. 30m.; dep. Rs. 3,164.4m. (June 30th, 1971); Gov. GHULAM ISHAQ KHAN; Deputy Gov. ABDUL LATIF.

PAKISTANI BANKS

Australasia Bank Ltd.: 2nd Floor, Gardee Trust Bldg., Napier Rd., P.O.B. 450, Lahore; f. 1942; cap. Rs. 5.4m.; dep. Rs. 338.8m. (Dec. 1970); Chair. FAROOQ A. SHEIKH; Gen. Man. M. A. K. YOUSUFI.

Bank of Bahawalpur Ltd.: P.I.D.C. House, Kutchery Rd., Karachi; a subsidiary of National Bank of Pakistan; f. 1947; cap. Rs. 5m.; Chair. and Man. Dir. (vacant).

Habib Bank Ltd.: Habib Bank Plaza, Karachi 21; f. 1941; cap. p.u. Rs. 90m.; res. Rs. 60m.; dep. Rs. 4,521m. (Dec. 1971); several hundred brs. throughout Pakistan and 27 overseas brs.; Pres. RAZZAK H. MOHAMMED; Chair./Man. Dir. RASHID D. HABIB.

Habib Bank (Overseas) Ltd.: Habib Square, Karachi 2; f. 1952; cap. Rs. 5m.; res. Rs. 4.6m.; dep. Rs. 395m. (Dec. 1971); Exec. Vice-Pres. G. A. MIRZA; Man. Dir. HYDER M. HABIB.

Lahore Commercial Bank Ltd.: Bank Mansion, 30 Napier Rd., Lahore; Man. Dir. M. A. FAROOQUE.

Muslim Commercial Bank Ltd.: Adamjee House, I. I. Chundrigar Rd., Karachi; f. 1948; cap. p.u. Rs. 27.0m.; dep. Rs. 1,495.4m. (Dec. 1971); Chair. A. W. ADAMJEE; Gen. Man. E. A. GARDA.

National Bank of Pakistan: I. I. Chundrigar Rd., Karachi; f. 1949; cap. p.u. Rs. 30m.; dep. Rs. 3,971.5m. (Dec. 1971); Man. Dir. A. JAMIL NISHTER.

United Bank Ltd.: American Life Building, I.I. Chundrigar Rd., Karachi; f. 1959; cap. Rs. 48m.; dep. Rs. 3,884.8m. (Dec. 1971); Chair. HABIB I. RAHIMTOOLA; Pres. AGHA HASAN ABEDI, S.PK.

FOREIGN BANKS

Afghan National Bank (Pakistan) Ltd. (*Banke Mille Afghan*): Kabul; Karachi.

Algemene Bank Nederland, N.V.: Vijzelstraat 32, Amsterdam; Karachi; Man. W. J. VAN DER MEI.

American Express International Travel Division: New York; Oriental Bldg., I. I. Chundrigar Rd., P.O.B. 4847, Karachi 2.

Bank of America N.T. and S.A.: Karachi.

Bank of India Ltd.: Bombay; Bunder Road, Karachi.

Bank of Tokyo: Tokyo; Karachi.

Chartered Bank, The: London; Karachi; also subsidiary Eastern Bank.

Commerce Bank: Karachi.

First National City Bank: New York, N.Y.; P.O.B. 4889, Karachi; Resident Vice-Pres. M. A. CALLAN; Man. M. R. HARDING-JONES; Lahore Branch: P.O.B. 612; Man. S. CRABTREE.

National and Grindlays Bank Ltd.: London; P.O.B. 5556, I. I. Chundrigar Rd., Karachi 2.

State Bank of India: Bombay; Karachi, Lahore.

Sumitomo Bank Ltd.: Tokyo; 111, Qamar House, Bunder Rd., Karachi 2.

United Commercial Bank Ltd.: Calcutta; Bunder Rd., P.O.B. 4811, Karachi.

CO-OPERATIVE BANKS

Co-operative Banks: 130 branches throughout Pakistan.

DEVELOPMENT FINANCE ORGANIZATIONS

Agricultural Development Bank of Pakistan: Shafi Court, Merewether Rd., Karachi; f. 1961; provides credit facilities to agriculturists and cottage industrialists in the rural areas and for allied objects; cap. authorized Rs. 200m.; total loans paid up (Sept. 1972) Rs. 1,536m.; Chair. RIAZUDDIN AHMED; Dep. Gen. Man. F. H. ABBASI; 11 regional offices and 89 field offices.

Investment Corporation of Pakistan: National Bank of Pakistan Bldg., P.O.B. 5410, Karachi-2; f. 1966 by the Government "to encourage and broaden the base of investments and to develop the capital market"; auth. cap. Rs. 200m., cap. p.u. Rs. 50m.; Chair. AKHTER HUSAIN, Man. Dir. N. M. QURESHI.

National Investment (Unit) Trust: 6th Floor, National Bank Bldg., I. I. Chundrigar Rd., Karachi; mobilizes domestic savings to meet the requirements of growing economic development and enables investors to share in the industrial and economic prosperity of the country; assets total £48.9m.

Pakistan Industrial Credit and Investment Corporation Limited (P.I.C.I.C.): Jubilee Insurance House, McLeod Rd., Karachi 2; f. Oct. 1957 as an industrial development bank to provide financial assistance for the establishment of new industries and balancing/modernization of existing ones in the private sector; auth. cap. Rs. 150m.; cap. p.u. Rs. 50m.; public joint stock company with 60 per cent and 40 per cent shareholdings of local and foreign investors respectively; Chair. A. W. ADAMJEE; Man. Dir. SAID AHMED; publ. *PICIC News* (quarterly).

STOCK EXCHANGE

Karachi Stock Exchange Ltd.: Kallian Rd., off McLeod Rd., Karachi 2; f. 1947; 200 mems.; Pres. KASIM DADA, S.K.; Sec. S. M. ASLAM KHAN, B.SC., A.C.A.

INSURANCE

On March 19th, 1972, all insurance companies—39 Pakistan and 4 foreign—were nationalized.

GENERAL INSURANCE

Pakistan Insurance Corporation: Pakistan Insurance Building, Bunder Road, Karachi-2; f. 1953 by the Government of Pakistan under the Pakistan Insurance Corporation Act 1952; a reinsurance corporation handling all forms of fire, marine and life reassurance; assisting the launching of new insurance companies in Pakistan; developing the insurance industry in the country; training insurance personnel; majority of shares held by the Government of Pakistan; Chair. M. A. MAJID; Man. Dir. A. G. RIZA.

Adamjee Insurance Co. Ltd.: Adamjee House, McLeod Rd., Karachi.

Alpha Insurance Co. Ltd.: State Life Square, State Life Bldg. No. 2, I. I. Chundrigar Rd., P.O.B. 4359, Karachi 2; f. 1951; Gen. Man. and Sec. V. C. GONSALVES.

Co-operative Insurance Society of Pakistan Ltd.: Co-operative Insurance Bldg., G.P.O. Square, Sharah Quaid-e-Azam, Lahore; Gen. Man. M. M. RAFIQUE

Crescent Star Insurance Co. Ltd.: Nadir House, McLeod Road, Karachi.

Eastern Federal Union Insurance Co. Ltd.: Qamar House, Bunder Rd., Karachi-2; f. 1932; Chair. A. G. H. HABIB; Man. Dir. R. ALI BHIMJEE.

Habib Insurance Co. Ltd.: P.O.B. 5217, Insurance House, No. 1 Habib Square, M. A. Jinnah Rd., Karachi; f. 1942; Chair. YUSUF QASIM; Chief Gen. Man. M. H. MAHOMED.

International General Insurance Co. of Pakistan Ltd.: Finlay House, I. I. Chundrigar Rd., Karachi 2; f. 1953; Exec. Dir. and Gen. Man. Gen. Dept. YUSUF J. HASWARY.

Khyber Insurance Co. Ltd.: 719-726 Muhammadi House, McLeod Rd., Karachi.

Mercantile Fire and General Insurance Co. of Pakistan Ltd.: 17 Chartered Bank Chambers, I. I. Chundrigar Rd., Karachi 2, f. 1958, Man. Dir. FAKHRUDDIN A. LOTIA, Dir. and Gen. Man. AHMED HASAN.

Muslim Insurance Co. Ltd., The: Bank Square, Sharae-Quaid-e-Azam, Lahore; f. 1934; Administrator MOHAMED ISHAQUE KHAN.

National Craft Underwriters: Khori Garden, P.O.B. 216, Karachi 2; f. 1946.

New Jubilee Insurance Co. Ltd.: Jubilee Insurance House, I. I. Chundrigar Rd., P.O.B. 4795, Karachi; f. 1953; Man. Dir. S. C. SUBJALLY.

Pakistan General Insurance Co. Ltd.: P.O.B. 1364, Bank Square, Shahrah-e-Quaid-e-Azam, Lahore; f. 1948; Gen. Man. Air Commdr. ZAFAR MASUD.

Pakistan Mutual Insurance Co. Ltd., The: 17/B Shah Alam Market, Lahore; f. 1946; Chair. FATEH MOHD.; Gen. Man. ALI AHMAD KHAN; Man. Dir. AZIZ AHMAD.

Premier Insurance Co. of Pakistan Ltd.: Premier Insurance Bldg., Wallace Rd., Karachi 2; f. 1952; Chair. M. M. BASHIR; Man. Dir. MAQBUL AHMED.

Sterling Insurance Co Ltd.: 26 Sharah-e-Quaid-e-Azam, Lahore, P.O.B. 119; f. 1949; Man. Sir. S. A. RAHIM; Gen. Man. S. A. MAHMUD; Man. Head Office M. A. NIAZ.

Since March 1972, all life insurance companies and the life departments of composite companies have been merged into *State Life Insurance Corporation of Pakistan.* As such, life insurance companies have ceased to exist as individual entities.

LIFE INSURANCE

State Life Insurance Corporation of Pakistan: State Life Insurance Bldg., I.I. Chundrigar Rd., Karachi 2; Chair. H. U. BEG.

INSURANCE ASSOCIATIONS

Insurance Association of Pakistan: Jamshed Kafrak Chambers, Machi Miani, P.O.B. 4932, Karachi 2; f. 1948; membership comprises 66 companies (Pakistan and foreign) transacting accident, fire, life, and marine insurance in Pakistan; issues tariffs and establishes rules for insurance in the country; Chair. S. C. SUBJALLY; Vice-Chair. M. M. RAFIQUE; Sec. M. MAROOF; brs. at Lahore.

Pakistan Insurance Institute: Karachi; f. 1951 to encourage insurance education among insurance personnel; affiliated to the Chartered Insurance Institute, London.

TRADE AND INDUSTRY

GOVERNMENT-SPONSORED ORGANIZATIONS

Board of Industrial Management: N.S.C. Bldg., Moulvi Tamizuddin Rd., Karachi; f. 1972; responsible for the management of a number of nationalized companies; Chair. J. A. RAHIM (Minister of Presidential Affairs, Commerce and Production).

National Economic Council: Planning Division, Secretariat, Block P, Islamabad; supreme economic body with the President as Chairman. The Governors of the four Provinces, Deputy Chairman of Planning Commission, Chairman of Planning and Development Board of Government of Pakistan are its members.

Planning Commission: Islamabad; f. 1959; Chair. (vacant); Deputy Chair. M. RASCHID, S.PK., S.Q.A.

Cotton Board, Government of Pakistan: 3rd floor, Luxmi Bldg., M. A. Jinnah Rd., Karachi 2; f. 1950; Chair. ASHRAF W. TABANI; Sec. FASIHUDDIN.

Indus Basin Development Board: Karachi; functions as a development working party to make recommendations to the Economic Committee of the Cabinet Economic Council in respect of schemes included in the Indus Basin Development Fund Agreement.

Oil and Gas Development Corporation: 4th Floor, Central Hotel Bldg., Club Rd., Karachi 4; f. 1961; Man. Dir. J. A. FARUQI; Sec. Lt.-Col. T. H. BASHIR.

Pakistan Industrial Development Corporation (PIDC): PIDC House, Karachi; f. 1962 by Act of Parliament; semi-autonomous; manufacturers of cement, fertilizers, machine tools, woollen textiles, carpets, chemicals, heavy machinery; Chair. A. R. FARIDI.

Pakistan Industrial Technical Assistance Centre (PITAC): Ferozepur Rd., POL-322, Lahore 16; f. 1958 by the Government to introduce modern industrial techniques by training and demonstration programmes; Chair. K. U. FAROOQI; Gen. Man. MUSTAFA HASAN.

Pakistan Steel Mills Corporation Ltd.: 5th Floor, P.I.D.C. House, Dr. Ziauddin Ahmad Rd., Karachi 4; f. 1968 to implement all activity connected with the manufacture of iron and steel in Pakistan, as well as to build up steel mill projects at Karachi and Kalabagh with an annual capacity of about 2 million tons of steel; Chair. A. R. FARIDI; Deputy Man. Dirs. S. S. ALI, Dr. AHAMEDULLA KHAN; Deputy Sec. R. A. ZOBERI.

Trading Corporation of Pakistan: Karachi; f. July 1967 for trade with Socialist countries and to undertake imports of some bulk items from other countries in competition with the private sector; handles a substantial portion of Pakistan's import and export of basic commodities.

Small Industries Corporation (SICS): 310 A. M. Preedy St., Saddar, Karachi 3; Dir. SYED SHAHID HUSAIN.

Pakistan Water and Power Development Authority: WAPDA House, Shara-e-Quaid-e-Azam, Lahore; f. 1958; for development of irrigation, water supply and drainage, building of replacement works under the World Bank sponsored Indo-Pakistan Indus Basin Treaty; flood-control and watershed management; reclamation of waterlogged and saline lands; inland navigation; generation of hydroelectric and thermal power and its transmission and distribution; Chair. I. A. KHAN; publ. *Indus* (English, monthly), *Barqab* (Urdu, monthly), *Wapda Weekly, Annual Report* (English).

CHAMBERS OF COMMERCE

Federation of Pakistan Chambers of Commerce and Industry, The: Lalji Lakhmidas Building, Bellasis St., Karachi; f. 1950; 71 mems.; Sec.-Gen. TUFAIL AHMAD KHAN.

AFFILIATED CHAMBERS

Chamber of Commerce and Industry: Aiwan-e-Tijarat, P.O.B. 4158, Nicol Rd., Karachi; f. 1960; 1,300 mems.; Pres. KASAM USMAN KANDAWALA; Sec. ASHA M. GHOUSE.

Hyderabad Chamber of Commerce and Industry: P.O.B. 99, Bungalow 6, Unit No. 3, Shah Latifabad, Hyderabad; Pres. INAYATULLAH BARKAT BHAI; Sec. ABDUL SALIM.

The Lahore Chamber of Commerce and Industry: P.O.B. 597, 11 Race Course Rd., Lahore; f. 1923; 1,800 mems.; Pres. Mian Tajammal Hussain; Sec. Mian Maqbool Ahmad.

Multan Chamber of Commerce and Industry: P.O.B. 90, Kutchery Rd., Multan; Pres. Shaikh Maqbool Ahmad; Sec. A. D. Malik.

Overseas Investors Chamber of Commerce and Industry: Chamber of Commerce Bldg., P.O.B. 4833, Talpur Rd., Karachi 2; 150 mems.; Pres. Masud Karim; Sec. P. T. Ensor, m.b.e.

Rawalpindi Chamber of Commerce and Industry: Chamber House, 108 Adamjee Rd., Rawalpindi; Pres. Shaikh Ishrat Ali; Sec. Mushtaq Ahwad.

Sarhad Chamber of Commerce and Industry: Sarhad Chamber House, G.T. Rd., Panj Tirath, Peshawar; f. 1958; 400 mems., including three Trade Groups and one Town Association; Pres. Haji Abdul Aziz Savul; Sec. Agha Muhammad.

Sukkur Chamber of Commerce and Industry: New Cloth Market, Sukkur; Pres. Mohammad Hafeez Yazdani; Sec. Mirza Iqbal Beg.

EMPLOYERS' AND TRADE ASSOCIATIONS

All- Pakistan Textile Mills Association: Muhammadi House, 3rd Floor, I. I. Chundrigar Rd., Karachi 2; Chair. A. Razak Adamjee; Sec. S. M. Usman.

Karachi Cotton Association Ltd., The: The Cotton Exchange, I. I. Chundrigar Rd., Karachi; Chair. A. H. M. Dadabhoy; Sec. Mrs. E. Davids.

Pakistan Banks' Association: National Bank of Pakistan Bldg., P.O.B. 4937, I. I. Chundrigar Rd., Karachi; Pres. Jamil Nishtar; Sec. Sheikh Lal Jani.

Pakistan Cotton Ginners' Association: Bungalow 159, Block 'C', Unit 2, Shah Latifabad, Hyderabad; Chair. Kh. Mohammad Masud; Sec. Syed Abbas Hussain.

Pakistan Film Producers' Association: Regal Cinema Bldg., Shahrah Quaid-e-Azam, Lahore; Pres. Niazi Malik; Sec. Shaukat Sheikh.

Pakistan Iron and Steel Merchants' Association: 2nd floor, Writers' Chambers, Dunolly Rd., Karachi; Pres. Maher H. Alavi; Sec. S. Z. Alam.

Pakistan Paint Manufacturers' Association: P.O.B. 3602, Block 14, Federal 'B' Area; f. 1953; Chair. Nasim Alam Khan; Sec. Abdur Rahman.

Pakistan Pharmaceutical Manufacturers' Association: 130–131 Hotel Metropole Club Rd., Karachi; Chair. Mahmood Ali; Sec. Syed Abbas.

Pakistan Shipowners' Association: Ralli Bros. Bldg., Wood St., Karachi 2; Chair. A. D. Ahmad Sqa; Sec. A. S. Wahedna.

Pakistan Silk and Rayon Mills' Association: 10 Bank House, 3 Habib Square, M. A. Jinnah Rd., Karachi; f. 1959; Chair. Alamgir Patel; Sec. M. H. K. Burney.

Pakistan Steel Re-rolling Mills' Association: Karachi Chambers, 6-Link McLeod Rd., Lahore; Chair. Mohammad Aslam; Sec. Sq. Ldr. Kh. M. Ikram.

Pakistan Sugar Mills' Association: 328-29 Al-Falah Bldg., Shahrah-e-Quaid-e-Azam, Lahore; Pres. M. Akram; Sec. Ali Ahmed.

Pakistan Vanaspati Manufacturers' Association: 404 Muhammadi House, I. I. Chundrigar Rd., Karachi 2; Chair. Rafiq Ghulam Husain; Sec. Wing Commdr. (Retd.) A. Habib Ahmad.

Pakistan Wool and Hair Merchants' Association: 27 Idris Chambers, Wood St., Karachi; Pres. Sheikh Seraj Din.

TRADE UNIONS

Pakistan National Federation of Trade Unions: 406 Qamar House, M.A. Jinnah Rd., Karachi; f. 1962; 270 unions with total of 130,000 mems.; Pres. Mohamed Sharif; Sec.-Gen. Rashid Mohammad; Publ. *PNFTU News.*

The principal affiliated Federations are:

All-Pakistan Railwaymen's Federation: 110 McLeod Rd., Lahore; f. 1948; 8 unions; 88,522 mems.; Pres. Mehboob-ul-Haq; Gen. Sec. Ch. Umar Din.

Maghrabi Pakistan Khet Mazdoor Federation: 1 Brandreth Rd., Lahore; f. 1954; plantation workers; about 14,000 mems.

Pakistan Transport Workers' Federation: 110 McLeod Rd., Lahore; 17 unions; 92,512 mems.; Pres. Mehboob-ul-Haq; Gen. Sec. Ch. Umar Din.

Sind Hari Federation (SHF): P.O. Umarkot, Sind; 18 unions; about 23,000 mems.; plantation workers; Pres. A. G. Sarhandi; Sec.-Gen. L. H. Palli.

Pakistan Mazdoor Federation: Landa Bazar, Lahore; f. 1951; 38 affiliated unions; 71,324 mems.; Pres. Khwaja Mohammed Hussain; Sec. Malik Fazal Ilahi Qurban.

United Trade Unions Federation of Pakistan: 1 Swami Narain Trust Bldg., Frere Rd., Karachi; 17 affiliated unions; about 15,000 mems.; Pres. Mirza Farooq Beg.

TRANSPORT

RAILWAYS

Commissioner of Railways: M. A. Karim, p.r.s., Ministry of Political Affairs and Communications, Islamabad.

Chairman of Pakistan Railway Board: A. M. Akhoond (Head Offices at Lahore).

The Pakistan rail system is state-owned, mostly broad gauge, and has a route mileage of 5,383 miles.

ROADS

The total of main roads in 1972 was 11,599 km., while secondary roads totalled 8,635 km. The new Karachi-Hyderabad road was opened in May 1970.

Government assistance comes from the Road Fund, financed from a share of the excise and customs duty on sales of petrol and from development loans.

Sind Road Transport Corporation: 3-Modern Housing Society, Drigh Rd., Karachi-8; Chair. B. A. Khan, p.s.p.

Automobile Association of Pakistan, The: P.O.B. 76, 8h Multan Rd., Lahore; Chair. Nawabzada Syed Iqbal Hassan; Sec. Zia Ullah Shaikh, t.k.

Karachi Automobile Association: Oriental Bldg., I. I. Chundrigar Rd., Karachi 2; f. 1958; Pres. Habib I. Rahimtoola; Sec.-Gen. Roshen Ali Bhimjee.

RIVERS, CANALS AND IRRIGATION

A score of large canals and hundreds of small ones criss-cross the territory of Pakistan watered by the rivers Sutlej, Ravi, Chenab, Jhelum, Indus and Swat. Many new canals and water works have been constructed.

In 1960 the Indus Basin Development Fund was established to finance irrigation in Pakistan and India. This project is now in its final stages and consists of two dams, six barrages and eight link canals. The last stage of the scheme, the Tarbela dam, should be operational by late 1974.

SHIPPING

The chief port is Karachi. In January 1974 the Government announced its intention of taking a controlling interest in maritime shipping companies.

National Shipping Corporation: NSC Bldg., Moulvi Tamizuddin Khan Rd., Karachi; f. 1963; 29 ships; cargo services to U.S.A., U.K., and Far East; five directors nominated by the Government, four elected by shareholders; Chair. Justice AMIN AHMED; Man. Dir. Commdr. AKHTAR HANIF, P.N.

MAJOR SHIPPING COMPANIES

Gulf Shipping Corporation Ltd.: Steel House, West Wharf Rd., Karachi; 4 dry-cargo vessels; Man. Dirs. F. M. MILLWALA, I. M. MILLWALA, A. E. MILLWALA.

Muhammadi Steamship Co. Ltd.: Valika Chambers, Altaf Hussain Rd., (P.O.B. 4128), Karachi 2; f. 1947; 5 cargo vessels; Chair./Man. Dir. F. VALIBHAI; services to Sri Lanka, Burma, India and U.S.A.

Pan-Islamic Steamship Co. Ltd., The: Writers' Chambers, Dunolly Rd., Karachi; f. 1950; Man. Dir. A. D. AHMED, S.Q.A.; Special Dir. ALI MOHAMMED MOOSA; 10 cargo/passenger vessels; services: coastal, U.S.A., and Pakistan/Saudi Arabia (Pilgrim Service); Karachi/Red Sea ports (cargo service).

Transoceanic Steamship Co. Ltd.: 260 R.A. Lines, Karachi; Chair. G. M. KANDAWALA; 5 cargo vessels; services: coastal trade.

United Oriental Steamship Co.: Baksh Chambers, Nicol Rd., Karachi; 7 cargo vessels; Man. Dirs. S. M. ANWAR, S. M. IQBAL.

CIVIL AVIATION

The Department of Civil Aviation comes under the Ministry of Defence; Dir.-Gen. M. R. RIZVI.

Karachi is an international airport.

Pakistan International Airlines Corpn.: PIA Bldg., Karachi Airport; f. 1955; operates domestic services and international services to Afghanistan, Abu Dhabi, the Netherlands, Dubai, Doha, Bahrain, Iran, Turkey, Saudi Arabia, Syria, Iraq, Egypt, Kuwait, Japan, the Philippines, Italy, Lebanon, Federal Republic of Germany, Malaysia, Singapore, Oman, Switzerland, France, Austria, Greece, Sri Lanka, U.S.A., United Kingdom, Thailand, the People's Republic of China, Tanzania, Oman and Yemen; fleet of 8 Boeing 707s, 3 720s, 7 F.27s; Chair. Air Marshal (retd.) M. NUR KHAN.

FOREIGN AIRLINES

The following foreign airlines are represented in Pakistan: Aeroflot, Air Ceylon, Air France, Alitalia, British Airways, East African Airlines, Garuda Indonesian Airways, Gulf Aviation, Iran Air, Iraqi Airways, JAL, KLM, Kuwait Airways, Lufthansa, Pan American, SAS, Saudi Arabia Airlines, Philippine Airlines, Royal Jordanian Airlines, Swissair, Syrian Arab Airlines, UTA.

TOURISM

Pakistan Tourism Development Corpn.: Hotel Metropole, Karachi 4; f. 1956; Dir.-Gen. Khwaja MASRUR HUSAIN, S.K.; brs. in Lahore, Peshawar, Rawalpindi, Kaptai, Gilgit, Quetta, Moenjodaro, Murree, Saidu Sharif and Abbottabad.

CULTURAL ORGANIZATIONS

Arts Council of Pakistan: Karachi; Exec. Dir. IRFAN HUSAIN; *Pakistan Arts Council*, Lahore: Pres. Justice S. A. RAHMAN; *Pakistan Arts Council*, Rawalpindi: Exec. Dir. AGHA BABAR.

ATOMIC ENERGY

Pakistan Atomic Energy Commission: P.O.B. 1114, Islamabad; responsible for organizing training and research centres in the field of nuclear science and technology and for installing and commissioning nuclear power and desalination plants; nuclear power plant at Kanupp; Chair. Dr. MUNIR AHMAD KHAN.

Atomic Energy Minerals Centre: P.O.B. 658 Lahore; f. 1961; research and development in the nuclear minerals field; equipped with analytical, mineralogical, mineral processing laboratories; Dir. M. ASLAM.

Atomic Energy Agricultural Research Centre: Tandojam;

f. 1963; research in plant physiology, genetics, entomology, soil science; Dir. Dr. A. R. AZMI.

Karachi Nuclear Power Station: equipped with a reactor of 137 MW (critical in August 1971); fully operational October 1972; on power refuelling started in 1973; availability during first year of operation (October 1972 to September 1973) 79 per cent.

Pakistan Institute of Nuclear Science and Technology: Nilhore, Rawalpindi; f. 1961; research; equipped with 5 MW swimming-pool-type reactor (critical 1966); Dir. Dr. ISHFAQ AHMAD.

UNIVERSITIES

University of Islamabad: 77-E Satellite Town, Rawalpindi; 80 teachers, 447 students.

University of the Punjab: Lahore; 25 professors, 35,409 students (incl. affiliated colleges).

University of Sind: Hyderabad; 3,170 students.

Pakistan Agricultural University: Lyallpur; 300 teachers, 1,565 students.

Pakistan University of Engineering and Technology: 145 teachers, 2,202 students.

University of Karachi: University Campus, University Rd., Karachi 32; 244 teachers, 3,506 students.

University of Peshawar: Peshawar; 552 teachers, 8,756 students.

PANAMA

INTRODUCTORY SURVEY

Location, Climate, Language, Religion, Flag, Capital

The Republic of Panama is a narrow strip of territory at the southern end of the isthmus separating North and South America. It is bounded to the west by Costa Rica and to the east by Colombia in South America. The Caribbean Sea is to the north and the Pacific to the south. The climate is tropical and the Caribbean coast receives up to 150 inches of rainfall per year. The tropical rain forest of the north coast gives way to savannah grassland on the south coast. Spanish is the official language and Roman Catholicism the religion of most of the people. The national flag (proportions 3 by 2) has four quarters: on the top row the left-hand quarter is white with a five-pointed blue star in the centre, while the right-hand quarter is red; on the bottom row the left quarter is blue and the right quarter is white with a five-pointed red star in the centre. The capital is Panama City.

Recent History

In October 1968, after only eleven days in office, the elected President, Dr. Arnulfo Arias Madrid, was deposed and Col. (now Gen.) Omar Torrijos Herrera, commander of the National Guard, emerged as the country's leader. The formation of political parties remained illegal and in October 1972 the National Assembly of Community Representatives conferred extraordinary powers on Gen. Torrijos as Chief of Government; at the same time a President and Vice-President with purely formal powers were elected. Considerable agrarian reform has been undertaken under the present administration.

The terms of the treaty by which the Panama Canal Zone was ceded to the United States, two weeks after Panama's emergence as an independent nation in 1903, have bedevilled relations between the two countries ever since. Early in 1974, however, it was announced that both Panama and the United States had agreed on principles for a new treaty which would eventually terminate United States jurisdiction in the Canal Zone. Panama is a member of the Organization of American States.

Government

In October 1972 General Omar Torrijos formally took office for a six-year term as Chief of Government, with almost unlimited powers. He is assisted by a Cabinet of Ministers.

Defence

There is a National Guard of some 11,000 men, commanded by General Omar Torrijos, but a military force is assembled only in emergencies.

Economic Affairs

The Panama Canal contributes some 14 per cent to the country's Gross National Product; direct and indirect contributions to the economy are estimated to total U.S. $175 million annually. Although the country has developed its potential as a banking and commercial centre, the economy is based on the land with rice, sugar and maize as principal crops. Cocoa, hemp, coconuts and bananas are also grown. Industry is mainly concerned with the manufacture of sugar, alcoholic beverages, clothing and shoes, cement and petrol refining. Shrimp fishing is important. There are timber resources, notably mahogany. Chief exports are refined petroleum, sugar, meat, bananas and shrimps, with the United States as the principal customer. Much revenue comes from shipping registration fees.

Transport and Communications

There is a government-owned railway and two others which are United States-owned. Roads extend for 6,859 kilometres of which 3,907 are unpaved. The Pan-American Highway is to be extended from Panama City to Colombia by 1976 ,thus making the highway complete. The merchant marine is one of the world's largest with over seven million gross tons. Most of the vessels are foreign-owned but registered in Panama.

Social Welfare

Social welfare is being developed with insurance benefits for unemployment, sickness and retirement. Employees contribute to the scheme, which is government-operated.

Education

There is compulsory education for children between seven and fifteen years. There are two universities.

Tourism

There is some tourism though most travellers are in transit through the Panama Canal. Panama City on the Pacific coast is the main resort.

Visas are not required to visit Panama by nationals of Costa Rica, El Salvador, Federal Republic of Germany, Honduras, Italy, Spain and Switzerland, for a stay of less than 3 months, and of the United Kingdom for a stay less than 30 days.

Sport

Baseball and basketball are the most popular games.

Public Holidays

1974: August 15th (Foundation of Panama City), October 11th (Revolution Day), November 3rd (Independence from Colombia), November 4th (National Flag Day), November 28th (Independence from Spain), December 8th (Immaculate Conception), December 25th (Christmas).

1975: January 1st (New Year's Day), January 9th (National Martyrs' Day), February 11th (Shrove Tuesday), March 28th (Good Friday), May 1st (Labour Day).

Weights and Measures

Both the metric and the imperial systems of weights and measures are in use. In 1972 the Government announced the gradual extension of the metric system to replace all other systems by 1982.

Currency and Exchange Rates

100 centésimos = 1 balboa (B).

Exchange rates (April 1974):

£1 sterling = 2.36 balboas;
U.S. $1 = 1.00 balboa.

STATISTICAL SURVEY

AREA AND POPULATION

AREA	POPULATION (Census of May 10th, 1970)			
	Total	Panama City (capital)	Birth Rate (per '000)	Death Rate (per '000)
75,650 sq. km. (excluding the Panama Canal Zone)	1,428,082	348,704	37.1	7.1*

Death registration is incomplete.

Total Population: 1,523,500 (July 1st, 1972).

AGRICULTURE

	AREA ('000 hectares)		PRODUCTION ('000 quintals)	
	1970–71	1971–72	1970–71	1971–72
Beans	18.6	12.0	72.7	72.9
Coffee	21.6	21.8	97.8	123.7
Maize	64.9	63.1	1,243.8	1,192.2
Rice	93.1	95.6	2,891.5	3,002.1
Sugar	24.0	28.4	29,270.7	2,609.4
Tobacco	1.2	1.2	22.6	25.7

INDUSTRY

		1969	1970	1971	1972
Beer and Spirits	million litres	40.2	42.0	43.6	34.0
Condensed, Evaporated, Powdered Milk	short tons	10,853.7	11,074.2	13,129.3	17,851.4
Salt	,, ,,	12,594.9	7,837.2	8,674.5	12,101.2
Tomato Derivatives	,, ,,	5,231.1	3,542.1	3,938.7	5,144.4
Sugar	,, ,,	79,410.1	78,278.8	89,290.0	87,836.1
Electricity	'000 kWh.	549,508.0	480,009.0	506,693.0	508,317.0
Gas	'000 cu. ft.	845,027.0	683,925.0	650,823.0	556,507.0

FINANCE

100 centésimos = 1 balboa (B).

Coins: 1, 5, 10, 25 and 50 centésimos; 1 balboa (United States coinage is also legal tender).

Notes: 1, 2, 5, 10, 20, 50 and 100 U.S. dollars (there are no Panamanian bank notes).

Exchange rates (April 1974): £1 sterling = 2.36 balboas; U.S. $1 = 1.00 balboa.

100 balboas = £42.35 = $100.00.

BUDGET

('000 balboas)

REVENUE	1972	1973	EXPENDITURE	1972	1973
Direct Taxes	75,497	77,250	National Assembly	406	986
Indirect Taxes	85,952	100,779	Inspectorate of Taxes	3,289	3,254
Income from Assets	3,040	3,963	President's Office	4,160	4,274
Income from State Enter-			Home Affairs and Justice	26,382	29,466
prises	23,145	29,306	Foreign Affairs	3,903	4,128
Other Sources of Income	30,757	12,937	Treasury	5,203	5,004
Current Transfers	2,609	4,797	Education	47,592	52,889
			Public Works	13,415	14,311
			Agriculture and Livestock	7,285	6,975
			Price Control Office	395	368
			Health	25,065	25,594
			Commerce and Industry	2,405	2,086
			Labour and Social Security	2,119	2,038
			Law Courts	2,094	2,088
			Public Services	1,252	1,234
			Electoral Tribunal	1,489	1,096
			External Debt	25,900	30,712
			Internal Debt	19,500	21,458
			Current Transfers	22,391	20,273
			Investments	6,809	—
TOTAL	221,000	229,032	TOTAL	221,000	228,234

COST OF LIVING INDEX

(1962 = 100)

	1968	1969	1970	1971	1972
Food	110.5	112.8	116.1	118.9	124.4
Housing	105.1	106.0	106.3	108.6	112.8
Clothing	103.5	104.3	104.8	107.5	111.5
Miscellaneous	103.9	106.6	113.2	114.2	123.6
GENERAL INDEX	106.7	108.6	112.0	114.2	120.3

This table is based on a study of families in Panama City with a monthly income of less than 600 balboas.

NATIONAL ACCOUNTS
(million balboas)

	1970	1971	1972
GROSS DOMESTIC PRODUCT	1,045.8	1,157.0	1,311.7
Income paid abroad	—26.4	—31.3	—35.1
GROSS NATIONAL PRODUCT . .	1,019.4	1,125.7	1,276.6
Balance of imports and exports of goods and services	34.6	45.1	71.6
AVAILABLE RESOURCES . . .	1,080.4	1,202.1	1,383.3
of which:			
Private consumption expenditure .	654.7	716.1	792.7
Central government consumption expenditure . .	149.8	164.0	185.8
Private fixed capital formation . .	187.9	232.9	292.7
Public fixed capital formation . .	14.6	28.8	27.2
Central government fixed capital formation	53.1	39.0	61.8
Increase in stocks	20.3	21.3	23.1

RESERVES
('ooo balboas)

	1969	1970	1971	1972
Gross International Reserves . . .	77,819.8	54,549.5	93,182.4	322,181.8
of which:				
Gold	10.0	10.0	10.0	10.0
Foreign currency	16,606.9	22,638.2	22,884.0	28,367.3
of which:				
U.S. coin	327.1	571.4	506.1	1,171.5
U.S. notes	16,249.6	22,049.2	22,360.2	27,150.2
Bank deposits (incl. Canal Zone) . .	60,672.5	30,614.7	69,561.7	291,739.8

Note: U.S. treasury notes and coins form the bulk of the currency in circulation in Panama.

BALANCE OF PAYMENTS
('ooo balboas)

	1971*			1972*		
	Credit	Debit	Balance	Credit	Debit	Balance
Goods and Services:						
Merchandise f.o.b.	137,780	363,007	—225,227	146,369	406,436	—260,067
Non-monetary gold . . .	4	946	— 942	—	570	— 570
Freight and insurance . . .	30	38,507	— 38,477	70	40,980	— 40,910
Transportation . . .	49,923	15,593	34,330	60,729	16,618	44,111
Travel	80,751	23,952	56,799	82,926	26,432	56,494
Investment income . . .	27,975	59,398	— 31,423	41,002	72,945	— 31,943
Government transactions n.e.s. .	10,675	7,561	3,114	10,871	9,356	1,515
Miscellaneous services . .	143,403	18,003	125,400	153,881	20,249	133,632
Total	450,541	526,967	— 76,426	495,848	593,586	— 97,738
Transfer Payments:						
Private	9,177	12,707	— 3,530	10,169	17,498	— 7,329
Government	9,532	1,569	7,963	10,040	1,808	8,232
Total	18,709	14,276	4,433	20,209	19,306	903
CURRENT BALANCE . . .	469,250	541,243	— 71,993	516,057	612,892	— 96,835
Capital and Monetary Gold:						
Private long-term . . .	39,616	4,414	35,202	60,680	3,688	56,992
Private short-term . . .	13,960	20,797	— 6,387	—	19,014	— 19,014
Government . . .	58,315	27,672	30,643	68,095	28,210	39,885
Gold and share holdings in central monetary institutions . . .	5,462	8,252	— 2,790	3,682	7,416	— 3,734
Gold and share holdings in other monetary institutions . . .	218,134	175,183	42,951	534,294	471,291	63,003
CAPITAL BALANCE . . .	335,487	236,318	99,169	666,751	529,619	137,132
Net Errors and Omissions . . .			— 27,176			— 40,297

* Preliminary figures.

BALANCE OF PAYMENTS BY AREA
('000 balboas)

Goods and Services:	1971*		1972*	
	Panama Canal Zone	Other Countries	Panama Canal Zone	Other Countries
Merchandise f.o.b.	18,197	—243,424	19,710	—279,777
Non-monetary gold	—	— 942	—	— 570
Freight and insurance	—816	— 37,661	—888	— 40,022
Transportation	—220	34,550	—245	44,356
Travel	38,566	18,233	39,108	17,386
Investment income	—	— 31,423	—	— 31,943
Government transactions n.e.s.	5,190	— 2,076	5,317	— 3,802
Miscellaneous services	81,510	43,890	83,282	50,350
Total	142,427	—218,853	146,284	—244,022
Transfer Payments	8,692	— 4,259	9,608	— 8,705

* Preliminary figures.

FOREIGN LOANS TO PANAMA
('000 balboas)

LOANS TO AUTONOMOUS AGENCIES	1970	1971	1972
Inter-American Development Bank:			
Institute for Economic Development	5,694	8,084	8,197
Institute of Housing and Town Planning	12,492	15,088	14,334
Institute of Aqueducts and Water Supply	4,755	5,031	5,138
Banco Nacional de Panamá	2,912	3,650	3,474
International Bank for Reconstruction and Development:			
Institute for Hydraulic Resources and Electrification	3,819	5,183	15,330
International Development Agency:			
Savings Bank (Caja de Ahorros)	1,718	1,598	1,478
Institute of Aqueducts and Water Supply	11,079	14,544	16,864
Institute of Housing and Town Planning	2,876	2,820	2,707
Franklin National Bank:			
Banco Nacional de Panamá	—	2,500	2,187
National Bank of North America:			
Banco Nacional de Panamá	—	2,500	2,187
TOTAL	45,345	60,998	71,896

EXTERNAL TRADE
(balboas)

	1969	1970	1971	1972
Imports	278,669,177	322,551,487	358,973,983	401,117,552
Exports	108,821,451	106,253,424	114,879,931	121,114,317

PRINCIPAL COMMODITIES
(balboas)

IMPORTS	1969	1970	1971	1972
Foodstuffs	20,889,715	24,591,279	34,227,035	33,926,524
Cereals and Manufactures	5,342,915	5,248,017	11,656,946	8,146,494
Fruits and Vegetables	4,873,560	6,418,010	7,033,400	7,628,575
Beverages and Tobacco	2,930,999	3,116,911	3,518,700	2,927,865
Inedible Raw Materials	1,635,100	2,774,455	2,731,472	2,952,172
Mineral Fuels and Lubricants	60,572,066	62,108,432	66,183,928	68,109,575
Crude Petroleum	58,595,520	59,664,412	63,677,813	65,080,221
Vegetable and Animal Oils and Fats	1,793,866	3,209,093	5,067,522	3,669,737
Chemical Products	26,752,382	29,164,917	31,942,845	40,365,981
Medical and Pharmaceutical Products	7,669,700	8,932,009	9,761,236	15,962,293
Basic Manufactures	63,351,443	74,040,626	82,722,654	89,893,864
Paper and Cardboard	12,380,173	15,011,272	15,032,676	16,008,797
Textile Fibres and Manufactures	17,977,356	21,017,048	24,202,848	30,669,607
Metal Manufactures	8,416,743	10,486,379	13,674,033	12,118,343
Machinery and Transport Equipment	68,134,038	89,860,310	90,353,712	112,846,310
Machinery, excl. Electrical	29,021,736	36,077,411	35,501,743	56,044,114
Transport Equipment	21,855,837	32,202,677	32,662,005	34,098,799
Miscellaneous Manufactures	32,292,214	36,924,693	41,818,414	46,217,590
Clothing	8,407,157	8,909,973	8,825,978	10,045,368
Miscellaneous Commodities n.e.s.	317,354	561,116	407,701	257,934

EXPORTS	1969	1970	1971	1972
Foodstuffs	80,087,520	81,082,517	85,742,537	94,736,800
Fresh and Preserved Fish	9,802,336	10,170,640	12,024,260	15,083,927
Fresh Bananas	61,248,395	60,919,946	63,115,181	64,832,488
Sugar	5,580,610	5,109,947	6,329,582	5,906,555
Coffee	1,101,403	1,704,813	1,553,162	2,501,975
Beverages and Tobacco	170,389	25,658	104,775	130,379
Crude Materials, inedible	1,531,743	1,773,424	1,208,759	1,509,059
Mineral Fuels and Lubricants	24,067,579	21,504,554	25,171,528	21,591,389
Petroleum Derivatives	24,055,459	21,464,765	25,125,933	n.a.
Animal and Vegetable Oils and Fats	55,038	58,943	248,365	270,986
Chemical Products	120,721	105,850	312,138	366,527
Basic Manufactures	1,927,596	1,299,538	1,790,337	1,969,299
Machinery and Transport Equipment	40,934	21,430	4,763	12,992
Miscellaneous Manufactures	819,731	381,510	296,729	526,936

PRINCIPAL COUNTRIES
('000 balboas)

IMPORTS	1970	1971	1972	EXPORTS	1970	1971	1972
Free Zone of Colón	40,524	46,356	56,077	Canada	4,200	3,501	3,379
German Federal Rep.	9,883	8,770	9,605	German Federal Rep.	17,296	20,704	22,662
Japan	20,481	27,069	33,802	Japan	349	1,696	657
United Kingdom	7,933	11,039	8,565	Netherlands	4,392	6,417	10,040
United States	129,027	128,043	136,344	United Kingdom	420	1,218	172
Venezuela	59,856	63,278	53,501	United States	66,441	55,868	53,385

Tourism (1972—preliminary): 162,785 visitors; Total Expenditure 31,661,000 balboas.

Railways (1972): Passengers carried 465,517, Freight 24,525 tons.

Roads (1972): Cars 53,629, Buses 3,253, Lorries 14,498, Others 104.

Shipping (1972—preliminary): 164 tankers of 3,139,286 gross registered tonnage, 5,275 others of 11,247,565 gross registered tonnage.

Civil Aviation (1972): Passengers arriving 452,556, departing 468,366.

EDUCATION
(1972)

Type	Number	Teachers	Pupils
Infant . .	170	329	9,259
Primary .	2,127	10,689	305,651
Secondary .	213	5,066	99,063
Universities .	7	668	18,280

Source: Dirección de Estadística y Censo, Panama.

THE CONSTITUTION

The draft of the new constitution was released in April 1972. It provides for a National Assembly of Community Representatives, comprising 505 *corregidores* to be elected by popular vote every six years. This assembly meets once a year when it elects a National Assembly composed of 25 members. It also elects the President, Vice-President and Chief of Government from a list submitted by the latter. The President and Vice-President have purely ceremonial duties. The Chief of Government (General Omar Torrijos) may stand for re-election for three consecutive six-year terms of office. He may appoint and discharge ministers from the cabinet and judiciary, nominate members of the National Assembly and formulate the nation's economic, social and administrative policies. There is a provision enabling the Government to issue its own paper currency and there are clauses requiring managers and executives to be Panamanian-born wherever possible. Bishops and priests of churches of all denominations are also required to be Panamanian-born.

THE GOVERNMENT

President: Ing. Demetrio Basilio Lakas Bahas.

Vice-President: Lic. Arturo Sucre Pereira.

Chief of Government and Supreme Leader of the Panamanian Revolution: Gen. Omar Torrijos Herrera.

CABINET
(*April* 1974)

Minister of the Interior and Justice: Lic. Juan Materno Vásquez.

Minister of Foreign Affairs: Lic. Juan Antonio Tack.

Minister of Public Works: Arq. Edwin Fábrega.

Minister of Finance: Lic. Miguel Sanchiz.

Minister of Agricultural Development: Ing. Gerardo González.

Minister of Commerce and Industry: Lic. Fernando Manfredo.

Minister of Public Health: Dr. Abraham Saied.

Minister of Labour and Social Welfare: Lic. Rolando Murgas.

Minister of Education: Dr. Aristides Royo.

Minister of Housing: Lic. José Antonio de la Ossa.

Minister of Planning and Economic Policy: Dr. Nicolás Ardito Barletta.

General Secretary to the Presidency: Lic. Roger Decerega.

Comptroller-General: Lic. Damián Castillo.

DIPLOMATIC REPRESENTATION

EMBASSIES ACCREDITED TO PANAMA
(In Panama City unless otherwise stated)

Argentina: Edificio de la Caja de Ahorros, Calle 17 y Avda. Central, Apdo. 1271; *Ambassador:* Teodoro J. Ricciardi Acosta.

Austria: Bogotá, Colombia.

Belgium: San José, Costa Rica.

Bolivia: Guatemala City, Guatemala.

Brazil: Calle Elvira Méndez y Calle 52 No. 24; *Ambassador:* (vacant).

Canada: San José, Costa Rica.

Chile: Edificio Grecia, Apdo. 1, Calle 49 No. 13, Apdo. 7341, Panamá 5; *Ambassador:* (vacant).

China (Taiwan): Avda. 9 No. 34, La Cresta, Apdo. Postal 4285, Panamá 5; *Ambassador:* Lt.-Gen. Jen Lin Huang.

Colombia: Edificio Bank of America, 4°, Calle 36 esq. Avda. Perú, Apdo. 4407, Panamá 5; *Ambassador:* Dr. Gustavo Serreno Gómez.

Costa Rica: Calle 34 No. 205, Apdo. 8963, Panamá 5; *Ambassador:* Román Ortega Castro.

Denmark: Mexico, D.F., Mexico.

Dominican Republic: Calle Elvira Méndez 30, Apdo. 6250, Panamá 5; *Ambassador:* Dr. Hans Paul Wiese Delgado.

Ecuador: Edificio Bank of America, 3°, Avda. Perú, Apdo. 530, Panamá 1; *Ambassador:* Dr. John Dunn Barreiro.

Egypt: Apdo. 7080; *Ambassador:* Moshen Fathi Abel-fattah.

El Salvador: Vía España 124, 4°, oficina 408, Apdo. 4434, Panamá 5; *Ambassador:* José Fernando Sigui Olivares.

France: Plaza de Francia 1–06, Apdo. 869; *Ambassador:* Mme Marcelle Campana.

Germany, Federal Republic: Edificio Universal, 2°, Calle 50 esq. Calle 70, Apdo. 4228; *Ambassador:* Gunter Schlegelberger.

Greece: Mexico D.F., Mexico.

Guatemala: Apdo. 1018; *Ambassador:* Col. Ariel Rivera Siliezar.

Haiti: Calle Aquilino de la Guardia 18, Apdo. 1134; *Ambassador:* (vacant).

Honduras: Avda. Balboa y Calle 30 No. 1-18, Apdo. 8704, Panamá 5; *Ambassador:* Dr. H. Silva Argüello.

India: Edificio Dorchester, Vía España 117; *Ambassador:* Placido Piedade d'Souza.

Israel: Apdo. 6357, Panamá 5; *Ambassador:* Mordechai Arbell.

Italy: Edificio Cemento Panamá, Avda. Eusebio A. Morales y Manuel Espinosa B., Apdo. 2024; *Ambassador:* Marquis Gio Paolo de Ferrar.

Jamaica: Ottawa, Canada.

Japan: Calle 46 No. 10 Apdo. 1411, Panamá 1; *Ambassador:* (vacant).

Korea, Republic: Edificio Interseco, Calle Elvira Méndez 10, Apdo. 8358, Panamá 7; *Ambassador:* Chung Nan Lee.

Lebanon: Mexico D.F., Mexico.

Mexico: Vía Espana 120, 2°, Apdo. 8373, Panamá 7; *Ambassador:* Col. Vicente Herrera.

Netherlands: San José, Costa Rica.

Nicaragua: Avda. Federico Boyd y Calle 50, Apdo. 933; *Ambassador:* Dr. D. Sierra Herrero.

Norway: Caracas, Venezuela.

Pakistan: Mexico D.F., Mexico.

Paraguay: San Salvador, El Salvador.

Peru: Avda. Federico Boyd y Calle 47 No. 1, Apdo. 4516; *Ambassador:* Felix Alvarez Brun.

Poland: Mexico D.F., Mexico.

Portugal: San José, Costa Rica.

Romania: New York, U.S.A.

Spain: Plaza Belisario Porras y Avda. Perú, Apdo. 1857, Panamá 1; *Ambassador:* Rafael Gómez Jordana y Prats.

Sweden: Bogotá, Colombia.

Switzerland: Guatemala City, Guatemala.

Turkey: Mexico D.F., Mexico.

United Kingdom: Avda. 7 España 120, 5°, Apdo. 889; *Ambassador:* D. Malcolm.

U.S.A.: Avda. Balboa entre Calles 37 y 38 Este, Apdo. 1099; *Ambassador:* William J. Jordan.

Uruguay: Edificio Aseguradora Mundial, Avda. Cuba esq. Calle 34, Apdo. 8898, Panamá 5; *Ambassador:* Alfredo Platas.

Vatican: Punta Paitilla, Apdo. 1763 (Apostolic Nunciature); *Apostolic Delegate:* Most Rev. Mgr. Edoardo Rovida.

Venezuela: Avda. Venezuela y Calle 46, Apdo. 661, Panamá 1; *Ambassador:* L. I. Sánchez Tirado.

Yugoslavia: Mexico D.F., Mexico.

PRESIDENT

On September 18th, 1972, the National Assembly of Community Representatives (*Asamblea Nacional de Representantes de Corregimientos*) elected Demetrio Basilio Lakas President of the Republic. Arturo Sucre Pereira was elected Vice-President. Their term of office began on October 12th, 1972.

NATIONAL ASSEMBLY

The National Assembly is composed of 25 members of the National Assembly of Community Representatives which meets every six years.

President: Elías Castillo.

POLITICAL PARTIES

In the elections to the National Assembly of Community Representatives in August 1972, no candidate was allowed to represent a political party.

JUDICIAL SYSTEM

The Supreme Court comprises nine magistrates, a new magistrate being appointed every two years for an eighteen-year term.

President of the Supreme Court and President of the Penal Chamber: Lic. Ramón A. Palacios P.

President of the Civil Chamber: Lic. José María Anguizola.

President of the Chamber for Administrative Disputes: Pedro Moreno Céspedes.

RELIGION

There is no official religion, although the majority of the population is Roman Catholic. Minorities include the Protestant, Anglican and Jewish faiths.

ROMAN CATHOLIC CHURCH

Metropolitan See: Arzobispado, Apdo. 6386, Panamá 5; Mgr. Marcos G. McGrath.

Suffragan Sees:

Chitré: Mgr. José María Carrizo Villareal.
David: Mgr. Daniel Enrique Núñez.
Santiago de Veraguas: Mgr. Martín Legarra Tellechea.

THE PRESS

DAILIES

Crítica: Vía Fernández de Córdoba, Apdo. 665, Panamá 9A; f. 1959; morning; tabloid; Spanish; Editor Gricelda López de Romero; circ. 27,000.

La Estrella de Panamá: Calle Demetrio H. Brid 7-38, Panamá; morning; Spanish; Editor Aristides G. Typaldos; circ. 25,175.

La Hora: Calle Luis Felipe Clement, Apdo. 1764, Panamá 1; f. 1947; daily; opposition; Spanish; Editor Iván Zurita; circ. 18,000.

El Panamá América: Vía Fernández de Córdoba, Apdo. B-4, Panamá 9A; f. 1929; evening; Spanish; Editor Antonio A. de León; circ. 25,000.

Panama-American: Vía Fernández de Córdoba, Apdo. B-4, Panamá 9A; f. 1925; evening; English; circ. 11,000.

La Prensa: Calle A y Calle 22 Oeste, Apdo. 8380, Panamá; morning; Editor Luis M. Botello; circ. 14,000.

La Razón: Avda. Bolívar 5361, David; f. 1946; evening; Spanish; Editor Manuel J. García; circ. 2,500.

The Star and Herald: Calle Demetrio H. Brid 7-38, Panamá; f. 1849; morning; English; Editor Luis Noli; circ. 12,270.

PERIODICALS

Panama City

Comercio, Industria y Turismo: Cámara de Comercio y Junta Nacional de Turismo, Apdo. 3743; monthly.

Estadística Panameña: f. 1941; published by the Contolaría General de la República; statistical survey in series according to subjects; Comptroller-Gen. Lic. Damián Castillo D.; Dir. of Statistics and Census Juan Manuel Caballero D.

Industria: Apdo. 952; organ of the Sindicato de Industriales de Panamá; Pres. Camilo J. Amado; Sec.-Gen. Guillermo Manfredo.

The Panama Tribune: Avda. 6 No. 26-13, Apdo. 3407; f. 1928; weekly; English-Spanish; Editor-Publisher George W. Westerman; circ. 7,000.

PRESS ASSOCIATION

Sindicato de Periodistas de Panamá: Calle 33A y Avda. Ecuador, Apdo. 2096, Panamá 1; Pres. RAMÓN JIMÉNEZ VÉLEZ.

PRESS AGENCIES

FOREIGN BUREAUX

Agence France Presse: Dir. ARQUIMÉDES FERNÁNDEZ.

Agencia "F": Avda. Balboa Apdo. Postal 479, Panamá 9A; Dir. Z. MARTÍNEZ DE LA VEGA.

ANSA: c/o "La Estrella de Panamá" Apdo. 159, Panamá; Chief LUIS ESPINOSA CASTILLO.

AP: Calle Demetrio H. Brid 2, Panamá; Correspondent LUIS C. NOLI.

Reuters: Dir. COLIN HALE.

UPI: Panamá; Chief PAUL WIATT.

Tass also maintains an office in Panama.

PUBLISHERS

PANAMA CITY

Librería Cultural Panameña, S.A.: Vía España 16, Apdo. 2018; education; Man. Dir. A. J. FRAGUELA REBELLEDO.

Editorial "La Estrella de Panamá": Avda. 9A Sur 7-38, Apdo. 159.

Editora de la Nación (*Government Publishing House*): Instituto Nacional de Cultural y Deportes Apdo. Postal 66A, Panamá 9A.

Editora Renovación S.A.: Vía Fernández de Córdoba, Apdo. B-4, Panamá 9A; newspapers; Man. Dir. HARMODIO ICAZA.

Fondo Educativo Interamericano: Apdo. 4289, Panamá 5; educational and reference; Dir. J. ALVARADO.

RADIO AND TELEVISION

RADIO

Dirección Técnica de Telecomunicaciones: Apdo. 3421, Panamá 1; Dir.-Gen. ARTURO PANZIA; Dir. Tec. Ing. FRANCISCO LAMPARERO.

Asociación Panameña de Radiodifusión: Apdo. 7387, Panamá; Pres. J. E. SITTON.

There are two short-wave and 57 medium-wave stations. Most stations are commercial.

In 1971 there were 230,000 radio sets.

TELEVISION

Circuito R.P.C.: Apdo. 1795, Panamá; commercial; Dir.-Gen. F. ELETA A.

Televisora Nacional, S.A.: Apdo. 8371, Panamá; private commercial station; Man. RODOLFO GARCÍA DE PAREDES CH.

In 1971 there were 158,000 television sets.

FINANCE

BANKING

cap. = (capital; p.u. = paid up; dep. = deposits; m. = million; amounts in balboas)

Comisión Nacional Bancaria (*National Banking Commission*): Panamá; f. 1966 to license and control banking activities on Panamian territory; Commissioners: Pres. Minister of the Treasury; mems. Man. of the Banco Nacional de Panamá and five others, three of whom represent private banking; Sec. FERNANDO DE J. ALBA.

NATIONAL BANK

Banco Nacional de Panamá: Avda. 5A Cuba y Calle 33, Apdo. 5220, Panamá 5; f. 1904; government-owned; cap. 15.4m., dep. 147.6m. (Dec. 1972); Pres. RAFAEL ALEMÁN; Gen. Man. RICARDO DE LA ESPRIELLA, Jr.

Banco Fiduciario de Panamá, S.A.: Vía España 200, Apdo. 1774, Panamá; f. 1948; cap. 3m., dep. 77.7m. (Dec. 1971); Chair. Dr. J. J. VALLARINO; Man. JEAN GIRARD; 7 brs. in Panama City and on Colón.

DEVELOPMENT BANK

Banco de Desarrollo Agropecuario—BDA: Apdo. 5282, Panamá; f. 1973; government-sponsored agricultural and livestock credit organization; Gen. Man. FERNANDO AMADO RAMOS.

SAVINGS BANKS

Caja de Ahorros: Apdo. 1740, Panamá; f. 1934; savings accounts 34m. (Dec. 1970); Pres. Dr. EDUARDO ALFARO; Gen. Man. LUIS C. PABÓN; brs. at Colón, Chitré, David, Chorrera, Aguadulce, Santiago and Las Tablas.

Caja de Seguro Social: Apdo. 1393, Panamá; f. 1941; 149,233 mems.

FOREIGN BANKS

Banco-Alemán-Panameño: Panamá.

Banco de Bogotá: Panamá.

Bank of London and South America Ltd.: Nassau, Bahamas; Avda. Justo Arosemena 32-42, Apdo. 8522, Panamá 5.

Chase Manhattan Bank N.A.: New York, U.S.A.; Vía España, Apdo. 9A-76, Panamá 9A; Vice-Pres. and Gen. Man. LUIS H. MORENO, Jr.; 2 brs. in Panama City; also in Balboa, Colón, Chitré, David, Santiago, Las Tablas, La Chorrera and Aguadulce.

Deutsch-Südamerikanische Bank A.G.: Hamburg, Germany; Calle María Icaza 10, Panamá 5.

First National City Bank: New York, U.S.A.; Vía España 124, Apdo. 555, Panamá 9A.

STOCK EXCHANGE

Cía. General de Seguros: Apdo. 4592, Panamá; f. 1937; Pres. JUAN B. ARIAS.

Panama City Stock Exchange: Panamá; f. 1960.

INSURANCE

Cía. Internacional de Seguros: Edificio Hatillo, Avda. Cuba y Calles 35 y 36, Apdo. 1036, Panamá 1; f. 1910; Pres. TOMÁS ARIAS; Gen. Man. NOEL MORÓN A.

Cía. Internacional de Seguros de Vida: Edificio Hatillo, Avda. Cuba y Calle 35 Este, Apdo. 1036, Panamá 1; f. 1957; Pres. TOMÁS ARIAS; Gen. Man. NOEL MORÓN AROSEMENA.

Cía. Istmena de Seguros, S.A.: Apdo. 50, Panamá; f. 1951; Man. J. B. ARIAS A.

Cía. Nacional de Seguros, S.A.: Apdo. 5303, Panamá 5; f. 1957; Pres. Ralph J. Lindo; Gen. Man. G. Fernández G.

Cía. Panameña de Seguros S.A.: Apdo. 3065, Panamá 3; Chair. C. E. González de la Lastra.

TRADE AND INDUSTRY

INDUSTRIAL ORGANIZATIONS

Cámara de Comercio, Industria y Agricultura: Avda. Cuba 33A-18, Apdo. 74, Panamá 1.

Cámara Oficial Española de Comercio: Apdo. 1857, Panamá 7; Pres. Víctor Gómez B.; Sec.-Gen. Atiliano Alonso; publ. *Boletín.*

Industrial Development and Productivity Centre: Apdo. 7639, Panamá 5; f. 1956 as a department of the Ministry of Agriculture, Commerce and Industry to undertake feasibility studies, technical assistance, analyses and promotion; Dir. Julio E. Sosa.

TRADE UNIONS

Confederación de Trabajadores de la República de Panamá —CTRP (*Confederation of Workers of the Republic of Panama*): Apdo. 8929, Panamá 5; f. 1950; mems. 15,000 from 11 affiliated groups; admitted to ICFTU/ORIT; Pres. Santiago O'Donell; Sec.-Gen. Phillip Dean Butcher; publ. *El Obrero* (annual).

Acción Sindical Panameña—ASP (*Panamanian Syndical Action*): Apdo. 4060, Panamá; admitted to CISC/CLASC; Sec.-Gen. Carlos J. George.

A number of unions exist without affiliation to a national centre.

COLÓN ZONE

The Colón Free Zone, an area of 96 acres, is an autonomous agency of the Government of Panama, situated less than half a mile from the Piers of Cristóbal, the Atlantic Port for the Panama Canal, on the Caribbean Sea. Foreign merchandise may be landed without application of customs or tariff duties. It may be processed before re-exportation, which is also without duties. The Free Zone was created in 1948 and started operations in 1953.

General Manager: Enrique Townshend, Apdo. 1118, Colón.

TRANSPORT AND TOURISM

Ministry of Public Works: controls all transport in Panama.

RAILWAYS

Of the railways in Panama, two are owned by American companies, one being constructed primarily to carry fruit, and the other to work in conjunction with the Canal.

Chiriquí National Railroad: David, Chiriquí; government-owned; operates 169 km. of narrow-gauge track (914 mm.), running from Puerto Armuelles to David, via Concepción, with a branch line south to Pedregal; Pres. and Gen. Man. José A. Segovia F.

United Fruit Company: Panamá; operates two lines which run partly in Costa Rica: the Northern Line (Almirante, Bocas del Toro) with 177 km. of 914 mm. gauge and the Southern Line (Puerto Armuelles, Chiriquí) with 183 km. of 914 mm. gauge.

Panama Railroad: Apdo. 5067, Cristóbal, Canal Zone; owned by the Panama Canal Company; operates 190 km. of 1,524 mm. gauge. In the fiscal year 1970 the railway carried 967,000 passengers and 240,000 tons of freight; Pres. Maj.-Gen. David S. Parker; Dir. Transportation and Terminals Bureau Charles R. Clark; Man. Railroad Division Donald R. Brayton.

ROADS

There are some 6,800 km. of roads in Panama, about half of which are paved. The two most important highways are the National, which runs from Panama City westwards to Concepción in the Province of Chiriquí, and eastwards as far as Chepo; and the Boyd-Roosevelt or Trans-Isthmian, linking the cities of Panama and Colón. The Pan American Highway to Mexico City opened in 1963 with 545 km. in Panama. A highway to San José, Costa Rica, was completed in 1967.

SHIPPING

The Panamanian Merchant Marine is one of the world's largest and, in 1971, over six million gross tons of ships were registered under the Panamanian flag.

A number of lines make regular calls at Panamanian ports, including: Furness Withy, Grace, Holland America, New Zealand, Pacific Steam Navigation, Royal Mail, Shaw Saville and United Fruit.

CIVIL AVIATION

Air Panama International: Avda. Justo Aresemena y Calle 34, Apdo. 8612, Panamá; f. 1967; services from Panama City to Guatemala, Mexico City, Guayaquil, Lima, Bogotá, Quito, Miami and New York; Pres. Carlos Eleta A.; fleet: 2 Boeing 727-100.

Compañía Panameña de Aviación (COPA): Avda. Perú 25, Apdo. 1572, Panamá 1; f. 1944; services from Panama City to San José, Managua, San Salvador, Medellín and Barranquilla; Pres. Dr. Mariano J. Oteiza; Gen. Man. Capt. Hermes Carrizo; fleet: 1 Lockheed Electra, 2 HS-748, 2 DC-3, 1 CV-340.

International de Aviación (Inair): Edificio El Embajador, Calle 50 y Elvira Méndez, Apdo. 4509, Panamá; f. 1967; chartered passenger and cargo services between Panama City and Belize, Chetumal, Cozumel, Caracas, Maracaibo, Gali, Guayaquil, Lima and Manaus; Chair. Eduardo Wong; Gen. Man. Jorge Solis; fleet: Boeing 720, 3 DC-6B.

Rutas Aéreas Panameñas: Avda. Peru y Calle 29 Este 17, Apdo. 4931, Panamá 5; internal services.

Panama is also served by the following foreign airlines: ALM (Netherlands Antilles), Avianca (Colombia), Braniff, British Airways, Ecuatoriana, Iberia, KLM, Lacsa (Costa Rica), LAN-Chile, Pan Am, Sahsa (Honduras), TACA (El Salvador) and Viasa (Venezuela).

TOURISM

Instituto Panameño de Turismo: Edificio del First National City Bank, 5°, Vía España y Elvira Méndez, Apdo. 4421, Panamá 5; f. 1960; Dir.-Gen. José Rogelio Arias.

Overseas Office: U.S.A.: 630 Fifth Ave., New York 10020.

Asociación Panameña de Agencias de Viajes y Turismo APAVIT: Apdo. 5567, Panama City; Pres. David Eisenmann.

CULTURAL ORGANIZATIONS

Dirección Nacional de Cultura: Instituto Nacional de Cultura y Deportes, Apdo. 66A, Panamá 9A; Dir. Prof. Jaime Ingram; responsible for the following:

Museo Nacional: Dir. Dra. Reina Torres de Araúz.

Comisión Nacional de Arqueología y Monumentos: Dir. Dra. Reina de Araúz.

Biblioteca Nacional: Dir. Carmen C. Lasso.

Escuela de Artes Plásticas: Dir. Prof. Manuel Medina.

Instituto de Música: Dir. Prof. Damián Carles.

Escuela de Danzas: Dir. Prof. Julio Araúz.

Casa de la Escultura: Dir. Prof. Carlos Arboleda.

Orquesta Sinfónica Nacional: Dir. Prof. Eduardo Charpentier.

Asociación de Conciertos: Apdo. 7666, Panamá 9; f. 1962; organizes musical seasons with national and international artists; Dir. Prof. Jaime Ingram.

Asociación Teatro en Círculo de Panamá: Calle 53 No. 28, El Cangrejo, Apdo. 742, Panamá 9A; f. 1961; presents theatrical works and encourages interest in the theatre in Panama; grants to cultural associations amount to $21,750; Pres. Maritza Diez de Morales; Exec. Sec. Manonguita de Obaldía.

Instituto Panameño de Arte: Apdo. 4211, Panamá 5; an adjunct of the Department of Fine Arts of the Ministry of Education; sponsors all aspects of culture; Exec. Sec. Olga Zubieta de Oller.

THEATRE AND ORCHESTRA

Orquesta Sinfónica Nacional: Apdo. 9190, Panamá 6; Dir. Prof. Eduardo Charpentier.

Teatro Nacional: Dirección Nacional de Cultura, Apdo. 66A, Panamá; Dir. a.i. Gabriela Candanedo G.

ATOMIC ENERGY

Universidad de Panamá: Institute of Nuclear Studies, Apdo. 3277, Panamá; medical and agricultural research with radio-isotopes.

UNIVERSITIES

Universidad de Panamá: Estafeta Universitaria, Panamá; 625 teachers, 20,900 students.

Universidad Santa María la Antigua: Apdo. 2143, Panamá; 240 teachers, 1,057 students.

PANAMA CANAL ZONE

The Canal Zone is flanked on either side by the Republic of Panama. It stretches from Balboa on the Pacific to Cristóbal on the Caribbean and is 82 km. long and 16 km. wide.

AREA AND POPULATION

AREA			POPULATION, 1973 estimate		
Total	Land	Water	Total	U.S. Citizens	Non-U.S. Citizens
647·29 sq. miles	372·32	274·97	46,400	39,900	6,500

BIRTHS AND DEATHS

	BIRTH RATE PER '000	DEATHS	DEATH RATE PER '000
1970 . .	16.20	112	2.50
1971 . .	14.38	121	2.42
1972 . .	14.00	94	1.90

EMPLOYMENT
(1973)

CANAL ZONE GOVERNMENT EMPLOYEES		PANAMA CANAL COMPANY EMPLOYEES	
Paid at U.S. Wage Base	Paid at Canal Zone Wage Base	Paid at U.S. Wage Base	Paid at Canal Zone Wage Base
2,307	1,099	3,293	8,323

FINANCE

United States currency: 100 cents = 1 U.S. dollar.

Coins: 1, 5, 10, 25 and 50 cents; 1 dollar (Panamanian coinage also circulates).

Notes: 1, 2, 5, 10, 20, 50 and 100 dollars.

Exchange rates (April 1974): £1 sterling = U.S. $2.36; $1 = 42.35 pence.

1973 BUDGETS

CANAL ZONE GOVERNMENT:

Revenue $60,450,000   **Expenditure** $58,805,000 (Health $29,888,000).

PANAMA CANAL COMPANY:

Revenue $199,848,000.   **Expenditure** $201,175,000.

TRANSPORT

CANAL TRAFFIC
(1973)

THROUGH TRANSITS	CARGO (tons)	TOLLS AND TOLL CREDITS (U.S. $)
15,109	127,561,733	113,381,705

PRINCIPAL USERS
(1973)

	TONNAGE CARRIED
Greece	12,572,638
Japan	12,166,721
Liberia	25,937,307
Norway	15,991,479
United Kingdom	13,279,073

EDUCATION
(1973)

	Schools	Pupils	Teachers
United States .	20	11,458	646
Latin American .	5	1,348	113

Source: Panama Canal Company.

THE CONSTITUTION

Occupation and use of the Canal Zone was granted to the United States by the Republic of Panama under Articles II and III of the 1903 Treaty. In effect, the Canal Zone is a United States Government reservation devoted to the protection, maintenance and operation of the Panama Canal in which private enterprise is not permitted except that directly related to the waterway and its operation.

The Code of Laws applicable within the Canal Zone is enacted by the Congress of the United States.

Administration is in the hands of the Panama Canal Company and the Canal Zone Government. The two units are headed by one man who is President of the Company and Governor of the Canal Zone. His appointment as Governor is made by the President of the United States subject to confirmation by the Senate and he is *ex-officio* President of the Company.

THE GOVERNMENT

CANAL ZONE GOVERNMENT

Governor: Maj.-Gen. David S. Parker, Balboa Heights, C.Z.

The Canal Zone Government performs the usual functions of city, county and state governments, including police, schools, customs, ports, immigration, roads, health and justice.

PANAMA CANAL COMPANY

Chairman of the Board: Hon. Kenneth E. BeLiew.

President: Maj.-Gen. David S. Parker.

Secretary: Thomas M. Constant.

The Company's activities involve operating the Canal and the Panama Railroad. The Company is required to recover all costs of operation and maintenance, pay the net cost of the Canal Zone Government, and pay interest on the net investment of the United States in the Canal Company.

JUDICIARY AND RELIGION

Judicial System:

Magistrates' Courts: Balboa and Cristóbal. Jurisdiction in criminal cases where the fine and punishment, except for a few specified offences, does not generally exceed $100 or 30 days in jail or both, and in civil cases where the claim is under $500.

U.S. District Court: Ancon; hears appeals from the Magistrates' Courts; Civil and Criminal cases in excess of the limitations of the Magistrates' Court are tried in the District Court. Appeals from the District Court are filed with the *U.S. Fifth Circuit Court of Appeals* in New Orleans, and the final stage of the review is in the U.S. Supreme Court.

Pardon and Parole Board: five members appointed by the Governor; considers submissions for pardon and parole.

Religion: All religious affiliations, in proportions corresponding approximately to those of the U.S.

RADIO AND TELEVISION

There is one radio station (SCN) and one television station (SCN-TV), both operated by the U.S. Armed Forces as part of the Southern Command Network.

FINANCE

Banks: *First National City Bank*: New York; branch in the Canal Zone.

Chase Manhattan Bank: New York; branch in the Canal Zone.

TRANSPORT AND TOURISM

Canal: Opened 1914; 82 km. long; ships take an average of 8 hours to go through the Canal. Terminal ports are Cristóbal on the Caribbean and Balboa on the Pacific.

Railways: *Panama Railroad* runs cross-isthmus services from Colón to Panamá.

Civil Aviation: Panama International Airport, Tocumen, by agreement also serves as the commercial airport for the Canal Zone.

Tourism: Panama Canal Information Officer, Balboa Heights, C.Z.; about 233,100 persons visited the Canal in 1973.

PARAGUAY

INTRODUCTORY SURVEY

Location, Climate, Language, Religion, Flag, Capital

Paraguay is a landlocked state in central South America. Bolivia lies to the north, Brazil to the east and Argentina to the south and west. The climate is sub-tropical with a temperature range from an average maximum of 34.3°c (93.7°F) in January to an average minimum in June of 14°c (51°F). The official language is Spanish. Guaraní is also spoken. Roman Catholicism is the established religion and embraces 89 per cent of the population. There is a small Protestant minority. The national flag (proportions 2 by 1) has horizontal stripes of red, white and blue. The obverse side bears the state emblem in the centre of the white stripe, while the reverse side carries the seal of the Treasury. The capital is Asunción.

Recent History

Paraguay suffered heavy losses in manpower in the Chaco War with Bolivia in the 1930s, though she increased the size of her territory. The country has a long history of political revolt and only since the election of General Alfredo Stroessner as President in 1954 has there been comparative stability. In 1955 the President assumed extensive powers and many opposition leaders went into exile, but some have since returned. General Stroessner was re-elected by large majorities in 1963, 1968 and 1973. In 1969 relations between the Church and the Government became strained, due to the former's demands that political prisoners be brought to trial or released. Several clerics were expelled by the Government, accused of undermining the State. These difficulties have now been partly resolved. Paraguay is a member of the UN and LAFTA.

Government

Paraguay is a Republic and executive power is exercised by the President, assisted by a Council of State. The Legislature is the bi-cameral Chamber of Senators and Deputies elected for a five-year term. The President has power to dissolve the Chamber of Deputies and to remove the Councillors of State, but in the first case an election must be called within two months. He may also call a state of siege, renewable every 90 days, if the working of the Constitution is endangered.

Defence

The armed forces total 14,900 men. The army is composed of 11,000 men and the air force of 2,000 men. The navy, which operates on the rivers, has 1,900 men, including marines.

Economic Affairs

Livestock, crops and timber account for nearly 50 per cent of Paraguay's domestic product. High world beef prices have stimulated the export of frozen beef, and meat exports are no longer confined to tinned products. The main agricultural crops are oil-producing seeds, cassava, cotton, tobacco, coffee, maize, fruit and vegetables. The forests yield valuable timber, mainly hardwoods. The principal industries are meat processing and production of vegetable oils. Trade is mostly with Argentina, the Federal Republic of Germany, the United States, Brazil and the United Kingdom. There has been a balance of payments surplus for several years, resulting from the high prices received for exports of meat and agricultural products.

The 1971–75 Development Plan aims at improving export facilities, developing agriculture (especially in regional areas), and modernizing the technique of timber production. The Plan provides for an annual economic growth rate of 6 per cent. The country's hydroelectric potential is being exploited. The Acaray hydro-electric works already supply surplus to neighbouring areas of Argentina and Brazil, and Paraguay and Brazil are to carry out a project to develop the potential of the River Paraná between the Guairá falls and the mouth of the River Iguazú. Construction is scheduled to start in 1974 and the potential annual output is 10.7 million kWh. Similarly, Paraguay and Argentina are to develop the hydro electric complex at the Yacyretá rapids. This has a potential annual output of 3.5 million kWh. work is scheduled to begin in 1976.

Transport and Communications

There are 498 km. of railways and some 5,800 km. of roads. The Pan American Highway runs for over 700 km. in Paraguay and the Trans-Chaco Highway extends from Asunción to Bolivia. The paving of the first section of this highway started in November 1973. The river Paraguay is navigable from Asunción to Concepción and beyond for small vessels, and there is much traffic along the River Paraná through Argentina to the Atlantic at Buenos Aires and Montevideo. In 1967 Paraguay and Argentina agreed to grant free navigation to merchant vessels of the two countries on the Rivers Plate, Paraguay and Paraná; in addition Paraguay enjoys free transit facilities at Buenos Aires and free port facilities at Paranagua, Brazil, and Nueva Palmira, Uruguay. There is a modern airport at Asunción for internal and international air transport.

Social Welfare

A bilateral co-operative health service is in force with the U.S.A. and there are a number of large health centres. A five-year malaria eradication programme has been launched.

Education

Primary education is free and where possible compulsory but there are insufficient schools, particularly in the remote parts of the country. In 1973 there were 3,283 primary and secondary schools; there is one state and one Catholic university.

Tourism

Tourism is undeveloped but with the growth of air transport and the construction of new international highways efforts are being made to promote it.

Visas are not required to visit Paraguay by nationals of Argentina, Belgium, Brazil, Chile, Denmark, Ecuador,

Finland, France, the Federal Republic of Germany, Italy, Liechtenstein, Luxembourg, Mexico, the Netherlands, Norway, Spain, Sweden, Switzerland, the United Kingdom, the U.S.A. and Uruguay.

Sport

Football is the most popular sport.

Public Holidays

1974: August 15th (Founding of Asunción), August 25th (Constitution Day), September 29th (Battle of Boquerón), October 12th (Discovery of America), November 1st (All Saints' Day), December 8th (Immaculate Conception), December 25th (Christmas Day).

1975: January 1st (New Year's Day), February 3rd (St. Blaise's Day), March 1st (Heroes' Day), March 27th–28th (Easter), May 1st (Labour Day), May 8th (Ascension), May 14th (Independence), May 29th (Corpus Christi), June 12th (Peace of Chaco).

Weights and Measures

The metric system is in force.

Currency and Exchange Rates

100 céntimos = 1 guaraní (G).

Exchange rates (April 1974):
£1 sterling = 297.52 guaraníes;
U.S. $1 = 126.00 guaraníes.

STATISTICAL SURVEY

AREA AND POPULATION

AREA (sq. km.)	POPULATION (1971 Census)	
	Total	Asunción (capital)
406,752	2,354,071	392,753

BIRTHS, MARRIAGES AND DEATHS
(1972)

BIRTHS	MARRIAGES	DEATHS
83,410	13,063	13,448

AGRICULTURE
('000 metric tons)

	1969–70	1970–71	1971–72
Alfalfa	25.4	25.0	25.6
Cotton	37.2	16.7	40.5
Groundnuts	17.0	17.7	21.2
Maize	220.0	216.9	227.8
Sweet Potatoes	134.3	138.3	159.0
Rice (hulled)	41.9	39.5	41.4
Sugar Cane	1,093.5	1,202.9	1,240.0
Tobacco	18.0	17.4	19.0
Wheat	35.0	45.5	16.9
Cassava (Manioc)	1,665.4	1,707.0	1,727.5
Beans	29.4	27.3	28.7

LIVESTOCK

Cattle: (1970) 5.5 million; (1971) 5.6 million; (1972) 5.6 million.

ANIMALS SLAUGHTERED
(Live weight in metric tons)

	INDUSTRY		CONSUMPTION		TOTAL	
	Number	Live Weight	Number	Live Weight	Number	Live Weight
1970 . .	184,494	66,403	512,506	177,547	697,000	243,950
1971 . .	217,420	76,867	477,780	172,001	695,200	248,868
1972 . .	301,753	109,537	391,780	192,216	693,533	251,753

FORESTRY
(metric tons)

	1970	1971	1972
Tannin . .	15,200	15,700	16,100
Logs for Export .	132,600	91,100	14,800

INDUSTRY
(Metric tons, unless stated otherwise)

	1967	1968	1969	1970	1971	1972
Alcohol ('ooo litres) . .	3,717	3,813	3,901	3,886	3,894	4,250
Beer ('ooo litres) . .	10,373	11,483	15,716	17,554	16,496	15,053
Cigarettes ('ooo packets) . .	26,141	22,932	21,611	22,934	23,351	32,010
Cement (Portland) . .	14,400	23,800	37,353	62,869	81,293	75,369
Electricity ('ooo kWh) . .	163,626	176,796	203,400	217,700	245,800	273,000
Hides. .	15,287	15,054	14,317	15,377	15,300	15,323
Meat (tinned) . .	19,564	15,620	12,700	9,951	9,975	9,975
Oils:						
Coconut (edible) . .	5,153	6,068	6,302	7,024	9,175	7,402
Coco Pulp . .	4,200	5,600	6,335	6,976	7,204	7,635
Tung . .	14,000	14,200	11,507	11,805	18,113	20,500
Sugar	35,700	34,100	42,275	48,352	56,518	52,700
Textile:						
Cotton . . .	16,500	17,500	18,555	20,334	20,622	21,188
Matches . . .	17,000	17,800	18,671	22,522	22,796	17,420

FINANCE

100 céntimos = 1 guaraní (G).

Notes: 1, 5, 10, 50, 100, 500, 1,000, 5,000 and 10,000 guaraníes
(coins are issued only for commemorative purposes).

Exchange rates (April 1974): £1 sterling = 297.52 guaraníes; U.S. $1 = 126.00 guaraníes.
1,000 guaraníes = £3.36 = $7.94.

BUDGET
(1973—million Gs.)

REVENUE		EXPENDITURE	
Ordinary Revenue	9,921.3	Presidency	84.5
Special Revenue	1,093.2	Legislature	96.1
Agricultural Surpluses . . .	49.2	Judiciary	185.9
External Loans	1,498.9	Ministries:	
Other	772.6	Public Works	2,091.0
		Defence	2,336.0
		Interior	1,074.5
		Foreign Affairs	228.3
		Finance	521.7
		Education	2,191.8
		Agriculture	650.7
		Health	506.7
		Justice and Labour . . .	159.5
		Industry and Commerce . .	65.6
		Without Portfolio . . .	2.9
		Other	3,140.0
TOTAL	12,335.2	TOTAL	13,335.2

1974: Estimated Expenditure 37,051 million guaraníes.

COST OF LIVING INDEX
(1964 = 100)

	1970	1971	1972
Food	105.9	115.0	127.8
Housing	108.3	110.0	112.8
Clothing	110.1	111.2	115.1
Miscellaneous	124.2	126.7	142.9
General Index	110.5	116.0	126.7

The cost of living is based on the expenses of a working class family in Asunción.

RESERVES AND CURRENCY IN CIRCULATION
('000 U.S.$)

	1970	1971	1972
Gross convertible reserves . . .	10,291	10,978	19,168
Net reserve position (incl. IMF position and payments agreement balances) . .	4,770	4,770	4,770
Money supply	62,421	68,206	81,611

EXTERNAL TRADE
(U.S. $'000)

	1968	1969	1970	1971	1972
Imports . . .	61,495	70,429	63,835	70,273	69,849
Exports . . .	47,575	50,953	64,071	65,204	86,188

COMMODITIES
(U.S. $'000)

Imports	1971	1972	Exports	1971	1972
Machinery and Apparatus .	12,801	15,652	Meat Products (excluding Horse-meat)	20,796	29,788
Vehicles and Accessories . .	8,474	9,005	Timber	10,408	9,498
Drinks and Tobacco . .	7,212	6,117	Tobacco	4,765	6,681
Fuels and Lubricants . .	6,347	5,953	Cotton Fibre . . .	835	3,815
Wheat and Derivatives . .	3,664	3,535	Tung Oil	3,745	3,090
Chemicals and Pharmaceutical Products	4,198	3,576	Coconut Oil . . .	3,723	2,345
Iron, Steel and Manufactures .	5,078	4,377	Cattle Hides . . .	1,517	3,665
Textiles and Manufactures .	2,512	1,747	Oils (essential) . . .	2,315	3,006
Other Metals and Manufactures .	3,261	2,578	Quebracho Extract . .	2,215	2,396
Paper, Cardboard and Manufactures	2,025	2,457	Oilseeds	1,848	4,984
Other Food Products . .	2,023	2,031	Coffee	1,016	3,116
Agricultural Equipment . .	1,518	2,073	Yerba Maté . . .	105	312
Others	11,160	10,748	Fruit	1,372	579
			Others	10,544	12,913
Total Imports .	70,273	69,849	Total Exports .	65,204	86,188

COUNTRIES

	Imports		Exports	
	1971	1972	1971	1972
Argentina	10,119	10,757	17,846	15,678
Belgium	428	488	2,934	4,210
France	1,953	1,327	3,014	3,167
Germany, Federal Republic .	8,155	9,998	3,602	14,057
Netherlands . . .	563	569	4,990	6,181
Spain	785	938	2,417	3,216
United Kingdom . .	6,940	5,770	3,623	7,478
U.S.A.	17,900	13,703	14,418	12,799
Uruguay	1,157	1,175	1,355	621
Others	22,272	24,093	15,005	18,781

TOURISM

	1969	1970	1971	1972
Number of visitors	111,643	119,239	123,676	93,023
Revenue ('000 U.S.$)	13,280	14,190	14,720	11,070

TRANSPORT

RAILWAYS

	Passengers	Freight (metric tons)
1970	195,447	126,592
1971	192,362	120,721
1972	200,503	160,938

ROADS
(1972)

Cars	9,517
Buses	2,106
Lorries	3,760
Vans	10,392
Jeeps	1,331
Total . . .	27,106

CIVIL AVIATION

	Passengers	Freight (metric tons)
1970	99,108	1,599
1971	116,876	1,217
1972	124,903	1,070

EDUCATION
(1972)

	Schools	Teachers	Students
Primary . . .	2,641	14,001	448,153
Secondary . .	642	6,883	62,552
Higher . . .	24	1,778	11,404

Source: Banco Central del Paraguay, Asunción.

THE CONSTITUTION

Following the presidential elections of February 1968, the 1940 constitution was replaced by one formulated in 1967.

The preamble to the Constitution states that Paraguay is an independent republic whose form of government is representative democracy. The powers accorded to the legislature, executive and judiciary are exercised separately and independently. The official religion of Paraguay is Roman Catholicism.

All citizens of Paraguay are equal before the law and have the right to freedom of conscience, travel, residence and religion. The freedom of association is guaranteed as is the right of workers to organize and strike. Political parties are free to operate providing they do not advocate the destruction of the republican representative system. All Paraguayans may vote in elections after the age of eighteen. No laws may be retrospective in application.

The legislature is composed of the Senate and the Chamber of Deputies. The Senate is made up of at least thirty members, the Chamber of Deputies of at least sixty members. Legislation concerning national defence and international agreements may be initiated in the Senate. Financial, electoral and municipal legislation may be initiated in the Chamber of Deputies. Both chambers of Congress are elected for a period of five years subject to dissolution.

Executive power is discharged by the President of the Republic, who must be a Roman Catholic. He is elected by direct vote for a five-year term of office. The President formulates legislation and enacts it. He is the commander-in-chief of the armed forces and may dissolve Congress.

The Supreme Court is composed of five members who are appointed for five years by the President. The Supreme Court has the power to declare legislation unconstitutional.

THE GOVERNMENT

HEAD OF STATE

President: Gen. Alfredo Stroessner.

COUNCIL OF MINISTERS
(April 1974)

Minister of the Interior: Dr. Sabino Augusto Montanaro.

Minister of Foreign Affairs: Dr. Raúl Sapena Pastor.

Minister of Finance: Gen. César Barrientos.

Minister of Education and Worship: Dr. Raúl Peña.

Ministry of Industry and Commerce: Dr. Delfín Ugarte Centurión.

Minister of the Treasury: Gen. César Barrientos.

Minister of Public Works and Communications: Gen. Juan Antonio Cáceres.

Minister of Defence: Gen. Marcial Samaniego.

Minister of Public Health: Dr. Adán Godoy Jiménez.

Minister of Justice and Labour: Dr. Saúl González.

Minister of Agriculture and Livestock: Ing. Hernando Bertoni.

Minister without Portfolio: Arq. Tomás Romero Pereira.

DIPLOMATIC REPRESENTATION

EMBASSIES AND LEGATION ACCREDITED TO PARAGUAY

(Asunción unless otherwise stated)

(E) Embassy; (L) Legation.

Argentina: Avda. Mcal. López 2335 (E); *Ambassador:* José María Rosa.

Austria: Buenos Aires, Argentina (E).

Belgium: Montevideo, Uruguay (E).

Bolivia: Juan de Salazar 1875 (E); *Ambassador:* Herberto Castedo Lladó.

Brazil: Rio de Janeiro 920 (E); *Ambassador:* Fernando de Alencar.

Canada: Buenos Aires, Argentina (E).

Chile: Eligio Ayala 1907 (E); *Ambassador:* Gen. Rolando González A.

Colombia: Mexico 513 (E); *Ambassador:* César Garrido.

Denmark: Buenos Aires, Argentina (E).

Ecuador: Yegros 837 (E); *Ambassador:* José Joaquín Silva.

Egypt: Montevideo, Uruguay (E).

El Salvador: Avda. Mcal. López 2435 (E); *Ambassador:* (vacant).

Finland: Buenos Aires, Argentina (E).

France: Avda. España 676 (E); *Ambassador:* Laurent Giovangrandi.

Germany, Federal Republic: Brasil 243 (E); *Ambassador:* Christoph Becker von Sothen.

Greece: Buenos Aires, Argentina (E).

Guatemala: Buenos Aires, Argentina (E).

India: Buenos Aires, Argentina (E).

Israel: Alberdi 221 (E); *Ambassador:* Shlomo Z. Katz.

Italy: Avda. Mcal. López 1104 (E); *Ambassador:* Dr. Luigi Ciotti.

Japan: Avda. Mcal. López 1099 (E); *Ambassador:* Kazuo Futamata.

Korea, Republic: Buenos Aires, Argentina (E).

Lebanon: Buenos Aires, Argentina (L).

Mexico: Eduardo Víctor Haedo 295 (E); *Ambassador:* Dr. Manuel Alcalá.

Netherlands: Buenos Aires, Argentina (E).

Nicaragua: Rio de Janeiro, Brazil (E).

Norway: Buenos Aires, Argentina (E).

Pakistan: Rio de Janeiro, Brazil (E).

Panama: Tte. Ruiz 696 (E); *Chargé d'Affaires:* Lic. Max Arosemena Ycaza.

Peru: Avda. Mcal. López 3873 (E); *Ambassador:* César A. de la Fuente.

Philippines: Buenos Aires, Argentina (E).

Portugal: Buenos Aires, Argentina (E).

South Africa: Montevideo, Uruguay (E).

Spain: 25 de Mayo 171 (E); *Ambassador:* Carlos Manuel Fernández Shaw.

Sweden: Buenos Aires, Argentina (E).

Switzerland: Estrella 625, 5° piso (E); *Ambassador:* Dr. Auguste Humi.

Thailand: Buenos Aires, Argentina (E).

United Kingdom: 25 de Mayo 171, 1° piso (E); *Ambassador:* Henry Bartlett.

U.S.A.: Avda. Mcal. López 1776 (E); *Ambassador:* George Landau.

Uruguay: Boquerón 590 (E); *Ambassador:* (vacant).

Vatican: Avda. Mcal. López 1750 (Apostolic Nunciature); *Nuncio:* Dr. José Mees.

Venezuela: Azara 1879 (E); *Ambassador:* Dr. Gilmer Urdaneta.

Yugoslavia: Buenos Aires, Argentina (E).

PRESIDENT AND CONGRESS

PRESIDENTIAL ELECTION

(*February 11th*, 1973)

CANDIDATES	VOTES
Gen. Alfredo Stroessner (Colorado) . .	681,306
Dr. Gustavo Adolfo Riart (Liberal Radical)	98,096
Dr. Carlos Levi Ruffinelli (Liberal) . .	24,611

CONGRESS

Under the Constitution the party gaining a majority of votes in the presidential election obtains two-thirds of the seats in both the thirty-member Senate and the sixty-member Lower House.

PARTY	SEATS	
	Senate	Chamber of Deputies
Colorado	20	40
Liberal Radical . . .	8	16
Liberal	2	4

COUNCIL OF STATE

Consists of the Ministers in charge of Government Departments, the Rector of the National University, the Archbishop of Asunción, one representative of commerce, two for agriculture and one for industry, the Presidents of the Banco Central del Paraguay and the Banco Nacional de Fomento, and two retired officers, one from the army and the other from the navy.

President: Dr. Juan Ramón Chávez.

POLITICAL PARTIES

Asociación Nacional Republicana (*Partido Colorado—National Republican Party*): the party of President STROESSNER, who has been in power since 1954; Chair. Dr. JUAN R. CHÁVEZ; Sec. Dr. PEDRO PEÑA.

Directorado Revolucionario del Partido Liberal: Ayolas 939, Asunción; Leader Dr. CARLOS LEVI RUFFINELLI.

Partido Liberal Radical: Yegros y Manuel Domínguez, Asunción; f. 1887; governed 1904–36, 1937–40; Presidential candidate in 1973 Gen. GUSTAVO ADOLFO RIART; Leader Dr. JUSTO PASTOR BENÍTEZ; publ. *El Radical*.

Partido Demócrata Cristiano: refused recognition by the electoral commission 1971, boycotted the 1973 election; Pres. Dr. HERMÓGENES ROJAS SILVA.

Partido Revolucionario Febrerista: an Opposition party; recognized in 1964, boycotted the 1973 election; Chair. MANUEL BENÍTEZ GONZÁLEZ.

JUDICIAL SYSTEM

The Supreme Court is composed of five judges chosen by the President with the approval of the Council of State.

President: Dr. JUAN FÉLIX MORALES.

Under the Supreme Court are the Courts of Appeal, the Tribunal of Jurors and Judges of First Instance, the Judges of Arbitration, the Magistrates (*Jueces de Instrucción*), and the Justices of the Peace.

RELIGION

All sects are tolerated, but 89 per cent of the population is Roman Catholic.

Metropolitan See:
Asunción . . Rt. Rev. ISMAEL BLÁS ROLÓN.

Suffragan Sees:
Concepción . . Rt. Rev. ANÍBAL MARICEVICH FLEITAS.

San Juan Bautista de las Misiones . . Rt. Rev. RAMÓN BOGARÍN ARGAÑA.

Villarrica . . Rt. Rev. FELIPE SANTIAGO BENÍTEZ AVALOS.

THE PRESS

DAILIES
Asunción

ABC: Yegros 745; f. 1967; Dir. ALDO ZUCCOLILLO.

Patria: organ of the Colorado Party; f. 1946; Dir. Dr. EZEQUIEL GONZÁLEZ ALSINA; circ. 25,000.

La Prensa: Iturbide 1169; evening; Dir. Dr. ALBERTO DUARTE.

La Tribuna: General Díaz 637; f. 1925; independent; Dir. CARLOS A. RUIZ APEZTEGUÍA; circ. 30,000.

Ultima Hora: Benjamín Constant 662; evening; Dir. ISAAC KOSTIANOVSKY.

PERIODICALS
Asunción

El Agricultor: Eligio Ayala 1033; agricultural affairs.

Así Es: 15 de Agosto 364; monthly; non-political.

Comercio: Estrella 540.

Diálogo: Luis Alberto de Herrera 1280; weekly; general interest.

El Enano: liberal; weekly; Publ. and Editor ROBERTO VÍCTOR ACOSTA ROLÓN.

Paraguay Industrial y Comercial: Casilla 900, Asunción; monthly; Dir. VENANCIO DUARTE SOSA.

El Radical: political weekly.

Revista del Comercio: fortnightly.

Sendero: official organ of the Bishops of Paraguay.

PRESS ASSOCIATION
Asociación Paraguaya de Prensa: Asunción; Pres. DANTE CAZAL.

FOREIGN BUREAUX
ANSA: Cerro Corá 1645, Asunción; Agent VÍCTOR E. CARUGATI.

EFE: 25 de Mayo y Yegros, Asunción; Rep. ATILIO R. FERNÁNDEZ.

Latin-Reuter: Yegros 652, Asunción.

UPI: General Díaz 865, Asunción.

PUBLISHERS

La Colmena, S.A.: Presidente Franco 328, Casilla 302, Asunción; Dir. DAUMAS LADOUCE.

Ediciones Diálogo: Calle Brasil 1391, Asunción; fine arts, history, sciences, fiction, paperbacks.

Ediciones Nizza: Estrella 721, Asunción; medicine.

ASSOCIATION
Cámara Paraguaya del Libro: Librería Internacional, Estrella 380, Asunción.

RADIO AND TELEVISION

RADIO
Administración Nacional de Telecomunicaciones: Administración General, Alberdi y General Díaz, Casilla 84, Asunción; f. 1926; Dir.-Gen. Lt.-Col. FELICIANO DUARTE; Tech. Dir. Ing. J. C. MARTÍNEZ R.

Number of radio receivers (1971): 175,000.

GOVERNMENT STATION
Radio Nacional: Oliva y Alberdi, 6° piso, Asunción; Dir. A. CÁCERES ALMADA.

COMMERCIAL STATIONS
Radio Concepción ZP8: Oliva y Schreiber, Concepción; f. 1963; Dir. Prop. SERGIO E. DACAK.

Radio Encarnación: General Artigas 728, Encarnación; commercial but government-owned; Man. J. GÓMEZ.

Radio Guairá: Alejo García y Pte. Franco, Villarica; Dir. E. TRAVERSI VÁSQUEZ.

Radio Guaraní: Avda. José F. Bogardo y 7A, Asunción; Dir. Esteban Cáceres Almada.

Radio Ñanduti: Antequera 654, Asunción; f. 1962; Dir. Humberto Rubin.

Radio Paraguay: Avda. Dr. Gaspar R. de Francia 343-38, Asunción; Dir.-Gen. Gerardo Halley Mora.

Radio Presidente Stroessner: Puerto Pte. Stroessner; Dir. Maria Bernabé.

Radio Charitas: Luis A. de Herrera 364, Casilla 1313, Asunción; Dir. Rev. Saturnino Urbistondo.

There are 14 other commercial stations.

TELEVISION

Televisión Cerro Corá S.A.: Avda. Carlos A. López 572, Asunción; commercial; Gen. Man. Ricardo Sánchez Abdo.

Number of television receivers (1972): 52,500.

FINANCE

BANKING

(cap.=capital; p.u.=paid up; dep.=deposits; m.=million; amounts in guaraníes)

Superintendencia de Bancos: Superintendent Dr. Víctor J. Beckelmann.

Central Bank

Banco Central del Paraguay: Independencia Nacional y 25 de Mayo, Asunción; f. 1925; cap. and res. 54.3m. (Dec. 1973); Pres. Dr. César Romeo Acosta; Gen. Man. Dr. Augusto A. Colmán.

Banco de Asunción: Independencia Nacional y Azara, Asunción.

Banco Nacional de Fomento: Independencia Nacional esq. 25 de Mayo y Cerro Corá, Asunción; f. 1961 to supply medium- and long-term industrial and agricultural credits; cap. 2.6m.; Pres. Alberto González (acting); 21 brs. and 16 agencies throughout the country.

Banco Nacional de Trabajadores (BNT): Asunción; f. 1973 to make credit available to workers and to encourage savings; initial cap. 100m.

Banco Paraguayo de Comercio "Sudameris" S.A.: Independencia Nacional esq. Cerro Corá, Asunción; f. 1958; savings and commercial bank; subsidiary of Banco Francés e Italiano para la América del Sud—Sudameris; cap. 178m., dep. 635m.; Pres. Dr. Ramiro Rodríguez Alcalá; Man. Dr. Antonino Monte.

Cooperativa Central de Producción: Asunción; f. 1969 to offer savings and credit facilities to co-operatives.

Foreign Banks

Banco Alemán Transatlántico: 14 de Mayo casi Estrella, Asunción.

Banco de la Nación Argentina: Buenos Aires; Chile y Palma, Asunción.

Banco do Brasil: Rio de Janeiro; Oliva y Nuestra Señora de la Asunción, Apdo. 667, Asunción; Man. José Nunes de Faria.

Banco Exterior S.A.: Madrid; 23 de Mayo esq. Yegros, Asunción; f. 1968; cap. 151m., dep. 1,000m. (Dec. 1971); Pres. Manuel Arburúa de la Miyar.

Banco Holandés Unido (*Hollandsche Bank-Unie*): Amsterdam; Palma y Nuestra Señora de la Asunción, Apdo. 1180, Asunción; Man. Peter van Dijk.

Bank of America N.T. & S.A.: San Francisco; Estrella 621, Asunción.

Bank of London and South America: London; Palma y J. E. O'Leary, Apdo. 696, Asunción; Man. George Camburn.

Dresdner Bank: c/o Banco Germánico de la América del Sud, Asunción.

First National City Bank: New York; Chile esq. Presidente Franco, Apdo. 1174, Asunción; Man. Guillermo H. Howard.

Banking Association

Asociación de Bancos Privados del Paraguay: Edificio Banco Exterior, 2° piso, Oficina 3, 25 de Mayo y Yegros, Asunción; mems.: Paraguayan banks and foreign banks with brs. in Asunción; Pres. Máximo Arnoldo Reutemann.

INSURANCE

Asunción

América S.A. de Seguros: Chile y 14 de Julio, Casilla 865; cap. 50m.; Pres. Dr. Hassel Aguilar Sosa; Gen. Man. Valentín Gamarra Velázquez; fire, car, aviation, accident, theft, etc.

El Comercio Paraguayo: Alberdi 453; f. 1947; Pres. Enrique Cazenave; life, fire, car, accident, liability, marine, aviation, glass, burglary.

La Consolidada S.A. de Seguros y Reaseguros: Chile 719, Casilla 1182; f. 1961; cap. 8.3m.; Pres. Dr. Francisco Esculies; Gen. Man. Dr. J. Manuel Ferreira; fire, car, accident, marine, plate glass, transport, life, burglary, general.

Cumbre S.A. de Seguros y Reaseguros: Oliva 393, Casilla 244; f. 1961; Man. César Avalos; fire, car, marine, glass, liability, accident.

Guaraní: Palma 685; f. 1946; Pres. Dr. José Demetrio Ayala; Man. Mario A. Iaffei; fire, car, marine, burglary, accident, liability, life.

Institución Paraguaya Aseguradora, S.A.: Alberdi 149, Casilla 735; Pres. R. Buzó; fire, marine, hull, car, accident.

La Paraguaya S.A. de Seguros: Estrella 625; f. 1905; Pres. Dr. Oscar Pérez Uribe; fire, car, accident, liability, glass, marine, life.

Rumbos S.A. de Seguros: Estrella 851; Pres. Dr. A. Soljanic; fire, car, transport, marine, livestock, health, life.

La Rural del Paraguay: 15 de Agosto 608, Casilla 21; f. 1920; Pres. E. Cazenave; fire, car, glass, liability, marine, accident, burglary, general.

Seguros Generales (SEGESA): Oliva 393, Casilla 802; Man. César Avalos; life, fire, car, marine, burglary, liability, water damage, guarantee.

TRADE AND INDUSTRY

INDUSTRIAL AND DEVELOPMENT ORGANIZATIONS

Secretaría Técnica de Planificación de la Presidencia de la República: Iturbide y Eligio Ayala, Asunción; government body responsible for overall planning.

Administración Nacional de Almacenes, Silos y Frigoríficos: Asunción; f. 1969 to organize a national network of storage installations; financed by a U.S. $6m. loan from the IADB.

Centro de Desarrollo y Productividad (*Centre for Development and Productivity*): Asunción; f. 1966 by *Unión Industrial* and *Feprinco*; supported by Ministry of Industry and Commerce; technical and financial assistance from U.S.A.I.D. advisory board; has mems. from 20 public and private sector institutions connected with the centre's activities.

Consejo Nacional de Coordinación Económica: Asunción; directs negotiations between workers and employers.

Consejo Nacional para el Desarrollo de la Ganadería: Asunción; f. 1964; government council representing public and private bodies in the cattle industry.

Consejo Nacional de Desarrollo Industrial (*National Council for Industrial Development*): Asunción; national planning institution.

Federación de la Producción, Industria y Comercio (FEPRINCO): 15 de Agosto 341 (altos), Asunción.

Instituto de Bienestar Rural: Asunción; responsible for rural welfare and colonization.

Instituto Nacional de Tecnología y Normalización: Avda. General Roa y General Aguiar, Asunción; national standards institute.

Instituto de Previsión Social: Asunción; responsible for employees' welfare and health insurance scheme.

TRADE UNIONS

Confederación Paraguaya de Trabajadores—CPT (*Confederation of Paraguayan Workers*): Yegros y Simón Bolívar, Asunción; f. 1951; mems. 20,000 (est.) from 113 affiliated groups; Dir.-Gen. Víctor Pinasco; Sec.-Gen. Nicanor Fleitas; publ. *La Voz de Trabajo* (fortnightly).

Confederación Paraguaya de Trabajadores en el Exilio (*Confederation of Paraguayan Workers in Exile*): Montevideo, Uruguay; f. 1959 as CPT in exile; admitted to ICFTU/ORIT; Sec.-Gen. Heriberto Román Berganza.

TRANSPORT

RAILWAYS

Ferrocarril Presidente Carlos Antonio López: Mexico 145, Casilla 453, Asunción; f. 1854 by a British company, purchased by Paraguayan Government in 1961; 441 km. open (1,435 mm. gauge); Gen. Man. Dr. Modesto Ali.

ROADS

In 1973 there were 1,673 km. of paved roads, 1,041 km. of gravelled roads and 3,128 km. of dirt roads. A 500 km. span of the Trans-Chaco highway is being paved.

Motorists' Organization

Touring y Automóvil Club Paraguayo: 25 de Mayo y Brasil, Casilla 1204, Asunción; f. 1924; 4,000 mems.; Pres. Dr. Ramón Codas; Sec. Amado A. Artaza.

SHIPPING

Administración Nacional de Navegación y Puertos (*National Shipping and Ports Department*): Colón e Isabel la Católica, Asunción; f. 1965; responsible for ports services and maintaining navigable channels in rivers and for improving navigation on the River Paraguay.

In 1967 Paraguay's merchant fleet had a total gross registered tonnage of 18,925.

Inland Waterways

Flota Mercante del Estado: Asunción; state-owned; boats and barges up to 1,000 tons displacement on Paraguay and Paraná rivers; cold storage ships for use between Asunción–Buenos Aires–Montevideo.

Ocean Shipping

Compañía Paraguaya de Navegación de Ultramar: Asunción; f. 1963 to operate between Asunción, U.S.A. and European ports; two ships of 1,135 tons each.

Vessels of the Compañía Argentina de Navegación Fluvial, Holland Pan-American Line and Lloyd Brasileiro also operate services. Lamport & Holt Line Ltd. and the Rotterdam South America Line have direct monthly and fortnightly services from Europe to Asunción, which eliminate the need for trans-shipment at Buenos Aires. The vessels which are used on this route are of 600–1,000 tons.

CIVIL AVIATION

The main airport is at Asunción.

National Airlines

Lineas Aéreas Paraguayas: Oliva 467, Asunción; f. 1962; services to Buenos Aires, Lima and Montevideo from Asunción; Pres. Lt.-Col. Adrian Jara; Exec. Man. Col. Enrique M. Nardi; fleet: 3 Lockheed Electra, 2 CV-240, 1 DC-3.

Transporte Aéreo Militar: Oliva 467, Asunción; domestic passenger and cargo services; Gen. Man. Col. M. Britez; fleet: 7 DC-3.

Foreign Airlines

Paraguay is also served by the following foreign airlines; Aerolíneas Argentinas, Braniff, Iberia, LAN (Chile), Lufthansa, Pluna (Uruguay) and Varig (Brazil).

TOURISM

Dirección General de Turismo: Ministerio de Obras Públicas y Comunicaciones, Oliva y Alberdi, Asunción; Dir. Dr. Alejandro Brugada Guanes.

Asociación de Agencias de Viajes del Paraguay: Apdo. 959, Asunción; Pres. Ricardo Fustagno.

ATOMIC ENERGY

Comisión Nacional de Energía Atómica: Ministerio de Relaciones Exteriores, Asunción; f. 1960; maintains no laboratories or installations; Pres. Prof. Dr. José Danilo Pecci.

Universidad Nacional de Asunción: Asunción; atomic research in medicine, mathematics, physics, chemistry and agronomy; the university does not possess special equipment.

Instituto Nacional de Investigaciones Científicas: P.O.B. 1141, Asunción; laboratory facilities for basic experiments in nuclear and atomic physics; Dir. Dr. Fabio Rivas A.

UNIVERSITIES

Universidad Católica "Nuestra Señora de la Asunción": Independencia Nacional y Comuneros, Asunción; 320 teachers, 4,370 students.

Universidad Nacional de Asunción: España 1098, Asunción; 500 teachers, 6,000 students.

PERU

INTRODUCTORY SURVEY

Location, Climate, Language, Religion, Flag, Capital

Peru is an Andean country situated on the Pacific coast of South America. It is bordered by Ecuador and Colombia to the north, Brazil and Bolivia to the east and Chile to the south. The climate varies with altitude, average temperatures being some 7°c (20F°) lower in the mountains than in the coastal region. The official language is Spanish but Quechua and Aymará are spoken by many of the Indian population. Most of the population is Roman Catholic and there is a Protestant minority. The national flag (proportions 3 by 2) has vertical stripes of red, white and red, with the state shield on the centre stripe. The capital is Lima.

Recent History

In October 1968 a military *coup* deposed President Fernando Belaúnde Terry after five years in office and established Gen. Juan Velasco Alvarado as President. Congress was suspended and a military cabinet appointed. President Velasco's Government has sought to enact reforms to expropriate foreign interests in the agricultural, industrial and mining sectors in favour of the peasants. Efforts to lessen the country's economic dependence on the United States and the repeated nationalization of American companies led initially to a marked decrease in foreign investment, but since 1970 the situation has recovered.

Early in 1974 the giant Cerro de Pasco Corporation was expropriated, but a lump sum payment in compensation has been agreed with the Corporation and with other American companies nationalized in past years. Support for President Velasco's measures is not unanimous, however, and in January 1974 widespread strikes and street demonstrations obliged the Government to declare a state of siege in Arequipa and Puno and a state of emergency in Cuzco, and to suspend constitutional guarantees in these cities.

Government

Executive power is vested in the President, assisted by a Cabinet. Congress was suspended in 1968; government is by decree, pending a new constitution and subsequent elections. The country is divided into 24 Departments administered by Prefects.

Defence

Armed forces consist of an Army, Navy and Air Force. The Army numbers about 39,000 men. All male citizens from eighteen to twenty-four years of age are liable to compulsory military training and some, chosen by ballot, have to do regular service for two years.

Economic Affairs

Peru has a diversified agricultural economy, the chief crops being sugar, potatoes, rice, coffee and cotton. Livestock is raised, particularly in the mountains. Fishing is an important factor in the economy and Peru's fishmeal industry is the largest in the world, although activities were almost completely suspended during 1972–73 because of the disappearance of *anchoveta* stocks due to temporary climatic changes and over-fishing. To combat deficiencies in the industry, all private firms producing fishmeal and its derivatives were expropriated in May 1973 and a state corporation, Pescaperú, created to control the processing and production of fishmeal and oil. Fishing recommenced, on a quota basis, in March 1974.

Minerals include silver, petroleum, iron ore, copper, phosphates and potash. Foreign exchange income earned by the mining industry reached record levels in 1973. Following the expropriation of the Cerro de Pasco Corporation, the Government is now in control of more than 50 per cent of national mineral production. Preliminary results from oil wells drilled in the Amazon jungle and off-shore have been promising and several foreign companies have entered into partnership with the state oil company, Petroperú, to exploit these reserves. Depending on the final results of these exploratory drillings, a 880-km. pipeline is to be laid through the Amazon region and over the Andes. It is anticipated that this will be in service by 1976. Plans have been drawn up for the establishment of worker-owned and controlled companies throughout the Peruvian economy. Peru is a member of the UN, Latin American Free Trade Association (LAFTA) and Andean Group, which has its headquarters in Lima.

Transport and Communications

Transport is made difficult by the terrain and internal air services are an important means of transport. There are some 2,100 km. of railways. The road system is centered on the 3,400 km. long Peruvian section of the Pan American Highway which is crossed by the Trans-Andean Highway running from Lima. A new 480 km. road, part of the Trans-Andean Highway, connecting Lima and Callao with the headwaters of the Amazon, is due for completion in 1980. European shipping lines call regularly at Peruvian ports, the chief of which is Callao. Internal air transport is provided by three local airlines and international services are provided by several major airlines.

Social Welfare

Social insurance is compulsory and benefits cover sickness, disability and old age. Labour legislation guarantees conditions of employment. Special schemes are in force for women and children.

Education

Primary education is free and where possible compulsory between the ages of six and fourteen. There are a number of fee-paying schools. Secondary education is both public and private. Educational reforms which became effective from April 1972 included nutrition and health courses for parents, compulsory vocational training for two years after the age of fifteen and instruction in Quechua as well as Spanish for the Andean Indians. There are thirty universities.

Tourism

Peru is famous for the relics of Inca and pre-Inca civilizations. There is spectacular mountain scenery including Lake Titicaca, situated at an altitude of 3,850 metres, and forest and jungle areas. Many of the towns have interesting examples of Spanish Colonial architecture and culture.

Visas are not required to visit Peru by nationals of the following countries: Argentina, Austria, Belgium, Brazil, Canada, Denmark, France, the Federal Republic of Germany, Italy, Liechtenstein, Luxembourg, the Netherlands, Norway, the Philippines, Portugal, Spain, Switzerland, the United Kingdom and the U.S.A.

Sport

Football is the most popular sport and basketball, baseball, horse-racing and bull- and cock-fighting are widely followed. There are opportunities for hunting and deep-sea fishing.

Public Holidays

1974: August 30th (St. Rose of Lima), October 9th (Day of National Dignity), November 1st (All Saints' Day), December 8th (Immaculate Conception), December 25th (Christmas Day).

1975: January 1st (New Year's Day), March 27th–28th (Easter), May 1st (Labour Day), June 29th (SS. Peter and Paul), July 28th–29th (Anniversary of Independence).

Weights and Measures

The metric system is in force.

Currency and Exchange Rates

100 centavos = 1 sol.

Exchange rates (April 1974):

£1 sterling = 91.38 soles;
U.S. $1 = 38.70 soles.

STATISTICAL SURVEY

AREA AND POPULATION

(Census of June 4th, 1972)

TOTAL AREA (sq. km.)	POPULATION
1,285,215.6	13,567,939*

* Excluding Indian jungle inhabitants and an allowance for underenumeration.

PRINCIPAL TOWNS

(Population at June 30th, 1970)

Lima (capital) . .	2,541,300*	Chiclayo . . . 140,800
Callao . .	335,400	Piura . . . 111,400
Arequipa .	194,700	Cuzco . . . 108,900
Trujillo . .	156,200	Chimbote . . 102,800

* Metropolitan area (Gran Lima).

ECONOMICALLY ACTIVE POPULATION

(1967—'000)

Agriculture and fishing 1,772.5, mining 80.3, manufacturing 529.8, construction 149.5, electricity, gas, water and sanitary services 9.9, commerce 354.2, transport 135.5, services 615.8, others 128.7. Total: 3,776.3.

AGRICULTURE

PRODUCTION OF PRINCIPAL CROPS
('ooo metric tons)

	1966	1967	1968	1969	1970	1971
Barley . . .	154	172	146	164	170	159
Coffee . . .	52	53	65	68	65	71
Cotton (lint) . .	332	264	385	255	248	269
,, (seed) . .	125	97	106	95	92	100
Maize . . .	581	591	553	590	615	616
Potatoes . . .	1,499	1,712	1,592	1,856	1,929	1,968
Rice (hulled) . .	374	461	286	444	587	591
Sugar . . .	8,463	7,943	7,272	6,412	7,591	8,309
Tobacco . . .	3	5	4	3	2	2
Wheat . . .	145	152	119	137	125	122
Tea . . .	7	7	n.a.	9	7	10

FISHING INDUSTRY
('ooo metric tons)

LIVESTOCK
(1971—'ooo)

Cattle . . .	4,310
Pigs . . .	2,071
Sheep . .	16,918

	1968	1969	1970
Total Catch . . .	10,440	9,143	12,481
Industrial Production .	2,291	1,799	2,516
Fishmeal . .	1,922	1,611	2,253
Fish Oil* . .	323	141	200
Frozen Fish . .	21	21	24
Tinned Fish . .	25	27	35
Others . . .	5,958	5,545	7,444

1971: Total catch 10,611,400 metric tons.   * Exported.

MINING*

	UNIT	1969	1970	1971
Crude Petroleum	'ooo metric tons	3,519	3,550	3,053
Natural Gas	million cu. metres	485	476	n.a.
Iron Ore	'ooo metric tons	5,853	6,119	n.a.
Copper	metric tons	210,387	205,928	212,900
Lead	,, ,,	162,139	156,596	n.a.
Zinc	,, ,,	313,203	320,670	n.a.
Tungsten†	,, ,,	869	1,014	966
Molybdenum	,, ,,	374	607	808
Mercury	,, ,,	124	108	62
Silver	,, ,,	1,116	1,239	1,194
Gold	kilogrammes	2,865	2,954	n.a.

* Figures for metallic minerals refer to metal content only.   † Exports only.

INDUSTRY

	UNITS	1968	1969	1970
Cigarettes	million	2,575	n.a.	n.a.
Motor Spirit (Petrol) . . .	'000 barrels	10,209	9,704	9,489
Kerosene	'000 metric tons	500	488	510
Distillate Fuel Oils . .	,, ,, ,,	905	948	929
Residual Fuel Oils . .	,, ,, ,,	1,230	1,173	1,231
Liquefied Petroleum Gas .	,, ,, ,,	44	20	27
Cement	,, ,, ,,	1,098	1,132	1,144
Refined Copper . . .	metric tons	38,500	32,061	32,641
Unwrought Lead . . .	,, ,,	86,383	77,923	72,510
Unwrought Zinc . . .	,, ,,	65,788	55,813	64,096
Passenger Cars (assembly) . .	number	7,700	12,600	10,300
Electricity	million kWh.	5,008	5,017	5,529

FINANCE

100 centavos = 1 sol.

Coins: 5, 10, 20, 25 and 50 centavos; 1, 5 and 10 soles.

Notes: 5, 10, 50, 100, 200, 500 and 1,000 soles.

Exchange rates (April 1974): £1 sterling = 91.38 soles (exchange certificate rate) or 102.43 soles (free rate);

U.S. $1 = 38.70 soles (exchange certificate rate) or 43.38 soles (free rate).

100 soles = £1.094 = $2.584 (exchange certificate rates).

BUDGET

The biennial budget for 1971–72 estimated the expenditure of 115,600 million soles and revenue of 114,800 million soles. Expenditure for the two years 1973–74 is forecast to be 143,200 million soles.

NATIONAL ACCOUNTS

(million soles)

	1967	1968	1969
GROSS NATIONAL PRODUCT . . .	153.75	181.24	198.32
Balance of exports and imports . .	8.47	2.58	−0.87
AVAILABLE RESOURCES . . .	162.22	183.82	197.45
of which:			
Private consumption expenditure .	113.49	137.67	149.84
Government consumption expenditure .	17.72	19.38	20.43
Gross fixed investment . . .	23.39	24.09	25.36
Increase in stocks . . .	7.62	1.69	1.82

BALANCE OF PAYMENTS

(million U.S. $—minus sign indicates debit)

	1965	1966	1967	1968	1969	1970
Goods and Services	−164	−253	−319	− 41	− 8	110
Trade Balance f.o.b.	32	− 14	− 74	177	207	337
Freight and Merchandise Insurance .	− 84	− 96	− 88	− 61	− 58	− 56
Investment Income	− 91	−128	−148	−139	−146	−135
Other	− 21	− 15	− 9	− 18	− 11	− 36
Transfer Payments:						
Private	5	7	6	6	3	15
Government	11	13	17	26	28	75
Capital Movements:						
Private	122	129	80	53	− 1	−111
Government	85	106	129	75	53	19
Commercial Banks:						
Assets	− 7	− 37	26	− 6	21	63
Liabilities	1	—	12	—	1	− 2
Allocation of SDRs . . . −	—	—	—	—	—	14
Monetary Authorities	− 15	23	34	15	− 37	−183
Monetary Gold	—	2	45	—	− 5	− 15
SDR Holdings	—	—	—	—	—	14
IMF Accounts	—	− 2	12	4	25	− 18
Foreign Exchange	− 15	22	− 27	11	− 53	−137
Other Liabilities	—	6	3	9	− 4	1
Other Claims	—	− 5	1	− 9	—	—
Net Errors and Omissions . . .	− 38	12	15	−128	− 60	n.a.

CONSUMER PRICE INDEX

(Lima and Callao; 1966 = 100)

	1968	1969	1970	1971	1972
Food and Drink . . .	129.66	136.89	141.14	150.75	161.88
Housing . . .	128.42	139.33	154.26	164.35	176.38
Clothing . . .	122.45	128.43	136.86	149.87	166.58
Miscellaneous . . .	143.54	153.79	157.80	166.05	171.80
General Index . .	130.74	138.88	145.85	155.78	166.98

EXTERNAL TRADE

('000 U.S. $)

	1969	1970	1971	1972*
Imports c.i.f. . . .	600,825	618,843	752,631	796,581
Exports f.o.b. . . .	865,631	1,047,779	892,733	944,430

* Preliminary.

COMMODITIES
('000 soles)

IMPORTS	1971	1972	EXPORTS	1971	1972
Animals and Animal Products .	1,872,031	2,286,771	Cotton	1,745,627	1,832,215
Vegetable Products . . .	2,491,262	2,343,182	Sugar and Derivatives . .	2,738,082	3,039,927
Mineral Products . . .	1,364,769	2,067,307	Wool	91,650	235,904
Chemical Products . . .	4,175,748	4,451,813	Petroleum and Derivatives .	210,609	296,418
Natural and Synthetic Rubber			Fish and Derivatives . .	13,048,738	10,854,771
and Plastics . . .	1,609,728	1,574,407	Coffee	1,371,505	1,811,774
Textiles and Manufactures .	1,184,778	947,216	Zinc	1,809,866	2,670,995
Metals and Manufactures .	3,365,059	2,848,551	Copper	6,583,883	7,296,493
Machinery, incl. Electrical .	7,227,424	8,039,872	Lead	1,052,328	1,284,491
Transport Equipment . .	1,691,064	1,995,460	Iron	2,405,307	2,513,577
			Gold	57,223	52,022
			Silver	1,827,633	2,384,087

COUNTRIES
('000 soles)

	IMPORTS				EXPORTS			
	1969	1970	1971	1972	1969	1970	1971	1972
Argentina . . .	2,404,726	1,547,048	851,412	750,482	592,629	539,048	817,160	574,438
Belgium . . .	555,562	571,420	537,869	668,566	1,659,956	1,864,550	1,394,326	1,273,239
Canada	554,944	1,086,096	1,443,530	1,231,323	74,290	144,593	72,276	280,216
Chile	216,026	431,360	396,923	326,203	368,764	257,824	222,208	497,952
Ecuador . . .	96,483	94,401	285,572	301,108	107,696	110,538	160,811	166,547
German Federal Republic	2,642,769	2,917,624	3,521,839	3,661,016	4,051,926	6,084,425	5,316,868	4,101,445
Italy . . .	636,796	699,345	889,249	955,772	877,621	973,695	905,183	907,085
Japan . . .	1,673,618	1,893,031	2,782,818	2,374,276	5,413,090	5,490,564	4,277,629	5,074,586
Netherlands . .	513,091	507,373	657,308	713,247	2,721,990	3,892,230	2,566,812	2,499,680
Switzerland . .	471,585	447,051	752,156	878,910	83,529	116,549	132,036	108,297
United Kingdom .	1,020,217	1,037,561	1,526,644	1,313,606	1,047,873	1,019,277	1,021,070	965,576
U.S.A. . . .	7,196,204	7,697,596	8,521,529	9,193,282	11,560,503	13,334,878	9,803,984	12,046,552

TRANSPORT
Roads

	1969	1970
Passenger Cars . . .	220,140	230,412
Lorries . . .	45,068	47,384
Buses	17,664	21,341
Other Motor Vehicles .	78,939	84,050

Railways (1970): Passenger-km. 248 million, Ton-km. 595 million.

Shipping (1970): Merchant tonnage registered 27,386,607 metric tons; Goods imported 2,127,874 metric tons, Goods exported 14,334,308 metric tons.

Civil Aviation (1969): Passengers carried 1,021,431, Freight 157,994 metric tons, Mail 23,020 metric tons.

Tourism (1970): Visitors: arrivals 88,289, departures 83,271; revenue U.S. $21.6m.

Sources: Dirección Nacional de Estadística y Censos, Lima; Banco Central de Reserva del Perú, Lima.

THE CONSTITUTION

The Republic of Peru, formerly the chief Spanish vice-royalty in South America, declared its independence on July 28th, 1821, but it was not until 1824, when all Spanish forces were obliged to leave, that the country gained its freedom from Spanish rule.

The existing Constitution was promulgated on April 9th, 1933. It has been amended from time to time.

Under the general guarantees some of the functions of the modern State are defined. Mines, lands, forests, waters, and, generally, all natural sources of wealth belong to the State. Conditions of their exploitation, either by the State or by means of concessions to private persons, will be fixed by law. In industry, the State will support profit-sharing schemes, and will legislate concerning the organization of industry, safety measures for workers, accident compensation, minimum wages, maximum hours and general conditions of work. In agriculture, the State will favour the preservation of the small rural property and may expropriate, with compensation, and subdivide land which is not being exploited economically.

Article 53 provides that the legal existence of political parties with international connections is not recognized, and those belonging to such parties may not hold political office.

Liberty of conscience and of beliefs is inviolable, and no one may be persecuted for his ideals. Freedom of the press is guaranteed, but compensation may be sought through legal channels by an injured party against the editor and author of a publication. Article 65 provides for the censorship of public spectacles. The principle of *habeas corpus* is recognized.

When the security of the State demands, the Executive may suspend wholly or in part, in the whole or in a part of the national territory, certain constitutional guarantees of the individual. If such suspension is decreed while Congress is in session, the Executive must inform Congress immediately. The suspension will be for thirty days only, and another decree will be needed for any further extension. The powers of the Executive during the suspension of guarantees will be fixed by law.

Voting for men and women between the ages of 21 and 60 is compulsory; after 60, voting is optional.

The Legislative Power. The Constitution provides for a bi-cameral legislature. Both the Senate of 45 members, and the Chamber of Deputies, consisting of 140 members, are elected for six years. Congress begins its sessions on July 28th, and continues in ordinary session for 120 days. The President, with the agreement of his Cabinet, may convoke extraordinary sessions. Congress legislates, interprets, modifies and repeals laws; examines alleged infringements of the Constitution; imposes and repeals taxes; and approves or rejects the national and departmental budgets. However, any Congressional action to impose or repeal taxes or vote expenditure must be taken on the initiative of the Executive Power. Congress authorizes the Executive to negotiate State loans and provide funds for amortization. It approves or rejects the President's recommendations for the advancement of higher officers of the armed forces, and establishes the strength of those forces, and approves or withholds approvals of treaties negotiated by the Executive.

The Executive Power. The President is elected for a six-year term, which begins on July 28th of the year of election. First and Second Vice-Presidents are elected simultaneously with the President. The last-named is not eligible for re-election until after the lapse of at least one presidential term. This provision of the Constitution may not be reformed or repealed, and any person attempting to do so must retire from office, and will be permanently incapacitated from holding any public office. The President may not command the armed forces without the permission of Congress. On taking up such a command, he becomes subject to military laws and regulations. His tasks include the drafting of laws and the making of resolutions and decrees promulgating laws, the maintenance of internal order and external security, the convoking of presidential and congressional elections, and of extraordinary sessions of Congress. It is his duty to see that the resolutions of the Judicial Power are carried out. He organizes and distributes the armed forces, administers the finances of the State, negotiates treaties, appoints and removes the members of his Cabinet and, with the approval of his Cabinet, appoints members of the diplomatic corps, and selects candidates of Peruvian birth for archbishoprics and bishoprics, whose names are submitted to the Vatican.

The Judiciary. The Supreme Court, with its seat in Lima, consists of the President and 10 members, whose appointments have to be approved by Congress. Higher Courts function in certain departments determined by law, and Courts of First Instance in provincial capitals. There are justices of peace in all towns. Members of the Higher Courts are nominated by the President from a list submitted by the Supreme Court. Appointments to the lower courts must be ratified by the Supreme Court.

The Constitution provides that in each ministry there shall be one or more Consultative Commissions consisting of specialists in the various branches of activity of the ministry; and also provides for a Council of National Economy whose members shall represent the interests of consumers, capital, labour and the liberal professions.

Regional Administration. The country is divided into 24 Departments administered by Prefects. The Departments are divided into provinces, which in turn are divided into districts.

Municipal Councillors are nominally elected by direct vote, and foreigners are eligible, but for some years municipal bodies have been appointed without election. The Municipal Elections Law provides for elections every three years.

Indigenous Communities. The Constitution recognizes the legal existence and juridical personality of the indigenous communities, whose property may not be alienated except in the public interest, when compensation must be given. The State is responsible for the civil, penal, economic and administrative laws regulating these communities.

This constitution has remained only partially in force during the several periods of military government since it was promulgated, including the present one.

THE GOVERNMENT

HEAD OF STATE

President: Gen. Juan Velasco Alvarado.

THE CABINET

(April 1974)

Prime Minister and Minister of War: Gen. Edgardo Mercado Jarrín.

Minister for the Navy: Rear-Adm. Luis E. Vargas Caballero.

Minister for the Air Force: Gen. (Air Force) Rolando Gilardi Rodríguez.

Minister of the Interior: Gen. Pedro Richter Prada.

Minister of Foreign Affairs: Gen. Miguel de la Flor Valle.

Minister of Economics and Finance: Gen. Guillermo Marcó del Pont.

Minister of Education: Gen. Alfredo Carpio Becerra.

Minister of Health: Gen. Fernando Miró Quesada.

Minister of Labour: Lt.-Gen. Pedro Sala Osorio.

Minister of Agriculture: Gen. Enrique Váldez Angulo.

Minister of Industry and Tourism: Rear-Admiral Alberto Jiménez de Lucio.

Minister of Transport and Communications: Gen. Raúl Meneses Arata.

Minister of Energy and Mines: Gen. Jorge Fernández Maldonado.

Minister of Housing: Rear-Admiral Ramón Arróspide Mejía.

Minister of Fisheries: Gen. Javier Tantaleán Vanini.

Minister of Commerce: Gen. Luis Barandiarán Pagador.

DIPLOMATIC REPRESENTATION

EMBASSIES ACCREDITED TO PERU

(Lima unless otherwise stated)

(E) Embassy.

Argentina: Avda. Inca Garcilaso de la Vega 911, 10° piso (E); *Chargé d'Affaires a.i.:* Germán Pedro Sánchez.

Australia: Plaza Bldg., 6° piso, Natalio Sánchez 220, (E); *Chargé d'Affaires a.i.:* Rodney B. Hodgson.

Austria: Avda. Javier Prado 1702, San Isidro (E); *Ambassador:* Dr. Erich Maximillian Schmidt.

Belgium: Avda. Angamos 380, Misaflores (E); *Ambassador:* Ronald Watteeuw (also accred. to Bolivia).

Bolivia: Avda. Arequipa 2650, San Isidro (E); *Ambassador:* Dr. Jorge Escobari Cusicanqui.

Brazil: Avda. Comandante Espinar 181, Miraflores (E); *Ambassador:* Manuel Antonio de Pimentel Brandão.

Bulgaria: Paul Harris 289, urb. Santa Mónica, San Isidro (E); *Ambassador:* Mladen Nikolov.

Canada: Natalio Sánchez 125, Avda. Arequipa (E); *Ambassador:* Pierre Trottier.

Chile: Avda. Javier Prado Oeste, San Isidro (E); *Ambassador:* Dr. Luis Jérez Ramírez.

China, People's Republic: Avda. Javier Prado 1415, San Isidro (E); *Ambassador:* Chaio Jo-yu.

Colombia: Avda. Arequipa 2685 (E); *Ambassador:* Jaime Parra Ramírez.

Costa Rica: Camino Real 159, oficina 400, San Isidro (E); *Ambassador:* Lic. Julio Alberto Ortiz López.

Cuba: Coroner Portillo 110, San Isidro (E); *Ambassador:* Dr. Antonio Núñez Jiménez.

Cyprus: New York, U.S.A. (E).

Czechoslovakia: Avda. Salaverry 3119, San Isidro (E); *Ambassador:* Josef Mejstrik.

Denmark: Camino Real 479, 8° piso, San Isidro (E); *Ambassador:* Johan Frederick Holck Colding.

Dominican Republic: Migues de Cervantes 200, San Isidro (E); *Ambassador:* Dr. Ciro Amaury Dargam Cruz.

Ecuador: Avda. Garcilaso de la Vega 1218, oficina 905 (E); *Ambassador:* Dr. Alfredo Luna Tobar.

Egypt: Avda. José Pardo 273, Miraflores (E); *Ambassador:* M. Samir Ahmed.

El Salvador: Las Acacias 230, Miraflores (E); *Ambassador:* Col. César Yanes Urías.

Finland: Los Eucaliptos 291, 7° piso, San Isidro (E); *Ambassador:* Dr. Karl Torsten Tikanvaara (also accred. to Bolivia and Ecuador).

German Democratic Republic: Avda. Javier Prado Oeste 2291, San Isidro (E); *Ambassador:* Edgar Fries.

Germany, Federal Republic: Avda. Arequipa 4202, Miraflores (E); *Ambassador:* Norbert Berger.

Greece: Buenos Aires, Argentina (E).

Guatemala: Nicolás de Rivera 495, San Isidro (E); *Ambassador:* Enrique Castellanos Carrillo (also accred. to Bolivia).

Haiti: Barcelona 635, 8° piso, San Isidro (E); *Chargé d'Affaires a.i.:* Isner N. Champagne.

Honduras: Avda. Jorge Chávez 174, Miraflores (E); *Ambassador:* Col. Armando Velásquez Cerrato.

Hungary: Los Eucaliptos 395, San Isidro (E); *Ambassador:* János Kracsek.

India: Paseo de la República 291, oficina 1201 (E); *Chargé d'Affaires a.i.:* Pascal Alan Nazareth.

Israel: Edificio Pacífico-Washington, 6° piso, Natalio Sánchez 125 (E); *Ambassador:* Moshe Avidan (also accred. to Bolivia).

Italy: Avda. Petit Thouars 355–369 (E); *Ambassador:* Dr. Emilio Savorgnan.

Japan: Avda. San Felipe 356, Jesús María (E); *Ambassador:* Shigeto Nikai.

Korea, Republic: Avda. Arequipa 3362, San Isidro (E); *Ambassador:* Sangjin Chyun.

Lebanon: Bogotá, Colombia (E).

Malta: Avda. Arequipa 4651, Miraflores (E); *Ambassador:* Dr. FERNANDO ESPÁ Y CUENCA.

Mexico: Avda. Inca Garcilaso de la Vega 1456, 8° piso (E); *Ambassador:* JULIO ZAMORA BÁTIZ.

Netherlands: Las Camelias 780, 10° piso, San Isidro (E); *Ambassador:* P. J. F. DANIËLS.

New Zealand: Avda. Salaverry 3006, San Isidro (E); *Chargé d'Affaires a.i.:* J. PHILIP COSTELLO.

Nicaragua: Camino Real 479, 7° piso, San Isidro (E); *Ambassador:* JOSÉ LEÓN SANDINO.

Norway: Santiago, Chile (E).

Panama: Avda. Orrantia 350, San Isidro (E); *Ambassador:* RÉGULO FRANCESCHI C.

Paraguay: Avda. Tacna 685, 17° piso (E); *Ambassador:* Dr. FERMÍN DOS SANTOS SILVA.

Poland: Avda. Salaverry 3307, San Isidro (E); *Ambassador:* EUGENIUSZ SZLEPER.

Portugal: Avenida Orrantia 718, San Isidro (E); *Ambassador:* Dr. ADRIANO ANTÓNIO DE CARVALHO.

Romania: Avda. Orrantia 690, San Isidro (E); *Ambassador:* MIRCEA NICOLAESCU.

Spain: Avda. República de Chile 120 (E); *Ambassador:* PEDRO SALVADOR DE VICENTE.

Sweden: Las Camelias 780, San Isidro (E); *Ambassador:* TORSTEN C. BJÖRCK.

Switzerland: Las Camelias 780, San Isidro (E); *Ambassador:* Dr. WILLIAM FREI.

Thailand: Brasília D.F., Brazil (E).

Trinidad and Tobago: Caracas, Venezuela (E).

Turkey: Santiago, Chile (E).

U.S.S.R.: Avda. Salaverry 3424, Orrantia del Mar, San Isidro (E); *Ambassador:* YURI V. LEBEDEV.

United Kingdom: Edificio Pacífico-Washington, 12° piso, Plaza Washington (E); *Ambassador:* HUGH TRAVERS MORGAN.

U.S.A.: Avda. Inca Garcilaso de la Vega (E); *Ambassador:* ROBERT W. DEAN.

Uruguay: Avda. Larco 886, Miraflores (E); *Chargé d'Affaires a.i.:* Dr. CARLOS GONZÁLEZ DEMARE.

Vatican: Avda. Salaverry esq. Nazca (Apostolic Nunciature); *Nuncio:* Mgr. CARLO FURNO.

Venezuela: Avda. Arequipa 298 (E); *Ambassador:* Dr. RAFAEL LEÓN MORALES.

Yugoslavia: Avda. Santa Cruz 330, San Isidro (E); *Ambassador:* KOLE CASULE.

CONGRESS

Elections were held in August 1967 which resulted in victory for a coalition between the Alianza Popular Revolucionaria (APRA) and the Unión Nacional Odriísta (UNO). Congress was suspended indefinitely on October 3rd, 1968.

POLITICAL PARTIES

Partido Acción Popular (AP): Nicolás de Piérola 677, Lima; f. 1956; government party 1963–68; Leader EDGARDO SEOANE CORRALES.

Partido Demócrata Cristiano (PDC): Apdo. 4682, Lima; f. 1956; Pres. LUIS GÓMEZ SÁNCHEZ BOZA; Sec.-Gen. Dr. CARLOS BLANCAS BUSTAMANTE; publs. *Pensamiento Político, Democracia.*

Alianza Popular Revolucionaria Americana (APRA): f. in Mexico 1924, in Peru 1930; legalized 1945; democratic left-wing party; Founder VÍCTOR RAÚL HAYA DE LA TORRE; Sec.-Gen. RAMIRO PRIALE; 700,000 mems.

Unión Nacional Odriísta (UNO): Jirón Callao 535, Lima; f. 1960; social reform party formerly allied to APRA; 160,000 mems.; publ. *U.N.O.*

Partido Social Demócrata: f. 1968; splinter of *Unión Nacional Odriísta*; Leader JULIO DE LA PIEDRA.

Partido Popular Cristiano: f. 1968; splinter group of *Partido Demócrata Cristiano*; Leader Dr. BEDOYA REYES.

Frente Liberal Nacional (FLN): f. 1961; extreme left wing movement.

The following parties are not legally recognized:

Vanguardia Revolucionaria: extreme left-wing guerrilla movement.

Movimiento Izquierdista Revolucionario (MIR): extreme left-wing guerrilla movement; Leader FERNANDO GONZÁLEZ GASCO.

The communist party is also banned.

JUDICIAL SYSTEM
SUPREME COURT
LIMA

Chief Justice: Dr. CÉSAR AUGUSTO LENGUA.

Judges: Dr. CARLOS TORRES MALPICA, Dr. RICARDO BUSTAMANTE CISNEROS, Dr. NAPOLEÓN VÁLDEZ TUDELA, Dr. CARLOS A. MAGUIÑA SUERO, Dr. JOSÉ I. TELLO VÉLEZ, Dr. ALBERTO EGUREN BRESANI, Dr. ROBERTO GARMENDIA, Dr. RAÚL ALVA, Dr. OCTAVIO CEBREROS, Dr. DOMINGO GARCÍA RADA.

DISTRICT COURTS

Courts 18, Judges 442, District Attorneys 266.

RELIGION

The Catholic Church

Nearly all inhabitants of the Republic of Peru belong to the Catholic Church. The State supports the Catholic religion, but recognizes civil marriages.

Freedom of worship is permitted to all religions. The President is consulted in the appointment of Bishops and other dignitaries.

Archbishoprics:

Lima	.	H.E. Cardinal JUAN LANDÁZURI RICKETTS.
Arequipa	.	Mgr. LEONARDO JOSÉ RODRÍGUEZ BALLÓN.
Ayacucho	.	Mgr. OTONIEL ALCEDO.
Cuzco	.	Mgr. RICARDO DURAND FLÓREZ.
Huancayo	.	Mgr. EDUARDO PICHER PEÑA.
Piura	.	Mgr. ERASMO HINOJOSA HURTADO.
Trujillo	.	Mgr. CARLOS MARÍA JURGENS BYRNE.

Bishoprics:

Abancay	.	Mgr. ENRIQUE PÉLACH Y FELIU.
Cajamarca	.	Mgr. JOSÉ ANTONIO DAMMERT BELLIDO.
Chachapoyas	.	Mgr. MANUEL PRADO PÉREZ-ROSAS.

Chiclayo .	Mgr. Ignacio María de Orbegozo y Goicoechea.
Huacho .	Mgr. Lorenzo León Alvarado.
Huancavelica .	Mgr. Florencio Coronado Romani.
Huánuco .	Mgr. Ignacio Arbulú Pineda.
Huaraz . .	Mgr. Fernando Vargas Ruiz de Somocurcio.
Ica . .	Mgr. Guido Breña López.
Puno . .	Mgr. Jesús Calderón Barrueto.
Tacna . .	Mgr. Oscar Rolando Cantuarias Pastor.

THE PRESS

DAILIES

LIMA

El Comercio: Miró Quesada 304; f. 1839; morning; independent; Editor Augusto Zimmermann Zacala; circ. 90,000 weekdays, 155,000 Sundays.

Correo: Avda. Wilson 1255; f. 1963; morning; independent; Editor Fernando Flores A.; circ. 75,000; also published in Arequipa, Huancayo, Piura and Tacna.

Expreso: Ica 646; f. 1961; morning; leading opposition daily; Dir. Guillermo Córtez Núñez; circ. 110,000.

Extra: f. 1964; evening edition of *Expreso*; circ. 134,000.

La Nueva Crónica: Avda. Tacna 665, Apdo. 928; f. 1912; morning and evening; illustrated; democratic; independent; publ. by Empresa Editora La Crónica y Variedades S.A.; Pres. Carlos Moreyra y Paz Soldán; Man. Dir. Gustavo Prado H.; circ. 149,000.

Ojo: f. 1968; morning; independent; Editor-in-Chief Raúl Villarán; circ. 180,000.

El Peruano (Diario Oficial): Quilca 556, Apdo. Postal 303; f. 1825; morning; official State Gazette; circ. 75,000.

La Prensa: Baquijano 745; f. 1903; morning; independent liberal; Dir. Pedro Beltrán Ballén; circ. 98,000.

La Tribuna: f. 1923; morning; Dir. Manuel Solano; circ. 26,000.

Ultima Hora: Unión 745; f. 1950; evening; independent, Dir. Bernardo Ortiz de Zevallos Thorndike; circ. 130,000.

AREQUIPA

Noticias: f. 1927; morning; conservative; independent; Dir. Gaston Aguirre; circ. 5,000.

El Pueblo: Sucre 213, Apdo. 35; f. 1905; morning; independent; Editor E. Hegarra Ballón; circ. 10,000.

CAJAMARCA

El Ferrocarril: f. 1932. evening.

CERRO DE PASCO

El Minero: f. 1896; evening; Dir. G. Patino López; circ. 3,000.

CHICLAYO

La Industria: f. 1954; Dir. Benigno Febres; circ. 5,000.

El País: f. 1918; evening; Dir. Víctor Mendoza E.; circ. 5,250.

El Tiempo: Casilla 66; f. 1918; morning; independent; Dir. Julio A. Hernández; circ. 4,800.

CHINCHA

La Voz de Chincha: evening; Editor Juan E. Ortiz.

CUZCO

El Comercio: Casilla 70; f. 1896; evening; independent; Dir. César Lomellini, circ. 6,000.

El Sol: Mesón de la Estrella 172; f. 1901; morning; Dir. Hugo Pacheco G.; circ. 5,000.

HUACHO

El Imparcial: evening; f. 1891; Dir. J. T. García.

La Verdad: Jirón Colón 130, Apdo. 61; f. 1930; popular; Dir. José M. Carvajal Manrique; circ. 3,700.

HUANCAYO

El Tiempo: f. 1920; evening; Dir. Benjamín Gutiérrez V.

La Voz de Huancayo: f. 1912; morning; Dir. César Augusto Arauco A.; circ. 3,500.

HUÁNUCO

La Voz de Huánuco: f. 1914; Dir. F. R. Aguirre.

ICA

La Opinión: Callao 176, Apdo. 19; f. 1922; evening; independent; Dir. Gonzalo Tueros Ramírez.

La Voz de Ica: f. 1918; evening; Dir. Octavio Nieri Boggiano; circ. 4,000.

IQUITOS

El Eco: Jirón Lima 100-108, Apdo. 170; f. 1924; evening; independent; Dir. F. Reátegui; circ. 6,000.

El Oriente: Morona 153, Casilla 161; f. 1905; evening; Editor P. Salazar; circ. 7,000.

MOLLENDO

El Eco de Mollendo: evening.

PACASMAYO

La Unión: 2 de Mayo 27-29; f. 1913; evening; independent; Dir. Manuel Pastor R.; circ. 3,000.

PISCO

La Independencia: f. 1940; morning; Dir. Alfredo Pérez F.

Ultimas Noticias: Dir. Luis Reyes M.; circ. 1,500.

PIURA

Ecos y Noticias: Libertad 902 y Ayacucho 307, Casilla 110; f. 1934; morning; independent; Man. Dir. José del C. Rivera; circ. 4,000.

La Industria: f. 1917; morning; independent; Dir. Elmer Núñez; circ. 5,000.

El Tiempo: Ayacucho 751; f. 1916; morning; independent; Dir. Víctor M. Helguero Checa; circ. 35,000.

PUNO

Los Andes: Lima 775, Casilla 110; f. 1928; morning; Dir. Dr. Samuel Frisancho Pineda; circ. 10,000.

El Eco: f. 1898; Dir. Rosendo A. Huirse.

El Siglo: evening; circ. 2,000.

TACNA

La Voz de Tacna: f. 1936; morning; Dir. Carlos García Delgado; circ. 3,000.

TRUJILLO

El Liberal: f. 1918; morning; Dir. Antonio Silva S.; circ. 2,000.

La Gaceta: Bolívar 945; f. 1965; morning; Editor Oscar Castaneda A.; circ. 75,000.

La Industria: Gamarra 443; f. 1895; morning; independent; Editor Daniel Gardillo; circ. 8,000.

La Nación: Francisco Pizarro 511; f. 1931; morning; democratic, independent; Dir. WASHINGTON CHICO HERRERA; circ. 5,000.

PERIODICALS AND REVIEWS
LIMA

Auto Aéreo: air and road transport monthly.

Caretas: Camaná 615, oficina 308; twice monthly; general interest; Editor ENRIQUE ZILERI; circ. 40,000.

Cultura Peruana: Casilla 5247; f. 1941; quarterly; illustrated; organ of the Instituto Nacional de Cultura.

Economista Peruano: monthly economic review.

Ecos: Apdo. 3758; f. 1962; monthly; illustrated cultural review; Dir. JOSÉ ALEJANDRO VALENCIA-ARENAS; circ. 5,000.

Hora del Hombre: Casilla 2378; f. 1943; monthly; cultural and political journal; illustrated; Dir. JORGE FALCÓN.

Industria Peruana: Edificio Pizarro, Unión 150; monthly publication of the Sociedad Nacional de Industrias.

El Mercurio: Edificio San Pedro 202; f. 1932; weekly; Peruvian agriculture, commerce and industry; Propr. and Dir. EDUARDO MARISCA.

Mercurio Peruano: Apdo. 1000; f. 1918; monthly; social science, letters; Dir. and Founder VÍCTOR ANDRÉS BELAÚNDE; Editor DOMINGO GARCÍA BELAÚNDE.

Ondas: Apdo. 3758; f. 1959; monthly cultural review; Dir. JOSÉ ALEJANDRO VALENCIA-ARENAS; circ. 5,000.

Panoramas: monthly review.

PeruvianTimes: Carabaya 928, Apdo. 531; weekly; English language; Publisher DONALD GRIFFIS; Editor NICHOLAS ASHESHOV; circulates internationally as *Andean Times*.

Revista de Economía y Finanzas: monthly economic and financial review.

Revista Peruana: monthly.

Síntesis Semanal: economic journal of the Corporación Nacional de Comerciantes.

La Vida Agrícola: Jirón Antonio Miró Quesada 191, Apdo. 1159; f. 1924; monthly review of agriculture and stock-raising; Dir. Ing. Agr. RÓMULO A. FERRERO; circ. 7,500.

Vanguardia: Lima; anti-communist; Editor EUDOCIO RAVINES.

JOURNALISTS' ASSOCIATION

Federación de Periodistas del Perú: Cailloma 109, Lima; Pres. GENARO CARNERO CHECA.

PRESS AGENCIES
FOREIGN BUREAUX

ANSA: 2 de Mayo 370, San Isidro, Lima; Chief MARCELLO ONGANIA.

AP: Apdo. 119 Lima; Chief JOE MCGOWAN Jr.

Jewish Telegraphic Agency: Jirón Unión 554, Lima; Man. Mrs. TRUDI SCHYDLOWSKY.

UPI: Casilla 1536 Jirón Puno 271, oficina 601, Lima; Man. GUILLERMO MARTÍNEZ.

The Jiji Press, Reuters and Tass also have bureaux in Lima.

PUBLISHERS

LIMA

Librerías ABC S.A.: Avda. Corpac 282, San Isidro; f. 1956; history, Peruvian art; Man. Dir. J. K. H. HARRIMAN, O.B.E.

Empresa Editora Ara y Cía: Camaná 950; belles-lettres, fiction.

Editorial Arica S.A.: Paseo de la República 3285, San Isidro; f. 1958; literature, educational, technical; Man. Dir. BORIS A. ROMERO.

Biblioteca Nacional: Avda. Abancay, Apdo. 2335; general non-fiction.

Asociación Editorial Bruno: Avda. Arica 751, Breña; educational; Man. Dir. F. ALVAREZ PENELAS.

Editorial Andrés López Dominovich: Riva Aguero 251, Apdo. 1971; f. 1923; publishers of *Guía Lascano del Peru*, a commercial, industrial and professional directory; also political and economic directories; Man. ANDRÉS LÓPEZ DOMINOVICH.

Editorial Carlos Fabbri, S.A.: Ayacucho 360; geography, ethnography, travel, guide-books.

"Field" Servicio de Informaciones Comerciales del Perú: f. 1935; publs. of *Directorio Gremial del Perú* (*Peruvian Trade Directory*); Dir. FEDERICO FIELD STORACE.

Editorial Labrusa S.A.: Pasco de la República 3277, San Isidro; literature, educational; Man. Dir. BENJAMÍN A. ROMERO.

Editorial Magisterio S.A.: Germán Schreiber, San Isidro; f. 1973; literature, educational; Man. Dir. BENJAMÍN A. ROMERO.

Editora Música Maldonado: Apdo. 6; music, dancing, theatre.

Editorial Laureano Martínez Música: Puno 370; music, dancing, theatre.

Librería Editorial Juan Mejía Baca: Azángaro 722; f. 1945; medicine and general.

Editorial Domingo Miranda: Carabayo 546; belles-lettres, fiction.

Empresa Editora Nacional: Junín 458; politics, law, economics.

Casa Editorial Nuevo Tesoro Escolar: Carabaya 719; education, textbooks; Dir. Dr. VÍCTOR E. VIVAR.

Editorial Manuela R.D. de Río: Húarez 347; belles-lettres, fiction.

Editorial Andrés Rosales Valencia: E. Villar 542; education, textbooks.

Sirob Ediciones S.A.: Las Golondrinas 117, San Isidro; f. 1969; catalogues, technical; Man. Dir. FERNANDO BOSSIO.

Sociedad Universitaria Peruana S.A.: Avda. Nicolás de Piérola 798; f. 1920; education, scientific and medical textbooks; Man. PEDRO JARQUE DE LEIVA.

Sociedad Bíblica Peruana A.C.: Petit Thouars 991, Apdo. 448; f. 1821; theology and bibles; Dir. ABELARDO ARISTA.

Librería Studium: Jirón Camaná 939–943, Apdo. 2139; textbooks, architecture, engineering, technology, economics.

Editorial Universo S.A.: Avda. Nicolás Arriola 2285, La Victoria; literature, technical, educational; Man. Dir. BORIS A. ROMERO.

Universidad de San Marcos: Depto. de Publicaciones, Avda. República de Chile 295, 8°, oficina 809; textbooks, education.

ASSOCIATION

Cámara Peruana del Libro: Calle Washington 1206, oficina 508, Apdo. 3744, Lima.

RADIO AND TELEVISION

The Government has a 25 per cent share in all radio stations and holds 66 per cent of the capital of Telecentro, a joint venture established in 1973 to control the production and purchase of all television programmes.

Dirección de Telecommunicaciones: Garcilaso de la vega esq. 28 de Julio, Lima; Dir.-Gen. C. A. ROMERO SANJINES.

Associación de Radioemisoras del Perú: Colmena 624, Lima; Gen. Sec. Dr. P. TELLO.

RADIO
GOVERNMENT STATION

Radio Nacional de Perú: Petit Thouars 441, Lima; f. 1937; stations at Lima, Tumbes, Iquitos, Puno and Tacna; five medium-wave and twelve short-wave transmitters; Dir. G. LAZARTE E.

There are 2 other government stations and 8 cultural stations.

PRINCIPAL COMMERCIAL STATIONS

Radio América: Casilla 1192, Lima; Dirs. N. GONZÁLEZ, J. ANTONIO UMBERT.

Radio El Sol: Avda. Uruguay 355, Lima; Dir. Ing. A. PEREYRA.

Radio Panamericana: Avda. Arequipa 1110, Casilla 4392, Lima; Dir. H. DELGADO PARKER.

There are 188 other commercial stations in Peru. In 1971 there were about 1,825,000 radio receivers.

TELEVISION

Ministerio de Educación Pública: Dirección de Cultura, Avda. Nicolás de Piérola, Lima; daily cultural programmes; Dir.-Gen. R. GARRIDO M.

Teleducación Universidad de Lima-Canal 13: Avda. Javici Prado Este, Monterrico, Lima; Gen. Man. ENRIQUE PINILLA.

COMMERCIAL STATIONS

Televisora América—Canal 4: esq. de Montero Rosas y Mariano Carranza, Lima; Dir. N. GONZÁLEZ; station at Huacho.

Televisora Bego: Avda. Manco Capac 333, Lima; f. 1963; Gen. Man. A. BELMONT.

Televisora Arequipa—Canal 6: Avda. J. Gálvez 1040, Arequipa.

Televisora El Sol-Canal 9: Avda. Uruguay 335, Lima; Dir.-Gen. A. PEREIRA.

Televisora Panamericana: Avda. Arequipa 1110, Lima; Dir.-Gen. G. DELGADO; stations at Trujillo, Piura, Chiclayo, Chimbote.

The **Organización Regional de Televisión del Perú** plans to establish commercial stations in 13 towns.

Number of television sets (1972): 411,000.

FINANCE

BANKING

(cap.=capital; p.u.=paid up; res.=reserves; dep.= deposits; m.=million; amounts in soles.)

Superintendencia de Banca y Seguros: Lima; Superintendent Dr. MAXIMILIANO GAMARRA FERREYRA.

CENTRAL BANK

Banco Central de Reserva del Perú: esq. Villalta y Carrera, Lima; f. 1922; refounded 1931; cap. and res. 169.4m., dep. 9,095.1m. (Aug. 1972); Pres. EMILIO BARRETO; publ. *Reseña económica* (quarterly), *Boletín del Banco Central del Perú* (monthly).

DEVELOPMENT BANK

Corporación Financiera de Desarrollo (Cofide): Garcilaso de la Vega 1456, 16° piso; f. 1971; directs investments in state enterprises; gives technical and financial help to private companies; Pres. Dr. LUIS BARVA CASTAÑEDA.

COMMERCIAL BANKS
Lima

Banco Central Hipotecario del Perú: Carabaya 429; f. 1929; cap. and res. 48m.; Pres. LUIS G. MIRANDA; Man. F. GONZÁLEZ DEL RIEGO.

Banco Comercial del Perú: Avda. Nicolás de Piérola 1065; f. 1947; cap. p.u. 165m., dep. 2,160m. (Dec. 1972); Pres. B. MONTEBLANCO; Man. Foreign Dept. DENIS ENGLISH.

Banco Continental: Apdo. 3849; f. 1951; cap. 600m., dep. 7,540m. (Sept. 1973); Chair. Dr. SALVADOR VELARDE; Gen. Man. FEDERICO CHIAPPINA; Mans. Int. Div. CAMILLO BOZZOLO, DAVID DUNCAN; publs. *Report on the Economic Situation Of Peru* (quarterly), *Monthly Economic Index, News Letter*.

Banco de Crécito del Perú: Jirón Lampa 401–499; f. 1889; cap. p.u. 901.3m., dep. 18,225m. (Dec. 1971); Chair. Dr. LIZARDO ALZAMORA PORRAS; Gen. Man. Dr. PAULO CUCCHIARELLI.

Banco de Fomento Agropecuario del Perú: Apdo. 2638; f. 1931; cap. and res. 803m.; loans to farmers for agricultural development.

Banco Industrial del Perú: Jirón Ucayali 388, Apdo. 1230; f. 1936; cap. and res. 878m.; Pres. EUGENIO A. ISOLA; Man. Dir. RICARDO MADUEÑO.

Banco Internacional del Perú: Plaza de la Merced; f. 1897; cap. 600m., dep. 8,380m. (Dec. 1972); Pres. DAVID LANDEO H.

Banco de Lima: esq. Carabaya y Puno, Casilla 3181; f. 1952; cap. 150m., dep. 2,046m. (Dec. 1971); Pres. MANUEL PABLO OLAECHEA.

Banco Minero del Perú: Apdo. 2565; f. 1941; cap. and res. 719m. (1973); Pres. Dr. CARLOS DONGO SORIA; Gen. Man. Ing. CÉSAR FUENTES LÍBANO.

Banco de la Nación: Avda. Abancay 491, Apdo. 1895; f. 1966; government-owned fiscal agent; auth. cap. 1,000m.; carries out all commercial banking operations with official government agencies.

Banco Popular del Perú: Casilla 143; f. 1899; cap. and res. 630.7m., dep. 8,318m. (Dec. 1971); Gen. Man. PIERO ODDONE COPPO; 134 brs.

Banco del Progreso: Avda. Abancay 491, Apdo. 4687; f. 1961; cap. 150m., dep. 1,329m. (Dec. 1970); Chair. and Gen. Man. Dr. MARCOS PERELMAN.

Banco de la Vivienda del Perú: Camaná 488, Apdo. 5425; f. 1962; Pres. MANUEL VALEGA SAYÁN; Gen. Man. ALFREDO TAPIA GARCÍA.

Banco Wiese Ltdo.: Apdo. 1235, Cuzco 245; f. 1943; cap. 25om., dep. 5,350m. (June 1973); Pres. and Chair. Dr. GUILLERMO WIESE DE OSMA; Mans. LUIS ALCÁZAR F., JORGE UTRILLA RÍOS, ANTONIO MORENO O.

PROVINCIAL BANKS

Banco Amazónico: Sargento Lores 171, Iquitos; f. 1962; Gen. Man. EDUARDO M. POWER.

Banco de Los Andes: Cuzco; f. 1962; Pres. J. CÉSAR LOMELLINI T.; Man. ALFREDO MADUEÑO P.

Banco Nor-Perú S.A.: esq. Gammarra y Bolívar, Trujillo; f. 1961; Chair. Dr. GUILLERMO GANDEZA V.; Gen. Man. LUIS GONZALES-VIGIL V.; 13 brs.

Banco Regional del Centro: Huancayo.

Banco Regional del Norte: Piura; f. 1960.

Banco del Sur del Perú: Arequipa.

SAVINGS BANK

Caja de Ahorros de la Sociedad de la Beneficencia Pública de Lima: f. 1868; cap. p.u. 140m., dep. 3,014m.; Pres. Dr. OSCAR URTEAGA BALLÓN; Mans. JUAN RAFFO, VÍCTOR PANCORVO.

FOREIGN BANKS

Bank of America National Trust and Savings Association: San Francisco; Antonio Miró Quesada 327, Lima.

Bank of London and South America Ltd.: London; Carabaya 442, Casilla 2639, Lima; Man. J. P. GENASI.

Deutsch-Südamerikanische Bank A.G. and **Dresdner Bank A.G.:** Hamburg; A. Miró Quesada 327, 5° piso, Lima; joint representation.

First National City Bank: New York City; Avda. Nicolás de Piérola 1062, Lima; Man. ERIC Y. REYNAL.

The Royal Bank of Canada: Montreal; Apdo. 2337, Lima; Man. B. V. KELLY.

STOCK EXCHANGE

Bolsa de Valores de Lima: Jirón Miró Quesada 265, Lima 1; f. 1860; Pres. FERNANDO VIDAL RAMÍREZ; Man. PEDRO GUZMÁN GOMERO; 150 mems.; publs. *Boletín Diario* (daily).

INSURANCE
Lima

Cía. de Seguros Atlas: Apdo. 1751; f. 1896; Chair. Ing. E. A. ISOLA.

Cía. de Seguros La Colmena: Apdo. 2238; f. 1942; Pres. Dr HERNANDO DE LAVALLE VARGAS; Man. Dir. JOSÉ LEDVINKA D.

Cía. de Seguros La Fénix Peruana: Apdo. 1356; f. 1928; Gen. Man. CARLOS ORTEGA.

Cía. de Seguros La Nacional: Minería 189; f. 1906; Pres. FRANCISCO ECHENIQUE; Man. ENRIQUE MAGÁN R.

Cía. de Seguros Rimac: Augusto N. Wiese 499; f. 1896; Pres. E. AYULO PARDO; Gen. Man. J. GRAÑA ACUÑA.

Cía. Internacional de Seguros del Perú: San José 323; f. 1895; Man. Dir. JOSÉ TAGLE BUENAÑO.

Cía. Italo-Peruana de Seguros Generales: Jirón Puno 279, Apdo. 395; f. 1930; Man. Dir. HUMBERTO BERTELLO.

Compañías Unidas de Seguros: Apdo. 327; f. 1916; Pres. ERNESTO NICOLINI PESCHIERA; Gen. Man. ARRIGO FANO MAYER.

El Pacífico, Compañía de Seguros y Reaseguros: Apdo. 595; f. 1943; Chair. ENRIQUE PARDO HEEREN.

Popular y Porvenir, Compañía de Seguros: Apdos. 220–237; f. 1904; Man. Dir. BENJAMÍN MONTEBLANCO.

Reaseguradora Peruana: f. 1966; cap. 6m.; all forms of reinsurance.

TRADE AND INDUSTRY

CHAMBERS OF COMMERCE

Federación Nacional de Cámaras de Comercio del Perú: Avda. Abancay 291, Lima; Pres. GUSTAVO EGUREN; Man. Dr. MANUEL LUGO; publ. *Integración* (fortnightly).

Cámara de Comercio de Lima (*Lima Chamber of Commerce*): Avda. Abancay 291, Lima; f. 1888; Pres. GUSTAVO EGUREN; Dir. Dr. MANUEL LUGO, 3,000 mems ; publs. *Boletín Semanal* (weekly), *Boletín de Protestos* (fortnightly), *Revista Mensual* (monthly).

There are also Chambers of Commerce in Arequipa, Cuzco, Callao and many other cities.

Cámara Algodonera del Perú (*Cotton Chamber*): Apdo. 1605, Lima; f. 1940; Pres. RODOLFO SELEM; publ. *Algodón*.

Cámara de Comercio Peruano-Mexicana: Lima; f. 1965 under the auspices of the Corporación Nacional de Comerciantes.

Cámara Internacional de Comercio: Avda. Abancay 291, 2° piso, Lima; f. 1966; Man. Dr. MANUEL LUGO.

INDUSTRIAL ORGANIZATIONS

Sociedad Nacional de Industrias (SNI) (*National Industrial Association*): Los Laureles 365, San Isidro, Apdo. 632, Lima; f. 1896; Pres. ALFREDO OSTOJA D.; Sec. FER-

NANDO REYES F.; 47 dirs. (reps. of firms); over 3,377 mems.; many provincial branches; publs. *Directorio Industrial* (annual), *Perú Exporta* (annual), *Memoria* (annual), *Industria Peruana* (monthly), *Horizonte Económico* (monthly).

The Association comprises Permanent Commissions covering all aspects of industry. These include:

> Agricultura
> Aguas
> Aranceles de Aduana (Customs)
> Asociación Latinoamericana de Libre Comercio (LAFTA).
> Contribuciones
> Eléctricos Nacionales
> Especialización Nacional
> Ferias y Exposiciones (Fairs and Exhibitions)
> Industrias
> Investigación y Planeamiento Integral de la Educación
> Marina Mercante
> Normas Técnicas
> Petróleo
> Promoción Industrial
> Seguro Social del Empleado
> Vivienda

There are industrial associations in Arequipa and Sicuani.

Sociedad Nacional Agraria (*National Agricultural Society*): A. Miró Quesada 327, Apdo. Postal 350, Lima; Pres. ALBERTO SACIO LEÓN.

Sociedad Nacional de Pesquería (*National Fisheries Association*): Inca Garcilaso de la Vega 911, 2° Piso, Lima; f. 1952; Pres. LUIS BANCHERO.

STATE CORPORATIONS

Corpac (*Commercial Aviation*): Aeropuerto Internacional Jorge Chávez; Pres. Gen. HUMBERTO CAMPODÓNICO; Man. PEDRO MADGE.

Electroperú (*Electricity*): Centro Cívico, Paseo de la República 114, Lima; Exec. Pres. Gen. PEDRO FUENTE REVILLA; Man. Ing. LUIS RATTO CHUECA.

Entelperú (*Telecommunications*): Las Begonias 375, San Isidro, Lima; Pres. Col. JORGE MIRÓ QUESADA CÁCERES; Man. Ing. MIGUEL COLINA.

Epsa (*Agriculture*): Cahuide 805, Jesús María; Pres. Dr. ALFONSO ELEJALDE ZEA; Exec. Dir. Ing. MANUEL DÍAZ CANO.

Epsep (*Fishing*): Sinchi Roca 2728, Lince; Pres. Gen. GUILLERMO ARBULÚ GALLIANI; Exec. Dir. Col. LUIS VILLACORTA B.

Induperú (*Industry*): Avda. 2 de Mayo 1675, Lima; Pres. Maj. EDUARDO VILLA SALCEDO; Man. ITALO ZOLEZZI.

Mineroperú (*Mining*): Avda. Arequipa 1649, Casilla 4332, Lima 14; Pres. Gen. JUAN BOSSIO.

Pescaperú: Lima; f. 1973 to solve the crisis in the fishmeal industry.

Petroperú (*Petroleum*): Paseo de la República 3361, San Isidro, Lima; Pres. Gen. MARCO FERNÁNDEZ BACA.

Siderperú (*Iron and Steel*): Avda. Tacna 543, 11° piso, oficina 111, Lima; Pres. Rear-Adm. JORGE LUNA GARCÍA; Man. Major LUIS CÁCERES GRACIANI.

EMPLOYERS' ASSOCIATIONS

Asociación Automotriz del Perú (*Association of Importers of Motor Cars and Accessories*): Germán Schreiber 296, Apdo. 1248, Lima; f. 1926; 166 mems.; Pres. CARLOS DONGO SORIA; Vice-Pres. JOHN F. BECK.

Asociación de Comerciantes del Perú (*Association of Shopkeepers*): Avda. Nicolás de Piérola 214, Lima; Pres. LUCIANO HART TERRÉ; Sec. R. V. MIRANDA.

Asociación de Comerciantes en Materiales de Construcción (*Association of Traders in Building Materials*): Avda. Colmena 214, Lima; Pres. ROSELLO TRUEL; Sec. RICARDO V. MIRANDA.

Asociación de Ganaderos del Perú (*Association of Stock Farmers of Peru*): Pumacahua 877, 3° piso, Jesús María, Lima; f. 1915; Gen. Man. Ing. MIGUEL J. FORT; publ. *Ganado*.

Cámara Sindical de Propietarios (*Estate Owners' Association*): Plaza San Martín 966, Lima; 567 mems.; Pres. Dr. GUILLERMO DONAYRE-BARRIOS.

Comité de Minería de la Cámara de Comercio e Industria de Arequipa (*Mining Association*): Casilla 508, Arequipa; Pres. F. CH. WILLFORT.

Confederación Pesquera del Perú (*Peru Fish Meal Employers' Confederation*): Lima.

Instituto Peruano del Café: f. 1965; representatives of government and industrial growers.

TRADE UNIONS

Confederación General de Trabajadores del Perú: Plaza 2 de Mayo 4, Lima; Sec.-Gen. GUSTAVO ESPINOZA.

There are a number of independent unions.

TRANSPORT

RAILWAYS

Empresa Nacional de Ferrocarriles del Perú (Enaferperú): Ancash 207, Apdo. 1379, Lima; the Peruvian National Railways were formed in September 1972 and taken over by the Government in December 1972; 1,628 km. open; Pres. Ing. JOSÉ DEL CASTILLO; Man. Ing. GERMÁN TITO GUTIÉRREZ; operates the following lines:

Central Railway (*Ferrocarril Central del Perú*): Casilla 391, Lima; 493 km. open; Man. M. SUÁREZ.

Southern Railway (*Ferrocarril del Sur*): Casilla 194, Aréquipa; 1,073 km. open; also operates steamship service on Lake Titicaca; Man. E. DUTHURBURU.

Tacna–Arica Railway (*Ferrocarril Tacna–Arica*): A. Aldarracín 484, Tacna; 62 km. open (1,435 mm. gauge); Admin. R. SANTA MARÍA.

Guaqui–La Paz (Bolivia) Railway (*Ferrocarril Guaqui–La Paz*): bought from the Bolivian Government in 1910 and supervised by the Southern Railway; 96 km. open; to be modernized under a technical co-operation agreement signed by the Peruvian and Bolivian governments.

Cerro de Pasco Railway: La Oroya; 212 km. open (1,435 mm. gauge); Supt. CIRO A. ODIAGA ANDRADE.

Cia. de Ferrocarril y Muelle de Pimentel: Pimentel, Chiclayo; 56 km. ope(n 914 mm. gauge); Pres. RODOLFO MONTENEGRO.

Empresa de Ferrocarril de Supe-Barranca Alpas: Barranca, Supe; 40 km. open (600 mm. gauge).

Ferrocarril Chimbote-Huallanca: government-owned; 169 km. open (914 mm. gauge); Man. CARLOS F. CHRISTEN.

ROADS

There are more than 43,000 km. of roads in Peru, of which 4,500 km. are asphalted and 6,500 km. surfaced; there are some 20,000 km. of tracks. The Pan American Highway runs southward from the Ecuadorean border along the coast to Lima and the 800 km. Trans-Andean Highway runs from Lima to Pucallpa on the River Ucayali via Oroya, Cerro de Pasco, and Tingo María.

SHIPPING

Empresa Nacional de Puertos (ENAPU): Terminal Marítimo del Callao, Edificio Administrativo, 3° piso, Lima; government agency administering all coastal, river and lake ports; Chair. Rear-Adm. JORGE PARRA DEL RIEGO.

Asociación Marítima del Perú: Lima; association of international shipping companies using Peruvian ports; Pres. ALEJANDRO MORENO.

Comisión Nacional de Marina Mercante: Ministerio de Marina, Avda. Salaverry s/n, Jesus María, Lima; f. 1962; promotes the development of the merchant navy; Pres. Minister for the Navy; Sec.-Gen. Capt. CARLOS BADANI SOUZA PEIXOTO.

Compañía Peruana de Vapores, S.A.: Gamarra 676, Chucuito, Casilla 208, Callao; government-owned; 161,256 d.w.t.; operates five regular services to U.S. Gulf, U.S. Atlantic and U.S. Pacific ports, Japan and Europe; Chair. Rear Adm. FEDERICO SALMÓN DE LA JARA; Gen. Man. Lt.-Commdr. P. N. ROQUE SALDÍAS BRAVO (Retd.); European Agents Karl Geuther & Co., 28 Bremen Martinstrasse, 58-Bremen, Federal Republic of Germany.

Among the European lines serving Peru are the Pacific Steam Navigation Company, the Norwegian Knutsen Line, the Swedish Johnson Line, the Italian Societá per Azioni di Navigazione "Italia", the French Compagnie Générale Transatlantique, the Royal Netherlands Steamship Company, the German Hamburg Amerika, Norddeutscher Lloyd and Westfal Larsen Lines. Several United States lines operate between the U.S. and Peru, the most prominent being Grace Line and Moore McCormack Line. The Kawasaki Kisen Kaisha Line operates services to Australia and the Bank Line serves India. The Booth Line serves the Peruvian reaches of the Amazon. The Compañía Sudamericana de Vapores and the Flota Gran Columbiana serve Peruvian ports but carry no passengers.

Most trade is through the port of Callao, but there are seven deep-water ports in northern Peru, including Salaverry, Pacasmayo and the new port of Paita, and four in the south, including the iron ore port of San Juan. A new port is in operation at Pejerrey, near Pisco. It cost some U.S. $25m. and provides a terminal for the 225-km. road to Ayacucho which is under construction.

Peru's merchant fleet totalled 27,386,607 g.r.t. in 1970.

CIVIL AVIATION
DOMESTIC AIRLINES

Aeroperú: Plaza San Martín 910, Lima; f. 1973 as the national airline following the re-organization of SATCO (Servicio Aéreo de Transportes Comerciales), the transport section of the Peruvian Air Force; operates internal services and plans include the opening of routes throughout Latin America and to the United States, Europe, South Africa and Japan; Pres. Gen. CARLOS SOTO VERA; Man. JORGE CABIESES.

Aeronaves del Perú: Aeropuerto Internacional Jorge Chávez, oficina 11; f. 1965; scheduled cargo services between Lima and Miami via Iquito and Pucallpa; Man. Dir. JULIO CÁCERES BREIDING.

Compañía de Aviación Faucett: Edificio Hotel Bolívar, Jirón Unión 926, Apdo. 1429, Lima; f. 1928; scheduled internal passenger services and cargo services to Miami; Pres. EDUARDO DIBOS; Chief Exec. ANTONIO BENTIN; fleet: 1 Boeing 727-100, 2 BAC-111/475, 6 DC-6B, 4 DC-4, 1 DC-3.

The following international airlines also serve Peru, Aerolíneas Argentinas, Air France, Air Panama, Alitalia: Avianca (Colombia), British Airways, Braniff, Canadian Pacific, Ecuatoriana, Iberia, KLM, LAB (Bolivia), LAN (Chile), Lufthansa, Pan American, Varig (Brazil), Viasa (Venezuela).

TOURISM

Empresa Nacional de Turismo (Enturperú): Conde de Superunda 298, Apdo. 4475, Lima; f. 1964; Pres. PEDRO MANUEL GARCÍA MIRÓ.

Touring y Automóvil Club del Perú: Avda. César Vallejo 699, Lince, Casilla 2219, Lima; f. 1924; 16,000 mems.; offices in Piura, Chiclayo, Trujillo, Arequipa, Tacna, Callao; Pres. ALFONSO BRYCE L.; Man. CARLOS PORTOCARRERO.

Asociación Peruana de Agencias de Viajes y Turismo (APAVIT): Avda. Nicolás de Piérola 757, oficinas 409–414, Casilla 755, Lima; f. 1947; 37 mems.; Pres. SIXTILIO DALUMAU; Man. HÉCTOR VIGIL.

PRINCIPAL THEATRES

Teatro "Felipe Pardo y Aliaga": Ministerio de Educación, Parque Universitario, Lima; Dir. CÉSAR MIRÓ.

Teatro Universitario de San Marcos: Lampa 833, Lima; Dir. GUILLERMO UGARTE CHAMORRO.

There are also several private theatre companies.

PRINCIPAL ORCHESTRAS

Orquesta Sinfónica Nacional: Instituto Nacional de Cultura, Ancash 390, Lima; f. 1938; Dirs. CARMEN MORAL, LEOPOLDO DA ROSA; weekly concerts and regional tours; 100 musicians.

Coro del Estado: Casa de la Cultura, Ancash 390, Lima; Dir. MANUEL CUADROS.

There are also two professional chamber orchestras.

ATOMIC ENERGY

Junta de Control de Energía Atómica: Avda. Nicolás Piérola 611, Apdo. 914, Lima; Pres. Dr. ENRIQUE MONGE GORDILLO; mems. include representatives of the various Ministries.

Instituto Superior de Energía Nuclear: Lima; specialist centre for nuclear sciences and technology; uses the research facilities of the Junta de Control de Energía Atómica and co-operates with the universities of the country; Dir. Ing. IGNACIO FRISANCHO PINEDA; publ. *Boletín de Información* (bi-monthly).

Universidad Agraria: Apdo. 456, Lima; applications of nuclear research to agriculture.

Universidad Nacional de Ingeniería: Casilla 1301, Lima; laboratory of atomic and nuclear physics in the Science Faculty.

UNIVERSITIES

Pontificia Universidad Nacional Católica del Perú: Apdo. 1761, Lima; f. 1917; 650 teachers, 5,500 students.

Universidad Agraria: Apdo. 456, La Molina, Lima; f. 1902; 378 teachers, 3,000 students.

Universidad Agraria de la Selva: Apdo. 156, Tingo María, Huánuco; f. 1965; 28 teachers, 226 students.

Universidad Femenina del Sagrado Corazón: Marconi 420, San Isidro, Apdo. 3604, Miraflores, Lima; f. 1962; 57 teachers, 539 students.

Universidad de Lima: Nazca 548, Campo de Marte, Lima; f. 1963.

Universidad Nacional de la Amazonia Peruana: Apdo. 496, Iquitos; f. 1961; 81 teachers, 1,181 students.

Universidad Nacional del Centro del Perú: Calle Real 160, Apdo. 77, Huancayo; f. 1962; 184 teachers, 3,000 students.

Universidad Nacional "Federico Villareal": Avda. Uruguay 262, Lima; f. 1963; 643 teachers, 13,450 students.

Universidad Nacional de Ingeniería (*National University of Engineering*): Casilla 1301, Lima; f. 1955; 779 teachers, 6,999 students.

Universidad Nacional Mayor de San Marcos de Lima: Apdo. 454, Lima; f. 1551; 2,052 teachers, 20,294 students.

Universidad Nacional de San Agustín: Calle Santa Catalina 117, Apdo. 23, Arequipa; f. 1828; 346 teachers, 7,414 students.

Universidad Nacional de San Antonio Abad del Cuzco: Apdo. 367, Cuzco; f. 1962; 500 teachers, 5,900 students.

Universidad Nacional de San Cristóbal de Huamanga: Apdo. 120, Ayacucho; f. 1677; 134 teachers, 2,955 students.

Universidad Nacional "San Luis Gonzaga": Bólívar 232, Ica; f. 1961; 250 teachers, 5,750 students.

Universidad Nacional Técnica del Altiplano: Ciudad Universitaria, Casilla 291, Puno; f. 1961; 113 teachers, 939 students.

Universidad Nacional Técnica de Cajamarca: Jirón Arequipa 289, Cajamarca; f. 1962; 100 teachers, 1,600 students.

Universidad Nacional de Trujillo: Diego de Almagro 396, Apdo. 315, Trujillo; f. 1824; 300 teachers, 5,544 students.

Universidad del Pacífico: Avda. Salaverry 2020, Lima; f. 1962; 63 teachers, 1,182 students.

Universidad Particular "Gran Chimu": Jirón San Martín, 8A Cuadra, Trujillo; f. 1965.

Universidad Particular "San Martín de Porres": Convento de Santo Domingo, Camaná 164–168, Lima; f. 1965; 180 teachers, 7,000 students.

Universidad Pedagógica Particular "Inca Garcilaso de la Vega": Avda. Arequipa 3610, Lima; f. 1964; 200 teachers, 5,000 students.

Universidad Peruana "Cayetano Heredia": Carretera Ancón, Lima; f. 1961; 356 teachers, 620 students.

Universidad Santa María: San Camilo 410, Apdo. 491, Arequipa; f. 1961.

THE PHILIPPINES

INTRODUCTORY SURVEY

Location, Climate, Language, Religion, Flag, Capital

The Republic of the Philippines lies in the Pacific Ocean east of South-East Asia. The principal islands of the Philippine archipelago are Luzon in the north and Mindanao in the south. The island chain stretches 1,150 miles from north to south and is 690 miles wide. Borneo is to the south-west and New Guinea to the south-east. The climate is maritime and tropical with high humidity. Rainfall is abundant and typhoons frequently inflict damage. There are numerous language groups. Pilipino (Tagalog), based on Malayan, is the native national language. English is widely spoken and some Spanish. Ninety per cent of the population is Christian (80 per cent Roman Catholic) and 5 per cent Muslim. The national flag (proportions 2 by 1) has two equal horizontal bands of blue and red with a gold sun and three stars on a white triangle next to the staff. Since the early 1960s Quezon City has been the official capital, but Manila continues to remain the administrative capital. Both cities are on Luzon island.

Recent History

After some 350 years as a Spanish colony, nearly 50 years of United States domination and Japanese occupation during the Second World War, the Philippines became an independent republic in 1946. A succession of Presidents under the control of U.S. economic interests and the Filipino landowning class, and corrupt, incompetent administrations did little to help the peasant majority or to curb disorder and political violence.

The election of Ferdinand Marcos as President in 1965 was followed by rapid development of the infrastructure and the introduction of high-yield rice, bringing rural prosperity, but by 1969 inflation, student unrest and Marcos' support for the U.S.A. in Viet-Nam had brought about a breakdown of law and order.

While Marcos gradually replaced the apparatus of democracy with martial law and rule by decree, two serious armed rebellions broke out. In the north the Communist New People's Army and in the south a Muslim separatist movement, said to be supported by Malaysia, each began guerrilla wars which the army has been unable to suppress. The introduction of a new constitution in 1973 has had no practical effect, the President claiming to have received a mandate to continue martial law and to enforce his economic and social reforms.

Government

The main features of the new Constitution relate to the powers of the Prime Minister and to the transitional provisions as they affect the President. Though the Prime Minister is C.-in-C. of the armed forces and can grant amnesties, reprieves or pardons, these powers are greatly limited because the transitional provisions give the incumbent President (i.e. Marcos), the *combined* authority of the Presidency (under the old Constitution) and of the Premiership under the new Constitution. This in effect enables the President to rule by decree. The interim National Assembly has been entirely replaced by extra-parliamentary "Citizens' Assemblies", at urban and rural level, whose functions include approval of a continuation of martial law and of those economic and political reforms already announced.

Defence

The armed forces of the Philippines include an army of 19,300, navy of 12,200 and air force of 11,200 men. A constabulary of 27,000 and 57,000 other security forces maintain internal order.

Economic Affairs

Agriculture, forestry and fisheries provided 30 per cent of domestic product in 1972 and employ about 50 per cent of the labour force. The major food-producing area is the central plain of Luzon. Rice forms the most important single item in the agricultural system but its predominance is less marked than in other South-East Asian countries, and in some of the islands maize is the leading food crop. Production of rice has, however, increased at a fast rate, mainly due to the introduction of high-yield strains, and the Philippines has attained self-sufficiency in that commodity and now exports a small surplus. The major export crops comprise coconuts, sugar, abaca (Manila hemp) and tobacco. Timber is an important natural resource, and a wide range of metallic minerals is found, including copper, gold, silver, chromite, manganese and iron ore. Mining, food processing, building materials (particularly timber and cement) and the processing of imported raw materials are developing industries, and the country's first integrated steel mill was inaugurated in 1968. High priority is given to the development of power resources, with major projects at Angat, Iligan and on the Bataan peninsula.

Trade is conducted mainly with the U.S.A. but Japan and the Federal Republic of Germany are becoming increasingly important trading partners. President Marcos announced in March 1972 that trade relations would be opened with Communist and socialist countries including the U.S.S.R. and China.

In October 1972 a six-point programme of economic reforms was announced. This included the creation of a National Economic Development Authority, the revision of the tax structure, customs and tariffs, the lowering of duties on capital goods and the banning of imported luxuries. Further reforms followed, most notably the suspension of capital gains tax and a radical land redistribution plan affecting over 600,000 small farmers, enabling them to own 12.5 acres each. These reforms have helped to produce rapid economic growth, at the cost of high inflation. The failure of the 1973 rice crop and underemployment have produced much discontent among the peasants and the growing urban proletariat.

Transport and Communications

In the period 1965 to 1971, 38,000 kilometres of new roads were built including 18,000 kilometres in 1971. There are railways on several of the larger islands but these carry mainly freight. The most widely used form of inland transport is bus services. Shipping plays a considerable part in carrying passengers and cargo between the islands. There are 77 national and 282 municipal ports. Philippine Air Lines maintains domestic and international air services and there is an international airport at Manila.

Social Welfare

Government social insurance provides cover for retirement and life. Employed persons contribute to the scheme from their wages. Public health services such as inoculation and vaccination are provided free in the State Dispensaries.

Education

There is free education in all primary schools of which there were 41,823 with nearly 7m. pupils (1971). Over 2 million students were enrolled in the 5,000 secondary schools, universities and colleges. Instruction is in English. There are 40 universities and some 700 colleges.

Tourism

In 1972 166,000 visitors spent an estimated 38 million U.S. dollars in the Philippines. Chief attractions are the warm climate, the tropical setting of the islands and the cosmopolitan city of Manila.

Sport

Basketball is the most popular game, closely followed by baseball.

Public Holidays

1974: November 30th (National Heroes' Day), December 25th (Christmas), December 30th (Rizal Day).

1975: January 1st (New Year's Day), March 27th–28th (Maundy Thursday and Good Friday), April 9th (Bataan Day), May 1st (Labour Day), June 12th (Independence Day), July 4th (Philippine-American Friendship Day).

Weights and Measures

The metric system is in force.

Currency and Exchange Rates

100 centavos = 1 Philippine peso.

Exchange rates (April 1974):

£1 sterling = 16.01 pesos;
U.S. $1 = 6.78 pesos.

STATISTICAL SURVEY

AREA AND POPULATION

AREA OF ISLANDS
(sq. miles)

TOTAL 7,100 islands and islets	LUZON	MINDANAO	SAMAR	NEGROS	PALAWAN	PANAY	MINDORO	LEYTE	CEBU	BOHOL	MASBATE
115,600	40,814	36,906	5,050	4,905	4,550	4,446	3,759	2,785	1,703	1,492	1,262

Source: Bureau of the Census and Statistics.

POPULATION

CENSUS ENUMERATIONS				MID-YEAR ESTIMATES			1972 DENSITY (per sq. km.)
February 15th, 1960	May 6th, 1970			1970	1971	1972	
	Male	Female	Total				
27,087,685	18,250,351	18,434,135	36,684,486	36,849,000	37,919,000	39,046,000	130

Latest Estimate: 40,730,000 (December 31st, 1973).

Source: Bureau of the Census and Statistics.

PRINCIPAL TOWNS
(1970 Census)

Manila	. . . .	1,330,780	Davao	323,020
Quezon City (capital)		754,452	Iloilo	209,738
Cebu	. . . .	347,116	Basilan	143,829

EMPLOYMENT (May 1972)

Agriculture, Forestry, Fisheries	Mining and Quarrying	Construction	Manufacturing	Commerce	Services*
7,166,000	58,000	456,000	1,467,000	1,674,000	2,397,000

* Includes all other industries.

Source: Bureau of the Census and Statistics: Philippine Statistical Survey of Households.

AGRICULTURE

PRINCIPAL CROPS
('ooo metric tons)

	1967–68	1968–69	1969–70	1970–71*	1971–72†
Rice . . .	4,561	4,445	5,233	5,343	5,100
Maize . . .	1,619	1,733	2,008	2,005	2,013
Coffee . . .	44	44	49	50	52
Tobacco. . .	65	57	61	56	56
Cocao . . .	4	4	4	4	4
Sugar Cane . .	12,191	12,224	18,835*	19,957	17,719
Copra . . .	1,542	1,516	1,656	1,574	1,703
Abaca (Manila hemp)	103	106	122	105	110

* Revised.   † Preliminary.

Years=Crop Years (July 1st–June 30th).

Source: Bureau of Agricultural Economics; Sugar Quota Administration.

LIVESTOCK
('ooo)

	1970	1971†	1972†
Cattle . . .	1,679	1,795	1,933
Horses . . .	294	n.a.	n.a.
Pigs . . .	6,456	7,050	7,742
Goats . . .	772	924	1,083
Buffaloes . .	4,432	4,556	4,711

† Preliminary.

Source: Bureau of Agricultural Economics.

FORESTRY

	1970	1971	1972
Logs (million board ft.) .	4,551	4,168	3,370
Lumber (million board ft.) .	324	501	563

Source: Bureau of Forestry.

FISHING
('000 metric tons)

	1969	1970	1971*	1972†
Commercial Fishing . . .	369	382	382	440
Fish Ponds	95	96	98	102
Municipal Fisheries and Sustenance Fishing	477	511	543	581
TOTAL	941	989	1,023	1,123

* Revised.   † Preliminary.

Source: Philippine Fisheries Commission.

MINING

		1968	1969	1970	1971	1972
Manganese .	('000 metric tons)	66	20	5	5	2
Iron . .	(,, ,, ,,)	1,353	1,562	1,870	2,250	2,205
Copper .	(,, ,, ,,)	110	131	160	197	197
Lead . .	(,, ,, ,,)	0.1	0.1	0.1	—	—
Chrome .	(,, ,, ,,)	439	469	566	430	430
Coal . .	(,, ,, ,,)	32	53	42	40	40
Salt . .	(,, ,, ,,)	217	231	210	235	235
Mercury . .	(flasks)	3,543	3,478	4,647	5,020	5,020
Silver . .	(fine ounces)	1,574,782	1,561,312	1,701,899	1,954,511*	1,954,511
Gold . .	(,, ,,)	527,355	571,145	602,715	639,877*	639,877

* Revised.

Source: Bureau of Mines.

INDUSTRY

		1969	1970	1971	1972
Sugar .	('000 metric tons)	1,596	1,927	2,058	1,815
Cement .	(,, ,, ,,)	2,950	2,447	3,117	2,903
Tobacco . .	(metric tons)	763	681	713	n.a.
Cigarettes .	(millions)	37,808	39,671	41,988	n.a.
Cotton Yarn .	(metric tons)	18,287*	22,154*	21,346	26,231
Cotton Fabrics .	(million metres)	172*	143*	161	188

* Revised.

Source: Central Bank of the Philippines.

FINANCE
100 centavos = 1 Philippine peso.
Coins: 1, 5, 10, 25 and 50 centavos; 1 peso.
Notes: 1, 2, 5, 10, 20, 50 and 100 pesos.

Exchange rates (April 1974): £1 sterling = 16.01 pesos; U.S. $1 = 6.78 pesos.
100 Philippine pesos = £6.25 = $14.75.

BUDGET (1972—ACTUAL)
(million pesos)

REVENUE		EXPENDITURE	
Excise Taxes	541.3	Education	1,404.0
Licence and Business Taxes . .	1,264.0	Health	281.6
Income Taxes	1,419.4	Agriculture and Natural Resources . .	539.6
Import Duties	1,086.8	Transport and Communications . .	792.6
Other	799.3	National Defence	601.6
		Government	725.4
TOTAL	5,110.8	TOTAL (incl. others) . . .	5,588.2

FISCAL PLAN 1971–73
(million pesos)

	1972 (Actual)	1973 (Revised Estimate)	1974
Agricultural and Natural Resources .	540	740	979
Commerce and Industry . .	93	575	544
Transport and Communications .	793	1,157	1,443
Education	1,404	1,517	1,884
Public Health . . .	282	356	472
Labour and Welfare . .	81	166	85
Other Economic Projects . .	464	457	447
TOTAL . . .	3,657	4,968	5,854

NATIONAL ACCOUNTS
(million pesos—at current prices)

	1970*	1971*	1972*
GROSS DOMESTIC PRODUCT (AT MARKET PRICES)	40,055	50,415	55,200
NET DOMESTIC PRODUCT (AT FACTOR COST) .	34,305	40,298	45,433
of which:			
Agriculture	12,476	14,700	15,812
Mining and quarrying . .	845	924	1,070
Manufacturing . . .	6,540	7,989	9,715
Construction	849	1,036	1,368
Transportation, communications and storage utilities . . .	1,230	1,388	1,459
Commerce	4,868	5,720	6,500
Services	7,497	8,541	9,509
Income from abroad . . .	(799)	(648)	(855)
Depreciation allowance . .	4,158	5,357	6,327
GROSS NATIONAL INCOME . . .	37,664	45,007	50,905
Less: Depreciation allowances . .	4,158	5,357	6,327
NET NATIONAL INCOME . . .	33,506	39,650	44,578
Indirect taxes less subsidies . .	3,515	4,525	4,990
NET NATIONAL PRODUCT . . .	37,021	44,175	49,568
Depreciation allowance . .	4,158	5,357	6,327
GROSS NATIONAL PRODUCT (AT MARKET PRICES)	41,179	49,532	55,895
Less: Balance of exports and imports of goods, services and borrowings (income from abroad) . . .	(974)	(774)	(1,348)
Less: Statistical discrepancy . .	1,923	(235)	1,550
AVAILABLE RESOURCES . .	40,230	50,541	55,693
of which:			
Private consumption expenditure .	28,239	35,863	40,133
Government consumption expenditure .	3,379	4,132	4,508
Gross domestic capital formation .	8,612	10,546	11,052

* Revised estimates as of February 12th, 1973.

Source: National Economic Development Authority.

GOLD RESERVES AND CURRENCY IN CIRCULATION
(At December 31st)

	1970	1971	1972
Gold Reserves (million U.S.$) . . .	56.4	67.1	70.7
Foreign Exchange Holdings of the Central Bank (million U.S.$) . . .	194.5	308.3	478.0
Currency in circulation (million pesos) . .	2,410.0	2,650.0	3,434.6
Money Supply (million pesos) . . .	5,047.4	5,567.4	6,796.6

BALANCE OF PAYMENTS
(million U.S.$)

	1969	1970	1971	1972
Merchandise	−277	− 28	− 58	−151
Other Goods and Services . . .	−112*	−120	− 68	− 25
Transfer Payments	155*	119	134	188
CURRENT BALANCE . . .	−234	− 29	8	12
Long-term Capital Movements . .	156	137	71	141
Short-term Capital Movements . .	134	134	95	− 8
Changes in Reserves	69	− 95	− 31	− 38
CAPITAL BALANCE . . .	359	176	135	95
Errors and Omissions	−125	−147	−143	−107

* Revised.

INTERNATIONAL INVESTMENTS
(1972—million U.S. $)

	DIRECT* PRIVATE LONG-TERM	INDIRECT			
		Public		Private	
		Long-Term	Short-Term	Long-Term	Short-Term
Net Foreign Investments in the Philippines:					
United States and Canada . .	−10.81	48.60	−40.48	26.81	−42.28	−18.16
OECD Member Countries . .	− 0.76	77.49	−17.52	−44.22	67.84	82.83
All Other Countries . . .	− 0.25	− 2.30	—	− 3.61	13.90	7.74
International Institutions . .	—	26.80	—	1.97	—	28.77
Unallocated	− 0.20	11.10	0.12	0.49	16.29	27.80
TOTAL FOREIGN LIABILITIES .	−12.02	161.69	−57.88	−18.56	55.75	128.98

* Represents direct investments reported through the banking system. This does not include investments made in the form of machinery and equipment.

Source: Central Bank of Philippines.

EXTERNAL TRADE
(million U.S. dollars)

	1969	1970	1971	1972
Imports . .	1,131.5	1,090.1	1,186.0	1,229.6
Exports . .	854.6	1,061.7	1,136.4	1,106.0

COMMODITIES
('000 U.S. dollars)

IMPORTS	1969	1970	1971	1972
Textile Yarns and Fabrics . .	33,576	23,895	23,372	24,257
Mineral Fuels and Lubricants .	106,726	118,948	141,233	148,825
Non-electric Machinery . .	258,533	235,218	255,118	239,930
Base Metals . . .	116,280	144,410	90,726	112,450
Transport Equipment . .	124,883	106,040	122,173	123,691
Dairy Products . . .	37,373	32,403	38,497	45,564
Cereals	38,055	32,526	65,098	84,253
Textile Fibres . . .	41,813	40,177	48,836	45,754
Electric Machinery . .	60,244	59,209	66,286	84,008
Explosives . . .	41,666	49,755	56,366	45,754

EXPORTS	1968	1969	1970	1971	1972
Copra	123,029	87,295	80,077	114,040	110,480
Sugar	144,048	148,796	187,653	212,348	208,639
Abaca (Manila Hemp) .	11,209	14,279	15,342	12,989	13,099
Logs and Lumber . .	216,630	225,988	249,766	225,907	174,444
Dessicated Coconut . .	24,605	16,146	19,449	20,741	17,551
Coconut Oil . . .	77,311	50,565	95,585	103,451	84,669
Iron Ore . . .	1,882	1,893	3,183	1,461	1,401
Plywood . . .	21,478	19,481	19,666	24,115*	33,717
Copper Concentrates . .	89,249	132,810	185,190	185,135*	190,867
Canned Pineapple . .	9,376	17,225	21,398	19,683	19,552

* Revised.

TRADING PARTNERS
('000 U.S. dollars)

	IMPORTS			EXPORTS		
	1970	1971	1972	1970	1971	1972
Australia	50,138	47,069	58,573	4,443	4,818	7,495
Belgium and Luxembourg . .	7,606	11,067	7,897	1,743	941	1,040
Canada	17,997	37,037	25,365	3,458	4,034	7,627
China (Taiwan) . . .	13,693	23,230	16,465	19,543	19,051	20,267
France	17,881	10,213	28,742	2,864	2,887	4,560
Germany, Federal Republic .	63,889	87,657	61,233	19,841	32,192	40,592
Hong Kong . . .	11,702	13,075	13,056	11,402	15,038	14,133
India	2,617	1,613	1,710	828	248	718
Indonesia . . .	26,017	29,333	8,594	1,726	3,468	4,099
Italy	15,048	10,951	10,147	8,415	7,203	6,141
Japan	344,879	359,100	390,785	420,753	391,408	373,449
Malaysia and Singapore .	30,628	28,925	25,108	7,854	17,328	8,860
Netherlands . . .	21,529	20,686	18,293	43,969	76,935	75,586
Spain	1,625	1,388	1,474	7,422	3,719	3,839
Switzerland . . .	9,392	9,356	7,495	273	222	259
United Kingdom . .	46,825	66,847	47,408	10,749	13,863	30,128
United States . . .	315,083	340,000	318,685	440,172	452,741	446,551

Source: Central Bank of Philippines.

TRANSPORT
RAILWAYS

		1969*	1970*	1971	1972†
Passengers . . .	(thousands)	6,050	5,628	5,362	4,036
Passenger-kilometres . .	(million)	668	455	686	703
Freight . .	('ooo metric tons)	559	354	386	283
Ton-kilometres . . .	(million)	106	47	83	40

* Revised.   † Provisional.

Source: Philippine National Railways.

VEHICLES IN USE

	1969	1970	1971	1972
Passenger Cars	272,183	279,172	285,063	312,137
Commercial Vehicles . . .	174,229	179,115	183,097	204,391

Source: Land Transportation Commission.

CIVIL AVIATION

		1969	1970	1971
Kilometres Flown .	(thousands)	27,130	24,795	18,650
Passenger-kilometres .	(,,)	854,572	838,269	842,685
Cargo Ton-kilometres .	(,,)	9,117	8,354	8,429
Mail Ton-kilometres .	(,,)	356	276	295

Source: Civil Aeronautics Board.

SHIPPING

		1969	1970	1971	1972
Vessels Entered .	('ooo metric tons)	9,259	8,550	8,267	9,317
Vessels Cleared .	(,, ,, ,,)	8,254	7,778	7,617	8,814
Goods Loaded .	(,, ,, ,,)	14,408	15,792	16,148	15,123
Goods Unloaded .	(,, ,, ,,)	12,580	12,539	13,462	13,363

Sources: Customs Bureau; Census and Statistics Bureau.

TOURISM

	1969	1970	1971	1972
Number of Visitors ('ooo) .	123	144	144*	166
Average stay (days) . .	7.2	7.3	7.3*	7.3
Estimated spending ('ooo U.S. dollars) . .	27,070	32,077	32,133	38,271

* Estimated.

Source: Bureau of Travel and Tourist Industry.

COMMUNICATIONS MEDIA

	1972
Radio Transmitters	313
Television Transmitters . . .	26
Telephones	329,323
Daily Newspapers	21*
Total Circulation	159,489*

* Preliminary.

Source: Bureau of the Census and Statistics.

EDUCATION
(1971)

	SCHOOLS	TEACHERS	PUPILS
Kindergarten .	447	1,499	51,279
Primary . .	41,823	243,821	6,968,978
Secondary .	3,883	50,835	1,719,386
Collegiate .	728	30,093	651,514
Special Vocational	625	2,361	106,099
Others . .	—	20	—

Source: Department of Education.

THE CONSTITUTION

(Proclaimed January 17th, 1973)

The following is a summary of the main features of the Constitution.

BASIC PRINCIPLES

Sovereignty resides in the people; defence of the State is a prime duty and all citizens are liable for military or civil service; war is renounced as an instrument of national policy; the State undertakes to strengthen the family as a basic social institution, promote the well-being of youth, maintain adequate social services, promote social justice, assure the rights of workers and guarantee the autonomy of local government.

Other provisions guarantee the right to life, liberty and property, freedom of abode and travel, freedom of worship, freedom of speech, of the press and of petition to the Government, the right of *habeas corpus* except in cases of invasion, insurrection or rebellion, and various rights before the courts.

SUFFRAGE

All citizens of the Philippines over the age of 18 years, not disqualified by law, resident in the Philippines for at least one year and in their voting district for at least six months, are eligible to vote.

THE PRESIDENT

The President is elected from among the members of the National Assembly for a six-year term, by a majority vote; he ceases to be a member of the Assembly or of any political party; he must be at least 50 years of age; he may not receive any emolument other than that entitled to as the President; he can dissolve the National Assembly, call general elections and, when appropriate, accept the resignation of the Cabinet.

THE NATIONAL ASSEMBLY

Legislative power is vested in the National Assembly; members are elected for six years and must be natural-born citizens, over 25 years of age, literate and registered voters in their district.

Regular elections are to be held on the second Monday of May; the Assembly convenes on the fourth Monday of July for its regular session; it elects a Speaker from among its members; the election of the President and Prime Minister precedes all other business following the election of the Speaker.

Various provisions define the procedures of the Assembly and the rights of its members, among them that the Assembly may withdraw its confidence in the Prime Minister by a majority vote; that no bill shall become law until it has passed three readings on separate days; that every bill passed by the Assembly shall be presented to the Prime Minister for approval, upon the withholding of which, the Assembly may reconsider a bill and, by a majority vote of two-thirds, enable it to become law.

THE PRIME MINISTER AND CABINET

Executive power is exercised by the Prime Minister with the assistance of the Cabinet; the Prime Minister is elected from the members of the National Assembly by a majority vote; he appoints the members of the Cabinet.

The Prime Minister is Commander-in-Chief of the armed forces; he may suspend the writ of *habeas corpus* and proclaim martial law; all powers vested in the President under the 1935 Constitution are vested in the Prime Minister unless the National Assembly provides otherwise.

THE JUDICIARY

The Supreme Court is composed of a Chief Justice and 14 Associate Justices, and may sit *en banc* or in two divisions.

LOCAL GOVERNMENT

The National Assembly shall enact a local government code which shall establish a more responsive and accountable local government structure.

CONSTITUTIONAL COMMISSIONS

These are the Civil Service Commission, the Commission on Elections and the Commission on Audit. The Commission on Elections enforces and administers all laws relating to the conduct of elections and registers and accredits political parties.

THE NATIONAL ECONOMY

The National Assembly shall establish a National Economic Development Authority which shall recommend co-ordinated social and economic plans to the National Assembly and all appropriate governmental bodies. Various provisions relating to the public interest in economic matters are set forth.

AMENDMENTS

Amendments and revisions to the Constitution may be proposed by the National Assembly upon a vote of three-quarters of its members, or by a constitutional convention. Any amendment or revision is valid when ratified by a majority of votes cast in a plebiscite.

TRANSITIONAL PROVISIONS

There shall be an *interim* National Assembly, convened by the incumbent President, who shall continue to exercise his powers under the 1935 Constitution until he calls on the *interim* National Assembly to elect the *interim* President and the *interim* Prime Minister, who shall then exercise their respective powers under the new Constitution. All proclamations, orders, decreees and acts of the incumbent President shall remain valid and binding even after the lifting of martial law or the ratification of this Constitution. The present Judiciary shall continue to exercise its powers and functions. This Constitution shall take effect immediately after its ratification by a majority of the votes cast in a plebiscite called for the purpose.

Note: When President Marcos proclaimed the ratification of the new Constitution on January 17th, 1973, following a plebiscite, he also proclaimed the suspension of the *interim* National Assembly envisaged by the Constitution and the continuation of martial law, in force since September 23rd, 1972. In a referendum held on July 27th–28th, 1973, a majority voted that President Marcos should continue in office beyond 1973 and complete the reforms he had initiated under martial law.

THE GOVERNMENT

HEAD OF THE STATE

President: FERDINAND EDRALIN MARCOS (inaugurated December 1965, re-elected November 1969, term of office extended by referendum July 1973).

THE CABINET

(April 1974)

President and Prime Minister: FERDINAND EDRALIN MARCOS.

Secretary of Foreign Affairs: Brig.-Gen. CARLOS P. ROMULO.

Secretary of Finance: CÉSAR VIRATA.

Secretary of Justice: VICENTE A. SANTOS.

Secretary of Agriculture and Natural Resources: ARTURO TANCO.

Secretary of Public Works and Communications: DAVID M. CONSUNJI.

Secretary of Education: JUAN L. MANUEL.

Secretary of Labour: BLAS F. OPLE.

Secretary of Agrarian Reform: CONRADO F. ESTRELLA.

Secretary of Nationa Defence: JUAN P. ENRILE.

Secretary of Health: CLEMENTE S. GATMAITAN.

Secretary of Trade and Industry: TROADIO P. QUIAZON, Jr.

Executive Secretary: ALEJANDRO MELCHOR.

Secretary of General Services: CONSTANCIO CASTAÑEDA.

Secretary of Social Welfare: ESTEFANIA ALDABA-LIM.

Secretary of Public Information: FRANCISCO TATAD.

Chairman, National Economic Development Authority: GERARDO SICAT.

Secretary of Local Government and Community Development: JOSE ROÑO.

Chairman, National Science Development Board: FLORENCIO MEDINA.

Commissioner of National Integration: MAMA SINSUAT.

Budget Commissioner: FAUSTINE SY-CHANGOO.

DIPLOMATIC REPRESENTATION

EMBASSIES ACCREDITED TO THE PHILIPPINES

(In Manila unless otherwise stated)

Argentina: Oledan Building, 131–133 Ayala Ave., Makati, Rizal; *Ambassador:* Dr. MARCO AURELIO LINO BENÍTEZ.

Australia: L. & S. Building, 1414 Roxas Blvd.; *Ambassador:* J. C. INGRAM.

Austria: Bangkok, Thailand.

Belgium: Makati Building, 127 Ayala Ave., Makati, Rizal; *Ambassador:* JACQUES LEBACQ.

Brazil: Tokyo, Japan.

Burma: Jakarta, Indonesia.

Canada: *Ambassador:* FRANK B. CLARK.

Chile: Tokyo, Japan.

China (Taiwan): 2038 Roxas Blvd.; *Ambassador:* SUN PI-CHI.

Denmark: Jakarta, Indonesia.

Egypt: Gochangco Building, 610 T. M. Kalaw St., Ermita; *Ambassador:* AHMED MOHAMED ABOU ZEID.

Finland: Tokyo, Japan.

France: 181 Balagtas St., Pasay City; *Ambassador:* CHARLES DE LESTRANGE.

Germany, Federal Republic: L. & S. Building, 1414 Roxas Blvd.; *Ambassador:* JOBST VON BUDDENBROCK.

Greece: Tokyo, Japan.

India: 1856 Jorge B. Bocobo St., Malate; *Ambassador:* B. DEVA RAO.

Indonesia: 2456 Taft Ave.; *Ambassador:* KUSNO UTOMO.

Iran: Tokyo, Japan.

Israel: Metropolitan Building, Ayala Ave., Makati, Rizal; *Ambassador:* ABRAHAM KIDRON.

Italy: 84–86 Libertad, Pasay City; *Ambassador:* EUGENIO RUBINO.

Japan: L. & S. Building, 1414 Roxas Blvd.; *Ambassador:* TOSHIO URABE.

Khmer Republic: 1840 Leveriza St., Pasay City; *Ambassador:* HEM PHANRASY.

Korea, Republic: Rufino Building, Ayala Ave., Makati, Rizal; *Ambassador:* CHI RYANG CHANG.

Laos: Bangkok, Thailand.

Malaysia: Far East Bank Building, Intramuros; *Ambassador:* AHMAD ZAINAL ABIDIN bin MOHAMED YUSOF.

Mexico: L. & S. Building, 1414 Roxas Blvd.; *Ambassador:* ERNESTO MADERO Y VASQUES.

Netherlands: Metropolitan Building, 142 Ayala Ave., Makati, Rizal; *Ambassador:* ROBERT SAMUEL NAPIER Baron VAN DER FELTZ.

Norway: L. & S. Building, 1414 Roxas Blvd.; *Ambassador:* IVAR MELHUUS.

Pakistan: 2332 Roxas Blvd.; *Ambassador:* (vacant).

Portugal: Philamlife Building, United Nations Ave.; *Ambassador:* ANTÓNIO NOVAIS MACHADO.

Saudi Arabia: *Ambassador:* OKAIL MOHAMED OKAIL.

Singapore: Manila; *Ambassador:* Tuan Haji YA'ACOB bin MOHAMED.

Spain: 1320 Marquez de Comillas; *Ambassador:* JOSÉ PÉREZ DEL ARCO.

Sri Lanka: Tokyo, Japan.

Sweden: Jakarta, Indonesia.

Switzerland: Gochangco Building, 610 T. M. Kalaw St.; *Ambassador:* Dr. OSCAR ROSSETTI.

Thailand: Oledan Building, 131–133 Ayala Ave., Makati, Rizal; *Ambassador:* KLOS VISESSURAKARN.

United Kingdom: L. & S. Building, 1414 Roxas Blvd., P.O.B. 295; *Ambassador:* J. A. TURPIN.

U.S.A.: Roxas Blvd.; *Ambassador:* WILLIAM SULLIVAN.

Vatican: 2140 Taft Ave. (Apostolic Nunciature); *Apostolic Nuncio:* Mgr. BRUNO TORPIGLIANI.

Viet-Nam, Republic: 554 Vito Cruz, Malate; *Ambassador:* DUONG HOANG THANH.

Note: Full diplomatic recognition was extended to Bangladesh in February 1972. In March 1972 diplomatic relations were established with Yugoslavia and Romania. In September 1973 the Philippines decided to establish diplomatic relations with Czechoslovakia, the German Democratic Republic, Hungary and Poland, and in December with Bulgaria. The Philippines also has diplomatic relations with Turkey.

NATIONAL ASSEMBLY

Following the suspension of Congress in September 1972 and the proclamation of martial law, a new Constitution (*q.v.*) was proclaimed in January 1973, which provided for an elected National Assembly. This was also suspended, however, in January 1973.

POLITICAL PARTIES

Nacionalista Party: Manila; f. 1907; The party represents the right wing of the former *Partido Nacionalista*, which split in two in 1946; Pres. Senator GIL J. PUYAT.

Liberal Party: The party represents the centre-liberal opinion of the old *Partido Nacionalista*, which split in 1946; Leader Senator GERARDO ROXAS.

Christian Social Movement: Manila; f. 1968; campaigning for liberal social reforms; Pres. RAUL MANGLAPUS.

National Citizen's Party: Manila; Pres. LORENZO TANADA.

JUDICIAL SYSTEM

Supreme Court: Composed of a Chief Justice and 14 Associate Justices. For the purpose of declaring a law or treaty unconstitutional and of imposing the death penalty, at least 10 Justices must concur. For other purposes, the concurrence of 8 Justices is enough.

Chief Justice: ROBERTO CONCEPCIÓN.

Court of Appeals. Consists of a Presiding Justice and twenty-three Associate Justices.

Presiding Justice: SALVADOR ESGUERRA.

In addition to the Supreme Court and the Court of Appeals, several lower courts exist, such as Courts of the First Instance, presided over by district judges, Circuit Criminal Courts, Juvenile and Domestic Relations Courts, City courts and Municipal courts.

Note: All members of the Philippine Bench are appointed by the President with the consent of the Commission on Appointments.

RELIGION

ROMAN CATHOLIC CHURCH

Roman Catholicism is the predominant religion of the Philippines, its adherents numbering approximately 80 per cent of the population.

Metropolitan See of Manila: Most Rev. ANTONIO G. CASAS, D.D., Vicar Capitular.

Metropolitan See of Cebu: H.E. Cardinal JULIO R. ROSALES. Auxiliary Bishop: Most Rev. NICHOLAS M. MONDEJAR.

Metropolitan See of Nueva Segovia: Most Rev. JUAN C. SISON.

Metropolitan See of Caceres: Most Rev. TEOFISTO ALBERTO Y VALDERRAMA.

Metropolitan See of Lingayen-Dagupan: Most Rev. MARIANO A. MADRIAGA.

Metropolitan See of Jaro: Most Rev. JOSÉ MARIA CUENCO.

Metropolitan See of Cagayan de Oro: Most Rev. PATRICK H. CRONIN.

Metropolitan See of Zamboanga: Most Rev. LINO R. GONZAGA Y RASDESALES.

Dipolog: Most Rev. FELIX S. ZAFRA, D.D.

Iglesia Filipina Independiente (*Philippine Independent Church*): 1327 Alfredo St., Sta. Cruz, Manila; f. 1902; 2.9 million mems. (8 per cent of the population); The Most Rev. Isabelo de los Reyes, Jr., s.t.d., d.d., Head Bishop; Rt. Rev. Macario V. Ga, Bishop Gen. Sec.; Rt. Rev. Federico R. Rico, Bishop Gen. Treas.; publ. *Christian Register*.

PROTESTANT CHURCHES

Union Church of Manila: P.O.B. 184 Makati, Rizal.

United Church of Christ in the Philippines: P.O.B. 718, Manila; Gen. Sec. Bishop Estanislao Q. Abainza;

175,000 mems.; publs. *United Church Letter, Church and Community*.

There are about 3,000,000 Protestants.

MUSLIMS

Chief Imam: Hadji Madki Alonto, Governor of Lansao del Sur.

There are about 1,500,000 Muslims.

OTHERS

There are about 43,000 Buddhists and 400,000 Animists and persons of no religion.

THE PRESS

The Philippines had a large and diverse press, with about 15 metropolitan dailies and 175 weeklies, before the imposition of martial law by President Marcos in September 1972, when all newspapers and radio stations were shut down. The President claimed that he had "silenced the media because some were undermining Philippine society and giving aid and comfort to the Communists". A number of reporters, editors and publishers were arrested, and before publication could be resumed the Government's Mass Media Council had to screen staff and give its authorization. The strict controls on content and comment were gradually relaxed, and the Mass Media Council was replaced in May 1973 by a Media Advisory Council, composed of representatives of the various media. The Press is now expected to exercise self-restraint, and its subservience is assured by the system of certificates of operation, renewable every six months only after being approved by the President. Newspapers are expected to publish only what the President described as news of "positive national value" and to eschew sensationalism.

DAILIES

Bulletin Today: Muralla St., Intramuros, Manila; English; Publisher Hans Menzi; Editor Ben F. Rodriguez.

Daily Express: 371 Bonifacio Drive, Port Area, Manila; f. 1971; English and Pilipino editions; Publisher Juan A. Perez, Jr.; Editor Enrique P. Romualdez; circ. 60,000.

The Times Journal: Meralco Ave., Corner Tektite Rd., Pasig, Rizal; English; published by Philippine Journalists Inc.; Editor Ricardo T. Torres.

United Daily News: 818 Benavides St., Manila; f. 1973; Chinese and English; Publisher Ralp Nubla; Editor Sy Yinchow; circ. 20,000.

PERIODICALS

Bannawag: Ramón Roces Building, 1655 Soler St., Manila; weekly; Ilocano; published by Liwayway Publishing Inc.; Editor David D. Campanano; circ. 50,000.

Bisaya: Ramón Roces Building, 1655 Soler St., Manila; weekly; Cebu-Visayan; published by Liwayway Publishing Inc.

Focus Philippines: P.O.B. 478, 3rd Floor, Med-di Building, Intramuros, Manila; Editor Kerima Polotan.

Government Report: P.O.B. 4201, Intramuros, Manila; published by The National Media Production Center; Man. Editor Max T. Ramos.

Hiligaynon: Ramón Roces Building, 1655 Soler St., Manila; f. 1934; weekly; Ilongo; published by Liwayway Publishing Inc.; Editor Francis J. Jamolangue.

Liwayway: Ramón Roces Building, 1655 Soler St., Manila; weekly; Pilipino; published by Liwayway Publishing Inc.; circ. 80,000.

Philippine News: P.O.B. 4201, Intramuros, Manila; published by The National Media Production Center.

Philippines Today: P.O.B. 4201, Intramuros, Manila; published by The National Media Production Center.

The Republic: 8th Floor, Beneficial Life Building, Solana St., Intramuros, Manila; published by The Bureau of National and Foreign Information.

NEWS AGENCIES

Philippines News Agency: P.O.B. 3396, Manila; f. 1973; Man. Jose L. Pavia; Man. Editor Renato B. Tiangco.

Foreign Bureaux

AP: L. and S. Building, 1515 Roxas Blvd., P.O.B. 2274, Manila; Chief of Bureau John E. Nance.

Central News Agency of China: P.O.B. 3585, Room 706, Bank of Philippine Island Building, Manila.

United Press International: 701 Trinity Bldg., 636 T. M. Kalaw St., Ermita, Manila; Man. Patrick J. Killen.

Antara, Reuters and Tass also have bureaux in Manila.

PRESS ASSOCIATION

National Press Club of the Philippines: Magallanes Drive, Manila; Pres. Primitivo Mijares; Sec.-Gen. Stephen F. Sergio.

Philippine Press Council: Manila; f. 1966; Chair. (*Acting*) Justice Pastor Endencia.

Philippine Press Institute: f. 1965; Manila; Dir. E. R. Sánchez.

PUBLISHERS

Abiva Publishing House: 942 Misericordia, Santa Cruz, Manila; f. 1949; Chair. Mrs. A. Q. Abiva; Pres. L. Q. Abiva.

Associated Publishers Inc.: 63 Quezon Blvd. Extension, Quezon City, P.O.B. 449, Manila; f. 1952; law, medical and educational books; Pres. J. V. Roxas.

Benipayo Publishers: 664 Misericordia, Manila; short stories; Man. Donato D. Benipayo, Jr.

Bookman Printing House: 49 Quezon Blvd. Extension, Quezon City.

A. G. Briones & Co.: Room 301 Marvel Bldg., No. 1, 258 Juan Luna Street, Manila; publishes *AB Commercial Directory of the Philippines.*

Bustamente Press Inc.: 155 Panay Ave., Quezon City; f. 1949; textbooks on English, sciences and mathematics; Man. Pablo N. Bustamente, Jr.

Capitol Publishing House Inc.: 54 Don Alejandro A. Roces Ave., Quezon City.

Carmelo & Bauermann Inc.: E. de los Santos Ave., Makati, Rizal.

Filipino Publishing House Inc.: Scout Reyes St., Quezon City.

R. M. Garcia Publishing House: 903 Quezon Blvd. Ext., Quezon City; f. 1951; distributor and publisher of textbooks and Filipiniana books; Pres. and Gen. Man. R. M. Garcia.

L. J. Gonzalez Publishers: P.O.B. 3501, 2 Broadway, Quezon City; f. 1956; magazines and brochures; Man. Luz J. Gonzalez.

Industry & Trade Publishers: 5 Martelino St., Quezon City.

Lawyers' Co-operative Publishing Company (Phil.) Inc.: 63 Quezon Blvd. Extension, Quezon City, P.O.B. 449, Manila; Head Office: The Lawyers' Co-operative Publishing Co., Rochester, New York 14603, U.S.A.; estab. in Manila 1913; law, medical and educational books; Pres. Jaime V. Roxas.

Macaraig Publishing Co. Inc.: 1144 Vermont St., Paco, Manila; f. 1926; textbooks; Pres. Serafin E. Macaraig.

Manor Press: 715 Evangelista St., Quiapo, Manila.

Martinez, Roberto & Sons: 3 Expaña, Quezon City.

Philippine Arts and Architecture: 1346 U.N. Ave., Ermita, Manila.

Philippine International Publishing Co.: 1789 A. Mabini St., Ermita, Manila.

Regal Printing Co. Inc.: 1729 J. P. Laurel, Sr., St., Manila.

Tamaraw Publishing Co.: Cebu Avenue, Quezon City.

University Publishing Co.: Central Office, 1128 Washington, Sampaloc, Manila; f. 1936; Dirs. Dr. José M. Aruego and Mrs. Constancia E. Aruego.

RADIO AND TELEVISION

Radio Control Office: Dept. of Public Works, Transportation and Communication; regulates the installation, construction and operation of all radio stations, transmitters and receivers; Chief Ceferino S. Carreon.

RADIO

The following are the principal companies operating:

Philippine Broadcasting Service (PBS): G.S.I.S. Bldg., Manila D-406; owned and operated by the Republic of the Philippines; *Stations:* Manila: DZFM, DZRP, DZRM, DZCP, DUB4, DUH2; FM stations: DZFM-FM, DZRP-FM, DZRM-FM; Provincial: DZMQ—Dagupan, DZEQ—Baguio City, DYMR—Cebu City, DXRP—Davao City, DXSO—Marawi City, DXSM—Jolo, Sulu; Gen. Man. Simoun Almario; Production Man. Nick Aragon; Sr. Exec. Asst. Pedro Prado; Dir. Engineering Luis Quintos.

Far East Broadcasting Company: P.O.B. 2041, Manila; f. 1948; operates a home service 24 hours a day, a cultural music station, seven provincial stations, an overseas service throughout Asia in 31 languages; Pres. Robert H. Bowman; Dir. Fred M. Magbanua, Jr.; publ. *The Signal* (bi-monthly).

Manila Broadcasting Company: 141 Ayala Ave., Makati, Rizal.

Mascom Network: Dumaguete City and Manila; educational and religious broadcasts; commercial radio stations subsidized by INTERMEDIA, NCCUSA; owned by National Council of Churches in the Philippines (NCCP); Man. DYSR—Dumaguete City B. V. Magdamo; Man. DZCH—Manila J. T. Pia, Jr.

The ABS-CBN Broadcasting Corpn.: Broadcast Center, Quezon City; f. 1946; Pres. Eugenio Lopez, Jr.; Vice-Pres. and Gen. Man. Augusto Almeda Lopez; Vice-Pres. and Asst. Gen. Man. Filemon Delfino; Vice-Pres. Manila Radio Nestor Escano; Vice-Pres., Television Januario Jison.

Philippine Broadcasting Corporation: Radio Center, 964 Taft Ave., Manila; Pres. Manuel Elizade, Sr.

Radio-Republic Broadcasting System: E. de los Santos Ave., Diliman, Quezon City; Dir.-Gen. Loreto F. Stewart.

Voice of America: U.S. Information Agency, Washington 20547, U.S.A.; medium- and short-wave relay transmitters at Poro.

The Voice of Philippines: 141 Ayala Ave., Makati; operates DZRH, the public service and drama station of the Elizalde Tri-media network.

In 1971 there were 1,520,000 radio sets.

TELEVISION

Philippine Broadcasting Service: G.S.I.S. Bldg., Manila 10401; owned and operated by the Republic of the Philippines; Station DZRP-TV; Gen. Man. Simoun Almario.

Bolinao Electronics Corporation: ABS Building, Roxas Blvd., Manila; Stations DYBC-TV, DZAQ-TV; Exec. Vice-Pres. E. López, Jr.

Chronicle Broadcasting Network: Aduana St., Manila; Station DZXL-TV; Pres. E. López, Jr.

Feati University: Helios Station, Santa Cruz, Manila.

Inter-Island Broadcasting Corporation, TV-13: 2nd Floor Sikatuna Bldg., Ayala Ave., Makati; f. 1958; 6 stations, Baguio, Manila, Cebu, Davao, Cagayan de Oro City, Bacolod, Naga; Pres. Juan de Ibazeta; Exec. Vice-Pres. and Gen. Man. Henry R. Canoy.

Manila Times Publishing Co.: TVT Bldg., Florentino Torres St., Manila; Publisher: Joaquin P. Roces.

Metropolitan Broadcasting Co. (Channel 11): 141 Ayala Ave., Makati, Rizal.

Republic Broadcasting System: E. de Los Santos Ave., Diliman, Quezon City; Station DZBB-TV; Dir.-Gen. R. L. Stewart.

In 1971 there were 421,000 television sets.

FINANCE

(cap. = capital, p.u. = paid up, dep. = deposits, m. = million, amounts in pesos)

BANKING

The banking structure of the Philippines consists of (1) the Central Bank, (2) commercial banks, (3) savings and mortgage banks, (4) building and loan associations, (5) development banks, (6) rural banks. In addition, three banks with specific functions, the Philippines Veterans Bank for war veterans, the Land Bank for financing the land reform programme, and the National Cottage Industries Bank for small industries, were established in the early 'sixties although they are considered commercial banks.

CENTRAL BANK

Central Bank of the Philippines: Aduana St., Intramuros, Manila; f. 1949; cap. 10m.; dep. 1,235.5m. (Dec. 1970); Presiding Officer (Monetary Board) Cesar Virata; Gov. Gregorio S. Licaros.

PRINCIPAL COMMERCIAL BANKS

Bank of the Philippines Islands: P.O.B. 777, 150 Plaza Cervantes, Manila; f. 1851; cap. p.u. 50m.; dep. 449m. (Sept. 1972); Pres. Alberto de Villa-Abrille; Vice-Pres. E. U. Miranda, G. D. Del Rosario, C. V. Francisco, M. T. Celestino.

China Banking Corporation: Corner Dasmariñas and Juan Luna, P.O.B. 611, Manila; f. 1920; cap. 120.2m.; dep. 462.7m. (June 1973); Chair. and Gen. Man. Albino Z. Sy Cip; Pres. George Dee Sekiat.

Commercial Bank and Trust Co. of the Philippines: Ayala Ave., Makati, Rizal; f. 1954; total resources 672.3m. (Sept. 1973); Chair. Manuel J. Marquez; Pres. Fernando R. Reyes; Exec. Vice-Pres. Vicente A. Pacis, Jr.

Far East Bank and Trust Co.: Far East Bank Bldg., Muralla, Intramuros, Manila (P.O.B. 1411); f. 1960; cap. 52m.; dep. 521m. (Sept. 1973); Chair. and Pres. José B. Fernandez, Jr.

General Bank and Trust Co.: P.O.B. 4040, 560 Rosario St.. Binondo, Manila D-405; f. 1963; Pres. and Chair. Dr, Clarencio S. Yujuico; Vice-Pres. Salvador D. Tenorio, Irineo P. San Luis, Regnar C. Rivera; cap. 23.7m.; dep. 70.4m. (1970); 16 brs.

Manufacturers Bank and Trust Co.: P.O.B. 1324, Manila; f. 1957; cap. 16.0m.; dep. 71.0m.; 15 brs.; Pres. Antonio de las Alas; Vice-Pres. and Gen. Man. Macario C. Tiu.

Metropolitan Bank and Trust Co.: Ayala Ave., Makati, Rizal; f. 1962; cap. 52.1m.; dep. 433.5m. (Sept. 1973); Chair. Emilio Abello; Pres. Andres V. Castillo.

Pacific Banking Corporation: 460 Quinton Paredes St., Manila; f. 1955; cap. 61.6m.; dep. 439.4m. (Sept. 1973); Chair. Antonio Roxas Chua; Pres. and Gen. Man. Chester G. Babst.

People's Bank and Trust Co.: Muelle del Banco Nacional, Corner T. Pinpin St., Manila; f. 1926; cap. 30m.; dep. 88.0m. (March 1971); Pres. Vicente C. Aquino.

Philippine Bank of Commerce: 6756 Ayala Avenue, Makati, Rizal; f. 1938; cap. 20m.; dep. 202m. (Dec. 1972); Pres. Juan Cojuangco.

Philippine Commercial and Industrial Bank: Antonio Building, T. M. Kalaw St., Ermita, Manila; f. 1960; cap. 89.8m.; dep. 502.3m. (Sept. 1973); Chair. A. Montelibano; Pres. Ramon S. Orosa, Jr.

Philippine National Bank (PHILNABANK): P.O.B. 1844, Manila; Government controlled; f. 1916; cap. 700m.; dep. 3,904m. (Sept. 1973); Pres. Panfilo O. Domingo; Exec. Vice-Pres. Mario Consing; 160 brs. and agencies; 9 overseas offices.

Philippine Trust Co.: Plaza Lacson, Manila; f. 1916; cap. 20m.; dep. 91.7m. (June 1973); Pres. and Chair. Paterno M. Sisante; Vice-Pres. Ricardo G. Verzosa; Asst. Vice-Pres. Paciencia M. Pineda.

Rizal Commercial Banking Corpn.: 219 Buendia Ave., Makati, Rizal; f. 1963; cap. 26.1m.; dep. 69.5m. (Dec. 1970); Chair. A. T. Yuchengco; Pres. F. E. V. Sison.

RURAL BANKS

Small private banks established with the encouragement and assistance (both financial and technical) of the Government in order to promote and expand the rural economy in an orderly manner. Conceived mainly to combat usury and to stimulate the productive capacities of small farmers, small merchants, and small industrialists in rural areas, their principal objectives are to place within easy reach and access of the people credit facilities on reasonable terms and, in co-operation with other agencies of the Government, to provide advice on business and farm management and the proper use of credit for production and marketing purposes. The nation's rural banking system now consists of 344 units spread over the different cities and municipalities of the country.

CO-OPERATIVE BANK

Philippine National Co-operative Bank: Dña. Amparo Bldg., Manila; f. 1960 to assist the people to develop their enterprises on a co-operative basis, to strengthen their economic independence by the promotion of organized methods of industrial production, marketing, distribution and credit.

SPECIAL BANKS

Land Bank: 4th Floor, RM Centre, Roxas Blvd., Manila; f. 1967; semi-government corporation; finances the acquisition of landed estates for redistribution to farmer lessees, bought up by the Government as part of the Land Reform programme; Chair. BENJAMIN DEL ROSARIO.

Philippine Veterans Bank: Boniface Drive, Port Area, Manila; f. 1964; loans granted to both veterans and non-veterans; auth. cap. 100m.; dep. 149.8m. (March 1970); Chair. ALEJO SANTOS; Pres. ESTEBAN B. CABANOS.

DEVELOPMENT BANKS

Development Bank of the Philippines: P.O.B. 800, Makati Commercial Centre, D-708; Buendia, Makati, Rizal; f. 1947; wholly owned by the Government; provides long-term loans for agricultural and industrial development; 17 brs.

In addition there are 24 private development banks.

OTHER DEVELOPMENT ORGANIZATIONS

Agricultural Credit Administration (ACA): 2544 Taft Ave., Manila; wholly government-owned corporation; provides credit extension to farmers.

National Development Company (NDC): Pureza St., Sta. Mesa, Manila; f. 1919; wholly Government-owned corporation engaged in the organization, financing and management of subsidiaries and corporations including commercial, industrial, mining, agricultural and other enterprises which may be necessary or contributory to the economic development of the country; Chair. CONSTANTE L. FARIÑAS; Gen. Man. CARLOS P. MORALES.

National Economic Development Authority (NEDA): Padre Faura, Manila; f. 1972; to ensure better utilization of public resources and to increase efficiency; Chair. GERARDO SICAT.

Philippine Rural Reconstruction Movement (PRRM): Manila; a non-profit-making, private, civic agency; f. 1952; operates social laboratories in 200 Philippine villages in which new and creative approaches to rural development are tested and validated; Pres. ARMANDO BALTAZAR.

Private Development Corporation of the Philippines (PDCP): PDCP Bldg., Ayala Ave., Makati, Rizal; f. 1963 with World Bank assistance; assists private enterprise development in the Philippines, especially of capital markets and managerial skills, total loans 1963–Dec. 1972: foreign currency loans U.S. $81m., peso currency loans 95.7m. pesos; Chair. and Pres. ROBERTO T. VILLANUEVA.

FOREIGN BANKS

Bank of America National Trust and Savings Association: San Francisco, Calif., U.S.A.; Manila, P.O.B. 935, 231 Juan Luna St., Manila; Vice-Pres. and Man. R. D. H. WILMER.

Chartered Bank, The: London; 223 Juan Luna St., Manila; Man. H. D. N. M. SHEDDEN.

First National City Bank: P.O.B. 615, Manila; Vice-Pres. S. R. EASTABROOKS.

Hongkong and Shanghai Banking Corporation, The: Hong Kong; 6780 Ayala Ave., Makati, Rizal, Manila.

ASSOCIATION

Bankers Association of the Philippines: 12th Floor, Philbanking Corpn. Bldg., Port Area, Manila; Pres. J. B. FERNANDEZ, Jr.

STOCK EXCHANGES

Manila Stock Exchange: Manila Stock Exchange Bldg; Muelle de la Industria and Prensa Sts., Binondo, Manila; f. 1927; 43 mems.; Pres. ENRIQUE SANTAMARÍA;

Vice-Pres. PEDRO UY-TIOCO; Sec. LUIS ONGPIN; Treas. MARIANO U. GODINEZ; publs. *MSE Monthly Review, Manual of Philippine Securities.*

INSURANCE

Alliance Insurance & Surety Co. Inc.: Room 301-303, Choong Bldg., 224 Desmarinos, Sta. Mesa, Manila.

Asian Surety and Insurance Co. Inc.: W. L. Yao Bldg., Manila; Pres. W. LI YAO; fire, casualty, car, marine, personal accident.

Associated Insurance & Surety Co., Inc.: David-M. de Banco. Nacional, Manila; Pres. E. A. SUAREZ.

Capital Insurance and Surety Co. Inc.: P.O.B. 1613, Escolta, Manila; f. 1949; Pres. J. G. GARRDIO; Chair. J. MUÑOZ; fire, casualty, marine, life.

Central Surety & Insurance Co.: 110th Floor, Philippine Banking Building, Port Area, Manila; auth. cap. 5m. pesos; Pres. (acting) SANTOS MARTINEZ; Sec. Treas. Mrs. T. T. CASTAÑEDA; Vice-Pres. and Gen. Man. B. B. MANAÑGAN; bonds, fire, marine, casualty, motor car, workmen's compensation.

Commercial Insurance and Surety Co., Inc.: 469 Solana St., Intramuros, Manila; non-life insurance.

Commonwealth Insurance Co.: Warner Barnes Bldg., 2900 Faraday Cnr. South Expressway, Makati, Rizal; f. 1935; cap. 3m. pesos; Pres. A. ROXAS; Vice-Pres. and Treas. E. ESTEBAN.

Domestic Insurance Company of the Philippines: Domestic Insurance Bldg., Port Area, Manila; f. 1946; Pres. A. L. ACHAVAL; Man. C. F. Uy, Jr.; fire, marine, motor car, fidelity and surety and allied lines.

Empire Insurance Co.: Prudential Bank Bldg., Ayala Ave., Makati, Rizal; f. 1949; Chair. A. A. SANTOS; fire, bonds, marine, accident, extraneous perils.

Equitable Insurance and Casualty Co. Inc., The: Equitable Bank Bldg., Juan Luna St., P.O.B. 1103, Manila; Pres. Dr. ROQUE D. YAP; fire, marine, accident, workmen's compensation, car.

Far Eastern Surety and Insurance Co. Inc.: Martinez Bldg., P.O. Box 345, Manila; f. 1934; Pres. ANTONIO TAN KIANG.

FGU Insurance Corporation: Insular Life Bldg., 6781 Ayala Ave., Makati, Rizal, P.O.B. 70, Makati; f. 1963; Chair. E. ZOBEL.

Fidelity and Surety Co. of the Philippines, Inc.: Plaza Lacson, Manila; f. 1912; Pres. PATERNO M. SISANTE.

First Continental Assurance Co. Inc.: Concepcion Bldg., corner Victoria and Muralla Streets, Intramuros, Manila; f. 1960; Pres. C. B. LICAROS, Jr.; fire, marine, motor car, accident, workmen's compensation, bonds.

First National Surety & Assurance Co. Inc.: Insurance Center Bldg., 633 Gen. Luna St., Intramuros, Manila; f. 1950; Pres. and Gen. Man. D. L. MERCADO; all kinds of non-life insurance, bonds and investments.

General Insurance & Surety Corporation: 5th Floor, Plywood Industries Bldg., T. Kalaw, Ermita, Manila; Pres. G. P. NAVA.

The Insular Life Assurance Co. Ltd.: Insular Life Bldg., 6781 Ayala Ave., Makati, Rizal, P.O.B. 128, Manila; incorporated 1910; Pres. MAX VELHAGEN.

Luzon Surety Co. Inc.: 180 David St., Manila; f. 1929; Pres. E. RODRIGUEZ, Sr.

Malayan Insurance Co. Inc.: P.O.B. 3389, 484 Rosario St., Manila; f. 1949; industrial and commercial; Pres. ALFONSO YUCHENGCO; cap. 2,500,000 pesos.

Manila Insurance Company, Inc.: 119 Dasmariñas Street, Binondo, Manila; f. 1917; Pres. JOSÉ P. FERNÁNDEZ; Vice-Pres. CARLOS P. FERNANDEZ.

Manila Surety & Fidelity Co., Inc.: 66 P. Florentino, Quezon City; f. 1945; Pres. Dr. PRECIOSO S. PEÑA; Vice-Pres. Dr. ELISA V. PEÑA.

Manila Underwriters Insurance Co. Inc.: 221 Natividad Bldg., Escolta, Manila; f. 1949; Pres. T. R. FLORO.

Metropolitan Insurance Company: Elizalde Bldg., 141 Ayala Ave., Makati, Rizal; f. 1933; Pres. MANUEL ELIZALDE; Vice-Pres. and Man. G. A. REEDYK; non-life.

National Life Insurance Company of the Philippines: 306 Regina Bldg., Escolta, Manila; Chair. J. V. MACUJA; Pres. E. S. SEVILLA.

Paramount Surety and Insurance Co. Inc.: Paramount Bldg., 434 Rosario St., Manila; Pres. TION SIM; fire, marine, casualty, car.

People's Surety & Insurance Co., Inc.: Trade Center Bldg., Cnr. P. Faura and A. Mabini Sts., Manila; f. 1950; Chair. Dr. A. LIBORO; non-life, surety, fidelity.

Philippine American Accident Insurance Co. Inc.: Philamlife Bldg., U.N. Ave., Manila; f. 1961; Chair. E. CARROLL; Pres. M. CAMPOS; Exec. Vice-Pres. W. E. WINEBRENNER; all classes of general insurance.

Philippine American General Insurance Group: Philamlife Bldg., U.N. Ave., Manila; f. 1950; Chair. E. CARROLL; Pres. M. CAMPOS; Exec. Vice-Pres. W. E. WINEBRENNER; all classes of general insurance.

Philippine American Life Insurance Co.: Philamlife Bldg., United Nations Ave., Ermita, Manila; f. 1947; Chair. and Chief Exec. Pres. EARL CARROLL; life.

The Philippine Guaranty Co. Inc.: Insular Life Bldg., 6781 Ayala Ave., Makati, Rizal, P.O.B. 70, Commercial Centre, Makati; f. 1917; Chair. E. ZOBEL.

Philippine Prudential Life Insurance Co. Inc.: Insurance Center Bldg., 633 Gen. Luna St., Intramuros, Manila; f. 1963; Pres. and Gen. Man. D. L. MERCADO; life, health and accident.

Philippine Reinsurance Corporation: 516–517 Bank of Philippine Islands Bldg., Plaza Cervantes, Manila; f. 1958; Chair. SERGIO CORPUS; reinsurance in all branches.

Philippine Surety & Insurance Co. Inc.: 224 Natividad Bldg., Escolta, Manila; Pres. C. MARTIN.

Philippine Underwriters Corpn.: General managers for: Sterling Life Assurance Corpn., Filriters Guaranty Assurance Corpn., F.G.R. Bldg., Buendia Ave., Makati, Rizal; Chair. LUZ B. MAGSAYSAY; Pres. ATTY H. V. RODIS; general insurance.

Pioneer Insurance and Surety Corpn.: Pioneer House, 320 Nueva Corner, Escolta, Manila; f. 1954; cap. p.u. 10m.; Chair. JOHNNY CHENG; Pres. ROBERT COYIUTO.

Plaridel Surety & Insurance Company: 459 Plaza Sta. Cruz, Manila-D-404; f. 1946; Pres. HERMOGENES R. DIMAGIBA; Gen. Man. BONIFACIO L. HILARIO.

Provident Insurance Company of the Philippines: 416 Natividad Bldg., Escolta, Manila; Gen. Man. JOSE DE LEON.

Reinsurance Company of the Orient, Inc.: Rico Bldg., 533 United Nations Avenue, Ermita, Manila; f. 1956; Pres. J. G. BARRERA; Vice-Pres. A. PADILLA; Gen. Man. M. P. CRUZ; all classes.

Republic Surety & Insurance Co., Inc.: 206/210 Koh Bldg., Plaza Sta. Cruz, Manila; Pres. and Gen. Man. F. T. KOH.

Rico General Insurance Corporation: Third Floor, RICO Bldg., 535 United Nations Ave., Ermita, Manila; f. 1964; Chair. and Pres. Justice CARMELINO G. ALVENIDA; Gen. Man. ROMEO A. MALLARI.

Rico Life Insurance Co., Inc.: RICO Bldg., 533 United Nations Ave., Ermita, Manila; Chair. CARMELINO G. ALVENDIA; Pres. Hon. JAIME HERNANDEZ; Officer-in-charge MIGUEL P. CRUZ.

Rizal Surety and Insurance Co.: Roman R. Santos Building, Plaza Goiti, Manila; f. 1939; Chair. A. A. SANTOS.

South Sea Surety and Insurance Co. Inc.: 55 M. de Binondo, Manila; f. 1947; Pres. V. L. Co CHIEN.

Standard Insurance Co. Inc.: 5th Floor, Cardinal Bldg., cnr. F. Agoncillo and Herran Sts., Manila; f. 1958; Pres. Mrs. LOURDES T. ECHAUZ.

State Bonding & Insurance Co. Inc.: Jacinto Bldg., 375 Escolta, Manila; cap. p.u. 2.2m.; Chair. N. JACINTO.

Tabacalera Insurance Co., Inc.: Rufino Bldg., Ayala Ave., Makati, Rizal; f. 1937; Pres. ALEJANDRO ROS DE LACOUR; Chair. MANUEL P. MANAHAN.

Traders' Insurance & Surety Co.: 277 Juan Luna St., Manila; Pres. J. V. LIMPE; Gen. Man. J. T. LIMPE.

Union Surety & Insurance Co., Inc.: Metropolitan Theatre Bldg., Plaza Lawton, Manila; Pres. R. F. NAVARRO.

United Insurance Co., Inc.: Padillade los Reyes Bldg., Manila; Pres. I. K. YANG.

Universal Reinsurance Corporation: Insular Life Bldg., 6781 Ayala Ave., Makati, Rizal, P.O.B. 70, Commercial Center, Makati; f. 1971; Chair. ENRIQUE J. ZOBEL; Pres. SALVADOR ESTRADA.

Visayan Surety and Insurance Corpn.: Vista Bldg., Quiapo, Manila; Pres. F. Go CHAN.

Workmen's Insurance Co., Inc.: 6th Floor, G. E. Antonino Bldg., T.M. Kalaw, Ermita, Manila; f. 1961; Chair. FELIPE LIWANAG, Sr.; Pres. and Gen. Man. FIRMO O. LIWANAG; fire, motor vehicle, marine cargo and hull, transportation, accidents, casualty, workmen's compensation, bonds.

World-Wide Insurance & Surety Co. Inc.: 4th Floor, Cardinal Bldg., Corner Herran and F. Agoncillo Streets, Ermita, Manila; f. 1950; affiliated with Standard-Cardinal Life Insurance Companies; Pres. ROMEO R. ECHAUZ; fire, marine, motor car, accident, workmen's compensation, loans, mortgages, bonds, aviation.

The majority of the larger British, American and Canadian insurance companies are represented in Manila.

TRADE AND INDUSTRY

TRADING CORPORATION

National Export Trading Corporation: NETRACOR Bldg., Buendia Ave., Cnr. Tindalo St., Makati, Rizal; f. 1968; government-run agency, gives financial aid to producer-exporters, promotes exports generally; 91 employees; Pres. E. D. VILLATUYA; Gen. Man. J. A. RIVERA.

CHAMBERS OF COMMERCE AND INDUSTRY

Chamber of Agriculture and Natural Resources of the Philippines: 9th Floor, Manila Bank Bldg. Ayala Ave., Makati, Rizal.

Chamber of Commerce of the Philippines: Magallanes Drive, Manila; f. 1903; 1,420 mems.; Pres. WIGBERTO P. CLAVECILLA; Sec.-Treas. BENITO F. MEDINA; publ. *Commerce.*

Federation of Filipino-Chinese Chambers of Commerce Inc.: P.O.B. 23, 6th Floor, Federation Centre, Muelle de Binondo, Manila; Pres. RALPH NUBLA.

International Chamber of Commerce of Iloilo: 2nd Floor, Masonic Temple Bldg., Plaza Libertad, Iloilo; Pres. ANTONIO HECHANOVA.

Manila Chamber of Commerce Inc.: P.O.B. 763, Room 410, Shurdut Bldg., Intramuros, Manila; f. 1898; 56 mems.; Pres. M. V. BANE; Vice-Pres. M. N. LITTLE, B. R. C. HARRISON.

Mandaluyong Chamber of Commerce and Industry: Mandaluyong, Rizal.

Philippines Chamber of Industries: 6th Floor, L & S Bldg., 1515 Roxas Blvd., Manila; f. 1950; 650 mems.; Pres. EMILIO ABELLO; publ. *Industrial Philippines.*

Philippine Chinese Chamber of Commerce: 1122 Soler, Manila.

San Juan Chamber of Commerce and Industry: San Juan, Rizal.

There are other Philippine Chambers of Commerce in all the more important towns and seaports.

American Chamber of Commerce of the Philippines Inc.: P.O.B. 1836, Manila.

Cámara Oficial Española de Comercio (*Spanish Chamber of Commerce*): 510 Romero Salas, Ermita, Manila; f. 1899; Pres. ALEJANDRO ROS; Vice-Pres. LUIS ANTÚNEZ; publ. *Spanish Economic News* (weekly).

French Chamber of Commerce: P.O.B. 3095, Manila.

EMPLOYERS' ASSOCIATIONS

Base Metals Association of the Philippines: Manila Banking Corpn. Bldg., Ayala Ave., Makati, Rizal; 12 mems.; Chair. JESÚS S. CABARRUS; Pres. SEBASTIAN UGARTE; Sec. H. T. CAWILE.

Filipino Shipowners' Association: R.212 Magsaysay Bldg., T. M. Kalaw St., Ermita, Manila; f. 1950; 18 mems.; Chair. and Pres. GENEROSO F. TANSECO; Exec. Sec. ANTONIO A. TORRES.

National Federation of Sugar Cane Planters: Rm. 414, Gonzaga Bldg., Rizal Ave., Manila; f. 1928; Pres. Dr. TRINO MONTINOLA; Sec. EDUARDO L. LEDESMA.

Philippine Sugar Association: Suite 809, Sikatuna Building, Ayala Ave., Makati, Rizal; f. 1922; Pres. MANUEL ELIZALDE; Sec.-Treas. JOSÉ E. ROMERO; 19 mems.

Pulp and Paper Manufacturers' Association Inc.: Room 302, Magsaysay Bldg., Teodoro M. Kalan St., Ermita, Manila; f. 1959; Pres. FRANCISCO P. MONGE.

Sugar Producers' Co-operative Marketing Association, Inc.: 6th Floor, Philsugin Building, North Ave., Diliman, Quezon City; P.O.B. 3839, Manila; Pres. CIRO LOCSIN; Sec. JOSE MORAS.

Textile Mills Association of the Philippines, Inc. (Texphil): Manila Hotel Annex, Manila; f. 1956; 21 mems.; Pres. RAYMUNDO LORENZANA.

TRADE UNIONS

FEDERATIONS

Confederation of Citizens Labor Unions (CCLU): R.303 Free Press Building, 708 Rizal Ave., Manila; f. 1951; 21 affiliated unions; Pres. LEON O. TY.

Confederation of Unions in Government Corporations (CUGC): 10 Roosevelt Ave., Diliman, Quezon City; f. 1956; about 12 affiliates; Pres. EMMANUEL CLAVE.

Federation of Free Workers (FFW): Suite E, Ysmael Apts., 1845 Taft Ave., Manila; f. 1950; affiliated to the Brotherhood of Asian Trade Unions and the WCL; about 370 affiliated unions and 200,000 mems.; Pres. JOHNNY C. TAN; Exec. Vice-Pres. RAMON JABAR.

National Association of Trade Unions (NATU): Suite 401, San Luis Terraces, Ermita, Manila; f. 1954; about 27,000 mems.; Pres. IGNACIO P. LACSINA.

National Labour Union Inc.: 3199 Sta. Mesa Blvd., Manila; f. 1929; Pres. EULOGIO R. LERUM; Sec. ANTONIO V. POLICARPIO; 100,000 mems.; publ. *National Labor Unionist* (quarterly).

Philippines Association of Free Labor Unions (PAFLU): 1233 Tecson-Tindalo, Tondo, Manila; f. 1951; 380 affiliated unions, about 75,000 mems.; Pres. CIPRIANO CID; Exec. Sec. ISRAEL DE C. BOCOBO.

Philippines Trade Union Council (PTUC): 302–303 Cu Unjieng Bldg., Escolta, Manila; f. 1954; 49 affiliated unions, about 238,000 mems.; affiliated to ICFTU; Pres. CIPRIANO CID; Gen. Sec. JOSÉ J. HERNANDEZ.

Philippine Transport and General Workers' Organization (PTGWO): Port Area, Manila; 180 affiliates; 45,000 mems.; Pres. PEDRO D. FERNANDEZ; Sec. ALEJANDRO D. LAZARO.

Textile and Allied Workers' Federation: Cu Unjieng Bldg., Escolta, Manila; 3,400 mems.; Pres. V. L. ARNIEGO.

Trade Union Congress of the Philippines: Suite 613, Shurdut Bldg., Intramuros, Manila; affiliates include PTGWO, CUGCO, PCWF, etc.; 1 million mems.

TRANSPORT AND TOURISM

RAILWAYS

Philippine National Railways: 943 Claro M. Recto Ave., Manila; f. 1892; Government owned; 1,067 km. of tracks (1971); the northern line runs from Manila to San Fernando, La Unión, and the southern line from Manila to Legaspi, Albay; Chair. Col. SALVADOR T. VILLA; Vice-Chair./Man. Dir. Col. NICANOR T. JIMENEZ.

Philippine Railway Co.: P.O.B. 300, Iloilo City, Panay; f. 1907; under Development Bank of the Philippines; operates in Panay Island only; 116 km.; Man. ANATOLIO T. VIRAY.

ROADS

Bureau of Public Highways: Manila; there are 21,316 km. of national roads, 46,739 km. of municipal and provincial roads, 14,378 km. feeder roads and 6,715 km. city roads; Commissioner BALTAZAR AQUINO.

Philippine Motor Association: P.O.B. 999, Manila; Pres. MANUEL LIM; Vice-Pres. JUAN E. TUASON.

SHIPPING

NATIONAL LINES

Botelho Bulk Transport Corpn.: 8th Floor, Antonino Building, T. M. Kalaw St., Ermita, Manila; f. 1966; 5 vessels; Pres. A. A. R. BOTELHO.

De La Rama Steamship Co., Inc.: P.O.B. 1800, Rizal D-708; Chair. and Pres. ESTEBAN R. OSMENA; services to U.S.A., Hong Kong and Japan.

Eastern Shipping Lines, Inc.: UPL Bldg., Intramuros, Manila; 6 vessels; Pres. Cong. JAMES L. CHIONGBIAN; services to Japan and Philippines.

Lusteveco (Luzon Stevedoring Co.): Tacoma and Second Sts., Port Area, P.O.B. 582, Manila; f. 1909; worldwide tanker and towage operations; fleet of 36 tankers, 182 tugs and 674 barges; Chair. VINCENTE G. PUYAT; Pres. DONALD I. MARSHALL.

Magsaysay Lines, Inc.: Magsaysay Building, 520 T. M. Kalaw St., Ermita, Manila (P.O.B. 21); 4 vessels; Chair. ROBERT C. F. HO; Pres. MIGUEL A. MAGSAYSAY; Shipping agents and brokers.

Maritime Company of the Philippines: 105 Dasmarinas St., (P.O.B. 805), Manila; 9 cargo vessels; Chair. J. P. FERNANDEZ; Man. WILLIAM R. PALOU.

Philippine Ace Lines, Inc.: 203-6 Development Bank of the Philippines Bldg., Port Area, Manila; 3 vessels; Chair. CLEMENTE V. TANKEH; cargo and liner services to Japan and U.S.A.

Philippine President Lines Inc.: 1022-1024 United Nations Ave., Manila; 12 cargo vessels; Chair. A. MONTELIBANO; Pres. E. T. YAP; services: U.S.A., Japan, Europe.

Sweet Lines, Inc.: Arellano cor Manalib Extension, Cebu City; 13 passenger-cargo vessels; Pres. L. POH; Gen. Man. P. C. LIM.

Transocean Transport Corpn.: Magsaysay Bldg., 520 T. M. Kalaw St., Ermita, Manila (P.O.B. 3050); 5 cargo vessels; Pres. MIGUEL A. MAGSAYSAY.

United Philippine Lines, Inc.: UPL Bldg., Santa Clara St., Intramuros, Manila; Chair. and Pres. Col. GENEROSO F. TANSECO; Sen. Vice-Pres. and Treas. RENATO M. TANESCO; services to Japan, Hong Kong, and U.S.A.

William Lines, Inc.: P.O.B. 147, Cebu City; passenger and cargo inter-island service; 11 pass/cargo vessels; Pres. W. L. CHIONGBIAN; Gen. Man. A. S. CHIONGBIAN.

CIVIL AVIATION

In addition to the international airport at Manila, there are eight trunk airports, 23 secondary airports and 90 airstrips in the domestic system.

Air Manila*: Manila International Airport, Pasay City; f. 1964; domestic and regional services; fleet of 9 Fairchild F-27, 2 Boeing 707, 8 DC-3; Chair. RICARDO C. SILVERIO.

Filipinas Orient Airways Inc.*: Head Office: Domestic Terminal, Manila International Airport, Pasay City; f. 1965; Pres. HONORIO POBLADOR Jr.; domestic routes; fleet of four YS-11, seven DC-3, one DC-6 B, two Boeing 707.

Philippine Air Lines Inc. (PAL): PAL Bldg., Ayala Ave., Makati, Rizal, P.O.B. 954 Manila; f. 1946; Chair. and Pres. BENIGNO P. TODA, Jr.; internal services; and to San Francisco, Honolulu, Sydney, Melbourne, Singapore, Hong Kong, Taipei, Tokyo, Bangkok, Karachi, Rome, Amsterdam, Frankfurt; fleet of two DC-3, two DC-8-63, two DC-8-50, two DC-8-30, three One-Eleven 500, thirteen HS 748.

Manila is also served by the following airlines: Allegheny Airlines, Air France, Alitalia, China Air Lines, Cathay Pacific Airways Ltd. (CPA), EgyptAir, JAL, KLM, Northwest Orient Airlines (NWA), Pan American, PIA, Qantas, SAS, Singapore Airlines, Swissair, Thai International and Air Viet-Nam.

* Merged with PAL from April 1st, 1973.

TOURISM

Department of Tourism: 8th Floor, Plywood Industries Bldg., T. M. Kalaw St., Ermita, Manila (P.O.B. 3451, Manila); Department of Tourism Sec. JOSE D. ASPIRAS.

Philippine Tourist and Travel Association, Inc.: Plywood Industries Bldg., T. Kalaw St., Ermita, Manila; Pres. MANUEL H. NIETO, Jr.

PRINCIPAL THEATRE COMPANIES

Bayanihan Philippine Dance Company: Philippine Women's University, Taft Ave., Manila; f. 1957; regular programmes; efforts towards a folk dance revival and the emergence of a native dance tradition; occasional subsidies from the Board of Travel and Tourist Industry, government grants for foreign tours; Music Dir. LUCRECIA R. KASILAG; Artistic Dir. JOSE LARDIZABAL.

Filippinescas Dance Company: 41 Timog (South) Ave., Quezon City; f. 1957; private company; folkloric ballets in native dance styles; Founder-Dir. Madame LEONOR OROSA GOQUINGCO.

PNC Baranggay Folk Dance Troupe: Philippine Normal College, Taft Ave., Manila; f. 1946; study and propagation of Philippine folk dances, songs and games; national and international performances; Founder-Dir. Mrs. PAZ-CIELO A. BELMONTE.

PRINCIPAL ORCHESTRAS

The Manila Symphony Orchestra: P.O.B. 664, Manila; f. 1926; regular symphonic, opera and ballet programmes; encourages young artists; Music Dir. and Conductor OSCAR C. YATCO.

National Philharmonic Orchestra: Suite B, 2nd Floor, Metropolitan Theatre Bldg., Plaza Lawton, Manila; f. 1960; seasonal symphony concerts; sponsors inter-national operas and ballets; privately financed; Pres., Musical Dir. and Conductor REDENTOR ROMERO.

Celebrity Concerts: Suite B, 2nd Floor, Metropolitan Theatre Bldg., Plaza Lawton, Manila; f. 1964; sponsors appearances of top international concert artists and group attractions not accommodated within the regular season of the National Philharmonic Society of the Philippines; Pres. REDENTOR ROMERO.

ATOMIC ENERGY

National Science Development Board: Bicutan, Taguig, Rizal; the policy-making body for science and technology; the Philippine Atomic Energy Commission and the National Institute of Science and Technology and 5 others are its implementing agencies, while 7 others are attached to it; Chair. FLORENCIO A. MEDINA; Vice-Chair. PEDRO G. AFABLE.

Philippine Atomic Energy Commission: Commonwealth Ave., Diliman, Quezon City, D-505; f. 1958; the official body dealing with nuclear energy activities in the Philippines, under the supervision of the National Science Development Board. It has a 1,000-kW. swimming pool research reactor for research, training and production of radioisotopes. Its research centre conducts studies in agriculture, biology, medicine, chemistry, physics and nuclear engineering. Technical assistance is received mainly from International Atomic Energy Agency, United States Agency for International Development, Colombo Plan and through bilateral agreements with other nations. Commissioner Dr. LIBRADO D. IBE.

UNIVERSITIES

Adamson University: Manila; 336 teachers, 10,144 students.

Aquinas University: Legazpi City; 155 teachers, 4,000 students.

Araneta University: Rizal; 180 teachers, 3,700 students.

Arellano University: Manila; 233 teachers, 7,745 students.

Ateneo de Manila University: Manila; 460 teachers, 7,402 students.

University of Banguio: Banguio City; 232 teachers, 8,282 students.

Bicol University: Legazpi City; 400 teachers, 12,522 students.

Central Luzon State University: Munoz; 168 teachers, 3,000 students.

Central Mindanao University: Bukidnon; 141 teachers, 1,820 students.

Central Philippine University: Iloilo City; 247 teachers, 6,457 students.

Centro Escolar University: Manila; 308 teachers, 10,836 students

De La Salle College: Manila; 190 teachers, 3,400 students.

Divine Word University: Tacloban City.

University of the East: Manila; 1,548 teachers, 64,500 students.

University of the Eastern Philippines: Catarman, Samar.

Far Eastern University: Manila; 1,300 teachers, 52,194 students.

Feati University: Manila; 595 teachers, 25,532 students.

Foundation University: Dumaguete City: 121 teachers, 3,500 students.

University of Manila: Manila; 356 teachers, 10,000 students.

Manila Central University: Manila; 202 teachers, 6,187 students.

Mindanao State University: Marawi City; 317 teachers, 5,777 students.

University of Mindanao: Davao City; c. 200 teachers, 18,300 students.

National University: Manila.

University of Negros Occidental-Recoletos: Bacolod; 222 teachers, 6,930 students.

University of Northern Philippines: Ilocos Sur; 126 teachers, 1,633 students.

Notre Dame University of Cotabate: Cotabate City; 122 teachers, 3,445 students.

University of Nueva Caceres: Naga City; 258 teachers, 6,497 students.

University of Pangasinan: Dagupan City; 333 teachers, 10,986 students.

Philippine Women's University: Manila; 549 teachers, 8,145 students.

University of the Philippines: Quezon City; 2,452 teachers, 17,886 students.

Manuel L. Quezon University: Manila; 489 teachers, 8,426 students.

Saint Louis University: Baguio City; 270 teachers, 13,500 students.

University of San Agustin: Iloilo City; 314 teachers, 10,086 students.

University of San Carlos: Cebu City; 301 teachers, 9,042 students.

University of Santo Tomás: Manila; 1,436 teachers, 33,587 students.

Silliman University: Dumaguete City; 340 teachers, 5,248 students.

University of Southern Philippines: Cebu City; 166 teachers, 5,877 students.

South Western University: Cebu City; 350 teachers, 12,527 students.

University of the Visavayas: Cebu City; 508 teachers, 19,946 students.

Xavier University: Cagayan de Oro City; 212 teachers, 4,128 students.

PORTUGUESE OVERSEAS TERRITORIES

STATES
ANGOLA (Portuguese West Africa), MOZAMBIQUE (Portuguese East Africa)

PROVINCES
THE CAPE VERDE ISLANDS, GUINEA (BISSAU), MACAO, PORTUGUESE TIMOR, SÃO TOMÉ AND PRÍNCIPE

INTRODUCTION

In May 1972 a new Organic Law for the Overseas Territories was enacted by the Portuguese National Assembly, becoming effective in January 1973. Under this law Angola and Mozambique are designated as States, each headed by a Governor-General who has the status of a Minister of State and who can attend Cabinet meetings. Together with Angola and Mozambique, each Province has a Legislative Assembly and a Consultative Council which have more autonomy in internal administration than the previous Legislative Council had. The Assemblies meet twice a year for periods not exceeding four months; they legislate on home affairs, collect taxes and are responsible for their respective budgets. A Governor is appointed to each Province by the President of Portugal. Elections to the Legislative Assemblies throughout the Overseas Territories were held in March 1973.

Courts of First Instance administer the Legal Code of Metropolitan Portugal. Cases may be finally referred to the Court of Second Instance and the Supreme Court in Lisbon.

Following the military *coup* in Lisbon in April 1974 and the consequent change in government, negotiations have taken place with several of the liberation movements active in the Overseas Territories on the question of their future status. The new President, Gen. António de Spínola, has promised the native populations the right to decide their own future.

The *Acção Nacional Popular*, the political party which formerly represented the Portuguese Government in the Overseas Territories, was abolished after the April 1974 *coup*.

Minister for Interritorial Co-ordination: Dr. ANTÓNIO DE ALMEIDA SANTOS.

ANGOLA (PORTUGUESE WEST AFRICA)

Angola lies on the west coast of Africa between Zaire and South West Africa (Namibia), and is bordered by Zambia on the east. Since 1961, Portuguese forces have been fighting nationalist guerrilla forces on several fronts (*see* Political Parties p. 1234), and some 55,000 Portuguese troops are stationed in Angola.

STATISTICAL SURVEY

AREA AND POPULATION

AREA (sq. km.)	POPULATION (1970 Census)	
	Total	Luanda (capital)
1,246,700	5,673,046*	475,328†

* In addition over 600,000 Angolan refugees live in exile, mostly in Zaire, and nationalist-held areas may contain over 100,000 people.

† Of which: 124,817 Whites, 37,974 Mestiços, 312,240 Blacks.

BIRTHS, MARRIAGES AND DEATHS (1971)

CHURCH BAPTISMS	REGISTERED MARRIAGES	REGISTERED DEATHS
116,314	23,968	15,136

DISTRIBUTION OF POPULATION BY DISTRICT
(1970)

DISTRICT	AREA (sq. km.)	POPULATION	DENSITY (per sq. km.)
Cabinda	7,270	80,857	11.12
Zaire	40,130	41,766	1.04
Uíge	55,818	386,037	6.91
Luanda	33,789	560,589	16.59
Cuanza Norte	27,106	298,062	10.99
Cuanza Sul	59,269	458,592	7.73
Malanje	101,028	558,630	5.52
Lunda	167,786	302,538	1.80
Benguela	37,808	474,897	12.56
Huambo	30,667	837,627	27.31
Bié	71,870	650,337	9.04
Moxico	199,786	213,119	1.06
Cuando-Cubango	192,079	112,073	0.58
Moçâmedes	55,946	53,058	0.94
Huíla	166,348	644,864	3.87
TOTAL	1,246,700	5,673,046	4.55

OTHER MAIN TOWNS
POPULATION (1970 Census)

Nova Lisboa	61,885	Sá da Bandeira . 31,674
Lobito	59,528	Malange . . 31,599
Benguela	40,996	Cabinda . . 21,124

AGRICULTURE
PRINCIPAL CROPS

	AREA ('ooo hectares)			PRODUCTION ('ooo metric tons)			YIELD (100 kg. per hectare)		
	1969	1970	1971	1969	1970	1971	1969	1970	1971
Wheat	20.0*	20.0*	20.0*	14.0	20.0	20.0*	7.0*	10.0*	10.0*
Maize	600.0*	500.0*	500.0*	540.0	456.0	404.0	9.0*	9.1*	8.1*
Millet and Sorghum	91.0*	93.0*	93.0*	78.0	78.0	78.0	8.6*	8.4*	8.4*
Rice	15.0*	25.0*	22.0*	16.0	39.0	34.0*	10.5*	15.5*	15.5*
Potatoes	5.0*	5.0*	5.0*	34.0	34.0	34.0*	63.0*	63.0*	63.0*
Sweet Potatoes, Yams	17.0*	18.0*	n.a.	145.0	147.0	n.a.	85.0*	82.0*	n.a.
Cassava (Manioc)	120.0*	120.0*	n.a.	1,590.0	1,600.0	n.a.	133.0*	133.0*	n.a.
Dry Beans	120.0*	120.0*	120.0*	64.0	66.0	65.0*	5.3*	5.5*	5.4*
Oranges, Tangerines	n.a.	n.a.	n.a.	81.0	82.0	82.0*	n.a.	n.a.	n.a.
Palm Kernels	n.a.	n.a.	n.a.	17.5	16.6	13.5	n.a.	n.a.	n.a.
Palm Oil	n.a.	n.a.	n.a.	38.0	38.0	38.0*	n.a.	n.a.	n.a.
Groundnuts	47.0*	47.0*	47.0*	32.0	32.0	32.0*	6.8*	6.8*	6.8*
Cottonseed	72.0	79.0	89.0	47.0	61.0	72.0	6.5	7.7	7.4
Sesame Seed	6.0*	6.0*	6.0*	2.0*	2.0*	2.0*	3.3*	3.3*	3.3*
Castor Beans	13.0*	13.0*	13.0*	5.0	5.0	5.0*	3.8*	3.8*	3.8*
Coffee	n.a.	n.a.	n.a.	215.0	204.0	228.0	n.a.	n.a.	n.a.
Tobacco	5.0	6.0	6.0	4.1	5.0	5.5	7.8	7.7	8.5
Cotton (lint)	72.0	79.0	89.0	23.0	30.0	33.0	3.3	3.8	3.7
Kenaf	2.0*	2.0*	2.0*	2.0*	2.0*	2.0*	10.0*	10.0*	10.0*
Sisal	70.0*	70.0*	n.a.	67.5	68.4	53.0	9.6*	9.8*	n.a.
Sugar Cane†	14.0*	14.0*	15.0*	684.6	683.0	764.0	489.0*	488.0*	499.0*

* FAO estimate.   † Crop year ending in year stated; 1971/72: 880,128 metric tons.

Source: FAO, *Production Yearbook 1971.*

COTTON PRODUCTION
(tons)

		UNGINNED COTTON	COTTON FIBRE
1961	. . .	13,099	4,323
1962	. . .	22,500	7,425
1963	. . .	13,700	4,521
1964	. . .	13,609	4,491
1965	. . .	19,506	6,437
1966	. . .	20,308	6,719
1967	. . .	27,361	9,032
1968	. . .	38,867	12,826
1969	. . .	60,057	19,820
1970	. . .	81,555	28,819
1971	. . .	86,013	35,478

COFFEE PRODUCTION
(tons)

VARIETIES	1969	1970	1971
Robusta:			
Ambriz . .	147,000	131,400	
Amboim . .	41,100	42,100	
Cazengo . .	17,000	21,300	n.a.
Cabinda . .	1,800	1,800	
Arábica . .	8,100	7,400	
TOTAL . .	215,000	204,000	228,000

DAIRY PRODUCE

		1971	1972
Milk (litres)	. . .	22,948,000	n.a.
Butter (kg.)	. . .	456,000	439,000
Cheese (kg.)	. . .	1,444,000	2,022,000

LIVESTOCK

		1971
Cattle	. .	3,797,000
Goats	. .	1,848,000
Pigs .	. .	1,343,000
Sheep	. .	361,000

Chickens: 4,500,000 (FAO estimate for 1970/71).

FORESTRY
ROUNDWOOD PRODUCTION
('ooo cu. metres)

1969	. . .	6,459
1970	. . .	7,065
1971	. . .	7,340

FISHING
TOTAL CATCH
(metric tons)

1970	. . .	377,770
1971	. . .	316,329
1972	. . .	599,110

MINING
(metric tons)

		1968	1969	1970	1971
Haematite Iron Ore	. . .	3,218,212	5,477,657	6,090,888	6,157,819
Manganese Ore	. . .	9,150	29,070	23,000	23,000
Crude Petroleum	. . .	749,514	2,457,512	5,065,105	5,721,331
Diamonds (carats)	. . .	1,667,133	2,021,532	2,395,552	2,413,021
Asphalt Rock	. . .	30,603	39,282	36,956	56,100
Sea Salt	. . .	72,496	80,181	87,743	90,284
Gypsum	. . .	10,160	n.a.	n.a.	n.a.

PORTUGUESE OVERSEAS STATES—ANGOLA

INDUSTRY
(metric tons)

	1970	1971	1972
Sugar	78,766	76,073	84,215
Beer ('000 litres)	70,794	81,907	93,884
Fishmeal	74,151	72,488	128,599
Cement	446,249	529,594	624,394
Cotton Blankets (number)	579,000	679,000	759,000
Flour	68,439	72,023	78,637
Soap	14,810	15,168	19,735
Tobacco	2,025	2,188	2,468
Butane	7,382	7,043	8,136
Fuel Oil	391,679	388,847	377,685
Gas Oil	98,377	100,807	104,514
Motor Spirit	56,118	52,385	48,065
Paraffin	n.a.	n.a.	n.a.
Asphalt	13,499	16,733	27,446

FINANCE

100 centavos = 1 Angolan escudo; 1,000 escudos are known as a *conto*.

Coins: 10, 20 and 50 centavos; 1, 2½, 10 and 20 escudos.

Notes: 20, 50, 100, 500 and 1,000 escudos.

Exchange rates (April 1974): £1 sterling = 59.45 escudos; U.S. $1 = 25.125 escudos.

100 Angolan escudos = £1.68 = $3.98.

ORDINARY BUDGET
('000 escudos)

ORDINARY RECEIPTS	1971	1972	ORDINARY EXPENDITURE	1971	1972
Direct Taxes	1,155,001	1,283,501	Provincial Debt	546,330	616,848
Indirect Taxes	1,833,000	2,163,000	Governments, etc.	38,840	45,394
Special Duties	1,140,201	1,766,399	Pensions, etc.	110,000	125,000
Dues, Service Returns	538,006	641,666	Administration	2,363,249	2,941,054
State Enterprises, etc.	401,120	371,940	Treasury	215,272	242,586
Capital Returns, etc.	84,760	74,670	Justice	145,003	154,309
Repayments, etc.	148,296	175,173	Development	3,097,620	3,517,854
Miscellaneous	3,390,534	3,756,359	Defence	796,176	876,970
			Navy	50,058	51,701
			Miscellaneous	1,317,370	1,648,016
			Other	11,000	12,976
TOTAL	8,690,918	10,232,708	TOTAL	8,690,918	10,232,708

DEVELOPMENT EXPENDITURE
(1968–73—million escudos)

Agriculture, Forestry and Fishing . . .	2,041
Mining	11,600
Transport and Communications . . .	3,779
Manufacturing Industry . . .	3,361
Education and Research . . .	1,358
Power Supplies . . .	1,238
Other Development	2,007
	25,384

MILITARY EXPENDITURE 1971
(million escudos)

SOURCE OF FINANCING	
Territory's Ordinary Budget . . .	580.0
Autonomous Bodies . . .	249.2
Extraordinary Tax for Defence of Angola .	350.0
Special Credit to be Authorized During 1971	270.8
Overseas Military Defence Fund .	67.0
Contribution from Portugal's Extraordinary Budget	250.0
Other	151.0
TOTAL	1,918.0

In addition, territorial budget estimates for 1971 include 618.0 million escudos for other military and security expenditure.

Source: UN General Assembly document A/8723/Add. 3, September 1st, 1972.

BALANCE OF PAYMENTS
(million escudos)

	1970			1971		
	Credit	Debit	Balance	Credit	Debit	Balance
Goods	9,196	10,271	−1,075	9,166	11,388	−2,222
Tourism	40	506	− 466	44	556	− 512
Transport	924	332	592	878	308	570
Insurance	17	21	− 4	20	23	− 3
Capital Earnings . . .	43	671	− 628	13	210	− 197
Official Transfers . . .	744	213	531	625	347	278
Private Transfers . . .	12	342	− 330	14	324	− 310
Other Services . . .	1,274	1,255	19	1,316	803	513
CURRENT ACCOUNT . . .	12,250	13,611	−1,361	12,076	13,959	−1,883
Capital Account . . .	1,058	457	601	877	807	70
COMBINED CURRENT AND CAPITAL ACCOUNT	13,308	14,068	− 760	12,953	14,766	−1,813

EXTERNAL TRADE
(excluding gold)
('000 escudos)

	1968	1969	1970	1971	1972
Imports	8,709,858	9,261,398	10,594,665	12,127,640	10,688,549
Exports	7,787,946	9,387,420	12,172,187	12,147,051	13,915,496

PRINCIPAL COMMODITIES

('ooo escudos)

IMPORTS	1970	1971	1972
Vehicles and Accessories	1,017,683	1,392,909	1,184,316
Iron and Steel	849,372	996,453	942,975
Textiles	523,239	516,007	n.a.
Wine	578,796	405,457	291,728
Tractors	223,820	290,492	221,770
Clothing	173,000	268,054	n.a.
Wheat	139,690	160,220	142,200
Locomotives, etc.	72,117	57,768	n.a.
Medicaments	363,698	318,862	409,503
Fuel Oil	187,238	206,919	n.a.
Excavating Machinery . . .	195,386	243,124	n.a.
Olive Oil	116,834	161,863	n.a.
Fertilizers	79,436	138,648	n.a.

EXPORTS	1970	1971	1972
Coffee	3,879,997	4,029,018	3,834,941
Crude Petroleum	1,397,378	1,811,551	3,535,396
Diamonds	2,340,087	1,523,239	1,583,059
Iron Ore	1,422,529	1,188,231	1,011,666
Raw Cotton	421,711	648,538	284,210
Sisal	237,640	221,192	332,037
Fish Meal for Cattle . . .	288,716	209,340	n.a.
Wood	198,679	189,273	175,072
Maize	314,588	181,809	142,760
Fuel Oil	117,639	155,465	125,367
Dried Fish	107,055	128,097	138,793
Wood Pulp	111,465	114,636	n.a.
Palm Oil	62,491	63,849	42,637
Tobacco and Products . . .	53,864	61,455	n.a.
Fresh Fish	50,114	114,979	n.a.
Bananas	118,366	174,806	264,082
Manioc	49,132	28,494	15,922
Sugar	42,158	32,915	42,431
Dried Beans	42,668	77,944	n.a.

TRADE BALANCE BY PRINCIPAL AREAS

(1965–72—million escudos)

	1965	1966	1967	1968	1969	1970	1971	1972
Foreign Countries . .	708.1	636.6	− 735.1	−399.0	−199.6	901.5	−380.2	1,782.2
Portugal . . .	−638.3	−278.1	− 518.1	497.8	75.8	444.8	−170.2	1,147.5
Other Portuguese Territories . . .	− 28.9	− 49.5	36.5	− 14.4	73.5	20.9	− 58.2	121.5
Others* . . .	105.3	102.8	145.8	189.3	176.8	210.3	269.6	n.a.
NET TRADE BALANCE .	146.2	411.8	−1,070.9	−921.9	126.0	1,577.5	−339.7	3,226.9

* Includes mainly supplies to navigation.

PRINCIPAL COUNTRIES

IMPORTS	1970	1971	1972
Portugal	3,728,308	3,832,299	2,485,084
Mozambique	187,321	247,158	
Macao	112,404	198,299	} 226,026
Other Portuguese Territories . . .	3,427	2,918	
Belgium-Luxembourg . . .	305,248	393,944	401,538
Denmark	128,994	111,745	n.a.
France	570,618	556,849	636,290
Germany, Federal Republic . .	1,185,282	1,378,987	1,320,282
Iran	145,691	180,154	320,153
Italy	336,552	453,729	480,580
Japan	459,426	673,776	616,510
Netherlands	144,880	266,777	n.a.
Norway	95,444	114,689	n.a.
South Africa	419,761	443,460	490,336
Spain	84,387	167,175	n.a.
Sweden	146,981	155,743	208,707
Switzerland	118,051	152,365	n.a.
United Kingdom	992,597	1,092,233	956,129
U.S.A.	1,149,957	1,339,616	1,364,151

EXPORTS	1970	1971	1972
Portugal	4,173,095	3,698,708	3,632,551
Mozambique	206,585	210,661	
Cape Verde Islands . . .	52,581	119,563	
São Tomé and Príncipe . .	50,337	41,663	} 347,510
Other Portuguese Territories . .	14,554	14,777	
Belgium-Luxembourg . . .	125,191	182,085	n.a.
Canada	249,538	704,741	1,636,992
Denmark	407,664	407,357	59,341
France	151,723	193,734	417,568
Germany, Federal Republic . .	771,648	319,521	581,540
Italy	79,760	93,112	n.a.
Japan	797,606	1,294,901	1,386,974
Netherlands	1,318,157	828,952	545,428
South Africa	146,493	161,144	152,858
Spain	560,689	404,254	612,772
Trinidad and Tobago . . .	21,906	261,563	n.a.
United Kingdom	431,783	178,353	479,304
U.S.A.	1,898,618	2,379,666	2,273,897
Zaire	143,507	144,155	n.a.

TRANSPORT

RAILWAYS

	PASSENGERS CARRIED		FREIGHT (metric tons)	
	1971	1972	1971	1972
Luanda Railway . .	693,285	728,307	400,686	319,066
Moçâmedes Railway . .	272,128	333,000	6,405,607	4,863,860
Benguela Railway . .	1,214,503	1,412,825	2,050,183	2,688,979

ROADS
(Motor Vehicles)

	1971	1972
Cars	102,604	115,452
Lorries . . .	23,604	24,958
Motor Cycles . .	18,386	19,017
Tractors . . .	8,108	8,795
TOTAL	152,702	168,222

SHIPPING
('ooo metric tons)

	LUANDA		LOBITO		MOÇÂMEDES		ANGOLA	
	1970	1971	1970	1971	1970	1971	1970	1971
Goods Loaded . .	966.5	798.6	935.5	957.2	6,253.3	5,481.7	12,623.7	12,431.7
Goods Unloaded . .	704.4	712.7	738.7	962.1	154.1	183.3	1,720.3	2,033.5

Vessels handled: (1971) 5,769; (1972) 6,084.

CIVIL AVIATION
(Angola Airlines—TAAG)

	1971	1972
Passengers Carried .	174,380	169,560
Freight Transported (tons) .	2,768	2,437
Mail Transported (tons) .	892	855
Kilometres Flown . .	4,720,743	4,726,330

EDUCATION
(1971–72)

	SCHOOLS	TEACHERS	PUPILS
Primary	5,103	11,887	493,276
Secondary . . .	241	3,834	66,319
University . . .	1	273	2,435
Ecclesiastic . . .	3	28	131

Source: Direcção Provincial dos Serviços de Estatística, Luanda.

THE CONSTITUTION

By special decrees of February 1955 and April and October 1961, Angola was divided into 15 districts as follows: Cabinda, Uíge, Zaire, Luanda, Cuanza Norte, Cuanza Sul, Malanje, Lunda, Benguela, Huambo, Bié, Cuando Cubango, Moxico, Moçâmedes and Huíla. Each district is again divided into regions supervised by an administrator who acts as the resident magistrate. In 1971 the 15 districts became 16, with the addition of Cunene.

The Governor-General holds office for four years, with possible extensions for further two-year periods. Angola has its own Legislative Assembly with 53 members. The Legislative Assembly meets twice annually for periods not exceeding four months. Although the Governor-General retains the right to veto, the Legislative Assembly can, by a two-thirds majority, block projects put forward to them, thereby invoking arbitration by the central Government. The Angola Legislative Assembly legislates on all home affairs, collects taxes, and is responsible for the budget. The central Government retains the right of appointing diplomatic representatives and making treaties with foreign states. It also supervises the administration and economy of Angola, and is responsible for defence.

THE GOVERNMENT

Governor-General: Gen. SILVINO SILVÉRIO MARQUES.

LEGISLATIVE ASSEMBLY

The Legislative Assembly was set up by the Organic Law for the Overseas Territories, enacted in May 1972. Elections took place in March 1973. Thirty-two out of the 53 members were elected by direct suffrage. The remainder were elected by "interest groups" such as the public services, religious groups and corporative bodies. Official voting figures were that, out of an electorate of 584,000 (population of Angola is 5.7 million), 85.6 per cent of the electorate voted. The racial composition of the Legislative Assembly is 29 white and 24 black.

CONSULTATIVE COUNCIL

The Consultative Council assists the Governor-General in the day-to-day business of government. Elections to the Consultative Council took place by direct suffrage within economic and social groups in March 1973.

POLITICAL PARTIES

Conferência das Organizações Nacionais das Colónias Portuguesas (CONCP): 18 rue Dirah, Hydra, Algiers, Algeria; f. 1961; central organization for MPLA, Angola, FRELIMO, Mozambique, PAIGC, Guinea, CLSTP, São Tomé.

Concelho Supremo de Libertação de Angola (CSLA) (*Angola Supreme Liberation Council*): Kinshasa, Zaire; f. 1972 by a union of the FNLA and the MPLA; meets at least twice a year; Pres. ROBERTO HOLDEN; Vice-Pres. Dr. AGOSTINHO NETO.

Frente Nacional de Libertação de Angola (FNLA) (*Angolan National Liberation Front*): Kinshasa, Zaire; f. 1962 by union of the *União dos Populações de Angola* and the *Partido Democrático Angolano*; have set up a Government-in-exile (GRAE); Leader ROBERTO HOLDEN.

Movimento Popular de Libertação de Angola (MPLA) (*Angola Popular Liberation Movement*): P.O.B. 1595, Lusaka, Zambia; f. 1956; Pres. Dr. AGOSTINHO NETO.

União Nacional para a Independência Total de Angola (UNITA) (*National Union for the Complete Independence of Angola*): Headquarters in Bié province; f. 1966; Leader Dr. JONAS SAVIMBI.

União das Populações de Angola (UPA): Kinshasa, Zaire; f. 1954; formed the FNLA with *Partido Democrático Angolano* in 1962; Leader ROBERTO HOLDEN.

JUDICIAL SYSTEM

Courts of First Instance. These administer the Legal Code of Metropolitan Portugal. Cases may be finally referred to the Court of Second Instance and the Supreme Court in Lisbon.

RELIGION

Most of the population follows traditional beliefs.

ROMAN CATHOLIC CHURCH

Metropolitan See:
Archbishop of Luanda . Most Rev. MANUEL NUNES GABRIEL, Caixa Postal 1230, Luanda.

Suffragan Sees:
Benguela . (vacant), Caixa Postal 670, Benguela.

Carmona-São Salvador . Rt. Rev. FRANCISCO DA MATA MOURISCA, Caixa Postal 239, Carmona.

Luso . . Rt. Rev. FRANCISCO ESTEVES DIAS, Caixa Postal 88, Luso.

Malanje . . Rt. Rev. EDUARDO ANDRÉ MUACA, Caixa Postal 192, Malanje.

Nova Lisboa . Rt. Rev. AMÉRICO HENRIQUES, Caixa Postal 10, Nova Lisboa.

Sá da Bandeira Rt. Rev. EURICO DIAS NOGUEIRA, Caixa Postal 231, Sá da Bandeira.

São Tomé e Príncipe . (vacant), Caixa Postal 146, São Tomé.

Silva Porto . Rt. Rev. MANUEL ANTÓNIO PIRES, Caixa Postal 16, Silva Porto.

There are 225 missions with a personnel of 1,441; Roman Catholics number 2,793,668.

The Baptists and Methodists have a number of missionary stations. There are about 800,000 Protestants.

THE PRESS

DAILIES

Boletim Oficial de Angola: Caixa Postal 1306, Luanda; f. 1845.

Diario de Luanda: Caixa Postal 1290, Rua Serpa Pinto, Luanda; f. 1930; owned by Gráfica Portugal; Editor Dr. FRANCISCO DA SILVEIRA PINTO; evenings and Sunday; circ. 18,000.

O Lobito: Caixa Postal 335, Lobito; published by Organização Publicitaria e Artística; Editor SAUL QUEIROZ; evening; circ. 12,000.

A Provincia de Angola: Caixa Postal 1312; f. 1923; owned by the Empresa Gráfica de Angola; Editor JAIME DE FIGUEIREDO; mornings and Sunday; circ. 41,000.

PERIODICALS

Actualidade Economica: Caixa Postal 16462, Luanda; weekly; Dir. ANTÓNIO PIRES.

Angola Norte: Caixa Postal 339, Malanje; weekly; Dir. Dr. ALBERTINA VICENTE VIEIRA.

O Apostolado: Caixa Postal 1230, Luanda; weekly; published by the Catholic Missions of Portugal; Dir. Rev. HENRIQUE ALVES.

Cuanza Sul: Caixa Postal 202, Novo Redondo; weekly; Dir. J. BARBOSA LOUREIRO.

Ecos do Norte: Caixa Postal 402, Malanje; twice weekly; Dir. TIMÓTEO DE ABREU COSTA.

Jornal de Benguela: Caixa Postal 17, Benguela; twice weekly; Dir. HORÁCIO SILVA.

Jornal do Congo: Caixa Postal 329, Carmona; weekly; Dir. Dr. CUSTÓDIO PEREIRA GOMES.

Jornal da Huila: Caixa Postal 1322, Sá da Bandeira; weekly; Dir. VENNÁCIO GUIMARÃES SOBRINHO.

Jornal Magazine: Luanda; weekly; Dir. Dr. VÍTOR HOMEM DE ALMEIDA.

O Moxico: Caixa Postal 362, Luso; f. 1966; fortnightly; Dir. E. DIAS.

O Namibe: Caixa Postal 328, Moçâmedes; twice weekly; Dir. MANUEL JOAO TENREIRO CARNEIRO.

Noticia: Calçada Gregório Ferreira, Luanda; weekly; Dir. Dr. HELDER DUARTE DE ALMEIDA.

A Palavra: Rua Dr. João das Regras, Luanda; weekly; Dir. Dr. CARLOS M. PEREIRA DE CARVALHO.

O Planalto: Caixa Postal 96, Nova Lisboa; three times weekly; Dr. ALTINO VAZ MONTEIRO.

Prisma: Luanda; monthly; Dir. ILÍDIO INÁCIO ESTEVES.

Revista de Angola: Luanda; fortnightly; Dir. F. DE ARAÚJO RODRIGUES.

Semana Ilustrada: Caixa Postal 2039, Luanda; weekly; Dir. A. BORGES DE MELO.

Sul: Benguela; weekly; Dir. VITÓRIO PEREIRA.

Tribuna dos Muceques: Rua Francisco Newton, Luanda; weekly; Dir. JAYME RAMOS MONTEIRO.

A Voz do Bié: Caixa Postal 131, Silva Porto; f. 1961; weekly; Dir. FRANCISCO JOSÉ DOS REIS RAMOS.

PUBLISHERS

Empresa Gráfica de Angola: Caixa Postal 1312, Luanda; f. 1923; Dir. RUY CORREIA DE FREITAS; publ. *A Província de Angola* (daily).

Empresa Gráfica do Uige, Lda.: Caixa Postal 329, Carmona; f. 1958; Editor LUIZ M. RODRIGUES; publ. *Jornal do Congo* (weekly).

Gráfica de Benguela: Benguela.

Gráfica Portugal, Lda.: Caixa Postal 1290, Rua Serpa Pinto, Luanda; f. 1930; owners of *Diario de Luanda*.

Imprensa Nacional de Angola: Caixa Postal 1306, Luanda; f. 1845; Gen. Man. Dr. ANTÓNIO DUARTE DE ALMEIDA E CARMO.

Industrias A.B.C.: Caixa Postal 1245, Luanda.

Lello and Cia, Lda.: Caixa Postal 1300, Luanda; general fiction and non-fiction.

NEA—Nova Editorial Angolana, S.A.R.L.: Caixa Postal 1225, Luanda; f. 1935; Man. M. POMBO FERNANDES.

Neográfica Lda.: Caixa Postal 6518, Luanda; publ. *Noticia*.

RADIO AND TELEVISION

RADIO

Emissora Oficial de Angola: Caixa Postal 1329, Luanda; f. 1953; government station; Dir. JOÃO ANTÓNIO DE OLIVEIRA PIRES.

Rádio Clube de Angola: Caixa Postal 229, Luanda; commercial station; Pres. Com. M. DE ALBUQUERQUE E CASTRO.

Rádio Clube Português: Rua Vasco da Gama, Luanda; commercial station.

Rádio Ecclésia—Emissora Católica de Angola: Luanda; religious station; Dir. Padre J. M. PEREIRA.

Voz de Angola: Avda. Norton de Matos, Luanda.

There are 12 other commercial stations.

There were 100,000 radio receivers in 1971.

There is no television.

FINANCE

(cap. =capital; dep. =deposits; m. =million; res. =reserves; amounts in escudos)

BANKING

Banco de Angola: Rua da Prata 10, Lisbon; Avda. Paulo Dias de Novais, Luanda; central bank; f. 1926; cap. and res. 1,000m., dep. 22,900m. (1972); Gov. Dr. MÁRIO ANGELO MORAIS DE OLIVEIRA.

Banco Comercial de Angola: Praça de Portugal, Caixa Postal 1343, Luanda; f. 1956; cap. and res. 438.6m., dep. 8,000m. (Dec. 1972); Pres. A. CUPERTINO DE MIRANDA; Gen. Man. Dr. J. MANUEL NUNES DA GLORIA.

Banco de Crédito Comercial e Industrial: Avda. dos Restauradores de Angola 79-83, Caixa Postal 1395, Luanda; f. 1965; cap. 200m., dep. 4,937m. (Dec. 1972); Chair. Dr. MIGUEL GENTIL QUINA; Man. Ing. ANIBAL TASSO DE FIGUEIREDO FARO VIANA; 61 brs. in Angola, 44 in Mozambique.

Banco de Fomento Nacional: Caixa Postal 6191, Luanda.

Banco Interunidos: formed by Banco Espíritu Santo e Comercial de Lisboa and First National City Bank.

Banco Pinto e Sotto Mayor, S.A.R.L.: Rua Áurea 28, Lisbon; Avda. Paulo Dias de Novais 86, Luanda; f. 1914; cap. 500m., dep. 31,140.6m. (Dec. 1971); Pres. EDUARDO FURTADO; 57 brs. in Angola, 45 brs. in Mozambique.

Banco Totta-Standard de Angola: Avda. Paulo Dias de Novais 127, Caixa Postal 5554, Luanda; f. 1966; associate of Totta and Açores and Standard and Charter Banking Group; cap. 150m., dep. 3,120m. (Dec. 1972); Joint Man. Dirs. J. J. H. VERMEULEN, Dr. M. QUARTIN BASTOS.

Caixa de Crédito Agro-Pecuário de Angola: Caixa Postal 6080, Luanda; f. 1961; cap. U.S. $8.5m.; agricultural loan bank; Gen. Man. Dr. PEDRO DE OLIVEIRA SIMÕES.

INSURANCE

Cia. de Seguros Angola, S.A.R.L.: Avda. Paulo Dias de Novais 37, 1°, Caixa Postal 721-C, Luanda; f. 1946; cap. 10m.; Dir.-Gen. Dr. FERNANDO MOUZACO DIAS.

Cia. de Seguros Angolana, S.A.R.L.: Avda. Paulo Dias de Novais 84, Caixa Postal 738, Luanda; f. 1946; cap. and res. 70m.; Dir. S. CARDOSO DE PINA.

Cia. Seguros Garantia Africa, S.A.R.L.: Caixa Postal 2726, Luanda; f. 1954; cap. and res. 8om.; Man. Dir. Dr. J. J. GOMES PEREIRA.

Cia. de Seguros A Nacional de Angola, S.A.R.L.: Avda. Paulo Dias de Novais 89, Caixa Postal 2921, Luanda; f. 1957; cap. 27.5m.; Admin. A. LEITE DE MAGAKHÃES; sub-Dirs. FRANCISCO A. RIBEIRO, A. RODRIGUES MOREIRA.

Cia. de Seguros Náuticos de Angola, S.A.R.L.: Rua Governador Eduardo Costa 69, Caixa Postal 5059, Luanda.

Cia. de Seguros Universal de Angola, S.A.R.L.: Caixa Postal 2987 and 12010-M, Luanda; f. 1957; cap. 15m.; Gen. Man. MANUEL MARIA DA FONSECA FREITAS; Dir. LUIS JOSÉ PAIVA DE CARVALHO.

Confiança Mundial de Angola—Seguros: Avda. Paulo Dias de Novais 93, Caixa Postal 500, Luanda.

Montepio Geral de Angola (*Mutual Aid Association*): Largo D. João IV 16, Caixa Postal 402, Luanda; f. 1933; Pres. RAFAEL GARCIA IBOLEON, Jr.; Sec. ALTINO AMADEU MAMEDE DE SOUSA E SILVA.

There are a number of Portuguese companies represented in Angola.

TRADE AND INDUSTRY

COMMISSIONS AND NATIONAL BOARDS

Direcção dos Serviços de Comércio (*Department of Trade*): Largo Diogo Cão, Caixa Postal 1337, Luanda; f. 1970; Dir. ANTÓNIO AUGUSTO DE ALMEIDA; brs. throughout Angola.

Instituto do Algodão de Angola (*Cotton Institute*): Caixa Postal 74, Luanda; f. 1938; Dir. M. A. CORRÊA DE PINHO.

Instituto do Café de Angola (*Coffee Institute*): Caixa Postal 342, Luanda; Dir. E. DE A. NORONHA.

Instituto dos Cereais de Angola (*Cereals Institute*): Caixa Postal 65, Luanda; Dir. M. DO VALE.

Instituto das Industrias de Pesca (*Fishing Institute*): Caixa Postal 83, Luanda; Dir. Com. LUIS GONZAGA CLEMENTE DOS REIS.

EMPLOYERS' AND LABOUR ORGANIZATIONS

Associação dos Agricultores de Angola (*Agriculturists' Association*): Luanda; Pres. Dr. ANTONIO MANUEL DA SILVA FERREIRA.

Associação Comercial de Luanda: Caixa Postal 1275, Luanda; f. 1864; Pres. J. F. VIEIRA; Sec. SÉRGIO ROMÃO PERES.

Associação Industrial de Angola: Caixa Postal 999C, Luanda; f. 1930; Gen. Sec. CARLOS A. PEREIRA SOARES; publ. *Boletim da Associação Industrial de Angola* (weekly).

Associação dos Lojistas de Luanda: Caixa Postal 1278, Luanda.

Labour is organized in four national syndicates:

Sindicato Nacional dos Constructores Civis e Mestres de Obras (*National Syndicate of Civil Construction and Contractors*): Caixa Postal 5072, Luanda; mems. nearly 2,000; Pres. ANTÓNIO MARTINS NOGUEIRA.

Sindicato Nacional dos Empregados Bancários de Angola: Rua Salvador Correia 194, Luanda.

Sindicato Nacional dos Empregados do Comercio e da Industria da Provincia de Angola—SNECIPA (*National Syndicate of Workers of Commerce and Industry*): Caixa Postal 28, Luanda; f. 1897; mems. 45,991 (24,746 in central br.); 16 brs. (1970); Chair. Dr. FERNANDO

DAVID LAIMA; Sec.-Gen. JOSÉ CELESTINO BRAVO-MARTINS.

Sindicato Nacional dos Motoriatas, Ferroviarios e Metalurgicos (*National Syndicate of Motor Transport, Railroad and Metal Workers*): Caixa Postal 272, Luanda; mems. about 2,000; Pres. ANTÓNIO DE ALMEIDA CRUZ.

Liga Geral dos Trabalhadores de Angola (LGTA): Kinshasa, Congo; in exile.

TRADE FAIR

Feira Internacional de Luanda (*International Trade Fair of Luanda*): Caixa Postal 1296, Luanda; f. 1969; organized by the Associação Industrial de Angola; annually in October.

TRANSPORT

RAILWAYS

The total length of track operated is over 3,000 km

STATE-OWNED

Porto e Caminhos de Ferro de Luanda: Direcção de Exploração do Porto e Caminhos de Ferro de Luanda, Caixa Postal 1229, Luanda; f. 1886; serves an iron, cotton and sisal-producing region between Luanda and Malange; 608 km. of 1.067 m. gauge. Under the Development Plan it is proposed to continue the line 97 km. from Malange to Lui and eventually to the Zaire border; Dir. Eng. LUIS HENRIQUE ERVEDOSA ABREU.

Caminho de Ferro de Moçâmedes: Moçâmedes; 858 km. main line from Moçâmedes to Serpa Pinto via Sá da Bandeira, Matala and Entrocamento, with a 38 km. branch from Chanja to Chela; branches to Cassinga North (16 km.) and Cassinga South (94 km.) carry 6 million tons of iron ore a year to Salazar Harbour, Moçâmedes; Gen. Man. JOAQUIM ALBINO ANTUNES DA CUNHA.

PRIVATELY-OWNED

Companhia do Caminho de Ferro de Benguela (*Benguela Railway Company*): Head Office: Rua do Ataide 7, Lisbon, Portugal; African Management: Caixa Postal 32, Lobito, Angola; London Office: 6 John St., London, WC1N 2ES; f. 1902; runs from the port of Lobito across Angola via Nova Lisboa and Luso to the Zaire border where it connects with the K.D.L. system which in turn links with Zambia Railways, thus providing the shortest West Coast route for Central African trade; 1,067 mm. gauge; principal export freights carried: copper, cobalt, zinc, manganese ore and maize; principal import freights carried: general cargo, petrol and oils; length of track 1,415 km.; Chair. Dr. LUIS SUPICO PINTO; Man. Dir. Dr. MANUEL FERNANDES.

Companhia do Caminho de Ferro do Amboim: Porto Amboim: f. 1922; serves a coffee region between Amboim and Gabela; 123 km. of 0.60 m. gauge; Dir. FERNANDO M. TOURET.

ROADS

Angola has over 8,000 km. of asphalted roads. Plans include a highway from Luanda to Cape Town, and another from Carmona to Quimbele, ultimately to be extended to the Zaire border, is under construction.

SHIPPING

Companhia Nacional de Navegação: Head Office: Rua do Comércio 85, Lisbon; Caixa Postal 20, Rua Governador Eduardo Costa 33, Luanda; regular cargo and passenger services from Portugal to Angola and Mozambique; monthly cargo services from Hamburg, Bremen, Rotterdam, London, Liverpool and Mediterranean ports to Angola.

Companhia de Servicos Maritimos—COSEMA: Caixa Postal 1360, Rua Direita 3A, Luanda; f. 1950; brs. in Lobito, Porto Amboim, Moçâmedes, São Tomé; Dir. Commdt. MANUEL ALBUQUERQUE E CASTRO; Gen. Man. ALVARO FONTES.

FOREIGN SHIPPING AGENCIES

Robert Hudsons & Sons (Pty.) Ltd.: Caixa Postal 6426, Luanda; suppliers of vehicles, agricultural, industrial and earth-moving equipment, aircraft and general goods; international forwarding agents at Luanda and Lobito; brs. and workshops in all main Angolan towns; agents in Angola for Clan Line, Texaco Overseas Tankship Ltd., etc.

Hull, Blyth (Angola) Ltd.: Caixa Postal 1214, Luanda; London Office: 1 Lloyds Ave., E.C.3; agents in Angola for Cie. Maritime Belge, Elder Dempster Lines Ltd., B.P. Tanker Co. Ltd., and others; Chair. Viscount LEATHERS; Sec. G. B. WOODHOUSE, F.C.I.S.

CIVIL AVIATION
ANGOLA AIRLINE

Transportes Aéreos de Angola—TAAG: Avda. Luis de Camões 123, Luanda; f. 1938; internal services, and services from Luanda to Windhoek (South West Africa) and São Tomé; Chair. Dr. EDUARDO PALMA; fleet of six F-27 and six DC-3.

OTHER AIRLINES SERVING LUANDA

Transportes Aéreos Portugueses S.A.R.L. (T.A.P.): Lisbon; Avda. Paulo Dias Novais 79-80, Caixa Postal 118, Luanda; f. 1953; Principal Officials: Eng. ALFREDO QUEIROZ VAZ PINTO, Cte. JULIO SCHOLZ, Eng. EDUARDO MENDES BARBOSA, Dr. LUIS FORJAZ TRIGUEIROS; services to Africa, Europe, North and South America.

South African Airways (S.A.A.): Head Office: S.A. Airways Centre, Johannesburg; Avda. Paulo Dias de Novais 123, Luanda; services between Luanda and Johannesburg.

TOURISM

Centro de Informação e Turismo de Angola—CITA: Caixa Postal 1240, Luanda; Dir. Col. J. F. M. ILHARCO.

UNIVERSITY

Universidade de Luanda: Caixas Postais 815 e 1350, Luanda; f. 1963; 121 teachers, 2,385 students.

MOZAMBIQUE (PORTUGUESE EAST AFRICA)

Mozambique lies on the east side of Africa, and is bordered by Tanzania to the north, Malawi, Zambia and Rhodesia to the west, and South Africa and Swaziland to the south. Since 1964, Portuguese forces have been fighting nationalist guerrilla forces in the north and west of Mozambique (*see* Political Parties, p. 1240), and there are now some 60,000 Portuguese troops stationed there.

STATISTICAL SURVEY
AREA AND POPULATION

AREA (sq. km.)	POPULATION (1970)	
	Total	Lourenço Marques (capital)
786,763	8,168,933	378,348

* Provisional figures.

Agriculture (principal crops—'000 metric tons) (1972—estimates): Tea 17.8, Raw Sugar 326, Cashew 203, Sisal 22, Rice 111, Maize 400, Cotton Lint 40, Cottonseed 80, Copra 64.6 (exports), Wood 286 ('000 sq. m.).

Livestock (1972): Cattle 1,315,613, Sheep 129,604, Goats 568,330, Pigs 178,558 Asses, Horses and Mules 18,408.

Fishing (1971—metric tons): Fish 7,483, Prawns 2,438, Molluscs 386, Other Crustaceans 116. (1972) 10,412 metric tons.

INDUSTRY AND MINING
('000 contos)

	1969	1970	1971		1969	1970	1971
Sugar	894	1,015	1,147	Chemical Products . .	460	524	679
Beer	282	347	405	Petroleum Derivatives .	619	593	705
Tobacco . . .	312	380	436	Cement	226	287	321
Textiles . . .	1,352	1,330	1,169	Transport Equipment .	175	222	172
Clothing and Footwear .	205	207	239	Coal	34	59	43

PORTUGUESE OVERSEAS STATES—MOZAMBIQUE

FINANCE

100 centavos=1 Mozambique escudo; 1,000 escudos are known as a *conto*.

Coins: 10, 20 and 50 centavos; 1, 2½, 5, 10 and 20 escudos.

Notes: 50, 100, 500 and 1,000 escudos.

Exchange rates (April 1974): £1 sterling=59.45 escudos; U.S. $1=25.125 escudos.

100 Mozambique escudos=£1.68=$3.98.

Budget (1972): *Estimated expenditure:* 8,893.1m. escudos; 1,076.3m. escudos were to be spent on the armed forces.

CURRENCY IN CIRCULATION
(contos)

	1969	1970	1971*
Notes	1,851,329	2,025,729	2,325,000
Coin	268,063	268,524	309,000
TOTAL . . .	2,119,392	2,294,253	2,634,000

* Provisional.

BALANCE OF PAYMENTS
(1970, contos)

	CREDIT	DEBIT	BALANCE
Goods and Services:			
Merchandise	4,230,090	8,190,466	−3,960,376
Tourism	459,455	287,721	171,734
Transport . . .	2,179,782	189,688	1,990,094
Insurance . . .	34,467	56,834	− 22,367
Capital returns . .	1,786	289,187	− 287,401
Government . . .	222,152	31,153	190,999
Other services . .	1,309,958	510,961	798,997
Total . . .	8,437,690	9,556,010	−1,118,320
Transfer Payments . .	50,995	251,517	− 200,522
CURRENT BALANCE . .			−1,318,842
Capital Operations:			
Private capital operations . .	519,338	729,765	− 210,427
Public capital operations . .	2,917	43,606	− 40,689
Total	522,255	773,371	− 251,116
Deficit			−1,569,958

EXTERNAL TRADE
(contos)

	1970	1971*	1972*
Imports. . . .	9,291,374	9,638,749	8,911,824
Exports. . . .	4,506,346	4,612,861	4,768,031

* estimates

PRINCIPAL COMMODITIES
('ooo contos)

IMPORTS	1969	1970	1971	EXPORTS	1969	1970	1971
Food, Beverages and Tobacco	506	598	485	Raw Cotton	795	739	657
Vegetable Products	375	423	442	Sisal	123	118	127
Mineral Products	671	739	1,010	Timber	207	197	190
Chemical Products	557	657	726	Vegetable Oils	430	545	496
Textiles	1,069	1,080	1,011	Cashew Nuts	780	855	993
Machinery	1,210	1,822	1,744	Petroleum Derivatives	318	337	340
Transport Equipment	1,064	1,444	1,281	Sugar and Molasses	558	578	708
				Tea	234	234	275

PRINCIPAL COUNTRIES
('ooo contos)

	IMPORTS			EXPORTS		
	1970	1971	1972	1970	1971	1972
Portugal	2,563	2,552	2,131	1,722	1,726	1,826
Portuguese Overseas Territories	329	311	276	244	250	177
Australia	167	155	140	13	42	52
Belgium-Luxembourg	173	173	130	30	44	57
France	310	337	685	60	43	121
German Federal Republic	713	816	791	118	91	104
Iraq	363	486	499	65	—	—
Italy	275	408	369	81	62	72
Japan	572	530	629	43	63	110
Netherlands	141	154	83	94	119	65
South Africa	1,373	1,423	1,312	467	434	387
United Kingdom	754	769	665	220	200	248
U.S.A.	912	709	460	416	623	613

TRANSPORT

Railways (1972): Passengers carried 5,103,600, Freight carried 18,239,000 metric tons.

Roads (1971): Cars 83,841, Lorries and Buses 20,215, Motor Cycles 4,081,

Inland Waterways (1972): Passengers carried 880,010; Freight carried 105,384 metric tons.

Shipping (1972): Lourenço Marques and Beira: vessels entered 2,923; freight unloaded 4,361,751, freight loaded 10,426,012 metric tons.

Civil Aviation (1972): Planes arrived 44,003; Passenger arrivals 316,254, Freight loaded 6,407 metric tons.

Pipeline: A pipeline 311 km. long links Beira with the Rhodesian oil refineries. It has not been used since December 1965, as a result of the international embargo on oil exports to Rhodesia, imposed in November 1965.

TOURISM

1971: 583,341 visitors.

EDUCATION
(1970)

	SCHOOLS	TEACHERS	PUPILS
Primary	4,274	6,855	526,962
Secondary			
Technical	23	744	11,458
Teacher Training	12	117	1,164
Universities	1	220	1,071

Sources: Instituto Nacional de Estatística, Lisbon; Banco Nacional Ultramarino, Lisbon.

THE CONSTITUTION

In January 1973 the new Organic Law came into effect. Mozambique was renamed a "State" with a new Legislative Assembly and Consultative Council which exercise more autonomy in the administration of Provincial affairs. The Legislative Assembly will meet twice a year, although not for more than four months at a time, and the Governor-General now has the status of a metropolitan Minister of State and may attend Cabinet meetings. Elections to the new 50-seat legislature were held in March 1973; the Parliament is currently comprised of 28 members from the Province, 19 from metropolitan Portugal, two from the Portuguese State of India (Goa) and one from Macao.

THE GOVERNMENT

Governor-General: Dr. HENRIQUE SOARES DE MELO.

Commander-in-Chief of Portuguese Armed Forces in Mozambique: Gen. TOMAZ BASTOS MACHADO.

Legislative Assembly. Composed of 50 members, of which 20 are directly elected, the remainder being elected indirectly by corporative electors.

Consultative Council. Replaces the former Legislative Council; assists the Governor in the running of affairs.

POLITICAL PARTIES

Frente de Libertação de Moçambique (FRELIMO) (*Mozambique Liberation Front*): P.O.B. 15274, Dar es Salaam, Tanzania; Pres. SAMORA MACHEL; Vice-Pres. MARCELINO DOS SANTOS.

FRELIMO was formed in 1962 by the merger of three existing nationalist parties: the *União Democrática Nacional de Moçambique* (UDENAMO), f. 1960; the Mozambique African Nationalist Union (MANU), f. 1961; and the *União Africana de Moçambique Independente* (UNAMI). The first President and Vice-President of FRELIMO were Dr. Eduardo Mondlane and Uria Simango.

FRELIMO launched its military campaign in September 1964, when small groups of guerrillas infiltrated into Mozambique from the north. By 1971 the situation in the province had deteriorated so far that the Portuguese had imposed strict military rule and ordered all travellers to move only with military convoys.

The Portuguese now have at least 60,000 troops in Mozambique, with possibly another 40,000 trained and armed Africans. FRELIMO claims control of a fifth of the territory, where it has set up clinics, primary schools and agricultural production units.

Comité Revolucionário de Moçambique (COREMO): (*Mozambique Revolutionary Commission*): Lusaka, Zambia; f. 1965 as fusion of three nationalist parties; Pres. Sec. PAULO GUMANE.

Mozambique Liberation Movement (MOLIMO): Dar es Salaam; f. 1970; splinter group of FRELIMO; Sec. Gen. HENRIQUES NYANKALE.

JUDICIAL SYSTEM

Courts of First Instance. These administer the Legal Code of Metropolitan Portugal. Cases may be finally referred to the Court of Second Instance and the Supreme Court in Lisbon.

RELIGION

The population is mainly animist, but there are about 815,000 Muslims and 960,000 Christians (660,000 Roman Catholics).

ROMAN CATHOLIC CHURCH

Metropolitan See:

Lourenço Marques	Rt. Rev. CUSTÓDIO ALVIM PEREIRA, Caixa Postal 258, Lourenço Marques.

Suffragan Sees:

Beira . .	(vacant); Caixa Postal 544, Beira.
Inhambane. .	Rt. Rev. ERNESTO GONÇALVES DA COSTA, Caixa Postal 178, Inhambane.
João Belo .	Rt. Rev. FÉLIX NIZA RIBEIRO.
Nampula	Rt. Rev. MANUEL VIEIRA PINTO; Caixa Postal 84, Nampula.
Porto Amélia	Rt. Rev. JOSÉ DOS SANTOS GARCIA, Caixa Postal 12, Porto Amélia.
Quelimane .	Rt. Rev. FRANCISCO NUNES TEIXEIRA, Caixa Postal 292, Quelimane.
Tete . .	Rt. Rev. A. C. ALVES FERREIRA DA SILVA, Caixa Postal 218, Tete.
Vila Cabral	Rt. Rev. L. G. FERREIRA DA SILVA, Caixa Postal 111, Villa Cabral.

THE PRESS

DAILIES

Diario: Caixa Postal 536, Lourenço Marques; f. 1905; Editor Dr. JOAQUIM LUIS DOS SANTOS, O.P.; circ. 11,000.

Noticias: Caixa Postal 327, Lourenço Marques; f. 1926; morning; Editor AVELINO DE ARAÚFO TASITAS; circ. 13,000.

Noticias de Beira: Caixa Postal 81, Beira; f. 1918; morning; Editor VITOR GOMES; circ. 6,000.

A Tribuna: Caixa Postal 1822, Lourenço Marques; f. 1962; evening; Editor Dr. FERNANDO AMARO MONTEIRO; circ. 15,000.

PERIODICALS AND MAGAZINES

LOURENÇO MARQUES

Boletim Oficial da Provincia de Moçambique: Caixa Postal 275; f. 1854; three times weekly; government and official announcements.

Boletim da Sociedade de Estudos: Caixa Postal 1138; f. 1930; six times a year; Pres. ANTÓNIO SILVA DE SOUSA; circ. 1,000.

Brado Africano: Avda. 24 de Julho 315, Caixa Postal 461; f. 1918; weekly; published by Associação Africana de P. de Moçambique; circ. 1,500.

Renovação: Caixa Postal 1016; f. 1961; weekly; Dir. ADÉRITO PEREIRA SOARES.

Voz de Moçambique: Caixa Postal 888; f. 1960; fortnightly; Dir. Eng. HOMERO DA COSTA BRANCO.

BEIRA

EM—Economia de Moçambique: Caixa Postal 81; Dir. Dr. MÁRIO PEDRO SIMONETE; monthly; economics and finance.

Voz Africana: Rua D. João de Mascarenhas; Dir. JOSÉ ANTÓNIO DE TRINDADE; Editor P. COSTA.

PUBLISHERS

Lourenço Marques

Imprensa Nacional da Provincia de Moçambique: Caixa Postal 275; f. 1854; publs. *Boletim Oficial, Anuário Estatístico, Comércio Externo, Estatística Agrícola, Censo da Populaçõo, Estatística Industrial, Revista de Entomologia*, and other statistical information and reports.

A. W. Bayly & Cia. Lda.: Avda. da República 195–197, Caixa Postal 185.

Editora Minerva Central: Rua Consiglieri Pedroso 84, Caixa Postal 272; f. 1908; stationers and printers, educational, technical and medical textbooks; Propr. J. A. Carvalho & Co. Ltd.

Empresa Moderna Lda.: Avda. da República 13, Caixa Postal 473; f. 1937; fiction, history, textbooks; Dirs. Louis Galloti, Eurico Bento, A. R. Ferreira.

Papeleria e Tipografia Colonial, Lda.: Rua Salazar 41, Caixa Postal 1077.

RADIO

Emissôra do Aero Clube da Beira: Caixa Postal 3, Beira; private commercial station; f. 1936; programmes in Portuguese and local languages; Dir. F. J. Silvério Moiteira.

Radio Clube de Moçambique: Caixa Postal 594, Lourenço Marques; non-profit organization; programmes in Portuguese, English, Afrikaans and local dialects; Dir.-Gen. Humberto das Neves.

Radio Mocidade: Caixa Postal 219, Lourenço Marques; programmes in Portuguese; Man. Dr. J. A. Almeida Nogueira.

Radio Pax: Caixa Postal 594, Beira; f. 1954; religious station administered by Franciscans; programmes in Portuguese and local languages; Dir. Rev. Antonio Gonçalves.

There were 100,000 radio receivers in 1971.

Television services are to start in 1974, covering Lourenço Marques, Beira and Nampula, and are to extend to other cities by 1977.

FINANCE

(cap. = capital; dep. = deposits; res. = reserves; m. = million; amounts in escudos)

BANKING

Issuing Banks

Banco Nacional Ultramarino: Rua do Comércio 84, Lisbon; Caixa Postal 423, Lourenço Marques; f. 1864; cap. 1,000m., dep. 21,640m. (Dec. 1972); Gov. Dr. João Dias Rosas; Vice-Govs. Dr. J. E. Gomes da Silva, Dr. L. Pereira Coutinho.

Banco Comercial de Angola: Praça de Portugal, Caixa Postal 1343, Luanda, Angola; Rua Consiglieri Pedroso 99, Caixa Postal 4002, Lourenço Marques; cap. and res. 438.6m., dep. 8,000m. (Dec. 1972); Chief Gen. Man. R. R. de Brito.

Banco de Crédito Comercial e Industrial: Avda. dos Restauradores de Angola 79–83, Caixa Postal 1395, Luanda, Angola; Praça 7 de Marco 45, Lourenço Marques; f. 1965; cap. 200m., dep. 4,937m. (Dec. 1971); Man. Dir. Teixeira Abreu; 47 brs. in Mozambique.

Banco Pinto e Sotto Mayor S.A.R.L.: Rua Áurea 28, Lisbon; Lourenço Marques; f. 1914; Pres. Eduardo Furtado; cap. 500m., dep. 31,141m. (Dec. 1971); 45 brs. in Mozambique.

Banco Standard Totta de Moçambique S.A.R.L.: Praça 7 de Março 1, Caixa Postal 1119, Lourenço Marques; f. 1966; associate of Banco Totta Açores and the Standard Bank Ltd.; cap. 112.5m., dep. 2,118m.; Man. Dir. Dr. F. M. P. Norton de Matos; 33 brs.

Casa Bancária de Moçambique: Avda. Pêro de Anaia, Hotel Moçambique, Caixa Postal 1690, Beira; f. 1972; Dir. Carlos Abel de Sousa e Brito.

Investment Bank

Banco de Fomento Nacional: Rua Monzinho da Silveira 26, Lisbon 2; Avda. da República 988, Caixa Postal 2077, Lourenço Marques; f. 1959; cap. 2,393.2m., dep. 6,913.7m.

INVESTMENT ASSOCIATION

Sociedade Moçambicana de Administração e Gestão de Bens, S.A.R.L.: Avda. da República 1675, Caixa Postal 2732, Lourenço Marques; f. 1967; minimum cap. 20m. contos; aims to administer and negotiate the total goods and real estate which make up the *Fundo de Investimentos Ultramarino* (Overseas Investment Fund), as well as issuing certificates; Chair. Dr. V. J. da Costa.

INSURANCE

Inspecção de Crédito e Seguros da Provincia de Moçambique: Lourenço Marques.

Mozambique Companies

Companhia de Seguros "Lusitana", S.A.R.L.: Caixa Postal 1165, Lourenço Marques; f. 1947; cap. 30m.; Chair. Armando de Matos Ribeiro; Man. Dir. Carlos António Sereno.

Companhia de Seguros A Mundial de Moçambique S.A.R.L.: Caixa Postal 514, Beira; f. 1857; cap. 10m.; Dir. Dr. Armindo dos Santos Pinho.

Companhia de Seguros Náuticus: Edificio Náuticus, Avda. da República 1383, Caixa Postal 696, Lourenço Marques; f. 1943; cap. 6om.; general; Chair. Dr. António Manuel de Mascarenhas Gaivão.

Companhia de Seguros Tranquilidade de Moçambique: Avda. de República 1203, Caixa Postal 9, Lourenço Marques; cap. 20m.; Chair. Dr. J. Pereira Martinho.

There are a large number of Portuguese companies represented in the Province.

TRADE AND INDUSTRY

REGULATING COMMISSIONS

Junta de Comércio Externo (*Board of External Trade and Economic Co-ordination*): Praça 7 de Março, Caixa Postal 654, Lourenço Marques; f. 1956; Man. Dr. Fernando Catalão Dionisio.

Instituto dos Cereais de Moçambique (*Mozambique Cereals Institute*): Praça Heróis das Campanhas de Africa, Lourenço Marques 8.

Instituto do Algodão de Moçambique (*Cotton Institute of Mozambique*): Caixa Postal 806, Lourenço Marques; f. 1938; Chair. Eng. Eugénio Paulo.

LABOUR ORGANIZATIONS

Sindicato Nacional des Empregades Bancarios da Provincia de Moçambique (*National Syndicate of Bank Employees of Mozambique*): Avda. da República 49, 6°, Lourenço

Marques; f. 1946; 1,020 mems.; Pres. José Joaquim Couto de Oliviera; Sec. Olívio Malheiro Vaz.

Sindicato Nacional dos Empregados do Comércio e da Indústria da Provincia de Moçambique (*National Syndicate of Commercial and Industrial Employees of Mozambique*): Avda. Pinheiro Chagas 1267, Caixa Postal 394, Lourenço Marques; f. 1898; about 15,000 mems.; Pres. José Pereira Lopes; Sec. Dr. Secundino Alonso.

Sindicato Nacional dos Operarios da Construção Civil e Oficios Correlativos (*National Syndicate of Civil Construction and Related Services*): Avda. Luciano Cordeiro 937–945, Lourenço Marques; f. 1949; about 19,000 mems.; Pres. Alfredo da Costa Lemos; Sec. Crispim da Silva Teixeira.

Sindicato Nacional dos Ferroviários de Manica e Sofala e do Pessoal do Porto da Beira (*National Syndicate of Railways of Manica and Sofala and of Personnel of the Port of Beira*): Caixa Postal 387, Beira; f. 1945; over 2,521 mems.; Pres. Domingos Viera Martins; Sec. João Batista Pereira.

Sindicato Nacional dos Motoristas e Oficios Correlativos (*National Syndicate of Motor Transport Operators and Related Services*): Avda. 24 de Julho 133, Lourenço Marques; f. 1948; about 3,500 mems.; Pres. José Zeferino; Sec. Armando Luís da Costa.

TRANSPORT

RAILWAYS

The total length of track is 3,703 km. excluding the Sena Sugar Estates Railway (90 km. of 0.92 m. gauge), which serves only the company's properties. The railways are now all State-owned, with the exception of the Trans-Zambesia Railway Company.

State-Owned Railways

Direcção dos Portos, Caminhos de Ferro e Transportes de Moçambique: Caixa Postal 276, Lourenço Marques; government department administering the following railways:

The Lourenço Marques System: consisting of the following main lines: (1) Lourenço Marques–Ressano Garcia; connects with the South African Railway system at the Transvaal border, and provides with that system through-railway transport to Johannesburg, the Rand area and Botswana; (2) Lourenço Marques–Goba; provides a rail link with the Swaziland iron mines of Bomvu Ridge; (3) Lourenço Marques–Malvérnia (on the Rhodesian border), providing through transport to Rhodesia, Zambia and south-eastern Zaire; 783 km. open (1,067 mm. gauge).

Mozambique System: Caixa Postal 16, Nampula; Nacala to Entre-Iagos; br. from Nova Freixo to Vila Cabral; br. from Lumbo to Rio Monapo; also an extension to Malawi through Nova Freixo.

Beira System: Caixa Postal 472, Beira; the main line runs from Beira to the Rhodesian town of Umtali via Vila de Manica and Vila Pery providing through transport to Rhodesia and Zambia; 318 km. open (1,067 mm. gauge). The system also includes:

  Tete Railway: Dona Ana to the Moatize coal mines; 254 km. open (1,067 mm. gauge).

Dondo-Malawi Line: from Dondo through Sena to Malawi frontier, connecting with Blantyre and including branch line from Inhamitanga to Marromeu; 423 km. open.

Inhambane and Gaza System: Caixa Postal 5, Inhambane; from Inhambane to Inharrime (91 km. of 1,067 mm. gauge); from João Belo to Chicomo, and a branch from Manjacaze to Marão (101 km. of 0.75 m. gauge).

Quelimane System: Caixa Postal 73, Quelimane from Quelimane to Mocuba (145 km. of 1,067 mm. gauge).

Private Railway

Trans-Zambesia Railway Co. Ltd.: Avda. de Liberdade 227, 7°, Lisbon 2; Predio Tamega, Caixa Postal 61, Beira; London Office: 40–42 Cannon St., E.C.4; runs from Dondo to Sena on the south bank of the Zambezi; 288 km. open (1,067 mm. gauge); Chair. and Man. Dir. Vivian L. Oury (London); Man. Dir. in Lisbon J. B. Correa da Silva; Resident Man. Dir. Eng. Fernando Pinto Teixeira.

ROADS

There were, in 1972, 38,354 km. of roads in Mozambique, of which 3,715 km. were classified as first-class roads, 7,595 as second class. There were also 14,510 km. of local routes and 12,534 km. of unclassified routes.

SHIPPING

Lourenço Marques, Beira and Nacala are the principal ports. Three new ports are to be built along the Zambezi.

Companhia Moçambicana de Navegação: Avda. da República, Caixa Postal 786, Lourenço Marques; f. 1969; agents: Navetur-Soc. de Agencias de Turismo e Transportes de Moçambique; Dir. Dr. B. de Almeida.

Companhia Nacional de Navegação: General agents: Navetur—Soc. de Agencias de Turismo e Transportes de Moçambique, Caixa Postal 2694, Lourenço Marques.

Empresa do Limpopo: Rua Araujo, Caixa Postal 145, Lourenço Marques; f. 1905; cargo and passenger services along Portuguese East African coast from Lourenço Marques to Mocimboa da Praia; Man. Dir. João Sá Nogueira.

CIVIL AVIATION

Mozambique Air Line

Direcção de Exploração dos Transportes Aéreos (DETA): Caixa Postal 2060, Aeroporto de Lourenço Marques; f. 1936; operates domestic services and on the following international routes: Lourenço Marques–Johannesburg; Lourenço Marques–Durban; Lourenço Marques–Manzini, Swaziland; Beira–Salisbury; Beira–Blantyre; fleet: three Fokker F27, four Boeing 737-200; Dir. Abel Neves de Azevedo.

Mozambique is also served by the following airlines: Air Madagascar, Air Rhodesia, SAA and TAP.

TOURISM

Centro de Informação e Turismo: Caixa Postal 614, Lourenço Marques.

UNIVERSITY

Universidade de Lourenço Marques: Caixa Postal 257, Lourenço Marques; f. 1962; 260 teachers, 2,455 students.

THE CAPE VERDE ISLANDS

The Cape Verde province consists of ten islands and five islets. There are two groups, the Barlavento, with the islands of São Vicente, Santo Antão, São Nicolau, Santa Luiza, Sal and Boa Vista, and the Sotavento, with the islands of São Tiago, Maio, Fogo, and Brava. The Cape Verde groups lie in the Atlantic west of Senegal. Capital: Praia (São Tiago). Chief Port: Mindello (São Vicente).

STATISTICAL SURVEY

Area: 3,929 sq. km. (1,517 sq. miles).

Population: 272,071 (1970 census). Vital statistics (1971): births 9,493, deaths 4,147.

Agriculture: *Principal crops* are coffee, castor oil, maize, peanuts, sugar cane, vegetables (mainly potatoes, tomatoes, pimentoes, beans) and fruit (largely bananas). *Livestock* (1971): Horses, Mules and Asses 15,000, Cattle 14,804, Sheep 1,649, Goats 47,482, Pigs 25,051.

Fishing: 5,234 metric tons (1971).

Industry (1971—contos): Food Industries 28,990, Beverages 4,035, Tobacco 2,128.

Production (1971): Honey 6,745 metric tons, Salt 32,937 metric tons, Frozen Fish 825 metric tons, Soft Drinks 138,976 litres.

Finance: 100 centavos=1 Cape Verde escudo; 1,000 escudos are known as a *conto*. Coins: 5, 10, 20 and 50 centavos; 1, 2½, 5 and 10 escudos. Notes: 20, 50, 100 and 500 escudos. Exchange rates (April 1974): £1 sterling=59.45 escudos; U.S. $1=25.125 escudos; 100 Cape Verde escudos=£1.68=$3.98.

Currency in Circulation (1971—contos): Notes 154,245, Coins 5,728.

Balance of Payments (1971—'000 contos): Balance of import and export of goods and services: −475; Current balance: 139; Capital balance: 290; Net balance: −46.

Budget (1971—contos): Ordinary receipts 249,495, Extraordinary receipts 264,133, Total 513,628; Ordinary expenditure 195,394, Extraordinary expenditure 264,133, Total 459,527.

Military Budget (1972—contos): 32,700.

External Trade (1971—contos): *Imports:* Live animals and animal products 20,107, Textiles 58,252, Food and drink 74,283, Machinery 39,708, Total 573,984; *Exports:* Live animals and animal products 11,007, Textiles 1,113, Food and drink 12,931, Machinery 1,262, Total 45,638.

Transport: *Roads* (1971): Cars 1,818, Lorries and buses 533, Motorcycles 683, Total 3,034. *Shipping* (1971): Vessels entered 1,113, Freight loaded 300,000 metric tons, Passengers transported 103,726. *Civil Aviation* (1971): Planes landed 2,540, Passengers landed 13,875 Freight entered and cleared 452,442 kg.

Education (1971): *Primary:* Schools 354, Teachers 826, Pupils 48,972. *Secondary:* Schools 9, Teachers 130, Pupils 3,060. *Technical:* Schools 1, Teachers 34, Pupils 321.

THE GOVERNMENT

Governor: Maj. LOUREIRO SANTOS.

Note: Elections were held in late March 1973 to the new Legislative Assembly of 22 members. 20 native members and 2 from Metropolitan Portugal were elected.

POLITICAL PARTIES

Conferência das Organizações Nacionais das Colónias Portuguesas (CONCP): 18 rue Dirah, Hydra, Algiers, Algeria; f. 1961; central organization for MPLA, Angola, FRELIMO, Mozambique, PAIGC, Guinea and Cape Verde, CLSTP, São Tomé; Pres. SAMORA MACHEL.

Partido Africano da Independencia da Guiné e Cabo Verde (PAIGC) (*African Party for Independence in Guinea and Cape Verde*): B.P. 298, Conakry, Guinea; Sec.-Gen. ARISTIDES PEREIRA (For further details *see* Guinea (Bissau) chapter).

Unión Democrática do Cabo Verde: f. 1974; Pres. JOÃO BAPTISTA MONTEIRO.

RELIGION

ROMAN CATHOLIC

Suffragan See, São Tiago de Cabo Verde (attached to the Metropolitan See of Lisbon): Praia, São Tiago; Rt. Rev. JOSÉ FELIPE DO CARMO COLAÇO. There are about 206,000 Roman Catholics.

THE PRESS

O Arquipélago: Caixa Postal 118, Praia, São Tiago; weekly; publication of the official tourism department; Dir. Dr. BENTO LEVY.

Boletim Oficial: Caixa Postal 113, Praia, São Tiago; official.

Noticias de Cabo Verde: Caixa Postal 15, São Vicente; f. 1932; fortnightly; independent; Dirs. MANUEL RIBEIRO DE ALMEIDA, RAUL RIBEIRO.

RADIO

Rádio Barlavento: Caixa Postal 29, São Vicente; government station; Pres. FRANCISCO LOPES DA SILVA.

Rádio Clube de Oabo Verde: Caixa Postal 26, Praia, São Tiago; private station; Pres. ANIBAL FONSECA.

Rádio Clube Mindelo: Caixa Postal 101, São Vicente; private station; Dir.-Gen. F. J. MARTINS.

There were 10,500 radio receivers in use at the end of 1972. There is no television service.

FINANCE

ISSUING BANK

Banco Nacional Ultramarino: Rua do Comércio 84, Lisbon; Praia; 3 brs. in Cape Verde Islands.

INSURANCE

Many leading Portuguese insurance companies have agents in the Cape Verde Islands.

TRANSPORT

ROADS

There were 1,500 km. of roads in 1965.

SHIPPING

Companhia Nacional de Navegação: agent in São Tiago: João Benoliel de Carvalho, Ltda., Caixa Postal 56, Praia.

Companhia Colonial de Navegação: agent in São Tiago: Francisco José da Costa, Rua Sá da Bandeira 40–48, Praia (Head Office: Rua Instituto Vergilio Machado, Lisbon).

CIVIL AVIATION

Transportes Aéreos de Cabo Verde (TACV): Caixa Postal 1, Rua da República, Praia; f. 1955; connects São Vicente, Praia, Sal, São Nicolau, Boavista, Fogo and Maio; Gen. Man. VASCO DE OLIVEIRA E MELO; fleet: three Dove, two BN-2A Islander.

South African Airways call at Sal on the Europe–South Africa route. T.A.P. services to Lisbon and Bissau, Guinea.

TOURISM

Centro de Informação e Turismo: Caixa Postal 118, Praia, São Tiago; official tourism department.

GUINEA (BISSAU)

Portuguese Guinea, known as Guinea (Bissau), includes the adjacent archipelago of Bijagoz and the island of Bolama, between Senegal and the Republic of Guinea. Capital and Chief Port: Bissau (estimated population 65,000 in 1971). Other ports: Bolama, Bubaque and Cacheu. Since 1961, Portuguese forces have been fighting nationalist guerrillas, who claim control of a large area of the country.

STATISTICS

Area: 36,125 sq. km. (13,948 sq. miles).

Population (1970 Portuguese census): 487,448. In addition to this figure, there are about 20,000 Metropolitan Portuguese troops in Guinea. Nearly 90,000 refugees live in Senegal, and nationalist-held areas may contain anything between 40,000 and the 400,000 claimed by the PAIGC.

Agriculture: *Principal Crops* (1971—metric tons): Groundnuts 65,000, Cassava 37,000 (1970), Rice 35,000, Palm Kernels 12,000 (exports only), Palm Oil 8,000, Rubber 100 (exports only). *Livestock* (1970–71): Cattle 270,000, Goats 175,000, Pigs 150,000, Sheep 65,000, Asses 3,000.

Industry: (1972—metric tons): Rice 2,660, Groundnuts 9,764, Vegetable Oils 3,254.

Finance: 100 centavos=1 Guinea escudo; 1,000 escudos are known as a *conto*. Coins: 10, 20 and 50 centavos; 1, 2½, 5, 10 and 20 escudos. Notes: 50, 100, 500 and 1,000 escudos. Exchange rates (April 1974): £1 sterling= 59.45 escudos; U.S. $1=25.125 escudos; 100 Guinea escudos=£1.68=$3.98.

Budget (1972—contos): Ordinary receipts 567,567,836, Extraordinary receipts 135,447,576, Total 703,015,412; Ordinary expenditure 555,206,403, Extraordinary expenditure 209,423,400, Total 764,633,803.

Currency in circulation (1972): Notes 286,358 contos, Coins 38,569 contos, Total 324,927 contos.

External Trade (1972—contos): Imports 866,843; Exports 69,035.

Commodities: *Imports* (1972): Vegetable Products 92,736, Food, Beverages and Tobacco 154,195, Mineral Products 57,209, Textiles and Products 128,313. *Exports:* (1972) Vegetable Products 57,412, Beverages and Tobacco 1,964, Wood, Timber and Coal 3,680.

Countries: *Imports* (1972): Portugal 498,085; Portuguese Overseas Provinces 46,403; Foreign Countries 303,049. *Exports* (1972): Portugal 61,060; Portuguese Overseas Provinces 4,760; Foreign Countries 3,215.

Transport: *Roads* (1972): Cars 3,268, Lorries and Buses 1,098, Motor Cycles 1,937, Total 6,302. *Shipping* (1972): Vessels entered 97, Freight unloaded 149,277 tons. *Civil Aviation* (1972): Passengers landed 15,106, Freight entered 180 metric tons.

Education (1972–73): *Primary:* Schools 509, Teachers 1,148, Pupils 48,007; *Secondary:* Schools 7, Teachers 176, Pupils 4,133.

Health (1972): Hospitals 10, Dispensaries and Maternity Homes 93, Doctors 83.

THE GOVERNMENT

Governor: Gen. JOSÉ BETTENCOURT RODRIGUES.

Legislative Assembly: Comprises 17 members elected for periods of four years assisted by a Consultative Council.

People's Congress: Held every year since 1970, in several sessions, with the participation of the traditional leaders of the various ethnical groups—designed to promote a permanent dialogue between the Government and the people.

Note: A new political-administrative statute for Portuguese Guinea came into effect on January 1st, 1973. The territory is represented at the Portuguese National Assembly and the Corporative Chamber in Lisbon.

POLITICAL PARTIES

Partido Africano da Independência da Guiné e Cabo Verde (PAIGC)(*African Party for Independence in Guinea and Cape Verde*): B.P. 298, Conakry, Guinea; Sec.-Gen. ARISTIDES PEREIRA; publs. *Liberação* (monthly, Portuguese), *PAIGC Actualités* (monthly, French).

The PAIGC is the most successful of the liberation movements in Portuguese Africa. It was formed in 1956 by Dr. Amílcar Cabral and Raphael Barbosa. In 1960 the PAIGC established itself in Conakry and in 1963 full-scale attacks began on Portuguese army installations and on towns. By 1972, despite the presence of up to 30,000 Portuguese and African troops, the PAIGC claimed control of some two-thirds of the territory, with the Portuguese and their supporters confined mainly to fortified garrisons and villages. The organization has military bases scattered along the boundaries of the neighbouring countries of Senegal and the Republic of Guinea, and receives considerable support from the signatory countries of the Warsaw Pact. The PAIGC have placed great emphasis on improving the quality of life of the people, and schools and hospitals have been set up in the liberated areas, as well as citizen's committees. In January 1973 the party leader, Dr. Cabral, was assassinated in Conakry and Aristides Pereira appointed as his successor.

Frente para a Libertação e Independencia da Guiné (FLING) (*National Independence Front*): Consists of *Mouvement de libération de la Guinée dite portugaise* (*MLG*) led by FRANÇOISE MENDY, and *Union des populations de Guinée dite portugaise* (*UPG*), leader BENJAMIM PINTO-BULL; based in Dakar, Senegal (*illegal in Guinea-Bissau*).

Note: On September 26th, 1973, nationalist elements declared the creation of the Republic of Guinea-Bissau, comprising those territories under nationalist control. The Republic has been recognized by several African states, but was dismissed by the former Caetano régime as an "act of propaganda".

RELIGION

Several religious creeds are professed: Animism (about 63 per cent), Islam (35 per cent), Catholicism (0.9 per cent) and other Christian religions in minor groups.

ROMAN CATHOLIC

Apostolic Prefecture Bissau: Caixa Postal 20, Bissau; Apostolic Prefect Mgr. AMÂNDIO DOMINGUES NETO.

INFORMATION

Centro de Informação e Turismo: Caixa Postal 294, Bissau; official Tourism and Information Department.

THE PRESS

Boletim Cultural da Guiné Portuguesa: Bissau; quarterly.

Boletim Oficial: weekly; official government gazette.

A Voz de Guiné: Editor Father CRUZ DE AMARAL.

RADIO

Emissora Regional da Emissora Nacional: Caixa Postal 191, Bissau; government station; programmes in Portuguese, French and local dialects.

There were 4,071 radio licences at the end of 1971. Arrangements are being made for the establishment of television in the near future.

FINANCE

ISSUING BANK

Banco Nacional Ultramarino: Rua do Comércio 84, Lisbon; Caixa Postal 38, Bissau; f. 1917; Man. ALBERTO DE ALMEIDA COELHO.

DEVELOPMENT

The Government Investment Plan of 1968–73 was established with an expenditure of 1,259,300,000 escudos to finance development. A new five-year plan became operational in 1974.

INSURANCE

The following Portuguese insurance companies have agents in Portuguese Guinea:

Comércio e Industria, S.A.R.L.: Caixa Postal 23, Bissau (Head Office: Rua Arco da Bandeira 22, Lisbon 2).

Império: Casa Gouvêa, Caixa Postal 44 (Head Office: Rua Garrett 56, Lisbon 2).

Tagus, S.A.R.L.: agent in Portuguese Guinea: José Lopes Abreu, Caixa Postal 86, Bissau (Head Office: Rua do Comércio 40–64, Lisbon).

Ultramarina, S.A.R.L.: Avda. Gov. Carvalho Viegas, Caixa Postal 257, Bissau (Head Office: Rua da Prata 108, Lisbon).

TRANSPORT

ROADS

There were over 3,500 km. of roads in 1972, of which 540 km. were tarred.

SHIPPING COMPANIES

Companhia Colonial de Navegação: agents at Bissau: Sociedade Comércial Ultramarina, Caixa Postal 23, Bissau (Head Office: Rua de S. Julião 63, Lisbon 2).

Companhia Nacional de Navegação: agents at Bissau: Guinémar (*q.v.*) (Head Office: Rua do Comércio 85, Lisbon).

Guinémar: Sociedade de Agências e Transportes du Guiné, Lda., Rua Dr. Oliveira Salazar 4, Bissau.

Sociedade Geral de Comércio, Industria e Transportes: agents at Bissau: Empresa Antonio Silva Gouvêa, S.A.R.L. (Head Office: Rua dos Douradores 11, Lisbon).

CIVIL AVIATION

There is an airport at Bissau and a regular service is provided by T.A.P. from Cape Verde and Lisbon.

Transportes Aéreos da Guiné Portuguesa: Caixa Postal 111, Bissau; internal flights; Dir. JOSÉ LEMOS FERREIRA; fleet of one Dornier Skyservant, two Dornier 27, three Cessna U206 and one Cessna F172.

MACAO

Macao consists of the peninsula of Macao and the two smaller adjacent islands of Taipa and Coloane, near Hong Kong. The capital is Macao.

STATISTICAL SURVEY

Area: 16 sq. km.

POPULATION

	TOTAL	BIRTHS	DEATHS	MARRIAGES
1969 .	244,100	2,878	1,474	99
1970 .	248,636	2,670	1,516	116
1971 .	n.a.	2,687	1,543	135

Industry (1970—'000 patacas): Furniture 4,071, Mineral Products 6,145, Shoes and Clothing 114,823, Textiles 62,100, Tobacco 729, Firecrackers 18,243, Optical Products 9,539, Beverages 4,378, Paper Industry 1,032.

Fishing (1972—'000 tons): 3,780 Fish; 6,361 Shellfish.

Finance: 100 avos=1 pataca. Coins: 5, 10 and 50 avos; 1 and 5 patacas. Notes: 10, 50, 100 and 500 patacas. Exchange rates (April 1974): 1 pataca=5.00 Portuguese escudos; £1 sterling=11.89 patacas; U.S. $1= 5.025 patacas; 100 patacas=£8.41=$19.90. The Hong Kong dollar (April 1974: £1 sterling=H.K. $11.98; U.S. $1=H.K. $5.08) also circulates freely in the province and is interchangeable with the pataca.

Budget (1972): 73,410,143 patacas.

Portuguese Intermediate Development Plan (1968–73): Investment in Macao (1970) 40 million escudos.

CURRENCY IN CIRCULATION

('000 patacas)

	NOTES	COINS	TOTAL
1970 . .	58,278	7,152	65,430
1971 . .	64,851	8,269	73,120
1972 . .	80,860	9,486	90,346

EXTERNAL TRADE

('000 patacas)

	IMPORTS	EXPORTS
1971 . .	447,211	291,118
1972 . .	592,525	409,734
1973 . .	750,300	497,100

COMMODITIES

('000 patacas)

IMPORTS	1971	1972
Live Animals . . .	48,665	54,647
Textiles . . .	149,130	233,215
Food . . .	92,371	109,844
Machinery . . .	28,720	30,910

EXPORTS	1971	1972
Live Animals . . .	19,654	19,678
Textiles . . .	187,782	306,051
Food and Drink . .	11,809	13,750
Machinery . . .	163	215

COUNTRIES

('000 patacas)

IMPORTS	1971	1972
Portugal . . .	4,144	6,152
Portuguese Overseas Territories . .	14	159
Other Countries . .	443,053	586,214

EXPORTS	1971	1972
Portugal . . .	33,177	34,148
Portuguese Overseas Provinces . . .	61,236	41,432
Foreign Countries . .	196,705	334,154

TRANSPORT

	1971	1972
Vehicles in Use:		
Cars . . .	3,949	4,861
Lorries and Buses . .	759	1,010
Motor Cycles . .	1,638	2,576
TOTAL .	6,346	8,447
Shipping:		
Vessels Entered . .	17,028	19,691

EDUCATION

	1970	1971
Primary:		
Schools	86	88
Teachers . . .	833	886
Pupils . . .	23,355	25,052
Secondary:		
Schools	29	30
Teachers . . .	485	505
Pupils . . .	7,280	8,229
Technical:		
Schools . . .	16	18
Teachers . . .	91	143
Pupils . . .	2,802	3,795

Sources: Instituto Nacional de Estatistica, Lisbon; Repartição dos Serviços de Economia, Macao; Banco Nacional Ultramarino, *Boletim Trimestral.*

THE GOVERNMENT

Governor: Gen. JOSÉ MANUEL DE SOUSA E FARO NOBRE DE CARVALHO.

POLITICAL PARTY

Note: Elections were held in March 1973 to the new Legislative Assembly of 13 members. Eleven native members and 2 from Metropolitan Portugal were elected.

JUDICIAL SYSTEM

Courts of First Instance. These administer the Legal Code of Metropolitan Portugal. Cases may be finally referred to the Court of Second Instance and the Supreme Court in Lisbon.

RELIGION

ROMAN CATHOLIC

Suffragan See (attached to Metropolitan See of Goa): Macao; Rt. Rev. PAULO JOSÉ TAVARES.

There are 21 missions with a total personnel of 641; Roman Catholics number about 25,000.

THE PRESS

PORTUGUESE

Notícias de Macau: Calçada do Tronco Velho 6, Macao; f. 1947; daily; independent; Dir. Maj. ACÁCIO CABREIRA HENRIQUES.

Boletim Oficial: Caixa Postal 33, Macao; f. 1838; weekly; government publication; Dir. JAIME ROBARTS.

Gazeta Macaense: Avenida Infante de Henrique 3, Macao; daily; Dir. Arq. JOSÉ PEREIRA CHAN.

O Clarim: Rua Central 26, Macao; f. 1948; twice weekly; Dir. Father RAMIRO DOS ANJOS MARÍA.

CHINESE

Ou Mun: Macao.

Si Man: Macao.

Wa Kio: Macao.

Tai Chung: Macao.

Sing Pou: Macao.

RADIO

Emissora de Radiodifusão de Macau: Macao; government station; programmes in Portuguese (6 hours daily) and Chinese; (4 hours daily); Dir. LUÍS GONZAGA GOMES.

Emissora Vila Verde: Rua Francisco Xavier Pereira 123, Macao; private commercial station; programmes in Chinese; Dir. HO YIN.

In 1971 there were 12,000 radio receivers in Macao.

There is no television in Macao.

FINANCE

ISSUING BANK

Banco Nacional Ultramarino: f. 1864; Lisbon; 2 Avenida Almeida Ribeiro, Macao.

FOREIGN BANKS

Banco Tai Tung: Av. Alm. Ribeiro 28, Macao.

Bank of Canton: Rua 5 de Outubro 126, Macao.

Hong Kong and Shanghai Banking Corporation Ltd.: 6 Gracechurch St., London, E.C.3; Rua da Praia Grande No. 2, Apartado 476, Macao.

INSURANCE

The following Portuguese companies are represented in Macao:

Companhia de Seguros Comércio e Indústria, S.A.R.L.: Agents: H. Nolasco & Cia. Lda., P.O.B. 223, Macao (Head Office: Rua Arco do Bandeira-12, Lisbon).

Companhia de Seguros Tagus, S.A.R.L.: Agents: F. Rodrigues (Suc. Res.) Lda., Rua da Praia Grande 71, P.O.B. 2, Macao (Head Office: Rua do Comércio 40-64, Lisbon).

Companhia de Seguros Ultramarina, S.A.R.L.: Agents: H. NOLASCO & Cia. Lda., P.O.B. 223, Macao (Head Office: Rua da Prata 108, Lisbon).

TRADE AND INDUSTRY

In recent years, a considerable number of new industrial establishments have been set up in Macao, and many factories already in operation have expanded and improved their equipment with the introduction of modern machinery. In the first six months of 1973, the principal export markets for Macao products were the United States, France, the Federal Republic of Germany, Portugal and the Portuguese Overseas Provinces, Belgium, Luxembourg, Italy, Japan, Sweden and Holland. Principal items of export are textiles, firecrackers, optical goods, footwear, leather goods, Chinese wine, porcelain ware, plastic goods, teak and camphor wood articles, incense, and metal wares.

Manufacturas Texteis de Macau: Avenida Coronel Mesquita 79, Macao.

CHAMBER OF COMMERCE

Associação Comercial de Macau: Chair. Yo HIN.

Associação dos Exportadores de Macau: Pres. UNION TRADING.

Associação Industrial de Macau: Pres. LOU PIU.

TRANSPORT

ROADS

There were 32 km. of roads in 1973.

SHIPPING

There are 20 shipping agencies for international lines.

Hydrofoils operate every half-hour during daylight between Macao and Hong Kong.

TOURISM

Centro de Informação e Turismo: Government Palace, Rua da Praia Grande, Macao; there were 2.2 million visitors to Macao in 1972.

Macao Tourist Information Bureau: 1525 Star House, Kowloon, Hong Kong.

PORTUGUESE TIMOR

Portuguese Timor includes the eastern part of the island of Timor, the territory of Oe-Cusse and the adjacent islands of Pulo Jako and Atauro, between Indonesia and Australia. The capital and chief port is Dili, with a population of about 20,000.

STATISTICAL SURVEY

Area: 14,925 sq. km. (5,763 sq. miles).

POPULATION

	TOTAL (July 1st)	BIRTHS	DEATHS	MARRI-AGES
1972 .	639,051	11,311	7,650	1,267

AGRICULTURE

PRINCIPAL CROPS
(metric tons)

	1972
Beans .	7,762
Coffee .	4,701
Copra .	1,993
Groundnuts .	521
Maize .	8,730
Manioc .	6,734
Rice .	16,145
Rubber .	121
Sweet Potatoes .	10,882
Tobacco .	37

LIVESTOCK
(1972)

Cattle	.	63,143	Goats .	.	156,773
Sheep	.	40,501	Pigs .	.	171,395

Finance: 100 centavos=1 Timor escudo; 1,000 escudos are known as a *conto*. Coins: 10, 20 and 50 centavos; 1, 2½, 5 and 10 escudos. Notes: 20, 50, 100, 500 and 1,000 escudos. Exchange rates (April 1974): £1 sterling =59.45 escudos; U.S. $1=25.125 escudos; 100 Timor escudos=£1.68=$3.98.

Budget (1973): 195,872 contos.

Portuguese Intermediate Development Plan, 1968–73: Investment in Portuguese Timor (1973) 187,745 contos.

EXTERNAL TRADE
(contos)

	1972
Imports .	200,211
Exports .	140,551

IMPORTS	1972
Food Products .	30,115
Minerals .	18,269
Chemical Products .	15,954
Textiles .	24,240
Machinery .	20,204

EXPORTS	1972
Vegetable Products .	139,048
Animal and Vegetable Oils .	497
Durable Goods .	391
Skins and Furs .	225
Metals and Ores .	14

TRANSPORT

ROAD TRAFFIC

	1972
Cars .	820
Lorries and Buses .	477
Motor Cycles .	1,022

SHIPPING

	1972
Registered Vessels .	359
Freight Loaded ('000 tons) .	12
Freight Unloaded ('000 tons) .	31

CIVIL AVIATION

	1972
Arrivals	1,512
Departures	1,512
Passengers Embarked . . .	13,785
Passengers Disembarked . .	14,453
Freight Loaded (tons) . . .	65,058
Freight Unloaded (tons) . .	66,232

Education: *Primary:* schools 342, teachers 697, pupils 33,884; *Secondary:* schools 5, teachers 39, pupils 930; *Technical:* schools 1, teachers 14, pupils 197.

Source: Instituto Nacional de Estatística.

GOVERNMENT

Governor: Col. FERNANDO ALVES ALDEIA.

Note: Elections were held in March 1973 to the new Legislative Assembly of 20 members. Sixteen native members and from 4 Metropolitan Portugal were elected.

RELIGION

ROMAN CATHOLIC CHURCH

Suffragan See (attached to Metropolitan See of Goa): Dili; Rt. Rev. JOSÉ JOAQUIM RIBEIRO.

There are 3 parishes and 16 missions with a total personnel of 868; Roman Catholics number about 196,570.

THE PRESS

Boletim Oficial: Dili; Government publication.

Seara: Dili; Father MARTINHO DA COSTA LOPES.

Voz de Timor: Dili; Dir. MANUEL ANTÓNIO LOURENÇO PEREIRA.

RADIO

Emissora de Radiodifusão de Timor: Dili; Government Station; programmes in Portuguese, Chinese and Tetum; Dir.-Gen. JAIME JOAQUIM DAS NEVES.

In 1972 there were 3,145 radio receivers. There is no television in Timor.

FINANCE

ISSUING BANK

Banco Nacional Ultramarino: Lisbon; Dili.

INSURANCE

The following Portuguese insurance firms are represented in Portuguese Timor:

Companhia de Seguros Tagus, S.A.R.L.: Dili; (Head Office: Rua do Comércio 40-64, Lisbon).

Companhia de Seguros Ultramarina, S.A.R.L.: agent in Dili: Sociedade Agrícola Pátria e Trabalho, Lda.; (Head Office: Rua da Prata 108, Lisbon).

TRANSPORT

ROADS

There were 2,896 km. of roads in 1972, of which 2,198 km. were classified (654 km. 1st class) and 1,540 km. seasonal tracks.

SHIPPING

Companhia Colonial de Navegação: agent in Dili: Sociedade Agrícola Pátria e Trabalho, Lda. (Head Office: Rua de S. Julião 63, Lisbon).

Companhia Nacional de Navegação: agent in Dili: Sociedade Agrícola Pátria e Trabalho, Lda. (Head Office: Rua de Comércio 85, Lisbon).

Koninklijke Paketvaart Maatschappij: agent in Dili: Banco Nacional Ultramarino.

CIVIL AVIATION

AOA Zamrud Aviation Corp.: Djl. Merdeka III/I, Kupang; Agent JACK SINE.

Transportes Aéreos de Timor: Dili; f. 1946; services between Kupang (Indonesia) and Darwin and Dili and Kupang and domestic services within Timor; Gen. Man. JOSÉ MARIA M. F. DE CASTRO.

Trans-Australia Airlines: services between Baucau and Darwin.

SÃO TOMÉ AND PRÍNCIPE

These islands lie in the Gulf of Guinea, West Africa. Capital: São Tomé (population over 7,000).

STATISTICAL SURVEY

Area: 964 sq. km. (372 sq. miles).

Population (1972): 76,430; Births 3,392, Marriages 141, Deaths 840.

Agriculture: *Principal crops* (metric tons—1972): Copra 5,152, Coconuts 879, Cocoa 10,395, Coffee 144. *Livestock* (1972): Horses, Mules and Asses 262, Cattle 2,750, Sheep 1,542, Goats 650, and Pigs 2,952.

Fishing (1972): 890 metric tons.

Industry (1972—metric tons): Maize Flour 103, Lime 564, Palm Oil 754, Soap 670, Meat Preparations 28, Dried Fish 31.

Finance: 100 centavos=1 Guinea escudo; 1,000 escudos are known as a *conto*. Coins: 10, 20 and 50 centavos; 1, 2½, 5, 10 and 20 escudos. Notes: 20, 50, 100, 500 and 1,000 escudos. Exchange rates (April 1974): £1 sterling =59.45 escudos; U.S. $1=25.125 escudos; 100 Guinea escudos=£1.68=$3.98.

Budget (1971): Receipts 173,394 contos, Expenses 184,897 contos.

Development Plan (1972): Investment 93,598 contos.

Currency in Circulation (1972): Notes 40,390 contos, Coins 11,739 contos.

External Trade (1972—contos): Imports 214,907; Exports 198,466.

Commodities (1972): *Imports:* Vegetable Products 28,000, Food, Beverages and Tobacco 44,757, Mineral Products 16,850, Chemicals and Products 22,838, Textiles and Products 24,766. *Exports:* Vegetable Products 24,394, Food, Beverages and Tobacco 171,858.

Countries (1972): *Imports:* Portugal 102,412, Portuguese Overseas Provinces 56,267, Foreign Countries 56,228. *Exports:* Portugal 62,562, Portuguese Overseas Provinces 3,996, Foreign Countries 131,908.

Transport: *Roads* (1972): Cars 1,483, Lorries and Buses 258, Motor Cycles 326. *Shipping* (1972): Vessels entered 114, Freight entered 20,535 metric tons, Freight cleared 30,817 metric tons. *Civil Aviation* (1972): Passengers landed 7,267, Freight entered and cleared 117 metric tons.

Education (1972): *Primary:* Schools 46, Teachers 303, Pupils 10,015; *Secondary:* Schools 2, Teachers 86, Pupils 2,114; *Technical:* Schools 3, Teachers 30, Pupils 256.

THE GOVERNMENT

Governor: Col. JOÃO CECÍLIO GONÇALVES.

Note: Elections were held in late March 1973 for the new Legislative Assembly which is currently composed of nine natives from the Province and six members from metropolitan Portugal.

POLITICAL PARTIES

Comité de Libertação de São Tomé e Príncipe (*Committee for the Liberation of São Tomé*): Sec.-Gen. TOMÁS MEDEIROS.

RELIGION

ROMAN CATHOLIC

São Tomé and Príncipe: Suffragan See, S. Tomé (Metropolitan See of Luanda—*see* under Angola); Bishop (vacant), Caixa Postal 146, São Tomé.

THE PRESS

Imprensa Nacional: Caixa Postal 28, S. Tomé; f. 1836; weekly; Dir. MANUEL LOPES DE SÁ.

A Voz de São Tomé: Caixa Postal 93; weekly; Dir. Dr. RICARDO JORGE RIBEIRO BRAVO.

RADIO

Emissora Regional de Sao Tomé e Príncipe da Emissora Nacional de Radiodifusao: Avda. Infante D. Henrique, Caixa Postal 44, S. Tomé; f. 1958; official station; Pres. CARLOS ALBERTO FERREIRA DIAS.

There were 6,200 radio licences current at the end of 1970. There is a closed circuit television service.

FINANCE

ISSUING BANK

Banco Nacional Ultramarino: Rua do Comércio 84, Lisbon; São Tomé; sub-agency at Príncipe.

DEVELOPMENT ORGANIZATION

Caixa de Crédito de São Tomé e Príncipe: Caixa Postal 168; f. 1965 to finance the development of agriculture and industry; cap. $54,545, dep. $83,636; Man. Dir. Dr. JOSÉ FREDERICO FERREIRA EPIFANIO DA FRANCA; publ. *Annual Report.*

INSURANCE

The following Portuguese insurance companies have agents in São Tomé and Príncipe:

Fidelidade: Largo do Corpo Santo 13, Lisbon; S. Tomé.

A Mundial, S.A.R.L.: Largo do Chiado 8, Lisbon; S. Tomé; agents: Auspício de Meneses, Lda.

Tagus, S.A.R.L.: Rua do Comércio 40–64, Lisbon; S. Tomé; agents: Silva & Gouveia, Lda.

Tranquilidade, S.A.R.L.: Rua Cándido dos Reis 105, Oporto; S. Tomé.

TRANSPORT

ROADS

There were 288 km. of roads in 1970.

SHIPPING

Companhia Nacional de Navegação: agents in S. Tomé: Lima & Gama Ltd. (Head Office: Rua do Comércio 85, Lisbon).

Companhia de Serviços Maritimos (COSEMA): agency in S. Tomé.

CIVIL AVIATION

Transportes Aéreos de São Tomé: São Tomé Airport Salazar, Caixa Postal 45, Sao Tomé; a government airline with regular services to Príncipe and Porto Alegre, Brazil; freight services to Luanda; Chief Exec. A. A. GROMICHO; fleet: Piper Navajo, DH Heron, Auster D4/180.

Also D.T.A. services to Ambrizete and Luanda, Angola.

PUERTO RICO

INTRODUCTORY SURVEY

Location, Climate, Language, Religion, Flag, Capital

The Commonwealth of Puerto Rico lies 50 miles east of Hispaniola (Haiti and the Dominican Republic) in the outer Caribbean. The climate is maritime-tropical with temperatures ranging from 63°F (17°C) to 96°F (36°C). The official language is Spanish and English is widely spoken. About 85 per cent of the population are Roman Catholic, the remainder belonging to Protestant denominations. The national flag (proportions 5 by 3) has five alternating red and white horizontal stripes, with a blue triangle containing a white star next to the staff. The capital is San Juan.

Recent History

Puerto Rico was a Spanish colony for 400 years until 1898 when, by the Treaty of Paris ending the Spanish-American War, it was ceded to the U.S.A. American citizenship was granted in 1917 and in 1947 Puerto Rico was given the right to elect its own Governor. In 1952 a Constitution was promulgated by which the island attained the status of a self-governing "Commonwealth" associated with the United States. In a plebiscite held in 1967, 60.5 per cent of voters ratified a continuation of Commonwealth status in preference to independence (0.6 per cent) or incorporation as a State of the United States (39 per cent). Emigration to the United States, once at a high rate in the 1940s and 1950s, has now almost ceased. The Constitution was amended by referendum in 1970 to reduce the minimum voting age to 18. In the general elections of 1972 the Popular Democratic Party, under the leadership of Rafael Hernández Colón, regained the governorship and legislative control from the New Progressive Party, which had been in power from 1968.

Government

Executive power is vested in a Governor, elected for a four-year term, and a Cabinet of ten Secretaries. The Legislature is the bi-cameral Legislative Assembly consisting of the Senate of 29 members and the House of Representatives of 54 members elected for four-year terms. A Resident Commissioner, elected for a four-year term, represents Puerto Rico in the U.S. House of Representatives. Puerto Ricans are citizens of the United States.

Defence

The United States and Puerto Rico have a common defence policy.

Economic Affairs

An intensive government-sponsored programme of industrialization has changed the country's economy from an agricultural to a mixed one. The main crops are sugar, tobacco and coffee. Industry now provides a greater income than agriculture and includes cigars, alcohol, chemicals, food-processing and household appliances. The United States provides the principal market for Puerto Rican imports and exports. In 1970–71 net income amounted to $4,296 million and per capita income was $1,564; the net income has been increasing consistently at a rate of about 10 per cent a year during the last decade. Tourism is an important source of revenue.

Transport and Communications

There are no railways on Puerto Rico. Roads total over 6,000 miles. There are ten ports, the chief ones being San Juan, Ponce and Mayagüez. Internal and international air services are provided by over thirty local American and foreign lines.

Social Welfare

Puerto Rico is included in the U.S. social security programme and also has a system of its own covering health, accident, disability and unemployment. About 30 per cent of the budget is devoted to social welfare and public health.

Education

The public education system is centrally administered by the Department of Education. Education is compulsory beteen the ages of 6 and 16. In the academic year 1970–71 there were 2,225 public day schools with a total of 687,877 pupils and 305 private schools with 101,842 pupils. The 12-year curriculum is subdivided into six grades of elementary school, three years junior high school and three years senior high school. Vocational schools at the high school level and kindergartens also form part of the public education system. Instruction is conducted in Spanish but English is a required subject at all levels. The Department of Education operates an island-wide radio and television educational network. About 40 per cent of the annual budget is devoted to education.

Public higher education policy is formulated by the Council on Higher Education which appoints the President of the University of Puerto Rico and Chancellors for the principal campuses. The State University system consists of four principal campuses and four regional colleges with a combined enrolment of 50,939 students. There are 35,334 students enrolled at private universities and colleges.

Tourism

There has been a sharp increase in tourism in recent years and it now forms a major source of income ($235.4 million in 1970). Attractions include the mountain scenery in the interior and fine beaches and game fishing in coastal waters. In 1973 there were 8,503 hotel rooms available and a total of 1,322,258 people visited the island.

United States laws and regulations apply to foreign visitors to Puerto Rico.

Sport

Baseball, basketball, boxing and cockfighting are the most popular sports.

Public Holidays

1974: September 3rd (Labour Day), October 8th (Discovery of America), October 22nd (Veterans' Day), November 19th (Discovery of Puerto Rico), November

22nd (Thanksgiiving Day), December 25th (Christmas Day).

1975: January 1st (New Year's Day), January 6th (Epiphany), January 11th (Birthday of Eugenio María de Hostos), February 18th (Birthday of George Washington), March 22nd (Emancipation of the Slaves), March 28th (Good Friday), April 16th (Birthday of José de Diego), May 28th (Memorial Day), July 4th (U.S. Independence Day), July 17th (Birthday of Luis Muñoz Rivera), July 25th (Constitution Day), July 27th (Birthday of José Celso Barbosa).

Weights and Measures

The United States system is officially in force and some old Spanish weights and measures are used in local commerce.

Currency and Exchange Rates

United States currency:
100 cents=1 U.S. dollar.
Exchange rates (April 1974):
£1 sterling=U.S. $2.36;
U.S. $1=42.35 pence.

STATISTICAL SURVEY

AREA AND POPULATION

AREA (square miles)

Total	Puerto Rico	Culebra	Vieques	Mona
3,423	3,336	11	57	20

POPULATION (Census of April 1st, 1970)

Total	San Juan* (capital)	Ponce	Mayagüez	Arecibo	Bayamón
2,713,147	824,758	158,981	85,857	73,468	156,192

* Includes Metropolitan Area.

Total Population (estimate at December 31st, 1972): 2,852,000.

BIRTHS, MARRIAGES AND DEATHS

Rate per '000	1969	1970	1971	1972
Births	25.2	25.0	25.6	24.1
Marriages	19.6	19.6	23.1	23.5
Deaths	6.6	6.7	6.5	6.7

EMPLOYMENT
('000)

	1970–71	1971–72	1972–73
Agriculture, Forestry and Fishing	66	62	58
Manufacturing	142	150	151
Trade	145	144	157
Government	119	138	153
Other	283	289	291
Total	755	783	810

AGRICULTURE

	Unit	1971	1972	1973†
Sugar (raw)	million short tons	4.5	4.4	3.6
Coffee	thousand cwt.	340	240	260
Tobacco	„ „	47	70	50
Pineapples	tons	57.5	48.3	44.5
Molasses	million gallons	31	28	24

† Preliminary.

Livestock (1971): Cattle 530,000, Pigs 198,070, Chickens 4,373,389.

INDUSTRY

	UNIT	1971	1972	1973
Sugar (Refined) . . .	thousand short tons	222	n.a.	n.a.
Distilled Spirits . .	thousand proof gallons	15,206	n.a.	n.a.
Rum (Bottled) . .	,, ,,	15,927	17,446	15,845
Beer	,, ,,	15,660	18,697	21,516
Cement . . .	thou. barrels of 376 lb.	9,883	10,452	10,548
Electricity . .	million kWh.	8,507	10,155	11,727

There were 1,829 government-aided factories in Puerto Rico in December 1970.

FINANCE

United States currency: 100 cents = 1 U.S. dollar ($).

Coins: 1, 5, 10, 25 and 50 cents; 1 dollar.

Notes: 1, 2, 5, 10, 20, 50 and 100 dollars.

Exchange rates (April 1974): £1 sterling = U.S. $2.36; U.S. $1 = 42.35 pence.

BUDGET, 1972 (Estimates)
($'000)

REVENUE		EXPENDITURE	
Surplus brought forward . . .	36,807	General Administration . . .	185,602
Property Taxes	40,918	Personal and Property Protection . .	202,265
Income Taxes . . .	414,304	Industrial, Agricultural and Commercial	
Inheritance and Gift Taxes . . .	13,558	Development . . .	146,344
Excise Taxes . . .	226,595	Health and Public Welfare . .	334,551
Licences, Permits, Fees, Business Charges	22,679	Education . . .	535,653
Lottery Proceeds . . .	31,710	Transport and Communications .	54,350
Miscellaneous . . .	160,886	Bond Redemption . . .	58,340
U.S. Grant-in-aid . . .	267,575	Other . . .	91,210
Bonds	175,095		
Customs . . .	42,692		
TOTAL . . .	1,432,819	TOTAL . . .	1,608,315

BALANCE OF PAYMENTS—ALL COUNTRIES
(million dollars)

	1972			1973		
	Credit	Debit	Balance	Credit	Debit	Balance
Goods and Services:						
Merchandise	1,982	3,065	− 1,083	2,579	3,481	− 902
Transportation . . .	111	375	− 264	119	431	− 312
Travel . . .	259	194	65	317	226	91
Investment income . .	255*	652†	− 397	261*	762†	− 501
Total . . .	2,703	4,423	−1,720	3,387	5,034	−1,647
Transfer Payments . .	582	—	582	636	—	636
CURRENT BALANCE . .	3,285	4,423	−1,138	4,023	5,034	−1,011
Capital and Monetary Gold:						
Long-term loans and investments .	1,311	27	1,284	880	102	778
Short-term loans and investments .	25	195	− 170	40	101	− 61
CAPITAL BALANCE . .	1,336	222	1,114	839	202	717
Net Errors and Omissions . .			− 25			− 31

* Includes operational disbursements of federal agencies and income on investments.

† Corresponds to income on investments.

PUERTO RICO—(STATISTICAL SURVEY)

EXTERNAL TRADE

(million dollars)

	1971	1972	1973
IMPORTS:			
From U.S.A.	2,202	2,270	2,538
From Foreign Countries	647	809	929
From Virgin Islands	29	28	29
Total	2,878	3,108	3,996
EXPORTS:			
To U.S.A.	1,578	1,744	2,184
To Foreign Countries	126	149	202
To Virgin Islands	92	81	80
Total	1,796	1,974	2,466

IMPORTS FROM AND EXPORTS TO THE U.S.A.

(1971-72: $'000)

	IMPORTS	EXPORTS
Food and Live Animals	485,238	271,661
Beverages and Tobacco	90,438	168,658
Crude Materials, Inedible, except Fuels	22,666	11,994
Mineral Fuels, Lubricants and Related Products	19,232	206,893
Animal and Vegetable Oils and Fats	17,527	7
Chemicals	243,782	419,060
Manufactured Goods classified chiefly by material	633,764	198,527
Machinery and Transport Equipment	584,231	292,527
Miscellaneous Manufactured Articles	381,673	558,574
Other Commodities and Transactions	59,239	2,777

IMPORTS AND EXPORTS BY COUNTRIES

(dollars)

	1971-72		1970-71	
	Imports	Exports	Imports	Exports
Belgium and Luxembourg	15,898,978	7,140,184	11,694,140	8,760,799
Canada	45,589,655	4,295,367	50,109,431	5,124,313
Dominican Republic	18,727,022	26,608,777	25,971,658	38,881,441
France	19,758,046	1,880,935	18,704,504	822,153
Germany, Federal Republic	42,503,497	2,336,269	43,301,051	1,568,861
Italy	18,386,356	1,998,272	20,691,126	3,550,038
Mexico	7,958,367	1,090,553	11,264,327	2,108,192
Netherlands Antilles	36,138,827	10,818,580	41,978,823	16,030,337
Spain	45,530,057	1,661,304	53,287,606	2,779,174
United Kingdom	38,642,403	5,608,195	25,959,078	3,986,976
U.S.A.	2,270,216,674	1,743,863,922	2,537,790,594	2,183,725,278
Venezuela	207,077,333	12,001,264	221,517,700	19,978,487

PUERTO RICO—(Statistical Survey)

TOURISM

	1970–71	1971–72	1972–73
Total Visitors . . .	1,095,119	1,172,885	1,322,258
From United States	860,754	888,706	1,011,485
From Other Countries . .	212,456	284,178	310,773
Expenditures (million $)	235	259	317
Rooms Available . . .	7,563	7,907	8,503

TRANSPORT
ROADS

	Cars		Trucks		Light Trucks	Others	Total
	Private	For Hire	Private	For Hire			
1970 . .	481,168	13,358	16,474	4,435	64,596	34,231	614,202
1971 . .	435,962	10,191	11,577	1,620	56,446	19,007	534,803
1972 . .	541,764	12,449	13,362	4,043	67,343	35,090	624,051

SHIPPING

	1970–71	1971–72	1972–73
Passengers Arriving . .	28,208	27,841	23,915
Passengers Departing . .	29,096	21,609	23,771
Freight (million tons) .	25.0	n.a.	n.a.

CIVIL AVIATION

	1969–70	1970–71	1971–72
Passengers Arriving . .	2,203,089	2,240,609	2,385,642
Passengers Departing . .	2,254,444	2,223,671	2,284,790
Freight (tons) . .	87,918	84,479	91,243

EDUCATION

Students and Teachers	1972	1973
Total Number of Students . . .	851,433	892,786
Public Day Schools . .	697,410	713,166
Private Schools (accredited) .	83,563	93,849
University of Puerto Rico .	43,609	50,439
Private Colleges and Universities .	26,851	35,334
Number of Teachers* . . .	23,859	28,919

* School teachers only   † August.

Source: Department of State, San Juan.

THE CONSTITUTION

On July 3rd, 1950, the United States Congress adopted an Act (Public Law No. 600) which was to allow "the people of Puerto Rico to organize a government pursuant to a constitution of their own adoption". This Act was submitted to the voters of Puerto Rico in a referendum and was accepted in the summer of 1951. A new Constitution was drafted in which Puerto Rico was styled as a commonwealth, or *estado libre asociado*, "a state which is free of superior authority in the management of its own local affairs", though it remained in association with the United States. This Constitution, with its amendments and resolutions, was ratified by the people of Puerto Rico on March 3rd, 1952, and by the Congress of the United States on July 3rd, 1952; and the Commonwealth of Puerto Rico was established on July 25th, 1952.

Under the terms of the political and economic union between the United States and Puerto Rico, United States citizens in Puerto Rico enjoy the same privileges and immunities as if Puerto Rico were a member state of the Union. Puerto Rican citizens are citizens of the United States and may freely enter and leave that country.

The Congress of the United States has no control of, and may not intervene in, the internal affairs of Puerto Rico.

Puerto Rico is exempted from the tax laws of the United States. While it has no representation in the United States Congress, the Puerto Rican Resident Commisioner to the United States, elected for a four-year term, enjoys the privileges of membership, without voting, of the House of Representatives of the United States Congress.

There are no customs duties between the United States and Puerto Rico. Foreign products entering Puerto Rico—with the single exception of coffee, which is subject to customs duty in Puerto Rico, but not in the United States—pay the same customs duties as would be paid on their entry into the United States.

The United States social security system is extended to Puerto Rico except for unemployment insurance provisions. Laws providing for economic co-operation between the Federal Government and the States of the Union for the construction of roads, schools, public health services and similar purposes are extended to Puerto Rico. Such joint programmes are administered by the Commonwealth Government.

Amendments to the Constitution are not subject to approval by the U.S. Congress, provided that they are consistent with the U.S. Federal Constitution, the Federal Relations Act defining federal relations with Puerto Rico, and Public Law No. 600. Subject to these limitations, the Constitution may be amended by a two-thirds vote of the Puerto Rican Legislature and by the subsequent majority approval of the electorate.

The Constitution starts with a definition of democracy and continues with a Bill of Rights.

BILL OF RIGHTS

No discrimination shall be made on account of race, colour, sex, birth, social origin or condition, or political or religious ideas. Suffrage shall be direct, equal and universal for all over the age of 18. Public property and funds shall not be used to support schools other than State schools. The death penalty shall not exist. The rights of the individual, of the family and of property are guaranteed. The Constitution establishes trial by jury in all cases of felony, as well as the right of *habeas corpus*. Every person is to receive free elementary and secondary education. Social protection is to be afforded to the old, the disabled, the sick and the unemployed.

THE LEGISLATIVE POWER

The Legislative Assembly consists of two houses, whose members are elected by direct vote for a four-year term. The Senate is composed of 27 members, the House of Representatives of 51 members. Senators must be over 30 years of age, and representatives over 25 years of age. The Constitution guarantees the minority parties additional representation in the Legislature, which may fluctuate from a quarter to a third of the seats in each house.

The Senate elects a President and the House of Representatives a Speaker from their respective members. The sessions of each house are public. A majority of the total number of members of each house constitutes a quorum. Either house can initiate legislation, though Bills for raising revenue must originate in the House of Representatives. Once passed by both Houses, a Bill is submitted to the Governor, who can either sign it into law or return it, with his reasons for refusal, within ten days. If it is returned, the Houses may pass it again by a two-thirds majority, in which case the Governor must accept it.

The House of Representatives, or the Senate, can impeach one of its members for treason, bribery, other felonies and "misdemeanours involving moral turpitude". A two-thirds majority is necessary before an indictment may be brought. The cases are tried by the Senate. If a representative or senator is declared guilty, he is deprived of his office and becomes punishable by law.

THE EXECUTIVE

The Governor, who must be at least 35 years of age, is elected by direct suffrage and serves for four years. He is responsible for the execution of laws, is commander-in-chief of the militia, and has the power to proclaim martial law. At the beginning of every regular session of the assembly, in January, he presents a report on the state of the treasury, and on proposed expenditure. To assist him, the Governor chooses his Secretaries of Departments, subject to the approval of the Legislative Assembly. These are led by the Secretary of State, who replaces the Governor at need.

LOCAL GOVERNMENT

The island is divided into 78 municipal districts for the purposes of local administration. The municipalities comprise not only urban areas but also the surrounding neighbourhood. The are governed by a mayor and a municipal assembly, both elected for a four-year term.

THE GOVERNMENT

HEAD OF THE STATE

Governor: Rafael Hernández Colón.

(Election, November 7th, 1972)

	Votes
Rafael Hernández Colón (Popular Democratic Party)	658,894
Luis A. Ferré (New Progressive Party)	563,582
Noel Colón Martínez (Independence Party)	69,653
Alfredo Nazario (People's Party)	4,007
Antonio J. González (Union Party)	3,214
Jorge Luis Landing (Soberanist Authentic Party)	433

EXECUTIVE

Governor: Rafael Hernández Colón.
Secretary of State: Víctor M. Pons, Jr.
Secretary of Justice: Francisco de Jesús Schuck.
Secretary of the Treasury: Salvador Casellas.
Secretary of Education: Ramón A. Cruz.
Secretary of Labour: Luis Silva Recio.
Secretary of Transportation and Public Works: Dennis W. Hernández.
Secretary of Health: José Alvarez de Choudens.
Secretary of Agriculture: Antonio González Chapel.
Secretary of Commerce: Damián Folch.
Secretary of Social Services: Elisa Díaz González.
Secretary of Housing: José E. Arrarás.
Secretary of Natural Resources: Cruz A. Matos.
Secretary of Addiction Services: Rafael Santos del Valle.
Secretary of Consumer Affairs: Federico Hernández Denton.

Resident Commissioner, Washington: Jaime Benítez.

LEGISLATIVE ASSEMBLY

SENATE
(29 members)

President of the Senate: Juan Cancel Ríos.

Vice-President of the Senate: Miguel Hernández Agosto.

Secretary of the Senate: Manuel Santana.

Composition: P.D.P. 20 seats, P.N.P. 8 seats, P.I.P. 1 seat (1972 elections).

HOUSE OF REPRESENTATIVES
(54 members)

Speaker of the House: Luis E. Ramos Yordán.

Vice-President of the House: Severo Colberg.

Secretary of the House: Enrique Piñero.

Composition: P.D.P. 37 seats, P.N.P. 15 seats, P.I.P. 2 seats (1972 elections).

POLITICAL PARTIES

Partido Nuevo Progresista (*New Progressive Party*): f. 1967; advocates eventual inclusion of Puerto Rico as a federated state of the United States of America; Leader Luis A. Ferré.

Partido Popular Democrático (*Popular Democratic Party*): f. 1938; supports continuation and improvement of the present Commonwealth status of Puerto Rico; Leader Rafael Hernández Colón.

Partido Independentista Puertorriqueño (*Puerto Rico Independence Party*): f. 1946; seeks immediate independence for Puerto Rico with the object of establishing a socialist democratic republic; Leader Rubén Berríos.

*Partido Auténtico Soberanista (*Soberanist Authentic Party*): f. 1971; seeks immediate independence for Puerto Rico by peaceful means and with special financial concessions from the United States; Leader Jorge Luis Landing.

*Partido del Pueblo (*People's Party*): f. 1968; supports continuation and improvement of the present Commonwealth status; Leader Roberto Sánchez Vilella.

*Partido Unión Puertorriqueña (*Puerto Rican Union Party*): f. 1971; seeks immediate independence for Puerto Rico by peaceful means and with special financial concessions from the United States; Leader Antonio González.

The **Partido Nacionalista** (*Nationalist Party*) and other entities favouring Puerto Rican independence are not organized or registered as political parties and advocate independence through non-electoral means.

The **Partido Socialista Puertorriqueño** (*Puerto Rican Socialist Party*) was formerly in that category, but is now in the process of registering to participate in future elections; Leader Juan Mari Bras.

* Obtained less than 5 per cent of total votes in 1972 elections; must re-register by petition of voters to participate in future elections.

JUDICIAL SYSTEM

The Judiciary is vested in a Supreme Court and other courts as may be established by law. The Supreme Court is composed of a Chief Justice and eight Associate Justices, appointed by the Governor with the consent of the Senate. The lower Judiciary consists of Superior and District Courts and Justices of the Peace equally appointed.

Chief Justice of the Supreme Court: PEDRO PÉREZ PIMENTEL.

There is also a Federal District Court, whose judges and attorney are appointed by the President of the United States.

District Judges: HIRAM CANCIO, JOSÉ V. TOLEDO, HERNÁN PESQUERA.

District Attorney: JULIO MORALES SÁNCHEZ.

RELIGION

There is no established Church in Puerto Rico. Eighty-five per cent of the population is Roman Catholic.

The Protestant churches represented include the Episcopalian, Baptist Presbyterian, Seventh Day Adventist, Lutheran and Christian Science.

There is a Jewish Community Centre in San Juan.

ROMAN CATHOLIC CHURCH

Archbishop:

San Juan: H.E. Cardinal LUIS APONTE MARTÍNEZ.

Bishops:

Arecibo: Most Rev. ALFRED F. MÉNDEZ.
Caguas: Most Rev. RAFAEL GROVAS-FÉLIX.
Ponce: Most Rev. JUAN FREMIOT TORRES OLIVER.

Episcopalian: Bishop: Rt. Rev. FRANCISCO REUS FROYLÁN.

Evangelical Council of Puerto Rico: Pres.: Rev. BENJAMÍN SANTANA.

Jewish Community Center: 903 Ponce de León Ave., Santurce, San Juan; Rabbi: SOLOMON WALDENBERG.

THE PRESS

With a literacy rate of more than 80 per cent, Puerto Rico has good readership of its few newspapers and magazines, as well as of mainland United States periodicals. However, radio and television are well organized, maintaining mainland U.S. standards, and offer a popular alternative. Several newspapers have large additional readerships in New York amongst the immigrant communities.

DAILIES
San Juan

El Mundo: P.O.B. 2408; f. 1919; morning; independent; Editor TOM C. HARRIS; circ. 136,495, Sunday 131,083.

El Nuevo Día: P.O.B. 297; f. 1909; morning (except Sunday); Spanish; independent; Publisher ANTONIO LUIS FERRÉ; Dir. PEDRO A. VÁZQUEZ; circ. 111,033, Saturday 82,308.

The San Juan Star: P.O.B. 4187; f. 1959; morning; English; independent; Editor ANDREW VIGLUCCI; circ. 56,000, Sunday 51,200.

PERIODICALS

Angela Luisa: P.O.B. 1807, Hato Rey; f. 1967; Spanish; monthly; Dir. ANGELA LUISA TORREGROSA; circ. 20,000.

Asomante: P.O.B. 1142, San Juan, 00902; f. 1945; Spanish; literary review; quarterly; published by Women Alumnae Association of the University of Puerto Rico; Chief Editor VENUS LYDIA SOTO.

Avance: 55 San Juan Bautista St., Puerto de Tierra; f. 1972; Spanish; weekly; Editor PEDRO ZERVIGÓN; circ. 40,000.

Bohemia: P.O.B. 1522, Hato Rey; Spanish; weekly; Editor CARLOS ROMERO GONZÁLEZ; circ. 50,000.

Boletín de la Academia de Artes y Ciencias de Puerto Rico: 716 Ponce de León Ave., Hato Rey, 00917; f. 1961; Spanish and English; quarterly; arts, sciences, history; Editor WASHINGTON LLORÉNS; circ. 2,000.

Caribbean Studies: Institute of Caribbean Studies, University of Puerto Rico; quarterly, in Spanish, English and French; Man. Editor SYBIL LEWIS; circ. 1,500.

Carta de Puerto Rico: Department of State, San Juan; f. 1965; weekly newsletter; English and Spanish editions; directed to overseas news media; Editor JOSÉ TORO ROMANACCE.

Educación: Department of Education, Hato Rey; f. 1960; Spanish; quarterly; Editor EDELMIRA GONZÁLEZ MALDONADO; circ. 25,000.

Isla Literaria: P.O.B. 1992, San Juan; f. 1969; Spanish; quarterly; literary review; Editor ERNESTO JUAN FONFRÍAS; circ. 4,000.

Qué Pasa in Puerto Rico: P.O.B. BN, San Juan, 00936; f. 1948; English; monthly tourist guide; Editor PATRICIA O'REILLY; circ. 60,000.

Revista de Ciencias Sociales U.P.R.: Facultad de Ciencias Sociales, University of Puerto Rico, Río Piedras; f. 1957; Spanish; quarterly; social sciences; Dir. PEDRO A. VALES HERNÁNDEZ; circ. 2,000.

Revista Colegio de Abogados de Puerto Rico: P.O.B. 1900, San Juan; f. 1940; Spanish; quarterly; law; Editor CARMELO DELGADO CINTRÓN; circ. 3,000.

Revista del Colegio de Ingenieros, Arquitectos y Agrimensores de Puerto Rico: P.O.B. 3845, San Juan, 00936; f. 1940; quarterly; architecture and engineering; Editor CARLOS DEL VALLE; circ. 5,500.

Revista del Instituto de Cultura Puertorriqueña: P.O.B. 4184, San Juan; f. 1958; Spanish; quarterly; arts, literature, Puerto Rican culture; Editor RICARDO ALEGRÍA; circ. 5,500.

La Torre: P.O.B. 22841, U.P.R. Station, San Juan; f. 1953; Spanish; quarterly; arts and literature; published by the University of Puerto Rico; Dir. ARTURO MORALES CARRIÓN; Editor M. MILLARES VÁZQUEZ; circ. 1,500.

PRESS AGENCIES

FOREIGN PRESS BUREAUX

A.P. P.O.B. 4187, San Juan, 00936; Chief JORGE ARFERD.

U.P.I. (*U.S.A.*): P.O.B. 5135, Puerto da Tierra Station; Division Man. FRANCIS M. McCARTHY.

PUBLISHERS

División Editorial Departamento de Instrucción Publica: Avda. Teniente César González, esquina Calaf, Urb. Tres Monjitas, Hato Rey, 00919; Dir. ANGEL ROSADO.

Editorial Biblioteca de Autores Puertorriqueños: P.O.B. 582, San Juan.

Editorial Club de la Prensa: P.O.B. 2229, San Juan; travel, fiction, folklore, essays.

Editorial Coquí: P.O.B. 21992, U.P.R., Río Piedras.

Editorial Cordillera, Inc.: P.O.B. 170, Hato Rey, 00919; f. 1964; Chair. MIGUEL A. SERRANO; Vice-Chair. HÉCTOR E. SERRANO.

Editorial Cultural Inc.: 51 Roble St., Río Piedras, 00925; f. 1947; Dir. F. VÁQUEZ ALAMO.

Editorial Edil, Inc.: 1001 Ponce de Léon Ave., P.O.B. 23008, Río Piedras; f. 1968; university texts, literature, technical and official publications; Dir. NORBERTO LUGO RAMÍREZ.

Editorial Instituto de Cultura Puertorriqueña: P.O.B. 4184, San Juan; history, literature, art, music, folklore.

Editorial Universitaria: University of Puerto Rico, Río Piedras, San Juan; science, medicine, philosophy, politics, textbooks.

RADIO AND TELEVISION

Radio and television in Puerto Rico are commercially operated, except for the government radio and television educational networks. There is a communications satellite (COMSAT) station in Cayey.

Broadcasters' Association of Puerto Rico: P.O.B. 96, Aguadilla; 50 mems.; Pres. HÉCTOR REICHARD.

RADIO

There are 81 commercial radio stations. The Puerto Rico Department of Education operates the WIPR educational radio network.

Number of radio receivers in 1972: 800,000.

TELEVISION

There are 17 commercial television stations. The Puerto Rico Department of Education operates the WIPR-TV education network. All television stations transmit in colour.

Number of television receivers in 1972: 680,000.

FINANCE

BANKING

(cap. = capital; res. = reserves; dep. = deposit; brs. = branches; amounts in dollars)

San Juan

Government Development Bank for Puerto Rico: P.O.B. 4748, San Juan, 00936; f. 1942; cap. 57m. (Dec. 1973). An autonomous government agency, this Bank acts as fiscal agent (borrowing agent) to the Commonwealth Government, its political subdivisions and its public corporations. It also supplies long- and medium-term loans for the establishment and expansion of private businesses. In addition, the bank serves as local settling agent for cheque clearing among Puerto Rico's commercial banks. Pres. JUAN A. ALBORS.

Banco Cooperativo de Puerto Rico: P.O.B. Ay, Hato Rey, 00936; f. 1974; Pres. Lic. ANTONIO GONZÁLEZ GEIGEL.

Banco Economías: P.O.B. BV; f. 1881; cap. 14.9m., dep. 212.9m. (Dec. 1973); Pres. LUIS A. MARTÍNEZ ALMO-DÓVAR; 12 brs.

Banco Mercantil de Puerto Rico: 1 Mercantil Plaza, Hato Rey; f. 1966; cap. 5m., dep. 79m., total resources 91m.; Pres. LUIS A. ABUDO; 3 brs.

Banco Obrero de Ahorro y Préstamo de Puerto Rico: P.O.B. BO, Hato Rey; f. 1961; cap. 7.4m., dep. 60.3m. (Oct. 1973); Pres. RAMÓN A. FIGUEROA; 3 brs.

Banco Popular de Puerto Rico: Banco Popular Center, P.O.B. 2708, Hato Rey; f. 1893; cap. 68m., dep. 878.6m. (Oct. 1973); Pres. JOSÉ LUIS CARRIÓN; 64 brs. in Puerto Rico, 7 in New York City.

Banco de San Juan: 1205 Ponce de Léon Ave., P.O.B. 9267, Santurce; f. 1927; cap. 14.6m., dep. 149.1m. (Oct. 1973); Pres. ROBERTO MARTÍN; 13 brs.

Banco de la Vivienda: P.O.B. 345, Hato Rey; f. 1962; cap. 7.1m., surplus 1.2m., total res. 17.6m. (Dec. 1971); Pres. JENARD BAQUERO; 7 brs.

First National Bank of Puerto Rico: P.O.B. 2139, Hato Rey; f. 1972; cap. 1.9m., dep. 15.7m.; Pres. ROBERTO LÓPEZ ALVAREZ.

Ponce

Banco Crédito y Ahorro Ponceño: Plaza Degetau, P.O.B. 4467; f. 1895; cap. 52.7m., dep. 667.4 (Oct. 1973); Pres. ANGEL M. RIVERA; Chair. of the Board ALFONSO VALDÉS; 49 brs. in Puerto Rico, 1 in New York City.

Banco de Ponce: Plaza Degatau, P.O.B. 3108; f. 1917; cap. 49.9m., dep. 495.5m. (Oct. 1973); Pres. ROBERTO DE JESÚS TORO; Exec. Vice-Pres. JULIO A. TORRES; Chair. FÉLIX JUAN SERRALLES; 26 brs. in Puerto Rico, 9 in New York City.

Humacao

Roig Commercial Bank: P.O.B. 457; f. 1922; cap. 4.8m., dep. 42.9m. (Oct. 1973); Pres. J. ADALBERTO ROIG; 6 brs.

AMERICAN AND CANADIAN BANKS IN PUERTO RICO

San Juan

Bank of Nova Scotia: P.O.B. 352; dep. 80.3m.; Man. KEVIN S. ROWE, 4 brs.

Chase Manhattan Bank N.A., The: P.O.B. 1990; Vice-Pres. and Gen. Man. FRANCISCO DE JESÚS TORO; 8 brs.

First National City Bank: P.O.B. 4106, 00936; Vice-Pres. FRANK QUEEN; 13 brs.

Royal Bank of Canada: P.O.B. 4987; District Man. D. MICHIE; 6 brs.

SAVINGS AND LOAN ASSOCIATIONS

Bayamón Federal Savings and Loan Association of Puerto Rico: P.O.B. 1435, Bayamón, 00619; f. 1960; cap. and dep. 93.2m., surplus 4.9m; Pres. GUILLERMO S. MARQUÉS; 9 brs.

Caguas Federal Savings and Loan Association of Puerto Rico: P.O.B. 666, Caguas; f. 1959; cap. 52m., surplus 4.2m., res. 1,080m.; Pres. JOSÉ M. FELICIANO.

Central Federal Savings and Loan Association of Puerto Rico: P.O.B. 735, Arecibo; cap. and dep. 16.5m., surplus 500,000 (Dec. 1971); Pres. FRANCISCO M. SUSONI.

First Federal Savings and Loan Association of Puerto Rico: P.O.B. 9146, Santurce; f. 1948; dep. 88.6m., surplus 16.3m., total resources 278.6m. (Dec. 1972); Pres. HORACE E. DÁVILA; 6 brs.

Oriental Federal Savings and Loan Association of Puerto Rico: P.O.B. 804, Humacao, 00661; cap. and dep. 11.2m., surplus 705,400 (Dec. 1972); Pres. CRISTOBAL RUIZ.

United Federal Savings and Loan Association of Puerto Rico: P.O.B. 2647, San Juan, 00936; f. 1957; cap. 81.5m., surplus and res. 6.1m., total resources 109.6m.; Pres. RAFAEL V. PÉREZ; 6 brs.

Western Federal Savings and Loan Association of Puerto Rico: P.O.B. 1180, Mayagüez; cap. 21.6m., surplus 2.5m., dep. 2.5m.; Pres. MIGUEL A. GARCÍA MÉNDEZ; 4 brs.

INSURANCE
San Juan

American International Life Insurance Co. of Puerto Rico: P.O.B. 3587; Pres. LUIS RODRÍGUEZ OLMO; life.

Atlantic Southern Insurance Co.: P.O.B. 2889, 00936; f. 1945; cap. p.u. 1m., assets 9.9m.; Chair. and Pres. W. W. GOODNER; Sec. MAURICE DORAN; life.

Caribbean Insurance Co.: Plaza Bldg.; Pres. I. RODRÍGUEZ MORENO; fidelity, surety.

Cooperativa de Seguros de Vida de Puerto Rico: Agents: Cafeteros Insurance Agency Inc., G.P.O. Box 3428; life.

La Cruz Azul de Puerto Rico: P.O.B. 4431; health.

Fortaleza Insurance Co.: P.O.B. 5634.

Insurance Company of Puerto Rico: Agents: Atlantic Insurance Underwriters of San Juan Inc., P.O.B. 5206, Puerta de Tierra.

International Life Insurance Co. of The Americans: P.O.B. 1869, 00936; f. 1957; Pres. W. W. GOODNER; Sec. LUIS F. QUIÑONES; life.

Puerto Rican—American Insurance Co.: P.O.B. 112, 00902; f. 1920; total assets 24.3m.; Pres. RAFAEL A. ROCA; Sec. RODOLFO E. CRISCUOLO.

Puerto Rico Fire and Casualty Co.: 701 Ponce de León Ave., Suite 208, Santurce; f. 1965; cap. and surplus $685,533; Pres. CARLOS M. BENÍTEZ; agents: Lippitt and Simonpietri Inc., P.O.B. 1112, 00902.

San Juan Mercantile Corp.: Muelle 6.

Security National Life Insurance Co.: P.O.B. 1873, Hato Rey, 00919; Pres. JORGE SOTO GARCÍA.

Seguros de Agricultores de Puerto Rico, Inc.: Agents: Cafeteros Insurance Agency Inc., P.O.B. 1511, Ponce.

Triple S: P.O.B. Box 3628, 00936; health.

There are over 15 principal agents, representing Puerto Rican, American and foreign companies.

TRADE AND INDUSTRY
CHAMBERS OF COMMERCE

Chamber of Commerce of Puerto Rico: Chamber of Commerce Bldgs., Tetuán 100, P.O.B. 3789, San Juan, 00904; f. 1913; 1,300 mems.; membership covers all towns in the island; Pres. HERMINIO FERNÁNDEZ TORRECILLAS; Treas. RAÚL PEÑAGARÍCANO; publs. *The Maritime Register* (monthly bulletin), *Comercio y Producción* (monthly).

Chamber of Commerce of Bayamón: 25 Dr. Barbosa St., Bayamón; 262 mems.; Pres. JUAN SANTIAGO; publ. *La Voz de Bayamón* (fortnightly).

Chamber of Commerce of Ponce: P.O.B. 2029, Ponce; f. 1887; 207 mems.; Pres. ROBERTO BACÓ; Sec. Mrs. MARTHA GERMAIN.

Chamber of Commerce of Río Piedras: 1057 Ponce de León Ave., Río Piedras; f. 1960; 300 mems.; Pres. NEFTALÍ GONZÁLEZ PÉREZ.

Chamber of Commerce of the West of Puerto Rico: P.O.B. 9, Mayagüez, 00708; f. 1962; over 450 mems.; Pres. ROBERTO FERRER; publ. *La Gaceta* (monthly).

Official Chamber of Commerce of Spain: Comercio 452, 2°, San Juan; f. 1966; 144 mems.; Pres. ULPIANO RODRÍGUEZ DEL VALLE.

DEVELOPMENT ORGANIZATION

Commonwealth of Puerto Rico Economic Development Administration—EDA: P.O.B. 2350, San Juan, 00936; 1290 Ave. of the Americas, New York, N.Y. 10019; public agency, with the Industrial Development Company and the Government Development Bank, in charge of the government-sponsored industrial development programme; Administrator TEODORO MOSCOSO.

PROFESSIONAL, INDUSTRIAL AND COMMERCIAL ASSOCIATIONS

Asociación de Industriales de Puerto Rico (*Puerto Rico Manufacturers' Association*): Suite 404–07, Midtown Condominium, 420 Ponce de León Ave., Hato Rey, 00918; f. 1934; 900 mems.; Pres. RAFAEL CEBOLLERO; Exec. Dir. HÉCTOR JIMÉNEZ JUARBE; publ. *Industrial Puerto Rico* (bi-monthly).

Asociación de Productores de Azúcar de Puerto Rico (*Sugar Producers' Association*): P.O.B. 9006, Santurce; f. 1909; 3 mems.; Pres. RAFAEL MARTÍNEZ; Sec. and Treas. PURA E. PADILLA.

Home Builders' Association of Puerto Rico: 1605 Ponce de León Ave., Condominium San Martín, Santurce; f. 1951; 199 mems.; Pres. EDUARDO FERRER.

Puerto Rico Bar Association: P.O.B. 1900, San Juan; f. 1840; 3,000 mems.; Pres. ELFREN BERNIER; Exec. Dir. RURICO E. RIVERA; publ. *Revista* (quarterly).

Puerto Rico Broadcasters' Association: P.O.B. 96, Aguadilla; f. 1947; 50 mems.; Pres. HÉCTOR REICHARD.

Puerto Rico Farmers' Bureau: P.O.B. 8114, Santurce; f. 1925; over 15,000 mems.; Pres. ORESTE RAMOS.

Puerto Rico Hotel Association: 1120 Ashford Ave., San Juan; 32 mems.; Pres. TOM SMITH; Exec. Dir. MIGUEL DOMENECH.

Puerto Rico Institute of Engineers, Architects and Surveyors: P.O.B. 3845, 00936; f. 1938; 4,100 mems.; Pres. RAFAEL LÓPEZ VEGA; publ. *Revista* (quarterly).

Puerto Rico Medical Association: P.O.B. 9387, Santurce; f. 1902; 1,900 mems.; Pres. JOSÉ RIGAU; publ. *Boletín Médico* (monthly).

Puerto Rico Rum Producers' Association, Inc.: P.O.B 3266, Old San Juan, 00904; f. 1943; 7 mems.; Pres. ANTONIO RODRÍGUEZ MAURA; Exec. Sec. CARLOS L. YORDÁN; publ. monthly and annual statistical reports.

Puerto Rico Teachers' Association: P.O.B. 1088, Hato Rey; f. 1911; 23,115 mems.; Pres. JOSÉ ELIGIO VÉLEZ; Exec. Sec. AGUSTÍN GARCÍA ESTRADA; publ. *El Sol* (monthly).

Puerto Rico United Retailers Center: P.O.B. 127, Hato Rey, 00919; f. 1891; 4,000 mems.; Pres. José A. Rivera; publ. *El Detallista* (monthly).

CO-OPERATIVES

Cooperativa de Cafeteros de Puerto Rico (*Coffee Growers' Co-operative*): P.O.B. 1511, Bo. Cuatro Calles, Ponce; f. 1924; 4,080 mems.; Chair. Damian Bennazar; Gen. Man. and Sec. Ramiro L. Colón, Jr.; publ. *Revista del Café* (monthly).

Puerto Rico Co-operative League: P.O.B. 707, San Juan, 00936; f. 1948; 372 mems.; Pres. Abimael Hernández.

TRADE UNIONS

American Federation of Labor—Congress of Industrial Organizations: 804 Ponce de León Ave., Santurce; Regional Dir. Agustín Benítez.

Confederación General de Trabajadores de Puerto Rico (*General Confederation of Workers of Puerto Rico*): 620 San Antonio St., Santurce; f. 1939; 35,000 mems.; Pres. Francisco Colón Gordiany.

Federación del Trabajo de Puerto Rico (*Puerto Rico Federation of Labour*): 1st floor, 274 Central Ave., Hyde Park, Río Piedras; f. 1952; 200,000 mems.; largest labour union in the country, affiliated with the ORIT and with the CIOSL; Pres. Hipólito Marcano; Sec.-Treas. Clifford W. Depin.

Federación Libre de los Trabajadores de Puerto Rico (*Free Federation of Labour of Puerto Rico*): First Federal Condominium, Santurce; f. 1899; about 105,000 mems.; Pres. Nicolás Nogueras Rivera.

Puerto Rico Industrial Workers' Union, Inc.: P.O.B. 22014, UPR Station, Río Piedras, 00928; Pres. David Muñoz Vázquez.

Sindicato de Equipo Pesado, AFL-CIO: RFD No. 3, P.O.B. 98, Río Piedras; f. 1954; 2,000 mems.; Pres. Félix Morales.

Sindicato de Obreros Unidos del Sur de Puerto Rico: P.O.B. 106, Salinas; f. 1961; 52,000 mems.; Pres. José Caraballo.

Unidad General de Trabajadores de Puerto Rico (*General Centre of Workers of Puerto Rico*): Calle Cerra 611, Parada 15, Santurce; f. 1948; 2,500 mems.; Pres. Adolfo Martínez.

TRANSPORT AND TOURISM

TRANSPORT

There are no railways in Puerto Rico.

ROADS

Paved roads totalled 6,553 miles in 1972. A modern highway system links all cities and towns along the coast and cross-country. In response to the demand for road expansion due to industrial growth, the Highways Authority was created in 1965 to design and build roads, highways and bridges. The annual investment in 1971–72 was $130m.

SHIPPING

There are ten ports in the island, the principal ones being San Juan, Ponce and Mayagüez. San Juan, one of the finest and longest all-weather natural harbours in the Caribbean, is the principal port of entry for foodstuffs and raw materials and for shipping finished industrial products. Sugar is shipped in bulk mostly through special piers located near production sites. Ocean passenger traffic is limited to tourist cruises since most travel to and from Puerto Rico is made by air.

The Puerto Rico Ports Authority regulates maintenance and use of port facilities, both governmental and private.

AMERICAN LINES SERVING PUERTO RICO

Gulf Puerto Rico Lines Inc.: P.O.B. 3628, San Juan; service: fully containerized, Puerto Rico–U.S. Gulf of Mexico ports.

Motorship of Puerto Rico, Inc.: 63 Fortaleza, San Juan; service: steamship agency; automobile carrier, Puerto Rico–Toronto.

Sea Land Service Inc.: P.O.B. 2648, San Juan, 00936; trailership and car-carrier services linking Puerto Rico with the Virgin Islands, Dominican Republic, Jamaica, Haiti, Trinidad, Curaçao, St. Maarten, St. Kitts, Antigua, U.S. East and West Coast ports, Europe and the Far East.

Seatrain Lines, Inc.: P.O.B. 4552, San Juan; service: trailership, Puerto Rico–New York–Philadelphia– Norfolk–Baltimore–Charleston–Virgin Islands–Santo Domingo–Europe–Haiti–Jamaica.

South Atlantic & Caribbean Line, Inc.: P.O.B. 5174, San Juan; service: army terminal docking facilities, roll on-roll off vessels from Jacksonville and Miami; Man. R. Whitehouse.

TMT Trailer Ferry, Inc.: P.O.B. 3921, San Juan; service: roll on-roll off, Puerto Rico–Florida.

Transamerican Trailer Transport Inc.: P.O.B. 3928, San Juan; service: trailerships (roll on-roll off), Puerto Rico–New York–Baltimore.

AGENTS FOR FOREIGN LINES

Antilles Shipping Corporation: Pier 8, San Juan; agents for: W. Llewellyn Wall & Co., Nordana Line.

Caribe Shipping Company: P.O.B. 3267, San Juan; agents for: W. Bruns and Co., Silver Line, Atlantic Transportation Co. Ltd., New York Navigation Co., Royal Mail Lines, Pacific Steam Navigation Co., Royal Netherlands S.S. Co., Mitsui O.S.K. Line, New Zealand Shipping Co., Aloca Steamship Co., Lloyd Brasileiro, Mardina Lines, Peninsular Oriental Steam Navigation, Royal Interocean Lines, Flota Mercante Grancolombiana, Companhia Nacional de Navegação, J. Lauritzen, Nopal Lines, Holland-America Line, Commodore Cruise Line, Sun Line, Lloyd Triestino, Cunard Line, Italian Line, Epirotiki Line and Exprinter.

Fred Imbert, Inc.: P.O.B. 4424, San Juan; agents for: Belfran Line, Fabre Line, French Line, Horn Line, Kawasaki, Kisen, Kaisha Ltd., Surinam Navigation Co. Ltd.

Gulf Puerto Rico Line: P.O.B. 3628, San Juan; agents for: Hapag-Lloyd.

International Shipping Agency, Inc.: P.O.B. 2748, San Juan; agents for: Caribbean Pioneers Line, Compañía Transatlántica Española, Nipon Yusen Kaisha Line, Saguenay Shipping Co. Ltd.

San Juan Mercantile Corporation: P.O.B. 4352, San Juan; agents for: Seaboard Shipping Co., Canadian Transport, Continental Line, Companhia Colonial de Navegação.

San Juan Trading Company: P.O.B. 3231, San Juan, 00936; agents for Royal Netherlands, Flota Mercante Gran Colombiana.

CIVIL AVIATION

Puerto Rican Airlines

Air Indes: Eastern Building, Santurce; regular routes from San Juan to Mayagüez, Ponce, St. Thomas and St. Croix; Pres. Harold Olson; fleet: 4 DC-3, 6 Twin Otter.

North Cay Airways: P.O.B. 3309, San Juan International Airport, 00904; scheduled passenger and cargo services between San Juan and St. Thomas (U.S. Virgin Islands); fleet: 4 DC-3, 20 BN-2A Islander.

Prinair: San Juan International Airport; regular routes from San Juan to Mayagüez, Ponce, and to several islands in the Caribbean; Pres. James S. Carrión.

Puerto Rico is also served by the following airlines: Aerovías Quisqueyanas (Dominican Republic), Air France, ALM (Netherlands Antilles), American, Avianca (Colombia), BWIA (Trinidad), Delta, Dominicana (Dominican Republic), Eastern, Iberia, Mexicana, Pan American, Viasa (Venezuela) and others.

San Juan International ranks among the airports with the highest passenger and cargo traffic in the world. Airports and seaports in Puerto Rico are operated by the Commonwealth's Ports Authority.

TOURISM

Tourism Development Company: Fomento Bldg., Hato Rey; P.O.B. BN, San Juan, 00936; f. 1970 as a public corporation to replace the Department of Tourism; Exec. Dir. Roberto Bouret.

Overseas Offices:

U.S.A.: 1290 Ave. of the Americas, New York, N.Y. 10019; 5455 Wilshire Blvd., Suite 1814, Los Angeles, Calif. 90036; Dupont Plaza Center, Suite 709-12, Miami, Fla. 33131; 11 East Adams St., Suite 1600, Chicago, Ill. 60603; 607 Boylston St., Boston, Mass.; 6 Penn Center, Philadelphia, Pa.; 235 Peachtree St. N.E., Atlanta, Ga. 30303.

Canada: Fidelity Bldg., 34 King St. East, Toronto, Ont.

Asociación Portorriqueña de Agencias de Viaje: 602 Muñoz Rivera Ave., Hato Rey; Pres. Charles Hastrup.

ATOMIC ENERGY

Puerto Rico Nuclear Center: Bio-Medical Bldg., Caparra Heights Station, San Juan; f. 1957; operated by the University of Puerto Rico for the U.S. Atomic Energy Commission; graduate-level research and training centre for Latin Americans; operates a pool-type 2-megawatt research reactor, and a L-77 homogeneous training reactor, and a sub-critical assembly; educational programmes at graduate level, and advanced training in radiation therapy, radiological physics, clinical uses of radioisotopes, radioecology, radiobiology and virology, radiation chemistry and physics; Acting Dir. Lawrence Ritchie.

UNIVERSITIES

Bayamón Central University: Bayamón; 60 teachers, 900 students.

Colegio Universitario Sagrado Corazón: Santurce: 93 teachers, 1,467 students.

Inter-American University of Puerto Rico: San Germán; 476 teachers, 8,732 students.

Universidad Católica de Puerto Rico: Santa María, Ponce; 318 teachers, 6,949 students.

University of Puerto Rico: Río Piedras; 2,919 teachers, 47,533 students.

QATAR
INTRODUCTORY SURVEY

Location, Climate, Language, Religion, Flag, Capital

The State of Qatar occupies a peninsula on the west coast of the Arabian Gulf. The climate is exceptionally hot and humid in the summer and mild in the winter. Rainfall is negligible. The official language is Arabic, though English is spoken in business, official and government circles. Almost all the inhabitants are Wahabi Muslims. The national flag (proportions 30 by 11) is maroon, with a white serrated border at the hoist. The capital is Doha.

Recent History

Qatar became an independent, sovereign state on September 1st, 1971, after being protected since 1916 by treaties and agreements with Britain. In February 1972 the Prime Minister, Sheikh Khalifa bin Hamad al-Thani, deposed his cousin the Amir, Sheikh Ahmad, in a bloodless *coup d'état*, and began implementing wide-ranging social and economic reforms.

Government

A new provisional constitution came into effect in July 1970. Executive power resides in the Cabinet, which also appoints three members of the Consultative Assembly, the remaining members being elected. An Advisory Council with 20 nominated members was set up in April 1972.

Economic Affairs

Qatar's economy is almost wholly dependent on oil. Although petroleum was first discovered in the mid-1930s, the first exports were not made until December 1949. At present oil production is carried out by only two companies, the Qatar Petroleum Company Ltd. (QPC), and Shell Company of Qatar, which together produced over 22 million long tons of crude oil in 1972, from which the

Government received 947 million riyals in royalties. Under an agreement signed in February 1974, the Government is to increase its share in QPC and Shell Qatar to 60 per cent. From October 1973 until March 1974 an embargo was placed on all exports of oil to the Netherlands and the U.S.A.

Education

Education is free at all levels and has been expanding at a rapid rate since the inception of a state educational system in 1956. Total school attendance in 1972/73 was over 20,000, while 615 Qatari students attended foreign colleges and universities.

Public Holidays

1974: August 18th* (Leilat Al Meiraj, Ascension of the Prophet), September 3rd (National Day), September 19th* (Ramadan begins), October 16th–19th* (Id ul Fitr, End of Ramadan), December 24th–26th (Christmas, also Id ul Adha).

1975: January 1st (New Year's Day), January 14th (Muslim New Year), January 24th* (Ashoura), March 26th (Mouloud, Birth of the Prophet).

* Religious holidays, which are dependent on the Muslim lunar calendar, and may differ from the dates given.

Weights and Measures

The imperial and metric systems are both in use.

Currency and Exchange Rates

100 dirhams = 1 Qatar riyal.
Exchange rates (April 1974):

£1 sterling = 9.35 riyals;
U.S. $1 = 3.947 riyals.

STATISTICAL SURVEY
AREA AND POPULATION

AREA	POPULATION (1972 Estimates)	
	TOTAL	DOHA (capital)
4,000 sq. miles	170,000	130,000

OIL

QATAR PETROLEUM COMPANY CRUDE OIL PRODUCTION

	LONG TONS		LONG TONS
1964	9,978,000	1969	9,366,000
1965	9,158,000	1970	8,882,000
1966	9,059,000	1971	10,400,000
1967	9,070,000	1972	11,368,000
1968	9,018,000	1973	11,730,000

SHELL QATAR CRUDE OIL PRODUCTION

	LONG TONS (million)
1970	7.4
1971	9.9
1972	11.5
1973	16*

* Approximately.

FINANCE AND TRADE

100 dirhams = 1 Qatar riyal (QR).

Coins: 1, 5, 10, 25 and 50 dirhams.

Notes: 1, 5, 10, 25, 50 and 100 riyals.

Exchange rates (April 1974): £1 sterling = 9.35 riyals; U.S. $1 = 3.947 riyals.

100 Qatar riyals = £10.695 = $25.333.

In May 1973 Qatar issued its own currency, the Qatar riyal (QR), with the same parity and exchange value as the old currency, the Qatar/Dubai riyal. Value in this Statistical Survey is expressed in the old currency.

Budget: The budget for the Muslim year 1392 (February 16th, 1972, to February 3rd, 1973) totalled 700 million Q/D riyals, of which 300 million were allocated to capital projects.

OIL REVENUES
('000 Q/D riyals)

	1970–71 (1390)	1971–72 (1391)
Payments by Qatar Petroleum Co.	327,985	517,911
Payments by Shell Qatar	267,016	429,200

EXTERNAL TRADE
IMPORTS ('000 Q/D riyals)

1969	252,179
1970	305,491
1971	515,869
1972	607,000*

* provisional.

Exports: Non-oil exports are negligible, and the customs do not provide figures, but there is a flourishing re-export trade with other Gulf States.

PRINCIPAL TRADING PARTNERS
('ooo Q/D riyals)

IMPORTS	1969	1970	1971	1972
United Kingdom	56,894	73,939	193,213	160,575
U.S.A.	31,606	30,865	50,298	63,149
Japan	19,365	28,492	54,108	76,108
Germany, Federal Republic . .	17,563	17,053	23,532	31,856
Lebanon	15,317	19,949	28,394	42,033
India	11,293	18,583	14,727	12,453
Bahrain	10,866	6,991	8,421	11,871
Iran	9,355	10,429	6,232	12,576
France	9,116	11,954	12,343	50,682
Netherlands	8,326	9,516	12,188	12,416

EXPORTS	1972
Saudi Arabia . . .	37,366
United Arab Emirates . .	14,153
Iran . . .	3,669
Kuwait . . .	2,794
Bahrain . . .	1,887
Oman . . .	1,696
Lebanon . . .	1,627
Japan . . .	1,431

EDUCATION

	PUPILS		TEACHERS	
	1969/70	1970/71	1969/70	1970/71
Primary	13,665	14,479	762	752
Preparatory General . .	2,183	2,537	120	141
Secondary General . .	769	911	62	80
Teacher Training . .	205	237	24	38
Commercial School . .	74	66	10	10
Technical School . .	170	143	34	34
Religious Institutions	157	158	16	16

THE CONSTITUTION

A new provisional constitution came into effect in July 1970. Executive power is put in the hands of the Cabinet, which will appoint three members to a twenty-three member Consultative Assembly; the other twenty members are to be elected. All fundamental democratic rights are guaranteed.

THE GOVERNMENT

HEAD OF STATE

Amir: Sheikh KHALIFA BIN HAMAD AL-THANI.

COUNCIL OF MINISTERS

(May 1974)

Prime Minister: Sheikh KHALIFA BIN HAMAD AL-THANI.

Minister of Finance and Petroleum: Sheikh ABDUL-AZIZ BIN KHALIFA AL-THANI.

Minister of Foreign Affairs: Sheikh SUHEIM BIN HAMAD AL-THANI.

Minister of Education, Culture and Youth Care: Sheikh JASIM BIN HAMAD AL-THANI.

Minister of Public Health: KHALED BIN MOHAMMED AL-MANAI.

Minister of the Economy and Commerce: Sheikh NASSER BIN KHALID AL-THANI.

Minister of Electricity and Water: Sheikh JASIM BIN MUHAMMAD AL-THANI.

Minister of Justice: Sheikh ABDEL RAHMAN BIN SAUD AL-THANI.

Minister of the Interior: Sheikh KHALID BIN AHMED AL-THANI.

Minister of Industry and Agriculture: Sheikh FAISAL BIN THANI AL-THANI.

Minister of Public Works: KHALID BIN ABDULLAH AL-ATIYYAH.

Minister of Information: ISA GHANIM AL-KUWARI.

Minister of Municipal Affairs: Sheikh MOHAMMED BIN JABER AL-THANI.

Minister of Labour and Social Affairs: ALI BIN AHMAD AL-ANSARI.

Minister of Transport and Communications: ABDULLAH BIN NASSER AL-SUWAIDI.

DIPLOMATIC REPRESENTATION

EMBASSIES ACCREDITED TO QATAR

Egypt: *Ambassador:* SALEH ZAGHLOUN.

France: *Chargé d'Affaires:* B. LOPINOT.

Germany, Federal Republic: *Ambassador:* HANS HELMUT FREUNDT.

India: *Ambassador:* OMAR QUMRAIN.

Iran: *Ambassador:* HOUSHING MOKADDAM.

Iraq: *Ambassador:* DAHHAM AL-ALOUSI.

Jordan: *Ambassador:* HASHIM ABU AMARA.

Kuwait: *Ambassador:* SULAIMAN SANEH.

Lebanon: *Ambassador:* MARCELLE NAMMOOR.

Pakistan: *Ambassador:* HAKIM MOHAMED AHSOON.

Saudi Arabia: *Ambassador:* Sheikh AHMED BIN ALI AL-MUBARAK.

Somalia: *Ambassador:* ABDULLAH HAJI ABDEL-RAHMAN.

Sudan: *Ambassador:* MOHAMMAD UTHMAN SHENDI.

Tunisia: *Ambassador:* MAHMOOD SHARSPHOOR.

United Kingdom: *Ambassador:* EDWARD HENDERSON.

Yemen Arab Republic: *Ambassador:* ABDULLA HIJIRI.

Qatar also has diplomatic relations with Afghanistan, Algeria, Austria, Chad, Denmark, Finland, Japan, the Netherlands, Norway, Pakistan, Senegal, Sweden, Syria, Trinidad and Tobago, the U.S.A. and Venezuela.

JUDICIAL SYSTEM

Justice is administered by five courts (Higher Criminal, Lower Criminal, Civil, Appeal and Labour) on the basis of codified laws. In addition traditional Sharia courts apply the Holy Law in certain cases. Non-Muslims are invariably tried by a court operating codified law. Independence of the judiciary is guaranteed by the provisional Constitution.

RELIGION

The indigenous population are Muslims of the Sunni sect, most being of the strict Wahabi persuasion.

PRESS

Al-Doha Magazine: Ministry of, P.O.B. 2324, Doha; f. 1969; monthly; Arabic.

Dar Al-Ouroba: Newspaper Printing and Publishing, Doha; publ. daily Arabic newspaper *Al-Arab*, weekly Arabic magazine *Al-Ouroba* and weekly English magazine *Gulf News*.

RADIO AND TELEVISION

Radio Qatar: P.O.B. 1414, Doha; f. 1968; government service, transmitting for 12 hours daily in Arabic; an English language programme was introduced early in 1972.

Qatar Television: P.O.B. 1944, Doha; f. 1970; two 5 kW transmitters began beaming programmes throughout the Gulf in March 1972.

FINANCE

BANKING

Qatar Monetary Agency: P.O.B. 1234, Doha; f. 1966 as Qatar and Dubai Currency Board; became Qatar Monetary Agency 1973 when Qatar issued its own currency, the Qatar riyal; currency in circulation (Dec. 1973) QR 129 million; Governor MAJED AL-MAJED.

Qatar National Bank, S.A.Q.: Doha, P.O.B. 1000; f. 1964; cap. and res. Q. riyals 57.3m., dep. 267m. (1973); Chair. Sheikh ABDUL AZIZ BIN KHALIFER ALTHANI.

Arab Bank Ltd.: Amman, Jordan; Doha, P.O.B. 172; Man. SHARIF AL JA'ABARY.

Banque de Paris et des Pays-Bas: Paris; Doha.

British Bank of the Middle East, The: Doha, P.O.B. 57; Man. R. R. REES.

Chartered Bank: London; P.O.B. 29, Doha.

First National City Bank: P.O.B. 2309, Doha.

National and Grindlays Bank Ltd.: London; Doha, P.O.B. 2001; Man. L. B. CANT.

United Bank of Pakistan: P.O.B. 242, Doha.

INSURANCE

Qatar Insurance Co.: P.O.B. 666, Doha; f. 1964; assets and reserves 5m. Q/D riyals (1971); branch in Dubai; Man. FATHI I. GABR.

COMMERCE

Qatar Chamber of Commerce: P.O.B. 402, Doha; f. 1963; 13 mems. appointed by decree; Pres. AHMED MUHAMMAD AL SOWAIDI; Sec. KAMAL ALI SALEH.

OIL

Qatar National Petroleum Company: f. April 1972; owns 20 per cent of shares of *Qatar Petroleum Co.* and *Shell Qatar*, and 50 per cent of shares of *Qatar Oil Co.* (*Japan*); in line with OPEC policy the Government agreed a participation agreement with the Qatar Petroleum Company and Shell Qatar in January 1974 to secure Qatar's interest. On February 20th, 1974 the Government signed a further agreement which gives it a 60 per cent interest in QPC and Shell Qatar. It has taken over the National Oil Distribution Co., which handles distribution and marketing.

Qatar Oil Co. Ltd (Japan): Doha; formed by a consortium of Japanese companies; granted an 8,500 square mile offshore concession in March 1969; drilling began in January 1971. The company discontinued its search for oil and returned the concession rights to the Government in May 1974.

Qatar Petroleum Co.: Doha; an associate of Iraq Petroleum Co. and 75 per cent shareholder in the operating Company producing and exporting crude oil from the Dokhan oilfield (onshore). Under a participation agreement signed in 1974 the Government became a 60 per cent interest holder in the QPC Concession and crude oil production facilities effective from January 1st, 1974. Since that date the operations in Qatar have been carried out on behalf of the interest holders by QPC as interim operator. Total production from the Dukhan field in 1973 was 91.65 million barrels (11.73 million long tons).

Shell Company of Qatar: P.O.B. 47, Doha; holds an offshore concession. A Government participation agreement was signed in February 1974 (*see* above); Man. Dir. B. R. SUTTILL. Total production in 1973 was approx. 16m. long tons.

TRANSPORT

ROADS

There are some 600 miles of surfaced road linking Doha and the oil centres of Dukhan and Umm Said with the northern end of the peninsula. A 65-mile long road from Doha to Salwa was completed in 1970, and joins one leading from Al Hufuf in Saudi Arabia, giving Qatar land access to the Mediterranean. A 260-mile highway, built in conjunction with Abu Dhabi, links both states with the Gulf network. Road construction is a continual process throughout the peninsula.

PIPELINES

Oil is transported by pipeline from the oilfield at Dukhan to the loading terminal at Umm Said. Natural gas is brought by pipeline from Dukhan to Doha where it is used as fuel for a power station and water distillation plant.

SHIPPING

Qatar National Navigation and Transport Co. Ltd.: P.O.B. 153, Doha; shipping agents, lighterage contractors ship chandlers, clearing and forwarding agents at the ports of Qatar.

Doha Port: A four-berth quay costing £10 million was completed in 1969; it is linked with Doha Town by a 3,600-ft. causeway. A new expansion project, estimated to cost QR 162 million is expected to double the size of the port.

Umm Said Harbour: Although accommodating smaller tankers (up to 60,000 d.w.t.) Umm Said still has the country's main oil terminal. A 220,000 ton capacity tank farm is connected by a series of pipelines with QPC's three main gathering stations. A 700 ft. wide jetty is linked to a grain mill and a newly constructed fertilizer plant.

CIVIL AVIATION

Doha international airport is equipped to receive jumbo jets; its runway was extended to 15,000 ft. in 1970. Plans for a new civil airport, which will have one of the longest runways in the world (14,993 ft.) are under consideration.

Gulf Air Co. Ltd.: jointly owned by Bahrain, Qatar, Abu Dhabi and British Airways (*see* Bahrain—Civil Aviation).

Gulf Helicopters: 76 per cent owned by Gulf Air, 24 per cent by a British Airways Group; fleet of four Sikorsky S.62A.

Doha is served by the following airlines: Alia (Jordan), British Airways, EgyptAir, Gulf Air, Iranian Airways, Iraqi Airways, Kuwait Airways, MEA, Pakistan International Airlines, Saudia, Syrian Arab Airlines, TMA, Yemen Airlines.

RHODESIA
(SOUTHERN RHODESIA)

INTRODUCTORY SURVEY

Location, Climate, Language, Religion, Flag, Capital

Rhodesia lies in south-central Africa with Mozambique to the east, Zambia to the north-west, Botswana to the south-west and South Africa to the south. Climate is tropical, modified considerably by altitude. The official language is English; the main African languages are Sindebele and Chishona. About 20 per cent of the population are Christian. Of the European and Coloured population, 33 per cent are Anglican, 11 per cent Presbyterian, 15 per cent Roman Catholic, 9 per cent Dutch Reformed and 9 per cent Methodist. Most of the Africans follow traditional beliefs, while the Asians are almost equally Muslim or Hindu. The official flag is an ensign with a sky blue background, with the Union Jack in the top left corner and the Rhodesia badge, consisting of a green shield with a gold pick and a red lion between two thistles. In November 1968 the Smith regime adopted a new national flag (proportions 2 by 1): three vertical stripes of green, white and green, with the Rhodesian coat of arms on the central white stripe. The capital is Salisbury.

Recent History

The British government and the white settlers grouped Southern and Northern Rhodesia and Nyasaland into the Central African Federation in 1953, but the Federation broke up in 1963 in the face of successful nationalist movements in Northern Rhodesia and Nyasaland, which achieved independence as Zambia and Malawi in 1964. The 1961 Constitution, drawn up for Southern Rhodesia by the British and white settler governments, provided for ultimate majority rule. In order to prevent such an eventuality the government of Prime Minister Ian Smith, on November 11th, 1965, unilaterally declared Rhodesia independent of the British Crown. Britain terminated all trading and other relations with Rhodesia, while the UN applied economic sanctions against the regime. However, through the evasion of sanctions by certain countries, the assistance of South Africa and Portugal and the diversification of the economy, the Smith regime was able to maintain itself in power.

The country was declared a republic on March 2nd, 1970, and the first elections under the new constitution were held in April 1970, when the Rhodesian Front won all 50 seats on the European roll.

All attempts at settlement between the British government and the Smith régime failed until November 1971, when a proposed settlement based on an amended form of the Smith regime's 1969 republican constitution, was agreed, subject to acceptance by the Rhodesian people as a whole. Public opinion was tested by a commission appointed by the British government which found that the settlement proposals were not acceptable to the people of Rhodesia. The Africans rejected them, and criticized the absence of African representation at the settlement negotiations. The great majority of the European population accepted the proposals, which had qualified support from the Coloureds and Asians. Sanctions have remained in force, while the Smith regime has continued to operate the 1969 Constitution.

The Smith regime has progressively moved closer to the South African system of *apartheid* with the introduction of more discriminatory legislation. It now has powers to impose collective fines, without trial or charge, on an entire community. A bill regulating residential areas by race was passed in December 1972.

In 1972 Rhodesian troops and police mounted a large operation against African guerrilla forces, which continued in 1973. In January the deaths of several Europeans as a result of guerrilla activity provided the pretext for the closure of the border with Zambia to all rail traffic except Zambia's copper exports. President Kaunda of Zambia reacted on January 11th by sealing the border completely, and announcing that Zambia would find other outlets for its copper. Mr. Smith re-opened the border on February 3rd but the Zambian authorities kept it closed. Meanwhile guerrilla activity continued.

Security laws were tightened in May 1973, and there was evidence of South African military assistance to the regime. During 1973 the regime detained numerous top officials of the African National Council (ANC) without trial. Sanctions were renewed by an overwhelming vote in the House of Commons in October 1973. Riots at the University of Rhodesia, more guerrilla attacks and a fall in white immigration created an uncertain situation. The regime reacted by extensive resettling of thousands of Africans, the hanging of several guerrillas, increasing its powers of detention, and a considerable increase in military expenditure. In April 1974 guerrilla activity was was continuing unabated and the security position on Rhodesia's borders appeared to be deteriorating further while diplomatic and economic pressure on the regime from the Organization of African Unity (OAU) and the UN were maintained.

Ian Smith's Rhodesian Front again won all 50 seats on the white roll in July elections.

Government

Since November 1965 the Smith regime has made a number of constitutional changes culminating in the republican constitution which is now in force. Under this there is a President, a 23-man Senate and an Assembly of 66 members. Fifty of these are Europeans elected on a European roll, eight are Africans elected on an African roll and another eight Africans are chosen by electoral colleges of chiefs, headmen and other government-paid officials.

A state of emergency has existed since November 1965 and powerful security legislation, extended in 1973 and 1974, remains in force.

Defence

The strength of the army is estimated at 3,500, of the air force 1,200, and of the reserves 10,000. The para-military British South African Police numbers over 8,000 with a further 35,000 in reserve. The Rhodesian forces have high standards of equipment, mobility and training. In

1971 it was announced that military service for white Rhodesians was to be increased to a year and a major expansion of the armed forces together with the extension of military service has been announced.

Economic Affairs

Rhodesia's minerals include notably gold, asbestos, coal and chrome, but copper and other minerals are mined. Despite sanctions, 1973 was a record year for the Rhodesian mining industry. Under an amendment to the U.S. Military Procurement Act of 1971, the United States has imported more than $13 million worth of "strategic and critical commodities", particularly nickel and chrome, from Rhodesia since January 1972 and despite attempts to repeal it, the amendment still remains in force. A nickel mine is to be developed at Shangani at an estimated cost of R$17 million and production is expected to begin in 1975. Manufactures now surpass mining in importance, particularly food processing, metals, engineering and textiles. Tea, maize, potatoes and sugar are the main crops apart from tobacco, which has been severely affected by UN sanctions, and there is much stock-raising. Agricultural output was adversely affected by the drought in 1973 though it has since improved. Maize, groundnuts, cotton and Oriental tobacco are the chief crops grown by African farmers, who have exclusive rights to half the land area of Rhodesia. The wage gap between Europeans and Africans widened considerably between 1965 and 1971 though unemployment has decreased. The dam on Lake Kariba provides most of the country's electricity. Trade between Britain and Rhodesia has ceased since the declaration of independence, and trade with many other countries has been restricted. This has led to considerable diversification of the Rhodesian economy and an energetic search for new outlets. Much Rhodesian merchandise is shipped from South Africa and Mozambique as exports from those countries and there has been widespread breaking of sanctions. The closure of the border with Zambia has curtailed Rhodesia's trade with Zaire and Zambia. The Rhodesian economy is likely to be hard hit by the Arab oil embargo, particularly as it extends to Portugal and South Africa on whom Rhodesia relies for supplies. Petrol rationing was re-introduced in February 1974.

Transport and Communications

Good rail services link Salisbury with South African and Portuguese ports, particularly Beira and Lourenço Marques in Mozambique. Major trunk roads are likewise of high standard. International and domestic air services connect most of the larger towns. There are also numerous charter and private aircraft used by mining companies, farmers and others. Over R$16 million is to be spent from 1973 to 1976 on roads and bridges, particularly in areas subjected to guerrilla attack. A large thermal power station costing an estimated R$250 million is to be built at Wankie.

Social Welfare

There is no statutory provision for social security, though government and industrial schemes exist. The Social Welfare Department deals with child welfare and delinquency for all races. For Whites, the Department also deals with marriage guidance, alcoholics, care of the aged, and relief of distress.

Education

Estimated expenditure for 1973-74 for African education was R$24m., for non-African R$21.7m. There were 784,874 African pupils in 1973 and 70,266 non-Africans in primary and secondary schools. The University College of Rhodesia at Salisbury provides multi-racial higher education.

Tourism

The principal tourist attractions are the Victoria Falls, the Kariba Dam and the Wankie Game Reserve and National Park. Zimbabwe Ruins near Fort Victoria and World's View in the Matopos Hills are of special interest. In the Eastern Districts around Umtali there is trout fishing and climbing. Safaris and game-watching holidays can be arranged. There has recently been a fall in the number of tourists visiting Rhodesia.

Sport

The climate is suitable for almost every form of sport. Football, cricket, tennis, golf, baseball, swimming, athletics and horse-racing are catered for, and gliding, yachting, camping and game hunting are also popular.

Public Holidays

1974: September 12th (Pioneers' Day), November 11th (Independence Day), December 25th–26th (Christmas and Boxing Day).

1975: January 1st (New Year's Day), March 28th–31st (Easter), May 19th (Whit Monday), July 14th (Rhodes' and Founders' Day).

Weights and Measures

The imperial system is in use.

Currency and Exchange Rates

100 cents = 1 Rhodesian dollar (R$).

Unofficial exchange rates (April 1974):

£1 sterling = R$ 1.398;
U.S. $1 = 59.21 Rhodesian cents.

STATISTICAL SURVEY

AREA AND POPULATION

AREA (sq. kilometres)	ESTIMATED POPULATION (June 1973)			
	TOTAL	AFRICANS	EUROPEANS	OTHERS
390,581	5,890,000	5,590,000	270,000	27,600

CHIEF TOWNS (Dec. 1972 est.)

Salisbury (capital)	.	490,000	Wankie . .	22,000
Bulawayo	.	296,000	Shabani . .	17,000
Gwelo	.	54,000	Sinoia . .	16,000
Umtali .	.	52,000	Fort Victoria .	14,000
Que Que .	.	39,000	Marandellas .	12,000
Gatooma .	.	30,000	Redcliff . .	11,000

LAND DISTRIBUTION

(1973—'000 hectares)

European Area:		African Area:	
Forest Land .	755	Forest Land .	172
Parks and Wild Life Land	1,774	Parks and Wild Life Land	255
General Land	15,619	Purchase Land .	1,485
Specially Designated Land	8	Tribal Trust Land .	16,181
		Specially Designated Land	119
Total European Area .	18,156	*Total African Area* .	18,212

National Area . . .	2,667
TOTAL . .	39,035

MIGRATION

	EUROPEANS*		ASIANS AND COLOUREDS*		NON-INDIGENOUS AFRICAN ADULT MALES†	
	Immigrants	Emigrants	Immigrants	Emigrants	Immigrants	Emigrants
1963 . . .	7,000	18,000	206	110	45,220	51,300
1964 . . .	7,000	15,710	130	228	40,370	48,600
1965 . . .	11,128	8,850	178	172	26,920	30,300
1966 . . .	6,418	8,510	131	160	17,430	33,630
1967 . . .	9,618	7,570	201	118	16,280	20,960
1968 . . .	11,864	5,650	149	149	19,350	21,910
1969 . . .	10,929	5,890	146	113	15,880	18,020
1970 . . .	12,227	5,890	118	128	13,000	22,270
1971 . . .	14,743	5,340	138	81	10,500	20,250
1972 . . .	13,966	5,150	119	102	8,640	16,290

* Exclusive of migration with Malawi and Zambia during the year 1963.

† Figures for years prior to 1965 include some juvenile males.

EMPLOYMENT

	1970		1971		1972*	
	Africans	Others	Africans	Others	Africans	Others
Agriculture, Forestry and Fishing . .	290,500	4,590	303,400	4,640	337,500	4,680
Mining and Quarrying . . .	53,300	3,740	53,900	3,670	54,200	3,650
Manufacturing	99,500	18,490	105,300	19,720	112,600	21,250
Building and Construction . .	42,500	7,490	47,000	7,890	51,200	7,830
Electricity and Water . . .	4,200	1,440	4,200	1,590	4,400	1,690
Distribution, Restaurants and Hotels .	46,200	19,970	50,770	21,000	57,600	21,890
Finance, Insurance and Real Estate .	2,800	6,550	2,800	7,070	2,900	7,740
Transport and Communications . .	17,000	10,240	18,700	10,490	19,200	10,740
Public Administration . . .	27,100	11,530	26,900	12,170	26,800	12,450
Education	24,400	6,580	24,400	6,600	24,900	6,920
Health	7,500	3,180	7,900	3,480	8,100	3,790
Private Domestic Service . .	108,400	} 9,860	114,200	} 10,030	120,100	} 10,160
Other Services . . .	23,800		25,100		27,500	
Total (rounded) . . .	747,000	103,700	785,000	108,400	847,000	112,800

* Provisional.

AGRICULTURE

PRINCIPAL CROPS
(production, 'ooo metric tons)

	1969	1970	1971
Wheat	30*	40*	40*
Maize.	1,020*	700*	1,179
Millet.	250*	220*	220*
Sorghum	55*	50*	50*
Sugar Cane†	1,050*	1,140*	1,250*
Potatoes	22	22	23*
Dry Beans	24*	24*	25*
Oranges and Tangerines . .	20*	20*	20*
Lemons, Limes, etc.‡ . .	4*	4*	4*
Groundnuts (in shell) . .	122	132	122*
Cottonseed	86	86	86*
Sunflower Seed . . .	3*	3*	3*
Tea§	2.3	2.3	2.3*
Tobacco	62.3	62.3	62.3
Cotton (lint) . . .	43	43	43

1972 ('ooo metric tons): Maize 1,400, Groundnuts 130,* Tea 2.3,* Tobacco 66.0, Cotton (lint) 43.*

*FAO estimate.
†Crop year ending in year stated.
‡Production on farms and estates only.
§Twelve months ending on September 30th of year stated.

Source: Mainly FAO, *Production Yearbook 1971*.

SALES OF PRINCIPAL CROPS AND LIVESTOCK
(R$ million)

	1969	1970	1971	1972
European Production . .	122.9	117.9	148.2	185.3
African Production . .	11.1	8.3	13.1	20.5
Total . . .	134.0	126.3	161.3	205.8

AGRICULTURAL OUTPUT
(R$ million)
EUROPEAN PRODUCTION

	1968	1969	1970	1971	1972
Gross Output	134.7	168.0	167.3	208.3	231.7

AFRICAN PRODUCTION

	1968	1969	1970	1971	1972
Sales through official Marketing Authorities . .	6.8	13.5	10.8	16.3	25.1
Approximate Consumption by Rural Households . .	48.3	50.7	56.7	55.4	55.1
TOTAL VALUE . .	55.1	64.2	67.5	71.7	80.2

AFRICAN-OWNED LIVESTOCK

	1969	1970	1971	1972
Cattle	2,482,000	2,623,000	2,786,000	2,879,000
Sheep	377,000	431,000	438,000	451,000
Pigs	106,000	107,000	107,000	96,000
Goats	1,326,000	1,545,000	1,735,000	1,861,000

EUROPEAN-OWNED LIVESTOCK

	1969	1970	1971	1972
Cattle	2,268,877	2,514,173	2,708,997	2,683,955
Sheep	362,876	356,139	327,013	272,706
Pigs	80,635	91,519	79,842	82,946
Equines	8,117	8,193	8,151	8,711
Goats	35,467	38,976	35,027	33,773

ELECTRICITY CONSUMPTION
(million kWh.)

	1969	1970	1971	1972
Agriculture and Forestry . .	182.1	233.7	256.3	323.1
Mining and Quarrying .	602.0	704.6	769.9	882.7
Manufacturing Industries .	1,219.0	1,440.5	1,544.1	2,004.0
Domestic Consumers .	550.7	599.5	636.2	681.7
Others . .	341.4	388.4	420.1	480.4
TOTAL . .	2,895.2	3,366.7	3,626.6	4,371.9

MINERAL PRODUCTION
(R$ '000)

	1963	1964	1965
Gold . . .	14,202	14,456	13,790
Asbestos . .	11,994	13,696	17,050
Chrome Ore . .	3,790	4,438	5,248
Coal . . .	6,156	6,864	7,744
Copper . . .	6,468	8,312	12,566
TOTAL (incl. others) .	47,470	53,508	64,000

1966 total: 65,200; 1967 total: 66,800; 1968 total: 67,400;
1969 total: 87,000; 1970 total: 98,700; 1971 total: 101,200;
1972 total: 108,000; 1973 total (Jan.–Nov.): 123,000.

(tons)

	1963	1964	1965
Gold ('000 fine oz.) .	566	574	550
Asbestos . .	142,255	153,451	176,151
Chrome Ore . .	412,394	493,371	645,500
Coal . . .	3,020,889	3,351,000	3,868,385
Copper . . .	18,488	18,341	19,819

INDUSTRY
(R$'000)

	1968*	1969*	1970*
Mining and Quarrying	84,728	105,730	122,888
Meat Industry	32,470	34,365	39,790
Grain Mill Products	35,081	35,618	46,062
Bakery Products	14,249	15,552	17,483
Dairy and Other Food Products . .	36,154	38,193	41,736
Alcoholic Beverages	15,398	17,455	20,115
Soft Drinks	6,059	6,384	7,340
Tobacco Manufacturing . . .	13,620	16,621	16,816
Clothing and Footwear . . .	34,897	38,537	45,330
Other Textiles	42,723	57,924	57,544
Wood Industries, except Furniture . .	9,442	11,097	13,583
Furniture, except Metal . . .	7,186	8,326	10,562
Pulp, Paper and Board . . .	11,713	13,366	15,564
Printing and Publishing . . .	13,509	15,793	18,523
Fertilizers and Pesticides . . .	25,887	32,826	37,559
Soap Preparations and Pharmaceuticals .	15,665	16,317	19,180
Other Chemical Products, including Plastic and Rubber	24,143	27,048	31,432
Cement, Bricks and other Non-Metal Products .	17,380	20,003	24,592
Metal Industries, except Machinery .	58,943	75,164	102,814
Machinery, including Electrical . .	23,945	28,933	37,332
Transport and Equipment . . .	28,085	35,757	38,675
Other Industries	4,445	5,481	6,272
TOTAL MANUFACTURING INDUSTRIES . .	470,996	550,760	648,304
Electricity Generation and Distribution .	45,059	48,813	54,530
Water Supply	6,943	6,412	7,270
TOTAL ALL INDUSTRIES . . .	607,726	711,715	832,992

* Year ending June 30th.

FINANCE

100 cents = 1 Rhodesian dollar (R$).

Coins: bronze ½c., 1c.; cupronickel 2½c., 5c., 10c., 20c., 25c.

Notes: R$1, R$2, R$10.

Unofficial exchange rates (April 1974): £1 sterling = R$1.398; U.S. $1 = 59.21 Rhodesian c.
R$100 = £71.53 = U.S. $168.89.

BUDGET
(R$'000)

	1969–70	1970–71	1971–72	1972–73*	1973–74*
Revenue	203,952	213,440	242,102	272,000	310,000
Expenditure	201,895	213,832	234,718	290,429	318,000
Surplus or Deficit	2,057	—392	7,384	—18,429	—8,000

*Estimate.

BUDGET ESTIMATES
(1972–73—R$'000)

REVENUE		EXPENDITURE	
Basic Tax on Income or Profits	123,750	Agriculture (incl. Research and Specialist Services)	30,203
Customs and Excise	48,450	Public Works	8,616
Sales Tax	40,000	Treasury (Supply Services)	28,494
Betting Tax	580	Pensions (mainly Civil and Defence)	9,164
Stamp Duties and Fees	5,150	British S.A. Police	17,466
Business Licences	1,600	Conservation and Extension	2,198
Education Fees	3,805	Internal Affairs	11,448
Health Services	2,100	Labour and Social Welfare	2,782
Aviation and Landing Fees	900	Health	21,200
Agricultural Services	525	Roads and Road Traffic	8,817
Interest, etc.	22,500	Civil Aviation	2,068
Pension Contributions of Government Employees	6,750	Education (European, Coloured and Asian)	20,102
Rent of Government property	1,800	Mines and Lands, National Parks, etc.	5,963
Estate Duties	625	Water Development	2,145
Share of Profits: Reserve Bank of Rhodesia	1,750	African Education	22,470
Mining Fees and Royalties	1,250	Service of Debt	32,107
Other Revenue	10,465	Veterinary Services	3,347
		Army, Air Force	23,778
		Local Government and Housing	1,458
		Old-Age Pensions	2,301
		Other Expenditure	34,302
TOTAL	272,000	TOTAL	290,429

NATIONAL ACCOUNTS
(million R$)

	1970	1971	1972*
GROSS DOMESTIC PRODUCT (factor cost) . .	994.9	1,124.8	1,260.6
of which:			
Wages and salaries	551.1	618.1	694.6
Income from unincorporated enterprise .	150.7	174.0	195.1
Gross operating profits	269.1	307.3	341.7
Income from property	23.9	26.4	29.1
Income from abroad	−19.4	−27.6	−31.0
GROSS NATIONAL INCOME . . .	975.5	1,097.2	1,229.6
Indirect taxes *less* subsidies . .	82.5	97.3	97.8
GROSS NATIONAL PRODUCT (market prices) .	1,058.0	1,194.5	1,327.4
Balance of imports and exports of goods and services	8.5	−24.2	41.0
Private consumption	642.1	742.3	817.2
African rural household consumption . .	63.8	66.0	70.1
Government current expenditure . .	120.4	138.1	147.6
Gross fixed capital formation . .	171.7	219.8	240.7
Increase in stocks	37.7	43.9	14.8

* Provisional.

INDUSTRIAL ORIGIN OF THE GROSS DOMESTIC PRODUCT
(percentage distribution)

	1970	1971	1972*
Agriculture	16.1	16.9	17.3
Mining	6.8	6.1	5.7
Manufacturing	22.2	22.7	23.2
Construction	6.2	5.8	5.9
Electricity and Water . . .	3.1	2.9	2.7
Transport and Communications . .	6.7	7.0	6.9
Wholesale and Retail Trade . .	14.0	13.9	14.0
Banking, Insurance, Real Estate .	5.1	5.0	5.3
Public Administration, Health and Education	10.8	10.9	10.8
Services	9.1	8.7	8.3
Gross Domestic Product (i) %	100.0	100.0	100.0
(factor cost) (ii) R$ million .	994.9	1,124.8	1,260.6

* Provisional.

COMPOSITION OF GROSS DOMESTIC EXPENDITURE 1972*

	R$ MILLION	%
Private Consumption (Money Economy) .	817.2	62.0
Private Non-Profit Making Bodies . .	27.0	2.0
African Rural Household Consumption .	70.1	5.3
Government Current Expenditure . .	147.6	11.2
Gross Fixed Capital Formation . .	240.7	18.3
of which:		
Land Improvement . . .		
Mine Development . . .	n.a.	n.a.
Building and Works . . .		
Plant, Machinery, etc. . . .		
Net Increase in Stocks . . .	14.8	1.1
Gross Domestic Expenditure . .	1,317.3	100.0
Net Exports of Goods and Services .	41.0	—
Gross Domestic Product at market prices .	1,358.4	—

*Provisional.

Note: "African rural household consumption" is an estimate of the market value of production for own consumption in the subsistence economy.

GOLD RESERVES OF RESERVE BANK OF RHODESIA
(R$'000—Nov. 1965)*

Gold	7,280
Foreign Assets	36,738
Total . . .	44,018

*Latest available figure.

CURRENCY IN CIRCULATION
(million R$—June 1970)

	Notes	Coin	Total
In Public Circulation.	29.7	3.7	33.4

December 1972 total: R$ 44.4 m.

EXTERNAL TRADE
(million R$)

	1969	1970	1971	1972
Imports	199.4	234.9	282.4	274.2
Exports and Re-exports, excl. gold .	219.0	253.6	277.2	328.5

No detailed official trade figures have been published since 1965.

COMMODITIES
(R$'000)

Imports	1964	1965	Exports	1964	1965
Food	19,400	18,688	Food		
Beverages and Tobacco . .	7,470	6,960	Fresh and Frozen Meat .	23,930	29,308
Tobacco . .	5,548	5,270	Canned Meat and Meat Pre-	5,984	8,456
Crude Materials, inedible .	10,934	9,780	parations . . .	4,100	5,046
Mineral Fuels and Lubricants .	12,374	11,822	Sugar	6,970	6,964
Petroleum Products .	11,538	11,056	Beverages and Tobacco .	83,958	99,610
Animal and Vegetable Oils .	1,112	2,606	Tobacco . . .	78,444	93,936
Chemicals . . .	23,032	26,900	Crude Materials, inedible .	33,626	38,784
Fertilizer . . .	6,300	8,698	Asbestos Fibre . .	20,030	21,522
Machinery and Transport .	62,478	76,020	Chrome Ore . .	5,000	7,620
Machinery, except Electrical .	28,034	31,864	Mineral Fuels and Lubricants .	12,872	18,978
Railway Engines and Vehicles .	3,224	4,676	Coal . . .	3,314	4,446
Motor Vehicles and Spares .	17,466	24,288	Animal and Vegetable Oils .	700	632
Miscellaneous Items . .	79,674	86,802	Chemicals . . .	9,086	9,152
Paper and Board . .	5,144	5,492	Machinery and Transport .	12,686	17,168
Textiles . .	16,612	19,916	Miscellaneous Items .	59,784	71,278
Iron and Steel . .	10,490	10,302	Clothing . .	10,614	10,834
			Refined Copper . .	7,104	12,112
			Pig Iron . .	5,100	4,946

TOURISM
Total Number of Tourist Arrivals*

1967	.	.	.	193,707
1968	.	.	.	217,542
1969	.	.	.	254,441
1970	.	.	.	270,659
1971	.	.	.	317,381
1972	.	.	.	339,210

*Excludes visitors in transit.

TRANSPORT

RAIL TRAFFIC

Rhodesia Railways (including operations in Botswana)

	1970–71*	1971–72*	1972–73†
Total Number of Passengers ('000) . .	2,782	3,013	2,766
Net Metric Tons ('000) . . .	11,686	12,676	10,380
Gross Ton-Kilometres (million) . .	14,283	15,308	12,677
Net Ton-Kilometres (million) . .	6,293	6,802	5,564
Financial Statistics:			
Total Revenue (R$'000) . . .	65,295	69,895	56,703
Total Expenditure (R$'000) . .	60,916	71,821	65,031
Net Surplus (R$'000) . . .	4,379	−1,926	−8,328

*Year ending June 30th.   †Ten months ending April 30th.

ROAD TRAFFIC
(est.)

	1966*
Passenger	113,123
Commercial	28,979
Motor Cycles and Scooters . .	8,363
Others (excluding Caravans and Trailers) .	9,252

* May.

AIR TRAFFIC*
Air Rhodesia

	KILOMETRES FLOWN		LOAD TON-KILOMETRES FLOWN		PASSENGERS CARRIED '000
	Aircraft '000	Passenger '000	Passenger '000	Cargo and Mail '000	
1970	5,151	155,836	12,988	983.1	263.4
1971	5,668	175,528	14,597	959.7	300.3
1972	6,073	196,320	16,288	973.4	344.3
1973	6,337	202,146	16,770	912.4	362.8

* Year ending June 30th.

COMMUNICATIONS MEDIA

	1972
Telephones	151,199
Radio Licences	32,058
Concessionary Radio Licences . .	135,035
Combined Radio and Television Licences .	56,788
Daily Newspapers	2

EDUCATION

AFRICAN EDUCATION

	SCHOOLS		PUPILS		TEACHERS	
	1972	1973	1972	1973	1972	1973
Primary	3,516	3,518	715,835	751,085	17,230	18,143
Secondary	140	150	29,170	33,789	1,418	1,673
Vocational/Technical/Teacher-Training	34	32	3,106	3,197	173	189
Agricultural College . .	1	1	80	77	14	14
Evening and Part-time Schools	76	85	2,977	5,838	n.a.	195
Special (Physically Handicapped) .	8	8	583	651	65	67

EUROPEAN, ASIAN AND COLOURED

	SCHOOLS		PUPILS		TEACHERS	
	1972	1973	1972	1973	1972	1973
Primary	187	180	40,654	41,018	1,670	1,718
Secondary	48	50	28,153	29,248	1,608	1,679
Technical/Teacher-Training .	3	3	3,963	4,443	214	229
Agricultural College . .	1	1	85	82	18	17
University*	1	1	978	1,076	195	194

* Multi-racial.

Source: Central Statistical Office, Salisbury.

THE CONSTITUTION

CONSTITUTIONAL DEVELOPMENT

THE British South Africa Company administered Rhodesia from 1889 to 1923 when the colony became self-governing after the settlers had voted against entering the Union of South Africa. The 1923 Constitution reserved powers including legislation affecting African interests to the British Secretary of State. In 1953 the Federation of Rhodesia and Nyasaland came into existence and under the Federal Constitution various internal powers with the exception of African affairs, internal security and industrial relations, were transferred to the Federal Government.

The 1961 Constitution

In 1959 the Southern Rhodesian Government proposed that the Constitution of Southern Rhodesia should be revised, with a view to transferring to Southern Rhodesia the exercise of the powers vested in the British Government. Following consultations between the two Governments an Order in Council embodying a new constitution was made on December 6th, 1961. This eliminated all the reserved powers save for matters including sections of the Constitution relating to the Declaration of Rights, Appeals to the Privy Council, the Judiciary, increasing franchise qualifications and racial limitation on the ownership or occupation of land. It also conferred on Southern Rhodesia wide powers for the amendment of her own Constitution and contained a number of important additional features such as a Declaration of Rights and the creation of a Constitutional Council designed to give confidence to all the peoples of Southern Rhodesia that their legitimate interests would be safeguarded.

Unilateral Declaration of Independence (U.D.I.)

On November 11th, 1965, the Smith Government, elected by the almost exclusively white electorate, unilaterally declared Rhodesia independent of the British Crown and with the assumption of independence, the Constitution of Rhodesia 1965 was issued by the new régime to replace that of 1961, and provisions under the Southern Rhodesian Order in Council, 1961, were held to be of no effect. The Queen, acting through her representative the Governor, dismissed the Government of Rhodesia, and the British Parliament passed the Southern Rhodesia Act, which declares that Southern Rhodesia (the legal name of the country now, although "Rhodesia" remains in common usage) continues to be part of Her Majesty's dominions and that the Government and Parliament of the United Kingdom continue to have responsibility and jurisdiction for and in respect of it. The Southern Rhodesia Constitution Order 1965 which was made under this Act declares that any constitution which the regime in Rhodesia may purport to promulgate is void and of no effect. The Order also prohibits the Legislative Assembly from making laws or transacting any other business and declares any proceedings in defiance of this prohibition void and of no effect. It also suspends the ministerial system, empowers the Governor to exercise his functions without seeking ministerial advice and empowers a Secretary of State as well as the Governor to exercise the executive authority of Rhodesia on Her Majesty's behalf.

The Five (Six) Principles

Successive British Conservative Governments have been guided in their approach towards the problem of granting Rhodesia independence by five principles (the 1964–70 Labour Government also recognized a sixth):

1. The principle and intention of unimpeded progress to majority rule, already enshrined in the 1961 Constitution, would have to be maintained and guaranteed.

2. There would also have to be guarantees against retrogressive amendment of the Constitution.
3. There would have to be immediate improvement in the political status of the African population.
4. There would have to be progress towards ending racial discrimination.
5. The British Government would need to be satisfied that any basis proposed for independence was acceptable to the people of Rhodesia as a whole.
6. It would be necessary to ensure that, regardless of race, there was no oppression of majority by minority or of minority by majority.

REPUBLICAN CONSTITUTION

(*November* 1969)

In a referendum held on June 20th, 1969, the constitutional proposals of the Rhodesian Front were approved by 54,724 votes to 20,776. At the same time the predominantly white electorate also approved the proposal to declare Rhodesia a republic by 61,130 to 14,327 votes. The relevant constitutional legislation giving effect to these proposals received the necessary two-thirds majority in the Legislative Assembly in November 1969: this legislation consisted of the Constitution of Rhodesia Bill, the Electoral Bill, the Land Tenure Bill and the High Courts (Amendments) Bill. The Constitutional Bill was signed by the Officer Administering the Government on November 29th, 1969, but did not come into operation until after the first general election under the new constitutional and electoral arrangements in April 1970.

PROVISIONS OF THE REPUBLICAN CONSTITUTION

There is a President in and over Rhodesia, who is Commander-in-Chief of the Armed Forces of Rhodesia. The term of office is five years, and a second term is permissible but not a third.

Legislative power is vested in a legislature consisting of the President and Parliament, and Parliament consists of a Senate and a House of Assembly.

The Senate comprises 23 members, ten Europeans elected by the European members of the House of Assembly, and ten African chiefs, elected by an electoral college consisting of the members of the Council of Chiefs. Five of these African Senators shall be chiefs in Matabeleland and five chiefs in Mashonaland.

The remaining three Senators are appointed by the President.

The House of Assembly initially consists of 66 members, 50 Europeans, elected by voters on the European roll, and 16 African members. Half of these, four from Mashonaland and four from Matabeleland, are elected by Africans on an African voters roll, the other half, again drawn equally from Matabeleland and Mashonaland are elected by electoral colleges made up from African chiefs, headmen and councillors from African councils.

When the aggregate of income tax assessed on the income of Africans exceeds sixteen sixty-sixths of that assessed on the income of Europeans and Africans then the number of African members in the House of Assembly will increase in proportion but only until the number of African members equals that of the European members.

To advise the President there is an Executive Council, consisting of the Prime Minister and other such persons, being Ministers as the President, on the advice of the Prime Minister may appoint.

The President appoints as Prime Minister the person, who, in his opinion, is best able to command the support of a majority of the members of the House of Assembly and acting on the advice of the Prime Minister, he appoints other Ministers.

LAND TENURE ACT

The Land Tenure Bill was passed by the Legislative Assembly in November 1969, and received the signature of the Officer Administering the Government on November 29th.

The Act, which repeals the Land Apportionment Act, regulates the ownership, leasing and occupation of land in all areas on racial grounds and preserves the special status of the Tribal Trust Land within the African area.

The total extent of Rhodesia is approximately 96.5 million acres which was divided by the Land Apportionment Act as follows: European Area 35.6 million acres, Tribal Trust Land 40.1 million acres, Native Purchase Area 4.3 million acres, National Land 105 million acres, Unreserved Land 6.0 million acres.

Previously only Tribal Trust Lands were specially protected under the Constitution. The Native Purchase Area and European Area enjoyed no such protection.

Under the new Act all areas are similarly protected, but there are now only three areas which are: European Area 44.95 million acres, African Area 44.95 million acres, National Area—reserved for the purpose of Wild Life Conservation and National Parks—6.6 million acres.

Exchange of land between one area and the other are controlled by two Boards of Trustees, one of which watches over the interests of Europeans and the other the interests of Africans.

ANGLO-RHODESIAN CONSTITUTIONAL PROPOSALS

(November 1971)

In November 1971 the British Foreign Secretary (Sir Alec Douglas-Home) and Lord Goodman met Mr. Ian Smith and agreed on a settlement. The settlement was subject to it being acceptable to Rhodesians as a whole in the opinion of the Pearce Commission, which tested opinion in Rhodesia between January and March 1972.

The settlement proposed that the number of African seats (now 16) will increase as more Africans meet voting qualifications, until they equal the Europeans' present 50 seats. The creation of new African seats will depend on the growth of a new higher African electoral roll, the qualifications being the same as those for Europeans. Two seats will be added for each 6 per cent rise in the higher African roll, but half the new seats will be filled by indirect election by the College of Chiefs. When the 50-50 parity has been achieved, an independent commission will recommend whether or not 10 Common Roll seats should be added, to be voted for by all on the European and higher African rolls. By this time both rolls should have about the same numbers. As more Africans qualified, they could out-vote

the Europeans and produce an African majority in the Assembly. An agreed blocking mechanism will prevent retrogressive legislation. An independent commission will examine racial discrimination. Britain and Rhodesia will join in a £100 million development and educational programme and Africans will get more land. Once the British Government is satisfied by Rhodesian action on the franchise, discrimination and detainees, Parliament will be asked to grant Rhodesia independence and to end sanctions.

On May 23rd, 1972 the report of the Pearce Commission was presented to the House of Commons by the Foreign Secretary. The conclusion of the Commission was that "the people of Rhodesia as a whole did not regard the proposals as acceptable as a basis for independence". Whilst expressing the hope that a solution within the five principles could be found in the future, the Foreign Secretary said that the British Government accepted the verdict of the Commission and that sanctions would continue and they are still in force.

THE GOVERNMENT

President: CLIFFORD WALTER DUPONT.

THE CABINET

(June 1974)

Prime Minister: IAN DOUGLAS SMITH.

Deputy Prime Minister and Minister of Finance and Posts: JOHN JAMES WRATHALL.

Minister of Roads and Traffic, Transport and Power: ROGER TANCRED ROBERT HAWKINS.

Minister of Foreign Affairs, Defence and Public Service: JOHN HARTLEY HOWMAN.

Minister of Internal Affairs: LANCE BALES SMITH.

Minister of Information, Immigration and Tourism: PIETER KENYON FLEMING VOLTELYN VAN DER BYL.

Minister of Justice, Law and Order: DESMOND WILLIAM LARDNER-BURKE.

Minister of Health, Labour and Social Welfare: IAN FINLAY MCLEAN.

Minister of Commerce and Industry: BERNARD HORACE MUSSETT.

Minister of Local Government and Housing: WILLIAM IRVINE.

Minister of Agriculture: DAVID COLLVILLE SMITH.

Minister of Education: ARTHUR PHILIP SMITH.

Minister of Lands, Natural Resources and Water Development: MARK HENRY HEATHCOTE PARTRIDGE.

Minister of Mines: IAN BIRT DILLON.

Minister without Portfolio: Sen. PHILIP VAN HEERDEN.

DIPLOMATIC REPRESENTATION

No country has yet recognized Rhodesia. South Africa has an accredited Diplomatic Mission in Salisbury and Portugal has a Consul-General.

PARLIAMENT
LEGISLATIVE ASSEMBLY
Speaker: Col. G. H. HARTLEY. **Clerk of the House:** L. J. HOWE-ELY.

GENERAL ELECTIONS (April 1970)

AFRICAN ROLL	VOTES	SEATS	EUROPEAN ROLL	VOTES	SEATS
Centre Party	2,147	7	Rhodesian Front . . .	39,028	49*
National People's Union .	1,000	1	Centre Party	5,629	—
Rhodesia African Party .	301	—	Republican Alliance . .	1,633	—
United National Progressive Party.	70	—	Independents . . .	4,538	—
All African People's Party .	63	—	Rhodesia Party . . .	—	1†
Independents . . .	747	—			
TOTAL . . .	4,328	8*	TOTAL . . .	50,828	50

* In 1974 3 of the 8 African M.P.s were supporters of the ANC.

* 13 of these seats were uncontested.
† Resigned from Rhodesian Front.

In the election of July 1974 the Rhodesian Front gained all 50 seats on the European roll. On the African roll Independent African National Council candidates and their allies gained 7 seats and the Centre Party 1.

Note: Another 8 African members are elected by electoral colleges of chiefs, headmen and councillors.

COUNCIL OF CHIEFS
Twenty-six elected members. **President:** Chief ZWIMBA of Sinoia District.

POLITICAL PARTIES

Rhodesian Front: P.O.B. 242, Salisbury; governing party with 49 seats (1970); aims to maintain Rhodesia's independence; Pres. IAN D. SMITH; Chair. D. FROST.

African National Council (ANC): Salisbury; f. March 1972, after originally having been formed in December 1971 as an *ad hoc* organization to campaign for the rejection of the Anglo-Rhodesian settlement proposals; 3 M.P.s are associated with the party; Chair. Bishop ABEL MUZOREWA; Vice-Pres. ELLIOT GABELLAH; Gen. Sec. C. C. NGCEBETSHA (detained); Rep. in Britain ESHMAEL MLAMBO; Rep. at United Nations Miss JUDITH TODD.

Centre Party: 22 Jameson Ave., Salisbury; f. August 1968; stands for united, independent Rhodesia, with one parliament for all Rhodesians, advancement by merit, and the eradication of racial discrimination; multi-racial and withdrew support for the Anglo-Rhodesian settlement proposals when the Rhodesian Front enacted new discriminatory legislation; Pres. (vacant).

African Progressive Party: f. 1974; aims for settlement with Britain on Anglo-Rhodesian 1971 terms; Leader CHAD CHIPUNZA.

*African Settlement Convention: f. 1973; aims for settlement with Britain on Anglo-Rhodesian 1971 terms; Chair. GEORGE CHARAMBARARA.

National Association of Coloured People: Chair. GERRY RAFTOPOULOS.

National People's Union: Salisbury; f. 1969; one seat in Assembly; Leader CHAD CHIPUNZA; Pres. G. CHAVUNDUKA (defunct).

Rhodesia Party: f. 1972; supports qualified franchise and "responsible" government, opposes Rhodesian Front policies on detention without trial, control of the media and racially discriminatory laws; Chair. LOUIS GELMAN; Pres. ALAN SAVORY.

Rhodesian Electoral Union: P.O.B. 1552, Bulawayo; f. 1970; Pres. R. C. MAKAYA; Vice-Pres. E. J. MHLANGA (defunct).

*Rhodesian Settlement Forum: aims to persuade Africans to accept Anglo-Rhodesian settlement terms; Leader HENRY CHIOTA.

Settlement Association of Rhodesia: f. 1973; aims for settlement on Anglo-Rhodesian 1971 terms; Leader FINLAY BABDA.

United Front Against Surrender: Salisbury; f. February 1972; supports "overriding principle that the white man's position must be supreme for all time".

Zimbabwe African People's Union (ZAPU): P.O.B. 20128, Dar es Salaam, Tanzania; f. 1961; African nationalist party advocating universal adult suffrage; Leader JOSHUA NKOMO (held without trial); Chair. JASON MOYO; Gen. Sec. EDWARD NDHLOVU: banned September 1962 now operating from Lusaka, Zambia; joined with ZANU in March 1973 to unify African resistance to the Smith regime by setting up a joint military command and political council.

Zimbabwe African National Union (ZANU): f. 1963 after split in ZAPU; African nationalist; Leader Rev. N. SITHOLE (imprisoned); (*banned*); joined with ZAPU in March 1973; Chair. HERBERT CHITEPO.

* The African Settlement Convention and the Rhodesian Settlement Forum plan to merge to form the National Settlement Convention.

JUDICIAL SYSTEM

The legal system is Roman-Dutch, based on the system which was in force in the Cape at the time of the occupation. Cape Ordinances form the basis of much of the early legislation.

The High Court has two Divisions, General and Appellate. The Appellate Division is the superior court of record, and the supreme Court of Appeal under the terms of the 1969 Constitution. It consists of the Chief Justice, the Judge President, and a number of judges of appeal.

The General Division of the High Court comprises the Chief Justice and appointed puisne judges. Below the High Court are Regional Magistrates' Courts with civil jurisdiction only and Magistrates' Courts with both civil and criminal jurisdiction.

Chief Justice: Rt. Hon. Sir Hugh Beadle, P.C., C.M.G., O.B.E.

Judge President: Mr. Justice H. N. Macdonald.

Judge of Appeal: Mr. Justice J. V. R. Lewis.

Judges: Mr. Justice E. W. G. Jarvis, C.M.G., Mr. Justice H. E. Davies, Mr. Justice B. Goldin, Mr. Justice J. Greenfield, Mr. Justice J. B. Macaulay, Mr. Justice C. E. L. Beck.

RELIGION

AFRICAN RELIGIONS
Most Africans follow traditional beliefs.

CHRISTIANS

ANGLICANS

PROVINCE OF CENTRAL AFRICA

Archbishop of Central Africa: Most Rev. Donald S. Arden (Kasupe, Malawi).

CATHOLICS

There are 504,259 Roman Catholics in Rhodesia.

Archbishop of Salisbury: Most Rev. Francis Markall, S.J., P.O.B. 8060, Causeway, Salisbury.

Catholic Secretariat: P.O.B. 2591, Salisbury.

OTHER DENOMINATIONS

Dutch Reformed Church: P.O.B. 967, 35 Jameson Ave., Salisbury; est. in Rhodesia 1891; the Central African Synod comprises Rhodesia and Malawi; 17 parishes, 12,500 adherents; Gen. Sec. Rev. P. W. de Wet.

Evangelical Lutheran Church: P.O.B. 2175, Bulawayo; est. in Rhodesia 1963 (mission since 1903); Sec. Bishop S. B. Strandvik; 22,000 mems.; publ. *Chiedza Chirepo*, monthly.

Methodist Church: First Church est. in Salisbury in 1891; Chair. and Gen. Supt. Rhodesia District, Rev. Andrew M. Ndhlela, P.O.B. 8298, Salisbury; membership 51,755 (Jan. 1973); Methodist Community approx. 113,000 (Jan. 1973).

Presbyterian Church: P.O.B. 50, Salisbury City; f. 1904; Ministers Rev. A. C. Milne, B.A., Rev. W. H. Watson, D.D., Rev. D. B. Henderson; Session Clerk G. Cooper; Sec. Miss M. W. Robinson, M.A.; membership 19,000.

Salvation Army (Rhodesia Territory): f. 1891; Territorial Commander Colonel Richard Atwell; P.O.B. 14, Salisbury; Staff: 1,200 officers and employees, 40,000 (approx.) members.

United Congregational Church of Southern Africa: P.O.B. 31083, Braamfontein, Transvaal; Moderator for Rhodesia Rev. J. R. Danisa; Sec. for Rhodesia Rev. G. O. Lloyd.

United Methodist Church: f. 1890; P.O.B. 8293, Causeway, Salisbury; Bishop of Rhodesia Abel Muzorewa; membership 45,000.

JEWS

Central African Jewish Board of Deputies: P.O.B. 1456, Bulawayo; Pres. Hon. A. E. Abrahamson; approx. 5,000 adherents; publs. *The Board, Central African Zionist Digest*.

THE PRESS

DAILIES

Chronicle, The: P.O.B. 585, Bulawayo; f. 1894; Bulawayo and throughout Matabeleland; English; Editor R. J. Fothergill; circ. 27,645.

Rhodesia Herald, The: P.O.B. 396, Salisbury; f. 1891; Salisbury and elsewhere in Central Africa; English; Editor R. Meier; circ. 64,496.

Umtali Post: P.O.B. 96, Umtali; f. 1893; Mondays, Wednesdays and Fridays; Editor Eric Richmond.

PERIODICALS

African Times: fortnightly; Editor R. Lotz.

Avondale Observer: P.O.B. 1160, Salisbury; monthly; circ. 5,000.

Central African Journal of Medicine: P.O.B. 2073, Salisbury; f. 1955; monthly; Editor Dr. M. Gelfand.

Chamber of Mines Journal: Thomson Newspapers Rhodesia (Pvt.) Ltd., P.O.B. 1683, Salisbury; f. 1960; monthly.

Citizen, The: P.O.B. 1160, Beatrice Rd., Salisbury; f. 1953; weekly; English; Editor C. Theo.

Country Times: Country Times Press (Pvt.) Ltd., 208 Birmingham Rd., Marandellas; twice-monthly.

Development Magazine: P.O.B. 1622, Salisbury; f. 1948; monthly; English; Man. Editor E. Roy Wright; circ. 3,000.

Die Rhodesier: P.O.B. M.P. 88, Mount Pleasant, Salisbury; Afrikaans; monthly.

Enterprise: P.O.B. 638, Salisbury; monthly.

Fort Victoria Advertiser: P.O.B. 138, Fort Victoria; f. 1959; independent; general; weekly; Editor STUART ROGERS; circ. 1,200.

Gatooma Mail: P.O.B. 550, Gatooma; f. 1912; Thursdays; Man. Editor D. BURKE; Editor V. SMEDA.

Greendale News: P.O.B. 1160, Salisbury; monthly; circ. 4,000.

Gwelo Times: P.O.B. 66, 51 Fifth St., Gwelo; f. 1897; Thursdays; Editor B. K. CHARLESWORTH; circ. 2,900.

Hatfield Record: P.O.B. 1160, Salisbury; monthly; circ. 2,200.

Highlands Times: P.O.B. 1160, Salisbury; monthly; circ. 4,400.

Homecraft: P.O.B. 8263, Causeway, Salisbury; published by the National Federation of Womens' Institutes of Rhodesia in English, Shona and Ndebele; f. 1962; monthly; Editor MARY LEDINGHAM; circ. 7,000.

Look and Listen: P.O.B. H.G. 200, Highlands, Salisbury; weekly; Editor BARBARA MILLER.

M. & M. Gazette: P.O.B. 1160, Salisbury; monthly; circ. 4,000.

Makoni Clarion: P.O.B. 17, Rusape; monthly.

Mashoko é Que Que: P.O.B. 186, Que Que; f. 1965; monthly; African; Editor O. R. ASHTON; circ. 2,000.

Midlands Observer: P.O.B. 186, Que Que; f. 1953; Fridays; English; Man. Editor O. R. ASHTON; circ. 1,700.

Mining in Rhodesia: Thomson Newspapers Rhod. (Pvt.) Ltd., P.O.B. 1683, Salisbury.

Modern Farming: P.O.B. 1622, Salisbury; f. 1964; Man. Editor PETER SMYTH; circ. 7,500.

Moto (*Fire*): P.O.B. 779, Gwelo; f. 1958; weekly; Shona and English; political, cultural, religious; Editors ALBERT PLANGGER, J. NYOKA, ONESIUS MAKAUI, JOHN ZACHARY, MENARD MASVINGISE; circ. 25,000.

Motor Trader and Fleet Operator: Thomson Newspapers Rhod. (Pvt.) Ltd., P.O.B. 1683, Salisbury; official organ of the Rhodesian Motor Trade Association.

Mt. Pleasant Courier: P.O.B. 1160, Salisbury; monthly; circ. 4,000.

Murimi: P.O.B. 1622, Salisbury; monthly; Editor CORNELIUS WOTYORKA.

National Observer: P.O.B. 2473, Bulawayo; monthly; Editor ELIZA MAHAJA.

News of Hartley: Citizen Press, P.O.B. 1160, Salisbury; weekly; circ. 750.

Outpost: P.O.B. H.G. 106, Highlands, Salisbury; f. 1911; monthly; English; Editor A. P. STOCK; circ. 6,000.

Parade and Foto-Action: P.O.B. 3798, Salisbury; f. 1953; monthly; English; Editor LEONIS M. LAMBIRIS.

Qua: P.O.B. 2377, Salisbury; monthly.

Rhodesia Agricultural Journal: P.O.B. 8108, Causeway, Salisbury; f. 1903; six per year; Editor W. B. CLEGHORN; circ. 1,500.

Rhodesia Calls: P.O.B. 8045, Causeway, Salisbury; f. 1960; every two months; Editor A. GERRARD ABERMAN; travel; circ. 18,000.

Rhodesian Caravaner: P.O.B. 8045, Causeway, Salisbury; f. 1969; every two months; Publisher A. GERRARD ABERMAN; Editor CLIVE WILSON; circ. 2,500.

Rhodesian Farmer: P.O.B. 1622, Salisbury; f. 1928; weekly journal of the Rhodesia National Farmers' Union and Rhodesia Tobacco Association and affiliated bodies; English; circ. 7,500; Editor D. H. B. DICKIN.

Rhodesian Financial Gazette: P.O.B. UA 345, Union Ave., Salisbury; weekly; broadly pro-government; Editor R. HAYNES; circ. 5,700.

Rhodesian Insurance Review: Thomson Newspapers Rhod. (Pvt.) Ltd., P.O.B. 1683, Salisbury; f. 1955; monthly.

Rhodesian Property & Finance: P.O.B. 2266, Salisbury; f. 1956; monthly; Editor WILFRED BROOKS; circ. 6,200.

Rhodesia Railways Magazine: P.O.B. 596, Bulawayo; f. 1952; monthly; Editor J. BRYANT; circ. 9,000.

Rhodesian Tobacco Journal: Thomson Newspapers Rhod. (Pvt.) Ltd., P.O.B. 1683, Salisbury; f. 1949; monthly.

Rhodesian Woman: P.O.B. U.A. 439, Salisbury; f. 1950; monthly; English; Editor JOANMARIE FOBBS.

Shield: P.O.B. 3194, Salisbury; monthly; English; Editor F. MEALING.

Sitima: P.O.B. 596, Bulawayo; official organ for African staff of the Rhodesia Railways in Rhodesia and Botswana; monthly; Editor J. BRYANT; circ. 10,000.

Sunday Mail: P.O.B. 396, Salisbury; f. 1935; English; Editor J. A. ROBERTSON; circ. 79,469.

Sunday News: P.O.B. 585, Bulawayo; f. 1930; English; Editor P. H. C. J. TUDOR-OWEN; circ. 23,630.

Teacher in New Africa: 107 Moffat St., P.O.B. 3513, Salisbury; f. 1964; monthly; English; Man. V. R. COHEN.

Umbowo: P.O.B. 7024, Umtali; United Methodist Church newspaper.

Waterfalls Sentinel: P.O.B. 1160, Salisbury; monthly; circ. 2,000.

Weekly Express: P.O.B. 1160; circ. 17,500 (African readership).

NEWS AGENCIES

Inter-African News Agency (Pvt.) Ltd.: P.O.B. 785, Salisbury; f. 1964; subsidiary of the South African Press Association; Chair. L. K. S. WILSON; Editor K. B. MOBBS.

FOREIGN BUREAUX

Agence France—Presse: 604 Robinson House, Union Ave., Salisbury (P.O.B. 2023); Rep. IAN MILLS.

UPI: 604 Robinson House, Union Ave., Salisbury (P.O.B. 2023); Rep. IAN MILLS.

Reuters are also represented in Salisbury.

PUBLISHERS

A. C. Braby (Rhod.) (Pvt.) Ltd.: P.O.B. 1027, Bulawayo; telephone directory publishers.

B. & T. Directories (Rhodesia) (Private) Ltd.: P.O.B. 2119, Bulawayo.

Burke Enterprises (Pvt.) Ltd.: P.O.B. 550, Gatooma.

The Citizen Press (Pvt.) Ltd.: P.O.B. 1160, Salisbury.

Dominion Press (Pvt.) Ltd.: P.O.B. 1160, Salisbury.

Kingstons Limited: P.O.B. 2374, Salisbury; wholesale and retail stationers and booksellers; brs. in Bulawayo, Gwelo, Que Que and Umtali.

Lomagundi Printing (Pvt.) Ltd.: P.O.B. 110, Sinoia.

Longman Rhodesia (Pvt.) Ltd.: P.O.B. S.T. 125, Southerton, Salisbury; f. 1964; member of the Longman group; representing Oliver and Boyd, Livingstone, Churchill, Penguin Books Ltd.

Mambo Press: P.O.B. 779, Gwelo; f. 1958; religion, education and fiction in English and African languages; Dir. ALBERT PLANGGER; Man. JAMES AMREIN.

Mercantile Publishing House (Pvt.) Ltd.: P.O.B. 1561, Salisbury.

Morris Publishing Co. (Pvt.) Ltd.: P.O. Box 1435, Salisbury.

Oxford University Press: Roslin House, Baker Ave., Salisbury; br. of London firm.

Publications (C.A.) (Pvt.) Ltd.: P.O.B. 1027, Bulawayo; trade directories.

Rhodesian Farmer Publications: P.O.B. 1622, Salisbury; farming books for Southern Africa.

The Rhodesian Printing and Publishing Co. Ltd.: P.O.B. 396, Salisbury; P.O.B. 96, Umtali; P.O.B. 585, Bulawayo.

Rhodesian Publications (1969) (Pvt.) Ltd.: P.O.B. 3745, Salisbury.

Thomson Newspapers Rhod. (Pvt.) Ltd.: P.O.B. 1683, Salisbury; trade journals.

Vision Publications: P.O.B. 1532, Salisbury; f. 1954.

RADIO AND TELEVISION

Rhodesia Broadcasting Corpn.: P.O.B. 444, Highlands, Salisbury; f. 1964; Chair. J. M. HELLIWELL; Dir.-Gen. J. C. NEILL.

RADIO

GENERAL AND COMMERCIAL SERVICES: news, information and entertainment; the main centre is in Salisbury, but there are studios in Bulawayo and Umtali. The Corporation broadcasts 20 news services daily.

AFRICAN SERVICE: broadcasts in three vernacular languages and English; studios in Salisbury and Bulawayo.

In 1974 there were 225,000 radio receivers.

TELEVISION

Rhodesia Broadcasting Corpn.: Stations at Salisbury, Bulawayo, Gwelo and Umtali.

Rhodesia Television Ltd.: P.O.B. H.G. 200, Highlands, Salisbury; programme contractors; commercial organization; studios in Salisbury and Bulawayo.

Ministry of Education: The Secretary for African Education, P.O.B. 8022, Causeway, Salisbury; and The Secretary for Education, P.O.B. 8024, Causeway, Salisbury.

There are 62,367 television receivers.

FINANCE

BANKING
(cap.=capital, p.u.=paid up, dep.=deposits, m.=million)

CENTRAL BANK

Reserve Bank of Rhodesia: P.O.B. 1283, Salisbury; f. May 1964; sole right of issue; cap. R$2m.; Gov. N. H. B. BRUCE; Britain has appointed Sir HENRY HARDMAN as Governor and Trustee to R.B.R.

COMMERCIAL BANKS

Barclays Bank International Ltd.: London; Local Head Office: Manica Road, Salisbury; 37 brs., 111 agencies; Gen. Man. S. J. BALES.

National and Grindlays Bank Ltd.: London; Local Head Office: 64 Baker Ave., Salisbury; 11 brs., 24 sub-brs. and agencies; Man. Dir. R. S. CORDINGLEY.

Rhodesian Banking Corporation Ltd.: P.O.B. 3198, Salisbury; incorporated in Rhodesia; cap. R$3,337,837; 18 brs., 11 agencies; Chair. R. S. WALKER, M.B.E.; Man. Dir. G. H. M. BEAK.

Standard Bank Ltd.: London; Administrative Office: P.O.B. 373, Salisbury; over 100 offices; Gen. Man. F. H. DITTMER.

MERCHANT BANKS

Merchant Bank of Central Africa Ltd.: P.O.B. 3200, Century House West, Baker Ave., Salisbury; f. 1956; cap. p.u. R$2.5m.; Chair. G. C. V. COPPEN; Man. Dir. K. DEWAR.

Neficrho Acceptances Ltd.: P.O.B. U.A. 130, Salisbury; cap. R$1m.; Chair. R. S. WALKER, M.B.E.; Man. Dir. J. F. J. SEKET.

Rhodesian Acceptances Ltd.: Rhodesian Acceptances House, 67 Jameson Ave., Salisbury; f. 1956; cap. p.u. R$1.5m.; Chair. Sir KEITH ACUTT, K.B.E.; Man. Dir. L. P. NORMAND.

Standard Merchant Bank of Rhodesia Ltd.: P.O.B. 60, Salisbury; f. 1971; cap. R$1.4m.; dep. R$9,151,000 (May 1974); Chair. E. R. CAMPBELL, C.B.E.; Gen. Man. J. S. DAVIDSON.

DISCOUNT HOUSES

British and Rhodesian Discount House Ltd.: P.O.B. 3321, Southampton House, Union Ave., Salisbury; f. 1959; cap. p.u. R$300,000; dep. R$24,998,000 (Dec. 1972); Chair. D. G. NICHOLSON; Man. M. G. GISBORNE.

Discount Company of Rhodesia Ltd.: P.O.B. 3424, Fanum House, Jameson Ave., Central, Salisbury; f. 1959; cap. p.u. R$450,000; dep. R$24,773,000 (Dec. 1972); Chair. G. ELLMAN-BROWN, C.M.G.; Man. Dir. G. WILDE.

INSURANCE

Insurance Corpn. of Rhodesia Ltd.: I.C.R. House, Cnr. Manica Rd./Angwa St., P.O.B. 2417, Salisbury; Man. ERIC WILDER.

Old Mutual Fire and General Insurance Company of Rhodesia (Pvt.) Ltd.: Mutual House, Speke Ave., P.O.B. 2101, Salisbury; f. 1958; cap. R$2,186,952; assets R$1,726,179; Chair. R. F. HALSTED, I.C.D., C.B.E.; Gen. Man. W. H. EDWARDS.

TRADE AND INDUSTRY

CHAMBERS OF COMMERCE

Associated Chambers of Commerce of Rhodesia: 5th Floor, Electricity Centre, Jameson Ave., P.O.B. 1934, Salisbury; f. 1919; 2,100 mems.; 17 constituent chambers of commerce throughout Rhodesia; Gen. Sec. M. BRITTEN; publ. *Commerce* (monthly). Constituent Chambers in: Bindura, Bulawayo, Chipinga, Gwanda, Gwelo, Gatooma, Kariba, Karoi, Lowveld, Que Que, Marandellas, Victoria, Hartley, Salisbury, Sinoia, Umtali and Victoria Falls.

Salisbury Chamber of Commerce: 5th Floor, Electricity Centre, Jameson Ave., P.O.B. 1934, Salisbury; f. 1894; 1,100 mems.; Pres. M. E. ROBINSON; Sec. G. W. TYLER.

INDUSTRIAL AND EMPLOYERS' ASSOCIATIONS

Confederation of Employers: Salisbury.

African Turkish Tobacco Growers' Association: Salisbury; f. 1960; membership open to growers in all territories.

Agricultural Marketing Authority: P.O.B. 8094, Causeway, Salisbury; f. 1967.

Association of Rhodesian Industries: Friern House, 7 Speke Ave., Salisbury; f. 1957; represents the interests of industry in Rhodesia; Pres. S. M. HARRIS; Dir. J. C. GRAYLIN, I.C.D., C.M.G.

B.I.F.O.R. (Building Industry's Federation of Rhodesia): P.O.B. 3794, Salisbury; Pres. W. L. WALENN.

Bulawayo Agricultural Society: P.O. Famona, Bulawayo; sponsors of Trade Fair Rhodesia; Pres. Sir FREDERICK CRAWFORD, G.C.M.G., O.B.E.; Gen. Man. P. ST. A. ROACH, F.I.E., A.I.V.(S.A.).

Bulawayo Chamber of Industries: P.O.B. 2317; f. 1931; 374 mems.; Pres. G. F. J. HANDOVER, O.L.M.

Bulawayo Landowners' and Farmers' Association: P.O.B. 9003, Hillside, Bulawayo.

Bulawayo Master Builders' and Allied Trades' Association: P.O.B. 1970, Bulawayo; f. 1919; 142 mems.; Pres. A. P. GLENDINNING; Sec. E. FRIEND.

Chamber of Mines of Rhodesia, The: P.O.B. 712, Salisbury; f. 1939; Pres. I. M. COWAN; Gen. Man. K. A. VANDERPLANK; publs. *Annual Report, Chamber of Mines Journal* (monthly).

Gatooma Farmers' and Stockowners' Association: P.O.B. 100, Gatooma; 108 mems.; Chair. W. BIRRELL; Sec. P. L. JAMES, F.C.I.S., F.C.C.S.

Industrial Council of the Meat Trade (Bulawayo Area): P.O.B. 1149; Bulawayo; Sec. QUICK & JOHNS (PVT.) LTD.

Industrial Council of the Motor Industry of Matabeleland: P.O.B. 1149, Bulawayo; Sec. QUICK & JOHNS (PVT.) LTD.

Industrial Development Corporation of Rhodesia Ltd.: P.O.B. 8531, Causeway, Salisbury; f. 1963; Chair. N. CAMBITZIS.

Manicaland Chamber of Industries: P.O.B. 78, Umtali; f. 1945; 55 mems.; Sec. T. W. STEPHENSON.

Midlands Chamber of Industries: P.O.B. 142, Gwelo; 70 mems.; Sec. C. RAMPF.

National Industrial Council of the Building Industry of Rhodesia: St. Barbara House, Baker Ave./Moffat St., Salisbury; Sec. R. D. W. DUTTON.

National Industrial Council of the Engineering and Iron and Steel Industry: 5th Floor, Chancellor House, Jameson Ave., P.O.B. 1922, Salisbury; f. 1943; Chair. C. W. LANDER, C.B.E.; Gen. Sec. A. G. MAYCOCK, F.I.ARB.(LOND.).

Que Que Farmers' Association: P.O.B. 240, Que Que; f. 1928; 80 mems.; Sec. B. KAULBACK.

Rhodesia National Farmers' Union: P.O.B. 1241, Salisbury; f. 1942; 6,200 mems.; Administrator J. R. HUMPHREYS; publs. *The Rhodesian Farmer* (weekly), *Modern Farming* (quarterly).

Rhodesian Smallworkers' Association: P.O.B. 100, Gatooma; f. 1906; 34 mems.; Chair. P. M. MAY; Hon. Sec. P. L. JAMES, F.C.I.S., F.C.C.S.

Rhodesia Tobacco Association: P.O.B. 1781, Salisbury; 1,700 mems.; Pres. V. HURLEY; Chief Exec. Officer J. M. MORTEN; publ. *The Rhodesian Farmer* (weekly, with Rhodesian National Farmers' Union).

Rhodesian Tobacco Corporation: Salisbury; f. 1966 to market the tobacco crop; total received from sales (1966) £11.5m. approx., government subsidy £5m. approx.

Rhodesian Tobacco Marketing Board: P.O.B. 1781, Salisbury; Chair. R. A. GRIFFITH, M.B.E.; Gen. Man. H. G. STONHILL.

Salisbury Chamber of Industries: Salisbury; Pres. C. W. DEWHURST.

Salisbury Master Builders' and Allied Trades' Association: P.O.B. 1502, Salisbury; f. 1921; 254 mems.; Chair. W. G. WELSH; Sec. JAS. Y. GILCHRIST.

Tobacco Export Promotion Council of Rhodesia: R.T.A. House, Baker Ave., P.O.B. 1781, Causeway, Salisbury.

Umtali District Farmers' Association: P.O.B. 29, Umtali; 97 mems.; Chair. J. WOOD; Sec. Mrs. J. FROGGATT.

TRADE UNIONS

African Trade Union Congress: 65 Sinoia St., Salisbury; f. 1957; Gen. Sec. E. V. WATUNGWA; there are 9 affiliated unions with a total membership of 29,198.

Main affiliates:

Commercial and Allied Workers' Union: Kingsway, Salisbury; 4,000 mems.; Pres. J. ZENDAH.

Engineering and Metal Workers' Union: 12 Kilmarnock Bldg., Fife St., Bulawayo; 732 mems.; Pres. A. F. TSOKA.

Railway Associated Workers' Union: P.O.B. 2276, Bulawayo; 11,000 mems.; Pres. S. T. MASHINGAIDZE; Gen. Sec. A. J. MHUNGU.

Trade Union Congress of Rhodesia: P.O.B. 556, Bulawayo; f. 1954; 16,359 mems.; Pres. H. B. BLOOMFIELD; Gen. Sec. (vacant).

Main affiliates:

Associated Mine Workers of Rhodesia: P.O.B. 384, Salisbury; 5,400 mems.; Pres. H. B. BLOOMFIELD.

Rhodesian Railway Workers' Union: P.O.B. 556, Bulawayo; 4,500 mems.; Pres. (vacant); Gen. Sec. (vacant).

Typographical Union of Rhodesia: P.O.B. 27, Bulawayo; and P.O.B. 494, Salisbury; 1,500 mems.; Sec. (Bulawayo) J. TAYLOR; Sec. (Salisbury) A. C. CAIN.

United Steelworkers' Union of Central Africa (USUCA): Schattil's Bldg., Musgrave Rd., Redcliffe; 1,100 mems.; Pres. D. JOUBERT; Sec. J. EVANS.

National African Federation of Unions: Salisbury; f. 1965; 14,669 mems; Pres. S. S. NKOMO; Gen. Sec. MATHIAS KAVIYA.

Main affiliates:

Agricultural and Plantation Workers' Union: P.O.B. 1806, Bulawayo; 9,000 mems.; Pres. F. NGWENYA.

Building and Woodworkers' Union: Kingsway, Salisbury; 1,700 mems.; Pres. N. L. KARAMBWA; Gen. Sec. MORRIS CHIRONDA.

Municipal Workers' Union: 1676 4th St., 9th Rd., Makokoba, Bulawayo; 1,800 mems.; Pres. D. C. GAMBI; Gen. Sec. C. D. CHIKWANA.

Principal non-affiliated unions:

Air Transport Union: P.O.B. AP 40, Salisbury Airport, Salisbury; f. 1956; 320 mems.; Pres. J. B. DEAS; Gen. Sec. R. A. WINZER.

Amalgamated Engineering Union: 23 15th Ave., P.O.B. 472, Bulawayo; 3,000 mems.; Gen. Sec. D. V. MULLER.

National Association of Local Government Officers and Employees: P.O.B. 2956, Salisbury; Pres. P. E. COLE; Sec. Mrs. W. W. BEATON.

Salisbury Municipal Employees' Association: P.O.B. 448, Salisbury; 1,900 mems.; Chair. P. E. COLE; Sec. Mrs. M. W. BEATON.

Tailors' and Garment Workers' Union: P.O.B. 9019, Harare, Salisbury; 2,241 mems.; Pres. P. B. MOYO; Gen. Sec. G. ELIA.

Transport Workers' Union: P.O.B. 1936, Bulawayo; Chair. S. P. BHEBHE.

TRADE FAIR

Trade Fair Rhodesia: P.O. Famona, Bulawayo; f. 1960; Pres. Sir FREDERICK CRAWFORD, G.C.M.G., O.B.E.; Gen. Man. P. ST. A. ROACH, F.E.I., A.I.V.(S.A.).

TRANSPORT

RAILWAYS

Rhodesia Railways: P.O.B. 596, Bulawayo; originally f. 1899 and reconstituted 1967 when joint operation by Rhodesia and Zambia ceased and each became responsible for its own system; Chair. W. N. WELLS; Gen. Man. T. A. WRIGHT.

Trunk lines run from Bulawayo south through Botswana to the border with the Republic of South Africa, connecting with the South African Railways; north-west to the Victoria Falls, where there is a connection with Zambia Railways though since January 1973 the border with Zambia has been closed to all rail traffic; and north-east to Salisbury and Umtali connecting with the Mozambique Railways' line from Beira. From a point near Gwelo, a line runs to the south-east, making a connection with the Mozambique Railways' Limpopo line and with the port of Lourenço Marques. The present lines total 2,024 miles.

ROADS

The Road system in Rhodesia totals 49,045 miles of which 5,295 miles are designated main roads.

MOTORISTS' ORGANIZATION

Automobile Association of Rhodesia: Fanum House, 57 Jameson Ave. Central, P.O.B. 585, Salisbury; f. 1923; 54,000 mems.; Pres. Mrs. W. J. CHAMPION, M.B.E.; Gen. Man. J. R. SORRIE.

CIVIL AVIATION

Air Rhodesia Corporation: Salisbury Airport; f. 1967; services to Johannesburg, Beira, Durban, Lourenço Marques, Vilanculos and Blantyre; Chair. R. WILLIAMSON; Gen. Man. Capt. P. A. TRAVERS; fleet of 7 Viscount 700, 3 DC-3; 3 Boeing 720.

Rhodesian Air Services (Pvt.) Ltd.: c/o Protea Airways (Pty.) Ltd., Johannesburg; associate of Protea Airways (Pty.) Ltd., Johannesburg, South Africa.

Rhodesia United Air Carriers (Pvt.) Ltd.: Salisbury Airport; f. 1960; aircraft charter; branches at Bulawayo and Victoria Falls; Man. Dir. C. MYERS.

The following international airlines also serve Salisbury: Air Malawi, D.E.T.A., S.A.A., T.A.P.

TOURISM

Rhodesia National Tourist Board: 95 Stanley Ave., P.O.B. 8052, Causeway, Salisbury; f. 1963; Dir. M. V. GARDNER; publ. *Rhodesia Calls*.

FOREIGN OFFICES

Mozambique: Predio Santos Gil, 5° Andar, Avenida da República, P.O.B. 2229, Lourenço Marques.

South Africa: Carlton Centre, Commissioner St., P.O.B. 9398, Johannesburg; 2219 Trust Bank Centre, Corner Adderley and Riebeeck Streets, P.O.B. 2465, Cape Town; 315 Smith St., Durban Club Place; P.O.B. 1689, Durban.

U.S.A.: 535 Fifth Ave., New York, N.Y. 10017.

UNIVERSITY

University of Rhodesia: P.O.B. M.P. 167, Mount Pleasant, Salisbury; 209 teachers, 1,472 students.

RWANDA

INTRODUCTORY SURVEY

Location, Climate, Language, Religion, Flag, Capital

Rwanda is a small, landlocked state in Central Africa just south of the equator, bounded by Zaire to the west, Uganda to the north, Tanzania to the east and Burundi to the south. The climate is tropical with an average temperature of 64°F (18°c). French and Kinyarwanda, the native language, are both in official use. About half the population follow animist beliefs, most of the remainder being Roman Catholic. There are Protestant and Muslim minorities. The national flag (proportions 3 by 2) has three vertical stripes of red, yellow and green, the yellow band bearing a black letter R. The capital is Kigali.

Recent History

Rwanda was formerly part of the Belgian-administered Trust Territory of Ruanda-Urundi. Tribal dissensions have long been rife and in 1959 led to serious disturbances and the establishment of a state of emergency. In 1961 it was decided by referendum to abolish the monarchy and set up a Republic. Internal autonomy was granted in 1961 and full independence followed in 1962. Tribal strife broke out again in December 1963 and large-scale killings (estimated at 20,000) were carried out by the Hutu against their former overlords the Tutsi. During 1964–65 large numbers of displaced Rwandese were resettled in neighbouring countries. President Kayibanda was re-elected in 1969 for a third four-year term, and all 47 seats in the Assembly were retained by the governing party, the Mouvement démocratique républicain (also known as *Parmehutu*).

At the end of 1972 tribal tension between Hutu and Tutsi flared up again and continued throughout February 1973. In July 1973 the Minister of Defence and head of the National Guard, Maj.-Gen. Juvénal Habyalimana, led a bloodless *coup* and set up a military commission. This ruled until August, when a new cabinet, with Gen. Habyalimana as President, was formed. The normal legislative processes have been held in abeyance and all political activity banned since the *coup*.

Government

Rwanda is a Republic, executive power being exercised by the President assisted by a Cabinet of 13 Ministers. Legislation was carried out by the Legislative Assembly of 47 members (elected by universal adult suffrage) until the *coup*, when it was dissolved. At the same time the *Parmehutu* was suspended. The country is divided into ten Prefectures, which comprise numerous communes or municipalities.

Defence

Until independence in 1962 defence was the responsibility of Belgium. Since the withdrawal of Belgian troops a small national force has been built up and now consists of a national guard of 2,750, a gendarmerie of 400 and a civil police of 800.

Economic Affairs

The economy is agricultural, mainly at subsistence level. Coffee, tea, cotton and pyrethrum are the principal crops. Livestock is widely raised and hides and skins are exported. Minerals include cassiterite (tin ore) and some gold, tantalite, wolfram and beryl, and exports are mainly to the U.S.A. and EEC countries. Natural gas reserves have also recently begun to be exploited. Industry is on a small scale, mainly the processing of food, although small textile, chemical and engineering interests are developing. Financial aid from Belgium and the United Nations has been necessary to balance the budget. Trade is chiefly with neighbouring states, Belgium, other EEC countries and the U.S.A. Rwanda severed economic ties with Burundi after the failure of their economic union in January 1964. A five-year economic stabilization plan, including devaluation of the Rwanda franc, was implemented in April 1966. Its main objectives, development of export crops and increase of mineral production, were only partly realized. The currency was devalued again in January 1974. A second Five-Year Plan is expected to emphasize Rwanda's economic infrastructure and the development of the productive sectors, agriculture absorbing a large portion of the budget.

Transport and Communications

There are no railways. The main roads are asphalted and there are highways linking Rwanda with Burundi, Tanzania and Kenya. In 1972 there were some 6,500 kilometres of roads. The rivers are not navigable but there is traffic on Lake Kivu. There are three airfields and an international airport at Kigali. Regular flights are made to Burundi and Belgium.

Social Welfare

State schemes cover family allowances, accidents and pensions. The Government-assisted Native Welfare Fund provides community centres and medical services. Religious missions also provide socio-medical services.

Education

Primary education is free and compulsory for children aged 7–11. Schools are run by the State and by Missions but cannot yet provide education for all children. Over 435,000 children were at school in 1972. There is a university at Butare but a few students go to Zaire or Belgium for higher education.

Tourism

Tourism has not been developed although there is attractive mountain scenery.

Sport

Football is the most popular sport.

Public Holidays

1974: August 15th (Assumption), September 25th (Kamparampaka Day), October 26th (Armed Forces Day), November 1st (All Saints' Day), December 25th (Christmas).

1975: January 1st (New Year), January 28th (Democracy Day), March 31st (Easter), May 1st (Labour Day), May 19th (Whit Monday), July 1st (National Holiday), July 5th (National Peace and Unity Day).

Weights and Measures

The metric system is in force.

Currency and Exchange Rates

100 centimes = 1 Rwanda franc.

Exchange rates (April 1974):

£1 sterling = 219.22 Rwanda francs;

U.S. $1 = 92.84 Rwanda francs.

STATISTICAL SURVEY

AREA AND POPULATION

AREA (sq. km.)	POPULATION (1967)				
	Total (1970)	Tribes			Capital
		Hutu	Tutsi	Twa	Kigali
26,338*	3,735,585	2,520,000	500,000	20,000	25,000

* 10,169 sq. miles.

Mid-1972 Population: 3,896,000.

Births and Deaths (1970): Registered births totalled 187,899 (birth rate 51.1 per 1,000) and registered deaths 81,809 (death rate 22.2 per 1,000). Registration is not, however, complete. UN estimates for 1965–70 put the average annual birth rate at 51.8 per 1,000 and the death rate at 23.3 per 1,000.

EMPLOYMENT
(1968)

Agriculture	.	.	.	.	18,097
Mining	.	.	.	.	11,135
Manufacturing	.	.	.	.	11,077
Building	.	.	.	.	3,538
Water, Electricity, Sanitation	.	.		2,614
Commerce	.	.	.	.	3,815
Transport	.	.	.	.	1,322
Services	.	.	.	.	12,981
Civil Service	.	.	.	.	1,751
Technical Assistance	.	.		490
Education	.	.	.	.	6,781
Domestic Work*	.	.	.	.	10,000
TOTAL	.	.	.	.	83,600

* Estimate.

Total Labour Force (1970): In an estimated population of 3,609,000 (probably an under-estimate), the economically active numbered 1,955,000, including 1,775,000 engaged in agriculture (ILO and FAO estimates).

AGRICULTURE
LAND USE, 1970
('000 hectares)

Arable Land	.	.	.	522
Under Permanent Crops	.	.	182
Permanent Meadows and Pastures	.	.	817
Forest Land	.	.	.	328
Other Land	.	.	.	675
Inland Water	.	.	.	110
TOTAL AREA	.	.	.	2,634

PRINCIPAL CROPS
(metric tons)

	1969	1970	1971
Maize	41,000	64,000	60,000
Sorghum	126,000	156,000	140,000*
Potatoes	129,000	126,000	126,000*
Sweet Potatoes and Yams . .	324,225	417,000	400,000*
Cassava (Manioc)	282,500	345,000	n.a.
Dry Beans	146,124	144,000	140,000*
Dry Peas	60,948	65,000	63,000*
Bananas and Plantains . . .	1,638,000	n.a.	1,679,000
Groundnuts (in shell) . . .	7,000	6,000*	6,000
Coffee	14,200	15,700	15,000
Tea	800	1,245	1,700
Tobacco	900	800*	800*

1972: Coffee 13,500 metric tons.

* FAO estimate.

Source: mainly FAO, *Production Yearbook 1971.*

LIVESTOCK
('000)

	1968–69	1969–70	1970–71*
Cattle . .	680	710	740
Sheep . .	227	228*	230
Goats . .	620*	600*	600
Pigs . .	47	54	60
Chickens . .	600	510	550

* FAO estimate.

Source: FAO, *Production Yearbook 1971.*

LIVESTOCK PRODUCTS
(metric tons)

	1968	1969	1970	1971*
Cows' Milk	35,000	37,000	39,000*	40,000
Goats' Milk . . .	7,000*	6,000*	6,000*	6,000
Beef and Veal . . .	8,000*	8,000*	8,000*	n.a.
Mutton, Lamb and Goats' Meat .	3,000*	3,000*	3,000*	n.a.
Hen Eggs	300*	300*	300*	300
Cattle Hides (dry) . . .	540	480	579	n.a.
Sheep Skins . . .	174*	179*	168	n.a.
Goat Skins . . .	500*	470*	450*	n.a.

* FAO estimate.

Source: FAO, *Production Yearbook 1971.*

Forestry (1967–70): An estimated 4.5 million cubic metres of roundwood were removed for fuel each year. In addition, 6,000 cubic metres of logs for industrial wood were taken in 1967. Other forest products (1967): 30 metric tons of bamboo.

FISHING
(metric tons)

1968 . . .	900
1969 . . .	1,000
1970 . . .	1,300
1971 . . .	1,300

Source: FAO, *Yearbook of Fishery Statistics 1971.*

MINING
(metric tons)

	1968	1969	1970
Cassiterite* . .	1,797	1,784	2,156
Wolframite† . .	624	486	1,004
Beryl . .	149	267	307
Colombo-tantalite .	28	30	34

Natural gas: about one million cubic metres per year.

* Tin metal content (metric tons): 1,340 in 1968; 1,320 in 1969; 1,320 in 1970; 1,320 in 1971.

† Tungsten trioxide content (metric tons): 407 in 1968; 319 in 1969; 410 in 1970; 455 in 1971.

INDUSTRY

	1969	1970	1971
Beer ('000 hectolitres) .	129	148	168
Radio Receivers (number) .	3,720	4,200	4,770

In 1966 there were 14 manufacturing enterprises, with a total of 3,000 employees.

Electric energy production (million kWh.): 10.8 in 1963 (including 10.3 from hydroelectricity); 48.1 in 1966 (hydroelectricity 46.8).

FINANCE

100 centimes = 1 franc rwandais (Rwanda franc).

Coins: 50 centimes; 1, 2, 5 and 10 francs.

Notes: 20, 50, 100, 500 and 1,000 francs.

Exchange rates (April 1974): £1 sterling = 219.22 Rwanda francs;
U.S. $1 = 92.84 Rwanda francs.
1,000 Rwanda francs = £4.56 = $10.77.

(*Note:* Between April 1966 and August 1971 the Rwanda franc was valued at 1 U.S. cent.)

BUDGET
(million Rwanda francs)

REVENUE	1969	1970	1971	EXPENDITURE	1969	1970	1971
Direct Taxes . . .	460	494	536	Education . . .	} 1,697	{ 491	578
Import Duties . . .	390	521	546	Other Current			
Export Duties . . .	142	508	265	Expenditure . .		{ 1,265	1,595
Other Indirect Taxes .	210	290	345	Extraordinary			
Grants . . .	109	} 131	151	Expenditure . .	80	112	186
Other Revenue . .	111						
TOTAL ORDINARY RECEIPTS . .	1,422	1,944	1,843	TOTAL EXPENDITURE .	1,777	1,868	2,359

Source: UN Economic Commission for Africa, *Statistical Yearbook 1972.*

1972 Budget (proposals): Ordinary Receipts and Current Expenditure to balance at 2,138 million francs.

EXTERNAL TRADE
(million R.F.)

	1967	1968	1969	1970	1971	1972
Imports . . .	2,022.2	2,245.8	2,362.4	2,909.9	3,298.3	3,223.6
Exports . . .	1,399.9	1,472.4	1,410.0	2,461.3	2,233.3	1,755.9

PRINCIPAL COMMODITIES
('ooo R.F.)

IMPORTS	1967	1968	1969
Food and Live Animals	153,190	198,400	260,560
Cereals and preparations	79,590	72,970	133,240
Beverages and Tobacco	24,100	83,310	140,300
Tobacco and manufactures . .	5,690	47,870	105,920
Petroleum Products	122,160	141,020	150,190
Chemicals	100,130	137,830	155,960
Basic Manufactures	802,310	933,880	807,830
Textile yarn, fabrics, etc. . . .	360,190	443,400	335,340
Cotton yarn and fabrics . .	115,020	174,700	125,650
Synthetic and regenerated yarn, fabrics .	183,160	233,620	158,170
Iron and steel	137,790	147,610	141,570
Machinery and Transport Equipment .	456,100	418,720	464,870
Machinery (non-electric) . . .	125,200	108,790	106,370
Electrical equipment . . .	60,070	94,350	93,060
Transport equipment . . .	270,830	215,570	265,438
Road vehicles . . .	216,910	202,720	257,080
Miscellaneous Manufactured Articles	182,460	118,220	186,380
TOTAL (incl. others) . . .	2,022,150	2,245,770	2,362,370

1970 (million Rwanda francs): Cereals and preparations 224.4, Petroleum products 159.5, Cotton yarn and fabrics 149.5, Synthetic yarn and fabrics 162.9, Machinery (non-electric) 146.4, Electrical equipment 91.7, Transport equipment 260.3, Total 2,909.9.

EXPORTS	1967	1968	1969
Food and Live Animals	805,270	914,370	728,510
Barley	3,230	17,560	1,860
Coffee (green and roasted) . . .	774,350	846,790	656,069
Tea	23,600	46,900	69,331
Hides and Skins (undressed) . . .	24,700	13,250	25,630
Tin Ores and Concentrates . . .	416,460	343,900	438,570
Tungsten Ores and Concentrates . .	100,710	159,350	154,110
Pyrethrum	29,480	17,420	36,004
Cinchona Bark	4,440	9,540	11,640
TOTAL (incl. others) . . .	1,399,920	1,472,410	1,409,990

Source: mainly United Nations, *Yearbook of International Trade Statistics 1969.*

1970 (million Rwanda francs, provisional): Coffee 1,407.1, Tea 96.0, Tin 471.2, Tungsten 379.8, Pyrethrum 29.2, Total 2,480.6.

1971 (million Rwanda francs): Coffee 1,114.9, Tea 130.4, Tin 454.0, Tungsten 365.9, Pyrethrum 59.8, Total 2,233.3.

1972 (million Rwanda francs): Coffee 797.7, Tin 489.9, Total 1,755.9.

PRINCIPAL COUNTRIES
('ooo R.F.)

IMPORTS	1967	1968	1969
Belgium/Luxembourg . . .	561,470	407,700	362,442
Burundi	77,650	50,940	37,630
France	117,490	89,450	121,340
Germany, Federal Republic . .	186,740	265,090	257,723
Hong Kong	34,750	37,690	45,560
Italy	22,540	31,190	39,665
Japan	248,090	305,050	328,719
Kenya	55,660	123,590	176,216
Netherlands	33,420	37,050	32,699
Uganda	272,540	309,270	275,051
United Kingdom	71,250	102,130	133,590
U.S.A.	138,990	153,050	156,258
Zaire	18,170	67,080	70,300
TOTAL (incl. others) . .	2,022,150	2,245,770	2,362,370

Source: mainly United Nations, *Yearbook of International Trade Statistics 1969.*

EXPORTS*	1967	1968	1969
Belgium/Luxembourg . . .	435,530	347,590	417,450
Burundi	33,100	25,480	26,320
France	7,590	35,170	8,510
Japan	21,590	22,560	15,950
Kenya	7,270	33,600	91,100
Netherlands	11,040	16,230	21,290
Uganda	62,110	104,340	107,030
United Kingdom	11,300	39,570	34,020
U.S.A.†	n.a.	n.a.	n.a.
Zaire	11,650	21,320	2,850
TOTAL (incl. others) . .	1,399,920	1,472,410	1,409,990

* Including certain goods consigned at Mombasa, in Kenya, for which the distribution by country is not known. The value of these exports (in 'ooo Rwanda francs) was: 591,850 in 1967; 818,720 in 1968; and 664,150 in 1969.

† The United States received more than 49 per cent (by value) of Rwanda's exports in 1965, but figures for subsequent years are not available.

Source: United Nations, *Yearbook of International Trade Statistics 1969.*

TRANSPORT

ROAD MOTOR VEHICLES
(in use at December 31st)

	1968	1969	1970	1971
Passenger Cars	2,880	3,400	3,872	4,300
Commercial Vehicles . . .	1,514	1,900	2,159	2,600
TOTAL	4,394	5,300	6,031	6,900

Shipping (1962): Lake Kivu freights 70,000 metric tons.

CIVIL AVIATION

	1968	1969	1970	1971
Freight Loaded (metric tons) . .	77	73	185	610
Freight Unloaded (metric tons) . .	41	50	104	293
Passenger Arrivals ('000) . .	9	11	12	14
Passenger Departures ('000) . .	9	10	10	11

Source: UN Economic Commission for Africa, *Statistical Yearbook 1972*.

COMMUNICATIONS

Telephones (at January 1st): 1,389 in 1969; 1,433 in 1970; 2,000 in 1971.

Radio: 31,000 receivers in use at December 31st, 1971.

EDUCATION
(1971–72)

	TEACHERS	PUPILS
First Level . .	7,328	425,000
Second Level . .	816	10,577
Third Level . .	136	1,166*

* Of whom 658 were in Rwanda and 508 abroad.

THE CONSTITUTION*

(*promulgated November* 1962)

The Republic of Rwanda was proclaimed in January 1961, following the abolition by public referendum of the Monarchy.

The Republic. Rwanda is a democratic, social and sovereign State. There is equality among citizens, who exercise national rights through their representatives.

Civil Rights. Fundamental liberties as defined in the Declaration of Human rights are guaranteed.

The Executive. Executive power is exercised by the President and his Ministers. The President is elected for four years by direct universal suffrage and may be re-elected. The President, who nominates and dismisses Ministers, presides over the Council of Ministers; negotiates and terminates all treaties; promulgates laws; may suspend but not dissolve the National Assembly; exercises the prerogative of mercy; and is the Commander-in-Chief of the Armed Forces.

Legislative power. Exercised jointly by the National Assembly and the President. The National Assembly, which is elected by universal direct suffrage, votes laws and the budget.

The Judiciary. The Supreme Court is the guardian of the Constitution. It has sole jurisdiction over penal matters affecting the President, Ministers or Deputies if indicted by a three-quarter majority of the National Assembly.

Revision of the Constitution. Both the President and the National Assembly may initiate Constitutional reforms.

*The military *coup* of July 1973 has meant that parts of this constitution are in abeyance.

THE GOVERNMENT

Head of State: Gen. JUVÉNAL HABYALIMANA, President of the Committee for National Peace and Unity.

COUNCIL OF MINISTERS
(*April* 1974)

Premier and Minister of National Defence: Gen. JUVÉNAL HABYALIMANA.

Minister of Interior and Civil Service: Lieut.-Col. ALEXIS KANYARENGWE.

Minister of National Education: THADDÉE BAGARAGAZA.

Minister of Agriculture and Livestock: SEDECIAS MUGAMBIRA.

Minister of Economic and Financial Affairs: J. CHRYSOSTOME NDUHUNGIREHE.

Minister of Planning and Natural Resources: J.-M. VIANNEY SHINGIRO MBONYUMUTWA.

Minister of Public Works and Equipment: ANDRÉ KATABARWA.

Minister of Foreign Affairs and International Co-operation: Lt.-Col. ALOYS NSEKALIJE.

Minister of Posts, Telecommunications and Transport: MARTIN BUCYANA.

Minister of Information: Major ALOYS SIMBA.

Minister of Justice: BONAVENTURE HABIMANA.

Minister of Public Health and Social Welfare: Dr. CLAUDIEN KAMILINDI.

Minister of Sports and Youth: Cmdr. CÉLESTIN RWAGAFILITA.

DIPLOMATIC REPRESENTATION

EMBASSIES ACCREDITED TO RWANDA

Austria: Kinshasa, Zaire.

Belgium: B.P. 81, Kigali; *Ambassador:* FRANS BAEKE-LANDT.

Burundi: B.P. 714, Kigali; *Ambassador:* GABRIEL NDICUN-GUYE.

Cameroon: Kinshasa, Zaire.

Canada: Kinshasa, Zaire.

Chad: Kinshasa, Zaire.

China, People's Republic: B.P. 1345, Kigali; *Ambassador:* HUANG SHIH-HSIEH.

Czechoslovakia: Dar es Salaam, Tanzania.

Egypt: Kampala, Uganda.

Ethiopia: Kinshasa, Zaire.

France: B.P. 53, Kigali; *Ambassador:* ROBERT PICQUET.

German Democratic Republic: Kampala, Uganda.

Germany, Federal Republic: B.P. 355, Kigali; *Ambassador:* Dr. WALTER FROEWIS.

Ghana: Kinshasa, Zaire.

Guinea: Kinshasa, Zaire.

India: Kampala, Uganda.

Israel: (Diplomatic relations severed October 9th, 1973).

Italy: Kampala, Uganda.

Japan: Kinshasa, Zaire.

Korea, Democratic People's Republic: Bujumbura, Burundi.

Korea, Republic: Kampala, Uganda.

Netherlands: Kinshasa, Zaire.

Nigeria: Kampala, Uganda.

Romania: Dar es Salaam, Tanzania.

Senegal: Kinshasa, Zaire.

Spain: Kinshasa, Zaire.

Switzerland: B.P. 597, Kigali; *Ambassador:* RICHARD PESTALOZZI.

Tanzania: Kinshasa, Zaire.

Uganda: Kigali; *Ambassador:* Lt.-Col. MICHAEL ENDEMA OMBIA.

U.S.S.R. B.P. 40, Kigali; *Ambassador:* GRIGORI ZHILIAKOV.

United Kingdom: Kampala, Uganda.

U.S.A.: B.P. 28, Kigali; *Ambassador:* ROBERT E. FRITTS.

Vatican: B.P. 261, Kigali; *Apostolic Nuncio:* Mgr. WILLIAM A. CAREW.

Yugoslavia: Kampala, Uganda.

Zaire: B.P. 169, Kigali; *Ambassador:* MOTO-BALUTI.

Zambia: Dar es Salaam, Tanzania.

Rwanda also has diplomatic relations at consular level with Denmark.

LEGISLATIVE ASSEMBLY

The Legislative Assembly was dissolved after the military *coup* of July 1973. At the elections in October 1969 all 47 seats had been won by the then governing party, MDR—*Parmehutu*.

POLITICAL PARTY

Mouvement démocratique républicain—Parmehutu (*Republican Democratic Movement Parmehutu*): P.O.B. 19, Gitarama; f. 1959 by Grégoire Kayibanda; supported by the Hutu people. The *Parmehutu* party was suspended after the military *coup* of July 1973.

JUDICIAL SYSTEM

The judiciary is independent of the Executive. Codified law is administered by the Courts of First Instance and the Court of Appeal. Traditional law is administered by the Supreme Court.

CODIFIED LAW

Court of Appeal: Kigali.

Courts of First Instance: there are ten Courts of First Instance.

TRADITIONAL LAW

Supreme Court of Rwanda: Nyabisindu; five sections for administration of Lower Courts, Constitutional Law, Council of State, Cassation, and Public Accounts; Pres. FULGENCE SEMINEGA.

RELIGION

AFRICAN RELIGIONS

Traditional belief is mainly in a God "Imana". About half the population are followers of traditional beliefs.

CHRISTIANITY

ROMAN CATHOLIC

Archdiocese of Kabgayi: B.P. 715, Kigali; f. 1900; Archbishop Most Rev. ANDRÉ PERRAUDIN; Suffragan Sees: Bishop of Nyundo Rt. Rev. VINCENT NSENGIYUMVA, Bishop of Kibungo Rt. Rev. JOSEPH SIBOMANA, Bishop of Butare Rt. Rev. JEAN BAPTISTE GAHAMANYI, Bishop of Ruhengeri Rt. Rev. PHOCAS NIKWIGIZE.

There are 1,900,000 adherents and 387 priests in Rwanda.

ANGLICANS

Under the Province of Uganda:

Archbishop of Uganda: Most Rev. ERICA SABITI, D.D.

Bishop of Rwanda: Rt. Rev. ADONIYA SEBUNUNGURI, B.P. 61, Kigali.

There are about 120,000 adherents in Rwanda.

BAPTISTS

Eglise Baptiste, Nyantanga, B.P. 59, Butare.

OTHER PROTESTANTS

About 250,000; there is a substantial Seventh Day Adventist minority.

ISLAM

There are a few Muslims.

PRESS AND RADIO

PERIODICALS

Imhavo: B.P. 63, Kigali; twice monthly; Kinyarwanda; circ. 40,000.

Hobe: B.P. 761, Kigali; f. 1955; monthly; Kinyarwanda; Dir. S. M. L. Moulart; circ. 35,500.

Kinya Mateka: Archevêché de Kabgayi, B.P. 761, Kigali; f. 1933; twice a month; Dir. S. M. L. Moulart; circ. 6,500.

Rwanda-Carrefour d'Afrique: B.P. 83, Kigali; publ. by Ministry of Foreign Affairs; monthly; French.

BROADCASTING

Radiodiffusion de la République Rwandaise: B.P. 83, Kigali; broadcasts daily programmes in Kinyarwanda, Swahili, French and English; Chief of Programmes Aloys Rukebesha; Dir. Ismael Amri Sued.

Deutsche Welle Relay Station Africa: Kigali; broadcasts daily in German, English, French, Hausa, Swahili and Amharic.

There were 31,000 radio receivers in 1971.

FINANCE

(cap.=capital; p.u.=paid up; m.=million; res.=reserves; amounts in Rwanda francs)

BANKING

CENTRAL BANK

Banque Nationale du Rwanda: B.P. 531, Kigali; f. 1964; Gov. M. Hattori; Vice-Gov. J. Birara.

SAVINGS BANK

Caisse d'Épargne du Rwanda: Kigali; f. 1964.

COMMERCIAL BANKS

Banque Commerciale du Rwanda S.A.R.L.: Kigali; f. 1963; brs. in Butare, Byumba, Cyangugu and Gisenyi; cap. 65m.; Res. 6m.; Man. for Rwanda L. Roegiers.

Banque de Kigali: B.P. 175, Kigali; f. 1966; cap. and res. 59.6m.; dep. 379m.; Pres. I. Hakizimana; Man. L. Degroot.

DEVELOPMENT BANK

Banque Rwandaise de Développement: Kigali; f. 1967; cap. p.u. 50m.

TRADE AND TRANSPORT

TRADE UNIONS

Confédération générale du travail du Rwanda (CGTR): Kigali; union for Banya-Rwanda workers.

Union des Travailleurs du Rwanda (UTR): Kigali.

RAILWAYS

There are no railways.

ROADS

In 1972 there were about 6,500 km. of roads, of which nearly half were main roads. Rwanda's first asphalt road, now under construction, will link Kigali with Kabale in south-west Uganda. Rwanda is also linked by road to the Tanzanian railways system.

INLAND WATERWAYS

There are services on Lake Kivu from Kibuye to Zaire.

CIVIL AVIATION

There are airfields at Butare, Gisenyi and Gabiro; the international airport is at Kigali. Rwanda is served by the following foreign airlines: Air Zaire, EAAC and Sabena.

TOURISM

Ministère de l'Information et du Tourisme: B.P. 83, Kigali; Minister, Major Aloys Simba.

UNIVERSITY

Université Nationale du Rwanda: B.P. 117, Butare; f. 1963; 60 teachers, 525 students.

SAUDI ARABIA

INTRODUCTORY SURVEY

Location, Climate, Language, Religion, Flag, Capital

Saudi Arabia occupies the greater part of the Arabian peninsula, with the Yemen Arab Republic and the Red Sea to the west and the Persian Gulf and the United Arab Emirates to the east. Jordan, Iraq and Kuwait are to the north and Oman and the Yemen People's Democratic Republic to the south. Much of the country is desert. In summer temperatures range from 100° to 120°F (38°–49°C) in coastal regions and humidity is high. Temperatures sometimes reach 130°F (54°C) in the interior. Winters are mild, except in the mountains. The language is Arabic. The great majority of the population are Sunni Muslims, and in the Najd there is a preponderance of members of the Wahhabi sect. The national flag (proportions 3 by 2) is green and bears, in white, an Arabic inscription ("There is no God but God and Muhammad is the prophet of God") above a white sword. The royal capital is Riyadh and the administrative capital is Jeddah.

Recent History

Saudi Arabia has been a member of the Arab League since 1945. King Saud ibn Abdul Aziz succeeded his father in 1953 but in 1964 full executive powers passed into the hands of Crown Prince Faisal, the Prime Minister since 1962. In November 1964 the Council of Ministers asked King Saud to resign in favour of his brother. King Faisal continued in the office of Prime Minister, and now rules the country directly through the Council of Ministers. For several years the Saudi Government supported the deposed Imam of the Yemen in his effort to regain the throne he lost in 1962. This led to strained relations with Egypt and other Arab republics, but these have since improved. Saudi Arabia did not directly participate in the 1967 war, but the government has adopted a strongly anti-Israeli policy. During 1973 Faisal became increasingly more militant in the Arab cause, and in October the Saudi Government reduced oil production by 10 per cent, at one time reaching a peak of more than 30 per cent, and placed an embargo on the export of oil to the United States between October 1973 and March 1974. Saudi troops were sent to the Syrian front in October 1973 during the war between the Arab States and Israel.

Government

Constitutionally, the King rules in accordance with the *Sharia*, or sacred law of Islam. A Council of Ministers is appointed by the King, and decisions of the Council of Ministers are reached by majority vote but require royal sanction. The principal administrative divisions are Najd, Hijaz, 'Asir, Najran, and Eastern Province. The organs of local government are the General Municipal Councils, the District Council and the tribal and village Councils.

Defence

Military forces number over 40,000; in addition to tanks and coastal patrol boats there are about 70 combat aircraft.

Economic Affairs

Saudi Arabia is the largest producer of crude oil in the Middle East; its crude oil production in 1973 exceeded 2,700 million barrels. The income from oil constitutes over 90 per cent of the budget receipts and accounts for 95 per cent of foreign exchange exchange earnings. The country is thought to possess the world's largest oil reserves. There is little industry but an iron and steel plant and an oil refinery were established at Jeddah in 1967. An oil lubricating plant is also under construction there. Agreement has been reached with a United States firm for the establishment of grain silos and flour mills in Jeddah. Apart from oil the chief activity is agriculture. The principal products are dates, wheat, barley, fruit, hides and wool. Camels, horses, donkeys and sheep are raised. Another source of revenue is the income from religious pilgrims, who come from all parts of the Muslim world to the holy cities of Mecca and Medina. Much attention is being given to underground water resources and to desalination projects. The Government is distributing land to former nomads.

Transport and Communications

There is a railway from Dammam to Riyadh and the rebuilding of the railway from Medina to Damascus has been completed on Saudi territory. Asphalted roads link Jeddah to Mecca and Medina, Medina to Yanbu, Taif to Mecca, Riyadh to al-Kharj, and Dammam to Hofuf. A new road has been opened between Riyadh and Jeddah. The road flanking the Trans-Arabian Pipeline from Dhahran to the Mediterranean is being rebuilt. Saudia (Saudi Arabian Airlines) operate internal and external air services. The principal ports are Jeddah, on the Red Sea, and Ras Tanura and Dammam, on the Gulf.

Social Welfare

Oil revenues have enabled the Saudi Arabian government to provide free medicine and medical care for all citizens and foreign residents. A far reaching new Labour Act and Social Security Ordinance were passed in 1969. In 1974 the country had more than 50 hospitals, containing between 8,000 and 9,000 beds, and more than 500 health centres.

Education

Elementary, secondary and higher education is free but not compulsory. In 1973 more than 600,000 boys and more than 200,000 girls were attending primary schools, and there were about 10,000 students at the country's four universities.

Tourism

All devout Muslims try to pay at least one visit to the holy cities of Medina, the burial place of Muhammad, and Mecca, his birthplace. More than 607,000 pilgrims visited Saudi Arabia in the Muslim year 1393 (1973–74).

Visas are not required for visits to Saudi Arabia by nationals of Kuwait.

Sport

The main sports are football, bicycle racing, hawking and horse-riding.

Public Holidays

1974: October 16th–18th (Id ul Fitr), December 26th–29th (Id ul Adha).

1975: January 14th (Muslim New Year), March 26th (Mouloud, Birth of the Prophet).

Weights and Measures

The metric system is in force.

Currency and Exchange Rates

100 halalah = 20 qursh = 1 Saudi riyal.

Exchange rates (April 1974):

£1 sterling = 8.40 Saudi riyals;

U.S. $1 = 3.55 Saudi riyals.

STATISTICAL SURVEY

AREA AND POPULATION

Area (estimated)	Mid-year Population (UN estimates)†					
	1968	1969	1970	1971	1972	1973
830,000 sq. miles*	7,317,000	7,524,000	7,740,000	7,965,000	8,199,000	8,443,000

* 2,149,690 square kilometres.

† A census was held in 1962–63 but the results have been officially repudiated.

PRINCIPAL TOWNS
(estimated population in 1965)

Riyadh (royal capital) . .	. .	225,000
Jeddah (administrative capital)	. .	194,000
Mecca	. .	185,000

Medina: 72,000 in 1962.

SAUDI ARABIA-IRAQ NEUTRAL ZONE

The Najdi (Saudi Arabian) frontier with Iraq was defined in the Treaty of Mohammara in May 1922. Later a Neutral Zone of 7,000 sq. km. was established adjacent to the western tip of the Kuwait frontier. No military or permanent buildings were to be erected in the zone and the nomads of both countries were to have unimpeded access to its pastures and wells. A further agreement concerning the administration of this zone was signed between Iraq and Saudi Arabia in May 1938.

SAUDI ARABIA-KUWAIT PARTITIONED ZONE

A Convention signed at Uqair in December 1922 fixed the Najdi (Saudi Arabian) boundary with Kuwait. The Convention also established a Neutral Zone of 5,770 sq. km. immediately to the south of Kuwait in which Saudi Arabia and Kuwait held equal rights. The final agreement on this matter was signed in 1963. Since 1966 the Zone has been divided between the two countries and each administers its own half, in practice as an integral part of the state. However, the oil wealth of the whole Zone remains undivided and production from the on-shore oil concessions in the Partitioned Zone is shared equally between the two states' concessionaires (Aminoil and Getty).

AGRICULTURE AND INDUSTRY

Agriculture (estimates, metric tons): Wheat 15,000, Maize 21,000, Millet and Sorghum 6,000, Barley 13,000, Rice 2,000, Dates 200,000. Other crops include alfalfa, vegetables, coffee and henna.

Livestock: Sheep 3,600,000, Goats 1,900,000, Asses 22,000.

Industry: Building, Date Packing, Cement (703,000 tons in 1971–72), Soap, Sugar, Rugs, Marble, Gypsum, Nails, Soft Drinks, Industrial Gases, Electricity (763 million kWh. in 1971–72).

OIL
CRUDE OIL PRODUCTION BY COMPANY
(million barrels)

	TOTAL	ARAMCO	GETTY OIL	ARABIAN OIL
1938 . . .	0.5	0.5	—	—
1946 . . .	59.9	59.9	—	—
1955 . . .	356.6	352.2	4.4	—
1966 . . .	950.0	873.3	30.2	46.5
1967 . . .	1,023.8	948.1	25.1	50.6
1968 . . .	1,114.0	1,035.8	23.2	55.0
1969 . . .	1,173.9	1,092.4	22.7	58.8
1970 . . .	1,386.3	1,295.3	28.3	62.7
1971 . . .	1,740.8	1,641.6	33.7	65.5
1972 . . .	2,201.7	2,098.4	28.3	75.0
1973 . . .	2,772.7	2,677.4	23.4	71.9

OIL REVENUES BY SOURCE
(million U.S. $)

	TOTAL	ARAMCO	GETTY OIL	ARABIAN OIL	OTHER COMPANIES
1939 . . .	3.2	3.2	—	—	—
1946 . . .	10.4	10.4	—	—	—
1955 . . .	340.8	338.2	2.6	—	—
1965 . . .	662.6	618.4*	23.8	20.4	—
1966 . . .	789.7	745.5*	20.6	22.3	1.3
1967 . . .	909.1	859.4*	17.8	31.8	0.1
1968 . . .	926.8	872.0	13.6	34.3	6.9
1969 . . .	949.0	895.2	15.2	37.1	1.5
1970 . . .	1,214.0	1,148.4	17.2	40.3	3.8
1971 . . .	1,884.9	1,806.4	20.6	44.2	13.7
1972 . . .	2,734.1	2,632.7†	28.0	68.7	4.7

* Including certain special payments.

† Including $45.2 million for the value of royalty oil delivered to PETROMIN.

Royalties from Aramco totalled $4,215.5 million in 1973.

FINANCE

100 halalah = 20 qursh = 1 Saudi riyal.

Coins: 1, 5, 10, 25 and 50 halalah; 1, 2 and 4 qursh.*

Notes: 1, 5, 10, 50 and 100 riyals.

Exchange rates (April 1974): £1 sterling = 8.40 Saudi riyals; U.S. $1 = 3.55 Saudi riyals.

100 Saudi riyals = £11.90 = $28.17.

* The coins of 1, 2 and 4 qursh are being gradually withdrawn from circulation.

BUDGET
(million riyals)

REVENUE	1972–73	1973–74	EXPENDITURE	1972–73	1973–74
Oil Royalties . . .	2,529	5,336	Defence	1,427	1,711
Income Tax (inc. tax on oil receipts) . . .	9,674	15,930	Interior	1,071	1,267
Customs . . .	315	330	Education	1,300	1,677
Other Items . . .	682	1,214	Health	375	499
			Development Projects .	6,718	14,263
			General Budgetary Reserve .	300	452
			Other Items . . .	2,009	2,941
TOTAL . . .	13,200	22,810	TOTAL . . .	13,200	22,810

SAUDI ARABIA—(Statistical Survey)

DEVELOPMENT EXPENDITURE
(million riyals)

	1970–71	1971–72	1972–73	1973–74
Ministry of Communications	523.6	1,333.7	1,246.1	2,051.7
Civil Aviation	79.9	127.3	223.9	466.8
Ministry of Agriculture and Water Resources	230.1	456.0	572.5	855.0
Ministry of Petroleum and Mineral Resources	39.6	82.3	86.7	136.3
Ministry of Commerce and Industry	9.2	28.9	29.9	46.0
Ministry of Labour and Social Affairs	8.2	24.1	26.4	36.4
Ministry of Education and Educational Institutions	24.9	125.9	255.1	565.5
Ministry of Health	10.9	29.2	45.4	84.2
Ministry of Interior (Municipalities)	190.1	438.8	640.5	1,575.3
Ministry of Hajj and Awqaf	9.4	28.2	45.7	57.5
Ministry of Information	28.2	48.8	82.2	158.5
Others	1,441.9	2,312.5	3,463.2	8,229.8
Total	2,596.0	5,035.7	6,717.6	14,263.0

Currency in Circulation (million riyals): 1969–70, 1,566.9; 1970–71, 1,655.8; 1971–72, 1,788.2; 1972–73, 2,163.9; 1973–74, 2,751.5.

NATIONAL ACCOUNTS
(million riyals—at current factor cost)

	1968–69	1969–70*	1970–71*	1971–72*
Agriculture, Forestry, Fishing	974.4	1,002.7	1,035.9	1,084.7
Mining and Quarrying:				
Crude petroleum and natural gas	7,201.0	8,238.0	11,350.3	15,235.1
Other mining and quarrying	41.9	42.1	44.5	52.6
Manufacturing:				
Petroleum refining	946.5	1,207.8	1,440.5	1,483.9
Other manufacturing	299.0	332.0	371.8	428.5
Construction	837.8	841.4	890.0	1,051.6
Electricity, Gas, Water, and Sanitary Services	196.0	212.5	231.6	241.3
Transport, Storage and Communications	1,198.1	1,307.1	1,433.7	1,584.9
Wholesale and Retail Trade	1,180.4	1,252.3	1,322.7	1,477.4
Banking, Insurance, and Real Estate	102.7	109.7	117.7	138.7
Ownership of Dwellings	601.0	654.5	712.8	790.2
Public Administration and Defence	1,195.1	1,247.0	1,313.3	1,445.3
Services:				
Education	426.0	453.2	508.8	589.9
Medical and health	140.2	141.2	143.8	173.8
Other services	320.6	329.6	358.9	411.8
Gross Domestic Product at Factor Cost	15,660.7	17,371.1	21,276.3	26,189.7
less: Net factor income payments to the rest of the world	3,390.3	3,961.0	5,346.6	6,988.5
Gross National Product	12,270.4	13,410.1	15,929.7	19,201.2
less: Depreciation	1,227.0	1,341.0	1,593.0	1,920.1
National Income	11,043.4	12,069.1	14,336.7	17,281.1

* Provisional.

1299

BALANCE OF PAYMENTS
(million U.S. $—estimates)

	1970	1971	1972
Receipts:			
Exports, f.o.b.	2,179	3,621	5,250
Oil royalties from companies other than Aramco	66	79	101
Pilgrimage	102	112	156
Miscellaneous	91	106	161
Total	2,438	3,918	5,668
Payments:			
Imports, c.i.f.	892	939	1,397
Non-monetary gold	18	9	15
Investment income payments	893	1,433	2,050
Government expenditures abroad, n.e.s.	268*	274*	299*
Travel and personal transportation, n.e.s.	123	144	179
Tapline expenditures abroad	16	47	47
Other services	166	177	275
Total	2,376	3,023	4,262
Current Balance	62	895	1,406
Capital and Financing Account:			
Direct investment capital	− 3	−109	−359
Other capital	−99	138	253
Gold, foreign exchange holdings, and investments of SAMA	87	794	1,322
Commercial banks' net foreign position	23	23	179
Errors and Omissions	54	49	11
Capital Balance	62	895	1,406

* Includes aid paid to Arab countries.

EXTERNAL TRADE
(million riyals—Muslim calendar)

	1966–67	1967–68	1968–69	1969–70	1970–71*
Imports	2,288	2,212	2,804	3,213	3,465
Exports	7,654	7,853	8,953	9,449*	10,600

* Provisional.

(million riyals—Gregorian calendar)

	1969	1970	1971	1972
Imports	3,377	3,197	3,667	4,708
Exports	9,496	10,907	17,302	22,761

PRINCIPAL COMMODITIES
(million riyals)

Imports	1970	1971	1972	Exports	1970	1971	1972
Foodstuffs	1,011	1,097	1,222	Crude Oil } Aramco	6,798	11,490	16,937
Textiles and Clothing	142	203	344	Refined Oil } only	1,342	1,470	1,647
Machinery, Transport	1,018	1,099	1,686				
Building Materials	384	463	480				
Chemical Products	180	240	244				
Miscellaneous	462	565	732				
Total	3,197	3,667	4,708	Total (incl. others)	10,907	17,302	22,761

* Provisional

PRINCIPAL COUNTRIES
(million riyals)

	IMPORTS		EXPORTS	
	1970	1971	1970	1971
North America . . .	575.6	629.2	146.4	733.3
U.S.A. . . .	568.5	615.1	97.8	589.5
Western Europe . . .	1,080.8	1,218.3	4,820.3	8,386.1
Belgium . . .	65.0	90.6	248.2	351.0
France . . .	88.0	78.6	691.6	1,661.8
Germany, Federal Republic .	312.8	289.0	222.3	577.8
Italy . . .	142.8	161.0	1,178.6	1,767.4
Netherlands . . .	139.7	169.3	992.5	1,568.8
Spain . . .	3.5	4.0	465.7	453.1
United Kingdom . .	230.9	327.7	827.6	1,510.2
Middle East . . .	636.2	810.0	608.6	805.7
Bahrain . . .	46.8	78.7	511.7	646.4
Jordan . . .	45.5	40.7	31.5	51.6
Lebanon . . .	362.9	473.9	30.4	69.9
Africa . . .	127.4	152.4	473.7	758.9
Asia . . .	610.8	711.9	3,339.4	4,413.7
India . . .	102.1	68.5	130.9	222.1
Japan . . .	314.2	414.2	2,323.4	2,783.1
Malaysia . . .	23.8	21.9	211.1	83.9
South America . . .	1.0	1.0	445.0	973.9

PILGRIMAGE TO MECCA

NUMBER OF PILGRIMS BY COUNTRIES
(Muslim years)

	1388 (1968–69)	1389 (1969–70)	1390 (1970–71)	1391 (1971–72)	1392 (1972–73)	1393 (1973–74)
Afghanistan . . .	8,744	9,125	13,663	10,744	17,447	6,220
Egypt . . .	12,413	10,875	11,490	29,171	39,606	36,452
Indonesia . . .	17,062	10,615	14,633	22,753	22,659	40,668
India . . .	16,154	16,057	16,470	16,657	18,306	19,879
Iran . . .	13,642	15,132	48,367	30,299	45,298	57,230
Iraq . . .	24,875	24,902	19,482	17,628	24,681	35,567
Jordan . . .	5,179	6,376	10,909	15,933	25,819	12,851
Libya . . .	16,565	13,547	11,835	16,861	23,774	30,705
Malaysia . . .	6,591	8,353	10,361	10,650	10,395	12,983
Morocco . . .	9,449	10,943	10,640	15,163	22,425	14,923
Nigeria . . .	16,177	24,185	35,187	44,061	48,981	38,869
Pakistan . . .	27,402	28,535	38,256	23,344	95,968*	65,875*
Sudan . . .	21,649	20,495	14,865	29,004	29,506	33,222
Syria . . .	12,814	22,383	42,329	27,045	31,777	10,448
Turkey . . .	51,055	56,578	13,269	23,922	27,235	36,258
Yemen . . .	51,577	54,658	50,269	60,358	60,250	59,082
Others . . .	63,436	73,554	69,245	85,476	101,055	101,523
TOTAL . . .	374,784	406,295	431,270	479,339	645,182	607,755

* Including 6,595 pilgrims in 1972–73 and 5,187 in 1973–74 from Bangladesh.

Source: General Directorate of Passports and Nationality, Ministry of Interior.

TRANSPORT

Roads (1970): 42,161 cars, 3,833 buses and coaches, 30,662 goods vehicles.

Railways (1966): 52.1 million kilometre tons, 96,000 passengers; length of track 610 km. standard gauge (1972).

EDUCATION

(Academic year 1971–72)

	SCHOOLS	TEACHERS	PUPILS
Kindergarten	45	192	6,349
Elementary	2,154	19,577	475,007
Intermediate	486	4,193	83,729
Secondary	141	944	23,014
Teacher Training	63	949	14,453
Technical	7	257	899
Schools for Deaf, Dumb, Blind . .	10	299	1,287
Adult Education	624	*	46,034
Higher Education	19	975	9,471
Night Schools	†	†	†

* Includes day school teachers teaching in other schools.

† Included in figures for day schools, by level.

Educational budget for financial year 1971–72: 1,150m. riyals.

Educational budget for financial year 1972–73: 1,585m. riyals.

THE CONSTITUTION

After Ibn Saud had finally brought the whole of present-day Saudi Arabia under his control in 1925, the territory was made into a dual kingdom.

Six years later, in 1932, the realm was unified by decree and became the Kingdom of Saudi Arabia. Saudi Arabia as a whole has in practice been developing, in the last six years or so particularly, from monarchical towards ministerial rule. The power of the Cabinet was further increased in May 1958, when several ministries were delegated to the Crown Prince. In December 1960, however, the Crown Prince resigned and King Saud assumed the Prime Ministership. In 1962, Prince Faisal resumed the Prime Ministership. In 1964 King Saud was relieved of his duties and his brother Prince Faisal was proclaimed King.

The organs of local government are the General Municipal Councils, the District Council and the tribal and village councils. A General Municipal Council is established in the towns of Mecca, Medina and Jeddah. Its members are proposed by the inhabitants and must be approved by the King. Functioning concurrently with each General Municipal Council is a General Administration Committee, which investigates ways and means of executing resolutions passed by the Council. There are also elected district councils under the presidency of local chiefs, consisting of his assistant, the principal local officials and other important persons of the district. Every village and tribe has a council composed of the sheikh, who presides, his legal advisers and two other prominent personages. These councils have power to enforce regulations.

The principal administrative divisions are as follows:

Najd: capital Riyadh. Najd is sub-divided as follows:
1. The principality of Riyadh, to which are associated Wadi al-Dawasir, al-Aflaj, al-Hariq, al-Kharj, al-'Aridh, al-Washm and Sudair.
2. The principality of al-Qasim, comprising 'Unaizah, Buraidah, al-Ras and their villages, and al-Mudhannab and its dependencies.
3. The Northern principality (capital Hayil). This includes the tribes of Shammar, 'Anzah, al-Dhafir and Mutair, the Town of Taima in the south and some northerly towns.

Hijaz: capital Mecca. Includes the principalities of Tabuk, al-'Ula, Dhaba, al-Wajh, Amlaj, Yanbu', Medina, Jeddah, al-Lith, al-Qunfundhah, Baljarshi and Tayif.

'Asir: capital Abha. Includes Abha, Qahtan, Shahran, Rijal Alma', Rijal al-Hajr, Banu Shahr, Mahayil, Bariq and Bisha.

Najran and its villages.

Eastern Province (*Al Hasa*): capital Dammam. Includes Hofuf, Al-Mubarraz, Qatif, Dhahran, Al-Khobar and Qaryat al-Jubail.

THE GOVERNMENT

HEAD OF STATE

H.M. King Faisal ibn Abdul Aziz al Sa'ud, g.b.e., k.c.m.g.

(Acceded to the throne November 2nd, 1964)

Crown Prince: Khalid ibn Abdul Aziz.

COUNCIL OF MINISTERS

(*January* 1974)

Prime Minister and Foreign Minister: H.M. King Faisal ibn Abdul Aziz.

Deputy Prime Minister: H.R.H. Prince Khalid inb Abdul Aziz.

Second Deputy Prime Minister and Minister of the Interior: H.R.H. Prince Fahd ibn Abdul Aziz.

Minister of Finance and National Economy: H.R.H. Prince Musa'id ibn Abdul Rahman.

Minister of Defence and Aviation: H.R.H. Sultan ibn Abdul Aziz.

Minister of Oil and Mineral Wealth: Sheikh Ahmed Zaki Yamani.

Minister of Agriculture and Water: Sheikh Hassan Al Mushari.

Minister of Pilgrimage Affairs and Endowments: Hassan Kutbi.

Minister of Communications: Sheikh Muhammad Umar Tawfiq.

Minister of Education: Sheikh Hasan ibn Abdulla Al Ash-Shaykh.

Minister of Labour and Social Affairs: Sheikh Abdul Rahman Aba Al-Khayl.

Minister of Commerce and Industry: Sheikh Muhammad Ali al Awadi.

Minister of Justice: Sheikh Muhammad Al-Harakan.

Minister of Health: Abdel-Aziz Abdulla al-Khuwaitir.

Minister of Information: Sheikh Ibrahim Al-Angari.

Special Councellor to H.M. King Faisal: Dr. Rashad Faroun.

Minister of State for Finance and National Economy: Sheikh Mohamed Ali Aba Al Khail.

Minister of State for Foreign Affairs: Sayid Omar Al Sakkaf.

Ministers of State without Portfolio: Hisham Muhyi al Din Nazir, Abdul Aziz al Kuraishi, Abdul Wahhab Ahmad Abdul Wasi, Salih bin Abdul Rahman al Husain.

DIPLOMATIC REPRESENTATION

EMBASSIES ACCREDITED TO SAUDI ARABIA

(All in Jeddah)

Afghanistan: *Ambassador:* Mohamed Younesse.

Algeria: *Ambassador:* Mohamed Kadri.

Argentina: *Ambassador:* (vacant).

Austria: *Ambassador:* Dr. Heinrich Winter.

Belgium: *Chargé d'Affaires:* Gilbert Boonen.

Brazil: *Ambassador:* Murillo Gurgel Valente.

Chad: *Ambassador:* Souleiman Outman.

China (Taiwan): *Ambassador:* Tien Pao-tai.

Egypt: *Ambassador:* Khaled Fawzi.

Ethiopia: Osman Mohammed.

France: *Ambassador:* Georges de Boutellief.

Germany, Federal Republic: *Chargé d'Affaires:* Peter Metzger.

Ghana: *Ambassador:* Osborne Heney Kwest Brew.

Greece: *Ambassador:* Georgios Yannie Kalitsounakis.

Guinea: *Ambassador:* Touré Fodé Mamadou.

India: *Ambassador:* Sri Zahir Ahmed.

Indonesia: *Ambassador:* H. Rus'an.

Iran: *Ambassador:* Jaafar Raed.

Iraq: *Ambassador:* Ahmad Dhafar Mahmoud al-Ghailani.

Italy: *Ambassador:* Alberto Ramasso Valacca.

Japan: *Ambassador:* Kanji Takasugi.

Jordan: *Ambassador:* Sheikh Muhammad Amin Shanqiti.

Kenya: *Ambassador:* Farid Mburak Aly Hinawy.

Korea, Republic: *Ambassador:* Kyong Do-Koon.

Kuwait: *Chargé d'Affaires:* Bader al-Haddad.

Lebanon: *Ambassador:* Rashid Fakhouri.

Libya: *Ambassador:* Mohieddin Messaudi.

Malaysia: *Ambassador:* Ahmad bin Mohamed Hashim.

Mauritania: *Ambassador:* Wild Jado.

Morocco: *Ambassador:* Abdul Rahman Badu.

Netherlands: *Ambassador:* Jacopus Johannes Derksen.

Nigeria: *Ambassador:* Haj Bello Mallabo.

Oman: *Ambassador:* Sulaiman Bin Ali-Khalili.

Pakistan: *Ambassador:* Saifur Rehman.

Qatar: *Ambassador:* Addul-Aziz bin Sa'ad al-Sa'ad.

Senegal: *Ambassador:* Hamet Diop.

Somalia: *Ambassador:* Ahmad Sheikh Muhammad Issa.

Spain: *Ambassador:* Alberto de Mestas.

Sudan: *Ambassador:* Al Khitm al-Sanoussi.

Switzerland: *Ambassador:* Max Casanova.

Syria: *Ambassador:* Abdul Hamid Darkal.

Tunisia: *Ambassador:* Muhammad Ruwaisi.

Turkey: *Ambassador:* Ciladet Qiyassi.

United Kingdom: *Ambassador:* Alan Keir Rothnie.

U.S.A.: *Ambassador:* James E. Akins.

Venezuela: *Ambassador:* Francisco Nillan Delpretti.

Yemen Arab Republic: *Ambassador:* Ismail Ahmad al-Jarafi.

Saudi Arabia also has diplomatic relations with Canada, Denmark, Mali, Mexico, Norway, the Philippines and Sierra Leone.

JUDICIAL SYSTEM

Justice throughout the kingdom of Saudi Arabia is administered according to Islamic law by a Chief Judge, who is responsible for the Department of Sharia Affairs. Sentences in the kingdom are given according to the Koran and the Sunna of the Prophet.

The judicial system provides for three grades of court and a Judicial Supervisory Committee:

The Judicial Supervisory Committee. The Committee consists of three members and a president appointed by the King. It supervises all the other courts and is situated at Mecca.

Chief Justice, Mecca: Sheikh ABDULLAH IBN HASSAN.

Courts of Appeal (Courts of Cassation). There are several courts of appeal in Hijaz and Najd, having jurisdiction to hear appeals from the *Mahkamat al-Sharia al-Koubra*.

Mahkamat al-Sharia al-Koubra. The competence of these courts extends to all cases not covered by the above. They are situated in Mecca, Medina and Jeddah. Appeal may be made to the Courts of Cassation.

Mahkamat al-Omour al Mosta'jalah. These courts, which are held throughout the country, deal with cases of minor misdemeanours and actions in which the value does not exceed S.R. 30. Other branches of these courts deal exclusively with affairs of the Bedouin tribes with the same competence. The decisions of these courts are final.

RELIGION

Arabia is the centre of the Islamic faith and includes the holy cities of Mecca and Medina. Except in the Eastern Province, where a large number of people follow Shi'a rites, the majority of the population are of the Sunni faith. The last fifty years have seen the rise of the Wahhabi sect, who originated in the eighteenth century, but first became unified and influential under their late leader King Ibn Saud. They are now the keepers of the holy places and control the pilgrimage to Mecca.

Mecca: Birthplace of the Prophet Muhammad, seat of the Great Mosque and Shrine of Ka'ba visited by a million Muslims annually.

Medina: Burial place of Muhammad, second sacred city of Islam.

Chief Qadi and Grand Mufti: (Vacant).

THE PRESS

Since 1964 most newspapers and periodicals have been published by press organizations administered by boards of directors with full autonomous powers, in accordance with the provisions of the Press Law. These organizations, which took over from small private firms, are privately owned by groups of individuals widely experienced in newspaper publishing and administration (*see* Publishers).

There are also a number of popular periodicals published by the government and by the Arabian American Oil Co. and distributed free of charge. The press is subject to no legal restriction affecting freedom of expression or the coverage of news.

DAILIES

al-Bilad: King Abdul Aziz St., Jeddah; f. 1934; Arabic; published by al-Bilad Publishing Corporation; Editor ABDULMAJID AL-SHUBUKSHI; circ. 20,000.

al-Medina al-Munwara: Jeddah, P.O.B. 807; f. 1937; Arabic; published by al-Medina Publishing Organization; Editor OSMAN HAFEZ; circ. 20,000.

al-Nadwah: Mecca; f. 1958; Arabic; published by Mecca Press and Information Organization; Editor HAMED MUTAWI'E; circ. 10,000.

Replica: P.O.B. 2043, Jeddah; English; daily newsletter from Saudi newspapers and broadcasting service.

al-Riyadh: P.O.B. 851, Riyadh; Arabic; published by Yamamah Press Organization; Editor AHMED HOSHAN; circ. 10,000.

al Ukadh: Jeddah; circ. 3,500.

WEEKLIES

Akhbar al-Dhahran (*Dhahran News*): Dammam; f. 1958; Editor 'ABD AL-AZIZ AL-ISA; circ. 1,500.

al-Dawa: Riyadh; Arabic.

al-Jazirah: P.O.B. 354, Apt. 88, Municipality Bldg., Safat, Riyadh; Arabic; circ. 5,000.

al-Khalij al-'Arabi (*The Arabian Gulf*): Al-Khobar; f. 1958; Editor 'ABD ALLAH SHUBAT; circ. 1,200.

Arabian Sun: Aramco, Dhahran; English; published by the Arabian American Oil Co.

News from Saudi Arabia: Press Dept., Ministry of Information, Jeddah; f. 1961; news bulletin; English; Editor IZZAT MUFTI; circ. 22,000.

News of the Muslim World: Mecca; English and Arabic; published by Muslim World League; Editor FUAD SHAKER.

Oil Caravan Weekly: Aramco, Dhahran; Arabic; published by the Arabian American Oil Co.

al-Qasim: Riyadh; f. 1959; Editor 'ABD ALLAH AL SANE'; circ. 1,000.

Quraish: Mecca; f. 1959; Editor AHMED SIBA'I; circ. 1,000.

al-Ra'id: Jeddah; f. 1959; Editor 'ABDUL-FATTAH ABU MADYAN; circ. 2,000.

al-Riyadhah: Mecca; f. 1960; for young men; Editor MUHAMMAD 'ABD ALLAH MALIBARI; circ. 500.

Umm al-Qura: Mecca; f. 1924; Editor ABDUL RAHMAN SHIBANI; published by the Government; circ. 5,000.

al-Yamamah: Riyadh; f. 1952; Dir. AHMED EL-HOSHAN; circ. 1,000.

al-Yaum (*Today*): P.O.B. 565, Dammam; f. 1965; Dir. ABDUL AZIZ AL-TURKY.

PERIODICALS

al-Manhal: 44 Arafat Street, Jeddah; f. 1937; monthly; literary; Editor 'ABDUL QUADDOS ANARIS; circ. 3,000.

al-Mujtama: P.O.B. 354, Apt. 88, Municipality Bldg., Safat, Riyadh; f. 1964; Arabic; monthly; Dir.-Gen. SALEH SALEM.

al-Tijarah: Jeddah; f. 1960; monthly; for businessmen; Editor AHMAD ISA TAHKANDI; circ. 1,300.

Hajj (*Pilgrim*): Mecca; f. 1947; Arabic and English; Editor MUHAMMAD SAID AL 'AMOUDI; published by the Government Ministry of Pilgrimage and Endowments; circ. 5,000.

PUBLISHERS

al-Bilad Publishing Organization: King Abdul Aziz St., Jeddah; publishes *al-Bilad*; Dir.-Gen. ABDULLAH DABBAGH.

Dar al-Yaum Press and Publishing Establishment: P.O.B. 565, Damman; publishes *al-Yaum*; Dir.-Gen. OMAR ZAWAWI.

al-Jazirah for Press Printing and Publishing: P.O.B. 354, Riyadh; f. 1964; 28 mems.; publishes *al-Jazirah* (weekly) and *al-Mujtama* (monthly); Dir.-Gen. SALEH SALEM.

al-Medina Publishing Organization: P.O.B. 807, Jeddah; publishes *al-Medina al-Munwara*; Dir.-Gen. AHMED SALAH JAMJOON.

Saudi Publishing House: 30–31 Shurbatly Bldg., Gabel St., P.O.B. 2043, Jeddah; books in Arabic and English; Man. Dir. MUHAMMAD SALAHUDDIN.

al-Yamamah Press Establishment: Riyadh; publishes *al-Riyadh*, *al-Yamamah* and *She*; Dir.-Gen. ABDULLAH QAR'AWI.

RADIO AND TELEVISION

RADIO

Saudi Arabian Broadcasting Co.: Ministry of Information, Airport Rd., Jeddah; three stations at Jeddah, Riyadh and Dammam broadcast programmes in Arabic and English; overseas service in Urdu, Indonesian, Persian and Swahili; Dir.-Gen. Sheikh A. F. GHAZAWI.

ARAMCO Radio: Dhahran; broadcasts programmes in English for the entertainment of employees of Arabian American Oil Company.

There are about 87,000 radio receivers.

TELEVISION

Saudi Arabian Government Television Service: Information Ministry, Riyadh; stations at Riyadh, Jeddah, Medina, Dammam, and Qassim operate 6 hours daily; major stations and relay points are under construction to serve all principal towns; Dir.-Gen. A. S. SHOBAIL.

ARAMCO-TV: P.O.B. 96, Dhahran; f. 1957; non-commercial, private company; 12 kW. transmitter at Dhahran, limited range transmitter at Hofuf; Producer S. A. AL-MOZAINI; 4–5 hours a day.

There are about 120,000 TV sets.

FINANCE

BANKING

The Saudi Arabian banking system consists of the Saudi Arabian Monetary Agency as central note-issuing and regulatory body, three national banks, one specialist bank (The Agricultural Credit Bank) and ten foreign banks. Charter for an industrial Bank and a Bank for people of small means have been drawn up; both are expected to be set up in the near future.

Saudi Arabia had no central monetary authority until 1952. Previous to this, foreign merchant companies (Gellatly Hankey, Netherlands Trading Society) had acted as bankers to the government, with such functions as the issue of currency being the responsibility successively of the General Finance Agency (set up in the late 1920s) and the Ministry of Finance (established 1932).

The rising volume of oil revenues imposed a need for modernization of this system, and in 1952 on American advice the Saudi Arabian Monetary Agency (SAMA) was established in Jeddah, SAMA complies with a Muslim law prohibiting the charging of interest. Instead, its services are paid for by a commission charged on all transactions. SAMA's functions include: bankers to the government;

stabilization of the value of the currency; administration of monetary reserves; issue of coin and notes; and regulation of banking.

From 1959 all banks were obliged to hold with SAMA a sum equivalent to 15 per cent of their deposit liabilities. This figure was reduced to 10 per cent between 1962 and 1966, when a new banking law came into force, which reintroduced the 15 per cent level. This could, however, be varied, at the Agency's discretion within the limits of 10 and 17.5 per cent. In addition every bank must maintain a liquid reserve of not less than 15 per cent of its deposit liabilities, which may be increased to 20 per cent by the SAMA. In addition banks must be organized as limited liability companies, and may not trade for purposes other than banking. A minimum of RIs 2.5m. equivalent is set for paid-up capital; banks' deposit liabilities may not exceed 15 times their paid-up capital and reserves; and all banks must plough back 25 per cent of profits before dividends to build up their reserve funds.

The intention of the 1966 law, besides strengthening the control of SAMA, is to encourage foreign banks to open branches in Saudi Arabia in an atmosphere of financial stability and assured growth potential.

(cap.=capital; p.u.=paid up; dep.=deposits; m.=million; amounts in Saudi Riyals)

CENTRAL BANK

Saudi Arabia Monetary Agency: P.O.B. 394, Airport St., Jeddah; f. 1952; gold, foreign exchange and investments 11,147.2m. (Oct. 1973); Pres. and Gov. ANWAR ALI; Vice-Gov. Sheikh KHALID MOHAMMAD ALGOSAIBI; Controller-Gen. ABDUL WAHAB M. S. SHEIKH; publs. *Statement of Affairs* (bi-weekly), *Annual Report, Statistical Summary*; 10 brs.

Agricultural Credit Bank: Jeddah; f. 1964; cap. 31.5m.; Dir.-Gen. IZZAT HUSNI AL-ALI.

Ibrahim I. Zahran Bank: Jeddah.

National Commercial Bank: P.O.B. 104, King Abdulaziz St., Jeddah; f. 1938; cap. 30m.; dep. 1,003m. (Feb. 1972); Partners Sheikh SALEH ABDULLAH MOSA ALKAAKI, Sheikh ABDULAZIZ MUHAMMAD ALKAAKI, Sheikh SALIM BIN MAHFOOZ (Gen. Man.); 22 brs.

Riyad Bank Ltd.: P.O.B. 1047, Jeddah; f. 1957; cap. p.u. 37.5m., total resources 1,008m. (Aug. 1972); Chair. H.E. Sheikh ABDULLAH IBN ADWAN; Man. Dir. H.E. Sheikh ABDUL RAHMAN AL-SHEIKH; Gen. Man. P. D. BREWER; 21 brs.

FOREIGN BANKS

Algemene Bank Nederland, N.V.: P.O.B. 67, Jeddah; Alkhobar; Dammam; head office: Amsterdam, Netherlands.

Arab Bank Ltd.: Amman, Jordan; Jeddah; 6 brs.

Bank Melli Iran: Ferdawsi Ave., Tehran; Jeddah.

Banque de l'Indochine: Paris; Jeddah; P.O.B. 1.

Banque du Caire: Cairo; Riyadh; 2 brs.

Banque du Liban et d'Outre-Mer S.A.: Beirut, Lebanon; Jeddah.

British Bank of the Middle East: head office: 20 Abchurch Lane, London EC4N 7AY; Jeddah; Dammam; Alkhobar.

First National City Bank: New York; Riyadh, P.O.B. 833, Al Batha St.; Man. W. L. ROBERTS, Jr.; Jeddah, P.O.B. 490; Man. M. Y. WYSKIEL; 2 brs.

National Bank of Pakistan: Karachi; Jeddah; principal foreign branches in London, New York, Hong Kong (2), Birmingham and Manchester; Man. Sheikh Inayat Ali.

United Bank Ltd.: Dammam.

INSURANCE COMPANY

Saudi National Insurance Co. Ltd.: P.O.B. 106, Al-Khobar; f. 1958; Pres. Hamad Ahmad Algosaibi; Gen. Man. A. A. Algosaibi.

TRADE AND INDUSTRY

CHAMBERS OF COMMERCE

Chamber of Commerce and Industries: Jeddah, P.O.B. 1264; f. 1950; Pres. (vacant); Dir. Yousuf M. Bannan; publ. *Al-Tijara*.

Chamber of Commerce and Industry: S. G. Saleh Tuimi, P.O.B. 596, Riyadh; f. 1961; acts as "arbitrator" in business disputes; Chair. Sheikh Abdul Aziz Muqairen; publ. monthly journal.

Dammam Chamber of Commerce: P.O.B. 719, Dammam.

Mecca Chamber of Commerce: P.O.B. 2, Mecca.

Medina Chamber of Commerce: P.O.B. 443, Medina.

CO-OPERATIVE SOCIETIES

Trade unions are prohibited but since 1962 several Co-operative Societies have been formed by workers in particular trades.

OIL

General Petroleum and Mineral Organization (PETROMIN): Riyadh; f. 1962 to establish oil and mineral industries and collateral activities in Saudi Arabia; Gov. Dr. Abdul Hadi Taher.

The following projects have been set up by Petromin:

Arabian Drilling Co.: f. 1964; shareholding 51 per cent, remainder French private capital; undertakes contract drilling for oil, minerals and water; working offshore concessions in Neutral Zone and Red Sea coast areas.

Arabian Geophysical Survey Co. (ARGAS): f. 1966; shareholding 51 per cent, remainder provided by *Cie. Générale de Géophysique*; exploration and discovery of natural resources; is setting up a nation-wide geodetic survey network.

Jeddah Refining Co.: Jeddah; f. 1968; shareholding 75 per cent, remainder held by Saudi Arabian Refining Co. (SARCO); the refinery at Jeddah, Japanese-built and American-staffed, has a capacity of 12,000 bbl./day; distribution in the Western Province is undertaken by Petromin's **Department for Distribution of Oil Products.**

Petromin Oil Lubricating Co.: Jeddah; f. 1968; joint venture with Mobil to set up a blending plant handling 75,000 bbl./year.

Saudi Arabian Fertilizer Co. (SAFCO): Dammam; f. 1965; 49 per cent shareholding, remainder open to public subscription; the plant at Dammam has a capacity of about 1,100 tons of urea and 35 tons of sulphur a day; construction and management have been undertaken by Occidental Petroleum Co. of U.S.A.

FOREIGN CONCESSIONAIRES

Arabian-American Oil Co. (Aramco): Dhahran; f. 1933, holds the principal working concessions in Saudi Arabia; covering approx. 85,000 square miles; production (1973) 2,677.4 million barrels; Saudi Government acquired 60 per cent participation, June 1974; Pres. F. Jungers; Chair. L. F. Hills.

Arabian Oil Co. Ltd.: P.O.B. 335, Riyadh; f. 1958; holds concession for offshore exploitation of Saudi Arabia's half interest in the Kuwait-Saudi Arabia Partitioned Zone; production (1973) 71.9 million barrels; Chair. T. Ishizaka; Dir. in Saudi Arabia Takashi Hayashi.

Getty Oil Co.: P.O.B. 363, Riyadh; office in Mina Saud; f. 1928; holds concession for exploitation of Saudi Arabia's half-interest in the Saudi Arabia-Kuwait Partitioned Zone, both on-shore and in territorial waters; total Zone production (1973) 23.5 million barrels; Pres. J. P. Getty.

REFINERIES

The following refineries are in operation:

Location	Capacity (bbl./day)
Ras Tanura	255,000
Mina Saud	50,000
Khafji	30,000
Jeddah	12,000
Projected but not built:	
Riyadh	15,000

TRANSPORT

RAILWAYS

Saudi Government Railroad Organization: Dammam; Gen. Man. Khalid M. Algosaibi.

The Saudi Government Railroad is a single track, standard gauge line 610 km. long. The main line, 577 km. long, connects the Port of Dammam and the Gulf with the capital Riyadh. The Organization is an independent entity with a board of directors headed by the Minister of Communications. In addition to working the railways the Organization also manages the Port of Dammam.

The historic Hedjaz railway running from Damascus to Medina has been the subject of a reconstruction project since 1963; however, little progress has been made since the war of June 1967.

ROADS

Asphalted roads link Jeddah to Mecca, Jeddah to Medina, Medina to Yanbu, Taif to Mecca, Riyadh to al-Kharj, and Dammam to Hofuf as well as the principal communities and certain outlying points in Aramco's area of operations. Work is proceeding on various other roads, including one which will link Medina and Riyadh, and one from Taif to Jizan in the south, near the Yemeni border. 1967 saw completion of the trans-Arabian highway, which links Damman, Riyadh, Taif, Mecca and Jeddah. In 1971 there were 8,759 kilometres of asphalted roads.

SHIPPING

The deep-water port of Jeddah is the main port of the kingdom and the port for pilgrims to Mecca. An expansion scheme providing for nine new piers for large ships, costing £20 million was completed in January 1973. Yanbu, the port of Medina, has been extended and modernized, with new docks, storage space and a special Pilgrim centre; other ports on the Red Sea are Muwaih, Wejh and Rabigh. On the Gulf there are the small ports of Alkhobar, Qatif and Uqair, suitable only for small local craft, and a deep-water port at Ras Tanura built by the Arabian American Oil Co. for its own use. The deep-water Dammam Port, which was also built by the Arabian American Oil Co. and is operated by the Saudi Government Railroad, lies approximately 12 km. from the coast and is connected to the mainland by a railway causeway. Expansion of the port was completed in 1961 at a cost of over U.S. $20 million. Further expansion is planned.

Khedivial Steamship Co.: Jeddah; services to Egypt.

Saudi Lines: P.O.B. 66, Jeddah; regular cargo and passenger services between all Red Sea ports and transport of pilgrims from the Philippines, Bangkok and Thailand; 2 cargo and 3 passenger ships.

CIVIL AVIATION

In August 1971 the government announced that an international airport was to be constructed near Hail in the centre of Saudi Arabia.

Saudia-Saudi Arabian Airlines: Head Office: SDI Bldg., P.O.B. 620, Jeddah; f. 1945; regular internal services to all major cities of Saudi Arabia; regular international services to London, Frankfurt, Geneva, Beirut, Rabat, Algiers, Tunis, Tripoli, Bombay, Karachi, Istanbul, Port Sudan, Khartoum, Cairo, Kuwait, Baghdad, Damascus, Amman, Doha and Asmara; fleet of 24 aircraft, principally Boeing 707, Boeing 720B, Boeing 737, Douglas DC-9, DC-6, and Convair 340; Dir.-Gen. Sheikh Kamil Sindi; Asst. Dir.-Gen. Melvin L. Milligan; Gen. Man. Technical T. Morgan; Gen. Man. External Affairs Rida Hakeem.

Saudi Arabia is also served by the following foreign airlines: Air Algérie, Air France, ALIA, Alitalia, AUA, British Airways, CSA, EgyptAir, Iranair, Iraqi Airways, KLM, Lufthansa, MEA, PIA, Sabena, Sudan Airways, and Syrian Arab Airlines.

ATOMIC ENERGY

Saudi Arabia joined the International Atomic Energy Agency in January 1963. Radioisotopes are used in the oil industry and are being introduced into state-controlled agricultural schemes.

UNIVERSITIES

Islamic University: Medina; f. 1961; 57 teachers, 1,007 students.

Riyadh University: Riyadh; f. 1957; 365 teachers, 4,369 students.

King Abdulaziz University: P.O.B. 1540, Jeddah; f. 1967; Rector Dr. Ahmad Ali; 163 teachers, 440 students.

College of Petroleum and Minerals: Dharan; f. 1963; 105 teachers, 974 students.

SENEGAL

INTRODUCTORY SURVEY

Location, Climate, Language, Religion, Flag, Capital

Senegal lies on the west coast of Africa, bounded to the north by Mauritania, to the east by Mali and to the south by the Republic of Guinea and the Portuguese province of Guinea (Bissau). In the southern part of the country The Gambia forms a narrow enclave extending some 200 miles inland. The climate of Senegal is tropical, with a long dry season followed by a short wet season. Average annual temperature is about 29°C (84°F). French is the official language but there are numerous native tongues of which Wolof and Toucouleur are the most widespread. Over 80 per cent of the population is Muslim and about 10 per cent Christian, mostly Roman Catholic. The remainder follow traditional beliefs. The national flag (proportions 3 by 2) has three vertical stripes of green, gold and red, the gold stripe bearing a five-pointed green star. The capital is Dakar.

Recent History

After 300 years as a French colony, Senegal became a self-governing member state of the French Community in November 1958. In April 1959 it joined with the former French Sudan to form the Mali Federation, which became independent in June 1960 but was dissolved two months later. The independent Republic of Senegal was proclaimed, and in September Léopold Sédar Senghor was elected President. In December 1962 the Prime Minister, Mamadou Dia, was imprisoned and the President added the office of Prime Minister to his own responsibilities. In March 1963 a new Constitution, incorporating this innovation, was adopted. Later that year the governing Party, *Union progressiste sénégalaise* (UPS), won a decisive victory in elections for the National Assembly. Riots against alleged electoral fraud were harshly quashed. By 1966 all opposition parties had been either outlawed or incorporated into the UPS. A general strike in 1968, after protests by students and workers, was resolved by the introduction of reforms, but a similar crisis in 1969 was more summarily dealt with, as the Government was stronger. In 1970 a constitutional amendment recreated the post of Prime Minister, and this was given to a young man, Abdou Diouf. The President both encourages young militants and supports the traditional Muslim leaders, whose influence is strong in rural areas. In January 1973 President Senghor, as sole candidate for the Presidency, was re-elected, and the UPS, as sole party, won all 100 seats in the National Assembly. In the same month there were clashes between radical students and government supporters, which were followed by arrests and the banning of the teachers' union. In 1974, however, the Government felt strong enough to free all political prisoners, including notably the former Prime Minister, Mamadou Dia.

Fighting between African nationalists and Portuguese troops in Guinea (Bissau) has driven about 70,000 refugees into Senegal, and has led to border incidents between Portuguese and Senegalese forces. Senegalese relations with the Republic of Guinea have also been strained. The Organization of Senegal River States broke up in 1971, but in March 1972 the Organization for the Development of the Senegal River (OMVS) was formed, without Guinea, by Senegal, Mali and Mauritania. Senegal also has co-operation agreements with The Gambia, Cameroon, and Algeria and is a member of the OAU, CEAO and OCAM. In 1974 Senegal renegotiated its co-operation agreements with France, but links between the two countries are still strong.

Government

The President is elected for a five-year term by universal direct suffrage and is eligible for re-election. He exercises executive power with the assistance of ministers nominated and chosen by himself. Legislative power is vested in the National Assembly, which is also elected for a five-year term at the time of the presidential election.

Defence

Senegal has an army of 5,500 men, a navy of 200 and an air force of 200. All men are liable to five years' active and 20 years' reserve national service. France provides technical and material aid, but under a new agreement signed in 1974 France is to hand over her military bases in Senegal and to begin withdrawing military and technical personnel.

Economic Affairs

About 70 per cent of the population is engaged in agriculture and stock rearing, and the economy is dominated by the production and processing of groundnuts. Groundnuts and groundnut products provide between a third and a half of total export earnings. Attempts to diversify have so far had little success, and poor groundnut harvests in 1971 and 1973, caused by drought, have had a serious effect on the economy. However, the fishing industry is expanding rapidly and the development of mining, industry and tourism are priorities of the 1973–77 five-year plan. At present only phosphates are mined on a large scale, but a considerable deposit of iron ore is known to exist at Falemé and traces of copper and gold have been found. Industry is fairly well developed and includes textiles, chemicals, building materials and various light industries, including food processing. After years of stagnation, industrial production increased in 1972, when it accounted for 20 per cent of the Gross Domestic Product, and a steady annual growth rate of 5 per cent is planned. One important project is for a naval repair centre for giant tankers at Dakar. With the aim of attracting foreign companies and providing employment, an Industrial Free Zone is being established near Dakar. Foreign firms operating there will be free of taxes, duties and bureaucratic controls. In the rest of Senegal, on the other hand, a policy of "Senegalization" is increasing state control and native management of affairs. A rise in tourist visits from an estimated 100,000 in 1973 to 190,000 in 1977 is envisaged in the present development plan, and this would make tourism a major sector of the economy. For the present, however, Senegal faces inflation, a balance of payments problem and a budgetary deficit, and remains heavily dependent on foreign investment and aid.

Transport and Communications

The main railway line runs east from Dakar into Mali and another line runs north to St. Louis along the coast, with a branch to Linguera, totalling 1,034 km. The road network is good with over 7,000 km. passable at all seasons. The Senegal river is used to transport goods by both Senegal and Mauritania. Dakar is the largest port in West Africa and serves both Senegal and Mauritania. There is an international airport at Dakar and numerous small airports.

Social Welfare

Social services include a state medical service and certain family and maternity benefits for workers. There are 4 teaching hospitals with about 2,600 beds, 4 regional hospitals with 600 beds, 32 health centres with 950 beds, 46 maternity hospitals with 1,250 beds and nearly 400 dispensaries.

Education

Education is compulsory for all children between six and fourteen years old, although facilities exist for only 40 per cent of this age group to attend school. Since 1971 education has been re-orientated towards practical subjects. Secondary school pupils have been encouraged to follow science-based courses and school-leavers directed to take up professional training in fields where personnel are needed. In line with the policy of "negritude", the university specializes in local studies, and half its teachers are Africans.

Tourism

There is a wild game reserve in the Nikolo-Koba National Park, and there are fine beaches. The island of Goré, near Dakar, is of great historical interest. Tourists provide a valuable source of foreign currency and encourage traditional crafts, and hotel accommodation is being increased. Senegal is a member of the Office Inter-Etats du Tourisme Africain.

Visas are not required by nationals of countries in the EEC or OCAM.

Sport

Football is the most popular game. Many forms of sport are practised, particularly watersports, hunting, golf and riding.

Public Holidays

1974: August 15th (Assumption), October 18th (Korité—end of Ramadan), November 1st (All Saints' Day), December 25th (Christmas), December 26th (Tabaski—Feast of the Sacrifice).

1975: January 1st (New Year's Day), March 26th (Mouloud—Birth of the Prophet), March 31st (Easter), May 1st (Labour Day), May 8th (Ascension Day), May 19th (Whitsun), July 14th (Day of Association).

Weights and Measures

The metric system is in force.

Currency and Exchange Rates

100 centimes=1 franc de la Communauté financière africaine (CFA).

Exchange rates (April 1974):
1 franc CFA=2 French centimes;
£1 sterling=579.75 francs CFA;
U.S. $1=245.625 francs CFA.

STATISTICAL SURVEY

AREA AND POPULATION

AREA (sq. km.)	POPULATION (1970)			
	Total	African	French and others	Dakar (capital and Commune du Grand Dakar)
196,192	3,822,000	3,777,000	45,000	693,000

Mid-1972 Population: 4,122,000 (UN estimate).

Principal Ethnic groups (1960 census): Wolof 709,000, Fulani 324,000, Serer 306,000, Toucouleur 248,000, Diola 115,000.

Chief Towns (1970): Dakar 436,000, Kaolack 96,000, Thiès 91,000, Saint-Louis 81,000, Ziguinchor 46,000.

Births and Deaths: Average annual birth rate 46.3 per 1,000; death rate 22.8 per 1,000 (UN estimates for 1965–70).

EMPLOYMENT

Total Labour Force (1970): Economically active population 1,705,000, including 1,288,000 in agriculture (ILO and FAO estimates).

AGRICULTURE

PRODUCTION
(metric tons)

	1969–70	1970–71	1971–72*
Millet and Sorghum . .	634,833	400,876	601,735
Cow Peas . .	22,584	17,777	21,875
Rice . . .	155,989	90,545	101,700
Maize . . .	48,840	38,746	n.a.
Cassava (Manioc) .	176,773	133,100	n.a.
Potatoes . .	16,255	9,718	n.a.
Cotton . . .	11,500	11,610	21,170

About 6,000 tons of Gum Arabic are produced annually.

* Provisional.

GROUNDNUTS
('000 tons)

	1967–68	1968–69	1969–70
Total Production . .	1,005	830	789
Production not Marketed (incl. Seeds) . .	163	232	194
Deliveries to Oil Mills .	558	461	509
Deliveries to Shelling Plants . . .	284	137	85
Exports (shelled) . .	197	95	58

Total Production: (1970/71) 583,000 tons; (1971/72—provisional) 917,500 tons, (1972/73—estimate) 500,000 tons.

Source: Bulletin de la B.C.E.A.O.

LIVESTOCK
('000 head)

	1969	1970	1971
Cattle	2,530	2,165	2,700
Sheep and Goats . .	2,607	2,700	2,800
Pigs	109	168	175
Horses . . .	197	200	202
Asses	178	185	191
Camels . . .	7	7	7

FISHING
('000 metric tons)

	1969	1970	1971
Local Fishermen . .	126	133	179
Tuna Fishing . .	11	12	18
Trawler Fishing . .	25	28	23
TOTAL CATCH .	162	163	220

1972 total catch: 248,000 tons.

MINING
('000 metric tons)

	1969	1970	1971
Aluminium Phosphate .	164	130	147
Lime Phosphate . .	1,035	998	1,454

1972: Lime phosphate 1,250,000 tons, sea salt 116,000 tons.

INDUSTRY

	UNIT	1969	1970	1971
Groundnut Oil	'000 metric tons	158	177	117
Sugar	,, ,, ,,	21	21	30
Cement	,, ,, ,,	207	241	241
Beer	'000 hectolitres	91	106	104
Cotton Fabrics . . .	'000 metres	1,140	7,200	7,693
Electricity (consumption) .	million kWh.	279	287	303

FINANCE

100 centimes = 1 franc de la Communauté financière africaine.
Coins: 1, 2, 5, 10, 25, 50 and 100 francs CFA.
Notes: 100, 500, 1,000 and 5,000 francs CFA.
Exchange rates (April 1974): 1 franc CFA = 2 French centimes.
£1 sterling = 579.75 francs CFA; U.S. $1 = 245.625 francs CFA.
1,000 francs CFA = £1.725 = $4.071.

Budget (1972–73) (million francs CFA): Balanced in revenue and expenditure at 56,500, of which 15,500 was extraordinary expenditure.

Budget (1973–74) (million francs CFA): Balanced in revenue and expenditure at 57,000. Major allocations of expenditure to Ministries include: National Education 7,928, Armed Forces 1,597, Interior 3,779, Health 3,656, Finance 3,252, Rural Development 2,299, Public Works 2,672.

FOREIGN OFFICIAL PUBLIC AID
('000 million francs CFA)

	1966	1967	1968
Transfers . . .	8.0	7.5	7.7
of which:			
French Technical Assistance . .	6.1	6.3	6.2
Grants . . .	3.6	4.0	2.7
Loans . . .	1.0	0.7	2.1
Total . . .	12.5	12.2	12.5

EXTERNAL AID, 1970
(million francs CFA)

France (EDF)	76,170
U.S.A. (1965)	1,786
German Federal Republic . . .	3,660
U.S.S.R.	1,650
UN (dollars)	240,000

EXTERNAL TRADE
(million francs CFA)

	1967	1968	1969	1970	1971	1972
Imports . . .	40,401	44,527	51,294	53,552	60,512	70,289
Exports . . .	33,890	37,369	31,907	42,181	34,702	54,412

PRINCIPAL COMMODITIES

Imports	1970	1971	1972	Exports	1970	1971	1972
Milk Products .	1,585	2,130	2,151	Groundnuts . .	2,691	1,785	n.a.
Rice . . .	3,335	4,639	4,252	Groundnut Oil .	12,971	7,409	20,385
Sugar . . .	2,518	2,907	4,341	Oilcake . .	4,594	3,138	7,392
Petroleum Products	2,723	3,763	4,232	Calcium Phosphate .	3,300	3,785	4,408
Wood . . .	742	748	n.a.	Wheat Flour .	736	186	n.a.
Paper . . .	1,745	1,765	1,912	Fish (preserved) .	1,732	2,788	2,585
Textiles . .	3,273	4,125	n.a.	Gum Arabic . .	1,392	1,428	n.a.
Metal Goods .	2,937	1,936	n.a.	Phosphatic			
Machinery .	4,829	4,493	7,923	Fertilizers . .	367	707	n.a.
Electrical Apparatus	2,270	2,583	3,010	Cotton Fabrics .	1,831	779	1,185
Vehicles and Spares .	3,345	4,442	n.a.				

PRINCIPAL COUNTRIES

	Imports			Exports		
	1969	1970	1971	1969	1970	1971
France	20,800	27,499	28,697	19,230	22,962	17,971
Germany, Federal Republic . .	5,800	3,464	3,540	633	928	528
Italy	1,624	1,727	1,906	935	1,079	1,509
Netherlands . . .	1,345	1,267	1,636	1,638	2,945	2,358
Nigeria	1	4	657	33	238	259
United Kingdom . . .	498	751	990	645	847	1,122
U.S.A.	3,246	2,555	3,631	87	173	180

TRANSPORT

RAILWAYS

	1969	1970	1971
Passenger-km. (million)	264	245	322
Net ton-km. (million) .	183	179	194

ROADS
Motor Vehicles in Use

	1969	1970	1971
Passenger Cars . .	35,965	38,235	40,417
Goods Vehicles . .	16,910	17,481	18,087
Buses and Coaches .	3,337	3,407	3,629

Source: World Road Statistics 1973.

INTERNATIONAL SEA-BORNE SHIPPING

	1969	1970	1971
Vessels Entered ('000 net tons) . . .	18,669	20,890	19,705
Goods Loaded ('000 metric tons) . .	1,777	2,804	2,013
Goods Unloaded ('000 metric tons) . .	2,630	2,470	2,585

CIVIL AVIATION
Scheduled Services
('000)

	1969	1970	1971
Kilometres Flown .	1,374	1,526	1,593
Passengers Carried .	38	51	54
Passenger-km. .	62,000	68,000	77,000
Freight ton-km. .	5,457	5,698	7,053

Source (unless otherwise stated): UN, *Statistical Yearbook 1972.*

EDUCATION
(1970–71)

	Students		Teachers	Matriculation Exam Passes
	Male	Female		
Primary . . .	164,932	101,451	6,500*	21,030
Secondary . . .	35,529	13,376	n.a.	5,766
Teacher Training . .	424	197	n.a.	n.a.
Dakar University . .	3,804*	886*	n.a.	1,962†

* 1971–72. † Passes in all university examinations.

Sources: Direction de la Statistique, Ministère des Finances et des Affaires Économiques, Dakar; and *Spotlight on Senegal,* Ministry of Information, Dakar, 1972.

THE CONSTITUTION

(Promulgated March 7th, 1963, revised June 20th, 1967)

Preamble: Affirms the Rights of Man, liberty of the person and religious freedom. National sovereignty belongs to the people who exercise it through their representatives or by means of referenda. There is universal, equal and secret suffrage. French is the official language.

The President: The President of the Republic is elected by direct universal suffrage for a five-year term and is eligible for re-election. He holds executive power and conducts national policy with the assistance of ministers chosen and nominated by himself. He is Commander of the Armed Forces and responsible for national defence. He may, after consultation with the President of the National Assembly and with the Supreme Court, submit any draft law to referendum. In circumstances where the security of the State is in grave and immediate danger, he can assume emergency powers and rule by decree. The President of the Republic can be impeached only on a charge of high treason or by a secret ballot of the National Assembly carrying a three-fifths majority.

The National Assembly: Legislative power is vested in the National Assembly which is elected by universal direct suffrage for a five-year term at the same time as the Presidential election. The Assembly discusses and votes legislation and submits it to the President of the Republic for promulgation. The President can direct the Assembly to give a second reading to the bill, in which case it may be made law only by a three-fifths majority. The President of the Republic can also call upon the Supreme Court to declare whether any draft law is constitutional and acceptable. Legislation may be initiated by either the President of the Republic or the National Assembly.

Amendments: The President of the Republic and Deputies to the National Assembly may propose amendments to the Constitution. Draft amendments are adopted by a three-fifths majority vote of the National Assembly. Failing this they are submitted to referendum.

Judicial Power: The President appoints the members of the Supreme Court of Justice, on the advice of the Superior Court of Magistrates, which determines the constitutionality of laws. A High Court of Justice, appointed by the National Assembly from among its members, is competent to impeach the President or members of the Government.

Local Government: Senegal is divided into seven regions, each having a Governor and an elected Local Assembly.

On February 26th, 1970, the Constitution was amended. The President can now stand for only two successive five-year terms of office, and the office of Prime Minister is recreated to apply policies determined by the President. The President retains control of foreign affairs, the army and certain judicial matters.

THE GOVERNMENT

HEAD OF STATE

President: LÉOPOLD SÉDAR SENGHOR

COUNCIL OF MINISTERS

(March 1974)

Prime Minister: ABDOU DIOUF.

Minister of State for the Armed Forces: AMADOU CLÉDOR SALL.

Minister of Foreign Affairs: ASSANE SECK.

Minister of Justice: ALIOUNE BADAR MBENGUE.

Minister of the Interior: JEAN COLLIN.

Minister of Finance and Economic Affairs: BABACAR BA.

Minister of National Education: DOUDOU N'GOM.

Minister of Rural Development: ADRIEN SENGHOR.

Minister of Higher Education: OUSMANE CAMARA.

Minister of Industrial Development: LOUIS ALEXANDRENNE.

Minister of Planning and Co-operation: OUSMANE SECK.

Minister of Public Works, Town Planning and Transport: DIARAF DIOUF.

Minister of Culture: ALIOUNE SÈNE.

Minister of Public Health and Social Affairs: COUMBA N'DOFFÈNE DIOUF.

Minister of the Civil Service, Labour and Employment: AMADOU LY.

Minister of Information, Posts and Telecommunications: Dr. DAOUDA SOW.

Minister in charge of Relations with the National Assembly: MAGATTE LÔ.

Secretary of State at the Prime Minister's Office for Youth and Sport: JOSEPH MATHIAM.

Secretary of State for Foreign Affairs: ADAMA N'DIAYE.

General Delegate for Tourism: MOUSTAPHA FALL.

General Delegate for Science and Technology: DJIBRIL SÈNE.

General Delegate for Social Improvement: BEN MADY CISSÉ.

DIPLOMATIC REPRESENTATION

EMBASSIES ACCREDITED TO SENEGAL

(In Dakar unless otherwise stated)

Algeria: 5 rue Mermoz, B.P. 3233; *Ambassador:* AZIZ HACENE.

Argentina: Imm. B.I.A.O. 1er étage, Place de l'Indépendance (E); *Ambassador:* OSWALDO GUILLERMO G. PINEIRO.

Austria: 24 blvd. Pinet-Laprade, B.P. 3247 (E); *Ambassador:* AUGUST TARTER.

Bangladesh: 22 rue Carnot (E); *Ambassador:* MOHAMED ANWARUL HAQ.

Belgium: route de la Corniche, B.P. 524 (E); *Ambassador:* RENÉ THIMSTER.

Brazil: Imm. B.I.A.O., 2e. étage, Place de l'Indépendance, B.P. 136 (E); *Ambassador:* JOÃO CABRAL DE MELO NETO.

Bulgaria: (E); *Ambassador:* IANLHO CHRISTOV IVANOV.

Canada: Imm. Daniel Sorano, blvd. de la République (E); *Ambassador:* RAOUL JEAN GRENIER (also accred. to Mauritania).

China, People's Republic: (E); *Ambassador:* WANG CHIN-CHUAN.

Denmark: Rabat, Morocco.

Egypt: Imm. Daniel Sorano, 45 blvd. de la République, B.P. 474 (E); *Ambassador:* NEGUIB KADRI.

Ethiopia: 24 blvd. Pinet-Laprade, 2e étage, B.P. 379 (E); *Ambassador:* ZENEBE HAILE.

Finland: Lagos, Nigeria (E).

France: 1 rue Thiers, B.P. 4035 (E); *Ambassador:* XAVIER DAUFRESNE DE LA CHEVALERIE.

Gabon: Abidjan, Ivory Coast.

Gambia: 5 ter. rue de Thiong, B.P. 3248; *Ambassador:* SAMUEL JONATHAN OKIKI SARR.

Germany, Federal Republic: 43 ave. A. Saurraut, B.P. 2100 *Ambassador:* ALEXANDER TOROK.

Ghana: 23 ave. Maginot, 1er étage (E); *Ambassador:* Dr. KUBIAA TAYLOR.

Haiti: 55 ave. Albert-Sarraut, B.P. 1552 (E); *Ambassador:* MARTIN CELESTIN DELENOIS.

India: 45 blvd. de la République, B.P. 398 (E); *Ambassador:* HARI KRISHNA SINGH.

Iran: (E); *Ambassador:* MONTEZA ADLE TABATABAI.

Italy: 26 ave. Roume, B.P. 348; *Ambassador:* LUDOVICI ARTENISIO.

Japan: Imm. B.I.A.O., Place de l'Indépendance, B.P. 3140; *Ambassador:* TOKISO ARAKI.

Korea, Democratic People's Republic: Paris, France (E).

Korea, Republic: Paris, France (E).

Lebanon: 18 blvd. de la République, B.P. 2345 (E); *Ambassador:* Dr. ISSAM HAIDAK.

Liberia: 21 ave. Faidherbe, B.P. 2110 (E).

Mali: 48 ave. Maginot, B.P. 7007; *Ambassador:* ZANGUÉ DIARRA.

Mauritania: 37 blvd. du Général de Gaulle, B.P. 12019; *Ambassador:* OULD ABDERRAHMANE.

Mexico: Addis Ababa, Ethiopia (E).

Morocco: Imm. Daniel Sorano, B.P. 490, 45 blvd. de la République; *Ambassador:* FADEL BENNANI.

Netherlands: 5 ave. Carde, B.P. 3262; *Ambassador:* J. P. ENGELS.

Nigeria: 9 ave. Roume, B.P. 3129 (E); *Ambassador:* Alhaji A. TAFAWA BALEWA.

Norway: Abidjan, Ivory Coast (E).

Poland: Point-E, Canal IV, Route de Ouakam, B.P. 3192; *Ambassador:* TADEUSZ MATYSIAK.

Romania: (E); *Ambassador:* NICOLAE IOAN DANCEA.

Saudi Arabia: rues Béranger Féraud et Masclary (E); *Ambassador:* FARID YOUSSEF BASRAWI.

Sierra Leone: Banjul, The Gambia (E).

Somalia: (E).

Spain: Imm. Daniel Sorano, 45 blvd. de la République, B.P. 2091; *Ambassador:* JOSÉ LUIS OCHOA Y OCHOA.

Sweden: 43 ave. Albert-Sarraut, B.P. 2052; *Ambassador:* LARS VON CELSING.

Switzerland: 1 rue Victor Hugo, B.P. 1772 (E); *Ambassador:* JEAN RICHARD.

Trinidad and Tobago: Addis Ababa, Ethiopia.

Tunisia: rue El-Hadj Seydou Nourou Tall, B.P. 3127 (E); *Ambassador:* ABDELHAMID AMMAR.

Turkey: Imm. B.I.A.O., Appt. Fls. 1er étage, Place de l'Indépendance, B.P. 6060, Etoile (E); *Ambassador:* ZIYA TEPEDELEN.

U.S.S.R.: ave. Jean-Jaurès, B.P. 3180 (E); *Ambassador:* GEORGI TER-GAZARYANTS.

United Kingdom: 20 rue du Dr. Guillet, B.P. 6025 (E); *Ambassador:* DENZIL DUNNET (also accred. to Dahomey and Mauritania).

U.S.A.: Imm. B.I.A.O., place de l'Indépendance, B.P. 49; *Ambassador:* RUDOLPH AGGREY.

Upper Volta: (E); *Ambassador:* EMILE OUTTARA.

Vatican: rue I, Cité Fann, B.P. 5076 (Apostolic Internunciature); *Apostolic Delegate for West Africa:* Mgr. GIOVANNI MARIANI.

Viet-Nam, Democratic Republic: *Ambassador:* VAN BA KIEM.

Yugoslavia: Rocade Fann-Bel-Air, route de Ouakam (E); *Ambassador:* ACO SOPOV.

Zaire: Imm. Daniel Sorano, 2e. étage, B.P. 2251 (E); *Ambassador:* FERDINAND KAYAKWA KIMOTO.

Zambia: (E); *Ambassador:* SITEKE G. MWALE.

Senegal also has diplomatic relations with Bahrain, Greece, Ivory Coast, Kuwait, Luxembourg, Monaco, Panama, Uganda, Uruguay and the Royal Government of Khmer National Union (Cambodia).

NATIONAL ASSEMBLY

President: Amadou Cissé Dia.

ELECTION, JANUARY 1973

All 100 seats were won by the *Union progressiste sénégalaise*, which presented the only list of candidates.

POLITICAL PARTY

Union progressiste sénégalaise (UPS): national section of the *Parti fédéraliste africaine* (PFA); government party; Sec.-Gen. Léopold Sédar Senghor; Permanent Sec. Karim Fall.

In 1966 the sole legal opposition party still in existence, *Parti de regroupement africain*, was incorporated by agreement into the UPS. Only clandestine opposition groups are still active, notably the two sections (pro-Chinese and pro-Soviet) of the *Parti africaine de l'indépendence* and supporters of former Prime Minister Mamadou Dia.

DEFENCE

There is a total armed force of 5,900 of which the standing army numbers 5,500 men in units of parachutists, engineers, signals, motorized infantry and gendarmerie. All males between the ages of 20 and 60 are liable for national service. The army is closely involved in government development projects. The air force is equipped with light reconnaissance aircraft and helicopters. The navy is composed of two coastal patrol-boats. Para-military forces number 1,600.

Army Chief-of-Staff: Lt.-Col. Idrissa Fall.

JUDICIAL SYSTEM

Supreme Court: f. 1960; Pres. Kéba M'Baye; Sectional Pres. Menoumbé Sar, Laïty Niang Bruno Cheramy.

High Court of Justice: f. 1962; composed of members of the National Assembly.

High Council of the Magistrature: f. 1960; Pres. Léopold Sédar Senghor (*President of the Republic*); Vice-Pres. Amadou Clédor Sall.

Court of Appeal: Dakar; Pres. Abdoulaye Diop.

Public Prosecutor's Office: Attorney General Ousmane Goundiam; Advocate General Charles Henry Dupuy-Dourreau; Public Prosecutor Oumar N'Diaye.

RELIGION

Muslim

About 76 per cent of the population are Muslims. The three principal brotherhoods are the *Tijaniyya*, the *Qadiriyya* and the *Mouride*.

Grand Imam: Alhaji Amadou Lamine Diene.

Native Beliefs

About 14 per cent of the population follow traditional beliefs, mainly animist.

Christianity

About 10 per cent of the population are Christian, mainly Roman Catholics.

Roman Catholic: Archbishop of Dakar: Mgr. Hyacinthe Thiandoum, B.P. 1908, Dakar.

Suffragan Bishops:
Kaolack: B.P. 58; Mgr. Théophile Albert Cadoux.
St. Louis du Sénégal: rue Neuville; (vacant).
Thiès: B.P. 4; Mgr. Francesco Saverio Dione.
Ziguinchor: B.P. 23; Mgr. Augustin Sagna.

Protestant Church: 49 rue Thiers, Dakar, B.P. 847; 42 rue Carnot, Dakar.

THE PRESS

DAKAR—DAILIES

L'Information Africaine: 38 ave. W.-Ponty, B.P. 338; f. 1950; daily; Editors E. Lalanne, J. Peillon; circ. 15,000.

Journal officiel de La République du Sénégal: Dakar; government paper.

Le Soleil: Société Sénégalaise de Presse et de Publication, B.P. 92; f. 1970; national; sponsored by the *Union progressiste sénégalaise*; Editor Bara Diouf; circ. 15,000.

DAKAR—PERIODICALS

Africa: 30 blvd. Pinet Lapade, B.P. 1826; f. 1957; economic review of West Africa; circulates throughout francophone west Africa; six issues a year.

Afrique Médicale: 30 blvd. Pinet Lapade; f. 1960; medical review; circulates throughout francophone tropical Africa and beyond.

Afrique, Mon Pays: 24 ave. Gambetta.

Awa: Imprimerie Diop, rue de Reims, angle rue Dial Diop.

Bafila: 26 ave. Gambetta, B.P. 1845.

Bingo: 17 rue Huart, B.P. 176; f. 1952; illustrated monthly; Editor Joachim Paulin; circ. 100,000.

Médecine d'Afrique Noire: 38 ave. William-Ponty; Dakar; f. 1952; monthly; Dir. Emile Lalanne; circ. 10,000.

Le Moniteur Africain du Commerce et de l'Industrie: Société Africaine d'Edition, B.P. 1877; f. 1961; weekly; Editor-in-Chief Jean Thibault; circ. 10,000; to be taken over by the governments of Senegal and the Ivory Coast in 1974.

L'Observateur Africain: 29 rue Paul Holle.

Revue Française d'Etudes Politiques Africaines: Société Africaine d'Edition, B.P. 1877; f. 1966; monthly; Dir. P. Biarnes; Editor-in-Chief Ph. Decraene.

La Semaine à Dakar.

Sénégal d'Aujourd'hui: 58 blvd. de la République, B.P. 546; monthly.

Terre Sénégalaise: B.P. 269; monthly; Dir. J. B. Graulle.

L'Unité Africaine: 72 blvd. de la République, B.P. 1077; weekly; organ of the U.P.S.; Editor Ousmane N'Gom.

La Voix des Combattants: Ecole El Hadj-Malick Sy.

PRESS AGENCIES

Agence de Presse Sénégalaise: Imm. Maginot, Dakar; f. 1959; state-owned; provides subscribers with daily teleprinted information; Dir. Barra Dioff; publ. *Info-Sénégal* (daily).

FOREIGN BUREAUX

A.F.P. (France): B.P. 363, Dakar; Dir. E. Makedonsky.

Novosti (U.S.S.R.): B.P. 3180, Corner Ave. Jean-Jaurès and rue Carnot, Dakar.

Other foreign bureaux in Dakar: Agencia Nazionale Stampa Associata (ANSI), Associated Press, Deutsche Presse Agentur (DPA), Reuters, Tass (U.S.S.R.), United Press International.

PUBLISHERS

Clairafrique: B.P. 2005, rue Sandiniery 2, Dakar; politics, law, sociology.

Grande Imprimerie Africaine: 9 rue Thiers, B.P. 51, Dakar; f. 1917; law, administration; Dir. Henry O'Quin.

Institut Fondamental d'Afrique Noire (IFAN): B.P. 206, Dakar; scientific and humanistic studies of Black Africa.

Maison du Livre, La: B.P. 2060, Dakar; fiction and belles-lettres.

Nouvelles Editions Africaines: Dakar; f. 1972; shareholders include the Sengalese Government (52 per cent), Hachette, Seuil, Fernand Nathan, Armand Colin and other French and African publishers; wide range of material.

Société Africaine d'Editions et de Publication: rue de Reims, Dakar.

Société d'Edition et de Presse Africaine: 17 rue Huart, Dakar.

RADIO AND TELEVISION

Radiodiffusion du Sénégal: B.P. 1765, Dakar; government-owned; broadcasts in French and four vernacular languages; international service in Arabic, English and Portuguese; Dir.-Gen. Alioune Fall.

There are about 275,000 radio sets.

Télévision du Sénégal: B.P. 2375, Dakar; f. 1964; Government-sponsored educational service; pilot project with one 50-kW transmitter began regular broadcasting at the end of 1973.

There are 1,650 television sets.

FINANCE

(all amounts in francs CFA, unless otherwise stated)

BANKS

Central Bank

Banque Centrale des Etats de l'Afrique de l'Ouest: 29 rue de Colisée, Paris 8e, France; ave. W.-Ponty, B.P. 3159, Dakar; Bank of Issue and Central Bank for 7 West African States including Senegal; f. 1955; cap. and res. 3,923m.; Pres. Babacar Ba; Gen. Man. Robert Julienne; Dir. in Dakar François Eliard.

Banque Internationale pour l'Afrique Occidentale: 9 ave. de Messine, Paris, France; place de l'Indépendance, B.P. 129, Dakar.

Banque Internationale pour le Commerce et l'Industrie du Sénégal: B.P. 392, 2 ave. Roume, Dakar; f. 1962; cap. 625m.; Pres. Djime Guibril N'diaye; Man. Dir. E. Mouterde; Gen. Man. P. Escoubeyron.

Banque Nationale de Développement du Sénégal: B.P. 319, 7 ave. Roume, Dakar; f. 1964; cap. 1,360m.; Dir.-Gen. Hamet Diop.

Banque Sénégalaise de Développement (B.S.D.): Dakar, 2 bis rue Béranger Féraud; f. 1960; cap. 1,000m.; Dir. Louis Kandé.

Banque Sénégalo-Koweitienne: f. 1974; cap. 1,000m.; Pres. El Hadj Babacar Kébé; Dir.-Gen. Mohamed Sabek.

Crédit Populaire Sénégalais: Dakar, 35 rue Carnot; cap. 360m.

Société Générale de Banques au Sénégal S.A.; 19 ave. Roume B.P. 323, Dakar; f. 1962; cap. 500m.; Chair. Roger Duchemin; Man. Dir. D. P. Meraud.

Union Sénégalaise de Banque pour le Commerce et l'Industrie (U.S.B.): 17 blvd. Pinet-Laprade, B.P. 56, Dakar; f. 1961; cap. 1,000m.; Pres. Tanor Thiendella Fall; Gen. Man. A. Sow.

BANKING ASSOCIATION

Association Professionelle de Banques et des Etablissements Financiers du Sénégal: Dakar.

INSURANCE

Comité des Sociétés d'Assurances du Sénégal: 43 ave. A. Sarraut, B.P. 1766, Dakar; Pres. Pierre Henri Delmas; Sec. Jean-Pierre Cairo.

Société Africaine d'Assurances: B.P. 508, Dakar; f. 1945; cap. 9 million; Dir. Pierre Vernet.

A considerable number of major French insurance companies have offices in Dakar.

TRADE AND INDUSTRY

CHAMBERS OF COMMERCE

Chambre de Commerce, d'Industrie et d'Artisanat de la Région du Fleuve: rue Bisson, Saint-Louis-du-Sénégal, B.P. 19; f. 1869; Pres. El Hadji Momar Sourang; publ. *Weekly Bulletin.*

Chambre de Commerce, d'Industrie et d'Artisanat de la Région du Sine Saloum: Kaolack, B.P. 203; Pres. Georges Laffont.

Chambre de Commerce, d'Industrie et d'Artisanat de la Casamance: B.P. 26, Ziguinchor; f. 1908; Pres. Youssouph Seydi.

Chambre de Commerce, d'Industrie et d'Artisanat de la Région de Thiès: ave. Foch, Thiès, B.P. 20; f. 1883; 32 mems.; Pres. El Hadji Diagne; Sec.-Gen. René Barbères.

Chambre de Commerce, d'Industrie et d'Artisanat de la Région du Cap Vert: B.P. 118, Dakar; Sec.-Gen. B. Niang.

Chambre de Commerce, d'Industrie et d'Artisanat de la Région de Diourbel: Diourbel; Pres. Cheikh Diongue.

Chambre de Commerce, d'Industrie et d'Artisanat de la Région du Sénégal Oriental: Tambacounda; Pres. Amadou Gaye.

PRINCIPAL EMPLOYERS' ASSOCIATIONS

Dakar

Délégation de la Fédération des Industries Mécaniques et Transformatrices des Métaux: 43 ave. Maginot, B.P. 1858; Pres. M. Barraqué.

Syndicat des Agents Maritimes de la Côte Occidentale de l'Afrique: 8-10 allées Canard, B.P. 167 and 138.

Syndicat des Commerçants Importateurs et Exportateurs de l'Ouest Africain: 14 ave. Albert-Sarraut, B.P. 806.

Syndicat des Entrepreneurs de Bâtiment et de Travaux Publics de l'Ouest Africain: 12 ave. Albert-Sarraut, B.P. 593; f. 1930; 45 mems.; Pres. Pierre Meyneng.

Syndicat des Entrepreneurs de Transports et Transitaires de l'Afrique Occidentale: 47 ave. Albert Sarraut, B.P. 233; Pres. J. Nègre.

Syndicat des Entreprises de Manutention des Ports d'Afrique Occidentale (SEMPAO): 8 allées Canard, B.P. 164.

Syndicat des Fabricants d'Huile et de Tourteaux du Sénégal: 11 allées Canard, B.P. 131; Pres. J. L. Oudeyrat.

Syndicat Patronal des Industries de Dakar et du Sénégal: 12 ave. Albert-Sarraut, B.P. 593; f. 1944; 103 mems.; Pres. MARC DELHAYE.

Union Fédérale des Syndicats Industriels et Commerciaux et Artisanaux: B.P. 281, 2 ave. Gambetta; Pres. CHARLES GRAZIANI.

Union Intersyndicale d'Entreprises et d'Industries de l'Ouest Africain: 12 ave. A. Sarraut, B.P. 593; Pres· MARC DELHAYE.

TRADE UNION FEDERATIONS

Confédération Nationale des Travailleurs Croyants: B.P. 1474, Dakar; 3,000 mems.; Pres. DAVID SOUNAH; Sec.-Gen. CHARLES MENDY.

Confédération Nationale des Travailleurs Sénégalais (CNTS): f. 1969; affiliated to Union progressiste sénégalaise; Pres. DOUDOU N'GOM.

Union Nationale des Travailleurs du Sénégal (UNTS): B.P. 840, Dakar; affiliated to Union Générale des Travailleurs d'Afrique Noire; 100,000 mems.; absorbed Confédération Sénégalaise du Travail 1966; Gen.-Sec. MAGATTE THIAW.

TRADE FAIR

Foire Internationale de Dakar: B.P. 3329, Dakar; the first Dakar International Fair will be held from November 28th to December 15th 1974.

TRANSPORT

RAILWAYS

There are 1,034 km. of main line including 70 km. of double track, and 152 km. of secondary line. One line runs from Dakar north to St. Louis (262 km.) with a branch to Linguera (129 km.); the main line runs to Bamako (Mali) and the Niger (643 km. in Senegal). All the locomotives are diesel-driven.

Régie des Chemins de Fer du Sénégal: P.O.B. 23-840, Dakar; Man. KHALILOU SALL.

ROADS

In 1971 there were 15,422 km. of roads, of which 2,294 km. were bitumenized. The third development plan ending in 1973 aimed to increase the road network to 2,646 km. of bitumenized roads, 866 km. of laterite roads ready to be surfaced with bitumen, and 4,800 km. of tracks passable throughout the year.

MOTORISTS' ORGANIZATION

Automobile-Club du Sénégal: B.P. 295, Chambre de Commerce, place de l'Indépendance, Dakar.

INLAND WATERWAYS

Senegal has three navigable rivers: the Senegal, navigable for three months of the year as far as Kayes (Mali), for six months as far as Kaédi (Mauritania) and all year as far as Rosso and Podor, and the Saloun and Pasamance.

Société des Messageries du Sénégal: 35 blvd. Pinet-Laprade, B.P. 209, Dakar; river traffic on the Senegal; also coastal services.

SHIPPING

Dakar is the largest port in West Africa. Its port installations can serve vessels of up to 100,000 tonnes, and it has extensive facilities for fishing vessels and fish processing.

Port Autonome de Dakar: B.P. 3195, Dakar, blvd. de la Libération; state-owned port authority; Pres. ISSA DIOP; Dir. MAMADOU M. GUEYE.

Ste. pour le Développement de l'Infrastructure de Chantiers Maritimes du Port de Dakar (DAKARMARINE): ave. Roume, Dakar; f. 1971; to set up facilities for the repair of giant tankers and other large vessels; Dir. ISSA DIOP.

Dakar

Cie. Sénégalaise de Navigation (COSENA): B.P. 3315, 11–13 rue Malenfant; Dir. GUY DELMAS; Man. Dir. P. PICARD.

Royal Interocean Lines: Peyrissac-Sénégal, rue Parchappe 9, Dakar, B.P. 193.

Scandinavian East Africa Line: c/o Ets. Buhan et Teisseire, place Kermel.

Société Ouest Africaine d'Entreprises Maritimes (Sénégal): B.P. 835; Dir. GEORGES GUIMONT.

Union Maritime et Commerciale (Umarco): 53 blvd. Pinet-Laprade; agents for Farrell Lines, Scindia Steam Navigation Co., Henry Abram Ltd., Van Nievelt, Goudriaan and Co.; Man. GEORGES GUIMONT.

Union Sénégalaise d'Industries Maritimes (USIMA): B.P. 164, 8–10 allées Canard; f. 1937; agents for Cie. de Navigation Parquet (CNP), Société Navale Chargeurs Delmas-Vieljeux, Compagnie Fabre-SGTM, Compagnie Générale Transatlantique, Compagnie des Croisières Paquet, Elder Dempster Lines, Cie de Navigation d'Orbigny, Cie. Navale des Chargeurs de l'Ouest, Armement Martin, Deutsche Afrika Line (Hamburg), Gulf West Africa Line (Oslo); Pres. PATRICE VIELJEUX; Dir.-Gen. GUY DELMAS.

CIVIL AVIATION

The international airport is Dakar—Yoff which can accommodate large jet aircraft, and there are other major airports at Ziguinchor and Tambacourda, in addition to about twelve smaller aerodromes.

SONATRA—Air Sénégal: Aéroport de Yoff, B.P. 8010, Dakar; f. 1971; 50 per cent owned by the Senegal Government, 40 per cent by Air Afrique; extensive internal services linking Dakar with all parts of Senegal; fleet of two DC-3, two Twin Otter, two DH Doves, one Aztec, one Cherokee and two Pawnee; Gen. Man. FERNAND BRIGAUD.

Air Afrique: B.P. 3132, Dakar; Senegal has a 6 per cent share in Air Afrique; see under Ivory Coast.

Senegal is also served by the following foreign airlines: Aeroflot, Air Zaire, Air France, Air Guinée, Air Mali, Air Mauritanie, Alitalia, ČSA, Ghana Airways, Lufthansa, Nigeria Airways, PAA, Pan American, Royal Air Maroc, Sabena and Swissair.

TOURISM

Délégation Général au Tourisme: 1 bis place de la République, B.P. 2018, Dakar; Delegate Gen. MOUSTAPHA FALL.

ARTS FESTIVAL

World Festival of Negro Art: ave. du Barachois, B.P. 3201, Dakar; f. 1965; bi-annual; Bureau Pres. ALIOUNE DIOP; Sec.-Gen. DJIBRIL DIONE.

UNIVERSITY

Université de Dakar: Fann Parc, Dakar; f. 1949; 237 teachers, 4,580 students.

SIERRA LEONE

INTRODUCTORY SURVEY

Location, Climate, Language, Religion, Flag, Capital

Sierra Leone lies on the west coast of Africa with Guinea to the north and east and Liberia to the south. The climate is hot and humid with an average temperature of 80°F (21°C); the rainy season lasts from May to October. English is the official language and Krio, Mende and Temne are widely spoken. The vast majority of the population follow animist beliefs and there are Muslim and Christian minorities. The national flag (proportions 3 by 2) has horizontal stripes of green, white and blue. The capital is Freetown.

Recent History

Formerly under British rule, Sierra Leone became independent in April 1961. Elections were held in 1962 and won by the Sierra Leone People's Party (SLPP) led by Sir Milton Margai. In 1964 Sir Milton Margai died, and was succeeded as premier by his brother Mr. (later Sir) Albert Margai, several members of whose government were later convicted on charges of corruption. Following disputed elections in March 1967, the army assumed control of the country and set up a National Reformation Council. The Governor-General was forced to leave the country. A second army revolt in April 1968 led to the restoration of civilian government and the return to power of the Prime Minister elected in 1967, Dr. Siaka Stevens. A state of emergency was declared on November 20th, 1968, after disorders in the Eastern and South-Eastern regions just before parliamentary by-elections were due to be held. The emergency was revoked on February 26th, 1969, and the elections held in March.

In April and May 1970 several of those who took part in the army coup of 1967 were tried and sentenced for treason. A defence agreement was reached with Guinea in March 1971 after another unsuccessful army attempt to overthrow Dr. Stevens led by Brigadier John Bangura. Guinean troops were flown in to assist loyal sections of the Sierra Leone army in protecting Dr. Stevens and restoring law and order. In April a republican constitution was introduced and Siaka Stevens became Executive President.

By-elections held in September 1972 were not contested by the opposition SLPP, six of whose members, including their leader, Salia Jusu-Sheriff, had been detained on charges of murder. They were later released on bail and the charge changed to conspiracy. In February 1973 one of the SLPP leaders was re-arrested. Elections were held in May 1973, when SLPP members were prevented from standing and claimed intimidation, and there is now no opposition in Parliament. Sierra Leone has strengthened its ties with communist countries. Internally the regime has become more authoritarian and a state of emergency remains in force.

Government

Sierra Leone is a republic within the Commonwealth. There is an Executive President with a Cabinet headed by a Prime Minister, who is also Vice-President. The House of Representatives consists of 85 members elected by direct universal suffrage, and twelve Paramount chiefs.

The country is divided into four regions: the Northern, Eastern and Southern Provinces, and the Western Area.

Defence

The Sierra Leone military forces consist of an infantry battalion and headquarters with a total strength of 1,500. There is a navy of 100. Police number about 2,100.

Economic Affairs

The economy is based on agriculture and mining, the chief products being palm kernels, coffee, cocoa, rice, timber, diamonds, and iron ore. Sierra Leone is striving to reach self-sufficiency in rice. Diamonds are the nation's principal export on which the country's economy is heavily dependent. In 1973 the value of diamond exports rose considerably but smuggling is a major problem. Since December 1969 the Government has taken a 51 per cent control in the four companies responsible for mining diamonds, iron ore, rutile and bauxite. Industry is on a small scale, covering palm oil, furniture and weaving. A Ten-Year Plan was launched in 1962 to develop industry and plantation agriculture. Trade remains largely controlled by foreign firms and immigrant communities. Sierra Leone adheres to a free trade agreement with Guinea, Ivory Coast and Liberia, signed in 1965, but largely ineffective owing to differences between the Ivory Coast and Guinea, and also to currency problems. In October 1973 Sierra Leone and Liberia concluded the Mano River Agreement which is to establish the economic union of the two countries in two stages, the first to be completed by 1977. The agreement will involve a local free trade area, the establishment of a Union Secretariat and a Customs Training School in Monrovia. The economy has been hard hit by the rise in world oil prices.

Transport and Communications

The railway system is being closed down and the road network considerably expanded. A road linking Freetown to Monrovia in Liberia is being planned by the African Development Bank. Inland waterways total 789 kilometres much of it navigable for only three months in the year. The chief ports are Freetown and Pepel. Internal air transport is well developed and international air services are provided by Sierra Leone Airways and eleven foreign lines. There is an international airport at Lungi which has been modernized.

Social Welfare

There is no state scheme for social security, but the Division of Social Welfare provides community developments centres, youth clubs and maternity welfare centres. Sierra Leone signed a two-year agreement with China which is to provide medical personnel.

Education

Education is private but nearly all schools are Government-assisted. Illiteracy, however, is estimated at 80 per cent. In 1973 there were 1,465 students at the University of Sierra Leone.

Tourism

The Tourist Board was set up in 1962 to develop Sierra Leone's tourist potential. The main attractions are the beaches, the mountains, jungle and wild life.

Visas are not required to visit Sierra Leone by nationals of Belgium, Denmark, Iceland, Ireland, Italy, Liechtenstein, Luxembourg, Netherlands, Norway, San Marino, Spain, Sweden, Turkey and United Kingdom and Commonwealth.

Sport

The most popular sports are football, cricket, athletics, lawn tennis and boxing. The National Sports Council supervises and encourages sport.

Public Holidays

1974: August 7th (Bank Holiday), October 18th (Id ul Fitr), December 25th–26th (Christmas, Boxing Day and Id ul Adha).

1975: January 1st (New Year's Day), March 26th (Mouloud, Birth of the Prophet), March 28th–31st (Easter), April 28th (Independence Day), May 19th (Whit Monday).

Muslim religious holidays dependent on the lunar calendar may differ slightly from the dates given.

Weights and Measures

The metric system is in force.

Currency and Exchange Rates

100 cents = 1 leone.

Exchange rates (April 1974):

£1 sterling = 2.00 leone;

U.S. $1 = 84.70 S.L. cents.

STATISTICAL SURVEY

AREA AND POPULATION

AREA (square miles)			POPULATION (1963 Census)*		
TOTAL	FREETOWN AND RURAL AREAS	PROVINCES	TOTAL	FREETOWN AND RURAL AREAS	PROVINCES
27,699	215	27,484	2,180,355	195,023	1,985,332

*Excluding an adjustment for underenumeration, estimated to have been 5 per cent.

Estimated Population: 2,627,000 (July 1st, 1972).

Main Tribes: Mende 673,000, Temne 550,000.

Chief Towns: Freetown (capital) 170,000, Bo 26,000, Kenema 13,000, Makeni 12,000.

AGRICULTURE

PRODUCTION
('000 metric tons)

CROP	1969	1970	1971	1972
Rice (Paddy)	407.0	425.0	372.0	321.5
Cocoa (Beans) . . .	4.0	5.0	6.6	4.6
Coffee . . .	5.4	7.5	9.2	1.0
Groundnuts (in shell) . .	9.0*	9.0*	1.3	9.0
Palm Kernels (exports) . .	48.0	60.0	48.0	50.0
Palm Oil	45.0	53.0	50.0	33.0
Maize	12.0	14.0	16.5	12.8

* FAO estimate.

Source: United Nations, *Statistical Yearbook 1971*, and Government Information Services, Freetown.

LIVESTOCK
(FAO estimates)

	1968–69	1969–70	1970–71
Cattle	230,000	240,000	250,000
Pigs	28,000	29,000	30,000
Sheep	55,000	57,000	58,000
Goats	153,000	156,000	158,000
Chickens . . .	2,850,000	2,900,000	3,000,000
Ducks	12,000	12,000	12,000

Source: FAO, *Production Yearbook 1971.*

Fisheries (1965): 6,000 tons.

MINING

	1969	1970	1971	1972
Diamonds ('000 metric carats) . .	1,989	2,050	1,945	1,800
Bauxite ('000 metric tons) . .	454	443	590	369
Iron Ore ('000 metric tons)* . .	2,336	2,259	2,540	3,762
Rutiles ('000 metric tons) . .	28	44	11	13

*Figures refer to gross weight. The iron content (in '000 metric tons) was: 1,425 in 1969; 1,377 in 1970; 1,528 in 1971.

INDUSTRY*

	Unit	1971	1972
Cigarettes	million sticks	731	828
Acetylene	'000 cu. ft.	829	608
Oxygen	,, ,, ,,	2,089	1,928
Carbon Dioxide . . .	'000 lb.	195	171
Paint	'000 imp. gal.	92	103
Spirit	,, ,, ,,	22	11
Beer and Stout . . .	,, ,, ,,	1,304	1,409
Confectionery . . .	'000 lb.	2,339	2,923
Salt	,, ,,	11,272	16,537
Matches	gross boxes	51,750	7,300
Plastic footwear . . .	'000 pairs	522	600
Nails	cwt.	11,484	n.a.
Motor Spirit . . .	m. imp. gal.	11.9	13.0
Gas, Diesel and Fuel Oils .	,, ,, ,,	49.0	79.4
Kerosene	,, ,, ,,	9.3	7.4

* Cleared through excise authorities.

Source: Bank of Sierra Leone.

FINANCE

100 cents = 1 leone.

Coins: ½, 1, 5, 10, 20 and 50 cents.

Notes: 50 cents; 1, 2 and 5 leone.

Exchange rates (April 1974): £1 sterling = 2.00 leone; U.S. $1 = 84.70 Sierra Leone cents.

100 leone = £50.00 = $118.06.

Budget (1972–73): *Estimated Revenue:* Le. 59.1 million; *Estimated Expenditure:* Le. 56.2 million.

Budget (1973–74): *Estimated Revenue:* Le. 65.9 million; *Estimated Expenditure:* Le. 55.8 million; in 1973–74 Development Expenditure was estimated at 17.4 million leones.

EXTERNAL TRADE
(Le. '000)

	1968	1969	1970	1971	1972
Imports . .	75,474	93,134	97,263	94,268	95,365
Exports* . .	79,720	87,754	85,540	83,384	91,611

* Including re-exports.

PRINCIPAL COMMODITIES

IMPORTS	1970	1971	1972
Food . . .	20,464	18,184	16,746
Beverages and Tobacco.	2,841	3,548	3,241
Crude Materials .	1,107	986	838
Mineral Fuels .	4,554	6,934	7,111
Oils and Fats .	1,087	855	1,276
Chemicals . .	6,161	6,780	6,730
Manufactures .	25,981	24,029	25,122
Machinery . .	24,970	22,751	23,390
Miscellaneous Goods .	8,781	8,713	9,284
Other Items .	1,317	1,488	1,627
TOTAL . .	97,263	94,268	95,365

EXPORTS	1970	1971	1972
Kola Nuts . .	120	197	288
Coffee . .	4,215	3,457	8,727
Cocoa Beans .	3,321	2,683	3,249
Ginger . .	352	339	202
Palm Kernels .	6,999	5,915	3,855
Iron Ore . .	10,169	11,430	10,164
Bauxite . .	1,130	2,516	3,274
Piassava . .	462	532	522
Diamonds . .	52,803	49,978	56,740
Other Items .	4,903	5,021	2,495
Re-exports . .	1,066	1,316	2,095
TOTAL (incl. re-exports) .	85,540	83,384	91,611

PRINCIPAL COUNTRIES

IMPORTS	1970	1971	1972
United Kingdom . .	28,717	27,170	22,060
Other Commonwealth Countries	11,119	12,601	n.a.
Japan. . .	9,009	9,619	9,464
Netherlands .	3,255	4,281	5,558
Fed. Repub. of Germany	6,780	5,742	9,123
U.S.A. . .	8,421	6,710	6,149
France . .	3,950	4,901	6,094
Italy . . .	1,497	1,427	1,827
Other Countries .	24,515	21,816	n.a.
TOTAL .	97,263	94,268	95,365

EXPORTS	1970	1971	1972
United Kingdom . .	54,570	51,529	58,410
Other Commonwealth Countries	191	641	n.a.
Netherlands . .	8,301	7,754	6,332
Fed. Repub. of Germany	2,802	4,512	222
Other Countries . .	18,610	17,632	n.a.
TOTAL (excl. re-exports)	84,474	82,068	88,416

Source: mainly *Standard Bank Review.*

TRANSPORT
Railways (1964): 43 million passenger-km.; freight: 16 million net ton-km.

ROAD MOTOR VEHICLES
(number in use)

	1968	1969	1970
Passenger Cars	16,000	21,200	23,400
Commercial Vehicles . . .	6,800	7,700	9,200
TOTAL . . .	22,800	28,900	32,600

INTERNATIONAL SEA-BORNE SHIPPING
('000 metric tons)

	GOODS LOADED*			GOODS UNLOADED*		
	1967	1968	1969	1967	1968	1969
Freetown	} 2,408	{ 3,052	3,001	} 629	{ 745	737
Other Ports		8	5		—	—
TOTAL . .	2,408	3,060	3,006	629	745	737

*Including trans-shipments.

CIVIL AVIATION

	1968	1969	1970
Freight Loaded (metric tons) . .	154	157	238
Freight Unloaded (metric tons) . .	317	287	323
Passenger Arrivals . . .	15,000	20,000	14,000
Passenger Departures . . .	17,000	22,000	15,000

Source: UN Economic Commission for Africa, *Statistical Yearbook 1972*.

COMMUNICATIONS

	1967	1968	1969
Books (titles published) . .	73	75	n.a.
Telephones	6,100	7,000	8,200
Radio Sets	n.a.	135,000	140,000
Television Sets	2,500	3,000	3,500

Daily Newspapers: 5 in 1969 (combined average circulation 40,000 copies per issue).

Sources: United Nations, *Statistical Yearbook 1971*; UN Economic Commission for Africa, *Statistical Yearbook 1972*.

EDUCATION
(1969–70)

	ESTABLISHMENTS	STUDENTS
Primary	1,023	154,898
Secondary . . .	81	29,058
Technical . . .	4	860
Teacher Training . . .	9	879
Higher	2	1,116

Source (unless otherwise stated): Government Information Services, Freetown.

THE CONSTITUTION

(*April* 1971)

The Constitution provides for an Executive President, elected for five years, with a maximum of two terms, and a Cabinet headed by a Prime Minister, who is also Vice-President. Not more than three Ministers may be appointed from outside the House of Representatives. The House of Representatives consists of a Speaker and Deputy Speaker, and a total of 85 elected members (with effect from May 1973) and 12 Paramount Chiefs who do not stand for office under party auspices. Constitutional provisions are designed to safeguard certain fundamental democratic liberties, concerning the House of Representatives, elections, appointments, the Supreme Court, the office of Paramount Chief and the independence of the judiciary.

Under the 1961 Constitution a general election was required for approval of any fundamental constitutional change. However, since the new Constitution is basically the same as the republican constitution approved by the House of Representatives during Sir Albert Margai's term of office, the Government considered the March 1967 general election to have provided the necessary approval for the changeover to a republic which took place in April 1971. Certain clauses of the Margai Constitution which the present Government does not agree with and which could not be altered under the 1961 procedure for constitutional amendments are to be changed as the need arises. The state of emergency was renewed in October 1973.

THE GOVERNMENT

President: Dr. Siaka Probyn Stevens.

CABINET

(*July* 1974)

Vice-President and Prime Minister: Sorie Ibrahim Koroma.

Minister of Finance: Christian A. Kamara-Taylor.

Minister of Agriculture and National Resources: S. A. T. Koroma.

Minister of the Interior: Bangali Mansary.

Minister of External Affairs: Desmond E. Fashole-Luke.

Attorney-General: L. A. M. Brewah.

Minister of Mines: S. B. Kawusu Conteh.

Minister of Trade and Industry: F. Minah.

Minister of Works: N. A. P. Buck.

Minister of Information and Broadcasting: A. B. M. Kamara.

Minister of Development and Planning: S. A. J. Pratt.

Minister of Transport and Communications: E. J. Kargbo.

Minister of Education: A. J. Sandy.

Minister of Social Welfare: A. B. S. Janneh.

Minister of Housing and Country Planning: D. F. Shears.

Minister of Labour: J. C. O. Hadson-Taylor.

Minister of Health: A. G. Sembu-Forna.

Minister of Lands: F. B. Turay.

Minister of Tourism and Culture: J. Barthes-Wilson.

Leader of the House: S. D. Koroma.

Minister of State, Northern Province: S. A. Fofona.

Minister of State, Southern Province: G. Gobio Lamin.

Minister of State, Eastern Province: S. W. Gandi-Capio.

Ministers of State: Paramount Chiefs Bai Koblo Pathbana II, Jaia Kai Kai, M. N. Torto.

DIPLOMATIC REPRESENTATION

HIGH COMMISSIONS, LEGATION AND EMBASSIES ACCREDITED TO SIERRA LEONE

(In Freetown unless otherwise stated)

(HC) High Commission; (E) Embassy; (L) Legation.

Algeria: Conakry, Guinea (E).

Belgium: Accra, Ghana (E).

Bulgaria: Conakry, Guinea (E).

Canada: Lagos, Nigeria (HC).

China, People's Republic: 29 Wilberforce Loop (E); *Ambassador:* Chao Cheng-yi.

Cuba: 8 Pultney St. (E); *Ambassador:* A. C. Crabb.

Egypt: 20 Pultney St. (E); *Ambassador:* Hussein Helmy Bolbol.

France: 2 Pademba Rd. (E); *Ambassador:* André Mahoudeau-Campoyer.

The Gambia: 3 George St. (HC); *High Commissioner:* S. J. O. Sarr.

German Democratic Republic: Conakry, Guinea (E).

Germany, Federal Republic: 18 Siaka Stevens St. (E); *Ambassador:* Dr. S. H. Kanu.

Ghana: 18 Pultney St. (HC); *High Commissioner:* Alhaji Yakubu Talli.

Guinea: 4 Liverpool St. (E); *Ambassador:* Alpha Camara.

Hungary: Conakry, Guinea (E).

India: Accra, Ghana (HC).

Italy: The Maze, Congo Cross (E); *Ambassador:* Domenico Bochetto.

Ivory Coast: 1 Wesley St. (L); *Chancellor:* George Anoma.

Japan: Accra, Ghana (E).

Korea, Democratic People's Republic: Conakry, Guinea (E).

Lebanon: Leone House, Siaka Stevens St. (E); *Chargé d'Affaires:* Gilbert Ghazi.

Liberia: 30 Brookfields Rd. (E); *Ambassador:* George T. Brewer Jnr.

Madagascar: Paris, France (E).

Netherlands: Monrovia, Liberia (E).

Nigeria: 21 Charlotte St. (HC); *High Commissioner:* J. Tanko Yusuf.

Pakistan: Accra, Ghana (E).

Philippines: Lagos, Nigeria (E).

Poland: Conakry, Guinea (E).

Senegal: Banjul, Gambia (E).

Spain: Accra, Ghana (E).

Tanzania: Conakry, Guinea (HC).

Tunisia: Dakar, Senegal (E).

U.S.S.R.: 13 Walpole St. (E); *Ambassador:* I. F. Filippov.

United Kingdom: Standard Bank Building, Wallace Johnson St. (HC); *High Commissioner:* I. B. Watt, C.M.G.

U.S.A.: Walpole St. (E); *Ambassador:* Clinton L. Olson.

Yugoslavia: Conakry, Guinea (E).

Zambia: Abidjan, Ivory Coast (HC).

Sierra Leone also has diplomatic relations with Czechoslovakia, Dahomey, Ethiopia, Republic of Korea, Lesotho, Mali, Mauritania, Niger, Sweden, Switzerland, Uganda and Upper Volta.

HOUSE OF REPRESENTATIVES

Speaker: Justice Percy Davies.

Elections, May 1973

Party	Seats
All-People's Congress (APC) . . .	84
Independent	1

The election was boycotted by the Sierra Leone People's Party. The Independent joined the APC and there is now no Opposition in the legislature.

POLITICAL PARTIES

All-People's Congress (APC): 39 Siaka Stevens St., Freetown; won a small majority in the 1967 election, but prevented from taking power by the military *coup*; Leader Dr. Siaka Probyn Stevens; Vice-President Sorie I. Koroma.

Sierra Leone People's Party (SLPP): Freetown; f. 1951; formed the government party (in alliance with United Progressive and People's National Parties) until 1967; Leader Salia Jusu-Sheriff.

United Democratic Party: f. Sept. 1970; merged with four-month-old National Democratic Party; leader Dr. John Karefa-Smart. (*Banned October 1970.*)

JUDICIAL SYSTEM

The Chief Justice heads the structure of the Supreme, Appeal, High, Magistrate and Local Courts. The laws applicable in Sierra Leone are local statutes, statutes of general application in England on January 1st, 1880, and Common Law and Equity. There is provision also for some cases to be tried by a judge alone.

The Supreme Court: Replaces the Privy Council and is the highest and final judicial tribunal in the land.

Chief Justice: Christopher Okoro E. Cole.

Supreme Court Judges: S. C. W. Betts, E. Livesley Luke, S. J. Forster, c.b.e., N. E. Browne-Marke.

The Court of Appeal: Is the Court of Appeal for all subordinate courts and any appeal against its own decisions may be made to the Supreme Court.

Appeal Court Judges: C. A. Harding, O. B. R. Tejan, Mrs. Agnes V. A. Macaulay, S. Beccles Davies.

High Courts have jurisdiction in civil cases:

(*a*) in the Freetown District "on any cause or matter which may lawfully be brought before them", and

(*b*) in the Provinces, in any matter (except libel or slander) between or involving non-natives or between a native and the holder of a trading licence (whether a native or not).

High Court Judges: Ken O. During, S. C. E. Warne, F. A. Short, M. E. A. Cole, E. C. Thompson-Davies, G. Okoro Idogu, S. M. F. Kutubu, S. T. Navo, Rowland E. A. Harding, A. O. Lawrence-Hume.

Magistrates' Courts: In criminal cases the jurisdiction of the Magistrates' Courts is limited to summary cases and to preliminary investigations to determine whether a person charged with an offence triable by the Supreme Court shall be committed for trial.

Native Courts have jurisdiction, according to native law and custom, in all matters between natives which are outside the jurisdiction of other courts (*see* above).

Attorney-General: L. A. M. Brewah.

Master and Registrar, Supreme Court: O. M. Golley.

RELIGION

AFRICAN RELIGIONS

Beliefs, rites and practices are very diverse, varying from tribe to tribe and family to family.

ISLAM

Islam is widespread throughout Sierra Leone with Muslims being of greater numerical strength than Christians. There was a government-sponsored pilgrimage to Mecca in 1972 and assistance is to be given to pilgrims for the 1973/74 pilgrimage.

Malikiya Sect.

Sierra Leone Muslim Congress: Pres. Alhaji Buhari.

The Islamic Council: Pres. S. A. T. Koroma.

Ahmadiyya Sect: 13 Bath St., Brookfields (Headquarters); Amir and Missionary-in-charge Maulvi A. B. Shams.

CHRISTIANITY

Christian Council of Sierra Leone: P.O.B. 404, Freetown.

Bible Society: P.O.B. 1169, Freetown.

Anglicans

Archbishop of the Province of West Africa and Bishop of Sierra Leone: Most Rev. M. N. C. O. Scott, c.b.e., d.d., dip.th., Bishopscourt, P.O.B. 128, Freetown.

Roman Catholics

Archbishop of Freetown and Bo: Most Rev. Thomas Joseph Brosnahan, P.O.B. 98, Freetown.

Methodists

Methodist Conference: 11 Gloucester St., Freetown; Pres. Rev. S. Leslie Wallace.

United Methodist Church: Training Institute, Bo; Head Bishop Howard.

THE PRESS

DAILIES

Daily Mail: 29–31 Rawdon St., P.O.B. 53, Freetown; f. 1931; Government-owned; Editor Clarence E. Labor; circ. 10,000.

Nation: Town Hall Building, Lightfoot Boston St., Freetown; f. 1971, replacing *Unity Independent*, which was earlier closed by the Government; Government-owned; Editor Sam Short.

PERIODICALS

Advance: Endrina Sq., 72 Dambara Rd., Bo; f. 1948; twice weekly; Editor S. E. Labor Jones.

African Crescent: P.O.B. 353, Freetown; f. 1955; monthly; English; Editor Maului Mansoor; circ. 1,000.

Akera Ka Kathemne: Provincial Literature Bureau, P.O.B. 28, Bo; f. 1962; monthly; Themne; Editor Joseph E. Tucker.

Gospel Bells: 5 Frederick St., P.O.B. 868, Freetown; weekly; English; religious.

Konomanda: Koidu; f. 1969; All-People's Congress-sponsored news-sheet.

Kono Spark, The: The Spark Publications, Sina Town Rd., P.O.B. 81, Koidu Town; f. 1967; African Nationalist with strong Pan-African leanings; twice weekly, Mon. and Thurs.; Editor Kai Abdul Forday; circ. 1,500.

Leone Woman's Magazine: P.O.B. 987, Freetown; Editor Mrs. Daisy Bona.

Madora: Walpole St., Freetown; weekly; English.

Seme Loko: Provincial Literature Bureau, P.O.B. 28, Bo; f. 1938; monthly; Mende; Editor Joseph E. Tucker.

Sierra Fashion: 21 East St., P.O.B. 459, Freetown; monthly; Editor Miss Rosamond Jones; circ. 5,000.

Sierra Leone Observer: 3 Hospital Rd., Bo; weekly; circ. 4,000.

Sierra Leone Outlook: P.O.B. 1169, Freetown; six a year; English; Editor Rev. S. A. Warratie.

Sierra Leone Trade Journal: Ministry of Information and Broadcasting, Water St., Freetown; f. 1961; quarterly; circ. 3,000.

Sunday Flash: 29–31 Rawdon St., P.O.B. 987, Freetown; Editor Mrs. Daisy Bona.

Sunday We Yone: Fort St., Freetown; twice weekly; in English; APC party newspaper; Editor Arika Awuta-Coker.

West African Star: Freetown; f. 1962; religious and general; weekly; Editor Rigsby Tom Davies; circ. 3,000.

NEWS AGENCY

Foreign Bureau

Tass, Hsinhua and Agence France-Presse are the only foreign bureaux in Freetown.

PUBLISHER

The Government Printer: Government Printing Dept., George St., Freetown.

RADIO AND TELEVISION

Radio and television services are to undergo a complete modernization under an agreement signed with an Italian company in 1974.

RADIO

Sierra Leone Broadcasting Service: New England, Freetown; f. 1934 and since 1958 has been operated by the Department of Broadcasting of the Sierra Leone Government. There are two short-wave transmitters and receiving stations in Freetown. Broadcasts are made in English and four Sierra Leonean languages, Mende, Limba, Temne and Krio. There is also a weekly broadcast in French. Dir. of Broadcasting Joseph W. O. Finlay, Jr.

There are about 60,000 radio sets.

TELEVISION

Sierra Leone Broadcasting Service: The television service was established in 1963 and is now an integral part of the Broadcasting Service. Transmissions are limited to a radius of 15 miles around Freetown; 4 hours of programmes daily.

There are about 6,000 television sets.

FINANCE

BANKING

(cap.=capital; res.=reserves; Le.=Leone.)

Bank of Sierra Leone: P.O.B. 30, Freetown; f. 1964; central bank; cap. Le.1.5m.; res. Le.39,326,000; Governor S. L. Bangura; Deputy Gov. A. S. C. Johnson; Gen. Man. M. R. Tejan-Cole.

Barclays Bank of Sierra Leone Ltd.: Head Office: P.O.B. 969, Freetown; Chair. and Gen. Man. D. E. Hughes; 11 brs. and sub-brs. and 2 agencies.

National Commercial Bank: Freetown; f. 1973.

National Development Bank Ltd.: Leone House, 21–23 Siaka Stevens St., P.M.B., Freetown; f. 1968; provides medium- and long-term finance and technical assistance to viable enterprises likely to contribute to Sierra Leone's development; major shareholders include the African Development Bank, Bank of Sierra Leone, other commercial banks, and insurance, trading and mining companies operating in Sierra Leone; auth. cap. Le.1m., subordinated interest free loan of Le.1m. from Government of Sierra Leone; Man. Dir. Abayomi Tejan.

Sierra Leone Commercial Bank Ltd.: 30 Walpole St., Freetown; f. 1933; cap. Le.1m.; Gen. Man. C. J. Smith.

Standard Bank of Sierra Leone Ltd.: Head Office: 9 Wallace Johnson St., P.O.B. 1155, Freetown; 11 other branches throughout the country; cap. Le.4m.

INSURANCE

The principal British companies are represented, and a Sierra Leonean company has been established by the Government.

National Insurance Co. Ltd.: 21–23 Siaka Stevens St., Freetown; Government owned.

TRADE AND INDUSTRY

CHAMBER OF COMMERCE

Chamber of Commerce of Sierra Leone: P.O.B. 502, Freetown; f. 1961; Pres. T. F. Hope.

GOVERNMENT ORGANIZATIONS

Government Diamond Office: P.O.B. 421, Freetown; f. 1959; all diamonds are exported through this office; Chair. Executive Board G. L. V. Williams, c.b.e.

National Trading Co. Ltd.: has import monopoly for sugar, tinned milk, corned beef, sardines, baked beans, cooking oil, onions, tomato paste, tea and coffee; Man. Dir. J. C. D. Solomon.

Sierra Leone Investments Ltd.: A. Momodu Allie House, P.O.B. 263, Freetown; f. 1961 to stimulate economic activity.

Sierra Leone Produce Marketing Board: Queen Elizabeth II Quay, Freetown; f. 1949 to secure the most favourable arrangements for the marketing of Sierra Leone produce and to stimulate agricultural development; has subsidiary in London for sale of palm kernels, coffee, cocoa and ginger; handles all agricultural export products; Chair. Paramount Chief Kenewa Gamanga, m.b.e., j.p.; Man. Dir. J. Teesdale (Head Office, Freetown).

Sierra Leone Rice Corpn.: Freetown; f. 1965 to assist farmers with rice cultivation; mills and markets locally grown rice; also imports to augment local product of rice; Sec. E. J. SILLAH.

EMPLOYERS' ASSOCIATIONS

Sierra Leone Employers' Federation: P.O.B. 562, Freetown; Chair. A. D. WURIE, C.B.E.; Exec. Officer A. E. BENJAMIN.

Association of Builders and Building Contractors: 18 mems.

Sierra Leone Chamber of Mines: P.O.B. 456, Freetown; comprises the four principal mining concerns.

TRADE UNIONS

Artisans, Ministry of Works Employees and General Workers' Union: 4 Pultney St., Freetown; f. 1946; 5,600 mems.; Pres. IBRAHIM LANGLEY; Gen. Sec. TEJAN A. KASSIM.

Sierra Leone Labour Congress: 53 Bathurst St., Freetown; f. 1966; approx. 18,000 mems. (20 per cent of all wage and salary earners) in 12 affiliated unions; Pres. G. A. CARAMBA-COKER; Vice-Pres. A. W. HASSAN; Sec.-Gen. C. E. PALMER.

Principal affiliated unions:

Clerical, Mercantile and General Workers' Union: 19 Pultney St., Freetown; f. 1945; 3,600 mems.; Gen. Sec. M. S. LAHAI.

Railway Workers' Union: The Technical Institute, 11 Dan St., Freetown; f. 1919; 510 mems.; Gen. Sec. O. ATERE ROBERTS.

Sierra Leone Dockworkers' Union: 182 Fourah Bay Rd., Freetown; f. 1962; 2,650 mems.; Sec.-Gen. O. CONTEH.

Sierra Leone Maritime and Waterfront Workers' Union: 4 Pultney St., Freetown; f. 1946; 5,600 mems.

Sierra Leone Motor Drivers' Union: 17 Charlotte St., Freetown; f. 1960; 1,900 mems.; Pres. A. W. HASSAN; Gen. Sec. YAMBA SESAY.

Sierra Leone Transport and General Workers' Union: 4 Pultney St., Freetown; f. 1946; 1,600 mems.; Gen. Sec. H. N. GEORGESTONE.

United Mineworkers' Union: 4 Pultney St., Freetown; f. 1944; 6,500 mems.; Gen. Sec. J. B. KABBIA.

Also affiliated to the Sierra Leone Labour Congress: General Union of Construction Workers, Sherbro Amalgamated Workers' Union, Sierra Leone Articled Seamen's Union, Sierra Leone Seamen's Union.

The following unions are not affiliated to the Sierra Leone Labour Congress: Sierra Leone Plantation Workers' Union, The Southern and Eastern Provincial General Workers' Union, Sierra Leone Teachers' Union (1,600 mems.).

CO-OPERATIVES AND MARKETING BOARDS

Very rapid progress has been made in the field of co-operatives. In 1973 there were 936 primary co-operatives with a total membership of 45,684. In addition there are 640 thrift and credit co-operative societies, 7 consumer co-operatives, 284 marketing societies, 3 producer co-operatives, and a Central Bank for all co-operatives.

The Co-operative Department is a separate entity under the Ministry of Trade and Industry with the Registrar of Co-operatives as head of the Department and Co-operative movement, and is based in Freetown with eight area offices spread throughout the provinces. Total shares paid by societies amount to Le.20,550.

TRANSPORT

RAILWAY

Sierra Leone Government Railway: Clinetown; f. 1899; three sections of the railway have already been closed, and the Government intends to phase out the whole system; Gen. Man. RICHARD W. R. NORMAN (acting).

There are also 93 km. of track owned by the Sierra Leone Development Company, used for carrying iron ore from Marampa to Pepel.

ROADS

All Government and most other roads are motorable throughout the year although occasionally ferries may be closed for a few days by abnormal flooding. There are 3,176 km. of first-class roads maintained by the Public Works Dept., 3,480 km. of roads maintained by local authorities, and 282 km. owned and maintained by private companies.

Construction of a new road between Bo and Kenema, 69 km. long and including a 213 metre bridge, started in 1972. A bridge is to be constructed over the Mano river. The 120 km. road between Tonkolili and Kono has been completed. Work on the road between Bo and Taiama and the road between Bauya and Yonibana is nearing completion; and a new 320 km. road linking Liberia and Sierra Leone will be built with aid from the World Bank, the British Government, the Federal German Government and the UNDP. The Freetown–Waterloo road is to be reconstructed with aid from the Federal Republic of Germany.

Director of Road Transport: E. B. M. SAVAGE.

Sierra Leone Road Transport Corporation: Blackhall Rd., P.O.B. 1008, Freetown; f. 1965; majority government shareholding; operates transport services throughout the country. A road haulage service was inaugurated in 1971 which has replaced the railway network; a fleet of about 50 Mercedes Benz buses serves the whole country. Chair. Dr. N. A. COX-GEORGE; 380 employees.

INLAND WATERWAYS

Recognized launch routes, including the coastal routes from Freetown northward to the Great and Little Scarcies rivers and southward to Bonthe, total almost 800 km. Some of the upper reaches of the rivers are only navigable for three months of the year (July to September). Nevertheless a considerable volume of traffic uses the rivers.

SHIPPING

Sierra Leone National Shipping Company Ltd.: Deep Water Quay, P.O.B. 935, Freetown; shipping, clearing and forwarding agency.

Sierra Leone Ports Authority: Freetown; operates the Port of Freetown, which has full facilities for ocean-going vessels; Gen. Man. Capt. A. R. MACAULAY.

Sierra Leone Shipping Agencies Ltd.: P.O.B. 74, Freetown; shipping, clearing and forwarding agency; agents for some 60 foreign shipping companies of which about 20 call regularly at Freetown; Gen. Man. J. E. HUGHES.

The following shipping lines also maintain offices in Freetown: Chargeurs Line, Delta Line, Deutsche Afrika Linien und Woermann Linie, Gold Star Line, Guinea Gulf Line, Hanseatic Africa Line, Hoegh Nedlloyd Lines, Lloyd Triestino S.P.A., Royal Interocean Lines, Scandinavian West Africa Line, United West Africa Service.

CIVIL AVIATION

Director of Civil Aviation: R. R. WRIGHT, A.R.AE.S.

Sierra Leone Airways: Leone House, Siaka Stevens St., Freetown (Head Office); Freetown International Airport, Lungi; operates daily services from Hastings Aerodrome, Freetown, to principal points in the country; handles all types of aircraft at international airport; operates flights to London and Monrovia, and twice weekly BAC 1-11 service Freetown/Robertsfield/Accra/Lagos; all operated by British Caledonian; fleet of 2 Britten-Norman Islanders; Chair. O. L. A. GORDON; Gen. Man. Capt. T. C. S. LEECE.

FOREIGN AIRLINES

The following foreign airlines provide services to Freetown: Air Afrique, Air Mali, British Caledonian, C.S.A., EgyptAir, Ghana Airways, Interflug, K.L.M., M.E.A., Nigeria Airways and U.T.A.

TOURISM

Ministry of Culture and Tourism: Lightfoot-Boston St., Freetown.

Tourist and Hotels Board: 28 Siaka Stevens St., Freetown.

UNIVERSITY

University of Sierra Leone: Freetown; f. 1967; incorporates the following colleges:

Fourah Bay College: P.O.B. 87, Freetown; f. 1827; 117 teachers, 936 students.

Njala University College: Private Mail Bag, Freetown; f. 1965; 120 teachers, 429 students.

SINGAPORE

INTRODUCTORY SURVEY

Location, Climate, Language, Religion, Flag, Capital

The Republic of Singapore comprises one main island and several offshore islands, situated approximately 77 miles north of the equator. The country is flanked by Malaysia in the north, with the Philippines to the north-east and Indonesia to the south. It is linked to the Malay Peninsula by a causeway. The climate is equatorial with a uniformly high daily and annual temperature varying between 75°F and 80°F (24°C–27°C). Relative humidity is high, and the average annual rainfall is 96 in. There are no well-defined wet and dry seasons. The national language is Malay, and there are four official languages—Malay, Chinese (Mandarin), Tamil and English. The language of administration is English. There is complete religious freedom: the main religions practised are Islam, Christianity, Buddhism, Hinduism, Confucianism and Taoism. The national flag (proportions 3 by 2) has two equal horizontal stripes of red and white, with a white crescent moon and five white stars in the top left. The capital is Singapore City.

Recent History

After the Second World War, Singapore was governed by the British Military Administration. When civil rule was restored in 1946, Singapore was detached from the other Straits Settlements and became a separate crown colony. A new constitution in 1955 introduced some measure of self-government, and in 1959 the state achieved complete internal self-government with Lee Kuan Yew as Prime Minister. The Federation of Malaysia came into being in September 1963, with Singapore as a constituent state. In August 1965, the association was ended and Singapore was separated from Malaysia and became a fully independent and sovereign nation. In December 1965 it became a Republic with a President as Head of State. In May 1973 the last major ties with Malaysia, currency and finance, were broken. In January 1971 Singapore was host to the first ever Commonwealth Conference to be held outside Great Britain. In September 1972 Lee Kuan Yew's ruling People's Action Party (PAP) won all the 65 parliamentary seats in the general election, also contested by five opposition parties. Singapore has achieved considerable political stability though the ruling PAP exercises strong control over the media. Lee Kuan Yew has taken a staunchly anti-Communist stand for years and this has led Singapore to maintain close ties with Britain and its Commonwealth partners in South-East Asia and to support a strong U.S. military presence in the area. With continuing economic prosperity in Singapore the massive unemployment and economic recession predicted after the 1971 withdrawal of British forces never materialized.

Government

Singapore is a Republic within the Commonwealth. The Head of State is the President, who must be a citizen of Singapore. The legislature comprises a Parliament elected by universal adult suffrage and there is a Cabinet presided over by the Prime Minister.

Defence

The United Kingdom withdrew her main forces in 1971. Defence is now co-ordinated under a consultative pact on external defence signed in April 1971 between Singapore and Malaysia, Australia, New Zealand and the United Kingdom forming a combined ANZUK force. There is a British, Australian and New Zealand presence in Singapore though it is Australian government policy to withdraw its troops in 1974 and reduce its ANZUK liability. The British commitment to ANZUK was also under review in 1974. In 1974 the Singapore armed forces totalled 20,600 troops: 19,000 in the army, 1,000 in the navy and 600 in the air force. Para-military and citizen defence forces and army reserves total nearly 40,000 and 1972/73 defence expenditure was S$693 million.

Economic Affairs

Strategically situated both for trade and defence, Singapore is the entrepôt for Malaysia and other South-East Asian states. It handles most of West Malaysia's external trade and is the world centre of the rubber and tin markets. The main commodities in trade are rubber and petroleum products, whilst foodstuffs form a quarter of retained imports. While the entrepôt trade and related services still account for 16 per cent of national income and employ a quarter of the labour force, the processing and manufacturing industries are receiving increasing attention, and manufactured domestic exports are increasing. Many new industries have been established to produce for export markets and there are rapidly growing industrial estates. Notable among the new industries is the Jurong Shipyard; the Sembawang Shipyard, the former British naval base, is also being developed for commercial ship repair.

Less than a quarter of the land area is under cultivation, and the primary sector accounts for about 4 per cent of national income and employs about 8 per cent of the workforce. Fruit and vegetable market gardening and offshore fishing are the major activities in this sector.

The growth rate of gross domestic product was over 14 per cent in 1971, 15.5 per cent in 1972 and 11 per cent in 1973. Singapore enjoys one of the highest per capita incomes in Asia. Intensive searches for submarine oil resources led to the completion of the first Singapore-built oil-rig. A fourth oil refinery was opened in February 1971 with a capacity of 81,000 barrels a day and in 1972 petroleum refining made considerable progress. The Pulau Bukom refinery will have Shell's largest crude oil distillation capacity when it is completed.

During 1973 vast foreign investment continued to flow into industry, and more than 50,000 new jobs were created. In 1973 there was another large balance of payments surplus and a rapid expansion in manufacturing industry. Although Singapore faces higher oil prices it has a strong currency backed 100 per cent by gold and foreign assets. The problem of unemployment has been forcefully tackled and there is now a shortage of labour. In 1974 Singapore's reserves stood at S$5,707.5 million. The Government is promoting Singapore as an international banking centre.

Transport and Communications

Singapore is the fourth largest port in the world, in terms of tonnage entering and leaving, and is used by more than 200 major shipping lines as well as by local coastal services. Shipbuilding employs 25,000 workers. A new container port became fully operational in late 1973. Singapore International Airport has been expanded to handle Boeing 747s and in 1971 a satellite communications centre came into operation.

Social Welfare

The Social Welfare Department, aided by local voluntary bodies, provides a wide range of welfare services to individuals and families in need. These services include direct financial assistance, day care and foster home care for children and institutional care for the handicapped, destitute, sick and aged. There are no state social insurance systems but there is a Central Provident Fund into which contributions must be paid by employers and employees. Since self-government in 1959 155,000 houses have been built and 40 per cent of the population are in low-cost flats. There has been immense progress in slum clearance and modernization of the city districts.

Education

Primary and secondary education is available in the four official languages of Malay, Chinese, Tamil and English. Government schools are either integrated schools with two or three language streams in one building under one administration or schools with only one language stream as is the case with government-aided and private schools. In June 1972 there were 414 primary schools with 354,748 students, and 111 secondary schools with 144,145 students. Outside the school system there are several higher education centres and vocational institutes providing craft level industrial training and technical institutes providing advanced craft training. There is a technical college, a polytechnic, a teacher training college and two universities. Adult education courses are conducted by a statutory board.

Tourism

In 1972 there were 783,015 tourists. The diverse population of the country offers opportunities to see a number of Asian cultures. Singapore has 72 hotels.

Visas to enter Singapore are not required by British subjects, Commonwealth citizens, British protected persons, holders of Thai diplomatic and service passports, or Philippine diplomatic and special passports, nor by nationals of Ireland, Liechtenstein, Monaco, Netherlands, San Marino and Switzerland; also citizens of the U.S.A., Federal Republic of Germany, Denmark, Italy, Belgium, Finland, France, Iceland, Luxembourg, Norway and Sweden who are in transit or making only a temporary visit.

Sport

Facilities exist for all types of sport.

Public Holidays

1974: August 9th (National Day), October 17th and 18th (Hari Raya Puasa, end of Ramadan), November 13th (Deepavali), December 24th (Hari Raya Haji), December 25th (Christmas).

1975: January 1st (New Year's Day), February 10th (Chinese New Year), March 28th (Good Friday), May 1st (Labour Day), May 6th (Wesak Day).

Weights and Measures

In addition to imperial weights and measures, the following are in use:

Weight: 16 Tahils=1 Kati=$1\frac{1}{3}$ lb.
100 Katis=1 Picul=$133\frac{1}{3}$ lb.
40 Piculs=1 Koyan=$5,333\frac{1}{3}$ lb.

Capacity: 1 Chupak=1 Quart.
1 Gantang=1 Gallon.

Currency and Exchange Rates

100 cents=1 Singapore dollar (S$).

Exchange rates (April 1974):
S$1=1 Brunei dollar;
£1 sterling=S$5.734;
U.S. $1=S$2.43.

STATISTICAL SURVEY

AREA
(square km.)

	Total	Singapore Island	Offshore Islands	Singapore City
	584.3	545.5	38.8	97.4

LAND USE
(1972—square km.)

Built-up*	Agricultural	Cultivable Waste	Forest	Marsh and Tidal Waste	Inland Water	Other
193.2	112.7	95.8	32.4	32.4	15.5	104.4

* Includes new industrial sites.

POPULATION

('000—mid-1972 estimate)

	Male	Female	Total
Chinese	823.7	810.9	1,634.6
Malays	164.4	158.8	323.2
Indians	89.3	60.3	149.6
Others	20.6	19.4	40.0
Total	1,098.0	1,049.4	2,147.4

Total Population: 2,203,500 (December 31st, 1973).

Capital: Singapore City (population 1,287,900 at July 1st, 1972).

BIRTHS AND DEATHS

	Live Births	Deaths
1967 . . .	50,560	10,523
1968 . . .	47,241	10,982
1969 . . .	44,562	10,224
1970 . . .	45,934	10,717
1971 . . .	47,088	11,329
1972 . . .	49,678	11,522

EMPLOYMENT

	1972 (March)	1972 (September)
Agriculture, Forestry, Hunting and Fishing .	2,466	2,568
Mining and Quarrying	1,867	2,055
Manufacturing	172,126	190,290
Construction	27,312	30,883
Electricity, Gas, Water and Sanitary Services .	15,689	15,378
Commerce	114,947	119,066
Transport, Storage and Communications .	48,601	51,358
Services	131,397	136,371
Total All Industries . .	514,405	547,969

Note: Data on employment have been collected under the Employment Act 1968, which covers all categories of workers, including working proprietors, self-employed workers, unpaid family workers and employees. Domestic servants, hawkers and members of the Armed Forces are excluded.

AGRICULTURE

	Area (hectares)				Production		
	1970	1971	1972		1970	1971	1972
Rubber	4,047	3,482	3,294	metric tons	2,012	1,680	1,530
Coconuts	2,631	2,610	2,600	million	11	10	10
Fruits	2,509	2,585	2,588	metric tons	4,501	4,375	4,750
Mixed Vegetables . .	1,437	1,329	1,367	,, ,,	30,480	61,730	65,810
Root Crops . . .	951	1,080	1,013	,, ,,	11,684	8,630	7,900
Tobacco . . .	364	372	243	,, ,,	490	500	317

FISHERIES

FISH LANDED AND AUCTIONED
(metric tons)

1967	1968	1969	1970	1971	1972
10,092	10,159	43,704	60,671	62,324	61,855

Note: Since 1969 with the opening of the Jurong Fish Central Market all fresh fish auctioned has been centralized and the coverage of fish auctioned is now comprehensive.

INDUSTRY

		1970	1971	1972
Rubber Smoked Sheets	metric tons	10,909	12,566	10,331
Remilled Crepe	,, ,,	96,474	110,511	92,590
Paints	kilolitres	9,377.4	10,451.4	11,574.5
Broken Granite	'ooo cu. metres	1,497.0	1,665.3	1,822.5
Bricks	'ooo pieces	94,069	103,441	117,744
Cigarettes	'ooo kg.	2,786.7	2,611.2	2,866.9
Cheroots	,, ,,	85.7	86.6	74.5
Soft Drinks	'ooo litres	86,304.3	93,330.6	110,892.0
Coconut Oil	metric tons	31,052	28,683	28,062
Vegetable Cooking Oil	,, ,,	36,762	41,458	42,494
Animal Fodder	,, ,,	324,183	365,368	368,873
Electricity	million kWh.	2,205.3	2,585.3	3,143.6
Gas	million cu. ft.	263.5	299.7	321.0

FINANCE

100 cents=1 Singapore dollar (S$).

Coins: 1, 5, 10, 20 and 50 cents; 1 dollar.

Notes: 1, 5, 10, 50, 100 and 1,000 dollars.

Exchange rates (April 1974): S$1=1 Brunei dollar; £1 sterling=S$5.734; U.S. $1=S$2.43.

S$100=£17.44=U.S. $41.15.

ORDINARY BUDGET
(S$ million—estimates for year ending March 31st, 1975)

REVENUE		EXPENDITURE	
Direct Taxes	989.2	General Services	128.4
Indirect Taxes and Taxes on Outlay	675.2	Defence and Justice	637.7
Reimbursements and Sales on Goods and		Social and Community Services	573.4
Services	317.1	Economic Services	123.0
Income from Investments and Property	164.7	Public Debt	321.4
Others	176.8	Unallocable	35.5
		Add: Transfer to Development Fund	480.0
TOTAL	2,323.0	TOTAL	2,299.4

DEVELOPMENT BUDGET
(S$ million—estimates for 1973–74)

EXPENDITURE	
Transport and Communications . .	40.6
Defence	65.3
Education	37.3
Health	10.5
Finance	27.4
Information and Social Affairs . .	11.8
Reclamation and Urban Redevelopment .	22.7
Public Works	27.4
Environment	36.2
Loans to:	
Industrial and Commercial Enterprises .	154.6
Jurong Town Corporation . .	140.2
Public Utilities Board . .	68.3
Housing and Development Board .	349.0
Sentosa Development Corporation .	57.0
Urban Renewal Authority . .	29.0
Other Heads	99.9
TOTAL	**1,177.2**

CURRENCY RESERVES ESTIMATES
(S$ million)

	MARCH 31ST 1972	DEC. 31ST 1972*
Total External Reserves of Monetary Authority (including gold tranche)†	1,843.9	2,729.3
Total External Reserves of Singapore Government and Statutory Authorities . . .	2,625.4	2,958.9

* Preliminary.

† Figure for March 1972 includes Singapore's estimated share of the foreign assets of the Board of Commissioners of Currency, Malaya and British Borneo.

BALANCE OF PAYMENTS
(S$ million—estimates)

	1971	1972†	1973*
Current Account:			
Merchandise:			
Import f.o.b.	8,090.5	8,909.3	11,901.6
Exports f.o.b.	5,075.0	5,738.9	8,430.6
Trade Balance	−3,015.5	−3,170.4	−3,471.0
Service Payments (net) . . .	845.6	799.2	900.8
Total Goods and Services (net receipts) .	−2,169.9	−2,371.2	−2,570.2
Transfers (net receipts) . . .	− 35.5	− 18.8	− 19.8
BALANCE ON CURRENT ACCOUNT . .	−2,205.4	−2,390.0	−2,590.0
Capital Movements:			
Private Long Term (net) . . .	406.5	552.2	577.1
Official Long Term (net) . . .	75.5	187.9	45.4
Net Errors and Omissions . . .	2,301.5	2,232.5	2,301.1
TOTAL CAPITAL MOVEMENTS . .	2,783.5	2,972.6	2,923.6
Net Surplus or Deficit . . .	578.1	582.6	333.6

* Preliminary.   † Revised.

EXTERNAL TRADE
(S$ million)

	1970	1971	1972	1973
Imports	7,533.8	8,664.0	9,538.0	12,562.0
Exports	4,755.8	5,371.3	6,149.4	8,914.0

PRINCIPAL COMMODITIES
(including trade with West Malaysia)
(S$ million)

	IMPORTS			EXPORTS		
	1970	1971	1972	1970	1971	1972
Food and Live Animals	950.5	984.1	1,036.6	549.6	541.9	554.1
Beverages and Tobacco	127.9	137.3	128.2	71.6	69.0	66.0
Crude Materials, inedible, excluding Fuels	858.8	781.6	822.5	1,430.3	1,190.3	1,132.5
Mineral Fuels and Lubricants	1,014.9	1,240.6	1,385.3	822.5	1,145.8	1,168.1
Animal and Vegetable Oils and Fats	126.0	197.1	148.8	140.2	208.1	150.7
Chemicals	386.9	437.1	501.7	128.9	184.6	218.8
Manufactured Goods classified chiefly by Materials	1,650.9	1,848.8	1,914.5	423.1	534.6	595.6
Machinery and Transport Equipment	1,718.4	2,209.1	2,648.4	520.9	740.5	1,220.6
Miscellaneous Manufactured Articles	538.7	644.8	727.9	247.9	343.4	497.2
Commodities and Transactions n.e.s.	160.8	183.4	224.1	420.8	413.2	545.8

PRINCIPAL TRADING PARTNERS*
(S$ million)

	IMPORTS			EXPORTS		
	1970	1971	1972	1970	1971	1972
Australia	340.5	367.7	385.9	160.0	257.2	294.8
China, People's Republic	385.5	406.7	399.1	69.4	46.6	57.4
East Malaysia	286.1	304.8	327.2	351.0	386.8	370.2
Germany, Federal Republic	253.2	339.9	368.7	136.2	113.7	171.3
Hong Kong	188.5	200.8	242.8	194.0	289.1	373.4
Japan	1,458.0	1,699.6	1,874.5	361.5	379.8	392.4
Thailand	149.4	174.4	269.3	156.8	159.6	214.4
United Kingdom	569.1	633.5	635.9	324.5	333.7	339.4
U.S.A.	814.8	1,102.3	1,339.8	527.3	634.8	949.1
West Malaysia	1,117.4	1,138.9	1,180.5	688.7	841.8	907.3

* No figures are available for trade with Indonesia.

TRANSPORT
RAILWAYS

The Malayan Railway system also serves Singapore; for combined statistics for Singapore and Malaysia *see under* Malaysia.

ROADS—VEHICLES REGISTERED

	End 1971	End 1972
Private Cars	155,956	168,991
Motor Cycles and Scooters	109,655	115,619
Motor Buses	2,681	2,936
Goods Vehicles (incl. private)	38,071	41,805
Total Vehicles on Register	699,637	732,745

SHIPPING
(Vessels of over 75 net registered tons)

	SHIPS ENTERED	SHIPS CLEARED	CARGO DISCHARGED ('ooo tons)	CARGO LOADED ('ooo tons)
1970 . .	18,422	18,269	26,439.4	15,720.4
1971 . .	19,073	18,723	28,817.6	19,269.0
1972 . .	18,624	18,628	35,651.8	21,412.4

CIVIL AIR TRAFFIC

	PASSENGERS			Mail ('ooo Kilograms)		Freight ('ooo Kilograms)	
	Arrived	Departed	In Transit	Landed	Despatched	Landed	Despatched
1969 . .	527,384	534,905	264,669	1,193	1,488	6,326	8,615
1970 . .	682,284	688,630	304,098	1,365	1,716	8,243	12,821
1971 . .	825,712	835,796	344,775	1,282	1,514	10,305	15,401
1972 . .	1,029,214	1,039,252	466,875	1,311	1,589	13,098	17,431

TOURISM
TOURIST EXPENDITURE
(S$ million)

1970	1971	1972
276	328	398*

* Preliminary.

In May 1973, there were 72 gazetted tourist hotels, having some 8,949 rooms in operation. Another 4,843 rooms are presently under construction, and will be completed between 1973 and 1975.

COMMUNICATIONS MEDIA

Radio Licences issued: (1971) 78,223; (1972) 72,924.

Radio and Television Licences issued: (1972) 204,847.

Rediffusion Subscribers (at Dec. 31st, 1972): 68,903.

DAILY NEWSPAPERS (1972)

Chinese . .	4	228,552	combined circ.	
English . .	2	140,516	,,	,,
Malay . .	1	15,906		
Tamil . .	2	5,041	,,	,,
Malayalam .	1	1,926		
TOTAL . .	10	391,941	,,	,,

EDUCATION
(End—June 1972)

	INSTITUTIONS*	STUDENTS	TEACHERS
Primary	414	354,748	10,858
Secondary:			
Academic . . .	111	144,145	5,648
Technical . . .	9	14,859	689
Commercial . . .	1	2,367	61
Technical and Vocational Institutes† . . .	10	5,841	593
Universities and Colleges .	5	15,318	1,543
TOTAL . . .	550	537,278	19,392

* A full school conducting both primary and secondary classes is treated as one primary and one secondary school.

† Including enrolment at Industrial Training Centres and the Boys' Town Trade School.

Source: Department of Statistics, Singapore.

THE CONSTITUTION

THE CABINET

The Cabinet consists of twelve Ministers headed by the Prime Minister.

THE LEGISLATURE

The Legislature consists of a Parliament of sixty-five members, presided over by a Speaker who may be elected from the members of Parliament themselves or appointed by Parliament although he may not be a member of Parliament. Members of Parliament are elected by universal suffrage.

A Constitutional Amendment Act was passed in December 1969 setting up a 21-Member Presidential Council chaired by the Chief Justice. This exists to examine legislation to see whether it contains elements which differentiate between racial or religious communities or contains provisions inconsistent with the fundamental liberties of Singapore citizens and report and advise the Government thereon.

CITIZENSHIP

The present principal qualifications for citizenship are:

1. Birth in Singapore, or
2. Descent from a father who was a Singapore citizen, or
3. By registration which would have required residence in Singapore for ten years during the twelve years preceding the application for registration as a citizen.

THE GOVERNMENT

HEAD OF THE STATE

President: Dr. Benjamin Henry Sheares.

THE CABINET

(*July* 1974)

Prime Minister: Lee Kuan Yew.

Deputy Prime Minister and Minister of Defence: Dr. Goh Keng Swee.

Minister for Science and Technology: Dr. Toh Chin Chye.

Minister for Finance: Hon Sui Sen.

Minister for Foreign Affairs: Sinnathamby Rajaratnam.

Minister for Labour: Ong Pang Boon.

Minister for Education: Dr. Lee Chiaw Meng.

Minister for Communications: Yong Nyuk Lin.

Minister for the Environment: Lim Kim San.

Minister for Law and National Development: E. W. Barker.

Minister for Culture: Jek Yeun Thong.

Minister for Social Affairs: Enche Othman bin Wok.

Minister for Health and Home Affairs: Chua Sian Chin.

DIPLOMATIC REPRESENTATION

EMBASSIES AND HIGH COMMISSIONS ACCREDITED TO SINGAPORE

(In Singapore City unless otherwise indicated)

(E) Embassy; (HC) High Commission

Australia: 201 Clemenceau Ave. (HC); *High Commissioner:* Robert Birch.

Austria: Bangkok, Thailand (E).

Belgium: 6E Asia Insurance Bldg., P.O.B. 2248 (E); *Ambassador:* Jan Hellemans.

Brazil: 267 Cantonment Rd. (E); *Ambassador:* J. de Oliveira Maia.

Bulgaria: 40C Goldhill Towers, Goldhill Ave. (E); *Chargé d'Affaires a.i.:* Bogomil Todorov.

Burma: 15 St. Martin's Drive (E); *Chargé d'Affaires a.i.:* Ohn Gyaw.

Canada: 11th Floor, International Bldg., 360 Orchard Rd. (HC); *High Commissioner:* C. R. Gallow.

Denmark: Rooms 10, 13/14 Supreme House, 10th Floor, Penang Rd. (E); *Chargé d'Affaires a.i.:* Leif Donde.

Egypt: 20C and 22C Paterson Rd. (E); *Chargé d'Affaires a.i.:* Amin Samy.

France: 5 Gallop Rd. (E); *Ambassador:* Jacques Gasseau.

Germany, Federal Republic: 6th Floor, International Bldg., 360 Orchard Rd. (E); *Ambassador:* Hans Dietrich.

Greece: 5th Floor, Chartered Bank Chambers, Battery Rd. (E); *Ambassador:* Basil Vitsaxis.

Hungary: New Delhi, India (E).

India: India House, 31 Grange Rd. (HC); *High Commissioner:* Prem Bhatia.

Indonesia: "Wisma Indonesia", 1st Floor, 435 Orchard Rd. (E); *Ambassador:* Soenarso.

Iran: Bangkok, Thailand (E).

Israel: 319A Bukit Timah Rd., "City Towers" (E); *Ambassador:* Yehoshua Almog.

Italy: Rooms 810–812, 8th Floor, Supreme House, Penang Rd. (E); *Ambassador:* Dr. Roberto De Cardona.

Japan: 16 Nassim Rd. (E); *Ambassador:* Yasuhiko Nara.

Khmer Republic: 35 Balmoral Rd. (E); *Ambassador:* Khong Roeum Lert Wongsanith.

Malaysia: Malayan Banking Chambers, 5th Floor, Fullerton Sq. (HC); *High Commissioner:* Dato ABDULLAH BIN ALI.

Nepal: Rangoon, Burma (E).

Netherlands: 10th Floor, International Bldg., 360 Orchard Rd. (E); *Ambassador:* RUDOLPH CARL PEKELHARING.

New Zealand: 13 Nassim Rd. (HC); *High Commissioner:* ROGER E. B. PEREN.

Norway: Room C4, 2nd Floor, Hongkong Bank Chambers, Collyer Quay (E); *Ambassador:* OYVIND SCOTT-HANSEN.

Pakistan: 603 Shaw House, Orchard Rd. (E); *Ambassador:* MOHAMMED SULTANUL ISLAM.

Philippines: Rooms D-F, 5th Floor, Thong Teck Bldg., 15 Scotts Rd. (E); *Ambassador:* DELFIN REUTO GARCIA.

Poland: 1st Floor, Bank of China Bldg. (E); *Ambassador:* WIKTOR KINECKI.

Romania: Jakarta, Indonesia (E).

Spain: c/o 10th Floor, Maxwell House, Maxwell Rd. (E); *Ambassador:* EL MARQUÉS DE VILLADARIAS.

Sri Lanka: c/o U.S. De Silva & Sons, 12B Collyer Quay (HC); *High Commissioner:* HALUKIRTHI OLIVER WIJEGOONARWARDENA.

Sweden: Room 43, Bank of China Bldg., Battery Rd. (E); *Ambassador:* ERIC OTTO GUNNARSSON VIRGIN.

Switzerland: Room 305, Shaw House, Orchard Rd. (E); *Chargé d'Affaires a.i.:* JAKOB ETTER.

Thailand: 370 Orchard Rd. (E); *Ambassador:* NIBBON WILAIRAT.

Trinidad and Tobago: New Delhi, India (HC).

Turkey: Bangkok, Thailand (E).

U.S.S.R.: 24 Cluny Rd. (E); *Ambassador:* BORIS VASSILYEVICH BEZRUKAVNIKOV.

United Kingdom: Phoenix Park, Tanglin Rd. (HC); *High Commissioner:* Sir SAMUEL FALLE.

U.S.A.: 30 Hill St. (E); *Ambassador:* EDWIN CRONK.

Yugoslavia: Jakarta, Indonesia (E).

Note: Singapore has established full diplomatic relations with Bangladesh, the German Democratic Republic, the Democratic Republic of Viet-Nam and the Republic of Viet-Nam.

PARLIAMENT

The Speaker: YEOH GHIM SENG, B.B.M., J.P.

A General Election was held in September 1972. The People's Action Party (P.A.P.) was returned in 57 out of the 65 constituencies and in the remaining 8 constituencies, P.A.P. candidates were returned unopposed.

POLITICAL PARTIES

The following participated in the 1972 general election:

People's Action Party: 143–145 Orchard Rd.; f. 1954; first formed the government of the State of Singapore in 1959; re-elected to power 1963, 1968 and 1972 as government of independent Republic of Singapore; Chair. Dr. TOH CHIN CHYE; Sec.-Gen. LEE KUAN YEW.

Socialist Front (*Barisan Sosialis Malaya*): 436-C Victoria St., Singapore 7; f. 1961; left-wing; formerly members of People's Action Party; seeks to abolish national service, provide free medical services for the poor, reduce taxes and relax the citizenship laws; Chair. Dr. LEE SIEW CHOH; publs. *Barisan* (Chinese), *Plebeian* (English).

Singapore Malays' National Organization (S.M.N.O.): 218E Changi Rd.; reorganized 1967; formerly the United Malays' National Organization in Singapore; seeks to improve conditions for the Malays, to promote Islam and Malay culture, to encourage democracy and racial harmony, to work against colonialism; Chair. Encik AHMAD bin HAJI TAFF.

United National Front: f. 1970; aims to abolish the Internal Security Act, release political detainees and promote a common market between Malaysia and Singapore.

Workers' Party: f. 1971; seeks a new democratic constitution, closer relations with Malaysia and the establishment of immediate diplomatic relations with the People's Republic of China; Leader J. B. JEYARETNAM.

People's Front: f. 1971; favours an independent democratic socialist republic and withdrawal of Singapore from the 5 power defence arrangements; Chair. LUI BOON POH.

JUDICIAL SYSTEM

A Supreme Court consisting of the High Court, the Court of Appeal and the Court of Criminal appeal was established by the Supreme Court of Judicature Act. The High Court exercises original criminal and civil jurisdiction in appeals from the Subordinate Courts. An appeal from the High Court lies to the Court of Criminal Appeal or the Court of Appeal which exercises appellate jurisdiction. In certain cases, a further appeal lies from the decision of the Court of Criminal Appeal or Court of Appeal, as the case may be, to the Judicial Committee of the Privy Council.

The Lower Courts consist of: Magistrates' Courts which have limited criminal jurisdiction; Criminal District Courts which have jurisdiction to try all offences for which the maximum term of imprisonment does not exceed seven years; and Civil District Courts which exercise limited civil jurisdiction.

There are also two Industrial Arbitration Courts, intended to regulate labour relations.

Trial by jury for capital offences was abolished in 1970. Prior to this, trial by jury in cases other than for capital offences had been abolished for the last ten years. Presently, the Criminal Procedure Code (Amendment) Act, 1969, enacts that in all cases where the accused is charged with an offence in respect of which punishment by death is authorized by law, the accused shall be tried by a court consisting of two Judges of the High Court, one of whom shall be the presiding Judge. The decision of the Court as to the guilt of the accused in respect of such a charge shall be arrived at unanimously.

The Government Proceedings Ordinance, 1965, enables an individual to sue the Government in tort and contract. Provision is also made for the right of the Government to sue if it has a claim against any person which would, if such claim had arisen between subject and subject, afford ground for civil proceedings.

The administration of justice in Singapore extends also to persons of limited means. There is an Ordinance to make legal aid and advice in Singapore more readily available to persons of limited means, to enable the cost of legal aid or advice to persons to be defrayed wholly or partly out of monies provided by Parliament. Provisions are also made for persons of limited means to apply for legal aid in defence of criminal cases and criminal appeals in which they are the accused.

In its administration of justice, Singapore adheres to "The Rule of Law" as defined in the United Nations Declaration of Human Rights.

Chief Justice: Mr. Justice WEE CHONG JIN.

Puisne Judges: Mr. Justice TAN AH TAH, Mr. Justioe F. A. CHUA, Mr. Justice A. V. WINSLOW, Mr. Justice T. KULASEKARAM, Mr. Justice CHOOR SINGH, Mr. Justice DENIS DE COTTA.

RELIGION

The majority of Chinese are Buddhists, Confucians or Taoists. The Malays and Pakistanis are almost all Muslims, while the Europeans and Eurasians are overwhelmingly Christian. Most of the Indian community are Hindu.

BUDDHISM

The Singapore Buddhist Sangha Organization: Headquarters: Pho Kark See, Bright Hill Drive, Thomson Rd., Singapore 20.

The Buddhist Union: 28 Jalan Senyum, Singapore 14.

The Buddhist Federation: Yan Kit Rd., Singapore.

World Fellowship of Buddhists: 387 Guilemard Rd., Singapore.

CHRISTIANITY

Anglican Church:

Diocese of Singapore: Bishop of Singapore and Dean of St. Andrew's Cathedral: The Rt. Rev. BAN IT CHIU, LL.B., Bishopsbourne, 4 Bishopsgate, Singapore 10.

Vicar of St. Andrew's Cathedral: (vacant), St. Andrew's Cathedral, Singapore 6.

Archdeacon of Singapore: The Ven. LAU TEIK OON, Church of the Good Shepherd, 2 Dundee Rd., Singapore 3.

Secretary of Synod: CHEONG HOCK HAI, P.O.B. 131, Tanglin Post Office, Singapore 10.

Roman Catholic Church—Archdiocese of Singapore: His Grace the Archbishop Mgr. MICHEL OLÇOMENDY, Archbishop's House, 31 Victoria St., Singapore. Archbishop's Secretary: Rev. S. FERNANDEZ.

Methodist Church: Bishop for Malaysia and Singapore: Dr. YAP KIM HAO, P.O.B. 483, Singapore; Comptroller YONG NGIM DJIN.

Brethren Assemblies: Bethesda Gospel Hall, 77 Bras Basah Rd., Singapore 7; f. 1864; Hon. Sec. LIM TIAN LEONG; Bethesda (Katong) Church, 17 Pennefather Rd., Singapore 15; Chair. of Elders and Deacons, Dr. B. CHEW.

Presbyterian Church: Minister Rev. E. M. WHITE, B.A., "B" Orchard Rd., Singapore; f. 1856; 327 mems.; publ. *St. Andrew's Outlook* (twice yearly).

THE PRESS

DAILIES
ENGLISH LANGUAGE

In 1974 the Government put forward a bill providing for compulsory government vetting of newspaper management. It obliges all newspaper companies to go public.

New Nation: Times House, River Valley Rd., Singapore 9; f. 1971; Proprs. New Nation Publishing Pte. Ltd.; Independent; Editor DAVID KRAAL; circ. 27,900.

Straits Times: Times House, River Valley Rd.; f. 1845; Proprs. The Straits Times Press (M) Bhd.; Man. Editor KHOO TENG SOON; circ. 121,000 (Singapore only).

CHINESE LANGUAGE

Min Pao Daily: 19B Amoy St.; Man. Dir. LAI KOK WAH; circ. 52,000.

Nanyang Siang Pau: 307 Alexandra Rd.; f. 1923; morning; Chair. LEE EU SENG (*under arrest*); Editor SHAMSUDDIN TUNG TAO CHANG; circ. 131,000 (weekdays).

Sin Chew Jit Poh: 128 Robinson Road; f. 1929; morning; Exec. Dir. AW IT HAW; Man. LIAO SUNG YANG; Editor WONG SZU; circ. 169,799 (average daily net sale 1972).

MALAY LANGUAGE
(Roman Script)

Berita Harian: Times House, River Valley Rd.; f. 1957; morning; Editor MUSTAPHA SUHAIMI; circ. 15,800.

MALAYALAM LANGUAGE

Malaysia Malayali: 12 Kinta Rd.; Man. Editor V. P. ABDULLAH; circ. 2,000.

TAMIL LANGUAGE

Tamil Malar: 430 Race Course Rd.; Editor T. SELVAGANA-PATHY; circ. 9,044.

Tamil Murasu: 139–141 Lavender St.; f. 1936; Editor G. SARANGAPANY; circ. 24,426.

Tamil Nesan: 167 Clemenceau Ave.; Editor MURUGU SUBRAMANIAN.

SUNDAY PAPERS
ENGLISH LANGUAGE

Sunday Mail: Times House, River Valley Rd.; Props. The Straits Times Press (Malaya) Bhd.; f. 1959; Editor P. J. JOSHUA (acting); circ. 17,500 (Singapore only).

Sunday Times: Times House, River Valley Rd.; Props. The Straits Times Press (Malaya) Bhd.; f. 1931; Editor DAVID TAMBYAH; circ. 135,000 (Singapore only).

CHINESE LANGUAGE

Nanyang Siang Pau: 307 Alexandra Rd.; f. 1923; Editor SZE CHUSIAN; circ. 156,000.

Sin Chew Jit Poh: 128 Robinson Rd.; f. 1929; Dir. Dato AW KOW; Man. LIAO SUNG YANG; Editor WONG SZU; circ. 78,000.

MALAY LANGUAGE

Berita Harian: Times House, Kim Seng Rd.; f. 1957; Editor SAMAD ISMAIL; circ. 13,000.

TAMIL LANGUAGE

Tamil Malar (Sunday Edition): 430 Race Course Rd.; Editor T. SELVAGANAPATHY; circ. 20,660.

Tamil Murasu (Sunday Edition): 139-141 Lavender St.; f. 1936; Editor G. SARANGAPANY; circ. 27,460.

PERIODICALS

About 300 periodicals are published in the various languages. The principal ones only are given here.

ENGLISH LANGUAGE

The Asia Magazine: International Bldg., Orchard Rd., 9; f. 1961; distributed by leading English language newspapers in Asia; Editor GEORGE V. LIU.

Eastern Trade: P.O.B. 21, Thomson Rd., Singapore 20; f. 1961; business newspaper; fortnightly; Editor Mrs. M. V. GILL.

Her World: "Times House", 390 Kim Seng Rd.; f. 1960; woman's monthly; Editor OSWALD HENRY.

Journal of the Singapore Paediatric Society: André Publications, Tanglin, P.O.B. 7, Singapore 10; twice-yearly, April and October.

Republic of Singapore Government Gazette: Singapore National Printers (Pte.) Ltd., P.O.B. 485; weekly (Friday).

Singapore Medical Journal: André Publications, Tanglin, P.O.B. 7, Singapore 10; quarterly.

Singapore Trade and Industry: Times Publishing Sdn. Bhd., 422 Thomson Rd.; Editor ILSA M. SHARP.

MALAY LANGUAGE

Medan Sastera: 745–747 North Bridge Rd., Singapore 7; f. 1964; quarterly; Editor HARUN AMINURRASHID; circ. 4,000.

PUNJABI LANGUAGE

Navjiivan National Punjabi News: 5 Albert House, Albert St., P.O.B. 2146; f. 1951; twice weekly, Wednesday and Saturday; Voice of the Sikhs in South-East Asia; Editor DEWAN SINGH RANDHAWA.

NEWS AGENCIES
FOREIGN BUREAUX

AP: 89/95 Anson Rd.; Correspondent MORT ROSENBLUM.

Agence France-Presse: 63 Robinson Rd.; Correspondent M. K. MENON.

Antara News Agency: 106A Grange Rd.; Correspondent M. ANWAR RAWY.

Central News Agency of China: 72B Robinson Rd., 2nd Floor; Correspondent YING YI CHUAN.

Czechoslovak News Agency ČETEKA: 1st Floor, M.S.A. Bldg., 77 Robinson Rd.; Correspondent Dr. MIROSLAV OPLT.

Jiji Press: 14K Asia Insurance Bldg.; Correspondent JEHEI TACHIBANA.

Kyodo News Service: c/o Reuters Ltd., 13 Peck Hay Rd.; Correspondent YOICHI YOKOBORI.

Reuters: 13 Peck Hay Rd.; S.E. Asian Man. DEREK BLACKMAN.

Tass News Agency: 17B Tomlinson Rd.; Correspondent VLADIMIR N. DUSHENKIN.

UPI: M.S.A. Bldg., First Floor, 77 Robinson Rd.; Man. B. C. ONG; Reg. Man. MAX VANZI.

PUBLISHERS

ENGLISH LANGUAGE

André Publications: Tanglin, P.O.B. 7, Singapore 10; publishes various guides to Asian cities.

Asia Pacific Press Pte. Ltd.: Liat Towers, 514 Orchard Rd., Singapore 9; f. 1969; fiction, religion, university textbooks; Chair. JOHN EDE.

Chopmen Enterprises: 47 The Arcade, Singapore 1; f. 1966; social science, history, textbooks, reference, fiction; Man. Dir. N. T. S. CHOPRA.

Eastern Universities Press Sdn. Bhd.: 9-D D'Almeida St., (P.O.B. 1742); 1; f. 1958; biography, history, textbooks; Man. RAYMOND YUEN.

Federal Publications Sdn. Bhd.: Times House, River Valley Rd., Singapore 9; educational books; Gen. Man. KOH HOCK SENG.

Jay-Birch & Co. Ltd.: 22B Penang Lane, P.O.B. 66; publishers to H.M. Forces.

University Education Press: Newton, P.O.B. 96, Singapore 11; Office: 37 Somerset Rd., 6th Floor B, Summer Centre, 9; Man. ANDREW S. K. LEE; publishers and publishers' representatives; books on E. and S.E. Asia, humanities and social sciences; publ. *Journal of Southeast Asian Social Science* (twice a year).

MALAY LANGUAGE

Al-Ahmadiah Press: 101 Jalan Sultan; religious books and periodicals; Propr. A. ARIFF.

H.M. Ali Press: P.O.B. 1484, Singapore; books and magazines.

Malaysia Press Ltd. (formerly Royal Press): 745-747 North Bridge Rd., Singapore 7; f. 1962; printers and publishers of Malay school textbooks; Dir. and Man. ABU TALIB ALLY.

Pustaka Melayu: 745–747 North Bridge Rd., Singapore 7; f. 1956; Malay educational books; Chief Editor HARUN AMINURRASHID.

CHINESE LANGUAGE

Commercial Press Ltd., The: incorporated in China; Singapore branch: 309 North Bridge Road; f. 1897; publishers, stationers and booksellers; school text-

books and magazines; Attorney and Manager DAVID C. N. HSU, F.B.A.A.

Hong Seng Press: 520 North Bridge Rd.; Man. P. Y. LOOI.

Nanyang Book Co. Ltd.: 20 North Bridge Rd.; f. 1935; school textbooks; publications on South-East Asia; Journal of South Seas Society; Dir. TAN YEOK SEONG.

INDIAN LANGUAGE

India Publishing House: 458 Race Course Rd., Singapore 8.

RADIO AND TELEVISION

RADIO

Radio Singapore: Ministry of Culture, P.O.B. 1902; f. 1959; broadcasts in English, Chinese (Mandarin and six dialects), Malay and Tamil, over four networks; each language channel broadcasts over one hundred hours weekly; Dir. KWA SOON CHUAN.

Rediffusion (Singapore) Private Ltd.: P.O.B. 608; subsidiary of Rediffusion International Ltd., London; f. 1949; commercial wired broadcasting service, originating two programmes in numerous Chinese dialects and English; over 75,000 subscribers; Man. Dir. J. SNOWDEN.

In 1974 there were 290,000 radio sets and 218,000 television sets.

Far East Broadcasting Co.: c/o Far East Broadcasting Associates, 130-S Sophia Rd., Singapore 9; Singapore Dir. LAUW KIM GUAN.

TELEVISION

Television Singapore: Ministry of Culture, P.O.B. 1902, Singapore; one station with two separate channels started operations in 1963; weekly average of 109 hours per channel; education service of 53 hours weekly; services in Malay, Chinese, Tamil and English; Dir. HSU TSE-KWANG.

FINANCE

(cap.=capital; p.u.=paid up; dep.=deposits; m.=million; S$=Singapore dollars; brs.=branches.)

BANKING

The Singapore monetary system is co-ordinated by the Ministry of Finance and embraces such bodies as the Currency Board of Singapore (*see* below), Accountant-General's Banking Department, Commissioner for Banking, Commissioner for Finance Companies, Registrar of Loans, Registrar of Companies, Department of Overseas Investments and Exchange Control.

Board of Commissioners of Currency, Singapore: Empress Place, Singapore 6; currency issuing authority for the Republic of Singapore; Chair. The Minister of Finance, HON SUI SEN.

MAJOR COMMERCIAL BANKS

Chung Khiaw Bank Ltd.: 59 Robinson Rd.; f. 1950; became a subsidiary of the *United Overseas Bank* (q.v.) in 1971; cap. p.u. S$10m.; dep. S$494.3m. (Dec. 1971); Vice-Chair./Man. Dir. WEE CHO YAW; 30 brs.

Four Seas Communications Bank Ltd: 57 Chulia St., 1; incorporated in Singapore 1906; auth. cap. S$50m.; cap. p.u. S$20m.; dep. S$163.4m. (Dec. 1972); Chair./Man. Dir. TAN SIAK KEW, P.J.G.; Deputy Chair./Gen. Man. LEE HIOK SIANG.

Industrial and Commercial Bank Ltd., The: ICB Bldg., 2 Shenton Way; f. 1954; cap. p.u. S$6m.; res. S$4.2m. (Dec. 1972); Chair. TAN KIM CHEONG; Man. Dir. Y. K. HWANG; Exec. Dir. Dr. TAN POH LIN; Gen. Man. C. H. HSU.

Lee Wah Bank Ltd.: 63 Robinson Rd., Singapore 1; f. 1920; cap. p.u. S$7.7m.; dep. S$163m. (June 1973); Man. Dir. RICHARD K. M. EU; Gen. Man. W. F. CHEN.

Oversea-Chinese Banking Corporation Ltd.: Head Office Bldg., Upper Pickering St.; f. 1932; auth. cap. S$100m.; cap. p.u. S$60m.; group assets S$1,614m. (Dec. 1972); Chair. TAN SRI TAN TUAN; Dir. and Gen. Man. LIN JO YAN; 29 overseas brs.; 42 brs. in Singapore, Malaysia and overseas.

Overseas Union Bank Ltd.: Meyer Chambers, Raffles Place; f. 1949; auth. cap. S$50m.; cap. p.u. S$20m.; dep. S$594.2m. (Dec. 1971); Chair. and Man. Dir. LIEN YING CHOW; 40 brs.

United Overseas Bank Ltd.: 175–179 Cecil St.; f. 1935; cap. p.u. S$25m.; dep. S$487.6m. (Dec. 1971); Chair. WEE KHENG CHIANG; Vice-Chair./Man. Dir. WEE CHO YAW; 22 brs. in Singapore and 2 overseas.

DEVELOPMENT BANK

Development Bank of Singapore Ltd., The: DBS Bldg., Shenton Way, Singapore 1; f. September 1968; functions: providing finance to manufacturing, processing, service and other industries in the form of term loans, equity participation and guarantees; hire-purchase financing and leasing; providing a wide range of merchant banking facilities including underwriting share, debenture and bond issues, syndicating loans, providing advice on corporate structure and financial planning; providing a complete commercial banking service to both corporate and individual clients; cap. S$100m.; dep. S$153m. (Dec. 1971); Pres. HOWE YOON CHONG; publ. *Annual Report*.

FOREIGN BANKS

Algemene Bank Nederland N.V. (*General Bank of the Netherlands*): 2 Cecil St.; Man. W. A. J. VAN OENE.

Banca Commerciale Italiana: Shenton Way, Shing Kwan House, 1; f. 1971.

Bangkok Bank Ltd.: 55 New Bridge Rd.; Vice-Pres./Branch Man. ADISORN TANTIMEDH.

Bank of America N.T. & S.A.: 31 Raffles Place; Man. D. F. STIEBER.

Bank of Canton Ltd.: 18 Chulia St.; Man. C. P. HUO.

Bank of East Asia Ltd.: 24-25 South Canal Rd.; Man. KAN YUET FAI.

Bank of India: 132-136 Robinson Rd.; Man. V. M. NADKARNI.

Bank of Tokyo Ltd.: 6/10 Phillip St.; Man. K. HAYASHI.

Banque de l'Indochine: P.O.B. 246, Afro-Asia Bldg., 63 Robinson Rd., Singapore 1; f. 1905; Man. R. PH. MARTIN.

Chartered Bank, The: 28-30 Battery Rd.; Man. T. M. ATTWOOD, C.B.E.; 20 brs.

Chase Manhattan Bank, N.A.: 4 Shenton Way, 541 Orchard Rd., 505 Yung An Rd., Jurong; Vice-Pres. and Gen. Man. ROBERT GJERLOW.

Dresdner Bank AG: 138 Robinson Rd.; Man. JUNG JOHANN.

First National Bank of Chicago: 49 Robinson Rd., 1; Vice Pres. J. Y. ROBERTSON.

First National City Bank: UIC Bldg., Shenton Way, P.O.B. 444; also at Yen San Bldg., Orchard Rd.; 189 Block 1, Corporation Drive, Jurong Town, and 5th Floor, UIC Bldg., Shenton Way; Vice-Pres. WONG NANG JANG, JOHN NEWBOLD; Man. CHIA CHEE YOONG.

Hongkong and Shanghai Banking Corporation: 21 Collyer Quay; Man. for Singapore and West Malaysia S. F. T. B. LEVER; 7 brs.

Indian Bank: 4 D'Almeida St.; Agent R. M. MUTHIAH.

Indian Overseas Bank: 1 and 3 Collyer Quay; Man. R. RAMACHANDRAN.

Malayan Banking Bhd.: Malayan Bank Chambers, Fullerton Square, 1; Man. LIM TECK CHONG.

Mercantile Bank Ltd.: 21 Raffles Place; Man. M. P. LANGLEY.

Mitsui Bank: 6 Robinson Rd.; Man. T. ASANUMA.

Republic National Bank of Dallas: Head Office: Dallas, Texas; 2 Shenton Way.

United Commercial Bank Ltd.: 2 D'Almeida St.; Man. R. A. NARAYANAN.

United Malayan Banking Corporation Bhd.: 66-68 South Bridge Rd.; Man. KERMIN TSANG.

STOCK EXCHANGE

Stock Exchange of Singapore: 601 Clifford Centre, Raffles Place, Singapore 1; f. 1936; 69 mems.; Chair. NG SOO PENG; Gen. Mans. LIM CHOO PENG, LIM HUA MIN; publs. *Singapore Stock Exchange Journal*, etc.

INSURANCE

Life Business Only:

Asia Life Assurance Society Ltd.: Asia Insurance Bldg., Finlayson Green, P.O.B. 76, Singapore 1; f. 1948; Man. Dir. NG AIK HUAN.

First Life Insurance Co. (Pte) Ltd., The: First Life Bldg., 96-98 Robinson Rd., Singapore 1.

Public Life Assurance Co. Ltd.: 59 Robinson Rd., Singapore 1; f. 1954; Man. FUNG LOK NAM.

General Business Only:

Asia Insurance Co. Ltd.: Asia Insurance Bldg., Finlayson Green, P.O.B. 76, Singapore 1; f. 1923; Man. Dir. NG AIK HUAN.

Industrial and Commercial Insurance Co. Ltd., The: Industrial and Commercial Bank Bldg., 2 Shenton Way, Singapore 1; f. 1958; Man. Dir. Y. K. HWANG.

Insurance Corporation of Singapore Ltd.: Podium 416, DBS Bldg., 6 Shenton Way, Singapore 1; f. 1969; Gen. Man. CHEW LOY KIAT.

Malayan Motor and General Underwriters (Pte.) Ltd.: 3rd Floor, M & G Centre, 154-170 Clemenceau Ave., Singapore 9; f. 1954; Gen. Man. D. A. KEIGHLEY.

Nanyang Insurance Co. Ltd.: 25-26 Circular Rd., Singapore 1; f. 1956; Man. LIM SI HUI.

Overseas Union Insurance Ltd.: 43-47 New Bridge Rd., Singapore 1; f. 1956; Dir. and Gen. Man. MAURICE C. LEE.

People's Insurance Co. of Malaya Ltd.: 66-68 Cecil St., Singapore 1; f. 1957; Man. CHEW CHENG HOI.

Public Insurance Co. Ltd.: 59 Robinson Rd., Singapore 1; f. 1950; Man. FUNG LOK NAM.

Life and General Business:

Great Eastern Life Assurance Co. Ltd.: Great Eastern Life Bldg., 12-16 Cecil St., Singapore 1; f. 1908; Dir. and Gen. Man. N. N. HANDA.

Singapore International Insurance Brokers (Pte.) Ltd.: 10th Floor, Singapore Airlines Bldg., 77 Robinson Rd., Singapore 1; f. 1969; Dir. and Gen. Man. TAN CHENG KAI; Man. Marine Dept. V. RAJARAM.

Overseas Assurance Corporation Ltd.: 5 Malacca St., Singapore 1; f. 1920; Gen. Man. TAN HOAY GIE.

General, Marine and Aviation Business:

Pacific and Orient Underwriters (Pte.) Ltd.: P and O Bldg., Corner Market and Cecil Sts., Singapore 1; f. 1965; Dir. RUDOLPH MENDEZ.

In addition, many foreign insurance companies have offices in Singapore.

TRADE AND INDUSTRY

CHAMBERS OF COMMERCE

Malay Chamber of Commerce, The: No. 101 Jalan Sultan, Singapore 7; Chair. Inche GHAZALI CAFFOOR; Vice-Chair. Y. M. RAJA MOHD. YUSOF; Hon. Treas. Inche MUSA ABDUL RAHMAN; Hon. Sec. Inche ALWEE ALKAFF.

Singapore Chinese Chamber of Commerce: 47 Hill St.; Sec. C. M. WONG.

Singapore Indian Chamber of Commerce: 55-A Robinson Rd., P.O.B. 1038, Singapore 1; f. 1937; 454 mems.; Pres. G. RAMACHANDRAN; Sec. S. N. DORAI; Hon. Treas. MOEZ NOMANBHOY.

Singapore International Chamber of Commerce: Denmark House, Raffles Quay; f. 1837; Chair. R. E. L. WINGATE, M.B.E.; Exec. Dir./Sec. T. EAMES HUGHES, C.B.E., B.A., HON. LL.D.; publs. *Economic Bulletin* (monthly), Annual and other Reports.

GOVERNMENT DEVELOPMENT ORGANIZATIONS

Economic Development Board: Second Floor, Fullerton Bldg., P.O.B. 2692; f. 1961; statutory organization planning and implementing Government's industrialization programme; Chair. CHAN CHIN BOCK; Dir. P. Y. HWANG.

Housing and Development Board: National Development Bldg., Maxwell Rd., P.O.B. 702, Singapore 2; f. 1960; Chair. LEE HEE SENG.

Intraco Ltd.: 2nd Floor, Industrial Commercial Bank Bldg., 2 Shenton Way, Singapore 1; f. Nov. 1968; an international trading organization out to develop export markets for domestic manufactures and produce on a widely diversified world basis; Chair. SIM KEE BOON.

INDUSTRIAL AND TRADE ASSOCIATIONS

Malayan Pineapple Industry Board: Malayan Bank Chambers, Battery Rd., Singapore 1 and 5th Mile, Jalan Scudai, Jahore Bahru; f. 1957; controls pineapple cultivation, canning, and marketing; Chair. Dato AZIZ bin ISMAIL (acting).

Rubber Association of Singapore: Rooms 604 and 606, 6th Floor, Chinese Chamber of Commerce Bldg., 47 Hill St., 6; incorporated Oct. 1967; to support, develop and maintain the rubber industry in general, and to conduct a market in Singapore for the sale and purchase of rubber under the arrangements and regulations formulated by the Corporation; Chair. TAN ENG JOO; Exec. Sec. GNOH CHONG HOCK.

Singapore Association of Shipbuilders and Repairers: c/o Keppel Shipyard Pte. Ltd., P.O.B. 2169, Singapore; Pres. CHUA CHOR TECK.

Singapore Manufacturers' Association: Colombo Court Bldg., Rooms 213–216, 2nd Floor, North Bridge Rd., Singapore 6; f. 1932; Chair. ONG LENG CHUAN; Deputy Chair. LIM HONG KEAT, PHUA KOK TEE; publ. *S.M.A. Directory* (annual).

EMPLOYERS' ORGANIZATIONS

The principal ones are:

The Singapore Employers' Federation: 23A Amber Mansions, Orchard Rd.; f. 1948; Pres. E. G. WALLER; Exec. Dir. E. R. BAUM.

Singapore Importers' and Exporters' Association: 76c Robinson Rd.; f. 1947; 150 mems.; Chair. TAY THIAN SOO; Sec. ALBERT TAN.

Singapore Maritime Employers' Federation: P.O.B. 247; f. 1955; Chair. Capt. M. S. WRIGHT.

Singapore Shipping Association: 76c Robinson Rd.; f. 1953; 28 mems.; Chair. TAY BENG CHUAN; Sec. LAU HAN CHEONG.

TRADE UNIONS

Singapore National Trades Union Congress (S.N.T.U.C.): Trade Union House, Shenton Way, Singapore; Pres. PHEY YEW KOK; Sec.-Gen. C. V. DEVAN NAIR.

In September 1972 there were 150 registered employees' and employers' unions of which 98 were employees' trade unions (total membership 150,000), half of which are affiliated to the SNTUC.

CO-OPERATIVES

Singapore has 106 co-operative societies, made up of 42 Thrift and Loan Societies, 8 Employees' Credit Societies, 22 Thrift and Investment Societies, 13 Consumers' Societies, 6 Marketing Societies, 4 Rural Credit Societies, 2 Housing Societies, 2 Co-operative Banks, 1 Co-operative Union and 6 Miscellaneous Societies. These societies have a combined membership of 40,480 with S$19,420,903 as their working capital and S$910,156 as Reserve Fund.

TRANSPORT AND TOURISM

Singapore owes much of its wealth to its situation as a natural centre for sea and air routes.

RAILWAYS

The Malayan Railway system, which is owned by the Government of the Federation of Malaysia, also serves Singapore. There are sixteen miles of metre-gauge track and four railway stations in Singapore. A 12-mile link between the Jurong industrial estate and the Malayan Railway was opened in 1965.

ROADS

(At December 31st, 1972)

	MILES
Major Arterial Roads	152
Collector Roads	70
Local Improved Roads	761
Local Unimproved Roads . . .	303
TOTAL	1,286

Major arterial roads: rural highways and expressways entering the city area. principal road network for through traffic, and roads linking principal areas of traffic generation.

Collector roads: distributor and collector roads serving traffic between major arterial roads and local streets, and also roads used mainly for traffic movements between adjacent residential, commercial and industrial areas.

Local roads: used primarily for access to residential, commercial and industrial areas.

All roads are maintained by the Public Works Department, 10th Floor, National Development Bldg., Maxwell Rd., Singapore 2.

SHIPPING

Port of Singapore Authority: P.O.B. 300; Chair./Gen. Man. HOWE YOON CHONG; Dir. Operations and Dir. Management Services CHUNG KEK CHOO; Dir. Finance BILLIE CHENG SHAO-CHI; Dir. General Services LOH HENG KEE; Dir. Eng. Services A. VIJIARATNAM; Sec. (Admin.) GOON KOK LOON.

Container port facilities comprise 914 metres of marginal wharves (13.8 metres LWOST) for container vessels, the first 610 metres of which became operational in December 1972, and a feeder service berth of 213 metres (10.8 metres LWOST) completed in October 1970.

MAJOR SHIPPING LINES

Neptune Orient Lines Ltd.: ICB Bldg., 2 Shenton Way, Singapore 1; f. 30 Dec. 1968; operate liner services on the Far East Freight Conference and Straits/Australia routes; operate tankers and dry cargo vessels on charter; own 22 ships (Nov. 1973) with 2 under construction; total tonnage (including 2 ships under construction) 633,169 d.w.t.; Chair. M. WONG PAKSHONG; Man. Dirs. ERIC KHOO CHENG LOCK, GOH CHOK TONG.

Austasia Line Pte. Ltd.: 1st Floor, 62 Robinson Rd., (P.O.B. 1946); 3 vessels; passenger/cargo services to Australasia and the Far East; Man. N. W. HORNBY.

Chip Hwa Shipping & Trading Co. Pte. Ltd.: 45 Telok Ayer St.; tramp service; Man. Dir. KIAT BIN LAU.

Guan Guan Shipping (Pte.) Ltd.: 23 Telok Ayer St., Singapore 1; shipowners and agents.

Heap Eng Moh Steamship Company Pte. Ltd.: 1 Finlayson Green; weekly cargo and passenger services to Sarawak; 2 motor vessels.

Hua Siang Steamship Co. Ltd.: 16 Winchester House (1st Floor), Collyer Quay; services to Sarawak—Malaysia, Phnom Penh (Khmer Republic); 3 cargo vessels.

Kie Hock Shipping (1971) Pte. Ltd.: 48 Cecil St., Singapore 1; cargo services throughout Indonesia, Malaysia, Far East, Middle East and East Africa; 5 cargo vessels; Man. Dir. TAY HOCK GWAN.

Pacific International Lines Pte.: Phoenix Bldg., Palmer Rd.; coastal services to Malaysia and Thailand; 13 cargo and passenger vessels; Chair. R. E. L. WINGATE.

Straits Steamship Co. Ltd.: P.O.B. 596, Phoenix Bldg.; services to Thailand, Brunei, East and West Malaysia; 24 vessels; Chair. R. E. L. WINGATE; Sec. T. S. ONG, B.COMM. (MELB.), A.A.S.A.

CIVIL AVIATION

Singapore Airlines Ltd. (SIA): SIA Bldg., 77 Robinson Rd., Singapore; f. Jan. 1972; became operational Oct. 1972; services to London via Bangkok, Colombo, Bombay, Bahrain, Athens, Rome, Zurich, Amsterdam and Frankfurt; to Tokyo and Osaka via Kuala Lumpur, Saigon, Taipei, Hong Kong and Bangkok; to Sydney via Jakarta; to Brunei, Manila, Madras, Medan, Perth and Melbourne direct from Singapore; fleet of nine Boeing 707s, five 737s, two 747s (on order one 747); Chair. J. Y. M. PILLAY; Man. Dir. LIM CHIN BENG; Deputy Man. Dir. LYE KHAY FONG.

Singapore is also served by the following foreign airlines: Aeroflot, Air Cambodge, Air Ceylon, Air India, Alitalia, Air New Zealand, Air Vietnam, Bouraq Indonesia, British Airways, Cathay Pacific Airways, China Air Lines, Czechoslovakian Airlines, Garuda Indonesian Airways, JAL, KLM, Lufthansa, Malaysia Airlines System, PIA, Qantas, Sabena, SAS, Swissair, Thai International, UTA.

TOURISM

Singapore Tourist Promotion Board: Tudor Court, Tanglin Rd.; f. 1964; Chair. RUNME SHAW; Dir. LAM PENG LOON; publs. *Singapore Travel News* (monthly in English and Japanese), *Singapore Weekly Guide* (English).

OVERSEAS OFFICES

Singapore Government Tourist Information Office:

Australia:
8th Floor, Goldfields House, 1 Alfred St., Sydney Cove, Sydney 2000, N.S.W.

Federal Republic of Germany:
5 Friedenstrasse, Frankfurt/Main 6.

Japan:
Room 2163, Imperial Hotel, East Bldg., 1-1-1 Uchisaiwai-cho, Chiyoda-ku, Tokyo 100.

United Kingdom:
143/147 Regent St., London, W1R 7LB.

U.S.A.:
251 Post St., San Francisco, California 94108.

CULTURAL ORGANIZATIONS

The Singapore Arts Council: c/o National Theatre, Clemenceau Ave., Singapore 9; aims to promote cultural activities and the integration of the Malay, Chinese, Tamil and English cultures; to maintain and improve standards in all forms of art and to serve as co-ordinating body for all cultural societies and associations in the Republic; Pres. LEE KHOON CHOY; Hon. Sec. M. LOGANATHAN.

National Theatre Trust: Clemenceau Ave., Singapore 9; f. 1960; responsible for the management of the National Theatre and the encouragement and development of culture in the Republic; Chair. KWA SOON CHUAN. The Trust established a **National Theatre Company** in 1968.

People's Association: Kallang, Singapore 14; a statutory corporation set up in 1960 for the organization of leisure, the promotion of youth activities and group participation in social, cultural, educational, vocational and athletic activities; operates a network of 181 community centres.

UNIVERSITIES

University of Singapore: Singapore 10; 446 teachers, 5,353 students.

Nanyang University: Singapore 22; 160 teachers, 2,596 students.

SOMALIA

INTRODUCTORY SURVEY

Location, Climate, Language, Religion, Flag, Capital

The Somali Democratic Republic lies on the east coast of Africa, with Ethiopia to the north-west and Kenya to the west. There is a short frontier with the French Territory of the Afars and the Issas (formerly French Somaliland) by the Gulf of Aden. The climate is dry and hot with a mean temperature of 80°F (20°C) rising to 108°F (42°C) inland. The national language and sole official written language is Somali. English, Italian and Arabic are also widely spoken. The population is mainly Muslim but there is a small Christian community, mostly Roman Catholic. The national flag (proportions 3 by 2) is pale blue, with a large five-pointed white star in the centre. The capital is Mogadishu.

Recent History

After the defeat of the Italian forces in 1941, the Somali territories now forming the Republic were placed under British military administration. The Somaliland Protectorate reverted to British Colonial Office rule in 1948 and the former Italian Somaliland was placed under United Nations trusteeship with Italy as the administering authority in 1950. In British Somaliland the protectorate was ended on June 26th, 1960, after which the two territories united to form the independent Republic of Somalia in July 1960. The frontier dispute between Britain and Somalia over the Kenya Northern Frontier District resulted in the breaking off of diplomatic relations by Somalia in March 1963. A further dispute over frontiers with Ethiopia led to fighting in 1964. Somalia resumed diplomatic relations with Kenya and the United Kingdom in January 1968, although relations with Ethiopia have deteriorated and the dispute over the Ogaden district flared up again in 1973. Somalia has pledged support for the Eritrean Liberation Front (ELF) and this has led to further bitterness in relations with Ethiopia. In October 1969, the President of the Republic, Abdi Rashid Ali Shermarke, was assassinated and the police and army seized power. The 1960 constitution was suspended and a new government was formed by a Supreme Revolutionary Council (S.R.C.). On the first anniversary of the revolution in October 1970 the Head of State, General Mohamed Siad Barre, declared Somalia a "socialist state". The S.R.C. has launched a campaign against tribalism. Somalia has become more aligned with the eastern block, though the détente with Kenya has continued.

Government

Government is by the Supreme Revolutionary Council, all former army officers, headed by the President, and a Cabinet of 14 Secretaries of State. There are 15 regions and 78 districts.

Defence

The armed forces total 17,300 men, of whom the army has 15,000, the navy 300 and the air force 2,000. These are supplemented by 6,000 police, 3,000 people's militia and 500 para-military border guards. The armed forces are equipped by the U.S.S.R.

Economic Affairs

The economy is mainly pastoral and 70 per cent of the country's export earnings come from livestock and livestock products. Seventy-five per cent of the inhabitants are nomadic, dependent on their flocks of sheep, goats and camels. Settled agriculture, which is limited to the irrigable river valleys, is now being developed. There has been a gradual increase in the cultivable areas along the Shebélle and Juba rivers, as well as in dry areas. There are two large state farms, financed by the U.S.S.R. Cash crops are grown where rainfall permits, and where irrigation is possible. The economy has been supported by aid from several countries including the U.S.S.R., the People's Republic of China, Bulgaria and the Federal Republic of Germany. Under the S.R.C.'s policy of "scientific socialism" the centrally controlled state farm is the main basis of agricultural progress. Nationalization of foreign banks, oil companies, education and the trade sector in the 1971–73 Development Programme and the balancing of the budget in 1971 were positive steps towards the self-sufficiency aimed for in the new 1974–78 National Development Plan. The Famde dam project is due for completion with Soviet aid by 1975.

Transport and Communications

There are no railways, and roads, though generally poor, provide the principal means of transport. There is an extensive road development programme, with Chinese and World Bank aid, designed to link north and south and all the main towns and villages. Nomads rely on pack transport. The ports of Mogadishu and Kismayu are connected by regular services with ports of Eastern Africa and Italy. There are eight airfields.

Social Welfare

There is no state system of social insurance but plans are under way for improving social welfare facilities. Medical treatment is free at Government hospitals and dispensaries.

Education

Elementary education and some intermediate education are free for all children able to secure places in Government schools. The illiteracy rate is high (90 per cent), partly because there was until very recently no generally accepted orthography for the Somali language. Some 1,500 students are studying abroad and there is a university institute in Mogadishu, a teachers' training college and several technical colleges. Numerous new schools have been established and a universal syllabus incorporating the Somali language will be in force by 1974/75. A Somali Language Commission was formed in 1973 to train teachers and civil servants in the new Somali script.

Tourism

Tourism in Somalia is undeveloped.

Visas are required by nationals of all countries.

Sport

Football is the most popular game. Other sports are basketball, volleyball, boxing, shooting and swimming.

Public Holidays

1974: October 18th (Id ul Fitr), October 24th (UN Day), December 26th (Id ul Adha).

1975: January 24th (Ashoura), March 26th (Mouloud), June 26th (Independence Day), July 1st (Foundation of the Republic).

Muslim religious holidays dependent on the lunar calendar may differ slightly from the dates given.

Weights and Measures

The metric system is in force in six provinces and the imperial system in the two northern provinces.

Currency and Exchange Rates

100 centesimi = 1 Somali shilling.

Exchange rates (April 1974):
£1 sterling = 14.717 Somali shillings;
U.S. $1 = 6.233 Somali shillings.

STATISTICAL SURVEY

Area: 246,201 square miles (637,657 square kilometres).

Population: 2,941,000 (July 1st, 1972); Mogadishu (1966) 172,000; Hargeisa (1966) 60,000; Kismayu (1966) 60,000; Merca (1965) 56,000; Berbera (1966) 50,000; Giamama (1964) 22,000. 1973 est.: Mogadishu 350,000.

Births and Deaths: Average annual birth rate 45.9 per 1,000; death rate 24.0 per 1,000 (UN estimates for 1965–70).

Employment (1970): Total economically active population 1,085,000, including 893,000 in agriculture (ILO and FAO estimates).

AGRICULTURE
PRINCIPAL CROPS
(FAO estimates, metric tons)

	1968	1969	1970	1971
Maize	42,000	40,000	35,000	35,000
Millet and Sorghum . . .	67,000	63,000	50,000	50,000
Sugar Cane*	277,000†	393,000†	450,000	450,000
Sweet Potatoes and Yams .	2,000	3,000	3,000	n.a.
Cassava (Manioc) . . .	23,000	23,000	25,000	26,000
Dry Beans	2,000	2,000	2,000	2,000
Citrus Fruit	4,000	4,000	4,000	4,000
Bananas	140,000†	150,000	150,000	124,000†
Groundnuts (in shell) . .	2,000	2,000	2,000	2,000
Cottonseed	2,000	2,000	2,000	2,000
Cotton (Lint)	1,000	1,000	1,000	1,000
Sesame Seed	6,000	6,000	6,000	6,000
Tobacco	100	100	100	100

* Crop year ending in year stated.   † Official estimate.

Source: FAO, *Production Yearbook 1971.*

LIVESTOCK
('000—FAO estimates)

	1968–69	1969–70	1970–71
Cattle . .	2,800*	2,800*	2,850
Sheep . .	3,900	3,900	3,950
Goats . .	4,800	4,900	5,000
Pigs† . .	6	7	7
Asses . .	24	23	22
Mules . .	20	20	21
Camels . .	3,000	3,000	3,000*
Chickens . .	1,900	2,000	2,100

* Official estimate.
† In former Italian Somaliland only.

Source: FAO, *Production Yearbook 1971.*

Forestry (1967–70): 560,000 cubic metres of roundwood removed each year.

Sea Fishing (1968–71): Total catch 5,000 metric tons each year (FAO estimate).

LIVESTOCK PRODUCTS
(FAO estimates, metric tons)

	1968	1969	1970
Cows' Milk . .	88,000	89,000	91,000
Goats' Milk . .	65,000	64,000	63,000
Beef and Veal . .	15,000	15,000	15,000
Mutton and Lamb* .	15,000	15,000	15,000
Edible Offal . .	11,000	11,000	11,000
Other Meat . .	25,000	25,000	25,000
Hen Eggs . .	1,400	1,500	1,600
Cattle Hides . .	2,420	2,420	2,500
Sheep Skins . .	1,980	1,875	2,175
Goat Skins . .	4,450	4,538	4,625

1971: Cows' milk 92,000; goats' milk 63,000; hen eggs 1,700.

Dairy Produce (official estimates, 1970): Butter 45 metric tons; Cheese 2 metric tons.

* Including goats' meat.

Sources: FAO, *Production Yearbook 1971;* United Nations, *The Growth of World Industry.*

INDUSTRY

RAW SUGAR
(metric tons)

1967	.	.	32,000
1968	.	.	36,000
1969	.	.	51,000
1970	.	.	50,000

ELECTRIC ENERGY
(million kWh.)

1967	.	.	19.0
1968	.	.	22.0
1969	.	.	26.0
1970	.	.	20.2

Note: Figures refer to production for public use in Mogadishu, Merca, Giohar and Hargeisa.

OTHER PRODUCTS, 1970

Tinned Meat . . .	metric tons	1,973
Condensed Milk and Cream .	metric tons	227
Ethyl Alcohol . . .	hectolitres	41,000
Soft Drinks . . .	hectolitres	3,000
Leather Footwear . .	pairs	27,000
Soap . . .	metric tons	197
Concrete Products . .	cubic metres	14,000

Source: United Nations, *The Growth of World Industry.*

In 1969 there were 127 manufacturing establishments with five or more persons engaged. Their combined staff was 4,300 and the gross output for the year was 108,800,000 Somali shillings.

FINANCE

100 centesimi = 1 Somali shilling.

Coins: 1, 5, 10 and 50 centesimi; 1 shilling.

Notes: 5, 10, 20 and 100 shillings.

Exchange rates (April 1974): £1 sterling = 14.717 Somali shillings; U.S. $1 = 6.233 Somali shillings.

100 Somali shillings = £6.795 = $16.04.

BUDGET
('000 Somali Shillings)

EXPENDITURE	1970	1971	1972
Defence	80,153	81,253	92,000
Interior	54,435	6,869*	7,268*
Finance	18,450	19,409	17,181
Public Works . .	94,499	18,114	17,186
Health and Labour . .	27,939	23,551	21,694
Education . . .	23,787	20,970	20,216
TOTAL (including others) .	409,495	407,664	507,000†

* Does not include police; in 1971 43,750,000 shillings were apportioned to police expenditure, in 1972 42,494,100 shillings.

† Includes 163,278,000 shillings for development programmes.

1973 Budget (million shillings): Estimated revenue and other receipts 774, of which Ordinary Revenue 457; Estimated expenditure 774, of which Ordinary expenditure 396.1, Local Councils 52 and Development Programme 325.

THREE-YEAR PLAN 1971–73

Total outlay (million shillings): 999.9; transport and communications 353.1; water resources 119.5; agriculture 107.7; industry 87.8; health 71.2; livestock 59.4; education 48.6; irrigation 38.9; electricity and power 23.6; mining 17.5; forestry 14.3; tourism 13.5; housing 11.6; other 33.2.

Total finance (million shillings): internal sources 201.6; foreign sources 798.3.

The Government's four-year plan 1974–78 gives increased attention to agricultural development.

Currency in Circulation (December 31st, 1972): 221.2 million Somali shillings.

BALANCE OF PAYMENTS
(million Somali Shillings)

	1968	1969	1970	1971
Current Account:				
Trade Balance	−115	−125	−98	−127
Travel	20	2	−7	−16
Central Government (n.e.s.)	1	9	5	23
Other Services	—	7	−34	−11
Private Transfers	4	10	6	15
Central Government Transfers	137	74	87	122
CURRENT BALANCE	6	−23	−41	6
Capital Account:				
Private	17	7	32	21
Central Government	27	73	52	24
CAPITAL BALANCE	44	80	84	45
Net Errors and Omissions	1	7	−4	−9
Net Surplus or Deficit	50	57	39	42
Allocation of Special Drawing Rights	—	—	{ 18 / −57	14 / −56

EXTERNAL TRADE
('ooo Somali Shillings)

	1966	1967	1968	1969	1970	1971	1972
Imports	300,300	286,400	339,800	369,798	322,170	447,563	523,884
Exports	213,900	198,500	212,000	231,910	224,346	246,441	299,930

PRINCIPAL COMMODITIES
('ooo Somali Shillings)

IMPORTS	1967	1968	1969	1970	1971
General manufactured goods	77,902	103,293	82,565	76,085	111,524
Yarn, fabrics and clothing*	34,453	43,413	24,615	25,525	36,406
Cereals and cereal products	35,264	34,962	48,828	55,006	104,777
Transport equipment	48,769	64,829	46,591	32,925	28,727
Non-electrical machinery	20,338	23,096	31,484	14,027	19,003
Mineral fuels	15,217	14,339	19,149	20,266	18,949
Sugar	810	7,953	1,011	933	1,048
Chemicals	n.a.	n.a.	26,413	21,747	28,727
Vegetable Oils and Fats	n.a.	n.a.	8,896	16,217	15,614

EXPORTS	1967	1968	1969	1970	1971
Bananas	68,370	59,684	55,723	62,813	63,827
Livestock	97,876	124,395	132,014	119,268	123,376
Hides and Skins	8,904	11,742	17,080	14,835	18,061
Wood and Charcoal	11,405	4,980	5,791	15	6
Fish Products	491	239	2,964	1,511	2,638
Meat and Meat products	2,393	2,976	2,965	6,670	21,408

* Also included in General manufactured goods.

PRINCIPAL COUNTRIES
('ooo Somali Shillings)

Imports	1969	1970	1971	Exports	1969	1970	1971
Arabian Peninsula .	12,319	16,708	11,584	Arabian Peninsula .	154,852	143,341	147,869
Ethiopia .	12,047	8,880	n.a.	Egypt . . .	614	1,527	5,569
Federal Republic of				Italy . . .	61,827	58,555	55,148
Germany . .	31,134	29,434	33,524	Kenya . . .	1,098	4,760	4,737
India . . .	4,430	4,568	4,134	U.K. . . .	1,534	607	612
Iran . . .	4,870	7,568	n.a.	U.S.S.R. . .	155	3,376	15,525
Italy . . .	114,409	94,955	121,191	U.S.A. . . .	4,833	1,537	291
Japan . . .	30,455	23,914	23,470				
Kenya . . .	16,941	16,946	n.a.				
U.K. . . .	33,358	20,076	29,219				
U.S.S.R. . .	13,052	21,428	29,100				
U.S.A. . . .	39,894	25,502	29,979				

Other major imports in 1971 were from: Thailand 34.5 million Somali shillings, Singapore 21 million Somali shillings.

TRANSPORT
ROAD MOTOR VEHICLES
(number in use)

	1966	1967	1968
Passenger Cars	5,300	6,700	8,200
Commercial Vehicles	6,600	7,800	10,000
Total	11,900	14,500	18,200

SHIPPING
MERCHANT FLEET
(Registered at June 30th each year)

	Displacement (gross tons)
1968 . .	59,000
1969 . .	295,000
1970 . .	369,000
1971 . .	593,000

International Sea-borne Shipping	1970	1971	1972
Vessels Entered ('ooo net reg. tons) . .	1,285	1,614	n.a.
Goods Loaded ('ooo metric tons) . .	264	294	395
Goods Unloaded ('ooo metric tons) . .	251	398	328

Shipping statistics are for the major harbours of Berbera, Mogadishu, Kismayu and Merca.

CIVIL AVIATION
Scheduled Services

	1967	1968	1969	1970
Kilometres Flown ('ooo) . . .	565	710	860	730
Passenger-km. ('ooo) . . .	7,240	8,440	12,750	9,890
Cargo ton-km. ('ooo) . .	95	90	100	90

Communications (1970): 50,000 radio receivers; 5,000 telephones.

EDUCATION

(Student numbers 1972–73)

Elementary	53,465
Intermediate	24,668
Secondary	9,457
TOTAL	87,590

During 1972–73 all private schools were taken over by the Government.

Source (unless otherwise stated): Central Statistical Department, Ministry of Planning and Co-ordination, Mogadishu.

THE CONSTITUTION

No new Constitution has been produced since the coup in 1969.

THE GOVERNMENT

The Government is comprised of the Supreme Revolutionary Council and the Council of the Secretaries of State.

SUPREME REVOLUTIONARY COUNCIL

President and Head of State: Maj.-Gen. MOHAMED SIAD BARRE.

Vice-Presidents: Maj.-Gen. HUSSEIN KULMIYE AFRAH, Maj.-Gen. MOHAMED ALI SAMATER (also Commander of the National Army), Col. ISMAIL ALI ABOKER.

MEMBERS

Brig.-Gen. ABDULLA MOHAMED FADIL.
Col. AHMED SULIMAN ABDULLAH.
Col. MOHAMED SHEIKH OSMAN.
Col. MOHAMED ALI SHIRREH.
Col. ALI MATTAN HASHI.
Col. MOHAMOUD MIRREH MUSA.
Lt.-Col. MOHAMOUD GHELLE YUSEF.
Lt.-Col. FARAH WAIS.
Lt.-Col. MUSA RABILEH GHOD.

Lt.-Col. AHMED MOHAMOUD FARAH.
Lt.-Col. AHMED HASSAN MUSA.
Lt.-Col. OSMAN MOHAMED JELLE.
Maj. ABDIRAZAK MOHAMED ABOKUR.
Maj. ABDI WARSAMA ISSAK.
Maj. ABDULCADIR HAJI MOHAMED.
Maj. MOHAMED YUSUF ELMI.
Maj. MOHAMED OMER GES.

COUNCIL OF SECRETARIES OF STATE

(*April* 1974)

Secretary of State for Foreign Affairs: OMER ARTEH GHALIB.

Secretary of State for the Interior: Maj.-Gen. HUSSEIN KULMIA AFRAH.

Secretary of State for Defence: Maj.-Gen. MOHAMED ALI SAMATER.

Secretary of State for Information and National Guidance: Col. ISMAIL ALI ABOKER.

Secretary of State for Industry: ABDIKASSIM SALAD HASSAN.

Secretary of State for Public Works: Col. MOHAMED SHEIKH OSMAN.

Secretary of State for Transport: Lt.-Col. MUSA RABILEH GHOD.

Secretary of State for Posts, Telegraphs and Telephones: Lt.-Col. AHMED MOHAMOUD FARAH.

Secretary of State for Education: Maj. ABDIRAZAK MOHAMED ABOKU.

Secretary of State for Justice and Religious Affairs: ABDUL SALAAM SHEIKH HUSSEIN.

Secretary of State for Finance: MOHAMED YUSUF WEIREH.

Secretary of State for Culture and Higher Education: Dr. MOHAMED ADAN MOHAMOUD.

Secretary of State for Livestock, Forestry and Pastures: Lt.-Col. OSMAN MOHAMOUD JELLE.

Secretary of State for Internal Trade: AHMED MOHAMED MOHAMOUD.

Secretary of State for External Trade: MOHAMED WARSAMA ALI.

Secretary of State for Labour and Sport: ABDULAZIZ NUR HERSI.

Secretary of State for Planning and Co-ordination: Ibrahim Megag Samater.

Secretary of State for Agriculture: Omer Saleh Ahmed.

Secretary of State for Minerals and Water Survey: Mohamed Buraleh.

Secretary of State for Health: Dr. Mohamed Ali Nur.

Secretary of State for Tourism and National Parks: Maj. Mohamed Omer Ges.

Secretary of State for Fisheries and Sea Transport: Osman Jama Ali.

DIPLOMATIC REPRESENTATION

EMBASSIES ACCREDITED TO SOMALIA

(In Mogadishu unless otherwise stated)

(E) Embassy.

China, People's Republic: Via Scire Uarsama (E); *Ambassador:* Fan Tsu-kai.

Czechoslovakia: Via Londra (E); *Ambassador:* Miroslav Novotný.

Egypt: Via Agostino Franzoi (E); *Ambassador:* Abdul Aziz Gamil.

Ethiopia: Via Benedetti (E); *Ambassador:* Ayalew Mandefro.

France: Corso Primo Luglio (E); *Ambassador:* Robert Duvauchelle.

German Democratic Republic: (E); *Ambassador:* Werner Herklotz.

Germany, Federal Republic: Via Muhammad Habi (E); *Ambassador:* Joseph Holick.

India: Via Balad (E); *Ambassador:* (vacant).

Iraq: (E); *Ambassador:* (vacant).

Italy: Via Trevis (E); *Ambassador:* Giulio Terruzzi.

Kenya: (E); *Ambassador:* J. K. Ilako.

Korea, Democratic People's Republic: (E); *Ambassador:* Kwak Chol Su.

Netherlands: (E); *Ambassador:* (vacant).

Pakistan: (E); *Ambassador:* Com. Abdul Hameed.

Saudi Arabia: Vardiglei Burhindi (E); *Ambassador:* Ali Awad.

Sudan: Via Cavour (E); *Ambassador:* Muawiya Ibrahim Sourig.

Syria: Via Washington (E); *Ambassador:* Baha-Addin Naqqar.

Tunisia: Addis Ababa, Ethiopia (E).

U.S.S.R.: Corso Italia (E); *Ambassador:* Alexei S. Pasiutin.

United Kingdom: Via Londra (E); *Ambassador:* John Shaw.

U.S.A.: Corso Primo Luglio (E); *Ambassador:* Matthew J. Looram Jnr.

Viet-Nam, Democratic Republic: (E); *Ambassador:* Luu Quy Tan.

Yemen Arab Republic: Corso Primo Luglio (E); *Ambassador:* Muhammad Abdulla Alfusayil.

Yemen, People's Democratic Republic: (E); *Ambassador:* Luu Abdul Barri Kassim.

Yugoslavia: (E); *Ambassador:* Sinisa Kosutic.

Somalia also has diplomatic relations with Austria, Belgium, Bulgaria, Hungary, Indonesia, Japan, Jordan, Kuwait, Lebanon, Libya, Malta, Nigeria, Poland, Sweden, Turkey and the United Arab Emirates.

NATIONAL ASSEMBLY

The National Assembly was dissolved when the Government was overthrown on October 21st, 1969.

POLITICAL PARTIES

All political parties were banned after October 21st, 1969.

JUDICIAL SYSTEM

The Judiciary is independent of the executive and legislative powers.

Laws and acts having the force of law must conform to the provisions of the Constitution and to the general principles of Islam.

Supreme Revolutionary Court: Mogadishu; as the highest judicial organ, has jurisdiction over the whole territory of the State in civil, penal, administrative and accounting matters.

National Security Court: Mogadishu; established following the 1969 coup to try members of the former government and their officials; Pres. Muhammad Sheikh Osman.

Military Supreme Court: established 1970 to try members of the armed forces; Pres. Muhammad Ali Sherman.

Courts of Appeal: There are Courts of Appeal in Mogadishu and Hargeisa, with two Sections: General and Assize.

Regional Courts: There are eight Regional Courts, with two Sections: General and Assize.

District Courts: There are 48 District Courts, with two Sections: Civil and Criminal. The Civil Section has jurisdiction over all controversies where the cause of action has arisen under Sharia Law (Muslim Law) or Customary Law and any other Civil controversies where the value of the subject matter does not exceed 3,000 Shillings. The Criminal Section has jurisdiction with respect to offences punishable with imprisonment not exceeding three years, or fine not exceeding 3,000 Shillings, or both.

Qadis: Civil matters such as marriage and divorce are handled by District Qadis under the Sharia (Islamic) law and other traditional laws.

A new Civil Code Law, to replace the remaining British and Italian laws still in force, came into operation in July 1973. It related to house rents, inheritance agreements, trade agreements and contracts.

The National Security Court was set up by the Supreme Revolutionary Council in April 1970; it is open to the public and is presided over by three military judges led by Col. Mohamed Sheikh Osman. Appeal lies only to the Supreme Council.

RELIGION

ISLAM

Islam is the State religion. Most Somalis are Sunni Muslims.

ROMAN CATHOLICS

Vicar Apostolic: (vacant), P.O.B. 273, Mogadishu.

The Apostolic Vicariate was established in 1928. There are about 1,500 Catholics in Somalia, mostly of Italian origin.

PRESS

Hidigta October: publ. by the Ministry of Information and National Guidance; in Somali; only daily newspaper.

NEWS AGENCIES
Foreign Bureaux

ANSA: Ambasciata d'Italia, Mogadishu.

Novosti: P.O.B. 963, Mogadishu; Chief V. Bulimov.

SONNA: Somali National News Agency.

Tass also has a bureau in Mogadishu.

RADIO

National Broadcasting Service: Radio Mogadishu, Voice of the Somali Democratic Republic, Mogadishu; main government service; broadcasts in Somali, English, Italian, Arabic, Swahili, Amharic, Galla and Affar; Dir. of Broadcasting Hussein Mohamed Bullaleh.

Radio Hargeisa: P.O.B. 14, Hargeisa; Northern Region Government station; broadcasts in Somali, and relays Somali and Amharic transmission from Radio Mogadishu; Dir. of Radio Idris Egal.

Number of radio receivers: 65,000, some of which are used for public address purposes in small towns and villages.

There is no television service.

FINANCE

BANKING

(cap.=capital; dep.=deposits; m.=million; (funds in Somali Shillings).

On May 7th, 1970, all banks were nationalized.

Central Bank

Banca Nazionale Somala: P.O.B. 11, Mogadishu; f. 1960; Central Bank and currency issuing authority; brs.

in Baidoa, Belet Uen, Berbera, Bosaso, Burao, Galcaio, Gardo, Giamama, Hargeisa, Kismayu and Merca; cap. 1m., reserves 15m. (1969); Gov. Dr. Abdwahman Nur Hersi; Man. Dir. Dr. Omar Ahmed Omar.

Commercial Banks

Somali Commercial Bank: P.O.B. 26, Mogadishu; f. 1971 to take over nationalized branches of National and Grindlays Bank Ltd., Banco di Roma, and Banco di Napoli; cap. 52.5m.; Gen. Man. Said Mohamed Ali.

Somali Credit and Savings Bank: Piazza Scerif Abo, Mogadishu.

Foreign Banks

All foreign banks in Somalia were nationalized under an order of the Supreme Revolutionary Council on May 7th, 1970. They became agencies of the Somali National Bank. The banks then operating in Somalia were the Banco di Napoli, Banco di Roma, Banque de Port Said and National and Grindlays Bank. Recently the Somali Savings and Credit Bank and the Somali Commercial Bank were formed to take over the agencies from the Somali National Bank. Though it retains a commercial section to co-operate with these banks, it operates solely as a central bank.

Development Bank

Somali Development Bank: P.O.B. 79, Mogadishu.

INSURANCE

Cassa per le Assicurazioni Sociali della Somalia: P.O.B. 123, Mogadishu; f. 1950; workmen's compensation; Pres. Haji Osman Mohammed; Dir.-Gen. Dr. Mohammed Ahmed Mohammed.

TRADE AND INDUSTRY

CHAMBER OF COMMERCE

Chamber of Commerce, Industry and Agriculture: P.O.B. 27, Mogadishu; Dir. Dr. Athos Bartolucci.

TRADE ORGANIZATION

National Agency of Foreign Trade: P.O.B. 602, Mogadishu; principal foreign trade agency; state owned; branch in Berbera and over 150 centres throughout the country.

DEVELOPMENT CORPORATION

Agricultural Development Corporation: Mogadishu; f. 1971; by amalgamation of previous agricultural and machinery agencies and grain marketing board; supplies farmers with equipment and materials at reasonable prices.

TRANSPORT

There are no railways in Somalia.

ROADS

In 1971 there were 17,223 km. of roads of which 1,053 were asphalted, the rest mainly gravel. Many roads were destroyed in the heavy floods of 1961. An ambitious road building and maintenance project was launched in 1965. Projects to build a road connecting Hargeisa and Berbera which is financed by the World Bank, and a road between Jowhar and Bulo Burti are expected to be completed in 1974. Work will begin on the Hargeisa–Borama road in late 1973. The International Development Association helped to finance a 216 km. road project linking Afgoi (near Mogadishu) with Baidoa. A highway to link Belet Uen with Burao will be built with Chinese aid and its estimated cost is 75 million Somali Shillings. It is the second largest Chinese aid project in Africa. There were 13,900 licensed vehicles in 1969.

SHIPPING

Merca, Berbera, Mogadishu and Kismayu are the chief ports. New deep-water extensions to Berbera harbour, constructed by the Soviet Union, were opened early in 1969, and the facilities at Kismayu have been extended with American assistance. Construction work began in 1973 to construct a new port with modern shipping berths at Mogadishu. The estimated cost is 155 million Somali shillings and the Somali Government have been assisted by loans. The project is scheduled for completion in 1976.

Brocklebank Line: monthly service Oct. to April from United Kingdom to Berbera; agents A. Besse and Co. (Somalia) Ltd., P.O.B. 121, Berbera.

Clan Line: regular calls at Berbera Oct. to April; agents A. Besse and Co. (Somalia) Ltd., P.O.B. 121, Berbera.

Lloyd Triestino: regular passenger and cargo service to Italy; agents Agenzia Marittima, P.O.B. 126, Mogadishu.

Other lines call irregularly at Somali ports.

Somali "Dhows" sail between East Africa, Aden and Arabia.

CIVIL AVIATION

Mogadishu has an international airport with landing facilities for aircraft up to DC-8 class. A new international airport is under construction at Kismayu with similar facilities. Work began in November 1972 and is scheduled to be completed in September 1974. Hargeisa airport can accommodate aircraft up to Viscount class. A new airport was constructed in Baidoa during 1973.

Somali Airlines: Piazza della Solidarietà Africana, P.O.B. 726, Mogadishu; 51 per cent government-owned and 49 per cent owned by Alitalia; operates internal passenger and cargo services and international services to Aden, Djibouti and Nairobi and due to be extended to London in 1974; fleet of one Boeing 720B, two Viscount 700, three DC-3, two Cessna 206, one Cessna 180; Pres. Hussein Mohamud Mohamed; Vice-Pres. Dr. M. Delmonte; Dir.-Gen. Abdullahi Ahmed Shire.

Foreign Airlines

The following foreign airlines serve Somalia: Aeroflot, Alitalia, Democratic Yemen Airlines, EAA., EgyptAir.

UNIVERSITY

Universitá Nazionale della Somalia: P.O.B. 15, Mogadishu; f. 1959; 23 teachers, 791 students.

SOUTH AFRICA

INTRODUCTORY SURVEY

Location, Climate, Language, Religion, Flag, Capital

The Republic of South Africa occupies the southern extremity of the African continent. To the north-west lies South West Africa (Namibia), with Botswana and Rhodesia to the north, Mozambique to the north-east, and Swaziland to the east. South African territory encircles the independent state of Lesotho. The climate is warm and sunny, with average temperatures about 63°F (17°C). The official languages are Afrikaans and English; the principal African languages are Xhosa, Zulu and Sesotho. The population is mainly Christian. The politically influential Dutch Reformed Church is adhered to by 55 per cent of the white population. About a fifth of the African Christians belong to African Separatist Churches and others are Methodists and Anglicans. Most Asians are Hindus. The national flag (proportions 3 by 2) is a horizontal tricolour of orange, white and blue, charged in the centre of the white stripe with the Union Jack, the old Orange Free State flag, and the old Transvaal Vierkleur. The administrative capital is Pretoria, the legislative capital is Cape Town and the judicial capital is Bloemfontein.

Recent History

The National Party came to power in 1948 and has ruled South Africa ever since. One of its major aims was the establishment of a Republic and, after a narrow majority of the white electorate had approved, this was achieved in May 1961. The main architect of *apartheid* (in theory the separate but equal development of all racial groups, in practice leading to white, particularly Afrikaner, supremacy) was Dr. Hendrik Verwoerd, Prime Minister from 1958 to 1966, when he was assassinated. *Apartheid* has been internationally condemned with the result that South Africa has been increasingly ostracized. This has led to its expulsion from many international bodies, and its withdrawal from the Commonwealth in 1961.

The South African Government has established "homelands" for African ethnic groups as an integral part of the *apartheid* policy, and promises to make them independent by stages. However, the mass of discriminatory laws which regulate the lives of the Republic's African, Coloured and Asian populations and stringent security legislation have led to the detention without trial of many of the Government's opponents, the banning of African political organizations outside the homelands, a large prison population and the forced removal of hundreds of thousands of Africans under the Group Areas Act and the homelands policy. Verwoerd's successor, Balthazar Vorster, has continued Verwoerd's basic policies while being somewhat less inflexible. His attempt to develop a dialogue with other African states has petered out. But since Rhodesia's unilateral declaration of independence in 1965 the white-ruled states of Southern Africa have drawn closer together. The International Court of Justice and the UN have declared South Africa's presence in South West Africa (Namibia) illegal. UN contacts with South Africa over South West Africa were terminated by the Security Council in December 1973 and a state of deadlock over the territory's status prevails.

The parliamentary majority of the National Party increased in each election since 1948 until 1970 when the opposition United Party (UP), which supports a white-ruled federal system with segregation less harshly applied, made small gains. These were lost in the April 1974 election, which the Nationalists won convincingly. The small anti-*apartheid* Progressive Party made gains at the UP's expense but the chance of ousting the Government, and thereby of achieving significant change within the present system, continues to appear remote.

Government

The State President of the Republic is elected by the members of the Senate and House of Assembly. Executive power is vested in an Executive Council (Cabinet) appointed by the State President. The Senate (54 members) includes representatives of each Province and one representative of the Cape Province Coloured people. Members of the Senate must be white. The House of Assembly (171 members) includes six members representing South West Africa (Namibia). Members of the House of Assembly must be white. Only whites are allowed to vote. A Coloured Persons Representative Council was introduced in 1969.

The country is divided into four Provinces each having an Administrator appointed by the State President and a unicameral Provincial Council elected by whites. South West Africa (Namibia) is governed by an Administrator appointed by the State President aided by an Executive of four chosen from an elected Assembly of 18 members. In 1963 the first Transkei Legislative Assembly was constituted for the Xhosa people and in 1974 it was announced that the Transkei is to request "independence" from the South African Government within five years. Legislative Assemblies have also been created for most of the other homelands.

Defence

All male white citizens from seventeen to sixty-five are liable to military service. The South African Defence Force consists of regular units of the army, navy and air force and units of the Citizen Force attached to each arm. The Citizen Force consists of volunteer, part-time officers and non commissioned officers and national servicemen. The regular army has about 10,000 men, compared with about 80,000 in the Citizen Force; the navy has 2,500 men and the air force 5,500. The Citizen Force may be employed on combat duty or in aid of the civil power. A second territorial unit, the Commandos, 75,000 strong, are voluntary infantry for internal security duties. Defence expenditure in 1973-74 is estimated at R481 million. A 1973 Defence Amendment Bill provided for the secondment of South African troops to Rhodesian forces, and an unidentified number of South African para-military police are already supporting Rhodesian defence forces.

Economic Affairs

South Africa has successfully diversified its economy and about one-third of the national income is now derived from manufacturing. The establishment of the South African

Iron and Steel Industrial Corporation (ISCOR) and the South African Coal, Oil and Gas Corporation (SASOL) laid the foundations of the heavy engineering, chemical and petroleum industries. The textile and food processing industries are also growing. Mining still contributes largely to the economy and gold is the most profitable export, accounting for about a third of the total, and the recent huge rise in the price of gold has led to record gold revenues and increased gold and foreign reserves. In 1973 inflation reached 10 per cent and remains a serious problem. Uranium is mined with gold. Much of the mining labour force comes from Lesotho, Botswana and Malawi. Industrial development is dependent on the white population for capital, management and higher technical skill, with the Africans, Coloureds and Asians providing most of the unskilled labour force who are the backbone of the economy. Much criticism, particularly from abroad, has been levelled at the low wages paid to African workers which resulted in 1973 in a series of widespread strikes for more pay. African trade unions are still not recognized by the Government. Much livestock is reared in South Africa and there are valuable fruit, wine and fishing industries. The export of wool, maize, sugar and karakul pelts is important. South Africa has large oil reserves but the economy is likely to be adversely affected by the embargo imposed by the Arabs states after the 1973 Middle East War. South Africa's huge reserves of coal are likely to increase in importance and the country may well use its valuable supplies of gold as a bargaining counter so the effect of the embargo is not expected to be at all catastrophic.

Transport and Communications

Railways, ports, airways and harbours are administered by the state. There are no navigable rivers. Private omnibus services are regulated to dove-tail with the railways. Roads are good and a national highway system is being built. There are many internal and international air services and much ocean shipping traffic, particularly since the closing of the Suez Canal.

Social Welfare

Social welfare services protect the old, the blind, the war disabled, the unemployed and those injured at work. Medical services are administered by the Provinces. These reach a high standard.

Education

For Whites, schooling is compulsory from seven to sixteen in English-medium or Afrikaans-medium schools; for Coloureds it is compulsory from seven to sixteen in Natal and seven to fourteen in the Cape Province where possible; for Asians provision has been made for compulsory school attendance where possible since April 1966. Schooling is not compulsory for Africans although four out of five attend school for varying periods. Africans' education is in their own languages and the curriculum is limited. Segregation is enforced by the Government in all universities though a few non-white individuals attend specialized courses at "white" universities.

Tourism

Tourism is an important industry and there were over half a million visitors to South Africa in 1972. South Africa's attractions are the climate, the scenery and wild-life. The great game reserves, of which the Kruger National Park is the largest, attract thousands of visitors from Europe, America and Africa. South Africa, Malawi, Mauritius, Portugal and Swaziland are members of a regional tourist council for Southern Africa.

Visas are not required to visit South Africa by white nationals of Australia, Canada, Ireland, Lesotho, Malawi, Rhodesia, Swaziland and United Kingdom and Colonies, or by nationals of Liechtenstein and Switzerland.

Sport

Sport is very popular, but is strictly racially segregated. Rugby football is the national game but many games are played, such as soccer, tennis, cricket, bowls, golf and baseball. Although South Africa has produced numerous outstanding sportsmen, the country is almost completely isolated in world sport because of *apartheid*, and the country is barred from competing in the Olympic Games.

Public Holidays

1974: September 3rd (Settlers' Day), October 10th (Kruger Day), December 16th (Day of the Covenant), December 25th–26th (Christmas Day and Boxing Day/ Family Day).

1975: January 1st (New Year's Day), March 28th–31st (Easter), May 8th (Ascension Day), May 31st (Republic Day).

Weights and Measures

The metric system is in use.

Currency and Exchange Rates

100 cents = 1 rand (R).

Exchange rates (April 1974):

£1 sterling = 1.581 rand;
U.S. $1 = 67.11 S.A. cents.

STATISTICAL SURVEY
AREA AND POPULATION
(Census of May 6th, 1970)

	TOTAL*	CAPE PROVINCE	NATAL	TRANSVAAL	ORANGE FREE STATE
AREA (sq. miles) . .	471,445	278,380	33,578	109,621	49,866
POPULATION ('000) .	21,448	4,236†	2,140†	6,389†	1,649†
Whites . .	3,751	1,102	442	1,890	296
Bantu . .	15,058	1,360†	1,116†	4,267†	1,317†
Asiatics . .	620	22	515	81	—
Coloureds . .	2,019	1,752	67	151	36

* Excludes Walvis Bay, which has an area of 434 sq. miles and a population of 12,648 (1960), which is administered as part of South West Africa (Namibia).

† Numbers exclude Africans in the homelands. During 1974 the Government dropped the label "Bantu" for Africans, who are now known officially as "Blacks".

Estimated Population: 22,987,000 (July 1st, 1972).

CHIEF TOWNS
POPULATION (1970)

Cape Town (capital) .	1,096,597	Bloemfontein (capital)	180,176
Pretoria (capital) .	561,703	Benoni . . .	162,794
Johannesburg .	1,432,643	Springs . . .	104,090
Durban . .	843,327	East London . .	123,294
Port Elizabeth .	468,577	Pietermaritzburg .	158,921
Germiston .	139,472	Welkom . . .	131,767

Transkei (Bantu Homeland) in the south-east of the Republic: Area: 15,831 square miles; Population (1970) 1,751,142 (Bantu 1,733,931, White 9,556, Coloureds 7,645, Asian 10); Capital Umtata.

POPULATION GROUPS
(1970—'000)

Zulu	4,026
Xhosa	3,930
Tswana	1,719
Sepedi (North Sotho) . .	1,604
Seshoeshoe (South Sotho) .	1,452
Swazi	499
Shangaan . . .	737
Venda	358
South Ndebele . . .	233
North Ndebele . . .	182
Other Bantu . . .	318
Whites	3,751
Coloureds . . .	2,019
Asians	620
TOTAL . . .	21,448

CENSUS RETURNS

	ALL RACES TOTAL	WHITES		
		Total	Male	Female
1936	9,619,000	2,009,000	1,021,000	988,000
1946	11,449,000	2,380,000	1,198,000	1,182,000
1951	12,716,000	2,647,000	1,325,000	1,322,000
1960	16,002,797	3,088,492	1,539,103	1,539,000
1970	21,448,169	3,751,328	1,867,850	1,883,478

	TOTAL NON-WHITES			BLACKS		ASIATICS		COLOUREDS AND MALAYS	
	Total	Male	Female	Male	Female	Male	Female	Male	Female
1936	7,610,000	3,832,000	3,778,000	3,324,000	3,293,000	120,000	101,000	389,000	383,000
1946	9,068,000	4,623,000	4,445,000	4,007,000	3,844,000	149,000	137,000	467,000	464,000
1951	10,068,000	5,128,000	4,940,000	4,386,000	4,208,000	190,000	178,000	553,000	555,000
1960	12,914,305	6,504,390	6,409,915	5,488,000	5,392,000	241,637	235,488	747,000	754,000
1970	17,696,841	8,693,295	9,003,546	7,390,246	7,667,706	309,433	311,003	993,616	1,024,837

BIRTHS*

	TOTAL REGISTERED			RATE (per 1,000)		
	Whites	Asiatics	Coloureds	Whites	Asiatics	Coloureds
1965 . . .	81,488	17,140	77,416	24.0	32.2	44.2
1966 . . .	82,548	17,429	78,644	23.7	31.9	43.6
1967 . . .	81,635	16,833	80,410	22.9	30.0	43.3
1968 . . .	84,100	18,815	76,508	23.2	31.7	39.3
1969 . . .	85,758	21,116	75,120	23.2	34.4	37.6
1970 . . .	88,886	21,082	74,429	23.5	33.3	36.3
1971 . . .	89,596	22,129	74,459	23.1	34.0	35.5

DEATHS*

	TOTAL REGISTERED			RATE (per 1,000)		
	Whites	Asiatics	Coloureds	Whites	Asiatics	Coloureds
1966 . . .	29,962	3,999	26,948	8.6	7.3	14.9
1967 . . .	32,015	4,251	29,276	9.0	7.6	15.7
1968 . . .	32,078	4,263	27,898	8.9	7.2	14.3
1969 . . .	32,391	4,314	27,882	8.7	7.0	13.9
1970 . . .	34,452	4,376	28,938	9.1	6.9	14.1
1971 . . .	33,321	4,468	27,919	8.6	6.9	13.3

* Statistics for births and deaths for Blacks are not available.

IMMIGRATION AND EMIGRATION
(Whites only)

Country of Birth or Destination	Immigrants			Emigrants		
	1971	1972	1973	1971	1972	1973
United Kingdom	15,725	15,912	9,196	2,268	2,494	2,217
Federal Republic of Germany .	2,611	2,067	1,622	10	495	526
The Netherlands	1,024	993	822	256	227	242
Italy	591	551	353	92	74	88
Rhodesia	2,030	1,408	1,946	3,073	2,491	1,580
Zambia	778	458	449	27	27	12
Malawi	66	45	65	13	20	5
Kenya	89	73	48	4	—	2
Mozambique	105	96	81	9	22	7
U.S.A.	218	237	185	140	38	111
Canada	299	246	120	60	50	123
Australasia	1,318	759	481	1,192	1,024	703
Total (incl. others) .	30,694	27,114	18,652	8,291	7,803	6,290

EMPLOYMENT

	Whites		Non-Whites		Total	
	1971	1972	1971	1972	1971	1972
Mining . . .	61,021	60,231	586,502	567,198	647,523	627,429
Manufacturing . .	278,700	282,000	923,800	946,000	1,202,500	1,228,000
Construction . .	60,100	58,600	323,700	326,100	383,800	384,700
Transport . .	112,382	110,854	115,169	116,798	227,551	227,652
Communications .	40,781	40,519	18,522	19,558	59,303	60,077
Public Authorities .	246,194	251,310	416,699	398,917	662,893	650,227

In 1969 about 1,700,000 of the population were engaged in agriculture, of which 1,455,000 Blacks, 118,000 Whites.

AGRICULTURE
PRINCIPAL CROPS
('000 metric tons)

	1968	1969	1970	1971	1972
Maize	5,316	5,339	6,133	8,600	9,630
Sorghum	207	232	445	650	n.a.
Wheat	1,270	1,328	1,396	1,670	1,615
Barley	34	18	33	35	36
Oats	143	110	122	97	103
Dry Beans . . .	58	50	49	51	56*
Cotton (lint) . .	15	23	19	17	22
Sugar Cane† . .	13,720	14,788	12,144	n.a.	n.a.
Tobacco . . .	38.2	38.3	34.4	32.4	30.1
Potatoes . . .	480	447	586	650*	640*
Groundnuts (in shell) .	227	368	318	404	402

* FAO estimate. † Cane crushed for sugar.

Sources: FAO, *Production Yearbook 1971* and *Monthly Bulletin of Agricultural Economics and Statistics.*

FRUIT

Deciduous Fruit (metric tons)				Citrus Fruit (Exports—units of 35 lb.)		
	1970	1971	1972*		1969	1970
Apples . . .	123,589	132,174	179,632	Oranges . . .	16,030,074	15,428,000
Grapes . .	27,695	33,760	33,334	Grapefruit . .	3,794,391	3,711,000
Peaches . .	1,184	1,262	1,413	Lemons . .	421,297	305,000
Pears . .	26,286	30,246	36,501	Tangerines . .	2,155	2,347

* Estimates.

LIVESTOCK
('000 head)

	1967/68	1968/69	1969/70	1970/71
Cattle . . .	12,145	11,780	12,251	12,320*
Pigs . . .	1,290	1,240	1,289	1,350*
Sheep . . .	35,978	36,059	33,136	30,671
Goats . . .	5,450*	5,500*	5,550*	5,600*
Horses . .	460*	450*	440*	430*
Asses . . .	295*	290*	290*	280*
Mules . . .	40*	40*	40*	40*
Chickens† . .	11,800*	12,000*	12,300*	12,400*

Beehives: 45,000 in 1970 (FAO estimate).
* FAO estimate. † On farms and estates only.
Source: FAO, Production Yearbook 1971.

LIVESTOCK PRODUCTS
(metric tons)

	1968	1969	1970
Beef and Veal . . .	355,000	390,000	390,000*
Mutton, Lamb and Goats' Meat .	177,000	201,000	200,000*
Pig Meat	87,000	102,000	100,000*
Poultry Meat . . .	38,000*	40,000*	41,000*
Edible Offal . . .	124,000*	126,000*	127,000*
Lard	3,600*	3,800*	4,000*
Tallow, etc. . . .	11,000*	11,000*	12,000*
Cows' Milk . . .	2,808,000	2,850,000	2,820,000
Butter (factory production)† .	53,000	55,000	47,000
Cheese† . . .	21,000	24,000	20,000
Condensed and Evaporated Milk† .	38,000	42,000	36,000
Dried Milk† . . .	19,000	19,000	16,000
Hen Eggs . . .	108,700	128,800	140,000*
Honey . . .	400*	410*	400*
Wool: Greasy . . .	142,300	145,100	117,900
Clean . .	69,200	70,500	57,300
Cattle Hides and Calf Skins (salted) .	34,300	34,000*	33,880*
Sheep Skins (fresh) . .	30,300	31,500*	32,250*
Goat Skins (fresh) . .	2,000	2,000*	2,030*

* FAO estimate. † Twelve months ending September 30th of year stated.
Source: FAO, Production Yearbook 1971.

FISHING*
('ooo metric tons)

	1969	1970	1971
Freshwater Fish	0.1	0.1	0.1
Marine Fish	1,889.5	1,554.7	1,085.7
Cape Hakes (Stokvisse) . . .	100.3	91.1	111.4
Maasbanker	31.7	14.7	150.0
Sardinellas	48.4	350.0†	
South African Pilchard . . .	1,159.7	554.4	334.7
Cape Anchovy	397.4	403.7	370.3
Chub Mackerel	92.8	77.7	54.5
Other Marine Animals‡ . . .	13.4	13.1	9.7
Aquatic Bird Guano . . .	5.3	4.5	4.3
Seaweeds	3.1	2.6	3.6
TOTAL CATCH‡ . . .	1,911.4	1,575.0	1,103.4

* Including figures for South West Africa (Namibia), where the total catch (all marine) was 65,800 metric tons in 1969 and 20,000 metric tons in 1970.

† FAO estimate.   ‡ Excluding seals. In 1971 the number of Cape fur seals caught was 76,502.

Source: FAO, *Yearbook of Fishery Statistics 1971.*

MINING*
(Rand 'ooo)

	1968	1969	1970	1971	1972
Gold	777,532	829,126	830,336	892,831	1,159,900
Uranium	n.a.	n.a.	n.a.	n.a.	n.a.
Silver	5,000	4,392	4,567	3,546	4,114
Iron Ore	29,536	27,610	28,961	31,275	30,314
Copper	99,427	115,464	139,137	108,256	116,591
Manganese Ore . . .	23,559	26,857	26,579	36,667	37,297
Chrome Ore . . .	8,913	10,112	11,023	14,820	12,809
Tin (metal concentrates) . .	4,078	4,293	3,418	3,230	n.a.
Coal	97,283	106,082	109,914	119,377	126,782
Asbestos	31,714	30,948	34,568	38,213	38,031
Diamonds	193,600	221,300	175,600	166,000	n.a.
Lime and Limestone. . .	13,610	15,295	17,165	19,578	n.a.

* Exports.

1973 gold revenue: R1,787,000.

MINERAL PRODUCTION
('ooo metric tons)

	1970	1971	1972
Antimony . . .	28.8	23.9	n.a.
Asbestos . . .	287.4	319.4	321.0
Chrome . . .	1,427.3	1,644.0	1,483.0
Coal . . .	56,611.7	58,866.0	58,440.0
Copper . . .	149.2	157.4	162.0
Fluorspar . . .	173.0	238.9	211.0
Iron Ore . . .	9,272.0	10,946.3	11,223.0
Manganese . . .	3,053.5	3,155.7	3,373.0
Phosphates, Crude .	1,684.9	1,729.5	1,966.0
Vanadium . . .	4.3	4.0	n.a.
Diamonds ('ooo carats) .	8,111.5	7,031.2	7,395.0
Gold (metric tons) . .	1,000.4	976.3	909.6

INDUSTRY
GROSS SALES
(Rand '000)

	1970	1971	1972
Processed Foodstuffs	1,087,171	1,150,105	1,317,831
Beverages and Tobacco	472,218	522,961	570,674
Textiles	387,881	405,584	444,855
Clothing and Knitted Products . .			
Footwear . . . . . . }	442,353	449,858	490,413
Wood and Wood Products . . .	131,978	135,894	126,619
Furniture	129,833	127,301	134,394
Paper and Paper Products . . .	257,138	262,991	371,314
Printing, Publishing and Allied Industries .	182,990	191,652	204,456
Leather and Leather Products . . .	38,515	39,209	46,486
Rubber Products	143,734	146,180	166,876
Chemicals and Chemical Products .	563,998	607,989	664,413
Non-metallic Mineral Products . .	345,462	379,026	393,892
Basic Metals	654,438	669,081	758,082
Metal Products	546,683	633,654	676,901
Machinery (except Electrical Machinery) .	370,184	397,513	389,047
Electrical Machinery and Equipment .	299,842	305,308	342,215
Transport Equipment . . .	661,852	681,105	773,905
TOTAL (incl. others) . .	7,144,850	7,572,942	8,393,195

FINANCE

100 cents = 1 rand (R).

Coins: ½, 1, 2, 5, 10, 20 and 50 cents.

Notes: 1, 2, 5, 10 and 20 rand.

Exchange rates (April 1974): £1 sterling = 1.581 rand; U.S. $1 = 67.11 S.A. cents.

100 rand = £63.27 = $149.00.

BUDGET ESTIMATES
(million rand, year ending March 31st)

REVENUE	1973–74	EXPENDITURE	1973–74
Revenue on Existing Basis of Taxation .	3,179	Printed Estimates	3,392
Foreign Currency Adjustment Account .	56	Forward Contracts Contingency Account .	30
Company Licences, Taxation Royalties, Excise Duties, etc.	17	Deficit on S.W.A. (Namibia) Account for 1972–73	22
	3,252	Social Pensions	11
Less: Sales Duty, Investment Allowance, Transfer Duty, Exporters Allowance, Pension Contribution, Tax Surcharge, etc.	89	Export Promotion	6
TOTAL	3,163	TOTAL . . .	3,461

GROSS DOMESTIC PRODUCT BY KIND OF ECONOMIC ACTIVITY
(Rand million)

	1969	1970	1971*	1972*
BUSINESS ENTERPRISES:				
Agriculture, forestry and fishing . .	1,009	1,021	1,221	1,442
Mining and quarrying	1,247	1,236	1,230	1,610
Manufacturing	2,521	2,828	3,047	3,267
Electricity, gas and water .	277	307	352	400
Construction (contractors)	424	507	599	688
Wholesale and retail trade, catering and accommodation	1,541	1,655	1,750	1,928
Transport, storage and communication .	992	1,074	1,214	1,266
Finance, insurance, real estate and business services	1,008	1,221	1,378	1,596
Community, social and personal services .	200	233	257	286
Sub-Total	9,309	10,082	11,048	12,482
General Government	969	1,123	1,359	1,502
Other Producers (non-profit institutions and domestic servants)	408	451	524	601
GROSS DOMESTIC PRODUCT AT FACTOR COST .	10,686	11,657	12,930	14,586

* Provisional.

GOLD RESERVES AND CURRENCY IN CIRCULATION
(At year's end—Rand million)

	1969	1970	1971	1972	1973
S.A. Reserve Bank—Gold Reserves . .	790	472	331.6	529.7	561
S.A. Reserve Bank—Foreign Exchanges .	91	209	132.3	406.9	235
TOTAL GOLD RESERVES AND FOREIGN EXCHANGES	881	681	463.9	936.6	796
Coin and Banknotes in Circulation .	458	513	570	627	748
Demand Deposits	1,766	1,749	1,878	2,085	2,639
Other Short- and Medium-Term Deposits .	1,551	1,722	1,828	1,151	2,596
TOTAL MONEY AND NEAR-MONEY . .	3,775	3,984	4,276	4,863	5,983

BALANCE OF PAYMENTS
(including South West Africa (Namibia))
(million rand)

	1971*	1972*	1973*
Current Account:			
Merchandise:			
Imports f.o.b.	−2,890	−2,817	−3,495
Exports f.o.b.	1,538	2,197	2,546
Trade Balance	−1,352	− 620	− 849
Net Gold Output	922	1,161	1,770
Service Payments (net) . . .	−1,224	−1,326	−1,578
Service Receipts	640	730	920
Transfers (net receipts) . . .	40	62	33
Balance on Current Account . . .	− 974	7	196
Capital Movements:			
Private Sector	539	306	− 116
Long Term	326	493	206
Short Term	186	− 125	− 188
Errors and Unrecorded Transactions .	27	− 62	− 134
Central Government and Banking Sector .	196	91	− 95
Long Term	111	96	6
Short Term	85	5	− 101
Total Capital Movements (net flow) . .	735	397	− 211
Change in Gold and Foreign Exchange Reserves as a result of Balance of Payments Transactions	− 239	404	− 15
SDR Allocations and Valuation Adjustments .	83	33	− 96
Total Change in Gold and Foreign Exchange Reserves	− 156	437	− 111

* Provisional.

EXTERNAL TRADE*
(million rand)

		1968	1969	1970	1971	1972	1973
Imports f.o.b. .	.	1,880.1	2,136.8	2,542.5	2,879.4	2,820.5	3,301.1
Exports f.o.b.† .	.	1,506.3	1,528.3	1,534.5	1,530.3	2,003.1	2,410.6

* Including data for South West Africa (Namibia), Botswana, Lesotho and Swaziland.　　　† Excluding gold.

COMMODITIES
(million rand)

Imports	1970	1971	1972
Vegetable Products	60.8	54.1	53.3
Mineral products	144.9	214.6	223.7
Chemicals and Products . . .	160.8	186.9	199.5
Plastic and Rubber Products . .	99.4	103.3	96.7
Paper and Products	87.7	86.0	87.8
Textiles and Articles	241.1	257.8	250.4
Base Metals and Products . . .	201.8	236.0	162.4
Machinery and Electrical Equipment .	706.6	786.2	771.9
Transport Equipment	467.5	582.9	575.6
Optical and Measuring Instruments .	98.1	98.5	106.7
Others	273.8	273.1	292.5
Total	2,542.5	2,879.4	2,820.5

COMMODITIES—*Continued*].

EXPORTS	1970	1971	1972
Vegetable Products	138.5	151.7	250.5
Prepared Foodstuffs	139.4	141.7	255.3
Mineral Products	218.6	222.3	232.5
Chemicals and Products	52.9	55.1	70.9
Hides and Skins	39.5	36.4	58.8
Paper and Products	32.7	36.9	48.2
Textiles and Articles	95.0	71.3	144.8
Precious Stones	187.2	193.7	322.2
Base Metals and Products	257.0	219.2	286.0
Machinery and Electrical Equipment . .	53.7	69.4	94.2
Others	320.0	332.6	239.7
TOTAL	1,534.5	1,530.3	2,003.1

Source: Standard Bank Review, March 1974.

COUNTRIES

(Including data for South West Africa (Namibia), Botswana, Lesotho and Swaziland)

(Rand '000)

IMPORTS	1969	1970	1971	1972
Australia	39,251	60,437	62,141	70,600
Belgium	23,953	33,990	37,969	35,500
Canada	53,063	70,495	47,305	41,300
France	61,196	88,097	104,718	99,300
Federal Republic of Germany . .	292,913	373,993	408,869	413,000
Italy	84,856	104,342	105,221	94,400
Japan	188,425	220,759	292,118	267,100
Netherlands	41,408	58,414	58,379	62,400
Sweden	37,865	45,096	43,932	43,800
Switzerland	40,803	49,584	56,050	62,700
United Kingdom	499,562	561,221	670,574	590,500
U.S.A.	370,487	423,379	469,767	466,600

(Rand '000)

EXPORTS	1969	1970	1971	1972
Australia	13,211	12,774	14,285	16,400
Belgium	63,088	55,788	56,928	81,600
Canada	28,280	28,175	38,897	50,600
France	42,992	37,822	38,338	57,000
Federal Republic of Germany . .	102,829	109,521	110,167	116,600
Hong Kong	22,435	23,968	26,363	34,100
Italy	44,536	43,176	37,144	77,300
Japan	151,240	181,152	182,170	259,300
Netherlands	32,369	34,939	36,381	55,800
Spain	15,952	13,920	14,728	40,700
United Kingdom	510,722	446,589	417,939	530,900
U.S.A.	108,243	128,917	118,516	147,000

TOURISM

Visitors from	1970	1971	1972	1973
Africa	225,221	239,050	258,237	294,904
Europe	116,813	152,917	171,876	197,731
Asia	3,098	4,490	5,190	6,247
America	30,235	44,981	50,723	55,148
Australasia . . .	14,327	18,040	22,664	26,104
Total . . .	389,694	459,478*	508,690	580,134

* Includes 61 "Other".

TRANSPORT
RAILWAYS

	1970	1971	1972
Freight traffic ('000 tons) . .	115,077	116,846	122,201
Passenger journeys ('000) . .	521,529	552,032	559,691

ROADS
Vehicles Licensed 1971 (estimate)

Cars	Buses	Commercial Vehicles	Motor Cycles
1,660,195	42,471	498,032	132,000*

* 1970 estimate.

SHIPPING*
(Year ended 31st March)

Cargo Handled ('000 tons)					Vessels Handled		
	Landed	Shipped	Total (including cargo transhipped)			Number	Registered Tonnage ('000 cubic metres)
							Net	Gross

Cargo Handled ('000 tons)				Vessels Handled		
	Landed	Shipped	Total (including cargo transhipped)	Number	Net	Gross
1969 . .	18,227	19,118	37,796	21,652	198,291	342,405
1970 . .	21,556	18,005	39,957	20,044	205,146	350,757
1971 . .	27,979	18,881	47,218	21,241	225,563	380,735
1972 . .	28,353	22,343	51,049	19,134	227,735	379,998

* Includes South West Africa (Namibia).

CIVIL AVIATION

	Kilometres Flown	Passengers Carried	Passenger Kilometres ('000)	Air Freight (kg.)	Air Freight Ton-Kilometres	Air Mail (kg.)	Air Mail Ton-Kilometres
Internal Services							
1970	18,190,777	1,244,780	1,056,724	13,401,636	12,338,547	2,565,850	2,488,090
1971	21,152,257	1,337,551	1,125,537	15,446,728	14,090,398	2,492,759	2,415,852
1972	21,018,766	1,463,058	1,229,024	17,847,716	16,243,290	2,579,356	2,482,277
International Regional Services							
1970	1,823,445	75,613	69,886	639,014	634,316	108,099	87,544
1971	2,118,218	100,512	89,154	979,357	908,229	161,402	124,220
1972	2,590,241	132,093	113,553	1,524,682	1,420,307	161,882	118,099
International Overseas Services							
1970	21,247,744	178,437	1,690,978	4,277,969	43,119,758	639,418	6,602,252
1971	24,596,231	199,387	1,857,078	4,689,773	47,235,455	737,350	7,457,638
1972	22,357,267	249,135	2,193,542	6,288,654	57,835,229	746,739	6,821,696

COMMUNICATIONS MEDIA

	Daily Newspapers	Circulation	Telephones	Licensed Radios
1969 .	22	n.a.	1,311,864	1,770,486
1970 .	20	1,382,609	1,572,709	2,014,311

EDUCATION
(1970)

	Institutions		Teachers		Students	
	White	Non-White	White Institutions	Non-White Institutions	White	Non-White
Primary and Secondary . .	2,664	10,150	41,603	56,242	864,407	3,595,552*
Teacher Training	18	40	966	713	12,532	8,706*
Residential Universities and University Colleges . . .	10	5	9,889	929	53,131	5,880
University of South Africa (correspondence)	1		961		13,831	4,039

* Of these, the figures for Africans included in the totals are 1968.

Sources (except where otherwise stated): South African Reserve Bank, *Quarterly Bulletin*; South Africa House, London; Standard Bank *Annual Economic Review: South and South West Africa*, July 1971, *South Africa*, March 1974.

THE CONSTITUTION

The Union of South Africa, embracing the Cape Colony, Natal, the Transvaal and the Orange River Colony in a dominion under the British Crown, was established May 31st, 1910. Following the Statute of Westminster of 1931 the South African Parliament in 1934 passed the Status of the Union Act, which defined the Union as a 'sovereign independent state' with eventual right of secession from the Commonwealth. Since then the representation of non-Whites in Parliament has gradually been reduced with the implementation of the policy of 'separate development' (*see* Bantu Homelands below). In 1936 Cape Africans were removed from the common voters' roll. In 1948 the Indians' right to elect three White representatives under an Act of 1946 was abolished; and a year later the Whites in the mandated territory of South West Africa were given 6 seats in the South African Assembly and 4 in the Senate. In 1956, a bill to remove the Cape Coloureds from the common voters' roll was passed. Africans lost their limited representation in Parliament in 1959. On May 31st, 1961, the Republic of South Africa was established after a majority (849,176) of the 1,633,772 White voters registered their approval in a referendum held in October 1960 and at the same time South Africa left the Commonwealth. The only major change the Republican Constitution made was to substitute a State President for the Queen. English and Afrikaans retained their equal status as the official languages. In 1968 the elimination of the remaining non-White representatives from Parliament, the members elected for the Coloured people, was provided for.

Executive Power

Executive power is vested in a State President, acting on the advice of Ministers of State or the Cabinet, composed of a Prime Minister and 17 other Ministers. The President is elected by an electoral college of members of the Senate and House of Assembly, presided over by the Chief Justice or a Judge of Appeal. He holds office for a seven-year term and is not eligible for re-election unless "it is otherwise decided" by the electoral college. He is Head of State and Commander-in-Chief of the Armed Forces. The Ministers are members of the Executive Council and they are appointed to administer such departments of State as are established by the State President-in-Council. Deputy Ministers, not exceeding eight in number, may be appointed by the State President to assist Ministers in the administration of departments of State. Deputy Ministers are not members of the Executive Council.

Parliament

The Parliament of the Republic consists of the State President, a Senate and a House of Assembly. The State President has power to summon, prorogue and dissolve Parliament, either both Houses simultaneously or the House of Assembly alone. There must be a session of Parliament at least every twelve months.

The Senate

Senators must be nationals of European descent, at least 30 years of age, qualified as voters, and resident at least five years within the Republic.

The Senate, as constituted in December 1965, consists of 54 white members: 41 elected by the electoral colleges of the four provinces (14 for the Transvaal, 11 for the Cape Province, 8 each for the Orange Free State and Natal) and two similarly elected for South West Africa. Eleven members are nominated by the State President, two for each of the four provinces and South West Africa (of whom half are chosen for their thorough knowledge of the reasonable wants and wishes of the non-White people) and one special representative of the interests of the Cape Coloured people.

The House of Assembly

Members of the House of Assembly must be nationals of European descent, must be registered voters and resident for at least five years in the Republic. The House of Assembly continues for five years unless previously dissolved.

All White persons over the age of 18 are entitled to vote, except those who have been convicted of treason, murder, or any other offence punishable by a term of imprisonment without option of a fine.

The House consists of 171 White members; 165 directly elected by White citizens, aged 18 years or over, to represent the electoral divisions of the Republic, and 6 similarly elected to represent the electoral divisions of South West Africa.

Representation of Coloureds

The Coloured Persons Representative Council Act of 1964 established a Council for Coloured Affairs whose function is to advise the Government in regard to matters affecting the interests of the Coloured people of the Republic. This Council has become a self-governing body for the Coloured people with certain legislative and administrative powers and consists of 40 members elected by Coloured voters and 20 nominated members. It is called the Coloured Person's Representative Council. First elections took place in September 1969. All Coloured men and women over 21 are able to vote.

Representation of Blacks

Five of eleven nominated Senators are selected for their thorough acquaintance with the reasonable wants and wishes of the African peoples.

The Native Affairs Act, 1920, made provisions for the establishment in African areas of local and general councils with minor powers of local self-government.

The Representation of Natives Act, 1936, transferred Cape Africans from the same voters' lists as Whites to the Cape Native Voters' Roll and, as a *quid pro quo* for their rights to participate in ordinary elections, empowered them to elect three members of the House of Assembly and two members of the Cape Provincial Council. Special representation for the African population of the Republic as a whole was provided for in that, through electoral colleges Africans could elect four Senators to represent their interests in Parliament, and could also elect some members of the Natives Representative Council, established by the Act.

(For development of the Bantustans and present representation of Africans *see* section at end of chapter.)

Procedure

Money Bills must originate in the House of Assembly, which may not pass a Bill for taxation or appropriation unless it has been recommended by message from the State President during the session. The amendment of money Bills by the Senate is restricted and such Bills, when passed by the House of Assembly in any session, may become law even if the Senate in the same session fails to pass them or passes them with amendments to which the House of Assembly cannot agree. Other Bills, with the exception of those which alter or repeal the provisions of sections 108 and 118 of the Republic of South Africa Constitution Act, may in the event of disagreement between the two Houses, become law after rejection by the Senate in two successive sessions. The provisions of sections 108 and 118 of the Republic of South Africa Constitution Act, relating to the equality of the two official languages of the Republic and the amendment of that Act, may not be altered or repealed unless the Bill embodying the alteration or repeal is passed by both Houses of Parliament sitting together, and at the third reading is agreed to by not less than two-thirds of the total number of members of both Houses.

The State President may assent to, or withhold assent from, a Bill. Two copies of every law, one in English and one in Afrikaans, are to be enrolled on record in the office of the Registrar of the Appellate Division of the Supreme Court of South Africa. In case of conflict between the two copies, that signed by the State President shall prevail.

Each member of each House must make an Oath or Affirmation of Allegiance. A member of one House cannot be elected to the other, but a Minister and a Deputy-Minister may sit and speak, but not vote, in the House of which he is not a member.

Provincial Government

Provision is made for the appointment of an administrator in each province, who holds office for a term of five years. In each province there is also a provincial council consisting of the same number of members as are elected in the province for the House of Assembly, but in no case is the membership to be less than 25. A member of a provincial council ceases to be a member on being elected to either House of the Central Parliament. The powers of the provinces, which relate chiefly to the administration of local affairs (mainly roads, hospitals and education) are subordinate to the powers of the Central Parliament and all provincial ordinances require the consent of the State President-in-Council.

An executive committee of four persons, not necessarily members of the council, together with the administrator as chairman, is elected by the provincial council at its first meeting after each general election. This committee carries on the administration of affairs on behalf of the provincial council. The administrator may, and when required to do so must, act on behalf of the State President-in-Council in regard to all matters in respect of which no powers are reserved or delegated to the provincial council.

THE GOVERNMENT

State President: Rt. Hon. JACOBUS J. FOUCHÉ.

CABINET

(*July* 1974)

Prime Minister: Rt. Hon. BALTHAZAR J. VORSTER.

Minister of Transport: Hon. STEPHANUS L. MULLER.

Minister of National Education: Hon. JOHANNES P. VAN DER SPUY.

Minister of Finance: Dr. the Hon. NICOLAAS D. DIEDERICHS.

Minister of Agriculture: Hon. HENDRIK SCHOEMAN.

Minister of Defence: Hon. PIETER W. BOTHA.

Minister of Tourism and Indian Affairs: Hon. J. C. HEUNIS.

Minister of Foreign Affairs: Dr. the Hon. HILGARD MULLER.

Minister of Health, Coloured and Rehoboth Affairs: Dr. the Hon. SCHALK W. VAN DER MERWE.

Minister of Labour, Posts and Telegraphs: Hon. MARAIS VILJOEN.

Minister of Bantu Administration and Development and Bantu Education: Hon. MICHIEL C. BOTHA.

Minister of Justice and of Police and of Prisons: Hon. J. T. KRUGER.

Minister of Mines, Immigration, Sports and Recreation: Dr. the Hon. P. G. J. KOORNHOF.

Minister of the Interior, Information, Social Welfare and Pensions: Dr. the Hon. CORNELIUS P. MULDER.

Minister of Community Development and of Public Works: Hon. ABRAHAM H. DU PLESSIS.

Minister of Planning and Statistics: Hon. JAN J. LOOTS.

Minister of Economic Affairs: Sen. OWEN P. F. HORWOOD.

Minister of Water Affairs and Forestry and Power: Hon. STEPHANUS P. BOTHA.

DEPUTY MINISTERS

Deputy Minister of Transport: J. W. RALL.

Deputy Minister of Finance and of Economic Affairs: (vacant).

Deputy Minister of Bantu Administration and Education: T. N. H. JANSON.

Deputy Minister of Agriculture: J. J. MALAN.

Deputy Minister of the Interior: C. W. CRUYWAGEN.

Deputy Minister of Coloured Affairs and of Social Welfare and Pensions: H. SMIT.

Deputy Minister of Bantu Development: A. J. RAUBENHEIMER.

DIPLOMATIC REPRESENTATION

EMBASSIES AND LEGATIONS ACCREDITED TO SOUTH AFRICA
(In Pretoria)
(E) Embassy; (L) Legation.

Argentina: 1059 Church St., Hatfield (E); *Ambassador:* F. DEL SOLAR DORREGO.

Australia: 302 Standard Bank Buildings, Church Square (E); *Ambassador:* C. T. MOODIE.

Austria: 10th Floor, Apollo Centre, 405 Church St. (E); *Ambassador:* Dr. E. HESSENBERGER.

Belgium: 275 Pomona St., Muckleneuk (E); *Ambassador:* M. W. J. SWINNEN.

Brazil: 22nd Floor, 2243 Poynton Centre, Church St. West (L); *Minister:* M. A. DA SALVO COIMBRA.

Canada: Netherlands Bank Centre, Cnr. Church and Beatrix Sts. (E); *Ambassador:* A. G. CAMPBELL (also accred. as HC to Botswana, Lesotho and Swaziland).

Finland: 310 Sunnyside Galleries, Sunnyside (L); *Chargé d'Affaires:* K. UGGELDAHL.

France: 807 George Ave., Arcadia (E); *Ambassador:* M. LEGENDRE.

Germany, Federal Republic: 180 Blackwood St., Arcadia (E); *Ambassador:* E. STRÄTLING.

Greece: 995 Pretorius St. (E); *Ambassador:* (vacant).

Israel: 496 Walter Lanham St. (E); *Ambassador:* M. MICHAEL.

Italy: 796 George Ave. (E); *Ambassador:* Dr. A. PIERANTONI.

Malawi: 99 Burns St., Colbyn; *Ambassador:* A. O. C. FUNSANI.

Netherlands: 1st Floor, Netherlands Bank Building, Church St. (E); *Ambassador:* A. H. HASSELMAN.

Portugal: 261 Devenish St. (E); *Ambassador:* Dr. J. E. DE MENESES ROSA.

Spain: 286 Bosman St. (E); *Ambassador:* Count PEÑARRUBIAS.

Sweden: 521 Pretorius St., P.O.B. 1664 (L); *Minister:* Baron C. J. M. RAPPE.

Switzerland: 818 George Ave., P.O.B. 2289 (E); *Ambassador:* T. CURCHOD.

United Kingdom: Greystoke, 6 Hill St. (E); *Ambassador:* Sir JAMES R. A. BOTTOMLEY, K.C.M.G.

U.S.A.: Thibault House, Pretorius St. (E); *Ambassador:* JOHN G. HURD.

South Africa also has relations with China (Taiwan), Denmark, Iran, Japan, Norway and Uruguay.

PARLIAMENT
(Cape Town)

THE SENATE
President: Senator the Hon. JAN DE KLERK.

ELECTION APRIL 1974

	NATIONAL PARTY	UNITED PARTY
Transvaal . . .	12	3
Cape Province . .	8	3
Orange Free State . .	8	
Natal . . .	2	6
South West Africa . .	2	—

There are 10 nominated members.

THE HOUSE OF ASSEMBLY
Speaker: (vacant).

ELECTION APRIL 1974

	SEATS
National Party	123
United Party	41
Progressive Party	7
Herstigte Nasionale Party . . .	—
Democratic Party	—

Of the white voters on the electoral roll in the 125 seats which were contested in 1974 1,134,338 went to the polls. Votes and percentages for each main party were: National Party 636,585 (57.1 per cent), United Party 363,459 (32.7 per cent), Progressive Party 58,768 (5.3 per cent), Herstigte Nasionale Party 39,568 (3.6 per cent), Democratic Party 10,449 (0.9 per cent).

COLOURED PEOPLE'S REPRESENTATIVE COUNCIL
Chairman: TOM SWARTZ.

ELECTION JULY 1972

	SEATS
Labour Party	22
Federal Coloured Peoples' Party . .	31*
National Coloured Peoples' Party . .	1
Republican Coloured Party . .	1
Independent	4
Conservative Coloured Peoples' Party .	—
TOTAL . .	59

* Elected membership of the Council is 40. The remaining 20 seats were filled by the Government with supporters of the Federal Party, which is pro-Government. The Federal Party therefore secured a majority in the Council over the Labour Party, which opposes *apartheid*, and Tom Swartz, leader of the Federal Party, was appointed Chairman.

THE BANTU HOMELANDS
See separate section at end of chapter.

POLITICAL PARTIES

National Party: P.O.B. 245, Pretoria; f. 1912; aims: (1) to safeguard the White nation in its South African homeland; (2) to lead the Black nations to effective self-government in their homelands; (3) to give all nations equal opportunity to develop the social and political organizations best suited to their own particular characteristics and aspirations; (4) to raise living standards in White and Black homelands alike. Leader BALTHAZAR J. VORSTER.

United Party: National Mutual Building, Church Square, Cape Town; f. 1934; seeks a solution of racial problems through the creation of a Federation of Races governed by a Central Parliament in which all racial groups will be represented. The United Party believes in the necessity to maintain overall white political control. Leader Sir DE VILLIERS GRAAFF.

Progressive Party: 6th Floor, Garmor House, Plein St., Cape Town; f. 1959 by breakaway from United Party; aim: a new Constitution based on the principles of maintenance of western civilization and protection of fundamental human rights, irrespective of race, colour, or creed; 7 representatives in Parliament; Leader COLIN W. EGLIN; Nat. Chair. HARRY G. LAWRENCE; Chair. Nat. Exec. R. A. F. SWART.

Herstigte Nasionale Party: Pretoria; f. Oct. 1969 by M.P.s expelled from National Party; believes in word of God as defined by Calvinism, that *apartheid* must be more strictly applied, that external relations must not affect South Africa's sovereignty and that immigration must be controlled to preserve Christian national civilization, favours Afrikaans becoming the National language; Leader Dr. ALBERT HERTZOG; Deputy Leader JAAP MARAIS.

Democratic Party: formed to provide a moderate centre group in South African politics; Chair. THEO GERDENER.

African National Congress of South Africa: f. 1912; aims to establish a non-racial society in co-operation with left-wing and liberal organizations of other races; banned April 1960 after Sharpeville shootings; Pres. NELSON MANDELA (detained for life on Robben Island); Acting Pres. OLIVER TAMBO; Sec.-Gen. ALFRED NZO.

Pan-Africanist Congress of Azania: f. 1959; splinter group from the African National Congress; believes that a democratic society can only come through African and not multiracial organizations; banned April 1960 after Sharpeville shootings; Pres. ROBERT SOBUKWE (banned).

Black People's Convention: f. 1972; first non-tribal black political movement to emerge since 1960; membership limited to Africans; Pres. SIPHO BUTHELEZI.

Indian National Congress of South Africa: f. 1896; Indian organization working with African National Congress in exile; Acting Pres. Dr. DAIDOO.

DEFENCE

Out of total armed forces of 18,000 regulars, the army has 10,000, the navy 2,500 and the air force 5,500. Military training is compulsory for all white citizens. The period of service is a minimum of 12 months continuous service with five further annual training periods. A Coloured Cadet Corps has been established. The Citizen Force reserve totals 92,000 of which the army has 80,000, the navy 9,000 and the air force 3,000. Para-military forces number 75,000 Kommandos, organized and trained as a home guard. There is limited military service for Coloureds and the Government announced plans in May 1973 to establish a service battalion for Asians to be a naval unit, based on Salisbury Island near Durban in 1976. The strength of non-commissioned members of the South African Police Force at December 31st, 1971, was 30,397, of which 15,067 were white. A number of para-military South African police are permanently stationed in Rhodesia, and several have been killed in clashes with African guerrillas near the border with Zambia. Their presence in Rhodesia has been controversial, as is the South African military presence in South West Africa (Namibia) which has been declared illegal by the UN.

Head of South African Defence Forces: Admiral H. H. BIERMANN.

Head of the Army: Lt.-Gen. M. A. DE MALAN, S.M.

Head of the Navy: Vice-Admiral J. JOHNSON, S.M., D.S.C.

Head of the Air Force: Lt.-Gen. J. P. VERSTER.

Chief of the Security Police: Maj.-Gen. G. L. PRINSLOO.

Chairman of the Armaments Board: Prof. SAMUELS.

JUDICIAL SYSTEM

The common law of the Republic of South Africa is the Roman-Dutch law, the uncodified law of Holland as it was at the time of the cecession of the Cape in 1806. The law of England is not recognized as authoritative, though the principles of English law have been introduced in relation to civil and criminal procedure, evidence and mercantile matters. In all other matters, however, Roman Dutch law prevails.

The Supreme Court consists of an Appellate Division; three Provisional Divisions in the Cape Province, one Provincial and one Local Division in each of the provinces of the Transvaal and Natal and one Provincial Division in the Orange Free State and South West Africa. Except for the fact that the local divisions in the Transvaal and Natal have no jurisdiction to hear appeals, they exercise within limited areas the same jurisdiction as Provincial Divisions.

The provinces are further divided into districts and regions with Magistrates' Courts, whose criminal and civil jurisdiction is clearly defined. From these courts appeals may be taken to the Provincial and Local Divisions of the Supreme Court, and thence to the Appellate Division.

THE SUPREME COURT

APPELLATE DIVISION

Chief Justice: Hon. FRANS L. H. RUMPFF.

Judges of Appeal: Hon. D. H. BOTHA, Hon. P. J. VAN BLERK, Hon. E. L. JANSEN, Hon. G. N. HOLMES, Hon. P. J. WESSELS, Hon. H. J. POTGIETER, Hon. W. G. TROLLIP, Hon. P. J. RABIE, Hon. G. VAN R. MULLER.

PROVINCIAL AND LOCAL DIVISIONS

Judge President (*Cape of Good Hope*): Hon. J. T. VAN WYK.

Judge President (*Transvaal*): Hon. P. M. CILLIÉ.

Judge President (*Natal*): Hon. N. JAMES.

Judge President (*Orange Free State*): Hon. J. N. C. DE VILLIERS.

Judge President (*Eastern Cape*): Hon. A. G. JENNETT.

Judge President (*South West Africa*): Hon. F. H. BADENHORST.

Judge (*North-West Cape*): Hon. G. F. DE VOS HUGO.

RELIGION

The South African Council of Churches: Pharmacy House, P.O.B. 31190, Braamfontein, Johannesburg; Gen. Sec. JOHN C. REES.

The Christian Institute of Southern Africa: P.O.B. 31134, Braamfontein, Johannesburg; Head Dr. BEYERS NAUDE.

THE DUTCH REFORMED CHURCH
(Nederduitse Gereformeerde Kerk)

The churches in the four provinces are governed by a synod in each province, united in 1962 under a General Synod which will meet every four years. There are 953 Dutch Reformed Churches in the Union with a membership of 1,695,951 (1960).

CAPE PROVINCE
Moderator: Dr. J. S. GERICKE.

Secretary of Synod and Director of Information Bureau: Rev. W. A. LANDMAN, P.O.B. 930, Cape Town.

NATAL
Moderator: Rev. C. COLYN, Private Bag 9030, Pietermaritzburg.

Commissioner: Rev. S. J. DU TOIT, Gus Brown Ave., Warner Beach.

ORANGE FREE STATE
Moderator: Rev. Dr. A. VAN DER MERWE, P.O.B. 263, Kroonstad.

Scriba Synodi: Rev. Dr. A. J. MINAAR, 110 Andries Pretorius St., Bloemfontein.

NORTHERN TRANSVAAL
Moderator: Dr. F. E. O'BRIEN GELDENHUYS, 325 Hay St., Brooklyn, Pretoria.

Commissioner: Rev. J. E. POTGIETER, P.O.B. 433, Pretoria.

SOUTHERN TRANSVAAL

Moderator: Rev. D. P. M. BEUKES, 18 Central Rd., Lynden East, Johannesburg.

Commissioner: Rev. S. J. ELOFF, 55 President St., Potchefstroom.

THE CHURCH OF THE PROVINCE OF SOUTH AFRICA

The Church of the Province of South Africa is one of the many autonomous branches of the Anglican Communion constituted outside England. It is (like the Church of Ireland, the Protestant Episcopal Church of the U.S.A., and the Church of England in Australia) in full communion with the Church of England. Approx. 1,500,000 mems.

Church of the Province of South Africa: Church House, 1 Queen Victoria St., P.O.B. 1932, Cape Town; Sec. and Treas. G. D. ABERNETHY, B.COM., C.A. (S.A.).

Archbishop of Cape Town and Metropolitan of the Province: Most Rev. BILL BURNETT, D.D., Bishopscourt, Claremont, Cape.

THE ROMAN CATHOLIC CHURCH

In 1970 there were 1,413,196 members of the Roman Catholic Church in South Africa.

Southern Africa Catholic Bishops' Conference (S.A.C.B.C.): P.O.B. 941, Standard Bank Buildings, Church Square, Pretoria.

PROVINCE OF CAPE TOWN

Archbishop of Cape Town: H.E. Cardinal OWEN MCCANN, D.D., D.PH., B.COM., D.LITT.; 12 Bouquet Street, Cape Town.

PROVINCE OF DURBAN

Archbishop of Durban: Most Rev. Archbishop DENIS E. HURLEY, O.M.I., D.D.; 408 Innes Rd., Durban.

PROVINCE OF PRETORIA

Archbishop of Pretoria: Most Rev. Archbishop JOHN C. GARNER, D.D., D.PH.; 125 Main St., Waterkloof, Pretoria.

PROVINCE OF ORANGE FREE STATE

Archbishop of Bloemfontein: Most Rev. Archbishop JOSEPH P. FITZGERALD, O.M.I., D.D.; P.O.B. 362, Bloemfontein.

THE EVANGELICAL LUTHERAN CHURCH

The Federation of Evangelical Lutheran Churches in Southern Africa (FELCSA), formed in 1966 and meeting every three years, is a general synod embracing 13 European and non-European Lutheran churches, including three in South West Africa and one in Rhodesia. Each church has its own leader, who is either a bishop or a president (präses). In 1960 there were 499,246 Lutherans in South and South West Africa.

The German mission societies (the Berliner, Hermannsburger, Rheinische und Herrnhuter) are also important. The German Lutheran congregations in Southern Africa are united in various Evangelical-Lutheran churches which together with other Lutheran congregations of European background form the United Evangelical Lutheran Church in Southern Africa.

OTHER CHURCHES

Bantu Presbyterian Church of South Africa: P.O. Mpolweni, Natal; Gen. Sec. Rev. A. V. NZIMANDE.

Baptist Union of South Africa: 210 Transafrica Building, Wolmarans St., Johannesburg; f. 1877; Pres. Rev. A. S. GILFILLAN; Gen. Sec. Rev. T. M. SWART; 46,511 mems.; publ. *South African Baptist*; circ. 4,579.

Church of England in South Africa: P.O.B. 1530, Cape Town; began with the British occupation of the Cape at the beginning of the nineteenth century, and continued to exist after the secession of the Church of the Province of South Africa in 1870; 20 European Churches (including 3 in Rhodesia), 2 Coloured and over 150 African; Bishops: Rt. Rev. S. C. BRADLEY, L.TH.; Rt. Rev. P. P. CHAMANE; Rt. Rev. W. D. DOUGLAS; Registrar H. HAMMOND, M.A.; publ. *Church News*; circ. 3,000.

Methodist Church of South Africa, The: Methodist Connectional Office, P.O.B. 2256, Durban, Natal; f. 1883; Pres. Rev. J. C. MVUSI; Sec. Rev. CYRIL WILKINS; 386,868 mems.; publ. *Dimension*.

Moravian Church: P.O.B. 11, Lansdowne, Cape Province; Head Bishop SCHABERG.

Nederduitsch Hervormde Kerk Van Afrika: P.O. Box 2368, Pretoria; governed according to Presbyterian Church regulation by a General Church Assembly; Administrator A. B. VAN N. HERBST, 210 Jacob Maré Street, Pretoria; total membership 190,342.

Presbyterian Church of Southern Africa: Head Office: Saambou Building, 112 Commissioner St., P.O.B. 11347, Johannesburg; f. 1897; Gen. Sec. and Clerk of the Assembly, Rev. E. S. PONS, M.A.; 63,000 mems.; publs. *The Christian Leader* (circ. 16,000), *Yearbook* Vols. 1 and 2.

Reformed Church in South Africa (Die Gereformeerde Kerk): P.O.B. 20004, Northbridge, Potchefstroom; f. 1859; publishes ecclesiastical and missionary periodicals; Principal Officer I. J. LESSING, P.O.B. 20004, North Bridge; total membership 141,743, all races.

United Congregational Church of Southern Africa: P.O.B. 31083, Braamfontein, Transvaal; f. 1799; Chair. Rev. B. H. M. BROWN; Secs. Rev. JOSEPH WING, Rev. J. F. THORNE; Regional Secs. Rev. A. A. F. LOCK (Botswana), Rev. B. SPONG (Central), Rev. J. T. PARSONS (Eastern Cape), Rev. B. K. DLUDLA (Natal), Rev. G. O. LLOYD (Rhodesia), Rev. G. NORMANTON (Western Cape); 120,000 mems.; publ. *The Christian Leader*.

JEWISH COMMUNITY

The Jews have been associated with South Africa since its earliest days. There was a party of Jews among the 1820 settlers. An organized Jewish community was founded at Cape Town in 1841 and there are now about 200 congregations in the country, most of them having their own synagogues. The official representative of the World Zionist Organization (and of its various funds and institutions in South Africa) is the South African Zionist Federation.

South African Jewish Board of Deputies: P.O.B. 1180, Johannesburg; f. 1912; is the representative institution of South African Jewry; is composed of all the important congregational and Jewish institutions in South Africa; there are about 118,000 Jews in South Africa; Pres. MAURICE PORTER; Chair. D. K. MANN.

THE PRESS

DAILIES

CAPE PROVINCE

Argus, The: 122 St. George's St., P.O.B. 56, Cape Town; f. 1857; evening; English; Independent; circ. 118,585; Editor W. W. MACKENZIE.

Burger, Die: 30 Keerom St., P.O.B. 692, Cape Town; f. 1915; morning; Afrikaans; supports National Party; circ. 64,263; Editor P. J. CILLIÉ.

Cape Times: 77 Burg St., Cape Town; f. 1876; morning; English; Independent; circulation 75,407; Editor A. H. HEARD.

Daily Dispatch: 33 Caxton St., P.O.B. 131, East London; f. 1872; morning; English; Liberal Independent; circ. 25,897; Editor D. J. WOODS.

Daily Representative: 64 Cathcart Rd., Queenstown; f. 1859; evening; English; circ. 1,723; Man. Dir. F. L. GREEN; Editor M. ARNOT.

Diamond Fields Advertiser: P.O.B. 610, Kimberley; f. 1878; morning; English; Editor M. B. LLOYD.

Eastern Province Herald: Newspaper House, 19 Baakens St., P.O.B. 1117, Port Elizabeth; f. 1845; morning; English; Independent; circ. 29,729; Editor H. E. O'CONNOR.

Evening Post: 19 Baakens St., P.O.B. 1121, Port Elizabeth; f. 1947; afternoon; Independent; English; circ. 24,000 daily edition, 51,000 weekend edition; Editor J. G. SUTHERLAND.

Grocott's Mail: 40 High St., P.O.B. 179, Grahamstown; English; Independent; Editor A. TEMPLE.

Oosterlig, Die: P.O.B. 525, Port Elizabeth; f. 1937; pro-Government; Editor D. J. VAN ZYL; readership approx. 50,000.

NATAL

Daily News, The: 85 Field St., Durban; f. 1878; evening; English; Editor J. M. W. O'MALLEY.

Natal Mercury: 12 Devonshire Place, P.O.B. 950, Durban; f. 1852; morning; English; circ. 76,305; Editor-in-Chief JOHN D. ROBINSON.

Natal Witness: 244 Longmarket St., P.O.B. 362, Pietermaritzburg; f. 1846; morning; English; Editor S. R. ELDRIDGE.

ORANGE FREE STATE

Friend, The and Goldfields Friend: 21 Charles St., P.O.B. 245, Bloemfontein; f. 1850; morning; English; Independent; Editor P. MULLER.

Volksblad, Die: P.O.B. 267, Bloemfontein; f. 1904; evening; Afrikaans; pro-government; circ. daily edition 36,260, weekend edition 31,426; Editor S. F. ZAAIMAN.

TRANSVAAL

Hoofstad: Hoofstad Pers Bpk., P.O.B. 442, Pretoria; Afrikaans; supports Nationalist Party; Man. W. P. M. SCHOOMBEE.

Pretoria News: 216 Vermeulen St., P.O.B. 439, Pretoria; f. 1898; evening; English; Independent; Editor A. T. MYBURGH; Man. R. J. R. GITTINS.

Rand Daily Mail: P.O.B. 1138, 171 Main St., Johannesburg; f. 1902; morning; English; Independent, strongly anti-Government; circ. 140,000; Editor RAYMOND LOUW; Man. J. N. McCLURG.

Star, The: 47 Sauer St., P.O.B. 1014, Johannesburg; f. 1887; evening; English; Independent; Editor J. P. JORDI.

Transvaler, Die: 8 Empire Rd. Extension, Auckland Park, P.O.B. 5474, Johannesburg; f. 1937; morning; Afrikaans; supports National Party; circ. 43,000; Editor C. F. NÖFFKE.

Vaderland, Die: 8 Empire Rd. Extension, Auckland Park, Johannesburg; f. 1914; Afrikaans; supports National Party; circ. 51,532; Editor A. M. VAN SCHOOR; Man. Dir. M. V. JOOSTE.

World, The: P.O.B. 6663, Johannesburg; f. 1932 as a weekly; daily in 1962; English language newspaper catering exclusively for the African people; circ. approx. 110,308; Editorial Dir. C. E. STILL.

WEEKLIES AND FORTNIGHTLIES

CAPE PROVINCE

Cape Herald, The: P.O.B. 56, Cape Town; weekly; Editor D. WIGHTMAN; circ. 83,614.

Courier: Bank St., P.O.B. 64, Beaufort West; f. 1869; Friday; Editor RUFUS DERCKSEN.

District Mail, The: P.O.B. 58, Somerset West; f. 1928; Friday morning; local news; Editor NORMAN McLEOD.

Eikestadnuus: P.O.B. 28, Stellenbosch; Friday; English and Afrikaans; Editor J. L. WEPENER.

Graaff-Reinet Advertiser: P.O.B. 31, Graaff-Reinet; f. 1864; rural; twice weekly; Independent; Editor A. R. KNOTT-CRAIG.

Huisgenoot: P.O.B. 1802, Cape Town; f. 1916; weekly; Editor P. A. JOUBERT.

Imvo Zabantsundu (*Bantu Opinion*): P.O.B. 190, King-williamstown; f. 1884; Editor J. G. GEURTSE.

Jongspan, Die: P.O.B. 1802, Cape Town; f. 1935; only Afrikaans juvenile weekly in South Africa; Editor C. MOSTERT.

Kerkbode, Die: P.O.B. 4539, Cape Town; f. 1849; official organ of the Dutch Reformed Church of South Africa; Editor Dr. W. J. G. LUBBE.

Mafeking Mail and Botswana Guardian: P.O.B. 64, Mafeking; f. 1899; English and Afrikaans; Fri.; Editor J. PODBREY; circ. 1,600.

Mercury, The: P.O.B. 122, King-williamstown; f. 1875; Thursday; general; English; Editor D. J. WOODS.

Midland News and Karroo Farmer: P.O. Box 101, Cradock; f. 1891; English; weekly; Editor J. B. FINLAISON.

Paarl Post: Upper New St., P.O.B. 248, Paarl; f. 1875; Tuesdays and Fridays; Afrikaans and English; Independent; Editor M. HENDLER.

South African Medical Journal: P.O.B. 643, Cape Town; weekly; organ of the Medical Association of South Africa; Editor P. J. VAN BILJON, M.B., CH.B., M.D.

South Western Herald: 119 York St., George; f. 1881; twice weekly; Man. S. R. BELL.

Uitenhage Chronicle: P.O.B. 44, 122 Caledon St., Uitenhage; f. 1880; weekly; general; English and Afrikaans; Editor E. M. HARPER.

Uitenhage Times, The: P.O.B. 46, Uitenhage; f. 1864; bilingual; Prop. and Editor J. S. HULTZER.

Umthunywa: Owen St., P.O.B. 129, Umtata; f. 1937; English and Xhosa; Editor J. D'OLIVEIRA.

Uniondale and Langkloof Medium: P.O.B. 31, Graaff Reinet; f. 1937; general news; Editor R. C. KNOTT-CRAIG.

Weekend Argus, The: P.O.B. 56, Cape Town; f. 1857; Saturday; English; circ. 156,072; Editor W. W. MACKENZIE.

NATAL

Darling: P.O.B. 83, Mobeni, Durban; f. 1952; fortnightly; Editor MARILYN HATTINGH.

Farmers' Weekly: P.O.B. 83, Mobeni, Natal; f. 1911; Wednesday; agriculture; Editor E. C. HAVINGA.

The Graphic: P.O.B. 2339, Durban; English; f. 1950; weekly; Editor M. S. ACHARY.

Ilanga: 128 Umgeni Rd., Durban; f. 1903; weekly; Zulu; Editorial Dir. A. J. KONIGKRAMER.

Indian Opinion: Private Bag, Durban; f. 1903; English and Gujerati; Editor Mrs. SUSHILA M. GANDHI.

Ladysmith Gazette: P.O.B. 500, Ladysmith; f. 1902; Thursday; circ. 3,200; Editor and Advt. Man. R. M. ROBINSON.

Leader, The: P.O.B. 2471, Durban; f. 1940; Ind.; English; weekly; Indian newspaper; Editor S. S. R. BRAMDAW.

Newcastle Advertiser: P.O.B. 144, Newcastle; f. 1901; weekly; English and Afrikaans; Gen. Man. M. W. D. POPE.

Personality: 1322 South Coast Rd., Mobeni, Durban; f. 1957; Friday; national fortnightly; Editor MARILYN HATTINGH.

Scope: 1322 South Coast Rd., Mobeni, Durban; f. 1966; Friday; national weekly news magazine; Group Editor JACK SHEPHERD-SMITH; Editor LEON BENNETT.

Sunday Tribune: P.O.B. 1491, Durban; f. 1947; English; Independent; Editor J. E. C. SCOTT.

Umafrika: P.O. Mariannhill, Natal; Zulu weekly; f. 1911; circ. 11,000; Editor CRISPIN GRAHAM, C.M.M.

ORANGE FREE STATE

Bethlehem Express: 10 Muller St., P.O.B. 555, Bethlehem; f. 1905; bilingual; farming and commercial; circ. 2,075; Editor T. C. ROFFE, M.C.

Noordeltke Stem, Die/The Northern Times: Murray St., P.O.B. 309, Kroonstad; English and Afrikaans; Friday; Editor E. J. DE LANGE.

People's Weekly: P.O.B. 286, Bloemfontein; f. 1911; English; Independent; circ. 6,500.

TRANSVAAL

African Jewish Newspaper: 25 Davies Street, Doornfontein, Johannesburg; f. 1931; Friday; Yiddish; Editor LEVI SHALIT.

Boksburg Advertiser and Boksburg Volksblad: P.O.B. 136, Boksburg; English and Afrikaans; Friday; Editor S. GILL.

Brandwag, Die: 20 Simmonds St. South, Selby, P.O.B. 48092, Johannesburg; f. 1971; weekly; Afrikaans; pro-government; Editor JOHAN FOURIE; circ. 80,000.

Germiston Advocate and Germiston Koerant: P.O.B. 7, Germiston; f. 1923; weekly; English and Afrikaans; Editor and Man. S. GILL.

Middelburg Observer: P.O.B. 36, Middelburg; f. 1903; weekly; coal mining, farming and educational.

Northern Review: P.O.B. 45, Pietersburg; English and Afrikaans; Friday.

Post: P.O.B. 6663, Johannesburg; f. 1935; general weekly; Editor C. R. VINEALL.

Potchefstroom Herald: 3B Olën Lane, Potchefstroom; f. 1908; weekly; English and Afrikaans; Editor R. W. INGRAM.

Pronk: 20 Simmonds St. South, Selby, P.O.B. 48092, Johannesburg; f. 1971; fortnightly; Afrikaans; Editor JOHAN FOURIE; circ. 92,000.

Rapport: Cnr. Menton Rd. and Empire Rd. Extension, Auckland Park; P.O.B. 8422, Johannesburg; f. 1971; Afrikaans Sunday newspaper with pro-government leanings; Editor W. J. WEPENER.

Rustenburg Herald: P.O.B. 170, Rustenburg; f. 1924; weekly; English and Afrikaans; Prop. Rustenburg Herald (Pty.) Ltd.; Managing Editor H. M. WULFSE.

S.A. Mining and Engineering Journal: Balgownie House, 66 Commissioner St., Johannesburg; f. 1891; technical journal; Gen. Manager P. H. CLARK; Editor G. M. THAIN.

The South African Financial Gazette: P.O.B. 8161, Johannesburg; f. 1964; weekly; English; Editor MARTIN SPRING.

South African Jewish Times (incorp. the **Rhodesian Jewish Journal**): P.O.B. 2878, Johannesburg; f. 1936; English-Jewish weekly; circ. 13,000; Editor ARTHUR MARKO-WITZ.

Stage and Cinema: P.O.B. 1556, Johannesburg; f. 1946; cinema, entertainment, fashion; fortnightly; Man. Editor S. A. DAVID; circ. 30,000.

Sunday Express: 171 Main St., P.O.B. 1067, Johannesburg; f. 1934; English; Independent; circ. 205,000; Editor M. A. JOHNSON.

Sunday Times: 171 Main St., P.O.B. 1090, Johannesburg; f. 1906; English; Independent; circ. 470,000; Editor JOEL MERVIS.

Uitspan: 20 Simmonds St. South, Selby, P.O.B. 48092, Johannesburg; f. 1971; weekly; Afrikaans; Editor VERA GIBSON; circ. 56,000.

Vereeniging and Vanderbijlpark News: P.O.B. 122, Vereeniging; f. 1915; Thursday; circ. 8,000; Editor B. BYRNE-DALY.

Weekend World: P.O.B. 6663, Johannesburg; f. 1968; general weekly; Editor C. E. STILL; circ. 177,396.

West Rand Review-Koerant: P.O.B. 171, Krugersdorp; f. 1898; Editor P. V. J. WALT.

West Rand Times and Westrander: Grand Chambers, Ockerse St., P.O.B. 93, Krugersdorp; f. 1934; bilingual; Editor S. GILL.

Westelike Stem, Die: 110 King Edward St., Potchefstroom; f. 1915; Afrikaans newspaper; circ. 3,000.

Zionist Record: P.O.B. 150, Johannesburg; f. 1908; weekly; English; circ. 10,000; Editor A. BEN-VERED.

MONTHLIES
CAPE PROVINCE

Commercial Opinion (*Journal of the Association of Chambers of Commerce of South Africa*): P.O.B. 566, Cape Town; f. 1923; circ. 15,060; Editor W. B. WEST, B.COM.

Education: 15 Grove Bldg., Grove Ave., Claremont, Cape Town; f. 1890; organ of the South African Teachers' Association; circ. 2,750; Editor W. T. FERGUSON; Man. Editor J. A. CLARKSON.

New African, The: P.O.B. 2068, Cape Town; politics and the arts.

South African Banker, The: P.O.B. 61510, Marshalltown, Transvaal; published by The Institute of Bankers in South Africa; f. 1904; circ. 14,500; Editor PETER KRAAK.

South African Outlook: Outlook Publications (Pty.) Ltd., P.O.B. 245, Rondebosch; f. 1870; ecumenical and racial affairs; Editor FRANCIS WILSON

South African Shipping News and Fishing Industry Review: P.O.B. 80, Cape Town; f. 1946; Editor Michael Stuttaford.

Unie, Die: P.O.B. 196, Cape Town; f. 1905; educational; organ of the South African Teachers' Union; Editor M. J. L. Olivier.

Wamba: 1 Leeuwen St., Cape Town; educational; publ. in seven African languages; Editor C. P. Senyatsi.

Wynboer, Die: Kaapag Trust (Pty.) Ltd., P.O.B. 115, Stellenbosch; f. 1931; devoted to the interest of viti-culture and the wine and spirit industry of South Africa; Editor G. R. F. Meyer.

NATAL

Home Front: c/o Mercury Bldg., Devonshire Place, P.O.B. 950, Durban; f. 1928; ex-Service magazine; Editor E. Gray.

Natal Review: 413 Paynes Bldgs., West St., P.O.B. 2434, Durban; English; trade review.

Reality: P.O.B. 1104, Pietermaritzburg; f. 1969; general political; Liberal; every two months.

South African Garden and Home: P.O.B. 83, Mobeni, Durban; f. 1947; monthly; Editor W. M. Hyman.

ORANGE FREE STATE

Merino: P.O.B. 402, Bloemfontein; f. 1941; circ. 23,000; Editor S. H. J. van Vuuren.

TRANSVAAL

Commercial Transport and Freight: P.O.B. 8308, Johannesburg; f. 1946; monthly; Editor D. Mearns.

Ditaba: P.O.B. 164, Potgietersrus; f. 1959; English and Sotho; Editor Daniel Tsebe.

Drum: 62 Eloff St. Extension, Johannesburg; f. 1951; twice monthly; circ. 80,000 in southern Africa, 400,000 throughout the continent; Editor P. Selwyn-Smith.

Financial Times and Industrial Press: P.O.B. 6620, Johannesburg; monthly; Editor D. Tommey.

Food Industries of South Africa: P.O.B. 8308, Johannesburg; f. 1948; Editor I. Philip.

Forum, The: P.O.B. 7108, Johannesburg; Editor N. A. G. Caley.

Journal of the South African Institute of Mining and Metallurgy: P.O.B. 61019, Marshalltown, Transvaal; f. 1894; circ. 2,300; Editor Dr. H. Glen.

Mining and Industrial Review: P.O.B. 9259, Johannesburg; f. 1907; Editor Leo Lavoo.

Ons Jeug: P.O.B. 2406, Pretoria; f. 1951; religious; Editor G. van der Westhuizen; circ. 12,000.

Photography and Travel: P.O.B. 8620, Johannesburg; f. 1963; monthly; Editor Cecil Holmes; circ. 8,000.

Postal and Telegraph Herald: P.O.B. 9186, Johannesburg; f. 1904; English and Afrikaans; circ. 12,000; Editor L. J. van der Linde.

Railway Engineering: P.O.B. 8308, Johannesburg; f. 1957; twice monthly; Editor Ken Milward.

S.A. Engineer and Electrical Review: P.O.B. 8308, Johannesburg; f. 1918; trade and technical; Joint Editors C. Waller, A. Waters.

S.A. Mining and Engineering Journal: P.O.B. 8308, Johannesburg; f. 1891; trade and technical; Editor P. Holz.

South African Architectural Record: 75 Howard House, Loveday Street, Johannesburg; f. 1915; journal of the Institute of South African Architects; Editor W. Duncan Howie, A.R.I.B.A., M.I.A.

South African Builder: Federated Insurance House, Cnr. Harrison St. and De Villiers St., P.O.B. 11359, Johannesburg; f. 1923; official journal of Building Industries Federation (South Africa); circ. 4,800; Editor G. De C. Malherbe.

South African Mechanical Engineer, The: P.O.B. 61019, Marshalltown, Johannesburg; f. 1892; journal of the South African Institution of Mechanical Engineers; Hon. Tech. Editor E. A. Bunt; Prod. Editor Mrs. L. Kraft.

South African Mining Review: 709-711 Union House, Main St., Johannesburg; f. 1907; Editor D. I. Haddon.

South African Nursing Journal: P.O.B. 1280, Pretoria; f. 1935; official organ of the South African Nursing Association; circ. 33,450; Editor Barbara L. Alford.

South African Philatelist: P.O.B. 375, Johannesburg; published by the Philatelic Federation of Southern Africa; Hon. Editor J. M. Weinstein.

Southern African Financial Mail: P.O.B. 9959, Carlton Centre, Commissioner St., Johannesburg; f. 1959; circ. 21,000; Editor George Palmer.

SASSAR (South African Railways Magazine): P.O.B. 1111, Johannesburg; f. 1910; Man. Editor P. le F. Strydom.

Utlwang: P.O. Box 170, Rustenburg; Tswana (Bantu); Prop. Utlwang Tswana Publications (Pty.) Ltd.; Managing Editor H. M. Wulfse.

Wings over Africa: P.O.B. 68585, Bryanston, Transvaal; f. 1941; the aviation news magazine of Africa; Editor and Man. Dir. J. K. Chilwell.

QUARTERLIES
CAPE PROVINCE

South African Law Journal: P.O.B. 30, Cape Town; f. 1884; Editor Ellison Kahn, B.Com., LL.M.

TRANSVAAL

Lantern: P.O.B. 1758, Pretoria; organ of the Foundation for Education, Science and Technology (formerly S.A. Assoc. for Advancement of Knowledge and Culture); Managing Editor V. C. Wood.

Motorist, The: P.O.B. 7068, Johannesburg; f. 1902; official journal of the Automobile Association of S.A.; quarterly; Editor A. Bezuidenhout; circ. 490,000.

South African Journal of Economics: P.O.B. 31213, Braamfontein; English and Afrikaans; Man. Editor Prof. D. J. J. Botha.

South African Journal of Medical Sciences: Witwatersrand University Press, Jan Smuts Ave., Johannesburg; f. 1935; Editor Prof. H. B. Stein.

South African Journal of Physiotherapy: P.O.B. 11151, Johannesburg; official journal of South African Society of Physiotherapy; Editor Miss E. M. Botting.

NEWS AGENCIES

South African Press Association: P.O.B. 7766, Mutual Buildings, Harrison St., Johannesburg; f. 1938; 28 mems.; Chair. D. P. de Villiers; Man. R. A. Wilson; Editor E. H. Linington.

FOREIGN BUREAUX

Agence France-Presse: P.O.B. 3462, Lydney House, 99 Goud St., Johannesburg; Bureau Man. Edmond Marco.

AP: 701-3 Union Centre, 31 Pritchard St., Johannesburg; Chief Kenneth L. Whiting.

Jewish Telegraphic Agency: De Villiers and Banket Sts., Johannesburg.

Reuters General News Division: P.O.B. 2662, Mutual Building, Harrison St., Johannesburg; also has offices in Cape Town, Durban and Port Elizabeth.

Reuters Ltd.: P.O.B. 2662, Glencairn, Market St., Johannesburg.

UPI: P.O.B. 2385, Standard Bank Chambers, 1st Floor, 33 Troye St., Johannesburg; Man. MICHAEL KEATS.

DPA also has an office in South Africa.

PRESS ASSOCIATION

Newspaper Press Union of South Africa: P.O.B. 10537, 914 9th Floor, B.P. Centre, 36 Kerk St., Johannesburg; f. 1882; 173 mems.; Pres. L. E. A. SLATER; Sec. G. G. A. UYS.

PUBLISHERS

Argus Printing and Publishing Co. Ltd.: P.O.B. 1014, 47 Sauer St., Johannesburg; f. 1889; newspapers; Chair. and Man. Dir. L. E. A. SLATER; Gen. Mans. J. D. ST. C. HENNESSY and C. L. C. HEWITT.

Balkema, A. A.: 93 Keerom St., Cape Town; science, literature, history, architecture, fine arts.

Buren Publishers: P.O.B. 673, Cape Town; general fiction and non-fiction.

Butterworth and Co. (South Africa) (Pty.) Ltd.: P.O.B. 792, Durban.

Cape and Transvaal Printing and Publishing Co. Ltd.: 77 Burg St., P.O.B. 81, Cape Town; Chair. C. S. CORDER; Man. Dir. G. M. C. CRONWRIGHT.

Central News Agency Ltd.: P.O.B. 1033, Johannesburg.

Christian Publishing Co.: P.O.B. 132, Roodepoort, Transvaal; f. 1939; religious books and children's books in colour; Principal Officers TIMO CROUS, MAURICE SPIES, Mrs. M. M. CROUS.

Combined Publishers (Pty.) Ltd.: subsidiary of the Argus Printing and Publishing Co., 5th Floor, Star Building, 47 Sauer St., P.O.B. 8620, Johannesburg; reference books.

Constantia Publishers: P.O.B. 5, Cape Town; general fiction and non-fiction.

Da Gama Publishers (Pty.) Ltd.: 311 Locarno House, Loveday St., Johannesburg; prestige, industrial and travel books and journals; Man. Dir. FRANK DE FREITAS.

David Philip Publishers: 3 Scott Rd., Claremont, Cape Town; general, academic, educational, juvenile.

Die Kinderpers: P.O.B. 2652, Cape Town; juvenile and educational.

Goeie Hoop-Uitgewers (Bpk.): P.O.B. 972, Johannesburg.

Government Printer: Bosman St., Pretoria.

H.A.U.M.: 58 Long St., P.O.B. 1371, Cape Town; general educational and juvenile.

Hugh Keartland Publishers Ltd.: P.O.B. 9221, Johannesburg; general fiction and non-fiction.

Human and Rousseau (Pty.) Ltd.: P.O.B. 5050, Cape Town; English and Afrikaans books; Dirs. J. J. HUMAN, L. ROUSSEAU, D. J. OPPERMAN, F. J. DAVIN.

Janda (Pty.) Ltd.: P.O.B. 2177, Cape Town; limited editions, art and flowers; Dirs. DAVID SCHRIRE, J. P. SCHRIRE, R. B. DEVITT.

Juta and Co. Ltd.: P.O.B. 30, Cape Town; f. 1853; Dirs. J. A. B. COOPER, T. G. DUNCAN, Q.C., J. D. DUNCAN, G. F. LAURENCE, J. E. CALDER, B. W. PARIS, J. E. DUNCAN, legal, technical, educational, general.

J. P. van der Walt en Seun (Edms.) Bpk.: P.O.B. 123, Pretoria; f. 1947; general; Man. Dir. J. P. VAN DER WALT.

Longman Southern Africa (Pty.) Ltd.: P.O.B. 1616, Cape Town; education and general; representing Longman Group, Penguin Books, Oliver and Boyd, Churchill/Livingstone and Ladybird Books.

Lovedale Press: Lovedale, C.P.

McGraw-Hill Book Co.: P.O.B. 23423, Joubert Park, Johannesburg; educational and general.

Macmillan S.A. (Publishers) Ltd.: P.O.B. 31487, Braamfontein; f. 1966; educational and general; Man. Dir. D. MITCHELL.

Maskew Miller Ltd.: 7-11 Burg St., P.O.B. 396, Cape Town; f. 1893; educational, scientific, general and fiction; Chair. B. W. MASKEW MILLER.

Nasionale Boekhandel: P.O.B. 119, Parow, Cape Province; fiction, general (English and Afrikaans).

Nasou Ltd.: P.O.B. 105, Parow; educational.

Oxford University Press: P.O.B. 1141, Cape Town; Gen. Man. N. C. GRACIE.

Perskor Publishers: P.O.B. 845, Johannesburg; f. 1971; general and educational; Gen. Man. D. S. VAN DER MERWE.

President Publishers: P.O.B. 1774, Johannesburg; Afrikaans fiction.

Pro Rege Press: P.O.B. 343, Potchefstroom; educational, religious and general.

Reijger Publishers: P.O.B. 2153, Cape Town; general fiction and non-fiction.

Romantica Press: P.O.B. 799, Cape Town; general fiction and non-fiction.

Shuter and Shuter (Pty.) Ltd.: P.O.B. 109, Pietermaritzburg; f. 1921; educational in English and Zulu, general; Chair. F. B. OSCROFT.

C. Struik Publishers (Pty.) Ltd.: P.O.B. 1144, Cape Town; specialists in all books dealing with Africa; Dirs. G. STRUIK, Mrs. J. W. STRUIK VAN HARTINGSVELDT, P. STRUIK.

Tafelberg Uitgewers: P.O.B. 879, Cape Town; f. 1950; children's books, fiction and non-fiction, historical books, etc.; Man. Dir. H. G. JAEKEL.

Thomson Publications, South Africa (Pty.) Ltd.: P.O.B. 8308, Johannesburg; trade and technical; Chair. B. PAVER.

Timmins, Howard: P.O.B. 94, Cape Town; f. 1937.

University Publishers and Booksellers (Pty.) Ltd.: P.O.B. 29, Stellenbosch, C.P.; educational and children's books.

Van Schaik, J. L., Ltd.: P.O.B. 724, Pretoria; f. 1914; fiction, general, educational; English, Afrikaans and vernacular; Man. Dir. JAN J. VAN SCHAIK.

Via Afrika Ltd.: P.O.B. 1097, Bloemfontein; Bantu educational.

White, A. C., Printing and Publishing Co. (Pty.) Ltd.: P.O.B. 286, Bloemfontein.

William Heinemann (South Africa) (Pty.) Ltd.: P.O.B. 11190, Johannesburg; f. 1967; fiction, general, educational, specialists in African Studies; Man. Dir. A. STEWART.

Witwatersrand University Press: Jan Smuts Ave., Johannesburg; f. 1938; academic; Publ. Officer N. H. WILSON.

World Printing and Publishing Co. (Pty.) Ltd.: P.O.B. 6663, Johannesburg; f. 1932; publishers of *The World, Weekend World, Ilanga*, newspapers serving the African market; Chair. L. E. A. SLATER; Man. Dir. J. D. St. C. HENNESSY; Editorial Dirs. C. E. STILL, A. KONIGKRAMER.

South African Publishers' Association: P.O.B. 122, Parow; founded in 1946 the Association affords book publishers the means of dealing collectively with many problems.

It represents publishers in dealing with government departments, local authorities and other institutions. Chair. H. G. JAEKEL; Sec. P. G. VAN ROOYEN.

PUBLICATIONS CONTROL BOARD

South African Publications Control Board: P.O.B. 9069, Cape Town; f. 1963; controls all entertainments and reading matter except daily and weekly newspapers; Chair. J. J. KRUGER.

RADIO AND TELEVISION

RADIO

South African Broadcasting Corporation: P.O.B. 8606, Johannesburg; Chairman of Control Board Dr. P. J. MEYER; Dir. Gens. J. N. SWANEPOEL, C. D. FUCHS.

Broadcasting in South Africa is carried on exclusively by the South African Broadcasting Corporation, a public utility organization established on August 1st, 1936, in terms of the Broadcasting Act No. 22. In 1949 the Act was amended to empower the SABC to broadcast to South-West Africa and to foreign countries. The SABC derives its revenue from licences and advertising. It is government-controlled.

Licences (1972): approx. 2,350,000 licence holders.

DOMESTIC SERVICES

English Service; Afrikaans Service; Springbok Radio (the three national services); Radio Highveld; Radio Port Natal; Radio Good Hope (the three regional advertising services).

Radio South Africa: includes all-night service from 12.00 midnight to 5.00 a.m.

Radio Bantu: broadcasts in Zulu, Xhosa, Southern Sotho, Northern Sotho, Tswana, Tsonga, Venda, Ndonga, Kuanyama, Nama/Damara and Herero.

Lourenço Marques Radio: This station is owned by the Radio Club of Mozambique but the youth-oriented programmes and advertising service are managed by the SABC. It broadcasts nationwide on shortwave and medium wave for 168 hours per week.

EXTERNAL SERVICE

Voice of South Africa: Bloemendal, near Johannesburg; short-wave station; broadcasting in English, Afrikaans, French, Portuguese, Dutch, German, Tsonga, Swahili and Chichewa.

Orlando Rediffusion Service (Pty.) Ltd.: 110-112 Denhil, Corner Bertha and Jorissen Sts., Braamfontein, Johannesburg; subsidiary of Rediffusion Ltd., London; f. 1952; wired broadcasting system distributing special "Bantu" programmes of the South African Broadcasting Corporation in the African township of Orlando; programmes 16 hours daily; Man. R. D. RAMSAY; 10,400 subscribers (1962).

TELEVISION

Services will begin in 1976, and will be run by the South African Broadcasting Corporation. Initially there will be a service of about 37 hours a week on one channel only, in English and Afrikaans. Later a decision will be taken on separate services in English, Afrikaans and the main Bantu languages.

FINANCE

BANKING

(cap.=capital; p.u.=paid up; dep.=deposits; m.=million; R.=Rand)

In May 1973 the Government announced plans for the nationalization of all banks over the next ten years though these have since been considerably modified and in November 1973 the Finance Minister said that though foreign banks would be required to reduce their shareholdings to 50 per cent by 1983, they would no longer be forced to reduce them further to 10 per cent.

CENTRAL BANK

South African Reserve Bank: Church Square, Pretoria; f. 1920; cap. p.u. R.2m.; dep. R.961m. (July 1973); Gov. Dr. T. W. DE JONGH; Sen. Deputy Gov. Dr. D. G. FRANZSEN; Deputy Govs. Dr. G. P. C. DE KOCK, H. O. DE VILLIERS; publs. *Quarterly Bulletin, Annual Economic Report*.

COMMERCIAL BANKS

Bank of Lisbon and South Africa Ltd.: 286 Bosman St., Pretoria, and four branches; f. 1965; cap. 80m. escudos.

Barclays National Bank Ltd.: P.O.B. 1153, Johannesburg; Chief Gen. Man. H. S. MORONY, O.B.E.; cap. and res. R.83m.; publ. *Barclays National Review*.

First National City Bank (South Africa) Ltd.: 60 Market St., Johannesburg; a subsidiary of First National City Bank of New York (U.S.A.); eight branches; Man. Dir. G. L. BENNETT.

French Bank of Southern Africa Ltd.: 50 Marshall St., Johannesburg, and ten branches; f. 1949; subsidiary of Banque de l'Indochine, Paris; cap. p.u. R.2.3m.; dep. R.105m. (Dec. 1972); Man. Dir. R. M. B. AGIER; Asst. Gen. Mans. L. J. G. GIRAUD, P. H. CAVARD.

Nedbank Ltd.: Nedbank Central, 81 Main St., Johannesburg; f. 1888; South African owned; cap. R.12.5m.; dep. R.577m. (Sept. 1971); Man. Dir. G. S. MULLER; Sen. Gen. Mans. D. T. NICHOLSON, R. J. N. ABRAHAMSEN.

South African Bank of Athens Ltd., The: 103 Fox St., Johannesburg; f. 1947; cap. R.1m.; dep. R.10.6m.; Man. Dir. JOHN ZOUNGOS.

Standard Bank of South Africa Ltd., The: 78 Fox St., Johannesburg; f. 1962; cap. p.u. R.38,180,200 (1970); Chief Gen. Man. G. M. F. OXFORD; publ. *Standard Bank Review* (monthly).

The Stellenbosch District Bank Ltd.: Bird St., Stellenbosch; f. 1882; cap. p.u. R.97,700; dep. R.14m. (1972); Chair. P. K. MORKEL.

Volkskas Ltd.: P.O.B. 578, 229 Van Der Walt St., Pretoria; f. 1935; cap. R.14m.; dep. R.699m. (March 1971); Chair. Dr. J. A. HURTER; Man. Dir. D. P. S. VAN HUYSSTEEN; 502 offices.

GENERAL BANKS

Nefic Ltd.: Cnr. Church and Andries Sts., Pretoria; a wholly owned subsidiary of the Netherlands Bank of S.A. Ltd.; cap. p.u. R.2.5m.; provides medium- and long-term finance; Chair. F. J. C. CRONJE.

Rand Bank Ltd.: Rand Bank Centre, Cnr. Jorissen and Melle Sts., Johannesburg; f. 1966; cap. p.u. and res. R.6.4m.; dep. R.91.9m.; specializes in shipping and confirming, the financing of the movement of goods, etc.; Chief Exec. E. T. J. VAN RENSBURG.

Santam Bank Ltd.: Cnr. Burg and Castle Sts., P.O.B. 653, Cape Town; Chair. C. H. J. VAN ASWEGEN; Man. Dir. I. J. STEYN.

FINANCE HOUSES

Central Finance Corporation of South Africa Ltd.: Commissioner St., Johannesburg; f. 1956; merchant bankers; Chair. M. S. LOUW; Gen. Man. and Sec. J. A. VENTER.

Credit Corporation of South Africa Ltd.: Hollard Place, 71 Fox St., Johannesburg; f. 1946; a registered banking institution; 12 brs. throughout South Africa; provides medium-term instalment finance for the purchase or leasing of machinery, office equipment; commercial vehicles, automobiles, etc.; Letters of Credit established for direct imports by instalment buyers; Chair. Dr. B. H. HOLSBOER.

Industrial Development Corporation of South Africa Ltd.: P.O.B. 6905, Johannesburg; f. 1940 as Statutory Body; Chair. J. J. KITSHOFF.

Industrial Finance Corporation of South Africa Ltd.: P.O.B. 8575, Johannesburg; f. 1957; provides capital for development of industry in South Africa; mems. include principal mining groups, commercial banks and life assurance companies operating in the Republic, the South African Reserve Bank and the Industrial Development Corporation of South Africa Ltd.; Sec. K. L. KINGMA.

Land and Agricultural Bank of South Africa: Cnr. of Paul Kruger and Visagie Sts., P.O.B. 375, Pretoria.

National Industrial Credit Corporation Ltd.: 12 New St. South, Johannesburg; finance and discounting business; cap. p.u. R.2.2m.; Chair. C. F. TODD.

Sentrale Aksepbank Bpk. (Central Merchant Bank Ltd.): 18 Fox St., Johannesburg; cap. p.u. R.10m.; dep. R.136m.; Chair. (vacant); Man. Dir. H. P. DE VILLIERS.

South African Scottish Finance Corp. Ltd.: P.O.B. 7482, Johannesburg; subsidiary of Credcor Bank Ltd.; cap. p.u. R.600,000; dep. R.6m. (1971); 12 branches throughout South Africa; provides medium-term instalment finance for the purchase or leasing of machinery, office equipment, commercial vehicles, automobiles, etc.; Letters of Credit established for direct imports by instalment buyers; Chair. Dr. B. H. HOLSBOER.

Trade & Industry Acceptance Corporation Ltd.: 4th Floor, Standard Chambers, 158 Jeppe St., P.O.B. 1055, Johannesburg; finance for business to acquire machinery and equipment on deferred payment or lease.

Trust Bank of Africa Ltd.: The Trust Bank Centre, P.O.B. 2116, Cape Town; f. 1954; banking investment and insurance services, including international finance and trade; cap. p.u. and reserves R.39m.; dep. R.600m. (1971); Chair. and Chief Exec. Officer Dr. JAN S. MARAIS; Man. Dir. A. P. J. BURGER.

Union Acceptances Ltd.: Carlton Centre, P.O.B. 582, Johannesburg; brs. at Cape Town, Durban, Port Elizabeth; f. 1955; total assets R.337m. (Syfrets-UAL Group, Dec. 1972); funds under administration R.1,500m.; registered merchant bank providing banking facilities, investment advice, economic research, and handling new issues, mergers, amalgamations, take-over bids, investment management of portfolios, closed-end trusts and mutual fund, company and financial analysis, economic research, shipping, export finance, deposits and foreign exchange, insurance broking; Chair. L. G. ABRAHAMSE; Man. Dir. A. N. D. BRYCE.

UDC Bank Ltd.: 10th Floor, Unicorn House, Cnr. Marshall & Sauer Sts., Johannesburg; f. 1937; money accepted on deposit; acceptance credits; non-recourse import and export financing; term loans; finance for hire purchase or leasing of plant, machinery, private and commercial vehicles; cap. R.2,500,000; dep. R.66,872,383; Chair. C. W. DACE; Man. Dir. I. R. SUMMERS.

Western Bank Ltd.: Schlesinger Centre, P.O.B. 1066, Braamfontein, Johannesburg; f. 1968; cap. p.u. R.2.3m.; dep. R.207.9m. (June 1973); Chair. M. D. MOROSS; Man. Dir. D. B. SANGER.

MERCHANT BANKS

City Merchant Bank Ltd.: Head Office, Johannesburg.

The Hill Samuel Group (S.A.) Ltd.: 70 Fox St., Johannesburg; a subsidiary of Hill Samuel & Co. Ltd., London; specialize in full range of merchant banking facilities, general insurance broking and pension fund consulting; cap. R.7.2m.; dep. R.20.6m.; Chair. G. V. RICHDALE; Chief Exec. F. J. LEISHMAN.

SAVINGS BANK

Post Office Savings Bank: The Postmaster-General, Dept. of Posts and Telegraphs, General Post Office, Pretoria.

DISCOUNT HOUSES

The Discount House of South Africa Ltd.: 60 Market St., Johannesburg; cap. p.u. R.2m.; Chair. G. C. FLETCHER, M.C.; Man. Dir. C. J. H. DUNN.

The National Discount House of South Africa Ltd.: Loveday St., Johannesburg; cap. p.u. R.2,410m.; dep. R.198m. (1971); Chair. D. L. KEYS; Man. Dir. K. J. B. SINCLAIR; total assets R.206m. (1971).

National Finance Corporation: Reserve Bank Bldg., P.O.B. 427, Pretoria.

DEVELOPMENT ORGANIZATIONS

Standard Bank Development Corporation of S.A. Ltd.: 78 Fox St., Johannesburg; cap. p.u. R.12,000,000 (1970); Man. Dir. J. A. ROGAN.

Standard Bank Investment Corporation Ltd.: 78 Fox St., Johannesburg; f. 1969; cap. p.u. R.38,181,000 (1970); Man. Dir. H. P. DE VILLIERS; publs. *Standard Bank Review* (monthly), *International Business Report* (fortnightly).

BANKING ORGANIZATION

Institute of Bankers in South Africa: P.O.B. 61510, Marshalltown, Johannesburg; f. 1904; 10,000 mems.; Sec. Gen. PETER KRAAK; publ. *The South African Banker*.

STOCK EXCHANGE

Johannesburg Stock Exchange: P.O.B. 1174, Johannesburg; f. 1887; market value of listed shares in 1,088 companies: R.34,663,659,000 (June 1973); Pres. RICHARD LURIE.

INSURANCE

A.A. Mutual Life Assurance Association Ltd.: Automutual House, 20 Wanderers St., P.O.B. 1653, Johannesburg; Chair. PHILIP SCEALES; Gen. Man. W. H. PLUMMER.

African Life Assurance Society Ltd.: African Life Centre, 117 Commissioner St., P.O.B. 1114, Johannesburg; f. 1904; Chair. M. D. MOROSS; Chief Gen. Man. R. A. L. CUTHBERT.

African Mutual Trust & Assurance Co. Ltd.: 34 Church St., P.O.B. 27, Malmesbury; f. 1900; Chief Gen. Man. R. A. L. CUTHBERT.

Atlantic & Continental Assurance Co. of South Africa Ltd.: A.C.A. Building, 102 Commissioner St., P.O.B. 5813, Johannesburg; f. 1948; Man. Dir. R. C. HELLIG.

Aviation Insurance Co. of Africa Ltd.: 9th Floor, St. Andrew's Bldg., 39 Rissik St., Johannesburg; Gen. Man. D. TILLEY.

Bastion Insurance Co. Ltd.: Netherlands Insurance Centre, Smit, Eloff and Wolmarans St., Braamfontein, Johannesburg; Gen. Man. N. Ross.

Commercial Union Assurance Co. of South Africa Ltd.: Commercial Union House, Cnr. Rissik and Main Sts., P.O.B. 222, Johannesburg; Gen. Man. J. W. BIRKINSHAW.

Credit Guarantee Insurance Corpn. of Africa Ltd.: Avril Malan Building, 57/59 Commissioner St., P.O.B. 9244, Johannesburg; f. 1956; Gen. Man. M. DE KLERK.

Federated Employers' Insurance Co. Ltd.: Federated Insurance House, 1 de Villiers St., P.O.B. 666, Johannesburg; f. 1944; Chair. J. A. BARROW; Man. Dir. H. J. S. EVERETT.

General Accident Insurance Co. South Africa Ltd.: General Assurance Building, 86 St. George's St., P.O.B. 558, Cape Town; Gen. Man. D. A. BLACK.

Guarantee Life Assurance Co. Ltd.: Schlesinger Centre, 222 Smit St.; Chair. M. D. MOROSS; Man. Dir. Dr. S. PEER.

Guardian Assurance Company South Africa Ltd.: Guardian Liberty Centre, 39 Wolmarans St., Braamfontein, P.O.B. 8777, Johannesburg; Gen. Man. G. H. WATSON.

Hollandia Reinsurance Company of South Africa Ltd.: 404 Pearl Assurance House, Foreshore, P.O.B. 3238, Cape Town; f. 1953; Chair. R. J. RUMBELOW; Deputy Chair. E. J. SLAGER; Man. T. P. J. M. PLATTENBURG.

Incorporated General Insurances Ltd.: Auckland House, 18 Biccard St., Braamfontein, Johannesburg; Gen. Man. I. M. A. LEWIS.

Liberty Life Association of Africa Ltd.: Guardian Liberty Centre, 39 Wolmarans St., Braamfontein, P.O.B. 10499, Johannesburg; f. 1958; mem. of the world-wide Guardian Royal Exchange Assurance Group.

Malmesbury Board of Executors and Trust and Fire Assurance Company: Hill St., Malmesbury.

Marine and Trade Insurance Company Ltd.: Harmain House, 26 Harrison St., P.O.B. 10509, Johannesburg; f. 1953; Chair. E. MELAMED; Gen. Man. L. D. GODDARD.

Maritime and General Insurance Co. Ltd.: 3rd Floor, Howard House, 23 Loveday St., Johannesburg; Gen. Man. D. P. GALLIMORE.

Metlife: Metropolitan Life Building, Central Square, Pinelands, Cape Province.

Momentum Life Assurers Ltd.: AVL-Buildings, 83 Devinsh St., Sunnyside, Pretoria.

Mutual & Federal Insurance Co. Ltd.: Standard Bank Centre, Fox St., P.O.B. 1120, Johannesburg; Man. Dir. A. J. van RYNEVELD.

National Employers' General Insurance Co. Ltd.: Amcor House, Marshall St. (between Harrison and Simmonds Sts.), Johannesburg, and P.O.B. 61286, Marshalltown, Transvaal; Man. Dir. R. H. HYDE, F.C.I.I.

National Employers' Life Assurance Co. of South Africa Ltd.: Amcor House, Marshall St. (between Harrison and Simmonds Sts.), P.O.B. 61286, Marshalltown, Transvaal; Gen. Man. T. R. USHER, B.A., A.C.I.I.

Netherlands Insurance Co. of South Africa Ltd.: Netherlands Insurance Centre, Smit, Eloff and Wolmarans St., Braamfontein; Gen. Man. A. J. HUNINK; Asst. Gen. Man. N. Ross.

Norwich Union Insurance Society of South Africa Ltd.: Norwich Union House, 91 Commissioner St., Johannesburg; Gen. Man. F. L. BULL, F.C.I.I.

Old Mutual (South African Mutual Life Assurance Soc.): Mutualpark, Jan Smuts Drive, P.O.B. 66, Cape Town; f. 1845; Chair. Brig. G. C. G. WERDMULLER, C.B.E., E.D., J.P.; Man. Dir. J. G. van der HORST; Gen. Man. J. C. PIJPER.

President Insurance Co. Ltd.: 6th Floor, Rentmeester Building, 52 Commissioner St., Johannesburg; Gen. Man. Dr. H. BRINK.

Protea Assurance Co. Ltd.: Protea Assurance Building, Greenmarket Sq., P.O.B. 646, Cape Town; Man. Dir. H. A. W. ANSCOMBE.

Provincial Insurance Co. of Southern Africa Ltd.: 1201 Parkade, Strand St., P.O.B. 1335, Cape Town; Gen. Man. J. H. HARRIES, F.C.I.I.

The Rand Mutual Assurance Co. Ltd.: Chamber of Mines Buildings, Main and Hollard Sts., P.O.B. 61413, Marshalltown, Johannesburg; f. 1894; Chair. R. A. PLUMBRIDGE; Man. W. D. MOLTENO.

Reinsurance Union of South Africa Ltd.: 6th Floor, Sage Centre, Fraser St., P.O.B. 6325, Johannesburg; f. 1950; Chair. H. J. S. EVERETT; Gen. Man. T. N. PEACE; Sec. W. H. GREENWOOD.

Rondalia Assurance Corporation of South Africa Ltd.: Rondalia Bldg., Visagie St., P.O.B. 2290, Pretoria; f. 1943.

Royal Insurance Co. of South Africa Ltd.: Standard Bank Centre, 78 Fox St., P.O.B. 1120, Johannesburg; Man. Dir. A. J. van RYNEVELD.

Santam Insurance Co. Ltd.: Burg St., P.O.B. 653, Cape Town; f. 1918; Chair. C. H. J. van ASWEGEN; Man. Dir. I. J. STEYN.

Shield Insurance Co. Ltd.: Shield Insurance House, Main Rd., Rosebank, P.O.B. 1520, Cape Town; Gen. Man. E. W. MESSENGER.

Shield Life Insurance Ltd.: 227 Main Rd., P.O.B. 10142, Cape Town; Man. Dir. JULIEN C. KARNEY.

South African Eagle Insurance Co. Ltd.: Eagle Star House, 70 Fox St., P.O.B. 61489, Marshalltown, Transvaal; Chair. Sir BRIAN MOUNTAIN; Chief Gen. Man. F. N. HASLETT, F.C.I.I.

South African Mutual Fire and General Insurance Co. Ltd.: Standard Bank Centre, Fox St., P.O.B. 1120, Johannesburg; f. 1921; Man. Dir. A. J. van RYNEVELD.

South African Trade Union Assurance Society Ltd.: Traduna House, 58 Frederick Street, P.O. Box 8791, Johannesburg; f. 1941; Chair. C. H. CROMPTON; Gen. Man. A. SUMNER.

Southern Insurance Association Ltd.: Allied Bldg., 46 St. George's St., P.O.B. 297, Cape Town; Gen. Man. S. H. H. BRADBURN.

The Southern Life Association: Great Westerford, Rondebosch, Cape Town; f. 1891; Chair. F. C. ROBB; Man. Dir. A. J. BURFORD.

Standard General Insurance Co. Ltd.: Standard General House, 12 Harrison St., P.O.B. 4352, Johannesburg; f. 1943; Chair. LEIF EGELAND; Vice-Chair. and Man. Dir. C. G. CAVALIERI.

Stenhouse (Pty.) Ltd.: 5th Floor, Hill Samuel House, Field St., Durban; f. 1964.

Suid-Afrikaanse Phoenix Assuransie Maatskappy Beperk: Phoenix House, 42 Burg St., P.O.B. 1827, Cape Town; Gen. Man. P. W. HOLT.

Swiss South African Reinsurance Co. Ltd.: 10th Floor, Swiss House, 86 Main St., P.O.B. 7049, Johannesburg; f. 1950; Chair. H. BYLAND; Gen. Man. W. STRICKER.

U.B.S. Insurance Co. Ltd.: 6th Floor, United Buildings, cnr. Fox and Eloff Sts.; Chair. P. W. SCEALES; Gen. Man. J. L. S. HEFER.

Union National South British Insurance Co. Ltd.: 107 Commissioner St., P.O.B. 5277, Johannesburg; Gen. Man. C. R. FORMBY; Deputy Gen. Man. and Sec. K. NILSSON.

Union and South-West Africa Insurance Co. Ltd.: United Buildings, Kaiser St., Windhoek, S.W.A.; P.O.B. 908, Cape Town; Gen. Man. A. J. ASSITER.

Westchester Insurance Co. (Pty.) Ltd.: Suite D, 8th Floor, 41 Hans Strijdom Ave., Cape Town.

Woltemade Insurers Ltd.: Constantia Buildings, Andries Street, Pretoria; Man. Dir. A. J. MARAIS.

TRADE AND INDUSTRY

CHAMBERS OF COMMERCE

Association of Chambers of Commerce: P.O.B. 566, Cape Town and P.O.B. 694, Johannesburg; f. 1892; 119 principal chambers of commerce and local chambers are members; Pres. N. D. SEMPILL; Exec. Dir. H. S. MABIN; publ. *Commercial Opinion*.

PRINCIPAL MEMBERS

Chamber of Commerce of the O.F.S.: P.O.B. 87, Bloemfontein; f. 1883; Exec. Sec. Mrs. R. KIBUR; 700 mems.

Chamber of Commerce: P.O.B. 204, Cape Town; Sec. B. MACLEOD; 1,200 mems.

Chamber of Commerce: P.O.B. 1506, Durban; Man. K. W. HOBSON; 3,500 mems.

Chamber of Commerce: P.O.B. 93, East London; Sec. K. C. WHITFIELD; 364 mems.

Chamber of Commerce: P.O.B. 65, Pietermaritzburg; Sec. Mrs. M. Y. HARRIS; 473 mems.

Chamber of Commerce: P.O.B. 48, Port Elizabeth; Sec. A. H. L. MASTERS; 696 mems.

Chamber of Commerce: P.O.B. 72, Pretoria; Sec. W. JACOBSON; 460 mems.

Chamber of Commerce and Industry: P.O.B. 201, Springs; Man. A. B. HUTCHISON; 255 mems.

Johannesburg Chamber of Commerce: P.O.B. 687, Johannesburg; Exec. Dir. H. J. VAN DER MERWE; 2,400 mems.

Zululand Chamber of Commerce: P.O.B. 99, Empangeni; Sec. A. BOZAS; 247 mems.

INDUSTRIAL ORGANIZATIONS

South African Federated Chamber of Industries: P.O.B. 4516, 4th Floor, Nedbank Centre, Cnr. Kerk and Beatrix Sts., Pretoria; f. 1917; Pres. H. C. MORCOMBE; Dir. Dr. H. J. J. REYNDERS; Alt. Dir. J. M. BURGER; Deputy Dir. J. VAN R. MAARTENS; publ. *F.C.I. Viewpoint*; mems. affiliated to the Federated Chamber of Industries.

Border Chamber of Industries: P.O.B. 27, East London; f. 1919; Sec. C. G. POTGIETER; 50 mems.

Cape Chamber of Industries: P.O.B. 1536, 5th Floor, Broadway Industries Centre, Heerengracht, Cape Town; f. 1904; Dir. R. M. LEE, B.A., LL.B.; 868 mems.

Chamber of Mines of South Africa: 5 Hollard St., P.O.B. 809, Johannesburg; f. 1889; Pres. R. A. PLUMBRIDGE; 136 mems.

Electricity Supply Commission (ESCOM): P.O.B. 1091, Johannesburg; Chair. Dr. R. L. STRASZACKER.

Federation of Master Printers of South Africa: P.O.B. 1200, Johannesburg; f. 1916; Dir. C. R. THOMPSON; 874 mems.

Footwear Manufacturers' Federation of South Africa: P.O.B. 2228, Port Elizabeth; f. 1944; Dir. A. G. EVERINGHAM; 40 mems.

Industrial Development Corporation of South Africa Ltd.: P.O.B. 6905, Johannesburg; f. 1940; issued cap. R.295m.; Chair. J. J. KITSHOFF.

Leather Industry Suppliers' Association: Secs. Midland Chamber of Industries, P.O.B. 2221, Port Elizabeth; f. 1949; 19 mems.; Chair. H. GERSTEL.

Midland Chamber of Industries: P.O.B. 2221, S.A. Wool Board Bldg., Grahamstown Rd., Port Elizabeth; f. 1917; Dir. I. L. KRIGE; 350 mems.

Natal Chamber of Industries: P.O.B. 1300, Durban; f. 1904; Sec. R. V. FREAKES, B.A.; 1,002 mems.

National Association of Automobile Manufacturers of South Africa: P.O.B. 2221, Port Elizabeth; f. 1935; Dir. F. N. LOCK.

National Association of Woolwashers and Carbonizers of South Africa: Secs. Midland Chamber of Industries, P.O.B. 2221, Port Elizabeth; f. 1952.

National Chamber of Milling, Inc.: Head Office: 801 Siemens House, Biccard St., Braamfontein (P.O.B. 8609), Johannesburg; f. 1936; Man. and Sec. J. BARENDSE; the Chamber comprises all principal commercial wheat millers in South Africa, with wheat-milling plants in all parts of the Republic, and is representative of practically the whole of commercial wheat milling in South Africa.

National Clothing Federation of South Africa: P.O.B. 8107, Johannesburg; f. 1945; handles all matters of economic importance to the industry; Dir. F. H. WHITAKER.

National Textile Manufacturers' Association: P.O.B. 1300, Durban; f. 1947; Sec. R. V. FREAKES, B.A.; 13 mems.

Northern Transvaal Chamber of Industries: P.O.B. 933, Pretoria; f. 1929; Dir. J. G. TOERIEN; 200 mems. (secondary industries).

Orange Free State Chamber of Industries: P.O.B. 1140, Bloemfontein; Pres. D. S. POOLEY.

Pietermaritzburg Chamber of Industries: P.O.B. 365, Pietermaritzburg; f. 1910; Secs. Messrs. Deloitte and Co.; 81 mems.

Plastic Converters' Association of South Africa: P.O.B. 4516, Pretoria; f. 1972; Secs: Federated Chamber of Industries; 180 mems.

Southern African Breweries Institute: 2 Jan Smuts Ave., Braamfontein, Johannesburg; Dir. J. A. H. VAN NIEKERK.

Southern Oil Exploration Corporation (SOEKOR): P.O.B. 3087, Johannesburg; Chair. D. P. DE VILLIERS.

South African Cement Producers' Association: P.O.B. 2832, Johannesburg; Dir. V. L. HOURELD.

South African Coal, Oil and Gas Corporation (SASOL): P.O.B. 1, Sasolburg, O.F.S.; produces oil from coal; the process has assumed new importance as a result of the energy crisis and rise in the price of oil; Chair. Dr. P. ETIENNE ROUSSEAU.

South African Dried Fruit Co-op. Ltd.: P.O.B. 508, Wellington.

South African Fish Canners' Association (Pty.) Ltd. P.O.B. 2066, Pearl Assurance House, Foreshore, Cape Town; f. 1953; Chair. K. PIETERSEN; Man. P. J. O'SULLIVAN; 15 mems.

South African Fruit and Vegetable Canners' Association (Pty.) Ltd.: 810-812 Tulbagh Centre, Hans Strijdom Ave., Cape Town; f. 1953; Sec. G. S. GLENDINING; 26 mems.

South African Institute of the Boot and Shoe Industry, Inc.: P.O.B. 2240, Port Elizabeth; f. 1939; 341 mems.; publs. on technology of shoe manufacture (educational); Hon. Sec. K. W. T. RICHES.

South African Iron and Steel Corporation (ISCOR): P.O.B. 450, Pretoria; giant iron and steel producing corporation; Chair. Dr. T. F. MULLER.

South African Lumber Millers' Association: P.O.B. 1602, Johannesburg; f. 1941; Dir. D. H. ELOFF; 143 mems.

South African Oil Expressers' Association: P.O.B. 17222, Hillbrow, Johannesburg; f. 1937; Sec. J. W. H. FICK; 14 mems.

South African Soap Detergent and Candle Manufacturers' Association: P.O.B. 17222, Hillbrow, Johannesburg; f. 1928; Sec. J. W. H. FICK; 24 mems.

South African Sugar Association: P.O.B. 507, Durban; Gen. Man. P. SALE.

South African Tanners' Association: P.O.B. 2221, Port Elizabeth; f. 1944 (regd. 1946); Secs. Midland Chamber of Industries; 14 mems.

South African Tyre Manufacturers' Conference: P.O.B. 7490, Johannesburg; Sec. W. S. KIRK.

South African Wool Combers Trade Association: Secs. Midland Chamber of Industries, P.O.B. 2221, Port Elizabeth; f. 1953.

South African Wool Commission: f. 1960, to stabilize wool prices.

South African Wool Textile Council: Secs. Midland Chamber of Industries, P.O.B. 2221, Port Elizabeth; f. 1953.

Transvaal Chamber of Industries: P.O.B. 4581, Johannesburg; f. 1910; Dir. I. G. MURRAY; 900 mems.

EMPLOYERS' ORGANIZATIONS

Association of Balanced Feed Manufacturers: Siems House, Wolmarans St., Braamfontein, Johannesburg; Sec. J. W. H. FICK.

Associated Commercial Employers: P.O.B. 694, Johannesburg; f. 1944; Sec. H. S. MABIN; 11 mem. associations.

Association of Electric Cable Manufacturers of South Africa: P.O.B. 1338, Johannesburg; 9 mems.

Association of Manufacturers of Gates, Fences, Wire Products and Light Metal Sections: P.O.B. 1536, Cape Town; Sec. J. F. ROOS.

Bespoke Tailoring, Dressmaking and Fur Garment Employers' Association: P.O.B. 9478, Johannesburg; f. 1933; Sec. B. KIEL; 398 mems.

Boatbuilders' and Shipwrights' Association of South Africa: P.O.B. 1536, Cape Town; Sec. J. F. ROOS.

Building Industries Federation (South Africa): P.O.B. 11359, Johannesburg; f. 1904; Dir. G. DE C. MALHERBE, B.ECON.; 3,164 mems.; publs. *South African Builder* (monthly), *Building and Allied Trades Official Handbook* (annually).

Bus Owners' Association: 7 Stratford Rd., Durban; f. 1931; Sec. R. MAHABEER; 170 mems.

Business Equipment Association of South Africa: Allied Building, Cnr. Bree and Rissik Sts., P.O.B. 4581, Johannesburg; f. 1936; Sec. J. L. R. WOOD; 61 mems.

Cigar and Tobacco Manufacturers' Association: 73 Carlisle St., Durban; f. 1942.

Dairy Products Manufacturers' Association: P.O.B. 265, Pretoria; f. 1945; Sec. P. H. LISHMAN; 59 mems.

Electrical Engineering and Allied Industries' Association: P.O.B. 1338, Johannesburg; f. 1936; 216 mems.

Employers' Association of the Cinematograph and Theatre Industry of South Africa: 501-503 H.M. Buildings, Joubert St., Johannesburg; f. 1945; Sec. J. A. PERL.

Engineers' and Founders' Association (Transvaal, Orange Free State and Northern Cape): P.O.B. 1338, Johannesburg; f. 1945; 579 mems.

Grain Milling Federation: P.O.B. 8609, Johannesburg; f. 1944; Sec. J. BARENDSE.

Iron and Steel Producers' Association of South Africa: P.O.B. 1338, Johannesburg; 11 mems.

Light Engineering Industries Association of South Africa: P.O.B. 1338, Johannesburg; f. 1936; 234 mems.

Master Diamond Cutters' Association of South Africa: 510 Diamond Exchange Building, Cnr. De Villiers and Quartz Sts., Johannesburg; f. 1928; 44 mems.

Motor Industries Federation: P.O.B. 3478, Johannesburg; f. 1910; Dir. R. G. DU PLESSIS; 6,500 mems.; publ. *The Automobile in South Africa.*

Motor Transport Owners' Association of South Africa: 501-502 Sanlam Bldgs., 29 Loveday St., Johannesburg; f. 1941; Sec. J. J. WEDDERBURN.

National Association of Biscuit Manufacturers of South Africa: P.O.B. 3137, Cape Town; f. 1927; Sec. P. H. COATES; 5 mems.

National Association of Grain Milling Employers: P.O.B. 8609, Johannesburg; f. 1945; Sec. J. BARENDSE; 96 mems.

National Federation of Hotel and Accomodation Establishments (Non-Liquor) of South Africa: Protea Assurance Building, 102 St. George's St., Cape Town; f. 1941; Sec. A. SEBBA.

Newspaper Press Union of South Africa: P.O.B. 10537, Johannesburg; f. 1882; Pres. L. E. A. SLATER; Sec. G. G. A. UYS; 173 mems.

Non-ferrous Metal Industries' Association of South Africa: P.O.B. 1338, Johannesburg; f. 1943; 30 mems.

Plastics Manufacturers' Association of South Africa: P.O.B. 1338, Johannesburg; f. 1948; 92 mems.

Precision Manufacturing Engineers' Association: P.O.B. 1338, Johannesburg; f. 1942; 96 mems.

Radio, Appliance and Television Association of South Africa: P.O.B. 1300, Durban; f. 1942; 96 mems.

Sheet Metal Industries' Association of South Africa: P.O.B. 1338, Johannesburg; f. 1948; 151 mems.

Society of Automotive Importers, Assemblers and Distributors of South Africa: 134 London House, 21 Loveday St., Johannesburg; f. 1949; Pres. J. COBB; 62 mems.

South African Agricultural and Irrigation Machinery Manufacturers' Association: P.O.B. 1338, Johannesburg; f. 1944; 38 mems.

South African Association of Shipbuilders and Repairers: P.O.B. 1338, Johannesburg; 20 mems. Also at P.O.B. 1536, Cape Town; Sec. J. F. Roos.

South African Brewing Industry Employers' Association: P.O.B. 4581, Johannesburg; f. 1927; Sec. M. E. ROBERTSON; 2 mems.

South African Brick Association: Paillard House, Cnr. Smit and De Beer Sts., Braamfontein, Transvaal; Dir. P. J. REYNOLDS.

South African Electroplating Industries' Association: P.O.B. 1338, Johannesburg; f. 1942; 18 mems.

South African Federation of Civil Engineering Contractors: Private Bag 1, Halfway House, Tvl.; f. 1940; Dir. K. LAGAAY; 150 mems.; publ. *The Civil Engineering Contractor* (monthly); circ. 2,000.

South African Foreign Trade Organization—SAFTO: Netherlands Bank Bldg., 80 Fox St., P.O.B. 9039, Johannesburg; f. 1963; Chief Exec. W. B. HOLTES; 400 mems.

South African Insurance Employers' Association: P.O.B. 1141, Johannesburg.

South African Master Dental Technicians' Association: P.O.B. 9478, Johannesburg; f. 1946; Sec. W. A. DAVIDSON (Pty.), Ltd.

South African Ophthalmic Optical Manufacturers' Association: P.O.B. 4581, Johannesburg; f. 1945; Secs. Transvaal Chamber of Industries; 24 mems.

South African Radio and Television Manufacturers' Association: P.O.B. 1338, Johannesburg; 17 mems.

South African Reinforced Concrete Engineers' Association: P.O.B. 1338, Johannesburg; f. 1944; 50 mems.

South African Tube Makers' Association: P.O.B. 1338, Johannesburg; f. 1942; 14 mems.

South African Wire and Wire-rope Manufacturers' Association: P.O.B. 1338, Johannesburg; f. 1943; 4 mems.

South African Wool Board: P.O.B. 1378, Pretoria; f. 1946; Chair. GIDEON J. JOUBERT; Man. Dir. S. P. VAN WYK; the Board consists of 16 members. They are 10 representatives of woolgrowers and six appointed by the Minister of Agriculture. One scientific adviser is a co-opted member.

Steel and Engineering Industries' Federation of South Africa: P.O.B. 1338, Johannesburg; f. 1947; 2,000 mems.

Sugar Manufacturing and Refining Employers' Association: 1100 Norwich Union House, Durban Club Place, Durban; f. 1947; Sec. D. R. WOODROFFE.

Tobacco Employers' Organisation: P.O.B. 4581, Johannesburg; f. 1941; Sec. Mrs. M. ROBERTSON; 3 mems.

Transvaal Coal Owners' Association: P.O.B. 1197, Johannesburg; f. 1907; Man. Dir. A. D. TEW.

TRADE UNIONS

The Industrial Conciliation Act of 1956 provides for the registration of Trade Unions and Employers' Organizations, for the establishment of Industrial Councils on which employers and employees have equal representation and for the settlement of disputes by conciliation and arbitration. The Act provides for the setting up of racially separate Trade Unions. In cases where separate Unions cannot be formed the mixed Unions must divide into separate branches for each race, while the Union Executive must be composed of white members only. The same act also prohibits the affiliation of Trade Unions with political parties. The Native Labour (Settlement of Disputes) Act, 1953, prohibits strikes by African workers and gives the Native Labour Officer ultimate authority in settling disputes involving such workers. The Act was amended in May 1973 to give Africans the right to strike but only in tightly controlled circumstances. African trade unions are not officially recognized by the Government. The only trade union federation with a high proportion of African members, the South African Congress of Trade Unions (f. 1955), which is completely non-racial, has been severely hampered by government bannings and detentions under the Suppression of Communism Act. The Trade Union Council of South Africa (TUCSA), which lost 14 member trade unions during 1968 after it reaffirmed its policy on African workers, decided in February 1969 to debar Africans from membership. In December 1972 White, Coloured and Asian members of TUCSA voted for the extension of full trade union rights for African workers. In October 1973 a British Trade Union Congress delegation visited South Africa to examine the status of African workers. Their recommendations were: that the TUC and ICFTU should establish an office in South Africa to organize African trade unions on a large scale; that the TUC should set up an appeal fund for victimized African trade unionists; that British investment in South Africa should be opposed unless British companies recognized African trade unions; that the TUC's General Council should discourage the emigration of white workers to South Africa. The South African Confederation of Labour (SACL) rejected the report whereas TUCSA regarded it as balanced. TUCSA is to consider the re-admission of African unions expelled in 1969. In March 1974 the Report of the House of Commons Parliamentary Select Committee investigating the pay and conditions of the 355,000 African workers employed by British companies in South Africa recommended that British companies in South Africa should aim to pay their African workers not less than the Minimum Effective Level (estimated at 50 per cent higher than subsistence level wages) and should set a timetable to achieve this.

South African Confederation of Labour—SACL: P.O.B. 31105, Braamfontein; f. 1957 (reconstituted 1968); allows affiliation by Federations as well as individual white unions; representing approx. 200,000 workers; Pres. IVAN D. MARTIN; Hon. Sec. C. P. GROBLER.

COMMITTEES

Confederation of Metal and Building Unions: P.O.B. 9692, Johannesburg; 75,500 mems. in 8 organizations; Chair. E. H. McCANN.

Electricity Supply Commission Unions' Joint Committee: 803 Amaleng, 8 de Villiers St., Johannesburg; f. 1959; 47,785 mems. in 7 organizations; Chair. B. NICHOLSON; Gen. Sec. R. F. BUDD.

Federation of Mining Unions (FMU): 803 Amaleng, 8 de Villiers St., P.O.B. 9692, Johannesburg; f. 1937; 35,000 mems. in 6 organizations; Chair. R. F. BUDD; Sec. B. NICHOLSON.

Federation of Salaried Staff Associations of S.A.: P.O.B. 61069, Marshalltown, Transvaal; f. 1959; 23,959 mems. in five associations; Pres. C. J. PRETORIUS.

Garment Workers' Unions' Consultative Committee: P.O.B. 7288, Johannesburg; f. 1960; 42,321 mems. in four unions; Chair. ANNA SCHEEPERS; Gen. Sec. JOHANNA CORNELIUS.

National Industrial Council for the Iron, Steel, Engineering and Metallurgical Industry: 412 B.P. Centre, Kerk St., Johannesburg; Parties to the Council: 33 employer organizations and 10 trade union organizations; Gen. Sec. W. R. GLASTONBURY.

National Liaison Committee of Engineering Trade Unions: Plein St., Johannesburg; 70,000 mems.; 7 organizations; Chair. E. H. McCANN; Gen. Sec. W. BORNMAN.

Pulp and Paper Industries' Joint Committee: 803 Amaleng, 8 de Villiers St., Johannesburg; f. 1958; 37,567 mems. in four unions; Chair. T. P. MURRAY; Gen. Sec. R. F. BUDD.

South African Council of Transport Workers—SACTW: 202 Vulcan House, 88 Anderson St., Johannesburg; 6,000 mems. in 8 affiliates; Sec. A. H. HAMMON.

S.A. Federation of Leather Trade Unions: 22 Trades Hall, Kerk St., Johannesburg; 18,000 mems. in 8 unions; Pres. L. ALLEN; Sec.-Treas. L. C. M. SCHEEPERS.

FEDERATIONS

African Leather Workers' Benefit Fund: P.O.B. 3039, Port Elizabeth; Sec. F. J. J. JORDAAN; 4,000 mems.

Co-ordinating Council of South African Trade Unions—CCSATU (*Die Koordinerende Raad van Suid Afrikaanse Vakverenigings*): 273 Pretorius-straat, P.O.B. 978, Pretoria; f. 1948; 52,000 mems. in 12 unions; Chair. D. J. JACOBS; Sec. J. A. VAN WYK; publ. *S.A. Worker.*

Federal Consultative Council of South African Railways and Harbours Staff Associations—FCC: 40 Ameshoff St., Braamfontein; 82,987 mems. from 7 unions; Chair. I. D. MARTIN; Sec. J. R. BENADE.

Trade Union Council of South Africa—TUCSA: P.O.B. 5592, Johannesburg; f. 1954; 194,288 mems. from 69 unions; Pres. L. C. SCHEEPERS; Gen. Sec. J. ARTHUR GROBBELAAR.

PRINCIPAL REGISTERED TRADE UNIONS

Amalgamated Engineering Union of South Africa: 8 de Villiers Street, P.O. Box 1168, Johannesburg; f. 1890; Sec. E. H. McCANN; 32,000 mems.; publ. *The Metal Worker* (monthly).

Amalgamated Society of Woodworkers: P.O. Box 1095, Johannesburg; f. 1881; Sec. H. B. BULL; 3,000 mems.

Amalgamated Union of Building Trade Workers of South Africa (Executive Council): 107-110 Vulcan House, 88 Anderson St., P.O.B. 5378, Johannesburg; f. 1916; Sec. E. SCOTT; 11,000 mems.

Artisan Staff Association: "Lowliebenhof", 193 Smit Street, Johannesburg; f. 1924; represents artisans and trade hands of the South African Railways, Airways and Harbours; Pres. J. ZURICH; Sec. C. P. GROBLER; 20,000 mems.

Bank Employees' Union: P.O.B. 1647, Pretoria; 5,000 mems.; Sec. J. P. STEYN.

European Liquor and Catering Trades Employees' Union: 508 Scott's Bldgs., Plein Street, Cape Town; f. 1960; Chair. J. J. FOURIE; Gen. Sec. Mrs. N. G. FORSYTH; 875 mems.

Federation of Furniture and Allied Trade Unions: P.O.B. 2040, Johannesburg; f. 1959; Sec. J. F. KLOPPER; 7,000 mems.

Food and Canning Workers' Union: 101/104 City Centre, 18 Corporation Street, Cape Town, P.O. Box 2678; f. 1941; 8,837 mems.; Gen. Sec. Mrs. LIZ ABRAHAMS.

Garment Workers' Union of S.A.: Garment Centre, 75 End St., P.O.B. 6779, Johannesburg; f. 1928; Sec. JOHANNA CORNELIUS; 11,000 mems.

Garment Workers' Union of Western Province: P.O.B. 3259, Cape Town; 40,000 mems.; Sec.-Treas. LOUIS A. PETERSEN.

Hotel, Bar and Catering Trade Employees' Association: 309 Exchange Bldg., 28 St. George's St., Cape Town; Sec. G. MUNSOOK; 1,500 mems.

Ironmoulders' Society of South Africa: P.O.B. 3322, Johannesburg; f. 1896; Gen. Sec. C. H. CROMPTON; 2,425 mems.

Johannesburg Municipal Transport Workers' Union: 2nd Floor, Vulcan House, 88 Anderson St., Johannesburg; Gen. Sec. D. J. SCHUTTE; 1,500 mems.

Mine Surface Officials' Association of South Africa: P.O.B. 6849, Johannesburg; f. 1919; Gen. Sec. and Man. R. H. BOTHA; 1,000 mems.; publ. *M.S.O.A. Journal.*

Mineworkers' Union: P.O.B. 2525, Johannesburg; f. 1903; Sec. P. J. PAULUS; 17,000 mems.; publ. *The Mineworker* (fortnightly).

Motor Industry Combined Workers' Union: 112 Vulcan House, 88 Anderson St., Johannesburg; f. 1960; 7,033 mems.; Pres. H. FABE; Gen. Sec. R. C. WEBB; publ. *Newsletters.*

Motor Industry Employees' Union of South Africa: 11 Biccard St., Johannesburg; f. 1939; Gen. Sec. P. J. PIENAAR; 22,950 mems.

Motor Transport Workers' Union: 315 Dalbree House, 300 Bree St., Johannesburg; f. 1934; Gen. Sec. G. H. VAN DER WALT; 1,100 mems.

National Union of Clothing Workers: P.O.B. 7288, Johannesburg; 4,000 mems.; Sec. Mrs. L. MVUBELO.

National Union of Distributive Workers: Boston House, Cape Town; f. 1936; Gen. Sec. J. R. ALTMAN; Pres. M. KAGAN; 14,500 mems.; publ. *New Day* (quarterly).

National Union of Furniture and Allied Workers of South Africa: Meubel Sentrum, Cnr. Eloff St. and Anderson St., Johannesburg; Pres. W. J. HOLMES; Sec. C. A. BOTES; 7,100 mems.

National Union of Leather Workers: P.O.B. 3039, Port Elizabeth; Sec. F. J. J. JORDAAN; 18,000 mems.

National Union of Liquor and Catering Trades Employees: P.O.B. 290, Durban; f. 1953; 15,000 mems. in six affiliated unions; Chair. W. CRAWFORD; Asst. Gen. Sec. A. C. REDDY.

National Union of Operative Biscuit Makers and Packers of South Africa: P.O.B. 4141, Cape Town; 1,200 mems.; Sec. A. SOLOMON.

Operative Bakers', Confectioners' and Conductors' Union: P.O.B. 3259, Cape Town; Sec. F. W. McLEOD.

Postal and Telegraph Association of South Africa: P.O.B. 9186, Johannesburg; f. 1902; Gen. Sec. L. J. VAN DER LINDE; 12,000 mems.

Running and Operating Staff Union: 40 Ameshoff St., Braamfontein, Johannesburg; f. 1928; 12,000 mems.; Gen. Sec. and Editor JOHANN R. BENADÉ; publ. *Headlight*; circ. 10,000.

South African Association of Municipal Employees: P.O.B. 62, Pretoria; f. 1921; Gen. Sec. J. T. SMIT; 35,000 mems.

South African Boilermakers', Iron and Steel Workers', Ship Builders' and Welders' Society: 3rd Floor, Vulcan House, 88 Anderson St., P.O.B. 9645, Johannesburg; f. 1916; Sec. T. P. MURRAY; 25,000 mems.; publ. *The Crucible* (monthly).

South African Electrical Workers' Association: 6th Floor, Amaleng, No. 8 de Villiers St., Johannesburg; f. 1937; Gen. Sec. R. COWLEY; 15,000 mems.

South African Engine Drivers', Firemen's and Operators' Association: 507-510 Vulcan House, 88 Anderson St., Johannesburg; f. 1894; Sec. KENNETH WILLEM DU PREEZ; 4,538 mems.

South African Footplate Staff Association: 105 Simmonds St., P.O.B. 31100, Braamfontein, Johannesburg; Pres. S. C. BOTHA; Sec. S. STEYN; 9,500 mems.

South African Hairdressers' Employees' Industrial Union: 42 Harvard Buildings, 49 Joubert St., Johannesburg; f. 1943; Sec. J. DANIEL; 4,000 mems.

South African Iron, Steel and Allied Industries Union: 430 Church St. West, P.O.B. 19299, Pretoria; f. 1936; Sec. W. BORNMAN; 35,000 mems.

South African Postal Association: P.O.B. 2004, Johannesburg; f. 1902; Gen. Sec. T. P. VAN NIEKERK; 4,100 mems.; publ. *Postal Journal.*

South African Railways and Harbours Employees' Union: Atkinson Building, Strand St., Cape Town; f. 1924; Gen. Sec. J. H. COETZEE; 8,300 mems.; publ. *Emplo Review* (monthly).

South African Railways and Harbours Salaried Staff Association: P.O.B. 6753, Johannesburg; f. 1918; Gen. Sec. F. A. SMIT; 24,000 mems.

South African Railways Police Staff Association: P.O.B. 31308, Braamfontein, Johannesburg; 2,321 mems.; Sec. B. J. S. REINECKE.

South African Society of Bank Officials: P.O.B. 31537, Braamfontein; f. 1916; Sec. T. M. M. ALEXANDER; 18,000 mems.

South African Teachers' Association: 15 Grove Buildings, Grove Ave., Claremont, Cape Town; f. 1862; Gen. Sec. J. A. CLARKSON, B.COM.; 2,000 mems.

South African Technical Officials Association: P.O.B. 7060, Johannesburg; Gen. Sec. H. MALLET-VEALE; 4,000 mems.

South African Theatre and Cinema Employees' Union: P.O.B. 8752, Johannesburg; Sec. A. E. NICHOLSON; 1,731 mems.

South African Typographical Union: S.A.T.U. House, 166 Visagie Street, P.O. Box 1993, Pretoria; f. 1898; Sec. E. VAN TONDER; 23,000 mems.

Teachers' Educational and Professional Association: Cape Town; 2,000 mems.; Sec. A. I. JACOBS.

Textile Workers' Industrial Union (S.A.): P.O.B. 4141, Cape Town; f. 1934; 4,080 mems.; Gen. Sec. N. J. DANIELS.

Tobacco Workers' Industrial Union: Oxford St., Oudtshoorn; Sec. J. J. BOTES.

Tramway and Omnibus Workers' Union: P.O.B. 1562, Cape Town; f. 1916; Sec. D. C. BENADÉ; 1,600 mems.

Transvaal Leather and Allied Trades Industrial Union: Meubelsentrum, Cnr. Eloff and Anderson Sts., 5th Floor, P.O.B. 3400, Johannesburg; Sec. L. C. SCHEEPERS; 3,000 mems.

Underground Officials' Association of South Africa: P.O.B. 5965, Johannesburg; f. 1918; 9,000 mems.; Sec. P. J. MALAN.

Western Province Building Workers' Union: P.O.B. 2013, Cape Town; 3,000 mems.; Sec. J. DOHERTY.

Witwatersrand Tea Room, Restaurant and Catering Trade Employees' Union: P.O.B. 6041, Johannesburg; Sec. Mrs. M. YOUNG; 1,000 mems.

TRANSPORT

RAILWAYS

South African Railways and Harbours Board: Union Bldgs., Pretoria; Chair. Minister of Transport the Hon. B. J. SCHOEMAN, M.P.; Deputy Minister of Transport the Hon. J. W. RALL, M.P.; Railway Commissioners Dr. J. H. BOTHA, P. J. C. DU PLESSIS, C. V. DE VILLIERS.

With a few minor exceptions the South African Railways and Harbours Administration owns and operates all the railways in the Republic and in South West Africa. The Administration also operates an extensive network of road transport services, which serves primarily to develop rural areas, but also acts as feeder to the railways. The fleet consists of some 46 vessels, mainly tugs and dredgers, which does not include minor harbour craft. The Administration spent approximately R.362 million on improvements during the year ended March 31st, 1973. This is part of the modernization programme which started just after the war. In June 1973 South African Railways ordered R.42 million worth of stock and its fleet is to increase to 1,000 diesel-electric and 1,600 electric locomotives.

ROUTE DISTANCE:

Owned and operated by South African Railways:

1. In Republic, 19,856 kilometres.
2. In South West Africa, 2,340 kilometres.

Privately-owned lines operated by South African Railways, 53 kilometres.

The electrified distance totals 4,501 kilometres.

ROADS

National Transport Commission: P.O.B. 415, Pretoria; responsible for location, planning, design, construction and maintenance of national roads.

On March 31st, 1973, there were approximately 2,000 km. completed national roads, and approximately 320,000 km. provincial roads of all categories. Of the 320,000 km. of rural roads, about 38,000 km. are tarred. A new road programme was announced in May 1973 with an estimated cost of R.1,316 million.

The Automobile Association of South Africa: A.A. House, 42 de Villiers St., Johannesburg; f. 1930; Pres. and Chair. E. P. NUPEN; Dir.-Gen. E. P. TURK; publ. *The Motorist* (every 3 months), circ. 500,000.

SHIPPING

South African Shipping Board: Secretariat: Dept. of Commerce, Private Bag 84, Pretoria; f. 1929; an advisory body to the Ministry of Economic Affairs upon any matter connected with sea transport to, from or between any of the Republic ports, particularly with regard to freight rates.

The principal harbours of the Republic are at Cape Town, Mossel Bay, Port Elizabeth, East London and Durban; South West Africa (Nambia): Walvis Bay. A new port at Richards Bay is under construction and Saldanha Bay is expected to become a major port in future years.

More than twenty-eight shipping lines serve South African ports among which are the following: Bay of Bengal/Africa Line, Blue Star Line (South Africa) (Pty.) Ltd., British India Steam Navigation Co. Ltd., Christensen Canadian African Lines, Clan Line Steamers Ltd., Companhia Colonial de Navegação, Compass Line (Pty) Ltd., Ellerman and Bucknall (Proprietary) Ltd., Farrell Lines, Hain Norse Management Ltd., Hall Line Ltd., Harrison Line, Houston Line, Interocean Lines (Pty.) Ltd., Lauro Lines, Lloyd Triestino Line, Lykes Bros., Mitsui OSK Lines Ltd., Nedlloyd SA Pty., Oriental African Line, Moore McCormack Lines Inc., Shaw Savill Line, South African Lines Ltd., South African Marine Corporation Ltd., Transatlantic SS Co. Ltd. of Gothenburg, Unicorn Shipping Lines Pty., Union Castle Mail Steamship Co. Ltd., West Coast of South America Line.

CIVIL AVIATION

All civil aviation in South Africa is controlled by the Minister of Transport under the Aviation Act of 1962. The National Transport Commission is responsible for licensing and control of air services. Executive and administrative work of the National Transport Commission is carried out by the Department of Transport.

Director of Civil Aviation: Private Bag X193, Pretoria; Dir. L. C. du Toit.

South African Airways (SAA): South African Airways Centre, Johannesburg; f. 1934; Chief Exec. J. Adam. There are daily passenger services linking all the principal towns of South Africa; regular services to Rhodesia; eleven services per week between Johannesburg and Lourenço Marques in partnership with DETA, and six per week to Gaborone and four per week to Francistown, five per week to Blantyre in partnership with Air Malawi, six per week to Manzini in partnership with Swazi-Air, weekly to Tananarive in partnership with Air Madagascar and four times per week to Mauritius.

South African Airways operates regular services to Europe and Australia, a weekly service to New York via Rio de Janeiro, a fortnightly service between Cape Town and Buenos Aires; operates eight Boeing 707, nine Boeing 727, six Boeing 737, three HS 748, five Boeing 747B; unduplicated route mileage 100,793.

Air Lowveld: 14th Floor, Union Sq. 80, Plein St., Johannesburg; separate internal services.

Avna Airways: P.O.B. 72, Airport, Dundee, Natal; separate internal services.

COMAIR (Commercial Airways (Pty.) Ltd.): Hangar No. 4, Rand Airport, P.O.B. 2245, Johannesburg; flies daily DC-3 schedules from Rand Airport to Welkom, Phalaborwa and Skukuza, and operates safaris to Kruger Park in conjunction with its scheduled services.

Margate Air Services: P.O.B. 231, Margate, South Coast, Natal; separate internal services.

Namakwaland Lugdiens (Edms) Bpk.: P.O.B. 28, Springbok C.P., and 1917 Sanlam Centre, Cape Town; internal services.

FOREIGN AIRLINES

The following foreign airlines also operate services to South Africa, Johannesburg being the principal centre: Air Madagascar, Air Malawi, Air Rhodesia, Alitalia, British Airways, Botswana National Airways, DETA Mozambique, El Al, Iberia, KLM, Lufthansa, Luxair, Olympic, PAA, Qantas, Sabena, SAS, Swazi-Air, Swissair, TAP, UTA and Varig.

TOURISM

South Africa is a member of the Southern Africa Regional Tourism Council (SARTOC) together with Malawi, Swaziland, Portugal and Mauritius. In 1973 there were 580,134 tourists in South Africa.

South African Tourist Corporation: 10th Floor, Arcadia Centre, 130 Beatrix St., Private Bag X164, Pretoria; 10 brs. in 9 countries; Dir. T. C. Owen.

ATOMIC ENERGY

Atomic Energy Board: Private Bag X256, Pretoria; f. 1948; 12 mems.; Pres. Dr. A. J. A. Roux; publs. *Annual Report, Nuclear Active* (half-yearly).

The National Nuclear Research Centre: Pelindaba, Private Bag X-256, Pretoria; f. 1961; 20 MW O.R.R. type research reactor (SAFARI-I) critical 1965; 3MeV Van de Graaff accelerator.

National Institute for Metallurgy: Private Bag 7, Auckland Park, Johannesburg; f. 1966; includes a pilot plant for the production of nuclear-grade uranium metal and compounds. The Institute is equipped and organ-ized to deal with all phases of the examination and recovery of valuable constituents from minerals and ores. It is the home of the Extraction Metallurgy Division of the Atomic Energy Board and is thus responsible for all work on the processing of raw materials for nuclear power; Dir. Gen. Dr. R. E. Robinson; publs. *Minerals Science and Engineering, Annual Report, NIM Abstracts.*

South Africa is a founder member of the International Atomic Energy Agency. Plans were recently announced for the construction of the country's first nuclear power station in the Western Cape.

UNIVERSITIES

The University Apartheid Act of 1959, strongly opposed by the four English-speaking universities, extended the *apartheid* system to the universities of South Africa.

University of Cape Town: P.O.B. 594, Cape Town; f. 1829; 500 teachers, 7,790 students (English).

University of Fort Hare: Private Bag 314, Alice, Cape Province; f. 1916; 107 teachers, 615 students (Xhosa and African only).

University of Natal: King George V Ave., Durban, Natal; f. 1909; 726 teachers, 7,171 students (English).

University of the North: P.O. Sovenga, Pietersburg; f. 1959; 98 teachers, 811 students (Tsonga, Sotho and Venda).

University of the Orange Free State: P.O.B. 339, Bloemfontein; f. 1855; 360 teachers, 5,841 students.

University of Port Elizabeth: P.O.B. 1600, Port Elizabeth; f. 1964; 186 teachers, 1,602 students (mainly Afrikaans).

Potchefstroom University for Christian Higher Education: Potchefstroom, Transvaal; f. 1869; 344 teachers, 5,891 students (Afrikaans).

University of Pretoria: Hillcrest, Pretoria; f. 1908; 939 teachers, 14,158 students (Afrikaans).

Rand Afrikaans University: P.O.B. 524, Johannesburg; f. 1966; 173 teachers, 2,037 students (Afrikaans).

Rhodes University: P.O.B. 94, Grahamstown; f. 1904; 195 teachers, 2,203 students (English).

University of South Africa: P.O.B. 392, Pretoria; f. 1873; 548 teachers, 31,873 students (all external).

University of Stellenbosch: Stellenbosch, Cape Province; f. 1918; 567 teachers, 8,100 students (Afrikaans).

University of the Western Cape: Private Bag, P.O. Kasselsvlei, Bellville; f. 1960; 107 full-time, 34 part-time teachers, 1,570 students (Coloureds only).

University of the Witwatersrand: 2 Jan Smuts Ave., Milner Park, Johannesburg, Transvaal; f. 1922; 768 teachers, 10,150 students (English).

University of Durban-Westville: Private Bag 4001, Westville, Durban; f. 1960; 225 teachers, 2,302 students (Indians only).

University of Zululand: Private Bag, Kwa-Dlangezwa, Via Empangeni, Natal; f. 1960; 98 teachers, 815 students (Zulu and Swazi).

THE BANTU HOMELANDS

AREA	POPULATION (1970)
57,933 sq. miles	7,034,125

1973 est. 6.9 million.

The Bantu Self-Government Act, 1959, which repealed the Representation of Natives Act, 1936, accepts the natural division of the African population into eight national units. The Transkei Territorial Authority was set up in 1962 and it received limited internal 'self-government' in 1963, this being the next step to independence which the South African government has promised the homelands. In 1971 the Bantu Homelands Constitutional Bill empowered the South African Government to grant self-government, on a similar basis to that already granted to the Transkei, to any African area which had a Territorial Authority, at its request. Bophuthatswana (June 1972), the Ciskei (August 1972), Lebowa (October 1972), Gazankulu (February 1973), VhaVenda (February 1973) and KwaZulu (April 1973) have since been granted 'self-government'. For more detailed information on the Bantu Homelands see *Africa South of the Sahara*, Europa Publications).

ORGANIZATION

Minister of Bantu Administration and Development, and Bantu Education: Hon. M. C. BOTHA.

Director of Bantu Development: L. A. PEPLER, B.SC.AG.

Commissioners General:

Transkei, Ciskei: J. H. ABRAHAM.

KwaZulu: H. TORLAGE.

Lebowa: G. P. C. BEZIDENHOUT.

VhaVenda: M. D. C. DE WET NEL.

Gazankulu: Prof. E. F. POTGIETER.

Bophuthatswana: Dr. J. S. KLOPPERS.

Basotho Quaqwa: N. C. VAN R. SADIE.

Chief Ministers and Chief Executives of the Homelands:

The Transkei (Xhosa): Chief KAIZER MATANZIMA.

The Ciskei (Xhosa): LENNOX SEBE.

Kwazulu (Zulu): Chief GATSHA BUTHELEZI.

Lebowa (Sepedi): CEDRIC N. PHATUDI.

Vhavenda (Venda): Chief PATRICK MPHEPHU.

Gazankulu (Shangaan): Prof. H. W. E. NTSANWISI.

Bophuthatswana (Tswana): Chief LUCAS M. MANGOPE.

Basotho Quaqwa (Seshoeshoe): Chief WESSEL MOTA.

THE TRANSKEI

AREA AND POPULATION

AREA (sq. miles)	POPULATION (1970)†
15,831	1,751,142

† Including 9,556 whites, 7,645 coloureds, 10 Asians (Capital Umtata).

Flag: The flag of the Transkei consists of equal horizontal stripes, green, white and ochre.

BUDGET 1973–74
(Rand '000)

EXPENDITURE	
Development and Conservation of Land . . .	1,027
Settlement of Population	268
Income Generation and Creation of Employment .	12,748
Development of Human Potential . . .	14,418
Provision of Social Services . . .	15,870
Overhead Administrative Services . . .	5,236
Overhead Capital Services	6,413
TOTAL	55,980

Budget: (1968–69) Revenue R.20,496,000; Expenditure R.19,977,000.
(1969–70) Revenue R.20,344,000; Expenditure R.23,570,000.
(1970–71) Revenue R.23,944,000; Expenditure R.26,261,000.
(1971–72) Revenue R.31,676,000; Expenditure R.32,381,000.

Although the *Bunga* had voted to accept the Bantu Authorities system in 1955, the imposition of this system, along with other grievances such as soil conservation schemes and increased taxation, resulted in violent opposition by the people, beginning in February 1960. There was a full-scale revolt in East Pondoland, and in November the Government introduced a state of emergency which has been in force ever since. No meeting can take place without the permission of the Bantu Commissioner; free speech is restricted; entry and exit in the Transkei is strictly controlled; chiefs have the power to apprehend persons described as "communists" by the Minister of Bantu Administration. In January 1961 the Government stated that 4,769 Africans had been arrested in Pondoland and 2,067 actually tried; 25 Africans had been murdered in Pondoland, two of whom were chiefs; and 15 Africans had been killed by the police in "self-defence". Most of the troops were withdrawn in May 1961.

Despite the state of emergency in the first Bantustan elections ever held, the elections in the Transkei in November 1963, 38 of the 45 elected members supported the anti-Government chief, Victor Poto, and only 7 the pro-Government candidate, Kaizer Matanzima. However, when the full Assembly, including 64 chiefs, met, Matanzima was elected Chief Minister, by 54 votes to Poto's 49 with the 14 chiefly votes of the pro-Government chief of the East Pondoland being crucial.

The Constitution of the Transkei was promulgated in the South African Parliament in May 1963, and came into force in December of the same year.

Recent Developments: In November 1973, six homeland leaders agreed on the federation of their homelands after they had attained "independence" and renewed their call for more land which the Government has consistently refused. In 1974, the first "Homeland Summit" between Mr. Vorster, who has rejected the idea of federation, and the eight homeland leaders took place. Talks were described as "brutally frank" but no agreement emerged on the controversial land issue.

THE GOVERNMENT

THE CABINET
(*April* 1974)

Chief Minister and Minister of Finance: Paramount Chief KAIZER MATANZIMA.

Minister of Justice: Chief GEORGE M. MATANZIMA.

Minister of Education: A. N. JONAS.

Minister of the Interior: Miss S. N. SIGCAU.

Minister of Agriculture and Forestry: Z. M. MABANDLA.

Minister for Roads and Works: Chief G. S. NDABANKULU.

Minister of Health: Chief JEREMIAH D. MOSHESH.

LEGISLATIVE ASSEMBLY
(Third Election, November 1973)

Elected Members: 45 (Transkei National Independence Party 25, Democratic Party 10, Independents 8 and 2 vacant).

Speaker: M. H. CANCA.

Deputy Chairman: M. E. DYARVANE.

Chief Whip: T. KA-TFHUNUNGWA.

Members: Chief MBUNGWA LANGASIKI, Chief MAKOSONKE SIGCAU, Chief JONGILIZWE NTOLA.

Non-Elected Members: Four Paramount Chiefs, 60 office-holding Chiefs in nine Regions (56 of the 64 Chiefs support the ruling party).

POLITICAL PARTIES

Transkei National Independence Party: f. 1964; accepts policy of apartheid; aims at Transkeian independence and called for complete independence in its 1968 election manifesto, won 7 of 45 elected seats in Assembly in 1963 elections, 28 in 1968 and 25 in 1973; Leader Chief KAIZER MATANZIMA.

Democratic Party: f. 1964; rejects apartheid in favour of the Transkei's status as a province within South Africa, with equal rights for both races in the Republic; won 38 of 45 elected seats in Assembly in 1963, 14 in 1968 and 10 in 1973; Leader KNOWLEDGE GUZANA.

Transkei People's Freedom Party: Umtata; f. 1966; aims at immediate independence from the Republic; Leader S. M. SINABA.

JUDICIARY

Transkei High Court: Chief Justice G. A. A. MUNNIK. The High Court was established in August 1973.

RELIGION

Church of the Province of South Africa: Bishop of St. John's Rt. Rev. JAMES LEO SCHUSTER, M.A., Bishopsmead, Umtata.

Roman Catholic Church: Bishop of Umtata (Province of Durban) Rt. Rev. ERNEST HEINRICH KARLEN.

RADIO

Radio Bantu: broadcasts in Zulu, Xhosa, Southern Sotho, Northern Sotho, Tswana, Tsonga, Venda, Ndonga, Kuanyama, Nama/Damara and Herero.

FINANCE

Xhosa Development Corporation: P.O.B. 618, East London; Man. Dir. F. MARITZ; cap. R.33m.; deals with promoting the economy of the Transkei and Ciskei.

Barclays National Bank Ltd.: Umtata.

Standard Bank of South Africa Ltd., The: Umtata.

TRADE AND INDUSTRY

DEVELOPMENT ORGANIZATIONS

Bantu Investment Corporation of S.A. Ltd.: P.O.B. 213, Pretoria; f. 1959 to develop Bantu areas; Chair. Dr. S. P. DU TOIT VILJOEN; Man. Dir. Dr. J. ADENDORFF.

Transkei Industrial Development Corporation: P.O.B. 103, Umtata; f. 1965; controlled by S.A. Government; intended to establish finance and develop industries in Transkei.

EDUCATION

In 1971 there were 1,679 state schools together with 38 private schools controlled by the church. Of the state schools, 1,602 are primary, 52 are secondary, 14 are high schools, four are vocational schools and five are schools for teacher training.

SOUTH WEST AFRICA
(NAMIBIA)

South West Africa is a mandated territory administered by South Africa. In 1966 the UN General Assembly terminated the League of Nations mandate and set up a committee to recommend means by which the territory should be administered. On June 12th, 1968, the UN renamed the Territory "Namibia". The South African Government has refused to allow the UN Committee on Namibia to enter the Territory. In June 1971 the International Court of Justice ruled in an advisory opinion that South Africa's presence in the Territory is illegal and talks with the UN on the future status of the Territory have broken down.

STATISTICAL SURVEY

AREA AND POPULATION
(1960 census and 1970* census)

AREA (sq. miles)	AFRICAN RESERVES (sq. miles)	TOTAL POPULATION	WHITES	AFRICAN	COLOUREDS	WINDHOEK (capital)
—	81,500	526,004	73,464	428,575	23,963	35,916 (whites 19,200)
317,827	84,774	746,328	90,658	627,395	28,275	64,700 (whites 35,700)

The principal port, Walvis Bay, is an enclave of South Africa. The summer capital is Swakopmund.

* Preliminary.

PRINCIPAL TRIBAL DIVISIONS
(1970 census*)

Ovambo	342,455
Damara	64,973
Kavango	49,577
Herero	49,203
Nama.	32,853
East Caprivians . . .	25,009
Bushmen	21,909
Rehobothers . . .	16,474

*Preliminary.

The Ovambo, who have some agriculture, form the chief source of labour in the Territory. The Bushmen are still primitive hunters while the other tribes are mainly semi-nomadic cattle raisers and stock hands.

HOMELANDS

	AREA (hectares)
Ovambo	5,607,200
Kavango	4,170,050
Kaokoland . . .	4,898,219
Damaraland . . .	4,799,021
Hereroland . . .	5,899,680
East Caprivi . . .	1,153,387
Tswanaland . . .	155,400
Bushmenland . . .	2,392,671
Rehoboth Gebied . .	1,386,029
Namaland	2,167,707
TOTAL . . .	32,629,364

AGRICULTURE
LIVESTOCK

	1966	1967	1968	1970*
Cattle . . .	2,261,000	2,196,792	1,407,658	1,662,000
Sheep . . .	4,067,542	3,802,415	3,678,733	3,738,000
Goats . . .	1,513,059	1,423,249	1,552,465	1,518,000

* Estimate.

LIVESTOCK PRODUCTS
('000 R.)

	1968	1969
Karakul Pelts . . .	19,156	21,900
Beef Cattle	23,354	22,856
Beef Cattle slaughtered locally	3,440	6,077
Small Stock exported . .	1,715	1,689

DAIRY PRODUCE
('000 lb.)

	1968	1969
Butterfat . . .	3,486,936	2,577,509
Butter . . .	4,250,616	3,135,357
Cheese . . .	254,820	150,455
Casein . . .	524,526	382,278

SOUTH WEST AFRICA (NAMIBIA)

KARAKUL PELTS
(Exports)

	Number	Rands Million
1968	4,870,248	27.1
1969	5,323,774	31.6
1970	5,148,396	29.8

FISHERIES

	1967	1968	1969
Canned Pilchards (short tons)	81,000	60,000	66,800
Fish Meal (short tons)	189,386	262,208	224,669
Fish Oil (centals)	37,684	67,324	44,342
Rock Lobster (short tons)	1,771	3,027	2,666

1969: Total value of catch R.36,303,000; Total catch 943,000 tons.

1972: Total catch 567,000 tons.

MINING

		1969	1970	1971	1972
Copper Ore*	'ooo metric tons	25.5	22.8	25.9	17.0
Lead Concentrates*	,, ,, ,,	75.7	70.5	73.2	59.0
Zinc Concentrates*	,, ,, ,,	38.2	46.1	48.9	25.0
Manganese Ore*	,, ,, ,,	7.0	6.0	n.a.	n.a.
Salt	,, ,, ,,	110.0	110.0	n.a.	n.a.
Tin Concentrates*	metric tons	1,024.0	1,045.0	965.0	800.0
Silver	,, ,,	39.6	38.0	44.0	n.a.
Vanadium	,, ,,	450.0	360.0	n.a.	n.a.
Diamonds	'ooo carats	2,024.0	1,865.0	1,900.0	n.a.

Asbestos: 90,000 metric tons in 1969; Iron Ore: 51,000 metric tons (gross weight) in 1967; Tungsten Concentrates: 106 metric tons (metal content) in 1966.

* Figures refer to the metal content of ores and concentrates.

Finance: *South African currency:* 100 cents=1 rand (R). Coins: ½, 1, 2, 5, 10, 20 and 50 cents. Notes: 1, 2, 5, 10 and 20 rand. Exchange rates (April 1974): £1 sterling = 1.581 rand; U.S. $1=67.11 S.A. cents; 100 rand=£63.27 =$149.00. *Budget* (1973–74): Revenue R.56,394,100, Expenditure R.72,640,500. An extra R.110 million is to be spent on services and development.

External Trade: Total Mineral exports: (1963) R.65m., (1964) R.93m., (1965) R.115m., (1966) R.128m., (1970) R.130m. Two-thirds of the total is accounted for by diamonds, some of which are mined off-shore.

Exports to U.K.: (1967) £21,343,000; (1968) £24,464,000; (1971) £23,341,522; (1972) £23,329,000; Imports from U.K.: (1967) £2,135,000; (1968) £1,478,000; (1971) £1,656,288; (1972) £993,000.

1970: Total imports R.150m.; Total exports R.220m.

Transport: *Roads* (1966): Registered vehicles 41,526; *Shipping (Walvis Bay)* (1965): Passengers 1,062, Freight 1,231,767 tons; (1966) Freight 1,187,824 tons; *Civil Aviation* (1966): To Republic of S. Africa 21,842 passengers, from Republic of S. Africa 21,769 passengers; 2,662 arrivals on international flights, 8,402 departures.

EDUCATION
Schools—1966

	Primary and Secondary
European	69
Coloured	57
African	417

Source: Bureau of Statistics, Pretoria.

ADMINISTRATION

The administration of South West Africa was vested by Mandate of the League of Nations, dated December 17th, 1920, in the Government of South Africa. The Territory was granted a constitution in 1925. The government consists of an Administrator appointed by the State President of the Republic, a Legislative Assembly of eighteen elected members and an Executive of four members chosen by the Assembly from its own ranks. The Parliament of the Republic is the supreme legislative authority and the Republic government is the chief executive authority. The South West Africa Legislative Assembly has wide powers except in matters of defence, railways and harbours, civil aviation, native affairs and certain legal affairs.

In 1949 the South African Parliament passed the South West African Affairs Amendment Act by which South West Africa was authorized to elect six members to the South African House of Assembly, and two members to the South African Senate. Two further senators are appointed by the State President. Non-Whites are not part of the Electorate for the South West Africa Legislative Assembly.

In October 1966 South Africa's security and apartheid laws were applied to the Territory, retrospective to 1950. The Development of Self-Government for Native Nations Act of 1968, provided for the establishment of Bantustans, and the South West Africa Affairs Act of 1969, removed control over all the major areas of administration from the Legislative Assembly to the relevant ministries in Pretoria. Its effect was to incorporate the territory as a fifth province of South Africa.

The United Nations have made annual recommendations that, as a former League of Nations Mandate, South West Africa should be placed under United Nations Trusteeship.

In 1950 the International Court of Justice advised that South Africa was not under a legal obligation to place South West Africa under the trusteeship system of the United Nations Organization. However, the court proceeded to hold unanimously that the mandate survived the dissolution of the League of Nations. It held further that the United Nations had, on the dissolution of the League of Nations, became vested with supervisory powers in respect of the mandate.

This opinion was followed by two further advisory opinions in 1955 and 1956, both of them concerned with the interpretation of the 1950 opinion.

In 1960 the governments of Ethiopia and Liberia, acting in the capacity of states which were members of the former League of Nations, brought before the International Court of Justice various allegations of contraventions of the League of Nations mandate for South West Africa by the Republic of South Africa. Final judgement was given on 18th July, 1966, when the International Court rejected the application of the plaintiff states on the grounds that they could not be considered to have established any legal rights or interests in the subject matter of their claims on South West Africa.

In 1966 the UN General Assembly terminated the League of Nations mandate and established the Council for Namibia which was entrusted with the task of recommending means by which the territory should be administered, and of acting as a government during an interim period before Namibian independence. The South African Government, which does not recognize the Council, refused to allow it to enter the territory.

In June 1971 the International Court of Justice in an advisory opinion ruled that South Africa's presence in the Territory was illegal and that she should withdraw immediately. In December 1971 there was a widely observed strike in Windhoek of Ovambo contract labourers. The strikers were sent home, mainly to Ovambo in the north of the Territory and the widespread outbreaks of opposition to the Government that followed led to a declaration of a state of emergency in Ovambo. No visitors or reporters were allowed into the area and many Africans were killed and arrested. The UN Secretary-General, Dr. Waldheim and the UN special envoy to Namibia, Dr. Escher, visited the Territory in 1972 and had talks with the South African Prime Minister, Mr. Vorster. Controversy surrounded statements issued after the talks with Dr. Escher. In March 1973 Mr. Vorster created a multi-racial "Advisory Council" which was to provide a forum for spokesmen of all races on the political future of the Territory. Its establishment was opposed by the influential Paramount Chief of the Herero Clemens Kapuoo and by SWAPO, and the Namas, Basters and Kakaolanders refused to be represented on it.

In late 1973 the detention and public floggings of numerous SWAPO supporters by Government-backed tribal authorities caused much criticism of the administration of the Territory. Contacts between the UN and the South African Government over the Territory's status, initiated in February 1972, were unanimously terminated by the UN Security Council in December 1973. The UN appointed a Commissioner for Namibia, and in December 1973 the UN General Assembly recognized SWAPO as "the authentic representative of the Namibian people."

HOMELANDS

The Odendaal Commission in 1964 recommended setting up ten Homelands for the major non-White peoples. But with the exception of the Ovambo and Rehobothers, the majority of each African group actually resides outside the area of their homeland. In 1970, out of 64,973 Damara, 7,736 lived in Damaraland.

The Ovambo Legislative Council of up to 42 members (nominated by the territory's seven tribal authorities) was formally opened in October 1968. There is also a seven-man Executive Council. In 1970 Kavango also obtained a Territorial Authority, and in 1972 the East Caprivi Legislative Council was formally opened. In June 1972 it was announced that the Ovambo homeland would be given "self-government" in 1973. In September 1972 the Chairman of the Damara Council of Headmen, Mr. Justus Garoeb, said that the Damaras were unwilling to request or accept a Legislative Council.

In August 1973, the South African Government arranged elections for Ovamboland. These were boycotted by the Ovambo electorate, only 2.3 per cent voting, and the low poll was attributed to the campaign for a boycott by SWAPO. Considerable unrest accompanied the elections; on several occasions the police charged into unarmed crowds. One man was shot dead and 264 arrested. Voting in the election for Kavango in September 1973 in which all candidates stood as independents owing to the absence of Kavango political parties, resulted in a high poll.

UN Commissioner for Namibia: SEAN MCBRIDE.

(April 1974)

Commissioner-General for the Indigenous People's of South West Africa: J. DE WET.

Administrator: B. J. VAN DER WALT.

Executive Committee: D. F. MUDGE, Adv. E. VAN ZIJL, J. W. F. PRETORIUS.

Legislative Assembly: E. T. MEYER (Chairman).

ELECTION, APRIL 1974

The National Party won all 18 seats contested in the Legislative Assembly. Africans are not allowed to participate in these elections.

POLITICAL PARTIES

EUROPEAN

National Party: P.O.B. 354, Windhoek; organized on a federal basis with the National Party in the Republic of South Africa; Leader A. H. DU PLESSIS, M.P.; Sec. A. J. LOUW; won all six seats in the South African Parliament and all 18 in the Legislative Assembly of S.W. Africa in the elections of March 30th, 1966, and subsequently of April 1970 as well as in the April 1974 election.

United South West Africa Party: f. 1927; official Opposition Party; amalgamated in 1971 with United Party in Republic of South Africa; Leader Adv. J. P. DE M. NIEHAUS; Chair. D. J. PRETORIUS; Sec. L. BADENHORST.

COLOURED

South West Africa Coloured People's Organisation: f. 1959; 4,000 mems. (estimate).

AFRICAN

South West African People's Organisation of Namibia: f. 1958; P.O.B. 1071, Windhoek; London Office: 10 Dryden Chambers, 119 Oxford St., London, W.1.; formerly Ovambo People's Organisation; aims at removal of racial discrimination and full and unconditional independence for Namibia as one unitary state, active in Namibia; Pres. SAM NUJOMA (*based in Dar es Salaam*); Vice-Pres. BRANDON SIMBWAYE (*in restriction since 1964*); Chair. DAVID MERORO; London Rep. P. H. KATJAVIVI; 150,000 mems.

Democratic Development Co-operative Party: anti-apartheid, supports immediate independence for Namibia; Leader JOHANNES NANGUTUUALA; Sec. ANDREAS NUUKWAWO.

South West Africa National Union: supported by Pan-African Congress; the acting president, GERSON VEIL, was imprisoned in 1967.

JUDICIAL SYSTEM

The Territory is divided into 18 magisterial districts and three detached assistant magistracies. Ovambo and Kaokoveld and the Kavango Native Territory are separate magisterial districts under the control of the Minister of Bantu Administration and Development. Some magistrates are also Bantu affairs commissioners and such hold courts in cases solely affecting Africans. From the Magistrates Courts appeal lies to the Supreme Court of South Africa (South West Africa Division) which has jurisdiction over the whole of South West Africa.

The Supreme Court of South Africa (South West Africa Division):

Judge-President: Hon. F. H. BADENHORST.

Puisne Judge: Hon. G. G. HOEXTER.

Master: K. J. WATTRUS.

Registrar: M. VAN DER WESTHUYZEN.

Attorney-General: S. C. TERBLANCHE, S.C.

DEFENCE

An unknown number of South African troops and police are stationed in South West Africa (Namibia) and there have been frequent clashes with members of the People's Liberation Army of Namibia (PLAN).

RELIGION

The Europeans and substantial numbers of the African and coloured populations are Christians. The principal missionary societies are Lutheran (321,000 adherents), Roman Catholic (46,000 adherents) and Anglican (5,000 adherents).

EVANGELICAL LUTHERAN

NON-WHITE CHURCHES

Ovambo-Kavango Church: Bishop LEONARD AUALA, Oniipa, P.O. Ondangwa.

Rhenish Mission Church: P.O.B. 5069, Windhoek; f. 1967; Pres. Prases Dr. L. DE VRIES; publ. *Immanuel* (monthly).

WHITE CHURCH

German Evangelical Lutheran Church in South West Africa: President: Rev. Landespropst K. KIRSCHNEREIT, P.O.B. 233, Windhoek.

ANGLICAN

Province of South Africa, Diocese of Damaraland: Rt. Rev. COLIN O'BRIEN WINTER, M.A., Church of St. Edmund the King, Lombard St., London, E.C.3. Exiled from Namibia in March 1972. Suffragan Bishop Rt. Rev. RICHARD WOOD.

ROMAN CATHOLIC

Keetmanshoop Vicariate: Rt. Rev. EDWARD SCHLOTTERBACK, O.S.F.S., P.O.B. 88, Keetmanshoop.

Windhoek Vicariate: Most Rev. Bishop RUDOLF KOPPMANN, O.M.I., D.D., Titular Bishop of Dalisanda, P.O.B. 272, Windhoek.

METHODIST

African Methodist Episcopal Church: Rev. KARVARA, P.O.B. 558, Windhoek.

THE PRESS

Allgemeine Zeitung: P.O.B. 2127, Windhoek; f. 1915; daily; German; Editor K. DAHLMANN; circ. 5,200.

Immanuel: Evangelical Lutheran Church in South West Africa (Rhenish Mission Church), P.O.B. 54, Karibib; f. 1961; Lit. Sec. U. POENNIGHAUS; monthly; circ. 3,500.

Namib Times: P.O.B. 706, Walvis Bay; twice-weekly (Tues. and Fri.); English, Afrikaans, German; Editor P. VINCENT.

Namibia News: 10 Dryden Chambers, 119 Oxford St., London, W.1; f. 1968; every two months; circ. 2,500.

Namibia Today: P.O.B. 2603, Dar es Salaam, Tanzania; f. 1960; every two months; circ. 1,500.

Official Gazette of South West Africa: Secretary for South West Africa, P.O.B. 292, Windhoek; fortnightly; Government publication.

Die Suidwes Afrikaner: P.O.B. 337, Windhoek; Tues. and Fri.; Editor J. A. ENGELBRECHT.

Die Suidwester: P.O.B. 766, Windhoek; f. 1945; Mon.–Fri.; Afrikaans; Man. F. L. VAN ZIJL.

Windhoek Advertiser: P.O.B. 2127, Windhoek; f. 1919; English; daily; circ. 3,512.

PUBLISHERS

Deutscher Verlag (Pty.) Ltd.: P.O.B. 56, Windhoek; f. 1939; newspaper publishers.

John Meinert (Pty.) Ltd.: P.O.B. 56, Windhoek; f. 1924; newspaper publishers.

RADIO

Radio R.S.A.: P.O.B. 4559, Johannesburg; f. 1966; external short wave service of South African Broadcasting Corporation, broadcasting in English, Afrikaans, French, Portuguese, German, Dutch, Swahili and Chichewa to Africa, the Middle East, Europe, North America, Madagascar, Mauritius and Australasia. Transmitted from international short-wave station at Bloemendal, nr. Johannesburg.

FINANCE

BANKING

Bank of South West Africa: auth. cap. R.5m.; Chair. J. H. van der Wath.

Barclays National Bank Ltd.: Local Head Office in South West Africa: P.O.B. 195, Windhoek; Regional Gen. Man. I. A. C. van Niekerk; 23 brs.

Land and Agricultural Bank of South Africa: Private Bag 13208, Branch Office, Windhoek; f. 1922; Man. F. Neethling.

Nedbank Ltd.: P.O.B. 370, Windhoek.

Prifinger and Roll (Pty.) Ltd. P.O.B. 7, Windhoek; f. 1933.

Standard Bank of South Africa Ltd.: Chief Office in South West Africa: Windhoek.

Volkskas Ltd.: Chief Office in South West Africa: P.O.B. 2121, Windhoek.

INSURANCE

African Life Assurance Society Ltd.: Windhoek; Man. B. T. Hattingh.

Employers Liability Assurance Corporation Ltd.: Continental Buildings, Kaiser St., Windhoek; Man. H. K. Borchardt.

Mutual and Federal Insurance Co. Ltd.: P.O.B. 151, Windhoek; Man. A. J. van Ryneveld.

Protea Assurance Co. Ltd.: Windhoek; Man. I. N. Martin.

Prudential Assurance Co.: P.O.B. 365, Windhoek.

TRADE AND INDUSTRY

ADVISORY BOARDS

Various Advisory Boards have been established by the Administration to advise it on the development of industries, and to promote them. The most important are the Karakul Industry Advisory Board, the Diamond Board and the Fisheries Development Board.

LABOUR ORGANIZATIONS

SWANLA, the South West African Native Labour Association at Grootfontein, and the recruiting organization to obtain African labour from the north under contract for mines, fisheries and farms, was abolished as from January 31st, 1972. It was replaced by South African Government recruiting stations at Ondangua in Ovambo, and Runtu in Kavango.

TRANSPORT

RAILWAYS

South African Railways: railways in South West Africa are administered by South African Railways. The main lines are from De Aar in the Republic of South Africa to Luderitz on the coast, Windhoek to Walvis Bay and Tsumeb. Total rail tracks are 2,340 route kilometres.

ROADS

There are about 54,400 km. of roads, of which some 33,600 are maintained by the South West Africa Administration. More than 69 Railway Motor Services operate over 8,406 km. of road.

SHIPPING

Walvis Bay and Luderitz are the only ports. Walvis Bay harbour has been extended.

CIVIL AVIATION

Suidwes Lugdiens (Edms) Bpk.: P.O.B. 731, Windhoek; f. 1946; subsidiary of Safmarine; Chair. A. Lombard; fleet of two DC-4, two DC-3, one Cessna 402, two Cessna 310, two Aztec, four Twin Commanche.

South West Airways provide a service three times a week between Cape Town, Walvis Bay, Luderitz and Windhoek and once per week between Windhoek and Grootfontein. Regular Fly-In Safari Tours to the Etosha National Park are also available.

TOURISM

The Etosha Pan is one of the finest game reserves in Africa and in 1972 an estimated 250,000 tourists visited South West Africa's game parks, an increase of 34,000 over 1971 and 59,000 over 1970.

SPANISH AFRICA

SPANISH SAHARA   CEUTA AND MELILLA   OTHER POSSESSIONS

SPANISH SAHARA

INTRODUCTION

Spanish Sahara lies on the Atlantic coast of North Africa, with Morocco to the north and Mauritania to the east and south. There is also a small boundary with Algeria. While the economic prospects are bright, with the colony likely to become the world's leading producer of phosphates, Spanish Sahara is virtually a military colony. Between 10,000 and 20,000 Spanish troops are stationed there, though there are only about 30,000 settled, as against nomadic, inhabitants. Opposition to the colonial regime has grown in recent years. At the beginning of 1969 a movement for the liberation of Sekia el Hamra and Río de Oro was formed. Known as *Sidam* in Arabic, the movement is reported to have been responsible for the anti-Spanish demonstration in Al-Aaiún in June 1970 during which Spanish troops killed at least 10 civilians.

Just before this, Morocco, Mauritania and Algeria had agreed on a common policy towards the liberation of Spanish Sahara, and in December of the same year the UN Committee on Trusteeship and the Non-Self-Governing Territories called on Spain to hold a referendum as soon as possible in Spanish Sahara so that the indigenous population could exercise its right to self-determination. In February 1973 the UN passed a resolution calling on Spain, in consultation with Morocco and Mauritania, to grant the territory independence.

STATISTICS

Area: approx. 266,000 sq. km. (Sur 184,000 sq. km.; Nordeste 56,000 sq. km.; Norte 26,000 sq. km.).

Population (Census of December 31st, 1970): 76,425, including 16,648 Europeans. There are also about 15,000 Spanish soldiers. Towns: Al-Aaiún (capital) 24,048 (12,238 non-Europeans, 11,810 Europeans); Villa Cisneros 5,454. The number of nomads entering the territory during the rainy season is indeterminable. Estimated total population at July 1st, 1973: 102,000.

Agriculture (1972): 700 palm trees.

Livestock (1971): 60,200 camels, 145,900 goats, 17,500 sheep, 38 cows, 2,120 asses.

Fishing (1972): Weight of catch 5,012 tons.

Mining: Phosphate deposits at Bucraa estimated at 1,700 million tons are exploited by Fosfatos de Bucraa, S.A., a state-controlled company. In April 1972 the first shipment of phosphate ore was loaded at Al-Aaiún.

Industry (1972): Production of electric energy: 8,854,000 kWh.; Buildings constructed: 106 (92 for habitation).

Finance: Spanish currency: 100 céntimos=1 peseta. Coins: 10 and 50 céntimos; 1, 2½, 5, 25, 50 and 100 pesetas. Notes: 100, 500 and 1,000 pesetas. Exchange rates (April 1974): £1 sterling=138.50 pesetas; U.S.$1 =58.725 pesetas; 1,000 Spanish pesetas=£7.22= $17.03.

Budget (1972): Expenditure 1,214,783,421 pesetas. The territory receives substantial aid from Spain.

External Trade (1972): Imports ('000 pesetas): 918,924 (Foodstuffs 297,010, Manufactures 608,192); Exports are negligible.

Transport: *Roads:* 6,500 km. roads and tracks; 4,966 (1972): Passengers disembarked 6,875, freight entered 341,632 metric tons; *Civil Aviation* (1972): Passengers entered 78,459, Passengers leaving 79,899; Freight unloaded 12,280 metric tons.

Tourism (1971): 21,163 tourists.

Education (1972): *Pre-primary:* 368 pupils; *Primary:* 3,405 Spanish, 614 Saharan pupils; 84 Spanish and 60 Saharan teachers; *Secondary:* about 1,500 pupils at Al-Aaiún and Villa Cisneros.

Health (1972): Hospital beds 262, doctors 22.

THE GOVERNMENT

Spanish Sahara was recognized as a Province in 1958. It is divided into three regions: Sur (184,000 sq. km.), Nordeste (56,000 sq. km.) and Norte (26,000 sq. km.). A *Yemáa* (General Assembly) of 103 members (Pres. JATRI ULD SAID ULD YUMANI) and a *Cabildo* or local council (Pres. SEILA ULD ABEIDA) are the main representative bodies of the province. The province is represented in the Spanish *Cortes* by 6 *procuradores*.

There was an election to the General Assembly in January 1971.

Governor-General: Gen. FERNANDO DE SANTIAGO Y DÍAZ DE MENDIVIL.

Director-General for Promotion of the Sahara: D. EDUARDO JUNCO MENDOZA (resident in Madrid).

Religion: Muslim; the Europeans are nearly all Catholics.

Radio: *Radio Aaiún*, Apt. 7, Al-Aaiún; government station; Dir. EDUARDO GONZALEZ RUIZ.
Radio Villa Cisneros, Apt. 60, Villa Cisneros; government station; Dir. E. PONCE RAMOS.

Television: retransmission stations in Al-Aaiún and Smara.

Transport: Airfields at Villa Cisneros (the chief seaport) and Al-Aaiún, with passenger services to Madrid and Las Palmas operated by Iberia. There are also landing-strips at Smara, La Güera, Hagunía, Auserd, Aargub, Bir Enzarán, Anech and Agracha. A 3,500 metre loading pier has been constructed at Al-Aaiún to handle phosphate exports. A 72-km. conveyor brings the phosphate ores from the mines at Bucraa.

CEUTA

Ceuta is a North African port opposite Gibraltar. It has been held by Spain since 1580.

Area: 19 square km.

Population (1971): 66,900.

External Trade: Ceuta is a duty-free port. Trade is chiefly with Spain, the Balearic and Canary Islands and Melilla.

Transport: Much of the traffic between Spain and Morocco passes through Ceuta; there are ferry services to Algeciras, Spain.

Education (1970): Primary: 205 schools, 6,750 pupils; Secondary: 2,206 pupils.

Government: A Mayor administers the town and he is also a member (under the title *Procurador*) of the Spanish Parliament in Madrid. Procurador SERAFINO BECERRA.

Religion: Most Africans are Muslims; Europeans are nearly all Catholics; there are a few Jews.

Radio: *Radio Ceuta*, Alfau 20, Ceuta; commercial; owned by Sociedad Española de Radiodifusión.

MELILLA

Melilla is a Mediterranean port about 320 km. east of Ceuta and has been held by Spain since 1497. It now forms part of the province of Málaga.

Area: 12.3 square km.

Population (1971): 64,307.

External Trade: Melilla is a duty-free port. Most imports are from Spain but over 90 per cent of exports go to non-Spanish territories. Chief exports: fish and iron ore from Moroccan mines.

Transport: There is a daily ferry service to Málaga and a weekly service to Almería. Melilla airport is served by a daily service to Málaga, operated by Iberia.

Education (1970): Primary: 196 schools, 6,174 pupils; Secondary: 2,675 pupils.

Government: A mayor administers the town.

Radio: *Radio Melilla*, O'Donell 26, Melilla; commercial; owned by Sociedad Española de Radiodifusión.

OTHER POSSESSIONS

Peñón de Vélez de la Gomera and Villa Sanjurjo on the Mediterranean coast between Ceuta and Melilla—and the Chafarinas Islands lying east of Melilla near the Algerian border. Peñón de Vélez de la Gomera and Villa Sanjurjo are small towns. The Chafarinas Islands have no permanent inhabitants.

SRI LANKA

INTRODUCTORY SURVEY

Location, Climate, Language, Religion, Flag, Capital

The Republic of Sri Lanka (formerly called Ceylon) lies 50 miles east of the southern tip of India. The climate is tropical, average temperature 80°F (26°C); the south-west around Colombo receives heavy monsoon rains. The official language, Sinhala, is spoken by about 70 per cent of the people; Tamil and English are also widely used. More than 66 per cent of the population are Buddhist, about 18 per cent are Tamil-speaking Hindus and there are important Christian (mostly Roman Catholic) and Muslim minorities. The national flag (proportions 35 by 18) is dark crimson with a yellow border, in each corner of which a Bo leaf is depicted. In the centre is a gold lion and at the left are two vertical stripes of green and orange. The capital is Colombo.

Recent History

In 1948 Ceylon attained independence while remaining a member of the British Commonwealth. During the 1950s and 1960s two main political groupings alternated in forming the Government. The United National Party (U.N.P.), which held office from 1948 to 1956 and from 1965 to 1970, with a brief period of office in 1960, took a liberal position and was often in coalition with parties concerned to protect the rights of the Tamils, who are Hindus of Indian origin living in the north of the country. The Sri Lanka Freedom Party (S.L.F.P.), by contrast, has pursued socialist policies, forming coalitions with other socialist groups and the Communist Party, and has laid emphasis on the national heritage, thereby winning the support of anti-Tamil groups that advocate the recognition of Sinhala as the only official language and the establishment of Buddhism as the state religion. Led first by Solomon Bandaranaike and then, following his assassination in 1959, by his widow, Sirimavo Bandaranaike, the S.L.F.P. held office from 1956 to 1965, except for a three-month interruption in 1960, and has been the leading partner in the United Front coalition which came to power in 1970.

In the 1970 election campaign the United Front had won the support of radical elements, but in 1971 violent disturbances broke out which were blamed on the militant radicals of the Janatha Vimukti Peramuna (People's Liberation Front). The uprisings were very firmly suppressed and a state of emergency was declared which remained in force ever since. The Government strengthened its position in various ways in 1971 and 1972 by abolishing the upper house of the parliament and bringing in legislation to modify the judicial process and restrict the freedom of the press. Curfew restrictions have also been imposed to stifle political activity. Popular discontent with the Government was evinced in April 1973 by the wave of national feeling that accompanied the death of Dudley Senanyake, the leader of the opposition U.N.P. Earlier, in May 1972, Ceylon became a republic and adopted its present name.

No government since independence has effectively handled the country's economic problems of inflation,

unemployment and dependence on foreign aid. Food subsidies have been a permanent feature of the economy, and in October 1973, with food shortages becoming critical, the Government was forced to cut rice and flour rations and launch an emergency campaign for the production of food. The world oil crisis in the following months added extra urgency to the situation and, although missions to India, China, Pakistan and the U.S.S.R. in 1974 all secured promises of food and technological supplies on generous terms, the outlook remained bleak.

In foreign policy Sri Lanka has adopted a non-aligned role. Judicial ties with Britain were severed when the republic was proclaimed in 1972. Negotiations have been held with India since 1964 on the repatriation of stateless Tamils of Indian origin. In February 1974 India agreed to accept half of the 150,000 Tamils in question.

Government

Under the present constitution, executive power is vested in the Cabinet, whose Prime Minister is appointed by the President. Parliament is uni-cameral and has a six-year term. The National State Assembly comprises 157 members, 151 of whom are elected by universal suffrage and 6 of whom are nominated. The country is divided into 21 administrative districts in charge of government agents appointed by the central government.

Defence

In 1947 Ceylon signed a mutual defence pact with the United Kingdom. This continues to operate. In 1973 the armed forces totalled 12,500: army 8,500, navy 2,300, air force 1,700.

Economic Affairs

About one-third of Sri Lanka's national income is derived from the cultivation, processing and export of tea, rubber and coconuts. Sri Lanka is the world's second largest producer of tea. Most of the tea and rubber is cultivated on estates, while coconuts are predominantly a smallholders' crop. Somewhat under half of the 51 per cent of the labour force officially classified in the agricultural sector is employed on estates. Rice is the staple food. Because of foreign exchange difficulties, rice imports, totalling about 1.4 million tons annually, were to have ended in 1973 but a grave shortage of food supplies forced Sri Lanka to seek supplies of rice from China, Pakistan and India in 1974. Under the Five-Year Plan (1972–76), self-sufficiency in rice is expected to be achieved by 1976. Sri Lanka's population is predominantly rural, with only about 15 per cent of the population living in towns, and a rapidly expanding population, concentrated in the south and south-west, has created heavy pressure on the densely populated zones.

The only commercially important mineral is graphite, although there are also deposits of iron ore, monazite, ilmenite sands, limestone, clay and kaolin. Lacking other forms of power, Sri Lanka is developing her water resources and the Maskeli Oya and Samanalawewa projects are expected to produce sufficient power to meet immediate domestic requirements. There is a possibility that oil may be found near Kachchativu island, ownership of which is disputed by Sri Lanka and India. Manufacturing and handicraft industries at present supply mainly the domestic market, and the three traditional primary products continue to account for nearly 90 per cent of all export earnings. The United Kingdom is Sri Lanka's principal trading partner, followed by the People's Republic of China, with which a rice-rubber barter agreement has been concluded.

The government sector extends over many branches of economic activity. There are fifteen state-sponsored industrial corporations, and insurance, some transport facilities and oil distribution have been nationalized.

Transport and Communications

Much of Sri Lanka is hilly, thickly wooded, and of difficult access by road and rail. The railways are state-owned with about 1,000 miles of track. The state also runs a national omnibus service. Air Ceylon connects the main towns of the north and east to Colombo, and there are international services. The port of Colombo is one of the most important in the East.

Social Welfare

There is an island network of hospitals, clinics and dispensaries where treatment is free. An institute for training and research in community development was set up in 1966. Rice, the staple food, is subsidized by the state.

Education

Education is compulsory and free between the ages of five and fourteen. There are nearly 10,000 primary and secondary schools, with 2.8 million pupils, and 27 teacher training colleges with over 7,000 students. There are five universities and many technical colleges.

Tourism

As a stopping place for luxury cruises and by virtue of the spectacle of its Buddhist festivals, ancient monuments and natural scenery, Sri Lanka is one of Asia's most important tourist centres. Good motor roads connect Colombo to the main places of interest.

In 1971 an estimated 40,000 visitors came to Sri Lanka.

Visas are not required to visit Sri Lanka by nationals of Australia, Austria, Canada, Denmark, Finland, France, Federal Republic of Germany, Ireland, Italy, Malaysia, Netherlands, New Zealand, Norway, Pakistan, Singapore, Sweden, Switzerland, U.S.A.

Sport

Football and cricket are the most popular games.

Public Holidays

1974: September 26th (Bandaranaike Commemoration Day), October 17th (Id-ul-Fitr), November 13th (Deepavali Festival Day), December 25th (Christmas Day).

1975: March 26th (Milad-un-Nabi), March 28th and 31st (Easter), April (Sinhalese New Year), May 1st (May Day), May 22nd (Republic Day).

Note: A number of Hindu, Muslim and Buddhist holidays occur throughout the year, the precise dates of which depend on lunar sightings.

Weights and Measures

Imperial weights and measures are in standard use.

Currency and Exchange Rates

100 cents=1 Sri Lanka rupee.

Exchange rates (April 1974):

£1 sterling=15.60 rupees;

U.S. $1=6.607 rupees.

STATISTICAL SURVEY

AREA AND POPULATION

AREA (sq. km.)	POPULATION (Census of October 9th, 1971)				
	Total	RACES ('000)			
		Sinhalese	Ceylon Tamil	Indian Tamil	Ceylon Moors
65,610	12,711,143	9,147	1,416	1,195	824

Estimated Population: 13,033,000 (July 1st, 1972).

Towns (1971):* Colombo (capital) 562,160, Dehiwala-Mount Lavinia 128,000 (1970 estimate), Jaffna 107,663, Kandy 93,602, Galle 72,720.

* Provisional.

Births and Deaths (1971): 381,780 births registered (birth rate 29.9 per 1,000); 96,328 deaths registered (death rate 7.6 per 1,000).

SRI LANKA—(Statistical Survey)

EMPLOYMENT*

	Total ('000)	Per cent
Professional, Technical and Related Workers	174.5	4.8
Administrative, Executive, Managerial and Related Workers	41.8	1.2
Clerical Workers	147.3	4.1
Sales Workers	254.3	7.1
Workers in Agriculture, Forestry, Hunting and Fishing	1,826.7	50.8
Miners, Quarrymen and Related Workers	17.5	0.5
Workers in Transport and Communication Occupation	134.1	3.7
Service, Sport and Recreational Workers	265.3	7.4
Craftsmen, Production Process Workers and other Labourers	727.9	20.2
Unspecified	6.0	0.2
Total	3,595.4	100.0

* 1970 estimates; detailed figures relating to the 1971 Census are not yet available.

AGRICULTURE

LAND USE, 1970
('000 hectares)

Arable Land	895
Under Permanent Crops	1,084
Permanent Meadows and Pastures*	439
Forest Land	2,899
Other Land	1,157
Total Land Area	6,474
Inland Water	87
Total	6,561

* Including scrub.
Source: FAO, *Production Yearbook 1971.*

PRINCIPAL CROPS (1971*)

Tea	'000 lb.	470,107
Rubber	tons	138,729
Rice	'000 bushels	66,895
Kurakkan	million bushels	495
Cassava	cwt.	7,600,000†
Sweet Potatoes	,,	1,129,000
Potatoes	,,	801,000†
Onions	,,	819,000
Maize	,,	455,000
Oil Crops	,,	132,000†
Chillies	,,	564,000
Ginger	,,	70,000
Pulses	'000 bushels	255,000
Cocoa	cwt.	50,000†
Cashew	,,	18,000†
Sorghum	,,	1,000†
Sugar	tons	8,000†
Cinnamon	,,	3,000†
Pepper	'000 cwt.	233,000

* Provisional. † 1970.

LIVESTOCK
(herds at June each year)

	1970	1971
Buffaloes	735,708	730,580
Cattle	1,593,306	1,624,954
Sheep	26,697	28,737
Goats	556,362	546,272
Pigs	108,356	89,669
Chickens	6,856,000	n.a.
Ducks	25,000	n.a.

LIVESTOCK PRODUCTS
(metric tons)

	1968	1969	1970	1971*
Beef, Veal and Buffalo Meat . .	16,000	17,000	16,000	17,000
Poultry Meat	2,900	2,800	2,900	n.a.
Cows' Milk	137,000	126,000	131,000	132,000
Buffaloes' Milk	41,000	38,000	36,000	34,000
Goats' Milk	5,000*	5,000*	5,000*	5,000
Hen Eggs	20,000	19,400	19,400	20,300

* FAO estimate.

Source: FAO, *Production Yearbook 1971.*

FORESTRY
('ooo cubic metres)

	1969	1970	1971
Roundwood Removals . . .	4,570	4,645	4,700
Sawnwood Production . .	145	150	155

Source: FAO, *Yearbook of Forest Products 1971.*

FISHING*

	CATCH (metric tons)			VALUE OF LANDINGS ('ooo rupees)		
	1969	1970†	1971	1969	1970†	1971
Indian Ocean:						
Redfishes, Basses, Jacks, Mullets, etc. .	31,000	20,800	17,900	n.a.	39,098	31,961
Herrings, Sardines, Anchovies, etc. .	27,100	22,300	17,700	34,420	27,023	22,043
Tunas, Bonitos, Mackerels, etc. . .	41,500	27,500	25,800	n.a.	59,403	61,313
Sharks, Rays, etc. . . .	19,800	12,500	9,600	22,963	14,884	10,802
Other Marine Fish	2,300	2,600	3,200	2,712	2,189	3,140
TOTAL MARINE FISH .	121,700	85,700	74,200	n.a.	142,597	129,259
Crustaceans	5,400	3,500	3,000	16,813	8,234	9,037
Molluscs	600	600	700	n.a.	1,340	1,287
TOTAL SEA CREATURES .	127,700	89,800	77,900	231,598	152,171	139,583
Freshwater Fish	8,500	10,100	9,800	7,537	7,334	4,341
TOTAL	136,700	99,900	87,700	239,135	159,505	143,924

* Excluding (a) quantities landed by Sri Lanka craft in foreign ports, and (b) quantities landed by foreign craft in Sri Lanka ports.

† For 1970 a change was made in the method of estimating the total catch by mechanized boats. This resulted in a total production estimate for 1970 which is 31 per cent less than that for 1969.

Source: FAO, *Yearbook of Fishery Statistics 1971.*

MINING

	1968	1969	1970	1971
Graphite (tons) . . .	10,631	11,238	9,631	7,633
Common Salt (cwt.) . .	1,952,711	2,247,060	1,447,020	1,695,580

INDUSTRY

		1968	1969	1970	1971
Beer and Stout .	'ooo galls.	1,566	2,491	1,949	1,750
Cigarettes . .	million	2,805	2,930	3,035	3,183
Cotton Yarn .	'ooo lb.	4,787	5,105	4,049	6,440
Cotton Fabrics .	'ooo sq. yds.	17,985	18,137	15,328	16,195
Footwear . .	'ooo pairs	5,046	5,686	5,592	5,796
Cement . .	'ooo metric tons	222	279	321	385
Sugar. . .	tons	8,087	13,310	14,409	13,365

FINANCE

100 cents = 1 Sri Lanka rupee.

Coins: 1, 2, 5, 10, 25 and 50 cents; 1 rupee.

Notes: 2, 5, 10, 50 and 100 rupees.

Exchange rates (April 1974): £1 sterling = 15.60 rupees; U.S. $1 = 6.607 rupees.

100 Sri Lanka rupees = £6.41 = $15.14.

BUDGET

(Rs. million, fifteen months ending December 31st)

REVENUE	1971–72	EXPENDITURE	1971–72
CURRENT RECEIPTS:		*Administration:*	
Personal and Corporate Income Tax .	576.0	Civil	514.0
Taxes on Production and Expenditure:		Defence	187.1
General Sales and Turnover Tax .	477.5		
Selective Sales Tax . . .	414.5	TOTAL ADMINISTRATION . .	701.1
Import Duties . . .	334.2	*Social Services:*	
Receipts from Sale of FEECs* .	533.0	Education	657.9
Export Duties . . .	356.9	Health	315.2
Licence Taxes . . .	63.9	Others	36.3
Property Transfer Taxes . .	25.8		
Surplus of Government Monopolies .	200.0	TOTAL SOCIAL SERVICES .	1,009.4
Profits from Food Sales . .	134.0	*Economic Services:*	
		Agriculture and Irrigation . .	95.0
Total Taxes on Production and Expenditure . . .	2,539.8	Communication . . .	37.3
Interest and Dividends . .	135.7	Others	56.3
Gross Receipts from Trading Enterprises	431.3	TOTAL ECONOMIC SERVICES .	188.6
Other Current Receipts . .	175.3	*Gross Payments of Trading Enterprises* .	321.9
		Intra-Governmental Payments . .	5.0
TOTAL CURRENT RECEIPTS .	3,858.1	*Transfer Payments:*	
CAPITAL RECEIPTS:		Food Subsidies . . .	822.8
Transfers from Capital Accounts of Domestic Sector . . .	42.8	Other Subsidies . . .	87.9
		Interest on Public Debt . .	484.1
Other Capital Receipts . .	43.6	Pensions	284.8
		Households . . .	67.9
TOTAL CAPITAL RECEIPTS .	86.4	Local Authorities . . .	77.2
		Other	79.5
		TOTAL TRANSFER PAYMENTS .	1,904.2
TOTAL REVENUE . . .	3,944.5	TOTAL EXPENDITURE . .	4,160.4†

* Foreign Exchange Entitlement Certificates.   † Includes unallocable FEECs amounting to Rs. 30.2 million.

Source: Central Bank of Ceylon, *Annual Report 1971.*

FOREIGN EXCHANGE RESERVES
(U.S. $ million at December 31st)

	1967*	1968	1969	1970	1971	1972†	1973
Central Bank	44	40	28	33	40	33	60
Government and Official . . .	11	12	12	10	10	11	11
Total	55	52	40	43	50	44	71

* Foreign assets and liabilities were revalued during November 1967.
† Excluding allocation of IMF Special Drawing Rights.
Source: IMF, *International Financial Statistics.*

CURRENCY IN CIRCULATION
(million rupees at December 31st)

1967 . .	980
1968 . .	1,066
1969 . .	1,084
1970 . .	935
1971 . .	1,115
1972 . .	1,200
1973 . .	1,437

Source: IMF, *International Financial Statistics.*

COST OF LIVING
Consumer Price Index, Colombo
(base: 1963 = 100)

	1962	1964	1966	1968	1969	1970	1971	1972	1973*
All Items . . .	97.7	103.1	103.2	111.7	119.9	127.0	130.4	138.7	155.7
Food Only . . .	98.0	103.3	105.9	117.6	124.2	132.5	135.1	143.2	165.4

* Average for the month of September.
Source: United Nations, *Monthly Bulletin of Statistics.*

GROSS DOMESTIC PRODUCT BY ORIGIN
(million rupees)

	1969	1970	1971
Agriculture, Hunting, Forestry and Fishing .	3,990	4,244	4,227
Mining and Quarrying	75	78	91
Manufacturing	1,082	1,164	1,253
Electricity, Gas and Water	56	73	83
Construction	739	836	781
Trade, Restaurants and Hotels . .	1,793	2,090	2,118
Transport and Communications . .	1,042	1,161	1,194
Other Services	2,047	2,181	3,541*
G.D.P. at Factor Cost . . .	10,824	11,827	n.a.
Indirect Taxes	1,617	1,736	} n.a.
Less Subsidies	−664	−637	
G.D.P. at Purchasers' Values . .	11,777	12,926	13,288

* Includes net indirect taxes.
Source: mainly United Nations, *Monthly Bulletin of Statistics.*

BALANCE OF PAYMENTS 1972
(Rs. million)

	Credit	Debit	Net
Goods and Services:			
Merchandise	1,962.5	2,265.4	−302.9
Freight and Merchandise Insurance	9.3	12.1	− 2.8
Other Transportation	129.3	33.6	95.7
Travel	32.0	13.0	19.0
Investment Income	11.9	148.5	−136.6
Government Expenditure n.e.s.	40.2	28.0	12.2
Other Services	126.2	127.8	− 1.6
Total Goods and Services	2,311.4	2,628.4	−317.0
Transfer Payments	106.7	58.8	47.9
Total Current Account	2,418.1	2,687.2	−269.1
Capital:			
Non-Monetary Sector:			
Direct Investment	12.5	8.2	4.3
Other Private Long-term	1.4	1.4	—
Other Private Short-term	37.0	28.9	8.1
Central Government	1,081.7	792.3	289.4
Monetary Sector:			
Commercial Banks—Liabilities	86.9	18.9	68.0
Commercial Banks—Assets	31.2	166.3	−135.1
Central Bank—Liabilities	119.4	117.8	1.6
Central Bank—Assets	43.8	91.0	− 47.2
Net IMF Position	128.9	116.2	12.7
Special Drawing Rights	61.8	—	61.8
Errors and Omissions	16.6	11.1	5.5

Source: Central Bank of Ceylon, *Bulletin.*

EXTERNAL TRADE
(million rupees, excluding gold)

	1965	1966	1967	1968	1969	1970	1971	1972
Imports	1,474	2,028	1,738	2,173	2,543	2,313	1,986	2,064
Exports	1,949	1,700	1,690	2,035	1,916	2,021	1,946	1,939

Source: Central Bank of Ceylon, *Bulletin.*

PRINCIPAL COMMODITIES
(Provisional figures)

1970 (million rupees): Total exports 2,033, of which: Tea 1,120; Rubber 440; Coconut Products 237.

1971 (million rupees): Total exports 1,947, of which: Tea 1,145; Rubber 307; Coconut Products 276.

TEA EXPORTS
('000 lb.)

	1969	1970	1971
United Kingdom	131,273	156,100*	103,400
Australia	34,017	28,800*	32,500
Canada	15,057	14,900	13,300
New Zealand	14,755	14,100	13,800
South Africa	45,337	25,900*	26,800
Egypt	15,456	18,000	1,000
U.S.A.	45,334	39,700	49,900
Others	143,082	162,600	217,000
Total	444,311	460,100	457,700

* Revised.

TRADING PARTNERS
('ooo Rs.)

	EXPORTS*		IMPORTS	
	1970	1971	1970	1971
United Kingdom	454,659	332,545	329,762	247,033
India	21,087	10,400	225,647	207,975
Japan	66,744	65,809	195,193	169,878
Burma	2,371	2	89,002	98,848
Australia	71,989	90,817	112,162	117,750
United States	143,806	164,297	132,111	101,067
Germany, Federal Republic . .	81,451	74,262	139,819	139,197
China, People's Republic . .	251,523	180,483	289,324	161,077
Netherlands	34,344	33,037	25,791	23,684
France	16,915	18,924	62,115	76,395
Belgium	6,337	6,126	19,145	27,618
Pakistan	42,314	110,149	57,887	67,010
Italy	39,193	32,409	26,669	24,256
South Africa	80,416	72,855	4,156	2,615
Canada	52,046	44,018	67,810	38,947
TOTAL (including other countries) .	1,995,315	1,929,220	2,313,307	1,985,563

* Excluding re-exports.

TOURISM
FOREIGN VISITORS

	1969	1970	1971
North America	5,863	5,826	3,936
U.S.A.	5,264	5,155	3,336
Latin America and Caribbean .	130	127	127
West Europe	19,415	22,924	23,263
France	3,220	4,480	3,618
Germany, Federal Republic .	4,143	5,771	5,888
United Kingdom . . .	5,445	5,484	4,865
East Europe	404	486	569
Africa	276	332	295
Middle East	349	292	253
Asia	12,571	14,882	10,130
India	8,841	10,686	6,097
Australia	1,203	1,378	1,081
TOTAL	40,211	46,247	39,654

Source: Ceylon Tourist Board, *Annual Statistical Report 1971.*

Tourist Expenditure ('ooo rupees): 1969, 17,032; 1970, 21,503; 1971, 20,276.

TRANSPORT
RAILWAYS
(Year ending September 30th)

	1966–67	1967–68	1968–69	1969–70	1970–71
Passengers carried ('ooo) . . .	78,731.5	82,026.8	85,543.3	85,508.7	84,210.4
Passenger-miles (million) . . .	1,584.9	1,678.3	1,781.2	1,825.7	1,757.0
Freight ('ooo tons) . . .	1,802.6	1,820.5	1,791.6	1,699.8	1,788.4
Freight ton-miles ('ooo) . . .	211,945.0	221,484.0	220,013.0	228,276.0	262,405.0

Source: Ceylon Statistical Pocket Book 1972.

ROADS
Vehicles Registered

	1967	1968	1969	1970	1971
Cars	83,743	84,678	86,520	87,682	88,319
Motor-cycles . .	17,704	18,043	18,994	20,239	21,125
Buses . . .	8,840	9,151	9,688	10,423	10,892
Goods Vehicles* .	32,241	33,410	35,525	37,611	38,147

* Including ambulances.

Source: Ceylon Statistical Pocket Book 1972.

SHIPPING
('ooo net tons)

	1967	1968	1969	1970
Entered:				
Merchant Vessels (except bunkering) .	4,589	4,102	8,097	7,308
,, ,, (bunkers) . .	3,139	3,698	95	104
Other . . .	77	103	—	—
Total	7,805	7,903	8,192	7,412
Cleared:				
Merchant Vessels (except bunkering) .	3,845	2,572	7,425	6,315
,, ,, (bunkers) .	3,072	3,698	95	106
Other . . .	77	103	—	—
Total	6,994	6,373	7,520	6,421

CIVIL AVIATION

	1968	1969	1970	1971
Passengers . .	96,137	104,856	116,772	97,325
Freight (kg.) . .	798,274	941,999	1,009,833	916,176
Mail (kg.) . .	245,868	271,216	273,898	231,501

EDUCATION
(1971)

	Schools	Pupils	Staff
Primary and Secondary . .	9,502	2,803,182	94,858
Teacher Training . .	27	7,239	562
Special . . .	28	1,645	193

Sources (unless otherwise stated): Department of Census and Statistics, Colombo; Central Bank of Ceylon, Colombo (Foreign Aid Statistics).

THE CONSTITUTION

The Constitution of the new Republic of Sri Lanka (Ceylon) was adopted and enacted by the Constituent Assembly of the People of Sri Lanka on May 22nd, 1972.

The Constituent Assembly which was formed after the general elections in May 1970 drafted the new Constitution to make Ceylon a Unitary State known as the Republic of Sri Lanka where the sovereignty of the people is to be exercised through a National State Assembly of elected representatives of the people.

A summary of the main provisions of the new Constitution follows.

THE NATIONAL STATE ASSEMBLY

The Assembly consists of 157 representatives and exercises:

(a) the legislative power of the people;

(b) the Executive power of the people, including the defence of Sri Lanka, through the President and Cabinet Ministers; and

(c) the Judicial Power of the people through Courts and other institutions created by law, except in the case of matters relating to its powers and privileges, wherein the judicial power of the people may be exercised directly by the National State Assembly.

The normal life of the Assembly is six years and there is universal adult suffrage. The age limit for elections is over 18 years.

EXECUTIVE GOVERNMENT

A cabinet of Ministers is vested with the direction and control of the government of the Republic and is collectively responsible to the National State Assembly and answerable to the National State Assembly on all matters for which they are responsible. The Prime Minister determines the number of Ministers and Ministries and the assignment of subjects and functions to Ministers. The Prime Minister and other Ministers of the Cabinet and Deputy Ministers are appointed by the President.

OTHER PROVISIONS

Buddhism: Buddhism has the foremost place among religions and it is the duty of the State to protect and foster Buddhism, at the same time allowing every citizen the freedom to adopt the religion of his choice.

Language: Sinhala is the official language and all laws shall be made or enacted in Sinhala. The use of Tamil, the language of the largest minority community, continues to be protected under the Tamil Language Act of 1958.

State Policy: The Republic is pledged to carry forward the progressive advancement towards the establishment in Sri Lanka of a socialist democracy.

President: The President of the Republic is the Head of State. He appoints the Prime Minister and the other Ministers.

Control of Finance: The National State Assembly has full control over public finance.

Creation of Courts: The National State Assembly may create and establish institutions for the administration of justice and the settlement of industrial and other disputes.

THE GOVERNMENT

President: WILLIAM GOPALLAWA, M.B.E.

THE CABINET

(April 1974)

Prime Minister and Minister of Defence, Foreign Affairs, Planning, Economic Affairs and Plan Implementation: Mrs. SIRIMAVO RATWATTE DIAS BANDARANAIKE.

Minister of Irrigation, Power and Highways and Leader of the House: MAITHRIPALA SENANAYAKE.

Minister of Foreign and Internal Trade: TIKIRI BANDA ILLANGARATNE.

Minister of Education: BADIUDIN MAHMUD.

Minister of Shipping and Tourism: PUNCHI BANDAGUNATILAKA G. KALUGALLA.

Minister of Labour: MICHAEL PAUL DE ZOYSA SIRIWARDENE.

Minister of Public Administration, Justice, Local Government and Home Affairs: FELIX REGINALD DIAS BANDARANAIKE.

Minister of Industries and Scientific Affairs: TIKIRI BANDA SUBASINGHE.

Minister of Finance: Dr. NANAYAKKARAPATHIRAGE MARTIN PERERA.

Minister of Communications: LESLIE SIMON GOONEWARDENE.

Minister of Plantation Industry and Constitutional Affairs: Dr. COLVIN REGINALD DE SILVA.

Minister of Agriculture and Lands: HECTOR SENERATH RAJAKARUNA BANDA KOBBEKADUWA.

Minister of Fisheries: GEORGE RAJAPAKSE.

Minister of Housing and Construction: PIETER GERALD BARTHOLOMEUS KEUNEMAN.

Minister of Posts and Telecommunications: CHELLIAH KUMARASURIER.

Minister of Health: WEGLIGAMA POLWATTEGE G. ARIYADASA.

Minister of Information and Broadcasting: RANAWAKEARACHIGE SOLMON PERERA.

Minister of Social Services: TIKIRI BANDA TENNEKOON.

Minister of Cultural Affairs: SEMAGE SALMAN KULATILEKE.

Minister of Parliamentary Affairs, Sports and Chief Government Whip: KIRI BANDA RATNAYAKE.

DIPLOMATIC REPRESENTATION

HIGH COMMISSIONS, EMBASSIES AND LEGATION ACCREDITED TO SRI LANKA

(HC) High Commission; (E) Embassy; (L) Legation.

Afghanistan: Islamabad, Pakistan (E).

Argentina: New Delhi, India (E).

Australia: 3 Cambridge Place, Colombo 7 (HC); *High Commissioner:* H. G. MARSHALL.

Austria: New Delhi, India (E).

Belgium: 100/3A Horton Place, Colombo 7 (E); *Ambassador:* C. H. KERREMANS.

Brazil: New Delhi, India (E).

Bulgaria: 168/1 Inner Flower Rd., Colombo 3 (E); *Chargé d'Affaires a.i.:* GEORGI KONSTANTINOV.

Burma: 53 Rosmead Place, Colombo 7 (E); *Ambassador:* U OHN KHIN.

Canada: 6 Gregory's Rd., Colombo 7 (HC); *High Commissioner:* Miss MARION ADAMS MACPHERSON.

China, People's Republic: 191 Dharmapala Mawata, Colombo 7 (E); *Ambassador:* HUANG MING-TA.

Cuba: New Delhi, India (E).

Czechoslovakia: 47/47A Horton Place, Colombo 7 (E); *Ambassador:* FRANTIŠEK MALIK.

Denmark: New Delhi, India (E).

Egypt: 15 Wijeramg Mawatha, P.O.B. 1419, Colombo 7 (E); *Ambassador:* MOHAMED ATEF ELNAWAWY.

Finland: New Delhi, India (E).

France: 89 Rosmead Place, Colombo 7 (E); *Ambassador:* JOSEF LAMBROSCHINI.

German Democratic Republic: 101 Rosmead Place, Colombo 7 (E); *Ambassador:* KRAFT BUMBEL.

Germany, Federal Republic: 16 Barnes Place, Colombo 7 (E); *Ambassador:* Dr. HILDEGUNDE FEILNER.

Ghana: New Delhi, India (HC).

Greece: New Delhi, India (E).

Hungary: New Delhi, India (E).

India: 18-3/1 Sir Baron Jayatileke Mawatha, Colombo 1 (HC); *High Commissioner:* V. H. COELHO.

Indonesia: 23 Alfred Place, Colombo 3 (E); *Ambassador:* Mr. SOEKIRMAN.

Iran: Islamabad, Pakistan (E).

Iraq: 49 Dharmapala Mawatha, Colombo 3 (E); *Ambassador:* BASHIR ISMAEL AL-TALIB.

Italy: 586 Galle Rd., Colombo 3 (E); *Ambassador:* Dr. FABRIZIO FABBRICOTTI.

Japan: 10 Ward Place, Colombo 7 (E); *Ambassador:* SASHICHIRO MATSUI.

Jordan: New Delhi, India (E).

Kuwait: New Delhi, India (E).

Laos: New Delhi, India (E).

Lebanon: New Delhi, India (E).

Malaysia: 63A Ward Place, Colombo 7 (HC); *High Commissioner:* His Highness TENGKU INDRA PETRA.

Maldives: 25 Melbourne Ave., Colombo 4 (E); *Ambassador:* HUSSAIN ALI DIDI.

Mexico: New Delhi, India (E).

Mongolia: New Delhi, India (E).

Nepal: New Delhi, India (E).

Netherlands: New Delhi, India (E).

New Zealand: New Delhi, India (HC).

Nigeria: New Delhi, India (HC).

Norway: New Delhi, India (E).

Pakistan: 17 Sir Ernest de Silva Mawatha, Colombo 7 (E); *Ambassador:* ABDUR RAUF KHAN.

Philippines: 5 Torrington Place, Colombo 7 (E); *Ambassador:* LIBRADO D. CAYCO.

Poland: 137 New Buller's Rd., Colombo 4 (E); *Ambassador:* WIKTOR KINECKI.

Portugal: 22 Maitland Crescent, Colombo 7 (L); *Chargé d'Affaires a.i.:* Dr. GIL PESANHA ALCOFORADO SALDANHA.

Romania: New Delhi, India (E).

Singapore: New Delhi, India (HC).

Spain: New Delhi, India (E).

Sudan: New Delhi, India (E).

Sweden: New Delhi, India (E).

Switzerland: No. 7 Upper Chatham St., Colombo 1 (E); *Ambassador:* FRANÇOIS P. CHATELAIN.

Thailand: 10 Sir Ernest de Silva Mawatha, Colombo 7 (E); *Ambassador:* OWART SUTHIWART-NARUEPUT.

Trinidad and Tobago: New Delhi, India (HC).

Turkey: New Delhi, India (E).

U.S.S.R.: 62 Sir Ernest de Silva Mawatha, Colombo 7 (E); *Ambassador:* RAFIK NISHANOV.

United Kingdom: Galle Rd., Kollupitiya, Colombo 3 (HC): *High Commissioner:* H. SMEDLEY.

U.S.A.: 44 Galle Rd., Colombo 3 (E); *Ambassador:* CHRISTOPHER VAN HOLLEN.

Viet-Nam, Democratic Republic: 106 Havelock Rd., Colombo 5 (E); *Ambassador:* HOANG THANH TRAI.

Yugoslavia: 32 Cambridge Place, Colombo 7 (E); *Ambassador:* SLOBADAN MARTINOVIC (designate).

PARLIAMENT

NATIONAL STATE ASSEMBLY

Speaker: STANLEY TILAKARATNE.

After the general election of 1970 the newly elected House of Representatives functioned as a Constituent Assembly with the aim of adopting a new Constitution. The new Constitution was finally approved in May 1972, and vested sovereignty exclusively in the new unicameral National State Assembly of 157 representatives. The National State Assembly is elected for a six-year term, and it was decided that the existing House of Representatives elected in 1970 would have an extended term of that duration.

GENERAL ELECTION, MAY 1970

	SEATS	VOTES
United National Party . .	17	1,879,996
Sri Lanka Freedom Party .	90	1,817,349
Federal Party . .	13	245,747
Lanka Sama Samaja Party (Trotskyists) . . .	19	443,224
Sri Lanka Freedom Socialist Party . . .	—	n.a.
Communist Party . .	6	169,149
Tamil Congress . .	3	115,557
Mahajama Eksath Peramuna (People's United Front)		
Jatika Vimukti Peramuna (National Liberation Front) .	—	n.a.
Independents and Others . .	2	292,747

POLITICAL PARTIES

The main political parties are:

Sri Lanka Freedom Party: 407 Galle Rd., Colombo 7; f. Oct. 1951 by the former Premier, Hon. S. W. R. D. BANDARANAIKE; Socialist; stands for a neutralist foreign policy; nationalization of certain industries but not immediately of the foreign-owned estates; Sinhalese as the official language, with safeguards for minorities; Pres. Mrs. SIRIMAVO R. D. BANDARANAIKE.

United National Party: "Siri Kotha", Kollupituya, Colombo; Democratic Socialist party; aims at a neutralist foreign policy; Sinhalese as the official language and State-aid to denominational schools; is opposed to nationalization of foreign-owned estates; Pres. J. R. JAYEWARDENE; publ. *U.N.P. Journal* (weekly in Sinhala).

Federal Party: 16 Alfred House Gdns., Colombo 3; f. 1949; principal Tamil party; stands for a Federal constitution; Leader S. J. V. CHELVANAYAKAM, Q.C.; Parliamentary Whip V. DHARMALINGAM, M.P.; Pres. S. M. RASAMANIKAM; 457 Union Place, Colombo 2; Hon. Sec. S. KATHIRAVELUPPILLAI.

Lanka Sama Samaja Party (*Trotskyist Party*): f. 1935; stands for nationalization of estates and other foreign-owned companies, opposed to communalism; Leader Dr. N. M. PERERA; Sec. BERNARD SOYSAL; publs. *Sumasamajaya, Samadharmam* and *Samasamajist* (Trotskyist weeklies in Sinhala, Tamil and English respectively).

Mahajama Eksath Peramuna (*People's United Front*): 53, 2/7 Mansoor Bldg., Main St., Colombo 11; f. 1960, coalition 1965; left wing; stands for nationalization of foreign estates; strongly Sinhalese and Buddhist; scientific socialist; non-aligned; includes the former **Viplavakari Lanka Sama Samaja** (**VLSSP**); 1,500 active mems.; 8,000 Youth Leaguers; Pres. DINESH GUNAWARDENE; Sec. SHANTHA LOKUPITIYA; publ. *Mahajana Eksath Peramuna* (weekly), *Pahara* (weekly).

Communist Party: 91 Cotta Rd., Colombo 8; f. 1943; Chair. Dr. S. A. WICKRAMASIHHE; Gen. Sec. N. SANMUGATHASAN; National Organizer V. A. SAMARAWICKRAMA; Gen. Treasurer C. KUMARASAMY; 9,500 mems.; publs. *Maubima, Desabhimani, Forward* (weeklies in Sinhalese, Tamil and English respectively), *Aththa* (Sinhalese daily), *NavaLogaya* (Sinhala monthly).

Lanka Prajathanthravadi Pakshaya (*Ceylon Democratic Party*): f. 1959 by the former Premier W. DAHANAYAKE; is opposed to the nationalization of foreign-owned estates, State take-over of denominational schools and interference with Buddhist organizations; Leader W. DAHANAYAKE.

Sri Lanka Freedom Socialist Party: Colombo; f. 1964; breakaway group from Sri Lanka Freedom Party; Leader (vacant).

Tamil Congress: strongly represented in northern and eastern Ceylon; Leader G. G. PONNAMBALAM.

JUDICIAL SYSTEM

THE SUPREME COURT
AND
COURT OF CRIMINAL APPEAL OF SRI LANKA

Chief Justice: Hon. H. N. G. FERNANDO, O.B.E.

Puisne Judges: Hon. G. P. A. SILVA, Hon. A. L. S. SIRIMANE, Hon. A. C. A. ALLES, Hon. G. T. SAMARAWICKREME, Q. C., Hon. C. G. WEERAMANTRY, Hon. O. L. DE KRETSER, Hon. S. R. WIJAYATILAKE, Hon. V. T. THAMOTHERAM.

Commissioners of Assize: E. R. DE FONSEKA, C. B. WALGAMPAYA, D. Q. M. SIRIMANE, T. W. RAJARATNAM.

Registrar: N. NAVARATNAM.

COURT OF APPEAL

Legislation to establish a Court of Appeal and abolish the right of appeal to the Privy Council in London was introduced in 1971 and passed in the following year, the Court holding its inaugural session on March 9th, 1972.
President: T. S. FERNANDO, Q.C.

DISTRICT COURTS

There are twenty-eight District Courts in Sri Lanka. They have unlimited original civil jurisdiction and criminal jurisdiction in respect of all offences which are not within the exclusive jurisdiction of the Supreme Court. In the exercise of their criminal jurisdiction, District Courts try only cases committed to them for trial by Magistrates' Courts.

MAGISTRATES' COURTS

There are thirty-four Magistrates' Courts in Sri Lanka. A Magistrates' Court may not pass a sentence heavier than the following, except where an Ordinance has specially empowered it to do so:

(a) Imprisonment up to six months.
(b) Fine up to Rs.100.
(c) Whipping if the offender is under 16 years.

COURTS OF REQUESTS AND RURAL COURTS

There are thirty Courts of Requests in the island, and they have original civil jurisdiction in all actions in which the debt, damage or demand, or the value of land in dispute, does not exceed a stipulated amount. The courts, with the exception of the Colombo Court, are presided over by a District Judge or a Magistrate, who acts as a Commissioner of Requests in addition to his duties as a District Judge or Magistrate. The Colombo Court is presided over by a separate Commissioner. There are forty-five Rural Courts in Sri Lanka.

CRIMINAL JUSTICE COMMISSIONS ACT

The Criminal Justice Commissions Act, passed in April 1972, set up a specially constituted Judicial Commission to try offences in connection with any rebellion, insurrection or any widespread breakdown of law and order, currency offences and sabotage of industrial plants.

CONSTITUTIONAL COURT

The new Constitution adopted in May 1972 provided for a Constitutional Court of five persons, appointed by the President, charged with ruling on the validity of legislation enacted within the National Assembly. Jurisdiction in these matters is now outside the sphere of ordinary courts.

RELIGION

BUDDHISM

Seventy-five per cent of the population are Theravada Buddhist. Buddhism was introduced into Ceylon in the third century B.C. by Prince Mahinda, son of the Indian King Asoka. There are 12,000 Buddhist Bhikkhus (monks), living in 6,000 temples on the island. They are educated in Pirivenas (temple schools), numbering 150. Two Pirivenas founded 85 years ago were raised to university status by Act of Parliament in 1959, in order to provide higher education for both Bhikkhus and laymen in the medium of the Sinhala language.

Ceylon Regional Centre of the World Fellowship of Buddhists: 6 Paget Rd., Colombo 5; Sec. W. P. DALUWATTA.

Buddhist Congress: Pres. JINADASA SAMARAKKODI.

HINDUISM

The Tamil population of Sri Lanka, including those long settled in the island as well as the immigrants from India, are Hindus. The Hindu population numbers over two million.

ISLAM

The majority of the Muslims in Sri Lanka are styled Moors or Moormen, and claim descent either from Arab immigrants or the Indian traders from the mainland who settled in the island. The rest are Malays, mostly descended from soldiers and labourers from Java and Sumatra introduced into the island by the Dutch. There are a few Afghans and other Muslim settlers. Arab merchants dominated trade in the island until the appearance of the Portuguese in the sixteenth century. The total Muslim population is over 600,000.

CHRISTIAN CHURCHES

CHURCH OF CEYLON

Bishop of Kurunagala: Rt. Rev. CYRIL LAKSHMAN WICKRE-MASINGHE; Bishop's House, Kandy Road, Kurunagala.

Bishop of Colombo: CYRIL ABEYNAYAKE; Bishop's House, Stewart Place, Colombo, 3.

METHODIST CHURCH IN SRI LANKA

President of Conference: Rev. G. DENZIL DE SILVA, B.D.

THE PRESBYTERY OF SRI LANKA

The Dutch Reformed Church in Sri Lanka.

Moderator: Rev. R. N. WEIMAN, B.D., M.TH.

CHURCH OF SOUTH INDIA

The Church of South India came into being in 1947 by a union of four Anglican Dioceses, four Methodist Districts and eight Councils of the South India United Church. About 5,000 members.

Bishop: Rt. Rev. D. J. AMBALAVNAR, B.A., B.D., M.TH. Jaffna Diocese, Vaddukoddai.

ROMAN CATHOLIC CHURCH

Archbishop: H.E. THOMAS Cardinal COORAY, O.M.I., B.A., PH.D., D.D., Metropolitan; Archbishop's House, Colombo 8. There are 12 Bishops.

THE PRESS

NEWSPAPERS

DAILIES

Newspapers are published in Sinhala, Tamil and English. There are three main newspaper publishing groups: Associated Newspapers of Ceylon Ltd., Independent Newspapers Ltd. and Times of Ceylon Ltd. In February 1973 legislation was passed setting up a Press Council of five members and imposing controls on newspapers, notably on the publication without official approval of Cabinet proceedings. In July 1973 ownership of Associated Newspapers was transferred by legislation, the Public Trustee acquiring 75 per cent of the shares for sale to the public, co-operative societies, trade unions, journalists and newspaper employees, but not to other newspaper groups. In April 1974 the Government ordered the offices of Independent Newspapers Ltd. to be closed.

Aththa: 95 Cotton Rd., Colombo 8; Sinhalese; Communist; circ. 41,000; Editor B. A. SIRIWARDENE.

Ceylon Daily Mirror: P.O.B. 159, Colombo 1; London Office: Stuart House, 1 Tudor St., E.C.4; f. 1961; English; published by the Times of Ceylon Ltd.; Independent; Editor R. MICHAEL; circ. 31,500; Sunday edition, *Sunday Mirror*.

Ceylon Daily News: Lake House, P.O.B. 248, Fort, Colombo; f. 1918; morning; published by the Associated Newspapers of Ceylon Ltd.; Editor M. DE SILVA; circ. 67,537.

Ceylon Observer: Lake House, P.O.B. 248, Fort, Colombo; f. 1834; evening and weekly; published by the Associated Newspapers of Ceylon Ltd.; Editor PHILIP COOREY; circ. evening 8,151; weekly 83,632.

Dawasa: 5 Gunasena Mawatha, Colombo 12; Sinhalese; published by Independent Newspapers Ltd.; Editor D. KARUNARATNE; circ. 76,000.

Dinamina: Lake House, P.O.B. 248; Fort, Colombo; f. 1909; morning; Sinhalese; published by the Associated Newspapers of Ceylon Ltd.; Editor S. SUBASINGHE; circ. 123,784.

Dinapathi: 5 Gunasena Mawatha, Colombo 12; Tamil; published by Independent Newspapers Ltd.; Editor S. T. SIVA NAYAGAM; circ. 34,400.

Eelanaadu: f. 1959; published by Eelanaadu Ltd.; Man. Editor K. P. Haran; Editor N. Sabaratnam.

Janadina: 47 Jayantha Weerasekera Mawatha, Colombo 10; Sinhalese; published by Suriya Printers and Publishers Ltd.; Editor Wimalaweera Perera.

Janata: Lake House, P.O.B. 248, Fort, Colombo; London Office: 151 Fleet Street, London, E.C.4; f. 1953; evening; Sinhalese; published by the Associated Newspapers of Ceylon Ltd.; Editor D. F. Kariyakarawana; circ. 37,908.

Lankadipa: Times Building, Colombo; publ. by Times of Ceylon Ltd.; London Office: Stuart House, Tudor St., E.C.4; f. 1947; Sinhalese; Editor D. H. Abeysinghe; circ. 510,000.

Mithran: 185 Grandpass Rd., Colombo 14; Tamil; published by Express Newspapers Ltd.; Editors K. V. S. Vas, K. Sivapragasam.

Rasavahini: Bristol St., Colombo 1; Sinhalese; published by the Times of Ceylon Ltd.; Editor D. H. Abeysinghe.

Riviresa: 5 Gunasena Mawatha, Colombo 12; Sinhalese; published by Independent Newspapers Ltd.; Editor G. Liyanage; circ. 170,000.

Sawasa: 5 Gunasena Mawatha, Colombo 12; Sinhalese; published by Independent Newspapers Ltd.; Editor M. Karunaratne; circ. 17,000.

Sun: Colombo; f. 1965; English; Editor Dr. Gamini Wijeyewardene.

Thanthi: 5 Gunasena Mawatha, Colombo 12; Tamil; published by Independent Newspapers Ltd.; Editor V. K. P. Nathan; circ. 7,050.

Thinakaran: Lake House, P.O.B. 1217, Fort, Colombo; London Office: 151 Fleet Street, London, E.C.4; f. 1932; morning; Tamil; published by the Associated Newspapers of Ceylon Ltd.; Editor R. Sivagurunathan; circ. daily 35,081.

Times of Ceylon: P.O.B. 159, Colombo 1; London Office: Stuart House, 1 Tudor St., London, E.C.4; f. 1846; evening except on Sundays; published by the Times of Ceylon Ltd.; Independent; Editor H. E. R. Abayasekara; circ. evening 15,000, Sunday 36,000.

Virakesari: 185 Grandpass Rd., Colombo 14 (P.O.B. 160); f. 1930; morning; Tamil; Chief Editor K. V. S. Vas; Ass. Editor K. Sivapragasam; circ. 24,680.

Sunday Papers

Observer (*Magazine Edition*): f. 1923 (see *Ceylon Observer* above).

Shri Lankadipa: Times Building, Colombo; publ. by Times of Ceylon Ltd.; f. 1951; Sinhalese; Editor D. H. Abeysinghe; circ. 120,000.

Silumina: Lake House, P.O.B. 248, Fort, Colombo; London Office: 151 Fleet St., London .E.C.4; f. 1930; illustrated; Sinhalese; Editor; D. D. Wettasinghe; circ. 366,000.

Sunday Times: P.O.B. 159, Colombo 1; f. 1923; illustrated; Independent; Editor H. E. R. Abayasekara; circ. 36,000.

Thinakaran Vaara Manjari: Lake House, P.O.B. 1217, Fort, Colombo; f. 1948; Editor R. Sivagurunathan; circ. (Sunday edition) 39,247.

Weekend Sun: 5 Gunasena Mawatha, Colombo.

PERIODICALS
Weeklies

Ceylon Catholic Messenger: Catholic Press, Colombo 8; f. 1868; Editor Rev. Fr. Manik Muttukumaru, b.a., d.c.l. (Rome); circ. 13,500.

Ceylon Government Gazette: Government Press, P.O.B. 500, Colombo; f. 1802; official Government publication; circ. 54,364.

Ceylon News: Lake House, P.O.B. 248, Fort, Colombo; f. 1938; articles from the *Ceylon Observer* and the *Ceylon Daily News*; published by the Associated Newspapers of Ceylon Ltd.

Chintamani: 5 Gunasena Mawatha, Colombo 12; Tamil; published by Independent Newspapers Ltd.; Editor S. T. Siva Nayagam; circ. 55,700.

Desabhimani: 91 Cotta Road, Colombo; Tamil; published by the Communist Party; Editor K. Ramanathan; circ. 10,000.

Forward: Colombo; English; Communist; circ. 9,000.

Gnanartha Pradipaya: Colombo Catholic Press, Colombo 8; Sinhalese; National Catholic paper; Editors Rev. Fr. Joe E. Wickramasinghe, P. Dharmaratne, Norbert Mawalage; circ. 36,500.

Janasathiya: 47 Jayantha Weerasekara Mawatha, Colombo 10; Sinhalese; published by Suriya Printers and Publishers Ltd.; Editor Nimal Horana.

Maubima: 91 Cotta Road, Colombo; Sinhalese; published by the Communist Party; circ. 18,000.

Mihira: Lake House, Fort, Colombo; children's magazine.

Morning Star: American Ceylon Mission Press, Manipay; f. 1841; English and Tamil; Editors L. S. Kulathungam (English), Rev. N. Subramaniam (Tamil).

Samadharmam: 47 Driebergs Ave., Colombo 10; Tamil; organ of the Lanka Samaja Party, section of the Fourth International.

Sarasaviya: Lake House, P.O.B. 248, Fort, Colombo; f. 1963; Sinhalese; circ. 38,000.

Sathiaveda Pathukavalan: Jaffna; published by St. Joseph's Catholic Press; f. 1876; Tamil; Editor S. M. J. Louis.

Sinhala Bauddhaya: Maha Bodhi Mandira, 13 Maligakanda Rd., Colombo 10; f. 1906; published by The Maha Bodi Society of Ceylon; Editor-in-Chief Raja V. Ekanayaka; circ. 25,000.

Siyarata: 532 Galle Road, Colombo 3; f. 1947; Sinhalese and English editions; Editor of Sinhalese edition P. A. Jinadasa Niyathapala; Editor of English edition Alwyn F. Perera.

Sutantiran: 194A Silversmith Street, Colombo; f. 1947; Tamil; Editor S. T. Sivanayagam.

U.N.P. Journal: organ of the United National Party.

Vanitha Viththi: Times Building, Colombo; London Office: Stuart House, Tudor Street, E.C.4; f. 1957; Sinhalese women's magazine; Editor M. Disanayake; circ. 40,000.

Virakesari (*Weekly Illustrated edition*): 185 Grandpass Rd., Colombo 14 (P.O.B. 160); f. 1930; Editor K. V. S. Vas; circ. 25,110.

Fortnightlies, Monthlies, etc.

Baptist Messenger: 44 Kynsey Rd., Colombo 8; Sinhalese and English; twice a month; organ of the Baptist Churches of Ceylon and published by the Sri Lanka Baptist Sangamaya; Editor Rev. Carlyle Pietersz; Business Man. H. B. Welagedera.

Bosat, The: Vajirarama, Bambalapitiya, Colombo; f. 1937; Buddhist English monthly; Board of Editors Vens. Narada, Piyadassi and Vinita and J. S. Gomes.

Ceylon Business Express, The: 23 Canal Row, Colombo; f. 1940; policy to extol private enterprise and teach business efficiency; monthly; Editor D. J. S. Peiris.

Ceylon Causerie, The: Nadaraja Bldg., Galle Road, Colombo 3; f. 1929; illustrated monthly; English; Editor ALEXIS ROBERTS.

Ceylon Commerce: Ceylon National Chamber of Commerce, 2nd Floor YMBA Bldg., Main St., (P.O.B. 1375), Colombo 1; fortnightly.

Ceylon Estate News: Lochiel, Nalluruwa, Pandura.

Ceylon Journal of Adult Education: 1 Maliban Street, Colombo; published by Ceylon Literacy Campaign; Socialist; monthly; Editor T. P. ANERASINGHE, B.A., F.R.ECON.S.

Ceylon Law Recorder: Kotte; f. 1919; legal miscellany and law report of Ceylon; monthly; Editorial Board: N. E. WEERASOORIA, Q.C., W. S. WEERASOORIA, LL.B., PH.D.

Ceylon Teacher, The: 95 Main Street, Jaffna; monthly journal of the All-Ceylon Union of Teachers; Editor A. E. TAMBER, B.SC.

Ceylon Trade Journal: Department of Commerce, P.O. Box 1507, Colombo; f. 1935; published by the Department of Commerce, Colombo; monthly; Editor-in-Chief Dir. of Commerce.

Ceylon Woman: 5 Castle Terrace, Colombo 8; English; monthly; Editor SITA JAYAWARDANA.

Duthaya: Colombo Catholic Press, Colombo; monthly; Editor Rev. Fr. OSWALD GOMIS.

Financial Times, The: 323 Union Place, P.O.B. 330, Colombo 2; quarterly; commercial and economic affairs; Man. Editor CYRIL GARDINER; Deputy Editor J. A. ALOYSIUS; Business Man. P. M. ALOYSIUS.

Guvan Viduli Sangarawa: P.O.B. 574, Colombo; Sinhalese; fortnightly; magazine of Sri Lanka Broadcasting Corporation.

Industrial Ceylon: Ceylon National Chamber of Industries, No. 2-1/12a, Bristol Bldg., Colombo 1; quarterly.

Janakavi: 47 Jayantha Weerasekera Mawatha, Colombo 10; Sinhalese; fortnightly; Associated Editors WIMALAWEERA PERERA and NIMAL HORANA.

Messenger of the Sacred Heart for Ceylon: Colombo Catholic Press, Colombo 8; f. 1920; monthly; Editors Rt. Rev. Mgr. MANIK MUTTUKUMARU, B.A., D.C.L. (Rome) (English), Rev. Fr. OSWALD GOMIS (Sinhalese); circ. 4,500.

Navalokaya: Gampaha, W.P.; f. 1941; Sinhalese; monthly; articles on literature, art, politics, education, science, etc.; Managing Editor Rev. U. SARANANKARA.

Nava Yugaya: Lake House, Colombo; f. 1956; fortnightly; Sinhalese; circ. 17,753.

Public Opinion: 723 Maradana Road, Colombo 10; monthly; Editor N. G. L. MARASINGHE.

Radio Times: P.O.B. 574, Colombo; English; fortnightly; magazine of Sri Lanka Broadcasting Corporation.

Rasavahini: Times Bldg., Colombo; London Office: Stuart House, Tudor Street, E.C.4; f. 1956; Sinhalese monthly; Editor M. DISANAYAKE.

Sri Lanka Methodist Church Record: Wesley Press, Wellawatte, Colombo 6; f. 1892; published by the Methodist Church, Sri Lanka; monthly; Editor JILL F. NEWSHAM, B.SC.; circ. 300.

Textiles: 15 Fifth Cross Street, Colombo 11; f. 1946; twice a month; Ceylon textile journal; circ. 3,000; Editor G. P. KARIYAWASAM.

Vanoli Mangari: P.O.B. 574, Colombo; Tamil; fortnightly; magazine of Sri Lanka Broadcasting Corporation.

QUARTERLIES, ETC.

Ceylon Journal of Medical Science: c/o The Librarian, University of Sri Lanka, P.O.B. 1698, Colombo 3.

Ceylon Journal of Science (*Biological Sciences*): f. 1924; twice yearly; published by the University of Sri Lanka; Gen. Editor Prof. H. CRUSZ.

Coconut Journal: Printing House, 16, 1/17 Baillie St., Colombo; f. 1956; quarterly; Editor VALENTINE S. PERERA.

Journal of the Ceylon Medical Association: 6 Wijerama Mawatha, Colombo 7; f. 1888; quarterly; Editors Prof. N. D. W. LIONEL, Dr. N. PARAMESHWARAN.

Poultry Journal: Printing House, 16, 1/17 Baillie St., Colombo 1; f. 1963; Editor VALENTINE S. PERERA.

Symposium: 36 Vajira Road, Colombo; English; literature, art and films; quarterly; Editor W. B. C. SILVA.

Trade Directory for Ceylon and Overseas: Printing House, 16, 1/17 Baillie St., Colombo 1; f. 1958; quarterly; Editor VALENTINE S. PERERA.

Tropical Agriculturist, The: P.O. Box 636, Colombo; f. 1881; research quarterly published by the Department of Agriculture; circ. 750.

PRESS AGENCIES

Co-operative Press Trust of Ceylon: Negris Bldg., P.O.B. 131, Colombo; National Co-operative news agency of Sri Lanka; receives international and Asian news which is distributed to subscribers; Chair. C. E. L. WICKREMESINGHE; Gen. Man. A. ARULPIRAGASAM.

FOREIGN BUREAUX

The following are represented: Deutsche Presse-Agentur (DPA), Reuters, Tass.

PUBLISHERS

Architecture and Arts Publication Co.: 75 Ward Place, Colombo 7.

Associated Newspapers of Ceylon Ltd.: Lake House, P.O.B. 248, Colombo; f. 1926; Chair. A. K. PREMADASA; Dirs. M. A. A. DE ABREW, W. SIRIWARDENA, C. H. HULUGALLE, MERVYN DE SILVA; Sec. S. R. T. DHARMARATNE.

W. E. Bastian and Co.: 23 Canal Row, Fort, Colombo 1; f. 1904; Man. Propr. W. D. E. BASTIAN.

H. W. Cave and Co. Ltd.: P.O.B. 25, Gaffoor Bldgs., Colombo 1; f. 1876; printers, publishers, booksellers, office equipment dealers, music dealers and stationers, etc.; Dirs. C. J. S. FERNANDO, B. J. L. FERNANDO.

Ceylon Printers Ltd.: 20 Sir Chittampalam A. Gardiner Mawatha, Colombo 2, P.O.B. 305.

Christian Literature Society Book Shop: Front St., Colombo 11.

Colombo Catholic Press: 3rd Division, Maradana, Colombo; f. 1865; liturgical books; Man. Rev. Fr. O. GOMIS.

Colombo Co-operative Society Printers Ltd.: 72 Kew Rd., Colombo 2.

Express Newspapers (Ceylon) Ltd.: 185 Grandpass Rd., Colombo 14; publishers of *Virakesari Daily, Virakesari Weekly, Mithran Daily, Mithran Weekly*; Chief Editor K. V. S. VAS, M.A.

M. D. Gunasena and Co. Ltd.: 217 Olcott Mawata, Colombo 11; f. 1915; educational and general.

Hansa Publishers Ltd.: Hansa House, Clifford Ave., Colombo 3; general.

Independent Newspapers Ltd.: 5 Gunasena Mawatha, Colombo 12.

J. K. G. Jayawardena and Co.: B.T.S. Bldg., 203, 1/13 Olcott Mawatha, Colombo 11.

Karunaratne and Co.: 145 Olcott Mawatha, Colombo 11.

Lake House Printers and Publishers Ltd.: 41 W.A.D. Ramanayake Mawatha, P.O.B. 1458, Colombo 2; educational and general.

Printing House: 16, 1/17 Baillie St., Colombo 1; printers, publishers, booksellers, etc.; publishers of *Ceylon Who's Who* (annually), *Coconut Journal, Trade Directory for Ceylon and Overseas, Poultry Journal* (all quarterly); Editor Valentine S. Perera.

Ratnakara Press Ltd.: 74 Dam St., Colombo 12.

Saman Publishers Ltd.: 49/16 Iceland Bldgs., Colombo 3.

Sandesa Ltd.: 44A Alfred House Gardens, Colombo 3; 185 Grandpass Rd., Colombo 14.

K. V. G. de Silva and Sons: 415 Galle Rd., Colombo 4.

Sri Lanka Publishing Co.: 209 Norris Rd., Colombo 11.

Times of Ceylon Ltd.: 3 Bristol St., Fort, Colombo.

The Union Press: 169 Union Place, Colombo 2.

Union Printing Works: 210 Srimath Bennett Soysa Vidiya, Kandy; printers, publishers, bookbinders; Propr. Mrs. Leelawathie Guneratne.

RADIO

National

Sri Lanka Broadcasting Corporation: Torrington Square, P.O.B. 574, Colombo 7; f. 1967; under Ministry of Information and Broadcasting; controls all broadcasting in Sri Lanka; 551 broadcasting hours a week, of which Sinhala National and Commercial 170 hours, Tamil National and Commercial All Asia 140 hours, Hindi All Asia Commercial 58 hours, English National and Commercial All Asia 160½ hours, Education Service 22½ hours; Chair. and Dir.-Gen. R. Tillekeratne.

Voice of America: Programmes in English (7¾ hours), Hindi (1 hour), Urdu (1 hour).

Commercial

Sri Lanka Broadcasting Corporation: P.O.B. 1510, Colombo; *Domestic Services:* 191¼ hours (Sinhala 78¾ hours; Tamil 43¾ hours; English 68¾ hours); *Overseas Services:* 117 hours (Hindi 52 hours; English 46¼ hours; Tamil 18½ hours); Reps. in India, Great Britain and U.S.A.; Chair. and Dir. Gen. R. Tillekeratne Dir. English Services J. Barucha; Dir. Sinhala Services Thevis Guruge; Dir. Tamil Services K. S. Nadarajah.

Ceylon Rediffusion Service Ltd.: P.O. Box 1002, 299 Union Place, Colombo; f. 1951; subsidiary of Rediffusion Ltd., London; four programme wired broadcasting networks in Colombo and district and Kandy; relays all Sri Lanka Broadcasting Corporation programmes including commercial to about 18,000 subscribers; Gen. Man. W. Macdonald.

In 1971 there were 500,000 radio licences.

There is no television in Sri Lanka.

FINANCE

(cap. p.u.=capital paid up; dep.=deposits; Rs.=rupees; m.=million).

BANKING

The government has announced that all domestic and foreign banks are to be nationalized.

Note: An export-import bank is to be set up to handle the financing of all foreign trade. It will be formed through an amalgamation of the foreign departments of the *People's Bank* and the *Central Bank of Ceylon (see below)* and is to be a wholly owned subsidiary of both banks.

Central Bank

Central Bank of Ceylon: P.O.B. 590, 34–36 Queens St., Colombo; f. 1950 by Act of Parliament; cap. Rs. 15m.; Rs. 746.1m. (Dec. 1971); Gov. and Chair. of the Monetary Board H. E. Tennekoon; Deputy Govs. Dr. G. Corea, Dr. W. M. Tilakaratna; publs. *Monthly Bulletin, Annual Report.*

National Banks

Bank of Ceylon: Head Office: 41 Bristol St., Colombo; cap. p.u. Rs. 4.5m.; dep. Rs. 1,227.7m. (Dec. 1971); Chair. K. Shinya; Gen. Man. S. M. Sirimanne.

Bank of Chettinad Ltd.: 256 Sea St., Pettah, Colombo; Man. P. M. Palaniappa Chettiar.

Batticaloa Co-operative Provincial Bank Ltd.: Advocate's Rd., Batticaloa; f. 1942; Chair. T. Mylvaganam; Gen. Man. R. S. B. Beadle.

  Kalmunai Branch: Town Hall, Kalmunai; Man. R. C. D. Balthazaar.

Colombo Co-operative Provincial Bank Ltd.: 9 Duke St., Fort, Colombo; f. 1931; cap. Rs. 223,600; dep. Rs. 11.5m.; Pres. W. M. Fonseka, j.p.u.m.; Gen. Man. K. L. E. R. Pintoe.

Commercial Bank of Ceylon Ltd.: Head Office: 57 Sir Baron Jayatilaka Mawatha, P.O.B. 148, Colombo; cap. Rs. 5m.; dep. Rs. 64.6m. (Dec. 1971); Chair. S. F. Amerasinghe.

Galle Co-operative Town Bank Ltd.: Galle; Pres. M. A. Fernando.

Hatton National Bank Ltd.: 481 Darby Rd., Colombo; f. 1970; cap. Rs. 2.7m.; Chair. E. J. Cooray; Gen. Man. Dir. M. Dharmaraja.

Jaffna Co-operative Provincial Bank Ltd.: 59 Main St., Jaffna; f. 1929; cap. p.u. Rs. 259,800; dep. Rs. 8m.; Pres. T. K. Rajasekaran; Gen. Man. D. Sellakandu.

Kandy Co-operative Urban Bank Ltd.: 210 Colombo St., Kandy; Pres. P. Mapalagama; Treas. Francis Guneratne.

People's Bank: G.C.S.U. Bldg., Sir Chittampalam Gardiner Mawatha, Colombo 2; f. 1961; cap. Rs. 5.7m.; total resources Rs. 1,830.5m.; Chair. H. Abhayavardhana; Gen. Man. D. D. W. Kannangara.

State Development Banks

Agricultural and Industrial Credit Corpn. of Ceylon: P.O.B. 20, 292 Galle Rd., Colombo 3; f. 1943; loan cap. Rs. 30m.; Chair. S. E. Satarasinghe; Gen. Man. H. S. F. Goonewardena.

Ceylon State Mortgage Bank, The: 91 Horton Place Colombo; f. 1931; Chair. N. S. Perera; Gen. Man. H. B. Kapuwatte.

Development Finance Corpn. of Ceylon: 9 Horton Place, Colombo 7; f. 1955; Chair. N. E. WEERASOORIA; Gen. Man. S. KANAGARATNAM.

FOREIGN BANKS

Chartered Bank, The: 38 Bishopsgate, London, E.C.2; 17 Queen St., Colombo; f. 1853; Man. P. J. McNAMARA.

Habib Bank (Overseas) Ltd.: Karachi, Pakistan; Ceylon Office: 163 Keyzer Street, Colombo (P.O. Box 1088).

Hongkong and Shanghai Banking Corporation, The: Hong Kong; 24 Sir Baron Jayatilaka Mawatha, Fort, Colombo; Man. A. R. KELLY.

Indian Bank: P.O.B. 1384, Madras 1; P.O.B. 624, 48 Muldalige Mawatha, Colombo 1.

Indian Overseas Bank: Madras; 139 Main St., Overseas Bank Bldg., Pettah, Colombo 11.

Mercantile Bank Ltd.: London; 16 Queen Street, Fort, Colombo.

National and Grindlays Bank Ltd.: 23 Fenchurch St., London, E.C.3; 37 York St., P.O.B. 112, Colombo 1; 11 York St., Colombo 1; Agents: Clark Spence & Co. Ltd., Galle.

State Bank of India: Colombo; 16 Sir Baron Jayatilaka Mawatha, Fort, Colombo 1; Agent: E. R. A. DA CUNHA.

STOCK EXCHANGE

Colombo Brokers' Association, The: P.O.B. 101, Colombo; Produce and share brokers.

INSURANCE

Insurance Corporation of Ceylon: Head Office: 288 Union Place, Colombo 2; f. 1961; General Insurance Dept., Gaffoor Bldgs., Leyden Bastian Rd., Fort, Colombo 1; Chair. H. J. SAMARAKKODY, B.SC.; Dirs. Dr. N. P. RAJENDRA, M.B.B.S., D.CH., S. S. WIJERATNE, B.A., LL.B., Dr. S. T. G. FERNANDO.

Lloyds: London; Agents in Colombo: Aitken Spence & Co. Ltd., P.O.B. 5; Cable Address: "Aitken Colombo", Tel. 27861-7; Telex 1142.

TRADE AND INDUSTRY

CHAMBERS OF COMMERCE

Ceylon Chamber of Commerce: Lower Chatham St., Fort, Colombo (P.O.B. 274); est. 1839; incorp. 1895; Chair. P. C. S. FERNANDO; Sec. C. DIAS, M.A., LL.B.

Ceylon Moor Chamber of Commerce: 14 China St., Colombo 11; Pres. Sir RAZIK FAREED, O.B.E., M.P.; Admin. Sec. A. I. L. MARIKAR.

Ceylon National Chamber of Commerce: Macan Markar Bldgs., Prince St., P.O.B. 1375, Colombo 1; f. 1950; Pres. H. R. FERNANDO; Hon. Sec. M. A. NAWAZ CAFFOOR; Admin. Sec. T. SENEVIRATNE publ. *Ceylon Commerce.*

Ceylonese National Council of the International Chamber of Commerce: 17 Alfred Place, Colombo 3; Chair. S. AMBALAVANAR; Hon. Sec. A. K. NESARATNAM; Hon. Treas. P. R. SAMUEL.

Indian Chamber of Commerce: 65 Bankshall St., Colombo 11.

Sinhala Chamber of Commerce: 203 1/12, Olcott Bldg., Olcott, Mawatha, Colombo 11; f. 1937; 2,500 mems.; Pres. K. A. G. PERERA; Hon. Sec. B. A. PERERA, Hon. Treas. B. S. KOTTEGODA, J.P.; publ. *Sinhala Chamber of Commerce Bulletin* (monthly in Sinhala).

Subsidiary Organizations: Admin. Sec. RANJITH MENDIS.
Sinhala Development Fund: f. 1969.
Trade and Services Division.
Educational Division.

Building Development Corporation Ltd.: f. 1958 engaged in Trade and Industrial Engineering.

TRADE AND INDUSTRIAL ORGANIZATIONS

Industrial Development Board of Ceylon: No. 615 Galle Rd., Katubedda, Moratuwa; f. 1966 under Ministry of Industries and Scientific Affairs for the encouragement, promotion and development of the small-scale industries sector.

All Ceylon Small Industries Association: 146/4 First Cross St., Colombo 11.

All Ceylon Trade Chamber, The: 212/45, 1/3 Gas Works St., Colombo 11.

Ceylon Association of Manufacturers: c/o Ceylon Chamber of Commerce, P.O.B. 274, Colombo; f. 1955; Chair. M. A. S. M. MOHIDEEN; Sec. C. DIAS; The Secretary, The Ceylon Chamber of Commerce (*ex-officio*).

Ceylon Hardware Merchants Association: 449 Old Moor St., Colombo 12.

Ceylon Merchants' Chamber: De Mel Building, Chatham St., Colombo; f. 1926.

Ceylon National Chamber of Industries: 2-1-12A, Bristol Bldg., Colombo 1; f. 1960; 370 mems.; Chair. E. J. COORAY; Deputy Chair. H. E. P. DE MEL; Chief Exec. P. SANGARAPPILLAI. Publ. *Industrial Ceylon* (quarterly).

Ceylon Pharmaceutical Traders Association: P.O.B. 875, Colombo 12; represents Ceylon Pharmaceutical Manufacturers, Importers and Wholesale and Retail Chemists; Pres. J. CAMILLUS; Hon. Sec. M. PEIRIS.

Ceylon Planters' Society, The: P.O.B. 46, Kandy; f. 1936; 1,376 mems.; Chair. H. G. R. DE MEL, F.C.I.P.; Sec. D. F. ABEYESEKERA, B.A.; 21 branch organizations; publ. *The Bulletin* (quarterly).

Ceylon Tea Propaganda Board: P.O.B. 295, 574 Galle Rd., Colombo 3; f. 1932 to promote demand for Ceylon tea in world markets; offices in various countries; Chair. B. WARUSAVITARNE; Exec. Dir. E. M. O. MARTENSTYN; Asst. Exec. Dir. T. G. PEIRIS; Sec. V. J. T. PERERA; publ. *Annual Report.*

Ceylon Textile Chamber: Australia Buildings, Colombo 1; f. 1942; 118 mems.; Chair. L. E. J. FERNANDO LAKRAJA-SINGHA, J.P.; Admin. Sec. LAMBERT DE SILVA.

Ceylonese Textile Traders' Association: 5, 2nd Cross Street, Colombo.

Chamber of Ceylonese Merchants by Descent: 146, 9/1 First Cross St., Colombo 11.

Coconut and General Products Exporters' Association: c/o The Ceylon Chamber of Commerce, P.O.B. 274, Colombo; Chair. W. KARUNARATNE; Sec. C. DIAS; The Secretary, The Ceylon Chamber of Commerce (*ex-officio*).

Coconut Marketing Board: 11 Duke St., Colombo 1; f. 1972; Board appointed under statute by Minister of Plantation Industry; Chair. Dr. S. TILAKARATNE; Gen. Man. S. GUNASEKERA; Addl. Gen. Man. J. EDIRISINGHE.

Colombo Brokers' Association, The: P.O.B. 101, 59 Janadipathi Mawatha, Colombo 1; f. 1904.

olombo Lighterage Co's Association: 140–142 Prince Street, Fort, Colombo.

Colombo Rubber Traders' Association, The: P.O.B. 274, Colombo; f. 1918; Chair. P. A. SILVA; Sec. C. DIAS; The Secretary, Ceylon Chamber of Commerce (ex-officio).

Colombo Tea Traders' Association: P.O.B. 274, Colombo; f. 1894; Chair. S. N. SENARATNE; Sec. C. DIAS; The Secretary, Ceylon Chamber of Commerce (ex-officio).

Export Promotion Council of Ceylon: 5 Charlemont Rd., Colombo 6; f. 1960; commercial consultants and job placement bureau; Sec. DINKAR MUTHA KRISHNA; publ. *Directory of Manufacturers and Industrialists* (annually).

Low-Country Products Association of Ceylon: 40 1/1 Upper Chatham St., Colombo 1; f. 1908; Chair. D. E. HETTIARACHCHI, J.P.; Hon. Sec. M. H. G. A. BRITO-MUTUNAYAGAM; 140 mems.

Mercantile Chamber of Ceylon: 99-2/62 Gaffoor Building, 2nd Floor, Main St., Colombo 1; f. 1930; 350 mems.; Admin Sec., K. T. SHANMUGAM.

Sri Lanka Importers, Exporters and Manufacturers' Association: 26 Reclamation Rd., P.O.B. 1050, Colombo 11; f. 1955; Pres. J. OLIVER PERERA, J.P.; Hon. Gen. Sec. FRANK HAMER.

Sri Lanka State Trading Corporation: Colombo; f. 1971; handles all export and import trading.

Tea Research Institute of Ceylon: St. Coombs, Talawakele; f. 1925 to research into all aspects of tea production and manufacture, and to provide and publish information derived from this research; 4 brs.; 60 research workers; Chair. S. PATHMANATHAN; Dir. Dr. L. H. FERNANDO; publs. *The Tea Quarterly, Annual Report, Advisory Pamphlets*, Monographs on Tea Production in Ceylon, Wall Charts.

THE CO-OPERATIVE MOVEMENT

The most important organizations on the consumer side are the Wholesale Stores Unions, which handle all food-stuffs and miscellaneous goods supplied by the Co-operative Wholesale Establishment, as well as running a large number of retail stores. The Co-operative Wholesale Establishment is at the head of the consumer co-operative movement. It was founded in 1943 and is administered by an autonomous Board of Directors.

EMPLOYERS' ORGANIZATIONS

Ceylon Estates Employers' Federation: 73/1 Kollupitiya Rd., Colombo 3 (P.O.B. 473); f. 1944; 338 mems.; Pres. S. M. DIAS; Deputy Pres. L. NAMASIVAYAM; Sec. T. R. R. WIJEWICKREMA.

Planters' Association of Ceylon: Colombo; Chair. C. WIJENAIKE.

Employers' Federation of Ceylon: P.O.B. 858, 73/1 Kollupitiya Rd., Colombo 3; f. 1929; mem. International Organization of Employers; Chair. HENRY PIERIS; Vice-Chair. G. M. TOPEN; Sec. E. S. APPADURAI.

COUNCIL REPRESENTATIVES

Agency House and Brokers' Mercantile Employers: S. CUMARASAMY.

Coconut Manufacturing and Export Trade Employers: J. W. B. PERERA.

Commercial Banks' Employers: J. A. CRUICKSHANK.

Engineer Employers: I. G. H. JAYESURIA.

Fertilizer Employers: S. COOMARASWAMY.

General Trades Mercantile Employers: H. L. E. COORAY.

Hotel Employers: C. E. GUFFROY.

Importer, Distributor and General Employers: J. D. RASIAH.

Manufacturing Employers: S. K. WICKREMASINGHE.

Master Printers' Employers: C. P. DE SILVA.

Motor Employers: A. L. PERERA.

Port Employers: M. L. D. CASPERSZ.

Rubber and General Produce Store Employers: J. A. LEEMBRUGGEN.

Tea Stores Employers: S. E. SATARASINGHE.

TRADE UNIONS

All Ceylon Federation of Free Trade Unions (ACFFTU): 94; 1/6 York Bldg., York St., Colombo 1; 6 affiliated unions, 65,000 mems.; Pres. W. K. WIJEMANNE; Gen. Sec. ANTONY LODWICK.

Ceylon Federation of Labour (CFL): No. 108 Kew Rd., Colombo 2; 25 affiliated unions; 125,700 mems.; Pres. Dr. N. M. PERERA; Gen. Sec. D. G. WILLIAM.

Ceylon National Trade Union Confederation (CNTUC): 63, 1/7 Hidramani Bldg., Chatham St., Colombo 1; f. 1966; combined membership 457,000; Gen. Sec. V. ANNAMALAY.

Ceylon Trade Union Federation (CTUF): 123 Union Place, Colombo; f. 1941; 24 affiliated unions; 35,271 mems.; Sec.-Gen. N. SANMUGATHASAN.

Ceylon Workers' Congress (CWC): 72 Ananda Coomaraswamy Mawatha, Colombo 7; f. 1940; mainly plantation workers; 395,775 mems.; Pres. S. THONDAMAN; Sec. M. S. SELLASAMY; publs. *Congress News* (fortnightly in English), *Congress* (weekly in Tamil).

Democratic Workers' Congress (DWC): 14 Sunethra Lane, Thimbirigasyaya Rd., Colombo 5; f. 1956; 398,165 mems.; Pres. ABDUL AZIZ; Sec. V. P. GANESAN.

Government Workers' Trade Union Federation (GWTUF): 22 affiliated unions; 100,000 mems.; controlled by the Lanka Sama Samaja Party.

Public Service Workers' Trade Union Federation (PSWTUF): 120 affiliated unions; 100,000 mems.; Pres. P. ADHIPOLA; Gen. Sec. W. PERERA.

Sri Lanka Independent Trade Union Federation (SLITUF): 213 Dharmapala Mawatha, Colombo 7; f. 1960; 35 affiliated unions; 65,132 mems.; Pres. HERBERT WICKRAMASINGHE; Gen. Sec. ANANDA DASSANAYAKE.

Union of Post and Telecommunication Officers: 11/4 Duke St., P.O.B. 15; Colombo 1; f. 1945; Pres. L. G. D. WICKREMASINGHE; Gen. Sec. U. S. JAYASEKERA; publ. *Postmark*.

TRANSPORT

RAILWAYS

Ceylon Government Railway: P.O.B. 355, Colombo 10; 9 diesel electric shunting locomotives, 110 diesel hydraulic locomotives, 29 diesel hydraulic shunting locos, 15 diesel electric rail cars, 39 diesel electric locos, 884 broad gauge, 99 narrow gauge carriage stock, 4,116 wagons; operates a network of about 954 miles, of which about 87 miles are narrow gauge; gross receipts (1969–70) Rs. 117.8m., expenses Rs. 144.1m.; Gen. Man. V. T. NAVARATNE; Additional Gen. Mans. (Administration) B. POLWATTE, (Technical) P. RAJAGOPAL.

All railways are state-owned.

ROADS

Public Works Department: Ministry of Irrigation, Power, and Highways, Colombo; this Ministry maintains about 21,990 km. (1972) of roads. There is a national omnibus service with about 3,000 vehicles.

Ceylon Transport Board: 200 Kirula Rd., Colombo 5; f. 1957; nationalized organization reponsible for road passenger transport services; Chair. ANIL MOONESINGHE; Vice-Chair. P. EHELIYAGODA; Sec. MAHINDA ELAYAPERUMA; publ. *Transport News* and *Transport Management*.

SHIPPING

Colombo is one of the most important ports in the East and is situated at the junction of the main trade routes. The other main ports of Sri Lanka are Trincomalee, Galle and Jaffna. Trincomalee is the main port for shipping out tea.

Ceylon Association of Steamer Agents: 1st Floor, Mackinnon's Bldg., York St., Colombo 1; f. 1966; primarily a consultative organization; represents members in dealings with Government Authorities; 33 mems.; Chair. M. L. D. CASPERSZ; Sec. B. C. JAYASURIYA.

Port (Cargo) Corporation: P.O.B. 595, Colombo 1; f. 1958; responsible for all cargo handling operations in the Ports of Colombo, Galle and Trincomalee; Chair. and Chief Exec. S. M. B. DOLAPIHILLA; Gen. Man. K. G. D. D. PATHIRATNE, C.A.S.

SHIPPING COMPANIES

Ceylon Ocean Lines Ltd.: 99-2/4, 2/67 Gaffoor Buildings, P.O.B. 1276, Colombo 1; agents for Polish, Russian, East German, Romanian, Chinese and Bulgarian lines; also charter vessels; Chair. L. G. GUNASEKARA, B.A., LL.B.; Sec. N. N. GUNEWARDENE.

Ceylon Shipping Lines Ltd.: P.O.B. 891, Prince St., Colombo 1; controlling interest by State and the Ceylon Shipping Corporation Ltd.; Chair. P. B. KARANDAWALA.

Eastern Star Lines Ltd.: 2nd Floor, National Bank Bldg., Fort, Colombo; services to Middle East, Persian Gulf and Indian coast; fleet of fourteen ships.

Messageries Maritimes Co.: 12 Sir Baron Jayatidlaka Mawatha, Colombo; representative for India, Pakistan, Sri Lanka and Burma.

Shipping Corporation of Ceylon Ltd.: No. 6 Sir Baron Jayatileke Mawatha, Colombo 1; f. 1969, became government corporation 1971; Chair. P. B. KARANDAWALA; Gen. Man. A. GIRAGAMA.

INLAND WATERWAYS

There are 104 miles of canals open for traffic.

CIVIL AVIATION

The control of Civil Aviation is in the hands of the Department of Civil Aviation.

There are airports at Bandaranaike, Gal Oya, Jaffna, Batticaloa, Anuradhapura and Trincomalee.

Air Ceylon Ltd.: Lower Chatham St., P.O.B. 692, Colombo 1; f. 1947; operates daily internal services and international services between Colombo and Bombay, Madras, Tiruchirapalli, Karachi, London, Rome, Singapore, Kuala Lumpur, Bangkok, Paris, Jakarta; Chair. S. H. SILVA; Gen. Man. E. DE S. WICKREMARATANE; fleet of one DC-850, one Trident 1E, one HS 748, two DC-3.

The following foreign airlines are represented in Colombo: Aeroflot, Air France, Air India, British Airways, Indian Airlines (IA), Pakistan International Airlines Corpn. (PIA), Qantas, Singapore Airlines, Swissair, Trans World Airlines Inc. (TWA)., Union de Transports Aériens (UTA).

Gal Oya, Jaffna, Batticaloa, Anuradhapura and Trincomalee are served by Air Ceylon.

TOURISM

Ceylon Tourist Board: P.O.B. 1504, 25 Galle Face, Centre Rd., Colombo 3; f. 1966; Chair. DHARMASIRI SENANAYAKE; Dir. Publicity T. B. ELANGASINGHE.

There were 40,200 tourists in 1969, 46,247 in 1970, 39,654 in 1971, and 56,047 in 1972.

CULTURAL ORGANIZATIONS

Department of Cultural Affairs: 135 Dharmapala Mawatha, Colombo 7; Dir. DONALD ABEYSINGHE.

Arts Council of Ceylon: 135 Dharmapala Mawatha, Colombo 7; Pres. D. G. DAYARATNE; Gen. Sec. W. B. RATNAYAKE.

National Theatre Trust: Department of Cultural Affairs, 135 Dharmapala Mawatha, Colombo 7; promotes development of theatre; Pres. P. H. PREMAWARDHANA; Sec. H. H. BANDARA; publ. monthly bulletin of theatre news in Sinhalese.

Sri Lanka Sanskutika Mandalaya (*Cultural Council of Ceylon*): 135 Dharmapala Mawatha, Colombo 7; f. 1971; Dir. and Admin. Trustee H. A. P. ABEYWARDENA, M.A., C.A.S.

UNIVERSITIES

University of Sri Lanka, Colombo Campus: f. 1967; 255 teachers, 3,365 students.

University of Sri Lanka, Katubedda Campus: f. 1966; 105 teachers, 2,100 students.

University of Sri Lanka, Peradeniya Campus: f. 1942; 432 teachers, 5,302 students.

University of Sri Lanka, Vidyalankara Campus: f. 1959; 152 teachers including 30 part-time, 1,420 students.

University of Sri Lanka, Vidyodaya Campus: f. 1959; 142 teachers, 2,548 students.

THE SUDAN

INTRODUCTORY SURVEY

Location, Climate, Language, Religion, Flag, Capital

The Democratic Republic of the Sudan is the largest country in Africa. Its border with Egypt to the north is the second cataract of the Nile; Khartoum is at the junction of the Blue Nile and White Nile. To the east is Ethiopia and the Red Sea, to the west the Central African Republic and Chad, and to the south Kenya, Uganda and Zaire. The climate shows a marked transition from the desert of the north to the rainy equatorial south. Temperatures vary with height and latitude. The overall average is about 70°F (21°C). Arabic is the main language but English is widely understood. Most Sudanese are Muslims with animists as the next largest group. There is a Christian community of more than 400,000. The national flag, introduced in 1970, has three horizontal stripes of red, white and black, with a green triangle at the hoist. The capital is Khartoum.

Recent History

The Sudan became an independent republic with a parliamentary system in 1956. Following a *coup d'état* in 1958 the Army took control of the state, suspending Parliament and abolishing political parties. A Supreme Council of the Armed Forces was set up and ruled until October 1964, when it was overthrown in a civilian revolution. The governments which followed failed to improve the economic situation or to deal with the problem of the southern provinces, and in May 1969 the Mahgoub government was overthrown by a group of officers and civilians led by Col. (later Maj.-Gen.) al-Nemery. All existing political institutions and organizations were abolished and the "Democratic Republic of the Sudan" was proclaimed with supreme authority in the hands of the Revolutionary Command Council. A more militant policy towards Israel was adopted and, in line with this, co-ordination committees with Egypt and Libya were established in December 1969. In November 1970 the Presidents of Egypt and Libya and President Nemery agreed in principle to political union between their countries, but internal opposition to Nemery prevented the Sudan joining the Federation of Arab Republics which was formed in January 1972 with Syria as the third member.

On July 19th, 1971, a section of the army, led by communists, overthrew the Nemery régime. However, President Nemery regained power in a counter-*coup* three days after being ousted. A massive purge of Communists followed, and fourteen people were executed almost immediately.

In a referendum held in October 1971 to confirm Gen. Nemery's nomination as President, Nemery received almost four million votes, with only 56,000 "no" votes. A new government was formed, the Revolutionary Command Council was dissolved, and the Sudanese Socialist Union was recognized as the Sudan's only political party.

From May 1969 onwards the Nemery government had made attempts to settle the problem of the three racially and culturally different southern provinces, where rebellion against rule from the north had first broken out in 1955. Fighting continued until March 1972. A permanent constitution was endorsed in April 1973. Elections to the Regional People's Assembly for the Southern Sudan took place in November 1973 and for the national People's Assembly in April 1974. The peaceful reconciliation between the North and South, after years of instability and civil war, has been a triumph for President Nemery who remains firmly in power.

In late 1972 the Sudan's relations with Egypt worsened when President Nemery refused to allow Libyan troops to be transported to Uganda over the Sudan and dropped pro-Egyptian Ministers in a cabinet reshuffle. Sudanese troops were withdrawn from the Suez Canal War Zone as a result and the Sudan's role in the October 1973 Middle East War was mainly passive.

In January 1973 an attempted anti-government plot was foiled by security forces. Sudanese foreign policy is no longer orientated towards the Eastern bloc.

Government

Under the Constitution of April 1973 executive power is vested in the President and Cabinet whom he may appoint. There is a national People's Assembly and a Regional People's Assembly in the South.

The Regional Constitution for the Southern Sudan grants the three southern provinces of the Sudan a large degree of autonomy from the central government.

Defence

The armed forces total 38,600, of which the army has 37,000, the navy 600 and the air force 1,000. Sudan has a defence agreement with the Arab League Unified Military Command.

Economic Affairs

Since the 1969 revolution the economy has become increasingly nationalized, including the cotton industry, but recently the Government has been forced to change its policy in an attempt to attract private investment from overseas. Over 80 per cent of the Sudanese people derive their living from the land.

Long-staple cotton, grown under irrigation, is overwhelmingly Sudan's most valuable export. The recent increase in the value of Sudanese cotton exports has been of great assistance to its economy. A 15-year plan with an estimated capital investment of £564.7 million to expand textile production was launched in June 1973. The vast Gezira scheme has been expanded and now covers nearly two million acres of which half is cultivated for cotton and the rest for wheat, dura, bean lubia, groundnuts and other foods. The Khashm El Girba Dam on the Atbara River serves 300,000 acres. The principal food crop is millet, but coffee, tobacco, rice and sugar are also grown. Nomadic tribes breed cattle, sheep, goats and camels. The vast forest areas provide timber and 80 per cent of the world's supply of gum arabic (an important export). Industry is confined mainly to the manufacture of food and vegetable oils. The 1961/62–1970/71 plan had as its main objects an increase in agricultural output, the establishment of industries for import substitution, improvements in education and social services and a higher rate of increase in national income than population growth. A new development programme, the Five-Year Economic Plan 1970–75 has similar objectives. Two dams are under construction on the Atbara river and the Blue Nile. In 1972 the Sudan had an external debt totalling some £S102.6 million. The UN contributed $20.7 million to assist the 150,000 refugees who returned to the Southern Region after the war. This vast relief operation was completed in October 1973.

Transport and Communications

There are 4,756 kilometres of railways owned by the state. Generally roads are only cleared tracks impassable immediately after rain. Hard-surfaced roads are no longer confined to urban areas. Highways from the capital to the provinces are under construction and plans have been drawn up for a network of highways in the Western Sudan. Sudan Railways operate passenger and freight steamer services on navigable reaches of the Nile. These are linked to the railway services of Egypt, Uganda and Kenya. Sudan Airways, the Government airline, maintains internal and external services.

Social Welfare

The Ministry of Health organizes the public health services. There are 81 hospitals, 60 health centres, 1,244 dispensaries and over 500 doctors.

Education

The Government provides elementary education from the ages of seven to eleven, intermediate from ages eleven to fifteen and secondary from fifteen upwards. Nevertheless, only about 20 per cent of Sudanese are literate. In 1967 there were 3,359 schools and about 600,000 pupils. Pupils from secondary schools are accepted at the University of Khartoum. subject to their reaching the necessary standards. Cairo University also has a Khartoum branch and there is an Islamic university at Omdurman.

Tourism

The rain forests in the south teem with wild game and attract hunters and observers from all over the world. In the north are the sites of several temples and pyramids of ancient Sudanese civilizations.

Visas are required by nationals of all countries.

Sport

Football is the most popular game. Sudanese athletes have competed at the Olympic and the Pan Arab and African Games.

Public Holidays

1974: October 12th (Republic Day), October 18th (Id ul Fitr), December 25th (Christmas), December 26th (Id ul Adha).

1975: January 1st (Independence Day), January 14th (Muslim New Year), March 3rd (Unity Day), March 26th (Mouloud, Birth of the Prophet), May 25th (Anniversary of the May Revolution).

The dates of the Muslim holidays may be slightly different from those given above. The holiday "Sham el Nassim" is variable in April each year.

Weights and Measures

The metric system is gradually replacing traditional weights and measures.

Currency and Exchange Rates

1,000 millièmes = 100 piastres = 1 Sudanese pound (£S). Exchange rates (April 1974):

£1 sterling = 822.29 millièmes;
U.S. $1 = 348.24 millièmes.

STATISTICAL SURVEY

AREA AND POPULATION

Total Area	Arable Land	Pasture	Forest	Total Population (July 1st, 1973)
967,500 sq. miles*	71,000 sq. kilometres	240,000 sq. kilometres	914,999 sq. kilometres	16,901,000

* 2,505,813 sq. kilometres.

PROVINCES
(July 1st, 1971)

	Area (sq. miles)	Population		Area (sq. miles)	Population
Bahr el Ghazal	82,530	1,499,000	Khartoum	8,097	922,000
Blue Nile	54,880	3,315,000	Kordofan .	146,930	2,954,000
Darfur .	191,650	1,779,000	Northern .	184,200	1,190,000
Equatoria	76,495	1,369,000	Upper Nile	91,190	1,346,000
Kassala .	131,528	1,712,000	TOTAL .	967,500	16,087,000

PRINCIPAL TOWNS

	POPULATION (1971)
Khartoum (capital)	280,431
Omdurman	273,268
Khartoum North	138,014
Port Sudan	116,366
Wadi Medani	79,364
El Obeid	76,420
Atbara	58,939

Because of the flooding of the Wadhi Halfa and adjacent areas by the Aswan High Dam, over 50,000 inhabitants have been resettled in Khashm el Girba, on the Atbara River.

Births and Deaths (1966): Registered births 143,052 (birth rate 10.1 per 1,000); registered deaths 13,416 (death rate 1.0 per 1,000). Birth registration is believed to be about 20 per cent complete and death registration 5 per cent complete. UN estimates for 1965–70 put the

TRIBAL DIVISIONS
(1956 Census)

	'000	%
Arab	3,989	39
Southerners (Nilotic, Nilo-Hamitic, Sudanic) . . .	3,056	30
Western People	1,315	13
Beja	646	6
Nuba	573	6
Nubiyin	330	3
Miscellaneous . . .	94	1

The remaining 2 per cent was made up of 260,000 foreigners.

average annual birth rate at 48.9 per 1,000 and the death rate at 18.4 per 1,000.

Employment (1970): Total economically active population 5,016,000, including 4,007,000 engaged in agriculture (ILO and FAO estimates).

AGRICULTURE
COTTON CROP
(1 feddan = 1.038 acres = 4,201 sq. metres)

	AREA (feddans)			PRODUCTION (tons)		
	1968–69	1969–70	1970–71	1968–69	1969–70	1970–71
Long Staple . . .	775,159	824,662	828,306	548,707	566,667	618,314
Medium Staple . . .	138,917	138,041	184,953	78,361	82,234	89,675
Short Staple . . .	240,867	295,208	200,729	28,548	33,583	18,537
TOTAL . .	1,154,943	1,257,911	1,213,988	655,616	682,484	726,526

Production of lint (metric tons): 184,000 in 1968; 225,000 in 1969; 246,000 in 1970; 245,000 in 1971; 239,000 in 1972.

OTHER CROPS
(metric tons)

	1968	1969	1970	1971
Wheat	88,000	123,000	115,000	135,000
Maize	16,000	36,000	23,000	40,000*
Millet	267,000	384,000	460,000	325,000
Sorghum (Durra) . . .	870,000	1,499,000	1,529,000	2,152,000
Rice	1,000	3,000	6,000	7,000*
Sugar Cane†	969,000	939,000	780,000*	750,000*
Potatoes	25,000*	26,000*	26,000*	26,000*
Sweet Potatoes and Yams .	11,000*	11,000*	12,000*	n.a.
Cassava (Manioc) . . .	132,000	140,000	140,000	n.a.
Onions	18,000	20,000	20,000*	n.a.
Dry Beans	4,000	6,000	6,000*	6,000*
Dry Broad Beans . . .	13,000	11,000	12,000*	13,000*
Chick-Peas	2,000	2,000	2,000*	2,000*
Other Pulses	42,000*	43,000*	40,000*	46,000*
Oranges and Tangerines . .	1,000*	1,000*	1,000*	1,000*
Dates	70,000	72,000*	72,000*	n.a.
Bananas	10,000*	10,000*	10,000*	n.a.
Groundnuts (in shell) . .	197,000	383,000	337,000	381,000
Cottonseed	334,000	421,000	460,000	458,000*
Sesame Seed	122,000	201,600	282,000	271,000*
Castor Beans	15,000	12,000	18,000	18,000*

1968: Mangoes 15,000 tons; Guavas 4,000 tons.
* FAO estimate.   † Crop year ending in year stated.

LIVESTOCK
('000)

	1968–69	1969–70*	1970–71*
Cattle . . .	13,326	13,500	13,650
Sheep . . .	12,678	13,000	13,200
Goats . . .	10,036	10,050	10,100
Pigs	6*	7	7
Horses . . .	20*	20	19
Asses	610*	630	640
Camels . . .	2,918	3,000	3,100
Chickens . . .	18,200*	18,500	18,800

* FAO estimate.

Source: FAO, *Production Yearbook 1971.*

LIVESTOCK PRODUCTS
(FAO estimates, metric tons)

	1968	1969	1970
Cows' Milk	1,330,000	1,350,000	1,360,000
Sheep's Milk . . .	120,000	125,000	130,000
Goats' Milk . . .	425,000	440,000	450,000
Beef and Veal . . .	129,000	142,000	140,000
Mutton, Lamb and Goats' Meat .	64,000	71,000	72,000
Poultry Meat . . .	10,000	10,000	10,000
Edible Offal . . .	40,000	43,000	43,000
Other Meat . . .	52,000	54,000	56,000
Tallow . . .	6,000	6,000	6,000
Hen Eggs . . .	16,200	16,400	16,700
Cattle Hides (salted) .	11,760	11,840	11,760
Sheep Skins (dry) . .	2,760	3,120	3,280
Goat Skins (dry) . .	360	368	360

1971 (metric tons): Cows' Milk 1,370,000; Sheep's Milk 140,000; Goats' Milk 450,000; Hen Eggs 17,000.

Source: FAO, *Production Yearbook 1971.*

FORESTRY
ROUNDWOOD REMOVALS
(cubic metres)
Twelve months ending June 30th

1966–67	20,984,000
1967–68	20,982,000

Source: FAO, *Yearbook of Forest Products.*

FISHING
(metric tons)

	1969	1970	1971
Inland waters . .	21,000	21,400	21,400
Sea . . .	800	800	800
TOTAL CATCH .	21,800	22,200	22,200

Source: FAO, *Yearbook of Fishery Statistics 1971.*

MINING

PRODUCTION

	UNIT	1966	1967	1968	1969
Iron Ore*	'ooo tons	14	39	—	—
Manganese Ore* . . .	tons	2,500	1,500	5,000	850
Chromium Ore* . . .	,,	25,000	17,391	22,086	23,944
Gold	ounces	—	111	29	—
Magnesite . . .	tons	4,000	4,000	7,000	1,000
Unrefined Salt . . .	'ooo tons	57	43	50	51

1971: Salt 63,000 tons.

* Figures relate to gross weight. Metal content (in metric tons) was as follows:

Iron: 20,000 in 1966; 7,000 in 1967.

Manganese: 600 in 1966; 600 in 1967; 2,000 in 1968; 340 in 1969; more than 500 in 1970.

Chromium oxide: 10,100 in 1966; 9,043 in 1967; 11,485 in 1968; 12,451 in 1969; 13,866 in 1970.

INDUSTRY

PRODUCTION

	UNIT	1967–68	1968–69	1969–70	1970–71
Cement	'ooo tons	128.7	140.7	194.0	229.0
Flour of Wheat . . .	,, ,,	48.8	51.5	111.6	176.0
Sugar	,, ,,	93.3	82.1	75.3	72.5
Soap	,, ,,	18.4	19.3	23.7	27.9
Wine	'ooo litres	1,634.6	1,453.0	2,450.0	3,357.0
Beer	,, ,,	7,447.6	7,159.0	4,534.0	7,245.0
Cigarettes	'ooo kilos	660.9	532.0	660.9	741.8
Matches	billion	4.0	3.9	4.9	4.4
Shoes	million pairs	9.5	10.7	6.7	8.5
Textiles	yards	93,122.0	101,350.0	n.a.	n.a.
Alcohol	'ooo litres	552.6	464.0	n.a.	n.a.
Oil	'ooo tons	36.0	46.0	n.a.	n.a.

PETROLEUM PRODUCTS
(metric tons)

	1967	1968	1969	1970
Motor Spirit	82,000	62,000	70,000	90,000
Naphtha	34,000	12,000	25,000	26,000
Jet Fuels	57,000	70,000	} 76,000	82,000
Kerosene	19,000	53,000		
Distillate Fuel Oils . . .	428,000	184,000	234,000	234,000
Residual Fuel Oils . . .	233,000	195,000	224,000	239,000
Liquefied Petroleum Gas . . .	1,000	1,000	2,000	2,000

Source: United Nations, *Statistical Yearbook 1971.*

ELECTRICITY OUTPUT

	INSTALLED CAPACITY (kW.)	UNITS GENERATED ('ooo kWh.)	UNITS SOLD ('ooo kWh.)
1967 . .	91,976	317,865	254,468
1968 . .	97,412	333,795	293,851
1969 . .	130,893	528,176	430,173
1970 . .	116,966	392,421	367,900

FINANCE

1,000 millièmes = 100 piastres = 1 Sudanese pound (£S).
Coins: 1, 2, 5 and 10 millièmes; 2, 5 and 10 piastres.
Notes: 25 and 50 piastres; £S1, £S5 and £S10.
Exchange rates (April 1974): £1 sterling = 822.29 millièmes; U.S. $1 = 348.24 millièmes.
£S100 = £121.612 sterling = $287.156.

BUDGET ESTIMATES FOR CURRENT REVENUE AND EXPENDITURE
(£S, twelve months ending June 30th)

REVENUE	1969–70	1970–71	EXPENDITURE	1969–70	1970–71
Direct Taxation .	17,500,000	18,870,000	Ministry of Agriculture and Forests . .	3,558,739	3,655,280
Indirect Taxation . .	63,201,000	73,636,797	Ministry of Communications and Tourism	4,239,999	4,258,324
Fees and Charges, etc. .	8,129,786	10,289,597	Ministry of Education .	9,803,319	8,667,390
Proceeds from Government Enterprises .	42,395,227	43,542,204	Ministry of Health . .	6,585,877	7,910,532
Interest and Dividends .	1,217,037	1,169,460	Ministry of Works Works . .	3,826,839	2,046,554
Pension Contributions .	1,373,964	1,554,000	Mechanical Transport .	2,434,941	2,494,414
Reimbursement and Inter-Departmental Services .	7,203,271	7,208,673	Ministry of Irrigation .	3,852,513	4,037,261
Other Sources . .	1,093,435	1,745,629	Department of Stores and Equipment .	1,104,171	915,310
			Other Ministries and Departments .	65,083,411	77,558,732
			General Administration .	40,623,911	38,781,043
			Koranic Studies . .	—	91,520
			TOTAL EXPENDITURE	141,113,720	150,416,360
			SURPLUS . .	1,000,000	7,600,000
TOTAL REVENUE .	142,113,720	158,016,360		142,113,720	158,016,360

1972–73 Budget Estimate: Revenue £S191.3m.; Expenditure £S255.5m.
1973–74 Budget Estimate: Revenue £S220.8m.; Expenditure £S217.1m.
1974–75 Budget Estimate: Revenue £S277.5m.; Expenditure £S268.3m.

Five-Year Plan (1970–75): £S217.3 million capital investment by public sector.

NATIONAL ACCOUNTS
(£S'000, years ending June 30th)

	1968–69	1969–70
Wages and Salaries . .	366,460	286,948
Operating Surplus . .	125,791	186,676
Domestic Factor Incomes .	492,251	473,624
Wages and Salaries Paid Abroad (net) . .	−2,412	−1,500
Property and Entrepreneurial Income Paid Abroad (net) .	−3,689	−1,600
Indirect Taxes . .	59,960	88,242
Less Subsidies . .	−3,742	−9,027
National Income at Market Price . .	542,369	550,739
Other Current Transfers to the Rest of the World (net) .	−1,616	−1,100
National Disposable Income .	540,752	549,639
National Disposable Income per capita (£S) . .	37.3	37.9

FIVE-YEAR PLAN 1970/71–74/75

The Plan has as its main objectives a sustained annual growth rate of the G.N.P. of 7.6 per cent; the raising of per capita income to £S46.6 by 1974/75; increasing agricultural output by 60.8 per cent; increasing the level of investment in education and culture by 60 per cent, in health by 82 per cent and in public utilities by 58 per cent; developing urban and rural water networks; increasing livestock production by 75.5 per cent; increasing the volume of trade by value to £S340 million.

TOTAL INVESTMENT, BY PUBLIC SECTOR BY 1974/75
(£S '000)

Agriculture	80,000
Industry and Power	49,200
Transport and Communications . .	29,630
Education and Culture . . .	14,580
Health and Public Utilities . .	21,420
Central Administration . . .	6,440
Technical Assistance and Grants . .	9,800
Unallocated and Others	3,930
TOTAL	215,000

BALANCE OF PAYMENTS ESTIMATES
(£S million)

	1970–71	1971–72*
Receipts:		
Cotton exports . .	61.3	47.2
Other exports . .	45.3	41.7
Invisible . .	16.4	13.8
Foreign loans . .	12.1	11.8
Other short-term capital	18.0	10.0
	153.1	124.5
Payments:		
Government imports .	43.8	28.4
Private sector imports .	75.3	68.7
Invisible . .	27.4	23.7
Repayments of capital .	11.5	7.0
	158.0	127.8
Deficit . . .	4.9	3.3

* July to April.

EXTERNAL TRADE
(£S million)

	1967	1968	1969	1970	1971	1972*
Imports . . .	74.3	83.8	89.3	100.1	115.4	108.2
Exports . . .	74.6	85.6	86.2	103.4	114.4	101.2

* Estimate.

PRINCIPAL COMMODITIES
(£S '000)

IMPORTS	1969	1970	1971	EXPORTS	1969	1970	1971
Sugar . . .	2,715	5,143	9,247	Animals . .	2,332	2,317	1,959
Tea . . .	2,210	4,955	4,004	Cotton, Ginned .	49,498	65,052	69,424
Coffee . . .	453	1,907	1,635	Cotton Seed .	1,489	1,728	1,422
Wheat Flour . .	1,125	657	226	Cotton Seed Oil .	920	771	4,501
Textiles . .	16,561	15,119	26,462	Durra . . .	43	60	1,136
Clothing . .	749	672	911	Groundnuts .	5,991	5,466	9,324
Footwear . .	585	127	102	Gum Arabic .	8,699	8,969	8,425
Sacks and Jute .	2,611	3,013	3,694	Oilseed Cake .	3,879	n.a.	n.a.
Cement . .	47	33	70	Sesame . .	8,017	5,087	7,996
Fertilizers . .	1,397	1,658	1,937	Hides and Skins .	1,803	1,590	1,806
Machinery, Apparatus, Vehicles . .	22,790	28,788	23,312				
Tyres . . .	1,485	1,384	1,937				
Petroleum Products .	8,809	9,025	8,918				
Pharmaceuticals .	2,200	3,387	2,760				
Iron and Steel .	4,594	4,612	4,794				

COTTON EXPORTS BY COUNTRIES
(tons)

	1969	1970	1971
Germany, Federal Republic . .	21,034	15,769	13,328
India	29,913	30,462	37,001
Italy	28,596	28,509	13,620
Japan	15,663	15,900	11,260
United Kingdom . . .	15,038	14,670	10,581
People's Republic of China . .	13,735	17,821	35,221
U.S.A.	935	2,388	2,549
U.S.S.R.	8,319	57,564	39,158
Romania	6,126	2,221	7,437
France	2,925	7,006	4,834
Netherlands . . .	859	1,006	328
Hungary	3,124	4,981	4,983
Poland	4,839	4,999	6,593
TOTAL (all countries) . .	172,425	203,296	206,903

PRINCIPAL COUNTRIES
(£S '000)

	IMPORTS				EXPORTS*			
	1968	1969	1970	1971	1968	1969	1970	1971
Belgium	1,830	2,094	2,076	1,708	2,206	1,957	1,996	2,080
China, People's Republic .	5,993	4,876	4,030	7,733	4,838	6,430	6,000	10,785
Egypt	3,516	3,848	5,323	6,814	2,402	3,914	4,981	5,700
France	3,325	3,351	1,716	4,234	2,061	1,307	2,223	3,090
Germany, Federal Republic .	4,647	5,771	7,802	7,069	12,256	10,142	9,855	8,779
India	9,342	9,063	14,226	22,677	7,946	10,133	14,226	11,997
Italy	4,990	4,327	2,430	2,351	9,713	10,777	10,190	9,775
Japan	8,113	7,153	5,629	4,796	6,652	8,010	9,250	8,332
Netherlands . . .	2,346	3,512	2,892	3,038	4,276	3,359	3,319	4,155
Poland	1,498	1,789	1,916	1,873	1,786	1,544	1,660	2,111
U.S.S.R.	6,223	4,486	8,328	7,858	4,818	3,389	17,242	18,351
United Kingdom . . .	15,831	16,944	17,929	15,757	4,800	5,762	5,834	4,885
U.S.A.	1,945	2,605	2,822	2,910	2,760	3,010	4,026	3,014
Yugoslavia . . .	639	770	1,140	2,201	831	989	986	1,006
Others	19,471	21,887	30,774	24,417	13,489	14,901	9,827	20,314
TOTAL . .	89,709	92,476	109,033	115,436	80,834	85,624	101,615	114,374

* Excluding re-exports.

TRANSPORT

RAILWAYS
(1968–69)

Passengers ('000)	3,548
Freight ('000 tons)	2,669

ROADS
(1969)

Passenger Vehicles	29,094
Goods Vehicles	21,413
Motor Cycles	1,973

SHIPPING

	1966	1967	1968	1969	1970
Ships calling at Port Sudan . .	1,223	1,004	845	770	760
Total Inward Tonnage . .	1,427,743	1,528,183	1,594,019	1,582,369	1,845,215
Total Outward Tonnage . .	941,317	866,948	952,449	950,975	1,014,757

CIVIL AVIATION

(Sudan Airways—International Traffic)

	1965	1966	1967	1968	1969
Passengers	45,793	50,673	31,367	36,975	65,293
Freight (kg.)	492,871.2	402,227.8	501,231.5	344,338	837,966

EDUCATION

(1969)

	TEACHERS	STUDENTS		
		MALE	FEMALE	TOTAL
Pre-Primary	266	7,927	7,958	15,885
Primary	12,370	410,023	200,775	610,798
Secondary: General . .	9,030	126,617	45,869	172,486
Vocational .	151	1,181	—	1,181
Teacher-Training .	156	1,439	852	2,291
Tertiary	1,107	10,304	1,387	11,691

Source: United Nations, *Statistical Yearbook 1971.*

Source: Department of Statistics, H.Q. Council of Ministers, Khartoum, except where otherwise stated.

THE CONSTITUTION

A Provisional Constitution was introduced by the Revolutionary Command Council in August 1971. A People's Council, including various categories of the people's working forces, was called to draft and ratify a permanent constitution. It was endorsed by the People's Assembly in April 1973 as the Permanent Constitution of the Sudan.

The President

The President must be a Sudanese of at least 35 years of age. He is nominated by the Sudanese Socialist Union, is Head of State, and is responsible for maintaining the Constitution. He may appoint Vice-Presidents, a Prime Minister and Ministers who are responsible to him. He is the Supreme Commander of the People's Armed Forces and Security Forces, and the Supreme Head of the Public Service.

If satisfied that a national crisis exists, the President may declare a State of Emergency, which may entail the suspension of any or all freedoms and rights under the Permanent Constitution other than that of resort to the courts. In the event of the President's death, the First Vice-President will temporarily assume office for a period not exceeding 60 days.

The People's Assembly

The President may appoint up to a tenth of the members of the Assembly. The duration of a sitting is four years and sittings are held in public. A quorum consists of half the number of members. Amendments to the Constitution may be proposed by the President or one third of the membership of the People's Assembly. An amendment to the Constitution must have a two-thirds majority of the People's Assembly and the assent of the President.

Judiciary

The State is subject to the rule of law which is the basis of government. The judiciary is an independent body directly responsible to the President and judges are appointed by the President.

Religion

Unrestricted freedom of religion is allowed and mention is specifically made of the Islamic and Christian religions.

Southern Region

Under the Regional Constitution for the Southern Sudan, the three southern provinces form a single region, with its own regional executive in Juba headed by a president who is also a Vice-President of the whole Republic. The regional executive is responsible for all matters outside national defence, external affairs, communications, currency and foreign trade regulation. The regional President will be appointed by and responsible to a regional People's Assembly. The Assembly may postpone legislation of the central Government which it considers adverse to the interests of the South, though the President is not compelled to accede to its request. The Regional Constitution can be amended only by a four-fifths majority of the central People's Assembly, where southerners will be proportionally represented.

The People's Assembly is to have 250 seats, which include 70 for the people's working forces alliance, 30 for the administrative units to be filled both by election and selection, 25 appointed by the President and 125 for the geographical areas. The regional People's Assembly will consist of 60 members of whom 30 will represent the geographical areas, 21 the people's working forces alliance and 9 the administrative units. They will be elected by direct secret ballot.

THE GOVERNMENT

President: Gen. JAAFIR AL NEMERY (*elected October* 1971).
First Vice-President: Maj.-Gen. MUHAMMAD EL-BAQHIR AHMED.
Vice-President and President of the High Executive Council for the Southern Region: ABEL ALIER.

MINISTERS (*July* 1974)

Minister of Foreign Affairs: Dr. MANSOUR KHALID.

Minister of Defence: Gen. AWAD KHALAFALLA.

Minister of Local Government and Community Development: Dr. GAAFAR ALI BAKHEIT.

Minister of Finance and National Economy: IBRAHIM MONEIM MANSOUR.

Minister of Education: Sir EL KHATIM EL KHALIFA.

Minister of Agriculture, Food and Natural Resources: WADIE HABASHI.

Minister of Culture and Information: OMER EL HAG MUSA.

Minister of Health and Social Welfare: ABUL GASIM MOHAMED IBRAHIM.

Minister of Transport and Communications: Dr. BASHIR ABADI.

Minister of Industry and Mining: MUSA AWAD BALLAL.

Minister of Interior: ABDALLAH EL HASSAN EL KHIDER.

Minister of Public Services and Administrative Reform: ABDEL RAHMAN ABDALLAH.

Attorney General: Dr. ZAKI MUSTAFA.

Minister for Egyptian Affairs in the Sudan: SALAH ABDEL AAL MABROUK.

Auditor General: IBRAHIM HASSAN ALLAM.

MINISTERS OF STATE

Minister of State for Foreign Affairs: GAMAL MOHAMED AHMED.

Minister of State for Irrigation: YAHIA ABDEL MAGGED.

Minister of State for Local Government: SAMUEL LUBAI.

Minister of State Information: BONA MALWAL.

Minister of State for Trade: HASSAN MOHAMED ALI BILEIL.

Minister of State for Agricultural Production: Dr. KAMAL ABDALLA AGABAWI.

Minister of State for General Education: Dr. MOHAMED KHEIR OSMAN.

Minister of State for the Government Secretariat: AHMED BABIKER BISA.

Minister of State for Construction and Public Works: MUSTAFA OSMAN.

Minister of State for Presidential Affairs: FAISAL MOHAMED ABDEL RAHMAN.

Minister of State for Research and Services: Dr. HUSSEIN IDRIS.

Minister of State for Head of Government Affairs: Dr. BAHA EDDIN MOHAMED IDRIS.

HIGH EXECUTIVE COUNCIL FOR THE SOUTHERN REGION

There are twelve Regional Ministers.

President: ABEL ALIER.

Secretary-General: CLETO HASSAN.

DIPLOMATIC REPRESENTATION

EMBASSIES ACCREDITED TO THE SUDAN
(In Khartoum unless otherwise stated)

Algeria: Junction Mek Nimr St. and 67th St., P.O.B. 80; *Ambassador:* ABDEL AZIZ BEN HUSAIN.

Belgium: St. 3, New Extension, P.O.B. 969; *Chargé d'Affaires:* THÉO LANSLOOT.

Bulgaria: El Mek Nimr St. South 7, P.O.B. 1690; *Chargé d'Affaires a.i.:* STAMEN STIANOV.

Central African Republic: Africa Rd., P.O.B. 1723; *Ambassador:* GILBERT BANDIO.

Chad: St. 47, New Extension; *Ambassador:* MOULI SAID.

China, People's Republic: 69 31st St., P.O.B. 1425; *Ambassador:* YANG SHOU-CHENG.

Czechoslovakia: 1, 5GE, Khartoum Central, P.O.B. 1047; *Ambassador:* MIROSLAV NOVOTNÝ.

Egypt: Mogram St.; *Ambassador:* MOHAMMED EL TABIE MOHAMMED.

Ethiopia: 6, 11A St. 3, New Extension, P.O.B. 844; *Ambassador:* DAWIT ABDOU.

France: 6H East Plot 2, 19th St., P.O.B. 377; *Ambassador:* HENRI COSTILHES.

German Democratic Republic: P4 (3) B2, Khartoum West, P.O.B. 1089; *Ambassador:* HERBERT DENZLER.

Germany, Federal Republic: Baladiya St., P.O.B. 970; *Ambassador:* MICHAEL JOVY.

Greece: Block 74, 31st St., P.O.B. 1182; *Ambassador:* NICOLAS FILOPOULOS.

Hungary: Block 11, Plot 12, 13th St., New Extension, P.O.B. 1033; *Ambassador:* LAJOS BENCZEKOVITS.

India: El Mek Nimr St., P.O.B. 707; *Ambassador:* INDU PRAKASH SINGH.

Iran: Baladiya St.; *Ambassador:* ARSALAN NAYER NURI.

Iraq: St. 5, New Extension; *Ambassador:* NAZIM JAWAD EL ARIDH.

Italy: 39th St., P.O.B. 793; *Ambassador:* GIULIO BILANCIONI.

Japan: 14-16, Block 5HE, P.O.B. 1649; *Ambassador:* TOSHIO KAWASHIMA.

Jordan: 25 7th St., New Extension; *Ambassador:* ALI KHRAIS.

Korea, Democratic People's Republic: 2-10 BE, 7th St., New Extension, P.O.B. 332; *Ambassador:* KIM DOK SU.

Kuwait: 9th St., New Extension; *Ambassador:* Mohammed Salem El Balhan.

Lebanon: 60 St. 49; *Ambassador:* Bulind Beydoun.

Libya: Africa Rd. 50, P.O.B. 2091; *Ambassador:* (vacant).

Morocco: *Chargé d'Affaires a.i.:* Mohamed Ibn Idris.

Netherlands: P.O.B. 391; *Chargé d'Affaires a.i.:* J. W. Bertens.

Niger: St. 1, New Extension, P.O.B. 1283; *Ambassador:* El Hag Omarou Amadou.

Nigeria: P.O.B. 1538; *Ambassador:* El Haji Nuhu Mohammed.

Pakistan: 29, 9AE, St. 3, New Extension, P.O.B. 1178; *Ambassador:* S. A. H. Ahsani.

Poland: 73 Africa Rd., P.O.B. 902; *Ambassador:* Janos Leordviske.

Qatar: St. 15, New Extension; *Ambassador:* Ali Abdul Rahman Muftah.

Romania: St. 47, Plot 67, P.O.B. 1652; *Ambassador:* Florian Stoica.

Saudi Arabia: Central St., New Extension, P.O.B. 852; *Ambassador:* (vacant).

Somalia: Central St., New Extension; *Ambassador:* Jalle Mohamed Hagi Nuir.

Spain: 52 39th St., P.O.B. 2621; *Ambassador:* Jose Manuel del Moral Y Gracia Saez.

Switzerland: Aboulela Bldg., P.O.B. 1707; *Ambassador:* Hans Karl Frey.

Syria: 3rd St., New Extension; *Ambassador:* (vacant).

Tanzania: P.O.B. 6080, *Chargé d'Affairs:* O. A. Tesha.

Tunisia: *Ambassador:* Mohammed bin Fadl.

Turkey: 71 Africa Rd., P.O.B. 771; *Ambassador:* (vacant).

Uganda: Cairo, Egypt.

U.S.S.R.: B1, A10 St., New Extension, P.O.B. 1161; *Ambassador:* Felix Fedotov.

United Arab Emirates: St. 3, New Extension; *Ambassador:* Khalifa Ahmed Abdel Aziz Al Mubarak.

United Kingdom: New Abulela Bldg., P.O.B. 801; *Ambassador:* John F. S. Phillips.

U.S.A.: Gumhouria Ave.; *Ambassador:* (recalled).

Vatican: El Safeh City, Shambat, P.O.B. 623; *Apostolic Pro-Nuncio:* Ubaldo Calabresi.

Yemen Arab Republic: St. 35, New Extension; *Ambassador:* Mohammed Abdul Wasse.

Yemen, People's Democratic Republic: St. 51, New Extension; *Chargé d'Affaires a.i.:* Mohamed Awad El Tahs.

Yugoslavia: St. 31, 79-A, Khartoum 1, P.O.B. 1180; *Ambassador:* Ljubomir Drndić.

Zaire: Gumhouria Ave.; *Ambassador:* Losso Lisongi.

Sudan also has diplomatic relations with Afghanistan, Argentina, Australia, Austria, Brazil, Cameroon, Canada, Chile, Cyprus, Denmark, Finland, Gabon, Guinea, Indonesia, Kenya, Malaysia, Mali, Mauritania, Norway, Senegal, Sri Lanka, Sweden, the Democratic Republic of Viet-Nam, and Zambia.

PEOPLE'S ASSEMBLY

A People's Assembly is provided for under the Permanent Constitution, elections to it were held in April 1974 and the Assembly opened in May 1974.

POLITICAL ORGANIZATION

Sudanese Socialist Union: Khartoum; f. 1971; only recognized political organization; consists of National Conference, Central Committee, Political Bureau and Secretariat-General.

Political Bureau (*June* 1974): Pres. Jaafir Al Nemery*, Mohamed El Baghir Ahmed, Abel Alier, Abul Gasim Mohamed Ibrahim*, Bahr Eddin Mohamed Ahmed Suliman*, El Rasheed El Taher Bakr*, Ahmed Abdel Halim*, Luigi Adok*, Mahdi Mustafa, Abdallah El Hassan El Khider, Gen. Awad Khalafalla, Gaafar Mohamed Ali Bakheit, Hilleri Paulo Logali, Ibrahim Moneim Mansour, Joseph Oduho, Lawrence Wol, Dr. Mansour Khalid, Omer El Hag Musa.

* Member also of the Secretariat-General.

JUDICIAL SYSTEM

The administration of justice is the function of the judiciary, as a separate and independent department of state. The general administrative supervision and control of the judiciary is vested in the Higher Judiciary Council headed by the President of the Republic. The members are the President of the Supreme Court, his three deputies and the Attorney-General.

Civil Justice: is administered by the courts constituted under the Civil Justice Ordinance, namely the Supreme Court, Court of Appeal and Other Courts. The Supreme Court consists of a president and one or more vice-presidents and sufficient number of judges. It is the custodian of the constitution under the Permanent Constitution of the Sudan of 1973.

Criminal Justice: is administered by the courts constituted under the Code of Criminal Procedure, namely Major Courts, Minor Courts and Magistrates' Courts. Serious crimes are tried by Major Courts which are composed of a president and two members and have power to pass the death sentence. Major Courts are as a rule presided over by a judge of the High Court appointed to a Provincial Circuit, or a Province Judge. There is a right of appeal against any decision or order of a Major Court and all findings and sentences of a Major Court are subject to confirmation.

Lesser crimes are tried by Minor Courts consisting of three magistrates and presided over by a second class magistrate and by Magistrates' Courts consisting of a single magistrate, or a bench of lay magistrates.

Local Courts: try a substantial portion of the criminal

and civil cases in the Sudan and work in parallel to some extent with the State Courts.

Chief Justice: KHALAFALLA EL RASHEED.

ISLAMIC LAW COURTS

Justice in personal matters for the Muslim population is administered by the Law Courts, which form the Sharia Division of the Judiciary. These courts consist of the Court of Appeal, High Courts and Qadis' Courts. The religious Law of Islam is administered by these courts in matters of inheritance, marriage, divorce, family relationships and charitable trusts.

Mufti: AWADALLA SALIH.

RELIGION

The majority of Sudanese are vigorous followers of Islam, but some communities in the south practise animism or fertility worship. It is estimated that there are more than 9 million Muslims and over 400,000 Catholics.

MUSLIM COMMUNITY
(Mainly divided into the following sects:)

Qadria: Heads of important local sub-sections include:
Sheikh AHMED EL GAALI.
Sheikh IBRAHIM EL KABASHI.
YOUSIF EL SHEIKH OMER EL OBEID.
KHALIFA BARAKAT EL SHEIKH.
Sheikh HAMAD EL NIL ABD EL BAGI.
Sheikh ABD EL BAGI EL MUKASHFI.

Shadhlia: Heads of local sub-sections include:
Sheikh EL MAGDOUB EL BESHIR.
Sheikh GAMAR EL DAWLA EL MAGDOUB.

Idrisia: Heads of local sub-sections include:
Sheikh EL HASSAN EL IDRISI.

Khatmiya: MUHAMMAD OSMAN EL MIRGHANI.

Sammania: Sheikh FATEH GHARIBALLA.

Ismaila: Sayed JAYAL ASFIA EL SAYED EL MEKKI.
Ansari.

Christian Council: P.O.B. 317, Khartoum.

Bible Society: P.O.B. 532, Khartoum.

Sudan Interior Mission: P.O.B. 220, Khartoum.

CHRISTIAN COMMUNITIES

Coptic Orthodox Church: Bishop of Nubia, Atbara and Omdurman: Rt. Rev. BAKHOMIOS.
Bishop of Khartoum, S. Sudan and Uganda: Rt. Rev. ANBA YOUANNIS.

Greek Orthodox Church: Metropolitan of Nubia: Archbishop SINESSIOS.

Greek Evangelical Church.

Evangelical Church: P.O.B. 57, Khartoum; Chair. Rev. RADI ELIAS; about 500 mems.

Episcopal Church in the Sudan: Clergy House, P.O.B. 135, Khartoum; Bishop in the Sudan: The Rt. Rev. ELINANA NGALAMU; Asst. Bishops: The Rt. Rev. YEREMAYA DOTIRO, The Rt. Rev. BUTRUS SHUKAI, The Rt. Rev. BENJAMIN YUGUSUK.

Catholic Church:
Roman Rite:
Vicariate Apostolic of Khartoum: P.O.B. 49, Khartoum; Rt. Rev. Bishop AUGUSTINE BARONI.
Vicariate Apostolic of Wau: P.O.B. 29, Wau; Rt. Rev. Bishop IRENEUS WIEN DUD.
Vicariate Apostolic of Juba: P.O.B. 32, Juba; Rt. Rev. PAOLINO DOGGALE, Apostolic Administrator.
Vicariate Apostolic of El Obeid: P.O.B. 386, El Obeid; Rt. Rev. Mgr. FRANCESCO CAZZANIGA, Apostolic Administrator.
Vicariate Apostolic of Rumbek: Catholic Church, Rumbek; Rev. Fr. DOMINIC MATONG, Vicar Del.
Prefecture Apostolic of Malakal: P.O.B. 27, Malakal; Rt. Rev. Mgr. PIUS YUKWAN DENG, Apostolic Administrator.
Prefecture Apostolic of Mupoi: Catholic Church, Tombora; Rt. Rev. JOSEPH GASI, Apostolic Administrator.

Maronite Church: P.O.B. 244, Khartoum; Rev. Fr. YOUSEPH NEAMA.

Greek Catholic Church: P.O.B. 766, Khartoum; Archimandrite: BASILIOS HAGGAR.

Presbyterian Church: Malakal.

Jewish Community: Chief Rabbi: (vacant).

THE PRESS

The Press was nationalized on August 27th, 1970. A General Corporation for Press, Printing and Publications was set up with two publishing houses, the Al-Ayam (P.O.B. 363, Khartoum), and the Al-Rai Al-Amm (P.O.B. 424, Khartoum). These two houses publish all the following newspapers and magazines with the exception of those produced by other ministries.

DAILIES

Al-Ayam: P.O.B. 363, Khartoum; Arabic.

Al-Sahafa: P.O.B. 424, Khartoum; f. 1961; Arabic.

PERIODICALS

El Guwat El Musallaha: armed forces publication; weekly.

Huna Omdurman: f. 1942; Arabic; weekly; Sudan Broadcasting Service Magazine; published by Ministry of Communications.

Khartoum: P.O.B. 424, Khartoum; Arabic; monthly.

Nile Mirror: English; twice-weekly; published by High Executive Council for the Southern Region (*suspended from August* 1973).

El Rai El Amm: P.O.B. 424, Khartoum; Arabic; weekly.

Sudan Cotton Bulletin: P.O.B. 1672, Khartoum; English; monthly; published by Cotton Public Corporation.

Sudan Cotton Review: P.O.B. 1672, Khartoum; English; annually; published by Cotton Public Corporation.

El Sudan El Gadid: P.O.B. 363, Khartoum; Arabic; weekly.

Sudanese Economist: Khartoum; English; monthly; economic and commercial review.

NEWS AGENCIES

Sudan National News Agency: P.O.B. 624, Khartoum; f. 1971; daily and weekly summaries in English and Arabic; Man. ABDUL KARIM OSMAN EL MAHDI.

FOREIGN BUREAUX

Middle East News Agency: Dalala Bldg., P.O.B. 740, Khartoum.

Tass also has a bureau in Khartoum.

PUBLISHERS

African Printing House: Press House, P.O.B. 1228, Khartoum; f. 1960; publishers of *Al-Sahafa*; also African News Service; Gen. Man. ABDUL RAHMAN MUKHTAR.

Ahmed Abdel Rahman El Tikeina: P.O. Box 299, Port Sudan.

Al Ayam Press Co. Ltd.: Aboul Ela Building, United Nations Square, P.O. Box 363, Khartoum; f. 1953; Man. Dir. BESHIR MUHAMMAD SAID; newspapers, pamphlets and books.

Al-Rai Al-Amm: P.O.B. 424, Khartoum.

Al Sahafa Publishing House: government publications and short stories.

Al Salam Co. Ltd.: P.O.B. 197, Khartoum.

Central Office of Information: Khartoum; government publishing office; publications include the *Sudan Almanac.*

Claudios S. Fellas: P.O. Box 641, Khartoum.

Fuad Rashed: Wadi Halfa.

Khartoum University Press: P.O.B. 321, Khartoum; f. 1967; scholarly works; Dir. (vacant).

RADIO AND TELEVISION

Sudan Broadcasting Service: P.O.B. 572, Omdurman; a government-controlled radio station which broadcasts daily in Arabic, English and Somali; Dir. EL TIGANI EL TAYIB.

There are 200,000 radio receivers. A radio station is to be constructed in the Southern Region.

Sudan Television Service (STS): P.O.B. 1094, Omdurman; f. 1962; thirty-five hours of programmes per week; Dir.-Gen. MEKKI AWAD EL NUR.

There are 62,500 television receivers.

FINANCE

BANKING

(cap. =capital; p.u. =paid up; dep. =deposits; m. =million)

Under the Nationalization of Banks Act 1970, all banks have been nationalized.

CENTRAL BANK

Bank of Sudan: P.O. Box 313, Khartoum; f. 1960; acts as banker and financial adviser to the Government and has sole right of issue of Sudanese banknotes; cap. p.u. £S1.5m.; Chair. IBRAHIM MOHAMMED NIMIR; Deputies EL FAKI MUSTAFA, EL BAGHIR YOUSIF MUDAWI; 7 brs.; publs. *Economic and Financial Bulletin* (quarterly), *Foreign Trade Statistical Digest* (quarterly), *Annual Report.*

COMMERCIAL BANKS

El Nilein Bank: P.O.B. 466, Khartoum; f. 1965 as a partnership between the Bank of Sudan and the Crédit Lyonnais; cap. p.u. £S53m.; 8 brs.; Chair. IBRAHIM ELIAS.

Juba-Omdurman Commercial Bank: Khartoum; f. 1973; formerly Juba Commercial Bank and Omdurman National Bank; Gen. Man. DIRDAZI IBRAHIM.

People's Co-operative Bank: P.O.B. 922, Khartoum; formerly the Misr Bank; 6 brs.; deals with all operations

and facilities of the Sudan co-operative movement; Gen. Man. AHMED ABDEL RAHMAN EL SHEIKH.

Red Sea Commercial Bank: Khartoum; formerly the Arab Bank; 3 brs.; Gen. Man. TAG EL SIR ABDULLA.

State Bank for Foreign Trade: P.O.B. 1008, Khartoum; formerly Barclays Bank D.C.O.; £S35,551,000 (Dec. 1972); 24 brs.; Gen. Man. HUSSEIN ABDEL GADIR.

Sudan Commercial Bank: P.O.B. 1116, Khartoum; f. 1960; cap. p.u. £S1,099,611; dep. £S8,280,000; Chair. and Gen. Man. MOHAMED YAHIA SALIH; 6 brs.

DEVELOPMENT BANKS

Agricultural Bank of Sudan: P.O. Box 1363, Khartoum; f. 1957; cap. £S7m.; provides agricultural credit; Chair. and Man. Dir. MIRGHANI EL AMIN EL HAG.

Estate Bank of Sudan: P.O.B. 313, Khartoum; Gen. Man. MOHAMMED MEKKI KANANI.

Industrial Bank of Sudan: P.O.B. 1722, Khartoum; f. 1962; cap. £S2m.; Gen. Man. MAHDI AHMED.

INSURANCE COMPANIES

There are over forty foreign insurance companies operating in the Sudan.

TRADE AND INDUSTRY

Sudan Gezira Board: H.Q. Barakat; Sales Office, P.O.B. 884, Khartoum; Chair. and Man. Dir. Dr. ABBAS ABDEL MAGID SINADA; Deputy Man. Dir. AWAD EL KARIM; Financial Controller ABDALLA IMAM; Agricultural Man. HASSAN ABDALLA HASHIM; Sales Man. BESHIR MEDANI; Sec. YOUSIF EL KARIB.

The Sudan Gezira Board is responsible for Sudan's main cotton producing area.

The Gezira Scheme represents a partnership between the Government, the tenants and the Board. The Government, which provides the land and is responsible for irrigation, receives 36 per cent of the net proceeds; the tenants, about 100,000 in 1971, receive 49 per cent. The Board receives 10 per cent, the local Government Councils in the Scheme area 2 per cent and the Social Development Fund, set up to provide social services for the inhabitants, 3 per cent.

The total possible cultivable area of the Gezira Scheme is over 5 million acres and the total area under systematic irrigation is now almost 2 million acres. In addition to cotton, groundnuts, sorghum, wheat and millet are grown for the benefit of tenant farmers.

Publications: *Annual Report, Annual Statement of Accounts, El Gezira News* (weekly), *Weekly Bulletin*.

State Cotton Marketing Corpn.: P.O.B. 1672, Khartoum; f. June 1970; the Corporation now supervises all cotton marketing operations through the following four main cotton companies:

Port Sudan Cotton and Trade Co. Ltd.: P.O.B. 590, Khartoum.

National Cotton and Trade Co. Ltd.: P.O.B. 1552, Khartoum.

Sudan Cotton Trade Co. Ltd.: P.O.B. 2284, Khartoum.

Alaktan Trading Co. Ltd.: P.O.B. 2607, Khartoum.

Offices Abroad:

Democratic Republic of Sudan Consulates, Sudan Cotton Section, 3 rue de Marché, 1204 Geneva, Switzerland.

Sudan Cotton Centre, P.O.B. 152, Osaka, Japan.

State Trading Corporation: Gen. Man. MOHAMED ABDEL KARIM ABBAS.

The Food Industries Corporation: P.O.B. 2341, Khartoum; produces dehydrated onion and pepper, dried vegetables, gum arabic, etc; dates, canned fruit and vegetables; wheat bran and sweets.

CHAMBER OF COMMERCE

Sudan Chamber of Commerce: P.O.B. 81, Khartoum; f. 1908; Pres. ABDEL SALAM ABOUL ELA; Hon. Treas. TH. APOSTOLOU; Hon. Sec. SAYED SALEH OSMAN SALEH.

TRADE UNIONS
FEDERATIONS

Federation of Sudanese Workers' Unions (F.S.W.U.): P.O.B. 2258, Khartoum; f. 1963; includes 135 affiliates totalling 450,000 mems.; affiliated to the International Confederation of Trade Union Federations and the All-African Trade Union Federation; currently being reformed and individual unions reconstituted; Pres. AWADALLA IBRAHIM; Sec.-Gen. (vacant); publs. *Al Talia* (Arabic weekly), *Bulletin* (English and Arabic, monthly).

PRINCIPAL UNIONS

In 1958 all Trade Unions were dissolved, but legislation in 1961 permitted registration of Trade Unions satisfying certain conditions.

Central Electricity and Water Administration Trade Union: P.O.B. 1380, Khartoum; 3,000 mems.; Pres. ALI SAID; Sec.-Gen. MAHJUB SID AHMAD.

Department of Agriculture Trade Union: Khartoum Workers' Club, Khartoum; 1,170 mems.; Pres. ABDAL-KARIM SADALLAH; Sec.-Gen. ABDULLAM IBRAHIM.

Egyptian Irrigation Department Trade Union: Khartoum; 1,210 mems.; Pres. FADL ABD-AL-WAHAB; Sec.-Gen. MUHAMMAD AL SAIYID MUHAMMAD.

Forestry Department Trade Union: c/o Forests Department, Al Suke; f. 1961; 2,510 mems.; Pres. IMAN UMAR; Sec.-Gen. MUHAMMED IBRAHIM AHMED.

Gezira Board Non-Agricultural Workers' Union: c/o Gezira Board, Wad Medani; f. 1961; 6,600 mems.; Pres. SULAYMAN ABD-AL-FARAJ; Sec.-Gen. MIRGHANI ABD-AL-RAHIM.

Khartoum Municipality Trade Union: c/o Khartoum Municipal Council, P.O. Box 750, Khartoum; 891 mems.; Pres. MUHAMMAD ABDULLAH AHMAD; Sec.-Gen. UTHMAN MUHAMMAD AL SHAIKH.

Khartoum University Trade Union: Khartoum University, P.O.B. 321, Khartoum; f. 1947; 1,400 mems.; Pres. MAHJUB AHMAD AL-ZUBAYR.

Mechanical Transport Department Trade Union: Khartoum Workers' Club, P.O.B. 617, Khartoum; 2,593 mems.; Pres. MADARRI MUHAMMAD AYD; Sec.-Gen. IBRAHIM BABALLAH.

Ministry of Education Trade Union: Khartoum Workers' Club, Khartoum; 679 mems.; Pres. MUHAMMAD HAMDAN; Sec.-Gen. UTHMAN AL-SIDDIQ.

Ministry of Health Trade Union: c/o Khartoum Hospital, Khartoum; 3,592 mems.; Pres. ABDAL RAZIQ UBAYD; Sec.-Gen. IBRAHIM UMAR ALHAJ.

Ministry of Irrigation and Hydro-Electric Power Trade Union: Medani Workers' Club, Wad Medani; 15,815 mems.; Pres. YAHYA HASAN AL-RAU.

Ministry of Public Utilities Trade Union: Khartoum Workers' Club, Khartoum; 607 mems.; Pres. AWADAL-LAH IBRAHIM; Sec.-Gen. HASSAN ABDEL GADIR.

Posts and Telegraphs Trade Union: Khartoum Workers' Club; 700 mems.; Pres. ABD-AL-MONEIM AHMAD; Sec.-Gen. FADL AHMAD FADL.

Sudan Textile Industry Employees Trade Union: Khartoum North; f. 1968; 3,750 mems.; Sec. MUKHTAR ABDALLA.

Sudan Railway Workers' Union (S.R.W.U.): Sudan Railway Workers' Union Club, Atbara; f. 1961; 28,000 mems.; Pres. MUSA AHMED MUTTAI; Sec. MUHAMMAD OSMAN ALI EL MUDIR.

CO-OPERATIVE SOCIETIES

There are some 600 co-operative societies in the Sudan, of which 570 are formally registered.

TRANSPORT AND TOURISM

RAILWAYS

Sudan Railways: Atbara; Gen. Man. Mohammed Abdel Rahman Wasfi.

The total length of railway in operation is 4,756 route-kilometres. The main line runs from Wadi Halfa, on the Egyptian border to El Obeid, via Khartoum. Lines from Atbara and Sennar connect with Port Sudan on the coast. There are lines from Sennan to Roseires on the Blue Nile (225 km.) and from Aradeiba to Nyala in the south-western province of Darfur (689 km.), with a 445 km. branch line from Babanousa to Wau in the Bahr el Ghazal Province.

ROADS

Ministry of Transport and Communications: P.O.B. 300, Khartoum; Dir. of Roads and Bridges Ahmed Omer Khalafalla.

Roads in the Northern Sudan, other than town roads, are only cleared tracks and often impassable immediately after rain. Motor traffic on roads in the Upper Nile Province is limited to the drier months of January–May. There are several good gravelled roads in the Equatoria and Bahr el Ghazal Provinces which are passable all the year round, but in these districts some of the minor roads become impassable after rain. Rehabilitation of communications in the Southern Sudan is a major priority as the civil war completely destroyed 1,600 km. of roads and 70 bridges.

The through route from Juba to Khartoum is open from mid-November to mid-April.

Over 48,000 km. of tracks are classed as "motorable", but only 333 km. are asphalt.

INLAND WATERWAYS

Ministry of Transport and Communications: P.O.B. 300, Khartoum.

The total length of navigable waterways served by passenger and freight services is 4,068 km. From the Egyptian border to Wadi Halfa and Khartoum navigation is limited by cataracts to short stretches but the White Nile from Khartoum to Juba is navigable at almost all seasons. The Blue Nile is not navigable. River transport was badly hit by the civil war. A new harbour is to be constructed at Suakin.

The Sudan Railways operate 2,500 km. of steamer services on the navigable reaches of the Nile, touching Juba, Gambeila, Wau, Shellal (in Egyptian territory),

and Dongola. These services connect with the Egyptian main railway services and the Nile river services of Uganda.

The construction of the Egyptian High Dam has flooded the Wadi Halfa. The Sudan and Egypt operate river services in the Wadi Halfa/Aswan reach by deep-draught vessels suitable to sail in the big lake thus created.

SHIPPING

Sudan Railways: Atbara; responsible for operating Port Sudan.

Port Sudan, on the Red Sea, 784 km. from Khartoum, is the only seaport. There are eleven fully equipped berths, with a total length of 7,461 metres, and two secondary berths. There are also two berths with a total length of 1,560 metres.

River Navigation Corporation: Khartoum; f. 1970; jointly owned by the Egyptian and Sudan governments; operates services between Aswan and Wadi Halfa.

Sudan Shipping Line: P.O.B. 426, Port Sudan; f. 1960; four vessels operating between the Red Sea, North Europe and the United Kingdom; Gen. Man. Yousif Bakheit Arabi.

CIVIL AVIATION

The airports at Juba and Malakal in Southern Sudan are to be repaired and new airports built at Wau and Port Sudan.

Sudan Airways: Gumhouria Ave., P.O.B. 253, Khartoum; f. 1947; this airline is owned by the Sudan Government; regular services throughout the Sudan and external services to Aden, Chad, Egypt, Ethiopia, Greece, Kenya, Uganda, Italy, Lebanon, Libya, Saudi Arabia, and the U.K.; Charter and Survey based at Khartoum; fleet of two Boeing 707, five Fokker F-27A, one DC-3, and three Twin Otters; two Boeing 707 are to be purchased in 1974; Chair. Abdel Bagi Mohamed; Gen. Man. Mohammed El Amir El Amin.

The Sudan is also served by the following foreign airlines: Aeroflot, Alitalia, British Airways, EgyptAir, Ethiopian, Interflug, Libyan Arab, Lufthansa, MEA, Saudia and Swissair.

TOURISM

Sudan Tourist Corporation: P.O.B. 2424, Khartoum; f. 1959; Dir. Abdul Rahman I. Kebeda; Deputy Dir. Tawfik Nur El Din; publs. *Views From Sudan* and other tourist brochures.

UNIVERSITIES

University of Khartoum: P.O.B. 321, Khartoum; f. 1956; 358 teachers, 2,600 students.

Cairo University Khartoum Branch: P.O.B. 1055, Khartoum; f. 1955; 80 teachers, 5,100 students.

SWAZILAND

INTRODUCTORY SURVEY

Location, Climate, Language, Religion, Flag, Capital

The Kingdom of Swaziland is bounded on the north, west and south by the Republic of South Africa's Transvaal province and by the Natal province and Mozambique on the east. Rainfall ranges from 40 to 90 inches a year on the Highveld to between 20 and 25 inches in the sub-humid Lowveld. English and siSwati are the official languages. Some 60 per cent of the population are Christian. The national flag (proportions 3 by 2) is blue, with a yellow-edged horizontal crimson stripe (half the depth) in the centre. On this stripe is a black and white Swazi shield, superimposed on two spears and a staff. Mbabane is the administrative capital and Lobamba, the traditional capital of the Swazi people, is to become the country's legislative capital.

Recent History

Swaziland's first constitution, drafted by Britain, was published in May 1963, and the general election to choose members for the first Legislative Council was held in June the following year. It resulted in an overwhelming victory for the Imbokodvo National Movement, which supports the traditional Swazi way of life allied to progressive evolution. From the very first meeting of the council, the Imbokodvo pressed for a revised constitution and this eventually resulted in the introduction of internal self-government on April 25th, 1967. Simultaneously Britain changed the country's status to that of a protected state, with the Paramount Chief (*Ngwenyama*) recognised as King of Swaziland and Head of State. At General Elections in April 1967 the Imbokodvo National Movement won all seats in the new National Assembly. Britain's protection continued until Swaziland became independent on September 6th, 1968. Swaziland is a member of the Commonwealth, the UN and the Organization of African Unity, where its policies have been basically conservative. In the May 1972 elections the Imbokodvo National Movement lost three seats to the Ngwane National Liberatory Congress, but support for the monarchy in the country as a whole is strong. In April 1973 the King repealed the constitution, suspended all political activity and took over all judicial, legislative and executive powers himself. In November 1973 the first summit between the leaders of Botswana, Lesotho and Swaziland was held in Gaborone, Botswana.

Government

The executive authority is vested in the King and is exercised through a Cabinet presided over by the Prime Minister and consisting of the Prime Minister, the Deputy Prime Minister and up to eight other Ministers. Parliament consists of the Senate and the House of Assembly. The House of Assembly has 30 members—24 elected from 8 three-member constituencies, and 6 appointed by the King—and the Attorney-General, who has no vote. The Senate has 12 members, 6 elected by the House of Assembly and 6 appointed by the King. The constitution was repealed in April 1973 and all political activity has been suspended. This remained unchanged in early 1974.

Defence

Swaziland has a para-military police force and there is a small army.

Economy

Sugar cane is the principal agricultural item in the economy and the 1972 crop was about 1.5 million tons, producing 180,000 tons of raw sugar. The marketing arrangements with South Africa were terminated in December 1964, and Swaziland became a member of the Commonwealth Sugar Agreement. Cattle form the main wealth of the Swazi people, while citrus fruits, cotton, rice and maize are important agricultural products. There are considerable mineral reserves, especially asbestos, iron ore and coal. Iron ore is an important export and in 1971 sales of this commodity, all to Japan, were worth R.11,031,000, though they have since declined. Manufacturing industries are concerned mainly with processing agricultural, livestock and forestry products. In 1964 the territory's first industrial estate was opened at Matsapa and several secondary industries have become established there.

Swaziland has a favourable balance of trade. Sugar and wood pulp and other forest products account for more than 40 per cent of all export earnings, and asbestos and iron ore for over 30 per cent. British private investment and grants-in-aid from the British Government helped until recently to balance the annual budget. The 1969 Customs Union agreement between South Africa, Botswana, Lesotho and Swaziland increased customs revenue for Swaziland from R2.0 million in 1968–69 to R8.5 million in 1971–72. The United Kingdom still provides substantial development aid.

Although company tax remains low and the country is anxious to attract foreign capital, Africanization was speeded up in Swaziland during 1973 with a series of radical measures. These included more participation in the mining industry, part-nationalization of the two main banks, a monopoly of insurance, extra taxes on sugar in the form of a heavy levy on producers and more taxes on the thriving hotel industry as well as a Land Speculation Act. Swaziland's second National Development Plan (1973–77) was announced in June 1973 and provides for an estimated expenditure totalling R42 million in 1973–75 with particular emphasis on agriculture, on which R8 million is to be spent.

Transport and Communications

The 224 km. Swaziland railway runs from the iron ore mine at Ngwenya, near Mbabane, on the western border through the middle of Swaziland to the Mozambique border near Goba, where it connects with the Mozambique line to the port of Lourenço Marques. Swaziland has 1,336 km. of main roads, and 984 km. of secondary roads. Swaziland plans to have a comprehensive bitumenized system of roads by 1977 at a cost of R9 million. The main airport is at Matsapa, near Manzini, and there are scheduled flights three times a week to Johannesburg and Durban and twice a week to Lourenço Marques.

Education

There are 392 primary schools with a total enrolment of more than 76,000. In 1972 there were more than 10,000 pupils in a total of 62 secondary schools. There are two teacher training colleges. Post-secondary education is provided by the University of Botswana, Lesotho and Swaziland, which is in Lesotho. Vocational and other training is provided by the Swaziland Industrial Training Institute, the Swaziland Agricultural College and University Centre and the Government's Staff Training Institute.

Tourism

Swaziland is benefiting from the South African tourist trade; 45,000 tourists visited the country in 1973.

Visas are not required to visit Swaziland by nationals of Belgium, Denmark, Finland, France, Greece, Iceland, Israel, Italy, Luxembourg, the Netherlands, Norway, Portugal, San Marino, South Africa, Spain, Sweden, the United Kingdom and Commonwealth, the U.S.A. and Uruguay.

Sport

The most popular sport is football. Other sports are athletics, golf and tennis.

Public Holidays

1974: August 26th (Umhlanga (Reed Dance) Day), September 6th (Somhlolo (Independence) Day), October 24th (United Nations Day), December 25th–26th (Christmas and Boxing Day).

1975: January 1st (New Year's Day), March 28th–31st (Easter), April 25th (National Flag Day), May 8th (Ascension Day), June 2nd (Commonwealth Day).

The holiday "Ncwala" is variable each year.

Weights and Measures

The metric system is in use.

Currency

South African currency: 100 cents = 1 rand (R).

Exchange rates (April 1974):

$£1$ sterling = 1.581 rand;
U.S. $1 = 67.11 S.A. cents.

From September 1974 Swaziland will also issue its own currency: 100 cents = 1 lilangeni (plural emalangeni). The lilangeni will be equal to, and freely convertible into, the rand.

STATISTICAL SURVEY

AREA AND POPULATION

Area: 6,704 square miles.

POPULATION
(1966 Census)

	MALE	FEMALE	TOTAL
Africans . .	172,291	190,076	362,367†
Europeans	4,370	3,617	7,987
Other Non-Africans .	2,134	2,083	4,217
Absentees* .	13,512	7,055	20,567
TOTAL‡ . .	192,307	202,831	395,138

* Mainly Africans working in South Africa.

† Latest estimate: 434,000 Africans (July 1st, 1972).

‡ Excluding 126 persons (108 males, 18 females) in transit.

EMPLOYMENT

About 60,000 people are in paid employment. This figure, which includes self-employed, is just over 30 per cent of the working-age population—people between 15 and 64—which at the 1966 census was 183,000.

Main Towns (1966 population): Mbabane (capital) 13,803; Manzini 6,081.

RECRUITMENT FROM SWAZILAND FOR MINING IN SOUTH AFRICA

	TOTAL PERSONNEL	
	GOLD MINES	COAL MINES
1969 . . .	7,941	326
1970 . . .	9,035*	291
1971 . . .	6,653*	312
1972 . . .	6,901	314

*Includes 215 persons recruited in 1970 and 180 in 1971 for platinum mines.

Source: Mine Labour Organization.

Births and Deaths: Average annual birth rate 52.3 per 1,000; death rate 23.5 per 1,000 (UN estimates for 1965–70).

AGRICULTURE

PRINCIPAL CROPS

(metric tons)

	1970	1971	1972
Maize	63,000	104,695	120,291
Rice	7,347	8,105	5,346
Sugar Cane†	1,429,000	1,735,835	1,480,711
Citrus Fruits	64,397	51,152	73,250
Cotton seed	4,868	6,490	7,059
Cotton (lint)	2,397	3,344	3,636

† Crop year ending in year stated.

Source: Central Statistical Office, Mbabane; FAO, *Production Yearbook 1971.*

PRODUCTION OF PROCESSED AGRICULTURAL PRODUCTS

	UNITS ('000)	1969	1970	1971	1972
Sugar Products:					
Sugar, milled	metric tons	153.6	156.5	176.0	180.6
Molasses	,, ,,	42.8	40.2	44.8	52.9
Cotton Products:					
Cotton Lint	,, ,,	1.4	0.9	2.1	3.1
Cotton Seed	,, ,,	2.8	1.8	6.2	5.8
Fruit Products:					
Canned Fruit	kg.	5,291.4	*	*	*
Jams and Juices	,,	28.6	*	*	*
Meat Products:					
Canned Meat	,,	213.7	392.9	355.5	355.0
Offal	,,	913.9	730.1	564.3	727.9
Other Meat	,,	2,831.3	2,784.2	3,435.2	3,846.4
Dairy Products:					
Butter	,,	106.1	29.9	n.a.	n.a.
Wood Products:*					
Sawn Timber	cu. metres	57.4	75.5	78.7	75.5
Boxes and Woodwork	,, ,,	12.3	11.8	10.6	10.3
Mine Timber	,, ,,	49.4	47.0	18.7	27.6
Block Board	sq. metres	129.7	173.8	400.3	186.0
Poles	cu. metres	5.8	10.3	11.4	24.5
Wattle	metric tons	1.8	n.a.	1.8	2.0
Eucalyptus Oil	litres	n.a.	8.2	37.2	38.0

* By agreement with the companies concerned the quantities of wood pulp and canned fruit are no longer published. The estimated production of chemical wood pulp (in metric tons) was: 90,000 in 1968; 95,000 in 1969; 98,000 in 1970.

LIVESTOCK

	1971	1972
Cattle	571,785	589,220
Goats	261,534	252,037
Sheep	43,089	37,247
Horses	2,172	1,871
Mules	273	272
Donkeys	15,078	15,704
Poultry	399,309	379,222
Pigs	11,369	14,493

MINERAL PRODUCTION

	UNIT	1969	1970	1971	1972
Chrysolite Asbestos . .	'ooo metric tons	36.4	32.8	38.1	33.5
Iron Ore*	,, ,, ,,	2,302.0	2,348.4	2,264.3	1,983.7
Coal	,, ,, ,,	114.7	138.2	150.5	143.0
Pyrophyllite . . .	,, ,, ,,	0.5	0.2	0.2	0.1
Barytes	,, ,, ,,	0.5	0.2	0.1	0.2
Kaolin	,, ,, ,,	1.5	1.4	2.1	2.2
Quarried Stone . .	'ooo cu. metres	51.6	42.1	23.3	45.3

* Figures relate to gross weight. The metal content (in 'ooo metric tons) was: 1,468 in 1969; 1,469 in 1970; 1,480 in 1971.

FINANCE

South African currency: 100 cents = 1 rand.
Coins: ½, 1, 2, 5, 10, 20 and 50 cents.
Notes: 1, 2, 5, 10 and 20 rand.
Exchange rates (April 1974): £1 sterling = 1.581 rand; U.S. $1 = 67.11 South African cents.
100 rand = £63.27 = $149.000.

BUDGET
Twelve months ending March 31st
(Rand)

REVENUE	1970–71	1971–72	EXPENDITURE	1970–71	1971–72
Customs and Excise . .	6,731,283	8,523,018	Public Debt . . .	887,421	889,799
Income Tax . .	4,615,233	5,332,902	Statutory Expenditure .	742,768	773,071
Taxes and Duties . .	1,029,899	1,156,942	Civil List . . .	61,763	62,610
Licences . . .	416,376	446,903	Parliament . . .	119,069	125,482
Earnings of Departments .	1,543,199	1,776,509	Prime Minister . .	919,603	1,225,546
Reimbursements and Loan			Police . . .	931,272	1,057,529
Repayments . .	186,459	171,677	Deputy Prime Minister .	981,700	497,797
Land and Minerals . .	271,753	291,147	Finance, Commerce and In-		
Judicial Fines . .	51,959	70,998	dustry . . .	3,531,414	2,642,149
Miscellaneous . .	488,513	463,342	Local Administration .	693,296	903,417
Loans . . .	325,916	216,228	Education . . .	2,623,204	3,081,400
			Health . . .	1,320,590	1,501,880
	15,660,590	18,449,666	Works, Power and Communi-		
			cations . . .	1,920,867	2,269,078
IMF . . .	821,428	—	Agriculture . .	1,586,465	1,531,334
			Judiciary . . .	92,505	108,264
			Law Office . . .	33,743	36,880
			Public Service Commission .	30,470	23,527
			Audit . . .	38,213	40,619
			Overseas Service Aid Scheme	—	
			Other Provisions . .	64,903	623,101
			Appropriation for Capital		
Capital Revenue . .	1,956,034	—	Budget . . .	1,640,034	735,000
TOTAL . . .	18,438,052	18,449,666	TOTAL . . .	18,219,300	18,128,483

1973-74 Budget: Recurrent Revenue R.28.1m.; Recurrent Expenditure R.23.9m.

Gross Domestic Product (million rand, July 1st to June 30th): 57.0 in 1968-69; 75.3 in 1969-70; 80.1 in 1970-71.

BRITISH AID
('ooo Rand)

	1966–67	1967–68	1968–69	1969–70	1970–71
Grants-in-Aid	1,200	1,760	3,296	428	—
Development Aid . . .	1,603	3,315	1,634	1,863	n.a.
OSAS	64	240	378	289	218
Other Technical Assistance .	113	n.a.	690	418	n.a.
TOTAL . . .	2,980	5,315	5,998	2,998	n.a.

EXTERNAL TRADE
('ooo Rand)

	1969	1970	1971	1972
Imports . . .	38,000	42,749	47,824	53,309
Exports . . .	48,000	50,202	56,034	65,485

PRINCIPAL COMMODITIES
(1972—'ooo Rand)

IMPORTS		EXPORTS	
Food	4,737	Sugar	19,217
Beverages and Tobacco . . .	2,652	Citrus Fruit	7,216
Crude Materials	543	Iron Ore	9,322
Fuels, Oils and Fats . . .	4,348	Wood pulp	11,069
Chemicals	5,933	Asbestos	9,554
Machinery and Transport Equipment .	13,812	Wood and Wood Products . . .	3,023
Manufactures classified by material	9,363	Meat and Meat Products . .	2,022
TOTAL (incl. others) . .	53,309	TOTAL (incl. others) . .	65,485

Principal Countries: The United Kingdom and South Africa have traditionally been Swaziland's principal trade partners, taking respectively R 12,631,000 and R 10,563,700 of Swazi exports in 1970. However, with the increase in iron ore production, Japan has become an important client, taking the whole of Swaziland's iron ore exports, valued at R 11,031,000 in 1970, among total exports to Japan of R 12,071,000 in that year.

EDUCATION
(1972)

	SCHOOLS	TEACHERS	PUPILS
Primary	392	2,015	76,343
Secondary	62	491	10,681
Teacher Training Colleges . .	2	n.a.	322
Technical and Vocational Training	3	n.a.	359
Universities	I	n.a.	200*

* Including students at universities abroad, but excluding students at U.B.L.S. in Swaziland.

Source: Central Statistical Office, Mbabane (unless otherwise stated).

THE CONSTITUTION

The constitution seeks to maintain a non-racial state in which everyone will be treated equally without discrimination, regardless of race, colour or creed, and securing to everyone freedom and justice and inviolability of their property.

The King of Swaziland, called the *Ngwenyama* (the Lion) in siSwati, is Head of State. If the King is absent from Swaziland or incapacitated, the Queen Mother—*Ndlovukazi* (She-Elephant)—acts in his place. Succession is governed by Swazi law and custom. The executive authority is vested in the King and exercised through a Cabinet presided over by the Prime Minister and consisting of him, the Deputy Prime Minister and other ministers.

Parliament consists of the Senate and the House of Assembly. The House of Assembly has the exclusive power to initiate legislation on taxation and financial matters. Parliament has no power to legislate in respect of Swazi law and custom, unless authorized by the Swazi National Council. The Senate has power to initiate legislation on matters other than taxation and finance and Swazi law and custom.

The Swazi National Council, which consists of the King, the Queen Mother and all adult male Swazi, advises the King on all matters regulated by Swazi law and custom and connected with Swazi traditions and culture.

In April 1973 King Sobhuza repealed the constitution and took over all judicial, legislative and executive powers himself. In September 1973 he announced the appointment of a Royal Constitutional Commission to draw up a new Constitution.

THE GOVERNMENT

Head of State: H.M. King Sobhuza II, K.B.E.

CABINET

(April 1974)

Prime Minister: Prince Makhosini Jameson Dlamini.

Deputy Prime Minister: Zonke Amos Khumalo.

Minister of Finance: Robert P. Stephens.

Minister of Local Administration: Prince Masitsela Dlamini.

Minister of Works, Power and Communications: Dr. Allen Nxumalo.

Minister of Health and Education: Dr. P. S. P. Dlamini.

Minister of Agriculture: Abednego K. Hlophe.

Minister of Industry, Mines and Tourism: Simon S. Nxumalo.

Minister for the Civil Service: Khanyakwezwe H. Dlamini.

Minister of Justice: Senator Polycarp Mafeletiven Dlamini.

Minister of State for Foreign Affairs: Stephen Matsebula.

Minister of Commerce and Co-operatives: Prince Mfanasibili Dlamini.

DIPLOMATIC REPRESENTATION

EMBASSIES AND HIGH COMMISSIONS ACCREDITED TO SWAZILAND

(In Mbabane unless otherwise stated)

(E) Embassy; (HC) High Commission.

Austria: Pretoria, South Africa (E).

Belgium: Pretoria, South Africa (E).

Canada: Johannesburg, South Africa (HC).

China (Taiwan): P.O.B. 56 (E); *Ambassador:* (vacant).

France: Lusaka, Zambia (E).

Germany, Federal Republic: Limbe, Malawi (E).

India: Blantyre, Malawi (HC).

Iran: Johannesburg, South Africa (E).

Israel: P.O.B. 146 (E); *Chargé d'Affaires:* Pinhas Gonen.

Italy: Pretoria, South Africa (E).

Japan: Lusaka, Zambia (E).

Korea, Republic: Nairobi, Kenya (E).

Netherlands: Pretoria, South Africa (E).

Portugal: Morris St. (E); *Ambassador:* Dr. Antonio Leite Cruz.

Switzerland: Pretoria, South Africa (E).

United Kingdom: Allister Miller St. (HC); *High Commissioner:* Eric Le Tocq.

U.S.A.: Allister Miller St. (E); *Ambassador:* C. J. Nelson.

Zambia: Gaborone, Botswana (HC).

PARLIAMENT*

THE SENATE

Consists of 12 members, 6 appointed by the King and 6 elected by the members of the House of Assembly.

HOUSE OF ASSEMBLY

Consists of 24 elected members, 6 members appointed by the King, and the Attorney-General, who has no vote.

ELECTIONS (May 1972)

	VOTES	SEATS
Imbokodvo National Movement	164,493	21
Ngwane National Liberatory Congress	38,276	3

POLITICAL PARTIES*

Imbokodvo National Movement: P. B. Mbabane; f. 1964; Leader Prince MAKHOSINI DLAMINI.

Ngwane National Liberatory Congress: P.O.B. 326, Mbabane; f. 1962; opposed to white settlers and to the "African Feudalist alliance" which it sees as represented by the Imbokodvo Party; Pres. Dr. AMBROSE P. ZWANE. (The Congress split into two rival factions during 1971, but it is Dr. ZWANE's section which was represented in the House of Assembly. The rival section is led by Mr. SAMKETI).

Swaziland Progressive Party: P.O.B. 6, Mbabane; f. 1929 as Swazi Progressive Association; Pres. J. J. NQUKU.

Swaziland United Front: P.O.B. 14, Kwaluseni; f. 1962; offshoot of Mr. Nquku's party; Leader O. M. MABUZA.

* All political activity is in abeyance following a royal proclamation in April 1973.

DEFENCE

In March 1973 King Sobhuza announced plans for the formation of an army and its present strength is estimated at 600. There are at present some para-military police units.

JUDICIAL SYSTEM

The judiciary is headed by the Chief Justice. There is a High Court (which is a Superior Court of Record) with five subordinate courts in all the administrative districts, and there is a Court of Appeal which sits at Mbabane.

There are 17 Swazi Courts, including two Courts of Appeal and a Higher Court of Appeal, which have limited jurisdiction on civil and criminal cases. They have no jurisdiction over Europeans.

Chief Justice: Mr. Justice RONALD HILL.

RELIGION

About 40 per cent of the adult Swazi hold traditional beliefs. Nearly all the rest of the adult population is Christian.

Council of Churches: P.O.B. 333, Mbabane; Head Dr. DAVID HYND.

Bible House: P.O.B. 550, Manzini; Head Mr. VILAKAZI.

ANGLICAN

CHURCH OF THE PROVINCE OF SOUTH AFRICA

Bishop of Swaziland: Rt. Rev. A. G. W. HUNTER, P.O.B. 118, Mbabane.

ROMAN CATHOLIC

In 1970 there were 33,000 Roman Catholics in Swaziland.

Bishop of Manzini and Swaziland: Rt. Rev. GIROLAMO M. CASALINI, P.O.B. 19, Manzini.

METHODIST

The Methodist Church of South Africa: Mbabane.

PRESS

Times of Swaziland: P.O.B. 28, Mbabane; f. 1897; English; weekly; Editor J. SPICER, M.B.E.; circ. 8,900.

Umbiki (*The Reporter*): Broadcasting House, Morris St., P.O.B. 464, Mbabane; f. 1968; siSwati; fortnightly; Swaziland Government Information Services; circ. 5,000.

RADIO

Swaziland Broadcasting Service: P.O.B. 338, Mbabane; f. 1967; broadcasts in English and siSwati; Broadcasting and Information Officer R. MABILA. Radio listeners also tune in to stations in South Africa and Mozambique.

Number of radio sets (1974): 51,000.

FINANCE

BANKING

The Swaziland Government has negotiated a 40 per cent shareholding in Barclays Bank and the Standard Bank.

Barclays Bank International Ltd.: Head Office, London; 6 brs.; 10 agencies; Chief Office in Swaziland P.O.B. 667, Mbabane; Man. A. G. TUCKER.

Standard Bank Ltd.: Head Office: London; brs. in Mbabane (head office for Swaziland) and Manzini; 12 agencies; Swaziland Man. A. R. CHILTONE-JONES.

Swaziland Development and Savings Bank: formerly Swaziland Credit and Savings Bank, f. 1974; 5 brs.; auth. cap. R5m.; agencies throughout country; Gen. Man. J. D. OWEN, F.C.I.S., A.I.B.

INSURANCE

Swaziland Royal Insurance Company: sole legal insurance company since January 1974, 51 per cent government owned; auth. cap. R500,000.

TRADE AND INDUSTRY

National Industrial Development Corporation of Swaziland (NIDCS): P.O.B. 866, Mbabane; handles investment and business enquiries.

Swaziland Citrus Board: P.O.B. 343, Mbabane; f. 1956 for development of citrus industry.

Swaziland Co-operative Rice Co. Ltd.: handles rice grown in Mbabane and Manzini areas.

Swaziland Tobacco Co-operative Co.: P.O.B. 2, Nhlangano; handles all tobacco crops.

There are 19 registered trade unions.

TRANSPORT

RAILWAY

Construction of a railway line from the iron ore deposits at Bomvu Ridge, near Mbabane, to the border to link with the Portuguese East Africa railway system was completed in 1964, and a spur line to serve Matsapa Industrial Area near Manzini in 1965. The main traffic is iron ore, which is being exported to Japan through Lourenço Marques, and wood pulp and sugar.

Swaziland Railway Board: Mbabane; f. 1963; Chair. D. STEWART.

ROADS

Ministry of Works, Power and Communications: P.O.B. 58, Mbabane; Permanent Sec. J. MAGAGULA; Chief Roads Engineer J. LAWSON, M.B.E., C.ENG., F.I.MUN.E.

Most roads are of gravel surface and 228 km. of tarred trunk roads had been laid by the end of 1972, mostly on a new 179 km. trans-territorial highway which, according to present plans, will be completely tarred by 1975. Good road connections exist with Lourenço Marques, Piet Retief, Carolina, Breyten and Ermelo. There are 1,280 km. of main roads and 1,120 km. of branch roads.

CIVIL AVIATION

The main airport, Matsapa, has a 4,800-ft. runway and can take twin-engined and some four-engined aircraft. Scheduled flights are in operation jointly by South African Airways and Swazi-Air Ltd. from Durban and Johannesburg and by D.E.T.A. from Lourenço Marques. There are about 20 privately owned grass landing strips distributed throughout the country, used by light aircraft.

Swazi-Air Ltd.: P.O.B. 552, Manzini; f. 1965; until 1971 a subsidiary of National Airways Corpn. of South Africa; services to Johannesburg, Durban and neighbouring countries; fleet of one DC-4 and three DC-3; Chair. P. WILHELMI; Gen. Man. T. J. GERAGHTY.

The following airlines operate services to Swaziland: DETA Mozambique, SAA.

UNIVERSITY

The University of Botswana, Lesotho and Swaziland: Swaziland Campus, P.O.B. Luyengo; f. 1964; 36 teachers, 276 students.

SYRIA

INTRODUCTORY SURVEY

Location, Climate, Language, Religion, Flag, Capital

The Syrian Arab Republic lies on the eastern shore of the Mediterranean Sea, with Turkey to the north, Iraq to the east and Jordan to the south. The Lebanon and Israel are to the south-west. Much of the country is mountainous and semi-desert. The coastal climate is hot in summer with mild winters. The inland plateau and plains are hot and dry but cold in winter. Average temperatures in Damascus are 36°F. to 53°F. in January and 64°F. to 99°F. in August. The national language is Arabic, with Kurdish a minority language. More than 80 per cent of the population are Muslims but there is an important Christian minority of various sects. The national flag (proportions 2 by 1) is a horizontal tricolour of red, white and black, the central stripe being charged with three five-pointed green stars. The capital is Damascus.

Recent History

In February 1958 Syria united with Egypt to form the United Arab Republic but following an army *coup d'état* in September 1961 Syria seceded and formed the independent Syrian Arab Republic. After a short period of civil rule a further army *coup* took place in March 1962, followed by a third in March 1963. Further changes of government in 1963 brought the army leader, Major-Gen. Amin al-Hafiz, to the Presidency of the National Revolutionary Council, with a predominantly Baath party cabinet under his own premiership. Since that time the economy has been centralized. The Baath (Arab Nationalist) party is still in power, though divided into factions. In February 1966, after a number of cabinet changes, the army, in a violent *coup d'état* instigated by Baathist extremists, deposed the government of President Hafiz, replacing him by Dr. Nureddin al-Atasi. However, in November 1970, after a bloodless *coup*, the military (moderate) wing of the Baath party seized power, led by Lt.-Gen. Hafiz al-Asad, who was elected President in March 1971. The border tension between Syria and Israel became increasingly severe after March 1962 with a series of armed conflicts and was a major influence leading to the six-day war which broke out on June 5th, 1967. An uneasy peace lasted from June 1967 until October 1973, and all attempts by outside powers to arrange a peace settlement met with failure. War broke out again in October 1973, with fierce fighting in the Golan Heights area, and it was not until the end of May 1974 that the U.S. Secretary of State, Dr. Henry Kissinger, secured an agreement for the disengagement of forces.

Since January 1972 Syria has been joined with Egypt and Libya in the Federation of Arab Republics, although the union has had little practical effect.

Government

Syria has a Republican form of Government with an elected President and a Council of Ministers. In February 1971 a People's Council was formed, the first legislative body since 1966 when the National Assembly was dissolved. In March 1973 a new constitution was adopted.

Defence

Syria has an army, navy and air force. The strength of the army is officially estimated at 120,000, the navy at 2,000 and the air force at 10,000. Para-military forces now number about 9,500 and reserves 203,500. National service is compulsory, and lasts for two and a half years except for persons with special qualifications, who serve for one and a half years. Syria is a member of the Arab League Unified Military Command. The U.S.S.R. is the principal supplier of arms, and the Soviet fleet makes frequent use of the port at Latakia. Defence expenditure for 1973 was £S800 million, 70 per cent of total revenue.

Economic Affairs

More than half of the working population are engaged in agriculture, forestry and fishing. These provided 26 per cent of the gross domestic product in 1972. Wheat and cotton, quantities of which are exported, are the chief crops. Oil has been discovered in the north-east, and oil exports began in 1968. Textiles and food processing are the most important industries. Aleppo and Damascus are thriving commercial centres, and revenue from the transit trade to Iraq, Jordan and the Lebanon, and from the oil pipelines which pass through Syria, help to cover the trade deficit. Many foreign companies and private businesses have been nationalized. The second five-year plan (1966–70) provided for the investment of £S4,995 million to finance the development of transport, communications, power and certain key industries. Of the total investment 67.46 per cent came from local sources and 32.54 per cent from foreign governments, almost all Soviet and East European. The first stage of the Euphrates dam, also financed under the plan, was completed in 1973, with considerable Soviet help. The third five-year plan (1971–75) provides for capital investment of £S7,290 million, mostly allocated to the public sector.

The damage caused by the October 1973 war has been estimated at £S1,200 million, but the economy was recovering during 1974.

Transport and Communications

Railways run between Homs, Hama and Aleppo and to Beirut in the Lebanon and Amman in Jordan. There is a line from Homs to Tripoli in the Lebanon, and lines from Aleppo to Turkey and Iraq. A 200 km. line between Damascus and Homs is being built. There is a network of 6,000 km. of main roads and all the principal towns are connected by road. The chief ports are Banias, the oil terminal, and Latakia. The Iraq Petroleum Company's oil pipeline from Iraq crosses Syria to Banias. The Arabian American Oil Co. pipeline (TAPLINE) from Saudi Arabia crosses Syria to Sidon in the Lebanon. International services to Damascus and Aleppo are provided by Syrian Airways and major foreign companies.

Social Welfare

State hospitals provide free medical care for persons unable to afford private medical attention. Over 30 government and 50 private hospitals are in existence. Old age pensions, and other benefits, are provided by law.

Education

The government aims to provide sufficient schools to ensure universal primary education. More than 850,000 children receive primary education and over 270,000 secondary education. There are universities at Damascus and Aleppo.

Tourism

Syria's tourist attractions include an attractive Mediterranean coastline, the mountains, the town bazaars and the antiquities of Damascus and Palmyra.

Visas are not required to visit Syria by nationals of the following countries: Arab League states, Chad, Cyprus, Mauritania, Somalia and the U.S.S.R.

Sport

The principal sports are football, basketball, volleyball, tennis and swimming.

Public Holidays

1974: October 18th* (Id ul Fitr), December 25th (Christmas Day), December 26th* (Id ul Adha).

1975: January 1st (New Year's Day), January 14th* (Muslim New Year), February 22nd (Unity Day), March 8th (National Day), March 31st (Easter), April 17th (Evacuation Day).

* Muslim religious holidays which may vary slightly from the dates given, depending on sightings of the moon.

Weights and Measures

The metric system is in force.

Currency and Exchange Rates

100 piastres = 1 Syrian pound (£S).

Exchange rates (April 1974):
£1 sterling = £S8.678;
U.S. $1 = £S3.675.

STATISTICAL SURVEY

AREA AND POPULATION

Total Area	Arable Land	Pastures	Forest	Population*
185,180 sq. km.	87,240 sq. km.	54,340 sq. km.	4,400 sq. km.	6,879,000

* July 1st, 1973.

	Births	Marriages	Deaths
1969 . .	181,925*	56,268	26,327
1970 . .	191,728	82,222	29,783
1971 . .	207,564	50,495	29,014

* The drop in 1969 is due to an increase in the number of non-registered births.

CHIEF TOWNS
(1970)

Damascus (capital) .	836,000	Latakia . . . 126,000
Aleppo . . .	639,000	Deit-ez-Zor . . 66,000
Homs . . .	216,000	Hasakeh . . . 32,000
Hama . . .	137,000	

AGRICULTURE
AREA AND PRODUCTION OF PRINCIPAL CROPS

	1970		1971	
	Hectares	Metric tons	Hectares	Metric tons
Wheat . . .	1,341,000	625,000	1,274,000	662,000
Barley . . .	1,126,000	235,000	435,000	123,000
Maize . . .	5,600	7,900	6,500	8,500
Millet . . .	25,800	13,500	25,300	19,400
Lentils . . .	139,600	57,500	111,500	61,3c0
Cotton . . .	249,300	382,600	250,400	407,900
Tobacco . . .	10,200	6,700	12,983	7,500
Sesame . . .	6,200	2,700	10,000	4,300
Grapes . . .	66,000	206,000	67,000	209,000
Olives . . .	124,000	85,000	125,000	117,000
Figs . . .	23,000	44,000	20,000	55,000
Apricots . . .	10,000	22,000	10,000	31,000
Apples . . .	7,000	17,700	8,000	34,200
Sugar Beet . .	9,000	227,500	8,600	232,200
Pomegranates . .	2,900	16,400	3,300	24,5c0
Onions . . .	6,100	65,300	7,300	90,400
Tomatoes . . .	16,400	192,400	20,200	248,400
Potatoes . . .	5,900	65,300	5,900	72,500

LIVESTOCK
('ooo head)

	1969	1970	1971
Cattle .	363	385	368
Horses . .	64	68	66
Camels . .	6	3.9	8.6
Asses .	243	235	244
Sheep .	5,963	6,112	5,230
Goats .	770	771	701
Hens and Chickens .	3,585	3,669	4,785

DAIRY PRODUCE

		1969	1970	1971
Milk .	'ooo tons	524	451	441
Cheese .	tons	27,418	24,355	27,758
Butter .	,,	1,819	1,827	2,045
Honey .	,,	257	202	279
Ghee .	,,	10,097	7,197	5,530
Eggs .	'ooo	354,338	274,119	301,801

INDUSTRY

		1970	1971	1972
Cotton Yarn	'ooo tons	20.0	23.4	27.9
Silk and Cotton Textiles . .	,, ,,	27.0	29.1	29.7
Woollen Fabrics . .	million metres	6.1	5.7	n.a.
Cement	'ooo tons	964.0	910.0	1,004.0
Natural Asphalt . .	,, ,,	23.6	24.6	21.0
Glass	,, ,,	15.9	15.2	15.8
Soap	,, ,,	21.2	23.3	25.9
Sugar	,, ,,	123.7	130.4	137.2
Salt	,, ,,	46.3	13.5	49.5
Edible Oils . . .	,, ,,	25.1	26.2	27.4
Manufactured Tobacco . .	,, ,,	4.2	4.4	4.7
Electricity . . .	million kWh.	946.9	1,049.0	1,223.0
Beer	'ooo litres	3,047.8	3,470.0	3,784.8
Wine	,, ,,	235.0	269.6	n.a.
Arak	,, ,,	548.0	654.3	n.a.

FINANCE

100 piastres = 1 Syrian pound (£S).

Coins: 2½, 5, 10, 25 and 50 piastres; 1 pound.

Notes: 1, 5, 10, 25 50, 100 and 500 pounds.

Exchange rates (April 1974): £1 sterling = £S8.678; U.S. $1 = £S3.675.

£S100 = £11.52 sterling = $27.21.

ORDINARY BUDGET*
(£S million)

	1969	1970	1971
National Defence	661.6	671.6	675.5
Cultural and Social Affairs . . .	251.2	285.2	318.5
Communications and Public Works .	32.3	48.1	29.0
Economic Affairs and Planning .	137.4	250.7	265.0
Administrative Affairs	116.5	128.9	107.0
TOTAL	1,199.0	1,384.5	1,395.0

* The Syrian budget is published at the end of the year in question.

CONSOLIDATED BUDGET
(£S million)

A new consolidated budget has been issued incorporating
both ordinary and development budgets

	1970	1971	1972
Justice and Public Authorities . .	45.2	62.9	71.6
National Security	679.3	690.6	795.0
Culture and Information . .	293.4	324.5	364.3
Social Welfare	59.3	71.0	84.1
Economy and Finance . . .	276.2	304.7	282.2
Agriculture and Land Reclamation . .	554.5	523.2	536.5
Industry and Mining	443.6	517.4	500.3
Public Works, Utilities and Communications	371.6	343.0	473.7
Other Expenditure and Revenue . .	56.9	48.2	80.3
TOTAL	2,780.0	2,886.2	3,188.0

The 1973 budget totalled £S3,413 million.

THIRD FIVE-YEAR PLAN
(1971–75—£S million)

	INVESTMENT (Public Sector)	%
Euphrates Dam Project .	1,593.0	24.7
Irrigation and Land Improvement . . .	211.7	3.3
Agriculture . . .	436.1	6.8
Industry . . .	1,173.0	18.2
Power and Fuel . . .	1,013.8	15.7
Transport and Communications . . .	783.0	12.1
Towns and Buildings .	585.9	9.1
Public Services . .	525.8	8.2
Local Trade . . .	124.7	1.9
TOTAL . . .	6,447.0	100.0

OIL

FLOW OF OIL ACROSS SYRIA
('000 long tons)

	TOTAL	To BANIAS	To SIDON (Lebanon)	To TRIPOLI (Lebanon)
1968 . .	73,389	29,533	23,543	20,313
1969 . .	68,351	29,875	16,138	22,338
1970 . .	60,679	29,977	8,036	22,666
1971 . .	64,544	27,712	16,407	20,425
1972 . .	50,477	22,213	21,053	7,193

EXTERNAL TRADE
(£S '000)

	1967	1968	1969	1970	1971	1972
Imports . . .	1,009,091	1,193,635	1,411,324	1,374,637	1,677,038	2,060,648
Exports . . .	591,271	673,978	789,918	775,343	743,353	1,097,601

COMMODITIES (£S million)

IMPORTS	1969	1970	1971	1972
Cotton textiles, other textile goods and silk . .	158.9	120.6	112.2	202.3
Mineral fuels and oils	144.9	106.9	102.3	91.4
Lime, cement and salt	16.6	8.5	27.6	28.0
Cereals	28.5	146.0	231.7	96.8
Vegetables and fruit	50.8	60.1	81.3	81.0
Oilseeds and medical plants . . .	7.4	4.7	6.0	8.3
Machinery, apparatus and electrical materials .	226.3	174.1	222.2	374.8
Precious metals and coins	7.3	3.4	3.5	2.7
Base metals and manufactures . . .	212.7	207.7	201.2	308.1
Vehicles	104.1	57.5	50.1	65.0
Chemical and pharmaceutical products . .	64.5	73.3	74.5	112.0
Preserved foods, beverages and tobacco .	49.1	69.7	141.1	169.0
Other products	340.2	342.1	423.3	521.2

EXPORTS	1969	1970	1971	1972
Cotton (raw, yarn, textiles)	325.9	332.1	} 412.1	536.2
Other textile goods	58.3	57.2		
Cereals	39.8	22.2	0.1	94.9
Vegetables and fruit	46.0	24.1	39.1	51.2
Precious metals	0.8	0.6	0.5	0.3
Preserved foods, beverages and tobacco .	44.8	47.2	35.8	63.4
Live animals	99.6	70.8	25.2	60.0
Dairy products	4.0	2.7	0.9	2.1
Other Products	170.7	218.4	229.6	289.5

Oil Exports: (1971) £S176 million; (1972) £S200 million.

COUNTRIES (£S million)

IMPORTS	1969	1970	1971	1972
Belgium	26.2	25.0	31.1	50.3
Cuba	20.1	33.9	52.3	86.4
France	93.7	64.3	99.0	119.6
Germany, Federal Republic	99.4	93.7	107.7	160.0
Iraq	88.1	88.7	101.6	83.7
Italy	123.1	89.5	116.4	166.3
Japan	59.6	80.2	72.9	130.8
Lebanon	72.1	86.5	143.5	138.4
Netherlands	28.4	24.4	42.5	48.1
U.S.S.R.	125.9	105.7	104.9	154.3
United Kingdom	64.9	54.2	55.5	99.0
U.S.A.	50.9	47.2	112.1	92.4

EXPORTS	1969	1970	1971	1972
China	43.7	60.6	24.2	70.3
Czechoslovakia	11.4	11.5	9.2	24.7
France	26.4	39.7	29.0	35.7
Germany, Federal Republic	7.6	17.3	29.3	33.3
Italy	96.6	167.0	208.8	116.7
Japan	11.3	54.3	20.9	16.3
Jordan	41.7	29.1	15.0	18.5
Kuwait	21.3	13.5	9.0	13.9
Lebanon	112.2	89.2	55.8	150.5
Romania	22.0	4.9	4.5	7.6
Saudi Arabia	12.4	4.3	14.7	24.6
U.S.S.R.	136.0	67.6	112.4	221.3
United Kingdom	8.9	3.4	3.3	22.0
U.S.A.	5.1	2.9	5.8	7.5

TRANSPORT

RAILWAYS

	1970	1971
Passenger-km. . .	86,459	83,735
Freight, '000 tons .	1,406	1,136

ROADS

	1970	1971
Passenger Cars . .	30,592	31,476
Buses . . .	1,760	1,639
Lorries, Trucks, etc. .	17,793	17,598
Motor-cycles .	8,122	8,580

SHIPPING
PORT OF LATAKIA

	1968	1969	1970	1971
Number of steam vessels entering harbour . .	1,527	1,697	1,642	1,629
Number of sailing vessels entering harbour . .	206	216	258	134
Cargo unloaded ('000 tons) . . .	1,612	1,597	1,847	1,717
Cargo loaded ('000 tons) . . .	364	526	478	264

CIVIL AVIATION
(Damascus Airport)

	1969		1970		1971	
	ARRIVE	DEPART	ARRIVE	DEPART	ARRIVE	DEPART
Aircraft	3,640	3,644	4,640	4,639	5,282	5,284
Passengers	124,607	123,662	118,726	116,240	139,598	139,633

TOURISM

	JORDANIANS AND LEBANESE	TOTAL VISITORS
1967	576,794	864,600
1968	471,348	772,452
1969	524,596	797,272
1970	504,692	870,276
1971	943,011	1,322,862

Tourist Accommodation: 19,952 tourist hotel beds (1969).

EDUCATION
(1970–71)

	PUPILS		TEACHERS	
	Public	Private	Public	Private
Pre-School . .	—	26,438	—	723
Primary . .	868,957	32,842*	23,298	1,216
Preparatory .	211,928	15,185*	} 12,226	897
Secondary .	71,511	7,983		
Vocational .	10,089	42	1,124	3
Teacher Training .	2,424	—	250	—
Universities .	38,734	—	1,123	—

* Excluding UNRWA schools.

Source: Statistical Yearbook of Damascus and Aleppo Universities.

Source: Central Bureau of Statistics, Office of the Prime Minister, Damascus.

THE CONSTITUTION

A new and permanent constitution was endorsed by 97.6 per cent of the voters in a national referendum on March 12th, 1973. The 157-article constitution defines Syria as a "Socialist popular democracy" with a "pre-planned Socialist economy". Under the new constitution, Lt.-Gen. al-Asad remains President, with the power to appoint and dismiss his Vice-President, Premier and Government Ministers, and also becomes Commander-in-Chief of the armed forces, secretary-general of the Baath Socialist Party and President of the National Progressive Front. This is the country's first permanent constitution since 1961, when Syria ended its union with Egypt. The provisional constitution introduced in 1969 was never formally promulgated.

THE GOVERNMENT

HEAD OF STATE

President: Lt.-Gen. HAFIZ AL-ASAD (elected March 12th, 1971, for a seven-year term).
Vice-President: MAHMOUD AL-AYOUBI.

CABINET

(January 1974)

(B) Baath, (SU) Socialist Union, (ASU) Arab Socialist Union.

Prime Minister: MAHMOUD AL-AYOUBI (B).

Deputy Prime Minister and Minister of Foreign Affairs: ABDEL HALIM KHADDAM (B).

Deputy Prime Minister and Minister of the Economy and External Trade: MOHAMMED HAIDAR (Independent).

Minister of Agriculture: AHMED HASSAN AL ASSAD (B).

Minister of Municipal and Rural Affairs: ABDEL RAZZAK ABDEL BAKI (SU).

Minister of Justice: ADIB AL-NAHAWI (ASU).

Minister for the Euphrates Dam: MUNIR WANNOUS (B).

Minister of Education: Dr. SHAKER AL-FAHAM (B).

Minister of Defence: Maj.-Gen. MUSTAFA TLAS (B).

Minister of Health: Dr. MADANI AL KHYAMI (Independent).

Minister of Information: GEORGE SADIKNI (B).

Minister of the Interior: Brig. ALI ZAZA (B).

Minister of Supply and Internal Trade: MOHAMED QABALAN.

Minister of Public Works and Water Resources: ABDLE-GHANI KANNOUT (ASU).

Minister of Higher Education: Dr. MOHAMED ALI HASHEM (B).

Minister of Petroleum, Electricity and Mineral Resources: JABER AL KAFRY (B).

Minister of Finance: NOURALLAH NOURALLAH (Independent).

Minister of Culture and National Guidance: FAWZI KAYYALI (ASU).

Minister of Labour and Social Affairs: HUSSEIN AHMED KOUEIDER (B).

Minister of Local Administration: ADIB MELHEM (B).

Minister of Industry: SHTEWI SEIFO (B).

Minister of Religious Affairs: Sheikh ABDEL SATTAR AL-SAYED (Independent).

Minister of Communications: Ing. OMAR SIBAI (Communist).

Minister of Tourism: ABDALLAH AL KHANI (Independent).

Minister of State for Village Affairs at the Front: MOUAYEN JAZZAN (B).

Minister of Planning: MOUSTAPHA HALLAJE (SU).

Minister of State for the Premiership: FAYEZ NASIR (B).

Ministers of State: ZOUHAIR ABDEL SAMAD (Communist), ANWAR HAMADEH (ASU).

DIPLOMATIC REPRESENTATION

EMBASSIES ACCREDITED TO SYRIA

(In Damascus unless otherwise stated)

(E) Embassy

Algeria: Rue Nouri Pacha (E); *Ambassador:* ALARABI SAADOUNI.

Argentina: Raouda, Rue Ziad ben Abi Soufian, Imm. Ab Kérim Abul (E); *Ambassador:* ENRIQUE LUPIZ.

Austria: Beirut, Lebanon (E).

Belgium: Rue Ata Ayoubi, Imm. Hachem (E); *Ambassador:* LUC SMOLDEREN.

Brazil: 76 Rue Ata Ayoubi (E); *Ambassador:* ROBERTO DE ARAÚJO.

Bulgaria: 4 Rue Chahbandar (E); *Ambassador:* METODI POPOV.

Canada: Rue Clemenceau, Imm. Alpha (E); *Ambassador:* JACQUES GIGNAC.

Chad: (E); *Ambassador:* MARON HAYMARI.

Chile: Beirut, Lebanon (E); *Ambassador:* GUILLERMO OVALLE.

China, People's Republic: Avenue Al Jala'a (E); *Ambassador:* CHIN CHIA-LIN.

Cuba: 81 Avenue Al Jala'a (E); *Ambassador:* CARLOS ALVAREZ VARELA.

Czechoslovakia: Place Aboul-Alaa (E); *Ambassador:* MIROSLAV POKORNY.

Denmark: Beirut, Lebanon (E); *Ambassador:* MOGENS WARBERG.

Egypt: Rue Misr, Imm. Malki (E); *Ambassador:* MAMDOUH GOBBA.

France: Rue Ata Ayoubi (E); *Ambassador:* ANDRÉ NÈGRE.

German Democratic Republic: 60 Avenue Adran el Malki (E); *Ambassador:* WOLFGANG KONSCHEL.

Greece: 57 Rue Ata Ayoubi (E); *Ambassador:* JEAN TSAOUSSI.

Hungary: 13 Rue Ibrahim Hanano (Imm. Roujoulé) (E), *Ambassador:* JÁNOS VERES.

India: 40/46 Avenue Al Malki (E); *Ambassador:* PRANAB KUMAR GUHA.

Indonesia: 19 Rue Al-Amir Ezzeddine (E); *Ambassador:* BAHRUDDIN UBANI.

Iran: Avenue Al-Jala'a, Imm. Wazzan (E); *Ambassador:* ARDACHIR NOURAZAR.

Iraq: Avenue Al Jala'a (Imm. Coudsi) (E); *Ambassador:* AUDA AHMED AL-BAYATI.

Italy: 82 Avenue Al Mansour (E); *Ambassador:* UBERTO BOZZINI.

Japan: 62 Rue Rawdak (E); *Ambassador:* SHIGETO NIKAI.

Korea, Democratic People's Republic: 89 Avenue Al Jala'a (E); *Ambassador:* HAN SU IK.

Kuwait: Rue Ibrahim Hanano (E); *Ambassador:* AHMED HUSSEIN.

Libya: Place Al Malki, 10 Avenue Mansour (E); *Ambassador:* MUHAMMAD RAMADAN MAHMOUD.

Mauritania: (address not available) (E); *Ambassador:* ABDALLAHI OULD EREBIH.

Morocco: Abou Roumaneh (E); *Ambassador:* IDRIS BENOUNA.

Netherlands: Rue Ziad Ben Abi Soufian (E); *Ambassador:* ANDRÉ M. E. BRINK.

Pakistan: Avenue Al Jala'a (E); *Ambassador:* MUHAMMAD SALIMALLA.

Poland: Rue Georges Haddad, Imm. Chahine (E); *Ambassador:* LONGIN ARABSKI.

Romania: (address not available) (E); *Ambassador:* EMILIAN MANIER.

Saudi Arabia: Avenue Al Jala'a (E); *Ambassador:* MUHAMMAD ABDULLA AL-MUTLAQ.

Spain: 14 Rue Misr (E); *Ambassador:* NUNO AGUIRE DE CARCER.

Sudan: Rue Hanano (E); *Ambassador:* HASSAN EL HASSAN.

Sweden: Damascus (E); *Ambassador:* AAKE JONSSON.

Switzerland: 12 Rue Georges Haddad (E); *Ambassador:* ALBERT DUBOIS.

Tunisia: (to be appointed).

Turkey: 58 Avenue Ziad Bin Abou Soufian (E); *Ambassador:* FAHIR ALACAM.

U.S.S.R.: Boustan El-Kouzbari, Rue d'Alep (E); *Ambassador:* NOUREDDIN MOHIEDDINOV.

United Arab Emirates: (address not available) (E); *Ambassador:* MUHAMMAD ABDER-RAHMAN AL-BAKR.

United Kingdom: *Ambassador:* DAVID ARTHUR ROBERTS.

Uruguay: (address not available) (E); *Ambassador:* RODOLFO COMAS-ARMARO.

Vatican: Rue Nasr (*Apostolic Nunciature*): RAPHAEL FORNI.

Venezuela: Abou Roomaneh, Rue Nouri Pacha (E); *Chargé d'Affaires:* J. QUINTANA.

Viet-Nam, Democratic Republic: (E); *Ambassador:* HOANG DUC PHONG.

Yemen Arab Republic: Avenue Al Jala'a (E); *Ambassador:* YAHYA MUDWAHI.

Yugoslavia: Avenue A. Jala'a (E); *Ambassador:* VOJISLAV PEKIC.

Syria also has diplomatic relations with Colombia, Cyprus, Finland, Guyana, Jordan and the U.S.A.

PEOPLE'S COUNCIL

A new People's Council was elected in May 1973 under the terms of the new Constitution. 140 out of the 186 seats were won by the Progressive Front, a grouping of the parties listed below, 42 seats were won by Independents, and the remainder by the Opposition.

Chairman: MUHAMMAD AL-HALABI.

POLITICAL PARTIES

The National Progressive Front, headed by President Asad, was formed in March 1972 by the grouping of the five parties listed below;

Arab Socialist Renaissance (Baath) Party: Arab socialist party; in power since 1963; supports militant Arab unity; Sec.-Gen. Pres. HAFIZ AL-ASAD.

Syrian Arab Socialist Union: Nasserite; Leader Dr. JAMAL ATASI; Sec.-Gen. FAUZI KAYYALI.

Socialist Union: Leader SAMI SOUFAN.

Arab Socialist Party: a breakaway socialist party; Leader ABDEL GHANI KANNOUT.

Communist Party of Syria: Sec.-Gen. KHALID BAGDASH.

JUDICIAL SYSTEM

Court of Cassation: Damascus; is the highest court of appeal.

Courts of Appeal: 13 Courts of Appeal in the 13 Prefectures try all criminal cases subject to appeal, as well as all other cases within their competence by virtue of the law in force; some of them are composed of several chambers; decisions are given by three judges, one of them being the President.

Summary Courts: 110 Summary Courts try civil, commercial and penal cases within their competence; a Summary Court is constituted by one judge known as a "Judge of the Peace".

First Instance Courts: 14 First Instance Courts, constituted by one judge, deal with all cases other than those within the competence of special tribunals. In some Prefectures are several Chambers.

Chief Justice of Syria: Ibrahim Al Faraji.

PERSONAL STATUS COURTS

For Muslims: each court consists of one judge, the "Qadi Shari'i", who deals with marriage, divorce, etc.

For Druzes: one court consisting of one judge, the "Qadi Mazhabi".

For non-Muslim Communities: for Catholics, Orthodox, Protestants, Jews.

OTHER COURTS

Courts for Minors: their constitution, officers, sessions, jurisdiction and competence are determined by a special law.

Military Court: Damascus.

RELIGION

In religion the majority of Syrians follow a form of Sunni orthodoxy. There is also a considerable number of religious minorities: Muslim Shi'ites; the Ismaili of the Salamiya district, whose spiritual head is the Aga Khan; a large number of Druzes, the Nusairis or Alawites of the Jebel Ansariyeh and the Yezidis of the Jebel Sinjar.

MUSLIMS

Grand Mufti: Ahmad Kuftaro.

Most Syrians are Muslims. Nearly all are Sunnites with a small number of Ismailis and Shi'ites.

CHRISTIANS

Greek Orthodox Patriarch: Elias IV.

Greek Catholic Patriarch: H.E. Maximos V. Hakim; Bab-Sharki, Damascus; P.O.B. 7181, Beirut, Lebanon.

Syrian Orthodox Patriarch: His Holiness Ignatius Yacob III.

THE PRESS

Since the coming to power of the Baath Arab Socialist Party the structure of the press has been modified according to socialist patterns. Most publications are published by organizations such as political, religious, or professional associations, trade unions, etc. and several are published by government ministries. Anyone wishing to establish a new paper or periodical must apply for a licence.

The major dailies are *al-Baath* (the organ of the party) and *al-Thawrah* in Damascus, *al-Jamahir al-Arabia* in Aleppo, and *al-Fida* in Hama.

PRINCIPAL DAILIES

Aravelk: Aleppo; Armenian; morning; Editor Dr. A. Angykian; circ. 3,500.

al-Baath (*Renaissance*): rue el Barazil, Damascus; Arabic; morning; organ of the Baath Arab Socialist Party; circ. 20,000.

Barq al-Shimal: rue Aziziyah, Aleppo; Arabic; morning; Editor Maurice Djandji; circ. 6,400.

al-Fida: rue Kuwatly, Hama; political; Arabic; morning, Publishing concession holder Osman Alouini; Editor A. Aulwani; circ. 4,000.

al-Jamahir al-Arabia: El Ouedha Printing and Publishing Organization, Aleppo; political; Arabic; Chief Editor Mortada Bakach; circ. 10,000.

al-Shabab: rue al Tawil, Aleppo; Arabic; morning; Editor Muhammad Talas; circ. 9,000.

al-Thawrah: El Ouedha Printing and Publishing Organization, Damascus; political; Arabic; morning; circ. 20,000.

WEEKLIES AND FORTNIGHTLIES

al-Ajoua: Compagnie de l'Aviation Arabe Syrienne, Damascus; aviation; Arabic; fortnightly; Editor Ahmad Allouche.

Arab Press Digest: Syrian Documentation Papers, P.O.B. 2712, Damascus.

al-Esbou al-Riadi: ave. Firdoisse, Tibi Bldg., Damascus; sports; weekly; Publisher Mounir Bakir; Dir. and Editor Kamel El Bounni.

Hadarat al-Islam: B.P. 808, Jadet Halbouni, Jadet El Raby, Damascus; religious; Arabic; fortnightly; Publisher Moustapha Essibai; Dir. Ahmad Farhat; Editor Muhammad Adib Saleh.

Homs: Homs; literary; Arabic; weekly; Publisher and Dir. Adib Kaba; Editor Philippe Kaba.

Jaysh al-Shaab: P.O.B. 3320, blvd. Palestine, Damascus; f. 1946; army magazine, Arabic; weekly; published by the Political Department.

Kifah al-Oummal al-Ishtiraki: Fédération Générale des Syndicats des Ouvriers, Damascus; labour; Arabic; weekly; Published by General Federation of Trade Unions; Editor Said El Hamami.

al-Majalla al-Batriarquia: B.P. 914, Syrian Orthodox Patriarchate, Damascus; f. 1962; religious; Arabic; monthly; Dir. and Editor Samir Abdoh; circ. 3,000.

al-Maukef al-Riadi: El Ouehda Organization, Damascus; sports; Arabic; weekly; Published by El Ouehda Printing and Publishing Organization; circ. 5,000.

al-Nass: B.P. 926, Aleppo; f. 1953; Arabic; weekly; Publisher Victor Kalous.

Nidal al-Fellahin: Fédération Générale des Laboureurs, Damascus; peasant workers; Arabic; weekly; Published by General Federation of Workers; Editor Mansour Abu El Hosn.

Revue de la Presse Arabe: 67 Place Chahbandar, Damascus; French; twice weekly.

al-Riada: B.P. 292, near Electricity Institute, Damascus; sports; Arabic; weekly; Dir. Noureddine Rial; Publisher and Editor Ourfane Ubari.

al-Sakafe al-Isboui: B.P. 2570, Soukak El Sakr, Damascus; cultural; Arabic; weekly; Publisher, Dir. and Editor Madhat Akkache.

al-Talia (*Vanguard*): B.P. 3031, the National Guard, Damascus; Arabic; fortnightly; Editor Sohdi Khalil.

al-Tamaddon al-Islami: Darwichillé, Damascus; religious; Arabic; fortnightly; Published by Tamaddon al-Islami Association; Dir. Muhammad El Khatib; Editor Ahmad Mazar El Adme.

al-Thawrah al-Ziraia (*Agricultural Revolution Review*): Ministry of Agrarian Reform, Damascus; f. 1965; agriculture; Arabic; monthly; circ. 7,000.

al-Yanbu al-Jadid: al-Awkaf Bldg., Homs; literary; Arabic; weekly; Publisher, Dir. and Editor Mamdou El Kousseir.

MONTHLIES

al-Dad: rue El Tital, Wakf El Moiriné Bldg., Aleppo; literary; Arabic; Dir. Riad Hallak; Publisher and Editor Abdallah Yarki Hallak.

Ecos: P.O.B. 3320, Damascus; monthly review; Spanish.

Flash: P.O.B. 3320, Damascus; monthly review; English and French.

al-Irshad al-Zirai: Ministry of Agriculture, Damascus; agriculture; every two months.

al-Kalima: Al-Kalima Association, Aleppo; religious; Arabic; Publisher and Editor FATHALLA SAKAL.

al-Kanoun: Ministry of Justice, Damascus; juridical; Arabic.

al-Maarifa: Ministry of Culture and National Guidance, Damascus; f. 1962; literary; Arabic; Editor MOHIDDEEN SOBHIJ.

al-Majalla al-Askaria: P.O.B. 3320, blvd. Palestine, Damascus; f. 1950; official military magazine; Editor NAKHLI KALLAS.

al-Majalla al-Toubilla al-Arabilla: Al-Jalla's St., Damascus; Published by Arab Medical Commission; Dir. Dr. SHAMSEDDIN EL JUNDI; Editor Dr. ADNAN TAKRITI.

al-Majma al Ilmi al-Arabi: The Arab Academy, Bab el Barid, Damascus; f. 1921; Islamic culture and Arabic literature (three a year).

Monthly Survey of Arab Economics: B.P. 2306, Damascus and B.P. 6068, Beirut; f. 1958; English and French editions; published Centre d'Etudes et de Documentation Economiques, Financières et Sociales; Dir. Dr. CHAFIC AKHRAS.

al-Mouallem al-Arabi (*The Arab Teacher*): Ministry of Education; Damascus; f. 1948; educational and cultural; Arabic.

al-Mouhandis al-Arabi: 8 Parliament St., Damascus; published by Union of Asscns. of Syrian Engineers; engineering, scientific and cultural; Dir. SAMIH FAKHOURY; Editor KASSEM SHAWAF.

al-Moujtama al-Arabi al-Ishtiraki: Ministry of Social Affairs, Damascus; social security; Arabic; Editor SAMI ATFE.

al-Oumran: Ministry of Municipal and Rural Affairs, Damascus; fine arts; Arabic.

Rissalat al-Kimia: B.P. 669, El Abid Bldg., Damascus; scientific; Arabic; Publisher, Dir. and Editor HASSAN EL SAKA.

Saut al-Forat: Deir-Ezzor; literary; Arabic; Publisher, Dir. and Editor ABDEL KADER AYACH.

al-Shourta: Directorate of Public Affairs and Moral Guidance, Damascus; juridical; Arabic.

Souriya al-Arabilla: Ministry of Information, Damascus; publicity; in four languages.

Syrie et le Monde Arabe: P.O.B. 3550, Place Chahbandar, Damascus; economic and political review.

al-Yakza: Sisi St., Al Yazka Association, Aleppo; f. 1935; Dir. and Editor PAUL GENADRI.

QUARTERLY

Les Archives Litteraires du Moyen Orient: Syrian Documentation Papers, P.O.B. 2712, Damascus.

ANNUALS

Bibliography of the Middle East: Syrian Documentation Papers, P.O.B. 2712, Damascus.

General Directory of the Press and Periodicals in the Arab World: Syrian Documentation Papers, P.O.B. 2712, Damascus.

PRESS AGENCIES

Agence Arabe Syrienne d'Information: Damascus; f. 1966; supplies bulletins on Syrian news to foreign news agencies.

FOREIGN BUREAUX

ANSA: P.O.B. 827, rue Salhié, Immeuble Tibi-Selo; f. 1962; Chief KHALIL NABKI.

UPI: 3 Argentine St., Hafez Bldg.; Chief ADNAN INAYEH. DPA, Reuter and Tass also have bureaux in Damascus.

PUBLISHERS

Arab Advertising Organization: 28 Moutanabbi St., P.O.B. 2842 and 3034, Damascus; f. 1963; publishes Directory of Commerce and Industry, Damascus International Fair Guide and Daily Bulletin of Official Tenders; Dir.-Gen. GEORGE KHOURY.

Bureau des documentations syriennes et arabes: B.P. 451, 67 place Chahbander, Damascus; f. 1948; affiliated with the *Office arabe de presse et de documentation* (see below) in 1966, Dir.-Gen. SAMIR A. DARWICH, publs. include *Répertoire Permanent des Lois et Réglements Syriens, Tarif Permanent des Douanes de Syrie, Recueil des Accords Internationaux conclus par la Syrie* and monographs, legislative texts and other documents concerning Syria and the Arab world.

Damascus University Press: Damascus; art, geography, education, history, engineering, medicine, law, sociology, school books.

Office Arabe de Presse et de Documentation: P.O.B. 3550, Damascus; f. 1964; numerous periodical books and surveys on political and economic affairs; Dir.-Gen. SAMIR A. DARWICH.

al-Ouedha Printing and Publishing Organization (*Institut al-Ouedha pour l'impression, édition et distribution*): Damascus and Aleppo; published *al-Jamahir al-Duroubah* and *al-Thawrah* (dailies) and *al-Maukef al-Riadi* (weekly).

Syrian Documentation Papers: P.O.B. 2712, Damascus; f. 1968; publishers of *Bibliography of the Middle East* (annual), *General Directory of the Press and Periodicals in the Arab World* (annual), *Les Archives Littéraires du Moyen Orient* (quarterly), *Arab Press Digest* (weekly), and numerous publications on political, economic and social affairs and literature and legislative texts concerning Syria and the Arab world; Dir.-Gen. LOUIS FARÉS.

al-Tawjih Press: P.O.B. 3320, Palestine St., Damascus.

Other publishers include: *Dar El-Yakaza El-Arabia, Dar El-Hahda El-Arabia, Dar El-Filez, Dar El-Fatah, Dubed, El-Mouassassa El-Sakafieh.*

RADIO AND TELEVISION

General Directorate of Broadcasting and Television: Omayyad Square, Damascus; f. 1945; Gen. Dir. KHODR AL SHA'AR; Dirs. AHMAD AYASS, BACHAR AKHRASS, GEORGE BOULAD; publ. *Here is Damascus* (fortnightly).

RADIO

Broadcasts in Arabic, French, English, Russian, German, Spanish, Polish, Turkish, Bulgarian.

There were 851,000 receivers in use at the end of 1973.

TELEVISION

Services started in 1960.

There were 178,700 receivers in use at the end of 1973.

FINANCE

BANKING

(cap. = capital; p.u. = paid up; dep. = deposits; m. = millions; amounts in £S)

CENTRAL BANK

Central Bank of Syria: 29 Ayar Square, Damascus; f. 1956; cap. 10m.; Gov. NASSOUH DACACK; Deputy Gov. Dr. MUHAMMAD AL ATRASH; Sec.-Gen. Dr. HICHAM KHATIB; 7 brs.

OTHER BANKS

Agricultural Bank: Baghdad St., Damascus; f. 1924; Dir.-Gen. Dr. HANNA KHOURY.

Commercial Bank of Syria S.A.: P.O.B. 933, Moawia St., Damascus; f. 1967; 20 brs.; cap. 50m.; total resources 1,932m. (1973); Pres. and Gen. Man. Dr. DIB ABU ASSALI.

Industrial Bank: Damascus; f. 1959; nationalized bank providing finance for industry; cap. 12.5m., dep. 53.4m., total investments (Feb. 1971) 106.8m.; brs. in Aleppo and Homs; Chair. and Gen. Man. Dr. A. S. KANAAN.

Popular Credit Bank: Darwishieh, Harika, P.O.B. 2841, Damascus; f. 1967; governmental bank; cap. 3m., dep. 95m. (Dec. 1973).

Real Estate Bank: Damascus; f. 1966; cap. 25m.

INSURANCE

Société d'Assurances Syrienne: Taghiz St., Damascus; f. 1953; operates throughout Syria, with branches in Jordan and Lebanon; Chair. and Gen. Man. Dr. AZIZ SAKR.

TRADE AND INDUSTRY

CHAMBERS OF COMMERCE

Damascus Chamber of Commerce: B.P. 1040, Mou'awiah St., Damascus; f. 1914; 3,800 mems.; Pres. BADRED-DINE SHALLAH; Gen. Dir. MUHAMMAD THABET Gh. MAHAYNI; publ. *Economic Bulletin* (quarterly).

Aleppo Chamber of Commerce: Al-Moutanabbi Str., Aleppo; f. 1885; Pres. KASSEM NOUR-EL-DINE; Dir. FADEL ANIS.

Hama Chamber of Commerce and Industry: Sh. Bachoura, Hama; f. 1934; Pres. ABDUL-HAMID KAMBAZ.

Homs Chamber of Commerce: Sh. Aboul-Of, Homs; Pres. ABDUL HASIB RUSLAN.

Latakia Chamber of Commerce: Sh. Al-Hurriyah, Latakia; Pres. JULE NASRI.

CHAMBERS OF INDUSTRY

Aleppo Chamber of Industry: Sh. Wara el-Jameh, Aleppo; Pres. SAMI AL-DAHR.

Damascus Chamber of Industry: P.O.B. 1305, Harika-Mouawiya St., Damascus; Pres. SHAFIC SOUCCAR; Gen. Man. ABDUL HAMID MALAKANI; publ. *Al Siniye* (Industry) (irregularly).

EMPLOYERS' ORGANIZATIONS

FEDERATIONS

Fédération Générale à Damas: Damascus; f. 1951; Dir. TALAT TAGLUBI.

Fédération de Damas: Damascus; f. 1949.

Fédération des Patrons et Industriels à Lattaquié: Latakia; f. 1953.

TRADE UNIONS

Ittihad Naqabat al-'Ummal al-'Am fi Suriya (*General Federation of Labour Unions*): Qanawat Street, Damascus; f. 1948; Pres. FAWZI BALI; Sec. MAHMUD FAHURI.

FEDERATIONS

Fédération de la Mécanique: Aleppo; f. 1956.

Fédération de l'Electricité: Damascus; f. 1956.

Fédération de l'Imprimerie: Damascus; f. 1956.

Fédération des Administrations de L'Etat: Damascus; f. 1955.

Fédération des Chemins de Fer de L'Etat: Damascus; f. 1951.

Fédération des Tabacs: Damascus; f. 1949.

Fédération du Pétrole: Homs; f. 1956.

Fédération du Tissage à Bras: Damascus; f. 1956.

Fédération du Tissage Mécanique: Damascus; f. 1956.

Teachers' Federation: Damascus; Chair. AHMED AL KHATIB.

TRADE

Foire Internationale de Damas: 67 blvd. de Baghdad, Damascus; held annually from July 25th to August 20th.

OIL

General Petroleum Company: P.O.B. 2849, Damascus; f. 1958; state agency; holds the oil concession for all Syria; exploits the Suwadiyah, Karachuk and Rumaila oilfields; production in 1973 4.5 million metric tons; also organizes refining, storage and distribution of petroleum; Dir. Engineer GHASSAN MOUHANNA.

TRANSPORT AND TOURISM

TRANSPORT

RAILWAYS

Syrian Railways: Registered Office: B.P. 182, Aleppo; Pres. of the Board of Administration Ing. OMAR SIBAI Gen. Man. ABDELJABBAR KOUNDAKJI.

The present railway system is composed of the following network:

Meydan Ekbez (Turkish frontier)–Aleppo; Çoban-bey (Turkish frontier)–Aleppo; Qamishliya (Turkish frontier)–Jaroubieh (Iraq frontier); Aleppo–Homs; Koussair (Lebanese frontier)–Aleppo; Homs–Akkari (Lebanese frontier); there are 555 km. of normal gauge and 313 km. of narrow gauge track. Lines from Latakia to Aleppo (partially completed) and Djezira are under construction, and work on a line between Homs and Damascus (204 km.) is planned.

Syrian Railways: Northern Lines: 248 km, Southern Lines: 295 km.

Hejaz Railways (narrow gauge): 301 km. in Syria; the historic railway to Medina is the subject of a reconstruction project jointly with Jordan and Saudi Arabia, but little progress has been made since the June 1967 war.

ROADS

Arterial roads run across the country linking the north to the south and the Mediterranean to the eastern frontier. The main arterial networks are as follows: Sidon (Lebanon)-Quneitra-Sweida-Salkhad-Jordan border: Beirut (Lebanon)-Damascus - Khan Abu Chamat - Iraq border - Baghdad; Tartous - Tell Kalakh - Homs - Palmyra; Banias - Hama - Salemie; Latakia-Aleppo-Rakka-Deirezzor-Abou Kemal-Iraq border; Tripoli (Lebanon)-Tartous-Banias-Latakia; Turkish border - Antakya; Amman (Jordan) - Dera'a - Damascus-Homs-Hama-Aleppo-Azaz (Turkish border); Haifa (Palestine)-Kuneitra-Damascus-Palmyra-Deirezzor-Hassetche-Kamechlie.

Asphalted roads: 6,000 km, macadam roads: 1,300 km, earth roads: 6,000 km.

Touring Club de Syrie: P.O.B. 28, Aleppo; f. 1950; the principal Syrian motoring organization; Pres. ALFRED GIRARDI.

PIPELINES

The oil pipelines which cross Syrian territory are of great importance to the national economy, representing a considerable source of foreign exchange. One of the pipelines runs from the Iraq Petroleum Company's installations in Kirkuk to Tripoli in the Lebanon, cutting through approximately 300 miles of Syrian territory. Another line also crosses Syria *en route* to Sidon (Lebanon). Another line, completed in 1968, runs from Karatchouk, through Homs to a terminal at Tartous.

Following the Iraq Government's nationalization of the Iraq Petroleum Company, the Syrian Government nationalized the IPC's pipelines, pumping stations and other installations in Syria, setting up a new company to administer them:

Syrian Company for Oil Transport (SCOT): Dir.-Gen. Hanna Haddad.

SHIPPING

The port of Latakia has developed and the construction of a deep water harbour was completed in 1959. A new port at Tartous is under construction.

The Iraq Petroleum Company has built a harbour at Banias to handle the oil transported in underground pipelines from Kirkuk.

CIVIL AVIATION

A new international airport for Damascus was opened in the summer of 1969.

Syrian Arab Airlines: P.O.B. 417, Red Crescent Bldg., Yousef-Al-Azmeh Square, Damascus; f. 1946; refounded 1961 after revocation of merger with Misrair forming U.A.A.; domestic services and routes to Abu Dhabi, Athens, Baghdad, Benghazi, Cairo, Delhi, Dhahran, Doha, Dubai, Jeddah, Karachi, Kuwait, London, Munich, Nicosia, Paris, Prague, Rome, Sharjah and Teheran; fleet of four Caravelle and one DC-6B; Chair. Major-Gen. Assad Moukayed; Man. Dir. Air Brig.-Gen. Ahmad Antar.

Foreign Companies Operating Services Through Syria

The following foreign airlines serve Syria: Aeroflot, Air France, Alitalia, Ariana Afghan Airlines, Balkan (Bulgaria), British Airways, ČSA, EgyptAir, Interflug, Iraqi Airways, KLM, Kuwait Airways, Lufthansa, Malev, Pan American, Pakistan International Airlines, Qantas, SAS, Saudia and Swissair.

TOURISM

Ministry of Tourism: Abou Firas El-Hamadani St., Damascus; f. 1972; Minister of Tourism Abdallah Khani; Vice-Minister B. Kassab Hassan; Dir. of Tourist Relations Ihsan Chichakli.

Youth Tourism and Travel Organization: Av. 29 Mai, B.P. 201, Damascus; f. 1966; Dir. Mohamed D'Adouch; 3 brs.

UNIVERSITIES

University of Aleppo: f. 1960; 420 teachers; 12,180 students.

Damascus University: Damascus; f. 1923; 678 teachers; 31,053 students.

TANZANIA*

INTRODUCTORY SURVEY

Location, Climate, Language, Religion, Flag, Capital

The United Republic of Tanzania consists of Tanganyika and the islands of Zanzibar and Pemba. Tanganyika lies on the east coast of Africa with Uganda and Kenya to the north, Zaire to the west and Zambia, Malawi and Mozambique to the south. Zanzibar and Pemba are in the Indian Ocean about 40 km. off the coast north of Dar es Salaam. The climate varies with altitude, ranging from tropical in Zanzibar and on the coast and plains to semi-temperate in the highlands. The official languages are Swahili and English and there are a number of tribal languages. There are Christian, Hindu and Muslim communities. Many Africans follow traditional beliefs. The national flag (proportions 3 by 2) is green and blue, divided by a yellow-edged dark brown diagonal stripe from lower left to upper right. The capital is Dar es Salaam.

Recent History

Formerly a United Nations Trusteeship Territory under British administration, Tanganyika became independent in 1961. The first general election was held in 1958, and in 1960 Julius Nyerere became Chief Minister when his party, the Tanganyika African National Union (TANU), won 70 of the 71 seats in the National Assembly. In 1962 Tanganyika became a Republic and Dr. Nyerere the first President. Zanzibar, a British Protectorate since 1890, became independent in 1963. Following an armed uprising by the African Afro-Shirazi Party in January 1964, the Zanzibar Government signed an Act of Union with Tanganyika in April 1964, thus creating the United Republic. At general elections in October 1965 and October 1970, President Nyerere was re-elected by 96.5 and 97 per cent of the votes respectively. Tanzania is a member of the East African Community (established December 1967 with Uganda and Kenya) and of the British Commonwealth. In June 1968 Britain ended all financial and technical aid to Tanzania after it had been announced that Tanzania would cease to pay pensions to British officials who worked for the pre-independence governments of Tanganyika and Zanzibar. However, in 1968 diplomatic relations with Britain, broken off in 1965 over Rhodesia, were resumed and aid was resumed in 1974. Tanzania's relations with Uganda became strained after the downfall of Dr. Milton Obote's Government there in January 1971. There were several border incidents during the year, and the running of the East African Community was hampered until the mediation of President Kenyatta of Kenya helped improve Tanzanian-Ugandan relations at the end of 1971. In September 1972, however, Uganda's military régime claimed that an armed force of Obote supporters and Tanzanians had crossed the border into Uganda. President Nyerere also strongly condemned Uganda's arbitrary expulsion of thousands of Asians. Ugandan aircraft bombed border areas of Tanzania, but, after Somali mediation, a peace pledge was signed between Tanzania and Uganda in October at Modadishu. Early in 1973, however, Uganda claimed that the Mogadishu agreement

was being broken and that Tanzania was training guerrilla forces to be sent into Uganda. Although President Nyerere's granting of sanctuary to Dr. Obote remains a source of tension, relations between Uganda and Tanzania have improved since August 1973, leading to a revival of the deteriorating co-operation within the East African Community.

In April 1972 Sheikh Abeid Karume, leader of Zanzibar and First Vice-President of the United Republic, was assassinated. Aboud Jumbe, appointed his successor, reorganized the government of the island in August 1972 by extending the powers of the Afro-Shirazi party. Zanzibar remains under the rigid, brutal and dictatorial rule which has characterized it since the 1964 uprising.

Government

An Interim Constitution, making the mainland a one-party state, was introduced in 1965. Executive power is in the hands of a President, who is elected by universal suffrage. The legislative organ is the unicameral National Assembly of up to 204 members who translate into action the policy of TANU as decided by the National Executive of the Party. A Presidential election must be held whenever the Assembly is dissolved and new Assembly elections held. The country is divided into 20 Regions, each with a Commissioner. Chiefs wishing to hold official posts must relinquish their tribal authority. There are no reserved seats for Europeans and Asians under the new Constitution.

Defence

The People's Defence Forces in Tanzania were formed in 1961 and consist of units of the former Tanganyika Rifles and the People's Liberation Army of Zanzibar. There is selective conscription. Total armed forces numbered 11,600 in 1973, 10,000 of whom were in the Army. There are also air and naval forces, and a para-military police marine unit. In 1973 Tanzania announced a comprehensive plan to improve her defences.

Economic Affairs

The economy is mainly agricultural and much of the farming is at subsistence level. Tanzania's Government has changed the economic system through the development of the communal *ujaama* villages. By 1974 one million people were settled in 5,500 *ujaama* villages and in 1973 the ruling TANU party proposed settling the entire rural population in *ujaama* villages by 1976. For its development programmes. Tanzania has relied overwhelmingly on foreign aid, the largest donor being Sweden; between 1961 and 1972 Tanzania received 1,430,000 million shillings in aid.

The main crops are coffee, cotton, sisal and cashew nuts. Cloves are grown on the islands, chiefly on Pemba, and Zanzibar relies on them for almost its entire foreign exchange earnings. Diamonds are an important export and other minerals are gold, tin and salt.

* See also **East African Community** in Vol. I.

Increasing Africanization is Government policy, although there is still substantial reliance on expatriates. President Nyerere has decreed widespread nationalization and, as a result, foreign private investment has been minimal, the high rates of taxation also being prohibitive. In November 1973 the Government nationalized 50 privately owned farms in the biggest land take-overs since 1967. The projected move of the capital to Dodoma is likely to cost 3,700 million shillings. The Second Five-Year Development Plan (1969–74) provides for total investment of 8,085 million shillings. Over half of the Government's contribution of 3,055 million shillings has been allocated to developing agriculture and communications. The 1969 Convention between the East African Community (comprising Kenya, Uganda and Tanzania) and the EEC provides for quotas for exports of coffee, cloves and pineapples to the EEC.

Transport and Communications

Railways and harbours are administered jointly with Uganda and Kenya and the services include lake shipping. Tanzania has 2,560 km. of railways and 16,742 km. of roads. An intergovernmental authority, the Tanzania-Zambia Railway Authority, has been formed to deal with the proposed rail link between the two countries which a Chinese team is expected to complete in 1974. Sweden, the World Bank and the International Development Association are financing the rebuilding of 500 km. of the Tanzam Highway, a 1,930 km. road running from central Zambia to Dar es Salaam. The three main sea ports are Dar es Salaam, Tanga and Mtwara and the chief port on Lake Victoria is Mwanza. Air services link the towns and international air transport is provided by East African Airways Corporation (operated jointly by Tanzania, Uganda and Kenya) and foreign lines. There are also private and charter services and the larger farms and plantations have their own aircraft.

Social Welfare

The state-sponsored Rural Development Division exists to improve educational, labour and health conditions in small communities. The state operates hospitals and health centres and Christian Missions also provide medical care.

Education

Most schools receive state aid, the remainder being organized by missions and other voluntary agencies. There are not yet enough schools to provide universal primary education. School fees were abolished in the 1973–74 budget, which allocated 48 million shillings more to education than the 1972–73 budget. The University College of Dar es Salaam forms part of the University of East Africa.

Tourism

The principal tourist attractions are the scenery and wild-life. The famous Serengeti National Park contains a great variety of game, and safari-parties come from all over the world. Mount Kilimanjaro (19,340 ft.) is the highest mountain in Africa. In 1972 100,000 tourists visited Tanzania.

Visas are not required to visit Tanzania by nationals of Denmark, Finland, Ireland, Norway and Sweden.

Sport

Organized sports include football, cricket, athletics and tennis. There is also fishing and swimming.

Public Holidays

1974: October 18th (Id ul Fitr), December 9th (Independence Day), December 25th (Christmas), December 26th (Id ul Adha).

1975: January 12th (Zanzibar Revolution Day), March 26th (Mouloud, Birth of the Prophet), March 28th–31st (Easter), April 26th (Union Day), May 1st (International Workers' Day), July 7th (Saba Saba Day).

Weights and Measures

The metric system is in force.

Currency and Exchange Rates

100 cents = 1 Tanzanian shilling.

Exchange rates (April 1974):

£1 sterling = 16.845 Tanzanian shillings;
U.S. $1 = 7.143 Tanzanian shillings.

STATISTICAL SURVEY

AREA AND POPULATION

AREA (square miles)		POPULATION 1967 Census—Private Households)	
Mainland .	341,150	African . . .	11,481,595
Zanzibar and Pemba.	1,021	Asian . . .	75,015
Water . .	20,650	Arabs . . .	29,775
Lake Victoria .	13,450	European . .	16,884
Lake Tanganyika .	5,150	Others . . .	839
Lake Rukwa .	1,100	Not Stated . .	159,042
TOTAL . .	362,821	TOTAL . .	11,763,150

1967 Census: Total population 12,313,469 (Mainland 11,958,654; Zanzibar and Pemba 354,815); 1973 estimate of total population: 14,376,600.

Principal Tribes of Tanganyika (1957 census): Sukuma 12.45%, Nyamwezi 4.13%, Makonde 3.80%, Haya 3.70%, Chagga 3.62%, Gogo 3.41%, Ha 3.30%, Hehe 2.86%, Nyakusa 2.50%, Nyika 2.41%, Luguru 2.30%, Bena 2.23%, Turu 2.23%, Sambaa 2.21%, Zaramo 2.09%.

Chief Towns: (1967) Dar es Salaam (capital) 272,821, Tanga 61,058, Mwanza 34,861, Arusha 32,452; (1970) Dar es Salaam 343,911.

REGIONS OF TANGANYIKA

(1967 Census)

Region	Population	Region	Population
Arusha	610,474	Mtwara	1,041,146
Coast	784,327	Mwanza	1,055,883
Dodoma	709,380	Ruvuma	393,043
Iringa	689,905	Shinyanga	899,468
Kigoma	473,443	Singida	457,938
Kilimanjaro	652,722	Tabora	562,871
Mara	544,125	Tanga	771,060
Mbeya	969,053	West Lake	658,712
Morogoro	685,104		

EMPLOYMENT

	1969	1970*	1971*
Agriculture, Forestry and Fishing	112,888	107,368	109,692
Mining and Quarrying	5,919	6,096	5,552
Manufacturing	40,323	43,746	54,714
Construction	52,767	54,569	52,658
Electricity and Water	9,755	11,296	10,618
Commerce	19,072	20,617	22,508
Transport and Communications	32,398	33,813	39,984
Finance	4,257	4,835	5,681
Services	90,556	93,295	100,505
Total	367,935	375,635	401,912

* Provisional.

Total Labour Force (1967 census): Tanganyika had an economically active population of 5,748,613.

AGRICULTURE

LAND USE, 1966

('000 hectares)

Arable Land	10,734
Under Permanent Crops	968
Permanent Meadows and Pastures	44,754
Forest Land	31,074
Other Land	1,092
Total Land Area	88,622
Inland Water	5,348
Total Area	93,970

Source: FAO, Production Yearbook 1971.

PRINCIPAL CASH CROPS*

	1970		1971†		1972§	
	Production ('ooo metric tons)	Value (million sh.)	Production ('ooo metric tons)	Value (million sh.)	Production ('ooo metric tons)	Value (million sh.)
Sisal	202.2	157.3	181.1	142.5	156.8	140.5
Cotton‡	76.4	244.6	65.3	220.2	79.8	260.6
Coffee	49.7	265.8	45.8	231.3	51.6	275.8
Groundnuts . .	6.2	6.6	6.7	6.6	7.4	8.0
Cashew Nuts . .	111.2	102.7	121.5	113.5	137.7	119.8
Tea	8.5	48.5	10.6	57.7	12.7	73.6
Tobacco . . .	11.0	48.8	11.9	49.2	14.2	69.9
Pyrethrum Extract .	2.3	8.6	3.7	13.2	4.3	15.9

* Cotton, cashew nuts and tobacco based on crop year, others based on calendar year.
† Revised.
‡ Figures attribute quantity to cotton lint and value to seed cotton.
§ Provisional.

LIVESTOCK

('ooo)

	1967–68	1968–69	1969–70	1970–71*
Cattle	12,345	12,862	13,206	13,300
Sheep	2,828	2,825	2,823	2,800
Goats	4,374	4,417	4,456	4,450
Pigs	19	20	21	22
Asses	160	160	160	160
Poultry	19,372	20,049	20,405	20,600

* FAO estimate.

Source: FAO, *Production Yearbook 1971.*

LIVESTOCK PRODUCTS

(metric tons)

	1968	1969	1970	1971*
Cows' Milk . . .	640,000	691,000	709,000	720,000
Goats' Milk . . .	48,000	46,000	48,000	50,000
Beef and Veal† . .	103,000*	121,000*	127,000*	128,000
Mutton and Lamb† . .	29,000	27,000	27,000	27,000
Hen Eggs . . .	13,600	14,100	14,400	15,000
Cattle Hides . . .	20,244*	23,919*	22,890*	n.a.
Sheep Skins . . .	1,478*	1,575*	1,590*	n.a.
Goat Skins . . .	3,400*	3,000*	3,000*	n.a.

* FAO estimate.

† Meat from indigenous animals only, including the meat equivalent of exported live animals. Figures for mutton and lamb include goats' meat.

Source: FAO, *Production Yearbook 1971.*

FORESTRY
ROUNDWOOD REMOVALS
('ooo cubic metres)

	CONIFEROUS (Soft Wood)		BROADLEAVED (Hard Wood)		TOTAL	
	1969	1970*	1969	1970*	1969	1970*
Sawlogs, Veneer Logs and Logs for Sleepers . . .	87	95	313	345	400	440
Other Industrial Wood . . .	3	3	622	652	625	655
Fuel Wood	50	50	29,450	30,450	29,500	30,500
TOTAL . . .	140	148	30,385	31,447	30,525	31,595

* Unofficial figures.

Source: FAO, *Yearbook of Forest Products 1970.*

TIMBER*
(cubic metres)

	1969	1970	1971	1972†
Sawlogs:				
Hard Wood	123,100	132,419	110,340	72,251
Soft Wood	36,464	27,038	26,669	32,301
Total . . .	159,564	159,457	137,009	104,552
Poles	15,961	20,501	22,062	28,940
Firewood	524,763	576,061	712,405	686,515

* Output of forest produce from public lands and forest reserves.   † Provisional.

OTHER FOREST PRODUCTS
(metric tons)

	1968	1969
Bark and Other Tanning Materials	10,115	11,340
Materials for Plaiting (non-bamboo) . . .	59	59
Natural Gums, Resins, etc. (non-rubber) . . .	206	454
Waxes	318	680

Source: FAO, *Yearbook of Forest Products.*

ZANZIBAR—CLOVE SHIPMENTS
(million shillings)

	1970	1971	1972
India . . .	0.2	2.9	—
U.S.S.R. . .	—	—	—
Pakistan . .	0.4	0.2	—
Indonesia . .	1.4	107.4	222.4
United Kingdom .	0.9	—	0.1
Sudan . . .	0.4	0.5	0.2
Japan . . .	1.8	0.8	0.7
Hong Kong . .	15.3	18.0	—
Singapore . .	81.7	45.9	14.1
Kuwait . . .	0.9	1.1	0.5
TOTAL (incl. others)	109.4	179.0	240.3

FISHING
(metric tons)

	1967	1968	1969	1970
Inland Waters	99,000	120,100	123,200	166,400
Indian Ocean	29,400	32,000	27,000	28,600
TOTAL CATCH . .	128,400	152,100	150,200	195,000
Value of Landings (T£'ooo) .	4,440	4,910	4,747	5,608

1971: Total catch 199,100 metric tons (FAO estimate).

Source: FAO, *Yearbook of Fishery Statistics.*

MINING

	1970 Production	1970 Export Value (million sh.)	1971 Production	1971 Export Value (million sh.)	1972 Production	1972 Export Value (million sh.)
Diamonds ('000 grammes) .	141.6	106.2	167.4	136.3	127.2	n.a.
Gold ('000 grammes) . .	244.4	2.3	5.2	0.05	6.6	0.09
Salt (metric tons) . .	41,944.0	2.6	37,378.2	4.4	44,247.2	4.0
Tin Concentrate (metric tons)	215.0	6.4	195.0	3.2	67.1	1.1

Asbestos: 397,000 metric tons in 1969.

INDUSTRIAL PRODUCTION

	Unit	1970	1971	1972
Beer	litres	38,601	53,916	64,823
Textiles . . .	sq. metres	58,412	67,010	89,365
Cigarettes . . .	'000	2,599	2,923	3,285
Paints	litres	1,648	1,952	2,208
Plywood . . .	'000 sq. metres	1,122	1,228	1,139
Sisal Twine . . .	metric tons	20,404	20,135	22,575

FINANCE

100 cents = 1 Tanzanian shilling.

Coins: 5, 20 and 50 cents; 1 and 5 shillings.

Notes: 5, 10, 20 and 100 shillings.

Exchange rates (April 1974): £1 sterling = 16.845 Tanzanian shillings; U.S. $1 = 7.143 Tanzanian shillings.
100 Tanzanian shillings = £5.94 = $14.00.

Note: Between July 1973 and January 1974 the exchange rate was U.S. $1 = 6.90 Tanzanian shillings. Prior to July 1973 the dollar/shilling exchange rate was the same as at present. In terms of sterling, the exchange rate between November 1967 and August 1971 was £1 = 17.14 Tanzanian shillings. In this survey the term "Tanzanian £" is used to denote amounts of 20 Tanzanian shillings, equivalent to £1.19 sterling in April 1974.

BUDGET

RECURRENT REVENUE AND EXPENDITURE
(million sh.)

REVENUE	1969–70	1970–71	1971–72	EXPENDITURE	1969–70	1970–71	1971–72
Recurrent Revenue				Recurrent Expenditure			
Direct Taxes .	352.0	447.6	532.0	Economic Services .	307.2	349.4	376.0
Indirect Taxes .	827.1	916.6	898.6	Social Services . .	434.5	501.6	560.3
Income from Property	116.2	111.9	131.9	General Administration . .	480.0	533.0	543.5
Miscellaneous .	130.7	146.8	182.7	Other Purposes .	305.0	247.4	300.8
Revenue and Capital Transfers .	150.9	60.2	114.0				
				Total Recurrent Expenditure .	1,526.7	1,631.4	1,780.6
				Surplus . .	50.2	51.7	78.6
TOTAL .	1,576.9	1,683.1	1,859.2	TOTAL .	1,576.9	1,683.1	1,859.2

Budget (1974–75): Estimated Revenue: 3,535 million sh.

Budget (1974–75): Estimated Expenditure: 3,661 million sh.

SECOND FIVE-YEAR DEVELOPMENT PLAN
(1969-74)
TOTAL CONTRIBUTION BY SECTORS (million sh.)

Central Government . . .	3,055
State Organization Co-operatives . .	2,300
TOTAL PUBLIC SECTOR .	5,355
East African Community . .	580
Private Sector	2,150
TOTAL	8,085

GROSS DOMESTIC PRODUCT
(at current factor cost—million shillings)

	1971	1972
Agriculture, Forestry and Fishing	3,494	3,956
Mining and Quarrying . .	121	124
Manufacturing . . .	893	973
Construction . . .	481	501
Electricity, Water . .	91	107
Trade, Restaurants, Hotels .	1,170	1,280
Transport and Communications .	788	867
Finance, Insurance, etc. .	921	1,052
Public Administration and Other Services . . .	1,018	1,142
SUB-TOTAL .	8,977	10,002
Less Imputed Bank Service Charges . . .	—131	—152
GROSS DOMESTIC PRODUCT	8,846	9,850

BALANCE OF PAYMENTS
(Current Account—million shillings)

	1969		1970		1971	
	Credit	Debit	Credit	Debit	Credit	Debit
Goods and Services:						
Merchandise	1,754.0	1,790.1	1,809.7	2,359.6	1,945.8	2,810.4
Freight and transport . . .	242.8	93.6	328.7	112.5	452.9	103.5
Travel	83.8	80.3	96.0	91.3	98.1	153.7
Investment income . . .	76.0	96.6	76.6	101.5	67.4	87.7
Government transactions n.e.s. .	40.0	27.1	32.4	22.9	47.8	31.5
Other services . . .	49.4	69.0	83.0	77.7	80.6	116.9
Total . . .	2,246.0	2,156.7	2,426.4	2,765.5	2,692.6	3,303.7
Transfer Payments . .	213.4	152.6	265.8	177.1	260.8	208.4
TOTAL CURRENT ACCOUNT . .	2,459.4	2,309.3	2,692.2	2,942.6	2,953.4	3,512.1

EXTERNAL TRADE*
(million shillings)

	1970	1971	1972	1973†
Imports	1,939	2,414	2,598	3,074
Exports	1,702	1,792	2,063	2,058

*Excluding trade with Kenya and Uganda in local produce and locally manufactured goods.

† Provisional.

PRINCIPAL COMMODITIES

IMPORTS		1971	1972	1973*	EXPORTS		1971	1972	1973*
Transport equipment	.	370	310	n.a.	Coffee beans	. . .	227	383	494
Machinery other than					Raw cotton	. . .	245	336	340
electric . . .		400	362	n.a.	Diamonds	. . .	209	124	n.a.
Electrical machinery .		154	157	n.a.	Sisal	. . .	134	145	216
Iron and steel . .		191	260	308	Cloves	. . .	179	240	233
Chemicals . .		109	116	n.a.	Cashew nuts	. .	120	150	141
Crude petroleum .		112	104	238	Distillate fuels	. .	64	79	36
Food . . .		79	171	n.a.	Tea		49	54	54
Cotton fabric . .		11	4	28					
Clothing . . .		27	21	n.a.					

* Provisional.

PRINCIPAL COUNTRIES

IMPORTS		1971	1972	1973*	EXPORTS		1971	1972	1973*
China, People's Republic		601	508	682	China, People's Republic		84	135	98
France . . .		38	91	99	Germany, Fed. Repub.		69	123	151
Germany, Fed. Repub.		181	206	256	Hong Kong . .		132	130	148
India . . .		51	42	51	India . . .		144	171	151
Iran . . .		138	166	240	Japan . . .		46	76	87
Italy . . .		125	214	156	United Kingdom .		424	324	248
Japan . . .		151	162	281	U.S.A. . .		135	137	181
Netherlands . .		105	68	108	Zambia . . .		139	182	71
United Kingdom .		487	461	494					
U.S.A. . .		105	140	96					

* Provisional.

INTER-EAST AFRICAN TRADE

		IMPORTS FROM KENYA AND UGANDA	EXPORTS TO KENYA AND UGANDA
1969	.	291	104
1970	.	335	148
1971	.	311	197
1972	.	332	133

TRANSPORT
EAST AFRICAN RAIL TRAFFIC

		UNIT	1970	1971	1972*
Goods Traffic	. .	million ton-miles	645	687	600
Passengers	. .	'000	3,160	3,133	3,100
Rolling Stock:					
Locomotives .	. .	number	155	153	167
Carriages	. .	,,	111	111	110
Wagons†	. .	,,	3,334	3,348	3,340

Source: E.A. Railways and Harbours. * Provisional.

† This is the basic Tanzanian stock. In addition, other units are in constant circulation between the three East African countries and are consequently available for use in Tanzania.

TANZANIA—(Statistical Survey)

ROAD TRAFFIC
LICENSED MOTOR VEHICLES

	1970	1971	1972*
Motor Cars	32,362	33,238	33,141
Light Commercial Vehicles . . .	13,899	14,273	14,784
Private Motor Cycles . . .	9,028	9,407	10,048
Lorries and Trucks . . .	12,525	13,183	14,217
Government Vehicles . . .	6,629	7,850	8,454
Tractors, Tankers, etc. . .	4,389	4,750	5,290
Others	6,595	6,546	7,079
TOTAL	85,427	89,247	93,013

* Provisional.

SEA TRAFFIC*

	1970	1971	1972
Number of Ships	1,651	1,496	1,675
Net Registered Tonnage ('000 tons) .	5,601	5,250	5,715
Number of Passengers† . . .	31,351	52,071	57,056
Cargo Handled ('000 deadweight tons):			
Imports	1,765	2,195	2,473
Exports	1,092	1,030	1,104
Total‡	2,867	3,249	3,606

* Through Dar es Salaam, Tanga and Mtwara.
† Including embarked and disembarked.
‡ Including export/import transhipment.

CIVIL AIR TRAFFIC

	1970	1971	1972
Ton-km. sold ('000) . . .	100,112	106,356	101,791
Passengers carried ('000) . .	511	564	564
Passenger km. ('000) . . .	800,144	860,575	860,338
Mail ton-km. ('000) . . .	2,884	3,445	3,238
Cargo ton-km. ('000) . . .	28,198	27,685	23,971
Passenger load factor (%) . .	45.3	41.7	43.7
Gross Revenue (million sh.) . .	320	403	416*

* Traffic Revenue only.

TOURISM

	HOTELS	BEDS
1969	80	3,623
1970	100	5,445
1971	103	5,460
1972	104	5,715

Tourist Arrivals (1972): 100,000.

EDUCATION
TANGANYIKA
(1971)

	SCHOOLS	TEACHERS	PUPILS
Primary . .	4,133	19,786	902,609
Secondary* .	141	2,199	32,603
Vocational .	4	n.a.	n.a.
Teacher Training .	22	327	4,471
University .	1	308	2,060

Zanzibar (1966): Primary pupils 35,000, Secondary pupils 1,700.

* Including Higher Secondary Schools.

Source: Bureau of Statistics, Dar es Salaam.

THE CONSTITUTION

Tanganyika became a Republic, within the Commonwealth, on December 9th, 1962, with an executive President, elected by universal suffrage, who is both the Head of State and Head of the Government. A presidential election will be held whenever Parliament is dissolved. Tanzania is governed as a democratic society in which the Government is responsible to a freely-elected Parliament, representative of the people, and in which the courts of law are independent and impartial.

The structure of the legislative, executive and judicial organs of the Government are set out in the Interim Constitution of 1965, which made provisional constitutional arrangements for the Union between Tanganyika and Zanzibar.

The legislative powers are exercised by a Parliament of the United Republic, which is vested by the Constitution with complete sovereign powers, and of which the present National Assembly is the legislative house. The Assembly also enacts all legislation concerning the mainland. Internal matters in Zanzibar are the exclusive jurisdiction of the Zanzibar executive and the Revolutionary Council of Zanzibar.

The National Assembly comprises 107 Elected Members, 20 *ex-officio* Members (the Regional Commissioners) 15 National Members elected by statutory bodies, 10 Members appointed by the President, up to 32 Members of the Zanzibar Revolutionary Council, and up to 20 other Zanzibar members appointed by the President in agreement with the President of Zanzibar. Provision is made for the total to reach 204 members.

The President has no power to legislate without recourse to Parliament. The assent of the President is required before any Bill passed by the National Assembly becomes law. Should the President withhold his assent and the Bill be re-passed by the National Assembly by a two-thirds majority, the President is required by law to give his assent within 21 days unless, before that time, he has dissolved the National Assembly, in which case he must stand for re-election.

To assist him in carrying out his functions the President appoints two Vice-Presidents from the elected members of the National Assembly. The First Vice-President is also the President of Zanzibar. The Second Vice-President, who is chosen from the elected members of the National Assembly, is the leader of Government business in the Assembly. The Vice-Presidents and ministers comprise the Cabinet, which is presided over by the President.

The independence of the judges is secured by provisions which prevent their removal, except on account of misbehaviour or incapacity, after investigation by a judicial tribunal. The Interim Constitution also makes provision for a Permanent Commission of Enquiry which has wide powers to investigate any abuses of authority.

Members of Parliament are elected for five years unless the President dissolves Parliament at an earlier date. Appointed members of Parliament hold their seats until dissolution unless their appointments are revoked by the President. The President must stand for re-election each time Parliament is dissolved. The Presidential candidate is chosen by an electoral convention of TANU and the Afro-Shirazi parties. Their choice is then presented to the people for confirmation by a yes-no vote. If the convention's first choice is rejected by a majority of the voters, another candidate must be chosen and submitted to the vote.

Mainland Tanzania is divided into 107 constituencies, although for the 1970 elections another 13 were created. In each of these areas TANU, the official party, puts forward two candidates chosen by the TANU membership. Then all adult citizens of the area, whether TANU members or not, vote to decide which of the candidates will represent them in Parliament. The constitution of TANU is incorporated as part of the Interim Constitution.

The National Executive of TANU is the supreme policy making body of the Party and the Government subject only to approval of a bi-annual National Conference, but it is the role of the National Assembly to translate party policy into legislation. The assembly deliberates independently and has on occasion amended or refused to approve government proposals.

The National Executive is a parallel body to the National Assembly and its members are democratically chosen by party members throughout the country. Both National Executive and National Assembly members are paid at the same rate from government funds.

The Afro-Shirazi party plays a similar role in Zanzibar and Pemba, giving effect to its policies through the Zanzibar Revolutionary Council.

The Constitution also makes provision for the attainment of citizenship in accordance with the principles already approved by the National Assembly.

The Constitution can be amended by an act of the Parliament of the United Republic, when the proposed amendment is supported by the votes of not less than two thirds of all the members of the Assembly.

ARUSHA DECLARATION

The Arusha Declaration of February 1967 (approved by the National Executive Committee of TANU at the end of January) laid down that every TANU and Government leader must be a peasant or a worker; that no such leader should hold shares or directorships in any company; that no leader should receive two or more salaries; and that no leader should own houses rented out to others. In addition, the Declaration urges the Government to take further steps in the implementation of the policy of socialism, especially in ensuring that the major means of production are under the control and ownership of the peasants and workers (through the Government and the co-operatives); to put emphasis on national self-reliance rather than depending on foreign loans and grants for development, and to put great emphasis on raising the standards of living of the peasants.

THE GOVERNMENT

HEAD OF STATE

President: Mwalimu Dr. JULIUS K. NYERERE.

THE CABINET

(July 1974)

President and Commander-in-Chief of the Armed Forces: Mwalimu Dr. JULIUS K. NYERERE.

First Vice-President: ABOUD JUMBE.

Prime Minister and Second Vice-President: RASHIDI M. KAWAWA.

Minister of Foreign Affairs: JOHN W. S. MALECELA.

Minister of Finance: CLEOPA MSUYA.

Minister of Commerce and Industries: AMIR H. JAMAL.

Minister of Home Affairs: Alhaji O. A. MUHAJI.

Minister of Agriculture: JOSEPH MUNGAI.

Minister of Economic Affairs and Development Planning: Dr. WILBERT CHAGULA.

Minister of Defence and National Service: EDWARD SOKOINE.

Minister of Natural Resources and Tourism: HASNU MAKAME.

Minister of National Education: Rev. SAIMON CHIWANGA.

Minister of Communications and Works: JOB LUSINDE.

Minister of State, First Vice-President's Office: HASSAN MOYO.

Minister of Lands, Housing and Urban Development: MUSOBI MAGENI.

Minister of Water Development and Power: ISAEL ELINAWINGA.

Minister of Health: HASSAN MWINYI.

Minister of Labour and Social Welfare: ALFRED TANDAU.

Minister of Information and Broadcasting: DAUDI MWAKAWAGO.

Minister of National Culture and Youth: Major-Gen. SARAKIKYA.

Ministers of State, President's Office: PETER SIYOVELWA, Chief ADAM SAPI.

JUNIOR MINISTERS

Office of the Prime Minister and Second Vice-President: PATRICK QORRO, MUSSA MASOMO.

Foreign Affairs: TAWAKALI KHAMIS TAWAKALI, I. A. SEPETU.

Defence and National Service: GEOFFREY MHAGAMA.

Communications and Works: ROBERT NG'ITU.

Health: MUSTAFA NYANG'ANYI.

Agriculture: STEPHEN M. WASIRA.

TANGANYIKA AFRICAN NATIONAL UNION (TANU)

TANU on the mainland and the *Afro-Shirazi Party* in Zanzibar and Pemba determine the broad lines of Government policy.

President: Mwalimu Dr. JULIUS K. NYERERE.

National Executive: supreme policy-making body of the Government and subject only to approval of bi-annual National Conference; Party headed by President; chooses Party leadership, with the exception of the President, who is selected by an electoral convention.

DIPLOMATIC REPRESENTATION

EMBASSIES AND HIGH COMMISSIONS ACCREDITED TO TANZANIA

(In Dar es Salaam unless otherwise stated)

(E) Embassy; (HC) High Commission.

Algeria: P.O.B. 2963, 34 Upanga Rd. (E); *Ambassador:* TAHAR GAID.

Australia: P.O.B. 2996, 4th Floor, National Bank of Commerce Bldg., Independence Ave. (HC); *High Commissioner:* J. A. FORSYTHE.

Austria: Nairobi, Kenya (E).

Belgium: Flat No. 7, NIC Bldg., Mirambo St. (E); *Ambassador:* EGARDUS P. VERHILLE.

Brazil: Nairobi, Kenya (E).

Bulgaria: P.O.B. 9260, Plot No. 232, Malik Rd., Upanga (E); *Ambassador:* DECHO D. STAMBOLIEV.

Burundi: Lugalo Rd., Upanga (E); *Ambassador:* ANDRÉ YANDA.

Cameroon: Addis Ababa, Ethiopia (E).

Canada: P.O.B. 1022, The Pan African Insurance Co. Ltd. Bldg. (HC); *High Commissioner:* J. R. BARKER.

China, People's Republic: P.O.B. 1649, 2, Kajificheni Close/Toure Drive (E); *Ambassador:* LI YAO-WEN.

Cuba: P.O.B. 9282, Plot No. 313, Upanga; *Ambassador:* ALIPIO ZORRILLA.

Czechoslovakia: P.O.B. 3054, Jubilee Mansion, 69 Upanga Rd. (E); *Ambassador:* Dr. JOSEF GANDEL.

Denmark: P.O.B. 9171, I.P.S. Bldg., Independence Ave./Azikiwe St. (E).

Egypt: P.O.B. 1668, 24 Garden Ave. (near Pamba House) (E); *Ambassador:* AHMED HATATA.

Ethiopia: Nairobi, Kenya (E).

Finland: P.O.B. 2455, Tanesco Bldg., Independence Ave. (E); *Ambassador:* MARTTI AHTISAARI.

France: P.O.B. 2349, Bagamoyo Rd. (E); *Ambassador:* JEAN DESPARMET.

Germany, Federal Republic: P.O.B. 9541, N.B.C. House, 1st Floor, Azikiwe St., City Drive (E); *Ambassador:* BURKARD Baron VON MUELLENHEIM RECHBERG.

Guinea: P.O.B. 2969, 35 Haile Selassie Rd., Oyster Bay (E); *Ambassador:* MAMADOU BOBO BALDE.

Hungary: P.O.B. 672, 40 Bagamoyo Rd. (E); *Ambassador:* MIKLÓS BARD.

India: P.O.B. 2684, 28 Independence Ave. (HC); *High Commissioner:* J. S. MEHTA.

Indonesia: P.O.B. 572, 299 Upanga Rd. (E); *Ambassador:* L. M. ABDULKADIR.

Italy: P.O.B. 2106, Plot 316, Lugalo Rd. (E); *Ambassador:* GIAN GIORGIO FABRI TRISSINO DA LODI.

Ivory Coast: Addis Ababa, Ethiopia (E).

Jamaica: Addis Ababa, Ethiopia (HC).

Japan: P.O.B. 2577 (E); *Ambassador:* NOBOYUKI NAKASHIMA.

Korea, Democratic People's Republic: P.O.B. 2690, Plot 297, Upanga Rd. (E); *Ambassador:* JAWG IL MAN.

Lesotho: (HC); *High Commissioner:* J. R. L. KOTSOKOANE.

Liberia: Nairobi, Kenya (E).

Mongolia: (E); *Ambassador:* BALJINGUIN LOCHIN.

Morocco: Addis Ababa, Ethiopia (E).

Netherlands: P.O.B. 1174, I.P.S. Bldg., 10th Floor (E); *Ambassador:* (vacant).

Norway: Nairobi, Kenya (E).

Pakistan: P.O.B. 2925, Plot 149, Malik Rd., Upanga (E); *Ambassador:* BASHIR AHMAD.

Poland: P.O.B. 2188, 4 Upanga Rd. (E); *Ambassador:* JULIAN TWOROG.

Romania: P.O.B. 590, Plot 11, Ocean Rd. (E); *Ambassador:* ION DRINCEANU.

Rwanda: P.O.B. 2918, Plot 32, Upanga Rd. (E); *Ambassador:* Major JEAN NEPOMUCENE MUNYANDEKWE.

Senegal: Addis Ababa, Ethiopia (E).

Somalia: P.O.B. 2031, Plot 31, Upanga Rd. (E); *Ambassador:* ABDULRAHMAN HUSSEIN MOHAMED.

Spain: P.O.B. 842, I.P.S. Bldg., 7th Floor; *Charge d'Affaires:* LUIS MARINAS.

Sudan: P.O.B. 2266, "Albaraka", 64 Upanga Rd. (E); *Ambassador:* EL NUR ALI SULIMAN.

Sweden: P.O.B. 9274, I.P.S. Bldg., 9th Floor, Independence Ave. (E); *Ambassador:* KNUT GRANSTEDT.

Switzerland: P.O.B. 2454, 17 Kenyatta Drive (E); *Ambassador:* LUCIEN MOSSAZ.

Syria: P.O.B. 2442, Plot 276, Upanga East (E); *Ambassador:* MOHAMED TALL.

Turkey: Nairobi, Ethiopia (E).

U.S.S.R.: P.O.B. 1905, Plot No. 73, Kenyatta Drive (E); *Ambassador:* S. A. SLIPCHENKO.

United Kingdom: P.O.B. 9200, Permanent House (HC); *High Commissioner:* A. R. H. KELLAS.

U.S.A.: P.O.B. 9123, National Bank of Commerce House (4th Floor), City Drive (E); *Ambassador:* W. BEVERLY CARTER, JR.

Vatican: P.O.B. 480, Plot 462, Msasani Peninsula; *Apostolic Nuncio:* Archbishop FRANCO BRAMBILLA.

Viet-Nam, Democratic Republic: P.O.B. 2194, 9 Ocean Rd. (E); *Ambassador:* DUONG THIET SON.

Viet-Nam, Provisional Revolutionary Government of the Republic of South: P.O.B. 21503, 21 Mzinga Way (E); *Ambassador:* TRAN NINH.

Yemen, People's Democratic Republic: P.O.B. 349, 353 United Nations Rd. (E); *Ambassador:* ABDUL BARI KASSIM.

Yugoslavia: P.O.B. 2838, Plot 35/36, Upanga Rd. (E); *Ambassador:* MARKO KOSIN.

Zaire: P.O.B. 975, 438 Malik Rd., Upanga (E); *Ambassador:* MWENDA M'SIRI MUKANDABANTU.

Zambia: P.O.B. 2525, Plot 442, Malik Rd., Upanga (HC); *High Commissioner:* R. S. MAKASA.

Tanzania also has diplomatic relations with Albania, Botswana, the Royal Government of Khmer National Union (Cambodia) Cyprus, the German Democratic Republic, Greece, Mexico, Sierra Leone, Swaziland, Trinidad and Tobago, and Tunisia.

PARLIAMENT

NATIONAL ASSEMBLY

Speaker: Chief ERASTO MANG'ENYA.

Elected Members: 120.

Nominated Members: The President may nominate up to 30 members; 20 from Zanzibar and 10 from the mainland. In December 1973 13 had been nominated from Zanzibar and 10 from the mainland.

Ex-Officio Members: 22. The majority of ex-officio members are the Regional Commissioners.

National Members: 15.

ELECTIONS, OCTOBER 1970

PARTY	SEATS
Tanganyika African National Union* (TANU)	198†

18 members represent the Zanzibar regional assembly and the Afro-Shirazi Party.

* Two candidates may contest each seat.

† December 1973.

POLITICAL PARTIES

Tanganyika African National Union (TANU): P.O.B. 9151, Dar es Salaam; f. 1954; aims to develop a socialist democratic state by self-help at all levels; 3,000,000 mems. (est.); since Arusha Declaration of February 1967 leaders must be workers or peasants and members must be fully dedicated to the objects and beliefs of the Party; Pres. JULIUS K. NYERERE.

There are also organizations for the Party Elders, for the women (UWT), for youth (TYL) and for parents (TAPA); and the co-operatives and the trade union are also affiliated.

Afro-Shirazi Party: P.O.B. 389, Zanzibar; f. 1957; mainly African party, dominant in the Zanzibar Revolutionary Council; est. mems. 100,000; Pres. ABOUD JUMBE.

JUDICIAL SYSTEM

Under a Bill introduced into the Assembly in December 1969 chiefs are no longer permitted to exercise any power under traditional or customary law.

From the beginning of 1970 People's Courts have been established in Zanzibar. Magistrates are elected by the people and have two assistants each. Defence lawyers are normally not permitted and Zanzibaris have no right of appeal to the Court of Appeal for East Africa.

The Court of Appeal for East Africa: P.O.B. 30187, Nairobi; Pres. Mr. Justice C. D. NEWBOLD, C.M.G.; Vice-Pres. Mr. Justice W. A. H. DUFFUS; Justices of Appeal J. F. SPRY, E. J. E. LAW; Registrar R. GAFFA. Hears appeals from Uganda, Kenya and Tanganyika.

Permanent Commission of Enquiry: P.O.B. 2643, Dar es Salaam; Chair. Col. KITUNDU (Official Ombudsman); Sec. H. K. KATUA.

The High Court: Has final jurisdiction in both criminal and civil cases, subject only to the right of appeal to the East African Court of Appeal. Its headquarters are at Dar es Salaam but it holds regular sessions in all Regions. It consists of a Chief Justice and thirteen Judges.

Chief Justice: Mr. Justice AUGUSTINE SAIDI.

Judges: Mr. Justice M. C. E. P. BIRON, Mr. Justice M. P. K. KIMICHA, Mr. Justice G. ONYIUKE, Mr. Justice L. MFALILA, Mr. Justice L. M. MAKAME, Mr. Justice Z. N. EL-KINDY, Mr. Justice R. H. KISANGA, Mr. Justice P. M. JONATHAN, Mr. Justice C. E. BRAMBLE, Mr. Justice J. B. PATEL, Mr. Justice N. S. MNZAVAS, Mr. Justice J. M. M. MWAKASENDO (acting), Mr. Justice M. H. A. KWIKIMA.

Registrar: R. B. MAGANGA (acting).

Senior Deputy Registrar: M. J. MWAKIBETE.

District Courts: These are situated in each district and are presided over by either a Resident Magistrate or District Magistrate. They have limited jurisdiction and there is a right of appeal to the High Court.

Primary Courts: These are established in every district and are presided over by Primary Court Magistrates. They have limited jurisdiction and there is a right of appeal to the District Courts and then to the High Court.

Attorney-General of Zanzibar: WOLF DOURADO.

RELIGION

ANGLICAN

Archbishop:

Province of Tanzania: Most Rev. JOHN SEPEKU, Bishop of Dar es Salaam; P.O.B. 25016, Ilala, Dar es Salaam.

ROMAN CATHOLIC

The Catholic Church was established in Tanganyika in 1868. There are some 2,228,600 Catholics in Tanzania.

Archbishop:

Dar es Salaam: Cardinal LAUREAN RUGAMBWA, P.O.B 167, Dar es Salaam.

Archbishop:

Tabora: Most Rev. MARK MIHAYO, Private Bag, P.O. Tabora.

LUTHERAN

Evangelical Lutheran Church in Tanzania: P.O.B. 3033, Arusha; 568,444 mems.; Head: Bishop STEFANO R. MOSHI, D.D. (HON.); Exec. Sec. JOEL NGEIYAMU; publ. *Uhuru na Amani.*

GREEK ORTHODOX

Archbishop of East Africa: NICADEMUS OF IRINOUPOULIS, Nairobi. (Province covers Kenya, Uganda and Tanzania.)

OTHER CHURCHES

Baptist Mission of East Africa: P.O.B. 20395, Dar es Salaam.

Christian Missions in Many Lands (CMML): P.O.B. 524, Mtwara.

Church Missionary Society: Private Bag, Dodoma.

Ismalia Provincial Council: P.O.B. 460, Dar es Salaam. A large proportion of the Asian community are Ismaelis.

Moravian Church: P.O.B. 32, Tukuyu, with missions in Mbeya, Chunya and Tabora.

Muslim Association: P.O.B. 605, Tanga. Islam is the dominant religion in Zanzibar.

Pentecostal Church: P.O.B. 34, Kahama.

Presbyterian Church: P.O.B. 2510, Dar es Salaam.

THE PRESS

DAILIES

Daily News: P.O.B. 9033, Dar es Salaam; f. 1972; TANU Newspaper; Editor-in-Chief Pres. JULIUS NYERERE; Man. Editor BEN MKAPA; circ. 23,108.

Kipanga: P.O.B. 199, Zanzibar; Swahili; Publr. Information and Broadcasting Services.

Ngurumo: P.O.B. 937, Dar es Salaam; Swahili; Editor S. B. THAKER; circ. 15,000.

Uhuru: P.O.B. 9221, Dar es Salaam; official organ of TANU; Swahili; Editor F. RUHINDA; circ. 21,000.

SUNDAY PAPERS

Mzalendo: P.O.B. 9221, Dar es Salaam; f. 1972; weekly organ of TANU in Swahili.

Sunday News: P.O.B. 9033, Dar es Salaam; f. 1954; Editor-in-Chief Pres. JULIUS NYERERE; Editor BEN MKAPA; circ. 6,000.

PERIODICALS

The African Review: P.O.B. 35042, Dar es Salaam; f. 1971; politics etc.; quarterly.

Gazette of the United Republic: P.O.B. 2483, Dar es Salaam; weekly; official Government publication.

Government Gazette: P.O.B. 261, Zanzibar; f. 1964; official announcements; weekly.

Jenga: P.O.B. 2669, Dar es Salaam; journal of the National Development Corporation; circ. 6,000.

Kiongozi (*The Leader*): P.O.B. 9400, Dar es Salaam; f. 1950; Swahili; fortnightly; Editor C. H. B. HAKILI; circ. 23,000.

Kweupe: P.O.B. 1178, Zanzibar; Swahili; Publr. Information and Broadcasting Service; weekly.

Mbioni: P.O.B. 9193, Dar es Salaam; English language monthly journal of the political education college, Kivukoni College; circ. 4,000.

Mewnge (*Firebrand*): P.O.B. 52, Peramiho, Songea; f. 1937; monthly; Editor JOHN MAHUNDI; circ. 12,800.

Nchi Yetu: P.O.B. 9142, Dar es Salaam; f. 1964; Swahili; weekly; Editor: Director of Information Services.

Nyota Afrika: P.O.B. 9010, Nairobi; f. 1963; Swahili; monthly; circ. 50,000.

Spotlight on South Africa: Dar es Salaam; organ of the African National Congress (South Africa).

Taamuli: P.O.B. 35042, Dar es Salaam; journal of political science; Publr. Department of Political Science of University of Dar es Salaam; twice-yearly.

Taifa Tanzania: P.O.B. 9010, Nairobi, Kenya; weekly; Man. Editor BOAZ OMORI.

Tanzania Trade and Industry: P.O.B. 234, Dar es Salaam; English; quarterly; circ. 4,500.

Uhuru na Amani: P.O.B. 25, Soni; publication of Evangelical Lutheran Church; Swahili; circ. 12,000.

Ukulima wa Kisasa: P.O.B. 2308, Dar es Salaam; f. 1955; Swahili; monthly; agricultural; Editor C. C. RWECHUNGURA; circ. 27,000.

Ushirika: Co-operative Union of Tanzania, P.O.B. 2567, Dar es Salaam; weekly.

NEWS AGENCIES
FOREIGN BUREAUX

Novosti: P.O.B. 2271, Dar es Salaam; Chief V. P. SIDENKO; publishes Swahili weekly: *Urusi Leo.*

Četeka, Prensa Latina, Reuters and Tass (Dar es Salaam and Zanzibar) also have bureaux in Tanzania.

PUBLISHERS

East African Literature Bureau: P.O.B. 1408, Dar es Salaam; literature, education, technology, textbooks.

East African Publishing House: P.O.B. 3209, Dar es Salaam.

Kantis Printing Works: P.O.B. 455, Dar es Salaam; fiction, art, children's books, science, education.

Longman Tanzania Ltd.: P.O.B. 3164, Dar es Salaam.

Oxford University Press: P.O.B. 21039, Maktaba Rd., Dar es Salaam.

Tanzania Publishing House: P.O.B. 2138, Dar es Salaam; f. 1966; 60 per cent owned by National Development Corporation of Tanzania; publishes educational and general books in Swahili and English; Gen. Man. WALTER BGOYA.

RADIO

Radio Tanzania: P.O.B. 9191, Dar es Salaam; f. 1956; Dir. P. A. SOZIGWA.

Broadcasts internally in Swahili; Radio Tanzania's external service broadcasts in English, and in African languages of Mozambique, Rhodesia, South Africa and South West Africa (Namibia).

Radio Tanzania Zanzibar: P.O.B. 1178, Zanzibar; f. 1964; Broadcasting Officer OMAR M. OMAR.

Broadcasts in Swahili in three wavelengths.

There are over 500,000 radio sets in use (1974).

There is no television on the mainland but in January 1973 a colour service, the first in black Africa, began on Zanzibar.

FINANCE
BANKING

On February 6th, 1967, all banks in Tanzania were nationalized.

CENTRAL BANK ORGANIZATION

Bank of Tanzania: P.O.B. 2939, Mirambo St., Dar es Salaam; f. 1966; sole issuing bank; government-owned; Gov. E. I. M. MTEI; Dir.-Gen. C. M. NYIRABU; cap. 20m. sh.

OTHER STATE BANKS

The National Bank of Commerce: P.O.B. 1255, Dar es Salaam; f. 1967, by Act of Parliament, to take over branches in Tanzania of National and Grindlays Bank Ltd., Standard Bank Ltd., Barclays Bank D.C.O., Algemene Bank Nederland N.V., Bank of India Ltd., Bank of Baroda Ltd., Commercial Bank of Africa Ltd., National Bank of Pakistan and Tanzania Bank of Commerce; on October 24th, 1970, the business of the National Co-operative and Development Bank was absorbed by the N.B.C. under a Presidential Decree of October 10th; 49 branches, 21 sub-branches and 164 agencies throughout Tanzania; cap. p.u. 50m. sh; gen. res. 71.8m. sh.; total dep. 2,379,000 sh. (Feb. 1974); all types of banking business transacted; Chair. and Gen. Man. AMON JAMES NSEKELA; Gen. Man. SAIDI KASSIM.

People's Bank of Zanzibar: P.O.B. 1173, Forodhani, Zanzibar; f. 1966; state-controlled private concern; Chair. and Man. ERNEST C. WAKATI.

Tanganyika Post Office Savings Bank: P.O.B. 9300, Dar es Salaam; f. 1927; dep. 64m. sh.; 185 brs. serve 320,000 depositors in mainland Tanzania; Man. F. T. KISSIMA.

Tanzania Housing Bank: P.O.B. 1723, Dar es Salaam; provides medium and long-term loans for housing projects; Exec. Chair. L. A. SAZIA; Gen. Man. D. A. YONA.

Tanzania Investment Bank: P.O.B. 9373, Dar es Salaam; f. 1970; cap. 108.3m. sh.; provides medium and long-term finance and technical assistance for economic development; Chair. and Man. Dir. G. F. MBOWE; Gen. Man. C. KAHANGI.

Tanzania Rural Development Bank: P.O.B. 268, Dar es Salaam; f. 1971; cap. 100m. sh.; provides medium and long term finance for rural development; Chair. and Man. Dir. P. A. MAGANI; Gen. Man. Z. MAGINA.

INSURANCE

National Insurance Corporation: P.O.B. 9264, Dar es Salaam; f. 1966; nationalized 1967; handles all types of insurance business.

Some forty foreign insurance companies are represented in Tanzania.

TRADE AND INDUSTRY

CHAMBERS OF COMMERCE

Tanganyika Chambers of Commerce: P.O.B. 41, Dar es Salaam; Pres. J. T. LUPEMBE.

Arusha Chamber of Commerce and Agriculture: P.O.B. 141, Arusha.

Dar es Salaam Chamber of Commerce: P.O.B. 41, Dar es Salaam.

Dar es Salaam Merchants' Chamber: P.O.B. 12, Dar es Salaam.

Mtwara Region Chamber of Commerce and Agriculture: P.O.B. 84, Mtwara.

Southern Region Chamber of Commerce and Agriculture: P.O.B. 1063, Lindi.

Tanga Chamber of Commerce: P.O.B. 331, Tanga.

Tanga Region Chamber of Commerce and Agriculture: P.O.B. 543, Tanga.

ASSOCIATE MEMBERS

Co-operative Union of Tanganyika Ltd.: P.O.B. 2567, Dar es Salaam.

Lint and Seed Marketing Board: P.O.B. 9161, Dar es Salaam.

Tanganyika Coffee Growers Association Ltd.: P.O.B. 102, Moshi.

MARKETING AND PRODUCER ASSOCIATIONS AND BOARDS

Cashew Authority of Tanzania: P.O.B. 9234, Dar es Salaam.

Copra Board: f. 1950; administers the proceeds of a levy on exported copra products for the benefit of the copra industry.

General Agricultural Products Export Corporation: P.O.B. 9172, Dar es Salaam.

National Agricultural and Food Corporation: P.O.B. 903, Dar es Salaam; Gen. Man. G. ISHENGOMA.

National Milling Corporation (NMC): P.O.B. 9502, Dar es Salaam.

Tanganyika Coffee Board: P.O.B. 732, Moshi; Chair. O. A. MAKULE.

Tanganyika Pyrethrum Board: P.O.B. 41, Dar es Salaam.

Tanganyika Tea Growers' Association: P.O.B. 2177, Dar es Salaam; Chair. D. I. C. HOPKINS; Sec. A. J. FOSTER.

Tanzania Cotton Authority: f. 1973; replaced the Lint and Seed Marketing Board.

Tanzania Sisal Authority: f. 1973; replaced the Tanganyika Sisal Marketing Board and the Tanganyika Sisal Marketing Association Ltd.

Tanzania Tea Authority: P.O.B. 2663, Dar es Salaam; Chair. J. B. M. MWAKANGALE.

DEVELOPMENT CORPORATIONS

Commonwealth Development Corporation: London and Dar es Salaam; finances agricultural and industrial development projects.

National Development Corporation of Tanzania: P.O.B. 2669, Dar es Salaam; f. 1965; government-owned; initial cap. 20m. sh.; principal instrument of expansion and progress in the fields of production and investment; Chair. A. H. JAMAL, M.P.; Gen. Man. E. A. MULOKOZI.

Tanganyika Development Finance Company Ltd.: P.O.B 2479, Dar es Salaam; f. 1962; issued share cap. £2,000,000 taken up equally by the National Development Corporation of Tanzania, the Commonwealth Development Corporation and agencies of the Federal German and Netherlands Governments; to assist economic development; Man. M. A. BOYD.

Economic Development Commission: Dar es Salaam; f. 1962; Government-owned; to plan the development of the country's economy.

TRADE UNIONS

Minimum wages are controlled by law and there is also compulsory arbitration under the Trades Disputes (Settlement) Act. This Act makes strikes and lockouts illegal unless the statutory conciliation procedure has been followed. In 1964 the existing 13 trade unions were dissolved by legislation and the National Union of Tanganyika Workers (NUTA) was substituted. Wage increases are to be linked with productivity. In early 1974 NUTA had some 330,000 members.

National Union of Tanganyika Workers: Dar es Salaam; f. 1964; sole Trade Union organization, no international affiliation, regional affiliation to AATUF; about 290,000 mems.; Gen. Sec. ALFRED TANDAU; Deputy Gen. Sec. C. TUNGARAZA.

INDUSTRIAL SECTIONS

East African Community Workers' Section:

East African Community Corporations: Asst. Sec.-Gen. Mr. KALUWA.

East African Secretariat and General Fund Services: Asst. Sec.-Gen. Mr. MPANGALA.

Railways (EAR and TAZARA): Asst. Sec.-Gen. Mr. SAGAWALA.

Transport, Mines and Domestic Section:

Industries and Mines: Asst. Sec.-Gen. Mr. KAINDOA.

Commerce, Transport and Construction: Asst. Sec.-Gen. Mr. MWAMBUMA.

Domestic, Hotels and General Workers: Asst. Sec.-Gen. D. PAZZI.

Government Civil Servants' Section: Asst. Sec.-Gen. Mr. PALLAHANI.

Agricultural Workers' Section: P.O.B. 2087, Tanga; Asst. Gen. Sec. Mr. ZIMBIHILE.

Teachers' Section: Asst. Sec.-Gen. M. P. BESHA.

PRINCIPAL UNAFFILIATED UNION

Workers' Department of the Afro-Shirazi Party: P.O.B. 389, Vikokotoni, Zanzibar; f. 1965.

CO-OPERATIVES

The co-operative movement plays a central role in the Tanzanian economy, handling almost all of the country's exports (except sisal) and acting as middleman between farmers and the marketing boards which buy most of the country's agricultural produce. The movement has made considerable incursions into the transport, distribution and retail trade. The co-operatives obtain their trade commodities from the importing agencies which are mostly now para-statal organizations.

The movement is composed of some 1,670 primary marketing societies under the aegis of about 40 co-operative unions. The Co-operative Union of Tanganyika is the national organization (affiliated with the ruling TANU party) to which all unions belong.

Co-operative Development Office: Zanzibar; f. 1952; encourages and develops co-operative societies.

Co-operative Union of Tanganyika Ltd.: P.O.B. 2567, Dar es Salaam; f. 1962; the Co-operative Association was formed in 1962; Sec.-Gen. B. NGWILULUPI; 700,000 mems.

PRINCIPAL SOCIETIES

Bukoba Co-operative Union Ltd.: P.O.B. 5, Bukoba; 74 affiliated societies; 75,000 mems.

Kilimanjaro Native Co-operative Union Ltd.: f. 1932; 42 affiliated societies; 40,000 mems.

Zanzibar State Trading Corporation: P.O.B. 26, Zanzibar; state enterprise since 1964, sole exporter of cloves, markets clove oil, chillies, cocoa, lime juice, lime oil and clove pomanders, sole shipping agent for the port of Zanzibar.

TRANSPORT AND TOURISM

TRANSPORT

RAILWAYS

East African Railway Corporation: P.O.B. 30121, Nairobi, Kenya; self-financing corporation within the East African Community; Dir. Gen. Dr. E. N. GAKUO; Tanzanian Regional Man. F. K. BURENGELO.

TANZANIAN LINES				KILOMETRES
Tanga–Moshi	.	.	.	350
Moshi–Arusha	.	.	.	85
Dar es Salaam–Kigoma	.	.	1,248
Mnyusi–Ruvu	.	.	.	187
Kilosa–Kidatu	.	.	.	109
Tabora–Mwanza	.	.	.	377
Kaliuwa–Mpanda	.	.	.	210

Tanzania-Zambia Railway Authority (TAZARA): Head Office: P.O.B. 2834, Dar es Salaam; Branch Office: P.O.B. 1784, Lusaka, Zambia; Construction work on the 1,860 km. of railway line to link the towns of Dar es Salaam in Tanzania and Kapiri Mposhi in Zambia was formally inaugurated in October 1970 and was scheduled to be completed by 1977. Track laying was completed to Tunduma on the joint border in August 1973. The Project is executed under technical and financial assistance from the People's Republic of China and costs about sh. 3,000 million; Exec. Officer L. E. KAWESHA; Sec. C. P. SHENGENA.

ROADS

A network of passenger and goods road services (4,188 km.) is operated in the Southern Highlands, providing a link with Zambia, and there is a through service to Nairobi in Kenya.

KILOMETRES (1969)			
National/Main Roads	.	.	5,421
Regional/Secondary Roads	.	.	1,459
Other Roads	.	.	9,862
TOTAL	.	.	16,742

Zanzibar has 619 km. of road, of which 442 km. are bitumen surfaced, and Pemba has 363 km., 130 of which are bitumen surfaced. A new road has been built between Zambia and Tanzania with aid from U.S.A., the World Bank Group and the Government of Sweden.

INLAND WATERWAYS

Lake marine services operate on Lakes Tanganyika and Victoria. Steamers connect with Kenya, Uganda, Zaire, Burundi and Zambia.

SHIPPING

East African Harbours Corporation: P.O.B. 9184, Dar es Salaam; responsible for the harbours functions formerly exercised by the now defunct East African Railways and Harbours Administration; Chair. P. K. KINYANJUI; 3 brs.

Harbours: Dar es Salaam (eight deep-water berths, one oil jetty and for super oil tankers up to 100,000 m.t.), Mtwara (two deep-water berths), Tanga (lighterage), Mombasa, Kenya (largest port in East Africa, 13 deep-water berths, two oil jetties and an explosives jetty).

National Shipping Agency (NASACO): State-owned shipping company with which all foreign shipping lines have had to deal exclusively since February 1974.

The following shipping lines are among the shipping lines serving East African ports: British India Line, Canadian City Lines, Christensen Canadian Lines, Clan Line, Cie Maritime Belge, Deutsche Ost Afrika Linie, East Africa National Shipping Line, Farrell Lines, Harrison Line, Indian African Line, Koninklijke Nedlloyd N.V., Lloyd Triestino, Lykes Lines, Maritime Co. of Tanzania Ltd., Mitsui OSK Lines, Moore-McCormack, Nedlloyd Line, Nippon Yusen Kaisha Line, Oriental Africa Line, Osaka Shosen Kaisha, Scandinavian East Africa Line, Southern Lines, Sovereign Marine Lines, Svedel Lines, Swedish East Africa Line, Union Castle Line.

CIVIL AVIATION

The only major international airport is at Dar es Salaam, 8 miles from the city centre. Flights are made to Kenya from Arusha/Kilimanjaro, Musoma, Mwanza, Tanga and Zanzibar, and to Uganda from Bukoba and Mwanza. There are 13 other airports on internal air routes. An airport at Kilimanjaro was opened in 1971, and in 1973 a new airport was constructed at Pemba at a cost of 20 million sh.

East African Airways Corporation: Head Office: Nairobi, Kenya (see chapter on Kenya); offices in Tanzania: Airways Terminal, Tancot House, P.O.B. 543, Dar es Salaam; P.O.B. 773, Zanzibar.

Tanzania is also served by the following airlines: Aeroflot, Air Comores, Air India, Air Zaire, Air France, Air Madagascar, Alitalia, British Airways, Ethiopian Airlines, KLM, Lufthansa, PAA, SAS, Sabena, Swissair, TWA and Zambia Airways.

TOURISM

East Africa Tourist Travel Association: Headquarters P.O.B. 2013, Nairobi, Kenya.

Tanzania Tourist Corporation: Headquarters P.O.B. 2485, Dar es Salaam; State-owned; offices at IPS Bldg., Maktaba/Independence Ave.

Tanzania Wildlife Safaris: P.O.B. 602, Arusha; subsidiary of Tanzania Tourist Corpn.

UNIVERSITY

University of Dar es Salaam: P.O.B. 35091, Dar es Salaam; f. 1961; 308 teachers, 2,060 students.

THAILAND

INTRODUCTORY SURVEY

Location, Climate, Language, Religion, Flag, Capital

The Kingdom of Thailand is situated in South-East Asia and extends far south down the narrow Kra peninsula to Malaya (West Malaysia). It is bordered to the west and north by Burma, to the north-east by Laos and to the south-east by the Khmer Republic. The climate is tropical and humid with an average temperature of 85°F (29°C). The language is Thai. Hinayana Buddhism is the predominant religion and there are a number of Muslim Malays to the south. There is a Christian minority, mainly in Bangkok and the north. The national flag (proportions 3 by 2) has horizontal stripes of red, white, blue, white and red, the central blue stripe being twice the width of the others. The capital is Bangkok.

Recent History

Formerly known as Siam, Thailand took its present name in 1939. The army seized power in a *coup* in 1947 and Field Marshal Pibul Songgram took control. His influence declined during the 1950s and, despite the superficial restoration of normal political processes in 1957, he was overthrown that same year in a bloodless *coup* led by Field Marshal Sarit Thanarat. Elections were held but in 1958 martial law was declared and all political parties dissolved. Following the death of Sarit in 1963, Gen. (later Field Marshal) Thanom Kittikachorn became Prime Minister. After ten years of military rule, a constitution was introduced in June 1968. Seven political parties secured seats in the parliamentary elections of February 1969, the majority being won by the party formed by the military government.

Following renewed Communist insurgency and internal political unrest, Field Marshal Thanom proclaimed military rule in November 1971. A five-member National Executive Council took charge, chaired by Thanom, and, although an interim constitution was promulgated in December 1972, dissolving the Council, establishing a Council of Ministers and an Assembly and paving the way for a new constitution, power remained effectively with Thanom. Failure to produce the new constitution to deal with the perennial problems of inflation, corruption, insurgency and a continued U.S. military presence led to student riots, culminating in bloodshed, which brought down the Government in October 1973. A mainly civilian government was formed under Dr. Sanya Thammasak. After submitting a draft constitution in February 1974, he and his cabinet resigned in May. Dr. Sanya agreed to stay in office and formed a new cabinet.

In foreign policy Thailand, close to the battleground in Indochina, committed itself to the U.S. camp and sent troops to fight in South Viet-Nam. A rethink in 1970, however, caused these troops to be withdrawn. In 1972 the Government began to explore the possibility of relations with the People's Republic of China.

Government

Under the interim constitution in force since 1972 the King is Head of State and appoints the executive authority, the Cabinet, whose members must not be members of parliament. The unicameral parliament comprises a National Legislative Assembly of 299 members, chosen by a national governmental convention which was nominated by the King. The country is divided into 71 Changwat (provinces), each under a Governor.

Defence

The armed forces totalled 180,000 in 1973: army 125,000, navy 20,000, air force 35,000. Military service lasts two years between the ages of twenty-one and thirty.

Economic Affairs

Agriculture contributed about 25 per cent of gross domestic product in 1972. About a quarter of the total area of the country is under cultivation and some three-quarters of the working population are engaged in agriculture. Thailand is one of the world's major rice exporters (although the volume was reduced in 1973); rubber, kenaf and tapioca products are also valuable export items; and maize production and export have risen steeply in recent years, in response to government encouragement. Forestry and fisheries are important elements in the economy. Of a variety of minerals extracted, tin is the most important; others include tungsten, lead, antimony and iron ore. In 1973 it was reported that there were indications of small oil and natural gas finds. Thailand is self-sufficient in cement, refined sugar and refined petroleum, and light manufacturing industries are of some significance in the economic structure. Many industries have been established to manufacture products using domestic raw materials.

The economy is organized along free-enterprise lines, with the private sector contributing about 85 per cent of gross national product. The Third Development Plan (1972–76) envisages an annual growth rate of 7.0 per cent. Of 100,284 million bahts to be spent on development projects under the Plan, 69,500 million is to be raised through the budget, 13,854 million from state enterprises and local authorities and 16,930 million from foreign grants and loans.

Provisional figures for 1973 indicated that gross domestic product rose in real terms by 8.7 per cent over the 1972 figure. The most important factor was the revival of crop production after the failure of the 1972 harvests. Paddy production increased by about 16 per cent. The manufacturing sector showed a 9.5 per cent increase.

Transport and Communications

There are 8,207 km. of state railways which have been extended and modernized with the help of a World Bank loan of U.S. $22 million. There were over 17,000 km. of roads in 1971. The port of Bangkok is an important ocean junction in South-East Asia and also serves Laos. 430 million bahts have been allocated to improve Klong Toey which includes the building of a deep-water quay. Air transport is provided by Thai Airways, Thai Air International and numerous foreign lines.

Social Welfare

A new Labour Law became effective in April 1972 which establishes minimum wage rates, authorizes the Ministry of the Interior to rule on labour disputes and, where necessary, impose fines or terms of imprisonment.

Education

Education between the ages of seven and fifteen is compulsory, wherever possible. There are approximately 30,000 schools, 6 million students and 200,000 teachers. There are seven universities.

Tourism

Thailand is noted for its temples, palaces and pagodas. The Royal Palaces of Bangkok are world famous. Over one million tourists visited Thailand in 1973.

Visas are not required by nationals of the U.S.A.

Sport

Football, golf, badminton, Thai boxing (in which the feet are also used) and kite-flying are the most popular sports.

Public Holidays

1974: August 12th (The Queen's Birthday), October 23rd (Chulalongkorn Day), December 5th (The King's Birthday —National Day), December 10th (Constitution Day), December 31st (New Year's Eve).

1975: January 1st (New Year's Day), February 7th (Makha Bucha), April 6th (Chakri Day), April 13th (Sangkran Day), May 1st (May Day), May 5th (Coronation Day), May 6th (Wisakha Bucha), May 7th (State Ploughing Ceremony), June 23rd (Asalaha-Bucha), June 24th (Buddhist Lent).

Weights and Measures

The metric system is in force, but a number of traditional measures are also used.

Currency and Exchange Rates

100 satangs=1 baht.

Exchange rates (April 1974):

£1 sterling=47.225 bahts;
U.S. $1=20.00 bahts.

STATISTICAL SURVEY

AREA AND POPULATION

AREA (sq. km.)	POPULATION	
	1960 Census	1970 Census
514,000	26,257,916	34,397,374

Mid-1972 Population: 36,286,000 (UN estimate).
Bangkok (Municipal area): 2,228,144 (June 1970).

AGRICULTURE

DISTRIBUTION OF LAND
(1961—'000 hectares)

GOVERNMENT FOREST AND GRAZING	CULTIVATED	OTHER FOREST	SWAMP
26,470	10,295	14,427	207

RICE (PADDY) PRODUCTION

AREA ('000 hectares)				PRODUCTION ('000 metric tons)			
1968	1969	1970	1971	1968	1969	1970*	1971
7,088	7,584	7,494	7,526	12,500	13,410	18,540	13,740

*long tons

OTHER CROPS
('000 metric tons)

	COTTON	SUGAR CANE	COCONUTS	PEANUTS	SOYA BEANS	MUNG BEANS	SESAME	MAIZE	TOBACCO	RUBBER
1965	60	4,480	1,170	131	19	125	18	1,021	76	217
1966	89	3,827	1,069	220	38	132	20	1,122	88	218
1967	81	4,526	1,084	132	53	123	23	1,212	78	219
1968	132	5,879	1,099	158	45	184	22	1,500	90	259
1969*	128	6,741	1,111	181	61	202	22	1,700	92	282
1970*	53	7,387	1,113	185	62	210	22	1,950	95	287
1971*	81	8,473	1,200	200	90	250	30	2,300	99	325

* Estimated.

LIVESTOCK
('ooo head)

	1967	1968*	1969*	1970*	1971*
Buffaloes	7,061	7,500	7,650	7,850	8,000
Cattle	5,173	6,200	6,250	6,350	6,450
Chickens	35,101	37,000	39,000	42,000	45,500
Pigs	4,143	4,200	4,800	5,100	5,500

* Estimated.

FISHING
('ooo metric tons)

	FRESH-WATER	SEA	TOTAL
1967 . .	85.3	762.2	847.4
1968 . .	85.2	1,004.1	1,089.3
1969 . .	90.4	1,179.6	1,270.0
1970 . .	122.7	1,335.7	1,448.4
1971 . .	116.8	1,470.3	1,587.1

FORESTRY
(cubic metres)

	1965	1966	1967	1968	1969	1970*	1971
Teak	223,393	134,416	182,067	263,514	326,671	233,942	298,869
Other timbers . .	1,848,713	1,934,566	2,147,989	2,312,388	2,144,188	1,404,353	2,514,383

*Revised

MINING AND INDUSTRY
(metric tons)

	1967	1968	1969	1970	1971	1972
Tin Metal	31,196	32,766	28,793	29,731	29,609	30,125
Wolfram Ore . . .	839	965	1,267	1,378	4,865	6,486
Lead Ore . . .	8,180	6,477	4,230	3,034	5,525	4,306
Antimony Ore . .	2,280	423	1,561	5,544	8,397	11,265
Iron Ore . . .	549,180	499,506	477,393	22,523	39,532	27,817
Cement	1,733,909	2,168,202	2,403,385	2,629,912	2,779,004	3,391,527
Electricity Generated ('ooo kWh.) .	2,331,650	2,980,239	3,660,399	4,405,819	5,083,236	n.a.
Sugar	232,412	188,777	318,120	406,640	580,000	585,557

FINANCE

100 satangs (stangs)=1 baht.
Coins: ½, 1, 5, 10, 20, 25 and 50 satangs; 1 baht.
Notes: 50 satangs; 1, 5, 10, 20, 100 and 500 bahts.
Exchange rates (April 1974): £1 sterling=47.225 bahts; U.S. $1=20.00 bahts.
100 bahts=£2.12=$5.00.

Note: Between October 1963 and July 1973 the exchange rate was U.S. $1=20.80 bahts.

BUDGET* (1970 Fiscal Year)
(million baht)

REVENUE					EXPENDITURE				
Taxes and Duties	.	.	.	16,968.3	Economic Services	.	.	.	6,822.8
Customs	.	.	.	6,439.3	Agriculture	.	.	.	2,845.9
Income Tax	.	.	.	2,171.1	Power and Fuel	.	.	.	302.5
Other	.	.	.	8,357.9	Industry	.	.	.	194.4
Sales of Goods and Services	.	.	430.6	Transport, Communications	.	.	3,250.4
State Enterprises	.	.	.	613.4	Other	.	.	.	229.7
Other Sources	.	.	.	1,090.6	Education Services	.	.	.	4,453.3
					Defence	.	.	.	5,024.5
					Debt Service	.	.	.	2,340.2
					Public Health and Social Services	.		2,913.6
					Public Health	.	.	.	800.4
					Social Welfare	.	.	.	1,030.1
					Miscellaneous Social Services	.	.	1,083.1
					Justice, Police and Corrective Services	.	1,724.7
					General Administrative Services	.	.	2,697.6
					Miscellaneous Expenditure	.	.	1,323.2
TOTAL	.	.	.	19,102.9	TOTAL	.	.	.	27,299.9

Budget Expenditure: (1971) 27,195 million baht, *of which:* economic services 7,205m., social services 7,477m., defence 5,416m., general administration and services 3,838m., others 3,229m.; (1972) 29,000 million baht; (1973) 31,000 million baht.

Source: National Statistical Office.   * Revised.

DEVELOPMENT PLANS
(million baht)

REVENUE	SECOND PLAN (1967–71)	THIRD PLAN (1972–76)
Domestic Sources	41,440	83,354
Foreign Assistance	14,435	16,930
TOTAL . . .	55,875	100,284
EXPENDITURE		
Agriculture and Co-operatives . .	11,300	
Industry and Mining . . .	885	
Power	3,540	
Communications, Transport . .	17,080	
Community Development and Public Utilities	10,250	n.a.
Public Health	2,570	
Education	6,520	
Commerce	180	
Reserve	3,550	
TOTAL	55,875	100,284

GROSS NATIONAL PRODUCT
AT 1962 PRICES
(million baht)

	1969*	1970†	1971†
Agriculture	40,752	38,800	41,298
Crops	28,420	26,912	28,868
Livestock	5,315	4,801	4,795
Fisheries	4,099	4,288	4,880
Forestry	2,918	2,799	2,755
Mining and Quarrying . . .	2,519	2,832	3,060
Manufacturing	19,811	21,795	23,649
Construction	8,229	8,329	8,319
Electricity and Water Supply .	1,409	1,622	1,918
Transport and Communication .	7,628	8,270	8,780
Wholesale and Retail Trade .	22,434	25,623	26,302
Banking, Insurance and Real Estate .	4,737	5,627	6,322
Ownership of Dwellings . .	2,578	2,739	2,917
Public Administration and Defence .	5,519	6,115	6,677
Services	12,950	14,197	15,318
GROSS DOMESTIC PRODUCT (G.D.P.) .	128,566	135,949	144,560
Net factor from income abroad .	226	379	30
GROSS NATIONAL PRODUCT (G.N.P.) .	128,792	136,328	144,590

* Revised.   † Preliminary.

Source: National Development Board.

BALANCE OF PAYMENTS
(million baht)

	1969	1970	1971*
Goods and Services:			
Merchandise . . .	−11,298	−12,258	−10,065
Freight and Insurance . .	134	110	155
Travel	766	903	914
Investment income . . .	226	380	29
Government . . .	4,591	4,445	4,115
Other Services . .	237	199	189
Total . . .	− 4,156	− 5,210	− 3,757
Transfer Payments . .	1,187	1,012	904
CURRENT BALANCE . .	− 2,969	− 4,198	− 2,853
Capital and Monetary Gold:			
Private Investment . .	2,915	2,400	1,501
Government Investment . .	157	62	236
IMF Position . . .	—	203	—
Other Monetary Movements .	913	− 2,652	− 335
Net Errors and Omissions .	345	96	1,388

* Preliminary.

EXTERNAL TRADE
(million baht)

	1966	1967	1968	1969	1970	1971	1972
Imports	25,347	22,188	24,103	26,891	27,009	26,794	30,875
Exports (including re-exports)	14,310	14,166	13,679	14,722	14,772	17,281	22,491

THAILAND—(Statistical Survey)

PRINCIPAL COMMODITIES IMPORTED
(million baht)

	1970	1971
Food	1,091	1,032
Beverages and Tobacco . .	303	521
Crude Materials . . .	1,400	1,757
Mineral Fuels and Lubricants .	2,329	2,721
Animal and Vegetable Oils and Fats	35	39
Chemicals	3,505	3,723
Manufactured Goods . .	6,458	5,869
Machinery	9,536	8,949
Other	2,352	2,183
Total . . .	27,009	26,794

PRINCIPAL COMMODITIES EXPORTED
(million baht)

	1969	1970	1971	1972
Rice	2,945	2,516	2,901	4,434
Rubber	2,664	2,232	1,901	1,894
Tin Metal	1,631	1,618	1,561	1,643
Kenaf and Jute	781	719	933	1,074
Maize	1,674	1,857	2,251	1,939
Teak and Other Woods . . .	216	206	296	330
Tapioca Products	876	1,223	1,229	1,560

TRADING PARTNERS
(million baht)

	IMPORTS				EXPORTS			
	1969	1970	1971	1972	1969	1970	1971	1972
Germany, Fed. Republic	2,354	2,288	2,075	2,177	510	533	640	556
Hong Kong . . .	411	374	314	417	1,156	1,113	1,152	1,672
Indonesia . . .	195	400	145	n.a.	273	342	248	n.a.
Japan	9,515	10,107	10,093	11,402	3,192	3,770	4,277	4,660
Malaysia . . .	248	145	456	491	1,079	830	731	1,119
Netherlands . . .	583	368	316	n.a.	1,030	1,276	1,386	n.a.
Singapore . . .	294	263	215	433	1,154	1,018	1,225	1,954
United Kingdom . .	2,034	2,014	2,054	1,620	406	305	435	368
United States . .	3,922	4,011	3,807	4,838	2,168	1,985	2,264	2,834

TRANSPORT

RAILWAYS
('000)

	1967	1968	1969	1970	1971
Passenger-kilometres .	3,614,478	3,883,592	3,961,723	4,112,611	4,259,666
Freight (ton kilometres) .	1,941,129	2,082,671	1,978,704	2,209,473	2,381,480
Freight tons carried .	5,236	5,462	4,829	5,131	5,073

ROADS
('ooo)

	1967	1968	1969	1970
Cars . . .	115.4	125.6	167.7	212.9
Lorries and Buses	99.5	102.4	119.8	146.2

SHIPPING
(Port of Bangkok)

	VESSELS ENTERED (number)	NET REGISTERED TONNAGE (in ballast)	VESSELS CLEARED (number)	NET REGISTERED TONNAGE (in ballast)	CARGO TONS UNLOADED	CARGO TONS LOADED
1969 . .	1,685	1,550,850	1,732	3,614,349	8,297,613	4,707,989
1970 . .	1,616	1,554,973	1,744	3,677,742	8,681,952	4,963,682
1971 . .	1,566	2,122,036	1,917	3,609,033	9,525,599	6,370,711

CIVIL AVIATION
(International and Internal Flights of Thai Airways)

	KILOMETRES FLOWN	TOTAL LOAD TON/ KILOMETRES	PASSENGERS CARRIED		FREIGHT CARRIED	
			Number	Passenger kilometres	Tons	Ton/ kilometres
1969 . .	14,840,521	6,076,266	569,222	571,391,762	4,878.5	5,212,101
1970 . .	16,269,838	8,395,616	766,561	717,557,636	6,778.0	7,465,527
1971 . .	17,651,323	14,507,596	700,783	916,738,167	7,777.1	13,273,994

SERVICES

Number of Telephones (Bangkok and Thonburi only) (1969)	103,988
Number of Radio Sets (1971) . .	2,800,000
Number of Television Sets (1971) . .	230,000
Number of Daily Papers (1972) . .	17

EDUCATION
(1969)

	SCHOOLS	TEACHERS	STUDENTS*
Kindergarten	71	954	26,296
Elementary (Ministry of Education)	569	7,684	184,124
Elementary (Provincial Authority) .	25,304	117,050	4,175,144
Municipal	497	8,446	267,360
Secondary	496	10,888	219,346
Private Regular . . .	2,408	43,294	1,079,537
Private Special . . .	1,206	4,257	115,952
Vocational	265	5,985	96,833
TOTAL . . .	30,816	198,558	6,164,952

* 1972 enrolment: primary schools 5,796,187; secondary schools 582,466; universities 45,237.

Source: National Statistical Office, Bangkok (unless otherwise stated).

THE CONSTITUTION

(Promulgated December 15th, 1972, as an interim Constitution, pending the drafting of a new Constitution by the National Legislative Assembly.)

SUMMARY

Article 1. Thailand is a Kingdom with the King as Head of State and Commander-in-Chief of the Armed Forces.

Article 2. The sovereign power emanates from the Thai people. The King, as Head of State, exercises such power according to the provisions of the Constitution.

Article 3. The King uses legislative power through the National Legislative Assembly, executive power through the Cabinet and judicial power through the Court.

Article 4. The person of the King is sacred and inviolable.

Article 5. There is a Privy Council consisting of not more than nine persons who can be appointed and relieved of their duties at the King's pleasure.

Article 6. The National Legislative Assembly consists of 299 members whom the King appoints from among Thai nationals. The term of the National Legislative Assembly is three years.

Article 7. In accordance with the resolution of the National Legislative Assembly, the King appoints from among its members a President and one or more Vice-Presidents.

Article 8. Subject to Articles 10 and 11, the National Legislative Assembly may adopt procedural rules on the election and duties of its officers, on parliamentary business and on consideration of constitutional matters. A quorum comprises at least one-third of its membership, subject to Article 10.

Article 9. The King enacts laws with the advice and consent of the National Legislative Assembly. Only members of the National Legislative Assembly or the Cabinet can present Bills. Members of the Cabinet only can submit financial Bills. The President of the Assembly decides in case of doubt.

Articles 10–11. The adoption of a Constitution.

Article 12. Any Minister may be questioned by a member of the National Legislative Assembly except where matters of national security or particular national interest are involved.

Article 13. The principle of parliamentary privilege applies not only to private utterances by members but also to deliberations of the Assembly and where applicable to published reports of parliamentary proceedings. Where criminal proceedings are pending against a detained or arrested member, that member can be released or trial proceedings suspended at the request of the President of the Assembly.

Article 14. The King appoints the Prime Minister and an appropriate number of Ministers forming the Council of Ministers responsible for the national administration. The Prime Minister and Ministers have the right to attend sittings of the National Legislative Assembly to make factual statements or express opinions, but they cannot vote.

Article 15. In the case of a threat to the security of the Kingdom or of national disaster or in the event of special financial legislation, the King has power to issue a royal decree which, if submitted to and approved by the National Legislative Assembly, becomes law. Whether approved or not, it is announced in the Official Gazette.

Article 16. The King has the power to issue any royal decree not inconsistent with law.

Article 17. During the coming into effect of the Constitution, the Prime Minister is empowered by Cabinet resolution to issue orders or take appropriate measures to safeguard national security, the Throne or the economy or to counter actions designed to subvert public morals, law and order.

Article 18. All orders, decrees or laws enacted must be countersigned by the Prime Minister or a Minister. A Prime Ministerial appointment must be countersigned by the President of the National Legislative Assembly.

Articles 19–23. Judicial independence is recognized.

THE GOVERNMENT

HEAD OF THE STATE

King Bhumibol Adulyadej (King Rama IX), born December 5th, 1927; succeeded to the throne on the death of his brother King Ananda Mahidol, on June 9th, 1946. The Heir-Apparent is Prince Vajiralongkorn, born July 28th, 1952.

PRIVY COUNCIL

H.H. Prince Dhani Nivat Kromamun Bidyalabh (President).
Gen. Luang Kampanart Sanyakorn.
Mom Chao Vongsanuvat Devakul.
Gen. Luang Suranarong.

Sri Sena Sampatasiri.
Phya Manavarat Sevi.
Chao Phya Sri Dhamathibet.
M. L. Dej Snitwongsa.

THE CABINET

(July 1974)

Prime Minister: Dr. Sanya Thammasak.
Deputy Prime Minister: Dr. Prakob Hutasingh.
Minister Attached to the Office of the Prime Minister: Manoon Borisutdhi.
Minister of Foreign Affairs: Charoonphan Israngkoon Na Ayudhaya.
Minister of Finance: Sommai Hoontrakul.
Minister of Commerce: Vicharn Nivatvongs.
Minister of Industry: Aroon Sorathesn.
Minister of Defence: Gen. Kruan Suthanin.
Minister of Agriculture and Co-operatives: Prince Chakraphan Pensiri Chakraphan.
Minister of Communications: Chaovana Na Sylvanta.
Minister of the Interior: Pol. Maj.-Gen. Atthasit Sithisoonthorn.
Minister of Justice: Kitti Sihanon.
Minister of Education: Kriang Kiratikorn.
Minister of Public Health: Dr. Udom Posakrisana.
Minister of State University Bureau: Kasem Suwanakul.

Deputy Minister of Foreign Affairs: Maj.-Gen. Chartchai Chunhawan.
Deputy Minister of Finance: Sanan Ketudat.
Deputy Minister of Commerce: Prasong Sukhum.
Deputy Minister of Industry: Prakaiphet Inthusophon.
Deputy Ministers of Defence: Admiral Thavil Rayananonda, Air Chief Marshal Bua Sirisup.
Deputy Ministers of Agriculture and Co-operatives: Dr. Thalerng Thamrong Navasawat, Phanlert Buranasilpin.
Deputy Minister of Communications: Sribhumi Sukhanetr.
Deputy Ministers of the Interior: Pol. Gen. Prachuab Suntrangkoon, Thien Ashakul, Pol. Lt.-Gen. Chumpon Lohachala.
Deputy Minister of Justice: Sompob Hotrakitya.
Deputy Ministers of Education: Dr. Kaw Swasdi Panich, Jirayu Nopawong.
Deputy Minister of Public Health: Dr. Sem Pringpuangkao.

DIPLOMATIC REPRESENTATION

EMBASSIES ACCREDITED TO THAILAND
(In Bangkok unless otherwise stated)

Afghanistan: Islamabad, Pakistan.
Argentina: 5th Floor, Thaniya Bldg., 62 Silom Rd.; *Ambassador:* Carlos de Posada (also accred. to Republic of Viet-Nam).
Australia: 7th Floor, Anglo-Thai Bldg., 64 Silom Rd.; *Ambassador:* Thomas Kingston Critchley, c.b.e.
Austria: Maneeya Bldg. (3rd Floor), 518 Ploenchit Rd., P.O.B. 27; *Ambassador:* Walter de Comtes (also accred. to Republic of Viet-Nam and Malaysia).
Bangladesh: *Ambassador:* Khweja Mohammad Kaiser.
Belgium: 44 Soi Phya Phipat; *Ambassador:* Luc Leermakers (also accred. to Laos).
Brazil: 5th Floor, Maneeya Bldg., 518 Ploenchit Rd.; *Ambassador:* Jorge de Oliveira Maia (also accred. to Republic of Viet-Nam).
Burma: 132 Sathorn Nua Rd.; *Ambassador:* U Tun Win.

Canada: Thai Farmers Bank Bldg., 142 Silom Rd., P.O.B. 2090; *Ambassador:* Gordon G. Riddell.
China (Taiwan): 1126 New Phetchburi Rd.; *Ambassador:* Admiral Ma Chi-chuang.
Cuba: Tokyo, Japan.
Denmark: 10 Soi Attakarn Prasit, Sathorn Tai Rd.; *Ambassador:* Albert Kønigsfeldt (also accred. to Republic of Viet-Nam, Philippines and Laos).
Dominican Republic: Taipeh, Taiwan.
Egypt: 49 Soi Ruam Rudee, Ploenchit Rd.; *Ambassador:* Moustafa Fahmy El-Essawy.
Finland: New Delhi, India.
France: Custom House Lane, New Rd.; *Ambassador:* Jean-Louis Toffin.
Germany, Federal Republic: 9 Sathorn Tai Rd.; *Ambassador:* Ulrich von Rhamm (also accred. to Laos).

Greece: New Delhi, India.

India: 139 Pan Rd.; *Ambassador:* ROMESH BHANDARI.

Indonesia: 600–602 Phetchburi Rd.; *Ambassador:* Maj.-Gen. SOETARTO SIGIT.

Iran: Shell Bldg., 140 Wireless Rd., 9th Floor; *Ambassador:* Dr. MOHESN S. ESFANDIARY.

Iraq: Karachi, Pakistan.

Israel: 31 Soi Lang Suan, Ploenchit Rd.; *Ambassador:* REHAVAM AMIR (also accred. to Laos).

Italy: 92 Sathorn Nua Rd.; *Ambassador:* DIEGO SORO.

Japan: 1674 New Phetchburi Rd.; *Ambassador:* FUJISAKI MASATO.

Jordan: New Delhi, India.

Khmer Republic: 185 Rajdamri Rd.; *Ambassador:* TIM NGON.

Korea, Republic: 956 Rama IV Rd., Olympia Thai Bldg., 1st floor; *Ambassador:* YUN YOUNG LIM (also accred. to The Maldives).

Laos: 193 Sathorn Tai Rd.; *Ambassador:* KÈO VIPHAKONE (also accred. to Philippines, Burma, Pakistan and Malaysia).

Lebanon: 23/48 Panch Sheel Marg., Chanakya Puri, New Delhi 21, India.

Malaysia: 35 Sathorn Tai Rd.; *Ambassador:* Gen. Tan Sri ABDUL HAMID bin BIDIN.

Nepal: 189 Soi Pueng Suk, Sukhumvit 71; *Ambassador:* BHARAT RAJ BHANDARY.

Netherlands: 106 Wireless Rd.; *Ambassador:* FRANS VAN DONGEN (also accred. to Laos).

New Zealand: Anglo-Thai Bldg., 64 Silom Rd.; *Ambassador:* Hon. E. J. HALSTEAD, T.D. (also accred. to Laos).

Nigeria: New Delhi, India.

Norway: 16 Surasak Rd.; *Ambassador:* OLAF TEILEFSEN.

Pakistan: 31 Soi Nana Nua, Sukhumvit Rd.; *Ambassador:* ABDUL GHAYUR. (also accred. to Laos).

Philippines: 760 Sukhumvit Rd.; *Ambassador:* Gen. MANUEL T. YAN.

Portugal: 26 Bush Lane; *Chargé d'Affaires:* Dr. MANUEL SÁ NOGUEIRA.

Saudi Arabia: 2nd Floor, 385 Silom Rd.; *Ambassador:* ABDULRAHMAN AL-OMRAN.

Singapore: 90 Sathorn Nua Rd.; *Ambassador:* CHI OWYANG.

Spain: 104 Wireless Rd.; *Ambassador:* MARIANO SANZ BRIZ (also accred. to Republic of Viet-Nam).

Sri Lanka: 22/1 Soi Sukothai 3, Rajvithee Rd.; *Ambassador:* H. O. WIJEGOONAWARDENA.

Sweden: 197/1 Silom Rd.; *Ambassador:* ERIC VIRGIN (also accred. to Republic of Viet-Nam and Laos).

Switzerland: 35 North Wireless Rd.; *Ambassador:* RUDOLF HARTMANN.

Turkey: 352 Phaholyothin Rd.; *Ambassador:* TÜRGUT ILKAN (also accred. to Republic of Viet-Nam, Singapore and Laos).

U.S.S.R.: 108 Sathorn Nua Rd.; *Ambassador:* BORIS I. ILYECHEV.

United Kingdom: Ploenchit Rd.; *Ambassador:* DAVID L. COLE.

U.S.A.: 95 Wireless Rd.; *Ambassador:* W. KINTNER.

Vatican: 217/1 Sathorn Tai Rd.; *Apostolic Pro-Nuncio:* The Most Rev. GIOVANNI MORETTI.

Viet-Nam, Republic: 83/1 Wireless Rd.; *Ambassador:* Lt.-Gen. TRAN NGOC TAM.

Yugoslavia: 15 Soi 61, Sukhumvit Rd.; *Ambassador:* AZEM ZULFICARI.

Thailand also has diplomatic relations with Hungary, Mongolia, Poland and Romania.

PARLIAMENT

NATIONAL LEGISLATIVE ASSEMBLY

Under the Constitution the legislature comprises a single-chamber of 299 members. The Assembly was dissolved by the King in December 1973, and a new one was appointed in the same month by a national government convention.

POLITICAL PARTIES

Political parties are in the process of being formed.

JUDICIAL SYSTEM

COURTS OF FIRST INSTANCE

Magistrates' Courts (*Sarn Kwaeng*): Function is to dispose of small cases with minimum formality and expense. Judges sit singly.

Juvenile Courts (*Sarn Kadee Dek Lae Yaochon*): original jurisdiction over juvenile delinquency and matters affecting children and young persons. One judge and one woman associate judge form a quorum. There are four courts in Bangkok, Songkla, Nakhon Ratchasima and Chiang Mai.

Civil Court (*Sarn Paeng*): Court of general original jurisdiction in civil and bankruptcy cases in Bangkok and Thonburi. Two judges form a quorum.

Criminal Court (*Sarn Aya*): Court of general original jurisdiction in criminal cases in Bangkok and Thonburi. Two judges form a quorum.

Provincial Courts (*Sarn Changvad*): Exercise unlimited original jurisdiction in all civil and criminal matters, including bankruptcy, within its own district which is generally the province itself. Two judges form a quorum. At each of the five Provincial Courts in the South of Thailand where the majority of the population are muslims (i.e., Pattani, Yala, Betong, Satun, and Narathiwat), there are two Dath Yutithum or Kadis (muslim judges). A Kadi sits with two trial judges in order to administer Islamic laws and usages in civil cases involving family and inheritance where all parties concerned are muslims. Questions on Islamic laws and usages which are interpreted by a Kadi are final.

COURT OF APPEALS

Sarn Uthorn: Appellate jurisdiction in all civil, bankruptcy and criminal matters; appeals from all of the Courts of First Instance throughout the country come to this Court. Two judges form a quorum.

SUPREME COURT

Sarn Dika: The final court of appeal in all civil, bankruptcy and criminal cases. The quorum in the Supreme Court consists of three judges. The Court sits in plenary session occasionally to determine cases of exceptional importance and cases where there are reasons for reconsideration or overruling of its own precedents. The quorum for the full Court is half the total number of judges in the Supreme Court.

RELIGION

Buddhism is the prevailing religion. Besides Buddhists, there are some Muslim Malays. Most of the immigrant Chinese are Confucians.

Christians are found mainly in Bangkok and Northern Thailand and number about 149,655, of whom 116,011 are Roman Catholics.

BUDDHIST

Supreme Patriarch of Thailand: (to be appointed following the death of the former Supreme Patriarch in December 1973).

The Buddhist Association of Thailand: 41 Phra Aditya St., Bangkok; under royal patronage; f. 1934; 3,879 mems.; Pres. Dr. SANYA THAMMASAK.

ROMAN CATHOLIC

Bangkok: Archbishop: Most Rev. JOSEPH KHIAMSUN NITTAYO, 51 Oriental Ave., Bangkok 5.

Tharé and Nonseng: Archbishop: Most Rev. MICHEL KIEN SAMOPHITHAK.

Catholic Association of Thailand: 12 Convent Rd., Bangkok.

PROTESTANT

The Church of Christ in Thailand: 14 Pramuan Rd., Bangkok; f. 1934; communicant mems. 24,000; Moderator Rev. CHAROON WICHAIDIST; Gen. Sec. WICHEAN WATAKEECHAROEN; affiliated mission mems.: United Presbyterian (U.S.A.), Disciples of Christ Mission American Baptist, German Lutheran (Marburger), Presbyterian Church of Korea, Church of South India, United Church of Christ in Japan, Member of the World Presbyterian Alliance, East Asia Christian Conference and W.C.C.

THE PRESS

(In Bangkok unless otherwise stated)

DAILIES
THAI LANGUAGE

Ban Muang: 35 Phya Thai Rd.; Editor MANA PRAEPHAN; circ. 100,000.

Bangkok News (formerly *Kiattisakdi*): 297 Hua Mark Rd.; Editor CHARN SINSOOK; circ. 45,000.

Chao Thai: Thai Samaki Co. Ltd., 555 Chakrapatpong Rd., Siyaek Maensrie; f. 1947; Editor CHALERM WUTHI-KOSIT; circ. 10,000.

Daily News: 423 Siphya Rd.; Editor-in-Chief SANIT EKACHAI; circ. 150,000.

Khao Panich (Daily Trade News): Ministry of Commerce, Memorial Bridge; Editor SOPHON EAMKEO; f. 1950; circ. 15,000.

Prachathipatai: 161/4 Soi Mahadlekluang 3, Rajadamri; Editor SAWAI PHROMMI; circ. 12,000.

Siam Rath: Mansion 6, Rajdamnern Ave.; Editor NOPPORN BUNYARIT; circ. 100,000.

Thai Rath: 1 Super Highway Rd.; Editor KAMPOL VACHA-RAPOL; circ. 500,000.

ENGLISH LANGUAGE

Bangkok Post: Post Publishing Co. Ltd.. Mansion 4, Rajdamnern Ave.; Editor MICHAEL J. GORMAN; circ. over 17,000.

Bangkok World: Post Publishing Co. Ltd., Mansion 4, Rajdamnern Ave.; f. 1957; Editor CHARLES KIRKWOOD; circ. 13,000.

The Nation: 861/3 New Rd.; Editor THAMNOON MAHA-PANIYA.

CHINESE LANGUAGE

Chia Pao (Tang Nam): 1017 Siphya Rd.

Sakol: 21/1 New Rd.; Editor EIENGLIEAK SAE-THEA; circ. 10,000.

Siang Sian Yit Pao Daily News: 267 New Rd.; Editor JAMES ENG; circ. 50,000.

Siri Nakorn: 984–8 New Rd.; Editor PRASIT VAREEVES; circ. 40,000.

Tong Hua: 877–9 New Rd.; Editor SOON SAE-TUNG; circ. 15,000.

WEEKLIES
THAI LANGUAGE

Arthit (The Sun): 58 Soi 36, Sukumvit Rd.

Bangkok: 33–9 Lan Luang Rd.; Editor VICHIT ROJANA-PRABHA.

Bangkok Time: 37 Bamrung Muang Rd.; Editor CHAROON KUVANONDH.

Dara Thai: 9 Soi Bampen, Tung Mahamek; Editor SURAT PUKAVES.

Darunee (Lady): 7/2 Soi Watanawonge, Rajprarope Rd.; f. 1953; magazine for ladies; Principal Officer CHIT KANPAI; Editor WEERAWAN SUWANVIPATH; circ. 100,000.

Khun Ying: 215 Soi Saynamthip, Svkumvit Rd.; women's magazine.

Mae Sri Ruen: 13/22 Prachatipok Rd.; Editor Mrs. NANTRA RATANAKOM.

Nakorn Thai: 13–22 Soi Wat Hivanruchee, Prachatipok Rd.

Phadung Silp: 163 Soi Thesa, Rajborpit Rd.; Editor AKSORN CHUAPANYA.

Sakul Thai: 58 Soi 36, Sukumvit Rd.; Editor PRAYOON SONGSERM-SWASDI.

Satri Sarn: 83–86 Arkarntrithosthep 2, Prachathipatai Rd.; f. 1948; women's magazine; Editor Miss NILAWAN PINTHONG.

See Ros: 612 Luke Luang Rd.; Editor MANI CHINDANONDH.

Siam Rath Weekly Review: Mansion 6, Rajadamnern Ave.; Editor SAMRUEY SINGHADET.

Sri Sapadah: Soi Sri Yan 1, Nakorn Chaisri Rd.; Editor M. L. Y. CHITTI NOPAWONGSE.

ENGLISH LANGUAGE

Financial Post: Mansion 4, Rajdamnern Ave., Bangkok.

FORTNIGHTLIES

Catholic Association Newsletter: 12 Convent Rd.

Chaiya-Pruek: 599 Maitrichit Rd.; f. 1953; Editor ANUJ APAPIROM.

Mae Barnkarn Ruan: 612 Luke Luang Rd.; Editor Mrs. THONG MUAN CHINDANONDH.

Nakorn Thai: 13/3 Prachatipok Rd.; Editor SAKDI RATANAKOM.

Pharp Khao Taksin: 226 Samsen Rd.; Editor LUAN VIRAPHAT.

Saen Sook: 553/9 Sriayuthya Rd.; Editor SUCHATI AMONKUL.

Sena Sarn: Army Auditorium, Ministry of Defence; Editor Lt.-Col. FUEN DISYAVONG.

MONTHLIES

Anusarn Aor Sor Tor: The Tourist Organization of Thailand, Rajdamnern Ave.

Bangkok Chamber of Commerce: 150 Rajbopit Rd.; Editor SANT SRONG-PRAPHA.

Chao Krung: Mansion 6, Rajadamnern Ave.; Editor NOP-PHORN BUNYARIT.

Chaiyapruek: Maitri Chit Rd.; Editor PLUANG NA-NAKORN.

Chang Akhas (*Thai Engineers' Digest*): Air Force Engineering Dept., Sapan Daeng; Editor Wing-Commdr. PRASIT PRAPASANOBOL.

The Dharmacakshu (*Dharma-vision*): Foundation of Mahamakut Rajavidyalaya, Wat Bovaranives, Banglumpoo, Bangkok 2; f. 1894; Buddhism and related subjects; Editor Group Capt. MEGH AMPHAICHARIT; circ. 5,000.

The Investor: Siam Publications Ltd., P.O.B. 1946, Bangkok; f. Dec. 1968; English language; business, industry, finance and economics in Thailand; Editor Dr. AMNUAY VIRAVAN; Man. Dir. ALAN DARBY; circ. 6,000.

Kasikorn: Dept. of Agriculture, Rajdamnern Ave.; Editor PAIROJ POLPRASID.

Kosana Sarn: Public Relations Dept., Rajadamnern Ave.; f. 1948; radio and TV magazine, Editor Mrs. CHA-OOM YAMNGARM.

The Lady: 77 Rama V Rd.; Editor Princess NGARMCHITR PREM PURACHATRA.

Navikasart: Royal Thai Navy, Thonburi; Editor Commodore YONG-YUT ANCHAVAKOM.

Satawa Liang: 689 Wang Burapa Rd.; Editor THAMRONG-SAK SRICHAND.

Thai T.V. Mirror: Thai T.V. Co. Ltd., 73-75 Sow Ching Cha Square; f. 1954; Editor ARCHIN PUNJAPHAN; circ. 20,000.

Thailand Illustrated: Government Relations Dept., Rajadamnern Ave., Bangkok 2; f. about 20 years ago; Thai and English; Editor Mrs. PAWA WATANASUPT; circ. 2,000.

Thammachak: Maha Makut Rajavithayalai, Prasumern Rd.

Villa Wina Magazine: 3rd Floor, Chalerm Ketr Theatre Bldg.; Editor BHONGSAKDI PIAMLAP.

Vithayu Sueksa: Ministry of Education, Rajdamnern Ave.; Editor PLUANG NA-NAKORN.

EVERY TWO MONTHS

Silpakon (*Fine Arts*): Records Section, National Archives Division, Fine Arts Dept., Na Pra That Rd.; f. 1957; Editor PRAPAT TRINARONG; circ. 1,000.

PRESS AGENCIES
FOREIGN BUREAUX

Agence France-Presse: P.O.B. 1567, Bangkok; Correspondent JACQUES J. ABELOUS.

AP: 103 Pat Pong Rd., Bangkok; Correspondent PETER O'LOUGHLIN.

Central News Agency Inc.: 25 Soi 2, St. Louis, Sathorn South Rd., Bangkok; Chief of Bureau CONRAD LU.

Antara, The Jiji Press, Reuters and UPI also have bureaux in Bangkok.

PRESS ASSOCIATION

Press Association of Thailand: 299 Nakorn Rassima North Rd., Bangkok; f. 1941.

There are other regional Press organizations and two journalists' organizations.

PUBLISHERS

Aksorn Charoen Tasna Ltd.: Bamrung Muang Road 195, Bangkok.

Chalermnit Press: 108 Sukumvit Soi 53, Bangkok; f. 1957; dictionaries, history, literature, guides to Thai language, books on Thailand; Mans. Brig.-Gen. M. L. M. JUMSAK and Mrs. JUMSAI.

Post Publishing Co. Ltd.: Mansion 4, Rajadamnern Ave., Bangkok; f. 1964; publishers of *The Bangkok Post* and *The Financial Post*; Chair. PRASIT LULITANON; Man. Dir. MICHAEL GORMAN.

Pra Cha Chang & Co. Ltd.: Talad Noi 861-3, New Rd., Bangkok.

Prae Pittaya Ltd.: P.O.B. 914, 718 Wang Burapa Rd., Bangkok; publishers, stationers, booksellers and general distributors.

Pramuansarn Publishing House: 703/15-16 Petchaburi Road, Bangkok; f. 1955; general books, fiction and non-fiction, paperbacks, guidebooks, children's books; Man. LIME TAECHATADA.

Ruamsarn: Wang Burapha, Bangkok.

Siam Directory: 535 Samsen, St., cnr. Wat Rajathivas, Bangkok; history, politics, economics, directories.

Sie Kan Ka Co. Ltd.: Prayurawong Mansion 198, Mansion 1, Thonburi.

Social Science Association Press: Chula Soi 2, Phya Thai Rd., Bangkok; f. 1961; scholarly books, quarterly magazine; Man. and Editor SULAK SIVARAKSA.

Suekanka Ltd.: Practatipok Road 198, Thonburi.

Suksapan Panit (*Business Organization of Teachers' Institute*): Mansion 9, Rajdamnern Ave., Bangkok; f. 1950; textbooks, children's books, pocketbooks; Man. KAMTHON SATHIRAKUL.

Suriwongs Book Centre: P.O.B. 44, Chiengmai; br. offices: 79-81 Chang Klan St., 33 Rajdamnern Rd.; f. 1954; textbooks and general books in Thai; wholesalers and retailers of Thai and foreign books; Man. Proprietor CHAI JITTIDECHARAKS.

Thai Commercial Printing Press: Bangkok; law, administration, politics, economics, industry.

Thai Inc.: Mansion 96, Rajadamnern Ave. 2, Bangkok.

Thai Vatnapanis: Maitrijit Road 599, Bangkok; children's books, picture books.

RADIO AND TELEVISION

RADIO

Thai National Broadcasting Station: Public Relations Dept., Rajdamnern Ave., Bangkok; f. 1938; under full Government control; Deputy Dir.-Gen. Dr. W. Siwasariyanond; services in Thai, English, French, Vietnamese, Chinese, Malay, Laotian and Cambodian.

Ministry of Education Broadcasting Service: Division of Educational Information, Ministry of Education, Bangkok; f. 1954; Dir. of Division Mom Luang Chintana Navawongs; evening programmes for general public; daytime programmes for schools including music, social studies and English.

Pituksuntiradse Radio Stations: Two at Paruksakavun Palace and Bangkhen, Bangkok, two at Nakorn, Rajsima and one at Chiengmai; Dir.-Gen. Suchart P. Sakorn; programmes in Thai.

Radio Station HS1JS: Bang-Sue, Bangkok; controlled by Government, permits advertising; Dir.-Gen. K. Kengradomying.

Voice of Free Asia: Ayutthaya Province; established 1968; 1,000 kW. broadcasting station; operated to broadcast programmes for the Royal Thai and U.S. Governments in Thai, English and several other languages used in the area.

In 1971 there were 2,800,000 radio sets.

TELEVISION

Television of Thailand: Government Public Relations Department, Bangkok; Government controlled; three stations; programmes 12.00 p.m.–16.00 p.m.

Thai Television Co. Ltd.: Mansion B., Rajdamnern Ave., Bangkok; transmissions from 1955, commercial programmes 4.45–12.00 p.m. daily, 10.00 a.m.–12.00 p.m. weekends; Dir.-Gen. Gen. K. Punnagunta.

Royal Thai Army HSA-TV: Pahol-yodhin St., Sanam Pao, Bangkok; transmissions over a 75 mile radius since Jan. 1958; daily 18.00–23.00 hours; Sundays 09.00–12.00 and 17.00–23.00 hours; Dir.-Gen. P. Cheunbonn.

In 1971 there were about 230,000 TV receivers in use.

FINANCE

(cap. =capital; p.u. =paid up; dep. =deposits; m. =million; res. =reserves; amounts in baht).

BANKING

CENTRAL BANK

Bank of Thailand: 273 Bang Khunprom, P.O.B. 154, Bangkok; f. 1942; Government-owned; cap. 20m.; dep. (Government and banks) baht 6,316m. (Dec. 1971); Gov. Bishudi Nimmanhaemin.

BANKS INCORPORATED IN THAILAND

Bangkok Bank Ltd., The: 3–9 Suapa Rd., Bangkok; f. 1944; cap. 500m.; dep. 14,051m. (Dec. 1971); Pres. Gen. Prapas Charusathiara; Pres. Chin Sophon Panich.

Bangkok Bank of Commerce Ltd.: 171 Surawongse Rd., Bangkok; f. 1944; cap. p.u. 50m.; dep. 1,963m. (Dec 1971); Chair. M. R. Boonrub Phinijchonkadi; Vice-Chair. Kukrit Pramoj; Man. Dir. Ajavadis Diskul.-

Bangkok Metropolitan Bank Ltd.: 84–96 Rajawongse Rd., Bangkok; f. 1950; cap. 10m.; dep. 2,310m. (June 1972); Chair. Phya D. Montri; Man. Dir. Udane Tejapaibul; 31 brs.

Bank of Asia for Industry and Commerce Ltd.: 601 Charoen Krung Rd., Bangkok, P.O.B. 112; f. 1939; cap. 62m.; dep. 1,573m. (Dec. 1972); Chair. Charoon Euarchukiati; Man. Sathien Tejapaibul.

Bank of Ayudhya Ltd.: P.O.B. 491, Bangkok; f. 1945; cap. p.u. 150m.; res. 94m.; dep. 3,470m. (June 1972); Chair. Pol. Gen. Prasert Rujiravongs; Man. Dir. Chuan Ratanaraks.

Government Savings Bank of Thailand: 470 Phaholyodhin Rd., Bangkok 4; f. 1913; dep. 6,642m (Dec. 1971); 346 brs.; Chair. Air Chief Marshal Boonchoo Chandrubeska; Dir.-Gen. Thongtang Thongtaem; publs. *Savings Bank Journal* (bi-monthly), *Annual Report*.

Krung Thai Bank Ltd. (*State Commercial Bank of Thailand*): 260 Yawaraj Rd., Bangkok 1; f. 1966; cap. p.u. 250m.; total resources 9,759m. (June 1972); Dir.-Gen. Man. Chamras Chaturabatara; 102 brs.

Laem Thong Bank Ltd.: P.O.B. 131, 289/9 Suriwongse Rd., Bangkok; f. 1948; cap. 12m.; dep. 760m. (June 1973); Man. Dir. Baisal Nandhabiwat; Chair. Phya Prichanusat.

Siam Commercial Bank Ltd., The: 1060 Bhejrburi Rd., Bangkok 4, P.O.B. 15; f. 1906; cap. p.u. and res. 244.6m.; dep. 3,516.6m.; Chair. Nai Poonperm Krairiksh; Gen. Man. Prachitr Yossundara.

Thai Danu Bank Ltd.: 943 Mahachai Rd., Bangkok; f. 1949; cap. p.u. 20m.; dep. 663m. (Dec. 1971); Chair. H.S.H. Prince Upalisan Jumbala; Gen. Man. Chalerm Prachuabmoh.

Thai Farmers' Bank Ltd.: 142 Silom Rd., Bangkok; f. 1945; cap. p.u. 100m.; dep. 4,946m. (June 30th, 1973); Pres. Bancha Lamsam; Chair. Phra Nitikarn-Prasom.

Thai Military Bank Ltd.: Mansion 2, Rajdamnern Ave., Bangkok; f. 1957; cap. p.u. 10m.; dep. 1,081m. (June 1970); Chair. Field Marshal Thanom Kittikachorn; Pres. Sukum Navapan.

Union Bank of Bangkok Ltd.: 624 Jawarad Rd., Bangkok; f. 1949; cap. p.u. 50m.; dep. 1,582m. (Dec. 1971); Chair. Gen. Kricha Punnakanta; Man. Dir. Banjurd Cholvijarn.

Wang Lee Chan Bank Ltd.: 1128 Chiengmai Rd., Wat Wat Thong Thammachat, Thonburi; f. 1933; cap. p.u. 0.25m.; dep. 11m. (Dec. 1970); Chair. and Man. Dir. Tan Siew Ting.

FOREIGN BANKS WITH BRANCHES IN BANGKOK

Bank of America National Trust and Savings Association: San Francisco; 297 Surawongse Rd., P.O.B. 158, Bangkok 5; Man. M. L. Greeberg.

Bank of Canton Ltd.: 270–274 Yawarad Rd., Bangkok; Man. C. Y. Sun.

Bank of Tokyo Ltd.: 62 Thaniya Bldg., Silom Rd., Bangkok; Man. Kiyohiko Wada.

Banque de l'Indochine S.A.: Paris; 140 Wireless Rd., P.O.B. 303, Bangkok; Man. J. L. Moulène.

Chartered Bank, The: London; Rama IV Rd., Saladaeng Circle, Bangkok; Man. W. C. L. BROWN.

Chase Manhattan Bank, N.A.: New York; 965 Rama I Rd., P.O.B. 525, Bangkok; Gen. Man. JOHN D. TAYLOR.

Four Seas Communications Bank Ltd.: 231 Rajawongse Rd., Bangkok; Man. TAN PUAY LIANG.

Hongkong and Shanghai Banking Corporation, The: Hong Kong; P.O.B. 57, 2 Bush Lane, Siphya, Bangkok; Man. P. M. RYAN.

Indian Overseas Bank: Madras; 221 Rajawongse Rd. Bangkok; Man. T. M. U. MENON.

International Commercial Bank of China: Tapei; 95 Suapa Rd., Bangkok; Man. JAMES C. C. CHENG.

Manufacturers Hanover Trust Co.: Dusit Thani Office Bldg., Saladaeng Circle, Rama IV Rd., P.O.B. 1660, Bangkok; Vice-Pres. C. E. HARKNESS.

Mercantile Bank Ltd.: Hongkong; P.O.B. 45, Silom Rd., Bangkok; Man. W. G. G. MCKERRON.

Mitsui Bank, The: Tokyo; 4-6 Nava Bldg., New Rd., Bangkok; Man. T. ASANUMA.

United Malayan Banking Corpn. Ltd.: Kuala Lumpur; 147-151 Suapa Rd., Bangkok; Man. JOHN C. LING.

INDUSTRIAL FINANCE ORGANIZATIONS

Industrial Finance Corporation of Thailand (I.F.C.T.): 101 Naret Rd., Bangkok; f. 1959 to assist industrial establishment, expansion, modernization and financing; a national private financial institution; makes medium- and long-term loans, underwriting shares and securities and guaranteeing loans; cap. p.u. baht 100m. (Dec. 1970); loans granted 1,179m. on 220 projects (Dec. 1972); Chair. RENOO SUVARNSIT; Gen. Man. SOMMAI HOONTRAKOOL.

Board of Investment: 88 Mansion 2, Rajdamnern Ave., Bangkok; Sec.-Gen. SOMPORN PUNYAGUPTA.

Thai Development Bank Ltd.: 20 Yukhon 2 Rd., P.O.B. 75, Bangkok; Cable address: Patanabank; cap. 150m.; 48 brs. throughout Thailand; Man. Dir. CORO TEJAPAIBUL.

STOCK EXCHANGE

Bangkok Stock Exchange: 6th Floor, Silom Bldg., 197/1 Silom Rd., Bangkok; f. 1963; 50 registered mems.; Chair. ISAAC DJEMAL; Pres. KRIANG JIARAKUL; Sec. P. D. HOWARD.

INSURANCE

Bangkok Insurance Co. Ltd.: The Bangkok Insurance Bldg., 302 Silom Rd., Bangkok; f. 1947; non-life insurance; Chair. CHIN SOPHONPANICH; Man. Dir. CHUMPON RUNGSOPINKUL.

Bangkok Union Insurance Co. Ltd.: 27-29 Yukon 1 Rd., Bangkok; f. 1967; Chair. PHORN LIEWPHAIRATANA; Man. Dir. Y. K. TU; Gen. Man. BOONYONG TAYJASANANT.

Borisat Arkanay Prakan Pai Jamkat (*South-East Insurance Co. Ltd.*): South East Insurance Bldg., 315 Silom Rd., Bangkok; f. 1946; Chair. and Exec. Dir. R. S. JOTIKASTHIRA; Exec. Dirs. P. SRIKARNCHANA, V. VATHANAKUL; cap. p.u. 10m.; life, marine, accident, fire, etc.

China Insurance Co. (Siam) Ltd.: 95 Suapa Rd., Bangkok; f. 1948; fire and marine underwriters; cap. (1971) baht 18.5m.; Man. K. Y. CHAN.

International Assurance Co. Ltd., The: 291-293 Rajawongse Rd., Bangkok; f. 1952; Chair. Gen. P. BORIBHANDH YUDDHAKICH; Man. Dir. V. S. SAMAN; cap. p.u. 2.5m.; fire, marine, general.

International Life Assurance (Thailand) Ltd., The: 52/4-5-6 Surawongse Rd., Bangkok; f. 1951; Chair. KRIS SRIVARA; Gen. Man. SURIYON RAIWA; cap. baht 15m.; life.

Luang Lee Insurance Co. Ltd.: 4219-4225 Chiengmai Rd., Klongsarn, P.O.B. 97, Bangkok-Thonburi Metropolitan City; f. 1933; non-life insurance; cap. baht 5m.; res. baht 8.9m.; Chair. TAN SIEW TING WANGLEE; Man. Dir. SUCHIN WANGLEE.

Ocean Insurance Company Ltd.: 1666 Krung Kasem Rd., Bangkok; Man. Dir. PHONGSAK ASSAKUL; accident, fire, life, marine, motor car.

Shiang Ann Insurance Co. Ltd.: 40-42 Chalermkhet Soi 3, Plabplachai Rd., Bangkok 1; f. 1929; non-life insurance; cap. baht 9m.; res. baht 2m.; Chair. CORO TEJA-PHAIBUL; Dir. K. P. YU.

Sinswad Assurance Co. Ltd.: 167/3-4 Wireless Rd., Bangkok; f. 1946; Chair. B. SUKANICH; Man. Dir. C. PRYPIROONROJN; cap. p.u. 10m.; fire, casualty, marine.

Syn Mun Kong Insurance Co. Ltd.: 385 Silom Rd., Yong Vanich Bldg. 3rd Floor, Bangkok 5; f. 1951; fire, automobile and personal accident underwriters; Man. Dir. TANAVIT DUSDEESURAPOT.

Thai Commercial Insurance Co. Ltd.: 133/19 (6th Floor) Rajdamri Rd., Bangkok; f. 1940; fire and casualty insurance; cap. baht 5.0m.; res. baht 1.4m.; unearned premium res. baht 1.9m.; Mans. SUCHIN WANGLEE, SURAJIT WANGLEE.

Thai Insurance Co. Ltd.: 933 Maha Chai Rd., Bangkok; est. 1939; Man. Dir. CHALOR THONGSUPHAN.

Thai Life Insurance Co. Ltd.: Mansion 8, Rajdamnern Ave., Bangkok; f. 1942; Man. Dir. SMIT YAMASMIT.

Thai Prasit Insurance Co. Ltd.: 295 Sriphya Rd., Bangkok f. 1947; fire, marine, automobile and life insurance Chair. TAN ENG GHEE; Man. Dir. SAENG LIMPAN ONDA.

Wilson Insurance Co. Ltd.: 70-76 Annuwongse Rd., Bangkok; f. 1951; fire, marine insurance; Chair. CHIN SOPHONPANICH; Man. Dir. CHOOMPORN RUNSOPINKUL.

TRADE AND INDUSTRY

CHAMBERS OF COMMERCE

Thai Chamber of Commerce: 150 Rajbopit Rd., Bangkok; f. 1946; 520 mems.; Pres. Nai Charoon Sibunruang; Vice-Pres. Nai Ob Vasuratna, Nai Preecha Tanprasert, Dr. Somphob Sussangkarn; Hon. Sec. Gen. Nai Dej Boon-Long; Asst. Hon. Sec. Gen. Nai Photipong-Lamsam; publs. *Thai Chamber of Commerce Journal* (monthly), *Thai Chamber of Commerce Directory*.

Chiengrai Chamber of Commerce: Chiengrai, North Thailand.

Cholburi Chamber of Commerce: Cholburi, South-East Thailand.

Foreign chambers of commerce:

American Chamber of Commerce in Thailand: 7th Floor, 140 Wireless Rd., Bangkok.

British Chamber of Commerce: 2nd Floor, Bangkok Insurance Bldg., 302 Silom Rd., Bangkok 5.

Chambre de Commerce Franco-Thaïe: 9th Floor, Shell House, 140 Wireless Rd., Bangkok.

Chinese Chamber of Commerce: 233 Sathorn Tai Rd., Bangkok 5.

German-Thai Chamber of Commerce: 699 Silom Rd., P.O.B. 1728, Bangkok 5.

Indian Chamber of Commerce: 13 Attakarnprasit Lane, Sathorn Tai Rd., Bangkok.

Japanese Chamber of Commerce and Industry: 67 Sathorn Tai Rd., Bangkok.

GOVERNMENT ORGANIZATIONS

Forest Industry Organization: 76 Rajadamnern Nok Ave., Bangkok 1; f. 1947; has wide responsibilities concerning all aspects of Thailand's forestry and wood industries; Man. Dir. Krit Samapuddhi.

Rubber Estate Organization: Visuthikasat Rd., Bangkok.

Thai Sugar Organization: Luang Rd., Bangkok.

INDUSTRIAL AND TRADE ASSOCIATIONS

The Association of Thai Industries: "Suriyothai" Bldg., 5th Floor, 260 Phaholyothin Rd., Bangkok 4; f. Nov. 1967, serving as a grouping of operators of all types of industry in Thailand; centre for mems. in the exchange of ideas contributory to industrial efforts; building and promoting fellowship among industrial operators; conducting research, publicity, promotion and training of modern technical know-how pertaining to industrial manufacture and commerce to enhance the progress of industry and commerce in Thailand in order to compete with foreign products; bringing about solidarity among mems. for the purpose of protecting, preserving and promoting the stability of all industries in the country; encouraging the graduation of young industrialists and the lifting of their efficiency standards; performing charity work; engaging in other industries that would promote the prosperity of domestic industries; mems.: 280; Pres. Maj.-Gen. Pramarn Adireksarn; Vice-Pres. Bunjerd Cholvicharn, Thavorn Pornprapha, Pong Sarasin; Hon. Sec.-Gen. Sqn. Ldr. Prakaipet Indhusophon; Office Man. Prachuab Udomsilpa.

Jute Association of Thailand: 335 New Rd., Bangkok.

Mineral Industry Association of Thailand: 26 Bangkok Rd., Puket.

Pharmaceutical Association of Thailand: 150 Rajbopit Rd., Bangkok.

Rice Mill Association of Thailand: 233 South Sathorn Rd., Bangkok.

Rice Traders Association of Thailand: 120 Sathorn Rd., Bangkok.

Rubber Trade Association of Thailand: 150 Rajbopit Rd., Bangkok.

Sawmill Association of Siam: 258/1 Visuthykasat Rd., Bangkok.

The Tapioca Association of Thailand: 291-293 Rajawongse Rd., Bangkok.

Thai Maize and Produce Exporters Association: 52/17-18 Surawongse Rd., Bangkok.

Thai Silk Association: c/o Industrial Promotion Dept., Ministry of Industry, Rama VI Rd., Bangkok.

Thailand Lac Association: 66 Chaleamkatt 1, Bangkok.

Timber Exporters Association: 119/1 Nr. Huachang Bridge, P.O.B. 240, Phaya Thai Rd., Bangkok.

The Union Textile Merchants Association of Thailand: 121/1 Rajawongse Rd., Bangkok.

TRADE UNIONS

All trade unions were abolished in November 1958 and workers were forbidden to organize new ones.

TRANSPORT

RAILWAYS

Thailand State Railways: Yosse, Bangkok; f. 1891; made autonomous 1951; 21,918 permanent employees, 13,776 temporary (Sept. 1970); 3,765 km. of open lines, 3,885 km. of running track and 557 km. of siding track; gauge 1 metre; Chair. Gen. Kruen Suddhanindra; Gen. Man. Ahna Kamyananda; Sec. Prayoon Kasemsuwan; publ. *Railway Monthly Magazine* (Thai).

ROADS

Total length of primary and secondary roads at the end of 1971 was 17,105 km., of which, 67 per cent were paved.

SHIPPING

Port Authority of Thailand: Bangkok; 16 vessels; Chair. Admiral Prajum I. Mokaves, r.t.n.; Dir. Admiral Abhai Sitakalin, r.t.n.

Bangkok United Mechanical Co. Ltd.: 144 Sukumvit Rd., Bangkok; coastal services; Pres. P. Prasarttong-Orsoth; Man. C. W. Chaikomin; 1 tanker.

Keat Navigation Co. Ltd.: 19 Thalang Rd., Phuket; Gen. Man. C. Upatising; 1 cargo vessel.

Oceanic Transport Co. Ltd.: 197/1 Silom Rd., Bangkok; tanker services; Chair. C. J. Huang; Man. Dir. C. D. Shiah; 4 tanker vessels.

Oil Fuel Organization of Thailand: Bangkok; river transport; 1 tanker vessel.

Thai Maritime Navigation Co. Ltd.: 59 Yanawa, Bangkok; services from Bangkok to Far Eastern ports; 3 vessels; Chair. Air Chief Marshal DAWEE CHULASAPYA; Gen. Man. G. SAMANANDA.

Thai Mercantile Marine Ltd.: Bangkok Bank Bldg., 4th Floor, P.O.B. 905, 300 Silom Rd., Bangkok; f. 1967; four dry cargo vessels on liner service between Japan and Thailand; Chair. H. E. THANAT KHOMAN; Vice-Chair. CHIN SOPHONPANICH.

Thai Navigation Co. Ltd.: 721 Hongkong Bank Lane, Siphya, Bangkok; f. 1940; services (passenger and freight) between Thailand, Singapore, Malacca and Penang; Man. a.i. Commodore SAWAENG KARNJANA-KANOK.

Thai Petroleum Transports Co. Ltd.: Air France Bldg., 3 Patpong Rd., Bangkok; coastal tanker services; Chair. C. CHOWKWANYUN; Man. Capt. A. MACKAY; 5 vessels.

CIVIL AVIATION

Note: Work has started on a new international airport at Nong Ngu Hao. Costing 2,000–3,000 million baht, it will be completed by 1977. The existing Don Maung airport will be used for military purposes and domestic services from 1977.

Thai Airways International Ltd.: 1043 Phaholyothin Rd., Bangkok 4; f. 1959; international services from Bangkok to Hong Kong, Bali, Calcutta, Dacca, Delhi, Jakarta, Kathmandu, Kuala Lumpur, Manila, Osaka, Penang, Rangoon, Saigon, Singapore, Taipei, Tokyo, Sydney and Copenhagen; Chair. Air Chief Marshal BOONCHOO CHANDRUBEKSA; Man. Dir. Air Marshal SUAN SUKSERM; 1 DC-8-62, 5 DC-8-33.

Thai Airways Co. Ltd.: 6 Larn Luang Rd., Bangkok; f. 1951; operates domestic services; Chair. and Acting Man. Dir. Air Chief Marshal SUAN SUKSERM; Deputy Man. Dir. K. A. KRISTIANSEN; fleet of 9 HS-748, 5 DC-3.

Air-Siam (*Air-Siam Air Co. Ltd.*): P.O.B. 4-155, Rajprasong Trade Centre, Bangkok; f. 1965; 2 DC-8-50, 1 BAC 1-11, 3 DC-4 freighters; principal routes: Bangkok–Hong Kong–Tokyo–Honolulu–Los Angeles, freighters operating Bangkok–Hong Kong; Chair. H.H. Princess SUDASIRISOBHA; Man. Dir. V. VANNAKUL; fleet of 5 B.707, 3 DC-4.

Bangkok is also served by the following airlines: Aeroflot, Air Cambodge, Air Ceylon, Air France, Air India, Air Viet-Nam, Alitalia, British Airways, Burma Airway Corpn., Cathay Pacific Airways, China Airlines, EgyptAir, Garuda Indonesian Airways, Japan Air Lines Co., KLM, Korean Airlines, Lufthansa, Pan American, Philippine Air Lines, Qantas, Royal Air Lao, Royal Nepal Airlines, SAS, Singapore Airlines, Swissair, Trans World Airlines, UTA.

TOURISM

The Tourist Organization of Thailand (TOT): Head Office, Mansion 2, Ratchadamnoen Ave., Bangkok 2; f. 1960; Dir.-Gen. Lt.-Gen. CHALERMCHAI CHARUVASTR; Deputy Dir.-Gen. Col. SIRISAK SUNTAROVAT, Col. SOMCHAI HIRANYAKIT; publs. *Thailand Travel Talk* (monthly, English), *Holiday Time in Thailand* (quarterly, English), *TOT's Magazine* (monthly, Thai), *Newsletter* (English); overseas offices in New York, Los Angeles, Frankfurt and Tokyo.

North Thailand Tourist Promotion Asscn.: Chuang Mai; Pres. Prof. MOMLUANG TUI XUMSAI.

ATOMIC ENERGY

Office of Atomic Energy for Peace: Srirubsook Rd., Bangkhen, Bangkok 9; Chair. the Prime Minister; Sec.-Gen. Dr. SVASTI SRISUKH.

The National Energy Administration maintains a research reactor and a nuclear institute.

Note: Thailand's first nuclear electricity plant is to be established at Ao Pai in Si Racha district by 1981.

UNIVERSITIES

Chiengmai University: Chiengmai; f. 1963; 662 teachers; 6,580 students.

Chulalongkorn University: Phya Thai Rd., Bangkok; 1,515 teachers, 12,308 students.

Kasetsart University: Bangkhen, Bangkok; 680 teachers, 6,234 students.

Khonkaen University: Khonkaen; f. 1966; 190 teachers, 1,686 students.

Mahidol University: Siriraj Hospital, Thonburi, Bangkok; c. 900 teachers, c. 4,320 students.

Silpakorn University: Na Pra Dhat Rd.; 1,090 students.

Thammasat University: Bangkok; 10,389 students.

TOGO

INTRODUCTORY SURVEY

Location, Climate, Language, Religion, Flag, Capital

The Republic of Togo lies on the coast of West Africa forming a narrow strip stretching north to Upper Volta with Ghana to the west and Dahomey to the east. The climate is hot and humid, temperatures averaging 27°C (80°F) on the coast and 30°C (97°F) in the drier north. The official language is French and there are a number of native tongues. The majority of the population follow animist beliefs; there are about 300,000 Christians and 75,000 Muslims. The national flag (proportions 3 by 2) has five stripes of alternate green and yellow, with a square red canton, containing a five-pointed white star, in the upper hoist. The capital is Lomé.

Recent History

Formerly a United Nations Trust Territory administered by France, Togo became an autonomous republic within the French Union in 1956 and achieved independence in 1960.

The leading political figure and first President of Togo, Sylvanus Olympio, was assassinated by military insurgents early in 1963 and Nicolas Grunitzky returned from exile to become President. In May 1963 a popular referendum approved his appointment and elected a new National Assembly from a single list of candidates. President Grunitsky was overthrown in January 1967 by an army *coup d'état*, led by Lt.-Col. (later Major-Gen.) Étienne Gnassingbe Eyadéma. The National Assembly was dissolved and the Constitution abolished, and in April 1967 Eyadéma took over the Presidency. In the same year all political parties were dissolved. The President has repeatedly announced his resolve to return Togo to civilian rule, but has been met by popular demands that the army should remain in power. In 1969 a political party, the *Rassemblement du peuple togolais*, was founded with Gen. Eyadéma as president. It is the only party in Togo and contributes greatly to the radical style of political life, especially by the organization of petitions and demonstrations in favour of the Government. A referendum held in January 1972 produced a massive vote of support for the President. In January 1974 Gen. Eyadéma narrowly escaped death in an aeroplane crash, which he maintained was an assassination attempt by the *Compagnie togolaise des mines du Bénin*, one of the major foreign companies operating in Togo. Soon afterwards the company was taken over by the State.

Togo favours a broad association of African states on a basis of shared interests, to replace the present groupings determined by a shared colonial past. Thus Togo maintains close relations with Ghana, Nigeria and Zaire as well as with the former French colonies of West Africa. Togo is a member of the United Nations, the Organization of African Unity, OCAM and the Conseil de l'Entente.

Government

Following the army *coup d'état* of January 1967, the constitution was suspended. Executive power is in the hands of a President and a Cabinet. The *Rassemblement du peuple togolais*, the only political party in Togo, mobilizes support for the Government. The country is divided into four Regions, each administered by an Inspector assisted by an elected council.

Defence

Togo's armed forces total about 2,500, including an infantry battalion and a small naval force. Under military agreements with France, Togo is helped with training and equipment.

Economic Affairs

Agriculture is the leading sector of the economy. It engages 90 per cent of the working population and provides 40 per cent of the Gross Domestic Product. The chief food crops are yams, millet, cassava and maize. Livestock breeding and fishing also contribute to the internal economy. The chief cash crops are coffee, cocoa, cotton, groundnuts and palm kernels. In 1971 coffee accounted for 18 per cent of export earnings and cocoa for 31 per cent. With the exception of cocoa, agricultural production has not expanded significantly in recent years. The industrial sector is small but rapidly growing. It comprises mainly the processing of agricultural produce and the production of consumer goods. The most important project in hand is the construction of a large-scale cement plant, which is due to begin production in 1974. Deposits of phosphates, limestone and marble are exploited. Phosphates are the country's leading export. It is estimated that almost 2.5 million tons were exported in 1973, providing more than 50 per cent of total export earnings. Phosphates are the country's leading export. It is estimated, that almost 2.5 million tons were exported in 1973, after a long struggle to extend its control over capital and marketing and to increase its revenue from phosphates, the Government finally took complete control of the company. The 1971–75 development plan envisages an annual economic growth rate of 7.7 per cent. Togo has a large balance of trade deficit and receives much foreign aid, but it possesses considerable unexploited resources and good potential for growth.

Transport and Communications

There are 498 km. of railways, including three lines running inland from Lomé and a coastal line which joins with the Dahomey system. There are 7,125 km. of roads, of which about 1,300 km. are all-weather roads. There are several airfields in Togo, and an international airport at Lomé served by Air Togo, Air Afrique and UTA.

Social Welfare

Medical services are provided by the Government and in 1971 there were 6 hospitals and many medical centres and clinics, with a total of 3,151 beds.

Education

About half the schools provide free education and there are places for over 40 per cent of children of school age. Mission schools are important and educate almost half of the pupils. There is a university at Lomé and scholarships are available to French universities.

Tourism

Big game hunting and fishing are the main attractions.

Visas are not required to visit Togo by nationals of Cameroon, the Central African Republic, Chad, Congo (Brazzaville), Dahomey, France, Gabon, Federal Republic of Germany, Israel, Italy, Ivory Coast, Madagascar, Mauritania, Niger, Nigeria, Senegal, Upper Volta and Zaire.

Sport

There is little organized sport but football and lawn tennis are popular.

Public Holidays

1974: August 15th (Assumption), November 1st (Memorial Day), December 25th (Christmas).

1975: January 1st (New Year's Day), January 13th (Liberation Day), March 31st (Easter Monday), April 27th (Independence Day), May 1st (Labour Day), May 8th (Ascension Day), May 19th (Whit Monday).

Weights and Measures

The metric system is in force.

Currency and Exchange Rates

100 centimes= 1 franc de la Communauté financière africaine (CFA).

Exchange rates (April 1974):

1 franc CFA =2 French centimes;

£1 sterling=579.75 francs CFA;

U.S. $=245.625 francs CFA.

STATISTICAL SURVEY

AREA AND POPULATION

Official estimate at June 30th, 1973

Area	Population
56,000 sq. km.*	2,111,000

* 21,600 square miles.

MAIN TRIBES
(1964)

Ewe	.	.	185,000
Ouatchi	.	.	152,000
Kabre	.	.	236,000

PRINCIPAL TOWNS
(1971)

Lomé (capital)	.	.	200,100	Tsevie	.	.	13,600
Sokodé	.	.	30,100	Anécho	.	.	11,400
Palimé	.	.	20,900	Mango	.	.	9,600
Atakpamé	.	.	17,800	Bafilo	.	.	9,100
Bassari	.	.	16,000	Taligbo	.	.	4,400

Births and Deaths (1968): Registered births 71,930 (birth rate 40.7 per 1,000); registered deaths 14,444 (death rate 8.2 per 1,000). Registration is not, however, complete. UN estimates for 1965–70 put the average annual birth rate at 50.9 per 1,000 and the death rate at 25.5 per 1,000.

AGRICULTURE
PRINCIPAL CROPS
('000 metric tons)

	1968	1969	1970	1971
Maize	120*	125	100*	100*
Millet, Sorghum and Fonio . .	193	160	130*	130*
Rice	17	21	22	22*
Sweet Potatoes and Yams .	1,160*	1,150	1,152*	1,152*
Cassava (Manioc) . . .	1,120*	1,150	1,170*	1,173*
Dry Beans . . .	17	25	19*	20*
Other Pulses . . .	8*	8*	7*	7*
Palm Kernels† . . .	12.9	18.8	17.1	18.0*
Groundnuts (in shell) . .	18	18	18	18*
Cottonseed . . .	4	10	12	12*
Cotton (lint) . . .	2	5	6	6*
Castor Beans . . .	—	—	1	1*
Copra	0.5	1.0	1*	1*
Coffee	16.8	13.2	12.0	12.0
Cocoa Beans‡ . . .	18.0	18.4	24.0	27.9

Coconuts: 18 million nuts in 1968; 21 million in 1969. Palm oil (1968–71): 2,800 metric tons each year (FAO estimate).

  * FAO estimate.   † Exports only.

  ‡ Twelve months ending September of year stated. 1971/72: 29,400 metric tons.

Source: mainly FAO, *Production Yearbook 1971.*

LIVESTOCK
ANIMALS REGISTERED FOR TAXATION
('000)

	1969	1970	1971
Cattle . . .	176	194	192
Sheep and Goats* .	1,130	1,192	972
Pigs . . .	231	139	204
Horses . .	0.8	0.9	1.5
Asses . .	2.0	2.2	1.8
Poultry . .	1,874	1,991	2,076

  * Similar numbers of sheep and goats are kept.

LIVESTOCK PRODUCTS
(FAO estimates—metric tons)

	1968	1969	1970	1971
Cows' Milk	13,000	14,000	14,000	15,000
Beef and Veal* . . .	4,000	4,000	4,000	4,000
Mutton, Lamb and Goats' Meat* .	3,000	3,000	3,000	3,000
Pork*	3,000	3,000	3,000	3,000
Poultry Meat . . .	3,000	3,000	3,000	n.a.
Other Meat . . .	4,000	4,000	4,000	n.a.
Hen Eggs . . .	1,200	1,400	1,500	1,800
Cattle Hides . . .	190	220	210	n.a.

  * Meat from indigenous animals only, including the meat equivalent of exported live animals.

Source: FAO, *Production Yearbook 1971.*

FORESTRY
ROUNDWOOD REMOVALS*
('ooo cubic metres)

	1968	1969	1970
Industrial Wood . .	90	95	102
Fuel Wood . . .	1,060	1,090	1,120
TOTAL . .	1,150	1,185	1,222

* Unofficial figures.

Source: FAO, Yearbook of Forest Products.

FISHING
(metric tons)

	1968	1969	1970	1971
Atlantic Ocean . . .	7,300	7,500	1,800	7,600
Inland Waters . . .	2,700	3,000	2,500	3,000
TOTAL CATCH .	10,000	10,500	4,300	10,600

Source: FAO, Yearbook of Fishery Statistics 1971.

MINING
(metric tons)

	1968	1969	1970	1971
Natural Phosphate Rock . . .	1,375,000	1,473,000	1,508,000	1,715,000
Phosphate of Lime . . .	1,114,000	1,194,000	1,200,000	n.a.

INDUSTRY

	1969	1970	1971
Beer (hectolitres)	92,491.3	94,048.9	97,693.3
Electric Energy (million kWh.) .	57.1	63.7	80.6

FINANCE

100 centimes=1 franc de la Communauté financière africaine.
Coins: 1, 2, 5, 10, 25, 50 and 100 francs CFA.
Notes: 100, 500, 1,000 and 5,000 francs CFA.
Exchange rates (April 1974): 1 franc CFA=2 French centimes;
£1 sterling=579.75 francs CFA; U.S. $1=245.625 francs CFA.
1,000 francs CFA=£1.725=$4.071.

GENERAL BUDGET ESTIMATES
(million francs CFA)

REVENUE	1970	1971	1972	EXPENDITURE*	1970	1971	1972
Taxes on Income	1,485.0	1,904.0	2,114.0	Interest on Public Debt	193.5	208.7	245.9
Other Direct Taxes	14.2	14.0	15.0	Subsidies to Enterprises	217.6	253.6	265.6
Import Duties	1,850.0	2,100.0	2,448.0	Transfers to Income Account of Households	198.9	269.3	388.8
Export Duties	525.0	615.0	1,000.0	Current Transfers to Local Governments	139.2	36.4	—
Other Indirect Taxes	2,830.0	3,385.0	4,817.0	Current Transfers to Abroad	130.8	172.3	187.1
Other Receipts	1,276.0	1,982.1	1,889.3	Current Expenditure on Goods and Services (net)	6,066.4	7,363.8	9,224.6
				Gross Fixed Capital Formation	1,033.8	1,696.0	1,971.3
TOTAL	7,980.2	10,000.1	12,283.3	TOTAL	7,980.2	10,000.1	12,283.3

*Expenditure includes (in million francs CFA):

	1970	1971	1972
Education	1,114.8	1,436.5	1,921.7
Public Health	640.3	684.4	799.5
Social Services	151.7	114.3	147.6
Defence	849.1	897.2	1,104.4

Capital Budget (1974): 2,000 million francs CFA, of which Communications and Tourism 565.6 million; Rural sector 468.0 million; Socio-cultural programmes 446.7 million; Industrial, Commercial and Crafts 303.5 million; Administration 216.0 million.

1973 estimate: General Budget balanced at 13,434 million francs CFA.

Source: United Nations, *Statistical Yearbook 1972.*

Currency in Circulation (December 31st, 1973): 6,059 million francs CFA.

SECOND DEVELOPMENT PLAN (1971–75)
(Estimates—million francs CFA)

SOURCE OF FINANCE				INVESTMENT EXPENDITURE		
Togolese Public Sources			20,000	Transport and Communications		26,947
Togolese Private Sources			9,800	Industry, Craft and Trade		15,536
Foreign Public Sources			36,000	Town Planning		11,000
Foreign Private Sources			10,000	Tourism		11,000
				Rural Development		11,000
TOTAL			75,800	TOTAL (incl. others)		75,890

EXTERNAL TRADE

(million francs CFA)

	1966	1967	1968	1969	1970	1971	1972	1973
Imports . .	11,668	11,133	11,623	14,572	17,928	19,455	21,384	21,398
Exports . .	8,872	7,894	9,549	11,477	15,176	13,626	12,659	12,648

PRINCIPAL COMMODITIES

IMPORTS	1967	1968	1969
Food and Live Animals . . .	1,549	1,326	1,816
Fish, fresh and simply preserved . .	364	198	419
Cereals and preparations . . .	377	333	453
Sugar and honey	268	319	293
Beverages and Tobacco . . .	988	862	1,366
Alcoholic beverages	326	334	441
Tobacco and manufactures . .	650	514	902
Cigarettes	513	467	849
Petroleum Products	495	526	668
Chemicals	837	1,015	1,048
Medicinal and pharmaceutical products .	309	397	443
Basic Manufactures . . .	3,873	4,090	4,818
Woven cotton fabrics . . .	2,098	2,191	1,972
Lime, cement, etc. . . .	252	278	375
Iron and steel	400	328	497
Machinery and Transport Equipment . .	2,240	2,572	3,309
Machinery (non-electric) . .	884	1,005	1,454
Electrical machinery, appliances, etc. .	470	516	482
Road motor vehicles . . .	771	922	1,203
Passenger cars . . .	334	188	468
Lorries and trucks . . .	298	347	472
Miscellaneous Manufactured Articles . .	756	704	914
TOTAL (incl. others) . . .	11,133	11,620	14,567

1970 (million francs CFA): Woven Cotton Fabrics 2,413; Total 17,928.

EXPORTS	1968	1969	1970	1971
Coffee (green and roasted) . .	1,602	1,749	2,657	2,435
Cocoa Beans	2,314	4,063	6,336	4,246
Oil-seeds, Oil-nuts, etc. . . .	860	747	n.a.	n.a.
Groundnuts (green) . . .	164	188	219	267
Palm nuts and kernels . .	573	481	656	517
Raw Cotton (excl. linters) . .	340	154	323	272
Natural Calcium Phosphates .	3,237	3,356	3,720	4,787
Chemicals	114	72	n.a.	n.a.
Woven Cotton Fabrics . .	169	192	n.a.	n.a.
Diamonds (non-industrial) . .	370	725	277	n.a.
Machinery (non-electric) . .	306	97	n.a.	n.a.
TOTAL (incl. others) .	9,550	11,476	15,176	13,626

Source: mainly *Overseas Associates, Foreign Trade* (Statistical Office of the European Communities, Luxembourg). The totals for 1968 and 1969 differ slightly from those given in the summary table, which are provided by the national statistical authority.

COUNTRIES

IMPORTS	1969	1970	1971
China, People's Republic . . .	405	437	352
France	4,657	5,283	6,687
Germany, Federal Republic . .	984	1,455	1,700
Ghana	371	653	501
Italy	774	678	498
Japan	1,045	1,067	943
Netherlands	812	1,303	1,235
U.S.S.R.	349	377	567
United Kingdom . . .	1,779	2,424	2,270
U.S.A.	754	1,022	1,030
Venezuela	236	215	482
TOTAL (incl. others) .	14,572	17,928	19,455

EXPORTS	1969	1970	1971
Belgium/Luxembourg . . .	1,123	1,039	765
France	3,913	4,284	4,298
Germany, Federal Republic . .	1,795	3,040	1,830
Italy	390	609	276
Japan	439	399	364
Netherlands	2,714	3,933	3,496
U.S.S.R.	256	873	1,334
United Kingdom . . .	306	361	208
TOTAL (incl. others) .	11,477	15,176	13,626

TRANSPORT

RAILWAYS

	1969	1970	1971
Passengers ('000) .	1,727	1,583	1,466
Passengers—km. (million) .	86.5	84.1	70.8
Freight ('000 tons) .	124	105.3	83.9
Freight (million ton—km.)	13	12.3	9.8
Total receipts (million francs CFA) . .	372	383	326.1

INTERNATIONAL SEA-BORNE SHIPPING

	1969	1970	1971
Vessels Entered . .	504	524	547
Displacement ('000 net tons)	1,489	1,477	1,690
Freight Unloaded ('000 metric tons) . .	233	255	284
Freight Loaded ('000 metric tons) . .	1,544	1,576	1,895
Passenger Arrivals .	646	181	69
Passenger Departures .	535	127	11

ROADS
MOTOR VEHICLES IN USE

	1968	1969	1970	1971
Passenger Cars . . .	5,800	6,800	8,200	9,600
Commercial Vehicles . .	2,000	2,300	2,700	3,000

CIVIL AVIATION

	1971	1972
Aircraft Arrivals and Departures	1,821	1,891
Freight Unloaded (tons) . .	498	477
Freight Loaded (tons) . .	450	413
Passenger Arrivals . .	16,249	19,350
Passenger Departures . .	16,528	19,156

COMMUNICATIONS

	1969	1970	1971
Telephones . . .	4,600	5,000	6,000
Radio Sets . . .	40,000	n.a.	45,000

Newspapers: 3 in 1970 (combined average circulation 13,000 copies for issue).

EDUCATION
(1971–72)

	SCHOOLS	TEACHERS	PUPILS
Primary .	934	4,403	257,877
Secondary .	71*	778	24,521
Technical .	19†	214	2,506
Higher (University)	1	93	1,369‡

* Includes four *lycées* and six colleges.
† Including one *lycée* and four colleges.
‡ In addition 689 students study abroad.

Source: Direction de la Statistique, Lomé (except where otherwise stated).

THE CONSTITUTION

The Constitution promulgated in May 1963 was suspended in January 1967. A Constitutional Committee began meeting in October 1967 to draft a new constitution which was completed in 1969 but has not been promulgated.

THE GOVERNMENT

HEAD OF STATE

President: Maj.-Gen. Gnassingbe (*formerly* Étienne) Eyadéma.

THE CABINET
(*April* 1974)

Minister of National Defence: Maj.-Gen. Gnassingbe Eyadéma.

Minister of Public Health and Social Affairs: Lt.-Col. Albert Djafalo Alidou.

Minister of Foreign Affairs: Joachim Hunlédé.

Minister of Public Works, Transport, Mines and Posts and Telecommunications: Alex Mivedor.

Minister of the Interior: Joseph Ogamo Bagnah.

Minister of National Education: Benoît Malou.

Minister of Finance and the Economy: Edouard Kodjo.

Minister of the Civil Service, Justice and Labour: Nanamalé Gbégbéni.

Minister of Rural Economy: Saibou Dermane Fofana.

Minister of Youth, Sport, Culture and Scientific Research: Mathieu Koffi.

Minister of Trade and Industry: Jean Tévi.

Minister of Planning: Henri Dogo.

Minister of Information, Press, Radio and Television: Michel Eklo.

High Commissioner for Tourism: Michel Ahyi.

ECONOMIC AND SOCIAL COUNCIL

An advisory council was created in 1967 and has been active since March 1968. Its 25 members include five trade unionists, five representatives of industry and commerce, five representatives of agriculture, five economists and sociologists, and five technologists.

President: Gervais Djondo.

DIPLOMATIC REPRESENTATION

EMBASSIES ACCREDITED TO TOGO
(In Lomé unless otherwise stated)

Algeria: Accra, Ghana.

Belgium: Abidjan, Ivory Coast.

Brazil: Accra, Ghana.

Canada: Accra, Ghana.

China, People's Republic: *Ambassador:* Wei Pao-sgien.

Czechoslovakia: Accra, Ghana.

Denmark: Accra, Ghana.

Egypt: Angle blvd. Circulaire et route d'Anèche; B.P. 8; *Ambassador:* Riad Moawad.

France: rue Paul Mahoux, B.P. 91; *Ambassador:* Jean-Pierre Campredon.

Gabon: Abidjan, Ivory Coast.

Germany, Federal Republic: rue d'Aflao, B.P. 289; *Ambassador:* Hermann Haferkamp.

Ghana: Tokoin—route de Palimé; *Ambassador:* Ben Forjoe.

Haiti: Dakar, Senegal.

Hungary: Accra, Ghana.

India: Lagos, Nigeria.

Italy: Accra, Ghana.

Japan: Abidjan, Ivory Coast.

Korea, Republic: Abidjan, Ivory Coast.

Lebanon: Accra, Ghana.

Liberia: Accra, Ghana.

Netherlands: Abidjan, Ivory Coast

Niger: Cotonou, Dahomey.

Nigeria: Accra, Ghana.

Pakistan: Accra, Ghana.

Poland: Lagos, Nigeria.

Spain: Abidjan, Ivory Coast.

Switzerland: Accra, Ghana.

Tunisia: Abidjan, Ivory Coast.

Turkey: Accra, Ghana.

U.S.S.R.: route d'Atakpamé, B.P. 634; *Ambassador:* Pyotr K. Slyusarenko.

United Kingdom: Angle blvd. Circ. et blvd. de la République, B.P. 892; *Ambassador:* Alan James Brown.

U.S.A.: 68 ave. de la Victoire; *Ambassador:* Nancy V. Rawls.

Viet-Nam, Republic: Abidjan, Ivory Coast.

Yugoslavia: Accra, Ghana.

Zaire: *Ambassador:* Itsindo Bosila Mpela.

Togo also has diplomatic relations with Congo (Brazzaville), the German Democratic Republic and the Democratic People's Republic of Korea.

NATIONAL ASSEMBLY

The National Assembly was dissolved in January 1967. Elections were then promised within three months, but none have so far been held and a new constitution has yet to be promulgated.

POLITICAL PARTY

Rassemblement du peuple togolais (RPT): Lomé; f. 1969; holds a Congress every three years, and its central committee meets at least every three months; Pres. Maj.-Gen. Gnassingbe Eyadéma.

Political Bureau: Maj.-Gen. Eyadéma, Lt.-Col. Albert Djafalo, Edouard Kodjo, Henri Dogo, Gervais Djondo, Benoît Bédou, Joachim Hunlédé, Benoît Malou, Louis Amega, Barthélémy Lambony, Prof. Valentin Mawupe-Vovor, Alphonse Kortho, Prof. Jean Kekeh, Fousseni Mama, Nanamalé Gbegbeni, Michel Eklo (Exec. Sec.).

JUDICIAL SYSTEM

The independence of the judiciary is assured by the Conseil Supérieur de la Magistrature, set up in 1964, consisting of the President as Chairman, the Minister of Justice, the President and Vice-President of the Supreme Court, one Deputy, two Magistrates, and another person chosen for his "independence and competence".

Cour Suprême: Lomé f. 1964; consists of four chambers: constitutional, judicial, administrative and auditing; Pres. Dr. Louis Amega.

CRIMINAL LAW

Cour d'Appel: Lomé; f. 1961; Pres. Brigitte Kekeh.

Tribunal Correctionnel: Lomé and three other centres.

Tribunal de Simple Police: Lomé and seven other centres.

Cour de Securité de l'Etat: f. Sept. 1970 to judge crimes against internal and external state security.

CIVIL AND COMMERCIAL LAW

Cour d'Appel: Lomé; f. 1961; Pres. M. Puech.

Tribunal de Droit Moderne: Lomé; sections at Sokodé, Anécho and Atakpame.

Tribunal Coutumier de Premier Instance: Lomé and seven other centres.

ADMINISTRATIVE LAW

Tribunal Administratif: Lomé.

LABOUR LEGISLATION

Tribunal de Travail: Lomé.

RELIGION

It is estimated that about 60 per cent of the population follow traditional Animist beliefs, some 40 per cent are Christians (with Roman Catholics comprising 20 per cent of the total population) and 10 per cent are Muslims.

Roman Catholic Missions: In the archdiocese of Lomé there are over 5,407 mission centres; publ. *Présence Chrétienne* (fortnightly, circ. 2,500).

Archbishop of Lomé: B.P. 348, Lomé; Mgr. Robert Dosseh Anyron.

Bishop of Atakpamé: B.P. 11, Atakpamé; Mgr. Bernard Oguki-Atakpah.

Bishop of Dapango: B.P. 61, Dapango; Mgr. Pierre Barthélémy Hanrion.

Bishop of Sokodé: B.P. 55, Sokodé; Mgr. Chrétien Bakpessi Matawo.

Protestant Missions: There are about 170 mission centres with a personnel of some 230, affiliated to European and American societies and run by a *Conseil Synodal* presided over by a *moderateur*.

PRESS

DAILIES

Journal Officiel de la République du Togo: EDITOGO, B.P. 891, Lomé.

Togo-Presse: EDITOGO, B.P. 891, Lomé; f. 1962; French and Ewe; political, economic and cultural; official government publication; Editor Polycarpe Johnson; circ. 10,000.

PERIODICALS

Akuavi: Lomé; produced by women's organization; French; Dir. Nabédé Pala.

Bulletin de la Chambre de Commerce: B.P. 360, Lomé; monthly.

Bulletin de Statistiques: B.P. 118, Lomé; published by Service de la Statistique Générale, Ministère des Finances et des Affaires Économiques; monthly.

Espoir de la Nation: EDITOGO, B.P. 891, Lomé; produced by Ministry of Information; monthly; Dir. M. Awesso; circ. 3,000.

Gamesu: Lomé; produced by Ministries of Education and Social Affairs; local language monthly for newly literate people in country areas.

Image du Togo: Lomé; monthly; circ. 2,000.

Le Lien: Office of Education, Lomé; cultural; monthly; circ. 600.

Présence Chrétienne: B.P. 1205, Lomé; f. 1960; French, Roman Catholic fortnightly; Dir. R. P. Alexis Oliger; o.f.m.; circ. 2,500.

Réalités Togolaises: Lomé; monthly.

NEWS AGENCIES

Foreign Bureaux

Agence France-Presse: B.P. 314, Lomé; Chief Jean Marie Wetzel.

D.P.A. also has a bureau in Lomé.

RADIO AND TELEVISION

Radiodiffusion du Togo: B.P. 434, Lomé; f. 1953; Government station; programmes on four wavelengths in French, English and vernacular languages; Dir. Prosper Amouzougah; Tech. Dir. Lucien Poenou.

There are 45,000 radio sets.

Télévision du Togo: f. 1973; programmes in French and vernacular languages; from 7.30 p.m. to 11 p.m. each evening.

FINANCE

(amounts in francs CFA unless otherwise stated).

BANKING

Central Bank

Banque Centrale des Etats de l'Afrique de l'Ouest: Head Office 29 rue du Colisée, 75008 Paris, France; B.P. 120, Lomé; f. 1955; the bank of issue in Togo and several other West African states; cap. and reserves 3,923m.; Pres. Edouard Kodjo; Gen. Man. Robert Julienne; Man. in Lomé Patrice Lawson; publs. *Bulletin Mensuel d'Information et Statistiques* (monthly), *Rapports d'Activité* (annual).

National Banks

Banque Commerciale du Ghana (SA) Togo: 14 rue du Commerce, B.P. 1321, Lomé; cap. 118m.

Banque Togolaise pour le Commerce et l'Industrie: 9 rue du Commerce, Lomé; f. 1974.

Caisse Centrale de Coopération Economique: Avenue de la Victoire, B.P. 33, Lomé; Man. Jean Boyer.

Caisse Nationale de Crédit Agricole: B.P. 1386, Lomé; Dir. Pierre Mazna.

Union Togolaise de Banque: B.P. 359, Lomé; f. 1964 by Republic of Togo, Deutsche Bank A.G., Crédit Lyonnais and Banca Commerciale Italiana; cap. 300m.; Pres. Boukari Djkbo; Gen. Man. Pédro D'Almeida; brs. at Atakpamé, Sokodé and Palimé.

Foreign Banks

Banque Internationale pour l'Afrique Occidentale: Head Office 9 avenue de Messine, Paris 8e, France; B.P. 346, Lomé.

Banque Nationale de Paris: Head Office 16 boulevard des Italiens, Paris 9e, France; 9 rue du Commerce, B.P. 363, Lomé; Man. in Lomé Jacques Guinard.

Development Banks

Banque Togolaise de Développement: B.P. 65, Lomé; f. 1967; cap. 300m.; Dir.-Gen. Bawa Mankoubi.

Société Nationale d'Investissements: Lomé; f. 1971; cap. 300m.

INSURANCE

Some thirty of the major French and British insurance companies are represented in Lomé.

TRADE AND INDUSTRY

CHAMBER OF COMMERCE

Chambre de Commerce, d'Agriculture et d'Industrie du Togo: Ave. Albert-Sarraut, B.P. 360; f. 1921; Pres. Albert Djabaku; Sec. Gen. Mme. Trénou; publ. *Bulletin Mensuel.*

EMPLOYERS' ORGANIZATIONS

Groupement Interprofessional des Entreprises du Togo (Gito): B.P. 345, Lomé; Pres. Clarence Olympio.

Syndicat des Commerçants Importateurs et Exportateurs de la République Togolaise: B.P. 345, Lomé; Pres. Ernest Wurtz.

TRADE UNIONS

Confédération Nationale des Travailleurs du Togo: Lomé; f. 1973 after the dissolution of the central bodies of all Togolese trade unions in December 1972 by the RPT central committee.

MARKETING BOARD

Office des Produits Agricoles du Togo (OPAT): Angle rue Branly et ave. numéro 3, Lomé, B.P. 1334; f. 1964; controls prices and export sales of coffee, cocoa, cotton, ground nuts, palm oil, copra, kapok, karite and castor oil, and is the sole exporter of these products; promotes development in agriculture, finances research and grants loans; is supervised by the Minister of Trade and Industry; Dir.-Gen. Joseph Bagna.

TRANSPORT

RAILWAYS

Chemin de Fer Togolais: B.P. 340, Lomé; f. 1905; total length 498 km., metre gauge, including three lines from Lomé—to Palimé (119 km.), to Anécho (44 km.) and to Atakpamé and Blitta (280 km.); Dir. W. Röhr.

ROADS

There are approximately 1,662 km. of main roads, of which 700 km. are bitumenized and 5,357 km. of "dry season" roads. Principal roads run from Lomé to the borders of Ghana, Nigeria, Upper Volta and Dahomey, and it is intended that the whole length of the north-south route be bitumenized by 1975.

SHIPPING

(Lomé)

The Port of Lomé completed a new deep water harbour in April 1968 which gives it a handling capacity of 400,000 tons and enables 1.5 million tons of goods to pass through per annum. Capacity was reached in 1972 and further works are under way.

Port Autonome de Lomé: B.P. 1225; Pres. Hézékiah Creppy.

Société Navale Chargeurs Delmas Vieljeux: ave. Gallieni, B.P. 34.

Holland West Africa Line: c/o S.C.O.A., B.P. 347.

John Holt and Co. Ltd.: B.P. 343, Lomé; merchandise importers; Lloyds agents.

Jugolinija: SOCOPAO, B.P. 821.

Société Navale de L'Ouest: S.O.A.E.M., B.P. 207.

CIVIL AVIATION

The main airport is at Tokoin near Lomé, and there are smaller ones at Sokodé, Sansanné-Mango, Dapango, Atakpamé.

Air Afrique: B.P. 111, Lomé; Togo has a 6 per cent share; *see* under Ivory Coast.

Air Togo: 1 ave. de la Libération, B.P. 1090, Lomé; f. 1963; scheduled internal services between Lomé, Sokodé, Mango and Dapango and external service to Lagos; fleet of two Cessna 402; Gen. Man. Isaac Ade Amadou.

Lomé is also served by UTA.

TOURISM

Office National Togolais du Tourisme: B.P. 1177, Lomé; Dir. M. Agbekodo.

Organisation pour le Développement du Tourisme en Afrique (Odta): Lomé; Chair. Karim Dembélé.

CULTURAL ORGANIZATIONS

Ministry of National Education: Lomé; in charge of promoting cultural activities.

Comité National des Foires et Expositions: Ministry of Commerce, Industry and Tourism, Lomé; in charge of overseas representation of Togo's cultural achievements; Pres. Jean Agbémégnan.

THEATRE GROUP

Groupement du Théâtre et du Folklore Togolais (G.T.F.T.): Direction de la Jeunesse et des Sports, Lomé; f. 1962; comedy and African ballet; Dir. Mathias Aithnard.

UNIVERSITY

Université du Bénin: B.P. 1515, Lomé; f. 1965; 121 teachers, 1,529 students.

TONGA

INTRODUCTORY SURVEY

Location, Climate, Language, Religion, Flag, Capital

The Kingdom of Tonga comprises about 150 islands in the south-west Pacific, 400 miles east of Fiji. The Tonga (or Friendly) Islands are divided into three main groups: Vava'u, Ha'apai and Tongatapu. Only 36 of the islands are permanently inhabited. The climate is mild for most of the year, though hot and humid from January to March. The languages are Tongan, a Polynesian language, and English. Tongans are predominantly Christians of the Wesleyan faith. The flag (proportions 2 by 1) is red, with a rectangular white canton containing a red cross. The administrative capital is Nuku'alofa, on Tongatapu Island.

Recent History

The foundations of the constitutional monarchy were laid in the nineteenth century. The kingdom was neutral until 1900 when it became a British Protected State. The treaty establishing the Protectorate was revised in 1958 and 1967, giving Tonga increasing control over its affairs, and on June 4th, 1970, it became fully independent, joining the Commonwealth on the same date.

Government

The present constitution is based on one adopted in 1875, providing for a government, consisting of a Sovereign, a Privy Council, a Cabinet and a Legislative Assembly, and for a Judiciary.

Defence

Tonga has its own defence force consisting of both regular and reserve units.

Economic Affairs

The majority of the islands have an inherently fertile soil and the economy is based mainly on agriculture, the two chief crops, coconuts and bananas, accounting for the bulk of Tonga's exports. Two Five-Year Development Plans, 1965–70 and 1970–75, have both aimed at stimulating the coconut industry and tourism and at improving internal and external communications.

Social Welfare

The Government operates three public hospitals and a number of dispensaries. A new hospital was provided for in the first Five-Year Development Plan (1965–70).

Education

Free state education is compulsory between the ages of 6 and 14, while the Government and other Commonwealth countries offer scholarship schemes enabling students to go abroad for higher education. There is one teacher training college.

Tourism

Tourism is considered an industry likely to expand. The first Five-Year Development Plan (1965–70) provided Tonga with its first modern tourist hotel, and the second plan (1970–75) included the upgrading of Fua'amotu airport to medium jet standard.

Sport

Boxing, rugby, football, cricket and basketball are all very popular, in addition to a number of traditional games.

Public Holidays

1974: November 4th (Constitution Day), December 25th, 26th (Christmas).

1975: January 1st (New Year's Day), March 28th, 31st (Easter), April 15th (ANZAC Day), May 4th (H.R.H. the Crown Prince's Birthday), June 4th (Emancipation Day), July 4th (H.M. the King's Birthday).

Weights and Measures

Tonga uses the imperial system of weights and measures.

Currency and Exchange Rates

100 seniti = 1 pa'anga (Tongan dollar).
Exchange rates (April 1974):
£1 sterling = $T1.585;
U.S. $1 = 67.23 seniti.

STATISTICAL SURVEY

Area: 270 square miles (Tongatapu 99.2). There are about 150 islands.

Population: 92,000 (estimate, December 31st, 1972); Nuku'alofa (capital) 25,000.

Agriculture (1971): Bananas 153,817 cases, Copra 15,746 tons; *Livestock:* Pigs 31,029, Horses 6,172, Cattle 3,141.

Currency: 100 seniti (cents) = 1 pa'anga (Tongan dollar). Coins: 1, 2, 5, 10, 20 and 50 seniti; 1 and 2 pa'anga. Notes: 50 seniti; 1, 2, 5 and 10 pa'anga. Exchange rates (April 1974): £1 sterling = $T1.585; U.S. $1 = 67.23 Tongan cents. $T100 = £63.10 = U.S. $148.75.

Budget (1971): Revenue $T2,731,691; Expenditure $T3,001,947.

External Trade (1971): *Imports* $T6,304,917 (mainly food and textiles); *Exports* $T2,200,232 (mainly copra and bananas). Trade is chiefly with the Commonwealth.

Transport: *Roads* (1971): Commercial Vehicles 634, Private Vehicles 341, Motor Cycles 321; *Shipping* (1971): Tonnage entered and cleared 412,230 tons; *Civil Aviation* (1971): Aircraft arriving 250.

THE CONSTITUTION

The Constitution of Tonga is based on that granted in 1875 by King George Tupou I. It provides for a government consisting of the Sovereign, a Privy Council and Cabinet, a Legislative Assembly and a Judiciary. Limited law-making power is vested in the Privy Council and any legislation passed by the Executive is subject to review by the Legislature.

The Privy Council is appointed by the Sovereign and consists of the Sovereign and the Cabinet.

The Cabinet consists of a Prime Minister, a Deputy Prime Minister, other Ministers and the Governors of Ha'apai and Vava'u.

The Legislative Assembly consists of the Speaker (President), the Cabinet, the Representatives of the Nobles (7) and the elected Representatives of the People (7). Franchise is open to all male literate Tongans of 21 and over who pay taxes, and all female literate Tongans aged 21 and over. There are elections every three years, and the Assembly must meet at least once very year.

Note: The next elections are due in 1974.

THE GOVERNMENT

The Sovereign: H.M. King TAUFA'AHAU TUPOU IV, G.C.V.O., K.C.M.G., K.B.E.

CABINET

Prime Minister, Minister of Foreign Affairs, Agriculture, Tourism and Telegraphs and Telephones: H.R.H. Prince FATAFEHI TU'IPELEHAKE, C.B.E.

Deputy Prime Minister and Minister of Lands: Hon. TUITA.

Minister of Police: Hon. 'AKAU'OLA.

Minister of Education and Works: Hon. Dr. S. LANGI KAVALIKU.

Minister of Industries, Commerce and Labour: Hon. the Baron VAEA.

Minister of Health and Acting Minister of Finance: Hon. Dr. S. TAPA.

Governor of Ha'apai: Hon. VA'EHALA.

Governor of Vava'u: Hon. MA'AFU TUPOU.

DIPLOMATIC REPRESENTATION

High Commissioner for Tonga in the U.K.: I. F. FALETAU.

Australian High Commissioner: H. W. BULLOCK (Resident in Suva, Fiji).

Belgian Ambassador: H. MATSAERT (Resident in Wellington, New Zealand.

British High Commissioner: HUMPHREY ARTHINGTON-DAVY (Resident in Wellington, New Zealand.)

Canadian High Commissioner: J. A. DOUGAN (Resident in Wellington, New Zealand).

French Ambassador: CHRISTIAN DE NICOLAY (Resident in Wellington, New Zealand).

Indian High Commissioner: BHAGWAN SINGH (Resident in Suva, Fiji).

Japanese Ambassador: TOSHIO MITSUDO (Resident in Wellington, New Zealand).

Korean Ambassador: CHOONG SIK MIN (Resident in Canberra, Australia).

New Zealand High Commissioner: W. E. THORP (Resident in Apia, Western Samoa).

JUDICIAL SYSTEM

The system of the Courts in Tonga is based on the British model. There are the following Courts: Magistrates Courts, Land Court, Supreme Court and Court of Appeal.

There are eight Magistrates, and appeals from the Magistrates Courts are heard by the Supreme Court. In cases which come before the Supreme Court the accused, or either party in a civil suit, may elect for a jury trial. The Chief Justice is resident in Tonga and appeals from the Supreme Court are heard by the Privy Council as a Court of Appeal. The Chief Justice and Puisne Judge are also Judges of the Land Court in which the trial judge sits with a Tongan assessor.

Chief Justice and Judge of the Land Court: H. STEAD ROBERTS.

Puisne Judge: (vacant).

RELIGION

The Tongans are Christian, 77 per cent belonging to sects of the Wesleyan faith.

PRESS AND RADIO

Press: *The Chronicle:* A weekly newspaper, sponsored by the Government; f. 1964; Editor S. H. FONUA; circ. (Tongan) 3,500, (English) 1,000.

There is a regular issue of Church newspapers by the various missions.

Radio: *Tonga Broadcasting Commission:* P.O.B. 36, Nuku'alofa; started operating July 1961, government and commercially sponsored; programmes from two 10 kW. medium wave 1020 kHz transmitters in English and Tongan with some Fijian and Samoan; Man. ALFRED E. F. SANFT. In 1972 there were 8,000 receivers.

FINANCE

BANKING

Treasury Banking Division: Box 165, Nuku'alofa; current accounts and all transactions in foreign exchange.

Government Savings Bank: Box 165, Nuku'alofa; saving accounts; no interest paid on deposits exceeding $T4,000.

There are no commercial banks.

TRADE AND INDUSTRY

Tonga Copra Board: P.O.B. 27, Nuku'alofa; f. 1941; non-profit making board controlling the export of coconut and all coconut products; Chair. Minister of Agriculture; Man. (acting) SIONE KINAHOI.

Tonga Construction Company: P.O.B. 28, Nuku'alofa; f. 1958 to carry out the construction programme of the Copra Board as well as those of government, local bodies and private concerns; commission agents for imports and exports; Chair. H.R.H. Prince TU'IPELEHAKE, C.B.E.; Man. T. M. 'OFA (acting).

Tonga Produce Board: P.O.B. 84, Nuku'alofa; formerly the Tonga Banana Board; non-profit making organization controlling the export of bananas, pineapples and me\ons; Man./Sec. A. JOHANSSON.

TRANSPORT

ROADS

There are about 120 miles of all-weather metalled roads on Tongatapu and 44 miles on Vava'u. Total mileage in Tonga including fair weather only dirt roads: 271.

SHIPPING

Regular services are maintained by:

Union Steam Ship Co. of New Zealand Ltd.: P.O.B. 4, Nuku'alofa; f. 1875; fortnightly passenger and cargo services between Auckland, Fiji, Samoa and Tonga; six-weekly cargo service from Australia to Fiji, Samoa and Tonga.

Bank Line: Burns Philp (South Sea) Co. Ltd., Nuku'alofa; approximately six-weekly cargo services to the United Kingdom.

Pacific Navigation Co.: P.O.B. 81, Nuku'alofa; formerly Tonga Shipping Agency; maintains a service from Sydney (Australia) to Nuku'alofa with the vessel

Tauloto, a monthly scheduled service between Suva (Fiji) and Nuku'alofa and local inter-island services.

Cruise ships of the following lines call at Tonga: P & O, Chandris, China Navigation, Sitmar, Swedish American West Line, American President, Princess Cruises, Lloyd Tristino, Pacific Far East and Royal Viking.

CIVIL AVIATION

There is a good airport on Tongatapu and limited seaplane facilities at Nuku'alofa and an airstrip at Vava'u. There is a five flights a week service from Fiji, run by Pacific Island Airways and a four flights a week service from Samoa run by Polynesian Airlines Ltd.

Air Pacific: Suva; agents in Tonga E. M. Jones Ltd., P.O.B. 34, Nuku'alofa; fleet comprises HS 747, BAC 1-11.

Polynesian Airlines Ltd.: Apia, W. Samoa; agents in Tonga E. M. Jones Ltd.; all bookings through Polynesian Airlines, Apia; Cables, Polynesian Apia.

TRINIDAD AND TOBAGO

INTRODUCTORY SURVEY

Location, Climate, Language, Religion, Flag, Capital

Trinidad, the southernmost of the Caribbean islands, lies within sight of the Venezuelan coast. The much smaller companion island of Tobago is 20 miles to the north-east. The climate is tropical with a dry season from January to May. Rainfall averages sixty-four inches per year. Average daytime temperature is 84°F (29°C). The language is English. Most of the population are Christians with Roman Catholics as the largest single group. There are Hindu and Muslim communities. The national flag (proportions 5 by 3) is deep red, divided by a white-edged black diagonal stripe, running from upper left to lower right. The capital is Port of Spain.

Recent History

Trinidad and Tobago, formerly a British colonial possession, became a member in 1958 of the newly established Federation of the West Indies and in the following year achieved full internal self-government. With the secession of Jamaica from the Federation in 1961, Trinidad and Tobago withdrew and the Federation collapsed. In 1962 Trinidad and Tobago became an independent state within the Commonwealth, and in 1967 became a member of the Organization of American States. "Black Power" riots in April 1970 and a mutiny in the army which lasted for six months resulted in the declaration of a state of emergency; subsequent unrest has culminated in guerrilla warfare. Against this background elections were held to the House of Representatives in May 1971, resulting in a complete victory for the People's National Movement under Dr. Eric Williams, the Prime Minister. Two members have since joined the United Progressive Party, although retaining their seats in the House. The elections were boycotted by the main opposition groups; a commission set up to examine the constitutional difficulties arising from this situation was due to make its findings public in 1973. Dr. Williams has postponed his threatened resignation until these findings are published.

Government

Legislative power is vested in a Parliament, consisting of the Senate and the House of Representatives. Representatives are elected for a five-year term by universal adult suffrage. Members of the Senate are nominated by the Governor-General in consultation with, and on the advice of, the Prime Minister and the Leader of the Opposition. The Governor-General is appointed by the Queen on the advice of the Prime Minister.

Defence

There is an army of about 1,000 enlisted troops.

Economic Affairs

Oil is of paramount importance in Trinidad's economy. At the end of the 1960s production from on-shore wells fell, but the discovery of off-shore oil fields has revived confidence in the nation's future as an oil-producing and refining country. As the leading Caribbean oil-producer, Trinidad has recently benefited from the world-wide increase in oil prices. The Government intends to use these revenues to off-set inflation (consumer prices rose by 23 per cent in 1973) and also for the longer-term purposes of job creation and economic restructuring, including direct government participation in the ownership of the petroleum sector. In 1972 a TT $1,200 million scheme for the development of natural gas resources was announced. A liquefied natural gas plant and pipeline network are to be built, as well as a fleet of tankers to export the gas. Apart from the oil industry, the manufacture of sugar, rum, molasses, fruit juices and cotton textiles are important, and Trinidad is a major world producer of asphalt. The Government is to acquire and resuscitate over 7,000 acres of cultivable land for growing rice and vegetables to combat worsening food shortages. Trinidad is a founder member of the Caribbean Free Trade Area (CARIFTA) and in 1973 was one of twenty-two Latin American and Caribbean countries to sign an agreement to form OLADE, a Latin American Energy Organization.

Transport and Communications

Road transport is widely used for passengers and freight and there are many buses and lorries. There are 2,630 miles of roads, of which 340 miles are major urban roads and 550 miles are major rural roads. Port of Spain has a deep-water wharf and there are regular sailings to all parts of the world. Numerous airlines use Piarco international airport.

Social Welfare

Old age pensions are paid, and there is some unemployment relief. State medical services are free. In April 1972 the National Insurance System was inaugurated. The System is run by an independent board and its provisions are similar to those contained in the British system introduced in 1948.

Education

Primary and secondary education is free and attendance is compulsory between the ages of six and twelve. Entrance to secondary schools is determined by the Common Entrance Examination. Many schools are run jointly by the state and religious bodies. The Trinidad campus of the University of the West Indies is at St. Augustine, Trinidad. Other institutions of higher education are the Polytechnic Institute and the East Caribbean Farm Institute.

Tourism

The climate and coastline of Trinidad attract tourists and Tobago is also receiving a growing number of visitors.

Visas are not required to visit Trinidad and Tobago by nationals of Belgium, Denmark, Finland, France, Iceland, Ireland, Italy, Liechtenstein, Luxembourg, Netherlands, Norway, San Marino, South Africa, Spain, Sweden, Switzerland, Turkey, the United Kingdom and Commonwealth and the U.S.A.

Sport

Cricket and football are the most popular games.

Public Holidays

1974: August 5th (Discovery Day), August 31st (Independence Day), December 25th, 26th (Christmas).

1975: January 1st (New Year's Day), March 28th (Good Friday), March 31st (Easter Monday), May 19th (Whit Monday), May 29th (Corpus Christi), June 19th (Labour Day).

The Hindu and Moslem festivals of Divali and Eid ul Fitr are also observed as public holidays.

Weights and Measures

The imperial system of weights and measures is in force.

Currency and Exchange Rates

100 cents = 1 Trinidad and Tobago dollar (TT $).
Exchange rates (April 1974):

£1 sterling = TT $4.80;
U.S. $1 = TT $2.03.

STATISTICAL SURVEY

AREA AND POPULATION

AREA (square miles)		POPULATION (1971 estimates)			
Trinidad	Tobago	Total	Port of Spain (capital)	San Fernando	Arima
1,864	116	1,032,500	70,000	31,300	11,000 (1960)

Africans 43%, East Indians 37%, Europeans 2%, Chinese 1%, Others 17%.

EMPLOYMENT

	1970	1971
Agriculture, Forestry, Hunting and Fishing .	81,800	71,800
Mining, Quarrying and Manufacturing . .	66,800	64,000
Construction	38,400	47,800
Commerce	43,600	44,300
Transport and Communications . .	21,700	21,100
Services	68,000	72,500
TOTAL	320,300	321,500

AGRICULTURE
(tons)

	1968	1969	1970	1971	1972
Sugar . .	239,100	237,400	216,000	213,200	228,300
*Cocoa . .	5,794	3,850	6,001	3,550	5,116
Coconuts and Copra .	13,470	14,019	11,015	12,253	12,346
*Citrus Fruits .	3,874	2,229	2,390	1,707	1,955

* Exports.

MINING

		1969	1970	1971	1972
Crude Petroleum . .	(barrels)	57,429,000	51,047,000	47,147,000	51,212,000
Asphalt . . .	(tons)	122,495	128,319	121,903	113,627

INDUSTRY

		1969	1970	1971	1972
Cement	tons	239,500	266,300	251,800	281,900
Cigarettes	lbs.	1,748,700	1,817,900	1,774,400	1,785,500
Rum	proof gals.	1,911,000	1,726,500	1,886,600	2,473,600
Bay Rum	,,	31,500	18,700	16,200	19,000
Beer	gals.	2,705,000	3,213,000	3,643,000	3,930,000

FINANCE

100 cents = 1 Trinidad and Tobago dollar (TT $).
Coins: 1, 5, 10, 25 and 50 cents; 1 dollar.
Notes: 1, 5, 10 and 20 dollars.
Exchange rates (April 1974): £1 sterling = TT $4.80; U.S. $1 = TT $2.03.
TT $100 = £20.83 = U.S. $49.19.

BUDGET
(1971 estimate—million TT $)

REVENUE			EXPENDITURE	
Income Tax, Purchase Tax, etc.	268.3		Recurrent	305.7
Non-tax Revenue	58.4		Other	122.2
Other	15.4			
TOTAL	342.1		TOTAL	427.9

Development Plan (1969–73): Total Planned Expenditure TT $375m.

COST OF LIVING INDEX
(September 1960 = 100)

	WEIGHTING	1970	1971	1972
Food	490	132.9	139.0	155.0
Drink and Tobacco	77	158.6	160.3	179.0
Rent	25	126.1	128.4	132.9
Maintenance	52	137.9	141.4	155.2
Fuel and Lighting	29	125.8	129.3	137.6
Clothing	99	118.1	120.4	128.3
Household Supplies	67	122.2	125.2	132.2
Services	142	144.3	149.9	158.3
Drugs and Toilet Articles	19	126.1	129.0	139.8
ALL ITEMS	1,000	134.1	138.8	151.7

NATIONAL ACCOUNTS*
(million TT$)

	1965	1966	1967	1968
GROSS DOMESTIC PRODUCT (factor cost)	1,188.0	1,326.5	1,422.6	1,533.5
of which:				
Agriculture, forestry, fishing, quarrying	101.7	103.9	110.4	127.0
Oil and asphalt	284.1	313.6	350.4	379.0
Manufacturing and construction	258.5	299.6	313.4	318.1
Others, including government	543.7	609.4	648.4	709.2

* Provisional.

RESERVES AND CURRENCY IN CIRCULATION
(T.T. $'000)

	1970	1971	1972
Foreign Exchange Reserve	106,600	155,900	110,300
of which:			
IMF gold tranche	13,100	13,100	13,100
Currency in Circulation	68,630	84,903	106,513

BALANCE OF PAYMENTS
(TT $'000)

	1971			1972*		
	Credit	Debit	Balance	Credit	Debit	Balance
Goods and Services:						
Merchandise	1,060.7	1,310.0	−249.3	1,142.3	1,444.5	−302.2
Transport	146.2	60.5	85.7	143.0	60.9	82.1
Travel	70.5	48.6	21.9	80.4	52.1	28.3
Investment income . . .	10.8	129.6	−118.8	11.0	139.2	−128.2
Government n.e.s. . . .	14.0	2.0	12.0	18.0	2.7	15.3
Other miscellaneous services .	14.9	13.8	1.1	8.5	6.3	2.2
Total	1,317.1	1,564.5	−247.4	1,403.2	1,705.7	−302.5
Transfer Payments:						
Private	6.5	2.0	4.5	6.5	2.2	4.3
Official	—	13.2	− 13.2	0.5	12.0	− 11.5
Total	6.5	15.2	− 8.7	7.0	14.2	− 7.2
Total Current Account . .	—	256.1	−256.1	—	309.7	−309.7
Capital:						
Private Sector:						
Direct investment . . .	234.0	11.3	222.7	172.7	4.0	188.7
Public Sector:						
Loans and repayments . . .	38.6	34.7	3.9	46.3	7.5	38.8
Subscriptions to international organizations	—	2.7	− 2.7	—	2.7	− 2.7
Other assets	27.9	—	27.9	—	1.4	− 1.4
Total Capital Account . .	300.5	48.7	251.8	219.0	15.6	203.4
Errors and Omissions . . .	33.9	—	33.9	47.4	—	47.4
Overall Surplus or Deficit . .	—	42.9	− 42.9	45.6	—	45.6

* Provisional.

EXTERNAL TRADE
(TT $'000)

Imports: (1969) 968,477.8; (1970) 1,086,969.8; (1971) 1,329,258.0; (1972) 1,471,098.8.
Exports: (1969) 950,264.9; (1970) 963,050.3; (1971) 1,041,627.0; (1972) 1,071,481.4.

COMMODITY GROUPS
(TT $'000)

	IMPORTS			EXPORTS		
	1970	1971	1972	1970	1971	1972
Food	103,448.4	114,541.1	132,923.0	81,630.7	80,087.8	92,386.5
Beverages and Tobacco . .	8,079.0	10,884.5	10,563.8	2,830.1	3,143.2	3,445.3
Crude Materials, inedible . .	13,032.1	13,252.0	16,553.7	6,879.6	5,143.1	5,259.8
Mineral Fuels and Lubricants	578,473.6	665,521.1	704,779.2	743,853.7	805,163.9	833,050.0
Animal and Vegetable Oils and Fats	8,971.8	8,132.4	8,951.0	1,014.0	1,024.1	166.9
Chemicals	47,415.8	52,088.5	64,608.8	76,203.6	72,940.6	77,920.1
Basic Manufactures . .	139,447.9	196,539.4	201,819.9	19,603.5	20,317.9	19,593.8
Machinery and Transport Equipment	135,356.5	201,122.3	256,769.9	9,354.4	27,908.2	9,242.0
Miscellaneous Manufactures .	46,259.4	61,374.8	68,852.2	18,806.0	22,596.1	26,669.6
Miscellaneous Transactions, Commodities n.e.s. . . .	6,485.4	5,801.9	5,277.4	2,874.8	3,197.5	3,247.6
TOTAL . . .	1,086,969.8	1,329,258.0	1,471,098.8	963,050.3	1,041,627.0	1,071,481.4

PRINCIPAL COUNTRIES

IMPORTS	1970	1971	EXPORTS	1970	1971
United Kingdom . .	144,173.0	171,158.0	Sweden . . .	61,856.6	101,210.3
United States . .	176,084.0	227,874.2	United Kingdom . .	92,612.0	92,905.6
Venezuela . . .	267,471.3	133,723.1	United States . .	446,175.0	421,675.7
Others . . .	766,713.0	—	Others	1,316,613.0	—

TRANSPORT

Roads (1972): Motor vehicles registered: 104,006.

Shipping (1971): Entered 26,296,000 tons; Cleared 26,110,000 tons.

Civil Aviation (1972): Passengers arriving 237,590; Passengers departing 240,490.

TOURISM
(1972)
Holiday and transit visitors 147,390.

EDUCATION
(1971)

	PRIMARY	GOVERNMENT AND ASSISTED SECONDARY
Schools	470	45
Teachers	6,408	1,343
Students	227,580	28,457

Source: Central Statistical Office, Port of Spain.

THE CONSTITUTION

Trinidad and Tobago attained independence on August 31st, 1962. The Constitution provides for a Parliament consisting of Her Majesty, a Senate and a House of Representatives.

The Senate consists of 24 members appointed by the Governor-General; thirteen on the advice of the Prime Minister, four on the advice of the Leader of the Opposition and seven on the advice of the Prime Minister after the Prime Minister has consulted those religious, economic or social bodies or associations from which the Prime Minister considers that such Senators should be elected.

The House of Representatives consists of 36 members elected by universal adult suffrage. The duration of a Parliament is five years.

The Cabinet, presided over by the Prime Minister, is responsible for the general direction and control of the Government. It is collectively responsible to Parliament. No more than two members of the Cabinet, apart from the Attorney-General, can be drawn from the Senate. The Cabinet must include the Attorney-General.

THE GOVERNMENT

Head of State: H.M. Queen ELIZABETH II.

Governor-General: Sir ELLIS EMMANUEL INNOCENT CLARKE, T.C., G.C.M.G.,

THE CABINET
(*July* 1974)

Prime Minister and Minister of External and West Indian Affairs: Dr. the Rt. Hon. ERIC WILLIAMS.

Minister in charge of the Administration and Operation of External and West Indian Affairs: Hon. Dr. CUTHBERT JOSEPH.

Minister of Finance: Hon. GEORGE CHAMBERS.

Minister of Industry and Commerce: ERROL MAHABIR.

Minister of Health and Local Government: Hon. KAMALUDDIN MOHAMMED.

Minister of Planning, Development and Housing: Hon. BRENSLEY BARROW.

Minister of Works: Hon. VICTOR CAMPBELL.

Minister of Education and Culture: Hon. CARLTON GOMES.

Attorney-General and Minister of Legal Affairs: Hon. BASIL PITT.

Minister in the Prime Minister's Office responsible for Public Relations and Minister for Public Utilities: Hon. SHAM MOHAMMED.

Minister of Labour, Social Security and Co-operatives: Hon. HECTOR McCLEAN.

Minister in the Prime Minister's Office in charge of Community Development and Youth: (vacant).

Minister of Petroleum and Mines: Sen. the Hon. FRANCIS PREVATT.

Minister of National Security: Hon. OVERAND PADMORE.

Minister of Agriculture, Lands and Fisheries: Hon. LIONEL ROBINSON.

Minister for Tobago Affairs: Hon. WILBERT WINCHESTER.

DIPLOMATIC REPRESENTATION

HIGH COMMISSIONS AND EMBASSIES ACCREDITED TO TRINIDAD AND TOBAGO

(All in Port of Spain)

(HC) High Commission; (E) Embassy

Argentina: 2nd floor, 34 Queen's Park West (E); *Chargé d'Affaires:* RAÚL E. PERAZZO NAON.

Brazil: 6 Elizabeth St., St. Clair (E); *Ambassador:* PAULO NABUCO DE GOUVEA.

Canada: Colonial Bldg., 72 South Quay (HC); *High Commissioner:* DAVID CHALMER REECE (also accred. to Barbados).

France: Furness House, 90 Independence Square (E); *Ambassador:* PAUL LE MINTIER DE LEHELEC.

Germany, Federal Republic: Furness House, 90 Independence Square (E); *Ambassador:* HANS HERMANN HAFERKAMP.

India: 87 Cipriani Blvd. (HC); *High Commissioner:* S. M. AGA.

Jamaica: 2 Newbold St., St. Clair (HC); *High Commissioner:* V. COURTNEY-SMITH.

Netherlands: Furness House, 90 Independence Square (E); *Ambassador:* S. D. EMANUELS.

United Kingdom: Furness House, 90 Independence Square (HC); *High Commissioner:* C. E. DIGGINES.

U.S.A.: 15 Queen's Park West (E); *Ambassador:* LLOYD I. MILLER.

Venezuela: 18 Victoria Ave. (E); *Ambassador:* Dr. CARLOS IRAZÁBAL.

Trinidad and Tobago also has diplomatic relations with Australia, Belgium, Colombia, Cuba, Ghana, Indonesia, Israel, Italy, Lebanon, Pakistan, Romania, Senegal and Switzerland.

PARLIAMENT

SENATE
President: Dr. WAHID ALI.
Vice-President: C. SPENSER.

HOUSE OF REPRESENTATIVES
Speaker: A. C. THOMASOS.
Deputy Speaker: H. GHANY.

ELECTION, MAY 1971

PARTY	SEATS
People's National Movement .	34
United Progressive Party .	2

POLITICAL PARTIES

People's National Movement: 1 Tranquillity St., Port of Spain; f. 1956; nationalist party; holds 34 seats in the House of Representatives; Leader Dr. ERIC WILLIAMS; Chair. F. C. PREVATT.

United Progressive Party (U.P.P.): f. 1972; Leader of the Opposition: J. R. F. RICHARDSON.

Democratic Action Congress: f. 1971; Leader A. N. RAYMOND ROBINSON.

Democratic Labour Party: 115 Charlotte St., Port of Spain; opposition party; Leader VERNON JAMADAR.

Liberal Party: 6 Ajax St., Port of Spain; minor opposition party; Leader P. G. FARQUHAR.

West Indian National Party: Leader A. SINANAN.

JUDICIAL SYSTEM

Supreme Court: The Supreme Court of Judicature of Trinidad and Tobago consists of the High Court of Justice and the Court of Appeal. The High Court consists of the Chief Justice, who is *ex officio* a Judge of the High Court, and nine High Court Judges. Its jurisdiction corresponds to that of the English High Court of Justice.

The Court of Appeal consists of the Chief Justice who is President and four other Judges. The Court of Appeal is deemed to be fully constituted if it consists of an uneven number of Judges, not less than three.

Appeal lies from the High Court of Justice to the Court of Appeal and to the Privy Council.

Chief Justice: His Lordship Sir ISAAC HYATALI.

Court of Appeal: The Hons. I. E. HYATALI, CLEMENT E. G. PHILLIPS, M. CORBIN, E. REES, K. P. DE LA BASTIDE.

Puisne Judges: The Hons. G. M. SCOTT, N. HASSANALI, D. MALONE, K. C. McMILLAN, J. A. BRAITHWAITE, R. NARINE, P. T. GEORGES, G. DES ILES, M. BOURNE.

District Courts: The Chief Magistrate, 4 Senior and 21 stipendiary magistrates preside over the District Courts established in various parts of the country. In these Courts the work of the Petty Civil Courts (which have jurisdiction to try civil matters where the cause of action does not exceed $1,200), the Magistrates' Courts and the Coroners' Courts is conducted.

Industrial Court: Chair. J. A. M. BRAITHWAITE.
Registrar: G. R. BENNY.
Attorney-General: BASIL PITT.

RELIGION

Roman Catholics 192,570, Anglicans 150,000, other Christians 67,283, Hindus 135,345, Muslims 32,615.

ANGLICAN
Bishop of Trinidad: Hayes Court, Port of Spain; Rev. CLIVE ORMINGTON ABDULLAH.

ROMAN CATHOLIC CHURCH
Archbishop of Port of Spain: Most Rev. GORDON ANTHONY PANTIN; 27 Maraval Rd., Port of Spain.

Christian Council of Trinidad and Tobago: Port of Spain; f. 1967; church unity organization formed by Roman Catholic, Anglican, Presbyterian, Methodist, Moravian, Lutheran Mission and Salvation Army, with Ethiopian Orthodox and Baptist Union as observers.

THE PRESS

DAILIES
Evening News: 22–26 Vincent St., Port of Spain; f. 1936; independent; evening; Editor COMPTON DELPH; London Office: c/o C. Turner Ltd., 122 Shaftesbury Ave., W.1; circ. 49,727.

Trinidad Guardian: 22 St. Vincent St., Port of Spain; f. 1917; independent; morning; Editor L. CHONGSING; London Office: c/o C. Turner Ltd., 122 Shaftesbury Ave., W.1; circ. 60,416.

Trinidad and Tobago Express: 35 Independence Square, Port of Spain; f. 1967; Editor DAVID RENWICK.

PERIODICALS
Annual Statistical Digest: 2 Edward St., Port of Spain; f. 1952; issued by the Central Statistical Office.

Caribbean Herald: 46 Henry St., Port of Spain; weekly.

Caribbean Medical Journal: General Hospital, Port of Spain; f. 1938; quarterly.

Catholic News: 34 Belmont Circular Rd., Port of Spain; f. 1892; weekly; Editor Rev. Fr. P. J. TIERNAN, O.P.; circ. 16,298.

Chiao Sheng: 10 Charlotte St., Port of Spain; Chinese; weekly.

The Democrat: 4 Wrightson Rd., Port of Spain; monthly.

Medi-News Caribbean: Trinidad and Tobago Medical Association, Medico-Dental House, Abercromby St., Port of Spain.

The Nation: 27 Pembroke St., Port of Spain; weekly; organ of the People's National Movement; political and cultural; Chair. FITZ BLACKMAN; Editor I. MERRITT; circ. 12,000.

Observer: 91 Queen St., P.O.B. 136, Port of Spain; f. 1941; monthly; Editor H. P. SINGH; circ. 3,000.

Quarterly Economic Report: 2 Edward St., Port of Spain; f. 1950; quarterly; issued by the Central Statistical Office.

Sunday Guardian: 22 St. Vincent St., Port of Spain; f. 1917; independent; morning; Editor J. A. INCE;

London Office: c/o C. Turner Ltd., 122 Shaftesbury Ave., W.1; circ. 97,216.

Trinidad and Tobago Gazette: 2 Victoria Ave., Port of Spain; weekly; official government paper.

Tropical Agriculture: c/o IPC Science and Technology Press Ltd., Iliffe House, 32 High St., Guildford, Surrey, England; f. 1924; journal of the Imperial College of Tropical Agriculture, University of the West Indies, St. Augustine, Trinidad; quarterly; Gen. Editor H. K. ASHBY; Faculty Editor C. K. ROBINSON, University of the West Indies.

PUBLISHERS

Longman Caribbean Ltd.: Port of Spain; f. 1970; general; Dir. PERCY CEZAIR.

Marshal Muir Ltd.: 64 Marine Square, P.O.B. 126, Port of Spain.

Trinidad Publishing Co. Ltd.: 22-26 St. Vincent St., Port of Spain; law, politics.

University of the West Indies: St. Augustine; education, textbooks.

RADIO AND TELEVISION

RADIO

NBS Radio 610: 17 Abercromby St., P.O.B. 610, Port of Spain; f. 1957; AM and FM transmitters at Chaguanas, Cumberland Hill; Gen. Man. P. A. PITTS; Dir. of Programmes L. DE LEON; est. regular audience 450,000.

Radio Trinidad: Broadcasting House, 11B Maraval Rd., Port of Spain; f. 1947; subsidiary of Rediffusion Ltd., London; island-wide commercial broadcasting service; two programmes; Man. P. E. M. HESKETH.

Rediffusion (Trinidad) Ltd.: Broadcasting House, 11B Maraval Road, Port of Spain; f. 1947; subsidiary of Rediffusion International Ltd., London; commercial wired service in Port of Spain and other built-up areas; two programmes, one relaying Radio Trinidad, one (Voice of Rediffusion) also originating; 6,700 subscribers (1971); rental and retail sales of television receivers; Man. B. M. ROSTANT.

Receiving sets (1971): 240,000.

TELEVISION

Trinidad-Tobago Television Co. Ltd.: Television House, Maraval Rd., Port of Spain; f. 1962; commercial station; Gen. Man. F. A. RAWLINS.

Receiving sets (1974): 94,000.

FINANCE

(cap.=capital; dep.=deposits; res.=reserves; m.=million; amounts in TT$)

BANKING

Central Bank: Independence Square, P.O.B. 1250, Port of Spain; f. 1964; Gov. VICTOR E. BRUCE; cap. 2m., dep. 58.7m.; publs. *Statistical Digest, Economic Bulletin* (monthly in English), *Annual Report*.

Agricultural Development Bank: 86 Duke St., Port of Spain; bill for establishment passed 1968; provides long, medium and short term loans to farmers;

eventually to be owned and operated by farmers; Chair. GEORG J. FULLER.

Industrial Development Bank: legislation for the foundation of a development bank was passed in 1966, but operations were suspended pending the establishment of a Caribbean area development bank.

National Commercial Bank of Trinidad and Tobago: 60 Independence Square, P.O.B. 718, Port of Spain; f. 1970; cap. 5m., dep. 26.3m.; Chair. CYRIL DUPREY.

Trinidad Co-operative Bank Ltd.: 80-84 Charlotte St., Port of Spain; f. 1914; Chair. PHILIP ROCHFORD; 2 brs.

BANKS

Barclays Bank of Trinidad and Tobago Ltd.: P.O.B. 1153, Port of Spain; f. 1970; cap. 5.5m.; Man. Dir. C. A. J. DEVAUX; Man. P. R. DAVIES-EVANS; 32 offices in Trinidad, 1 in Tobago.

Canadian Imperial Bank of Commerce: Head Office: 25 King St., West, Toronto 1, Ontario; Port of Spain Office: P.O.B. 69, 72 Independence Square; Area Man. K. G. HOUSE; 14 brs.

Chase Manhattan Bank: Head Office: 1 Chase Manhattan Plaza, New York, N.Y. 10015; Port of Spain Office: 53 Independence Square; Man. F. P. CAMACHO.

First National City Bank: Head Office: 399 Park Ave., New York, N.Y. 10022; Port of Spain Office: 74 Independence Square, P.O.B. 1249; 3 brs.

Royal Bank of Trinidad and Tobago Ltd.: 1st floor, 55 Independence Square, P.O.B. 287, Port of Spain; Chair. and Man. Dir. C. P. DE SOUZA; 15 brs.

STOCK EXCHANGE

The Caribbean Stock Exchange and Bond Trinidad Ltd.: 16 Vincent St., Port of Spain, Trinidad.

INSURANCE

National companies in Port of Spain:

Caribbean Home Insurance Co. Ltd.: 19–21 Chacon St.; f. 1973; initial cap. 1m.; Chair. SYDNEY KNOX; general except life.

Colonial Life Insurance Co. Ltd.: Colonial Life Bldg., 29 St. Vincent St.; f. 1936; Man. C. O. MONSANTO.

Trinidad & Tobago Insurance Ltd.: 82–86 Duke St., P.O.B. 1004.

Trinidad Distributors Ltd.: 7–9 Marli St., P.O.B. 617.

Trinidad Friendly Life Insurance Society: 30A St. Vincent St.

Trinidad Motor Insurance Co. Ltd.: 25 Edward St.; Man. E. J. MARSDEN.

Trinidad Trading Co. Ltd.: 84–88 Independence Square, P.O.B. 660; Man. Dir. IGNATIUS S. FERREIRA; agents for a number of foreign companies.

The principal British and a number of U.S. and Canadian companies have agencies in Port of Spain.

TRADE AND INDUSTRY

CHAMBER OF COMMERCE

Trinidad and Tobago Chamber of Industry and Commerce (Inc.): P.O.B. 499, Port of Spain; f. 1973; Pres. GEORGE GUY; Gen. Man. FRANK DOWDY; Sec. FRANK McKENZIE-COOK.

Southern Division: P.O.B. 80, San Fernando; Pres. ECCLES BIDESHI; Man. CAROL TRABOULAY; 450 mems.

ASSOCIATIONS

British Caribbean Citrus Association Ltd.: P.O.B. 174, Port of Spain; f. 1955; mems. Citrus Growers' Associations in Jamaica, Belize, Dominica and Trinidad and Tobago; Chair. Sir HAROLD ROBINSON; Sec. G. DE VERTEUIL.

Cocoa Planters' Association of Trinidad Ltd.: P.O.B. 346, Port of Spain; f. 1915; 165 mems.; Pres. J. GASTON DE GANNES; Man. ARTHUR C. DE SILVA.

Coconut Growers' Association Ltd.: P.O.B. 229, Port of Spain; f. 1936; 341 mems.; Pres. F. AGOSTINI, H.E.C.

Co-operative Citrus Growers' Association of Trinidad and Tobago Ltd.: P.O.B. 174, Port of Spain; f. 1932; 600 mems.; Pres. Hon. Sir H. E. ROBINSON; Sec. G. DE VERTEUIL.

Pan Trinbago: 72–74 Queen St., Port of Spain; official body for Trinidad and Tobago Steelbandsmen; Pres. ROY AUGUSTUS; Sec. DENNIS LE GENDRE.

Shipping Association of Trinidad and Tobago: Room D, 1st floor, Salvatori Bldg., Port of Spain; f. 1938; Pres. A. A. C. LAWLOR; Exec. Sec. B. R. DE LEON.

Sugar Manufacturers' Association of Trinidad Ltd.: 80 Abercromby St., Port of Spain; f. 1920; 3 mems.; Chair. G. H. MAINGOT; Sec. M. Y. KHAN.

Sugar Technologists' Association of Trinidad and Tobago: 80 Abercromby St., Port of Spain; f. 1967; 214 mems.; Chair. G. H. MAINGOT; Sec. M. Y. KHAN.

Trinidad Island-wide Cane Farmers' Association Inc.: San Fernando; f. 1957; Chair. SEURADGE SOOKHOO; Man. S. NORMAN GIRWAR; Sec. HARRY OUTAR; publ. *The Cane Farmer* (monthly).

Trinidad Manufacturers: permanent exhibition at 1 Anderson Terrace, Maraval, Port of Spain.

DEVELOPMENT

National Housing Authority: P.O.B. 555, Port of Spain; f. 1962; Chair. IVAN WILLIAMS; Deputy Chair. LANCE MURRAY; Sec. VERNON CAMPS; Exec. Dir. VERNON CARRINGTON.

Point Lisas Industrial Port Development Corporation Ltd.: P.O.B. 80, San Fernando; f. 1969; Chair. R. C. MONTANO; at present building liquefied natural gas plant with deep-water harbour facilities and iron ore direct reduction plant, both scheduled for completion in 1977.

Trinidad and Tobago Industrial Development Corporation: Corner Duncan St. and Independence Square; f. 1959; encourages new industries and hotels and develops industrial estates; operates loan funds; Chair. BERNARD V. PRIMUS; Gen. Man. ELDON G. WARNER.

TRADE UNIONS

Trinidad and Tobago Labour Congress: Port of Spain; f. 1966 as the result of a merger between the *National Federation of Labour* and the *Trinidad and Tobago National Trades Union Congress*; affiliated to the Caribbean Congress of Labour and ICFTU; about 55,000 mems.; Pres. NATHANIEL CRICHLOW; Gen. Sec. CYRIL GONZALES.

PRINCIPAL AFFILIATES

All Trinidad Sugar Estates and Factory Workers' Trade Union: 8 Mon Chagrin St., San Fernando; about 8,000 mems.; Acting Pres. DICKSON EMERY; Gen. Sec. RAMPRATAP SINGH.

Amalgamated Workers' Union: 16 New St., Port of Spain; about 7,000 mems.; Pres. CYRIL LOPEZ; Acting Sec. FLAVIUS NURSE.

Communication Workers' Union: 54 Duke St., Port of Spain; about 1,800 mems.; Pres. CARLTON SAVARY; Gen. Sec. CARL TULL.

Public Services Association: 89 Abercromby St., Port of Spain; about 9,000 mems.; Pres. Mrs. URSULA GITTENS; Gen. Sec. JAMES I. A. MANSWELL.

Seamen and Waterfront Workers' Trade Union: 1D Wrightson Rd., Port of Spain; about 7,000 mems.; Pres.-Gen. VERNON GLEAN; Acting Sec.-Gen. PETER BUDD.

Union of Commercial and Industrial Workers: 130 Henry St., Port of Spain; about 5,000 mems.; Pres. V. A. STANFORD; Sec. I. S. GONZALES.

NON-AFFILIATED UNIONS

National Union of Government and Federated Workers: 145 Henry St., Port of Spain; about 20,000 mems.; Pres. NATHANIEL E. CRICHLOW; Gen. Sec. SELWYN JOHN.

Oilfield Workers' Trade Union: Leader GEORGE WEEKES.

TRANSPORT

ROADS

There are 2,630 miles of roads in Trinidad and Tobago, of which 1,740 miles are classified as minor roads, 340 miles as major urban roads and 550 miles as major rural roads.

Public Transport Service Corporation: Railway Bldgs., South Quay, P.O.B. 391, Port of Spain; f. 1965 to operate road and rail transport; Chair. EMMANUEL B. ANNISETTE; Gen. Man. CECIL ST. HILL; operates a fleet of 368 buses; 33,677,829 passengers were transported by bus in 1972.

There are no longer any operational railways in Trinidad.

SHIPPING

The chief ports are Port of Spain in Trinidad and Scarborough in Tobago.

Port Authority of Trinidad and Tobago: Wrightson Rd., Port of Spain; Gen. Man. HAROLD MOYLAN (acting).

West Indies Shipping Service: c/o West Indies Shipping Corporation, 1 Richmond St., Port of Spain.

The chief foreign shipping lines which call at Port of Spain are: Atlantic Lines, Booth Line, Furness Lines, Great Lakes Transcaribbean Line, Hamburg-America Line, Harrison Line, Lauro Line, P. & O. Orient Lines, Royal Netherlands Steamship Co., Saguenay Shipping Ltd.

CIVIL AVIATION

Arawak Airlines: Port of Spain; services to Tobago.

British West Indian Airways: Sunjet House, 26–30 Edward St., Port of Spain; incorporated 1948; 90 per cent of shares held by the Government of Trinidad and Tobago; points served include Trinidad, Tobago, Barbados, St. Lucia, Puerto Rico, Jamaica, Guyana, Toronto, Miami, New York, London and Havana; fleet of 7 Boeing 707; Chair. DODDRIDGE ALLEYNE; Sec. TREVOR BERTIE.

The following foreign airlines serve Trinidad and Tobago: Air Canada, Air France, ALM (Netherlands Antilles), British Airways, Caribair (Puerto Rico), Cubana, KLM, LAV (Venezuela), LIAT (Antigua), Pan Am, Surinam Airways and Viasa (Venezuela).

TOURISM

Trinidad and Tobago Tourist Board: 56 Frederick St., P.O.B. 222, Port of Spain; f. 1958; statutory board with 7 mems. appointed by the Governor in Council, some on the recommendation of the various organizations representing the tourist industry; Chair. Jack de Lima; Gen. Man. Donald Bain.

Overseas Offices

Canada: Suite 1006, 110 Yonge St., Toronto, Ontario.

U.S.A.: Suite 712–714, 400 Madison Ave., New York, N.Y. 10017.

There are approximately 1,500 hotel rooms available.

CULTURAL ORGANIZATIONS

Annual Art and Music Festivals are held in Trinidad. The following are some of the cultural associations in Port of Spain:

The Arts Festival Association: Extra Mural Dept., 113 Frederick St.; Sec. Mrs. D. Sampson.

Trinidad Dramatic Club: 4 River Rd., Maraval; Pres. Mrs. D. Butt.

Trinidad Light Operatic Society: 55 Observatory St.; Sec. L. Woodruffe.

Trinidad Music Association: 18 Mary St., St. Clair; Pres. Mrs. Robert Johnstone.

Trinidad and Tobago Association of Calypso Singers and Composers: 68 Henry St.; Sec. R. Joseph.

The Trinidad and Tobago Art Society: Art Society Centre, French St., Woodbrook; Sec. Mrs. M. Neehall.

Queen's Hall: St. Ann's, Port of Spain; f. 1959; statutory body financed by the Government; Pres. Peter Rochford; Man. Otto Massiah.

Naparima Bowl: Paradise Pasture, San Fernando; f. 1962; government-sponsored; consists of an Auditorium, open-air Amphitheatre, and various exhibition and meeting rooms; Chair. of the Board Dr. Arthur E. Chen; Man. Grace M. Abdool, m.m., a.t.c.l., m.b.e.

Pan Trinbago: 72–74 Queen St., Port of Spain; official body for Trinidad and Tobago Steelbandsmen; Pres. Roy Augustus; Sec. Dennis le Gendre.

UNIVERSITY

University of the West Indies: St. Augustine, Trinidad; other faculties in Jamaica and Barbados; 250 teachers, 1,850 students.

TUNISIA

INTRODUCTORY SURVEY

Location, Climate, Language, Religion, Flag, Capital

The Republic of Tunisia lies on the southern shore of the Mediterranean Sea, between Algeria and Libya. The climate is temperate on the coast, with winter rain, and hot and dry in the southern desert. Arabic is the official language and French is widely used. Islam is the state religion and embraces the vast majority of the population. There are Jewish, Roman Catholic, Greek Orthodox and Protestant minorities. The national flag (proportions 3 by 2) is red, charged with a white disc containing a red crescent moon and a five-pointed red star. The capital is Tunis.

Recent History

Formerly a French Protectorate, Tunisia became autonomous in 1955 and achieved independence the following year. In 1957 the monarchy was abolished and Habib Bourguiba became the first President. In 1961, following repeated demands by President Bourguiba that France should withdraw its troops from the naval base at Bizerta, a blockade was set up. French reinforcements were sent and heavy fighting broke out. After discussion in the United Nations a cease-fire was arranged and French evacuation negotiated in October 1963. In May 1964 Tunisia appropriated all foreign-owned lands, and France in retaliation withdrew most of her economic aid. Economic aid from France recommenced after a cultural agreement was signed in 1966. The Government's socialist agricultural policy provoked resistance amongst the rural population and in 1969 Ahmed Ben Salah, the Minister largely responsible for the drive towards co-operative farming, was dismissed and imprisoned. In 1973 he escaped and from abroad accused the Government of favouring the rich and foreign capitalists. Students and workers have also clashed with the Government. President Bourguiba's hold on power seems firm, however, despite his ill health.

Tunisian foreign policy is noted for its moderate position on the Israel question and for good relations with the U.S.A. In 1973 Tunisia tried to initiate negotiations for a peaceful settlement of the Arab-Israeli dispute, and Bourguiba gave only half-hearted support to the Arab cause in the October War. In January 1974, it was announced that Tunisia and Libya were to form a united Islamic Arab Republic. Subsequently Bourguiba postponed the project, although he reiterated support for the principle of Arab unity. Mohamed Masmoudi, the Minister for Foreign Affairs, was dismissed for his part in arranging the union and for his general anti-American line.

Government

Executive power is vested in the President, elected for a five-year term by direct suffrage, and a Cabinet. The legislative organ is the unicameral National Assembly of 101 members, which is elected by universal suffrage for five years at the same time as the Presidential elections. All citizens of twenty or over are entitled to vote.

Defence

The national army numbers about 20,000 men. Officer-training is carried out in the U.S.A. and France as well as in Tunisia. The navy and air force have only recently been brought into existence and consist of training cadres of 2,000 men each.

Economic Affairs

Agriculture and mining are the basis of the economy. The chief agricultural products are wheat, olive oil, wine and fruits. Market gardening and livestock breeding are being encouraged. Between 1965 and 1969 a system of co-operative farming was promoted, but its failure has left agriculture divided into a large-scale modernized sector, both State and private, and a traditional sector of small peasant holdings. Rural depopulation is a serious problem as young people desert the country for the towns.

Phosphates, iron ore and lead are the principal minerals, and petroleum production was nearly 4 million tons in 1972. Industry is expanding rapidly. There is a large steel works, and chemical, textile and paper industries are well-developed. An important industrial complex, with a large freight port, a cement works, phosphate processing plant and other industries, is being built at Gabès in the south.

Tunisia has a serious unemployment problem, aggravated by a high rate of population increase, and a permanent balance of payments deficit. To help cope with these problems a law of April 1972 made the whole country a virtual Free Zone for foreign export-oriented industries. Tourism is of growing importance as a source of employment and foreign currency. There were over 670,000 tourist visitors in 1971. Some 150,000 Tunisians work abroad, and the number is increasing. Their remittances are worth about 10 million dinars annually.

Transport and Communications

The total length of railways is 2,305 km., of which 1,998 km. are State-owned. 10,483 km. of highways and roads connect all the major commercial centres. There are four major ports and a special petroleum port at La Skhirra. Air transport is provided by Tunis Air and several foreign lines.

Social Welfare

A state system of social security provides benefits for sickness, maternity and old age. Free health services are available to 80 per cent of the population. Regional committees for social security care for the aged, needy and orphaned.

Education

Approximately 72 per cent of children of school age receive education in Tunisia, the majority in state-run schools, and the proportion is continually rising. Higher and adult education are also expanding rapidly, and in all almost one person in five in Tunisia attends some sort of school. Arabic is the first language of instruction in primary schools but is gradually replaced by French in the higher grades. In 1971 about 33 per cent of the budget was devoted to education.

Tourism

The main tourist attractions are the magnificent sandy beaches, oriental architecture and remains of the Roman Empire. Tunisia contains the site of the ancient city of

Carthage. Tourism has expanded rapidly in Tunisia following extensive government investment in hotels, improved roads and other facilities.

Sport

Football, swimming and boxing are the most popular sports.

Public Holidays

1974: August 3rd (Birthday of President Bourguiba), August 13th (Women's Day), September 3rd (Commemoration of September 3rd, 1934), October 15th (Evacuation of Bizerta), October 18th (Id ul Fitr—end of Ramadan), December 25th (Christmas), December 26th (Id ul Adha).

1975: January 1st (New Year's Day), January 14th (Muslim New Year), January 18th (National Revolution Day), March 20th (Independence Day), March 26th (Mouloud—Birth of the Prophet), April 9th (Martyrs' Day), May 1st (Labour Day), June 1st (National Day), July 25th (Republic Day).

Weights and Measures

The metric system is in force.

Currency and Exchange Rates

1,000 millimes = 1 Tunisian dinar.

Exchange rates (April 1974):

£1 sterling = 1.028 dinars;
U.S. $1 = 435.2 millimes.

STATISTICAL SURVEY

AREA AND POPULATION

AREA (sq. km.)	POPULATION	
	Total (July 1st, 1973)	Tunis (capital) (1966 census)
164,150	5,509,000	468,997

	1969	1970	1971*
Births .	194,940	185,756	182,749
Deaths .	52,872	45,435	48,762
Marriages	33,764	34,318	37,642

* Provisional figures.

Chief Towns: Sfax 100,000, Sousse 90,000, Bizerta 70,000, Kairouan 50,000, Gabès 40,000, Monastir 40,000, Menzel-Bourguiba 35,000.

AGRICULTURE

PRINCIPAL CROPS
('000 metric tons)

	1968	1969	1970	1971
Soft Wheat . .	73	91	150	200
Hard Wheat . .	310	245	299	400
Barley . .	130	81	151	140
Esparto Grass . .	108	74	84	79
Citrus Fruits . .	66	97	n.a.	77
Dates . .	39	59	18	39
Sugar Beet . .	27	34	30	27
Olives . .	275	125	400	900

Olive production: (1972) 350,000 metric tons; (1973) 675,000 metric tons.

LIVESTOCK
(1970—'000)

CATTLE	ASSES	SHEEP	HORSES	MULES	GOATS	CAMELS
670	185	3,100	98	60	450	280

Source: FAO Production Yearbook, 1971.

Fishing: Total catch including Shellfish (1968) 27,972 tons, (1969) 29,668 tons, (1970) 24,376 tons, (1971) 27,040 tons.

MINING

		1967	1968	1969	1970	1971
Iron Ore . .	('000 metric tons)	1,003	1,016	945	774	940
Lead Ore . .	(,, ,, ,,)	28	24	38	35	33
Calcium Phosphate	(,, ,, ,,)	2,810	3,361	2,599	3,021	3,162
Zinc . . .	(metric tons)	5,635	7,165	16,692	21,500	20,800

Petroleum: Production from the El Borma field totalled approximately 3,191,000 tons in 1968, 3,707,000 tons in 1969, 4,151,000 tons in 1970, 4,096,000 tons in 1971, 3,970,000 tons in 1972.

INDUSTRY

		1968	1969	1970	1971
Superphosphates . .	('000 metric tons)	376	333	382	422
Cement . . .	(,, ,, ,,)	491	582	522	554
Lead	(,, ,, ,,)	14	24	22	21
Electric Power . .	(million kWh.)	546	624	680	768
Natural Gas . .	('000 cubic metres)	9,443	9,299	4,740	936
Town Gas . .	(,, ,, ,,)	19.5	19.3	19.1	17.6
Beer . . .	('000 hectolitres)	237	169	201	280
Cigarettes . . .	(millions)	2,975	3,253	3,286	3,549
Wine	('000 hl.)	912	843	559	966
Olive Oil . .	('000 metric tons)	51	55	25	90

FINANCE

1,000 millimes = 1 Tunisian dinar.

Coins: 1, 2, 5, 10, 20, 50, 100 and 500 millimes.

Notes: 500 millimes; 1, 5 and 10 dinars.

Exchange rates (April 1974): £1 sterling = 1.028 dinars; U.S. $1 = 435.2 millimes.

100 Tunisian dinars = £97.31 = $229.78.

BUDGET
('000 dinars)

REVENUE	1969	1970	EXPENDITURE	1969	1970
Direct Taxes . . .	26,819	30,545	Education	35,721	44,367
Indirect Taxes . . .	80,163	81,582	Finances and National		
Other Taxes . . .	3,448	3,829	Economy . . .	41,630	31,239
Internal Revenue and Services	6,090	5,528	Public Health . .	12,350	13,708
Revenue from Investments .	9,567	18,523	Interior . . .	10,200	10,637
Others and Reinvestments .	5,263	6,493	National Defence . .	7,000	9,509
			Public Works and Housing .	6,530	6,088
			Others	17,919	30,952
TOTAL . . .	131,350	146,500	TOTAL . . .	131,350	146,500

Budget Estimates: 154 million dinars (1971); 175 million dinars (1972); 208 million dinars (1973).

NATIONAL ACCOUNTS
(million dinars, at 1966 prices)

	1969	1970	1971*
Agriculture	77.8	80.1	100.7
Food and Agricultural Industries . . .	20.6	19.3	26.0
Petroleum	22.5	26.0	24.0
Mining	9.1	8.7	9.1
Public Utilities	n.a.	n.a.	n.a.
Other Industry	32.1	33.9	35.8
Building and Public Works . . .	42.9	44.4	49.3
Transport and Telecommunications . .	45.0	51.3	45.8
Rent	46.7	47.4	48.3
Commerce	56.0	72.5	84.8
Tourism	14.8	16.6	25.2
Other Services including Government .	132.8	142.6	145.2
Gross Domestic Product at Factor Cost	518.6	561.6	615.0
Indirect Taxes	83.7	88.2	94.8
Gross Domestic Product at Market Prices	602.3	649.8	709.8
Imports of Goods and Services *less* Exports .	46.0	49.9	57.1
Total Resources	648.3	699.7	766.9
Private Consumption	399.4	421.7	469.9
Government Consumption . . .	110.5	122.9	121.4
Gross Fixed Capital Formation . .	135.3	145.7	173.4
Increase in Stocks	3.1	9.4	2.2

* Provisional.

EXTERNAL TRADE
('ooo dinars)

	1966	1967	1968	1969	1970	1971	1972
Imports	131,224	137,087	114,497	139.777	160,396	179,958	222,200
Exports	73,684	78,355	82,829	86,960	95,804	113,304	150,300

PRINCIPAL COMMODITIES
('ooo dinars)

Imports	1968	1969	1970
Machinery, non-electric	15,324	16,818	20,048
Cereals	11,301	15,493	18,016
Iron and Steel	6,530	9,598	10,996
Electric Machinery . . .	8,067	9,402	10,699
Road Transport Equipment . . .	6,332	7,564	9,824
Animal and Vegetable Oils and Fats .	3,631	6,182	8,926
Petroleum Products . . .	3,422	6,780	7,704
Sugar and Sugar Preparations . .	2,927	3,587	4,804

Principal Commodities—*continued*]

Exports				1969	1970	1971
Crustaceans and Molluscs	.	.	.	696	1,131	1,075
Oranges	.	.	.	3,040	1,590	1,302
Dates	.	.	.	990	1,399	2,228
Dried Almonds	.	.	.	638	1,488	1,362
Other Fruit and Nuts	.	.	.	262	215	1,669
Wine	.	.	.	3,443	4,754	1,316
Pulp and Waste Paper	.	.	.	1,856	1,884	1,889
Natural Phosphates	.	.	.	8,699	10,529	11,554
Iron	.	.	.	1,745	1,946	2,834
Crude Petroleum	.	.	.	21,158	23,451	28,733
Motor Spirit and Gas Oil	.	.	.	1,165	1,673	1,450
Other Petroleum Products	.	.	.	1,450	n.a.	n.a.
Olive Oil	.	.	.	9,964	8,394	24,019
Phosphatic Fertilizers	.	.	.	8,161	8,611	9,634
Lead	.	.	.	2,226	3,215	1,925
Total (incl. others)	.	.		86,960	95,804	113,304

PRINCIPAL COUNTRIES
('ooo dinars)

Imports				1969	1970	1971
Belgium/Luxembourg	.	.	.	1,833	3,059	3,674
Brazil	.	.	.	952	2,303	3,249
France	.	.	.	46,196	55,557	64,827
Germany, Federal Republic	.	.		10,512	13,619	12,239
Iraq	.	.	.	2,094	2,584	3,216
Italy	.	.	.	12,489	11,566	15,497
Netherlands	.	.	.	2,522	3,480	3,742
Poland	.	.	.	2,698	4,856	2,970
United Kingdom	.	.	.	4,105	4,557	5,836
U.S.A.	.	.	.	28,208	27,134	26,230
Total (incl. others)	.	.		139,777	160,396	179,958

Exports				1969	1970	1971
Algeria	.	.	.	2,236	4,045	1,724
France	.	.	.	23,173	23,383	21,884
Germany, Federal Republic	.	.		12,088	9,293	14,857
Italy	.	.	.	11,745	19,781	22,146
Libya	.	.	.	6,362	8,873	11,212
Poland	.	.	.	2,360	3,523	3,459
U.S.S.R.	.	.	.	2,525	1,460	3,721
United Kingdom	.	.	.	2,736	2,503	1,770
Total (incl. others)	.	.		86,960	95,804	113,304

TRANSPORT
ROADS

Vehicles Licensed	1969	1970	1971
Private Cars . .	62,280	66,438	72,056
Buses . .			
Lorries . }	34,889	37,246	41,506
Commercial Vehicles			
Motor Cycles .	9,808	9,904	10,063

SHIPPING

	1968	1969	1970	1971
Vessels Entered* ('ooo net reg. tons)	12,379	13,547	13,124	25,137
Passengers . . . (number)	163,700	229,100	213,800	252,200
Goods Loaded ('ooo metric tons)	5,147	4,655	4,799	5,043
Goods Unloaded (,, ,, ,,)	2,931	3,417	3,459	3,472

* Including vessels leaving.

CIVIL AVIATION

	1969	1970	1971
Passenger ('ooo) . .	695.5	785.0	1,047.2
Freight (metric tons) .	4,294	4,475	4,756
Mail (metric tons) .	775	896	921

TOURISM

PRINCIPAL NATIONALITIES OF VISITORS
('ooo)

	1968	1969	1970	1971
Federal Germany . . .	71.7	66.5	84.2	163.7
France	66.6	93.5	113.8	138.1
United Kingdom . . .	48.2	60.8	47.0	73.0
Italy	34.9	50.3	58.6	63.4
Libya	31.7	31.0	36.3	54.4
Sweden	22.6	23.9	17.8	22.5
Switzerland	22.6	27.1	20.6	28.9
Algeria	14.4	7.5	8.9	11.8
U.S.A.	11.8	16.9	17.2	15.5
Morocco	9.7	11.6	5.8	5.1
TOTAL (incl. others) .	384.3	455.3	482.0	673.1

Tourist Accommodation: 6,800 beds in officially classified hotels (total capacity in 1971: 42,996 beds including hostels and holiday villages).

Tourist Spending: (1969) 26m. dinars, (1970) 29m. dinars, (1971) 54m. dinars.

EDUCATION

	INSTITUTIONS	PUPILS		TEACHERS	
		1968–69	1969–70	1968–69	1969–70
Primary	2,131	859,927	912,646	16,194	18,000
Secondary	88	135,947	163,353	3,818	6,931
Secondary Technical . .	80	n.a.	n.a.	2,141	
Teacher Training . . .	5	n.a.	n.a.	n.a.	
University of Tunis . . .	1	7,668	9,413	304	539
Students Abroad . . .	—	2,816	n.a.	—	—

The ratio of boys to girls is approx. 2 : 1 in primary schools, 3 : 1 in secondary schools and 4 : 1 at the University.

THE CONSTITUTION

Tunisia, which had been a French Protectorate since 1881, achieved full internal autonomy in September 1955, and was finally recognized as a fully independent sovereign State by the Protocol of Paris of March 20th, 1956, by which France abrogated the former treaties and conventions.

NATIONAL ASSEMBLY

The Constitution was proclaimed by the Constituent Assembly on June 1st, 1959. Tunisia is a free, independent and sovereign republic. Legislative power is exercised by the National Assembly which is elected (at the same time as the President) every five years by direct universal suffrage. Every citizen who has had Tunisian nationality for at least five years and who has attained twenty years of age has the vote. The National Assembly shall hold two sessions every year, each session lasting not more than three months. Additional meetings may be held at the demand of the President or of a majority of the deputies.

HEAD OF STATE

The President of the Republic is both Head of State and Head of the Executive. He must be not less than forty years of age and is not permitted to serve more than three terms consecutively. The President of the Republic is also the Commander-in-Chief of the army and makes both civil and military appointments.

COUNCIL OF STATE

Comprises two judicial bodies: (1) an administrative body dealing with legal disputes between individuals and State or public bodies; (2) an audit office to verify the accounts of the State and submit reports.

ECONOMIC AND SOCIAL COUNCIL

Deals with economic and social planning and studies projects submitted by the National Assembly. Members are grouped in seven categories representing various sections of the community.

THE GOVERNMENT

HEAD OF STATE

President of the Republic: Habib Bourguiba (*re-elected for a third five-year term on November 2nd, 1969*).

THE CABINET
(*April* 1974)

Prime Minister: Hedi Nouira.
Minister responsible to Prime Minister: Mohamed Sayah.
Minister, Director of the President's Office: Shadli Klibi.
Minister of Justice: Slaheddine Bali.
Minister for Foreign Affairs: Habib Chatti.
Minister of the Interior: Tahar Belkhodja.
Minister of Defence: Mohamed Hédi Khefacha.
Minister in charge of the Plan: Mansour Moalla.
Minister of Finance: Mohamed Fitouri.
Minister of the Economy: Chedly Ayari
Minister of Agriculture: Dr. Dhaoui Hannablia.
Minister of Education: Driss Guiga.
Minister of Cultural Affairs: Mahmoud Messadi.
Minister of Public Health: Mohamed Mzali.

Minister of Supply: Abdallah Farhat.
Minister of Social Affairs: Mohamed Ennaceur.
Minister of Transport and Communications: Lasaad Ben Osman.
Minister of Youth and Sport: Fouad M'Bazâa.
Secretary of State for the Plan: Mustapha Zaanouni.
Secretary of State for the National Economy: Mekki Zidi.
Secretary of State for Education: Hamed Zghal.
Secretaries of State for Agriculture: Mohamed Ghedira and Abderrahman Ben Messaoud.
Secretaries of State for Supply: Adbel-hamid Sassi and Larbi Mallakh.
Secretary of State for Defence: Ahmad Bennour.
Secretary of State for Information: Slaheddine Abdellah.

DIPLOMATIC REPRESENTATION

EMBASSIES ACCREDITED TO TUNISIA

(In Tunis unless otherwise indicated)

Algeria: 18 rue du Niger; *Ambassador:* Tedjeni Haddam.

Argentina: Rabat, Morocco.

Austria: 17 ave. de France; *Ambassador:* Hans Pasch.

Belgium: 47 rue du 1er Juin; *Ambassador:* Jacques Gérard.

Brazil: rue Sayouti, El Menzah; *Ambassador:* Adolpho J. Bezerra de Menezesi.

Bulgaria: 137 ave. de la Liberté; *Ambassador:* Bogomil Nonev.

Cameroon: 3 ave. de Lesseps; *Ambassador:* Ferdinand Léopold Oyono.

Canada: 3 rue Didon, Notre Dame de Tunis, Cité al Mahdi; *Ambassador:* Henri Gaudefroy.

Central African Republic: 10 rue Imam Muslim, El Menzah; *Ambassador:* Jean Charlie Mokamenede.

China, People's Republic: 41 ave. Lesseps; *Ambassador:* Hou Yeh-feng.

Costa Rica: *Ambassador:* Miguel Yamuni Tabush.

Czechoslovakia: 98 rue de la Palestine; *Ambassador:* Jan Janik.

Denmark: 138 ave. de la Liberté; *Ambassador:* Ditlov Scheel.

Egypt: 1 rue Dr. Calmette; *Ambassador:* HASSEN ABDEL ALI EL NAÏL.

Finland: 23 rue Baudelaire, El Omrane; *Ambassador:* SUNNELL JUHANI OSSI.

France: pl. de l'Indépendance; *Ambassador:* GEORGES GAUCHER.

Gabon: Paris, France.

German Democratic Republic: 16 rue Es-Soyouti, El Menzah; *Ambassador:* HEINZ DIETER WINTER.

Germany, Federal Republic: 18 rue Félicien Challaye; *Ambassador:* Dr. HEINZ NAUPERT.

Ghana: 103 ave de la Liberté.

Greece: 78 ave. Mohamed V; *Ambassador:* GEORGES J. GAVAS.

Guinea: Algiers, Algeria.

Hungary: Algiers, Algeria.

India: 13 rue du Dr. Burnet; *Ambassador:* V. M. M. NAIR.

Indonesia: Algiers, Algeria.

Iran: 10 rue Dr. Burnet, Belvédère; *Ambassador:* (vacant).

Iraq: 125 ave. de la Liberté; *Ambassador:* MEDLOUL NAJI EL MOHANNEH.

Italy: 37 rue Abdennasser; *Ambassador:* SALVATORE SARACENO.

Ivory Coast: 1 pl. Pasteur; *Ambassador:* CHARLES AILLOT ABOUT.

Japan: 16 rue Jugurtha; *Ambassador:* YASUO YANO.

Jordan: 16 rue El Moutanabi, El Menzah; *Ambassador:* (vacant).

Korea, Republic: 85 ave. de la Liberté; *Ambassador:* KYU SAP CHUNG.

Kuwait: rue Jacques Cartier, Belvédère; *Ambassador:* MOJRANE AHMED EL HAMAD.

Lebanon: 18 ave. Charles Nicolle; *Ambassador:* JOSEPH SALAMA.

Libya: 48bis rue du 1er Juin; *Commissioner General:* FRAJ BEN GILEIL.

Mali: Paris, France.

Malta: Tripoli, Libya.

Mauritania: 18 ave. Charles Nicolle; *Ambassador:* (vacant).

Mexico: Rome, Italy.

Morocco: 5 rue Didon, Notre Dame; *Ambassador:* (vacant).

Netherlands: 2 rue d'Artois; *Ambassador:* J. D. VAN DEN BRANDELER.

Niger: Algiers, Algeria.

Nigeria: Paris, France.

Norway: 7 ave. Habib Bourguiba; *Ambassador:* OLAVE MOLTTHE HANSEN.

Oman: 129 ave. de Lesseps; *Chargé d'Affaires:* MOHAMED HARTHI.

Pakistan: 20 rue Imam Muslim, El Menzah; *Ambassador:* N. KHAN KHATTAK.

Peru: *Ambassador:* FELIPE VALDIVIESO BELAÚNDE.

Poland: 12 rue Didon, Notre Dame.

Romania: 6 rue Magon, Notre Dame; *Ambassador:* MARIN RADOI.

Saudi Arabia: 16 rue de l'Autriche; *Ambassador:* ABDEL-RAHMAN EL BASSAM.

Senegal: 122 ave. de la Liberté; *Ambassador:* Lt.-Gen. CLAUDE MADEMBA-SY.

Spain: 14 ave. des Etats-Unis d'Amérique; *Ambassador:* ROMÁN OYARZÚN.

Sudan: Cairo, Egypt.

Sweden: 17 ave. de France; *Ambassador:* MARC GIRON.

Switzerland: 17 ave. de France; *Ambassador:* RENÉ STOUDMANN.

Syria: 128 ave. de Lesseps.

Thailand: Madrid, Spain.

Turkey: 47 ave. Mohamed V; *Ambassador:* ADNAN BULAK.

U.S.S.R.: 31 rue du 1er Juin; *Ambassador:* BORIS L. KOLOKOLOV.

United Kingdom: 5 pl. de la Victoire; *Ambassador:* JOHN MARNHAM.

U.S.A.: 144 ave. de la Liberté; *Ambassador:* TALCOTT WILLIAMS SEELYE.

Viet-Nam, Republic: 23 rue Jacques Cartier; *Ambassador:* TRAM VAN MINTH.

Yugoslavia: 4 rue du Libéria; *Ambassador:* DRAGOMIR PETROVIC.

Zaire: 5 rue du Niger; *Ambassador:* GEYRO TE KULE.

Tunisia also has diplomatic relations with Afghanistan, Albania, Chad, Kenya, Madagascar, Monaco, Panama, Somalia, Syria, Uganda, the Upper Volta, the Vatican City, Venezuela, the Democratic Republic of Viet-Nam and the Yemen Arab Republic.

NATIONAL ASSEMBLY

President: SADOK MOKADDEM.

First Vice-President: FERDJANI BELHADJ AMMAR.

ELECTION, NOVEMBER 1969

All 101 seats were won by the Destour Socialist Party. There were no opposition candidates, but some seats were contested by more than one member of the governing party.

POLITICAL PARTIES

Destour Socialist Party (*Parti socialiste destourien—PSD*): 10 rue de Rome, Tunis; f. 1934 by Habib Bourguiba, as a splinter party from the old *Destour* (Constitution) Party; moderate left-wing republican party, which achieved Tunisian independence; 8th Congress held Oct. 1971; Pres. HABIB BOURGUIBA.

Political Bureau: 14 members, elected by the Central Committee, including:
President: HABIB BOURGUIBA.
Secretary: HEDI NOUIRA.
Deputy Secretary-General: MANSOUR MOALLA.
General Treasurer: ABDALLAH FARHAT.
Deputy-General Treasurer: JELLOULI FARES.
Director of Party: MOHAMED SAYAH.

Central Committee: 56 members.

JUDICIAL SYSTEM

Cour de Cassation: Tunis; has three civil and one criminal sections.

There are three Courts of Appeal, at Tunis, Sousse and Sfax, and thirteen courts of First Instance, each having three chambers except the Court of First Instance of Tunis which has eight chambers.

Cantonal Justices have been set up in 48 areas.

RELIGION

The Constitution of 1956 recognizes Islam as the State religion, with the introduction of certain reforms, such as the abolition of polygamy. Minority religions are Jews (20,000), Roman Catholics (20,000), Greek Orthodox and a number of French and English Protestants.

Grand Mufti of Tunisia: Sheikh MOHAMMED HEDI BEL-CADHI.

Roman Catholic Prelature: 4 rue d'Alger, Tunis; *Titular Archbishop of Mossori:* Mgr. MICHEL CALLENS.

THE PRESS

DAILIES

TUNIS

L'Action: 10 rue de Rome; f. 1932; organ of the Destour Socialist Party; French; Chief Editor ABDELHAY SEGHAÏER; circ. 32,000.

al-Amal (*Action*): 10 rue de Rome; f. 1934; organ of the Destour Socialist Party; Arabic; Chief Editor LARBI ABDERRAZAK; circ. 25,000.

Dar Assabah: 4 rue Ali Bach-Hamba; f. 1951; Dir. HABIB CHEKH ROUHOU; circ. 50,000.

La Presse de Tunisie: 6 rue Ali Bach-Hamba; f. 1936; French; Dir. ABDELHAKIM BELKHIRIA; Chief Editor NOUREDDINE TABKA; circ. 35,000.

PERIODICALS

TUNIS

ach-Chaab: Place M'Hamed Ali; Trade union publication; Arabic; fortnightly.

ach-Chabab: 10 rue de Rome, publ. of the Union of Tunisian youth; Arabic language; monthly.

Bulletin Annuel: Institut National de Statistique, B.P. 65.

Bulletin de la Chambre de Commerce de Tunis: 1 avenue Habib Thameur, Palais Consulaire; monthly; Dir. SLIMANE AGHA.

Conjoncture: Banque Centrale de Tunisie, 7 place de la Monnaie; economic and financial surveys; quarterly.

Il Corriere di Tunisi: 4 rue de Russie; Italian; weekly; Dir. M. FINZI.

Etudiant Tunisien: B.P. 286, 13 rue Gamal Abdel Nasser; f. 1953; French and Arabic; Chief Editor MOUNIR BEJI.

al-Fikr (*Thought*): B.P. 556; f. 1955; cultural review; Arabic; monthly; Dir. MOHAMED MZALI.

Ibla: 12 rue Jamâa el Haoua; f. 1937; social and cultural review on Maghreb and Muslim-Arab affairs; French and Arabic; twice yearly; Dir. A. DEMEERSEMAN.

al-Idhaa wa Talvaza (*Radio and Television*): 71 ave. de la Liberté; broadcasting magazine; Arabic language; fortnightly; Editor ABDELMAJID ENNAIFAR; circ. 15,000.

al-Jaich: National Defence publication; Arabic language.

Journal Officiel Tunisien: 42 rue du 18 Janvier 1952; the official gazette; f. 1860; French and Arab editions published twice weekly by the Imprimerie Officielle (The State Press); Pres./Gen. Man. MOHIEDDINE DEROUICHE.

al-Maraa (*The Woman*): 56 boulevard Bab Benat; f. 1961; issued by the National Union of Tunisian Women; Arabic; political, economic and social affairs; monthly; circ. 10,000.

Le Sport: 9 ave. de la Liberté; French language; weekly; Pres. MAHMOUD ELLAFI; circ. 20,000.

Statistiques Financières: Banque Centrale de Tunisie, 7 place de la Monnaie; statistical tables; monthly.

Tunisie Actualités: Centre de Documentation Nationale, 2 rue d'Alger, Tunis; f. 1966; quarterly; French; official journal.

La Tunisie Economique: 32 rue Charles-de-Gaulle; French; every 2 months; published by the Union Tunisienne de l'Industrie, du Commerce et de l'Artisanat; circ. 2,000.

SFAX

Bulletin Economique de la Chambre de Commerce du Sud: 21–23 rue Habib Thameur; f. 1949; monthly; French and Arabic.

SOUSSE

Bulletin de la Chambre de Commerce du Centre: every two months in French and Arabic; Dir. HEDI BOUSLAMA.

NEWS AGENCIES

Tunis Afrique Presse (TAP): 25 ave. Habib Bourguiba, Tunis; f. 1961; Pres. and Dir.-Gen. SLAHEDDINE BEN HAMIDA.

FOREIGN BUREAUX

AFP (*France*): 45 ave. Habib Bourguiba, Tunis; Chief MARIO BIANCHI.

AP (*U.S.A.*): 35 rue Garibaldi, Tunis; Chief F. VENTURA.

Novosti (*U.S.S.R.*): APN office, 108 ave. de la Liberté, Tunis; Chief O. BOGUSHEVICH.

Reuters (*U.K.*): 45 ave. Habib Bourguiba; Chief GUSTAVE DEJEANNE.

Tanjug (*Yugoslavia*): 4 rue du Libéria, Tunis.

TASS (*U.S.S.R.*): 2 rue Gounot, Tunis; Chief VARDAN NADIRIAN.

UPI (*U.S.A.*): 28 rue Gamal Abdul Nasser, Tunis; Chief MICHEL DELLRÉ.

Visnews: 33 rue Lénine, Tunis.

PUBLISHERS

Coopérative Ouvrière Publication Impression "C.O.O.P.I.": rue du Marché and ave. Taieb M'hiri, Sfax.

Dar Al Kitab: 5 ave. Habib Bourguiba, Sousse.

Dar Assabah (*Société Tunisienne de Presse, d'Edition et d'Impression*): 37 rue de Marseille, Tunis; f. 1951; 48 mems.; publishes daily papers which circulate throughout Tunisia, North Africa and France.

Hedi Abdelghani: ave. de France, Tunis.

Maison Tunisienne d'Edition (M.T.E.): 54 ave. de la Liberté, Tunis.

Service des statistiques du Secrétariat d'Etat au plan et à l'économie nationale: Tunis; publishes a variety of annuals, periodicals and papers concerned with the economic policy and development of Tunisia.

S.L.I.M. (Société Librairie Imprimerie Messagerie): blvd. Président Bourguiba, El Kef.

Société Anonyme de Papeterie et Imprimerie: 12 rue de Vesoul, Tunis.

Société d'Arts Graphiques, d'Edition et de Presse: la Kasbah, Tunis; f. 1966; publishes daily papers, magazines, books etc.

Société Nationale d'Edition et de Diffusion: 5 ave. de Carthage, Tunis.

RADIO AND TELEVISION

RADIO

Radiodiffusion Télévision Tunisienne: 71 ave. de la Liberté, Tunis; government station; broadcasts in Arabic, French and Italian; Dir.-Gen. Slaheddine Ben Hamida.

Number of radio receivers 277,145.

TELEVISION

Television was introduced in northern and central Tunisia in January 1966, and by 1972 transmission reached all the country. A relay station to link up with European transmissions was built at El Haouaria in 1967.

Number of television receivers 147,104.

FINANCE

(cap.=capital, p.u.=paid up, dep.=deposits, m.=million)

BANKING

Central Bank

Banque Centrale de Tunisie: 7 Place de la Monnaie, Tunis; f. 1958; cap. 1.2m. dinars, assets 160m. dinars (Dec. 1973); Gov. Mohamed Ghenima; Dir.-Gen. Mohamed Bousbia; publs. *Conjoncture* (quarterly), *Statistiques Financières* (monthly), *Rapport Annuel*.

Banque de Développement de l'Economie de la Tunisie: 68 ave. Habib Bourguiba, Tunis; f. 1959; development bank, now the main source of long term and equity finance for industrial and tourist enterprises; received $35m. loan from World Bank in 1967; cap. 14m. dinars; Pres. and Gen. Man. Habib Bourguiba, Jr.

Banque Franco-Tunisienne: 13 rue d'Alger, Tunis; Gen. Man. Habib Ben Youssef.

Banque Nationale de Tunisie: 19 ave. de Paris, Tunis; f. 1959; cap. p.u. 1.6m. dinars, dep. (1971) 32,394m. dinars; Pres./Gen. Man. Abdelaziz Lasram; Dir.-Gen. Tahar Farah; 28 brs.; publ. *Report* (annual).

Banque du Sud: 14 ave. de Paris, Tunis; f. 1968; cap. 2.5m. dinars, dep. 30.7m. dinars (Dec. 1973); Pres. Saïd Chenik; Sec.-Gen. Mongi Ben Othman; publs. *rapport annuel, bulletin trimestriel*.

Banque de Tunisie: 3 avenue de France, Tunis; f. 1884; cap. 1.5m. dinars, dep. 33.35m. dinars (Dec. 1973); Pres. Boubaker Mabrouk; Gen. Man. Abderrazak Rassaa.

Caisse d'Epargne Nationale Tunisienne: blvd. 9 Avril 1938, Tunis.

Compte Cheques Postaux: blvd. 5 Avril 1938, Tunis.

Société Tunisienne de Banque: 1 ave. Habib Thameur, Tunis; f. 1958; cap. p.u. 3m. dinars (July 1972); Chair. M. Hassen Belkhodja.

Union Bancaire pour le Commerce et l'Industrie: 7-9 rue Gamal Abdel Nasser, Tunis; f. 1961; cap. p.u. 1.65m. dinars, dep. 33.6m. dinars; incorporates Banque d'Escompte et de Crédit à l'Industrie en Tunisie; Pres. and Dir.-Gen. Abdesselam Ben Ayed.

Union Internationale de Banques: 65 ave. Habib Bourguiba, Tunis; f. 1963 as a merging of Tunisian interests by the Société Tunisienne de Banque with the Crédit Lyonnais and other foreign banks; cap. 2m. dinars; Pres. and Gen. Man. Tawfik Torgeman.

Foreign Banks

Arab Bank Ltd., Tunis Branch: Amman, Jordan; 21 rue Al-Djazira, Tunis.

British Bank of the Middle East: London; 70 avenue Habib Bourguiba, Tunis.

Crédit Foncier et Commercial de Tunisie: 13 ave. de France, Tunis.

Société Marseillaise de Crédit: Marseilles; 12 avenue de France, Tunis.

A national Stock Exchange was opened during 1967.

INSURANCE

Astrée, Compagnie Franco-Tunisienne d'Assurances Tous Risques et de Réassurances, S.A.: 43-45 ave. Habib Bourguiba, Tunis; f. 1950; Pres. Abderrazak Rassaa; Dir.-Gen. Mohammed Hachicha.

Caisse Tunisienne d'Assurances Mutuelles Agricoles: 6 ave. Habib Thameur, Tunis; f. 1912; Pres. Moktar Bellagha, Dir.-Gen. Slaheddine Ferchiou.

Lloyd Tunisien: 7 ave. de Carthage, Tunis; f. 1945; Pres. M. Zerdzeri; fire, accident, liability, marine, life.

Société Tunisienne d'Assurances et de Réassurances: ave. de Paris, Tunis; f. 1958; Pres./Dir.-Gen. Hedi Ennifer; all kinds of insurance.

Foreign Companies

About thirty of the major French, Swiss and British insurance companies are represented in Tunisia.

TRADE AND INDUSTRY

CHAMBERS OF COMMERCE

Tunis

Chambre de Commerce de Tunis: Palais Consulaire, 1 ave. Habib Thameur, Tunis; f. 1925; 25 mems.; Pres. Mahmoud Zerzeri; publ. *Bulletin* (monthly).

Sousse

Chambre de Commerce du Centre: rue Chadly Khaznadar, Sousse; Pres. Hédi Bouslama; Sec.-Gen. Mohamed Ben Cherifa; publ. *Bulletin Economique* (every two months in French and Arabic).

Sfax

Chambre de Commerce du Sud: 21-23 rue Habib Thameur; f. 1895; 8 mems.; publ. *Bulletin Economique*.

Bizerta

Chambre de Commerce du Nord: 12 rue Ibn Khaldoun, Bizerte; f. 1903; 8 mems.; Pres. Mohamed Terras; Sec.-Gen. Mme Sfaxi Rachida; publ. *Bulletin Economique*.

ECONOMIC ORGANIZATION

Union Tunisienne de l'Industrie, du Commerce et de l'Artisanat (U.T.I.C.A.): 32 rue Charles-de-Gaulle, Tunis; f. 1946 by Ferdjani ben Hadj Ammar; mems. about 250,000 in 13 regional unions and federations (Industry, Commerce, Handicrafts); Pres. Ferdjani Ben Hadj Ammar; First Vice-Pres. Habib Majoul; publs. *La Tunisie Economique* (monthly), *Economic Yearbook* (annual).

TRADE UNIONS

Union Générale des Etudiants de Tunisie (U.G.E.T.): 11 rue d'Espagne, Tunis; f. 1953; 600 mems.; Sec.-Gen. Mohamed Ben Ahmed; publ. *L'Etudiant Tunisien*.

Union Générale Tunisienne du Travail (U.G.T.T.): 29 place M'Hamed Ali, Tunis; f. 1946 by Farhat Hached; affiliated to ICFTU; mems. 150,000 in 23 affiliated unions; Sec.-Gen. Habib Achour.

Union Nationale des Femmes de Tunisie (U.N.F.T.): 56 blvd. Bab-Benat, Tunis; f. 1956; 35,000 mems.; Pres. Mme. Fathia Mzali; Sec.-Gen. Mme. Dordana Masmoudi.

TRADE FAIR

International Fair in Tunis: Mohammed V St., Tunis; May 3rd–June 8th, 1975.

TRANSPORT

RAILWAYS

Société Nationale des Transports: Tunis; controls the electrified line from Tunis to La Marsa (39 km.); operates over 100 local and long-distance domestic bus routes.

Société Nationale des Chemins de Fer Tunisiens: 67 ave. Farhat Hached, Tunis; f. 1957; State organization controlling 1,998 km. of railways; acquired *Chemin de Fer Gafsa* (a line specializing in the transport of phosphate) in Jan. 1967; Pres. M. A. Souissi; publs. monthly and annual reports.

In 1969 the total length of railways was 2,305 km.

ROADS

In 1971 there were 18,267 km. of roads. Of these 10,483 km. were main roads and 5,603 km. secondary roads.

SHIPPING

Tunisia has 4 major ports: Tunis–La Goulette, Bizerta, Sousse and Sfax. There is a special petroleum port at La Skhirra. A complex of three ports, with separate facilities for general merchandise, minerals and oil, is under construction at Gabès.

Compagnie Tunisienne de Navigation: P.O.B. 40, 5 avenue Dag Hammarskjoeld, Tunis; brs. at Bizerta, La Skhirra, Sfax and Sousse.

CIVIL AVIATION

There are two international airports, Tunis-Carthage and Tunis-El Aouina. Other airports are at Jerba, Monastir, Sfax, Gabès and Tozeur.

Tunis Air (*Société Tunisienne de l'Air*): 113 ave. de la Liberté, Tunis; f. 1948; flights to Algeria, Belgium, France, Fed. Rep. of Germany, Italy, Libya, Luxemberg, Morocco, Netherlands, Saudi Arabia, Switzerland and U.K. and internal flights; fleet of four Boeing 727, four Caravelles, one Nord 262; Pres. Abdel-Aziz Znaïdi.

Société Tunisienne de Réparations Aéronautiques et de Constructions: Aérodrome de Tunis-Carthage, Tunis; f. 1952; internal charter flights for oil companies.

FOREIGN AIRLINES

Aeroflot, Air Afrique, Air Algérie, Air France, Air India, Alitalia, Austrian Airlines, Balkan, British Caledonian, CSA, EgyptAir, Interflug, JAT, KLM, Libyan Arab, LOT (Poland), Lufthansa, Malev Hungarian, Royal Air Maroc, Sabena, SAS, Swissair, Tabso (Bulgaria), TWA, and UTA also serve Tunis.

TOURISM

Office National du Tourisme et du Thermalisme: ave. Mohammed V, Tunis; Dir.-Gen. A. Bouraoui.

Direction de l'Information: 2 rue d'Alger, Tunis; Dir. Abdelkrim Moussa.

Tunisian Hotel and Tourism Association: 2 ave. de France, Tunis; Dir. Saheb Ettaba; publ. *Voyages* 2,000.

CULTURAL ORGANIZATIONS

Ministry of Cultural Affairs: Tunis; departments organize all national cultural events; Minister Chedli Klibi.

International Cultural Centre: Hammamet; f. 1962; has built an amphitheatre at Hammamet and maintains a summer drama school for actors and students; Dir. Naceur Chlioui.

PRINCIPAL THEATRES

Théâtre Municipal de Tunis: Tunis; subsidized by the state.

Hammamet Theatre: Hammamet; open air theatre built 1963; organized by International Cultural Centre of Tunis.

CULTURAL FESTIVALS

Carthage Festival: Ministry of Cultural Affairs, Tunis; international festival of arts; held every year at the site of the ancient city and in Tunis; next Festival October, 1974.

Maghreb Theatre Festival: Monastir; f. 1964; open to theatrical groups from Algeria, Libya, Morocco and Tunisia.

ATOMIC ENERGY

Institut de Recherche Scientifique et Technique: Tunis-Carthage; f. 1969; attached institute of the University of Tunis; Dir. Taoufik Ben Mena.

UNIVERSITY

Université de Tunis: 94 bvd. du 9 Avril 1938, Tunis; f. 1960; 681 teachers, 10,849 students.

UGANDA*

INTRODUCTORY SURVEY

Location, Climate, Language, Religion, Flag, Capital

The Republic of Uganda is an equatorial country in East Africa, bordered by Sudan to the north, Zaire to the west, Kenya to the east and Rwanda, Tanzania and Lake Victoria to the south. The climate is tropical with temperatures, moderated by the altitude of the country, varying between 60° and 85°F. The official language is English and there are many local languages, the most important of which is Luganda. More than half the population follow Christian beliefs. There is a small Muslim minority. The national flag (proportions 3 by 2) has six horizontal stripes: black, gold, red, black, gold and red. In the centre is a white disc containing a crested crane. The capital is Kampala.

Recent History

Formerly a British Protectorate, Uganda became independent in 1962. In October 1963 Uganda became a republic, with the Kabaka of Buganda as first President and Dr. Milton Obote, leader of the Uganda People's Congress (UPC), continuing as Prime Minister. By 1966 rivalry between the UPC and the followers of the Kabaka was intense, and in February Obote led a pre-emptive *coup* against the President. Heavy fighting followed his introduction of a provisional constitution with himself as executive President, and the Kabaka fled to Britain, where he later died. In 1967 a new definitive constitution was introduced, and the Kingdom of Buganda brought under control of the central government. In 1969 all opposition parties were banned.

President Obote was overthrown in January 1971 by the Army, led by Maj.-Gen. (later Gen.) Idi Amin Dada. The beginning of Amin's rule was marked by the massacre of troops from Obote's Lango tribe and of the Acholi. Dr. Obote fled to Tanzania, whose support for him led to disputes within the East African Community and clashes between Ugandan and Tanzanian troops on the border. In March the government decreed a ban on political activities for two years, and in May took additional powers of detention against anti-government elements. Early in 1972 Amin expelled the Israeli military mission in Uganda and in August 1972 proclaimed an "economic war" which he claimed would free Uganda from foreign domination, particularly that of Britain and of British Asians resident in Uganda. The mass expulsion of non-citizen Asians, and the confiscation of their property without compensation, caused relations with Britain to become very strained. In September 1972 an attempted invasion of Uganda by supporters of Obote was repulsed, and border clashes with Tanzania, whose government denied supporting the attack, continued until a peace was signed in October between the two states. General Amin has used various pretexts for purging his military and civilian opponents. The army (now increasingly composed of mercenaries, Nubians and Southern Sudanese to give the Muslim element dominance) and the "Police Safety Unit" have liquidated numerous opponents of Amin. Many have vanished without trace and atrocities have continued unabated.

General Amin's bizarre statements and policies have caused speculation about his mental stability. His initial popularity within Uganda has now been eroded.

During 1974, in a report to the UN, the International Commission of Jurists accused Gen. Amin's régime of murdering between 25,000 and 250,000 people since January 1971 and claimed that there had been a complete breakdown of law in Uganda.

Government

Under the 1967 Constitution, executive authority is vested in the President and may be exercised through the Cabinet. There are 18 administrative districts. A state of emergency still exists in Buganda. General Amin has recently divided Uganda into nine provinces under governors from the army, prisons and police force.

Defence

The defence forces consist of an army of 12,000 men and an air force of 600, with 21 combat aircraft.

In February 1971, General Amin announced that a Defence Council would supervise the administration and discipline of the Armed Forces. The Soviet Union has supplied considerable amounts of military equipment including a squadron of MiG fighters. By 1974 the armed forces had control over almost the entire judicial system in Uganda.

Economic Affairs

Agriculture, the most important factor in Uganda's economy, provides a livelihood for about 85 per cent of the population. The chief plantation and export crops are coffee, cotton, tea and tobacco. The most important mineral is copper, mined at Kilembe, and exported to Japan. In 1970 coffee accounted for 56 per cent of Uganda's export earnings. In 1971, exports to Kenya and Tanzania, Uganda's partners in the East African Community, fell sharply and inter-state trade within the Community declined further in 1972. In 1970, before his downfall, President Obote had announced that the Government was acquiring 60 per cent of the shares of all banks, oil companies, manufacturing and plantation industries and the Kilembe copper mine which, in late 1973, faced an acute shortage of technicians.

General Amin has embarked on a policy of mass nationalization of foreign firms without compensation. The mass expulsion of non-citizen Asians, who had a predominant share in commerce, and Gen. Amin's erratic political policies have left the economy in total limbo. Many of the Asians' assets were distributed among soldiers and military police. Many of the Asians' jobs have been taken over by Libyans. British aid to Uganda was suspended in November 1972 and many skilled foreign personnel have left or been expelled. Food prices have risen sharply. In 1973 Uganda faced a grave shortage of foreign exchange, unemployment was increasing and the business sector was stagnant, owing to shortages of skilled manpower and imported goods. By 1974 the situation had worsened, despite high world coffee prices in 1973. The estimated 1974 coffee crop

* See also East African Community in Vol. I.

is far lower than that of 1973 and the lack of foreign aid, high unemployment and shortages of skilled manpower remain problems. The tourist trade has been severely hampered and the continuation of the economy as a viable force largely depends on coffee and cotton, farmed by Africans and largely unaffected by the Asians' expulsion.

Transport and Communications

There are 845 km. of railways, operated under the East African Community. The total length of made roads is 24,024 km. By 1974 the transport system had deteriorated since the expulsion of the Asians who largely controlled it and this has led to problems in the distribution of food. Steamers ply on Lake Victoria linking Uganda ports with those in Kenya and Tanzania. Air transport from Entebbe airport is provided by East African Airways Corporation and fourteen other lines.

Social Welfare

Benefits are available for industrial accidents, sickness and unemployment. There are 26 Government hospitals with 4,857 beds and a large teaching hospital was opened at Kampala in 1962 but at the end of 1973 most hospitals were two-thirds understaffed. A social security act was introduced in 1967. The health service has been adversely affected by the departure of foreign personnel in 1972. In April 1973 Gen. Amin banned doctors from leaving Uganda.

Education

Education is sponsored by the Government and by Missions, most schools being Government-financed or aided. There is a severe shortage of teachers. The national university is Makerere University in Kampala. In 1972 Gen. Amin banned the National Union of Ugandan Students and severe harrassment of students and teachers at Makerere University and the murder of its Vice-Chancellor has led to chaos in higher education.

Tourism

The forests, lakes and mountains are the main tourist features. Since Gen. Amin came to power in 1971 the tourist trade has suffered heavily. Tourists were banned from visiting Uganda between September 1972 and September 1973.

Visas are required to visit Uganda by nationals of all countries.

Sport

Football is the most popular sport.

Public Holidays

1974: October 9th (Independence Day), October 18th (Id ul Fitr, end of Ramadan), December 25th (Christmas), December 26th (Id ul Adha).

1975: January 1st (New Year's Day), January 25th (Anniversary of the Second Revolution), March 28th–31st (Easter), May 1st (Labour Day), July 10th (National Day), September 8th (Republic Day).

Weights and Measures

The metric system is in force.

Currency and Exchange Rates

100 cents = 1 Uganda shilling.

Exchange rates (April 1974):

£1 sterling = 16.853 Uganda shillings;
U.S. $1 = 7.143 Uganda shillings.

STATISTICAL SURVEY

AREA AND POPULATION

AREA (sq. km.)*			POPULATION (Census of August 18th, 1969)†					
Total	Land	Water	Total	African	Asian‡	Arab	European	Others
236,860	197,400	39,459	9,548,847	9,456,466	74,308	3,238	9,533	5,302

* *Source:* Lands and Surveys Department.

† Includes 13,796 people enumerated in Karasuk, a part of Kenya which was administered by Uganda at the time of the census. The administration of Karasuk has since reverted to Kenya.

‡ Defined as persons from India and Pakistan (including Bangladesh) only. Other persons from non-Arab countries in Asia are included among "Others".

MID-YEAR POPULATION

(estimates)

1970 . . .	9,806,400
1971 . . .	10,127,400
1972 . . .	10,461,500

AFRICAN POPULATION BY NATIONALITY
(1969 Census)

	MALE	FEMALE	TOTAL
Uganda	4,462,898	4,507,394	8,970,292
Rwanda . . .	108,826	53,127	161,953
Kenya	68,889	48,744	117,633
Sudan	34,639	30,601	65,240
Zaire	39,380	24,618	63,998
Burundi . . .	30,730	9,294	40,024
Tanzania . . .	22,454	11,164	33,618
Others . . .	711	362	1,073
Not Stated . . .	1,336	1,299	2,635
TOTAL . .	4,769,863	4,686,603	9,456,466

MAIN TRIBES OF UGANDA
(1959 Census)

TRIBE	MALE	FEMALE	TOTAL
Baganda . . .	508,735	536,143	1,044,878
Iteso . . .	257,134	267,582	524,716
Basoga . . .	246,182	255,739	501,921
Banyankore . .	253,993	265,290	519,283
Banyaruanda . .	212,434	166,222	378,656
Bakiga . . .	220,936	238,683	459,619
Lango . . .	180,694	183,113	363,807
Bagisu . . .	163,923	165,334	329,257
Acholi . . .	141,643	143,286	284,929
Lugbara . . .	116,114	120,156	236,270
Banyoro . . .	93,907	94,467	188,374
Batoro . . .	103,436	104,864	208,300
Karamojong . .	63,747	67,966	131,713
TOTAL (incl. others) .	3,236,902	3,212,656	6,449,558

PRINCIPAL TOWNS
(1969 census)

Kampala (capital)	330,700
Jinja and Njeru	52,509
Bugembe Planning Area . . .	46,884
Mbale	23,544
Entebbe	21,096
Gulu	18,170

Births and Deaths: Average annual birth rate 43.2 per 1,000; death rate 17.6 per 1,000 (UN estimates for 1965–70). These estimates, prepared before the final results of the 1969 census were known, assume an average natural increase rate of 25.6 per 1,000 each year. More recent official estimates, though, put the annual rate of population increase at 3.3 per cent (33 per 1,000).

EMPLOYMENT

(1970)

	PRIVATE INDUSTRY	PUBLIC SERVICES	TOTAL
Agriculture	44,224	7,045	51,269
Cotton Ginning	6,587	—	6,587
Coffee Curing	5,113	—	5,113
Forestry, Fishing and Hunting . . .	557	2,951	3,508
Mining and Quarrying	7,855	43	7,898
Manufacture of Food Products . . .	15,218	—	15,218
Miscellaneous Manufacturing Industries .	24,413	309	24,722
Construction	14,855	32,801	47,656
Commerce	14,981	156	15,137
Transport and Communications . .	4,856	8,102	12,958
Government	—	21,428	21,428
Local Government	—	23,623	23,623
Educational and Medical Services . .	31,861	30,054	61,915
Miscellaneous	12,328	2,876	15,204
TOTAL . . .	182,848	129,388	312,236

The total includes 298,598 Africans (of whom 46,000 were born outside Uganda). In addition more than 3,000,000 Africans not in employment are economically active in agriculture.

AGRICULTURE

LAND USE, 1967

('000 hectares)

Arable Land	3,772
Under Permanent Crops . . .	1,116
Permanent Meadows and Pastures .	5,000
Forest Land	9,172*
Other Land	305
TOTAL LAND AREA . .	19,365
Inland Water . . .	4,239
TOTAL AREA . .	23,604

*Data taken from the world forest inventory carried out by the FAO in 1963.

Source: FAO, *Production Yearbook 1971.*

PRINCIPAL CROPS
('ooo metric tons)

	1968	1969	1970	1971
Maize	333	338	335	335*
Millet	626	630	630*	630*
Sorghum	254	332	332*	332*
Rice (paddy)	3	3	6	6*
Sugar Cane†	1,672	1,550*	1,700*	1,700*
Potatoes	23*	23*	24*	24*
Sweet Potatoes and Yams .	666	710*	710*	713*
Cassava (Manioc) . . .	1,945	2,321	2,150*	2,200*
Onions	10*	10*	10*	n.a.
Dry Beans	260*	260*	260*	270*
Dry Peas	2	4*	4*	4*
Pigeon Peas	27	50	34*	40*
Cow Peas	64	56	70*	63*
Groundnuts (in shell) . .	234	234	210	200
Cottonseed	169	187	165	165
Cotton (lint)	77	85	75	74
Sesame Seed	23	23*	23*	23*
Castor Beans‡	2	2	3	3*
Coffee	133.0	247.2	222.1	195.0
Tea	15.2	17.6	18.2	18.0
Tobacco	4.6	3.5	3.4	4.3

* FAO estimate.   † Crop year ending in year stated.   ‡ Exports only.

1972 ('ooo metric tons): Groundnuts 215, Cottonseed 200, Cotton Lint 87, Coffee 200*, Tea 23.7, Tobacco 5.4.

Source: mainly FAO, *Production Yearbook 1971.*

LIVESTOCK
('ooo)

	1968–69	1969–70	1970–71*
Cattle . . .	3,857	4,145	4,400
Sheep . . .	766	855	880
Goats . . .	1,873	1,911	1,940
Pigs . . .	53	68*	77
Asses . . .	17*	17*	16
Chickens . .	9,500*	10,000*	10,200

*FAO estimate.

Source: FAO, *Production Yearbook 1971.*

LIVESTOCK PRODUCTS
(FAO estimates, metric tons)

	1968	1969	1970
Cows' Milk . .	251,000	258,000	275,000
Goats' Milk .	10,000	11,000	12,000
Beef and Veal .	52,000	53,000	57,000
Mutton and Lamb† .	9,000	10,000	10,000
Poultry Meat . .	5,900	6,200	6,500
Edible Offal . .	12,700	13,900	14,100
Other Meat . .	12,000	12,000	12,000
Hen Eggs . .	8,700*	9,000*	11,000
Cattle Hides .	9,790	9,980	10,690
Sheep Skins .	520	533	598
Goat Skins .	1,280	1,409	1,435

1971 (FAO estimates, metric tons): Cows' milk 293,000; Goats' milk 12,000; Hen eggs 11,200.

* Official estimate.

† Including goats' meat.

Source: FAO, Production Yearbook 1971.

FORESTRY
(Twelve months ending June 30th)
ROUNDWOOD REMOVALS
(cubic metres)

1968–69 . .	11,250,000
1969–70 . .	13,810,000
1970–71 . .	14,195,000

Source: FAO, Yearbook of Forest Products.

SAWNWOOD PRODUCTION
(cubic metres)

	1968–69	1969–70	1970–71
Broadleaved (hard wood)	58,726	62,634	69,057
Coniferous (soft wood) .	2,594	2,310	4,086

FISHING
(inland waters)

	1968	1969	1970	1971
Total Catch (metric tons) . .	108,400	125,300	129,000	137,000
Value of Landings (U£'000) . .	6,127	6,525	6,950	9,350

Source: FAO, Yearbook of Fishery Statistics 1971.

MINING
(metric tons)

	1969	1970	1971
Copper Ore*	16,500	17,600	15,900
Tin Concentrates* . . .	166	122	117
Tungsten Concentrates* . .	110	153	137
Salt (unrefined) . . .	5,000	2,000	3,000
Natural Phosphate Rock . .	206,000	30,000	24,000

* Figures relate to the metal content of ores and concentrates.

INDUSTRY

		1969	1970	1971
Raw Sugar	metric tons	151,000	156,000	154,000
Beer	hectolitres	210,140	277,670	349,620
Cigarettes and Cigars . .	million	1,332	1,536	1,583
Pipe Tobacco	metric tons	137	127	126
Woven Cotton Fabrics* . .	'000 sq. metres	47,193	49,555	46,178
Soap†	metric tons	11,964	12,925	13,613
Cement	,, ,,	172,940	191,072	205,110
Crude Steel	,, ,,	20,000	19,500	16,400
Blister Copper . . .	,, ,,	16,564	16,958	n.a.
Electric Energy . . .	million kWh.	731	734	n.a.

* After undergoing finishing processes.

† Including washing powders and detergents.

Source: mainly United Nations, Statistical Yearbook 1971; and Bank of Uganda, Annual Report.

FINANCE

100 cents = 1 Uganda shilling.

Coins: 5, 10, 20 and 50 cents; 1, 2 and 5 shillings.

Notes: 10, 20, 50 and 100 shillings.

Exchange rates (April 1974): £1 sterling=16.853 Uganda shillings; U.S. $1=7.143 Uganda shillings.

100 Uganda shillings=£5.93=$14.00.

Note: Between July 1973 and January 1974 the exchange rate was U.S. $1=6.90 Uganda shillings. Prior to July 1973 the par value of the Uganda shilling was 14 U.S. cents (U.S. $1=7.143 shillings), the same as the value in operation since January 1974. In terms of sterling, the exchange rate between November 1967 and August 1971 was £1=17.14 Uganda shillings. In this survey the term "Uganda £" is used to denote amounts of 20 Uganda shillings, equivalent to £1.20 sterling in September 1973.

BUDGET

(million shillings, twelve months ending June 30th)

Government Revenue	1969–70	1970–71		Budgetary Recurrent Expenditure	1969–70	1970–71	1971–72*
Income Tax	178.4	226.0		Education	242.8	282.4	292.8
Development Tax	24.9	24.2		Public Health	90.8	101.2	102.7
Export Tax	203.9	249.0		Other Social Services	45.1	46.2	42.0
Customs	267.7	269.5		Agriculture	58.6	71.0	68.8
Excise	134.1	211.8		Works, Communications			
Transfer Taxes	3.8	6.2		and Housing	45.6	56.1	56.4
Sales Tax	179.8	179.9		Other Economic Services	53.7	50.8	60.7
Service and Production Fees	3.7	3.8		Defence	121.7	114.8	145.0
Fees and Licences	36.1	36.4		Police Force	71.2	77.8	72.7
Interest	4.6	4.7		Public Service and Local			
Miscellaneous	18.9	25.5		Administration	53.0	57.2	56.6
Appropriation-In-Aid, Net	5.7	6.7		Other General Services	122.5	131.9	127.8
				Other Expenditure	135.3	188.2	224.0
Total Recurrent Revenue	1,061.6	1,243.3					
Development Budget Revenue	22.2	44.7					
Grand Total	1,083.8	1,288.0		Total	1,040.3	1,177.6	1,249.5

* Estimates.

Budget (1972–73): Revenue 1,006 million shillings; Expenditure 1,429 million shillings.

Budget (1973–74) Estimated Revenue 1,241 million shillings; Estimated Expenditure 1,241 million shillings.

Source: Bank of Uganda, *Annual Report.*

DEVELOPMENT PLAN

Third Five-Year Plan (1971–76): Total investment is provisionally set at 7,700 million shillings, with spending in the public sector at 1,600 million shillings, over half of which is to be financed from local resources. G.D.P. is planned to rise in real terms at 5 per cent annually.

DEVELOPMENT EXPENDITURE
(million shillings)

	1969–70	1970–71	1971–72†
General Services . . .	156.7	313.1	247.1
Education . . .	59.3	61.4	43.3
Health . . .	56.2	57.4	19.1
Other Social Services .	13.0	34.4	10.9
Economic Services .	177.7	277.6	246.5
Other Expenditure .	0.1	14.9	2.7
Total . .	463.0	758.8	569.6

† Estimate.

Source: Bank of Uganda, *Annual Report.*

Currency in Circulation (December 31st, 1972): 620 million Uganda shillings.

NATIONAL ACCOUNTS

GROSS DOMESTIC PRODUCT
million shillings (current prices)

	1969	1970	1971	1972*
Monetary Sector:				
Agriculture	1,691	2,021	2,022	1,671
Forestry, fishing and hunting . . .	123	155	146	89
Mining and quarrying . . .	145	144	129	111
Manufacturing	686	774	778	551
Electricity	84	90	97	103
Construction	124	116	122	95
Transport and communications . . .	269	263	309	330
Government	385	447	512	582
Miscellaneous services . . .	738	767	853	500
Trade, restaurants and hotels . .	989	1,051	1,189	961
Non-Monetary Sector:				
Agriculture	1,821	2,224	2,629	1,866
Forestry, fishing and hunting . . .	152	191	229	161
Construction	30	31	33	33
Owner-occupied dwellings . . .	242	254	268	264
Gross Domestic Product at Factor Cost .	7,479	8,528	9,316	7,317

* Forecast at 1966 prices.

BALANCE OF PAYMENTS
(million shillings)

	1966	1967	1968	1969	1970*	1971†
Goods and Services (net) . .	−116.0	− 72.3	− 18.8	− 27.1	183.7	−587.6
Merchandise	133.5	177.9	166.8	149.3	402.0	−294.6
Investment income . . .	−124.4	−134.7	−119.9	−125.6	−107.4	−158.0
Other current account payments.	−125.1	−115.5	− 65.7	− 50.8	−110.9	−135.0
Transfer Payments (net) . .	7.5	0.1	− 3.2	− 16.7	38.6	− 30.0
Capital Account (net) . . .	268.9	163.5	88.2	124.2	−152.8	255.8
Private	85.0	58.1	− 1.7	− 40.6	−258.7	70.7
Official	183.9	105.4	89.9	170.2	105.9	185.1
SDR's Allocations . . .	—	—	—	—	38.4	36.1
Errors and Omissions . . .	− 11.4	− 20.1	9.8	− 10.4	—	—
Net Monetary Movements . .	149.0	− 71.2	− 76.0	− 70.0	− 30.7	+362.4

(+ = Decrease in Net Foreign Assets; − = Increase in Net Foreign Assets)
* Revised. † Provisional.
Source: Bank of Uganda.

EXTERNAL TRADE*
(million shillings)

	1968	1969	1970	1971	1972	1973†
Imports	876	909	865	1,362	812	674
Exports	1,327	1,412	1,772	1,680	1,861	2,192

* Excluding trade in local produce and locally manufactured goods with Kenya, Tanganyika and (since 1968) Zanzibar.
† Provisional.
Source: United Nations, Monthly Bulletin of Statistics.

INTER-COMMUNITY TRADE
(U £'000)

	IMPORTS FROM KENYA AND TANZANIA	EXPORTS TO KENYA AND TANZANIA
1970 . .	18,179	12,043
1971 . .	21,045	8,840
1972 . .	17,275	7,874
1973 . .	23,170	4,903

COMMODITIES
('000 shillings)

IMPORTS*	1971	1972†	1973‡
Paper and Paper Products . . .	41,900	24,260	26,460
Cotton Fabrics, other than grey . . .	11,680	7,180	9,040
Iron and Steel	72,860	34,180	34,060
Other Metals and Metal Products .	108,280	64,900	41,860
Machinery, incl. agricultural machinery .	285,280	261,860	} 231,680
Transport Equipment . . .	246,240	83,420	
All other articles	595,800	336,880	331,320
TOTAL	1,362,040	812,680	674,420

EXPORTS*	1971	1972†	1973‡
Coffee, not roasted	982,340	1,128,280	1,508,600
Cotton, raw	351,900	368,480	336,100
Copper, unwrought . . .	137,740	112,780	109,520
Tea	95,440	125,960	108,820
Hides, skins, etc.	21,020	42,640	31,340
Other	83,780	73,260	93,140
Re-exports	8,160	9,720	4,360
TOTAL	1,680,380	1,861,120	2,191,880

* Excluding inter-Community trade.   † Adjusted.   ‡ Provisional.

Source: Standard Bank Review.

PRINCIPAL COUNTRIES*
('000 shillings)

IMPORTS	1971	1972	1973‡
Belgium/Luxembourg . . .	17,321	12,040	11,680
Canada	7,490	n.a.	n.a.
China, People's Republic . . .	14,549	4,900	10,400
Denmark	13,402	n.a.	n.a.
France	55,801	24,640	26,780
Germany, Federal Republic . .	131,771	69,200	86,620
Hong Kong	27,086	8,340	8,200
India	64,753	39,540	37,880
Israel	25,855	n.a.	n.a.
Italy	75,010	41,940	27,800
Japan	183,673	82,740	61,480
Netherlands	55,110	19,480	18,540
Pakistan	14,359	9,760	1,780
Sweden	17,685	n.a.	n.a.
Switzerland	12,686	n.a.	n.a.
U.S.S.R.	19,461	n.a.	n.a.
United Kingdom	439,414	273,180	197,820
U.S.A.	96,558	77,060	21,640
TOTAL (incl. others) . .	1,362,049	812,680	674,420

‡ Provisional.

Exports†	1969	1970	1971
Australia	51,046	43,497	43,183
Canada	56,138	49,678	44,025
China, People's Republic . . .	8,889	10,907	10,197
Germany, Federal Republic . . .	44,824	80,257	113,344
Greece	247	44,444	—
Hong Kong	55,880	62,356	19,075
Hungary	20,485	32,520	—
India	48,413	75,429	136,350
Israel	21,513	16,285	10,657
Japan	222,588	205,937	181,969
Netherlands	32,786	32,015	41,656
Poland	16,959	35,522	13,541
Romania	25,445	26,108	11,132
Spain	13,609	50,972	29,487
Sudan	17,981	37,316	34,036
Sweden	16,054	47,777	31,975
Thailand	20,957	7,885	—
U.S.S.R.	15,868	20,844	—
United Kingdom	315,798	358,949	404,391
U.S.A.	330,747	362,472	373,190
Total (incl. others) . .	1,456,470	1,758,718	1,680,392

* Excluding inter-Community trade.   † Excluding re-exports.

Source: Annual Trade Reports.

TOURISM†

TOURIST ARRIVALS BY COUNTRY OF RESIDENCE

	1968	1969	1970
Germany, Federal Republic . . .	2,023	2,517	2,897
India	1,727	2,025	2,333
Italy	1,049	2,000	1,788
United Kingdom	10,114	12,585	10,754
U.S.A.	7,507	11,474	10,940
Others	5,716	7,266	6,675
Unspecified	25,827	36,113	44,976
Total	53,963	73,980	80,363

Source: United Nations, *Statistical Yearbook.*

† Between September 1972 and September 1973 tourists were banned from Uganda.

TRANSPORT

Railways: (*see* Tanzania chapter).

ROADS

	Cars	Commercial Vehicles	Other Vehicles
1968 .	25,609	15,534	6,815
1969 .	28,236	13,758	6,765
1970 .	29,120	13,993	7,306

CIVIL AVIATION
TOTAL SCHEDULED SERVICES*

			1968	1969	1970
Kilometres Flown ('000)	.	.	5,209	6,096	6,340
Passenger-km. ('000)	.	.	222,189	233,428	267,630
Cargo ton-km. ('000)	.	.	7,529	8,847	9,626
Mail ton-km. ('000)	.	.	1,000	1,045	961

* Including one-third of the traffic of the East African Airways Corporation and Caspair Ltd., which operate services on behalf of Kenya, Tanzania and Uganda.

EXTERNAL AIR TRAFFIC

		PASSENGERS		FREIGHT (kg.)	
		Arrival	Departure	Unloaded	Loaded
1968	. .	26,129	26,947	581,704	1,118,521
1969	. .	33,876	37,675	774,166	1,546,820
1970	. .	34,901	40,280	1,151,200	1,414,817

EDUCATION
(1970—Aided Schools only)

				ESTABLISHMENTS	TEACHERS	PUPILS
Primary	.	.	.	2,755	21,471	720,127
Senior Secondary	.	.	.	73	1,816	40,697
Vocational Secondary		.	.	14	114	1,524
Technical Secondary		.	.	5	113	1,451
Teacher Training	.	.	.	26	298	4,450
Technical and Commercial Colleges		.		2	83	1,272
University	.	.	.	1	350	1,949

Higher Education Abroad (1972): 1,804.

Source (unless otherwise stated): Statistics Division, Ministry of Planning and Economic Development, Entebbe.

THE CONSTITUTION

Uganda achieved independence on October 9th, 1962, as a dominion with a federal structure. A year later, on October 9th, 1963, the country became a republic, with a nominal President and an executive Prime Minister. The Constitution was suspended on February 24th, 1966, by the Prime Minister, Dr. Milton Obote, who abolished the office of President in the following month. A provisional Constitution, which ended the federal system and introduced an executive President, came into force on April 15th, 1966, but was replaced by a new definitive Constitution on September 8th, 1967. According to this, the Republic of Uganda has an executive President who is Head of State, Leader of the Government and Commander-in-Chief of the Armed Forces. The Parliament is the supreme legislature, and consists of the President and a National Assembly of 82 elected members. The Constitution provides for some specially elected members as may be required to give the party having the greatest numerical strength of elected members a majority of not more than ten of all the members of the National Assembly.

There are 18 Administrative Districts of Acholi, Ankole, Bugisu, Bukedi, Bunyoro, Busoga, East Mengo, Karamoja, Kigezi, Lango, Madi, Masaka, Mubende, Sebei, Teso, Toro, West Mengo and West Nile.

This Constitution was not revoked by General Amin, but in February 1971 he ordered the suspension of Uganda's legal system, and the concentration of legislative powers in his own hands, with the assistance of a Council of Ministers nominated by him.

General Amin has divided Uganda into nine provinces: Buganda, Busoga, Central, Eastern, Karamoja, Northern, Southern, Western and West Nile.

THE GOVERNMENT

HEAD OF STATE

President: General Alhaji IDI AMIN DADA, V.C., D.S.O., M.C.*

CABINET

(July 1974)

President and Minister of Defence: Gen. IDI AMIN DADA.

Minister of Provincial Administration: Brig. MOSES ALI.

Minister of Internal Affairs: MATHEW L. OBADO.

Minister of State for Finance: S. KIYINGI.

Secretary to the Treasury: S. IKARA (acting).

Minister of Planning and Economic Development: EMMANUEL B. WAKWHEYA.

Minister of Agriculture and Forestry and Animal Resources: J. M. BYAGAGAIRE (acting).

Minister of Co-operatives and Marketing: MUSTAFA RAMADHAN.

Minister of Education: Brig. BARNABAS KILI.

Minister of Labour: L. KATGYIRA (acting).

Minister of Information and Broadcasting: Major JUMA ORIS ABDALLA.

Minister of Commerce and Industry: E. L. ATHIYO.

Minister of Health: HENRY KYEMBA (acting).

Minister of Foreign Affairs: ELIZABETH BAGAYA.

Minister of State for Foreign Affairs: PAUL O. ETIANG (acting).

Minister of Justice: J. S. LULE.

Minister of Works and Housing: Lt.-Col. S. LUKAKAMWA (acting).

Minister of Culture and Community Development: Maj.-Gen. FRANCIS NYANGWESO.

Minister of Land and Water Resources: E. W. ORYEMA.

Minister of Power and Communications: J. J. OBBO (acting).

Minister of Public Services and Cabinet Affairs: R. B. NSHEKANABO.

Minister without Portfolio: A. C. K. OBOTH-OFUMBI.

* Ugandan decorations.

DIPLOMATIC REPRESENTATION

HIGH COMMISSIONS AND EMBASSIES ACCREDITED TO UGANDA

(In Kampala unless otherwise indicated)

(HC) High Commission; (E) Embassy.

Algeria: Dar es Salaam, Tanzania (E).

Australia: Nairobi, Kenya (HC).

Austria: Nairobi, Kenya (E).

Belgium: Nairobi, Kenya (E).

Botswana: Lusaka, Zambia (HC).

Brazil: Nairobi, Kenya (E).

Burundi: P.O.B. 4379 (E); *Ambassador:* ANDRÉ YANDA.

Canada: Nairobi, Kenya (HC).

China, People's Republic: P.O.B. 4106 (E); *Ambassador:* KE PU-HAI.

Czechoslovakia: P.O.B. 522 (E); *Chargé d'Affaires:* KAREL KRUTINA.

Denmark: Nairobi, Kenya (E).

Egypt: P.O.B. 4280 (E); *Ambassador:* ABBAS EFFAT.

Ethiopia: Nairobi, Kenya (E).

Finland: Addis Ababa, Ethiopia (E).

France: P.O.B. 7212 (E); *Ambassador:* ALBERT THABAULT.

German Democratic Republic: P.O.B. 7294 (E); *Ambassador:* HANS FISCHER.

Germany, Federal Republic: Embassy House, P.O.B. 7016 (E); *Ambassador:* Dr. WILHELM KOPF.

Ghana: P.O.B. 4062 (HC); *High Commissioner:* Brig. A. A. CRABBE.

Greece: Nairobi, Kenya (E).

Guinea: Dar es Salaam, Tanzania (E).

Hungary: Nairobi, Kenya (E).

India: P.O.B. 7040 (HC); *High Commissioner:* H. K. SINGH.

Iraq: P.O.B. 7137 (E); *Ambassador:* KARIM SHINTAF.

Italy: P.O.B. 4646 (E); *Ambassador:* RENZO FALASCHI.

Ivory Coast: Addis Ababa, Ethiopia (E).

Japan: Nairobi, Kenya (E).

Korea, Democratic People's Republic: P.O.B. 5885 (E); *Ambassador:* SIN BONG ON.

Korea, Republic: Baumann House, P.O.B. 3717 (E); *Ambassador:* YOO DONG HAN.

Lesotho: Nairobi, Kenya (HC).

Liberia: Nairobi, Kenya (E).

Libya: P.O.B. 6079 (E); *Ambassador:* MAHMOUD SAAD.

Mali: Dar es Salaam, Tanzania (E).

Morocco: Addis Ababa, Ethiopia (E).

Netherlands: Nairobi, Kenya (E).

Nigeria: P.O.B. 4338 (HC); *High Commissioner:* M. O. ADEFOPE.

Norway: Nairobi, Kenya (E).

Pakistan: Nairobi, Kenya (E).

Poland: P.O.B. 3011 (E); *Chargé d'Affaires:* M. J. LUKASIK.

Rwanda: P.O.B. 2468 (E); *Ambassador:* UBALIJORO BONAVENTURE.

Saudi Arabia: (E); *Ambassador:* ABDULLAH HABABI.

Senegal: Addis Ababa, Ethiopia (E).

Somalia: P.O.B. 7113 (E); *Chargé d'Affaires:* H. HAJI ALI.

Spain: Nairobi, Kenya (E).

Sudan: P.O.B. 3200 (E); *Chargé d'Affaires:* K. A. DAWOOD.

Swaziland: Nairobi, Kenya (HC).

Sweden: Nairobi, Kenya (E).

Switzerland: Nairobi, Kenya (E).

Tunisia: Addis Ababa, Ethiopia (E).

Turkey: Nairobi, Kenya (E).

U.S.S.R.: P.O.B. 7022 (E); *Ambassador:* A. V. ZAKHAROV.

United Kingdom: P.O.B. 7070 (HC); *Acting High Commissioner:* J. P. I. HENNESSY, O.B.E.

Vatican: P.O.B. 7177; *Apostolic Pro-Nuncio:* LUIGI BELLOTTI.

Yugoslavia: P.O.B. 4370 (E); *Ambassador:* MIRO KALE-ZIC.

Zaire: P.O.B. 4972 (E); *Ambassador:* MUKAMBA K. NZEMBA.

Zambia: Nairobi, Kenya (HC).

Uganda also has diplomatic relations with Cameroon, Cuba and the U.S.A.

PARLIAMENT

The National Assembly was dissolved on February 2nd, 1971, when Gen. Amin declared himself Head of State and took over all legislative, executive and military powers.

POLITICAL PARTIES

These were suspended after the *coup* of January 1971. There is a guerrilla organization, the Front for National Salvation (FRONASA), founded in 1973, whose aim is the overthrow of Gen. Amin whom it accuses in its manifesto of 83,000 deaths and the ruin of the Ugandan economy as well as the most savage and repressive rule over Uganda.

JUDICIAL SYSTEM

The Court of Appeal for East Africa: P.O.B. 30187, Nairobi; Pres. Mr. Justice W. A. H. DUFFUS; Justices of Appeal J. F. SPRY, E. J. E. LAW, LUTTA A. MUSTAFA, S. MUSOKE; Registrar T. T. M. ASWANI. Hears appeals from Uganda, Kenya and Tanganyika.

The High Court: f. 1902; it has full criminal and civil jurisdiction over all persons and matters in the country.

Appeals from the High Court of Uganda lie to the Court of Appeal for East Africa, except in constitutional matters.

The High Court consists of a Chief Justice and 14 Puisne Judges.

Magistrates' Courts: Their present status and rights are established under the Magistrates' Courts Act of 1970.

The country is divided into magisterial areas, presided over by a Chief Magistrate. Under him there are Magistrates Grades I, II, and III with powers of sentence varying accordingly. The Magistrates preside alone over their courts and have limited jurisdiction. Appeals lie to the Chief Magistrate's Court, and from there to the High Court.

General Amin has not proclaimed martial law but military tribunals have been authorizing public executions in Uganda, the first occurring in February 1973. Military courts were given official status to try anyone accused of violent or subversive crimes in June 1973. In August 1973, Gen. Amin gave extra powers to the military police and reduced the period after which a

person is presumed dead from seven years to three. There is an acute shortage of trained lawyers and magistrates.

Chief Justice: S. WAMBUZI.

Puisne Judges: P. V. PHADKE, S. MUSOKE, A. W. K. MUKASA, M. SAIED, BANKEY ASTHANA, D. L. K. LUBOGO, M. OPU, M. C. KANTINI, P. NYAMUCHONCHO, S. T. MANYIND, P. A. P. J. ALLEN.

RELIGION

About a half of the African population is Christian. There is a Muslim minority and the remainder follow various forms of traditional religion. President Amin announced in October 1972 that he wanted Ugandanization of the churches. In January 1973 he announced measures to implement this. In June 1973 twelve religious sects were banned.

CHRISTIANS
ROMAN CATHOLICS
Archbishop: Archbishop of Kampala: Most Rev. EMMANUEL NSUBUGA, P.O.B. 14125, Mengo, Uganda.

There are more than 4 million Roman Catholics in Uganda.

ANGLICANS
Archbishop: Archbishop of Uganda, Rwanda, Burundi and Boga-Zaire: Most Rev. JANANI LUWUM, P.O.B. 14123, Kampala.

There are about 1.8 million Anglicans in Uganda.

MUSLIMS
The Uganda Muslim Supreme Council: P.O.B. 3247, Kampala; Chief Kadhi Sheikh ABDUL RAZAK MATOVU.

BAHAI
There are 3,223 centres, 3 schools and 2 teaching institutes of the Bahai faith in Uganda; Headquarters: P.O.B. 2662, Kampala.

THE PRESS

DAILIES
Munno (*Your Friend*): P.O.B. 14125, Kampala; f. 1911; Luganda; Roman Catholic; Editor (vacant); circ. 18,000.

Omukulembeze (*The Leader*): P.O.B. 7142, Kampala; f. 1963; government owned; general news and sport; Editor ALONI LUBWAMA; circ. 8,000.

Taifa Empya (*New Nation*): P.O.B. 1986, Kampala; f. 1953; Luganda; Editor MARK KIWANUKE ZAKE; circ. 12,000.

Voice of Uganda: P.O.B. 20081, Kampala; f. 1955; English; government; Editor (vacant); circ. 27,000.

WEEKLIES
Dwon Lwak (*Voice of the People*): P.O.B. 7142, Kampala; f. 1964; government publication; Editor P. ORYANG; circ. 7,000.

Mwebembezi (*The Leader*): P.O.B. 7142, Kampala; f. 1963; weekly; Editor C. B. ISINGOMA; circ. 3,000.

Sports Recorder: P.O.B. 3936, Kampala; f. 1972; weekly; Editor GRACE SEMAKULA.

Taifa Uganda Empya: P.O.B. 1986, Kampala; f. 1961; weekly; Man. Editor M. KIWANUKA ZAKE.

FORTNIGHTLIES

Apupeta (*News*): P.O.B. 7142, Kampala; f. 1945; government publication; Editor F. A. OTAI; circ. 10,000.

Dwan Lotino (*The Voice of Youth*): P.O.B. 200, Gulu; supplement to Lobo Mewa; monthly; circ. 4,000.

Erwom K'iteso (*Teso News*): P.O.B. 3025, Mbale Ngora; f. 1957; Roman Catholic; Ateso; Editor Fr. MICHAEL EKUMU; circ. 5,620.

Lobo Mewa (*Our Land*): P.O.B. 200, Gulu; f. 1952; Luo; fortnightly; Catholic; Editor Rev. Fr. GONZALEZ; circ. 12,000.

MONTHLIES

Amut (*News*): P.O.B. 49, Lira; f. 1953; Lango; Editor Y. W. APENYO; circ. 4,000.

Musizi: P.O.B. 14152, Mengo, Kampala; f. 1955; Roman Catholic; Luganda; Editor Fr. J. M. KISABWE; circ. 30,000.

Runyunyuzi: P.O.B. 34, Hoima; f. 1971; Runyoro/Rutoro; Editor Msqr. E. WANDERA.

OTHERS

E.A. Journal of Rural Development: Dept. of Rural Economy, P.O.B. 7062, Kampala; Editor Prof. V. F. AMANN; circ. 800; twice a year.

Uganda Dairy Farmer: Kampala.

NEWS AGENCIES
FOREIGN BUREAUX

Novosti and Tass have bureaux in Kampala and Reuters, AP and UPI are represented.

PUBLISHERS

Longman Uganda Ltd.: P.O.B. 3409, Kampala; f. 1965; Man. Dir. MUSTAFA MUTYABA.

Uganda Publishing House: P.O.B. 2923, Kampala.

RADIO AND TELEVISION
RADIO

Radio Uganda: Ministry of Information and Broadcasting, P.O.B. 7142, Kampala; transmits daily programmes in English, Luganda, Luo, Runyoro/Rutoro and Ateso and Runyankore/Rukiga, Lusoga, Lumasaba, Lunyole/Lusamia/Lugwe, Ngakarimojong, Madi, Alur, Kupsabiny, Lugbara, Rukonjo, Dhupadhola, Kumam and Kakwa; Chief Engineer FRANCIS KATENDDE; Controller of Programmes R. SEMPA.

There were 250,000 radio receivers in use at the end of 1973.

TELEVISION

Uganda Television Service: P.O.B. 4260, Kampala; f. 1962; commercial service operated by the Ministry of Information and Broadcasting; transmits over a radius of 200 miles from Kampala; 5 relay stations have been built, others are under construction; Controller of Programmes J. DEAN; Controller of Engineering J. M. A. OBO; Commercial Man. (vacant).

There are an estimated 68,000 television receivers.

FINANCE
BANKING
CENTRAL BANK

Bank of Uganda: P.O.B. 7120, Parliament Avenue, Kampala; f. 1966; bank of issue; authorized cap. Sh. 40m.; dep. Sh. 532m.; Gov. ONEGI OBEL; Gen. Man. D. K. TAMALE.

STATE BANKS

Uganda Commercial Bank: P.O.B. 973, Kampala; f. 1965; cap. p.u. Sh. 30m.; dep. Sh. 335m. (Sept. 1972); 17 brs.; Man. Dir. H. M. KAJURA; Deputy Man. Dir. C. M. KABENGE, A.C.I.S., A.C.C.S.

Uganda Co-operative Development Bank Ltd.: P.O.B. 6863, Kampala; f. 1970; cap. Sh. 45m.; Gen. Man. E. KAMULEGAYA.

Uganda Development Bank: P.O.B. 7210, Kampala; f. 1972; cap. Sh. 130m.; Chair. Prof. J. S. OLOYA; Man. Dir. Z. K. BUKENYA.

REGIONAL BANK

East African Development Bank: P.O.B. 7128, Kampala; f. 1967; provides financial and technical assistance to promote industrial development within the East African Community and to make the economies of the three members more complementary in the industrial field; authorized cap. Sh. 400m.; funds committed for investment (July 1972) Sh. 158m.; Dir.-Gen. and Chair. IDDI SIMBA; publs. *Guide to Investors, Annual Report.*

FOREIGN BANKS

Bank of Baroda (Uganda) Ltd.: Head Office: P.O.B. 7197, Kampala; merged with Bank of India (Uganda) Ltd. in July 1972; Man. Dir. N. B. DESAI.

Barclays Bank of Uganda Ltd.: Head Office: 16 Kampala Rd., Kampala; Man. Dir. F. H. MacDOUGALL.

Commercial Bank of Africa Ltd.: Dar es Salaam, Tanzania; Embassy House, Parliament Avenue, P.O.B. 4224, Kampala.

Grindlays Bank (Uganda) Ltd.: Head Office: 45 Kampala Rd., Kampala; Gen. Man. D. A. G. FORBES.

Libyan Arab Uganda Bank for Foreign Trade and Development: f. 1972; majority Libyan shareholding.

Standard Bank Uganda Ltd.: P.O.B. 311, Kampala; f. 1970; associated bank of the Standard Bank Ltd.; Chief Man. P. W. CROSSLEY.

INSURANCE

East Africa General Insurance Co. Ltd.: 14 Kampala Rd., P.O.B. 1392, Kampala; life, fire, motor, marine and accident insurance; cap. authorized Sh. 5m.; cap. p.u. Sh. 2,694,600; appropriated by the State in 1972, to be placed in African ownership.

Uganda American Insurance Co. Ltd.: f. 1970; auth. cap. Sh. 10m.

About six of the leading insurance companies are represented in Uganda.

TRADE AND INDUSTRY

Uganda Advisory Board of Trade.

CHAMBERS OF COMMERCE

Jinja Chamber of Commerce and Industry: P.O.B. 167, Jinja; f. 1925.

Mbale Chamber of Commerce: P.O.B. 396, Mbale.

National Chamber of Commerce and Industry: P.O.B. 2369, Kampala.

DEVELOPMENT CORPORATIONS

National Housing Corporation: Ambassador House, P.O.B. 659, Kampala; f. 1964; Govt. agent for building works; aims to improve living standards, principally by building residential housing; Chair. J. BIKANGAGA; Chief Exec. A. S. N. KIWANA.

Uganda Development Corporation Ltd.: 9–11 Parliament Ave., P.O.B. 442, Kampala; f. 1952; Man. Dir. S. NYANZI; publ. *Crane* (Jan. and June).

TRADE UNIONS

Legislation providing for the establishment of the National Organization of Trade Unions to which all trade unions registered under the law would be affiliated was passed in December 1973.

Uganda Trades Union Congress: P.O.B. 2889, Kampala; affiliated to the ICFTU; about 102,000 mems. and 23 affiliated unions; Pres. H. LUANDE; Gen. Sec. D. G. NKUUTE.

Principal Affiliate:

National Union of Plantation and Agricultural Workers: P.O.B. 4327, Kampala; f. 1952; 31,450 mems.; Pres. SILAS EDYAU; Gen. Sec. R. N. IMANYWOHA.

Federation of Uganda Trade Unions: P.O.B. 3460, Jinja; f. 1964; 20,000 mems.; Pres. E. R. KIBUKA; Sec. J. W. TWINO.

Principal Affiliate:

Uganda Public Employees' Union: P.O.B. 3460, Kampala; f. 1961; 17,000 mems.; Pres. Z. BIGIRWENKYA; Gen. Sec. E. KIBUKA.

MARKETING AND CO-OPERATIVE SOCIETIES

Lint Marketing Board: P.O.B. 7018, Kampala; statutory authority for sale of all cotton lint and cotton seed. Sales of lint to countries with State-controlled economies negotiated directly by the Board, but for others lint is sold through auction to members of East African Cotton Exporters Ltd., P.O.B. 3980, Kampala; Chair. C. H. M. BARLOW; Sec. E. J. H. KITAKA-GAWERA.

Coffee Marketing Board: P.O.B. 7154, Kampala; statutory authority for sale of all processed coffee produced in Uganda. Sales of coffee to ICA quota and non-quota markets are made directly by the Board. Chair. R. J. MUKASA; Sec. B. S. LUKWAGO.

There are 2,500 co-operative unions including the following:

Bwavumpologoma Growers' Co-operative Union Ltd.: P.O.B. 501, Masaka; f. 1953; 100 mem. socs.; Pres. JOSEPH MWANJE; coffee, cotton and agricultural produce marketing association.

Bugisu Co-operative Union Ltd.: 2 Court Road, P.O. Mbale; f. 1954; handles the Bugisu *Arabica* crop; 83 mem. socs.

East Mengo Growers' Co-operative Union Ltd.: P.O.B. 7092, Kampala; f. 1968; general products growers' union; 137 mem. socs.; Chair. D. MAWEJJE.

Masaka District Growers' Co-operative Union Ltd.: P.O.B. 284, Masaka; f. 1951; 200 coffee-growing societies; Pres. A. KIWANUKA; Gen. Man. ALLEN M. KERA.

Mubende District Co-operative Union: coffee growers' association.

Nkoba Za Mbogo Farmers' Co-operative Association: coffee growers' association.

Wamala Growers' Co-operative Union Ltd.: P.O.B. 99, Mityana; f. 1968; general products growers' union; 75 mem. socs.; Chair. C. SEMPALA.

West Mengo Growers' Co-operative Union Ltd.: P.O.B. 7039, Kampala; f. 1948; general products growers' union; 105 mem. socs.; Chair. B. K. KAUMI.

TRANSPORT AND TOURISM

TRANSPORT
RAILWAYS
See East African Railways (Kenya Chapter).

ROADS
The Ministry of Works maintains 832 km. of tarmac road and 9,779 km. of all-weather road. There are a further 35,344 km. of lesser dirt roads.

INLAND WATERWAYS
Regular steamer services operate on Lake Victoria.

CIVIL AVIATION
Uganda's international airport is at Entebbe, on the shores of Lake Victoria some 40 km. from Kampala. Distances within the country are too short for air transport to be used to advantage in general, but there are several small airstrips.

East African Airways Corporation (EAAC): Head Office: Sadler House, Koinange St., P.O.B. 41010, Nairobi, Kenya; joint national airline for Uganda, Kenya and Tanzania (*see* under East African Community and Kenya).

The following foreign airlines also serve Entebbe: Aeroflot, Air Zaire, Air India, Alitalia, British Airways, British Caledonian, Caspair (an EAAC associate), Ethiopian Airlines, Lufthansa, Sabena, SAS, and Sudan Airways.

TOURISM
Uganda Tourist Development Corporation.

Uganda Tourist Board: Chair. Mr. SSEMWEZI.

No tourists were permitted to enter Uganda between September 1972 and September 1973 and few have entered since the ban has been lifted. General Amin has appealed to Ugandans to treat visitors with the hospitality "for which the country is renowned".

UNIVERSITY

Makerere University: P.O.B. 7062, Kampala; f. 1922; 350 teachers, 3,501 students.

UNITED ARAB EMIRATES

INTRODUCTORY SURVEY

Location, Climate, Language, Religion, Flag, Capital

The United Arab Emirates (formerly known as Trucial Oman or the Trucial States) extend along the coast of the Arabian Gulf from the base of Qatar to the border with Oman. The climate is exceptionally hot and humid in the summer and mild in the winter. The official language is Arabic, but English is spoken in business circles. Islam is the principal religion. The national flag has horizontal stripes of green, white and black, with a vertical red stripe at the hoist. The capital is Abu Dhabi.

Recent History

Federation of what were then the Trucial States was proposed by the rulers in 1968, when Britain announced its intention of withdrawing its troops from the area by the end of 1971. The proposals originally included Bahrain and Qatar, as well as the seven Trucial States, but negotiations on the participation of the two larger and more developed states eventually broke down in 1971, and they opted for separate independence from British protection. Abu Dhabi, Dubai, Sharjah, Umm al Quwain, Ajman and Fujairah then formed the United Arab Emirates on December 2nd, 1971. Ras al Khaimah refused to join the Union until February 1972, when it had become clear that neither Britain nor any Arab government was prepared to take action on Iran's seizure of the two Tumb islands in the Gulf belonging to the sheikhdom. A treaty of friendship between Britain and the United Arab Emirates was signed in December 1971. The U.A.E. joined the UN and the Arab League. Abu Dhabi is a member of OAPEC.

In January 1972 the Ruler of Sharjah, Sheikh Khalid, was killed by rebels led by his cousin, Sheikh Saqr, who had been deposed as Ruler in 1965. The rebels were rounded up, and Sheikh Sultan succeeded his brother as interim Ruler.

During the 1973 Middle East War Abu Dhabi strongly supported the Arab cause to which she has promised $1,000 million in aid. The sheikhdoms remain among the most politically conservative of the Arab states.

Government

Below the President and Vice-President of the United Arab Emirates there is a Supreme Council of the Unions consisting of the rulers of the seven sheikhdoms in which the rulers of Abu Dhabi and Dubai have the power of veto. There is also a Union Cabinet and a Federal National Assembly, which met for the first time in February 1972. Abu Dhabi has its own Consultative Assembly, appointed by the Ruler. Otherwise each ruler has absolute control over his own subjects.

Defence

The Abu Dhabi Defence Force numbers about 10,000, that of Dubai 1,000, Ras al Khaimah 300 and Sharjah 250, and the Union Defence Force over 2,000. It receives British assistance in the form of personnel and equipment. In 1974 Abu Dhabi signed a contract with France for MiG jets.

Economic Affairs

Abu Dhabi's economy is almost entirely dependent on oil, and earnings from it have made the state the richest in the world in terms of income per head. Dubai is also rich in oil but its reserves have yet to be fully developed. In March 1974 Abu Dhabi was offered a 60 per cent holding by the major oil-producing companies in the oil concessions. In December 1972 an agreement with the oil companies gave it a 25 per cent share which was to rise to 51 per cent by 1982. The huge increase in oil prices and the resultant importance of oil-producing states is of great benefit to the U.A.E. as a Union and to Abu Dhabi and Dubai in particular. Dubai remains the principal commercial centre and entrepôt port and plans for a £91 million supertanker dry dock are going ahead. The rulers of the northern sheikhdoms have all signed exploration agreements but, for the present, traditional and very impoverished economic activity, based on fishing and pearling, persists. The U.A.E. became a member of the World Bank and the International Monetary Fund in 1972. In October 1973 Abu Dhabi was the first state to announce a total ban on oil exports to the U.S. and Dubai followed suit. The ban was also extended to the Netherlands as a protest against its pro-Israeli stance in the October Middle East War. Supplies have since resumed since March 1974.

Transport and Communications

A metalled, all-weather road runs from Dubai to Ras al Khaimah. Abu Dhabi is linked to the mainland by a £1 million bridge, opened in 1968, and to the Buraimi Oasis by a dual-carriageway road. Dubai is the main port, and now has the largest harbour in the Middle East which is undergoing a huge expansion and modernization programme which began in late 1973. The port of Abu Dhabi is also being substantially developed. Dubai also has a new international airport and there are smaller international airports at Abu Dhabi and Sharjah.

Social Welfare

Social services are still in their infancy and scarcely existed before the oil boom. A large hospital was opened in Sharjah in 1973, and Abu Dhabi has free medical services.

Education

Education is little developed beyond the primary level. It is now compulsory and numerous new schools are being built, particularly in Abu Dhabi. Kuwait has given assistance in the development of educational facilities. In 1973/74 there were 50,000 pupils enrolled in schools throughout the U.A.E.

Tourism

No tourist industry exists.

Visas are not required to visit the U.A.E. by nationals of Bahrain, Oman, Qatar and Saudi Arabia.

Public Holidays

1974: August 6th* (Accession of the Ruler of Abu Dhabi), August 18th* (Leilat al Meiraj), October 16th*–

18th* (Id ul Fitr), December 25th* (Christmas), December 26th* (Id ul Adha).

1975: January 14th* (Muslim New Year), January 24th* (Ashoura), March 26th* (Mouloud).

* Muslim religious holidays which may vary slightly from the dates given.

Weights and Measures

The imperial, metric and local systems are all in use.

Currency and Exchange Rates

1,000 fils = 1 U.A.E. dirham.

Exchange rates (April 1974):

£1 sterling = 9.305 dirhams;

U.S. \$1 = 3.947 dirhams.

STATISTICAL SURVEY

AREA AND POPULATION

AREA (sq. miles)		POPULATION			
Total	Abu Dhabi (estimate)	Total (1972 est.)	Abu Dhabi (1968 Census)	Dubai (1972 est.)	Sharjah (1968 Census)
32,000	25,000	230,000	46,375	75,000	31,480

Population estimates (1970) for the other sheikhdoms are as follows: Ras al Khaimah 24,500, Fujairah 10,000, Ajman and Umm al Quwain 4,000 each.

OIL

PRODUCTION OF CRUDE OIL
(metric tons)

	ABU DHABI MARINE AREAS LTD.	ABU DHABI PETROLEUM CO. LTD.	DUBAI PETROLEUM COMPANY
1968 . .	8,878,089	15,156,700	—
1969 . .	11,728,264	16,815,000	523,000
1970 . .	12,686,029	20,080,000	4,305,000
1971 . .	16,833,341	27,160,000	6,252,000
1972 . .	22,409,000	28,833,735	7,500,000

FINANCE

1,000 fils = 1 U.A.E. dirham.

Coins: 1, 5, 10, 25, 50 and 100 fils.

Notes: 1, 5, 10, 50, 100 and 1,000 dirhams.

Exchange rates (April 1974): £1 sterling = 9.305 dirhams; U.S. \$1 = 3.947 dirhams.

100 U.A.E. dirhams = £10.747 = \$25.333.

Note: The dirham was introduced on May 20th, 1973, replacing the Bahrain dinar in Abu Dhabi and the Qatar riyal in other states.

Budget: The 1973 budget totalled £49 million; among the largest allocations were £10.9 million for development projects, £8.3 million for education, £4.9 million for defence, £5.3 million for health services and £3.5 million for water and electricity supplies.

EXTERNAL TRADE
DUBAI
IMPORTS
('ooo Qatar/Dubai riyals)

COMMODITIES	1968	1969	1970	1971
Household Goods	179,411	202,150	179,391	208,137
Foodstuffs	117,634	114,142	132,498	150,080
Garments	147,812	164,910	145,278	134,140
Machinery	150,880	187,173	155,606	102,001
Building Materials	73,947	101,000	139,151	142,154
Electrical, Radio and Allied Goods . .	30,560	44,021	62,992	54,970
Stationery	5,024	6,980	5,581	7,314
Photographic Goods	2,413	3,969	5,870	3,793
Cosmetics	6,591	6,871	8,925	8,986
Medicines and Chemicals . . .	5,141	8,694	9,230	19,263
Fuel and Oil	12,088	27,979	27,031	26,710
Arms and Ammunition . . .	1,369	5,543	17,622	10,078
Oil Field Materials	25,550	45,192	64,436	90,347
Liquor and Wine	2,657	4,317	6,279	11,063
TOTAL	761,077	922,941	959,890	996,036

PRINCIPAL COUNTRIES	1969	1970	1971	1972
Switzerland	105,722	82,678	93,724	110,249
Japan	179,012	162,668	181,699	308,157
United Kingdom	161,227	169,990	186,450	191,314
United States	75,594	88,304	127,394	200,483
India	42,007	56,048	47,010	54,026
Pakistan	34,603	20,721	25,282	29,336
China	32,672	30,111	33,887	46,535
Germany, Federal Republic . . .	39,260	31,514	36,252	43,259
Hong Kong	28,741	32,323	35,562	57,604
Netherlands	19,962	25,743	32,018	41,518
Saudi Arabia	23,443	23,245	22,792	77,399

EXPORTS AND RE-EXPORTS
(Qatar/Dubai riyals)

1969 . .	93,074,606
1970 . .	120,800,256
1971 . .	136,827,297

There is a large and officially authorized trade in gold which is not, however, included in the official trade statistics for Dubai.

ABU DHABI

IMPORTS
(Bahrain dinars)

COMMODITIES	1972
Food and Live Animals . . .	6,873,324
Beverages and Tobacco . . .	1,322,442
Crude Materials (excl. oil) . . .	821,420
Gas and Fuels	2,692,447
Chemicals	2,619,487
Machinery and Transport . .	36,271,769
Manufactured Goods . . .	18,156,141
Animal and Vegetable Fats . . .	447,559

('ooo Bahrain dinars)

COUNTRIES	1971	1972
Australia . . .	1,070	1,444
Dubai	4,316	n.a.
France	1,009	5,569
Germany, Federal Republic .	2,135	436
Italy . . .	1,193	2,002
Japan . . .	2,556	11,786
Lebanon . . .	1,012	2,152
Netherlands . .	1,649	213
United Kingdom . .	14,541	18,138
U.S.A. . . .	10,687	10,395

TOTAL IMPORTS

(Bahrain dinars)

1969	. .	59,277,212
1970	. .	35,245,328
1971	. .	46,941,551
1972	. .	75,761,951

THE CONSTITUTION

The constitution of the United Arab Emirates was set up in December 1971. This laid the foundation for the federal structure of the Union of the seven sheikhdoms, previously known as the Trucial States. The Rulers of the United Arab Emirates have absolute control over their own subjects. Abu Dhabi has a National Consultative Assembly, formed in 1971, whose 50 members are nominated by the Ruler.

The Supreme Council, the highest authority of the Union, on which all the Rulers are represented, meets at least twice a year to discuss problems of mutual interest. There is also a Union Cabinet and a National Consultative Assembly.

THE GOVERNMENT

HEAD OF STATE

President: Sheikh ZAYED BIN SULTAN AL-NHAYYAN.

Vice-President: Sheikh RASHID BIN SAID AL-MAKTUM.

SUPREME COUNCIL OF THE UNION

(with each ruler's date of accession)

Ruler of Sharjah: Sheikh SULTAN BIN MUHAMMAD AL-QASIMI (1972).

Ruler of Ras al Khaimah: Sheikh SAQR BIN MUHAMMAD AL-QASIMI (1948).

Ruler of Umm al Quwain: Sheikh AHMAD BIN RASHID AL-MU'ALLA, M.B.E. (1929).

Ruler of Ajman: Sheikh RASHID BIN HUMAID AL-NU'AIMI (1928).

Ruler of Dubai: Sheikh RASHID BIN SAID AL-MAKTUM (1958).

Ruler of Abu Dhabi: Sheikh ZAYED BIN SULTAN AL-NHAYYAN (1966).

Ruler of Fujairah: Sheikh MUHAMMAD BIN HAMAD AL-SHARQI (1940).

CABINET

(*January* 1974)

Prime Minister: Sheikh MAKTUM BIN RASHID AL-MAKTUM.

Deputy Prime Minister: KHALIFAH BIN ZAYED AL-NHAYYAN.

Minister of Finance and Industry: HAMDAN BIN RASHID AL-MAKTUM.

Minister of Public Works: HAMDAN BIN MUHAMMED AL-NHAYYAN.

Minister of the Interior: MUBARAK BIN MUHAMMED AL-NHAYYAN.

Minister of Defence: MUHAMMAD BIN RASHID AL-MUKTUM.

Minister of Foreign Affairs: AHMAD KHALIFAH AS-SUWAIDI.

Minister of Economy and Commerce: Sultan BIN AHMAD AL-MU'ALLA.

Minister of Health: SAIF BIN MUHAMMAD AL-NHAYYAN.

Minister of Labour and Labourers: MUHAMMAD BIN SULTAN AL-QASIMI.

Minister of Education: ABDULLAH IMRAN TARYAM.

Minister of Petroleum and Mineral Resources: MANI' SAID AL-UTAIBAH.

Minister of Social Affairs: ABDUL AZIZ BIN RASHID AL-NU'AIMI.

Minister of Electricity and Water: ABDULLAH BIN HUMAID AL-QASIMI.

Minister of Justice: AHMAD BIN SULTAN AL-QASIMI.

Minister of Information: AHMAD BIN HAMED.

Minister of Agriculture and Fishing Resources: HAMAD BIN MUHAMMAD AL-SHARQI.

Minister of Housing: SAID BIN SALMAN.

Minister of Islamic Affairs and Awqaf: THANI BIN ISA BIN HAREB.

Minister of Youth and Sports: RASHID BIN HUMAID.

Minister of Planning: MUHAMMED AL-KINDI.

Minister of State for the Supreme Council's Affairs: ABDUL MALEK KAYED AL-QASIMI.

Minister of State for Interior Affairs: HAMMUDAH BIN ALI.

Minister of State for Foreign Affairs: SAIF SAID GHUBASH.

Minister of State for Information Affairs: SAID AL-GHAITH.

Ministers of State: HAMAD BIN SAIF ASH-SHARQI, AHMAD BIN SULTAN BIN SLAYYEM.

The Abu Dhabi Cabinet resigned in December 1973 and some of its functions have been transferred to the Federal Cabinet and others to local administration departments. Abu Dhabi established a State Council in January 1974.

DIPLOMATIC REPRESENTATION

EMBASSIES ACCREDITED TO THE UNITED ARAB EMIRATES

(Abu Dhabi unless otherwise stated.)

Australia: Teheran, Iran.

Afghanistan: Baghdad, Iraq.

Egypt: *Ambassador:* SAAD MORTADA.

France: Kuwait City, Kuwait.

Germany, Federal Republic: Kuwait City, Kuwait.

India: Kuwait City, Kuwait.

Iran: *Ambassador:* MANOUCHEHR BENHAM.

Iraq: *Ambassador:* TAWFIQ AL MOUMEN.

Italy: Kuwait City, Kuwait.

Japan: Kuwait City, Kuwait.

Jordan: *Ambassador:* MANSOUR BATAINEH.

Kuwait: *Ambassador:* (vacant).

Lebanon: *Ambassador:* HASSIB AL-ABDULLAH.

Libya: *Ambassador:* MUHAMMAD BASHIR AL-MUGHAYRIBI.

Netherlands: Kuwait City, Kuwait.

Pakistan: *Ambassador:* Jamil Eddin Hasan.

Somalia: *Chargé d'Affaires:* Abdi Nur Ali Yussuf.

Spain: Kuwait City, Kuwait.

Sudan: *Ambassador:* (vacant).

Syria: *Ambassador:* Mounib al Rifai.

Tunisia: *Ambassador:* Al Hashimi Wanas.

United Kingdom: *Ambassador:* Daniel John MacCarthy, C.M.G.

United States: Kuwait City, Kuwait (E).

Yemen Arab Republic: (E); *Ambassador:* Muhammad Said Qubati.

The United Arab Emirates also has diplomatic relations with Bangladesh, Canada, Chad, Greece, Norway and Zaire.

ASSEMBLIES

U.A.E. FEDERAL NATIONAL ASSEMBLY

This was formed according to the temporary constitution. It has 40 members. It met for the first time on February 13th, 1972, when it was opened by the U.A.E. President, Sheikh Zaid.

ABU DHABI CONSULTATIVE ASSEMBLY

Formed on September 1st, 1971, it has 50 members, all nominated by the Ruler, Sheikh Zaid. None of the members belongs to the ruling family, though many of them represent tribal interests.

The Assembly can make recommendations on draft laws to the Council of Ministers before they are submitted for the Ruler's approval.

The Assembly met for the first time in October 1971. Its term is two years.

DEFENCE

Total Armed For ces: 13,550: Union Defence Force 2,000; Abu Dhabi 10,000; Dubai 1,000; Ras al Khaimah 300; Sharjah 250.

JUDICIAL SYSTEM

U.A.E. subjects and citizens of all Arab and Muslim states are subject to the jurisdiction of the local courts. In the local courts the rules of Islamic law generally prevail. A modern code of law is being produced for Abu Dhabi.

In Dubai there is a court run by a *qadi*, while in some of the other states all legal cases are referred immediately to the Ruler or a member of his family, who will refer to a *qadi* only if he cannot settle the matter himself. In Abu Dhabi a professional Jordanian judge presides over the Ruler's Court.

The 95th article of the provisional constitution of 1971 provided for the setting up of a Union Supreme Court and Union Primary Tribunals.

The Union has exclusive legislative and executive jurisdiction over all matters that are concerned with the strengthening of the Federation such as foreign affairs, defence and Union armed forces, security, finance, communications, construction, traffic control, education, public health, currency, measures, standards and weights, electricity, matters relating to nationality and emigration, Union information, etc.

The individual emirates maintain jurisdiction in all matters not assigned to the exclusive jurisdiction of the Union as stated in the constitution.

RELIGION

Most of the inhabitants are Muslims of the Sunni and Shi'ite sects.

THE PRESS

Abu Dhabi Chamber of Commerce Review: P.O.B. 662, Abu Dhabi; monthly; Arabic.

al-Ittihad (*Unity*): Abu Dhabi; f. 1972; first daily paper in the U.A.E.

al-Wahdah: Abu Dhabi; f. 1973; independent; daily.

United Arab Emirates: Ministry of Information and Tourism, P.O.B. 17, Abu Dhabi; weekly; English.

Akhbar Dubai: Department of Information, Dubai Municipality, P.O.B. 1420, Dubai; f. 1965; weekly; Arabic.

Dubai External Trade Statistics: P.O.B. 516, Dubai; monthly; English.

Dubai Official Gazette: P.O.B. 516, Dubai; Arabic and English; quarterly or as necessary.

---

al Sharooq (*The Sunrise*): Sharjah; f. 1970; monthly; Dir.-Gen. Tareem Omran; Editor Yousef al Hassan; circ. 3,000.

Akhbar Ras al Khaimah: Ras al Khaimah; monthly; Arabic.

RADIO AND TELEVISION

There are radio stations in Abu Dhabi, Dubai, Ras al Khaimah and Sharjah and television stations in Abu Dhabi and Dubai.

Voice of the United Arab Emirates: f. 1972; stations in Abu Dhabi, Dubai, Ras al Khaimah and Sharjah; broadcasts daily in Arabic over a wide area ; commercial. It is estimated that there are 50,000 radio receivers and 16,000 television receivers in the U.A.E.

FINANCE

BANKING

Committee of Clearing Bankers: Abu Dhabi; f. 1971 by the banks operating in Abu Dhabi; Chair. Hazim Chalabi.

Arab Bank: Amman, Jordan; P.O.B. 875, Abu Dhabi; P.O.B. 1650, Dubai; P.O.B. 130, Sharjah; Ras al Khaimah (2 brs.).

Bank of Cairo: P.O.B. 533, Abu Dhabi.

Bank of Credit and Commerce International S.A.

Bank of Oman Ltd.: P.O.B. 2111, Dubai; f. 1967; cap. p.u. 6.7m. dirhams (May 1974); brs. at Abu Dhabi, Alain, Doha, Ajman, Hor-Al-Anz, Naif Rd. and Dubai Side; Gen. Man. Abdulla al-Ghurair.

British Bank of the Middle East, The: London; brs. in Dubai, Sharjah, Khor Fakkhan, Ras al Khaimah, Abu Dhabi, Fujairah, Kalba, Diba.

Chartered Bank: London; P.O.B. 240, Abu Dhabi; P.O.B. 999 and 1125, Dubai; P.O.B. 5, Sharjah.

Commercial Bank of Dubai: P.O.B. 1709, Dubai; f. 1969; owned by Chase Manhattan Bank, Commerzbank A.G. and the Commercial Bank of Kuwait; br. in Sharjah.

Dubai Bank: P.O.B. 2545, Deira, Dubai; f. 1970; control is held by local interests, but British, French and American banks are also participating; p.u. cap. 11.5m. dirhams.

First National City Bank: New York; P.O.B. 749, Dubai; P.O.B. 346, Sharjah; P.O.B. 999, Abu Dhabi.

Habib Bank (Overseas): Karachi; P.O.B. 888, Dubai; P.O.B. 300, Sharjah; P.O.B. 14, Ajman; P.O.B. 32, Umm al Quwain; P.O.B. 205, Ras al Khaimah; P.O.B. 897, Abu Dhabi; P.O.B. 1317, Al Anin.

Melli Bank (Iran): P.O.B. 1894, Dubai; P.O.B. 459, Sharjah.

National and Grindlays Bank Ltd.: London; P.O.B. 241 and 1100, Abu Dhabi; P.O.B. 225, Ras al Khaimah; P.O.B. 357, Sharjah; P.O.B. 4166, Dubai.

National Bank of Abu Dhabi: P.O.B. 4, Abu Dhabi; f. 1968; auth. cap. 10m. Dh; res. 7.5m. Dh; dep. 600m. Dh; Gen. Man. D. G. SUTCLIFFE.

National Bank of Dubai: P.O.B. 777, Dubai; brs. in Abu Dhabi and Umm al Quwain; Gen. Man. D. W. MACK, M.B.E.

Rafidain Bank (Iraq): Ras al Khaimah.

Sedarat Bank (Iran): P.O.B. 7000, Abu Dhabi; P.O.B. 4182, Dubai; other brs. at Sharjah and Ras al Khaimah.

United Bank: P.O.B. 1000, Dubai; P.O.B. 237, Abu Dhabi; eight other brs.

INSURANCE

Abu Dhabi National Insurance Co.: f. 1972; cap. 500,000 BD subscribed 25 per cent by the Government of Abu Dhabi and 75 per cent by the private sector.

Arab Commercial Enterprises (Abu Dhabi) Ltd.: P.O.B. 585; Man. MANSOUR ABDUL RAHMAN.

Arab Commercial Enterprises (Dubai) Ltd.: P.O.B. 1100, Dubai; Man. TOUFIC H. BARAKEH.

Arabia Insurance Co. Ltd.: P.O.B. 1050, Dubai; Rep. WALEED H. JISHI.

Sharjah Insurance Co.: P.O.B. 792, Sharjah; f. 1970; monopoly of local insurance business.

A large number of foreign insurance companies are represented in the United Arab Emirates.

COMMERCE

Abu Dhabi Chamber of Commerce and Industries: P.O.B. 662, Abu Dhabi; f. 1969; mems. 1,200; Pres. AHMED MASSOUD; publ. monthly magazine in Arabic.

Dubai Chamber of Commerce: Gamal Abdul Nasser Square, P.O.B. 1457, Dubai; f. 1965; 2,300 mems. Pres. SAIF AHMED ALGHURAIR.

Ras al Khaimah Chamber of Commerce, Industry and Agriculture: P.O.B. 87, Ras al Khaimah; registers trademarks in Ras al Khaimah; publ. quarterly magazine in Arabic and English.

Sharjah Chamber of Commerce and Industry: P.O.B. 580, Sharjah; f. 1970; Pres. MOHAMMED BIN OBAID AL-SHAMSI.

DEVELOPMENT

The activities of the former Trucial States Development Office were taken over by the Government in 1972 and assigned to various ministries.

Capital Projects include inter-state roads, urban water and electricity schemes, housing and other urban development, rural water supplies, agricultural extension schemes and harbour works. Investigations into water resources, mineral prospects, soil, agricultural marketing and fisheries have been conducted. An Arab economic development fund, with a capital of BD 50 million, was set up by Abu Dhabi in 1971.

Planning and Co-ordination Department: Abu Dhabi; under Ministry of Cabinet Affairs, supervises Abu Dhabi's Development Programme; Dir. MAHMOUD HASSAN JUMA.

OIL

In line with OAPEC policy the Government was to acquire a 51 per cent holding in all oil concessions by 1983. It is to pay $152 million for its initial 25 per cent share of ADMA and ADPC operations. Owing to recent developments in the Middle East Abu Dhabi has now been offered 60 per cent holding by the major companies.

ABU DHABI

Department of Petroleum Affairs and Industry: B.P. 9, Abu Dhabi; State supervisory body; Dir. MANI AL OTAIBA.

Abu Dhabi Marine Areas (ADMA): P.O.B. 303, Abu Dhabi; Britannic House, Moor Lane, London, EC2Y 9BU, England; operates a concession 50 per cent owned by the British Petroleum Co. Ltd., and Japan Oil Development Co., 25 per cent by Compagnie Française des Petroles, and 25 per cent by Abu Dhabi National Oil Company. The concession lies in the Abu Dhabi offshore area and currently produces oil from Zakum and Umm Shaif fields; also acts as operator on behalf of al-Bundug Co. Ltd.; production (1973) 23,938,949 long tons; Chief Rep. and Gen. Man. Dr. A. J. HORAN.

Abu Dhabi Gas Liquefaction Company: operated by Abu Dhabi Marine Areas (ADMA); owned mainly by Mitsui (36 per cent), BP (26.2 per cent) and ADNOC (20 per cent); to utilize natural gas produced in association with oil from offshore fields, the liquefied gas facilities are planned to come on stream in mid-1976 at an estimated cost of $300 million.

Abu Dhabi National Oil Company (ADNOC): Abu Dhabi; consortium of three Japanese oil companies, Maruzen, Daikyo and Nihon Kogyo; holds offshore concession; oil strikes reported in September 1969 and January 1970; in 1973 announced plans to build an industrial complex in Abu Dhabi.

Abu Dhabi Petroleum Company Ltd. (ADPC): P.O.B. 270, Abu Dhabi; engaged in production and export of crude oil from on-shore areas of Abu Dhabi. Export started from Bab Field in December 1963. The terminal is at Jebel Dhanna. The annual production capacity was raised to 12 million tons during 1965 by the connection of Bu Hasa field to Jebel Dhanna. Facilities installed to raise annual production capacity to 40 million tons were completed in December 1972; took over local distribution of all petroleum products in July 1973; production (1972) 28,900,000 long tons; Chair. C. M. DALLEY; Man. Dir. G. G. STOCKWELL; U.A.E. Government nominated Dir. MANI SAEED AL-UTAIBA; Gen. Man. A. TURNER.

Middle East Oil Company Ltd: Abu Dhabi; formed 1968 by the Mitsubishi group; holds concessions covering some 15,000 square km. on land.

Phillips Petroleum: P.O.B. 6, Abu Dhabi; heads consortium with the Italian AGIP Company (each with a 50 per cent interest); holds 9,686 square km. concession on land; Gen. Man. E. D. COOPER.

United Petroleum Development (Japan): Abu Dhabi; f. 1970; association of four Japanese companies, in association with British Petroleum, to develop the Bunduq oilfield.

DUBAI

Petroleum Affairs Department: P.O.B. 707, Dubai; government supervisory body; Dir. MAHDI AL TAJIR.

Dubai Marine Areas: Dubai; holds offshore concession agreement signed in 1963, with a 50 per cent holding in production; British Petroleum sold its two-thirds interest in the company to Compagnie Française des Pétroles in October 1969.

Dubai Petroleum Company: Dubai; subsidiary of Continental Oil Co. (U.S.A.) in partnership with Compagnie Française des Pétroles, Hispanoil (Spain), Sun Oil Co. (U.S.A.), Deutsche Texaco AG (Germany), Wintershall AG (Germany); holds offshore concession which began production in 1969; production in 1972 7.7m. tons; 1973 10.8m. tons.

RAS AL KHAIMAH

Union Oil of California, Peninsula Petroleum GB Ltd. and Vitol Exploration have concessions.

SHARJAH

John Mecom Ltd. have held a concession since 1964. In January 1969 the Ruler of Sharjah signed two exploration agreements with Shell interests, and in December 1969 he also granted an offshore exploration concession to the Buttes Oil and Gas Co. of California. Crescent Petroleum has a 500,000 acre concession in Abu Musa where it made a significant find in 1973.

FUJAIRAH

Bochumer Mineralöl G.m.b.H., owned by the Federal German Bomin Group, has held a concession covering the whole of the land area and territorial waters of the sheikhdom since 1966.

AJMAN

Occidental Petroleum has a concession.

UMM AL QUWAIN

An offshore concession was granted to Occidental Petroleum in November 1969 but this has recently been withdrawn. John Mecom Ltd. and Shell also hold concessions.

TRANSPORT

ROADS

Until very recently there was no proper system of roads except in Dubai town, but the desert tracks are often motorable. In 1965 plans were made for a £1 million all-weather metalled road to be built from Dubai to Ras al Khaimah, to be financed by the Trucial States Development Office. The Dubai/Sharjah section of this was opened in September 1966. Work has now been completed on the Sharjah/Ras al Khaimah section at the expense of the Saudi Arabian Government. In 1968 Abu Dhabi opened a £1 million bridge linking the town with the mainland. The town is also linked with the Buraimi Oasis by a dual-carriageway motor road built mainly for political reasons. The oil companies have constructed roads in the area in which they operate. An underwater tunnel linking Dubai Town and Deira with a dual carriageway and pedestrian subway is to be built by a British firm at a cost of £7.5 million. There is a road linking Dubai and Abu Dhabi, and also a road between Fujairah and Khor Fakkan. Roads between Dhaid (Sharjah) and Fujairah and between Qatar and Abu Dhabi are under construction.

SHIPPING

Dubai is the main port. The British India Steam Navigation Co. Ltd. maintains a weekly scheduled service to Dubai on the Bombay–Basra run. The ships of British India Line and F. Strick & Co. call at Dubai and Abu Dhabi several times a month. Other lines which call regularly are D. D. G. Hansa, Johnson Line, Holland–Persian Gulf, Maersk Line, and Jugolinÿa. Work began in 1970 on a new four-mile channel which will make the port of Abu Dhabi accessible to sea-going vessels including tankers. The Port Rashid project was completed a year ahead of schedule in October 1972; with fifteen deep-water berths it makes Dubai harbour the biggest in the Middle East. A dry dock scheme costing £91 million began in 1973; it will have two docks capable of handling 500,000-ton tankers, seven repair berths and also a third dock able to accommodate one million ton tankers, which will make Dubai the biggest supertanker complex in the Gulf. There is also a smaller port in Sharjah.

CIVIL AVIATION

The new air terminal at Dubai was opened in 1971 by Sheikh Rashid. The £4m. terminal was the first in the Middle East to have facilities for handling Jumbo Jets. There are smaller international airports at Abu Dhabi and Sharjah and an internatoinal airport is being built at Ras al Khaimah.

Gulf Air Dubai: Dubai National Air Travel Agency, P.O.B. 1515, Dubai; Omeir Travel Agency, Abu Dhabi; Sharjah Aircraft Handling Agency, Sharjah; daily service Bahrain–Doha–Abu Dhabi–Muscat and twice weekly from Dubai to Shiraz, Bandar Abbas, Bombay and Kuwait; four times weekly from Dubai to Karachi and Salalah.

Gulf Air Sharjah: Sharjah Aircraft Handling Agency, P.O.B. 8; Oman Travel Agency, P.O.B. 15; Kanoo Travel Agency; weekly flight Shiraz–Muscat, weekly flight Abu Dhabi–Doha–Bahrain–Sharjah.

Alia, Air India, British Airways, Iran Air, Kuwait Airways, Middle East Airlines, PIA, KLM, Gulf Air, Iraqi Airways, Saudia, Syrian Arab Airlines and TMA all serve Dubai and Abu Dhabi, while Gulf Air and TMA serve Sharjah.

TOURISM

Ministry of Information and Tourism: Government of Abu Dhabi, P.O.B. 17, Abu Dhabi.

Ministry of Information and Tourism: Government of Dubai, P.O.B. 67, Dubai.

Ministry of Information and Tourism: Government of Sharjah, P.O.B. 55, Sharjah.

UNITED STATES OF AMERICA

INTRODUCTORY SURVEY

Location, Climate, Language, Religion, Flag, Capital

The United States of America occupies the North American continent between Canada and Mexico. Alaska, to the north-west of Canada, and Hawaii, in the central Pacific, are two of the 50 States of the U.S. The climate is continental inland, temperate at the coasts, New York ranging from 0° to 90°F (−18° to 32°C), but subtropical conditions prevail in the south. Much of Texas and Arizona is desert. The language is English, and Christianity is the predominant religion. In 1970 more than 11 per cent of the population were black Americans (Negroes), most of them Christians. There are over six million Jews. The national flag (proportions 19 by 10) has 13 alternating stripes (seven red and six white) with a dark blue rectangular canton, containing 50 white five-pointed stars, in the upper hoist. The capital is Washington.

Recent History

By means of gigantic programmes of aid, including the rehabilitation of Japan and the Marshall Plan for Europe, the U.S.A. financed the post-war recovery of much of the world. From 1950 to 1953 the U.S. provided most of the men, money and materials required by the United Nations forces in the Korean War. Throughout the 1950s relations with the U.S.S.R. were poor. However, since the Cuban missile crisis of 1962, when President John Kennedy forced the removal of Soviet-built missiles from the island, relations between the two countries have improved.

In November 1963 President Kennedy was assassinated in Dallas, Texas. His successor, President Lyndon Johnson, carried through Congress a wide programme of Federal intervention on behalf of under-privileged sectors of the community, though racial tensions erupted in violence in the summers of 1965, 1966, 1967 and 1968. Abroad, President Johnson committed huge quantities of military and financial aid to the Saigon Government in South Viet-Nam. 1968 was also marked by the violent deaths of the civil rights leader Martin Luther King and of the aspiring Democratic Presidential candidate Robert Kennedy. In 1968 Richard Nixon was elected President and in 1972 was re-elected with one of the largest majorities ever achieved in a presidential election. A Treaty for Non-Proliferation of Nuclear Weapons, jointly sponsored by the U.S.A. and the U.S.S.R., was ratified simultaneously by the two countries in 1969. After protracted negotiations a Viet-Nam peace treaty was signed in January 1973, although continued fighting in Laos delayed the withdrawal of troops and the return of prisoners of war. Fighting in South Viet-Nam was still continuing in the middle of 1974.

During Nixon's presidency, progress was made in *détente* with both the People's Republic of China and, especially, the U.S.S.R., both of which the President visited and with both of whom trade has increased considerably.

American diplomatic leadership, in the person of the Secretary of State, Dr. Henry Kissinger, contributed towards an agreement for disengagement between Syrian and Israeli forces in June 1974, after months of fighting and negotiations.

Domestically, the main preoccupations of 1973 and early 1974 were a series of scandals and crises involving the presidency and senior administration officials in charges of corruption and obstruction of justice. By June 1974, half a dozen former presidential aides and a former attorney-general had all been implicated and sentenced and the Vice-President, Spiro Agnew, had resigned on unrelated charges of tax evasion. The President's obstructive handling of investigations had led by June 1974 to a growing clamour for his impeachment or resignation.

Government

The U.S.A. is a federal republic. Each of the fifty member states exercises a measure of internal self-government. Defence, foreign affairs, coinage, posts, the higher levels of justice, and internal security are the responsibility of the Federal Government. The President is head of the executive and is elected for a four-year term by a college of representatives elected directly from each state. The President nominates the other members of the executive. The Congress is the seat of legislative power and consists of the Senate and the House of Representatives. Two Senators are chosen by direct election in each state, to serve a six-year term, and one third of the membership is renewable every two years. Representatives are elected by direct and universal suffrage for a two-year term. Judicial power is vested in the Supreme Court, which has the power to veto legislation which it regards as incompatible with the Constitution.

Defence

In 1972 United States active forces comprised 811,000 army, 726,000 air force, 588,000 navy and 198,000 marine corps. Military conscription ended in January 1973. The Strategic Air Command and Polaris nuclear submarines are equipped with nuclear weapons. The defences of the United States are organized on a global basis. It is a member of the NATO, SEATO and ANZUS Pact defensive organizations and co-operates closely with the Central Treaty Organization (CENTO). In 1970 the defence budget was cut by the closing of military bases abroad, and the reduction of the armed forces. The 1973–74 defence budget was $88,200 million and the proposed budget for 1974–75 was $95,000 million, which represents 29 per cent of the federal budget, compared with 44 per cent in 1968–69.

Economic Affairs

The United States of America is the world's leading economic power. Its chief imports are petroleum, non-ferrous metals, coffee, machinery, vehicles and newsprint. In most other materials the country is self-supporting. This is reflected in the extreme diversification of the economy. Leading industries include steel, motor vehicles, aerospace industries, telecommunications, chemicals, electronics and all kinds of consumer goods. There are more than 30 million employed in services. Agriculture accounts for only 5 per cent of employment, but for over

20 per cent of exports. The chief agricultural products are cereals, cotton and tobacco. The principal mineral deposits are of oil, coal, copper, iron, uranium and silver. American business corporations have built up very large interests abroad during this century, and particularly since 1950. The value of the U.S. dollar, fixed in 1934, was reduced twice, in December 1971 and in February 1973. During 1973, in common with other major industrialized countries, the U.S.A. experienced a high rate of inflation, which was still running at 10 per cent a year in the middle of 1974. The U.S.A. was particularly badly affected by the oil-producing states' embargo on supplying oil during the 1973 Middle East crisis and the subsequent large increase in the price of oil. In December 1973 a programme with the aim of making the U.S.A. self-sufficient in energy within ten years was instituted.

The 1974–75 budget is mildly expansionary and forecasts are for a low growth rate and continuing inflation in the first half of 1974, followed by growth and a slower rate of inflation later in the year.

Transport and Communications

There is a comprehensive network of railways operated by private companies; the network retains its lead as a freight transporter but passenger services have been greatly affected by competition from private cars and airlines, and accordingly many services have been cut. Long-distance buses provide swift and cheap travel to all parts of the country. Water transport is used on the Mississippi and other rivers and on the Great Lakes. Major ports include New York, Boston, Baltimore, New Orleans, Galveston, San Diego, San Francisco and Seattle. Chicago at the head of Lake Michigan handles large quantities of agricultural freight. Domestic air services are extensively used and frequent international services are provided by a large number of home and foreign companies.

Social Welfare

Provision of welfare and medical services is being progressively standardized and extended by federal legislation: formerly benefits varied considerably between states. Despite opposition from the medical profession to "socialized medicine" there is now a far more comprehensive scheme of publicly funded medical care available. By 1975, provision by employers of health insurance for employees will be mandatory, and a comprehensive national insurance scheme is to be instituted. The 1971–75 budget provides $26,300 million for health programmes. Social security benefits were increased by 70 per cent between 1969 and 1974.

Education

Education is still largely the concern of individual states, but the 1965 Education Bill makes federal funds available for general improvement of primary and secondary schools. There is a plan for federal scholarships for college students. All states have elementary, junior high, and high schools and 47 states have kindergartens. Education is free except in private schools. The period of compulsory education varies between states; in 37 states the minimum school-leaving age is 16, in 7 states 17 and in 4 states 18. There are over 1,600 universities and colleges with over 8 million students.

Tourism

The U.S. affords every kind of interest to tourists from winter sports to tropical beaches. The natural marvels include the Grand Canyon, Niagara Falls and the large protected parks of the north-west. Modern architecture, museums and art galleries, night life in the big cities, these are only a few of the innumerable attractions. The U.S. has now begun to arrange inexpensive all-in tours for foreign visitors.

Visas are not required to visit the U.S. by nationals of Canada.

Sport

The most popular sports are baseball, American football, basketball and volleyball. Athletics, golf, tennis, boxing and horse racing are also widely followed and there are facilities for many other sports.

Space Research

The first space vehicle successfully launched by the U.S.A. was *Explorer I*, an earth-orbiting satellite launched in January 1958. The first manned earth-orbiting flight by the U.S.A. took place in 1962, in a series of flights named Project Mercury. Space exploration by the United States included the launching of a number of weather satellites and space observatories in 1964 and 1965. In 1967 *Ranger 7* relayed pictures of the moon back to earth. The *Apollo* series of flights was directed towards a manned landing on the moon, which was accomplished in July 1969. Four more successful manned landings followed; one failed. The *Apollo* programme for the 1970s has had to be curtailed since the space budget has been cut from $5,250m. in 1965 to $3,151 m. in 1971. No further manned Moon landings are planned beyond 1972. In November 1971 the unmanned *Mariner* 9 orbited Mars. In March 1972 *Pioneer* 10 was launched to travel beyond Jupiter, and in April 1972 *Apollo* 16 made a successful moon landing. In August the last orbiting astronomical observatory was launched and in May 1973 Sky Lab was put into orbit. The current budget for space research is $310 million a year, half the allocation being made in the mid-60s. The Viking mission plans to land equipment for detecting the existence of life in any form on Mars in 1976.

Public Holidays

1974: September 2nd (Labour Day), October 28th (Veterans' Day), November 28th (Thanksgiving), December 25th (Christmas Day).

1975: January 1st (New Year's Day), February 12th (Lincoln's Birthday), February 17th (Washington's Birthday), March 28th (Good Friday), May 26th (Memorial Day), July 4th (Independence Day).

Weights and Measures

With certain exceptions, the imperial system is in force. One U.S. billion equals one thousand million; one U.S. cwt. equals 100 lb.; long ton equals 2,240 lb.; short ton equals 2,000 lb.

Currency and Exchange Rates

100 cents=1 United States dollar ($).

Exchange rates (April 1974):
£1 sterling=U.S. $2.36;
U.S. $1=42.35 pence.

STATISTICAL SURVEY

AREA AND POPULATION

AREA (sq. miles)			CENSUS POPULATION†		
Land	Inland Water	Total	April 1st, 1950	April 1st, 1960	April 1st, 1970
3,536,855	78,267	3,615,122*	151,325,798	179,323,175	203,235,298

* 9,363,123 square kilometres.

† Figures relate to resident population, excluding members of the U.S. armed forces serving overseas (estimated at 609,720 in 1960) and civilian citizens absent from the U.S.A. for an extended period of time (estimated at 764,701 in 1960). The census totals also exclude any adjustment for net underenumeration, estimated to have been at least 2.5 per cent in 1950 and about 3 per cent in 1960.

MID-YEAR POPULATION*

(official estimates for July 1st)

1968	1969	1970	1971	1972	1973
200,706,000	202,677,000	204,879,000	207,045,000	208,842,000	210,404,000

* Estimates of the resident population, based on census results, excluding adjustment for net underenumeration (about 3 per cent in 1960). The figures include U.S. armed forces overseas but exclude civilian citizens absent for an extended period.

STATE	GROSS AREA (LAND AND WATER) ('000 sq. miles)	RESIDENT POPULATION* July 1973 ('000)	STATE	GROSS AREA (LAND AND WATER) ('000 sq. miles)	RESIDENT POPULATION* July 1973 ('000)
Alabama	51.6	3,539	Montana	147.1	721
Alaska	586.4	330	Nebraska	77.2	1,542
Arizona	113.9	2,058	Nevada	110.5	548
Arkansas	53.1	2,037	New Hampshire	9.3	791
California	158.7	20,601	New Jersey	7.8	7,361
Colorado	104.2	2,437	New Mexico	121.7	1,106
Connecticut	5.0	3,076	New York	49.6	18,265
Delaware	2.1	576	North Carolina	52.6	5,273
District of Columbia	0.1	746	North Dakota	70.7	640
Florida	58.6	7,678	Ohio	41.2	10,731
Georgia	58.9	4,786	Oklahoma	69.9	2,663
Hawaii	6.5	832	Oregon	97.0	2,225
Idaho	83.6	770	Pennsylvania	45.3	11,902
Illinois	56.4	11,236	Rhode Island	1.2	973
Indiana	36.3	5,316	South Carolina	31.1	2,726
Iowa	56.3	2,904	South Dakota	77.0	685
Kansas	82.3	2,279	Tennessee	42.2	4,126
Kentucky	40.4	3,342	Texas	267.3	11,794
Louisiana	48.5	3,764	Utah	84.9	1,157
Maine	33.2	1,028	Vermont	9.6	464
Maryland	10.6	4,070	Virginia	40.8	4,811
Massachusetts	8.3	5,818	Washington	68.2	3,429
Michigan	58.2	9,044	West Virginia	24.2	1,794
Minnesota	84.1	3,897	Wisconsin	56.2	4,569
Mississippi	47.7	2,281	Wyoming	97.9	353
Missouri	69.7	4,757	TOTAL	3,615.1	209,851

* Excluding armed forces overseas.

MAIN CITIES
(Greater metropolitan areas)

(POPULATION—1972 estimates)

Washington, D.C., Md.–Va. (capital)	2,998,900	Bridgeport, Conn.	793,900
New York, N.Y.	9,943,800	Albany-Schenectady-Troy, N.Y.	792,900
Chicago, Ill.–Ind.	7,084,700	Providence-Pawtucket, R.I.–Mass.	782,600
Los Angeles, Calif.	6,999,600	Toledo, Ohio	780,600
Philadelphia, Pa.–N.J.	4,877,500	Birmingham, Ala.	778,500
Detroit, Mich.	4,488,900	New Haven, Conn.	760,800
Boston, Mass.	3,417,000	Greensboro-Winston-Salem, N.C.	745,100
San Francisco, Calif.	3,131,800	Salt Lake City, Utah	744,300
Nassau-Suffolk, N.Y.	2,597,300	Oklahoma City, Okla.	735,800
St. Louis, Mo.–Ill.	2,399,800	Nashville, Tenn.	715,700
Pittsburgh, Pa.	2,395,900	Fort Lauderdale-Hollywood, Fla.	684,900
Dallas, Tex.	2,378,353*	Norfolk-Portsmouth, Va.	682,600
Baltimore, Md.	2,125,000	Akron, Ohio	682,200
Newark, N.J.	2,082,000	Honolulu, Hawaii	660,100
Cleveland, Ohio	2,045,500	Worcester, Mass.	644,700
Houston, Tex.	1,999,316*	Gary-Hammond-E. Chicago, Ind.	644,100
Minneapolis-St. Paul, Minn.	1,995,800	Syracuse, N.Y.	643,400
Atlanta, Ga.	1,683,600	Jacksonville, Fla.	635,500
Anaheim-Santa Ana-Garden Grove, Calif.	1,527,300	Northeast Pennsylvania	631,500
San Diego, Calif.	1,443,100	Jersey City, N.J.	610,600
Milwaukee, Wis.	1,423,200	Allentown-Bethlehem, Pa.	607,900
Seattle, Wash.	1,399,600	New Brunswick, N.J.	595,600
Cincinnati, Ohio–Ky.	1,391,400	Springfield-Chicopee-Holyoke, Mass.–Conn.	591,100
Buffalo, N.Y.	1,353,100	Charlotte-Gastonia, N.C.	569,200
Miami, Fla.	1,331,100	Omaha, Nebr.–Iowa	568,800
Denver, Colo.	1,309,200	Tulsa, Okla.	559,600
Kansas City, Mo.–Kans.	1,303,600	Richmond, Va.	552,600
St. Petersburg, Fla.	1,189,000	Grand Rapids, Mich.	548,500
San Bernardino Riverside, Calif.	1,178,500	Youngstown-Warren, Ohio–Pa.	544,100
Indianapolis, Ind.	1,128,000	Flint, Mich.	521,200
San Jose, Calif.	1,126,700	Wilmington, Del.–N.J.	512,400
New Orleans, La.	1,076,600	Orlando, Fla.	506,200
Columbus, Ohio	1,057,700	Greenville-Spartanburg, S.C.	497,100
Phoenix, Ariz.	1,053,000	Long Branch-Asbury Park, N.J.	478,600
Portland, Oreg.-Wash.	1,036,300	Paterson-Clifton-Passaic, N.J.	464,300
Rochester, N.Y.	968,600	Fall River, Mass.-R.I.	457,200
San Antonio, Tex.	888,197*	Raleigh-Durham, N.C.	438,700
Louisville, Ky.–Ind.	887,700	Lansing-East Lansing, Mich	436,900
Dayton, Ohio	857,300	Fresno, Calif.	430,500
Sacramento, Calif.	851,300	Harrisburg, Pa.	422,100
Hartford, Conn.	833,800	Knoxville, Tenn.	420,800
Memphis, Tenn.	847,100	Tacoma, Wash.	405,300

* 1970 Census.

EXPANSION OF POPULATION
('000)

	ALL CLASSES	WHITE	NEGRO	INDIAN	OTHERS
1900	76,014	66,809	8,834	237	114
1910	91,973	81,732	9,828	266	147
1920	105,710	94,821	10,463	244	182
1930	122,775	110,287	11,891	332	265
1940	131,670	118,215	12,866	334	255
1950	150,697	134,942	15,042	343	370
1960	179,323	158,832	18,872	523	1,096
1970*	203,166	177,612	22,672	791	2,880

* Provisional figures.

UNITED STATES OF AMERICA—(STATISTICAL SURVEY)

BIRTHS, MARRIAGES, DEATHS

	BIRTHS		MARRIAGES		DEATHS	
	Number ('ooo)	Rate (per 'ooo)	Number ('ooo)	Rate (per 'ooo)	Number ('ooo)	Rate (per 'ooo)
1968 . .	3,502	17.4	2,059	10.3	1,923	9.6
1969 . .	3,571	17.7	2,146	10.6	1,916	9.5
1970 . .	3,718	18.2	2,179	10.7	1,921	9.4
1971 . .	3,571	17.3	2,196	10.6	1,926	9.3
1972* . .	3,256	15.6	2,269	10.9	1,962	9.4

* Preliminary figures.

IMMIGRATION 1951–1972

COUNTRY OF LAST PERMANENT RESIDENCE	1951–60	1966	1967	1968	1969	1970	1971	1972
All Countries .	2,515,579	323,040	361,972	454,448	358,579	373,326	370,478	384,685
Europe . . .	1,328,293	115,898	128,775	129,347	120,086	188,106	91,509	86,321
France . .	51,121	4,173	4,904	4,815	2,024	2,477	2,844	2,870
Germany . .	121,189	17,661	16,595	16,590	9,289	9,684	8,646	7,760
Austria . .	160,729	1,446	1,484	2,022	758	888	1,945	2,251
Great Britain .	191,564	18,775	23,004	26,752	15,014	14,158	12,302	11,521
Greece . .	47,668	8,221	14,194	12,185	17,724	16,464	15,002	10,452
Irealnd . .	57,332	2,603	1,991	2,268	1,989	1,562	1,173	1,423
Italy . .	185,491	26,449	28,487	25,882	23,617	24,973	22,818	22,413
Netherlands .	52,277	1,922	1,786	2,051	1,303	1,457	1,092	979
Poland . .	9,985	8,470	4,356	3,676	4,052	3,585	1,928	3,770
Portugal . .	19,588	8,481	13,400	11,827	16,528	13,195	10,545	9,465
Spain . .	7,894	4,944	4,562	7,904	3,916	4,139	3,661	4,284
Switzerland .	17,675	1,995	2,279	2,187	691	1,051	1,066	999
Yugoslavia .	8,225	1,611	2,753	2,705	8,686	8,575	3,265	2,767
Asia . . .	147,553	40,112	57,574	55,973	73,621	92,816	98,062	115,978
America . .	996,944	162,552	170,235	262,736	156,341	56,436	171,680	173,165
Canada . .	377,952	37,223	34,768	41,716	18,582	151,087	22,709	18,596
Mexico . .	299,811	47,217	43,034	44,716	44,623	13,804	50,324	64,209
West Indies .	123,091	37,999	61,987	29,376	59,395	44,469	25,129	24,171
Africa . . .	140,092	1,967	2,577	3,220	5,876	8,115	5,844	5,472
Australia, New Zealand .	11,506	1,890	2,128	2,374	1,878	2,280	2,357	2,550
Not specified .	12,493	444	534	659	764	922	868	964

ECONOMICALLY ACTIVE POPULATION*
(official estimates for 1972)

	MALES	FEMALES	TOTAL
Agriculture, Forestry, Hunting and Fishing	3,031,000	670,000	3,701,000
Mining and Quarrying	573,000	44,000	616,000
Manufacturing	14,952,000	6,070,000	21,022,000
Construction	5,420,000	307,000	5,728,000
Electricity, Gas, Water and Sanitary Services	1,052,000	146,000	1,198,000
Commerce	12,272,000	9,680,000	21,952,000
Transport, Storage and Communications .	3,419,000	1,031,000	4,449,000
Services	12,240,000	14,959,000	27,198,000
Armed Forces	2,406,000	43,000	2,449,000
TOTAL	55,364,000	32,950,000	88,314,000

* Figures exclude 677,000 persons seeking work for the first time but include other unemployed persons, totalling 4,163,000 (2,328,000 males and 1,835,000 females).

AGRICULTURE

LAND UTILIZATION 1969*

	MILLION ACRES	%
In Farms	1,064	47
Cropland	387	17.1
Grassland Pasture . .	540	23.8
Woodland Pasture . .	62	2.7
Woodland not Pastured . .	50	2.2
Farmsteads, Roads, other Land	25	1.1
Not in Farms	1,200	53.0
Grazing Land . . .	287	12.6
Forest Land not Grazed .	476	21.1
Other Land	437	19.3
TOTAL . . .	2,264	

* Provisional.

CROP PRODUCTION

	Harvest units	1970			1971 (preliminary)		
		Acreage ('000)	Harvest	Value ($ million)	Acreage ('000)	Harvest	Value ($ million)
Maize . .	million bushels	57,224	4,099	5,441	63,819	5,540	5,896
Wheat . .	,, ,,	44,141	1,370	1,826	48,453	1,640	2,168
Oats . .	,, ,,	18,524	909	581	15,734	876	538
Barley . .	,, ,,	—	410	—	—	463	—
Rice . .	million cwt.	1,815	84	433	1,818	84	440
Sorghum .	,, bushels	13,732	696	798	16,601	895	925
Cotton Lint .	,, cwt.	—	10	—	—	10	—
Cotton Seed .	'000 short tons	11,160	4,000	1,119	—	4,244	—
Hay . .	,, ,, ,,	62,911	127,000	3,100	63,265	131,000	3,333
Beans, dry .	million cwt.	—	18	—	—	16	—
Soybeans .	,, bushels	42,056	1,124	3,205	42,409	1,169	3,465
Potatoes .	,, lb.	1,420	326	712	1,380	316	626
Tobacco .	,, ,,	892	1,908	1,390	843	1,751	1,368
Peanuts .	,, ,,	—	2,979	—	—	3,003	—
Sugar Beet .	'000 short tons	1,413	26,000	391	1,336	27,044	414
Rye . .	million bushell	—	39	—	—	51	—

FRUIT PRODUCTION

		1970	1971	1972*
Apples	million lb.	6,294	6,081	5,828
Peaches	,, ,,	3,011	2,863	2,443
Pears	'000 tons	537	702	610
Grapes	,, ,,	3,119	3,997	2,567
Oranges	'000 boxes	189,640	194,790	195,370
Grapefruit . . .	,, ,,	53,910	60,560	63,840
Lemons	,, ,,	15,120	16,450	16,680

* Preliminary.

UNITED STATES OF AMERICA—(Statistical Survey)

LIVESTOCK
('ooo head)

	1969	1970	1971	1972
All Cattle	109,885	112,303	114,470	117,916
Pigs	60,632	56,655	67,449	62,972
Stock Sheep . . .	18,332	17,411	16,968	15,767
Chickens (million) . . .	420	434	435	n.a.
Turkeys	6,604	6,769	7,715	n.a.

LIVESTOCK PRODUCE
(million lb.)

	1970	1971	1972
Beef	21,651	21,868	22,381
Veal	588	546	458
Lamb and Mutton . .	551	555	543
Pork	13,427	14,783	13,617
Eggs (million) . . .	70,023	70,082	69,804
Milk ('ooo million lb.) .	117	119	120
Butter	1,137	1,144	1,110
Cheese	2,201	2,373	n.a.

FORESTRY

		1968	1969	1970*	1971*
Soft Wood . .	million board ft.	28,936	28,133	27,439	30,283
Hard Wood . .	,,	7,188	7,316	7,023	6,356
Wood Pulp . .	million cu. ft.	3,385	3,585	3,865†	3,880
Paper and Paperboard	,,	51,245	54,187	53,329	54,150

* Preliminary.   † Actual figure.

SEA AND INLAND FISHERIES
(million lb.)

	1967	1968	1969	1970	1971	1972*
Cod . . .	43	49	58	53	53	46
Haddock . .	98	71	46	27	22	12
Herring, Sea .	85	108	88	79	87	102
Mackerel . .	40	59	48	57	65	53
Menhaden . .	1,166	1,381	1,548	1,837	2,190	1,939
Salmon . .	206	328	246	410	312	217
Tuna and similar Fish	329	294	323	393	348	378
Ocean Perch . .	72	62	56	55	60	59
Crabs . . .	316	238	246	277	276	281
Shrimp . .	312	292	317	367	388	385
Oysters . .	58	56	52	54	55	53
Total (incl. others)	4,062	3,226	3,019	3,619	4,656	1,710

* Preliminary.

MINING

		1969	1970	1971	1972
Bitumen	'ooo short tons	1,919	1,981	1,669	n.a.
Coal	mill. short tons	561	603	552	590
Natural Gas	'ooo mill. cu. ft.	20,698	21,921	22,493	n.a.
Crude Oil	mill. barrels	3,372	3,517	5,098	5,483
Phosphate Rock	'ooo short tons	37,725	38,739	38,886	n.a.
Sulphur	'ooo long tons	6,551	6,419	9,120	8,620
Bauxite	,,	1,843	2,082	1,988	1,416*
Iron Ore	,,	89,854	87,176	80,762	75,286*
Copper	'ooo short tons	1,546	1,720	1,522	1,505
Lead	,,	509	572	578	574*
Zinc	,,	553	534	503	447*
Uranium	'ooo lb.	23,748	24,682	24,520	n.a.
Gold	'ooo troy oz.	1,733	1,743	1,495	1,317*
Silver	,,	41,906	45,005	41,564	34,992*
Molybdenum	'ooo lb.	103,009	110,381	109,592	97,235
Nickel	'ooo short tons	17,056	15,993	17,036	n.a.

* Provisional figures.

INDUSTRY
PRINCIPAL MANUFACTURES
(Added Value—$ million)

	1969	1970	1971
Food and Beverages	30,120	31,895	34,110
Beverages	5,676	5,927	6,557
Tobacco Products	2,385	2,488	2,560
Textile Products	9,672	9,251	9,995
Apparel	11,639	11,601	12,448
Lumber and Wood Products	6,359	5,859	6,761
Furniture and Fixtures	5,056	4,842	5,227
Paper and Allied Products	11,284	11,530	11,682
Printing and Publishing	16,615	17,265	18,086
Newspapers	4,979	5,214	5,537
Chemicals and Allied Products	27,177	27,946	29,432
Basic Chemicals	8,718	n.a.	n.a.
Petroleum and Coal Products	5,725	5,444	5,617
Petroleum Refining	4,946	4,561	4,614
Rubber and Plastic Products	8,495	8,460	9,521
Leather and Products	2,944	2,806	2,761
Stone, Clay and Glass Products	10,049	9,867	10,758
Primary Metal Industries	22,714	21,370	21,119
Steel Rolling and Finishing	11,280	n.a.	n.a.
Iron and Steel Foundries	3,187	2,845	3,016
Non-Ferrous Rolling and Drawing	3,470	3,445	3,347
Fabricated Metal Products	20,841	20,708	21,966
Structural Metal Products	5,474	n.a.	6,237
Machinery, excluding Electrical	31,983	31,752	30,681
Construction	4,949	4,930	5,032
Metalworking	5,403	4,915	4,248
Industrial	4,492	4,551	4,280
Electrical Machinery	28,275	27,797	27,874
Household	3,067	3,045	3,174
Communications Equipment	8,059	8,287	7,939
Transport Equipment	35,068	28,889	34,845
Motor Vehicles	18,356	14,524	20,506
Aircraft and Parts	12,829	10,303	9,805
Instruments and Related Products	7,589	7,891	8,386
Miscellaneous Manufactures, incl. Ordnance	11,918	10,616	10,309

FINANCE

100 cents = 1 United States dollar ($).

Coins: 1, 5, 10, 25 and 50 cents; 1 dollar.

Notes: 1, 2, 5, 10, 20, 50 and 100 dollars.

Exchange rates (April 1974): £1 sterling = U.S. $2.36; U.S. $100 = £42.35.

FEDERAL BUDGET

($'000 million, year ending June 30th)

REVENUE	1973-74†	1974-75*	EXPENDITURE	1973-74†	1974-75*
Individual Income Taxes . .	118.0	129.0	National Defence . . .	80.6	87.7
Corporation Income Taxes .	43.0	48.0	International Affairs and Finance	3.9	4.1
Social Insurance Taxes and Contributions . . .	77.9	85.6	Space Research and Technology .	3.2	3.3
Excise Taxes . . .	17.1	17.4	Agriculture and Rural Development . . .	4.0	2.7
Estate and Gift Taxes . .	5.4	6.0	Natural Resources and Environment . . .	0.6	3.1
Customs Duties . .	3.5	3.8	Commerce and Transportation .	13.5	13.4
Other Receipts . . .	5.0	5.2	Community Development and Housing . . .	5.4	5.7
			Education and Manpower . .	10.8	11.5
			Health	23.3	26.3
			Income Security . . .	85.0	100.1
			Veterans' Benefits and Services .	13.3	13.6
			Interest	27.8	29.1
			General Government . .	6.8	6.8
TOTAL . . .	270.0	295.0	TOTAL . .	274.7	304.4
			Deficit . . .	4.7	9.4

† Revised estimate.   * Proposed.

STATE AND LOCAL GOVERNMENT BUDGETS

($ million, year ending June 30th)

REVENUE	1969-70	1970-71	EXPENDITURE	1969-70	1970-71
From Federal Government .	21,857	26,146	General	131,332	150,674
From State and Local Govt. .	128,248	139,945	Education . . .	52,718	59,413
General, net of Intergovernmental	108,898	118,782	Higher Institutions . .	12,924	14,785
Taxes	86,795	94,975	Local Schools . . .	37,461	41,766
Property . . .	34,054	37,852	Highways . . .	16,427	18,095
Sales and gross receipts .	30,322	33,233	Public Welfare . . .	14,679	18,226
Individual income . .	10,812	11,900	Health	1,806	2,119
Corporation income .	3,738	3,424	Hospitals . . .	7,863	9,086
Other . . .	7,868	8,567	Police	4,494	5,228
Charges and Miscellaneous .	22,103	23,807	Fire Service . . .	2,024	2,303
Utility and Liquor Stores .	8,614	9,359	Natural Resources . .	2,732	3,082
Insurance Trust Revenue .	10,736	11,804	Sanitation . . .	3,413	4,087
Employee Retirement .	6,493	7,451	Housing and Urban Renewal .	2,138	2,554
Unemployment Compensation .	3,101	3,096	Local Parks and Recreation .	1,888	2,109
			Financial Administration .	2,030	2,271
			General Control . .	2,652	3,027
			Interest on General Debt .	4,374	5,089
			Utility and Liquor Stores Expenditure . .	9,447	10,300
			Insurance Trust Expenditure .	7,273	9,793
			Employee Retirement .	3,629	4,155
			Unemployment Compensation .	2,723	4,708
TOTAL . . .	150,106	166,090	TOTAL . . .	148,052	170,766

COST OF LIVING INDEX
(1967 = 100)

	1969	1970	1971	1972
Food	108.6	114.9	118.4	123.5
Housing	110.8	118.9	124.3	129.2
Rent	105.7	110.1	115.2	119.2
House ownership	116.0	128.5	133.7	n.a.
Fuel and Utilities	103.6	107.6	115.1	120.1
Furnishings and maintenance . .	109.0	113.4	118.1	121.0
Clothes	111.5	116.1	119.8	122.3
Transport	107.2	112.7	118.6	119.9
Health and Recreation . . .	110.3	116.2	122.2	n.a.
Medical care	113.4	120.6	128.4	132.5
Personal care	109.3	113.2	116.8	119.8
Reading and recreation . . .	108.7	113.4	119.3	122.8
Other goods and services . . .	109.1	116.0	120.9	125.5
Total	109.8	116.3	121.3	125.3

NATIONAL ACCOUNTS
($'ooo million)

	1969	1970	1971	1972*
Net National Income . . .	766.0	798.6	855.7	934.7
of which:				
Agriculture, forestry and fisheries . .	24.8	25.5	26.5	29.1
Mining and construction . .	47.7	50.5	54.1	57.8
Manufacturing	222.3	216.3	223.2	248.3
Transport	28.7	29.7	32.5	35.7
Communications and public utilities .	15.8	16.8	18.2	20.9
Wholesale and retail trade . .	114.8	121.2	130.8	140.2
Finance and real estate . . .	84.5	90.0	98.7	105.9
Services	94.7	102.7	110.6	121.6
Government	114.3	126.8	137.9	150.1
Taxes *less* subsidies . . .	82.7	191.5	100.9	113.4
Net National Product . . .	848.7	890.1	956.5	1,048.1
Capital consumption allowances . .	81.6	86.3	93.8	103.7
Gross National Product . . .	930.3	976.4	1,050.4	1,151.8
of which:				
Business	794.1	826.3	884.7	970.6
General government . . .	103.8	114.7	124.8	136.1
Households and institutions . .	28.1	30.9	33.9	37.8
Rest of world	4.3	4.6	6.9	7.3
Balance of exports and imports of goods and services	1.9	3.6	0.7	−4.2
Available Resources . . .	932.2	980.0	1,051.1	1,147.6
of which:				
Private consumption expenditure . .	579.5	616.8	664.9	721.0
Government consumption expenditure .	213.7	226.1	234.2	246.2
Gross domestic investment . .	139.0	137.1	152.0	180.4

* Preliminary.

GOLD RESERVES AND CURRENCY IN CIRCULATION
($ million in December)

	1969	1970	1971	1972
Gold Stock . . .	10,367	11,105	10,132	10,410
Foreign Currency Holdings . .	2,781	629	276	241
Currency in Circulation . .	53,591	57,013	61,063	66,060

BALANCE OF PAYMENTS—ALL FOREIGN COUNTRIES
($ million)

	1970			1971		
	Credit	Debit	Balance	Credit	Debit	Balance
Goods and Services:						
Merchandise . . .	41,963	39,637	2,326	42,769	45,241	— 2,472
Non-monetary gold . .	—	162	— 162	—	221	— 221
Freight and transport .	3,627	4,034	— 407	3,708	4,303	— 595
Travel	2,319	3,973	— 1,454	2,457	4,294	— 1,837
Investment income . .	12,455	5,490	6,965	13,845	5,307	8,538
Other government services .	2,342	5,439	— 3,097	2,862	5,422	— 2,560
Other private services .	3,113	859	2,254	3,607	963	2,644
Total	65,818	59,592	6,226	69,249	65,752	3,497
Transfer Payments . .	409	3,765	3,356	436	4,165	3,729
Current Balance . .	66,227	63,357	2,870	69,685	69,917	— 232
Capital and Monetary Gold:						
Non-Monetary Sector:						
Direct investment . .	—	5,884	— 5,884	—	7,450	— 7,450
Other private long-term .	1,774	—	1,774	1,497	—	1,497
Other private short-term .	892	—	892	—	1,119	— 1,119
Central government . .	—	2,018	— 2,018	—	2,378	— 2,378
Total	—	5,236	— 5,236	—	9,450	— 9,450
Monetary Sector:						
Deposit money banks . .	—	7,164	— 7,164	—	9,878	— 9,878
Total Capital Account .	—	12,400	—12,400	—	19,328	—19,328
Allocation of IMF Special Draw-						
ing Rights . . .	867	—	867	717	—	717
Revenues and Related Items .	9,839	—	9,839	29,766	—	29,766
Liabilities . . .	7,362	—	7,362	27,417	—	27,417
Assets	2,477	—	2,477	2,349	—	2,349
Net Errors and Omissions .	—	—	— 1,174	—	—	—10,923

INTERNATIONAL INVESTMENTS
($ million)

	1968	1969	1970	1971
U.S. Assets Abroad	146,772	158,100	166,900	180,600
Non-liquid	131,062	138,500	150,000	164,400
Private	102,519	107,700	117,800	130,200
Long-term	89,529	96,300	105,000	115,600
Direct investments	64,983	71,000	78,200	86,000
Portfolio	24,546	25,300	26,800	29,600
Short-term	12,990	11,400	12,800	14,700
U.S. Government	26,543	30,700	32,200	34,200
Long-term credits	25,940	28,200	29,700	31,800
Foreign currencies and other claims .	2,603	2,500	2,500	2,400
Liquid: U.S. monetary reserve assets .	15,710	19,600	16,900	16,200
Gold	10,892	—	—	—
Convertible currencies	3,528	—	—	—
IMF gold tranche position . . .	1,290	—	—	—
U.S. Liabilities to Foreigners . . .	81,248	90,800	97,700	122,800
Non-liquid	47,634	44,900	50,700	54,900
Private	42,890	42,500	48,700	53,400
Long-term	40,353	39,600	44,800	49,600
Direct investments	10,815	11,800	13,300	13,700
Portfolio	29,538	27,800	31,500	35,900
Short-term	2,537	2,900	3,900	3,800
U.S. Government	4,744	2,400	2,000	1,500
Liquid	33,614	45,900	47,000	67,900
To private foreigners . . .	20,103	17,100	22,600	16,600
To foreign official agencies . . .	13,511	4,000	24,400	51,200
Net International Investment Position of U.S. .	65,524	67,200	69,200	57,900

INTERNATIONAL INVESTMENTS, BY AREA
($ million)

AREA AND TYPE OF INVESTMENT	1970		1971		1972	
	Receipts	Payments	Receipts	Payments	Receipts	Payments
Total, All Areas	9,507	5,056	10,729	4,809	11,447	5,803
Direct	6,001	441	7,286	621	7,948	604
Other Private	2,597	3,591	2,556	2,344	2,693	2,515
U.S. Government . . .	909	1,024	887	1,844	806	2,684
Canada	1,781	591	1,875	553	1,942	578
Direct	944	39	1,000	88	967	91
Other Private	836	378	873	258	971	243
U.S. Government . . .	1	174	2	207	4	244
Latin America	1,770	482	1,797	298	1,652	284
Direct	1,057	22	1,124	28	974	28
Other Private	553	446	517	243	532	247
U.S. Government . . .	160	14	156	27	146	9
Western Europe	2,251	3,079	2,374	3,058	2,468	3,567
Direct	1,390	363	1,659	466	1,820	427
Other Private	500	2,169	470	1,462	463	1,590
U.S. Government . . .	361	547	245	1,130	185	1,550
Other Countries	3,706	904	4,683	904	5,389	1,376
Direct	2,610	17	3,503	40	4,187	58
Other Private	708	599	696	384	728	436
U.S. Government . . .	388	288	484	480	474	882

FOREIGN AID
($ million)

	TOTAL 1945–66	1969	1970	1971	1972*
International Organizations	1,190	184	234	246	271
ADB	10	10	10	—	17
IDB	190	126	165	175	180
IBRD	635	—	—	—	1
IDA	320	48	58	71	73
IFC	35	—	—	—	—
Military Grants	36,786	2,888	2,634	3,180	4,235
Western Europe . . .	n.a.	62	66	51	64
Near East and South Asia .	n.a.	266	200	253	216
Africa	n.a.	26	19	25	13
Far East and Pacific . .	n.a.	2,495	2,321	2,824	3,912
Americas	n.a.	36	25	21	25
Not Specified	n.a.	4	4	6	5
Non-Military Assistance . .	68,949	3,558	2,910	3,634	3,452
Western Europe . . .	23,574	142	−278	−142	−158
Austria	1,089	−12	−6	9	—
France	4,142	−3	−27	5	34
Germany, Federal Republic .	2,849	−4	−16	6	3
Italy	2,793	224	−8	−7	−15
United Kingdom . . .	6,450	−42	−143	−138	−208
Yugoslavia	2,009	−28	−36	26	55
Eastern Europe . . .	1,606	−27	7	−2	70
Near East and South Asia .	16,723	1,048	946	1,622	1,115
Greece	1,656	6	−24	−10	−9
India	5,901	464	431	467	112
Pakistan	2,804	209	239	216	154
Turkey	1,888	84	88	109	171
U.A.R.	1,106	4	—	106	−6
Africa	2,625	279	275	348	259
Far East and Pacific . .	15,499	1,144	985	978	1,219
China, (Taiwan) . . .	2,150	12	14	14	26
Japan	2,587	22	−54	−66	−60
Korea, Republic . . .	4,037	260	198	194	221
Philippines	1,151	29	63	51	70
Viet-Nam, Republic . .	2,831	446	418	427	539
Americas	6,327	605	541	407	460
Brazil	1,892	99	92	98	53
Other International Organizations and Unspecified Areas	2,595	368	435	433	488

* Preliminary.

EXTERNAL TRADE

(\$ million, excluding gold)

	1968	1969	1970	1971	1972	1973
Imports f.o.b.	33,226	36,043	39,952	45,563	55,583	69,121
Exports f.o.b.	34,636	38,006	43,224	44,130	49,779	71,314

PRINCIPAL COMMODITIES

(\$ million)

	IMPORTS			EXPORTS		
	1970	1971	1972	1970	1971	1972
Food and Live Animals	5,375	5,529	6,362	4,356	4,367	5,665
Meats and Preparations	1,014	1,050	1,223	175	192	252
Grains and Preparations	—	—	92	2,596	2,449	3,505
Fruits and Nuts	447	460	496	406	430	526
Vegetables	289	287	350	178	182	209
Beverages and Tobacco	855	876	1,010	702	709	908
Raw Materials, excl. Fuels	3,307	3,382	3,860	4,605	4,329	5,029
Soybeans	—	—	—	1,216	1,327	1,508
Woodpulp	480	482	490	464	351	358
Textile Fibres and Wastes	202	158	196	543	777	751
Metal Ores and Scrap	1,149	1,044	1,022	940	486	508
Mineral Fuels and Related Materials	3,075	3,715	4,799	1,595	1,497	1,554
Coal	—	—	—	962	902	984
Petroleum and Products	2,764	3,323	4,300	488	479	445
Animal and Vegetable Oils and Fats	160	172	180	493	615	507
Chemicals	1,450	1,612	2,015	3,826	3,836	4,134
Chemical Elements and Compounds	—	—	—	1,642	1,645	1,698
Organic Chemicals	355	400	509	137	140	157
Medical and Pharmaceutical Products	87	119	149	420	396	474
Plastic Materials and Resins	—	—	—	653	656	696
Uranium Oxide	—	—	—	—	—	—
Machinery and Transport Equipment	11,172	13,873	17,400	17,882	19,460	21,514
Machinery, excl. Electrical	3,103	3,504	4,541	8,686	8,772	9,871
Agricultural	173	181	237	182	180	249
Office Machines	505	566	700	1,104	1,261	1,341
Metalworking	164	107	140	396	405	410
Electrical Apparatus	2,271	2,555	3,375	2,999	3,067	3,699
Power Machinery	247	263	356	611	679	787
Transport Equipment	5,798	7,814	9,484	6,197	7,621	7,944
Motor Vehicles	5,068	6,776	7,946	3,245	3,879	4,470
Other Manufactures	13,285	14,929	18,332	7,636	7,147	8,094
Paper and Manufactures	1,087	1,157	1,261	622	685	726
Metals and Manufactures	4,508	5,114	6,004	2,978	2,183	2,314
Iron and Steel Mill Products	1,952	2,615	2,743	1,188	760	800
Non-ferrous Base Metals	1,502	1,431	1,754	893	597	n.a.
Metal Manufactures	825	837	1,144	744	754	n.a.
Textiles	1,135	1,391	1,528	603	632	n.a.
Clothing	1,269	1,521	1,883	227	216	n.a.
Scientific Apparatus	356	381	513	857	885	n.a.

PRINCIPAL COUNTRIES
($ million)

AREA AND COUNTRY	IMPORTS			EXPORTS		
	1970	1971	1972	1970	1971	1972
Western Hemisphere . . .	*16,928*	*18,730*	*21,912*	*15,612*	*16,850*	*19,695*
Canada	11,092	12,692	14,909	9,079	10,365	12,415
Mexico	1,219	1,262	1,632	1,704	1,620	1,982
Guatemala . . .	87	95	108	100	98	102
El Salvador . . .	48	52	49	64	62	74
Honduras . . .	102	121	116	89	84	79
Nicaragua . . .	61	70	82	77	63	75
Costa Rica . . .	117	109	130	95	103	110
Panama	76	66	55	208	209	216
Bahamas	82	229	247	173	141	144
Jamaica	187	170	181	218	216	221
Dominican Republic . .	184	175	232	143	164	183
Trinidad and Tobago .	232	215	251	84	117	122
Netherlands Antilles . .	416	386	400	126	119	122
Colombia	269	239	284	395	378	317
Venezuela . . .	1,082	1,216	1,298	759	787	924
Surinam	56	68	69	35	36	37
Ecuador	109	90	126	127	134	134
Peru	340	274	334	214	258	292
Bolivia	25	23	26	35	45	45
Chile	157	91	83	300	224	187
Brazil	670	762	942	840	966	1,243
Uruguay	19	11	8	41	32	37
Argentina . . .	172	176	201	441	391	400
Europe	*11,395*	*12,741*	*15,740*	*14,817*	*14,562*	*16,160*
Sweden	399	454	601	543	470	472
Norway	142	175	241	196	185	213
Denmark	284	286	367	227	253	258
United Kingdom . .	2,194	2,499	2,986	2,536	2,369	2,658
Ireland	135	125	152	112	138	125
Netherlands . . .	528	534	639	1,651	1,786	1,851
Belgium/Luxembourg .	696	844	968	1,195	1,077	1,138
France	942	1,088	1,369	1,483	1,373	1,610
Germany, Federal Republic .	3,127	3,650	4,249	2,741	2,831	2,811
Austria	120	128	173	74	101	96
Czechoslovakia . . .	24	24	28	23	39	49
Switzerland . . .	459	493	619	700	627	672
Finland	114	123	142	99	90	91
Poland	98	108	139	70	73	112
U.S.S.R.	72	57	95	119	162	547
Spain	353	458	600	712	627	930
Portugal	92	113	150	126	142	212
Italy	1,316	1,406	1,756	1,353	1,314	1,430
Yugoslavia . . .	96	96	150	168	174	169
Greece	52	57	90	203	275	250
Turkey	70	67	106	315	307	317

(continued on next page)

PRINCIPAL COUNTRIES—*continued*

AREA AND COUNTRY	IMPORTS			EXPORTS		
	1970	1971	1972	1970	1971	1972
Asia	9,621	11,780	15,112	10,027	9,855	11,300
Lebanon	13	13	21	64	93	130
Iran	67	136	199	326	482	559
Israel	150	173	222	592	707	558
Kuwait	25	36	49	62	84	111
Saudi Arabia	20	99	194	141	164	314
India	298	329	427	572	648	350
Pakistan	80	77	40	325	211	183
Thailand	100	97	116	150	144	170
Viet-Nam, Republic	1	2	2	352	297	318
Malaysia and Singapore	161	213	566	301	387	513
Indonesia	182	207	278	266	263	308
Philippines	472	496	484	373	340	366
Korea, Republic	370	462	708	643	681	735
Hong Kong	944	991	1,249	406	424	489
China, People's Republic*	—	—	30	—	49	60
China (Taiwan)	549	817	1,294	527	510	631
Japan	5,875	7,259	9,064	4,652	4,055	4,965
Australia and Oceania	871	895	1,145	1,189	1,168	1,035
Australia	611	619	807	986	1,004	843
New Zealand and Western Samoa	222	230	277	135	111	137
Africa	1,113	1,236	1,595	1,580	1,694	1,577
Morocco	10	7	11	89	102	58
Algeria	10	20	104	62	82	98
Libya	39	51	116	108	78	85
Egypt	23	19	17	77	63	76
Ghana	91	106	80	59	55	44
Nigeria	71	130	271	129	168	114
Angola	68	89	90	38	36	26
Liberia	51	49	53	46	43	71
Zaire	41	45	43	62	84	37
Ethiopia	67	61	58	26	26	24
South Africa	290	287	325	563	622	602
Kenya	23	26	27	34	41	26
Uganda	48	43	49	4	7	3

* 1973: Imports $60 million; exports $840 million.

TOURISM

		1968	1969	1970	1971	1972*
Overseas Visitors		2,042,666	2,382,198	3,020,359	3,127,678	n.a.
Canadian Visitors		n.a.	n.a.	n.a.	n.a.	n.a.
Receipts from Visitors . .	($ million)	2,022	2,361	2,696	2,889	3,200
Expenditure by Americans .	(,, ,,)	4,722	5,365	6,153	6,633	7,716
Expenditure in Canada .	(,, ,,)	829	900	1,049	1,111	1,036

Source: OECD.   * Preliminary.

TRANSPORT
RAILWAYS

		1968	1969	1970	1971
Passengers Carried .	million	301	302	289	276
Passenger-Miles . .	,,	13,164	12,214	10,785	8,863
Revenue Tons Originated	,,	1,515	1,558	1,572	1,472
Freight Revenue . .	million dollars	9,942	10,538	11,124	11,996
Passenger Revenue .	,, ,,	447	442	423	384

ROADS
Motor Vehicles Registered ('000)

	1969	1970	1971	1972
Passenger Cars and Taxis .	86,855	89,230	92,799	96,397
Trucks and Buses . .	18,221	19,145	20,200	21,209
Motor Cycles . . .	2,316	2,824	3,345	3,787

INLAND WATERWAYS
(million ton-miles)

	1968	1969	1970	1971
Atlantic Coast Rivers. . . .	25,938	26,603	28,572	28,620
Gulf Coast Rivers . . .	25,757	27,808	28,582	30,473
Pacific Coast Rivers . . .	7,303	8,061	8,397	8,525
Mississippi* . . .	120,339	125,195	138,534	142,385
Great Lakes System . . .	112,073	115,235	114,475	105,027
Total . . .	291,409	302,901	318,560	315,030

* Includes other waterways and canals, and Alaskan waterways.

OCEAN SHIPPING
Sea-going Merchant Vessels
(displacement in '000 gross registered tons)

	1971		1972	
	Number Registered	Gross Tonnage	Number Registered	Gross Tonnage
Cargo Ships . . .	1,014	11,515	792	9,366
Tankers . . .	293	7,848	283	8,047
Total (incl. others) .	1,478	20,474	1,233	18,412

UNITED STATES OF AMERICA—(STATISTICAL SURVEY)

VESSELS ENTERED AND CLEARED IN FOREIGN TRADE IN ALL PORTS

	ENTERED		CLEARED	
	Number	Displacement ('000 net tons)	Number	Displacement ('000 net tons)
1969	52,642	238,085	51,670	237,986
1970	53,293	254,154	52,195	253,136
1971	51,443	255,779	50,400	258,082
1972	54,147	295,281	55,005	307,110

CIVIL AVIATION
SCHEDULED AIR CARRIERS

		1970		1971	
		Domestic	International	Domestic	International
Miles Flown . . .	million	2,028	391	2,001	376
Passengers . . .	,,	153	16	156	18
Passenger-miles . .	,,	104,147	27,563	106,294	29,358
Freight ton-miles .	,,	3,158	2,216	3,574	2,275
Mail ton-miles . .	,,	715	549	707	457

COMMUNICATIONS MEDIA

	1968	1969	1970	1971
Telephones (at December 31st) .	109,256,000	115,222,000	120,218,000	125,142,000
Radio Sets	n.a.	275,000,000	290,000,000	336,000,000
Television Sets . . .	n.a.	81,000,000	84,600,000	93,000,000
Books published (titles)* .	26,384	23,408	35,415	36,038
Daily Newspapers† . .	n.a.	1,758	1,773	1,749
Newspaper Circulation† . .	n.a.	62,060,000	62,108,000	62,231,000

* Figures cover only the commercial production of the book trade, excluding government publications, university theses and other non-trade book production.

† Figures relate to English language dailies only.

EDUCATION
PUPILS ENROLLED ('000)

	1969	1970	1971	1972
Kindergarten	3,276	2,726	2,778	3,135
Elementary	33,788	33,950	33,507	32,242
High School	14,553	14,715	15,183	15,169
Colleges	7,435	7,413	8,087	8,313
TOTAL . . .	59,053	58,804	59,555	58,859

Sources: Statistical Abstract of the United States; International Monetary Fund, *Balance of Payments Year Book; Bureau of the Census Population Estimates and Projections; World Almanac.*

THE CONSTITUTION

The form of Government set up during the American Revolution by the thirteen original States which declared their independence in 1776 soon proved inadequate. After several earlier attempts to reform these "Articles of Confederation" the thirteen States finally sent delegates to a Convention which met at Philadelphia in 1787, and which framed the Constitution of the United States. This Constitution was ratified by the requisite number of States in 1789 and remains in force to the present day. Although the federal nature of the Government that was being set up was made quite clear, Article VI of the Constitution declared it to be the "supreme law of the land", and the central authority was given the right to raise taxes, pay debts and provide defences and to "make all laws necessary and proper to this end". The Constitution was created for a population of under 4,000,000 in a mere 100,000 miles of inhabited territory. It confines itself to laying down general principles and is often lacking in precision, but has for this reason been capable of adaptation, by interpretation and by amendment, to the conditions of the nineteenth and twentieth centuries.

TEXT OF THE CONSTITUTION

Preamble

We, the people of the United States, in order to form a more perfect Union, establish justice, insure domestic tranquillity, provide for the common defence, promote the general welfare, and secure the blessings of liberty to ourselves and our posterity, do ordain and establish this Constitution for the United States of America.

Article I

Section 1

All legislative powers herein granted shall be vested in a Congress of the United States, which shall consist of a Senate and House of Representatives.

Section 2

1. The House of Representatives shall be composed of members chosen every second year by the people of the several States and the electors in each State shall have the qualifications requisite for electors of the most numerous branch of the State Legislature.

2. No person shall be a Representative who shall not have attained to the age of twenty-five years and been seven years a citizen of the United States and who shall not, when elected, be an inhabitant of that State in which he shall be chosen.

3. Representatives and direct taxes shall be apportioned among the several States which may be included within this Union according to their respective numbers, which shall be determined by adding to the whole number of free persons, including those bound to service for a term of years, and excluding Indians not taxed, three-fifths of all other persons. The actual enumeration shall be made within three years after the first meeting of the Congress of the United States, and within every subsequent term of ten years, in such manner as they shall by law direct. The number of Representatives shall not exceed one for every thirty thousand, but each State shall have at least one Representative; and until such enumeration shall be made, the State of New Hampshire shall be entitled to choose 3; Massachusetts 8; Rhode Island and Providence Plantations 1; Connecticut 5; New York 6; New Jersey 4; Pennsylvania 8; Delaware 1; Maryland 6; Virginia 10; North Carolina 5; South Carolina 5, and Georgia 3.*

4. When vacancies happen in the representation from

* See Article XIV Amendments.

any State, the Executive Authority thereof shall issue writs of election to fill such vacancies.

5. The House of Representatives shall choose their Speaker and other officers and shall have the sole power of impeachment.

Section 3

1. The Senate of the United States shall be composed of two Senators from each State, chosen by the Legislature thereof, for six years; and each Senator shall have one vote.

2. Immediately after they shall be assembled in consequence of the first election, they shall be divided as equally as may be into three classes. The seats of the Senators of the first class shall be vacated at the expiration of the second year, of the second class at the expiration of the fourth year, and of the third class at the expiration of the sixth year, so that one-third may be chosen every second year; and if vacancies happen by resignation or otherwise, during the recess of the Legislature or of any State, the Executive thereof may make temporary appointment until the next meeting of the Legislature, which shall then fill such vacancies.

3. No person shall be a Senator who shall not have attained to the age of thirty years, and been nine years a citizen of the United States, and who shall not, when elected, be an inhabitant of that State for which he shall be chosen.

4. The Vice-President of the United States shall be President of the Senate, but shall have no vote unless they be equally divided.

5. The Senate shall choose their other officers, and also a President pro tempore, in the absence of the Vice-President, or when he shall exercise the office of the President of the United States.

6. The Senate shall have the sole power to try all impeachments. When sitting for that purpose, they shall be on oath or affirmation. When the President of the United States is tried, the Chief Justice shall preside; and no person shall be convicted without the concurrence of two-thirds of the members present.

7. Judgment of cases of impeachment shall not extend further than to removal from office, and disqualification to hold and enjoy any office of honour, trust, or profit under the United States; but the party convicted shall nevertheless be liable and subject to indictment, trial, judgment, and punishment, according to law.

Section 4

1. The times, places and manner of holding elections for Senators and Representatives shall be prescribed in each State by the Legislature thereof; but the Congress may at any time by law make or alter such regulations, except as to places of choosing Senators.

2. The Congress shall assemble at least once in every year, and such meeting shall be on the first Monday in December, unless they shall by law appoint a different day.

Section 5

1. Each House shall be the judge of the elections, returns, and qualifications of its own members, and a majority of each shall constitute a quorum to do business; but a smaller number may adjourn from day to day, and may be authorised to compel the attendance of absent members in such manner and under such penalties as each House may provide.

2. Each House may determine the rules of its proceedings, punish its members for disorderly behaviour, and with the concurrence of two-thirds, expel a member.

3. Each House shall keep a journal of its proceedings, and from time to time publish the same, excepting such parts as may in their judgment require secrecy; and the yeas and nays of the members of either House on any question shall, at the desire of one-fifth of those present, be entered on the journal.

4. Neither House, during the session of Congress shall, without the consent of the other, adjourn for more than three days, nor to any other place than that in which the two Houses shall be sitting.

Section 6

1. The Senators and Representatives shall receive a compensation for their services to be ascertained by law, and paid out of the Treasury of the United States. They shall in all cases, except treason, felony, and breach of the peace, be privileged from arrest during their attendance at the session of their respective Houses, and in going to and returning from the same; and for any speech or debate in either House they shall not be questioned in any other place.

2. No Senator or Representative shall, during the time for which he was elected, be appointed to any civil office under the authority of the United States which shall have been created, or the emoluments whereof shall have been increased during such time; and no person holding any office under the United States shall be a member of either House during his continuance in office.

Section 7

1. All bills for raising revenue shall originate in the House of Representatives, but the Senate may propose or concur with amendments, as on other bills.

2. Every bill which shall have passed the House of Representatives and the Senate shall, before it becomes a law, be presented to the President of the United States; if he approve, he shall sign it, but if not he shall return it, with his objections, to that House in which it shall have originated, who shall enter the objections at large on their journal and proceed to reconsider it. If after such reconsideration two-thirds of that House shall agree to pass the bill, it shall be sent, together with the objections, to the other House, by which it shall likewise be reconsidered; and if approved by two-thirds of that House it shall become a law. But in all such cases the votes of both Houses shall be determined by yeas and nays, and the names of the persons voting for and against the bill shall be entered on the journal of each House respectively. If any bill shall not be returned by the President within ten days (Sundays excepted) after it shall have been presented to him, the same shall be a law in like manner as if he had signed it, unless the Congress by their adjournment prevent its return; in which case it shall not be a law.

3. Every order, resolution, or vote to which the concurrence of the Senate and House of Representatives may be necessary (except on a question of adjournment) shall be presented to the President of the United States, and before the same shall take effect shall be approved by him, or being disapproved by him shall be repassed by two-thirds of the Senate and the House of Representatives, according to the rules and limitations prescribed in the case of a bill.

Section 8

1. The Congress shall have power:

To lay and collect taxes, duties, imposts, and excises, to pay the debts and provide for the common defence and general welfare of the United States; but all duties, imposts, and excises shall be uniform throughout the United States.

2. To borrow money on the credit of the United States.

3. To regulate commerce with foreign nations, and among the several States and with the Indian tribes.

4. To establish a uniform rule of naturalisation and uniform laws on the subject of bankruptcies throughout the United States.

5. To coin money, regulate the value thereof, and of foreign coin, and fix the standard of weights and measures.

6. To provide for the punishment of counterfeiting the securities and current coin of the United States.

7. To establish post-offices and post-roads.

8. To promote the progress of science and useful arts by securing for limited times to authors and inventors the exclusive rights to their respective writings and discoveries.

9. To constitute tribunals inferior to the Supreme Court.

10. To define and punish piracies and felonies committed on the high seas, and offences against the law of nations.

11. To declare war, grant letters of marque and reprisal, and make rules concerning captures on land and water.

12. To raise and support armies, but no appropriation of money to that use shall be for a longer term than two years.

13. To provide and maintain a navy.

14. To make rules for the government and regulation of the land and naval forces.

15. To provide for calling forth the militia to execute the laws of the Union, suppress insurrections, and repel invasions.

16. To provide for organizing, arming, and disciplining the militia, and for governing such part of them as may be employed in the service of the United States, reserving to the States respectively the appointment of the officers, and the authority of training the militia according to the discipline prescribed by Congress.

17. To exercise exclusive legislation in all cases whatsoever over such district (not exceeding ten miles square) as may, by cession of particular States and the acceptance of Congress, become the seat of Government of the United States, and to exercise like authority over all places purchased by the consent of the Legislature of the State in which the same shall be, for the erection of forts, magazines, arsenals, dry-docks, and other needful buildings.

18. To make all laws which shall be necessary and proper for carrying into execution the foregoing powers and all other powers vested by this Constitution in the Government of the United States, or in any department or officer hereof.

Section 9

1. The migration or importation of such persons as any of the States now existing shall think proper to admit shall not be prohibited by the Congress prior to the year one thousand eight hundred and eight, but a tax or duty may be imposed on such importations, not exceeding ten dollars for each person.

2. The privilege of the writ of habeas corpus shall not be suspended, unless when in cases of rebellion or invasion the public safety may require it.

3. No bill or attainder or *ex post facto* law shall be passed.

4. No capitation or other direct tax shall be laid, unless in proportion to the census or enumeration hereinbefore directed to be taken.

5. No tax or duty shall be laid on articles exported from any State.

6. No preference shall be given by any regulation of commerce or revenue to the ports of one State over those of another, nor shall vessels bound to or from one State be obliged to enter, clear, or pay duties to another.

7. No money shall be drawn from the Treasury but in consequence of appropriations made by law; and a regular statement and account of the receipts and expenditures of all public money shall be published from time to time.

8. No title of nobility shall be granted by the United States. And no person holding any office of profit or trust under them shall, without the consent of the Congress, accept of any present, emolument, office, or title of any kind whatever from any king, prince, or foreign state.

Section 10

1. No State shall enter into any treaty, alliance or confederation, grant letters of marque and reprisal, coin money, emit bills of credit, make anything but gold and silver coin a tender in payment of debts, pass any bill of attainder, *ex post facto* law, or law impairing the obligation of contracts, or grant any title of nobility.

2. No State shall, without the consent of the Congress, lay any impost or duties on imports or exports, except what may be absolutely necessary for executing its inspection laws, and the net produce of all duties and imposts, laid by any State on imports or exports, shall be for the use of the Treasury of the United States; and all such laws shall be subject to the revision and control of the Congress.

3. No State shall, without the consent of Congress, lay any duty of tonnage, keep troops or ships of war in time of peace, enter into agreement or compact with another State, or with a foreign power, or engage in war, unless actually invaded, or in such imminent danger as will not admit of delay.

Article II

Section 1

1. The Executive power shall be vested in a President of the United States of America. He shall hold his office during the term of four years, and, together with the Vice-President chosen for the same term, be elected as follows:

2. Each State shall appoint, in such manner as the Legislature thereof may direct, a number of electors equal to the whole number of Senators and Representatives to which the State may be entitled in the Congress; but no Senator or Representative or person holding an office of trust or profit under the United States shall be appointed an elector.

3. The electors shall meet in their respective States and vote by ballot for two persons, of whom one at least shall not be an inhabitant of the same State with themselves. And they shall make a list of all the persons voted for, and of the number of votes for each, which list they shall sign and certify and transmit, sealed, to the seat of the Government of the United States, directed to the President of the Senate. The President of the Senate shall, in the presence of the Senate and House of Representatives, open all the certificates, and the votes shall then be counted. The person having the greatest number of votes shall be the President, if such number be a majority of the whole number of electors appointed, and if there be more than one who have such a majority, and have an equal number of votes, then the House of Representatives shall immediately choose by ballot one of them for President; and if no person have a majority, then from the five highest on the list the said House shall in like manner choose the President. But in choosing the President, the vote shall be taken by States, the representation from each State having one vote. A quorum, for this purpose, shall consist of a member or members from two-thirds of the States, and a majority of all the States shall be necessary to a choice. In every case, after the choice of the President, the person having the greatest number of votes of the electors shall be the Vice-President. But if there should remain two or more who have equal votes, the Senate shall choose from them by ballot the Vice-President.*

4. The Congress may determine the time of choosing the electors and the day on which they shall give their votes, which day shall be the same throughout the United States.

5. No person except a natural born citizen, or a citizen of the United States, at the time of the adoption of the Constitution, shall be eligible to the office of President; neither shall any person be eligible to that office who shall not have attained to the age of thirty-five years and been fourteen years a resident within the United States.

6. In case of the removal of the President from office, or of his death, resignation, or inability to discharge the powers and duties of the said office, the same shall devolve on the Vice-President, and the Congress may by law provide for the case of removal, death, resignation, or inability, both of the President and Vice-President, declaring what officer shall then act as President, and such officer shall act accordingly until the disability be removed or a President shall be elected.

7. The President shall, at stated times, receive for his services a compensation which shall neither be increased nor diminished during the period for which he shall have been elected, and he shall not receive within that period any other emolument from the United States, or any of them.

8. Before he enter on the execution of his office he shall take the following oath or affirmation:

"I do solemnly swear (or affirm) that I will faithfully execute the office of President of the United States, and will, to the best of my ability, preserve, protect, and defend the Constitution of the United States."

Section 2

1. The President shall be Commander-in-Chief of the Army and Navy of the United States, and of the militia of the several States when called into the actual service of the United States; he may require the opinion, in writing, of the principal officer in each of the executive departments upon any subject relating to the duties of their respective offices, and he shall have power to grant reprieves and pardons for offences against the United States except in cases of impeachment.

2. He shall have power by and with the advice and consent of the Senate to make treaties, provided two-thirds of the Senators present concur; and he shall nominate and by

*This clause is amended by Article XII and Article XX, Amendments.

and with the advice and consent of the Senate shall appoint ambassadors, other public ministers and consuls, judges of the Supreme Court, and all other officers of the United States whose appointments are not herein otherwise provided for, and which shall be established by law; but the Congress may by law vest the appointment of such inferior officers as they think proper in the President alone, in the courts of law, or in the heads of departments.

3. The President shall have power to fill up all vacancies that may happen during the recess of the Senate by granting commissions, which shall expire at the end of their next session.

Section 3

He shall from time to time give to the Congress information of the state of the Union, and recommend to their consideration such measures as he shall judge necessary and expedient; he may, on extraordinary occasions, convene both Houses, or either of them, and in case of disagreement between them with respect to the time of adjournment, he may adjourn them to such time as he shall think proper; he shall receive ambassadors and other public ministers; he shall take care that the laws be faithfully executed, and shall commission all the officers of the United States.

Section 4

The President, Vice-President, and all civil officers of the United States shall be removed from office on impeachment for and conviction of treason, bribery or other high crimes and misdemeanours.

Article III

Section 1

The judicial power of the United States shall be vested in one Supreme Court, and in such inferior courts as the Congress may from time to time ordain and establish. The judges, both of the Supreme and inferior courts, shall hold their offices during good behaviour, and shall at stated times receive for their services a compensation which shall not be diminished during their continuance in office.

Section 2

1. The judicial power shall extend to all cases in law and equity arising under this Constitution, the laws of the United States, and treaties made, or which shall be made, under their authority; to all cases affecting ambassadors, other public ministers and consuls; to all cases of admiralty and maritime jurisdiction; to controversies to which the United States shall be a party; to controversies between two or more States, between a State and citizens of another State, between citizens of different States, between citizens of the same State claiming lands under grants of different States, and between a State, or the citizens thereof, and foreign States, citizens, or subjects.

2. In all cases affecting ambassadors, other public ministers, and consuls, and those in which a State shall be party, the Supreme Court shall have original jurisdiction. In all the other cases before mentioned the Supreme Court shall have appellate jurisdiction both as to law and fact, with such exceptions and under such regulations as the Congress shall make.

3. The trial of all crimes, except in cases of impeachment, shall be by jury, and such trials shall be held in the State where the said crimes shall have been committed; but when not committed within any State the trial shall be at such place or places as the Congress may by law have directed.

Section 3

1. Treason against the United States shall consist only in levying war against them, or in adhering to their enemies, giving them aid and comfort. No person shall be convicted of treason unless on the testimony of two witnesses to the same overt act, or on confession in open court.

2. The Congress shall have power to declare the punishment of treason, but no attainder of treason shall work corruption of blood or forfeiture except during the life of the person attained.

Article IV

Section 1

Full faith and credit shall be given in each State to the public acts, records, and judicial proceedings of every other State. And the Congress may by general laws prescribe the manner in which such acts, records, and proceedings shall be proved, and the effect thereof.

Section 2

1. The citizens of each State shall be entitled to all privileges and immunities of citizens in the several States.

2. A person charged in any State with treason, felony, or other crime, who shall flee from justice, and be found in another State, shall, on demand of the Executive authority of the State from which he fled, be delivered up, to be removed to the State having jurisdiction of the crime.

3. No person held to service or labour in one State, under the laws thereof, escaping into another shall in consequence of any law or regulation therein, be discharged from such service or labour, but shall be delivered up on claim of the party to whom such service or labour may be due.

Section 3

1. New States may be admitted by the Congress into this Union; but no new State shall be formed or erected within the jurisdiction of any other State, nor any State be formed by the junction of two or more States, or parts of States, without the consent of the Legislatures of the States concerned, as well as of the Congress.

2. The Congress shall have power to dispose of and make all needful rules and regulations respecting the territory or other property belonging to the United States; and nothing in this Constitution shall be so construed as to prejudice any claims of the United States, or of any particular State.

Section 4

The United States shall guarantee to every State in this Union a Republican form of government, and shall protect each of them against invasion, and on application of the Legislature, or of the Executive (when the Legislature cannot be convened) against domestic violence.

Article V

The Congress, whenever two-thirds of both Houses shall deem it necessary, shall propose amendments to this Constitution, or, on the application of the Legislatures of two-thirds of the several States, shall call a convention for proposing amendments, which in either case, shall be valid to all intents and purposes, as part of this Constitution, when ratified by the Legislatures of three-fourths of the several States, or by conventions in three-fourths thereof, as the one or the other mode of ratification may be proposed by the Congress, provided that no amendment which may be made prior to the year one thousand eight hundred and eight shall in any manner affect the first and fourth clauses in the Ninth Section of the First Article; and that no State, without its consent, shall be deprived of its equal suffrage in the Senate.

Article VI

1. All debts contracted and engagements entered into before the adoption of this Constitution shall be as valid against the United States under this Constitution as under the Confederation.

2. This Constitution and the laws of the United States which shall be made in pursuance thereof and all treaties made, or which shall be made, under the authority of the

United States, shall be the supreme law of the land, and the judges in every State shall be bound thereby, anything in the Constitution or laws of any State to the contrary notwithstanding.

3. The Senators and Representatives before mentioned, and the members of the several State Legislatures, and all executive and judicial officers, both of the United States and of the several States, shall be bound by oath or affirm-ation to support this Constitution; but no religious test shall ever be required as a qualification to any office or public trust under the United States.

Article VII

The ratification of the Conventions of nine States shall be sufficient for the establishment of this Constitution between the States so ratifying the same.

AMENDMENTS TO THE CONSTITUTION

Ten Original Amendments, in force December 15th, 1791

Article I

Congress shall make no law respecting an establishment of religion, or prohibiting the free exercise thereof; or abridging the freedom of speech or of the Press; or the right of the people peaceably to assemble and to petition the Government for a redress of grievances.

Article II

A well-regulated militia being necessary to the security of a free State, the right of the people to keep and bear arms shall not be infringed.

Article III

No soldier shall, in time of peace, be quartered in any house without the consent of the owner, nor in time of war but in a manner to be prescribed by law.

Article IV

The right of the people to be secure in their persons, houses, papers, and effects, against unreasonable searches and seizures, shall not be violated, and no warrants shall issue but upon probable cause, supported by oath or affirmation, and particularly describing the place to be searched, and the persons or things to be seized.

Article V

No person shall be held to answer for a capital or other infamous crime unless on a presentment or indictment of a Grand Jury, except in cases arising in the land or naval forces, or in the militia, when in actual service, in time of war or public danger; nor shall any person be subject for the same offense to be twice put in jeopardy of life or limb; nor shall be compelled in any criminal case to be a witness against himself, nor be deprived of life, liberty, or property, without due process of law; nor shall private property be taken for public use without just compensation.

Article VI

In all criminal prosecutions, the accused shall enjoy the right to a speedy and public trial, by an impartial jury of the State and district wherein the crime shall have been committed, which districts shall have been previously ascertained by law, and to be informed of the nature and cause of the accusation; to be confronted with the witnesses against him; to have compulsory process for obtaining witnesses in his favour, and to have the assistance of counsel for his defense.

Article VII

In suits at common law, where the value in controversy shall exceed twenty dollars, the right of trial by jury shall be preserved, and no fact tried by a jury shall be otherwise re-examined in any court of the United States than according to the rules of the common law.

Article VIII

Excessive bail shall not be required, nor excessive fines imposed, nor cruel and unusual punishments inflicted.

Article IX

The enumeration in the Constitution of certain rights shall not be construed to deny or disparage others retained by the people.

Article X

The powers not delegated to the United States by the Constitution, nor prohibited by it to the States, are reserved to the States respectively, or to the people.

Article XI, became part of the Constitution February 1795

The judicial power of the United States shall not be construed to extend to any suit in law or equity, commenced or prosecuted against one of the United States, by citizens of another State, or by citizens or subjects of any foreign State.

Article XII, ratified June 1804

The Electors shall meet in their respective States, and vote by ballot for President and Vice-President, one of whom at least shall not be an inhabitant of the same State with themselves; they shall name in their ballots the person voted for as President, and in distinct ballots the person voted for as Vice-President; and they shall make distinct list of all persons voted for as President, and of all persons voted for as Vice-President, and of the number of votes for each, which list they shall sign and certify, and transmit, sealed, to the seat of the Government of the United States, directed to the President of the Senate; the President of the Senate shall, in the presence of the Senate and House of Representatives, open all the certificates and the votes shall then be counted; the person having the greatest number of votes for President shall be the President, if such number be a majority of the whole number of Electors appointed; and if no person have such majority, then from the persons having the highest number, not exceeding three, on the list of those voted for as President, the House of Representatives shall choose immediately, by ballot, the President. But in choosing the President, the votes shall be taken by States, the representation from each State having one vote; a quorum for this purpose shall consist of a member or members from two-thirds of the States, and a majority of all the States shall be necessary to a choice. And if the House of Representatives shall not choose a President, whenever the right of choice shall devolve upon them, before the fourth day of March next following, then the Vice-President shall act as President, as in the case of the death or other constitutional disability of the President. The person having the greatest number of votes as Vice-President shall be the Vice-President if such number be a majority of the whole number of Electors appointed, and if no person have a majority, then, from the two highest numbers on the list the Senate shall choose the Vice-

President; a quorum for the purpose shall consist of two-thirds of the whole number of Senators, and a majority of the whole number shall be necessary to a choice. But no person constitutionally ineligible to the office of President shall be eligible to that of Vice-President of the United States.

Article XIII, ratified December 1865

1. Neither slavery nor involuntary servitude, except as a punishment for crime whereof the party shall have been duly convicted, shall exist within the United States, or any place subject to their jurisdiction.

2. Congress shall have power to enforce this article by appropriate legislation.

Article XIV, ratified July 1868

1. All persons born or naturalized in the United States, and subject to the jurisdiction thereof, are citizens of the United States and of the State wherein they reside. No State shall make or enforce any law which shall abridge the privileges or immunities of citizens of the United States, nor shall any State deprive any person of life, liberty, or property without due process of law, nor deny to any person within its jurisdiction the equal protection of the laws.

2. Representatives shall be apportioned among the several States according to their respective numbers, counting the whole number of persons in each State excluding Indians not taxed. But when the right to vote at any election for the choice of Electors for President and Vice-President of the United States, Representatives in Congress, the executive and judicial officers of a State, or the members of the Legislature thereof, is denied to any of the male inhabitants of such State, being twenty-one years of age, and citizens of the United States, or in any way abridged, except for participation in rebellion, or other crime, the basis of representation therein shall be reduced in the proportion which the number of such male citizens shall bear to the whole number of male citizens twenty-one years of age in such State.

3. No person shall be a Senator or Representative in Congress, or Elector of President and Vice-President or hold any office, civil or military, under the United States, or under any State, who, having previously taken an oath as member of Congress or as an officer of the United States, or as a member of any State Legislature, or as an executive or judicial officer of any State, to support the Constitution of the United States, shall have engaged in insurrection or rebellion against the same, or given aid and comfort to the enemies thereof. But Congress may, by a vote of two-thirds of each House, remove such disability.

4. The validity of the public debt of the United States, authorized by law, including debts incurred for payment of pensions and bounties for services in suppressing insurrection and rebellion, shall not be questioned. But neither the United States nor any State shall assume or pay any debt or obligation incurred in aid of insurrection or rebellion against the United States, or any claim for the loss or emancipation of any slave; but all such debts, obligations, and claims shall be held illegal and void.

5. The Congress shall have power to enforce by appropriate legislation the provisions of this article.

Article XV, ratified February 1870

1. The right of the citizens of the United States to vote shall not be denied or abridged by the United States or by any State on account of race, colour, or previous condition of servitude.

2. The Congress shall have power to enforce the provisions of this article by appropriate legislation.

Article XVI, ratified February 1913

The Congress shall have power to lay and collect taxes on incomes, from whatever sources derived, without apportionment among the several States, and without regard to any census or enumeration.

Article XVII, ratified April 1913

1. The Senate of the United States shall be composed of two Senators from each State, elected by the people thereof, for six years; and each Senator shall have one vote. The electors in each State shall have the qualifications requisite for electors of the most numerous branch of the State Legislature.

2. When vacancies happen in the representation of any State in the Senate, the executive authority of such State shall issue writs of election to fill such vacancies: Provided that the Legislature of any State may empower the Executive thereof to make temporary appointment until the people fill the vacancies by election as the Legislature may direct.

3. This amendment shall not be so construed as to affect the election or term of any Senator chosen before it becomes valid as part of the Constitution.

Article XVIII, ratified January 1919*

1. After one year from the ratification of this article the manufacture, sale, or transportation of intoxicating liquors within, the importation thereof into, or the exportation thereof from the United States, and all territory subject to the jurisdiction thereof for beverage purposes is hereby prohibited.

2. The Congress and the several States shall have concurrent power to enforce this article by appropriate legislation.

3. This article shall be inoperative unless it shall have been ratified as an amendment to the Constitution by the Legislatures of the several States, as provided in the Constitution, within seven years from the date of the submission hereof to the States by the Congress.

Article XIX, ratified August 1920

1. The right of citizens of the United States to vote shall not be denied or abridged by the United States or by any State on account of sex.

2. Congress shall have power, by appropriate legislation, to enforce the provisions of this article.

Article XX, ratified January 1933

Section 1

The terms of the President and Vice-President shall end at noon on the 20th day of January, and the terms of Senators and Representatives at noon on the 3rd day of January, of the years in which such terms would have ended if this article had not been ratified; and the terms of their successors shall then begin.

Section 2

The Congress shall assemble at least once in every year, and such meeting shall begin at noon on the third day of January, unless they shall by law appoint a different day.

Section 3

If, at the time fixed for the beginning of the term of the President, the President elect shall have died, the Vice-President elect shall become President. If a President shall not have been chosen before the time fixed for the beginning of his term, or if the President elect shall have failed to qualify, then the Vice-President elect shall act as President until a President shall have qualified; and the Congress may by law provide for the case wherein neither a President elect nor a Vice-President elect shall have qualified, declaring who shall then act as President, or the manner in which one who is to act shall be selected, and such person shall act accordingly until a President or Vice-President shall have qualified.

* Repealed by Article XXI.

Section 4

The Congress may by law provide for the case of the death of any of the persons from whom the House of Representatives may choose a President whenever the right of choice shall have devolved upon them, and for the case of the death of any of the persons from whom the Senate may choose a Vice-President whenever the right of choice shall have devolved upon them.

Section 5

Sections 1 and 2 shall take effect on the 15th day of October following the ratification of this article.

Section 6

This article shall be inoperative unless it shall have been ratified as an amendment to the Constitution by the legislature of three-fourths of the several States within seven years from the date of its submission.

Article XXI, ratified December 1933

Section 1

The eighteenth article of amendment to the Constitution of the United States is hereby repealed.

Section 2

The transportation or importation into any State, Territory or Possession of the United States for delivery or use therein of intoxicating liquors, in violation of the laws thereof, is hereby prohibited.

Section 3

This article shall be inoperative unless it shall have been ratified as an amendment to the Constitution by conventions in the several States, as provided in the Constitution, within seven years from the date of the submission hereof to the States by the Congress.

Article XXII, ratified February 1951

No person shall be elected to the office of President more than twice, and no person who has held the office of President, or acted as President, for more than two years of a term to which some other person was elected President shall be elected to the office of President more than once. But this article shall not apply to any person holding the office of President when this Article was proposed by Congress, and shall not prevent any person who may be holding the office of President, or acting as President, during the term within which this Article becomes operative from holding the office of President or acting as President during the remainder of such term.

Article XXIII, ratified March 1961

Section 1

The District constituting the seat of Government of the United States shall appoint in such manner as the Congress may direct:

A number of electors of President and Vice-President equal to the whole number of Senators and Representatives in Congress to which the District would be entitled if it were a State, but in no event more than the least populous State; they shall be in addition to those appointed by the States, but they shall be considered, for the purposes of the election of President and Vice-President, to be electors appointed by a State; and they shall meet in the District and perform such duties as provided by the twelfth article of amendment.

Section 2

The Congress shall have power to enforce this article by appropriate legislation.

Article XXIV, ratified January 1964

Section 1

The right of citizens of the United States to vote in any primary or other election for President or Vice-President, for electors for President or Vice-President, or for Senator or Representative in Congress, shall not be denied or abridged by the United States or any State by reason of failure to pay any poll tax or other tax.

Section 2

The Congress shall have power to enforce this article by appropriate legislation.

Article XXV, ratified February 1967

Section 1

In the case of the removal of the President from office or of his death or resignation, the Vice-President shall become President.

Section 2

Whenever there is a vacancy in the office of the Vice-President, the President shall nominate a Vice-President who shall take office upon confirmation by a majority vote of both Houses of Congress.

Section 3

Whenever the President transmits to the President *pro tempore* of the Senate and the Speaker of the House of Representatives his written declaration that he is unable to discharge the powers and duties of his office, and until he transmits to them a written declaration to the contrary, such powers and duties shall be discharged by the Vice-President as Acting President.

Section 4

Whenever the Vice-President and a majority of either the principal officers of the executive departments or of such other body as Congress may by law provide, transmit to the President *pro tempore* of the Senate and the Speaker of the House of Representatives their written declaration that the President is unable to discharge the powers and duties of his office, the Vice-President shall immediately assume the powers and duties of the office as Acting President.

Thereafter, when the President transmits to the President *pro tempore* of the Senate and the Speaker of the House of Representatives his written declaration that no inability exists, he shall resume the powers and duties of his office unless the Vice-President and a majority of either the principal officers of the executive department or of such other body as Congress may by law provide, transmit within four days to the President *pro tempore* of the Senate and the Speaker of the House of Representatives their written declaration that the President is unable to discharge the powers and duties of his office. Thereupon Congress shall decide the issue, assembling within forty-eight hours for that purpose if not in session. If the Congress, within twenty-one days after receipt of the latter written declaration, or, if Congress is not in session, within twenty-one days after Congress is required to assemble, determines by two-thirds vote of both Houses that the President is unable to discharge the powers and duties of his office, the Vice-President shall continue to discharge the same as Acting President; otherwise, the President shall resume the powers and duties of his office.

Article XXVI, ratified July 1971

Section 1

The right of citizens of the United States, who are 18 years of age or older, to vote shall not be denied or abridged by the United States or by any State on account of age.

Section 2

The Congress shall have power to enforce this article by appropriate legislation.

NOTE: *By Article IV, Section 3 of the Constitution, implemented by vote of Congress and referendum in the territory concerned, Alaska was admitted into the United States on January 3rd, 1959, and Hawaii on August 21st, 1959.*

THE EXECUTIVE

HEAD OF STATE

President: Richard Milhous Nixon (inaugurated for a second term January 20th, 1973).

Vice-President: Gerald R. Ford.

THE CABINET
(*July* 1974)

Secretary of State: Dr. Henry A. Kissinger.

Secretary of the Treasury: William E. Simon.

Secretary of Defense: James Schlesinger.

Attorney-General: William B. Saxbe.

Secretary of the Interior: Rogers C. B. Morton.

Secretary of Agriculture: Earl L. Butz.

Secretary of Commerce: Frederick B. Dent.

Secretary of Labor: Peter J. Brennan.

Secretary of Health, Education and Welfare: Caspar W. Weinberger.

Secretary of Housing and Urban Development: James T. Lynn.

Secretary of Transportation: Claude S. Brinegar.

EXECUTIVE OFFICE OF THE PRESIDENT

Executive Office Building, 17th Street and Pennsylvania Avenue, N.W., Washington, D.C.

The White House Office; 1600 Pennsylvania Avenue, Washington, D.C. 20500; detailed activities relating to the President's immediate office; the Assistants to the President are personal aides; Press Sec. Ronald L. Ziegler.

Office of Management and Budget; Dir. Roy L. Ash.

Domestic Council; members: the Cabinet; Dir. Melvin Laird.

Office of Consumer Affairs; New Executive Office Building, 17th and H Sts., N.W.; Dir. Virginia H. Knauer.

Council of Economic Advisers; Chair. Herbert Stein.

Council on International Economic Policy; Exec. Dir. Peter M. Flanigan.

National Security Council; members: The President, The Vice-President, Secretary of State, Secretary of Defense, Director of the Office of Emergency Preparedness; Special Assistant to the President for National Security Affairs Dr. Henry A. Kissinger.

Central Intelligence Agency; Washington 25; Dir. William E. Colby.

Special Action Office for Drug Abuse Prevention; 712 Jackson Place; Dir. Robert Du Pont.

National Aeronautics and Space Council; members: Secretary of State, Secretary of Defense, Administrator of NASA, Chair. Atomic Energy Commission; Exec. Sec. William A. Anders.

Office of Economic Opportunity; administers federal programmes for alleviation of poverty; Dir. Alvin J. Arnett.

Office of Emergency Preparedness; Dir. George A. Lincoln.

Office of Science and Technology; Executive Office Building; supervises development of policies for science and technology; Dir. Edward E. David, Jr.

Office of the Special Representative for Trade Negotiations; Special Representative for Trade Negotiations William D. Eberle.

Council on Environmental Quality; Chair. Russell Train.

Office of Telecommunications Policy; 1800 East St., N.W.; Dir. Clay T. Whitehead.

DEPARTMENT OF STATE

2201 C Street, N.W., Washington, D.C. 20520

Secretary of State: Dr. Henry A. Kissinger.

Deputy Secretary: Kenneth Rush.

Agency for International Development; Administrator John Hannah.

United States Mission to the United Nations; 799 U.N. Plaza, New York City, N.Y.; Representative to the United Nations and the Security Council George H. Bush.

DEPARTMENT OF DEFENSE

The Pentagon, Washington, D.C. 20301

Secretary: James Schlesinger.

Deputy Secretary: William P. Clements.

Department of the Army: Secretary Howard H. Callaway.

Department of the Navy: Secretary William Middendorf.

Department of the Air Force: Secretary John C. McLucas.

INDEPENDENT AGENCIES
(Washington unless otherwise stated)

Action: 806 Connecticut Ave., N.W., 20525; Dir. MICHAEL P. BALZANO.

Appalachian Regional Commission: 1666 Conn. Ave., N.W., 20235; Fed. Co-Chair. DONALD W. WHITEHEAD.

Atomic Energy Commission: Washington 20545; Chair. DIXY LEE RAY.

Civil Aeronautics Board: Universal Building, 1825 Connecticut Avenue, N.W., 20428; Chair. ROBERT D. TIMM.

Commission on Civil Rights: 1121 Vermont Ave., N.W., 20425; Staff Dir. JOHN A. BUGGS.

Commission of Fine Arts: 706 Jackson Place, N.W., 20006; Chair. J. CARTER BROWN.

District of Columbia: District Building, Pennsylvania Ave. and 14th St., N.W.; Chair. GILBERT HAHN.

Environmental Protection Agency: 401 M St., N.W., 20460; Admin. RUSSELL E. TRAIN.

Equal Employment Opportunity Commission: 1800 G St., N.W., 20506; Chair. WILLIAM H. BROWN, III.

Export-Import Bank of the United States: 811 Vermont Ave., N.W., 20571; Pres. and Chair. HENRY KEARNS.

Farm Credit Administration: 485 L'Enfant Plaza West, S.W., 20578; Chair. J. HOMER REMSBERG.

Federal Communications Commission (FCC): 1919 M St., N.W., 20554; Chair. DEAN BURCH.

Federal Deposit Insurance Corporation: 550 17th St., N.W., 20429; Chair. FRANK WILLE.

Federal Home Loan Bank Board: 101 Indiana Avenue, N.W., 20552; Chair. CARL O. KAMP.

Federal Maritime Commission: 1405 I St., N.W., 20573; Chair. HELEN DELICH BENTLEY.

Federal Mediation and Conciliation Service: Dept. of Labor Building, 20427; Dir. W. J. USERY.

Federal Power Commission: General Accounting Office Bldg., 441 G St., N.W., 20426; Chair. JOHN N. NASSIKAS.

Federal Reserve System: 20th St. and Constitution Ave., N.W., 20551; Chair. of Board of Governors Dr. ARTHUR F. BURNS.

Federal Trade Commission: Pennsylvania Ave. at 6th St. N.W.; Chair. LEWIS A. ENGMAN.

Foreign Claims Settlement Commission of the U.S.A.: 1111 20th St., N.W., 20579; Chair. LYLE S. GARLOCK.

General Services Administration (GSA): General Service Bldg., 18th St., N.W., 20406; Admin. ARTHUR F. SAMPSON (acting).

Indian Claims Commission: 1730 K St., N.W., 20006; Chair. JEROME K. KUYKENDAL.

Interstate Commerce Commission: 12th St. and Constitution Ave., N.W., 20423; Chair. GEORGE M. STAFFORD.

National Aeronautics and Space Administration (NASA): Washington D.C. 20546; Admin. JAMES C. FLETCHER.

National Foundation on the Arts and the Humanities: 806 15th St., N.W., 20506; Arts Chair. NANCY HANKS; Humanities Chair. RONALD S. BERMAN.

National Labor Relations Board: 1717 Pennsylvania Ave., N.W., 20570; Chair. EDWARD B. MILLER.

National Mediation Board: 1230 16th St., N.W., 20572; Chair. DAVID H. STOWE.

National Science Foundation: 1800 G. St., N.W., 20550; Dir. H. GUYFORD STEVER.

Railroad Retirement Board: 844 Rush St., Chicago 11, Ill.; Chair. JAMES L. COWEN.

Securities and Exchange Commission (SEC): 500 North Capitol St., 20549; Chair. G. BRADFORD COOK.

Selective Service System: 1724 F St., N.W., 20435; Dir. BYRON V. PEPITONE.

Small Business Administration: 1441 L St.; Admin. THOMAS S. KLEPPE.

Smithsonian Institution: Smithsonian Institution Building, 1000 Jefferson Drive, 20560; Chancellor of Board of Regents Chief Justice WARREN E. BURGER; Sec. S. DILLON RIPLEY.

Tennessee Valley Authority (TVA): New Sprankle Building, Knoxville, Tennessee 37901; Woodward Building, 15th and H Streets, N.W., 20444; Chair. AUBREY J. WAGNER.

U.S. Arms Control and Disarmament Agency: Department of State Building, Washington; Dir. FRED C. IKLE.

U.S. Civil Service Commission: 1900 East St., N.W., 20415; Chair. ROBERT E. HAMPTON.

U.S. Information Agency: 1750 Pennsylvania Ave., N.W., 20547; Dir. JAMES KEOGH.

United States Postal Service: 1200 Pennsylvania Ave., N.W., 20260; Postmaster Gen. E. T. KLASSEN.

U.S. Tariff Commission: East St., between 7th and 8th Streets, N.W., 20436; Chair. CATHERINE BEDELL.

Veteran's Administration: Vermont Ave., at H St., N.W., 20420; Admin. DONALD JOHNSON.

DIPLOMATIC REPRESENTATION

EMBASSIES ACCREDITED TO THE UNITED STATES
(In Washington)

Afghanistan: 2341 Wyoming Ave., N.W.; *Ambassador:* ABDULLAH MALIKYAR (also accred. to Argentina, Canada and Mexico).

Algeria: 2118 Kalorama Rd., N.W.; *Ambassador:* (vacant) (also accred. to Mexico).

Argentina: 1600 N. Hampshire Ave., N.W.; *Ambassador:* ALEJANDRO JOSÉ LUIS ORFILA.

Australia: 1601 Massachusetts Ave., N.W.; *Ambassador:* Sir PATRICK SHAW.

Austria: 2343 Massachussetts Ave., N.W.; *Ambassador:* ARNO HALUSA.

Bahamas: 600 New Hampshire Ave., N.W.; *Ambassador:* LIVINGSTON B. JOHNSON.

Bangladesh: 2123 California St., N.W.; *Ambassador:* M. HOSSAIN ALI.

Barbados: 2144 Wyoming Ave., N.W.; *Ambassador:* VALERIE T. McCOMIE.

Belgium: 3330 Garfield St., N.W.; *Ambassador:* WALTER LORIDAN.

Bolivia: 1145 19th St., N.W. *Ambassador:* EDMUNDO VALENCIA-IBÁÑEZ (also accred. to Canada).

Botswana: 1825 Connecticut Ave., N.W.; *Ambassador:* AMOS M. DAMBE (also accredited to Canada).

Brazil: 3006 Massachusetts Ave., N.W.; *Ambassador:* JOÃO AUGUSTO DE ARAÚJO CASTRO.

Bulgaria: 2100 16th St., N.W. (Legation); *Chargé d'Affaires:* VLADIMIR VELCHEV.

Burma: 2300 S St., N.W.; *Ambassador:* U WIN.

Burundi: 2717 Connecticut Ave., N.W.; *Ambassador:* JOSEPH NDABANIWE.

Cameroon: 2349 Massachussetts Ave., N.W.; *Ambassador:* FRANÇOIS XAVIER TCHOUNGUI.

Canada: 1746 Massachusetts Ave., N.W.; *Ambassador:* MARCEL CADIEUX.

Central African Republic: 1618 22nd St., N.W.; *Ambassador:* GASTON BANDA-BAFIOT (also accred. to Canada).

Chad: 1132 New Hampshire Ave., N.W.; *Chargé d'Affaires:* ABDELKERIM MAHAMAT.

Chile: 1736 Massachusetts Ave., N.W.; *Ambassador:* WALTER HEITMANN.

China (Taiwan): 2311 Massachusetts Ave., N.W.; *Ambassador:* JAMES SHEN.

Colombia: 2118 Leroy Place, N.W.; *Ambassador:* Dr. DOUGLAS BOTERO-BOSHELL.

Costa Rica: 2112 South St., N.W.; *Ambassador:* RODOLFO SILVA.

Cyprus: 2211 R St., N.W.; *Ambassador:* NICOS G. DIMITRIOU.

Czechoslovakia: 3900 Linnean Ave., N.W.; *Ambassador:* Dr. DUSAN SPACIL.

Dahomey: 2737 Cathedral Ave., N.W.; *Ambassador:* TIAMIOU ADJIBADE (also accred. to Canada).

Denmark: 3200 Whitehaven St., N.W.; *Ambassador:* EYVIND BARTELS.

Dominican Republic: 1715 22nd St., N.W.; *Ambassador:* S. SALVADOR ORTIZ.

Ecuador: 2535 15th St., N.W.; *Ambassador:* ALBERTO QUEVODO-TORO.

Egypt: 2310 Decatur Place, N.W., 20008; *Ambassador:* ASHRAF A. GHORBAL.

El Salvador: 2308 California St., N.W.; *Ambassador:* Dr. FRANCISCO BERTRAND GALINDO.

Ethiopia: 2134 Kalorama Rd., N.W.; *Ambassador:* KIFLE WODAJO.

Fiji: 1629 K St., N.W.; *Ambassador:* S. K. SIKIVOU.

Finland: 1900 24th St., N.W.; *Ambassador:* LEO TUOMINEN.

France: 2535 Belmont Rd., N.W.; *Ambassador:* JACQUES KOSCIUSKO-MORIZET.

Gabon: 4900, 16th St. N.W., 20011; *Ambassador:* VINCENT MAVOUNGOU.

Germany, Federal Republic: 4645 Reservoir Rd., N.W.; *Ambassador:* BERND VON STADEN.

Ghana: 2460 16th St., N.W.; *Ambassador:* HARRY R. AMONOO (also accred. to Mexico).

Greece: 2221 Massachusetts Ave., N.W.; *Ambassador:* Dr. CONSTANTINE P. PANAYOTACOS.

Guatemala: 2220 R St., N.W.; *Ambassador:* JULIO ASENSIO-WUNDERLICH (also accred. to Canada).

Guinea: 2112 Leroy Place, N.W.; *Ambassador:* SADAN MOUSSA TOURÉ (also accred. to Canada).

Guyana: 2490 Tracy Place, N.W.; *Ambassador:* FREDERICK HILBORN TALBOT

Haiti: 4400 17th St., N.W.; *Ambassador:* GERARD S. BOUCHETTE.

Honduras: 4715 16th St., N.W.; *Ambassador:* ROBERTO GALVES BARNES (also accred. to Canada).

Hungary: 2437 15th St., N.W.; *Ambassador:* KÁROLY SZABÓ.

Iceland: 2022 Connecticut Ave., N.W.; *Ambassador:* HARALDUR KROYER (also accred. to Canada, Cuba and Mexico).

India: 2107 Massachusetts Ave., N.W.; *Ambassador:* TRILOKI NATH KAUL.

Indonesia: 2020 Massachusetts Ave., N.W.; *Ambassador:* SJARIF THAJEB.

Iran: 3005 Massachusetts Ave., N.W.; *Ambassador:* ARDESHIR ZAHEDI.

Ireland: 2234 Massachusetts Ave., N.W.; *Ambassador:* JOHN G. MOLLOY.

Israel: 1621 22nd Ave., N.W.; *Ambassador:* SIMCHA DINITZ.

Italy: 1601 Fuller St., N.W.; *Ambassador:* EGIDIO ORTONA.

Ivory Coast: 2424 Massachusetts Ave., N.W.; *Ambassador:* T. N. AHOUA.

Jamaica: 1666 Connecticut Ave., N.W.; *Ambassador:* DOUGLAS V. FLETCHER.

Japan: 2520 Massachusetts Ave., N.W.; *Ambassador:* TAKESHI YASUKAWA.

Jordan: 2319 Wyoming Ave., N.W.; *Ambassador:* ABDULLAH SALAH (also accred. to Canada).

Kenya: 2249 R St., N.W.; *Ambassador:* LEONARD OLIVER KIBINGE.

Khmer Republic: 4500 16th St., N.W.; *Ambassador:* UM SIM.

Korea, Republic: 2320 Massachusetts Ave., N.W.; *Ambassador:* PYONG-CHOON HAHM.

Kuwait: 2940 Tilden St., N.W.; *Ambassador:* SALEM S. AL-SABAH (also accred. to Canada).

Laos: 2222 South St., N.W.; *Ambassador:* PHAGNA PHÈNG NORINDR.

Lebanon: 2560 28th St., N.W.; *Ambassador:* NAJATI KABBANI.

Lesotho: 1601 Connecticut Ave., N.W.; *Ambassador:* EPHRAIM TSEPA MANARE (also accred. to Canada).

Liberia: 5201 16th St., N.W.; *Ambassador:* EDWARD PEAL (also accred. to Canada).

Libya: 2344 Massachusetts Ave., N.W.; *Chargé d'Affaires:* HUSSEIN ZAGAAR.

Luxembourg: 2210 Massachusetts Ave., N.W.; *Ambassador:* JEAN WAGNER (also accred. to Canada and Mexico).

Madagascar: 2371 Massachusetts Ave., N.W.; *Ambassador:* HENRI RAHARIJAONA (also accred. to Canada and Korea Republic).

Malawi: 2362 Massachusetts Ave., N.W.; *Ambassador:* ROBERT B. MBAYA.

Malaysia: 2401 Massachusetts Ave., N.W.; *Ambassador:* MOHAMED KHIR JOHARI.

Mali: 2130 R St., N.W.; *Ambassador:* SEYDOU TRAORÉ (also accred. to Canada).

Malta: 2017 Connecticut Ave., N.W.; *Ambassador:* JOSEPH ATTARD KINGSWELL.

Mauritania: 2129 Leroy Place, N.W.; *Ambassador:* AHMEDOU OULD ABDALLAH.

Mauritius: 2308 Wyoming Ave., N.W.; *Ambassador:* PIERRE G. C. BALANCY (also accred. to Canada).

Mexico: 2829 16th St., N.W.; *Ambassador:* JOSÉ JUAN DE OLLOQUI.

Morocco: 1601 21st St., N.W.; *Ambassador:* BADDREDDINE SENOUSSI (also accred. to Mexico).

Nepal: 2131 Leroy Place, N.W.; *Ambassador:* YADU NATH KHANAL (also accred. to Canada).

Netherlands: 4200 Linnean Ave., N.W.; *Ambassador:* Baron RIJNHARD BERNHARD VAN LYNDEN.

New Zealand: 19 Observatory Circus, N.W.; *Ambassador:* LLOYD WHITE (also accred. to Argentina).

Nicaragua: 1627 New Hampshire Ave., N.W.; *Ambassador:* GUILLERMO SERVILLA-SACASA (also accred. to Canada).

Niger: 2204 R St., N.W.; *Ambassador:* ABDOULAYE DIALLO.

Nigeria: 1333 16th St., N.W.; *Ambassador:* JOHN M. GARBA.

Norway: 3401 Massachusetts Ave., N.W.; *Ambassador:* SØREN CHRISTIAN SOMMERFELT.

Oman: 2342 Massachusetts Ave., N.W.; *Ambassador:* AHMED MACKI.

Pakistan: 2315 Massachusetts Ave., N.W.; *Ambassador:* SAHABZADA YAQUB KHAN (also accred. to Mexico and Venezuela).

Panama: 2862 McGill Terrace, N.W.; *Ambassador:* NICOLAS GONZALEZ-REVILLA (also accred. to Canada).

Paraguay: 2400 Massachusetts Ave., N.W.; *Ambassador:* MIGUEL SOLANO-LÓPEZ.

Peru: 1700 Massachusetts Ave., N.W.; *Ambassador:* FERNANDO BERCKEMEYER.

Philippines: 1617 Massachusetts Ave., N.W.; *Ambassador:* EDUARDO Z. ROMUALDEZ.

Poland: 2640 16th St., N.W.; *Ambassador:* WITOLD TRAMPCZYNSKI.

Portugal: 2125 Kalorama Rd., N.W.; *Ambassador:* JOÃO MANUEL HALL THEMIDO.

Qatar: 2721 Connecticut Ave., N.W.; *Ambassador:* ABDULLAH S. AL-MANA.

Romania: 1607 23rd St., N.W.; *Ambassador:* CORNELIU BOGDAN.

Rwanda: 1714 New Hampshire Ave., N.W.; *Ambassador:* JOSEPH NIZEYIMANA.

Saudi Arabia: 1520 18th St., N.W.; *Ambassador:* IBRAHIM AL-SOWAYEL.

Senegal: 2112 Wyoming Ave., N.W.; *Ambassador:* ANDRÉ JEAN COULBARY (also accred. to Canada and Mexico).

Sierra Leone: 1701 19th St., N.W.; *Ambassador:* PHILIP J. PALMER (also accred. High Commission to Canada).

Singapore: 1824 R St., N.W.; *Ambassador:* Dr. ERNST STEVEN MONTEIRO.

Somalia: 1875 Connecticut Ave., N.W.; *Ambassador:* ADBULLAHI AHMED ADDOU.

South Africa: 3051 Massachusetts Ave., N.W.; *Ambassador:* JOHAN S. F. BOTHA.

Spain: 2700 15th St., N.W.; *Ambassador:* MANUEL FRAGA.

Sri Lanka: 2148 Wyoming Ave., N.W.; *Ambassador:* NEVILLE KANAKARATNE (also accred. to Mexico).

Sudan: 3421 Massachusetts Ave., N.W.; *Ambassador:* ABDEL AZIZ AL NASRI HAMZA (also accred. to Canada).

Swaziland: 4301 Connecticut Ave., N.W.; *Ambassador:* J. L. F. SIMELANE (also accred. to Canada).

Sweden: 600 New Hampshire Ave., N.W.; *Ambassador:* WILHELM WACHTMEISTER.

Switzerland: 2900 Cathedral Ave., N.W.; *Ambassador:* FELIX SCHNYDER.

Tanzania: 2010 Massachusetts Ave., N.W.; *Ambassador:* PAUL BOMANI.

Thailand: 2300 Kalorama Rd., N.W.; *Ambassador:* ANAND PANYARACHUN.

Togo: 2208 Massachusetts Ave., N.W.; *Ambassador:* EMPHANE AYI MAWUSSI (also accred. to Canada).

Trinidad and Tobago: 2209 Massachusetts Ave., N.W.; *Ambassador:* VICTOR McINTYRE.

Tunisia: 2408 Massachusetts Ave., N.W.; *Ambassador:* ALI HEDDA (also accred. to Mexico).

Turkey: 1606 23rd St., N.W.; *Ambassador:* MELIH ESEMBEL.

Uganda: 5909 16th St., N.W.; *Ambassador:* S. M. NSUBUGA.

U.S.S.R.: 1125 16th St., N.W.; *Ambassador:* ANATOLY F. DOBRYNIN.

United Kingdom: 3100 Massachusetts Ave., N.W.; *Ambassador:* Sir PETER RAMSBOTHAM.

Upper Volta: 5500 16th St., N.W.; *Ambassador:* TELESPHORE YAGUIBOU (also accred. to Canada).

Uruguay: 1918 F St., N.W.; *Ambassador:* Dr. HÉCTOR LUISI (also accred. to Canada).

Venezuela: 2445 Massachusetts Ave., N.W.; *Ambassador:* ANDRÉS AGUILAR.

Viet-Nam, Republic: 2251 R St., N.W.; *Ambassador:* TRAN KIM PHOUNG.

Yemen Arab Republic: 600 New Hampshire Ave., N.W.; *Ambassador:* YAHYA H. GEGHMAN.

Yugoslavia: 2410 California St., N.W.; *Ambassador:* TOMA GRANFIL.

Zaire: 1800 New Hampshire Ave., N.W.; *Ambassador:* MBEKA MAKOSSO.

Zambia: 2419 Massachusetts Ave., N.W.; *Ambassador:* SITEKE GIBSON MWALE.

The United States also has diplomatic relations with Bahrain, Bhutan, Congo (Brazzaville), Equatorial Guinea, the Gambia, Latvia (government-in-exile), Lithuania (government-in-exile), Monaco, Nauru, San Marino, Tonga, United Arab Emirates and Western Samoa.

CONGRESS

(*November* 1973)

SENATE

President: JAMES O. EASTLAND.

Democrats	57 seats	
Republicans	43 seats	

Majority Leader: MIKE MANSFIELD (Montana).

Minority Leader: HUGH SCOTT (Pennsylvania).

Senators' terms are for 6 years, one-third of the Senate being elected every two years.

MEMBERS

With party and date term expires.

Alabama

JAMES B. ALLEN	Dem.	1975
JOHN SPARKMAN	Dem.	1979

Alaska

MIKE GRAVEL	Dem.	1975
TED STEVENS	Rep.	1979

Arizona		
Barry Goldwater	Rep.	1975
Paul J. Fannin	Rep.	1977
Arkansas		
J. William Fulbright	Dem.	1975
John L. McClellan	Dem.	1979
California		
Alan Cranston	Dem.	1975
John V. Tunney	Dem.	1977
Colorado		
Peter H. Dominick	Rep.	1975
Floyd K. Haskell	Dem.	1979
Connecticut		
Abraham Ribicoff	Dem.	1975
Lowell P. Weicker	Rep.	1977
Delaware		
Joseph R. Biden, Jr.	Dem.	1979
William V. Roth	Rep.	1977
Florida		
Edward J. Gurney	Rep.	1975
Lawton Chiles	Dem.	1977
Georgia		
Herman E. Talmadge	Dem.	1975
Sam Nunn	Dem.	1979
Hawaii		
Daniel K. Inouye	Dem.	1975
Hiram L. Fong	Rep.	1977
Idaho		
Frank Church	Dem.	1975
James A. McClure	Rep.	1979
Illinois		
Adlai E. Stevenson	Dem.	1975
Charles H. Percy	Rep.	1979
Indiana		
Birch Bayh	Dem.	1975
Vance Hartke	Dem.	1977
Iowa		
Harold E. Hughes	Dem.	1975
Dick Clark	Dem.	1979
Kansas		
Robert J. Dole	Rep.	1975
James B. Pearson	Rep.	1979
Kentucky		
Marlow W. Cook	Rep.	1975
Walter Huddleston	Dem.	1979
Louisiana		
Russell B. Long	Dem.	1975
J. Bennett Johnson, Jr.	Dem.	1979
Maine		
William D. Hathaway	Dem.	1979
Edmund S. Muskie	Dem.	1977
Maryland		
C. McC. Mathias, Jr.	Rep.	1975
J. Glenn Beall	Rep.	1977
Massachusetts		
Edward W. Brooke	Rep.	1979
Edward M. Kennedy	Dem.	1977
Michigan		
Robert P. Griffin	Rep.	1979
Philip A. Hart	Dem.	1977
Minnesota		
Walter F. Mondale	Dem.	1979
Hubert Humphrey	Dem.	1977

Mississippi		
James O. Eastland	Dem.	1979
John Stennis	Dem.	1977
Missouri		
Thomas F. Eagleton	Dem.	1975
Stuart Symington	Dem.	1977
Montana		
Lee Metcalf	Dem.	1979
Mike Mansfield	Dem.	1977
Nebraska		
Carl T. Curtis	Rep.	1979
Roman L. Hruska	Rep.	1977
Nevada		
Alan Bible	Dem.	1975
Howard W. Cannon	Dem.	1977
New Hampshire		
Norris Cotton	Rep.	1975
Thomas J. McIntyre	Dem.	1979
New Jersey		
Clifford P. Case	Rep.	1979
H. A. Williams, Jr.	Dem.	1977
New Mexico		
Pete V. Domenici	Rep.	1979
Joseph M. Montoya	Dem.	1977
New York		
Jacob K. Javits	Rep.	1975
James L. Buckley	Con.	1977
North Carolina		
Sam J. Ervin, Jr.	Dem.	1975
Jesse A. Helms	Rep.	1979
North Dakota		
Milton R. Young	Rep.	1975
Quentin N. Burdick	Dem.	1977
Ohio		
William B. Saxbe	Rep.	1975
Robert Taft	Rep.	1977
Oklahoma		
Henry Bellmon	Rep.	1975
Dewey F. Bartlett	Rep.	1979
Oregon		
Robert W. Packwood	Rep.	1975
Mark O. Hatfield	Rep.	1979
Pennsylvania		
Richard S. Schweiker	Rep.	1975
Hugh Scott	Rep.	1977
Rhode Island		
Claiborne Pell	Dem.	1979
John O. Pastore	Dem.	1977
South Carolina		
Ernest F. Hollings	Dem.	1975
Strom Thurmond	Rep.	1979
South Dakota		
George McGovern	Dem.	1975
James Abourezk	Dem.	1979
Tennessee		
Howard H. Baker, Jr.	Rep.	1979
William E. Brock	Rep.	1977
Texas		
John G. Tower	Rep.	1979
Lloyd M. Bentsen	Dem.	1977
Utah		
Wallace F. Bennett	Rep.	1975
Frank E. Moss	Dem.	1977

Vermont		
George D. Aiken	Rep.	1975
Robert T. Stafford	Rep.	1977

Virginia		
William Lloyd Scott	Rep.	1979
Harry F. Byrd, Jr.	Ind.	1977

Washington		
Warren G. Magnuson	Dem.	1975
Henry M. Jackson	Dem.	1977

West Virginia		
Jennings Randolph	Dem.	1979
Robert C. Byrd	Dem.	1977

Wisconsin		
Gaylord Nelson	Dem.	1975
William Proxmire	Dem.	1977

Wyoming		
Clifford P. Hansen	Rep.	1979
Gale W. McGee	Dem.	1977

HOUSE OF REPRESENTATIVES
(June 1974)

Speaker: Carl Albert.

Democrats	245 seats
Republicans	189 seats
Independent	1 seat

Majority Leader: John McFall.
Minority Leader: John J. Rhodes.

A new House of Representatives is elected every two years.

STATE GOVERNMENTS
(November 1973)

With expiration date of Governors' current term of office.

Alabama
Governor: George Wallace; Dem.; Jan. 1975.
Lieutenant-Governor: Jere Beasley; Dem.
Senate: Dem. 33, Rep. 0.
House: Dem. 99, Rep. 2.

Alaska
Governor: William Egan; Dem.; Dec. 1974.
Lieutenant-Governor: H. A. Boucher; Dem.
Senate: Dem. 9, Rep. 11.
House: Dem. 20, Rep. 19.

Arizona
Governor: Jack Williams; Rep.; Jan. 1975.
Senate: Dem. 12, Rep. 18.
House, Dem. 22, Rep. 38.

Arkansas
Governor: Dale Bumpers; Dem.; Jan. 1975.
Lieutenant-Governor: Robert C. Riley; Dem.
Senate: Dem. 34, Rep. 1.
House: Dem. 99, Rep. 1.

California
Governor: Ronald Reagan; Rep.; Jan. 1975.
Lieutenant-Governor: Ed Reinecke; Rep.
Senate: Dem. 19, Rep. 19, 1 vacancy.
House: Dem. 50, Rep. 29.

Colorado
Governor: John A. Love; Rep.; Jan. 1975.
Lieutenant-Governor: John D. Vanderhoof; Rep.
Senate: Dem. 13, Rep. 22.
House: Dem. 28, Rep. 37.

Connecticut
Governor: Thomas J. Meskill; Rep.; Jan. 1975.
Lieutenant-Governor: T. Clark Hull; Rep.
Senate: Dem. 13, Rep. 23.
House: Dem. 53, Rep. 98.

Delaware
Governor: Sherman W. Tribbitt; Dem. Jan. 1977.
Lieutenant-Governor: Eugene D. Bookhammer; Rep.
Senate: Dem. 10, Rep. 11.
House: Dem. 20, Rep. 21.

Florida
Governor: Reubin Askew; Dem.; Jan. 1975.
Lieutenant-Governor; Tom Adams; Dem.
Senate: Dem. 25, Rep. 14.
House: Dem. 77, Rep. 43.

Georgia
Governor: Jimmy Carter; Dem.; Jan. 1975.
Lieutenant-Governor: Lester G. Maddox; Dem.
Senate: Dem. 48, Rep. 8.
House: Dem. 151, Rep. 29.

Hawaii
Governor: John A. Burns; Dem.; Dec. 1975.
Lieutenant-Governor: George R. Ariyoshi; Dem.
Senate: Dem. 17, Rep. 8.
House: Dem. 35, Rep. 16.

Idaho
Governor: Cecil D. Andrus; Dem.; Jan. 1975.
Lieutenant-Governor: Jack M. Murphy; Rep.
Senate: Dem. 12, Rep. 23.
House: Dem. 19, Rep. 51.

Illinois
Governor: Daniel Walker; Dem.; Jan. 1977.
Lieutenant-Governor: Neil F. Hartigan; Dem.
Senate: Dem. 29, Rep. 30.
House: Dem. 89, Rep. 88.

Indiana
Governor: Otis R. Bowen; Rep.; Jan. 1977.
Lieutenant-Governor: Robert D. Orr; Rep.
Senate: Dem. 21, Rep. 29.
House: Dem. 27, Rep. 73.

Iowa
Governor: Robert D. Ray; Rep.; Jan. 1975.
Lieutenant-Governor: Arthur A. Neu; Rep.
Senate: Dem. 22, Rep. 28.
House: Dem. 44, Rep. 56.

Kansas
Governor: Robert Docking; Dem.; Jan. 1975.
Lieutenant-Governor: David Owen; Rep.
Senate: Dem. 13, Rep. 27.
House: Dem. 45, Rep. 80.

Kentucky
Governor: WENDELL FORD; Dem.; Dec. 1975.
Lieutenant-Governor: JULIAN CARROLL; Dem.
Senate: Dem. 25, Rep. 11.
House: Dem. 72, Rep. 27, 1 vacancy.

Louisiana
Governor: EDWIN EDWARDS; Dem.; May 1976.
Lieutenant-Governor: JAMES E. FITZMORRIS; Dem.
Senate: Dem. 38, Rep. 1.
House: Dem. 101, Rep. 4.

Maine
Governor: KENNETH CURTIS; Dem.; Jan. 1975.
Senate: Dem. 11, Rep. 22.
House: Dem. 72, Rep. 79.

Maryland
Governor: MARVIN MANDEL; Dem.; Jan. 1975.
Lieutenant-Governor: BLAIR LEE III; Dem.
Senate: Dem. 33, Rep. 10.
House: Dem. 121, Rep. 21.

Massachusetts
Governor: FRANCIS W. SARGENT; Rep.; Jan. 1975.
Lieutenant-Governor: DONALD DWIGHT; Rep.
Senate: Dem. 33, Rep. 7.
House: Dem. 186, Rep. 52.

Michigan
Governor: WILLIAM G. MILLIKEN; Rep.; Dec. 1975.
Lieutenant-Governor: JAMES H. BRICKLEY; Rep.
Senate: Dem. 19, Rep. 19, 1 vacancy.
House: Dem. 60, Rep. 50.

Minnesota
Governor: W. R. ANDERSON; Dem.; Jan. 1975.
Lieutenant-Governor: RUDY PERPICH; Dem.
Senate: 67 non-partisan.
House: 134 non-partisan.

Mississippi
Governor: WILLIAM WALER; Dem.; Jan. 1976.
Lieutenant-Governor: WILLIAM WINTER; Dem.
Senate: Dem. 50, Rep. 2.
House: Dem. 119, Rep. 2, Independent 1.

Missouri
Governor: CHRISTOPHER BOND; Rep.; Jan. 1977.
Lieutenant-Governor: C. PHELPS; Rep.
Senate: Dem. 21, Rep. 13.
House: Dem. 97, Rep. 66.

Montana
Governor: THOMAS L. JUDGE; Dem.; Jan. 1977.
Lieutenant-Governor: WILLIAM CHRISTIANSEN; Dem.
Senate: Dem. 27, Rep. 13.
House: Dem. 54, Rep. 46.

Nebraska
Governor: J. JAMES EXON; Dem.; Jan. 1975.
Lieutenant-Governor: FRANK MARSH; Rep.
Legislature: unicameral body composed of 49 senators elected on a non-partisan ballot.

Nevada
Governor: MIKE O'CALLAGHAN; Dem.; Jan. 1975.
Lieutenant-Governor: HARRY M. REID; Dem.
Senate: Dem. 14, Rep. 6.
Assembly: Dem. 25, Rep. 15.

New Hampshire
Governor: MELDRIM THOMSON, Jr.; Rep.; Jan. 1975.
Senate: Dem. 10, Rep. 14.
House: Dem. 138, Rep. 261.

New Jersey
Governor: WILLIAM T. CAHILL; Rep.; Jan. 1974.
Senate: Dem. 16, Rep. 22.
Assembly: Dem. 67, Rep. 83.

New Mexico
Governor: BRUCE KING; Dem.; Jan. 1975.
Lieutenant-Governor: ROBERT A. MONDRAGON; Dem.
Senate: Dem. 30, Rep. 13.
House: Dem. 51, Rep. 19.

New York
Governor: NELSON A. ROCKEFELLER; Rep.; Jan. 1975.
Lieutenant-Governor: MALCOLM WILSON; Rep.
Senate: Dem., 23 Rep. 37.
Assembly: Dem. 67, Rep. 83.

North Carolina
Governor: JAMES E. HOLSHOUSER, Jr.; Rep.; Jan. 1977.
Lieutenant-Governor: JAMES B. HUNT, Jr.; Dem.
Senate: Dem. 35, Rep. 15.
House: Dem. 85, Rep. 35.

North Dakota
Governor: ARTHUR A. LINK; Dem.; Jan. 1977.
Lieutenant-Governor: WAYNE SANSTEAD; Dem.
Senate: Dem. 10, Rep. 41.
House: Dem. 23, Rep. 79.

Ohio
Governor: JOHN G. GILLIGAN; Dem.; Jan. 1975.
Lieutenant-Governor: JOHN W. BROWN; Rep.
Senate: Dem. 15, Rep. 17.
House: Dem. 58, Rep. 41.

Oklahoma
Governor: DAVID HALL; Dem.; Jan. 1975.
Lieutenant-Governor: GEORGE NIGH; Dem.
Senate: Dem. 38, Rep. 10.
House: Dem. 75, Rep. 26.

Oregon
Governor: TOM McCALL; Rep.; Jan. 1975.
Lieutenant-Governor: CLAY MYERS; Rep.
Senate: Dem. 18, Rep. 12.
House: Dem. 33, Rep. 27.

Pennsylvania
Governor: MILTON J. SHAPP; Dem.; Jan. 1975.
Lieutenant-Governor: ERNEST P. KLINE; Dem.
Senate: Dem. 25; Rep. 24.
House: Dem. 96, Rep. 106.

Rhode Island
Governor: PHILIP W. NOEL; Dem.; Jan. 1975.
Lieutenant-Governor: J. JOSEPH GARRAHY; Dem.
Senate: Dem. 37, Rep. 13.
House: Dem. 73, Rep. 27.

South Carolina
Governor: JOHN C. WEST; Dem.; Jan. 1975.
Lieutenant-Governor: EARL E. MORRIS; Dem.
Senate: Dem. 43, Rep. 3.
House: Dem. 103, Rep. 21.

South Dakota
Governor: RICHARD S. KNEIP; Dem.; Jan. 1975
Lieutenant-Governor: WILLIAM DOUGHERTY; Rep.
Senate: Dem. 18, Rep. 17.
House: Dem. 35, Rep. 35.

Tennessee
Governor: WINFIELD DUNN; Dem.; Jan. 1975.
Senate: Dem. 19, Rep. 13, American Party 1.
House: Dem. 51, Rep. 48.

Texas
Governor: DOLPH BRISCOE; Dem.; Jan. 1975.
Lieutenant-Governor: WILLIAM P. HOBBY; Dem.
Senate: Dem. 28, Rep. 3.
House: Dem. 133, Rep. 17.

Utah
Governor: CALVIN L. RAMPTON; Dem.; Jan. 1977.
Lieutenant-Governor: CLYDE L. MILLER.
Senate: Dem. 13, Rep. 16.
House: Dem. 31, Rep. 44, Independent 1.

Vermont
Governor: THOMAS P. SALMON; Dem.; Jan. 1975.
Lieutenant-Governor: JOHN S. BURGESS; Rep.
Senate: Dem. 8, Rep. 22.
House: Dem. 60, Rep. 89.

Virginia
Governor: LINWOOD HOLTON; Rep.; Jan. 1974.
Lieutenant-Governor: HENRY E. HOWELL, Jr., Ind.
Senate: Dem. 33, Rep. 7.
House: Dem. 71, Rep. 25, Independent 1.

Washington
Governor: DANIEL J. EVANS; Rep.; Jan. 1977.
Lieutenant-Governor: JOHN A. CHERBERG; Dem.
Senate: Dem. 30, Rep. 19.
House: Dem. 57, Rep. 41.

West Virginia
Governor: ARCH A. MOORE, Jr.; Rep.; Jan. 1977.
Senate: Dem. 24, Rep. 10.
House: Dem. 57, Rep. 43.

Wisconsin
Governor: PATRICK J. LUCEY; Dem.; Jan. 1975.
Lieutenant-Governor: MARTIN J. SCHREIBER.
Senate: Dem. 15, Rep. 18.
Assembly: Dem. 62, Rep. 37.

Wyoming
Governor: STANLEY K. HATHAWAY; Rep.; Jan. 1975.
Senate: Dem. 13, Rep. 17.
House: Dem. 17, Rep. 44, Independent 1.

POLITICAL PARTIES AND GROUPS

Republican National Committee: f. 1854; 310 First St., S.E., Washington, D.C. 20003.
Chairman: GEORGE BUSH.
Co-Chairman: Miss JANET J. JOHNSTON.
Vice-Chairmen: RAY C. BLISS, Mrs. HOPE McCORMICK, BERNARD M. SHANLEY, R. J. SHAW, Mrs. PAULA F. HAWKINS, GEORGE P. STADELMAN, Mrs. ISABEL C. MOBERLY, Mrs. J. W. MARRIOTT.
Secretary: Mrs. JACK L. STACY.
Treasurer: JOHN M. CHRISTIE.
General Counsel: HARRY S. DENT.

Democratic National Committee: 1625 Massachussetts Ave., N.W., Washington, D.C. 20036.
Chairman: ROBERT S. STRAUSS.
Vice-Chairmen: BASIL PATERSON, CAROLINE WILLIAMS.
Secretary: Mrs. DOROTHY VREDENBURGH BUSH.
Treasurer: C. PETER McCOLOUGH.

Prohibition National Committee: f. 1869; P.O.B. 2635 Denver, Colorado.
National Chairman: CHARLES WESLEY EWING.
Executive Secretary: EARL F. DODGE.
National Secretary: ROGER C. STORMS.
America's oldest minor party; publ. *The National Statesman.*

Social Democrats, U.S.A.: f. 1901; 1182 Broadway, New York, N.Y. 10001.
Co-Chairmen BAYARD RUSTIN, CHARLES S. ZIMMERMAN.
National Secretary: JOAN SUALL.
Claims local groups in 22 States. Name changed from Socialist Party 1972.
Publication *New America* (2 a month).

Greenback Party: f. 1872; 1522 Northwest 58th Street, Seattle, Wash. 98107.
National Chairman: FRED C. PROEHL.
Advocates monetary reform and opposes the Federal Reserve System.

Socialist Labor Party of America: f. 1890; 116 Nassau St., Brooklyn, N.Y. 11201.
National and Financial Secretary: NATHAN KARP.
Claims local organizations in 18 States.
Publications *Weekly People, New York Labor News.*

Socialist Workers Party: 14 Charles Lane, New York, N.Y. 10014.
National Chairman Emeritus: JAMES P. CANNON.
National Secretary: JACK W. BARNES.
Organization Secretary: BARRY F. SHEPPARD.

Communist Party (Marxist-Leninist): f. 1965; P.O.B. 72116, Watts Station, Los Angeles, Calif. 90002.
Representative: MICHAEL LASKI.
Formerly Communist Party of the U.S.A.; 2,500 mems. claimed (1970).

Conservative Party of the State of New York: 468 Park Ave. South, New York, N.Y. 10016.
Chairman: J. D. MAHONEY.
Secretary: HENRY S. JORIN, Jr.
Executive Director: SERPHIN R. MALTESE.

Liberal Party of New York State: f. 1944; 1560 Broadway, New York, N.Y. 10036.
Chairman: Dr. DONALD S. HARRINGTON.
First Vice-Chairman: DAVID DUBINSKY.
Vice-Chairmen: ALEX ROSE, TIMOTHY W. COSTELLO, BENJAMIN F. McLAURIN, FILENO DE NOVELLIS, LOUIS BROIDO, EDWARD A. MORRISON, HENRY FONER, WILLIAM W. COWAN, VICTOR A. LORD, LAWRENCE WRIGHT, JACOB LOFT, SYLVIA BLOOM, EUGENE P. KLUMPP.
Secretary and Exec. Director: BEN DAVIDSON.
Assistant Secretary: JOSEPHINE L. GAMBINO.

Americans for Democratic Action: 1424 16th St., N.W., Washington, D.C. 20036.
National Chairman: DONALD M. FRASER.
Chairman Executive Committee: CUSHING DOLBEARE.
National Director: LEON SHULL.

Committee on Political Education, AFL-CIO: AFL-CIO Building, Washington, D.C. 20006.
Chairman: GEORGE MEANY.
Secretary-Treasurer: LANE KIRKLAND.
National Director: ALEXANDER E. BARKAN.

National States' Rights Party: f. 1948; P.O.B. 1211, Marietta, Georgia 30061.
Chairman: J. B. STONER.
Secretary: EDWARD R. FIELDS.
Treasurer: PETER XAVIER.
Publication *The Thunderbolt* (monthly).
Right-wing, racist, anti-Communist party, 13,000 mems.

John Birch Society: f. 1958; 395 Concord Ave., Belmont, Mass. 02178.
President: ROBERT WELCH.
Claimed membership 100,000 (1968).
Publications *American Opinion* (monthly), *The Review of the News* (weekly).

JUDICIAL SYSTEM

Each State has a judicial system similar to the Federal system listed below, with a Supreme Court and subsidiary courts, to deal with cases arising under State Law.

SUPREME COURT OF THE UNITED STATES

(Washington, D.C. 20543)

The Supreme Court is the only Federal Court set up by the Constitution. It is the highest court in the nation. Since 1869 the Supreme Court has consisted of the Chief Justice and eight Associate Justices.

Chief Justice: WARREN E. BURGER (appointed 1969).

Associate Justices: WILLIAM O. DOUGLAS (1939), WILLIAM J. BRENNAN, Jr. (1956), POTTER STEWART (1958), BYRON R. WHITE (1962), THURGOOD MARSHALL (1967), HARRY A. BLACKMUN (1970), LEWIS F. POWELL, Jr. (1972), WILLIAM H. REHNQUIST (1972).

Clerk: MICHAEL RODAK, Jr.

Marshal: FRANK M. HEPLER.

Reporter of Decisions: HENRY PUTZEL, Jr.

Librarian: H. CHARLES HALLAM, Jr.

U.S. COURTS OF APPEAL

The country is divided into ten judicial circuits, in each of which there is one Court of Appeals and a number of District Courts (which total ninety-two).

There is also a U.S. Court of Appeals in the District of Columbia, which is regarded as a judicial circuit. By statute, most Federal suits must first be tried in the District Courts.

District of Columbia Circuit: DAVID L. BAZELON (Chief Judge); J. SKELLY WRIGHT, CARL McGOWAN, EDWARD ALLEN TAMM, HAROLD LEVENTHAL, SPOTTSWOOD W. ROBINSON III, ROGER ROBB, GEORGE E. MacKINNON, MALCOLM R. WILKEY.

First Circuit (Maine, Massachusetts, New Hampshire, Rhode Island, Puerto Rico); FRANK M. COFFIN (Chief Judge), EDWARD M. McENTEE, LEVIN H. CAMPBELL.

Second Circuit (Connecticut, New York, Vermont); HENRY J. FRIENDLY (Chief Judge), IRVING R. KAUFMAN, PAUL R. HAYS, WILFRID FEINBERG, WALTER R. MANSFIELD, WILLIAM H. MULLIGAN, JAMES L. OAKES, WILLIAM H. TIMBERS.

Third Circuit (Delaware, New Jersey, Pennsylvania, Virgin Islands): COLLINS J. SEITZ (Chief Judge), RUGGERO J. ALDISERT, FRANCIS L. van DUSEN, ARLIN M. ADAMS, JOHN J. GIBBONS, MAX ROSENN, JAMES ROSEN, JAMES HUNTER III, JOSEPH F. WEIS.

Fourth Circuit (Maryland, North Carolina, South Carolina, Virginia, West Virginia); CLEMENT F. HAYNSWORTH, Jr. (Chief Judge); HERBERT S. BOREMAN, JOHN D. BUTZNER, Jr., HARRISON L. WINTER, J. BRAXTON CRAVEN, Jr., DONALD RUSSELL, JOHN A. FIELD, Jr., H. EMORY WIDENER.

Fifth Circuit (Alabama, Florida, Georgia, Louisiana, Mississippi, Texas, Canal Zone): JOHN R. BROWN (Chief Judge), JOHN GODBOLD, ROBERT A. AINSWORTH, Jr., JOHN MINOR WISDOM, WALTER PETTUS GEWIN, GRIFFIN B. BELL, HOMER THORNBERRY, JAMES P. COLEMAN, IRVING L. GOLDBERG, DAVID W. DYER, BRYAN SIMPSON, LEWIS R. MORGAN, CHARLES CLARK. JOE McDONALD INGRAHAM, PAUL H. RONEY.

Sixth Circuit (Kentucky, Michigan, Ohio, Tennessee): HARRY PHILLIPS (Chief Judge), JOHN W. PECK, WADE HAMPTON McCREE, PAUL C. WEICK, GEORGE CLIFTON EDWARDS, Jr., ANTHONY J. CELEBREZZE, WILLIAM E. MILLER, W. WALLACE KENT, PIERCE LIVELY.

Seventh Circuit (Illinois, Indiana, Wisconsin); LUTHER SWYGERT (Chief Judge), WALTER J. CUMMINGS, Jr., THOMAS E. FAIRCHILD, OTTO KERNER, ROGER J. KILEY, WILBUR F. PELL, JOHN PAUL STEPHENS, ROBERT A. SPRECHER.

Eighth Circuit (Arkansas, Iowa, Minnesota, Missouri, Nebraska, North Dakota, South Dakota): M. C. MATTHES (Chief Judge), PAT MEHAFFY, FLOYD R. GIBSON, DONALD P. LAY, GERALD W. HEANEY, MYRON H. BRIGHT, DONALD R. ROSS, ROY L. STEPHENSON.

Ninth Circuit (Arizona, California, Idaho, Montana, Nevada, Oregon, Washington, Alaska, Hawaii, Guam): RICHARD H. CHAMBERS (Chief Judge), CHARLES M. MERRILL, M. OLIVER KOELSCH, JAMES R. BROWNING, BEN CUSHING DUNIWAY, WALTER ELY, SHIRLEY M. HUFSTEDLER, EUGENE A. WRIGHT, OZELL M. TRASK, HERBERT Y. C. CHOY, J. CLIFFORD WALLACE, ALFRED T. GOODWIN.

Tenth Circuit (Colorado, Kansas, New Mexico, Oklahoma, Utah, Wyoming): DAVID T. LEWIS (Chief Judge), DELMAS C. HILL, OLIVER SETH, WILLIAM J. HOLLOWAY, Jr., ROBERT H. McWILLIAMS, JAMES E. BARRETT, WILLIAM E. DOYLE.

U.S. COURT OF CLAIMS

(717 Madison Place, N.W., Washington, D.C. 20005)

Set up in 1855; deals exclusively with money claims against the Government; holds one term annually, commencing on the first Monday in October.

Chief Judge: WILSON COWEN, Maryland.

Associate Judges: OSCAR H. DAVIS, BYRON SKELTON, PHILIP NICHOLS, Jr., SHIRO KASHIWA, ROBERT L. KUNZIG, MARION T. BENNETT.

Senior Judges: MARVIN JONES, Texas, J. WARREN MADDEN, Pennsylvania.

U.S. CUSTOMS COURT

(1 Federal Plaza, New York, N.Y. 10007)

Chief Judge: NILS A. BOE, South Dakota.

Judges: MORGAN FORD, North Dakota; SCOVEL RICHARDSON, Missouri; FREDERICK LANDIS (Indiana); JAMES L. WATSON, New York; HERBERT N. MALETZ, Massachusetts; BERNARD NEWMAN, New York; EDWARD D. RE, New York, PAUL P. RAO.

Senior Judges: CHARLES D. LAWRENCE, New York; DAVID J. WILSON, Utah; MARY H. DONLON, New York; SAMUEL M. ROSENSTEIN, Kentucky.

COURT OF CUSTOMS AND PATENT APPEALS

(Courts Bldg., Lafayette Square, Washington, D.C. 20439)

Chief Judge: HOWARD T. MARKEY.

Associate Judges: GILES S. RICH, New York; J. LINDSAY ALMOND, Jr., Virginia; PHILLIP B. BALDWIN, Texas; DONALD E. LANE, Maryland.

TAX COURT OF THE UNITED STATES

(12th Street and Constitution Ave., N.W., Washington, D.C. 20044)

Chief Judge: WILLIAM M. DRENNEN, West Virginia.

Judges: HOWARD A. DAWSON, Jr., WILLIAM M. FAY, BRUCE M. FORRESTER, AUSTIN HOYT, IRENE F. SCOTT, ARNOLD RAUM, WILLIAM A. GOFFE, CHARLES R. SIMPSON, THEODORE TANNENWALD, Jr., C. MOXLEY FEATHERSTON, LEO H. IRWIN, SAMUEL B. STERRETT, WILLIAM QUEALY, CYNTHIA H. HALL, DARRELL D. WILES.

RELIGION

RELIGIOUS DENOMINATIONS

There is no standard definition of membership and some statistics are accurately calculated whereas others are estimates; care should therefore be taken in making comparisons.

ADHERENTS (1973)

Protestant Bodies	71,713,000
Roman Catholic Church	48,390,990
Jewish Congregations	5,450,000
Eastern Churches	4,112,623
Old Catholic, Polish National Catholic and Armenian	646,000
Buddhists	100,000

PROTESTANT AND EASTERN ORTHODOX

National Council of the Churches of Christ in the United States of America: National Offices: 475 Riverside Drive, New York, N.Y. 10027.

A co-operative agency of 32 Protestant and Eastern Orthodox denominations with a constituency of 42 million members which carries on more than 80 interdenominational programmes. It is supervised and governed by a Governing Board of 266 members which meets twice yearly over a triennium. Members of the Governing Board are responsible for the policies and programmes of the Council and are appointed by the constituent denominations.

The work of the National Council is carried out through the three main Divisions: Church and Society, Education and Ministry and Overseas Ministries. Other major subdivisions are Commissions: Broadcasting and Film, Faith and Order, Regional and Local Ecumenism and Stewardship. Programmes include world relief, resettlement of refugees, overseas ministries and work in various areas relating to social justice and international affairs.

President Rev. W. STERLING CARY (United Church of Christ); First Vice-President Mrs. VICTOR BALTZELL (Christian Church, Disciples of Christ); Second Vice-President Most Rev. Archbishop TORKOM MANOOGIAN (Armenian Church of North America); Third Vice-President Rev. EUNICE SANTANA VELEZ (Christian Church, Disciples of Christ); Treas. CARL W. TILLER (American Baptist Churches in the U.S.A.); Gen. Sec. Dr. R. H. EDWIN ESPY; Recording Sec. Rev. JOHN S. GROENFELDT (Moravian Church in America).

Publs. *Tempo* (newsletter), *Spectrum* (quarterly), *Yearbook of American and Canadian Churches*.

BAPTISTS

Members (latest estimate) 26,315,235, in 21 bodies of which the following have over one million members:

Southern Baptist Convention: 460 James Robertson Parkway, Nashville, Tennessee 37219; f. 1845; 34,441 churches; 11,826,463 members; Exec. Sec. Dr. PORTER ROUTH.

National Baptist Convention of the U.S.A.: 915 Spain Street, Baton Rouge, La. 70802; f. 1880; 27,396 churches; 6,487,003 members; Pres. Rev. J. H. JACKSON; Sec. Rev. T. J. JEMISON.

National Baptist Convention of America: 1058 Hogan St., Jacksonville, Fla. 32202; f. 1880; 11,398 churches; 2,668,799 members; Pres. Dr. C. D. PETTAWAY; Corr. Sec. Rev. ROBERT H. WILSON.

American Baptist Churches in the U.S.A.: Valley Forge, Pa. 19481; f. 1907; 6,029 churches; 1,562,740 members; Pres. Rev. Dr. GENE E. BARTLETT; Gen. Sec. Rev. Dr. ROBERT C. CAMPBELL.

METHODISTS

Members (latest estimate) 12,930,573, in 13 bodies of which the following have the greatest number of members:

The United Methodist Church: 1100 W. 42nd St., Indianapolis, Ind. 46208; f. 1784; 39,626 churches; 10,334,521 members; Council of Bishops; Pres. Bishop CHARLES F. GOLDEN; Sec. Bishop RALPH T. ALTON.

African Methodist Episcopal Church: 2843 Princess Ann Rd., Norfolk, Va. 23540; f. 1816; 4,500 churches, 940,000 mems.; Bishops' Council; Pres. Bishop JOSEPH D. CAUTHEN; Gen. Sec. Dr. RUSSELL S. BROWN.

African Methodist Episcopal Zion Church: 741 South 44th St., Louisville, Ky. 40211; f. 1796; 1,035,421 mems.; Senior Bishop HERBERT SHAW.

LUTHERANS

Members (latest estimate) 8,833,232 in 7 bodies of which the following have over one million members:

Lutheran Church in America: 231 Madison Ave., N.Y. 10016; f. 1962; 3,023,219 members; Pres. Rev. ROBERT J. MARSHALL, D.D.; Sec. Rev. GEORGE F. HARKINS, D.D.

Lutheran Church: Missouri Synod; 500 No. Broadway, St. Louis, Mo. 63102; f. 1847; 5,886 churches; 2,886,207 members; Pres. Dr. J. A. O. PREUS; Sec. Dr. HERBERT MUELLER.

American Lutheran Church, The: 422 So. Fifth St., Minneapolis, Minn. 55415; f. 1961; Pres. Rev. Dr. DAVID PREUS; Sec. A. R. MICKELSON; 2,491,590 members.

U.S.A. National Committee of the Lutheran World Federation: 315 Park Ave. South, New York, N.Y. 10010; f. 1967 to succeed *National Lutheran Council*; an agency of the American Lutheran Church and the Lutheran Church in America for work relating to the Lutheran World Federation; Pres. LUVERN V. RIEKE; Gen. Sec. Dr. CARL H. MAU, Jr.

PRESBYTERIANS

Members (latest estimate) 4,134,806 in 7 bodies.

United Presbyterian Church in the U.S.A.: 475 Riverside Drive, New York, N.Y. 10027; f. 1958; 8,813 churches; 3,029,369 members; Moderator CLINTON M. MARSH; Ruling Elder WILLIAM P. THOMPSON.

Presbyterian Church in the U.S.: 341 Ponce de Leon Ave., N.E., Atlanta, Georgia 30308; 4,284 churches, 951,788 members; Moderator Rev. L. NELSON BELL; Stated Clerk Dr. JAMES A. MILLARD, Jr.

PROTESTANT EPISCOPAL CHURCH

Members (latest figures available) 3,385,436 in 7,506 churches.

815 Second Ave., New York, N.Y. 10017; f. 1789; Presiding Bishop and Pres. of the Executive Council Rt. Rev. JOHN ELBRIDGE HINES; Sec. of the General Convention Rev. Canon CHARLES M. GUILBERT.

EASTERN ORTHODOX CHURCHES

Members (latest estimate) 4,111,600 in 18 bodies. Leading Orthodox Churches:

Greek Orthodox Church of North and South America: 10 East 79th St., New York, N.Y. 10021; 490 churches, with 1,950,000 members; Primate The Most Rev. Archbishop IAKOVOS.

Romanian Orthodox Episcopate of America: 2522 Grey Tower Rd., Jackson, Mich. 49201; f. 1929; 50,000 members; Bishop His Grace VALERIAN D. TRIFA; Sec. Rev. Fr. EUGENE LAZAR.

Orthodox Church in America: 59 East and 2nd Street, New York, N.Y. 10003; f. 1794; 370 parishes; 80 missions; 1,000,000 members; His Beatitude, Metropolitan IRENEY Archbishop of New York, Metropolitan of All America and Canada.

ROMAN CATHOLIC CHURCH

There are 32 archbishoprics in the U.S.A. and 133 dioceses; 18,244 parishes, 48,390,990 members.

Apostolic Delegate to the United States: 3339 Massachusetts Ave., Washington 20008, D.C.

Cardinals

LEO C. BYRNE (St. Paul, Minn.), JOHN J. CARBERRY (St. Louis), JOHN PATRICK CODY (Chicago), TERENCE JAMES COOKE (New York), JOHN JOSEPH KROL (Philadelphia), LAWRENCE JOSEPH SHEHAN (Baltimore).

OTHER CHRISTIAN CHURCHES

Seventh-Day Adventists: 6840 Eastern Ave., N.W. Takoma Park, Washington, D.C. 20012; org. 1863; 3,278 churches, 448,888 mems. (worldwide); Pres. ROBERT H. PIERSON; Sec. C. O. FRANZ.

Assemblies of God: 1445 Boonville Ave., Springfield, Mo. 65802; f. 1914; 8,871 churches, 700,071 mems.; Gen. Supt. T. F. ZIMMERMAN; Gen. Sec. B. PETERSON.

Christian Churches, International Convention of Disciples of Christ: 222 South Downey Ave., Indianapolis, Ind.; f. 1809; 4,569 churches, 1,352,211 mems.; Moderator Dr. JAMES M. MOUDY; Pres. Dr. A. DALE FIERS.

Church of Christ, Scientist, The First (The Mother Church): Christian Science Center, Boston, Mass. 02115; f. 1879; approx. 2,369 churches; Pres. ROY GARRETT WATSON.

Church of Jesus Christ of Latter-Day Saints: 47 East S. Temple St., Salt Lake City, Utah 84111; f. 1830; Church membership of over 3,000,000; 5,394 wards (an ecclesiastical unit similar to a parish) and independent branches, and 101 missions in various parts of the world; Pres. SPENCER W. KIMBALL; Presiding Bishop VICTOR L. BROWN.

Friends, General Conference of the Religious Society of: 1520 Race St., Philadelphia, Pa. 19102; f. 1900; 32,124 mems.; Chair. C. LLOYD BAILEY; Sec. HOWARD W. BARTRAM.

Jehovah's Witnesses: 124 Columbia Heights, Brooklyn, New York, N.Y. 11201; f. 1884; 431,179 mems.; Pres. N. H. KNORR.

Moravian, Northern Province: 69 W. Church St., Bethlehem. Pa. 18018; f. 1740; 99 churches, 34,044 mems.; Pres. Dr. J. S. GROENFELDT, D.D.

Moravian Church, Southern Province: Drawer O, Salem Station, Winston-Salem, N.C. 27108; f. 1753; 49 churches, 22,784 mems.; Pres. Dr. CLAYTON H. PERSONS; Sec.-Treas. RONALD R. HENDRIX.

Nazarene, Church of the: 6401 The Paseo, Kansas City, Mo. 64131; f. 1908; 4,681 churches, 404,732 mems.; Gen. Sec. B. EDGAR JOHNSON; Gen. Treas. NORMAN O. MILLER.

Reformed Church in America, General Synod of: 475 Riverside Drive, New York, N.Y. 10027; f. 1628; 939 churches, 375,546 mems.; Gen. Sec. Rev. MARION DE VELDER, D.D.

Salvation Army, The: 120–130 West 14th St., New York, N.Y. 10011; estab. in U.S.A. 1880; 335,684 mems.; U.S. Nat. Commander, Commissioner PAUL J. CARLSON; Nat. Chief Sec. Col. ERNEST W. HOLZ.

United Church of Christ: 297 Park Ave., South, New York City, N.Y. 10010; f. 1957; 6,635 churches, 1,895,016 mems.; Moderator Rev. DAVID G. COLWELL; Pres. Rev. ROBERT V. MOSS; Sec. Rev. JOSEPH H. EVANS.

JEWISH ORGANIZATIONS

There are an estimated 5,450,000 Jews in the U.S.A.

Synagogue Council of America, The: 235 Fifth Avenue, New York, N.Y. 10016; f. 1926; represents Orthodox, Conservative and Reform Judaism; its constituent members are the Central Conference of American Rabbis, the Rabbinical Assembly of America, the Rabbinical Council of America, the Union of American Hebrew Congregations, the United Synagogue of America, and the Union of Orthodox Jewish Congregations in America; Pres. Rabbi HENRY SIEGMAN; Exec. Vice-Pres. Rabbi HENRY SIEGMAN; Recording Sec. ROBERT L. ADLER; National Sec. Hon. HERBERT TANZER; Treas. MEYER H. ROBINSON; publ. *Highlights* (bimonthly).

Rabbis, Central Conference of American: 790 Madison Ave., New York, N.Y. 10021; f. 1889; Pres. Rabbi DAVID POLISH; Exec. Vice-Pres. Rabbi JOSEPH B. GLAZER; 1,100 mems.; publs. *Yearbook, CCAR Journal.*

Rabbinical Assembly, The: 3080 Broadway, New York, N.Y. 10027; f. 1901; Pres. Rabbi JUDAH NADICH; Exec. Vice-Pres. Rabbi WOLFE KELMAN; 1,050 mems.; publs. include *Quarterly Journal, Annual Proceedings.*

Hebrew Congregations, Union of American: 838 Fifth Ave., New York, N.Y. 10021; f. 1873; 1,000,000 mems.; Pres. Rabbi MAURICE N. EISENDRATH; Vice-Pres. Rabbi ALEXANDER M. SCHINDFLER; 710 congregations; publs. *Keeping Posted* (monthly); *Compass* (quarterly); *Reform Judatsm* (monthly).

United Synagogue of America: 3080 Broadway, New York, N.Y. 10027; f. 1913; Pres. JACOB STEIN; Exec. Dir. Dr. BERNARD SEGAL; 800 Conservative synagogues, 1,400,000 mems.; Publ. *United Synagogue Review* (quarterly).

Union of Orthodox Jewish Congregations of America: 116 East 27th St., New York, N.Y. 10016; f. 1898; Pres. HAROLD M. JACOBS; National Dir. Rabbi DAVID COHEN; publs. *Jewish Life* (quarterly), *Jewish Action* (monthly), *Reporter* (monthly), *Jewish Youth* (two-monthly); representing 3,100 orthodox congregations.

BAHA'I

National Spiritual Assembly of the Bahá'ís of the United States: 536 Sheridan Rd., Wilmette, Ill. 60091; f. 1844 in Persia; Bahá'u'lláh was the prophet-founder of Bahá'i Faith, which teaches the oneness of God, of religion and of mankind; over 14,100 assemblies in the U.S.A.; Chair. Dr. FIRUZ KAZEMZADEH; Vice-Chair. Dr. DANIEL JORDAN; Sec. Mr. GLENFORD E. MITCHELL; publs. *Bahá'i News* (monthly), *World Order* (quarterly magazine), *American Bahá'i* (monthly), *National Bahá'i Review* (monthly), *World Order Magazine* (quarterly).

THE PRESS

The U.S. publishes more newspapers and periodicals than any other country. Most dailies give a greater emphasis to local news because of the strong interest in local and regional affairs and the decentralized structure of many government services. These factors, together with the distribution problem inherent in the size of the country, are responsible for the lack of national newspapers. Almost every small town has its own paper.

In September 1972, there were 1,728 English language daily newspapers (322 morning, 1,378 evening and 15 "all day") with a combined circulation of 62,353,381 copies per issue. The Sunday press is an important and distinctive feature of U.S. newspaper publishing; many Sunday newspapers run to over a 100 pages. In 1972, there were 585 Sunday newspapers with a total circulation of 50,391,861.

The famous tradition of press freedom in the U.S. is grounded in the First Amendment to the Constitution which declares that "Congress shall make no law ... abridging the freedom of speech or of the Press ..." and confirmed in the legislations of many states which prohibit any kind of legal restriction on the dissemination of news.

Legislation affecting the Press is both state and federal. A source of controversy between the Press and the courts has been the threat of the encroachment by judicial decrees on the area of courtroom and criminal trial coverage. Since 1963 an average of 35 per cent of congressional committee meetings in Washington have been held in secret. In July 1972 the Supreme Court ruled that journalists were not entitled to refuse to give evidence before grand juries on information they have received confidentially. Since then the frequent issuing of subpoenas to journalists and the jailing of several reporters for refusing to disclose sources has led to many "shield" bills being put before Congress calling for immunity for journalists from both federal and state jurisdiction.

In recent years, increased prices and the competition of radio and television have subjected the industry to considerable economic strain, resulting in mergers and take-overs, a great decline in competition between dailies in the same city, and the appearance of inter-city dailies catering for two or more adjoining centres. Suburban dailies have thrived at the expense of the large city dailies, the largest being *Newsday*, the New York State newspaper.

The aggregate circulation of the **9,573** periodicals is approximately **210** million. Some 100 of them have a national readership.

All newspapers subscribe to the Associated Press (AP) co-operative news agency, the United Press International (UPI), or the Los Angeles Times-Washington Post News Service, which, while giving access to a large quantity of news, limit the variety of presentation.

One consequence of modern economic trends has been the steady growth of newspaper groups or chains, of which there are some 163 controlling some 750 dailies. This figure represents an increase of twenty groups since 1962 when 188 of the group-owned dailies had an aggregate circulation of 27.4 million, or just less than half of the total for all dailies. The six largest groups are the following:

Newhouse Newspapers Group (Pres. SAMUEL NEWHOUSE): 1 Star Square, Long Island City, Queens, N.Y. 11101; owns twenty-one newspapers, six of them in New York. The main dailies include *Cleveland Plain Dealer* (407,916), *Long Island Daily Press* (418,028), and *St. Louis Globe Democrat* (291,074), the total circulation being over 6 million; also two large magazine chains, one French and one Italian magazine.

Scripps-Howard Newspapers Group (Pres. JACK R. HOWARD; Chair of Board CHARLES E. SCRIPPS): owns sixteen dailies, including *Cleveland Press* (382,687), and *Pittsburg Press* (292,288).

Hearst Newspapers Group (Editor-in-Chief WILLIAM RANDOLPH HEARST, Jr.): owns eight dailies, including *Los Angeles Herald Examiner* (474,020), and *Boston Record American* (369,873); two Sunday papers, including *Boston Sunday Advertiser*, and thirteen magazines, three of which are in the U.K.; a large comics syndicate.

Tribune Company Group (Pres. of Tribune Co. H. F. GRUMHAUS): owns seven dailies, including *Chicago Tribune* (735,734), *Chicago Today* (441,775) and *New York News* (2,092,603).

Other major newspaper groups are *Knight Newspapers, Gannett Newspapers* and *Ridder Publications.*

Time-Life Group (Pres. JAMES A. LINEN): the largest of the magazine chains, and includes *Time* (U.S. edition 4,341,978), *Sports Illustrated* (2,201,222), *Fortune* (583,897).

Times Mirror Co. (Pres. A. V. CASEY): owns four newspapers, including *Los Angeles Times*; Newsday Inc., Orange Coast Publishing Company and Times Herald Printing Company.

Owing to the regionalism mentioned above there is no truly national press corresponding to major West European dailies. Most influential and highly respected among the few newspapers which may claim a national distribution are the *New York Times* (notably the main sections of its massive Sunday edition), *Washington Post*, *Los Angeles Times*, and *Wall Street Journal*, the financial and news daily with editions in New York City, California, Illinois and Texas. The *International Herald Tribune* printed in Paris, which recently absorbed the European edition of *New York Times*, has an important following in Europe.

Thirty-five daily papers have circulations of over 250,000 copies, including five in New York and five in Chicago. Among the largest of these in daily circulation are

New York News (2,092,603 daily), *Wall Street Journal* (1,313,146 total of four editions), *Los Angeles Times* (1,024,721), *New York Times* (877,962), *Chicago Tribune* (735,734), *New York Post* (630,621), *Detroit News* (683,452) and *Philadelphia Bulletin* (611,634).

Of the large weekly news magazines *Time* (4.3m.) and *Newsweek* (2.7m.), with a world distribution, provide a serious, comprehensive coverage of current affairs; the *New Yorker* (478,414) also includes fiction and among the larger monthly periodicals *McCall's* (7.5m.) and *Fortune* (583,000) are widely respected for their treatment of literary topics and business and industrial affairs respectively; the lighter and more varied *Reader's Digest* (17.9m.) and *National Geographic Magazine* (7.7m.) have the distinction of world distribution; women's interests are extensively catered for, the most popular magazine being *Ladies Home Journal* (7.0m.), while *Playboy* (6.9m.) and *Esquire* (1.2m.) appeal specifically to men, and *Ebony* (1.2m.) is directed particularly to a Negro readership.

PRINCIPAL DAILY AND SUNDAY NEWSPAPERS

(Ind. = politically independent; Dem. = Democrat; Rep. = Republican; D. = all day; E. = evening; M. = morning; S. = Sunday; ex. = excluding; Publr. = Publisher.)

In general, only newspapers with circulations of 40,000 and over are included, except in Wyoming, where the newspaper with the largest circulation is listed.

ALABAMA

Birmingham News: 2200 North 4th Avenue, Birmingham, Ala. 35202; f. 1888; Publr. C. B. HANSON, Jr.; Man. Editor JOHN W. BLOOMER; Ind.; E.S.; circ. 181,051 (E.), 223,626 (S.).

Birmingham Post-Herald: 2200 North 4th Ave., Birmingham, Ala. 35202; f. 1888; Publr. Birmingham Post Co.; Editor DUARD LE GRAND; Ind.; M.; circ. 77,059.

Huntsville Times: 2317 Memorial Parkway, S.W., Huntsville, Ala. 35807; f. 1910; Editor and Publr. LEROY A. SIMMS; Ind.-Dem.; circ. 53,363 (E)., 55,852 (S.E.).

Mobile Register (M.) f. 1830, **Mobile Press** (E.) f. 1929, **Mobile Press-Register** (S.), 304 Government St., Mobile, Ala. 36602; Pres. WILLIAM J. HEARIN; Exec. Vice-Pres. LUIS M. WILLIAMS; Exec. Editor FALLON TROTTER; Ind.-Dem.; circ. 43,483 (M.), 60,948 (E.), 96,860 (S.).

Montgomery Advertiser: 200 Washington Ave., Montgomery, Ala. 36102; f. 1828; Publr. HAROLD MARTIN; Exec. Editor BEN DAVIS; Ind.-Dem.; M.S.; circ. 58,471 (M.), 78,814 (S.).

ALASKA

Anchorage Times: 820 Fourth Ave., Anchorage, Alaska 99501; f. 1915; Publr. and Editor ROBERT B. ATWOOD; Ind.; E.; circ. 43,000.

ARIZONA

Arizona Daily Star (M.S.) Ind.-Dem., **Tucson Daily Citizen** (E) Ind.-Rep.; 208 N. Stone, Tucson, Ariz. 85703; f. 1877; Editor (Citizen) PAUL A. McKALIP, Editor (Star) M. E. PULITZER; circ. 66,534 (M.), 52,455 (E.).

Arizona Republic (M.S.) f. 1890, **Phoenix Gazette** (E.) f. 1880; 120 E. Van Buren St., Phoenix, Ariz. 85004; Publr. EUGENE C. PULLIAM; Editor (Republic) F. S. MARQUARDT, (Gazette) L. MEEK; Ind.; circ. 194,511 (M.), 111,405 (E.), 300,000 (S.).

ARKANSAS

Arkansas Democrat: Capitol Ave. and Scott, Little Rock, Ark.; f. 1871; Publr. C. S. BERRY; Editor MARCUS B. GEORGE; Ind.; E.S.; circ. 74,305 (E.), 92,280 (S.).

Little Rock Arkansas Gazette: 112 West Third St., Little Rock, Ar.; f. 1819; Publr. HUGH B. PATTERSON, Jr.; Gen. Man. J. R. WILLIAMSON; Ind.-Dem.; M.S.; circ. 115,576 (M.), 141,125 (S.).

CALIFORNIA

Bakersfield Californian: (E.S.), 1707 Eye St., Bakersfield, Calif. 93302; f. 1866; Pres. B. C. FRITTS; Exec. Dir. D. H. FRITTS; Dem.; (E.); circ. 50,093 (E), 45,886 (S).

Fresno Bee: 1559 Van Ness Ave., Fresno, Calif. 93721; f. 1922; Pres. ELEANOR McCLATCHY; Exec. Editor WALTER P. JONES; Ind.; E.S.; circ. 115,589 (E), 140,716 (S).

Long Beach Independent—Press-Telegram (M.E.S.): Twin Coast Newspapers, Inc., 604 Pine Ave., Long Beach, Calif. 90844; Publr. DANIEL H. RIDDER; Editor MILES E. SINES; Man. Editor LARRY ALLISON; Ind.; circ. 160,613 (combined daily), 146,269 (S.).

Los Angeles Herald-Examiner: Box 2416, Terminal Annex, Los Angeles, Calif. 90054; f. 1871; Publr. GEORGE R. HEARST, Jr.; Man. Editor DONALD GOODENOW; Ind.; circ. 474,020 (E), 483,649 (S.).

Los Angeles Times: Times Mirror Co., Times Mirror Square, Los Angeles, Calif. 90053; f. 1881; Publr. OTIS CHANDLER; Editor WILLIAM F. THOMAS; Ind.; M.S.; circ. 1,036,911 (M.), 1,226,132 (S.). A separate edition is published for Orange County at Costa Mesa.

Modesto Bee: McClatchy Newspapers, 14th and H, Modesto, Calif.; f. 1884; Pres. ELEANOR McCLATCHY; Editor WALTER P. JONES; Ind.; circ. 51,426 (E.), 55,559 (S.).

Oakland Tribune: Box 509, Oakland, Calif. 94604; f. 1874; Rep., E.S.; circ. 191,149 (E), 221,844 (S.).

Palo Alto Times: Peninsula Newspapers Inc., 245 Lytton Ave., Palo Alto, Calif.; Editor A. BODI; E.; circ. 45,171.

Pasadena Star News: Twin Coast Newspapers Inc., 525 East Colorado Blvd., Pasadena, Calif. 91109; f. 1886; Publr. BERNARD J. RIDDER; Editor CHARLES CHERNISS; Ind.-Rep.; S.; circ. 72,179.

Pomona Progress-Bulletin: 300 S. Thomas St., Pomona, Calif.; Publr. R. G. BUSH; E.S.; circ. 42,765 (E.), 43,158 (S.).

Riverside Press-Enterprise: 3512 14th St., Riverside, Calif. 92502; Publrs. A. A. CULVER, H. H. HAYS, Jr.; Editor H. H. HAYS, Jr.; S.; circ. 83,618.

Sacramento Bee: McClatchy Newspapers, 21st and Q, Sacramento, Calif. 95816; f. 1857; Pres. ELEANOR McCLATCHY; Editor WALTER P. JONES; Ind. E.S.; circ. 190,000 (E.), 220,000 (S.).

Sacramento Union: 301 Capitol Ave., Sacramento, Calif. 95812; f. 1851; Publr. and Gen. Man. CARLYLE REED; Editor PETER J. HAYES; Ind.; M.S.; circ. 99,231 (M.), 90,985 (S.).

San Bernardino Sun (M.), **San Bernardino Evening Telegram** (E.), **San Bernardino Sun-Telegram** (S.): 399 D. St., San Bernardino, Calif. 92401; f. 1894; Pres. MARVIN W. REIMER; Editor and Publr. JAMES GEEHAN; Ind.; circ. 71,378 (M.), 15,807 (E.), 91,296 (S.).

San Diego Union (M.S.) f. 1868; Rep., **San Diego Evening Tribune** (E.) f. 1895; Ind.: 940 Third Ave., San Diego, Calif. 92112; Publr. HELEN C. COPLEY; Editor (Union) GENE GREGSTON, (Tribune) FRED KINNE; circ. 175,298 (M.), 124,712 (E.), 289,911 (S.).

San Francisco Chronicle (M.), **San Francisco Sunday Examiner and Chronicle** (S.): 901 Mission St., San Francisco 19, Calif. 94119; f. 1865; Publr. and Editor CHARLES DE YOUNG THIERIOT; Man. Editor G. PATES; Ind.-Rep.; M.S.; circ. 461,164 (M.), 661,016 (S.).

San Francisco Examiner (E.) 110 Fifth St., San Francisco, Calif. 94119; Publ. CHARLES GOULD; Editor EDMUND J. DOOLEY; Ind.; circ. 179,010.

San Gabriel Valley Tribune: 2037 W. San Barnardino Rd., West Covina, Calif. 91723; f. 1955; Man. Editor R. E. TRACY; Ind.; E.S.; circ. 81,828 (E.), 82,958 (S.).

San Jose Mercury (M.) f. 1851, **San Jose News** (E.) f. 1883, **San Jose Mercury-News** (S.): 750 Ridder Park Drive, San Jose, Calif. 95131; Publr. JOSEPH B. RIDDER; Exec. Editor KENNETH S. CONN; Man. Editor OSCAR LIDEN (M.S.); PAUL E. CONROY (E.); Ind.; circ. 134,214 (M.), 77,519 (E.), 214,452 (S.).

San Mateo Times and Daily News Leader: Amphlett Printing Co., 1080 S. Amphlett Blvd., San Mateo, Calif. 94402; f. 1889; Publr. and Editor J. HART CLINTON; Ind.-Rep.; circ. 43,961 (E.).

San Rafael Independent-Journal: California Newspapers Inc., 1040 B. St. San Rafael, Calif. 94902; f. 1861; Publr. WISHARD A. BROWN; Editor JACK CRAEMER; Rep.; circ. 43,649 (E.).

Santa Ana Register: 625 N. Grand Ave., Santa Ana, Calif.; f. 1905; Publr. R. C. HOILES; Exec. Editor M. J. DEAN; Man. Editor M. C. MALONEY; Ind., M.E.S.; circ. 60,062 (M.), 113,980 (E.), 201,871 (S.).

Santa Rosa Press-Democrat: 427 Mendocino Ave., Santa Rosa, Calif. 95402; Publr. Mrs. ERNEST L. FINLEY; Co-Publr. EVERT B. PERSON; Editor DAN BOWERMAN; Dem.; E.S.; circ. 47,228 (E.), 49,133 (S.).

South Bay Breeze: S. Calif. Assoc. Newspapers, 5215 Torrance Blvd., Torrance, Calif. 90503; f. 1894; Publr. HUBERT L. KALTENBACH; Editor S. C. STEWART; Ind.-Rep.; circ. 75,000 (E.), 76,000 (S.).

Stockton Record: 530 E. Market St., P.O.B. 900, Stockton Calif. 95201; f. 1895; Publr. R. VECKER; Man. Editor N. S. DEMOTTE; Ind.; circ. 54,788 (E.), 52,645 (S.).

Valley News and Green Sheet: 14539 Sylvan St., P.O.B. 310, Van Nuys, Calif. 91406; f. 1911; Publr. MAURICE W. MARKHAM; Editor FERDINAND MENDENHALL; Ind.; M. ex. Mon., Wed., Sat.; circ. 55,433 paid, 206,895 controlled, total 262,328.

Wall Street Journal: (Pacific Coast Edition; *see under* New York); circ. 239,958.

COLORADO

Colorado Springs Gazette-Telegraph: Freedom Newspapers. 30 S. Prospect, Colorado Springs; f. 1872; Publr HARRY H. HOILES; Man. Editor MAURICE D. WHITNEY; Ind.; E. (Mon.–Fri.), M. (Sat.–S.); circ. 60,296 (E.), 62,495 (S.).

Denver Post: 650 15th St., Denver, Colo. 80202; f. 1895; Publr. and Editor CHARLES R. BUXTON; Exec. Editor WILLIAM H. HORNBY; Ind.; E.S.; circ. 256,439 (E.), 368,912 (S.).

Pueblo Star-Journal and Chieftain: 825 West 6th St. Pueblo, Colo.; f. 1871, 1901; Publr. FRANK S. HOAG, Jr.; Gen. Man. ROBERT H. RAWLINGS; Editor JOHN F. JAMES; Ind.-Rep.; S.; circ. 46,484.

Rocky Mountain News: 400 W. Colfax Ave., Denver, Colo. 80204; Editor VINCENT M. DWYER; Ind.; M.S.; circ. 194,124 (M.), 202,000 (S.).

CONNECTICUT

Bridgeport Post: 410 State St., Bridgeport, Conn. 06602; Man. Editor LEONARD E. GILBERT; Ind.; E.S.; circ. 82,342 (E.), 88,968 (S.).

Hartford Courant: 285 Broad St., Hartford, Conn. 06115; f. 1764; Chair. JOHN R. REITMEYER; Pres. EDMUND W. DOWNES; Editor and Publr. BOB EDDY; Rep.; M.S.; circ. 170,459 (M.), 219,365 (S.).

Hartford Times: 10 Prospect St., Hartford, Conn. 06101; f. 1817; Publr. ROGER C. CORYELL; Executive Editor CHARLES A. BETTS; E.S.; circ. 123,376 (E.), 122,857 (S.).

New Haven Register: 367 Orange St., New Haven, Conn. 06503; Publr. LIONEL S. JACKSON; Editor ROBERT J. LEENEY; Ind.; E.S.; circ. 106,000 (E.), 126,830 (S.).

DELAWARE

Morning News f. 1880, **Evening Journal** f. 1871: 831 Orange St., Wilmington, Del. 19899; Pres. and Editor RICHARD P. SANGER; Ind.; circ. 46,849 (M.), 89,397 (E.).

DISTRICT OF COLUMBIA

Washington News: 1013 13th St., N.W., Washington, D.C. 20005; f. 1921; Pres. RAY F. MACK; Editor RICHARD HOLLANDER; Ind.; E.; circ. 223,627.

Washington Post: 1150 15th St., N.W. Washington, D.C. 20005; f. 1877; Publr. KATHARINE GRAHAM; Pres. J. PRESCOT; Exec. Editor BENJAMIN C. BRADLEE; Ind.; M.S.; circ. 532,008 (M.), 701,671 (S.).

Washington Star: 225 Virginia Ave., S.E., Washington, D.C. 20003; f. 1852; Pres. JOHN H. KAUFFMANN; Editor NEWBOLD NOYES; Ind.; E.S.; circ. 305,297 (E.), 345,019 (S.).

FLORIDA

Florida Times-Union (M.S.), **Jacksonville Journal** (E): 1 Riverside Ave., P.O.B. 1949, Jacksonville, Fla. 32201; f. 1864 (Times-Union), 1887 (Journal); Exec. Editor JOHN S. WALTERS; Man. Editor ARTHUR B. MANNING (Times-Union), E. G. HENSON (Journal); Ind.-Dem.; circ. 147,763 (M.), 63,392 (E.), 179,258 (S.).

Fort Lauderdale News: 320 S.E. First Ave., Fort Lauderdale, Fla.; f. 1911; Publr. and Editor JACK W. GORE; Ind.-Dem.; E.S.; circ. 95,534 (E.), 113,898 (s.).

Miami Herald: 1 Herald Plaza, Miami, Fla. 33101; f. 1910; Pres. ALVAH H. CHAPMAN; Editor DON SHOEMAKER; Ind.; M.S.; circ. 405,855 (M.), 508,956 (s.).

Miami News: Box 615, Miami, Fla. 33152; Publr. JAMES M. Cox, Jr.; Editor J. FAIN; Dem.; E.S.; circ. 72,955 (E.).

Orlando Sentinel (M.S.) f. 1885, **Orlando Star** (E.) f. 1876: 633 N. Orange Ave., Orlando, Fla. 32801; Publr. and Editor W. G. CONOMOS; Exec. Editor NORMAN WOLFE; Ind.; circ. 138,807 (M.), 42,760 (E.), 209,291 (s.).

Palm Beach Post-Times: 2751 South Dixie Highway, West Palm Beach, Fla.; f. 1922; Publr. CECIL B. KELLEY; Editor ROBERT H. KIRKPATRICK; Ind.; s.; circ. 76,868.

Pensacola Journal (M.), **Pensacola News** (E.), **Pensacola News-Journal** (s.): 101 E. Romana St., Pensacola, Fla. 32501; f. 1895 (News), 1898 (Journal); Publr. BRADEN L. BALL; Exec. Editor EARLE BOWDEN; Ind.; circ. 64,223 (M.); 28,159 (E.), 94,517 (s.).

St. Petersburg Times (M.S.) f. 1884, **St. Petersburg Independent** (E.) f. 1906; P.O.B. 1121, St. Petersburg, Fla. 33731; Pres. and Editor EUGENE PATTERSON; Man. Editor R. HAIMAN; Ind.; circ. 199,443 (M.), 31,114 (E.), 239,671 (s.).

Tampa Tribune: Tribune Bldg., Tampa, Fla. 33601; f. 1895; Pres. ALAN S. DONNAHOE; Editor J. A. CLENDINEN; Ind.; M.S.; circ. 177,350 (M.), 212,706 (s.).

Today: P.O.B. 1330, Cocoa, Fla.; f. 1966; Pres. JAMES H. JESSE; Man. Editor BUDDY BALCH; Ind.; circ. 62,345 (M.)., 68,632 (s.).

GEORGIA

Atlanta Constitution (M.), **Atlanta Journal** (E.), **Atlanta Journal-Constitution** (s.): Box 4689, Atlanta, Ga. 30302; Editor (Constitution) REGINALD MURPHY, (Journal) JACK SPALDING; Ind.-Dem.; circ. 214,252 (M.), 259,292 (E.), 579,783 (s.).

Augusta Chronicle (M.), **Augusta Herald** (E.), **Augusta Chronicle-Herald** (s.): 725 Broad St., Augusta, Ga. 30903; Publr. W. S. MORRIS III; Exec. Editor (Chronicle-Herald) L. C. HARRIS; Ind.; circ. 48,177 (M.), 19,866 (E.), 65,839 (s.).

Columbus Ledger-Enquirer: 17 W. 12th St., Columbus, Ga. 31902; f. 1930; Pres. M. R. ASHWORTH; Exec. Editor CARLTON M. JOHNSON; Ind.-Dem.; daily circ. 65,903, s. 59,533.

Macon Telegraph (M.), **Macon News** (E.), **Macon Telegraph-News** (s.): 120 Broadway, Macon, Ga.; f. 1826 (Telegraph), 1884 (News); Pres. JAMES L. KNIGHT; Exec. Editor DON CARTER; Editor (News) JOSEPH B. PARHAM; Gen. Man. BERT STRUBY; Dem.; circ. 51,729 (M.), 23,561 (E.), 73,430 (s.).

Savannah Morning News: 105-111 West Bay St., Savannah, Ga. 31402; f. 1850; Pres. W. S. MORRIS, III; Exec. Editor WALLACE M. DAVIS, Jr.; Ind.; M.S.; circ. 56,481 (M.), 67,658 (s.).

HAWAII

Honolulu Advertiser (M.) f. 1856, **Honolulu Star-Bulletin** (E.) f. 1912, **Honolulu Star-Bulletin & Advertiser** (s.): 605 Kapiolani Blvd., Honolulu, Hawaii 96818; Editor (Advertiser) GEORGE CHAPLIN, (Star-Bulletin) A. A. SMYSER; Ind.; circ. 74,799 (M.), 129,561 (E.), 187,648 (s.).

IDAHO

Idaho Statesman: Federated Publications Inc., 6th and Bannock Streets, Boise, Idaho; Publr. ROBERT B. MILLER, Jr.; Man. Editor RICHARD P. HRONEK; Ind.-Rep.; M.S.; circ. 53,581 (M.), 60,286 (s.).

ILLINOIS

Bloomington Pantagraph: 301 W. Washington St., Bloomington, Ill.; f. 1846; Publr. DAVIS U. MERWIN; Editor HAROLD V. LISTON; Ind. D.S.; circ. 48,372 (D.), 44,572 (s.).

Chicago Daily News: Field Enterprises Inc., Newspaper Div., 401 N. Wabash St., Chicago, Ill. 60611; f. 1876; Editor DARYLE FELDMEIR; Ind.; E.; circ. 442,250.

Chicago Sun-Times: Field Enterprises Inc., Newspaper Div., 401 N. Wabash St., Chicago, Ill. 60611; f. 1947; Editor JAMES F. HOGE, Jr.; Ind.; circ. 567,139 (M.), 779,390 (s.).

Chicago Today: 441 N. Michigan Ave., Chicago, Ill. 60611; f. 1900; Publr. LLOYD WENDT; Ind.; E.S.; circ. 430,208 (E.), 441,775 (s.).

Chicago Tribune: Tribune Tower, Chicago, Ill. 60611; f. 1847; Publr. HAROLD F. GRUMHAUS; Editor MAXWELL McCROHON; Ind.-Rep.; M.S.; circ. 735,734 (M.), 1,106,947 (s.).

Decatur Herald-Review: 365 N. Main Street, Decatur, Ill.; f. 1877-79; Editor M. L. MILAVETZ; Ind.; s.; circ. 58,709. (s.).

Herald-News: The Copley Press Inc., 78 N. Scott St., Joliet, Ill. 60431; f. 1838; Publr. and Editor W. BLACKBURN; circ. 47,144 (E.), 48,059 (s.).

Illinois State Journal (M.) f. 1831; Rep., **Illinois State Register** (E.) f. 1836; Dem., **Illinois State Journal & Register** (s.) f. 1961: 313 South 6th St., Springfield, Ill.; Editor (Journal) J. P. CLARKE; (Register) E. H. ARMSTRONG; circ. 54,918 (M.), 25,238 (E.), 71,186 (s.).

Peoria Journal-Star: War Memorial Drive, Peoria, Ill. 61614; f. 1855; Publr. HENRY P. SLANE; Editor CHARLES L. DANCEY; Ind.; M.E.S.; circ. 44,358 (M.), 60,830 (E.), 114,447 (s.).

Rock Island Argus: 1724 Fourth Ave., Rock Island, Ill. 61202; f. 1851; Publrs. M. F. POTTER; Exec. Editor LYNN L. ASH; Ind.; circ. 26,507 (E.).

Star, The (M.S.), **Register-Republic, The** (E.): 99 East State St., Rockford, Ill. 61105; Member of the Gannett Group; f. 1855; Pres. Publr. COVE HOOVER; Ind. circ. 57,916 (M.), 29,592 (E.), 84,515 (s.).

Wall Street Journal: (Midwest Edition; *see under* New York): circ. 408,347.

INDIANA

Evansville Courier (M.), **Evansville Press** (E.), **Evansville Sunday Courier-Press** (s.): 201 N.W. 2nd St., Evansville. Ind. 47701; f. 1845 Courier), 1906 (Press), 1939 (Courier-Press); Editor (Courier) LENORD U. KREUGER, (Press) MICHAEL GREHL, (Sunday Courier-Press) JAMES MARGEDANT; Ind.; circ. 65,786 (M.), 46,604 (E.), 113,631 (s.).

Fort Wayne Journal-Gazette (M.S.) f. 1863; Editor L. ALLEN; Ind.-Dem., **Fort Wayne News-Sentinel** (E.) f. 1833; Editor ERNEST E. WILLIAMS; Ind.-Rep.: 600 W. Main St., Fort Wayne, Ind. 46802; circ. 141,472 (comb. M. and E.), 106,394 (s.).

Gary Post-Tribune: 1065 Broadway, Gary, Ind. 46402; f. 1909; Editor J. E. RASMUSEN; Ind.; circ. 81,000 (E.), 81,000 (s.).

Indianapolis Star (M.S.), **Indianapolis News** (E.): 307 N. Pennsylvania St., Indianapolis, Ind. 46206; f. 1869 (News), f. 1903 (Star); Editor (Star) FRANK H. CRANE, (News) M. STANTON EVANS; Ind.; circ. 229,156 (M.), 176,273 (E.), 371,059 (S.).

Lafayette Journal & Courier: 221 North 6th St., Lafayette, Ind. 47901; f. 1829; Publr. GREGORY L. DELIYANNE; Editor B. P. LYONS; Ind.-Rep.; E.; circ. 45,000.

South Bend Tribune: 225 W. Colfax, South Bend, Ind. 46626; Publr. and Editor FRANKLIN D. SCHURZ; Ind.; E.S.; circ. 116,562 (E.), 125,849 (S.).

The Times: 417 Fayette St., Hammond, Ind.; f. 1906; Editor WILLIAM F. CHAPMAN; Ind.; E.S.; circ. 66,284 (E.), 70,424 (S.).

IOWA

Cedar Rapids Gazette: 500 Third Ave., S.E., Cedar Rapids, Iowa 52406; f. 1883; Publr. and Editor J. F. HLADKY, Jr.; Ind.; E.S.; circ. 74,391 (E.), 80,313 (S.).

Davenport Times-Democrat: 124 East 2nd St., Davenport, Iowa 52801; Publr. HENRY B. HOOK; Editor FORREST KILMER; D.S.; circ. 69,076 (D.), 81,281 (S.).

Des Moines Register (M.S.) f. 1849, **Des Moines Tribune** (E.) f. 1906: 715 Locust St., Des Moines, Iowa 50304; Pres. and Publr. DAVID KRUIDENIER; Editor KENNETH MACDONALD; Ind.; circ. 245,060 (M.), 107,325 (E.), 484,909 (S.).

Dubuque Telegraph-Herald: West 8th and Bluff Sts., Dubuque, Iowa 52001; f. 1836; Publr. F. W. WOODWARD; Editor JAMES GELADAS; Ind.; E.S. ex. Sat.; circ. 39,699 (E.), 41,112 (S.).

Sioux City Journal: 5th and Douglas Sts., Sioux City, Iowa 51102; f. 1870; Pres. ELIZABETH SAMMONS; Editor ERWIN SIAS; Ind.; D.S.; circ. 68,513 (D.), 54,721 (S.).

Waterloo Courier: 501 Commercial Street, Waterloo, Iowa; f. 1854; Gen. Man. and Exec. Editor ROBERT J. McCOY; Editor GENE THORNE; Ind.-Rep.; E.S.; circ. 53,457 (E.), 54,687 (S.).

KANSAS

Hutchinson News: 300 West 2nd St., Hutchinson, Kans.; Publr. and Editor STUART AWBREY; Ind.; D.S.; circ. 48,692 (D.), 48,507 (S.).

Topeka Capital (M.) f. 1879, **Topeka State Journal** (E.) f. 1874, **Topeka Capital-Journal** (S.): 6th & Jefferson Sts., Topeka, Kans.; Publr. O. S. STAUFFER; Exec. Editor L. PORTER; Ind.; circ. 63,028 (M.), 30,342 (E.), 73,227 (S.).

Wichita Eagle (M.), **Wichita Beacon** (E.), **Wichita Sunday Eagle and Beacon** (S.): 825 East Douglas St., Wichita, Kans. 67201; f. 1872; Publr. BRITT BROWN; Editor DON BOYETT; Ind.-Rep.; circ. 129,987 (M.), 59,604 (E.), 190,444 (S.).

KENTUCKY

Lexington Herald (M.) f. 1870; Dem., **Lexington Leader** (E.) f. 1888; Rep., **Lexington Herald and Leader** (Sat.), **Lexington Herald-Leader** (S.) f. 1937; Ind.: 227–239 W. Short St., Lexington, Ky.; Editor (Herald) DON MILLS, (Leader) FRED B. WACHS; circ. 53,922 (M.), 31,769 (E.), 78,446 (Sat.), 76,774 (S.).

Louisville Courier-Journal (M.S.) f. 1868, **Louisville Times** (E.) f. 1884: 525 W. Broadway 2, Louisville, Ky. 40202; Publr. and Editor BARRY BINGHAM, Jr.; Ind.; circ. 230,956 (M.), 176,022 (E.), 363,917 (S.).

LOUISIANA

Baton Rouge Advocate (M.S.), **Baton Rouge State Times** (E.): 525 Lafayette St., Baton Rouge 1, La. 70821; f. 1842; Publr. and Editor D. L. MANSHIP Sr.; Ind.-Dem.; circ. 62,500 (M.), 42,500 (E.), 98,000 (S.).

New Orleans Times-Picayune (M.S.) f. 1837; Editor A. F. FELT; **New Orleans States and Item** (E.): 3800 Howard Ave., New Orleans, La. 70140; f. 1880; Publr. ASHTON PHELPS; Editor W. G. COWAN; Ind.-Dem.; circ. 210,523 (M.), 127,353 (E.), 313,294 (S.).

Shreveport Journal: 222 Lake Street, Shreveport, La,; f. 1895; Publr. DOUGLAS F. ATTAWAY; Editor GEORGE W. SHANNON; Ind.; E.; circ. 45,564.

Shreveport Times: P.O.B. 222, Shreveport, La. 71130; f. 1871; Chair. R. E. BROWN; Exec. Editor RAYMOND L. MCDANIEL; Ind.; M.S.; circ. 92,075 (M.), 120,199 (S.).

MAINE

Bangor News: 491 Main St., Bangor, Maine 04401; f. 1834; Publr. RICHARD K. WARREN; Ind.; M.; circ. 77,625.

Portland Press Herald (M.) f. 1862, **Evening Express** (E.) f. 1882, **Maine Sunday Telegram** (s.) f. 1887: 390 Congress St., Portland, Maine 04104; Publr. ROBERT B. BEITH; Editor ERNEST W. CHARD; Ind.; circ. 52,957 (M.), 29,854 (E.), 110,795 (S.).

MARYLAND

Baltimore News-American: The Hearst Corpn. Inc., Lombard and South Streets, Baltimore, Md. 21203; f. 1872; Publr. MARK F. COLLINS; Editor-in-Chief W. R. HEARST, Jr.; Ind.; circ. 207,775 (E.), 294,565 (S.).

Baltimore Sun: Calvert and Center Streets, Baltimore, Md. 21203; f. 1837; Editor-in-Chief PRICE DAY; Ind.; circ. 169,185 (M.), 194,534 (E.), 356,108 (S.).

MASSACHUSETTS

Boston Globe: 135 Morrissey Blvd., Boston, Mass. 02107; Publr. W. D. TAYLOR; Editor THOMAS WINSHIP; circ. 280,281 (M.), 182,205 (E.), 608,325 (S.).

Boston Record American (M.), **Boston Advertiser** (S.): Hearst Corporation, 5 Winthrop Square, Boston, Mass.; f. 1961 (Record American), 1904 (Advertiser); Publr. H. G. KERN; Man. Editor (Record American) C. EDWARD HOLLAND; Man. Editor (Advertiser) SAM BORNSTEIN; Ind.; circ. 371,365 (M.), 503,045 (S.).

Brockton Enterprise and Times: 60 Main St., Brockton, Mass.; f. 1880; Publr. C. A. FULLER; Editor M. F. FULLER; Ind.; E.; circ. 51,765.

Christian Science Monitor: 1 Norway St., Boston, Mass; f. 1908; Editor JOHN HUGHES; Ind.; M.; circ. 196,849.

Fall River Herald-News: 207 Pocasset St., Fall River, Mass. 02722; f. 1877; Publr. D. TOOMEY; Man. Editor T. K. BRINDLEY.; Ind; E.; circ. 42,136.

Lawrence Eagle-Tribune: 100 Turnpike, Lawrence, Mass.; f. 1867; Editor IRVING E. ROGERS; Ind.; D.; circ. 46,220.

Lowell Sun: 15 Kearney Square, Lowell, Mass.; f. 1878; Pres. JOHN H. COSTELLO; Editor CLEMENT C. COSTELLO; Ind.; E.S.; circ. 51,432 (E.), 42,607 (S.).

New Bedford Standard Times: 555 Pleasant St., New Bedford, Mass.; f. 1850; Publr. GERALD T. TAELIE; Editor J. RICHARD EARLY; Ind.; E.S.; circ. 49,928 (E.), 74,282 (S.).

Patriot Ledger, The: 13-19 Temple St., Quincy, Mass.; f. 1837; Publr. G. PRESCOTT LOW; Editor DONALD C. WILDER; Ind. E.; circ. 72,839.

Springfield Union (M.) f. 1864; Rep., **Springfield News** (E.) f. 1880, Dem., **Springfield Republican** (S.) f. 1844; Ind.: 1860 Main St., Springfield, Mass. 01101; Editor (Union and Republican) JOSEPH W. MOONEY, (News) RICHARD GARVEY; circ. 81,519 (M.), 91,216 (E.), 132,913 (S.).

Worcester Telegram (M.), **Worcester Evening Gazette** (E.), **Worcester Sunday Telegram** (S.): 20 Franklin St., Worcester, Mass. 01613; Publr. RICHARD C. STEELE; Editor ROBERT C. ACHORN; Ind.; circ. 58,936 (M.), 93,874 (E.), 111,038 (S.).

MICHIGAN

Battle Creek Enquirer and News: Federated Publications Inc., 155 W. Van Buren St., Battle Creek, Mich. 49016; f. 1911; Publr. ROBERT B. MILLER; Editor W. S. SIMS; circ. 38,118 (E.), 42,145 (S.).

Detroit Free Press: Detroit, Mich. 48231; f. 1831; Publr. LEE HILLS; Editor MARK ETHRIDGE; Ind.; M.S.; circ. 605,216 (M.), 706,312 (S.).

Detroit News: 615 Lafayette Boulevard, Detroit, Mich. 48231; f. 1873; Publr. PETER B. CLARK; Editor MARTIN S. HAYDEN; Ind.; E.S.; circ. 667,500 (E.), 842,615 (S.).

Flint Journal: 200 East 1st St., Flint, Mich. 48502; f. 1883; Editor GLEN A. BOISSONNEAULT; Ind.; E.S.; circ. 114,323 (E.), 114,020 (S.).

Grand Rapids Press: Press Plaza, Vandenberg Center, Grand Rapids, Mich. 49502; f. 1892; Editor WERNER VEIT; Ind.; E.S.; circ. 130,636 (E.), 134,500 (S.).

Kalamazoo Gazette: 401 S. Burdick Street, Kalamazoo, Mich.; f. 1833; Editor DANIEL M. RYAN; Ind.; E.S.; circ. 57,287 (E.),59,993 (S.).

Lansing State Journal: 120 E. Lenawee St., Lansing, Mich. 48919; f. 1855; Pres. LOUIS A. WEIL, Jr.; Man. Editor K. L. GUNDERMAN; Ind.-Rep.; E.S.; circ. 76,589 (E.), 77,362 (S.).

Macomb Daily: Macomb Publishing Co., 67 Cass Ave., P.O.B. 707, Mount Clemens, Mich. 48043; Editor MAURICE A. VINCENT; E.; circ. 50,903.

Muskegon Chronicle: 981 Third Street, Muskegon, Mich.; f. 1857; Man. ROBERT A. MORSE; Editor ROBERT C. HERRICK; Ind.; circ. 49,208 (E.), 46,949 (S.).

Oakland Press: 48 W. Huron St., Pontiac, Mich.; f. 1843; Publr. PHILLIP J. MEEK; Editor BRUCE H. MCINTYRE; Ind.; E.; circ. 79,075.

Royal Oak Tribune: 210 East 3rd Street, Royal Oak; f. 1902; Editor GRANT W. HOWELL; Ind.; E.; circ. 58,445.

Saginaw News: 203 S. Washington Ave., Saginaw, Mich.; f. 1859; Editor RAYMOND L. GOVER; Ind.; E.S.; circ. 58,055 (E.), 59,319 (S.).

MINNESOTA

Duluth News Tribune (M.S.), **Duluth Herald** (E.): 424 W. 1st St., Duluth, Minn. 58802; f. 1868 (Tribune), 1883 (Herald); Publr. B. H. RIDDER, Jr.; Exec. Editor ORVILLE E. LOMOE; Ind.; circ. 55,733 (M), 24,067 (E.), 82,972 (S.).

Minneapolis Tribune (M.S.) f. 1867, **Minneapolis Star** (E.) f. 1878: 425 Portland Ave., Minneapolis, Minn. 55415; Pres. O. SILHA; Publr. R. W. SMITH; Editor (Star) ROBERT C. KING; (Tribune) CHARLES W. BAILEY; Ind.; circ. 233,025 (M.), 253,491 (E.), 639,134 (S.).

St. Paul Pioneer Press (M.S.), f. 1849, **St. Paul Dispatch** (E.) f. 1869: 55 East 4th St., St. Paul, Minn. 55101; Publr. T. L. CARLIN; Editor WILLIAM SUMNER; Ind.; circ. 108,675 (M.), 127,533 (E.), 235,890 (S.).

MISSISSIPPI

Jackson Clarion-Ledger (M.), **Jackson News** (E.), **Jackson Clarion Ledger-News** (S.): 311 East Pearl St., Jackson, Miss. 39205; Publr. R. M. HEDERMAN, Jr.; Editor (Clarion-Ledger) T. M. HEDERMAN, Jr., (News) JAMES WARD; Dem.; circ. 58,585 (M.), 47,918 (E.), 111,648 (S.).

MISSOURI

Kansas City Times (M.), **Kansas City Star** (E.S.): 1729 Grand Ave., Kansas City, Mo. 64108; f. 1880; Editor WILLIAM W. BAKER; Ind.; circ. 335,361 (M.), 315,560 (E.), 404,519 (S.).

St. Joseph Gazette (M. ex. SAT.); **St. Joseph News-Press** (E.S. ex. SAT.): f. 1845 (Gazette), 1879 (News-Press); Publr. DAVID R. BRADLEY; Editor (Gazette) HAROLD MILLS, (News-Post) MERRILL CHILCOTE; Ind.; circ. 45,102 (M.), 44,084 (E.), 51,393 (S.).

St. Louis Globe-Democrat: 12th Boulevard at Delmar, St. Louis, Mo. 63101; f. 1852; Publr. G. DUNCAN BAUMAN; Editor GEORGE A. KILLENBERG; Ind.; M. ex. Sat., Week-end; circ. 291,074 (M.), 295,040 (Week-end).

St. Louis Post-Dispatch: Pulitzer Publishing Co., 1133 Franklin Ave., St. Louis, Mo. 63101; f. 1878; Publr. and Editor JOSEPH PULITZER, Jr.; Ind.; E.S.; circ. 317,247 (E.), 530,750 (S.).

Springfield News (M.), **Springfield Leader and Press** (E.), **Springfield News and Leader** (S.): f. 1933; Editor DALE FREEMAN; Ind.; circ. 30,036 (M.), 48,555 (E.), 76,493 (S.).

MONTANA

Billings Gazette: 401 N. Broadway, Billings, Mont.; Publr. STRAND HILLEBOE; Editor DUANE W. BOWLER; circ. 43,917 (M.), 10,701 (E.), 55,381 (S.).

Great Falls Tribune (M.S.): 4th and 2nd Avenue, N., Great Falls, Mont.; f. 1887; Publr. WILLIAM A. CORDINGLEY; Man. Editor E. P. FURLONG; Ind.; circ. 41,353 (M.), 45,894 (S.).

NEBRASKA

Lincoln Star (M.), **Lincoln Journal** (E.), **Lincoln Journal-Star** (S.): Ninth and P Streets, Lincoln, Neb. 68501; f. 1867; Editor (Star) WILLIAM O. DOBLER, (Journal) J. R. SEACREST, (Journal-Star) DALE L. GRIFFING; Ind.; circ. 27,122 (M.), 46,984 (E.), 60,487 (S.).

Omaha World-Herald: World-Herald Sq., Omaha, Neb. 68102; f. 1885; Pres. HAROLD ANDERSEN; Exec. Editor LOUIS G. GERDES; Editor KEITH WILSON; Ind.; M.E.S.; circ. 128,613 (M.), 114,837 (E.), 284,076 (S.).

NEVADA

Las Vegas Review-Journal: 737 North Main St., Las Vegas, Nev. 89101; f. 1908; Publr. DONALD W. REYNOLDS; Editor DON DIGILLO; E.S.; circ. 57,479 (E.), 61,915 (S.).

Reno Nevada State Journal (M.S.), **Reno Gazette** (E.): 401 W. Second St., Reno, Nev. 89503; f. 1870 (Journal), 1876 (Gazette); Publr. RICHARD J. SCHUSTER; Editor (Journal) PAUL A. LEONARD; Man. Editor (Gazette) WARREN LERUDE; (Journal) Ind.-Dem., (Gazette) Ind.-Rep.; circ. 21,095 (M.), 23,236 (E.), 35,807 (S.).

NEW HAMPSHIRE

Manchester Union Leader (D.), **New Hampshire Sunday News** (S.): 35 Amherst St., Manchester, N.H. 03105; f. 1862; Publr. WILLIAM LOEB; Editor in Chief B. J. McQUAID; Man. Editor PAUL H. TRACY; Ind.; circ. 65,000 (D.), 61,000 (S.).

NEW JERSEY

Asbury Park Press: Press Plaza, Asbury Park, N.J. 07712; f. 1879; Publr. ERNEST W. LASS; Editor WAYNE D. MCMURRAY; Ind.; E.S.; circ. 85,296 (E.), 102,472 (S.).

Atlantic City Press: 1900 Atlantic Ave., Atlantic City, N.J. 08401; f. 1872; Editor CHARLES C. REYNOLDS; Ind.; M.S.; circ. 65,985 (M.), 59,651 (S.).

Courier-News: 1201, Route 22, Somerville, N.J. 08876; f. 1884; Man. Editor JOHN J. CURLEY; Ind.; E.; circ. 65,029.

Courier-Post: Southern N.J. Newspapers Inc., Camden, N.J. 08101; f. 1875; Publr. WILLIAM A. STRETCH; Editor T. P. FLYNN; Ind.; E.; circ. 125,670.

Elizabeth Journal: 295–299 Broad St., Elizabeth, N.J. 07207; f. 1779; Publr. D. A. KRENZ; Exec. Editor JOSEPH S. JENNINGS; E.; circ. 63,233.

Hackensack Record (E.), **Sunday Record Call** (S.): 150 River St., Hackensack, N.J.; f. 1895; Publr. MALCOLM A. BORG; Editor DONALD G. BORG; Ind.; circ. 155,726 (E.) 185,282 (S.).

Herald-News: 988 Main Ave., Passaic, N.J. 07055; Publr. RICHARD DRUKKER; Exec.-Editor ARTHUR G. McMAHON; Ind.-Rep.; E.; circ. 88,627.

Hudson Dispatch: 400 38th Street, Union City, N.J. 07087; f. 1873; Publr. JAMES J. McMAHON; Editor HENRY J. AVERY; Ind.-Dem.; M.; circ. 45,851.

Jersey Journal: 30 Journal Square, Jersey City, N.J. 07306; f. 1867; Publr. JAMES S. WEAR; Editor A. LOCKWOOD; Ind.; E.; circ. 87,767.

New Brunswick Home News: 123 How Lane, New Brunswick, N.J. 08903; f. 1786, daily since 1879; Exec. Editor ROBERT E. RHODES; Ind.; E.S.; circ. 57,990 (E.), 63,286 (S.).

Newark Star-Ledger: 217 Halsey St., Newark, N.J. 07101; f. 1832; Publr. S. I. NEWHOUSE; Editor MORT PYE; Ind.; M.S.; circ. 355,065 (M.), 576,902 (S.).

Paterson News: News Plaza, Paterson, N.J. 07509; f. 1890; Publr. and Editor EDWARD HAINES; Ind.; D.; circ. 75,304.

Trenton Times (E.), **Trenton Times-Advertiser** (s.): 500 Perry St., Trenton, N.J. 08618; f. 1882; Publr. and Editor JAMES KERNEY, Jr.; Ind.; circ. 81,157 (E.), 106,353 (S.).

Trentonian: Southard and Perry Sts., Trenton, N.J. 08602; f. 1946; Publr. DEAN A. KRENZ; Editor F. GILLMAN SPENCER; Ind.; M.; circ. 57,173.

NEW MEXICO

Albuquerque Journal (M.S.), **Albuquerque Tribune** (E.): 701 Silver St., S.W., Albuquerque, New Mex. 87117; f. 1880 (Journal), 1922 (Tribune); Pres. (Journal) T. H. LANG, (Tribune) FRANK B. POWERS; Editor (Journal) ROBERT A. BROWN, (Tribune) RALPH LOONEY; Ind.; circ. 75,067 (M.), 38,528 (E.), 104,037 (S.).

NEW YORK

Albany Times-Union (M.S.) f. 1856, **Albany Knickerbocker News-Union-Star** (E.) f. 1856: The Hearst Corporation, 645 Albany-Shaker Rd., Albany, N.Y. 12201; Publr. ROBERT J. DANZIG; Exec.-Editor (Times-Union) JOHN J. LEARY, Exec. Editor (Knickerbocker News) ROBERT G. FICHENBERG; Ind.; circ. 75,439 (M.), 70,517 (E.), 145,956 (S.).

Binghamton Press: Vestal Parkway East, Binghamton, N.Y. 13902; Editor LAURENCE S. HALE; Ind.; E.S.; circ. 75,640 (E.), 83,000 (S.).

Buffalo Courier-Express: 787 Main St., Buffalo, N.Y. 14203; f. 1845; Publr. and Editor WILLIAM J. CONNERS III; Ind.; M.S.; circ. 127,767 (M.), 292,280 (S.).

Buffalo Evening News: 1 News Plaza, Buffalo, N.Y. 14240; f. 1880; Man. Editor (Admin.) ELWOOD M. WARDLOW; Man. Editor (News) MURRAY B. LIGHT; Ind.-Rep.; E.; circ. 297,455 (D.), 278,332 (Sat.).

Elmira Star-Gazette (D.), **Elmira Telegram** (s.): 201 Baldwin St., Elmira, N.Y. 14902; f. 1853 (Advertiser), 1888 (Star), 1828 (Gazette), 1907 (Star-Gazette), 1879 (Telegram); Publr. COVE HOOVER; Man. Editor BURTON H. BLAZAR; Ind.; circ. 47,359 (D.), 52,927 (S.).

Newsday: 550 Stewart Ave., Garden City, N.Y. 11530; f. 1940; Pres. and Publr. WILLIAM ATTWOOD; Ind.; E.S.; circ. 444,407 (E.), 344,627 (S.).

Rochester Democrat and Chronicle (M.S.) f. 1832, **Rochester Times-Union** (E.) f. 1826: 55 Exchange St., Rochester 14, N.Y. 14614; Publr. PAUL MILLER; Man. Editor (Democrat and Chronicle) RICHARD B. TUTTLE, (Times-Union) PAUL MILLER; Ind.-Rep.; circ. 139,103 (M.), 142,235 (E.), 228,759 (S.).

Schenectady Gazette: 334 State St., Schenectady, N.Y. 12301; f. 1894; Editor JOHN E. N. HUME, Jr.; Ind.; M.; circ. 63,111.

Syracuse Herald-Journal (E.) f. 1877, **Syracuse Post-Standard** (M.), **Sunday Herald American** (s.) f. 1881: Clinton Square, Syracuse, N.Y. 13202; Publr. STEPHEN ROGERS; Editor W. D. COTTER; Ind.; circ. 129,531 (E.), 93,794 (M.), 246,530 (S.).

Troy Record (M.), **Troy Times-Record** (E.): Broadway and 5th Avenue, Troy, N.Y. 12181; f. 1896 (Record), 1899 (Times-Record); Publr. and Editor ALTON T. SLITER; Ind.; circ. 8,238 (M.), 42,161 (E.).

Utica Press (M.), **Utica Observer-Dispatch** (E.S.): 221 Oriskany Plaza, Utica, N.Y. 13503; f. 1882 (Press), 1922 (Observer-Dispatch); Publr. HERMAN E. MOECKER; Exec. Editor MASON C. TAYLOR; Ind.-Rep.; circ. 27,945 (M.), 42,352 (E.), 56,915 (S.).

Watertown Times: 260 Washington St., Watertown, N.Y. 13601; f. 1861; Editor JOHN B. JOHNSON; Ind.-Rep.; E; circ. 41,761.

Yonkers Herald Statesman: Larkin Plaza, Yonkers, N.Y. 10702; f. 1392; Pres. THOMAS P. DOLAN; Editor BARNEY WALTERS; Ind.-Rep.; E.; circ. 47,852.

NEW YORK CITY

Long Island Press: 92-20 168th St., Jamaica, N.Y. 11433; f. 1898; Publr. S. I. NEWHOUSE; Editor DAVID STARR; Ind.; E.S.; circ. 375,082 (E.), 352,389 (S.).

New York News: 220 East 42nd St., New York, N.Y. 10017; f. 1919; Publr. W. H. JAMES; Exec. Editor FLOYD BARGER; Ind.; M.S.; circ. 2,107,453 (M.), 2,894,359 (S.).

New York Post: 210 South St., New York, N.Y. 10002; f. 1801; Publr. and Editor-in-Chief DOROTHY SCHIFF; Exec. Editor PAUL SANN; Ind.-Dem.; E.S.; circ. 626,713 (E.), 395,607 (Sat.).

New York Times: 229 West 43rd St., New York, N.Y. 10036; f. 1851; Publr. ARTHUR OCHS SULZBERGER; Assoc. Editor CLIFTON DANIEL; Ind.; M.S.; circ. 877,962 (M.), 1,486,902 (S.).

Staten Island Advance: 950 Fingerboard Rd., Staten Island, New York, N.Y.; f. 1886; Publr. S. I. NEWHOUSE; Editor LES TRAUTMANN; Ind.-Dem.; E.S.; circ. 70,000 (E.), 70,100 (S.).

Wall Street Journal: 22 Cortlandt St., New York, N.Y. 10007; f. 1889; Man. Editor FRED TALYOR; Ind.; M.; circ. 1,300,000.

White Plains Reporter Dispatch: Westchester Rockland Newspapers Inc., 10 Church St., White Plains, N.Y. 10602; f. 1917; Editor IRVING LEVINE; Ind.-Rep.; circ. 47,685 (E.).

NORTH CAROLINA

Asheville Citizen (M.), **Asheville Times** (E.), **Asheville Citizen-Times** (S.): 14 O. Henry Avenue, Asheville, N.C. 28801; f. 1870; Publr. ROBERT BUNNELLE; Editor (Citizen) R. B. SATTERTHWAITE, (Times) PHILIP CLARK, Senior Editor (Citizen-Times) LUTHER B. THIGPEN; Ind.-Dem.; circ. 47,081 (M.), 22,220 (E.), 69,301 (S.).

Charlotte Observer (M.S.), **Charlotte News** (E.): 600 S. Tryon St., Charlotte, N.C. 28201; f. 1886 (Observer), 1888 (News); Publr. JAMES L. KNIGHT; Editor (Observer) STEWART SPENCER, (News) PERRY MORGAN; Ind. (Observer), (News); circ. 175,895 (M.), 69,163 (E.), 220,632 (S.).

Durham Herald (M.S.), **Durham Sun** (E.): 115 Market, Durham 1, N.C.; Publr. STEED ROLLINS; Exec. Editor H. B. WEBB; Dem.; circ. 42,187 (M.), 26,607 (E.), 51,511 (S.).

Greensboro Record (E.), **Greensboro News** (M.S.): 200-04 N. Davie St., P.O.B. 20848 Greensboro, N.C. 27420; f. 1890 (Record), 1909 (News); Editor WM. D. SNIDER; Exec. News Editor PORTER L. CRISP; Ind.; circ. 81,000 (M.), 35,000 (E.), 103,000 (S.).

Raleigh News and Observer (M.S.), **Raleigh Times** (E.): 215 S. McDowell St., Raleigh, N.C. 27601; Editor (News and Observer) CLAUDE SITTON (Times) HERBERT O'KEEF; Ind.-Dem.; circ. 135,065 (M.), 32,698 (E.), 157,811 (S.).

Winston-Salem Journal (M.) f. 1897, **Twin City Sentinel** (E.) f. 1885, **Winston-Salem Journal and Sentinel** (S.) f. 1928: 416-20 N. Marshall, Winston-Salem, N.C. 27102; Editor and Publr. WALLACE CARROLL; Pres. and Gen. Man. DONALD CHIPMAN; Ind.; circ. 77,752 (M.), 45,549 (E.), 97,152 (S.).

NORTH DAKOTA

Fargo Forum : 101 5th St. N., Fargo, N.D. 58102; Publr. WILLIAM C. MARCIL; Editor JOHN D. PAULSON; Ind.-Rep.; D.S.; circ. 60,775 (D.), 60,247 (S.).

OHIO

Akron Beacon Journal: 44 E. Exchange St., Akron, Ohio 44,328; f. 1839; Pres. and Editorial Chair. JOHN S. KNIGHT; Publr. BEN MAIDENBURG; Editor PERRY MORGAN; Ind.; E.S.; circ. 175,302 (E.), 214,375 (S.).

Canton Repository: 500 Market Ave., S., Canton, Ohio; f. 1815; Editor JOHN A. MAXWELL, Jr.; Rep.; E.S.; circ. 70,612 (E.), 82,768 (S.).

Cincinnati Enquirer: 617 Vine St., Cincinnati, Ohio 45201; f. 1841; Editor BRADY BLACK; Ind.; M.S.; circ. 194,945 (M.), 301,755 (S.).

Cincinnati Post and Times-Star: 800 Broadway St., Cincinnati, Ohio 45202; f. 1881; Editor WALTER FRIEDENBERG; Ind.; E.; circ. 209,118.

Cleveland Plain Dealer: 1801 Superior Ave., Cleveland, Ohio 44114; f. 1842; Publr. and Editor THOMAS VAIL; Ind.; M.S.; circ. 409,281 (M.), 514,756 (S.).

Cleveland Press: E. W. Scripps Co., 901 Lakeside Ave., Cleveland, Ohio 44114; f. 1878; Editor THOMAS L. BOARDMAN; Ind.; E.; circ. 378,532.

Columbus Citizen-Journal: 34 S. Third St., Columbus, Ohio 43216; f. 1899; Editor CHARLES EGGER; Ind.; M.; circ. 118,899.

Columbus Dispatch: Dispatch Printing Co., 34 S. Third St., Columbus, Ohio 43216; Publr. EDGAR T. WOLFE, Jr.; Exec. Editor CARL DE BLOOM; Ind.; E.S.; circ. 225,450 (E.), 346,133 (S.).

Dayton Journal Herald (M.), **Dayton News** (E.S.): 37 S. Ludlow St., Dayton, Ohio 45402; Editor (Journal-Herald) CHARLES T. ALEXANDER, (News) JAMES FAIN; Ind.-Rep. (Journal-Herald), Ind.-Dem. (News); circ. 113,117 (M.), 156,347 (E.), 226,806 (S.).

Lima News: 121 E. High St., Lima, Ohio; f. 1884 (E.), 1896 (S.); Publr. E. R. SMITH; Editor TOM MULLEN; Ind.; E.S.; circ. 40,535 (E.), 46,017 (S.).

Mansfield News Journal: 70 W. Fourth Street, Mansfield, Ohio; f. 1885; Editor D. K. WOODMAN; Ind.; E.S.; circ. 38,145(E.), 44,601 (S.).

Springfield Sun (M.), **Springfield News** (E.), **Springfield News-Sun** (S.): 202 N. Limestone, Springfield, Ohio; f. 1894 (Sun), 1817 (News), 1928 (News-Sun); Editor (Sun) MAYNARD KNISKERN, (News) LOREN G. SCHULTZ; Ind. (Sun), Ind.-Dem. (News); circ. 18,783 (M.), 29,187 (E.), 42,229 (S.).

Toledo Times (M. except Sat.), **Toledo Blade** (Sat. M., E.S.): 541 Superior St., Toledo, Ohio; f. 1835; Publrs. PAUL BLOCK, Jr., WILLIAM BLOCK; Exec. Editor JOSEPH O'CONOR; Ind.; circ. 29,565 (M.), 174,612 (E.), 204,700 (S.).

Warren Tribune Chronicle: 240 Franklin St., S.E., Warren, Ohio 44482; Publr. HELEN HART HURLBURT; Editor STANLEY E. HART; Rep.; E.; circ. 41,958.

Youngstown Vindicator: Vindicator Square, Youngstown, Ohio 44501; Publr. and Editor WILLIAM J. BROWN, Jr.; Ind.-Dem.; E.S.; circ. 103,013 (E.), 158,295 (S.).

OKLAHOMA

Daily Oklahoman (M.S.) **Oklahoma City Times** (E.): Box 25125, Oklahoma City 73125 Okla.; f. 1889; Pres. and Publr. E. K. GAYLORD; Exec. Vice-Pres. and Treas. EDWARD L. GAYLORD; Man. Editor CHARLES L. BENNETT; Ind.; circ. 192,478 (M.), 102,661 (E.), 309,408 (S.).

Oklahoma Journal: Oklahoma City, Okla.; f. 1964; Publr. and Editor W. P. BILL ATKINSON; Ind.; circ. 51,545 (M.), 44,473 (S.).

Tulsa World (M.S.) f. 1905, **Tulsa Tribune** (E.) f. 1904: Box 1770, Tulsa, Okla. 74102; Exec. Editor (World) SID STEEN; Editor (Tribune) JENKIN L. JONES; Ind. (World), Ind.-Rep. (Tribune); circ. 118,323 (M.), 79,711 (E.), 192,450 (S.).

OREGON

Eugene Register-Guard: 975 High St., Eugene, Ore. 97401; f. 1867; Publr. and Editor ALTON F. BAKER, Jr.; Ind.; Monday to Friday E., Saturday M., S.; circ. 56,588 (E.), 56,671 (M.), 58,772 (S.).

Portland Oregonian (M.S.) f. 1850; Ind.-Rep., **Oregon Journal** (E.) f. 1902; Ind.: 1320 S.W. Broadway, Portland, Ore. 97201; Pres. and Gen. Man. (Oregonian) FRED A. STICKEL; Publr. (Oregonian) ROBERT C. NOTSON; Editor (Journal) DONALD J. STERLING, Man. Editor (Oregonian) RICHARD NOKES; (Journal) ED. O'MEARA; circ. 244,868 (M.), 128,032 (E.), 407,076 (S.).

PENNSYLVANIA

Allentown Call (M.) f. 1883, **Allentown Chronicle** (E.) f. 1870, **Allentown Call-Chronicle** (S.): 101 North 6th St., Allentown, Pa. 18105; Editor (Call) GORDON B. FISTER, (Chronicle) NELSON A. WEISER, (Call-Chronicle) JOHN W. STEACY, Jr.; Ind.; circ. 127,868 (M.E.), 147,646 (S.).

Bucks County Courier Times: Route 13, Levittown, Pa. 19058; f. 1966; Pres. and Publr. S. W. CALKINS, Jr.; Editor SANDY OPPENHEIMER; E.; circ. 60,000.

Delaware County Daily Times: 18–26 East 8th St., Chester, Pa.; f. 1875; Gen. Man. RONALD A. HEDLEY; Exec. Editor ARTHUR MAYHEW; Ind.; E.; circ. 49,503.

Easton Express: 30 N. Fourth, Easton, Pa. 18042; f. 1855; Publr. J. L. STACKHOUSE; Editor DONALD W. DIEHL; Ind.; E.; circ. 52,947.

Erie News (M.), **Erie Times** (E.), **Erie Times-News** (S.): 20 E. 12th St., Erie, Pa. 16501; Publr. GEORGE J. MEAD; Editor JOSEPH MEAGHER; Ind.-Rep.; circ. 21,394 (M.), 49,215 (E.), 90,443 (S.).

Harrisburg Patriot (M.) f. 1854, **Harrisburg News** (E.) f. 1831, **Harrisburg Patriot-News** (S.) f. 1949: 812 Market St., Harrisburg, Pa. 17104; Pres. EDWIN F. RUSSELL; Exec. Editor JAMES R. DORAN; Ind.; circ. 47,094 (M.), 72,235 (E.), 168,128 (S.).

Johnstown Tribune-Democrat: Locust St., Johnstown, Pa. 15907; f. 1853; Publr. RICHARD H. MAYER; Editor G. FATTMAN; Ind.-Rep.; D.; circ. 59,555.

Lancaster Intelligencer Journal (M.), **Lancaster New Era** (E.), **Lancaster Sunday News** (S.): 8 W. King St., Lancaster, Pa. 17604; f. 1794 (Intelligencer), 1877 (New Era), 1923 (News), Publr. JOHN F. STEINMAN; Editor (Intelligencer) HARRY F. STACKS, (News) HAROLD J. EAGER, (New Era) DANIEL L. CHERRY; Ind.; circ. 36,746 (M.), 58,075 (E.), 118,469 (S.).

Philadelphia Bulletin: 30th and Market Streets, Philadelphia, Pa. 19101; f. 1847; Publr. ROBERT L. TAYLOR; Exec. Editor WILLIAM B. DICKINSON; Ind.; E.S.; circ. 611,634 (E.), 691,297 (S.).

Philadelphia Inquirer: 400 N. Broad St. Philadelphia, Pa. 19101; f. 1771; Pres. FREDERICK CHAIT: Vice-Pres. and Gen. Man. SAM S. McKEEL; Exec. Editor JOHN E. McMULLAN; Ind.; M.S.; circ. 450,293 (M.), 833,302 (S.).

Philadelphia News: 400 North Broad St., Philadelphia, Pa. 19101; f. 1925; Pres. FREDERICK CHALT; Editor ROLFE NEILL; Ind.; E.; circ. 250,697.

Pittsburgh Post-Gazette: 50 Blvd. of Allies, Pittsburgh, Pa. 15222; Publrs. WILLIAM BLOCK, PAUL BLOCK, Jr.; Editor FRANK N. HAWKINS; Ind.; M.; circ. 230,801.

Pittsburgh Press: 34 Blvd. of Allies, Pittsburgh, Pa. 15230; Editor JOHN TROAN; Ind.; E.S.; circ. 284,011 (D.), 701,622 (S.).

Reading Times (M.) f. 1858, **Reading Eagle** (E.S.) f. 1868: 345 Penn St., Reading, Pa. 19601; Publr. HAWLEY QUIER; Man. Editor THOMAS N. BOLAND (Eagle), RICHARD C. PETERS (Times); Ind.; circ. 40,000 (M.), 50,000 (E.), 90,124 (S.).

Scranton Times (E.), **Scranton Sunday Times** (S.): Penn and Spruce, Scranton, Pa. 18501; f. 1870; Editor EDWARD J. LYNETT, Jr.; Man. Editor H. MULLEN; Ind.; circ. 59,827 (E.), 57,753 (S.).

Scranton Tribune (M.) f. 1870, **Scrantonian** (S.) f. 1897: 338 N. Washington Ave., Scranton, Pa. 18501; Pres. (Tribune) N. GOODMAN, (Scrantonian) R. LITTLE, III; Editor ROBERT J. ARTHUR; Rep.; circ. 40,184 (M.), 51,691 (S.).

Wilkes-Barre Record (D.), **The Evening Times-Leader** (D.), **News** (D.): 15 North Main St., Wilkes-Barre, Pa. 18701; f. 1832 (Record), 1879 (Times-Leader), 1878 (News), Exec. Editor (Daily) PAUL J. ARTHUR, (Sunday) HARRISON H. SMITH; Ind.; circ. 72,803 (D.), 21,261 (S.).

York Dispatch: East Philadelphia St., York, Pa.; Publr. D. P. YOUNG; Man. Editor C. F. MOORE; E.; circ. 47,000.

RHODE ISLAND

Providence Journal (M.S.), **Providence Bulletin** (E.): 75 Fountain St.. Providence, R.I. 02902; f. 1829; Publr. JOHN C. A. WATKINS; Asst. Publr. EDWIN P. YOUNG; Editor CHARLES H. SPILMAN; Exec. Editor C. M. HAUSER; Ind.; circ. 67,975 (M.), 148,182 (E.), 206,826 (S.).

SOUTH CAROLINA

Anderson Independent (M.S.), **Anderson Mail** (E.), P.O.B. 2507, Anderson, S.C. 29621; Publr. JOHN GINN; Editor (Independent) L. S. HEMBREE, (Mail) J. B. HALL; Dem.; circ. 52,910 (M.), 8,420 (E.), 53,602 (S.).

Charleston News and Courier (M.S.), **Charleston Post** (E.): 134 Columbus St., Charleston, S.C. 29402; f. 1803 (Courier), 1894 (Post); Publr. PETER MANIGAULT; Editor (News and Courier) ARTHUR M. WILCOX, (Post) THOMAS R. WARING; Ind.; circ. 66,669 (M.), 41,260 (E.), 91,603 (S.).

Columbia State (M.S.) f. 1891; Editor W. E. RONE, **Columbia Record** (E.) f. 1897; Editor T. N. McLEAN: Stadium Rd., P.O.B. 1333, Columbia, S.C. 29202; Publr. AMBROSE G. HAMPTON; Ind.; circ. 109,629 (M.), 32,721 (E.), 126,164 (S.).

Greenville News (M.S.), **Greenville Piedmont** (E.): 305 S. Main St., Greenville, S.C. 29602; Publr. J. KELLY SISK; Editor (News) CARL D. WELMER, (Piedmont) WILLIAM C. MORRIS, circ. 88,746 (M.), 26,181 (E.), 97,908 (S.).

Spartanburg Herald (M.), **Spartanburg Journal** (E.), **Spartanburg Herald-Journal** (S.): 177 West Main St., Spartanburg, S.C. 29301; f. 1890 (Herald), 1844 (Journal), 1890 (Herald-Journal); Publr. PHIL BUCHHEIT; Editor (Herald) HUBERT HENDRIX, (Journal) T. A. SMITH, Man. Editor (Herald-Journal) SEYMOUR ROSENBURG; Dem. circ. 40,132 (M.), 10,492 (E.), 46,317 (S.).

SOUTH DAKOTA

Sioux-Falls Argus-Leader: 200 S. Minnesota, Sioux Falls, S.D. 57102; f. 1885; Publr. W. H. LEOPARD; Exec. Editor A. YEAGER; Ind.; circ. 53,537 (E.), 60,554 (S.).

TENNESSEE

Chattanooga Times (M.S.): 117 East 10th St., Chattanooga, Tenn. 37401; Publr. RUTH S. HOLMBERG; Pres. and Gen. Man. A. W. HOLMBERG; Editor NORMAN BRADLEY; Ind.-Dem.; circ. 65,674 (M.), 68,804 (S.).

Knoxville Journal: 208 W. Church Avenue, Knoxville, Tenn.; f. 1839; Publr. CHARLES H. SMITH, III; Editor WILLIAM CHILDRESS; Rep.; M.; circ. 63,756.

Knoxville News-Sentinel: 204 W. Church Ave., Knoxville, Tenn. 37901; f. 1886; Editor RALPH L. MILLETT, Jr.; Ind.; E.S.; circ. 109,099 (E.), 162,197 (S.).

Memphis Commercial Appeal (M.S.) f. 1840, **Memphis Press-Scimitar** (E.) f. 1880: 495 Union Ave., Memphis, Tenn. 38101; Editor (Commercial Appeal) GORDON HANNA, (Press-Scimitar) CHARLES H. SCHNEIDER; Ind.; circ. 221,325 (M.), 125,865 (E.), 286,708 (S.).

Nashville Banner: 1100 Broadway, Nashville 1, Tenn. 37203; Publr. JAMES G. STAHLMAN; Editor ALVAND C. DUNKLEBERGER; Ind.; E.; circ. 99,895.

Nashville Tennessean: 1100 Broadway, Nashville 1, Tenn. 37203; f. 1812; Pres. AMON CARTER EVANS; Publr. JOHN SEIGENTHALER; Dem.; M.S.; circ. 145,234 (M.), 246,498 (S.).

TEXAS

Abilene Reporter News: 100 Block Cypress St., Abilene, Tex. 79604; f. 1881; Publr. A. B. SHELTON; Editor E. N. WISHCAMPER; Ind.-Dem.; M.E.S.; circ. 41,663 (M.), 19,384 (E.), 54,263 (S.).

Amarillo News (M.), **Amarillo Globe Times** (E. ex. Sat.), **Amarillo News-Globe** (S.): 900 Harrison St., Amarillo, Tex. 79105; f. 1909 (News), 1924 (Globe); Editor (News) WES IZZARD, (Globe Times) T. THOMPSON; Man. Editor JIM CLARK; Ind.-Dem.; circ. 49,525 (M.), 35,513 (E.), 75,600 (S.).

Austin American (M.), **Austin Statesman** (E.), **Austin American-Statesman** (S.): 308 Guadalupe St., P.O.B. 670, Austin, Tex. 78767; f. 1914 (American), 1871 (Statesman), 1924 (American-Statesman); Publr. RICHARD F. BROWN; Editor SAM WOOD; Dem.; circ. 58,768 (M.), 32,725 (E.), 89,040 (S.).

Beaumont Enterprise (M.S.), **Beaumont Journal** (E.): 380 Walnut St., Beaumont, Tex. 77704; f. 1880 (Enterprise), 1889 (Journal); Editor BILL HARTMAN; Ind.-Dem.; circ. 63,471 (M.), 19,964 (E.), 75,675 (S.).

Corpus Christi Caller (M.), **Corpus Christi Times** (E.), **Corpus Christi Caller** (S.): 820 Lower Broadway, Corpus Christi, Tex. 78401; Editor and Publr. EDWARD H. HARTE, Exec. Editor JOHN L. STALLINGS; Ind.; circ. 68,514 (M.), 37,443 (E.), 91,655 (S.).

Dallas News: "Communications Center", Dallas, Tex. 75222; f. 1885; Pres. JOE M. DEALEY; Editor DICK WEST; Ind.-Dem.; M.S.; circ. 266,667 (M.), 310,530 (S.).

Dallas Times Herald: 1101 Pacific, Dallas, Tex. 75202; f. 1876; Publr. JAS. F. CHAMBERS, Jr.; Editor FELIX R. McKNIGHT; Ind.-Dem.; E.S.; circ. 244,326 (E.), 297,990 (S.).

El Paso Times (M.S.), **El Paso Herald-Post** (E.): 401 Mills St., El Paso, Tex. 79999; f. 1881; Pres. (Times) DORRANCE D. RODERICK, (Herald-Post) FRANK POWERS; Editor (Times) WILLIAM A. LATHAM, (Herald-Post) ROBERT W. LEE; Ind.; circ. 59,348 (M.), 43,867 (E.), 87,117 (S.).

Fort Worth Press: 507 Jones, Fort Worth, Tex. 76102; f. 1921; Editor DELBERT WILLIS; Ind.; E.S. (ex. Sat.); circ. 48,257 (E.), 52,456 (S.).

Fort Worth Star-Telegram: 400 W. 7th St., Fort Worth, Tex. 76101; Publr. AMON G. CARTER, Jr.; Editor JACK L. BUTLER; Ind.-Dem.; M.E.S.; circ. 235,687 (M.E.), 227,297 (S.).

Houston Chronicle: 512-20 Travis St., Houston, Tex. 77002; f. 1901; Editor EVERETT D. COLLIER; Ind.-Dem.; E.S.; circ. 297,482 (E.), 359,638 (S.).

Houston Post: 4747 Southwest Freeway, Houston, Tex. 77001; f. 1885; Exec. Editor W. P. HOBBY, Jr.; Ind.; M.S.; circ. 292,122 (M.), 344,716 (S.).

Lubbock Avalanche-Journal: 8th St. and Ave. J. Lubbock, Tex. 79408; Editor J. HARRIS; Exec. Editor D. KNAPP; Ind.; M.E.S.; circ. 59,321 (M.), 22,024 (E.), 76,102 (S.).

San Angelo Standard-Times: 34 West Harris St., San Angelo Tex. 76901; Publr. F. CONN; Editor BILL MARTIN; M.E.S. (ex. Sat.); circ. 40,452 (M.), 9,618 (E.), 43,313 (S.).

San Antonio Express (M.), **San Antonio News** (E.), **San Antonio Express-News** (S.): Ave. E. and 3rd St., San Antonio, Tex. 78205; f. 1865; Publr. HOUSTON H. HARTE; Exec. Editor C. O. KILPATRICK; Ind.; circ. 84,329 (M.), 63,048 (E.), 133,052 (S.).

San Antonio Light: Hearst Corpn., 5th and Broadway, San Antonio 6, Tex. 78206; f. 1881; Publr. and Editor F. A. BENNACK, Jr.; Ind.; E.S.; circ. 123,560 (E.), 170,121 (S.).

Waco News-Tribune (M.), **Waco Times-Herald** (E.), **Waco Tribune-Herald** (s.): 900 Franklin, Waco, Tex. 76703; f. 1895 (News-Tribune), 1891 (Times-Herald); Publr. PAT TAGGAGT; Editor HARRY PROVENCE; Ind.; circ. 27,304 (M.), 21,364 (E.), 51,054 (S.).

Wall Street Journal (Southwest Edition): *see under* New York; circ. 130,479.

Wichita Falls Record News (M., except Sunday), **Wichita Fall Times** (E.S.): 1301 Lamar St., Wichita, Tex. 76307; f. 1907; Publr. and Editor RHEA HOWARD; Dem.; circ. 31,404 (M.), 19,562 (E.), 46,359 (S.).

UTAH

Salt Lake City Deseret News: 34 East First St., Salt Lake City, Utah 84110; f. 1850; Editor W. B. SMART; Ind.; E.; circ. 79,965.

Salt Lake City Tribune: 143 South Main St., Salt Lake City, Utah 84111; f. 1871; Publr. J. W. GALLIVAN; Editor ARTHUR C. DECK; Ind.; M.S.; circ. 110,635 (M.), 185,847 (S.).

VERMONT

Burlington Free Press: 189 College St., Burlington, Vt. 05401; f. 1827; Publr. URBAN L. BERGERON; Editor GORDON T. MILLS; Ind.-Rep.; M.; circ. 48,223.

VIRGINIA

Newport News Daily Press (M.S.), **Newport News Times-Herald** (E.): 7505 Warwick Blvd., Newport Va. 23607; f. 1896 (Press) 1900 (Times-Herald); Editor Mrs. DOROTHY R. BOTTOM; Ind.-Dem.; circ. 51,259 (M.), 41,618 (E.), 81,410 (S.).

Norfolk Virginian-Pilot (M.S.) f. 1865, **Norfolk Ledger-Star** (E.) f. 1876: 150 W. Brambleton Ave., Norfolk, Va. 23501; Publr. FRANK BATTEN; Editor (Virginian-Pilot) ROBERT MASON, (Ledger-Star) GEORGE J. HEBERT; Ind.; circ. 129,793 (M.), 105,296 (E.), 186,293 (S.).

Richmond Times-Dispatch (M.S.) f. 1850, **Richmond News Leader** (E.) f. 1896: 333 E. Grace St., Richmond, Va. 23219; Publr. D. TENNANT BRYAN; Exec. Editor J. E. LEARD; Ind.; circ. 142,019 (M.), 121,063 (E.), 199,287 (S.).

Roanoke Times (M.S.), **Roanoke World-News** (E.): 201-209 W. Campbell Ave., Roanoke, Va. 24011; Publr. BARTON W. MORRIS, Jr.; Ind.; circ. 62,636 (M.), 50,428 (E.), 108,999 (S.).

WASHINGTON

Seattle Post-Intelligencer: Hearst Publishing Co., 6th and Wall Sts., Seattle, Wash. 98121; f. 1863; Publr. D. STARR; Editor J. DOUGHTY; Ind.; M.S.; circ. 200,451 (M.), 250,841 (S.).

Seattle Times: Fairview Ave N. and John, Seattle, Wash. 98111; f. 1896; Publr. J. A. BLETHEN; Man. Editor HENRY MacLEOD; Ind.; E.S.; circ. 234,971 (E.), 294,211 (S.).

Spokane Chronicle: West 926 Sprague, Spokane, Wash. 99210; f. 1881; Publr. W. H. COWLES; Editor H. C. CLEAVINGER; Ind.; E.; circ. 82,502.

Spokane Spokesman-Review: West 927 Riverside, Spokane Wash. 99210; f. 1883; Publr. W. H. COWLES 3rd.; Editor JAMES L. BRACKEN; Ind.-Rep.; M.S.; circ. 82,277 (M.), 126,138 (S.).

Tacoma News Tribune (E.) f. 1918, **Tacoma News Tribune and Sunday Ledger** (s.) f. 1907: 1950 S. State St., Tacoma, Wa. 98411; Publr. ELBERT H. BAKER II; Editor D. A. PUGNETTI; Ind.; circ. 97,232 (E.), 97,129 (S.).

WEST VIRGINIA

Charleston Gazette (M.), **Charleston Gazette-Mail** (S.): 1001 Virginia St. E., Charleston, W. Va. 25330; f. 1883 (Gazette), 1887 (Mail); Editor HARRY G. HOFFMAN; Ind.-Dem.; circ. 59,701 (M.), 105,699 (S.).

Charleston Mail: 1001 Virginia St. E., Charleston, W. Va. 25330; f. 1887; Editor J. D. MAURICE; Ind.-Rep.; E.; circ. 59,171.

Huntington Herald-Dispatch (M.), **Huntington Advertiser** (E.), **Huntington Herald-Advertiser** (S.): 946 5th Ave., Huntington, W. Va. 25701; f. 1927; Publr. (Herald-Dispatch, Advertiser) N. S. HAYDEN; Editor-in-Chief GEORGE H. CLARK; Man. Editor (Herald-Dispatch and Herald Advertiser) DONALD G. MAYNE, (Huntington Advertiser) DON HATFIELD; Rep. (Herald-Dispatch), Dem. (Advertiser), Ind. (Herald-Advertiser); circ. 55,000 (M.), 18,000 (E.), 62,000 (S.).

Wheeling Intelligencer (M.) f. 1852, **Wheeling News-Register** (E. ex. Sat., s.) f. 1890: News Publishing Co., 1500 Main St., Wheeling, W. Va.; Editor (Intelligencer) FRANCIS HOLLENDONNER (News-Register) HARRY HAMM; Rep. (Intelligencer), Ind.-Dem. (News-Register); circ. 25,577 (M.), 30,476 (E.), 65,351 (S.).

WISCONSIN

Green Bay Press-Gazette: 435 E. Walnut St., Green Bay, Wis. 54305; f. 1915; Editor DAVID A. YUENGER; Ind.; E.S.; circ. 49,913 (E.), 64,000 (S.).

Milwaukee Sentinel (M.) f. 1837, **Milwaukee Journal** (E.S.) f. 1882: 333 W. State St., Milwaukee, Wis. 53201; Publr. DONALD B. ABERT; Editor (Sentinel) Harvey W. SCHWANDNER, (Journal) RICHARD LEONARD; Ind.; circ. 180,349 (M.), 357,077 (E.), 551,017 (S.).

Post Crescent: 306 West Washington St., Appleton, Wis. 54911; Editor JOHN B. TORINUS; E.S.; circ. approx. 45,353 (E.), 49,345 (S.).

Wisconsin State Journal (M.S.) f. 1839; Ind.-Rep., **Capital Times** (E.) f. 1917; Ind.-Dem.: 115 South Carroll St., Madison, Wis. 53701; Publr. (Journal) J. MARTIN WOLMAN; Editor (Journal) WILLIAM C. ROBBINS; Publr. and Editor (Times) MILES McMILLIN; circ. 78,258 (M.), 46,788 (E.), 120,566 (S.).

WYOMING

Casper Star-Tribune: 111 South Jefferson, Casper, Wyo.; f. 1914; Publr. and Editor THOMAS W. HOWARD; Ind.; circ. 29,637 (D.), 30,727 (S.).

SELECTED PERIODICALS

(Q=quarterly; M=monthly; F=fortnightly; W=weekly)

AAUW Journal (*American Association of University Women*): 2401 Virginia Ave., N.W., Washington, D.C. 20037; f. 1882; Editor JEAN FOX; circ. 185,000; 7 a year.

Africa Report: 833 United Nations Plaza, Room 505, New York, N.Y. 10017; circ. 11,000; 6 a year.

Agricultural Situation: Statistical Reporting Service; Dept. of Agriculture, Washington, D.C. 20250; f. 1921; agricultural economics; Editor GERALDINE C. SCHUMACHER; circ. 170,000; M.

America: 106 West 56th St., New York, N.Y. 10019; f. 1909; Roman Catholic; Editor D. R. CAMPION; circ. 65,000; W.

American Anthropologist: 1703 New Hampshire Ave., N.W. Washington, D.C. 20009; Editor R. A. MANNERS; circ. 12,000; two-monthly.

American Artist: Billboard Publishing Co., Inc., 1 Astor Place, New York, N.Y. 10036; f. 1937; Editor SUSAN E. MEYER; circ. 89,677.

American Child, The: 419 Park Ave. South, New York, N.Y. 10036; f. 1919; Editor LILA ROSENBLUM; Lib.; M.

American Cinematographer: American Society of Cinematographers Inc., 1782 N. Orange Drive, Hollywood, Calif. 90028; f. 1920; Editor HERB A. LIGHTMAN; M.

American Economic Review: American Economic Asscn., Northwestern Univ., Evanston, Ill.; f. 1911; Editor GEORGE H. BORTS; circ. 26,000; Q.

American Federationist: A.F.L.-C.I.O., Washington, D.C. 20006; Editor GEORGE MEANY; M.

American Heritage: 1221 Ave. of the Americas, New York, N.Y. 10020; Editor O. JENSEN; circ. 210,000; 6 a year.

American Historical Review, The: 400 A St., S.E., Washington, D.C. 20003; Editor R. K. WEBB; circ. 25,000; 5 issues annually.

American Home: 641 Lexington Ave, New York 10022; f. 1928; Editor HUBBARD H. COBB; circ. 3,359,606; M.

American Journal of Cardiology, American Journal of Surgery, American Journal of Medicine: 666 Fifth Ave., New York, N.Y. 10019; Editor-in-Chief A. J. ANTENUCCI, M.D.; Editors W. J. GRACE, M.D. (Medicine), ROBERT M. ZOLLINGER, M.D. (Surgery), SIMON DACK, M.D. (Cardiology).

American Journal of International Law: 2223 Massachusetts Ave., N.W., Washington, D.C. 20008; f. 1906; Pres. W. D. ROGERS; Editor-in-Chief R. R. BAXTER; circ. 9,000; Q.

American Journal of Psychiatry: American Psychiatric Association, 1700 18th St., N.W., Washington, D.C. 20009; Editor FRANCIS J. BRACELAND, M.D.; circ. 26,290; M.

American Journal of Public Health: 1740 Broadway, New York, N.Y. 10019; f. 1911; Editor GEORGE ROSEN, M.D.; circ. 30,000; M.; also publish *The Nation's Health*, Editor PATRICK FLANAGAN.

American Legion Magazine: 1345 Ave. of the Americas, New York, N.Y. 10019; f. 1919; organ of the American Legion; Editor ROBERT B. PITKIN; circ. 2,500,000; M.

American Literature: Duke University Press, College Station, Box 6697, Durham, N.C. 27708; f. 1929; Editor ARLIN TURNER; circ. 5,800; Q.

American Motorist: AAA, 8111 Gatehouse Rd., Falls Church, Va. 22042; Editor GLENN T. LASHLEY; M.

American Observer: Scholastic Magazines Inc., 50 West 44th St., New York, N.Y. 10036; f. 1931; Editor LE ROY HAYMAN; also publish *Civic Leader*, Editor ANTON BERLE.

American Photograph: American Photographic Publishing Company, 421 Fifth Ave., Minneapolis, Minn.; f. 1889; Editor GEORGE WRIGHT; M.

American Political Science Review: 1527 New Hampshire Ave., N.W., Washington, D.C. 20036; Editorial Offices of Review, North Hall, University of Wisconsin, Madison, Wis. 53706; f. 1903; Editor NELSON POLSBY; circ. 16,000; Q.

American Scholar: 1811 Q. St., N.W., Washington, D.C. 20009; Editor P. GAY; circ. 47,000; Q.

American Sociological Review: American Sociological Association, 1722 N St., N.W., Washington, D.C. 20036; Editor JAMES F. SHORT, Jr.; circ. 18,000; two-monthly.

American Teacher: 1012 14th St., N.W., Washington, D.C. 20005; f. 1916; Editor DAVID A. ELSILA; circ. 450,000; M., excluding July and August.

Analytical Chemistry: American Chemical Society, 1155 16th St., Washington, D.C. 20036; f. 1928; Editor Prof. HERBERT A. LAITINEN; circ. 30,000; M.

Architectural Record: c/o McGraw Hill Inc., 1221 Ave. of the Americas, New York, N.Y. 10020; Editor WALTER F. WAGNER, Jr.; circ. 54,000; M.

Argosy Magazine: 205 East 42nd St., New York 10017; f. 1882; Editor HENRY STEEGER; circ. 1,348,000; M.

Armed Forces Journal International: 1710 Connecticut Ave., Washington, D.C. 20009; f. 1863; Publr. M. ERTEL; Editor BENJAMIN SCHEMMER; circ. 25,000; M.

Atlantic Monthly, The: 8 Arlington St., Boston, Mass. 02116; f. 1857; Editor ROBERT MANNING; Ind.; circ. 325,000; M.

Automotive Industries: Chilton Company, Radnor, Penna. 19089; f. 1895; Publr. E. H. JACOBS.; F.

Barrons National Business & Financial Weekly: 30 Broad St., New York 10004; Editor ROBERT M. BLEIBERG; circ. 492,627; W.

Better Homes and Gardens: Meredith Corporation, 1716 Locust St., Des Moines, Ia. 50336; f. 1922; Editor JAMES A. AUTRY; circ. 7,777,770; M.

Biological Abstracts: 2100 Arch St., Philadelphia, Pa. 19103; f. 1926; Dir. P. V. PARKINS.

Books Abroad: University of Oklahoma Press, Norman, Oklahoma; f. 1927; Editor IVAR IVASK; circ. 2,800; Q.

British-American Trade News: British-American Chamber of Commerce, 10 East 40th St., New York, N.Y.10016; f. 1964; Editor SADIE GOLD; Q.

Broadcasting: 1735 De Sales St., N.W., Washington, D.C. 20036; f. 1931; Chair. and Editor SOL TAISHOFF; Ind.; circ. 40,000; W.

Bulletin of the Atomic Scientists: c/o Educational Foundation for Nuclear Science, 935 E. 60th St., Chicago, Ill. 60637; Editor-in-Chief EUGENE RABINOWITCH; Man. Editor RICHARD S. LEWIS; circ. 26,000; 10 issues a year.

Business Week: 1221 Ave. of the Americas, New York 10020; f. 1929; Editorial Chair. LEWIS H. YOUNG; Ind.; circ. 725,000; W.

Changing Education: 1012 14th St., N.W., Washington, D.C. 20005; f. 1966; Editor DAVID A. ELSILA; circ. 425,000; Q.

Changing Times: 1729 H St., N.W., Washington, D.C. 20006; f. 1947; family economics and self-help; Publr. A. H. KIPLINGER; Editor R. W. HARVEY; circ. 1,500,000; M.

Chemical and Engineering News: American Chemical Society, 1155 16th St., N.W., Washington, D.C. 20036; f. 1923 Director RICHARD L. KENYON, Editor PATRICK P. McCURDY; circ. 135,000; W.

Chemical Week: 1221 Ave. of the Americas, New York, N.Y. 10020; f. 1914; Editor-in-Chief RALPH R. SCHULZ; circ. 55,000; W.

Child Life Magazine: 1100 Waterway Blvd., Indianapolis, Ind. 46202; f. 1921; Publr. RITA COOPER; circ. 210,000.

Childhood Education: Asscn. for Childhood Education International, 3615 Wisconsin Ave., N.W., Washington, D.C. 20016; f. 1924; Editor MONROE D. COHEN; circ. 27,000; 6 issues a year.

Christian Century, The: 407 S. Dearborn St., Chicago, Ill. 60605; f. 1908; Editor M. WALL; circ. 30,000; W.

Christian Herald: 40 Overlook Drive, Chappagua, N.Y. 10514; f. 1878; Editor K. L. WILSON; circ. 300,000; M.

Christianity Today: 1014 Washington Building, 15th and New York Ave. N.W., Washington, D.C. 20005; Editor and Publr. Dr. HAROLD LINDSELL; circ. 180,000; F.

Civil Engineering: 345 East 47th St., New York, N.Y. 10017; f. 1930; Editor K. A. GODFREY, Jr.; circ. 71,000.

Civil Liberties: American Civil Liberties Union, 22 East 40th St., New York, N.Y. 10016; f. 1920; Editor CLAIRE COOPER; circ. 200,000.

Congressional Digest: 3231 P St., N.W., Washington, D.C. 20007; f. 1921; Publr. N. T. N. ROBINSON III; Editor JOHN E. SHIELDS; M.

Consumer Reports: Consumers Union of U.S., Inc., 256 Washington St., Mount Vernon, N.Y. 10550; f. 1936; Pres. COLSTON E. WARNE; Exec. Dir. RHODA KARPATKIN; circ. 2,225,000; M.

Contemporary Psychology: American Psychological Asscn., 1200 17th St., N.W., Washington, D.C. 20036; Editor GARDNER LINDZEY; circ. 15,000; M.

Crisis, The: 1790 Broadway, New York, N.Y. 10019; f. 1910; Editor HENRY LEE MOON; M.

Cumulative Book Index: 950 University Ave., Bronx, N.Y. 10452; f. 1898; Editor NINA THOMPSON; M.

Current Biography: 950 University Ave., Bronx, N.Y. 10452; f. 1940; Editor CHARLES MORITZ; circ. 15,477; M. (except August).

Daedalus: 7 Linden, Harvard University, Cambridge, Mass. 02138; published by the American Academy of Arts and Sciences; Editor STEPHEN R. GRAUBARD; Man. Editor GENO A. BALLOTTI; circ. 60,000; Q.

Design: 1100 Waterway Blvd., Indianapolis, Ind. 46202; Publr. RITA COOPER; Editor RAYMOND E. GRAY; two-monthly.

Dun's: Dun and Bradstreet Publications Corp., 466 Lexington Ave., New York, N.Y. 10017; Editor RAYMOND J. BRADY; circ. 215,000; M.

Ebony: 820 S. Michigan, Chicago, Ill. 60605; f. 1945; news and illustrated; for Negroes; Editor HERBERT NIPSON; circ. 1,250,000; M.

Economic Geology: 91A Yale Station, New Haven, Conn. 06520; f. 1905; Editor B. J. SKINNER; 8 times a year.

Editor & Publisher: 850 Third Ave., New York 10022; f. 1884; Editor ROBERT U. BROWN; circ. 25,822; W.

Educational Record: American Council on Education, One Dupont Circle, Washington, D.C. 20036; f. 1920; Editor C. B. FAIR; circ. 10,000; Q.

Educational Screen and Audiovisual Guide: 230 E. Ohio St., Chicago 11, Ill.; f. 1922; Publr. H. S. GILLETTE; Editor PAUL C. REED; M.

Electricity on the Farm: 466 Lexington Ave., New York, N.Y. 10017; f. 1927; Publr. and Editorial Dir. H. J. HANSEN; circ. 500,000; M.

Electronics: 1221 Avenue of the Americas, New York City, N.Y., 87,500; W.

Elks Magazine: 386 Park Avenue South, New York 10016; Gen. Man. W. H. MAGRATH; circ. 1,361,455; M.

Esquire: 488 Madison Ave., New York City, N.Y. 10022; f. 1933; U.S. and International editions; Publr. ARNOLD GINGRICH; circ. 1,200,000; M.

Evergreen Review: Evergreen Review, Inc., 53 E. 11th St., New York, N.Y. 10003; Editor BARNEY ROSSET; literary; circ. 180,000; Q.

Export Trade: 20 Vesey St., New York 7, N.Y.; f. 1919; Editor REDINGTON FISKE; W.

Extension Service Review: U.S. Dept. of Agriculture, Washington, D.C. 20250; f. 1930; Editor MARY ANN WAMSLEY; M.; circ. 17,600.

Family Circle: New York Times Media Co., 488 Madison Ave., New York, N.Y. 10022; Editor ARTHUR HETTICH; circ. 8,000,000.

Farm Journal: Washington Square, Philadelphia, Pa. 19105; f. 1877; Editor LANE PALMER; circ. 1,750,000; M.

Federationist: American Federation of Labor and Congress of Industrial Organizations, 815 16th St., N.W. Washington, D.C. 20006; f. 1886; M.

Foreign Affairs: 58 East 68th St., New York City, N.Y. 10021; f. 1922; Editor W. P. BUNDY; circ. 75,000; Q.

Forest Industries: Miller Freeman Publications, 500 Howard St., San Francisco, Calif. 94105; Editor HERBERT G. LAMBERT; Vice-Pres. and Publr. JAMES C. WALLACE; circ. 23,000.

Fortune: Time and Life Building, New York City, N.Y. 10020; business and industry; Man. Editor ROBERT LUBAR; circ. 580,000; M.

Good Housekeeping: 959 8th Ave., New York City, N.Y. 10019; women's magazine; Editor WADE H. NICHOLS; circ. 5,800,000; M.

Graphic Arts Monthly, The: 7373 North Lincoln Ave., Chicago, Ill. 60646; f. 1929; Editor PAUL J. HARTSUCH; circ. 66,000; M.

Greek, Roman and Byzantine Studies: Duke University, Durham, N.C.; f. 1958; Sen. Editor WILLIAM H. WILLIS; Q.

Harper's Bazaar: 717 Fifth Ave., New York City, N.Y. 10022; women's fashion and general magazine; Editorial Dir. JAMES BRADY; circ. 430,000; M.

Harper's Magazine: 2 Park Ave., New York, N.Y. 10016; f. 1850; public affairs, literary; Editor ROBERT SHNAYERSON; circ. 325,000.

Harvard Business Review: Soldiers Field, Boston, Mass. 02163; f. 1922; Editor and Publr. RALPH F. LEWIS; circ. 140,000; two-monthly.

High Fidelity: The Billboard Publishing Co., Great Barrington, Mass. 01230; f. 1951; Editor LEONARD MARCUS; High Fidelity/Musical America Edition; circ. 250,000; M.

Highlights for Children: 2300 West Fifth Ave., Columbus, O. 43216; f. 1946; Editor W. B. BARBE; circ. 1,100,000.

Holiday: Curtis Publishing Co., 1100 Waterway Blvd., Indianapolis, Ind. 46202; f. 1946; Editor S. FLYTHE, Jr.; circ. 700,000; bi-monthly.

Horizon: 1221 Ave. of the Americas, New York, N.Y. 10020; Editor CHARLES L. MEE, Jr.; circ. 108,000; Q.

Hotel & Motel Management: 845 Chicago Ave., Evanston, Ill. 60202; Editor and Publisher ROBERT C. FREEMAN.

House & Garden: 350 Madison Ave., New York, N.Y. 10017; Editor-in-Chief MARY JANE POOL; circ. 1,007,999; M.

House Beautiful: 717 Fifth Ave., New York, N.Y. 10022; Editor WALLACE GUENTHER; circ. 912,000; M.

Industrial Marketing: Crain Communications Inc., 740 Rush St., Chicago, Ill. 60611; f. 1916; Man. Editor SALLY R. STRONG; circ. 23,000; M.

Industry Week: Penton Publishing Co., Penton Plaza, Cleveland, Ohio 44114; f. 1882; Editor STANLEY J. MODIC; W.; circ. 172,000.

Intellect: Society for the Advancement of Education, 1860 Broadway, New York, N.Y. 10023; f. 1915; Editor and Sec. Dr. WILLIAM W. BRICKMAN; circ. 9,000; M. (Oct.-May).

Journal of Abnormal Psychology: American Psychological Association, 1200 Seventeenth Street, N.W., Washington, D.C. 20036; f. 1906; Editor L. D. ERON; circ. 7,400; two-monthly.

Journal of Accountancy, The: 666 Fifth Ave., New York, N.Y. 10019; f. 1905; Editor WILLIAM O. DOHERTY; circ. 170,000; M.

Journal of the American Medical Association (JAMA): 535 North Dearborn St., Chicago, Ill. 60610; Editor R. H. MOSER, M.D.; circ. 230,204; W.

Journal of the American Society for Information Science (JASIS) c/o American Society for Information Science 1155 Sixteenth St., N.W., Washington, D.C. 20036; f. 1950; Editor ARTHUR W. ELIAS; circ. 6,600; two-monthly.

Journal of Applied Psychology: American Psychological Association, 1200 17th St., N.W., Washington, D.C. 20036; f. 1917; Editor EDWIN A. FLEISHMAN; circ. 7,600; two-monthly.

Journal of Criminal Law and Criminology: Northwestern University School of Law, 357 East Chicago Avenue, Chicago, Ill. 60611; f. 1910; Editor C. R. McKIRDY; circ. 4,000; Q.

Journal of Home Economics: American Home Economics Association, 2010 Massachusetts Ave., N.W., Washington, D.C. 20036; f. 1909; Editor MARY K. OVERHOLT; circ. 53,000; M. Sept. to May.

Journal of Marketing: American Marketing Association, 222 S. Riverside Plaza, Chicago, Ill. 60606; f. 1936; Exec. Dir. WAYNE A. LEMBURG; Editor E. W. CUNDIFF; circ. 18000; Q.; also publish *Journal of Marketing Research*.

Journal of Personality and Social Psychology: American Psychological Association, 1200 Seventeenth Street, N.W., Washington, D.C. 20036; f. 1965; Editor J. T. LANZETTA; circ. 6,000; M.

Journal of Philosophy: 720 Philosophy Hall, Columbia University, New York 10027; f. 1904; Editors JOHN H. RANDALL, Jr., BERNARD BEROFSKY, ARTHUR DANTO, SYDNEY MORGENBESSER, CHARLES D. PARSONS, JAMES J. WALSH; Man. Editor LEIGH S. CAUMAN; circ. 4,500; F.

Journal of Police Science and Administration: 357 East Chicago Ave., Chicago, Ill. 60611; f. 1973; Editor FRED E. INBAU; circ. 2,000; Q.

Journal of Religion: University of Chicago Press, 5801 Ellis Ave., Chicago, Ill. 60637; f. 1920; Editors NATHAN A. SCOTT, Jr., BRIAN GERRISH; Q.

Kenyon Review: Kenyon College, Gambier, Ohio 43022; f. 1939; Editor GEORGE LANNING; arts and letters; circ. 6,300; 5 times a year.

Labor: Labor Cooperative Educational & Publishing Society, 400 First Street, N.W., Washington 1, D.C.: f. 1919; Editor RUBEN LEVIN; F.

Ladies' Home Journal: Downe Publishing Co. Inc., 641 Lexington Ave., New York, N.Y. 10022; f. 1883; Editor John Mack Carter; circ. 7,000,000; m.

Library Journal: R. R. Bowker Company, 1180 Ave. of the Americas, New York 10036; f. 1876; Editor John N. Berry III; circ. 40,000; f.

McCall's Magazine: McCall Corporation, 230 Park Ave., New York, N.Y. 10017; f. 1870; Editor Patricia Carbine; circ. 7,500,000.

Management Adviser: 666 Fifth Ave., New York, N.Y. 10019; f. 1964; Editor Robert M. Smith; circ. 17,036; two-monthly.

Management Review: American Management Association, 135 West 50th St., New York, N.Y. 10020; f. 1923; Editor R. F. Guder; circ. 67,000; m.

Marketing/Communications: Decker Communications Inc., 501 Madison Ave., New York, N.Y. 10022; f. 1888; Editor Walter Joyce; circ. 71,000; m.

Materials Engineering: Reinhold Publishing Company, Inc., 600 Summer St., Stamford, Conn. 06904; f. 1929; Editor J. E. Hauck; m.

Mechanix Illustrated: 1515 Broadway, New York, N.Y. 10036; f. 1928; Editor Robert G. Beason; circ. 1,618,000; m.

Modern Packaging: 1221 Ave. of the Americas, New York, N.Y. 10020; f. 1927; Publr. J. C. Page; Editor Thomas M. Jones; circ. 53,000; m.

Motor: 250 West 55th Street, New York City, N.Y. 10019; m.

Ms: 370 Lexington Ave., New York, N.Y. 10017; f. 1972; Publr. Patricia Carbine; Editor Gloria Steinem; circ. 350,000.

Musical Quarterly, The: 866 Third Ave., New York, N.Y. 10022; f. 1915; Editor Christopher Hatch; q.

Museum News: 2233 Wisconsin Ave., N.W., Washington, D.C. 20007; f. 1924; Editor Roberta H. Faul; circ. 6,000; m.

Nation: 333 Sixth Ave., New York City, N.Y. 10014; Editor Carey McWilliams; politics and the arts; circ. 29,470; w.

Nation's Business: 1615 H St., N.W., Washington, D.C. 20006; f. 1912; Chamber of Commerce Journal; Editor Jack Wooldridge; circ. 875,000; m.

National Geographic Magazine: National Geographic Society, 17th and M Sts., N.W., Washington, D.C. 20036; f. 1888; Editor Gilbert M. Grosvenor; circ. 8,500,000.

National Review: 150 East 35th St., New York City, N.Y. 10016; f. 1955; Editor W. F. Buckley, Jr.; circ. 120,000; w.

Natural History Magazine: American Museum of Natural History, Central Park West at 79 St., New York 10024; Editor Alan Ternes; circ. 350,000; 10 a year.

New Republic: New Republic, Inc., 1244 19th St., N.W., Washington, D.C. 20036; f. 1914; Editor Gilbert A. Harrison; circ. 150,000; w.

New York Times Book Review: Times Square, New York City, N.Y.; w.

New Yorker: 25 West 43rd St., New York City, N.Y. 10036; fiction, commentary and humour; Editor William Shawn; circ. 473,275; w.

Newsweek: Newsweek Building, 444 Madison Ave., New York City, N.Y. 10022; f. 1933; Editor Osborn Elliott; European and Pacific editions; circ. 3,100,000; w.

Nursing World: Joseph Kruger Publications, 468 4th Ave., New York 16, N.Y.; f. 1888; Editor Virginia A. Turner, R.N.; m.

Office, The: 1200 Summer St., Stamford, Conn. 06904; f. 1935; Editor William R. Schulhof; circ. 117,699; m.

Outdoor Life: 380 Madison Avenue, New York, N.Y. 10017; f. 1898; Editor Chet Fish; circ. 1,900,000; m.

Paper Trade Journal: Lockwood Trade Journal Company, Inc., 49 West 45th St., New York, N.Y. 10036; f. 1872; Editor John C. W. Evans; w.

Parents' Magazine: Parents' Magazine Enterprises Inc., 52 Vanderbilt Ave., New York, N.Y. 10017; f. 1926; Publr. George J. Hecht; Editor Genevieve Millet Landau; circ. 2,000,000; m.

Parks and Recreation: 1601 North Kent St., Arlington Va. 22209; f. 1906; Editor Charles B. Fowler; circ. 30,000; m.

Partisan Review: 1 Richardson St., New Brunswick, N.J. 08903; f. 1934; Editor William Phillips; Associate Editor Steven Marcus; Lib.; circ. 10,000; q.

Personnel: American Management Associations, 135 W. 50th St., New York, N.Y. 10020; f. 1923; Exec. Editor Frances Fore; circ. 67,000; two-monthly.

Physics Today: 335 East 45th St., New York, N.Y. 10017; f. 1948; Editor Harold L. Davis; circ. 62,000; m.

Plant Operating Management: 205 East 42nd St., New York, N.Y. 10017; f. 1928; Editor Robert K. Moffett; m.

Plastics Industry Magazine: 342 Madison Avenue, New York 17, N.Y.; f. 1941; Editor Morrison S. Ricker; m.

Playboy: 919 North Michigan Ave., Chicago, Ill. 60611; f. 1953; men's magazine; Editor-Publisher Hugh M. Hefner; circ. 6,500,000; m.

Plays: 8 Arlington St., Boston, Mass. 02116; f. 1941; Editor A. S. Burack; circ. 29,400; 8 a year.

Poetry: 1228 North Dearborn Pkwy., Chicago, Ill. 60610; f. 1912; Editor Daryl Hine; circ. 10,000; m.

Political Science Quarterly: Academy of Political Science, 2852 Broadway, New York 10025; Editor D. Caraley; circ. 11,000; q.

Popular Mechanics: 224 West 57 St., New York, N.Y. 10019; subsidiary of the Hearst Corporation; f. 1902; Editor Jim Liston; circ. 1,750,000; m.

Popular Photography: 1 Park Ave., New York, N.Y. 10016; f. 1937; Editor Kenneth Poli; circ. 650,000; m.

Power: McGraw-Hill Inc., 1221 Avenue of the Americas, New York, N.Y. 10020; f. 1882; Editor-in-Chief James J. O'Connor; Publisher John E. Slater; m.

Practical Home Economics: Lakeside Publishing Company, 468 4th Ave., New York, N.Y. 10016; f. 1929; Editor Ruthanna Russell; m.

Printing Management: 19 Church St., Berea, Ohio 44017; f. 1894; Publr. P. B. Holder; Editor Jeremiah E. Flynn; circ. 30,000; m.

Product Engineering: McGraw-Hill Inc., 330 West 42nd St., New York, N.Y. 10036; f. 1930; Editor W. A. Stanbury; f.

Progressive Architecture: 600 Summer St., Stamford, Conn. 06904; Publr. Robert N. Sillars, Jr.; Editor John Morris Dixon; circ. 66,000; m.

Progressive Farmer, The: 820 Shades Creek Parkway, Box 2581, Birmingham, Ala. 35202; f. 1886; Editor-in-Chief Eugene Butler; circ. 1,252,544; m.

PTA Magazine: National Congress of Parents and Teachers, 700 North Rush St., Chicago 11, Ill.; Editor D. Mahoney; circ. 80,000; M.

Public Administration Review: American Society for Public Administration, 1225 Connecticut Ave., N.W., Washington, D.C.; f. 1940; Pres. Frank P. Sherwood; two-monthly; circ. 14,000; also publish *Public Administration News and Views*.

Public Management: International City Management Association, 1140 Connecticut Ave., N.W., Washington, D.C. 20036; f. 1919; Editor Mary Margaret Grant.

Public Opinion Quarterly: Journalism Building, Columbia University, New York, N.Y. 10027; f. 1937; Editor Bernard Roshco; Q.

Publishers Weekly: R. R. Bowker Company, 1180 Ave. of the Americas, New York, N.Y. 10036; f. 1872; Editor Arnold W. Ehrlich; circ. 32,483; W.

Q P Herald: Quigley Publishing Company, 1270 Ave. of the Americas, N.Y. 10020; London Office: Paramount House, 162-170 Wardour St., W.1, England; f. 1907; Publr. Martin Quigley, Jr.; Editor Richard Gertner; circ. 11,000; weekly.

QST: American Radio Relay League, 225 Main St., Newington, Conn. 06111; f. 1915; Editor John Huntoon; circ. 110,000; M.

Railway Age: Simmons-Boardman Publishing Corporation; 350 Broadway, New York, N.Y. 10013; f. 1856; Editor Luther S. Miller; W.

Reader's Digest: Pleasantville, N.Y. 10570; Chair. H. Lewis; Pres. W. W. Hitesman; circ. 29,728,098; M.

Redbook Magazine: 230 Park Ave., New York, N.Y. 10017; f. 1903; Editor Sey Chassler; circ. 4,700,000; M.

Review of Educational Research: American Educational Research Association, 1126 16th St., N.W., Washington D.C., 20036; f. 1933; Editor Samuel Messick; Q.; also *American Educational Research Journal* Q., *Educational Researcher* M.

Rotarian, The: Rotary International, 1600 Ridge Ave., Evanston, Ill. 60201; f. 1911; Editor W. L. White; circ. 454,000; M.

Rural Sociology: Rural Sociological Society, Pennsylvania State University, University Park, Penn.; f. 1936; Editor Robert C. Bealer; Q.

Saturday Review, The: 380 Madison Ave., New York, N.Y. 10017; f. 1924; Literary; Editor Nicholas H. Charney; circ. 750,000; W.

Scholastic Teacher: Scholastic Magazines, Inc., 50 West 44th St., New York, N.Y. 10036; f. 1946; Editor Loretta Hunt Marion; circ. 440,000; M. Sept.-May.

School & Community: Missouri State Teachers' Association, M.S.T.A. Building, Columbia, Mo. 65201; f. 1920; Editor Dr. Inks Franklin; M.

Science: 1515 Massachusetts Avenue, N.W., Washington, D.C. 20005; f. 1880; official organ of the American Association for the Advancement of Science; Editor Philip H. Abelson; circ. 161,099; W.

Science and Mechanics: Davis Publishing Co., 229 Park Ave. South, New York, N.Y. 10003; f. 1930; Editor Tony Hogg; circ. 300,000; M.

Science Books: 1515 Massachusetts Ave., N.W., Washington, D.C. 20005; f. 1965; scientific book review publication of the American Association for the Advancement of Science; Editor Kathryn Wolff; circ. 6,000; Q.

Science Digest: 224 West 57th St., New York 10019; f. 1937; Editor Richard F. Dempewolff; circ. 160,000; M.

Science News: Science Service, Inc., 1719 N St., N.W., Washington, D.C. 20036; f. 1922; Editor Kendrick Frazier; circ. 100,000; M.; also publish *Things of Science*.

Science World: 50 West 44th St., New York, N.Y., 10036; publ. by Scholastic Magazines and Book Services, Inc.; Editorial Dir. Eric Berger; circ. 535,000; F.

Scientific American: 415 Madison Ave., New York City, N.Y. 10017; f. 1845; popular science; Publr. Gerard Piel; Editor Dennis Flanagan; Gen. Man. Donald H. Miller, Jr.; circ. 450,000; M.

Social Casework: Family Service Association of America, 215 Park Ave. South, New York 3, N.Y.; f. 1920; Editor Cora Kasius; M.

Special Libraries: Special Libraries Association, 235 Park Ave. South, New York, N.Y. 10003; f. 1909; Editor Janet D. Bailey; M.

Sport: 205 East 42nd St., New York, N.Y. 10017; M.

Sports Illustrated: Time Inc., Rockefeller Center, New York, N.Y. 10020; Man. Editor R. Terrell; circ. 150,000; W.

Successful Farming: Meredith Publishing Corp., 1716 Locust St., Des Moines, Iowa 50336; f. 1902; Editor Dick Hanson; M.

Survey, The: Survey Associates Inc., 112 East 19th St., New York 3, N.Y.; f. 1912; Editor Paul U. Kellog; M.

Symposium: A Quarterly Journal in Modern Foreign Literatures: 210 H. B. Crouse Hall, Syracuse University, Syracuse, N.Y. 13210; Editor Prof. J. H. Matthews; Q.

Technical Book Review Index: Special Libraries Association, 235 Park Ave. South, New York, N.Y. 10003; Editor Albert F. Kamper; M.

Technology Week: American Aviation Publications, Inc., 1001 Vermont Ave., N.W., Washington, D.C. 20005; f. 1956; Editor W. J. Coughlin; circ. 45,000; W.

TV Guide: Radnor, Pa.; Editorial Dir. Merrill Panitt; Exec. Editor Alexander H. Joseph; Man. Editor Roger J. Youman; circ. 18,500,000; W.

TV Radio Mirror: 205 East 42nd St., New York, N.Y. 10017; M.

Textile World: McGraw-Hill Inc., 1175 Peachtree St., N.E., Atlanta, Ga. 30309; f. 1868; Editor Laurence Christiansen, Jr.; Publr. D. C. Billian; circ. 31,992; M.

Time: Time and Life Building, New York, N.Y. 10020; f. 1923 (Atlantic Edition; f. 1946); Man. Editor H. A. Grundwald; circ. 5,500,000; W.; also publish *Time Asia, Time South Pacific, Time Latin America, Time Canada, Time Atlantic*, and Military edition.

Today's Health: 535 North Dearborn St., Chicago, Ill. 60610; f. 1923; published by the Amer. Med. Asscn.; Editor David Sendler; circ. 710,000.

Town & Country: 717 Fifth Ave., New York, N.Y. 10022; f. 1846; Editor F. Zachary; circ. 120,000; M.

Trap & Field: 1100 Waterway Boulevard, Indianapolis, Indiana 46202; f. 1890; Publisher and Editor Betty Ann Foxworthy; M.

Travel: Travel Building, Floral Park, New York, N.Y. 11001; f. 1901; Editor R. H. Rufa; circ. 500,000; M.

True: 1515 Broadway, New York, N.Y. 10036; f. 1927; non-fiction; Editor Clare Conley; circ. 1,100,000; M.

True Story Magazine: MacFadden-Bartell Corp., 205 East 42nd St., New York 10017; f. 1919; Editor Suzanne Hilliard; circ. 2,500,000; M.

U.S. Camera: 9 E. 40th St., New York, N.Y. 10016; M.

U.S. News & World Report: 2300 N Street, N.W., Washington, D.C. 20037; f. 1933; Chair. JOHN H. SWEET; Editor HOWARD FLIEGER; Ind.; circ. 1,900,000; w.

Variety: 154 West 46th St., New York City, N.Y. 10036; films, television, theatres, radio, music, night clubs, vaudeville, drama, legit., news, reviews, etc.; f. 1905; Publr. SYD SILVERMAN; Man. Editor ROBERT J. LANDRY; Editor ABEL GREEN; circ. 45,000; w.

Village Voice: 80 University Pl., New York, N.Y. 10003; f. 1955; reviews; Editor DANIEL WOLF; Publr. EDWIN FANCHER; circ. 152,000; w.

Vital Speeches: Box 606 Southold, N.Y. 11971; f. 1934; Man. Editor THOMAS F. DALY III; F.

Vogue: 420 Lexington Ave., New York, N.Y. 10017; f. 1892; Editor GRACE MIRABELLA; circ. 450,000; F.

Washington Examiner: Washington, D.C.; f. 1967; Publisher O. ROY CHALK; Editor JACK LIMPERT; w.

Wilson Library Bulletin: 950 University Ave., Bronx, N.Y. 10452; f. 1914; Editor Wm. R. ESHELMAN; circ. 36,398; M. (excl. July and Aug.).

Woman's Day: 1515 Broadway, New York City, N.Y. 10036; Editor GERALDINE RHOADS; circ. 8,000,000; M.

World Aviation Directory including World Space Directory: Ziff-Davis Publishing Co., 1156 15th St., N.W., Washington, D.C. 20005; Editor and Publr. D. W. DEAN; circ. 8,300; twice-yearly (Feb. and Aug.).

World's Business Magazine: 342 Madison Avenue, New York 17, N.Y.; f. 1879; Editor ERNEST L. FARESE; M.

Writer's Digest: 9933 Alliance Rd., Cincinnati, Ohio 45242; f. 1920; Editor S. WEINER; M.; also publish *The Writer's Market* and *Writer's Yearbook*.

Yale Review: 1902A Yale Station, New Haven, Conn. 06520; Editor J. E. PALMER; circ. 6,000; Q.

Youth and Work: 419 Park Ave. South, New York 16; f. 1956; Exec. Editor LILA ROSENBLUM.

NEWS AGENCIES

Associated Press: 50 Rockefeller Plaza, New York, N.Y. 10020; f. 1848; Chair. PAUL MILLER (*Rochester Times Union*); Pres. WES GALLAGHER; Sec. HARRY T. MONTGOMERY; 4,200 U.S. members and 5,200 subscribers abroad.

Central News of America: 67 Wall St., New York City; Editor WALTER ZOUBECK; Man. J. P. REDINGTON.

Central Press Association: 1380 Dodge Court, Cleveland, Ohio 44114; Editor COURTLAND C. SMITH; Gen. Man. FRANK C. McLEARN.

Dow Jones & Co. Inc.: 30 Broad St., New York, N.Y. 10004; publishes the *Wall Street Journal* (circ. 1,239,544), *Barrons' National Business and Financial Weekly* (circ. 250,735), *The National Observer* (circ. 529,390) and the Dow Jones News Service; operates the AP-Dow Jones Economic Report and the AP-Dow Jones Financial Wire in association with Associated Press; the Dow Jones Broadcast Service established in 1967; Gen. Man. WARREN PHILLIPS.

Jewish Telegraphic Agency Inc.: 660 First Ave., New York, N.Y. 10016; f. 1917; Pres. ROBERT H. ARNOW; Editor MURRAY ZUCKOFF.

Newspaper Enterprise Association Service: 1200 West Third St., Cleveland, Ohio 44113; news features; f. 1902; Pres. and Editor R. R. METZ, 230 Park Ave. New York, N.Y. 10017; Vice-Pres. and Gen. Man. E. H. ANDERSON, Cleveland.

North American Newspaper Alliance: 220 East 42nd St., New York, N.Y. 10017; news features; f. 1922; Pres. W. C. PAYETTE; Exec. Editor SID GOLDBERG; 143 newspaper subscribers; circ. 24m.

United Press International: 220 East 42nd St., New York, N.Y. 10017; f. 1907; Chair. of the Board MIMS THOMASON; Pres. RODERICK W. BEATON; Vice-Pres. and Editor H. L. STEVENSON; serves clients in 114 countries and territories; in the United States it serves 1,140 newspapers and 3,234 radio stations and 593 television stations.

FOREIGN BUREAUX

Agence France-Presse: 914 National Press Building, Washington, D.C. 20004; Chief FERNAND MOULIER.

Agence Tunis Afrique Presse: 40 East 71st St., New York.

ANSA (Italian National News Agency): 220 East 42nd St., New York 17; North American Bureau Chief CARLO SCARSINI; 2475 Virginia Ave., N.W., Washington, D.C.; Washington Correspondent ALDO BAGNALASTA.

Canadian Press: 50 Rockefeller Plaza, New York, N.Y. 10020, Chief GEORGE KITCHEN; 1300 Connecticut, N.W., Washington, D.C. 202, Chief A. M. MACKENZIE.

Central News Agency of China: 1231 News Building, 220 East 42nd St., New York 10017; 549 National Press Building, Washington 4, D.C. 20004; 681 Market St., Room 772, San Francisco, Calif. 94105.

Četeka (Czechoslovak News Agency): 1444 Rhode Island Ave., N.W., Washington, D.C.

Ghana News Agency: 300 East 46th St., New York, N.Y. 10017.

Kyodo News Service: Room 1188, National Press Building, Washington, D.C. 20004, Chief TAKASHIGE OTSUKA; Room 811, AP Building, 50 Rockefeller Plaza, New York, N.Y. 10020, Chief ASAHI KAMEI.

Reuters: 1700 Broadway, New York, N.Y. 10019.

Tass: 50 Rockefeller Plaza, New York, N.Y. 10020.

Antara, DPA, Jiji Press, and Novosti, also have bureaux in the U.S.A.

NATIONAL ASSOCIATIONS AND CLUBS

American Newspaper Publishers Association: 750 Third Ave., New York, N.Y. 10017; f. 1887; Pres. and Gen. Man. STANFORD SMITH; over 1,000 daily newspapers.

American Society of Newspaper Editors: 750 Third Ave., New York, N.Y. 10017; Pres. C. A. McKNIGHT (*Charlotte Observer*); Exec. Sec. GENE GIANCARLO; 740 mems. publ. *Bulletin*.

Audit Bureau of Circulations: 123 N. Wacker Drive, Chicago, Ill. 60606; f. 1914; Chair. of Board H. A. LEHRTER; Sec. PRESTON W. BALMER; Pres. and Man. Dir. ALAN T. WOLCOTT; 3,900 mems.

Coordinating Council of Literary Magazines—C.C.L.M.: 80 Eighth Ave., New York 10011; f. 1967; aids noncommercial literary publishing; Chair. of the Board WILLIAM PHILLIPS; Exec. Dir. GAIL KONG; Sec. HOWARD McCORD.

Educational Press Association of America: Newhouse Communications Center, Syracuse University, Syracuse, New York; f. 1895; Pres. Miss BARBARA KROHN; Sec.-Treas. MARVIN REED; 800 mems.; publs. *Directory of Educational Periodicals* (biennially), *Edpress News Letter* (14 issues).

Gridiron Club: 315 National Press Bldg., Washington, D.C. 20004; f. 1885; Sec. JULIUS FRANDSEN; 50 active mems., 15 limited mems., associated membership varies.

Magazine Publishers' Association Inc.: 575 Lexington Ave., New York, N.Y. 10022; f. 1919; Pres. STEPHEN E. KELLY; Exec. Vice-Pres. ROBERT E. KENYON; Chair. HARRY C. THOMPSON; membership: 130 publishers of 450 magazines.

National Newspaper Association: 491 National Press Building, Washington, D.C. 20004; f. 1885; Exec. Vice-Pres. and Gen. Man. THEODORE A. SERRILL; 6,800 mems.; publs. *Publishers' Auxiliary*.

National Newspaper Publishers Association: 2400 South Michigan, Chicago, Ill. 60616; Pres. JOHN H. SENG-STACKE; Vice-Pres. GARTH C. REEVES; Sec. WILLIAM H. LEE; Exec. Dir. HOWARD H. MURPHY.

National Press Club: National Press Building, Washington 4, D.C.; f. 1908; Pres. ED. EDSTROM; approx. 5,000 mems.

The Newspaper Guild: 1125 16th St., N.W., Washington, D.C. 20005; affiliated to AFL-CIO, Canadian Labor Congress, International Federation of Journalists; Chair. BARNEY PETERSON; Pres. C. A. PERLIK, Jr.

Periodical Publishers Association of America: 575 Lexington Ave., New York, N.Y. 10022; Exec. Vice-Pres. ROBERT KENYON; 110 mems.

PUBLISHERS

Abelard-Schuman Ltd.: 257 Park Ave. South, New York, N.Y. 10010; Vice-Pres. FRANCES SCHWARTZ; juvenile, non-fiction; science.

Abingdon Press: 201 Eighth Ave., South Nashville, Tenn. 37202; f. 1789; Man. CHARLES O. McNISH; religious, juvenile, general, biography, music.

Harry N. Abrams, Inc.: 110 East 59th St., New York, N.Y. 10022; acquired by Times-Mirror Co. 1966; Pres. HARRY N. ABRAMS; art.

Academic Press, Inc.: 111 Fifth Ave., New York, N.Y. 10003; f. 1942; Pres. WALTER J. JOHNSON; scientific and technical books and journals.

Ace Books: 1120 Ave. of the Americas, New York, N.Y. 10036; Vice-Pres. E. P. THOMPSON; Senior Editors Mrs. E. B. GRIPPO; FREDERICK POHL; paperbacks, mainly fiction.

Addison-Wesley Publishing Company, Inc.: Reading, Mass. 01867; 3220 Porter Drive, Palo Alto, Calif.; f. 1942; Pres. MELBOURNE W. CUMMINGS; scientific, engineering, textbooks for universities, technical institutes, secondary and elementary schools.

Aldine Publishing Company: 529 South Wabash Ave., Chicago, Ill. 60605; Chair. and Publisher ALEXANDER J. MORIN; Pres. LAWRENCE I. GOLDBERG.

Allyn and Bacon, Inc.: 470 Atlantic Ave., Boston, Mass. 02110; Pres. W. B. ANSBRO; educational.

American Book Company: 450 West 33rd St., New York, N.Y. 10001; Pres. CHARLES W. PEPPER; college and school textbooks.

American Elsevier Publishing Co., Inc.: 52 Vanderbilt Ave., New York, 10017; Chair. Dr. E. VAN TONGEREN; Pres. PAUL B. HOEBER.

American Heritage Publishing Co. Inc.: 1221 Ave. of the Americas, New York, N.Y. 10020; Pres. PAUL GOTTLIEB; general non-fiction.

American Technical Society: 848 East 58th St., Chicago, Ill. 60637; Pres. D. N. McCARL; technical and vocational.

Appleton-Century-Crofts: 440 Park Ave. South, New York, N.Y. 10016; f. 1825; Gen. Man. CHARLES R. WALTHER; a division of Meredith Corporation; college texts, general programming materials and medical, scientific and reference books.

Arco Publishing Co., Inc.: 219 Park Ave. South, New York 10003; Pres. MILTON GLADSTONE; business, technical.

Association Press: 291 Broadway, New York, N.Y. 10007; Dir. ROBERT W. HILL; publication department of National Council of Y.M.C.A.s.

Atheneum Publishers: 122 E. 42nd St., New York, N.Y. 10017; Chair. ALFRED KNOPF, Jr.; Pres. SIMON MICHAEL BESSIE; fiction and non-fiction, poetry, drama.

Atlantic Monthly Press: 8 Arlington St., Boston, Mass. 02116; Dir. PETER DAVISON; fiction, biography.

Augsburg Publishing House: 426 South 5th St., Minneapolis, Minn. 55415; f. 1873; Gen. Man. ALBERT E. ANDERSON; religious.

Avon Book Division of Hearst Corpn.: 959 Eighth Ave., New York, N.Y. 10019; Publr. and Editor-in-Chief PETER MAYER; reprints and original.

Baker Book House: 1019 Wealthy St., S.E., Grand Rapids, Mich. 49506; f. 1939; Pres. HERMAN BAKER; Vice-Pres. RICHARD BAKER, PETER BAKER; religious (Protestant).

Ballantine Books, Inc.: 101 Fifth Ave., New York, N.Y. 10003; Pres. IAN BALLANTINE; fiction, non-fiction, originals and reprints.

Bantam Books, Inc.: 666 Fifth Ave., New York, N.Y. 10019; Pres. OSCAR DYSTEL; paperbacks.

A. S. Barnes & Co.: Forsgate Drive, Cranbury, N.J. 08512; f. 1838; Pres. JULIEN YOSELOFF; sports, outdoor, cinema and general books.

Barnes and Noble Books: 10 East 53rd St., New York, N.Y. 10022; a division of Harper and Row Publishers, Inc.; Vice-Pres. and Publr. TADASHI AKAISHI.

Clarence L. Barnhart Inc.: Box 250, Bronxville, N.Y. 10708; Pres. CLARENCE L. BARNHART; Vice-Pres. ROBERT K. BARNHART; educational, reference.

Richard W. Baron Publishing: 201 Park Ave. S., New York, N.Y. 10003; Pres. and Publr. R. W. BARON.

Basic Books, Inc.: 10 East 53rd St., New York, N.Y. 10022; f. 1953; Pres. E. A. GLIKES; social, physical and political sciences, natural history, behavioural sciences.

Beacon Press: 25 Beacon St., Boston, Mass. 02108; f. 1902; Dir. GOBIN STAIR; Business Man. PAUL SIDMAN; world affairs, ethics, liberal religion, general non-fiction.

Benefic Press: 10300 West Roosevelt Rd., Westchester, Ill. 60153; Pres. J. C. SINDELAR; textbooks.

W. A. Benjamin, Inc.: 2725 Sand Hill Rd., Menlo Park, Calif. 94025; Pres. DAVID C. BULL; Exec. Editor A. C. BARTLETT; science.

Benziger, Bruce and Glencoe, Inc.: 8701 Wilshire Blvd., Beverley Hills, California 90211; f. 1792; Pres. JACK E. WITMER; textbooks.

Berkley Publishing Corpn.: 200 Madison Ave., New York, N.Y. 10016; owned by G. P. Putnam & Sons; Pres. STEPHEN CONLAND; paperback originals and reprints.

The Bethany Press: 2640 Pine Blvd., Box 179, St. Louis, Mo. 63166.

Benjamin Blom, Inc.: 2521 Broadway, N.Y. 10025; f. 1963; Pres. BENJAMIN BLOM; Sec. and Treas. Miss ANETTE RENDAR; literature, the arts, humanities.

Bobbs-Merrill Co., Inc.: 4300 W. 62nd St., Indianapolis, Ind. 46268; f. 1838; subsidiary of Howard W. Sams & Co. Inc.; Pres. LEO C. GOBIN; fiction, biography, history, popular science, travel, children's books, religious, technical, law, education, paperbacks.

Bollingen Foundation: 140 East 62nd St., New York, N.Y. 10021.

The Book House for Children: Tangley Oaks Educational Center, Lake Bluff, Ill. 60044.

R. R. Bowker Co.: 1180 Ave. of the Americas, New York, N.Y. 10036; f. 1872; part of Xerox Corp.; Pres. RICHARD P. ZELDIN; publishing trade journals; reference and bibliography books.

George Braziller, Inc.: 1 Park Ave., New York, N.Y. 10016; Pres. GEORGE BRAZILLER; Vice-Pres. and Editor-in-Chief EDWIN SEAVER; high-quality fiction and non-fiction, art books.

The British Book Centre Inc.: 996 Lexington Ave., N.Y. 10021; Pres. Dr. J. H. HOLLOMON, distribute all British books not published in U.S.

Broadman Press: 127 Ninth Ave. N., Nashville, Tenn. 37234; religious, non-fiction.

Brookings Institution: 1775 Massachusetts Ave. N.W., Washington, D.C. 20036; Dir. of Publications ROLAND A. HOOVER; economics, government, foreign policy, social sciences.

Brown University Press: 129 Waterman St., Providence, R.I. 02912; Dir. GRANT DUGDALE; scholarly.

William C. Brown Co.: 135 South Locust St., Dubuque, Iowa 52001; Pres. WILLIAM C. BROWN; Vice-Pres. JOHN W. GORSUCH; college textbooks.

Bruce Publishing Co.: 866 Third Ave., New York, N.Y. 10022; f. 1891; br. in New York and Chicago; Chair. of Board WILLIAM C. BRUCE; Pres. WILLIAM G. BRUCE; general trade, biography, history, philosophy, textbooks, craft, juveniles, Catholic trade and textbooks.

Burgess Publishing Co.: 7108 Ohms Lane, Minneapolis, Minn. 55415; f. 1925; Pres. M. C. BURGESS; Exec. Vice-Pres. C. S. HUTCHINSON; college textbooks and manuals.

Butterworth, Inc.: 7300 Pearl St., Washington, D.C. 20014; medicine, science and law.

Callaghan & Co.: 6141 North Cicero Ave., Chicago, Ill. 60646; f. 1864; Pres. MICHAEL CUDAHY; law and tax materials.

Cambridge University Press: 32 E. 57th St., New York, N.Y. 10022; Dir. JACK SCHULMAN.

Catholic University of America Press: Affiliated to Consortium Press; 620 Michigan Ave., N.E., Washington, D.C. 20005.

The Caxton Printers Ltd.: Caldwell, Ida. 83605; Pres. JAMES H. GIPSON, Jr.; general non-fiction.

Chandler Publishing Company: 124 Spear St., San Francisco, Calif. 94105; Pres. and Man. Ed. H. CHANDLER; college texts.

The Child's World Inc.: Box 711, Mankato, Minn. 56001.

Children's Press: 1224 West Van Buren St., Chicago, Ill. 60607; Pres. TED WINTER.

Chilmark Press: 201 East 50th St., New York, N.Y. 10022; Pres. and Editor L. G. COWAN.

Chilton Book Co.: Chilton Way, Radnor, Pa. 19089; Gen. Man. WILLIAM D. BYRNE; Editor-in-Chief J. D. KELLY; arts and crafts, automotive, technical and trade.

The Christian Science Publishing Society: One Norway St., Boston, Mass. 02115; Man. ZADIE HATFIELD.

Citadel Press: 222 Park Ave., South, New York 10003; Vice-Pres. ALLAN J. WILSON, MORRIS SORKIN; general.

Coiner Publications Ltd.: 3066 M St., N.W., Washington, D.C. 20007; f. 1962; law books; Pres. MAYO L. COINER.

College and University Press: 263 Chapel St., New Haven, Conn. 06513; Pres. I. FREDERICK DODUCK; f. 1958; college and school textbooks, scholarly books and paperbacks.

P.F. Collier, Inc.: 866 Third Ave., New York 10022; Division of The Macmillan Co.; quality paperback books on all subjects.

Columbia University Press: 562 West 113 St., New York, N.Y. 10025; f. 1893; Chair. H. J. KELLY; Pres. and Dir. ROBERT G. BARNES; trade, educational, scientific, reference.

Commerce Clearing House, Inc.: 4025 West Peterson Ave., Chicago, Ill. 60646; Pres. ROBERT C. BARTLETT; Man. Editor GEORGE HARRIS; taxation and business law subjects.

F. E. Compton Co.: 425 North Michigan Ave., Chicago, Ill. 60611; division of Encyclopedia Britannica; Editor-in-Chief AUDREY MITCHELL; reference.

Concordia Publishing House: 3558 South Jefferson Avenue, St. Louis, Mo. 63118; Pres. R. L. REINKE; religious (Protestant).

Cooper Square Publishers, Inc.: 59 Fourth Ave., New York 10003; f. 1960; Pres. HENRY CHAFETZ; Vice-Pres. SIDNEY B. SOLOMON; scholarly, reference.

Cornell University Press: 124 Roberts Place, Ithaca, N.Y. 14850; f. 1869; Publr. ROGER HOWLEY; scholarly, non-fiction.

Council on Foreign Relations, Inc.: 58 East 68th St., New York, N.Y. 10021; f. 1921; Chair. of Board DAVID ROCKEFELLER; Pres. BAYLESS MANNING; Vice-Pres. and Sec. JOHN T. SWING; Vice-Pres. DAVID W. MAC-EACHRON; *Foreign Affairs*; q.; Editor WILLIAM BUNDY; Council Papers and Books.

Coward-McCann and Geoghegan, Inc.: 200 Madison Ave., New York, N.Y. 10016; f. 1928; Pres. JOHN J. GEOGHE-GAN; fiction, non-fiction, juveniles, plays, translations.

Creative Educational Society, Inc.: 123 South Broad St., Mankato, Minn. 56002; Pres. G. R. PETERSON, Jr.

Thomas Y. Crowell Company: 666 Fifth Ave., New York, N.Y. 10019; f. 1876; Pres. L. W. GILLENSON; reference, general fiction and non-fiction, juvenile, college texts, linguistics, art, music.

Crown Publishers, Inc.: 419 Park Ave. South, New York, N.Y. 10016; f. 1936; Pres. NAT WARTELS; general fiction and non-fiction, illustrated books, educational records, art and gift books, hard-cover reprints.

Dartnell Corporation, The: 4660 Ravenswood Ave., Chicago, Ill. 60640; Chair. of Board and Pres. W. H. FETRIDGE; business.

F. A. Davis Co.: 1915 Arch St., Philadelphia, Pa. 19103; f. 1879; Pres. ROBERT H. CRAVEN; medical and scientific.

John Day Co. Inc., The: 257 Park Ave. S., New York, N.Y. 10010; f. 1926; Pres. RICHARD J. WALSH, Jr.; fiction, non-fiction, juveniles.

John De Graff, Inc.: 34 Oak Ave., Tuckahoe, N.Y. 10707; Pres. JOHN G. DE GRAFF; non-fiction.

Marcel Dekker, Inc.: 95 Madison Ave., New York, N.Y. 10016; Pres. MARCEL DEKKER; scientific and reference.

Delacorte Press: 245 East 47th St., New York, N.Y. 10017; division of Dell Publishing Co.; Editorial Dir. Ross CLAIBORNE.

Dell Publishing Co., Inc.: 750 Third Ave., New York, N.Y. 10017; Pres. HELEN MEYER.

Delmar Publishers, Inc.: 50 Wolf Rd., Albany, N.Y. 12205; Exec. Vice-Pres. L. JACKEL; textbooks.

Devin-Adair Co., The: 1 Park Ave., Old Greenwich, Conn. 06870; f. 1911; Pres. DEVIN A. GARRITY; general fiction and non-fiction, Irish and health.

Dial Press: 750 Third Ave., New York, N.Y. 10017; a subsidiary of Dell Publishing Co., Inc.; Editors-in-Chief RICHARD MAREK; general fiction, non-fiction, children's books.

Dodd, Mead & Co.: 79 Madison Ave., New York, N.Y. 10016; f. 1839; Chair. of Board EDWARD H. DODD, Jr.; Pres. S. PHELPS PLATT, Jr.; Vice-Pres. WILLIAM M. OMAN; fiction, biography, belleslettres, juvenile.

Doubleday & Company Inc.: Garden City, N.Y. 11530; f. 1897; Pres. JOHN T. SARGENT; Exec. Vice-Pres. and Sec. NELSON DOUBLEDAY; general.

Dover Publications, Inc.: 180 Varick St., New York, N.Y. 10014; Pres. HAYWARD CIRKER; high quality paperback non-fiction.

Dow Jones Books: Box 300, Princeton, N.J. 08540; Pres. W. PHILLIPS.

Dufour Editions, Inc.: Chester Springs, Pa. 19425; Pres. Mrs. JEANNE H. DUFOUR; literary, art, English imports.

Duke University Press: Box 6697, College Station, Durham, N.C. 27708; f. 1922; Dir. A. G. BRICE; scholarly.

Duquesne University Press: Pittsburgh, Pa. 15219.

E. P. Dutton & Co.: 201 Park Ave., South, New York, N.Y. 10003; f. 1852; Pres. JOHN MACRAE III; Chair. JOHN MACRAE, Jr.; Editor-in-Chief HAL SCHARLATT.

East-West Center Press: 1777 East-West Rd., Honolulu, Hawaii 96872.

W. B. Eerdmans Publishing Co.: 255 Jefferson Ave., S.E., Grand Rapids, Mich. 49502; Pres. WILLIAM B. EERDMANS, Jr.; Vice-Pres. HERO BRATT; religious (Protestant), some fiction, juveniles.

Encyclopaedia Britannica, Inc.: 425 North Michigan Ave., Chicago, Ill. 60611; Chair. of Board R. P. GWINN; Pres. CHARLES E. SWANSON.

M. Evans & Company, Inc.: 216 East 49th St., New York, N.Y. 10017; f. 1960; Pres. and Treas. GEORGE C. DE KAY; Vice-Pres. and Editor-in-Chief HERBERT M. KATZ; adult and juvenile fiction and non-fiction.

Farrar, Straus & Giroux, Inc.: 19 Union Square West, New York, N.Y. 10003; Pres. ROGER W. STRAUS, Jr.; Vice-Pres. and Editor-in-Chief ROBERT GIROUX; general, special interest in new writers.

Fawcett World Library: 1515 Broadway, New York, N.Y. 10036; paperback fiction and non-fiction.

J. G. Ferguson Publishing Company: 6 No. Michigan Ave., Chicago, Ill. 60602; Pres. G. M. PLEWS; reference.

Field Educational Publications, Inc.: 2400 Hanover St., Palo Alto, Calif. 94304; Pres. A. W. BAIN, Jr.; textbooks.

Field Enterprises Educational Corpn.: 510 Merchandise Mart Plaza, Chicago, Ill. 60654; Pres. W. BRANHAM; Editorial Dir. Dr. W. H. NAULT; reference.

Follett Publishing Co.: 1010 West Washington Blvd., Chicago, Ill. 60607; Pres. ROBERT J. R. FOLLETT; Vice-Pres. and Editor C. ALLEN FORT; juveniles, dictionaries and reference books, sports books, Big Table books.

Fordham University Press: 2546 Belmont Ave., Bronx, N.Y. 10458; f. 1907; Dir. H. GEORGE FLETCHER; scholarly.

Fortress Press: 2900 Queen Lane, Philadelphia, Pa. 191290 Gen. Man. FRANK G. RHODY; religious education.

Franklin Book Programs, Inc.: 801 Second Ave., New York N.Y. 10017; f. 1952; Pres. JOHN H. KYLE; a non-profit organization for international book-publishing development.

The Free Press (Div. of Macmillan Co.): 866 Third Ave., New York, N.Y. 10022; non-fiction, college textbooks.

W. H. Freeman & Company, Publishers: 660 Market St., San Francisco, Calif. 94104; Pres. R. W. WARRINGTON; textbooks.

Samuel French, Inc.: 25 West 45th St., New York, N.Y. 10036; Man. Dir. ABBOTT VAN NOSTRAND; plays.

Friendship Press: 475 Riverside Drive, New York, N.Y. 10027; f. 1902; Exec. Dir. WILLIAM C. WALZER; books, maps, plays, filmstrips on the church and its work.

The Frontier Press Company: 250 East Town St., Columbus, O. 43215; Pres. WILLIAM H. SEIBERT; reference books.

Funk & Wagnalls Publishing Co. (a subsidiary of Dun and Bradsheet, Inc.); 53 East 77th St., New York, N.Y. 10021; f. 1877; Pres. and Chief Exec. FRANK J. SCULLY; dictionaries, general reference, trade, juvenile.

Gale Research Co.: Book Tower, Detroit, Mich. 48226; f. 1954; Pres. F. G. RUFFNER; Vice-Pres. and Editorial Dir. JAMES M. ETHRIDGE; reference, reprints.

Garrard Publishing Company: 1607 North Market St., Champaign, Ill. 61820; Pres. ROBERT J. GARRARD; juvenile.

Bernard Geis Associates: 128 East 56th St., New York, N.Y. 10022; general fiction and non-fiction.

Genealogical Publishing Co.: 521–523 St. Paul Place, Baltimore, Md. 21202; f. 1959; Pres. B. CHODAK; reprints of books on genealogy and heraldry.

General Learning Corporation: 250 James St., Morristown, N.J. 07960; textbooks, professional.

K. S. Giniger Co., Inc.: 1727 South Indiana Ave., Chicago, Ill. 60616; f. 1965; Pres. KENNETH S. GINIGER; joint imprint publishers of general non-fiction.

Ginn & Co.: 191 Spring St., Lexington, Mass. 02173; f. 1867; Pres. Dr. ROBERT F. BAKER; Senior Vice-Pres. ROBERT D. YEO; textbooks.

Golden Press: 850 Third Ave., New York, N.Y. 10022; a division of Western Publishing Co., Inc.; Gen. Man. and Vice-Pres. JOHN C. WORRELL; juveniles, encyclopaedias, reference, classics, art, periodicals.

Good Will Publishers, Inc.: P.O.B. 269, 1520 York Rd., Gastonia, N.C.

Gordon and Breach, Science Publishers, Inc.: One Park Ave., New York, N.Y. 10016; f. 1961; Pres. ENA ADAM; Vice-Pres. and Editor-in-Chief Dr. E. H. IMMERGUT; Chair. MARTIN B. GORDON; scientific and technical books and journals.

Stephen Greene Press: Box 100, Brattleboro, Vt. 05301.

Greenwood Press: 51 Riverside Ave., Westport, Conn. 06880; f. 1967; Pres. ROBERT HAGELSTEIN; journals, reprints, bibliographic, scholarly, original monographs, micropublishing, Index to Current Urban Documents.

Grolier Incorporated: 575 Lexington Ave., New York, N.Y. 10022; f. 1895; Chair. E. J. McCabe, Jr.; Pres. W. J. Murphy; encyclopaedias, reference, educational.

Grosset & Dunlap, Inc.: 51 Madison Ave., New York, N.Y. 10010; f. 1898; Pres. Harold Roth; original, reprint, adult, juvenile.

Grossman Publishers: 625 Madison Ave., New York, N.Y. 10022; f. 1962; Editorial Dir. Richard L. Grossman; Editor and Asst. Editorial Dir. D. Okrent; general fiction and non-fiction, poetry, photography and art.

Grove Press, Inc.: 53 East 11th St., New York, N.Y. 10003; Pres. Barney Rosset; fiction and non-fiction, college textbooks.

Grune & Stratton, Inc.: 381 Park Ave., S., New York, N.Y. 10016; Pres. Niels C. Buessem; medical.

Hafner Publishing Co., Inc.: 866 Third Ave., New York, N.Y. 10022; f. 1946; Dir. E. J. Quigley; science, technology, philosophy, medicine, mathematics.

Hamond Incorporated (C. S. Hammond & Co.): 515 Valley St., Maplewood, N.J. 07040; Pres. Stuart L. Hammond; maps, atlases.

Harcourt Brace Jovanovich Inc.: 757 Third Ave., New York 10017; f. 1919; Chair. William Jovanovich; Pres. Paul D. Corbett; textbooks, general.

Harlow Publishing Corporation: P.O.B. 898, 212 East Gray St., Norman, Okla. 73070.

Harper & Row: 10 East 53rd St., New York, N.Y. 10022, f. 1817; Chair. of Board John Cowles, Jr.; Pres. and Chief Exec. Officer Winthrop Knowlton; fiction, non-fiction, educational, medical, general.

Hart Publishing Company, Inc.: 15 West 4th St., New York, N.Y. 10012; Editor and Publr. Harold H. Hart; non-fiction.

Harvard University Press: 79 Garden St., Cambridge, Mass. 02138; British Agents, Oxford University Press; f. 1913; Dir. Arthur J. Rosenthal; educational, scientific, classics, fine arts, philosophy, religion, history and government.

Hastings House Publishers, Inc.: 10 East 40th St., New York, N.Y. 10016; f. 1936; Pres. and Editor Walter W. Frese; Exec. Vice-Pres. and Editor Russell F. Neale; general, regional, Americana, decorative and graphic arts, communications, photography, children's.

Hawthorn Books, Inc.: 70 Fifth Ave., New York, N.Y. 10011; f. 1952; Pres. and Chief Exec. Officer W. Clement Stone; Vice-Pres. and Gen. Man. A. Dale Timpe; general non-fiction, reference, business, religious, history, biography, cookery and juveniles.

Hayden Book Company Inc.: 50 Essex St., Rocheue Park, N.J. 07662; Pres. James S. Mulholland, Jr.; scientific, technical, professional.

D. C. Heath & Co.: 125 Spring St., Lexington, Mass. 02173.

James H. Heineman Inc.: 475 Park Ave., New York, N.Y. 10022; current affairs, history.

Hill and Wang: 19 Union Sq. W., New York, N.Y. 10011; Editor-in-Chief A. W. Sang; fiction, non-fiction, drama, history.

Hillary House Publishers: 450 Park Ave., South, New York, N.Y. 10016; division of Humanities Press Inc.

R. H. Hinkley Company: 575 Lexington Ave., New York, N.Y. 10022.

History Book Club: 40 Guernsey St., Stamford, Conn. 06904.

Holden-Day, Inc.: 500 Sansome St., San Francisco, Calif. 94111; Pres. Frederick H. Murphy; textbooks, scientific, reference.

Holiday House: 18 E. 56th St., New York, N.Y. 10022; Pres. John H. Briggs, Jr.; juveniles.

Holt, Rinehart and Winston, Inc.: 383 Madison Ave., New York, N.Y. 10017; f. 1866; subsidiary of C.B.S.; Chair. Ross D. Sackett; Pres. Kenneth Northrop; textbooks and general, magazines.

Houghton Mifflin Company: 2 Park St., Boston, Mass. 02107; f. 1832; Pres. H. T. Miller; Vice-Pres. Finance and Admin. Edward Reynolds, Jr.; general.

Humanities Press: 450 Park Ave. South, New York 10016; f. 1950; Pres. and Editor Simon Silverman; scholarly.

Indiana University Press: 10th and Morton Streets, Bloomington, Indiana 47401; f. 1950; Dir. Bernard B. Perry; trade and scholarly non-fiction.

Industrial Press: 200 Madison Ave., New York, N.Y. 10016.

Initial Teaching Alphabet Pubns., Inc.: 6 E. 43rd St., New York, N.Y. 10017; Pres. E. M. Crane Jr.; elementary reading series.

Intext Publishers Group: 257 Park Ave., South, New York 10010; Chair. R. W. Kislik; Pres. T. B. Dolmatch; college textbooks in engineering, business, humanities, natural and social sciences, adult and juvenile fiction and non-fiction, elementary textbooks.

Iowa State University Press: 5 State Ave., Ames, Ia. 50010; Dir. Merritt Bailey; agriculture, engineering, science, home economics, veterinary, journalism, economics, flight instruction.

Richard D. Irwin, Inc.: 1818 Ridge Rd., Homewood, Ill. 60430; f. 1933; Chair. of Board Richard D. Irwin; Pres. Irvin L. Grimes; economics, business.

Jewish Publication Soc. of America: 222 N. 15th St., Philadelphia, Pa. 19102; Pres. William S. Fishman.

Johnson Reprint Corpn.: 111 Fifth Ave., New York, N.Y. 10003; f. 1945; affiliated to the Academic Press Inc.; Pres. C. Hutt; Vice-Pres. J. K. Burgess; scientific reprints.

Johns Hopkins University Press: Baltimore, Md. 21218; f. 1878; Dirs. Harold E. Ingle, Jack G. Goellner; Editor-in-Chief M. A. Aronson; social sciences, humanities, science.

Augustus M. Kelley, Publishers: 305 Allwood Rd., Clifton, N.J. 07012; f. 1947; reprints of economic classics.

Kennikat Press Inc.: 90 South Bayles Ave., Port Washington, N.Y. 11050; f. 1963; Pres. and Editor Cornell Jaray; scholarly reprints and originals.

Alfred A. Knopf, Inc.: 201 East 50th St., New York, N.Y. 10022; f. 1915; merged with Random House Inc. 1960; Chair. William A. Kushland; Pres. R. Gottlieb; fiction, textbooks, general literature.

John Knox Press: 341 Ponce de Leon Ave., N.E., Atlanta, Georgia 30308; f. 1938; Publr. J. Howard Montgomery; Editor Richard A. Ray; religious.

Kraus Reprint Co.: Route 100 Millwood, New York, N.Y. 10546; a U.S. division of Kraus-Thomson Organization Ltd.

Laidlaw Brothers: Thatcher and Madison Streets, River Forest, Ill. 60305; a division of Doubleday.

Lancer Books Inc.: 18 East 41st St., New York, N.Y. 10017; Pres. W. Zacharius; Editors Robert Hoskins, Ruth Bronsteen, Evan Heyman; paperback reprints and originals.

Lea & Febiger: 600 Washington Square, Philadelphia, Pa. 19106; f. 1785; Editorial Adviser John F. Spahr; medical, dental, veterinary and other life sciences.

Lenox Hill Press: 419 Park Ave. S., New York, N.Y. 10016; a division of Crown Publishers, Inc.; light fiction, Gothic romances, westerns.

Lion Books: 52 Park Ave., New York, N.Y. 10016.

J. B. Lippincott Company: East Washington Square, Philadelphia, Pa. 19105; f. 1792; Pres. JOSEPH W. LIPPINCOTT, Jr.; Sec. W. B. ROUTT; fiction, biography, history, scientific, medical, educational, juvenile, religious.

Little, Brown and Company Inc.: 34 Beacon St., Boston, Mass. 02106; f. 1837; Chair. of Board and Pres. ARTHUR H. THORNHILL, Jr.; Sec. JAMES B. PLATE; fiction, biography, history, current affairs, general trade, juveniles, medical, law, college textbooks.

Louisiana State University Press: Baton Rouge, La. 70803; f. 1935; Dir. CHARLES EAST; Associate Dir. LESLIE E. PHILLABAUM; scholarly, regional and general.

Loyola University Press: 3441 N. Ashland Ave., Chicago, Ill. 60657; Dir. Rev. JOHN B. AMBERG.

Lyons and Carnahan: 407 E. 25th St., Chicago, Ill. 60616.

M.I.T. Press: 28 Carlton St., Cambridge, Mass. 02142; f. 1932; Dir. HOWARD R. WEBBER; Editor-in-Chief A. TOVELL; scholarly, advanced textbooks, research monographs, non-fiction trade books, paperbooks.

McCormick-Mathers Publishing Co. Inc.: 450 West 33rd St., New York 10001; Pres. CHARLES PEPPER; textbooks.

McCutchan Publishing Corporation: 2526 Grove St., Berkeley, Calif. 94704; college textbooks.

MacFadden-Bartell Corporation: 205 East 42nd St., New York, N.Y. 10017; Pres. ALBERT S. TRAINA; paperbound fiction and non-fiction.

McGraw-Hill Book Co.: 1221 Ave. of the Americas, New York, N.Y. 10020; f. 1909; Pres. HAROLD W. McGRAW, Jr.; college and school textbooks, technical, scientific and business, medical, legal, religious, art, fiction, general non-fiction and young people's books, encyclopaedias and reference books, text-films and film-strips, subscription and home-study books and programmes tapes, records, transparencies, science kits, instructional systems and tests, planetariums and special instructional equipment.

David McKay Co. Inc.: 750 Third Avenue, New York, N.Y. 10017, Pres. and Ed. KENNETT L. RAWSON; general fiction, non-fiction, juvenile, college texts, languages, dictionaries.

The Macmillan Co.: 866 Third Ave., New York, N.Y. 10011; a subsidiary of Crowell Collier and Macmillan Inc.; Pres. JEREMIAH KAPLAN; trade and professional books, college textbooks.

Macmillan, Inc.: 866 Third Ave., New York, N.Y. 10022; Pres. and Chair. of Board RAYMOND C. HAGEL; Exec. Vice-Pres. R. A. BARTON, J. KAPLAN, W. B. SMITH, J. F. BOND; reference, textbooks, trade, home study courses, professional magazines.

Macrae Smith Company: 225 S. 15th St., Lewis Tower Bldg., Philadelphia, Pa. 19102.

Meredith Corpn.: Book Division, 1716 Locust St., Des Moines, Iowa 50303; f. 1961; Corp. Vice-Pres. and Gen. Man. JACK BARLASS; Dir. Vice-Pres. ROBERT NELSON.

G. and C. Merriam Co.: 47 Federal St., Springfield, Mass. 01101; f. 1831; Pres. DAVID R. REPLOGLE; Vice-Pres. CRAWFORD LINCOLN, VICTOR W. WEIDMAN; affiliate of Encyclopaedia Britannica Inc.; Merriam-Webster dictionaries, reference.

Charles E. Merrill Publishing Co.: 1300 Alum Creek Drive, Columbus, Ohio 43216; f. 1842; a division of Bell and Howell; Pres. GARY D. EISENBERGER; textbooks and supplementary material.

Julian Messner: 1 West 39th St., New York, N.Y. 10018; a Div. of Simon and Schuster Inc.

Michigan State University Press: Box 550, East Lansing, Mich. 48823; Chair. of Board. LYLE BLAIR; Pres. RUSSEL B. NYE.

Monarch: 630 Fifth Ave., New York, N.Y. 10020; a division of Simon & Schuster Inc.; Dir. WILLIAM MLAWER.

Moody Press: 820 North La Salle St., Chicago, Ill. 60610; f. 1894; Dir. PETER F. GUNTHER; Editor LESLIE STOBBE; religious.

William Morrow & Co. Inc.: 105 Madison Ave. S., New York, N.Y. 10016; f. 1926; subsidiary of Scott, Foresman & Co.; Pres. LAWRENCE HUGHES; Exec. Vice-Pres. RIDLEY M. ENSLOW; fiction, non-fiction, juvenile.

C. V. Mosby Co.: 11830 Westline Industrial Drive, St. Louis, Mo. 36141; a subsidiary of The Times Mirror Co.; Chair. JOEL A. ROGERS; Pres. LEONARD A. BATTERSON; Editor-in-Chief Dr. JAMES B. FINN; Man. Dir. International Sales MANUEL L. PONTE; medical, dental, nursing education, nursing science, bio-sciences, physical education and social sciences books and journals.

National Academy of Sciences—National Academy of Engineering—Institute of Medicine—National Research Council: 2101 Constitution Ave., N.W., Washington, D.C. 20418; f. 1863; Pres. Dr. PHILIP HANDLER; scientific and technical reports, abstracts, bibliographies, catalogues.

Thomas Nelson Inc.: 405 Seventh Ave., South, Nashville TN37203; Pres. S. MOORE; religious, trade, juveniles.

The New American Library, Inc.: 1301 Ave. of the Americas, New York, N.Y. 10019; Chair. MARTIN P. LEVIN; Pres. H. K. SCHNALL; all categories except text; a subsidiary of Times-Mirror Co.

New Directions Pub. Corpn.: 333 Ave. of the Americas, New York, N.Y. 10014; f. 1936; Pres. and Editor JAMES LAUGHLIN; modern literature, poetry, criticism, belles lettres.

New York University Press: 62 Fifth Ave., New York 10011; f. 1916; Man. Editor ROBERT L. BULL; Sales, Advertising and Promotion Man. EDWIN M. SCRIBNER, Jr.; scholarly books.

Noble and Noble, Publishers, Inc.: 1 Dag Hammarskjold Plaza, New York, N.Y. 10017.

Northwestern University Press: 1735 Benson Ave., Evanston, Ill. 60201.

W. W. Norton & Co. Inc.: 55 Fifth Ave., New York, N.Y. 10003; f. 1924; Pres. GEORGE P. BROCKWAY; Vice-Pres. and Exec. Editor ERIC P. SWENSON; general fiction and non-fiction, college, science.

Oceana Publications Inc.: 40 Cedar St., Dobbs Ferry, N.Y. 10522; f. 1957; Pres. PHILIP F. COHEN; Vice-Pres. DAVID R. COHEN; trade, general, juveniles, law, politics, directories.

Octagon Books: 19 Union Square West, New York, N.Y. 10003; Editor-in-Chief HENRY G. SCHLANGER.

October House, Inc.: 160 Sixth Ave., New York, N.Y. 10013.

Ohio State University Press: 2070 Neil Ave., Columbus, O. 43210.

Ohio University Press: Admin. Annex, Ohio University, Athens, O. 45701.

Orbis Books: Maryknoll, N.Y. 10545; Editor-in-Chief PHILLIP SCHARPER; contemporary culture and religion; problems of the Third World.

Ottenheimer Publishers, Inc.: 1330 Reisterstown Rd., Baltimore, Md. 21208.

Oxford University Press Inc.: 200 Madison Ave., New York, N.Y. 10016; f. 1896; Pres. JAMES Y. HUWS-DAVIES; all non-fiction, trade books, religious, reference, Bibles, college textbooks, medical, music, technical.

Pantheon Books: 201 East 50th St., New York, N.Y. 10022; division of Random House Inc.; Man. Dir. ANDRÉ SCHIFFRIN; fiction, non-fiction, history, philosophy, art, juvenile, illustrated editions.

Paperback Library Inc.: 315 Park Ave. South, New York, N.Y. 10010; Pres. HY STEIRMAN; Editorial Dir. JERRY GROSS; paperback reprints and originals.

Parents' Magazine Press: 52 Vanderbilt Ave., New York, N.Y. 10017; Pres. EDWARD A. SAND.

Parnassus Press: 2721 Parker St., Berkeley, Calif. 94704.

Penguin Books Inc.: 7110 Ambassador Rd., Baltimore, Md. 21207; f. 1949; Vice-Pres. DEREK SHIPTON; reprints and originals.

Pennsylvania State University Press: University Press Building, University Park, Pa. 16802; f. 1956; Dir. C. W. KENTERA, Editorial Dir. J. M. PICKERING; scholarly non-fiction.

Pergamon Press Inc.: Fairview Park, Elmsford, N.Y. 10523; f. 1952; Pres. ROBERT MAXWELL; science, medicine.

Philosophical Library, Inc.: 15 East 40th Street, New York 10016; f. 1941; Pres. and Editor DAGOBERT D. RUNES, PH.D.; Editor REGEEN KIERNAN; educational and reference.

Pitman Publishing Corporation: 6 East 43 St., New York 10017; Chair. of Board MICHAEL PITMAN, Pres. E. M. CRANE; business education, technical, college, arts and crafts, and general non-fiction.

Plenum Publishing Corpn.: 227 West 17th St., New York, N.Y. 10011; Pres. EARL M. COLEMAN; scientific and technical books and journals, dictionaries, translations, music, Americana, exploration, art, architecture and general reprints.

Pocket Books Inc.: 630 Fifth Avenue, New York 10020; f. 1939; a division of Simon & Schuster Inc.; Pres. W. EWALD; reprints and originals.

Popular Library: 355 Lexington Ave., New York, N.Y. 10017; Editor-in-Chief P. O'CONNOR; reprints and originals.

Clarkson N. Potter, Inc.: 419 Park Ave. S., New York, N.Y. 10016.

Praeger Publishers, Inc.: 111 Fourth Ave., New York, N.Y. 10003; f. 1950; Pres. DAVID R. REPLOGLE; Editor-in-Chief ARNOLD DOLIN; general non-fiction.

Prentice-Hall Inc.: Engelwood Cliffs, N.J. 07632, and 70 Fifth Ave., New York, N.Y. 10011; f. 1913; Chair. PAUL R. ANDREWS; Pres. and Chief Exec. FRANK J. DUNNIGAN; scientific, industrial, educational, textbooks, general.

Press of Case Western Reserve University: Quail Bldg., Cleveland, O. 44106.

Princeton University Press: Princeton, New Jersey 08540; f. 1905; Dir. HERBERT S. BAILEY, Jr.; scholarly books.

The Psychological Corporation: 304 E. 45th St., New York, N.Y. 10017.

G. P. Putnam's Sons: 200 Madison Avenue, New York 10016; f. 1838; Pres. WALTER J. MINTON; general.

Pyramid Communications Inc.: 919 Third Ave., New York 10022; Pres. MATTHEW HUTTNER, Vice-Pres. and Asst. Publr. N. GOLDFIND; paperback reprints and originals.

Quadrangle Books, Inc.: 12 East Delaware Place, Chicago, Ill. 60611; history, politics; paperbacks.

Rand McNally & Co.: Box 7600, Chicago, Ill. 60680; f. 1856; Pres. ANDREW McNALLY III; Exec. Vice-Pres. WILLIAM BOLD, THOMAS J. HERMES; juvenile, non-fiction, school, college textbooks, atlases, maps.

Random House Inc.: 201 East 50th St., New York, N.Y. 10022; f. 1925; Chair. of Board DONALD S. KLOPFER; Pres. ROBERT L. BERNSTEIN; originals; reprints; paperbacks; juvenile, series, textbooks.

The Reader's Digest: 200 Park Ave., New York, N.Y. 10017.

Reader's Digest Association: Pleasantville, N.Y. 10570.

Henry Regnery Co.: 114 West Illinois St., Chicago, Ill. 60610; f. 1947; Chair. HENRY REGNERY; Pres. HARVEY PLOTNICK; general, non-fiction, poetry, fiction.

Reinhold Publishing Corporation: 430 Park Ave., New York, N.Y. 10022; Pres. JAMES F. MOTTERSHEAD; Vice-Pres. and Publishing Dir. JAMES B. ROSS; technical, architectural, art and craft books, chemical, scientific, engineering magazines.

Fleming H. Revell Co.: Old Tappan, N.J. 07675; f. 1870; Pres. WILLIAM R. BARBOUR, Jr.; religious.

Reynal & Company, Inc.: 221 E. 49th St., New York, N.Y. 10017.

The Richards Company: 635 Madison Ave., New York, N.Y. 10022.

Ward Ritchie Press: 3044 Riverside Drive, Los Angeles, Calif. 90039; f. 1932; Pres. JOSEPH SIMON; Sales Man. JAMES A. BARBER; Western Americana, Western travel guides to the U.S.A., cook books, wine books.

The Rockefeller University Press: York Ave. and 66th St., New York, N.Y. 10021.

Ronald Press Co., The: 79 Madison Ave., New York, N.Y. 10016; f. 1900; Pres. and Treas. PHILIP J. WARNER; Exec. Vice-Pres. EUGENE SIMONOFF; non-fiction, college textbooks, reference books.

Roy Publishers, Inc.: 30 East 74th Street, New York 10021; Pres. HANNA KISTER; fiction and non-fiction, juveniles.

Russell & Russell, Publishers (Division of Atheneum Publishers, Inc.): 122 East 42nd St., New York, N.Y. 10017; f. 1953; Man. Editor Mrs. E. SOSCHIN; reprints of scholarly books.

Rutgers University Press: 30 College Avenue, New Brunswick, N.J. 08903; Dir. WILLIAM SLOANE; Assoc. Dir. HELEN STEWART; scholarly and regional.

William H. Sadlier Inc.: 11 Park Place, New York, N.Y. 10007; f. 1832; Chief Exec. Officer F. SADLIER DINGER; Pres. FRANK M. POWER; elementary and secondary school textbooks.

St. Martin's Press Inc.: 175 Fifth Ave., New York, N.Y. 10010; f. 1952; Chair. F. WHITEHEAD; Pres. THOMAS J. McCORMACK; general and technical trade, textbooks.

Howard W. Sams & Co., Inc.: 4300 W. 62nd Street, Indianapolis, Ind. 46268; Pres. STANLEY S. SILLS; Vice-Pres. Sales THOMAS V. SURBER; Vice-Pres. Engineering and Technical Editorial LESTER H. NELSON; text and technical books.

W. B. Saunders Co.: West Washington Square, Philadelphia, Pa. 19105; f. 1888; Pres. T. VANDENBEEMT; Editor JOHN L. DUSSEAU; Exec. Vice-Pres. ROBERT R. ROWAN; medical, technical and scientific textbooks.

Scarecrow Press, Inc.: 52 Liberty St., Metuchen, N.J. 08840; Pres. ERIC MOON; reference, library science.

Schenkman Publishing Co. Inc.: 3 Mt. Auburn Place, Harvard Square, Cambridge, Mass. 02138; f. 1961; politics, sociology, economics, biology, trade.

Schocken Books, Inc.: 200 Madison Ave., New York, N.Y. 10016; Pres. THEODORE SCHOCKEN; primarily non-fiction.

Scholastic Magazines, Inc.: 50 West 44th St., New York, N.Y. 10036; f. 1920; Chair. MAURICE R. ROBINSON; Pres. JOHN P. SPAULDING; educational paperbacks and periodicals for elementary and secondary schools; includes Scholastic Book Services Division.

Science Research Associates, Inc.: 259 E. Erie St., Chicago, Ill. 60611; Pres. R. A. GIESEN; educational.

William R. Scott, Inc.: 333 Avenue of the Americas, New York, N.Y. 10014; f. 1938; Pres. and Treas. WILLIAM R. SCOTT; Vice-Pres. JOHN G. McCULLOUGH; Sec. and Editor CARLA STEVENS; juveniles.

Scott, Foresman & Co.: 1900 East Lake Ave., Glenview, Ill. 60025; f. 1896; Vice-Pres. International Sales J. T. HOLMES; textbooks.

Charles Scribner's Sons: 597 Fifth Ave., New York 10017; f. 1846; Chair. G. McKAY SCHIEFFELIN; Pres. CHARLES SCRIBNER, Jr.; general.

The Seabury Press Inc.: 815 Second Ave., New York 10017; Pres. WERNER MARK LINZ; religious, education, psychology, sociology, literature, juvenile.

Sheed & Ward: 475 Fifth Ave., New York, N.Y. 10017; Pres. and Editor J. F. ANDREWS; history, biography, juvenile, theology, sociology, philosophy, Catholic.

Shoe String Press Inc., The: 995 Sherman Ave., Hamden, Conn. 06514; f. 1952; Pres. and Man. Editor Mrs. FRANCES T. RUTTER; scholarly literature, reprints and originals, bibliography and documentation; publisher for Connecticut Academy of Arts and Sciences.

Simon & Schuster, Inc.: 630 Fifth Ave., New York 10020; f. 1924; Pres. SEYMOUR TURK; general.

The L. W. Singer Company, Inc.: 249 W. Erie Blvd., Syracuse, N.Y. 13201.

Peter Smith: 6 Lexington Ave., Gloucester, Mass. 01932; Pres. PETER SMITH; reprints.

Smithsonian Institution Press: Washington, D.C. 20560; academic.

Southern Illinois University Press: P.O.B. 3697 Carbondale, Ill. 62901; f. 1953; Dir. and Editor VERNON STERNBERG; scholarly non-fiction and standard fiction reprints.

Southern Methodist University Press: Dallas, Tex. 75222; f. 1937; Dir. ALLEN MAXWELL; Associate Dir. and Editor MARGARET L. HARTLEY.

The Southwestern Company: 1–65 Moores Lane, P.O.B. 820, Nashville, Tenn. 37202; Pres. S. HAYS; religious, educational.

South-Western Publishing Company: 5101 Madison Rd., Cincinnati, O. 45227; Pres. R. D. COOPER; textbooks.

Springer-Verlag New York, Inc.: 175 Fifth Ave., New York 10010; Exec. Vice-Pres. BERND GROSSMANN; scientific, technical, research and reference books.

Stackpole Books: Cameron and Kelker Streets, Harrisburg, Pa. 17105; f. 1930; Exec. Vice-Pres. and Editorial Dir. C. P. PETERS; outdoor, general-trade, politico-military, juvenile, gun care and repair.

Standard Educational Corporation: 130 North Wells St., Chicago, Ill. 60606; f. 1909; reference materials.

Stanford University Press: Stanford, Calif. 94305; f. 1925; Dir. LEON E. SELTZER; Editor J. G. BELL.

State University of New York Press: 99 Washington Ave., Albany, N.Y. 12210; f. 1966; Dir. NORMAN MANGOUNI; scholarly books and journals.

Steck-Vaughn Company: P.O.B. 2028, Austin, Tex. 78767.

Sterling Publishing Co., Inc.: 419 Park Avenue South, New York, N.Y. 10016; f. 1949; Pres. DAVID A. BOEHM; non-fiction, reference, textbooks.

Summy-Birchard Company: Evanston, Ill. 60204; f. 1872; Pres. DAVID K. SENGSTACK; education and music.

Swallow Press Inc., The: 1139 S. Wabash Ave., Chicago, Ill. 60605; f. 1940; Pres. MORTON P. WEISMAN; Vice-Pres. and Editor DURRETT WAGNER; poetry, fiction, criticism, biography, reprints and originals.

Syracuse University Press: P.O.B. 8, University Station, Syracuse, N.Y. 13210.

Taplinger Publishing Co. Inc.: 200 Park Ave. South, New York, N.Y. 10003; f. 1955; Pres. T. TAPLINGER; general.

Theatre Arts Books: 333 6th Ave., New York, N.Y. 10014.

Charles C. Thomas, Publisher: 301 East Lawrence Ave., Springfield, Ill. 62703; f. 1927; Pres. PAYNE E. L. THOMAS; medical, law, technical, textbooks.

Time-Life Books: Time & Life Building, Rockefeller Center, New York, N.Y. 10020; Publr. Mrs. JOAN D. MANLEY; Gen. Man. J. D. McSWEENEY; international political, cultural, social; U.S. history, science, art, music.

Times-Mirror Co.: Times-Mirror Square, Los Angeles, Calif. 90053; f. 1887; Division: Los Angeles Times; subsidiaries: Harry N. Abrams, Inc., Matthew Bender & Co., Inc., Fuller & Dees Marketing Group, Inc., The C. V. Mosby Co., Times Mirror Magazines, Inc., New American Library, Inc., New English Library Ltd., Southwestern Co., The World Publishing Co. Year Book Medical Publishers, Inc.; Chair. Dr. FRANKLIN D. MURPHY; Pres. ALBERT V. CASEY.

Tower Publications Inc.: 185 Madison Ave., New York, N.Y. 10016; f. 1960; Pres. HARRY SHORTEN; Editor in-Chief P. McCURTIN; paperback reprints and originals, fiction and non-fiction.

Twayne Publishers Inc.: Agent: 70 Lincoln St., Boston, Mass. 02111; f. 1949; Pres. JACOB STEINBERG; Exec. Editor T. T. BEELER; trade, literary criticism, textbooks and monographs.

Charles E. Tuttle Co., Inc.: 28 Main St., Rutland, Vt. 05701; f. 1832; Pres. CHARLES E. TUTTLE; books on the Orient, particularly Japan, language, art, culture, juveniles.

Frederick Ungar Publishing Co., Inc.: 250 Park Ave. South, New York, N.Y. 10003; f. 1940; Pres. FREDERICK UNGAR; Vice-Pres. and Exec. Editor Miss RUTH SELDEN; Asst. to Publr. BERTRAND T. UNGAR; reference works, non-fiction, literature and criticism, languages, engineering, mathematics.

The United Educators, Inc.: Tangley Oaks Educational Center, Lake Bluff, Ill. 60044.

United Nations: Sales Section, Publishing Service, New York, N.Y. 10017; Chief of Section W. SCOTT LAING; trade and textbooks on world and national economy, international trade, social questions, human rights, international law.

United States Naval Institute: Annapolis, Md. 21402.

Universal Publishing and Distributing Corpn.: 235 East 45th St., New York 10017; f. 1945; Pres. and Publr. ARNOLD E. ABRAMSON; Exec. Vice-Pres. ROBERT J. ABRAMSON; paperback originals and reprints, fiction and non-fiction.

University of Alabama Press: Drawer 2877, University, Ala. 35486; f. 1945; Dir. MORGAN L. WALTERS; Editor FRANCIS P. SQUIBB; scholarly books, especially political science, public administration, history, linguistics and philology, philosophy and religion.

University of Arizona Press: Box 3398, Tucson, Ariz. 85722; f. 1959; Dir. MARSHALL TOWNSEND; scholarly, popular regional.

University of California Press: Berkeley, Calif. 94720; f. 1893; Los Angeles Office: 60 Powell Library, U.C., Los Angeles, Calif. 90024; New York Office: 25 W. 45th St., New York, N.Y. 10036; f. 1893; Dir. AUGUST FRUGÉ; Assoc. Dir. PHILIP E. LILIENTHAL; L.A. Editor ROBERT ZACHARY.

University of Chicago Press: 5801 Ellis Ave., Chicago, Ill. 60637; f. 1891; Dir. MORRIS PHILIPSON; scholarly books and journals, textbooks, general.

University of Florida Press: 15 N.W. 15th St. Gainesville, Fla. 32601; f. 1945; Dir. WILLIAM B. HARVEY; Editor PAUL CHALKER; general, scholarly, regional.

University of Georgia Press: Athens, Ga. 30602; f. 1939; Dir. RALPH STEPHENS; academic, scholarly.

University of Hawaii Press: 535 Ward Ave., Honolulu, Hawaii 96814.

University of Illinois Press: Urbana, Ill. 61801; f. 1918; Dir. MIODRAG MUNTYAN; Editor RICHARD L. WENTWORTH; scholarly books and journals.

University of Kansas Press: 366 Watson Library, Lawrence, Kan. 66045.

University of Massachusetts Press: Amherst, Mass. 01002; f. 1964; Dir. LEONE STEIN; scholarly, poetry, regional, general.

University of Miami Press: Drawer 9088, Coral Gables, Fla. 33124.

University of Michigan Press, The: Ann Arbor, Mich. 48106; f. 1930; Dir. W. SEARS; Assoc. Dir. JOHN SCOTT MABON; non-fiction, textbooks, paperbacks.

University of Minnesota Press: 2037 University Ave. S.E., Minneapolis, Minn. 55455; f. 1927; Dir. JOHN ERVIN Jr.; Editor JEANNE SINNEN; scholarly, general.

University of Missouri Press: 107 Swallow Hall, Columbia, Mo. 65201.

University of Nebraska Press: Lincoln, Nebr. 68508; f. 1941; Acting Dir. F. M. LINKI; Editor VIRGINIA FAULKNER; general scholarly non-fiction, regional history.

University of New Mexico Press: Albuquerque, New Mex. 87106; f. 1931; Dir. H. W. TREADWELL; general, scholarly.

University of North Carolina Press: Box 2288, Chapel Hill, North Carolina 27514; f. 1922; Dir. MATTHEW HODGSON biographical, regional, general non-fiction, general college.

University of Notre Dame Press: Notre Dame, Ind. 46556; f. 1949; Chair. of Board Rev. PAUL E. BEICHNER; Dir. JOHN E. EHMANN (acting); scholarly in humanities and social sciences.

University of Oklahoma Press: Norman, Okla. 73069; f. 1928; Dir. ED SHAW; Editor MARY STITH; scholarly books in all fields.

University of Pennsylvania Press: 3933 Walnut St., Philadelphia, Pa. 19174; Acting Dir. R. L. WARREN; scholarly.

University of Pittsburgh Press: 127 North Bellefield Ave., Pittsburgh, Pa. 15260; f. 1936; Dir. FREDERICK A. HETZEL; scholarly books.

University Press of Kentucky: Lafferty Hall, University of Kentucky, Lexington, Ky. 40506; f. 1943; Dir. BRUCE F. DENBO; Editor JEROME CROUCH; scholarly, regional.

University Press of Virginia: Box 3608, University Sta., Charlottesville, Va. 22903; f. 1963; Dir. WALKER COWEN; bibliography.

University of South Carolina Press: Columbia, S.C. 29208; Dir. ROBERT T. KING; scholarly books.

University of Tennessee Press: Communications Bldg., Knoxville, Tenn. 37916.

University of Texas Press: P.O.B. 7819 Austin, Texas 78712; f. 1950; Dir. FRANK H. WARDLAW; Latin American studies, folklore, southwest regional, general scholarly.

University of Washington Press: Seattle, Wash. 98195; f. 1909; Dir. DONALD R. ELLEGOOD; Editor-in-Chief CHARLES E. CUNINGHAM; general, scholarly, non-fiction, reprints.

University of Wisconsin Press Ltd: Box 1379, Madison, Wis. 53701; Dir. THOMSON WEBB, Jr.; Assoc. Dir. EZRA DIMAN; non-fiction.

Vanderbilt University Press: Nashville, Tenn. 37235; Dir. and Editor DAVID HOWELL JONES

Vanguard Press, Inc.: 424 Madison Ave., New York, N.Y. 10017; Pres. EVELYN SHRIFTE.

D. Van Nostrand Reinhold Co.: 450 West 33rd St., New York, N.Y. 10001; f. 1848; Pres. ROBERT E. EWING; Vice-Pres. and Publr. JEAN KOEFOED; technical, scientific, general non-fiction.

The Viking Press, Inc.: 625 Madison Avenue, New York, N.Y. 10022; f. 1925; Pres. THOMAS H. GUINZBURG; fiction, non-fiction and juvenile.

Wadsworth Publishing Co., Inc.: Belmont, Calif. 94002; f. 1956; Chair. of Board RICHARD P. ETTINGER, Jr.; Pres. JAMES F. LEISY; college textbooks.

Henry Z. Walck, Inc.: 750 Third Ave., New York, N.Y. 10017; juveniles.

Walker & Co.: 720 Fifth Ave., New York, N.Y. 10019; f. 1959; a division of Walker Publishing Co. Inc.; Pres. SAMUEL S. WALKER, Jr.; Chair. SAMUEL W. MEEK; fiction, non-fiction and juvenile.

Washington Square Press: 630 Fifth Ave., New York, N.Y. 10020; f. 1959; a subsidiary of Simon and Schuster, Inc.; Exec. Editor LINDA LEWIN; Editor LAURIE BROWN; educational paperback books.

Franklin Watts, Inc.: 730 Fifth Ave., New York, N.Y. 10019; f. 1942; Pres. H. B. GRAHAM; Exec. Vice-Pres. M. T. BRINN; a division of Grolier, Inc.; juvenile, adult non-fiction.

Wayne State University Press: 5980 Cass Ave., Detroit, Mich. 48202.

Wesleyan University Press: Middletown, Conn. 06457.

Western Publishing Co., Inc.: 1220 Mound Ave., Racine, Wis. 53404; f. 1907; Chair., Chief Exec. and Pres. GERALD J. SLADE; juvenile, general.

The Westminster Press: Witherspoon Building, Juniper and Sansom Streets, Philadelphia, Pa. 19107; Gen. Man. CHARLES COLMAN III; Religious Editor PAUL L. MEACHAM; Juvenile Editor BARBARA BATES; juvenile, fiction, non-fiction, religious.

Weybright and Talley, Inc.: 750 Third Ave., New York, N.Y. 10017.

David White Company, Publishers: 60 E. 55th St., New York, N.Y. 10022.

John Wiley and Sons, Inc.: 605 Third Ave., New York, N.Y. 10016; f. 1807; Chair. W. BRADFORD WILEY; scientific, technical, medical and social science books, research monographs and periodicals under the imprints of Wiley, Wiley-Interscience, Hampton Publishing Co., Wiley Systems Inc. and Melville Publishing Co., including Audio-Visual materials.

Williams & Wilkins Co., The: 428 East Preston St., Baltimore, Md. 21202; f. 1925; Pres. CHARLES O. REVILLE, Jr.; medical, dental, veterinary, scientific.

H. W. Wilson Co.: 950 University Ave, Bronx, N.Y. 10452; f. 1898; Chair. of Board HOWARD HAYCRAFT; Pres. LEO M. WEINS; book and periodical indexes, library reference.

World Publishing Co., The: 2080 West 117th St., Lakewood, Ohio 44111 and 110 East 59th St., New York, N.Y.; acquired by Times-Mirror Co. of Los Angeles, Dec. 1963; Chair. MARTIN P. LEVIN; Pres. CHRISTOPHER J. H. M. SHAW; Exec. Vice-Pres. and Publr. LEONARD R. HARRIS; trade books, juvenile, art, fiction, biography, information, Bibles, dictionaries, religious.

Xerox College Publishing: 191 Spring St., Lexington, Mass. 02173; Publr. and Gen. Man. THEODORE CARIS; Vice-Pres. Editorial Development WILLIAM FROHLICH; college textbooks.

Yale University Press: 149 York Street, New Haven, Conn. 06511; f. 1908; Dir. CHESTER KERR; scholarly non-fiction.

Year Book Medical Publishers, Inc.: 35 E. Wacker Drive, Chicago, Ill. 60601; subsidiary of Times-Mirror Co.; Pres. WILLIAM F. KELLER.

Zondervan Corporation: 1415 Lake Drive, S.E. Grand Rapids, Mich. 49506; f. 1931; Pres. PETER KLADDER, Jr.; Chair. P. J. ZONDERVAN; religious.

ORGANIZATIONS AND ASSOCIATIONS

American Booksellers' Association: 800 Second Ave., New York, 10017; f. 1900; 4,100 mems.; Exec. Dir. G. ROYSCE SMITH.

American Educational Publishers Institute: 432 Park Ave. S., New York, N.Y. 10016; Pres. H. M. WARRINGTON.

Association of American Publishers, Inc.: 1 Park Ave., New York, N.Y. 10016; f. 1970; 245 mems.; Pres. T. HOOPES.

Association of American University Presses Inc.: 1 Park Ave., New York, N.Y. 10016; f. 1937; 67 mems.; Exec. Dir. JOHN B. PUTNAM; publ. *Directory*.

National Association of Book Editors: 59 4th Ave., New York, N.Y. 10003; f. 1962; 100 mems.; Pres. HANS SANTESSON; publ. *Nabe News* (monthly).

RADIO AND TELEVISION

Federal Communications Commissions (FCC): Washington, D.C. 20554; f. 1934; Seven Commissioners appointed by the President for seven years; regulates inter-state and foreign communication by radio, wire and cable; Chair. DEAN BURCH.

National Association of Broadcasters (NAB): 1771 N. St., N.W., Washington, D.C. 20036; f. 1922; over 4,000 mems.; a private body of Radio and TV stations and networks; lays down Operating Codes for Radio and TV, and provides other services; funds subscribed by members.

RADIO

Number of licensed and operating stations A.M. over 4,300, F.M. over 2,200. Number of radios; 336 million (1971).

COMMERCIAL NETWORKS

American Broadcasting Cos., Inc.: 1330 Ave. of the Americas, New York, N.Y. 10019; Chair. and Chief Exec. LEONARD H. GOLDENSON; Pres. and Chief Operating Officer ELTON H. RULE; 7 owned A.M./F.M. radio stations; 5 television stations; TV and radio networks.

Columbia Broadcasting System Inc.: 51 West 52nd St., New York, 10019; Chair. WILLIAM S. PALEY; Pres. ARTHUR TAYLOR; Pres. C.B.S. Radio Division S. COOK DIGGES; 7 owned and operated A.M., 7 owned and operated F.M., 243 affiliated stations.

Mutual Broadcasting System: 135 West 50th St., New York, N.Y. 10020; Pres. C. EDWARD LITTLE.

National Broadcasting Company Inc.: 30 Rockefeller Plaza, New York, N.Y. 10020; Chair. of Board DAVID C. ADAMS; Pres. JULIAN GOODMAN; 5 owned television stations, 220 television affiliated stations; 6 owned radio stations, 230 radio affiliated stations.

Keystone Broadcasting System: 111 W. Washington St., Chicago, Ill. 60602; and 527 Madison Ave., New York, N.Y. 10022; branches in Los Angeles, San Francisco and Detroit; transcription network for rural America; approx. 1,140 affiliated stations.

Westinghouse Broadcasting Company Inc.: 122 East 42nd St., New York, N.Y. 10017; Pres. D. H. McGANNON; Exec. Vice-Pres. R. V. TOOKE and L. H. ISRAEL; 6 AM, 3 FM, 5 VHF-TV owned and operated stations.

EDUCATIONAL

National Association of Educational Broadcasters: 1346 Connecticut Ave., N.W., Washington, D.C. 20036; f. 1925; Pres. WILLIAM G. HARLEY; 190 member educational radio stations, 5,000 individual members; publs. *Newsletter* (monthly), *Educational Broadcasting Review* (two-monthly), *Annual Directory of Educational Telecommunications*.

U.S. Office of Education: Washington, D.C. 20202; Asst; Sec. and Commr. of Education JAMES E. ALLEN, Jr.; 100 stations.

TELEVISION

Number of receiving sets: 93 million (1971).
Number of licensed and operating stations: 707 (1972).

COMMERCIAL

(*see also* Radio Section for full addresses)

American Broadcasting Companies, Inc.: New York; Chair. and Chief Exec. LEONARD H. GOLDENSON; Pres. and Chief Operating Officer ELTON H. RULE; 5 owned TV stations; 170 primary TV network affiliates; 119 secondary TV network affiliates.

American Broadcasting Company: Pres. of ABC Television Network THOMAS W. MOORE; 140 primary affiliates; 132 secondary TV network affiliates.

Columbia Broadcasting System Inc.: Pres. C.B.S. T.V. Network Division ROBERT D. WOOD; Pres. C.B.S. Television Stations D. THOMAS MILLER; 5 owned and operated, 205 affiliated stations.

Westinghouse Broadcasting Company: National T.V. Sales Man. ROBERT McGREDY; 5 stations.

EDUCATIONAL

U.S. Office of Education: Washington, D.C. 20202.

National Association of Educational Broadcasters: Washington; represents more than 135 educational television stations, 100 school closed-circuit television installations and 5,000 individuals (*see also* under Radio).

Public Broadcasting Service: H.Q.: 485 L'Enfant Plaza, S.W. Washington, D.C. 20024; non-profit-making; provides programming to 240 affiliated non-commercial educational television stations; Pres. H. N. GUNN Jr.

Net Television, Inc.: 2715 Pachard Rd., Ann Arbor, Mich.; videotape duplication-distribution and television post-production services.

Many universities and colleges have closed circuit systems.

FOREIGN RADIO SERVICES

GOVERNMENT

Voice of America: U.S. Information Agency, 330 Independence Ave., S.W. Washington, D.C. 20547; Dir. U.S. Information Agency JAMES KEOGH; Asst. Dir. (Broadcasting) KENNETH R. GIDDENS; broadcasts in 36 languages to all areas of the world.

Department of Defense, American Forces Radio and Television Service (AFRTS): Office of Information for the Armed Forces OASD (M and RA), Washington, D.C. 20305; *European Pacific and Southeast Asia Service:* American Forces Radio and Television Service, Washington, Office of Information for the Armed Forces OASD (M and RA), Washington, D.C. 22209; Commander LTC F. L. CASIPIT.

Radio and TV broadcasts in English to Europe, Middle and Far East, South-east Asia, Caribbean, North Atlantic, Pacific, North Africa.

PRIVATE

ABC International: 1330 Avenue of the Americas, New York, N.Y. 10019; subsidiary of American Broadcasting Company Inc.; Pres. RICHARD O'LEARY; 50 stations in Latin America, Japan, Australia; Canada etc.

KFRN: Ferney, Texas; f. 1960; operated by Globe Broadcasting Co.; serves Central and South America.

Radio Free Europe: Englischer Garten 1, Munich 22, Germany; Dir. RALPH WALTER; a division of Free Europe Inc., 2 Park Ave., New York, N.Y. 10016; Pres. WILLIAM P. DURKEE.

Broadcasts to Eastern Europe in Bulgarian, Czech, Slovak, Hungarian, Polish, Romanian.

Radio Liberty: 8 Munich 81, Arabellastrasse 18, Germany; Exec. Dir. WALTER K. SCOTT; supported by the Radio Liberty Committee Inc., whose funds are from private persons and organizations in the United States; 30 East 42nd St., New York, N.Y. 10017; Pres. HOWLAND H. SARGEANT.

Broadcasts 24 hours daily in 20 national languages of the Soviet Union.

Radio New York Worldwide Inc.: 485 Madison Ave., New York City, N.Y. 10022; Pres. and Gen. Man. JOHN C. MOLER; operates New York City stereo FM station WRFM.

Radio Station KGEI Inc. The Voice of Friendship: Friendship Station, Redwood City, Calif. 94063; f. 1939; owned and operated by Far East Broadcasting Co. Inc.; Pres. R. H. BOWMAN; Station Man. JIM R. BOWMAN; broadcasts in English, Spanish, Portuguese, Russian, Ukrainian, Japanese, Mandarin, Chinese.

FINANCE

BANKING

FEDERAL RESERVE SYSTEM

(Washington, D.C. 20551)

BOARD OF GOVERNORS

Chairman: Dr. ARTHUR F. BURNS.

Vice-Chairman: J. L. ROBERTSON.

Governors: GEORGE W. MITCHELL, J. DEWEY DAANE, JEFFREY M. BUCHER, ANDREW F. BRIMMER, JOHN E. SHEEHAM.

Executive Director: ROBERT C. HOLLAND.

Advisers to the Board: J. CHARLES PARTEE, ROBERT SOLOMON.

Assistants to the Board: HOWARD H. HACKLEY, (vacant), ROBERT L. CARDON, (vacant), EDWIN J. JOHNSON.

Special Assistants to the Board: JOSEPH R. COYNE, FRANK O'BRIEN, Jr., JOHN S. RIPPEY.

Secretary of the Board: TYNAN SMITH.

General Counsel: THOMAS J. O'CONNELL.

Director, Division of Research and Statistics: J. CHARLES PARTEE.

Director, Division of International Finance: RALPH C. BRYANT.

The Federal Reserve System comprises the Board of Governors, the Federal Open Market Committee, the Federal Advisory Council, the 12 Federal Reserve Banks with 24 branches, and the member banks. Founded 1913.

The Board of Governors is composed of seven members appointed by the President of the United States with the advice and consent of the Senate.

The Reserve Banks are empowered to issue Federal Reserve notes fully secured by the following assets, alone or in any combination: (1) Gold certificates; (2) U.S. Government securities; (3) Eligible paper as described by statute. The Reserve Banks may discount paper for member banks and make properly secured advances to member banks. At the direction of the Federal Open Market Committee

the Federal Reserve Banks engage in open market operations, chiefly concerned with U.S. Government securities; the Reserve Banks function as collectors and clearing houses for member banks and act as fiscal agents of the United States Government.

All national banks are members of the Federal Reserve System, and State-chartered banks may apply for membership and be admitted upon qualification.

The Comptroller of the Currency has primary supervisory authority over national banks, and the banking supervisors of the States have similar jurisdiction over banks organised under State laws. State member banks are examined by the Federal Reserve, and all member banks are subject to regulations issued by the Board of Governors.

FEDERAL RESERVE BANKS

Federal Reserve Bank of:	Chairman	President
Boston	James S. Duesenberry	Frank E. Morris
New York	Roswell L. Gilpatric	Alfred Hayes
Philadelphia	Bayard L. England	David P. Eastburn
Cleveland	Albert G. Clay	Willis J. Winn
Richmond	Robert W. Lawson, Jr.	Aubrey H. Heflin
Atlanta	John C. Wilson	Monroe Kimbrel
Chicago	Emerson G. Higdon	Robert P. Mayo
St. Louis	Frederico M. Peirce	Darryl R. Francis
Minneapolis	David M. Lilly	Bruce K. Maclaury
Kansas City	Robet W.Wagstaff	George H. Clay
Dallas	Charles F. Jones	Philip E. Coldwell
San Francisco	O. Meredith Wilson	(vacant)

COMPTROLLER OF CURRENCY
Comptroller: William B. Camp.

The Comptroller of Currency has supervisory control over all Federal chartered banks (the national banks), comprising more than half the U.S. banking system.

INTERNATIONAL BANK
First Washington Securities Corporation: Washington, D.C.; f. 1970; international finance, particularly in Europe, Latin America and the Far East.

EXPORT-IMPORT BANK
Export-Import Bank of the United States: 811 Vermont Ave., Washington, D.C. 20571; f. 1934, and made a permanent independent agency of the United States in 1945; auth. cap. stock $1,000,000,000; Board of Directors appointed by the President, finances and facilitates U.S. trade with other countries, general banking business in the foreign trade field, guarantees payment to American foreign traders and banks, extends credit to foreign government and private concerns; First Vice-Pres. and Vice-Chair. Walter C. Sauer; Dirs. M. P. Kobelinski, R. Alex McCullough, John C. Clark; Acting Exec. Vice-Pres. Warren W. Glick; Sen. Vice-Pres. Delio E. Gianturco, Rosemary A. Mazon.

COMMERCIAL BANKING SYSTEM
As might be expected the United States banking system is the largest and in most respects the most comprehensive and sophisticated in the world, and it includes the four largest banks in terms of deposits. Banking has, however, been largely subject to state rather than federal jurisdic-

tion, and this has created a structure very different from that in other advanced industrial countries. In general no bank may open branches or acquire subsidiaries in states other than that in which it is based. Some states also restrict banks to a single branch, or to operating only in certain counties of the state. The strict federal anti-trust laws also limit mergers of banks within a state. The effect of these measures has been to preserve the independence of a very large number of banks—over 13,500 in 1969. Nevertheless, the dominant banks are the main banks in the big industrial states; of the ten largest, six are based in New York, two each in California and Illinois.

BANKING AND THE INDIVIDUAL
The possession of bank accounts and the use of banking facilities are perhaps more widespread amongst all classes and regions than in any other country. This has had important effects on monetary theory and policy, as bank credit has become much more important than currency supply in the regulation of the economy. Use of current accounts and credit cards are so common that many authorities claim the U.S. can be regarded as effectively a cashless society.

EXPANSION OVERSEAS
Since 1960 the leading banks have rapidly built up substantial banking interests overseas. There were then only about 15 branches of U.S. banks in Europe and a negligible number elsewhere; by early 1970 some 400 branches had opened overseas (over 100 in Europe), owned by more than 40 banks. Over 300 of these are owned by the largest three banks; these three, and several others,

also own or have taken large minority interests in a number of foreign banks. Overseas branches as a whole are estimated to account for over 20 per cent of American bank deposits. The main factors behind the expansion overseas are the geographical limitations imposed by law at home; the rapid expansion of U.S. business interests abroad and their preference for dealing with an American bank; the faster economic growth of certain foreign countries; and finally the profitability of the "Euro-dollar" capital market in Europe.

COMMERCIAL BANKS

The following list is based on a minimum of $10 million capital. In states where no such bank exists the bank with the largest capital is listed.

(cap.=total capital including surplus, profits and reserve; dep.=deposits; m.=million.)

ALABAMA

First National Bank of Birmingham: P.O.B. 11007, Birmingham, Ala. 35288; f. 1873; cap. $77m.; dep. $881m. (June 1973); Chair. of the Board and Chief Exec. Officer ROBERT H. WOODROW, Jr.; Pres. M. E. MOORE, Jr.

ALASKA

National Bank of Alaska: Fourth and E, Box 600, Anchorage; f. 1916; cap. $17.6m.; dep. $226.1m. (June 1972); Chair. E. RASMUSON; Pres. D. L. MELLISH.

ARIZONA

First National Bank of Arizona: First National Bank Plaza, P.O.B. 20551, Phoenix 85036; f. 1877; cap. $104,100m.; dep. $1,520m. (Dec. 1973); Chair. S. HAZELTINE; Pres. R. D. WILLIAMS.

Valley National Bank of Arizona: 241 North Central Ave. Phoenix; f. 1899; cap. $124.6m.; dep. $1,952.2m. (June 1972); Chair. JAMES B. MAYER; Pres. G. F. BRADLEY.

ARKANSAS

Simmons First National Bank of Pine Bluff: Main and Fifth Streets, Pine Bluff, Ark.; f. 1903; cap. $3.5m.; dep. $130.8m. (Dec. 1973); Pres. and Chief Exec. Officer LOUIS L. RAMSAY, Jr.

CALIFORNIA

Bank of America National Trust and Savings Assen.: Bank of America Center, San Francisco, Calif. 94120; f. 1904; cap. $1,526m.; dep. $32,393m. (June 1971); 1,100 banking offices; Pres. A. W. CLAUSEN; Chair. of the Board C. J. MEDBERRY.

Bank of California, N.A.: 400 California St., San Francisco, Calif. 94120; f. 1864; cap. $100.6m.; dep. $1,678m. (June 1971); Chair. of Board CHARLES DE BRETTEVILLE.

Crocker National Bank: One Montgomery St., San Francisco, Calif. 94138; cap. $362m.; dep. $8.016m. (Dec. 1973); Chair. and Chief Exec. Officer EMMETT G. SOLOMON; Exec. Vice-Pres. International Div. A. TAAPKEN.

First Western Bank and Trust Co.: 548 South Spring St., Los Angeles, Calif. 90013; f. 1961; cap. $77m.; dep. $1,116m. (Dec. 1972); Chair. and Pres. STAFFORD R. GRADY; Senior Vice-Pres. and Man. International Div. JACOB SITSER.

Security Pacific National Bank: Sixth and Spring Sts., Los Angeles, Calif. 90013; f. 1929 as Security-First National Bank of Los Angeles; cap. $594m.; dep. $7,855m. (June 1971); Pres. CARL E. HARTNACK; Senior Vice-Pres. and Administrator International Banking Dept. RALPH E. BELVILLE.

Union Bank: 445 South Figueroa St., Los Angeles, Calif. 90017; f. 1914; cap. $218m.; dep. $3,614m. (Dec. 1973); Pres. GEORGE A. THATCHER.

United California Bank: 707 Wilshire Blvd., Los Angeles, Calif. 90017; f. 1903; cap. $410.6m.; dep. $6,386m. (June 1973); Chair. FRANK L. KING; Pres. NORMAN BARKER, Jr.

Wells Fargo Bank N.A.: 464 California St., San Francisco, Calif. 94104; f. 1960; cap. $502m.; dep. $7,000m. (Dec. 1973); Chair. of Board ERNEST C. ARBUCKLE.

COLORADO

United Bank of Denver N.A.: United Bank Center, 1740 Broadway, Denver 80217; f. 1958; cap. $44m.; dep. $5,860m. (June 1973); Chair. R. D. KNIGHT, Jr.; Vice-Chair. NEIL F. ROBERTS; Pres. JOHN D. HERSHNER.

CONNECTICUT

Connecticut Bank and Trust Co.: 1 Constitution Pl., Hartford, Conn. 06115; f. 1792; cap. $107m.; dep. $1,505m. (Dec. 1973); Pres. WALTER J. CONNOLLY, Jr.; Chair. JAMES F. ENGLISH, Jr.

Hartford National Bank and Trust Co.: 777 Main St., Hartford, Conn. 06115; f. 1792; cap. $18m.; dep. $1,523,817m. (Dec. 1973); Pres. C. E. LORD.

DELAWARE

Bank of Delaware: 300 Delaware Ave., Wilmington 19899; f. 1885; cap. $34m.; dep. $349m. (Dec. 1972); Chair. and Pres. JAMES H. DAWSON; Treas. FRANCIS J. KARPINSKI.

DISTRICT OF COLUMBIA

Riggs National Bank of Washington, D.C.: 1503 Pennsylvania Ave., N.W., Washington, D.C. 20013; f. 1836; cap. $93m.; dep. $1,006m. (Dec. 1972); Chair. JOHN M. CHRISTIE; Pres. VINCENT C. BURKE, Jr.

FLORIDA

First National Bank of Miami: 100 South Biscayne Blvd., Miami 33131; f. 1902; cap. $75m.; dep. $1,141m. (Dec. 1973); Chair. H. H. BASSETT; Pres. J. B. SHUMATE.

GEORGIA

Citizens and Southern National Bank, The: 35 Broad St. N.W., Atlanta, Ga. 30301; f. 1887; cap. $217.5m.; dep. $1,988.9m. (Dec. 1973); Pres. RICHARD L. KATTEL; Exec. Vice-Pres. Int. Dept. JAMES E. GREEN, Jr.

First National Bank of Atlanta: P.O.B. 4148, 2 Peachtree St., Five Points, Atlanta, Ga. 30302; f. 1865; cap. $84m.; dep. $1,039m. (June 1973); Chair. E. D. SMITH; Pres. T. R. WILLIAMS.

HAWAII

Bank of Hawaii: 111 South King St., Honolulu 96813; f. 1897; cap. $55m.; dep. $920m. (Dec. 1973); Chair. and Chief Exec. CLIFTON D. TERRY; Pres. WILSON P. CANNON, Jr.

IDAHO

Idaho First National Bank: P.O.B. 7009, Boise; f. 1867; cap. $36m.; dep. $591.6m. (June 1970); Pres. THOMAS C. FRYE; Chair. WILLIAM E. IRVIN.

ILLINOIS

American National Bank and Trust Co. of Chicago: La Salle St. at Washington, Chicago, Ill. 60690; f. 1928; cap. $175.3m.; dep. $1,261.5m. (Sept. 1973); Chair. A. P. STULTS; Pres. W. G. ERICSSON.

Continental Illinois National Bank and Trust Co. of Chicago:
231 South La Salle St., Chicago, Ill. 60693; f. 1857;
cap. $705m.; dep. $9,690.9m. (Dec. 1972); Chair. of
Board R. E. ANDERSON; Pres. J. H. PERKINS.

First Chicago Corporation: 1 First National Pl., Chicago,
Ill. 60670; f. 1893; cap. $696m.; dep. $10,670m.
(Sept. 1973); Chair. GAYLORD A. FREEMAN, Jr.; Pres.
JOHN E. DRICK.

Harris Trust and Savings Bank: 111 West Monroe St.,
Chicago, Ill. 60690; f. 1882; inc. 1907; cap. $225m.;
dep. $2,853m.; Chair. W. F. MURRAY.

Northern Trust Co., The: 50 South La Salle St., Chicago,
Ill. 60690; f. 1889; cap. $156m.; dep. $1,958m. (June
1972); Chair. EDWARD B. SMITH; Vice-Chair. DOUGLAS
R. FULLER.

INDIANA

Indiana National Bank, The: 1 Indiana Square, Indiana-
polis, Ind. 46204; f. 1834; cap. $89m.; dep. $1,225m.
(Dec. 1971); Chair. J. FRED RISK; Pres. JOHN R.
BENBOW.

Merchants National Bank and Trust Co. of Indianapolis:
11 South Meridan St., Indianapolis; f. 1865; cap.
$59m.; dep. $852m. (June 1973); Chair. of the Board
OTTO N. FRENZEL; Pres. D. TANSELLE.

IOWA

Iowa-Des Moines National Bank: 6th and Walnut Sts.,
Des Moines 50309; f. 1969; cap. $24m.; dep. $351m.
(Dec. 1972); Pres. JOHN R. FITZGIBBON; Exec. Vice-
Pres. HAROLD P. KLEIN.

KANSAS

Fourth National Bank and Trust Co., Wichita: Market St.
at Douglas Ave., Wichita, Kan. 67201; f. 1887; cap.
$11m.; dep. $279m. (June 1972); Pres. JORDAN L.
HAINES.

KENTUCKY

First National Bank of Louisville: 101 South 5th St.,
Louisville 40202; f. 1863; cap. $87.6m.; dep. $734.3m.
(Dec. 1973); Chair. HUGH M. SCHWAB; Pres. A. STEVENS
MILES.

LOUISIANA

First National Bank of Commerce, New Orleans: 210
Baronne St., New Orleans; f. 1933; cap. $46m.; dep.
$546m. (Dec. 1971); Pres. JAMES H. JONES; Vice-Pres.
EDWIN G. JEWETT, Jr.

MAINE

Maine National Bank: 400 Congress St., Portland 04112;
f. 1889; cap. $5.4m.; dep. $181.6m. (June 1971); Chair.
HUBERT H. HAUCK.

MARYLAND

First National Bank of Maryland: 25 South Charles St.,
Baltimore, Md. 21202; f. 1806; cap. $62.3m.; dep.
$665.7m. (Dec. 1971); Chair. of the Board ADRIAN L.
McCARDELL; Pres. J. OWEN COLE; publ. *International
Trade Winds* (two-monthly).

Maryland National Bank: Baltimore and Light Sts., Baltimore, Md. 21203; f. 1933; cap. $96m.; dep. $1,109m.
(Dec. 1971); Chair. R. D. H. HARVEY.

MASSACHUSETTS

First National Bank of Boston: 100 Federal St., Boston,
Mass. 02110; f. 1784; cap. $433m.; dep. $6,180m. (Dec.
1973); Chair. of the Board RICHARD D. HILL; Pres.
WILLIAM L. BROWN.

National Shawmut Bank of Boston: 40 Water St., Boston,
Mass. 02106; f. 1836; cap. $84m.; dep. $1,240m. (Dec.
1972); Chair. and Pres. D. THOMAS TRIGG; Sen. Vice-
Pres. International J. VAN VOLLENHOVEN.

State Street Bank and Trust Co.: 225 Franklin St., Boston,
Mass. 02101; f. 1792; cap. $95m.; dep. $1,045m. (Dec.
1971); Chair. and Pres. H. FREDERICK HAGEMANN, Jr.

MICHIGAN

Detroit Bank and Trust Co.: Fort at Washington, Detroit,
Mich. 48231; f. 1849; cap. $171.8m.; dep. $2,314m.
(Dec. 1972); Chair. RAYMOND T. PERRING; Pres. C.
BOYD STOCKMEYER.

Manufacturers' National Bank of Detroit: Mich. 48231; f.
1933; cap. $169m.; dep. $2,355m. (Dec. 1973); Pres.
L. G. ALLEN.

Michigan National Bank: Lansing; f. 1940; cap. $117m.;
dep. $1,294m. (June 1973); Chair. STANFORD C.
STODDARD; Pres. PAUL C. SOUDER; Controller H.
PERRY DRIGGS, Jr.

National Bank of Detroit: 611 Woodward Ave., Detroit,
Mich. 48232; f. 1933; cap. $354m.; dep. $5,567m.;
Chair. ROBERT M. SURDAM; Pres. C. T. FISHER III.

MINNESOTA

First National Bank of Minneapolis: 120 South Sixth St.,
Minneapolis, Minn. 55402; f. 1857; cap. $116m.; dep.
$1,165m. (Dec. 1973); Chair. of the Board and Pres.
GEORGE H. DIXON.

First National Bank of St. Paul: 332 Minnesota St., St.
Paul, Minn. 55101; f. 1853; cap. $7.4m.; dep. $769m.
(June 1971); Pres. PHILIP H. NASON.

Northwestern National Bank of Minneapolis: Seventh and
Marquette, Minneapolis, Minn. 55480; f. 1872; cap.
$108m.; dep. $1,043m. (June 1973); Chair. J. A. MOOR-
HEAD; Pres. P. B. HARRIS; Int. Dept. Vice-Pres. J. W.
JOHNSON.

MISSISSIPPI

Deposit Guaranty National Bank: 200 East Capitol St.,
Jackson, Miss. 39201; f. 1952; cap. $52m.; dep. $620m.
Chair. RUSS M. JOHNSON; Pres. J. H. HINES.

MISSOURI

First National Bank in St. Louis: Broadway, Olive, Locust
and Sixth, P.O. Box 267, St. Louis, Mo. 63166; f. 1919;
cap. $88m.; dep. $792m. (June 1973); Chair. and Chief
Exec. EDWIN S. JONES; Pres. CLARENCE C. BARKSDALE.

Mercantile Trust Co.: 721 Locust St., St. Louis, Mo. 63166;
f. 1855; cap. $120m.; dep. $989m. (June 1972); Chair.
DONALD E. LASATER; Pres. HARRISON F. COEVER.

United Missouri Bank of Kansas City, N.A.: P.O.B. 226,
10th and Grand Ave., Kansas City, Mo. 64141; f. 1913;
cap. $38.8m.; dep. 390.5m. (Sept. 1973); Pres. J. H.
SCOTT.

MONTANA

First National Bank: 101 North Main St., Butte; f. 1877;
cap. $2.8m.; dep. $45.6m.; Pres. WILLIAM R. TAIT.

NEBRASKA

Omaha National Bank: 17th and Farnam Sts., Omaha
68102; f. 1966; cap. $10m.; res. 508.3m. (June 1972);
Chair. MORRIS F. MILLER; Pres. F. O. STARR.

NEVADA

First National Bank of Nevada: One East First St., Reno;
f. 1903; cap. $53m.; dep. $807m. (Dec. 1973); Chair. of
Board and Chief Exec. A. M. SMITH; Pres. E. MARTIN-
ELLI.

New Hampshire

Concord National Bank: 43 North Main St., Concord 03301; f. 1864; cap. $4.9m.; dep. $37m. (June 1973); Chair. and Pres. F. N. Southworth.

New Jersey

Commercial Trust Company of New Jersey: 15 Exchange Place, Jersey City 07302; f. 1899; cap. $27.9m.; dep. $222m. (Dec. 1973); Chair. of the Board and Chief Exec. Officer Harry C. Zimmer; Pres. Robert Swanson.

Midlantic National Bank: 744 Broad St., Newark, N.J. 07101; dep. $809.2m. (June 1973); Chair. Theron L. Marsh; Pres. R. van Buren.

New Mexico

Albuquerque National Bank: 123 Central Ave. N.W., Albuquerque 87101; f. 1924; cap. $3.9m.; dep. $205.3m. (Dec. 1969); Pres. Robert L. Tripp.

New York

Allied Bank International: 116 East St., New York, N.Y. 10022; f. 1968; cap. $27m.; dep. $307m. (Dec. 1971); Pres. Jacques R. Stunzi.

Bank of America: P.O.B. 466, Church St. Station, New York, N.Y. 10015; wholly owned subsidiary of Bank of American National Trust and Savings Association; f. 1950; cap. $1,526m.; dep. $27,820m. (June 1971); Chair. C. J. Medberry; Pres. A. W. Clausen.

Bank of New York, The: 48 Wall St., New York, N.Y. 10015; f. 1784; cap. $159.6m.; dep. $1,581.6m. (June 1971); Chair. and Chief Exec. Officer Samuel H. Woolley; Pres. Elliott Overett.

Bankers' Trust Company: 16 Wall St., New York City, N.Y. 10015; f. 1903; cap. $507m.; dep. $8,455m. (June 1971); Chair. of the Board William H. Moore.

Chase Manhattan Bank, N.A., The: 1 Chase Manhattan Plaza, New York, N.Y. 10015; f. 1955; cap. $1,418m.; dep. $21,227m. (Dec. 1970); Chair. of the Board David Rockefeller; Pres. Willard Butcher.

Chemical Bank: 20 Pine St., New York City, N.Y. 10015; f. 1824; cap. $868.5m.; dep. $13,047m. (Nov. 1973); Chair. D. C. Platten.

First National City Bank: 55 Wall St., New York, N.Y. 10015; f. 1812; subsidiary of First National City Corporation; cap. $1,724m.; dep. $23,170m. (June 1971); Chair. W. B. Wriston; Pres. W. I. Spencer; Chair. Exec. Cttee. E. L. Palmer.

Irving Trust Company: 1 Wall St., New York, N.Y. 10015; f. 1851; cap. $317m.; dep. $5,200m. (Dec. 1972); Chair. Gordon T. Wallis; Pres. Arthur G. Boardman, Jr.

Lincoln Rochester Trust Company: 183 East Main St., Rochester 3; f. 1893; cap. $66.6m.; dep. $863m. (Dec. 1971); Pres. Wilmot R. Craig.

Manufacturers' and Traders' Trust Company: 1 M and T Plaza, Buffalo, N.Y. 14240; f. 1856; cap. $77.9m.; dep. $734m. (Dec. 1969); Chair. and Pres. Claude F. Shuchter.

Manufacturers' Hanover Trust Company: 350 Park Ave., New York, N.Y. 10022; f. 1961; cap. $837m.; dep. $12,534m. (June 1971); Chair. Gabriel Hauge; Pres. John F. McGillicuddy.

Marine Midland Bank—New York: 140 Broadway, New York, N.Y. 10015; f. 1907; cap. $213m.; dep. $5,820m. (Sept. 1973); Chair. of Board and Pres. John S. Lawson.

Morgan Guaranty Trust Company of New York: 23 Wall St., New York, N.Y. 10015; 1959; cap. $1,060m.; dep. $12,838 (Dec. 1972); Chair. Ellmore C. Patterson; Pres. Walter H. Page.

National Bank of North America: 44 Wall St., New York, N.Y. 10005; f. 1967; cap. $197m.; dep. $2,133 (Dec. 1971); Chair. S. Friedman; Pres. J. H. Vogel.

United States Trust Company (of New York): 45 Wall St., New York, N.Y. 10005; f. 1853; cap. $73m.; dep. $424m. (Dec. 1972); Chair. Hoyt Ammidon; Pres. Charles W. Buek.

North Carolina

Wachovia Bank and Trust Company N.A.: Third and Main Sts., Winston-Salem, N.C. 27102; f. 1879; cap. $51m.; dep. $2,400m. (June 1972); Pres. John F. Watlington, Jr.

North Carolina National Bank: 200 South Tryon St., Charlotte; f. 1874; cap. $163.8m.; dep. $2,961m. (Dec. 1973); Chair. L. H. Hodges; Pres. H. L. McCull.

North Dakota

Bank of North Dakota: 700 First St., Bismarck, N.D. 58501; f. 1919; cap. $20.8m.; dep. $137m. (June 1971); owned and operated by the State of North Dakota; Pres. and Man. H. L. Thornda.

Ohio

Central National Bank of Cleveland: 800 Superior Ave., Cleveland, Ohio 44114; f. 1890; cap. $100m.; dep. $1,348m. (Dec. 1973); Chair. and Pres. John A. Gelbach.

Central Trust Company: Fourth and Vine Sts., Cincinnati, Ohio 45202; f. 1862; cap. $63m.; dep. $537.7m. (June 1972); Chair. Fletcher E. Nyce; Pres. O. W. Birckhead.

Cleveland Trust Company: 900 Euclid Ave., Cleveland, Ohio 44101; f. 1894; cap. $314m.; dep. $2,361m. (June 1972); Chair. G. F. Karch; Pres. Everett Ware Smith.

Fifth Third Bank: Fifth Third Center, Cincinnati, Ohio 45201; f. 1858; cap. $15m.; dep. $501m. (Sept. 1971); Chair. and Pres. W. S. Rowe.

First National Bank of Cincinnati, The: S.E. cnr. 4th and Walnut Sts., Cincinnati, Ohio 45202; f. 1863; cap. $87.2m.; dep. $684m. (Sept. 1973); Chair. William N. Liggett.

National City Bank: 623 Euclid Ave., Cleveland, Ohio 44114; f. 1845; cap. $171.9m.; dep. $1,754.8m. (Dec. 1973); Chair. Claude M. Blair; Pres. Julien L. McCall.

Society National Bank of Cleveland: 127 Public Square, Cleveland, Ohio 44114; f. 1849; cap. $73m.; dep. $942.4m. (Sept. 1973); Chair. Walter F. Lineberger, Jr.; Pres. J. Maurice Struchen.

Toledo Trust Company: 245 Summit St., Toledo, Ohio 43603; f. 1868; cap. $53.1m.; dep. $478.5m. (Dec. 1972); Chair. of the Board Donald M. Dresser; Pres. Samuel G. Carson.

Union Commerce Bank: 917 Euclid Ave., Cleveland, Ohio 44101; v. 1938; cap. $87m.; dep. $933m. (June 1972); Chair. Alfred L. Jones.

Oklahoma

First National Bank and Trust Co. of Oklahoma City: 120 N Robinson Ave., Oklahoma City 73102; f. 1889; cap. $63m.; dep. $532m. (Dec. 1972); Pres. Felix N. Porter.

OREGON

First National Bank of Oregon: 1300 S.W. Fifth Ave., Portland, Ore. 97208; f. 1865; cap. $147m.; dep. $1,891m. (June 1972); Pres. RALPH J. VOSS.

United States National Bank of Oregon: 309 S.W. Sixth Ave., Portland, Ore. 97208; f. 1891; subsidiary of U.S. Bancorp; cap. $177m.; dep. $2,069m. (Dec. 1973); Chair. LEROY B. STAVER; Pres. J. A. ELORRIAGA; Vice-Pres. and Man. Int. Div. R. L. GIBBS.

PENNSYLVANIA

First Pennsylvania Banking and Trust Co., The: 15th and Chestnut Sts., Philadelphia, Pa. 19101; f. 1782; cap. $400m.; dep. $3,493m. (Sept. 1973); Chair. JOHN R. BUNTING; Pres. JAMES F. BODINE.

Girard Trust Bank: 1 Girard Plaza, Philadelphia, Pa. 19101; cap. $204m.; dep. $2,526m. (Dec. 1972); Chair. STEPHEN S. GARDNER; Pres. WILLIAM B. EAGLESON, JR.

Mellon National Bank and Trust Company: Mellon Square, Pittsburgh, Pa. 15230; f. 1902; cap. $536m.; dep. $4,926m. (June 1971); Chair. JOHN A. MAYER; Pres. A. BRUCE BOWDEN.

Philadelphia National Bank: Broad and Chestnut Sts., Philadelphia, Pa. 19101; f. 1803; cap. $219m.; dep. $2,596m. (Sept. 1973); Chair. G. MORRIS DORRANCE, JR.

Pittsburgh National Bank: Pittsburgh National Bldg., Pittsburgh, Pa. 15222; f. 1864; cap. $181m.; dep. $1,535m. (June 1971); Chair. M. E. GILLIAND; Pres. ROBERT C. MILSOM.

Provident National Bank: Broad and Chestunt Sts., Philadelphia, Pa. 19101; f. 1847; cap. $84.2m.; dep. $920.9m. (Dec. 1969); Chair. WILLIAM G. FOULKE; Pres. ROGER S. HILLAS; Senior Vice-Pres. Int. Div. ALAIN DE MAYNADIER.

RHODE ISLAND

Industrial National Bank of Rhode Island: 111 Westminster St., Providence 02903; f. 1791; cap. $109m.; dep. $1,273m. (Sept. 1973); Pres. JOHN J. CUMMINGS, JR.; Exec. Vice-Pres. ROBERT D. KILMARX; LOUIS A. MCCARTEN; J. TERRENCE MURRAY.

SOUTH CAROLINA

South Carolina National Bank: P.O.B. 168, Columbia, S.C. 29202; f. 1834; cap. $66m.; dep. $724m. (Sept. 1973); Chair. JOHN H. LUMPKIN; Pres. CHARLES K. CROSS.

SOUTH DAKOTA

Northwestern National Bank of Sioux Falls: 9th and Main Sts., Sioux Falls; f. 1890; cap. $15m.; dep. $199m.; Pres. CURTIS A. LOVRE.

TENNESSEE

First American National Bank: 326 Union St., Nashville, Tenn. 37237; f. 1883; cap. $65m.; dep. $685m. (June 1972); Pres. SCOTT FILLEBROWN.

Union Planters National Bank of Memphis: 67 Madison Ave., Memphis 38147; f. 1869; cap. $78m.; dep. $971.8m. (Sept. 1973); Chair. of the Board C. BENNETT HARRISON.

TEXAS

Bank of the Southwest N.A.: P.O.B. 2629, Houston, Tex. 77001; f. 1907; cap. $85.5m.; dep. $822.4m. (Sept. 1973); Chair. and Chief Exec. Officer A. G. McNEESE, JR.; Vice-Pres. and Man. International Banking M. R. CROCKARD.

First City National Bank of Houston: P.O.B. 2557, Houston, Tex. 77001; est. 1956; cap. $123.8m.; dep. $180m. (Sept. 1973); Pres. N. S. ROGERS; Senior Vice-Pres. ROBERT C. HOWARD.

First National Bank of Dallas: P.O.B. 6031, Dallas, Tex. 75283; f. 1875; shareholder's equity $164.9m.; dep. $3,094.5m. (Dec. 1973); Chair. HARRY A. SHUFORD; Pres. J. RAWLES FULGHAM, JR.

Mercantile National Bank at Dallas: 1704 Main St., Dallas, Tex. 75201; f. 1916; cap. $74m.; dep. $625m. (June 1972); Chair. and Chief Exec. J. D. FRANCIS.

Republic National Bank in Dallas: Pacific and Ervay Sts., Dallas, Tex. 75222; f. 1920; $149m.; dep. $2,759m. (Dec. 1972); Chair. of Board JAMES W. ASTON; Pres. JAMES W. KEAY.

Texas Commerce Bank N.A.: 712 Main St., Houston, Tex. 77001; f. 1964; cap. $116m.; dep. $1,187.1m. (June 1972); Chair. and Chief Exec. Officer J. E. WHITMORE; Pres. B. F. LOVE; Sen. Vice-Pres. International Div. GEORGE W. EBANKS.

UTAH

First Security Bank of Utah National Association: P.O.B. 1289, Salt Lake City, Utah 84110; f. 1881; cap. $67.8m.; dep. $747m. (Dec. 1973); Pres. HAROLD J. STEELE.

VERMONT

Howard Bank of Vermont, The: 111 Main St., Burlington; f. 1870; cap. $9m.; dep. $145m. (June 1972); Pres. L. F. JOHNSON.

VIRGINIA

First and Merchants' National Bank: 827 East Main St., Richmond, Va. 23261; f. 1865; cap. $92m.; dep. $1,012m. (Dec. 1972); Chair. C. COLEMAN McGEHEE.

WASHINGTON (STATE)

National Bank of Commerce of Seattle: P.O.B. 3966, 1100 Second Ave., Seattle; f. 1889; cap. $35m.; dep. $1,798.4m. (Sept. 1973) Chair. R. TRUEX; Vice-Chair. ANDREW PRICE, JR.

Seattle-First National Bank: 1001 Fourth Ave., Seattle, Wash. 98124; f. 1870; cap. $192m.; dep. $2,754m. (Sept. 1973); Chair. WILLIAM M. JENKINS; Pres. ROBERT S. BEAUPRE.

WEST VIRGINIA

Security National Bank and Trust Co.: 1114 Market St., Wheeling 26003; f. 1962; cap. $7m.; dep. $41m. (June 1972); Pres. H. B. DAVIS.

WISCONSIN

First Wisconsin National Bank of Milwaukee: 743 North Water St., Milwaukee 2; f. 1853; cap. $99.5m.; dep. $1,467m. (June 1972); Chair. GEORGE F. KASTEN; Pres. HAL C. KUEHL.

WYOMING

First National Bank of Casper: P.O.B. 40, Casper 82601; f. 1889; cap. $7.1m.; dep. $84m. (June 1972); Chair. and Pres. ROBERT E. BRYANS.

BANKING ASSOCIATIONS

There is a State Bankers Association in each state.

The American Bankers Association: 1120 Connecticut Ave., N.W., Washington, D.C. 20036; f. 1875; 96 per cent of American banks are members; Exec. Vice-Pres. WILLIS W. ALEXANDER; Sec. GEORGE H. GUSTAFSON.

National Association of Mutual Savings Banks: 60 East 42nd St., New York, N.Y. 10017; f. 1920; Pres. SAMUEL W. HAWLEY; Exec. Vice-Pres. G. W. ENSLEY; 515 mems.

New York Clearing House Association: 100 Broad St., New York, N.Y. 1004; f. 1853; Pres. WILLIAM H. MOORE

(Chair. of the Board, Bankers Trust Co.); Exec. Vice-Pres. and Sec. JOHN F. LEE.

Securities and Exchange Commission: 500 N. Capitol, Washington, D.C. 20549; federal body which administers the Federal securities laws; Chair. G. BRADFORD COOK.

STOCK EXCHANGES

American Stock Exchange: 86 Trinity Place, New York, N.Y. 10006; f. 1849; Chair. of the Board FRANK P. KOLTON; Pres. R. M. BURDGE; mems. 650 regular, 190 associate.

Baltimore Stock Exchange: Baltimore Stock Exchange Building, Baltimore, Md. 21202.

Boston Stock Exchange: 53 State St., Boston, Mass. 02109; f. 1834; Pres. JAMES E. DOWD; Exec. Vice-Pres. R. E. HAUAGHAN; 196 mems.

Cincinatti Stock Exchange: 205 Dixie Terminal Building, Cincinnati, Ohio 45202; f. 1885; Pres. D. E. WESTON; Sec. D. R. GOODRICH.

Detroit Stock Exchange: 2314 Penobscot Building, Detroit, Mich. 48226; f. 1907; 63 mems.; Pres. PETER M. MAC-PHERSON; Exec. Vice-Pres. M. EDWARD DENNY.

Honolulu Stock Exchange: 843 Fort St., Honolulu, Hawaii 96813; f. 1898; Pres. P. C. T. LOO; 10 mems.

Midwest Stock Exchange: 120 South La Salle St., Chicago, Ill. 60603; f. 1882; Chair. of Board RICHARD W. SIMMONS; Pres. MICHAEL E. TOBIN; Sen. Vice-Pres. and Sec. JOHN G. WEITHERS; 435 mems.

Minneapolis-St. Paul Stock Exchange: Roanoke Building, Minneapolis, Minn. 55402.

National Stock Exchange: 91 Hudson St., New York, N.Y. 10013; registered 1960; opened 1962; Pres. JOHN D. GIRARD; Sec. MICHAEL J. GEOGHAN.

New Orleans Stock Exchange: 740 Gravier St., New Orleans, La. 71212.

New York Stock Exchange Inc.: 11 Wall St., New York, N.Y. 10005; f. 1792; Pres. J. J. NEEDHAM; Sec. JOHN J. MULCAHY, Jr.; 1,366 mems.

Pacific Stock Exchange: 301 Pine St., San Francisco, Calif. 94104; f. 1957; 207 mems.; Pres. THOMAS P. PHELAN; Sec. Treas. HOWARD R. HELWIG.

Philadelphia-Baltimore-Washington Stock Exchange: Stock Exchange, 17th St. and Stock Exchange Place, Philadelphia, Pa. 19103; f. 1790; Pres. ELKINS WETHERILL; Exec. Vice-Pres. and Sec. CHARLES L. WILSON.

Pittsburgh Stock Exchange: 333 Fourth Ave., Pittsburgh, Pa. 15222; org. 1895, inc. 1896; Pres. K. B. CUNNING-HAM; Sec. A. M. NEDBALETZ.

Richmond Stock Exchange: P.O.B. 77, Zone 1, Richmond, Va.; f. 1873; Pres. JOHN R. REYNOLDS; Vice-Pres. RICHARD W. HEWARD; Sec.-Treas. MYRL L. HAIRFIELD.

Salt Lake Stock Exchange: 39 Exchange Place, Salt Lake City, Utah 84111; f. 1888; Pres. ERNEST MUTH; Exec. Sec. MIKE GRAHAM.

San Francisco Mining Exchange: 249 Pine St., San Francisco, Calif. 92104; Pres. GEORGE J. FLACH.

Spokane Stock Exchange: Radio Central Building, Spokane 8, Wash.; f. 1927; Pres. BENJAMIN A. HARRISON; Sec. JOHN R. MEEK; 12 mems.

INSURANCE

INSURANCE COMPANIES

(With assets of $10,000,000 or more)

Acacia Mutual Life Insurance Company: 51 Louisiana Ave., N.W. Washington, D.C. 20001; f. 1869; Chair. of the Board and Pres. DANIEL L. HURSON; operating in 35 States and the District of Columbia.

Aetna Casualty & Surety Co.: 151 Farmington Ave., Hartford, Conn. 06115; f. 1907; Chair. J. H. FILER; operating in all States and Canada.

Aetna Insurance Company: 55 Elm St., Hartford, Conn. 06115; f. 1819; Pres. F. D. WATKINS.

Aetna Life Insurance Company: 151 Farmington Ave., Hartford, Conn. 06115; f. 1850; Chair. J. H. FILER; Pres. D. M. JOHNSON; operating in all States in the Union, the District of Columbia and Canada.

American Equitable Assurance Co. of New York: 92 William St., New York 38, N.Y.; f. 1918.

American General Insurance Co.: 2727 Allen Parkway, Houston, Texas; f. 1926; Chair. of Board B. N. WOODSON; Pres. W. D. STERLING; operating in Michigan, Pennsylvania, Tennsesee and Texas.

American Insurance Company: 15 Washington Street, Newark 1, N.J.; f. 1846; Pres. F. H. MERRILL.

American Mutual Liability Insurance Co.: Route 128 Wakefield, Mass.; f. 1887; Pres. R. E. ROBERSON.

American Mutual Life Insurance Company: Liberty Building, Des Moines 7, Iowa 50307; f. 1897; Pres. G. F. N. SMITH; Vice-Pres. and Treas. W. E. ENGEL; operating in 23 States.

American National Insurance Company: One Moody Plaza, Galveston, Tex.; f. 1905; Chair. of the Board and Pres. GLENDON E. JOHNSON; operating in 49 States, the District of Columbia, Canada, Western Europe, Puerto Rico and Guam.

American United Life Insurance Company: 1 West 26th St., Indianapolis, Indiana 46206; f. 1877; Chair. of Board and Pres. JACK E. REICH; Senior Vice-Pres. L. S. NORMAN; Sec. and Gen. Counsel K. B. WILSON; operating in 44 States, District of Columbia and Ontario, Canada; authorized reinsurer in all States.

American-Amicable Life Insurance Company: 4th Ave. and 23rd St. North, Birmingham 1, Alabama; f. 1909; Pres. MATHEW S. HOBBS; operating in 21 States, Panama Canal Zone and Japan.

Amica Mutual Insurance Company: 10 Weybosset St., P.O. Drawer 6008, Providence, R.I. 02904.

Arkwright-Boston Manufacturers Mutual Insurance Co.: 225 Wyman St., Waltham, Mass. 02154; f. 1850; Pres. and Chief Exec. Officer R. L. JOHNSTON.

Baltimore Life Insurance Company: Mount Royal Plaza, Baltimore 1, Md.; f. 1882; Pres. G. G. RADCLIFFE; operating in 7 States and the District of Columbia.

Bankers Life Company: 711 High St., Des Moines, Iowa 50307; f. 1879; Chair. H. G. ALLEN; Pres. R. N. HOUSER; operating in District of Columbia, all States and in Manitoba, Ontario, Alberta, Quebec, Canada.

Bankers' Life and Casualty Co.: 4444 Lawrence Ave., Chicago, Ill. 60630; f. 1880; Chair. and Pres. JOHN D. MACARTHUR; operates in the District of Columbia and all States except California, New Jersey and New York.

Bankers Life Nebraska: Cotner at O St., Lincoln, Nebraska 68501; f. 1887; Chair. GEORGE B. COOK; operating in 41 States and the District of Columbia.

Bankers' National Life Insurance Company: 1599 Littleton Rd., Parsippany, N.J. 07054; f. 1927; Chair. STANLEY GOLDBLUM; Pres. FRED LEVIN; Exec. Vice-Pres. W. F. GOOD, J. C. SMITH; Sec. S. B. LOWELL; Vice-Pres. and Actuary A. S. LEWIS; operating in 49 States, the District of Columbia and Puerto Rico.

Berkshire Life Insurance Company: 700 South St., Pittsfield, Mass.; f. 1851; Pres. LAWRENCE W. STRATTNER, Jr.; operating in 25 States and the District of Columbia.

Business Men's Assurance Company of America: B.M.A. Tower, 1 Penn Valley Park, Kansas City, Mo. 64141; f. 1909; Chief Exec. W. D. GRANT; operating in 48 States, Puerto Rico and the District of Columbia.

California-Western States Life Insurance Company: 2020 L St., Sacramento, Calif. 95814; f. 1910; Pres. H. S. HOOK; operating in 28 States and Canada.

Capitol Life Insurance Company: 1600 Sherman St., Denver, Colo.; f. 1905; Pres. HARLAND W. FARRAR; operating in 49 States, Europe and Puerto Rico.

Central Life Assurance Company: 611 Fifth Ave., Des Moines, Iowa 50306; f. 1896; Chair. and Chief Exec. Officer N. T. FUHLRODT; operating in 26 States and District of Columbia.

Colonial Life Insurance Company of America: P.O. Box 191, East Orange, New Jersey; f. 1897; Pres. RICHARD D. NELSON; operating in 40 States, District of Columbia, Puerto Rico and the Virgin Islands.

Columbus Mutual Life Insurance Company: East Broad St., Columbus 16, Ohio; f. 1907; Pres. RALPH E. WALDO; Vice-Pres. and Sec. ORVAL J. MILLER; operating in 27 States and the District of Colombia.

Commonwealth Life Insurance Company: Commonwealth Building, 4th and Broadway, Louisville, Ky. 40201; f. 1905; Chair. of Board WILLIAM H. ABELL; Pres. J. T. PARKER; operating in 7 States.

Connecticut General Insurance Company: Hartford, Conn. 06115; f. 1865; Pres. HENRY R. ROBERTS; operating in District of Columbia and all States of the U.S.A.; also in Canada and Puerto Rico.

Connecticut Mutual Life Insurance Company: 140 Garden St., Hartford, Conn. 06115; f. 1846; Pres. EDWARD B. BATES; operating in District of Columbia and all States in U.S.A. except North Dakota.

Continental American Life Insurance Company: 11th and King Street, Wilmington, Del. 19899; f. 1907; Pres. WILLIAM G. COPELAND; operating in 41 States and the District of Columbia.

Continental Assurance Company; Continental Casualty Company: 310 South Michigan Ave., Chicago, Ill. 60604; Chair. J. W. SAMMET; operating in all States, Canada and Puerto Rico.

Continental Insurance Company: 80 Maiden Lane, New York, N.Y. 10038; f. 1853; Chair. N. H. WENTWORTH; Pres. MILTON W. MAYS.

Country Life Insurance Co.: 1701 Towanda Ave., Bloomington, Ill.; f. 1928; Pres. HAROLD B. STEELE.

Country Mutual Insurance Co.: 1701 Towanda Avenue, Bloomington, Ill.; f. 1925; Pres. H. B. STEELE.

Equitable Life Assurance Society of the United States: 1285 Ave. of the Americas, New York, N.Y. 10019; f. 1859; Chair. J. HENRY SMITH; Pres. C. EKLOND; operating in all States, the District of Columbia, Puerto Rico and Canada.

Equitable Life Insurance Company: 3900 Wisconsin Ave., Washington, D.C. 20016; f. 1902; Chair. of Board C. E. PHILLIPS; Pres. G. C. BODDIGER; operating in 14 States and the District of Columbia.

Equitable Life Insurance Company of Iowa: 604 Locust St., Des Moines, Iowa 50306; f. 1867; Pres. K. R. AUSTIN; operating in 35 States and the District of Columbia.

Farmers' and Traders' Life Insurance Company: 960 James St., Syracuse, N.Y. 13203; f. 1912; Pres. MATTHIAS E. SMITH; Exec. Vice-Pres. WILLIAM T. BOLTON; operating in 27 States and the District of Columbia.

Farmers' Insurance Exchange: 4680 Wilshire Boulevard, Los Angeles, Calif. 90051; f. 1928.

Farmers New World Life Insurance Co.: Sunset Highway, Mercer Island, Wash. 98040; f. 1910; Pres. C. D. BESHEARS; operating in 25 States.

Federal Insurance Company: Millburn Township, N.J.; f. 1901; Chair. PERCY CHUBB; Pres. W. M. REES.

Federal Life Insurance Company: 6100 N. Cicero Avenue, Chicago 46; Ill.; f. 1899; Pres. and Chair. A. G. WILLIAMSON; operating in 32 States.

Fidelity & Casualty Company of New York: 80 Maiden Lane, New York, N.Y. 10038; f. 1875; Chair. N. H. WENTWORTH; Pres. M. W. MAYS.

Fidelity Mutual Life Insurance Company: Philadelphia, Pa. 19101; f. 1878; Pres. J. C. LADD; operating in 39 States.

Fireman's Fund Insurance Company: 3333 California Street, San Francisco, Calif. 94119; f. 1863; Pres. S. D. MENIST.

Fireman's Insurance Company of Newark, N.J.: 80 Maiden Lane, New York, N.Y. 10038; f. 1855; Chair. N. H. WENTWORTH; Pres. M. W. MAYS.

Franklin Life Insurance Company: Franklin Square, Springfield, Ill. 62705; f. 1884; Pres. and Chief Exec. Officer GEORGE E. HATMAKER; operating in the District of Columbia, Puerto Rico, the Virgin Islands, Canada and all States except New York.

General American Life Insurance Company: N.W. Corner 15th and Locust Streets, St. Louis, Mo. 63166; f. 1933; Pres. A. C. STALNAKER; operating in 49 States.

Great American Insurance Co.: 99 John Street, New York, N.Y. 10038; f. 1872; Chair. MARVIN FINELL.

Great Southern Life Insurance Co.: 3121 Buffalo Speedway, Houston, Tex. 77006; f. 1909; Chair. PAT M. GREENWOOD; operates in 14 States.

Guarantee Mutual Life Company: Guarantee Mutual Life Bldg., 8721 Indian Hills Drive, Omaha, Nebraska 68114; f. 1901; Pres. J. D. ANDERSON; operating in 22 States.

Guardian Life Insurance Company of America, The: 201 Park Avenue South, New York, N.Y. 10003; f. 1860; Pres. M. S. Hobbs; Chair. of Board E. G. Fitts; operating in all States of the Union, including the District of Columbia and Puerto Rico.

Gulf Insurance Co.: 4333 Madison, Kansas City, Missouri 64111; f. 1925; Pres. E. L. Kale.

Gulf Life Insurance Co.: 1301 Gulf Life Drive, Jacksonville, Fla. 32207; f. 1911; Pres. M. S. Hobbs; operates in 18 States and District of Columbia.

John Hancock Mutual Life Insurance Company: 200 Berkeley St., Boston, Mass. 02117; f. 1862; Chair. Gerhard D. Bleicken; Pres. Frank B. Maher; operates in all States.

Hanover Insurance Co.: 111 John Street, New York, N.Y. 10038; f. 1852; Pres. John Adam, Jr.

Hartford Life Insurance Co.: Hartford Plaza, Hartford, Conn. 06115; f. 1902; Pres. H. P. Schoen; operating in all States.

Hartford Steam Boiler Inspection & Insurance Co.: 56 Prospect St., Hartford, Conn. 06102; f. 1866; Vice-Pres. of Engineering E. L. Kemmler.

Home Beneficial Life Insurance Company: 3901 West Broad St., Richmond, Va. 23230; f. 1899; Hon. Chair. of Board W. E. Wiltshire; Chair. of Board M. D. Nunnally, Jr.; Pres. R. W. Wiltshire; operating in 6 States and the District of Columbia.

Home Fire & Marine Insurance Co. of California: 3333 California Street, San Francisco, Calif.; f. 1864.

Home Insurance Company Ltd.: 59 Maiden Lane, New York, N.Y. 10038; f. 1853; Chair. of Board J. H. Washburn.

Home Life Insurance Company: 253 Broadway, New York, N.Y. 10007; f. 1860; Pres. Gerald K. Rugger; operating in all States of the U.S.A. and Puerto Rico.

Indianapolis Life Insurance Company: 2960 North Meridian St., Indianapolis, Indiana 46208; f. 1905; Pres. Walter H. Huehl; operating in 31 States and the District of Columbia.

Insurance Company of North America: 1600 Arch St., Philadelphia, Pa. 19101; f. 1792; Pres. Charles K. Cox.

Integon Life Insurance Corpn.: 420 N. Spruce St., Winston-Salem, N.C. 27102; f. 1920; Pres. J. Edwin Collette; operating in 26 States.

Inter-Insurance Exchange of the Chicago Motor Club: 66 East South Water Street, Chicago 1, Ill.; f. 1917.

Jefferson Standard Life Insurance Company: Jefferson Square, Greensboro, N.C. 27401; f. 1907; Pres. W. Roger Soles; operating in 32 States, the District of Columbia, and Puerto Rico.

Kansas City Life Insurance Company: 3520 Broadway, Box No. 139, Kansas City 41, Mo.; f. 1895; Chair. of Board and Pres. Joseph R. Bixby; Exec. Vice-Pres. H. W. Kenney; Sen. Vice-Pres. D. W. Gilmore; Admin. Vice-Pres. W. E. Bixby, Jr. operating in 42 States and the District of Columbia.

Lamar Life Insurance Company: P.O. Box 880, 317 East Capitol Street, Jackson, Miss.; f. 1906; Pres. Harland L. Knight; operating in 11 States.

Liberty Life Insurance Company: Liberty Life Building, Wade Hampton Blvd., Greenville, S.C., 29602; f. 1905; Chair. of the Board Francis M. Hipp; Pres. Herman N. Hipp; licensed in 23 States, the District of Columbia and Puerto Rico.

Life and Casualty Insurance of Tennessee: Life and Casualty Tower, Nashville, Tenn.; f. 1903; Chair. B. N. Woodson; Pres. A. M. Steele; operating in 27 States, the District of Columbia, Puerto Rico and the Virgin Islands.

Life Insurance Co. of Georgia: Life of Georgia Tower, Atlanta, Ga. 30308; f. 1891; Chair. R. Howard Dobbs, Jr.; Pres. Rankin M. Smith; operates in 11 Southeastern States.

Life Insurance Company of Virginia: Capitol and 10th Streets, Richmond 9, Va.; f. 1871; Pres. Warren M. Pace; licensed in 26 States and the District of Columbia.

Lincoln National Life Insurance Company: South Harrison St. Fort Wayne, Indiana; f. 1905; Pres. T. A. Watson; operating in Panama Canal Zone, Philippine Islands, Canada, Guam, Puerto Rico, Virgin Islands, District of Columbia and all States of U.S. except New York.

Lutheran Mutual Life Insurance Company: First St., S.E., Waverly, Iowa; f. 1879; Pres. E. T. Koopman; operating in 30 States and the District of Columbia.

Manhattan Life Insurance Company: 111 West 57th St., New York, N.Y. 10019; f. 1850; Chair. Thomas E. Lovejoy, Jr.; operating in all 50 States and the District of Columbia.

Massachusetts Mutual Life Insurance Company: State St., Springfield, Mass.; f. 1851; Pres. James R. Martin; licensed in all States of the Union and the District of Columbia; also in Puerto Rico and the Dominion of Canada, with provincial licenses in Manitoba, Alberta, Ontario, New Brunswick, and Quebec.

Metropolitan Life Insurance Company: 1 Madison Ave., New York, N.Y. 10010; f. 1868; Chair. of the Board George P. Jenkins; Pres. and Chief Exec. Officer Richard R. Shinn; licensed in all States, District of Columbia, Puerto Rico, and Canada.

Midland Mutual Life Insurance Company, The: 250 E. Broad St., Columbus, Ohio 43216; f. 1905; Pres. James B. McIntosh; Vice-Pres. Gerald E. Mayo; Agency Vice-Pres. Ronald W. Allbee; operating in 23 States.

Minnesota Mutual Life Insurance Company: Victory Square, Saint Paul, Minn. 55101; f. 1880; Pres. Coleman Bloomfield; operating in all the Continental United States, also Canada and Puerto Rico.

Monarch Life Insurance Company: 1250 State St., Springfield, Mass. 01101; f. 1901; Chair. of Board William C. Giles, Jr.; Pres. Benjamin F. Jones; operating in 46 States and the District of Columbia.

Monumental Life Insurance Company: Charles and Chase Streets, Baltimore, Md. 21202; f. 1858; Chair. Frank Baker, Jr.; Pres. Donald H. Wilson, Jr.; operating in 20 States and the District of Columbia.

Mutual Benefit Life Insurance Company: 520 Broad St., Newark 1, N.J.; f. 1845; Pres. Robert V. van Fossan; operating in all States (except Alaska) and District of Columbia.

Mutual Life Insurance Company of New York: 1740 Broadway, New York 19, N.Y.; f. 1842; Chair. of Exec. Cttee. Lewis W. Douglas; operating in all States of the Union, the District of Columbia and Canada.

Mutual Trust Life Insurance Co.: 77 S. Wacker Drive, Chicago, Ill. 60606; f. 1904; Chair. V. F. Dowling; operates in 31 States and the District of Columbia.

National Guardian Life Insurance Company: 2 East Gilman St., Madison, Wis. 53703; f. 1909; Chair. and Chief Exec. Officer L. J. Larson; operating in 31 States.

National Life and Accident Insurance Company: National Life Center, Nashville, Tenn. 37203; f. 1898; Chair. of Board G. D. BROOKS; Pres. WILLIAM C. WEAVER, Jr.; operating in 23 States.

National Life Insurance Company: National Life Drive, Montpelier, Vt.; f. 1848; Pres. J. T. FEY; licensed for sale of life insurance in all States of the Union, including the District of Columbia.

Nationwide Mutual Insurance Co.: 246 North High St., Columbus, Ohio 43216; f. 1933.

New York Life Insurance Company: 51 Madison Ave., New York, N.Y. 10010; f. 1845; Pres. MARSHALL P. BISSELL; Chair. R. MANNING BROWN, Jr.; operating in all States, the District of Columbia, Canada and Puerto Rico.

Niagara Fire Insurance Co.: 80 Maiden Lane, New York 38, N.Y.; f. 1850.

North American Life Insurance Company of Chicago: 35 East Wacker Drive, Chicago, Ill. 60601; f. 1907; Pres. F. D. GUYNN; operating in 46 States including the District of Columbia.

North American Reassurance Company: 245 Park Ave., New York, N.Y. 10017; f. 1923; Pres. R. R. GALLAGHER; operating in all States and Canada (this office writes life reassurance business only but is included in this list because its assets exceed $10,000,000).

Northern Assurance Company of America: One Beacon St., Boston, Mass.; f. 1954; Pres. HENRY S. STONE.

Northwestern Mutual Life Insurance Co.: 720 East Wisconsin Ave., Milwaukee, Wis. 53202; f. 1857; Pres. FRANCIS E. FERGUSON; operates in all States, except Alaska, also in District of Columbia.

Northwestern National Insurance Co.: 731 North Jackson St., Milwaukee, Wis. 53202; f. 1869; Chair. CHARLES D. JAMES; Pres. T. PARKER LOWE; Sec. ROBERT P. FALAT.

Northwestern National Life Insurance Company: 20 Washington Ave. South, Minneapolis, Minn. 55440; f. 1885; Chair. T. PARKER LOWE; Pres. F. R. ELIASON; operating in 48 States and the District of Columbia.

Occidental Life Insurance Company of California: 12th St. at Hill and Olive at 12th St., Los Angeles, Calif. 90015; f. 1906; Chair. EARL CLARK; Pres. MENO T. LAKE; operating in 49 States, the District of Columbia and Puerto Rico, Canada, Australia, United Kingdom, Hong Kong and Japan.

Ohio National Life Insurance Company: W. Howard Taft Road at Highland Avenue, Cincinnati 1, Ohio; f. 1909; Pres. M. R. DODSON; operating in 34 States and the District of Columbia.

Ohio State Life Insurance Company: 100 East Broad St., Columbus, Ohio 43215; f. 1906; Pres. JAMES M. BATES; operating in 20 States and the District of Columbia.

Old Line Life Insurance Company of America: 707 N. 11th Street, Milwaukee 3, Wis.; f. 1931; Pres. F. D. GUYNN; Vice-Pres. FRANKLIN P. GRAF; operating in 29 States.

Pacific Mutual Life Insurance Company: 700 Newport Centre Drive, Newport Beach, Calif. 92663; f. 1868; Chair. STANTON G. HALE; Pres. WALTER B. GERKEN; operating in 49 States and the District of Columbia.

Pan-American Life Insurance Company: Pan American Life Building, 2400 Canal Street, New Orleans, La. 70119; f. 1911; Chair. of Board, Pres. and Chief Exec. G. FRANK PURVIS, Jr.; operating in 28 States and the District of Columbia and in Central and South America.

Penn Mutual Life Insurance Co.: Independence Square, Philadelphia, Penn. 19172; f. 1847; Pres. F. K. TARBOX; operates in all States and District of Columbia; also Alberta, British Columbia, Manitoba, New Brunswick, Nova Scotia, and Ontario, Canada.

People's-Home Life Insurance Company of Indiana and Federal Life and Casualty Company: 78 West Michigan Avenue, Battle Creek, Michigan 49016; f. 1906; Pres. J. T. GRIMALDI; operating in 50 States and the District of Columbia.

People's Life Insurance Company: 601 New Hampshire Avenue, N.W., Washington 7, D.C.; f. 1903; Chair. and Chief Exec. Officer W. T. LEITH; Pres. and Chief Oper. Officer E. L. HOGAN; operating in 10 States and the District of Columbia.

Philadelphia Life Insurance Company: 111 N. Broad Street, Philadelphia 7, Pa.; f. 1906; Pres. JOSEPH E. BOETTNER; operating in 25 States and the District of Columbia.

Phoenix Insurance Co.: 61 Woodland Street, Hartford, Conn. 06115; f. 1854; Pres. M. H. BEACH.

Phoenix Mutual Life Insurance Company: One American Row, Hartford, Conn. 06115; f. 1851; Pres. ROBERT T. JACKSON; operating in 45 States, District of Columbia and Puerto Rico.

Pilot Life Insurance Company: Greensboro, N.C.; f. 1890; Pres. L. C. STEPHENS, Jr.; operating in 26 States, the District of Columbia and Puerto Rico.

Protective Life Insurance Company: Protective Life Bldg., 2027 First Ave. North, Birmingham, Ala. 35203; f. 1907; Chair. of Board Col. WILLIAM J. RUSHTON; operating in 14 States and the District of Columbia.

Provident Life and Accident Insurance Company: Fountain Square, Chattanooga, Tenn. 37402; f. 1887; Pres. HUGH O. MACLELLAN; Chair. HENRY C. UNRUH; operating in 47 States of the Union; also Provinces of Ontario and Quebec, Canada.

Provident Mutual Life Insurance Company of Philadelphia: 4601 Market St., Philadelphia 1, Pa.; f. 1865; Pres. E. L. STANLEY; operating in 46 States and the District of Columbia.

Prudential Insurance Company of America, The: Prudential Plaza, Newark, N.J. 07101; f. 1875; Pres. C. K. FOSTER; operating throughout the U.S.A. and Canada.

Reliance Insurance Co.: 4 Penn Center Plaza, Philadelphia, Pa. 19103; f. 1817; Pres. A. ADDISON ROBERTS.

Reliance Standard Life Insurance Co.: 175 West Jackson Blvd., Chicago, Ill. 60604; Exec. Offices 4 Penn Center Plaza, Philadelphia, Pa. 19103; f. 1907 as Central Standard Life Insurance Co., name changed 1965; Chair. A. A. ROBERTS; operates in 47 States and the District of Columbia.

Paul Revere Life Insurance Co.: 18 Chestnut St., Worcester, Mass.; f. 1930; Pres. GEORGE L. HOGEMAN; operates in all States, District of Columbia and all Provinces in Canada except Newfoundland and Prince Edward Island.

SAFECO Corpn.: 4347 Brooklyn Ave. N.E., Seattle, Wash. 98105; Pres. G. H. SWEANY.

St. Paul Fire & Marine Insurance Co.: 385 Washington St., St. Paul, Minn. 55102; f. 1925; Chair. C. B. DRAKE, Jr.; Pres. W. G. SMITH.

Security Insurance Co. of Hartford: 1000 Asylum Ave., Hartford, Conn. 06101; f. 1841; Pres. and Chief Exec. D. H. GARLOCK.

Security Mutual Life Insurance Company of New York: Court House Square, Binghamton, N.Y. 13902; f. 1886; Chair. of Board RICHARD E. PILLE; Pres. ROBERT M. BEST; Exec. Vice-Pres. KENNETH P. LORD; operating in the District of Columbia and all States except Alaska, Colorado, Hawaii, Idaho, Kansas, Louisiana, Montana, Nebraska, Nevada, New Mexico, Oklahoma, Oregon, Texas, Utah, Washington, Wyoming.

Southland Life Insurance Company: Southland Center, Dallas 1, Texas; f. 1908; Pres. JAMES B. GOODSON; operating in 45 States, District of Columbia and Puerto Rico.

Southwestern Life Insurance Company: Southwestern Life Building, 1807 Ross Ave., Dallas, Tex. 75201; f. 1903; purchased Atlantic Life Insurance Co., Richmond, Va. in 1964; Chair. and Chief Exec. Officer WILLIAM H. SEAY; operating in 35 States and the District of Columbia.

Standard Insurance Company: P.O.B. 711, Portland, Oregon 97207; f. 1906; Pres. LOUIS B. PERRY; Sec. WM. F. GAARENSTROOM; operating in 10 States.

State Farm Life Insurance Co.: State Farm Insurance Building, 112 East Washington St., Bloomington, Ill.; f. 1929; Chair. EARLE B. JOHNSON; Pres. EDWARD B. RUST; operates in 48 States, District of Columbia and Canada (Alberta, British Columbia, Ontario and New Brunswick).

State Farm Mutual Automobile Insurance Co.: 112 East Washington St., Bloomington, Ill. 61701; f. 1922; Pres. EDWARD B. RUST.

State Life Insurance Company: 141 East Washington, Indianapolis, Indiana; f. 1894; Pres. WILLIAM J. SULLIVAN; operating in 26 States, and the District of Columbia.

State Mutual Life Assurance Company of America: 440 Lincoln Street, Worcester, Mass. 01605; f. 1844; Chair. of Board H. LADD PLUMLEY; Pres. W. DOUGLAS BELL; licensed in all States of the Union and the District of Columbia, Canada and Puerto Rico.

Sun Life Insurance Company of America: Sun Life Building, Baltimore, Md. 21201; f. 1890; Pres. S. Z. ROTHSCHILD, Jr.; operating in 31 States and the District of Columbia.

Travelers Insurance Company: One Tower Square, Hartford, Conn. 06115; f. 1864; Chair. of Board ROGER C. WILKINS; Pres. MORRISON H. BEACH; operating in all States of the Union, District of Columbia, Puerto Rico and Canada.

Unigard Insurance Group: 217 Pine St., Seattle, Wash. 98101; f. 1901.

Union Central Life Insurance Company: P.O.B. 179, Cincinnati, Ohio 45201; f. 1867; Hon. Chair. W. HOWARD COX; Pres. JOHN A. LLOYD; Vice-Pres. and Treas. ELMER R. BEST; Vice-Pres. Investments D. A. WARNER, Jr.; Vice-Pres. and General Counsel C. L. PETERSON; Vice-Pres. Sales ROBERT L. POPE; Sec. P. R. INSKEEP; operating in all 50 States of the Union and the District of Columbia.

Union Mutual Life Insurance Company: 2211 Congress St., Portland, Maine 04112; f. 1848; Pres. COLIN C. HAMPTON; operating in the District of Columbia, all States, in Puerto Rico and Canada.

United Benefit Life Insurance Company: Dodge at 33rd St., Omaha, Nebraska 68131; f. 1926; Chair. of the Board V. J. SKUTT; Pres. GALE E. DAVIS; Virgin Islands, Okinawa, Korea, Guam, Canal Zone, Panama, Puerto Rico, Europe, Japan, Taiwan and the Philippines.

United Life and Accident Insurance Company: United Life Building, 2 White Street, Concord, New Hampshire; f. 1913; Pres. T. BENSON LEAVITT; operating in 49 States and the District of Columbia.

United States Fidelity & Guaranty Co.: United States Fidelity & Guaranty Building, Baltimore, Md. 21203; f. 1896; Chair. and Pres. WILLIFORD GRAGG.

United States Life Insurance Company in the City of New York: 125 Maiden Lane, New York, N.Y. 10038; f. 1850; Pres. GORDON E. CROSBY, Jr.; operating in 50 States, the District of Columbia, and several foreign countries.

Victory Mutual Life Insurance Company: 5601 South State Street, Chicago, Ill. 60621; f. 1933; Pres. B. C. CYRUS; Vice-Pres. and Sec. M. A. MAHONE; operating in 5 States and the District of Columbia.

Volunteer State Life Insurance Company: Volunteer Building, Chattanooga 2, Tenn.; f. 1903; Chair. of the Board and Chief Exec. Officer J. H. DAVENPORT, Jr.; Pres. and Chief Admin. Officer CARTER J. LYNCH, Jr.; Agency Vice-Pres. S. RUSSELL McGEE, Jr., C.L.U.; operating in 42 States and District of Columbia.

Washington National Insurance Company: Chicago Ave., Evanston, Ill.; f. 1911; Chair. of Board G. P. KENDALL; Pres. J. L. ELLIOT; operating in all States, District of Columbia and Alberta and Ontario, Canada.

West Coast Life Insurance Company: 605 Market St., San Francisco 5, Calif.; f. 1906; Chair. FRANCIS V. KEESLING, Jr.; Pres. H. CURTIS REED; operating in 13 States.

Western Life Insurance Company: 385 Washington St., St. Paul, Minn.; f. 1910; Pres. RALPH E. YOUNG; operating in 49 States.

Western-Southern Life Insurance Company: 400 Broadway, Cincinnati, Ohio 45202; f. 1888; Pres. C. M. BARRETT; operating in 42 States and District of Columbia.

Wisconsin National Life Insurance Company: 220–222 Washington Ave., Oshkosh, Wis.; f. 1908; Pres. A. DEAN ARGANBRIGHT; operating in 23 States.

INSURANCE ORGANIZATIONS

AFIA: 1700 Valley Rd., Wayne, N.J. 07470; f. 1918; operates in over 80 countries for 10 members American capital stock insurance; Chair. of Board LOUIS W. NIGGEMAN; Vice-Chair. JOHN H. WASHBURN and A. ADDISON ROBERTS; Pres. F. A. MAYES.

American Institute of Marine Underwriters: 99 John St., New York 38, N.Y.; f. 1898; membership: 118 marine insurance companies represented by 248 individuals; Pres. G. DORNE McCARTHY; Exec. Vice-Pres. CARL E. McDOWELL; Sec. JOHN C. HERMAN.

American Insurance Association: 85 John St., New York, N.Y. 10038; f. 1866; Pres. T. LAWRENCE JONES; Sec. RICHARD C. MACHCINSKI.

American International Underwriters Corporation: 102 Maiden Lane, New York, N.Y. 10005; f. 1926; Chair. E. A. G. MANTON; Pres. J. J. ROBERTS; Exec. Vice-Pres. A. WEBER.

Casualty Actuarial Society: 200 East 42nd St., New York, N.Y. 10017; f. 1914; 545 mems.; Pres. P. S. LISCORD; Sec.-Treas. R. B. FOSTER.

Institute of Life Insurance: 277 Park Avenue, New York, N.Y. 10017; f. 1939; 158 mem. companies; Pres. BLAKE T. NEWTON, Jr., Exec. Vice-Pres. WILLIAM K. PAYNTER.

Insurance Services Office: 160 Water St., New York, N.Y. 10038.

Life Insurance Association of America: 277 Park Avenue, New York, N.Y. 10017; Pres. BENJAMIN F. SMALL.

Life Insurance Marketing and Research Association: 170 Sigourney St., Hartford, Conn. 06105; f. 1916; over 500 mems.; a world-wide sales research and service organization of life insurance companies; Chair. of Board W. J. CLARK; Pres. BURKETT W. HUEY.

Life Office Management Association: 100 Park Avenue, New York, N.Y. 10017; 500 mem. companies; Pres. L. MERRITT; Vice-Pres. and Sec.-Treas. ALDEN F. JACOBS.

National Association of Mutual Insurance Companies: 2511 East 46th St., Suite H, Indianapolis, Ind. 46205; 1,028 mems.; Pres. HAROLD W. WALTERS; Chair. of the Board O. C. LEE.

Society of Actuaries: 208 S. La Salle Street, Chicago 4, Ill.; f. 1949; 1,259 fellows, 940 associates; Pres. JOHN H. MILLER; Sec. W. L. GRACE; Treas. GATHINGS STEWART.

TRADE AND INDUSTRY

CHAMBERS OF COMMERCE

Chamber of Commerce of the United States: 1615 H St., N.W., Washington, D.C. 20006; f. 1912; Exec. Vice-Pres. ARCH N. BOOTH.

Membership: more than 3,700 organization mems. (Chambers of Commerce, associations, etc.), more than 33,000 business mems. (persons, firms and corporations).

British-American Chamber of Commerce: 10 East 40th St., New York, N.Y. 10016; f. 1920; Exec. Dir. DAVID FARQUHARSON; publs. *BAT News* (10 issues a year). *Yearbook, Directory.*

GENERAL
EMPLOYERS' ORGANIZATIONS

American Management Association: 135 W. 50th St., New York, N.Y. 10020; f. 1923; Pres. ALEXANDER B. TROWBRIDGE; 60,000 company and individual mems.

American Mining Congress: Ring Building, Washington, D.C. 20036; f. 1897; Pres. J. ALLEN OVERTON, Jr.; Sec. and Treas. HENRY I. DWORSHAK; publ. *Mining Congress Journal* (monthly).

Farmers Educational & Co-operative Union of America (National Farmers Union): 12025 East 45th Ave., P.O.B. 2251, Denver, Colo. 80201; Pres. TONY T. DECHANT.

National Association of Manufacturers: 277 Park Ave., New York, N.Y. 10017; f. 1895; Pres. W. P. GULLANDER; Chair. of Board M. P. VENEMA; Sec. JOHN McGRAW; Treas. A. F. AMBROSE; approx. 13,000 mems.

National Grange: 1616 H Street, N.W., Washington, 20006; f. 1867; farmers' organisation.

LABOUR ORGANIZATION

There are 181 Unions of which 116 are affiliated to the AFL-CIO (1972). Total membership 17,630,000; AFL-CIO membership 13,600,000. Only Unions with 50,000 members or more are listed below.

American Federation of Labor and Congress of Industrial Organisations: 815 16th St., N.W., Washington, D.C. 20006; Pres. GEORGE MEANY; Sec.-Treas. LANE KIRKLAND; publs. *AFL-CIO News* (weekly) and *Federationist* (monthly) (official magazine).

CHEMICALS
EMPLOYERS' ORGANIZATIONS

American Institute of Chemists, Inc.: 60 E. 42nd St., New York, N.Y. 10017; f. 1923; Pres. Dr. EMMETT B. CARMICHAEL; Treas. Dr. F. A. HESSEL; Editor V. F. KIMBALL; Sec. JOHN KOTRADY; publ. *The Chemist* (monthly); 3,100 mems.

American Pharmaceutical Association: 2215 Constitution Ave., N.W., Washington, D.C. 20037; f. 1852; 48,000 mems.; Exec. Dir. WILLIAM S. APPLE; publ. *Journal of the American Pharmaceutical Association* (monthly), *Journal of Pharmaceutical Science* (monthly).

Fertilizer Institute, The: 1015 18th St., N.W., Washington, D.C. 20036; inc. July 1955; Pres. EDWIN M. WHEELER; Sec.-Treas. GARY D. MYERS.

Manufacturing Chemists' Association, Inc.: 1825 Connecticut Ave., N.W., Washington, D.C. 20009; f. 1872; Pres. WILLIAM J. DRIVER; Sec.-Treas. GEORGE E. BEST; 179 mems.

National Association of Retail Druggists: One East Wacker Drive, Chicago, Ill. 60601; f. 1898; Exec. Sec. and Gen. Man. WILLARD B. SIMMONS; 36,000 mems.; publ. *N.A.R.D. Journal.*

National Paint and Coatings Association: 1500 Rhode Island Ave., N.W., Washington, D.C. 20005; f. 1888; 1,000 mems.; Exec. Vice-Pres. ROBERT A. ROLAND; Sec. ALLAN W. GATES.

National Wholesale Druggists' Association: 220 East 42nd St., New York City, N.Y. 10017; f. 1876; Exec. Vice-Pres. WILLIAM L. FORD; 800 mems.

Pharmaceutical Manufacturers Association: 1155 15th St., N.W., Washington, D.C. 20005; f. 1958; Chair. of Board R. M. FURLAUD; Pres. C. JOSEPH STETLER; mems. 115.

Soap and Detergent Association: 475 Park Ave. South, New York, N.Y. 10016; f. 1926; Pres. THEODORE F. BRENNER; Vice-Pres. ROBERT C. SINGER.

LABOUR ORGANIZATION

International Chemical Workers' Union: 1655 W. Market St., Akron, Ohio 44313; f. 1940; Pres. THOMAS E. BOYLE; Sec.-Treas. F. D. MARTINO; publ. *Chemical Worker.*

CONSTRUCTION
(see also Electricity and Engineering and Machinery)

EMPLOYERS' ORGANIZATIONS

Associated General Contractors of America: 1957 E St., N.W., Washington, D.C. 20006; f. 1918; mems. 9,500 (1973); Exec. Dir. J. M. SPROUSE; publ. *Constructor* (monthly).

Building Owners and Managers Association International: 224 South Michigan Ave., Chicago, Ill. 60604; f. 1908; Exec. Vice-Pres. THOMAS D. LANEY; 3,500 mems.; publ. *Skyscraper Management* (monthly).

International Association of Wall and Ceiling Contractors: 1775 Church St., N.W., Washington, D.C. 20036; f. 1918; 500 mems.; Pres. F. J. KRAFFT; Man. Dir. JOE M. BAKER, Jr.; publ. *The Hexahedron* (bi-monthly), *Walls and Ceilings* (monthly).

Mechanical Contractors Association of America, Inc.: 666 Third Avenue, Suite 1464, New York, N.Y. 10017; f. 1889; Exec. Vice-Pres. LEON B. KROMER, Jr.; publ. *Mechanical Contractor* (monthly).

National Association of Plumbing-Heating-Cooling Contractors: 1016 20th Street, N.W., Washington, D.C. 20036; f. 1883; 10,000 mems.; Exec. Dir. L. P. MUTTER.

Tile Contractors' Association of America, Inc.: Investment Building, Washington, D.C. 20005; f. 1928; Sec. FRED T. WINDSOR.

LABOUR ORGANIZATIONS

Bricklayers', Masons' and Plasterers' International Union of America: 815 15th St., Washington, D.C. 20005; Pres. THOMAS F. MURPHY; 155,255 mems.

International Brotherhood of Painters and Allied Trades: United Nations Bldg., 1750 New York Ave., N.W. Washington D.C. 20006; Gen. Sec. MICHAEL DISILVESTRO.

Laborers' International Union of North America: 905 16th St., N.W., Washington, D.C. 20006; f. 1903; Pres. PETER FOSCO; 429,279 mems.; publ. *The Laborer*.

Operative Plasters' and Cement Masons' International Association of the U.S. and Canada: 1125 Seventeenth St., N.W., Washington, D.C. 20036; f. 1864; Pres. J. T. POWER; Sec.-Treas. JOHN J. HAUCK; 68,000 mems.; publ. *The Plasterer and Cement Mason* (monthly).

Service Employees' International Union (AFL-CIO-CLC): 900 17th St., N.W., Washington, D.C. 20006; Pres. DAVID SULLIVAN; 425,000 mems.

United Brotherhood of Carpenters and Joiners of America: 101 Constitution Avenue. N.W., Washington 1, D.C.; f. 1881; 830,000 mems.; Gen. Pres. WILLIAM SIDELL; Gen. Sec. RICHARD E. LIVINGSTON; publ. *The Carpenter* (monthly).

United Cement, Lime and Gypsum Workers' International Union: 7830 West Lawrence Ave., Chicago, Ill. 60656; f. 1939; Pres. THOMAS F. MIECHUR; Sec.-Treas. REUBEN ROE; publ. *Voice*.

ELECTRICITY
(see also Construction, and Engineering and Machinery)

EMPLOYERS' ORGANIZATIONS

Edison Electric Institute: 750 Third Ave., New York, N.Y. 10017; f. 1933; Man. Dir. E. VENNARD.

Institute of Electrical and Electronics Engineers, Inc.: 345 East 47th St., New York, N.Y. 10017.

National Association of Electrical Distributors: 600 Madison Ave., New York, N.Y. 10022; f. 1908; Exec. Dir. ARTHUR W. HOOPER.

National Electrical Contractors' Association: 7315 Wisconsin Ave., N.W., Washington, D.C. 20014; f. 1901; Sec.-Treas. J. C. MCCREIGHT.

National Electrical Manufacturers' Association: 155 East 44th St., New York, N.Y. 10017; f. 1926; 540 mfrs. mems.; Pres. BERNARD H. FALK; Chair. of the Board W. H. SATTERFIELD; publ. *NEMA Report, Government News Bulletin*.

LABOUR ORGANIZATIONS

International Brotherhood of Electrical Workers: 1200 15th St., N.W., Washington 6, D.C.; 340,000 mems.; Pres. DAVID SULLIVAN.

International Union of Electrical, Radio and Machine Workers: 1126 16th St., N.W., Washington, D.C. 20036; f. 1949; 300,000 mems.; Pres. PAUL JENNINGS; Sec.-Treas. DAVID J. FITZMAURICE; publ. *IUE News* (monthly).

United Electrical, Radio and Machine Workers of America: 11 East 51st St., New York, N.Y. 10022; 165,000 mems.; Pres. ALBERT FITZGERALD; publ. *UE News*.

ENGINEERING AND MACHINERY
(see also Electricity and Construction)

EMPLOYERS' ORGANIZATIONS

Air-Conditioning and Refrigeration Institute: 1815 N. Fort Myer Drive, Arlington, Va. 22209; f. 1953; Pres. W. C. YOCUM; Man. Dir. L. N. HUNTER.

American Institute of Chemical Engineers: 25 West 45th Street, New York 36, N.Y.; f. 1908; over 20,000 mems.; Sec. F. J. VAN ANTWERPEN; publ. *Chemical Engineering Progress* (monthly), etc.

American Institute of Consulting Engineers: United Engineering Center, 345 East 47th Street, New York, N.Y. 10017; f. 1910; Pres. ROBERT B. RICHARDS; Sec. GILBERT I. ROSS; 435 mems.; publs. *Engineering Consultants, Consulting Engineering* (monthly).

American Institute of Mining, Metallurgical and Petroleum Engineers, Inc.: 345 East 47th St., New York, N.Y.; f. 1871; 48,303 mems.; Pres. JOHN S. BELL; Exec. Dir. JOE B. ALFORD; publs. *Journal of Metals, Mining Engineering, Journal of Petroleum Technology* (monthlies), *Society of Petroleum Engineers Journal* (quarterly), *Society of Mining Engineers Transactions Quarterly, Transactions of the Metallurgical Society* (quarterly).

American Pipe Fittings Association: Room 2122, 60 East 42nd St., New York, N.Y. 10017; f. 1938; Exec. Dir. RAY H. GOODRIDGE.

American Railway Engineering Association: 59 E. Van Buren St., Chicago, Ill. 60605; f. 1899; Exec. Man. E. W. HODGKINS; 3,400 mems. (international); publ. *AREA Bulletin*.

American Society of Civil Engineers: 345 East 47th St., New York, N.Y. 10017; f. 1852; 64,000 mems.; Pres. THOMAS M. NILES; Exec. Dir. W. H. WISELY; publ. *Civil Engineering*.

American Society of Heating, Refrigerating, and Air Conditioning Engineers: 62 Worth Street, New York 13, N.Y.; f. 1895; Exec. Sec. A. V. HUTCHINSON; 18,545 mems.; publs. *Air Conditioning and Refrigerating Data Books, Heating Ventilating Air Conditioning Guide* (annually), *ASHRAE Journal* (monthly).

American Society of Mechanical Engineers, The: United Engineering Center, 345 E. 47th St., New York, N.Y. 10017; f. 1880; Exec. Dir. and Sec. ROGERS B. FINCH.

American Society of Naval Engineers Inc.: Suite 807, 1012 14th St., N.W., Washington, D.C. 20005; f. 1888; 4,000 mems.; Sec.-Treas. Capt. FRANK G. LAW; publ. *Naval Engineers Journal* (every two months).

Engineering Foundation: United Engineering Center, 345 East 47th St., New York, N.Y. 10017; f. 1914; Sec. JOHN A. ZECCA; publs. *Engineering Foundation Newsletter, Annual Report*, etc.

Machinery and Allied Products Institute: 1200 18th St., N.W., Washington, D.C. 20036; long-range economic studies in capital goods industries for 22 associations; f. 1933; Pres. C. W. STEWART; publ. *Capital Goods Review*.

National Machine Tool Builders' Association: 7901 Westpark Drive, McLean, Va. 22101; f. 1902; Exec. Vice-Pres. JAMES A. GRAY; 280 mems.; publs. *Directory* *of Machine Tools, Training Texts* on *Blueprint Reading, Precision Measurement, Shop Theory* (I and II), *Instructor's Guide, Machine Tools . . . Today, Film Catalog, America's Muscles, Profile of a Distributor, Directory of NC Machine Tool and Related Products, Industrial Training for the Machine Tool Industry, NMTBA Training Tests, Economic Handbook of the Machine Tool Industry.*

Society of Automotive Engineers Inc.: 2 Pennsylvania Plaza, New York, N.Y. 10001; f. 1905; Pres. W. A. GEBHARDT; Sec. and Gen. Man. JOSEPH GILBERT; 27,000 mems.; publs. *Automotive Engineering* (monthly), *S.A.E. Transactions* and *S.A.E. Handbook* (annually).

Society of Motion Picture and Television Engineers: 9 East 41st St., New York, N.Y. 10017; f. 1916; Pres. WILTON R. HOLM; Exec. Sec. DENIS A. COURTNEY; 8,000 mems.; publ. *S M P T E Journal*; circ. 10,500.

Society of Naval Architects and Marine Engineers: 74 Trinity Place, New York, N.Y. 10006; f. 1893; Sec. ROBERT G. MENDE; 10,000 mems.

The Valve Manufacturers' Association: Room 310, 6845 Elm St., P.O.B. 539, McLean, Va. 22101; f. 1938; Exec. Vice-Pres. R. W. SULLIVAN.

World Safety Research Institute Inc.: 2 Pennsylvania Plaza, Suite 1500, New York, N.Y. 10001; worldwide co-operation in all accident prevention matters; Pres. THOMAS N. BOATE; Vice-Pres. ALBERT S. REGULA; Sec.-Treas. JOHN F. SCHWEITERS.

LABOUR ORGANIZATIONS

International Association of Bridge, Structural and Ornamental Iron Workers: 3615 Olive Street, St. Louis 8, Mo.; Pres. JOHN H. LYONS; 138,789 mems.

International Association of Machinists and Aerospace Workers: Machinists' Building, 1300 Connecticut Ave., N.W., Washington, D.C. 20036; f. 1889; International Pres. FLOYD E. SMITH; Gen. Sec.-Treas. EUGENE GLOVER; 922,199 mems.; publ. *The Machinist* (weekly).

International Brotherhood of Boilermakers, Iron Ship Builders, Blacksmiths, Forgers and Helpers: 8th at State Ave., Kansas City, Kan. 66101; org. 1880; Pres. H. J. BUOY; Sec.-Treas. E. F. MORAN; 130,000 mems.

International Molders' and Allied Workers' Union of North America: 1225 East McMillan Street, Cincinatti, Ohio 45206; f. 1859; Pres. D. DOYAL; Sec. W. F. CATES; 54,000 mems.

International Union, Allied Industrial Workers of America: 3520 West Oklahoma Avenue, Milwaukee, Wis. 53215; Pres. GILBERT JEWELL; 90,000 mems.

International Union of Operating Engineers: 1125 Seventeenth Street, N.W., Washington, D.C., 20036; f. 1896; 292,000 mems.; Gen.-Pres. HUNTER P. WHARTON, Gen. Sec.-Treas. NEWELL J. CARMAN; 300,000 mems.

International Union, United Automobile, Aerospace and Agricultural Implement Workers of America: 8000 East Jefferson Ave., Detroit, Mich. 48214; f. 1935; Pres. LEONARD WOODCOCK; Sec.-Treas. PAT GREAT-HOUSE; 1,400,000 mems.; publ. *UAW Solidarity.*

United Steelworkers of America: 1500 Commonwealth Bldg., Pittsburgh, Pa. 15222; f. 1936; Pres. I. W. ABEL; 1,200,000 mems.; publ. *Steel Labor* (monthly).

FOOD
EMPLOYERS' ORGANIZATIONS

American Meat Institute: 59 East Van Buren St., Chicago 5, Ill.; f. 1906; Dir. Public Relations HERBERT B. BAIN.

Boston Fisheries Association Incorporated: Administration Building, Fish Pier, Boston, Mass. 02210; f. 1959; Pres.

FRANCIS SHINNEY; Exec. Sec. HUGH F. O'ROURKE; 64 mems.

Distilled Spirits Institute: 1132 Pennsylvania Building, Washington, D.C. 20004; f. 1933; Pres. ROBERT W. COYNE; Exec. Vice-Pres. MALCOLM E. HARRIS.

D.F.A. of California: 303 Brokaw Rd., P.O.B. 270-A, Santa Clara, Calif. 95052; f. 1908; 37 mems.; Exec. Vice-Pres. W. W. DADA.

Grocery Manufacturers of America, Inc.: 1425 K St., N.W., Washington, D.C. 20005; f. 1908; Pres. GEORGE W. KOCH.

Millers' National Federation: 14 East Jackson Blvd., Chicago, Ill. 60604; Washington Office: 1114 National Press Building, Washington, D.C. 20004; f. 1902; Pres. C. L. MAST, Jr.

National-American Wholesale Grocers' Association Inc.: 51 Madison Ave., New York, N.Y. 10010; f. 1906; Chair. of Board G. W. McKAY; Pres. C. R. HOERR III; Exec. Vice-Pres. GERALD E. PECK.

National Association of Food Chains: 1725 Eye St., N.W., Washington, D.C. 20006; f. 1934; Pres. CLARENCE G. ADAMY; Chair. of Board J. B. DANZANSKY; publ. *Washington Food Industry Newsletter.*

National Association of Retail Grocers: 360 North Michigan Ave., Chicago 1, Ill.; f. 1893; Pres. RAY COWPER-THWAITE; Exec. Dir. Mrs. M. KIEFER.

National Canners Association: 1133 20th St., N.W., Washington, D.C. 20036; f. 1907; 600 mems.

National Confectioners Association: 36 S. Wabash Ave., Chicago, Ill. 60603; f. 1884; 400 mems.; Adm. J. E. MACK; Sec.-Treas. L. W. ELSTON; publ. *Confectio-NEWS* (monthly).

National Council of Farmer Cooperatives: 1200-17th Street, N.W., Washington, D.C.; f. 1929; Exec. Vice-Pres. KENNETH D. NADEN; Dir. of Public Relations RUSSELL O. TALL; 128 direct mems.

National Dairy Council: 111 North Canal St., Chicago, Ill. 60606; f. 1915; 3,000 mems.; Pres. M. F. BRINK, PH.D.

National Grain Trade Council: 604 Folger Building, Washington, D.C.; Pres. WILLIAM F. BROOKS.

National Live Stock and Meat Board: 36 S. Wabash Ave., Chicago, Ill. 60603; f. 1923; Pres. DAVID H. STROUD.

National Soft Drink Association: 1101 Sixteenth St., Washington, D.C. 20036; f. 1919; 1,939 mems.; Exec. Vice-Pres. THOMAS F. BAKER; publ. *National Soft Drink Bulletin* (monthly).

United Fresh Fruit and Vegetable Association: 1019-19th St., N.W., Washington, D.C. 20036; f. 1904; 2,800 mems.; Exec. Vice-Pres. B. J. IMMING; publs. *United Fresh Outlook, United Spudlight* (weeklies), etc.

United States Brewers' Association: 535 Fifth Ave., New York, N.Y. 10017; f. 1862; Pres. HENRY B. KING.

Vegetable Growers' Association of America Inc.: 1616 H St., N.W., Washington, D.C. 20006; f. 1908; Exec. Sec. A. E. MERCKER.

LABOUR ORGANIZATIONS

Amalgamated Meat Cutters and Butcher Workmen of N.A.: 2800 N. Sheridan Rd., Chicago, Ill. 60657; f. 1897; Sec.-Treas. PATRICK E. GORMAN.

American Bakery and Confectionery Workers' International Union: 1120 Connecticut Ave., N.W., Washington, D.C.; Pres. DANIEL E. CONWAY.

American Federation of Grain Millers: 4949 Olson Memorial Highway, Minneapolis 22, Minn.; Pres. ROY O. WELL-BORN; 60,000 mems.

Bakery and Confectionery Workers' International Union of America (AFL-CIO-CLC): 1828 L St., N.W., Washington, D.C. 20036; chartered 1886; Pres. Daniel E. Conway.

International Union of United Brewery, Flour, Cereal, Soft Drink, and Distillery Workers of America: 2347-51 Vine Street, Cincinnati, Ohio 45219; f. 1886; Pres. Karl F. Feller; Sec.-Treas. Arthur P. Gildea; 75,000 mems.

National Brotherhood of Packinghouse and Dairy Workers: 1201 East Court Ave., Des Moines, Iowa 50316; f. 1939; Nat. Pres. Don Mahon; Nat. Sec.-Treas. Chester C. Green.

United Packinghouse, Food and Allied Workers of America: 608 S. Dearborn Street, 1800 Transportation Building, Chicago 5, Ill.; f. 1937; Sec.-Treas. G. R. Hathaway.

IRON AND STEEL
EMPLOYERS' ORGANIZATIONS

American Hardware Manufacturers' Association: 2130 Keith Bldg., Cleveland, Ohio 44115; f. 1901; Man. Dir. F. A. Petersen.

American Iron and Steel Institute: 150 East 42nd St., New York, N.Y. 10017; 79 company mems., 2,700 individual mems.; Chair. Stewart S. Cort; Pres. John P. Roche; Vice-Pres., Sec. and Treas. E. O. Sommer, Jr.; publ. *Steel Facts* (five times a year).

Gray and Ductile Iron Founders' Society, Inc.: Cast Metals Federation Bldg., 20611 Center Ridge Rd., Rocky River, Ohio 44116; f. 1928; 200 mem. companies; Exec. Vice-Pres. D. H. Workman; Tech. Dir. C. F. Walton; publ. *Iron Castings Handbook, Cost Accounting, Manual for Foundries, Sources for Iron Castings.*

National Retail Hardware Association: 964 N. Pennsylvania St., Indianapolis, Ind. 46204; f. 1901; 18,000 mems.; Man. Dir. William G. Mashaw; publ. *Hardware Retailing* (monthly).

National Wholesale Hardware Association: 1900 Arch St., Philadelphia, Pa. 19103; f. 1894; Man. Dir. Thomas A. Fernley III; Exec. Sec. Thomas A. Fernley, Jr.

Steel Founders' Society of America: Cast Metals Federation Bldg., 20611 Center Ridge Rd., Rocky River, Ohio 44116; f. 1902; 128 mems.; Exec. Vice-Pres. Jack McNaughton.

LABOUR ORGANIZATIONS

Industrial Union of Marine and Shipbuilding Workers: 1126 16th St., N.W., Suite 100, Washington, D.C. 20036; f. 1933; Pres. Andrew A. Pettis; Vice-Pres. Eugene L. McCabe; Sec.-Treas. (vacant).

United Assen. of Journeymen and Apprentices of the Plumbing and Pipefitting Industry of the U.S. and Canada: 901 Massachusetts Ave., N.W., Washington, D.C. 20001; f. 1889; 250,000 mems.; Gen. Pres. Peter T. Schoemann; Sec.-Treas. Martin J. Ward; publ. *United Association Journal* (monthly).

LEATHER
EMPLOYERS' ORGANIZATIONS

American Footwear Industries Association Inc.: 1611 N. Kent St., Arlington, Va. 22209; Exec. Vice-Pres. and Sec. Maxwell Field.

American Footwear Manufacturers Association: 342 Madison Ave., New York, N.Y. 10017; f. 1905; Pres. Mark E. Richardson.

National Shoe Retailers' Association: 274 Madison Ave., New York City; Exec. Vice-Pres. E. J. McDonald.

Tanners' Council of America, Inc.: 411 Fifth Ave., New York, N.Y. 10016; f. 1917; Pres. Irving R. Glass.

LABOUR ORGANIZATION

United Shoe Workers of America: Suite 222, 120 Boylston St., Boston, Mass. 02116; f. 1937; 60,000 mems.; Pres. George Fecteau; Sec.-Treas. Angelo G. Georgian.

Upholsterers' International Union of North America: 25 North 4th St., Philadelphia, Pa. 19106; Pres. Sal B. Hoffman; 60,000 mems.

LUMBER
(see also Paper)
EMPLOYERS' ORGANIZATIONS

National Association of Furniture Manufacturers: 666 Lake Shore Drive, Chicago, Ill. 60611; f. 1928; 500 mems.; Exec. Vice-Pres. John M. Snow.

National Forest Products Association (*Federation of 25 associations*): 1619 Massachusetts Ave., N.W., Washington, D.C. 20036; f. 1902.

National Hardwood Lumber Association: 59 East Van Buren St., Chicago, Ill. 60605; f. 1898; 1,600 mems.; Sec.-Man. E. H. Gatewood.

National Home Furnishings Association Inc.: 1150 Merchandise Mart, Chicago, Ill. 60654; inc. 1921; Exec. Vice-Pres. and Sec. S. A. Johnson.

National Lumber and Building Material Dealers Association: Suite 302, Ring Bldg., 18th and M Sts., N.W., Washington, D.C. 20036; f. 1922; Pres. Samson Wiener; Exec. Vice-Pres. Loren F. Dorman; publ. *National News.*

National Wooden Pallet and Container Association: 1619 Massachusetts Ave., N.W., Washington, D.C. 20036; f. 1947; Exec. Vice-Pres. William H. Sardo, Jr.

North American Wholesale Lumber Association: 180 Madison Av., New York, N.Y. 10016; f. 1893; Exec. Vice-Pres. John J. Mulrooney.

Southern Forest Products Association: P.O.B. 52468, New Orleans, La. 70152; f. 1914; Exec. Vice-Pres. William R. Ganser; 125 mems.

LABOUR ORGANIZATIONS

International Woodworkers of America: 1622 N. Lombard Street, Portland 17, Ore.; f. 1936; Sec.-Treas. William Botkin.

United Furniture Workers of America: 700 Broadway, New York 3, N.Y.; f. 1937; 45,000 mems.; Pres. Morris Pizer; Sec.-Treas. Fred Fulford; publ. *Furniture Workers Press.*

METALS
EMPLOYERS' ORGANIZATIONS

Aluminium Association, The: 750 Third Ave., New York, N.Y. 10017; f. 1935; Exec. Vice-Pres. S. L. Goldsmith, Jr.; Exec. Sec. and Treas. Richard A. Lillquist.

American Society for Metals: Metals Park, Ohio 44073; f. 1913; Man. Dir. Allan Ray Putman; 40,000 mems.; publs. *Metal Progress, Metallurgical Transactions* (with TMS-AIME), *ASM News, Metals Abstracts and Index* (with Institute of Metals, Great Britain), *Metals Engineering Quarterly*, etc.

Copper and Brass Fabricators Council Inc.: 225 Park Ave., Room 315, New York, N.Y. 10017; f. 1964; Man. Dir. T. E. Veltfort.

Copper Institute: 26 Broadway, New York City. (R. R. Eckert.)

Lead Industries Association: 292 Madison Ave., New York, N.Y. 10017; f. 1928; Exec. Vice-Pres. P. E. ROBINSON; publ. *Lead* (quarterly).

Manufacturing Jewelers and Silversmiths of America, Inc.: 340 Howard Bldg., 155 Westminster St., Providence, R.I. 02903; f. 1880, inc. 1903; 1200 mems.; Exec. Dir. GEORGE R. FRANKOVICH; publ. *American Jewelry Manufacturer* (monthly).

Retail Jewelers of America: 551 Fifth Ave., New York 17, N.Y.; f. and inc. 1906; Exec. Vice-Pres. P. E. ROBINSON; 4,500 mems.; publ. *The RJA Bulletin* (monthly).

Zinc Institute Inc.: 292 Madison Ave., New York, N.Y. 10017; f. 1918; Exec. Vice-Pres. P. E. ROBINSON.

LABOUR ORGANIZATIONS

Sheet Metal Workers' International Association: 1750 New York Ave., N.W., Washington, D.C. 20006; f. 1888; Gen. Pres. EDWARD J. CARLOUGH; Gen. Sec.-Treas. DAVID S. TURNER.

United Steelworkers of America: 1500 Commonwealth Bldg., Pittsburgh, Pa.; Pres. I. W. ABEL.

PAPER
(see also Lumber)
EMPLOYERS' ORGANIZATIONS

American Paper Institute, Inc.: 122 East 42nd St., New York, N.Y. 10017; f. 1964; Chair. WILLIAM R. ADAMS; Pres. ROBERT E. O'CONNOR.

National Paper Box Association: 231 Kings Highway East, Haddonfield, N.J. 08033; f. 1918; Exec. Dir. NORMAN T. BALDWIN.

National Paper Trade Association Inc.: 220 East 42nd St., New York, N.Y. 10017; f. 1903; Pres. DONALD J. RAMAKER; Exec. Vice-Pres. GLENN LEACH.

National Office Products Association: Suite 1200, 1500 Wilson Blvd., Arlington, Va. 22209; Exec. Vice-Pres. WILLIAM W. GOSS.

Paperboard Packaging Council: 1800 K St. N.W., Suite 600, Washington, D.C. 20006; f. 1933; Pres. S. E. ICIEK.

The Wall Paper Institute: 509 Madison Ave., New York 22, N.Y.; f. 1935; 12 mems.; Sec. JOSEPH ROBY.

LABOUR ORGANIZATIONS

International Brotherhood of Pulp, Sulphite and Paper Mill Workers: John P. Burke Building, Fort Edward, New York 12828; f. 1901; Pres.-Sec. JOSEPH P. TONELLI.

United Papermakers and Paperworkers: 712–718 North Pearl St., Albany, N.Y. 12201; f. 1957; Pres. HARRY D. SAYRE; Sec.-Treas. WILLIAM L. FRANKS; 144,000 mems.

PETROLEUM AND COAL
EMPLOYERS' ORGANIZATIONS

American Petroleum Institute: 1801 K St., N.W., Washington, D.C. 20006; f. 1919; 8,000 mems.; Pres. FRANK N. IKARD; Sec. E. E. HAMMERBECK.

National Coal Association: Coal Building, 1130 17th St., N.W., Washington, D.C. 20036; f. 1917; Pres. C. E. BAGGE.

National Petroleum Refiners Association: 1725 Desales St., N.W., Washington, D.C. 20036; f. 1902; Pres. A. W. WINTER; 115 mems., 22 assoc. mems.

LABOUR ORGANIZATIONS

Oil Chemical and Atomic Workers International Union: P.O.B. 2812, 1636 Champa St., Denver, Colo. 80201; f. 1918; 175,000 mems.; Pres. A. F. GROSPIRON; Sec.-Treas. B. J. SCHAFER; publ. *OCAW Union News*.

United Mine Workers of America: United Mine Workers' Building, Washington, D.C. 20005; f. 1890; Pres. ARNOLD MILLER; Vice-Pres. MIKE TRBOVICH; Sec.-Treas. HARRY PATRICK.

PRINTING AND PUBLISHING
EMPLOYERS' ORGANIZATIONS

American Book Publishers Council, Inc.: 58 West 40th Street, New York 18, N.Y.; f. 1946; Man. Dir. DAN LACY; 181 mems.

American Booksellers' Association: 800 Second Ave., New York, N.Y. 10017; Exec. Dir. G. ROYSCE SMITH.

American Business Press Inc.: 205 East 42nd St., New York, N.Y. 10017; f. 1965; 86 member companies; Pres. CHARLES S. MILL.

Book Manufacturers' Institute: 161 East 42nd St., New York, N.Y. 10017; f. 1933; Pres. ROBERT A. WUNSCH; Exec. Dir. ROBERT M. PECK.

Lithographers National Association: 420 Lexington Ave., New York 17, N.Y.; f. 1888, org. 1906; Exec. Dir. W. F. MAXWELL; Sec. EDWARD D. MORRIS.

National Book Committee, Inc.: 58 West 40th Street, New York 18, N.Y.; f. 1954; 100 mems.; Chair. NORMAN H. STROUSE; Exec. Sec. MARGARET W. DUDLEY.

National Newspaper Association: 491 National Press Building, Washington, D.C. 20004; Exec. Vice-Pres. THEODORE A. SERRILL; Sec. and Gen. Counsel WILLIAM G. MULLEN; 6,800 mems.

Printing Industries of America, Inc.: 5223 River Rd., Washington, D.C. 20016; f. 1887 as United Typothetae of America; membership of over 7,000 commercial printing and allied industry firms in U.S.A., Canada and elsewhere; Chair. of Board JOSEPH H. HENNAGE; Pres. RODNEY L. BORUM; Vice-Chair. JAMES F. CONWAY; Treas. O. T. HAMILTON; Sec. FRANK LIEDTKE; publ. *Pia Bulletin* (monthly).

LABOUR ORGANIZATIONS

International Brotherhood of Bookbinders: 900 City Building, 1612 K St., N.W., Washington, D.C. 20006; f. 1892; 70,000 mems.; Pres. JOHN CONNOLLY; Sec.-Treas. WESLEY A. TAYLOR; publ. *International Bookbinder*.

International Printing Pressmen and Assistants' Union of North America: 1730 Rhode Island Ave., Washington, D.C. 20036; f. 1889; Sec.-Treas. ALEXANDER J. ROHAN; publs. *The American Pressman*, *The Speciality Worker* (monthly).

International Typographical Union: P.O. Box 157, Colorado Springs, Colo.; f. 1852; Pres. JOHN J. PILCH; Sec.-Treas. WILLIAM R. CLOUD; 122,376 mems.; publ. *The Typographical Journal*, *The Bulletin*, *ITU Review*.

Lithographers and Photoengravers International Union: 1900 L St., N.W., Washington, D.C. 20036; f. 1964; 59,000 mems.; Int. Pres. KENNETH J. BROWN; Exec. Vice-Pres. WILLIAM J. HALL.

PUBLIC UTILITIES
(see also Transport)
EMPLOYERS' ORGANIZATIONS

American Gas Association: 605 Third Ave., New York, N.Y. 10016; f. 1918; Pres. J. W. HEINEY; Man. Dir. F. DONALD HART; Sec. VAUGHAN O'BRIEN; 7,000 mems.

American Public Utilities Bureau: 280 Broadway, New York 7, N.Y.; organised to assist municipalities, other public bodies, and consumers in public utility matters, especially rates and policies in the public interest; Dir. JOHN BAUER; Sec. RUFUS H. REED.

American Public Works Association: 1313 East 60th St., Chicago, Ill. 60637; f. 1894; Exec. Dir. ROBERT D. BUGHER; 1,5000 mems.; the Association represents public works officials in the U.S. and foreign countries; publs. *APWA Reporter* (monthly), books on refuse collection, disposal, etc., research reports.

American Water Works Association: 6666 West Quincy Ave., Denver, Colorado 80235; f. 1881; Exec. Sec. ERIC F. JOHNSON; 23,000 mems.; publ. *Journal AWWA* (monthly).

Public Administration Service: 1313 East 60th Street, Chicago, Ill. 60637; f. 1933; Exec. Dir. E. F. RICKETTS.

State of New York Public Service Commission: 44 Holland Ave., Albany, N.Y. 12208; f. 1907; Chair. JOSEPH C. SWIDLER; Deputy Chair. WILLIAM K. JONES.

LABOUR ORGANIZATIONS

Alliance of Independent Telephone Unions: P.O.B. 5462, Hamden, Conn. 06518; Pres. JOHN W. SHAUGHNESSY, Jr.

American Federation of State, County and Municipal Employees: 1155 15th St., N.W., Washington, D.C. 20005; f. 1936; 525,000 mems.; Pres. JERRY WURF; Sec.-Treas. W. LUCY.

American Postal Workers Union—AFL-CIO: 817 14th St., N.W., Washington, D.C. 20005; f. 1906; Gen. Pres. and Editor FRANCIS S. FILBEY; Gen. Sec.-Treas. J. LOVE; 275,000 mems.; publ. *The American Postal Worker* (monthly).

National Association of Letter Carriers: 100 Indiana Ave., N.W., Washington, D.C. 20001; f. 1889; Pres. JAMES H. RADEMACHER; Sec.-Treas. A. B. CARLSON; 225,000 mems.; publ. *The Postal Record* (monthly).

National League of Postmasters of the U.S.: 927 Munsey Bldg., Washington, D.C. 20007; f. 1904; Pres. EUGENE DALTON; Exec. Vice-Pres. ALTON A. ELLIS; Sec.-Treas. WANDA FEIDNER; publ. *Postmaster's Advocate*.

Transportation-Communication Div., Brotherhood of Railway, Airline and Steamship Clerks, Freight Handlers, Express and Station Employees: 6300 River Rd., Rosemont, Ill. 60018; f. 1886; Grand Sec.-Treas. L. H. FREEMAN.

United Public Workers of America: New York, N.Y.; f. April 1946 by merger of State County and Municipal Workers of America and United Federal Workers of America; Sec.-Treas. EWART GUINIER.

Utility Workers' Union of America—AFL-CIO: 1875 Connecticut Ave., N.W., Washington, D.C. 20009; f. 1945; Pres. HAROLD T. RIGLEY; Sec.-Treas. MARSHALL M. HICKS.

RUBBER
EMPLOYERS' ORGANIZATIONS

National Tire Dealers and Retreaders Association Inc.: 1343 L St., N.W., Washington, D.C. 20005; f. 1921; 4,500 mems.; Exec. Vice-Pres. W. W. MARSH; publ. *Dealer News* (weekly).

Rubber Manufacturers' Association: 444 Madison Avenue, New York, N.Y. 10022; Pres. R. R. ORMSBY.

Rubber Trade Association of New York, Inc.: 15 William Street, New York 5, N.Y.; f. 1914; Pres. A. J. GARRY.

Tire Retreading Institute: 1343 L St., N.W., Washington, D.C. 20005; Dir. PHILIP H. TAFT.

LABOUR ORGANIZATION

United Rubber, Cork, Linoleum and Plastic Workers of America: 87 South High St., Akron 8, Ohio; f. 1935; Pres. PETER BOMMARITO; Vice-Pres. KENNETH OLDHAM; Sec.-Treas. I. GOLD, 212,000 mems.; publ. *The United Rubber Worker* (monthly).

STONE, CLAY AND GLASS PRODUCTS
EMPLOYERS' ORGANIZATIONS

American Glassware Association: 60 East 42nd St., New York, N.Y. 10017; f. 1934; Man. Dir. DONALD V. REED.

Glass Container Manufacturers' Institute: 1800 K St., N.W., Washington, D.C. 20006; Chair. D. L. SHEESLEY; Pres. and Gen. Man. LEIF OXAAL.

National Crushed Stone Association: 1415 Elliot Place, N.W., Washington, D.C. 20007; f. 1918; Pres. W. L. CARTER; Vice-Pres. Eng. F. P. NICHOLS, Jr.; publs. engineering and marketing bulletins.

National Lime Association: 5010 Wisconsin St., N.W., Washington, D.C. 20016; f. 1902, inc. 1922; Exec. Dir. ROBERT S. BOYNTON; Man. Tech. Service KENNETH A. GUTSCHICK.

National Sand and Gravel Association: 900 Spring St., Silver Spring, Md. 20910; f. 1917; Man. Dir. KENNETH E. TOBIN, Jr.

Structural Clay Products Institute: 1520 18th Street, N.W., Washington 6, D.C.; f. 1934; 160 mems.; Sec. J. J. CERMAK; publ. *SCPI News*.

LABOUR ORGANIZATIONS

Glass Bottle Blowers Association: 226 S. 16th St., Philadelphia, Pa. 19102; f. 1840; International Sec.-Treas. HARRY A. TULLEY.

United Glass, Ceramic Workers of America: 556 East Town St., Columbus, Ohio 43215; f. 1941; Pres. RALPH REISER.

TEXTILES
EMPLOYERS' ORGANIZATIONS

Affiliated Dress Manufacturers Inc.: 1440 Broadway, New York City.

American Carpet Institute, Inc.: 350 Fifth Ave., New York, N.Y. 10001; f. 1927; Pres. PAUL M. JONES.

American Textile Manufacturers Institute, Inc.: 1501 Johnston Building, Charlotte, N.C. 28281; Exec. Vice-Pres. ROBERT C. JACKSON; Sec.-Treas. F. SADLER LOVE.

Custom Tailors and Designers Association of America, The, Inc.: 400 Madison Avenue, New York 17, N.Y.; f. 1881; Sec. C. D. HUNTER; 850 mems.; publ. *The Custom Tailor* (every 2 months).

Hat Institute, Inc.: 358 5th Avenue, New York 1, N.Y.; f. 1929; Sec. WARREN S. SMITH.

International Association of Garment Manufacturers: 347 5th Avenue, New York 6, N.Y.; f. 1908; Exec. Dir. J. GOLDSTEIN.

Limited Price Variety Stores Association: 25 West 43rd Street, New York 18, N.Y.; f. 1933; Sec. J. J. MYLER.

Man-Made Fiber Producers Association Inc.: 1150 17th St., N.W., Washington, D.C. 20036; Pres. CHARLIE W. JONES; Exec. Asst. & Sec. Treas. L. K. MARTIN.

Menswear Retailers of America: 390 National Press Bldg., Washington, D.C. 20004; f. 1914; Exec. Dir. DON J. DeBOLT.

National Association of Hosiery Manufacturers: 468 Park Avenue South, New York 16, N.Y., and 901 Johnston Bldg., Charlotte 2, N.C.; f. 1905; Pres. REUBEN C. BALL; Sec. MATTHEW C. KURTZ.

National Association of Wool Manufacturers: 1200 17th St., N.W., Washington, D.C. 20036; New York Office: 386 Park Ave. South, New York 10016; f. 1864; Pres. JACK A. CROWDER.

National Board of the Coat and Suit Industry: 450 7th Ave., New York 1, N.Y.; f. 1935; 1,200 mems.

National Federation of Textiles Inc.: 389 Fifth Ave., New York 16, N.Y.; f. 1872; Exec. Dir. Miss IRENE L. BLUNT.

National Knitted Outerwear Association: 51 Madison Ave., New York, N.Y. 10010; f. 1918; Pres. GEORGE VARGISH; Chair. of Board JAMES F. NIELDS; Exec. Dir. and Counsel S. S. KORZENIK; Sec. EDWARD A. BRANDWEIN; publ. *Knitting Times* (weekly), and 3 annuals.

National Knitwear Manufacturers Association: 350 Fifth Ave., New York, N.Y. 10001; f. 1866; Pres. ROBERT D. MCCABE, C.A.E., J.D.

National Retail Merchants Association Inc.: 100 West 31st St., New York, N.Y. 10001; f. 1911; Chair. of Board C. V. MARTIN; Pres. J. J. WILLIAMS; Vice-Pres. International A. L. TROTTA; publ. *Stores* (monthly).

New York Coat and Suit Association, Inc.: 225 West 34th Street, New York 1, N.Y.; f. 1962 after merger of Industrial Council of Cloak, Suit and Skirt Manufacturers and Merchants Ladies Garment Association; Pres. DAVID ZELINKA; Exec. Dir. SAMUEL SANDHAUS.

Northern Textile Association: 211 Congress St., Boston, Mass. 02110; f. 1854; inc. 1894; Pres. WILLIAM F. SULLIVAN.

United Infants' and Children's Wear Association Inc.: 225 West 34th St. New York 1, N.Y.; f. 1933; Pres. HENRY RIEGEL; Exec. Sec. MAX H. ZUCKERMAN.

LABOUR ORGANIZATIONS

Amalgamated Clothing Workers of America, AFL-CIO-CLC: 15 Union Square, New York, N.Y. 10003; f. 1914; 365,000 mems.; Gen. Pres. MURRAY H. FINLEY; Gen. Sec.-Treas. JACOB SHEINKMAN; publ. *The Advance.*

International Ladies' Garment Workers' Union: 1710 Broadway, New York 19, N.Y.; f. 1900; Pres. LOUIS STULBERG.

Textile Workers Union of America: 99 University Place, New York 3, N.Y.; f. 1939; Pres. SOL STETIN; Sec.-Treas. W. M. DUCHESSI; publ. *Textile Labor* (monthly).

TOBACCO
EMPLOYERS' ORGANIZATIONS

Retail Tobacco Dealers of America, Inc.: Statler Hilton Hotel, 7th Avenue and 33rd Street, New York, N.Y. 10001; f. 1932; Man. Dir. MALCOM L. FLEISCHER; publ. *Tobacco Retailers Almanac.*

Tobacco Association of the United States: Raleigh, North Carolina.

Tobacco Merchants Association of the U.S.: Statler Hilton, Seventh Ave. and 33rd St., New York, N.Y. 10001; f. 1915; Exec. Dir. M. K. BLOOM; publ. *Tobacco Barometer, Tobacco Trade Barometer, International Tobacco Report, Tobacco Update.*

TRANSPORT
(see also Public Utilities)
EMPLOYERS' ORGANIZATIONS

Aerospace Industries Association of America, Inc.: 1725 De Sales St., N.W., Washington, D.C. 20036; f. 1919; Pres. KARL G. HARR, Jr.; Sec. SAMUEL L. WRIGHT; 49 mems.; publs. *Aerospace Facts and Figures*, etc.

Air Transport Association of America: 1709 New York Ave., Washington, D.C. 20006; f. 1936; Chair. of Board STUART G. TIPTON; Pres. PAUL R. IGNATIUS; Sec. FREDERICK DAVIS; 27 certificated airlines of U.S. and Canada; publs. *Air Transport Facts and Figures* (annual).

American Institute of Merchant Shipping: 1625 K St., N.W., Washington, D.C. 20006; f. 1969; Pres. J. J. REYNOLDS; Sec.-Treas. WILLIAM J. COFFEY; 35 mem. companies.

American Transit Association: 815 Connecticut Ave., N.W., Washington, D.C. 20006; f. 1882; Exec. Vice-Pres. and Gen. Sec. ROBERT SLOAN; publ. *Passenger Transport.*

American Trucking Associations: 1616 P St., N.W., Washington, D.C. 20036; f. 1933; Pres. WILLIAM A. BRESNAHAN; 50 affiliated State Associations and District of Columbia; publ. *Transport Topics* (weekly).

Association of American Railroads: American Railroads Bldg., 1920 L St., N.W., Washington, D.C. 20036; f. 1934; Pres. STEPHEN AILES; Exec. Asst. to Pres. and Sec.-Treas. R. E. KEEFER; mems. 82 system lines comprising 171 railroads; 77 associate mems. in U.S.A. Canada and Mexico, incl. 25 associate mems. outside North America.

Motor Vehicle Manufacturers Association: 320 New Center Bldg., Detroit, Mich. 48202; f. 1913; Chair. B. McCORMICK; Pres. FRANKLIN M. KREML; Vice-Pres. RUSSELL E. MACCLEERY; Sec. J. J. RICCARDO.

National Association of Motor Bus Owners: 1025 Connecticut Ave., Washington, D.C. 20036; f. 1926; Pres. C. A. WEBB; Sec. Man. S. WIEDER; 700 mems.; publ. *Bus Facts.*

National Automobile Dealers' Association: 2000 K St., N.W., Washington, D.C. 20006; f. 1917; 22,000 mems.; Pres. H. GIBSON.

Shipbuilders Council of America: Watergate Six Hundred, Washington, D.C. 20037; f. 1921; Pres. EDWIN M. HOOD; 40 mems.

LABOUR ORGANIZATIONS

Air Line Pilots Association: Munsey Bldg., 1329 E St., N.W. Washington, D.C. 20004; Pres. JOHN J. O'DONNELL; 30,000 mems. (Pilot division), 10,000 (Stewardess division).

Amalgamated Association of Street, Electric Railway and Motor Coach Employees of America: 5025 Wisconsin Avenue, N.W., Washington 16, D.C.; Pres. JOHN M. ELLIOTT; 134,000 mems.

Amalgamated Transit Union: 5025 Wisconsin Ave., N.W., Washington, D.C. 20016; chartered 1892; Pres. D. V. MARONEY; Sec.-Treas. JAMES J. HILL; 130,000 mems.

Brotherhood of Locomotive Engineers: Brotherhood of Locomotive Engineers' Building, Cleveland 14, Ohio; f. 1863; Pres. C. J. COUGHLIN; Gen. Sec.-Treas. J. F. SYTSMA.

Brotherhood of Maintenance of Way Employes: 12050 Woodward Avenue, Detroit, Mich. 48203; f. 1887; Pres. H. C. CROTTY; Sec.-Treas. B. L. SORAH; 115,000 mems.

Brotherhood of Railway, Airline and Steamship Clerks, Freight Handlers, Express and Station Employees: 6300 River Rd., Rosemont, Ill. 60018; Chief Exec. Officer GEORGE M. HARRISON; International Pres. C. L. DENNIS; International Sec.-Treas. D. J. SULLIVAN; 300,000 mems.

Brotherhood of Railway Carmen of the United States and Canada: 4929 Main St., Kansas City, Mo. 64112; f. 1888; Gen. Sec.-Treas. O. P. CHANNEL; 103,000 mems.

Communications Workers of America: 1925 K St., N.W., Washington, D.C. 20006; Pres. JOSEPH A. BEIRNE; Sec.-Treas. GLENN E. WATTS; 575,000 mems.; publ. *CWA News* (monthly).

International Brotherhood of Firemen and Oilers: 100 Indiana Ave., N.W., Washington 1, D.C.; Pres. and Sec.-Treas. ANTHONY MATZ.

International Brotherhood of Teamsters, Chauffeurs, Warehousemen and Helpers of America: 25 Louisiana Ave., N.W., Washington, D.C. 20001; f. 1903; Gen.-Pres. FRANK FITZSIMMONS; Gen. Sec.-Treas. MURRAY W. MILLER; 2,000,000 mems.; publ. *The International Teamster* (monthly).

International Longshoremen's Association: 265 West 14th Street, New York City, N.Y.; Sec.-Treas. HARRY R. HASSELGREN.

International Longshoremen's and Warehousemen's Union: 1188 Franklin St., San Francisco, Calif. 94109; f. 1937; Pres. HARRY BRIDGES; Sec.-Treas. LOUIS GOLDBLATT; publ. *Dispatcher* (bi-weekly).

International Union, United Automobile, Aerospace and Agricultural Implement Workers of America: *see* under Engineering and Machinery.

Seafarers' International Union of N.A.: 675 4th Ave., Brooklyn, New York, N.Y.; f. 1938; Pres. PAUL HALL; Sec.-Treas. J. D. GIORGIO.

Transport Workers' Union of America: 210 West 50th Street, New York 19, N.Y.; org. 1935, chartered 1937; Sec.-Treas. MATHEW GUINAN.

Transportation-Communication Div., Brotherhood of Railway, Airline and Steamship Clerks, Freight Handlers, Express and Station Employees: 6300 River Rd., Rosemont, Ill. 60018; Pres. A. R. LOWRY.

United Transportation Union: 15401 Detroit Ave., Cleveland, Ohio 44107; org. 1969; Pres. CHARLES LUNA; Gen. Sec.-Treas J. H. SHEPHERD; 280,000 mems.; publ. *UTU Transportation News* (weekly).

MISCELLANEOUS

EMPLOYERS' ORGANIZATIONS

American Advertising Federation: 1225 Connecticut Ave., N.W., Washington, D.C. 20036; f. 1905; Pres. HOWARD H. BELL; Chair. J. R. McCARTY; Sec.-Treas. D. R. CUNNINGHAM; 40,000 mems.; publs. *AAF Washington Report* and *AAF Exchange* (both 12 times a year).

American Brush Manufacturers' Association: 1900 Arch Street, Philadelphia 3, Pa.; f. 1917; Pres. PHILIP A. SINGLETON; Exec. Sec. ROBERT C. FERNLEY; 200 mems.

American Importers Association Inc.: 420 Lexington Ave., New York, N.Y. 10017; f. 1921; Exec. Vice-Pres. GERALD H. O'BRIEN.

American Institute of Certified Public Accountants: 666 Fifth Ave., New York, N.Y. 10019; f. 1887; Exec. Vice-Pres. W. E. OLSON; 97,321 mems.; publs. *The Journal of Accountancy* (monthly), *Management Advisor* (bi-monthly), *The Tax Advisor* (monthly).

American National Standards Institute, Inc.: 1430 Broadway, New York, N.Y. 10018; f. 1918 as American Engineering Standards Committee; Man. Dir. DONALD L. PEYTON; 170 national trade associations, technical and professional societies and consumer groups; U.S.A. member of the International Organisation for Standardisation and The International Electrotechnical Commission; 900 company mems.

American Society of Association Executives: 1101 16th St., N.W., Washington, D.C. 20036; f. 1920; Exec. Vice-Pres. JAMES P. LOW; 5,000 mems.

American Warehousemen's Association: 222 West Adams St., Chicago, Ill. 60606; Exec. Vice-Pres. D. E. HORTON.

Bowling Proprietors Association of America Inc.: P.O.B. 5802, Arlington, Texas, 76011; f. 1923; Pres. R. M. GOLOBIC; Exec. Dir. V. A. WAPENSKY; publ. *The Bowling Proprietor* (monthly).

Co-operative League Fund: 1828 L St., N.W., Suite 1100, Washington, D.C. 20036; f. 1944; Exec. Vice-Pres. Dr. ALLIE C. FELDER; publ. *Fund Report*.

Electronic Industries Association: 2001 Eye St., N.W., Washington, D.C. 20006; f. 1924; Pres. V. J. ADDUCI.

International Accountants' Society, Inc.: 209 West Jackson Boulevard, Chicago 6, Ill.; Pres. BYRON MENIDES.

Motion Picture Association of America, Inc.: 522 Fifth Ave., New York, N.Y. 10036; f. 1922; Pres. JACK J. VALENTI; Sec. SIDNEY SCHREIBER.

National Association of Accountants: 919 Third Ave., New York, N.Y. 10022; f. 1919; Exec. Dir. W. M. YOUNG, Jr.; 67,000 mems., 295 chapters in U.S., France, Italy, Switzerland, Colombia, Peru, Chile, Argentina, Brazil and Japan; publ. *Management Accounting* (monthly).

National Association of Broadcasters: 1771 N St., N.W., Washington, D.C. 20036; org. 1922; Pres. VINCENT T. WASILEWSKI; Sec.-Treas. E. E. REVERCOMB; 4,952 mems.

National Association of Purchasing Management: 11 Park Place, New York, N.Y. 10007; f. 1915; 19,500 mems.; Exec. Vice-Pres. G. W. H. AHL; publ. *Bulletin*(monthly), *Journal of Purchasing* (quarterly).

National Association of Realtors: 155 E. Superior St., Chicago, Ill. 60611; f. 1908; 115,000 mems.; Exec. Vice-Pres. H. JACKSON PONTIUS; Vice-Pres. Admin. W. R. MAGEL; publ. *Realtor's Headlines* (weekly newsletter).

National Education Association of the United States: 1201 16th St., N.W., Washington, D.C. 20036; f. 1857; Pres. H. D. WISE; Sec. TERRY HERNDON; 1,400,000 mems.; publs. educational periodicals and books.

National Funeral Director's Association of the United States, Inc.: 135 W. Wells St., Milwaukee, Wis. 53203; f. 1882; Exec. Dir. HOWARD C. RAETHER.

National Furniture Warehousemen's Association: 222 West Adams St., Chicago Ill. 60606; f. 1920; 1,300 mems.; Exec. Dir. ROBERT O. WOGSTAD; publ. *NFWA Direction* (monthly).

National Ice Association: 7979 Old Georgetown Rd., Washington, D.C. 20014; f. 1917; Pres. and Sec. J. MICHAEL PAYNE.

National Institute of Drycleaning: 909 Burlington Ave., Silver Spring, Maryland; f. 1907; Exec. Gen. Man. CHARLES R. RIGGOTT; 11,000 mems.

LABOUR ORGANIZATIONS

American Federation of Government Employees: 1325 Massachusetts Ave., N.W., Washington, D.C. 20005; Sec.-Treas. DOUGLAS H. KERSHAW; publ. *The Government Standard* (monthly).

American Federation of Musicians of the U.S. and Canada: 641 Lexington Ave., New York, N.Y. 10022; f. 1896; Pres. H. C. DAVIS; Sec.-Treas. STANLEY BALLARD, 220 Mt. Pleasant, Newark 4, N.J.; 320,000 mems.; publ. *International Musician* (monthly).

American Federation of Teachers: 1012 14th St., N.W., Washington, D.C. 20001; f. 1916; Pres. DAVID SELDEN; 400,000 mems.; publs. *The American Teacher, Changing Education.*

Associated Actors and Artistes of America: 165 West 46th St., New York, N.Y. 10036; Pres. F. O'NEAL; 70,000 mems.

Barbers, Beauticians and Allied Industries International Association: 7050 West Washington St., Indianapolis, Ind. 46241; f. 1887; Gen. Pres. R. A. PLUMB; publ. *Journeyman Barber and Beauty Culture.*

Hotel and Restaurant Employees' and Bartenders' International Union: 120 East Fourth St., Cincinnati,Ohio 45202; f. 1891; Sec. J. GIBSON.

International Association of Fire Fighters: AFL-CIO, CLC; 1750 New York Avenue, N.W., Washington, D.C. 20006; f. 1918; 166,944 mems.; Pres. WM. HOWARD McCLENNAN; Sec.-Treas. F. A. PALUMBO; publ. *International Fire Fighter.*

International Alliance of Theatrical, Stage Employees and Moving Picture Operators of U.S. and Canada: 1270 Ave. of the Americas, New York, N.Y. 10020; f. 1893; Internat. Pres. RICHARD F. WALSH; Gen. Sec.-Treas. PATRICK H. RYAN; Int. Rep. JOHN C. HALL Jr.

National Federation of Federal Employees: Ind.; 1737 H St., N.W., Washington, D.C.; f. 1917; Pres. NATHAN T. WOLKOMIR; Sec.-Treas. RITA M. HARTZ; publs. *The Federal Employee.*

Office and Professional Employees International Union: 265 West 14th St., New York, N.Y. 10011; Pres. HOWARD COUGHLIN; 85,000 mems.; publ. *White Collar.*

Retail Clerks International Association: Suffridge Building, Washington, D.C. 20006; f. 1888; Pres. JAMES T. HOUSEWRIGHT; Sec.-Treas. P. L. HALL.

Retail, Wholesale and Department Store Union: 100 West 42nd Street, New York 18, N.Y.; f. 1937; Pres. MAX GREENBERG.

Upholsterers' International Union of N.A.: 25 North 4th Street, Philadelphia, Pa. 19106; f. 1882; Pres. SAL B. HOFFMANN; Vice-Pres. M. L. GARBER; Treas. L. FORMAN; 60,000 mems.; publ. *U.I.U. Journal* (monthly).

TRANSPORT

INTERSTATE COMMERCE COMMISSION

Interstate Commerce Commission: 12th Street and Constitution Avenue, N.W., Washington, D.C.; f. 1887; federal body with regulatory authority over domestic surface common carriers; jurisdiction extends over rail, inland waterway, oil pipelines and motorised traffic; Chair. GEORGE M. STAFFORD.

PRINCIPAL RAILWAYS

(M.=average mileage operated; N.O.I.=net operating income in dollars.)

Amtrack: quasi public corporation; f. 1971; took over passenger services of 13 investor owned railroads.

Atchison, Topeka and Santa Fe Railway Co.: 80 East Jackson Blvd., Chicago, Ill. 60604: 120 Broadway, New York, N.Y. 10005; Chair. of Board, Pres. and Chief Exec. Officer JOHN S. REED; Vice-Pres. Exec. Dept. J. C. DAVIS; M. 12,653; N.O.I. 831,695,000

Baltimore and Ohio Railroad Co., The: Baltimore, Md. 21201; f. 1827; controlled by Chesapeake and Ohio Railway Co.; Chair. G. S. DeVINE; Pres. and Chief Exec. Officer H. T. WATKINS, Jr.; total line mileage operated 5,849.21; total track mileage 11,052.96; operating revenue (1970) $479 million.

Boston and Maine Corporation: 150 Causeway St., Boston, Mass. 02114; f. 1835; Pres. and Chief Exec. Officer R. J. MULHERN; First Vice-Pres. R. W. PICKARD; M. 1,573; N.O.I. 11,914,238.

Burlington Northern Inc.: Head Office: 176 East Fifth St., St. Paul, Minn. 55101; f. 1970; Chair.-Emeritus ROBERT S. MACFARLANE; Chair. and Chief Exec. Officer LOUIS M. MENK; Pres. ROBERT W. DOWNING; M. 23,873 (1970); serves 17 states; Diesel Units 1,987; Freight cars 116,694; Passenger cars 1,230.

Central of Georgia Railway: 227 West Broad Street, Savannah, Ga. 31401; Chair. of Board and Chief Exec. Officer W. GRAHAM CLAYTOR, Jr.; Pres. R. E. FRANKLIN.

Chesapeake and Ohio Railway Co.: Terminal Tower, Cleveland, Ohio 44101; Chair. and Chief Exec. H. T. WATKINS; Pres. J. W. HANIFIN; N.O.I. (1973) 1,124m.

Chicago, Milwaukee, Saint Paul and Pacific Railroad: Union Station, Chicago, Ill. 60606; Chair. of Board W. J. QUINN; Pres. WORTHINGTON L. SMITH; M. 10,200.

Chicago and North Western Railway Co.: 400 West Madison St., Chicago, Ill. 60606; Pres. L. S. PROVO; Vice-Pres. Finance J. M. BUTLER; M. 10,246; operating revenue (1972) $361m.

Chicago, Rock Island and Pacific Railroad Co.: La Salle St. Station, Chicago, Ill. 60605; Vice-Chair. and Chief Exec. THEODORE E. DESCH; Pres. W. J. DIXON; Gen. Man. W. C. HOENIG; M. 7,645.

Delaware and Hudson Railway Company: The Plaza, Albany, N.Y. 12207; Pres. C. B. STERZING Jr.; Vice-Pres. Traffic R. H. GEORGE; M. 750; N.O.I. 8,848,260.

Denver and Rio Grande Western Railroad Co.: One Park Central, 1515 Arapahoe St., Denver, Colo. 80202; Chair. G. B. AYDELOTT; Exec. Vice-Pres. and Gen. Man. W. J. HOLTMAN; Sec. W. G. PRESCOTT; M. 1,868.

Duluth, Missabe and Iron Range Railway: Missabe Building, Duluth, Minn. 55802; Pres. F. W. OKIE; Vice-Pres. and Gen. Man. D. B. SHANK; M. 516; net income after taxes 4,673,987.

Erie Lackawanna Railway Co.: Midland Building, Cleveland, Ohio 44115; Pres. and Chief Exec. Officer GREGORY W. MAXWELL; Senior Vice-Pres. J. R. NEIKIRK; M. 2,239.

Illinois Central Gulf Railroad Co.: Central Station, 135 East Eleventh Place, Chicago, Ill. 60605; inc. 1851; Chair. Exec. Cttee. WILLIAM B. JOHNSON; Pres. ALAN S.

BOYD; Vice-Pres. and Gen. Counsel JAMES N. OGDEN; M. 9,675; N.O.I. 25,394,062.

Lehigh Valley Railroad: 466 Lexington Ave., New York, N.Y. 10017; f. 1846; Pres. J. F. NASH; Vice-Pres. W. C. WIETERS (Operation), J. A. BROWN (Traffic); Treas. J. W. McDONNELL.

Louisville and Nashville Railroad: 908 West Broadway, Louisville, Ky. 40201; f. 1850; Pres. PRIME F. OSBORN III; M. 6,479; publ. *L. and N. Magazine.*

Maine Central Railroad Co.: 242 St. John St., Portland, Me.; Pres. and Chair. E. SPENCER MILLER; Vice-Pres. (vacant); M. 936.

Missouri-Kansas-Texas Railroad Co.: Katy Bldg., Dallas, Tex. 75202; Line originated 1870, inc. 1922; Chair. and Pres. R. N. WHITMAN; M. 2,918.

Missouri Pacific Railroad Co.: Missouri Pacific Bldg., St. Louis, Mo. 63103; f. 1849; Chair. of Board and Pres. D. B. JENKS; Chair. Exec. Cttee. J. M. KEMPER, Jr.; M. 8,978; N.O.I. 42,688,939.

Norfolk and Western Railway: Roanoke, Va.; f. 1896 Pres. and Chief Exec. officer J. P. FISHWICK; Exec. Vice-Pres. R. B. CLAYTOR.

Penn Central Transportation Co: Six Penn Center Plaza, Philadelphia, Pa. 19104; Pres. and Chief Exec. Officer WILLIAM H. MOORE; Sec. ROBERT W. CARROLL; Treas. JOHN H. SHAFFER.

Reading Company: Reading Terminal, Philadelphia, Pa. 19107; Pres. and Chief Exec. Officer C. E. BERTRAND; Vice-Pres. Law A. W. HESSE, Jr.; M. 1,286 owned, controlled and leased.

St. Louis-San Francisco Railway Company: 906 Olive St., St. Louis, Mo. 63101; f. 1916; Chair. J. E. GILLILAND; Pres. R. C. GRAYSON; Vice-Pres. Gen. Counsel J. E. McCULLOUGH; M. 5,034; operating revenue (1970) $194 million.

Seaboard Coast Line Railroad Co.: 3600 West Broad St., Richmond, Va. 23230 and 500 Water St., Jacksonville, Fla. 32202; Chair. of Board W. THOMAS RICE; Chair. of Exec. Cttee. WILLIAM E. McGUIRK, Jr.; Pres. PRIME F. OSBORN; M. 9,057 (Dec. 1972).

SOO Line Railroad Company: Minneapolis, Minn. 55440; f. 1961; Pres. LEONARD H. MURRAY; Exec. Vice-Pres. J. D. BOND; T. R. KLINGEL.

Southern Pacific Transportation Company: 1 Market St., San Francisco, Calif. 94105; Pres. B. F. BIAGGINI; M. 12,161 (1973); principal subsidiary: **St. Louis Southwestern Railway Company (Cotton Belt),** 1517 West Front St., Tyler, Tex. 75701; Chair. of Board B. F. BIAGGINI; Pres. R. M. NALL; M. 13,601 (1973).

Southern Railway System: 920 15th St , Washington, D.C. 20005; Pres. W. GRAHAM CLAYTOR Jr.; M. 10,400.

Union Pacific Railroad: 345 Park Ave., New York, N.Y. 10022; inc. Utah 1897; Chair. Board of Dirs. and Chief Exec. Officer F. E. BARNETT; Vice-Chair. Board of Dirs. J. H. EVANS; Chair. Exec. Cttee. E. T. GERRY; Pres. J. C. KENEFICK (Omaha, Neb.); M. 8,638; N.O.I. 83,546m. (1973).

Western Maryland Railway Co.: P.O.B. 1876, Baltimore, Md. 21203; f. 1852; Pres. W. P. COLITON; Vice-Pres. and Gen. Counsel N. C. MELVIN; M. 866; N.O.I. 6.794m. (1973).

Western Pacific Railroad Company: 526 Mission St., San Francisco, Calif. 94105; f. 1916; Chair. and Chief Exec. A. E. PERLMAN; Exec. Pres. R. G. FLANNERY; M. 1,513; N.O.I. 7.014m.

ASSOCIATIONS

Association of American Railroads: American Railroads Bldg., 1920 L Street; N.W., Washington, D.C. 20036;

f. 1934; Pres. and Chief Exec. Officer STEPHEN AILES; Exec. Vice-Pres. G. S. PRINCE; Sec.-Treas. and Exec. Asst. to Pres. R. E. KEEFER.

American Short Line Railroad Asscn.: 2000 Massachusetts Ave., N.W., Washington, D.C. 20036; f. 1913; Pres. and Treas. P. HOWARD CROFT; Vice-Pres. and Gen. Counsel C. H. JOHNS; 252 mems.

Eastern Railroad Association: 2 Penn Plaza, New York, N.Y. 10001; f. 1923; Chair. Exec. Cttee. E. SPENCER MILLER.

Public Relations Office, Western Railroad Association: 222 South Riverside Plaza, Suite 1200, Chicago, Ill. 60606; Dir. of Personnel and Public Relations FRANK J. STANTON.

ROADS

Federal Highway Administration of the U.S. Department of Transportation): Includes Bureau of Public Roads and Bureau of Motor Carrier Safety; Fed. Highway Administrator ROBERT T. TIEMAN; publs. *Public Roads, A Journal of Highway Research* (quarterly), *Highway Statistics* (annual).

There are 3,758,942 miles of roads, of which 2,983,072 are surfaced. State mileage 712,785 (rural), 77,386 (municipal), local 2,256,271 (rural), 515,661 (municipal), Federal (national parks, forest, etc.) 196,839 (Dec. 1971).

MOTORING ORGANIZATIONS

American Automobile Association: 1712 G St., N.W., Washington, D.C. 20006; f. 1902; 15,000,000 mems.; Pres. CHARLES J. GALLAGHER.

American Automobile Touring Alliance: 2040 Market St., Philadelphia, Pa. 19103; f. 1932; 1,000,000 mems.; Gen. Sec. JOHN K. SHOCKLEY.

National Automobile Club: 65 Battery St., San Francisco, Calif. 94111; 400,000 mems.; Gen. Man. G. HALLIBURTON.

INLAND WATERWAYS

Day Line, Inc. (Inc. 1962): Pier 81, Foot of West 41st St., New York 36, N.Y.; seasonal services on the Hudson River between New York and Bear Mt. State Park, West Pt. U.S. Military Academy and Poughkeepsie; Pres. FRANCIS J. BARRY.

Interlake Steamship Co.: 200 Union Commerce Bldg., Cleveland, Ohio 44115; Gen. Man. D. A. GROH; contractors for freight carriage on the Great Lakes; 19 vessels.

Federal Barge Lines, Inc.: 611 East Marceau Street, St. Louis 11, Mo.; f. 1918; year-round direct service on Lower Mississippi, Illinois and Warrior-Tombigbee Rivers; seasonal direct service on Upper Mississippi and Missouri Rivers; year-round connecting service on Ohio River system and Gulf Intra-coastal Waterway; Pres. PETER FANCHI, Jr.; Vice-Pres. J. F. LYNCH (Sales), J. S. McDERMOTT (Operations); B. O. CAPLENER (Marine Operation), Sec.-Treas. H. W. BRUNE.

Kinsman Marine Transit Co.: 1548 Rockefeller Bldg., Cleveland, Ohio 44113; bulk cargo on the Great Lakes; Pres. G. M. STEINBRENNER III.

Nicholson Lines: 1465 West Jefferson Ave., Detroit, Mich.; daily service across Lake Michigan for loaded road vehicles, petroleum tanker service; Pres. F. L. HEWITT; Vice-Pres. and Gen. Man. P. G. FINDLAY.

United States Steel Corporation, Lake Shipping: 600 Grant St., Pittsburgh, Pa.; Vice-Pres. C. F. BEUKEMA (Lake Shipping); Gen. Man. W. R. RANSOM; 50 vessels.

Wilson Marine Transit Company: 55 Public Square; Cleveland, Ohio 44113; services on the Great Lakes, Pres. J. C. RIEGER; 14 vessels

OCEAN SHIPPING

Federal Maritime Commission: 1405 I St., N.W., Washington, D.C. 20573; f. 1961 to regulate the waterborne foreign and domestic offshore commerce of the U.S.; Commission is composed of 5 mems., appointed by the President, with the advice and consent of the Senate.

Maritime Administration/Maritime Subsidy Board: Dept. of Commerce, Washington, D.C. 202350; concerned with administration of Government aid to shipbuilding, shipping and port development; Sec. JAMES S. DAWSON, Jr.

PRINCIPAL PORTS

The two largest ports in the U.S.A. in terms of traffic handled are the Port of New York, handling over 181 million tons in 1971, and New Orleans, Louisiana (120 million tons); many other large ports serve each coast, 37 of them handling between 9 and 68 million tons of traffic annually. The deepening of channels and locks on the St. Lawrence-Great Lakes Waterway, allowing the passage of large ocean-going vessels, has increased the importance of the Great Lakes ports, of which 12 handle over 10 million tons. The largest of the inland ports, Chicago, handled over 47 million tons in 1971.

PRINCIPAL COMPANIES

Alcoa Steamship Company, Inc.: Two Pennsylvania Plaza, New York, 10001; services worldwide; Pres. G. C. HALSTEAD; Vice-Pres. and Sec. O. A. SWENSON.

American Export Isbrandtsen Lines Inc.: 26 Broadway, New York, N.Y. 10004; break-bulk freight services: U.S. Atlantic, Great Lakes to Mediterranean; U.S. Atlantic to Red Sea, India, Pakistan, Far East; Great Lakes to Europe and England; container freight services: between Northern Europe, England and Mediterranean; passenger freighter services: to India and North Africa, Lebanon, Greece, Turkey, Spain; Chair. of Board Admiral JOHN M. WILL; Pres. MANUEL DIAZ; Exec. Dir. DONALD G. ALDRIGE; Sec. ROBERT P. WHITMAN, Jr.; 38 vessels.

American President Lines Ltd.: 601 California St., San Francisco, Calif. 94108; f. 1929; Services: east and west coasts N. America, Far East; Pres. N. SCOTT; Sec. J. D. KENNY; 25 vessels.

Amoco Shipping Co.: 500 North Michigan Ave., Chicago, Ill. 60680; Marine Transportation Dept.; Pres. R. S. HADDOW; Vice-Pres. C. D. PHILLIPS; Man. of Engineering C. J. BYSAROVICH.

Barber Steamship Lines Inc.: 17 Battery Place, New York, N.Y. 10004; services to the Mediterranean, Middle East, Far East, and West Africa; Pres. E. J. BARBER.

Bull & Co. (Inc.), A. H.: 115 Broad St., New York 4, N.Y.; Pres. M. F. BLOOMENSTIEL; Sec. J. HATGIS; 8 vessels.

Chevron Shipping Company: 555 Market St., San Francisco, Calif. 94120; world-wide tanker services; Pres. L. C. FORD; Vice-Pres. W. H. BANKS; Sec. Treas. R. W. MACAULAY; 59 tankers.

Columbia Transportation Division, Oglebay Norton Company: 1200 Hanna Bldg., Cleveland, Ohio 44115; services on the Great Lakes; Pres. JOHN J. DWYER; 19 vessels.

Delta Steamship Lines Inc. (Delta Line): P.O.B. 50250, 1700 International Trade Mart, New Orleans, La.; Chair. F. E. FARWELL; Pres. Capt. J. W. CLARK; 11 vessels.

Exxon Company, U.S.A.: Marine Dept., P.O.B. 1512, Houston, Tex. 77001; Gen. Man. E. A. HUMBLE; 18 tankers.

Farrell Lines Inc.: One Whitehall St., New York, N.Y. 10004; f. 1926; regular mail, passenger and freight services from New York and other U.S. Atlantic ports to South, East and West Africa, and from U.S. Atlantic ports and the Gulf to Australia, New Zealand; Chair. JAMES A. FARRELL, Jr.; Pres. THOMAS J. SMITH; Exec. Vice-Pres. C. W. SWENSON.

Global Marine Inc.: 811 West 7th St., Los Angeles, Calif. 90017; Chair. of Board R. F. BAUER; Pres. A J. FIELD; 13 vessels.

Hudson Waterways Corpn.: 1 Chase Manhattan Plaza, New York, N.Y. 10005; Pres. S. KAHN; Exec. Vice-Pres. N. KAHN; tramp services; 17 vessels and 4 containers.

Interocean Shipping Company: 25 Broadway, New York, N.Y. 10004; Pres. F. S. SHERMAN; carriage of bulk materials in foreign trade; 3 vessels.

Lykes Bros. Steamship Co. Inc.: Lykes Center, 300 Poydras St., New Orleans, La. 70130, and at Houston, Galveston, New York; f. 1900; routes to South America, Far East, South and East Africa and Europe; Chair. Jos T. LYKES, Jr.; Pres. W. J. AMOSS, Jr.; Exec. Vice-Pres. J. M. LYKES, Jr.; 41 vessels.

Marine Transport Line, Inc.: 60 Broad St., New York, N.Y. 10004; tanker and cargo services with 2 associated companies; Chair. C. Y. CHEN; 55 vessels.

Matson Navigation Company: 100 Mission St., San Francisco, Calif. 94105; inc. 1901; container and other freight services between U.S. West Coast and Hawaii; Pres. M. H. BLAISDELL.

Moore-McCormack Lines Inc.: 2 Broadway, New York, N.Y. 10004; services to North and South America, South and East Africa; Chair. and Pres. JAMES R. BARKER; 14 vessels.

Pacific Far East Line Inc.: One Embarcadero Center, San Francisco, Calif. 94111; container services to Guam, Pacific, Far East; Pres. L. C. ROSS; Vice-Pres. K. S. LYNCH; G. J. GMELCH.

Prudential-Grace Lines Inc.: 1 New York Plaza, New York, N.Y. 10004; Pres. S. S. SKOURAS; serves U.S.A.-Panama Canal, South and Central America, Caribbean, Mediterranean and Levant ports; 28 vessels.

States Marine International Inc.: High Ridge Park, P.O.B. 1540, Stamford, Conn. 06904; freight and passenger services to Far East, South East Asia, Persian Gulf and Mediterranean; Pres. D. D. MERCER; Chair. R. G. STONE, Jr.; 24 vessels.

United Fruit Company: (Steamship Service) (Inc. 1899): 30 St. James Avenue, Boston 16, Mass.; services New York to Latin America and Europe; Pres. JOHN M. FOX; Sec. FRANKLIN MOORE; 15 vessels.

United States Lines, Inc. (Del.): 1 Broadway, New York, N.Y. 10004; freight service to Europe, Far East; Pres. EDWARD J. HEINE; 41 vessels.

Waterman Steamship Corporation: 61 Saint Joseph St., Mobile, Ala.; services to Europe, the Far East; Pres. E. P. WALSH; Sec. R. S. WALSH; 16 vessels.

ASSOCIATIONS

American Steamship Owners' Mutual Protection and Indemnity Asscn. Inc.: 25 Broad St., New York City.

CIVIL AVIATION

Civil Aeronautics Board: Universal Building, Washington, D.C. 20428; f. 1938; five mems. appointed by the President with the consent of the Senate; regulates aspects of and promotes domestic and international civil aviation; Chair. ROBERT D. TIMM.

Federal Aviation Administration: Dept. of Transportation, 800 Independence Ave., S.W., Washington, D.C. 20591; f. 1958; promotes safety in the air; Administrator A. P. BUTTERFIELD.

PRINCIPAL SCHEDULED COMPANIES

American Airlines Inc.: 633 Third Ave., New York, N.Y. 10017; f. 1934; mail, express, freight and passengers; Chair. of Board and Chief Exec. GEORGE A. SPATER; Pres. GEORGE A. WARDE; fleet of 62 Boeing 707, 16 Boeing 747, 126 Boeing 727, 25 DC-10, and 15 BAC One-11.

Braniff Airways Inc.: Braniff Tower, P.O.B. 35001, Dallas, Tex. 75235; f. 1928; Chair of Board and Chief Exec. Officer HARDING L. LAWRENCE; Pres. and Chief Operating Officer C. EDWARD ACKER; serves U.S. Mainland and Hawaii, Mexico and South America; fleet of 65 Boeing 727, 11 Douglas DC8, 1 Boeing 747.

Continental Air Lines Inc.: Los Angeles International Airport, Los Angeles, Calif. 90009; f. 1934; Pres. R. F. SIX; Sen. Vice-Pres. and Gen. Man. A. DAMM; international and domestic services; fleet of 4 Boeing 747, 4 Boeing 707-320C, 8 Boeing 720B, 22 Boeing 727, 13 Douglas DC-9.

Delta Air Lines Inc.: Hartsfield, Atlanta International Airport, Atlanta, Ga. 30320; Chair. and Chief Exec. W. T. BEEBE; Pres. D. C. GARRETT; domestic services and services to Venezuela, Puerto Rico, Jamaica, Canada, Bermuda and the Bahamas; fleet of 75 DC-9, 34 DC-8, 41 Boeing 727, 5 DC-10, 5 Boeing 747, 4 Lockheed 1-1011, 2 FH-227.

Eastern Air Lines Inc.: Eastern Air Lines Bldg., 10 Rockefeller Plaza, New York, N.Y. 10020; f. 1938; Chair. F. D. HALL; Pres. SAMUEL L. HIGGINBOTTOM; serves entire eastern half of U.S., Texas, Seattle, Washington, Portland, Oregon, California, Nebraska, U.S. Virgin Islands and Puerto Rico; international services to Canada, Mexico, Bahamas, Jamaica and Bermuda; fleet of 36 DC-8, 34 Boeing 727, 17 Lockheed Electra, 11 Tri-Star.

Frontier Airlines: Stapleton International Airport, Denver, Colo. 80207; Pres A L. FELDMAN; fleet of 32 Convair 580, 13 Boeing 737.

Hawaiian Airlines Inc.: P.O.B. 9008, Honolulu International Airport, Honolulu, Hawaii 96820; Pres., Chair. and Chief Exec. JOHN H. MAGOON, Jr.; fleet of 10 Douglas DC-9.

Hughes Airwest: San Francisco International Airport, San Francisco, Calif. 94128; Vice-Pres. and Gen.-Man. IRVING T. TAGUE; fleet of 17 DC-9-30, 9 DC-9-10, 14 Fairchild F-27.

National Airlines Inc.: P.O.B. 2055, Airport Mail Facility, Miami, Fla. 33159; f. 1934; Chair. and Chief Exec. L. B. MAYTAG; Sec. J. M. LINDSEY; fleet of 5 DC-8, 38 Boeing 727, 2 Boeing 747, 13 Douglas DC-10.

Northwest Orient Airlines, Inc.: Minneapolis St. Paul International Airport, St. Paul, Minn. 55111; f. 1926; Pres. DONALD W. NYROP; coast to coast domestic services and services to Canada, Alaska, Japan, Hong Kong, Philippines, Okinawa, Taiwan and Hawaii; fleet of 32 Boeing 727-100, 24 Boeing 727-200, 23 320 B/C, 15 DC-10-40, 15 Boeing 747.

Pan American World Airways: The Pan Am. Bldg., New York 17, N.Y.; f. 1927; Chair. JOHN B. CONNALLY; Pres. WILLIAM T. SEAWELL; services connect 119 cities in 81 countries on all continents; fleet of 32 Boeing 747, 100 Boeing 707 and 24 Boeing 727, 4 Boeing 720.

Trans World Airlines Inc.: 605 Third Ave., New York, N.Y. 10016; f. 1925 as Western Air Express; Chair. CHARLES C. TILLINGHAST, Jr.; Pres. FORWOOD C. WISER; domestic and international services connecting 21 countries; fleet of 103 Boeing 707, 72 Boeing 727, 19 Boeing 747, 25 Convair 580, 19 Douglas DC-9, 6 Lockheed Tristar, 27 on order.

United Air Lines Inc.: P.O.B. 66100, Chicago, Ill. 60666; Pres. EDWARD E. CARLSON; Exec. Vice-Pres. and Gen. Man. C. F. McERLEAN; domestic services from coast to coast, Canada and to the Hawaiian Islands; fleet of 18 Boeing 747, 96 DC-8, 150 Boeing 727, 66 Boeing 737, 15 DC-8 Freighters, 18 DC-10.

Western Airlines Inc.: 6060 Avion Drive, P.O.B. 92005, Los Angeles, Calif. 90009; f. 1925; Chair. of Board FRED BENINGER; Vice-Chair. J. J. TAYLOR; Pres. ARTHUR F. KELLY; North American and Hawaiian services; fleet of 25 Boeing 720, 5 Boeing 707, 30 Boeing 737, 12 Boeing 727, 3 DC-10.

ASSOCIATION

National Aeronautic Association: 806 15th St., N.W., Washington 20005, D.C.; f. 1905; over 100,000 mems.; Chair. F. B. LEE; Pres. J. B. MONTGOMERY; publ. *National Aeronautics Magazine*.

TOURISM

United States Travel Service: U.S. Department of Commerce, Washington, D.C. 20230; f. 1961; Government Agency; Dir. C. L. WASHBURN.

OVERSEAS OFFICES

Canada: Toronto-Dominion Centre, Toronto, Ontario M5K 1K7.

France: 23, Place Vendome, 75001 Paris.

Germany (Federal Republic): 6 Frankfurt/Main, Boersenstrasse 1.

Japan: Kokusai Bldg., 3-1-1 Marunouchi, Chiyoda-Ku, Tokyo.

United Kingdom: 22 Sackville St., London W1X 2EA.

CONVENTION OFFICE

International Conventions Office: c/o American Embassy, Bldg. A, Room 211, 2 ave. Gabriel, Paris.

American Society of Travel Agents Inc.: 360 Lexington Ave., New York, N.Y. 10017; f. 1931; over 11,000 mems.; Exec. Vice-Pres. GEORGE L. FICHTENBAUM; publ. *ASTA Travel News; ASTA notes*.

Discover America Travel Organizations: 1100 Connecticut Ave., N.W. Washington, D.C. 20036; Pres. WILLIAM D. TOOHEY.

Travelers Aid Society of New York: 204 East 39th Street, New York 16, N.Y.; 5,800 mems.; Gen. Dir. J. J. RYAN.

CULTURAL ORGANIZATIONS

The communications media have played a crucial part in the development of a homogeneous American culture. Jazz, pop-rock music, advertising, comic-books, television and films are all aspects of America's popular culture which have had a great impact on the development of the arts both in the U.S.A. and the rest of the world.

New art museums open at the rate of two per month. There are over one thousand symphony orchestras, the most famous being in Boston, Philadelphia, New York, Cleveland and Chicago. The main theatrical centre is the area of New York City on and near Broadway, but there are also over five thousand community theatres and four hundred summer theatres. For the first fifty years of this century Hollywood, California was known as the film capital of the world although in recent years the cinema has suffered from competition with television.

National Foundation on the Arts and the Humanities: 806 15th St., N.W., Washington, D.C. 20506; f. 1965 to develop and promote national support for the arts and humanities in the U.S.; consists of the following bodies:

National Endowment for the Arts: supports the development and growth of cultural resources in the U.S by giving matched grants to non-profit organizations, and unmatched grants to individuals; Chair. NANCY HANKS.

National Endowment for the Humanities: supports research, teaching, public programmes, improved university curricula and state and community programmes to encourage development and appreciation of the humanities; Chair. RONALD S. BERMAN.

National Council on the Arts and **National Council on the Humanities:** advise the respective endowment Chairmen on policies and procedures; each Council has 26 members chosen by the President.

Federal Council on the Arts and the Humanities: co-ordinates the activities of the endowments with the work of other Federal agencies; Chair. JOHN RICHARDSON, Jr.

The Federal Government grants aid to the arts under the following programmes: literary and music programmes of the Library of Congress and the National Gallery, the Office of Education (Arts and Humanities Branch), John F. Kennedy Center for the Performing Arts. Direct aid to the arts is also granted as an incidental part of wider programmes, such as the Cultural Presentations Program, the cultural exchange agreements with the U.S.S.R., the Urban Renewal Program. The 1974 budget proposes doubling aid to $80 million.

Most states organize their own arts councils, which play a significant role in giving official support to the arts, notably in the states of New York, North Carolina and California. City and county governments have also developed a variety of channels for economic aid to the arts, and business corporations, charitable foundations and wealthy individuals frequently contribute at both state and county levels.

PRINCIPAL THEATRES

There are some 50 permanent professional theatre companies operating in the U.S.A., mostly created as non-profit undertakings. The following is a selection of the most important companies:

The Actors Studio Theater: New York, N.Y.; f. 1962; Dir. LEE STRASBERG.

The Actor's Workshop: San Francisco, Calif.

Alley Theatre: Houston, Tex.

The American Place Theater: 111 West 46th St., New York, N.Y. 10036; Dir. WYNN HANDMAN; Assoc. Dir. JULIA MILES.

The American Shakespeare Theater: East 31, Highway 95, Stratford, Conn.; 1,500 seats; April to Sept.

APA-Phoenix (formerly *Phoenix Theatre*): New York, N.Y.; f. 1953.

Arena Stage and the **Kreeger Theater:** 6th and M Sts. S.W., Washington, D.C.; f. 1950; Prod. Dir. ZELDA FICHANDLER.

Center Stage: Baltimore, Md.; Prod. Dir. J. CARTIER; Artistic Dir. JOHN STIX.

Cincinnati Playhouse in the Park: 962 Mt. Adams Circle, Cincinnati, Ohio 45202; Artistic Dir. H. SCOTT; Man. Dir. SARA O'CONNOR.

The Cleveland Play House: 2040 East 86th St., Cleveland, Ohio 44106; f. 1915; Dir. RICHARD OBERLIN.

The Guthrie Theater: Minneapolis/St. Paul, Minn.; Artistic Dir. MICHAEL LANGHAM; Man. Dir. DONALD SCHOENBAUM.

J. F. Kennedy Center for the Performing Arts: 726 Jackson Place, N.W., Washington, D.C. 20566; inaugurated 1971; has facilities for drama and all the performing arts; Gen. Dir. WILLIAM McCORMICK BLAIR.

Lincoln Center for the Performing Arts: Vivian Beaumont-Theater Bldg., 150 West 65th St., New York, N.Y. 10023; facilities for all the performing arts; Producer J. PAPP.

Milwaukee Repertory Theater: Milwaukee, Wis. 53202; f. 1954; Man. Dir. CHARLES R. McCALLUM; Artistic Dir. NAGLE JACKSON.

Minnesota Theater Company, Tyrone Guthrie Theater: 725 Vineland Place, Minneapolis, Minn. 55403; f. 1967.

New York Shakespeare Festival: 425 Lafayette St., New York, N.Y.; f. 1954; Producer JOSEPH PAPP; Assoc. Producer BERNARD GERSTEN; produces at several theatres, including a mobile theatre, throughout New York.

Ypsilanti Greek Theater: Ypsilanti, Mich.

There are 754 opera-producing groups in the U.S.A., the most important being the New York Metropolitan Opera (Pres. GEORGE S. MOORE), the New York City Opera, the Chicago Lyric Opera and the San Francisco Opera (Dir. MERCE CUNNINGHAM).

The New York City Ballet, under the direction of GEORGE BALANCHINE, the San Francisco Ballet, the National Ballet in Washington, are among the most important ballet companies. The world-famous modern dance company of Martha Graham has no permanent home.

PRINCIPAL ORCHESTRAS

There are over 1,400 symphony orchestras. The following are the major orchestras:

Atlanta Symphony Orchestra: Atlanta Memorial Arts Center, 1280 Peachtree St., N.E., Atlanta, Ga. 30309; f. 1945; Music Dir. Robert Shaw; Gen. Man. F. Ratka.

Baltimore Symphony: 120 W. Mt. Royal Ave., Baltimore, Md. 21201; f. 1916; Pres. Joseph Meyerhoff; Gen. Man. J. Leavitt; Conductor Sergiu Comissiona.

Boston Symphony: Boston, Mass.; f. 1881; Music Dir. Seiji Ozawa; Principal guest conductors, Colin Davis, Michael Tilson Thomas; **Boston Pops Orchestra,** Boston, Mass.; f. 1885; Conductor Arthur Fiedler.

Buffalo Philharmonic: Kleinhans Music Hall, 370 Pennsylvania St., Buffalo, N.Y. 14201; f. 1936; Conductor and Music Dir. Michael Tilson Thomas; Pres. Howard A. Bradley.

Chicago Symphony: 220 South Michigan Ave., Chicago, Ill. 60604; f. 1891; Pres. Stuart S. Ball; Chair. of Board Louis Sudler; Gen. Man. John S. Edwards; Music Dir. Sir Georg Solti.

Cincinnati Symphony: 1313 Central Trust Tower, Cincinnati, Ohio 45202; Resident conductor Erich Kunzel; Music Dir. Thomas Schippers; Gen. Man. Albert K. Webster.

Cleveland Orchestra: 11001 Euclid Ave., Cleveland, Ohio 44106; Musical Dir. Lorin Maazel; Gen. Man. Michael Maxwell.

Dallas Symphony: P.O.B. 26207, Dallas, Tex. 75226; f. 1900; Gen. Man. K. R. Meine.

Denver Symphony: 1615 California St., Denver, Colo. 80202; Conductor Brian Priestman; Man. David G. Kent.

Detroit Symphony: Ford Auditorium, Detroit, Mich. 48226; f. 1914; Music Dir. and Conductor Sixten Ehrling.

Houston Symphony: Jones Hall, Houston, Tex. 77002; f. 1913; Music Dir. Lawrence Foster.

Indianapolis Symphony: Clowes Memorial Hall, cap. 2200, 4600 Sunset Ave., Indianapolis, Ind. 46208; Musical Dir. Izler Solomon.

Kansas City Philharmonic: 210 W. 10th St., Kansas City, Mo. 64105; Exec. Dir. Howard Jarratt; Music Dir. Jorge Mester.

Los Angeles Philharmonic: 135 N. Grand Ave., Los Angeles, Calif. 90012; f. 1919; Conductor Zubin Mehta; Exec. Dir. Ernest Fleischmann.

National Symphony Orchestra: John F. Kennedy Center for the Performing Arts, Washington, D.C. 20566; f. 1931; Music Dir. Antal Dorati.

New Orleans Philharmonic-Symphony: New Orleans, La. 70130.

New York Philharmonic: New York, N.Y.; f. 1842; Music Dir. Pierre Boulez; Laureate Conductor Leonard Bernstein.

Philadelphia Orchestra: Philadelphia, Penn.; Musical Dir. Eugene Ormandy.

Pittsburgh Symphony: Pittsburgh, Penn.; Musical Dir. William Steinberg.

Rochester Philharmonic: Rochester, N.Y.; Music Advisor D. Zinman; Assoc. conductor I. Jackson.

San Antonio Symphony: 600 Hemisfair Plaza Way, San Antonio, Tex. 78205; f. 1939; Conductor Victor Alessandro.

San Francisco Symphony: 107 War Memorial Veteran's Bldg., San Francisco, Calif.; Music Dir. and Conductor Seiji Ozawa; Gen. Man. J. A. Scafidi.

Seattle Symphony: 305 Harrison St., Seattle, Wash. 98109; f. 1903; Pres. Dr. Ellsworth C. Alvord, Jr.; Gen. Man. Lanham Deal; Music Dir. and Conductor Milton Katims.

Utah Symphony Orchestra: 55 West First South, Salt Lake City, Utah 84101; Pres. Wendell J. Ashton; Exec. Dir. Herold L. Gregory.

There are also 29 metropolitan orchestras, with budgets between $100,000 and $250,000.

ATOMIC ENERGY

Atomic Energy Commission: Washington, D.C. 20545; Commissioners Dr. Dixy Lee Ray (Chair.), James T. Ramey, Clarence Larson, William O. Doub, (vacant).

FUNCTIONS

1. To conduct, assist and foster research and the development of atomic energy.
2. To disseminate unclassified, scientific and technical information.
3. To control the possession, use and production of atomic energy and special nuclear material.
4. To encourage widespread participation in the development and utilisation of atomic energy for peaceful purposes to the maximum extent consistent with the common defence and security and with the health and safety of the public.
5. To promote common defence and security and to make available to co-operating nations the benefits of peaceful applications of atomic energy as widely as common defence and security will allow.
6. To keep Congress informed.

At the beginning of 1973, there were 29 operable nuclear power plants with a capacity of 11,817,900 kW.; 55 plants under construction with a capacity of 3,992,100 kW.; and 76 plants planned with a capacity of 65,884,000 kW.

DEPARTMENTS

Environment and Safety: Divisions of Operational Safety, Environmental Affairs and Waste Management and Transportation.

Research: Divisions of Biology and Medicine, Controlled Thermonuclear Research, Physical Research.

Energy and Development: Divisions of Reactor Development and Technology, Space Nuclear Systems, Applied Technology, Nuclear Education and Training, International Programmes.

Administration: Divisions of Classification, Headquarters Services, Personnel, Security, Construction, Contracts, Labour Relations, Management Information.

Production and Management of Nuclear Materials: Production and Raw Materials, Management, Grand Junction Office.

National Security: Division of International Security Affairs, Military Application, Nuclear Materials Security, Naval Reactors.

Other Divisions: Planning and Analysis, Information, Congressional Relations and Inspection.

FIELD OFFICES

Albuquerque Operations Office: P.O. Box 5400, Albuquerque, N. Mex. 87115; Man. HAROLD C. DONNELLY.

Brookhaven Office: Upton, N.Y. 11973; Man. E. L. VAN HORN.

Chicago Operations Office: 9800 South Cass Ave., Argonne, Ill. 60439; Man. WESLEY M. JOHNSON (acting).

Grand Junction Office: Grand Junction, Colo. 81502; Man. ELTON A. YOUNGBERG.

Idaho Operations Office: P.O.B. 2108, Idaho Falls, Ida. 83401; Man. W. L. GINKEL.

Nevada Operations Office: P.O.B. 1676, Las Vegas Nev. 89101; Man. CHARLES E. WILLIAMS (acting).

Oak Ridge Operations Office: P.O.B. E, Oak Ridge, Tenn. 37830; Man. ROBERT J. HART.

Pittsburgh Naval Reactors Office: P.O.B. 1105, Pittsburgh, Pa. 15122; Man. LAWTON D. GEIGER.

Richland Operations Office: P.O.B. 550, Richland, Wash. 99352; Man. THOMAS A. NEMZEK.

San Francisco Operations Office: 2111 Bancroft Way Berkeley, Calif. 94704; Man. ROBERT D. THORNE.

Savannah River Operations Office: P.O.B. A. Aiken, S.C. 29802; Man. NATHANIEL STETSON.

Schenectady Naval Reactors Office: P.O.B. 1069, Schenectady, N.Y. 12301; Man. BARRY M. ERICKSON.

MAJOR RESEARCH AND
DEVELOPMENT INSTALLATIONS

Ames Laboratory: Ames, Iowa; Dir. Dr. ROBERT S. HANSEN.

Argonne National Laboratory: Argonne, Ill.; Dir. Dr. ROBERT B. DUFFIELD.

Bettis Atomic Power Laboratory: Pittsburgh, Pa.; Gen. Man. W. H. HAMILTON.

Brookhaven National Laboratory: Upton, Long Island, N.Y.; Dir. Dr. MAURICE GOLDHABER.

Burlington Plant: Burlington, Iowa; Man. R. B. JEWELL.

Feed Materials Production Center: Fernald, Ohio; Man. JAMES H. NOYES.

Hanford Facilities: Richland, Wash.; nine contracts, including Pacific Northwest Laboratory (*see below*).

Kansas City Plant: The Bendix Corp., Kansas City, Mo.; Gen. Man. R. J. QUIRK.

Knolls Atomic Power Laboratory: Schenectady, N.Y.; Gen. Man. H. E. STONE.

Los Alamos Scientific Laboratory: P.O.B. 1663, Los Alamos, N. Mex.; Dir. RONALD S. PAUL.

Mound Laboratory: Miamisburg, Ohio; Project Dir. H. K. NASON.

National Reactor Testing Station: Idaho Falls, Idaho; Nuclear Systems Man. Dr. J. W. MORFITT.

Nevada Test Site: Mercury, Nev.; Gen. Man. J. R. CROCKETT.

Notre Dame Radiation Laboratory: Notre Dame, Ind. 46556; Dir. Prof. MILTON BURTON.

Nuclear Materials and Propulsion Operation: P.O.B. 15132, Cincinnati, Ohio 45215; Man. W. H. LONG.

Nuclear Rocket Development Station: Jackass Flats, Nev.; Project Man. R. L. YORDY.

Oak Ridge National Laboratory: Oak Ridge, Tenn.; Dir. A. M. WEINBERG.

Oak Ridge Production Facilities: Paducah, Ky.; Vice-Pres. R. F. HIBBS.

Pacific Northwest Laboratory: 3000 Stevens Drive, P.O.B. 999, Richland, Wash. 99352; Dir. Dr. F. W. ALBAUGH.

Pantex Plant: Amarillo, Tex.; Man. R. B. JEWELL.

Portsmouth Gaseous Diffusion Plant: Piketon, Ohio; Gen. Man. C. H. REYNOLDS.

Princeton Plasma Physics Laboratory: James Forrestal Research Center, Princeton, N.J.; Dir. Dr. MELVIN B. GOTTLIEB.

Rocky Flats Plant: Rocky Flats, Colo.; Gen. Man. Dr. LLOYD M. JOSHEL.

Sandia Laboratory: Sandia Base, Albuquerque, N. Mex.; Pres. J. A. HORNBECK.

Savannah River Laboratory: Aiken, S.C.; Dir. F. E. KRUESI.

Stanford Linear Accelerator: Palo Alto, Calif.; Dir. W. K. H. PANOFSKY.

E. O. Lawrence Radiation Laboratory: Berkeley and Livermore, Calif.; Dir. (vacant).

UNIVERSITIES AND COLLEGES

Universities and colleges providing higher education to doctorate level with 6,000 and over students. Student and teaching staff numbers are for Spring 1973.

Adelphi University: Garden City, N.Y. 11530; 550 teachers, 8,000 students.

University of Akron: Akron, Ohio; 1,362 teachers, 18,139 students.

University of Alabama: University, Ala.; 763 teachers, 13,481 students.

University of Alaska: Fairbanks, Alaska; 517 teachers, 9,978 students.

American University: Washington, D.C.; 778 teachers, 12,097 students.

Arizona State University: Tempe, Arizona; 1,034 teachers, 27,322 students.

University of Arizona: Tucson, Arizona; 1,657 teachers, 26,786 students.

University of Arkansas: Fayetteville, Arkansas; 707 teachers, 10,784 students.

Auburn University: Auburn, Ala.; 897 teachers, 15,339 students.

Ball State University: Muncie, Indiana.; 776 teachers, 16,562 students.

Baylor University: Waco, Dallas and Houston, Texas; 413 teachers, 7,451 students.

Boston College: Chestnut Hill, Mass.; 914 teachers, 12,218 students.

Boston University: Boston, Mass.; 2,700 teachers, 21,925 students.

Bowling Green State University: Bowling Green, Ohio; 935 teachers, 15,900 students.

Brigham Young University: Provo, Utah; 1,060 teachers, 25,175 students.

Brown University: Providence, R.I.; 755 teachers, 6,269 students.

University of California: Berkeley, Calif. 94720; 14,638 teachers, 105,531 students.

Berkeley Campus: Berkeley, Calif.; 2,000 teachers, 27,770 students.

Davis Campus: Davis, Calif.; 906 teachers, 13,497 students.

Irvine Campus: Irvine, Calif.; 480 teachers, 5,845 students.

Los Angeles Campus: Los Angeles, Calif.; 1,945 teachers, 27,460 students.

Riverside Campus: Riverside, Calif.; 600 teachers, 5,125 students.

San Diego Campus: La Jolla, Calif.; 550 teachers, 6,630 students.

San Francisco Medical Center: San Francisco, Calif.; 1,100 teachers, 2,184 students.

Santa Barbara Campus: Santa Barbara, Calif.; 690 teachers, 12,100 students.

Santa Cruz Campus: Santa Cruz, Calif.; 357 teachers, 4,454 students.

Case Western Reserve University: University Circle, Cleveland, Ohio; 1,150 teachers, 8,466 students.

Catholic University of America: Washington, D.C.; 572 teachers, 6,667 students.

University of Chicago: Chicago, Ill.; 1,125 teachers, 9,083 students.

University of Cincinnati: Cincinnati, Ohio; 2,805 teachers, 29,506 students.

City University of New York: 11,727 teachers, 155,414 students.

Clemson University: Clemson, S. Carolina; 694 teachers, 9,587 students.

Colorado State University: Fort Collins, Col.; 1,125 teachers, 14,897 students.

University of Colorado: Boulder, Col.; 2,729 teachers, 30,428 students.

Columbia University: New York, N.Y.; 4,500 teachers, 14,475 students.

University of Connecticut: Storrs, Conn.; 1,213 full-time teachers, 19,972 students.

Cornell University: Ithaca, N.Y.; 1,907 teachers, 15,994 students.

University of Delaware: Newark, Del.; 1,125 teachers, 16,771 students.

University of Denver: Denver, Col.; 611 teachers, 7,780 students.

University of Detroit: Detroit, Mich.; 597 teachers, 8,672 students.

Drexel University: Philadelphia, Pa.; 298 teachers, 9,045 students.

Duke University: Durham, N.C.; 1,392 teachers, 8,682 students.

Duquesne University: Pittsburgh, Pa.; 450 teachers, 8,261 students.

East Texas State University: Commerce, Texas; 436 teachers, 8,958 students.

Florida State University: Tallahassee, Fla.; 1,272 teachers, 19,032 students.

University of Florida: Gainesville, Fla.; 2,260 teachers, 20,240 students.

Fordham University: New York, N.Y.; 811 teachers, 13,841 students.

George Washington University: Washington, D.C.; 1,175 teachers, 14,242 students.

Georgetown University: Washington, D.C.; 621 teachers, 9,430 students.

Georgia Institute of Technology: Atlanta, Ga.; 556 teachers, 7,199 students.

University of Georgia: Athens, Ga.; 2,100 teachers, 19,000 students.

University of Hartford: West Hartford, Conn.; 539 teachers, 7,959 students.

Harvard University: Cambridge, Mass.; 5,700 teachers, 22,000 students.

University of Hawaii: Honolulu, Hawaii; 1,612 teachers, 27,016 students.

University of Houston: Houston, Texas; 1,543 teachers, 25,727 students.

Howard University: Washington, D.C.; 1,532 teachers, 10,905 students.

Illinois Institute of Technology: Chicago, Ill.; 762 teachers, 7,067 students.

Illinois State University: Normal, Ill.; 1,038 teachers, 17,032 students.

University of Illinois: Urbana, Chicago, Ill.; 5,075 teachers, 54,684 students.

Indiana State University: Terre Haute, Indiana; 775 teachers, 14,472 students.

Indiana University: Bloomington and Indianapolis, Ind.; 2,999 teachers, 68,546 students.

Iowa State University: Ames, Iowa; 1,995 teachers, 17,251 students.

University of Iowa: Iowa City, Iowa; 2,655 teachers, 19,055 students.

Johns Hopkins University: Baltimore, Md.; 1,199 teachers, 9,023 students.

Kansas State University of Agriculture and Applied Science: Manhattan, Kansas; 748 teachers, 14,223 students.

University of Kansas: Lawrence, Kansas; 1,168 teachers, 19,026 students.

Kent State University: Kent, Ohio; 940 teachers, 17,816 students.

University of Kentucky: Lexington, Ky.; 1,750 teachers, 19,331 students.

Louisiana State University: Baton Rouge, La.; 3,686 teachers, 36,528 students.

University of Louisville: Louisville, Ky.; 1,402 teachers, 10,781 students.

Loyola University: Chicago, Ill.; 630 teachers, 13,787 students.

University of Maine: Orono, Maine; 545 teachers, 8,782 students.

Marquette University: Milwaukee, Wis.; 701 teachers 10,671 students.

University of Maryland: Baltimore, Md.; 6,000 teachers, 45,000 students.

Massachusetts Institute of Technology: Cambridge, Mass.; 950 teachers, 7,432 students.

University of Massachusetts: Amherst, Mass.; 1,558 teachers, 28,505 students.

University of Miami: Coral Gables, Fla.; 1,231 teachers, 13,056 students.

Michigan State University: East Lansing, Mich.; 3,201 teachers, 41,349 students.

University of Michigan: Ann Arbor, Mich.; 4,904 teachers, 41,178 students.

University of Minnesota: Minneapolis, Minn.; 6,659 teachers, 44,756 students.

Mississippi State University: State College, Miss.; 767 teachers, 9,111 students.

University of Mississippi: nr. Oxford, Miss.; 350 teachers, 8,300 students.

University of Missouri, Columbia: Columbia, Mo.; 1,587 teachers, 20,836 students.

University of Missouri, Kansas City: Kansas City, Mo.; 440 teachers, 9,439 students.

University of Missouri, Rolla: Rolla, Mo.; 400 teachers, 3,885 students.

University of Missouri, St. Louis: St. Louis, Mo.; 330 teachers, 10,724 students.

Montana State University: Bozeman, Mont.; 548 teachers, 8,113 students.

University of Montana: Missoula, Mont.; 450 teachers, 8,500 students.

University of Nebraska: Lincoln, Neb.; 1,103 teachers, 21,581 students.

University of Nevada: Las Vegas and Reno; 563 teachers, 10,478 students.

University of New Hampshire: Durham, N.H.; 734 teachers, 10,529 students.

University of New Mexico: Albuquerque, N.M.; 1,560 teachers, 18,583 students.

New Mexico State University: Las Cruces, N.M.; 490 teachers, 10,727 students.

State University of New York: Albany, N.Y.; 8,468 teachers, 142,751 students.

New York University: New York, N.Y.; 4,930 teachers, 35,129 students.

North Carolina State University, Raleigh: Raleigh, N.C.; 913 teachers, 12,829 students.

University of North Carolina, Chapel Hill: Chapel Hill, N.C.; 1,800 teachers, 19,500 students.

University of North Carolina at Greensboro: Greensboro, N.C.; 475 full-time teachers, 7,076 students.

North Dakota State University: Fargo, N. Dak; 350 teachers; 6,660 students.

University of North Dakota: Grand Forks, N.D.; 625 teachers, 8,282 students.

North Texas State University: Denton, Texas; 1,004 teachers, 14,582 students.

Northeastern University: Boston, Mass.; 1,800 teachers, 34,240 students.

University of Northern Colorado: Greeley, Col.; 561 teachers, 9,650 students.

Northern Illinois University: Dekalb; 1,400 teachers, 19,801 students.

Northwestern University: Evanston and Chicago, Ill.; 2,400 teachers, 14,418 students.

University of Notre Dame: Notre Dame, Indiana; 625 teachers, 8,344 students.

Ohio State University: Columbus, Ohio; 5,348 teachers, 45,074 students.

Ohio University: Athens, Ohio; 1,184 teachers, 19,327 students.

Oklahoma State University: Stillwater, Okla.; 904 teachers, 16,888 students.

University of Oklahoma: Norman, Okla.; 747 teachers, 19,115 students.

Oregon State University: Corvallis, Ore.; 1,520 teachers, 14,125 students.

University of Oregon: Eugene, Oregon; 1,390 teachers, 14,418 students.

Pennsylvania State University: University Park, Pa.; 2,939 teachers, 52,360 students.

University of Pennsylvania: Philadelphia, Pa.; 1,726 teachers, 17,339 students.

University of Pittsburgh: Pittsburgh, Pa.; 1,901 teachers, 25,562 students.

Purdue University: Lafayette, Ind.; 3,905 teachers, 35,864 students.

University of Rhode Island: Kingston, R.I.; 840 teachers, 10,049 students.

University of Rochester: Rochester, N.Y.; 2,143 teachers, 7,923 students.

Rutgers, The State University: New Brunswick, N.J.; 2,387 teachers, 35,229 students.

Saint John's University: Jamaica, N.Y.; 632 teachers, 13,113 students.

Saint Louis University: St. Louis, Mo.; 1,720 teachers, 9,542 students.

Seton Hall University: South Orange, N.J.; 500 teachers, 9,200 students.

University of South Carolina: Columbia, S.C.; 1,596 teachers, 23,080 students.

South Dakota State University: Brookings, S.D.; 305 teachers, 6,326 students.

University of South Dakota: Vermillion, S.D.; 485 teachers, 5,502 students.

University of Southern California: Los Angeles, Calif.; 2,425 teachers, 19,001 students.

Southern Illinois University: Carbondale, Ill.; 2,466 teachers, 18,398 students.

Southern Methodist University: Dallas, Texas; 726 teachers; 10,021 students.

University of Southern Mississippi: Hattiesburg, Miss.; 650 teachers, 7,900 students.

Stanford University: Stanford, Calif.; 1,289 teachers, 11,197 students.

Syracuse University: Syracuse, N.Y.; 834 teachers, 21,333 students.

Temple University: Philadelphia, Pa.; 2,900 teachers, 28,459 students.

University of Tennessee System: Knoxville, Tenn.; 2,755 teachers, 41,742 students.

Texas A. & M. University System: College Station, Texas; 1,300 teachers, 15,196 students.

Texas Christian University: Fort Worth, Tex.; 474 teachers; 6,388 students.

Texas Tech University: Lubbock, Texas; 1,329 teachers, 19,787 students.

University of Texas System: Austin, Texas; 6,379 teachers, 68,534 students.

University of Toledo: Toledo, Ohio; 670 teachers, 14,903 students.

Tulane University of Louisiana: New Orleans, La.; 830 teachers, 8,212 students.

Utah State University: Logan, Utah; 528 teachers, 7,900 students.

University of Utah: Salt Lake City, Utah; 1,094 teachers, 21,668 students.

Vanderbilt University: Nashville, Tenn.; 1,423 teachers, 6,467 students.

University of Vermont: Burlington, Vt.; 903 teachers, 9,359 students.

Virginia Polytechnic Institute: Blacksburg, Va.; 1,405 teachers, 13,976 students.

University of Virginia: Charlottesville, Va.; 1,200 teachers, 12,300 students.

Washington State University: Pullman, Wash.; 878 teachers, 13,770 students.

Washington University: St. Louis, Mo.; 1,180 teachers, 11,159 students.

University of Washington: Seattle, Wash.; 2,200 teachers, 30,765 students.

Wayne State University: Detroit, Mich.; 1,400 teachers, 32,154 students.

West Virginia University: Morgantown, W. Va.; 834 teachers, 15,203 students.

Wichita State University: Wichita, Kansas; 650 teachers, 12,896 students.

University of Wisconsin, Madison: Madison, Wis.; 3,000 teachers, 34,000 students.

University of Wisconsin, Milwaukee: Milwaukee, Wis.; 2,197 teachers, 22,466 students.

University of Wyoming: Laramie, Wyoming; 628 teachers, 8,026 students.

Yale University: New Haven, Conn.; 2,324 teachers, 9,912 students.

Yeshiva University: New York, N.Y.; 2,500 teachers, 6,648 students.

UNITED STATES EXTERNAL TERRITORIES

AMERICAN SAMOA   GUAM   TRUST TERRITORY OF THE PACIFIC ISLANDS
U.S. VIRGIN ISLANDS

AMERICAN SAMOA

American Samoa is an island group in the southern Central Pacific along latitude 14°S. at about longitude 170°W.

STATISTICAL SURVEY

Area: 76.1 square miles. (Seven islands).

Population (1970 census): Total 28,000; Ofu 411, Olosega 410, Ta'u 1,317, Tutuila 25,357, Swains 74, Rose (uninhabited); Pago Pago (capital, on Tutuila Island) 2,291.

Agriculture (1970) (lb.): Bananas 522,144, Taro 547,727, Vegetables 125,506, Fruit 90,942, Coconuts 943,973, Breadfruit 141,815. Papayas and pineapples are grown. There are about 112 cattle, 7,000 pigs and 27,000 chickens.

Industry (1970): Canned Fish $33,018,237, Pet Food $2,004,752, Electricity 36.7 million kWh (1969).

Currency: United States currency: 100 cents=1 U.S. dollar ($). Coins: 1, 5, 10, 25 and 50 cents; 1 dollar. Notes: 1, 2, 5, 10, 20, 50 and 100 dollars. Exchange rates (April 1974): £1 sterling=U.S. $2.36; $100= £42.35.

Budget (1972): Local Revenue $7,781,000, Congressional grants and direct appropriation $17,019,000.

Development Plan: $10.1 million appropriated for education, building, roads, services and health.

External Trade (1972—U.S. $): *Imports:* $19,556,873; *Exports:* $41,369,235.

Transport (1971): *Roads:* Cars 1,459, Trucks 207, Taxis 80, Motorcycles 130; *Shipping:* Ships entered 649, Passengers 7,450; *Civil Aviation:* Planes arriving at Pago Pago airport 3,369, Passengers 28,169.

THE CONSTITUTION

American Samoa is administered by the United States Department of the Interior. A new Constitution was proposed by the Constitutional Convention and the Secretary of the Interior and approved by a territory-wide election in November 1966. Executive power is vested in the Governor, who is appointed by the Secretary of the Interior, but the new Constitution limits his authority in favour of the legislature. The President of the Senate and the Speaker of the House of Representatives have an equal voice with the Governor in choosing heads of Departments. Local government is carried out by indigenous officials. The Fono (Legislature) consists of two Houses. The Senate is composed of 18 members elected according to Samoan custom from local Chiefs. The House of Representatives consists of 20 members elected by popular vote. The Fono meets twice a year, in February and July, for not more than 30 days and at such special sessions as the Governor may call.

THE GOVERNMENT

Governor: JOHN M. HAYDON.

Executive Departments: Administrative Services, Agriculture, Audit, Communications, Education, Information, Legal Affairs, Public Safety, Local Government, Medical Services, Personnel, Port Administration, Public Defender, Public Works and Development Planning Office.

JUDICIAL SYSTEM

High Court: Consists of four Divisions: Appellate, Trial, Probate and Land and Title. Appellate Division has limited original jurisdiction and hears appeals from the other three. Trial Division hears original cases $300 and over in civil as well as criminal cases. It serves as appellate court for 59 District Courts; Traffic Courts; Small Claims Court. Land and Title Division hears cases involving communal land questions and disposition of Matai titles to family litigants. Total caseload (1972) over 5,000 cases.

Chief Justice: WILLIAM J. McKNIGHT, III.

Associate Justice: LESLIE JOCHIMSEN.

RELIGION

The population is largely Christian. Roman Catholics come under the jurisdiction of the Vicar Apostolic for Samoa and the Tokelau Islands (Catholic Mission, Apia, Western Samoa) Mgr. GEORGE H. PEARCE, Titular Bishop of Attalea in Pamphilia. Protestant denominations active in the Territory include the Congregational Christian Church, the Methodist Church, the Church of Jesus Christ of the Latter-Day Saints, Assemblies of God, Church of the Nazarene, Seventh Day Adventists and Jehovah's Witnesses.

THE PRESS

Daily Bulletin: Office of Samoan Information, Pago Pago; English; daily; circ. 6,500.

Samoa News: P.O.B. 57, Pago Pago; twice a week; circ. 3,000.

RADIO AND TELEVISION
RADIO

Radio Station WVUV: Pago Pago; Government station administered by the Office of Samoan Information; programmes in English and Samoan; 112 hours a week; Man. NAFOA TAMASESE.

TELEVISION

KVZK: Pago Pago; f. 1964; Government-owned station administered by the Department of Education; programmes in English and Samoan; operates on channels 2, 4, 5, 8, 10 and 12 for seven hours a day, broadcasting instructional programme for school use; channels 4 and 5 for six hours daily for adult education, public information, entertainment; channel 4 for 10 hours, channel 5 for six hours, on Saturday and Sunday; Gen. Man. RICHARD W. STEVENS.

FINANCE

BANKING

Bank of Hawaii: Pago Pago; f. 1969; total assets $6,404,654 (June 1972); Pres. WILSON P. CANNON; Man. DENNIS K. PEARSON.

Development Bank of American Samoa: Pago Pago; f. 1969; cap. $2.5m.; a non-commercial undertaking; Chair. and Pres. MUNDEY JOHNSTON.

TRADE AND INDUSTRY

Copra Board of American Samoa: Pago Pago; Government-directed marketing medium.

Star-Kist Samoa Inc.: Employs 525 workers.

Van Camp Sea Food Company: Employs 675 workers.

DEVELOPMENT

American Samoa Development Corporation: Pago Pago, f. 1962; financed by Samoan private shareholders; a luxury hotel employing 115 people has been built.

INSURANCE

G.H.C. Reid and Co.

Burns Philp (SS) Company Ltd.

Hartford Insurance Co.

Richard Gebauer.

TRANSPORT

ROADS

Non-scheduled commercial buses operate a service over 42 miles of main and secondary roads.

SHIPPING

Pacific Far East Lines Inc.: ships call every three weeks *en route* from U.S.A. and Canada to New Zealand, Australia and Tasmania, and on return journey also.

A small container vessel calls every two weeks *en route* from New Zealand to Western Samoa and Tonga. A number of inter-island boats operate frequently between Western and American Samoa.

CIVIL AVIATION

Pan American World Airways: P.O.B. 728, Pago Pago; service to Honolulu, Tahiti and New Zealand.

Polynesian Airlines Ltd.: P.O.B. 280, Pago Pago; daily service to Western Samoa.

Air New Zealand: Pago Pago; twice-weekly service to New Zealand.

American Airlines: P.O.B. 280.

EDUCATION

Education is compulsory from the age of 6 to 18. The Government maintains 27 consolidated elementary schools, 4 senior high schools and 1 community college. It also operates 138 village early childhood education centres. Total enrolment in elementary and secondary public schools (1972–73): 8,207 pupils; 390 teachers. The community college has 223 full-time students and a staff of 25 full-time instructors. One thousand six hundred children are enrolled in 5 private schools. The new consolidated elementary school was completed in 1973.

GUAM

Guam is an unincorporated territory of the United States under the jurisdiction of the Department of the Interior. It is the southernmost and largest of the Mariana Islands, situated about 1,500 miles south-east of Manila (Philippines).

STATISTICAL SURVEY

Area: 209 square miles.

Population (1973): 104,572; Servicemen and dependants, about 30,952. Capital: Agaña.

Agriculture: Production (1972): Fruits and vegetables 2,504,000 lb.; Eggs 2,065,270 dozen; Pigs 8,325 head; Cattle 4,112 head; Fish 143,629 lb.

Industry: Construction companies, retail stores, watch assembly factories, soft drink bottling plants and tourist facilities are the major employers in private industry. The island's economy, once basically military-oriented, is quickly becoming civilian with the rapid growth in tourism. The Government of Guam is also a major employer.

Tourism: No. of visitors ('000): (1971) 119.1; (1972) 185.4; (1973—projected) 242.7.

FINANCE

United States currency: 100 cents=1 U.S. dollar ($).
Coins: 1, 5, 10, 25 and 50 cents; 1 dollar.
Notes: 1, 2, 5, 10, 20, 50 and 100 dollars.
Exchange rates (April 1974): £1 sterling=U.S. $2.36; $100=£42.35.

BUDGET
(1972—U.S. $ million)

REVENUE		EXPENDITURE	
Income Taxes	44.11	Current Operating Programmes:	
Gross Receipts Tax	13.77	General Government	11.94
Real Estate Property Tax	2.11	Public Safety	4.02
Other Local Taxes	0.35	Highways*	—
Licences and Permits	0.45	Personnel Benefits	2.90
Court Fines and Forfeits	0.27	Conservation of Health	2.32
Use of Money and Property	0.09	Social and Community Services†	4.39
Federal Grants-in-Aid	9.57	Public Schools	27.95
Charges for Current Services	3.91	Public Library	0.29
Other Revenues	0.35	Recreation	0.36
		Protection and Development of Resources	1.85
		Utilities, Hospitals and Other Enterprises	6.20
		Repayment of Rehabilitation Loans	1.88
		Previous Years' Operating Encumbrances	1.28
		Capital Improvement Projects	4.23
		Other Continuing Projects	1.13
		Appropriated Receipts	1.19
		TOTAL EXPENDITURE	71.93
TOTAL REVENUE	74.98	Overall Surplus	3.05

* 1972 Statement does not include this figure ($1,074,079) due to transfer to Government of Guam Revolving Fund.
† Includes sanitation and waste removal.

External Trade: Imports (1972) $166.8 million; Exports (1972) $16.4 million.

Shipping: Vessels entered (1972) 829; Freight (1972) entered 596,000 tons, cleared 117,300 tons, in transit 25,700 tons.

THE CONSTITUTION

Guam is governed under the Organic Act of Guam of 1950, which gave the island statutory local power of self-government and made its inhabitants citizens of the United States, although they cannot vote in national elections. Their Delegate to the House of Representatives is elected every two years. Executive power is vested in a civilian Governor, first elected in 1970. Elections for the governorship occur every four years. The government has 14 executive departments, whose heads are appointed by the Governor with the consent of the Guam Legislature. The Legislature consists of 21 members elected by popular vote every two years. It is empowered to pass laws on local matters, including taxation and fiscal appropriations.

THE GOVERNMENT

Governor: CARLOS GARCIA CAMACHO.

Lieutenant Governor: KURT SCOTT MOYLAN.

The 14 executive departments are as follows: Law, Revenue and Taxation, Labour, Public Safety, Public Works, Agriculture, Land Management, Commerce, Education, Public Health and Social Services, Commercial Port, Administration, Corrections and Public Utility Agency.

LEGISLATURE

Speaker: FLORENCIO T. RAMIREZ.

Elections: November 1972. The Democratic Party won 15 seats, the Republican Party six seats.

JUDICIAL SYSTEM

District Court of Guam: Judge appointed by the President. The court has the jurisdiction of a district court of the United States in all cases arising under the law of the United States and original jurisdiction over such other cases arising in Guam as the Guam Legislature does not transfer to courts of its own creation. Appeals may be made to the Court of Appeals for the Ninth Circuit and to the Supreme Court of the United States.

Presiding Judge: Hon. CRISTOBAL C. DUENAS.

Clerk of Court: EDWARD L. G. AGUON.

There are also the Island Court, the Police Court, Traffic Court, Juvenile Court and the Small Claims Court.

RELIGION

The population is largely Roman Catholic; Bishop of the Diocese of Agaña (Bishop's House, Cuesta San Ramon, Agaña) Most Rev. FELIXBERTO C. FLORES, O.F.M.CAP.; Apostolic Administrator, *sede plena*, of the Diocese of Agaña Mgr. JOSÉ LEÓN GUERRERO.

THE PRESS

Pacific Daily News: P.O.B. DN, Agaña; f. 1950; daily and Sunday; morning; Publisher ROBERT UDICK; circ. 20,600.

Pacific Dateline: P.O.B. DN, Agaña; f. 1970; daily; evening; Editor THOMAS BRISLIN; circ. 4,000.

Pacific Sunday News: P.O.B. DN, Agaña; f. 1950; Sunday; Editor GLENDA MOORE; circ. 19,000.

Pacific Voice: Agaña; Sunday; Ed. JOHN L. MITCHELL; circ. 5,500.

RADIO AND TELEVISION

RADIO

Radio Guam (KUAM): P.O.B. 368, Agaña; relays N.B.C. C.B.S. and A.B.C. programmes; Pres. H. SCOTT KILLGORE; Exec. Vice-Pres. WILLIAM B. NIELSEN.

There were 100,000 radio receivers in 1970.

TELEVISION

Guam-Agaña (KUAM-TV): P.O.B. 368, Agaña; relays N.B.C., C.B.S. and A.B.C. programmes; Pres. H. SCOTT KILLGORE; Exec. Vice-Pres. WILLIAM B. NIELSEN.

There were 10,000 television receivers in 1971.

BANKING

American Savings and Loan Association: P.O.B. 811, Agaña; Pres. WILLIAM THOMASSON.

Bank of America National Trust and Savings Association: San Francisco, Calif., U.S.A.; P.O.B. BA, Agaña; 2 agencies; Man. KARL HAEUSER.

Bank of Guam: P.O.B. 3988, Agaña; Pres. JESUS LEON GUERRERO.

Bank of Hawaii: Honolulu, Hawaii, U.S.A.; P.O.B. BH, Agaña, Guam 96910; Vice-Pres. and Man. W. M. ORD.

Chase Manhattan Bank of New York: P.O.B. AE, Agaña; Man. F. J. MCGINITY.

First National City Bank of New York: Agaña; Man. ROBERT S. WILCOX.

First Hawaiin Bank: Honolulu, Hawaii, U.S.A.; P.O.B. AD, Agaña; Vice-Pres. E. W. SCHAARTT.

Guam Savings and Loan Association: P.O.B. 216, Agaña; Pres. JOSEPH FLORES.

TRANSPORT

SHIPPING

Getz Bros. and Co. (U.S.): P.O.B. 6128 Tamuning, Guam 96911; General Agents for P & O Lines, American President Lines, American Pioneer Lines, Chandris Lines (Aust.) Pty., Eastern and Australian Steamship Co., Matson Navigation Co., Moore-McCormack Steamship Co., Nedlloyd Lines, U.S. Lines Inc., etc.; Gen. Agent R. M. ASH.

Micronesian Interocean Line Inc.: P.O.B. 365, Agaña; Man. FILEMON GO.

Pacific Navigation System: P.O.B. 7, Agaña; f. 1946; Pres. KENNETH T. JONES, Jr.

Pacific Far East Line (Guam) Ltd.: P.O.B. EE, Agaña; Gen. Man. J. PHILIP LOMAX.

Atkins Kroll (Guam) Ltd.: Agents: PNS, P.O.B. 7, Agaña; Man. DAVID PORTER.

AVIATION

Pan American World Airways: Skinner Plaza, P.O.B. BB, Agaña; Dir. JAMES L. BARTON.

Trans-World Airlines Inc.: P.O.B. 7297, Agaña; Gen. Man. G. H. HOLLENBECK.

Continental Airlines-Air Micronesia: P.O.B. 138, Saipan, Mariana Islands, 96950; Gen. Man. B. DUGGAN.

Japan Air Lines: P.O.B. 7659, Tamuning, 96911; Dir. TARO KANAI.

TOURISM

Guam Visitors Bureau: P.O.B. 3520, Agaña 96910; Man. Dir. BERT UNPINGCO.

EDUCATION

(1972–73)

Twenty-six elementary schools, 5 Junior High Schools, 3 Senior High Schools, a Vocational-Technical High School and a school for mentally retarded children; total enrolment 26,333.

The parochial and private systems have an additional 4,548 students.

UNIVERSITY

University of Guam: P.O.B. EK, Agaña, Guam 96910; 225 teachers, 3,275 students.

TRUST TERRITORY OF THE PACIFIC ISLANDS

The Trust Territory of the Pacific Islands consists of the Mariana Islands (except Guam), the Caroline Islands and the Marshall Islands in the Western Pacific. There are in all 2,141 islands, 90 of which are inhabited, grouped into 6 administrative districts.

STATISTICAL SURVEY

Area: Total area of the Territory: 3 million square miles; Land area: 700 square miles; the largest islands are Babelthuap (153 square miles) in Palau District and Ponape Island (129 square miles) in Ponape District.

Population (1972): Total 114,645; Mariana Islands 13,381, Marshall Islands 24,248, Palau 13,025, Ponape 23,723, Truk 32,738, Yap 7,536. Administration centre: Saipan, Mariana Islands.

Agriculture: The chief crops are Coconut, Breadfruit, Bananas, Taro, Yams, Cocoa, Pepper and Citrus. Sub-sistence crop production predominates and, except for copra from all districts and vegetables from the Mariana Islands, little is marketed. Estimated copra production for 1972 was 10,300 short tons.

Livestock (1972): Goats 5,831, Cattle 13,189, Carabao 135, Pigs 17,250, Poultry 150,750.

Fishing* (1972): Trochus Shells 103 short tons, Tuna and other fish n.a.

* Exports only.

FINANCE

United States currency: 100 cents = 1 U.S. dollar ($).

Coins: 1, 5, 10, 25 and 50 cents; 1 dollar.

Notes: 1, 2, 5, 10, 20, 50 and 100 dollars.

Exchange rates (April 1974): £1 sterling = U.S. $2.36; $100 = £42.35.

BUDGET
(1972—U.S.$)

Revenue		Expenditure	
Territorial Taxes, Fees and Licences .	3,416,815	General Administration . . .	4,181,774
Reimbursements	352,531	Construction	15,944,416
Direct U.S. Appropriation . .	608,300	Economic and Political Development .	6,661,025
Grant from U.S. Congress . .	59,371,700	Legal and Public Safety . .	1,889,852
Carried over	9,504,392	Health	6,175,038
		Education	11,077,341
		Miscellaneous . . .	3,056,846
Total	73,569,885	Total . . .	48,986,292

TRADE

External Trade (1972): *Imports:* $30 million est. (including foodstuffs $9.3 million, beverages $3.08 million, petroleum products $3.2 million, building materials $3.02 million). *Exports:* $2.6 million (copra, scrap metal, trochus shells, handicrafts, vegetables and fish).

TRANSPORT
(1972)

Roads: Privately owned vehicles (mostly sedans and pickups) are estimated at 6,983.

Shipping: Passengers 458 (Micronesia Interocean Line Inc.); Freight 134,348 tons; other American vessels also entered and cleared in external trade.

Civil Aviation: Passenger miles 72,974.

EDUCATION
(1972)

	Schools	Teachers		Pupils
		Indigenous	Others	
Elementary .	238	1,306	120	29,917
High School .	18	162	250	6,447

THE CONSTITUTION

The Trust Territory of the Pacific Islands is a United Nations Trusteeship administered by the United States of America. Executive and administrative authority is exercised by a High Commissioner, appointed by the President of the United States with the consent and approval of the U.S. Senate. The High Commissioner is under the direction of the Secretary of the Interior. The High Commissioner is represented in each district by a District Administrator and has his headquarters at Saipan, Mariana Islands.

Legislative authority is vested in the Congress of Micronesia, a bicameral legislature consisting of the Senate and the House of Representatives. There are twelve Senators, two elected at large from each of the six districts for a term of four years. The House of Representatives has twenty-one members elected for two-year terms from single-member election districts of approximately equal population. The present apportionment of Representatives is: Mariana Islands District, three; Marshall Islands District, four; Palau District, three; Ponape District, four; Truk District, five; and Yap District, two.

The Mariana Islands, Marshall Islands, Palau, Ponape, Truk, and Yap Districts have formally constituted legislatures. Local governmental units are the municipalities and villages. Elected Magistrates and Councils govern the municipalities. Village government is largely traditional.

THE GOVERNMENT

High Commissioner: The Hon. EDWARD E. JOHNSTON.

Deputy High Commissioner: The Hon. PETER T. COLEMAN.

Director of Resources and Development: EUSEBIO RECHUCHER.

Director of Public Works: JAMES R. WHEELER.

Director of Education: DAVID RAMARUI.

Director of Finance: RON PETERSON.

Director of Health Services: MASAO KUMANGAI, M.D.

Director of Personnel: ARTHUR AKINA.

Director of Public Affairs: STRIK YOMA.

Director of Transportation and Communications: JOSEPH BEADLES.

Attorney-General: RICHARD MIYAMOTO.

District Administrators: FRANCISCO C. ADA (Mariana Islands), OSCAR DE BRUM (Marshall Islands), THOMAS REMENGESAU (Palau), LEO A. FALCAM (Ponape; acting), JUAN A. SABLAN (Truk), LEONARD AGUIGUI (Yap).

CONGRESS OF MICRONESIA

President of the Senate: Hon. TOSIWO NAKAYAMA.

Speaker of the House of Representatives: Hon. BETHWEL HENRY.

DISTRICT LEGISLATURES

Mariana Islands District Legislature: 16 members serving for three years.

Marshall Islands District Legislature: 24 members serving for two years.

Palau District Legislature (*Olbiil era Kelulau*): 16 chiefs (non-voting members) and 28 elected representatives serving for four years.

Ponape District Legislature: 24 representatives elected for four years (terms staggered).

Truk District Legislature: 27 members, serving for three years.

Yap District Legislature: 20 members, 12 elected from the Yap Islands proper and 8 elected from the Outer Islands of Ulithi and Woleai, for a two-year term.

JUDICIAL SYSTEM

The Trust Territory laws derive from the Trusteeship Agreement, certain applicable laws of the United States and Executive Orders of the President, Secretarial Orders of the Secretary of the Interior, laws and regulations of the Government of the Trust Territory, District Administrator's orders and enactments of the Congress of Micronesia and district legislative bodies approved by the High Commissioner, and municipal ordinances. Recognized customary law has full force where it does not conflict with aforementioned laws.

High Court: Appellate and Trial Divisions; Chief Justice Hon. HAROLD W. BURNETT; Associate Justices Hon. ARVIN H. BROWN (Eastern Carolines), Hon. D. KELLY TURNER (Marshalls), Hon. ROBERT A. HEFNER (Eastern Carolines).

District Courts: 3 judges Mariana Islands; 3 Marshall Islands; 3 Palau; 5 Ponape; 4 Truk; 3 Yap.

Community Courts: a number in each District; 125 judges.

RELIGION

The population is predominantly Christian. Christian missionaries (Catholic and Protestant) number 150; there are 31 mission schools with 5,143 pupils.

Roman Catholicism: Vicar Apostolic for Caroline and Marshall Islands H.E. Bishop MARTIN NEYLON, S.J.; Bishop for Mariana Islands H.E. Bishop FELIXBERTO C. FLORES, D.D.

Protestantism: Marshall Islands and Eastern Caroline Islands: U.S. effort under the auspices of the United Church Board for World Ministries (475 Riverside Drive, New York City, N.Y. 10027); Pacific Regional Sec.: Rev. PAUL GREGORY.

Western Carolines: under auspices of the Liebenzell Mission of Germany and the U.S.A.; Rev. PETER ERMEL, Truk, Caroline Islands 96942.

THE PRESS

Highlights: newsletter from Office of the High Commissioner; semi-monthly; circ. 9,700.

Marianas Variety: f. 1922; P.O.B. 231, Saipan; Marianas district weekly; independent; English, Chamarro; circ. 2,000.

Micronesian Reporter: Public Information Office; journal of Micronesia; 4 times a year; circ. 5,300.

Micronitor: Marshall Islands; f. 1970; weekly; Editor JOE MURPHY (Marshalls); circ. 2,500 throughout Micronesia.

Tia Belau: P.O.B. 569, Koror, Palau; f. 1972; bi-weekly; independent; Editor MOSES ULUDONG; circ. 1,000.

RADIO AND TELEVISION

All stations are government owned, broadcasting between 6 a.m. and midnight daily.

Station KJQR: Saipan, Mariana Is. 96950; programmes in English and Chamorro; 1 kW; Man. R. SABLAN.

Station WSZA: Colonia, Yap, W. Caroline Is. 96943; programmes in English and Yapese; 1 kW; Man. A. YUG.

Station WSZB: Koror, Palau, W. Caroline Is. 96940; member of the Micronesian Broadcasting System; 1 kW; 18 hours a day; Man. H. RODAS.

Station WSZC: Moen, Truk, E. Caroline Is. 96942; programmes in English and Trukese; 5 kW; Man. K. PETER.

Station WSZD: Kolonia, Ponape, E. Caroline Is. 96941; programmes in English, Kusaiean and Ponapean; 10 kW; Man. H. JOHNNY (Acting).

Station WSZE-AM-FM: Saipan, Mariana Is.; commercial station owned by Micronesian Broadcasting Corpn.

Station WSZO: Majuro, Marshall Islands 96960; owned and operated by the Government of the Trust Territory of the Pacific Islands; programmes in English and Marshallese; 1 kW broadcasts on 1440 kc.; on the air 18 hours a day Monday to Friday, 16 hours on Sundays and holidays; Station Man. LAURENCE N. EDWARDS.

WSZE-TV: Saipan, Mariana Is. 96950; commercial station owned by Micronesian Broadcasting Corpn., broadcasts 6 hours of American shows daily.

In 1972 there were 48,250 radio receivers and 1,600 TV sets.

FINANCE

BANKING

Bank of America, National Trust and Savings Association: Saipan Branch, P.O.B. 67, Saipan, Mariana Islands 96950; Man. DALE BRANCHCOMB; brs. also in Truk and Majuro, Marshall Islands.

Bank of Hawaii: brs. in Kwajalein (Marshall Is.), Koror, Ponape, Saipan, Yap, Wake, Midway.

Banking services for the rest of the territory are available in Guam, Hawaii and on the U.S. mainland.

INSURANCE

There are two firms on Saipan which sell insurance:

Micronesian Insurance Underwriters Inc.

Microl Corporation: P.O.B. 267, Saipan, Mariana Islands 96950.

CO-OPERATIVES

Mariana Islands: Mariana Islands District Co-operative Association, Rota Producers, Tinian Producers Association.

Palau: Palau Fishermen's Co-operative, Palau Boatbuilders' Association, Palau Handicraft and Woodworkers' Guild.

Ponape: Ponape Federation of Co-operative Associations (P.O.B. 100, Ponape ECI, 96941), Ponape Handicraft Co-operative, Ponape Fishermen's Co-operative, Uh Soumwet Co-operative Association, Kolonia Consumers and Producers Co-operative Association, Kitti Minimum Co-operative Association, Kapingamarangi Copra Producers' Association, Metalanim Copra Co-operative Association, PICS Co-operative Association, Mokil Island Co-operative Association, Ngatik Island Co-operative Association, Nukuoro Island Co-operative Association, Kusaie Island Co-operative Association, Pingelap Consumers Co-operative Association.

Truk: Truk Co-operative, Faichuk Cacao and Copra Co-operative Association, Pis Fishermen's Co-operative, Fefan Women's Co-operative.

Yap: Yap Co-operative Association (P.O.B. 159, Colonia Yap 96943, Western Caroline Islands), Yap Shipping Co-operative Association.

Co-operative organizations have been set up for the sale of school supplies and sundries, one at the Truk High School and one at the Ponape High School.

TRANSPORT

ROADS

Macadam and concrete roads are found in the more important islands. Other islands have stone and coral surfaced roads and tracks.

SHIPPING

Most shipping in the Territory is government-organized. Six vessels are operated by Micronesia Interocean Lines Inc. and other private carrier services are being set up with government subsidies.

Micronesia Interocean Line Inc.: P.O.B. 468, Saipan, Mariana Islands 96950; f. 1968.

Marshall Islands Import-Export Co.: Marshall Islands District; service began 1956; carry more than half the inter-district trade; 2 motor vessels; deals with imports from U.S., Japan and Australia.

Ponape Federation of Co-operative Asscns.: P.O.B. 127, Kolonia, Ponape; inter-island tramp.

Saipan Shipping Co.: Mariana Islands District; services Saipan–Tinian–Rota–Guam and Northern Islands.

Transpacific Lines, Inc.: P.O.B. 468, Saipan.

Truk Transportation Co.: Box 99, Moen, Truk; f. 1967; inter-island tramp; Pres. MASATAKA MORI.

Yap Shipping Co-operative Asscn.: Palau and Yap; inter-island tramp.

CIVIL AVIATION

Air services in the Trust Territory is provided by *Air Micronesia*, a corporation which is jointly owned by Continental Air Lines, Aloha Air Lines, and the United Micronesia Development Association (U.M.D.A.).

Services: daily flight Guam–Saipan by Boeing 727-QC and/or DC-6 aircraft; four flights a week by DC-6 of B-727 from Guam to Yap–Palau; 4 times weekly by Boeing 727-QC from Guam to Ponape–Truk–Marshalls; Trust Territory now connected to Hawaii and Okinawa (Ryukyus) by this air service.

UNITED STATES VIRGIN ISLANDS

The U.S. Virgin Islands consist of three main islands (St. Thomas, St. John and St. Croix) and about 40 smaller islands (mostly uninhabited), situated at the eastern end of the Greater Antilles about 40 miles east of Puerto Rico in the Caribbean.

Recent History

The U.S. bought the Virgin Islands from Denmark in 1917, and they were administered through the Navy Department. In 1931 their administration was moved to the Department of the Interior and civilian as opposed to Naval Governors were appointed, usually of the same political allegiance as the President of the United States. The Democratic Party has been the majority party for many years, and Republican governors tended to be in conflict with the local Legislature, though over political rather than racial issues. In November 1970 the first gubernatorial election took place and was hotly contested by the three parties; the Republican incumbent, Melvin

Evans, retained office. 1971 was the tricentenary of Denmark's colonization of the Islands.

Since 1945 the Virgin Islands have become a popular tourist centre as well as a place of settlement for a rapidly increasing number of Americans. The tourist trade has brought a measure of prosperity, but at the same time, in conjunction with the increase in population, it has created serious social problems and a drastic labour shortage. The basic amenities have been unable to keep pace with the demand; there has been a sharp increase in crime, and the Black Power Movement, imported from America, has begun to make itself felt. Nearly a third of the population are aliens due to the importation of labour, and this has resulted in a serious problem for the U.S. Federal Immigration Service. At the same time, unless a regular supply of bona fide alien labour is established in most of the manual categories, the economy of the Islands is likely to receive a sharp set-back.

Area: 133 square miles.

Population (1970 census): St. Thomas 28,960, St. Croix 31,779, St. John 1,729; total 62,468 of whom more than 80 per cent are non-European.

Immigration: (est. total 1971 legally and illegally resident) 21,000; employed 16,000, of which 5,000 came from St. Kitts-Nevis-Anguilla; 2,840 from Antigua and 2,200 from Trinidad and Tobago.

FINANCE

United States currency: 100 cents = 1 U.S. dollar ($).

Coins: 1, 5, 10, 25 and 50 cents; 1 dollar.

Notes: 1, 2, 5, 10, 20, 50 and 100 dollars.

Exchange rates (April 1974): £1 sterling = U.S. $2.36; U.S. $100 = £42.35.

TWO-YEAR BUDGET
(1967–69 estimate—U.S. dollars)

Revenue				
Estimated Balance	.	.	.	500,000
General Fund	.	.	.	36,612,000
Matching Fund	.	.	.	12,000,000
Total Revenue	.	.	.	49,112,000

Expenditure			
Health	.	.	8,921,563
Education	.	.	8,896,662
Public Works	.	.	6,930,266
Public Safety	.	.	2,849,300
Welfare	.	.	2,713,343
Legislature	.	.	450,000
Commerce	.	.	1,716,726
Agriculture	.	.	2,044,868
Labour	.	.	431,056
Other Administrative Agencies	.	.	9,024,702
Total Expenditure	.	.	43,978,486

EXTERNAL TRADE
(U.S. $ million)

	1966	1967	1968	1969	1970	1971
Imports c.i.f.	.	138.2	172.2	260.2	327.2	410.6	551.9
Exports f.o.b.	.	56.3	92.3	153.9	200.0	262.2	327.1

Employment (1967): Mining and Manufacturing 1,969, Wholesale Trade 599, Retail Trade 3,954, Selected Services 2,945. (1971 est.) total labour force 38,000, of which 7,000 are in Government Service.

Agriculture: Some sugar is produced on St. Croix and vegetables on St. Croix and St. Thomas but most of the land is unsuitable for cultivation on a significant scale. Cattle are also raised on St. Croix, and meat is exported to Puerto Rico.

Fishing: Commercial fishing is on a small scale but there is considerable scope for game fishing, particularly for marlin.

Industry: The chief industries are tourism, watches, jewellery, metal articles and parts, rum distilling, textiles and petroleum products. Value of crushed stone produced in 1967 was $851,000.

Principal imports from U.S.A.: Food, building materials, motor vehicles, electrical equipment.

Principal exports to U.S.A.: Sugar cane, rum and gin, jewellery, watches, perfumery, woollen and worsted fabrics.

Tourism: Number of Tourists (1955) 90,000; (1968; 800,000; Money spent (1955) $7m.; (1968) $100m.) Hotel beds (1955) 1,351; (1968) 5,615.

Roads (number of vehicles: 1966): Cars 8,232, Lorries 1,920, Buses 120, Motorcycles and Scooters 407.

Shipping (1967): Vessels entered: St. Thomas 840, St., Croix 1,499; Cruise Ships arrivals (1955) 30; (1968) 300.

Civil Aviation (1966): Passengers: arrivals 436,775, departures 436,802.

EDUCATION
(1966)

	Schools	Teachers	Pupils
Public	.	26	359	10,850
Parochial	.	9	103	3,261
Private	.	2	22	208

THE CONSTITUTION

The government of the U.S. Virgin Islands is organised under the provisions of the Revised Organic Act of the Virgin Islands enacted by the Congress of the United States on July 22nd, 1954. Executive power was vested in a Governor, appointed by the President of the United States with the advice and consent of the Senate until 1968, when Congress passed an act providing for an elected Governor. The Governor appoints, with the advice and consent of the Legislature, the heads of the eleven executive Departments and may also appoint administrative assistants as his representatives on St. John and St. Croix. Legislative power is vested in the Legislature of the Virgin Islands, a unicameral body composed of fifteen Senators elected by popular vote. Legislation is subject to the approval of the Governor. Bills disapproved by the Governor may be passed over his veto by a two-thirds majority, but if a bill is vetoed twice by the Governor, it must be sent to the President of the United States for final approval or disapproval. All residents of the islands, who are citizens of the United States and aged over 21, have the right to vote in local elections. They do not send representatives to the Federal Congress nor participate in national elections. In January 1971, the first elected Governor assumed office and in April 1973 a Bill was passed allowing one non-voting delegate to be sent to the U.S. House of Representatives.

THE GOVERNMENT

Governor: MELVIN H. EVANS.

Lieutenant-Governor: DAVID E. MAAS.

Government Secretary: CYRIL KING.

Administrative Assistant for St. Croix: AUBREY ANDUZE.

Administrative Assistant for St. John: CARL NELTHROPE.

President of the Legislature: EARL B. OTTLEY.

Secretary of the Legislature: DAVID PURITZ.

The Senate: all fifteen seats are held by Democrats.

The eleven executive Departments (headed by Commissioners) are as follows: Agriculture, Labour, Education, Finance, Health, Property and Procurement, Public Safety, Public Works, Social Welfare and Commerce, Housing and Community Renewal.

POLITICAL PARTIES

Democratic Party: loosely connected with the Democratic Party in the U.S.; leader: Senator EARLE B. OTTLEY; 13,000 mems.

Republican Party: leader: MELVIN EVANS.

Independent Citizens Movement: leader: CYRIL KING.

JUDICIAL SYSTEM

District Court of the Virgin Islands: Local jurisdiction and jurisdiction of cases under Federal law; the judge and district attorney are appointed by the President of the United States with the advice and consent of the Senate. There is also one municipal court.

Judge of the District Court: Hon. ALMERIC L. CHRISTIAN (Chief Judge), Hon. WARREN H. YOUNG.

RELIGION

The population is mainly Christian. The main churches with followings in the Islands are the Roman Catholic, Anglican, Lutheran, Methodist, Moravian and Seventh-Day Adventists. There are also a number of Jews.

THE PRESS

Daily News: P.O.B. 644, St. Thomas; f. 1930; morning; Ind.; Editor ARIEL MELCHIOR; circ. 8,700.

Home Journal: P.O. Box 987, St. Thomas; f. 1950; evening except Mon.; Ind.; Editor EARLE B. OTTELY; circ. 2,000.

St. Croix Avis: P.O. Box 750, Christiansted; f. 1844; morning; Ind.; Man. Editor JEROME DREYER; circ. 1,790.

West End News: Frederiksted; f. 1912; morning; Ind.; Editor CEPHUS N. ROGERS; circ. 900.

RADIO AND TELEVISION

Caribbean Communications Corpn.: P.O.B. 2632 St. Thomas 00801.

H.R.H. Inc. (Station WIVI-STEREO): P.O.B. 310, Christiansted, St. Croix; commercial station; Pres. Mrs. HAZEL M. HIGDON; Vice-Pres. RAYMOND E. HIGDON; Gen. Man. WINONA L. PHAIRE.

Island Teleradio Service, Inc.: P.O. Box 1947, Charlotte Amalie, St. Thomas; commercial radio and TV stations; Pres. ROBERT MOSS.

Quality Telecasting Corpn.: Recovery Hill, Christiansted, St. Croix 00708; Man. R. BURTON.

Radio Station WSTA: P.O.B. 489, St. Thomas; commercial radio station; Gen. Man. A. C. OTTLEY.

Thousand Islands Broadcasting Corpn. WVWI: P.O.B. 5170, St. Thomas; commercial radio; Pres. R. E. NOBLE.

There were 75,000 television receivers and 16,500 radio receivers in 1971.

FINANCE

BANKING

Virgin Islands National Bank: 80 Kronprindsens Gade, Charlotte Amalie, St. Thomas 00801; affiliated to First Pennsylvania Banking and Trust Company of Philadelphia; f. 1935; cap. $400,000; dep. $135.0m. (1971); Pres. EDWARD C. BOWER.

Bank of America N.T. & S.A.: San Francisco; 1-B King St., Christiansted, St. Croix.

Bank of Nova Scotia: Charlotte Amalie, St. Thomas; Man. G. W. ROBINSON.

Barclays Bank D.C.O.: London; St. Thomas.

Chase Manhattan Bank, N.A.: New York; Charlotte Amalie, St. Thomas (4 brs.); Christiansted and Frederiksted, St. Croix (4 brs.); Cruz Bay, St. John.

First Federal Saving and Loan Association of Puerto Rico: St. Thomas branch: Veteran's Drive; Man. OSCAR A. HERNANDEZ; also a branch at St. Croix.

First National City Bank: St. Thomas.

INSURANCE

The principal American companies have agencies in the Virgin Islands.

TRADE AND INDUSTRY

St. Thomas-St. John Chamber of Commerce: Box 324, St. Thomas; Pres. HENRY WHEATLY.

St. Croix Chamber of Commerce: Christiansted, St. Croix; f. 1925; 450 mems.; Pres. VINCENT A. COLIANNI; Exec. Sec. JOHN K. THOMAS; publ. *Newsletter* (twice monthly).

TRANSPORT

ROADS

There are good roads on St. Thomas and St. Croix; the roads on St. John are being improved.

SHIPPING

Cruise ships and cargo vessels of the Alcoa Steamship Co., Atlantic Lines, Berwin Lines, Delta Line, Eastern Shipping Corporation, Florida Lines and Sea-Way Lines call at the Virgin Islands. Ships entering St. Thomas and Christiansted harbours can avail themselves of pilot services. A bi-monthly passenger service is maintained during the eight months tourist season between Miami and Charlotte Amalie.

CIVIL AVIATION

Antilles Air Boats: 39, Strand Street, Christiansted, St. Croix; inter-island seaplane services and connections with Puerto Rico and Marigot, St. Martin, FWI and Tortola, BVI.

There are international airports on St. Thomas and St. Croix., served by the following airlines: Caribair (Puerto Rico), Eastern Airlines, L.I.A.T. (Antigua) Pan Am, Prinair (Puerto Rico) and Trans Caribbean Airlines (U.S.A.).

TOURISM

Department of Commerce (Visitors' Bureau): Frederiksted (St. Croix); Office in New York: 16 West 49th St.; Office in Puerto Rico: 104 La Fortaleza, San Juan.

THE UPPER VOLTA

INTRODUCTORY SURVEY

Location, Climate, Language, Religion, Flag, Capital

Upper Volta is a landlocked state in West Africa surrounded by Mali, Niger, Dahomey, Togo, Ghana and the Ivory Coast. The climate is hot and mainly dry with temperatures averaging 27°C (83°F); humidity reaches 80 per cent in the south during the rainy season, which occurs between June and October but is often very short. French is the official language and there are three principal native tongues with many dialects. About 75 per cent of the population follow animist beliefs, some 20 per cent are Muslims and the remainder are Christians, chiefly Roman Catholics. The national flag (proportions 3 by 2) has three horizontal stripes of black, white and red. The capital is Ouagadougou.

Recent History

Formerly a province of French West Africa, Upper Volta became a self-governing Republic within the French Community in 1958, achieving full independence in 1960. In January 1966 Lt.-Col. (later Gen.) Sangoulé Lamizana deposed President Maurice Yaméogo, dissolved the National Assembly, suspended the constitution and assumed the position of Head of State. In December 1966 the Supreme Council of the Armed Forces announced that military rule would continue for four years. Restrictions on political activities were lifted in November 1969, and in June 1970 the Government introduced a new constitution which provided for a return to civilian rule after a four-year interim period of joint military and civilian administration. Elections for a 57-member National Assembly were held in December with the participation of all the political parties, and the *Union démocratique voltaïque* (UDV) won a majority of the seats. In January 1971 the President appointed as Prime Minister the UDV leader, Gérard Ouédraogo, under whom a government was formed a month later. This government aroused the opposition of the local chiefs, the trade unions and the students. In late 1973 differences between the Prime Minister and the Secretary-General of the UDV, Joseph Ouédraogo, led to calls for the Prime Minister's resignation but he refused to step down. Deadlock resulted between the Government and the National Assembly. In February 1974 the President, Gen. Lamizana, announced that the Army had assumed power. The National Assembly was dissolved and political activity banned. The new Government declared its intention of taking strenuous measures to deal with the critical economic situation.

Upper Volta follows a moderate foreign policy. The Republic has good relations with neighbouring countries and especially with Senegal, with whom agreements were signed in February 1973 on trade, industry and culture, together with a pledge to strive for West African economic union.

Government

In February 1974 the army assumed power and the June 1970 Constitution was suspended, the President dissolved the National Assembly and banned political activities. Freedom of the press, labour unions and worship were guaranteed. The establishment of a Government of National Renovation was promised, dedicated to social justice and the well-being of the people. Local administration is through eight "départements" divided and subdivided into small units.

Defence

Military service is compulsory and lasts for eighteen months. Liability for service lasts for twenty-eight years. Armed forces number 1,800, including an air force of 50, and there are also about 1,250 in the national guard and *gendarmerie*.

Economic Affairs

The economy is agricultural and most of the population are farmers or livestock-raising nomads. Settled agriculture is confined to the river valleys and oases and efforts are being made to extend the area of irrigated land. The chief crops are sorghum, millet, yams, beans, and maize, most of which are consumed within the country. Livestock, meat, poultry, hides, beans and karité nuts and butter are the principal exports. Several new projects financed by foreign aid and the UNDP were begun in 1973 to apply modern methods to agriculture and stock-rearing. However, lack of water, disease and soil erosion are constant problems. The main hope for future growth lies in the Liptako-Gourma development authority established in 1970 by the Upper Volta, the Niger and Mali to develop the mineral-rich area on their common borders. Its main projects are to improve infrastructure, to exploit the large deposits of manganese at Timbao, to mine phosphates for a fertilizer factory and limestone for a clinker factory, and to harness the River Niger for water supplies and hydro-electric power. By a policy of austerity, the economy has recovered remarkably since the country was near bankruptcy in 1966, and although 40 per cent of revenue comes from French aid, the country has enjoyed a budgetary surplus for many years. The Upper Volta remains, however, an exceptionally poor country even by Third World standards. The drought which began in 1971 and has continued into 1974 is having increasingly serious effects. A large part of the livestock herds has died and much of the population is on the brink of starvation. The Upper Volta has joined with other affected countries to organize the distribution of international aid.

It is a member of the Conseil de l'Entente, the OAU, CEAO, UMOA, OCAM and the Niger River Commission, and an associate member of the EEC.

Transport and Communications

The Abidjan-Niger railway, jointly operated with the Ivory Coast, extends for 517 km. into Upper Volta and gives an outlet to the sea at Abidjan (Ivory Coast). The first part of a tarred road to link Ouagadougou with the port of Tema (Ghana) was begun in 1972, and other major roads are being built or improved, especially in the northeast. There are about 17,700 km. of roads. of which over half are open all the year round. The international airports are at Ouagadougou and Bobo-Dioulasso, and there are

49 airfields used for internal transport. The national airline is Air Volta and the country is also a member of Air Afrique. In addition three foreign lines provide international flights.

Social Welfare

The Government provides hospitals and rural medical services. A special medical service for schools is in operation. There are three hospitals, which provide over 1,200 beds, 32 medical centres, 71 maternity clinics and 257 dispensaries, and an anti-tuberculosis centre has been established in Ouagadougou since 1970. There were 58 physicians, one for every 93,000 inhabitants, in 1970. An old-age and veterans' pension system was introduced in 1960, and extended workers' insurance schemes have been in operation since 1967.

Education

Education is free but not compulsory with about 10 per cent of children receiving some schooling. There is a Centre for Higher Education in Ouagadougou, and government grants are available for higher education in Europe and African universities. A rural radio service is being established to further general and technical education standards in rural areas.

Tourism

The principal tourist attraction is big game hunting in the East and South West and along the river banks of the Black Volta. There is a wide variety of wild animals in the game reserves. Between 1970 and 1971 tourist arrivals at hotels increased by 47 per cent to 6,369.

Visas are not required to visit Upper Volta by nationals of France, or, for visits of up to three months, by nationals of Belgium, the Netherlands and Luxembourg.

Sport

There is little organized sport but football and basketball are popular.

Public Holidays

1974: August 15th (Assumption), October 18th (Id ul Fitr, end of Ramadan), November 1st (All Saints' Day), December 11th (Proclamation of the Republic), December 25th (Christmas), December 26th (Id ul Adha).

1975: January 1st (New Year), January 3rd (January 1966 Revolution), March 26th (Mouloud, Birth of the Prophet), March 31st (Easter Monday), May 1st (May Day), May 8th (Ascension), May 19th (Whit Monday).

Weights and Measures

The metric system is in force.

Currency and Exchange Rates

100 centimes=1 franc de la Communauté financière africaine (CFA).

Exchange rates (April 1974):
1 franc CFA   =2 French centimes;
£1 sterling=579.75 francs CFA;
U.S. $1=245.625 francs CFA.

STATISTICAL SURVEY

AREA AND POPULATION

Area	Population
(sq. km.)	(1972 estimate)
274,122	5,541,000

PRINCIPAL TOWNS
(1970 estimates)

Ouagadougou (capital)	110,000	Kaya . . .	17,609
Bobo-Dioulasso . .	78,478	Ouahigouya . .	18,988*
Koudougou . .	41,200	Banfora . . .	8,500

* 1972 estimate.

MAIN TRIBES
(1970 estimates)

Mossi	2,604,480
Fulani	542,600
Lobi	379,820
Mandingo	374,394
Bobo-Dioulasso	363,542
Sénoufo	298,430
Gourounsi	287,578
Bissa	255,022
Gourmantché	244,170
Others	75,964

Births and Deaths: Average annual birth rate 49.4 per 1,000; death rate 29.1 per 1,000 (UN estimate for 1965–70).

EMPLOYMENT
Economically active population (1972–'000)

Total	Men	Women
2,797	1,350	1,446

More than 88 per cent of the labour force is in agriculture (FAO estimate for 1970).

AGRICULTURE

LAND USE, 1970
('000 hectares)

Arable Land	5,315
Under Permanent Crops	62
Permanent Meadows and Pastures	13,755
Forest Land	4,101
Other Land	4,147
Total Land Area	27,380
Inland Water	40
Total Area	27,420

Source: FAO, *Production Yearbook 1971.*

PRINCIPAL CROPS
(metric tons)

	1969	1970	1971	1972
Maize	60,000	55,000	42,000	37,996
Millet and Fonio	392,000	389,000	397,000	260,056
Sorghum	547,000	563,000	576,000	484,906
Rice (Paddy)	34,000	34,000	37,000	29,752
Sweet Potatoes and Yams	50,000*	52,000*	52,000*	n.a.
Cassava (Manioc)	41,000*	42,000*	n.a.	n.a.
Cow Peas	94,000*	96,000*	85,000*	n.a.
Other Pulses	80,000*	80,000*	80,000*	n.a.
Groundnuts (in shell)	71,000	68,000	68,000*	62,468
Cottonseed	18,000	16,000	23,000	20,000
Cotton (Lint)	12,000	11,000	15,000	12,000
Sesame Seed	3,800	6,300	6,300*	5,646
Tobacco	800*	800*	800*	n.a.

* FAO estimate.

Source: FAO, *Production Yearbook 1971*; and Direction de la Statistique et de la Mécanographie, Haut Commissariat au Plan, Ouagadougou.

LIVESTOCK
(FAO estimates—'000)

	1969–70	1970–71	1971–72
Cattle . .	2,800	2,900	2,958
Sheep . .	1,900	2,000	2,060
Goats . .	2,600	2,650	2,729
Pigs . . .	139	141	145
Horses . .	71	70	71
Asses . .	190	190	190
Camels . .	6	7	7

Chickens (1967–68 to 1970–71): 10,000,000 each year (official estimate).

Source: FAO, Production Yearbook 1971; and Direction de la Statistique et de la Mécanographie, Haut Commissariat au Plan, Ouagadougou.

LIVESTOCK PRODUCTS
(FAO estimates—metric tons)

	1968	1969	1970	1971
Cows' Milk	70,000	73,000	75,000	77,000
Goats' Milk	18,000	19,000	20,000	21,000
Beef and Veal* . . .	28,000	29,000	30,000	32,000
Mutton, Lamb and Goats' Meat* . .	13,000	14,000	14,000	14,000
Pork* . . .	4,000	4,000	4,000	4,000
Horse Meat . . .	2,300	2,300	2,300	n.a.
Poultry Meat . . .	7,300	7,200	7,900	n.a.
Edible Offal . . .	5,000	5,000	5,000	n.a.
Other Meat . . .	2,000	2,000	2,000	n.a.
Hen Eggs . . .	2,900	3,100	3,200	3,300
Cattle Hides . . .	2,232	2,250	2,250	n.a.
Sheep Skins . . .	120	126	180	n.a.
Goat Skins . . .	366	360	357	n.a.

* Meat from indigenous animals only, including the meat equivalent of exported live animals.

Source: FAO, Production Yearbook 1971.

FORESTRY
ROUNDWOOD REMOVALS
(cubic metres)

1969 . .	3,687,000
1970 . .	4,092,000
1971 . .	4,182,000

Source: FAO, Yearbook of Forest Products.

FISHING
(metric tons)

1969 . . .	5,000
1970 . . .	5,000
1971 . . .	5,000

Source: FAO, Yearbook of Fishery Statistics 1971.

INDUSTRY

	Unit	1969	1970	1971	1972
Soap	metric tons	2,711	2,301	2,786	2,854
Groundnut Oil . . .	,, ,,	630	377	884	852
Karité Butter . . .	,, ,,	1,222	945	843	858
Oil Cakes . . .	,, ,,	n.a.	454	1,167	1,176
Beer	hectolitres	57,923	59,243	65,194	n.a.
Soft Drinks . . .	,,	23,198	28,334	32,704	n.a.
Electric Power . . .	'000 kWh.	25,194	27,164	32,719	n.a.

FINANCE

100 centimes = 1 franc de la Communauté financière africaine.

Coins: 1, 2, 5, 10, 25, 50 and 100 francs CFA.

Notes: 100, 500, 1,000 and 5,000 francs CFA.

Exchange rates (April 1974): 1 franc CFA = 2 French centimes.

£1 sterling = 579.75 francs CFA; U.S. $1 = 245.625 francs CFA.

1,000 francs CFA = £1.725 = $4.071.

BUDGET
(million francs CFA)

REVENUE	1969	1970	1971*	EXPENDITURE	1969	1970	1971*
Direct Taxes	2,069	2,213	2,600	Current Budget	8,056	8,613	9,580
Import Duties		4,869	5,131	Capital Budget	1,554	1,588	940
Export Duties	6,525	213	213				
Other Indirect Taxes		1,566	1,926				
External Receipts	450	450					
Extraordinary Receipts	293	404	650				
Other Revenue	715	1,224					
TOTAL	10,052	10,939	10,520	TOTAL	9,610	10,201	10,520

* Estimates.

Source: UN Economic Commission for Africa, *Statistical Yearbook* 1972.

1972 Budget (million francs CFA): Revenue 10,833; Expenditure 8,858.

1973 Budget (million francs CFA): Revenue 11,726; Expenditure 9,525.

Second Development Plan (1972–75): Investment 62,133 million francs CFA; Rural Development 31.8 per cent, Modern Sector 20.4 per cent, Infrastructure 28 per cent.

EXTERNAL TRADE
('000 francs CFA)

	1967	1968	1969	1970	1971	1972
Imports	8,970,300	10,119,100	12,450,000	12,963,073	13,899,000	15,311,980
Exports	4,429,300	5,290,300	5,329,275	5,055,452	4,408,000	5,141,012

PRINCIPAL COMMODITIES
(million francs CFA)

IMPORTS	1970	1971	1972	EXPORTS	1970	1971	1972
Food, Beverages and Tobacco	2,526	2,402	3,406	Live Animals	1,578	1,602	2,099
Petrol and Oil	1,168	1,173	1,296	Hides and Skins	75	84	164
Other Raw Materials	832	n.a.	n.a.	Meat	204	264	193
Cotton, Textiles and Clothing	1,008	1,399	1,171	Cotton Fibre	1,298	834	1,021
Iron, Steel and Metal Products	1,044	760	7,974	Cotton Seed	194	76	94
Vehicles and Parts	1,626	1,649	715	Groundnuts (shelled)	318	447	373
Electrical Equipment	599	659	834	Karité Nuts and butter	601	277	132
Other Machinery	1,324	1,275	1,146	Sesame Seed	251	219	255
				Fruit and Vegetables	205	n.a.	111

PRINCIPAL COUNTRIES

Imports	1970	1971	1972		Exports	1970	1971	1972
Belgium and Luxembourg .	289	143	101		France	624	983	989
France	5,852	6,246	7,028		Rest of Franc Zone* . .	1,976	1,936	2,746
Rest of Franc Zone† .	3,371	3,434	3,202		Ghana	507	447	281
Federal Germany . .	785	767	702		Italy	454	440	364
Netherlands . . .	392	474	385		Japan	782	200	75
U.S.A.	590	714	378					

*About half of the franc zone trade is with the Ivory Coast.

TOURISM

	1970	1971
Tourist Arrivals . .	4,331	6,369

TRANSPORT

RAILWAYS

	1970	1971	1972
Passengers Carried . . .	2,565	2,631	2,595
Passenger-km. ('000) . .	380,942	454,854	519,542
Freight Carried ('000 metric tons) .	756	801	810
Ton-km. ('000) . . .	303,409	331,643	343,818

CIVIL AVIATION

	1970	1971	1972
Aircraft Arrivals and Departures . . .	2,690	3,317	3,416
Passenger Arrivals . .	15,983	16,140	18,605
Passenger Departures . .	12,295	14,446	19,442
Freight Unloaded (tons) .	747	845	837
Freight Loaded (tons) .	410	459	607

ROADS

	1969	1970	1971
Cars	5,824	6,428	7,063
Buses	144	156	162
Lorries	6,136	6,755	7,289
Tractors	389	415	318
Motor-bicycles . . .	1,292	1,393	1,459

EDUCATION

(1971–72)

	Schools		Students	
	Public	Private	Public	Private
Primary	609	28	107,643	4,404
Country Schools . .	783	—	26,992	—
Secondary . . .	25	33	5,267	3,730
Technical . . .	1	10	682	1,214
Teacher Training . .	3		1,212	—

The higher education centre (*Centre d'Enseignement Supérieur*) had 345 students in 1971–72.

In 1972–73 there were 108,000 pupils in primary schools and 10,400 in secondary schools.

Source: (except where otherwise stated) Direction de la Statistique et de la Mécanographie, Haut Commissariat au Plan, Ouagadougou.

THE CONSTITUTION

In February 1974 the army assumed power in the Upper Volta. President Lamizana made the following proclamation:

Article 1: The Constitution of June 21st, 1970, is suspended.

Article 2: The National Assembly is dissolved. A renovated institution in which all the vital forces of the nation will participate will be established.

Article 3: Political activities are formally banned.

Article 4: Freedom of the press and labour unions and freedom of worship which does not interfere with public order are guaranteed within the law.

Article 5: A National Renovation Government will be formed in the coming hours to help the Head of State, President of the Republic, and the Council of Ministers.

Article 6: The National Renovation Government will orient its action towards the well-being of our people and will adopt a policy based on our own means and will work for social justice for all.

Article 7: The army and the national security forces will ensure public order throughout the national territory.

Article 8: Any interference in our domestic affairs will not be tolerated.

Article 9: All international agreements and commitments will be respected.

THE GOVERNMENT

HEAD OF STATE

President: Gen. Sangoulé Lamizana.

COUNCIL OF MINISTERS

(April 1974)

President of the Council of Ministers and Minister of Justice: Gen. Sangoulé Lamizana.

Minister of the Interior and Security: Capt. Hounsouho Charles Bambara.

Minister of Foreign Affairs: Maj. Saye Zerbo.

Minister of National Defence and Ex-Servicemen: Col. Baba Sy.

Minister of Finance: Tiemoko Marc Garango.

Minister of Planning, Rural Development, the Environment and Tourism: Maj. Antoine Dakouré.

Minister of Trade, Industrial Development and Mines: Emmanuel Zoma.

Minister of Public Works, Transport and Town Planning: Capt. Mahamoudou Ouédraogo.

Minister of National Education: Ali Lankoandé.

Minister of Public Health and Social Affairs: Dr. Rasmane Sawadogo.

Minister of Civil Service and Labour: Guiliou Christophe Kam.

Minister of Information and Posts and Telecommunications: Lt.-Col. Bila Zagre.

Minister of Youth and Sports and Culture: Maj. Félix Tientaraboum.

Secretary of State for Justice: Capt. Bagnamou Bondé.

Secretary of State for Planning, Rural Development, the Environment and Tourism: Lt. Léonard Kalmogo.

SUPREME COUNCIL OF THE ARMED FORCES

Since 1966 the army has had the power to assume responsibility for making a final decision on State matters. It acts through a council consisting of army officers in the government, the Chief of Staff, staff-officers and regimental commanding officers. Its president is the Minister of National Defence.

DIPLOMATIC REPRESENTATION

EMBASSIES ACCREDITED TO THE UPPER VOLTA

(In Ouagadougou unless otherwise stated)

Algeria: Niamey, Niger.
Austria: Dakar, Senegal.
Belgium: Abidjan, Ivory Coast.
Bulgaria: Accra, Ghana.
Canada: Abidjan, Ivory Coast.
China, People's Republic: *Ambassador:* Tang-chih Hxieh.
Denmark: Accra, Ghana.
Egypt: Bamako, Mali.
Ethiopia: Abidjan, Ivory Coast.
France: B.P. 504; *Ambassador:* Paul Blanc.
Gabon: *Ambassador:* José Joseph Amiar.
Germany, Federal Republic: B.P. 600; *Ambassador:* Michael Schmidt.
Ghana: B.P. 212; *Ambassador:* Christian Charles Lokko.
Guinea: Bamako, Mali.
Hungary: Accra, Ghana.
India: Dakar, Senegal.
Italy: Abidjan, Ivory Coast.
Japan: Abidjan, Ivory Coast.
Korea, Republic: Abidjan, Ivory Coast.

Lebanon: Abidjan, Ivory Coast.
Mali: Abidjan, Ivory Coast.
Mauritania: Abidjan, Ivory Coast.
Morocco: Abidjan, Ivory Coast.
Netherlands: Abidjan, Ivory Coast.
Nigeria: Niamey, Niger.
Pakistan: Accra, Ghana.
Romania: Brussels, Belgium.
Senegal: Bamako, Mali.
Sierra Leone: Accra, Ghana.
Spain: Abidjan, Ivory Coast.
Sweden: Lagos, Nigeria.
Switzerland: Abidjan, Ivory Coast.
Tunisia: Abidjan, Ivory Coast.
U.S.S.R.: B.P. 643; *Ambassador:* Yakov Lazarev.
United Kingdom: Abidjan, Ivory Coast.
U.S.A.: B.P. 35; *Ambassador:* (vacant).
Viet-Nam, Republic: Abidjan, Ivory Coast.
Yugoslavia: Bamako, Mali.

Upper Volta also has diplomatic relations with the German Democratic Republic, the Ivory Coast, the Democratic People's Republic of Korea, Liberia and Luxembourg.

NATIONAL ASSEMBLY

The National Assembly was dissolved in February 1974. It is to be replaced by a National Consultative Council.

POLITICAL PARTIES

All political activity was formally banned in February 1974. The following parties were active at that date:

Groupement d'action populaire (GAP): Ouagadougou; f. 1966; a religious break-away faction from the UDV; Pres. Massa Nouhoun Sigué; Sec.-Gen. Saïdou Ouédraogo.

Mouvement de libération nationale (MLN): Ouagadougou; f. 1970; Sec.-Gen. Prof. Joseph Ki-Zerbo; publ. *L'Eclair* (fortnightly).

Parti du regroupement africain (PRA): Ougadougou; before February 1974 had 12 seats in the National Assembly and included two Ministers; Sec.-Gen. Laousséni-Ouédraogo.

Parti du regroupement national (PRN): Ouagadougou; Sec. Gen. Emmanuel Batiebo.

Parti travailliste voltaïque (PTV): Sec.-Gen. Georges Kaboré.

Union démocratique voltaïque (UDV): Ouagadougou; National section of the Rassemblement Démocratique Africain (R.D.A.); before February 1974 was majority party in the National Assembly and in the Council of Ministers; President Gérard Kango Ouédraogo; Sec.-Gen. Joseph Ouédraogo.

Union nationale des indépendents (UNI): Ouagadougou; f. 1973; Sec. Gen. Kassoum Kargougou.

Union pour la nouvelle république voltaïque (UNRV): f. 1970; break-away faction from PRA; Pres. Blaise Bassoleth; Sec.-Gen. Gansonré Bakary Traoré.

JUDICIAL SYSTEM

Supreme Court: Ouagadougou; has four chambers: Constitutional, Judicial, Administrative and Fiscal; Pres. Charles Traoré Sériba.

Other courts include a High Court of Justice, composed of deputies in the National Assembly; a Court of Appeal at Ouagadougou; and four courts of First Instance at Ouagadougou, Bobo-Dioulasso, Ouahigouya and Fada N'Gourma competent in criminal, commercial and civil law. For cases involving common law there is a court at Ouagadougou and several Magistrates' Courts in the *départements*.

In 1967 a Special Tribunal was set up under the jurisdiction of the Minister of Justice, to try crimes against internal and external security, crimes of embezzlement of public funds, corruption and theft.

RELIGION

Most people follow Animist beliefs. There are about a million Muslims and over 260,000 Catholics.

Roman Catholic Church: There are 85 parishes with 104 African priests and 350 non-African priests.

Archbishop of Ouagadougou: H. E. Cardinal Paul Zoungrana; B.P. 90, Ougadougou.

PRESS

DAILY

Bulletin Quotidien d'Information: B.P. 507, Ouagadougou; f. 1957; publ. by the Direction de l'Information; simultaneously published in Bobo-Dioulasso.

Bulletin Quotidien d'Information de la Chambre de Commerce: B.P. 502, Ouagadougou.

L'Observateur: Sonepress, Ouagadougou; f. 1973.

PERIODICALS

Bulletin Douanier et Fiscal: B.P. 502, Ouagadougou; 10 issues per year.

Bulletin mensuel de statistique: B.P. 374, Ouagadougou; published by National Statistics Office; monthly.

Carrefour Africain: B.P. 368, Ouagadougou; f. 1960; weekly; Government sponsored; Editor in Chief Alphonse Yaogho.

Courrier Consulaire de la Haute-Volta: B.P. 502, Ouagadougou; published by the Chamber of Commerce; monthly.

L'Eclair: MLN, Ouagadougou; fortnightly.

Journal Officiel de la République de Haute-Volta: B.P. 294, Ouagadougou; weekly.

Kibaré.

Le Soleil de Haute-Volta.

PRESS AGENCIES

Agence Voltaïque de Presse (A.V.P.): Ouagadougou; f. 1963 under UNESCO auspices.

Agence France-Presse: B.P. 391, Ouagadougou; Chief of Bureau Bernard Loth.

Tass also has a bureau in Ouagadougou.

RADIO AND TELEVISION

RADIO

Radio-Haute-Volta: B.P. 511, Ouagadougou; f. 1959; services in French and 13 vernacular languages; Dir. of Radio and Television Paul Ismael Ouédraogo; Dir. of Programmes Karim Konate. There is a second station at Bobo-Dioulasso.

There are 88,000 radio sets.

TELEVISION

Voltavision: B.P. 511, Ouagadougou; f. 1963; Government-owned; transmissions on two days a week; currently received only in Ouagadougou; public viewing centres are being set up; Dir. of Programmes O. Sanogoh.

There are about 3,000 television receivers.

FINANCE

(Amounts in francs CFA unless otherwise stated)

BANKS

Central Bank

Banque Centrale des Etats de l'Afrique de l'Ouest: 29 rue du Colisée, Paris 8e, France; B.P. 356, Ouagadougou; f. 1955; bank of issue of several West African states including Upper Volta; cap. 3,600m.; Pres. Edouard Kodjo; Gen. Man. Robert Julienne; Man. in Upper Volta Kassoum Congo; publs. *Notes d'information et statistiques* (monthly), *Rapport d'activité* (annual).

Banque Internationale pour le Commerce, l'Industrie et l'Agriculture de la Haute Volta: B.P. 8, Ougadougou.

Banque Nationale de Développement (B.N.D.): B.P. 148, Ouagadougou; f. 1961; cap. 355m., 63 per cent state-owned; Dir.-Gen. E. ZOMA.

Caisse Centrale de Coopération Economique: ave. de l'Indépendence, B.P. 529, Ouagadougou; Dir. RENÉ MALLORGA.

FOREIGN BANK

Banque Internationale pour l'Afrique Occidentale: 9 ave. de Messine, Paris 8, France; B.P. 362, Ouagadougou; branch at Bobo Dioulasso; Man. in Ouagadougou PIERRE GUIRIEC.

INSURANCE

Caisse de Compensation des Prestations Familiales: B.P. 333, Ouagadougou.

Several French insurance companies are also represented.

TRADE AND INDUSTRY

CHAMBERS OF COMMERCE

Chambre de Commerce, d'Agriculture et d'Industrie de la Haute-Volta: B.P. 502, Ouagadougou; Pres. ANDRÉ AUBARET; publ. *Bulletin Douanier et Fiscal, Courrier Consulaire.*

EMPLOYERS' ORGANIZATIONS

Syndicat des Entrepreneurs et Industriels de Haute-Volta: B.P. 446, Ouagadougou; Pres. KLÉBÉR JACOPIN.

Syndicat des Commerçants, Importateurs et Exportateurs (SCIMPEX): B.P. 552, Ouagadougou; mems. are commercial employers.

Syndicat d'Entreprises du Bâtiment et des Travaux Publiques: Ouagadougou.

Syndicat de Transportateurs Publiques: B.P. 198, Ouagadougou.

CO-OPERATIVE

SOVOLCOM: Ouagadougou; f. 1967 by the amalgamation of the Coopérative Centrale de Consommation and the government Office de Commercialisation; aims to supply peasants and sell their harvests.

TRADE UNIONS

Out of a total of 33,000 wage earners, trade union membership is about 12,500.

Comité inter-syndical: Pres. SALIF OUÉDRAOGO.

Confédération Africaine des Travailleurs Croyants (CATC): B.P. 445, Ouagadougou; f. 1950; 3,000 mems. in 10 affiliated unions; Pres. JOSEPH OUÉDRAOGO; Sec.-Gen. LUCIEN ZONGO.

Confédération nationale des travailleurs voltaïques (CNTV).

Fédération syndicale du commerce et de l'industrie.

Organization Voltaïque des Syndicats Libres (OVSL): B.P. 99, Ouagadougou; f. 1960 as Union Nationale des Syndicats des Travailleurs de Haute Volta; 2,500 mems. in 7 affiliated unions; affiliated to Int. Confed.

of Free Trade Unions; Sec.-Gen. FRANÇOIS DE SALLES KABORE.

Union Syndicale des Travailleurs Voltaïques (USTV): B.P. 381, Ouagadougou; f. 1958 as Union Générale des Travailleurs d'Afrique Noire; 4,300 mems. in 14 affiliated unions; affiliated to the All-African Trade Union Federation; Sec.-Gen. ZOUMANA TRAORÉ.

There are nine unaffiliated unions.

TRANSPORT AND TOURISM

TRANSPORT

RAILWAY

La Régie du Chemin de Fer Abidjan-Niger: B.P. 192, Ouagadougou; Head Office: Abidjan, Ivory Coast; 1,147 km. of track linking Ouagadougou via Bobo-Dioulasso with the coast at Abidjan (Ivory Coast); 517 km. of this railway are in Upper Volta.

It is planned to build a 360 km. extension to the Mali and Niger frontier and a branch line to the Tambao manganese deposits nearby.

ROADS

Compagnie Transafricaine: Bobo Dioulasso, B.P. 91.

Ghana-Upper Volta Road Transport Commission: Accra; set up to implement 1968 agreement on improving communications between the two countries.

There are about 9,000 km. of classified roads open all the year, including 4,450 km. of national roads, and also 8,000 km. of tracks not always passable in the wet season.

CIVIL AVIATION

There are two international airports at Ouagadougou and Bobo-Dioulasso, 49 small aerodromes and 13 private air fields.

Air Afrique: Upper Volta has a 6 per cent share; *see* under Ivory Coast.

Air Volta: rue Binger, B.P. 116, Ouagadougou; f. 1967; government airline with a monopoly of domestic services; fleet of one Piper Navajo, one Cherokee 6; Pres. F. LOMPO; Dir.-Gen. Adjoint R. MINGUEZ.

International services are also provided by Air Ghana, Air Mali and U.T.A.

TOURISM

Office National du Tourisme de la Haute-Volta: B.P. 624, Ouagadougou; Dir. PIERRE BANDÉE.

POWER

Société Voltaïque d'Electricité (VOLTELEC) S.A.: B.P. 54, Ouagadougou; f. 1968; cap. 80m. francs CFA of which 80 per cent state-owned.

Production and distribution of electricity and water. Dir. ROGER BECQUET.

URUGUAY

INTRODUCTORY SURVEY

Location, Climate, Language, Religion, Flag, Capital

Uruguay is the smallest of the South American republics. It lies on the north bank of the estuary of the River Plate with Brazil to the north and Argentina to the west. The climate is temperate with an average winter temperature of 14°–16°C (57°–61°F) and an average summer temperature of 21°–28°C (70°–82°F). The language is Spanish. There is no state religion but Roman Catholicism is predominant with Protestant minorities. The national flag (proportions 3 by 2) has nine horizontal stripes (five white and four blue, alternating) with a square white canton, containing a golden sun, in the upper hoist. The capital is Montevideo.

Recent History

Since the nineteenth century, the political scene has been dominated by two parties: the Colorados (Liberals) and the Blancos (Conservatives). Thanks to the progressive policies of José Batlle y Ordóñez, Colorado President from 1903 to 1907 and 1911 to 1915, Uruguay became the first welfare state in Latin America.

In December 1967, Jorge Pacheco Areco assumed the Presidency. His period in office was marked by massive increases in the cost of living, labour unrest and the spectacular and embarrassing exploits of the Tupamaro urban guerrilla movement. Despite the President's uncompromising attitude to the guerrillas, none of the country's problems had been solved when the presidential and congressional elections were held in November 1971. After accusations of fraud and a recount conducted by the army, the official Colorado candidate, Juan María Bordaberry Arocena, was declared the winner in February 1972, taking office in March. In order to suppress the Tupamaro guerrilla movement, the new Government passed a law declaring a "state of internal war" in April 1972. The army now took complete control of the campaign against the guerrillas. The increasingly independent and arbitrary role played by the army in civilian affairs brought about a clash between the President and the army chiefs in February 1973. After four days of confrontation, during which he lost the support of the navy, President Bordaberry accepted the army's "nineteen objectives" which included measures against corruption and for agrarian reform. This accession to army demands resulted in a conflict with Congress and led to the latter's dissolution and replacement by a Council of State of 25 members in June 1973. Trade union agitation caused serious economic disruption throughout 1973 and forced the Government to offer substantial pay rises to both state and private employees. Opposition campaigns to prevent the consolidation of military rule continued within Uruguay and outside, with renewed Tupamaro activity in the latter half of 1973. In December the Communist Party and 18 other left-wing groups were banned.

Government

Executive power is exercised by the President, elected every five years. He appoints a council of ministers to assist him. The legislative body is a Council of State of 25 members, which replaced the dissolved congress in June 1973. It is designed to control the executive and draft a plan for constitutional reform. There is also a National Security Council, under the chairmanship of the President, composed of selected cabinet ministers and the commanders-in-chief of the armed forces. For administrative purposes the country is divided into 19 Departments, each currently under the control of Government appointees.

Defence

The army consists of volunteers between the ages of 18 and 45 who contract for one or two years of service. There is a small navy, and an air force is being built up with U.S. assistance.

Economic Affairs

The raising of livestock, particularly cattle and sheep, is the chief source of wealth, 60 per cent of the area of the country being used for this purpose. The principal agricultural products are wheat, maize, sunflower seed, rice, linseed, barley and oats. In general, agricultural methods are not advanced. The principal industries are food processing (meat, sugar, milk, fruit, wine), hides and leather, textiles, construction, metallurgy and rubber, which is growing in importance. Most industries are concentrated in the Montevideo area; smaller centres are Paysandú, Río Negro, Lavalleja, Artigas and Colonia. Trade is mainly with the U.S.A. and the United Kingdom, the principal exports being wool and meat. Tourism ranks third after beef and wool as a major source of foreign currency. In April 1973 Uruguay signed a three-year non-preferential trade agreement with the EEC for promoting beef exports to Europe. A development plan formulated in 1973 aims at curbing inflation, stabilizing the economy in order to attract foreign investment, and improving productivity in the fishing and sugar cane industries. Two external loans have been granted for the building of fishing vessels and the improvement of port facilities.

Transport and Communications

The easy nature of the terrain and the small area of the country make for rapid communications within Uruguay and with neighbouring Argentina and Brazil. The railways are state-owned and there are 3,000 km. of track. The total length of roads is 44,800 km. of which 90 per cent can be used in all weathers. Inland waterways are an important means of transport and cargo and passenger services operate on the rivers Plate and Uruguay, which are navigable for 560 km. Internal air services link the principal towns and international services are provided by the national and a number of foreign airlines. A new airport was opened in Artigas in 1973.

Social Welfare

Uruguay is noted for its advanced scheme of social welfare, which covers professional accidents, industrial diseases, sickness, old age, maternity and child welfare.

Employment guarantees are in force and government subsidies are available for workers. The pension age is low (30 years' service, sometimes less); social charges faced by companies, however, are high (reaching 77½ per cent for the construction industry and more than 100 per cent in the wool industry and ports). There are also laws governing the protection of minors and women in employment, insurance against suspension from work, annual licences, redundancy payments, etc. Grants for families are provided by the Family Subsidies Fund.

Education

All education, including university education, is free and primary and the first stage of secondary schooling are compulsory. The programmes of instruction are the same in both public and private schools, but private schools are subject to certain state controls. According to the 1963 census, the rate of illiteracy was 8 per cent. There is one general and one technical university.

Tourism

The sandy beaches and lagoons on the coast and the forests of the interior with their variety of wild life and vegetation provide the main tourist attractions. Tourism is administered by the Ministry of Transport, Communications and Tourism.

Visas are not required to visit Uruguay for up to three months by nationals of Argentina, Austria, Belgium, Brazil, Canada, Chile, Denmark, Ecuador, Finland, France, Federal Republic of Germany, Greece, Israel, Italy, Liechtenstein, Luxembourg, Netherlands, Norway, Paraguay, Spain, Sweden, Switzerland, United Kingdom and Dependent Territories and United States. Citizens of the American Republics do not, as a rule, need a visa when proceeding to Uruguay direct from their own country.

Sport

Football is the most popular sport (Uruguay has won various Olympic and World titles), the main centre being in the capital, although there are stadia throughout the country. Basketball and horse-racing are important and rowing is popular on the rivers Uruguay and Negro. Swimming, cycling, boxing, volley-ball, tennis, golf, yachting and fishing are also practised.

Public Holidays

1974: August 25th (National Independence Day), October 12th (Discovery of America), November 2nd (All Souls' Day), December 8th (Blessing of the Waters), December 25th (Christmas Day).

1975: January 1st (New Year's Day), January 6th (Epiphany), April 19th (Landing of the 33 Patriots), May 1st (Labour Day), May 18th (Battle of Las Piedras), June 19th (Birth of General Artigas), July 18th (Constitution Day).

Many business firms close during Carnival week and Tourist week.

Weights and Measures

The metric system is in force.

Currency and Exchange Rate

100 centésimos=1 Uruguayan peso.

Exchange rate (April 1974):

£1 sterling=2,394 pesos;
U.S. $1=1,014 pesos.

STATISTICAL SURVEY

AREA AND POPULATION

AREA sq. km.	POPULATION July 1st, 1972	MONTEVIDEO (Capital), 1973 est.
177,508	2,956,000	1,450,000

OTHER TOWNS

POPULATION (1963 Census)

Salto	. . .	57,714	Melo . . .	33,741
Paysandú .	. .	51,645	Mercedes . . .	31,325
Rivera	. . .	41,266	Minas . . .	31,256
Las Piedras	. .	40,658		

ECONOMICALLY ACTIVE POPULATION*
(Census of October 16th, 1963)

	Male	Female	Total
Agriculture, Forestry, Hunting and Fishing .	176,888	6,790	183,678
Mining and Quarrying . . .	2,366	22	2,388
Manufacturing	159,758	58,594	218,352
Construction	54,964	433	55,397
Electricity, Gas, Water and Sanitary Services.	15,053	1,495	16,548
Commerce	103,352	26,087	129,439
Transport, Storage and Communication .	55,059	3,459	58,518
Services	134,463	134,976	269,439
Other Activities . . .	44,747	13,825	58,572
Total Economically Active .	746,650	245,681	992,331

* Excluding 19,936 persons seeking work for the first time.

AGRICULTURE

	1970–71		1971–72		1972–73	
	Area ('000 hectares)	Production ('000 metric tons)	Area ('000 hectares)	Production ('000 metric tons)	Area ('000 hectares)	Production ('000 metric tons)
Wheat	336.7	388.3	339.6	301.6	185.7	180.4
Linseed	91.5	41.9	73.6	42.5	47.7	26.3
Oats	82.9	78.0	69.0	60.0	65.0	57.4
Common Barley . . .	5.8	5.9	3.9	3.2	3.0	2.5
Brewing Barley . . .	35.6	39.5	48.1	28.6	26.1	25.8
Birdseed	3.2	1.8	4.0	2.1	2.3	1.5
Potatoes	24.0	150.4	23.3	106.1	n.a.	n.a.

Livestock (1970—'000): Cattle 8,564, Sheep 19,893, Goats 14,000,* Pigs 418, Horses 421.

* FAO estimate.

FINANCE

100 centésimos=1 Uruguayan peso.

Coins: 1, 5, 10, 20 and 50 pesos.

Notes: 50, 100, 500, 1,000, 5,000 and 10,000 pesos.

Exchange rates (April 1974): £1 sterling=2,361 pesos (buying rate) or 2,394 pesos (selling rate);
U.S. $1=1,000 pesos (buying rate) or 1,014 pesos (selling rate).

10,000 Uruguayan pesos=£4.177=$9.862 (selling rates).

CONSUMER PRICE INDEX
(1960=100)

	1970	1971	1972
Food .	3,347.3	4,167.2	8,077.2
Clothing .	6,498.4	8,420.1	13,606.6
Housing .	1,922.3	2,321.8	3,322.1
Miscellaneous	5,339.3	6,430.2	10,374.1
General Index	3,824.5	4,719.8	8,363.7

GOLD AND CURRENCY IN CIRCULATION
(at December 31st)

	1970	1971
Gold reserves (million U.S. $) . .	162	161
Notes and coins in circulation (million pesos) . . .	56,959	84,408

BALANCE OF PAYMENTS
(million U.S. $)

	1970			1971		
	Credit	Debit	Balance	Credit	Debit	Balance
Goods and Services:						
Merchandise	224.1	196.7	27.4	196.6	203.0	— 6.4
Non-monetary gold . . .	n.a.	n.a.	n.a.	0.2	—	0.2
Freight and insurance .	1.4	28.2	—26.8	1.0	30.9	—29.9
Transport	3.6	14.6	—11.0	4.1	15.7	—11.6
Travel	40.8	44.7	— 3.9	39.9	34.8	5.1
Investment income . . .	1.3	23.3	—22.0	0.8	22.4	—21.6
Government transfers . .	7.2	6.0	1.2	6.4	7.2	— 0.8
Other services . . .	3.4	10.0	— 6.6	4.5	11.3	— 6.8
Total	281.8	325.5	—41.7	253.5	325.3	—71.8
Transfer Payments	7.8	2.6	5.2	9.8	1.5	8.3
Current Balance . .	289.6	326.1	—36.5	263.3	326.8	—63.5
Capital and Monetary Gold:						
Non-Monetary Sector:						
Direct investment . .	n.a.	n.a.	n.a.	n.a.	n.a.	n.a.
Other private long-term .	n.a.	n.a.	n.a.	n.a.	n.a.	n.a.
Other private short-term .	20.1	2.9	17.2	75.7	3.9	71.8
Local government . .	—	0.2	— 0.2	—	0.3	— 0.3
Central government . .	7.2	8.5	— 1.3	26.4	9.2	17.2
Total . . .	27.3	11.6	15.7	102.1	13.4	88.7
Monetary Sector:						
Private institutions . .	2.4	—	2.4	—	41.0	—41.0
Central bank . . .	3.4	—	3.4	—	1.7	— 1.7
Total . . .	5.8	—	5.8	—	42.7	—42.7
Capital Balance . .	33.1	11.6	21.5	102.1	56.1	46.0
Net Errors and Omissions . .	—	26.5	—26.5	—	44.8	—44.8

EXTERNAL TRADE
(U.S. $'000)

	1966	1967	1968	1969	1970	1971	1972
Imports .	164,200	171,400	159,343	197,325	230,919	222,143	200,294
Exports .	185,800	158,600	179,158	200,336	232,709	205,693	214,077

PRINCIPAL COMMODITIES
(U.S. $'000)

IMPORTS	1971	1972	EXPORTS	1971	1972
Machinery in General and Parts	21,261.2	12,572.3	Meat and Meat Preparations .	69,630.6	102,909.0
Fuels and Lubricants . .	32,166.3	31,776.8	Wool	43,473.2	32,861.8
Motor Vehicles and Parts .	26,842.6	11,990.3	Textiles . . .	26,860.2	27,262.4
Drugs, Chemicals and Pharmaceuticals	9,378.8	9,752.7	Agricultural Products and Manufactures . . .	25,526.1	12,390.9
Buildings and Construction Material . . .	6,442.8	4,702.3	Hides and Animal Hair .	21,515.7	22,933.8
Fruit and Vegetables . .	2,863.2	1,808.1	Others . . .	18,686.8	15,719.5
Raw Materials . .	84,131.5	90,673.3			
Others . . .	27,729.7	23,735.5			
TOTAL . . .	222,192.8	200,294.1	TOTAL . . .	205,692.6	214,077.4

PRINCIPAL COUNTRIES
(U.S. $'000)

IMPORTS	1970	1971	1972	EXPORTS	1970	1971	1972
Argentina . .	26,291.1	31,926.8	27,490.3	Belgium . .	5,865.4	7,406.1	6,681.8
Brazil . .	35,074.2	35,782.1	35,929.5	Brazil . .	12,418.2	24,070.5	11,320.0
Germany, Federal Republic .	25,506.1	21,986.6	15,743.9	France . .	6,114.0	10,108.7	25,896.7
Italy. . .	5,895.5	6,319.7	4,535.4	Germany, Federal Republic . .	30,557.7	24,857.7	27,556.7
Kuwait . .	14,578.5	13,547.6	13,637.2	Greece . .	13,606.1	12,133.7	6,388.8
Nigeria . .	8,749.8	7,322.5	7,714.3	Italy. . .	22,865.3	22,186.0	14,719.3
United Kingdom	16,120.8	18,467.4	11,716.9	Netherlands .	20,088.0	14,915.5	13,844.1
U.S.A. . .	29,783.8	22,904.6	32,881.1	Spain . .	7,324.4	6,099.5	23,801.1
				United Kingdom	19,525.7	15,237.1	15,763.5
				U.S.A. . .	19,809.9	9,583.4	7,178.3
TOTAL (incl. others)	230,918.4	222,142.8	200,294.1	TOTAL (incl. others)	232,708.7	205,692.6	214,077.4

TRANSPORT
RAILWAYS

	1964	1965	1966
Passengers Carried . .	10,395,000	8,263,000	10,822,000
Freight Tonnage . .	1,762,000	1,500,000	1,600,000

Roads (1970 est.): 121,000 Cars, 88,000 Commercial Vehicles.

SHIPPING
MERCHANT FLEET
(gross registered tons—June 30th)

	1969	1970	1971
Oil Tankers . . .	42,000	71,000	93,000
Total . . .	112,000	141,000	163,000

INTERNATIONAL SEA-BORNE SHIPPING
(metric tons)

	1968	1969	1970
Goods Loaded . .	1,395,000	1,617,000	1,631,000
Goods Unloaded . .	2,543,000	2,235,000	2,412,000

CIVIL AVIATION
('000)

	1968	1969	1970
Kilometres Flown . .	2,995	2,284	2,315
Passenger-km. . .	75,118	66,455	63,207
Cargo ton-km. . .	211	171	285
Mail ton-km. . .	7	6	5

TOURISM
Foreign Exchange Receipts (1967): U.S. $50m. approx.
Number of Tourists (1967): 535,000.

EDUCATION
(1970)

	SCHOOLS	TEACHERS	STUDENTS
State Primary .	2,011	10,254	288,626
Private Primary .	301	1,755	65,470
State Secondary .	112	n.a.	109,187
Technical .	24	n.a.	8,806
University .	1	n.a.	6,442

Source: CENCI, Montevideo.

THE CONSTITUTION

The present constitution of Uruguay was ratified by plebiscite on November 27th, 1966, when the country voted to return to the presidential form of government after fifteen years of "collegiate" government. The main items of the Constitution are as follows:

General Provisions

Uruguay shall have a democratic republican form of government, sovereignty being exercised directly by the Electoral Body in cases of election, by initiative or by referendum, and indirectly by representative powers established by the constitution, according to the rules set out therein.

There shall be freedom of religion; there is no state religion; property shall be inviolable; there shall be freedom of thought. Anyone may enter Uruguay. There are two forms of citizenship: natural, being persons born in Uruguay or of Uruguayan parents, and legal, being people established in Uruguay with at least three years' residence in the case of those with family, and five years' for those without family. Every citizen has the right and obligation to vote.

Elections for both houses of the General Assembly, the President and Vice-President and for departmental governments shall take place every five years on the last Sunday in November, those elected to take office the following year.

Administration is by a central civil service, autonomous bodies and decentralized services.

Legislature

Legislative power is vested in the General Assembly, made up of two houses, which may act separately or together according to the dispositions of the constitution.

It is responsible for drawing up laws, establishing tribunals, arranging administration of justice and administrative litigation; expediting laws relating to the independence, security, peace and decorum of the Republic; laws relating to the protection of individual rights and development of agricultural, industrial and commercial life; it establishes fiscal contributions and the method of collection; it must approve accounts presented by the executive power, authorize the national debt, regulate public credit; it may declare war and approve or reject, by absolute majority, peace treaties and all international agreements made by the Executive; it has jurisdiction over the size of the armed force; it can create new Departments, by a two-thirds majority in each house; it can create or suppress public appointments; concede monopolies, by a two-thirds majority (absolute in the case of government departments).

It elects in joint session the members of the Supreme Court of Justice, of the Electoral Court, Tribunals,

Administrative Litigation and the Accounts Tribunal.

Elections for both houses, the President and the Vice-President and the departmental governments shall take place every five years on the last Sunday in November; sessions of the Assembly begin on March 15th each year and last until December 15th (October 15th in election years, in which case the new Assembly takes office on February 15th). Extraordinary sessions can be called only in cases of extreme urgency.

The Chamber of Representatives has 99 members elected by direct suffrage by the people according to the system of proportional representation, with at least two representatives to each Department. The number of representatives can be altered by law by a two-thirds majority in both houses. Their term of office is five years and they must be over 25 and natural citizens or legal citizens with 5 years' exercise of their citizenship. The members have the right to bring accusations against any member of the government or judiciary for violation of the Constitution or any other serious offence.

The Senate is made up of 30 members, elected directly by the people by proportional representation on the same lists as the representatives, for a term of 5 years. They must be natural citizens or legal citizens with seven years' exercise of their rights, and be over 30 years of age. The Senate is responsible for hearing any cases brought by the representatives and can deprive a guilty person of his post by a two-thirds majority.

The representatives and senators may not take any other paid state employment. The President and members of the Electoral Tribunal may not engage in party political activities. Any change in the civil or electoral registers requires a two-thirds majority in both Houses; any other changes require only a simple majority.

A permanent commission consisting of 4 senators and 7 representatives elected by proportional representation shall be set up to watch over the observance of the Constitution and laws of the land.

The Executive

Executive power is exercised by the President and the Council of Ministers. There shall be a Vice-President, who shall also be President of the General Assembly and of the Senate. The President and Vice-President are elected by simple majority of the people by means of the system of double simultaneous vote, and remain in office for five years. They must be over 35 and natural citizens of Uruguay.

The Council of Ministers is made up of the office holders in the 11 ministries or their deputies, and is responsible for all acts of government and administration. It is presided over by the President of the Republic who has a vote.

Autonomous bodies and decentralized services administer the industrial and commercial aspects of the country. A National Economy Council may be set up.

There shall be an Accounts Tribunal of 7 members, fulfilling the same qualifications as senators, designated by the General Assembly by a two-thirds majority. It shall be responsible to the General Assembly—both houses meeting together—for all matters connected with accounts of the State, government departments, autonomous bodies and decentralized services.

The Judiciary

Judicial Power shall be exercised by the Supreme Court of 5 members and by Tribunals and local courts; members of the Supreme Court must be over 40, natural citizens, or legal citizens with 10 years' exercise and 25 years' residence, and must be lawyers of 10 years' standing, 8 of them in public or fiscal ministry or judicature. Members serve for 10 years and can be re-elected after a break of 5 years. The Court nominates all other judges and judicial officials.

Administration

All government administration and services in the Departments except public security are in the hands of departmental juntas, consisting of 31 members, headed by a municipal intendant. Junta members must be over 23 years of age, natural citizens or legal with 3 years' exercise, and be a native of or resident in the Department for at least 3 years. They hold office for 5 years and election is by direct public vote. Intendants are elected under the same conditions as senators and hold office for 5 years, and may be re-elected once more, provided they resign at least three months before the elections. The intendant represents the Department in its relations with the state powers and with other Departmental governments.

There are also local juntas, with five members, in towns outside the departmental capitals.

There shall be an Administrative Litigation Tribunal, made up of 5 members; its jurisdiction is over all definitive administrative acts emanating from state and government bodies.

There shall be an Electoral Court, with direct jurisdiction over all electoral matters. It is made up of 9 members, 5 designated by the General Assembly by a two-thirds majority and 4 designated by the General Assembly as representatives of parties, two each from the two most popular lists.

THE GOVERNMENT

HEAD OF THE STATE

President: Juan María Bordaberry Arocena.

THE CABINET

(*May* 1974)

Minister of the Interior: (vacant).

Minister of Foreign Affairs: Dr. Juan Carlos Blanco.

Minister of Defence: Dr. Walter Ravenna.

Minister of Economy and Finance: Moisés Cohen (acting).

Minister of Public Health: Dr. Juan Bruno Irulegui.

Minister of Livestock and Agriculture: Benito Medero.

Minister of Industry and Commerce: José Echeverry Stirling.

Minister of Public Works: Ing. Eduardo Crispo Ayala.

Minister of Labour: Marcial Bugallo.

Minister of Education and Culture: Dr. Edmundo Narancio.

Minister of Transport, Communications and Tourism: Francisco María Ubillos.

Director of the Planning and Budget Office: Moisés Cohen.

DIPLOMATIC REPRESENTATION

EMBASSIES AND LEGATION ACCREDITED TO URUGUAY

(In Montevideo, unless otherwise stated)

(E) Embassy; (L) Legation.

Algeria: Buenos Aires, Argentina.

Argentina: Avda. Agraciada 3397; *Chargé d'Affaires a.i.:* José María Pico.

Australia: Buenos Aires, Argentina.

Austria: Sarandi 693, 3° piso; *Ambassador:* Dr. Karl Wolf.

Belgium: Leyenda Patria 2880, 4° piso; *Ambassador:* Jacques Vermer.

Bolivia: Río Branco 1320, 4° piso; *Chargé d'Afaires a.i.:* José Monje Roca.

Brazil: 20 de Setiembre 1415 (E); *Ambassador:* Arnaldo Vasconcellos.

Bulgaria: Rambla Mahatma Gandhi 647, 5° piso, Apdo. 11; *Chargé d'Affaires a.i.:* Stancho Popov.

Canada: Buenos Aires, Argentina (E).

Chile: Cuareim 1473 (E); *Ambassador:* Raúl Elgueta A.

China (Taiwan): Avda. Dr. Francisco Soca 1128, Apdo. 001; *Ambassador:* Tchen Hiong Fei.

Colombia: Hotel Victoria Plaza, oficinas 901/907 (E); *Ambassador:* Francisco Plata Bermúdez.

Costa Rica: Avda. Dr. Francisco Soca 1395-A, Apdo. 601; *Chargé d'Affaires a.i.:* Mrs. Ana Ramos de Pijuan.

Cyprus: Buenos Aires, Argentina.

Czechoslovakia: Luis B. Cavia 2996 (E); *Ambassador:* Dr. Václav Malosik.

Denmark: Buenos Aires, Argentina (E).

Dominican Republic: José Ellauri 581, Apdo. 901; *Ambassador:* Dr. Antonio Fernández Spencer.

Ecuador: 21 de Setiembre 2816 (E); *Ambassador:* Gonzalo Apunte Caballero.

Egypt: Antonio D. Costa 3469; *Ambassador:* Sayed Ezedeine Rifaat (also accred. to Paraguay).

El Salvador: Buenos Aires, Argentina (E).

Finland: Solís 1533 (E); *Ambassador:* Alexander Thesleff.

France: Avda. Uruguay 853 (E); *Ambassador:* Jean Français.

German Democratic Republic: Echevarriarza 3452; *Chargé d'Affaires a.i.:* Hermann Kuhne.

Germany, Federal Republic: Br. Artigas 1256 (E); *Ambassador:* Dr. Heinrich Adrian Loewe.

Greece: Buenos Aires, Argentina.

Guatemala: Dr. Francisco Soca 1397-A, 7° piso, Apdo. 703 (E); *Ambassador:* Lic. Juan Alfredo Rendón Maldonado.

Honduras: Br. España 2627; *Ambassador:* Dr. José Antonio Bermúdez Milla.

Hungary: Dr. Prudencio de Pena 2469; *Chargé d'Affaires a.i.:* Dr. János Domeny.

India: Buenos Aires, Argentina (E).

Indonesia: Juan Carlos Gómez 1492, 4° piso (E); *Ambassador:* M. Jusuf Ronodipuro.

Israel: Br. Artigas 1585; *Ambassador:* Dov Schmorak.

Italy: José B. Lamas 2857; *Ambassador:* Dr. Felice Benuzzi.

Japan: Rincón 487; *Ambassador:* Shiro Kondo.

Korea, Republic: Avda. Brasil 2385; *Ambassador:* Sung Wook Hong.

Lebanon: Francisco Solano Antuña 2882; *Chargé d'Affaires a.i.:* Dr. Raymond Heneine.

Lithuania: Ciudad de París 5836 6182 (L); *Chargé d'Affaires:* Anatolijus Grisonas.

Malta: Cerro Largo 761 (E); *Ambassador:* Maximilien Herode.

Mexico: Juncal 1305, 2° piso, oficinas 209/210; *Ambassador:* (vacant).

Netherlands: Leyenda Patria 2880, Apdo. 202 (E); *Chargé d'Affaires a.i.:* Joseph Zwalf.

Nicaragua: Juan M. Pérez 2996, Apdo. 201; *Ambassador:* Luis Mena Solorzano.

Norway: Buenos Aires, Argentina (E).

Pakistan: Buenos Aires, Argentina (E).

Panama: Juan Benito Blanco 1255, Apdo. 1101; *Ambassador:* Lt.-Col. Rodolfo U. Castrellón.

Paraguay: Colonia 1007, 1° piso; *Ambassador:* Atilio R. Fernández.

Peru: Cuareim 1537 (E); *Ambassador:* Fernán Cisneros.

Philippines: Buenos Aires, Argentina.

Poland: Jorge Canning 2389 (E); *Ambassador:* Mieczyslaw Wlodarek.

Portugal: Dr. Prudencio de Pena 2486; *Ambassador:* José M. de Noronha Gamito.

Romania: Lord Ponsonby 2550 (E); *Ambassador:* Valeriu Pop.

Senegal: Brasília, D.F., Brazil.

South Africa: Rincón 487, 2° piso; *Ambassador:* Pieter H. Jansen van Vuuren.

Spain: Avda. Brasil 2786 (E); *Ambassador:* Ramón Saenz de Heredia.

Sweden: Avda. Brasil 3079, 6° piso (E); *Ambassador:* Tore Högstedt.

Switzerland: Ing. Federico Abadie 2940, 11° piso; *Ambassador:* Roger Campiche.

Turkey: Buenos Aires, Argentina (E).

U.S.S.R.: Br. España 2471; *Ambassador:* Nikolai V. Demidov.

United Kingdom: Cerrito 420, 7° piso; *Ambassador:* Peter Oliver.

U.S.A.: Lauro Muller 1776; *Ambassador:* Ernest V. Siracusa.

Vatican: Br. Artigas 1270 (Apostolic Nunciature); *Apostolic Nuncio:* Mgr. Dr. Augustin J. Sepkinski.

Venezuela: Dr. Prudencio de Pena 2415; *Ambassador:* Dr. Luis Viloria Garbati.

Yugoslavia: 21 de Setiembre 2993 (E); *Ambassador:* Dragoljub Vujica.

Uruguay also has diplomatic relations with Morocco, New Zealand and Nigeria.

NATIONAL SECURITY COUNCIL
(Consejo de Seguridad Nacional)

Chairman: President Juan María Bordaberry Arocena.

Members: Minister of Defence, Minister of the Interior, Minister of Foreign Affairs, Minister of Economy and Finance, Director of the Planning and Budget Office, Commanders-in-Chief of the Navy, Army and Air Force.

Permanent Secretary: Gen. Gregorio Alvarez, Chief of the Joint General Staff.

COUNCIL OF STATE
(Consejo de Estado)

The Council of State came into existence in December 1973, replacing Congress which was dissolved in June 1973. It has 25 members and is to draft a plan for constitutional reform.

President: Senator Martín R. Echegoyen

POLITICAL PARTIES

The names of the two principal parties derive from the flags of the civil war of 1836, namely Blanco and Colorado. By tradition the Blanco Party is conservative and the Colorado Party more liberal.

Partido Colorado: The Party, which depends for its support largely on the urban area, controlled the executive for 94 years until the elections of 1958. It regained control in 1967 when Gen. Gestido became President under the new Constitution. In the elections of November 1971, there were two Colorado candidates. Juan María Bordaberry was the nominee of the outgoing President, Jorge Pacheco Areco. Jorge Batlle Ibáñez, leader of the splinter group, *Unidad y Reforma*, obtained fewer votes than Sr. Bordaberry and his votes were added to the Bordaberry vote for the purposes of selecting the President.

Partido Nacional (*Blanco*): The Party, with its substantially rural support, won the 1958 and 1962 elections but lost in 1966. In 1971 the Party's presidential candidate was Wilson Ferreira Aldunate, who was narrowly defeated.

Frente Amplio: This coalition was formed to fight the 1971 election and represented all shades of left-wing opinion. Its candidate was Líber Seregni.

Partido Demócrata Cristiano (PDC): formerly *Unión Cívica del Uruguay*; f. 1962; Pres. Arq. Juan Pablo Terra.

Partido Comunista: Leader José Luis Massero; Sec.-Gen. Rodney Arismendi.

Partido Socialista: Sec.-Gen. José Cardozo.

JUDICIAL SYSTEM

The Supreme Court of Justice has original jurisdiction in constitutional, international and admiralty cases and is the court of cassation for cases in which the decision has been altered or modified in lower appeal courts. It consists of five judges elected by the General Assembly. These hold office for ten years, and can be re-elected only after a five-year interval.

Supreme Court of Justice: Calle Ibicuy 1310, Montevideo; Pres. Dr. Rómulo Vago.

There are four *Courts of Appeal*, each with three judges.

In Montevideo there are 18 *Courts of the First Instance* (also dealing in commercial matters), 3 financial courts, 5 criminal instruction courts, 6 crime courts (formerly correctional courts), 2 juvenile courts and 1 customs court.

In the interior of the country there are Departmental Courts in the capitals of each of the 19 departments and also in other important towns; there are Justices of the Peace in each of the 226 judicial sections.

RELIGION

Under the Constitution, the Church and the State were declared separate and toleration for all forms of worship was proclaimed. Roman Catholicism predominates.

THE ROMAN CATHOLIC CHURCH

Metropolitan See: Arzobispado, Calle Treinta y Tres 1368, Montevideo; Most Rev. Carlos Parteli.

Suffragan Sees:

Canelones: Rt. Rev. Orestes S. Nuti Sanguinetti.

Florida: Rt. Rev. Humberto Tonna.

Maldonado: Rt. Rev. Antonio Corso.

Melo: Rt. Rev. Roberto Cáceres.

Mercedes: Rt. Rev. Enrique L. Cabrera Urdangarín.

Minas: Rt. Rev. Edmondo Quaglia Martínez.

Salto: Rt. Rev. Marcelo Mendiharat.

San José: Rt. Rev. Luis Baccino.

Tacuarembó: Rt. Rev. Miguel Balaguer.

PROTESTANT CHURCHES AND ASSOCIATIONS

Anglican-Methodist Church: Christ Church, Calle Reconquista 522, Montevideo; f. 1844; mems. approximately 200 families; Minister-in-Charge: Rev. Jonas E. White.

Federación de Iglesias Evangélicas del Uruguay: San José 1457, Montevideo; Sec. Marcos Rocchietti.

Iglesia Adventista (*Adventist*): Castro 167, Montevideo.

Iglesia Bautista (*Baptist*): Sierra y Paysandú, Montevideo.

Iglesia Evangélica Valdense (*Evangelical*): Avda. 8 de Octubre 3037, Montevideo.

THE PRESS

Censorship regulations are in force and include the prohibition of reports on the internal security situation. Many newspapers and periodicals suffer temporary closures.

DAILIES
MONTEVIDEO

Acción: Avda. General Rivera 3303; Colorado-Batllista; evening; Editors Julio M. Sanguinetti, Juan Adolfo Singer; circ. 65,000.

B.P. Color: San José 1116; f. 1878; mid-day; Dir. Edgardo Sason; circ. 30,000.

El Debate: J. C. Gómez 1380; f. 1931; morning; Herrera Nationalist; Editor WASHINGTON GUADALUPE; circ. 65,000.

El Día: Avda. 18 de Julio 1299; f. 1886; morning; Colorado-Batllista; Editor JOSÉ PEREIRA GONZÁLEZ; circ. 80,000.

El Diario: Bartolomé Mitre 1275; f. 1923; evening; Colorado Independent; Editor Dr. EUGENIO BAROFFIO; circ. 170,000.

Diario Español: Cerrito 551-555, Apdo. 899; f. 1905; morning (except Monday); Democratic-Republican; Editor MANUEL MAGARIÑOS; circ. 35,000.

Diario Oficial: Florida 1178; f. 1905; morning; publishes laws, official decrees, parliamentary debates and legal transactions; Dir. OSVALDO BUONO (publ. at the Govt. Printing Office).

Frente: San José 1116; f. 1969; left-wing.

Gaceta Comercial: Pl. Independencia 717; f. 1916; morning (except Sunday); Dir. MILTON SANS; Editor MARIO A. RAINERI; circ. 8,500.

La Mañana: Bartolomé Mitre 1275; f. 1917; morning; Colorado Independent; Editor Dr. CARLOS MANINI RÍOS; circ. 45,000, Sundays 120,000.

El País: Cuareim 1287; f. 1918; morning and evening; Independent-Blanco; Dirs. DANIEL RODRÍGUEZ LARRETA, MARTÍN AGUIRRE and ENRIQUE BELTRÁN; circ. 120,000.

El Plata: Pl. Libertad 1164; f. 1914; evening; Independent-Blanco; Dirs. JOSÉ ANTONIO RAMÍREZ, ALFREDO GARCÍA MORALES; circ. 90,000.

El Popular: Avda. 18 de Julio 948, 2° piso; morning; organ of the Central Committee of the Partido Comunista; Dir. EDUARDO VIERA.

Primera Hora: Juncal 1317; Dir. Ing. GUZMÁN ACOSTA Y LARA.

The Southern Star: Bartolomé Mitre 1361; non-partisan, in English; Editor RICHARD M. BUNZL.

La Tribuna: f. 1879; Blanco; circ. 75,000.

Vida Marítima: Apdo. 517; f. 1918; evening; commercial; Dir. RICARDO SERRANO.

PROVINCIAL DAILIES

COLONIA

El Ideal.

La Colonial.

FLORIDA

El Heraldo: f. 1919; evening; circ. 7,000.

MERCEDES

Acción: f. 1935; Editors F. FERNÁNDEZ and T. BALARINI; circ. 3,000.

El Día: Dir. JUAN JOSÉ LABADIE.

El Radical: Editor JUAN CARLOS GUIMARAENS.

PAYSANDÚ

El Telégrafo: 18 de Julio 1027; f. 1910; morning; independent; Dir. FERNANDO M. BACCARO; circ. 10,000.

PUNTE DEL ESTE

Punte del Este.

ROCHA

Ecos del Este.

La Palabra: Dir. CARLOS N. ROCHA.

SALTO

La Prensa: f. 1942; Editor ALFONSO CARDOZO; circ. 5,000.

Tribuna Salteña: J. Suárez 71; f. 1906; morning; Dir. M. J. LLANTADA; circ. 51,000.

SAN JOSÉ

Aquí Está: f. 1952; Monday to Friday with a monthly revue; Dir. ARIEL TARÓ CHABALGOÏTY.

PERIODICALS

MONTEVIDEO

Azus y Blanco.

Boletín Comercial: Colón 1580; monthly.

Boletín Informativo del Ministerio de Hacienda: monthly, commerce and statistics.

Comunidad: Catholic weekly; Editor ELISEO SOSA CONSTANTINI.

Gacetilla Austral: Coronel Alegre 1340; f. 1950; monthly; bibliography; Dir. CARLOS M. RAMA.

La Justicia Uruguaya: 25 de Mayo 555.

Marcha: Bartolomé Mitre 1414; f. 1939; weekly; independent; Dir. CARLOS QUIJANO; Editor HUGO ALVARO.

Montevidean: Ituzainago 1522; f. 1951; weekly; English; Editor Mrs. ILMA LEWIS.

Municipales: Treinta y Tres 1289.

Nacion.

Ovum: La Cruz de Carrasco, Casilla 2454; cultural; Editor CLEMENTE PADÍN.

Revista Militar y Naval: 25 de Mayo 279.

9 de Febrero.

PRESS AGENCIES

Agencia Nacional de Informaciones (A.N.I.): Montevideo; f. 1945.

FOREIGN BUREAUX

ANSA: Plaza Cagancha 1356, 2° piso, Montevideo; Chiefs AGUSTÍN FERNÁNDEZ CHAVES, SANDRO COLOMBO.

AP: Bartolome Mitre 1275, Montevideo; Correspondent FRANCISCO QUINTANS.

UPI: Avda. 18 de Julio 1224, 2° piso, Montevideo; Chief HÉCTOR MENONI.

DPA, Prensa Latina, Reuters and Tass also have bureaux in Montevideo.

PRESS ASSOCIATION

Asociación de Prensa Uruguaya: Plaza Cagancha 1356, Montevideo.

PUBLISHERS

MONTEVIDEO

Editorial Aguilar: Andes 1406; general.

Editorial Alfa: Cludadela 1393; f. 1957; literature, history; Dir. LEONARDO MILLA.

Librería y Distribuidora América Latina: 18 de Julio 2089; politics, economics, sociology.

Editorial Arca SRL: Colonia 1263; f. 1963; Man. Dir. A. RAMA; general literature.

Ediciones de la Banda Oriental: Yi 1364; Man. Dir. H. RAVIOLO; history, education, social science.

Barreiro y Ramos, S.A.: J. C. Gómez 1436; general; Dir. GASTÓN BARREIRO ZORRILLA.

Cenci-Uruguay: Misiones 1361; f. 1956; economics, statistics; principal officers LADISLAO VERTESI, CARLOS CANTA, Dr. ROBERTO PALAGYI; publs. *Aranceles de Aduana, Boletines y Estudios de Industrias en los países de la ALALC, Anuarios Estadísticos de Importación y Exportación, "EC-CO" Economía y Comercio de los países Iberoamericanos*, etc.

Editorial Ciencias: Duvimioso Terra 1461; medicine.

Librería Delta Editorial: Avda. Italia 2817; f. 1960; Man. Dir. A. Breitfeld; medicine, humanities.

Librería-Editorial Amalio M. Fernández: 25 de Mayo 477; f. 1951; law.

Fundación de Cultura Universitaria: 25 de Mayo 537, Casilla 1155; f. 1963; educational and scholarly.

Hemisferio Sur: Alzáiban 1328; f. 1966; agronomy and veterinary science.

Editorial Medina: Gaboto 1521; general.

Editorial Mentor: Uruguay 1325.

A. Monteverde & Cía S.A.: 25 de Mayo 577; educational.

Mosca Hnos.: 18 de Julio 1574; religion.

Nativa Libros SRL: Avda. Uruguay 1783; f. 1964; Man. Dir. V. Rovetta; politics.

Ediciones Pueblos Unidos: Tacuarembó 1494; f. 1943; Man. Dir. A. Pascale; general.

Editorial Tauro SRL: Misiones 1290; f. 1966; educational and social sciences.

Association

Cámara Uruguaya del Libro: Calle Ibicuy 1276, 1° piso, oficina 4, Montevideo; Sec. Marcos Medina Vidal; Man. Enrique F. Melantoni.

RADIO AND TELEVISION

RADIO

Dirección Nacional de Comunicaciones: Sarandi 472, Montevideo; Dir. Ing. Haroldo R. Paglieta.

Servicio Oficial de Difusión Radioeléctrica (SODRE): Mercedes 823, Montevideo; non-commercial; government owned; Tech. Dir. A. Silva.

Radio América: Pl. Independencia 846, Montevideo; non-commercial; Dir. L. Svirski.

Radio Ariel: Germán Barbato 1472, Montevideo.

Radio Carve: Mercedes 973, Montevideo; f. 1928; Dirs. Raúl Fontaina.

Radio El Espectador: Soriano 1287, Montevideo; Dir.-Gen. H. Amengual.

Radio Fénix: Canelones 1969, Montevideo; Dir. M. Racioppi.

CX4 Radio Rural: 18 de Julio 1513, Montevideo; Man. R. Barreto.

Commercial radio stations in the Montevideo area total 19 and there are stations in all but two of the 19 departments, with a total of 49.

In 1970 there were 1,081,000 radio receivers in Uruguay.

TELEVISION

Canal 9 del Este: Punta Ballena, Maldonado; commercial; Dir. F. Elices.

Monte Carlo TV: Avda. 18 de Julio 1855, Montevideo; commercial; Channel 4; Dir.-Gen. H. Romay Salvo.

Río Uruguay TV: Zorilla y Argentina, Fray Bentos; commercial; Dir. Daniel Romay Salvo.

Rosario Televisión: Avda. 18 de Julio 1855, Montevideo; commercial; Channel 8; Dir. A. W. Romay Salvo.

Saeta: Dr. Lorenzo Carnelli 1234, Montevideo; commercial; f. 1956; Pres. Raúl Fontaina; Dir. Jorge de Feo.

Servicio Oficial de Difusión Radioeléctrica (SODRE): Colorado 2362, Montevideo; f. 1961; state-owned.

Tele-Rocha: Avda. O. de los Santos 105, Rocha; commercial; Dir. Francisco Elices.

Televisora Larranaga, S.A.: Enriqueta Compte y Rique 1276, Montevideo; commercial; Pres. Carlos E. Scheck; Gen. Man. H. Scheck.

Televisora Melo: Montevideo 723, Melo; commercial; Channel 12; Dir. R. D. Lucas.

There were 305,000 TV sets in 1972.

Asociación Nacional de Broadcasters Uruguayos (A.N.D.E.B.U.): Calle Yi 1264, Montevideo; f. 1933; 94 mems.; Pres. Dr. Luis Alberto Solé; Sec. Walter Espiga; publ. *Memorándum Mensual*.

FINANCE

(cap. = capital; p.u. = paid up; dep. = deposit; m. = million; res. = reserves; amounts in pesos)

BANKING

Banco Central: Paysandú 1469, Montevideo; f. 1967; note-issuing bank, also controls private banking; Pres. Dr. Jorge Echevarría Leunda.

Banco de la Republica Oriental del Uruguay: Cerrito y Zabala, Montevideo; f. 1896; a state institution; cap. 1,500m.; Pres. Ing. Jorge Seré del Campo; Vice-Pres. Col. Abdón Raimúndez; Sec. Dr. Oscar Goldie Arenas.

Banco Hipotecario del Uruguay (*State Mortgage Bank*): Plaza de la Constitución, Montevideo; f. 1892; Pres. Edison Mozart Fradiletti.

Banco de Previsión Social: Mercedes 1852, Montevideo; autonomous service of the state; co-ordinates state welfare services and organizes social security; Pres. Dr. Julio C. Espínola.

Principal Commercial Banks

Montevideo

Banco Comercial: Cerrito 400; f. 1857; cap. 500m., dep. 41,723m. (Sept. 1973); Pres. Julio F. Braga Salvañach; Gen. Mans. Yamadú d'Elia, Horacio Porteiro.

Banco de Cobranzas: Sarandi 402; f. 1889; cap. 99.7m. (June 1970); Gen. Man. Jorge Anselmi.

Banco de Crédito: 18 de Julio 1451; f. 1908; cap. 65m., dep. 10,587m. (Dec. 1972); Pres. José Aldao.

Banco de Montevideo: Rincón esq. Misiones; f. 1941; cap. 228m., dep. 12,053m. (June 1973); Pres. Dr. Bernardo Supervieille; Gen. Man. Carlos Langwagen.

Banco del Plata: Zabala 1427; f. 1959; cap. 50m., res. 125m. (Sept. 1971); Pres. Jaime Querol Cladera; Gen. Man. Eduardo Rocca Couture.

Banco Financiero Sudamericano, S.A.: Rincón 550; f. 1910; Pres. Dr. Nilo Berchesi; Man. Carlos A. Tejería.

Banco Internacional: Zabala 1463; f. 1952; cap. and res. 112m., dep. 344m. (Jan. 1973); Man. Edmundo Martínez Peña.

Banco Israelita del Uruguay: Convención 1271; f. 1938; cap. 2m.; Pres. Bernardo Konicheckis.

Banco La Caja Obrera: 25 de Mayo 500; f. 1905; cap. 150m., dep. 19,045m. (Dec. 1972); Pres. Alberto Fernández Goyechea; Gen. Man. José Luis Cavezas.

Banco Mercantil del Río de la Plata: Zabala 1532; f. 1915; cap. 152.2m., res. 539m. (1970); Pres. Dr. Jorge Peirano Facio.

Banco Popular del Uruguay: 25 de Mayo 402; f. 1902; Pres. Arq. Carlos García Arocena.

Banco Rural: Avda. 18 de Julio 1317; f. 1957; cap. 17m.; Gen. Man. Luis O. Pérez Molea.

Unifín de Bancos del Uruguay: Calle 25 de Mayo 401; cap. and res. 662m., dep. 14,343m. (June 1973); Pres. C. Varela Collazo; Gen. Man. Leonidas Halarewicz.

Durazno

Banco de Durazno: Eusebio Píriz 850; f. 1914; Pres. Ernesto J. Filippini; Man. Hugo L. Despaux.

Florida

Banco de Florida: Independencia 718; f. 1951; Pres. Alcides V. Dos Santos; Man. Luis Medeglia.

San José

Banco de San José: 18 de Julio 509; f. 1909; cap. 18.5m.; Pres. Dr. Luis A. Sarazola; Man. Mario Pereda.

Paysandú

Banco del Litoral: 18 de Julio 1084; f. 1938; cap. 65m., dep. 4,870m. (Dec. 1972); Pres. Dr. Miguel Saralegui; Man. Tómas Sánchez.

Foreign Banks in Montevideo

Banco do Brasil: Rio de Janeiro; 25 de Mayo 628; Man. Laraje Cidade.

Banco Holandés Unido: Amsterdam; 25 de Mayo 501; Man. in Montevideo D. B. Baarslag.

Bank of America N.T. and S.A.: San Francisco; 25 de Mayo 552.

Bank of London and South America, Ltd.: London; Bank of London and South America Building, Zabala 1500, Apdo. 204; Resident Man. M. St. G. Johnston.

Banque Française et Italienne pour l'Amérique du Sud: Paris; Rincón 500.

Dresdner Bank A.G.: Frankfurt; Avda. 18 de Julio 1455, 6° piso.

First National City Bank: New York; Cerrito y Misiones, Casilla 690.

Development Bank

Banco de Producción y Consumo: Uruguay 883, Montevideo.

BANKERS' ASSOCIATION

Asociación de Bancos del Uruguay (*Bank Association of Uruguay*): Rincón 468; f. 1945; 27 mem. banks; Man. J. E. Oreggioni Pons; publ. *Resumen de los principales aspectos de la actividad económica del Uruguay* (annual).

STOCK EXCHANGE

Bolsa de Valores de Montevideo (*Stock Exchange*): Edificio de la Bolsa de Comercio, Misiones 1400; f. 1867; 80 mems.; Pres. José María de Cores; publs. *Boletín Diario de Operaciones y de Cierre del Mercado Bursátil, Información Oficial* (stock and shares information, quarterly), *Panorama del Mercado Bursátil* (annual), *Informe Anual.*

INSURANCE

Montevideo

Banco de Seguros del Estado (*State Insurance Organization*): Avda. Agraciada esq. Mercedes, Casilla 473; f. 1911.

Since the establishment of the State Insurance Organization in 1912 it has had a monopoly of certain types of insurance and no new companies are allowed to be set up.

La Uruguaya, S.A.: Florida 1251; f. 1900; Pres. Martín de la Force; Vice-Pres. Dr. Jorge Echevarría Liunda; Sec. Moises Hazán.

TRADE AND INDUSTRY

NATIONAL CHAMBERS OF COMMERCE

(Montevideo)

Cámara Nacional de Comercio (*National Chamber of Commerce*): Edificio de la Bolsa de Comercio, Misiones 1400; f. 1867; 760 mems.; Pres. Ing. Carlos R. Vegh Garzón; Sec. Gustavo Vilaró Sanguinetti; publ. *Memoria Anual.*

Cámara Mercantil de Productos del País (*Chamber of Commerce for Local Products*): Avda. General Rondeau 1908; f. 1891; 415 mems.; Pres. Antonio Otegui.

There are chambers of commerce in the following fields: shops and stores; agricultural and chemical products and seeds. There are associations or chambers of importers of: ironmongery; agricultural machinery; sewing machines; automobile parts and spares; electrical and radio articles; motor vehicles; motor cycles; office and school equipment; paper and cardboard; pharmaceutical specialities; photographic equipment; pumps; medical and scientific apparatus.

FOREIGN CHAMBERS OF COMMERCE

Montevideo

Cámara de Comercio Belgo-Uruguaya de Montevideo Casilla 666; f. 1935; 101 mems.; Pres. Claude Bragard; publ. *Bulletin Informatif* (quarterly).

Cámara de Comercio de los EE. UU. en el Uruguay: Rincón 723; f. 1935; 400 mems.; Pres. John H. Wells; Sec. Julio C. Brusa; publ. *Boletín Informativo* (fortnightly in Spanish and English).

Cámara de Comercio Francesa de Montevideo: Soriano 1203; f. 1882; 120 mems.; Pres. René Irion; Vice-Pres. Gilbert Mizrahi; Sec.-Gen. Fernand Hareau.

Cámara de Comercio Italiana del Uruguay: Paysandú 816.

Cámara de Comercio Suizo-Uruguaya: Avda. Agraciada 1641, 4° piso; f. 1944; 99 mems.; Pres. Luis A. Danero; Vice-Pres. Carlos J. Joos; publ. *Boletín* (monthly).

Cámara de Comercio Uruguayo-Alemana: Zabala 1379.

Cámara de Comercio Uruguayo-Argentina: Avda. 18 de Julio 1018; f. 1939; 200 mems.; Pres. José C. Cadenazzi.

Cámara de Comercio Uruguayo-Brasileña: Avda. 18 de Julio 984; f. 1917; 210 mems.; Pres. Antonio Otegui.

Cámara de Comercio Uruguayo-Británica: Avda. Agraciada 1641, 2° piso; f. 1935; Pres. Helios Maderni; Sec. José W. Maiztegui.

Cámara de Comercio Uruguayo-Chilena: 25 de Mayo 622.

Cámara de Comercio Uruguayo-Israelí: Buenos Aires 484.

Cámara Oficial Española de Comercio, Industria y Navegación: Calle Treinta y Tres 1315.

INTERNATIONAL TRADING ASSOCIATION

Consejo Interamericano de Comercio y Producción (*Inter-American Council of Commerce and Production*): Edificio de la Bolsa de Comercio, Misiones 1400, Montevideo; f. 1941; 507 mems.; Pres. John P. Phelps, Jr.; Sec.-Gen. Carlos Ons Cotelo; publs. *Boletín Informativo*, *Libre Empresa* (bi-monthly), *Informes y Documentos*.

GOVERNMENT ORGANIZATIONS
Montevideo

Administración Nacional de Combustibles Alcohol y Portland (ANCAP): Agraciada y Paysandú; is an autonomous government organization (f. 1931) concerned with the transport, refining and sale of crude petroleum and petroleum products, and the manufacture of alcohol, spirits, cement and sugar; owns research laboratories in Pando-Canelones, an agricultural experimental station in Juanicó and a sugar-factory and sugar-beet farms in Salto; Pres. Ing. Bertrand Grüss Dassain.

Frigorífico Nacional: Andes 1470; f. 1929; concerned with processing of meat and sub-products for internal consumption and export; monopoly in supply of Montevideo; Pres. Bernardo Ferreira Avila.

Obras Sanitarias del Estado (OSE): José Martí 3379; f. 1952; processing and distribution of drinking water, sinking wells, supplying industrial zones of the country; Pres. Dr. José Fernández Caiazzo.

Servicio Oceanográfico y de Pesca (SOYP): Julio H. y Obés 1467; autonomous body concerned with exploiting rivers and seas of the country; fishing, fish processing and sales, sealing, conservation of marine fauna; Dir.-Gen. Julio C. Franzini.

Usinas y Teléfonos del Estado (UTE): Paraguay 2431; autonomous state body; sole purveyor of electricity and telephones; owns a hydro-electric centre at Rincón del Bonete on the Río Negro; Pres. Ulises Pereira Reverbel.

EMPLOYERS' ORGANIZATIONS
Montevideo

Cámara de Industrias del Uruguay (*Chamber of Industry*): Avda. Agraciada 1670, 1° piso; f. 1898; Pres. Edgardo Héctor Abellá; Sec. Ing. Quim Luis C. Bonomi; publs. *Guía Industrial*, *Boletín Informativo*.

Comisión Patronal del Uruguay de Asuntos Relacionados con la O.I.T. (*Commission of Uruguayan Employers for Affairs of the ILO*): Edificio de la Bolsa de Comercio, Misiones 1400; f. 1954; mems. Cámara Nacional de Comercio, Cámara de Industrias, Asociación Comercial del Uruguay; Sec. and Man. Gustavo Vilaró Sanguinetti.

Asociación de Importadores y Mayoristas de Almacén (*Importers' and Wholesalers' Association*): Edificio de la Bolsa de Comercio, Misiones 1400; f. 1926; 38 mems.; Pres. José Luis Braba; publ. annual report.

Asociación Rural del Uruguay: Uruguay 864; f. 1871; 1,600 mems.; Pres. Ing. Francisco Haedo Terra; publ. *Revista Mensual*.

Federación Rural: 18 de Julio 965; f. 1915; 1,463 mems.; Pres. Ing. Antonio M. Durán Rubio.

TRADE UNIONS

All trade union activity has been under strict control since June 1973, when the central organization (*Confederación Nacional de Trabajadores*), which claims some 400,000 members, was declared illegal.

TRANSPORT

Ministerio de Transporte, Comunicaciones y Turismo: Agraciada 1409, Montevideo; formed under terms of constitution of 1967; exercises control over all state forms of transport: railways, airline, river and maritime fleets, urban transport system in Montevideo; also exercises some control over private transport companies; the Municipal Intendancies are responsible for urban and departmental transport.

RAILWAYS

Administración de los Ferrocarriles del Estado—AFE: La Paz 1095, Casilla 419, Montevideo; f. 1952; state organization; 2,976 km. of track (1,435mm. gauge) connecting all parts of the country; the system includes four lines formerly under British ownership; there are connections with the Brazilian network; Pres. Col. Martín E. Guarino.

ROADS

Uruguay has 44,800 km. of good roads, among the best in South America, which connect Montevideo with Colonia and Mercedes on the Río Negro, with the interior of the country as far as Paso Toros, and go eastwards, through Minas and Treinta y Tres, almost to the Brazilian frontier. Another road connects the holiday resorts, starting at Montevideo and ending at Punta del Este. The international bridge of the Yaguaron River, connecting the city of Yaguaron (Brazil) with Río Branco (Uruguay), is open. Long-distance motor buses and lorries ply in certain areas in competition with the trains.

Automóvil Club del Uruguay: Avda. Agraciada 1532, Montevideo; f. 1918; 14,777 mems.; Pres. Eduardo Iglesias Montero; Sec. Dr. Francisco Devincenzi.

INLAND WATERWAYS

Compañía Uruguaya de Navegación y Transportes Aéreos S.A.: Plaza Independencia 811, Montevideo; owns two vessels of 1,000 tons each; operates cargo services on the River Plate, and the Uruguay and Paraná rivers.

There are about 1,250 km. of navigable waterways, which provide an important means of transport.

A hydrofoil service to Buenos Aires was inaugurated in 1962.

SHIPPING

Administración Nacional de Puertos: Rambla Franklin D. Roosevelt 160, entre Macial y Guaraní, Montevideo.

Administración Nacional de Combustibles, Alcohol y Portland (ANCAP): Agraciada y Paysandú, Montevideo; Pres. Ing. Bertrand Grüss Dassain; tanker services, also river transportation.

Prefectura Nacional Naval: Rambla Roosevelt, Montevideo; Sec. Yamandu E. Legazcue.

Alamar (Asociación Latinoamericana de Armadores): 25 de Mayo 572, Montevideo; f. 1963 in Chile; private consultative organization with legal status in Chile and Uruguay; represents 65 Latin-American private and government shipowners from 11 Lafta countries; total tonnage registered: 4,215,891 d.w.t.; Pres. Jorge O. Petterson; Gen. Sec. Jorge Medina C. (Uruguay).

Dodero: Buenos Aires; Montevideo; passenger services between Argentina and Uruguay.

Uruguay's merchant fleet totalled 108,560 g.r.t. in 1967.

The following foreign shipping lines have offices in Montevideo:

Argentine, Bank, Blue Star, Brodin, Columbus, Compagnie Maritime Belge, Cia. Chilena, Delta, Greek South America, Hamburg-South American, Havenlijn, Houlder Brothers, Italia, Ivaran, Johnson, Lamport and Holt, Linea "C", Messageries Maritimes, Moore-McCormack, Nopal, O.S.K. Line, Rotterdam-South America, Royal Interocean, Royal Mail, Société Générale de Transports Maritimes, Torm, Westfal-Larsen, Ybarra.

CIVIL AVIATION

Domestic Airlines

Primeras Líneas Uruguayas de Navegación Aérea (P.L.U.N.A.): Colonia 1021 y Agraciada, Montevideo; f. 1936; operates internal services and services to Argentina and Paraguay under management of Uruguayan Air Force; Dir.-Gen. Col. Manuel E. Buadas; Traffic Man. Víctor Bello; fleet: 5 Viscount 700, 10 DC-3.

The following foreign airlines also serve Uruguay: Aerolíneas Argentinas, Air France, Alitalia, Austral (Argentina), Avianca, Canadian Pacific, Cruzeiro do Sul (Brazil), Iberia, KLM, LAN (Chile), Líneas Aéreas Paraguayas, Lufthansa, Pan American, Sabena, SAS, Swissair, Varig (Brazil).

TOURISM

Ministerio de Transporte, Comunicaciones y Turismo: Agraciada 1409, Montevideo; created by constitution of 1967, replacing former Comisión Nacional de Turismo; responsible for all aspects of tourism: lodgings and hotels, entertainments, fairs, price controls, etc.; visitors come mainly from Argentina and Brazil; revenue from tourism amounts to some U.S. $50m. a year; development plans include publishing more tourist literature and establishing tourism promotion offices in Argentina (eight offices in provincial capitals) and Brazil (four new offices); Minister Francisco María Ubillos; the Ministry maintains overseas offices in São Paulo and Porto Alegre, Brazil.

Comisión Nacional de Turismo: 18 de Julio 845, Montevideo.

Asociación Uruguaya de Agencias de Viajes Internacionales —AUDAVI: Hotel Victoria Plaza, oficina 502, Montevideo; Pres. Herbert Buencristiano.

ATOMIC ENERGY

Comisión Nacional de Energía Atómica: Sarandí 430, 3° piso, Montevideo; f. 1955; Pres. Dr. Alfonso C. Frangella; publ. *Boletín*.

Instituto de Endocrinología "Prof. Dr. Juan C. Mussio Fournier" del Ministerio de Salud Pública: Hospital Pasteur, Larravide 74, Montevideo; Dir. Prof. Dr. José M. Cerviño.

Instituto de Física: Parque Rodo, Montevideo; Dir. W. S. Hill.

Instituto de Investigación de Ciencias Biológicas: Avda. Italia 3318, Montevideo; Dir. Prof. Clemente Estable.

Instituto de Oncología: Avda. 8 de Octubre 3265, Montevideo; Prof. Dr. Alfonso Frangella.

Laboratorio MC³: Avda. 8 de Octubre 2874, Montevideo; medical application of radio isotopes; Dir. Dr. Walter S. Hill.

Universidad de la República: Apto. de Investigaciones Nucleares, Avda. J. Herrera y Reissig 565, 2° piso, Montevideo; atomic research in the faculties of engineering; chemistry and medicine; reactor physics; economics of nuclear power; design of research facilities including research reactor.

UNIVERSITIES

Universidad de la República: Avda. 18 de Julio 1824, Montevideo; 2,982 teachers, 16,500 students.

Universidad del Trabajo del Uruguay: Calle San Salvador 1674, Montevideo.

VENEZUELA

INTRODUCTORY SURVEY

Location, Climate, Language, Religion, Flag, Capital

The Republic of Venezuela ("Little Venice") lies on the north coast of South America and is bordered by Colombia to the west, Guyana to the east and Brazil to the south. The climate varies with altitude from tropical to temperate, the average temperature in Caracas being 21°c (69°F). The language is Spanish. There is no state religion, but most of the population are Roman Catholics. The national flag (proportions 3 by 2) has three horizontal stripes of yellow, blue and red, with seven five-pointed white stars, arranged in a semi-circle, in the centre of the blue stripe. The state flag has, in addition, the national coat of arms in the top left-hand corner. The capital is Caracas.

Recent History

Colonel (later Gen.) Marcos Pérez Jiménez seized power in December 1952 and took office as President in 1953. He remained in office until 1958 when he was overthrown by a military junta under Admiral Wolfgang Larrazábal. President Rómulo Betancourt was elected in the same year. In 1961 the Constitution now in force was promulgated and three years later President Betancourt became the first Venezuelan President to complete his term of office. Dr. Raúl Leoni was elected President in December 1963 and took office in March 1964. Supporters of ex-President Pérez staged an abortive military uprising in 1966. Dr. Rafael Caldera Rodríguez, elected in December 1968, became Venezuela's first Christian Democratic President in March 1969. He succeeded in stabilizing the country politically and economically, although political assassinations and abductions committed by underground organizations continued into 1974. In the elections held in December 1973 Carlos Andrés Pérez, candidate of *Acción Democrática*, the main opposition party, was chosen as successor to President Caldera. He took office in March 1974.

Government

Venezuela is a Federal Republic consisting of 20 states, a Federal District and two Federal Territories, each under a Governor. Executive power is vested in the President who is elected for a five-year term by universal suffrage and has wide powers. The legislative organ is Congress, consisting of a Senate and Chamber of Deputies. Both Houses of Congress are elected by universal suffrage.

Defence

Military service is compulsory for two years between ages 18 and 45. The strength of the army is 24,000 men and there is a small navy (including a body of marines) and air force.

Economic Affairs

Oil, of which Venezuela is one of the world's leading producers, is the country's greatest asset. Production in 1973 averaged some 3.3 million barrels per day. Income from oil in 1974 is expected to reach 42,000 million bolívares. Production from the old oil concessions in and around Lake Maracaibo is likely to stop in the mid-1980s. Other oil fields have been found (notably the Orinoco oil belt, thought to contain about 700,000 million barrels) but exploitation has not begun yet, owing to production difficulties and pressure from a strong conservationist faction in the country. Concessions to foreign companies expire in 1983. Bills for the nationalization of the industry were introduced by opposition parties in the Senate early in 1974, and the Government has since declared its intention of complete nationalization by the end of 1974 with appropriate compensation paid.

Although it contributes a large proportion of the country's revenue, the oil industry employs only 24,000 people, and with unemployment estimated at eight per cent, industrial diversification is a high government priority. Two liquefied natural gas plants are planned and in 1971 an 859 million bolívares contract was signed with a Belgian-German consortium for the construction of a steel rolled-products plant. A petro-chemical complex has been established at El Tablazo on Lake Maracaibo with foreign participation. Other important minerals found in Venezuela are iron-ore, bauxite, gold, coal, manganese, diamonds and copper. In 1971 the *Programa Integral de Desarrollo Agrícola* was announced. It is designed to raise the living standards and output of 63,000 rural families at a cost of U.S. $181.3 million. The new Government has promised large-scale investment in agriculture and measures to halt the flow of labour from rural areas to the towns. The country's chief crops are maize, coffee, cocoa, rice and cotton. Cattle farming is becoming increasingly important.

The first stage of the Guri dam project, begun in 1964, was completed in November 1968 and has a capacity of 525,000 kW. When the project is finally completed towards 1990, it will have a capacity of 6 million kW from 24 generators and will be one of the largest in the world; the cost is estimated at U.S. $73 million.

Venezuela is a member of the Andean Group, LAFTA, the OAS and OPEC.

Transport and Communications

The length of railway track is 175 km., and a 20-year National Railway Plan, inaugurated in 1950, has been extended. There are over 40,000 km. of all-weather roads. A 310 km. highway links Venezuela with Brazil. The River Orinoco is navigable for about 1,120 km. and there are steamer services on Lake Maracaibo. Internal air services are well developed and international air transport is provided by three national and a number of foreign airlines.

Social Welfare

Labour legislation protects workers and there are benefits for accidents, sickness and old age. A modified insurance scheme was introduced in 1967, entitling insured workers and their dependents to medical assistance, pensions etc.

Education

Primary education is free and compulsory between the ages of 7 and 13. By 1971 there were 10,491 primary schools with 1,918,655 pupils. Secondary education, received by 564,167 pupils in 1971, lasts for four years with a further year for admission to higher education. There are eight state and three private universities.

Tourism

The mountain peaks and the many forests and lakes form the main tourist attractions. Angel Waterfalls (3,212 feet) are reputed to be the highest in the world. In 1969 a state organization, CONAHOTU, was set up to promote tourism.

Visas are required by all visitors to Venezuela.

Sport

Football, tennis, golf, baseball and basketball are the most popular sports. Bullfighting also has a large following.

Public Holidays

1974: August 15th (Assumption), October 12th (Discovery of America), November 1st (All Saints' Day), December 8th (Immaculate Conception), December 17th (Death of Bolívar), December 24th–25th (Christmas), December 31st (New Year's Eve).

1975: January 1st (New Year's Day), January 6th (Epiphany), March 19th (St. Joseph), March 28th–31st (Easter), April 19th (Declaration of Independence), May 1st (Labour Day), May 8th (Ascension), May 29th (Corpus Christi), June 24th (Army Day), June 29th (St. Peter and St. Paul), July 5th (Independence Day), July 24th (Birth of Simón Bolívar).

Weights and Measures

The metric system is in force.

Currency and Exchange Rates

100 céntimos = 1 bolívar.

Exchange rates (April 1974):

£1 sterling = 10.15 bolívares.
U.S. $1 = 4.30 bolívares.

STATISTICAL SURVEY

AREA AND POPULATION

AREA (sq. km.)	POPULATION* (Census of November 2nd, 1971)				
	Total	Caracas (capital)	Maracaibo	Barquisimeto	Valencia
916,500	10,721,522	1,035,499	650,002	334,333	367,154

* Excluding Indian jungle inhabitants.

STATE POPULATIONS AND CAPITALS
(1971 Census)

Federal District	1,860,637	Caracas	1,035,499
Anzoátegui	506,297	Barcelona	76,410
Apure	164,705	San Fernando	38,960
Aragua	543,170	Maracay	255,134
Barinas	231,046	Barinas	56,329
Bolívar	391,665	Ciudad Bolívar	103,728
Carabobo	659,339	Valencia	367,154
Cojedes	94,351	San Carlos	21,029
Falcón	407,957	Coro	68,701
Guárico	318,905	San Juan	37,817
Lara	671,410	Barquisimeto	334,333
Mérida	347,095	Mérida	74,214
Miranda	856,272	Los Teques	62,747
Monagas	298,239	Maturín	121,662
Nueva Esparta	118,830	La Asunción	6,334
Portuguesa	297,047	Guanare	37,715
Sucre	469,004	Cumaná	119,751
Táchira	511,346	San Cristóbal	152,239
Trujillo	381,334	Trujillo	25,921
Yaracuy	223,545	San Felipe	43,801
Zulia	1,299,030	Maracaibo	650,002
Federal Territories			
Amazonas	21,696	Puerto Ayacucho	10,417
Delta Amacuro	48,139	Tucupita	21,417
TOTAL	10,721,522		

BIRTHS, MARRIAGES, DEATHS

	BIRTHS	MARRI-AGES	DEATHS
1969 . . .	397,003	58,130	67,784
1970 . . .	392,583	60,128	68,493
1971 . . .	406,476	65,772	70,478
1972 . . .	406,061	69,217	73,530

EMPLOYMENT
('ooo workers)

	1969	1970	1971*	1972*
Agriculture . . .	706	646	655	773
Petroleum . . .	24	24	23	}40
Mining . . .	9	36	32	
Manufacturing . .	496	561	573	482
Construction . .	176	146	186	226
Electricity . . .	31	45	45	52
Transport . . .	182	200	211	216
Commerce . . .	521	562	584	521
Services . . .	732	799	806	783
Total . . .	2,877	3,019	3,115	3,093
Unemployed . .	204	194	192	208
Labour Force . .	3,081	3,213	3,307	3,301

* Estimates.

AGRICULTURE
('ooo metric tons)

	1969	1970	1971	1972
Maize . . .	670.3	709.9	713.5	506.3
Rice (in hull) . .	243.8	226.2	175.4	164.6
Beans . . .	25.0	23.8	27.2	21.3
Wheat . . .	0.4	0.5	0.5	0.6
Potatoes . . .	123.7	125.0	130.7	109.3
Sesame . . .	82.5	125.6	n.a.	n.a.
Raw Cotton . .	41.0	39.9	42.4	57.2
Coffee . . .	60.6	60.5	62.8	40.4
Cocoa . . .	23.5	18.8	19.3	16.7
Tobacco . . .	9.5	11.9	13.6	12.5
Bananas . . .	980.2*	280.7	298.4	996.9*
Sugar Cane . .	4,216.8	5,052.0	5,450.0	5,475.5

* 'ooo stems.

LIVESTOCK
(head)

	1968	1969	1970	1971
Cattle . .	908,408	942,729	984,373	1,044,859
Pigs . .	835,136	856,002	972,848	979,754
Goats . .	382,410	383,847	385,320	386,880
Sheep . .	46,267	45,416	45,696	46,045
Poultry ('ooo) .	56,776	59,442	64,960	67,889

MILK, MEAT AND FISH PRODUCTION

		1969	1970	1971	1972
Milk	'ooo litres	888.4	1,018.3	1,109.3	1,048.5
Meat	'ooo metric tons	334.6	348.2	346.0	274.5
Fish	,, ,, ,,	134.2	126.3	140.0	150.0

MINING

PRODUCTION OF MINERALS

		1969	1970	1971	1972
Gold	kg.	603	680	596	615
Diamonds	'ooo carats	194	509	499	456
Iron Ore: gross weight	'ooo metric tons	17,916	22,200	19,570	17,326
metal content	,, ,, ,,	12,410	14,080	12,522	n.a.
Coal	,, ,, ,,	32	40	41	40

PETROLEUM PRODUCTION

		1969	1970	1971	1972
Crude Petroleum	'ooo bbl. per day	3,594	3,708	3,543	3,220
by oilfields:					
Maracaibo	,, ,, ,, ,,	2,919	3,001	2,880	2,594
Falcón	,, ,, ,, ,,	1	1	1	1
Apure	,, ,, ,, ,,	58	58	56	51
Oriental	,, ,, ,, ,,	616	648	612	574
Private Companies	,, ,, ,, ,,	3,563	3,662	3,497	3,159
Corporación Venezolana del Petróleo	,, ,, ,, ,,	31	46	52	61
Natural Gas*	million cu. metres	47,374	48,427	47,579	46,020
Liquid Gas	'ooo barrels	902	1,207	1,644	1,961
Derivatives	million barrels	422	472	455	412
of which:					
Fuel Oil	,, ,,	258	298	284	248
Motor Spirit	,, ,,	60	65	69	67
Diesel Oil	,, ,,	55	55	58	54
Other	,, ,,	49	54	44	43
Private Companies	,, ,,	418	466	448	405
Corporación Venezolana del Petróleo	,, ,,	4	6	7	7

* Gross production.

DESTINATION OF PETROLEUM EXPORTS
(million barrels)

	1970	1971	1972
Brazil	19	17	12
Canada	147	142	139
Netherlands Antilles	293	255	249
Puerto Rico	62	78	82
Trinidad and Tobago	51	26	15
United Kingdom	56	68	44
United States	410	409	385
Others	245	211	206

INDUSTRY

		1968	1969	1970	1791
Beer	('000 litres)	356,216	484,000	495,510	436,661
Soft Drinks	(,, ,,)	553,180	n.a.	667,510	711,700
Cigarettes	(million)	11,048	10,321	11,466	12,129
Sawn Timber	(cubic metres)	209,646	n.a.	n.a.	n.a.
Cement	(metric tons)	2,355,395	2,114,200	2,352,458	2,508,412
Electricity	('000 kWh.)	10,369,000	n.a.	12,923,614	13,246,305
Tyres	(number)	1,530,000	1,619,400	1,758,000	1,977,279
Textiles:					
Cotton Cloth	(metres)	66,850	77,708	118,707	n.a.
Rayon Cloth	(,,)	38,121	38,290	37,600	n.a.
Paint	(metric tons)	19,748	14,600	23,817	27,582
Animal Feeding Stuffs	(,, ,,)	537,109	596,700	797,096	810,540
Vegetable Oils and Fats	(,, ,,)	n.a.	n.a.	106,705	169,413
Salt	(,, ,,)	95,100	n.a.	48,436	50,080
Sugar	(,, ,,)	308,654	373,100	409,922	462,089

FINANCE

100 céntimos = 1 bolívar.

Coins: 5, 10, 25 and 50 céntimos; 1 and 2 bolívares.

Notes: 5, 10, 20, 50, 100 and 500 bolívares.

Exchange rates (April 1974): £1 sterling = 9.92 bolívares (petroleum export rate),

10.11 bolívares (other exports) or 10.15 bolívares (selling rate);

U.S. $1 = 4.20 bolívares (petroleum export rate), 4.28 bolívares (other exports) or 4.30 bolívares (selling rate).

100 bolívares = £9.85 = $23.26 (selling rates).

BUDGET 1970
(million bolívares)

REVENUE		EXPENDITURE	
Customs	607	Interior	1,867
Mines and Hydrocarbons	2,864	Foreign Affairs	84
Direct Taxes	4,603	Treasury	724
Indirect Taxes	842	Defence	923
Other Taxes	582	Development	266
Extraordinary Income	754	Public Works	2,220
		Education	1,654
		Health and Welfare	877
		Agriculture	767
		Labour	154
		Communications	323
		Justice	235
		Mining	201
TOTAL	10,252	TOTAL	10,295

Budget Estimates: (1971) Expenditure 10,987m. bolívares.

(1972) Expenditure 14,113m. bolívares.

(1973) Expenditure 13,858m. bolívares.

(1974) Expenditure 14,584m. bolívares.

Expenditure allocations to ministries for the 1974 Budget were announced as follows:

Interior	2,676	Agriculture	931
Foreign Affairs	110	Labour	150
Defence	1,500	Communications	357
Development	213	Justice	284
Public Works	2,299	Finance	2,012
Education	2,747	Mines and Hydrocarbons	223
Health and Welfare	1,046	Budget Adjustment	36

CONSUMER PRICES INDEX
(Caracas Metropolitan area)

	FOOD, DRINK AND TOBACCO	CLOTHING	HOUSEHOLD EXPENSES	MISCELLANEOUS	GENERAL INDEX
1968	100.0	100.0	100.0	100.0	100.0
1969	102.9	101.7	101.3	103.1	102.4
1970	104.3	105.4	102.3	106.7	104.6
1971	107.8	105.8	103.5	113.7	108.4
1972	114.1	109.0	104.8	116.5	111.8

(Base: 1968 = 100)

BALANCE OF PAYMENTS
(million U.S. $)

	1970	1971	1972
Current Transactions	— 116	— 11	— 124
Exports f.o.b.	2,658	3,128	3,798
Imports c.i.f.	—1,780	—1,985	—2,343
Commercial Balance	878	1,143	1,455
Transport and insurance	— 172	— 200	— 242
Other transport	— 15	— 14	— 19
Other insurance	— 9	— 14	— 14
Travel	— 90	— 82	— 105
Income and investments	— 556	— 693	—1,042
Government expenses	— 14	— 30	— 15
Others	— 46	— 36	— 47
Balance on services	— 902	—1,069	—1,484
Balance on Goods and Services	— 24	74	— 29
Unilateral Transfers	— 92	— 85	— 95
Non-monetary Capital	84	298	360
Private sector	— 48	113	125
Long term	39	— 10	55
Investments	— 25	12	58
Loans received	— 3	7	— 4
Share transactions	— 11	— 15	1
Short term	— 9	123	70
Government sector	132	185	235
Long term	127	180	239
Short term	5	5	— 4
Errors and Omissions	75	134	— 3
Balance on Current and Capital Transactions	43	421	— 233
Official Creation of Reserves	41	35	35
SDRs	42	35	35
Revaluation	—	—	35
Monetizations of gold	1	—	—
Monetary Movements	84	— 456	— 268
Liabilities	4	8	—
Monetary gold	20	— 6	—
Foreign exchange	— 41	— 416	— 167
SDRs	— 48	35	— 35
Position at IMF	— 28	6	—
Other Reserve Assets	9	— 13	— 66

EXTERNAL TRADE
(million U.S. $)

	1970	1971	1972
Imports . . .	1,780	1,985	2,225
Exports . . .	2,658	3,128	2,889

PRINCIPAL COMMODITIES
(million bolívares)

IMPORTS	1971	1972	EXPORTS	1971	1972
Foodstuffs	599	869	Food Products . . .	201.92	304.21
Drink and Tobacco . . .	76	112	Coffee	66.08	68.57
Raw Materials, except Fuels .	332	360	Cocoa	29.17	28.26
Fuels and Lubricants . .	74	74	Others	106.67	207.38
Oils and Fats . . .	73	63	Beverages and Tobacco . .	0.34	1.39
Chemicals	930	1,015	Crude Materials (inedible) . .	634.93	643.10
Manufactures (classified) . .	1,510	1,724	Iron Ore . . .	624.00	637.36
Manufactures (non-classified) .	619	772	Others . . .	10.93	5.74
Machinery and Transport Equipment	3,993	4,623	Mineral Fuels and Lubricants .	12,690.68	11,768.92
Live Animals, Special Transactions, Gold and Other Valuables	141	178	Petroleum and Derivatives .	12,690.68	11,768.92
			Others . . .	—	—
			Oils and Fats . . .	0.01	0.05
			Chemicals . . .	16.04	16.35
			Basic Manufactures . .	141.90	197.90
			Machinery and Transport Equipment . . .	6.86	10.07
			Miscellaneous Manufactures .	5.58	7.20
			Live Animals, Special Transactions, Gold and Other Valuables	1.00	1.87
			Gold	—	—
			Others . . .	1.00	1.87
			Re-exports . . .	70.81	72.71

PRINCIPAL COUNTRIES
(million bolívares)

	IMPORTS			EXPORTS		
	1970	1971	1972	1970	1971	1972
Argentina . . .	62	70	49	128	68	131
Belgium and Luxembourg	125	128	205	154	101	57
Brazil . . .	40	42	91	178	204	172
Canada . . .	331	407	344	1,543	1,655	1,674
Denmark . . .	56	34	28	30	20	2
France . . .	220	366	395	175	190	230
German Fed. Republic .	670	838	1,009	262	226	156
Italy . . .	360	420	532	146	161	191
Japan . . .	565	668	858	135	39	87
Netherlands . .	125	123	144	118	73	126
Spain . . .	115	122	164	160	148	128
United Kingdom . .	377	402	507	627	863	530
United States . .	3,550	3,861	4,202	5,282	6,630	4,159

TRANSPORT

SHIPPING

	DOMESTIC FREIGHT ('000 tons)	INTERNATIONAL FREIGHT ('000 tons)	IMPORTS ('000 tons)	EXPORTS ('000 tons)
1969 .	116.8	406.3	370.5	35.8
1970 .	139.1	468.3	440.2	28.0
1971 .	165.0	416.0	390.3	25.0

ROADS
VEHICLES IN USE

	PASSENGER CARS	BUSES	GOODS VEHICLES
1968 .	498,144	14,583	161,606
1969 .	534,449	14,253	164,128
1970 .	614,616	16,390	222,694

Source: IRF *World Road Statistics 1967–72.*

CIVIL AVIATION
(Internal)

	1969	1970	1971
No. of Passengers .	897.1	934.9	986.2
Cargo ('000 metric tons)	16.5	15.0	13.0

EDUCATION
(1971–72)

	ESTABLISHMENTS	TEACHERS	PUPILS
Kindergarten and Primary .	10,491	54,387	1,918,655
Secondary . . .	1,205	15,665	564,167
Higher . . .	12	9,105	99,745

Source: Dirección General de Estadística y Censos Nacionales, Caracas.

THE CONSTITUTION
(*January* 1961)

The Federal Republic of Venezuela is divided into States, a Federal District, Federal Territories and Federal Dependencies. The States are autonomous but must comply with the laws and constitution of the Republic.

The Legislative Power is exercised by Congress, divided into two Chambers: the Senate and the Chamber of Deputies.

Senators are elected by universal suffrage, two to represent each State, and two to represent the Federal District. There are in addition other Senators, their number being determined by law, who are selected on the principle of minority representation. Ex-Presidents of the Republic are also members of the Senate. Deputies are elected by universal suffrage, the number representing each State being at least two and for the Federal District one. Ordinary sessions of both Chambers shall commence on the second day of March of each year, and continue until the sixth day of the following July; thereafter, sessions are renewed from the first day of October to the thirtieth day of November, both dates inclusive. The Chamber of Deputies is empowered to initiate legislation. Congress also elects a Controller-General to preside over the Audit Office (*Contraloría de la Nación*), which investigates Treasury income and expenditure, and the finances of the autonomous institutes.

The Executive Power is vested in a President of the Republic elected by universal suffrage every five years; he may not serve two consecutive terms. The President is empowered to discharge the Constitution and the laws, to nominate or remove Ministers, to take supreme command of the Armed Forces, to direct foreign relations of the State, to declare a state of emergency and withdraw the civil guarantees laid down in the Constitution, to convene extraordinary sessions of Congress, to administer national finance and to nominate and remove Governors of the Federal District and the Federal Territories. The President also appoints an Attorney General to act as a legal arbiter for the state.

The Judicial Power is exercised by the Supreme Court of Justice and by the Tribunals. The Supreme Court forms the highest Tribunal of the Republic and the Magistrates of the Supreme Court are elected by both Chambers in joint session.

THE GOVERNMENT

HEAD OF THE STATE

President of the Republic: CARLOS ANDRÉS PÉREZ RODRÍGUEZ.

THE CABINET
(May 1974)

Minister of the Interior: Dr. LUIS PIÑERÚA ORDAZ.

Minister of Foreign Affairs: Dr. EFRAÍN SCHACHT ARISTI-GUIETA.

Minister of Finance: Dr. HÉCTOR HURTADO NAVARRO.

Minister of Defence: Gen. HOMERO LEAL TORRES.

Minister of Development: Dr. CARMELO LAURÍA LESSEUR.

Minister of Public Works: Ing. ARNOLDO JOSÉ GABALDÓN.

Minister of Education: Dr. LUIS MANUEL PEÑALVER.

Minister of Health and Social Assistance: Dr. BLAS BRUNI CELLI.

Minister of Agriculture: LUIS JOSÉ OROBEZA ALVAREZ.

Minister of Labour: Dr. ANTONIO LEIDENZ.

Minister of Communications: Dr. ARMANDO SÁNCHEZ BUENO.

Minister of Justice: Dr. OTTO MARÍN GÓMEZ.

Minister of Mines and Hydrocarbons: Ing. VALENTÍN HERNÁNDEZ ACOSTA.

Minister of State for Planning, in charge of Central Planning Office: Dr. GUMERSINDO RODRÍGUEZ.

Minister of State for Information: Dr. SIMÓN ALBERTO CONSALVI.

Secretary-General of the Presidency: Dr. RAMÓN ESCOVAR SALOM.

Governor of the Federal District: Dr. DIEGO ARRÍA SALICETTI.

Governor of Miranda State: Dr. MANUEL MANTILLA.

STATE GOVERNORS

STATE	GOVERNOR	STATE	GOVERNOR
Anzóategui	Dr. PEDRO TABATA GUZMÁN.	Monagas	Gen. MARTÍN MÁRQUEZ AÑEZ.
Apure	Dr. EDUARDO HERNÁNDEZ.	Nueva Esparta	Dr. VIRGILIO AVILA.
Aragua	Gen. ROBERTO MOREÁN SOTO.	Portuguesa	JOSÉ RAFAEL CASAL.
Barinas	Ing. Agr. JOSÉ ANGEL HERNÁNDEZ.	Sucre	Dr. GASTÓN NAVARRO DONA.
Bolívar	Dr. DOMINGO ALVAREZ.	Táchira	Ing. LUIS E. MOGOLLÓN CARRILLO.
Carabobo	Ing. EMILIANO AZCUNES.	Trujillo	Gen. ANTONIO BRICEÑO LINARES.
Cojedes	Dr. EGOR NUCETE.	Yaracuy	Dr. NELSON BRASCHI SANTOS.
Falcón	Dr. LEONCIO LÓPEZ.	Zulia	Dr. CARMELO CONTRERAS.
Guárico	Dr. MÁXIMO SALAZAR.	Distrito Federal	Dr. DIEGO ARRÍA SALICETTI.
Lara	Ing. HERNÁN RODRÍGUEZ ARAUJO.	Territorios Federales:	
Mérida	Dr. RIGOBERTO HENRÍQUEZ VERA.	Amazonas	Dr. PABLO ANDUZE.
Miranda	Dr. MANUEL MANTILLA.	Delta Amacuro	Ing. Agr. EMERY MATA MILLÁN.

DIPLOMATIC REPRESENTATION

EMBASSIES AND LEGATION ACCREDITED TO VENEZUELA
(In Caracas unless otherwise stated)
(E) Embassy; (L) Legation.

Algeria: Rio de Janeiro, Brazil (E).

Argentina: Edif. Capriles, Plaza Venezuela (E); *Ambassador:* JULIO AURELIO AMOEDO.

Australia: Brasília, D.F., Brazil (E).

Austria: Ciudad Comercial Tamanaco, Avda. La Estancia 10 (E); *Ambassador:* Dr. HARALD GÜDEL.

Belgium: Quinta Isaba, Avda. Principal del Bosque (E); *Ambassador:* HUGO WALSCHAP.

Bolivia: Avda. Principal de Chuao, Apdo. 4670 (E); *Ambassador:* FEDERICO ARANA SERRUDO.

Brazil: Quinta San Antonio, Avda. San Juan Bosco, esq. con Transversal 8, Altamira (E); *Ambassador:* LUCILLO HADDOCK-LOBO.

Canada: Edif. La Estancia, 16° piso, Avda. La Estancia 10, Ciudad Comercial Tamanaco (E); *Ambassador:* C. J. VAN TIGHEM.

Chile: Edif. Rupi, Of. 71-73, Calle El Recreo, esq. Avda. Casanova, Sabana Grande (E); *Chargé d'Affaires a.i.:* Col. FERNANDO PAREDES PIZARRO.

China (Taiwan): 3 Calle 9, Campo Alegre (E); *Ambassador:* WANG CHIH-CHEN.

Colombia: Avda. El Parque 18, Quinta Colombia, Campo Alegre (E); *Chargé d'Affaires a.i.:* Dr. VICENTE MARTÍNEZ EMILIANI.

Costa Rica: Edif. Blue Palace, 10° piso, Avda. de Los Palos Grandes (E); *Ambassador:* Dr. EMILIO VALVERDE VEGA.

Czechoslovakia: Quinta Lecuna, Calle Lecuna, Country Club (L); *Chargé d'Affaires a.i.:* JOSEF HROCH.

Denmark: Edif. Easo, Avda. Francisco de Miranda, Chacaíto (E); *Ambassador:* Dr. AXEL SERUP.

Dominican Republic: Quinta Quisqueyana, Avda. Los Samanes 21, La Florida (E); *Ambassador:* Dr. Rafael Bonilla Aybar.

Ecuador: Centro Comercial Cediaz, Torre Este, 7° piso, Avda. Casanova (E); *Ambassador:* Isidro de Ycaza Plaza.

Egypt: Quinta Cunury, Avda. Chama, Colinas de Bello Monte (E); *Ambassador:* Abbas Helmy Sidky.

El Salvador: Quinta San Antonio, Avda. Principal, Prados del Este (E); *Ambassador:* Héctor Palomo Salazar.

Finland: Lima, Peru (E).

France: Quinta Chuna, Calle la Cinta, Las Mercedes (E); *Ambassador:* André Rodocanachi.

Germany, Federal Republic: Edif. Panaven, 2° piso, Avda. San Juan Bosco, Apdo. 2078 (E); *Ambassador:* Dr. Rudolf Spang.

Ghana: Mexico, D.F., Mexico (E).

Greece: Brasília, D.F., Brazil (E).

Guatemala: Quinta Teocal, Calle Codazzi, esq. Calle Andalucía, Prados del Este (E); *Ambassador:* Julio Chocano Becerra.

Guyana: Edif. Continental, 17° piso, Calle Real Sabana Grande, esq. Avda. Los Jabillos (E); *Ambassador:* Samuel Rudolph Insanally.

Honduras: Quinta Coromotana, 3 Avda. y 4 Transversal, Santa Eduvigis (E); *Ambassador:* Ing. Agripino Flores Aguilar.

Hungary: Quinta Margit, Calle Las Colinas, Lomas de San Rafael, La Florida (E); *Ambassador:* János Beck.

India: Edif. Nuevo Centro, Avda. Libertador (E); *Ambassador:* A. R. Kakodkar.

Iran: Quinta Lourdes, Calle El Retiro, El Rosal (E); *Ambassador:* Manucher Farmanfarmaian.

Iraq: Edif. La Línea, 5° piso, Avda. Libertador (E); *Ambassador:* Dr. Hassan Tha Kittany.

Israel: Edif. Teatro Altamira, Entrada Este, Of. 32, Avda. Avila, Altamira Sur (E); *Ambassador:* Victor Eliachar.

Italy: Edif. Fedecámaras, 3° piso, Avda. El Empalme, El Bosque (E); *Ambassador:* Dr. Silvio Falchi.

Jamaica: Port-of-Spain, Trinidad (E).

Japan: Centro Capriles, 9° piso, Of. 902-3, Plaza Venezuela (E); *Ambassador:* Susumu Nakagawa.

Korea, Republic: Quinta Gladys María, Calle Ciega, Cerro Quintero, Las Mercedes (E); *Ambassador:* Song Kwang-Jung.

Kuwait: Washington, D.C., U.S.A. (E).

Lebanon: Quinta Assunta, Calle Guapure, Colinas de Bello Monte (E); *Ambassador:* Dr. Younes Rezk.

Mexico: Edif. Teatro Altamira, Avda. Avila, Altamira Sur (E); *Ambassador:* Jorge Eduardo Navarrete López.

Netherlands: Edif. La Estancia, 3° piso, Avda. La Estancia 10, Ciudad Comercial Tomanaco (E); *Ambassador:* Dr. Efraín Jonckheer.

Nicaragua: Quinta Graciela, Calle Andalucía, Prados del Este (E); *Ambassador:* William Barquero Montiel.

Norway: Edif. Torre Primera, 10° piso, Avda. Francisco de Miranda, esq. Campo Alegre (E); *Ambassador:* Arne Kapsto.

Panama: Quinta Trece, 4 Avda. y Calle 8, Los Palos Grandes (E); *Ambassador:* Humberto Jirón Soto.

Paraguay: Edif. Mercaderes, 2° piso, Of. 4 (E); *Ambassador:* Persio da Silva.

Peru: Avda. Páez 36, El Pinar, El Paraíso (E); *Ambassador:* Luis Barrios Llona.

Philippines: Edif. Jena, 10° piso, Lieja 8 (E); *Ambassador:* León María Guerrero.

Poland: Quinta Ambar, Avda. Nicolás Copernic, Sector Los Naranjos, Las Mercedes (E); *Ambassador:* Zdzislaw Szewczyk.

Portugal: Quinta Panorama, Calle Los Bambúes (E); *Ambassador:* João Morais da Cunha Matos.

Romania: Avda. Principal 42, La Castellana (E); *Ambassador:* Dr. Petrache Danila.

Saudi Arabia: Edif. Mobil, Of. 300, Avda. Francisco de Miranda (E); *Ambassador:* Sheikh Faisal Alhegelan.

Spain: Quinta La Carmela, Avda. Los Cedros, Country Club (E); *Ambassador:* Enrique Domínguez Passier.

Sweden: Edif. Panaven, 5° piso, Avda. San Juan Bosco, Altamira (E); *Ambassador:* Per-Bertil Kollberg.

Switzerland: Edif. Roraima, 1° piso, Avda. Francisco de Miranda (E); *Ambassador:* George Bonnant.

Syria: Edif. Easo, 3° piso, Letra B, Avda. Francisco de Miranda, Chacaíto (E); *Chargé d'Affaires a.i.:* Adnan Hamdoun.

Trinidad and Tobago: Quinta Serrana, 4 Avda., Altamira (E); *Ambassador:* Wilfred Sheikh Naimool.

Turkey: Quinta Turquesa, Calle La Vuelta del Zorro 6, Valle Arriba (E); *Ambassador:* Rifat Ayanlar.

U.S.S.R.: Quinta Goldy, Calle Las Lomas, Las Mercedes (E); *Ambassador:* Viktor Ivanovich Likhachev.

United Kingdom: Ciudad Comercial Tomanaco, Avda. La Estancia 10 (E); *Ambassador:* Sir Alexander Lees Mayall, K.C.V.O.

U.S.A.: Avda. Principal de La Floresta, esq. Francisco de Miranda, La Floresta (E); *Ambassador:* Robert McClintock.

Uruguay: Centro Empresarial Miranda, 2° piso, Avda. Miranda (E); *Chargé d'Affaires a.i.:* Jorge Durán Comparada.

Vatican: Avda. La Salle, Los Caobos (Apostolic Nunciature); *Apostolic Nuncio:* Mgr. Dr. Antonio del Giudice.

Yugoslavia: Quinto Los Trompillos, Avda. Principal 107, La Castellana (E); *Ambassador:* Lazar Lilic.

Venezuela also has diplomatic relations with Ethiopia, Guinea, Haiti, Libya, Morocco, Nigeria, Qatar and Tunisia.

CONGRESS

(Elections for both Chambers of Congress were held in December 1973)

SENATE

President: Dr. Gonzalo Barrios.

Party	Seats
Acción Democrática	28
COPEI	13
Movimiento al Socialismo . .	2
Movimiento Electoral del Pueblo . .	2
Cruzada Cívica Nacionalista . . .	1
Unión Republicana Democrática . .	1

CHAMBER OF DEPUTIES

President: Dr. González Ramírez Cubillán.

Party	Seats
Acción Democrática	102
COPEI	64
Movimiento al Socialismo . .	9
Movimiento Electoral del Pueblo . .	8
Cruzada Cívica Nacionalista . . .	7
Partido Comunista Venezolano . .	2
Movimiento Izquierdista Revolucionario .	1
Opinión Nacional . . .	1
Partido Nacional Integracionista . .	1

POLITICAL PARTIES

Acción Democrática-AD: Edif. No. 4, Calle Los Cedros, La Florida, Caracas; government party; Pres. Dr. Gonzalo Barrios; Sec.-Gen. Dr. Octavio Lepage.

Comité Pro Elecciones Independientes-COPEI: Edif. Celca, esq. Dr. Díaz, Caracas; f. 1946; Christian Socialist, main opposition party; Leaders Dr. Rafael Caldera, Luis Herrera Campins, Arístedes Beaujon; Sec.-Gen. Pedro Pablo Aguilar; Presidential candidate Dr. Lorenzo Fernández.

Nueva Fuerza: Apdo. 4003, Carmelitas, Caracas; electoral alliance composed of party and non-party groups (including MEP and PCV) to fight the 1973 elections; Presidential candidate Dr. J. A. Paz Galarraga.

Cruzada Cívica Nacionalista: f. 1965; Leader ex-Pres. Marcos Pérez Jiménez, whose candidature in the 1973 elections was declared unconstitutional.

Fuerza Democrática Popular-FDP: f. 1962; Sec.-Gen. Jorge Dáger; Presidential candidate Adm. Wolfgang Larrazábal.

Movimiento al Socialismo-MAS: f. 1970 by PCV dissidents; Sec.-Gen. Pompeyo Márquez; Presidential candidate Dr. José Vicente Rangel.

Movimiento Electoral del Pueblo-MEP: f. 1968; left-wing members of AD; Leader Dr. J. A. Paz Galarraga; Sec.-Gen. Adelso González Ordaneta.

Partido Comunista de Venezuela-PCV: Edif. Cantaclaro, esq. San Pedro, San Juan, Caracas; f. 1931; Leader Gustavo Machado; Sec.-Gen. Senator Jesús Faría.

Partido Revolucionario de Izquierda Nacionalista-PRIN: left-wing opposition party; Sec.-Gen. Dr. Raúl Ramos Giménez.

Unión Republicana Democrática-URD: Leader Jóvito Villalba.

JUDICIAL SYSTEM

THE SUPREME COURT OF JUSTICE

The Supreme Court of Justice decides whether the laws of Congress and the acts of the Executive are constitutional. It hears accusations against members of the government and high public officials, cases involving diplomatic representatives, and certain civil actions arising between the State and individuals.

President: Dr. Carlos Acedo Toro.

STATE COURTS

A Superior Court in each state hears appeals from the Courts of First Instance in that state.

RELIGION

Roman Catholicism is the religion of the majority of the population, but there is complete freedom of worship.

ROMAN CATHOLIC CHURCH

Metropolitan See:
Caracas . H.E. Cardinal José Humberto Quintero.

Suffragan Sees:
Calabozo . Rt. Rev. Miguel Antonio Salas.
Los Teques . Most Rev. Juan José Bernal Ortiz.
Maracay . Rt. Rev. Feliciano González Ascanio.
Valencia . Rt. Rev. Luis Eduardo Henríquez Jiménez.

Metropolitan See:
Barquisimeto Most Rev. Críspulo Benítez Fontúrvel.

Suffragan Sees:
Guanare . Rt. Rev. Angel Adolfo Polachini.
San Felipe . Rt. Rev. Tomás Enrique Márquez Gómez.

Metropolitan See:
Maracaibo . Most Rev. Domingo Roa Pérez.

Suffragan Sees:
Cabimas . Rt. Rev. Marcos Tulio Ramírez Roa.
Coro . . Rt. Rev. Francisco José Iturriza Guillén.

Metropolitan See:
Mérida . Most Rev. Angel Pérez Cisneros.

Suffragan Sees:
Barinas . Rt. Rev. Rafael Angel González Ramírez.
San Cristóbal Rt. Rev. Alejandro Fernández Feotinoco.
Trujillo . Rt. Rev. José León Rojas Chaparro.

Metropolitan See:
Ciudad Bolívar Most Rev. Crisanto Mata Cova.

Suffragan Sees:
Barcelona . Rt. Rev. Constantino Maradei Donato.
Cumaná . Rt. Rev. Mariano José Parra León.
Maturín . Rt. Rev. Antonio José Ramírez Salaverria.

THE PRESS

DAILIES

(Most daily newspapers in Venezuela publish a Sunday edition)

CARACAS

Daily Journal, The: Avda. Fuerzas Armadas, San Ramón a Crucecita 65, Apdo. 1408; f. 1945; morning; in English; Editor J. L. Waldman; circ. 15,200.

Extra: Torre de la Prensa, Plaza Panteón, Apdo. 1192; not Sundays; circ. 61,335.

Gaceta Oficial: Imprenta Nacional, San Lázaro a Puente Victoria 89; official gazerre.

Meridiano: Final Avda. San Martín, esq. La Quebradita; circ. 112,000.

El Mundo: Torre de la Prensa, Plaza Panteón, Apdo. 1192; f. 1959; evening; independent; Editor Miguel Angel Capriles; circ. 105,000.

El Nacional: Edificio El Nacional, Puente Nuevo a Puerto Escondido, Apdo. 209; f. 1943; morning; independent; Editor Dr. Arturo Uslar Pietri; circ. 108,400 (weekdays), 141,000 (Sunday).

La Religión: Torre a Madrices, Edif. Juan XXIII 5, Apdo. 1008; f. 1890; morning; Catholic; Editor Gustavo Echegaray; circ. 16,000.

Ultimas Noticias: Torre de la Prensa, Plaza Panteón, Apdo. 1192; f. 1941; morning; tabloid; independent; Editor Miguel Angel Capriles; circ. 141,365.

El Universal: Edif. El Universal, Avda. Urdaneta, Apdo. 1909; f. 1909; morning; Dir. Luis T. Nuñez; circ. 120,000.

La Verdad: Calle Real de Quebrada Honda 30-32, Apdo. 1089; f. 1965; morning; Dir. Dr. Nicomedes Zuloaga; circ. 35,000.

BARQUISIMETO

El Impulso: Edificio El Impulso; f. 1904; morning; independent; Dir. Gustavo A. Carmona; circ. 30,000.

El Informador: Calle 35 No. 19-48; Dir. Eleazar Arce.

BOLÍVAR

El Bolivarense: Calle Igualdad 8; f. 1957; independent; Dir. Dr. Alvaro Natera Febres.

CARORA

El Diario: Calle 3 No. 10-69; f. 1919; morning; independent; Editor Antonio Herrera Oropeza; circ. 12,000.

CARÚPANO

Agencia Comercial: Independencia 57; f. 1925; evening; independent; Editor Pedro A. Luciani.

MARACAIBO

La Columna: Calle 95 No. 7–11, Apdo. 420; f. 1924; morning; Catholic; Editor Pedro Hernández Hernández; circ. 10,000.

Crítica: Calle 92 No. 3–21; f. 1966; morning; independent; Editor Miguel Angel Capriles; circ. 52,000.

Panorama: Calle 96 No. 3–35, Apdo. 425; f. 1914; morning; Pres. Esteban Pineda Bellosa; circ. 60,370.

MÉRIDA

El Vigilante: Avda. 5; f. 1922; morning; religious; circ. 2,600.

PUERTO DE LA CRUZ

El Tiempo: Calle Boyacá 5; f. 1958; independent; Editor Jesús Alvarado; circ. 18,000.

SAN CRISTÓBAL

El Centinela: Calle 6 No. 7–27; f. 1938; independent; Editor Pbro. Pedro Arellano Roa; circ. 5,000.

Diario Católico: Carrera 4a No. 3-41; f. 1924; Catholic; Editor Pbro. Pedro Arellano Roa; circ. 7,500.

Diario de la Nación: Edif. Zetor, Calle 4, esq. Carrera 6; morning; circ. 16,100.

Valencia

El Carabobeño: Edificio Ayacucho, Avda. Urdaneta 99-60; Editor Eladio Alemán Sucre; circ. 30,000.

PERIODICALS AND REVIEWS

Caracas

Aeronaves: Edif. Zingg, Sociedad a Traposos, Avda. Universidad; f. 1945; aeronautical monthly; Dir. Miguel Angel García; circ. 5,000.

Agricultura Venezolana: Edif. Vandissel, 3° piso, Calle Chile, Las Acacias, Apdo. 8373; agricultural monthly; circ. 20,000.

Automóvil de Venezuela: Apdo. 50,045; automobile trade monthly; circ. 7,000.

Banca y Seguros: Edificio Zingg, Sociedad a Trapasos, Avda. Universidad; f. 1945; monthly; economics and banking; Dir. Miguel Angel García; circ. 4,000.

Billiken: Cruz Verde a Zamuro; f. 1919; literary fortnightly; Dir. Lucas Manzano.

Bohemia Venezolana: Ferrenquín a La Cruz 178, Apdo. 575; general interest weekly; circ. 164,200 (Venezuela and Caribbean countries).

Buenhogar: Ferrenquín a la Cruz 178, Apdo. 575; women's magazine; circ. 63,000.

Business Venezuela: Apdo. 5181; fortnightly; business and economics journal in English; edited by the American Chamber of Commerce of Venezuela; circ. 5,000.

Il Corriere di Caracas: Apdo. 2560; f. 1949; Sunday; Italian; Pres. Dir. Franco Pattarino; circ. 28,500.

Economía Prensa Económica: Edif. Vandissel, 3° piso, Calle Chile, Las Acacias, Apdo. 8373; monthly economics and business journal; circ. 10,000.

Elite: Torre de la Prensa, Apdo. 2976; f. 1925; general interest weekly; Editor Miguel Angel Capriles; circ. 61,980.

Ellas: Avda. La Trinidad, Quinta Leonor, Las Mercedes, Apdo. Central 491; women's weekly; circ. 28,000.

El Farol: Apdo. 889; f. 1939; organ of the Creole Petroleum Corpn.; 4 issues per year; Editor Omar Vera López; circ. 39,500.

Gaceta Hípica: Avda. Principal Los Ruices, Apdo. 2935; weekly horse-racing magazine; circ. 100,000.

Hipodromo: Torre de la Prensa, Apdo. 2976; f. 1968; racing weekly; Editor Miguel Angel Capriles; circ. 54,323.

El Independiente: f. 1936; democratic; Editor R. H. Ojeda Mazzareli.

Momento: Edif. La Línea, Avda. Libertador, Apdo. 9324; general interest weekly; Editor Carlos Ramírez MacGregor; circ. 50,000.

Páginas: Torre de la Prensa, Apdo. 2976; f. 1948; women's weekly; Editor Miguel Angel Capriles; circ. 68,410.

Petróleo: Edificio Zingg. Sociedad a Traposos, Avda. Universidad; f. 1948; petroleum monthly; Dir. Miguel Angel García; circ. 6,000.

Revista Nacional de Cultura: Instituto Nacional de Cultura y Bellas Artes; cultural monthly.

Semana: Edif. Nuevo Centro, 4° piso, Avda. Libertador, Apdo. 20-53; weekly; general news magazine; circ. 25,000.

Tópicos Shell: Compañía Shell de Venezuela Ltd., Edif. "La Estancia", Ciudad Comercial Tamanaco, Apdo. 809; f. 1939; monthly; house organ; Editor Richard Bailey Lazzari.

Variedades: Páez a Campo Elias 11, San Agustín del Norte; women's weekly; circ. 49,000.

Ve Venezuela: Edif. Kathryn, Calle Santa Lucia, El Bosque, Apdo. 141; tourism and travel magazine in English and Spanish; circ. 20,000.

Venezuela Gráfica: Torre de la Prensa, Apdo. 2976; f. 1951; weekly; illustrated news magazine; Editor Miguel Angel Capriles; circ. 70,043.

La Voce d'Italia: Torre a Gradillas-c-Caracas; twice weekly; Italian and Spanish editions; circ. 20,000.

Zona Franca: Edif. 9, 2° piso, Conde e Carmelitas, Apdo. 2976; literary fortnightly.

Ciudad Bolívar

Demos: Apdo. 5; f. 1960; monthly illustrated review; Dir. Mons. Dr. Constantino Maradei; circ. 4,000.

Cumaná

Renacimiento: Sucre 40, Apdo. 201; f. 1925; three times weekly; Dir. Juan José Acuna.

Maracaibo

Maracaibo: Edif. Nery 4, Apdo. 1308; weekly; genera interest; Dir. Héctor Hernández Calles.

Valencia

Valencia Económica: Edif. Libertador, 7° piso; economics and business magazine; circ. 3,000.

PRESS AGENCIES

A.N.S.A.: Torre de la Prensa, 13° piso, Plaza Panteón, Caracas; Chief Marcello Mancini.

A.P.: Edif. El Nacional, Puente Nuevo a Puente Escondido, Apdo. 1015, Caracas; Chief Thomas V. Brady.

U.P.I.: Residencia Avilanes, Entrada B, Avilanes al Río, Caracas; Bureau Man. John F. Virtue.

Reuters and Tass also have bureaux in Caracas.

PUBLISHERS

Caracas

Editorial El Ateneo: Sabana Grande, Transversal Las Delicias, Centro Comercial Notre Dame; scholarly and reference.

Editorial Ciudad Universitaria: Universidad Central de Venezuela, Ciudad Universitaria; f. 1961; education, textbooks, science, arts, religion; Dir. Rafael di Prisco.

Edisa S.A. Editores: Edif. Santiago de León, 3° piso, Avda. Casanova, esq. Calle El Recreo, Apdo. 8364.

Editorial Escolar, S.A.: Apdo. 552; juvenile, reference, textbooks.

Editorial González Porto: Edif. Reyes Pinal, Avda. Universidad 8, Apdo. 502.

Editorial Kapelusz Venezolana, S.A.: Edif. Camoruco; Avda. Urdaneta, Animas a Platanal, Apdo. 14234, f. 1963; Man. Dir. Horacio Perotti Beraldo.

Editorial Labor: Edif. Garten (Sector Maripérez), Avda. Andrés Bello; arts, science, education, textbooks.

Monte Avila Editores C.A.: Edif. Los Hermanos, 3° piso, Avda. Principal de los Cortijos de Lourdes, Apdo. 70712; f. 1968; general; Man. Dir. M. Fernández.

Ediciones Palante, S.A.: Avda. Francisco de Miranda.

Librería Editorial Salesiana S.A.: Paradero a Salesianos 6, Apdo. 369; f. 1960; education; Man. Aldo Manolino.

Ediciones Selectas, S.A.: Edif. Araure, Calle Real de Sabana Grande 181, Apdo. 8208.

Editorial Tiempo Nuevo S.A.: Apdo. 50304; f. 1970; literature; Man. Dir. Benito Milla.

Ediciones Vega S.R.L.: Edif. Saturno, Calle Sorbona, Colinas de Bello Monte; educational; Man. Dir. F. Vega Alonso.

ASSOCIATION

Cámara Venezolana del Libro: Edif. del Cine San Bernadino, Avda. Andrés Bello, Apdo. 2435, Caracas (4); Sec. E. Bordegué.

RADIO AND TELEVISION

Ministerio de Comunicaciones: Dirección de Telecomunicaciones, División de Radiodifusión y Televisión, Edif. Ramia, esq. Carmelitas, Caracas; controls all broadcasting and television; Dir. Gen. Amable Espina.

RADIO

Radio Nacional: Apdo. 3979, Caracas; f. 1946; state broadcasting organization; one medium wave, one short wave and two ultra short wave transmitters; foreign language programmes broadcast in French and English; Dir. R. Osorio Canales; publ. *Programme Bulletin*.

There are also one educational and 143 commercial stations, including the organizations in most large provincial towns.

In 1971 there were approximately 1,750,000 radio licences.

Cámara Venezolana Industria Radio y Televisión: Apdo. 3955, Caracas; Pres. A. José Isturiz.

TELEVISION

Televisora Nacional: Cerro Marín, Colinas de las Acacias, Apdo. 3979, Caracas; state television organization; one transmitter; Dir.-Gen. R. Osorio Canales.

Cadena Venezolana de Televisión: Apdo. 2739, Caracas; colour station; 8 repeaters; Dir.-Gen. Dr. Arnoldo Paolini R.

Ondas del Lago Televisión: Edif. Teleradiopolis, Calle 74, Apdo. 261, Maracaibo; commercial station; one transmitter; Dir.-Gen. N. Vale.

Radio Caracas Televisión: Edif. Radio Centro, Barcenas, Apdo. 2057, Caracas; commercial station; station in Caracas and 13 repeater stations throughout country; Dir.-Gen. Peter Bottome.

Radio Valencia Televisión: Apdo. 248, Valencia; commercial station; two transmitters; Dir.-Gen. M. Aché.

Teletrece: 1A Avda. Eduvigis, Caracas; Tech. Dir. M. Sapkowski.

Venevisión S.A.: Apdo. 6674, Caracas; commercial; 11 stations; Gen. Man. E. Cuscó.

In 1972 there were approximately 995,000 TV receivers.

FINANCE

BANKING

(cap.=capital; p.u.=paid up; dep.=deposits; res.= reserves; m.=million; amounts in bolívares)

CENTRAL BANK

Banco Central de Venezuela: esq. Carmelitas, Caracas; f. 1940; bank of issue and clearing house for commercial banks; cap. 5m., res. 559.9m. (1971); Pres. Dr. Alfredo Lafée.

CARACAS

Banco Agrario Nacional: State-owned; supplies credit to the agricultural sector.

Banco Agrícola y Pecuario: Socarrás a Salvador de León 40; f. 1928; state-owned; cap. 167m., dep. 72m.; administers government crop credit scheme for small farmers; Pres. Dr. Arnaldo Ron Pedrique; brs. in all main cities.

Banco Caracas, C.A.: Avda. Urdaneta 4; f. 1890; cap. 40m., dep. 473.9m. (Dec. 1972); Pres. Dr. Andrés Velutini.

Banco del Centro Consolidado, C.A.: Avda. Francisco de Miranda, Urb. La California Norte, Caracas-Petare; f. 1969; cap. 40m., dep. 402m. (Dec. 1971); Pres. Dr. José Alvarez Stelling; 10 brs., 30 agencies.

Banco de Comercio, S.A.: esq. San Jacinto, Apdo 2330; f. 1954; cap. 20m., res. 8.4m. (Dec. 1971); Gen. Man. Dr. Miguel A. Calvo.

Banco del Caribe, C.A.: Avda. Fuerzas Armadas, esq. Socarrás; f. 1954; Pres. N. D. Dao; Vice-Pres. Dr. Marco Tulio Henríquez.

Banco de la Construcción y de Oriente, C.A.: Edif. Seguros, Marrón a Dr. Paul, Apdo. 6719; f. 1955; cap. 29.9m., dep. 266.5m. (1971); Pres. Giacomo di Mase; Exec. Vice-Pres. Alfredo A. Azpurua.

Banco de los Trabajadores de Venezuela C.A.: f. 1968 to channel workers' savings for the financing of artisans and small industrial firms; cap. 20m., cap. p.u. 15.5m., dep. 73m.; Pres. Augusto Malave Villalba; Man. Silverio A. Narvaez; 4 agencies.

Banco de Venezuela, S.A.: Avda. Universidad, Sociedad a Traposos 7, Apdo. 6286; f. 1890; cap. 105m., dep. 1,877.4m. (Dec. 1972); Pres. E. Sosa Fernández.

Banco Exterior, C.A.: Avda. Urdaneta, Urapal a Rio, Apdo. 14278; f. 1958; cap. 28m., dep. 17.3m. (1971); Pres. José Antonio Cordido Freytes.

Banco de Fomento Comercial de Venezuela: Gradillas a San Jacinto 6–3, Apdo. 6734; f. 1949; cap. p.u. 13.7m.; Pres. Miguel Rottenberg; Vice-Pres. and Gen. Man. R. Velazio Troconis.

Banco La Guaira Internacional, S.A.: Torre a Madrices, Apdo. 3127; f. 1956; cap. 24m., res. 8.9m. (Dec. 1972); Pres. Alfredo Fernández; Gen. Man. Rafael Núñez Alemán.

Banco Hipotecario Unido, S.A.: Edif. Banco Hipotecario, Este 2, Los Caobos; f. 1961; mortgage and credit institution; cap. p.u. 12.5m.; Chair. SALVADOR SALVA-TIERRA S.

Banco Industrial de Venezuela, C.A.: Avda. Universidad, esq. Traposos; f. 1938; state-owned; cap. 160m.; Man. F. ACOSTA ESTRADA.

Banco Latino Americano de Venezuela C.A. "Sudameris": Edif. Sudameris, Avda. Urdaneta, Apdo. 2026; f. 1950; cap. and res. 105m. (Jan. 1973); Pres. ENRIQUE BENEDETTI; Man. Dir. DINO CARMINATI.

Banco Mercantil y Agrícola: Sociedad a San Francisco 5, Apdo. 789; f. 1925; cap. 72m., dep. 1,336m. (Nov. 1973); Pres. Dr. ALFREDO MACHADO GÓMEZ.

Banco Metropolitano, C.A.: Edif. Banco Metropolitano; f. 1953; cap. 30m., res. 15.4m. (June 1972); Pres. CARLOS BERACASA; Vice-Pres. and Man. A. FRANCESCHI.

Banco Nacional de Descuento, C.A.: Avda. Urdaneta, Conde a Carmelitas, Apdo. 2701; f. 1954; cap. 112m., dep. 1,211.9m. (Dec. 1972); Chair. and Pres. Dr. J. J. GONZÁLEZ GORRONDONA; Vice-Pres. Lic. HOMERO FARÍA.

Banco Obrero: Edif. Cruz Verde, esq. Cruz verde; f. 1926; state-owned; cap. 789m.; builds and administers government housing projects.

Banco Provincial de Venezuela C.A.: Edif. Provincial, Marrón a Pelota 10, Apdo. 1269; f. 1953; cap. 41m., res. 22.1m. (Dec. 1972); Pres. REMIGIO ELIAS PÉREZ; Gen. Man. R. LAFAILLE.

Banco Royal Venezolano C.A.: Sociedad a Camejo 31, Apdo. 1009; f. 1971 to take over brs. of Royal Bank of Canada; cap. 35m., dep. 365.6m. (Dec. 1972); Pres. A. J. LARA; Gen. Man. H. J. W. BROPHY.

Banco Unión, C.A.: Chorro a Dr. Díaz 45-47; f. 1946; cap. 150m., dep. 1,819m. (Dec. 1973); Pres. SALVADOR SALVATIERRA; Vice-Pres. and Man. RAMÓN ALLER ALBERDI.

Banco Venezolano de Crédito, S.A.: Sur 2 No. 7; f. 1925; cap. 52m., dep. 382.2m. (Dec. 1972); Pres. Dr. LUIS PÉREZ DUPUY.

H. L. Boulton & Co., S.A.: esq. del Chorro 24, Apdo. 929; cap. 12m., dep. 13.2m.; Dirs. H. L. BOULTON, A. BOULTON, A. W. BOULTON.

CUMANÁ

Banco de Fomento Regional de Oriente, C.A.: Edif. Banco de Fomento, Calle Mariño, f. 1951; cap. p.u. and res. 36m.; Pres. Dr. GIACOMO DI MASE; Gen. Man. MARIO CARRASCO ESPEJO.

MARACAIBO

Banco Comercial de Maracaibo, C.A.: 4-37 Calle 99; f. 1916; cap. 40m.; Pres. R. J. VILLASMIL; Vice-Pres. HERNÁN VILLASMIL B.

Banco de Fomento Regional Zulia, S.A.: Avda. 4 entre Calles 97 y 98; f. 1956; Pres. ANTONIO QUINTERO PARRA; Man. ARCÁNGELO VULPIS MILANO.

Banco de Maracaibo, C.A.: Avda. 5 de Julio, esq. Avda. 12; f. 1882; cap. p.u. 60m.; Pres. D. BELLOSO ROSSELL.

Banco Occidental de Descuento, C.A.: Apdo. 695; f. 1957; cap. 15m.; Pres. Dr. ALFREDO BELLOSO.

H. L. Boulton, Jr. and Co., S.A.: Avda. Bustamante, Apdo. 131, f. 1875; cap. 11m.; Dirs. A. BOULTON, A. W. BOULTON, H. L. BOULTON, Jr., Dr. H. BOULTON, R. BOULTON.

MARACAY

Banco Italo-Venezolano: Avda. Urdaneta 23, de Pelota a Punceres; f. 1952; cap. 30m., dep. 415m. (1971); Chair. Dr. FÉLIX MIRALLES.

PUERTO CABELLO

Calderón Hijos: Edif. Mercaderes, Apdo. 1946; f. 1906; cap. 350,000; Partners M. S. SALAS, FERMÍN CALDERÓN, FRANCISCO A. CALDERÓN.

"Rioka" S.A. Sucesora de R. & O. Kolster: Avda. 101 Norte (Comercio) 117; f. 1897; cap. p.u. 2.4 m.; Pres. LUIS GONZALO MARTURET; Exec. Dir. MIGUEL A. SCHÖN.

SAN CRISTÓBAL

Banco Táchira, C.A.: Calle 5 No. 47; f. 1944; cap. 20m.; Pres. F. R. VALE; Gen. Man. M. A. CONTRERAS.

FOREIGN BANKS

Banca Nazionale del Lavoro: Rome; T.I.E.C., Edif. Citibank, Carmelitas a Altagracias, Of. 205, Caracas.

Banco de Santander: Santander; Avda. de Urdaneta, esq. Las Ibarras, Edif. Central, Of. 104, Caracas.

Banco Germánico de la América del Sud (*Deutsch-Südamerikanische Bank* and *Dresdner Bank*): joint representation: Edif. Galipán, Entrada A, 1° piso, Of. B, Avda. Francisco de Miranda, El Rosal.

Banco Holandés Unido (*Hollandsche Bank-Unie, N.V.*): Amsterdam; Sociedad a San Francisco 6, Apdo. 909, Caracas; Local Man. J. VAN DER VEEN.

Chase Manhattan Overseas Banking Corporation: New York; Edif. Seguros Caracas, 7° piso, Marrón a Cují, Caracas; Rep. WALTER A. BUSTARD.

Deutsche Bank A.G.: Frankfurt; Apdo. 60568, Caracas; Rep. G. W. P. SOMMERLATTE.

First National City Bank: New York; Santa Capilla a Mijares 26, Caracas; Vice-Pres. GEORGE HAGERMAN.

Morgan Guaranty Trust Co. of New York: New York; Caracas.

STOCK EXCHANGES

Bolsa de Comercio de Caracas: Edif. Mercantil y Agrícola, 5° piso, esq. de San Francisco, Caracas; f. 1947; 30 mems.; Pres. JOSÉ MANUEL SÁNCHEZ; Man. Dr. HÉCTOR ESTEVES H.; publs. daily, weekly, monthly reports, bulletins.

Bolsa de Comercio del Estado Miranda: Edif. Easo, Loc. H., Avda. Miranda, Caracas.

Bolsa de Comercio de Valencia: Valencia.

INSURANCE

All companies must have at least 51 per cent Venezuelan participation in their capital.

NATIONAL COMPANIES

Adriática Venezolana de Seguros, C.A.: Edif. Venadria, Avda. Andrés Bello, Apdo. 1928, Caracas; f. 1952; Man. FRANCESCO DI VENERE.

Arauca, Compañía Anónima de Seguros: Edif. Torre del Banco Industrial de Venezuela, esq. Traposos, Apdo. 3178, Caracas; Gen. Man. WILLIAM R. PHELAN.

Avila, Compañía Anónima de Seguros: Edif. Banco Caracas, Avda. Urdaneta, Apdo. 1007, Caracas; f. 1936; Pres. ANDRÉS VELUTINI.

C.A. Seguros Catatumbo: Avda. 4 No. 83-49, Apdo. 1083, Maracaibo; f. 1957; Pres. L. URDANETA BRAVO.

Compañía Anónima de Seguros American International: Edif. Seguros Venezuela, 8° piso, Avda. Francisco de Miranda, Apdo. 61323, Chacao, Caracas; Pres. EDWARD C. DOBBS.

Compañía Anónima de Seguros Royal Caribe de Venezuela: Avda. Urdaneta, Apdo. 1609, Caracas; Chair. J. C. F. MILLER.

La Confederación del Canadá Venezolana, C.A.: Torre Phelps, 16° piso, Plaza Venezuela, Apdo. 51174, Sabana Grande, Caracas; incorporated as a Venezuelan co. 1967; Gen. Man. PATRICIO ESTEVEZ NAVARRO.

La Continental Venezolana, Compania Anónima: Torre Lincoln, Avda. A. Lincoln (Sabana Grande), Apdo. 6666, Caracas; f. 1956; Pres. G. A. LOVERA; Gen. Man. G. SCHARIFKER.

Co-operativa Central de Seguros: Avda. Urdaneta, esq. La Pelota, Apdo. 2655, Caracas; f. 1957.

Horizonte, C.A.: Edificio Banco Industrial, Avda. Universidad, esq. de Traposos, Apdo. 2357, Caracas; f. 1956; Gen. Man. Ing. GUSTAVO ROJAS VALERY.

La Metropolitana: Edif. "Seguros La Metropolitana", Avda. Universidad (Perico a Monroy), Apdo. 2197, Caracas; f. 1949; Pres. CARLOS BERACASA; Man. Dr. C. G. RANGEL.

C.A. de Seguros La Nacional: Edif. Torre Lincoln, esq. Avdas. Acacias y Lincoln, Sabana Grande, Apdo. 1028, Caracas; f. 1940; Pres. FRANCISCO RAFFALLI; Exec. Vice-Pres. HECTOR BELLOSO.

"Nuevo Mundo" Seguros Generales S.A.: Edif. Sudameris, Avda. Urdaneta y Fuerzas Armadas, Apdo. 2062, Caracas; f. 1956; Gen. Man. S. CACIAGLI.

La Occidental, C.A.: Edif. Boulton, Calle 98, Apdo. 131, Maracaibo; f. 1957; Gen. Man. J. MORENO MARTÍNEZ.

Patria, C.A.: Edif. Abril, Avda. Urdaneta, esq. Las Ibarras, Apdo. 6598, Caracas; f. 1957; Man. Dr. A. J. VILELA.

La Popular, C.A.: Edif. Urapal, esq. de Urapal, Avda. Urdaneta (este 1), Caracas; f. 1958.

"La Previsora", Compañía Nacional Anónima de Seguros: esq. de La Marrón, Apdo. 848, Caracas; f. 1914; Pres. RAMÓN E. TELLO.

Reaseguradora Nacional de Venezuela, C.A.: Avda. Altamira, Don Bosco, Apdo. 68064, Caracas 101; f. 1957; Gen. Man. A. S. OLMETA.

La Seguridad, C.A.: Edif. "C.A. La Seguridad", esq. Calle Ibarras a Maturín 21-23, Apdo. 473, Caracas; f. 1943; Man. Dir. Dr. E. ANZOLA MONTAUBÁN.

Seguros Los Andes, C.A.: Carrera 7 No. 9-40, Apdo. 168, San Cristóbal; f. 1956; Man. Dr. E. RAMÍREZ.

Seguros Carabobo: Avda. Díaz Moreno y Calle Rondón, Apdo. 138, Valencia; f. 1955; Gen. Man. RODOLFO NOVA.

Seguros Caracas, C.A.: Edif. "Seguros Caracas", Torre Norte 1° piso, Marrón a Cuji, Apdo. 981, Caracas; f. 1943; cap. 25m.; Gen. Man. R. MATTHIES.

Seguros La Paz, C.A.: Edif. "La Paz-Andrés Bello", Avda. Andrés Bello, Apdo. 3242, Caracas; f. 1918; Pres. Dr. S. TOVAR, Jr.

C.A. Seguros Lara: Edif. Seguros Lara, Calle 25 con Carrera 18, Apdo. 527, Barquisimeto; f. 1957; Pres. JOSÉ MARIO PARRA.

Seguros Orinoco, C.A.: Avda. Fuerzas Armadas, esq. Socarrás, Apdo. 6448, Caracas; f. 1957; Man. HERNÁN REBOLLEDO M.

Seguros Venezuela, C.A.: Avda. Francisco de Miranda, Chacao, Apdo. 60357, Caracas; Gen. Man. ARISTIDES BRICEÑO SOTOMAYOR.

S.A. General de Seguros y Reaseguros: Edif. Luz Eléctrica de Venezuela, 4° piso, esq. de Urapal, Avda. Urdaneta, Apdo. 1792, Caracas; f. 1953; Pres. Dr. ROBERTO DÍAZ HERNÁIZ; First Vice-Pres. Dr. RICARDO ZULOAGA.

Sud América, S.A.: Edif. Sudameris, Avda. Urdaneta, Apdo. 2959, Caracas; f. 1952; Chair. Dr. C. MORALES.

La Unión, Compañía Nacional de Seguros, S.A.: Edif. Seguros Venezuela, Avda. Francisco de Miranda, Apdo. 11331, Caracas; Mans. F. ANDRES, P. STOESSEL.

La Venezolana de Vida, C.A. de Seguros: Edif. Easo, Avda. Francisco de Miranda, Chacaíto, Apdo. 60815, Caracas; f. 1969; Pres. ARTURO BRILLEMBOURG; Man. Dir. MICHAEL V. CALANDRA.

TRADE AND INDUSTRY

CHAMBERS OF COMMERCE AND INDUSTRY

CARACAS

Federación Venezolana de Cámaras y Asociaciones de Comercio y Producción—FEDECAMARAS: Edif. Fede-cámaras, 5° piso, Avda. El Empalme, El Bosque, Apdo. 2568; f. 1944; 163 mems.; Pres. Dr. OSCAR DE GURU-CEAGA.

Cámara Agrícola de Venezuela: Altagracia a Salas 28.

Cámara de Comercio de Caracas: Avda. Este 2 No. 215, Los Caobos; f. 1893; 473 mems.; Pres. RAMÓN IMERY; Sec. Dr. FÉLIX MARTÍNEZ ESPINO O.

Cámara de Industriales de Caracas: Esquina de Puente Hidalgo; f. 1935; Sec. Dr. TULIO ZAMORA HIDALGO; 835 mems.

Cámara de la Industria del Petróleo: Edif. Easo, 10° piso, Avda. Francisco de Miranda, Local D.

Cámara Minera de Venezuela: Edif. Los Claveles, Transversal de Maripérez, Apdo. 3.

Cámara Nacional del Transporte: Edif. Caupolicán, 5° piso, Apdo. 43, Sordo a Guayabal.

Cámara de Productores de Azúcar de Venezuela (*Sugar Growers*): Sta. Teresa a Cipreses 73; f. 1943; 25 mems.; Pres. JESÚS M. GARCÍA, Jr.

Cámara Venezolana de la Construcción (*Building*): Centro Profesional del Este, 13° piso, Calle Villaflor, Sabana Grande.

There are chambers of commerce and industry in all major provincial centres.

STATE CORPORATIONS AND DEVELOPMENT ORGANIZATIONS

Cordiplan: Palacio Blanco, Avda. Urdaneta, Miraflores, Caracas; co-ordination and planning office; Pres. Dr. LUIS ENRIQUE OBERTO G.; Dir. Dr. ANTONIO CASAS GONZÁLEZ.

Corporación Andina de Fomento (CAF): Apdo. 5086, Caracas; f. 1968 following the constituent agreement signed by Bolivia, Chile, Colombia, Ecuador, Peru and Venezuela; financial organization of the sub-regional Andean integration programme; commenced activities in June 1970; authorized cap. U.S. $100m., cap. p.u. U.S. $25m., (Chile, Colombia, Peru, Venezuela U.S. $5.5m. each; Bolivia, Ecuador U.S. $1.5m. each); Exec. Pres. ADOLFO LINARES.

Corporación Venezolana de Fomento: Prolongación Edif. Norte, Centro Simón Bolívar, Apdo. 1129, Caracas; f. 1947; autonomous body under government direction to develop industry and natural resources; principal source of medium- and long-term credit, supplements private financing; cap. 1,820m.; Pres. Dr. EDUARDO GÓMEZ TAMAYO; Gen. Man. Dr. ALEJANDRO ALFONZO LARRAIN; publ. *Cuadernos*.

Corporación Venezolana de Guayana: Avda. La Estancia 10, 13° piso, Apdo. 7000, Caracas; development of Guayana area; Pres. RAFAEL ALFONZO RAVARD.

Corporación Venezolana del Petróleo: Edif. Selemar, Calle Real de Sabana Grande, Apdo. 51237, Caracas; f. 1960; autonomous body under government direction; Dir.-Gen. Dr. MAURICE VALERY N.

Instituto Agrario Nacional: Quinta Barrancas, La Quebradita, Caracas; f. 1945 under Agrarian Law to assure ownership of the land to those who worked on it; now authorized to expropriate and redistribute idle or unproductive lands; nearly 150,000 families had been settled by the end of 1967.

Instituto Venezolana de Petroquímica—I.V.P.: Edif. Aco, Avda. Principal, Las Mercedes, Caracas; involved in many joint U.S. projects for expanding petrochemical industry; total investment to 1970: U.S. $274.5m. I.V.P. contribution: U.S.$130m.; active in regional economic integration.

EMPLOYERS' ASSOCIATIONS
CARACAS

Alimentos Margarita, C.A.: (*Fishermen*): Edif. Cari, 2° piso, Avda. Principal de Boleíta, Apdo. 3673; Pres. EDUARDO OROPEZA CASTILLO; Gen. Man. Dr. HÉCTOR CROCKER R.

Asociación Nacional de Comerciantes e Industriales (*Tradesmen and Industrialists*): Apdo. 33; f. 1936; Pres. Dr. JUAN CARMONA; Sec. J. S. FLORES; 500 mems.; publ. *Comercio e Industria* (monthly).

Asociación Nacional de Droguerías de Venezuela (*Druggists*): Farmacia Los Rosales, Avda. Nueva Granada 2, Apdo. 3370.

Asociación Nacional de Ganaderos de Venezuela (*Cattle-Owners*): Altagracia a Cuartel Viejo 16.

Asociación Textil Venezolana: Pres. ARMANDO BRANGER.

Federación Nacional de Asociaciones de Productores Agropecuarios—Fedeagro: Edif. Casa d'Italia, 6° piso, Of. 11, Avda. La Industria, San Bernardino.

Federación Nacional de Ganaderos de Venezuela: Edif. Casa d'Italia, 7° piso, Avda. La Industria, San Barnardino.

Unión de Industriales Textiles y de la Confección: Edif. General Urdaneta, 2° piso, Marrón a Pelota.

Unión Nacional de Productores de Azúcar de Venezuela: Edif. Luz Eléctrica, 7° piso, esq. Urapal, Avda. Urdaneta.

Unión Patronal Venezolana del Comercio: Edif. General Urdaneta, 2° piso, Marrón a Pelota.

PROVINCIAL

Asociación de Comerciantes e Industriales: Maracaibo.

Asociación Nacional de Cultivadores de Algodón (*National Cotton Growers Association*): Edif. Sivira, 2° piso, Calle Páez Oeste, Apdo. 67, Maracay.

Asociación Nacional de Empresarios y Trabajadores de la Pesca: Apdo. 52, Cumana.

Unión Nacional de Cultivadores de Tabaco: Edif. Super Centro Moro, Avda. Miranda, Local 29, Maracay.

TRADE UNIONS

About half the labour force in Venezuela belongs to unions, of which over 5,000 are legally recognized.

Confederación de Trabajadores de Venezuela—CTV (*Confederation of Venezuelan Workers*): Sur 25, Los Caobos, Apdo. 8056, Caracas; f. 1959; 1,300,000 mems. from 23 regional and 16 industrial federations; Pres. JOSÉ GONZÁLEZ NAVARRO; Sec.-Gen. AUGUSTO MALAVÉ VILLALBA; publ. *La Jornada* (weekly).

Comité Unitario de Sindicalistas Cristianos de Venezuela—C.U.S.I.C.: Apdo. 6058, Caracas; f. 1959; Pres. DAGOBERTO GONZÁLEZ; Exec. Sec. RAMÓN H. SILVA J.; publ. *Pueblo* (periodical).

Comité de Sindicatos Autónomos—CODESA: Edif. Polar, Plaza Venezuela, Los Caobos, Caracas; Catholic organization.

Central Unitaria de Trabajadores de Venezuela—CUTV: Caracas; leftist union affiliated to WFTU.

TRANSPORT

RAILWAYS

Instituto Autónomo Administración de Ferrocarriles del Estado: Caño Amarillo, Caracas; state company which took over the lines of six private railway companies with a total length of 470 km.; 175 km. of 1,435 mm. gauge now open; Gen. Man. Ing. TOMÁS E. REYNA PLAZA.

Plans are under way for building an underground railway in Caracas. The first stage was to be completed by 1973.

ROADS

In 1971 there were 43,238 km. of classified roads, most of which are open throughout the year, and about 18,600 km. of which are paved.

Of the three great highways, the first (960 km.) runs from Caracas to Ciudad Bolívar. The second, the Pan-American Highway (1,290 km.), runs from Caracas to the Colombian frontier and is continued as far as Cúcuta. A branch runs from Valencia to Puerto Cabello. The third highway runs southwards from Coro to La Ceiba, on Lake Maracaibo. In 1962 an 8-km. bridge, connecting

the two shores of Lake Maracaibo, was completed, thereby greatly improving communications between Caracas and Maracaibo, and the first bridge across the Orinoco river was built in 1967, linking the industrial area of Quayana with the rest of the country.

A new Marginal Highway is under construction along the western fringe of the Amazon Basin in Venezuela, Colombia, Ecuador, Peru, Bolivia and Paraguay. The Venezuelan section now runs for over 440 km. and is fully paved.

INLAND WATERWAYS

Instituto Nacional de Canalizaciones: Edif. Atlantic, Avda. Andrés Bello, Los Palos Grandes, Caracas; semi-autonomous institution.

Compañía Anónima La Translacustre: Maracaibo; freight and passenger service serving Lake Maracaibo, principally from Maracaibo to the road terminal from Caracas at Palmarejo.

SHIPPING

The main port for imports is La Guaira, the port for Caracas; Puerto Cabello 72 km. to the west handles raw materials for the industrial region around Valencia and is being extended to provide full facilities for handling and storage, as well as a dry dock. Maracaibo is the chief port for the oil industry. Puerto Ordaz, on the Orinoco River, has also been developed to deal with the shipments of iron from Cerro Bolívar.

C.A. Venezolana de Navegación (*Venezuelan Line*): Edif. Central, 2° piso, Avda. Urdaneta, esq. Las Ibarras, Caracas; weekly service Baltimore, Philadelphia, New York–Venezuelan ports; weekly service Houston, New Orleans–Venezuelan ports; service every two weeks to Norfolk, Charleston–Savannah–Venezuelan ports; services to north European ports of Bremen, Hamburg, Antwerp, Rotterdam, Amsterdam and ports of Le Havre and Bilbao; associated services from Scandinavian, Baltic, Mediterranean and Japanese ports; 12 cargo vessels 69,500 g.r.t.; Pres. Dr. ALFONSO MÁRQUEZ AÑEZ.

Compañía de Petróleo Lago: Edif. Creole, Apdo. 889, Caracas; Creole Petroleum Corporation; 2 tankers each of 10,905 d.w.t.

Compañía Shell de Venezuela, Ltd.: Apdo. 809, Caracas; 6 vessels of 147,832 tons; Pres. K. WETHERELL.

Ferrys del Caribe, C.A.: operates ferry services (three times weekly) between Muaco and Guarano and the Netherlands Antilles.

The following foreign shipping lines call at Venezuelan ports:

Alcoa, Belfran, Fern-Ville, French Line, Grace Line, Grancolombiana, Grimaldi Siosa Lines, Hamburg Amerika Harrison, Horn-Linie, Italian, Johnson, K. Mitsui, Lauro Lykes Bros. Steamship Co., Mitsui OSK, Moore-McCormack Lines, Nordana Line, North German Lloyd, Olsen P. & O., Royal Mail Lines, Royal Netherlands Steamship Co., Saguenay Shipping Ltd., Salen, Sidarma, Transatlántica Española, Zim.

CIVIL AVIATION

Caracas's airport, Maiquetía, is being rebuilt to handle all types of supersonic aircraft. There are 63 commercial airports.

NATIONAL AIRLINES

Aerovías Venezolanas S.A. (AVENSA): Edif. 29, Avda. Universidad, esq. El Chorro, Apdo. 943, Caracas; f. 1943; routes flown: Caracas to Barcelona, Cumaná, Porlamar, Carúpano, Maturin, Ciudad Bolívar, Pto. Ordaz, Anaco, San Tomé, Canaima, Pto. Cabello, San Felipe, Barquisimeto, Coro Carora, Las Piedras, Valera, Mérida, Maracaibo, Sta. Barbara, Zulia, San Antonio, La Fría; Pres. ANDRÉS BOULTON; Vice-Pres. HENRY BOULTON; fleet: 1 DC-9-30, 2 DC-9-10, 7 CV-580, 4 CV-340, 1 DC-3.

Linea Aéropostal Venezolana (LAV): Bloque 1, El Silencio, Caracas; f. 1933; extensive domestic network, also flights to Curaçao, Aruba and Port-of-Spain; Pres. Dr. PABLO VILLAFANE; fleet: 1 DC-9-30, 3 DC-9-15, 3 Viscount 700, 4 HS-748, 7 DC-3, 2 C-46, 2 Fairchild C-123.

Venezolana Internacional de Aviación, S.A. (VIASA): Edif. Seguros Caracas, Marrón a Dr. Paúl, Apdo. 6857, Caracas; f. 1960; partly government-owned; international flights to S. America, Caribbean, Europe and N. America; Pres. Dr. OSCAR MACHADO ZULOAGA; fleet: 2 DC-8-63, 2 DC-8-50, 2 DC-8-30, 1 DC-9-14.

Venezuela is also served by the following foreign airlines: Air France, Alitalia, ALM (Netherlands Antilles), Avianca (Colombia), British Airways, Delta, Iberia, KLM, LIAT (Leeward Islands), Pan Am, Varig (Brazil).

TOURISM

Dirección de Turismo: Ministerio de Fomento, Edif. Sur, 9° piso, Centro Bolívar, Caracas; f. 1954; Dir. DIEGO ARRIA SALICETI.

    Offices in La Guaira and Puerto Cabello.

Venezuelan Government Tourist Bureau: 485 Madison Ave., New York; Acting Man. GUILLERMO ESPINOZA FERNÁNDEZ.

Oficina Central de Información: Palacio de Miraflores, Caracas; f. 1965; information on all aspects of Venezuelan life; publ. *Carta de Venezuela* (fortnightly in Spanish, monthly in English), cultural and scientific bulletins.

Sociedad Financiera para el Fomento del Turismo y de Recreo Público (FOMTUR): Caracas; f. 1962; government tourist development agency.

Corporación Nacional de Hoteles y Turismo (CONAHOTU): Apdo. 6651, Caracas; f. 1969; government agency; Pres. DIEGO ARRIA; publs. *Venezuela Suya* (quarterly).

PRINCIPAL ORCHESTRA

Sociedad Orquesta Sinfónica Venezuela: Departamento de Cultura y Bienestar Social, Caracas; f. 1930 under the auspices of the government of the Federal District and the Instituto Nacional de Cultura y Bellas Artes.

ATOMIC ENERGY

Instituto Venezolano de Investigaciones Científicas (IVIC): Altos de Pipe, Apdo. 1827, Caracas; research in biology, medicine, chemistry, physics, mathematics and technology; atomic research facilities include a nuclear reactor of 3-5 MW; Dir. Dr. RAIMUNDO VILLEGAS; Dep. Dir. Dr. GERMÁN CAMEJO.

Universidad Central de Venezuela: Ciudad Universitaria, Caracas; atomic research in plant physiology, chemistry, physics, quantity mechanics, physical chemistry, mining and engineering.

UNIVERSITIES

Universidad de Carabobo: Apdo. 129, Valencia; 504 teachers, 11,000 students.

Universidad Católica Andrés Bello: Apdo. 29068, Caracas; 466 teachers, 4,972 students.

Universidad Central de Venezuela: Ciudad Universitaria, Caracas; 2,700 teachers, 40,179 students.

Universidad Centro-Occidental: Barquisimeto, Lara; 100 teachers, 2,000 students.

Universidad de los Andes: Mérida; 1,090 teachers, 16,490 students.

Universidad de Oriente: Apdo. 105, Cumaná, Sucre; 659 teachers, 8,300 students.

Universidad de Santa Maria: El Paraíso, Caracas; 250 teachers, 3,500 students.

Universidad del Zulia: Apdo. 526, Maracaibo; 912 teachers, 12,540 students.

DEMOCRATIC REPUBLIC OF VIET-NAM

(NORTH VIET-NAM)

INTRODUCTORY SURVEY

Location, Climate, Language, Religion, Flag, Capital

The Democratic Republic of Viet-Nam forms the northern part of the former state of Viet-Nam, previously an associate member of the French Union. The 17th parallel separates the Democratic Republic from the southern part, now called the Republic of Viet-Nam. To the north is China, to the west Laos and to the east the South China Sea. The climate is hot and wet with a monsoon season from May to October. The language is Vietnamese. The principal religions are Buddhism, Taoism and Confucianism, with a small Roman Catholic minority. The national flag (proportions 3 by 2) is red, with a large five-pointed yellow star in the centre. The capital is Hanoi.

Recent History

Viet-Nam came under French colonial rule in the late nineteenth century and with Cambodia and Laos formed the Indochinese Union. During the Second World War the Japanese used Indochina for military purposes and in 1945 assumed direct authority over the colonies. With the surrender of the Japanese, the independent Democratic Republic of Viet-Nam was proclaimed in September 1945 and the Communist Viet-Minh quickly became the dominant force in the provisional government. Negotiations with the returning French authorities broke down in 1946 and armed hostilities began. The Viet-Minh were successful in retaining control over the north and centre of the country, while in the south the French came to terms with anti-Communist elements and in 1949 created the Associated State of Viet-Nam. The Geneva Agreements of 1954 brought the war to an end. Viet-Nam was partitioned into two military zones, with the Communist forces regrouped north of 17°N. latitude and the non-Communists south of it, pending a political settlement. The general elections throughout Viet-Nam, envisaged in the Geneva Agreements, have not taken place and the effect of the partition has been the continued existence of two governments in the country. From 1960 onwards the northern government has played an active part in the resistance movement in the south, greatly increasing this support after 1963. The U.S.A. intervened vigorously in the war in 1965, sending a large land-force to the south and bombing targets in the north. In November 1968 the bombing was halted and peace talks between the four participants in the war opened in Paris. In April 1971, 420 deputies were elected to the National Assembly. In April 1972, a major military offensive was launched against South Viet-Nam on several fronts. Following U.S. blockading and mining of North Vietnamese ports and the extension of U.S. bombing to include Hanoi and Haiphong, the offensive was halted in September. In October the North Vietnamese government rejected a draft U.S. peace agreement and in December U.S. bombing of the North was resumed with great intensity.

In late January 1973 a peace agreement was signed. This included a ceasefire throughout South Viet-Nam; U.S.

withdrawal from Viet-Nam; the establishment in the South of a National Council of National Reconciliation and Concord; reunification of Viet-Nam to be agreed between North and South by peaceful means without outside interference; and U.S. agreement to aid the North on post-war reconstruction.

Fighting continued unabated, however, and the International Commission of Control and Supervision, which had been set up to supervise the ceasefire in the South, was unable to perform its task. By the winter of 1973 the North Vietnamese had built up their supply routes along the Laotian and Cambodian borders and were thought to have built up their armaments also. In December North Vietnamese and United States' spokesmen met in Paris. The United States offered aid for the reconstruction of North Viet-Nam in return for the cancellation of an expected offensive against the Saigon Government's forces, an accounting of U.S. prisoners of war and a cessation of interference in the affairs of Laos and the Khmer Republic. There were indications in the early months of 1974 that this offer had been accepted. In April 1974 the cabinet was reshuffled, apparently with the aim of strengthening governmental machinery for post-war reconstruction.

Government

Legislative power is vested in the National Assembly elected for a four-year term by universal adult suffrage. The Assembly elects the President of the Republic for a similar period. Executive power is exercised by the Council of Ministers which is responsible to the National Assembly. There are seventeen provinces.

Defence

At the end of 1973, the armed forces totalled 578,000 men (army 564,750, navy 3,250, air force 10,000), with an additional half million militia and security troops. About 240,000 troops were believed to be deployed in South Viet-Nam in early 1974. Military service commences at 18 years of age. Considerable military aid has been received both from China and the Soviet Union.

Economic Affairs

The economy is governed by a five-year plan. About 85 per cent of agriculture is collectivized. The chief crops are rice (the staple crop), wheat, maize, sugar, coffee, tea, fruit, tobacco, cotton, soybeans and jute. The vast forests yield bamboo and teak. There are coal deposits scattered over 750 square miles and producing about 3 million tons annually. The most valuable deposit is the anthracite of Quang-Yen. Other minerals mined are tin, zinc, copper, chromium, iron, silver, mercury, gold and, most important, apatite (phosphate). Industries include iron and steel (at the Thai-Nguyen works), fertilizers, textiles, paper and food processing.

In February 1974 the Government announced details of plans for the reconstruction of the economy during the following two years.

Transport and Communications

There are 1,500 km. of railways based on Hanoi, of which about half are believed to be in operation. Roads, badly damaged during hostilities, have been rebuilt and now extend for some 13,400 km. Rivers are much used for transport. The main port is Haiphong. There are internal air services and a direct line to Canton.

Social Welfare

The state operates a system of social security. Hospitals, dispensaries and sanatoria number about 400. Mobile medical teams treat trachoma, malaria and other diseases.

Education

There is compulsory education, where possible, for 10 years. Pupils number about 7,000,000. There is one university, in Hanoi.

Tourism

There are mountains and seaside resorts but few foreign visitors.

Sport

The state encourages team games and athletics.

Weights and Measures

The metric system is in force.

Currency and Exchange Rates

100 xu = 10 hào = 1 dông.

Exchange rates (April 1974):
£1 sterling = 5.815 dông;
U.S. $1 = 2.463 dông.

STATISTICAL SURVEY

AREA AND POPULATION

AREA	Census (March 1st, 1960)	MID-YEAR POPULATION (UN estimates)				
		1969	1970	1971	1972	1973
158,750 sq. km.*	15,916,955	20,715,000	21,154,000	21,595,000	22,038,000	22,481,000

* 61,294 square miles.

PRINCIPAL TOWNS
(1960 census)

Hanoi (capital)	.	414,620*	Nam Dinh	.	86,132
Haiphong	.	182,490†	Vinh	.	43,954

* Greater Hanoi 643,576.   † Greater Haiphong 369,248.

Births and Deaths: Average annual birth rate 37.5 per 1,000; death rate 16.1 per 1,000 (UN estimates for 1965–70).

Employment (mid-1970): In a total population of 20,757,000, the economically active numbered 10,921,000, including 8,475,000 in agriculture (FAO and ILO estimates).

AGRICULTURE

LAND USE, 1966
('000 hectares)

Arable and Under Permanent Crops	.	2,018
Forest Land	.	7,900
Other Land and Inland Water	.	5,957
TOTAL AREA	.	15,875

Source: FAO, *Production Yearbook 1971.*

DEMOCRATIC REPUBLIC OF VIET-NAM—(Statistical Survey)

PRINCIPAL CROPS
(FAO estimates)

	Area Harvested ('000 hectares)				Production ('000 metric tons)			
	1968	1969	1970	1971	1968	1969	1970	1971
Maize	210	210	210	210	230	240	250	230
Rice (Paddy) . . .	2,500	2,500	2,500	2,400	4,920*	4,900	5,000	4,600
Sugar Cane†, ‡	19	19	19	19	600	600	600	600
Sweet Potatoes and Yams	188	190	190	n.a.	830	900	900	n.a.
Cassava (Manioc)	100	100	100	n.a.	700	700	730	n.a.
Dry Beans . . .	60	60	60	60	15	15	15	15
Soybeans . . .	36	38	38	38	17	18	19	19
Groundnuts (in shell) .	46	47	47	43	42	45	46	40
Cottonseed . . .	} 20	20	20	20	} 4	4	4	4
Cotton (Lint) . .					2	2	2	2
Sesame Seed .	7	7	7	7	3	3	3	3
Castor Beans .	4	4	4	4	2	2	2	2
Coffee	n.a.	n.a.	n.a.	n.a.	1	1	1	1
Tea†	12	12	13	13	2.7	2.7	2.8	2.8
Tobacco . . .	4	4	4	4	4	4	4	4
Kenaf	12	12	12	12	16	16	16	16

* Unofficial estimate quoted by FAO.
† Planted area.
‡ Crop year ending in year stated.

Source: FAO, *Production Yearbook, 1971.*

LIVESTOCK
('000—FAO estimates)

	1967–68	1968–69	1969–70	1970–71
Cattle	840	850	865	880
Pigs	6,200	6,400	6,600	6,800
Buffaloes . . .	1,620	1,680	1,700	1,700
Horses	56	57	58	59

Source: FAO, *Production Yearbook 1971.*

Forestry (1970): Timber 1,125,000 cubic metres (est).

MINING
('000 metric tons)

	1968	1969	1970	1971
Coal	3,000	3,000	3,000	3,000
Salt	150	150	150	150
Phosphate Rock .	1,050	1,230	1,050	n.a.

Source: Bureau of Mines, U.S. Department of the Interior.

Note: No recent data are available for the production of chromium ore (19,400 metric tons in 1960), tin or zinc.

INDUSTRY

ELECTRIC ENERGY
(million kWh)

1962	368
1963	460
1964	548
1965	660

CEMENT
(metric tons)

1966	750,000
1967	750,000
1968	495,000
1969	495,000
1970	495,000

Source: United Nations, *Statistical Yearbook 1972.*

OTHER COMMODITIES
('ooo metric tons unless otherwise specified)

	1960	1965 (Target)	% Change +
Pumps (units)	—	1,400	—
Phosphate Fertilizer	51	224	339
Fish	112.5	200	78
Fish Sauce (million litres)	29.6	60	103
Sugar and Molasses	25.3	50	97
Cigarettes (million packets)	73.4	160	118
Cotton and Silk Fabrics (million metres)	92.5	134	45
Paper	4.5	35.5	689
Bicycles ('ooo units)	27	100	270

FINANCE

100 xu = 10 hào = 1 dông.

Coins: 1, 2 and 5 xu.

Notes: 2 xu; 1, 2, and 5 hào; 1, 2, 5 and 10 dông.

Exchange rates (April 1974): £1 sterling = 5.815 dông; U.S. $1 = 2.463 dông.

100 dông = £17.20 = $40.61.

Note: Prior to August 1971 the dông was valued at 34 U.S. cents (U.S. $1 = 2.941 dông). From December 1971 to February 1973 the dông's value was 36.91 U.S. cents ($1 = 2.709 dông). In terms of sterling, the value of the dông between November 1967 and June 1972 was 2s. 10d. (14.17p), the exchange rate being £1 = 7.059 dông (or 12 dông = £1.70).

Budget (1963): Balanced at 1,779,288,000 dông; Gifts received under Five-Year Plan 88,893,000 dông; Loans received 167,259,400 dông.

AID FROM COMMUNIST COUNTRIES

The following tables, prepared by U.S. intelligence sources, show U.S. estimates of aid received by North Viet-Nam.

ECONOMIC AID
(million U.S. dollars)

Donor	1965	1966	1967	1968	1969	1970	1971
U.S.S.R.	225	450	600	720	750	1,035	945
China, People's Republic	150	225	240	300	270	180	300
Eastern Europe	45	150	240	360	405	615	655

MILITARY AID
(million U.S. dollars)

DONOR	1965	1966	1967	1968	1969	1970	1971
U.S.S.R.	630	1,080	1,515	870	360	210	300
China, People's Republic	180	285	435	300	315	225	225

Source: Asia Research Bulletin, May 1972.

EXTERNAL TRADE
NON-COMMUNIST COUNTRIES
(U.S. $'000)

	IMPORTS		EXPORTS	
	1967	1968	1967	1968
France	627	1,374	541	313
Germany, Federal Republic	521	664	122	172
Italy	550	143	71	107
Netherlands	473	46	99	128
Sweden	5	79	27	9
Switzerland	9	16	9	74
United Kingdom	185	254	207	122
Khmer Republic	484	432	627	306
Hong Kong	151	52	1,099	1,168
Japan	1,817	2,444	6,686	6,108
Malaysia	—	13*	229	100*
Singapore	1,228	1,232	1,447	1,375
Egypt	1	83†	97	55†
TOTAL	6,051	6,832	11,261	10,037

* Jan.–Oct.   † Jan.–Nov.

COMMUNIST COUNTRIES
(U.S.$'000)

	IMPORTS 1966	EXPORTS 1966
U.S.S.R.	68,200	25,300
Czechoslovakia	13,800	5,600
German Democratic Republic	16,500	5,000
Hungary	9,700	1,500
Poland	10,520	3,720
Romania	9,000	200
TOTAL	127,720	41,320

TRANSPORT
INTERNATIONAL SEA-BORNE SHIPPING
(metric tons)

	1968	1969
Goods Loaded	370,000	360,000
Goods Unloaded	850,000	915,000

Source: United Nations, Statistical Yearbook 1971.

Inland Waterways (1960): 27 million freight ton-km.

EDUCATION
(1966–67)

	GENERAL	SECONDARY VOCATIONAL	HIGHER
Schools	10,993	185	28
Teachers	86,495	4,194	5,004
Pupils and Undergraduates* . .	4,517,600	101,880	48,402
of which: in evening and correspondence courses	1,154,500	9,300	10,743

*1972: Number of students at all grades is 7 million.

Sources (unless otherwise indicated): *Nhan Dan* of May 3rd and 4th, 1963; text of the Five-Year Plan as presented to the National Assembly (end April 1963); trade statistics of partner countries; General Statistical Office of the Democratic Republic of Viet-Nam.

THE CONSTITUTION

The original constitution of the Democratic Republic was replaced by a revised constitution, adopted in 1960.

Main provisions:

Unity of Viet-Nam: The territory of Viet-Nam is an indivisible whole.

Economic Principles: The economy is directed by a plan, and the state relies on the organs of state, the trade unions and the co-operative sector to assist in fulfilling the plan. In the present transitional period, ownership of the means of production, may be by the state, by the co-operative sector, by individuals or by national capitalists.

President: elected for four years. He is responsible for most senior appointments, and promulgates laws and decrees. He represents the country in external affairs, and is the supreme commander of the armed forces.

Council of Ministers: consists of the Prime Minister (President), the Vice-Premiers, the Heads of State Commissions and the Director-General of the National Bank. The Council is responsible to the National Assembly.

Special Political Conference: *ad hoc* executive body convened to make important political decisions. The President of the state takes the chair.

National Assembly: elected for the same period as the President. The Assembly is to meet twice a year, or for extraordinary sessions. It elects a President of the Assembly, the President and Vice-President of the state, the Prime Minister and other officials. It discusses economic plans, and, among other functions, examines and approves the budget.

Standing Committee of the National Assembly: permanent executive body of the Assembly, and elected by it. It consists of a Chairman, Vice-Chairman, Secretary-General, and members. It is responsible to the National Assembly, and decides questions of election and franchise, and most appointments. It also supervises local government.

Local Government: the country is divided into provinces, and subdivided into districts, cities and towns. There are People's Courts at all these levels, elected locally.

Judicial System: consists of the Supreme People's Court, local People's Courts, and military courts. There are also People's Organs of Control, under the Supreme People's Organ of Control, to secure observance of the laws.

THE GOVERNMENT

President of the Republic: TON DUC THANG.
Vice-President: NGUYEN LUONG BANG.

THE CABINET
(*April* 1974)

Prime Minister: PHAM VAN DONG.

Deputy Premiers: NGUYEN DUY TRINH, LE THANH NGHI, Gen. VO NGUYEN GIAP, HUANG ANH, NGUYEN CON, TRAN HUU DUC, Brig. PHAN TRONG TUE, DANG VIET CHAU.

Deputy Premier, Minister of Building: DO MUOI.

Minister of National Defence: Gen. VO NGUYEN GIAP.

Minister of Foreign Affairs: NGUYEN DUY TRINH.

Minister of the Interior: DUONG QUOC CHINH.

Minister of Foreign Trade: PHAN ANH.

Minister of Internal Trade: HOANG HUOC THINH.

Minister of Electricity and Coal: (vacant).

Minister of Materials: TRAN DANH TUYEN.

Minister of Light Industry: KHA VANG CAN.

Minister of Finance: DANG VIET CHAU.

Minister of Communications and Transport: DUONG BACH LIEN.

Minister of Water Conservancy: HA KE TAN.

Minister of Grain and Food Products: NGO MINH LOAN.

Minister of Culture: HOANG MINH GIAM.

Minister of Education: NGUYEN VAN HUYEN.

Minister of Higher Education and Vocational Middle Schools: TA QUANG VUU.

Minister of Labour: (vacant).

Minister of Machinery and Metallurgy: NGUYEN CON.

Minister of Premier's Office: TRAN HUU DUC.

Minister of Public Health: NGUYEN VAN HUONG.

Minister of Public Security: TRAN QUOC HOAN.

Minister of Water: NGUYEN THANH BINH.

Minister Director of Premier's Office: PHAN MY.

Minister in Charge of Cultural Affairs and Education: TRAN QUANG HUY.

Ministers Vice-Chairmen of the Central Agricultural Commission: NGHIEM XUAN YEM, NGUYEN VAN LOC.

Ministers Vice-Chairmen of the State Planning Commission: NGUYEN VAN KHA, (vacant).

Minister with Special Responsibility for the Construction of the Da River Dam: HA KE TAN.

Minister without Portfolio: XUAN THUY.

Chairman of the Central Agricultural Commission: (vacant).

Chairman of the Central Nationalities Commission: LE KUANG BA.

Chairman of the National Bank: TA HOANG CO.

Chairman of the National Reunification Commission: DANG THI.

Chairman of the State Inspection Commission: NGUYEN VAN LOC.

Chairman of the State Planning Commission: LE THANH NGHI.

Chairman of the State Price Commission: (vacant).

Chairman of the State Scientific and Technical Commission: TRAN DAI NGHIA.

CENTRAL COMMITTEE OF THE LAO-DONG PARTY
First Secretary: LE DUAN.

DIPLOMATIC REPRESENTATION

Ambassadors accredited to the country include Dr. KLAUS WILLERDING (German Democratic Republic), BERNT ARNE BJÖRNBERG (Sweden), ANSOU KAMANO (Guinea), MOHAMMED CHERIF SAHLI (Algeria), ASSANE GUINDO (Mali), SALAH EL DEN A. EL ABD (Egypt), TUNJINGIYN MASHLAY (Mongolia), T. ZAMFIR (Romania), WANG YU-PING (People's Republic of China).

The Canadian and United Kingdom ambassadors had not yet presented their credentials by May 1974.

Diplomatic relations are also maintained with Argentina, Australia, Bangladesh, Cameroon, Canada, Denmark, Finland, France, India, Japan, Madagascar, Malaysia, Norway, Singapore, Switzerland, Syria, Tunisia, U.S.S.R., United Kingdom, Yemen (People's Democratic Republic) and Zambia.

The Democratic Republic of Viet-Nam has diplomatic relations at Ministerial level with Burma.

NATIONAL ASSEMBLY

GENERAL ELECTION, APRIL 1971

There were unopposed Communist candidates for roughly three-quarters of the 420 seats.

Chairman of the Standing Committee: TRUONG CHINH.

Secretary-General: TON QUANG PHIET.

POLITICAL PARTIES

Lao-Dong Party (*Viet-Nam Workers' Party*): Hanoi; controlling party in Viet-Nam Fatherland Front (Viet-Minh); successor to the Communist Party of Indochina; f. 1930; Chair. (vacant); First Sec. LE DUAN; 620,000 mems.; publ. *Nhan Dan*.

Socialist Party: Hanoi; f. 1951; consists mainly of intelligentsia; Gen. Sec. NGUYEN XIEN.

Democratic Party: Hanoi; f. 1944; party of the middle classes, businessmen and intelligentsia; Sec.-Gen. NGHIEM XUAN YEM.

POLITICAL ORGANIZATIONS

Ho Chi Minh Working Youth Union: 60 Ba Trieu, Hanoi; f. 1931; 2,600,000 mems.; Sec. VU QUANG.

Federation of Vietnamese Women: Hanoi; 3,500,000 mems.

Viet-Nam Fatherland Front: Hanoi; f. 1955; unites the three political parties and state organizations for political purposes; led by the Lao-Dong Party.

DEFENCE

Armed Forces and Equipment (1973): Total 578,000 of which army 564,750; navy 3,250; air force 10,000 (plus para-military forces of 445,000). Of the DRVN regular troops, about 200,000 are now deployed in South Viet-Nam, 63,000 in Laos and about 40,000 in Cambodia. Equipment is largely of Soviet and Chinese origin and includes 550 field guns, 390 tanks, 228 combat aircraft, 46 SAM(missile) battalions and 12 AA regiments. There are also about 1,000 Soviet military advisers in North Viet-Nam and 20,000 Chinese working on construction and engineering projects there and in Laos. A new agreement was signed in September 1972 between the Soviet Union and China for the transhipment of Soviet war material through China to North Viet-Nam to offset American mining and blockading of the country's ports and the renewed U.S. bombing campaign.

Military Service: Two years minimum.

Defence Expenditure: Estimated defence spending (1970): 2,150 million dông (U.S. $731 million).

Commander-in-Chief DRVN Armed Forces: General VO NGUYEN GIAP.

JUDICIAL SYSTEM

The Judicial System, based on French lines, has been thoroughly revised since 1954. The Supreme Court in Hanoi is the chief court and exercises civil and criminal jurisdiction over all lower courts. There are People's Courts in District towns, and a number of military courts. The observance of the laws is the concern of the People's Organs of Control, under a Supreme People's Organ of Control.

President of the Supreme Court: PHAM VAN BACH.

RELIGION

BUDDHISTS

Most of the population is Buddhist. It is estimated that about 200,000 Buddhists emigrated to South Viet-Nam in 1954.

CHRISTIANS (ROMAN CATHOLICS)

There are about two million Christians in Viet-Nam, mostly Roman Catholic. Following the Geneva Agreements of 1954, almost all the Catholics moved into the Southern part of Viet-Nam.

Archbishop of Hanoi: Most Rev. JOSEPH MARIE TRIN NHU KHUE, 40 Phô Nhà Chung, Hanoi.

THE PRESS

DAILIES

Nhan Dan (*People's Daily*): Hanoi; f. 1946; official organ of the Lao-Dong Party; circ. 100,000.

Thoi Moi: Hanoi; circ. 25,000.

Thu Do Hanoi: Hanoi; f. 1957; Editor Dinh Nho Khoi; circ. 30,000.

There are some 45 regional dailies.

PERIODICALS

Bulletin of the Medical Association of the Viet-Nam D.R.: Hanoi; illustrated annual in French and English.

Cuu Quoc (*National Salvation*): Hanoi; weekly; f. 1942; organ of the Fatherland Front; circ. 20,000; Chief Editor Nguyen Tieu.

Hoc Tap (*Studies*): 28 rue Tran binh Trong, Hanoi; monthly; f. 1955; organ of the Lao Dong Party; circ. 50,000.

Lao Dong (*Labour*): Hanoi; twice weekly; organ of Federation of Trade Unions; circ. 10,000.

Nhan Dan Nong Thong (*Peasantry*): Hanoi; twice weekly; agricultural supplement; circ. 21,000.

Quan Doi Nhan Dan (*People's Army*): f. 1957; published by the Army.

Tien Phong (*Avant Garde*): 15 rue Ho Xuan Huong, Hanoi; f. 1957; three times weekly; organ of the Youth Movement; circ. 16,000.

Viet-Nam: 79 Ly Thuong Kiet St., Hanoi; f. 1954; illustrated monthly; published by Committee for Cultural Relations with Foreign Countries; Vietnamese, Russian, Chinese, French, Spanish and English; circ. 86,000; Dir. Le Ba Thuyen.

Viet-Nam Courier: 46 Tran Hung Dao, Hanoi; weekly; Committee for Cultural Relations with Foreign Countries; English and French editions.

Vietnamese Studies: 46 Tran Hung Dao, Hanoi; quarterly publ. by Committee for Cultural Relations with Foreign Countries; English and French editions.

NEWS AGENCIES

Viet-Nam News Agency: Hanoi.

FOREIGN BUREAUX

Czechoslovak News Agency (Ceteka): 63 Hoang Dieu St., Hanoi.

Novosti Press Agency: APN Representation, 15 Thuyen Guang St., Hanoi.

Tass also has a bureau in Hanoi.

PUBLISHERS

Su That (*Truth*) **Publishing House:** Hanoi; controlled by the Government; Marxist classics, political and philosophical works.

Foreign Languages Publishing House: Hanoi; controlled by the Government.

Giao Duc (*Educational*) **Publishing House:** Hanoi; Ministry of Education.

Khoa Hoc (*Social Sciences*) **Publishing House:** Hanoi.

Lao Dong (*Labour*) **Publishing House:** Hanoi.

Literary Publishing House: Hanoi; State-controlled.

Pho Thong (*Popularization*) **Publishing House:** Hanoi.

Popular Army Publishing House: Hanoi.

Scientific Publishing House: Hanoi.

Y Hoc (*Medical*) **Publishing House:** Hanoi.

RADIO

Voice of Viet-Nam: 58 Quan-Su Street, Hanoi; controlled by the Council of Ministers; Home Service in Vietnamese; Foreign Service in English, Japanese, Korean, French, Cambodian, Laotian, Thai, Cantonese and Standard Chinese, and Indonesian; Dir.-Gen. T. Lam.

In 1971 there were 510,000 radio receivers.

There is no television.

FINANCE

BANKING

State Bank of the Democratic Republic of Viet-Nam (Vietbank): 7 Le-Lai St., Hanoi; f. 1951; central bank of issue; 350 branches; Min. Gen. Dir. Ta Hoang Co, Vice-Mins. Dep. Gen. Dir. Le Duc, Vu-Duy-Hieu Tran-Duong, Dinh-Van-Bay.

Bank for Foreign Trade of the Democratic Republic of Viet-Nam (Vietcombank): 47–49, Ly-Thai-To St., Hanoi; f. 1963; the only bank authorized to deal in the country with foreign currencies and international payments; Chair. Tran Duong; Vice-Chair. Dao Viet Doan, Mai Huu Ich.

INSURANCE

Viet-Nam Insurance Co. (Baoviet): 7 Ly Thuong Kiet, Hanoi; state company; marine insurance.

TRADE AND INDUSTRY

Chamber of Commerce of the Democratic Republic of Viet-Nam (Vietcochamber): 33 Ba Trieu St., Hanoi; attached organizations are:

Vinacontrol (*Goods Control Office*): 54 Tran Nhan Tong St., Hanoi.

Maritime Arbitration Committee: 33 Ba Trieu St., Hanoi; settles and exercises jurisdiction over disputes arising from sea transportation.

Foreign Trade Arbitration Committee: 33 Ba Trieu St., Hanoi; settles disputes arising from foreign trade transactions between Vietnamese and foreign economic organizations.

All foreign trade activities are directed and controlled by the State through the intermediary of the Ministry of Foreign Trade. To this effect, several National Import-Export Corporations have been set up (*see below*).

FOREIGN TRADE CORPORATIONS

Agrexport (*Viet-Nam National Agricultural Produce and Foodstuffs Export-Import Corporation*): 6 Trang Tien, Hanoi; imports and exports agricultural produce and foodstuffs.

Artexport (*Viet-Nam National Handicrafts and Arts Articles Export-Import Corporation*): 31–33 Ngo Quyen St., Hanoi; deals in craft products and art materials.

Machinoimport (*Viet-Nam National Machinery Export-Import Corporation*): 8 Trang Thi St., Hanoi; imports and exports machinery and tools.

Meranimex (*Viet-Nam National Marine and Animal Products Import and Export Corporation*): 17 Cu Chinh Lan St., Haiphong; exports live animals, salted and frozen meat, eggs, animal feeds, furs and skins, shellfish and seaweed.

Minexport (*Viet-Nam National Minerals Export-Import Corporation*): 35 Hai Ba Trung, Hanoi; exports minerals and metals, quarry products, building materials, chemical products, pharmaceutical products; imports coal, metals, pharmaceutical and chemical products, industrial and building materials, fuels and oils, asphalt, fertilizers, gypsum and cement bags.

Naforimex (*Viet-Nam National Forest and Native Produce Export-Import Corporation*): 19 Ba Trieu St., Hanoi; imports coconut products, rubber and wood and exports oils, forest products and miscellaneous products.

Technoimport (*Viet-Nam National Complete Equipment Import and Technical Exchange Corporation*): 16–18 Trang Thi St., Hanoi; imports industrial plant.

Tocontap (*Viet-Nam National Sundries Export-Import Corporation*): 36 Ba Trieu St., Hanoi; imports and exports consumer goods.

Transaf (*Viet-Nam National Foreign Trade Corporation*): 33 Ba Trieu St., Hanoi; import and export transactions with foreign co-operative societies and firms in consumer goods and foodstuffs; re-exports; compensation trade; agents for all commercial transactions.

Xunhasaba (*Viet-Nam State Corporation for Export and Import of Books, Periodicals and other Cultural Commodities*): 32 Hai Ba Trung, Hanoi.

Fafim (*Viet-Nam State Film Distribution Enterprise*): 49 Nguyen Trai, Hanoi; export and import of films; organization of film shows and participation of Vietnamese films in international film exhibitions.

All commercial and non-commercial payments to foreign countries are effected through the Bank of Foreign Trade of the Democratic Republic of Viet-Nam.

TRADE UNIONS

Tong Cong Doan Viet-Nam (T.C.D.) (*Viet-Nam Federation of Trade Unions*): 82 Tran Hung Dao, Hanoi; f. 1946; 1,200,000 mems.; Pres. HOANG QUOC VIET; Gen. Sec. NGUYEN DUC THUAN; publs. *Viet-Nam Trade Unions* (in English, French and Spanish), *Lao Dong*, *Cong Doan*.

TRANSPORT AND TOURISM

RAILWAYS

Viet-Minh National Railways: Hanoi; Government-owned; official information is not available, but lines reported to be in operation are: Hanoi–Haiphong (104 km.), Hanoi–Mukh Nam Quong (162 km.), Hanoi–Thanh Hoa (167 km.), Hanoi–Laokay (296 km.), Dong Anh–Thai Nguyen (51 km.).

ROADS

National Automobile Transport Undertaking: Hanoi; f. 1951; operates long distance and municipal bus services.

There are about 13,400 kilometres of motorable roads.

SHIPPING

Vietfracht (*Viet-Nam Foreign Trade Transportation Corporation*): 74 Nguyen Du St., Hanoi; in charge of all activities concerning sea transportation; charters vessels and books shipping space for principals at home and abroad; canvasses cargo for shipowners; provides regular services to and from South-East Asian ports, mainly Haiphong–Hong Kong–Singapore, Cambodian ports–Heungnam–Chungjin and main Japanese ports; provides services to and from the Black Sea and western and northern Europe.

Viet-Nam Ocean Shipping Agency (VOSA): 11 Tran Phu St., Haiphong; in charge of performing all such facilities as may be required for the coming and going of merchant shipping, of loading and unloading operations, lighterage, forwarding and reception of goods, tallying, weighing and measuring, warehousing, reconditioning and repacking of damaged goods; arranging the booking of cargo, the chartering, purchase and sale of vessels and the settlement of marine casualties and insurance.

CIVIL AVIATION

Civil Aviation of Viet-Nam (CAVN): Hanoi; f. 1954; Government-owned; controls all services but operates no aircraft; Gia Lam is the largest civil airport.

Civil Aviation Administration of China: operates services between Gia Lam and Canton.

Interflug Gesellschaft: operates services between East Berlin and Hanoi via Moscow, Tashkent and Dacca.

TOURISM

Vietnamtourism (*Viet-Nam Travel Service*): 54 Nguyen Du St., Hanoi.

UNIVERSITY

University of Hanoi: Hanoi; about 150 teachers; about 1,500 students.

REPUBLIC OF VIET-NAM
(SOUTH VIET-NAM)

INTRODUCTORY SURVEY

Location, Climate, Language, Religion, Flag, Capital

The Republic of Viet-Nam is situated in the eastern part of South-East Asia with the Democratic Republic of Viet-Nam to the north of the 17th parallel and the Khmer Republic to the west. The China Sea lies to the east. The climate is warm and humid with a monsoon season from May to October. The language is Vietnamese. Buddhism is the religion of most of the population. There are sizeable groups of Cao-Daiists, Hoa-Hao, Confucians, Taoists and Roman Catholics. The national flag (proportions 3 by 2) is deep yellow, with three horizontal crimson stripes in the centre. The capital is Saigon.

Recent History

(For the history of the country up to the partition of Viet-Nam in 1954 *see* the chapter on the Democratic Republic of Viet-Nam.)

Ngo Dinh Diem became Prime Minister of the State of Viet-Nam in 1954 and, following a referendum, proclaimed himself President of the Republic of Viet-Nam in 1955. The authoritarian nature of the Diem régime provoked a serious resistance movement in the south and the insurgents (mainly former members of the Viet-Minh) established the National Liberation Front (NLF) in December 1960. The People's Revolutionary (Communist) Party soon became a dominant element in the NLF. In November 1963 Diem was overthrown in a military *coup*, and a series of short-lived military régimes followed. The last of these was the National Leadership Committee, established in June 1965, with Lt.-Gen. Nguyen Van Thieu as Chairman and Air Vice-Marshal Nguyen Cao Ky as Prime Minister. This group introduced a new constitution in 1967, when presidential and parliamentary elections were held in government-controlled areas. With the NLF and "neutralist" candidates banned, Gen. Thieu was elected President, and Marshal Ky Vice-President, with 35 per cent of the popular vote. In 1971, after splitting with Marshal Ky, Thieu was re-elected unopposed after all other candidates withdrew.

The resistance movement in the south developed in the early 1960s into full-scale hostilities, and the North Vietnamese intervened to assist anti-government forces while the U.S.A. and allied powers gave enormous military and financial aid to the Saigon régime. Peace talks between the four participants in the war opened in Paris in November 1968. In June 1969 the NLF announced the formation of a Provisional Revolutionary Government (PRG) to administer "liberated" areas.

In early April 1972, North Vietnamese forces launched a major military offensive against South Viet-Nam on three fronts; in the north, in the central highlands and in the south. The U.S. resumed large-scale offensive bombing of North Viet-Nam and in May President Nixon announced a blockade and mining of all its ports. Martial law was proclaimed in the South. In late June President Thieu assumed emergency powers. In September the North Vietnamese offensive was stopped with the capture by Saigon troops of Quang Tri province.

In January 1973 a peace agreement was signed by the U.S.A., South Viet-Nam, North Viet-Nam and the PRG. The fighting in South Viet-Nam continued during 1973, however, and a second ceasefire in July was no more effective than the first. The North Vietnamese appeared to be preparing for a new offensive early in 1974 but, following offers of aid from the U.S.A., this offensive was not launched. Talks in Paris between representatives of the Saigon Government and the PRG to set up a National Council of National Reconciliation and Concord, and to arrange for elections, failed to make progress and were suspended in April 1974.

Senate elections in August 1973 strengthened President Thieu's position and in February 1974 the constitution was amended to extend his term of office.

Government

Legislative authority is vested in the National Assembly, consisting of a House of Representatives elected for four years by universal suffrage, and a Senate whose members are elected by list voting for six years. Executive authority resides in the President, who is elected by universal suffrage for four years. The President appoints the Prime Minister and, on the latter's proposal, the members of the Government. There is a Supreme Court, whose functions include the interpretation of the Constitution.

Defence

South Vietnamese armed forces, commanded by Vietnamese officers and trained under U.S. supervision, include 460,000 ground troops, 50,000 airmen, a navy of 45,000, 17,000 marines and 1.4 million local militia and police. Anti-government forces, which include North Vietnamese regular troops, are estimated at about 320,000.

Economic Affairs

The economy is dominated by agriculture. Rice is overwhelmingly the most important food crop, with about four-fifths of arable land under rice; maize, cassava and sweet potatoes are grown as a substitute for rice, while coffee and tea are also important. Rubber is the principal industrial crop, followed by sugar, coconut oil, copra and kenaf. Fishing provides a valuable supplement to the diet. Industry is confined to food processing, light machinery assembly, cement, paper, glass, beverages and textiles.

The war in South Viet-Nam has seriously affected the economy, however, making industrial development virtually impossible and disrupting agricultural production. Before the Second World War Viet-Nam was the world's third largest rice exporter but the Government in Saigon now imports rice to meet needs. About half the country, including most of the rubber-growing and some important rice-growing regions, was in the hands of the Provisional Revolutionary Government (PRG) at the end of 1973. The Saigon Government has been supported by massive aid from the U.S.A. for both military and economic purposes. The withdrawal of U.S. forces from Viet-Nam in 1973 and cuts in U.S. aid in 1974 therefore posed a considerable threat to the economy in areas controlled from Saigon. Inflation worsened in 1973 with rice and fuel prices rising especially rapidly. The trade deficit lessened slightly in 1973 but still remained enormous. In May 1973 President Thieu launched an eight-year programme, the first stage of which (1973–74) gave priority to relief operations, refugee aid, the reconstruction of the country's infrastructure and the resumption of production.

Transport and Communications

There are about 1,278 km. of railways, of which about half are open, and 20,027 km. of motorable roads. Inland waterways total 4,500 km., of which 2,200 km. are canals. Air Viet-Nam maintains internal and external services throughout South-East Asia and the Far East. Saigon is served by nine airlines.

Social Welfare

There are a number of general and field hospitals providing several thousand beds. In addition there are 615 village maternity clinics. There is a pension scheme for state workers.

Education

In 1969–70 there were 7,978 primary schools, half of them privately owned, and 886 secondary schools. There are five universities.

Tourism

The main centres of tourism are Saigon, the old city of Hué in the north-east and Dalat, a mountain resort. There is abundant wild game, which attracts many hunters.

Visas are required by all visitors, unless staying under 72 hours.

Sport

Football is the most popular game.

Public Holidays

1974: November 1st (National Day), December 25th (Christmas Day).

1975: January 1st (New Year's Day), January–February (*Têt*, Lunar New Year), March 28th (Easter), March 31st (Ancestors' Day), May 1st (Labour Day), May (Buddha's Birthday).

Weights and Measures

The metric system is in force.

Currency and Exchange Rates

100 centimes = 1 Viet-Nam piastre.

Exchange rates (April 1974):

£1 sterling = 1,428.56 piastres;
U.S. $1 = 605.00 piastres.

STATISTICAL SURVEY

AREA (sq. km.)		POPULATION (official estimates for July 1st)	
Central Lowlands	54,988	1966 . .	16,543,000
Central Highlands	49,921	1967 . .	16,973,000
South Viet-Nam (Cochinchina) .	68,900	1968 . .	17,414,000
		1969 . .	17,867,000
TOTAL	173,809*	1970 . .	18,332,000
		1971 . .	18,809,000
		1972 . .	19,373,000

* 67,108 square miles.

MAJOR CITIES
(1972)

Saigon (capital)	.	1,845,385	Can-Tho .	. .	170,931
Danang .	. .	457,979	Nha-Trang	. .	206,384
Hué	. .	198,064	Dalat .	. .	92,697
My-Tho .	. .	112,152			

Births and Deaths (1969): Annual birth rate 42.7 per 1,000; death rate 8.1 per 1,000 (*Source:* U.S. Department of Commerce, *International Statistical Programs Monthly Activities*, December 1971).

Employment (mid-1970): Total economically active population 9,441,000, including 7,015,000 in agriculture (ILO and FAO estimates).

AGRICULTURE

LAND USE, 1970
('ooo hectares)

Arable Land	2,702
Under Permanent Crops . . .	216
Permanent Meadows and Pastures . .	2,870
Forest Land	5,949
Other Land and Inland Water . .	5,644
TOTAL AREA . . .	17,381

Source: FAO, Production Yearbook 1971.

PRINCIPAL CROPS
(metric tons)

	1969	1970	1971	1972
Paddy Rice	5,115,000	5,715,500	6,324,200	6,348,200
Rubber	27,650	28,458	37,500	20,000
Maize	30,535	31,485	33,750	41,700
Coffee	3,550	3,925	4,400	3,900
Tea	4,900	5,545	5,800	5,100
Tobacco	7,790	8,420	8,600	8,800
Sweet Potatoes	225,560	219,750	230,300	240,500
Cassava (Manioc)	233,485	215,710	270,000	247,300
Kenaf	80	80	20	100
Sugar Cane	321,445	335,720	340,500	331,000
Water Melons	35,000	42,000	40,000	37,500
Dry Beans	12,000	11,000	13,000	18,700
Mulberries	2,600	1,600	600	190
Bananas	184,000	204,000	210,000	248,000
Pineapples	33,000	33,000	34,000	32,900
Soyabeans	6,000	7,000	8,400	7,100
Groundnuts (in shell) . .	34,000	32,000	37,000	38,900

Coconuts: 99 million in 1969; 118 million in 1970; 125 million in 1971; 116 million in 1972. Copra: 22,500 metric tons in 1967.

RUBBER PRODUCTION AND EXPORTS
(metric tons)

	1972
Production:	
Estates	18,675
Smallholdings	1,325
Total	20,000
Exports:	
U.S.A.	7
U.K.	1,069
Belgium/Luxembourg	20
France	13,287
Federal Republic of Germany .	1,356
Italy	288
Netherlands	341
Spain	1,213
Hong Kong	—
Japan	4,098
Singapore	574
Others	679
Total	22,932
Consumption	2,571
Stocks:	
Estates	551
Dealers	1,359
Total	1,910

LIVESTOCK

	1969–70	1970–71	1971–72	1972–73
Cattle	940,000	908,300	897,800	852,500
Pigs	3,772,000	3,847,500	4,071,500	4,275,000
Buffaloes. . . .	627,000	565,250	559,800	500,800
Sheep	10,000	12,000	12,840	18,530
Goats	29,000	43,000	43,500	38,200
Horses	9,000	8,000	8,340	8,070
Chickens	19,261,000	20,000,000*	19,000,000	23,250,000
Ducks	14,475,000	14,500,000*	16,500,000	18,170,000

* FAO estimate.

LIVESTOCK PRODUCTS
(metric tons)

	1968	1969	1970
Beef, Veal and Buffalo Meat* . .	19,000	23,000	16,000
Pork, including Bacon and Ham* .	56,000	94,000	81,000
Hen Eggs	27,500†	26,000†	25,000†
Cattle and Buffalo Hides . .	1,975	2,415	2,415

* Commercial production only, excluding farm slaughterings.   † FAO estimate.

Source: FAO, *Production Yearbook 1971.*

FORESTRY
SAWNWOOD PRODUCTION
(cubic metres)

	1968	1969	1970
Coniferous (soft wood)	15,000	35,000	44,000
Broadleaved (hard wood) . . .	176,000	273,000	226,000
TOTAL	191,000	308,000	270,000

Source: United Nations, *Statistical Yearbook 1971.*

FISHING
(metric tons)

1969	. .	463,800
1970	. .	577,400
1971	. .	587,490
1972	. .	677,718

MINING
SALT PRODUCTION
(metric tons)

1967	. .	157,000
1968	. .	158,000
1969	. .	118,000
1970	. .	167,610
1971	. .	134,182

INDUSTRY

		1970	1971	1972
Electricity	'ooo kWh.	1,214,512	1,340,829	1,482,126
Cotton Yarn	tons	11,742	13,368	9,398
Jute (Kenaf) Yarn . . .	„	1,522	1,399	1,061
Woven Cotton Fabrics . . .	'ooo metres	134,453	76,660	43,244
Rayon and Synthetic Fabrics . .	„	60,317	42,654	36,446
Refined Sugar	tons	124,443	235,967	225,379
Brown Sugar	„	2,974	3,287	2,821
Beer	hl.	1,486,666	1,468,910	1,431,790
Carbonated Drinks . . .	„	1,383,030	1,185,330	1,156,170
Tobacco Products	tons	9,670	12,163	11,759
Paper and Paper Preparations . .	„	42,823	48,537	46,375
Glass	„	18,783	20,779	24,458
Cement	„	285,751	263,316	243,172

FINANCE

100 centimes = 1 Viet-Nam piastre.
Coins: 1, 5 and 10 piastres.
Notes: 1, 5, 10, 20, 50, 100, 200, 500 and 1,000 piastres.
Exchange rates (April 1974): £1 sterling = 1,428.56 piastres; U.S. $1 = 605.00 piastres.
10,000 Viet-Nam piastres = £7.00 = $16.53.

BUDGET ESTIMATES
(million piastres)

REVENUE	1971	1972	EXPENDITURE	1971	1972
Direct Taxes	12,813	14,000	General Administration . .	3,347	4,186
Indirect Taxes	17,607	21,980	Foreign Affairs . . .	4,254	2,437
Customs	79,000	50,000	Justice	239	273
Excise	13,060	18,075	Information	3,057	3,428
Registration Fees . . .	7,120	8,000	Interior	24,192	29,302
Revenues of Various Ministries .	54,855	13,418	National Education . . .	12,938	20,398
Other Sources . . .	87,615	203,013	Health and Social Welfare .	6,248	9,250
			Labour	152	191
			Finance	1,328	2,404
			Economy	1,870	1,073
			Rural Affairs	14,169	22,386
			Public Works and Communications . . .	3,874	5,566
			Military and War Veterans .	177,549	228,262
			Common Expenditures .	6,820	12,962
			U.S. Aid Construction and Development Programmes . .	14,000	21,400
			Revolutionary Development .	225	1,102
			Ministry of Open Arms .	275	476
			Ministry of Ethnic Development	522	725
			Planning	11	91
TOTAL . . .	272,070	328,486	TOTAL . . .	272,070	365,912

GOLD RESERVES AND CURRENCY IN CIRCULATION
(million piastres—at 31 December)

	1968	1969	1970	1971	1972
Gold Reserves and Foreign Exchange:					
Tied up	} 21,514	17,410	17,611	18,892	105,790
Available					
Currency in Circulation . . .	99,618	114,113	131,954	174,444	196,073

BALANCE OF PAYMENTS
(million U.S. $)

	1971			1972		
	Credit	Debit	Balance	Credit	Debit	Balance
Goods and Services:						
Merchandise	14.7	802.7	788.0	23.8	736.0	712.2
Non-monetary gold . . .	—	—	—	—	—	—
Freight and insurance . .	22.8	12.4	10.4	12.4	7.6	4.8
Travel	2.5	29.3	— 26.8	3.9	31.2	— 28.3
Investment income . .	11.4	16.5	5.1	9.3	13.2	— 3.9
Government, n.e.s. . .	478.4	163.6	314.8	343.8	209.9	133.9
Other services . . .	15.6	11.0	4.6	42.7	11.0	31.7
Total	545.4	1,061.7	—516.3	435.9	1,008.9	—573.0
Transfer Payments . .	11.3	2.0	9.0	5.4	3.3	2.1
Current Balance . .	556.7	1,063.7	—507.0	441.3	1,012.2	—570.9
Net Errors and Omissions .	—	1.4	1.4	—	2.8	2.8

UNITED STATES ECONOMIC AID
(million U.S. $)
U.S. Fiscal Years—July–June

	1970	1971	1972	Total (1954–72)
Agency for International Development (AID)				
Grants and Loans	406.8	440.3	385.0	5,048.4
of which:				
Development Loans . .	—	—	—	39.0
Commercial Import Programme .	238.5	281.0	313.0	3,302.6
Other	168.3	159.3	72.0	1,795.8
Food for Peace (PL 580) . .	170.3	141.4	112.5	1,220.7
Title 1: Planned Grants and Loans	130.9	108.2	108.4	878.0
Title 2: Emergency Relief .				
Title 3: Voluntary Relief Agencies .	39.4	33.2	4.1	337.0
Total Economic Aid . . .	577.1	581.7	497.0	6,358.5
of which:				
Grants . . .	577.1	581.7	497.0	6,269.9
Loans . . .	—	—	—	95.6

EXTERNAL TRADE
(million piastres)

	1965	1966	1967	1968	1969	1970	1971	1972
Imports . . .	12,480	28,363	43,037	37,271	53,422	44,032	70,104	233,225
Exports . . .	1,242	1,491	1,313	936	955	916	944	5,467

PRINCIPAL COMMODITIES

IMPORTS	1971		1972	
	metric tons	'ooo piastres	metric tons	'ooo piastres
Dairy Products . . .	29,234	1,841,349	25,442	5,651,120
Wheat Flour . . .	61,870	1,939,514	48,084	1,780,661
Sugar	228,716	3,690,396	165,907	14,215,834
Rice	437,200	8,314,000	271,000	16,707,000
Tobacco and Cigarettes .	4,656	827,668	16,524	9,721,666
Cement	951,827	2,795,654	651,597	5,912,844
Petroleum Products . .	1,115,202	2,310,726	1,844,040	20,720,031
Chemicals	89,780	2,819,305	50,446	7,880,513
Pharmaceuticals . .	3,396	5,933,199	3,234	9,700,109
Fertilizers . . .	172,108	1,407,880	234,173	7,266,809
Rubber and Rubber Goods .	5,396	921,933	5,581	3,103,849
Paper and Cardboard . .	48,581	784,571	29,007	2,280,688
Textile Fabrics . . .	6,667	3,568,605	7,352	14,610,406
Yarn	13,522	2,612,560	13,895	8,495,548
Metallurgic Products . .	194,690	4,997,714	212,098	16,042,322
Machinery and Appliances .	28,764	9,365,364	20,514	20,873,680
Electrical Equipment . .	8,902	4,147,825	13,177	14,057,134
Motor Cars and Parts . .	12,906	1,231,434	15,259	4,590,401

EXPORTS	1971		1972	
	metric tons	'ooo piastres	metric tons	'ooo piastres
Shrimps, Crustaceans . .	377	94,102	1,872	1,599,883
Feathers for Beds . . .	439	43,203	424	113,031
Bones	—	—	517	10,720
Tea	134	7,811	601	123,283
Rubber	32,720	760,002	44,594	1,565,248
Ceramics	266	9,504	173	18,098

Note: Exports of rice are now insignificant.

PRINCIPAL TRADING PARTNERS
(million piastres)

IMPORTS	1971	1972	EXPORTS	1971	1972
U.S.A. . . .	28,412	96,000	France	436	1,065
China (Taiwan) . .	6,667	17,083	Germany, Federal Republic	98	144
Japan . . .	12,500	45,541	United Kingdom . .	40	155
Korea, Republic . .	1,720	4,660	Japan	143	1,650
France . . .	5,394	16,117	Singapore . . .	17	316
Germany, Federal Republic	3,873	4,528	Hong Kong . . .	29	1,340
India . . .	755	525	Italy	20	30
Italy . . .	1,713	4,169	U.S.A. . . .	37	229
United Kingdom . .	471	1,880	Netherlands . .	5	25
Portugal . .	53	198	Spain	7	47
Thailand . . .	782	5,650	China (Taiwan) . .	15	51
Singapore . .	2,453	18,914	Thailand . . .	51	9
TOTAL . . .	64,793	215,265	TOTAL . . .	898	5,061

TRANSPORT

RAILWAYS

	1971	1972
Passengers ('000 passenger-km.) .	85,657	65,672
Freight ('000 ton-km.) . . .	38,208	6,617

ROADS

	1971	1972
Passenger Cars . . .	74,000	74,600
Commercial Vehicles . . .	90,400	91,250

SHIPPING

	1970	1971	1972
Goods Loaded ('000 metric tons) . .	904	} 7,092	} 6,120
Goods Unloaded ('000 metric tons)	6,824		

CIVIL AVIATION

	1971	1972
INTERNATIONAL		
Flights . . .	18,039	15,219
Passengers . .	746,617	528,489
Freight (metric tons) .	72,717	105,753
Mail (,, ,,) .	4,334	7,702
DOMESTIC		
Flights . . .	85,169	89,572
Passengers . .	1,723,823	1,411,073
Freight (metric tons) .	9,116	7,622
Mail (,, ,,) .	825	1,335

EDUCATION
(1969–70)

	SCHOOLS	TEACHERS	PUPILS
Primary .	7,978	52,194	2,718,036
Secondary .	886	21,205	711,240
Higher .	7	1,221	56,608

Source: Institut National de la Statistique, Saigon.

THE CONSTITUTION

(Promulgated April 1st, 1967)

BASIC PROVISIONS, CITIZENS' RIGHTS

Viet-Nam is a territorially indivisible, unified and independent Republic, with sovereignty residing in the people. The State recognizes and guarantees the basic rights of all citizens. It will comply with those provisions of international law which are not contrary to its national sovereignty and will contribute to the maintenance of international peace and security.

All citizens are equal before the law, which will protect human rights and the lives, property and honour of every citizen.

The private life, home and correspondence of every citizen shall be respected; he is guaranteed the freedom to worship, pursue the kind of education suited to him, meet and form associations; the State recognizes the freedom of thought, speech and the press. It will strive to improve the social security system, being bound to establish regulations providing for assistance to the old, sick, disabled, orphans, widows and the victims of natural disasters and public misfortune.

Every citizen has the duty to defend the country and the Republic; to defend the Constitution and respect the law; to fulfil his military obligations as prescribed by law and to pay taxes in proportion to his means and in accordance with the provisions of the law.

THE LEGISLATURE

Legislative authority is vested by the people in the **National Assembly** which is made up of the Senate and the House of Representatives.

The **Senate** consists of between 30 and 60 members, elected by list voting for six years. Half of the Senate is elected every three years. Candidates must be 30 years old, enjoy the full rights of citizenship, have fulfilled military obligations and meet all the conditions prescribed in the Senatorial electoral law.

The **House of Representatives** consists of between 100 and 200 representatives, popularly elected from separate constituencies by direct and secret ballot; they will run as individual candidates. Candidates must be at least 25 years of age, enjoy the full rights of citizenship, have fulfilled military obligations and meet other conditions as specified in the electoral law. Representatives will serve for four years. They may be re-elected.

The Senate and the House of Representatives have the authority to vote legislation, approve treaties and international agreements, determine declarations of war and the holding of peace talks, determine declaration of a state of emergency, imposition of curfew over all or part of the territory of Viet-Nam, control the Government in the carrying out of national policy, propose the removal of part or all of the Government, pass on the validation of Senators and Representatives and decide territorial problems.

The National Assembly is empowered to investigate government agencies or officials at the central or local levels, and may propose the dismissal of ministers, secretaries, the Prime Minister or the entire Government by a two-thirds majority vote of the total membership of each house. This recommendation is binding unless the President has special reasons for rejecting it. In the event of rejection, the National Assembly can override this by a three-quarters majority vote of the total number of Representatives and Senators.

Representatives and Senators cannot be prosecuted, pursued, arrested or sentenced for any statement or vote in the National Assembly or its committees except in cases of flagrant violation of the law.

Bills may be introduced by Representatives, Senators or the President and must be submitted to the Office of the House of Representatives.

The National Assembly shall meet each year in two regular sessions, the first beginning on the first Monday in April, the second on the first Monday in October, each session lasting a maximum of 90 days. Special sessions may be called by request of the President or one third of the total membership of either house. Each house will elect its own Chairman and permanent officers.

THE EXECUTIVE

Executive authority is vested by the people in the President.

The President and Vice-President will run on one list and will be elected by the entire nation in a secret and direct ballot. The term of office of each is four years and they may be re-elected. To run for the Presidency a candidate must have Vietnamese citizenship from birth and continuous residence in Viet-Nam for ten years prior to the date of the election; he must be at least 35 years of age, have fulfilled military obligations, enjoy full rights of citizenship and be introduced by ten Representatives or Senators or by a political party.

The President promulgates legislation; laws will be promulgated within thirty days from the time the President receives bills approved by the National Assembly. He appoints the Prime Minister, and on the latter's proposal the Ministers, Secretaries and Under-Secretaries. He may reorganize part or all of the Government. The President, with the approval of the Senate, will appoint Justices of the Supreme Court, Chiefs of Diplomatic Missions, Rectors of Universities and will appoint and promote General Officers.

The President represents the Nation in international relations, and receives letters of accreditation of diplomatic envoys. With the approval of the National Assembly he shall declare war and ratify peace treaties. He is the Commander-in-Chief of the Armed Forces of the Republic; Chairman of the National Assembly Council. He shall prescribe national policy and with the assistance of the Vice-President, Prime Minister and Cabinet Ministers he shall carry out national policy and laws.

The Vice-President is Chairman of the Culture and Education Council, the Economic and Social Council, and the Ethnic Minority Council.

The Prime Minister directs the Government and the administrative agencies of the nation, and is responsible before the President for carrying out national policy. He and other government officials may participate in sessions of the Assembly or its committees to explain matters relating to national policy.

The President is Chairman of the National Security Council, which studies all matters relating to national defence, proposes measures for the maintenance of national security, and proposes the declaration of states of alert, curfew, emergency, or war, declarations of war, and the holding of peace talks.

Province chiefs, mayors, and the members of village, province, and municipal councils are elected by universal suffrage, whilst village chiefs are elected by village councils from among their members. The Government appoints two officials with the responsibility of assisting mayors, province chiefs, and village chiefs in administrative and security matters, as well as other administrative personnel. Members and heads of local government bodies may be dismissed by the President if they violate the Constitution, the law, or national policy.

THE JUDICIARY

The Judiciary is an independent branch of the Government, equal in status with the Executive and Legislative. Judicial power will be entrusted to judges and directed by the Supreme Court and lower courts; every court has to be established and organized according to law with an element which judges and an element which prosecutes. All courts are under the control of the Supreme Court.

The Supreme Court will consist of nine to fifteen judges, nine of them nominated by the High Judicial Council with the consent of the National Assembly and then appointed by the President; two will be nominated by the Senate and four by the House of Representatives for appointment by the President. The High Judicial Council will nominate 18 candidates for the Supreme Court, from which nine will be selected by the National Assembly. The members of the Supreme Court nominated by the High Judicial Council will hold office until they reach the statutory retirement age; those nominated by the Senate and the House of Representatives will serve for the same term as they would have in the respective houses. The President and Vice-President of the Supreme Court will be elected by its members.

The Supreme Court can review decisions by any lower court, but only in matters concerning the application of the law; it is empowered to decide on the validity of the Presidential and Vice-Presidential elections and proclaim their results. It will hold sessions to review the constitutionality of laws and decree laws, the constitutionality and legality of decrees and decisions issued by the Executive, to interpret the constitution in cases of conflict between Government agencies as to their responsibility and competence and to discuss the dissolution of a political organization.

The Supreme Court will have an autonomous budget and the right to determine its internal organization and procedures governing the management of the Judiciary; its organization and procedures will be determined by law.

The High Judicial Court will consist of one member of the Supreme Court, the Presiding Judges of the Courts of Appeal, one representative of the Ministry of Justice, the leader of the Association of Lawyers, and a number of elected members. The President and Vice-President will be elected by the Council's entire membership. It will have jurisdiction in promotions and disciplinary measures involving judges, the review of appointments and transfers of all judges, the nomination of certain judges for the Supreme Court, and advising the Government as well as the Supreme Court on all judicial matters.

The Judicial Council, which is elected by the judges from among their own number, proposes the appointment, promotion, transfer, and disciplining of judges, and advises the Supreme Court in matters relating to the judiciary.

SPECIAL INSTITUTIONS

Special Court: During each of its terms the National Assembly will elect five Senators and five Representatives to form a Special Court, chaired by the President of the Supreme Court; this Court will be empowered to judge the President and the Vice-President of the Republic, the Prime Minister, Ministers, Secretaries, Generals, members of the Inspectorate and Justices of the Supreme Court when charges of treason or high crimes are brought against them. Charges will be brought by a motion signed by more than half of the total membership of both the Senate and the House of Representatives, and that motion must be approved by a two-thirds majority of the total membership of both houses. In the case of the President or Vice-President, the motion must be signed by two-thirds of the total number and approved by three-quarters. The Special Court is to decide removal from office by a three-fourths vote of its membership (four-fifths in the case of the President and Vice-President).

The **Inspectorate** includes from nine to eighteen inspectors, one-third designated by the National Assembly, one-third by the President, and one-third by the Supreme Court, and is empowered to investigate personnel of all public and private agencies on suspicion of being directly or indirectly engaged in corruption, speculation, influence-peddling, or acts harmful to the national interest; to inspect accounts of public agencies and corporations; and to audit the property of personnel of public agencies, including the President, Vice-President, Prime Minister, National Assembly members, and the President of the Supreme Court. In the case of the Chairman and members of the Inspectorate, the audit of personal property would be conducted by the Supreme Court. The Inspectorate announces publicly the results of its investigations, and proposes disciplinary action against guilty persons or requests prosecution by competent courts.

The **Armed Forces Council** advises the President on matters relating to the Armed Forces, especially promotion, transfer, and disciplining of military personnel of all ranks.

A **Culture and Education Council** assists and stimulates the Government in carrying out an educational policy in keeping with the criteria set out in the Constitution; one-third of the members will be appointed by the President and two-thirds will represent public and private cultural and educational organizations, parents and student associations and youth organizations from throughout the country; their term of office is six years, one-third of the membership being renewed every two years.

The **Economic and Social Council** has the mission of initiating and developing ideas on economic and social matters in order to establish a self-sufficient and prosperous economy. One-third of the members will be chosen by the President from among experts in the field of economics and sociology and two-thirds will be elected separately by economic, commercial and industrial organizations; their term of office is for four years.

The **Ethnic Minority Council,** representing the ethnic minorities living on Vietnamese territory, has the mission of advising the Government on all matters affecting ethnic minorities, with the purpose of helping them to develop politically, economically, culturally and socially. It is composed of one third members appointed by the President from people knowledgeable about minority affairs, and two thirds elected by ethnic minority groups; its term of office will be four years.

POLITICAL PARTIES AND OPPOSITION

Political parties can be freely established and operate openly in the spirit of the law and non-violence; they must respect the constitution, the law and national sovereignty. The State will facilitate their establishment and progress and encourage and assist progress towards a two-party system. The State recognizes the principle of formalizing political opposition.

AMENDING THE CONSTITUTION

The President or an absolute majority of either the Senators or the Representatives may propose amendment of the constitution; no amendment may be made affecting the republican regime, the unity and the territorial integrity decided by the Constitution. A joint committee would study the proposed amendment and report to joint plenary sessions of the Assembly. A resolution to amend the Constitution must be approved by two-thirds of the total number of Representatives and Senators.

There will be a transitional period before the new constitution comes entirely into force; the Constituent Assembly elected in September 1966 will assume the legislative powers established by this constitution until a constitutional government and the first National Assembly have been established. The Assembly will be responsible for drafting a law governing elections, regulations governing the press, political parties and opposition.

THE GOVERNMENT
(*April* 1974)

President: Lieut.-Gen. NGUYEN VAN THIEU (re-elected unopposed October 3rd, 1971).

Vice-President: TRAN VAN HUONG.

In the Presidential election of October 3rd, 1971, Gen. THIEU received 5,776,074 votes (91.51 per cent of the total), all other candidates including Gen. DUONG VAN MINH and Air Vice-Marshal NGUYEN CAO KY withdrew.

THE CABINET
Prime Minister and Minister of Defence: Gen. TRAN THIEN KHIEM.

Deputy Prime Minister: Dr. NGUYEN LUU VIEN.

Deputy Prime Minister and Minister of Land Reclamation and Social Welfare: Dr. PHANG QUAN DAN.

Deputy Prime Minister in charge of National Development Programmes: Gen. TRAN VAN DON.

Minister of Foreign Affairs: VUONG VAN BAC.

Minister of Justice: DUONG DUC THUY.

Minister of the Interior: LE CONG CHAT.

Minister of Finance: CHAU KIM NANH.

Minister of Trade and Industry: NGUYEN DUC CUONG.

Minister of Youth and Education: NGO KHAC TINH.

Minister of Information and "Open Arms": HOANG DUC NHA.

Minister of Agriculture: TOI THAT TRINH.

Minister of Public Works and Communications: DUONG KICH NHUONG.

Minister of Labour: DAM SI HIEN.

Minister of Health: Dr. HUYNH VAN HUON.

Minister for Veterans Affairs: Dr. HO VAN CHAM.

Minister of Ethnic Minorities: NAY LUETT.

Secretary of State at the Prime Minister's Office: BUU VIEN.

Vice-Minister of National Education: Prof. BUI XUAN BAO.

DIPLOMATIC REPRESENTATION

EMBASSIES ACCREDITED TO THE REPUBLIC OF VIET-NAM

(In Saigon unless otherwise indicated)

(E) Embassy.

Argentina: Bangkok, Thailand (E).

Australia: Hotel Caravelle, Place Lam-Son (E); *Ambassador:* GEOFFREY PRICE.

Austria: Bangkok, Thailand (E).

Belgium: 13 Truong Minh Giang (E); *Ambassador:* WILLY TILEMANS.

Brazil: Bangkok, Thailand (E)..

China (Taiwan): 175 Hai Ba-Trung (E); *Ambassador:* HU-LIEN.

France: *Ambassador:* J.-M. MÉRILLON.

Gabon: Taipei, China (Taiwan) (E).

Germany, Federal Republic: 217 Vo Tanh (E); *Ambassador:* Dr. HORST VON ROM.

Greece: New Delhi, India (E).

Israel: *Ambassador:* YAIR ARAN.

Italy: 135 Pasteur (E); *Ambassador:* VINCENZO TORNETTA.

Japan: 13-17 Nguyen Hué (E); *Ambassador:* FUMIHIKO TOGO.

Khmer Republic: 185 Le van Duyet (E); *Ambassador:* NOU HACH.

Korea, Republic: 107 Nguyen Du (E); *Ambassador:* KIM YONG GWAN.

Laos: 93 Pasteur (E); *Ambassador:* NAKKHALA SOUVAN-NAVONG.

Malaysia: 118 Truong Minh Giang (E); *Chargé d'Affaires:* V. YOOGALINGAM.

Netherlands: 147 Phan Dinh Phung (E); *Ambassador:* W. THORN LEESON.

New Zealand: 45 Phung Khac Khoan (E); *Ambassador:* PAUL K. EDMONDS.

Philippines: 42 Doan Thi Diem (E); *Ambassador:* ANASTACIO B. BARTOLOME.

Spain: 104 Wireless Rd. (E); *Ambassador:* El Marqués de VILLADARIAS.

Sweden: Bangkok, Thailand.

Thailand: 77 Truong Minh Giang (E); *Ambassador:* SUBAN SAWETAMAL.

Turkey: Bangkok, Thailand (E).

United Kingdom: 25 Boulevard Thong Nhat (E); *Ambassador:* FRANCIS BROOKS RICHARDS.

U.S.A.: 4 Thong Nhat (E); *Ambassador:* GRAHAM MARTIN.

Vatican: 173 Hai Ba Trung (Delegation); *Apostolic Delegate:* Mgr. HENRI LEMAITRE.

The Republic of Viet-Nam also has diplomatic relations with Canada, Portugal and Singapore.

NATIONAL ASSEMBLY

HOUSE OF REPRESENTATIVES
Election, August 29th, 1971

One hundred and fifty-nine seats contested by 1,297 candidates, most of them standing as independents.

SENATE
Election, August 26th, 1973

Four lists, comprising 15 candidates, stood for election for 30 seats.

Chairman: Senator NGUYEN VAN HUYEN.

POLITICAL PARTIES

Under Decree Law 60 passed on December 27th, 1972, a political party could acquire legal status only with representation in no less than half of the 44 provinces or 6 of the 11 municipalities, and with at least 5 per cent of the voters in the capitals of the provinces enrolled as members and local representation in one-quarter of the villages or city wards in the political sub-division in question. Of the 28 parties previously existing, only the following 3 had met these requirements when the registration period closed on March 27th, 1973:

Dan Chu (*Democratic Party*): f. March 1973; Leader President NGUYEN VAN THIEU.

Tu Do (*Freedom Party*): Leader NGUYEN VAN HUYEN.

Dan Chu Xa Hoi (*Social-Democrat Party*): incorporated six existing groups.

Anti-Government Fronts

National Liberation Front (N.L.F.): Leader NGUYEN HUU

THO. On 10 June 1969 the N.L.F. announced the formation of a "Provisional Revolutionary Government of the Republic of South Viet-Nam". The members are (with special responsibilities):

HUYNH TAN PHAT (Prime Minister); Prof. NGUYEN VAN KIET (Deputy Prime Minister, Education and Youth); NGUYEN DOAN (Deputy Prime Minister); Dr. PHUNG VAN CUNG (Deputy Prime Minister, Interior); TRAN BUU KIEM (Minister in Prime Minister's Office); TRAN NAM TRUNG (Defence); Mme NGUYEN THI BINH (Foreign Affairs); CAO VAN BON (Economy and Finance); LIEU HUU PHUOC (Information and Culture); Mme. DUONG QUYNG HOA (Health and Social Affairs); TRUONG NHU TANG (Justice).

Alliance of National, Democratic and Peace Forces: Formation announced February 1968; Chair. TRINH DINH THAO.

JUDICIAL SYSTEM

The judicial system is based on the Constitution of April 1st, 1967. The Judiciary consists of the Supreme Court, a Special Court, a Council of State, an Administrative Court, Courts of Appeal and Lower Courts:

The Supreme Court: consists of fifteen Justices, serving a six-year term, who when chosen by the National Assembly from thirty Jurists elected by the Associations of Judges, Prosecutors and the Bar, are appointed by the President. Chief Justice: TRAN THUC LINH.

The Special Court: Comprises the Chief Justice as presiding judge, five Senators and five associate judges; is empowered to remove from office the most high-ranking persons in the Republic, including the President, in cases of treason and other high crimes.

The Council of State: reviews all sentences ruled in the first instance by the Administrative Court. Appeals may be made to the Administrative Cassation of the Supreme Court. Chair. DO QUANG HUE.

The Administrative Court: settles disputes between citizens and the Government. President: HA NHU VINH.

There are two Courts of Appeal in Hue and Saigon which decide on civil and criminal cases rendered by the Lower Courts. Judgements can be retried by the Civil or Criminal Cassation of the Supreme Court. Presidents (Saigon): DINH VAN HUAN. (Hue): PHAM VAN HIEN. The Lower Courts comprise eleven Courts of First Instance: twenty Courts of Peace with Extended Jurisdiction holding weekly and monthly circuit sessions in remote villages: eight Labour Courts; four Land Courts; four Juvenile Courts; eight Martial Courts, four in forward areas.

RELIGION

Buddhism: Became the official religion under the Ly dynasty (1009–1225). There are many sects.

Buddhist Unified Church: Saigon; f. 1963; Leader (vacant); split in 1966 into a militant faction (An Quang) from Central Viet-Nam, led by THICH TRI QUANG, the moderates, led by THICH TAM CHAU, comprising, since 1954, emigrants from the North and lastly, the non-political southerners.

Jetavana Vihara: 610 Phan-Dinh-Phung, Saigon; 10,000 mems.; Pres. Ven. NAGA MAHA THERA-BUU-CHON.

Caodaiism: Has attracted a substantial following since 1926 and (in 1969) claimed nearly 3 million adherents. Caodaiism is a synthesis of Buddhism, Confucianism, Taoism and Christianity, preaching that the principal founders of religion are the successive reincarnation of the Supreme God. Tay-Ninh at the foot of Mount Ba-Den is the principal shrine.

Hoa Hao: The Hoa Hao is a Buddhist sect which originated in 1919 in the village of Hoa Hao (Delta region). The sect was founded by HUYNH PHU SO.

Hoa Hao Buddhism numbers about 1.5 million adherents in the western part of the Republic of Viet-Nam.

Confucianism: Introduced from China during the era of Chinese domination.

Christianity: The first missionaries arrived in the sixteenth century. There are 1.7 million Roman Catholics, many of whom emigrated from North Viet-Nam after the Geneva Agreement of 1954. 1,256 schools and 41 hospitals are operated by Roman Catholics.

Archbishop of Saigon: Most Rev. PAUL NGUYEN VAN BINH (180 Phan-dinh-Phung, Saigon).

Archbishop of Hué: Most Rev. PHILIPPE NGUYEN KIM DIEN (6 Nguyen Truong To, Hué).

Taoism: The only indigenous religion of China. Initiated by LAO TSE (*c.* 500 B.C.) and developed by CHUANG TSE-TAO—the Way or the Path—is the true principle of life and is mystical and universal. Taoism later became associated with ritual and magic and consequently declined in importance.

THE PRESS

A new press code came into effect on August 5th, 1972. Under it daily newspapers must deposit within 30 days, U.S. $43,000 (20 m.piastres), periodicals 10m. piastres, to cover possible future fines and court charges arising out of the Government's Press regulations on "national security" matters; the maximum penalty for violation of which is 5 years in prison and a fine of 5m. piastres. Certain specialized journals and official political party organs are exempt. If any publication is confiscated for a second time, the Interior Ministry can close it down pending a court decision. Following a strike by a number of newspapers on August 22nd against these regulations, President Thieu closed all of them down in September.

DAILIES

Vietnamese

Anh Sang: 54 Vo-Tanh; Editor NGUYEN THANH MY; circ. 15,000.

Bao-Den: 260 Cong-Quynh; Editor TRAN DA TU; circ. 20,000.

Bo-Cau: 213 Pham-Ngu-Lao; Editor NHON KIM HOANH; circ. 10,000.

Cap Tien: 242 Ter Phan-Dinh-Phung; Editor VO-BINH SON; circ. 15,000.

Chinh-Luan: 82 Le-Lai; Editor DANG VAN SUNG; circ. 30,000.

Chuong-Viet: 82 A Yen-Do; Editor NGUYEN VAN OANH; circ. 20,000.

Cong-Luan: 24 Nguyen-An-Ninh; Editor TON THAT DINH; circ. 25,000.

Cuu-Long: 40 Nguyen-An-Ninh; Editor LE PHUOC SANG; circ. 25,000.

Dan: 207 Pham-Ngu-Lao; Editor DUONG VAN CHANH; circ. 15,000.

Dan-Chu-Moi: 25 Vo-Tanh; Editor HA THANH THO; circ. 20,000.

Dan-Keu: 255 Le-Thanh-Ton; Editor NGUYEN KIM CHINH; circ. 10,000.

Dan-Tien: 205 Pham-Ngu-Lao; Editor NGUYEN MINH CHAU; circ. 15,000.

Dan-Y: 224-283 Gia-Long; Editor TRAN TRONG NGHIA; circ. 25,000.

Dien-Tin: 101 Vo-Tanh; Editor HONG SON DONG; circ. 20,000.

Doc-Lap: 164 Vo-Tanh; Editor HO QUANG CHAU; circ. 25,000.

Dong Nai: 54 Vo-Tanh; Editor HUYNH-THANH-VI; circ. 17,000.

Duoc Nha Nam: Nguyen-Van-Thinh; Editor TRAN TAN QUOC; circ. 20,000.

Gio Nam: 99-B Gia-Long; Editor NGUYEN VAN XUNG. circ. 20,000.

Hau-Chien: 150 Gia-Long; Editor PHAN MY TRUC; circ. 20,000.

Hoa-Binh: 295 Pham-Ngu-Lao; Editor LINH MUC TRAN-DU; circ. 40,000 (*closed down*).

Lap-Truong: 156 Bui-Thi-Xuan; Editor VU TAI LUC; circ. 15,000.

Ngon-Luan: 109 Pham-Ngu-Lao; Editor PHAM TRONG VIEN; circ. 20,000.

Nhan Dan Mien Nam: 164 Minh-Mang (GD); Editor PHAN QUY BINH; circ. 20,000.

Saigon-Moi: 39 Pham-Ngu-Lao; Editor TO THI THAN; circ. 20,000.

Su That: 106 Gia-Long; Editor TRAN NGOC ANH; circ. 20,000.

Thach Do: 24 Pham-Hong-Thai; Editor DANG VAN BE; circ. 20,000.

Than-Phong: 86 Le-Lai; Editor NGUYEN THANH HOANG. circ. 20,000.

Thoi Dai Moi: 23 Tu-Do; Editor NGUYEN-THI-MIEN; circ; 18,000.

Tia-Sang: 45-47 Phat-Diem; Editor NGUYEN TRUNG THANH; circ. 20,000.

Tien Bo: 118 Hong-Thap-Tu; Editor TRAN VAN KY; circ. 25,000.

Tien-Tuyen: 103 Gia-Long; Editor PHAM XUAN NINH; circ. 15,000.

Tieng Vang: 223 Pham-Ngu-Lao; Editor NGUYEN VAN HANH; circ. 15,000.

Tieng Viet: 131 Cong-Quynh; Editor NGUYEN TRUNG NGON; circ. 12,000.

Tin Dien: 476 Su Van-Hanh; Editor VO VAN NINH; circ. 15,000.

Tin Mat: 205 Pham-Ngu-Lao; Editor NGUYEN THI MAN; circ. 15,000.

Tin-Sang: 124 Le-Lai; Editor NGO CONG DUC; circ. 40,000;

Tin-Som: 287 Pham-Ngu-Lao; Editor NGUYEN KIM CANG; circ. 15,000.

Tin Song: 54 Thu-Khoa-Huan; Editor PHUNG THI HANH; circ. 25,000.

Trang Den: 272 Le-Thanh-Ton; Editor PHAM THU TRUC; circ. 50,000.

Xay Dung: 9B/15 Thanh-Mau; f. 1964; Editor Rev. NGUYEN QUANG LAM; circ. 15,000.

CHINESE

A Chau: 129 Dong Khanh, Saigon; Editor LUU VINH; circ. 12,000.

Luan Dan: 18 Tran Dien, Saigon 5; f. 1965; Chief Editor TO-BINH; circ. 10,000.

Luan Dan Moi: 15 Tran Dien, Saigon 5; f. 1954; Chief Editor LAU-YAT-SENG; circ. 20,000.

Quang Hoa: 760 Ben Ham Tu; Editor LUONG PHU DIEN; circ. 10,000.

Thanh Cong: 31-33 Tran Hoa; Editor KHUU DAO; circ. 15,000.

FRENCH AND ENGLISH

Courrier d'Extrême-Orient: 35 Phu Kiêt, Saigon; French; Editor Mme M.-G. SAUVEZON-GOIS; circ. 8,000.

Saigon Daily News: 135 Nguyen Hue, Saigon; f. 1963; English; Editor NGUYEN LAU; circ. 10,000 (*closed down*).

Saigon Post: 339 Tran Hung Dao, Saigon; f. 1963; English; Editor BUI PHUONG THE; circ. 20,000.

Viet-Nam Guardian: 234 Pasteur St., Saigon; f. 1966; English; Editor/Publisher NGUYEN VAN TUOI; circ. 10,000 (*closed down*).

Le Viet-Nam Nouveau: 45 Bui Vien, Saigon; French.

WEEKLIES

Binh Dan: Saigon; circ. 11,000.

L'Information d'Indochine Economique et Financière: 12–22 Ton Thal Dam, Saigon; French; Editor MAURICE PANTONNIER.

Les Nouvelles du Dimanche: 157 Tu Do, Saigon; French; Editor MAURICE LOESCH; circ. 3,000.

Phu Nu Dien Dan: 70 Nguyen Du, Saigon; Editor Mrs NGUEN THI SANG; circ. 19,500.

Sang Doi Mien Nam: 214–219 Tran Quang Khai, Saigon; Editor NGUYEN VAN PHUONG.

Sunday Post: 339 Tran Hung Dao, Saigon; f. 1963; English; Editor BUI PHUONG THE; circ. 25,000.

Times of Viet-Nam: 26 Gia Long, Saigon; English; Editor NGUYEN LAU; circ. 8,000.

Tong Nha Thanh Nien: 5 Dinh Tien Hoang, Saigon; circ. 10,000.

Van Nghe Tien Phong: Saigon; circ. 15,100.

MONTHLIES

Bach-Khoa (Thoi-Dai): 160 Phan-dinh-Phung, Saigon; f. 1957; Editor LE NGO CHAU; circ. 8,500.

Dai Hoc: Vien Dai Hoc (Hué); Editor CAO VAN LUAN.

Free Pacific Magazine: 922 Nguyen Trai, Saigon; f. 1957; Chinese; circ. 15,000.

Front de la Liberté: B.P. 1035, Saigon; f. 1945; Asian People's Anti-Communist League; Editor R. J. DE JAEGHER; circ. 22,000.

Que Huong: 3 Phan ke Binh, Saigon; Editor NGUYEN CAO HACH.

Tim Hieu Thong Thieng Hoc: 72/6 Nguyen dinh Chu, Saigon; Theosophical Society of Viet-Nam; Editor NGUYEN VAN HUAN; circ. 6,500.

Viet-Nam Observer: 235-241 Hai Ba Trung, Saigon; f. 1966; Pubr. Mrs. NGUYEN THI NGA; Editor TRAN TRONG HUNG (*Phu Si*); circ. 5,000 (*suspended since 1969*).

Xay Dung Moi (*New Construction*): 29B Phan-dinh-Phung St., Saigon; technical magazine concerning architecture, building and town planning; Editor LE VAN LAM.

NEWS AGENCIES

Viet-Nam Thong Tan Xa (*Viet-Nam Press*): 116 Hong Thap Tu, Saigon 3; f. 1951; official news agency; supplies local, national and international news; Gen. Man. TRAN VAN NGO; Man. Editor PHAM TUNG; Administrative Dir. LE QUAN; publs. daily and weekly news, financial and economic bulletins twice daily, in 4 languages, *Who's Who in Vietnam* (Vietnamese and English, revised annually), etc.

Free Pacific News Agency: 922 Nguyen Trai, Cholon; f. 1957; Chinese language news agency; Dir. Rev. Fr. RAYMOND J. DE JAEGHER.

FOREIGN BUREAUX

AP: Room 422, Eden Bldg., Tu Do, Saigon; Chief GEORGE ESPER.

Kyodo News Service: 129A Nguyen Hue, Saigon; Chief ATSUO KANEKO.

UPI: 19 Ngo Duc Ke, Saigon; Chief ARTHUR HIGBEE.

AFP (*France*): 158-D Pasteur, Saigon; Chief JEAN-LOUIS ARNAUD.

Reuters: 15 Han Thuyen, Saigon; Chief PETER SHARROCK.

PRESS COUNCIL

Press Council of Viet-Nam: 25 Vo Tanh, Saigon; Chair. PHAM VIET TUYEN.

PUBLISHERS

Khai Tri: Blvd. Le Loi, Saigon.

Kim-Lai An Quan: Duong Nguyen Sieu 3, Saigon.

Tan-Viet: Saigon.

Thanh-Tan: Saigon.

Trung-Tam Hoc-Lieu (*Instructional Materials Centre*): 240 Tran-Binh-Trong, Saigon; f. 1958; provides educational materials for schools, producing television programmes and other audio-visual aids, as well as publishing about 100,000 textbooks a month; mems. 150; Dir. Nguyen Trung Nguon.

Zien Hong Publishing Co.: 80/8 Duong Ba Huyen Thanh Quan, P.O.B. 679, Saigon; f. 1947; textbooks, dictionaries, trade books, in Vietnamese and English; Man. Dir. Le Ba Kong.

RADIO AND TELEVISION

RADIO

Radio Viet-Nam (*Vo Tuyen Viet Nam—VTVN, The National Broadcasting System of Viet-Nam*): 3 Phan dinh Phung St., and 37 Nguyen Binh Khiem St., Saigon; 8 Regional Stations (Hué, Danang, Quang-Ngai, Qui-Nhon, Nha-Trang, Dalat, Ban-Me-Thuot, Can Tho); broadcasts in Vietnamese, Chinese, French, English, Cambodian, Thai; Dir.-Gen. Pham Hau; Asst. Dir.-Gen. Pham Ba Cato.

Radio V.O.F. (Voice of Freedom) and **A.F.R.S.** (in English only) also broadcast in South Viet-Nam. A Commercial Broadcasting Station was started in April 1967.

There were 5 million radio receivers in 1972.

TELEVISION

Television was introduced into Viet-Nam early in 1966 when the official government station THVN was established with American assistance. THVN is still the only Vietnamese station, broadcasting from five transmitters for about 6½ hours a day. However, many Vietnamese also watch programmes broadcast by AFVN, the U.S. Armed Forces network, although these are exclusively in English. In 1972 there were about 1.2 million receivers, many installed in public meeting places.

Truyen Hinh Viet-Nam (**THVN**): 9 Hong Thap Tu, Saigon; f. 1966; official state television station; Dir. Gen. Le Vinh Hoa.

FINANCE

BANKING

(cap.=capital; dep.=deposits; m.=million; figures are in Vietnamese piastres)

National Bank

Ngan Hang Quoc Gia Viet-Nam (*National Bank of Viet-Nam*): 17 Ben Chuong Duong, Saigon; f. 1955; central bank authorized to issue notes; cap. (Dec. 1972) 7,117m.; dep. 88,297m.; Gov. Le Quang Uyen.

Major Commercial Banks

Agricultural Development Bank: 7 bis Ben Chuong Duong, Saigon; f. 1967; cap. 200m.; Dir.-Gen. Dr. Nguyen Dang Hai.

Nong Cong Thuong Ngan Hang (*Agricultural, Industrial and Commercial Bank*): 115-119 Nguyen Cong Tru, Saigon.

Tin Nghia Ngan Hang: 50 Chuong Duong, Saigon.

Viet-Nam Cong Thuong Ngan Hang (*Commercial and Industrial Bank of Viet-Nam*): 93–95 Ham-Nghi St., Saigon 2; f. 1953; cap. 150m.; dep. 10,000m.

Viet-Nam Ngan Hang (*Bank of Viet-Nam*): 117 Nguyen-Hue, Saigon; f. 1927; cap. and reserves 609m.; dep. 7,490m. (June 1973); Chair. N. T. Lap; Dir.-Gen. N. N. Phat.

Viet-Nam Thuong-Tin (*Commercial Credit Bank of Viet-Nam*): 79 Ham-Nghi St., Saigon; 24 brs.; f. 1955; cap. 200m.; dep. 49,000m. (Dec. 1972); Chair. Le Quang Uyen; Gen. Man. Le Tan Loc; Asst. Gen. Mans. Pham Viet Gy, Dang Co, Lam Vo Hoang, Duong Hoang Danh.

Foreign

Bangkok Bank Ltd.: Bangkok; 44 Nguyen Cong Tru, Saigon; br. at Cholon and Cau Ong Lanh.

Bank of China: Taipei; 11 Chuong Duong, Saigon.

Bank of Communications: 87 Dai Lo Ham Nghi, Saigon; Man. Tchao Tse King.

Bank of East Asia: Hong Kong; 6 Vo-Di-Nguy, P.O.B. 90, Saigon.

Bank of Tokyo: Tokyo; 12-22 Ham Nghi, Saigon.

Banque Française de l'Asie: Paris; 29 Chuong Duong; f. 1875.

Banque Française pour le Commerce: Paris; 32 Dai Lo Ham Nghi, Saigon; 5 brs.

Banque Nationale de Paris: Paris; 36 Ton-That-Dam, Saigon.

Chartered Bank: London, 3-5 Vo-Di-Nguy, Saigon.

Chase Manhattan Bank, N.A.: New York; 27-8 Ben Bach Dang, P.O.B. R.6, Saigon, Viet-Nam; Second Vice-Pres. and Man. Cornelius Termijn.

Hongkong and Shanghai Banking Corporation: Hong Kong; f. 1865; 9 Ben Chuong Duong, Saigon.

Korea Exchange Bank: Seoul; 25 Vo-Di-Nguy, Saigon.

DEVELOPMENT ORGANIZATIONS

IDEBANK (*Investment and Development Bank*): 7-19 Vo-Di-Nguy St., Saigon 1; f. 1962 by a consortium of commercial banks and operating as an industrial financing institution and investment corporation; cap. 595m.; Gen. Man. Dr. Lam Van Si; publ. *IDEBANK Newsletter*.

Industrial Development Bank of Viet-Nam (IDB): 40 Nguyen-Hue blvd., Saigon; f. 1971; autonomous public institution dealing with industrial promotion and development; Dir.-Gen. KHUONG HUU DIEU.

Investment Service Center: 100 Tu Do, Saigon, P.O.B. 2816; f. 1972; government body providing investment services and supervising investment projects; Sec.-Gen. NGUYEN DANG KHOI; Dir. DO DUY LAM.

National Economic Development Fund of Viet-Nam (NEDEF): 17 Ben Chuong Duong; f. 1972; aims to promote economic development by co-ordinating and granting medium and long-term credit to private investment and by allocating financial aid from foreign countries; Pres. Dr. NGUYEN VAN HAO; Chair. LE QUANG UYEN.

INSURANCE

NATIONAL COMPANIES
Saigon

Cong-Ty Bao-Hiem Tai Bao-Hiem Viet-Nam (*Vietnamese Insurance and Re-Insurance Co.*): 26 Ton-That-Dam; f. 1960; all kinds of insurance except life insurance; cap. 120m.; Man. Dir. LE-VAN-DINH; Controller HUYNH-VAN-DIEM.

Dai Nam Bao-Hiem Cong-Ty: 4 Ton-That-Thiep; f. 1953; Pres. and Gen. Man. NGUYEN THANH DAI.

Hai-Ngoai Bao-Hiem Cong-Ty (Overseas Insurance Co.): 3, Nguyen Hue St., Saigon; Pres. ONG HONG.

Viet-Nam Bao Hiem Cong Ty (*Viet-Nam Motor Insurance Co.*): 19 Rue Phu Kiet; f. 1929; Dirs. NGUYEN THANH LAP, NGUYEN THANH DAI, LE VAN KINH; Man. Dir. LAM SANH TAI.

Viet-Nam Bao Hiem Phat Ba (*Viet-Nam Assurance*): 13 Pasteur St., f. 1952; Man. TRAN VAN HUE.

There are several foreign insurance companies operating in Saigon.

TRADE AND INDUSTRY

CHAMBERS OF COMMERCE

Saigon Chamber of Commerce and Industry: 69 Tu Do St., Saigon; f. 1955; mems. 45,406; Pres. NGUYEN VAN KHAI; Sec.-Gen. TRAN DUC UOC.

Danang Chamber of Commerce and Industry: 32 Doc Lap St., Danang; P.O.B. 102; f. 1970; mems. 22; Chair. LE HUU TRINH; Sec.-Gen. NGUYEN VAN MINH; publ. *Bulletin d'Information de la Chambre de Commerce et d'Industrie de Danang*.

French Chamber of Commerce: 177 Hai-Ba-Trung, B.P. 786, Saigon.

INDUSTRIAL ORGANIZATIONS

Confédération Générale de l'Industrie et du Commerce du Viet-Nam: 38 dai-lo Nguyen-Hué, Saigon.

Confederation of Industries and Handicrafts: Saigon.

Bureau Mixte des Syndicats Exportateurs de Céréales: 36 Maréchal de Lattre, Saigon; f. 1957; mems. 26; Pres. NGUYEN NGOC DAN; deals with all cereal products.

Manufactures Indochinoises de Cigarettes: 152 Dai-Lo Nguyen-Hoang, Saigon; Head Office: 1 rue de Paris, Djibouti; f. 1929; a member of British-American Tobacco Group; Pres. GASTON RUEFF.

Syndicat des Exportateurs de Caoutchouc: Saigon; deals with all rubber products.

TRADE UNIONS

Tong-Lien-Doan Lao-Cong (*Vietnamese Federation of Christian Labour*): 14 Le-van-Duyet, Saigon; f. 1948; Pres. TRAN QUOC BUU; Sec.-Gen. TRAN HUU QUYEN.

Trade Unions are affiliated to the Federation through Provincial Councils. Total membership: 500,000.

PRINCIPAL AFFILIATED FEDERATIONS

Federation of Plantation Workers: 14 Le-van-Duyet St., Saigon; 25,000 mems.; Gen. Sec. PHAM VAN VY.

Federation of Tenant Farmers: above address; 350,000 mems.; Gen. Sec. VO VAN GIAO.

Federation of Transport Workers: above address; 14,000 mems.; Gen. Sec. LUU VAN VINH.

Luc Luong Tho Thuyen Viet-Nam (*Viet-Nam Labour Union*): 133 Hai-Ba-Trung, Saigon; f. 1953; mems. 40,000 (est.); Chair. NGUYEN VAN NGAI; Sec.-Gen. LE HUA.

Tong Lien Doan Lao Dong Viet-Nam (*Confederation of Workers' Trade Unions of Viet-Nam*): 179 Duong Ly-thai-To, Cholon; f. 1952; present name adopted 1953; mems. approximately 30,000 in 28 affiliated unions.

TRANSPORT

RAILWAYS

Viet-Nam Railways: 2 Dien Hong Square, Saigon; Dir. NGUYEN-VAN-CHIEU; Deputy Dir. TRAN-MONG-CHAU; Chief Accountant LAM-NGOC-THACH; Chief Dept. of Operations TRINH-DINH-TUONG; Chief Engineer, Track, Buildings LE-DAC-BA; Chief Mechanical Dept. NGUYEN A MI; Chief Dept. Transportation, Navigation NGUYEN-THAI HOA.

State-owned; length of track 1,278 km.; dislocation caused by the war had reduced exploitable length of track to about 684 km. in 1973.

ROADS

There are 6,523 km. of national highways, 3,663 km. of secondary or regional roads, 10,731 km. of other roads; total 20,917.

SHIPPING

There are more than 4,500 km. of navigable waterways of which 2,200 km. are canals.

Nam-Hai: 20 Nguyen-Cong-Tru, Saigon.

Nam-Tien: 114 Vo-Di-Nguy, Saigon.

Viet-Nam Thuy-Bo-Van-Tai Cong-Ty: 10 Ton-Dam, Saigon.

The following foreign lines call at Saigon.

American President Lines: San Francisco, Calif.; Getz Bros. & Co. (Vietnam), 26–28 Ham Nghi, Saigon.

Compagnie des Messageries Maritimes: 46–48 Tu-Do, B.P. 11, Saigon.

Compagnie Maritime des Chargeurs Réunis: 27–28 Ben Bach Dang, B.P. 137, Saigon.

East Asiatic Company Ltd.: Copenhagen; Saigon.

CIVIL AVIATION

Air Viet-Nam: 27B Phan-Dinh-Phung St., P.O.B. 217, Saigon; f. 1951; The government holds 92.75 per cent of the stock and Air France 6 per cent; operates domestic routes and 5 international services to Laos,

Khmer Republic, Formosa, Japan, Philippines, Singapore, Malaysia, Hong Kong and Thailand; Chair. H. E. Tran-Van-Vien; Pres. Nguyen-Tan-Trung; Exec. Vice-Pres. Phan-Luong-Quang; fleet: two B-727, four DC-6, seven DC-4, nineteen DC-3, six C-46; 3,200 staff.

The following foreign airlines are also represented. Air Cambodge, Air France, Cathay Pacific, China Airlines, Pan American World Airways, Royal Air Lao, Singapore Airlines, Thai International, UTA.

TOURISM

Commission for Tourism in Viet-Nam: 1 Tu Do St., Saigon; Commissioner Phan Luong Quang.

Dalat Tourist Bureau: 12 Yersin St., Dalat.

Hué Tourist Bureau: 26 Ly-Thuong-Kiet, Hué.

ATOMIC ENERGY

Atomic Energy Office: 291 Phan-Thanh-Gian, P.O.B. Q-16, Saigon; f. 1958; Dir.-Gen. Prof. Le Van Thoi; government body responsible for atomic affairs; maintains a Nuclear Research Centre at Dalat.

Dalat Nuclear Research Centre: Dalat; f. 1961; 250 kW. Triga II reactor; laboratories: radiochemical, radiobiological, nuclear physics, health physics, electronics; reference library; Dir. Ngo Dinh Long.

UNIVERSITIES

University of Cantho: Dailo Hoabinh, Cantho; 105 teachers, about 3,600 students.

University of Dalat: rue de l'Université, Dalat; about 60 teachers, about 2,700 students.

University of Hué: 3 rue le Loi, Hué; 288 teachers, 3,409 students.

University of Saigon: 3 Cong-Tryong Chien-Si, Saigon; 670 teachers, 27,000 students.

Van-Hanh University: 222 Truong-Minh-Giang St., Saigon; 160 teachers, 4,500 students.

WEST INDIES ASSOCIATED STATES

ANTIGUA **DOMINICA** **ST. CHRISTOPHER*-NEVIS-ANGUILLA**

ST. LUCIA **ST. VINCENT**

A group of Caribbean islands sharing a common relationship with Britain and participating in regional co-operative organizations.

INTRODUCTION

Associate Status: During 1966 the British Government and each of the Windward and Leeward Islands, except Montserrat, concluded a number of agreements establishing a new non-colonial relationship between the United Kingdom and the following former colonies (dates of association in brackets): Antigua (February 27th, 1967), Dominica (March 1st, 1967), Grenada (March 3rd, 1967), St. Christopher-Nevis-Anguilla (February 27th, 1967), St. Lucia (March 1st, 1967), St. Vincent (October 27th, 1969). The association is free and voluntary and can be terminated unilaterally by either party. Association with Grenada was terminated on February 7th, 1974.

On July 28th, 1971, the United Kingdom Government adopted legislation which had the effect of restoring direct British rule to Anguilla. The island will remain part of St. Christopher-Nevis-Anguilla, however, so long as the latter retains its status of association with the U.K.

Defence and External Affairs: The British Government retains responsibility for defence and external affairs and there is a British Government Representative for the islands to supervise this aspect of the arrangements. External affairs and defence policy are conducted in close consultation with the governments of the Associated States, to whom authority may be delegated in the following affairs: membership of international organizations of which the United Kingdom is a member, trade agreements, agreements of local concern negotiated with Caribbean members of the Commonwealth, agreements of a financial, cultural or scientific nature with any Commonwealth member or with the U.S.A., and agreements relating to migration. The Associated States are to provide any defence facilities that might be requested by the British Government.

British Government Representative: Edgar Ord Laird, C.M.G., M.B.E. (resident in Castries, St. Lucia).

Internal Government: Each State exercises full internal self-government. The Queen is Head of State and is represented in each case by a Governor. The structure of internal government is regulated by separate constitutions for each island. Dominica, St. Kitts, St. Lucia and St. Vincent have unicameral parliaments of 10, 10, 11 and 13 members respectively, with three nominated members and one *ex-officio* member. Antigua has a bicameral legislature, consisting of an Upper and a Lower House. The life of parliament is five years in each case. The Premier and Cabinet of each State are responsible to the parliament.

Constitutional Amendments: The association agreements may be terminated at any time, either by an Associated State, after necessary legislation has been passed, or by the British Government, which may declare the State independent. Legislation terminating the association requires a two-thirds majority in the Lower House and a two-thirds majority in a referendum, except if the association is terminated for the purpose of joining a federation, union or association with an independent Commonwealth country in the Caribbean. Constitutional amendments may take place only in the territory concerned. Amendments involving basic clauses of the Constitutions (e.g. fundamental freedoms) would require approval of two-thirds of the members of the parliament or of two-thirds of the electorate. In the case of Antigua, both provisions would need to be satisfied before such an amendment could be passed.

Judicial System: A Regional Supreme Court of Judicature has been established for the five Associated States and is composed of a High Court of Justice and a Court of Appeal, the latter replacing the Eastern Caribbean Court of Appeal. The jurisdiction of the High Court includes fundamental rights and freedoms, membership of the parliaments, and matters concerning the interpretation of the constitutions of the Associated States.

Citizenship: Citizens of the Associated States continue to be citizens of the United Kingdom and colonies. Should the association be terminated, separate citizenship for each State will become operative, and will apply to those born in the territory, those whose fathers were citizens of the territory, and women married to citizens of the territory.

Other Provisions: The association arrangements also provide for the establishment of Police and Public Service Commissions, entrenched constitutional clauses on Human Rights, the continuation of British policies on trade, aid and immigration in the Associated States, and the prospect of future regional co-operation in the Caribbean area.

* While this island is officially named St. Christopher as part of the state, it is almost invariably abbreviated to St. Kitts.

REGIONAL COMMON SERVICES

WEST INDIES (ASSOCIATED STATES) COUNCIL OF MINISTERS

Bridge St., Castries, St. Lucia

The Council of Ministers is composed of the Premiers of the Associated States and the Chief Minister of Montserrat, and is responsible for such regional undertakings as broadcasting, seismological surveys, etc., and the initiation of further co-operative projects. A committee of the Council, appointed to define development priorities, advocated the establishment of a Regional Development Agency, now situated in Antigua. A Regional Development Bank was established in October 1969. Other recommendations include tourist development, the development and co-ordination of industry, agriculture and fisheries, the establishment of joint marketing boards and joint commercial bodies.

The Council meets regularly, the chairmanship rotating annually, and decisions are taken by a majority vote.

Chairman (1973): JAMES MITCHELL (St. Vincent).

The Secretariat is responsible for convening meetings, the transmission of Council decisions to member governments, the surveillance of the development of regional projects, and the administration of the overseas offices of the Council in London and Canada.

Executive Secretary: GEORGE ODLUM.

SUPREME COURT OF JUDICATURE

St. George's, Grenada

The West Indies Associated States Supreme Court was established by Order in Council in 1967, and its jurisdiction extends to the five Associated States, Grenada, Montserrat and the British Virgin Islands. It is composed of a High Court of Justice, and a Court of Appeal. The High Court is composed of the Chief Justice and six Puisne Judges. The Court of Appeal is presided over by the Chief Justice and includes two other Justices of Appeal. Jurisdiction of the High Court includes the general supervision of justice in the Associated States, Grenada, Montserrat and the British Virgin Islands, fundamental rights and freedoms, membership of the parliaments, and matters concerning the interpretation of the constitutions of the Associated States. Appeals from the Court of Appeal lie to the Privy Council.

Chief Justice: The Hon. Sir ALLEN MONTGOMERY LEWIS, Q.C.

PRESS

Caribbean Press Association: P.O.B. 45, St. George's, Grenada; f. 1947.

RADIO

Radio Grenada: Broadcasting House, St. George's, Grenada; f. 1972; medium-wave transmissions from Grenada, Dominica, St. Vincent, St. Lucia and Carriacou, and short-wave transmissions; Man. and Programme Dir. JEROME D. M. ROMAIN.

FINANCE

East Caribbean Currency Authority: St. Kitts; f. 1965; responsible for issue of currency in Antigua, Dominica, Grenada, Montserrat, St. Christopher-Nevis-Anguilla, St. Lucia, St. Vincent; Barbados ceased to be a member in April 1974; notes in circulation (March 1971): EC $57,213,594; Man. Dir. N. L. SMITH (acting).

CURRENCY

100 cents = 1 East Caribbean dollar (EC $).
Coins: 1, 2, 5, 10, 25 and 50 cents.
Notes: 1, 5, 20 and 100 dollars.
Exchange rates (April 1974):

£1 sterling = EC $4.80;
U.S. $1 = EC $2.03
EC $100 = £20.83 = U.S. $49.19.

TRADE AND INDUSTRY

REGIONAL DEVELOPMENT AGENCY

Established January 1968 in Antigua by the West Indies Associated States Council of Ministers and Barbados.

Executive Secretary: GEORGE E. WILLIAMS.

TRADE ORGANIZATIONS

Caribbean Association of Industry and Commerce (Inc.): 7-9 Harbour St., Kingston, Jamaica; Pres. AARON J. MATALON; Exec. Officer URBAN O. ARCHIBALD.

Federation of Primary Producers of the British Caribbean, Ltd.: Jamaica; Chair. R. L. M. KIRKWOOD.

West Indian Limes Association (Inc.): 2 Pasea St., St. Augustine, Trinidad; f. 1941; Pres. Dr. B. G. MONTSERIN; Sec. LEON VITAL.

West Indian Sea Island Cotton Association (Inc.): P.O.B. 77, Temple St., St. John's, Antigua; 6 mem. associations; Pres. H. A. L. FRANCIS; Sec. S. L. HENRY.

West Indies Sugar Association (Inc.): Broad St., P.O.B. 170, Bridgetown, Barbados; f. 1942; 5 mem. associations; Chair. Sir ROBERT KIRKWOOD, K.C.M.G.; Sec. R. NORRIS, M.B.E.; publs. *W.I.S.A. Handbook, Report of Proceedings of Meetings of W.I. Sugar Technologists*.

Windward Islands Banana Growers' Association: Castries, St. Lucia; Pres. I. H. SINSON; Gen. Man. D. A. PERRYMAN, M.B.E.; Sec. A. V. GRELL.

Windward Islands Cocoa Board: Grenada.

TRANSPORT

SHIPPING

West Indies Shipping Corporation: 1 Richmond St., Port-of-Spain, Trinidad; f. 1961; statutory body to manage and maintain services between the West Indian Islands; Gen. Man. O. J. ALONZO; 2 ships.

CIVIL AVIATION

British West Indian Airways (BWIA): Sunjet House, 30 Edward St., Port-of-Spain, Trinidad; f. 1948; scheduled passenger and cargo services throughout the Caribbean, and to New York, Toronto, Miami, Guyana and London.

Leeward Island Air Transport Services Ltd. (LIAT): Coolidge Airport, Antigua; f. 1956; operates scheduled passenger, cargo and mail services to 24 East Caribbean islands from Trinidad to Puerto Rico; fleet of 3 BAC 1-11/500, 6 HS-748, 5 BN-24 Islander; Man. Dir. M. A. WARWICK.

TOURISM

Association of Tourist Boards of the Eastern Caribbean (ATBEC): f. 1967; mems.: Antigua, Dominica, Grenada, Montserrat, St. Christopher-Nevis-Anguilla, St. Lucia and St. Vincent; London office: 10 Haymarket, London, S.W.1; Man. Mrs. WENDY JOLLY.

EAST CARIBBEAN COMMON MARKET
c/o Secretariat, St. John's, Antigua

In June 1968 an Agreement was signed in Grenada for the establishment of the East Caribbean Common Market. The signatory governments were: Antigua, Dominica, Grenada, St. Christopher-Nevis-Anguilla, St. Lucia and St. Vincent. Montserrat acceded to the agreement in April 1969.

The Associated States (with the exception of Antigua) are all members of the **Caribbean Common Market** (**CARIBCOM**), on which there is a separate chapter in Volume I of *The Europa Year Book*.

ANTIGUA AND BARBUDA

The island of Antigua at 17° 6′ N. 61° 45′ W., is some 108 square miles in extent.
The island of Barbuda lies about 25 miles to the north of Antigua and has an area of 62 square miles.

STATISTICS

Area: 170 sq. miles.

Population (1972): 66,000, St. John's (capital) 14,000 (1972 estimate).

Agriculture: Sugar (1970) 15,400 tons, (1971) 11,085 tons; Cotton (1969) 3,855 lb., (1971) 6,801 lb.

Finance: Budget (1973) Expenditure EC $39.5m.

External Trade (1968): Imports EC $39,247,907; Exports EC $5,780,113.

Tourism: (1972): 72,328. visitors

Education (1971): Schools 56, Pupils 22,000.

THE GOVERNMENT

Governor: Sir WILFRED E. JACOBS, O.B.E., Q.C.

CABINET
(May 1974)

Premier and Minister of Planning, Development and External Affairs: Hon. GEORGE HERBERT WALTER.

Minister of Agriculture, Lands and Fisheries: Hon. ROBERT VERNON LONGFORD HALL.

Minister of Finance, Industry and Tourism: Hon. SYDNEY U. PRINCE.

Minister of Public Works, Housing and Communications: Hon. VICTOR E. McKAY.

Minister of Education, Health and Culture: Hon. BASIL ALPHONSO PETERS.

Minister of National Security, Legal Affairs and Labour and Attorney-General: Hon. GERALD O. A. WATT.

SENATE

President: CLARENCE A. HARNEY.
Vice-President: J. OLIVER DAVIS.
Nominated Members: 10.

HOUSE OF REPRESENTATIVES

Speaker: CECIL HEWLETT.
Official Member: The Attorney-General.
Elected Members: 17.
Clerk: L. STEVENS.

ELECTIONS, FEBRUARY 1971

PARTY	SEATS
Progressive Labour Movement . . .	13
Antigua Labour Party	4

POLITICAL PARTIES

Antigua Labour Party: St. John's; Leader V. C. BIRD.

Antigua People's Party: St. John's; Leader J. ROWAN HENRY.

Progressive Labour Movement: St. John's; f. 1970; government party; Leader GEORGE HERBERT WALTER.

RELIGION

ANGLICAN

The Diocese of Antigua is made up of 12 islands, viz. Antigua, St. Kitts, Nevis, Anguilla, Barbuda, Montserrat, Dominica, Saba, St. Maarten, Aruba, St. Bartholomew and St. Eustatius; the total number of Anglicans is about 60,000. The See City is St. John's.

Bishop of Antigua: The Rt. Rev. ORLAND LINDSAY, Bishop's Lodge, P.O.B. 23, St. John's.

Publication: *The Angelus* (diocesan newspaper).

ROMAN CATHOLIC

The Diocese of St. John's was formerly part of Roseau (Dominica).

Bishop of St. John's: The Rt. Rev. JOSEPH OLIVER BOWERS, Catholic Offices, P.O.B. 836, St. John's.

THE PRESS

Antigua Star: Antigua Printery Ltd., 30 Long St., St. John's; f. 1936; Wednesday and Saturday; circ. Wed. 3,500, Sat. 4,500; Chair. M. BENJAMIN (acting); London Office: 122 Shaftesbury Ave., W.1.

The Antigua Times: St. John's; twice weekly; Chair. J. ROWAN.

The Worker's Voice: 46 North St., St. John's; f. 1944; daily; official organ of the Labour Party; circ. 1,500 weekdays, 2,000 Sundays; Editor A. FREELAND.

RADIO AND TELEVISION

Antigua Broadcasting Service: St. John's; f. 1956; Broadcasting Officer E. A. M. JOHN.

Radio Grenville Z.D.K.: f. 1970; Man. IVOR BIRD.

Leeward Islands Television Services Ltd. (ZAL TV): Antigua; affiliate of Columbian Broadcasting Service; f. 1964; operates three channels, one to Antigua, one to Montserrat and one to St. Maarten (Netherlands Antilles); Man. BRYANT MEADE.

FINANCE

Antigua Commercial Bank Ltd.: St. Mary's and Thames Sts., P.O.B. 95, St. John's; f. 1955; cap. $1m.; Man. C. W. DICKSON.

Bank of Nova Scotia: Head Office: 44 King St. West, Toronto; Antigua Office: High St., St. John's.

Barclays Bank International Ltd.: Head Office: 54 Lombard St., London, EC3P 3AH; two brs. in St. John's: P.O.B. 225 (Man. S. W. E. G. MAYNARD), and P.O.B. 740 (Man. M. J. KELLY); agency at All Saints.

Canadian Imperial Bank of Commerce: Head Office: Commerce Court, Toronto; High St., St. John's.

Royal Bank of Canada: Head Office: Place Ville Marie, Montreal; High St. and Market St., St. John's; Man. K. E. D. FISHER.

Virgin Islands National Bank: Head Office: Charlotte Amalie, U.S. Virgin Islands; Market St. and High St., St. John's.

Antigua-Barbuda Savings Bank: St. John's; Man. H. B. AMBROSE.

Antilles Bank and Trust Co. Ltd.: Head Office: Tortola, British Virgin Islands; Antigua Office: High St., St. John's; Man. PETER BAK.

TRADE AND INDUSTRY

Antigua Chamber of Commerce: Church St., St. John's; f. 1944; 66 mems.; Pres. CALVIN A. RODGERS; Man. A. C. DERRICK; publ. *News Bulletin* (monthly).

Antigua Cotton Growers' Association: P.D.O., St. John's; Chair. ANTHONY SHOUL.

TRADE UNIONS

Antigua Public Service Association: Antigua; 800 mems.; Pres. R. E. H. LAKE; Hon. Sec. E. A. M. JOHN.

Antigua Trades and Labour Union: 46 North Street, St. John's; f. 1940; about 300 mems.; Pres. LIONEL HURST.

Antigua Workers' Union: Antigua; f. 1967; 8,200 mems.; Pres. M. DANIEL; Gen. Sec. KEITHLYN SMITH.

TRANSPORT

RAILWAYS

There are 49.7 miles of narrow-gauge line used for moving sugar cane.

ROADS

There are 150 miles of main roads and 450 miles of secondary dry weather roads. Registered vehicles (1972) 7,976, motor cycles 401.

SHIPPING

The main harbour is the St. John's Deep Water Harbour. There are two tugs for the berthing of ships, and modern cargo handling equipment. The harbour can also accommodate three large cruise ships.

The following shipping lines use St. John's: Atlantic, Booker, Booth, French, Grimaldi Siosa, Harrison, Royal Netherlands, Saguenay and West Indies Shipping Service.

CIVIL AVIATION

Antigua's Coolidge Airport has been remodelled and extended to accommodate jet aircraft.

Leeward Islands Air Transport Services Ltd. (LIAT): (*see* under Regional Common Services—Transport).

Antigua is also served by the following foreign airlines: Air Canada, Air France, ALM (Netherlands Antilles), British Airways, BWIA (Trinidad), Eastern and Pan American.

TOURISM

Tourism is the main industry. There were 72,328 visitors in 1972. There are 32 hotels with a total of 1,124 rooms.

Antigua Tourist Board: Lower High St., P.O.B. 363, St. John's; Chair. Hon. SELVYN WALTER; Sec. Miss Y. MAGINLEY.

DOMINICA

Dominica is the most northerly of the Windward Islands, lying between Guadeloupe and Martinique. About a quarter of the total area of the island is under cultivation, exploitation being limited to the volcanic soils. The chief agricultural pursuit is the growing of bananas, followed closely by citrus fruit, particularly the lime, which besides producing edible fruit and juices, also yields various essential oils which are of value in pharmaceutical products. Oranges, cocoa, vanilla and coconuts are other crops. Production is mainly carried on from small holdings owned and worked by peasant farmers, who supply both home needs and an export trade.

STATISTICS

Area: 289.5 sq. miles.

Population (1970): 70,302; Roseau (capital) 10,157.

Agriculture (1968): Bananas 4,103,000 stems, Limes 3,856 barrels.

Finance: (1971): Revenue EC $17,007,374, Expenditure EC $17,541,493.

External Trade (1970): Imports EC $31,513,530, Exports EC $11,809,931.

Tourism: (1972) 15,294 visitors.

Education (1972): Primary Schools 57, Secondary Schools 5; Primary Pupils 21,500.

THE GOVERNMENT

The Governor: H.E. Sir LOUIS COOLS-LARTIGUE, O.B.E.

CABINET

(*May* 1974)

Premier: Hon. EDWARD O. LEBLANC.

Deputy Premier and Minister of Finance and Development: Hon. P. R. JOHN.

Minister for Home Affairs: Hon. A. C. ACTIVE.

Minister of Education and Health: Hon. H. L. CHRISTIAN, M.B.E.

Minister of Communications and Works: Hon. E. A. LESLIE.

Minister for Agriculture, Trade and Natural Resources: Hon. THOMAS ETIENNE.

Attorney-General: Hon. L. I. AUSTIN, O.B.E., Q.C.

Secretary to the Cabinet: C. A. SEIGNORET, O.B.E.

HOUSE OF ASSEMBLY

Speaker: Hon. EUSTACE FRANCIS.

Nominated Members: 3.

Official Member: 1.

Elected Members: 11.

Clerk: Mrs. M. DAVIS-PIERRE.

ELECTION, OCTOBER 1970

PARTY	
LeBlanc Labour Party	8
Dominica Freedom Party	2
Dominica Labour Party	1

POLITICAL PARTIES

LeBlanc Labour Party: Roseau; f. 1970 as a result of split in Dominica Labour Party; Leader Hon. E. O. LEBLANC.

Dominica Freedom Party: Roseau; Leader Miss M. E. CHARLES.

RELIGION
ROMAN CATHOLIC CHURCH

Bishop of Roseau, Dominica: Rt. Rev. ARNOLD BOGHAERT; Bishop's House, Roseau; 67,000 Catholics (1970).

There are also Methodist and Anglican Churches. The Anglican Bishop of the Windward Islands is resident in St. Vincent.

THE PRESS

Dominica Chronicle: (Bulletin Office), P.O.B. 124, Roseau; f. 1909; Catholic Democratic; Saturday; Man. S. A. W. BOYD; circ. 2,500.

Dominica Herald: 23 Hanover St., Roseau; f. 1955; Liberal weekly; Editor STAR LESTRADE; circ. 2,000.

The Educator: 69 Queen Mary St., Roseau; weekly; Editor EUSTACE FRANCIS; circ. 2,000.

Government Gazette: Government Printer, Roseau; weekly; circ. 500.

The Star: 26 Bath Rd., Roseau; weekly; literary and political; Editor PHYLLIS SHAND ALLFREY; circ. 2,000.

RADIO

Radio Dominica: Victoria St., Roseau; government station; 10 kW transmitter on the medium wave band; programmes received throughout Caribbean excluding Jamaica and Guyana.

FINANCE
BANKS

Dominica Co-operative Bank Ltd.: 9 Gt. Marlborough St., Roseau; f. 1941; Pres. and Man. Dir. J. B. CHARLES.

Barclays Bank International Ltd.: Head Office: 54 Lombard St., London, EC3P 3AH; two brs. in Roseau (P.O.B. 4 and P.O.B. 196); sub-br. in Portsmouth; agencies in Marigot and Grandbay; Senior Man. F. DUPIGNY.

Royal Bank of Canada: Head Office: Place Ville Marie, Montreal; br. in Roseau; Man. A. C. DA SILVA.

TRADE AND INDUSTRY

Agricultural Marketing Board: Roseau; Gen. Man. M. G. WHITE.

Co-operative Citrus Growers' Association: Roseau; Pres. C. J. L. DUPIGNY.

Dominica Banana Growers' Association: Roseau; Gen. Man. V. E. WHITE.

Dominica Chamber of Commerce: Love Lane, Roseau; Pres. C. A. MAYNARD; Sec. J. N. LIBURD.

TRADE UNIONS

Dominica Trade Union: 70-71 Queen Mary St., Roseau; f. 1945; 2,500 mems.; Pres. DEVERILL P. LAWRENCE; Gen. Sec. STEWART WILLIAMS.

Civil Service Association: 46 King George Vth St., Roseau; f. 1960; 1,200 mems.; Pres. C. MAXIMAE; Sec. C. A. SAVARIN.

Dominica Amalgamated Workers' Union: 49 Kennedy Ave., Roseau; f. 1960; 3,307 mems.; Gen. Sec. A. F. JOSEPH.

Waterfront and Allied Workers' Union: Upper Lane, Roseau; f. 1965; 2,300 mems.; Pres. LOUIS BENOIT; Gen. Sec. CURTIS AUGUSTUS.

MARKETING AND CO-OPERATIVE ORGANIZATIONS

There are 25 credit societies with about 15,000 members and share capital of approximately $1.6 million; loans granted in 1971 totalled some $1.3 million. There are also marketing and processing societies (lime juice, lime oil, fisheries, poultry, vegetables, bay oil and sugar cane) with share capital of $16,000, and two service societies (entertainment) with a membership of 110 and share capital of $6,500.

TRANSPORT
ROADS

There are 231 miles of first class, 163 miles of second class and 73 miles of third class motorable roads. There are also 282 miles of tracks. Extensive road development is taking place.

SHIPPING

Vessels of the following lines call at Roseau: Atlantic, Booker Line, Booth American, Caribbean Shipping Line, Geest Industries Ltd., Harrison, Hawthorn Enterprise Ltd., Jones Barbelmeir Clement Line, Linea C., Lamport and Holt, Royal Netherlands Steamship Ltd., Saguenay, St. Lucia Food Co., Seaways Line, West India Shipping Co., West Indies Shipping Services and West Indies Tramping Co.

Passengers (1970): 1,939 arrivals, 2,018 departures.

CIVIL AVIATION

Melville Hall Airport is served by LIAT (Antigua).

Passengers (1971): 22,798 arrivals, 20,995 departures, in transit 33,130; Freight (1971): entered 436,702 kg., cleared 563,747.3 kg.

TOURISM

Dominica Tourist Board: Roseau; Chair. C. A. BUTLER; Sec. Miss C. COOLS-LARTIGUE.

There were 15,294 visitors in 1972.

ST. CHRISTOPHER-NEVIS-ANGUILLA

STATISTICS

Area (sq. miles): 138 (St. Kitts 65, Nevis 36, Anguilla 35, Sombrero 2).

Population: St. Kitts (1970) 34,227; Nevis (1970) 11,230; Anguilla (1960) 5,568; Basseterre (capital) 15,726.

Agriculture: Sugar (1972) 23,800 tons.

Finance: Budget (1974) Estimated Expenditure EC $31.3m.

External Trade (1970): Imports EC $23,427m., Exports EC $8,290m.

Tourism (1972): 16,245 visitors.

ST. KITTS – NEVIS

St. Kitts (St. Christopher)

This island covers an area of about 65 sq. miles and is 28 miles long and 5 miles wide.

The economy of the island is based mainly on sugar. There is one sugar factory located in Basseterre. Sea Island cotton is also grown. Tourism is developing rapidly.

The chief port and capital of the island is Basseterre.

Nevis

This lies three miles to the south-east of St. Kitts and is 36 sq. miles in area.

Cultivation is confined to very small farms which once prospered exclusively on sugar, but because of competition from St. Kitts, Sea Island cotton and coconuts have become the staple crops, though some sugar is still produced.

THE GOVERNMENT

The Governor: H.E. Sir MILTON P. ALLEN, O.B.E.

CABINET

(May 1974)

Premier and Minister of Home and External Affairs: Hon. ROBERT L. BRADSHAW, J.P.

Deputy Prime Minister and Minister of Finance, Trade, Development and Tourism: Hon. C. A. P. SOUTHWELL, J.P.

Minister of Agriculture and Labour: Hon. L. E. ST. JOHN PAYNE.

Minister of Education, Health and Social Affairs: Hon. F. C. BRYANT, J.P.

Minister of Communications, Works and Transport: Hon. ROBERT L. BRADSHAW, J.P. (a.i.).

Minister without Portfolio: Hon. J. N. FRANCE.

Attorney-General: Hon. L. L. MOORE.

Director of Public Prosecutions: H. M. SQUIRES.

Cabinet Secretary: I. WALWYN, O.B.E.

HOUSE OF ASSEMBLY

The Speaker: Hon. W. F. GLASSFORD.

Elected Members: 9.

Nominated Members: 2.

ELECTIONS, MAY 1971

PARTY	SEATS
Labour Party . . .	7
People's Action Movement .	1
Nevis Reformation Party .	1

POLITICAL PARTIES

St. Kitts-Nevis-Anguilla Labour Party (Workers' League): Church St., Basseterre; f. 1932; Leader R. L. BRADSHAW; Sec. J. N. FRANCE.

People's Action Movement: Leader Dr. W. V. HERBERT.

United National Movement: Nevis; affiliated to the St. Kitts-Nevis-Anguilla Labour Party; Leader EUGENE WALWYN.

THE PRESS

Democrat: Cayon St., Basseterre; f. 1948; weekly; Dirs. Capt. J. L. WIGLEY, W. V. HERBERT, M.B.E.; Editor Miss V. FIEULLETEAU; circ. 3,540.

The Labour Spokesman: Masses House, Church St., Basseterre; f. 1957; daily; organ of St. Kitts-Nevis Trades and Labour Union; Editor G. ELROY LEWIS; circ. 1,200.

RADIO

ZIZ Radio and Television: Springfield, Basseterre; government controlled; radio from 1961, television from 1972; Gen. Man. EUSTACE L. JOHN.

FINANCE

Bank of America National Trust and Savings Association: Basseterre and Sandy Point; Man. JOHN D. TOPLEY.

Barclays Bank International Ltd.: Head Office: 54 Lombard St., London, EC3P 3AH; br. in Basseterre (P.O.B. 42, Man. J. C. O'SHEA) and Nevis (Man. H. R. WEATHERHEAD).

Nevis Co-operative Banking Co. Ltd.: Charlestown, Nevis; Man. Dir. D. R. WALWYN, O.B.E.

Royal Bank of Canada: Head Office: Place Ville Marie, Montreal; Basseterre: P.O.B. 91; Man. W. L. BECKETT.

St. Kitts-Nevis-Anguilla National Bank Ltd.: P.O.B. 343, Church St., Basseterre; Man. E. W. LAWRENCE.

TRADE AND INDUSTRY

St. Kitts-Nevis Chamber of Commerce (Inc.): Basseterre; f. 1938, incorporated 1949; 66 mems.; Pres. Capt. J. L. WIGLEY; Sec. J. D. QUINLAN.

St. Kitts Employers' Consultative Federation: Basseterre; represents most large employers in commercial, industrial and agricultural sectors; Sec. RALPH VANIER.

St. Kitts Sea Island Cotton Growers' Association Ltd.: P.O.B. 238, Basseterre; f. 1937; Pres. R. D. E. YEARWOOD; Sec. R. S. VANIER.

St. Kitts Sugar Association Ltd.: P.O.B. 238, Basseterre; f. 1941; 33 mems.; Pres. R. D. E. YEARWOOD.

Nevis Cotton Growers' Association Ltd.: Charlestown, Nevis; Pres. IVOR STEVENS.

TRADE UNIONS

St. Kitts-Nevis Trades and Labour Union: Masses House, Church St., Basseterre; f. 1940; affiliated Caribbean Congress of Labour; associated with St. Kitts-Nevis-Anguilla Labour Party; about 4,000 mems.; Pres. ROBERT BRADSHAW; Gen. Sec. JOS N. FRANCE; publ. *The Labour Spokesman* (daily).

St. Kitts-Nevis-Anguilla Civil Service Association: North Square St., Basseterre; about 270 mems.; Pres. Dr. E. O. JACOBS; Sec. GEORGE WARNER.

TRANSPORT
RAILWAYS

There are 36 miles of light railway on St. Kitts serving the sugar plantations.

ROADS

In St. Kitts there are approximately 60 miles of roads, in Nevis approximately 63 miles and in Anguilla 35 miles.

There are 3,224 registered vehicles.

SHIPPING

The Government maintains a commercial motor boat service between the islands and the following shipping lines call at the islands: Saguenay, West Indies Shipping Service, Harrison, Booth, Lamport and Holt, Royal Netherlands, Athel, Atlantic, Grimaldi Siosa and Lauro.

CIVIL AVIATION

The following airlines serve St. Kitts: LIAT (Antigua), Windward Island Airways (Netherlands Antilles). Nevis is served by LIAT.

TOURISM

St. Kitts-Nevis-Anguilla Tourist Board: P.O.B. 132, Basseterre.

There were 16,245 visitors to St. Kitts-Nevis and Anguilla in 1972.

ANGUILLA

Covering an area of some 35 square miles, Anguilla lies 70 miles to the north of St. Kitts and has an estimated population of 6,500 (1973).

Livestock raising, salt production, boat building and fishing play a major part in the economy. In recent years efforts have been made to diversify the economy and encourage the development of tourism. The unit of currency is the East Caribbean Dollar (EC$).

CONSTITUTION

Anguilla was a British colony from 1650 until 1967. In February 1967 St. Christopher-Nevis-Anguilla became a State in Association with the United Kingdom with four other former British colonies in the Eastern Caribbean. Under Associated Statehood the States became independent internally, while the British Government retained responsibility for external affairs and defence. Three months later the Anguillans repudiated government from St. Kitts. After attempts to repair the breach between St. Kitts and Anguilla had failed, British security forces were landed in Anguilla in March 1969 to install a British Commissioner. Following further fruitless negotiations the British Government decided upon an interim solution so that the island might be effectively administered; this was rejected by the State Government.

In July 1971 the Anguilla Bill received royal assent and an Order in Council made detailed provision for the administration of the territory. One clause in the Act provides that, should the Associated State of St. Kitts-Nevis-Anguilla initiate legislative steps to terminate the status of association, Her Majesty in Council may by order direct that Anguilla shall no longer form a part of that State.

At present, Anguilla is administered by Her Majesty's Commissioner, in consultation with the Anguilla Council. The Commissioner is empowered to make provision for public safety and public order in Anguilla, and generally to ensure the maintenance of good government on the island.

THE GOVERNMENT

Her Majesty's Commissioner for Anguilla: A. C. WATSON, The Valley, Anguilla.

The administration of Anguilla is conducted in consultation with the Anguilla Council. The leader of the Council is RONALD WEBSTER.

RADIO

Radio Anguilla: The Valley; f. 1969; owned and operated by the British Government; 250,000 listeners throughout the northern Caribbean; Dir. ROY G. DUNLOP.

TRANSPORT
CIVIL AVIATION

Anguilla is served by Windward Island Airways of St. Maarten (Netherlands Antilles).

SAINT LUCIA

Saint Lucia is one of the Windward Islands, lying between Martinique and St. Vincent. The principal crop raised on the island is bananas; there are many large plantations, together with numerous small holdings, and bananas represent four-fifths of all exports. Cocoa, citrus and coconuts are important secondary crops. The chief industries are the manufacture of rum, edible oils, cigarettes and mineral waters, the processing of citrus fruit and cotton ginning.

STATISTICS

Area: 238 sq. miles.

Population (1970): 101,100, Castries (capital) *c.* 45,000.

Agriculture (1971—exports in '000 EC$): Copra 469, Coconut Meal 75, Coconut Oil 1,287, Cocoa 188, Bananas 6,947, Spices 93, Fresh Fruit and Vegetables 79.

Finance: Budget (1974) Revenue EC$ 29,389,657, Expenditure EC$ 49,504,342.

External Trade (1968): Imports EC $29,452,000, Exports EC $12,553,000.

Tourism: (1972) 42,398 visitors.

Education (1972): St. Lucia's University Centre has been opened at Morne Fortune.

THE GOVERNMENT

The Governor: H.E. IRA MARCUS SIMMONS, I.S.O., M.B.E.

CABINET

(May 1974)

Premier and Minister of Finance, Planning and Development: Hon. JOHN G. M. COMPTON, LL.B.

Minister of Trade, Industry, Agriculture and Tourism: Hon. G. W. MALLET.

Minister of Education and Health: Hon. J. R. A. BOUSQUET.

Minister of Communications and Works: Hon. I. FELICIEN.

Minister of Housing, Community Development, Social Affairs and Labour: Hon. J. M. D. BOUSQUET.

Parliamentary Secretary to the Premier: (vacant).

Attorney-General: Hon. L. WILLIAMS (a.i.).

Cabinet Secretary: Dr. GRAHAM LOUISY, M.B.E.

HOUSE OF ASSEMBLY

Speaker: W. ST. CLAIR DANIEL.

Official Member: 1.

Nominated Members: 3.

Elected Members: 10.

Clerk: Mrs. U. RAVENEAU.

ELECTION, APRIL 1969

PARTY	SEATS
United Workers Party . .	6
St. Lucia Labour Party . .	3
United Front . . .	1

POLITICAL PARTIES

United Workers Party: Castries; f. 1964; comprises members of dissolved National Labour Movement and People's Progressive Party; Leader J. G. M. COMPTON.

St. Lucia Labour Party: Castries; Leader K. A. H. FOSTER.

United Front: Castries; f. 1969; Leader G. F. L. CHARLES.

RELIGION

Bishop of Castries (Roman Catholic): Rt. Rev. C. A. H. J. GACHET, F.M.I., C.B.E., Bishop's House, Castries.

Roman Catholics form at least 90 per cent of the population; there are also Anglican, Methodist, Baptist, Seventh Day Adventist and Bethel Tabernacle Churches and other sects. The Anglican Bishop of the Windward Islands is resident in St. Vincent.

THE PRESS

Castries Catholic Chronicle, The: Bishop's House, Castries; f. 1957; fortnightly; circ. 1,800.

The Voice of St. Lucia: P.O.B. 104, Castries; f. 1885; twice weekly; Editor R. WAYNE; circ. 9,000; London Office: Colin Turner (London) Ltd., Nassau House, 122 Shaftesbury Ave., W.1; U.S.A. Office: S.S. Koppe and Co., Inc., 610 Fifth Ave., Rockefeller Center, New York, N.Y. 10020.

West Indian Crusader: 19 St. Louis St., Castries; weekly; Editor Miss MIKEY CRICHLOW.

RADIO AND TELEVISION

RADIO

Radio Caribbean International: P.O.B. 121, Castries; f. 1961; subsidiary of Rediffusion Ltd., London; French and English services; Man. JOHN H. WHITMARSH.

There is also a government-owned station, Radio St. Lucia, which was formerly a sub-station of the Windward Islands Broadcasting Service (Grenada).

TELEVISION

St. Lucia Television Service Ltd.: P.O.B. 292, Castries; f. 1967; commercial station; Chair. GEORGE KILLIP; Man. J. B. HOLDEN.

FINANCE

BANKING

Agricultural and Industrial Bank: Castries; f. 1966; provides loan facilities to farmers and producers' associations; Chair. JOSEPH QUENTIN CHARLES.

Government Savings Bank: Treasury, Castries; Accountant-General NORMAN ETIENNE.

St. Lucia Co-operative Bank Ltd.: Castries; incorporated 1937; auth. cap. $500,000; Pres. JOSEPH QUENTIN CHARLES; Man. E. A. THEODORE; Sec. Mrs. URSULA RAVENEAU.

Bank of Nova Scotia Ltd.: Head Office: 44 King St. West, Toronto 1, Ontario, Canada; 6 William Peter Boulevard, Castries; Man. D. W. GALE.

Barclays Bank International Ltd.: Head Office: 54 Lombard St., London, EC3P 3AH; brs. in Castries, Soufrière and Vieux Fort; three agencies; Senior Man. A. G. SANDFORD.

Canadian Imperial Bank of Commerce: Head Office: Commerce Court, Toronto, Canada; William Peter Blvd., Castries.

Chase Manhattan Bank, N.A.: Head Office: 1 Chase Manhattan Plaza, New York, N.Y. 10015; P.O.B. 314, Castries; Man. R. M. VANDERPOEL.

Royal Bank of Canada: Head Office: Place Ville Marie, Montreal; P.O.B. 280, Castries; Man. P. J. JULY.

TRADE AND INDUSTRY

St. Lucia Agriculturists' Association Ltd.: Castries; Chair. and Man. Dir. IRA D'AUVERGNE; Sec. R. RAVENEAU.

St. Lucia Banana Growers' Association: Castries; f. 1953, became statutory corporation 1967; Chair. H. V. ATKINSON; Man. S. D. GAGE.

St. Lucia Chamber of Commerce: George Gordon Bldgs., 4 Bridge St., Castries; f. 1889; 81 mems.; Pres. CORNELL CHARLES; Sec. HILARY MODESTE.

St. Lucia Coconut Growers' Association Ltd.: P.O.B. 259, Castries; Man. Dir. M. C. SALLES-MIQUELLE; Sec. N. E. EDMUNDS.

TRADE UNIONS

St. Lucia Workers' Union: Reclamation Grounds, Castries; f. 1939; affiliated to ICFTU, ORIT, IFPAAW, PTTI and CCL; about 3,000 mems.; Pres. CHARLES AUGUSTIN; Sec. J. B. KING.

St. Lucia Civil Service Association: Castries; Pres. Dr. G. LOUISY; Sec. P. JOSIE.

St. Lucia Seamen and Waterfront Workers' Trade Union: Reclamation Grounds, P.O.B. 166, Castries; f. 1945; about 800 mems.; affiliated to ICFTU; Pres. A. ST. OMER; Sec. H. ANNEVILLE.

St. Lucia Teachers' Union: Castries; Pres. I. DUPRES; Sec. G. BURTON.

Vieux Fort Dock Workers' Union: Vieux Fort; Pres. JOSEPH EMMANUEL.

CO-OPERATIVE SOCIETIES

There are 11 co-operative societies.

TRANSPORT

ROADS

There is a total of approximately 500 miles of roads, of which 123 miles are main roads, 285 miles are feeder roads, and about 92 miles are unclassified roads.

SHIPPING

The ports at Castries and Vieux Fort are being fully mechanized. Castries has three berths with a total length of 1,735 ft.; Vieux Fort will have two berths available, each 535 ft. long. The port of Soufrière has a deep water anchorage but no alongside berth for ocean-going vessels.

In 1973 more than 100 passenger liners called at the three ports. Regular services are provided by the following lines: Atlantic, Booker, Booth, Federal, French, Geest, Harrison, Italia, Lamport and Holt, Royal Dutch Line, Saguenay, Seaway and West Indies Shipping Co.

Total cargo handled in 1973 was 210,000 tons (Castries), and 54,000 tons (Vieux Fort).

CIVIL AVIATION

There are two airports in use, Vigie near Castries, served by LIAT (Antigua) and Caribair (Puerto Rico) with a runway of 5,700 ft., and Hewanorra International (formerly Beane Field), near Vieux Fort, served by British Airways and Eastern Airlines with a runway of 9,000 ft.

TOURISM

St. Lucia Tourist Board: P.O.B. 221, Castries; Chair. P. BERGASSE; Sec. S. SALTIBUS; Man. I. SKEETE.

SAINT VINCENT

Saint Vincent is one of the Windward Islands, west of Barbados. As well as the main island, the state includes the St. Vincent Grenadines, the northerly part of an island group between St. Vincent and Grenada. The principal islands are Bequia, Canouan, Mustique, Mayreau and Union. The territory attained statehood within the Associated States in October 1969. Saint Vincent is the leading world producer of arrowroot, although bananas make up over half of the island's exports. Copra, coconuts, nutmegs, groundnuts, cocoa and cassava are also produced; about one-third of the island is suitable for cultivation.

STATISTICS

Area (sq. miles): 150.3 (St. Vincent 133, other islands 17).

Population (1972): 100,000, Kingstown (capital) 22,000.

Agriculture: Arrowroot (1968) 2,827,000 lb.; Bananas (1969) 75,745,000 lb.

Finance: Budget (1970) EC $18,517,150.

External Trade (1971): Imports EC $24,416,070, Exports EC $7,175,961.

Tourism (1972): 16,902 visitors.

Education (1968): Primary Schools 58, Secondary Schools 9; Primary Pupils 27,199, Secondary Pupils 2,817.

THE GOVERNMENT

The Governor: H.E. Sir RUPERT GODFREY JOHN.

CABINET

(May 1974)

Premier and Minister of Agriculture, Trade and Grenadine Affairs: Hon. JAMES F. MITCHELL.

Deputy Premier and Minister of Finance and Information: Hon. EBENEZER T. JOSHUA.

Minister of Home Affairs, Labour and Tourism: Hon. CLIVE TANNIS.

Minister of Communications and Works: Hon. D. R. SYLVESTER.

Minister of Health, Housing and Local Government: Hon. V. CUFFY.

Minister of Education, Community Development and Youth Affairs: Hon. ALFONSO DENNIE.

HOUSE OF ASSEMBLY

Speaker: Hon. E. J. LAMBERT.

Nominated Members: 2.

Official Members: 1.

Elected Members: 9.

Clerk: O. CUFFY.

WEST INDIES ASSOCIATED STATES

ELECTION, APRIL 1972

PARTY	SEATS
Labour Party	6
People's Political Party	6
Independent	1

POLITICAL PARTIES

The St. Vincent Labour Party: Kingstown; Leader R. M. CATO.

People's Political Party: Kingstown; left-wing; Leader E. T. JOSHUA.

JUDICIAL SYSTEM

Justice is administered by the Supreme Court of Judicature in Grenada, the Court of Summary Jurisdiction and the Magistrates' Courts.

Attorney-General: Hon. CARLISLE PAYNE.

RELIGION
ANGLICAN

Bishop of the Windward Islands: Rt. Rev. GEORGE CUTHBERT MANNING WOODROOFE, C.B.E., M.A., Bishop's House, P.O.B. 128, St. Vincent.

THE PRESS

Government Bulletin: Public Relations Dept., Kingstown; periodically; Editor Public Relations Officer; circ. 100.

Government Gazette: P.O.B. 12, Kingstown; f. 1868; Government Printer A. DOWERS; circ. 370.

The Vincentian: Lot 29, 113 Bay St., Kingstown; f. 1919; Independent; weekly; Man. Dir. C. DE BARNARD; Editor W. H. LEWIS; circ. 25,000; Great Britain Rep. R. H. Humphrey, 39 Brockenhurst Rd., Croydon, Surrey.

RADIO

The local radio station relays news from Grenada, St. Lucia and Dominica and provides limited local programmes. It is expected to expand to full-time programming eventually.

FINANCE
BANKING

Co-operative Bank: Kingstown; Gen. Man. O. C. FORDE

St. Vincent Agricultural and Co-operative Bank: Kingstown; government-owned; finances agriculture, fisheries and related industries; Man. C. C. SAMUEL.

St. Vincent Agricultural Credit and Loan Bank: Kingstown; Gen. Man. P. HULL.

Barclays Bank International Ltd.: Head Office: 54 Lombard St., London, EC3P 3AH; br. in Kingstown; Man. R. O. HAYDOCK; sub-brs. in Bequia, Georgetown and on Union Island.

Canadian Imperial Bank of Commerce: Head Office: Commerce Court, Toronto; Kingstown; Man. C. F. DAVIS.

Royal Bank of Canada: Head Office: Place Ville Marie, Montreal; Kingstown; Man. D. R. BERTRAND.

TRADE AND INDUSTRY

St. Vincent Chamber of Commerce (Inc.): Kingstown; Pres. DUNCAN PROVIDENCE.

St. Vincent Co-operative Arrowroot Association: Kingstown; Chair. Sir FRED PHILLIPS.

TRADE UNIONS

The Civil Service Association: Kingstown; f. 1943; 400 mems.; Pres. ARNIM EUSTACE; Sec. H. STEWART.

Commercial, Technical and Allied Workers' Union: Kingstown; affiliated to Caribbean Congress of Labour (C.C.L.), ICFTU, Fiet, P.T.T.I. and St. Vincent Trade Union Congress; Sec. J. BURNS BONADIE.

Federated Industrial and Agricultural Workers' Union: Kingstown: affiliated to ICFTU; about 3,000 mems.; Pres. Hon. E. T. JOSHUA; Sec. ALMA JOHNSON.

The Teachers' Union: Kingstown; members of Caribbean Union of Teachers affiliated to N.U.T., W.C.O.T.P. and C.C.L.; 600 mems.

The Secondary School Teachers' Association: Kingstown; 49 mems.; Gen. Sec. ALISON McINTOSH.

CO-OPERATIVE AND MARKETING
ORGANIZATIONS

There are 26 Agricultural Credit Societies who receive loans from the Government and 5 Registered Co-operative Societies.

TRANSPORT
ROADS

There are 568 miles of roads of which 178 miles are oiled, 235 miles rough motorable and 240 miles tracks and byeways.

SHIPPING

Two Federal ships provide a weekly cargo and passenger service. Monthly services are provided by the Royal Netherlands Steamships Co., Booth, American Shipping Co., Fratelli Grimaldi Line, James Nourse Line, Harrison Line, Atlantic Line, West Indies Shipping Co., Linea C., Saguenay Shipping Ltd. and Geest Line.

CIVIL AVIATION

There is a civilian airport at Arnos Vale, situated about two miles south-east of Kingstown, served by LIAT (Antigua).

TOURISM

St. Vincent Tourist Board: P.O.B. 834, Kingstown; Chair. D. E. FRANK

There were 16,902 visitors in 1972.

WESTERN SAMOA

Western Samoa became independent from New Zealand on January 1st, 1962, and is a member of the Commonwealth. It lies in the South Pacific 1,500 miles north of New Zealand and consists of two large and seven small islands; five islands are uninhabited. Following a general election in February 1970, Fiame Mata'afa Mulinuu, Prime Minister since 1959, was voted out of office. A new cabinet headed by Tupua Tamasese Lealofi was formed. In March 1973, however, Mata'afa won a resounding victory in a general election and became Prime Minister once more.

STATISTICAL SURVEY

AREA AND POPULATION

AREA
(square miles)

Total	Savai'i	Upolu
1,097	662	433

POPULATION
1966

Total	Upolu	Savai'i	Apia (capital)
131,552	95,344	36,208	25,391

Average annual rate of increase (1961–66): 2.8 per cent.
Population (census of November 3rd, 1971): 146,635.

EMPLOYMENT
(Nov. 1966)

Agriculture	26,160
Industry	1,364
Commerce	1,768
Transport and Communications .	842
Services	771
Other	4,387
TOTAL	35,292

Livestock (1966 estimate): Cattle 20,000; Pigs 40,000; Horses 2,600; Poultry 500,000.
Fishing (1966 estimate): 5,000 tons.

AGRICULTURE
(1971 est.)

	ACRES
Coconuts	55,000
Bananas	17,000
Cocoa	18,000
Food Crops	n.a.
Mixed Crops	n.a.

Industry: There are four saw mills, one tyre retreading plant, a soap factory, a bottling plant, a cabinet making industry, a biscuit factory and two garment factories and various small enterprises.

FINANCE

100 sene (cents) = 1 tala (Western Samoan dollar).
Coins: 1, 2, 5, 10, 20 and 50 sene.
Notes: 1, 2 and 10 tala.
Exchange rates (April 1974): £1 sterling = 1.408 tala; U.S. $1 = 59.62 sene.
100 tala = £71.04 = U.S. $167.74.

BUDGET
(W.S. $'000)

REVENUE		1971 (est.)	EXPENDITURE		1971 (est.)
Ordinary Revenue. . . .		6,478.2	Maintenance and Capital . .		6,518.4
Other Revenue:			Development		518.2
Grants		220			
Loans		—			
TOTAL		6,698.2	TOTAL		7,036.6

EXTERNAL TRADE
(W.S. $)

Imports*: 1969 total: 7.4 million (New Zealand supplied 28 per cent, Japan 11 per cent, and the U.K. 10 per cent).

 * Comprise: food products (25 per cent); manufactured goods (20 per cent) machinery and transport equipment (14 per cent).

Exports*: 1969 total: 4.6 million (New Zealand accounted for 31 per cent, German Federal Republic 25 per cent, and the Netherlands 20 per cent).
1970 estimates: *Imports:* 9.8 million; *Exports:* 3.3 million.

 * Copra, cocoa and bananas account for about 90 per cent of the total value of exports.

TRANSPORT
ROADS
Vehicles Registered—31 December 1970

Passenger Cars and Buses . . .	416
Private Cars and Lorries . . .	1,740
Motor-Cycles	221

EDUCATION
(1966)

	Number of Schools	Number of Pupils
Primary . . .	169	
Intermediate . .	39	34,000
Secondary . .	15	
Higher* . . .	4	420

* 1972

THE CONSTITUTION
(*January* 1962)

HEAD OF STATE

The office of Head of State is held by His Highness Malietoa Tanumafili, who will hold this post for life. After that the Head of State will be elected by the Legislative Assembly for a term of five years.

EXECUTIVE POWER

Executive power lies with the Cabinet, consisting of a Prime Minister, supported by the majority in the Legislative Assembly, and eight Ministers selected by the Prime Minister. Cabinet decisions are subject to review by the Executive Council, which is made up of the Head of State and the Cabinet.

LEGISLATIVE POWER

Since the General Election of February 25th, 1967 the Legislative Assembly has consisted of 47 members, two of whom are Europeans. It has a three-year term and the Speaker is elected from among the members. Samoans and Europeans have separate electoral rolls; the Europeans are elected by universal adult suffrage and the Samoans by the Matai (elected family leaders). There were changes of government in 1970 and 1973.

THE GOVERNMENT
HEAD OF STATE

O le Ao o le Malo: H.H. Malietoa Tanumafili II, c.b.e., Fautua of Maliena.

CABINET
(*April* 1974)

Prime Minister, Minister of Police, Immigration and Emigration, District Affairs, Labour and Civil Aviation: Fiame Mata'afa, c.b.e.

Minister of Finance: Sam Sa'ili.

Minister of Works and Marine: Laumea Matolu II.

Minister of Education: Alphonso Philipp.

Minister of Agriculture and Forestry: Muagututi'a Pinati.

Minister of Post Office: Tapua'i Ene.

Minister of Health: Seiuli Taulafo.

Minister of Lands and Land Registry: Lesatele Rapi.

Minister of Justice: Tupua Tamasese Lealofi IV.

DIPLOMATIC REPRESENTATION

EMBASSIES AND HIGH COMMISSIONS ACCREDITED TO WESTERN SAMOA
(In Wellington, New Zealand, unless otherwise indicated)
(E) Embassy; (HC) High Commission.

Australia: Suva, Fiji (HC); *High Commissioner:* H. W. Bullock.

Canada: (HC); *High Commissioner:* J. A. Dougan.

France: (E); *Ambassador:* Christian de Nicolay.

India: (HC); *High Commissioner:* P. S. Naksar.

New Zealand: Apia (HC); *High Commissioner:* W. G. Thorp.

United Kingdom: (HC); *High Commissioner:* H. A. Arthington-Davy, o.b.e.

U.S.A.: (E); *Ambassador:* Armistead B. Selden.

PARLIAMENT
LEGISLATIVE ASSEMBLY

Speaker: Hon. Toleafoa Taletimu.

Deputy Speaker: Hon. Teo Fetu.

Samoan Members: 45 representing 41 territorial constituencies.

Individual Voters: 2.

JUDICIAL SYSTEM

The **Supreme Court** consists of a Chief Justice and a Puisne Judge. It has full jurisdiction for both criminal and civil cases. Appeals lie with the Court of Appeal.

Chief Justice: G. J. Donne.

Puisne Judge: To be appointed.

Registrar: F. J. Thomsen.

The Court of Appeal consists of a President (the Chief Justice of the Supreme Court), and with such persons possessing qualifications prescribed by statute as may be appointed by the Head of State. Any three judges of the Court of Appeal may exercise all the powers of the Court. A Judge of the Court cannot sit on the hearing of an appeal from any decision made by him.

The Magistrates Court consists of a Magistrate and two senior Samoan Judges, assisted by seven junior Samoan Judges.

Magistrate: W. A. WILSON.

The Land and Titles Court has jurisdiction in respect of disputes over Samoan land and succession to Samoan titles. It consists of the President (who is also Chief Justice of the Supreme Court) assisted by five Samoan associate judges and assessors; P.O.B. 33, Apia.

Registrar: AUELUA F. ENARI.

RELIGION

The population is almost entirely Christian.

PROTESTANT CHURCHES

Congregational Christian Church in Samoa: Tamaligi, Apia; Elder Deacon FUIMAONO ASUEMU.

Methodist Church in Samoa: Pres. AMANI AMITUANA'I.

Church of Jesus Christ of Latter-Day Saints: Pres. RALPH RODGERS, L.D.S. Mission, P.O.B. 197, Apia.

Seventh-Day Adventist Church: Box 600, Apia; f. 1895; mission territory constituted by American Samoa and Western Samoa; adherents (1972 est.) 2,250; Pres. Pastor D. E. HAY; publs. two monthly magazines.

Congregational Church of Jesus in Samoa: Rev. SOLOMONA SIULAGI, Fataogo, Apia.

Anglican Church: Rev. H. H. BUTLER; P.O.B. 16, Apia.

ROMAN CATHOLIC COMMUNION

Bishop of Apia: H.E. Cardinal PIO TAOFINU'U, Cardinal's Residence, Box 532, Apia, Western Samoa.

THE PRESS

Samoa Times, The: Apia, Western Samoa, Pago Pago, Western Samoa; weekly; independent, bi-lingual newspaper; Editor FAALOGO PITO FAALOGO; circ. 7,000.

Savali: P.O.B. 193, Apia; f. 1904; fortnightly; government publication; Samoan and English; Man. and Editor KALATI MOSE; circ. 6,500.

South Seas Star: Box 242, Apia; f. 1971; weekly (Wed.); Man. Editor LEOTA PITA; English Editor S. FIGIEL; Samoan Editor POUVI SU'A; circ. 3,000.

TELECOMMUNICATIONS

Western Samoa Broadcasting Service: Broadcasting Dept., P.O.B. 200, Apia; commenced operation and broadcasts 1948; broadcasts in English and Samoan on 1420 kc./s. and 10.000 watts power; Dir. J. W. MOORE; Senior Programme Organizer C. H. J. SINCLAIR; Supervising Technician D. A. HENDERSON. In 1970, there were 20,000 radio sets.

There is a radio communication station at Apia. Radio telephone service connects Western Samoa with American Samoa, Fiji, New Zealand, Australia, Canada, U.S.A., U.K. and other overseas countries. Telephone subscribers numbered 1,800 in December 1970.

BANKING AND TRADE

Bank of Western Samoa: Apia; f. 1959; cap. p.u. $500,000; dep. $4,730,392 (Dec. 1972); Chair. D. O. WHYTE, C.B.E.; Man. W. W. ANSELL.

CO-OPERATIVES

In 1966 there were 8 registered co-operatives, and 13 credit unions.

TRANSPORT

Public Works Department: Apia; Dir. of Works L. McQUITTY.

VEHICLES REGISTERED

	1970	1971*
Passenger Cars and Buses .	416	761
Private Cars and Lorries .	1,740	1,438
Motor Cycles .	221	165

* Jan.-Oct.

ROADS

There are 496 miles of roads in the islands, of which 76 miles are bitumen surfaced. Main roads 242 miles, Secondary roads 103 miles, Plantation roads 151 miles.

SHIPPING

A regular fortnightly service from New Zealand via Fiji, Japan, linking U.K. and U.S.A. Also a direct service with Japan and U.K. Nauru state shipping line makes regular calls at Apia, Western Samoa.

CIVIL AVIATION

Polynesian Airlines Ltd.: P.O.B. 599, Beach Rd., Apia; daily air services to Pago Pago (capital of American Samoa) connect with services to Fiji, Tahiti, New Zealand, U.S.A.; four services weekly to Nadi (Fiji), one a week to Niue Island; three services weekly to Nuku'alofa (Tonga); aircraft: 2 HS 748; Chair. E. ANNANDALE; Gen. Man. M. R. STANTON.

YEMEN ARAB REPUBLIC

INTRODUCTORY SURVEY

Location, Climate, Language, Religion, Flag, Capital

The Yemen Arab Republic is situated in the south-west corner of the Arabian Peninsular, bounded to the north and east by Saudi Arabia, to the west by the Red Sea, and to the south and east by the People's Democratic Republic of Yemen (formerly Aden and the Protectorate of South Arabia). The climate in the semi-desert coastal strip is hot, with high humidity; inland, the climate is somewhat less hot, with heavy rainfall. The eastern plateau slopes into desert. The language is Arabic. The population is almost entirely Muslim split between the Shafai and Zaidi sects. The national flag (proportions 3 by 2) has three horizontal stripes of red, white and black, with a five-pointed green star in the centre. The capital is Sana'a.

Recent History

The Yemen Arab Republic was set up in 1962 after the overthrow of the Imam Muhammad al-Badr, a week after he had succeeded his late father, Ahmad. Civil war between Royalists and Republicans followed, with the Republicans eventually gaining the upper hand with the help of Egyptian forces. The Republican Government was recognized by most countries and the UN. After the British officially withdrew from Aden in 1967, trouble appeared in another guise; the National Liberation Front, having defeated the rival force—the Front for the Liberation of Occupied South Yemen (FLOSY)—introduced repressive measures and more than 300,000 Southern Yemenis fled to North Yemen. Backed by Saudi Arabia and Libya, many of these refugees joined mercenary organizations aimed at the overthrow of the Marxist régime in Southern Yemen and carried out raids across the border. Intermittent fighting, beginning in early 1971, flared into open warfare between the two Yemens in October 1972, with North Yemen receiving aid from Saudi Arabia and Southern Yemen being supported by Soviet arms. A ceasefire was arranged under the auspices of the Arab League, and in Cairo a week later (October 28th) both sides agreed to the union of the two Yemens, to be implemented within 18 months. Although numerous discussions took place during 1973 and early 1974, no clear decisions about implementing the union were made public. A ten-member Command Council, composed of army officers and led by Colonel Ibrahim al-Hamidi, seized control in a bloodless *coup* in June 1974.

Government

The National Congress, meeting (without the participation of the Royalists) at Khamer in May 1965, published an interim constitution, setting up a supreme Consultative Assembly with power to make laws, remove members of the Republican Council and nominate the President. A new constitution was promulgated in December 1970, and elections for a Consultative Council were held in 1971.

Defence

The total regular forces number 20,900 (army 20,000). There is a three-year period of military service.

Economic Affairs

Agriculture is the principal activity. In the highlands the land is terraced and irrigated and quite fertile. The chief crops are millet, maize, sorghum and oats. Oranges, plums, apricots, apples, bananas, quinces and lemons are grown, and dates are produced in low lying areas. High quality Moka coffee is the principal export crop. There is a little light industry. Agriculture suffers from drought.

Transport and Communications

There are no railways in the Yemen. Roads are being developed with Chinese, American and Soviet assistance. There are highways from Hodeida to Sana'a and from Moka to Taiz and Sana'a. Hodeida port has been considerably extended with Soviet aid. A direct road runs from Taiz to Sana'a. The Yemeni Airline Co. operates internal services and services to Cairo, and the new Sana'a airport was opened in August 1973.

Social Welfare

Under the Imamate there was little provision for social welfare. The Republicans intend to bring about a social revolution on the lines of that achieved in Egypt. By 1974 there were 180 doctors and pharmacists serving in 40 hospitals or clinics, with a total of 4,000 beds.

Education

Education before the revolution was in private hands. The Republican Government is establishing new schools run by the state, and by 1974 enrolment in primary, intermediate and general secondary schools had reached 76,000.

Tourism

Tourism is undeveloped.

Sport

The chief sports are football, hunting and hawking.

Public Holidays

1974: September 26th (Proclamation of the Republic), October 18th* (Id ul Fitr), December 26th* (Id ul Adha).

1975: January 14th* (Muslim New Year), March 26th* (Mouloud, Birth of the Prophet).

* Muslim religious holidays dependent on the lunar calendar, which may vary slightly from dates given.

Weights and Measures

Local weights and measures are used, and vary according to location.

Currency and Exchange Rates

40 buqsha=1 Yemeni riyal.
Exchange rates (April 1974):
$£1$ sterling=10.80 Yemeni riyals;
U.S. $1=4.575 Yemeni riyals.

STATISTICAL SURVEY

AREA AND POPULATION

AREA	TOTAL (July 1st, 1972)	SANA'A (capital)	TAIZ	HODEIDA
200,000 sq. km.	6,062,000	121,000	80,000	90,000

AGRICULTURE
PRINCIPAL CROPS

	1969–70		1970–71		1971–72	
	Area ('000 hectares)	Production ('000 metric tons)	Area ('000 hectares)	Production ('000 metric tons)	Area ('000 hectares)	Production ('000 metric tons)
Sorghum and Millet . . .	1,200	680	1,230	984	1,100	1,020
Wheat	35	30	30	33	50	54
Barley	145	160	140	154	143	178
Maize	4	9	16	32	50	80
Pulses	50	50	50	60	60	60
Potatoes	4	20	6	55	5	58
Vegetables	8	50	10	100	16	137
Grapes	4	10	6	30	7	35
Coffee	5	4	6	4	6	5
Cotton	5	2	10	10	15	15
Tobacco	4	2	4	3	4	5

LIVESTOCK
1971 ('000 head)

Cattle . . .	957
Sheep . . .	} 10,627
Goats . . .	
Camels . . .	69
Horses . . .	4
Donkeys . . .	672

Source: Ministry of Agriculture.

INDUSTRY
Industrial Production 1971
('000 riyals)

Mining and Quarrying . . .	3,597
Food Manufacturing . .	6,332
Soft Drinks . . .	6,877
Tobacco and Cigarettes . .	2,062
Textiles . . .	25,352
Wood Products . .	2,260
Printing and Publishing . .	1,042
Building Materials . .	4,178
Metal Products . .	3,077
Electricity . . .	9,256
Vehicle Maintenance . .	3,751
Others . . .	1,886

FINANCE

40 buqsha = 1 Yemeni riyal.

Coins: ½, 1 and 2 buqsha.

Notes: 10 and 20 buqsha; 1, 5, 10, 20 and 50 riyals.

Exchange rates (April 1974): £1 sterling = 10.80 Yemeni riyals; U.S. $1 = 4.575 Yemeni riyals.

100 Yemeni riyals = £9.26 = $21.86.

BUDGET
('000 riyals)

	REVENUE	EXPENDITURE
1970–71 . .	97,464	170,672
1971–72 . .	151,274	233,803
1972–73 . .	199,021	271,458

Source: Ministry of Treasury and Central Bank of Yemen.

EXTERNAL TRADE
('000 riyals)

	1969	1970	1971	1972
Imports . .	157,848	178,449	184,840	376,245
Exports . .	17,957	15,759	21,571	20,074

PRINCIPAL COMMODITIES
(riyals)

IMPORTS	1971	EXPORTS	1971
Foodstuffs	66,847,599	Cotton	7,986,195
Beverages and Tobacco . .	14,848,768	Coffee	4,582,409
Petroleum Products . . .	10,544,543	Qat	2,798,095
Chemicals	9,406,572	Rock Salt . . .	2,383,694
Manufactured Goods . .	39,167,487	Hides and Skins . .	2,039,483
Machinery . . .	14,127,654		
Transport Equipment . .	15,422,431		
Textiles	7,916,018		

Source: Central Bank of Yemen.

EXPORTS BY MAIN COUNTRY
(million riyals)

	1971	1972
Yemen, People's Dem. Rep. .	7.3	4.4
Japan	2.5	0.54
U.S.S.R. . . .	1.9	1.8
China	8.0	7.7

IMPORTS BY MAIN COUNTRY
(million riyals)

	1971	1972
Yemen, People's Dem. Rep. .	49.5	40.9
Japan	17.4	38.4
U.K. . . .	14.7	19.6
Australia . . .	13.9	47.0
U.S.S.R. . . .	13.5	14.8
Singapore . . .	8.4	9.6
Italy	8.5	9.6

Source: Central Bank of Yemen.

TRANSPORT

ROAD TRAFFIC 1972

Private cars 736, motor cycles 3,416, taxis 3,177, trucks 3,671.

SHIPPING			CIVIL AVIATION			
	VESSELS ENTERING HODEIDA PORT	TONNAGE UNLOADED			PASSENGERS CARRIED	FREIGHT (kilos)
1971 . .	367	4,618,301	1971		52,300	378,200
1972 . .	506	5,066,991	1972		58,000	582,600

EDUCATION
(1972–73)

	INSTITUTIONS	TEACHERS	PUPILS	
			Boys	Girls
Primary	1,442	4,053	136,977	17,630
Preparatory . . .	59	387	7,212	94
Secondary . . .	8	157	2,248	19
Commercial . . .	1	8	124	—
Technical . . .	1	42	250	—
Teacher Training . .	9	n.a.	201	738
University Colleges . .	4	41	391	48

Source (except where otherwise stated): Yemen Arab Republic Central Planning Organization.

THE CONSTITUTION*

(*Published December 28th, 1970*)

Yemen is an Islamic Arab independent sovereign Republic, with parliamentary democracy, forming part of the Arab nation. Islam is the state religion and Islamic Law the basis of all legislation. Sana'a is the capital.

The Constitution ensures equality of all before the law, freedom of expression, press, publication, public gatherings and trade union activity within the framework of the law. The people are the source of all authority, through their representatives in the Consultative Assembly.

The Consultative Assembly is composed of 179 members, 20 of whom will be appointed by the President and the rest elected by popular franchise every four years. The Assembly shall issue laws and regulations for the organization of the state, and approve the state budget and treaties and agreements concluded by the Government. The members of the Republican Council will be appointed by the Assembly, and may be withdrawn by a two-thirds majority vote of the Assembly.

The Republican Council may present bills to the Council of Ministers for presentation to the Consultative Assembly. Any motion submitted to the Council will require the support of at least 30 members and must be endorsed by a two-thirds majority. No reports are to be submitted to the President except through the Council of Ministers and all laws, orders and directions from the President will be issued through the Council of Ministers.

The Consultative Assembly will nominate the President. Duties of the President of the Republic include the signing of legislation approved by the Consultative Assembly.

The Council of Ministers, as executive and administrative authority in the state, is responsible *inter alia* for the execution of plans laid down by the follow-up committee of the national peace conference, set up to implement the conference resolutions.

The Constitution provides for an independent judiciary, a supreme Sharia Court, and local organs of government. Other provisions cover human rights and equality for women.

* suspended after the military *coup* of June 13th, 1974

THE GOVERNMENT

A ten-member Command Council, composed of army officers and led by Col. IBRAHIM AL-HAMIDI, took control in a *coup d'état* on June 13th, 1974. The cabinet of Prime Minister HASSAN MAKKI was asked to continue in office for the time being.

CABINET

(July 1974)

Prime Minister and Minister for Foreign Affairs: MOHSIN ALAINI.

Minister for Local Government: ABBULMALIK AL-TAIB.

Minister of Information: AHMED DAHMASH.

Minister of the Interior: YAHIA AL-METWAKEL.

Minister of Social Affairs: MOHAMMED AL-RUBAI.

Minister of Supplies: SULTAN AL-KIRSHI.

Minister for Wakfs: AHMED AL-KABAH.

Minister of Economy: ABDULWAHAB MAHMOUD ABDUL-HAMID.

Minister of Agriculture: ABDULKUDOSE AL-WAZIR.

Minister of State: AMEEN ABOU RASE.

Minister of State: ABDULKARIM ALAANSY.

Deputy Premier for Foreign Affairs: Dr. HASSAN MAKKI.

Deputy Premier for Communications: ABDULLAH AL-ASNAG.

Minister for Public Works: ABDULLATIF DAIFALLAH.

Minister of Finance: MOHAMMED AL-GONAID.

Minister of Education: AHMED JABER.

Minister of Justice: ALI AL-SAMAN.

Minister for Development: ABDULKARIM AL-IRYANI.

Minister of State: SALAH AL-MASRI.

DIPLOMATIC REPRESENTATION

EMBASSIES ACCREDITED TO THE YEMEN ARAB REPUBLIC

(In Sana'a unless otherwise stated)

Afghanistan: Cairo, Egypt.

Algeria: Ali Abdul Moghni St.; *Ambassador:* NOUIOUAT SAADEDDINE.

Austria: Jeddah, Saudi Arabia.

Belgium: Jeddah, Saudi Arabia.

Bulgaria: Cairo, Egypt.

China, People's Republic: Zubairy St.; *Ambassador:* CHANG TSAN-MING.

Czechoslovakia: Gamal Abdul Naser St.; *Chargé d'Affaires:* FRANTIŠEK KNOPACEK.

Egypt: Gamal Abdul Naser St.; *Ambassador:* AHMAD FOUAD ABDUL HAYE.

Ethiopia: Zubairy St.; *Ambassador:* FITAWRARI MOHAMED SIRAGE.

France: Building Yahya Al-Sunaidar; *Ambassador:* GEORGES GALLIÉ.

German Democratic Republic: 26 Sept St.; *Ambassador:* HEINZ BÜRGEL.

Germany, Federal Republic: Republican Palace St.; *Ambassador:* Dr. GUNTER HELD.

Greece: Jeddah, Saudi Arabia.

Hungary: Cairo, Egypt.

India: Al-Amir Building, Gamal Abdul Naser St.; *Ambassador:* SYED NAZIR HUSSAIN.

Iran: *Ambassador:* Dr. HASSAN SABETI.

Iraq: Building Mohamed Zehrah, Zubairy St.; *Ambassador:* MAHDI HUSSAIN EL-YASSERY.

Italy: Gamal Abdul Naser St.; *Ambassador:* LORENZO BARACCHI TUA DI PAULLO.

Japan: Jeddah, Saudi Arabia.

Jordan: *Ambassador:* Maj.-Gen. HAIDAR MUSTAFA.

Korea, Democratic People's Republic: Zubairy St.; *Ambassador:* KIM YONG IL.

Kuwait: 62 September St.; *Ambassador:* (vacant).

Lebanon: Airport Rd.; *Ambassador:* MUNIR AL-NASULI.

Libya: Airport Rd.; *Ambassador:* HUSSEIN ASSAYED ASHARIF.

Netherlands: Jeddah, Saudi Arabia.

Pakistan: Cairo, Egypt.

Poland: Cairo, Egypt.

Qatar: Jeddah, Saudi Arabia.

Romania: Cairo, Egypt.

Saudi Arabia: Arman Building; *Ambassador:* Sheikh MOUSSAID BIN AHMED AL-SUDAIRI.

Somalia: Jeddah, Saudi Arabia.

Spain: Cairo, Egypt.

Sweden: Jeddah, Saudi Arabia.

Switzerland: Jeddah, Saudi Arabia.

Syria: Zubairy St.; *Ambassador:* MUHAMMAD ADNAN MURAD.

Tunisia: Jeddah, Saudi Arabia.

Turkey: Jeddah, Saudi Arabia.

U.S.S.R.: 26 September St.; *Ambassador:* VASILI KORNEV.

United Arab Emirates: *Ambassador:* SAYYID SALIM AL SUWAIDI.

United Kingdom: 11/13 Republican Palace St.; *Ambassador:* D. C. CARDEN.

U.S.A.: Beit Al-Halali; *Ambassador:* WILLIAM R. CRAWFORD, Jr.

Viet-Nam, Democratic Republic: Cairo, Egypt.

CONSULTATIVE COUNCIL*

A Consultative Council was established as the supreme legislative body under the 1970 Constitution. It consists of 179 members, of whom 20 are appointed by the President and the remainder elected by popular vote every four years. Elections were first held in March 1971.

Speaker: Shaikh Abdullah Bin-Husain Al-Ahmar.

* Dissolved June 1974.

POLITICAL ORGANIZATION*

Yemeni Union: Sana'a; f. 1973 in anticipation of merging of two Yemens; Leader President Abdul Rahman Al-Iryani; Sec.-Gen. Abdulla Asnag.

* Dissolved June 1974.

LAW AND RELIGION

President of the People's Tribunal: Col. Ghalib Shari.

Public Prosecutor: Major Abdulla Barakat.

Sharia Court: Sana'a; f. 1964 to deal with political cases and to try senior government officials.

PRESS AND RADIO

Al Bilad: Sana'a; Arabic; weekly.

Al Iman: Sana'a; Arabic; Editor Abdul Karim Bin Ibrahim Al-Amir.

Al Nasr: Taiz; Arabic; Editor Muhammad Bin Hussein Musa.

Saba: Taiz; f. 1949; Arabic; fortnightly; political and social affairs; Editor Muhammad Abdu Salah Al-Shurjebi; circ. 10,000.

Al Thawra (*The Revolution*): Sana'a; daily.

Middle East News: Ali Abdel Ghani St., Ali Moh. Hamoud Al-Yamani, Sana'a.

Saba News Agency: Sana'a; f. 1970; Chair. Ahmad Muhammad Hadi.

Tass also has a bureau in Sana'a.

Radio Sana'a: Station controlled by the government which broadcasts in Arabic for thirteen hours daily; Dir. Gen. Ali Hamood Afif.

There are 250,000 receiving sets.

BANKING

Central Bank of Yemen: P.O.B. 59, Sana'a; f. 1971; cap. p.u. 10m. riyals; responsible for issuing currency, managing gold and foreign exchange reserves etc.; at end of December 1973 currency in circulation amounted to 457.5m. riyals; Gov. and Chair. Abdul Aziz Abdul Ghani; Deputy Gov. and Deputy Chair. Abdulla Sanabani; Gen. Man. Ahmed Muhammad Ali.

Yemen Bank for Reconstruction and Development: P.O.B. 541, Sana'a; f. 1962; cap. 10m. riyals; consolidated bank; 9 brs.; Chair. Mohsin Sirry.

British Bank of the Middle East: 20 Abchurch Lane, London, E.C.4; P.O.B. 3932, Hodeida: Man. D. C. Howells; P.O.B. 4886, Taiz: Man. I. W. Cutress.

TRADE AND INDUSTRY

Nationalized Organizations

General Cotton Organization: Sana'a.

Hodeida Electricity and Water Company: P.O.B. 3363, Hodeida; affiliate of Yemen Bank for Reconstruction and Development.

National Tobacco and Matches Co.: P.O.B. 571, Hodeida; f. 1964; monopoly importing and sales organization for tobacco and matches; now building a cigarette factory at Hodeida to use tobacco grown locally on the company's plantations; Chair. A. A. Nagi.

Yemen Company for Foreign Trade: Hodeida.

Yemen Petroleum Co.: P.O.B. 360, Hodeida; the sole petroleum supplier in the Yemen; Chair. Hussain Abdullah Al Makdani; Gen. Man. Abdul Rahman Yousef.

Yemen Printing and Publishing Co.: P.O.B. 1081, Sana'a; f. 1970; publishes ten newspapers (including two government newspapers), and undertakes many kinds of commercial printing; Chair. Ahmad Muhammad Hadi.

TRANSPORT

Roads: There are about 1,650 km. of main roads, of which about 450 km. are asphalted and the rest gravelled. Highways run from Hodeida to Sana'a, and from Moka to Taiz, Ibb and Sana'a. A highway from Sana'a to Saada is being built with Chinese aid. The Sana'a-Khamir section was opened in February 1972.

Shipping: Hodeida is a Red Sea port of some importance, and the Yemen Navigation Company runs passenger and cargo services to many parts of the Middle East and Africa.

Adafar Yemenite Line: Hodeida.

Middle East Shipping Co.: P.O.B. 700, Hodeida; br. in Moka.

Civil Aviation: Three airports—Al Rahaba at Sana'a, Al Ganad at Taiz and Hodeida Airport—are classified as being of international standard and are being developed following the end of the civil war. Federal Germany gave financial assistance towards the construction of the new Sana'a airport, which opened in August 1973.

Yemen Airways: Sana'a; internal services to Sana'a, Hodeida, Taiz, Beida, Hareeb, Barat and Saada, external services to Aden, Asmara, Cairo, Dharan, Djibouti, Jeddah and Kuwait; Chair. and Pres. Col. Ali Al-Ashwal; fleet of five DC-6, one Ilyushin Il-18, four DC-3.

The following airlines also serve the Yemen: Aeroflot, Democratic Yemen Airlines, Ethiopian Airlines and Saudi Arabian Airlines.

UNIVERSITY

University of Sana'a: Sana'a; f. 1974.

PEOPLE'S DEMOCRATIC REPUBLIC OF YEMEN

INTRODUCTORY SURVEY

Location, Climate, Language, Religion, Flag, Capital

The People's Democratic Republic of Yemen lies on the southern shore of the Arabian peninsula, with the Yemen Arab Republic to the north-west, Saudi Arabia to the north, and Oman to the east. The islands of Perim and Kamaran at the southern end of the Red Sea are also part of the Republic. The climate is hot and dry. Arabic is spoken and most of the population are Muslims. The national flag (proportions 3 by 2) has horizontal stripes of red, white and black, with a light blue triangle, containing a five-pointed red star, at the hoist. The capital, formerly known as Al Ittihad, has been renamed Madinat ash-Sha'b (People's City).

Recent History

The People's Republic of Southern Yemen was formed on November 30th, 1967, comprising Aden and the former Protectorate of South Arabia. Aden had been under British rule since 1839 and the Protectorate was developed by a series of treaties between Britain and local leaders. Prior to British withdrawal, two rival factions fought for control, the National Liberation Front (NLF) and the Front for the Liberation of Occupied South Yemen (FLOSY). The Marxist NLF eventually won and assumed power under the leadership of Qahtan ash-Sha'abi. He was forced out of office in 1969 and the country's present name was adopted in 1970. More than 300,000 Southern Yemenis fled to North Yemen when the NLF started rounding up dissident elements, including the FLOSY leader Abdullah al-Asnag, who became a cabinet minister in the neighbouring Yemen Arab Republic ("North Yemen"). A polarization of interests by then existed, with North Yemen establishing closer ties with the West and receiving aid from Saudi Arabia and Libya, while the extreme left-wing régime in Southern Yemen, isolated in the Gulf, began receiving aid from Communist China and the U.S.S.R. There were clashes with Saudi Arabia in 1969 and intermittent fighting with North Yemeni mercenaries on the border between the two Yemens in 1971. This erupted into open war in October 1972 and there was fierce fighting, including air raids, for about two weeks. Agreement on a ceasefire was eventually reached with Arab League mediation. At a meeting in Cairo on October 24th both sides proposed a union of the two Yemens, and a draft agreement to this effect was signed on October 28th, but although numerous discussions have since taken place between representatives of the two Yemens, few practical steps have been taken towards implementing the union.

Government

A 101-member Provisional Supreme People's Council exercises legislative power until a permanent Council can be elected. The country is divided into six Governorates.

Defence

The Republic has armed forces of 9,500 men and is engaged in training a small air force of 500 men. The army consists of 8,800 men, and the navy of 200 men. The U.S.S.R. is reported to be supplying military aid.

Economic Affairs

Before independence the economy of the area had depended to a considerable extent on revenues from Aden, an important free port which also benefited from the British forces expenditure. The political troubles brought about a decline in tourism, and the closure of the Suez Canal greatly reduced shipping traffic generally. The major oil refinery in Aden also suffered initially, but has since recovered owing to demand from Egypt following the destruction of the Suez refinery. The economy has otherwise declined since independence; British aid ceased in summer 1968, but aid from several Communist and Arab countries continues on an increasing scale. All important foreign business enterprises except the B.P. refinery were nationalized in November 1969. The hinterland depends on subsistence agriculture and fishing; the rich fishing grounds are so far largely unexploited. Some cotton is grown and this constitutes the country's major export.

Transport and Communications

When the Suez Canal is open Aden is the principal port of call for traffic between Europe and the Persian Gulf, India and the Far East. There are also good international air services. Few roads exist inland, and transport is mainly by camel and donkey, but China is helping in the construction of new roads.

Social Welfare

There is one general hospital, sixteen other hospitals and a number of clinics, medical units and dispensaries with a total of around 1,300 beds. Health services are also provided by the B.P. refinery and mission stations. No comprehensive system of social insurance yet exists.

Education

Educational facilities include 477 primary, 56 intermediate and 11 secondary schools, and total enrolment in 1972–73 was just under 100,000.

Tourism

Aden, a free port before independence, then attracted many visitors from shipping calling at the port, but there are no tourist facilities in the hinterland.

Public Holidays

1974: August 18th* (Leilat al Meiraj, Ascension of the Prophet), October 14th (National Day), October 18th* (Id ul Fitr, end of Ramadan), December 26th* (Id ul Adha).

1975: January 14th (Muslim New Year), January 23rd* (Ashoura).

* Muslim holidays, dependent on the lunar calendar, which may vary slightly from the dates given.

Weights and Measures

The imperial system is generally used in Aden, while the rest of the country still employs a variety of local weights and measures.

Currency and Exchange Rates

1,000 fils = 1 Yemeni dinar (YD).
Exchange rates (April 1974):
£1 sterling = 815.6 fils;
U.S. $1 = 345.4 fils.

STATISTICAL SURVEY

AREA AND POPULATION

AREA (sq. miles)		MID-YEAR POPULATION (official estimates)			
Aden	Hinterland	1970	1971	1972	1973
75	111,000	1,436,000	1,475,000	1,515,000	1,555,000

Capital: Madinat ash-Sha'b (population 29,000 in 1967).
Largest City: Aden (population 150,000 in 1964).

EMPLOYMENT
Aden
1967

TOTAL	PORT HANDLING	BUILDING	OIL REFINING	INDUSTRY	RETAIL AND WHOLESALE TRADE	GOVERN-MENT SERVICE	DOMESTIC SERVANTS	MISCEL-LANEOUS
42,417	5,172	473	2,943	8,425	3,730	12,632	8,000	1,042

In the rest of the country 90 per cent of the population are engaged in agriculture.

AGRICULTURE
PRINCIPAL CROPS

	AREA HARVESTED ('000 hectares)			PRODUCTION ('000 metric tons)		
	1969	1970	1971	1969	1970	1971
Wheat	6	7	8*	10	13	13*
Barley	1*	1	1*	4*	4	4*
Millet and Sorghum . . .	40	36	40*	81	58	75*
Dates	n.a.	n.a.	n.a.	8*	8*	n.a.
Cottonseed	} 20	12	14	9	9	11
Cotton (lint)				5	5	6
Sesame Seed	4*	4*	4*	29*	29*	29*

* FAO estimate.
Source: FAO, *Production Yearbook 1971.*

LIVESTOCK
(1970–71)

Cattle	92,000
Sheep	215,000
Goats	870,000
Camels	40,000

Source: FAO, *Production Yearbook 1971.*

FINANCE

1,000 fils = 1 Yemeni dinar (YD).
Coins: 1, 5, 25 and 50 fils.
Notes: 250 and 500 fils; 1, 5 and 10 dinars.
Exchange rates (April 1974): £1 sterling = 815.6 fils; U.S. $1 = 345.4 fils.
100 Yemeni dinars = £122.61 = $289.52.

BUDGET
(million dinars)

	REVENUE	FOREIGN AID	EXPENDITURE
1967–68	8.94	16.49	23.68
1968–69	8.96	4.91	15.83
1969–70	11.11	0.21	15.44
1970–71	13.22	1.85	17.56

THREE-YEAR PLAN 1971–74
('000 dinars)

Transport and Communications	13,184.3
Agriculture	10,495.0
Industry	9,865.3
Education	3,234.0
Geological Surveys	2,300.0
Health	750.0
Culture	7.0
Unallocated Reserve	864.7
	40,700.3

EXTERNAL TRADE
(million dinars)

	1967	1968	1969	1970	1971
Imports	72.1	84.5	90.9	83.7	64.9
Exports	49.0	45.8	59.8	60.8	43.6

COMMODITIES, 1970
(dinars)

	IMPORTS	EXPORTS
Live Animals	1,427,340	—
Dairy Produce, Eggs	2,533,358	72,057
Cereals	8,058,942	1,214,378
Fruit and Vegetables	1,571,888	148,547
Sugar, etc.	2,220,512	163,418
Coffee, Tea, Cocoa, Spices	2,803,054	801,856
Beverages and Tobacco	1,147,535	37,848
Oilseeds, Oil Nuts, etc.	1,277,443	389,440
Petroleum and Petroleum Products	34,390,272	44,991,450
Chemicals	3,029,368	256,496
Textiles	8,210,356	1,768,661
Machinery	1,572,333	117,019
Electrical Machinery	1,265,284	113,386
Transport Equipment	1,517,064	88,413
Manufactured Goods	5,055,902	696,195

COUNTRIES
(dinars)

IMPORTS	1969	1970	EXPORTS*	1969	1970
Iran	13,545,258	15,252,843	U.K. . . .	13,117,710	14,945,217
Kuwait . . .	12,327,134	11,106,192	Japan . . .	6,288,104	8,724,919
Japan . . .	11,899,701	8,820,657	Australia . .	4,217,861	3,664,670
U.K. . . .	5,078,864	4,579,634	Thailand . .	4,012,614	5,192,631
India . . .	4,281,988	3,470,064	Canary Is. .	2,905,417	3,041,468
Trucial States (now U.A.E.)	3,951,816	4,592,011	Yemen A.R. .	2,958,359	2,852,661
Hong Kong . .	2,496,129	2,239,319			

* Excluding the supply of ships' bunker oil (4,011,144 dinars in 1970).

TRANSPORT
ROAD TRAFFIC
(motor vehicles in use)

	1969	1970	1971
Passenger Cars . . .	9,600	10,200	13,000
Commercial Vehicles . .	2,100	2,400	3,900

Source: United Nations, *Statistical Yearbook 1972.*

INTERNATIONAL SEA-BORNE SHIPPING

	1969	1970	1971
Vessels Entered* ('000 net reg. tons) .	8,220	8,299	6,598
Goods Loaded ('000 metric tons) .	5,863	5,873	3,322
Goods Unloaded ('000 metric tons) .	7,194	6,998	4,286

* Including vessels in ballast.

Source: United Nations, *Statistical Yearbook 1972.*

CIVIL AVIATION
(1968)

AIRCRAFT MOVEMENTS	PASSENGERS			FREIGHT (kilos)	
	Arrivals	Departures	Transit	Inward	Outward
5,860	53,300	53,161	8,167	998,538	852,898

EDUCATION
NUMBER OF SCHOOLS
(1967–68)

Primary Schools			.	387
Intermediate Schools . . .			.	67
Secondary Schools . . .			.	16
Teachers' Colleges for Males .			.	4
Teachers' Colleges for Females .			.	2
Technical Institute . . .			.	1

Source: Ministry of National Guidance and Information, Aden.

THE CONSTITUTION

Before the new constitution was drawn up existing ordinances and regulations remained in force, with Presidential authority replacing the powers of the British and Federal Governments. The National Liberation Front general command, which had 41 members, formed the interim legislative authority. The country is divided into six administrative Governates. The two-year term of office granted to the National Liberation Front expired on November 30th, 1969, and was formally renewed for another year. Following the adoption of the new constitution on November 30th, 1970, a Provisional Supreme People's Council took over legislative powers. The 101 members were selected from the NLF, armed forces, professions, etc., with 15 workers elected by trade unions.

THE GOVERNMENT

HEAD OF STATE

President and Supreme Commander of the Armed Forces: SALEM RUBAI ALI.

PRESIDENTIAL COUNCIL

Chairman: SALEM RUBAI ALI.

Member and NLF Secretary-General: ABD-AL-FATTAH ISMAIL.

Member: ALI NASIR MUHAMMAD.

CABINET

(June 1974)

Prime Minister, Minister of Defence and Minister of Education: ALI NASIR MUHAMMAD.

Minister of Foreign Affairs: MUHAMMAD SALIH MUTI.

Minister of the Interior: SALEH MUSLEH.

Minister of Information: RASHED MUHAMMAD THABET.

Minister of Justice and Waqfs: ABDULLAH MOHAMED GHANEM.

Minister of Health: Dr. ABD-AL-AZIZ AL-DALI.

Minister of Public Works: HAIDAR ABU BAKR AL-ATTAS.

Minister of Communications: ANIS HASAN YAHYA.

Minister of Labour and Social Affairs: ALI ASSAD MUTANYA.

Minister of Finance: FADL MUHSIN ABDULLAH.

Minister of Agriculture and Agrarian Reform: MUHAMMAD SULAIMAN NASIR.

Minister of Economy and Industry: ABDEL-AZIZ ABDEL-WALI.

Minister of Culture and Tourism: ABDULLAH BADIB.

Minister of Planning: ALI SALEM BAID.

Minister of State (Presidential Affairs): ABDULLA KHAMERI.

DIPLOMATIC REPRESENTATION

EMBASSIES ACCREDITED TO THE PEOPLE'S DEMOCRATIC REPUBLIC OF YEMEN

(In Aden unless otherwise stated)

Austria: Addis Ababa, Ethiopia.

Bulgaria: Khormaksar; *Ambassador:* SIRAFIM SERAFIMOV.

China, People's Republic: 145 Andalus Gardens, Khormaksar; *Ambassador:* TSUI TSIEN.

Cuba: 36 Socotra Rd., Khormaksar; *Ambassador:* JACINTO VÁZQUEZ DE LA GARZA.

Czechoslovakia: Cairo, Egypt.

Egypt: Relief Rd., Ma'alla; *Ambassador:* MAHMOUD FAUZI KAMEL.

France: Sayhut St., Khormaksar; *Ambassador:* GEORGES DENIZEAU.

German Democratic Republic: Khormaksar; *Ambassador:* GUNTHER SCHARFENBERG.

Guinea: *Ambassador:* TASSIEN BANGURA (non-resident).

Hungary: Cairo, Egypt.

India: Premjee Mansion, Steamer Point; *Ambassador:* JAGDISH LAL MALHAUTRA.

Iraq: Sana'a, Yemen Arab Republic.

Italy: Tawahi; *Ambassador:* Dr. ALVARO VITO BELTRANI.

Korea, Democratic People's Republic: Khormaksar; *Ambassador:* KIM UNG.

Lebanon: Sana'a, Yemen Arab Republic.

Libya: Khartoum, Sudan.

Pakistan: 34 Kassim Hilal, Khormaksar; *Chargé d'Affaires:* HAMID ALI KHAN.

Poland: Cairo, Egypt.

Romania: Plot 49, Flat No. 1, Khoharien St., Khormaksar; *Ambassador:* CONSTANTIN BABEANU.

Somalia: Britannic Court, Dolphin Square, Ma'alla; *Chargé d'Affaires:* ABDI ALI HUSSEIN.

Spain: Addis Ababa, Ethiopia.

Sweden: Addis Ababa, Ethiopia.

Syria: *Ambassador:* ADNAN MURAD (non-resident).

Switzerland: Addis Ababa, Ethiopia.

U.S.S.R.: Beach Rd., Khormaksar; *Ambassador:* VLADIMIR POLYAKOV.

United Kingdom: 28 Shara Ho Chi Minh, Khormaksar; *Ambassador:* JAMES W. G. RAMAGE.

Yugoslavia: Mogadishu, Somalia.

The People's Democratic Republic of Yemen also has diplomatic relations with Ethiopia and the Provisional Revolutionary Government of the Republic of South Viet-Nam. The Kuwait Government has an office in Aden.

POLITICAL PARTY

National Liberation Front: Aden; f. 1963; socialist and Arab nationalist; Leader ABDUL FATTAH ISMAIL. The Central Committee has 31 members and 14 substitute members—all elected.

POLITICAL BUREAU

Secretary-General: ABD-AL-FATTAH ISMAIL.

Deputy Secretary-General: President SALEM RUBAI ALI

ALI SALIH OBAID.

ALI SALIM AL-BEIDH.

SALIH MUSLIH.

MUHAMMAD SALIH MUTI.

ALI NASIR MUHAMMAD.

JUDICIAL SYSTEM

The administration of justice is entrusted to the Supreme Court and Magistrates' Courts. In the former Protectorate States Muslim law and local common law (Urfi) are also applied.

President of the Supreme Court: ABD-AL-MAJID ABD-AL-RAHMAN.

RELIGION

The majority of the population are Muslim but there are small Christian and Hindu communities.

THE PRESS

DAILIES

al Akhbar: News House, P.O.B. 435, Aden; f. 1953; Arabic; Editor MUHAMMAD ALI LUQMAN, B.A., M.L.C.

Fatat ul Jezirah: Esplanade Rd., Crater, Aden; f. 1940; Arabic; Editor MUHAMMAD ALI LUQMAN; circ. approx. 10,000.

Fourteenth October: Aden.

WEEKLIES

Aden Chronicle: Esplanade Road, Crater, Aden; English; Editor FAROUK LUQMAN.

al Taleeah: P.O.B. 115, Mukalla; Arabic.

al-Thaqafa Al-Jadida: P.O.B. 1187, Aden; f. Aug. 1970; a cultural monthly review issued by the Ministry of Culture and Tourism; Arabic; circ. 3,000.

MONTHLIES

Angham: P.O.B. 555, Aden; f. 1956; Arabic; Editor ALI AMAN.

B.P. Aden Magazine: B.P. Refinery, P.O.B. 3003, Little Aden; f. 1960; English (publ. in Arabic as **Magallat Adan**); Editor The Public Relations Officer, B.P. Refinery.

NEWS AGENCY

Aden News Agency: Aden.

RADIO AND TELEVISION

RADIO

Democratic Yemen Broadcasting Service: P.O.B. 1264, Aden; transmits 76 hours a week in Arabic; Broadcasting Officer H. M. SAFI; there are about 80,000 receivers in the country.

TELEVISION

Democratic Yemen Broadcasting Service: P.O.B. 1264, Aden; programmes for three hours daily were introduced in 1964 on a commercial basis and extended to $4\frac{1}{2}$ hours in both English and Arabic, plus $2\frac{1}{2}$ hours weekly of programmes for schools. There are about 25,000 receivers.

FINANCE

CENTRAL BANK

Bank of Yemen: P.O.B. 4452, Aden; replaced Yemeni Currency Authority 1972; cap. p.u. 500,000 YD; Publ. *Annual Report.*

BANKS

All foreign banking interests were nationalized in November 1969 and thereafter amalgamated to form the National Bank of Yemen, the only commercial bank operating in the country.

National Bank of Yemen: P.O.B. 5, Crater, Aden; f. 1970 by nationalizing and amalgamating the local branches of the seven foreign banks then in Aden.

INSURANCE

All foreign insurance interests were nationalized in November 1969.

Arabian Trading Co. (Aden) Ltd.: P.O.B. 426, Aden; Dir. TAHER A. A. NABEE.

TRADE AND INDUSTRY

National Chamber of Commerce and Industry: P.O.B. 4345, Crater; Pres. ABDULREHMAN AL-SAILANI; Sec. HUSSEIN ALI ABDO.

Aden Merchants' Association: M. A. Luqman Rd., 1-11 Crater; f. 1932; 209 mems.; Pres. PHEROZESHAW P. PATEL; Secs. SORABJEE P. PATEL, M.B.E., ALI A. SAFFI.

National Company for Home Trade: Crater, Aden; f. 1969; importers of cars, electrical goods, agricultural machinery, building materials and general consumer goods; incorporates the main foreign trading businesses which were nationalized in 1970; Acting Gen. Man. SALEH AHMED SALEH.

EMPLOYERS' ASSOCIATIONS

Aden Hotel Proprietors' Association: c/o Crescent Hotel, Steamer Point, Aden.

Civil Contractors' Association: P.O. Box 307, Aden.

TRADE UNIONS

General Confederation of Workers of the People's Democratic Republic of Yemen: P.O.B. 1162, Ma'ala, Aden; f. 1956; affiliated to W.F.T.U. and I.C.F.T.U.; 35,000 mems.; Gen. Sec. FADHLE ALI ABDULLA; publ. *Sout A Omal* weekly, circ. approx. 4,500.

There are fifteen Registered Trade Unions, including the following:

General and Port Workers' Union.

Forces and Associated Organizations Local Employees' Union.

Government and Local Government Employees' Union.

General Union of Petroleum Workers.

Miscellaneous Industries Employees' Union.

Aden Port Trust Employees' Union.

Civil Aviation Employees' Union.

Banks Local Staff Union.

CO-OPERATIVES AND MARKETING

There are 65 co-operative societies, mostly for agricultural products; the movement was founded in 1965 and is now the responsibility of the Ministry for Agriculture and Agrarian Reform.

OIL

Yemeni National Petroleum Co.: P.O.B. 5050, Aden; sole oil concessionaire importer and distributor of oil products in Yemen P.D.R.; in receipt of technical and financial assistance from Algeria; Chair. and Gen. Man. ABDUL KARIM THABET.

TRANSPORT

RAILWAYS

There are no railways.

ROADS

Aden Bus Co. Ltd.: Adbusco Bldg., Ma'alla, P.O.B. 905, Aden; f. 1960; operates services within the Crater, Ma'alla, Steamer Point, Sheikh Othman and Al-Mansoura areas; Chair. and Gen. Man. SAEED FARA SALIM.

A new state transport monopoly, the Yemen Land Transport Company, is being formed to incorporate the Aden Bus Company and all other local public transport.

Aden has 140 miles of roads, of which 127 have bituminous surfacings. There are approximately 2,680 miles of rough tracks passable for motor traffic in the hinterland, but most of the transport is by camel and donkey.

SHIPPING

National Shipping Company: P.O.B. 1228, Steamer Point, Aden; founded by the amalgamation and nationalization of five foreign shipping companies in November 1969; freight and passenger services; branches or agents in Mukalla, Berbera (Somalia) and Mocha and Hodieda (Yemen Arab Republic).

Port of Aden Authority: Aden; f. 1889; state administrative body; Aden remained a free port (except for tariffs on petrol, alcohol and tobacco) until 1970, though trade has greatly declined since 1967. Aden Main Harbour has twenty first-class berths. Three of them are Dolphin berths accommodating vessels drawing up to 40 ft., and the remaining seventeen are buoy berths for vessels drawing up to 42 ft. There are 4 second-class berths for vessels drawing up to 28 feet, and six third-class berths for vessels whose draught does not exceed 18 feet. In addition to the above, there is ample room to accommodate vessels of light draught at anchor in the 18-foot dredged area. There is also 800 feet of cargo wharf accommodating vessels of 300 feet length and 18 feet draught. Aden Oil Harbour accommodates four tankers of 55,000 tons and up to 40 feet draught.

A programme of dredging to maintain the advertised depths, and of deepening some channels, began in April 1970 and was completed in 1971.

CIVIL AVIATION

Democratic Yemen Airlines Company: Aden; f. 1971 as wholly owned Corporation by the Govt.

Other companies operating services include the following: Aeroflot, Air Djibouti, Air India, EAAC, EgyptAir, Ethiopian Airways, Kuwait Airways, MEA, Pakistan International Airlines, Somali Airlines, Sudan Airways, Yemen Airlines.

Aden Civil Airport is at Khormaksar, 7 miles from the Port. It was established in 1952, and is operated by the Civil Aviation Department.

ZAIRE

INTRODUCTORY SURVEY

Location, Climate, Language, Religion, Flag, Capital

The Republic of Zaire, until October 1971 known as the Democratic Republic of the Congo, is a vast territory in the heart of Central Africa, bounded by the People's Republic of the Congo and the River Zaire to the northwest, by the Central African Republic and the Sudan to the north, by Uganda, Rwanda, Burundi and Tanzania to the east and by Zambia and Angola to the south. There is a short coastline at the outlet of the Zaire. The climate is tropical with an average temperature of 80°F (27°C) and an annual rainfall of 60 to 80 inches. French is the official language. Over 400 Sudanese and Bantu dialects are spoken, Swahili, Kiluba, Kikongo and Lingala being the most widespread. African religions are based on traditional beliefs. Christian missions have long been active. There are small Muslim and Jewish minorities. The flag is green and contains a central yellow disc in which a black hand holds a torch with a red flame. The capital is Kinshasa.

Recent History

The Congo regained independence from Belgium on June 30th, 1960. Five days later the armed forces mutinied. Belgian actions during the disorder that followed and her support for the secession of Katanga were condemned in the UN and UN troops were sent to the Congo to maintain order. Disagreement between Patrice Lumumba, the Congo's Prime Minister, and Dag Hammarskjöld, the UN Secretary-General, on the role of UN troops in ending Katangan secession led to preparations by Lumumba, with Soviet assistance, to send Congolese forces into Katanga. However, in September, the Head of State, Joseph Kasavubu, replaced Lumumba with Joseph Ileo, and the government later allied itself with Col. Joseph Mobutu's alternative régime of university-educated people, which he claimed would replace politicians. Lumumba was imprisoned by the government but his supporters set up a rival government in Stanleyville (Kisangani) which controlled Orientale, Kivu and northern parts of Kasai and Katanga.

In January 1961 Lumumba and two colleagues were murdered in Katanga. The strong reactions to this in Africa and the UN led to negotiations between Kasavubu and the followers of Lumumba which eventually produced a new government with Cyrille Adoula as Prime Minister. In September 1962, fighting broke out in Katanga between UN troops and the local gendarmerie, which included many Belgians and white mercenaries. Hammarskjöld was killed in a plane crash when flying to negotiate with Moïse Tshombe of Katanga. Katangan secession ended only in January 1963 after more fighting and with Tshombe going into exile.

During 1962 the Lumumbists left the government, which later assumed full powers, closing parliament, and arresting opposition elements. Early in 1964 revolt flared up in Kwilu under Pierre Mulele and fighting between his followers and the Congolese army spread to Orientale and Kivu. In July Kasavubu appointed Tshombe as an interim Prime Minister pending elections, and with American and mercenary support Tshombe was able to push back the rebels. Early in 1965 the revolt crumbled. Elections were held in June but irregularities prevented the National Assembly meeting. The struggle between Tshombe and Kasavubu for the new post as President brought about the seizure of power by the army under Mobutu in November. In July 1966 and 1967 there were two further revolts, by pro-Tshombe mercenaries and Katangan soldiers. In September 1968 Mulele returned to Kinshasa from Brazzaville after being promised a pardon but was almost immediately tried secretly and executed. Congo (Brazzaville) broke off diplomatic relations with Kinshasa and tension between the two countries, periodically inflamed by mutual accusations of interference in each other's affairs, continued. In October 1971 the Democratic Republic of the Congo became the Republic of Zaire.

In 1966 the use of European names alongside Congolese names for some towns was abandoned. Personal names not of African origin have to be changed to Zairian names. In 1971 the Congo River was unilaterally renamed the Zaire, and soon after provinces and other localities were also renamed, the most notable change being that from Lake Albert to Lake Mobutu Sese Seko. In September 1972 the Government of Zaire and the Executive Committee of the *Mouvement populaire de la Révolution* (MPR), Zaire's sole political party, merged into the National Executive Council. The latest Cabinet reshuffle took place in March 1974, when the number of State Commissioners was reduced from 24 to 21. At the same time the strength of the political bureau of the MPR was increased by four.

Government

A new constitution, the second since independence, was adopted by an overwhelming majority in a referendum held in June 1967. It provides for a Presidential régime, with a single legislative chamber elected by universal suffrage, and wide powers for the head of state who also heads the Government. There are eight Regions.

Defence

The armed forces, built up under Belgian rule as the *Force Publique*, are known as the *Armée Nationale Zaïroise* and consist of troops, parachutists and air and sea forces. Military service is compulsory. Total armed forces: 50,000. Defence expenditure in 1971 amounted to 38 million zaires.

Economic Affairs

The economy has only recently begun to show signs of recovery from the troubled beginnings of the independent state, and substantial aid has been given by the United Nations, Belgium, the U.S.A. and other countries. The country's chief riches lie in the Shaba copper mines. Manganese, zinc, uranium and other minerals are also mined and there are rich diamond deposits in Kasai. By 1968 the Government had taken over all Union Minière operations. Minerals form more than two-thirds of exports by value. Agricultural products, which have declined since 1960, include palm-oil, rubber, coffee, timber, manioc and bananas. Industry is still undeveloped but bricks, cement, clothing and cigarettes are manufactured. There are large reserves of hydro-electric power. In November 1972 the first phase of the Inga hydro-electric power complex was inaugurated, and the two-phase system, with a total design capacity of over 1,500 megawatts, is expected to be fully operational by early 1976, when part of the power will serve industrial needs in Lower Zaire and the rest the copper industry in the Shaba district. Further power schemes are to be developed with foreign assistance, at Kani and N'zilo in Shaba. In December 1966 the Union Minière was nationalized by governmental decree, and the Société Générale Congolaise des Minerais (GECOMIN) was set up in 1967 and nationalized in 1968. The company is now known as the Société Générale des Carrières et Mines du Zaïre (GECAMINES). In March 1968 oil deposits were found in the Lower Zaire province. Refineries are operated at Matadi and Moanda. In view of the downward movement in world copper prices since 1970, and the resulting decline in the growth rate of the G.D.P., Zaire is now turning to the development of other sectors of the economy, notably agriculture, but hopes to be refining all its own copper by 1980 instead of receiving Belgian assistance. Extensive plans for "zairisation" of the economy were announced by President Mobutu in November 1973. All but the largest companies have been made over to Zairians, and government offices have been set up to oversee the process. The agricultural, mining and shipping sectors have seen the most radical changes of administration. By 1975 all companies established over five years will be required to have Zairians as president and managing director.

In March 1968 the Congo formed an economic union with Chad and the Central African Republic, but the latter withdrew before the union became effective. Closer co-operation with Rwanda and Burundi began in 1969 and eventual economic union is planned.

Transport and Communications

Transport flows for the most part along the River Zaire and its tributaries, Zairian rivers being navigable above the Inga rapids for more than 8,500 miles. The chief port is Matadi, which is the highest point on the Zaire accessible from the sea. Parts of the railways were badly damaged during the period of unrest following independence, but the main rail link between Kinshasa and Shaba was reopened in 1963 and most mineral exports from Shaba use this route to Matadi. Most roads are in poor condition owing to inadequate maintenance. In 1971 they totalled about 145,000 kilometres, of which some 20,000 were main roads.

Social Welfare

There is an Institut National de la Sécurité Sociale guaranteeing insurance coverage for sickness, pensions and family allowances under an obligatory scheme of national insurance. In 1969 there were 496 doctors working in Zaire.

Education

There are primary, secondary, technical and agricultural schools. In 1970 there were more than 3.3 million children in subsidized schools. There are three universities and eleven colleges, with over 4,500 students. Compulsory civilian service for a two-year period was introduced in 1966 in order to enlist young intellectuals as teachers.

Public Holidays

1974: August 15th (Assumption), November 1st (All Saints' Day), November 17th (Army Day), November 24th (Anniversary of the new régime), December 25th (Christmas).

1975: January 1st (New Year's Day), January 4th (Commemoration of the Martyrs), May 8th (Ascension Day), June 30th (Independence Day).

Weights and Measures

The metric system is in force.

Currency and Exchange Rates

10,000 sengi = 100 makuta = 1 zaire.
Exchange rates (April 1974):

£1 sterling = 1.18 zaires;
U.S. $1 = 50.0 makuta.

STATISTICAL SURVEY
AREA AND POPULATION

Region	Area (sq. km.)	Population (July 31st, 1970)	Density (per sq. km.)
Bandundu	295,658	2,600,556	8.6
Bas-Zaire	53,920	1,504,361	27.6
Equateur	403,293	2,431,812	6.0
Haute-Zaire	503,239	3,556,419	6.6
Kasai Occidental . . .	156,967	2,433,861	15.5
Kasai Oriental	168,216	1,872,231	11.1
Kivu	256,662	3,361,883	13.1
Shaba (formerly Katanga) .	496,965	2,753,714	5.5
Kinshasa (city)* . . .	9,965	1,323,039	132.7
Total	2,344,885	21,637,876	9.2

* Including the commune of Maluku, with an area of 7,948.8 sq. km. and a population of 14,678.

Source: Institut National de la Statistique, *Bulletin Trimestriel des Statistiques Générales.*

Total Population (July 1st, 1971): 22,476,978.

PRINCIPAL TOWNS
(with 1970 population)

Kinshasa (capital)	1,323,039	Likasi	146,394
Kananga (formerly Luluabourg)	428,960	Bukavu	134,861
Lubumbashi	318,000	Kikwit	111,960
Mbuji-Mayi	256,154	Matadi	110,436
Kisangani	229,596	Mbandaka	107,910

1972: Kinshasa 1,623,760 (provisional estimate).

AGRICULTURE
LAND USE, 1962
('ooo hectares)

Arable and Under Permanent Crops	7,200
Permanent Meadows and Pastures	65,500
Forest Land	129,141*
Other Areas	32,700
Total	234,541

Source: FAO: *Forest Inventory 1963,* * *Production Yearbook 1971.*

PRINCIPAL CROPS
('ooo metric tons)

	1968	1969	1970	1971
Wheat	3	3	3	3*
Maize	250	350	375	306
Millet and Sorghum	18	30	38*	38*
Rice (Paddy)	130	130	188	195
Sugar Cane[1]	395	421	420	500*
Potatoes	50*	15	30*	30*
Sweet Potatoes and Yams	300*	350	350*	360*
Cassava (Manioc)	10,772	10,000	10,000*	10,500*
Onions (dry)	17	15	15*	n.a.
Tomatoes	24*	25	25*	n.a.
Cabbages	5*	5	5*	n.a.
Dry Peas and Other Pulses	80*	80*	80*	80*
Oranges and Tangerines	75*	90	90*	90*
Grapefruit	8*	8	8*	8*
Other Citrus Fruit	6*	5	5*	5*
Bananas	60*	80	80*	n.a.
Pineapples	27*	28	28*	n.a.
Palm Kernels	125	128	130	120
Groundnuts (in shell)	200*	200	180	180
Cottonseed	24	32	32	34*
Cotton (Lint)	12	16	17	17*
Sesame Seed	4*	3.5	5*	5*
Coffee	60	66	81	78
Cocoa Beans[2]	4.9	4.5	5.0	5.0
Tea	4.5	4.5	4.7*	4.7*
Tobacco	2.5*	2.0	2.0*	2.0*
Kenaf	6	6	6*	6*
Natural Rubber (Exports only)	40.9	36.5	32.3	40.0

1972 ('ooo metric tons): Palm Kernels 105; Groundnuts 180; Coffee 81.

Palm oil ('ooo metric tons): 196 in 1968; 179 in 1969; 180 in 1970; 197 in 1971.

* FAO estimate.
[1] Crop year ending in year stated.
[2] Twelve months ending in September of year stated. 1971–72: 5,000 metric tons.

Source: mainly FAO, *Production Yearbook 1971.*

LIVESTOCK
('000)

	1968–69	1969–70*	1970–71*
Cattle . . .	887	900	930
Sheep . . .	564	570	575
Goats . . .	1,545	1,600	1,650
Pigs . . .	433	442	450
Poultry . . .	5,400*	5,500	5,600

* FAO estimate.

Source: FAO, *Production Yearbook 1971.*

LIVESTOCK PRODUCTS
(FAO estimates, metric tons)

	1968	1969	1970
Cows' Milk . .	18,000	18,000	19,000
Beef and Veal .	16,000	18,000	18,000
Mutton and Lamb* .	6,000	6,000	6,000
Poultry Meat .	4,000	4,000	4,000
Edible Offal .	4,500	4,000	4,000
Other Meat .	120,000	120,000	120,000
Hen Eggs . .	4,100	4,200	4,200

1971 (FAO estimates): Cows' Milk 19,000 metric tons; Hen Eggs 4,400 metric tons.

* Including goats' meat.

Source: FAO, *Production Yearbook 1971.*

FORESTRY
('000 cubic metres)

ROUNDWOOD REMOVALS

	FUEL WOOD	OTHER WOOD	TOTAL
1968 . .	10,000	1,600	11,600
1969 . .	10,000	1,600	11,600
1970 . .	12,250	1,740	13,990
1971 . .	12,500	1,810	14,310

SAWNWOOD PRODUCTION

1968 . . .	145
1969 . . .	150
1970 . . .	160
1971 . . .	170

Source: FAO, *Yearbook of Forest Products.*

FISHING
(metric tons)

	1968	1969	1970	1971
Inland Waters . . .	97,800	100,000	110,000	133,800
Atlantic Ocean . .	12,400	12,000*	12,000*	12,000*
TOTAL . .	110,200	112,000*	122,000*	145,800*

* FAO estimate.

Source: FAO, *Yearbook of Fishery Statistics 1971.*

MINING

	UNIT	1969	1970	1971	1972†
Copper ore . . .	metric tons	364,132	387,116	407,064	424,000
Tin Concentrates . .	,, ,,	6,647	6,458	6,055	6,000
Manganese ore* . .	,, ,,	311,429	346,950	329,066	378,000
Coal . . .	,, ,,	84,235	101,739	119,295	119,600
Zinc Concentrates . .	,, ,,	95,503	104,338	109,201	109,000
Cobalt Ore . . .	,, ,,	10,596	13,958	14,518	13,043
Cadmium . . .	,, ,,	300	316	264	n.a.
Wolfram . . .	,, ,,	227	365	553	n.a.
Industrial Diamonds .	'000 carats	11,616	12,408	12,502	12,500
Gem Diamonds . .	,, ,,	2,500	1,655	673	1,000
Silver	kilogrammes	49,349	46,052	51,105	57,000
Gold	,,	5,516	5,630	5,314	5,000

* Figures relate to gross weight. The metal content (in metric tons) was: 165,000 in 1969; 156,000 in 1970; 148,100 in 1971.

† Estimate.

INDUSTRY

BASE METALS

(metric tons)

	1968	1969	1970	1971
Copper (unwrought): Smelter . .	327,094	340,093	385,500	387,058
Refined . .	238,412	236,053	274,615	279,097
Zinc (unwrought)	62,573	63,732	63,749	62,673
Cobalt Metal	10,160	10,600	12,100	8,092
Tin (unwrought)	1,922	1,882	1,396	1,393

Lead (unwrought): 2,458 metric tons in 1971.

OTHER PRODUCTS

	UNIT	1968	1969	1970	1971
Cigarettes	millions	2,972	3,478	4,422	4,031
Beer	'ooo hectolitres	2,233	2,706	3,287	3,740
Aerated drinks . . .	,, ,,	302	322	391	672
Sugar	metric tons	38,408	36,015	42,080	44,359
Margarine . . .	,, ,,	1,700	2,051	3,006	3,774
Sulphuric Acid . .	,, ,,	130,000	126,000	135,000	141,000
Explosives . . .	,, ,,	3,159	5,273	6,390	6,599
Cement . . .	,, ,,	294,148	323,000	426,000	461,000
Motor Spirit . .	,, ,,	81,334	104,114	120,276	108,839
Kerosene . . .	,, ,,	58,314	68,466	71,499	69,171
Distillate Fuel Oils . .	,, ,,	138,142	163,988	180,989	166,000
Residual Fuel Oils . .	,, ,,	264,300	316,693	293,642	296,000
Bottles . . .	'ooo units	18,500	12,488	23,311	25,038
Cotton Fabrics (plain) .	'ooo sq. metres	55,570	64,430	67,760	75,521
Printed Textiles . .	,, ,, ,,	36,490	36,620	43,150	49,823
Blankets . . .	'ooo units	1,611	1,300	1,748	2,076
Electricity . . .	million kWh	2,664	2,912	3,230	3,540

FINANCE

10,000 sengi = 100 makuta (singular, likuta) = 1 zaire.

Coins: 10 sengi; 1 likuta, 5 makuta.

Notes: 10, 20 and 50 makuta; 1, 5 and 10 zaires.

Exchange rates (April 1974): £1 sterling = 1.18 zaires; U.S. $1 = 50.0 makuta.

100 zaires = £84.70 = $200.00.

BUDGET

(million zaires)

REVENUE	1969	1970	1971	EXPENDITURE	1969	1970	1971
Direct Taxes . .	73.7	75.9	75.4	Defence . . .	25.6	38.3	38.1
Import Duties . .	41.3	44.0	52.0	Education . . .	46.5	52.1	62.8
Export Duties .	91.8	108.5	67.0	Transfers Overseas .	17.7	21.3	26.1
Other Customs Receipts	19.4	22.4	37.8	Other Ordinary Expenditure . .	140.5	174.2	178.5
Other Indirect Taxes .	41.7	43.6	47.9				
Other Ordinary Receipts*	1.5	21.0	8.7				
Transfers from Overseas	24.5	27.7	30.5	Total Current Budget	230.3	285.9	305.5
				Capital Budget .	68.9	86.1	91.7
TOTAL . .	294.0	343.0	319.3	TOTAL . .	299.3	372.0	397.2

* Including an adjustment.

Source: Banque du Zaïre, *Rapport Annuel 1971–1972.*

RESERVES AND CURRENCY
('000 zaires at June 30th)

	1969	1970	1971	1972	1973
Gold Reserves	21,433	27,644	25,050	27,485	30,850
Currency in Circulation . .	56,320	65,984	83,833	91,148	104,670

NATIONAL ACCOUNTS

GROSS DOMESTIC PRODUCT
(million zaires at current prices)

Economic Activity	1970	1971	1972*
Monetary Sector:			
Agriculture	107.6	107.1	107.1
Mining . . . . }	245.1	203.9	215.1
Metallurgy . . . . }			
Manufacturing	52.4	57.2	61.8
Energy	9.4	9.8	10.2
Building and public works . .	36.4	46.1	52.6
Transport and telecommunications .	52.2	57.6	58.8
Commerce	132.8	143.1	151.0
Banks, insurance and other services .	104.9	111.2	119.0
Sub-total (at factor cost) . .	740.8	736.0	775.6
Indirect taxation . . .	81.3	114.5	113.4
Sub-total (market prices) . }	822.1	850.5	889.0
Administration . . . . }			
State education . . . }	109.0	134.0	140.7
Defence . . . . }			
Total Monetary Product . . .	931.1	984.5	1,029.7
Non-Monetary Sector:			
Agriculture	80.1	84.9	n.a.
Construction	15.0	19.2	n.a.
Gross Domestic Product . . .	1,026.2	1,088.6	n.a.

* Estimated figures.
Source: Banque du Zaïre, Annual Report.

NATIONAL INCOME
(million zaires)

	At 1968 Prices			At Current Prices		
	1969	1970	1971	1969	1970	1971
Gross Domestic Product	794.6	871.6	918.8	902.4	1,026.2	1,088.6
Less: Net transfers abroad of interest and investment income	10.8	17.2	18.3	10.8	17.2	18.3
Net transfers abroad of private income	31.7	35.5	34.5	31.7	35.5	34.5
Gross National Product	752.1	818.9	866.0	859.9	973.5	1,035.8
Less: Indirect taxation, net of subsidies .	70.8	72.9	82.2	73.1	78.9	111.5
Amortizations.	92.9	99.9	109.5	96.6	113.9	139.1
National Income	588.4	646.1	674.3	690.2	780.7	785.2
Less: Direct taxation and export tax . .	158.6	172.7	148.6	181.3	202.1	158.2
National Disposable Income . . .	429.8	473.4	525.7	508.9	578.6	627.0

Source: Banque du Zaïre, Annual Report.

EXTERNAL TRADE

RECORDED TRANSACTIONS

(million zaires)

	1965	1966	1967	1968	1969	1970	1971*
Imports: Merchandise . .	160.7	171.6	128.1	154.8	225.9	266.5	313.4
Exports: Merchandise . .	168.0	232.4	217.9	252.6	339.6	390.6 }	342.4
Gold . . .	0.7	1.6	2.6	2.1	2.4	3.2	

* Provisional estimate.

TRANSACTIONS REPORTED BY TRADING PARTNERS

(merchandise only—million zaires)

	1965	1966	1967	1968	1969	1970
Imports . . .	137.0	145.8	128.7	160.4	202.5	250.5
Exports . . .	192.8	261.0	237.8	289.0	363.5	406.5

Source: International Monetary Fund, *International Financial Statistics.*

COMMODITIES

('000 zaires)

IMPORTS	1969*	1970	EXPORTS*	1969	1970
Fish and Fish Products .	6,944	8,257	Coffee	12,945	19,318
Dairy Produce . . .	2,741	4,498	Raw Cotton . . .	1,662	2,048
Cereals and derivatives .	9,030	13,825	Rubber	8,135	6,379
Coal, Coke, etc. . .	5,000	2,910	Palm Oil . . .	9,635	14,091
Petroleum Products . .	10,650	15,470	Palm Kernel Oil . .	4,992	6,304
Medicinal and Pharmaceutical			Copper	214,716	246,751
Products . . .	4,690	8,580	Diamonds . . .	17,082	22,973
Rubber Articles . .	4,603	6,370	Gold	2,411	3,194
Paper and Paperboard .	3,737	5,707	Cobalt	12,270	16,895
Printed Cotton Cloth .	8,318	8,813	Zinc (unrefined) . .	6,952	8,366
Clothing	2,983	4,555	Tin (unrefined) . .	3,097	1,977
Iron and Steel Bars and Sections .	2,752	6,307	Cassiterite . . .	8,247	7,555
Iron and Steel Plates and Sheets .	3,632	6,606			
Non-Electrical Machinery . .	24,372	34,335			
Electrical Machinery . .	13,011	16,350			
Railway Equipment . .	7,851	3,802			
Road Vehicles . . .	27,653	32,917			
Aviation Equipment . .	8,340	2,123			
TOTAL, including others .	205,130	266,491	TOTAL, including others .	324,657	370,896

* Provisional figures.

COUNTRIES
('000 zaires)

IMPORTS	1969*	1970	EXPORTS*	1969	1970 †
Belgium/Luxembourg .	48,452	65,172	Belgium/Luxembourg .	140,260	158,602
France . . .	15,888	21,615	France . . .	22,571	25,695
Germany, Federal Republic .	20,456	27,613	Germany, Federal Republic .	7,099	9,640
Italy	9,776	14,449	Italy . . .	39,500	42,212
Japan . . .	14,280	17,958	Netherlands . . .	7,731	7,595
Netherlands . .	13,160	11,112	United Kingdom . .	28,410	26,815
United Kingdom .	12,784	19,362	U.S.A. . . .	6,167	6,299
U.S.A. . . .	26,124	28,493	Others . . .	8,109	9,161
			Unspecified . .	64,810	84,858
TOTAL (incl. others) .	205,130	266,491	TOTAL . .	324,657	370,877

* Provisional figures.

† Excluding re-exports, valued at 18,800 zaires.

TOURISM

	1970	1971
Tourist arrivals . .	38,348	63,307

TRANSPORT

RAILWAYS
(1971)

	C.F.M.K. Network	B.C.K. Network
Freight carried ('000 tons) .	1,825	4,957
Freight ('000 ton-km.) .	511,182	1,971
Passengers ('000) .	1,372	2,636
Passenger-km. ('000) .	158,137	592,763

ROADS

	1967	1968*	1969*
Passenger Cars .	43,500	46,100	55,800
Commercial Vehicles .	23,200	26,200	43,100

* Provisional estimates.
Source: United Nations, *Statistical Yearbook.*

SHIPPING
(1971)

	MATADI	BOMA
Number of ships entering .	512	270
Number of ships departing .	513	274
Freight entering ('000 tons) .	541	46
Freight departing ('000 tons) .	932	69

	KINSHASA
Freight entering from Zaire Basin (tons) .	289,596
Freight leaving for Zaire Basin (tons) .	235,587
Freight entering from Kasai Basin (tons) .	389,832
Freight leaving for Kasai Basin (tons) .	210,163

CIVIL AVIATION
SCHEDULED SERVICES

	1969	1970	1971
Kilometres Flown ('000) . . .	10,051	12,689	12,222
Passenger-km. ('000) . .	367,214	464,826	528,000
Cargo ton-km. ('000) . .	11,234	14,848	17,314
Mail ton-km. ('000) . . .	1,254	1,282	1,133

Source: United Nations, *Statistical Yearbook 1972.*

EDUCATION
(1970–71)

	Schools	Teachers	Pupils
Primary .	4,756	69,999	3,088,011
Secondary .	1,201	11,755	253,234
Vocational .	n.a.	n.a.	n.a.
Higher .	33	1,386	12,363

Sources (unless otherwise stated): Institut National de la Statistique, Office Nationale de la Recherche et du Développement, B.P. 20 Kinshasa; Département de l'Economie Nationale, Kinshasa, Institut de la Statistique.

THE CONSTITUTION

A new constitution was adopted by national referendum in June 1967.

The Republic of Zaire is defined as a united, democratic and social state, composed of eight administrative regions and the city of Kinshasa.

HEAD OF STATE

The President of the Republic is elected for a seven-year term by direct universal suffrage. Candidates must be natives of Zaire and aged over 40. Under the Constitution, the Head of State is also the Head of the National Executive Council and acts as the chief executive, controls foreign policy and is Captain-General of the armed forces and the gendarmerie.

EXECUTIVE POWER

The programme and decisions of the National Executive Council are determined by the President and carried out by the State Commissioners who are heads of their departments. The National Executive Council is dissolved at the end of each Presidential term, though it continues to function until a new National Executive Council is formed. The members of the National Executive Council are appointed or dismissed by the President.

LEGISLATURE

Parliament consists of a single Chamber, the National Legislative Council, elected for five years by direct, universal suffrage with a secret ballot. Elections were held in 1970. The National Legislative Council will consist of the President, two Vice-Presidents and four Secretaries. The members of the National Executive Council have the right, and if required the obligation to assist at the meetings of the National Legislative Council. It will meet twice yearly, from April to July, and from October to January.

POLITICAL PARTIES

In May 1970 it was resolved that the MPR should be Zaire's only party.

REGIONAL GOVERNMENTS

The regional commissioners of the eight regions are appointed and dismissed by the President.

CONSTITUTIONAL COURT

The Constitutional Court consists of nine counsellors, three named by the President, three proposed by the National Legislative Council, and three proposed by the Supreme Court of Magistrates. The Counsellors have the right to judge all matters of dispute concerning the present Constitution.

JUDICIARY

The judiciary is wholly independent of the legislature and the executive. It is responsible to the Courts and Tribunals which apply statute and common law. The chief organs of justice are the Supreme Court of Justice, the Courts of Appeal, Military Courts and Tribunals.

FUNDAMENTAL RIGHTS AND DUTIES

All citizens are equal before the law, irrespective of social class, religion, tribe, sex, birth or residence. Every person shall enjoy the rights of personal respect, protection of life and inviolability of person. No person may be arrested or detained except within the prescribed form of the law. All citizens are entitled to freedom of expression, conscience and religion. Military service is obligatory, but can be replaced by alternative forms of public service under the conditions fixed by law. All natives of Zaire have the right and duty to work, and can defend their rights by trade union action. The right to strike is recognized and is exercised according to laws.

THE GOVERNMENT

HEAD OF STATE

President: General MOBUTU SESE SEKO.

NATIONAL EXECUTIVE COUNCIL

(*March* 1974)

Head of National Executive Council, State Commissioner of Defence, Ex-Servicemen and Planning: Gen. MOBUTU SESE SEKO.

State Commissioner of Political Affairs: ENGULU BAANGAMPONGO LOKANGA.

State Commissioner of Foreign Affairs: UMBA DI LUTETE.

State Commissioner of Information: SAKOMBI INONGO.

State Commissioner of Justice: MOZAGBA NGBUKA.

State Commissioner of Youth and Sport: SAMPASSA KAWETE MILOMBE.

State Commissioner of Finance: BARUTI WA NDWALI.

State Commissioner of National Economy: NAMWISI MA NKOI.

State Commissioner of Mines: Z'BO KALOGI.

State Commissioner of Agriculture: KAYINGA ONSI NDAL.

State Commissioner of Commerce: NDONGOLA TADI LEWA.

State Commissioner of National Education: MABOLIA INENGO TRA BWATO.

State Commissioner of Public Works and Territorial Administration: TAKIZALA LUYANU MUSIMBIMBI.

State Commissioner of Transport and Communications: EKETEBI MOYINDIBA MONDJOLOMBA.

State Commissioner of Lands: INONGA LOKONGO L'OME.

State Commissioner of Energy: MINTUKAKUBI TSHIONDO KABANZA WA MINTENGE.

State Commissioner of Public Health: KALONDA LUMEMA.

State Commissioner of Social Affairs: MATAA MKUMU WA BOWANDA ANGAN BIONO.

State Commissioner of Employment and Social Security: BINTU' A TSHIABOLA.

State Commissioner of Posts and Telecommunications: KABUITA NYAMABU.

State Commissioner of Culture and the Arts: BOKONGA EKANGA BOTOMBELE.

POLITICAL BUREAU OF THE M.P.R.

Gen. MOBUTU SESE SEKO
BO-BOLIKO LOKONGA
NGUZA KARL-I-BOND
ENGULU BAANGAMPONGO BOKOKELA LOKANGA
UMBA DI LUTETE
SAKOMBI INONGO

MOZAGBA NGBUKA
SAMPASSA KAWETA MILOMBE
KITHIMA BIN RAMAZANI
NZONDOMYO A'DOPKE LINGO
ILEO SOMBO AMBA
LUTAY-KANZA
MPANUMPANU-BI-BANDA

TSHIBANGU KANZA MUYEMBE
MPINGA
KAMBIMBI
NDATABAYE
KIWEWA FUMU NKOI
KIKONGI DI MWINSA LEKULA
BULUNDWE KITONGO PENGEMALI

DIPLOMATIC REPRESENTATION

EMBASSIES ACCREDITED TO ZAIRE

(In Kinshasa unless otherwise stated)

Belgium: Bldg. Le Cinquantenaire, Place du 27 octobre, B.P. 899; *Ambassador:* J. VANDEN BLOOCK.

Bulgaria: B.P. 967; *Ambassador:* (vacant).

Burundi: B.P. 1483; *Ambassador:* JEAN-MARIE DERY.

Cameroon: B.P. 3636; *Ambassador:* JEAN-CLAUDE NGOH.

Canada: B.P. 8341; *Ambassador:* (vacant).

Central African Republic: B.P. 7769; *Ambassador:* (vacant).

Chad: B.P. 9343; *Ambassador:* ALPHONSE MBAINOUNGAM.

Congo (Brazzaville): B.P. 9328; *Ambassador:* APOLLINAIRE BAZINGA.

Czechoslovakia: B.P. 8242; *Ambassador:* (vacant).

Dahomey: 11 ave. Pumbul, B.P. 3265; *Ambassador:* (vacant).

Denmark: B.P. 1446; *Ambassador:* (vacant).

Egypt: B.P. 8838; *Ambassador:* GAMAL EL DINE.

Equatorial Guinea: *Ambassador:* CLEMENTE ATEBA.

Ethiopia: B.P. 8435; *Ambassador:* BEKERE ABERRA.

France: 3 ave. des trois "Z", B.P. 3093; *Ambassador:* CLAUDE CHAYET.

Gabon: B.P. 9592; *Ambassador:* (vacant).

Germany, Federal Republic: 201 ave. Astrid, B.P. 4800; *Ambassador:* GÜNTHER FRANZ WERNER.

Ghana: B.P. 8446; *Ambassador:* Gen. H. D. TWUM-BARINA.

Greece: B.P. 478; *Ambassador:* (vacant).

Guinea: *Ambassador:* AHMADOU TITIANE SANO.

India: B.P. 1026; *Ambassador:* (vacant).

Italy: B.P. 1000; *Ambassador:* DIEGO SIMONETTI.

Ivory Coast: 68 ave. de la Justice, B.P. 8935; *Ambassador:* GASTON FIANKAN.

Japan: B.P. 1810; *Ambassador:* HIROSHI UCHIDA.

Kenya: B.P. 9667; *Ambassador:* (vacant).

Korea, Republic: B.P. 628; *Ambassador:* (vacant).

Liberia: B.P. 8940; *Ambassador:* JENKINS COOPER.

Morocco: B.P. 912; *Ambassador:* ABDELAZIZ BINNANI.

Netherlands: 11 ave. Zongo Ntolo, B.P. 3106; *Ambassador:* M. VERDONCK HUFFNAGEL.

Nigeria: B.P. 1700; *Ambassador:* EDWARD ENAHORD.

Poland: B.P. 7769; *Ambassador:* (vacant).

Romania: B.P. 2242; *Ambassador:* (vacant).

Rwanda: B.P. 967; *Ambassador:* (vacant).

Senegal: B.P. 7686; *Ambassador:* PASCAL ANTOINE SANE (also accred. to Gabon).

Somalia: Dar es Salaam, Tanzania.

Spain: B.P. 8036; *Ambassador:* LUIS DEPETROSO.

Sudan: B.P. 7347; *Ambassador:* SALAH EL DIN BABIR ZARROUG.

Sweden: B.P. 3038; *Ambassador:* HENRIK RAMEL.

Switzerland: B.P. 8724; *Ambassador:* J. P. EDMOND WEBER.

Tanzania: B.P. 1612; *Ambassador:* M. TIBAN.

Togo: *Ambassador:* ALEX SEIBUO NAPO.

Tunisia: B.P. 1488; *Ambassador:* MOHAMED AMAMOU.

Uganda: B.P. 1036; *Ambassador:* Lt.-Col. OMBIA.

U.S.S.R.: B.P. 1143; *Ambassador:* M. LAVROV.

United Kingdom: B.P. 8049; *Ambassador:* RICHARD STRATTON (also accred. to Burundi).

U.S.A.: B.P. 697; *Ambassador:* SHELDON B. VANCE.

Vatican: 81 rue Goma; *Nuncio:* Mgr. BRUNO TORPIGLIANI.

Viet-Nam, Republic: B.P. 9316; *Ambassador:* (vacant).

Yugoslavia: B.P. 619; *Ambassador:* ESAD CERIC.

Zambia: B.P. 1144; *Ambassador:* JORDAN MUNKANTA.

Zaire also has diplomatic relations with Argentina, Austria, China (People's Republic), Cyprus, German Democratic Republic, Hungary, Korea (Democratic People's Republic), Lebanon, Libya, Luxembourg, Norway, and Turkey.

PRESIDENT AND NATIONAL ASSEMBLY

PRESIDENTIAL ELECTION
(October 1970)

Total Registered Voters	10,101,330
Total Votes Cast	10,131,828
For General Mobutu Sese Seko	10,131,669
Against	157

The results show that 99.9985 per cent of the votes cast were in favour of Gen. Mobutu, the sole candidate.

NATIONAL LEGISLATIVE COUNCIL
(Legislative Elections, November 14th–15th, 1970)

Total Registered Voters	9,854,517
Votes for Party Candidates	9,691,132
Votes Against	72,378
Spoiled or Blank Papers	91,007

All 420 seats were won by the MPR, the sole party.

President: BOBOLIKO LOKONGAI.

REGIONAL GOVERNMENTS

Under the Loi Fondamentale there were 6 provinces in the Republic. This number was changed to 21 by a law promulgated in August 1962, and finally reduced to 8 by presidential decree from January 1967. These provinces were renamed "regions" in July 1972. Regional government is in the hands of a Regional Commissioner and 6 Councillors.

REGION	COMMISSIONER	REGION	COMMISSIONER
Shaba	DUGA KUGBETOLO	Lower Zaire	Mme. NZUZI WA MBOMBO
Kivu	NDEBO YA LUTETE	Equator	MBALA MBABU
Upper Zaire	ASUMARI BUSANYA LUKILI	Eastern Kasai	MATABISI IYUALEKE ILANDE
Bandundu	MULENDA SHAMWANYE MUTEBI	Western Kasai	NGOMA NTOTO MBUANGI

Governor of Kinshasa: N.DJOKU EYO'BABA (responsible directly to the National Department of the Interior).

POLITICAL PARTY

Mouvement populaire de la révolution (MPR): Kinshasa; f. 1967; stands for national unity, opposition to tribalism, and African socialism; political bureau of 15 members; Leader President MOBUTU; Sec. NGUZA KARL-I-BOND.

JUDICIAL SYSTEM

Under the terms of the 1967 Constitution there is a Supreme Court at Kinshasa, two Courts of Appeal at Kinshasa and Lubumbashi; eight Tribunals of First Instance in each region.

SUPREME COURT

First President: LIHAU EBUA LIBANA.

Second President: GUY BOUCHOMS.

Prosecutor-General: KENGO WADOND.

Advocate-General: VALENTIN PHANZU.

Secretary: MBEMBA, B.P. 7016, Kinshasa-Kalina.

APPEAL COURTS

Kinshasa: Pres. LUBAMBA.

Kisangani: Pres. ANDRÉ MOISE.

Lubumbashi: Pres. KALALA-ILUNGA.

RELIGION

AFRICAN RELIGIONS

About half the population follow traditional beliefs, which are mostly animistic, while most of the remainder are Roman Catholic.

CHRISTIANITY

ROMAN CATHOLIC CHURCH

Archbishop of Bukavu: MUTABESHA MULINDWA, B.P. 3324, Bukavu.

Archbishop of Mbandaka: PIERRE WIJNANTS, B.P. 1064, Mbandaka.

Archbishop of Lubumbashi: EUGÈNE KABANGA, B.P. 72, Lubumbashi.

Archbishop of Kinshasa: H.E. Cardinal JOSEPH MALULA, B.P. 8431, Kinshasa.

Archbishop of Kisangani: AUGUSTIN FATAKI, B.P. 505, Kisangani.

Archbishop of Kananga: MARTIN BAKOLE, B.P. 70, Kananga.

CHURCH OF CHRIST IN ZAIRE

Eglise de Christ au Zaïre: B.P. 3094, Kinshasa-Gombe; f. 1902 (as Zaire Protestant Council); Pres.-Gen. Rev. Dr. BOKELEALE I. B.; Vice-Pres. Rev. Dr. MASAMBA M.M.

There are 53 Zairian Protestant member communities with about 5 million mems. Depts.: Evangelization and the Life of the Church (including Christian Education, Family and Social Works, Chaplaincies to the Zairian Armed Forces); Protestant Education Bureau; Diaconate (including Medical, Development and Refugee sub-depts.).

ANGLICAN CHURCH
(Province of Uganda)

Diocese of Boga-Zaire: Bishop: The Rt. Rev. PHILIP RIDSDALE, B.P. 154, Bunia.

OTHER RELIGIONS

Muslims	115,500
Jews	1,520

Baha'i Faith: B.P. 181, Kinshasa; there are 710 centres of worship in Zaire.

THE PRESS

(French language, unless otherwise stated)

DAILIES

Documentation et Information Africaine: B.P. 2598, Kinshasa I.

Elima: ave. Kasavubu, B.P. 10.017, Kinshasa I; f. 1928; independent; Editor PASCAL KAPELLA; circ. 25,000.

Elombe: ave. de l'Université, B.P. 11498, Kinshasa I; Editor THU-RENÉ ESSOLOMWA.

Monano: B.P. 982, Kisangani; f. 1969; Editor FRÉDÉRIC-MARTIN MONZEMU; circ. 5,000.

Mwanga: B.P. 2474, Lubumbashi; published by La Presse Zairoise, S.Z.A.R.L.; circ. 20,000.

Nyoto: 10ème Rue, B.P. 1366, Lisete-Kinshasa; f. 1963; published by Société d'Edition Etoile du Zaire; circ. 25,000.

Salongo: Blvd. du 30 Juin, B.P. 78, Kinshasa VII; pro-governmental; Editor GABRIEL MAKOSSO.

Taifa: 490 ave. Mobutu, B.P. 525, Lubumbashi; f. 1927; independent; Editor JACQUES TSHILEMBE; circ. 10,000.

WEEKLIES

Actualités du Kivu: B.P. 475, Bukavu.

Afrique Chrétienne: B.P. 7653, Kinshasa I; Publisher Soc. Miss. St. Paul; Dir. L. KALONJI; circ. 50,000.

Dimukai: B.P. 1375, Mbuji Mayi.

Echo du Kasai Occidental: B.P. 1670, Kananga.

Epanza: 1 ave. Bangandanga, B.P. 8205, Kinshasa.

M'Bandaka: P.O.B. 349, Mbandaka; f. 1947; French and Lingala.

Michezo: Stade 20 Mai, B.P. 7853, Kinshasa.

Mwanga-Hebdo: 907 ave. Moero, B.P. 4425, Lubumbashi; f. 1959; Editor HAMICI POYO KIBEBYA; circ. 12,000.

Nkumu: ave. Badjoko 340, Matonge/Kinshasa; Editor GASTON N'SENGI BIEMBE.

La Semaine: rue de Luvungi 87, Kinshasa; Editor EMILE SOLET.

Tabalayi: 31 bis, rue Doruma, B.P. 6250, Kinshasa.

Uhaki-Verité: P.O.B. 1454, Lubumbashi; f. 1946; Swahili and French; Editor JULIUS KANSO MULENGA; circ. 6,000.

Le Zaïre: ave. Buskadingi, Grand Marché, B.P. 8203, Kinshasa I.

FORTNIGHTLIES

Nature, Parcs et Jardins: P.O.B. 3220, Kinshasa; Kalina; f. 1938; journal of the Société Congolaise des Sciences Naturelles.

Zaire Magazine: P.O.B. 8246, Kinshasa; f. 1960; official; publ. in French-Lingala, French-Kikongo, French-Kiswahili, French-Tshiluba; circ. 10,000.

PERIODICALS

Aequatoria: B.P. 276, Mbandaka; f. 1937; scientific native questions; Editor G. HULSTAERT, M.S.C.

Afrique et l'Europe: rue d'Itanga 81, Kinshasa.

Aliazo: B.P. 8085, Kinshasa; Editor ANDRÉ MASSAKI.

Asco: B.P. 8037, Kinshasa; Editor NSIALA ZINDUKA.

Les Bantous et la Culture: 20 rue Balari, Kinshasa-Bandalungwa; Editor SEBASTIEN NANGI.

Le Bon Berger: rue de Bosobolo 47, Kinshasa; Editor M. BAVELEDY.

Centre Afrique: Direction de l'Imprimerie Nationale Congolaise, Kinshasa.

Conscience: rue Bakongo 17, Kinshasa; Editor TSHIALA MWANA.

Dionga: 2ème Rue Dima, Immeuble Amassio, B.P. 8031, Kinshasa.

Le Drapeau Zaïrois: B.P. 235, Kinshasa XI; Editor D. B. Kathalay.

Les Droits de l'Homme: Africaine Import-Export, B.P. 991, Kinshasa, Editor Jean-Marie Malenge.

Echos du Bas-Zaïre: Avenue Kabambare No. 23, Kinshasa; Editor Raymond Bikebi.

Energie et Progrès: blvd. du 30 Juin, INSS Building, B.P. 500, Kinshasa I.

Equateur Mabenga: B. P. 243, ave. de Budja No. 45, Mbandaka; Editor Joseph Besembe.

Espoir: B.P. 903, Kinshasa; Editor Sakou Mamba.

Etudes Zaïroises: c/o Institut National d'Etudes Politiques, B.P. 2307, Kinshasa; Editor Louis Mandala.

Le Flambeau: ave. Mangembo 106, Kinshasa; Editor Camille Loboya.

Flash: B.P. 7969, Kinshasa; Editor Joseph Franssen.

Forum Universitaire: B.P. 799, Kinshasa XI; periodical for UNAZA students.

Le Grand Combat: B.P. 1129, Kinshasa; Editor Pascal Mvuemba.

Indépendance: B.P. 8201, Kinshasa; Editor Antoine Kiwewa.

Kibanguisme: 56 ave. d'Opala, Kinshasa; Editor P. Losolo.

Kin Malebo: B.P. 768, Kinshasa; Editor François-Ferdinand Diatako.

Lokole Lokiso: B.P. 245, Mbandaka; Editor Paul Ngoi.

Longle: B.P. 5835, Kinshasa.

Le Matin: B.P. 1301, Kinshasa; Editor Ignace Bolenge.

Le Messager du Salut: 275 ave. du Plateau, B.P. 8636, Kinshasa; journal of the Salvation Army; monthly; French, Lingala and Kikongo.

Misamu Gifumzi Gydu: B.P. 2186, Kinshasa; Editor Nabothe Nzamba.

Mission des Noirs: B.P. 8029, Kinshasa; Editor Simon Pierre M'Padi.

Mokano: Ministry of Information, B.P. 8246, Kinshasa.

Mon Opinion: rue Van Eetevelde 15/A, Kinshasa; Editor Cesaire Katembabisu.

Monaco: ave. Borns 9, Wangata, Kinshasa; Editor Paul Ebaka.

Mondo: B.P. 8085, Kinshasa; Editor Emmanuel Kounzika.

Notre Combat: E.N.D.A., Kinshasa; Editor Bonaventure Bibombe.

Nsamu Mbote: Baptist Mid Mission, B.P. 18, Kikwit; Editor H. Eicher.

Le Porte Feuille: B.P. 3473, Kinshasa-Kalina.

Le Progrès: B.P. 7074, Kinshasa; Editor Adrien Mokese.

Réalités: Institut Enseignement Médical, Kinshasa; Editor Michel Ngoma Ngimbi.

La Revue Juridique du Zaïre: Société d'Etudes Juridiques du Katanga; B.P. 510, Lubumbashi; f. 1924.

Solidarité Africaine: ave. Mgr. Kimbondo 488, Kinshasa, Bandalungwa; Editor F. Kimway.

Le Travailleur de l'Angola: Quartier Mongo 35/E, Kinshasa; Editor Ferdinand Mavunza.

Tribune du Travailleur: U.N.T.C., Kinshasa; Editor Valentin Muthombo.

Tribune Zaïroise: Kananga; Editor Medard Olongo.

Unidade Angolana: ave. Tombeur de Tabora 51, Kinshasa; Editor Mario de Andrade.

Voici l'Heure: ave. Kaviakere 3144, Kinshasa; Editor Roger Kassongo.

Voir et Savoir: 16 ave. Bangala, Kinshasa; Editor (vacant).

La Voix de la Nation Angolaise: rue d'Itanga No. 56, Kinshasa; Editor Roberto Holden.

La Voix de l'Orphelin: rue Tshuapa 58, Kinshasa; Editor Jules Pandamare.

La Voix du Kwilu: Kikwit; Editor Valère Nzanba.

Le Vrai Visage: 43 ave. des Colons, Kinshasa; Editor François Kupa.

Zaïre Afrique: B.P. 3375, Kinshasa; monthly; economic and cultural; organ of Centre d'Etudes pour l'Action Sociale; Editors René Beeckmans, Francis Kikassa.

Zaire News Letter: American Baptist Foreign Mission Society, B.P. 4728, Kinshasa II; f. 1910; English; Editor Mrs. Wesley H. Brown.

NEWS AGENCIES

Agence Zaïre-Presse (AZAP): B.P. 1595, Kinshasa; f. 1957; official agency; Dir.-Gen. Mpanu-Mpanu Bibanda.

Foreign Bureaux

Deutsche Presse-Agentur and Reuters have offices in Kinshasa.

All religious publications were banned by a decree of February 8th, 1973.

RADIO AND TELEVISION

Radiodiffusion-Télévision Nationale Zaïroise (RTNZ): B.P. 3171, Kinshasa-Kalina; f. 1940; regional stations at Kinshasa, Kisangani, Bukavu, Kananga, Mbandaka, Bakwanga, Mbuji-Mayi and Lubumbashi. Broadcasts in French and African languages; Dir. A. Kibongue.

International Service: B.P. 7699; Kinshasa broadcasts in French, English, Spanish, German and Portuguese; Chief A. Kongo.

TV-College: B.P. 7074, Collège S. François de Sales, 1700 avenue Wangermée, Lubumbashi; f. 1947; religious, educational; services in French, Swahili, Kibemba; radio services suspended 1968 but television service continues in collaboration with RTNZ; Dir.-Gen. M. Salesiens.

Radio Léo: B.P. 3165, Kinshasa; f. 1937; religious, educational; owned and operated by Collège Albert; services in French; Dir.-Gen. P. Wart.

Radiodiffusion Ufac: B.P. 97, Lubumbashi; services in French, English, Kiswahili.

La Voix de la Fraternité Africaine: Lubumbashi; f. 1965.

In 1971 there were 75,000 radio licences and 7,050 television licences.

FINANCE

(cap. = capital; dep. = deposit; m. = million; res. = reserves)

BANKING

CENTRAL BANK

Banque du Zaïre: B.P. 2697, Kinshasa; f. 1961; cap. 1m. Zaires, res. 9.5m. Zaires; Gov. SAMBWA PIDA NBAGUI.

COMMERCIAL BANKS

Banque Commerciale Zaïroise S.Z.A.R.L.: ave. des Wagenias, B.P. 2798, Kinshasa; f. 1909; cap. 4m. Zaires; 29 brs.; Man. Dirs. E. BONVOISIN, J. VERDICKT, M. H. DELVOIE.

Banque de Kinshasa: ave. Tombalbaye, Pl. du Marché, B.P. 2433, Kinshasa; f. 1969; br. in Lubumbashi; cap. and res. 1,764,135 Zaires, dep. 21,095,220 Zaires.

Banque de Paris et des Pays-Bas: Bldg. Unibra, ave. Col. Ebeya, B.P. 1600, Kinshasa; f. 1954; cap. 775,000 Zaires.

Banque du Peuple: blvd. du 30 Juin, Kinshasa; f. 1947; cap. 2,327,106 Zaires.

Banque Internationale pour l'Afrique au Zaïre (BIAZ): ave. de la Douane, B.P. 8725, Kinshasa; f. 1970; cap. 150,000 Zaires.

Banque Zaïroise pour le Développement: Kinshasa; f. 1966; Gov. M. MUSHIETTE.

Barclays Bank S.Z.A.R.L.: Head Office: 191 ave. de l'Equateur, B.P. 1299, Kinshasa; f. 1951; subsidiary of Barclays Bank International Ltd.; br. in Lubumbashi; cap. 40,000 Zaires, dep. 1,408,610 Zaires (Oct. 1972); Chair. Vicomte OBERT DE THIEUSIES; Man. Dir. M. J. ST. C. DYER.

Caisse Générale d'Epargne du Zaïre: ave. Prince Charles, Kalina-Kinshasa, B.P. 8147; f. 1950; Dir.-Gen. VICTOR MAKUNGU.

Caisse Nationale d'Epargne et de Crédit Immobilier: B.P. 11196, Kinshasa; f. 1971; cap. 2m. Zaires; dep.

700,000 Zaires; state-owned; Dir. Gen. BIANGALA ELONGA MBAÜ.

Compagnie Immobilière du Zaïre "Immozaire": P.O.B. 332, Kinshasa; f. 1962; cap. 150m. Zaires; Chair. A. S. GERARD; Man. Dir. M. HERALY.

Crédit Commercial Africain: Kinshasa.

Crédit Foncier de l'Afrique Centrale: B.P. 1198, Kinshasa; f. 1961; cap. 40,000 Zaires.

Crédit Foncier du Nord Est: Bukavu; f. 1961; cap. 10m. Zaires.

Crédit Hypothécaire du Nord Est: Bukavu; f. 1961; cap. 15m. Zaires.

First National City Bank-Zaire: 809 blvd. du 30 Juin, B.P. 9999, Kinshasa; f. 1971; cap. 250,000 Zaires; Man. Dir. C. SPINK; Man. D. PEPONIS.

Société de Crédit aux Classes Moyennes et à l'Industrie: B.P. 3105, Kinshasa-Kalina; f. 1947; cap. 500m. Zaires.

Société de Crédit Foncier: Lubumbashi; f. 1961.

Société Zaïroise de Banque S.Z.R.L.: blvd. 30 Juin, B.P. 400, Kinshasa; cap. 0.6m. Zaires; taken over by government in August 1971.

Société Zaïroise de Financement et de Développement (SOFIDE): f. 1970; cap. 2m. Zaires; partly state-owned; Pres. MAMBU MA KHENZU MAKUALA.

Union Zaïroise de Banques S.A.R.L.: 19 ave. de la Nation, Kinshasa; f. 1929; cap. 1,200,000 Zaires; dep. 13.5m.; Dir.-Gen. GÉRARD GODEFROID.

INSURANCE

Société Nationale d'Assurances (SONAS): Kinshasa; f. 1966; cap. 5m. Zaires; 8 brs.; state-owned.

All foreign insurance companies were closed by Presidential decree from December 31st, 1966.

TRADE AND INDUSTRY

CHAMBERS OF COMMERCE

Chambre de Commerce de Boma: Boma.

Chambre du Commerce de l'Equateur: B.P. 127, Mbandaka; f. 1926; 64 mem. societies; Pres. J. BOSEKOTA.

Chambre du Commerce, de l'Industrie et de l'Agriculture de l'Ituri: Bunia; f. 1932; Pres. LOUIS BEAUTHIER; Sec. HENRI GROVEN; publ. monthly bulletin in French.

Chambre de Commerce, d'Industrie et d'Agriculture du Kasai à Kananga: P.O.B. 194, Kananga; f. 1946; publ. monthly bulletin.

Chambre du Commerce et de l'Industrie du Shaba: B.P. 972, Lubumbashi; f. 1910; Pres. S. MAWAWA; Sec. A. HISETTE; 225 mems.; publ. monthly bulletin in French.

Chambre de Commerce et d'Industrie de Bukavu: P.O. Box 321, Bukavu; f. 1931; Chair. PH. MOREL DE WESTGAVER; Sec. R. BASTIN; publ. *Monthly Bulletin.*

Chambre de Commerce et d'Industrie de Kinshasa: P.O.B. 7247, 10 avenue des Aviateurs, Kinshasa; f. 1921; Pres. H. T. TUMBA; Sec. J. M. VAN LEEUW; 400 mems.; publ. bulletin in French.

Chambre de Commerce de Matadi: B.P. 145, Matadi; f. 1959; Chair. CH. VAN GOETHEM; Vice-Pres. A. WYNANT-VERPEUT; Sec. H. WAGEMANS; 103 mems.; publ. monthly *Bulletin.*

Chambre du Commerce, de l'Industrie et de l'Agriculture: P.O.B. 358, Kisangani; f. 1939; Pres. G. AUTRIQUE; 250 members; publ. monthly bulletin in French.

Chambre du Commerce et de l'Industrie du Tanganyika: B.P. 228, Kamina; 43 mems.; Pres. G. HOSLI; Sec. O. MUKALA.

DEVELOPMENT

MINERALS

La Générale des Carrières et Mines du Zaïre (GÉCAMINES): Lubumbashi; f. 1967; fully nationalized 1968; took over assets in the Congo of Union Minière du Haut Katanga; production (1972): 428,000 metric tons of copper; Pres. D. KANDOLO.

PETROLEUM

Société Zaïre-Italienne de Raffinage (SOZIR): B.P. 1478, Kinshasa; f. 1963 by agreement between Zairian Government and Italian ANIC; cap. 4,400m. Zaires; 500 employees.

Zaire Oil Co.: Kinshasa; subsidiary of Teikoku Oil, Japan; production to start mid-1974.

POWER

Società Italo-Zairese Attività Industriali—SIZAI: avenue Costermans 10, Kinshasa; f. 1963 to advise the Zaire Government on development of the power potential of the Inga rapids; ownership: IRI (Italian state) 60 per cent, Impresa Astaldi Estero 40 per cent; first contract awarded 1968 to Impresa Astaldi Estero for creation of a dam on the Van Duren tributary (now called Fwamalo) to produce power through six generators; four of the generators are operating (1973); the fifth and sixth are planned for 1974; SIZAI is now studying the development of a second power plant and an industrial area related to the project, which would include a steel plant.

Société Nationale d'Electricité (SNEL): 49 blvd. du 30 Juin, B.P. 500 Kin I, Kinshasa; state-owned; Gen. Man M. MUTONDO.

TRADE ASSOCIATIONS

Association des Entrepreneurs du Zaïre (ADEZ): B.P. 2361, Kinshasa.

Association Belgo-Zaïroise du Textile (ABZT): B.P. 3097, Kinshasa.

Association Nationale des Entreprises Zaïroises (ANEZA): 10 ave. des Aviateurs, B.P. 7247, Kinshasa; f. 1943; Pres. TUMBA TUNKADI.

　ANEZA-SUD: B.P. 1500, ave. du Kasai, Lubumbashi, Shaba.

　ANEZA-NORD EST: B.P. 1407, Kisangani, Upper Zaire.

　ANEZA-OUEST: B.P. 7247, Kinshasa.

MEMBERS

Association des Entreprises de l'Equateur (ADEQUA): B.P. 1052, Mbandaka.

Association des Entreprises de l'Est du Zaïre (AEEZ): B.P. 2467, Bukavu; Pres. M. GUERIN.

Association des Entreprises de l'Ouest du Zaïre (AEOZ): B.P. 8634, Kinshasa; 163 mems.

Association des Entreprises du Kasai (A.E.Kas.): B.P. 649; Kananga; Pres. M. BRUYNEEL.

Association des Entrepreneurs du Zaïre (ADEZ): c/o Sesomo, B.P. 2361, Kinshasa.

Association Belgo-Zaïroise du Textile (ABZT): B.P. 3097, Kinshasa.

Fédération d'Entreprises du Zaïre (FEZ): 82 blvd. du 30 Juin, B.P. 8634, Kinshasa.

TRADE UNIONS

Union Nationale des Travailleurs Zaïrois (UTZ): B.P. 8814, Kinshasa; f. 1967 as the sole syndical organization; Sec.-Gen. ANDRÉ BO-BOLIKO; publs. *Notre Droit, Formation.*

Principal Affiliated Unions:

Alliance des Prolétaires Indépendants du Zaïre (APIZ): 2 avenue de la Kéthule, B.P. 8721, Kinshasa; f. 1946; 6,400 mems.; Sec. JOSEPH KIMPIATU.

Centrale des Enseignants Zaïrois (CEZ): B.P. 8814, Kinshasa; f. 1957; 18,000 mems.; Sec. FERDINAND TOTO-ZITA; Publ. *Pedagogia.*

Centrale des Mines et Métallurgie: B.P. 8814, Kinshasa; f. 1965; 24,000 mems.; Sec. SEBASTIEN KALAIA.

Centrale des Plantations et Alimentation: B.P. 8814, Kinshasa; f. 1962; 24,000 mems.; Sec. DONAT MUTUMBO..

Centrale des Services Publics: B.P. 8814, Kinshasa; f. 1957, 12,000 mems.; Sec. CAMILLE IFELO.

Centrale des Travailleurs du Transport: B.P. 8814, Kinshasa; f. 1959; 38,000 mems.; Sec. JEAN LUYEYE.

Fédération Nationale des Agents sous Contrat de l'Etat (FNACE): B.P. 970, Kinshasa; f. 1964; 20,000 mems.; Pres. A. LINGULU; Sec. M. MONTINGIA.

Fédération Nationale des Employés Commerciaux et Cadres (FNECC): B.P. 970, Kinshasa; f. 1961; Pres. FRANÇOIS TOKO.

Fédération des Ouvriers des Mines du Zaïre (FOMIZ): Kisangani; f. 1964; Sec.-Gen. THOMAS KALOMBO

Syndicat du Bâtiment du Zaïre (SYBAZ): Ngiri-Ngiri, Kinshasa; f. 1961; Pres. JOSEPH MULOWAYE; Sec. ALPHONSE KADIMA.

Syndicat National des Travailleurs Zaïrois (SNTZ): 398 avenue van Eetveld, B.P. 2077, Kinshasa; f. 1959; 2,000 mems.; Pres. ALPHONSE KITHIMA.

TRADE FAIR

Kinshasa International Trade Fair: Kinshasa; held annually in July.

TRANSPORT AND TOURISM

RAILWAYS

Total length of railways: 5,174 km., including 500 km. of electrified rail. A link between Ilebo and Matadi is planned. The Zaire system is also linked to Lobito via the Benguela Railway, and Beira via Zambia, Rhodesia and Mozambique.

Compagnie des Chemins de Fer Kinshasa-Dilolo-Lubumbashi (KDL): P.O.B. 297, Lubumbashi; administers the following sections: Sakania Border–Bukama 710 km.; Bukama–Ilebo 1,123 km.; Tenke–Dilolo–Border 522 km.; Kamina–Kabongo 201 km. Of these 2,556 km., 859 km. are electrified; the non-electrified lines are equipped with diesel engines.

Soc. Zaïroise des Chemins de Fer des Grands Lacs (formerly *C.F.L.*): B.P. 230, Kalemie, Shaba; f. 1965; administers the Kisangani-Ubundu, Kindu-Kalemie and Kabalo-Kabongo lines; rail services, 1,086 km.; river

and Lake Tanganyika services; Dir.-Gen. ROBERT CHERRIER.

Office National des Transports au Zaïre (ONATRA): Regd. Office: B.P. 99, Kinshasa; operates the Kinshasa-Matadi rail link; Pres. MPETE LOMENA IKOTO.

Chemin de Fer de Matadi-Kinshasa (C.F.M.K.): Head Office: P.O.B. 98, Kinshasa; length of track, 403 km.; Gen. Man. BOMBUTSI ENTOMBO.

Chemin de Fer du Mayumbe (C.F.M.): Administrative offices in Boma; length of track, 136 km.; Dir. NKANV-NTEOLO-A-NKENDA.

Soc. des Chemins de Fer Vicinaux de Zaïre (C.V.Z.): Head Office: B.P. 499, Kinshasa; offices in Aketi and Isiro; length of track, 1,023 km.

Benguela Railway Co.: Rua do Ataide 7, Lisbon 2, Portugal; 781 ave. du Kasai, B.P. 1047, Lubumbashi; 2,093 km. to Lobito on Angolan coast.

ROADS

There are approximately 145,213 km. of motor roads in Zaire (approx. 94,300 cars and lorries in 1971). In general road conditions are poor, owing to inadequate maintenance since 1958.

ROAD TRANSPORT

Chief companies are:

Soc. Zaïroise des Chemins de Fer du Grand Lac (see Railways above): Road services between Cisumbura and Kigali and from Samba to Tongoni.

OTRAZ: Head Office: P.O.B. 98, Kinshasa; regular service between Kalunda (Uvira) and Bukavu (140 km.), Boma and Tshela (140 km.); Pres. L. M. CARLOS.

C.V.Z.: 5 rue de la Science, Brussels; Road Management: Isiro, Upper Zaire; passenger and goods service in the Upper Zaire and Kivu provinces; network of 14,973 km.

INLAND WATERWAYS

For over 1,600 km. the River Zaire (Congo) is navigable. Above the Stanley Falls the Zaire changes its name to Lualaba, and is used for shipping on a 965-km. stretch from Bubundu to Kindu and Kongolo to Bukama. (There is a railway from Matadi, the principal port on the lower Zaire, to Kinshasa.) The total length of inland waterways is 16,400 km.

Office Zaïrois des Chemins de Fer du Grand Lac (see Railways above): River Lualaba services, Bubundu–Kindu and Kongolo–Malemba N'kula; Lake Tanganyika services, Kamina – Kigoma – Kalundu – Moba–Mpulungu.

Zaire Network: services on the Luapula and Lake Mweru.

East African Railways and Harbours: services on Lake Mobutu Sese Seko.

Office d'Exploitation des Transports au Zaïre (OTRAZ): River Communications Office: boulevard du 30 juin, Kinshasa; passenger, mail and cargo services over 12,000 km.

SHIPPING

The principal seaports are Matadi, Banana and Boma on the lower Zaire. Matadi is linked by rail with Kinshasa. Much of the mineral trade is shipped from Lobito in Angola, however, and does not pass through Zaire's ports.

Compagnie Maritime Belge: B.P. 264, Matadi, and P.O.B. 33, Boma; weekly service Antwerp to Matadi and Boma, monthly service New York and Gulf ports to Matadi and Boma.

Compagnie Maritime Zaïroise: Matadi, P.O.B. 9496, Kinshasa; f. 1967; since 1973 owned wholly by Zaire (formerly part-owned by Belgium); services to Antwerp, North Continental Range to East Africa, U.S.A., Mediterranean ports to West Africa; Chair. LIONDJO FATAKI; Man. Dir. F. GUINOTTE.

Office d'Exploitation des Transports au Zaïre (OTRAZ): blvd. du 30 juin, Kinshasa; administers the port of Matadi.

CIVIL AVIATION

There are international airports at Kinshasa, Lubumbashi and Kamina.

Air Zaire, SARL: 4 ave. du Port, B.P. 10120, Kinshasa; f. 1960: national airline; Pres. JACQUES MASSANGU; operates four DC-8, one DC-10, two Caravelles and seven F-27; a second DC-10 is ordered for June 1973.

Agence et Messageries Aériennes Zaïroises (AMAZ) S.P.R.L.: B.P. 671, Kinshasa; charter and regular services; Man. Dirs. KANDE-DZAMBULATE, K.K., R. LINARD, P. DAVISTER.

FOREIGN AIRLINES

Air France, Air Afrique, Alitalia, British Airways, East Africa Airways, Iberian, KLM, Lufthansa, PAA, Sabena, Swissair and UTA provide services to Kinshasa.

TOURISM

Bureau International du Tourisme et des Echanges pour les Jeunes (BITEJ): Kinsako, Kinshasa; f. 1967; travel organization for young people in Zaire and abroad.

Commissariat Général au Tourisme de la République du Zaïre: blvd. du 30 juin, Building de la Rwindi, B.P. 9502, Kinshasa I.

Regional branches at Bukavu, Goma, Moanda and Bunia; office in Brussels.

CULTURAL ORGANIZATION

Centre Culturel du Zaïre: Balari No. 20, Bandalungwa, Kinshasa; aims to promote Bantu culture; publ. *Académie des Arts et Métiers.*

UNIVERSITIES

Université Lovanium de Kinshasa: B.P. 127, Kinshasa XI; f. 1954; 477 teachers, 3,285 students.

Université Officielle du Zaïre: B.P. 1825, Lubumbashi; f. 1955; 65 teachers, 1,250 students.

Université Libre du Zaïre: B.P. 2012, Kisangani; f. 1963; 75 teachers, 650 students.

ZAMBIA

INTRODUCTORY SURVEY

Location, Climate, Language, Religion, Flag, Capital

Zambia, in southern central Africa, is divided from (Southern) Rhodesia by the Zambezi River and Lake Kariba. To the east lie Mozambique and Malawi, to the north Tanzania, and to the south and west Botswana and Angola, while the country is almost split in half by an arm of Zaire territory in the north-west. The climate is tropical, modified by altitude with average temperatures of 65° to 75°F (18°–24°C). The official language is English; the African peoples speak Bantu dialects. Some Africans follow traditional beliefs. Christians make up about 80 per cent of the population, including all Europeans, and are roughly divided between Protestants and Roman Catholics. Asians are mostly Moslems, with a few Hindus. The national flag (proportions 3 by 2) is green, with a canton in the lower right having equal red, black and gold vertical stripes, surmounted by an osprey in flight. The capital is Lusaka.

Recent History

The Federation of Rhodesia and Nyasaland broke up in 1963 in the face of successful nationalist movements in Northern Rhodesia and Nyasaland, and Northern Rhodesia achieved independence as Zambia in October 1964. A state of emergency has existed since independence because of the activities of the white minorities in Rohdesia, Angola and Mozambique and the presence of refugees and southern African liberation movements in Zambia. In 1970 the Zambian President, Dr. Kenneth Kaunda, was elected chairman of the Assembly of Heads of State at the Organization of African Unity (OAU) and in September that year the summit of the non-aligned nations was held in Lusaka. A staunch opponent of racist policies, whether those of South Africa or Uganda, President Kaunda has propagated his philosophy of *Humanism* as the basis for a peaceful society in Zambia. Since 1969 he has attempted to reduce the influence of tribal loyalties in political life. Before the proclamation of a one-party state in December 1972 Zambian politics were characterized by outbreaks of politically-inspired violence, particularly on the Copperbelt. The decline of the main opposition party, the African National Congress (ANC), and internal disputes in United National Independence Party (UNIP) led to the formation of the United Progressive Party in 1971, though that was banned in 1972 and many of its leaders detained. The ANC opposed the formation of a one-party state but shortly afterwards the country united to face the potentially crippling effect of the closure of the border with Rhodesia.

Zambia is in the front line of the increasingly bitter struggle between the white-ruled states south of the Zambezi and the black North. It has consistently supported African liberation movements and by 1973 these groups posed a substantial threat to Rhodesia's border. The border with Rhodesia is now closed. There has been increasing guerrilla activity since the border closure, leading to more tension between Rhodesia and Zambia. In December 1973 a UN report revealed that Zambia housed 33,000 refugees from neighbouring white-ruled states.

Government

Zambia is an independent Republic within the Commonwealth and in December 1972 became a one-party participatory democracy. Executive power is vested in a President and a Cabinet, appointed by the President from among the members of the National Assembly. The National Assembly is to have 125 elected seats under the new Constitution. In addition, the President may nominate up to ten special members to the Assembly. An advisory House of Chiefs voices the interests of provincial chiefs. The former British Protectorate of Barotseland was incorporated within the Republic of Zambia at the assumption of independence in October 1964. In August 1969 Barotse Province, one of the seven making up Zambia, was renamed Western Province and Western Province became Copperbelt Province.

Defence

The Zambian Defence Force is centred on an army headquarters and a brigade headquarters. The Zambia air force headquarters administers transport aircraft in close co-operation with the army. The total strength of armed forces is 6,000, with 5,000 in the army and 1,000 in the air force. The police force numbers 6,250.

Economic Affairs

Zambia has applied, as far as she has been able, the UN sanctions against Rhodesia, although this has involved reducing her imports from Rhodesia, which in 1965 made up 34 per cent of her total imports, to less than 10 per cent of the total, and has necessitated great expenditure on alternative transport and communication routes.

The basis of Zambian wealth is mining in the rich Copperbelt whose mines employed 55,000 people in 1974. Copper amounts to 95 per cent of Zambia's mineral production and it is the world's fourth largest copper producer. In 1971 the Zambian Government acquired a 51 per cent share in the mines, and re-organized the structure of the industry. In August 1973 the Government announced it was taking full control of the two largest copper mining groups, Nchanga and Roan Consolidated Copper Mines. Zinc, cobalt, lead, manganese and substantial amounts of coal are also mined. Smelting and refining works have grown up around the mines and industry is developing swiftly. The majority of the population are still agriculturalists, however. The chief cash products are maize, cattle, groundnuts and tobacco. On the European farms tobacco is grown for export. Community development schemes are improving the quality of farming over most of the country. In 1966 a large coalfield was discovered at Siankandobo (the Maamba field), which is expected to make Zambia self-sufficient in coal for several years. The 1972–76 Development Plan aims at 7 per cent growth, expansion and diversification of industry and agriculture and enlargement of the social services. Work is in hand to build a dam and a hydro-electric scheme at Kafue and a power station on the Zambian side of Kariba, thus lessening Zambia's dependence on the Kariba system shared with but operated by Rhodesia. Since 1968 the important sectors of the economy have been put under the control of state corporations. Since 1969 retail trade has been restricted to Zambian ownership in Suburban areas. Zambianization of the transport services is also in hand. Zambia has applied for membership of the East African Community.

After the closure of the Rhodesian border in 1973 the Zambian economy faced a considerable challenge as half its vital copper exports were previously transported through Rhodesia to the Mozambique port of Beira which also handled most of Zambia's imports. The Government introduced stringent tax increases in January 1973, and import controls in February. In the 1974 budget, taxes were lowered but import controls remain. However, with considerable UN support, large aid donations by many friendly countries and help given by Tanzania in re-routing its trade, Zambia's economy came through 1973 with a record trade surplus, owing to the large increase in the world price of copper. The balance of payments and foreign reserve holdings were also improved and the Tan-Zam Railway was well ahead of schedule and likely to end Zambia's dependence on white-ruled southern Africa when it is completed in late 1974. Zambia's supply of crude oil is assured but the high oil price is likely to affect the Second National Development Plan adversely.

Transport and Communications

Zambia Railways connects Lusaka and the Copperbelt towns, Ndola and Kitwe, to the Zaire rail system and the Benguela railway in Southern Angola, and (by lake service) with East African Railways. Since Rhodesia's declaration of independence, Zambia has sought to develop a transport and communication network outside the control of both Rhodesia and Portugal. The existing Great North Road to Dar es Salaam in Tanzania has been supplemented by a pipeline from Ndola to Dar es Salaam, opened in August 1968; and construction of the Tan-Zam railway began in 1970 with Chinese aid and is expected to be completed ahead of schedule in 1974. A new international airport was opened at Lusaka in 1967 and work is in progress to extend other airports. Zambia Airways provides domestic and intercontinental links.

Social Welfare

The Department of Welfare and Probation services is resopnsible for relief of distress, care of the aged, pro-

tection of children, adoption and probation services. It gives grants for group welfare services including voluntary schemes. A form of pension is granted to aged residents with less than £300 annual income.

Education

In 1970 there were about 700,000 pupils at primary schools and 52,000 at secondary schools. There are teacher training colleges and technical colleges and the University of Zambia accepted its first students in 1966 and in 1972 had over 2,000. Agricultural research for Central Africa is centred at Mount Makulu near Lusaka, while veterinary research is carried on at Mazabuka Research Station. English is to become the medium of instruction in all schools.

Tourism

The numerous lakes, Victoria Falls, Kafue and Luangwa Valley game reserves, as well as the climate, attract an ever-increasing tourist traffic. Game-watching, camping, fishing and water-sports are available, while there are a number of excellent hotels and motels. In 1971 and 1972 over 60,000 tourists visited Zambia.

Visas are not required to visit Zambia by nationals of Commonwealth countries and the Republic of Ireland.

Sport

There are facilities for almost every kind of sport in Zambia. Athletic and football events are the subject of keen interest and competition. Many touring teams visit Lusaka.

Public Holidays

1974: August 12th (Youth Day), October 24th (Independence Day), December 25th (Christmas Day), December 26th (Boxing Day).

1975: January 1st (New Year's Day), March 28th–31st (Easter), May 1st (Labour Day), May 19th (Whit Monday), May 26th (Africa Freedom Day), July 7th (Heroes' Day), July 8th (Unity Day).

Weights and Measures

The metric system is in use.

Currency and Exchange Rates

100 ngwee—1 Zambian kwacha (K).

Exchange rates (April 1974):

£1 sterling=1.516 kwacha;
U.S. $1=64.3 ngwee.

STATISTICAL SURVEY

AREA AND POPULATION

AREA (sq. miles)	ESTIMATED POPULATION (June 30th, 1972)		
	Total	African	Others
290,586	4,515,000	4,457,000	58,000

Estimated Population (1973): 4,635,000.

Population (1969 Census): 4,056,995.

LAND DISTRIBUTION
(1968—'000 acres)

State Land	11,726
Freehold and Leasehold . . .	6,172
Townships	205
Protected Forest Areas and Forest Reserves	2,512
Under Tribal Occupation . . .	1,408
Inundated by Water . . .	375
Unalienated	1,053
Reserves	35,656
Trust Land	107,363
Western Province . . .	31,231
TOTAL	185,975

CHIEF TOWNS
(POPULATION 1973 ESTIMATE)

Lusaka (capital) .	381,000	Mufulira . .	130,000
Kitwe (incl. Kalulushi)	311,000	Luanshya . .	116,000
Ndola . .	216,000	Kabwe (Broken Hill)	89,000
Chingola (incl. Chilila-bombwe, formerly (Bancroft) .	194,000	Livingstone . .	54,000

Births and Deaths: Average annual birth rate 49.8 per 1,000; death rate 20.7 per 1,000 (UN estimates for 1965–70).

EMPLOYMENT
(1971)

	AFRICANS	OTHERS
Agriculture, Forestry and Fisheries	38,740	580
Mining and Quarrying .	52,800	5,360
Manufacturing . . .	39,020	3,000
Construction . . .	63,140	2,730
Electricity and Water .	3,590	450
Distribution and Catering .	33,350	4,580
Transport and Communications .	21,010	1,570
Business Services . .	8,610	1,950
Community and Social Services .	78,740	6,320
TOTAL . .	339,000	26,540

AGRICULTURE
LAND USE, 1962
('000 hectares)

Arable and Under Permanent Crops . .	4,800
Permanent Meadows and Pastures . .	33,800
Forest Land	34,000
Other Areas	2,661
TOTAL	75,261

Source: FAO, *Production Yearbook.*

PRINCIPAL CROPS
(metric tons)

	1968	1969	1970	1971
Maize	590,000*	655,000*	550,000*	750,000*
Millet and Sorghum .	260,000*	280,000*	250,000*	250,000*
Sugar Cane† . .	183,000	180,000	350,000*	322,000
Potatoes . .	2,000*	3,000	3,000	3,000*
Sweet Potatoes and Yams	13,000*	13,000*	13,000*	n.a.
Cassava (Manioc) .	145,000	145,000	143,000	145,000*
Groundnuts (in shell) .	47,000	62,000	42,000	103,000
Cottonseed . .	3,000	5,000	5,000	5,000
Cotton (Lint) . .	1,000	3,000	2,000	3,000
Tobacco . . .	6,700	5,300	5,100	6,500

* FAO estimate.   † Crop year ending in year stated.
Source: FAO, *Production Yearbook 1971.*

TOBACCO

	Unit	1970	1971	1972
Virginia Flue-cured:				
Crop sold	'ooo lb.	10,571	13,745	12,196
Value	K'ooo	3,001	4,306	4,145
Burley:				
Crop sold	'ooo lb.	561	855	848
Value	K'ooo	143	218	221
Turkish:				
Crop sold	'ooo lb.	19	10	n.a.
Value	K'ooo	4	2	n.a.

LIVESTOCK
FAO estimates ('ooo)

	1968–69	1969–70	1970–71
Cattle . . .	1,519*	1,550	1,600
Sheep . . .	29	28	28
Goats . . .	175	180	185
Pigs . . .	96	100	105
Poultry . . .	6,700	6,800	6,900

* Official estimate.

Source: FAO, *Production Yearbook 1971.*

LIVESTOCK PRODUCTS
(FAO estimates—metric tons)

	1968	1969	1970	1971
Cows' Milk	65,000	68,000	70,000	72,000
Beef and Veal*	23,000	24,000	27,000	27,000
Pork*	4,000	5,000	5,000	5,000
Poultry Meat	8,000	9,000	10,000	n.a.
Edible Offal	4,400	4,400	4,400	n.a.
Hen Eggs	7,300	8,000	8,400	8,700
Cattle Hides	4,221	4,423	4,893	n.a.
Sheep Skins	19	19	19	n.a.
Goat Skins	153	159	162	n.a.

Butter and Cheese: No recorded production since 1967.

* Meat from indigenous animals only, including the meat equivalent of exported live animals.

Source: FAO, *Production Yearbook 1971.*

FORESTRY
(cubic metres)

ROUNDWOOD REMOVALS		SAWNWOOD PRODUCTION	
1968 . .	4,022,000	1968 . .	45,000
1969 . .	4,008,000	1969 . .	45,000
1970 . .	4,747,000	1970 . .	40,000
1971 . .	4,931,000	1971 . .	23,000

Source: FAO, *Yearbook of Forest Products.*

FISHING
(inland waters)

	1968	1969	1970	1971
Total Catch (metric tons) . . .	41,300	44,000	48,400	39,300
Value of Landings ('000 kwacha) . .	2,358	2,400	3,000	n.a.

Source: FAO, *Yearbook of Fishery Statistics 1971*.

MINING
(metric tons)

	1969	1970	1971
Coal . . .	397,400	623,200	812,100
Cobalt Ore . .	1,811	2,400	2,080
Copper Ore* . .	719,467	684,064	651,396
Lead Ore . .	22,900	32,600	30,800
Silver† . .	42.8	47.6	n.a.
Tin Concentrates .	24	24	24
Zinc Ore* . .	68,160	65,800	68,700
Gold (kg.) . .	282	364	307

Gypsum: 1,075 metric tons in 1968.
Manganese: 13,444 metric tons in 1968.

* Figures relate to the content of concentrates.
† Recovery from refinery slimes.

Source: mainly United Nations, *The Growth of World Industry*.

1972 (metric tons): Coal 936,500; Cobalt 2,055; Copper 718,000; Tin 24; Zinc 75,600.

1973 (metric tons): Coal 940,100; Cobalt 1,929; Copper 706,600; Zinc 53,500.

INDUSTRY
SELECTED COMMODITIES
(metric tons)

	1970	1971	1972
Raw Sugar .	40,000	42,000	n.a.
Sulphuric Acid .	15,000	n.a.	n.a.
Cement . .	179,000	471,000	n.a.
Copper (unwrought):			
Smelter* .	683,371	633,450	698,000
Refined .	580,127	534,600	614,400
Lead (primary) .	27,205	27,700	25,900
Zinc (primary) .	53,456	57,000	55,900
Cobalt Metal .	2,052	2,079	2,055
Electric Energy (million kWh.)† .	949	1,168	n.a.

* Including some production at the refined stage.
† Net production, i.e. excluding station use.

Source: mainly Central Statistical Board, *Monthly Digest of Statistics*.

FINANCE

100 ngwee=1 Zambian kwacha (K).
Coins: 1, 2, 5, 10 and 20 ngwee.
Notes: 50 ngwee; 1, 2, 10 and 20 kwacha.
Exchange rates (April 1974): £1 sterling=1.516 kwacha; U.S. $1=64.3 ngwee.
100 Zambian kwacha=£65.98=$155.56.

BUDGET
(K million)

Revenue	1972	1973	Expenditure	1972	1973
Recurrent Revenue:			Development and Finance, National		
Company and Income Tax .	119.2	132.0	Guidance and Development		
Customs and Excise . .	99.0	98.5	Planning . . .	15.8	40.6
Mineral Royalties and Copper			Zambia Police . . .	15.9	16.7
Export Tax . . .	27.7	91.3	Provincial and Local Government .	8.0	7.5
Interest	0.9	0.7	Trade, Industry and Mines . .	8.4	13.0
			Health	25.8	28.3
			Power, Transport and Works .	29.7	28.2
			Education	60.9	65.6
			Rural Development . .	37.5	40.6
			Constitutional and Statutory .	129.5	119.6
Total (incl. others) . . .	315.2	384.9	Total (incl. others) . . .	350.3	394.3

Budget (1974): Estimated Revenue K499.7 million; Estimated Expenditure K436 million.

ZAMBIA—(Statistical Survey)

SECOND NATIONAL DEVELOPMENT PLAN
1972–76

	K million
Economic Facilities, Transport . . .	716.5
Industrial, Mining Development . .	655.0
Social Facilities	314.9
Education	117.5
Agriculture and Lands . . .	152.5
Total	1,956.4

Currency in Circulation (December 31st, 1973): 69,396,000 kwacha.

CONSUMER PRICE INDEX

	High Income Group		Low Income Group	
	All Items	Food	All Items	Food
1970 . .	105.0	103.0	102.6	102.1
1971 . .	110.9	109.4	108.8	108.8
1972 . .	118.3	118.7	114.5	113.8
1973 . .	126.0	127.4	121.2	120.4

GROSS DOMESTIC PRODUCT BY KIND OF ECONOMIC ACTIVITY
(K million)

	1970	1971*	1972*
Agriculture, Forestry and Fishing . . .	85.4	100.6	112.5
Mining and Quarrying	436.6	268.6	296.0
Manufacturing	127.4	143.6	164.5
Electricity, Gas and Water . . .	15.5	17.8	38.0
Construction	82.3	90.5	99.5
Wholesale and Retail Trade, Restaurants and Hotels	130.1	130.5	132.5
Transport, Storage and Communications .	52.0	70.0	78.5
Financial Institutions and Insurance .	41.8	45.0	46.0
Property	37.3	36.3	37.0
Business Services	16.7	17.5	18.0
Public Administration and Defence .	62.6	71.7	74.2
Education	40.4	49.2	53.8
Health Services	13.3	21.0	21.5
Other Services	28.4	27.6	25.0
All Industries	1,169.9	1,089.9	1,197.0
Import Duties	32.1	36.7	41.8
Less Imputed Bank Service Charge .	16.7	20.4	21.0
Gross Domestic Product . . .	1,185.3	1,106.2	1,217.8
of which:			
National Income (at market prices) .	1,029.5	1,012.2	1,029.5

* Provisional.

Source: Central Statistical Office, *Monthly Digest of Statistics.*

BALANCE OF PAYMENTS
(K million)

	1971			1972†		
	Credit	Debit	Balance	Credit	Debit	Balance
Goods, Services and Transfer Payments:						
Merchandise f.o.b. . . .	479.2	401.3	77.9	547.9	405.4	142.5
Travel, transport, freight, insurance .	16.2	97.3	− 81.1	18.3	109.5	− 91.2
Investment income . . .	22.3	65.9	− 43.6	13.6	64.6	− 51.0
Government and other services .	5.2	27.1	− 21.9	9.6	30.5	− 20.9
Private transfer payments .	2.0	110.6	−108.6	2.0	99.5	− 97.5
Government transfer payments .	1.9	1.1	0.8	3.0	2.5	0.5
Total	526.8	703.3	−176.5	594.4	712.0	−117.6
Capital Transactions:						
Private	111.2	142.7	− 31.5	—	—	—
Government . . .	43.0	—	43.0	—	—	—
Monetary movements* . .	179.2	7.6	171.6	93.9	—	93.9
Net Errors and Omissions . .	—	47.0	− 47.0	—	—	—

* Includes foreign government securities held by the Zambian Government and reserve position in the IMF.
† Provisional.

EXTERNAL TRADE
(K'000)

	1967	1968	1969	1970	1971	1972	1973
Imports . . .	306,350	325,184	311,797	340,711	399,274	402,471	340,561
Exports . . .	470,009	544,415	766,489	714,964	485,177	541,564	742,414

COMMODITIES
(K'000)

IMPORTS	1971	1972	1973	EXPORTS	1971	1972	1973
Food	48,193	37,138	24,026	Copper	450,200	490,900	699,000
Beverages and Tobacco .	1,417	1,250	1,039	Zinc	11,507	16,368	16,751
Crude Materials, inedible .	7,629	7,943	5,420	Lead	4,557	5,596	5,412
Mineral Fuels, Lubricants				Cobalt	4,125	8,590	4,797
and Related Materials .	32,235	26,523	24,448	Tobacco	3,512	2,737	4,756
Animal and Vegetable Oils				Timber	423	100	—
and Fats . . .	4,516	3,907	4,282	Others	5,687	11,752	7,602
Chemicals . . .	31,688	33,041	35,949	Re-exports . . .	5,166	5,521	4,096
Basic Manufactures .	84,786	87,918	78,078				
Machinery and Transport .	160,115	168,009	140,119				
Miscellaneous . . .	27,257	35,377	25,505				
Others . . .	1,448	1,365	1,695				
Total . . .	399,274	402,471	340,561	Total . . .	485,177	541,564	742,414

PRINCIPAL COUNTRIES
(K'000)

IMPORTS		1970	1971	1972	EXPORTS		1970	1971	1972
EEC†	. . .	43,868	59,570	61,564	EEC†	. . .	227,249	148,403	170,917
Germany, Fed. Rep.	.	16,478	17,558	21,539	Germany, Fed. Rep.	.	84,151	45,520	45,505
EFTA*†	. .	14,465	15,066	15,547	EFTA*†	. .	38,641	29,154	28,647
Soviet Bloc†	. .	6,217	3,358	6,048	Soviet Bloc†	. .	4,636	1,279	2,606
Latin America†	. .	1,098	2,267	643	Latin America†	. .	7,266	13,898	33,637
Japan	. . .	21,809	26,833	38,843	Japan	. . .	166,459	99,669	110,608
Other Asian Countries	.	25,248	32,415	50,469	Other Asian Countries	.	200,531	131,731	123,299
Rhodesia	. . .	737	21,128	11,558	Rhodesia	. .	20,618	354	1,135
South Africa	. .	59,097	60,891	59,308	South Africa	. .	8,682	10,447	10,804
United Kingdom	.	80,559	97,091	94,867	United Kingdom	.	160,074	79,187	107,650
U.S.A.	. . .	32,902	43,359	35,008	U.S.A.	. . .	1,442	4,557	2,288
TOTAL (incl. others)		340,711	399,282	402,471	TOTAL (incl. others)		714,964	485,177	541,564

* Excluding United Kingdom.
† Provisional.

ROAD MOTOR VEHICLES
(number in use)

	1969	1970	1971
Passenger Cars .	53,800	58,500	61,600
Commercial Vehicles	27,100	30,600	34,100
TOTAL . .	80,900	89,100	95,700

CIVIL AVIATION

	1969	1970	1971	1972
Aircraft arrivals . . .	23,964	22,036	26,836	21,212
Passenger arrivals . .	227,700	256,100	300,400	209,200
Passenger departures .	226,600	256,100	299,600	208,300
Freight loaded (metric tons) .	1,959	1,917	2,538	1,881
Freight unloaded (metric tons) .	6,828	8,242	10,155	5,880

EDUCATION
(1969)

	NUMBER OF INSTITUTIONS	PUPILS			NUMBER OF TEACHERS
		Male	Female	Total	
Primary . . .	2,550	367,986	293,295	661,281	13,569
Secondary . . .	114	32,575	15,582	48,157	2,071
Trades and Technical .	18	444	2	446	n.a.
Teacher Training . .	9	1,340	849	2,189	n.a.
University . . .	1	1,093	205	2,057*	352*

* 1972 figures.

Source: Central Statistical Office, Lusaka.

THE CONSTITUTION

On October 24th, 1964, Northern Rhodesia became an independent Republic within the Commonwealth and adopted the name of Zambia. The Constitution of January 1964 was amended in 1968 and in 1972, when it was officially announced that Zambia would become a one-party participatory democracy. A new Constitution was drawn up and received Presidential assent in August 1973. Its provisions are as follows:

The President: The President of the Republic of Zambia will be Head of State and Commander-in-Chief of the Armed Forces. His powers include the appointment of a Prime Minister, a Secretary-General of the Party, an Attorney General, a Director of Public Prosecutions, a Chief Justice and judges of the Supreme Court. Presidential nominations will not be valid unless they are supported by at least 200 registered voters from each of Zambia's eight provinces. There will be no limitation placed on the length of the term of office of the President. He will be head of the United National Independence Party (UNIP).

The Prime Minister: Appointment will be by the President and the Prime Minister will be the Leader of Government Business. He is to be an ex-officio member of the UNIP Central Committee.

The Secretary-General: He will be appointed by the President and must be an ex-officio member of the Cabinet. He will be responsible for the administration of UNIP.

The Central Committee: The new Constitution provides for a Central Committee for the only legal party, the United National Independence Party (UNIP). It will consist of not more than 25 members, 20 to be elected at the Party's General Conference, held every five years, and three to be nominated by the President. It has more powers than the Cabinet. It is to consist of eight sub-committees, whose members are appointed by the President from among the Central Committee and National Council members. All members must be full-time officials of UNIP's National Headquarters.

The Cabinet: This will be appointed by the President who may nominate non-elected ministers and appoint others from elected members of the National Assembly, in consultation with the Prime Minister. The decision of the Cabinet is to be subordinate to that of the UNIP Central Committee.

Legislature: Parliament will consist of the President and a National Assembly of 125 elected members. The President will have power to nominate up to 10 additional members of the National Assembly. There will be a Speaker and a Deputy Speaker. The normal life of Parliament is five years. To become law, a bill requires Presidential assent.

The House of Chiefs: The Constitution provides for a House of Chiefs numbering 27, four each from the Northern, Western, Southern and Eastern Provinces, three each from the North-Western, Luapula and Central Provinces and two from the Copperbelt Province. It may submit resolutions to be debated by the Assembly and consider those matters referred to it by the President.

Judiciary: The Attorney General will be appointed by the President, in consultation with the Prime Minister, and will be the principal legal adviser to the Government. The President will appoint the Director of Public Prosecutions who must vacate his office when he reaches the age of 60. The Supreme Court of Zambia will be the final Court of Appeal. The Chief Justice and other judges will be appointed by the President. Subsidiary to the Supreme Court will be the High Court which will have unlimited jurisdiction to hear and determine any civil or criminal proceedings under any Zambian law.

Citizenship: The qualifying period for Zambian citizenship will be increased from five to ten years. Every citizen of Zambia who is over the age of 18, and a registered voter, may vote.

Bill of Rights: The Constitution provides for a Bill of Rights in which the fundamental freedoms and rights of the individual are guaranteed. The President has the power to proclaim a State of Emergency at any time when he feels the security of the State is threatened.

THE GOVERNMENT

President: Dr. KENNETH DAVID KAUNDA.

CENTRAL COMMITTEE (UNIP)

(Consisting also of sub-committee heads and members)

Head: President KENNETH DAVID KAUNDA.
Prime Minister: M. MAINZA CHONA.

Secretary-General of UNIP: A. GREY ZULU.
Secretary to the Cabinet: PATRICK CHISANGA.

SUB-COMMITTEE HEADS

Defence and Security: President KENNETH DAVID KAUNDA.
Elections, Publicity and Strategy: SIKOTA WINA.
Economics and Finance: HUMPHREY MULEMBA.
Political, Constitutional, Legal and Foreign Affairs: ELIJAH H. K. MUDENDA.

New Appointments and Discipline: WESLEY P. NYIRENDA.
Social and Cultural: SOLOMON KALULU.
Rural Development: REUBEN KAMANGA.
Youth and Sports: ANDREW MUTEMBA.

MEMBERS

KENNETH KAUNDA, GREY ZULU, MAINZA CHONA, SIKOTA WINA, HUMPHREY MULEMBA, ELIJAH MUDENDA, WESLEY NYIRENDA, SOLOMON KALULU, REUBEN KAMANGA, ANDREW MUTEMBA, JETHRO MUTTI, DANIEL LISULO, SHADRECK SOKO, ALEX SHAPI,

ANANIAS CHONGO, SAMUEL MBILISHI, FINES BULA-WAYO, Mrs. CHIBESA KANKASA, BOB LITANA, STEPHEN SIKOMBE, FRANK CHITAMBALA, Mrs. MARY FULANO, BAUTIS KAPULU, Miss PETRONELLA KAWANDAMI, EDWARD LISO.

THE CABINET

(*May* 1974)

President and Minister of Defence: Dr. KENNETH DAVID KAUNDA.

Prime Minister and Minister of National Guidance and Culture: M. MAINZA CHONA.

Minister of Foreign Affairs: VERNON MWAANGA.

Minister of Local Government and Housing: PETER W. MATOKA.

Minister of Home Affairs: AARON MILNER.

Minister of Power, Transport and Works: ACKSON SOKO.

Minister of Labour and Social Services: HYDEN DINGIS-WAYO BANDA.

Minister of Planning and Finance: ALEXANDER CHIK-WANDA.

Minister of Education: FWANYANGA MULIKITA.

Minister of Rural Development: PAUL LUSAKA.

Minister of Lands, Natural Resources and Tourism: Dr. NEPHAS S. MULENGA.

Minister of Mines and Industry: ANDREW KASHITA.

Minister of Legal Affairs and Attorney-General: ANNEL M. SILUNGWE.

Minister of Health: Dr. (Mrs.) MUTUMBA BULL.

Minister of Commerce: RAJAH KUNDA.

Minister of Information and Broadcasting: C. M. MWANAN-SHIKU.

Ministers of State for Defence: Maj.-Gen. G. K. CHINKULI, Air Commodore PETER ZUZE.

MINISTERS FOR PROVINCES

Eastern Province: WILLIAM NKANZA.

Central Province: FINE LIBOMA.

Copperbelt Province: ACKSON CHALIKULIMA.

Western Province: JOSEPHAT B. SIYOMUNJI.

Luapula Province: BASIL KABWE.

Southern Province: WILLIE MWONDELA.

North-Western Province: AMOCK PHIRI.

Northern Province: UNIA G. MWILA.

DIPLOMATIC REPRESENTATION

EMBASSIES AND HIGH COMMISSIONS ACCREDITED TO ZAMBIA

(In Lusaka, unless otherwise stated)

(HC) High Commission.

Algeria: Dar es Salaam, Tanzania.

Australia: Dar es Salaam, Tanzania (HC).

Austria: Nairobi, Kenya.

Belgium: Leopard's Hill Rd., P.O.B. 1204; *Ambassador:* H. EDGAR VERHILLE.

Botswana: 2647 Haile Sellassie Ave., P.O.B. 1910 (HC); *High Commissioner:* E. M. ONTUMETSE.

Brazil: Nairobi, Kenya.

Bulgaria: Dar es Salaam, Tanzania.

Burundi: Dar es Salaam, Tanzania.

Cameroon: Addis Ababa, Ethiopia.

Canada: North End Branch, Barclays Bank, Cairo Rd., P.O.B. 1313 (HC); *High Commissioner:* ARTHUR F. BROADBRIDGE.

China, People's Republic: 19 Leopard's Hill Rd., Kabulonga, P.O.B. 1975; *Ambassador:* LI CHIANG-FEN.

Cuba: Dar es Salaam, Tanzania.

Czechoslovakia: 2278 Independence Ave., P.O.B. 59; *Ambassador:* STANISLAV KOHOUSEK.

Denmark: 352 Independence Ave., P.O.B. RW299; *Ambassador:* HANS KUNHE.

Egypt: Plot 5206, United Nations Ave., P.O.B. 2428; *Ambassador:* AHMED SALEH EL-ZAHID.

Ethiopia: Nairobi, Kenya.

Finland: Dar es Salaam, Tanzania.

France: Unity House, Cnr. of Katunjila Rd. and Freedom Way, P.O.B. 62; *Ambassador:* Comte GÉRARD DE LA VILLESBRUNNE.

Germany, Federal Republic: 350 Independence Ave., P.O.B. RW120; *Ambassador:* Dr. FRIEDRICH LANDAU.

Ghana: Nairobi, Kenya (HC).

Guinea: Dar es Salaam, Tanzania.

Guyana: Design House, 2 Dar es Salaam Place, P.O.B. 3889 (HC); *High Commissioner:* F. R. WILLS.

Hungary: Dar es Salaam, Tanzania.

India: Anchor House, Lusaka Square, P.O.B. 2111 (HC); *High Commissioner:* A. M. THOMAS.

Italy: Woodgate House, Nairobi Place, Cairo Rd., P.O.B. 1046; *Ambassador:* Dr. GIROLAMO TROTTA.

Ivory Coast: Kinshasa, Zaire.

Jamaica: Addis Ababa, Ethiopia (HC).

Japan: 342 Independence Ave., P.O.B. 3390; *Ambassador:* NOBUYASU NISHIMIYA.

Kenya: Kafue House, Nairobi Place, Cairo Rd., P.O.B. 3651 (HC); *High Commissioner:* E. K. MUGOLA.

Korea, Republic: 28 Joseph Mwilwa Rd., Fairview, P.O.B. 3230; *Ambassador:* JONG SONG GYU.

Liberia: Nairobi, Kenya.

Malawi: Woodgate House, Cairo Rd., P.O.B. RW425 (HC); *High Commissioner:* CALLISTO MATEKENYA MKONA.

Netherlands: 5028 United Nations Ave., P.O.B. 1905; *Ambassador:* Jonkheer Dr. M. A. BEELAERTS.

Nigeria: Zambia Bible House, Freedom Way, P.O.B. 2598 (HC); *High Commissioner:* LAWRENCE APALARA FABUNMI.

Norway: Nairobi, Kenya.

Pakistan: Dar es Salaam, Tanzania.

Poland: Dar es Salaam, Tanzania.

Romania: 2 Leopard's Hill Rd., Kabulonga, P.O.B. 1944; *Ambassador:* AUREL ARDELEANU.

Senegal: Addis Ababa, Ethiopia.

Sierra Leone: Addis Ababa, Ethiopia.

Somalia: Farm 913/377A Kabulonga Rd., P.O.B. 3251; *Chargé d'Affaires:* BASIL M. SUFI.

Spain: Dar es Salaam, Tanzania.

Sri Lanka: Nairobi, Kenya (HC).

Sudan: Nairobi, Kenya.

Swaziland: Nairobi, Kenya (HC).

Sweden: Anchor House, Cairo Rd., P.O.B. 788; *Ambassador:* FRITZ IWO DOLLING.

Switzerland: Dar es Salaam, Tanzania.

Syria: Dar es Salaam, Tanzania.

Tanzania: Ujaama House, Plot 5200 United Nations Ave., P.O.B. 1219 (HC); *High Commissioner:* OBED MBOGO KATIKAZA.

Trinidad and Tobago: Addis Ababa, Ethiopia (HC).

Turkey: Nairobi, Kenya.

U.S.S.R.: 2 Shakespeare Court, Ituna Rd., P.O.B. 2355; *Ambassador:* D. Z. BELOKOS.

United Kingdom: Stand No. 5210, Independence Ave., P.O.B. RW50 (HC); *High Commissioner:* J. S. R. DUNCAN.

U.S.A.: Cnr. of Independence and United Nations Ave., P.O.B. 1617; *Ambassador:* Miss JEAN MARY WILKOWSKI.

Vatican City: Brentwood Drive, P.O.B. 1445 (Apostolic Nunciature); *Apostolic Pro-Nuncio:* Archbishop LUCIANO ANGELONI.

Yugoslavia: Plot 5216, off Independence Ave., P.O.B. 1180; *Ambassador:* DJURO VUKOLIC.

Zaire: Plot 1124, Parirenyatwa St., P.O.B. 1287; *Ambassador:* BANDE LARITY NYARENDE.

Zambia also has diplomatic relations with the German Democratic Republic, Ireland, Madagascar and Togo.

PARLIAMENT

NATIONAL ASSEMBLY

Following the establishment of a one-party state with UNIP as the sole party, all M.P.s have to be members of UNIP. Elections under the new one-party system were held in December 1973. Elections were held in two stages; in the first stage party cadres elected up to three UNIP members. In the second stage the electorate as a whole had to choose between the candidates thus selected. In the new parliament there are 125 elected members, ten members nominated by the President, and the Speaker.

Speaker: ROBINSON NABULYATO.

(Elections, December 1968)

PARTY	SEATS
United National Independence Party (UNIP) .	81
African National Congress	23
Independent	1
Nominated	5

HOUSE OF CHIEFS

There are 27 Chiefs, four from the Northern, Western, Southern and Eastern Provinces, three from the North-Western, Luapula and Central Provinces, two from the Copperbelt province.

POLITICAL PARTIES

United National Independence Party (UNIP): f. 1959; the only legal party in Zambia since the proclamation of a one-party state in December 1972; Leader Dr. KENNETH KAUNDA; Gen. Sec. M. MAINZA CHONA.

The following political parties existed before December 1972:

The African National Congress: f. 1944; Leader HARRY NKUMBULA (now assimilated in UNIP after unsuccessfully opposing the creation of a one-party state).

The United Progressive Party: Pres. SIMON KAPWEPWE (now disbanded).

JUDICIAL SYSTEM

The law is administered in Zambia by a High Court, consisting of a Chief Justice and five Puisne Judges. Resident Magistrates' Courts are also established at various centres. The Local Courts deal mainly with customary law, though they have certain statutory powers in addition. A Zambian Court of Appeal was set up early in 1964. Under the new Constitution of August 1973 a Supreme Court will be the highest Court in Zambia and will serve as the high court of appeal and the right of appeal to the Privy Council was abolished in September 1973.

Chief Justice: The Hon. Justice BRIAN DOYLE.

Puisne Judges: Mr. Justice PICKETT, Mr. Justice RAMSAY, Mr. Justice EVANS, Mr. Justice MAGNUS, Mr. Justice GODFREY MUWO.

Justice of Appeal: (vacant).

Registrar of the High Court: J. J. HUGHES.

RELIGION

United Church of Zambia: Synod Headquarters, P.O.B. RW 122, Lusaka; f. 1965; Pres. Rev. J. MWAPE; Gen. Sec. D. M. MUSUNSA.

ANGLICANS
PROVINCE OF CENTRAL AFRICA

Archbishop of Central Africa: Most Rev. DONALD S. ARDEN, Kasupe, Malawi.

ROMAN CATHOLICS

Roman Catholic Church: P.O.B. RW 3, Lusaka; f. 1897; publs. *Cengelo*, *The Sun*.

METROPOLITAN ARCHBISHOPS

Lusaka: Most Rev. EMMANUEL MILINGO, P.O.B. RW3, Lusaka.

Kasama: Most Rev. ELIAS MUTALE, P.O.B. 66.

Salvation Army: Work in Zambia under control of Command H.Q.; P.O.B. RW 193, Lusaka; Social Service Centre: P.O.B. 75, Ndola; runs Chikankata hospital Leprosarium and Chikankata Secondary School, Caanga Clinic and a training college in Lusaka.

Watchtower Bible and Tract Society (Jehovah's Witnesses): P.O.B. 1598, Kitwe; 57,000 active members and about 100,000 adherents in Zambia where the proportion of witnesses to the total population is higher than in any other country.

Muslims: There are about 6,000 members of the Muslim Association in Zambia, and these include a number of Africans.

Baha'i: Headquarters P.O.B. 2319, Lusaka; 383 centres in Zambia.

THE PRESS

DAILY

Times of Zambia, The: P.O.B. 394, Lusaka; f. 1943; English; Editor MULIMO PUNABANTU; circ. 49,000.

Zambia Daily Mail: P.O.B. 1421, Lusaka; f. 1968; Editor-in-Chief VINCENT MIJONI; Man. Editor ALAN WATERIDGE; owned by government-controlled Zambia Publishing Co., Ltd.; circ. 25,000.

PERIODICALS

African Social Research: P.O.B. 900, Institute for African Studies, University of Zambia, Lusaka.

Farming in Zambia: P.O.B. RW 197, Lusaka; publ. by Ministry of Rural Development for commercial farmers; quarterly; Editor D. C. MARSHALL.

Icengelo: Chifuba Rd., P.O.B. 1581, Ndola; f. 1970; Bemba; monthly; published by the Franciscan Fathers; Editor Fr. ALEXANDER RICCIARELLI; circ. 8,500 (Oct. 1973).

Imbila: P.O.B. 1520, Ndola; Bemba; circ. 27,000.

Intanda: P.O.B. 182, Livingstone; f. 1958; general; fortnightly; published by Zambia Information Services; Chitonga; circ. 7,500.

Liseli: P.O.B. 80, Mongu; publ. by Zambia Information Services; Lozi; fortnightly.

Lukanga: P.O.B. 919, Kabwe; publ. by Zambia Information Services; Bemba, Lenje and Tonga; fortnightly.

Ngoma: P.O.B. 38, Solwezi; Lunda, Luvale, Kaonde; fortnightly.

Sun: Roman Catholic magazine; P.O.B. 8067, Lusaka; Editor SEÁN O'CONNOR.

Sunday Times of Zambia: P.O.B. 394, Lusaka; f. 1965; Sundays; English; Editor-in-Chief MULIMO PUNABANTU; circ. 41,750.

Tsopano (*Now*): P.O.B. 202, Chipata; f. 1958; fortnightly; published by Zambia Information Services; Nyanja; circ. 12,000.

Z.: P.O.B. RW 20, Lusaka; f. 1969; English; monthly; published by Zambia Information Services; Editor D. SIMPSON; circ. 10,000.

Zambia Government Gazette: P.O.B. 136, Lusaka; f. 1911; English; weekly; printed by Government Printer J. E. HARPER.

Zambia Law Journal: P.O.B. 2379, University of Zambia, Lusaka; publ. by School of Law at University of Zambia; Gen. Editor, Prof of Law.

Zambia Motor News: P.O.B. 717, Ndola; monthly.

Zambia Museum Journal: P.O.B. 498, Livingstone; f. 1970; yearly; Editor JOSEPH O. VOGEL, Livingstone Museum.

Zambian Review: P.O.B. 837, Ndola; monthly.

PRESS AGENCIES

Agence France-Presse: P.O.B. RW 157, Lusaka.

FOREIGN BUREAUX

D.P.A. and Reuters have bureaux in Lusaka.

PUBLISHERS

Directory Publications of Zambia Ltd.: P.O.B. 1659, Ndola.

Government Printer: P.O.B. 136, Lusaka; publisher of all official documents including statistical bulletins, laws, parliamentary debates, etc.

Ministry of Lands and Natural Resources: Survey Department, P.O.B. RW 397, Lusaka; publishers of atlases and maps of Zambia.

Multimedia Zambia: P.O.B. 8002, Woodlands, Lusaka; the communications organization of the Christian Council of Zambia; secular and religious material.

National Educational Publishing Company of Zambia (NECZAM): P.O.B. 2664, Lusaka; f. 1967; educational and general works; Gen. Man. S. D. Allison; Editor C. H. Chirwa.

Oxford University Press: P.O.B. 2335, Lusaka.

Zambia Information Services: Ministry of Information, Broadcasting and Tourism, P.O.B. RW 20, Lusaka.

Zambia Publishing Company Ltd.: P.O.B. 1059, Lusaka; f. 1960; publs. include *Zambia Daily Mail*; Man. Dir. Alan Wateridge.

University of Zambia: Publications Office, Institute for African Studies, P.O.B. 900, Lusaka; academic books, papers and journals.

RADIO AND TELEVISION

Zambia Broadcasting Services: P.O.B. RW 15, Ridgeway, Lusaka; P.O.B. 748, Kitwe; f. 1966; government controlled; manages sound broadcasting and television services; services in English and seven Zambian languages; Deputy Dir. Asaf Mvula.

In 1973 there were an estimated 260,000 radio receivers.

Television Zambia: P.O.B. RW 15, Ridgeway, Lusaka; P.O.B. 1106, Kitwe; programme contractors; Controller Neb Jere; taken over by the government in 1967.

In 1973 there were an estimated 22,500 television receivers.

Educational Broadcasting Unit: Headquarters: P.O.B. RW 231, Lusaka; radio broadcasts from Lusaka studies; television for schools from P.O.B. 1106, Kitwe; Controller of Educational Broadcasting and Television Wilfred Chilangwa.

FINANCE

Originally, in November 1970, it was announced that the Zambian Government was to take a majority interest in all banks operating in Zambia, and was to take over completely building society and insurance operations. However, the banking proposals were later modified, so that only the already state-owned National Commercial Bank Ltd., together with the Commercial Bank of Zambia Ltd., have the Government as majority shareholder, through FINDECO. The foreign-owned banks have had to become incorporated in Zambia, as from January 1st, 1972. In addition, capitalization of banks has to consist of not less than K500,000 in the case of any commercial bank wholly or partly owned by the Government and not less than K2 million in the case of any other commercial bank. Furthermore, at least half the directors of these latter banks have to be established residents of Zambia.

State Finance and Development Corporation (FINDECO): P.O.B. 1930, Lusaka; f. 1971; responsible for Zambia's state banking, investment, insurance, building society and industrial financing interests; authorized cap. K50 million; Chair. Minister of Finance.

Up to April 1972, FINDECO financed the Zambianization of small businesses, and now aims at encouraging import substitution, earning foreign exchange and creating employment. FINDECO has successfully financed Zambia's economic reforms and has facilitated the takeover by Zambians of small industrial and commercial activities in the Republic. FINDECO's new financial policy is one of encouraging the promotion of industries orientated to import substitution, foreign exchange earning and employment creation. With this in view, FINDECO has embarked on an ambitious rural ramification programme to promote rapid diversification of the rural economy.

BANKING
(cap.=capital; dep.=deposits)

Bank of Zambia: P.O.B. 80, Lusaka; f. 1964; central bank; cap. p.u. K2m., dep. K68.1m. (June 1973); Gov. B. R. Kuwani.

COMMERCIAL BANKS

Commercial Bank of Zambia Ltd.: P.O.B. 2555, Lusaka; f. 1965; auth. cap. K2m., p.u. K500,000, dep. K30m. (June 1973); brs. at Kitwe, Livingstone, Lusaka (2) and Ndola; Man. Dir. D. D. Speirs; Gen. Man. R. N. F. Fowler.

National Commercial Bank Ltd.: P.O.B. 2811, Lusaka; f. 1969; cap. p.u. K2m., dep. K57m.; 4 brs. at Lusaka (2), Ndola and Kitwe; Chair. G. M. Mukonge; Gen. Man. L. M. Nyambe.

National Savings and Credit Bank.

FOREIGN BANKS

Barclays Bank of Zambia Ltd.: Head Office: P.O.B. 1936, Lusaka; mem. of the Barclays Group; cap. p.u. K2m., dep. K119.6m.; Chair. and Man. Dir. J. H. C. Whicker; Gen. Man. K. H. Dickenson; 23 brs. and 17 subsidiary offices.

Grindlays Bank International (Zambia) Ltd.: Head Office: Woodgate House, Cairo Rd., P.O.B. 1955, Lusaka; fully owned subsidiary of National and Grindlays Bank Ltd., London; cap. p.u. K2m., dep. K25.3m.; nine brs., at Chingola, Kabwe, Kafue, Kitwe, Lusaka (2), Mkushi, Mufulira and Ndola; Chair. A. N. L. Wina; Gen. Man. H. Brown.

Standard Bank Zambia Ltd.: Head Office: Standard House, Cairo Rd., P.O.B. 2238, Lusaka; cap. p.u. K2m., dep. K118.6m.; 22 brs. in all main towns; Man. Dir. D. W. Bloxam.

DEVELOPMENT BANK

Development Bank of Zambia: f. 1974; 60 per cent Zambian government participation; to provide medium and long term loans and offer consultancy and research services to the business community.

INSURANCE

Zambia State Insurance Corporation Ltd.: 1st Floor, Kafue House, Cairo Rd., P.O.B. 894, Lusaka; took over all insurance transactions in Zambia on January 1st, 1972.

TRADE AND INDUSTRY
CHAMBERS OF COMMERCE

Chingola Chamber of Commerce and Industry: P.O.B. 1216, Chingola.

Kabwe Chamber of Commerce and Industry: P.O.B. 132, Kabwe.

Kitwe and District Chamber of Commerce and Industry: Zambia State Ins. Bld., Room 510, P.O.B. 672, Kitwe; 160 mems.; Sec. D. D. Trent.

Livingstone Chamber of Commerce and Industry: Livingstone; f. 1920; approx. 90 mems.; Pres. D. D. Steyn; Sec. Mrs. O. S. Woods.

Luanshya Chamber of Commerce and Industry: P.O.B. 47, Luanshya.

Lusaka Chamber of Commerce and Industry: P.O.B. 844, Lusaka; 200 mems.; Chair. G. J. Austin; Sec. L. R. Edwards.

Ndola and District Chamber of Commerce and Industry: P.O.B. 6041; f. 1930; 136 mems.; Pres. P. J. Redfern; Sec. I. K. Mehta.

INDUSTRIAL AND COMMERCIAL ASSOCIATIONS

Commercial Farmers' Bureau of Zambia: P.O.B. 395, Lusaka; 453 mems.; Pres. A. R. B. Landless; Sec. Mrs. E. M. M. Saunders.

Copper Industry Service Bureau Ltd.: P.O.B. 2100, Kitwe; formerly Chamber of Mines; f. 1941.

Zambian Industrial and Commercial Association: P.O.B. 844, Lusaka; 800 mems.; Chair. G. J. Austin; Sec. L. R. Edwards.

STATUTORY ORGANIZATIONS
Industry

Industrial Development Corporation of Zambia Ltd. (INDECO): P.O.B. 1935, Lusaka; f. 1960; auth. cap. K100m.; initiates and operates industrial projects, controls about 50 subsidiaries and associated companies dealing in brewing, chemicals, property, manufacturing; re-organized under the Ministry of Industry and Mining in 1974; Chair. Andrew Kashita.

Consumer Buying Corporation of Zambia Ltd.: P.O.B. 2162, Ndola; f. 1968; partially owned subsidiary of INDECO; undertakes retail trade; took over the Booker Group shops and stores 1968; Bookers (Zambia) Ltd. provide management services.

Mining and Development Corporation Ltd. (MINDECO): P.O.B. 90, Lusaka; controls administration of mines, handles other industrial projects; Chair. Andrew Kashita, m.p.; Man. Dir. B. C. Mulaisho.

National Import and Export Corporation: f. 1974.

Zambia Industrial and Mining Corporation (ZIMCO): P.O.B. 1935, Lusaka; established by government to hold its mining and industrial portfolio; holds 51 per cent of shares in all mining enterprises; Chair. President Kenneth Kaunda; operates through INDECO, FINDECO, NTC, NHC and MINDECO which are wholly-owned subsidiaries.

Agriculture

Cold Storage Board: P.O.B. 1915, Lusaka; Gen. Man. S. N. E. Chembe.

Dairy Produce Board: P.O.B. 124, Lusaka; major importer and distributor of dairy produce in Zambia.

Department of Community Development: P.O.B. 1958, Lusaka; under Ministry of Rural Development.

Department of Co-operatives: P.O.B. 1229, Lusaka; Dir. S. B. Mwamba; under Ministry of Rural Development.

National Agricultural Marketing Board of Zambia: P.O.B. 122, Lusaka.

Rural Development Corporation of Zambia Ltd.: P.O.B. 1957, Lusaka; f. 1969; formerly The Agricultural Development Corporation of Zambia Ltd., f. 1968; cap. K30m.; Man. Dir. B. P. Kapota.

Tobacco Board: P.O.B. 1963, Lusaka; Exec. Chair. M. J. Lumina.

TRADE UNIONS
(minimum membership, 1,000)

The Civil Servants' Association of Zambia: P.O.B. RW 12, Ridgeway, Lusaka; f. 1919; 1,500 mems.; Chair. G. A. Jarvis; publ. *Newsletter*.

Zambia Congress of Trade Unions: P.O.B. 652, Kitwe; f. 1965; 16 affiliated unions; 141,977 mems.; Pres. N. L. Zimba; Vice-Pres. L. Mulimba; Gen. Sec. B. R. Kabwe.

Principal Affiliates:

Airways and Allied Workers' Union: P.O.B. 272, Lusaka; Pres. M. E. Mwinga; Gen. Sec. S. K. Kongwa.

Hotel Catering Workers' Union of Zambia: P.O.B. 1627, Kitwe; 8,000 mems.; Pres. R. Kasokolo; Gen. Sec. E. J. Banda.

Mine Workers' Union of Zambia: P.O.B. 448, Kitwe; Pres. D. Mwila; Gen. Sec. E. S. Thawe.

National Union of Building, Engineering and General Workers: P.O.B. 1515, Kitwe; 12,000 mems.; Pres. F. Chiluba; Gen. Sec. B. Sitali.

National Union of Commercial and Industrial Workers: 87 Gambia Ave., P.O.B. 1735, Kitwe; 16,000 mems.; Pres. G. B. Zulu; Gen. Sec. J. W. Musonda.

National Union of Plantation and Agricultural Workers: P.O.B. 529, Kabwe; 4,500 mems.; Pres. I. B. Ikowa; Gen. Sec. S. C. Silwimba.

National Union of Postal and Telecommunication Workers: P.O.B. 751, Ndola; 1,300 mems.; Pres. Mr. Sampa; Gen. Sec. G. J. Titima.

National Union of Public Services' Workers: P.O.B. 2523, Lusaka; Gen. Sec. W. H. Mbewe.

National Union of Teachers: P.O.B. 1914, Lusaka; 2,120 mems.; Pres. N. L. Zimba; Gen. Sec. M. Mubita.

National Union of Transport and Allied Workers: P.O.B. 2431, Lusaka; Pres. J. Fulilwa; Gen. Sec. B. Daka.

Zambia Electricity Workers' Union: P.O.B. 859, Ndola; Pres. Mr. Ngoma; Gen. Sec. F. Mwanza.

Zambia Railways Amalgamated Workers' Union: P.O.B. 302, Kabwe; 5,950 mems.; Pres. E. J. Mwansa; Gen. Sec. A. H. Simwanza.

Zambia Typographical Union: P.O.B. 1439, Ndola; Pres. N. Tembo; Gen. Sec. B. M. Zaza.

Zambia Union of Financial Institutions: P.O.B. 1174, Lusaka; Gen. Sec. E. Nkole.

Zambia United Local Authorities Workers' Union: P.O.B. 575, Ndola; Pres. H. Bweupe; Gen. Sec. S. Lungu.

University of Zambia Staff Association: P.O.B. 2379, Lusaka; Pres. M. Mulizwa; Gen. Sec. Mr. Chipote.

Principal Independent Unions:

Zambian African Mining Union: Kitwe; f. 1967; 40,000 mems.

Zambian African Teachers' Association: Lusaka; Pres. M. M. Kaunda.

TRANSPORT

RAILWAYS

Zambia Railways: Head Office: P.O.B. 935, Kabwe; Gen. Man. H. J. FAST.

Total length of railways in Zambia is 1,297 kilometres.

Tanzania-Zambia Railway Authority (TAZARA): Head Office: P.O.B. 2834, Dar es Salaam; Branch Office: P.O.B. 1784, Lusaka; construction work on the 1,860 km. of railway line to link the towns of Dar es Salaam in Tanzania and Kapiri Mposhi, north of Lusaka, began in October 1970 and was scheduled to be completed by 1977 but is likely to be completed at the end of 1974. Track laying was completed to Tunduma on the joint border in August 1973. The Project is receiving technical and financial assistance from the People's Republic of China and costs are estimated at K300 million.

ROADS

There is a total of 34,366 kilometres of which 6,466 are main roads. The main arterial roads run from Beit Bridge to Tunduma (the Great North Road), through the copper mining area to Chingola and Chililabombwe (the Zaire Border Road), from Livingstone to the junction of the Kafue River and the Great North Road, and from Lusaka to the Malawi border (the Great East Road). The border is closed to road traffic at Chirundu (Beit Bridge), Kariba and Livingstone.

National Transport Corporation of Zambia Ltd.: P.O.B. 2607, Lusaka; state-owned freight and passenger transport service; Man. Dir. S. B. KAFUMUKACHE.

Zambia-Tanzania Road Services: P.O.B. 2581, Lusaka; f. 1966; over 1,000 trucks operating between Dar es Salaam, Tunduma (Tanzanian border), the Copperbelt and Lusaka; cap. K4m.

INLAND WATERWAYS

Zambezi River Transport Service Ltd.: P.O.B. 177, Livingstone; operates a passenger and goods service from Livingstone to Senanga. The route is by road to Mambova, thence by barge to Katima Mulilo, and by road to Senanga.

CIVIL AVIATION

A new international airport, 14 miles from Lusaka, was opened in 1967. Ndola airport is undergoing reconstruction.

Zambia Airways Corporation: City Airport, Lusaka, P.O.B. 272; f. 1967; management by Alitalia until 1976; internal services and flights to Kenya, Tanzania, Botswana, Cyprus, Malawi, Mauritius, Italy and U.K.; fleet of one DC-8, two BAC 1-11 and four H.S. 748; Chair. PETER A. SIWO; Man. Dir. SIMON C. KATILUNGU.

National Air Charter: f. 1973; operates air cargo and passenger transportation.

The following foreign airlines serve Zambia: Air Zaire, Air Malawi, Alitalia, Botswana Airways, British Airways, British Caledonian, East African Airways and UTA.

TOURISM

In 1972 61,638 tourists visited Zambia.

Zambia National Tourist Bureau: Century House, Cairo Rd., P.O.B. 17, Lusaka; established a Tour Operations Unit at the beginning of 1968.

National Hotels Corporation Ltd.: P.O.B. 3200/3210 Lusaka; subsidiary of ZIMCO.

UNIVERSITY

The University of Zambia: P.O.B. 2379, Lusaka; f. 1965; 352 teachers, 2,057 students (1972).

INDEX OF TERRITORIES

THE WORLD

Greenland (Den.)

Arctic Circle

Alaska

Greenland (Den.)

Iceland

Canada

Norway   Sweden   Finla

United   Den.   Hamburg
R. of   Kingdom   Berlin
Ireland   Birmingham   Manchester   Germany   Poland
London   NI   Czech
Paris   B   Budapest
France   Sw.   Aust.   Hung.   Romania
Yugo.   Bulgaria
Italy   Ista
Spain   Rome   Alb.
Madrid   Greece
Portugal   Athens   Cyp
Azores   Gibraltar   Malta
(Port.)   Alexandria
Morocco   Libya   Cairo
Egypt

50°

Montreal
Toronto
Detroit   Cleveland   Boston
Chicago   Pittsburgh   New York
San Francisco   United States of America   Philadelphia
St. Louis   Baltimore
Washington
Los Angeles

Bermuda
(U.K.)

Tropic of Cancer

Bahama
Islands
Mexico   Sp Sahara
Cuba   Algeria
Mexico   Haiti   Dom. Repub.   Mauritania   Niger   Chad   Sudan
City   Belize(U.K.)   Jamaica   Puerto Rico   Mali
Guatemala   Honduras   (U.S.A.)   Senegal
El Salvador   Nicaragua   Neths.   Gambia
Antilles   Barbados   Port.
Costa Rica   Grenada   Guinea   Guinea   Nigeria
Panama   Trinidad   S.L.   Ivory   Cent. Afr.
& Tobago   Liberia   Coast   Ghana   Cameroon   Rep.
Venezuela   Guyana   Equat.   U
Caracas   Surinam   Guiana   Guinea   Gabon
Bogota   Gr   Congo   Zaire   R
Colombia   B   Ta
Equator
Ecuador

Peru   Brazil   Angola

Lima   Zambia

Bolivia   Rhodesi.

Rio de Janeiro   S. W.
Paraguay   Tropic of Capricorn   Africa   Botswana
São Paulo   (Namibia)

Repub. of   Les
Chile   S. Africa   S

Santiago   Uruguay
Argentina   Buenos Aires

50°

Falkland Is.
(U.K.)

50°

100°   50°   0°

Oxford projection. Scale 1:65m. Equal-area.